IRREGULAR SERIALS & ANNUALS

An International Directory

**Seventh Edition
1982**

A Bowker Serials
Bibliography

Irregular Serials and Annuals: An International Directory
is compiled by R. R. Bowker Company
Serials Bibliography Department

Emery I. Koltay, Director, Serials Bibliography and Standards;
Leigh Carol Yuster, Manager, Sources and Services;
Jacqueline Mullikin, Project Coordinator;
Frank Zirpolo, Project Coordinator;
Diana McMorrow, Senior Editor;
Mike Fitzpatrick, Maria Giurdanella,
Deirdre Newton, Sylvia Sciotti and
Marina Zogbi, Editors;
Florentina Hart, Assistant Editor;
Terence Carlson, Margareta Leon, Richard Oosterom,
Milt Silver and Eline van de Poel,
Contributing Editors.

Programming and processing was done by the Bowker
Publications Systems Department:
Michael B. Howell, Business Systems Manager

Andrew H. Uszak, Vice President and Publisher,
Data Services Division

IRREGULAR SERIALS & ANNUALS
An International Directory

Seventh Edition 1982

A Bowker Serials Bibliography

R. R. BOWKER COMPANY
A Xerox Publishing Company
New York & London

Published by R.R. Bowker Company
(A Xerox Publishing Company)
1180 Avenue of the Americas, New York, N.Y. 10036

Copyright © 1982 by Xerox Corporation

All rights reserved. Reproduction of this list, in whole or in part, without permission of the publisher is prohibited.

International Standard Book Number 0-8352-1407-9
International Standard Serial Number 0000-0043
Library of Congress Catalog Card Number 67-25026

Printed and bound in the United States of America.

No payment is either solicited or accepted for the inclusion of entries in this publication. Every possible precaution has been taken to ensure that the information it contains is accurate, and the publishers cannot accept any liability for errors or omissions however caused.

Contents

PREFACE	vii
USER'S GUIDE	ix
ABBREVIATIONS	
General Abbreviations	xii
Abstracting and Indexing Services	xii
Money Symbols	xx
Micropublishers	xxi
Country of Publication Codes	xxiii
INTERNATIONAL STANDARD SERIAL NUMBER (ISSN)	xxv
NOTES ON SUBJECTS	xxvii
SUBJECTS	xxix
CROSS-INDEX TO SUBJECTS	xxxiii
CLASSIFIED LIST OF SERIALS	1
CESSATIONS	903
INDEX TO PUBLICATIONS OF INTERNATIONAL ORGANIZATIONS	
International Organizations	917
International Congress Proceedings	928
European Communities	933
United Nations	934
ISSN INDEX	941
TITLE INDEX	1267

From the Bowker Serials Bibliography Department
The Ulrich's Family of Directories

ULRICH'S INTERNATIONAL PERIODICALS DIRECTORY

No other periodicals reference source is as current and comprehensive as *Ulrich's*, which is one reason why the *American Reference Books Annual* calls it a "truly outstanding reference tool."

The current edition of *Ulrich's International Periodicals Directory* lists some 63,000 periodicals of all kinds from all over the world in some 270 subject areas. Each entry provides title, frequency of publication, publisher name and address, country of publication code, and Dewey Decimal Classification number. Additional bibliographic and buying information provided when available includes: ISSN, subscription price, year first published, language of text, if advertising and book reviews are included, where abstracted or indexed, corporate author, variant forms, whether or not available from a subscription agency, and more. Separate sections include a list of cessations, an index to publications of international organizations, and a title index.

IRREGULAR SERIALS AND ANNUALS

An International Directory

Designed as a companion to *Ulrich's International Periodicals Directory*, *Irregular Serials and Annuals* is worldwide in scope and provides data on some 35,000 serials, annuals, continuations, conference proceedings, and other publications issued irregularly or less frequently than twice a year. Entries are alphabetically by title under 270 subject headings, and data includes: frequency of issue, publisher, Dewey Decimal number, ISSN number, language of text, year first published, price, and editor.

In addition, the next edition of *Irregular Serials and Annuals* will include an ISSN index. All titles included in the Bowker Serials Bibliography data base, *Ulrich's*, *Irregular Serials and Annuals* and *Ulrich's Quarterly*, with ISSN are listed in this index.

ULRICH'S QUARTERLY

A Supplement to Ulrich's International Periodicals Directory *and* Irregular Serials and Annuals

This quarterly brings you continuous worldwide, up-to-date information on new serial titles, title changes, and cessations. It gives you all the data you need to keep current between editions of *Ulrich's International Periodicals Directory* and *Irregular Serials and Annuals*. It replaces the *Bowker Serials Bibliography Supplement*. Each issue lists some 2,000 new and newly-added (to our serials database) periodicals, irregular serials and annuals of all kinds from all over the world in all subject areas. It utilizes the same subject arrangement as the base volumes and provides the same full bibliographic annotation for each item.

The *Ulrich's Quarterly* arrangement follows the format of *Ulrich's International Periodicals Directory* and *Irregular Serials and Annuals*. Pagination is continuous within each volume, and title, title changes, and cessations are cumulated in each issue.

Ulrich's International Periodicals Directory, Irregular Serials and Annuals and Ulrich's Quarterly are "stand alone" bibliographic tools, but together they constitute a unique and valuable current serials bibliography reference work.

SOURCES OF SERIALS

International Serials Publishers and their Titles with Copyright and Copy Availability Information

This directory will provide comprehensive and authoritative *author/publisher* access to the world's periodicals. It enables the user to quickly and easily identify, locate, and contact more than 65,000 publishers and corporate authors of the approximately 96,600 titles listed in the latest editions of *Ulrich's International Periodicals Directory, Irregular Serials and Annuals*, and *Ulrich's Quarterly*.

The arrangement is first by country, then by publisher and/or corporate author. Under each publisher is a complete listing of all serial titles published. The publisher's full name and current address is provided. Cross references from corporate author are included when the publisher is not the corporate author of the serial. An International Serials Publishers alphabetical index is included.

Order from
R.R. BOWKER ORDER DEPARTMENT
Box 1807
Ann Arbor, Michigan 48106

Preface

The 7th edition of *Irregular Serials and Annuals* is here to bring you world-wide, up-to-date information on 35,000 serial publications currently published throughout the world. It updates and expands the base volume of the 6th edition and includes as well those irregular serials and annuals listed in *Ulrich's Quarterly* through Vol. V, No. 3.

Ulrich's Quarterly brings you up-to-date information on new serial titles, title changes and cessations, and keeps you current between the editions of *Ulrich's International Periodicals Directory* and *Irregular Serials and Annuals*, with timely information and cumulated indexes.

Irregular Serials and Annuals provides information which is often difficult to locate for serials and continuations such as proceedings, transactions, advances, progresses, reports, yearbooks, handbooks, annual reviews, and monographic series, which constitute the "twilight" area between books and serials.

Limitations of inclusiveness in a directory of this kind are determined by its expected use. Our aim is maximum title coverage and a subject breakdown which will satisfy the widest range of use. Because of the great number of serial publications, we have established certain criteria for inclusion. The directory includes: titles issued annually or less frequently than once a year, or irregularly; serials published at least twice under the same title, and those first publications which plan to have subsequent issues. Excluded are publications which are essentially administrative in content, such as membership directories, annual reports, house organs, or local interest publications.

Entries are arranged by subject. A "Cross-Index to Subjects," giving key words not used in the subject heading scheme, is provided in the front matter.

In addition to adding some 7,500 new entries, features started in the previous edition were further extended.

Information about microform availability is given, as well as the abbreviation for the microform publisher. (A list of microform publishers and abbreviations used in this edition is provided in the front matter.) When available and different from the main entry title, key title is included in the entry.

Coverage of abstracting and indexing information was also significantly extended. In addition to information received from publishers, holding lists of several major abstracting and indexing services were checked.

A special feature is the subheading "Abstracting, Bibliographies, Statistics" for each major subject group. Entries are listed within specific subject headings, with cross references under the general subject headings "Abstracting and Indexing Services," "Bibliographies," and "Statistics" when appropriate. This arrangement allows users searching in a subject to focus first on the abstracting and indexing, bibliographies, and statistics, before searching on specific titles.

The "Index to Publications of International Organizations" includes all titles listed in *Ulrich's* and *Irregular Serials and Annuals*. The "Index," divided into four sections, lists publications of International Organizations, International Congresses, the European Communities and the United Nations.

A continuing feature is the ISSN index for the titles included in *Ulrich's*, *Irregular Serials and Annuals*, and *Ulrich's Quarterly*. This ISSN index is a regular feature of all the forthcoming *Irregular Serials and Annuals*.

PREFACE

We have developed one of the most sophisticated, perhaps unique, systems for the maintenance of a machine-readable serials file. Through this system we are in contact with 65,000 publishers and corporate authors in 170 countries, who keep us informed on the status of 96,000 current serials, providing information on new titles, changes, mergers, splits and cessations.

The file is maintained by country, publisher and/or corporate author. This approach not only enables us to eliminate confusing and duplicate entries, which occur in a file maintained in title sequence, but also to build a unique publisher and corporate author name file by country.

In the fall of 1981, we published *Sources of Serials, International Serials Publishers and Their Titles with Copyright and Copy Availability Information*, a directory listing all titles in *Ulrich's International Periodicals Directory* and *Irregular Serials and Annuals* by country and within country by publisher and/or corporate author.

Ulrich's International Periodicals Directory, Irregular Serials and Annuals, Ulrich's Quarterly and *Sources of Serials* are "stand alone" bibliographic tools, but together they constitute a unique and valuable current serials bibliography reference work.

Ulrich's Quarterly, Sources of Serials, International Serials Publishers and Their Titles with Copyright and Copy Availability Information and the ISSN indexes represent our continuing commitment to the library world to provide improved bibliographic tools for improved serials control. These bibliographies join established serials reference works published by R. R. Bowker, including: *Ulrich's International Periodicals Directory* and *Irregular Serials and Annuals,* the two directories that served as the starting data base for the assignment of International Standard Serial Number (ISSN).

The improvement of any serial file is a continuous operation and requires the users' collaboration, comments and suggestions. We are looking forward to your participation.

Emery Koltay, Director
Serials Bibliography and Standards

User's Guide

CLASSIFIED LIST OF SERIALS.

Entries for selected, current serials are arranged alphabetically by title under 385 subject headings. The complete entry is listed under one subject heading. If a serial covers more than one subject, cross references direct the user from related subjects to the subject under which the complete entry is listed. The Key to Subjects gives page location for subject headings in the Classified List. Categories for religions and theology and abstracting and indexing have been revised; notes for the new and revised categories precede the Key to Subjects. In addition, the Cross-Index to Subjects provides references from related terms to headings in the Key to Subjects.

In the preparation of this edition, over 65,000 publishers were contacted by direct mail. Information about title changes and cessations that was not received by the deadline for this edition will appear in *Ulrich's Quarterly.*

Every entry contains the following basic information: title, frequency of publication, publisher name and address, country of publication code, Dewey Decimal Classification Number. The additional information, described below, is included whenever available.

Title Information
The main entry title, cataloged according to rules of entry based on the *Anglo-American Cataloging Rules,* is printed in upper case as the first item in the entry. The parallel language title, also printed in upper case, follows the main entry title and is separated from it by a slash. The ISSN and country of publication code appear on the line above the main entry title. Subtitle and variant title information provide further description of the main entry title. Former titles, the original title of a translation, and the translated edition titles are listed with the ISSN (ISSN are given only when available). The key title (the title to which the responsible center of the International Serials Data System assigns the ISSN) is listed only if it is different from the main entry title. Cataloging and filing rules are given in the Rules for Main Entry section of the User's Guide.

Buying and Ordering Information
In addition to the publisher name and address, the subscription address is included if it is different from the publisher's main or editorial office address. Information on sole distributor is given after publisher information.

Subscription price is generally given in the currency of the country of publication. U.S. rates for titles published outside the U.S. are included only if supplied by the publisher. If the annual rate is not known, the price per issue is given.

Frequency of publication is given preceding price information; year of first issue (or year and number of first known or of latest issue) precedes the frequency. Notations on availability of back issues are included. The symbol ‡ following a price indicates that the publication is not available from a subscription agency.

Format of the periodical and availability of alternative formats is also given. If a microform is available from another publisher, an abbreviation for the micropublisher follows the notation on microform availability. A listing of abbreviations with full names and addresses of micropublishers is given in the front of this directory.

Information on supplements and special issues is included. Main series titles are given for sub-series titles.

Abstracting and Indexing Information
Following the notation "Indexed:" abbreviations for services that abstract or index the periodical on a regular basis are listed. The listing of Abstracting and Indexing Services, in the Abbreviations section fol-

USER'S GUIDE

lowing the User's Guide, provides full titles for the abbreviated service.

Author and Editor Information

If the corporate author of the periodical is not the publisher, the name of the corporate author is given in parentheses. The abbreviation Ed. (editor) is used to indicate editor-in-chief, executive editor and managing editor. If there are three or more editors, the abbreviation Ed.Bd. (editorial board) is given. Generally, advanced degrees and titles of editors are omitted, with the exception of medical, military and clerical titles.

Contents of the Serial

A language note is given when the text is in a language other than the language of the country of publication, or when the text is multi-lingual.

Abbreviations are given to indicate if the periodical contains any of the following features: advertising, reviews (of books, films, plays, or other media), bibliography section, abstracts, charts, illustrations, patents, statistics, or trademarks. Availability of indexes is given. A brief subject annotation is included when the contents of the publication is not clearly defined by the title. Key words in italics are given on the last line of the entry as a scanning aid in broad subject categories of the Classified List.

RULES FOR MAIN ENTRY

Since the establishment of the International Serials Data System (ISDS) and the key title concept (1973) and the publication of the *International Standard Bibliographic Description for Serials* (1974), the *Anglo-American Cataloging Rules* have been revised.

In view of new developments in national and international standards, rules for entry in this edition have been developed to reflect traditional practices as well as trends toward key title. Whenever possible, main entry cataloging is done from a sample page of the most recent issue, according to the following rules:

Serials with distinctive titles are usually entered under title.

If the title consists only of the name of the issuing body and a generic term, or if the name of the issuing body clarifies the content of the publication, entry is under the name of the issuing body. For example:

Newsletter of the American Industrial Arts Association is entered as *American Industrial Arts Association. Newsletter.*

A title is considered nondistinctive if it consists of a subject modified generic term and the name of the issuing body and is entered under the name of the issuing body. For example:

Anthropological Notes of the Department of Anthropology of Duke University is entered as *Duke University. Department of Anthropology. Anthropological Notes.*

Government publications with nondistinctive titles are usually entered under the name of the government jurisdiction of the issuing body; distinctive titles of government issuing bodies are entered under title. For example:

Great Britain. Science Research Council. Report

but

Statistical Abstract of Wales

SAMPLE ENTRY

DEWEY DECIMAL CLASSIFICATION — 940
COUNTRY CODE — FR ISSN 1234-5679
MAIN ENTRY TITLE — ASSOCIATION DES HISTORIENS EUROPEENS. JOURNAL/ASSOCIATION OF EUROPEAN HISTORIANS. JOURNAL;
PARALLEL LANGUAGE TITLE
SUBTITLE — une revue d'histoire depuis la Renaissance jusqu'a present.
FREQUENCY OF PUBLICATION
PRICE
LANGUAGE NOTATION — (Text in French and English) 1952. a. 200 F.
CORPORATE AUTHOR — (Institute of European Studies)
YEAR FIRST PUBLISHED
PUBLISHER NAME AND ADDRESS — Timsitt Publications, 55 rue Desaix, 7500-Paris, France.
EDITOR — Ed. Richard Duprey.
SPECIAL FEATURES — bk.rev. bibl. illus. cum.index: 1952-1960 (vol. 9).
MICROPUBLISHER — also avail. in microfiche from UMI.
INDEX INFORMATION
INDEXED IN HISTORICAL ABSTRACTS — Indexed: Hist. Abstr. Key Title: Journal de l'Association des Historiens Europeens.
FORMER TITLE — Formerly: Review of Military History (ISSN 1232-5678)
ANNOTATION — Military History

Titles which begin with the initials of the issuing body are entered under the initials of the issuing body. Cross-references from full name of issuing body to initials in main entry are given in the Title Index. If a title consists only of a generic term and the name of issuing body, and the name of the issuing body includes a geographic name, entry will be under the name of the issuing body. For example:

> *University of Chicago. Graduate School of Business. Selected Papers,* not *Chicago. University. Graduate School of Business. Selected Papers.*

Multilingual titles are entered under the first title given on the title page (or first title reported by publisher if title page is not available). Titles in other languages are entered directly after the main entry title.

FILING RULES

Articles at the beginning of titles have been omitted. In Arabic and Hebrew titles, the articles, *al- el, ha- he-, an- ar- as-,* are bypassed in filing. Articles and prepositions within titles are alphabetized as words:

> *Journal of the West* precedes
> *Journal of Theological Studies*

Hyphenated words are treated as separate words:

> *Bio-Medical Review* precedes
> *Biography Index*

Titles entered under corporate author or government jurisdiction are sequenced before distinctive titles which begin with the same words:

> *Arizona. Water Resources Board. Quarterly Review* will precede *Arizona Land Surveys Conference Proceedings.*

Acronyms and initials are treated as such and are listed at the beginning of each letter of the alphabet with the exception of the abbreviations U.N. (United Nations), U.S. (United States), Gt. Britain (Great Britain), and St. (Saint) which are filed as words:

> *U. R. S. I. Information Bulletin*
> *Union List of Serials in Canadian Libraries*
> *U.N. Economic Commission. Report.*

Diacritical marks have been omitted. The German and Scandinavian umlaut has been replaced by the letter "e" following the vowels a, o, and u. In Danish, Norwegian, and Swedish texts, the letter å is sequenced as "aa" and the letter ø as "oe."

CESSATIONS

Entries for serials which have ceased or have been suspended since the last edition are listed here alphabetically by title. The cessation entry includes: title, Dewey Decimal Classification number, country of publication code, former frequency of publication, publisher name and address, and if available, ISSN, subtitle, corporate author, year of first issue and year ceased, former titles. If full information about a succeeding title is available, the ceased title is given in the succeeding title entry in the Classified List, and no entry appears in the Cessations section. A reference from the new title is given in the Title Index. *Ulrich's Quarterly* updates the cessations sections of both *Ulrich's* and *Irregular Serials and Annuals.* In addition, title changes for both these directories are given in a separate index in *Ulrich's Quarterly.*

INDEX TO PUBLICATIONS OF INTERNATIONAL ORGANIZATIONS

This index contains the current titles including titles listed in the 20th edition of *Ulrich's International Periodicals Directory* and *Ulrich's Quarterly.* Titles listed with page numbers refer to entries included in the Classified List of this directory. Titles listed without page numbers refer to entries in *Ulrich's* and *Ulrich's Quarterly.* Complexity of corporate author structure as well as title page variations in multilingual texts and editions compound the problems in cataloging international publications. This special index is provided so that the user may have one reference point for these titles. This index consists of four sections:

> International Organizations
> International Congress Proceedings
> European Communities
> United Nations

ISSN INDEX

Titles in the Bowker Serials Bibliography database, which are published in *Ulrich's, Irregular Serials and Annuals* and *Ulrich's Quarterly,* with ISSN, are listed in this index.

TITLE INDEX

Title index entries for all current and ceased periodicals listed in this directory include: title, ISSN and country code, name of issuing body if main entry title contains only the initials of the issuing body. Cross-references for variant titles, parallel language titles, and former titles are included. The page number where the complete entry appears is printed in italic type; page numbers in roman type indicate pages of related subject listings.

Emery Koltay, Director
Serials Bibliography and Standards

Abbreviations

General Abbreviations

a.	annual	irreg.	irregular
abstr.	abstracts	m.	monthly
adv.	advertising	mkt.	market prices
approx.	approximately	music rev.	music reviews
B.R.D.	Federal Republic of Germany	N.S.	New Series
bi-m.	every two months	pat.	patents
bibl.	bibliographies	play rev.	play reviews (theatre reviews)
bk.rev.	book reviews	Prof.	Professor
c-o	care of	q.	quarterly
charts	charts (diagrams, graphs, tables)	record rev.	record reviews
circ.	circulation	s-a.	twice annually
contr.	controlled	s-m.	twice monthly
cum.ind.	cumulative index	s-w.	twice weekly
Cy.	county	stat.	statistics
d.	daily	subscr.	subscription
D.D.R.	German Democratic Republic	tele.rev.	television reviews
dance rev.	dance reviews	3/m.	3 times a month
Dir.	Director	3/yr.	3 times a year
Ed., Eds.	Editor, Editors	tr.lit.	trade literature (manufacturers' catalogues, etc.)
Ed.Bd.	Editorial Board	tr.mk.	trade marks
film rev.	film reviews	w.	weekly
fortn.	fortnightly	‡	not available from a subscription agency
ISSN	International Standard Serial Number	*	not updated
illus.	illustrations		

Abstracting and Indexing Services

A.A.P.P.Abstr.	Amino Acids, Peptide & Protein Abstracts
A.B.C.Pol.Sci.	Advance Bibliography of Contents, Political Science & Government
ABTICS	Abstracts and Book Title Index
ACCESS	ACCESS
A.I.D.Res.Dev. Abstr.	A.I.D. (Agency for International Development) Research and Development Abstracts
A.S.&T.Ind.	Applied Science & Technology Index
ASCA	Automatic Subject Citation Alert
A-V Ind.	Audio-Visual Index
Abr.R.G.	Abridged Reader's Guide to Periodical Literature
Abstr. Anthropol.	Abstracts in Anthropology
Abstr.Bull.Inst. Pap.Chem.	Abstract Bulletin of the Institute of Paper Chemistry
Abstr.Comput. Lit.	Abstracts of Computer Literature (Ceased)
Abstr.Crim. &Pen.	Abstracts on Criminology and Penology (Formerly: Excerpta Criminologica)
Abstr.Engl.Stud.	Abstracts of English Studies
Abstr.Folk.Stud.	Abstracts of Folklore Studies
Abstr.Health Care Manage. Stud.	Abstracts of Health Care Management Studies
Abstr.Health Eff.Environ. Pollut.	Abstracts on Health Effects of Environmental Pollutants
Abstr.Hosp. Manage.Stud.	Abstracts of Hospital Management Studies

Abstr.Hyg.	Abstracts on Hygiene	Aus.Educ.Ind.	Australian Education Index
Abstr.J.Earthq. Eng.	Abstract Journal in Earthquake Engineering	Aus.Leg.Mon. Dig.	Australian Legal Monthly Digest
Abstr.Mil.Bibl.	Abstracts of Military Bibliography	Aus.P.A.I.S.	Australian Public Affairs Information Service
Abstr.N.Amer. Geol.	Abstracts of North American Geology	Aus.Sci.Ind.	Australian Science Index
Abstr.Pop.Cult.	Abstracts of Popular Culture	Aus.Speleo Abstr.	Australian Speleo Abstracts
Abstr.Soc.Work.	Abstracts for Social Workers (Now: Social Work Research & Abstracts)	Avery Ind. Archit. Per.	Avery Index to Architectural Periodicals of Columbia University
Abstr.Trop.Agri.	Abstracts on Tropical Agriculture		
Abstr.World Med.	Abstracts of World Medicine (Ceased)		
Access	Access: the Supplementary Index to Periodicals	B.C.I.R.A.	B.C.I.R.A. Abstracts of Foundry Literature
Afr.Abstr.	African Abstracts	B.P.I.	Business Periodicals Index
Agri.Ind.	Agriculture Index (Now: Biological & Agricultural Index)	B.R.I.	Bioresearch Index
		Bangladesh Agr.Sci. Abstr.	Bangladesh Agricultural Sciences Abstracts
Agrindex	Agrindex		
Air Un.Lib.Ind.	Air University Library Index to Military Periodicals	Ber.Biochem. Biol.	Berichte Biochemie und Biologie
Alt.Press Ind.	Alternative Press Index	Bibl.Agri.	Bibliography of Agriculture
Amer.Hist.& Life	America: History & Life	Bibl.& Ind.Geol.	Bibliography & Index to Geology
		Bibl.Engl.Lang. & Lit.	Bibliography of English Language and Literature
Amer.Hum.Ind.	American Humanities Index		
Amer.Stat.Ind.	American Statistics Index	Bibl.Ind.	Bibliographic Index
Anal.Abstr.	Analytical Abstracts	Bibl.Pflanz.	Bibliographie der Pflanzenschutzliteratur
Anbar	Anbar Publications Ltd.		
	Accounting & Data Processing Abstracts	Bibl.Repro.	Bibliography of Reproduction
	Marketing & Distribution Abstracts	Bibliogr.Bras. Odontol.	Bibliografia Brasileira Odontologia
	Personnel & Training Abstracts	Bioeng.Abstr.	Bioengineering Abstracts
	Top Management Abstracts	Biog.Ind.	Biography Index
	Work Study & O and M Abstracts	Biol.Abstr.	Biological Abstracts
		Biol.& Agr.Ind.	Biological & Agricultural Index (Formerly: Agricultural Index)
Anim.Behav. Abstr.	Animal Behavior Abstracts	Biol.Dig.	Biology Digest
Anim.Breed. Abstr.	Animal Breeding Abstracts	Bk.Rev.Dig.	Book Review Digest
		Bk.Rev.Ind.	Book Review Index
Apic.Abstr.	Apicultural Abstracts	Bk.Rev.Mo.	Book Reviews of the Month
Appl.Ecol.Abstr.	Applied Ecology Abstracts	Br.Archaeol. Abstr.	British Archaeological Abstracts
Appl.Mech.Rev.	Applied Mechanics Review		
Aqua.Sci. & Fish.Abstr.	Aquatic Sciences & Fisheries Abstracts	Br.Ceram. Abstr.	British Ceramic Abstracts
Archit.Per.Ind.	Architectural Periodicals Index	Br.Educ.Ind.	British Education Index
Arct.Bibl.	Arctic Bibliography	Br.Hum.Ind.	British Humanities Index
Art & Archeol. Tech.Abstr.	Art and Archaeology Technical Abstracts	Br.Tech.Ind.	British Technology Index
		Bull.Anal.Ent. Med. Vet.	Bulletin Analytique d'Entomologie Medicale et Veterinaire
Art Ind.	Art Index		
Arts & Hum. Cit.Ind.	Arts & Humanities Citation Index	Bull.Hyg.	Bulletin of Hygiene
		Bull.Inst. Pasteur	Bulletin de l'Institute Pasteur
Ash.G. Bot. Per.	Asher's Guide to Botanical Periodicals		
		Bull.Signal.	Bulletin Signaletique
Astron.& Astrophys. Abstr.	Astronomy and Astrophysics Abstracts	Bull. Thermodyn.& Thermochem.	Bulletin of Thermodynamics & Thermochemistry
Astron. Jahresber.	Astronomischer Jahresbericht	Bus.Educ.Ind.	Business Education Index

ABSTRACTING AND INDEXING SERVICES

CALL	Current Awareness—Library Literature
C.C.L.P.	Contents of Current Legal Periodicals (Now: Legal Contents)
C.C.M.J.	Contents of Contemporary Mathematical Journals
C.I.J.E.	Current Index to Journals in Education
CINAHL (also C.I.N.L.)	Cumulative Index to Nursing and Allied Health Literature
CIRF Abstr.	CIRF Abstracts
C.I.S. Abstr.	C.I.S. Abstracts on Cards
C.I.S. Ind.	Congressional Information Service Index
CJPI	Criminal Justice Periodical Index
C.P.I.	Current Physics Index
C.R.E.J.	Contents of Recent Economic Journals
C.R.I. Abstr.	Cement Research Institute of India Abstracts
Can.B.P.I.	Canadian Business Periodical Index (Now: Canadian Business Index)
Can.Educ.Ind.	Canadian Education Index
Can.Ind.	Canadian Periodical Index
Can.Ind.Geo.Sci.Data	Canadian Index to Geoscience Data
Canon Law Abstr.	Canon Law Abstracts
Cath.Ind.	Catholic Periodical & Literature Index (Formerly: Catholic Periodical Index)
Ceram.Abstr.	Ceramic Abstracts
Chem.Abstr.	Chemical Abstracts
Chem.Infd.	Chemischer Informationsdienst
Chem.Titles	Chemical Titles
Chicago Psychoanal.Lit.Ind.	Chicago Psychoanalytic Literature Index
Child Devel.Abstr.	Child Development Abstracts
Chir.Vet.Ref.Abstr.	Chirurgia Veterinaria Referate Abstracts
Chr.Per.Ind.	Christian Periodical Index
Coll.Stud.Pers.Abstr.	College Student Personnel Abstracts
Commer.Fish.Abstr.	Commercial Fisheries Abstracts
Commer.Ind.	Commercial Index
Commun.Abstr.	Communication Abstracts
Community Ment. Health Rev.	Community Mental Health Review
Comput.& Info.Sys.	Computer and Information Systems
Comput.Abstr.	Computer Abstracts
Comput.& Contr.Abstr.	Computer & Control Abstracts (See Science Abstracts)
Comput. Rev.	Computing Reviews
Concr.Abstr.	Concrete Abstracts
Consum.Ind.	Consumer's Index
Copper Abstr.	Copper Abstracts
Corros.Abstr.	Corrosion Abstracts
Crime Delinq. Abstr.	Crime and Delinquency Abstracts
Crime Delinq. Lit.	Crime & Delinquency Literature
Cum.Comput. Abstr.	Cumulative Computer Abstracts
Curr.Aus.N.Z. Leg.Lit.Ind.	Current Australian and New Zealand Legal Literature Index
Curr.Bibl. Aquatic Sci.& Fish.	Current Bibliography for Aquatic Sciences & Fisheries
Curr.Bk.Rev.Cit.	Current Book Review Citations
Curr.Cont.	Current Contents
Curr.Dig.Sov. Press	Current Digest of Soviet Press
Curr.Ind. Commonw. Leg.Per.	Current Index to Commonwealth Legal Periodicals
Curr.Ind.Stat.	Current Index to Statistics
Curr.Leather Lit.	Current Leather Literature
Curr.Lit.Blood	Current Literature of Blood
Curr.Pap.Phys.	Current Papers in Physics
Curr.Tit. Electrochem.	Current Titles in Electrochemistry
Curr.U.S.Gov. Per.Mfiche	Current U.S. Government Periodicals on Microfiche
D.A.	Dissertation Abstracts
DSH Abstr.	DSH Abstracts
Dairy Sci.Abstr.	Dairy Science Abstracts
Data Process.Dig.	Data Processing Digest
Deep Sea Res.& Oceanogr.Abstr.	Deep Sea Research & Oceanographic Abstracts
Dent.Abstr.	Dental Abstracts
Dent.Ind.	Index to Dental Literature
Diab.Lit.Ind.	Diabetes Literature Index
Doc.Abstr.	Documentation Abstracts (Now: Information Science Abstracts)
Doc.Geogr.	Documentatio Geographica
Dok. Arbeitsmed.	Dokumentation Arbeitsmedizin
Dok.Raum.	Dokumentation zur Raumentwicklung
Dok.Str.	Dokumentation Strasse
ERIC	Eric Clearinghouse (See also C.I.J.E.)
Ecol.Abstr.	Ecological Abstracts
Econ.Abstr.	Economic Abstracts (Now: Key to Economic Science)
Educ.Admin. Abstr.	Educational Administration Abstracts

ABSTRACTING AND INDEXING SERVICES

Educ.Ind.	Education Index
Ekist.Ind.	Ekistic Index
Elec. & Electron. Abstr.	Electrical & Electronic Abstracts
Elec.Eng.Abstr.	Electrical Engineering Abstracts (See Science Abstracts)
Electroanal. Abstr.	Electroanalytical Abstracts
Electron.Abstr.J.	Electronics Abstracts Journal (Now: Electronics and Communications Abstracts Journal)
Electron.& Communic. Abstr.J.	Electronics and Communications Abstracts Journal (Formerly: Electronics Abstracts Journal
Employ.Rel. Abstr.	Employment Related Abstracts (Now: Work Related Abstracts)
Endocrinol.Ind.	Endocrinology Index
Energy Ind.	Energy Index
Energy Info.Abstr.	Energy Information Abstracts
Energy Res.Abstr.	Energy Research Abstracts
Eng.Ind.	Engineering Index
Eng.Ind.India	Engineering Index of India
Entomol.Abstr.	Entomology Abstracts
Environ.Abstr.	Environmental Abstracts
Environ.Per. Bibl.	Environmental Periodicals Bibliography
Environ.Qual. Abstr.	Environmental Quality Abstracts
Ergon.Abstr.	Ergonomics Abstracts
Except.Child Educ.Abstr.	Exceptional Child Education Abstracts
Excerp.Bot.	Excerpta Botanica
Excerp. Criminol.	Excerpta Criminologica (Now: Abstracts on Criminology and Penology
Excerp.Med.	Excerpta Medica
Exec. Sci.Inst.	Executive Sciences Institute Operations Research/Management Science Abstract Services Quality Control and Applied Statistics
F.A.C.T.	Fuel Abstracts & Current Titles (Now: Fuel & Energy Abstracts)
Farm & Garden Ind.	Farm & Garden Index
Fert.Abstr.	Fertilizer Abstracts
Field Crop Abstr.	Field Crop Abstracts
Film Lit.Ind.	Film Literature Index
Fire Res.Abstr. & Rev.	Fire Research Abstracts and Reviews
Food Sci.& Tech.Abstr.	Food Science and Technology Abstracts
Foreign Leg. Per.	Index to Foreign Legal Periodicals
Forest.Abstr.	Forestry Abstracts
Fuel & Energy Abstr.	Fuel & Energy Abstracts (Formerly: Fuel Abstracts & Current Titles)
Fut.Abstr.	Future Abstracts
G. Indian Per. Lit.	Guide to Indian Periodical Literature
G.Perf.Arts	Guide to the Performing Arts
G.Rel.Per.	Guide to Religious Periodicals
G.Soc.Sci.& Rel.Per.Lit.	Guide to Social Science and Religion in Periodical Literature
Gard.Abstr.	Gardener's Abstracts
Gas Abstr.	Gas Abstracts
Gastroenterol: Abstr.& Cit.	Gastroenterology: Abstracts & Citations
Geneal.Per.Ind.	Genealogical Periodical Annual Index
Genet.Abstr.	Genetics Abstracts
Geo.Abstr.	Geographical Abstracts
Geophys.Abstr.	Geophysical Abstracts
Geosci.Doc.	Geoscience Documentation
Geotech.Abstr.	Geotechnical Abstracts
Geotimes	Geotimes
Graph.Arts Abstr.	Graphic Arts Abstracts
Helminthol. Abstr.	Helminthological Abstracts
Herb.Abstr.	Herbage Abstracts
Hisp.Press Ind.	Hispanic Press Index
Hist.Abstr.	Historical Abstracts
Hors.Abstr.	Horseman's Abstracts
Hort.Abstr.	Horticultural Abstracts
Hosp. Abstr.	Hospital Abstracts
Hosp.Abstr. Serv.	Hospital Abstracts Services
Hosp.Lit.Ind.	Hospital Literature Index
Hum.Ind.	Humanities Index
Human Resour. Abstr.	Human Resources Abstracts (Formerly: Poverty & Human Resources Abstracts)
Hwy.Res.Abstr.	Highway Research Abstracts Now:Transportation Research Abstracts)
I.B.S.A.	Indian Behavioural Science Abstracts
I.C.U.I.S. Abstr. Service	ICUIS Abstract Service (Institute on the Church in Urban Industrial Society)
I.M.M.Abstr.	IMM Abstracts (Institute of Mining & Metallurgy)
I.N.E.P.	Index to New England Periodicals
INIS Atomind.	INIS Atomindex

I.P.A.	International Pharmaceutical Abstracts
I.R.E.B.I.	Indices de Revista de Bibliotecologia
Ind.Agri.Am.Lat.Caribe	Indice Agricole de America Latina y el Caribe
Ind.Amer.Per.Verse	Index of American Periodical Verse
Ind.Artic.Jew.Stud.	Index of Articles on Jewish Studies
Ind.Chem.	Current Abstracts of Chemistry and Index Chemicus (Formerly: Index Chemicus)
Ind.Child.Mag.	Subject Index to Children's Magazines
Ind.Curr.Urb.Doc.	Index to Current Urban Documents
Ind.Develop.Abstr.	Industrial Development Abstracts
Ind.Econ.J.	Index of Economic Journals
Ind.Hyg.Dig.	Industrial Hygiene Digest
Ind.India	Index India
Ind.Islam.	Index Islamicus
Ind.Jew.Per.	Index to Jewish Periodicals
Ind.Lit.Amer.Indian	Index to Literature on the American Indian
Ind.Lit.Dent.	Indice de la Literatura Dental en Castellano
Ind. Little Mag.	Index to Little Magazines
Ind.Med.	Index Medicus
Ind.Med.Esp.	Indice Medico Español
Ind.N.Z.Per.	Index to New Zealand Periodicals
Ind.Per.Art.Relat.Law	Index to Periodical Articles Related to Law
Ind.Per.Blacks	Index to Periodical Articles by and about Blacks (Formerly: Index to Periodical Articles by and about Negroes)
Ind. Per. Lit.	Indian Periodical Literature
Ind. Per. Negroes	Index to Periodical Articles by & about Negroes (Now: Index to Periodical Articles by & about Blacks)
Ind. S.A. Per.	Index to South African Periodicals
Ind. Sci. Rev.	Index to Scientific Reviews
Ind. Sel. Per.	Index to Selected Periodicals (Now: Index to Periodical Articles by & about Blacks)
Ind.U.S.Gov.Per.	Index to U.S. Government Periodicals
Ind.Vet.	Index Veterinarius
Indian Lib.Sci.Abstr.	Indian Library Science Abstracts
Indian Psychol.Abstr.	Indian Psychological Abstracts
Indian Sci.Abstr.	Indian Science Abstracts
Indian Sci.Ind.	Indian Science Index
Inform.Sci.Abstr.	Information Science Abstracts (Formerly: Documentation Abstracts)
Instrum.Abstr.	Instrument Abstracts
Int.Abstr.Biol.Sci.	International Abstracts of Biological Sciences
Int.Abstr.Oper.Res.	International Abstracts in Operations Research
Int.Aerosp.Abstr.	International Aerospace Abstracts
Int.Bibl.Soc.Sci.	International Bibliography of the Social Sciences
Int.Build.Serv.Abstr.	International Building Services Abstracts (Formerly: Thermal Abstracts)
Int.Dredg.Abstr.	International Dredging Abstracts
Int.G.Class.Stud.	International Guide to Classical Studies
Int.Ind.	International Index (Now: Social Sciences Index and Humanities Index)
Int.Ind.Film Per.	International Index to Film Periodicals
Int.Nurs.Ind.	International Nursing Index
Int.Packag.Abstr.	International Packaging Abstracts
Int.Polit.Sci.Abstr.	International Political Science Abstracts
Int.Z.Bibelwiss.	Internationale Zeitschriften fuer Bibelwissenschaft und Grenzgebiete
J.Curr.Laser Abstr.	Journal of Current Laser Abstracts
J.of Doc.	Journal of Documentation
J. of Econ. Abstr.	Journal of Economic Abstracts
J. of Econ. Lit.	Journal of Economic Literature
Jap.Per.Ind.	Japanese Periodicals Index
Key to Econ.Sci.	Key to Economic Science
Key Word Ind. Wildl.Res.	Key Word Index to Wildlife Research
LISA	Library & Information Science Abstracts (Formerly: Library Science Abstracts)
Landwirt. Zentralbl.	Landwirtschaftliches Zentralblatt
Lang.& Lang. Behav.Abstr.	Language & Language Behavior Abstracts
Lang.Teach.& Ling.Abstr.	Language Teaching and Linguistics Abstracts

ABSTRACTING AND INDEXING SERVICES

Lead Abstr.	Lead Abstracts	Nutr. Abstr.	Nutrition Abstracts & Reviews
Leg. Per.	Index to Legal Periodicals		
Lib. Lit.	Library Literature		
Lib. Sci. Abstr.	Library Science Abstracts (Now: Library & Information Science Abstracts)	Occup. Saf. & Health Abstr.	Occupational Safety & Health Abstracts
Lit. Automat.	New Literature on Automation	Ocean. Abstr.	Oceanic Abstracts (Formerly: Oceanic Index)
		Ocean. Abstr. Bibl.	Oceanic Abstracts and Bibliography
MEDSOC	Medical Socioeconomic Research Sources	Ocean Ind.	Oceanic Index (Now: Oceanic Abstracts)
		Old Test. Abstr.	Old Testament Abstracts
M.H.B.R.I.	Mental Health Book Review Index	Oper. Res. Manage. Sci.	Operations Research/Management Science (See: Executive Sciences Institute)
M.L.A.	Modern Language Abstracts		
M.M.R.I.	Multi-Media Reviews Index (Now: Media Review Digest)	Ophthal. Lit.	Ophthalmic Literature
		Oral Res. Abstr.	Oral Research Abstracts (Ceased)
Manage. Abstr.	Management Abstracts		
Mar. Sci. Cont. Tab.	Marine Science Contents Tables	P.A.I.S.	Public Affairs Information Service
Mark. Res. Abstr.	Market Research Abstracts	PASCAL	Plan de Classement PASCAL
Math. R.	Mathematical Reviews	PHRA	Poverty & Human Resources Abstracts (Now: Human Resources Abstracts)
Med. Abstr.	Medical Abstract Service		
Med. Care Rev.	Medical Care Review		
Med. Res. Ind.	Medical Research Index		
Media Rev. Dig.	Media Review Digest (Formerly: Multi-Media Reviews Index)	P.I.R.A.	P.I.R.A. Marketing Abstracts
		P.N.I.	Pharmaceutical News Index
Ment. Retard. Abstr.	Mental Retardation Abstracts	Packag. Abstr.	Packaging Abstracts (Now: International Packaging Abstracts)
Met. Abstr.	Metal Abstracts (Formed by the merger of ASM Review of Metal Literature & Metallurgical Abstracts)	Past. Care & Couns. Abstr.	Pastoral Care & Counseling Abstracts
		Peace Res. Abstr.	Peace Research Abstracts
Met. Finish. Abstr.	Metal Finishing Abstracts	Peace Res. Rev.	Peace Research Reviews
		Percept. Cognit. Devel.	Perceptual Cognitive Development
Meteor. & Geo-astrophys. Abstr.	Meteorological & Geoastro-physical Abstracts	Periodex	Periodex
		Pers. Manage. Abstr.	Personnel Management Abstracts
Meth. Per. Ind.	Methodist Periodical Index		
Microbol. Abstr.	Microbiological Abstracts	Petrol. Abstr.	Petroleum Abstracts
		Petrol. Energy B.N.I.	Petroleum/Energy Business News Index
Mineral. Abstr.	Mineralogical Abstracts		
Mkt. Inform. Guide	Marketing Information Guide	Pharmacog. Tit.	Pharmacognosy Titles
		Phil. Ind.	Philosophers Index
Multi. Scler. Abstr.	Multiple Sclerosis Abstracts (Ceased)	Philip. Abstr.	Philippine Abstracts
		Photo. Abstr.	Photographic Abstracts
Music Artic. Guide	Music Article Guide	Photo. Ind.	Photography Index
		Phys. Abstr.	Physics Abstracts (See: Science Abstracts)
Music Ind.	Music Index		
Mycol. Abstr.	Mycological Abstracts	Phys. Ber.	Physikalische Berichte
		Pinpointer	Pinpointer
		Plant Breed. Abstr.	Plant Breeding Abstracts
Nav. Abstr.	Naval Abstracts	Plast. Abstr.	Plastic Abstracts
New Per. Ind.	New Periodicals Index	Pol. Tech. Abstr.	Polish Technical Abstracts
New Test. Abstr.	New Testament Abstracts	Pollut. Abstr.	Pollution Abstracts
Nucl. Sci. Abstr.	Nuclear Science Abstracts (Superseded by: INIS Atomindex)	Pop. Mus. Per. Ind.	Popular Music Periodicals Index
		Pop. Per. Ind.	Popular Periodicals Index

xvii

ABSTRACTING AND INDEXING SERVICES

Popul. Ind.	Population Index	Sage Pub. Admin. Abstr.	Sage Public Administration Abstracts
Potato Abstr.	Potato Abstracts	Sage Urb. Stud. Abstr.	Sage Urban Studies Abstracts
Poult. Abstr.	Poultry Abstracts	Sci. Abstr.	Science Abstracts
Psychol. Abstr.	Psychological Abstracts		A. Physics Abstracts
Psychol. R.G.	Psychological Reader's Guide		B. Electrical Engineering Abstracts
Psychopharmacol. Abstr.	Psychopharmacology Abstracts		C. Computer & Control Abstracts
Pub. Admin. Abstr.	Public Administration Abstracts and Index of Articles	Sci. & Tech. Aerosp. Rep.	Science & Technical Aerospace Reports
		Sci. Cit. Ind.	Science Citation Index
Qual. Contr. Appl. Stat.	Quality Control and Applied Statistics (See: Executive Sciences Institute)	Sci. Fiction Bk. Rev. Ind.	Science Fiction Book Review Index
		Sci. Res. Abstr.	Science Research Abstracts
		Sel. Water Res. Abstr.	Selected Water Resources Abstracts
RADAR	Repertoire Analytique de Revues de Quebec	Sinop. Odontol.	Sinopse de Odontologia
RAPRA	Rubber & Plastics Research Association of Great Britain	Soc. Sci. Ind.	Social Sciences Index
		Soc. Work. Res. & Abstr.	Social Work Research & Abstracts (Formerly: Abstracts for Social Workers)
R.G.	Readers' Guide to Periodical Literature		
RILA	RILA (International Repertory of the Literature of Art)	Sociol. Abstr.	Sociological Abstracts
		Sociol. Educ. Abstr.	Sociology of Education Abstracts
RILM	RILM Abstracts of Music Literature	Soils & Fert.	Soils & Fertilizers
Ref. Zh.	Referativnyi Zhurnal	Solid St. Abstr.	Solid State Abstracts
Rehabil. Lit.	Rehabilitation Literature	Speleol. Abstr.	Speleological Abstracts
Rel. & Theol. Abstr.	Religious & Theological Abstracts	Stand. Philip. Per. Ind.	Standard Philippine Periodicals Index
Rel. Ind. One	Religion Index One: Periodicals (Formerly: Index to Religious Periodicals)	Stat. Theor. Meth. Abstr.	Statistical Theory and Method Abstracts
		Sugar Ind. Abstr.	Sugar Industry Abstracts
Rel. Per.	Index to Religious Periodicals (Now: Religion Index One: Periodicals)		
		T.C.E.A.	Theoretical Chemical Engineering Abstracts
Rep. Biomed	Repertoire Biomed	Tech. Educ. Abstr.	Technical Education Abstracts
Res. Educ.	Research in Education		
Res. High. Educ. Abstr.	Research into Higher Education Abstracts	Tech. Zentralbl.	Technisches Zentralblatt
		Text. Tech. Dig.	Textile Technology Digest
Res. Indicat. Petrol.	Resumos Indicativos do Petroleo	Theol. & Rel. Ind.	Theological & Religious Index
		Therm. Abstr.	Thermal Abstracts (Now: International Building Services Abstracts)
Rev. Appl. Entomol.	Review of Applied Entomology		
Rev. Appl. Mycol.	Review of Applied Mycology	Tob. Abstr.	Tobacco Abstracts
Rev. Plant Path.	Review of Plant Pathology	Top Manage. Abstr.	Top Management Abstracts
Rheol. Abstr.	Rheology Abstracts		
Rural Recreat. Tour. Abstr.	Rural Recreation and Tourism Abstracts	Trans. Res. Abstr.	Transportation Research Abstracts (Formerly: Highway Research Abstracts)
		Trop. Abstr.	Tropical Abstracts
		Trop. Dis. Bull.	Tropical Disease Bulletin
S.A. Waterabstr.	S.A. (South Africa) Waterabstracts		
SSCI	Social Science Citation Index		
Saf. Sci. Abstr.	Safety Science Abstracts Journal	Urb. Aff. Abstr.	Urban Affairs Abstracts

Vert.File Ind.	Vertical File Index	Work Rel.Abstr.	Work Related Abstracts (Formerly: Employment Related Abstracts)
Vet.Bull.	Veterinary Bulletin		
Virol.Abstr.	Virology Abstracts		
Vis.Ind.	Vision Index	World Agri. Econ.& Rural Sociol.Abstr.	World Agricultural Economics & Rural Sociology Abstracts
		World Alum. Abstr.	World Aluminum Abstracts
W.R.C.Inf.	W.R.C. Information (Water Research Centre) (Formerly: Water Pollution Abstracts)	World Fish. Abstr.	World Fisheries Abstracts
		World Surf. Coat.	World Surface Coatings Abstracts
Water Pollut. Abstr.	Water Pollution Abstracts (Now: W.R.C. Information)	World Text. Abstr.	World Textile Abstracts
Water Resour. Abstr.	Water Resources Abstracts		
Weed Abstr.	Weed Abstracts		
Wild Life Rev.	Wild Life Review	Zent.Math.	Zentralblatt fuer Mathematik und ihre Grenzgebiete
Wom.Stud. Abstr.	Women's Studies Abstracts	Zoo.Rec.	Zoological Record

Money Symbols

SYMBOL	UNIT	COUNTRY
Arg.$	peso	Argentina
As.	annas	Pakistan
Aus.$	dollars	Australia
B.	bahts	Thailand
B.$	dollars	Borneo (Brunei)
Bl.	balboas	Panama
Bol.$	peso	Bolivia
Bs.	bolivares	Venezuela
C.$	cordobas	Nicaragua
Can.$	dollars	Canada
Col.	colones	Costa Rica, El Salvador
Col.$	peso	Colombia
Cr.$	cruzeiros	Brazil
ctms.	centimes; centimos; centesimos	various
cvs.	centavos	various
d.	pence	Great Britain
DH.	dirhams	Morocco
DM.	marks	West Germany
din.	dinars	Yugoslavia
$	dollars; pesos	various
Dr.	drachmas	Greece
EAs.	shillings	East Africa
Esc.	escudos	Portugal
Eth.$	dollars	Ethiopia
F.	franc	France
fl.	florins or guilders	The Netherlands, Surinam
FMG.	francs	Malagasy Republic
Fmk.	marks; markkas	Finland
Fr.	francs	Belgium, Switzerland
Fr. CFA	francs	African Financial Community
Ft.	forints	Hungary
Gde.	gourdes	Haiti
G.$	dollars	Guyana
g.	guaranies	Paraguay
HK.$	dollars	Hong Kong
I.D.	dinars	Iran, Iraq
Jam.$	dollar	Jamaica
K.	kwacha	Zambia
Kcs.	koruny	Czechoslovakia
Kop.	kopecks	U.S.S.R.
Kr.	kroner; kronor	Scandinavian countries
L.	lempira; lira	Honduras, Italy
Le.	Leones	Sierra Leone
lei	lei	Romania
lv.	leva	Bulgaria
M.	marks	East Germany
M.$	dollars	Malaya
Mex.$	pesos	Mexico
Mils.	mils	Cyprus
$m.n.	moneda nacional	various
n.	ngwee	Zambia
NC.	New Cedis	Ghana
NT.$	dollars	Taiwan
N.Z.$	dollars	New Zealand
p.	pesewas; pence	Ghana, Gt. Britain
P.	pesos	various
P.T.	piasters	Egypt, Syria, Turkey
pf.	pfennigs	Germany
£	pounds	Gt. Britain
£E	pounds	Egypt
I£	pounds	Israel
£L	pounds	Lebanon, Libya
£N	pounds	Nigeria
£S	pounds	Syria
ptas.	pesetas	Spain
Q.	quetzales	Guatemala
R.	rands	South Africa
RD.$	peso	Dominican Republic
Rhod.$	dollars	Rhodesia
Rps.	rupiahs	Indonesia
Rs.	riels; rupees; rials	Cambodia, Ceylon, India, Pakistan, Iran
Rub.	rubles	U.S.S.R.
S/	sucres, soles	Ecuador, Peru
S.	schillings	Austria
S.$	dollars	Singapore
s.	shillings	Gt. Britain
TL.	pounds	Turkey
T.T.$	dollars	Trinidad
Urg.$	Pesos	Uruguay
VN.$	dollars	Vietnam
Won	won (hwan)	Korea
Yen	yen	Japan
Zl.	zlotys	Poland

Micropublishers

AMS	AMS Press, Inc., 56 East 13th St., New York, NY 10003
BLH	Bell & Howell Micro Photo Division, Old Mansfield Rd., Wooster, OH 44691
BLI	Balch Institute, 1627 Fidelity Bldg., 123 S. Broad St., Philadelphia, PA 19109
CLA	Canadian Library Association, Microfilm Project, 151 Sparks St., Ottawa, Ont. K1P SE3, Canada
EDR	Eric Document Reproduction Service, National Institutes of Health, 19th and M Sts., Washington, D.C. 20208
FCM	Fairchild Microfilms, Visuals Division, Fairchild Publications, Inc., 7 East 12th St., New York, NY 10003
GLB	Gaylord Bros. Inc., P.O. Box 61, Syracuse, NY 13201
GMC	General Microfilm Co., 100 Inman St., Cambridge, MA 02139
HPL	Harvester Press Ltd., 2 Stanford Terrace, Hassocks, North Brighton, England
IDC	Inter Documentation Co. A.G., Poststr. 14, Zug, Switzerland
JAI	Johnson Associates, Inc., P.O. Box 1017, Greenwich, CT 06830
JOH	Johnson Reprint Microeditions, 111 Fifth Ave., New York, NY 10003
JRC	Johnson Research Corp., 2099 New Highway, Farmingdale, NY 11735
JSC	J.S. Canner & Co., 49-65 Lansdowne St., Boston, MA 02110
KTO	KTO Microform Division, Route 100, Millwood, NY 10546
LCP	The Library of Congress, Photoduplication Service, 10 First St., S.E., Washington, DC 20540
LIB	Library Microfilms, 737 Loma Verde Ave., Palo Alto, CA 94303
MCA	Microfilming Corporation of America, 21 Harristown Rd., Glen Rock, NJ 07452
MCE	Microcard Editions, 5500 South Valentia Way, Englewood, CO 80110
MIM	Microforms International Marketing Co. (subsidiary of Pergamon Press, Inc., Maxwell House, Fairview Park, Elmsford, NY 10523
MML	Micromedia Limited, Box 34, Station S, Toronto, Canada M5M 4L6
MMP	McLaren Micropublishing, P.O. Box 972, Station F, Toronto, Canada M4Y 2N9
NBI	Newsbank Inc., P.O. Box 645, 135 E. Putnam Ave., Greenwich, CT 06830
NTI	National Technical Information Service, 5285 Port Royal Rd., Springfield, VA 22151
NYT	New York Times Information Bank, 229 West 43rd St., New York, NY 10036
OMP	Oxford Microform Publications Ltd. (member of Blackwell Group), Blue Boar St., Oxford OX1 4EY, England
PMC	Princeton Microfilm Corp., Alexander Rd., Princeton, NJ 08540
RRI	Rothman Reprints, Inc., 57 Leuning St., South Hackensack, NJ 07606
TMI	Tennessee Microfilms, P.O. Box 1096, Nashville, TN 37202
UMI	University Microfilms International, 300 North Zeeb Rd., Ann Arbor, MI 48106 (University Microfilms International Ltd., 18 Bedford Row, WC1R 4EJ, London, England)
UNM	University of Michigan Library, Interlibrary Lending, Circulation Dept. Harlan Hatcher Graduate Library, Ann Arbor, MI 48104
UNW	University of Wisconsin Library, Interlibrary Loan Dept., 728 State St., Madison, WI 53706
WDS	William Dawson & Sons Ltd., Cannon House, Folkestone, Kent CT19 5EE England
WMP	World Microfilm Publications Ltd., 62 Queen's Grove, London NW8 6ER England

Country of Publication Codes

This list of countries and their codes has been taken from the list used by the Library of Congress in the MARC II format, 1972. The list used here is not the complete list of the MARC II format and is limited to presently existing national entities. The states of the United States, provinces and territories of Canada, divisions of the United Kingdom, and republics of the USSR are not listed separately.

The codes are mnemonic in most cases. The first letter of the two letter-code is the same as the first letter of the place name. Special codes not in the MARC format are used for publications of two international organizations: EI for European Communities and UN for United Nations and related organizations.

AA	Albania	CK	Colombia	GO	Gabon	LB	Liberia
AE	Algeria	CL	Chile	GP	Guadeloupe	LE	Lebanon
AF	Afghanistan	CM	Cameroon	GR	Greece	LH	Liechtenstein
AG	Argentina	CN	Canada	GT	Guatemala	LO	Lesotho
AN	Andorra	CR	Costa Rica	GU	Guam	LS	Laos
AO	Angola	CS	Czechoslovakia	GV	Guinea	LU	Luxembourg
AQ	Antigua	CU	Cuba	GW	Germany, West BRD	LY	Libya
AS	American Samoa	CX	Central African Republic	GY	Guyana (also British Guiana)	MC	Monaco
AT	Australia					MF	Mauritius
AU	Austria	CY	Cyprus			MG	Malagasy Republic (Madagascar)
AY	Antarctica	DK	Denmark	HK	Hong Kong		
BB	Barbados	DM	Benin	HO	Honduras	MH	Macao
BD	Burundi	DR	Dominican Republic	HT	Haiti	MK	Muscat and Oman
BE	Belgium			HU	Hungary	ML	Mali
BF	Bahamas	EC	Ecuador			MM	Malta
BG	Bangladesh	EG	Equatorial Guinea	IC	Iceland	MP	Mongolia
BH	Belize	EI	European Communities	IE	Ireland	MR	Morocco
BL	Brazil			II	India	MU	Mauritania
BM	Bermuda	ES	El Salvador	IO	Indonesia	MW	Malawi
BO	Bolivia	ET	Ethiopia	IQ	Iraq	MX	Mexico
BR	Burma			IR	Iran	MY	Malaysia
BS	Botswana	FG	French Guiana	IS	Israel	MZ	Mozambique
BT	Bhutan	FI	Finland	IT	Italy		
BU	Bulgaria	FJ	Fiji	IV	Ivory Coast	NA	Netherlands Antilles
BX	Brunei	FR	France				
CB	Cambodia	FT	Djibouti	JA	Japan	NE	Netherlands
CC	China, Mainland			JM	Jamaica	NG	Niger
CD	Chad	GE	Germany, East DDR	JO	Jordan	NL	New Caledonia
CE	Sri Lanka					NO	Norway
CF	Congo (Brazzaville)	GH	Ghana	KE	Kenya	NP	Nepal
		GI	Gibraltar	KN	Korea, North	NQ	Nicaragua
CH	China, Republic of	GL	Greenland	KO	Korea, South	NR	Nigeria
CJ	Cayman Islands	GM	Gambia	KU	Kuwait	NU	Nauru

xxiii

COUNTRY OF PUBLICATION CODES

NZ	New Zealand	SJ	Sudan	TU	Turkey	VE	Venezuela
		SL	Sierra Leone	TZ	Tanzania	VI	U.S. Virgin Islands
PE	Peru	SM	San Marino			VN	Vietnam
PH	Philippines	SO	Somalia	UA	Egyptian Arab		
PK	Pakistan	SP	Spain		Republic	WS	Western Samoa
PL	Poland	SQ	Swaziland	UG	Uganda		
PN	Panama	SR	Surinam	UI	United Kingdom	XC	Maldive Islands
PO	Portugal	SU	Saudi Arabia		Miscellaneous		
PP	Papua New Guinea	SW	Sweden		Islands	YE	Yemen
PR	Puerto Rico	SX	South-West Africa	UK	United Kingdom	YS	Southern Yemen
PY	Paraguay	SY	Syria	UN	United Nations		and Aden
		SZ	Switzerland		and Related	YU	Yugoslavia
					Organizations		
RE	Reunion						
RH	Zimbabwe	TG	Togo	UR	USSR	ZA	Zambia
RM	Rumania	TH	Thailand	US	United States	ZR	Zaire
RW	Rwanda	TI	Tunisia	UV	Upper Volta		
RY	Ryuku Islands	TO	Tonga	UY	Uruguay		
		TR	Trinidad and				
			Tobago				
SA	South Africa	TS	United Arab	VB	British Virgin Islands		
SG	Senegal		Emirates	VC	Vatican City		
SI	Singapore						

xxiv

International Standard Serial Number (ISSN)

1. *What is the ISSN?*

An internationally accepted, concise, unique and unambiguous code for the identification of serial publications. One ISSN represents one serial.

The ISSN consists of seven numbers with an eighth check digit calculated according to Modulus 11 and used to verify the number in computer processing. A hyphen is printed after the fourth digit, as a visual aid, and the abbreviation ISSN precedes the number.

A code indicating country of publication may be printed preceding the ISSN as an additional identifier; for example, UK ISSN 1234-5679.

2. *How did the ISSN evolve as an international system?*

The International Organization for Standardization Technical Committee 46 (ISO/TC 46) is the agency responsible for the development of the ISSN as an international standard. The organization responsible for the administration and assignment of ISSN is the International Center (IC) of the International Serials Data System (ISDS). The IC/ISDS, supported by the French government and Unesco, is located in Paris.

In the interim period between the ISO/TC 46 approval of the ISSN draft and the time when the international administrative system (IC/ISDS) became operative, 70,000 titles in the serials data base of the R. R. Bowker Company (*Ulrich's International Periodicals Directory* and *Irregular Serials and Annuals*) were assigned ISSN. The next serials data base numbered was the *New Serial Titles 1950–1970* cumulation listing 220,000 titles, cumulated, converted to magnetic tape and published by the R. R. Bowker Company in collaboration with the Serials Record Division of the Library of Congress. These two data bases were used as the starting base for the implementation of the ISSN.

3. *What types of publications are assigned ISSN?*

For assignment of ISSN, a serial is defined by the International Serials Data System as: "a publication in print or in non-print form, issued in successive parts, usually having numerical or chronological designations, and intended to be continued indefinitely."

4. *How will ISSN be used?*

ISSN, the tool for communication of basic information about a serial title with a minimum of error, will be used for such processes as ordering, billing, inventory control, abstracting, indexing, etc. Authors will use ISSN for copyright. In library processes, ISSN will be used in operations such as acquisitions, claiming, binding, accessioning, shelving, cooperative cataloging, circulation, interlibrary loans, retrieval of requests.

5. *May a publication have an International Standard Book Number (ISBN) and an ISSN?*

Yes! Monographic series (separate works issued indefinitely under a common title, generally in a uniform format with numeric designation) and annuals or titles planned to be issued indefinitely under the same title may be defined as serials. The ISSN is assigned to the serial title, while an ISBN is assigned to each individual title or monograph in the series.

A new ISBN is assigned to each volume or edition by the publisher, while the ISSN, which is assigned by the International Center, national or regional center, remains the same for each issue. Both numbers should be printed on the copyright page of each volume, with initials or words preceding each number for immediate identification. With the availability of both ISSN and ISBN, the problem of defining the overlap of serials and monographs has been resolved.

SAMPLE TITLE

Statistical Research Monographs
ISSN: 0081-5020

   I. Passage Problem for a Stationary Markov Chain
      J. H. B. Kemperman
      1961 Cloth ISBN 0-226-43050-2

  II. Statistical Inference for Markov Processes
      Patrick Billingsley
      1961 ISBN 0-226-05077-7

 III. Sequential Identification and Ranking Procedures
      Robert E. Bechhofer, Jack Kiefer
        and Milton Sobel
      1965 Cloth ISBN 0-226-04035-6

 IV. The Analysis of Frequency Data
      Shelby J. Haberman
      1974 Cloth ISBN 0-226-31184-8

6. *Where should the ISSN appear on the serial?*

In a prominent position on or in each issue of the serial, such as front cover, back cover, title or copyright pages. ISDS recommends that the ISSN of a periodical be printed, whenever possible, in the upper right corner of the front cover.

Promotional and descriptive materials about the serial should include the ISSN.

7. *When a title changes is a new ISSN assigned?*

The International Center, national or regional center of ISDS will determine if a new assignment is necessary. Publishers should report changes to their respective centers.

8. *How does a publisher apply for an ISSN?*

The national, regional or International Center of ISDS must be provided with bibliographic evidence of the serial, including a copy of the title page and cover.

Publishers should contact the national library or bibliographic center in the country where they are publishing, for details.

There is no charge to the publisher for the assignment of ISSN.

Notes On Subjects

Titles previously listed under the headings *Business and Industry, Economics, Medical Sciences* and *Religions and Theology* have been reclassified according to a more specific classification scheme. All titles related to these subjects were reviewed and titles reclassified according to the new scheme.

Advertising and Public Relations
Business and Economics
Business and Economics-Accounting
Business and Economics-Banking and Finance
Business and Economics-Chamber of Commerce Publications
Business and Economics-Cooperatives
Business and Economics-Domestic Commerce
Business and Economics-Economic Situation and Conditions
Business and Economics-Economic Systems and Theories, Economic History
Business and Economics-International Commerce
Business and Economics-International Development
Business and Economics-Investments
Business and Economics-Labor and Industrial Relations
Business and Economics-Macroeconomics
Business and Economics-Management
Business and Economics-Marketing and Purchasing
Business and Economics-Office Equipment and Services
Business and Economics-Personnel Management
Business and Economics-Production of Goods and Services
Business and Economics-Public Finance
Business and Economics-Small Business
Business and Economics-Trade and Industrial Directories

Consumer Education and Protection
Insurance
Labor Unions
Occupations and Careers
Patents, Trademarks and Copyrights
Real Estate

Birth Control
Drug Abuse and Alcoholism
Gerontology and Geriatrics
Medical Sciences
Medical Sciences-Allergology and Immunology
Medical Sciences-Anaesthesiology
Medical Sciences-Cancer
Medical Sciences-Cardiovascular Diseases
Medical Sciences-Chiropractics, Homeopathy, Osteopathy
Medical Sciences-Communicable Diseases
Medical Sciences-Dentistry
Medical Sciences-Dermatology and Venereology
Medical Sciences-Endocrinology
Medical Sciences-Experimental Medicine, Laboratory Technique
Medical Sciences-Forensic Sciences
Medical Sciences-Gastroenterology
Medical Sciences-Hematology
Medical Sciences-Hypnosis
Medical Sciences-Nurses and Nursing
Medical Sciences-Obstetrics and Gynecology
Medical Sciences-Ophthalmology and Optometry
Medical Sciences-Orthopedics and Traumatology
Medical Sciences-Otorhinolaryngology
Medical Sciences-Pediatrics
Medical Sciences-Psychiatry and Neurology

Medical Sciences-Radiology and Nuclear Medicine
Medical Sciences-Respiratory Diseases
Medical Sciences-Rheumatology
Medical Sciences-Surgery
Medical Sciences-Urology and Nephrology
Pharmacy and Pharmacology
Physical Fitness and Hygiene
Public Health and Safety

Ethnic Interests
Religions and Theology
Religions and Theology-Islamic
Religions and Theology-Judaic
Religions and Theology-Oriental
Religions and Theology-Protestant

Religions and Theology-Roman Catholic
Religions and Theology-Other Sects

Titles previously listed under the headings *Abstracting and Indexing Services*, *Bibliographies* and *Statistics* have been reclassified according to a more specific classification scheme. These titles were reviewed and reclassified to appear under the specific subject to which they relate. A new subdivision *Abstracting, Bibliographies, Statistics* appears under each heading. The main entry for each title appears under the specific subject and subdivision. Cross references appear under the general subject when appropriate. Titles which cover several subjects are listed under the primary subject with cross references under the additional subjects. Titles with universal subject coverage continue to appear under the general headings.

Subjects

ENGLISH	FRENCH	GERMAN	SPANISH
Abstracting and Indexing Services	Services d'Analyse et Indexage	Referate-und Indexdienste	Servicios de Extractos e Indices
Adventure and Romance	Aventure et Romance	Abenteuer und Liebesgeschichte	Aventura y Romance
Advertising and Public Relations	Publicité et Relations Publiques	Reklamewesen und Public Relations	Publicidad y Relaciones Públicas
Aeronautics and Space Flight	Aéronautique et Astronautique	Luft- und Raumfahrt	Aeronáutica y Vuelo Espacial
Agriculture	Agriculture	Landwirtschaft	Agricultura
Agricultural Economics	Agriculture Economique	Agrarökonomie	Economía Agrícola
Agricultural Equipment	Outillage Agricole	Gerate	Aparatos Agrícolas
Crop Production and Soil	Récolte et Terre	Produkte und Boden	Producción de Cosecha, Tierra
Dairying and Dairy Products	Production Laitière	Milchwirtschaft	Lechería y Productos Lácteos
Feed, Flour and Grain	Pature, Farine et Grain	Futter, Mehl und Getreide	Forraje, Granos y Harina
Poultry and Livestock	Elevage	Geflügel-und Viehwirtschaft	Ganaderia
Anthropology	Anthropologie	Anthropologie	Antropología
Archaeology	Archeologie	Archaeologie	Arqueología
Architecture	Architecture	Architektur	Arquitectura
Art	Art	Kunst	Arte
Astrology	Astrologie	Astrologie	Astrología
Astronomy	Astronomie	Astronomie	Astronomía
Beauty Culture	Soins de Beauté	Schönheitspflege	Belleza Personal
Perfumes and Cosmetics	Parfums et Cosmétiques	Kosmetik und Parfüme	Perfumes y Cosméticos
Beverages	Boissons	Getränke	Bebidas
Bibliographies	Bibliographies	Bibliographien	Bibliografías
Biography	Biographie	Biographie	Biografía
Biology	Biologie	Biologie	Biología
Biological Chemistry	Chimie Biologique	Biochemie	Química Biológica
Biophysics	Biophysique	Biophysik	Biofísica
Botany	Botanique	Botanik	Botánica
Cytology and Histology	Cytologie et Histologie	Zytologie und Histologie	Citología e Histología
Entomology	Entomologie	Entomologie	Entomología
Genetics	Génétique	Genetik	Genética
Microbiology	Microbiologie	Mikrobiologie	Microbiología
Microscopy	Microscopie	Mikroskopie	Microscopia
Ornithology	Ornithologie	Ornithologie	Ornitología
Physiology	Physiologie	Physiologie	Fisiología
Zoology	Zoologie	Zoologie	Zoología
Birth Control	Réglementation de la Natalité	Geburtenregelung	Reglamentación del Nacimiento
Blind	Aveugles	Blinde	Ciegos
Building and Construction	Batiment et Construction	Bauwesen	Edificios y Construcción
Carpentry and Woodwork	Charpenterie et Menuiserie	Zimmerhandwerk und Holzbau	Carpintería y Ebanistería
Hardware	Quincaillerie	Metallbaustoffe	Quincalla
Business and Economics	Affaires et Economie	Wirtschaft und Handel	Negocios y Economía
Accounting	Comptabilite	Rechnungswesen	Contabilidad
Banking and Finance	Banque et Finance	Bank-und Finanzwesen	Bancos y Finanzas
Chamber of Commerce Publications	Publications des Chambres de Commerce	Veröffentlichungen von Handelskammern	Publicaciones de las Cámaras de Comercio
Cooperatives	Coopératives	Genossenschaften	Cooperativos
Domestic Commerce	Commerce Interieur	Binnenhandel	Comercio Interior
Economic Situation and Conditions	Situations et Conditions Economiques	Wirtschaftliche Situation und Verhältnisse	Situaciones y Condiciones Económicas
Economic Systems and Theories, Economic History	Systemes et Théories Economiques, Histoire Economique	Ökonomische Systeme und Theorien, Wirtschaftsgeschichte	Sistemas y Teorías Económicos, Historia Ecónomica
International Commerce	Commerce International	Aussenhandel	Comercio Internacional
International Development and Assistance	Développement et Assistance Internationaux	Internationale Entwicklungshilfe	Desarrollo y Asistencia Internacionales
Investments	Investissements	Investitionen	Inversiones
Labor and Industrial Relations	Travail et Relations Industrielles	Arbeits- und Industrielle Beziehungen	Trabajo y Relaciones Industriales
Macroeconomics	Macroeconomique	Makroökonomie	Macroeconomía
Management	Gestion	Betriebsführung	Gerencia
Marketing and Purchasing	Cours et Achats	Marketing und Kauf	Compra y Venta
Office Equipment and Services	Matériel et Entretien de Bureaux	Büroeinrichtung und Service	Equipo y Servicios de Oficinas
Personnel Management	Direction de Personnel	Personal Führung	Dirección de Empleados
Production of Goods and Services	Production	Produktion	Producción
Public Finance, Taxation	Finance Publique, Impots	Staatsfinanzen, Steuerwesen	Finanza Publica, Impuestos
Small Business	Petites et Moyennes Affaires	Kleinbetrieb	Negocios Pequeños
Trade and Industrial Directories	Directoires de Commerce et Industrie	Firmenverzeichnisse	Directorios de Comercio y Industria
Ceramics, Glass and Pottery	Céramique, Verrerie et Poterie	Keramik, Glas und Töpferei	Cerámica, Vidrio y Porcelana
Chemistry	Chimie	Chemie	Química
Analytical Chemistry	Chimie Analytique	Analytische Chemie	Química Analítica
Crystallography	Cristallographie	Kristallographie	Cristalografía
Electrochemistry	Electrochimie	Elektrochemie	Electroquímica
Inorganic Chemistry	Chimie Inorganique	Anorganische Chemie	Química Inorgánica
Organic Chemistry	Chimie Organique	Organische Chemie	Química Orgánica
Physical Chemistry	Chimie Physique	Physikalische Chemie	Fisicoquímica
Children and Youth	Enfance et Adolescence	Kinder und Jugendliche	Niños y Jóvenes
About	Au Sujet de	Über	Acerca
For	Pour	Für	Para
Civil Defense	Defense Civile	Ziviler Bevölkerungsschutz	Defensa Civil
Classical Studies	Etudes Classiques	Klassische Studien	Estudios Clásicos
Cleaning and Dyeing	Nettoyage et Teinturerie	Reinigen und Farben	Limpieza y Tintura
Clothing Trade	Vêtement	Bekleidungsgewerbe	Industria de Vestidos
Fashions	Mode	Moden	Modas
Clubs	Clubs	Klubs	Clubes
College and Alumni	Université et Diplomés	Universitäten und Hochschul-Absolventen	Universidades y Exalumnos

SUBJECTS

Communications	Communications	Nachrichtentechnik	Comunicaciones
Postal Affairs	Postes	Postwesen	Correo
Radio and Television	Radio et Télévision	Rundfunk und Fernsehen	Radio y Televisión
Telephone and Telegraph	Téléphone et Télégraphe	Telephon und Telegraph	Teléfono y Telégrafo
Computer Technology and Applications	Technologie et Applications des Machines à Calculer	Computertechnik und Anwendung	Tecnología y Aplicaciones de Calculadoras
Conservation	Conservation	Landschaftsschutz	Conservación
Consumer Education and Protection	Protection de Consomateur	Verbraucherswirtschaftsschutz	Protección del Consumidor
Criminology and Law Enforcement	Criminologie et Police	Kriminologie und Strafvollzug	Criminología y Acción Policial
Dance	Danse	Tanz	Baile
Deaf	Sourds	Gehörlose	Sordos
Drug Abuse and Alcoholism	Toxicomanie et Alcoolisme	Rauschgiftsucht und Alkoholismus	Drogadismo y Alcoholismo
Earth Sciences	Sciences Géologiques	Wissenschaften der Erde	Ciencias Geológicas
Geology	Géologie	Geologie	Geología
Geophysics	Géophysique	Geophysik	Geofísica
Hydrology	Hydrologie	Hydrologie	Hidrología
Oceanography	Océanographie	Ozeanographie	Oceanografía
Education	Education	Bildungswesen	Educación
Adult Education	Enseignement des Adultes	Erwachsenenbildung	Enseñanza de Adultos
Guides to Schools and Colleges	Guides d'Ecoles et Colleges	Führer zur Schulen und Universitaten	Guías de Escuelas y Colegios
Higher Education	Enseignement Supérieur	Hochschulwesen	Enseñanza Superior
International Education Programs	Programmes d'Education Internationale	Internationale Erziehungs-Programme	Programas de Enseñanza Internacional
Organization and Administration	Organisation et Administration	Organisation und Verwaltung	Administración y Dirección
Special Education and Rehabilitation	Enseignement Special et Réhabilitation	Fachunterricht und Rehabilitierung	Enseñanza Especial y Rehabilitación
Teaching Methods and Curriculum	Méthodes Pédagogiques et Programmes Scolaires	Lehrmethoden und Lehrplan	Métodos de Enseñanza y Plan de Estudios
Electricity and Electrical Engineering	Electricité et Technique Electrique	Elektrizität und Elektrotechnik	Electricidad y Electrotécnica
Encyclopedias and General Almanacs	Encyclopédies et Almanachs Générales	Enzyklopädien und Allgemeine Nachschlagewerke	Enciclopedias y Almanaques Generales
Energy	Energie	Energie	Energía
Engineering	Génie	Ingenieurwesen	Ingeniería
Chemical Engineering	Génie Chimique	Chemieingenieurwesen	Ingeniería Química
Civil Engineering	Génie Civil	Bauingenieurwesen	Ingeniería Civil
Hydraulic Engineering	Génie Hydraulique	Wasserbau	Ingeniería Hidráulica
Mechanical Engineering	Génie Mécanique	Maschinenbau	Ingeniería Mecánica
Environmental Studies	Science de l'Environnement	Umweltschutz	Ciencias Ecológicas
Ethnic Interests	Publications de l'Orientation Ethnique	Veröffentlichungen von Minoritäten	Publicaciones de Temas Etnicos
Fire Prevention	Précaution contre l'Incendie	Brandbekaempfung	Prevención del Fuego
Fish and Fisheries	Poisson et Peche	Fische und Fischerei	Pesca y Pescados
Folklore	Folklore	Volkskunde	Folklore
Food and Food Industries	Alimentation et Industries Alimentaires	Nahrungsmittel und Lebensmittelindustrie	Alimentos e Industrias Alimenticias
Bakers and Confectioners	Boulangerie et Confiserie	Bäcker-und Konditorgewerbe	Panaderías y Dulcerías
Grocery Trade	Epicerie	Kolonialwarenhandel	Abacerías
Forest and Forestry	Forêts et Exploitation Forestière	Forstwesen und Waldwirtschaft	Bosques y Selvicultura
Lumber and Wood	Bois	Holz	Maderas
Funerals	Funérailles	Beerdigungen	Funerales
Gardening and Horticulture	Jardinage et Horticulture	Gartenpflege und Gartenbau	Jardinería y Horticultura
Florist Trade	Commerce des Fleurs	Blumenhandel	Floristas
Genealogy and Heraldry	Généalogie et Science Héraldique	Genealogie und Wappenkunde	Genealogía y Heráldica
General Interest Periodicals (Subdivided by country)	Publications d'Intérêt Général (Selon pays)	Allgemeine Zeitschriften (nach Land)	Periódicos de Interés General (por país)
Geography	Géographie	Geographie	Geografía
Gerontology and Geriatrics	Gérontologie	Gerontologie	Gerontologiá y Geriátrica
Giftware and Toys	Cadeaux et Jouets	Geschenkartikel und Spielwaren	Regalos y Juguetes
Heating, Plumbing and Refrigeration	Chauffage, Plomberie et Réfrigération	Heizung, Kühlung und Installation	Caletacción, Plomería y Refrigeración
History	Histoire	Geschichte	Historia
History of Africa	Histoire de l'Afrique	Geschichte-Afrika	Historia de Africa
History of Asia	Histoire de l'Asie	Geschichte-Asien	Historia de Asia
History of Australasia	Histoire de l'Australasie	Geschichte-Australasien	Historia de Australasia
History of Europe	Histoire de l'Europe	Geschichte-Europa	Historia de la Europa
History of North and South America	Histoire de l'Amérique du Nord et du Sud	Geschichte-Nord- und Südamerika	Historia de la América del Norte y de la del Sur
History of Near East	Histoire du Proche-Orient	Geschichte-Nahe Osten	Historia del Cercano Oriente
Hobbies	Passe-Temps	Hobbies	Pasatiempos
Antiques	Antiquités	Antiquitäten	Antiguedades
Needlework	Travaux à l'Aiguille	Nadelarbeiten	Bordados
Numismatics	Numismatique	Numismatik	Numismática
Philately	Philatélie	Philatelie	Filatelia
Home Economics	Economie Domestique	Hauswirtschaft	Economía Doméstica
Homosexuality	Homosexualisme	Homosexualität	Homosexualismo
Hospitals	Hôpitaux	Krankenhäuser	Hospitales
Hotels and Restaurants	Hôtels et Restaurants	Hotels und Restaurants	Hoteles y Restaurantes
Housing and Urban Planning	Lógement et Urbanisme	Wohnungswesen und Städteplanung	Viviendas y Urbanismo
Humanities: Comprehensive Works	Humanités: Oeuvres Comprehensives	Geisteswissenschaften	Humanidades: Obras Comprensivas
Industrial Health and Safety	Médecine du Travail et Prevention	Arbeitsmedizin und Arbeitsschutz	Sanidad y Seguridad del Trabajo
Instruments	Instruments	Instrumente	Instrumentos
Insurance	Assurances	Versicherungswesen	Seguros
Interior Design and Decoration	Agencements Intérieurs et Décoration	Innenarchitektur und Innenausstattung	Diseño del Interior y Ornamentación
Furniture and House Furnishing	Meubles et Articles pour la Maison	Möbel und Wohnungseinrichtung	Muebles y Articulos para el Hogar
Jewelry, Clocks and Watches	Bijouterie et Horlogerie	Schmuck und Uhren	Joyería y Relojería
Journalism	Journalisme	Journalismus	Periodismo
Labor Unions	Syndicalisme	Gewerkschaften	Sindicatos
Law	Droit	Recht	Derecho
International Law	Droit International	Völkerrecht	Derecho Internacional

SUBJECTS

Leather and Fur Industries	Maroquinerie et Pelleterie	Leder und Pelz	Pieles y Cuero
Library and Information Science	Bibliothéconomie et Informatique	Bibliothek-und Informationswissenschaft	Bibliotecología y Ciencia de la Información
Linguistics	Linguistique	Sprachwissenschaft	Lingüística
Literary and Political Reviews	Revues Littéraires et Politiques	Literarische und Politische Zeitschriften	Revistas Literarias y Políticas
Literature	Litterature	Literatur	Literatura
Poetry	Poésie	Poesie	Poesía
Machinery	Machines	Maschinenwesen	Maquinaria
Mathematics	Mathématiques	Mathematik	Matemática
Medical Sciences	Sciences Médicales	Medizinische Wissenschaften	Ciencias Médicas
Allergology and Immunology	Allergologie et Immunologie	Allergie und Immunologie	Alergología e Imunología
Anaesthesiology	Anesthésiologie	Anaesthesiologie	Anestesiología
Cancer	Cancer	Krebs	Cancer
Cardiovascular Diseases	Maladies Cardiovasculaires	Kreislauferkrankungen	Enfermedades Cardiovasculares
Chiropractics, Homeopathy, Osteopathy	Chiropraxie, Homépathie, Ostéopathie	Chiropraktik, Homöopathie, Osteopathie	Quiropractica, Homeopatía, Osteopatia
Communicable Diseases	Maladies Contagieuses	Infektiöse Krankheiten	Enfermedades Contagiosas
Dentistry	Dentisterie	Zahnmedizin	Dentistería
Dermatology and Venereology	Dermatologie et Maladies Vénériennes	Dermatologie und Geschlechtskrankheiten	Dermatología y Venereología
Endocrinology	Endocrinologie	Endokrinologie	Endocrinología
Experimental Medicine, Laboratory Technique	Médecine Expérimentale, Techniques de Laboratoire	Versuchsmedizin, Laboratoriumstechnik	Medicina Experimental, Tecnicas del Laboratorio
Forensic Sciences	Médecine Légale	Gerichtliche Medizin	Ciencias Forenses
Gastroenterology	Gastroentérologie	Gastroenterologie	Gastroenterologia
Hematology	Hématologie	Hämatologie	Hematología
Hypnosis	Hypnose	Hypnose	Hipnotismo
Nurses and Nursing	Personnel et Soins Infirmiers	Krankenpflege	Enfermeras y Enfermería
Obstetrics and Gynecology	Obstétrique et Gynécologie	Gynäkologie und Geburtshilfe	Obstetricia y Ginecología
Ophthalmology and Optometry	Ophtalmologie et Optométrie	Opthalmologie und Optometrie	Oftalmología y Optometría
Orthopedics and Traumatology	Orthopédie et Traumatologie	Orthopädie und Traumatologie	Ortopedia y Traumatología
Otorhinolaryngology	Otorhinolaryngologie	Otorhinolaryngologie	Otorinolaringología
Pediatrics	Pédiatrie	Pädiatrie	Pediatría
Psychiatry and Neurology	Psychiatrie et Neurologie	Psychiatrie und Neurologie	Psiquiatría y Neurología
Radiology and Nuclear Medicine	Radiologie et Médecine Nucléaire	Radiologie und Nuklearmedizin	Radiología y Medicina Nuclear
Respiratory Diseases	Maladies Respiratoires	Atmungskrankheiten	Enfermedades Respiratorios
Rheumatology	Rhumatologie	Rheumatologie	Reumatologia
Surgery	Chirurgie	Chirurgie	Cirugía
Urology and Nephrology	Urologie et Néphrologie	Urologie und Nephrologie	Urología y Nefrología
Meetings and Congresses	Réunions et Congrès	Tagungen und Kongresse	Conferencias y Congresos
Metallurgy	Métallurgie	Metallurgie	Metalurgia
Welding	Soudure	Schweissen	Soldadura
Meteorology	Météorologie	Meteorologie	Meteorología
Metrology and Standardization	Métrologie et Standardisation	Mass-und Gewichtskunde, Normung	Metrología y Normalización
Military	Militaires	Militärwesen	Militares
Mines and Mining Industry	Mines et Resources Minières	Bergbau und Hüttenwesen	Minas y Minerales
Motion Pictures	Cinéma	Film und Kino	Películas
Museums and Art Galleries	Musées et Galleries	Museen und Kunstgalerien	Museos y Galerías del Arte
Music	Musique	Musik	Música
Nutrition and Dietetics	Nutrition et Diététique	Ernährung und Diätetik	Nutrición y Dieta
Occupations and Careers	Occupations et Carrières	Berufe	Empleos y Ocupaciones
Oriental Studies	Etudes Orientales	Orientalistik	Estudios Orientales
Packaging	Emballage	Verpackung	Empaque
Paints and Protective Coatings	Couleurs et Peintures	Farben	Pinturas y Manos Protectores
Paleontology	Paléontologie	Paleontologie	Paleontología
Paper and Pulp	Papier et Pulpe	Papier und Papierstoff	Papel y Pasta
Parapsychology and Occultism	Parapsychologie et Occultisme	Parapsychologie und Okkultismus	Parapsicología y Ocultismo
Patents, Trademarks and Copyrights	Brevets, Marques de Fabrique et Droits d'Auteur	Patente, Schutzmarken und Urheberrechte	Patentes, Marcas de Fabrica y Derechos de Autor
Petroleum and Gas	Pétrole et Gas Naturel	Petroleum und Gas	Petróleo y Gas Natural
Pets	Animaux Familiers	Haustiere	Animales Domésticos
Pharmacy and Pharmacology	Pharmacie et Pharmacologie	Pharmazie and Pharmakologie	Farmacia y Farmacología
Philosophy	Philosophie	Philosophie	Filosofía
Photography	Photographie	Photographie	Fotografía
Physical Fitness and Hygiene		Gesundheitszustand und Hygiene	Salud Fisica e Higiene
Physics	Physique	Physik	Física
Heat	Chaleur	Wärme	Calor
Mechanics	Mécanique	Mechanik	Mecánica
Nuclear Energy	Energie Nucléaire	Kernphysik	Energía Nuclear
Optics	Optique	Optik	Optica
Sound	Son	Schall	Sonido
Plastics	Plastiques	Kunststoffe	Plásticos
Political Sciences	Sciences Politiques	Politische Wissenschaften	Ciencias Políticas
Civil Rights	Droits Civiques	Bürgerrechte	Derechos Civiles
International Relations	Relations Internationales	Internationale Beziehungen	Relaciones Internacionales
Population Studies	Démographie	Bevölkerungswissenschaft	Demografía
Printing	Imprimerie	Druck	Imprenta
Psychology	Psychologie	Psychologie	Psicología
Public Administration	Administration Publique	Öffentliche Verwaltung	Administración Pública
Municipal Government	Gouvernement Municipal	Kommunalverwaltung	Gobierno Municipal
Public Health and Safety	Santé Publique et Prevention	Öffentliche Gesundheitspflege	Salud Pública y Seguridad
Publishing and Book Trade	Edition et Commerce du Livre	Verlagswesen und Buchhandel	Editoriales y Librería
Real Estate	Immobilières	Grundbesitz und Immobilien	Bienes Raíces

SUBJECTS

Religions and Theology	Religions et Théologie	Religion und Theologie	Religión y Teologia
Islamic	Islamique	islamische	Islámico
Judaic	Judaique	Jüdäistische	Judaismo
Oriental	Oriental	orientalische	Oriental
Protestant	Protestant	evangelische	Protestante
Roman Catholic	Catholique romain	römisch-katholische	Catolico romano
Other Sects	Autres sectes	andere Sekte	Otras sectas
Rubber	Caoutchouc	Gummi	Caucho
Sciences: Comprehensive Works	Sciences: Oeuvres Comprehensives	Wissenschaften: Umfassende Werke	Ciencias: Obras Comprensivas
Shoes and Boots	Chaussures et Bottes	Schuhe und Stiefel	Zapatos y Botas
Social Sciences: Comprehensive Works	Sciences Sociales: Oeuvres Comprehensives	Sozialwissenschaften: Umfassende Werke	Ciencias Sociales: Obras Comprensivas
Social Services and Welfare	Service Social et Protection Sociale	Sozialpflege und Fürsorge	Asistencia Social
Sociology	Sociologie	Soziologie	Sociología
Sound Recording and Reproduction	Enregistrement et Reproduction du Son	Tonaufnahme und Tonwiedergabe	Grabaciones y Reproducciones Sonoras
Sports and Games	Sports et Jeux	Sport und Spiele	Deportes y Juegos
Ball Games	Jeux de Balle	Ballspiele	Juegos de Pelota
Bicycles and Motorcycles	Bicyclettes et Motocyclettes	Fahrräder und Motorräder	Bicicletas y Motocicletas
Boats and Boating	Bateaux et Canotage	Boote und Bootssport	Botes
Horses and Horsemanship	Equitation	Pferde und Reitsport	Caballos y Equitación
Outdoor Life	Vie en Plein Air	Im Freien	Vida de Campo
Statistics	Statistique	Statistik	Estadísticas
Technology: Comprehensive Works	Technologie: Oeuvres Comprehensives	Technologie: Umfassende Werke	Tecnologia: Obras Comprensivas
Textile Industries and Fabrics	Textiles	Textil	Textiles y Telas
Theater	Théâtre	Theater	Teatro
Tobacco	Tabac	Tabak	Tabaco
Transportation	Transports	Transport	Transporte
Air Transport	Transport Aérien	Luftverkehr	Transporte Aéreo
Automobiles	Automobiles	Kraftfahrzeugen	Automóviles
Railroads	Chemins de Fer	Eisenbahnen	Ferrocarriles
Roads and Traffic	Routes et Circulation	Strassen und Strassenverkehr	Caminos y Circulación
Ships and Shipping	Navires et Transport Maritimes	Schiffe und Schiffahrt	Barcos y Embarques
Trucks and Trucking	Transports Routiers	Lastkraftwagen	Camiones
Travel and Tourism	Voyages et Tourisme	Reisen und Tourismus	Viajes y Turismo
Veterinary Sciences	Science Vétérinaire	Tierheilkunde	Veterinaria
Water Resources	Ressources de l'Eau	Wasserwirtschaft	Recursos de Agua
Women's Interests	Publications d'Intérêt Feminin	Veröffentlichungen für Frauen	Publicaciones de Temas Femininas

Cross-Index to Subjects

Abortion see BIRTH CONTROL 131
Abrasives see MACHINERY 582
ABSTRACTING AND INDEXING SERVICES 1
Accident Prevention see INDUSTRIAL HEALTH AND SAFETY 495, see also TRANSPORTATION - Roads and Traffic 874
ACCOUNTING 167
Acoustics see PHYSICS - Sound 706
Activation Analysis see PHYSICS - Nuclear Energy 701
Actuarial Science see INSURANCE 497, see also MATHEMATICS 583
Acupuncture see MEDICAL SCIENCES 591
Addictions see DRUG ABUSE AND ALCOHOLISM 286
ADULT EDUCATION 328
ADVENTURE AND ROMANCE 4
ADVENTURE AND ROMANCE — Abstracting, Bibliographies, Statistics 4
ADVERTISING AND PUBLIC RELATIONS 4
ADVERTISING AND PUBLIC RELATIONS — Abstracting, Bibliographies, Statistics 6
Advertising Art see ADVERTISING AND PUBLIC RELATIONS 4
Aerodynamics see PHYSICS - Mechanics 700
AERONAUTICS AND SPACE FLIGHT 6, see also ENGINEERING - Mechanical Engineering 381, TRANSPORTATION - Air Transport 867
AERONAUTICS AND SPACE FLIGHT — Abstracting, Bibliographies, Statistics 11
Aerophysics see PHYSICS - Mechanics 700
Aerospace Medicine see MEDICAL SCIENCES 591
Aesthetics see ART 71, see also PHILOSOPHY 686
African History see HISTORY - History of Africa 438
African Studies see HISTORY - History of Africa 438
Agricultural Chemistry see AGRICULTURE 11, see also CHEMISTRY 245
AGRICULTURAL ECONOMICS 26
Agricultural Engineering see AGRICULTURE 11, see also ENGINEERING 365
AGRICULTURAL EQUIPMENT 32
Agricultural Marketing see AGRICULTURE - Agricultural Economics 26, see also FOOD AND FOOD INDUSTRIES - Grocery Trade 407
AGRICULTURE 11, see also FOOD AND FOOD INDUSTRIES 403, FORESTS AND FORESTRY 407, GARDENING AND HORTICULTURE 414
AGRICULTURE — Abstracting, Bibliographies, Statistics 23
AGRICULTURE — Agricultural Economics 26
AGRICULTURE — Agricultural Equipment 32
AGRICULTURE — Crop Production And Soil 32
AGRICULTURE — Dairying And Dairy Products 40
AGRICULTURE — Feed, Flour And Grain 41
AGRICULTURE — Poultry And Livestock 43
Agronomy see AGRICULTURE 11
Air Conditioning see HEATING, PLUMBING AND REFRIGERATION 429
Air Defense see MILITARY 638
Air Force see MILITARY 638
Air Law see AERONAUTICS AND SPACE FLIGHT 6, see also LAW 507, TRANSPORTATION - Air Transport 867
Air Navigation see AERONAUTICS AND SPACE FLIGHT 6
Air Pollution see ENVIRONMENTAL STUDIES 383
AIR TRANSPORT 867
Airplanes see AERONAUTICS AND SPACE FLIGHT 6, see also TRANSPORTATION - Air Transport 867
Airports see AERONAUTICS AND SPACE FLIGHT 6, see also TRANSPORTATION - Air Transport 867
Alcoholic Beverages see BEVERAGES 85
Alcoholism see DRUG ABUSE AND ALCOHOLISM 286
Algae see BIOLOGY - Botany 112

ALLERGOLOGY AND IMMUNOLOGY 603
Almanacs, General see ENCYLOPEDIAS AND GENERAL ALMANACS 87
Alumni see COLLEGE AND ALUMNI 263
Amateur Radio see COMMUNICATIONS - Radio and Television 266
Amusement Guides see COMMUNICATIONS - Radio and Television 266, see also MUSIC 656, THEATER 858, TRAVEL AND TOURISM 882
ANAESTHESIOLOGY 604
Analogue Computation see COMPUTER TECHNOLOGY AND APPLICATIONS 269
ANALYTICAL CHEMISTRY 249
Anatomy see MEDICAL SCIENCES 591
Ancient History see ARCHAEOLOGY 56, see also HISTORY 430
Angiology see MEDICAL SCIENCES - Cardiovascular Diseases 606
Animals see AGRICULTURE - Poultry and Livestock 43, see also BIOLOGY - Zoology 126, LEATHER AND FUR INDUSTRIES 524, PETS 682, SPORTS AND GAMES - Horses and Horsemanship 827, VETERINARY SCIENCE 893
ANTHROPOLOGY 47, see also ARCHAEOLOGY 56
ANTHROPOLOGY — Abstracting, Bibliographies, Statistics 55
Antibiotics see PHARMACY AND PHARMACOLOGY 683
ANTIQUES 476
Antiquities see CLASSICAL STUDIES 258
Apparel see CLOTHING TRADE 261
Appliances see ELECTRICITY AND ELECTRICAL ENGINEERING 351, see also HEATING, PLUMBING AND REFRIGERATION 429, INTERIOR DESIGN AND DECORATION - Furniture and House Furnishings 503
Applied Mechanics see ENGINEERING - Engineering Mechanics and Materials 377
Apprenticeship see OCCUPATIONS AND CAREERS 666
Aquariums see BIOLOGY - Zoology 126, see also FISH AND FISHERIES 395, PETS 682
ARCHAEOLOGY 56, see also ANTHROPOLOGY 47, ART 71, HISTORY 430
ARCHAEOLOGY — Abstracting, Bibliographies, Statistics 67
Archery see SPORTS AND GAMES 818
ARCHITECTURE 68, see also BUILDING AND CONSTRUCTION 133, ENGINEERING - Civil Engineering 374, HOUSING AND URBAN PLANNING 483
ARCHITECTURE — Abstracting, Bibliographies, Statistics 71
Archives see HISTORY 430, see also LIBRARY AND INFORMATION SCIENCES 525
Area Planning see HOUSING AND URBAN PLANNING 483
Armed Forces see MILITARY 638
ART 71
ART — Abstracting, Bibliographies, Statistics 80
Art Exhibitions see MUSEUMS AND ART GALLERIES 651
Art History see ART 71
Arteriosclerosis see MEDICAL SCIENCES - Cardiovascular Diseases 606
Arthritis see MEDICAL SCIENCES - Rheumatology 623
Arts see ART 71, see also DANCE 285, LITERATURE 558, MOTION PICTURES 648, MUSIC 656, THEATER 858
Asbestos see BUILDING AND CONSTRUCTION 133
Asian History see HISTORY - History of Asia 441
Asthma see MEDICAL SCIENCES - Respiratory Diseases 623
ASTROLOGY 80
Astronautics see AERONAUTICS AND SPACE FLIGHT 6
ASTRONOMY 80
ASTRONOMY — Abstracting, Bibliographies, Statistics 85
Astrophysics see ASTRONOMY 80
Atmospheric Sciences see METEOROLOGY 631
Atomic Energy see ENERGY 361, see also PHYSICS - Nuclear Energy 701

xxxiii

Audio-Visual Education see EDUCATION - Teaching Methods and Curriculum 347, see also MOTION PICTURES 648
Audiology see MEDICAL SCIENCES - Otorhinolaryngology 617
Auditing see BUSINESS AND ECONOMICS - Accounting 167
Automation see COMPUTER TECHNOLOGY AND APPLICATIONS 269
Automobile Racing see SPORTS AND GAMES 818
AUTOMOBILES 869
Aviation see AERONAUTICS AND SPACE FLIGHT 6, see also TRANSPORTATION - Air Transport 867
Aviculture see BIOLOGY - Ornithology 124
Bacteriology see BIOLOGY - Microbiology 123, see also MEDICAL SCIENCES - Communicable Diseases 607
Badminton see SPORTS AND GAMES 818
BAKERS AND CONFECTIONERS 406
BALL GAMES 823
Ballet see DANCE 285
BANKING AND FINANCE 168
Banking Law see BUSINESS AND ECONOMICS - Banking and Finance 168, see also LAW 507
Barbering see BEAUTY CULTURE 85
Baseball see SPORTS AND GAMES - Ball Games 823
Batteries see ELECTRICITY AND ELECTRICAL ENGINEERING 351, see also TRANSPORTATION - Automobiles 869
BEAUTY CULTURE 85
BEAUTY CULTURE — Perfumes And Cosmetics 85
Behavioral Sciences see PSYCHOLOGY 734, see also SOCIOLOGY 811
BEVERAGES 85, see also FOOD AND FOOD INDUSTRIES 403
BEVERAGES — Abstracting, Bibliographies, Statistics 86
Biblical Studies see RELIGIONS AND THEOLOGY 762
BIBLIOGRAPHIES 87, see also ABSTRACTING AND INDEXING SERVICES 1, LIBRARY AND INFORMATION SCIENCES 525, PUBLISHING AND BOOK TRADE 757
BICYCLES AND MOTORCYCLES 826
Billiards see SPORTS AND GAMES - Ball Games 823
Biochemistry see BIOLOGY - Biological Chemistry 110
Biocybernetics see MEDICAL SCIENCES 591
Bioenergetics see BIOLOGY 100, see also PHYSICAL FITNESS AND HYGIENE 694
BIOGRAPHY 96
BIOGRAPHY — Abstracting, Bibliographies, Statistics 99
BIOLOGICAL CHEMISTRY 110
BIOLOGY 100, see also MEDICAL SCIENCES 591
BIOLOGY — Abstracting, Bibliographies, Statistics 109
BIOLOGY — Biological Chemistry 110
BIOLOGY — Biophysics 112
BIOLOGY — Botany 112
BIOLOGY — Cytology And Histology 119
BIOLOGY — Entomology 120
BIOLOGY — Genetics 122
BIOLOGY — Microbiology 123
BIOLOGY — Microscopy 124
BIOLOGY — Ornithology 124
BIOLOGY — Physiology 125
BIOLOGY — Zoology 126
Biometeorology see METEOROLOGY 631
Biometry see BIOLOGY 100, see also STATISTICS 832
BIOPHYSICS 112
Birds see BIOLOGY - Ornithology 124, see also CONSERVATION 274, PETS 682
BIRTH CONTROL 131
BIRTH CONTROL — Abstracting, Bibliographies, Statistics 133
BLIND 133, see also EDUCATION - Special Education and Rehabilitation 345, MEDICAL SCIENCES - Ophthalmology and Optometry 615, SOCIAL SERVICES AND WELFARE 803
BLIND — Abstracting, Bibliographies, Statistics 133
Blood Transfusion see MEDICAL SCIENCES - Cardiovascular Diseases 606
BOATS AND BOATING 826
Bobsleighing see SPORTS AND GAMES - Outdoor Life 828
Bond Market see BUSINESS AND ECONOMICS - Investments 202
Book Collecting see PUBLISHING AND BOOK TRADE 757
Book Illustrating see PUBLISHING AND BOOK TRADE 757
Book Reviews see LITERATURE 558, see also PUBLISHING AND BOOK TRADE 757
Book Trade see BIBLIOGRAPHIES 87, see also PRINTING 733, PUBLISHING AND BOOK TRADE 757
Bookbinding see PUBLISHING AND BOOK TRADE 757
Bookkeeping see BUSINESS AND ECONOMICS - Accounting 167
Booksellers see PUBLISHING AND BOOK TRADE 757
BOTANY 112, see also AGRICULTURE - Crop Production and Soil 32, GARDENING AND HORTICULTURE 414
Bottling see BEVERAGES 85, see also PACKAGING 672
Bowling see SPORTS AND GAMES - Ball Games 823
Boxes see PACKAGING 672
Boxing see SPORTS AND GAMES 818
Braille see BLIND 133
Brass Instruments see MUSIC 656
Brewing see BEVERAGES 85
Bricks see BUILDING AND CONSTRUCTION 133, see also CERAMICS, GLASS AND POTTERY 243
Bridge see SPORTS AND GAMES 818
Bridge Construction see ENGINEERING - Civil Engineering 374
Broadcasting see COMMUNICATIONS - Radio and Television 266
Bryology see BIOLOGY - Botany 112
Buddhism see RELIGIONS AND THEOLOGY 762
BUILDING AND CONSTRUCTION 133, see also ARCHITECTURE 68, ENGINEERING - Civil engineering 374, HOUSING AND URBAN PLANNING 483
BUILDING AND CONSTRUCTION — Abstracting, Bibliographies, Statistics 140
BUILDING AND CONSTRUCTION — Carpentry And Woodwork 141

BUILDING AND CONSTRUCTION — Hardware 141
Bullfighting see SPORTS AND GAMES 818
Burns see MEDICAL SCIENCES - Orthopedics and Traumatology 616
Buses see TRANSPORTATION - Automobiles 869
Business Administration see BUSINESS AND ECONOMICS - Management 213
BUSINESS AND ECONOMICS 141
BUSINESS AND ECONOMICS — Abstracting, Bibliographies, Statistics 151
BUSINESS AND ECONOMICS — Accounting 167
BUSINESS AND ECONOMICS — Banking And Finance 168
BUSINESS AND ECONOMICS — Chamber Of Commerce Publications 178
BUSINESS AND ECONOMICS — Cooperatives 180
BUSINESS AND ECONOMICS — Domestic Commerce 181
BUSINESS AND ECONOMICS — Economic Situation And Conditions 182
BUSINESS AND ECONOMICS — Economic Systems And Theories, Economic History 191
BUSINESS AND ECONOMICS — International Commerce 192
BUSINESS AND ECONOMICS — International Development And Assistance 199
BUSINESS AND ECONOMICS — Investments 202
BUSINESS AND ECONOMICS — Labor And Industrial Relations 205
BUSINESS AND ECONOMICS — Macroeconomics 212
BUSINESS AND ECONOMICS — Management 213
BUSINESS AND ECONOMICS — Marketing And Purchasing 217
BUSINESS AND ECONOMICS — Office Equipment And Services 219
BUSINESS AND ECONOMICS — Personnel Management 219
BUSINESS AND ECONOMICS — Production Of Goods And Services 220
BUSINESS AND ECONOMICS — Public Finance, Taxation 226
BUSINESS AND ECONOMICS — Small Business 234
BUSINESS AND ECONOMICS — Trade And Industrial Directories 234
Business Law see BUSINESS AND ECONOMICS 141, see also LAW 507
Cables see COMMUNICATIONS - Telephone and Telegraph 269, see also ELECTRICITY AND ELECTRICAL ENGINEERING 351
Cafeterias see HOTELS AND RESTAURANTS 482
Calculating Machines see BUSINESS AND ECONOMICS - Accounting 167, see also COMPUTER TECHNOLOGY AND APPLICATIONS 269, ELECTRICITY AND ELECTRICAL ENGINEERING 351, MATHEMATICS 583
Calendars of Events see MEETINGS AND CONGRESSES 626, see also TRAVEL AND TOURISM 882
Calligraphy see ART 71
Camping see SPORTS AND GAMES - Outdoor Life 828, see also TRAVEL AND TOURISM 882
Canals see TRANSPORTATION - Ships and Shipping 876
CANCER 604
Candy see FOOD AND FOOD INDUSTRIES - Bakers and Confectioners 406
Canning and Preserving see FOOD AND FOOD INDUSTRIES 403, see also HOME ECONOMICS 479
Canoeing see SPORTS AND GAMES - Boats and Boating 826
Canon Law see RELIGIONS AND THEOLOGY 762
Canvas see TEXTILE INDUSTRIES AND FABRICS 854
Carboniferous Geology see EARTH SCIENCES - Geophysics 303
Cardiology see MEDICAL SCIENCES - Cardiovascular Diseases 606
CARDIOVASCULAR DISEASES 606
Cardiovascular Surgery see MEDICAL SCIENCES - Surgery 624
Careers see OCCUPATIONS AND CAREERS 666
Cargo Handling see TRANSPORTATION - Ships and Shipping 876
Caribbean History see HISTORY - History of North and South America 465
CARPENTRY AND WOODWORK 141
Carpets and Rugs see INTERIOR DESIGN AND DECORATION - Furniture and House Furnishings 503
Cartography see GEOGRAPHY 419
Cartoons see ART 71
Catering see HOTELS AND RESTAURANTS 482
Cattle see AGRICULTURE - Poultry and Livestock 43
Caves see EARTH SCIENCES - Geology 290
Cemeteries see FUNERALS 414
CERAMICS, GLASS AND POTTERY 243, see also ART 71, HOBBIES 475
CERAMICS, GLASS AND POTTERY — Abstracting, Bibliographies, Statistics 245
Cereals see AGRICULTURE - Feed, Flour and Grain 41, see also FOOD AND FOOD INDUSTRIES 403
Cerebral Palsy see MEDICAL SCIENCES - Psychiatry and Neurology 618
CHAMBER OF COMMERCE PUBLICATIONS 178
Chambers of Commerce see BUSINESS AND ECONOMICS - Chamber of Commerce Publications 178
Chaplains see MILITARY 638, see also RELIGIONS AND THEOLOGY 762
Charities see SOCIAL SERVICES AND WELFARE 803
CHEMICAL ENGINEERING 372
CHEMISTRY 245
CHEMISTRY — Abstracting, Bibliographies, Statistics 249
CHEMISTRY — Analytical Chemistry 249
CHEMISTRY — Crystallography 250
CHEMISTRY — Electrochemistry 251
CHEMISTRY — Inorganic Chemistry 251
CHEMISTRY — Organic Chemistry 252
CHEMISTRY — Physical Chemistry 254
Chemotherapy see BIOLOGY - Biological Chemistry 110, see also MEDICAL SCIENCES 591, PHARMACY AND PHARMACOLOGY 683
Chess see SPORTS AND GAMES 818
Chest Diseases see MEDICAL SCIENCES - Respiratory Diseases 623
Child Psychology see PSYCHOLOGY 734
Child Welfare see CHILDREN AND YOUTH - About 256, see also SOCIAL SERVICES AND WELFARE 803
CHILDREN AND YOUTH — About 256
CHILDREN AND YOUTH — Abstracting, Bibliographies, Statistics 257
CHILDREN AND YOUTH — For 257
CHIROPRACTICS, HOMEOPATHY, OSTEOPATHY 607
Chromatography see CHEMISTRY - Analytical Chemistry 249
Church History see RELIGIONS AND THEOLOGY 762
Cigarettes and Cigars see TOBACCO 860
Cinematography see MOTION PICTURES 648, see also PHOTOGRAPHY 692

xxxiv

Circulatory System see MEDICAL SCIENCES - Cardiovascular Diseases 606
Circus see THEATER 858
Cities and Towns see HOUSING AND URBAN PLANNING 483, see also PUBLIC ADMINISTRATION - Municipal Government 748
Citizenship see POLITICAL SCIENCE 707
Citrus Fruits see AGRICULTURE - Crop Production and Soil 32, see also FOOD AND FOOD INDUSTRIES 403, GARDENING AND HORTICULTURE 414
City Planning see HOUSING AND URBAN PLANNING 483
Civil Aeronautics see TRANSPORTATION - Air Transport 867
CIVIL DEFENSE 258, see also MILITARY 638
CIVIL ENGINEERING 374
CIVIL RIGHTS 718
Civil Service see OCCUPATIONS AND CAREERS 666, see also PUBLIC ADMINISTRATION 739
CLASSICAL STUDIES 258, see also ARCHEOLOGY 56, HISTORY 430, LINGUISTICS 539, LITERATURE 558
CLASSICAL STUDIES — Abstracting, Bibliographies, Statistics 261
CLEANING AND DYEING 261
CLEANING AND DYEING — Abstracting, Bibliographies, Statistics 261
Climatology see METEOROLOGY 631
Clinical Medicine see MEDICAL SCIENCES 591
CLOTHING TRADE 261
CLOTHING TRADE — Abstracting, Bibliographies, Statistics 262
CLOTHING TRADE — Fashions 262
CLUBS 262
Coaching see SPORTS AND GAMES 818
Coastal Engineering see ENGINEERING - Hydraulic Engineering 380
Cognitive Studies see PSYCHOLOGY 734
Coins see HOBBIES - Numismatics 477
Collectors and Collecting see HOBBIES 475
COLLEGE AND ALUMNI 263, see also CLUBS 262, EDUCATION - Higher Education 333
COLLEGE AND ALUMNI — Abstracting, Bibliographies, Statistics 263
College Management see EDUCATION - Higher Education 333, see also EDUCATION - School Organization and Administration 343
Colloids see CHEMISTRY - Physical Chemistry 254, see also PHYSICS 695
Combustion see CHEMISTRY - Physical Chemistry 254, see also PHYSICS - Heat 700
Commerce see BUSINESS AND ECONOMICS - Domestic Commerce 181, see also BUSINESS AND ECONOMICS - International Commerce 192
Commercial Art see ADVERTISING AND PUBLIC RELATIONS 4, see also ART 71
Commercial Education see EDUCATION - Teaching Methods and Curriculum 347
Commercial Law see BUSINESS AND ECONOMICS 141, see also LAW 507
COMMUNICABLE DISEASES 607
COMMUNICATIONS 263, see also JOURNALISM 504
COMMUNICATIONS — Abstracting, Bibliographies, Statistics 265
COMMUNICATIONS — Postal Affairs 266
COMMUNICATIONS — Radio And Television 266
COMMUNICATIONS — Telephone And Telegraph 269
Communism see BUSINESS AND ECONOMICS - Economic Systems and Theories, Economic History 191, see also POLITICAL SCIENCE 707
Community Affairs see PUBLIC ADMINISTRATION - Municipal Government 748
Comparative Psychology see PSYCHOLOGY 734
Compressed Air see ENGINEERING - Mechanical Engineering 381
COMPUTER TECHNOLOGY AND APPLICATIONS 269, see also LIBRARY AND INFORMATION SCIENCES 525
COMPUTER TECHNOLOGY AND APPLICATIONS — Abstracting, Bibliographies, Statistics 274
Conchology see BIOLOGY - Zoology 126
Confectioners see FOOD AND FOOD INDUSTRIES - Bakers and Confectioners 406
Congenital Abnormalities see BIOLOGY - Genetics 122, see also MEDICAL SCIENCES 591
Congresses see MEETINGS AND CONGRESSES 626
CONSERVATION 274, see also ENVIRONMENTAL STUDIES 383, FISH AND FISHERIES 395, FORESTS AND FORESTRY 407, WATER RESOURCES 895
CONSERVATION — Abstracting, Bibliographies, Statistics 279
Constitutional Law see LAW 507, see also POLITICAL SCIENCE 707
Construction see BUILDING AND CONSTRUCTION 133, see also ENGINEERING - Civil Engineering 374
Consumer Credit see BUSINESS AND ECONOMICS - Banking and Finance 168
CONSUMER EDUCATION AND PROTECTION 279
CONSUMER EDUCATION AND PROTECTION — Abstracting, Bibliographies, Statistics 280
Contact Lenses see MEDICAL SCIENCES - Ophthalmology and Optometry 615
Contraception see BIRTH CONTROL 131
Contractors see BUILDING AND CONSTRUCTION 133
Convention Dates see MEETINGS AND CONGRESSES 626
Cookery see HOME ECONOMICS 479, see also HOTELS AND RESTAURANTS 482
COOPERATIVES 180
Copying and Duplicating see PHOTOGRAPHY 692, see also PRINTING 733
Copyrights see PATENTS, TRADEMARKS AND COPYRIGHTS 676
Corporation Law see BUSINESS AND ECONOMICS - Management 213, see also LAW 507
Correspondence Education see EDUCATION - Adult Education 328
Corrosion see METALLURGY 626, see also PAINTS AND PROTECTIVE COATINGS 673
Cosmetics see BEAUTY CULTURE - Perfumes and Cosmetics 85
Counseling see EDUCATION 313, see also PSYCHOLOGY 734, SOCIAL SERVICES AND WELFARE 803
Credit Unions see BUSINESS AND ECONOMICS - Banking and Finance 168
Cricket see SPORTS AND GAMES 818
Criminal Law see CRIMINOLOGY AND LAW ENFORCEMENT 280, see also LAW 507
CRIMINOLOGY AND LAW ENFORCEMENT 280

CRIMINOLOGY AND LAW ENFORCEMENT — Abstracting, Bibliographies, Statistics 284
CROP PRODUCTION AND SOIL 32
Croquet see SPORTS AND GAMES - Ball Games 823
Cryogenic Engineering see ENGINEERING - Mechanical Engineering 381
Cryogenics see PHYSICS - Heat 700
CRYSTALLOGRAPHY 250
Currency see BUSINESS AND ECONOMICS - Banking and Finance 168
Curriculum and Methods see EDUCATION - Teaching Methods and Curriculum 347
Customs and Excise see BUSINESS AND ECONOMICS - Public Finance, Taxation 226
Cybernetic Medicine see MEDICAL SCIENCES 591
Cybernetics see COMPUTER TECHNOLOGY AND APPLICATIONS 269
Cystic Fibrosis see MEDICAL SCIENCES 591
CYTOLOGY AND HISTOLOGY 119
DAIRYING AND DAIRY PRODUCTS 40
DANCE 285, see also THEATER 858
DANCE — Abstracting, Bibliographies, Statistics 286
Data Processing see COMPUTER TECHNOLOGY AND APPLICATIONS 269
DEAF 286, see also EDUCATION - Special Education and Rehabilitation 345, MEDICAL SCIENCES - Otorhinolaryngology 617, SOCIAL SERVICES AND WELFARE 803
Decoration see INTERIOR DESIGN AND DECORATION 502
Defense see CIVIL DEFENSE 258, see also MILITARY 638
Delinquency see CHILDREN AND YOUTH - About 256, see also CRIMINOLOGY AND LAW ENFORCEMENT 280, SOCIAL SERVICES AND WELFARE 803
Demography see POPULATION STUDIES 725
DENTISTRY 608
Department Stores see BUSINESS AND ECONOMICS - Marketing andPurchasing 217
DERMATOLOGY AND VENEREOLOGY 610
Desalination see ENVIRONMENTAL STUDIES 383, see also WATER RESOURCES 895
Design see ART 71
Diabetes see MEDICAL SCIENCES - Endocrinology 611
Dialysis see MEDICAL SCIENCES - Urology and Nephrology 625
Diecasting see ENGINEERING 365
Diesel Engines see ENGINEERING - Mechanical Engineering 381
Dietetics see NUTRITION AND DIETETICS 665
Digestive System see MEDICAL SCIENCES - Gastroenterology 613
Diplomatic Service see POLITICAL SCIENCE - International Relations 719
Disarmament see MILITARY 638, see also POLITICAL SCIENCE 707
Distilling see BEVERAGES 85
Documentation see COMPUTER TECHNOLOGY AND APPLICATIONS 269, see also LIBRARY AND INFORMATION SCIENCES 525
Domestic Animals and Birds see PETS 682, see also VETERINARY SCIENCE 893
DOMESTIC COMMERCE 181
Drafting see ENGINEERING 365, see also TECHNOLOGY 849
Drama see LITERATURE 558, see also THEATER 858
Drawing and Sketching see ART 71
DRUG ABUSE AND ALCOHOLISM 286
DRUG ABUSE AND ALCOHOLISM — Abstracting, Bibliographies, Statistics 288
Drugs see PHARMACY AND PHARMACOLOGY 683
Dry Goods see CLOTHING TRADE 261, see also TEXTILE INDUSTRIES AND FABRICS 854
Dyes and Dyeing see CLEANING AND DYEING 261, see also TEXTILE INDUSTRIES AND FABRICS 854
E C G see MEDICAL SCIENCES - Cardiovascular Diseases 606
E E G see MEDICAL SCIENCES - Psychiatry and Neurology 618
EARTH SCIENCES 288
EARTH SCIENCES — Abstracting, Bibliographies, Statistics 290
EARTH SCIENCES — Geology 290
EARTH SCIENCES — Geophysics 303
EARTH SCIENCES — Hydrology 307
EARTH SCIENCES — Oceanography 309
Ecclesiastical Art see ART 71, see also RELIGIONS AND THEOLOGY 762
Ecclesiastical Law see RELIGIONS AND THEOLOGY 762
Ecology see BIOLOGY 100, see also CONSERVATION 274, ENVIRONMENTAL STUDIES 383
Economic Geology see EARTH SCIENCES - Geology 290
ECONOMIC SITUATION AND CONDITIONS 182
ECONOMIC SYSTEMS AND THEORIES, ECONOMIC HISTORY 191
ECONOMICS 313, see also BUSINESS AND ECONOMICS 141
EDUCATION 313, see also CHILDREN AND YOUTH - About 256
EDUCATION — Abstracting, Bibliographies, Statistics 325
EDUCATION — Adult Education 328
EDUCATION — Guides To Schools And Colleges 330
EDUCATION — Higher Education 333
EDUCATION — International Education Programs 342
EDUCATION — School Organization And Administration 343
EDUCATION — Special Education And Rehabilitation 345
EDUCATION — Teaching Methods And Curriculum 347
Educational Films see EDUCATION - Teaching Methods and Curriculum 347, also MOTION PICTURES 648
Educational Psychology see PSYCHOLOGY 734
Egyptology see ARCHAEOLOGY 56, see also ART 71, HISTORY - History of Africa 438
ELECTRICITY AND ELECTRICAL ENGINEERING 351, see also COMMUNICATIONS 263, PHYSICS 695
ELECTRICITY AND ELECTRICAL ENGINEERING — Abstracting, Bibliographies, Statistics 359
ELECTROCHEMISTRY 251
Electronics see ELECTRICITY AND ELECTRICAL ENGINEERING 351
Electroplating see ELECTRICITY AND ELECTRICAL ENGINEERING 351, see also METALLURGY 626

Electrotherapy see MEDICAL SCIENCES - Psychiatry and Neurology 618, see also MEDICAL SCIENCES - Radiology and Nuclear Medicine 622
Embroidery and Needlework see HOBBIES - Needlework 476
Embryology see BIOLOGY 100, see also MEDICAL SCIENCES 591
Emigration see POPULATION STUDIES 725
Emotionally Disturbed Children see EDUCATION - Special Education and Rehabilitation 345
Employment see BUSINESS AND ECONOMICS - Labor and Industrial Relations 205, see also OCCUPATIONS AND CAREERS 666
Encephalitis see MEDICAL SCIENCES - Psychiatry and Neurology 618
ENCYCLOPEDIAS AND GENERAL ALMANACS 360
ENCYCLOPEDIAS AND GENERAL ALMANACS — Abstracting, Bibliographies, Statistics 361
ENDOCRINOLOGY 611
ENERGY 361
ENERGY — Abstracting, Bibliographies, Statistics 364
ENGINEERING 365
ENGINEERING — Abstracting, Bibliographies, Statistics 371
ENGINEERING — Chemical Engineering 372
ENGINEERING — Civil Engineering 374
ENGINEERING — Engineering Mechanics And Materials 377
ENGINEERING — Hydraulic Engineering 380
ENGINEERING — Mechanical Engineering 381
Engines see ENGINEERING - Mechanical Engineering 381, see also TRANSPORTATION 861
English Language - Study and Teaching see LINGUISTICS 539
Engraving see ART 71, see also PRINTING 733
Entertainment see COMMUNICATIONS - Radio and Television 263, see also DANCE 285, MOTION PICTURES 648, MUSIC 656, SPORTS AND GAMES 818, THEATER 858, TRAVEL AND TOURISM 882
ENTOMOLOGY 120
Environmental Health see ENVIRONMENTAL STUDIES 383, see also PUBLIC HEALTH AND SAFETY 750
ENVIRONMENTAL STUDIES 383, see also CONSERVATION 274
ENVIRONMENTAL STUDIES — Abstracting, Bibliographies, Statistics 390
Enzymes see BIOLOGY - Biological Chemistry 110, see also MEDICAL SCIENCES 591
Ephemerides see ASTRONOMY 80
Epidemiology see PUBLIC HEALTH AND SAFETY 750
Epilepsy see MEDICAL SCIENCES - Psychiatry and Neurology 618
Ergonomics see BUSINESS AND ECONOMICS - Labor and Industrial Relations 205, see also PSYCHOLOGY 734
Erosion see AGRICULTURE - Crop Production and Soil 32, see also CONSERVATION 274
Esperanto see LINGUISTICS 539
ETHNIC INTERESTS 390
ETHNIC INTERESTS — Abstracting, Bibliographies, Statistics 394
Ethnography see ANTHROPOLOGY 47, see also SOCIOLOGY 811
Eugenics see BIOLOGY - Genetics 122
European History see HISTORY - History of Europe 448
Exceptional Children, Education see EDUCATION - Special Education and Rehabilitation 345
EXPERIMENTAL MEDICINE, LABORATORY TECHNIQUE 612
Exports and Imports see BUSINESS AND ECONOMICS - International Commerce 192
Extrasensory Perception see PARAPSYCHOLOGY AND OCCULTISM 676
Fabrics see TEXTILE INDUSTRIES AND FABRICS 854
Family Planning see BIRTH CONTROL 131
Farm Equipment see AGRICULTURE - Agricultural Equipment 32, see also MACHINERY 582
Farm Management see AGRICULTURE 11
FASHIONS 262
FEED, FLOUR AND GRAIN 41
Fellowships see EDUCATION - Higher Education 333
Feminist Movement see POLITICAL SCIENCE - Civil Rights 718, see also WOMEN'S INTERESTS 900
Fencing see SPORTS AND GAMES 818
Fertilizers see AGRICULTURE - Crop Production and Soil 32
Filmmaking see MOTION PICTURES 648
Finance see BUSINESS AND ECONOMICS - Banking and Finance 168, see also BUSINESS AND ECONOMICS - Investments 202
Fire Insurance see INSURANCE 497
FIRE PREVENTION 394
FIRE PREVENTION — Abstracting, Bibliographies, Statistics 395
Firearms see HOBBIES 475, see also SPORTS AND GAMES 818
First Aid see MEDICAL SCIENCES 591, see also PUBLIC HEALTH AND SAFETY 750
FISH AND FISHERIES 395, see also BIOLOGY - Zoology 126
FISH AND FISHERIES — Abstracting, Bibliographies, Statistics 401
Fishing, Sport see SPORTS AND GAMES - Outdoor Life 828
Flax see AGRICULTURE - Crop Production and Soil 32, see also TEXTILE INDUSTRIES AND FABRICS 854
Floor Coverings see INTERIOR DESIGN AND DECORATION - Furniture and House Furnishings 503
Floral Decorations see ART 71, see also GARDENING AND HORTICULTURE 414
FLORIST TRADE 416
Flowers see BIOLOGY - Botany 112, see also GARDENING AND HORTICULTURE 414
Fluid Power see ENGINEERING - Mechanical Engineering 381
Flying see AERONAUTICS AND SPACE FLIGHT 6, see also TRANSPORTATION - Air Transport 867
Flying Saucers see AERONAUTICS AND SPACE FLIGHT 6
FOLKLORE 401
FOLKLORE — Abstracting, Bibliographies, Statistics 403
FOOD AND FOOD INDUSTRIES 403
FOOD AND FOOD INDUSTRIES — Abstracting, Bibliographies, Statistics 406
FOOD AND FOOD INDUSTRIES — Bakers And Confectioners 406

FOOD AND FOOD INDUSTRIES — Grocery Trade 407
Football see SPORTS AND GAMES - Ball Games 823
Footwear see LEATHER AND FUR INDUSTRIES 524, see also SHOES AND BOOTS 795
Foreign Affairs see POLITICAL SCIENCE - International Relations 719
Foreign Aid see BUSINESS AND ECONOMICS - International Development and Assistance 199
Foreign Commerce see BUSINESS AND ECONOMICS - International Commerce 192
Foreign Legion see MILITARY 638
FORENSIC SCIENCES 612
Forest Fires see FORESTS AND FORESTRY 407
FORESTS AND FORESTRY 407
FORESTS AND FORESTRY — Abstracting, Bibliographies, Statistics 412
FORESTS AND FORESTRY — Lumber And Wood 412
Foundry Practices see METALLURGY 626
Fraternal Organizations see CLUBS 262
Freight see TRANSPORTATION 861
French Language - Study and Teaching see LINGUISTICS 539
Frequency Modulation see COMMUNICATIONS - Radio and Television 266, see also SOUND RECORDING AND REPRODUCTION 818
Fretted Instruments see MUSIC 656
Frozen Food see FOOD AND FOOD INDUSTRIES 403
Fruit see AGRICULTURE - Crop Production and Soil 32, see also FOOD AND FOOD INDUSTRIES 403, GARDENING AND HORTICULTURE 414
Fuel see ENERGY 361, see also HEATING, PLUMBING AND REFRIGERATION 429, MINES AND MINING INDUSTRY 641, PETROLEUM AND GAS 677
Fundraising see SOCIAL SERVICES AND WELFARE 803
FUNERALS 414
FUNERALS — Abstracting, Bibliographies, Statistics 414
Fur see LEATHER AND FUR INDUSTRIES 524
Furnaces see HEATING, PLUMBING AND REFRIGERATION 429, see also METALLURGY 626
FURNITURE AND HOUSE FURNISHINGS 503, see also HOME ECONOMICS 479
Galleries see MUSEUMS AND ART GALLERIES 651
Game Breeding see AGRICULTURE - Poultry and Livestock 43
Games see SPORTS AND GAMES 818
GARDENING AND HORTICULTURE 414, see also AGRICULTURE 11, BIOLOGY - Botany 112
GARDENING AND HORTICULTURE — Abstracting, Bibliographies, Statistics 416
GARDENING AND HORTICULTURE — Florist Trade 416
Gas Chromatography see CHEMISTRY - Analytical Chemistry 249
Gas Dynamics see PHYSICS - Mechanics 700
Gas Turbines see ENGINEERING - Mechanical Engineering 381
GASTROENTEROLOGY 613
Gastronomy see HOME ECONOMICS 479
GENEALOGY AND HERALDRY 416
GENEALOGY AND HERALDRY — Abstracting, Bibliographies, Statistics 418
GENERAL INTEREST PERIODICALS — Africa 418
GENERAL INTEREST PERIODICALS — Australasia 418
GENERAL INTEREST PERIODICALS — Bangladesh 418
GENERAL INTEREST PERIODICALS — Canada 418
GENERAL INTEREST PERIODICALS — Central America 418
GENERAL INTEREST PERIODICALS — Colombia 418
GENERAL INTEREST PERIODICALS — Germany, West 418
GENERAL INTEREST PERIODICALS — Great Britain 418
GENERAL INTEREST PERIODICALS — India 418
GENERAL INTEREST PERIODICALS — Indonesia 418
GENERAL INTEREST PERIODICALS — Italy 418
GENERAL INTEREST PERIODICALS — Libya 418
GENERAL INTEREST PERIODICALS — Malagasy Republic 418
GENERAL INTEREST PERIODICALS — Oceania 418
GENERAL INTEREST PERIODICALS — Pakistan 418
GENERAL INTEREST PERIODICALS — Peru 419
GENERAL INTEREST PERIODICALS — Puerto Rico 419
GENERAL INTEREST PERIODICALS — Singapore 419
GENERAL INTEREST PERIODICALS — South America 419
GENERAL INTEREST PERIODICALS — United States 419
GENERAL INTEREST PERIODICALS — Venezuela 419
GENERAL INTEREST PERIODICALS — West Indies 419
GENETICS 122
Geochemistry see EARTH SCIENCES - Geology 290
Geodesy see EARTH SCIENCES - Geophysics 303, see also GEOGRAPHY 419
GEOGRAPHY 419, see also TRAVEL AND TOURISM 882
GEOGRAPHY — Abstracting, Bibliographies, Statistics 428
GEOLOGY 290
Geomagnetism see EARTH SCIENCES - Geophysics 303
GEOPHYSICS 303
German Language - Study and Teaching see LINGUISTICS 539
GERONTOLOGY AND GERIATRICS 428
GERONTOLOGY AND GERIATRICS — Abstracting, Bibliographies, Statistics 428
GIFTWARE AND TOYS 429
Glaciology see EARTH SCIENCES - Geology 290
Glaucoma see MEDICAL SCIENCES - Ophthalmology and Optometry 615
Gliders see AERONAUTICS AND SPACE FLIGHT 6
Golf see SPORTS AND GAMES - Ball Games 818
Government see POLITICAL SCIENCE 707, see also PUBLIC ADMINISTRATION 739
Graphic Arts see ART 71, see also PRINTING 733
Graphology see PSYCHOLOGY 734
GROCERY TRADE 407
GUIDES TO SCHOOLS AND COLLEGES 330
Gymnastics see SPORTS AND GAMES 818
Gynecology see MEDICAL SCIENCES - Obstetrics and Gynecology 614

xxxvi

Hair Removal see BEAUTY CULTURE 85
Hairdressing see BEAUTY CULTURE 85
Handbags see CLOTHING TRADE 261, see also LEATHER AND FUR INDUSTRIES 524
Handicrafts see ART 71, see also HOBBIES 475
Harbors see TRANSPORTATION - Ships and Shipping 876
HARDWARE 141
Harnesses see LEATHER AND FUR INDUSTRIES 524
Health Insurance see INSURANCE 497
Hearing see DEAF 286, see also MEDICAL SCIENCES - Otorhinolaryngology 617
Heart Diseases see MEDICAL SCIENCES - Cardiovascular Diseases 606
HEAT 700
HEATING, PLUMBING AND REFRIGERATION 429, see also BUILDING AND CONSTRUCTION 133, ENGINEERING - Mechanical Engineering 381
Helicopters see AERONAUTICS AND SPACE FLIGHT 6
HEMATOLOGY 613
Heraldry see GENEALOGY AND HERALDRY 416
Herbs see AGRICULTURE 11, see also GARDENING AND HORTICULTURE 414
Heredity see BIOLOGY - Genetics 122
Hides see LEATHER AND FUR INDUSTRIES 524
HIGHER EDUCATION 333
Highways see ENGINEERING - Civil Engineering 374, see also TRANSPORTATION - Roads and Traffic 874
Histochemistry see BIOLOGY - Cytology and Histology 119
Histology see BIOLOGY - Cytology and Histology 119
Historic Sites see HISTORY 430, see also TRAVEL AND TOURISM 882
HISTORY 430, see also ARCHAEOLOGY 56, BIOGRAPHY 96, CLASSICAL STUDIES 258
HISTORY — Abstracting, Bibliographies, Statistics 437
HISTORY — History Of Africa 438
HISTORY — History Of Asia 441
HISTORY — History Of Australasia And Other Areas 447
HISTORY — History Of Europe 448
HISTORY — History Of North And South America 465
HISTORY — History Of The Near East 474
HOBBIES 475, see also SPORTS AND GAMES 818
HOBBIES — Abstracting, Bibliographies, Statistics 476
HOBBIES — Antiques 476
HOBBIES — Needlework 476
HOBBIES — Numismatics 477
HOBBIES — Philately 478
HOME ECONOMICS 479
HOME ECONOMICS — Abstracting, Bibliographies, Statistics 480
Homeopathy see MEDICAL SCIENCES - Chiropractics, Homeopathy, Osteopathy 607
HOMOSEXUALITY 480
HOMOSEXUALITY — Abstracting, Bibliographies, Statistics 480
Hormones see MEDICAL SCIENCES - Endocrinology 611
Horology see JEWELRY, CLOCKS AND WATCHES 503
HORSES AND HORSEMANSHIP 827
Horticulture see GARDENING AND HORTICULTURE 414
Hosiery see CLOTHING TRADE 261
Hospital Supplies see HOSPITALS 480, see also PHARMACY AND PHARMACOLOGY 683
HOSPITALS 480, see also MEDICAL SCIENCES 591
HOSPITALS — Abstracting, Bibliographies, Statistics 481
HOTELS AND RESTAURANTS 482
HOTELS AND RESTAURANTS — Abstracting, Bibliographies, Statistics 483
House Furnishings see INTERIOR DESIGN AND DECORATION - Furniture and House Furnishings 503
Household Management see HOME ECONOMICS 479
HOUSING AND URBAN PLANNING 483, see also BUILDING AND CONSTRUCTION 133, PUBLIC ADMINISTRATION 739, REAL ESTATE 761
HOUSING AND URBAN PLANNING — Abstracting, Bibliographies, Statistics 488
Human Ecology see SOCIOLOGY 811
Human Geography see GEOGRAPHY 419, see also POPULATION STUDIES 725
Humanism see PHILOSOPHY 686
HUMANITIES: COMPREHENSIVE WORKS 489
HUMANITIES: COMPREHENSIVE WORKS — Abstracting, Bibliographies, Statistics 495
Hunting see SPORTS AND GAMES - Outdoor Life 828
HYDRAULIC ENGINEERING 380
Hydroelectric Engineering see ELECTRICITY AND ELECTRICAL ENGINEERING 351
Hydrography see WATER RESOURCES 895
HYDROLOGY 307
Hygiene see INDUSTRIAL HEALTH AND SAFETY 495, see also PHYSICAL FITNESS AND HYGIENE 694, PUBLIC HEALTH AND SAFETY 750
Hypertension see MEDICAL SCIENCES - Cardiovascular Diseases 606
Illumination see ELECTRICITY AND ELECTRICAL ENGINEERING 351
Immigration see POPULATION STUDIES 725
Immunology see MEDICAL SCIENCES - Allergology and Immunology 603
Imports see BUSINESS AND ECONOMICS - International Commerce 192
Indexing Services see ABSTRACTING AND INDEXING SERVICES 1
Indoor Games and Amusements see HOBBIES 475, see also SPORTS AND GAMES 818
Industrial Arts see TECHNOLOGY 849
Industrial Chemistry see ENGINEERING - Chemical Engineering 372
Industrial Design see ENGINEERING 365, see also TECHNOLOGY 849
Industrial Engineering see BUSINESS AND ECONOMICS - Production of Goods and Services 220, see also ENGINEERING 365, TECHNOLOGY 849
INDUSTRIAL HEALTH AND SAFETY 495
INDUSTRIAL HEALTH AND SAFETY — Abstracting, Bibliographies, Statistics 496

Industrial Relations see BUSINESS AND ECONOMICS - Labor and Industrial Relations 205, see also BUSINESS AND ECONOMICS - Personnel Management 219
Industry see BUSINESS AND ECONOMICS - Production of Goods and Services 220
Infectious Diseases see MEDICAL SCIENCES - Communicable Diseases 607, see also PUBLIC HEALTH AND SAFETY 750
Information Science see COMPUTER TECHNOLOGY AND APPLICATIONS 269, see also LIBRARY AND INFORMATION SCIENCES 525
INORGANIC CHEMISTRY 251
Insects see BIOLOGY - Entomology 120
INSTRUMENTS 496
INSTRUMENTS — Abstracting, Bibliographies, Statistics 497
Insulation see BUILDING AND CONSTRUCTION 133, see also HEATING, PLUMBING AND REFRIGERATION 429
INSURANCE 497
INSURANCE — Abstracting, Bibliographies, Statistics 501
Intensive Care Medicine see MEDICAL SCIENCES 591
INTERIOR DESIGN AND DECORATION 502, see also HOME ECONOMICS 479
INTERIOR DESIGN AND DECORATION — Abstracting, Bibliographies, Statistics 502
INTERIOR DESIGN AND DECORATION — Furniture And House Furnishings 503
Internal Medicine see MEDICAL SCIENCES 591
International Affairs see BUSINESS AND ECONOMICS - International Development and Assistance 199, see also LITERARY AND POLITICAL REVIEWS 555, POLITICAL SCIENCE - International relations 719
INTERNATIONAL COMMERCE 192
INTERNATIONAL DEVELOPMENT AND ASSISTANCE 199
INTERNATIONAL EDUCATION PROGRAMS 342
INTERNATIONAL LAW 522
INTERNATIONAL RELATIONS 719
Interplanetary Flight see AERONAUTICS AND SPACE FLIGHT 6
INVESTMENTS 202
Ionization see CHEMISTRY - Electrochemistry 251
Irrigation see AGRICULTURE 11, see also CONSERVATION 274, ENGINEERING 365, WATER RESOURCES 895
ISLAM 769
Italian Language - Study and Teaching see LINGUISTICS 539
JEWELRY, CLOCKS AND WATCHES 503
Job Opportunities see BUSINESS AND ECONOMICS - Labor and Industrial Relations 205, see also OCCUPATIONS AND CAREERS 666
Jogging see PHYSICAL FITNESS AND HYGIENE 694
JOURNALISM 504
JOURNALISM — Abstracting, Bibliographies, Statistics 506
JUDAISM 770
Judo see SPORTS AND GAMES 818
Jute see TEXTILE INDUSTRIES AND FABRICS 854
Juvenile Delinquency see CHILDREN AND YOUTH - About 256, see also CRIMINOLOGY AND LAW ENFORCEMENT 280
Juvenile Literature see CHILDREN AND YOUTH- For 257, see also PUBLISHING AND BOOK TRADE 757
Karate see SPORTS AND GAMES 818
Kinetics see CHEMISTRY - Organic Chemistry 252, see also CHEMISTRY - Physical Chemistry 254, PHYSICS 695
Knit Goods see CLOTHING TRADE 261, see also TEXTILE INDUSTRIES AND FABRICS 854
Knitting see HOBBIES - Needlework 476
LABOR AND INDUSTRIAL RELATIONS 205
Labor Law see BUSINESS AND ECONOMICS - Labor and Industrial Relations 205, see also LAW 507
LABOR UNIONS 506
LABOR UNIONS — Abstracting, Bibliographies, Statistics 507
Laboratory Animals see MEDICAL SCIENCES - Experimental Medicine, Laboratory Techniques 612
LABORATORY TECHNIQUE 507
Laboratory Techniques see INSTRUMENTS 496, see also MEDICAL SCIENCES - Experimental Medicine, Laboratory Techniques 612
Land Reclamation see AGRICULTURE - Crop Production and Soil 32
Landscaping see ARCHITECTURE 68, see also GARDENING AND HORTICULTURE 414
Language, Study and Teaching see LINGUISTICS 539
Laryngology see MEDICAL SCIENCES - Otorhinolaryngology 617
Lasers see ELECTRICITY AND ELECTRICAL ENGINEERING 351, see also PHYSICS - Optics 705
Lathes see MACHINERY 582
Latin American History see HISTORY - History of North and South America 465
Latin Language and Literature see CLASSICAL STUDIES 258, see also LINGUISTICS 539
Laundries see CLEANING AND DYEING 261
LAW 507
LAW — Abstracting, Bibliographies, Statistics 521
Law Enforcement see CRIMINOLOGY AND LAW ENFORCEMENT 280
LAW — International Law 522
LEATHER AND FUR INDUSTRIES 524, see also SHOES AND BOOTS 795
LEATHER AND FUR INDUSTRIES — Abstracting, Bibliographies, Statistics 525
Legal Aid see LAW 507
Legislation see LAW 507, see also POLITICAL SCIENCE 707, PUBLIC ADMINISTRATION 739
Leprosy see MEDICAL SCIENCES - Communicable Diseases 607
Leukemia see MEDICAL SCIENCES - Hematology 613
Lexicography see LINGUISTICS 539
LIBRARY AND INFORMATION SCIENCES 525, see also BIBLIOGRAPHIES 87, COMPUTER TECHNOLOGY AND APPLICATIONS 269, PUBLISHING AND BOOK TRADE 757
LIBRARY AND INFORMATION SCIENCES — Abstracting, Bibliographies, Statistics 538

xxxvii

Library Bookbinding see LIBRARY AND INFORMATION SCIENCES 525, see also PUBLISHING AND BOOK TRADE 757
Lighting see ELECTRICITY AND ELECTRICAL ENGINEERING 351, see also INTERIOR DESIGN AND DECORATION - Furniture and House Furnishings 503
Limnology see EARTH SCIENCES - Hydrology 307
LINGUISTICS 539
LINGUISTICS — Abstracting, Bibliographies, Statistics 555
Liquor see BEVERAGES 85
LITERARY AND POLITICAL REVIEWS 555, see also LITERATURE 558
LITERARY AND POLITICAL REVIEWS — Abstracting, Bibliographies, Statistics 558
Literary Criticism see LITERARY AND POLITICAL REVIEWS 555, see also LITERATURE 558
LITERATURE 558, see also LINGUISTICS 539, LITERARY AND POLITICAL REVIEWS 555
LITERATURE — Abstracting, Bibliographies, Statistics 577
LITERATURE — Poetry 578, see also LITERARY AND POLITICAL REVIEWS 555
Lithography see PRINTING 733
Little Magazines see LITERARY AND POLITICAL REVIEWS 555
Livestock see AGRICULTURE - Poultry and Livestock 43, see also VETERINARY SCIENCE 893
Lubrication and Lubricants see ENGINEERING - Mechanical Engineering 381, see also PETROLEUM AND GAS 677
LUMBER AND WOOD 412, see also BUILDING AND CONSTRUCTION - Carpentry and Woodwork 141
Machine Translating see COMPUTER TECHNOLOGY AND APPLICATIONS 269, see also LINGUISTICS 539
MACHINERY 582, see also AGRICULTURE - Agricultural Equipment 32, ENGINEERING - Mechanical Engineering 381, TECHNOLOGY 849
MACROECONOMICS 212
Macromolecules see CHEMISTRY - Organic Chemistry 252
Magic see HOBBIES 475
Magnetism see ELECTRICITY AND ELECTRICAL ENGINEERING 351
Mail Order Business see BUSINESS AND ECONOMICS - Marketing and Purchasing 217
Malacology see BIOLOGY - Zoology 126
MANAGEMENT 213
Marijuana see DRUG ABUSE AND ALCOHOLISM 286
Marine Biology see BIOLOGY 100, see also EARTH SCIENCES - Oceanography 309
Marine Engineering see ENGINEERING 365, see also TRANSPORTATION - Ships and Shipping 876
Maritime Law see LAW 507
MARKETING AND PURCHASING 217
Marxism see BUSINESS AND ECONOMICS - Economic Systems and Theories, Economic History 191, see also POLITICAL SCIENCE 707
Mathematical Geography see GEOGRAPHY 419
Mathematical Physics see PHYSICS 695
MATHEMATICS 583
MATHEMATICS — Abstracting, Bibliographies, Statistics 591
Mechanical Drawing see ENGINEERING 365, see also TECHNOLOGY 849
MECHANICAL ENGINEERING 381, see also MACHINERY 582, TECHNOLOGY 849
Mechanical Handling see MACHINERY 582, see also TECHNOLOGY 849, TRANSPORTATION 861
Mechanical Translating see COMPUTER TECHNOLOGY AND APPLICATIONS 269, see also LINGUISTICS 539
MECHANICS 700
Medical Bacteriology see MEDICAL SCIENCES - Communicable Diseases 607
Medical Engineering see MEDICAL SCIENCES 591
Medical Jurisprudence see MEDICAL SCIENCES - Forensic Sciences 612
Medical Parasitology see MEDICAL SCIENCES - Communicable Diseases 607
MEDICAL SCIENCES 591, see also BIOLOGY 100, DRUG ABUSE AND ALCOHOLISM 286, GERONTOLOGY AND GERIATRICS 428, HOSPITALS 480, INDUSTRIAL HEALTH AND SAFETY 495, NUTRITION AND DIETETICS 665, PHARMACY AND PHARMACOLOGY 683, PHYSICAL FITNESS AND HYGIENE 694, PUBLIC HEALTH AND SAFETY 750
MEDICAL SCIENCES — Abstracting, Bibliographies, Statistics 601
MEDICAL SCIENCES — Allergology And Immunology 603
MEDICAL SCIENCES — Anaesthesiology 604
MEDICAL SCIENCES — Cancer 604
MEDICAL SCIENCES — Cardiovascular Diseases 606
MEDICAL SCIENCES — Chiropractics, Homeopathy, Osteopathy 607
MEDICAL SCIENCES — Communicable Diseases 607
MEDICAL SCIENCES — Dentistry 608
MEDICAL SCIENCES — Dermatology And Venereology 610
MEDICAL SCIENCES — Endocrinology 611
MEDICAL SCIENCES — Experimental Medicine, Laboratory Technique 612
MEDICAL SCIENCES — Forensic Sciences 612
MEDICAL SCIENCES — Gastroenterology 613
MEDICAL SCIENCES — Hematology 613
MEDICAL SCIENCES — Hypnosis 613
MEDICAL SCIENCES — Nurses And Nursing 613
MEDICAL SCIENCES — Obstetrics And Gynecology 614
MEDICAL SCIENCES — Ophthalmology And Optometry 615
MEDICAL SCIENCES — Orthopedics And Traumatology 616
MEDICAL SCIENCES — Otorhinolaryngology 617
MEDICAL SCIENCES — Pediatrics 617
MEDICAL SCIENCES — Psychiatry And Neurology 618
MEDICAL SCIENCES — Radiology And Nuclear Medicine 622
MEDICAL SCIENCES — Respiratory Diseases 623
MEDICAL SCIENCES — Rheumatology 623
MEDICAL SCIENCES — Surgery 624
MEDICAL SCIENCES — Urology And Nephrology 625
Medieval Studies see HISTORY - History of Europe 448, see also LITERATURE 558, PHILOSOPHY 686

MEETINGS AND CONGRESSES 626
Menswear see CLOTHING TRADE 261
Mental Hygiene see PUBLIC HEALTH AND SAFETY 750
Mental Retardation see EDUCATION - Special Education and Rehabilitation 345, see also MEDICAL SCIENCES - Psychiatry and Neurology 618, PSYCHOLOGY 734
Merchandising see BUSINESS AND ECONOMICS - Marketing and Purchasing 217
Metabolism see BIOLOGY - Physiology 125, see also MEDICAL SCIENCES 591
Metal Industries see METALLURGY 626
METALLURGY 626
METALLURGY — Abstracting, Bibliographies, Statistics 631
METALLURGY — Welding 631
Metaphysics see PHILOSOPHY 686
METEOROLOGY 631
METEOROLOGY — Abstracting, Bibliographies, Statistics 636
METROLOGY AND STANDARDIZATION 636
MICROBIOLOGY 123
Microfilming see PHOTOGRAPHY 692
Microphotography see PHOTOGRAPHY 692
MICROSCOPY 124
Microwaves see ELECTRICITY AND ELECTRICAL ENGINEERING 351
Midwifery see MEDICAL SCIENCES - Obstetrics and Gynecology 614
Migration see POPULATION STUDIES 725
MILITARY 638
MILITARY — Abstracting, Bibliographies, Statistics 641
Military Engineering see ENGINEERING 365
Military Law see LAW 507, see also MILITARY 638
Military Medicine see MEDICAL SCIENCES 591
Millinery see CLOTHING TRADE 261
Milling see AGRICULTURE - Feed, Flour and Grain 41
Mineral Resources see EARTH SCIENCES - Geology 290, see also MINES AND MINING INDUSTRY 641
Mineralogy see EARTH SCIENCES - Geology 290
MINES AND MINING INDUSTRY 641
MINES AND MINING INDUSTRY — Abstracting, Bibliographies, Statistics 648
Missiles see AERONAUTICS AND SPACE FLIGHT 6
Mobile Homes see HOUSING AND URBAN PLANNING 483, see also TRANSPORTATION 861
Models and Model Building see HOBBIES 475
Mollusca see BIOLOGY - Zoology 126
Morphology see BIOLOGY 100, see also MEDICAL SCIENCES 591
Mosses see BIOLOGY - Botany 112
Motels see HOTELS AND RESTAURANTS 482
MOTION PICTURES 648
MOTION PICTURES — Abstracting, Bibliographies, Statistics 651
Motor Scooters see SPORTS AND GAMES - Bicycles and Motorcycles 826
Motorcycles see SPORTS AND GAMES - Bicycles and Motorcycles 826
Mountaineering see SPORTS AND GAMES - Outdoor Life 828
Movies see MOTION PICTURES 648
Multiple Sclerosis see MEDICAL SCIENCES - Psychiatry and Neurology 618
MUNICIPAL GOVERNMENT 748
Municipal Law see LAW 507, see also PUBLIC ADMINISTRATION - Municipal Government 748
Municipal Transportation see TRANSPORTATION 861
MUSEUMS AND ART GALLERIES 651
MUSEUMS AND ART GALLERIES — Abstracting, Bibliographies, Statistics 656
MUSIC 656
MUSIC — Abstracting, Bibliographies, Statistics 665
Music Therapy see EDUCATION - Special Education and Rehabilitation 345, see also MUSIC 656
Mycology see BIOLOGY - Botany 112
Mysteries see ADVENTURE AND ROMANCE 4, see also LITERATURE 558
Mythology see FOLKLORE 401
Narcotics see DRUG ABUSE AND ALCOHOLISM 286, see also PHARMACY AND PHARMACOLOGY 683
Natural Food see NUTRITION AND DIETETICS 665
Natural Resources see CONSERVATION 274, see also ENVIRONMENTAL STUDIES 383
Naturalization see POLITICAL SCIENCE 707
Nautical Arts and Sciences see TRANSPORTATION - Ships and Shipping 876
Naval Architecture see TRANSPORTATION - Ships and Shipping 876
Naval Engineering see TRANSPORTATION - Ships and Shipping 876
Naval Medicine see MEDICAL SCIENCES 591
NEEDLEWORK 476
Nephrology see MEDICAL SCIENCES - Urology and Nephrology 625
Neurology see MEDICAL SCIENCES - Psychiatry and Neurology 618
Neurophysiology see MEDICAL SCIENCES - Psychiatry and Neurology 618
Neuroradiology see MEDICAL SCIENCES - Radiology and Nuclear Medicine 622
Neurosurgery see MEDICAL SCIENCES - Psychiatry and Neurology 618, see also MEDICAL SCIENCES - Surgery 624
North American History see HISTORY - History of North and South America 465
Notions see GIFTWARE AND TOYS 429
NUCLEAR ENERGY 701
Nuclear Medicine see MEDICAL SCIENCES - Radiology and Nuclear Medicine 622
Nudism see PHYSICAL FITNESS AND HYGIENE 694
NUMISMATICS 477
Nurseries see GARDENING AND HORTICULTURE - Florist Trade 416
NURSES AND NURSING 613
Nursing Homes see HOSPITALS 480, see also SOCIAL SERVICES AND WELFARE 803
NUTRITION AND DIETETICS 665, see also FOOD AND FOOD INDUSTRIES 403, HOSPITALS 480, PHARMACY AND PHARMACOLOGY 683, PHYSICAL FITNESS AND HYGIENE 694
NUTRITION AND DIETETICS — Abstracting, Bibliographies, Statistics 666
OBSTETRICS AND GYNECOLOGY 614
Occultism see PARAPSYCHOLOGY AND OCCULTISM 676

Occupational Therapy see EDUCATION - Special Education and Rehabilitation 345, see also MEDICAL SCIENCES 591
OCCUPATIONS AND CAREERS 666, see also BUSINESS AND ECONOMICS - Labor and Industrial Relations 205
OCCUPATIONS AND CAREERS — Abstracting, Bibliographies, Statistics 668
OCEANOGRAPHY 309
OFFICE EQUIPMENT AND SERVICES 219
Old Age see GERONTOLOGY AND GERIATRICS 428
Old Age Insurance see INSURANCE 497
Operations Research see COMPUTER TECHNOLOGY AND APPLICATIONS 269, see also MATHEMATICS 583
OPHTHALMOLOGY AND OPTOMETRY 615
OPTICS 705
Optometry see MEDICAL SCIENCES - Ophthalmology and Optometry 615
ORGANIC CHEMISTRY 252
ORIENTAL RELIGIONS 771
ORIENTAL STUDIES 668, see also HISTORY - History of Asia 441, LINGUISTICS 539, LITERATURE 558, PHILOSOPHY 686
ORIENTAL STUDIES — Abstracting, Bibliographies, Statistics 672
ORNITHOLOGY 124
Orthodontics see MEDICAL SCIENCES - Dentistry 608
ORTHOPEDICS AND TRAUMATOLOGY 616
Osteopathy see MEDICAL SCIENCES - Chiropractics, Homeopathy, Osteopathy 607
Otology see MEDICAL SCIENCES - Otorhinolaryngology 617
OTORHINOLARYNGOLOGY 617
OUTDOOR LIFE 828
PACKAGING 672
PACKAGING — Abstracting, Bibliographies, Statistics 672
PAINTS AND PROTECTIVE COATINGS 673
PAINTS AND PROTECTIVE COATINGS — Abstracting, Bibliographies, Statistics 673
Paleobotany see BIOLOGY - Botany 112
PALEONTOLOGY 673
PAPER AND PULP 675, see also FORESTS AND FORESTRY - Lumber and Wood 412
PAPER AND PULP — Abstracting, Bibliographies, Statistics 676
Papyrus see PAPER AND PULP 675
Parachuting see SPORTS AND GAMES 818
Paraplegia see MEDICAL SCIENCES - Psychiatry and Neurology 618
PARAPSYCHOLOGY AND OCCULTISM 676
Parasitology see BIOLOGY 100
Parent Teacher Associations see EDUCATION - School Organization and Administration 343
Parks and Recreation Areas see CONSERVATION 274, see also SPORTS AND GAMES - Outdoor Life 828, TRAVEL AND TOURISM 882
PATENTS, TRADEMARKS AND COPYRIGHTS 676
Peat see HEATING, PLUMBING AND REFRIGERATION 429
PEDIATRICS 617
Penology see CRIMINOLOGY AND LAW ENFORCEMENT 280
Pensions see BUSINESS AND ECONOMICS - Labor and Industrial Relations 205, see also INSURANCE 497, SOCIAL SERVICES AND WELFARE 803
PERFUMES AND COSMETICS 85
PERSONNEL MANAGEMENT 219
Pest Control see AGRICULTURE 11, see also BIOLOGY - Entomology 120, PUBLIC HEALTH AND SAFETY 750
PETROLEUM AND GAS 677
PETROLEUM AND GAS — Abstracting, Bibliographies, Statistics 682
Petrology see EARTH SCIENCES - Geology 290
PETS 682
PHARMACY AND PHARMACOLOGY 683, see also MEDICAL SCIENCES 591
PHARMACY AND PHARMACOLOGY — Abstracting, Bibliographies, Statistics 686
Philanthropy see SOCIAL SERVICES AND WELFARE 803
PHILATELY 478
Philology see LINGUISTICS 539
PHILOSOPHY 686
PHILOSOPHY — Abstracting, Bibliographies, Statistics 692
Phonetics see LINGUISTICS 539
Phonographs see MUSIC 656, see also SOUND RECORDING AND REPRODUCTION 818
Photogrammetry see GEOGRAPHY 419, see also PHOTOGRAPHY 692
Photographic Surveying see ENGINEERING - Civil Engineering 374
PHOTOGRAPHY 692, see also MOTION PICTURES 648
PHOTOGRAPHY — Abstracting, Bibliographies, Statistics 694
Photomechanical Processing see PRINTING 733
PHYSICAL CHEMISTRY 254
Physical Education see EDUCATION - Teaching Methods and Curriculum 347, see also SPORTS AND GAMES 818
PHYSICAL FITNESS AND HYGIENE 694
PHYSICAL FITNESS AND HYGIENE — Abstracting, Bibliographies, Statistics 695
Physical Therapy see MEDICAL SCIENCES 591
PHYSICS 695
PHYSICS — Abstracting, Bibliographies, Statistics 700
PHYSICS — Heat 700
PHYSICS — Mechanics 700
PHYSICS — Nuclear Energy 701
PHYSICS — Optics 705
PHYSICS — Sound 706
PHYSIOLOGY 125
Planned Parenthood see BIRTH CONTROL 131
Plant Breeding see AGRICULTURE - Crop Production and Soil 32, see also BIOLOGY - Botany 112, GARDENING AND HORTICULTURE 414
Plasma Physics see PHYSICS 695
Plastic Surgery see MEDICAL SCIENCES - Surgery 624
PLASTICS 706, see also CHEMISTRY - Physical chemistry 254, ENGINEERING - Chemical Engineering 372

Plays see LITERATURE 558, see also THEATER 858
Plumbing see HEATING, PLUMBING AND REFRIGERATION 429
POETRY 578
Poliomyelitis see MEDICAL SCIENCES - Psychiatry and Neurology 618
Political Reviews see LITERARY AND POLITICAL REVIEWS 555
POLITICAL SCIENCE 707, see also LITERARY AND POLITICAL REVIEWS 555, PUBLIC ADMINISTRATION 739
POLITICAL SCIENCE — Abstracting, Bibliographies, Statistics 717
POLITICAL SCIENCE — Civil Rights 718
POLITICAL SCIENCE — International Relations 719
Pollution see ENVIRONMENTAL STUDIES 383, see also PUBLIC HEALTH AND SAFETY 750
Polymers see CHEMISTRY 245, see also ENGINEERING - Chemical Engineering 372
POPULATION STUDIES 725
POPULATION STUDIES — Abstracting, Bibliographies, Statistcs 731
Ports see TRANSPORTATION - Ships and Shipping 876
Portuguese LANGUAGE - Study and Teaching see LINGUISTICS 539
POSTAL AFFAIRS 266
POULTRY AND LIVESTOCK 43
Power Plants see ELECTRICITY AND ELECTRICAL ENGINEERING 351, see also ENERGY 361
Pre-school Education see EDUCATION 313
Precision Mechanics see INSTRUMENTS 496
Prefabricated Houses see BUILDING AND CONSTRUCTION 133
Preventive Medicine see PUBLIC HEALTH AND SAFETY 750
PRINTING 733
Prisons see CRIMINOLOGY AND LAW ENFORCEMENT 280
Private Schools see EDUCATION - Guides to Schools and Colleges 330, see also EDUCATION - School Organization and Administration 343
PRODUCTION OF GOODS AND SERVICES 220
Programmed Instruction see EDUCATION - Teaching Methods and Curriculum 347
Programming, Automatic see COMPUTER TECHNOLOGY AND APPLICATIONS 269
Proofreading see JOURNALISM 504, see also PRINTING 733
Prosthetics see MEDICAL SCIENCES - Orthopedics and Traumatology 616
Protective Coatings see PAINTS AND PROTECTIVE COATINGS 673
PROTESTANTISM 771
Protozoology see BIOLOGY - Zoology 126
PSYCHIATRY AND NEUROLOGY 618
Psychic Phenomena see PARAPSYCHOLOGY AND OCCULTISM 676
Psychical Research see PARAPSYCHOLOGY AND OCCULTISM 676
Psychoanalysis see PSYCHOLOGY 734
Psychological Testing see PSYCHOLOGY 734
PSYCHOLOGY 734
PSYCHOLOGY — Abstracting, Bibliographies, Statistics 739
Psychosomatic Medicine see MEDICAL SCIENCES 591
Psychotherapy see MEDICAL SCIENCES - Psychiatry and Neurology 618
PUBLIC ADMINISTRATION 739, see also POLITICAL SCIENCE 707
PUBLIC ADMINISTRATION — Abstracting, Bibliographies, Statistics 747
PUBLIC ADMINISTRATION — Municipal Government 748
Public Affairs see POLITICAL SCIENCE 707, see also PUBLIC ADMINISTRATION 739, SOCIAL SCIENCES 795
PUBLIC FINANCE, TAXATION 226
PUBLIC HEALTH AND SAFETY 750, see also DRUG ABUSE AND ALCOHOLISM 286, ENVIRONMENTAL STUDIES 383, FIRE PREVENTION 394, FUNERALS 414, HOSPITALS 480, INDUSTRIAL HEALTH AND SAFETY 495, MEDICAL SCIENCES 591
PUBLIC HEALTH AND SAFETY — Abstracting, Bibliographies, Statistics 756
Public Relations see ADVERTISING AND PUBLIC RELATIONS 4
Public Utilities see ELECTRICITY AND ELECTRICAL ENGINEERING 351, see also PETROLEUM AND GAS 677, PUBLIC ADMINISTRATION 739
Public Welfare see SOCIAL SERVICES AND WELFARE 803
Public Works see BUILDING AND CONSTRUCTION 133, see also ENGINEERING - Civil Engineering 374, HOUSING AND URBAN PLANNING 483, PUBLIC ADMINISTRATION 739
Publicity see ADVERTISING AND PUBLIC RELATIONS 4
PUBLISHING AND BOOK TRADE 757, see also BIBLIOGRAPHIES 87, LIBRARY AND INFORMATION SCIENCES 525, PATENTS, TRADEMARKS AND COPYRIGHTS 676, PRINTING 733
PUBLISHING AND BOOK TRADE — Abstracting, Bibliographies, Statistics 760
Puppets see HOBBIES 475, see also THEATER 858
Puzzles see SPORTS AND GAMES 818
Quality Control see BUSINESS AND ECONOMICS - Management 213, see also METROLOGY AND STANDARDIZATION 636
Quantum Chemistry see CHEMISTRY - Physical Chemistry 254
Quarries see MINES AND MINING INDUSTRY 641
Race Relations see POLITICAL SCIENCE - Civil Rights 718, see also SOCIOLOGY 811
Radar see COMMUNICATIONS 263
Radiation see ASTRONOMY 80, see also BIOLOGY - Biophysics 112, CHEMISTRY - Physical Chemistry 254, MEDICAL SCIENCES - Radiology and Nuclear Medicine 622, PHYSICS - Nuclear Energy 701
Radio Advertising see ADVERTISING AND PUBLIC RELATIONS 4, see also COMMUNICATIONS - Radio and Television 266
RADIO AND TELEVISION 266
Radiobiology see BIOLOGY 100
Radiocarbon see PHYSICS - Nuclear Energy 701
RADIOLOGY AND NUCLEAR MEDICINE 622
Railroad Engineering see TRANSPORTATION - Railroads 872
RAILROADS 872
Railway Ties see FORESTS AND FORESTRY - Lumber and Wood 412, see also TRANSPORTATION - Railroads 872
Rare Earths see CHEMISTRY - Inorganic Chemistry 251
Reading Guides and Aids see ABSTRACTING AND INDEXING SERVICES 1, see also BIBLIOGRAPHIES 87, EDUCATION - Teaching Methods and Curriculum 347, LIBRARY AND INFORMATION SCIENCES 525

xxxix

REAL ESTATE 761, see also BUILDING AND CONSTRUCTION 133, HOUSING AND URBAN PLANNING 483
REAL ESTATE — Abstracting, Bibliographies, Statistics 762
Recorded Music see MUSIC 656, see also SOUND RECORDING AND REPRODUCTION 818
Recreation see DANCE 285, see also HOBBIES 475, SPORTS AND GAMES 818
Recreation Areas see CONSERVATION 274, see also TRAVEL AND TOURISM 882
Red Cross see SOCIAL SERVICES AND WELFARE 803
Refrigeration see HEATING, PLUMBING AND REFRIGERATION 429, see also PHYSICS - Heat 700
Regional Planning see HOUSING AND URBAN PLANNING 483
Rehabilitation see EDUCATION - Special Education and Rehabilitation 345, see also MEDICAL SCIENCES 591, SOCIAL SERVICES AND WELFARE 803
RELIGIONS AND THEOLOGY 762
RELIGIONS AND THEOLOGY — Abstracting, Bibliographies, Statistics 769
RELIGIONS AND THEOLOGY — Islamic 769
RELIGIONS AND THEOLOGY — Judaic 770
RELIGIONS AND THEOLOGY — Oriental 771
RELIGIONS AND THEOLOGY — Other Denominations And Sects 776
RELIGIONS AND THEOLOGY — Protestant 771
RELIGIONS AND THEOLOGY — Roman Catholic 773
Religious History see RELIGIONS AND THEOLOGY 762
Reproduction and Fertility see BIOLOGY 100, see also MEDICAL SCIENCES 591
Resins see PLASTICS 706
Resorts see HOTELS AND RESTAURANTS 482, see also TRAVEL AND TOURISM 882
RESPIRATORY DISEASES 623
Restaurants see HOTELS AND RESTAURANTS 482
Retailing see BUSINESS AND ECONOMICS - Marketing and Purchasing 217
Rheology see PHYSICS - Mechanics 700
RHEUMATOLOGY 623
Rhinology see MEDICAL SCIENCES - Otorhinolaryngology 617
ROADS AND TRAFFIC 874
Rockets see AERONAUTICS AND SPACE FLIGHT 6
Rodeo see SPORTS AND GAMES - Horses and Horsemanship 827
Roller Skating see SPORTS AND GAMES 818
ROMAN CATHOLICISM 773
RUBBER 777, see also ENGINEERING - Chemical Engineering 372, PLASTICS 706
RUBBER — Abstracting, Bibliographies, Statistics 778
Rugby see SPORTS AND GAMES - Ball Games 823
Safety Education see BUSINESS AND ECONOMICS - Labor and Industrial Relations 205, see also PUBLIC HEALTH AND SAFETY 750, TRANSPORTATION - Roads and Traffic 874
Sailing see SPORTS AND GAMES - Boats and Boating 826
Salesmanship see BUSINESS AND ECONOMICS - Marketing and Purchasing 217
Sanitary Engineering see PUBLIC HEALTH AND SAFETY 750
Sanitation see ENGINEERING - Civil Engineering 374, see also PHYSICAL FITNESS AND HYGIENE 694, PUBLIC HEALTH AND SAFETY 750
Scholarships see EDUCATION - Higher Education 333
SCHOOL ORGANIZATION AND ADMINISTRATION 343
Science Fiction see LITERATURE 558
SCIENCES: COMPREHENSIVE WORKS 778
SCIENCES: COMPREHENSIVE WORKS — Abstracting, Bibliographies, Statistics 794
Scooters see SPORTS AND GAMES - Bicycles and Motorcycles 826
Sculpture see ART 71
Seaweed see BIOLOGY - Botany 112, see also EARTH SCIENCES - Oceanography 309
Sediment Data see ENGINEERING - Hydraulic Engineering 380
Sedimentology see EARTH SCIENCES - Geophysics 303
Seismology see EARTH SCIENCES - Geophysics 303
Semantics see LINGUISTICS 539
Semiconductors see ELECTRICITY AND ELECTRICAL ENGINEERING 351
Service Stations see PETROLEUM AND GAS 677, see also TRANSPORTATION - Automobiles 869
Sewage and Waste Treatment see PUBLIC ADMINISTRATION 739, see also PUBLIC HEALTH AND SAFETY 750
Sewing see CLOTHING TRADE - Fashions 262, see also HOBBIES - Needlework 476
Sex Education see PHYSICAL FITNESS AND HYGIENE 694
Sheet Metal see METALLURGY 626
Shipbuilding see TRANSPORTATION - Ships and Shipping 876
SHIPS AND SHIPPING 876
SHOES AND BOOTS 795, see also LEATHER AND FUR INDUSTRIES 524
SHOES AND BOOTS — Abstracting, Bibliographies, Statistics 795
Shooting see SPORTS AND GAMES - Outdoor Life 828
Short Wave see COMMUNICATIONS - Radio and Television 266
Shorthand see BUSINESS AND ECONOMICS - Office Equipment and Services 219
Sign Manufacturing see ADVERTISING AND PUBLIC RELATIONS 4
Silicosis see MEDICAL SCIENCES 591
Skating see SPORTS AND GAMES 818
Skeet Shooting see SPORTS AND GAMES - Outdoor Life 828
Skiing see SPORTS AND GAMES - Outdoor Life 828
Slavonic Languages - Study and Teaching see LINGUISTICS 539
SMALL BUSINESS 234
Smoking see DRUG ABUSE AND ALCOHOLISM 286, see also PHYSICAL FITNESS AND HYGIENE 694, PUBLIC HEALTH AND SAFETY 750, TOBACCO 860
Soap see BEAUTY CULTURE - Perfumes and Cosmetics 85
Soccer see SPORTS AND GAMES - Ball Games 823
Social Insurance see INSURANCE 497, see also SOCIAL SERVICES AND WELFARE 803
Social Psychology see PSYCHOLOGY 734, see also SOCIOLOGY 811
SOCIAL SCIENCES: COMPREHENSIVE WORKS 795

SOCIAL SCIENCES: COMPREHENSIVE WORKS — Abstracting, Bibliographies, Statistics 802
Social Security see INSURANCE 497, see also SOCIAL SERVICES AND WELFARE 803
SOCIAL SERVICES AND WELFARE 803
SOCIAL SERVICES AND WELFARE — Abstracting, Bibliographies, Statistics 810
Socialism see BUSINESS AND ECONOMICS - Economic Systems and Theories, Economic History 191, see also POLITICAL SCIENCE 707
SOCIOLOGY 811, see also POPULATION STUDIES 725
SOCIOLOGY — Abstracting, Bibliographies, Statistics 818
Soft Drinks see BEVERAGES 85
Soil see AGRICULTURE - Crop Production and Soil 32, see also CONSERVATION 274, ENGINEERING - Civil Engineering 374
Solar Energy see ASTRONOMY 80, see also ENERGY 361, PHYSICS 695
Solar Energy Engineering see ENGINEERING - Mechanical Engineering 381
SOUND 706
SOUND RECORDING AND REPRODUCTION 818
SOUND RECORDING AND REPRODUCTION — Abstracting, Bibliographies, Statistics 818
South American History see HISTORY - History of North and South America 465
Space Flight see AERONAUTICS AND SPACE FLIGHT 6
Spanish Language - Study and Teaching see LINGUISTICS 539
Spearfishing see SPORTS AND GAMES - Outdoor Life 828
SPECIAL EDUCATION AND REHABILITATION 345
Spectroscopy see PHYSICS - Optics 705
Speech and Hearing Disorders see DEAF 286, see also EDUCATION - Special Education and Rehabilitation 345, MEDICAL SCIENCES - Psychiatry and Neurology 618
Speech - Study and Teaching see EDUCATION - Special Education and Rehabilitation 345, see also LINGUISTICS 539
Speleology see EARTH SCIENCES - Geophysics 303
Spices see FOOD AND FOOD INDUSTRIES 403
Spinning see HOBBIES - Needlework 476
Spiritualism see PARAPSYCHOLOGY AND OCCULTISM 676
Sporting Goods see SPORTS AND GAMES 818
SPORTS AND GAMES 818
SPORTS AND GAMES — Abstracting, Bibliographies, Statistics 823
SPORTS AND GAMES — Ball Games 823
SPORTS AND GAMES — Bicycles And Motorcycles 826
SPORTS AND GAMES — Boats And Boating 826
SPORTS AND GAMES — Horses And Horsemanship 827
SPORTS AND GAMES — Outdoor Life 828
Sports Cars see TRANSPORTATION - Automobiles 869
Sports Medicine see MEDICAL SCIENCES - Surgery 624
Sportswear see CLOTHING Trade 261
Stained Glass see ART 71, see also CERAMICS, GLASS AND POTTERY 243
Standards see METROLOGY AND STANDARDIZATION 636
Stationery and Office Equipment see BUSINESS AND ECONOMICS - Office Equipment and Services 219
STATISTICS 832, see also POPULATION STUDIES 725
Stenography see BUSINESS AND ECONOMICS - Office Equipment and Services 219
Sterilization see BIRTH CONTROL 131
Stock and Stock-Breeding see AGRICULTURE - Poultry and Livestock 43
Stocks and Bonds see BUSINESS AND ECONOMICS - Investments 202
Storage Batteries see ELECTRICITY AND ELECTRICAL ENGINEERING 351
Store Display and Promotion see ADVERTISING AND PUBLIC RELATIONS 4
Street Lighting see ELECTRICITY AND ELECTRICAL ENGINEERING 351, see also PUBLIC ADMINISTRATION - Municipal Government 748
Stress see PSYCHOLOGY 734
Student Aid see EDUCATION 313
Supermarkets see FOOD AND FOOD INDUSTRIES - Grocery Trade 407
Surfing see SPORTS AND GAMES - Outdoor Life 828
SURGERY 624
Surgical Instruments see MEDICAL SCIENCES - Surgery 624
Surveying see ENGINEERING - Civil Engineering 374, see also GEOGRAPHY 419
Swimming see SPORTS AND GAMES 818
Synthetic Fabrics see TEXTILE INDUSTRIES AND FABRICS 854
Table Tennis see SPORTS AND GAMES - Ball Games 823
Tailoring see CLOTHING TRADE 261
Talking Books see BLIND 133
Tape Recording see SOUND RECORDING AND REPRODUCTION 818
Tariffs see BUSINESS AND ECONOMICS - International Commerce 192, see also BUSINESS AND ECONOMICS - Public Finance, Taxation 226
TAXATION 849, see also BUSINESS AND ECONOMICS - Public Finance, Taxation 226
Taxicabs see TRANSPORTATION - Automobiles 869
TEACHING METHODS AND CURRICULUM 347
TECHNOLOGY: COMPREHENSIVE WORKS 849
TECHNOLOGY: COMPREHENSIVE WORKS — Abstracting, Bibliographies, Statistics 854
Telecommunications see COMMUNICATIONS 263, see also ELECTRICITY AND ELECTRICAL ENGINEERING 351
Telegraph see COMMUNICATIONS - Telephone and Telegraph 269
TELEPHONE AND TELEGRAPH 269
Television see COMMUNICATIONS - Radio and Television 266, see also MOTION PICTURES 648
Tennis see SPORTS AND GAMES - Ball Games 823
Textbooks see EDUCATION - Teaching Methods and Curriculum 347, see also PUBLISHING AND BOOK TRADE 757
TEXTILE INDUSTRIES AND FABRICS 854
TEXTILE INDUSTRIES AND FABRICS — Abstracting, Bibliographies, Statistics 857
Thanatology see MEDICAL SCIENCES 591
THEATER 858
THEATER — Abstracting, Bibliographies, Statistics 860
Theology see RELIGIONS AND THEOLOGY 762

Theosophy see PHILOSOPHY 686, see also RELIGIONS AND THEOLOGY 762
Thermodynamics see CHEMISTRY - Physical Chemistry 254, see also PHYSICS - Heat 700
Thoracic Surgery see MEDICAL SCIENCES - Surgery 624
Thrombosis see MEDICAL SCIENCES - Cardiovascular Diseases 606
Timber see FORESTS AND FORESTRY - Lumber and Wood 412
Timetables see TRANSPORTATION 861
Tires see RUBBER 777, see also TRANSPORTATION - Automobiles 869
TOBACCO 860
TOBACCO — Abstracting, Bibliographies, Statistics 861
Tools see MACHINERY 582
Touring see TRAVEL AND TOURISM 882
Tourist Camps see HOTELS AND RESTAURANTS 482, see also TRAVEL AND TOURISM 882
Town Planning see HOUSING AND URBAN PLANNING 483
Toxicology see MEDICAL SCIENCES 591, see also PHARMACY AND PHARMACOLOGY 683
Toys see GIFTWARE AND TOYS 429
Track and Field see SPORTS AND GAMES 818
Tractors see AGRICULTURE - Agricultural Equipment 32
Trade see BUSINESS AND ECONOMICS - Domestic Commerce 181, see also BUSINESS AND ECONOMICS - International Commerce 192
TRADE AND INDUSTRIAL DIRECTORIES 234
Trade Unions see LABOR UNIONS 506
Trademarks see PATENTS, TRADEMARKS AND COPYRIGHTS 676
Traffic see TRANSPORTATION - Roads and Traffic 874
Trailers see TRANSPORTATION 861
Transistors see ELECTRICITY AND ELECTRICAL ENGINEERING 351
Translation Services see LINGUISTICS 539
TRANSPORTATION 861
TRANSPORTATION — Abstracting, Bibliographies, Statistics 864
TRANSPORTATION — Air Transport 867
TRANSPORTATION — Automobiles 869
Transportation Law see LAW 507
TRANSPORTATION — Railroads 872
TRANSPORTATION — Roads and Traffic 874
TRANSPORTATION — Ships And Shipping 876
TRANSPORTATION — Trucks And Trucking 881
Trapshooting see SPORTS AND GAMES - Outdoor Life 828
Traumatology see MEDICAL SCIENCES - Orthopedics and Traumatology 616
TRAVEL AND TOURISM 882, see also GEOGRAPHY 419, HOTELS AND RESTAURANTS 482
TRAVEL AND TOURISM — Abstracting, Bibliographies, Statistics 893
Treaties see LAW - International Law 522
Trees see FORESTS AND FORESTRY 407, see also GARDENING AND HORTICULTURE 414
Tropical Diseases see MEDICAL SCIENCES - Communicable Diseases 607
Tuberculosis see MEDICAL SCIENCES - Respiratory Diseases 623
Typewriters see BUSINESS AND ECONOMICS - Office Equipment and Services 219
Typography see PRINTING 733
Ultrasonics see PHYSICS - Sound 706
Underground Periodicals see LITERARY AND POLITICAL REVIEWS 555, see also POLITICAL SCIENCE 707
Underwear see CLOTHING TRADE 261
Unemployment see BUSINESS AND ECONOMICS - Labor and Industrial Relations 205
Unidentified Flying Objects see AERONAUTICS AND SPACE FLIGHT 6
Unions see LABOR UNIONS 506
U. S. Armed Forces see MILITARY 638
Universities and Colleges see EDUCATION - Higher Education 333

Upholstery see INTERIOR DESIGN AND DECORATION - Furniture and House Furnishings 503
Urban Renewal see HOUSING AND URBAN PLANNING 483
UROLOGY AND NEPHROLOGY 625
Vaccines see PHARMACY AND PHARMACOLOGY 683
Vacuum Sciences see ENGINEERING - Mechanical Engineering 381, see also PHYSICS - Mechanics 700
Vegetarianism see NUTRITION AND DIETETICS 665
Vending Machines see BUSINESS AND ECONOMICS - Marketing and Purchasing 217
Venereology see MEDICAL SCIENCES - Dermatology and Venereology 610
Ventilation see HEATING, PLUMBING AND REFRIGERATION 429
Veterans see MILITARY 638
VETERINARY SCIENCE 893
VETERINARY SCIENCE — Abstracting, Bibliographies, Statistics 895
Virology see BIOLOGY - Microbiology 123
Vital Statistics see POPULATION STUDIES 725
Vitamins see PHARMACY AND PHARMACOLOGY 683
Viticulture see AGRICULTURE - Crop Production and Soil 32
Vocational Education see EDUCATION - Teaching Methods and Curriculum 313, see also OCCUPATIONS AND CAREERS 666
Volume Feeding see HOTELS AND RESTAURANTS 482
Wages see BUSINESS AND ECONOMICS - Labor and Industrial Relations 205
Waste Reclamation see ENVIRONMENTAL STUDIES 383
Water Pollution see ENVIRONMENTAL STUDIES 383
WATER RESOURCES 895, see also AGRICULTURE 11, CONSERVATION 274, ENVIRONMENTAL STUDIES 383, PUBLIC HEALTH AND SAFETY 750
WATER RESOURCES — Abstracting, Bibliographies, Statistics 900
Water Sports see SPORTS AND GAMES 818
Weather see METEOROLOGY 631
Weaving see HOBBIES - Needlework 476, see also TEXTILE INDUSTRIES AND FABRICS 854
Weights and Measures see METROLOGY AND STANDARDIZATION 636
WELDING 631
Welfare see SOCIAL SERVICES AND WELFARE 803
Wildlife see BIOLOGY 100, see also CONSERVATION 274
Window Covering see INTERIOR DESIGN AND DECORATION - Furniture and House Furnishings 503
Windows see BUILDING AND CONSTRUCTION 133, see also CERAMICS, GLASS AND POTTERY 243
Wine see BEVERAGES 85
Wire see MACHINERY 582, see also METALLURGY 582
Wit and Humor see LITERARY AND POLITICAL REVIEWS 555
WOMEN'S INTERESTS 900
WOMEN'S INTERESTS — Abstracting, Bibliographies, Statistics 901
Women's Liberation Movement see POLITICAL SCIENCE - Civil Rights 718, see also WOMEN'S INTERESTS 900
Women's Wear see CLOTHING TRADE 261
Wood see BUILDING AND CONSTRUCTION - Carpentry and Woodwork 141, see also FORESTS AND FORESTRY - Lumber and Wood 412
Wood Pulp see PAPER AND PULP 675
Woodwork see BUILDING AND CONSTRUCTION - Carpentry and Woodwork 141
Wrestling see SPORTS AND GAMES 818
Writers and Writing see JOURNALISM 504, see also LITERATURE 558, PUBLISHING AND BOOK TRADE 757
Yachting see SPORTS AND GAMES - Boats and Boating 826
Yoga see PHILOSOPHY 686, see also PHYSICAL FITNESS AND HYGIENE 694
Youth see CHILDREN AND YOUTH - About 256
Zoning see HOUSING AND URBAN PLANNING 483
ZOOLOGY 126

Classified List of Serials

ABSTRACTING AND INDEXING SERVICES

see also Bibliographies

A.E.T.F.A.T. INDEX; releve des travaux de phanerogamie systematique et des taxons nouveaux concernant l'Afrique au sud du Sahara et Madascar. (Association pour l'Etude Taxonomique de la Flore d'Afrique Tropicale) see BIOLOGY — Abstracting, Bibliographies, Statistics

A S M. BIBLIOGRAPHY SERIES. (American Society for Metals) see METALLURGY — Abstracting, Bibliographies, Statistics

ABSTRACT JOURNAL IN EARTHQUAKE ENGINEERING. see ENGINEERING — Abstracting, Bibliographies, Statistics

ABSTRACTS OF BELGIAN GEOLOGY AND PHYSICAL GEOGRAPHY. see EARTH SCIENCES — Abstracting, Bibliographies, Statistics

ABSTRACTS OF DOCTORAL DISSERTATIONS IN ANTHROPOLOGY. see MEDICAL SCIENCES — Abstracting, Bibliographies, Statistics

ABSTRACTS OF HEALTH CARE MANAGEMENT STUDIES. see HOSPITALS — Abstracting, Bibliographies, Statistics

011   US   ISSN 0363-065X
ACCESS: THE INDEX TO LITTLE MAGAZINES. 1976. a. $50. John Gordon Burke, Inc., Box 4901, Syracuse, NY 13221. (also avail. in microform (ISSN 0363-2822))

ACCOUNTANTS' INDEX. see BUSINESS AND ECONOMICS — Abstracting, Bibliographies, Statistics

ACCUMULATIVE VETERINARY INDEX. see VETERINARY SCIENCE — Abstracting, Bibliographies, Statistics

AEROSPACE RESEARCH INDEX. see AERONAUTICS AND SPACE FLIGHT — Abstracting, Bibliographies, Statistics

AGRONOMY ABSTRACTS. see AGRICULTURE — Abstracting, Bibliographies, Statistics

AMERICAN ASSOCIATION OF STRATIGRAPHIC PALYNOLOGISTS. ABSTRACTS OF PAPERS PRESENTED AT THE ANNUAL MEETINGS. see EARTH SCIENCES — Abstracting, Bibliographies, Statistics

AMERICAN HERITAGE INDEX. see HISTORY — Abstracting, Bibliographies, Statistics

ANGLO AMERICAN DIRECTORY OF MEXICO. see POPULATION STUDIES — Abstracting, Bibliographies, Statistcs

ASTRONOMY AND ASTROPHYSICS ABSTRACTS. see PHYSICS — Abstracting, Bibliographies, Statistics

AUSTRALIAN RENEWABLE ENERGY RESOURCES INDEX. see ENERGY — Abstracting, Bibliographies, Statistics

AVERY INDEX TO ARCHITECTURAL PERIODICALS. SUPPLEMENT. see ARCHITECTURE — Abstracting, Bibliographies, Statistics

B S B I ABSTRACTS; abstracts from literature relating to the Vascular plants of the British Isles. (Botanical Society of the British Isles) see BIOLOGY — Abstracting, Bibliographies, Statistics

BANGLADESH AGRICULTURAL SCIENCES ABSTRACTS. see AGRICULTURE — Abstracting, Bibliographies, Statistics

BARBADOS. STATISTICAL SERVICE. OVERSEAS TRADE REPORT. see BUSINESS AND ECONOMICS — Abstracting, Bibliographies, Statistics

BIOGRAPHICAL DICTIONARIES MASTER INDEX. see BIOGRAPHY — Abstracting, Bibliographies, Statistics

BIOSIS SEARCH GUIDE; BIOSIS previews edition. see BIOLOGY — Abstracting, Bibliographies, Statistics

BLACK LIST; the concise and comprehensive reference guide to black journalism, radio and television, educational and cultural organizations in the USA, Africa and the Caribbean. see ETHNIC INTERESTS — Abstracting, Bibliographies, Statistics

BOOK REVIEW INDEX: ANNUAL CLOTHBOUND CUMULATIONS. see LITERATURE — Abstracting, Bibliographies, Statistics

BOOK REVIEW INDEX TO SOCIAL SCIENCE PERIODICALS. see SOCIAL SCIENCES: COMPREHENSIVE WORKS — Abstracting, Bibliographies, Statistics

BUILDING ABSTRACTS SERVICE C I B. see BUILDING AND CONSTRUCTION — Abstracting, Bibliographies, Statistics

BULLETIN OF CHEMICAL THERMODYNAMICS (1977) see CHEMISTRY — Abstracting, Bibliographies, Statistics

BYGGNORMINDEX/SWEDISH BUILDING CODES AND STANDARDS INDEX. see BUILDING AND CONSTRUCTION — Abstracting, Bibliographies, Statistics

C I N D A; an index to the literature on microscopic neutron data. see PHYSICS — Abstracting, Bibliographies, Statistics

C I S ANNUAL. (Congressional Information Service) see PUBLIC ADMINISTRATION — Abstracting, Bibliographies, Statistics

011   US
CALIFORNIA PERIODICALS INDEX. 1977. a. $40. Gabriel Micrographics (Subsidiary of: Minnesota Scholarly Press, Inc.) Box 224, Mankato, MN 56001. Ed. Opal Kissinger. bk. rev. (also avail. in microfilm)

CANADA. GEOLOGICAL SURVEY. ABSTRACTS OF PUBLICATIONS. see EARTH SCIENCES — Abstracting, Bibliographies, Statistics

CANADA. GEOLOGICAL SURVEY. INDEX OF PUBLICATIONS OF THE GEOLOGICAL SURVEY OF CANADA. see EARTH SCIENCES — Abstracting, Bibliographies, Statistics

CANADIAN BUILDING ABSTRACTS. see BUILDING AND CONSTRUCTION — Abstracting, Bibliographies, Statistics

CANADIAN ESSAY AND LITERATURE INDEX. see LITERATURE — Abstracting, Bibliographies, Statistics

CANADIAN L P & TAPE CATALOGUE. see MUSIC — Abstracting, Bibliographies, Statistics

CANADIAN LOCATIONS OF JOURNALS INDEXED FOR MEDLINE/DEPOTS CANADIENS DES REVUES INDEXEES POUR MEDLINE. see *MEDICAL SCIENCES — Abstracting, Bibliographies, Statistics*

CATALOG OF MUSEUM PUBLICATIONS AND MEDIA; a directory and index of publications and audiovisuals available from U.S. and Canadian institutions. see *MUSEUMS AND ART GALLERIES — Abstracting, Bibliographies, Statistics*

CATHOLIC PERIODICAL AND LITERATURE INDEX. see *RELIGIONS AND THEOLOGY — Abstracting, Bibliographies, Statistics*

CHILDREN'S BOOK REVIEW INDEX. see *CHILDREN AND YOUTH — Abstracting, Bibliographies, Statistics*

CLIN-ALERT. see *PHARMACY AND PHARMACOLOGY — Abstracting, Bibliographies, Statistics*

COMBINED CUMULATIVE INDEX TO PEDIATRICS. see *MEDICAL SCIENCES — Abstracting, Bibliographies, Statistics*

011   US   ISSN 0194-0546
CONFERENCE PAPERS ANNUAL INDEX. a. $140. Data Courier Inc., 620 S. Fifth St., Louisville, KY 40202. Ed. Valerie MacLeod.
Formerly: Current Programs Annual Index.

CONSUMERS INDEX TO PRODUCT EVALUATIONS AND INFORMATION SOURCES. see *CONSUMER EDUCATION AND PROTECTION — Abstracting, Bibliographies, Statistics*

CONTENTS OF RECENT ECONOMICS JOURNALS. see *BUSINESS AND ECONOMICS — Abstracting, Bibliographies, Statistics*

CUMULATED ABRIDGED INDEX MEDICUS. see *MEDICAL SCIENCES — Abstracting, Bibliographies, Statistics*

CUMULATED INDEX MEDICUS. see *MEDICAL SCIENCES — Abstracting, Bibliographies, Statistics*

CUMULATIVE INDEX TO NURSING & ALLIED HEALTH LITERATURE. see *MEDICAL SCIENCES — Abstracting, Bibliographies, Statistics*

CURRENT ARTICLES ON NEOPLASIA. see *MEDICAL SCIENCES — Abstracting, Bibliographies, Statistics*

CURRENT CAREER AND OCCUPATIONAL LITERATURE. see *OCCUPATIONS AND CAREERS — Abstracting, Bibliographies, Statistics*

016 311   US   ISSN 0364-1228
CURRENT INDEX TO STATISTICS; applications-methods-theory. 1976. a. $18. American Statistical Association, 806 15th St., N.W., Washington, DC 20005. index. circ. 2,000.

D D R-PUBLIKATIONEN ZUR IMPERIALISMUSFORSCHUNG, AUSWAHLBIBLIOGRAPHIE. see *POLITICAL SCIENCE — Abstracting, Bibliographies, Statistics*

DEVINDEX; index to literature on third world economic and social development. see *BUSINESS AND ECONOMICS — Abstracting, Bibliographies, Statistics*

DIABETES-RELATED LITERATURE INDEX BY AUTHORS AND KEY WORDS IN THE TITLE. see *MEDICAL SCIENCES — Abstracting, Bibliographies, Statistics*

DIGEST OF LITERATURE ON DIELECTRICS. see *ELECTRICITY AND ELECTRICAL ENGINEERING — Abstracting, Bibliographies, Statistics*

011   AT   ISSN 0110-666X
DIRECTORY OF AUSTRALIAN ASSOCIATIONS. (Supplement Published Between Editions) 1978. every 30 mos. Aus.$39 (supplement Aus.$25) Australasia Reference Research Publications, 76 Annandale St., Keperra, Brisbane, Qld. 4054, Australia. Ed. B. Chan.

DIRECTORY OF SCIENTIFIC PERIODICALS OF PAKISTAN. see *SCIENCES: COMPREHENSIVE WORKS — Abstracting, Bibliographies, Statistics*

DIRECTORY OF THE CULTURAL ORGANIZATIONS OF THE REPUBLIC OF CHINA. see *EDUCATION — Abstracting, Bibliographies, Statistics*

DOKUMENTATION IMPFSCHAEDEN-IMPFERFOLGE. see *MEDICAL SCIENCES — Abstracting, Bibliographies, Statistics*

DOKUMENTATION RHEOLOGIE/ DOCUMENTATION RHEOLOGY. see *PHYSICS — Abstracting, Bibliographies, Statistics*

DOKUMENTATION TRIBOLOGIE/ DOCUMENTATION TRIBOLOGY; verschleiss, reibung und schmierung. see *ENGINEERING — Abstracting, Bibliographies, Statistics*

E F I NYTT/E F I NEWS. (Ekonomiska Forskningsinstitutet) see *BUSINESS AND ECONOMICS — Abstracting, Bibliographies, Statistics*

EIGHT PEAK INDEX OF MASS SPECTRA. see *PHYSICS — Abstracting, Bibliographies, Statistics*

ELECTRICAL ENGINEERING RESEARCH ABSTRACTS. CANADIAN UNIVERSITIES. see *ELECTRICITY AND ELECTRICAL ENGINEERING — Abstracting, Bibliographies, Statistics*

ENERGY INDEX. see *ENERGY — Abstracting, Bibliographies, Statistics*

ENGINEERING INDEX. NOTES & COMMENT. see *ENGINEERING — Abstracting, Bibliographies, Statistics*

ENGINEERING SCIENCES DATA UNIT INDEX. see *ENGINEERING — Abstracting, Bibliographies, Statistics*

F & S INDEX EUROPE. ANNUAL. see *BUSINESS AND ECONOMICS — Abstracting, Bibliographies, Statistics*

F & S INDEX INTERNATIONAL ANNUAL. see *BUSINESS AND ECONOMICS — Abstracting, Bibliographies, Statistics*

FEDERAL INDEX. ANNUAL. see *PUBLIC ADMINISTRATION — Abstracting, Bibliographies, Statistics*

FORESTRY ABSTRACTS. LEADING ARTICLE REPRINT SERIES. see *FORESTS AND FORESTRY — Abstracting, Bibliographies, Statistics*

GEZINSSOCIOLOGISCHE DOCUMENTATIE; Jaarboek. see *POPULATION STUDIES — Abstracting, Bibliographies, Statistcs*

GUIDE TO CHINESE PERIODICALS. see *PUBLISHING AND BOOK TRADE — Abstracting, Bibliographies, Statistics*

HEALTH EDUCATION INDEX; and Guide to Voluntary Social Welfare Organisations. see *PHYSICAL FITNESS AND HYGIENE — Abstracting, Bibliographies, Statistics*

HEALTH PHYSICS RESEARCH ABSTRACTS. see *PUBLIC HEALTH AND SAFETY — Abstracting, Bibliographies, Statistics*

HOME ECONOMICS RESEARCH ABSTRACTS. see *HOME ECONOMICS — Abstracting, Bibliographies, Statistics*

INDEX ASIA SERIES IN HUMANITIES. see *HUMANITIES: COMPREHENSIVE WORKS — Abstracting, Bibliographies, Statistics*

INDEX OF AMERICAN PERIODICAL VERSE. see *LITERATURE — Abstracting, Bibliographies, Statistics*

INDEX OF ARTICLES ON JEWISH STUDIES/ RESHIMAT MA'AMARIM BE-MADA'E HA-YAHADUT. see *RELIGIONS AND THEOLOGY — Abstracting, Bibliographies, Statistics*

INDEX OF BIOCHEMICAL REVIEWS. see *BIOLOGY — Abstracting, Bibliographies, Statistics*

636.4 016   UK
INDEX OF CURRENT RESEARCH ON PIGS. 1954. a. £1.90($4.50) (Agricultural Research Council) National Institute for Research in Dairying, Church Lane, Shinfield, Reading RG2 9AT, England. Ed. Dr. R. Braude. circ. 1,300.

INDEX OF ECONOMIC ARTICLES IN JOURNALS AND COLLECTIVE VOLUMES. see *BUSINESS AND ECONOMICS — Abstracting, Bibliographies, Statistics*

INDEX OF REVIEWS IN ORGANIC CHEMISTRY. see *CHEMISTRY — Abstracting, Bibliographies, Statistics*

INDEX OF RHEUMATOLOGY. see *MEDICAL SCIENCES — Abstracting, Bibliographies, Statistics*

INDEX TO CHINESE LEGAL PERIODICALS. see *LAW — Abstracting, Bibliographies, Statistics*

INDEX TO HOW TO DO IT INFORMATION; a periodical index. see *HOBBIES — Abstracting, Bibliographies, Statistics*

INDEX TO INDIAN PERIODICAL LITERATURE. see *SOCIAL SCIENCES: COMPREHENSIVE WORKS — Abstracting, Bibliographies, Statistics*

INDEX TO LITERATURE ON THE AMERICAN INDIAN. see *ETHNIC INTERESTS — Abstracting, Bibliographies, Statistics*

INDEX TO MODEL MAKING & MINIATURES. see *HOBBIES — Abstracting, Bibliographies, Statistics*

016 289.3   US   ISSN 0148-6586
INDEX TO MORMONISM IN PERIODICAL LITERATURE. (Text in various languages) 1976. a. $5. Church of Jesus Christ of Latter-Day Saints, Historical Department, 50 E. North Temple, E. Wing, Salt Lake City, UT 84150. Ed. Melvin Bashore. adv. bk. rev. film rev. index. circ. 120. (microfiche; back issues avail.)

029   NZ   ISSN 0073-5957
INDEX TO NEW ZEALAND PERIODICALS. 1940. 3/yr. (annual cumulations) NZ.$30 (annual cum. alone NZ. $15) National Library of New Zealand, Private Bag, Wellington, New Zealand. circ. 300. (also avail. in microfiche)

INDEX TO PERIODICAL ARTICLES BY AND ABOUT BLACKS. see *ETHNIC INTERESTS — Abstracting, Bibliographies, Statistics*

INDEX TO SOUTH AFRICAN PERIODICALS/ REPERTORIUM VAN SUID-AFRIKAANSE TYDSKRIFARTIKELS. see *PUBLISHING AND BOOK TRADE — Abstracting, Bibliographies, Statistics*

INDEX TO THAI NEWSPAPERS. see *JOURNALISM — Abstracting, Bibliographies, Statistics*

INDEX TO THAI PERIODICAL LITERATURE. see *SOCIAL SCIENCES: COMPREHENSIVE WORKS — Abstracting, Bibliographies, Statistics*

INDEX TO THE NATIONAL ASSEMBLY RECORDS/KUK HOE HOE EU ROK SAEGIN. see *LIBRARY AND INFORMATION SCIENCES — Abstracting, Bibliographies, Statistics*

INDIA. MINISTRY OF EDUCATION AND SOCIAL WELFARE. DEPARTMENT OF SOCIAL WELFARE. DOCUMENTATION SERVICE BULLETIN. see *SOCIAL SCIENCES: COMPREHENSIVE WORKS — Abstracting, Bibliographies, Statistics*

ABSTRACTING AND INDEXING SERVICES

INDIAN GEOLOGICAL INDEX. see *EARTH SCIENCES — Abstracting, Bibliographies, Statistics*

INDIAN INSTITUTE OF TECHNOLOGY, MADRAS. M.S., PH.D. DISSERTATION ABSTRACTS. see *TECHNOLOGY: COMPREHENSIVE WORKS — Abstracting, Bibliographies, Statistics*

INDIAN SCIENCE INDEX. see *SCIENCES: COMPREHENSIVE WORKS — Abstracting, Bibliographies, Statistics*

INDICE DE ARTICULOS DE PUBLICACIONES PERIODICAS EN EL AREA DE CIENCIAS SOCIALES Y HUMANIDADES. see *SOCIAL SCIENCES: COMPREHENSIVE WORKS — Abstracting, Bibliographies, Statistics*

574.5 016 MX
INDICE DE PROYECTOS EN DESARROLLO EN ECOLOGIA TROPICAL/INDEX OF CURRENT TROPICAL ECOLOGY RESEARCH. (Text in English, Spanish) 1976. irreg. Instituto Nacional de Investigaciones sobre Recursos Bioticos, Apdo. 63, Xalapa, Veracruz, Mexico.

011 CU
INDICE GENERAL DE PUBLICACIONES PERIODICAS CUBANAS. 1970. a. exchange. (Biblioteca Nacional Jose Marti, Departmento de Hemeroteca e Informacion de Humanidades) Ediciones Cubanas, Vice-Direccion de Exportacion, Apdo. 605, Havana, Cuba. index. circ. 2,000.

INDICE MEDICO COLOMBIANO. see *MEDICAL SCIENCES — Abstracting, Bibliographies, Statistics*

INSURANCE PERIODICALS INDEX. see *INSURANCE — Abstracting, Bibliographies, Statistics*

INTERNATIONAL BIOPHYSICS CONGRESS. ABSTRACTS. see *BIOLOGY — Abstracting, Bibliographies, Statistics*

INTERNATIONAL INDEX TO FILM PERIODICALS. see *MOTION PICTURES — Abstracting, Bibliographies, Statistics*

INTERNATIONAL RAYON AND SYNTHETIC FIBRES COMMITTEE. STATISTICAL YEARBOOK. see *TEXTILE INDUSTRIES AND FABRICS — Abstracting, Bibliographies, Statistics*

JAHRESVERZEICHNIS DER HOCHSCHULSCHRIFTEN DER DDR, DER BRD UND WESTBERLINS. see *EDUCATION — Abstracting, Bibliographies, Statistics*

KEY WORD INDEX OF WILDLIFE RESEARCH. see *SCIENCES: COMPREHENSIVE WORKS — Abstracting, Bibliographies, Statistics*

KOREA (REPUBLIC) BUREAU OF STATISTICS. REPORT ON MINING AND MANUFACTURING SURVEY/ KWANGGONGUP TONGGYE ZO SA BOGO SEO. see *MINES AND MINING INDUSTRY — Abstracting, Bibliographies, Statistics*

016 US
LATHROP REPORT ON NEWSPAPER INDEXES. 1979. a. $60. Norman Lathrop Enterprises, 2342 Star Dr., Box 198, Wooster, OH 44691.

LIBRARY LIT. see *LIBRARY AND INFORMATION SCIENCES — Abstracting, Bibliographies, Statistics*

M L A INTERNATIONAL BIBLIOGRAPHY OF BOOKS AND ARTICLES ON THE MODERN LANGUAGES AND LITERATURES. (Modern Language Association of America) see *BIBLIOGRAPHIES*

029.4 015 MY ISSN 0126-5040
MALAYSIAN PERIODICALS INDEX/INDEKS MAJALAH MALAYSIA. (Text in English and Malay) 1973. a. M.$20. National Library, Reference Division, Wisma Sachder/Thakurdas, 1st Fl., Jalan Raja Laut, Kuala Lumpur, Malaysia (Orders to: Parry's Book Centre, Box 960, Hotel Hilton, Kuala Lumpur, Malaysia) Ed. Siti Mariani Omar. circ. 200.

MEDIA REVIEW DIGEST; the only complete guide to reviews of non-book media. see *MOTION PICTURES — Abstracting, Bibliographies, Statistics*

MEDICAL RESEARCH INDEX. see *MEDICAL SCIENCES — Abstracting, Bibliographies, Statistics*

MISSISSIPPI STATE UNIVERSITY ABSTRACTS OF THESES AND DISSERTATIONS. see *EDUCATION — Abstracting, Bibliographies, Statistics*

N A A. (Nordic Archaeological Abstracts) see *ARCHAEOLOGY — Abstracting, Bibliographies, Statistics*

N.E.S.F.A. INDEX: SCIENCE FICTION MAGAZINES AND ANTHOLOGIES. (New England Science Fiction Association Inc.) see *ADVENTURE AND ROMANCE — Abstracting, Bibliographies, Statistics*

N I C E M INDEX TO EDUCATIONAL AUDIO TAPES. (National Information Center for Educational Media) see *EDUCATION — Abstracting, Bibliographies, Statistics*

N I C E M INDEX TO EDUCATIONAL OVERHEAD TRANSPARENCIES. (National Information Center for Educational Media) see *EDUCATION — Abstracting, Bibliographies, Statistics*

N I C E M INDEX TO EDUCATIONAL RECORDS. (National Information Center for Educational Media) see *EDUCATION — Abstracting, Bibliographies, Statistics*

N I C E M INDEX TO EDUCATIONAL SLIDES. (National Information Center for Educational Media) see *EDUCATION — Abstracting, Bibliographies, Statistics*

N I C E M INDEX TO EDUCATIONAL VIDEO TAPES. see *EDUCATION — Abstracting, Bibliographies, Statistics*

N I C E M INDEX TO ENVIRONMENTAL STUDIES-MULTIMEDIA. (National Information Center for Educational Media) see *ENVIRONMENTAL STUDIES — Abstracting, Bibliographies, Statistics*

N I C E M INDEX TO HEALTH AND SAFETY EDUCATION-MULTIMEDIA. (National Information Center for Educational Media) see *PHYSICAL FITNESS AND HYGIENE — Abstracting, Bibliographies, Statistics*

N I C E M INDEX TO PRODUCERS AND DISTRIBUTORS. (National Information Center for Educational Media) see *MOTION PICTURES — Abstracting, Bibliographies, Statistics*

371 016 US
N I C E M INDEX TO VOCATIONAL AND TECHNICAL EDUCATION-MULTIMEDIA. 1972. biennial. $55. National Information Center for Educational Media, University of Southern California, University Park, Los Angeles, CA 90007. abstr. bibl. cum.index (1934-1975) (also avail. in microfiche)

N I C E M INDEX TO 8MM MOTION CARTRIDGES. (National Information Center for Educational Media) see *EDUCATION — Abstracting, Bibliographies, Statistics*

N I C E M INDEX TO 16MM EDUCATIONAL FILMS. (National Information Center for Educational Media) see *EDUCATION — Abstracting, Bibliographies, Statistics*

N I C E M INDEX TO 35MM EDUCATIONAL FILMSTRIPS. (National Information Center for Educational Media) see *EDUCATION — Abstracting, Bibliographies, Statistics*

NEPAL DOCUMENTATION; occasional bibliography. see *BUSINESS AND ECONOMICS — Abstracting, Bibliographies, Statistics*

995 015 PP ISSN 0028-5161
NEW GUINEA PERIODICAL INDEX; guide to current periodical literature about New Guinea. 1968. a. K.10 (avail. also on exchange) ‡ University of Papua New Guinea, The Library, Box 4819, University Post Office, Papua New Guinea. circ. 500. (processed)

NEW PERIODICALS INDEX. see *LITERARY AND POLITICAL REVIEWS — Abstracting, Bibliographies, Statistics*

NURSING AND ALLIED HEALTH LITERATURE INDEX. see *MEDICAL SCIENCES — Abstracting, Bibliographies, Statistics*

PASTORAL CARE AND COUNSELING ABSTRACTS. see *RELIGIONS AND THEOLOGY — Abstracting, Bibliographies, Statistics*

PESTICIDE INDEX. see *AGRICULTURE — Abstracting, Bibliographies, Statistics*

PHARMINDEX. see *PHARMACY AND PHARMACOLOGY — Abstracting, Bibliographies, Statistics*

PHOTOGRAPHY INDEX. see *PHOTOGRAPHY — Abstracting, Bibliographies, Statistics*

PHYSICAL REVIEW INDEX. see *PHYSICS — Abstracting, Bibliographies, Statistics*

PLANT PROTECTION ABSTRACTS. SUPPLEMENT. see *BIOLOGY — Abstracting, Bibliographies, Statistics*

PLAY INDEX. see *LITERATURE — Abstracting, Bibliographies, Statistics*

POLISH ARCHAEOLOGICAL ABSTRACTS. see *ARCHAEOLOGY — Abstracting, Bibliographies, Statistics*

PREDICASTS F & S INDEX UNITED STATES. see *BUSINESS AND ECONOMICS — Abstracting, Bibliographies, Statistics*

PUBLIZISTIK WISSENSCHAFTLICHER REFERATEDIENST. see *JOURNALISM — Abstracting, Bibliographies, Statistics*

REFERENCE BOOK REVIEW INDEX. see *PUBLISHING AND BOOK TRADE — Abstracting, Bibliographies, Statistics*

RELIGIOUS & THEOLOGICAL ABSTRACTS. see *RELIGIONS AND THEOLOGY — Abstracting, Bibliographies, Statistics*

RHODESIA RESEARCH INDEX; register of current research in Rhodesia. see *SCIENCES: COMPREHENSIVE WORKS — Abstracting, Bibliographies, Statistics*

SCIENCE FICTION BOOK REVIEW INDEX. see *LITERATURE — Abstracting, Bibliographies, Statistics*

SEA GRANT PUBLICATIONS INDEX. see *EARTH SCIENCES — Abstracting, Bibliographies, Statistics*

SERIAL SOURCES FOR THE BIOSIS DATA BASE. see *BIOLOGY — Abstracting, Bibliographies, Statistics*

SHORT STORY INDEX; an index to stories in collections and periodicals. see *LITERATURE — Abstracting, Bibliographies, Statistics*

011 SI ISSN 0377-7928
SINGAPORE PERIODICALS INDEX. (Text in Malay, Chinese and English) 1969/70. biennial. price varies. National Library, Stamford Rd, Singapore 0617, Singapore. Ed. Lai Yeen Pong. circ. 450.

SOUTHERN BAPTIST PERIODICAL INDEX. see *RELIGIONS AND THEOLOGY — Abstracting, Bibliographies, Statistics*

SPAIN. INSTITUTO GEOLOGICO Y MINERO. CATALOGO DE EDICIONES. see *EARTH SCIENCES — Abstracting, Bibliographies, Statistics*

SPEECH INDEX; an index to 259 collections of orations and speeches for various occasions. see LINGUISTICS — *Abstracting, Bibliographies, Statistics*

SPORTS DOCUMENTATION CENTRE. AESTRACT JOURNAL HOLDINGS. see EDUCATION — *Abstracting, Bibliographies, Statistics*

SUBJECT INDEX TO CHILDREN'S MAGAZINES. see CHILDREN AND YOUTH — *Abstracting, Bibliographies, Statistics*

029   FI   ISSN 0081-9395
SUOMEN AIKAKAUSLEHTI-INDEKSI/INDEX TO FINNISH PERIODICALS. 1959. a. price varies. Turun Yliopisto, Kirjasto - University of Turku, SF-20500 Turku 50, Finland. Ed. Pirkko Sundstroem. circ. 300-400.

THEOLOGICAL AND RELIGIOUS INDEX. see RELIGIONS AND THEOLOGY — *Abstracting, Bibliographies, Statistics*

TOPICATOR; classified article guide to the advertising/communications/marketing periodical press. see ADVERTISING AND PUBLIC RELATIONS — *Abstracting, Bibliographies, Statistics*

TURKISH DISSERTATION INDEX. see SCIENCES: COMPREHENSIVE WORKS — *Abstracting, Bibliographies, Statistics*

U S S R REPORT: CYBERNETICS, COMPUTERS, AND AUTOMATION TECHNOLOGY. see COMPUTER TECHNOLOGY AND APPLICATIONS — *Abstracting, Bibliographies, Statistics*

U S S R REPORT: ELECTRONICS AND ELECTRICAL ENGINEERING. see ELECTRICITY AND ELECTRICAL ENGINEERING — *Abstracting, Bibliographies, Statistics*

U S S R REPORT: ENGINEERING AND EQUIPMENT. see ENGINEERING — *Abstracting, Bibliographies, Statistics*

U S S R REPORT: GEOPHYSICS, ASTRONOMY, AND SPACE. see EARTH SCIENCES — *Abstracting, Bibliographies, Statistics*

U S S R REPORT: MATERIALS SCIENCE AND METALLURGY. see ENGINEERING — *Abstracting, Bibliographies, Statistics*

U S S R REPORT: PHYSICS AND MATHEMATICS. see MATHEMATICS — *Abstracting, Bibliographies, Statistics*

U S S R REPORTS: CHEMISTRY. see CHEMISTRY — *Abstracting, Bibliographies, Statistics*

U.S. NATIONAL CENTER FOR HEALTH STATISTICS. CURRENT LISTING AND TOPICAL INDEX TO THE VITAL AND HEALTH STATISTICS SERIES. see PUBLIC HEALTH AND SAFETY — *Abstracting, Bibliographies, Statistics*

UNIVERSIDAD DE BUENOS AIRES. INSTITUTO DE ECONOMIA. BIBLIOGRAFIA SOBRE ECONOMIA NACIONAL. see BUSINESS AND ECONOMICS — *Abstracting, Bibliographies, Statistics*

URBAN MASS TRANSPORTATION ABSTRACTS. see TRANSPORTATION — *Abstracting, Bibliographies, Statistics*

VANDERBILT UNIVERSITY. ABSTRACTS OF THESES. see EDUCATION — *Abstracting, Bibliographies, Statistics*

VISION INDEX. see MEDICAL SCIENCES — *Abstracting, Bibliographies, Statistics*

WATER POLLUTION CONTROL FEDERATION CONFERENCE. ABSTRACTS OF TECHNICAL PAPERS. see ENVIRONMENTAL STUDIES — *Abstracting, Bibliographies, Statistics*

WEED SCIENCE SOCIETY OF AMERICA. ABSTRACTS. see AGRICULTURE — *Abstracting, Bibliographies, Statistics*

YEAR BOOK OF CANCER. see MEDICAL SCIENCES — *Abstracting, Bibliographies, Statistics*

YONSEI UNIVERSITY. GRADUATE SCHOOL. ABSTRACTS OF FACULTY RESEARCH REPORTS. see EDUCATION — *Abstracting, Bibliographies, Statistics*

ZAMBIA SCIENCE ABSTRACTS. see SCIENCES: COMPREHENSIVE WORKS — *Abstracting, Bibliographies, Statistics*

ACCOUNTING

see Business and Economics — Accounting

ADULT EDUCATION

see Education — Adult Education

ADVENTURE AND ROMANCE

808.83   US   ISSN 0362-7403
ANALOG ANNUAL. 1975. a. $1.50. Pyramid Books, 757 Third Ave., New York.

808.83   CN   ISSN 0702-1437
BAKKA MAGAZINE. no. 3, 1975. a. Can.$2 per no. Bakka Book Stores Ltd., 282-286 Queen St. West, Toronto, Ont. M5V 2A1, Canada. bibl.

CONTRIBUTIONS TO THE STUDY OF SCIENCE FICTION AND FANTASY. see LITERATURE

808   US   ISSN 0024-8886
MACABRE. 1957. irreg. $0.75 per no. c/o Joseph Payne Brennan, 26 Fowler St., New Haven, CT 06515. adv. bk. rev. circ. 200.

808.838
NEBULOUSFAN. 1977. irreg., no.9, 1979. per no. (Wing Nuts Wing Club) David Thayer, Ed. & Pub., 7209 DeVille Dr., Ft. Worth, TX 76118. bk. rev. illus. circ. 200.

810   US
TRUMPET. 1975. irreg., no. 12, latest. $3 per no. Trumpet Publications, 1131 White, Kansas City, MO 64126. Ed. Ken Keller. adv. circ. 2,000.
    Former titles: Nickelodeon; Trumpet.
    Science fiction

808.838   UK
WORLD BEST SF SHORT STORIES. 1974. a. £4.50. Elmfield Press, Elmfield Rd., Morley, Yorks. LS27 0NN, England. Ed. Donald Wollheim.

ADVENTURE AND ROMANCE — Abstracting, Bibliographies, Statistics

808.838   US   ISSN 0361-3038
N.E.S.F.A. INDEX: SCIENCE FICTION MAGAZINES AND ANTHOLOGIES. 1966. a. $5-12. New England Science Fiction Association Inc., Box G, MIT Branch P.O., Cambridge, MA 02139. Ed. Robert Spence. circ. 500-1,500.
    Formerly (1966-1970): Index to the Science Fiction Magazines (ISSN 0579-6059)

ADVERTISING AND PUBLIC RELATIONS

see also Business and Economics — Marketing and Purchasing

659.1   UK   ISSN 0065-3578
ADVERTISER'S ANNUAL. 1925. a. £30. Kelly's Directories Ltd., Windsor Court, East Grinstead House, East Grinstead, West Sussex RH19 1XB, England. adv. circ. 5,200.

659.1   US   ISSN 0065-3586
ADVERTISER'S GUIDE TO SCHOLARLY PERIODICALS. Cover title: Ad Guide. 1958. biennial. $50. American University Press Services, Inc., One Park Ave., New York, NY 10016.

ADVERTISING LAW ANTHOLOGY. see LAW

659.1   US
ADVERTISING RESEARCH FOUNDATION. YEARBOOK. a. Advertising Research Foundation, 3 E. 54th St., New York, NY 10022. Ed. Barry Pavelec. adv.

659.13   US
ADVERTISING SPECIALTY REGISTER: PRODUCT RESEARCH AND SOURCE DATA. a. Advertising Specialty Institute, NBS Bldg., Second and Clearview Ave., Trevose, PA 19047.

659.1   UK   ISSN 0065-3659
ADVERTISING STANDARDS AUTHORITY, LONDON. ANNUAL REPORT. 1962-63. a. 50p. Advertising Standards Authority Ltd., 15-17 Ridgemount St., London WC1E 7AW, England. circ. 4,000.

659.1   FR
ANNUAIRE GENERAL DES PUBLICITAIRES DE FRANCE. a. 250 F.($45) Nouvelles Editions de la Publicite, 9 rue Leo Delibes, 75116 Paris, France. Ed. Paul Le Hir. adv. circ. 2,000.
    Formerly: Annuaire G D P F.

659.1 741.67   JA
ANNUAL OF AD PRODUCTION IN JAPAN. (Text in Japanese and English) a. $30. Rikuyosha, 127 Banshu-cho, Shinju-ku, Tokyo, Japan. adv. illus. tr. lit.

741.67 659   JA   ISSN 0548-1643
ANNUAL OF ADVERTISING ART IN JAPAN/ NENKAN KOKOKU BIJUTSU. (Text in English and Japanese) 1957. a. $54. (Art Directors Club of Tokyo - Tokyo Ato Direkutazu Kurabu) Bijutsu Shuppan-sha, 15 Ichigaya, Honmura-cho, Shinjuku-ku, Tokyo 162, Japan. adv. circ. 4,000. (back issues avail.)
    Advertising art

659.1   BL   ISSN 0570-3956
ANUARIO BRASILEIRO DE PROPAGANDA. 1968. a. Cr.$1500. Publicacoes Informativas Ltda., Rua Caetes 139, 05016 Sao Paulo, Brazil. Ed. J.C. Salles Neto. adv. circ. 15,000.

070   HK
ASIAN PRESS AND MEDIA DIRECTORY. (Text in English) 1974. a. Syme Media Enterprises Ltd., Rm. 1301, World Trade Centre, Gloucester Rd., Causeway Bay, Hong Kong, Hong Kong. adv.

659.2   FR   ISSN 0066-9253
ASSOCIATION FRANCAISE DES RELATIONS PUBLIQUES. ANNUAIRE. 1963. a. Association Francaise des Relations Publiques, 8 rue Jean Goujon, 75008 Paris, France.

659.1   US   ISSN 0067-0537
AUDARENA STADIUM GUIDE AND INTERNATIONAL DIRECTORY. Variant title: Amusement Business's AudArena Stadium Guide. 1958. a. $30. Billboard Publications Inc., Amusement Business Division, Box 24970, Nashville, TN 37202. Ed. Steve Rogers. adv. circ. 8,895.
    Formerly: Arena, Auditorium, Stadium Guide (ISSN 0518-3979)

659.1   AT
B & T YEAR BOOK. 1958. a. Greater Publications Pty. Ltd., Box 2608, G.P.O., Sydney, N.S.W. 2001, Australia.
    Formerly: Broadcasting and Television Year Book

ADVERTISING AND PUBLIC RELATIONS

659.2 UK
B T A STUDYCARDS; journal of educational projects. 1952. a. free; avail. only in U.K. British Trades Alphabet Ltd., Alpha House Main St., East Ardsley, Wakefield, West Yorkshire WF3 2AR, England. Ed. A. Rothery. adv. circ. 30,000. (cards)
Formerly: British Trades Alphabet (ISSN 0068-2632)

659.1 US
BEST IN ADVERTISING. (Subseries of: Print Casebooks) 1975. a. $13.95. R C Publications, Inc., 355 Lexington Ave., New York, NY 10017 (Or 6400 Goldsboro Rd., Washington, DC 20034) illus.
Formerly: Best in Advertising Campaigns (ISSN 0360-8263)
Advertising art

659.1 US
BURRELLE'S MARYLAND/DELAWARE AND LOCAL WASHINGTON, D.C., MEDIA DIRECTORY. a. $21. Burrelle's Media Directories, 75 E. Northfield Ave., Livingston, NJ 07039.

659.1 US
BURRELLE'S NEW JERSEY MEDIA DIRECTORY. a. $30. Burrelle's Media Directories, 75 E. Northfield Ave., Livingston, NJ 07039. (Affiliate: New England Newsclip Agency, Inc.)
Formerly: New Jersey Media Directory.

659.1 US
BURRELLE'S NEW YORK STATE MEDIA DIRECTORY. a. $30. Burrelle's Media Directories, 75 E. Northfield Ave., Livingston, NJ 07039. (Affiliate: New England Newsclip Agency, Inc)
Formerly: New York State Media Directory.

659.1 US
BURRELLE'S PENNSYLVANIA MEDIA DIRECTORY. a. $28. Burrelle's Media Directories, 75 E. Northfield Ave., Livingston, NJ 07039.

659 US
BURRELLE'S SPECIAL GROUPS MEDIA DIRECTORY. 1980. a. $50. Burrelle's Media Directories, 75 E. Northfield Ave., Livingston, NJ 07039.

658.5 659 FR
CADEAU ET L'ENTREPRISE; les techniques de stimulation des ventes. a. 420 F. Agence de Diffusion et de Publicite, 24 Place du General Catroux, 75017-Paris, France.

659.2 US
CALIFORNIA PUBLICITY OUTLETS. 1972. a. $24.95. Unicorn Systems Company, Information Services Division, 3807 Wilshire Blvd., Suite 1102, Los Angeles, CA 90010. Ed. Barbara Quelle. adv. circ. 700. (back issues avail)

659.1 US
CECIL H. BRITE LECTURE SERIES IN ADVERTISING AND PUBLICATIONS MANAGEMENT. 1975. irreg. University of Oklahoma, H. H. Herbert School of Journalism, Norman, OK 73069. Ed. Robert L. Bryson.

659.1 US
CITY & REGIONAL MAGAZINE DIRECTORY. 1977. a. $19.95. Conference Management Corporation, 500 Summer St., Stamford, CT 06901.

659.1 US ISSN 0091-0473
COLLECTABLE OLD ADVERTISING.* (Blue book with current prices and photographs) a. $5.95. c/o Jim Cope, Box 1417, Orange, TX 77530. liius.

384 659 KO ISSN 0069-8067
COMPREHENSIVE MEDIA GUIDE: KOREA. 1969. a. $3.-$5. International Advertising Association, Korea Chapter, I.P.O. Box 3562, Seoul, S. Korea.

659.1 US
CONNECTICUT MEDIA DIRECTORY. a. $19. New England Newsclip Agency, Inc., 5 Auburn St., Framingham, MA 01701.

659 US
CREATIVE BLACK BOOK. 1970. a. $25. Friendly Publications, 80 Irving Place, New York, NY 10003. circ. 40,000.

740 US ISSN 0097-6075
CREATIVITY. 1971. a. $26.50. (Art Direction Magazine) Advertising Trade Publications, Inc., 10 E. 39th St., New York, NY 10016. Ed. Don Barron. circ. 6,500.
Supersedes (1960-1965): Advertising Directions.
Advertising art

659.1 US ISSN 0163-3392
CURRENT ISSUES AND RESEARCH IN ADVERTISING. 1978. a. price varies. University of Michigan, Graduate School of Business Administration, Division of Research, Monroe and Tappan St., Ann Arbor, MI 48109. Eds. James H. Leigh, Claude R. Martin, Jr. circ. 850. (back issues avail.)

659.1 DK ISSN 0070-2854
DANSKE REKLAMEBUREAUERS BRANCHEFORENING. OPLAGSTAL OG MARKEDSTAL. 1959. a. price varies. Danske Reklamebureauers Brancheforening - Danish Association of Advertising Agencies, Gl. Strand 44, DK-1202 Copenhagen, Denmark. circ. 450.

659.1 GW
DEUTSCHER WERBEKALENDER. 1964. a. DM.26. INFO-Verlag H. G. Thal, Macherscheider Str. 130, 4040 Neuss, W. Germany (B.R.D.) Ed. H. G. Thal. adv. circ. 6,000.
Formerly: Taschenbuch der Werbung (ISSN 0082-1802)

659 GW ISSN 0419-0637
DIALOG DER GESELLSCHAFT; Schriftenreime fuer Publizistik und Kommunikationswissenschaft. 1966. irreg., vol. 18, 1977. price varies. Verlag Regensberg, Daimlerweg 58, Postfach 6748/6749, 4400 Muenster, W. Germany (B.R.D.) Ed. Henk Packe.

659.1 US ISSN 0070-5365
DIRECTORY OF CORPORATE AFFILIATIONS. (Geographical Index avail.) 1967. a. $109. National Register Publishing Co., Inc., (Subsidiary of: Standard Rate & Data Service) 5201 Old Orchard Rd., Skokie, IL 60077. Ed. Bob Weicherding. circ. 12,000.

DIRECTORY OF MAILING LIST HOUSES. see BUSINESS AND ECONOMICS — Trade And Industrial Directories

606 659.152 US ISSN 0361-4255
DIRECTORY OF NORTH AMERICAN FAIRS AND EXPOSITIONS. Variant title: Amusement Business's Directory North American Fairs. 1888. a. $29.95. Billboard Publications, Inc., Amusement Business Box 24970, Nashville, TN 37202. Ed. Tom Powell. circ. 2,200.
Formerly (until 1972): Cavalcade and Directory of Fairs (ISSN 0069-1291)

659 BE ISSN 0531-2701
E A A A NEWSLETTER. 1969. irreg., latest June 1977. European Association of Advertising Agencies, c/o Nils Faernet, Ave. E. Cambier 19, 1030 Brussels, Belgium.

659 GW ISSN 0085-0349
EUROPA HANDBUCH DER WERBEGESELLSCHAFTEN. 1962. a. DM.64.50. Team Verlag GmbH und Fachzeitschriften KG, Auwanne 19, 8757 Karlstein, W. Germany (B.R.D.) Ed. Horst P. Czerner. adv. circ. 2,500.

659.1 US
GALLAGHER PRESIDENTS' REPORT. w. $120. Gallagher Communications, Inc., 230 Park Ave, New York, NY 10017. Ed. Cynthia A. Billings.

GRAPHIS ANNUAL; international annual of advertising and editorial graphics. see ART

GREATER BOSTON MEDIA DIRECTORY. see JOURNALISM

659 AT
GREY MATTER; Australian edition. 1970. irreg. Grey Advertising Pty. Ltd., 89 Berry St., North Sydney, N.S.W. 2060, Australia.

GROUPEMENT DES DIRECTEURS PUBLICITAIRES DE FRANCE. ANNUAIRE. see BUSINESS AND ECONOMICS — Management

GUIDE TO PUBLISHERS AND RELATED INDUSTRIES IN JAPAN. see PUBLISHING AND BOOK TRADE

659 US
HANDBOOK OF ADVERTISING AND MARKETING SERVICES. 1971. a. with mid-year update. $45. Executive Communications, Inc., 400 E. 54th St., New York, NY 10022. Ed. Sue Fulton. circ. 1,000. (back issues avail)

613 US
HEALTH MEDIA BUYER'S GUIDE. 1972. irreg. updates to 3 base vols. $90. Navillus Publishing Corporation, 1074 Hope St., Box 4790, Stamford, CT 06907. Ed. John W. Sullivan. circ. 500.

659.2 UK ISSN 0073-3059
HOLLIS PRESS AND PUBLIC RELATIONS ANNUAL. 1967. a. (with quarterly supplements) £18.50. Hollis Directories Ltd., Contact House, Lower Hampton Rd., Sunbury-On-Thames, Middlesex TW16 5HG, England. Ed. Robert Hollis. adv. bk. rev. bibl. illus. index. circ. 3,000 (back issues avail.)

659.1 UK ISSN 0538-4168
INTERNATIONAL ADVERTISING ASSOCIATION. UNITED KINGDOM CHAPTER. CONCISE GUIDE TO INTERNATIONAL MARKETS. 1966. irreg., latest edt. 1976. £20. ‡ Leslie Stinton & Partners, 39A London Rd., Kingston-Upon-Thames, Surrey KT2 6ND, England. Ed. Leslie Stinton. adv. circ. 1,000.

659.1 296 070 US
JEWISH PRESS IN AMERICA. 1970. biennial. $10. Joseph Jacobs Organization, 60 East 42nd Street, New York, NY 10017. Ed. Bruce Baff. circ. 2,000.

659.1 KE
KENYA MEDIA ADVERTISING REVIEW. 1973. a. EAs.750($100) Corcoran & Tyrrell Ltd., Box 44365, Nairobi, Kenya. Ed. Tony Corcoran. stat. circ. 60.

659.1 GE
LEIPZIGER MESSEJOURNAL. (Text in English) a. Leipziger Messeamt, Markt 11/15, 701 Leipzig, E. Germany (D.D.R.) Ed. Ines Schymura.

659.1 US ISSN 0076-2148
MADISON AVENUE HANDBOOK. 1958. a. $15. Peter Glenn Publications, Inc., 17 E. 48th St., New York, NY 10017. Ed. Peter Glenn. adv. circ. 21,000.

659.1 US
MAINE MEDIA DIRECTORY. a. $15. New England Newsclip Agency, Inc., Maine Clipping Service, 5 Auburn St., Framingham, MA 01701 (Subscr. to: Box 360, Winthrop, ME 04364)

659 GW ISSN 0085-3119
MARKEN-HANDBUCH DER WERBUNG UND ETATBETREUUNG. 1960. a. DM.59.50. Team Verlag GmbH und Fachzeitschriften KG, Auwanne 19, 8757 Karlstein 1, W. Germany (B.R.D.) Ed. Horst P. Czerner. adv. circ. 2,500.

MEDIA ENCYCLOPEDIA; working press of the nation. see JOURNALISM

659.1 DK ISSN 0076-5821
MEDIA SCANDINAVIA; a Scandinavian advertising media directory. (Text in Danish and English) 1952. a. Kr.250. Danske Reklamebureauers Brancheforening - Danish Association of Advertising Agencies, Gl. Strand 44, DK-1202 Copenhagen K, Denmark. Ed. Jesper Holm. adv. circ. 2,500.

659.1 US
METRO CALIFORNIA MEDIA. 1979. a. $59.50. Public Relations Plus, Inc., Box 327, Washington Depot, CT 06794. Ed. Harold D. Hansen. circ. 600.

659.1 BL
MIDIA. 1977. a. free. Editora Rural, Rua Gabriela 333, Porto Alegre, Brazil.

778.5 US
MINI-IMAGES. irreg. membership. Association for Multi-Image, 947 Old York Rd., Abington, PA 19001.

659.2 UK
MODERN PUBLICITY. 1924. a. £17.50. Studio Vista (Subsidiary of: Cassell Ltd.) 35 Red Lion Square, London WC1R 4SG, England. circ. 10,000.

659.1 CN ISSN 0077-5177
NATIONAL LIST OF ADVERTISERS. 1939. a. Can.$26. Maclean-Hunter Ltd., 481 University Ave., Toronto, Ont. M5W 1A7, Canada. Ed. Grace Hynes.

381 US
NEW DETROIT PROGRESS REPORT. a. New Detroit Inc., 719 Griswold, 1010 Commonwealth Bldg., Detroit, MI 48226.
Formerly: New Detroit Incorporated.

659.1 US
NEW ENGLAND MEDIA DIRECTORY. a. $27. New England Newsclip Agency, Inc., 5 Auburn St., Framingham, MA 01701.

659.1 US
NEW HAMPSHIRE MEDIA DIRECTORY. a. $15. New England Newsclip Agency, Inc., 5 Auburn St., Framingham, MA 01701.

659.2 US ISSN 0077-9024
NEW YORK PUBLICITY OUTLETS. 1954. a. $55. Public Relations Plus, Inc., Box 327, Washington Depot, CT 06794. Ed. Harold D. Hansen. circ. 2,000.
Guide for public relations people, covering key personnel on media located within a 50-mile radius of Columbus Circle

659.1 US
NO DEADLINE. 1965. irreg. $5. ‡ Robert Eastman, Ed. & Pub., P.O. Box 368, Ithaca, NY 14850. illus. circ. 800.

O'DWYER'S DIRECTORY OF PUBLIC RELATIONS EXECUTIVES. see BIOGRAPHY

659 US ISSN 0078-3374
O'DWYERS DIRECTORY OF PUBLIC RELATIONS FIRMS. 1969. a. $50. J. R. O'Dwyer Co., Inc., 271 Madison Ave., New York, NY 10016. adv. circ. 1,500.

070 659.1 UK ISSN 0078-7132
OVERSEAS MEDIA GUIDE. 1965. a. £5. Overseas Press and Media Association, 122 Shaftesbury Ave., London, W1V 8HA, England. Ed. Kay Stout. adv. circ. 5,000(controlled)

659.2 US ISSN 0300-7731
PLUS-PROFIT PUBLICITY; the public relations viewsletter. 1956. 4-6/yr. $3. P R Group, 16 E. 42nd St., New York, NY 10017. Ed. Bd. bk. rev. tr.lit. circ. 1,000. (processed)

659.2 US
PROFESSIONAL GUIDE TO PUBLIC RELATIONS SERVICES. 1968. a. $60. Public Relations Publishing Co., 888 Seventh Ave., New York, NY 10106. Ed. Richard Weiner.

659 IT
PUBBLICITA E ORGANIZZAZIONE OGGI. 1968. a (with q. supplements) Editre, Via Montenapoleone 18, 20121 Milan, Italy. Ed. Tancredi Capozza. adv. circ. 4,000.

659.1 IT ISSN 0079-7472
PUBBLICITA IN ITALIA; suggestione pubblicitaria. (Text and summaries in English, French, German and Italian) 1953/54. a. L.29700. Ufficio Moderno, Via V. Foppa 7, 20144 Milan, Italy. Ed. Antonio Palieri. adv.

659.13 CN ISSN 0706-8085
REACHING THE MANITOBA MARKET. 1977. a. free. Manitoba Community Newspapers Association, 401-280 Smith St., Winnipeg, Man. R3C 1K2, Canada. Ed. B.G. McCallum. adv. circ. 3,000.

659.2 FR ISSN 0080-1194
REPERTOIRE PRATIQUE DE LA PUBLICITE. 1968/69. a. 141 F. Editions Jacquemart, 19 rue des Pretres-Saint-Germain-l'Auxerrois, Paris 1, France.

RHODE ISLAND MEDIA DIRECTORY. see JOURNALISM

659.102 US ISSN 0081-4229
STANDARD DIRECTORY OF ADVERTISERS. (In 2 editions: Classified and Geographical) 1907. a. $109. National Register Publishing Co., Inc., (Subsidiary of: Standard Rate & Data Service) 5201 Old Orchard Rd., Skokie, IL 60077. Ed. Bob Weicherding. adv. circ. 11,000(classified edt.); 2,600(geographical edt.)

070 SZ
STREUDATEN DER SCHWEIZER PRESSE. (Text in German) 1968. triennial. 75 Fr.($40) Verband Schweizerischer Werbegesellschaften, Seestrasse 5, CH-8008 Zurich, Switzerland. circ. 250. (also avail. in magnetic tape)

659.1 US ISSN 0073-2893
UNITED STATES & CANADIAN MAILING LISTS. Title varies: Catalog of Mailing Lists. 1950. biennial. free. ‡ Fritz D. Hofheimer, Inc., 88 Third Avenue, Mineola, NY 11501. Ed. Irene Hofheimer. stat. circ. 175,000 (controlled)

V.I.P. DU MARKETING ET DE LA PUBLICITE. see BUSINESS AND ECONOMICS — Marketing And Purchasing

VERMONT MEDIA DIRECTORY. see JOURNALISM

WHERE SHALL I GO TO COLLEGE TO STUDY ADVERTISING? see EDUCATION — Guides To Schools And Colleges

WHO'S WHO IN ADVERTISING. see BIOGRAPHY

WHO'S WHO IN PUBLIC RELATIONS (INTERNATIONAL) see BIOGRAPHY

659 US ISSN 0568-0301
WORLD ADVERTISING EXPENDITURES. 1953. biennial. $35 non-members. ‡ International Advertising Association., 475 Fifth Ave., New York, NY 10017 (Dist. by Starch INRA Hooper, 420 Lexington Ave., New York, N.Y. 10017) adv.
Formerly: Biennial Survey of Advertising Expenditures Around the World (ISSN 0074-1272)

741.67 US
99 BASIC ADVERTISING LAYOUT DESIGNS. 1980. biennial. $50. Howard Spriggle Publishers, 1010 Chestnut St., Collingdale, PA 19023. Ed. H. Kenwood Spriggle. illus. circ. 2,500.
Advertising art

ADVERTISING AND PUBLIC RELATIONS — Abstracting, Bibliographies, Statistics

659.1 US ISSN 0162-3125
BACON'S PUBLICITY CHECKER. (In 2 vols.: Magazines & Newspapers) 29th edt., 1981. a. plus 3 suppl. $110. Bacon's Publishing Co., 14 E. Jackson Blvd., Chicago, IL 60604.

659 314 IE ISSN 0075-0531
IRELAND (EIRE) CENTRAL STATISTICS OFFICE. INQUIRY INTO ADVERTISING AGENCIES ACTIVITIES. a. Central Statistics Office, Earlsfort Terrace, Dublin 2, Ireland. Stencilled releases

MEDIA GUIDE INTERNATIONAL. AIRLINE INFLIGHT/TRAVEL MAGAZINES EDITION. see TRANSPORTATION — Abstracting, Bibliographies, Statistics

070 US ISSN 0164-1743
MEDIA GUIDE INTERNATIONAL. BUSINESS/PROFESSIONAL PUBLICATIONS EDITION. (Published in 4 regional vols.: Europe; Asia-Australasia-USSR; Latin America; Africa-Middle East) 1971. a. $60-70. Directories International, 1718 Sherman Ave., Evanston, IL 60201. Ed. Marilyn Justman. adv. circ. 1,000.
Former titles: Media Guide International. Business Publications Edition (ISSN 0098-9398); Newsmedia Guide International.

659 US ISSN 0093-9447
MEDIA GUIDE INTERNATIONAL. NEWSPAPERS/NEWSMAGAZINES EDITION. 1972. a. $65. Directories International, 1718 Sherman Ave., Evanston, IL 60201. Ed. Marilyn Justman. adv. circ. 1,300. Key Title: Media Guide International. Edition Newspapers-Newsmagazines.
Continues: Newsmedia Guide International.

MINORITY/ETHNIC MEDIA GUIDE; ethnic and minority media and markets in the U. S. see ETHNIC INTERESTS — Abstracting, Bibliographies, Statistics

384 016 659 US ISSN 0040-9340
TOPICATOR; classified article guide to the advertising/communications/marketing periodical press. 1965. bi-m. $95. Box 127, Golden, CO 80401. Ed. Carol Lillibridge. (processed)

AERONAUTICS AND SPACE FLIGHT

see also Transportation — Air Transport

629.1 US
A I A A/A S M E/S A E STRUCTURES, STRUCTURAL DYNAMICS, AND MATERIALS CONFERENCE. PROCEEDINGS. vol. 17, 1976. irreg. American Institute of Aeronautics & Astronautics, 1290 Ave. of the Americas, New York, NY 10019.

629.1 US
A I A A ATMOSPHERIC FLIGHT MECHANICS CONFERENCE PROCEEDINGS. a. American Institute of Aeronautics and Astronautics, 1290 Ave. of the Americas, New York, NY 10104.

629.1 621.384 US
A I A A COMMUNICATIONS SATELLITE SYSTEMS CONFERENCE. TECHNICAL PAPERS. (Subseries of: Progress in Astronautics and Aeronautics) 4th, 1972. irreg. price varies. American Institute of Aeronautics and Astronautics, 1290 Ave. of the Americas, New York, NY 10019.
Telecommunication

629.13 629.4 US ISSN 0065-8693
A I A A ROSTER. 1964. biennial. $50. American Institute of Aeronautics and Astronautics, 1290 Ave. of the Americas, New York, NY 10019. Ed. Nelson W. Friedman. adv. circ. 200.

629.4 US ISSN 0065-3373
ADVANCES IN SPACE SCIENCE AND TECHNOLOGY. SUPPLEMENT. 1963. irreg., 1965, no. 2. price varies. Academic Press, Inc., 111 Fifth Ave., New York, NY 10003.

629.13 BL
AERO. irreg. Cr.$150. J. Ribeiro de Mendonca, Av. Alfonso de Taunay, 143, Barra de Tijuca, Rio de Janeiro, Brazil. illus.

629.13 US ISSN 0065-3705
AERONAUTICS BULLETIN.* 1947. irreg. free. University of Illinois at Urbana-Champaign, Institute of Aviation, 318 Civil Engineering Bldg., Urbana, IL 61803. Ed. Gertrude Becker.

629 AG
AERONAVEGACION COMERCIAL ARGENTINA. irreg. price varies. Instituto Nacional de Estadistica y Censos, Hipolito Yrigoyen 250, Buenos Aires, Argentina. charts. stat.

629.13 BE ISSN 0065-3713
AERONOMICA ACTA. (Text in French, Flemish, Dutch or English, with preliminary material also in other languages) 1959. irreg., latest 1975. Institut d'Aeronomie Spatiale de Belgique, Ave. Circulaire 3, 1180 Brussels, Belgium.

AERONAUTICS AND SPACE FLIGHT

629.1   JA
AEROSPACE INDUSTRY YEARBOOK. (Text in Japanese) 1974. a. 7000 Yen. Society of Japanese Aerospace Companies, Inc. - Nihon Koku Uchu Kogyokai, Hibiya Park Bldg, 8-1 Yurakucho 1-chome, Chiyoda-ku, Tokyo 100, Japan. circ. 1,000.

629.1   BL
AEROSPACO.* 1972. irreg. Editora Imagem Nova, Rua da Graca, 201, Conj. 41, C.E.P. 01125, Sao Paulo, Brazil. illus.

387.7   CN   ISSN 0568-3424
AIR CANADA. ANNUAL REPORT. (Text in: English and French) a. Air Canada, 1 Place Ville Marie, Montreal, Que., Canada.

629.1 387.7   UK   ISSN 0143-4063
AIR TRANSPORT (LONDON) 1978. a. I P C Transport Press Ltd., Dorset House, Stamford St., London SE1 9LU, England.

629.1   UN   ISSN 0065-4876
AIRCRAFT ACCIDENT DIGEST. (Issued as a subseries of: Air Navigation. Series F: Circulars) (Edts. in English, French, Spanish) 1951. irreg.; latest issue, no. 20, 1974. price varies. International Civil Aviation Organization - Organisation de l'Aviation Civile Internationale, P.O. Box 400, Succursale: Place de l'Aviation Internationale, 1000 Sherbrooke Street West, Montreal, Quebec H3A 2R2, Canada.

629.13   US   ISSN 0065-4892
AIRCRAFT ENGINES OF THE WORLD. 1941. irreg. Paul H. Wilkinson, Ed. & Pub., 5900 Kingswood Rd., N.W., Washington, DC 20014. adv. circ. 2,000.

629.1   UK
AIRCRAFT ILLUSTRATED ANNUAL. a. price varies. Ian Allan Ltd., Terminal House, Shepperton, Middlesex TW17 8AS, England. Ed. Martin Horseman. circ. 9,500.

629.1 387.7   US
AIRMAN'S INFORMATION MANUAL (FALLBROOK) a. $5.50. Aero Publishers, Inc., 329 W. Aviation Rd., Fallbrook, CA 92028. illus. index.

629.133   US   ISSN 0065-8510
AMERICAN HELICOPTER SOCIETY. NATIONAL FORUM. PROCEEDINGS. 1943. a. price varies. American Helicopter Society, Inc., 1325 18th St., N.W., Washington, DC 20036. circ. 400.
   Helicopters

629.13 629.4   US   ISSN 0065-8685
AMERICAN INSTITUTE OF AERONAUTICS AND ASTRONAUTICS. A I A A LOS ANGELES SECTION. MONOGRAPHS. 1967. irreg., latest vol. 20. Western Periodicals Co., 13000 Raymer St., North Hollywood, CA 91605.

629.13 629.4   US   ISSN 0065-8707
AMERICAN INSTITUTE OF AERONAUTICS AND ASTRONAUTICS. PAPER. 1963. irreg.(according to meeting schedules) $2.50 non-members; $1.75 members. American Institute of Aeronautics and Astronautics, 1290 Ave. of the Americas, New York, NY 10019. (also avail. in microfiche) Indexed: Eng.Ind. Int.Aerosp.Abstr.
   Incorporates: Guidance Control and Flight Mechanics Conference. Proceedings (ISSN 0072-7946) & Aerodynamics Deceleration Systems Conference. Papers Presented (ISSN 0065-3675)

629.13 629.4   US   ISSN 0065-8715
AMERICAN INSTITUTE OF AERONAUTICS AND ASTRONAUTICS. SELECTED REPRINT SERIES. 1967. irreg., latest vol. 19. price varies. American Institute of Aeronautics and Astronautics, 1290 Avenue of the Americas, New York, NY 10019. Ed. Robert A. Gross. index.

ANCIENS ELEVES DE L'ECOLE TECHNIQUE D'AERONAUTIQUE ET DE CONSTRUCTION AUTOMOBILE. ANNUAIRE. see *TRANSPORTATION — Automobiles*

629.13   UK
ANGLO-AMERICAN AERONAUTICAL CONFERENCE. PROCEEDINGS. irreg., 15th. London 1977. Royal Aeronautical Society, 4 Hamilton Place, London W1, England.

340 387.7   CN   ISSN 0701-158X
ANNALS OF AIR AND SPACE LAW/ANNUAIRE DE DROIT AERIEN ET SPATIAL. 1976. a. Can.$25. McGill University, Institute of Air and Space Law, McGill University Press, Montreal, Que., Canada. Ed. Nicolas M. Matte. bk. rev.

ANNUAL BOOK OF A S T M STANDARDS. PART 25. PETROLEUM PRODUCTS AND LUBRICANTS (3); AEROSPACE MATERIALS. see *ENGINEERING — Engineering Mechanics And Materials*

629.13   FR
ASSOCIATION AERONAUTIQUE ET ASTRONAUTIQUE DE FRANCE. ANNUAIRE. 1961. a. Association Aeronautique et Astronautique de France, 80 rue Lauriston, 75116 Paris, France. adv. circ. 1,200.
   Formerly (1964-1974): Association Francaise des Ingenieurs et Techniciens de l'Aeronautique et de l'Espace. Annuaire (ISSN 0066-9245)

ASSOCIATION TECHNIQUE MARITIME ET AERONAUTIQUE, PARIS. BULLETIN. see *TRANSPORTATION — Ships And Shipping*

629.4   US   ISSN 0304-8705
ASTRONAUTICAL RESEARCH. Represents: International Astronautical Federation. Proceedings of the Congress. 1950. irreg., 21st, 1970. Pergamon Press, Inc., Maxwell House, Fairview Park, Elmsford, NY 10523. illus.
   Continues: International Astronautical Congress. Proceedings (ISSN 0074-1795)

629.13   GW   ISSN 0067-0685
AUSRUESTUNG IN LUFT- UND RAUMFAHRT. 1966. irreg. price varies. R. Oldenbourg Verlag GmbH, Rosenheimer Str. 145, Postfach 801360, 8000 Munich 80, W. Germany (B.R.D.) Ed. Karl H. Fischer.

387.1   AT
AUSTRALIA. AIR TRANSPORT GROUP. AERODROMES AND GROUND AIDS. irreg. Air Transport Group, Canberra, Australia. illus.

629.13   AT   ISSN 0084-7232
AUSTRALIAN AVIATION YEARBOOK.* 1960. a. $4.50. Pacific Yearbooks, Box C235, Clarence St., Sydney, N.S.W. 2000, Australia.

629.13   AT   ISSN 0084-7364
AUSTRALIAN GLIDING YEARBOOK. 1969. a. Aus.$1. ‡ Gliding Federation of Australia, Box 1650, Adelaide, S.A. 5001, Australia. Ed. Allan Ash. adv. bk. rev. circ. 4,000.
   Gliding

629.1   AT   ISSN 0311-628X
AUSTRALIAN TRANSPORT. 1973/74. a. Aus.$5.60. Australian Government Publishing Service, Box 84, Canberra, A.C.T. 2600, Australia. Ed. K. Williams. charts. illus. stat. circ. 5,000.
   Formerly: Australia. Department of Civil Aviation. Civil Aviation Report (ISSN 0572-0400)

629.1   US
AVIATION ANNUAL. 1974. a. $1.95. Werner & Werner Corporation, 606 Wilshire Blvd., Santa Monica, CA 90401. Ed. Steve Werner. adv. illus.

629.13   UK   ISSN 0143-1145
AVIATION EUROPE. 1947. a. £20. Sell's Publications Ltd., Sell's House, 39 East St., Epsom KT17 1BQ, Surrey, England. adv. bk. rev. circ. 5,000.
   Incorporating: Sell's British Aviation (ISSN 0080-8695)

616.98   US   ISSN 0067-2661
AVIATION MEDICAL EDUCATION SERIES. 1965. irreg. U. S. Federal Aviation Administration, Aviation Medicine Office, 800 Independence Ave., S.W., Washington, DC 20590.
   Aerospace medicine

629.1   US
AVIATION/SPACE WRITERS ASSOCIATION MANUAL. 1972. a. $25. ‡ Aviation-Space Writers Association, Cliffwood Rd., Chester, NJ 07930. Ed. William F. Kaiser. adv. circ. 6,000(controlled)

629.13 629.4   US   ISSN 0067-267X
AVIATION WEEK & SPACE TECHNOLOGY. MARKETING DIRECTORY. 1955. a. $4. ‡ McGraw-Hill Publications Co., 1221 Avenue of the Americas, New York, NY 10020. Ed. R. B. Hotz. adv. index. circ. 104,000. (also avail. in microform from UMI)

629.13   UK
AVIONICS DATA SHEETS. irreg. $110. Aviation Studies International, Sussex House, Parkside, Wimbledon, London SW19 5NB, England.

629.13   UY
C I D A. 1976. irreg. Direccion General de Aviacion Civil, Centro de Investigacion y Difusion Aeronautico Espacial, Yi 1182, Montevideo, Uruguay.

629.13   II   ISSN 0077-2968
CATALOGUE OF N A L TECHNICAL TRANSLATIONS. (Text in English) 1972. a. exchange basis. National Aeronautical Laboratory, Box 1779, Kodihalli, Bangalore 560017, India. (Affiliate: Council of Scientific and Industrial Research) Ed. C. V. Suryanara Yanan. (processed)

629.4   FR   ISSN 0069-2034
CENTRE NATIONAL D'ETUDES SPATIALES. RAPPORT D'ACTIVITE. 1962. a. free. Centre National d'Etudes Spatiales, 18 Ave. E. Belin, 31055 Toulouse Cedex, France. Ed. J. P. Bordet.

CIVIL JET TRANSPORT. AVIONIC EQUIPMENT. see *TRANSPORTATION — Air Transport*

629.4 341   US   ISSN 0069-5831
COLLOQUIUM ON THE LAW OF OUTER SPACE. PROCEEDINGS. 1958. a. $27.50. (International Institute of Space Law) University of California, Davis, School of Law, Davis, CA 95616 (Dist. by Fred B. Rothman & Co., 57 Leuning St., S. Hackensack, N.J. 07606) (Co-sponsor: International Astronautical Federation) Ed. Mortimer D. Schwartz. circ. 200. (back issues avail)

629.13   US   ISSN 0573-0872
COMMONWEALTH SPACE-FLIGHT SYMPOSIUM. PROCEEDINGS.* 1959. irreg. Academic Press, Inc., 111 Fifth Ave, New York, NY 10003.

629.8   US   ISSN 0090-5267
CONTROL AND DYNAMIC SYSTEMS: ADVANCES IN THEORY AND APPLICATIONS. a. Academic Press, Inc., 111 Fifth Ave., New York, NY 10003. Ed. Cornelius T. Leondes. illus. Indexed: Appl.Mech.Rev. Key Title: Control and Dynamic Systems.
   Continues: Advances in Control Systems (ISSN 0065-2466)

629.4   FR   ISSN 0084-9332
COSPAR TECHNIQUE MANUAL. 1967. irreg. price varies. Committee on Space Research, 51 Bd. de Montmorency, 75016 Paris, France.

629.4   FR   ISSN 0084-9340
COSPAR TRANSACTIONS. 1967. irreg. price varies. Committee on Space Research, 51 Boulevard de Montmorency, 75016 Paris, France.

387.7   US   ISSN 0096-3364
CURRENT AVIATION STATISTICS. irreg.? U.S. Federal Aviation Administration, Office of Management Systems, Information and Statistics Division, Washington, DC 20590.

629.13   GW
D F V L R-FORSCHUNGSBERICHTE UND D F V L R-MITTEILUNGEN. (Text in German; summaries in English and German) 1964. irreg. price varies. Deutsche Forschungs- und Versuchsanstalt fuer Luft- und Raumfahrt e.V., Linder Hoehe, Postfach 906058, 5000 Cologne 90, W. Germany (B.R.D.) index. Indexed: Appl.Mech.Rev.
   Formerly (until 1978): Duetsche Luft- und Raumfahrt. Forschungsberichte (ISSN 0070-4245)

629.13   GW   ISSN 0070-3966
D F V L R JAHRESBERICHT. 1969. a. price varies. Deutsche Forschungs- und Versuchsanstalt fuer Luft- und Raumfahrt e.V., Linder Hoehe, Postfach 906058, 5000 Cologne 90, W. Germany (B.R.D.)

629.13 629.4   GW   ISSN 0070-4083
D. G. L. R. JAHRBUECHER. 1952. a. price varies. Deutsche Gesellschaft fuer Luft und Raumfahrt e.V., Goethestr. 10, 5000 Cologne 51, W. Germany (B.R.D.) Eds. Werner Schulz, Werner Wilke. index.
Formerly: Wissenschaftliche Gesellschaft fuer Luft- und Raumfahrt. Jahrbuecher.

DEVELOPMENTS IN SOLAR SYSTEM AND SPACE SCIENCE. see *ASTRONOMY*

629.13   US
DIRECTORY OF AEROSPACE EDUCATION. 1975. biennial. $2.95. American Society for Aerospace Education, 821 15th St. N.W., Suite 432, Washington, DC 20005. Ed.Wayne R. Matson. circ. 200,000. (also avail. in microfilm)

629.13   FR
E S A SCIENTIFIC-TECHNICAL REPORTS, NOTES AND MEMORANDA. 1964. irreg. European Space Agency, 8-10 rue Mario Nikis, 75738 Paris Cedex 15, France.
Formerly (1964-1975): E S R O Scientific-Technical Reports, Notes and Memoranda.

ELECTRONICS AND AEROSPACE SYSTEMS CONVENTION. E A S C O N RECORD. see *ELECTRICITY AND ELECTRICAL ENGINEERING*

629.1   BE   ISSN 0531-2248
EUROCONTROL. 1965. biennial; vol. 4, no. 3, 1974. 150 Fr. for 2 nos. ‡ European Organization for the Safety of Air Navigation - Organisation Europeene pour la Securite de la Navigation Aerienne, 72 rue de la Loi, 1040 Brussels, Belgium. index.

629.1 621.38   FR   ISSN 0531-7444
EUROPEAN ORGANISATION FOR CIVIL AVIATION ELECTRONICS. GENERAL ASSEMBLY. ANNUAL REPORT. (Text in English and French) 1964. a. free. European Organization for Civil Aviation Electronics, 11 rue Hamelin, 75783 Paris Cedex 16, France. circ. 200.

629.13   UK   ISSN 0071-402X
FARNBOROUGH AIR SHOW (PUBLIC PROGRAMME) biennial. ‡ Society of British Aerospace Companies Ltd., 29 King St. St. James's, London, SW1Y 6RD, England.

341.46   US   ISSN 0533-0963
FEDERAL AVIATION REGULATIONS FOR PILOTS. a. $4. Aero Publishers, Inc., 329 W. Aviation Rd., Fallbrook, CA 92028. charts. illus. index.

629.13 350   US   ISSN 0198-6503
FEDERAL REPORTER. 1977. biennial. Federal Reporter Publishing Company, 323 S. Franklin, Suite 804D, Chicago, IL 60606. Ed. H. Zach Miller. circ. 500. (reprint service avail. from UMI)
Formerly: Federal Opportunity Research.

629.1 551.4   FI   ISSN 0355-2004
FINNISH METEOROLOGICAL INSTITUTE. OBSERVATIONS OF SATELLITES. VISUAL OBSERVATIONS OF ARTIFICIAL EARTH SATELLITES IN FINLAND. (Text in English) a., no. 19, 1979. Ilmatieteen Laitos - Finnish Meteorological Institute, Box 503, SF-00100 Helsinki 10, Finland (Orders to: Valtion Painatuskekus, Annankatu 44, Box 516, SF-00101 Helsinki 100, Finland)
Formerly (until no. 13, 1972): Visual Observations of Artificial Earth Satellites in Finland.

614.8   NZ
FLIGHT SAFETY. 1973. irreg. NZ.$2.50. Civil Aviation Division, Flight Operations Branch, Private Bag, Wellington 1, New Zealand. illus. circ. 7,200.

629.13   SW   ISSN 0081-5640
FLYGTEKNISKA FOERSOEKSANSTALTEN. MEDDELANDE/REPORT. (Text in English) 1944. irreg. price varies. (Aeronautical Research Institute of Sweden) Almqvist & Wiksell International, Box 62, S-101 20 Stockholm, Sweden. Ed. Brit Berg.

629.13   US   ISSN 0163-1144
FLYING ANNUAL & BUYERS' GUIDE. 1965. a. $2.50. Ziff-Davis Publishing Co., 1 Park Ave., New York, NY 10016 (Dist. by Sportshelf, Box 634, New Rochelle, NY 10802) Ed. Robert Parke. adv. circ. 165,000.
Former titles: Flying Annual and Pilots' Buying Guide; Flying Annual and Pilots' Guide (ISSN 0071-6286)

629.13   FR   ISSN 0078-3773
FRANCE. OFFICE NATIONAL D'ETUDES ET DE RECHERCHES AEROSPATIALES. ACTIVITIES. (Editions in English & French) 1965. a. free. ‡ Office National d'Etudes et de Recherches Aerospatiales, 29, Avenue de la Division-Leclerc, 92320 Chatillon, France. circ. 750(English edt.) 2,250 (French edt.)
Until 1968: France. Office National d'Etudes et de Recherches Aerospatiales. Recueil de Notes sur l'Activite de ONERA.

629.13   FR   ISSN 0078-3781
FRANCE. OFFICE NATIONAL D'ETUDES ET DE RECHERCHES AEROSPATIALES. NOTES TECHNIQUES. (Text in French; abstract in English) 1946. irreg.(about 20 per year) price varies. Office National d'Etudes et de Recherches Aerospatiales, 29 Ave. de la Division-Leclerc, 92320 Chatillon, France. Ed. Claude Sevestre. index. cum index: 1950-76. circ. 250. Indexed: Appl.Mech.Rev.

629.13   FR   ISSN 0078-379X
FRANCE. OFFICE NATIONAL D'ETUDES ET DE RECHERCHES AEROSPATIALES. PUBLICATIONS. (Text in French; abstract in English) 1946. irreg. (about 5 per year) price varies. Office National d'Etudes et de Recherches Aerospatiales, 29 Avenue de la Division-Leclerc, 92320 Chatillon, France. Ed. Claude Sevestre. index. cum index: 1947-1976. circ. 250. Indexed: Appl.Mech.Rev.

629.135   US   ISSN 0094-3975
FUNDAMENTALS OF AEROSPACE INSTRUMENTATION. Represents: Instrument Society of America. International I S A Aerospace Instrumentation Symposium. Tutorial Proceedings. a. price varies. Instrument Society of America, 400 Stanwix St., Pittsburgh, PA 15222.

629.13   UK   ISSN 0072-5595
GREAT BRITAIN. AERONAUTICAL RESEARCH COUNCIL. CURRENT PAPER SERIES. 1950. irreg. price varies. H.M.S.O., P.O. Box 569, London SE1 9NH, England.

629.13   UK   ISSN 0072-5609
GREAT BRITAIN. AERONAUTICAL RESEARCH COUNCIL. REPORTS AND MEMORANDA SERIES. irreg. price varies. H.M.S.O., P.O. Box 569, London SE1 9NH, England.

629.1 623   CN   ISSN 0708-4331
HIGH FLIGHT. At head of title: Canada's Wings. 1980. irreg. Can.$14. Box 393, Stittsville, Ont. K0A 3G0, Canada. illus.

387.7   US   ISSN 0018-2443
HISTORICAL AVIATION ALBUM. 1965. a. $10 per no. ‡ Paul R. Matt, Box 33, Temple City, CA 91780. Eds. Kenn C. Rust, Thomas G. Foxworth. charts. illus. stat. tr.mk. circ. 3,500. (tabloid format; also avail. in microform from UMI)

629.47   US
I E E E POWER ELECTRONICS SPECIALISTS CONFERENCE. RECORD. 1970. irreg. $15. Institute of Electrical and Electronics Engineers, Inc., Aerospace and Electronics Systems Society, 445 Hoes Lane, Piscataway, NJ 08854. illus.
Former titles, 1972: I E E E Power Processing and Electronics Specialists Conference. Record (ISSN 0090-2381); Continues: Power Conditioning Specialists Conference. Record (ISSN 0079-4414)

629.1   II
INDIA. DEPARTMENT OF SPACE. ANNUAL REPORT. (Editions in English & Hindi) 1973. a. controlled free circ. Department of Space, Janardhan, Residency Rd., Bangalore 560025, India. Ed. P. Nanda Kumar. circ. 3,500. (back issues avail)

629.13   US   ISSN 0073-6775
INDIANA. AERONAUTICS COMMISSION. ANNUAL REPORT. 1946. a. free. Aeronautics Commission, 100 N. Senate Ave., Indianapolis, IN 46204. circ. controlled.

629.1   SZ   ISSN 0074-1116
INTERAVIA A B C; world directory of aviation and astronautics. (Text in English, French, German, Italian, Spanish) 1935. a. 145 Fr.($78) Interavia S.A., 86 Av. Louis Casai, Case Postale 162, 1216 Cointrin-Geneva, Switzerland. Ed. J. Didelot. adv. index.

629.13   FR
INTERNATIONAL AERONAUTIC FEDERATION. ANNUAL INFORMATION BULLETIN. irreg. 50 F. International Aeronautic Federation, 6 rue Galilee, 75782 Paris Cedex 16, France.
Formerly: International Aeronautic Federation. General Conference Minutes(of the) Business Meetings (ISSN 0534-6509)

629.1   UN   ISSN 0074-2244
INTERNATIONAL CIVIL AVIATION ORGANIZATION. AIRWORTHINESS COMMITTEE. REPORT OF MEETING. (Edts. in English, French, Spanish, Russian) irreg; 10th, Montreal, 1973. price varies. International Civil Aviation Organization - Organisation de l'Aviation Civile Internationale, P.O. Box 400, Succursale: Place de l'Aviation Internationale, 1000 Sherbrooke Street West, Montreal, Quebec H3A 2R2, Canada.

629.1   UN   ISSN 0074-2333
INTERNATIONAL CIVIL AVIATION ORGANIZATION. ALL-WEATHER OPERATIONS PANEL. REPORT OF MEETING. (Editions in English, French, Russian, Spanish) irreg; 5th, Montreal, 1973. price varies. International Civil Aviation Organization - Organisation de l'Aviation Civile Internationale, P.O. Box 400, Succursale: Place de l'Aviation Internationale, 1000 Sherbrooke Street West, Montreal, Quebec H3A 2R2, Canada.

629.1   UN   ISSN 0074-2384
INTERNATIONAL CIVIL AVIATION ORGANIZATION. ASSEMBLY. REPORT OF THE TECHNICAL COMMISSION. irreg.; 18th, 1971. price varies. International Civil Aviation Organization - Organisation de l'Aviation Civile, P.O. Box 400, Succursale: Place de l'Aviation Internationale, 1000 Sherbrooke Street West, Montreal, Quebec H3A 2R2, Canada.

629.1   UN   ISSN 0074-2252
INTERNATIONAL CIVIL AVIATION ORGANIZATION. AUTOMATED DATA INTERCHANGE SYSTEMS PANEL. REPORT OF MEETING. (Editions in English, French, Russian, Spanish) irreg; 6th, Montreal, 1975. price varies. International Civil Aviation Organization - Organisation de l'Aviation Civile Internationale, P.O. Box 400, Succursale: Place de l'Aviation Internationale, 1000 Sherbrooke Street West, Montreal, Quebec H3A 2R2, Canada.

629.1   UN   ISSN 0074-252X
INTERNATIONAL CIVIL AVIATION ORGANIZATION. OBSTACLE CLEARANCE PANEL. REPORT OF MEETING. (Editions in English, French, Spanish) 1968. irreg; 3rd, Montreal, 1971. price varies. International Civil Aviation Organization - Organisation de l'Aviation Civile Internationale, P.O. Box 400, Succursale: Place de l'Aviation Internationale, 1000 Sherbrooke Street West, Montreal, Quebec H3A 2R2, Canada.

629.1   UN   ISSN 0074-2228
INTERNATIONAL CIVIL AVIATION ORGANIZATION. (PANEL ON) APPLICATION OF SPACE TECHNIQUES RELATING TO AVIATION. REPORT OF MEETING. (Editions in English, French, Spanish) irreg; 4th, Montreal, 1971. price varies. International Civil Aviation Organization - Organisation de l'Aviation Civile Internationale, P.O. Box 400, Succursale: Place de l'Aviation Internationale, 1000 Sherbrooke Street West, Montreal, Quebec H3A 2R2, Canada.

629.1   UN   ISSN 0074-2546
INTERNATIONAL CIVIL AVIATION ORGANIZATION. REPORT OF THE AIR NAVIGATION CONFERENCE. (Editions in English, French, Russian, Spanish) 1953. irreg; 8th, Montreal, 1974. price varies. International Civil Aviation Organization - Organisation de l'Aviation Civile Internationale, P.O. Box 400, Succursale: Place de l'Aviation Internationale, 1000 Sherbrooke Street West, Montreal, Quebec H3A 2R2, Canada.

AERONAUTICS AND SPACE FLIGHT

629.1   UN   ISSN 0074-2562
INTERNATIONAL CIVIL AVIATION ORGANIZATION. SONIC BOOM PANEL. REPORT OF THE MEETING. (Editions in English, French, Spanish) irreg; 2nd, Montreal, 1970. $1.50. International Civil Aviation Organization - Organisation de l'Aviation Civile Interntionale, P.O. Box 400, Succursale: Place de l'Aviation Internationale, 1000 Sherbrooke Street West, Montreal, Quebec H3A 2R2, Canada.

629.1   UN   ISSN 0074-2570
INTERNATIONAL CIVIL AVIATION ORGANIZATION. TECHNICAL PANEL ON SUPERSONIC TRANSPORT. REPORT OF MEETING. (Editions in English, French, Spanish, Russian) 1968. irreg; 5th, Montreal, 1974. price varies. International Civil Aviation Organization - Organisation de l'Aviation Civile Internationale, P.O. Box 400, Succursale: Place de l'Aviation Internationale, 1000 Sherbrooke Street West, Montreal, Quebec H3A 2R2, Canada.

629.1   UN   ISSN 0074-2589
INTERNATIONAL CIVIL AVIATION ORGANIZATION. VISUAL AIDS PANEL. REPORT OF MEETING. (Editions in English, French, Spanish) 1964, 3rd. irreg; 6th, Montreal, 1972. price varies. International Civil Aviation Organization - Organisation de l'Aviation Civile Internationale, P.O. Box 400, Succursale: Place de l'Aviation Internationale, 1000 Sherbrooke Street West, Montreal, Quebec H3A 2R2, Canada.

INTERNATIONAL CONFERENCE ON THE ENVIRONMENTAL IMPACT OF AEROSPACE OPERATIONS IN THE HIGH ATMOSPHERE. (PROCEEDINGS) see *ENVIRONMENTAL STUDIES*

629.1   US
INTERNATIONAL FLIGHT INFORMATION MANUAL. a. with q. supplements. $9. U.S. Federal Aviation Administration, 800 Independence Ave., S.W., Washington, DC 20591 (Orders to: Supt. of Documents, Washington, DC 20402)

629.13   US
INTERNATIONAL SERIES IN AERONAUTICS AND ASTRONAUTICS. DIVISION 1. SOLID AND STRUCTURAL MECHANICS. 1961. irreg. price varies. Pergamon Press, Inc., Maxwell House, Fairview Park, Elmsford, NY 10523. index.
Formerly: International Series of Monographs in Aeronautics and Astronautics. Division 1. Solid and Structural Mechanics (ISSN 0074-7947)

629.13   629.4   US
INTERNATIONAL SERIES IN AERONAUTICS AND ASTRONAUTICS. DIVISION 2. AERODYNAMICS AND ASTRONAUTICS. 1958. irreg., 1969, vol. 7. price varies. Pergamon Press, Inc., Maxwell House, Fairview Park, Elmsford, NY 10523. index.
Formerly: International Series of Monographs in Aeronautics and Astronautics. Division 2. Aerodynamics (ISSN 0074-7955)

629.13   629.4   US
INTERNATIONAL SERIES IN AERONAUTICS AND ASTRONAUTICS. DIVISION 3. PROPULSION SYSTEMS INCLUDING FUELS. 1957. irreg., 1970, vol. 6. price varies. Pergamon Press, Inc., Maxwell House, Fairview Park, Elmsford, NY 10523. index.
Formerly: International Series of Monographs in Aeronautics and Astronautics. Division 3. Propulsion Systems Including Fuels (ISSN 0074-7963)

629.4   US
INTERNATIONAL SERIES IN AERONAUTICS AND ASTRONAUTICS. DIVISION 7. ASTRONAUTICS. 1958. irreg., 1964, vol. 5. price varies. Pergamon Press, Inc., Maxwell House, Fairview Park, Elmsford, NY 10523. index.
Formerly: International Series of Monographs in Aeronautics and Astronautics. Division 7. Astronautics (ISSN 0074-7998)

629.13   629.4   US
INTERNATIONAL SERIES IN AERONAUTICS AND ASTRONAUTICS. DIVISION 9. SYMPOSIA. 1958. irreg., 1969, vol. 20. price varies. Pergamon Press, Inc., Maxwell House, Fairview Park, Elmsford, NY 10523.
Formerly: International Series of Monographs in Aeronautics and Astronautics. Division 9. Symposia (ISSN 0074-8005)

629.13   IS   ISSN 0075-0972
ISRAEL ANNUAL CONFERENCE ON AVIATION AND ASTRONAUTICS. PROCEEDINGS. 1958. a. $20. Technion-Israel Institute of Technology, Department of Aeronautical Engineering, Haifa, Israel. Indexed: Appl.Mech.Rev. Sci. & Tech.Aerosp.Rep.

629.133   UK   ISSN 0075-3017
JANE'S ALL THE WORLD AIRCRAFT. a. £40. Jane's Publishing Co., Paulton House, 8 Shepherdess Walk, London N.1., England. Ed. John W. R. Taylor.

JORNADAS NACIONALES DE DERECHO AERONAUTICO Y ESPACIAL. TRABAJOS. see *TRANSPORTATION — Air Transport*

629.13   SW
KUNGLIGA TEKNISKA HOEGSKOLAN. FLYGTEKNISKA INSTITUTIONEN. K T H AERO MEMO F I. (Text in English) irreg. Kungliga Tekniska Hoegskolan, Flygtekniska Institutionen, S-100 44 Stockholm 70, Sweden.

629.13   US   ISSN 0024-5704
LOCKHEED ORION SERVICE DIGEST. 1962. irreg., no. 32, 1976. free. ‡ Lockheed-California Co., Burbank, CA 91510. Ed. Wayne Cradduck. charts. illus. circ. 6,000(controlled)

629.4   358   US   ISSN 0460-3400
MCGRAW-HILL SERIES IN MISSILE AND SPACE TECHNOLOGY. 1958. irreg. price varies. McGraw-Hill Book Co., 8171 Redwood Highway, Novato, CA 94947.

MANAGEMENT (BALTIMORE); a continuing literature survey with indexes. see *BUSINESS AND ECONOMICS — Management*

629.1   US
MASSACHUSETTS INSTITUTE OF TECHNOLOGY. FLIGHT TRANSPORTATION LABORATORY. F T L REPORT. irreg. Massachusetts Institute of Technology, Flight Transportation Laboratory, Cambridge, MA 02139. Ed. Joseph Vittek. charts. illus.

629.1   US
MONOGRAPHS ON ROCKETS AND MISSILES. a. price varies. Gordon and Breach Science Publishers, One Park Ave., New York, NY 10016. Ed. J. Clemow.

629.13   US   ISSN 0077-3093
N A S A FACTS. irreg. National Aeronautics and Space Administration, Washington, DC 20546 (Orders to: Supt. Doc., Washington, DC 20402)

629.13   US   ISSN 0077-2623
N A S A-UNIVERSITY CONFERENCE ON MANUAL CONTROL (PAPERS) 1965. a. $3. National Aeronautics and Space Administration, 600 Maryland Ave. S.W., Washington, DC 20546 (Order from: National Technical Information Service, Springfield, VA 22161)

629.13   II   ISSN 0077-2976
NATIONAL AERONAUTICAL LABORATORY. ANNUAL REPORT. (Text in English) 1960/61. a. exchange basis. National Aeronautical Laboratory, Box 1779 Kodihalli, Bangalore 560017, India. (Affiliate: Council of Scientific and Industrial Research) circ. 500.

629.13   II   ISSN 0077-300X
NATIONAL AERONAUTICAL LABORATORY. TECHNICAL NOTE. (Text in English) 1960. irreg., latest issue 1978. exchange basis. National Aeronautical Laboratory, Box 1779, Kodihalli, Bangalore 560017, India. (Affiliate: Council of Scientific and Industrial Research) circ. 500. Indexed: Appl.Mech.Rev.

629.13   629.4   US   ISSN 0077-3085
NATIONAL AERONAUTICS AND SPACE ADMINISTRATION. N A S A FACTBOOK. 1971. irreg. 1975 2nd ed. $44.50. Marquis Academic Media, 200 E. Ohio St., Chicago, IL 60611. index.

629.13   US   ISSN 0499-9320
NATIONAL AERONAUTICS AND SPACE ADMINISTRATION. TECHNICAL MEMORANDUMS. irreg. U.S. National Aeronautics and Space Administration, Scientific and Technical Information Facility, Box 8757, Baltimore/Washington International Airport, MD 21240 (Order from: N T I S, Springfield, VA 22161) (also avail. in microfiche) Key Title: N A S A Technical Memorandum.

629.13   US   ISSN 0077-3131
NATIONAL AERONAUTICS AND SPACE ADMINISTRATION. TECHNICAL NOTES. irreg. U.S. National Aeronautics and Space Administration, Scientific and Technical Information Facility, Box 8757, Baltimore-Washington International Airport, MD 21240 (Order from: National Technical Information Service, Springfield, VA 22161) Indexed: Appl.Mech.Rev.

629.13   US   ISSN 0077-314X
NATIONAL AERONAUTICS AND SPACE ADMINISTRATION. TECHNICAL REPORTS. irreg. U. S. National Aeronautics and Space Administration, Scientific and Technical Information Facility, Box 8757, Baltimore-Washington International Airport, MD 21240 (Orders to: Supt. Doc., Washington, DC 20402) Indexed: Appl.Mech.Rev.

629.13   US   ISSN 0077-3158
NATIONAL AERONAUTICS AND SPACE ADMINISTRATION. TECHNICAL TRANSLATIONS. irreg. U.S. National Aeronautics and Space Administration, Scientific and Technical Information Facility, Box 8757, Baltimore-Washington International Airport, MD 21240 (Order from: National Technical Information Service, 5285 Port Royal Rd., Springfield, VA 22151) (also avail. in microfiche) Indexed: Appl.Mech.Rev.

629.4   US   ISSN 0065-373X
NATIONAL AEROSPACE AND ELECTRONICS CONFERENCE. RECORD. Abbreviated title: NAECON. a. Institute of Electrical and Electronics Engineers, Inc., 445 Hoes Lane, Piscataway, NJ 08854.

629.13   US
NATIONAL AEROSPACE MEETING. (PROCEEDINGS) irreg., 1977, Denver. Institute of Navigation, Suite 832, 815 15th St. N.W., Washington, DC 20005.

NATIONAL RESEARCH COUNCIL, CANADA. NATIONAL AERONAUTICAL ESTABLISHMENT. MECHANICAL ENGINEERING REPORTS. see *ENGINEERING — Mechanical Engineering*

629.13   CN   ISSN 0077-5541
NATIONAL RESEARCH COUNCIL, CANADA. NATIONAL AERONAUTICAL ESTABLISHMENT. AERONAUTICAL REPORT (L R SERIES) 1951. irreg. free. National Research Council of Canada, N A E - D M E Publications Section, Bldg. M-16, Ottawa K1A 0R6, Canada. circ. 300-1,200. Indexed: Appl.Mech.Rev. Eng.Ind. Sci.&Tech.Aerosp.Rep.

629.1388   CN   ISSN 0077-5592
NATIONAL RESEARCH COUNCIL, CANADA. SPACE RESEARCH FACILITIES BRANCH. REPORT. (SRFB SERIES) 1966. irreg. free. National Research Council of Canada, Ottawa, Ont. K1A 0R6, Canada. Ed. R.J. Colley. circ. 100. Indexed: Sci.&Tech.Aerosp.Rep.

629.13   US   ISSN 0092-9980
OKLAHOMA. AERONAUTICS COMMISSION. ANNUAL REPORT. 1964. a. free. Aeronautics Commission, 424 United Founders Tower Bldg., Oklahoma City, OK 73112. illus. circ. 1,000. Key Title: Annual Report - Oklahoma Aeronautics Commission.

629.13 US ISSN 0092-3591
OVERVIEW OF THE F A A ENGINEERING & DEVELOPMENT PROGRAMS. (Subseries of its Report no. FAA-EM) 1974. irreg., latest 1975. free to qualified personnel. U. S. Federal Aviation Administration, 800 Independence Ave., S.W., Washington, DC 20591. Ed. Eugene Rehrig. illus.

387.7 US
P N A H F JOURNAL. 1970. a. $2 to non-members. ‡ Pacific Northwest Aviation Historical Foundation, 400 Broad St., Seattle, WA 98109. Ed. Frederick A. Johnsen. adv. bk. rev. illus. charts. stat. circ. 1,000. (processed)

629.1 AT ISSN 0156-3726
PACIFIC AVIATION YEARBOOK. 1979. a. Aus.$40. Peter Isaacson Publications, 46-49 Porter St., Prahran, Vic. 3181, Australia. adv.

387.7
PENNSYLVANIA AIRCRAFT ACCIDENT AND VIOLATION ANALYSIS. 1972. irreg., latest, 1973. $1.06. Bureau of Aviation, Capital City Airport, New Cumberland, PA 17070. Ed. A.H. Childs. (tabloid format)

629.1 US ISSN 0376-0421
PROGRESS IN AEROSPACE SCIENCES. (Text in English and French) 1961. 4/yr. $110. Pergamon Press, Inc., Journals Division, Maxwell House, Fairview Park, Elmsford, NY 10523 (And Headington Hill Hall, Oxford OX3 0BW, England) Eds. J. A. Bagley, P. J. Finley. (also avail. in microform from MIM,UMI)
Formerly: Progress in Aeronautical Sciences (ISSN 0079-6026)

629.13 629.4 US ISSN 0079-6050
PROGRESS IN ASTRONAUTICS AND AERONAUTICS SERIES. (Vols. 1-8 published as Progress in Astronautics and Rocketry; Vols. 1-23 published by Academic Press) 1968. irreg; latest issue vol. 47. American Institute of Aeronautics and Astronautics, 1290 Ave. of the Americas, New York, NY 10019. Indexed: Appl.Mech.Rev.

RADIO TECHNICAL COMMISSION FOR AERONAUTICS. PROCEEDINGS OF THE ANNUAL ASSEMBLY MEETING. see *COMMUNICATIONS — Radio And Television*

629.13 629.4 GW
REUSS JAHRBUCH DER LUFT- UND RAUMFAHRT. 1951. a. DM.34.80. Suedwestdeutsche Verlagsanstalt GmbH, Am Marktplatz, Postfach 5760, 6800 Mannheim 1, W. Germany (B.R.D.) Ed. Tilman Reuss. adv. bk. rev. index.
Formerly: Jahrbuch der Luftfahrt und Raumfahrt (ISSN 0075-269X)

629.4 US ISSN 0080-3413
ROCKET AND SPACE SCIENCE SERIES. (Volume 1: Propulsion; Volume 2: Propellants) 1967. irreg. $4.25 per vol. Howard W. Sams & Co. Inc., 4300 W. 62nd St., Indianapolis, IN 46268.

629 JA ISSN 0485-2877
ROCKET NEWS. (Text in Japanese) 1957. irreg. exchange basis. Japanese Rocket Society - Nihon Roketto Kyokai, c/o Yomiuri Shinbunsha, 1-7-1 Ote-machi, Chiyoda-ku, Tokyo 100, Japan. abstr.

629.134 US ISSN 0583-9270
S.A.W.E. JOURNAL. (Former name of issuing body: Society of Aeronautical Weight Engineers) irreg. Society of Allied Weight Engineers, Box 60024, Terminal Annex, Los Angeles, CA 90060. illus.

629.1 SW ISSN 0080-5149
SAAB TECHNICAL NOTES. (Text in English) 1950. irreg. available on exchange. SAAB-SCANIA, Aerospace Division, S-581 88 Linkoeping, Sweden. Ed. O. Holme. circ. 600. Indexed: Appl.Mech.Rev.
Formerly: SAAB-SCANIA Technical Notes.

629.13 US
SMITHSONIAN STUDIES IN AIR AND SPACE. 1977. irreg. Smithsonian Institution Press, Washington, DC 20560. Ed. Albert L. Roffin, Jr. circ. 1,000. (reprint service avail. from UMI)

797 AT ISSN 0310-9399
SOARING IN THE A.C.T. (Australian Capital Territory) 1973. irreg. (Australian National University Gliding Club) Canberra Gliding Club, P.O. Box 1130, Canberra City, A.C.T. 2601, Australia.

629.1 US
SOCIETY OF FLIGHT TEST ENGINEERS. ANNUAL SYMPOSIUM PROCEEDINGS. vol. 4, 1973. a. $35. Society of Flight Test Engineers, Box 4047, Lancaster, CA 93534. illus.

629.1 NO
SPACE ACTIVITY IN NORWAY; report to COSPAR. (Text in English) 1963. a. free. Norges Teknisk-Naturvitenskapelige Forskningsraad, Space Activity Division - Royal Norwegian Council for Scientific and Industrial Research, Space Activity Division, Wdm. Thranesgt. 98, Oslo 1, Norway. illus.
Formerly: Norway. Komite for Romforskning. N.S.R.C. Report (ISSN 0452-3687)

629.41 US
SPACE FLIGHT TECHNOLOGY. a. price varies. Gordon and Breach Science Publishers, One Park Ave., New York, NY 10016. Ed. E. J. Durbin.

629.4 JA
SPACE IN JAPAN. biennial. 1500 Yen. Science and Technology Agency - Nihon Kagaku Gijutsucho, 2-2-1 Kasumigaseki, Chiyoda-ku, Tokyo 100, Japan (Subscr. to: KEIDANREN (Federation of Economic Organizations), 1-9-4 Otemachi, Chiyoda-ku , Tokyo 100, Japan) illus.

629.1 US
SPACE SCIENCE AND TECHNOLOGY TODAY. 1973. irreg. Goddard Space Flight Center, NASA Field Installation, Greenbelt, MD 20770 (Orders to: Supt. of Documents, Washington, DC 20402) illus.

629.1 US
SPACE SCIENCE TEXT SERIES. 1968. irreg., 1971, latest vol., unnumbered. price varies. John Wiley & Sons, Inc., 605 Third Ave., New York, NY 10016. Eds. A.J. Dessler, F.C. Michel.

SURINAM. CENTRAAL BUREAU LUCHTKARTERING. JAARVERSLAG. see *GEOGRAPHY*

001.94 CN ISSN 0707-7106
SWAMP GAS JOURNAL. 1978. irreg. contr. free circ. C. Rutkowski, Box 1918, Winnipeg General Post Office, Winnipeg, Man. R3C 3R2, Canada.
Unidentified flying objects

629.13 US ISSN 0082-0806
SYMPOSIUM ON ADVANCED PROPULSION CONCEPTS. PROCEEDINGS. 1957. irreg., 1967, 4th. $86 (2 vol. set) (U.S. Air Force, Office of Scientific Research) Gordon and Breach Science Publishers, 1 Park Avenue, New York, NY 10016. (Co-sponsor: General Electric Company)

629.4 US ISSN 0082-0857
SYMPOSIUM ON NONDESTRUCTIVE EVALUATION OF COMPONENTS AND MATERIALS IN AEROSPACE, WEAPONS SYSTEMS AND NUCLEAR APPLICATIONS. biennial. $25. (American Society for Nondestructive Testing, South Texas Section) Western Periodicals Co., 13000 Raymer St., N. Hollywood, CA 91506. (Co-sponsor: Southwest Research Center)
First through 4th titled: Symposium on Nondestructive Testing of Aircraft and Missile Components (ISSN 0082-0865)

629.13 IS ISSN 0072-9302
T. A. E. REPORT. (Text in English) 1959. irreg. $10. Technion-Israel Institute of Technology, Department of Aeronautical Engineering, Haifa, Israel. Indexed: Appl.Mech.Rev. Sci.&Tech.Aerosp.Rep.

629.132 CN ISSN 0316-2494
TAILSPINNER. 1972. irreg. Waterloo-Wellington Flying Club, Breslau, Ont., Canada.
Formerly: Talespinner (ISSN 0316-2540)

629.13 523.01 US ISSN 0564-6294
TOPICS IN ASTROPHYSICS AND SPACE PHYSICS. 1969. a. price varies. Gordon and Breach Science Publishers, One Park Ave., New York, NY 10016. Eds. A. G. W. Cameron, George B. Field.

001.94 US ISSN 0162-8046
U F O ANNUAL. (Unidentified Flying Objects) a. $1.50. Gambi Publications, Inc., 333 Johnson Ave., Brooklyn, NY 11206. illus.
Unidentified flying objects

001.94 UK
U F O INSIGHT. 1978. irreg. £1.80 for 6 nos. Federation U. F. O. Research, 2 Acer Ave., Crewe, Cheshire, England.
Unidentified flying objects

U S S R REPORT: SPACE BIOLOGY AND AEROSPACE MEDICINE. see *MEDICAL SCIENCES*

629.1 US
U.S. AERONAUTICAL INFORMATION PUBLICATION. Short title: U.S. A I P. biennial with q. amendments. $39. U.S. Federal Aviation Administration, 800 Independence Ave., S.W., Washington, DC 20591 (Orders to: Supt. of Documents, Washington, DC 20402)

629.13 600 US
U.S. NATIONAL AERONAUTICS AND SPACE ADMINISTRATION. RESEARCH AND TECHNOLOGY OPERATING PLAN (RTOP) SUMMARY. 1970. a. $9.25. U. S. National Aeronautics and Space Administration, Scientific and Technical Information Facility, Box 8757, Baltimore-Washington International Airport, MD 21240 (Orders to: National Technical Information Service, Springfield, VA 22161) circ. 600.
Supersedes: U.S. National Aeronautics and Space Administration. Research and Technology Program Digest. Flash Index (ISSN 0077-3115)

629.4 629.13 JA ISSN 0082-4828
UNIVERSITY OF TOKYO. INSTITUTE OF SPACE AND AERONAUTICAL SCIENCE. REPORT. (Text and summaries in English) 1964. irreg., 1970, vol. 35, no. 15. University of Tokyo, Institute of Space and Aeronautical Science - Tokyo Daigaku Uchu Koku Kenkyusho, 4-6-1 Komaba, Meguro-ku, Tokyo 153, Japan. Ed. Eiji Niki. index.

629.1388 CN ISSN 0082-5239
UNIVERSITY OF TORONTO. INSTITUTE FOR AEROSPACE STUDIES. PROGRESS REPORT. 1952. a. available on exchange. University of Toronto, Institute for Aerospace Studies, 4925 Dufferin St., Downsview, Ont. M3H 5T6, Canada. circ. 450.

629.1 CN ISSN 0082-5255
UNIVERSITY OF TORONTO. INSTITUTE FOR AEROSPACE STUDIES. REPORT. 1948. irreg. avail. on exchange. University of Toronto, Institute for Aerospace Studies, 4925 Dufferin St., Downsview, Ont. M3H 5T6, Canada. circ. 450.

629.1388 CN ISSN 0082-5247
UNIVERSITY OF TORONTO. INSTITUTE FOR AEROSPACE STUDIES. REVIEW. 1950. irreg. available on exchange. University of Toronto, Institute for Aerospace Studies, 4925 Dufferin St., Downsview, Ont. M3H 5T6 Canada. circ. 450.

629.1 CN ISSN 0082-5263
UNIVERSITY OF TORONTO. INSTITUTE FOR AEROSPACE STUDIES. TECHNICAL NOTE. 1954. irreg. available on exchange. University of Toronto, Institute for Aerospace Studies, 4925 Dufferin St., Downsview, Ontario M3H 5T6, Canada. circ. 450.

629.13 UK
VINTAGE AIRCRAFT DIRECTORY. a. $3.58. Battle of Britain Prints International Ltd., 3 New Plaistow Rd., Stratford, London E.15, England. illus.

629.1 NZ
WHITES AIR DIRECTORY & WHO'S WHO IN NEW ZEALAND AVIATION. (Including the South Pacific) 1947. a. NZ.$7.50. Modern Productions Ltd., P.O. Box 3159, Auckland 1, New Zealand. Ed. S. C. Niblock. adv. circ. 950.

WHO'S WHO IN SPACE; international edition. see *BIOGRAPHY*

AGRICULTURE

629.1   FR
WORLD AERONAUTICAL RECORDS. (Includes annual Updating) (Text in English and French) 1920. a; no. 113, 1974. 500 F. (for 5 years) International Aeronautic Federation, 6 rue Galilee, 75782 Paris, France. Ed. Bd. illus. stat. circ. 1,000.
Formerly: International Aeronautic Federation. Latest World Records.

629.13   GW   ISSN 0065-2024
ZUERL'S ADRESSBUCH DER DEUTSCHEN LUFT- UND RAUMFAHRT. 1950. a. DM.64. Luftfahrt-Verlag Walter Zuerl, Amselweg 6, 8031 Woerthsee-Steinebach, W. Germany (B.R.D.) Ed. Walter Zuerl. adv. bk. rev. circ. 3,000.

AERONAUTICS AND SPACE FLIGHT — Abstracting, Bibliographies, Statistics

629.1   016   UK
AEROSPACE RESEARCH INDEX. 1981. irreg. £54. Longman Group Ltd., Longman House, Burnt Mill, Harlow, Essex CM20 2JE, England (Dist. in U.S. and Canada by: Gale Research Co. Ltd., Book Tower, Detroit, MI 48226)

629.13   016   JA   ISSN 0454-191X
FOREIGN AERO-SPACE LITERATURE/ GAIKOKU KOKU UCHU BUNKEN MOKUROKU. (Text in Japanese and English) 1962. a. National Diet Library - Kokuritsu Kokkai Toshokan, 1-10-1 Nagata-cho, Chiyoda-ku, Tokyo 100, Japan.

INTERNATIONAL CIVIL AVIATION ORGANIZATION. INDEXES TO I C A O PUBLICATIONS. ANNUAL CUMULATION. see *TRANSPORTATION — Abstracting, Bibliographies, Statistics*

629.1   016   CN   ISSN 0077-5568
NATIONAL RESEARCH COUNCIL, CANADA. NATIONAL AERONAUTICAL ESTABLISHMENT. PUBLICATIONS LIST AND SUPPLEMENTS. 1965. irreg. free. National Research Council of Canada, N A E - D M E Publications Section, Bldg. M-16, Ottawa, Ont. K1A 0R6, Canada. circ. 1,800.

387.7   NZ
NEW ZEALAND CIVIL AVIATION STATISTICS. 1971. a. free. Civil Aviation Division, Private Bag, Wellington, New Zealand. stat. circ. 2,000.

AGRICULTURAL ECONOMICS

see *Agriculture—Agricultural Economics*

AGRICULTURAL EQUIPMENT

see *Agriculture—Agricultural Equipment*

AGRICULTURE

see also *Agriculture—Agricultural Economics; Agriculture—Agricultural Equipment; Agriculture—Crop Production and Soil; Agriculture—Dairying and Dairy Products; Agriculture—Feed, Flour and Grain; Agriculture—Poultry and Livestock; Food and Food Industries; Forests and Forestry; Gardening and Horticulture*

630   US
A. D. C. REPRINTS. 1973. irreg. free. Agricultural Development Council Inc., 1290 Ave. of the Americas, New York, NY 10019. charts. circ. 11,500.

630   ET
A R D U PUBLICATION. 1966. irreg. price varies. Arussi Rural Development Unit, Box 3376, Addis Ababa, Ethiopia. charts. cum.index.
Supersedes: C A D U Publications (ISSN 0069-3405)

630   UK   ISSN 0065-0285
ABERYSTWYTH MEMORANDA IN AGRICULTURAL, APPLIED AND BIOMETEOROLOGY. 1958. a. price varies. University College of Wales, Aberystwyth, Department of Geography, c/o J.A. Taylor, Llandinam Bldg., Penglais, Aberystwyth, Dyfed SY23 3DB, Wales.

631.0913   CU
ACADEMIA DE CIENCIAS DE CUBA. INSTITUTO DE INVESTIGACIONES FUNDAMENTALES EN AGRICULTURA TROPICAL. INFORME CIENTIFICO-TECNICO. (Text in Spanish; summaries in English) irreg., no. 77, 1978. exchange basis. Academia de Ciencias de Cuba, Instituto de Investigaciones Fundamentales en Agricultura Tropica, Calle 2 Esquina, Santiago de las Vegas, Havana, Cuba. bibl. charts. illus.

ACCADEMIA DELLE SCIENZE DI SIENA DETTA DE FISIOCRITICI. ATTI. see *MEDICAL SCIENCES*

ACTA AGROBOTANICA. see *BIOLOGY — Botany*

630   PL
ACTA PHYSIOLOGIAE PLANTARUM. (Text in English; summaries in Polish) 1978. irreg. 30 Zl. per no. (Polska Akademia Nauk, Wydzial Nauk Rolniczych i Lesnych) Panstwowe Wydawnictwo Naukowe, Miodowa 10, 00-251 Warsaw, Poland (Dist. by: Ars Polona, Krakowskie Przedmiescie 7, 00-068 Warsaw, Poland) circ. 510.

630   US
ADVANCED SERIES IN AGRICULTURAL SCIENCES. 1975. irreg., vol. 8, 1980. price varies. Springer-Verlag, 175 Fifth Ave., New York, NY 10010 (Also Berlin, Heidelberg, Vienna) Ed.Bd. (reprint service avail. from ISI)

630   US   ISSN 0065-2113
ADVANCES IN AGRONOMY. 1949. irreg., vol. 31, 1979. price varies. (American Society for Agronomy, Inc.) Academic Press, Inc., 111 Fifth Ave., New York, NY 10003. Ed. A. G. Norman. index. cum.index: vols. 1-15(1949-63) in vol. 16(1964) (also avail. in microfiche)

630   UK   ISSN 0305-7828
AETHER. vol. 3, no. 2; 1976. irreg. 20p. per issue. 3 Cairnleith Croft, Ythanbank, Ellon AB4 OUB, Scotland.

630   BL
AGENDA DOS CRIADORES E AGRICULTORES. 1976. a. Cr.$1000. Editora dos Criadores Ltda., Av. Pompeia 1214, Fundos B, Sao Paulo, Brazil. Ed. Luiz de Almeida Penna. adv. charts. illus. stat. mkt.
Cattle

630   NZ
AGLINK. 1977. irreg. free. Ministry of Agriculture and Fisheries, Information Services, Box 2298, Wellington, New Zealand.
Formed by the merger of: New Zealand Agriculture & Agricultural Science and Technology & Farm Production and Practice & Horticultural Produce and Practice.

AGRARSOZIALE GESELLSCHAFT. KLEINE REIHE. see *SOCIOLOGY*

AGRARSOZIALE GESELLSCHAFT. GESCHAEFTS- UND ARBEITSBERICHT. see *SOCIOLOGY*

AGRARSOZIALE GESELLSCHAFT. MATERIALSAMMLUNG. see *SOCIOLOGY*

630   370   US
AGRI EDUCATOR; the magazine for professionals teaching vocational agriculture. vol. 3, no. 1, 1978. $15. Agri Business Publications, Inc., Division of Century Communications, Inc., 5520 Touhy Ave., Suite G, Skokie, IL 60077. Ed. Lyle E. Orwig. adv.

630   IT
AGRICOLTORE VERONESE. a. Unione Provinciale Agricoltori di Verona, Via Locatelli 3, 37100 Verona, Italy.

630   SP
AGRICULTURA ESPANOLA EN (YEAR) (Supplement to - Panorama de Agricultura en (year)) a. Ministerio de Agricultura, Secretaria General Tecnica, Paseo Infante 1, Madrid 7, Spain. illus. charts. stat.
Formerly: Agricultura Espanola (ISSN 0065-440X)

AGRICULTURAL COMMODITIES INDEX; ready-reference guide to USDA statistical series. see *BIBLIOGRAPHIES*

630   US
AGRICULTURAL DEVELOPMENT COUNCIL. RESEARCH AND TRAINING NETWORK A.D.C.-R.T.N. 1972. irreg. free. ‡ Agricultural Development Council Inc., 1290 Ave. of the Americas, New York, NY 10019. charts. circ. 11,500.

354   MY
AGRICULTURAL DIRECTORY OF MALAYSIA. (Text in English) 1972. a. M.$10. University of Malaya, Agricultural Graduates Alumni, c/o Faculty of Agriculture, Lembah Pantai, Kuala Lumpur 22-11, Malaysia. illus.

630   920   CN   ISSN 0083-9744
AGRICULTURAL INSTITUTE OF CANADA. MEMBERSHIP DIRECTORY/INSTITUT AGRICOLE DU CANADA. LISTE DES MEMBRES. 1940. triennial. Agrican Publishers Inc., 151 Slater St., Suite 907, Ottawa, Ont. K1P 5H4, Canada. Ed. J. Watts. adv. circ. 5,000.
Formerly: Who's Who in the Agricultural Institute of Canada.

AGRICULTURAL REAL ESTATE VALUES IN ALBERTA. see *REAL ESTATE*

630   US
AGRICULTURAL RESEARCH CENTER. PROCEEDINGS OF THE ANNUAL MEETING. no. 37, 1976. a. Agricultural Research Center, Inc., 1305 E. Main St., Lakeland, FL 33801.

630   GY   ISSN 0065-4523
AGRICULTURAL RESEARCH GUYANA. 1967. irreg. free. ‡ Central Agricultural Station, Research Division, Mon Repos, E.C. Demerara, Guyana. bk. rev.

630   UK   ISSN 0065-4531
AGRICULTURAL RESEARCH INDEX; including forestry, fisheries and food. (2 Vols) irreg., 6th edt., 1977. ‡ Longman Group Ltd., Longman House, Burnt Mill, Harlow, Essex CM20 2JE, England (Dist. in U.S. and Canada by: Gale Research Co. Ltd., Book Tower, Detroit, MI 48226)

630   IS
AGRICULTURAL RESEARCH ORGANIZATION. PAMPHLET. (Text in English or Hebrew) 1925. irreg., 1976, no. 162. price varies. Agricultural Research Organization, P.O. Box 6, Bet Dagan, Israel. circ. 700.
Formerly: Agricultural Research Organization, Rehovot. Bulletin (ISSN 0083-6842)

631   CN   ISSN 0707-7793
AGRICULTURAL SCIENCE BULLETIN. 1964. irreg. free. ‡ University of Saskatchewan, Extension Division, Saskatoon, Sask., Canada. Ed. Bert Wolfe Writer. circ. 4,000.
Former titles: Agricultural Science (ISSN 0381-5927); Information (ISSN 0381-5919); Supersedes: Saskatchewan Farm Science (ISSN 0048-9174)

630   NE
AGRICULTURAL SCIENCE IN THE NETHERLANDS. (Text in English) 1953. triennial. $10. International Agricultural Centre, P.O. Box 88, Wageningen 6140, Netherlands. circ. 5,000. (tabloid format)

AGRICULTURE

631 AT
AGRICULTURAL SHOWS ANNUAL. 1972. a. free. Agricultural Societies Council of New South Wales, Agriculture House, 195 Macquarie Street, Sydney, N.S.W. 2000, Australia. Ed. Syd Giles. adv. circ. 2,000.
  Former titles: Country Shows Annual (ISSN 0311-1946); Country Shows Bulletin.

630 NR ISSN 0065-454X
AGRICULTURAL SOCIETY OF NIGERIA. PROCEEDINGS. 1962. a. free. Agricultural Society of Nigeria, c/o Dr. T. I. Ashaye, P. M. B. 5029, Ibadan, Nigeria. Ed. Q. B. Anthonio. adv. bk. rev. circ. 1,000.

630 UK ISSN 0065-4558
AGRICULTURAL STATISTICS, ENGLAND AND WALES. 1972. a. £4.25. H. M. S. O., P.O. Box 569, London SE1 9NH, England. (Co-sponsors: Ministry of Agriculture, Fisheries and Food; Department of Agriculture for Scotland; Ministry of Agriculture, N. Ireland)

630 BG ISSN 0065-4566
AGRICULTURAL STATISTICS OF BANGLADESH. (Text in English) 1973-1975 latest. a. Bureau of Statistics, Secretariat, Dacca 2, Bangladesh.

630 UK ISSN 0065-4582
AGRICULTURAL STATISTICS, SCOTLAND. 1912. a. price varies. Department of Agriculture and Fisheries, Chesser House, 500 Gorgie Rd., Edinburgh, Scotland (Avail. from H.M.S.O., 13a Castle St., Edinburgh EH2 3AR, Scotland)

630 UK ISSN 0065-4590
AGRICULTURAL STATISTICS, UNITED KINGDOM. 1972. a. £2.25. H. M. S. O., P.O. Box 569, London SE1 9NH, England. (Co-sponsor: Ministry of Agriculture, Fisheries and Food)

630 JA ISSN 0515-8672
AGRICULTURE ASIA/AJIA NOGYO. (Text in English) 1963. a. 3000 Yen($10) Association of Agricultural Relations in Asia - Ajia Nogyo Koryu Konwakai, 5-27-11 Sendagaya, Shibuya-ku, Tokyo 151, Japan. Ed. Shoken Yokoyama.

630 HK
AGRICULTURE HONG KONG. 1972. a. price varies. Government Information Services, Beaconsfield House, Queen's Rd., Central, Victoria, Hong Kong, Hong Kong.
  Supersedes: Agricultural Science Hong Kong (ISSN 0572-3221)

630 UK
AGRICULTURE IN SCOTLAND. 1912. a. £1.50. Department of Agriculture and Fisheries, Chesser House, 500 Gorgie Rd., Edinburgh, Scotland (Avail. from H.M.S.O., 13a Castle St., Edinburgh EH2 3AR, Scotland)

630 370 US ISSN 0515-7420
AGRICULTURE TEACHERS DIRECTORY AND HANDBOOK. 1953? a. price varies. 3042 Overlook, Montgomery, AL 36109.

630 CN ISSN 0065-4655
AGRO-NOUVELLES. (Text in French) 1965. irreg. Order of Agrologists of Quebec, 262 Ouest, Blvd. Henri-Bourassa, Montreal, Que. H3L 1N6, Canada.

630 US ISSN 0002-1822
AGROBOREALIS. 1969. 2-3/yr. free. ‡ University of Alaska, Agricultural Experiment Station, Fairbanks, AK 99701. Ed. A. L. Brundage. charts. illus. stat. circ. 4,000. Indexed: Curr.Cont.

630.23 BU
AGROFIZICHNI IZSLEDOVANIIA. (Text in Bulgarian; summaries in English and Russian) irreg., vol. 2, 1975. 1.62 lv. (Akademiia na Selskostopanskite Nauki) Publishing House of the Bulgarian Academy of Sciences, Ul. Akad. G. Bonchev, 1113 Sofia, Bulgaria. Ed. I. Vulev.

630 580 MZ ISSN 0044-6858
AGRONOMIA MOCAMBICANA. Represents: Instituto de Investigacao Agronomica de Mocambique. Comunicacoes. (Text in Portuguese; summaries in English and Portuguese) 1967. irreg. price varies. ‡ Instituto de Investigacao Agronomica de Mocambique, Centro de Documentacao Agraria, C. P. 3658, Maputo 11, Mozambique. charts. illus. stat. index. circ. 400-500. Indexed: Biol.Abstr. Chem.Abstr.

630 US ISSN 0065-4663
AGRONOMY: A SERIES OF MONOGRAPHS. 1949. irreg., 1972, nos. 15 & 16, 1976, no. 17. price varies. American Society of Agronomy, Inc., 677 South Segoe Rd., Madison, WI 53711.

630 PL
AKADEMIA ROLNICZA, KRAKOW. ROLNICTWO. irreg., 1975, no. 15. price varies. Akademia Rolnicza, Krakow, Al. Mickiewicza 21, 30-120 Krakow, Poland.

630 PL
AKADEMIA ROLNICZA, POZNAN. ROCZNIK. PRACE HABILITACYJNE. (Summaries in English and Russian) 1959. irreg. price varies. Akademia Rolnicza, Poznan, Ul. Wojska Polskiego 28, 60-637 Poznan, Poland. Indexed: Bibl.Agri.

630 PL
AKADEMIA ROLNICZA, POZNAN. ROCZNIK. ROLNICTWO. (Summaries in English and Russian) 1959. irreg. price varies. Akademia Rolnicza, Poznan, Ul. Wojska Polskiego 28, 60-637 Poznan, Poland. Indexed: Bibl.Agri.

AKADEMIA ROLNICZA, SZCZECIN. ZESZYTY NAUKOWE. see BIOLOGY — Botany

630 PL ISSN 0083-7296
AKADEMIA ROLNICZA, WARSAW. ZESZYTY NAUKOWE. SERIA HISTORYCZNA. (Text in Polish; summaries in French, Russian) 1963. irreg. price varies. Akademia Rolnicza, Warsaw, Ul. Rakowiecka 26/30, Warsaw, Poland (Dist. by: Ars Polona-Ruch, Krakowskie Przedmiescie 7, 00-068 Warsaw, Poland)

630 PL
AKADEMIA ROLNICZA, WROCLAW. ROLNICTWO. a. price varies. Akademia Rolnicza, Wroclaw, Norwida 25, 50-375 Wroclaw, Poland.
  Formerly: Wyzsza Szkola Rolnicza, Wroclaw. Rolnictwo.

630 PL ISSN 0324-9204
AKADEMIA ROLNICZO-TECHNICZNA. ZESZYTY NAUKOWE. 1956. irreg. price varies. Akademia Rolniczo-Techniczna, Blok 21, 10-957 Olsztyn-Kortowo, Poland (Dist. by Ars Polona-Ruch, Krakowskie Przedmiescie 7, Warsaw, Poland) Ed.Bd.
  Formerly: Wyzsza Szkola Rolnicza, Olsztyn. Zeszyty Naukowe (ISSN 0078-4583)

630 GW ISSN 0568-7594
AKTUELLE FRAGEN DES LANDBAUES. 1967. irreg., no. 8, 1971. price varies. Verlag Paul Parey (Hamburg), Spitalerstr. 12, 2000 Hamburg 1, W. Germany (B.R.D.) Ed. Ernst ter Veen. bibl. illus. index. (reprint service avail. from ISI)

630 CN ISSN 0065-597X
ALBERTA. DEPARTMENT OF AGRICULTURE. ANNUAL REPORT. 1905. a. ‡ Department of Agriculture, Printmedia Branch, 9718 107th St., Edmonton, Alta. T5K 2C8, Canada. circ. 500.
  Incorporating: Alberta. Water Resources Division Annual Report.

630 CN ISSN 0707-9818
ALBERTA RURAL DEVELOPMENT STUDIES. 1972. a. free contr. circ. Rural Education and Development Association, 9934 106th St., Edmonton, Alta. T5K 1C4, Canada.

630 II
ALL INDIA REPORT ON AGRICULTURAL CENSUS. (Text in English) 1970/71. a. Rs.19.50($7) Ministry of Agriculture and Irrigation, Department of Agriculture, Directorate of Economics and Statistics, A-2E-3 Kasturba Gandhi Marg Barracks, New Delhi 110001, India.

630 US ISSN 0066-0566
AMERICAN SOCIETY OF AGRONOMY. A S A SPECIAL PUBLICATION. 1963. irreg. American Society of Agronomy, Inc., 677 South Segoe Rd., Madison, WI 53711.

632 US
ANALYTICAL METHODS FOR PESTICIDES, PLANT GROWTH REGULATORS AND FOOD ADDITIVES. 1963. irreg., vol. 10, 1978. price varies. Academic Press, Inc., 111 Fifth Ave., New York, NY 10003. Ed. Gunter Zweig.

630 PL ISSN 0365-1118
ANNALES UNIVERSITATIS MARIAE CURIE-SKLODOWSKA. SECTIO E. AGRICULTURA. (Text in English or Polish; Summaries in English, French, German, Russian) 1946. a. Uniwersytet Marii Curie-Sklodowskiej, Plac Marii Curie-Sklodowskiej 5, 20-031 Lublin, Poland. Ed. A. Szember. Indexed: Biol.Abstr. Soils & Fert. Weed Abstr.

630 TI
ANNUAIRE AGRICOLE DE LA TUNISIE. (Text and summaries in Arabic and French) 1971. biennial. 3 din.($7.50) Agence Generale d'Edition et de Publicite, 19 Ave. de Carthage, Tunis, Tunisia. adv.

630 FR
ANNUAIRE DE L'AGRICULTURE. 1968. a. Centre de Documentation et d'Information Rurale, 92 rue du Des Sous des Berges, 75013 Paris, France. Ed. Robert Faure.

630 FR ISSN 0066-2534
ANNUAIRE DE LA FRANCE RURALE DANS LE MARCHE COMMUN. irreg., 1968, 5th ed. (Ministere de l'Agriculture) Euro-Publi Marcel Puget, 9 Bld. des Italiens, Paris 2e, France.

630 915.2 JA
ANNUAL REVIEW OF AGRICULTURE, KINKEI DISTRICT/KINKI NOGYO JOSEI HOKOKU. (Text in Japanese) 1964. a. Kinki Agricultural Administration Bureau - Kinki Nosei-kyoku, 102 Shimochoja-machi Saguru, Nishinotoin-dori, Kamigyo-ku, Kyoto 602, Japan.

630 658 BL ISSN 0518-0937
ANUARIO DOS CRIADORES. 1960. a. Cr.$1000. Editora dos Criadores Ltda., Av. Pompeia 1214, 05022 Sao Paulo, Brazil.

630 US ISSN 0570-4359
ANUARIO LATINOAMERICANO. 1965. a. Hacienda, Inc., Box 61-1197, 639 N.E. 125th St., North Miami, FL 33161. adv.

630 AG ISSN 0066-7242
ARGENTINA. ESTACION EXPERIMENTAL AGROPECUARIA MANFREDI. SERIE INFORMACION TECNICA. irreg. exchange basis. Instituto Nacional de Tecnologia Agropecuria, Estacion Experimental Agropecuaria Manfredi, 5988 Manfredi (Cordoba), Argentina.

630 AG
ARGENTINA. SECRETARIA DE ESTADO DE AGRICULTURA Y GANADERIA. COMUNICADO DE PRENSA. no. 107, Jun. 1979. irreg. Secretaria de Estado de Agricultura y Ganaderia, Paseo Colon 922, 1063 Buenos Aires, Argentina. stat. (processed)

630 AG
ARGENTINA. SERVICIO NACIONAL DE ECONOMIA Y SOCIOLOGIA RURAL. PUBLICACION E S R. irreg. Servicio Nacional de Economia y Sociologia Rural, Paseo Colon 974, Buenos Aires, Argentina.

630 622 US
ARIZONA LANDMARKS. a. State Land Department, Division of Forestry, Box 387, 3650 Lake Mead Rd., Flagstaff, AZ 86001. Ed. Jack Crowe. charts. illus.

630 020 CR ISSN 0074-0748
ASOCIACION INTERAMERICANA DE BIBLIOTECARIOS Y DOCUMENTALISTAS AGRICOLAS. BOLETIN ESPECIAL. 1966. irreg., no. 17, 1977. membership. Asociacion Interamericana de Bibliotecarios y Documentalistas Agricolas, Apdo. No. 74, Turrialba, Costa Rica. Ed. Ana Maria Paz de Erickson. circ. 800.

ASSOCIACAO BRASILEIRA DE EDUCAO AGRICOLA SUPERIOR. ANAIS DE REUNIAO ANUAL. see EDUCATION — Higher Education

630 070.48 FR
ASSOCIATION DES JOURNALISTES AGRICOLES. ANNUAIRE. a. Association des Journalistes Agricoles, 9 rue Papillon, 75009 Paris, France. circ. 2,000.

630 664 NE ISSN 0066-9040
ASSOCIATION EURATOM-ITAL. ANNUAL REPORT. 1961. a. free. ‡ Foundatin ITAL, Keyenbergseweg 6, Postbus 48, 6700 AA Wageningen, Netherlands.

AUSTRALIA. BUREAU OF AGRICULTURAL ECONOMICS. WHEAT: SITUATION AND OUTLOOK. see AGRICULTURE — Feed, Flour And Grain

338.1 AT
AUSTRALIA. BUREAU OF STATISTICS. VICTORIAN OFFICE. LAND UTILISATION AND CROPS. 1970. a. free. Australian Bureau of Statistics, Victorian Office, Box 2796Y, G.P.O., Melbourne, Vic. 3001, Australia. circ. 1,350.

630 AU ISSN 0067-2262
AUSTRIA. BUNDESMINISTERIUM FUER LAND- UND FORSTWIRTSCHAFT. TAETIGKEITSBERICHT. 1959. a. S.180. Stubenring 1, 1010 Vienna, Austria. circ. 1,600.

633.72 BG
BANGLADESH TEA RESEARCH INSTITUTE. ANNUAL REPORT. (Text in English) 1973. irreg. Tk.20. Bangladesh Tea Research Institute, 11-113 Motijheel, Dacca 2, Bangladesh.
    Tea

630 GW ISSN 0522-604X
BEHOERDEN UND ORGANISATIONEN DER LAND- FORST- UND ERNAEHRUNGSWIRTSCHAFT. approx. a. DM.88. B. Behr's Verlag GmbH, Averhoffstr. 10, 2000 Hamburg 76, W. Germany (B.R.D.)

630 BE ISSN 0303-9056
BELGIUM. RIJKSSTATION VOOR LANDBOUWTECHNIEK. MEDEDELINGEN. (Text mainly in Dutch; summaries in English, French and German) 1964. irreg. price varies. Rijksstation voor Landbowtechniek, Van Gensberghelaan 115, B-9220 Merelbeke, Belgium. circ. (controlled) (back issues avail.) Indexed: Biol. & Agr.Ind.

630 GW ISSN 0301-2689
BERICHTE UEBER LANDWIRTSCHAFT. SONDERHEFTE. (Text in German; summaries in English and German) irreg., no. 196, 1979. price varies. Verlag Paul Parey (Hamburg), Spitalerstr. 12, 2000 Hamburg 1, W. Germany (B.R.D.) circ. 2,000. (reprint service avail. from ISI) Indexed: Biol.Abstr. Curr.Cont.

630 GW ISSN 0405-6485
BETRIEBS- UND ARBEITSWIRTSCHAFT IN DER PRAXIS; eine Schriftenreihe fuer die Landwirtschaft. 1955. irreg., no. 21, 1976. price varies. Verlag Paul Parey (Hamburg), Spitalerstr. 12, 2000 Hamburg 1, W. Germany (B.R.D.) bibl. illus. index. (reprint service avail. from ISI)

630 II ISSN 0067-6454
BHARAT KRISHAK SAMAJ. YEAR BOOK. (Text in English) 1964. a. Rs.25($5) Bharat Krishak Samaj - Farmer's Forum, India, A-1 Nizamuddin West, New Delhi 110003, India.

630 BL ISSN 0067-6594
BIBLIOGRAFIA BRASILEIRA DE CIENCIAS AGRICOLAS. 1969. irreg. Cr.$300($15) Ministerio da Agricultura, Rio de Janeiro, Brazil. bk. rev. circ. 300.
    Supersedes: Bibliografia Brasileira de Agricultura.

630 634.9 GW ISSN 0067-5849
BIOLOGISCHE BUNDESANSTALT FUER LAND- UND FORSTWIRTSCHAFT, BERLIN-DAHLEM. MITTEILUNGEN. (Text and summaries in English and German) 1906. irreg. price varies. (Biologische Bundesanstalt fuer Land- und Forstwirtschaft in Berlin-Dahlem) Verlag Paul Parey (Berlin), Lindenstr. 44-47, 1000 Berlin 61, W. Germany (B.R.D.) illus. Indexed: Biol.Abstr.

BOL OG BY. see HISTORY — History Of Europe

630 AG ISSN 0084-7968
BOLSA DE CEREALES. REVISTA INSTITUCIONAL. NUMERO ESTADISTICO.* a. Bolsa de Cereales, Avda. Corrientes 127, 1043 Buenos Aires, Argentina.

630 BS ISSN 0068-0478
BOTSWANA. MINISTRY OF AGRICULTURE. ANNUAL REPORT.* (Reports available for various divisions of the Ministry of Agriculture) a. free. Ministry of Agriculture, Private Bag 3, Gaborone, Botswana.

630 334.683 BL
BRAZIL. INSTITUTO NACIONAL DE COLONIZACAO E REFORMA AGRARIA. ACAO ASSOCIATIVISTA. no. 2, 1976. irreg. Instituto Nacional de Colonizacao e Reforma Agraria, Palacico do Desenvolvimento, Brasilia, Brazil. chart. illus. stat.

630 334.683 BL
BRAZIL. MINISTERIO DA AGRICULTURA DEPARTAMENTO DE ASSISTENCIA AO COOPERATIVISMO SERIE CONTABILIDADE. no. 203, 1968. irreg. free. Ministerio da Agricultura, Departamento de Assistencia ao Cooperativismo, Rua do Carmo 88, Sao Paulo, Brazil.

630 334.683 BL
BRAZIL. MINISTERIO DA AGRICULTURA DEPARTAMENTO DE ASSISTENICA AO COOPERATIVISMO. SERIE INTEGRACAO. no. 1101, 1972. irreg. free. Ministerio da Agricultura, Departamento de Assistencia ao Cooperativismo, Rua do Carmo 88, Sao Paulo, Brazil.

630 338.4 BL
BRAZIL. MINISTERIO DA AGRICULTURA. ESCRITORIO DE ESTATISTICA. OLEOS E GORDURAS VEGETAIS. 1971. a. Ministerio da Agricultura, Escritorio de Estatistica, Espanada dos Ministerios, Bloco 8, 6 Andar, Brasilia 70000, Brazil. stat. circ. 800. (processed)

630 BL
BRAZIL. MINISTERIO DA AGRICULTURA. SUBSECRETARIA DE PLANEJAMENTO E ORCAMENTO. PRODUCAO E ABASTECIMENTO, PERSPECTIVAS E PROPOSICOES: SINTESE. irreg. Ministerio da Agricultura, Subsecretaria de Planejamento e Orcamento, Brasilia, Brazil. stat.

630 CN
BRITISH COLUMBIA. MINISTRY OF AGRICULTURE D.A.T.E. PROGRAM REPORT. 1974. a. Ministry of Agriculture, Victoria, B.C., Canada. Ed. Reg Miller. circ. 1,500.

BULLETIN OF AGRI-HORTICULTURE. see GARDENING AND HORTICULTURE

630 MW
BUNDA COLLEGE OF AGRICULTURE. RESEARCH BULLETIN. (Text in English) 1970. a. exchange basis. Bunda College of Agriculture, Research and Publications Committee, Box 219, Lilongwe, Malawi. Ed. Dr. M. J. Roberts. circ. 500. (processed)

630 AU
BUNDESVERSUCHSANSTALT FUER ALPENLAENDISCHE LANDWIRTSCHAFT GUMPENSTEIN. VERSUCHSERGEBNISSE. irreg. Bundesanstalt fuer Alpenlaendische Landwirtschaft Gumpenstein, Gumpenstein, Austria.
    Continues: Bundesanstalt fuer Alpine Landwirtschaft. Versuchsergebnisse.

630 GW ISSN 0525-2989
BUSS HANDBUCH EUROPAEISCHER PRODUKTENBOERSEN. 1949. irreg. DM.38. Hestra-Verlag, Holzhofallee 33, Postfach 4244, 6100 Darmstadt 1, W. Germany (B.R.D.) adv.

630 CN ISSN 0068-7340
CANADA. AGRICULTURE CANADA PUBLICATIONS. 1935. irreg. free. Agriculture Canada, Information Services, Ottawa, Ont. K1A 0C7, Canada.

630 CN
CANADA. AGRICULTURE CANADA. RESEARCH BRANCH. ANNUAL REPORT. 1958/61. biennial. Agriculture Canada, Research Station, Beaverlodge, Alberta, Canada.
    Incorporating: Canada. Agriculture Canada. Research Station, Beaverlodge, Alberta. Research Report (ISSN 0068-8096); Canada. Experimental Farm, Beaverlodge, Alberta. Research Report.

630 CN ISSN 0068-7472
CANADA. AGRICULTURE CANADA. RESEARCH STATION, MELFORT, SASKATCHEWAN. RESEARCH HIGHLIGHTS. ANNUAL PUBLICATIONS. 1953. a. free. ‡ Agriculture Canada, Research Station, Melfort, Saskatchewan, Box 1240, Melfort, Sask., Canada. Ed. Dr. S. E. Beacon. circ. 1,000.

630 CN ISSN 0068-7480
CANADA. EXPERIMENTAL FARM, ST. JOHN'S WEST, NEWFOUNDLAND. RESEARCH REPORT. 1956. a. free. Agriculture Canada, Attn: Jean Perrin, Neatby Bldg., Ottawa, Ont. K1A 0C6, Canada.

630 CN ISSN 0068-9688
CANADIAN SOCIETY OF AGRONOMY. ANNUAL MEETING. PROCEEDINGS.* 1952. a. $3. Canadian Society of Agronomy, c/o A. I. C., 151 Slater St., Ottawa 4, Ont., Canada. Indexed: Field Crop Abstr.

630 CN ISSN 0068-9718
CANADIAN SOCIETY OF RURAL EXTENSION. MEETING AND CONVENTION. PROCEEDINGS.* 1960. a. Canadian Society of Rural Extension, Agricultural Institute of Canada, No. 907, 151 Slater St., Ottawa 4, Ont. K1P 5H4, Canada.

630 NE ISSN 0069-2212
CENTER FOR AGRICULTURAL PUBLISHING AND DOCUMENTATION. AGRICULTURAL RESEARCH REPORTS. irreg., approx. 20 per year. price varies. Centre for Agricultural Publishing and Documentation, Marijkeweg 17, P.O. Box 4, 6700 AA Wageningen, Netherlands. circ. 700.

638.2 II ISSN 0304-6818
CENTRAL SERICULTURAL RESEARCH AND TRAINING INSTITUTE. ANNUAL REPORT. (Text in English) 1964. a. Central Sericultural Research and Training Institute, Manandavadi Rd., Srirampura, Mysorc 570008, India. circ. 200(controlled) Key Title: Annual Report - Central Sericultural Research and Training Institute.

354.69 MG
CENTRE NATIONAL DE RECHERCHES APPLIQUES AU DEVELOPPEMENT RURAL. DEPARTEMENT DE RECHERCHES AGRONOMIQUES. RAPPORT ANNUEL. a. Centre National de la Recherche Appliquee au Developpement Rural, Departement de Recherches Agronomiques, B. P. 1690, Antananarivo, Malagasy Republic.

630 MG
CENTRE NATIONAL DE RECHERCHES APPLIQUES AU DEVELOPPEMENT RURAL. DEPARTEMENT DE RECHERCHES AGRONOMIQUES. RAPPORT D'ACTIVITE. irreg. Centre National de la Recherche Appliquee au Developpement Rural, Departement de Recherches Agronomiques, B.P.1690, Antananarivo, Malagasy Republic.

630 MX ISSN 0084-8689
CENTRO DE INVESTIGACIONES AGRICOLAS DE TAMAULIPAS. CIRCULAR CIAT. 1968. a. free. Centro de Investigaciones Agricolas de Tamaulipas, Apartado Postal 172, Rio Bravo, Tamaulipas, Mexico.

630 MX ISSN 0084-8697
CENTRO DE INVESTIGACIONES AGRICOLAS DE TAMAULIPAS. INFORME ANUAL DE LABORES. 1968. a. free. Centro de Investigaciones Agricolas de Tamaulipas, A.P. 172, Rio Bravo, Tamaulipas, Mexico.

631.091　　　　　　BL
CENTRO DE PESQUISA AGROPECUARIA DO TROPICO UMIDO. BOLETIM TECNICO. (Text in Portuguese; summaries in English & Portuguese) 1976. irreg. (Centro de Pesquisa Agropecuaria do Tropico Umido) Empresa Brasileira de Pesquisa Agropecuaria, Caixa Postal 48, 66000 Belem-Para, Brazil. bibl, charts, stat.
Tropical agriculture

634　　　　　　CE　ISSN 0009-0816
CEYLON COCONUT PLANTER'S REVIEW. (Text in English) 1960. irreg. Rs.1.25($0.25) per no. Coconut Research Institute, Bandirippuwa Estate, Lunuwila, Sri Lanka. Ed. U. Pethiyagoda. adv. abstr. charts. illus. stat. cum.index. circ. 1,000. Indexed: Chem.Abstr. Field Crop.Abstr. Indian Sci.Abstr. Trop.Abstr.
Coconuts

630　　　　　　AT　ISSN 0084-8735
CHIASMA. 1963. a. Aus.$2. University of New England, Rural Science Undergraduates' Society, Armidale, N.S.W. 2351, Australia. Ed. David McLeod. adv. circ. 1,000. (also avail. in microfilm from UMI)

630　　　　　　CL
CHILE. INSTITUTO DE INVESTIGACIONES AGROPECUARIAS. MEMORIA ANUAL. 1965. a. exchange basis. Instituto de Investigaciones Agropecuarias, Casilla 5427, Santiago, Chile.

630　　　　　　CH
CHU CHEN. (Text in Chinese) 1975. irreg. Taiwan ta Hsueh Nung Tai Hui, Taipei, Taiwan, Republic of China. illus.

630　　　　　　PN
CIENCIA AGROPECUARIA. (Text in Spanish; summaries in English) 1978. a. $3.50 (or exchange) Instituto de Investigacion Agropecuaria, Departamento de Publicaciones, Apartado 58, Santiago de Veraguas, Panama. Ed. Elizabeth de Ruiloba. abstr. bibl. charts.

630　　　　　　UK　ISSN 0069-6897
COMMONWEALTH AGRICULTURAL BUREAUX. LIST OF RESEARCH WORKERS; in the agricultural sciences in the Commonwealth and the Republic of Ireland. 1966. triennial. Commonwealth Agricultural Bureaux, Farnham House, Farnham Royal, Slough SL2 3BN, England.

630　331.11　　　　US
CONDITION OF FARMWORKERS AND SMALL FARMERS. 1948. a. free. National Sharecroppers Fund & Rural Advancement Fund, 2128 Commonwealth Ave., Charlotte, NC 28205. Ed. James M. Pierce. (back issues avail.) Indexed: Vert.File. Ind.

630　　　　　　US
CONSUMER-FARMER COOPERATOR. 1938. a. free. ‡ Consumer Farmer Foundation, 101 E. 15th St., New York, NY 10003. Ed. Martin Young. charts. illus. circ. 5,000.

630　　　　　　US
CORNELL INTERNATIONAL AGRICULTURE MIMEOGRAPHS. 1963. irreg., 3-4/yr. single copies free; $0.25 for each additional copy. Cornell University, Program in International Agriculture, 252 Roberts Hall, Ithaca, NY 14853 (Orders to: Mailing Room, 7 Research Park, Ithaca, NY 14853) circ. 700.
Formerly: Cornell International Agricultural Development Mimeographs (ISSN 0070-0010)

630　　　　　　US
COUNCIL FOR AGRICULTURAL AND CHEMURGIC RESEARCH. PROCEEDINGS OF ANNUAL CONFERENCES. a. Council for Agricultural and Chemurgic Research, 350 Fifth Ave., New York, NY 10001.

630　　　　　　US
COUNTY AGENTS DIRECTORY; the reference book for agricultural extension workers. 1915. a. Century Communications Inc, 5520-G Touhy Ave., Skokie, IL 60077. Ed. Karma L. Orwig. adv.

CUBA. CENTRO DE INFORMACION Y DOCUMENTACION AGROPECUARIO. BOLETIN DE RESENAS. SERIE: GENETICA Y REPRODUCCION. see *BIOLOGY — Zoology*

631.091　　　　　　CU
CUBA. CENTRO DE INFORMACION Y DOCUMENTACION AGROPECUARIO. BOLETIN DE RESENAS. SERIE: ARROZ. 1974. irreg. $5. Centro de Informacion y Documentacion Agropecuario, Calle 11 no. 1057, Gaveta Postal 4149, Havana 4, Cuba.

630　　　　　　CY　ISSN 0070-2307
CYPRUS. AGRICULTURAL RESEARCH INSTITUTE. ANNUAL REPORT. 1962/63. a. free. ‡ Agricultural Research Institute, Nicosia, Cyprus. Ed.Bd. bk. rev. circ. 1,000.

630　　　　　　CY　ISSN 0070-2315
CYPRUS. AGRICULTURAL RESEARCH INSTITUTE. TECHNICAL BULLETIN. 1966. irreg., no. 30, 1980. free. Agricultural Research Institute, Nicosia, Cyprus. Ed.Bd. circ. 1,000.

630　　　　　　CY　ISSN 0379-0932
CYPRUS. AGRICULTURAL RESEARCH INSTITUTE. TECHNICAL PAPER. 1972. irreg., no. 17, 1979. free. Agricultural Research Institute, Nicosia, Cyprus. (processed)

630　　　　　　CY
CYPRUS. DEPARTMENT OF STATISTICS AND RESEARCH. AGRICULTURAL SURVEY. a. Mils.300. Department of Statistics and Research, Ministry of Finance, Nicosia, Cyprus.

DEVELOPMENTS IN AGRICULTURAL AND MANAGED FOREST ECOLOGY. see *FORESTS AND FORESTRY*

630　　　　　　FR
DICTIONNAIRE-ANNUAIRE DE L'AGRICULTURE; organismes-dirigeants-fournisseurs. Short title: Dic-Agri. 1966. a. 168 F. Agri-Editions, 92 rue du Dessous des Berges, 75013 Paris, France. Ed. Robert Faure. adv. index. circ. 15,000.

630　　　　　　CK
DIRECTORIO AGROPECUARIO DE COLOMBIA. a. Col.300($10) (Sociedad de Agricultores de Colombia) Editores y Distribuidores Asociados Ltda., Avda. Jimenez 4-49, Apdo. 14965, Bogota 1, Colombia.

630　　　　　　US　ISSN 0419-2400
DIRECTORY OF COMMUNICATORS IN AGRICULTURE.* irreg.; latest issue, 1973-74. $5. (United Dairy Industry Association) Agricultural Relations Council, c/o C. L. Mast, Jr., Exec. Sec., 2041 Vardon Lane, Flossmoor, IL 60422. (With: American Dairy Assn.; National Dairy Council; Dairy Research, Inc.) index.

630　334.683　　　　US
DIRECTORY OF FARMER COOPERATIVES. 1968. triennial. $10. National Council of Farmer Cooperatives, 1800 Massachusetts Ave., N.W., Washington, DC 20036. Ed. Donald K. Hanes. circ. 2,000.
Cooperative farming

630　　　　　　EI　ISSN 0537-6297
DOCUMENTATION EUROPEENNE - SERIE AGRICOLE. Italian ed.: Documentazione Europea - Serie Agricola (ISSN 0537-6300); German ed.: Europaeische Dokumentation - Schriftenreihe Landwirtschaft (ISSN 0537-6327) (Edition also in Dutch) 1968. irreg. Commission of the European Communities, Direction Generale de la Presse et Information, Rue de la Loi 200, 1049 Brussels, Belgium (Dist. in U.S. by European Community Information Service, 2100 M St. N.W., Suite 707, Washington D.C. 20037) circ. controlled.

334　　　　　　DQ
DOMINICA. REGISTRAR OF CO-OPERATIVE SOCIETIES. REPORT.* irreg. Ministry of Agriculture, Trade and Natural Resources, Roseau, Dominica, West Indies. charts.

630　　　　　　AG
E A G PUBLICACIONES. Secretaria de Estado de Agricultura y Ganaderia, Servicio Nacional de Economia y Sociologia Rural, Paseo Colon 922, 1063 Buenos Aires, Argentina. charts. stat. (processed)
Formed by the merger of: S E A G Boletin del Maiz (ISSN 0036-1232) & S E A G Boletin del Trigo (ISSN 0036-1240) & S E A G Boletin del Algodon (ISSN 0036-1224)

630　　　　　　UK
EAST OF ENGLAND SHOW CATALOGUE. 1968. a. £1. ‡ East of England Agricultural Society, East of England Showground, Peterborough PE2 OXE, England. Ed. Roy W. Bird. adv. circ. 3,500.

310　　　　　　ES
EL SALVADOR. DIRECCION GENERAL DE ECONOMIA AGROPCUARIA. ANUARIO DE ESTADISTICAS AGROPCUARIAS. a. Direccion General de Economia Agropecuaria, Boulevard de los Heroes, Edificio Latinoamericano, San Salvador, El Salvador.

630　　　　　　MX　ISSN 0425-3442
ESTUDIOS AGRARIOS. 1960. irreg (1-2/yr) Centro de Investigaciones Agrarias, Aquiles Serdan 28, Mexico, D. F., Mexico.

630　　　　　　UN　ISSN 0071-6960
F A O AGRICULTURAL DEVELOPMENT PAPERS. (Text in English, French and Spanish) irreg., 1969, no. 91. price varies. Food and Agriculture Organization of the United Nations, Distribution and Sales Section, Via delle Terme di Caracalla, 00100 Rome, Italy (Dist. in U.S. by: Unipub, 345 Park Ave. S., New York, NY 10010)

630　　　　　　UN　ISSN 0071-6987
F A O AGRICULTURAL STUDIES. (Text in English, French and Spanish) 1949. irreg., 1973, no. 91. price varies. Food and Agriculture Organization of the United Nations, Distribution and Sales Section, Via delle Terme di Caracalla, 00100 Rome, Italy (Dist. in U.S. by: Unipub, 345 Park Ave. S., New York, NY 10010)

350　630　　　　UN　ISSN 0071-7045
F A O LEGISLATIVE SERIES. (Text in English and French) 1957. irreg., 1970, no. 9. price varies. Food and Agriculture Organization of the United Nations, Distribution and Sales Section, Via delle Terme di Caracalla, 00100 Rome, Italy (Dist. in U.S. by: Unipub, 345 Park Ave. S., New York, NY 10010)

630　　　　　　UN　ISSN 0429-9353
F A O REGIONAL CONFERENCE FOR AFRICA. 1960. biennial, 10th 1978, Grusha, Tanzania. price varies. Food and Agriculture Organization of the United Nations, Distribution and Sales Section, Via delle Terme di Caracalla, I-00100 Rome, Italy (Dist. in U.S. by: Unipub, 345 Park Ave. S., New York, NY 10010)

630　　　　　　UN　ISSN 0427-8070
F A O REGIONAL CONFERENCE FOR ASIA AND THE FAR EAST. REPORT. (Included in FAO. Agriculture in Asia and the Far East) (Issued also in French as its Rapport) 1949. irreg., 14th 1978, Kuala Lumpur. price varies. Food and Agriculture Organization of the United Nations, Distribution and Sales Section, Via delle Terme di Caracalla, I-00100 Rome, Italy (Dist. in U.S. by: Unipub, 345 Park Ave. S., New York, NY 10010)

630　　　　　　UN
F A O REGIONAL CONFERENCE FOR EUROPE. REPORT OF THE CONFERENCE. (In cooperation with the UN Economic Commission for Europe) irreg., 11th 1978, Lisbon. price varies. Food and Agriculture Organization of the United Nations, Distribution and Sales Section, Via delle Terme di Caracalla, I-00100 Rome, Italy (Dist. in U.S. by: Unipub, 345 Park Ave. S., New York, NY 10010)

630　　　　　　UN
F A O REGIONAL CONFERENCE FOR LATIN AMERICA. REPORT. irreg., 14th 1974, Lima. price varies. Food and Agriculture Organization of the United Nations, Distribution and Sales Section, Via delle Terme di Caracalla, I-00100 Rome, Italy (Dist. in U.S. by: Unipub, 345 Park Ave. S., New York, NY 10010)

630　　　　　　UN　ISSN 0427-8089
F A O REGIONAL CONFERENCE FOR THE NEAR EAST. REPORT. 1962. irreg., 14th 1978, Damascus. price varies. Food and Agriculture Organization of the United Nations, Distribution and Sales Section, Via delle Terme di Caracalla, I-00100 Rome, Italy (345 Park Ave. S., New York, NY 10010)

630 UN ISSN 0532-0313
F A O TERMINOLOGY BULLETIN. Food and Agriculture Organization of the United Nations, Distribution and Sales Section, Via delle Terme di Caracalla, I-00100 Rome, Italy (Dist. in U.S. by: Unipub, 345 Park Ave., S., New York, NY 10010)

338.1 UK ISSN 0071-3910
FARM INCOMES IN ENGLAND AND WALES. 1950. a. price varies. H. M. S. O., P.O. Box 569, London SE1 9NH, England. (Co-sponsor: Ministry of Agriculture, Fisheries and Food)

630 CN
FARMER FORUMS. 1970. a. free. Saskatchewan Federation of Agriculture, Box 1637, 1601 McAra St., Regina, Sask. S4P 3C4, Canada. Es. Gary Carlson, Lenore Borgares. (processed)

630 CN ISSN 0381-2421
FARMERS' MARKET. 1974. irreg. free. Alberta Agriculture Farmers' Market Committee, Edmonton, Alta., Canada. Ed. Jocelyn Tennison. illus. circ. 300.

630 US
FERTILIZER INDUSTRY ROUND TABLE. PROCEEDINGS. 1955. a. $10 per copy. Fertilizer Industry Round Table, Glen Arm, MD 21057. Ed. Albert Spillman. (back issues avail.)

630 FJ ISSN 0071-4844
FIJI. MINISTRY OF AGRICULTURE & FISHERIES. ANNUAL REPORT. (Text in English) 1906. a. $0.90. Ministry of Agriculture & Fisheries, Box 358, Suva, Fiji.
Formerly: Fiji. Department of Agriculture. Annual Report.

630 FJ
FIJI. MINISTRY OF AGRICULTURE & FISHERIES. ANNUAL RESEARCH REPORT. (Text in English) N.S. 1969. a. $3.75 per no. Ministry of Agriculture & Fisheries, Box 358, Suva, Fiji.
Former titles: Fiji. Department of Agriculture. Annual Research Report; Fiji. Department of Agricultural Stations. Annual Report.

630 FJ
FIJI. MINISTRY OF AGRICULTURE & FISHERIES. BULLETIN. (Text in English) irreg. price varies. Ministry of Agriculture & Fisheries, Box 358, Suva, Fiji.
Formerly: Fiji. Department of Agriculture. Bulletin.

FLORIDA. DIVISION OF PLANT INDUSTRY. BIENNIAL REPORT. see *BIOLOGY — Botany*

630 UN ISSN 0532-0208
FOOD AND AGRICULTURE ORGANIZATION OF THE UNITED NATIONS. BASIC TEXTS. (Text in English., French and Spanish) 1960. Food and Agriculture Organization of the United Nations, Distribution and Sales Section, Via delle Terme di Caracalla, I-00100 Rome, Italy (Dist. in U.S. by: Unipub, 345 Park Ave. S., New York, NY 10010)

630 UN ISSN 0071-6944
FOOD AND AGRICULTURE ORGANIZATION OF THE UNITED NATIONS CONFERENCE. REPORT. biennial, 1975, 18th session. price varies. Food and Agriculture Organization of the United Nations, Distribution and Sales Section, Via delle Terme di Caracalla, Rome, Italy (Dist. in U.S. by: Unipub, 345 Park Ave. S., New York, NY 10010)

FORD ALMANAC; for farm and home. see *ENCYCLOPEDIAS AND GENERAL ALMANACS*

630 FR
FRANCE. MINISTERE DE L'AGRICULTURE. ENQUETE COMMUNAUTAIRE SUR LA STRUCTURE DES EXPLOITATIONS AGRICOLES. 1949. a. Ministere de l'Agriculture, Service Central des Enquetes et Etudes Statistiques, 44, Avenue de Sainte Mande, 75570 Paris Cedex 12, France. charts. stat. circ. 1,800.
Formerly (until 1975): France. Ministere de l'Agriculture et du Developpement Rural. Service Central des Enquetes et Etudes Statistiques. Statistique Agricole Annuelle (ISSN 0071-9080)

FREEDOM FROM HUNGER CAMPAIGN. BASIC STUDIES. see *FOOD AND FOOD INDUSTRIES*

630 JA
FUKUI UNIVERSITY. FACULTY OF EDUCATION. MEMOIRS. SERIES 5: APPLIED SCIENCE AND AGRICULTURAL SCIENCE. (Text in Japanese; summaries in English & Japanese) a. Fukui University, Faculty of Education, 9-1, 3-chome, Bunkyo, Fukui 910, Japan.

630 MX
GACETA AGRICOLA. 1958. irreg. exchange basis. Apdo. Postal 5-225, Guadalajara, Mexico.

630 575.1 JA ISSN 0435-1096
GAMMA FIELD SYMPOSIA. (Text in English; summaries in Japanese) 1962. a. exchange basis. Institute of Radiation Breeding - Norin-sho Nogyo Gijutsu Kenkyusho Hoshasen Ikushujo, Omiya-machi, Naka-gun, Ibaraki 319-22, Japan.

338 630 GW ISSN 0072-1565
GERMANY (FEDERAL REPUBLIC,1949-) BUNDESMINISTERIUM FUER ERNAEHRUNG, LANDWIRTSCHAFT UND FORSTEN. AGRARBERICHT DER BUNDESREGIERUNG. 1956. a. Bundesministerium fuer Ernaehrung, Landwirtschaft und Forsten, 5300 Bonn, W. Germany (B.R.D.)

630 GW ISSN 0343-7477
GERMANY(FEDERAL REPUBLIC, 1949-) BUNDESMINISTERIUM FUER ERNAEHRUNG, LANDWIRTSCHAFT UND FORSTEN. JAHRESBERICHT. FORSCHUNG IM GESCHAEFTSBEREICH DES BUNDESMINISTERS FUER ERNAEHRUNG, LA WIRTSCHAFT UND FORSTEN. 1962. a. DM.82. Bundesministerium fuer Ernaehrung, Landwirtschaft und Forsten, 5300 Bonn, W. Germany (B.R.D.) circ. 370.
Formerly: Germany(Federal Republic, 1949-) Bundesministerium fuer Ernaehrung, Landwirtschaft und Forsten. Jahresbericht. Forschung im Bereich des Bundesministers.

630 JA ISSN 0072-4513
GIFU UNIVERSITY. FACULTY OF AGRICULTURE. RESEARCH BULLETIN/GIFU DAIGAKU NOGAKUBA KENKYU HOKOKU. (Text and summaries in English or Japanese) 1951. irreg. 1969, no. 28. free. Gifu University, Faculty of Agriculture - Gifu Daigaku Nogakuba, 3-1 Naka Monzen-cho, Kagamihara, Gifu 504, Japan. Ed. Shosaku Senda. circ. 750.

630 UK ISSN 0072-6729
GREAT BRITAIN. MINISTRY OF AGRICULTURE, FISHERIES AND FOOD. TECHNICAL BULLETIN. irreg. price varies. H. M. S. O., P.O. Box 569, London SE1 9NH, England. (Co-sponsor: Ministry of Agriculture, Fisheries and Food)

630 UK
GREAT BRITAIN. REGIONAL AGRICULTURAL SERVICE. ANNUAL REPORT. 1976. a. H.M.S.O., P.O. Box 569, London SE1 9NH, England. illus.

630 GR
GREEK AGRICULTURAL DIRECTORY. (Text in Greek and English) 1977. a. Dr.300($10) International Contacts Office, Box 1381, Omonia, Athens, Greece. Ed. Demetrius Tsirimocos. adv. circ. 20,000.

630 UK ISSN 0017-4092
GREENSWARD. 1962. a. membership (non-members £ 2($6) ‡ South West Scotland Grassland Society, Auchincruive, Ayr, Scotland. Ed. R. D. Harkess. adv. abstr. charts. circ. 800.

630 BL
GUIA DA E M B R A P A E DE INSTITUICOES BRASILEIRAS DE PESQUISA AGROPECUARIA. 1976. a. (Instituicoes Brasileiras de Pesquisa Agropecuaria) Empresa Brasileira de Pesquisa Agropecuaria, Departamento de Informacao e Documentacao, Caixa Postal 1316, 70000 Brasilia, Brazil. illus.
Formerly: Directorio da E M B R A P A.

630 US ISSN 0073-098X
HAWAII AGRICULTURAL EXPERIMENT STATION, HONOLULU. RESEARCH BULLETIN.* irreg., 1969, no. 148. Hawaii Agricultural Experiment Station, College of Tropical Agriculture, University of Hawaii, Honolulu, HI 96822.

630 US ISSN 0073-0998
HAWAII AGRICULTURAL EXPERIMENT STATION, HONOLULU. RESEARCH REPORT.* irreg., 1970, no. 182. Hawaii Agricultural Experiment Station, College of Tropical Agriculture, University of Hawaii, Honolulu, HI 96822.

630 US ISSN 0073-1005
HAWAII AGRICULTURAL EXPERIMENT STATION, HONOLULU. TECHNICAL BULLETIN.* irreg., 1970, no. 81. Hawaii Agricultural Experiment Station, College of Tropical Agriculture, University of Hawaii, Honolulu, HI 96822.

630 US ISSN 0073-2230
HILGARDIA; a journal of agricultural science. 1924. irreg. exchange basis only. University of California, Berkeley, Agricultural Experiment Station, c/o Agricultural Publications, 1422 S. 10th St., Richmond, CA 94804. Indexed: Biol.Abstr. Biol. & Agr.Abstr. Chem.Abstr.

630 JA ISSN 0073-229X
HIROSAKI UNIVERSITY. FACULTY OF AGRICULTURE. BULLETIN/HIROSAKI DAIGAKU NOGAKUBU GAKUJUTSU HOKOKU. (Text in English or Japanese; summaries in English) 1955. a. exchange basis. Hirosaki University, Faculty of Agriculture - Hirosaki Daigaku Nogakubu, 3 Bunkyo-cho, Hirosaki 036, Japan. Ed. Ichiro Takayasu. bk. rev. circ. 500.

630 GW ISSN 0340-9783
HOHENHEIMER ARBEITEN. 1961. irreg., no. 77, 1975. (Universitaet Hohenheim) Verlag Eugen Ulmer, Wollgrasweg 41, Postfach 700561, 7000 Stuttgart 70, W. Germany (B.R.D.) bk. rev.

630 US ISSN 0098-5716
IDAHO. DEPARTMENT OF AGRICULTURE. ANNUAL REPORT. 1973. a. free. Department of Agriculture, Boise, ID 83708. stat. Key Title: Annual Report - Idaho State Department of Agriculture.

331.7 US
IDAHO. DEPARTMENT OF EMPLOYMENT. ANNUAL RURAL EMPLOYMENT REPORT. a. free. Department of Employment, Planning, Research and Evaluation Bureau, Box 35, Boise, ID 83735. illus. stat.
Former titles: Idaho. Department of Employment. Annual Rural Manpower Report; Idaho. Department of Employment. Annual Farm Labor Report (ISSN 0091-0732)

630 CL ISSN 0073-4675
IDESIA. (Text in Spanish; summaries in English) 1970. irreg. price varies. Universidad del Norte, Departamento de Agricultura, Arica, Chile. Ed. Raul Cortes. bk. rev. charts. bibl. illus. stat.

630 II ISSN 0084-781X
INDIAN AGRICULTURE IN BRIEF. (Text in in English) 1958. irreg. Rs.25.50. Ministry of Agriculture and Irrigation, Department of Agriculture, Directorate of Economics and Statistics, A-2E-3 Kasturba Gandhi Marg Barracks, New Delhi 110001, India. Ed. C. D. Sharma. circ. 2,000.

630 II
INDIAN REVIEW OF LIFE SCIENCES. (Text in English) 1981. a. $40. Impex India, 2/18 Ansari Rd., Daryaganj, New Delhi 110002, India. Ed. David N. San.

630 US ISSN 0073-6783
INDIANA. AGRICULTURAL EXPERIMENT STATION. INSPECTION REPORT. 1956. irreg. price varies. Purdue University, Agricultural Experiment Station, West Lafayette, IN 47907. Ed. Dallas L. Dinger.

630 US ISSN 0073-6791
INDIANA. AGRICULTURAL EXPERIMENT STATION. RESEARCH BULLETIN. 1957. irreg., 12-15/yr. single copy free. Purdue University, Agricultural Experiment Station, West Lafayette, IN 47907. Ed. Edward C. Ferringer. circ. 2,500.

AGRICULTURE

630 TI ISSN 0020-238X
INSTITUT NATIONAL DE LA RECHERCHE AGRONOMIQUE DE TUNISIE. DOCUMENTS TECHNIQUES. (Text in French; summaries in English) 1963. irreg., no.69, May 1975. price varies per no. Institut National de la Recherche Agronomique de Tunisie, Ariana, Tunisia.

630 ZR
INSTITUT NATIONAL POUR L'ETUDE ET LA RECHERCHE AGRONOMIQUE. RAPPORT ANNUEL. a. Institut National pour l'Etude et la Recherche Agronomique, B.P. 1513, Kisangani, Zaire. illus.

630 BG
INSTITUTE OF NUCLEAR AGRICULTURE. ANNUAL REPORT. (Text in English) irreg. Tk.40. Institute of Nuclear Agriculture, c/o Bangladesh Agricultural University, Mymensingh, Bangladesh.

630 BL
INSTITUTO BRASILEIRO DE ECONOMIA. CENTRO DE ESTUDOS AGRICOLAS. AGROPECUARIA. irreg. free. (Centro de Estudos Agricolas) Fundacao Getulio Vargas, Praia de Botafogo 190, Rio de Janeiro, Brazil (Orders to: Caixa Postal 9052, Rio de Janeiro, Brazil)

630 CK ISSN 0538-0391
INSTITUTO COLOMBIANO AGROPECUARIO. BOLETIN TECNICO. no. 45, 1977. irreg. Instituto Colombiano Agropecuario, Apdo. Aereo 151123, Bogota, Colombia. illus. circ. 2,500.

INSTITUTO DE INVESTIGACAO AGRONOMICA DE ANGOLA. DIVISAO DE METEOROLOGIA AGRICOLA. ANUARIO. see *METEOROLOGY*

630 AO ISSN 0078-2254
INSTITUTO DE INVESTIGACAO AGRONOMICA DE ANGOLA. RELATORIO. 1962. a. available on exchange. Instituto de Investigacao Agronomica de Angola, C.P. 406, Nova Lisboa, Angola. Indexed: Trop.Abstr.

630 AO ISSN 0078-2262
INSTITUTO DE INVESTIGACAO AGRONOMICA DE ANGOLA. SERIE CIENTIFICA. 1968. irreg.; no. 37, 1974. price varies. Instituto de Investigacao Agronomica de Angola, C.P. 406, Nova Lisboa, Angola. Indexed: Trop.Abstr.

630 AO ISSN 0078-2270
INSTITUTO DE INVESTIGACAO AGRONOMICA DE ANGOLA. SERIE TECNICA. 1968. irreg.; no. 44, 1970. price varies. Instituto de Investigacao Agronomica de Angola, C.P. 406, Nova Lisboa, Angola. Indexed: Trop.Abstr.

630 MZ ISSN 0077-1791
INSTITUTO DE INVESTIGACAO AGRONOMICA DE MOCAMBIQUE. CENTRO DE DOCUMENTACAS AGRARIA. MEMORIAS. (Summaries in English, French and Portuguese) 1966. irreg. price varies. ‡ Instituto de Investigacao Agronomica de Mocambique, Centro de Documentacao Agraria, C.P. 3658, Maputo 11, Mozambique. illus. index. circ. 500.

630 CR ISSN 0301-4355
INSTITUTO INTERAMERICANO DE CIENCIOS AGRICOLAS DE LA O E A. DOCUMENTOS OFICIALES. Issued with: Inter-American Institute of Agricultural Sciences. Reunion Anual de la Junta Directiva. Informe (ISSN 0538-3307) (Text in English, Spanish) 1971. irreg. free. Instituto Interamericano de Ciencias Agricolas de la O E A, Secretariado, Apdo. 55, Coronado, Prov. San Jose, Costa Rica. Ed. Carlos J. Molestina. circ. 1,500.

630 340 PE
INSTITUTO PERUANO DE DERECHO AGRARIO. CUADERNOS AGRARIOS. 1977. irreg. Instituto Peruano de Derecho Agrario, Apartado 11549, Jesus Maria, Lima, Peru.

630 RM
INSTITUTUL AGRONOMIC "DR. PETRU GROZA". BULETINUL. (Text in Romanian; summaries in English) 1975. a. $8. Institutul Agronomic "Dr. Petru Groza", Str. Manastur No. 3, Cluj-Napoca, Romania. Ed. Ioan Puia. circ. 600. Indexed: Biol.Abstr. Field Crop Abstr. Ind.Vet. Landwirt.Zentralbl.

630 RM ISSN 0075-3505
INSTITUTUL AGRONOMIC "ION IONESCU DE LA BRAD". LUCRARI STIINTIFICE. I. AGRONOMIE - HORTICULTURA. irreg. Institutul Agronomic "Ion Ionescu de la Brad", Aleea M. Sadoveanu, Nr. 3, Jassy, Romania.

630 CR ISSN 0538-3277
INTER-AMERICAN INSTITUTE OF AGRICULTURAL SCIENCES. INFORME ANUAL. (Editions in English, Spanish) 1942-43. a. free. Instituto Interamericano de Ciencias Agricolas de la O E A, Secretariado, Apdo. 55, Coronado, Prov. San Jose, Costa Rica. Ed. Carlos J. Molestina. circ. 1,800 Sp. edt.; 500 Eng. edt. (also avail. in microform)

630 CR
INTER-AMERICAN INSTITUTE OF AGRICULTURAL SCIENCES. TECHNICAL ADVISORY COUNCIL. JUNTA DIRECTIVA. REUNION ANUAL. RESOLUCIONES Y DOCUMENTOS. 1955. irreg. Instituto Interamericano de Ciencias Agricolas de la O E A, Technical Advisory Council, Apartado 10281, San Jose, Costa Rica. Ed. Carlos J. Molestina. circ. 1,500.
Formerly: Inter-American Institute of Agricultural Sciences. Technical Advisory Council. Report of the Meeting.

338.1 UK ISSN 0074-1736
INTERNATIONAL ASSOCIATION OF SEED CRUSHERS. PROCEEDINGS OF THE ANNUAL CONGRESS. 1910. a. £12. International Association of Seed Crushers, 8 Salisbury Square, London EC4P 4AN, England.

638.1 RM ISSN 0074-2007
INTERNATIONAL BEEKEEPING CONGRESS. REPORTS. biennial since 1963; 24th, Buenos Aires, Argentina, 1973. $15. International Federation of Beekeepers' Associations "Apimondia", Str. Pitar Mos Nr. 20, Bucharest, Romania.

630 CK
INTERNATIONAL CENTER OF TROPICAL AGRICULTURE. ANNUAL REPORT.* (Editions in English and Spanish) 1969. a. International Center of Tropical Agriculture, Office of Publication Services, Apartado Aereo 67-13, Cali, Colombia.

630 CK
INTERNATIONAL CENTER OF TROPICAL AGRICULTURE. INFORMATION BULLETIN.* (Editions in English or Spanish) 1973. irreg. International Center of Tropical Agriculture, Office of Publication Services, Apartado Aereo 67-13, Cali, Colombia.

630 CK
INTERNATIONAL CENTER OF TROPICAL AGRICULTURE. REFERENCE BULLETINS.* (Text in English and Spanish) 1972. irreg., 1973 no. 2. International Center of Tropical Agriculture, Office of Publication Services, Apartado Aereo 67-13, Cali, Colombia.

630 CK
INTERNATIONAL CENTER OF TROPICAL AGRICULTURE. TECHNICAL BULLETIN.* (Text in English and Spanish) 1971. irreg. avail. on exchange. International Center of Tropical Agriculture, Office of Publication Services, Apartado Aero 67-13, Cali, Colombia. charts. stat. circ. controlled.

INTERNATIONAL COMMISSION ON IRRIGATION AND DRAINAGE. REPORT. see *WATER RESOURCES*

338.1 FR ISSN 0074-5863
INTERNATIONAL FEDERATION OF AGRICULTURAL PRODUCERS. GENERAL CONFERENCE PROCEEDINGS. (Editions in English and French) 1946. approx. every 18 months; 23rd, Sorrento, Italy; 1979. International Federation of Agricultural Producers, 1, rue d'Hauteville, 75010 Paris, France.

338.1 UK
INTERNATIONAL WHEAT COUNCIL. ANNUAL REPORT. (Editions in English, French, Russian and Spanish) 1949/50. a. free. International Wheat Council, Haymarket House, 28 Haymarket, London SW1Y 4SS, England. stat.
Formerly: International Wheat Council. Report for Crop Year (ISSN 0539-1296)

338.1 UK ISSN 0539-130X
INTERNATIONAL WHEAT COUNCIL. RECORD OF OPERATIONS OF MEMBER COUNTRIES. 1960/61. a. free. International Wheat Council, Haymarket House, 28 Haymarket, London SW1Y 4SS, England. stat. circ. controlled. (processed)

338.1 UK ISSN 0539-1326
INTERNATIONAL WHEAT COUNCIL. SECRETARIAT PAPERS. 1961. irreg. free. International Wheat Council, Haymarket House, 28 Haymarket, London SW1Y 4SS, England. stat.

630 US ISSN 0021-0692
IOWA STATE UNIVERSITY. IOWA AGRICULTURE AND HOME ECONOMICS EXPERIMENT STATION. RESEARCH BULLETIN SERIES. 1911. irreg. free. ‡ Iowa State University, Publications Distribution Center, Printing and Publications Bldg., Ames, IA 50011. Ed. John F. Heer. charts. illus. stat. cum.index. circ. controlled. Indexed: Biol.Abstr. Chem.Abstr. Curr.Cont. Bibl.Agri.

630 US ISSN 0578-6258
IOWA STATE UNIVERSITY. IOWA AGRICULTURE AND HOME ECONOMICS EXPERIMENT STATION. SPECIAL REPORT. 1936. irreg. free. ‡ Iowa State University, Publications Distribution Center, Printing and Publications Building, Ames, IA 50011. (Co-sponsor: Iowa Cooperative Extension Service in Agriculture and Home Economics) Ed. John F. Heer. Indexed: Biol.Abstr. Curr.Cont. Bibl.Agri.

630 IQ ISSN 0075-0530
IRAQI JOURNAL OF AGRICULTURAL SCIENCE. (Text in English; summaries in Arabic) 1966. a. available on exchange. University of Baghdad, College of Agriculture, Abu-Ghraid, Baghdad, Iraq. Ed. K. H. Juma. circ. 500. (back issues avail.)

630 IE
IRELAND (EIRE) CENTRAL STATISTICS OFFICE. ESTIMATED GROSS AND NET AGRICULTURAL OUTPUT. a. Central Statistics Office, Earlsfort Terrace, Dublin 2, Ireland.
Formerly: Ireland (Eire) Central Statistics Office. Estimates of the Quantity and Value of Agricultural Output (ISSN 0075-0557)
Stencilled releases

IRELAND (EIRE) DEPARTMENT OF AGRICULTURE AND FISHERIES. JOURNAL. see *FISH AND FISHERIES*

630 IE ISSN 0075-0646
IRELAND (EIRE) DEPARTMENT OF AGRICULTURE AND FISHERIES. ANNUAL REPORT. a. price varies. Government Publications Sales Office, G.P.O. Arcade, Dublin 1, Ireland.

630 IE
IRISH COOPERATIVE ORGANIZATION SOCIETY. ANNUAL REPORT. 1895. a. £3. Irish Agricultural Organization Society Ltd., Plunkett House, 84 Merrion Square, Dublin 2, Ireland. Ed. J. Smith. circ. controlled.
Formerly: Irish Agricultural Organization Society. Annual Report (ISSN 0075-0719)

630 IS
ISRAEL. RURAL PLANNING AND DEVELOPMENT AUTHORITY. AGRICULTURAL AND RURAL ECONOMIC REPORT. (Text in Hebrew; summaries in English) a. free. Ministry of Agriculture, Rural Planning and Economic Development, P.O. Box 7011, Hakirya, Tel-Aviv, Israel. circ. 600.
Former titles: Israel. Rural Planning and Development Authority. Agricultural and Rural Development Report; Israel. Agriculture and Settlement Planning and Development Center. Agricultural and Rural Development Report; Israel. Agriculture and Settlement Planning and Development Center. Statistical Series for the Agricultural Year (ISSN 0075-0964); Israel. Agriculture and Settlement Planning and Development Center. Statistical Series of the Budgetary Year (ISSN 0075-1294)

630 IT ISSN 0075-1669
ITALY. ISTITUTO CENTRALE DI STATISTICA. ANNUARIO DI STATISTICA AGRARIA. 1965. a. L.9000. Istituto Centrale di Statistica, Via Cesare Balbo 16, Rome, Italy.

AGRICULTURE

630 634.9 JA ISSN 0446-5458
JAPAN. MINISTRY OF AGRICULTURE AND FORESTRY. ANNUAL REPORT/NORIN-SHO NENPO. (Text in Japanese) 1953. a. 6000 Yen. (Norin-sho Daijin Kanbo) Government Publications Service Center, 1-2-1 Kasumigaseki, Chiyoda-ku, Tokyo 100, Japan. illus. stat.
Continues: Norin Suisan Nenkan.

630 JO
JORDAN. DEPARTMENT OF STATISTICS. AGRICULTURAL STATISTICAL YEARBOOK AND AGRICULTURAL SAMPLE SURVEY. (Text in Arabic and English) 1966. a. $5. Department of Statistics, Amman, Jordan.

630 UK
JOURNAL OF AGRICULTURAL LABOUR SCIENCE. vol. 4, 1975. irreg. £4. British Society for Agricultural Labour Science, University of Reading, Earley Gate RG6 2AT, England. Ed. Bd.

630 US ISSN 0146-3071
JOURNAL OF SEED TECHNOLOGY. 1908. a. Association of Official Seed Analysts, Ohio Department of Agriculture Laboratory, Reynoldsburg, OH 43068. Ed. Dr. Lawrence O. Copeland. cum.index 1908-1937; 1938-1959. circ. 400. (back issues avail)
Formerly: Association of Official Seed Analysts Proceedings.

JOURNAL OF SOIL AND WATER CONSERVATION IN INDIA. see *CONSERVATION*

630 GW
K T B L-SCHRIFTEN. irreg. no. 205, 1976. price varies. Kuratorium fuer Technik und Bauwesen in der Landwirtschaft e.V., Bartningsstr. 49, 6100 Darmstadt 12, W. Germany (B.R.D.) charts. illus.

338.1 US
KANSAS. STATE BOARD OF AGRICULTURE. ANNUAL REPORT WITH FARM FACTS. 1872. a. free. State Board of Agriculture, 503 Kansas Ave., Topeka, KS 66603. Ed. W. R. Fitzgerald. illus. stat.
Continues: Kansas. State Board of Agriculture. Report; Formed by the merger of: Kansas. State Board of Agriculture. Annual Report & Farm Facts; Formerly: Kansas Agriculture Report (ISSN 0091-6900); Supersedes: Kansas. State Board of Agriculture. Biennial Report to the Governor.

630 TH ISSN 0075-5192
KASETSART JOURNAL. (Text in Thai or English) 1961. s-a. $2. Kasetsart University, Bangkok 9, Thailand. Ed. Phaitoon Ingkasuwan.

KONGELIGE VETERINAER- OG LANDBOHOEJSKOLE. AARSKRIFT. see *VETERINARY SCIENCE*

630 NE
KONINKLIJK INSTITUUT VOOR DE TROPEN. AFDELING AGRARISCH ONDERZOEK. ANNUAL REPORT. a. Koninklijk Instituut voor de Tropen, Mauritskade 63, 1092 AD Amsterdam, Netherlands. illus.

630 NE
KONINKLIJK INSTITUUT VOOR DE TROPEN. AFDELING AGRARISCH ONDERZOEK. COMMUNICATION. irreg. Koninklijk Instituut voor de Tropen, Mauritskade 63, 1092 AD Amsterdam, Netherlands. illus.

630 KO ISSN 0075-6865
KOREA (REPUBLIC) OFFICE OF RURAL DEVELOPMENT. AGRICULTURAL RESEARCH REPORT/KOREA (REPUBLIC) NONGCH'ON CHINHUNGCH'ONG. NONGSA SIHOM YON'GU POGO. (Text in Korean; summaries in English) 1958. a. free. Ministry of Agriculture & Fishery, Office of Rural Development, Seodun-Dong, Suweon, S. Korea. Ed. In Hwan Kim. circ. 1,230.

630 JA ISSN 0075-7373
KYOTO PREFECTURAL UNIVERSITY. SCIENTIFIC REPORTS: AGRICULTURE/KYOTO-FURITSU DAIGAKU GAKUJUTSU HOKOKU NAGAKU. (Text in Japanese; summaries in English) 1951. irreg., no. 28, 1976. available only on exchange. Kyoto Prefectural University - Kyoto-furitsu Daigaku, Shimogamo Hangi-cho, Sakyo-ku, Kyoto 606, Japan. Ed. Z. Hayashino. Indexed: Biol.Abstr.

630 JA
KYUSHU UNIVERSITY. INSTITUTE OF TROPICAL AGRICULTURE. BULLETIN. (Text in English and Japanese) 1975. irreg. on exchange basis. Kyushu University, Institute of Tropical Agriculture, 13 Hakazaki, Higashiku, Fukuoka 812, Japan. Ed. Bd. circ. 100. (back issues avail)

630 GT
LA ZONA NORTE. INFORMA. 1965. q. Instituto Interamericano de Ciencias Agricolas de la O E A, Apartado 1815, Guatemala, Guatemala.

630 GW ISSN 0455-2342
LANDARBEIT UND TECHNIK. irreg., no. 35, 1968. price varies. (Max-Planck-Institut fuer Landarbeit und Landtechnik) Verlag Paul Parey (Hamburg), Spitalerstr. 12, 2000 Hamburg 1, W. Germany (B.R.D.) Ed. Gerhardt Preuschen. bibl. illus. index. (reprint service avail. from ISI)

630 NE ISSN 0083-6990
LANDBOUWHOGESCHOOL, WAGENINGEN. MISCELLANEOUS PAPERS. 1968. irreg. price varies. (State Agricultural University) H. Veenman en Zonen, Box 7, Wageningen, Netherlands. (back issues avail.)

630 SR
LANDBOUWPROEFSTATION SURINAME. JAARVERSLAG/AGRICULTURAL EXPERIMENT STATION SURINAM. ANNUAL REPORT. (Text in Dutch; Summaries in English) Department of Agriculture and Fisheries, Landbouwproefstation, Box 160, Paramaribo, Surinam. charts. illus. stat.

LANDBRUKETS AARBOK. JORDBRUK, HAGEBRUK, SKOGBRUK. see *FORESTS AND FORESTRY*

LANDSCAPE HISTORY. see *HISTORY — History Of Europe*

630 NZ ISSN 0069-3839
LINCOLN COLLEGE. FARMERS' CONFERENCE. PROCEEDINGS. 1951. a. price varies. Lincoln College, Canterbury, New Zealand.

394.6 US ISSN 0093-0687
LOUISIANA FAIRS AND FESTIVALS. a. Department of Agriculture, Baton Rouge, LA 70804.

630 VE
LUZ. (Text in Spanish; summaries in English) 1968. irreg; 1975, vol. 3, no. 2. Universidad del Zulia, Facultad de Agronomia, Apartado 526, Maracaibo, Venezuela. Eds. Eovaldo Hernandez, Rodolfo Avila. bibl. charts.

630 MY
M A R D I RESEARCH BULLETIN. (Text in English; summaries in Malay) 1973. s-a. M.$3.50. Malaysian Agricultural Research and Development Institute, Box 208, Sungei Besi, Serdang, Selangor, Malaysia. bibl. illus.

630 LE ISSN 0076-2369
MAGON. SERIE SCIENTIFIQUE.* (Text and summaries in English and French) 1965. irreg., 1970, no. 33. free. Institut de Recherches Agronomiques, Laboratoire Regional Veterinaire, Fanar, Lebanon.

630 LE ISSN 0076-2377
MAGON. SERIE TECHNIQUE.* (Text in Arabic, English and French; summaries in English and French) 1965. irreg., 1970, no. 11. free. Institut de Recherches Agronomiques, Laboratoire Regional Veterinaire, Fanar, Lebanon.

630 HU ISSN 0076-2423
MAGYAR TUDOMANYOS AKADEMIA. AGRARTUDOMANYOK OSZTALYA. MONOGRAFIASOROZAT. (Text in Hungarian; occasional summaries in English, German, Italian or Russian) 1955. irreg. price varies. Akademiai Kiado, Publishing House of the Hungarian Academy of Sciences, P.O. Box 24, H-1363 Budapest, Hungary.

630 UG ISSN 0075-4730
MAKERERE UNIVERSITY. FACULTY OF AGRICULTURE. HANDBOOK.* 1963. irreg. Makerere University, Faculty of Agriculture, Box 7062, Kampala, Uganda.

630 UG ISSN 0075-4773
MAKERERE UNIVERSITY. FACULTY OF AGRICULTURE. TECHNICAL BULLETIN. 1962. irreg. ‡ Makerere University, Faculty of Agriculture, Box 7062, Kampala, Uganda.

630 MW
MALAWI. DEPARTMENT OF AGRICULTURAL RESEARCH. ANNUAL REPORT. a. K.4.60 price varies. Government Printer, P.O. Box 37, Zomba, Malawi.
Incorporates (from 1975): Agricultural Research Council of Malawi. Annual Report (ISSN 0065-4515); Formerly (1963/64-1969/70): Malawi. Department of Agriculture. Annual Report (ISSN 0076-3047)

630 MW
MALAWI. DEPARTMENT OF AGRICULTURAL RESEARCH. RESEARCH BULLETIN. 1975. irreg., latest no. 4, 1976. Department of Agricultural Research, Box 30134, Capital City, Lilongwe 3, Malawi. circ. 500.

630 MW ISSN 0085-3011
MALAWI. NATIONAL STATISTICAL OFFICE. COMPENDIUM OF AGRICULTURAL STATISTICS. 1971. irreg (approx. every 5 yrs.) K.4.50($5) ‡ National Statistical Office, Box 333, Zomba, Malawi. stat. (processed)

630 MW ISSN 0076-3292
MALAWI. NATIONAL STATISTICAL OFFICE. NATIONAL SAMPLE SURVEY OF AGRICULTURE. 1970. irreg. K.8.50($9.50) ‡ National Statistical Office, P.O. Box 333, Zomba, Malawi.

630 639.2 MY
MALAYSIA. MINISTRY OF AGRICULTURE. TECHNICAL AND GENERAL BULLETINS. 1957, N.S. 1973. irreg. Ministry of Agriculture - Kementerian Pertanian, Publications Officer, Swettenham Rd., Kuala Lumpur, Malaysia.
Former titles: Malaysia. Ministry of Agriculture. Technical Bulletins; Malaysia. Ministry of Agriculture & Rural Development. Technical Bulletins.

630 334.683 MY
MALAYSIAN MULTI-PURPOSE COOPERATIVE SOCIETY. REVIEW. Title varies: Majallah Syarikat Kerjasama Serbaguna Malaysia. (Text in Malaysian, Chinese, English) irreg. $24. Malaysian Multi-Purpose Cooperative Society, 67 Jalan Ampang, Kuala Lumpur, Malaysia. illus.

634 MY
MALAYSIAN PINEAPPLE. (Text and summaries in English) 1971. irreg. latest vol. 2, 1972. Malayan Pineapple Industry Board, Pineapple Research Station, Box 101, Pekan Nenas, Johor, Malaysia. illus. circ. 1,500.

630 338.1 MM
MALTA. CENTRAL OFFICE OF STATISTICS. CENSUS OF AGRICULTURE AND FISHERIES. a. £0.15. Central Office of Statistics, Auberge de Castille, Valletta, Malta (Subscr. to: Department of Information, Auberge de Castille, Valletta, Malta)
Formerly: Malta. Office of Statistics. Census of Agriculture (ISSN 0076-3454)

338.1 US ISSN 0092-9794
MASSACHUSETTS AGRICULTURAL STATISTICS. Cover title, 1973: Agricultural Statistics, Massachusetts. 1972. a. free. New England Crop and Livestock Reporting Service, 55 Pleasant St., Concord, NH 03301. (Co-sponsors: Massachusetts Department of Food & Agriculture; U.S. Department of Agriculture) illus. stat.

630 US ISSN 0076-5589
MAX C. FLEISCHMANN COLLEGE OF AGRICULTURE. PUBLICATIONS. B (SERIES) (Replaces: Agricultural Experiment Station Bulletins and Cooperative Extension Service Bulletins) 1964. irreg. University of Nevada Cooperative Extension Service, Max C. Fleischmann College of Agriculture, Reno, NV 89507.

630 US ISSN 0076-5597
MAX C. FLEISCHMANN COLLEGE OF
AGRICULTURE. PUBLICATIONS. C (SERIES)
(Supersedes: Agricultural Experiment Station
Circulars and Cooperative Extension Service
Circulars) irreg. University of Nevada Cooperative
Extension Service, Max C. Fleischmann College of
Agriculture, Reno, NV 89507.

630 US ISSN 0076-5600
MAX C. FLEISCHMANN COLLEGE OF
AGRICULTURE. PUBLICATIONS. R (SERIES)
irreg. University of Nevada Cooperative Extension
Service, Max C. Fleischmann College of
Agriculture, Reno, NV 89507.

630 US ISSN 0076-5619
MAX C. FLEISCHMANN COLLEGE OF
AGRICULTURE. PUBLICATIONS. T (SERIES)
(Supersedes: Agricultural Experiment Station
Technical Bulletins) 1964. irreg. University of
Nevada Cooperative Extension Service, Max C.
Fleischmann College of Agriculture, Reno, NV
89507.

630 UN ISSN 0532-0402
MEETING OF INTERNATIONAL
ORGANIZATIONS FOR THE JOINT STUDY
OF PROGRAMS AND ACTIVITIES IN THE
FIELD OF AGRICULTURE IN EUROPE.
REPORT. (Issued in the Meeting Report (Series) of
its Agriculture Division) 1955. irreg. Food and
Agriculture Organization of the United Nations,
Distribution and Sales Section, Via delle Terme di
Caracalla, I-00100 Rome, Italy.

630 AT ISSN 0085-3232
MELBOURNE NOTES ON AGRICULTURAL
EXTENSION. 1968. irreg. free. ‡ University of
Melbourne, Faculty of Agriculture and Forestry,
Parkville, Vic. 3052, Australia. (Co-Sponsor:
Victorian Department of Agriculture) Eds. Dr. H. S.
Hawkins, Dr. H. M. Russell. bk. rev. circ. 650.
Indexed: World Agri. Econ. & Rural Sociol. Abstr.

631 HU ISSN 0077-2658
NAGYUZEMI GAZDALKODAS KERDESEI. 1961.
irreg. price varies. (Magyar Tudomanyos Akademia)
Akademiai Kiado, Publishing House of the
Hungarian Academy of Sciences, P.O. Box 24, H-
1363 Budapest, Hungary.

630 CE ISSN 0547-3616
NATIONAL AGRICULTURAL SOCIETY OF
CEYLON. JOURNAL. (Text in English) 1964. a.
Rs.5.50($2) ‡ National Agricultural Society of
Ceylon, Faculty of Agriculture, University of Sri
Lanka, Peradeniya, Sri Lanka. Ed. Dr. Y. D. A.
Senanayake. adv. illus. circ. 250. Indexed:
Trop.Abstr.

631 JA ISSN 0077-4820
NATIONAL INSTITUTE OF AGRICULTURAL
SCIENCES, TOKYO. BULLETIN. SERIES A
(PHYSICS AND STATISTICS) (Text in English or
Japanese with English summary) 1951. irreg., no.
24, 1977. avail. on exchange basis only. National
Institute of Agricultural Sciences - Norin-sho Nogyo
Gijutsu Kenkyusho, 2-7-1 Nishigahara, Kita-ku,
Tokyo 114, Japan. Ed. Y. Takahasi.

631 JA ISSN 0077-4863
NATIONAL INSTITUTE OF AGRICULTURAL
SCIENCES, TOKYO. BULLETIN. SERIES H
(FARM MANAGEMENT, LAND
UTILIZATION, RURAL LIFE) (Text in English or
Japanese with English summary) 1951. irreg., no.
49, 1977. avail. on exchange basis only. National
Institute of Agricultural Sciences - Norin-sho Nogyo
Gijutsu Kenkyusho, 2-7-1 Nishigahara, Kita-ku,
Tokyo 114, Japan. Ed. F. Suzuki.

630 JA ISSN 0077-4871
NATIONAL INSTITUTE OF AGRICULTURAL
SCIENCES, TOKYO. MISCELLANEOUS
PUBLICATION. (Text in English or Japanese)
1974. irreg. avail. on exchange basis only. National
Institute of Agricultural Sciences - Norin-sho Nogyo
Gijutsu Kenkyusho, 2-7-1 Nishigahara, Kita-ku,
Tokyo 114, Japan. Ed. K. Sakai.

630 JA
NATIONAL RESEARCH INSTITUTE OF
AGRICULTURE. BIENNIAL REPORT/NOGYO
SOGO KENKYUSHO NENPO. (Text in Japanese)
1949. a. National Research Institute of Agriculture -
Norin-sho Nogyo Sogo Kenkyusho, 2-2-1
Nishigahara, Kita-ku, Tokyo 114, Japan.

630 CH ISSN 0077-5819
NATIONAL TAIWAN UNIVERSITY. COLLEGE
OF AGRICULTURE. MEMOIRS. (Text in
Chinese and English; summaries in English) 1936.
irreg. National Taiwan University, College of
Agriculture, Taipei, Taiwan, Republic of China.
Ed.Bd. circ. 500.

630 NP
NEPAL. DEPARTMENT OF AGRICULTURAL
EDUCATION AND RESEARCH. ANNUAL
REPORT.* (Text in English) a. Department of
Agricultural Education and Research, Lalitpur,
Nepal.

630 US ISSN 0077-832X
NEW HAMPSHIRE. AGRICULTURAL
EXPERIMENT STATION, DURHAM.
RESEARCH REPORTS. 1961. irreg; latest issue,
1976. free. University of New Hampshire,
Agricultural Experiment Station, Durham, NH
03824.

630 US ISSN 0077-8338
NEW HAMPSHIRE. AGRICULTURAL
EXPERIMENT STATION, DURHAM. STATION
BULLETINS. 1888. irreg; latest issue, 1976. free.
University of New Hampshire, Agricultural
Experiment Station, Durham, NH 03824. circ. 100
approx.

630 US ISSN 0077-846X
NEW JERSEY. DEPARTMENT OF
AGRICULTURE. HIGHLIGHTS OF THE
ANNUAL REPORT. 1961. a. free. Department of
Agriculture, P.O. Box 1888, Trenton, NJ 08625. Ed.
Amanda Q. Zich.

630 US ISSN 0548-5967
NEW MEXICO. AGRICULTURAL EXPERIMENT
STATION. RESEARCH REPORT. no. 348, 1977.
irreg. New Mexico State University, Agricultural
Experiment Station, Drawer 3AI, Las Cruces, NM
88003.

338.1 US ISSN 0077-8540
NEW MEXICO AGRICULTURAL STATISTICS.
1962. a. free. Department of Agriculture, Crop and
Livestock Reporting Service, P.O. Box 3189, Las
Cruces, NM 88001. (Co-Sponsor: U.S. Department
of Agriculture)

630 NZ ISSN 0110-4624
NEW ZEALAND. DEPARTMENT OF
STATISTICS. AGRICULTURAL STATISTICS. a.
NZ.$4.50. Dept. of Statistics, Private Bag,
Wellington, New Zealand (Subscr. to: Government
Printing Office, Publications, Private Bag,
Wellington, New Zealand)
Formerly: New Zealand. Department of Statistics.
Statistical Report of Farm Production (ISSN 0077-
9822)

630 JA ISSN 0549-4826
NIIGATA UNIVERSITY. FACULTY OF
AGRICULTURE. MEMOIRS/NIIGATA
DAIGAKU NOGAKUBU KIYO. (Text in Japanese
and English) 1961. a. exchange basis. Niigata
University, Faculty of Agriculture - Niigata Daigaku
Nogakubu, 8050 Igarashi 2, Niigata-Shi, 950-21,
Japan. circ. 500.

631.2 NO ISSN 0065-0218
NORGES LANDBRUKSHOEGSKOLE. INSTITUTT
FOR BYGNINGSTEKNIKK.
BYGGEKOSTNADSINDEKS FOR
DRIFTSBYGNINGER I JORDBRUKET.
PRISUTVIKLINGEN. (Bound with its Melding)
1958. a. free. Norges Landbrukshoegskole, Institutt
for Bygningsteknikk, Box 15, N-1432 Aas-NLH,
Norway.

630 US
NORTH CAROLINA SEED LAW. 1971. irreg. free.
Department of Agriculture, Raleigh, NC 27611.
circ. controlled. (tabloid format)

353.9 US
NORTH DAKOTA. DEPARTMENT OF
AGRICULTURE. BIENNIAL REPORT. biennial.
free. Department of Agriculture, Bismarck, ND
58501. illus. stat.
Formerly: North Dakota. Department of
Agriculture. Annual Report (ISSN 0093-8203)

630 UK
NORTH OF SCOTLAND COLLEGE OF
AGRICULTURE, ABERDEEN. BULLETIN. 1970.
irreg. North of Scotland College of Agriculture, 581
King St., Aberdeen AB9 1UD, England.

630 UK ISSN 0078-1746
NORTHERN IRELAND. DEPARTMENT OF
AGRICULTURE. ANNUAL REPORT ON
RESEARCH AND TECHNICAL WORK. 1963. a.
£10.50. ‡ Department of Agriculture, Dundonald
House, Upper Newtownards Rd., Belfast BT4 3SB,
N. Ireland. Ed. Dr. W. O. Brown. circ. 450.

630 UK ISSN 0078-1754
NORTHERN IRELAND. DEPARTMENT OF
AGRICULTURE. RECORD OF
AGRICULTURAL RESEARCH. 1963. irreg., vol.
28, 1980. £6.50. ‡ Department of Agriculture,
Dundonald House, Upper Newtownards Rd., Belfast
BT4 3SB, N. Ireland. Ed. Dr. W. O. Brown. circ.
425.

630 US ISSN 0078-3951
OHIO AGRICULTURAL RESEARCH AND
DEVELOPMENT CENTER, WOOSTER.
RESEARCH BULLETIN. irreg. single copies free.
Ohio Agricultural Research and Development
Center, Wooster, OH 44691. Ed. Edward H. Roche.

630 US ISSN 0078-396X
OHIO AGRICULTURAL RESEARCH AND
DEVELOPMENT CENTER, WOOSTER.
RESEARCH CIRCULAR. irreg. single copies free.
Ohio Agricultural Research and Development
Center, Wooster, OH 44691. Ed. Edward H. Roche.

631.091 UK ISSN 0048-1580
OIL PALM NEWS. 1966. irreg. £1.75 free to official
bodies in developing countries. ‡ Tropical Products
Institute, 56-62 Gray's Inn Rd., London WC1X
8LU, England. Ed. Dr. J.A. Cornelius. bk. rev.
abstr. stat. circ. 1,970.
Tropical

630 CN ISSN 0078-4664
ONTARIO. AGRICULTURAL RESEARCH
INSTITUTE. REPORT. 1962/63. a. Agriculture
Research Institute, Parliament Bldg, Toronto, Ont.,
Canada. Ed. Dr. J. C. Rennie.

OSSERVAZIONI DI METEOROLOGIA AGRARIA
DELLA PUGLIA E BASILICATA; dati
meteorologici della Puglia e Lucania. see
METEOROLOGY

630 636 US
OXFORD TROPICAL HANDBOOKS. irreg. price
varies. Oxford University Press, 200 Madison Ave.,
New York, NY 10016 (And Ely House, 37 Dover
St., London W1X 4AH, England)

630 PK ISSN 0078-8139
PAKISTAN. FOOD AND AGRICULTURE
DIVISION. YEARBOOK OF AGRICULTURAL
STATISTICS. (Issued in Pakistan. Food and
Agriculture Division. Agriculture Wing. Planning
Unit. Fact Series) (Text in English) a. Ministry of
Food, Agriculture and Rural Development, Food
and Agriculture Division, Agriculture Wing,
Planning Unit, 139-H, G 6-3, Islamabad, Pakistan.

630 PN
PANAMA. INSTITUTO DE INVESTIGACION
AGROPECUARIA. CARTA INFORMATIVA
AGRICOLA. 1978. irreg. free. Instituto de
Investigacion Agropecuaria, Apartado 58, Santiago,
Veraguas, Panama. Ed. Elizabeth de Ruiloba. charts.
illus.

630 PN
PANAMA. INSTITUTO DE INVESTIGACION
AGROPECUARIA. INFORME ANUAL. 1976. a.
Instituto de Investigacion Agropecuaria, Apartado
58, Santiago, Veraguas, Panama. Dir. Carmen
Damaris Chea.

630 PN
PANAMA. INSTITUTO DE INVESTIGACION
AGROPECUARIA. PUBLICACION TECNICA.
irreg. Instituto de Investigaciones Agropecuaria,
Apartado Postal 58, Santiago de Veraguas, Panama.
Ed. Elizabeth de Ruiloba. bibl. charts. illus. stat.

630 PN ISSN 0085-4654
PANAMA. MINISTERIO DE AGRICULTURA Y
GANADERIA. BOLETIN TECNICO.* irreg. free.
Ministerio de Agricultura y Ganaderia, Apartado
5390, Panama 5, Panama. stat.

630 SP
PANORAMA DE AGRICULTURA EN (YEAR) a.
300 ptas. Ministerio de Agricultura, Secretaria
General Tecnica, Paseo de Infanta Isabel 1, Madrid
7, Spain. charts. stat.

630 BL
PARANA, BRAZIL. SECRETARIA DE ESTADO
DA AGRICULTURA. PLANO DE ACAO. 1976.
a. free. Secretaria de Estado da Agricultura, Servico
de Documentacao e Biblioteca, Caixa Postal 464,
8000 Curitiba, Parana, Brazil. circ. 5,000.

630 AG ISSN 0325-1799
PERGAMINO, ARGENTINA. ESTACION
EXPERIMENTAL REGIONAL
AGROPECUARIA. INFORME TECNICO. 1960.
irreg. Estacion Experimental Regional Agropecuaria,
Centro Documental, Casilla de Correo 31, 2700
Pergamino, Argentina. (Affiliate: Instituto Nacional
de Tecnologia Agropecuaria) circ. 1,000.
  Formerly (until 1970): Pergamino. Estacion
Experimental Agropecuaria. Informe Tecnico (ISSN
0020-0832)

PHILIPPINE AGRICULTURAL METEOROLOGY
BULLETIN. see METEOROLOGY

630.7 PH
PHILIPPINES. BUREAU OF VOCATIONAL
EDUCATION. AGRICULTURAL EDUCATION
PROGRAM; INFORMATION AND
STATISTICAL GUIDE. (Text in English) irreg.
Bureau of Vocational Education, Manila,
Philippines. stat.

630 US
PIONEER QUARTERLY. 1938. q. $10 for 12 nos.
Paldor Publications, 225 E. Utah St., Fairfield, CA
94533. Ed. Paul Doerr. bk. rev. film rev. index.
  Formerly: Pioneer.

630 MY ISSN 0032-0951
PLANTER. 1920. a. M.$60. Incorporated Society of
Planters, No. 29, 31 & 33, Jalan Taman u Thant,
Kuala Lumpur 01-02, Malaysia. Ed. M. Rajadurai.
adv. bk. rev. circ. 2,500.

630 PO ISSN 0079-4139
PORTUGAL. INSTITUTO NACIONAL DE
ESTATISTICA. ESTATISTICAS AGRICOLAS.
(Text in Portuguese and French) a. $90. Instituto
Nacional de Estatistica, Av. Antonio Jose de
Almeida, Lisbon 1, Portugal (Orders to: Imprensa
Nacional, Casa da Moeda, Direccao Comercial, rua
D. Francisco Manuel de Melo 5, Lisbon 1, Portugal)

630 PL ISSN 0079-4708
POZNANSKIE TOWARZYSTWO PRZYJACIOL
NAUK. KOMISJA NAUK ROLNICZYCH I
KOMISJA NAUK LESNYCH. PRACE. (Text in
Polish; summaries in English or German) 1950. a.
price varies. Poznanskie Towarzystwo Przyjaciol
Nauk, Mielzynskiego 27/29, 61-725 Poznan, Poland
(Dist. by Ars Polona-Ruch, Krakowskie
Przedmiescie 7, Warsaw, Poland) (Co-sponsor:
Komisja Nauk Lesnych) bibl, charts, illus. Indexed:
Chem.Abstr.

338.1 CN
PRINCE EDWARD ISLAND. ECONOMICS,
MARKETING & STATISTICS BRANCH.
AGRICULTURAL STATISTICS. 1966. a. ‡
Department of Agriculture and Forestry, P.O. Box
2000, Charlottetown, P.E.I. C1A 7N8, Canada. (Co-
sponsor: Statistics Canada) illus. stat.

630 338 SP ISSN 0079-5895
PRODUCTO NETO DE LA AGRICULTURA
ESPANOLA. a. Ministerio de Agricultura,
Secretaria General Tecnica, Paseo Infante Isabel 1,
Madrid 7, Spain.

333 UN ISSN 0085-5197
PROGRESS IN LAND REFORM. (Report prepared
jointly by United Nations, Food and Agriculture
Organization of the United Nations, International
Labour Organization) (Editions in English, French,
Spanish) 1954. irreg.; 5th 1970. price varies. United
Nations Publications, Room LX-2300, New York,
NY 10017 (Or Distribtuion and Sales Section,
Palais des Nations, CH-1211 Geneva 10,
Switzerland)

QUEENSLAND. LAND ADMINISTRATION
COMMISSION. ANNUAL REPORT. see PUBLIC
ADMINISTRATION

630 AT ISSN 0085-5332
QUEENSLAND PRIMARY PRODUCERS' CO-
OPERATIVE ASSOCIATION. PRIMARY
PRODUCERS' GUIDE.* 1969. a. $1. Queensland
Primary Producers' Co-Operative Association, Box
186, Brisbane, Qld. 4001, Australia.

630 YU ISSN 0033-8583
RADOVI POLJOPRIVREDNOG FAKULTETA
UNIVERZITETA U SARAJEVU. (Summaries in
English and Dutch) 1953. irreg. $11.50. Univerzitet
u Sarajevu, Poljoprivredni Fakultet, Zagrebacka 18,
Sarajevo, Yugoslavia. Ed. Taib Saric. Indexed:
Chem.Abstr.

630 CN
RECHERCHES AGRONOMIQUES SOMMAIRE
DES RESULTATS. (Text in English and French)
no. 18, 1973. a. free. Conseil des Recherches
Agricoles du Quebec, Ministere de l'Agriculture,
Quebec, Canada. Ed. Bd. bibl. Indexed: Biol.Abstr.

630 570 US ISSN 0034-5261
RESEARCH IN THE LIFE SCIENCES. 1953. irreg.
free. ‡ University of Maine at Orono, Life Sciences
and Agriculture Experiment Station, Orono, ME
04469. (also avail. in microfilm) Indexed: Curr.Cont.
  Formerly: Maine Farm Research.

338.1 UK
REVIEW OF THE WORLD WHEAT SITUATION.
(Text in English; summaries in English, French,
Russian and Spanish) 1960. a. free. International
Wheat Council, Haymarket House, 28 Haymarket,
London SW1Y 4SS, England. charts. stat.
  Formerly: International Wheat Council. Review
of the World Grains Situation (ISSN 0539-1318)

630 AG ISSN 0080-2069
REVISTA AGRONOMICA DEL NOROESTE
ARGENTINO. 1953. irreg. $3. Universidad
Nacional de Tucuman, Facultad de Agronomia y
Zootecnia, Casilla de Correos 32, 4000 San Miguel
de Tucuman, Argentina. Indexed: Biol.Abstr.
Trop.Abstr.

630 PR
REVISTA DE AGRICULTURA DE PUERTO RICO.
1903. a. Department of Agriculture, Box 10163, San
Juan, PR 00908. charts. illus. Indexed: Chem.Abstr.

REVISTA DE DERECHO Y REFORMA
AGRARIA. see LAW

630 VE
REVISTA LATINOAMERICANA DE CIENCIAS
AGRICOLAS. (Text in Spanish, Portuguese;
summaries in English) 1961. a. Bs.43($10)
(Asociacion Latinoamericana de Ciencias Agricolas,
MX) Emp-Servi C.A., c/o Benilda Villalobos,
Apdo. 2224, Caracas, Venezuela. Eds. Luis
Marcano, Benilda Villalobos. charts. illus. stat.

630 PL ISSN 0080-3685
ROCZNIKI NAUK ROLNICZYCH. SERIA D.
MONOGRAFIE. (Text in Polish, English and
Russian; summaries in English and Russian) 1903.
irreg., 1976. vol. 158. price varies. (Polska
Akademia Nauk, Wydzial Nauk Rolniczych i
Lesnych) Panstwowe Wydawnictwo Naukowe, Ul.
Miodowa 10, Warsaw, Poland (Dist. by Ars Polona-
Ruch, Krakowskie Przedmiescie 7, Warsaw, Poland)
Ed. Bohdan Dobrzanski. bibl.

ROCZNIKI NAUK ROLNICZYCH. SERIA H.
RYBACTWO. see FISH AND FISHERIES

630 UK ISSN 0080-4134
ROYAL AGRICULTURAL SOCIETY OF
ENGLAND. JOURNAL. 1839. a. £2 to non-
members. Royal Agricultural Society of England,
National Agricultural Centre, Kenilworth,
Warwickshire, England. adv. index. circ. 19,000.

630 UK
ROYAL BATH & WEST SHOW CATALOGUE.
1852. a. £1. Royal Bath and West and Southern
Counties Society, The Showground, Shepton Mallet,
Somerset BA4 6QN, England. adv. circ. 4,500.
  Formerly: Bath & West Show Catalogue.

630 UK
ROYAL HIGHLAND AND AGRICULTURAL
SOCIETY OF SCOTLAND. SHOW GUIDE AND
REVIEW. 1969. a. 30p. Royal Highland and
Agricultural Society of Scotland, Ingliston,
Newbridge, Midlothian, Scotland. Ed. J. D. G.
Davidson. adv. circ. 16,000. (tabloid format)

338.01 AT ISSN 0067-2106
RURAL INDUSTRY DIRECTORY. 1958. a. free.
Department of Primary Industry, Canberra, A. C.T.
2600, Australia.
  Former titles: Australian Agriculture, Fisheries
and Forestry Directory; Australian Primary Industry
Organizations.

630 UK ISSN 0141-898X
RURAL TECHNOLOGY GUIDE. 1977. irreg. £0.90.
Tropical Products Institute, 56-62 Gray's Inn Rd.,
London WC1X 8LU, England.

630 AT ISSN 0080-5009
RUTHERGLEN, AUSTRALIA. RESEARCH
STATION. DIGEST OF RECENT RESEARCH.
1969. a. free. Department of Agriculture,
Information Officer, Treasury Gardens, Melbourne,
Victoria 3002, Australia. circ. 1,000.

630 NR ISSN 0080-5769
SAMARU MISCELLANEOUS PAPER. 1963. irreg.
price varies. Ahmadu Bello University, Institute for
Agricultural Research, P. M. B. 1044, Zaria,
Nigeria.

630 NR ISSN 0080-5777
SAMARU RESEARCH BULLETIN. 1960. price
varies. Ahmadu Bello University, Institute for
Agricultural Research, P.M.B. 1044, Zaria, Nigeria.

630 MY ISSN 0080-6420
SARAWAK. DEPARTMENT OF AGRICULTURE.
RESEARCH BRANCH. ANNUAL REPORT.
(Text in English) 1962/63. a, latest 1977. M.10. ‡
Department of Agriculture, Research Branch, P.O.
Box 977, Kuching, Sarawak, Malaysia.

630 CN ISSN 0080-648X
SASKATCHEWAN. DEPARTMENT OF
AGRICULTURE. FAMILY FARM
IMPROVEMENT BRANCH. TECHNICAL
BULLETIN. 1961. irreg. free. Department of
Agriculture, Family Farm Improvement Branch,
1318 Winnipeg St., Regina, Sask. S4R 1J6, Canada.

630 UK ISSN 0143-8654
SCHOOL OF AGRICULTURE, ABERDEEN.
ANNUAL REPORT. a. North of Scotland College
of Agriculture, 581 King St., Aberdeen AB9 1UD,
Scotland.
  Formerly: North of Scotland College of
Agriculture, Aberdeen. Annual Report (ISSN 0550-
8525)

630 340 AU
SCHRIFTENREIHE FUER AGRARWIRTSCHAFT.
irreg., vol. 14, 1979. price varies. Oesterreichische
Gesellschaft Agrarrecht, Peter Jordan Strasse 82, A-
1190 Vienna, Austria. Ed. Karl Korinek.

SEOUL NATIONAL UNIVERSITY. FACULTY
PAPERS. BIOLOGY AND AGRICULTURE
SERIES. see BIOLOGY

SHINSHU UNIVERSITY. FACULTY OF TEXTILE
SCIENCE AND TECHNOLOGY. JOURNAL.
SERIES A: BIOLOGY. see BIOLOGY

638.2 JA
SHINSHU UNIVERSITY. FACULTY OF TEXTILE
SCIENCE AND TECHNOLOGY. JOURNAL.
SERIES E: AGRICULTURE AND
SERICULTURE. (Text in Japanese and English)
1955. irreg. exchange basis. Shinshu University,
Faculty of Textile Science and Technology -
Shinshu Daigaku Sen'i Gakubu, 3-15-1 Tokida,
Ueda, Nagano 386, Japan.

AGRICULTURE

630   SA   ISSN 0002-1393
SOUTH AFRICA. DEPARTMENT OF AGRICULTURAL TECHNICAL SERVICES. AGRICULTURAL BULLETINS. (Editions in Afrikaans and English) 1925. 10-12/yr. price varies. ‡ Department of Agricultural Technical Services, Private Bag X144, Petoria 0001, South Africa (Orders to: Government Printer, Bosman St., Private Bag X85, Pretoria 0001, South Africa) charts. illus. stat. circ. 1,100. (reprint service avail. from UMI) Indexed: Biol.Abstr.

630   SA   ISSN 0081-2145
SOUTH AFRICA. DEPARTMENT OF AGRICULTURAL TECHNICAL SERVICES. AGRICULTURAL RESEARCH. (Each yr. consists of 5 sections) 1961. a. free. Department of Agricultural Technical Services, Private Bag X144, Pretoria 0001, South Africa (Orders to: Government Printer, Bosman St., Private Bag X85, Pretoria 0001, South Africa) Ed. P. Steyn. circ. 100. (reprint service avail. from UMI)

630   SA
SOUTH AFRICA. DEPARTMENT OF AGRICULTURAL TECHNICAL SERVICES. OFFICIAL LIST OF PROFESSIONAL RESEARCH WORKERS, LECTURING STAFF AND EXTENSION WORKERS IN THE AGRICULTURAL FIELD. 1965. a. free. ‡ Department of Agricultural Technical Services, Private Bag X144, Pretoria 0001, South Africa (Orders to: Government Printer, Bosman St., Private Bag X85, Pretoria 0001, South Africa) circ. controlled. (reprint service avail. from UMI)
Formerly: South Africa. Department of Agricultural Technical Services. List of Research Workers and Lecturing Staff in the Agricultural Field.

630   SA   ISSN 0081-2153
SOUTH AFRICA. DEPARTMENT OF AGRICULTURAL TECHNICAL SERVICES. REPORT OF THE SECRETARY FOR AGRICULTURAL TECHNICAL SERVICES. 1960/61. a. price varies. ‡ Department of Agricultural Technical Services, Private Bag X144, Pretoria 0001, South Africa (Orders to: Government Printer, Bosman St., Private Bag X85, Pretoria 0001, South Africa) circ. 1,000. (reprint service aval. from UMI)

630   SA   ISSN 0038-1934
SOUTH AFRICA. DEPARTMENT OF AGRICULTURAL TECHNICAL SERVICES. SCIENCE BULLETINS. (Text in Afrikaans & English) 1911. irreg. Department of Agricultural Technical Services, Private Bag X144, Pretoria 0001, South Africa (Orders to: Government Printer, Bosman St., Private Bag X85, Pretoria 0001, South Africa) charts. illus. stat. Indexed: Biol.Abstr. Chem.Abstr.

630   SA   ISSN 0081-2161
SOUTH AFRICA. DEPARTMENT OF AGRICULTURAL TECHNICAL SERVICES. SPECIAL PUBLICATION. irreg. Department of Agricultural Technical Services, Private Bag X144, Pretoria 0001, South Africa (Orders to: Government Printer, Bosman St., Private Bag X85, Pretoria 0001, South Africa) (reprint service avail. from UMI)

630   SA   ISSN 0081-217X
SOUTH AFRICA. DEPARTMENT OF AGRICULTURAL TECHNICAL SERVICES. TECHNICAL COMMUNICATION. 1960. irreg.; no. 118, 1974. free. ‡ Department of Agricultural Technical Services, Private Bag X144, Pretoria 0001, South Africa (Orders to: Government Printer, Bosman St., Private Bag X85, Pretoria 0001, South Africa) Ed. P. Steyn. circ. 1,100. (reprint service aval. from UMI)

630   AT
SOUTH AUSTRALIA. DEPARTMENT OF AGRICULTURE. FOCUS ON EXTENSION. 1977. irreg. free. Department of Agriculture, Box 1671, Adelaide, S.A. 5001, Australia. Ed. L. Coleman.
Formerly: South Australia. Department of Agriculture and Fisheries. Focus on Extension.

338.1   SP   ISSN 0085-6541
SPAIN. DIRECCION GENERAL DE CAPACITACION Y EXTENSION AGRARIAS RESUMEN DE ACTIVIDADES. 1963. a. free. ‡ Direccion General de Capacitacion y Extension Agrarias, Bravo Murillo 101, Madrid 20, Spain. charts. illus. stat. circ. 2,500.

630   SP
SPAIN. INSTITUTO NACIONAL DE INVESTIGACIONES AGRARIAS. ANALES. SERIE: GENERAL. (Text in Spanish; summaries in English, French, German) 1971. irreg (approx 1-2/yr) 300 ptas. per issue. Instituto Nacional de Investigaciones Agrarias, General Sanjurjo 56, Madrid 3, Spain. circ. 1,500.
Supersedes in part: Spain. Instituto Nacional de Investigaciones Agronomicas. Anales.

630 500   SP   ISSN 0210-3338
SPAIN. INSTITUTO NACIONAL DE INVESTIGACIONES AGRARIAS. ANALES. SERIE: RECURSOS NATURALES. (Subseries of Instituto Nacional de Investigaciones Agrarias. Anales) (Text in Spanish; summaries in English) irreg. 300 ptas. per no. Instituto Nacional de Investigaciones Agrarias, General Sanjurjo 56, Madrid 3, Spain. bibl. charts. illus. stat.

630   SP
SPAIN. INSTITUTO NACIONAL DE INVESTIGACIONES AGRARIAS. ANALES. SERIE: TECHNOLOGIA. (Text in Spanish; summaries in English, French, German) irreg. 300 ptas. per no. Instituto Nacional de Investigaciones Agrarias, General Sanjurjo 56, Madrid 3, Spain. bibl, charts, stat.

630   SP
SPAIN. INSTITUTO NACIONAL DE INVESTIGACIONES AGRARIAS. COMUNICACIONES. SERIE: GENERAL. (Text in English or Spanish) no. 3, 1978. irreg. Instituto Nacional de Investigaciones Agrarias, General Sanjurjo 56, Madrid 3, Spain. bibl. charts. illus.

630   SP   ISSN 0210-329X
SPAIN. INSTITUTO NACIONAL DE INVESTIGACIONES AGRARIAS. COMUNICACIONES. SERIE: PRODUCCION VEGETAL. no. 19, 1978. irreg. Instituto Nacional de Investigaciones Agrarias, General Sanjurjo 56, Madrid 3, Spain. bibl. charts.

630   UN   ISSN 0081-4539
STATE OF FOOD AND AGRICULTURE. (Text in English, French and Spanish) 1947. a. price varies. Food and Agriculture Organization of the United Nations, Distribution and Sales Section, Via delle Terme di Caracalla, Rome, Italy (Dist. in U.S. by: Unipub, 345 Park Ave. S., New York, NY 10010)

630   EI   ISSN 0081-4946
STATISTICAL OFFICE OF THE EUROPEAN COMMUNITIES. STATISTIQUE AGRICOLE. 1961. irreg., 6-8 issues per yr. 15000 Fr.($36.20) includes yearbook. B.P. 1907, Luxembourg, Luxembourg (Dist. in the U.S. by: European Community Information Service, 2100 M St., NW, Suite 707, Washington, DC 20037)

338.1 630   GW   ISSN 0072-1581
STATISTISCHES JAHRBUCH UEBER ERNAEHRUNG, LANDWIRTSCHAFT UND FORSTEN DER BUNDESREPUBLIK DEUTSCHLAND. 1956. a. DM.96. Bundesministerium fuer Ernaehrung, Landwirtschaft und Forsten, Abteilung 2, 5300 Bonn, W. Germany (B.R.D.) Ed. K. Haefner.

630   US   ISSN 0069-8997
STORRS AGRICULTURAL EXPERIMENT STATION. RESEARCH REPORT. 1964. irreg., no. 55, 1979. price varies, usually free. ‡ Storrs Agricultural Experiment Station, University of Connecticut, Storrs, CT 06268. circ. 550(approx.)

630   US
STORRS AGRICULTURAL EXPERIMENT STATION. BULLETIN. 1888. irreg., no. 452, 1979. price varies, usually free. Storrs Agricultural Experiment Station, University of Connecticut, Storrs, CT 06268. circ. 550.

SUGAR INDUSTRY'S WHO'S WHO AND DIRECTORY. see *BIOGRAPHY*

630   US   ISSN 0160-0680
SULPHUR IN AGRICULTURE. 1977. a. free to qualified personnel. Sulphur Institute, 1725 K Street, N.W., Washington, DC 20006. Ed. J. S. Platou. circ. 3,000. (back issues avail.)
Supersedes: Sulphur Institute Journal (ISSN 0039-4904)

630   SW
SVERIGES LANTBRUKSUNIVERSITET. INSTITUTIONEN FOER VAEXTODLING. RAPPORTER OCH ARHANDLINGAR. 1973. irreg. Sveriges Lantbruksuniversitet, Institutionen foer Vaextodling - Swedish University of Agricultural Sciences, Department of Plant Husbandry, Box 7043, S-750 07 Uppsala, Sweden.
Formerly (until 1977): Lantbrukshoegskolan Institutionen foer Vaextodling. Rapporter och Arhandlingar (ISSN 0346-7236)

338.1   SQ
SWAZILAND. CENTRAL STATISTICAL OFFICE. CENSUS OF INDIVIDUAL TENURE FARMS. 1968/69. a?, latest 1975/76. eO.25. Central Statistical Office, P.O. Box 456, Mbabane, Swaziland. stat. circ. 600. (processed)

354.68   SQ
SWAZILAND. MINISTRY OF AGRICULTURE. ANNUAL REPORT. 1967. a. Ministry of Agriculture, Mbabane, Swaziland. stat.

630 581   CH
TAIWAN AGRICULTURAL RESEARCH INSTITUTE. RESEARCH SUMMARY. irreg., latest June 1975. Taiwan Agricultural Research Institute, Taichung, Taiwan, Republic of China.

630   CH
TAIWAN AGRICULTURAL RESEARCH INSTITUTE. ANNUAL REPORT. (Text in Chinese) 1946. a. Taiwan Agricultural Research Institute, Taichung, Taiwan, Republic of China. charts. illus. stat.

630 581   CH
TAIWAN AGRICULTURAL RESEARCH INSTITUTE. BULLETIN. (Text in Chinese and English) 1950. irreg. Taiwan Agricultural Research Institute, Taichung, Taiwan, Republic of China. charts. illus. stat.

630   JA   ISSN 0082-156X
TAMAGAWA UNIVERSITY. FACULTY OF AGRICULTURE. BULLETIN. (Text in English, German and Japanese; summaries in English and German) 1960. a. available on exchange. Tamagawa University, Faculty of Agriculture - Tamagawa Daigaku Nogakubu, 6-1-1 Tamagawagakuen, Machida, Tokyo 194, Japan.

630 070   GW   ISSN 0082-1845
TASCHENBUCH FUER AGRARJOURNALISTEN. 1957. a. DM.29.50. (Verband der Agrarjournalisten) B. Behr's Verlag GmbH, Averhoffstr. 10, 2000 Hamburg 76, W. Germany (B.R.D.)

630   AT   ISSN 0082-1993
TASMANIA. DEPARTMENT OF AGRICULTURE. ANNUAL REPORT. a. free. ‡ Department of Agriculture, Box 192 B, G.P.O., Hobart, Tasmania, Australia.

630   IS   ISSN 0333-5879
TECHNION-ISRAEL INSTITUTE OF TECHNOLOGY. FACULTY OF AGRICULTURAL ENGINEERING. PUBLICATIONS. (Text in English & Hebrew) 1964. irreg. Technion-Israel Institute of Technology, Faculty of Agricultural Engineering, Haifa 32000, Israel. circ. controlled.

630   PE
TIERRA Y SOCIEDAD. 1978. irreg. Archivo del Fuero Agrario, Paita 429, Lima, Peru.

630   JA
TOHOKU UNIVERSITY. INSTITUTE FOR AGRICULTURAL RESEARCH. REPORTS. (Text in English) 1949. a. free. Tohoku University, Institute for Agricultural Research - Tohoku Daigaku Nogaku Kenkyusho, 2-1-1 Katahira, Sendai 980, Japan.
Formerly: Tohoku University. Research Institutes. Science Reports. Series D: Agriculture (ISSN 0082-4666)

631.3   DK   ISSN 0563-8887
TOOLS AND TILLAGE; a journal on the history of the implements of cultivation and other agricultural processes. (Text in English; summaries in German) 1968. a. Nationalmuseet, Oplysningsafdelingen, Ny Vestergade 10, DK-1471 Copenhagen K, Denmark. Ed. Bd. bk. rev. charts. illus.

630.7   JA   ISSN 0082-5360
TOTTORI UNIVERSITY. FACULTY OF AGRICULTURE. JOURNAL. (Text in European languages) 1951. a. exchange basis only. Tottori University, Faculty of Agriculture - Tottori Daigakubu, 1-1 Koyama-cho, Tottori 680, Japan. Ed.Bd.

TRAINING FOR AGRICULTURE AND RURAL DEVELOPMENT. see *EDUCATION — Adult Education*

630   TU   ISSN 0082-6928
TURKEY. DEVLET ISTATISTIK ENSTITUSU. TARIM ISTATISTIKLERI OZETI/SUMMARY OF AGRICULTURAL STATISTICS. (Text in Turkish and English) 1963. a. free or on exchange basis. State Institute of Statistics, Necatibey Caddesi 114, Ankara, Turkey.

630   TU   ISSN 0082-6936
TURKEY. DEVLET ISTATISTIK ENSTITUSU. TARIMSAL YAPI VE URETIM/ AGRICULTURAL STRUCTURE AND PRODUCTION. (Text in English and Turkish) 1951. a. free. State Institute of Statistics, Necatibey Caddesi 114, Ankara, Turkey.

630   II   ISSN 0067-3471
U A S EXTENSION SERIES. 1967. irreg., 1979, no. 8. University of Agricultural Sciences, Bangalore, Communication Centre, Hebbal, Bangalore 560024, Karnataka, India. Ed. B. V. Venkata Rao. circ. 500. (also avail. in microform from UMI; reprint service avail. from ISI and UMI)

630   II   ISSN 0067-348X
U A S MISCELLANEOUS SERIES. 1965. irreg., no. 26, 1975. price varies. University of Agricultural Sciences, Bangalore, Communication Centre, Hebbal, Bangalore 560024, Karnataka, India. Ed. B. V. Venkata Rao. circ. 500. (also avail. in microform from UMI; reprint service avail. from ISI and UMI)

U S-CANADIAN RANGE MANAGEMENT; a selected bibliography on ranges, pastures, wildlife, livestock, and ranching. see *BIBLIOGRAPHIES*

630   US
U S S R REPORT: AGRICULTURE. irreg. (approx. 53/yr.) $212. U.S. Joint Publications Research Service, 1000 N. Glebe Rd., Arlington, VA 22201 (Orders to: NTIS, Springfield, VA 22161)
Former titles: Translations on U S S R Agriculture; Translations on Soviet Agriculture.

630 370   FR   ISSN 0082-7711
UNION NATIONALE DE L'ENSEIGNEMENT AGRICOLE PRIVE. ANNUAIRE. 1968. a. Union Nationale de l'Enseignement Agricole Prive, 277 rue Saint-Jacques, 75005 Paris, France.

630.8   US   ISSN 0092-1785
U. S. AGRICULTURAL RESEARCH SERVICE. A R S-N C. 1972. irreg., no. 20, 1975. ‡ U.S. Science and Education Administration, North Central Region, 2000 W. Pioneer Parkway, Peoria, IL 61614. Ed. Lovell S. Glasscock. illus. Key Title: A.R.S. N.C. Agricultural Research Service. North Central Region.

630.8   US   ISSN 0092-1939
U. S. AGRICULTURAL RESEARCH SERVICE. A R S-S. irreg. U.S. Science and Education Administration, Southern Region, P. O. Box 53326, New Orleans, LA 70153. illus. Key Title: A.R.S. S. Agricultural Research Service. Southern Region.

630   US   ISSN 0082-9315
U. S. BUREAU OF THE CENSUS. CENSUS OF AGRICULTURE. 1840. quinquennial. price varies. U.S. Bureau of the Census, Dept. of Commerce, Washington, DC 20233 (Orders to: Supt. of Documents, Washington, DC 20402)

338.109   US   ISSN 0082-9714
U.S. DEPARTMENT OF AGRICULTURE. AGRICULTURAL STATISTICS. 1936. a. $5.15. U.S. Department of Agriculture., 14th St. & Independence Ave. S.W., Washington, DC 20250 (Orders to: Supt. of Documents, Washington, DC 20402)

630   US   ISSN 0065-4612
U.S. DEPARTMENT OF AGRICULTURE. AGRICULTURE HANDBOOK. 1940. irreg. price varies. U.S. Department of Agriculture, Washington, DC 20250.

630.82   US   ISSN 0065-4639
U.S. DEPARTMENT OF AGRICULTURE. AGRICULTURE INFORMATION BULLETIN. 1949. irreg. U.S. Department of Agriculture, Washington, DC 20250.

630   US
U.S. DEPARTMENT OF AGRICULTURE. ECONOMICS, STATISTICS AND COOPERATIVES SERVICE. COOPERATIVE INFORMATION REPORT. 1977. irreg. free. U.S. Department of Agriculture, Economics, Statistics and Cooperatives Service, 550 GHI Building, Washington, DC 20250.
Supersedes: U.S. Department of Agriculture. Farmer Cooperative Service. Information (Series) (ISSN 0082-9765)

631   US
U.S. DEPARTMENT OF AGRICULTURE. ECONOMICS, STATISTICS AND COOPERATIVES SERVICE. STATISTICS OF FARMER COOPERATIVES. a. free. U.S. Department of Agriculture, Economics, Statistics and Cooperatives Service, 550 GHI Building, Washington, DC 20250.
Supersedes: U.S. Department of Agriculture. Farmer Cooperative Service. Statistics of Farmer Cooperatives (ISSN 0081-5128)

630   US   ISSN 0082-9803
U. S. DEPARTMENT OF AGRICULTURE. REPORT OF THE SECRETARY OF AGRICULTURE. 1862. a. free. U. S. Department of Agriculture, Office of Communication, Washington, DC 20250.

630   US   ISSN 0082-9811
U.S. DEPARTMENT OF AGRICULTURE. TECHNICAL BULLETIN. 1927. irreg. U.S. Department of Agriculture., Washington, DC 20250.

630.58   US   ISSN 0084-3628
U.S. DEPARTMENT OF AGRICULTURE. YEARBOOK OF AGRICULTURE. 1894. a. price varies. U. S. Department of Agriculture, 14th St. & Independence Ave. S.W., Washington, DC 20250.

630   VE   ISSN 0041-8285
UNIVERSIDAD CENTRAL DE VENEZUELA. FACULTAD DE AGRONOMIA. REVISTA. (Text in Spanish; occasionally in English and French) 1952. irreg. free on exchange. Universidad Central de Venezuela, Facultad de Agronomia, Comision de Informacion y Documentacion, Apartado 4579, Maracay, Venezuela. Ed. Francisco Fernandez Yepez. bibl. charts. illus. stat. circ. 1,500. Indexed: Biol.Abstr. Chem.Abstr. Nutr.Abstr. Agrindex. Ind.Agr.Am.Lat.Caribe.

630   UY   ISSN 0077-1279
UNIVERSIDAD DE LA REPUBLICA. FACULTAD DE AGRONOMIA. PUBLICACION MISCELANEA.* 1956. irreg. Universidad de Uruguay, Facultad de Agronomia, Avda. Garzon 780, Montevideo, Uruguay.

630   UY   ISSN 0077-1260
UNIVERSIDAD DE URUGUAY. FACULTAD DE AGRONOMIA. BOLETIN. 1953. irreg. free on exchange. ‡ Universidad de Uruguay, Facultad de Agronomia, Avda. Garzon 780, Montevideo, Uruguay. circ. 1,000. Indexed: Biol.Abstr. Chem.Abstr.

630   BL   ISSN 0071-1276
UNIVERSIDADE DE SAO PAULO. ESCOLA SUPERIOR DE AGRICULTURA "LUIS DE QUEIROZ." ANAIS. (Text and summaries in English and Portuguese) 1944. a. $10 or on exchange. Universidade de Sao Paulo, Escola Superior de Agricultura "Luis de Queiroz", Library, P.O. Box 9, 13400 Piracicaba, Sao Paulo, Brazil. Ed.Bd. circ. 1,000.

630   BL   ISSN 0071-1292
UNIVERSIDADE DE SAO PAULO. ESCOLA SUPERIOR DE AGRICULTURA "LUIS DE QUEIROZ." BOLETIM DE DIVULGACAO. 1962. irreg., 1977, no. 23. $10 or on exchange. Universidade de Sao Paulo, Escola Superior de Agricultura "Luis de Queiroz", Box 9, 13400 Piracicaba, Sao Paulo, Brazil. circ. 500. Indexed: Biol.Abstr. Chem.Abstr. Bibl.Agri.

630   BL   ISSN 0084-8646
UNIVERSIDADE FEDERAL DO CEARA. ESCOLA DE AGRONOMIA. DEPARTAMENTO DE FITOTECNIA. RELATORIA TECNICO.* irreg. free. Universidade Federal do Ceara, Escola de Agronomia, Departamento de Filotecnia, Caixa Postal 354, Fortaleza, Ceara 60000, Brazil.

630   BL
UNIVERSIDADE FEDERAL DO RIO GRANDE DO SUL. FACULDADE DE AGRONOMIA. BOLETIM TECNICO. (Text in Portuguese; summaries in English) irreg. Universidade Federal do Rio Grande do Sul, Faculdade de Agronomia, Bento Goncalves 7712, Caixa Postal 776, 90000 Porto Alegre, R.S., Brazil. charts. illus. circ. 300. Indexed: Biol.Abstr. Chem.Abstr. Field Crop Abstr.

630   IT   ISSN 0082-6871
UNIVERSITA DELGI STUDI DI TORINO. FACOLTA DI SCIENZE AGRARIE. ANNALI. (Text in Italian; summaries in English) 1962. a. available on exchange. Universita degli Studi di Torino, Facolta di Scienze Agrarie, Via P. Giuria 15, 10126 Turin, Italy. Ed. Italo Currado. index. circ. 600. Indexed: Biol.Abstr.

630   AU
UNIVERSITAET FUER BODENKULTUR IN WIEN. DISSERTATIONEN. 1972. irreg., no. 9, 1978. price varies. (Universitaet fuer Bodenkultur in Wien) Verband der Wissenschaftlichen Gesellschaften Oesterreichs, Lindengasse 37, A-1070 Vienna, Austria.
Formerly: Hochschule fuer Bodenkultur in Wien. Dissertationen.

630   GW   ISSN 0075-4609
UNIVERSITAET GIESSEN. ERGEBNISSE LANDWIRTSCHAFTLICHER FORSCHUNG. 1956. irreg. Universitaet Giessen, Landgraf-Philipp-Platz 4, 6300 Giessen, W. Germany (B.R.D.)

630   GW
UNIVERSITAET KIEL. AGRARWISSENSCHAFTLICHE FAKULTAET. SCHRIFTENREIHE. 1950. irreg., no. 59, 1978. price varies. Verlag Paul Parey (Hamburg), Spitalerstr. 12, 2000 Hamburg 1, W. Germany (B.R.D.) bibl. illus. index. (reprint service avail. from ISI)

630   SQ
UNIVERSITY COLLEGE OF SWAZILAND. AGRICULTURAL RESEARCH DIVISION. ANNUAL REPORT. 1970. a. University College of Swaziland, Agricultural Research Division, Swaziland Campus, P.O. Luyengo, Swaziland.
Former titles: University of Botswana, Lesotho and Swaziland. Agricultural Research Division. Annual Report; University of Botswana, Lesotho and Swaziland. Faculty of Agriculture. Research Division. Annual Report; Swaziland. Department of Agriculture. Research Division. Report.

630   II   ISSN 0067-3455
UNIVERSITY OF AGRICULTURAL SCIENCES, BANGALORE. ANNUAL REPORT. 1964-65. a. Rs.15. University of Agricultural Sciences, Bangalore, Communication Centre, Hebbal, Bangalore 560024, Karnataka, India. Ed. B. V. Venkata Rao. circ. 1,000. (also avail. in microform from UMI; reprint service avail. ISI and UMI)

630   II
UNIVERSITY OF AGRICULTURAL SCIENCES, BANGALORE. COLLABORATIVE SERIES. (Text in English) 1968. irreg., no. 3, 1976. price varies. University of Agricultural Sciences, Bangalore, Communication Centre, Hebbal, Bangalore 560024, Karnataka, India. (reprint service avail. from ISI and UMI)

AGRICULTURE

630   II
UNIVERSITY OF AGRICULTURAL SCIENCES, BANGALORE. EDUCATIONAL SERIES. (Text in English) 1969. irreg., no. 7, 1981. price varies. University of Agricultural Sciences, Bangalore, Communication Centre, Hebbal, Bangalore 560024, Karnataka, India. (reprint service avail. from ISI and UMI)

630   II
UNIVERSITY OF AGRICULTURAL SCIENCES, BANGALORE. INFORMATION SERIES. (Text in English) irreg., no. 9, 1981. price varies. University of Agricultural Sciences, Bangalore, Communication Centre, Hebbal, Bangalore 560024, Karnataka, India. (reprint service avail. from ISI and UMI)

630   II
UNIVERSITY OF AGRICULTURAL SCIENCES, BANGALORE. RESEARCH MONOGRAPH SERIES. irreg., no. 9, 1981. price varies. University of Agricultural Sciences, Bangalore, Communication Centre, Hebbal, Bangalore 560024, Karnataka, India. (reprint service avail. from ISI and UMI)

630   II   ISSN 0067-3463
UNIVERSITY OF AGRICULTURAL SCIENCES, BANGALORE. RESEARCH SERIES. 1968. irreg., no. 15, 1973. price varies. University of Agricultural Sciences, Bangalore, Communication Centre, Hebbal, Bangalore 560024, Karnataka, India. Ed. B. V. Venkata Rao. circ. 500. (also avail. in microform from UMI; reprint service avail. from ISI and UMI)

630   II
UNIVERSITY OF AGRICULTURAL SCIENCES, BANGALORE. TECHNICAL INFORMATION SERIES. (Text in Kannada) 1975. irreg. price varies. University of Agricultural Sciences, Bangalore, Communication Centre, Hebbal, Bangalore 560024, Karnataka, India. (reprint service avail. from ISI and UMI)

630   II
UNIVERSITY OF AGRICULTURAL SCIENCES, BANGALORE. TECHNICAL SERIES. (Text in English) 1973. irreg., latest issue no. 36. price varies. University of Agricultural Sciences, Bangalore, Communication Centre, Hebbal, Bangalore 560024, Karnataka, India. (reprint service avail. from ISI and UMI)

630   US   ISSN 0072-1271
UNIVERSITY OF GEORGIA. COLLEGE OF AGRICULTURE EXPERIMENT STATIONS. BULLETIN. irreg. free controlled circ. ‡ University of Georgia, College of Agriculture Experiment Stations, Barrow Hall, Athens, GA 30602. Ed. Nancy B. Bowen.

630   US   ISSN 0072-128X
UNIVERSITY OF GEORGIA. COLLEGE OF AGRICULTURE EXPERIMENT STATIONS. RESEARCH REPORTS. irreg., 1969, no. 43. controlled free circ. ‡ University of Georgia, College of Agriculture Experiment Stations, Barrow Hall, Athens, GA 30602. Ed. Nancy B. Bowen.

631.091   US   ISSN 0073-1161
UNIVERSITY OF HAWAII. COLLEGE OF TROPICAL AGRICULTURE. COOPERATIVE EXTENSION SERVICE. CIRCULAR. 1939. irreg., no. 486, 1975. University of Hawaii, College of Tropical Agriculture, Cooperative Extension Service, Honolulu, HI 96822 (Order Information Available from Publications and Information Office, 2500 Dole St., Univ. of Hawaii, Honolulu, HI 96822) circ. 1,000-10,000.
Tropical

631.091   US   ISSN 0073-117X
UNIVERSITY OF HAWAII. COLLEGE OF TROPICAL AGRICULTURE. COOPERATIVE EXTENSION SERVICE LEAFLET. 1963. irreg., no. 193, 1975. University of Hawaii, College of Tropical Agriculture, Cooperative Extension Service, Honolulu, HI 96822 (Order Information Available from Publications and Information Office, 2500 Dole St., Univ. of Hawaii, Honolulu, HI 96822) circ. 1,000-50,000.
Tropical

631.091   US   ISSN 0073-1188
UNIVERSITY OF HAWAII. COLLEGE OF TROPICAL AGRICULTURE. COOPERATIVE EXTENSION SERVICE. MISCELLANEOUS PUBLICATION. 1960. irreg., no. 121, 1975. University of Hawaii, College of Tropical Agriculture, Cooperative Extension Service, Honolulu, HI 96822 (Order Information Available from Publications and Information Office, 2500 Dole St., Univ. of Hawaii, Honolulu, HI 96822) circ. 300-2,000.
Tropical

630   NR   ISSN 0579-7195
UNIVERSITY OF IFE. FACULTY OF AGRICULTURE. ANNUAL RESEARCH REPORT. 1967. a. £N1.50. University of Ife Press, Ile-Ife, Nigeria. circ. 500.

630   US
UNIVERSITY OF ILLINOIS AT URBANA-CHAMPAIGN. AGRICULTURAL EXPERIMENT STATION. RESEARCH PROGRESS. 1888. biennial. free. University of Illinois at Urbana-Champaign, Agricultural Experiment Station, 212 Mumford Hall, Urbana, IL 61801 (Or 1301 W. Gregory Dr., Urbana, IL 61801)

630   US   ISSN 0073-5299
UNIVERSITY OF ILLINOIS AT URBANA-CHAMPAIGN. COLLEGE OF AGRICULTURE. AGRICULTURAL COMMUNICATIONS RESEARCH REPORT. 1960. irreg. free. ‡ University of Illinois at Urbana-Champaign, College of Agriculture, Office of Agricultural Communications, Urbana, IL 61801. Ed. James F. Evans. circ. 300.

630   US   ISSN 0073-5205
UNIVERSITY OF ILLINOIS AT URBANA-CHAMPAIGN. COLLEGE OF AGRICULTURE. SPECIAL PUBLICATION. 1960. irreg; no. 46, 1977. price varies. ‡ University of Illinois at Urbana-Champaign, College of Agriculture, Urbana, IL 61801. Ed. A. W. Janes.

630   CN   ISSN 0076-4051
UNIVERSITY OF MANITOBA. FACULTY OF AGRICULTURE. PROGRESS REPORT ON AGRICULTURAL RESEARCH AND EXPERIMENTATION. 1954. a. University of Manitoba, Faculty of Agriculture, Winnipeg, Man., Canada.

630.7   US   ISSN 0548-0906
UNIVERSITY OF NEBRASKA. DEPARTMENT OF AGRICULTURAL EDUCATION. REPORT.* 1967. irreg. University of Nebraska- Lincoln, Department of Agricultural Education, Lincoln, NE 68503.

630   US   ISSN 0077-8400
UNIVERSITY OF NEW HAMPSHIRE. INSTITUTE OF NATURAL AND ENVIRONMENTAL RESOURCES. RESEARCH REPORTS. irreg., latest issue, 1974. free. University of New Hampshire, Agricultural Experiment Station, Durham, NH 03824.

630 574   JA   ISSN 0474-7852
UNIVERSITY OF OSAKA PREFECTURE. BULLETIN. SERIES B: AGRICULTURE AND BIOLOGY/OSAKA-FURITSU DAIGAKU KIYO, B NOGAKU, SEIBUTSUGAKU. (Text in Japanese and European languages) 1951. a. exchange basis. University of Osaka Prefecture - Osaka-furitsu Daigaku, 4-804 Mozuume-machi, Sakai-shi, Osaka 591, Japan.

630   PH
UNIVERSITY OF THE PHILIPPINES AT LOS BANOS. AGRARIAN REFORM INSTITUTE. OCCASIONAL PAPERS. 1975. irreg. University of the Philippines at Los Banos, Agrarian Reform Institute, Laguna 3720, Philippines.

630   JA   ISSN 0485-7828
UNIVERSITY OF THE RYUKYUS. COLLEGE OF AGRICULTURE. SCIENCE BULLETIN/ RYUKYU DAIGAKU NOGAKUBU GAKUJUTSU HOKOKU. (Text in English or Japanese) a. University of the Ryukyus, College of Agriculture - Ryukyu Daigaku Nogakubu, 3-1 Tonokura-cho, Shuri, Naha 903, Okinawa, Japan.

338.1   UV
UPPER VOLTA. SERVICE DES STATISTIQUES AGRICOLES. ANNUAIRE. a. Service des Statistiques Agricoles, Ministere du Plan, du Developpement Rural, de l'Environnement et du Tourisme, Ouagadougou, Upper Volta.

630   US
UTAH. STATE DEPARTMENT OF AGRICULTURE. BIENNIAL REPORT. 1970. biennial. free. Department of Agriculture, 147 North 200 West, Salt Lake City, UT 84103.

338.1   VE   ISSN 0083-5366
VENEZUELA. MINISTERIO DE AGRICULTURA Y CRIA. DIRECCION DE ECONOMICA Y ESTADISTICA AGROPECUARIA. ANUARIO ESTADISTICO AGROPECUARIO. 1961. a. free. Ministerio de Agricultura y Cria, Direccion de Planificacion y Estadistica, Division de Estadistica, Piso 11, Torre Norte-Caracas, Venezuela.

630   US   ISSN 0083-5706
VERMONT. AGRICULTURAL EXPERIMENT STATION, BURLINGTON. RESEARCH REPORT. 1951. irreg., no. 105, 1979. free. Vermont Agricultural Experiment Station, University of Vermont, Burlington, VT 05405. Ed. Thomas J. McCormick.
Before 1968: Vermont, Agricultural Experiment Station, Burlington. Miscellaneous Publications Series.

630   US   ISSN 0083-5714
VERMONT. AGRICULTURAL EXPERIMENT STATION, BURLINGTON. STATION BULLETIN SERIES. 1887. irreg., no. 685, 1980. free. Vermont Agricultural Experiment Station, University of Vermont, Morrill Hall, Burlington, VT 05405. Ed. Thomas J.McCormick.

630   US   ISSN 0083-5722
VERMONT. AGRICULTURAL EXPERIMENT STATION, BURLINGTON. STATION PAMPHLET SERIES. 1943. irreg., no. 41, 1978. free. Vermont Agricultural Experiment Station, University of Vermont, Burlington, VT 05405. Ed. Thomas J. McCormick.

630   US   ISSN 0362-3661
VIRGINIA. DIVISION OF PRODUCT AND INDUSTRY REGULATION. INSPECTION SERVICE SECTION. ANNUAL REPORT. a. Department of Agriculture and Commerce, Division of Product and Industry Regulation, 203 N. Governor St., Room 304, Richmond, VA 23219. Key Title: Annual Report - Inspection Service Section.

630.8   US   ISSN 0097-1510
VIRGINIA POLYTECHNIC INSTITUTE AND STATE UNIVERSITY. RESEARCH REPORT. irreg. Virginia Polytechnic Institute and State University, Research Division, Blacksburg, VA 24061. Key Title: Research Division Report - Virginia Polytechnic Institute and State University.

630 634.9   US
WEST VIRGINIA. AGRICULTURAL AND FORESTRY EXPERIMENT STATION. BULLETIN. 1888. free. West Virginia University, Agricultural and Forestry Experiment Station, College of Agriculture and Forestry, Morgantown, WV 26506.

630 634.9   US
WEST VIRGINIA. AGRICULTURAL AND FORESTRY EXPERIMENT STATION. RESOURCE MANAGEMENT SERIES. 1971. irreg. free. West Virginia University, Agricultural and Forestry Experiment Station, College of Agriculture and Forestry, Morgantown, WV 26506.

630   US   ISSN 0083-8381
WEST VIRGINIA. AGRICULTURAL EXPERIMENT STATION, MORGANTOWN. CURRENT REPORT. 1952. irreg., 1976, no. 67. free. West Virginia University, Agricultural Experiment Station, Morgantown, WV 26506. Ed. John Luchok. circ. 5,000.

630   AT
WESTERN AUSTRALIA. DEPARTMENT OF AGRICULTURE. BULLETIN. 1905? irreg. Department of Agriculture, Jarrah Rd., South Perth, WA 6151, Australia.

AGRICULTURE — ABSTRACTING, BIBLIOGRAPHIES, STATISTICS

630   AT   ISSN 0083-8675
WESTERN AUSTRALIA. DEPARTMENT OF AGRICULTURE. TECHNICAL BULLETIN. 1969. irreg. free. ‡ Department of Agriculture, Jarrah Rd., South Perth W.A. 6151, Australia. Ed. L. English. circ. 350-600. (back issues avail.) Indexed: Aus.Sci.Ind.

630   US
WHAT'S DEVELOPING IN ALASKA. irreg. University of Alaska, Cooperative Extension Service, Fairbanks, AK 99701.

630   CN
WHO'S WHO IN BRITISH COLUMBIA AGRICULTURE. 1978. a. Can.$5. Country Life Ltd., 1345 Johnston Rd., White Rock, B.C. V4B 3Z3, Canada.

630   UK
WHO'S WHO IN WORLD AGRICULTURE. (2 Vols.) 1979. irreg. £75. Longman Group Ltd., Longman House, Burnt Mill, Harlow, Essex CM20 2JE, England (Dist. in U.S. and Canada by: Gale Research Co. Ltd., Book Tower, Detroit, MI 48226)

630   US   ISSN 0084-313X
WYOMING. AGRICULTURAL EXPERIMENT STATION, LARAMIE. BULLETIN. irreg. University of Wyoming, Agricultural Experiment Station, Box 3354, Laramie, WY 82071.

630   US   ISSN 0084-3148
WYOMING. AGRICULTURAL EXPERIMENT STATION, LARAMIE. RESEARCH JOURNAL. 1962. irreg., 1968, no. 20. $0.35. Univ. of Wyoming, Agricultural Experiment Station, Box 3354, Laramie, WY 82071. Ed. Dana Boucher.

630   US   ISSN 0084-3156
WYOMING. AGRICULTURAL EXPERIMENT STATION, LARAMIE. SCIENCE MONOGRAPH. 1966. irreg., 1971, no. 23. $1. University of Wyoming, Agricultural Experiment Station, Box 3354, Laramie, WY 82071. Ed. Dana Boucher.

630   CN   ISSN 0084-3865
YEARBOOK OF MANITOBA AGRICULTURE. 1963. a. Department of Agriculture, Publications Distribution Centre, 411 York Ave., Winnipeg, Man. R3C 3M1, Canada. circ. 4,000.

630   ZA   ISSN 0084-4853
ZAMBIA. MINISTRY OF AGRICULTURE. ANNUAL REPORT.* 1964. a. Government Printer, P.O. Box 136, Lusaka, Zambia.

630   PL   ISSN 0084-5477
ZESZYTY PROBLEMOWE POSTEPOW NAUK ROLNICZYCH. (Text and summaries in English, French, German, Polish and Russian) 1956. irreg., 1970, vol. 110. price varies. (Polska Akademia Nauk, Wydzial Nauk Rolniczych i Lesnych) Panstwowe Wydawnictwo Naukowe, Miodowa 10, Warsaw, Poland (Dist. by Ars Polona-Ruch, Krakowskie Przedmiescie 7, Warsaw, Poland) Ed. Janusz Haman.

630   RH
ZIMBABWE. CENTRAL STATISTICAL OFFICE. AGRICULTURAL PRODUCTION IN TRIBAL TRUST LAND IRRIGATION SCHEMES AND TILCOR ESTATES. 1970. a. Rhod.$0.50. Central Statistical Office, Box 8063, Causeway, Salisbury, Zimbabwe. circ. 130.
Formerly: Rhodesia. Central Statistical Office. Agricultural Production in Tribal Trust Land Irrigation Schemes.

AGRICULTURE — Abstracting, Bibliographies, Statistics

630   338.1   GR   ISSN 0065-4574
AGRICULTURAL STATISTICS OF GREECE. (Text in Greek and English) 1961. a., latest 1976. $2.50. National Statistical Service, Publications and Information Division, 14-16 Lycourgou St., Athens 112, Greece.

630   016   US   ISSN 0065-4671
AGRONOMY ABSTRACTS. 1950. a. $2 to non-members. American Society of Agronomy, Inc., 677 South Segoe Rd., Madison, WI 53711. circ. 8,000.

338.1   US   ISSN 0065-5694
ALASKA AGRICULTURAL STATISTICS. 1960. a. free. ‡ Crop and Livestock Reporting Service, P.O. Box 799, Palmer, AK 99645. Ed. DeLon A. Brown.
Formerly (1960-62): Alaska Farm Production (ISSN 0516-4850)

338.1   318   AG   ISSN 0066-7269
ARGENTINA. JUNTA NACIONAL DE CARNES. SINTESIS ESTADISTICA. Title varies; issued 1956-59, 1961-69 as: Argentine Republic. Junta Nacional de Carnes. Resena. 1934. a. Arg.$9600. ‡ Junta Nacional de Carnes, Biblioteca, San Martin 459 1 Piso, Buenos Aires, Argentina. index. circ. 2,000.

338.1   318   AG
ARGENTINA. SECRETARIA DE ESTADO DE AGRICULTURA Y GANADERIA. AREA DE TRABAJO DE LECHERIA. RESENA ESTADISTICA. 1964. irreg. free. Secretaria de Estado de Agricultura y Ganaderia, Area de Trabajo de Lecheria, Paseo Colon 922, 1063 Buenos Aires, Argentina. stat. circ. 1,000. (processed; also avail. in cards)

638.1   338.1   AT
AUSTRALIA. BUREAU OF STATISTICS. BEE KEEPING. 1972-73. a. free. Australian Bureau of Statistics, P.O. Box 10, Belconnen, A.C.T. 2616, Australia. circ. 1,200.
Formerly: Australia. Bureau of Statistics. Bee Farming. (ISSN 0587-5781)

338.1   AT
AUSTRALIA. BUREAU OF STATISTICS. DAIRYING AND DAIRY PRODUCTS. a. free. Australian Bureau of Statistics, P.O. Box 10, Belconnen, A.C.T. 2616, Australia. illus. circ. 769.
Formerly: Australia. Bureau of Statistics. Dairying Industry (ISSN 0312-6447)

636   319.4   AT
AUSTRALIA. BUREAU OF STATISTICS. LIVESTOCK STATISTICS. a. free. Australian Bureau of Statistics, Box 10, Belconnen, A.C.T. 2616, Australia. stat. circ. 2,300.

630   319.4   AT
AUSTRALIA. BUREAU OF STATISTICS. RURAL LAND USE, IMPROVEMENTS AND LABOUR. 1971. a. free. Australian Bureau of Statistics, P.O. Box 10, Belconnen, A.C.T. 2616, Australia. stat. circ. 2,300.
Formerly: Australia. Bureau of Statistics. Rural Land Use, Improvements, Agricultural Machinery and Labour.

AUSTRALIA. BUREAU OF STATISTICS. SOUTH AUSTRALIAN OFFICE. RURAL PRODUCTION. see BUSINESS AND ECONOMICS — Abstracting, Bibliographies, Statistics

634   319.4   AT
AUSTRALIA. BUREAU OF STATISTICS. TASMANIAN OFFICE. FRUIT. a. Australian Bureau of Statistics, Tasmanian Office, Box 66A, Hobart, Tasmania 7001, Australia. illus. circ. 620.
Formerly: Australia. Bureau of Statistics. Tasmanian Office. Fruit Production (ISSN 0314-1667)

631.5   319.4   AT
AUSTRALIA. BUREAU OF STATISTICS. TASMANIAN OFFICE. POTATO PRODUCTION. a. Australian Bureau of Statistics, Tasmanian Office, Box 66A, Hobart, Tasmania 7001, Australia. illus. circ. 580.
Formerly: Australia. Bureau of Statistics. Tasmanian Office. Potato Statistics (ISSN 0519-5373)

338.1   AT
AUSTRALIA. BUREAU OF STATISTICS. VALUE OF AGRICULTURAL COMMODITIES PRODUCED. a. free. Australian Bureau of Statistics, P.O. Box 10, Belconnen, A.C.T. 2616, Australia. circ. 1,066.
Formerly: Australia. Bureau of Statistics. Value of Primary Production, Excluding Mining, and Indexes of Quantum and Unit Gross Value of Agricultural Production (ISSN 0312-6242)

636   AT
AUSTRALIA. BUREAU OF STATISTICS. VICTORIAN OFFICE. LIVESTOCK. 1951. a. free. Australian Bureau of Statistics, Victorian Office, Box 2796Y, G.P.O., Melbourne, Vic. 3001, Australia. circ. 1,500.

338.1   319   AT
AUSTRALIA. BUREAU OF STATISTICS. VICTORIAN OFFICE. VALUE OF PRIMARY COMMODITIES PRODUCED (EXCLUDING MINING) 1967. a. free. Australian Bureau of Statistics, Victorian Office, Box 2796Y, G.P.O., Melbourne, Vic. 3001, Australia. circ. 750.
Formerly: Australia. Bureau of Statistics. Victorian Office. Value of Primary Production.

630   AT
AUSTRALIA. BUREAU OF STATISTICS. WESTERN AUSTRALIAN OFFICE. AGRICULTURAL STATISTICS (GENERAL SUMMARY) 1946. a. free. Australian Bureau of Statistics, Western Australian Office, 1-3 St. George's Terrace, Perth, W.A. 6000, Australia. Ed. E. Binns. circ. 500. (processed)
Formerly: Australia. Bureau of Statistics. Western Australian Office. Agricultural and Pastoral Statistics (ISSN 0067-1231)

636   AT
AUSTRALIA. BUREAU OF STATISTICS. WESTERN AUSTRALIAN OFFICE. CATTLE AND PIGS: WESTERN AUSTRALIA. a. Australian Bureau of Statistics, Western Australian Office, 1-3 St. George's Terrace, Perth, W.A. 6000, Australia.

631.7   319.4   AT
AUSTRALIA. BUREAU OF STATISTICS. WESTERN AUSTRALIAN OFFICE. RURAL LAND UTILISATION. a. Australian Bureau of Statistics, Western Australian Office, 1-3 St. George's Terrace, Perth, W.A. 6000, Australia. Ed. E. Binns. circ. 500.

631.8   AT   ISSN 0312-6269
AUSTRALIA. BUREAU OF STATISTICS. WESTERN AUSTRALIAN OFFICE. WESTERN AUSTRALIA: ARTIFICIAL FERTILISER USED ON RURAL HOLDINGS. 1964. a. free. Australian Bureau of Statistics, Western Australian Office, 1-3 St George's Tce., Perth, W.A. 6000, Australia. Ed. E. Binns. circ. 400. (processed)

630   AU
AUSTRIA. STATISTISCHES ZENTRALAMT. ERGEBNISSE DER LANDWIRTSCHAFTLICHEN MASCHINENZAEHLUNG. (Subseries of: Beitraege zur Oesterreichischen Statistik) 1953. irreg. S.130. Oesterreichische Staatsdruckerei, Vienna, Austria. circ. 500.

630   314   AU   ISSN 0067-2327
AUSTRIA. STATISTISCHES ZENTRALAMT. ERGEBNISSE DER LANDWIRTSCHAFTLICHEN STATISTIK. (Subseries of: Beitraege zur Oesterreichischen Statistik) 1946. a. S.120. ‡ Oesterreichische Staatsdruckerei, Vienna, Austria. circ. 500.

630   016   BG
BANGLADESH AGRICULTURAL SCIENCES ABSTRACTS. Other title: B A S A. (Text in English) 1974. biennial. Tk.50($20) Bangladesh Agricultural University Old Boys' Association, c/o Dept. of Soil Science, Bangladesh Agricultural University, Mymensingh, Bangladesh. (Co-sponsor: Bangladesh Agricultural Research Council) Ed. M. Eaqub. abstr. circ. 500.

630   CL
BIBLIOGRAFIA AGRICOLA CHILENA. 1977. a. $15. Instituto de Investigaciones Agropecuarias, Programa de Informacion y Documentacion, Casilla 5427, Santiago, Chile. Eds. Sonia Elso, Veronica Bravo. (back issues avail.)

633.1   016   BL
BIBLIOGRAFIA DO ARROZ. 1975. irreg. Empresa Brasileira de Assistencia Tecnica e Extensao Rural, Sistema Nacional de Informacao Rural, Brasileira, Brazil.

AGRICULTURE — ABSTRACTING, BIBLIOGRAPHIES, STATISTICS

630 016   US   ISSN 0190-7077
BIBLIOGRAPHY OF AGRICULTURAL BIBLIOGRAPHIES. irreg. U.S. Science and Education Administration, Technical Information Systems, Beltsville, MD 20705.

338.1 318   BL
BRAZIL. ESCRITORIO DE ESTATISTICA. PECUARIA, AVICULTURA, APICULTURA, SERICICULTURA. a. free. Ministerio da Agricultura, Escritorio de Estatistica, Esplanada dos Ministerios, Bloco 8-6 Andar, Rio de Janiero, Brazil. stat.

338.1 318   BL
BRAZIL. MINISTERIO DA AGRICULTURA. ESCRITORIO DE ESTATISTICA. CADASTRO DAS EMPRESAS PRODUTORAS DE OLEOS, GORDURAS VEGETAIS E SABPRODUTOS. 1970. triennial. free. Ministerio da Agricultura, Escritorio de Estatistica, Esplanada dos Ministerios, Bloco 8, 6 Andar, Brasilia 7000, Brazil. circ. 800. (processed)

338.1   US   ISSN 0527-2181
CALIFORNIA FRUIT AND NUT ACREAGE. a. California Crop and Livestock Reporting Service, Box 1258, Sacramento, CA 95814. stat.
Formerly: Production and Marketing California Grapes, Raisins and Wine (ISSN 0095-411X)

338.1   US   ISSN 0361-9095
CALIFORNIA LIVESTOCK STATISTICS. a. California Crop and Livestock Reporting Service, Box 1258, Sacramento, CA 95806.

338.1 317   CN   ISSN 0068-712X
CANADA. STATISTICS CANADA. FARM NET INCOME/REVENU NET AGRICOLE. (Catalog 21-202) (Text in English and French) 1940. a. Can.$4.50($5.40) Statistics Canada, Publications Distribution, Ottawa, Ont. K1A 0V7, Canada. (also avail. in microform from MML)

338.17   CN   ISSN 0383-008X
CANADA. STATISTICS CANADA. FRUIT AND VEGETABLE PRODUCTION/PRODUCTION DE FRUITS ET DE LEGUMES. (Catalogue 22-003) (Text in English and French) 1932. irreg(seasonal) Can.$25($30) Statistics Canada, Publications Distribution, Ottawa, Ont. K1A 0V7, Canada. (also avail. in microform from MML)

630   CN   ISSN 0068-7146
CANADA. STATISTICS CANADA. INDEX OF FARM PRODUCTION/INDICE DE LA PRODUCTION AGRICOLE. (Catalog 21-203) (Text in English and French) 1948. a. Can.$3($3.60) Statistics Canada, Publications Distribution, Ottawa, Ont. K1A 0V7, Canada. (also avail. in microform from MML)

636   CN   ISSN 0068-7154
CANADA. STATISTICS CANADA. LIVESTOCK AND ANIMAL PRODUCTS STATISTICS/STATISTIQUE DU BETAIL ET DES PRODUITS ANIMAUX. (Catalog 23-203) (Text in English and French) 1909. a. Can.$6($7.20) Statistics Canada, Publications Distribution, Ottawa, Ont. K1A 0V7, Canada. (also avail. in microform from MML)

338.1 317 633.6   CN   ISSN 0317-9672
CANADA. STATISTICS CANADA. PRODUCTION AND VALUE OF MAPLE PRODUCTS/PRODUCTION ET VALEUR DES PRODUITS DE L'ERABLE. (Catalogue 22-204) (Text in English and French) 1938. a. Can.$3($3.60) Statistics Canada, Publications Distribution, Ottawa, Ont. K1A 0V7, Canada. (also avail. in microform from MML)

636.5   CN   ISSN 0068-7189
CANADA. STATISTICS CANADA. PRODUCTION OF POULTRY AND EGGS/PRODUCTION DE VOLAILLE ET OEUFS. (Catalog 23-202) (Text in English and French) 1936. a. Can.$4.50($5.40) Statistics Canada, Publications Distribution, Ottawa, Ont. K1A 0V7, Canada. (also avail. in microform from MML)

338.1   CN   ISSN 0527-6179
CANADA. STATISTICS CANADA. SHORN WOOL PRODUCTION/PRODUCTION DE LAINE TONDUE. (Catalog 23-204) (Text in English and French) 1931. a. Can.$3($3.60) Statistics Canada, Publications Distribution, Ottawa, Ont. K1A 0V7, Canada. (also avail. in microform from MML)

338 633.83   II
CARDAMOM STATISTICS. (Text in English) irreg. Cardamom Board, Chittoor Rd., Cochin 682018, India.

338.1 016   UK   ISSN 0305-1552
COMMONWEALTH BUREAU OF AGRICULTURAL ECONOMICS. ANNOTATED BIBLIOGRAPHIES SERIES A. 1971. irreg. price varies. Commonwealth Agricultural Bureaux, Farnham House, Farnham Royal, Slough SL2 3BN, England. abstr. bibl. index. circ. 2,000. Indexed: Sociol.Abstr. Geo.Abstr.

338.1 016   UK   ISSN 0305-1552
COMMONWEALTH BUREAU OF AGRICULTURAL ECONOMICS. ANNOTATED BIBLIOGRAPHIES. SERIES B: AGRICULTURAL POLICY AND RURAL DEVELOPMENT IN AFRICA. 1971. irreg. price varies. Commonwealth Agricultural Bureaux, Farnham House, Farnham Royal, Slough SL2 3BN, England. Ed. M. A. Bellamy. abstr. bibl. index. Indexed: Sociol.Abstr. Afr.Abstr. Geo.Abstr.

631.4 016   UK   ISSN 0305-2524
COMMONWEALTH BUREAU OF SOILS. ANNOTATED BIBLIOGRAPHIES. 1965. irreg. price varies. Commonwealth Bureau of Soils, Rothampstead Experimental Station, Harpenden, Herts AL5 2JQ, England.

633   US   ISSN 0070-0681
COTTON GINNINGS IN THE UNITED STATES. 1900. a. $0.75. U. S. Bureau of the Census, Subscriber Services Section (Publications), Washington, DC 20233.
Formerly: Cotton Production in the United States.

338.1 314   DK   ISSN 0070-3559
DENMARK. DANMARKS STATISTIK. LANDBRUGSSTATISTIK HERUNDER GARTNERI OG SKOVBRUG/STATISTICS ON AGRICULTURE, GARDENING AND FORESTRY. (Subseries of its Statistiske Meddelelser) 1936. a. Kr.12.80. Danmarks Statistik, Sejroegade 11, 2100 Copenhagen OE, Denmark. index.

338.1 314   NE
E E G VADEMECUM/SELECTED AGRI-FIGURES OF THE E.E.C. (Text in Dutch, English, French, and German) 1960. biennial. free. Ministerie van Landbouw en Visserij, Statistics and Documentation Section - Ministry of Agriculture and Fisheries, Kon. Julianaplein 3, The Hague, Netherlands.
Formerly: Geselecteerde Agrarische Cijfers van de E E C (ISSN 0072-4211)

633 310   ES
EL SALVADOR. DIRECCION GENERAL DE ECONOMIA AGROPECUARIA. PROGNOSTICO DE ZAFRA. irreg. Direccion General de Economia Agropecuaria, Boulevard de los Heroes, Edificio Lationamericano, San Salvador, El Salvador. stat.

016 630   UN   ISSN 0532-0291
F A O LIBRARY LIST OF RECENT ACCESSIONS. Food and Agriculture Organization of the United Nations, Distribution and Sales Section, Via delle Terme di Caracalla, I-0010 Rome, Italy.

338.1 314   UK
FARM BUSINESS STATISTICS FOR SOUTH EAST ENGLAND. 1969. a. price varies. Wye College (University of London), School of Rural Economics & Related Studies, Farm Business Unit, Nr. Ashford, Kent, England. Ed. Bd. charts. stat. circ. 800.

338.1   NZ   ISSN 0110-084X
FARMING STATISTICS. a. free. Department of Lands and Survey, Wellington, New Zealand. circ. 150.

631.8   II   ISSN 0430-327X
FERTILISER ASSOCIATION OF INDIA. FERTILISER STATISTICS. (Text in English) 1956. a. Rs.25. Fertiliser Association of India, Near Jawaharlal Nehru University, New Delhi 110067, India. Ed. Bd. charts. stat.

630   UN
FOOD AND AGRICULTURE ORGANIZATION OF THE UNITED NATIONS. ASIA AND THE FAR EAST COMMISSION ON AGRICULTURAL STATISTICS. PERIODIC REPORT. irreg. free. Food and Agriculture Organization of the United Nations, Regional Office for Asia and the Far East, Milawan Mansion, Phra Atit Rd., Bangkok 2, Thailand.

GERMANY (FEDERAL REPUBLIC, 1949-) STATISTISCHES BUNDESAMT. FACHSERIE 16, REIHE 1: ARBEITERVERDIENSTE IN DER LANDWIRTSCHAFT. see *BUSINESS AND ECONOMICS — Abstracting, Bibliographies, Statistics*

314 338.1   GW   ISSN 0072-3681
GERMANY (FEDERAL REPUBLIC, 1949-) STATISTISCHES BUNDESAMT. FACHSERIE 3, REIHE 2: BETRIEBS-, ARBEITS- UND EINKOMMENSVERHAELTNISSE. (Consists of several subseries) irreg. price varies. W. Kohlhammer-Verlag GmbH, Abt. Veroeffentlichungen des Statistischen Bundesamtes, Philipp-Reis-Str. 3, Postfach 421120, 6500 Mainz 42, W. Germany (B.R.D.)

633 338.1 314   GW
GERMANY (FEDERAL REPUBLIC, 1949-) STATISTISCHES BUNDESAMT. FACHSERIE 3, REIHE 3: PFLANZLICHE ERZEUGUNG. 1961. a. price varies. W. Kohlhammer-Verlag GmbH, Abt. Veroeffentlichungen des Statistischen Bundesamtes, Philipp-Reis-Str. 3, Postfach 421120, 6500 Mainz 42, W. Germany (B.R.D.)
Formerly: Germany(Federal Republic, 1949-) Statistisches Bundesamt. Fachserie 3, Reihe 3: Gartenbau und Weinwirtschaft.

636 338.1   GW
GERMANY (FEDERAL REPUBLIC, 1949-) STATISTISCHES BUNDESAMT. FACHSERIE 3, REIHE 4: TIERISCHE ERZEUGUNG. m, s-a, a. price varies. W. Kohlhammer-Verlag GmbH, Abt. Veroeffentlichungen des Statistischen Bundesamtes, Philipp-Reis-Str. 3, Postfach 421120, 6500 Mainz 42, W. Germany (B.R.D.)

338.1 314   GW   ISSN 0072-3894
GERMANY (FEDERAL REPUBLIC, 1949-) STATISTISCHES BUNDESAMT. FACHSERIE 17, REIHE 1: PREISE UND PREISINDIZES FUER DIE LAND- UND FORSTWIRTSCHAFT. m. DM.44.40. W. Kohlhammer-Verlag GmbH, Abt. Veroeffentlichungen des Statistischen Bundesamtes, Philipp-Reis-Str. 3, Postfach 421120, 6500 Mainz 42, W. Germany (B.R.D.)

630 314   HU   ISSN 0441-4683
HUNGARY. KOZPONTI STATISZTIKAI HIVATAL. MEZOGAZDASAGI STATISZTIKAI ZSEBKONYU. a. 30 Ft. Statisztikai Kiado Vallalat, Kaszas U.10-12, P.O.B.99, 1300 Budapest 3, Hungary.

338.1   US   ISSN 0094-1271
IDAHO AGRICULTURAL STATISTICS. 1972. a. Department of Agriculture, Crop and Livestock Reporting Service, Box 1699, Boise, ID 83701. circ. 2,500.

631.8   II
INDIAN FERTILIZER STATISTICS. (Text in English) 1967. a. free. Ministry of Chemicals and Fertilizers, Economics and Statistics Division, New Delhi, India. stat. circ. controlled.

630 016   CK   ISSN 0073-7151
INDICE AGRICOLA COLOMBIANO. 1961-62. a. Col.250($30.) Instituto Colombiano Agropecuario, Apartado Aereo 7984, Bogota, D.E., Colombia.

630 016   CK
INSTITUTO COLOMBIANO AGROPECUARIO. CATALOGO DE PUBLICACIONES PERIODICAS. 1975. a (with irreg supplements) Instituto Colombiano Agropecuario, Biblioteca Agropecuaria, Division de Comunicacion Rural, Apartado Aereo 151123, Bogota, Colombia. Eds. Guadalupe Bustamante, Candace Walker. circ. 1,000.

630 016   CR   ISSN 0301-438X
INTER-AMERICAN CENTRE FOR AGRICULTURAL DOCUMENTATION AND INFORMATION. DOCUMENTACION E INFORMACION AGRICOLA. (Text in various languages) 1973. irreg. free on exchange. Instituto Interamericano de Ciencias Agricolas de la O E A, Secretariado, Apdo. 55, Coronado, Prov. San Jose, Costa Rica. Ed. Hugo Caceres. bk. rev. circ. 800. (also avail. in microform)
Formed by the merger of: Inter-American Institute of Agricultural Sciences. Center for Training and Research. Bibliotecologia y Documentacion (ISSN 0074-0926) & Inter-American Institute of Agricultural Sciences. Bibliografias (ISSN 0085-1949)

631   PH
INTERNATIONAL BIBLIOGRAPHY OF CROPPING SYSTEMS. 1976. a. $25.50. International Rice Research Institute, Library and Documentation Center, Box 933, Manila, Philippines.

633 016   PH   ISSN 0074-2031
INTERNATIONAL BIBLIOGRAPHY OF RICE RESEARCH. 1963. a. $48. International Rice Research Institute, Library and Documentation Center, Box 933, Manila, Philippines. cum.index every 5 years.

637 016   BE   ISSN 0538-7086
INTERNATIONAL DAIRY FEDERATION. CATALOGUE OF I D F PUBLICATIONS. CATALOGUE DES PUBLICATIONS DE LA F I L. (Text in English and French) 1973. a. free. International Dairy Federation, Square Vergote, 41, 1040 Brussels, Belgium. bk. rev. circ. 3,000. (processed)

631.6 016   NE   ISSN 0074-6436
INTERNATIONAL INSTITUTE FOR LAND RECLAMATION AND IMPROVEMENT. BIBLIOGRAPHY. (Text in English) 1960. irreg. price varies; free on exchange. International Institute for Land Reclamation and Improvement, P.O. Box 45, 6700 AA Wageningen, Netherlands.

338.1   US   ISSN 0360-5841
INVENTORY OF AGRICULTURAL RESEARCH. a. U.S. Science and Education Administration, Technical Information Systems, Beltsville, MD 20705.

636 314   IE
IRELAND. CENTRAL STATISTICS OFFICE. DISTRIBUTION OF CATTLE AND PIGS BY SIZE OF HERD. biennial. Central Statistics Office, Earlsfort Terrace, Dublin 2, Ireland. charts. stat.

636.4 314   IE
IRELAND. CENTRAL STATISTICS OFFICE. PIG ENUMERATION. 1974. a. Central Statistics Office, Earlsfort Terrace, Dublin 2, Ireland. charts. stat.

636 314   IT   ISSN 0390-6426
ITALY. ISTITUTO CENTRALE DI STATISTICA. ANNUARIO STATISTICO DELLA ZOOTECNIA, DELLA PESCA E DELLA CACCIA. 1963. a. L.5000. Istituto Centrale di Statistica, Via Cesare Balbo 16, 00100 Rome, Italy. circ. 1,050.
Formerly: Italy. Istituto Centrale di Statistica. Annuario Statistiche Zootecniche (ISSN 0075-1774)

630 310   IV
IVORY COAST. MINISTERE DE L'AGRICULTURE. STATISTIQUES AGRICOLES. 1970. a. Ministere de l'Agriculture, Abidjan, Ivory Coast.

338.1   US
KENTUCKY AGRICULTURAL STATISTICS. 1948. a. free. Crop and Livestock Reporting Service, Frankfort, KY 40601. illus.

338.1   LB
LIBERIA. MINISTRY OF AGRICULTURE. PRODUCTION ESTIMATES OF MAJOR CROPS. a. Ministry of Agriculture, Monrovia, Liberia. (Co-sponsor: Ministry of Planning and Economic Affairs)
Formerly: Liberia. Ministry of Agriculture. National Rice Production Estimates.

338.1 630   II   ISSN 0304-6184
MADHYA PRADESH. DIRECTORATE OF AGRICULTURE. AGRICULTURAL STATISTICS. (Text in English) Directorate of Agriculture, Bhopal, India. Key Title: Agricultural Statistics, Madhya Pradesh.

NETHERLANDS. CENTRAAL BUREAU VOOR DE STATISTIEK. STATISTIEK DER LONEN IN DE LANDBOUW. STATISTICS OF WAGES IN AGRICULTURE. see BUSINESS AND ECONOMICS — Abstracting, Bibliographies, Statistics

630   NE   ISSN 0077-7145
NETHERLANDS. CENTRAAL BUREAU VOOR DE STATISTIEK. STATISTIEK VAN DE LAND- EN TUINBOUW. STATISTICS OF AGRICULTURE. (Text in Dutch and English) 1949. a. fl.18.65. Centraal Bureau voor de Statistiek, Prinses Beatrixlaan 428, Voorburg, Netherlands (Orders to: Staatsuitgeverij, Christoffel Plantijnstraat, The Hague, Netherlands)

631.4 016   NZ
NEW ZEALAND. SOIL BUREAU. BIBLIOGRAPHIC REPORT. 1971. irreg. Soil Bureau, Private Bag, Lower Hutt, New Zealand.

630 627   NZ   ISSN 0111-0829
NEW ZEALAND AGRICULTURAL ENGINEERING INSTITUTE. CURRENT PUBLICATIONS. a. free. New Zealand Agricultural Engineering Institute, Lincoln College, Canterbury, New Zealand.

338.1 317   US   ISSN 0078-1541
NORTH DAKOTA CROP AND LIVESTOCK STATISTICS. 1956. a. single copy free. North Dakota Crop and Livestock Reporting Service, Box 3166, Fargo, ND 58102. Ed. J. R. Price. circ. 4,000.

630   NO   ISSN 0078-1894
NORWAY. STATISTISK SENTRALBYRAA. JORDBRUKSSTATISTIKK/AGRICULTURAL STATISTICS. (Subseries of its Norges Offisielle Statistikk) (Text in Norwegian and English) 1937. a. Kr.15. Statistisk Sentralbyraa, Box 8131 Dep., Oslo 1, Norway. circ. 2,000.

016 632   US
OHIO AGRICULTURAL RESEARCH AND DEVELOPMENT CENTER, WOOSTER. LIBRARY. LIST OF REFERENCES: MAIZE VIRUS DISEASES AND CORN STUNT. Running title: Maize Virus Information Service. 1971. irreg. free. Ohio Agricultural Research and Development Center, Wooster, OH 44691. Ed. R. M. Ritter. circ. controlled.

631.4 016   CX   ISSN 0538-2769
ORGANIZATION OF AFRICAN UNITY. INTER-AFRICAN BUREAU FOR SOILS. BIBLIOGRAPHIE. 1951. irreg. $20. Organization of African Unity, Inter- African Bureau for Soils, B.P. 1352, Bangui, Central African Republic. Ed. M.A. Rasheed.

632.95 016   US
PESTICIDE INDEX. irreg., 5th edt. 1976. price varies. Entomological Society of America, 4603 Calvert Rd., College Park, MD 20740.

630 314   PL
POLAND. GLOWNY URZAD STATYSTYCZNY. ROCZNIK STATYSTYCZNY ROLNICTWAI GOSPODARKI ZYWNOSCIOWEJ. YEARBOOK OF AGRICULTURAL STATISTICS. (Issued in its Seria Roczniki Branzowe. Branch Yearbooks) irreg. Glowny Urzad Statystyczny, Al. Niepodleglosci 208, 00-925 Warsaw, Poland.
Formerly: Poland. Glowny Urzad Statystyczny. Rolniczy Rocznik Statystyczny. Yearbook of Agricultural Statistics (ISSN 0079-2810)

631 314   PL   ISSN 0079-2861
POLAND. GLOWNY URZAD STATYSTYCZNY. UZYTKOWANIE GRUNTOW I POWIERZCHNIA ZASIEWOW ORAZ ZWIERZETA GOSPODARSKIE. (Subseries of its: Statystyka Polski) 1966. a. 23 Zl. Glowny Urzad Statystyczny, Al. Niepodleglosci 208, 00-925 Warsaw, Poland.

636.5 310   US   ISSN 0565-1980
POULTRY MARKET STATISTICS. a. U.S. Agricultural Marketing Service, Washington, DC 20250.
Poultry

318 338.1   VE
PRODUCCION AGRICOLA - PERIODO DE INVIERNO. 1965. irreg.; latest issue 1976. free. Ministerio de Agricultura y Cria, Direccion de Planificacion y Estadistica, Division de Estadistica, Torre Norte, Centro Simon Bolivar, Caracas, Venezuela.

338.1 016   US
RURAL DEVELOPMENT BIBLIOGRAPHY SERIES. 1977. irreg. Southern Rural Development Center, Box 5406, Mississippi State, MS 39762.

318 338.1   AG
SANTIAGO DEL ESTERO. DIRECCION GENERAL DE INVESTIGACIONES ESTADISTICA Y CENSOS. ESTADISTICA AGRICOLA-GANADERA. irreg. free. Direccion General de Investigaciones Estadistica y Censos, Palacio de los Tribunales, Santiago del Estero, Argentina. Dir. Jose H. Alegre.

338.1 316   SA
SOUTH AFRICA. DEPARTMENT OF AGRICULTURAL ECONOMICS AND MARKETING. DIVISION OF AGRICULTURAL MARKETING RESEARCH. ABSTRACT OF AGRICULTURAL STATISTICS. (Text in English and Afrikaans) 1958. a, latest 1980. free. ‡ Department of Agricultural Economics and Marketing, Division of Agricultural Marketing Research, Private Bag X246, Pretoria 0001, South Africa. circ. controlled.

630 338.1   SA
SOUTH AFRICA. DEPARTMENT OF STATISTICS. REPORT ON AGRICULTURAL AND PASTORAL PRODUCTION. (Report No. 06-01). a, latest 1976. price varies. Department of Statistics, Private Bag X44, Pretoria 0001, South Africa (Orders to: Government Printer, Bosman St., Private Bag X85, Pretoria 0001,South Africa)

630 310   SP
SPAIN. MINISTERIO DE AGRICULTURA. SECRETARIA GENERAL TECNICA. ANUARIO DE ESTADISTICA AGRARIA. 1972. a. Ministerio de Agricultura, Secretaria General Tecnica, Servicio de Publicaciones Agrarias, Paseo de Infante Isabel, 1, Madrid-7, Spain. charts.

630 338.1   SP
SPAIN. MINISTERIO DE AGRICULTURA. SECRETARIA GENERAL TECNICA. CUENTAS DEL SECTOR AGRARIO. no. 4, 1979. irreg. Ministerio de Agricultura, Secretaria General Tecnica, Paseo Infante 1, Madrid 7, Spain. charts. stat.

630   SW   ISSN 0082-0199
SWEDEN. STATISTISKA CENTRALBYRAAN. JORDBRUKSSTATISTISK AARSBOK. (Text in Swedish; summaries in English) 1965. a. Kr.47. Liber Foerlag, Fack, S-162 89 Vaellingby, Sweden. circ. 1,500.

630 314   SW   ISSN 0082-0288
SWEDEN. STATISTISKA CENTRALBYRAAN. STATISTISKA MEDDELANDEN. SUBGROUP J (AGRICULTURE) (Text in Swedish; table heads and summaries in English) 1963 N.S. irreg. Kr.130. Liber Foerlag, Fack, S-162 89 Vaellingby, Sweden. circ. 1,175.

338.1   US   ISSN 0091-1550
TEXAS LIVESTOCK STATISTICS. (Subseries of: Texas Department of Agriculture. Bulletin) 1968. a. free. Crop and Livestock Reporting Service, P. O. Box 70, Austin, TX 78767. Dir. Eldon Johnson. charts. illus. mkt. stats. circ. 2,800.

633 317   US   ISSN 0091-4673
TEXAS SMALL GRAINS STATISTICS. (Subseries of Texas. Department of Agriculture. Bulletin) 1968. a. free. Crop and Livestock Reporting Service, P.O. Box 70, Austin, TX 78767. Dir. Lloyd Garrett. charts. illus. mkt. stats. circ. 2,500.

636 317 US
U.S. DEPARTMENT OF AGRICULTURE.
ANIMAL AND PLANT HEALTH INSPECTION
SERVICE. COOPERATIVE STATE-FEDERAL
BRUCELLOSIS ERADICATION PROGRAM:
STATISTICAL TABLES. a. free. U.S. Animal and
Plant Health Inspection Service, 6505 Belcrest Rd.,
Federal Center Bldg., Hyattsville, MD 20782. stat.

636 317 US
U.S. DEPARTMENT OF AGRICULTURE.
ANIMAL AND PLANT HEALTH INSPECTION
SERVICE. COOPERATIVE STATE-FEDERAL
BOVINE TUBERCULOSIS ERADICATION
PROGRAM: STATISTICAL TABLES. a. free. U.S.
Animal and Plant Health Inspection Service, 6505
Belcrest Rd., Federal Center Bldg., Hyattsville, MD
20782. stat.

338.1 317 US ISSN 0091-3502
U.S. DEPARTMENT OF AGRICULTURE.
ECONOMICS, STATISTICS, AND
COOPERATIVES SERVICE. AGRICULTURAL
FINANCE STATISTICS. 1973. a. U. S.
Department of Agriculture, Economics, Statistics,
and Cooperatives Service, Information Staff,
Fourteenth Street and Independence Ave., S.W.,
Washington, DC 20250 (Orders to: Supt. of
Documents, Washington, DC 20402) Key Title:
Agricultural Finance Statistics.
 Formerly: Agricultural Finance Review
Supplement.

338.1 382 317 US
U.S. FOREIGN AGRICULTURAL TRADE
STATISTICAL REPORT, CALENDAR YEAR.
(Supplement to the Monthly: Foreign Agricultural
Trade of the United States) 1971. a. free. U.S.
Department of Agriculture, Economics, Statistics,
and Cooperatives Service, Information Staff,
Publications Unit, Washington, DC 20250.

338.1 382 317 US
U.S. FOREIGN AGRICULTURAL TRADE
STATISTICAL REPORT, FISCAL YEAR.
(Supplement to the monthly: Foreign Agricultural
Trade of the United States) a. free. U.S. Department
of Agriculture, Economics, Statistics, and
Cooperatives Service, Information Staff, Publications
Unit, Washington, DC 20250.

630 317 US
UTAH AGRICULTURAL STATISTICS. 1971. a.
free. Department of Agriculture, 147 North 200
West, Salt Lake City, UT 84103. (Co-Sponsor: U.S.
Department of Agriculture, Statistical Reporting
Service)

338.1 318 VE ISSN 0085-7653
VENEZUELA. MINISTERIO DE AGRICULTURA
Y CRIA. DIRECCION DE ECONOMIA Y
ESTADISTICA AGROPECUARIA. DIVISION
DE ESTADISTICA. PLAN DE TRABAJO.* a.
Ministerio de Agricultura y Cria, Direccion de
Economia y Estadistica Agropecuaria, Division de
Estadistica, Caracas, Venezuela.

338.1 US ISSN 0095-4330
WASHINGTON AGRICULTURAL STATISTICS.
irreg. Crop and Livestock Reporting Service, 909
First Ave., Room 3039, Seattle, WA 98174.

632.58 632 US
WEED SCIENCE SOCIETY OF AMERICA.
ABSTRACTS. 1956. Weed Science Society of
America, 309 W. Clark St., Champaign, IL 61820.
(reprint service avail. from UMI,ISI)
 Formerly (until 1967): Weed Society of America.
Abstracts (ISSN 0511-4144)

633.18 016 LB
WEST AFRICA RICE DEVELOPMENT
ASSOCIATION. CURRENT BIBLIOGRAPHY.
(Text in English and French) 1974. irreg. West
Africa Rice Development Association, Box 1019,
Monrovia, Liberia.

338.1 UK ISSN 0512-3844
WORLD WHEAT STATISTICS. (Text in English,
French, Russian and Spanish) 1955. a. £7.50($17) ‡
International Wheat Council, Haymarket House, 28
Haymarket, London SW1Y 4SS, England.

316 630 ZA
ZAMBIA. CENTRAL STATISTICAL OFFICE.
AGRICULTURAL AND PASTORAL
PRODUCTION (COMMERCIAL AND NON-
COMMERCIAL) 1965/66. a, latest 1975
(preliminary report) K.1. Central Statistical Office,
P.O. Box 1908, Lusaka, Zambia.
 Supersedes in part: Zambia. Central Statistical
Office. Agricultural and Pastoral Production (ISSN
0080-1305)

338.1 ZA
ZAMBIA. CENTRAL STATISTICAL OFFICE.
AGRICULTURAL AND PASTORAL
PRODUCTION (COMMERCIAL FARMS) a.
Central Statistical Office, P.O. Box 1908, Lusaka,
Zambia.
 Supersedes in part: Zambia. Central Statistical
Office. Agricultural and Pastoral Production (ISSN
0080-1305)

630 ZA
ZAMBIA. CENTRAL STATISTICAL OFFICE.
AGRICULTURAL AND PASTORAL
PRODUCTION (NON-COMMERCIAL) 1972. a,
latest 1975. Central Statistical Office, P.O. Box
1908, Lusaka, Zambia.
 Supersedes in part: Zambia. Central Statistical
Office. Agricultural and Pastoral Production (ISSN
0080-1305)

630 ZA
ZAMBIA. CENTRAL STATISTICAL OFFICE.
QUARTERLY AGRICULTURAL STATISTICAL
BULLETIN. q. K.0.50. Central Statistical Office,
P.O. Box 1908, Lusaka, Zambia.

AGRICULTURE — Agricultural Economics

630 338.1 US
A.D.C. STAFF PAPERS. 1973. irreg. free.
Agricultural Development Council Inc., 1290 Ave.
of the Americas, New York, NY 10019. bibl. illus.

338.1 UK ISSN 0065-4337
AGRARIAN DEVELOPMENT STUDIES. 1965.
irreg. price varies. Wye College (University of
London), School of Rural Economics and Related
Studies, Nr. Ashford, Kent, England. Ed. Dr. E. S.
Clayton. bk. rev. index.

338.1 GW ISSN 0065-4345
AGRARMARKT-STUDIEN. 1966. irreg., no. 27,
1978. price varies. (Universitaet Kiel, Institut fuer
Agrarpolitik und Marktlehre) Verlag Paul Parey
(Hamburg), Spitalerstr. 12, 2000 Hamburg 1, W.
Germany (B.R.D.) Ed. Hans Stamer. illus. bibl.
index. (reprint service avail. from ISI)

338.1 GW ISSN 0065-4353
AGRARPOLITIK UND MARKTWESEN. 1963.
irreg., no. 14, 1974. price varies. Verlag Paul Parey
(Hamburg), Spitalerstr. 12, 2000 Hamburg 1, W.
Germany (B.R.D.) Ed. Bd. bibl. illus. index.
(reprint service avail. from ISI)

338.1 332.6 US ISSN 0065-4396
AGRI-BUSINESS BUYERS REFERENCE. 1943. a.
$3.50. Grain and Farm Service Centers, 2150 Board
of Trade, Chicago, IL 60604. Ed. Dean Clark.
index. circ. 19,077.

630 338.1 UK ISSN 0142-4998
AGRICULTURAL CO-OPERATION IN THE
UNITED KINGDOM: SUMMARY OF
STATISTICS. 1970. a. £2($3.50) Plunkett
Foundation for Co-Operative Studies, 31 St. Giles,
Oxford OX1 3LF, England. (Co-sponsors: Central
Council for Agricultural and Horticultural Co-
Operation; Federation of Agricultural Co-
Operatives(U.K.)) circ. 1,200.

338.1 MW
AGRICULTURAL DEVELOPMENT AND
MARKETING CORPORATION. ANNUAL
REPORT AND STATEMENT OF ACCOUNTS.
a. free. ‡ Agricultural Development and Marketing
Corporation, Box 5052, Limbe, Malawi. stat.
 Supersedes: Agricultural Development and
Marketing Corporation. Annual Report &
Agricultural Development Corporation. Balance
Sheet and Accounts; Which was formerly: Farmers
Marketing Board. Balance Sheet and Accounts.

338.1 332 PK ISSN 0065-4426
AGRICULTURAL DEVELOPMENT BANK OF
PAKISTAN. ANNUAL REPORT AND
STATEMENT OF ACCOUNTS. a. Agricultural
Development Bank of Pakistan, Shafi Court,
Merewether Rd., Karachi, Pakistan.

338.1 UN ISSN 0065-4434
AGRICULTURAL ECONOMICS BULLETIN FOR
AFRICA. 1967, no. 9. irreg., no. 15, 1975. price
varies. United Nations Economic Commission for
Africa - Commission Economique pour l'Afrique,
Box 3001, Addis Ababa, Ethiopia (Dist. by: United
Nations Publications, Room LX-2300, New York,
NY 10017; or Distribution and Sales Section, Palais
des Nations, CH-1211 Geneva 10, Switzerland)

338.1 PK ISSN 0065-4469
AGRICULTURAL ECONOMIST. (Vols. 1-3 include
proceedings of the Annual Conference of
Agricultural Economists) (Text in English) 1958.
irreg. Rs.5 per. no. Agricultural Economics Society
of Pakistan, 154 Government Quarters, Lawrence
Rd., Karachi, Pakistan.

338.1 BG
AGRICULTURAL PRODUCTION LEVELS IN
BANGLADESH. (Text in English) 1976. a. free.
Bureau of Statistics, Secretariat, Dacca 2,
Bangladesh. Ed. A.K.M. Ghulam Rabbani. charts.
stat.

338.1 UK ISSN 0065-4493
AGRICULTURAL PROGRESS. 1924. a. £8.
Agricultural Education Association, c/o Ed. & Pub.
A. R. Staniforth, 5 Capel Close, Oxford OX2 7LA,
England. adv. bk. rev. circ. 1,000.

630 338.1 MY
AGRICULTURAL STATISTICS OF SABAH. (Text
in English) 1971. a. contr. free circ. Department of
Agriculture, Economics and Statistics Division, Kota
Kinabalu, Sabah, Malaysia. charts. stat. circ. 500.

630 338.1 MY
AGRICULTURAL STATISTICS OF SARAWAK.
1971. a, latest 1978. M.$5. Department of
Agriculture, Research Branch, Agricultural Research
Centre, Semongok, Box 977, Kuching, Sarawak,
Malaysia.

338.1 331 II ISSN 0084-6066
AGRICULTURAL WAGES IN INDIA. (Text and
summaries in English) 1950. a. Rs.105. Ministry of
Agriculture and Irrigation, Department of
Agriculture, Directorate of Economics and
Statistics, A-2E-3 Kasturba Gandhi Marg Barracks,
New Delhi 110001, India. Ed. C. D. Sharma. circ.
300.

333 NR ISSN 0065-4744
AHMADU BELLO UNIVERSITY. INSTITUTE OF
ADMINISTRATION. TRADITIONAL LAND
TENURE SURVEYS. 1963. irreg. $4. Ahmadu
Bello University, Institute of Administration, Zaria,
Nigeria.

338.1 NE
AKKERBOUW. irreg. Landbouw-Economisch
Instituut, Afdeling Landbouw, Conradkade 175,
2517 CL The Hague, Netherlands.

338.1 CK
ALMANAQUE CREDITARIO. vol. 29, 1975. a. free.
Caja de Credito Agrario, Oficina de Divulgacion,
Carrera 8a No. 16-88, Apdo. Aereo 12035, Bogota,
Colombia. Dir. Alejandro Bonilla Bonilla. illus. circ.
200,000.

338.1 US
AMERICAN AGRICULTURAL ECONOMICS
ASSOCIATION. HANDBOOK. quinquennial. $15.
American Agricultural Economics Association, c/o
Sydney C. James, Department of Economics, Iowa
State University, Ames, IA 50011.

ANNALES D'ECONOMIE ET DE SOCIOLOGIE
RURALES. see SOCIOLOGY

338.1 630 JA ISSN 0546-109X
ANNUAL REPORT OF THE DEVELOPMENT OF
AGRICULTURE IN JAPAN/NIHON NOGAKU
SHIMPO NEMPO. (Text in English) 1951-52. a.
Science Council of Japan - Nihon Gakujutsu Kaigi,
7-22-34 Roppongi, Minato-ku, Tokyo 106, Japan.

AGRICULTURE — AGRICULTURAL ECONOMICS

338.1   SP
ANUARIO HORTOFRUTICOLA ESPANOL. 1968-69. a. 600 ptas. Sucro S.A., Hernan Cortes, 5, Valencia 4, Spain. circ. 5,000.

338.1   BL
ASPECTOS GERAIS E PRINCIPAIS TENDENCIAS DA AGROPECUARIA PARAIBANA. a. Comissao Estadual de Planajamento Agricola, Paraiba, Brazil. illus.

338.1 633   AT   ISSN 0311-0788
AUSTRALIA. BUREAU OF AGRICULTURAL ECONOMICS. COARSE GRAINS: SITUATION AND OUTLOOK. 1954. a. price varies. ‡ Australian Government Publishing Service, P.O. Box 84, Canberra, A.C.T. 2600, Australia.
    Supersedes in part: Australia. Bureau of Agricultural Economics. Coarse Grains and Oilseeds Situation (ISSN 0084-702X); Australia. Bureau of Agricultural Economics. Coarse Grain Situation.

338.1 637   AT
AUSTRALIA. BUREAU OF AGRICULTURAL ECONOMICS. DAIRY PRODUCTS: SITUATION AND OUTLOOK. 1954. a. price varies. ‡ Australian Government Publishing Service, P.O. Box 84, Canberra, A.C.T. 2600, Australia.
    Supersedes: Australia. Bureau of Agricultural Economics. Dairy Situation (ISSN 0084-7038)

338.1 637.5   AT
AUSTRALIA. BUREAU OF AGRICULTURAL ECONOMICS. EGGS: SITUATION AND OUTLOOK. 1955. a. price varies. ‡ Australian Government Publishing Service, P.O. Box 84, Canberra, A.C.T. 2600, Australia.
    Supersedes: Australia. Bureau of Agricultural Economics. Egg Situation (ISSN 0084-7046)

338.1   AT   ISSN 0311-2950
AUSTRALIA. BUREAU OF AGRICULTURAL ECONOMICS. FIBRE REVIEW. 1972. irreg. price varies. ‡ Australian Government Publishing Service, P.O. Box 84, Canberra, A.C.T. 2600, Australia.
    Supersedes: Australia. Bureau of Agricultural Economics. Fibres Other Than Wool (ISSN 0045-0200)

338.1 636.2   AT   ISSN 0311-0885
AUSTRALIA. BUREAU OF AGRICULTURAL ECONOMICS. MEAT: SITUATION AND OUTLOOK. 1953. a. price varies. ‡ Australian Government Publishing Service, P.O. Box 84, Canberra, A.C.T. 2600, Australia.
    Supersedes: Australia. Bureau of Agricultural Economics. Meat Situation; Australia. Bureau of Agricultural Economics. Beef Situation (ISSN 0084-7011); Australia. Bureau of Agricultural Economics. Mutton and Lamb Situation (ISSN 0084-7054)

338.1   AT
AUSTRALIA. BUREAU OF AGRICULTURAL ECONOMICS. OCCASIONAL PAPERS. no. 36, 1976. irreg. price varies. ‡ Australian Government Publishing Service, P.O. Box 84, Canberra, A.C.T. 2600, Australia. charts. illus.

338.1 633   AT
AUSTRALIA. BUREAU OF AGRICULTURAL ECONOMICS. OILSEEDS: SITUATION AND OUTLOOK. a. price varies. ‡ Australian Government Publishing Service, P.O. Box 84, Canberra, A.C.T. 2600, Australia.
    Supersedes in part: Australia. Bureau of Agricultural Economics. Coarse Grains and Oilseeds Situation (ISSN 0084-702X)

338.1 319   AT   ISSN 0314-1659
AUSTRALIA. BUREAU OF STATISTICS. TASMANIAN OFFICE. AGRICULTURAL INDUSTRY. 1949-50. a. free. Australian Bureau of Statistics, Tasmanian Office, Box 66A, G.P.O., Hobart, Tasmania 7001, Australia. circ. 680. (processed)
    Formerly: Australia. Bureau of Statistics. Tasmanian Office. Primary Industries (Excluding Mining) (ISSN 0067-1053)

338.1   PE
BANCO AGRARIO DEL PERU. MEMORIA. no. 45, 1976. a. Banco Agrario del Peru, c/o Axel Pflucker Otoya, Augusto Wiese 543-547, Lima, Peru.

338.1   BG   ISSN 0070-8143
BANGLADESH. DIRECTORATE OF AGRICULTURAL MARKETING. AGRICULTURAL MARKETING SERIES.* (Text in English) irreg. Directorate of Agricultural Marketing, Dacca, Bangladesh.

338.1   BL
BRAZIL. SUPERINTENDENCIA DO DESENVOLVIMENTO DO NORDESTE. DEPARTAMENTO DE AGRICULTURA E ABASTECIMENTO. PROGRAMA DE TRABALHO PARA A AGRICULTURA NORDESTINA. irreg. Superintendencia do Desenvolvimento do Nordeste, Departamento de Agricultura e Abastecimento, Recife, Brazil.

630 338.1   VE
CALENDARIO AGRICOLA. 1970. irreg. free. Ministerio de Agricultura y Cria, Direccion de Planificacion y Estadistica, Division de Estadistica, Torre Norte, Centro Simon Bolivar, Caracas, Venezuela. stat.

338.1   CN   ISSN 0068-7286
CANADA. AGRICULTURE CANADA. ECONOMICS BRANCH. TRADE IN AGRICULTURAL PRODUCTS. (Issued as subseries of Dept's Economic Branch Bulletin) a. free. Agriculture Canada, Economics Branch, Ottawa, Ont. K1A 0C5, Canada.

CANADA. GRAIN COMMISSION. ECONOMICS AND STATISTICS DIVISION. VISIBLE GRAIN SUPPLIES AND DISPOSITION. see *AGRICULTURE — Feed, Flour And Grain*

338.1 636   CN
CANADA. MARKETING AND TRADE DIVISION. ANIMAL AND ANIMAL PRODUCTS; OUTLOOK. irreg. free. Agriculture Canada, Marketing and Trade Division, Ottawa, Ont. K1A 0C5, Canada. illus.

330   CN   ISSN 0383-414X
CANADA. NATIONAL FARM PRODUCTS MARKETING COUNCIL. ANNUAL REPORT. (Text in French) no. 5, 1976/77. a. National Farm Products Marketing Council, 165 Sparks St., Booth Bldg., 7th Floor, Ottawa, Ont. K1P 5B9, Canada.

338.1   CN   ISSN 0707-4808
CANADIAN AGRICULTURAL ECONOMICS SOCIETY. PROCEEDINGS OF THE WORKSHOP. 1968. a. Canadian Agricultural Economics Society, 151 Slater St., Ottawa, Ont. K1P 5H4, Canada.

338.1   IS
CENTER FOR AGRICULTURAL ECONOMIC RESEARCH, REHOVOT. WORKING PAPERS. 1969. irreg. Center for Agricultural Economic Research, Box 12, Rehovot, Israel.

630 338.1   CR
CIFRAS SOBRE PRODUCCION AGROPECUARIA. 1975. a. free. Banco Central de Costa Rica, Avenida Central, Calles 2 y 4, Apdo 10058, San Jose, Costa Rica. charts. circ. 400.

338.1 636   EI
COMMISSION OF THE EUROPEAN COMMUNITIES. MARCHES AGRICOLES: SERIE "PRIX". PRODUITS ANIMAUX. 1970. 6-9/yr. free. Commission of the European Communities, Services de Renseignement et de Diffusion des Documents, Rue de la Loi 200, 1049 Brussels, Belgium (Dist. in the U.S. by: European Community Information Service, 2100 M St., NW, Suite 707, Washington, DC 20037) circ. controlled.
    Supersedes a publication issued under the same title from 1965, no. 4-1969. Numbered alternately with its Marches Agricoles: Serie "Prix" Produits Vegetaux (EI ISSN 0423-7323)

338.1 633   EI
COMMISSION OF THE EUROPEAN COMMUNITIES. MARCHES AGRICOLES: SERIE "PRIX". PRODUITS VEGETAUX. 1970. 6-9/yr. free. Commission of the European Communities, 31049 Brussels, Rue de la Loi 200, 1049 Brussels, Belgium (Dist. in the U.S. by: European Community Information Service, 2100 M St., NW, Suite 707, Washington, DC 20037) circ. controlled.
    Supersedes a publication issued under the same title from 1965 no. 4-1969, numbered alternately with its Marches Agricoles: Serie "Prix" Produits Animaux. (EI ISSN 0531-366X) Issued 1962-1965, no. 3 in a single edition with Produits Animaux as its Marches Agricoles: Series "Prix" (EI ISSN 0423-7323)

630 338.1   EI   ISSN 0069-6722
COMMISSION OF THE EUROPEAN COMMUNITIES. ETUDES: SERIE INFORMATIONS INTERNES SUR L'AGRICULTURE.* 1964. irreg. limited distribution. Office for Official Publications of the European Communities, C.P. 1003, Luxembourg, Luxembourg (Dist. in the U.S. by European Community Information Service, 2100 M St. W.W., Suite 707, Washington DC 20037)

630 338.1   EI   ISSN 0069-6765
COMMISSION OF THE EUROPEAN COMMUNITIES. STUDIES: AGRICULTURAL SERIES.* 1960. irreg. price varies. Office for Official Publications of the European Communities, C.P. 1003, Luxembourg, Luxembourg (Dist. in U.S. by: European Community Information Service, 2100 M St., NW, Suite 707, Washington, DC 20037)

333   AT   ISSN 0069-746X
COMMONWEALTH SCIENTIFIC AND INDUSTRIAL RESEARCH ORGANIZATION. DIVISION OF LAND USE RESEARCH. TECHNICAL PAPER. 1959. irreg (approx. 2/yr) Aus.$0.80 per issue. C. S. I. R. O., Division of Land Use Research, 314 Albert St., E. Melbourne 3002, Victoria, Australia.

333   AT   ISSN 0069-7648
COMMONWEALTH SCIENTIFIC AND INDUSTRIAL RESEARCH ORGANIZATION. LAND RESEARCH SERIES. 1952. irreg. Aus.$7.50 per issue. C. S. I. R. O., 314 Albert St., E. Melbourne 3002, Victoria, Australia.

338.1   US   ISSN 0069-9179
CONSORTIUM FOR THE STUDY OF NIGERIAN RURAL DEVELOPMENT. C S N R D WORKING PAPER. 1967. irreg., 1969, no. 11. Michigan State University, 204 Ag. Hall, East Lansing, MI 48823.

338.1   US
CORNELL INTERNATIONAL AGRICULTURAL DEVELOPMENT SERIES. BULLETINS REPORTING RESEARCH ON THE ECONOMICS OF ASIAN AGRICULTURE. (Subseries of its Bulletin) irreg. Cornell University, Department of Agricultural Economics, Ithaca, NY 14850.

338.1   US
CORNELL UNIVERSITY. DEPARTMENT OF AGRICULTURAL ECONOMICS. PRICES, EMPLOYMENT AND INCOME DISTRIBUTION RESEARCH PROJECT. OCCASIONAL PAPERS. 1967. irreg; no. 72, 1974. Cornell University, Department of Agricultural Economics, Ithaca, NY 14850. (Co-sponsor: U.S. Agency for International Development)

338.7   II   ISSN 0304-6907
COTTON CORPORATION OF INDIA. ANNUAL REPORT. (Text in English) a. Cotton Corporation of India, Air India Building, P.B. No. 1350, Bombay 400021, India. Key Title: Annual Report--Cotton Corporation of India.

630 338.1   UK   ISSN 0307-689X
DIRECTORY OF AGRICULTURAL CO-OPERATIVES IN THE UNITED KINGDOM. 1970. a. £3.50($5.25) Plunkett Foundation for Co-Operative Studies, 31 St. Giles, Oxford OX1 3LF, England. (Co-sponsors: Central Council for Agricultural and Horticultural Co-Operation; Federation of Agricultural Co-Operatives (U.K.)) circ. 900.

AGRICULTURE — AGRICULTURAL ECONOMICS

338.1   CN   ISSN 0070-5527
DIRECTORY OF FARMERS' ORGANIZATIONS AND MARKETING BOARDS IN CANADA. 1955. a. free. Agriculture Canada, Information Services, Ottawa, Ont. K1A 0C7, Canada.

338.1   US   ISSN 0070-8615
ECONOMIC QUESTIONS FOR ILLINOIS AGRICULTURE. 1969. irreg., 1971, EQ-5. free. University of Illinois at Urbana-Champaign, Cooperative Extension Service, Urbana, IL 61801. Ed. H. D. Guither.

338.1   NZ
ECONOMIC REVIEW OF NEW ZEALAND AGRICULTURE. 1974. a. free. Ministry of Agriculture and Fisheries, Economic Division, Box 19062, Wellington, New Zealand. circ. controlled.

338.1   II   ISSN 0085-0160
ECONOMIC SURVEY OF INDIAN AGRICULTURE. (Text and summaries in English) 1961. a. Rs.6.25. Ministry of Agriculture and Irrigation, Department of Agriculture, Directorate of Economics and Statistics, A-2E-3 Kasturba Gandhi Marg Barracks, New Delhi 110001, India (Order from: Controller of Publications, Civil Lines, Delhi 110054, India) Ed. C. D. Sharma. circ. 700.

634 338.1   UK   ISSN 0070-8763
ECONOMICS OF FRUIT FARMING. 1949. irreg. price varies. ‡ Wye College (University of London), School of Rural Economics and Related Studies, Near Ashford, Kent, England.

338.1   FR   ISSN 0068-4899
ECONOMIES ET SOCIETES. SERIE AG. PROGRES ET AGRICULTURE. 1962. irreg. 42 F. Institut de Sciences Mathematiques et Economiques Appliquees, Paris, Institut Henri Poincare, 11 rue Henri et Marie Curie, 75005 Paris, France. Ed.Bd. circ. 1,600.

630 338.1   VE
ENCUESTA AGROPECUARIA. 1969. a. free. Ministerio de Agricultura y Cria, Direccion de Planificacion y Estadistica, Division de Estadistica, Caracas, Venezuela. stat.

338.1   PN
ESTADISTICA PANAMENA. SITUACION ECONOMICA. SECCION 312. SUPERFICIE SEMBRADA Y COSECHA DE ARROZ Y MAIZ. 1954. a. Bol.$.30. Direccion de Estadistica y Censo, Contraloria General, Apartado 5213, Panama 5, Panama. circ. 1,500.

338.1   UN   ISSN 0071-7002
F A O COMMODITY REVIEW AND OUTLOOK. (Text in English, French and Spanish) 1961. a. price varies. Food and Agriculture Organization of the United Nations, Distribution and Sales Section, Via delle Terme di Caracalla, 00100 Rome, Italy (Dist. in U.S. by: Unipub, 345 Park Ave. S., New York, NY 10010)

338.1   UK   ISSN 0306-719X
FARM BUSINESS REVIEW. 1975. a. £0.75. University of Exeter, Agricultural Economics Unit, Exeter EX4 4QJ, England. Ed. W. J. K. Thomas. illus. stat.

338.1   UK   ISSN 0071-3848
FARM CLASSIFICATION IN ENGLAND AND WALES. 1963. a. price varies. H. M. S. O., P.O. Box 569, London SE1 9NH, England. (Co-sponsor: Ministry of Agriculture, Fisheries and Food)

338.1   UN   ISSN 0430-084X
FARM MANAGEMENT NOTES FOR ASIA AND THE FAR EAST. 1965. Food and Agriculture Organization of the United Nations, Regional Office for Asia and the Far East, Regional Working Party on Farm Management for Asia and the Far East, Maliwan Mansion, Phra Atit Rd., Bangkok 2, Thailand.

338.1   UK
FARM MANAGEMENT POCKETBOOK. irreg., no.11,1981. price varies. Wye College (University of London), School of Rural Economics and Related Studies, Farm Business Unit, Nr. Ashford, Kent, England.

338.1   UK
FARMING IN THE EAST MIDLANDS. FINANCIAL RESULTS. 1947-48. a. £1.30($3) (approx.) ‡ University of Nottingham, School of Agriculture, University Park, Nottingham NG7 2RD, England. Eds. H.W.T. Kerr, H.W. Johnson. circ. 1,000.

630 338.1   UN   ISSN 0532-0194
FOOD AND AGRICULTURE ORGANIZATION OF THE UNITED NATIONS. AGRICULTURAL PLANNING STUDIES. 1963. Food and Agriculture Organization of the United Nations, Distribution and Sales Section, Via delle Terme di Caracalla, I-00100 Rome, Italy (Dist. in U.S. by: Unipub, 345 Park Ave. S., New York, NY 10010)

338.1   UN   ISSN 0071-6928
FOOD AND AGRICULTURE ORGANIZATION OF THE UNITED NATIONS. COMMODITY POLICY STUDIES. (Text in English, French, and Spanish) 1953. irreg., 1971, no. 22. price varies. Food and Agriculture Organization of the United Nations, Distribution and Sales Section, Via delle Terme di Caracalla, Rome, Italy (Dist. in U.S. by: Unipub, 345 Park Ave. S., New York, NY 10010)

338.1   UN   ISSN 0071-7118
FOOD AND AGRICULTURE ORGANIZATION OF THE UNITED NATIONS. PRODUCTION YEARBOOK. (Text in English, French and Spanish) 1947. a. price varies. Food and Agriculture Organization of the United Nations, Distribution and Sales Section, Via delle Terme di Caracalla, Rome, Italy (Dist. in U.S. by: Unipub, 345 Park Ave. S., New York, NY 10010)

338.1 382   UN   ISSN 0071-7126
FOOD AND AGRICULTURE ORGANIZATION OF THE UNITED NATIONS. TRADE YEARBOOK. (Text in English, French and Spanish) 1947. a. price varies. Food and Agriculture Organization of the United Nations, Distribution and Sales Section, Via delle Terme di Caracalla, Rome, Italy (Dist. in U.S. by: Unipub, 345 Park Ave. S., New York, NY 10010)

FRANCE. CAISSE NATIONALE DE CREDIT AGRICOLE. RAPPORT SUR LE CREDIT AGRICOLE MUTUEL. see *BUSINESS AND ECONOMICS — Banking And Finance*

630 338.1   FR
FRANCE. MINISTERE DE L'AGRICULTURE. COLLECTIONS DE STATISTIQUE AGRICOLE, SERIE ETUDES. 1965. irreg. 200 F. Ministere de l'Agriculture, 4 Av. de Saint Mande, 75570 Paris Cedex 12, France.

630 338.1   FR
FRANCE. MINISTERE DE L'AGRICULTURE. INFORMATION RAPIDES STATISTIQUES DES ENTREPRISES. irreg. 30 F. (per year) Ministere de l'Agriculture, Service Central des Enquetes et Etudes Statistiques, 4 Av de Saint Mande, 75570 Paris Cedex 12, France.
    Formerly: France. Ministere de l'Agriculture. Informations Rapides Agro-Alimentaires.

641   UN   ISSN 0532-6370
FREEDOM FROM HUNGER CAMPAIGN. F F H C REPORT. Food and Agriculture Organization of the United Nations, Distribution and Sales Section, Via delle Terme di Caracalla, I-00100 Rome, Italy.

338.1   GM   ISSN 0301-8423
GAMBIA. PRODUCE MARKETING BOARD. ANNUAL REPORT. 1971. a. free. Produce Marketing Board, Box 284, Marina Foreshore, Banjul, Gambia. illus.
    Continues: Gambia. Oilseeds Marketing Board. Report.

338.1   US
GIANNINI FOUNDATION OF AGRICULTURAL ECONOMICS. INFORMATION SERIES. 1964. irreg. University of California, Berkeley, Giannini Foundation of Agricultural Economics, 207 Giannini Hall, Berkeley, CA 94720.
    Formerly: Information Series on Agricultural Economics (ISSN 0073-7887)

338.1   US   ISSN 0575-4208
GIANNINI FOUNDATION OF AGRICULTURAL ECONOMICS. MONOGRAPH. no. 10, 1961. irreg., no. 36, 1978. University of California, Berkeley, Giannini Foundation of Agricultural Economics, 207 Giannini Hall, Berkeley, CA 94720.

338.1   US
GIANNINI FOUNDATION OF AGRICULTURAL ECONOMICS. PAPER. no. 273,1967. irreg., no. 492, 1978. University of California, Berkeley, Giannini Foundation of Agricultural Economics, 207 Giannini Hall, Berkeley, CA 94720.

338.1   US   ISSN 0072-4459
GIANNINI FOUNDATION OF AGRICULTURAL ECONOMICS. RESEARCH REPORT. 1930. irreg., no. 325, 1978. free. ‡ University of California, Berkeley, Giannini Foundation of Agricultural Economics, 207 Giannini Hall, Berkeley, CA 94720. Indexed: Amer.Bibl.Agri.Econ. World Agri.Econ. & Rural Sociol.Abstr.

338.9 636   UK   ISSN 0072-6672
GREAT BRITAIN. MINISTRY OF AGRICULTURE. FISHERIES AND FOOD. FATSTOCK GUARANTEE SCHEME. (Joint publication with the Dept. of Agriculture and Fisheries for Scotland and the Ministry of Agriculture, Northern Ireland) 1954-55. a. price varies. H. M. S. O., P.O. Box 569, London SE1 9NH, England. (Co-sponsor: Ministry of Agriculture, Fisheries and Food)

338.1   GT
GUATEMALA. BANCO NACIONAL DE DESARROLLO AGRICOLA. MEMORIA. 1971. a. Banco Nacional de Desarrollo Agricola, 9 Calle No. 9-47, Zona 1, Guatemala, Guatemala. stat.

338.1   US
I B M AGRIBUSINESS SYMPOSIUM. PROCEEDINGS. irreg. price varies. International Business Machines Corp., Data Processing Division, 112 E. Post Rd., White Plains, NY 10601.

630 338.1   SP
INDICADORES SOCIO-ECONOMICOS DEL CAMPO ESPANOL. (Subseries of the Confederation's's Publicaciones) irreg. 900 ptas. Confederacion Espanola de Cajas de Ahorros, Fonda para la Investigacion Economica y Social, Alcal27, Madrid 14, Spain. illus. stat.

338.1   US   ISSN 0073-7887
INFORMATION SERIES IN AGRICULTURAL ECONOMICS. (University of California. Division of Agricultural Sciences. Bulletin Series) 1963. irreg., 1-5/yr. free. University of California, Berkeley, Agricultural and Resource Economics, Cooperative Extension Service, 207 Giannini Hall, Berkeley, CA 94720. (Co-Sponsor: Giannini Foundation of Agricultural Economics) Indexed: Amer.Bibl.Agri.Econ. World Agri.Econ. & Rural Sociol.Abstr.

338.1   EI   ISSN 0073-7895
INFORMATION SERVICE OF THE EUROPEAN COMMUNITIES. NEWSLETTER ON THE COMMON AGRICULTURAL POLICY.* irreg.(approx. 20 nos. per year) Press and Information Service of the European Communities, 224 rue de la Loi, 1004 Brussels, Belgium.

338.1 338.9   CM
INSTITUT PANAFRICAIN POUR LE DEVELOPPEMENT. TRAVAUX MANUSCRITS. 1972. irreg. price varies. ‡ Pan- African Institute for Development, B.P. 4078, Douala, Cameroon. circ. 200.

338.1   SZ   ISSN 0074-2856
INTERNATIONAL CONFEDERATION FOR AGRICULTURAL CREDIT. ASSEMBLY AND CONGRESS REPORTS.* irreg., 1973, 5th Congress, Milan. International Confederation for Agricultural Credit, 24 Beethovenstr., 8002 Zurich, Switzerland.

338.13   US   ISSN 0074-2902
INTERNATIONAL CONFERENCE OF AGRICULTURAL ECONOMISTS. PROCEEDINGS. 1929. triennial, 17th, 1979, Baniff, Canada. ‡ International Association of Agricultural Economists, c/o World Bank, 1818 H St., Washington, DC 20433 (901 N. 17th St., Lincoln, NE 68588) Eds. Glenn L Johnson, A. H. Maunder. circ. 2,000 (approx.) Indexed: World Agri.Econ. & Rural Sociol.Abstr.

AGRICULTURE — AGRICULTURAL ECONOMICS

331.88 SZ ISSN 0538-7477
INTERNATIONAL FEDERATION OF PLANTATION, AGRICULTURAL AND ALLIED WORKERS. REPORT OF THE SECRETARIAT TO THE I F P A A W WORLD CONGRESS. irreg., 4th, 1976, Geneva. International Federation of Plantation, Agricultural and Allied Workers, 17 rue Necker, CH-1201 Geneva, Switzerland.

333 JA
IWATE UNIVERSITY. MOUNTAINS LAND USE RESEARCH LABORATORY. BULLETIN. (Text in Japanese and English) 1968. irreg. exchange basis. Iwate University, Mountains Land Use Research Station - Iwate Daigaku Nogakubu Fuzoku Sanchi Riyo, 3-18-8 Ueda, Morioka 020, Iwate, Japan.

338.1 US ISSN 0075-5303
KEEPING TRACK, CURRENT NEWS FROM THE DEPARTMENT OF AGRICULTURAL ECONOMICS AT PURDUE. 1966. a.(with bi-w. supplement) free. Purdue University, Department of Agricultural Economics, Krannert Bldg., West Lafayette, IN 47907. Ed. Patty Cassidy. circ. 300.

333 US ISSN 0075-7837
LAND ECONOMICS MONOGRAPHS. 1966. irreg. ‡ (University of Wisconsin-Madison, Land Tenure Center) University of Wisconsin Press, 114 N. Murray St., Madison, WI 53715.

333 US ISSN 0084-0785
LAND TENURE CENTER. NEWSLETTER. Short title: L T C Newsletter. 1962. irreg., no. 58, 1977. free. University of Wisconsin-Madison, Land Tenure Center, 1525 Observatory Dr., 310 King Hall, Madison, WI 53706. Ed. Jane B. Knowles. cum.index.

333 630 US ISSN 0084-0793
LAND TENURE CENTER. PAPER. Short title: L T C Paper. (Some texts in Spanish and Portuguese) 1965. irreg., no. 119, 1978. $0.75 in North America (excluding Mexico) and Western Europe; free elsewhere. University of Wisconsin-Madison, Land Tenure Center, 310 King Hall, Madison, WI 53706. Ed. Jane B. Knowles.

333 US ISSN 0084-0815
LAND TENURE CENTER. RESEARCH PAPER. (Some texts in Spanish and Portuguese) 1964. irreg., no. 73, 1978. $1 in North America (excluding Mexico) and Western Europe; free elsewhere. University of Wisconsin-Madison, Land Tenure Center, 310 King Hall, Madison, WI 53706. Ed. Jane B. Knowles.

338.1 NE
LANDBOUW-ECONOMISCH INSTITUUT. BEDRIJFSUITKOMSTEN IN DE LANDBOUW. a. price varies. Landbouw-Economisch Instituut, Afdeling Landbouw, Conradkade 175, 2517 CL The Hague, Netherlands. stat.

338.1 NE
LANDBOUW-ECONOMISCH INSTITUUT. STAFAFDELING. LANDBOUW-ECONOMISCH BERICHT. (Summary in English) 1972. a. price varies. Landbouw-Economisch Instituut, Conradkade 175, 2517 CL The Hague, Netherlands.

630 338.1 LB
LIBERIA. MINISTRY OF AGRICULTURE. STATISTICAL HANDBOOK. triennial. Ministry of Agriculture, Monrovia, Liberia.

338.1 NZ ISSN 0110-7720
LINCOLN COLLEGE. AGRICULTURAL ECONOMICS RESEARCH UNIT. DISCUSSION PAPER. 1968. irreg., no. 47, 1979. $2 per no; also avail. on exchange. Lincoln College, Canterbury, New Zealand.

338.1 NZ ISSN 0069-3790
LINCOLN COLLEGE. AGRICULTURAL ECONOMICS RESEARCH UNIT. RESEARCH REPORT. 1964. irreg., no. 104, 1979. $4 per no; also avail. on exchange. Lincoln College, Canterbury, New Zealand. Indexed: Bibl.Agri. World Agri.Econ. & Rural Sociol.Abstr.

338.1 US ISSN 0085-2929
M. OLIVER NEWSLETTER.* 1972. irreg. Michael Oliver, Box 485, Carson City, NV 89701.

338.7 II ISSN 0304-7245
MADHYA PRADESH STATE AGRO-INDUSTRIES DEVELOPMENT CORPORATION LTD. ANNUAL REPORT. (Text in English) a. Madhya Pradesh State Agro-Industries Development Corporation Ltd., New Market, T. T. Nagar, Bhopal, India. Key Title: Annual Report-Madhya Pradesh State Agro-Industries Development Corporation Ltd.

381.41 CN ISSN 0527-6624
MARKETING BOARDS IN CANADA/OFFICES DE COMMERCIALISATION AU CANADA. (Text in English and French) 1973. a. Agriculture Canada, Economics Branch, Sir John Carling Building, Carling Ave., Ottawa K1A 0C5, Canada.

381.45 US ISSN 0094-2510
MARKETING CALIFORNIA DRIED FRUITS: PRUNES, RAISINS, DRIED APRICOTS & PEACHES. irreg. free. Federal-State Market News Service, 1220 N St., Sacramento, CA 95814. stat. Key Title: Marketing California Dried Fruits.

338.1 US ISSN 0098-8928
MARKETING CALIFORNIA PEARS FOR FRESH MARKET. a. free. Federal-State Market News Service, 1220 N St., Sacramento, CA 95814.

630 338.1 MX
MEXICO. SECRETARIA DE AGRICULTURA Y RECURSOS HIDRAULICOS. INFORME ESTADISTICOS. 1946. irreg., no. 85, 1977. Secretaria de Agricultura y Recursos Hidraulicos, Direccion General de Distritos y Unidades de Riego, Mexico, D.F., Mexico.

338.1 US ISSN 0065-4442
MICHIGAN STATE UNIVERSITY. AGRICULTURAL ECONOMICS REPORT. 1965. irreg.(approx. 10/yr.) free. Michigan State University, Department of Agricultural Economics, 202 Agriculture Hall, E. Lansing, MI 48824. circ. 3,000. (processed) Indexed: Bibl. & Ind.Geol. World Agri.Econ. & Rural Social.Abstr.

331.7 338.1 US
MICHIGAN STATE UNIVERSITY. CENTER FOR RURAL MANPOWER & PUBLIC AFFAIRS. REPORT. 1966. irreg., no. 53, 1978. Michigan State University, Center for Rural Manpower & Public Affairs, Agricultural Economics Dept., 41 Agriculture Hall, East Lansing, MI 48824.
Formerly: Michigan State University. Rural Manpower Center. R M C Report (ISSN 0076-826X)

338.1 SA
NATIONAL FRESH PRODUCE MARKET, JOHANNESBURG. ANNUAL TRADING RESULTS/JAARLISKE HANDELSYFERS. 1935. a. free. National Fresh Produce Market, Box 577, Johannesburg 2000, South Africa. stat. circ. 750.

338.1 636 NZ ISSN 0078-0197
NEW ZEALAND POULTRY BOARD. REPORT AND NEW ZEALAND MARKETING AUTHORITY REPORT AND STATEMENT OF ACCOUNTS. 1953. a. free. ‡ New Zealand Poultry Board, 56 Victoria St., P.O. Box 379, Wellington, New Zealand. circ. 1,000.

333 NO ISSN 0065-0242
NORGES LANDBRUKSHOEGSKOLE. INSTITUTT FOR JORDSKIFTE OG EIENDOMSUTFORMING. MELDING. 1956. irreg. (2-4/yr.); no. 3l, 1979. price varies. Norges Landbrukshoegskole, Institutt for Jordskifte og Eiendomsutforming, Box 29, N-1432 Aas-NLH, Norway.

338.1 NO
NORGES LANDBRUKSOEKONOMISKE INSTITUTT. DRIFTSGRANSKINGER I JORD- OG SKOGBRUK. a. free. Norges Landbruksoekonomiske Institutt, Postboks 8024 Oslo-Dep, Oslo 1, Norway.
Formerly: Norges Landbruksoekonomiske Institutt. Driftsgranskinger i Jordbruker (ISSN 0078-1223)

630 570 JA
OKAYAMA UNIVERSITY. OHARA INSTITUTE FUER LANDWIRTSCHAFTLICHE BIOLOGIE. BERICHTE. Japanese edition: Nogaku Kenkyu (ISSN 0029-0874) (Text in English) 1916. irreg. exchange basis. Okayama University, Ohara Institute fuer Landwirtschaftliche Biologie - Ohara Institute for Agricultural Biology, 2-20-1 Chuo, Kurashiki 710, Japan.

330 338.1 GW ISSN 0078-6888
OSTEUROPASTUDIEN DER HOCHSCHULEN DES LANDES HESSEN. REIHE 1. GIESSENER ABHANDLUNGEN ZUR AGRAR- UND WIRTSCHAFTSFORSCHUNG DES EUROPAEISCHEN OSTENS. 1957. irreg. price varies. (Universitaet Giessen, Zentrum fuer Kontinentale Agrar- und Wirtschaftsforschung) Duncker und Humblot, Dietrich-Schaefer-Weg 9, Postfach 410329, 1000 Berlin 41, W. Germany (B.R.D.) circ. 400-600.

338.1 UK
OXFORD AGRARIAN STUDIES. 1933. a. £5.50. University of Oxford, Agricultural Economics Institute, Dartington House, Little Clarendon St., Oxford, Eng. Ed. G. T. Jones. bibl. charts. stat. index. index. circ. 900. Indexed: Nutr.Abstr. World Agri.Econ. & Rural. Sociol.Abstr.
Formerly: Farm Economist (ISSN 0014-7931) *Economics*

PAKISTAN. EXPORT PROMOTION BUREAU. FRESH FRUITS. see *BUSINESS AND ECONOMICS — International Commerce*

338.1 BL
PERNAMBUCO, BRAZIL. SECRETARIA DA AGRICULTURA. PLANO ANUAL DE TRABALHO. a. Secretaria da Agricultura, Recife, Brazil.
Formerly: Brazil. Departamento de Agricultura e Abastecimento. Plano Anual de Trabalho do D A A.

338.1 PH
PHILIPPINES. BUREAU OF AGRICULTURAL ECONOMICS. CROP AND LIVESTOCK STATISTICS. (Text in English) 1954. a. Bureau of Agricultural Economics, Del Santos Bldg., Quezon Blvd. Ext., Quezon City, Philippines. Ed. J. C. Alix. circ. 500.
Formerly: Philippines. Bureau of Agricultural Economics. Crop, Livestock and Natural Resources Statistics (ISSN 0079-1512)

338.1 PH ISSN 0079-1520
PHILIPPINES. BUREAU OF AGRICULTURAL ECONOMICS. REPORT. (Text in English) 1953. a. Bureau of Agricultural Economics, Delos Santos Bldg., Quezon Blvd. Ext., Quezon City, Philippines. Ed. J. C. Alix. circ. 500.

630 338.1 PH
PHILIPPINES. DEPARTMENT OF AGRARIAN REFORM. PLANNING SERVICE. ANNUAL REPORT. (Text in English) 1973. a. Department of Agrarian Reform, Planning Service, Manila, Philippines.

338.1 PH
PHILIPPINES. NATIONAL ECONOMIC AND DEVELOPMENT AUTHORITY. FOOD BALANCE SERIES. irreg., latest no. 3. National Economic and Development Authority, Box 1116, Manila, Philippines.

PLUNKETT DEVELOPMENT SERIES. see *BUSINESS AND ECONOMICS — International Development And Assistance*

630 338.1 UK ISSN 0551-0910
PLUNKETT FOUNDATION FOR CO-OPERATIVE STUDIES. OCCASIONAL PAPERS. 1952. irreg. price varies. Plunkett Foundation for Co-Operative Studies, 31 St. Giles St., Oxford OX1 3LF, England.

630 338.1 UK ISSN 0142-5005
PLUNKETT FOUNDATION FOR CO-OPERATIVE STUDIES. STUDY SERIES. 1978. irreg. price varies. Plunkett Foundation for Co-Operative Studies, 31 St. Giles St., Oxford OX1 3LF, England.

AGRICULTURE — AGRICULTURAL ECONOMICS

338.1 633   UK   ISSN 0079-4309
POTATO MARKETING BOARD, LONDON.
ANNUAL REPORT AND ACCOUNTS. a. Potato Marketing Board, 50 Hans Crescent, Knightsbridge, London SW1X 0NB, England.

338.1   BL   ISSN 0302-5195
PRECOS PAGOS PELOS AGRICULTORES. 1969. a. (Instituto Brasileiro de Economia, Centro de Estudos Agricolas) Fundacao Getulio Vargas, Praia de Botafogo 190, Rio de Janeiro, Brazil (And C.P. 9052, 20000 Rio de Janeiro RJ, Brazil) stat.

338.1   BL   ISSN 0100-5219
PRECOS RECEBIDOS PELOS AGRICULTORES. 1970. a. (Instituto Brasileiro de Economia, Centro de Estudos Agricolas) Fundacao Getulio Vargas, Caixa Postal 9052, 20000 Rio de Janeiro R.J., Brazil.

338.1   CN   ISSN 0708-3017
PROCESSING & MANUFACTURING GUIDE. 1977. biennial. Agricultural Processing Branch, 423 Legislative Bldg., Edmonton, Alta. T5K 2B6, Canada. charts. illus.
Formerly: Agricultural Processing & Manufacturing Guide (ISSN 0708-3025)

338.1   AT
PROFESSIONAL FARM MANAGEMENT GUIDEBOOK. 1967. irreg; (approx. 1/yr) Aus $2.50. University of New England, Agricultural Business Research Institute, Armidale, N.S.W. 2351, Australia. circ. 4,000.

338.1   UK
READING/LEGON JOINT RESEARCH PROJECT IN VILLAGE DEVELOPMENT, SOUTH EAST GHANA. REPORT. (Subseries of Reading, Eng. University. Dept. of Agricultural Economics and Management. Development Studies) 1971. irreg. 50p. ‡ University of Reading, Department of Agricultural Economics & Management, Reading, England. illus. stat.

338.1   SP
RED CONTABLE AGRARIA NACIONAL. irreg. Ministerio de Agricultura, Secretaria General Tecnica, Paseo de Infanta Isabel 1, Madrid 7, Spain. charts. stat.

338.1   HU
RESEARCH INSTITUTE FOR AGRICULTURAL ECONOMICS. BULLETIN. (Text in English) irreg. exchange basis. Agrargazdasagi Kutato Intezet, Zsil u. 3, P.O.B. 5, 1355 Budapest, Hungary.
Formerly: Hungarian Academy of Sciences. Research Institute for Agricultural Economics. Bulletin.

338.1   MY   ISSN 0034-6403
REVIEW OF AGRICULTURAL ECONOMICS MALAYSIA. (Text in English) 1967. irreg. M.$5. ‡ Federal Agricultural Marketing Authority, 17 & 19 Jalan Selangor, Petaling Jaya, Selangor, Malaysia. Ed. Abu Bakar bin Hamid. adv. charts. tr.lit. circ 1,000. Indexed: Trop.Abstr.

338.1 300   US
ROCKEFELLER FOUNDATION. WORKING PAPERS. 1974. irreg. free. Rockefeller Foundation, 1133 Ave. of the Americas, New York, NY 10036.

338.1   PL   ISSN 0080-3715
ROCZNIKI NAUK ROLNICZYCH. SERIA G. EKONOMIKA ROLNICTWA. (Text in Polish; summaries in English, Russian or Polish) 1903. irreg., 1975, vol. 80, no.4. price varies. (Polska Akademia Nauk, Komitet Ekonomiki Rolnictwa) Panstwowe Wydawnictwo Naukowe, Miodowa 10, Warsaw, Poland (Dist by Ars Polona-Ruch, Krakowskie Przedmiescie 7, Warsaw, Poland) Ed. Z. Grochowski. bibl. charts.

630   UG   ISSN 0080-4851
RURAL DEVELOPMENT RESEARCH PAPER. 1965. irreg. price varies. Makerere University, Department of Rural Economy and Extension, P.O. Box 7062, Kampala, Uganda. (Co-sponsor: Makerere Institute of Social Research)

338.1   CY
SALES OF VINE PRODUCTS MANUFACTURED IN CYPRUS. a. Mils.200. Department of Statistics and Research, Ministry of Finance, Nicosia, Cyprus.

381   CN   ISSN 0381-3223
SASKATCHEWAN FARMERS' MARKETS ANNUAL REPORT. 1975. a. Department of Agriculture, Marketing and Economics Branch, Administration Bldg., Regina, Sask. S4S 0B1, Canada. charts. illus.

338.1   CN
SASKATCHEWAN FARMSTART CORPORATION. ANNUAL REPORT. a. Saskatchewan Farmstart Corporation, Regina, Sask., Canada.

SCANDINAVIAN INSTITUTE OF AFRICAN STUDIES. RURAL DEVELOPMENT. see *ANTHROPOLOGY*

338.1   UK   ISSN 0080-7966
SCOTTISH AGRICULTURAL ECONOMICS; SOME STUDIES OF CURRENT ECONOMIC CONDITIONS IN SCOTTISH FARMING. 1950. a. price varies. Department of Agriculture and Fisheries, Chesser House, 500 Gorgie Rd., Edinburgh, Scotland (Avail. from H.M.S.O., 13a Castle St., Edinburgh EH2 3AR, Scotland)

338.1   BL
SOCIEDADE BRASILEIRA DE ECONOMISTAS RURAIS. ANAIS DA REUNIAO.* irreg.
Sociedade Brasileira de Economistas Rurais, Rua Anchieta, 41, 10 Andar, Sao Paulo, Brazil.

SORGO - UMA ALTERNATIVA ECONOMICA. see *AGRICULTURE — Feed, Flour And Grain*

338.1   SA
SOUTH AFRICA. DIVISION OF SURVEYS. REPORT OF THE DIRECTOR-GENERAL OF SURVEYS. 1974/75. a. Division of Surveys, Rhodes Ave., Mowbray, South Africa.

630 301.35   SP
SPAIN. INSTITUTO NACONAL DE INVESTIGACIONES AGRARIAS. ANALES. SERIE: ECONOMIA Y SOCIOLOGICA AGRARIAS. (Text in Spanish; summaries in English, French, German) 1971. irreg (approx 1/yr) 300 ptas. per issue. Instituto Nacional de Investigaciones Agrarias, General Sanjurjo 56, Madrid 3, Spain. bk. rev. circ. 1,500.
Supersedes in part: Spain. Instituto Nacional de Investigaciones Agronomicas, Anales.

338.1   SP   ISSN 0081-3478
SPAIN. SERVICIO DE EXTENSION AGRARIA. SERIE TECNICA. 1953. irreg; latest issue, no. 52, 1974. 50 ptas. Servicio de Extension Agraria, Ministerio de Aricultura, Bravo Murillo 101, Madrid 20, Spain.

338.1   GW   ISSN 0081-7198
STUDIEN ZUR AGRARWIRTSCHAFT. 1967. irreg., no. 20, 1980. price varies. I F O Institut fuer Wirtschaftsforschung, Poschingerstr. 5, 8000 Munich 80, W. Germany (B.R.D.) circ. 500.

333 338.1   UK   ISSN 0081-8453
STUDIES IN RURAL LAND USE. 1954. irreg., 1972, no. 11. price varies. Wye College (University of London), School of Rural Economics and Related Studies, Countryside Planning Unit, Nr. Ashford, Kent, England. circ. 1,000. Indexed: Geo.Abstr. World Agri.Econ.&Rural Sociol.Abstr.

338.1 636.5   II
STUDIES IN THE ECONOMICS OF POULTRY FARMING IN PUNJAB. (Text in English) 1972. a. Rs.14. Ministry of Agriculture and Irrigation, Department of Agriculture, Directorate of Economics and Statistics, A-2E-3 Kasturba Gandhi Marg Barracks, New Delhi 110001, India. Ed. G. S. Sandhu. charts. illus. stat.

338.1 630   SJ
SUDAN YEARBOOK OF AGRICULTURAL STATISTICS. (Text in English) 1974. a. Department of Agricultural Economics, Statistics Division, Khartoum, Sudan.
Supersedes: Bulletin of Agricultural Statistics of the Sudan.

338.1   GW
TECHNISCHE UNIVERSITAET BERLIN. INSTITUT FUER SOZIALOEKONOMIE DER AGRARENTWICKLUNG. ANNUAL REPORT (ABRIDGED VERSION) 1965. a. Technische Universitaet Berlin, Institut fuer Sozialoekonomie der Agrarentwicklung, Podbielskiallee 64-66, 1000 Berlin 33 (Dahlem), W. Germany (B.R.D.) circ. 350. (processed)

338.1   GW
TECHNISCHE UNIVERSITAET BERLIN. INSTITUT FUER SOZIALOEKONOMIE DER AGRARENTWICKLUNG. JAHRESBERICHT. 1960. a. free. Technische Universitaet Berlin, Institut fuer Sozialoekonomie der Agrarentwicklung, Podbielskiallee 64-66, 1000 Berlin 33 (Dahlem), W. Germany (B.R.D.) circ. 300. (processed)
Formerly (until 1976): Technische Universitaet Berlin. Institut fuer Sozialoekonomie der Agrarentwicklung. Taetigkeitsbericht (ISSN 0067-6039)

338.1 633   US   ISSN 0082-3392
TEXAS COTTON REVIEW. (Since 1960/61 issued in its Research Reports) 1949/50. a. free. University of Texas at Austin, Natural Fibers Economic Research, Box 8180, University Station, Austin, TX 78712. (Co-sponsor: Natural Fibers & Food Protein Commission of Texas)
Cotton

338.1   MY
UNITED PLANTING ASSOCIATION OF MALAYSIA. ANNUAL REPORT. (Text in English) 1968. a. M.$2.50. United Planting Association of Malaysia, Box 272, Kuala Lumpur 01-02, Malaysia. circ. 1,100.

338.1   US   ISSN 0002-1601
U.S. CROP REPORTING BOARD. AGRICULTURAL PRICES. m. with annual summary. free. U.S. Crop Reporting Board, U.S. Dept. of Agriculture Statistical Reporting Service, 14th and Independence Ave. S.W., Washington, DC 20250.

338.1   US   ISSN 0083-0445
U.S. DEPARTMENT OF AGRICULTURE. AGRICULTURAL ECONOMICS REPORT. 1961. irreg. U.S. Department of Agriculture, Washington, DC 20250.
Reports 1-233 (1916-1972) issued as: U.S. Department of Agriculture. Economic Research Service. Agricultural Economics Report.

630 338.1   US   ISSN 0148-7094
U.S. DEPARTMENT OF AGRICULTURE. ECONOMICS, STATISTICS, AND COOPERATIVES SERVICE. AFRICA AND WEST ASIA AGRICULTURAL SITUATION. a. single copy free. U. S. Department of Agriculture, Economics, Statistics, and Cooperatives Service, Information Staff, Publications Unit, Washington, DC 20250.
Formerly: Agricultural Situation in Africa and West Asia (ISSN 0094-5528)

338.1   US   ISSN 0501-9117
U.S. DEPARTMENT OF AGRICULTURE. ECONOMICS, STATISTICS, AND COOPERATIVES SERVICE. AGRICULTURAL FINANCE OUTLOOK. 1961. a(in December) single copy free. U.S. Department of Agriculture, Economics, Statistics, and Cooperatives Service, Information Staff, Publications Unit, Washington, DC 20250.

338.1   US   ISSN 0002-1466
U.S. DEPARTMENT OF AGRICULTURE. ECONOMICS, STATISTICS, AND COOPERATIVES SERVICE. AGRICULTURAL FINANCE REVIEW. 1938. a. free. U. S. Department of Agriculture, Economics, Statistics, and Cooperatives Service, Information Staff, Washington, DC 20250 (Orders to: Supt. of Documents, Washington, DC 20402) bk. rev. charts. mkt. stat. index. circ. 3,000. Indexed: J. of Econ.Abstr.

AGRICULTURE — AGRICULTURAL ECONOMICS

630 338.1 US ISSN 0098-4000
U.S. DEPARTMENT OF AGRICULTURE. ECONOMICS, STATISTICS, AND COOPERATIVES SERVICE. AGRICULTURAL SITUATION IN EASTERN EUROPE. a. single copy free. U. S. Department of Agriculture, Economics, Statistics, and Cooperatives Service, Information Staff, Publications Unit, Washington, DC 20250.

630 338.1 US ISSN 0566-9502
U.S. DEPARTMENT OF AGRICULTURE. ECONOMICS, STATISTICS, AND COOPERATIVES SERVICE. AGRICULTURAL SITUATION IN THE FAR EAST AND OCEANIA. a. single copy free. U. S. Department of Agriculture, Economics, Statistics, and Cooperatives Service, Information Staff, Publications Unit, Washington, DC 20250.

630 338.1 US
U.S. DEPARTMENT OF AGRICULTURE. ECONOMICS, STATISTICS, AND COOPERATIVES SERVICE. AGRICULTURAL SITUATION IN THE PEOPLE'S REPUBLIC OF CHINA. a. single copy free. U. S. Department of Agriculture, Economics, Statistics, and Cooperatives Service, Information Staff, Publications Unit, Washington, DC 20250.

630 338.1 US ISSN 0360-4098
U.S. DEPARTMENT OF AGRICULTURE. ECONOMICS, STATISTICS, AND COOPERATIVES SERVICE. AGRICULTURAL SITUATION IN THE SOVIET UNION. a. single copy free. U. S. Department of Agriculture, Economics, Statistics, and Cooperatives Service, Information Staff, Publications Unit, Washington, DC 20250.

630 338.1 US ISSN 0501-9257
U.S. DEPARTMENT OF AGRICULTURE. ECONOMICS, STATISTICS, AND COOPERATIVES SERVICE. AGRICULTURAL SITUATION IN THE WESTERN HEMISPHERE. a. U. S. Department of Agriculture, Economics, Statistics, and Cooperatives Service, Information Staff, Publications Unit, Washington, DC 20250.

630 338.1 US
U.S. DEPARTMENT OF AGRICULTURE. ECONOMICS, STATISTICS, AND COOPERATIVES SERVICE. AGRICULTURAL SITUATION IN WESTERN EUROPE. a. single copy free. U. S. Department of Agriculture, Economics, Statistics, and Cooperatives Service, Information Staff, Publications Unit, Washington, DC 20250.

338.1 US ISSN 0092-9530
U.S. DEPARTMENT OF AGRICULTURE. ECONOMICS, STATISTICS AND COOPERATIVES SERVICE. COST OF STORING AND HANDLING COTTON AT PUBLIC STORAGE FACILITIES. 1964. irreg. free. U. S. Department of Agriculture, Economics, Statistics, and Cooperatives Service, Information Staff, Publications Unit, Washington, DC 20250. stat. Key Title: Cost of Storing and Handling Cotton at Public Storage Facilities.

668 US
U.S. DEPARTMENT OF AGRICULTURE. ECONOMICS, STATISTICS, AND COOPERATIVES SERVICE. FERTILIZER SITUATION. 1971. a. free. U. S. Department of Agriculture, Economics, Statistics, and Cooperatives Service, Information Staff, Washington, DC 20250. stat. circ. 3,500.

338.14 US ISSN 0082-9781
U.S. DEPARTMENT OF AGRICULTURE. MARKETING RESEARCH REPORT. 1952. irreg. U.S. Department of Agriculture, Washington, DC 20250.

338.1 US ISSN 0082-979X
U.S. DEPARTMENT OF AGRICULTURE. PRODUCTION RESEARCH REPORTS. 1956. irreg. U.S. Department of Agriculture., Washington, DC 20250.

338.1 332 US
U. S. DEPARTMENT OF AGRICULTURE, ECONOMICS, STATISTICS, AND COOPERATIVES SERVICE. FARM REAL ESTATE TAXES, RECENT TRENDS AND DEVELOPMENTS. 1961. a. free. U. S. Department of Agriculture, Economics, Statistics, and Cooperatives Service, Information Staff, Publications Unit, Washington, DC 20250. Ed. W. Fred Woods. circ. 3,000.
Formerly: Farm Real Estate Taxes (ISSN 0071-4003)

332.71 338.1 334 US
U.S. FARM CREDIT ADMINISTRATION. ANNUAL REPORT OF THE FARM CREDIT ADMINISTRATION AND THE COOPERATIVE FARM CREDIT SYSTEM. 1933. a. $1.20 price varies. U.S. Farm Credit Administration., 490 l'Enfant Plaza, Suite 4000, Washington, DC 20578 (Orders to: Supt. Doc., Washington, DC 20402)
Formerly: U.S. Farm Credit Administration. Annual Report of the Farm Credit Administration on the Work of the Cooperative Farm Credit System (ISSN 0083-0542)

338.1 382 US ISSN 0083-0976
U. S. FOREIGN AGRICULTURAL SERVICE. FOOD AND AGRICULTURAL EXPORT DIRECTORY. a.(approx.) free controlled circ. U. S. Foreign Agricultural Service, Information Service Staff, Room 5918, Department of Agriculture, Washington, DC 20250.

630 US ISSN 0083-0992
U. S. FOREIGN AGRICULTURAL SERVICE. MISCELLANEOUS REPORTS. 1956. irreg. contr. free circ. U. S. Foreign Agricultural Service, Infomation Service Staff, Room 5918, Department of Agriculture, Washington, DC 20250. (also avail. in microfilm; back issues avail)

338.1 IT
UNIVERSITA DEGLI STUDI DI TRIESTE. ISTITUTO DI RICERCHE ECONOMICO AGRARIE. PUBBLICAZIONE. 1971. irreg. Universita degli Studi di Trieste, Istituto di Ricerche Economico-Agrarie, Trieste, Italy.

338.1 301 CN
UNIVERSITY OF ALBERTA. DEPARTMENT OF RURAL ECONOMY. BULLETIN. irreg. University of Alberta, Department of Rural Economy, Edmonton, Alta. T6G 2H1, Canada. illus.
Formed by the merger of: University of Alberta. Department of Agricultural Economics and Rural Sociology. Agricultural Economics and Rural Sociology Research Bulletin (ISSN 0065-6046) & University of Alberta. Department of Agricultural and Rural Sociology. Agricultural Economics Technical Bulletin & University of Alberta. Department of Agricultural Economics and Rural Sociology. Agricultural Economics Special Report.

338.1 US
UNIVERSITY OF FLORIDA. FOOD AND RESOURCE ECONOMICS DEPARTMENT. ECONOMIC INFORMATION REPORT. 1969. irreg., no. 123, 1979. free. ‡ University of Florida, Institute of Food and Agricultural Sciences, c/o Dr. Leo Polopolus, Chairman, Food and Resource Economics Department, Gainesville, FL 32611. Ed. Cecil N. Smith. circ. 2,500.
Former titles: University of Florida. Food and Resource Economics Department. Economics Report; University of Florida. Institute of Food and Agricultural Sciences. Agricultural Economics Series.

338.1 US ISSN 0073-5213
UNIVERSITY OF ILLINOIS AT URBANA-CHAMPAIGN. DEPARTMENT OF AGRICULTURAL ECONOMICS. AGRICULTURAL FINANCE PROGRAM REPORT. 1970. irreg. price varies. ‡ University of Illinois at Urbana-Champaign, Department of Agricultural Economics, Urbana, IL 61801.

338.1 US
UNIVERSITY OF ILLINOIS AT URBANA-CHAMPAIGN. DEPARTMENT OF AGRICULTURAL ECONOMICS. LANDLORD AND TENANT SHARES. 1961. a. free. University of Illinois at Urbana-Champaign, Department of Agricultural Economics, Urbana, IL 61801. Ed. Franklin J. Reiss. stat. circ. controlled.

338.1 US ISSN 0073-523X
UNIVERSITY OF ILLINOIS AT URBANA-CHAMPAIGN. DEPARTMENT OF AGRICULTURAL ECONOMICS. RESEARCH REPORT. 1954. irreg. ‡ University of Illinois at Urbana-Champaign, Department of Agricultural Economics, Urbana, IL 61801.

338.1 CN ISSN 0076-4000
UNIVERSITY OF MANITOBA. DEPARTMENT OF AGRICULTURAL ECONOMICS AND FARM MANAGEMENT. OCCASIONAL PAPERS. 1960. irreg. price varies. University of Manitoba, Department of Agricultural Economics and Farm Management, Winnipeg, Manitoba R3T 2N2, Canada.

338.1 UK ISSN 0557-6911
UNIVERSITY OF READING. DEPARTMENT OF AGRICULTURAL ECONOMICS AND MANAGEMENT. FARM BUSINESS DATA. 1974. a. £1. ‡ University of Reading, Department of Agricultural Economics, Reading, England. Ed. R. H. Tuck. bibl. charts. stat.

338.1 UK ISSN 0486-0845
UNIVERSITY OF READING. DEPARTMENT OF AGRICULTURAL ECONOMICS. MISCELLANEOUS STUDIES. 1973, no. 55. irreg. price varies. ‡ University of Reading, Department of Agricultural Economics, Reading, England. charts.

338.1 AT ISSN 0313-8704
UNIVERSITY OF SYDNEY. DEPARTMENT OF AGRICULTURAL ECONOMICS. AGRICULTURAL EXTENSION BULLETIN. 1976. irreg., no. 5, 1978. price varies. University of Sydney, Department of Agricultural Economics, Sydney, N.S.W. 2006, Australia. circ. 200.

338.1 AT ISSN 0082-0563
UNIVERSITY OF SYDNEY. DEPARTMENT OF AGRICULTURAL ECONOMICS. RESEARCH BULLETIN. 1957. irreg. price varies. ‡ University of Sydney, Department of Agricultural Economics, Sydney, N.S.W. 2006, Australia. circ. 400.

338.1 AT
UNIVERSITY OF SYDNEY. DEPARTMENT OF AGRICULTURAL ECONOMICS. RESEARCH REPORT. 1957. irreg., no. 7, 1978. price varies. ‡ University of Sydney, Department of Agricultural Economics, Sydney, N.S.W. 2006, Australia. circ. 400. (processed)
Formerly: University of Sydney. Department of Agriculture Economics. Mimeographed Report. (ISSN 0082-0555)

338.1 US ISSN 0082-3384
UNIVERSITY OF TEXAS, AUSTIN. NATURAL FIBERS ECONOMIC RESEARCH. RESEARCH REPORT. 1947. irreg. free. University of Texas at Austin, Natural Fibers Economic Research, Box 8180, University Station, Austin, TX 78712. (Co-sponsor: Natural Fibers & Food Protein Commission of Texas)

333 US ISSN 0084-0807
UNIVERSITY OF WISCONSIN, MADISON. LAND TENURE CENTER. REPRINT. (Some numbers in Spanish) 1965. irreg., no. 136, 1978. free. University of Wisconsin-Madison, Land Tenure Center, 310 King Hall, Madison, WI 53706. Ed. Jane B. Knowles.

333 US ISSN 0084-0823
UNIVERSITY OF WISCONSIN, MADISON. LAND TENURE CENTER. TRAINING AND METHODS SERIES. (Text of no. 1-P Portuguese; other numbers have bibliographical entries in Spanish, Portuguese) 1964. irreg., no. 27, 1978. $1 in North America (excluding Mexico) and western Europe; free elsewhere. University of Wisconsin-Madison, Land Tenure Center, 310 King Hall, Madison, WI 53706. Ed. Theresa Anderson.

338.1 VE
VENEZUELA. INSTITUTO DE CREDITO AGRICOLA Y PECUARIO. INFORME ANUAL. a. Instituto de Credito Agricola y Pecuario, Carrera 23 con Calle 30, Barquisimento, Venezuela.

AGRICULTURE — AGRICULTURAL EQUIPMENT

630 338.1 VE
VENEZUELA. MINISTERIO DE AGRICULTURA Y CRIA. DIRECCION DE PLANIFICACION Y ESTADISTICA. ESTADISTICAS AGROPECUARIAS DE LAS ENTIDADES FEDERALES. 1962. biennial. free. Ministerio de Agricultura y Cria, Direccion de Planificacion y Estadistica, Division de Estadistica, Caracas, Venezuela.

338.1 UR
VOPROSY EKONOMIKI SEL'SKOGO KHOZYAISTVA DAL'NEGO VOSTOKA. irreg. 0.57 Rub. Akademiya Nauk S.S.S.R., Dal'nevostochnyi Nauchnyi Tsentr, Ul. Leninskaya 50, Vladivostok, U.S.S.R.

630 AT
WESTERN AUSTRALIA. DEPARTMENT OF AGRICULTURE. RURAL ECONOMICS AND MARKETING SECTION. REPORT ON THE MARKET MILK INDUSTRY IN WESTERN AUSTRALIA. irreg. Department of Agriculture, Rural Economics and Marketing Section, Perth, W.A., Australia.

WESTERN AUSTRALIAN POTATO MARKETING BOARD. ANNUAL REPORT. see AGRICULTURE — Crop Production And Soil

338.1 UK
WYE COLLEGE (UNIVERSITY OF LONDON). AGRARIAN DEVELOPMENT UNIT. OCCASIONAL PAPER. 1974. irreg. price varies. Wye College (University of London), School of Rural Economics and Related Studies, Agrarian Development Unit, Nr. Ashford, Kent, England.

338.1 631 UK
WYE COLLEGE (UNIVERSITY OF LONDON). SCHOOL OF RURAL ECONOMICS & RELATED STUDIES. FARM BUSINESS UNIT. OCCASIONAL PAPER. 1978. irreg. price varies. Wye College (University of London), School of Rural Economics and Related Studies, Farm Business Unit, Nr. Ashford, Kent, England.

630 338.1 UK ISSN 0142-498X
YEAR BOOK OF AGRICULTURAL CO-OPERATION. 1927. a. £5.50($11.50) Plunkett Foundation for Co-Operative Studies, 31 St. Giles St., Oxford OX1 3LF, England. (Co-sponsor: International Co-Operative Alliance) circ. 500.

AGRICULTURE — Agricultural Equipment

631.3 CU
ACTUALIDADES DE LA INGENIERIA AGRONOMICA. irreg.; 1971, no. 23. exchange. Universidad de la Habana, Centro de Informacion Cientifica y Tecnica, Havana, Cuba. Ed. Bd. charts. stat.

631.3 CU
CUBA. CENTRO DE INFORMACION Y DOCUMENTACION AGROPECUARIO. BOLETIN DE RESENAS. SERIE: MECANIZACION. 1974. irreg. $5. Centro de Informacion y Documentacion Agropecuario, Calle 11 no. 1057, Gaveta Postal 4149, Havana 4, Cuba.

631.3 DK ISSN 0302-5349
DANSK MASKINHANDLERFORENING. HANDBOG. 1966. irreg. Dansk Maskinhandlerforening, Aboulevard 48, 2200 Copenhagen V, Denmark.

631.3 UK ISSN 0071-3880
FARM AND GARDEN EQUIPMENT GUIDE. 1969. a. £5.50. I P C Agricultural Press Ltd., Surrey House, 1 Throwley Way, Sutton, Surrey SM1 4QQ, England (Dist. in the U.S. by Iliffe- N.T.P. Inc., Sales Division, 205 E. 42 St., New York, N.Y. 10017).
Formerly: Farm Equipment Buyers Guide; Which was formed by the merger of: Farm Equipment Directory & Farm Implement Buyers Guide.

631.3 JA ISSN 0071-3937
FARM MACHINERY YEARBOOK/NOGYO KIKAI NENKAN. (Text in Japanese; summary, contents and statistical section in English) 1943. a. 8500 Yen. Shin-Norinsha Co., Ltd., 2-7 Kanda Nishikicho, Chiyoda-ku, Tokyo 101, Japan. Ed. Yoshisuke Kishida. adv. circ. 10,000.

631.3 FR
FICHES TECHNIQUES R.T.D. APPLICATIONS AGRICOLES. (Revue Technique Diesel) irreg. price varies. Editions Techniques pour l'Automobile et l'Industrie, 20-22 rue de la Saussiere, 92100 Boulogne-Billancourt, France. charts. illus. (looseleaf format)

631.3 UK ISSN 0017-3932
GREEN BOOK; the authority on tractors and farm equipment. 1951. a. £15($25) Industrial Newspapers Ltd., Queensway House, Queensway, Redhill, Surrey RH1 1QS, England. Ed. H. Catling. adv. illus. circ. 4,000.

631.3 FR
GUIDE-ANNUAIRE DE L'EQUIPEMENT AGRICOLE; catalogue officiel du Salon International de la Machine Agricole. (Text in French; Summaries in English, German, Spanish, Italian) 1922. a. 7 F. ‡ Salon International de la Machine Agricole, 95 rue Saint-Lazare, 75441 Paris, France. adv. index.

631.372 US ISSN 0073-5566
IMPLEMENT & TRACTOR PRODUCT FILE. a. $5. Intertec Publishing Corp., 9221 Quivira Rd., Box 12901, Overland Park, KS 66212. Ed. Pat Blanton.

631.3 US ISSN 0073-5574
IMPLEMENT & TRACTOR RED BOOK. a. $5. Intertec Publishing Corp., 9221 Quivira Rd., Box 12901, Overland Park, KS 66212. Ed. Charles G. Ewing.

631.3 IS
INSTITUTE OF AGRICULTURAL ENGINEERING, BET DAGAN. SCIENTIFIC ACTIVITIES. (Text in English) irreg. Institute of Agricultural Engineering, Bet Dagan, Israel. illus.

621 631 PL ISSN 0137-6918
POLITEKNIKA POZNANSKA. ZESZYTY NAUKOWE. MASZYNY ROBOCZE I POJAZDY. (Text in Polish; Summaries in English and Russian) 1956. irreg., no. 12, 1972. price varies. Politechnika Poznanska, Pl. Curie-Sklodowskiej 5, Poznan, Poland. Ed. Kazimierz Niewiarowski. circ. 150.
Formerly: Politeknika Poznanska. Zeszyty Naukowe. Mechanizacja i Elektryfikacja Rolnictwa (ISSN 0076-5805)

631.3 AT ISSN 0079-4422
POWER FARMING TECHNICAL ANNUAL. 1937. a. Aus.$8.50. Pacific Publications (Australia) Pty. Ltd., G.P.O. Box 3408, Sydney, N.S.W. 2001, Australia. Ed. Barry Badger. adv.

631.3 JA
PRODUCT FILE FOR AGRICULTURAL MACHINERY AND RELATED MATERIAL. (Text in Japanese) 1972. a. 7000 Yen. Farm Machinery Industrial Research Corp., Shin-Norin Bldg., 27-2-chome, Nishi-Shimbashi, Chiyoda-ku, Tokyo 101, Japan. Ed. Y. Kishida. adv.

631.3 PL ISSN 0080-3677
ROCZNIKI NAUK ROLNICZYCH. SERIA C.TECHNIKA ROLNICZA. (Text in Polish; summaries in English, Polish, Russian) 1903. irreg., 1975, vol. 72, no. 1. price varies. (Polska Akademia Nauk, Komitet Techniki Rolniczej) Panstwowe Wydawnictwo Naukowe, Miodowa 10, Warsaw, Poland (Dist. by Ars Polona-Ruch, Krakowskie Przedmiescie 7, Warsaw, Poland) Ed. Janusz Haman. bibl. charts. illus.
Title Varies: Roczniki Nauk Rolniczych. Seria C. Mechanizacja Rolnictwa.

631.3 FR ISSN 0082-5662
TRACTOCATALOGUE; guide technique de mecanique agricole. 1955. a. 100 F. Editions Gozlan, 94 rue Saint-Lazare, 75442 Paris Cedex 9, France.

631.3 US
TRACTOR PERFORMANCE POCKET BOOK. 1975. a. $1.50. Continental Publishing Co., Inc., Box 27347, 210 Hillcrest Bldg., Ralston, NE 68127. adv. illus. circ. 175,455.

631.3 UK ISSN 0084-2184
WORLD PLOUGHING CONTEST. OFFICIAL HANDBOOK. (Text in English and in language of country in which the contest is held) 1954. a. £1. World Ploughing Organization, Foulsyke, Loweswatwer, Cockermouth, Cumberland, England. Ed. Alfred Hall. adv. index. circ. 10,000.

AGRICULTURE — Crop Production And Soil

see also Agriculture—Feed, Flour and Grain; Gardening and Horticulture; Rubber; Tobacco

630 PL ISSN 0065-0919
ACTA AGRARIA ET SILVESTRIA. SERIES AGRARIA. (Text in Polish; summaries in English and Russian) 1961. irreg., 1972, vol. 12. price varies. (Polska Akademia Nauk, Oddzial w Krakowie, Komisja Nauk Rolniczych i Lesnych) Panstwowe Wydawnictwo Naukowe, Miodowa 10, Warsaw, Poland (Dist. by Ars Polona-Ruch, Krakowskie Przedmiescie 7, Warsaw, Poland) Ed. Eugeniusz Gorlach.

631 US ISSN 0065-4477
AGRICULTURAL ENGINEERS YEARBOOK. 1954. a. $25 to non-members. ‡ American Society of Agricultural Engineers, 2950 Niles Rd., St. Joseph, MI 49085. Ed. Joan Baxter.
Agricultural engineering

631 US
AGRICULTURAL RESEARCH CENTER. ANNUAL REPORT. 1952. a. free. ‡ Agricultural Research Center, Inc., 1305 East Main Street, Lakeland, FL 33801. circ. 160.
Formerly: Annual Report Soil Science Foundation.

630.24 668.6 NE
AGRO CHEMIE-KOERIER. Dutch edition of: Pflanzenschutz-Kurier. 1959. 3/yr. free. ‡ Bayer Nederland B.V., Postbus 105, 6800 AC Arnhem, Netherlands (Main office: Bayer Pflanzenschutz, Leverkusen, W. Germany (B.R.D.)) charts. illus. circ. 30,900 (controlled)
Agricultural chemistry

631.4 NR ISSN 0065-4728
AHMADU BELLO UNIVERSITY. INSTITUTE FOR AGRICULTURAL RESEARCH. SOIL SURVEY BULLETIN. 1956. irreg. 1969, no. 39. price varies. Ahmadu Bello University, Institute for Agricultural Research, P.M.B. 1044, Zaria, Nigeria.

631.7 PL
AKADEMIA ROLNICZA, POZNAN. ROCZNIK. MELIORACJE WODNE. (Summaries in English and Russian) 1972. irreg. price varies. Akademia Rolnicza, Poznan, Ul. Wojska Polskiego 28, 60-637 Poznan, Poland. Indexed: Bibl.Agri. Forest.Abstr.

631.5 368 CN ISSN 0319-3535
ALBERTA HAIL AND CROP INSURANCE CORPORATION. ANNUAL REPORT. 1970. a. Alberta Hail and Crop Insurance Corporation, 1110 First Street, S.W., Calgary, Alberta T2R OV2, Canada.

631.4 CN ISSN 0080-1593
ALBERTA RESEARCH COUNCIL. PRELIMINARY REPORTS. SOIL SURVEYS. 1957. irreg. Can.$1 approx. Alberta Research Council, 11315 87th Ave., Edmonton, Alta. T6G 2C2, Canada.

630.281 US
ANIMAL AGRICULTURE SERIES. irreg. price varies. Interstate Printers & Publishers, Inc., 19-27 N. Jackson St., Danville, IL 61832.

634 338.1 FR ISSN 0066-3131
ANNUAIRE FRUCTIDOR; annuaire international des fruits, legumes, primeurs, derives et industries annexes. 1935. a. 350 F. Editions Fructidor, 20 bis Avenue des Deux-Routes, Avignon (Vaucluse), France.

AGRICULTURE — CROP PRODUCTION AND SOIL

ANNUAL BOOK OF A S T M STANDARDS. PART 19. NATURAL BUILDING STONES; SOIL AND ROCK; PEATS, MOSSES, AND HUMUS. see *ENGINEERING — Engineering Mechanics And Materials*

631.8   UN   ISSN 0084-6546
ANNUAL FERTILIZER REVIEW. (Tables in English and French with Spanish glossary; text in English, French and Spanish) 1951. a. price varies. Food and Agriculture Organization of the United Nations, Distribution and Sales Section, Via delle Terme di Caracalla, 00100 Rome, Italy (Dist. in U.S. by: Unipub, 345 Park Ave. S., New York, NY 10010)
    Formerly: Fertilizers: an Annual Review of World Production, Consumption and Trade (ISSN 0071-464X); Annual Review of World Production, Consumption and Trade of Fertilizers.
    Fertilizers

464.8   AG   ISSN 0066-5207
ANUARIO F.H.I. ARGENTINA: FRUTAS Y HORTALIZAS INDUSTRIARIZADAS Y FRESCAS/F. H. I. ANNUAL: FRESH AND INDUSTRIALIZED FRUITS AND VEGETABLES. (Text in Spanish; summaries in English) 1965. irreg. $10. Riccardo Luchini, Ed. & Pub., 2455 Canning, 1425 Buenos Aires, Argentina. adv. bk. rev. circ. 1,500.

631   AG
ARGENTINA. INSTITUTO NACIONAL DE TECNOLOGIA AGROPECUARIA. SUELOS. irreg. Instituto Nacional de Tecnologia Agropecuaria, Centro de Investigaciones de Recursos Naturales, Rivadavia 1439, Buenos Aires, Argentina.

631.5   BL
ARMAZENAGEM. irreg. Companhia Brasileira de Armazenamento, Palacio do Desenvolvimento, Brasilia, Brazil. illus.

630   FR
ASSOCIATION DES INGENIEURS ET ANCIENS ELEVES DE L'ECOLE SUPERIEURE D'INGENIEURS ET TECHNICIENS POUR L'AGRICULTURE. ANNUAIRE. a. Association des Ingenieurs et Anciens Eleves de l'Ecole Superieure d'Ingenieurs et Techniciens pour l'Agriculture., 38, rue des Ecoles, 75005 Paris, France. adv.

632   US   ISSN 0066-9431
ASSOCIATION OF AMERICAN PESTICIDE CONTROL OFFICIALS. OFFICIAL PUBLICATION. 1964/65. a. $6. Association of American Pesticide Control Officials, Inc., Iowa Department of Agriculture, State Capitol, Des Moines, IA 50319.

631.5   US
ASSOCIATION OF OFFICIAL SEED CERTIFYING AGENCIES. PRODUCTION PUBLICATION. 1959. irreg., no. 21, 1970. Association of Official Seed Certifying Agencies, Plant & Animal Science Building, Room 265, Clemson University, Clemson, SC 29631.
    Formerly: International Crop Improvement Association. Production Publication (ISSN 0538-7043)

338.1   AT
AUSTRALIA. BUREAU OF STATISTICS. CROP STATISTICS. 1971-72. a. free. Australian Bureau of Statistics, P.O. Box 10, Belconnen, A.C.T. 2616, Australia. circ. 2,400.

AUSTRALIA. BUREAU OF STATISTICS. VICTORIAN OFFICE. LAND UTILISATION AND CROPS. see *AGRICULTURE*

AUSTRALIA. BUREAU OF STATISTICS. WESTERN AUSTRALIAN OFFICE. WESTERN AUSTRALIAN CEREAL CROP FORECAST. see *AGRICULTURE — Feed, Flour And Grain*

634.11   AT
AUSTRALIA. BUREAU OF STATISTICS. WHEAT STATISTICS. 1936. a. free. Australian Bureau of Statistics, P.O. Box 10, Belconnen, A.C.T. 2616, Australia. charts. circ. 920. (processed)
    Formerly: Australia. Bureau of Statistics. Wheat Industry (ISSN 0043-4698)
    Wheat

633   AT   ISSN 0313-3192
AUSTRALIAN PLANT INTRODUCTION REVIEW. 1975. irreg. free. C. S. I. R. O., Division of Plant Industry, P. O. Box 1600, Canberra City, A.C.T. 2601, Australia.
    Supersedes: Commonwealth Scientific and Industrial Research Organization. Division of Plant Industry. Plant Introduction Review.

632   AT
AUSTRALIAN WEED CONTROL HANDBOOK. 1973. biennial. price varies. Plant Press, 3A Ipswich St., Toowoomba, Qld 4350, Australia. Ed. J. T. Swarbrick. circ. 2-3,000.

631.5   BG   ISSN 0070-8151
BANGLADESH. DIRECTORATE OF AGRICULTURE. SEASON AND CROP REPORT.* (Text in English) a. Directorate of Agriculture, Dacca, Bangladesh.

633.18   BG
BANGLADESH RICE RESEARCH INSTITUTE. ANNUAL REPORT. (Text in English) a. Tk.30. Bangladesh Rice Research Institute, Joydebpur, Dacca, Bangladesh. stat.

630   US   ISSN 0084-7747
BEAN IMPROVEMENT COOPERATIVE. ANNUAL REPORT. 1959. a. $6 for 2 years. Bean Improvement Cooperative, c/o M.H. Dickson, Ed., Department of Seed and Vegetable Sciences, New York State Agricultural Experiment Station, Geneva, NY 14456. circ. 350.

630   CE
BIBLIOGRAPHICAL SERIES ON COCONUT. (Text in English) 1967. a. Rs.15($2.55) Coconut Research Institute, Bandirippuwa Estate, Lunuwila, Sri Lanka. Ed. M.J.C. Perera. circ. 100. (processed)

631.4   US   ISSN 0081-1890
BOOKS IN SOILS AND THE ENVIRONMENT. 1967. irreg., vol. 8, 1975. price varies. Marcel Dekker, Inc., 270 Madison Ave., New York, NY 10016. Ed. A. D. McLaren.
    Formerly: Soil Science Library.

631 663 340   BL
BRAZIL. INSTITUTO DO ACUCAR E DO ALCOOL. CONSELHO DELIBERATIVO. COLETANEA DE RESOLUCOES (E) PRESIDENCIA. COLETANEA DE ATOS. 1972. irreg. Instituto do Acucar e do Alcool, Divisao de Estudo e Planejamento, Divisao Administrativa, Servico de Documentacao, Caixa Postal 420, Rio de Janeiro, Brazil. (Affiliate: Brazil. Ministerio da Industria e do Comercio)
    Formed by the merger of: Brazil. Instituto do Acucar e do Alcool. Conselho Deliberativo. Coletanea de Resolucoes & Brazil. Instituto do Acucar e do Alcool. Presidencia. Coletanea de Actas.
    Laws and regulations governing sugar and alcohol

631.7   BL   ISSN 0100-123X
BRAZIL. SERVICO NACIONAL DE LEVANTAMENTO E CONSERVACAO DE SOLOS. BOLETIM TECNICO. 1966. irreg. free to qualified personnel. Servico Nacional de Levantamento e Conservacao de Solos, Rua Jardim Botanico 1024, 22460 Rio de Janeiro RJ, Brazil. illus.
    Formerly: Brazil. Departamento Nacional de Pesquisa Agropecuaria. Divisao de Pesquisa Pedologica. Boletim Tecnico.

631.5   CN   ISSN 0705-5757
BRITISH COLUMBIA. MINISTRY OF AGRICULTURE. NURSERY PRODUCTION GUIDE. 1978. a. free. Ministry of Agriculture, Publications Office, Parliament Bldg., Victoria, B.C. V8W 2Z7, Canada.

633   AG   ISSN 0068-3418
BUENOS AIRES. INSTITUTO DE FITOTECNIA. BOLETIN INFORMATIVO. (Text in Spanish; summaries in English) 1954. irreg.; no. 39, 1980. available on exchange. Instituto Nacional de Tecnologia Agropecuaria, Centro de Investigaciones en Ciencias Agronomicas, Departamento de Genetica, Casilla de Correo No. 25, 1712 Castelar, Argentina.

633   JA   ISSN 0068-4090
BULLETIN OF SUGAR BEET RESEARCH. SUPPLEMENT/TENSAI KENKYU HOKOKU HOKAN. Also known as: Proceedings of Sugar Beet Research. (Text in Japanese; summaries in English) 1963. a. free. Sugar Beet Institute, Japan Sugar Beet Improvement Foundation, Hitsujigaoka 1, Sapporo, Hokkaido 062, Japan.

631   MX   ISSN 0047-701X
C I A B CIRCULAR. 1962. irreg. free. Centro de Investigaciones Agricolas de el Bajio, Apdo. 112, Celaya Gto, Mexico. Ed. Ramon F. Hijar. circ. 2,000.

632   CN
CANADA. AGRICULTURE CANADA. RESEARCH INSTITUTE. RESEARCH BRANCH REPORT. 1951/56. a., since 1966. free. Agriculture Canada, Research Institute, University Sub Post Office, London, Ont. N6A 3KO, Canada.
    Formerly: Canada. Research Institute, London, Ontario. Research Report (ISSN 0068-807X)

632   CN   ISSN 0068-7898
CANADA. COMMITTEE ON PESTICIDE USE IN AGRICULTURE. PESTICIDE RESEARCH REPORT. (Text mainly in English; occasionally in French.) 1962. a. controlled circulation. ‡ Agriculture Canada, Pesticide Technical Information Office, K. W. Neatby Bldg., Ottawa, Ont. K1A 0C6, Canada. Ed. E. Y. Spencer.

630   CN
CANADA. DEPARTMENT OF AGRICULTURE. ENGINEERING & STATISTICAL RESEARCH INSTITUTE, OTTAWA. RESEARCH REPORT. 1960-66. irreg. contr.free circ. ‡ Agriculture Canada, Engineering & Statistical Research Institute, Ottawa, Ont. K1A 0C6, Canada. circ. 300.
    Formerly: Canada. Department of Agriculture. Engineering Research Service, Ottawa. Research Report (ISSN 0068-7294)
    Agricultural engineering

631.7   CN
CANADA. DEPARTMENT OF REGIONAL ECONOMIC EXPANSION. ANNUAL REPORT ON PRAIRIE FARM REHABILITATION AND RELATED ACTIVITIES/RAPPORT ANNUEL: RETABLISSEMENT AGRICOLE DES PRAIRIES ET TRAVAUX CONNEXES. Cover title: P F R A Annual Report. 1936-37. a. free. Prairie Farm Rehabilitation Administration, Information Division, Ottawa, Ontario, Canada. stat. circ. 3,000.
    Land reclamation

632   CN   ISSN 0068-8185
CANADIAN AGRICULTURAL INSECT PEST REVIEW. 1923. a. free. Agriculture Canada, Research Program Services, c/o J. S. Kelleher, Neatby Bldg., Rm. 1133, Ottawa K1A 0C6, Canada. index: annual. cum.index every 10 years.
    Formerly: Canadian Insect Pest Review.

632   CN   ISSN 0065-4485
CANADIAN PEST MANAGEMENT SOCIETY PROCEEDINGS. 1954. a. Can.$5. Canadian Pest Management Society, c/o Agriculture Canada, 4134 Neatley Bldg., Ottawa, Ont. K1A 0C6, Canada. Ed. J. A. Scott. circ. 200. Indexed: Chem.Abstr. Pollut.Abstr. Rev.Appl.Entomol.
    Continues: Agricultural Pesticide Society. Annual Meeting. Proceedings (ISSN 0065-4485)

631.5   CN   ISSN 0068-9610
CANADIAN SEED GROWERS ASSOCIATION. ANNUAL REPORT. 1903-04. a. Canadian Seed Growers Association, P.O. Box 8455, Ottawa, Ont. K1G 3T1, Canada. circ. 6,000.

632.9   US
CEREAL RUST BULLETIN. 1963. irreg. free. University of Minnesota, Cereal Rust Laboratory, St. Paul, MN 55108. Ed. Alan P. Roelfs. circ. 500. (looseleaf format)

634   US   ISSN 0412-6300
CITRUS ENGINEERING CONFERENCE. TRANSACTIONS. 1955. a. $7.50. Citrus Engineering Conference, Bailey Motor Equipment Co., Box 3386, Orlando, FL 32802.

COMMISSION OF THE EUROPEAN COMMUNITIES. MARCHES AGRICOLES: SERIE "PRIX". PRODUITS VEGETAUX. see *AGRICULTURE — Agricultural Economics*

AGRICULTURE — CROP PRODUCTION AND SOIL

COMMONWEALTH BUREAU OF HORTICULTURE AND PLANTATION CROPS. RESEARCH REVIEW. see *GARDENING AND HORTICULTURE*

COMMONWEALTH BUREAU OF HORTICULTURE AND PLANTATION CROPS. TECHNICAL COMMUNICATIONS. see *GARDENING AND HORTICULTURE*

633   UK   ISSN 0069-701X
COMMONWEALTH BUREAU OF PASTURES AND FIELD CROPS. BULLETIN. 1948. irreg. price varies. (Commonwealth Bureau of Pastures and Yield Crops) Commonwealth Agricultural Bureaux, Farnham House, Farnham Royal, Slough SL2 3BN, England.

631.4   UK   ISSN 0069-7036
COMMONWEALTH BUREAU OF SOILS. TECHNICAL COMMUNICATIONS. 1929. irreg., no. 55, 1975. price varies. Commonwealth Bureau of Soils, Commonwealth Agricultural Bureaux, Rothamsted Experimental Station, Harpenden, Herts. AL5 2JQ, England. adv. circ. 1,000-3,500.

631.5   AT
COMMONWEALTH SCIENTIFIC AND INDUSTRIAL RESEARCH ORGANIZATION. DIVISION OF PLANT INDUSTRY. REPORT. 1980. biennial. free. ‡ C. S. I. R. O., Division of Plant Industry, P.O. Box 1600, Canberra City, A.C.T. 2601, Australia.
Supersedes: Commonwealth Scientific and Industrial Research Organization. Division of Plant Industry. Annual Report (ISSN 0069-7540)

631.5   AT   ISSN 0069-7567
COMMONWEALTH SCIENTIFIC AND INDUSTRIAL RESEARCH ORGANIZATION. DIVISION OF PLANT INDUSTRY. TECHNICAL PAPER. 1952. irreg. free. C. S. I. R O., Division of Plant Industry, Box 1600, Canberra City, A.C.T. 2601, Australia.

631.4   AT   ISSN 0069-7583
COMMONWEALTH SCIENTIFIC AND INDUSTRIAL RESEARCH ORGANIZATION. DIVISION OF SOILS. BIENNIAL REPORT. 1949. biennial. free. C. S. I. R. O., Division of Soils, Private Bag No. 2, Glen Osmond, S.A. 5064, Australia (Subscr. to: CSIRO, Editorial & Publications Service, Box 89, East Melbourne, Vic. 3002, Australia) circ. 1,500. Indexed: Soils & Fert.

631.4   AT
COMMONWEALTH SCIENTIFIC AND INDUSTRIAL RESEARCH ORGANIZATION. DIVISION OF SOILS. DIVISIONAL REPORT. 1975. irreg. free. C. S. I. R. O., Division of Soils, Private Bag 2, Glen Osmond, S.A. 5064, Australia.

631.4   AT
COMMONWEALTH SCIENTIFIC AND INDUSTRIAL RESEARCH ORGANIZATION. DIVISION OF SOILS. TECHNICAL PAPERS. 1971. irreg. Aus.$2. C. S. I. R. O., Division of Soils, Private Bag 2, Glen Osmond, S. A. 5064, Australia (Subscr. to: CSIRO, Editorial & Publications Service, Box 89, East Melbourne, Vic. 3002, Australia)

631.5 581   AT
COMMONWEALTH SCIENTIFIC AND INDUSTRIAL RESEARCH ORGANIZATION. DIVISION OF TROPICAL CROPS AND PASTURES. TECHNICAL PAPER. 1961. irreg. Aus.$0.80 per issue. C. S. I. R. O., Division of Tropical Crops and Pastures, 314 Albert St., E. Melbourne 3002, Victoria, Australia.
Formerly: Commonwealth Scientific and Industrial Research Organization. Division of Tropical Pastures. Technical Paper (ISSN 0069-7613)

632.9   CN
COMPENDIUM OF PEST CONTROL PRODUCTS REGISTERED IN CANADA; volume RP: Registered Pesticides. (Text in English and French) 1979. irreg. Can.$30($36) per no. Agriculture Canada, Pesticides Division, 960 Carling Ave., Ottawa, Ont. K1A 0C6, Canada (Subscr. to: Supply and Services Canada, Publishing Centre, Hull, Que. K1A 0S9, Canada) Ed. J. A. Scott. (looseleaf format)
Pest control

633   US   ISSN 0069-9993
CORN ANNUAL. 1970. a. free. Corn Refiners Association, Inc., 1001 Connecticut Ave. N.W., Washington, DC 20036. Ed. Joyce A. Mattis. circ. 8,500.

631   US
CORNELL RECOMMENDATIONS FOR COMMERCIAL VEGETABLE PRODUCTION. 1969. a. $1.75 per no. ‡ New York State College of Agriculture and Life Sciences, Cornell University, Ithaca, NY 14853. Ed. Roger F. Sandsted.
Formerly: Vegetable Production Recommendations.

631.8   PE   ISSN 0589-7742
CORPORACION NACIONAL DE FERTILIZANTES. MEMORIA ANUAL. 1963. a. Corporacion Nacional de Fertilizantes, Lima, Peru.

630.24   BL
CORREIO AGRICOLA (BRAZIL) 1960. irreg., no. 3, 1974. free. Bayer do Brasil Industrias Quimicas S.A., C.P. 22-523-ZP-18, 01000 Sao Paulo, Brazil. Ed. Sergio Malta Cardoso. adv. charts. illus. circ. 50,000(controlled)

630.24   PO
CORREIO AGRICOLA (PORTUGAL) Portuguese edition of: Pflanzenschutz-Kurier. 1964. irreg. free. Bayer Portugal S A R L, Apartado 2365, Lisbon, Portugal (Main Office: Bayer Pflanzenschutz, Leverkusen, W. Germany (B.R.D.)) Ed. J. C. Silva Dias. charts. illus. circ. controlled.

630.24   GW
CORREO FITOSANITARIO (INTERNATIONAL) English edition: Crop Protection Courier(International) (ISSN 0590-1243); Crop Protection Courier (South Africa) German edition: Pflanzenschutz-Kurier (ISSN 0405-0738) 1960. 3/yr. free. Bayer AG, 5090 Leverkusen-Bayerwerk, W. Germany (B.R.D.) Ed. Matthias Willig. charts. illus. circ. 46,000(controlled)

630.24   GW   ISSN 0590-1243
CROP PROTECTION COURIER (INTERNATIONAL) German edition: Pflanzenschutz-Kurier (ISSN 0405-0738); South African edition: Crop Protection Courier (South Africa) Spanish edition: Correo Fitosanitario(International) 1960. 3/yr. free. Bayer AG, 5090 Leverkusen-Bayerwerk, W. Germany (B.R.D.) Ed. Matthias Willig. charts. illus. circ. 33,500(controlled)

630.24   GW
CROP PROTECTION COURIER (SOUTH AFRICA) English international edition: Crop Protection Courier(International) (ISSN 0590-1243); German edition: Pflanzenschutz-Kurier (ISSN 0405-0738) 1964. 3/yr. free. Bayer AG, 5090 Leverkusen-Bayerwerk, W. Germany (B.R.D.) Ed. Matthias Willig. charts. illus. circ. 65,000(controlled)

631   CN
CROPS GUIDE. (Supplement to Country Guide) 1972. a. Public Press Ltd., 1760 Ellice Ave., Winnipeg, Man. R3H OB6, Canada. circ. 163,509. (microform; also avail. in microfilm from UMI)

634   CU
CUBA. CENTRO DE INFORMACION Y DOCUMENTACION AGROPECUARIO. BOLETIN DE RESENAS SERIE: CITRICOS. 1974. irreg. $5. Centro de Informacion y Documentacion Agropecuario, Calle 11 no. 1057, Gaveta Postal 4149, Havana 4, Cuba.

631   CU
CUBA. CENTRO DE INFORMACION Y DOCUMENTACION AGROPECUARIO. BOLETIN DE RESENAS. SERIE: PROTECCION DE PLANTAS. 1974. irreg. $5. Centro de Informacion y Documentacion Agropecuario, Calle 11 no. 1057, Gaveta Postal 4149, Havana 4, Cuba.

631.7   CU
CUBA. CENTRO DE INFORMACION Y DOCUMENTACION AGROPECUARIO. BOLETIN DE RESENAS. SERIE: RIEGO Y DRENAJE. 1974. irreg. $5. Centro de Informacion y Documentacion Agropecuario, Calle 11 no. 1057, Gaveta Postal 4159, Havana 4, Cuba.

631.7   CU
CUBA. CENTRO DE INFORMACION Y DOCUMENTACION AGROPECUARIO. BOLETIN DE RESENA. SERIE: SUELOS Y AGROQUIMICA. 1974. irreg. $5. Centro de Informacion y Documentacion Agropecuario, Calle 11 no. 1057, Gaveta Postal 4149, Havana 4, Cuba.

631   CY   ISSN 0070-234X
CYPRUS. DEPARTMENT OF AGRICULTURE. SOILS AND PLANT NUTRITION SECTION. REPORT. (Text in English) 1959. biennial. free. ‡ Department of Agriculture, Soils and Plant Nutrition Section, Nicosia, Cyprus.

631.7 627   BL
D N O C S-FINS E ATIVIDADES. irreg. Departamento Nacional de Obras Contra as Secas, Fortaleza, Ceara, Brazil. illus.

632   UK   ISSN 0305-2680
DESCRIPTIONS OF PLANT VIRUSES. a. £5($11.50) Commonwealth Agricultural Bureaux, Farnham House, Farnham Royal, Slough, England (U.S. subscr. to: Unipub, 345 Park Ave. S., New York, NY 10010) (back issues avail)

632.9   ET   ISSN 0418-761X
DESERT LOCUST CONTROL ORGANIZATION FOR EASTERN AFRICA. ANNUAL REPORT. 1962/1963. a, latest 1974/75. Desert Locust Control Organization for Eastern Africa, P.O. Box 4255, Addis Ababa, Ethiopia.
Supersedes: East Africa High Commissions Desert Locust Survey. Report.

631.4   NE
DEVELOPMENTS IN SOIL SCIENCE. 1972. irreg., vol. 9, 1979. price varies. Elsevier Scientific Publishing Co., Box 211, 1000 AE Amsterdam, Netherlands.

631   VE
DIRECTORIO INDUSTRIAL AZUCARERO. 1972. a. Bs.50. Distribuidora Venezolana de Azucares, Departamento de Promocion Industrial, Edificio Torre Europa, Av. de Miranda, Caracas 106, Venezuela. adv. charts. stat.

633.83   II
DIRECTORY OF CARDAMOM PLANTERS. (Text in English) 1974. irreg. Rs.50. Cardamom Board, Chittoor Rd., Cochin 682018, India.

631.4   FR   ISSN 0180-9555
DOCUMENTS PEDOZOOLOGIQUES. (Text in French; summaries in English) 1979. irreg. free to qualified personnel. Institut National de la Recherche Agronomique, Laboratoire de Zooecologie du Sol, 17 rue Sully, 21034 Dijon Cedex, France. Ed. M. B. Bouche. circ. 300. Indexed: Chem.Abstr. PASCAL. Zoo.Rec.

631.8   GW
DUENGUNGSRATSCHLAEGE FUER DEN BAUERNHOF. 1938. irreg. DM.2. Fachverband Stickstoffindustrie, Sternstr. 9-11, 4000 Duesseldorf 1, W. Germany (B.R.D.) Ed. Helmut Nieder. circ. 50,000.

633.491   NE
E A P R ABSTRACTS OF CONFERENCE PAPERS. (Text in English, French, German) 1961 (1st Conference in 1960) triennial. $23. European Association for Potato Research, Box 20, 6700 AA Wageningen, Netherlands.
Formerly (until 1975): European Association for Potato Research. Proceedings of the Triennial Conference (ISSN 0071-2507)

630   CN   ISSN 0012-7892
E R D A. (Engineering Research and Development in Agriculture) (Supplements) 1968. irreg. contr.free circ. ‡ Agriculture Canada, Engineering & Statistical Research Institute, Ottawa, K1A 0C6, Ont., Canada. Ed. G. F. Montgomery. charts. illus. index. circ. 1,100. (looseleaf format)
Agricultural engineering

ECONOMICS OF FRUIT FARMING. see *AGRICULTURE — Agricultural Economics*

630.24 668.6   EC
ECUADOR. INSTITUTO NACIONAL DE INVESTIGACIONES AGROPECUARIAS. INFORME TECNICO. irreg. Instituto Nacional de Investigaciones Agropecuarias, Departamento de Comunicacion, Casilla 2600, Quito, Ecuador.

AGRICULTURE — CROP PRODUCTION AND SOIL

630.24   CN
ELEVATOR MANAGER, FARM CHEMICAL & FERTILIZER DEALER. 1976. a. Can.$30. Agri-Book Publishing Co. Ltd., Box 1060, Exeter, Ont. N0M 1S0, Canada. Ed. Peter Darbishire. adv. (back issues avail.)
Agricultural chemistry

631.5   II   ISSN 0085-0314
ESTIMATES OF AREA AND PRODUCTION OF PRINCIPAL CROPS IN INDIA. SUMMARY TABLES. (Text and summaries in English) 1951-52. a. Rs.22. Ministry of Agriculture and Irrigation, Department of Agriculture, Directorate of Economics and Statistics, A-2E-3 Kasturba Gandhi Marg Barracks, New Delhi 110001, India. Ed. C. D. Sharma. circ. 700.

632   FR   ISSN 0071-2388
EUROPEAN AND MEDITERRANEAN PLANT PROTECTION ORGANIZATION. E P P O BULLETIN/BULLETIN O E P P. (Text in English and French) 1951; n.s. 1971. irreg. 160 F.($40) ‡ European and Mediterranean Plant Protection Organization - Organisation Europeenne et Mediterraneenne pour la Protection des Plantes, 1, rue le Notre, 75016 Paris, France. Ed. Dr. G. Mathys. circ. 800. (back issues avail.) Indexed: Rev.Appl.Entomol. Rev. Plant. Path.
    Formerly: European and Mediterranean Plant Protection Organization. Publications. Series A; Reports of Technical Meetings; Incorporates: European and Mediterranean Plant Protection Organization. Publications. Series C: Reports of Working Parties (ISSN 0071-240X)

632   FR   ISSN 0071-2396
EUROPEAN AND MEDITERRANEAN PLANT PROTECTION ORGANIZATION. PUBLICATIONS. SERIES B: PLANT HEALTH NEWSLETTER. (Editions in English and French) 1950 N.S. 1970. irreg., 1973, no. 75. free contr. circ. ‡ European and Mediterranean Plant Protection Organization, 1 rue le Notre, 75016 Paris, France. Ed. G. Mathys. (processed)
    Formerly: Surveys of the Position of Various Pests and Diseases in Europe and the Mediterranean Area.

633   BE   ISSN 0071-2825
EUROPEAN GRASSLAND FEDERATION. PROCEEDINGS OF THE GENERAL MEETING. 1965. irreg., 7th, 1978, Belgium. 48 Fr. European Grassland Federation, c/o Society for Grassland and Fodder Groups, Van Gansberghelaan 96, B-9220 Merelbeke, Belgium (Inquiries to: J. W. Minderhoud, Department of Field Crops and Grassland Husbandry, State Agricultural University, Haarweg 33, Wageningen, Netherlands) circ. 340.
    Proceedings published in host country

630.24   668.6   US   ISSN 0430-0750
FARM CHEMICALS HANDBOOK. 1914. a. $18.50. Meister Publishing Co., 37841 Euclid Ave., Willoughby, OH 44094. Ed. Gordon L. Berg. adv. circ. 9,000.
    Supersedes: American Fertilizer Handbook.

631   UK   ISSN 0071-3961
FARMING IN THE EAST MIDLANDS. a. £1.30. University of Nottingham, School of Agriculture, University Park, Nottingham NG7 2RD, England.
    Formerly: Farm Management Notes.

633   CK
FEDERACION NACIONAL DE CAFETEROS DE COLOMBIA. INFORME DE LABORES DE LOS COMITES DEPARTAMENTALES DE CAFETEROS. irreg. Federacion Nacional de Cafeteros de Colombia, Av. Jimenez 7-65, Bogota, Colombia. illus.
    Coffee trade

631.8   UN   ISSN 0071-4615
FERTILIZER INDUSTRY SERIES. irreg., no. 9, 1977. price varies. United Nations Industrial Development Organization, Lerchenfelderstrasse 1, Box 707, A-1011 Vienna, Austria (Orders from Europe, Africa and Middle East to: Distribution and Sales Section, Palais des Nations, 1211 Geneva 10, Switzerland. Orders from Asia, the Pacific and North and South America to: United Nations Publications, Room LX-2300, New York, NY 10017)

631.8   US   ISSN 0071-4623
FERTILIZER SCIENCE AND TECHNOLOGY SERIES. 1968. irreg., vol. 2, part 4, 1979. price varies. Marcel Dekker, Inc., 270 Madison Ave., New York, NY 10016. Ed. A. V. Slack.
    Fertilizers

631.8   US   ISSN 0071-4631
FERTILIZER TRENDS. 1956. biennial. free. Tennessee Valley Authority, National Fertilizer Development Center, Muscle Shoals, AL 35660. circ. 8,000.
    Fertilizers

FIJI SUGAR YEAR BOOK. see FOOD AND FOOD INDUSTRIES

632.3   UN
FOOD AND AGRICULTURE ORGANIZATION OF THE UNITED NATIONS. PLANT PROTECTION COMMITTEE FOR SOUTHEAST ASIA AND PACIFIC REGION. INFORMATION LETTER. irreg. free. Food and Agriculture Organization of the United Nations, Regional Office for Asia and the Far East, Maliwan Mansion, Phra Atit Rd., Bangkok 2, Thailand.
    Contains information on plant importation regulations in the region

631   UN   ISSN 0428-9765
FOOD AND AGRICULTURE ORGANIZATION OF THE UNITED NATIONS. PLANT PROTECTION COMMITTEE FOR SOUTHEAST ASIA AND PACIFIC REGION. TECHNICAL DOCUMENT. (Text and summaries in English) 1958. 6-8/yr. free. Food and Agriculture Organization of the United Nations, Regional Office for Asia and the Far East, Maliwan Mansion, Phra Atit Rd., Bangkok 2, Thailand. circ. 400(controlled)

631.4   UN   ISSN 0532-0437
FOOD AND AGRICULTURE ORGANIZATION OF THE UNITED NATIONS. SOILS BULLETINS. 1965. irreg.; 1972, no. 17. unpriced. Food and Agriculture Organization of the United Nations, Distribution and Sales Section, Via delle Terme di Caracalla, I-00100 Rome, Italy (Dist. in U.S. by: Unipub, 345 Park Ave., S., New York, NY 10010) bibl.

631.4   UN   ISSN 0532-0488
FOOD AND AGRICULTURE ORGANIZATION OF THE UNITED NATIONS. WORLD SOIL RESOURCES REPORTS.* 1961. irreg. Food and Agriculture Organization of the United Nations, Distribution and Sales Section, Via delle Terme di Caracalla, I-00100 Rome, Italy.

630   GW   ISSN 0301-2727
FORTSCHRITTE DER PFLANZENZUECHTUNG/ ADVANCES IN PLANT BREEDING. (Supplement to: Zeitschrift fuer Pflanzenzuechtung) (Text in English or German; summaries in English, French, German) 1971. irreg., no. 10, 1979. price varies. Verlag Paul Parey (Berlin), Lindenstr. 44-47, 1000 Berlin 61, W. Germany (B.R.D.) Indexed: Biol.Abstr. Curr.Cont.

630   GW   ISSN 0301-2735
FORTSCHRITTE IM ACKER- UND PFLANZENBAU/ADVANCES IN AGRONOMY AND CROP SCIENCE. (Supplement to: Zeitschrift fuer Acker- und Pflanzenbau) (Text and Summaries in English or German) 1973. irreg. price varies. Verlag Paul Parey (Berlin), Lindenstrasse 44-47, 1000 Berlin 61, W. Germany (B.R.D.) Ed. A. Scheibe. Indexed: Biol.Abstr. Curr.Cont.

380.1   FR
FRUCTIDOR INTERNATIONAL. 1931. a. 300 F. Presses de Provence, 14 Boulevard Montmartre, Paris, France. Ed. Betty Monter. adv. circ. 6,000.

632.9   US
FUNGICIDE AND NEMATICIDE TESTS. (Text in English and Spanish) a. $7. American Phytopathological Society, 3340 Pilot Knob Rd., St. Paul, MN 55121 (Orders to: Dr. Arthur W. Engelhard, Agricultural Research & Education Center, University of Florida, 5007 60th St. East, Bradenton, FL 33505) Ed. Charles W. Averre. index. circ. 2,200. (back issues avail.)
    Pest control

630.24   BE
GORSAC KOERIER. Belgian/Dutch edition of: Pflanzenschutz-Kurier. irreg. free. N.V. Bayer Gorsac S.A., St. Truiden, Belgium (Main Office: Bayer Pflanzenschutz, Leverkusen, W. Germany (B.R.D.)) Ed. Victor Sweldens. charts. illus. circ. 34,200(controlled)

633   UK   ISSN 0072-5552
GRASSLAND RESEARCH INSTITUTE, HURLEY, ENGLAND (BERKSHIRE) TECHNICAL REPORTS. 1965. irreg. price varies. (Agricultural Research Council) Grassland Research Institute, Hurley, Maidenhead, Berks SL6 5RL, England.

633   SA   ISSN 0072-5560
GRASSLAND SOCEITY OF SOUTHERN AFRICA. PROCEEDINGS OF THE ANNUAL CONGRESSES. (Text and summaries in Afrikaans or English) 1966. a. R.9. ‡ Grassland Society of Southern Africa, Box 29718, Sunnyside 0132, South Africa. cum.index. circ. 400. Indexed: Biol.Abstr. Biol. & Agr.Ind. Biol. & Agri.Abstr. Bibl.Agri. Herb.Abstr.

633   AT
GRASSLAND SOCIETY OF VICTORIA. NEWSLETTER. 1960. irreg. Aus.$10 to members; students Aus. $5. Grassland Society of Victoria, 191 Royal Parade, Parkville, Vic. 3052, Australia. Ed.Bd. bk. rev. circ. 800.

632.9   UK   ISSN 0307-9082
GREAT BRITAIN. CENTRE FOR OVERSEAS PEST RESEARCH. REPORT. 1973. a (approx.) price varies. Centre for Overseas Pest Research, College House, Wrights Lane, London W8 5SJ, England. bibl. illus. circ. 550. (back issues avail.)

632   UK   ISSN 0072-6486
GREAT BRITAIN. PEST INFESTATION CONTROL LABORATORY. REPORT. 1958. irreg. price varies. Ministry of Agriculture, Fisheries and Food, Slough Laboratory, London Rd., Slough SL3 7HJ, England (Avail. from H.M.S.O., c/o Liaison Officer, Atlantic House, Holborn Viaduct, London EC1P 1BN, England) Ed. Miss G. M. Williams. circ. 4,000.

631.4   UK   ISSN 0072-7180
GREAT BRITAIN. SOIL SURVEY OF ENGLAND AND WALES. RECORDS. 1970. irreg., no. 70, 1981. 70p. Soil Survey of England and Wales, Rothamsted Experimental Station, Harpenden, Herts AL5 2JQ, England. Indexed: Geo.Abstr. Soils & Fert.

631.4   UK   ISSN 0072-7199
GREAT BRITAIN. SOIL SURVEY OF ENGLAND AND WALES. REPORT. 1967. a. £1. Soil Survey of England and Wales, Rothamsted Experimental Station, Harpenden, Herts AL5 2JQ, England.

631.4   UK   ISSN 0072-7202
GREAT BRITAIN. SOIL SURVEY OF ENGLAND AND WALES. SPECIAL SURVEYS. 1969. irreg., no. 13, 1981. price varies. Soil Survey of England and Wales, Rothamsted Experimental Station, Harpenden, Herts AL5 2JQ, England. Indexed: Geo.Abstr. Soils & Fert.

631.4   UK   ISSN 0072-7210
GREAT BRITAIN. SOIL SURVEY OF ENGLAND AND WALES. TECHNICAL MONOGRAPHS. 1969. irreg., no. 15, 1981. price varies. Soil Survey of England and Wales, Rothamsted Experimental Station, Harpenden, Herts AL5 2JQ, England. Indexed: Geo.Abstr. Soils & Fert.

631   SA
GUIDE TO THE USE OF INSECTICIDES AND FUNGICIDES IN SOUTH AFRICA. (Editions in English and Afrikaans) 1960. a. R.1.25. Department of Agricultural Technical Services, Private Bag X144, Pretoria 0001, South Africa (Orders to: Government Printer, Bosman St., Private Bag X85, Pretoria 0001, South Africa) circ. 1,000. (reprint service avail. from UMI)

AGRICULTURE — CROP PRODUCTION AND SOIL

632.9 US
GUIDELINES FOR THE USE OF INSECTICIDES TO CONTROL INSECTS AFFECTING CROPS, LIVESTOCK, HOUSEHOLDS, STORED PRODUCTS, FOREST & FOREST PRODUCTS. (Subseries of U.S.D.A. Agriculture Handbook) 1957. a. ‡ U.S. Department of Agriculture, Fourteenth St. and Independence Ave. S.W., Washington, DC 20250. (Prepared jointly by: U.S. Agricultural Research Service and U.S. Forest Service) Ed. Paul Schwartz, Jr. (looseleaf format)

633.6 GY
GUYANA SUGAR CORPORATION. ANNUAL REPORTS AND ACCOUNTS. 1976. irreg. Guyana Sugar Corporation, 22 Church St., Georgetown, Guyana. illus.

633.6 US ISSN 0073-1358
HAWAIIAN PLANTERS' RECORD. 1909. irreg.(quarterly until 1956) exchange basis only. Hawaiian Sugar Planter's Association, Experiment Station, Box 1057, Aiea, HI 96701. index. Indexed: Chem.Abstr.

633.6 US ISSN 0073-1366
HAWAIIAN SUGAR PLANTERS' ASSOCIATION EXPERIMENT STATION. ANNUAL REPORT. 1947. a. exchange basis only. Hawaiian Sugar Planter's Association, Experiment Station, Box 1057, Aiea, HI 96701.

633.491 US ISSN 0018-1986
HINTS TO POTATO GROWERS. 1920. irreg., 2-4/yr. membership (non-members $10) New Jersey State Potato Association, Box 231 Blake Hall, Cook College, Rutgers University, New Brunswick, NJ 08903. Ed. Dr. Melvin Henninger. charts. stat. circ. 150. (processed)
Potatoes

631.4 JA ISSN 0073-2923
HOKKAIDO NATIONAL AGRICULTURAL EXPERIMENT STATION. SOIL SURVEY REPORT/HOKKAIDO NOGYO SHIKENJO DOSEI CHOSA HOKOKU. (Text and summaries in Japanese or English) 1951. a. available on exchange. Hokkaido National Agricultural Experiment Station, 1 Hitsujigaoka, Toyohira-ku, Sapporo 061-01, Japan (Dist. in U.S. by: New York Agricultural Experiment Station, Geneva, NY 14456) circ. 800. (also avail. in microform)

631 SZ
I P I BULLETIN. 1974. irreg., no. 5, 1978. 4 Fr.($3.35) International Potash Institute, Postfach, CH-3048 Worblaufen-Berne, Switzerland.

631 SZ
I P I RESEARCH TOPICS. 1976. irreg., no. 4, 1978. price varies. International Potash Institute, Postfach, CH-3048 Worblaufen-Berne, Switzerland.

631.8 FR
I S M A TECHNICAL CONFERENCE. PROCEEDINGS. (Published by host country; 1976, Netherlands) biennial. $57.50. International Superphosphate Manufacturers Association, Ltd., 28 rue Marbeuf, 75008 Paris, France. Ed. L.J. Carpentier.
Fertilizers

633.3 US ISSN 0085-1701
IDAHO PEA AND LENTIL COMMISSION. ANNUAL REPORT. 1966. irreg. Idaho Pea & Lentil Commission, P.O. Box 8566, Moscow, ID 83843.

INDIA. CARDAMOM BOARD. ANNUAL REPORT. see *PUBLIC ADMINISTRATION*

633 II ISSN 0073-649X
INDIAN INSTITUTE OF SUGARCANE RESEARCH, LUCKNOW. ANNUAL REPORT. (Text in English) 1954. a. exchange basis. Indian Institute of Sugarcane Research, Indian Council of Agricultural Research, Lucknow 2, Uttar Pradesh, India.

633 IS
INSTITUTE OF FIELD AND GARDEN CROPS. SCIENTIFIC ACTIVITIES. (Text in English) irreg. Institute of Field and Garden Crops, Bet Dagan, Israel.

633 PO
INSTITUTO DO AZEITE E PRODUTOS OLEAGINOSOS. BOLETIM. (Text in Portuguese; summaries in Portuguese, French and English) irreg. Esc.100($3) Instituto do Azeite e Produtos Oleaginosos, Av. de Sidonio Pais, 10, Lisbon 1, Portugal. bibl. charts. stat.

633.491 RM ISSN 0074-0373
INSTITUTUL DE CERCETARI PENTRU CULTURA CARTOFULUI SI SFECLEI DE ZAHAR, BRASOV. ANALE. CARTOFUL. (Text in Romanian; summaries in English and French) 1969. a. 80 lei. Institutul de Cercetari Pentru Cultura Cartofului si Sfeclei de Zahar, Str. Fundaturii, Nr. 2, Brasov, Romania.

633.41 RM ISSN 0074-0381
INSTITUTUL DE CERCETARI PENTRU CULTURA CARTOFULUI SI SFECLEI DE ZAHAR, BRASOV. ANALE. SFECLA DE ZAHAR. (Text in Romanian; summaries in English and French) 1968. a. 80 lei. Institutul de Cercetari Pentru Cultura Cartofului si Sfeclei de Zahar, Str. Fundaturii, Nr. 2, Brasov, Romania.

631.6 NE ISSN 0511-0688
INSTITUUT VOOR CULTUURTECHNIEK EN WATERHUISHOUDING. JAARVERSLAG. a. Instituut voor Cultuurtechniek en Waterhuishouding - Institute for Land and Water Management Research, Box 35, 6700 AA Wageningen, Netherlands.

631.6 NE ISSN 0074-0411
INSTITUUT VOOR CULTUURTECHNIEK EN WATERHUISHOUDING. MEDEDELING. (Text in Dutch; summaries in English) 1958. irreg., no. 156, 1979. free. ‡ Instituut voor Cultuurtechniek en Waterhuishouding - Institute for Land and Water Management Research, P.O. Box 35, 6700 AA Wageningen, Netherlands. Ed. E. W. Schierbeek. circ. 1,200. Indexed: Bull.Signal. Field Crop Abstr. Herb.Abstr. Hort.Abstr. Meteor. & Geostrophys.Abstr. Water Resour.Abstr. World Agri. Econ & Rural Sociol. Abstr.

631.6 NE ISSN 0074-042X
INSTITUUT VOOR CULTUURTECHNIEK EN WATERHUISHOUDING. TECHNICAL BULLETIN/INSTITUTE FOR LAND AND WATER MANAGEMENT RESEARCH. TECHNICAL BULLETIN. (Text in English) 1958. irreg., no. 116, 1980. free. ‡ Instituut voor Cultuurtechniek en Waterhuishouding - Institute for Land and Water Management Research, P.O. Box 35, 6700 AA Wageningen, Netherlands. Ed. E. W. Schierbeek. circ. 1,300. (back issues avail.) Indexed: Bull.Signal. Field Crop Abstr. Herb.Abstr. Hort.Abstr. Meteor. & Geostrophys.Abstr. Water Resour.Abstr. World Agri.Econ. & Rural Sociol.Abstr.

631.6 NE ISSN 0074-0438
INSTITUUT VOOR CULTUURTECHNIEK EN WATERHUISHOUDING. VERSPREIDE OVERDRUKKEN/INSTITUTE FOR LAND AND WATER MANAGEMENT RESEARCH. MISCELLANEOUS REPRINTS. (Text in Dutch, English and German; summaries occasionally in English) 1962. irreg., no. 252, 1980. free. ‡ Instituut voor Cultuurtechniek en Waterhuishouding - Institute for Land and Water Management Research, P.O. Box 35, 6700 AA Wageningen, Netherlands. Ed. E. W. Schierbeek. circ. 1,100. Indexed: Bull.Signal. Field Crop Abstr. Herb.Abstr. Hort.Abstr. Meteor. & Geostrophys.Abstr. Water Resour.Abstr. World Agri. Econ. & Rural Sociol.Abstr.

632 581 NE ISSN 0074-0446
INSTITUUT VOOR PLANTENZIEKTENKUNDIG ONDERZOEK. JAARVERSLAG. Dutch edition: Institute of Phytopathological Research. Annual Report. (Editions in Dutch and English) 1950. a. price varies. Instituut voor Plantenziektenkundig Onderzoek, P.O. Box 42, 6700 AA Wageningen, Netherlands. Ed. G. S. Roosje.

632 581 NE ISSN 0019-0349
INSTITUUT VOOR PLANTENZIEKTENKUNDIG ONDERZOEK. MEDEDELING/INSTITUTE OF PHYTOPATHOLOGICAL RESEARCH. COMMUNICATIONS. (Text in Dutch, English, French or German; summaries in Dutch or English) 1950. irreg., no. 670, 1974. price varies. Instituut voor Plantenziektenkundig Onderzoek, P.O. Box 42, 6700 AA Wageningen, Netherlands. Ed. G. S. Roosje. Indexed: Bull.Signal. Abstr. Plant Breed.Abstr. Rev.Appl.Mycol.

632 CM ISSN 0534-4859
INTER-AFRICAN PHYTO-SANITARY COMMISSION. PUBLICATION.* irreg. Inter-African Phyto-Sanitary Commission, Route de l' Hippodrome, B. P. 4170, Yaounde, Cameroon.

631.8 SZ ISSN 0074-2171
INTERNATIONAL CENTRE OF FERTILIZERS. WORLD CONGRESS. ACTS.* irreg., 1972, 7th, Vienna and Baden. International Centre of Fertilizers, Beethovenstr. 24, 8002 Zurich, Switzerland.
Fertilizers

631.8 US
INTERNATIONAL COLLOQUIUM ON PLANT ANALYSIS AND FERTILIZER PROBLEMS. PROCEEDINGS. irreg., 6th, 1971. price varies. Gordon and Breach Science Publishers, 1 Park Ave., New York, NY 10016.

630 FR ISSN 0074-2694
INTERNATIONAL COMMISSION OF AGRICULTURAL ENGINEERING. REPORTS OF CONGRESS. (Proceedings published by organizing committee) 1930. irreg.; 9th, 1979, East Lansing, Michigan. International Commission of Agricultural Engineering, 17-21 rue de Javel, 75015 Paris, France.
Agricultural engineering

633 US
INTERNATIONAL COTTON ADVISORY COMMITTEE. COUNTRY STATEMENTS PRESENTED IN CONNECTION WITH THE PLENARY MEETINGS. 35th, 1976. a. $10. International Cotton Advisory Committee, South Agriculture Bldg., Washington, DC 20250. stat. (back issues avail)

633 UR ISSN 0074-6185
INTERNATIONAL GRASSLAND CONGRESS. PROCEEDINGS. 1927. irreg., 1974, 12th, Moscow. International Grassland Congress, Inquire: Dr. V. Igloviv, All-Union Research Forage Institute, Moscow Region, Lugovaya, USSR.

668.65 US
INTERNATIONAL I U P A C CONGRESS OF PESTICIDE CHEMISTRY. PROCEEDINGS. irreg., 2nd, Tel Aviv, 1971. $199 (6 vols.) Gordon and Breach Science Publishers, Park Ave., New York, NY 10016. Ed. A.S. Tahori. bibl. illus.
Agricultural chemistry

631.6 NE ISSN 0074-6428
INTERNATIONAL INSTITUTE FOR LAND RECLAMATION AND IMPROVEMENT. ANNUAL REPORT. (Text in English) 1960. a. free on exchange. International Institute for Land Reclamation and Improvement, P.O. Box 45, 6700 AA Wageningen, Netherlands.

631.6 NE ISSN 0074-6444
INTERNATIONAL INSTITUTE FOR LAND RECLAMATION AND IMPROVEMENT. BULLETIN. (Text in English) 1958. irreg. price varies; free on exchange. International Institute for Land Reclamation and Improvement, P.O. Box 45, 6700 AA Wageningen, Netherlands.

631.6 NE ISSN 0074-6452
INTERNATIONAL INSTITUTE FOR LAND RECLAMATION AND IMPROVEMENT. PUBLICATION. (Text in English) 1958. irreg. price varies; free on exchange. International Institute for Land Reclamation and Improvement, P.O. Box 45, 6700 AA Wageningen, Netherlands.

AGRICULTURE — CROP PRODUCTION AND SOIL

633.6　　　　　BE　ISSN 0074-6460
INTERNATIONAL INSTITUTE FOR SUGAR BEET RESEARCH. REPORTS OF THE WINTER CONGRESS. Variant title: I I R B Winter Congress Proceedings. (Text and summaries in English, French or German) 1958. a. 700 Fr. International Institute for Sugar Beet Research, 47 rue Montoyer, B-1040 Brussels, Belgium. adv. circ. 700(approx.) (back issues avail.)

634.63　　　　　SP　ISSN 0074-7173
INTERNATIONAL OLIVE GROWERS FEDERATION. CONGRESS REPORTS. 1957. irreg., 1969, 21st, Madrid. International Olive Growers Federation, Juan Bravo 10, Madrid 6, Spain.

631.8　　　　　FI　ISSN 0355-1008
INTERNATIONAL PEAT SOCIETY. BULLETIN/ INTERNATIONALE MOOR- UND TORF-GESELLSCHAFT. MITTEILUNGEN. (Text in English) 1972. irreg. (approx. a) $8. International Peat Society, Bulevardi 31, 00180 Helsinki 18, Finland. adv. bk. rev. charts. illus. circ. 1,000.

631.8　　　　　SZ　ISSN 0074-7491
INTERNATIONAL POTASH INSTITUTE. COLLOQUIUM. COMPTE RENDU. 1963. irreg., 13th, 1977. International Potash Institute, Postfach, CH-3048 Worblaufen-Berne, Switzerland.
Fertilizers

631.8　　　　　SZ　ISSN 0074-7505
INTERNATIONAL POTASH INSTITUTE. CONGRESS REPORT. irreg., 11th, 1978, Berne. International Potash Institute, Postfach, CH-3048 Worblaufen-Berne, Switzerland.
Fertilizers

338.1　　　　　UK　ISSN 0074-8706
INTERNATIONAL SUGAR ORGANIZATION. ANNUAL REPORT. a. free. International Sugar Organization, 28 Haymarket, London SW1Y 4SP, England.

668.62　631.85　　UK　ISSN 0074-8714
INTERNATIONAL SUPERPHOSPHATE AND COMPOUND MANUFACTURERS ASSOCIATION LIMITED. TECHNICAL MEETING. PROCEEDINGS.* (Text in English and French) 1947. biennial. membership (non-members L.25) International Superphosphate and Compound Manufacturers Association Ltd., 121 Gloucester Pl, London W1, England.
Issued formerly under previous name of organization: International Superphosphate Manufacturers Association. Technical Meeting. Proceedings.

631.5　　　　　BE
INTERNATIONAL SYMPOSIUM ON CROP PROTECTION. PROCEEDINGS. (Published in Rijksuniversiteit te Gent. Faculteit Landbouwwetenschappen. Mededelingen) (Text and summaries in English, Dutch, French, German) 1948. a., 33rd, 1981, Ghent. $40. Rijksuniversiteit te Gent, Faculteit Landbouwwetenschappen, Coupure Links 533, B-9000 Ghent, Belgium. circ. 250. Indexed: Chem.Abstr. Agri.Ind. Helminthol.Abstr.
Formerly: International Symposium on Crop Protection. Communications (ISSN 0074-8803)

633　　　　　US
IOWA CROP AND LIVESTOCK REPORTING SERVICE. PLANTING TO HARVEST. WEATHER AND FIELD CROPS. 1964. a. Crop and Livestock Reporting Service. Planting to Harvest. Annual Crop Weather Summary, c/o Agricultural Statistician, Federal Bldg., Rm. 833, 210 Walnut St., Des Moines, IA 50309. (Co-sponsors: Iowa Department of Agriculture; United States Department of Agriculture) illus. stat. circ. 3,500.
Supersedes: Iowa. Crop and Livestock Reporting Service. Planting to Harvest. Weather and Field Crops (ISSN 0163-4976)

631.5　636　　　IE
IRELAND (EIRE) CENTRAL STATISTICS OFFICE. CROPS AND PASTURE AND NUMBERS OF LIVESTOCK. a. Central Statistics Office, Earlsfort Terrace, Dublin 2, Ireland.
Formerly: Ireland (Eire) Central Statistics Office. Crops and Livestock Numbers. (ISSN 0075-0549)
Stencilled releases

633.61　　　　　JM
JAMAICAN ASSOCIATION OF SUGAR TECHNOLOGISTS. PROCEEDINGS. a. membership. Jamaican Association of Sugar Technologists, c/o Sugar Industry Research Institute, Agricultural Division, Mandeville, Jamaica.

631　　　　　US　ISSN 0094-2391
JOURNAL OF AGRONOMIC EDUCATION. 1972. a. $6 non-members: $4 to members. American Society of Agronomy, Inc., 677 S. Segoe Rd., Madison, WI 53711. Ed. R. K. Fendall. adv. bk. rev.

631.7　　　　　KE　ISSN 0075-5915
KENYA. NATIONAL IRRIGATION BOARD. REPORTS AND ACCOUNTS. 1967. irreg; latest issue, 1973-74. free to recognized institutions. National Irrigation Board, Lenana Rd., P.O. Box 30372, Nairobi, Kenya.

668.65　　　　　US　ISSN 0099-1929
LOUISIANA. DEPARTMENT OF AGRICULTURE. ANALYSIS OF OFFICIAL PESTICIDE SAMPLES; ANNUAL REPORT. a. Department of Agriculture, Box 44345, Capitol Station, Baton Rouge, LA 70804. Key Title: Analysis of Official Pesticide Samples.
Agricultural chemistry

MANITOBA CROP INSURANCE CORPORATION. ANNUAL REPORT. see *INSURANCE*

633.6　　　　　MX　ISSN 0464-882X
MANUAL AZUCARERO MEXICANO. 1958. a. Mex.$250($13) Compania Editora del Manual Azucarero S.A., Balderas 44, Mexico 1 D.F., Mexico. adv. stat. circ. 1,500.

631.4　　　　　UN　ISSN 0543-3770
MEETING ON SOIL CORRELATION FOR NORTH AMERICA. (REPORT) (Subseries of Food and Agriculture Organization of the United Nations. World Soil Resources Reports) 1965. irreg. Food and Agriculture Organization of the United Nations, Distribution and Sales Section, Via delle Terme di Caracalla, I-00100 Rome, Italy.

631.4　　　　　UN　ISSN 0543-3789
MEETING ON SOIL SURVEY CORRELATION AND INTERPRETATION FOR LATIN AMERICA. REPORT. 1962. irreg. Food and Agriculture Organization of the United Nations, Distribution and Sales Section, Via delle Terme di Caracalla, I-00100 Rome, Italy.

MEGADRILOGICA. see *BIOLOGY — Zoology*

631.7　　　　　CN
MERITE DU DEFRICHEUR. RAPPORT DE L'ORDRE DU MERITE AGRICOLE. 1950. a. free contr. circ. Editeur Officiel du Quebec, 1283 Bd. Charest ouest, Quebec G1N 2C9, Canada. Ed. Benoit Roy. circ. 5,000.
Formerly: Merite du Defricheur. Rapport de l'Ordre du Merite du Defricheur (ISSN 0076-6577)

631　　　　　MX
MEXICAN SOCIETY FOR SOIL MECHANICS MEETING. PROCEEDINGS. (Text in Spanish) biennial. price varies. Sociedad Mexicana de Mecanica de Suelos, Londres 44, Coyoacan, Mexico 21, D.F., Mexico.

631.8　　　　　US　ISSN 0077-4510
NATIONAL FERTILIZER DEVELOPMENT CENTER. ANNUAL REPORT. 1966. a. free. Tennessee Valley Authority, National Fertilizer Development Center, Muscle Shoals, AL 35660. circ. 8,000. Indexed: Amer.Stat.Ind.
Continues: Tennessee Valley Authority. Agricultural and Chemical Development Annual Report.

638　　　　　UK　ISSN 0077-4782
NATIONAL INSTITUTE OF AGRICULTURAL BOTANY, CAMBRIDGE, ENGLAND. ANNUAL REPORT OF THE COUNCIL AND ACCOUNTS. 1919. a. £2.50. National Institute of Agricultural Botany, Huntingdon Rd., Cambridge CB3 0LE, England. circ. 7,000.

631　　　　　UK
NATIONAL INSTITUTE OF AGRICULTURAL BOTANY, CAMBRIDGE, ENGLAND. FARMERS LEAFLETS. a. price varies. National Institute of Agricultural Botany, Huntingdon Rd., Cambridge CB3 0LE, England.

630　　　　　UK　ISSN 0077-4790
NATIONAL INSTITUTE OF AGRICULTURAL BOTANY, CAMBRIDGE, ENGLAND. JOURNAL. 1922. a. £5. National Institute of Agricultural Botany, Huntingdon Rd., Cambridge CB3 0LE, England. index. circ. 5,000.

631　　　　　UK
NATIONAL INSTITUTE OF AGRICULTURAL BOTANY, CAMBRIDGE, ENGLAND. TECHNICAL LEAFLETS. 1979. a. price varies. National Institute of Agricultural Botany, Huntingdon Rd., Cambridge CB3 0LE, England.

631　　　　　UK
NATIONAL INSTITUTE OF AGRICULTURAL BOTANY, CAMBRIDGE, ENGLAND. VEGETABLE GROWERS LEAFLETS. a. price varies. National Institute of Agricultural Botany, Huntingdon Rd., Cambridge CB3 0LE, England.

631　　　　　UK　ISSN 0077-4812
NATIONAL INSTITUTE OF AGRICULTURAL ENGINEERING, SILSOE, ENGLAND. TRANSLATIONS. 1956. irreg. price varies. ‡ National Institute of Agricultural Engineering, Wrest Park, Silsoe, Bedford MK45 4HS, England. Ed. E. Harris.
Agricultural engineering

631.8　　　　　JA　ISSN 0077-4839
NATIONAL INSTITUTE OF AGRICULTURAL SCIENCES, TOKYO. BULLETIN. SERIES B (SOILS AND FERTILIZERS) (Text in English or Japanese with English summary) 1952. irreg., no. 29, 1977. avail. on exchange basis only. National Institute of Agricultural Sciences - Norin-sho Nogyo Gijutsu Kenkyusho, 2-7-1 Nishigahara, Kita-ku, Tokyo 114, Japan. Ed. Y. Matsuzaka.

634　　　　　US　ISSN 0092-2633
NATIONAL PEACH COUNCIL. PROCEEDINGS. a. $6. National Peach Council, Box 1085, Martinsburg, WV 25401. adv. illus.

631.7　　　　　US　ISSN 0085-3879
NEBRASKA. AGRICULTURAL EXPERIMENT STATION, NORTH PLATTE. FALL CROPS AND IRRIGATION FIELD DAY.* a. University of Nebraska, North Platte Agricultural Experiment Station, North Platte, NE 69101. circ. 400.

631.8　　　　　NE　ISSN 0077-7595
NETHERLANDS NITROGEN TECHNICAL BULLETIN. (Text in English) 1966. irreg. free. Nederlandse Tikstofmeststoffen Industrie, Landbouwkundig Bureau - Netherlands Nitrogen Fertilizer Industry, Agricultural Bureau, Thorbeckelaan 360, Postbus 6695, The Hague 2025, Netherlands.

338.1　　　　　US　ISSN 0098-9541
NEW JERSEY ORCHARD AND VINEYARD SURVEY. irreg., approx. quinquennial. Crop Reporting Service, Rm. 204, Health and Agriculture Bldg., Trenton, NJ 08625. illus.

633　　　　　US　ISSN 0077-8966
NEW YORK AGRICULTURAL STATISTICS. a. free. ‡ New York Crop Reporting Service, c/o Department of Agriculture and Markets, State Campus, Albany, NY 12235. circ. 1,800.

631.4　　　　　NZ　ISSN 0077-9644
NEW ZEALAND. SOIL BUREAU. BULLETIN. 1948. irreg. price varies. Department of Scientific and Industrial Research, Box 9741, Wellington, New Zealand.

631.4　　　　　NZ
NEW ZEALAND. SOIL BUREAU SCIENTIFIC REPORT. 1971. irreg. Soil Bureau, Private Bag, Lower Hutt, New Zealand. bibl.

630　627　　　NZ　ISSN 0077-9520
NEW ZEALAND AGRICULTURAL ENGINEERING INSTITUTE. ANNUAL REPORT. 1965-66. a. exchange basis. New Zealand Agricultural Engineering Institute, Lincoln College, Canterbury, New Zealand.
Agricultural engineering

AGRICULTURE — CROP PRODUCTION AND SOIL

631.4   US   ISSN 0078-1320
NORTH AMERICAN FOREST SOILS CONFERENCE. PROCEEDINGS. 1958. quinquennial. $18.90. Society of American Foresters, 1010 16th St. N.W., Washington, DC 20036. (Co-sponsors; Soil Science Society of Canada; Canadian Institute of Forestry) (also avail. in microform from UMI)

630.24   668.6   US   ISSN 0065-4418
NORTH CAROLINA AGRICULTURAL CHEMICALS MANUAL. 1948. a. $3.50. North Carolina State University, School of Agriculture-Life Sciences, Box 5125, Raleigh, NC 27607. index.
Agricultural chemistry

631.4   US   ISSN 0078-1517
NORTH CAROLINA STATE UNIVERSITY. DEPARTMENT OF CROP SCIENCE. RESEARCH REPORT. 1962. irreg., no. 50, 1974. North Carolina State University, Department of Crop Science, Raleigh, NC 27607.

631   US   ISSN 0078-1703
NORTHEASTERN WEED SCIENCE SOCIETY. PROCEEDINGS. 1946. a. $11 ($2 for supplement) Northeastern Weed Science Society, c/o R.R. Hahn, Sec.-Treas., Department of Agronomy, Cornell University, Ithaca, NY 14853. Ed. C. B. Coffman. index. circ. 700.
Formerly: Northeastern Weed Control Conference.

634   CN   ISSN 0078-2386
NOVA SCOTIA FRUIT GROWERS ASSOCIATION. ANNUAL REPORT AND PROCEEDINGS. 1874. a. Nova Scotia Fruit Growers Association, Kentville, N. S., Canada. adv. circ. 500. Indexed: Chem.Abstr.

631   551   CN
ONTARIO INSTITUTE OF PEDOLOGY. DEPARTMENT OF LAND RESOURCE SCIENCE. PROGRESS REPORT. irreg. Ontario Institute of Pedology, Department of Land Resource Science, Blackwood Hall, University of Guelph, Guelph, Ont. N1G 2W1, Canada.

630   US   ISSN 0078-6128
ORGANIC DIRECTORY. 1970. irreg. $2.95. Rodale Press, Inc., 33 E. Minor St., Emmaus, PA 18049.

OSSERVATORIO REGIONALE PER LE MALATTIE DELLA VITE. OSSERVAZIONI DI METEOROLOGIA, FENOLOGIA E PATOLOGIA DELLA VITE. see *BIOLOGY — Botany*

631.5   PK   ISSN 0078-7930
PAKISTAN CENTRAL COTTON COMMITTEE. AGRICULTURAL SURVEY REPORT.* (Text in English) 1960, no. 2. irreg. Pakistan Central Cotton Committee, Secretary, Moulvi Tamizuddin Khan Rd., Karachi 1, Pakistan.

631.5   PK   ISSN 0078-7949
PAKISTAN CENTRAL COTTON COMMITTEE. TECHNOLOGICAL BULLETIN. SERIES A.* (Head of title: Pakistan Institute of Cotton Research and Technology) (Text in English) 1960. irreg. Pakistan Central Cotton Committee, Secretary, Moulvi Tamizuddin Khan Rd., Karachi 1, Pakistan.

631.5   PK   ISSN 0078-7957
PAKISTAN CENTRAL COTTON COMMITTEE. TECHNOLOGICAL BULLETIN. SERIES B.* (Head of Title: Pakistan Institute of Cotton Research and Technology) (Text in English) 1959. irreg. Pakistan Central Cotton Committee, Secretary, Moulvi Tamizuddin Khan Rd., Karachi 1, Pakistan.

631.4   FR   ISSN 0378-181X
PEDOFAUNA. (Text in English, French, and German) 1964 N.S. irreg. $5. International Society of Soil Science, Third Commission, c/o Dr. M. Bouche, Station de Recherches sur la Faune du Sol, 7 rue Sully, 21 Dijon, France. bk. rev. circ. 500.
Formerly (until vol. 23, 1976): Biologie du Sol (ISSN 0067-8805)

338.1   US   ISSN 0079-046X
PENNSYLVANIA CROP AND LIVESTOCK ANNUAL SUMMARY. a. free. Crop Reporting Service, 2301 N. Cameron St., Harrisburg, PA 17120. circ. 5,000.
Formerly: Pennsylvania Crop Reporting Service. C.R.S. (ISSN 0079-0478); Incorporates: Pennsylvania's Machinery Custom Rates.

632.9   US
PESTICIDE DICTIONARY. a. $5. Meister Publishing Co., 37841 Euclid Ave., Willoughby, OH 44094. Ed. John Hardesty.

632   US
PESTICIDE HANDBOOK-ENTOMA. biennial. Entomological Society of America, 4603 Calvert Rd., College Park, MD 20740.

632   US   ISSN 0079-1148
PESTICIDE REVIEW. 1953. a. free. ‡ U.S. Agricultural Stabilization and Conservation Service, Box 2415, Washington, DC 20013. Ed. D. Lee Fowler. circ. 6,500.
Formerly: Pesticide Situation.

632.9   II
PESTICIDES ANNUAL. (Text in English) a. Rs.60. Colour Publications Pvt. Ltd., 126-A Dhuruwadi, Off Dr. Nariman Rd., Bombay 400025, India. illus.

630.24   GW   ISSN 0405-0738
PFLANZENSCHUTZ-KURIER. English edition: Crop Protection Courier (International) (ISSN 0590-1243); South African edition: Crop Protection Courier (South Africa) Spanish edition: Correo Fitosanitario(International) 1956. 3/yr. free. Bayer AG, 5090 Leverkusen-Bayerwerk, W. Germany (B.R.D.) Ed. Matthias Willig. charts. illus. circ. 168,000(controlled)

630.24   GW   ISSN 0079-1342
PFLANZENSCHUTZ-NACHRICHTEN BAYER. (Editions in English and German) 1948. irreg. (2-3/yr) free. ‡ Bayer AG, 5090 Leverkusen-Bayerwerk, W. Germany (B.R.D.) Ed. Maria Middendorf. Indexed: Anal.Abstr.   Biol.Abstr.   Rev.Appl.Mycol.

354.599   PH
PHILIPPINE COCONUT AUTHORITY. AGRICULTURAL RESEARCH DEPARTMENT. ANNUAL REPORT. (Text in English) 1974. a. Philippine Coconut Authority, Agricultural Research Department, Box 295, Davao, Philippines. illus. stat.

631   663   340   BL
PLANO DA SAFRA ACUCAR E ALCOOL. irreg. Instituto do Acucar e do Alcool, Praca Quinze de Novembro 42, Rio de Janeiro, Brazil. (Affiliate: Brazil. Ministerio da Industria e do Comercio)
Laws and regulations governing sugar and alcohol

631.5   UK   ISSN 0079-2225
PLANT BREEDING INSTITUTE, CAMBRIDGE. ANNUAL REPORT. 1959. a. L.1. (Agricultural Research Council) Plant Breeding Institute, Trumpington, Cambridge, England. Ed. Dr. E. S. Bunting. circ. 1,000. Indexed: Plant Breed.Abstr.

631.8   US
PLANT FOOD DICTIONARY. a. $5. Meister Publishing Co., 37841 Euclid Ave., Willoughby, OH 44094. Ed. John Hardesty.

630   635   CH
PLANT PROTECTION CENTER. ANNUAL REPORT. (Text in English) 1973. a. Plant Protection Center, Chung Cheng Rd., Wuffeng, Taichung Hsien, Taiwan, Republic of China.

631.4   PL   ISSN 0079-2985
POLISH JOURNAL OF SOIL SCIENCE. (Text in English; summaries in Polish and Russian) 1968. irreg., 1971, vol. 4, no. 2. price varies. (Polska Akademia Nauk, Komitet Gleboznawstwa i Chemii Rolnej) Panstwowe Wydawnictwo Naukowe, Ul. Miodowa 10, Warsaw, Poland (Dist. by Ars Polona-Ruch, Krakowskie Przedmiescie 7, Warsaw, Poland) Ed. B. Dobrzanski. bibl. charts. illus. Indexed: Chem.Abstr.

POTATO MARKETING BOARD, LONDON. ANNUAL REPORT AND ACCOUNTS. see *AGRICULTURE — Agricultural Economics*

631.5   IS
PROFITABILITY OF CITRUS GROWING IN ISRAEL/HA-RIVHIYUT SHEL GIDUL HADAVIM. (Issued as the Institute's Publications. Series F) (Text in Hebrew; summaries in English) 1968-69. a. I£150($6) Institute of Farm Income Research, 6 Hachashmonaim Blvd., Tel Aviv, Israel.

631.5   IS   ISSN 0079-595X
PROFITABILITY OF COTTON GROWING IN ISRAEL/HA-RIVHIYUT SHEL GIDUL HAKUTNAH. (Issued as the Institute's Publications. Series C) (Text in Hebrew; summaries in English) 1964-1965. a. I£150($6) per issue. Institute of Farm Income Research, 6 Hachashmonaim Blvd., Tel Aviv, Israel.

631.5   IS   ISSN 0079-5976
PROFITABILITY OF SUGARBEET GROWING IN ISRAEL/HA-RIVHIYUT SHEL GIDUL SELEK HA-SUKAR. (Issued as the Institute's Publications, Series A.) (Text in Hebrew; summaries in English) 1964-65. a. I£150($6) per issue. Institute of Farm Income Research, 6 Hachashmonaim Blvd., Tel Aviv, Israel.

631   BL   ISSN 0100-526X
PROGNOSTICO. 1972. a. Instituto de Economia Agricola, Av. Miguel Stefano, Caixa Postal 8114, C E P 04301 Sao Paulo S.P., Brazil. stat. circ. controlled.
Formerly: Prognostico da Agricultura Paulista.

631.5   BL   ISSN 0100-5316
PROGNOSTICO REGIAO CENTRO-SUL. 1974. a. exchange basis. Instituto de Economia Agricola, Av. Miguel Stefano 3900, Caixa Postal 8114, C E P 04301, Sao Paulo S.P., Brazil. stat. circ. controlled.

630   PL   ISSN 0079-7154
PRZEGLAD NAUKOWEJ LITERATURY ROLNICZEJ I LESNEJ. GLEBOZNAWSTWO. CHEMIA ROLNA. OGOLNA UPRAWA ROLI I ROSLIN I SIEDLISKA LESNE. 1955. a. price varies. Panstwowe Wydawnictwo Naukowe, Miodowa 10, Warsaw, Poland (Dist. by Ars Polona-Ruch, Krakowskie Przedmiescie 7, Warsaw, Poland) Ed. W. Trzcinski.

631   IO
RESEARCH INSTITUTE FOR ESTATE CROPS, BOGOR. COCOA STATISTICS/BALAI PENELITIAN PERKEBUNAN, BOGOR. STATISTIK COKLAT. (Text in Indonesian and English) 1969. a. Rps.2000. Research Institute for Estate Crops - Balai Penelitian Perkebunan Bogor, Jl. Taman Kencana 1, Box 81, Bogor, Indonesia. (Co-sponsor: Central Bureau for Statistics) circ. 200. Indexed: Hort.Abstr.   RAPRA.   Trop.Abstr.

631   315   IO
RESEARCH INSTITUTE FOR ESTATE CROPS, BOGOR. COFFEE STATISTICS/BALAI PENELITIAN PERKEBUNAN, BOGOR. STATISTIK KOPI. (Text in Indonesian and English) 1968. a. Rps.2000. Research Institute for Estate Crops - Balai Penelitian Perkebunan Bogor, Jl. Taman Kencana 1, Box 81, Bogor, Indonesia. (Co-sponsor: Central Bureau for Statistics) circ. 200. Indexed: Hort.Abstr.   RAPRA.   Trop.Abstr.

631   IO
RESEARCH INSTITUTE FOR ESTATE CROPS, BOGOR. COMMUNICATIONS. (Text in English) 1971. irreg. Research Institute for Estate Crops - Balai Penelitian Perkebunan Bogor, Jl. Taman Kencana 1, Box 81, Bogor, Indonesia. Indexed: Hort.Abstr.   RAPRA.   Trop.Abstr.

631   315   IO
RESEARCH INSTITUTE FOR ESTATE CROPS, BOGOR. RUBBER STATISTICS/BALAI PENELITIAN PERKEBUNAN, BOGOR. STATISTIK KARET. (Text in Indonesian and English) 1968. a. Rps.2000. Research Institute for Estate Crops - Balai Penelitian Perkebunan Bogor, Jl. Taman Kencana 1, Box 81, Bogor, Indonesia. (Co-sponsor: Central Bureau for Statistics) circ. 200. Indexed: Hort.Abstr.   RAPRA.   Trop.Abstr.

632   JA   ISSN 0557-7527
REVIEW OF PLANT PROTECTION RESEARCH. (Text in English) 1968. a. $15. Japanese Society of Applied Entomology and Zoology, c/o National Institute of Agricultural Sciences, 2-1-7 Nishigahara, Kita-ku, Tokyo 114, Japan. (Co-sponsors: Phytopathological Society of Japan; Pesticide Science Society of Japan) abstr. circ. 1,000.

AGRICULTURE — CROP PRODUCTION AND SOIL

633 NE
RIJKSINSTITUUT VOOR HET RASSENONDERZOEK VAN CULTUURGEWASSEN. JAARVERSLAG. 1955. a. free. Rijksinstituut voor het Rassenonderzoek van Cultuurgewassen - Government Institute for Research on Varieties of Cultivated Plants, Postbus 32, 6700 AA Wageningen, Netherlands. circ. 230.
Formerly: Instituut voor Rassenonderzoek van Landbouwgewassen. Jaarverslag (ISSN 0080-3057)

633 NE
RIJKSINSTITUUT VOOR HET RASSENONDERZOEK VAN CULTUURGEWASSEN. MEDEDELINGEN. (Text and summaries in Dutch, English, French or German) 1949. irreg., 1969, no. 57. free. Rijksinstituut voor het Rassenonderzoek van Cultuurgewassen - Government Institute for Research on Varieties of Cultivated Plants, Postbus 32, 6700 AA Wageningen, Netherlands. circ. 2,000-3,000.
Formerly: Instituut voor Rassenonderzoek van Landbouwgewassen. Mededelingen (ISSN 0080-3065)

631.4 PL ISSN 0080-3642
ROCZNIKI GLEBOZNAWCZE. (Text mainly in Polish; summaries in English& Russian) 1950. q. $26. (Polskie Towarzystwo Gleboznawcze) Panstwowe Wydawnictwo Naukowe, Ul. Miodowa 10, Warsaw, Poland (Dist. by: Ars Polona-Ruch, Krakowskie Przedmiescie 7, Warsaw, Poland) Ed. Wladyslaw Trzcinski.

633 635 PL ISSN 0080-3650
ROCZNIKI NAUK ROLNICZYCH. SERIA A. PRODUKCJA ROSLINNA. (Text in Polish; summaries in English, Polish, Russian) 1903. irreg., 1975, vol. 101, no. 2. price varies. (Polska Akademia Nauk, Komitet Uprawy i Hodowli Roslin) Panstwowe Wydawnictwo Naukowe, Miodowa 10, Warsaw, Poland (Dist. by Ars Polona-Ruch, Krakowskie Przedmiescie 7, Warsaw, Poland) Ed. Stanislaw Starzycki. bibl. charts.

632.9 PL ISSN 0080-3693
ROCZNIKI NAUK ROLNICZYCH. SERIA E. OCHRONA ROSLIN. (Text in Polish; summaries in English and Russian) 1970. irreg., 1976, vol. 5, no. 2. price varies. (Polska Akademia Nauk, Komitet Ochrony Roslin) Panstwowe Wydawnictwo Naukowe, Ul. Miodowa 10, Warsaw, Poland (Dist. by Ars Polona-Ruch, Krakowskie Przedmiescie 7, Warsaw, Poland) Ed. Wladyslaw Wegorek. bibl. charts. illus.

631.4 PL ISSN 0080-3707
ROCZNIKI NAUK ROLNICZYCH. SERIA F. MELIORACJI I VZYTKOW ZIELONYCH. (Text in Polish; summaries in English and Russian) 1903. irreg., 1970, vol. 77. price varies. (Polska Akademia Nauk, Komitet Melioracjii, Lakarstwa i Torfoznawstwa) Panstwowe Wydawnictwo Naukowe, Miodowa 10, Warsaw, Poland (Dist. by Ars Polona-Ruch, Krakowskie Przedmiescie 7, Warsaw, Poland) Ed. Jerzy Ostromecki.

631.4 US ISSN 0081-1904
S S S A SPECIAL PUBLICATION SERIES. 1967. irreg., no. 7, 1975. price varies. Soil Science Society of America, 677 South Segoe Rd., Madison, WI 53711. (Affiliate: American Society of Agronomy)

631.5 US ISSN 0080-8504
SEED TRADE BUYER'S GUIDE. 1917. a. $8. Scranton Gillette Communications, Inc., 380 Northwest Highway, Des Plaines, IL 60016. Ed. Laura Stepanek.

633.6 CU
SERIE CANA DE AZUCAR. (Text in Spanish; summaries in English) 1967. irreg. exchange. Academia de Ciencias de Cuba, Instituto de Investigaciones de la Cana de Azucar, San Jose de los Lajas, Havana, Cuba. illus. circ. 5,000. (back issues avail.)

630 US
SERIES IN GEOTECHNICAL ENGINEERING. 1951. irreg., unnumbered, latest, 1980. price varies. John Wiley & Sons, Inc., 605 Third Ave., New York, NY 10016. Eds. T. William Lambe, Robert V. Whitman.
Formerly: Soil Engineering Series.

631 MW
SMALLHOLDER TEA AUTHORITY. ANNUAL REPORT. a. Smallholder Tea Authority, Box 80, Thyolo, Malawi.

632 JA ISSN 0081-170X
SOCIETY OF PLANT PROTECTION OF NORTH JAPAN. ANNUAL REPORT/KITANIHON BYOGAICHU KENKYUKAI KAIHO. (Summaries in English) 1950. a. 500 Yen($1.50) Society of Plant Protection of North Japan - Kita Nihon Byogaichu Kenkyukai, c/o Tohoku National Agricultural Experiment Station, 3 Shimofurumichi, Yotsuya, Omagari 014-01, Japan. Ed. Yukio Koshimizu. cum.index: 1950-1959, 1960-1969.

631.4 CE
SOIL SCIENCE SOCIETY OF CEYLON. JOURNAL. (Text in English) 1970. a. Rs.5($1) Soil Science Society of Ceylon, Faculty of Agriculture, University of Sri Lanka, Peradeniya, Sri Lanka. Ed. N. W. Thenabadu. bk. rev. circ. 150.

631.4 AT ISSN 0081-1912
SOILS AND LAND USE SERIES. 1949. irreg. Aus.$5 free. C. S. I. R. O., Division of Soils, Private Bag No. 2, Glen Osmond, S.A. 5064, Australia (Subscr. to: CSIRO, Editorial & Publications Service, Box 89, East Melbourne, Vic. 3002, Australia) circ. 700. Indexed: Aus.Sci.Ind. Soils & Fert.

631.4 AT
SOILS NEWS. 1957? irreg. Australian Society of Soil Science, c/o G. J. Hamilton, Ed., Soil Conservation Service, P.O. Box 249, Cowra, N.S.W. 2794, Australia. bk. rev. circ. 700.

SOUTH AFRICAN SUGAR YEAR BOOK. see FOOD AND FOOD INDUSTRIES

630.24 US ISSN 0362-4463
SOUTHERN WEED SCIENCE SOCIETY. PROCEEDINGS. a. $10. Southern Weed Science Society, c/o Ed. James F. Miller, University of Georgia, Extension Agronomy Department, Athens, GA 30602. (back issues avail) Key Title: Proceedings - Southern Weed Science Society.

633 US
SOYA BLUEBOOK. 1946. a. $25. ‡ American Soybean Association, Box 27300, St. Louis, MO 63141. Ed. Melissa Kennedy. adv. charts. stat. circ. 3,500. (back issues avail.)
Formerly (until 1980): Soybean Digest Blue Book (ISSN 0081-3222)

633 SP
SPAIN. DIRECCION GENERAL DE LA PRODUCCION AGRARIA. CAMPANA ALGODONERA. irreg. Ministerio de Agricultura, Direccion General de la Produccion Agraria, Madrid, Spain.

632 SP
SPAIN. INSTITUTO NACIONAL DE INVESTIGACIONES AGRARIAS. ANALES. SERIE: PROTECCION VEGETAL. (Text in Spanish; summaries in English, French, German) 1971. irreg (approx 1-2/yr) 300 ptas. per issue. Instituto Nacional de Investigaciones Agrarias, General Sanjurjo 56, Madrid 3, Spain. bibl, charts, illus. circ. 1,500.
Supersedes in part: Spain. Instituto Nacional de Investigaciones Agronomicas. Anales & Boletin de Patologia Vegetal y Entomologia Agricola.

631 SP
SPAIN. INSTITUTO NACIONAL DE INVESTIGACIONES AGRARIAS. ANALES. SERIE: PRODUCCION VEGETAL. (Text in Spanish; summaries in English, French, German) irreg. 300 ptas. per no. Instituto Nacional de Investigaciones Agrarias, General Sanjurjo 56, Madrid 3, Spain. bibl. charts. illus.

SPRENGER INSTITUUT. COMMUNICATIONS. see FOOD AND FOOD INDUSTRIES

SPRENGER INSTITUUT. JAARVERSLAG/ ANNUAL REPORT. see FOOD AND FOOD INDUSTRIES

631.8 GW ISSN 0081-5535
DER STICKSTOFF. 1963. irreg. free. Fachverband Stickstoffindustrie, Sternstr. 9-11, 4000 Duesseldorf 1, W. Germany (B.R.D.) Ed. Helmut Nieder. circ. 10,000.
Fertilizers

631 SJ ISSN 0562-5068
SUDAN COTTON REVIEW. (Text in English) 1958. a. Cotton Public Corporation, Box 1672, Khartoum, Sudan.

631.8 US ISSN 0081-9255
SULPHUR INSTITUTE. TECHNICAL BULLETIN. 1963. irreg., no. 22, 1977. single copy free. Sulphur Institute, 1725 K St. N.W., Washington, DC 20006. Ed. J. Platou. circ. 2,500.

630 PL ISSN 0082-1276
SZCZECINSKIE TOWARZYSTWO NAUKOWE. WYDZIAL NAUK PRZYRODNICZO-ROLNICZYCH. PRACE. (Text in Polish; summaries in English, German and Russian) 1959. irreg. price varies. Szczecinskie Towarzystwo Naukowe, Wydzial Nauk Przyrodniczo-Rolniczych, Rycerska 3, 70-537 Szczecin, Poland (Dist. by: Ars Polona-Ruch, Krakowskie Przedmiescie 7, Warsaw, Poland)

633 CH
TAIWAN SUGAR RESEARCH INSTITUTE. ANNUAL REPORT. (Text in English) a. Taiwan Sugar Research Institute, Tai-Wan Tang Yeh Yen Chiu So, Tainan, Taiwan, Republic of China. illus.

631 II ISSN 0082-1586
TAMIL NADU. DEPARTMENT OF STATISTICS. SEASON AND CROP REPORT. (Text in English) 1902-03. a. Rs.5. Director of Statistics, Madras 600006, India (Subscription to: Government Publication Depot, 166 Anna Road, Madras 600006, India)

631.5 GW ISSN 0082-1799
TASCHENBUCH DER PFLANZENARZTES. 1951. a. DM.26. Landwirtschaftsverlag GmbH, Marktallee 89, Postfach 480210, 4400 Muenster-Hiltrup, W. Germany (B.R.D.)

TEA RESEARCH ASSOCIATION. MEMORANDUM. see BEVERAGES

TEA RESEARCH ASSOCIATION. OCCASIONAL SCIENTIFIC PAPERS. see BEVERAGES

TEA RESEARCH ASSOCIATION. SCIENTIFIC ANNUAL REPORT. see BEVERAGES

TEXAS COTTON REVIEW. see AGRICULTURE — Agricultural Economics

633 US ISSN 0092-153X
TEXAS FIELD CROP STATISTICS. (Subseries of Texas. Dept. of Agriculture. Bulletin) 1968. a. free. Department of Agriculture, P.O. Box 12847, Austin, TX 78711. charts. illus. mkt. stats. circ. 3,600.

631.8 TH ISSN 0085-7246
THAILAND. DIVISION OF AGRICULTURAL CHEMISTRY. REPORT ON FERTILIZER EXPERIMENTS AND SOIL FERTILITY RESEARCH.* (Text in English) 1966. irreg. Ministry of Agriculture, Division of Agricultural Chemistry, Bangkok 9, Thailand.

354.54 II
TOBACCO EXPORT PROMOTION COUNCIL. ANNUAL REPORT AND ACCOUNTS. (Text in English) a. Tobacco Export Promotion Council, World Trade Centre, 123-C Mount Rd., Madras 600006, India. stat.

632 TZ ISSN 0082-6642
TROPICAL PESTICIDES RESEARCH INSTITUTE. ANNUAL REPORT. 1957. a. 15 available on exchange. Tropical Pesticides Research Institute, P.O. Box 3024, Arusha, Tanzania.

633 US ISSN 0363-8561
U.S. CROP REPORTING BOARD. CROP PRODUCTION. m. with annual summary. free. U.S. Crop Reporting Board, Washington, DC 20250. Key Title: Crop Production.

632 US ISSN 0083-0518
U. S. ENVIRONMENTAL PROTECTION AGENCY. PESTICIDES ENFORCEMENT DIVISION. NOTICES OF JUDGEMENT UNDER FEDERAL INSECTICIDE, FUNGICIDE, AND RODENTICIDE ACT.* irreg. free. U.S. Environmental Protection Agency, M St. N.W., Washington, DC 20460 (Orders to: Supt. Doc., Washington, DC 20402)

633 US ISSN 0083-064X
U.S. FEDERAL CROP INSURANCE CORPORATION. ANNUAL REPORT TO CONGRESS. 1939. a. U.S. Federal Crop Insurance Corporation., U.S. Dept. of Agriculture, Washington, DC 20250 (Orders to: Supt. Doc., Washington, DC 20402) Ed. George Vohs.

631.4 US ISSN 0083-3304
U. S. SOIL CONSERVATION SERVICE. NATIONAL ENGINEERING HANDBOOK. irreg. U.S. Soil Conservation Service, c/o Dept. of Agriculture, Washington, DC 20250 (Orders to: Supt. of Documents, Washington, DC 20402) (also avail. in microfiche)

631.4 US ISSN 0083-3320
U. S. SOIL CONSERVATION SERVICE. SOIL SURVEY INVESTIGATION REPORTS. 1967. irreg. U. S. Soil Conservation Service, Department of Agriculture, Washington, DC 20250 (Orders to: Supt. Doc., Washington, DC 20402)

631.4 US ISSN 0083-3339
U. S. SOIL CONSERVATION SERVICE. TECHNICAL PUBLICATIONS. irreg. U.S. Soil Conservation Service, U. S. Dept. of Agriculture, Washington, DC 20250.

631.7 PE
UNIVERSIDAD NACIONAL AGRARIA. TALLER DE ESTUDIOS ANDINOS. SERIE ANDES CENTRALES. no. 4, 1977. irreg. Universidad Nacional Agraria, Taller de Estudios Andinos, La Molina, Peru.

631 PE
UNIVERSIDAD NACIONAL AGRARIA. TALLER DE ESTUDIOS ANDINOS. SERIE: COSTA CENTRAL. 1978. irreg. Universidad Nacional Agraria, Taller de Estudios Andinos, Departamento de Ciencias Humanas, Apdo. 456, La Molina, Lima, Peru.

632 IT ISSN 0078-8619
UNIVERSITA DEGLI STUDI DI PALERMO. ISTITUTO DI ENTOMOLOGIA AGRARIA. BOLLETTINO.* (Text in Italian; summaries in Italian, English, French) 1955. biennial. Universita degli Studi di Palermo, Istituto di Entomologia Agraria, Viale delle Scienze, 90128 Palermo, Italy.

631.4 CN ISSN 0085-1329
UNIVERSITY OF GUELPH. DEPARTMENT OF LAND RESOURCE SCIENCE. PROGRESS REPORT. 1954. a. free. University of Guelph, Department of Land Resource Science, Guelph, Ont. N1G 2W1, Canada. bibl. charts. illus. circ. 1,000. (processed)

632.9 PH
UNIVERSITY OF THE PHILIPPINES AT LOS BANOS. RODENT RESEARCH CENTER. ANNUAL REPORT. 1969. a. free. University of the Philippines at Los Banos, Rodent Research Center, College, Laguna 3720, Philippines. circ. 2,000. Indexed: Biol.Abstr.

633 TR
UNIVERSITY OF THE WEST INDIES. ANNUAL REPORT ON COCAO RESEARCH. a. University of the West Indies, St. Augustine, Trinidad. bibl. illus.

630.24 SW
VAEXTSKYDDS-KURIREN. Swedish edition of: Pflanzenschutz-Kurier. 1960. irreg. free. Bayer (Sverige) AB, Agro-Kemi, Bjuroegatan 42, S-211 24 Malmoe, Sweden. Ed. Olof Skioeld. charts. illus. circ. 40,000(controlled)

632 US ISSN 0507-6773
VERTEBRATE PEST CONFERENCE. PROCEEDINGS. 1962. biennial. Vertebrate Pest Council, c/o California Department of Food & Agriculture, 1220 N St., Rm. A-357, Sacramento, CA 95814. circ. 1,000.

630 UR
VSESOYUZNYI NAUCHNO-ISSLEDOVATEL'SKII INSTITUT ZERNOVOGO KHOZYAISTVA. TRUDY. 1964. irreg. price varies. (Vsesoyuznaya Akademiya Sel'skokhozyaistvennykh Nauk im. V. I. Lenina) Izdatel'stvo Kolos, Sadovaya - Spasskaya, 18, 107807 Moscow, U.S.S.R. bibl. illus. circ. 2,000-5,000.

632 US ISSN 0511-411X
WEED CONTROL MANUAL AND HERBICIDE GUIDE. a. Meister Publishing Co., 37841 Euclid Ave., Willoughby, OH 44094.

WEED SOCIETY OF NEW SOUTH WALES. PROCEEDINGS. see BIOLOGY — Botany

631.4 UK ISSN 0083-7938
WELSH SOILS DISCUSSION GROUP. REPORT. 1960. a. £1.60. Welsh Soils Discussion Group, c/o Soil Survey of England & Wales, University College, Swansea, Wales. circ. 400. Indexed: Chem.Abstr. Soils & Fert.

633.18 LB
WEST AFRICA RICE DEVELOPMENT ASSOCIATION. ANNUAL REPORT. a. West Africa Rice Development Association, Box 1019, Monrovia, Liberia.

631 636.3 AT
WESTERN AUSTRALIA. DEPARTMENT OF AGRICULTURE. DIVISION OF PLANT PRODUCTION. ANNUAL REPORT. a. Department of Agriculture, Wheat and Sheep Division, Perth, W.A., Australia.
Formerly: Western Australia. Department of Agriculture. Wheat and Sheep Division. Annual Report.

633 AT ISSN 0310-897X
WESTERN AUSTRALIA. DEPARTMENT OF AGRICULTURE. RANGELAND MANAGEMENT SECTION. RANGELAND BULLETIN. 1971? irreg. Department of Agriculture, Rangeland Management Section, Jarrah Rd., South Perth, WA 6151, Australia.

WESTERN AUSTRALIA VEGETABLES. see GARDENING AND HORTICULTURE

631 658.8 AT
WESTERN AUSTRALIAN POTATO MARKETING BOARD. ANNUAL REPORT. a. Western Australian Potato Marketing Board, Perth, W.A., Australia.

661 UK
WORLD DIRECTORY OF FERTILIZER MANUFACTURERS. irreg. $200. British Sulphur Corp. Ltd., Parnell House, 25 Wilton Rd., London SW1V 1NH, England. (reprint service avail. from UMI)

661 UK
WORLD DIRECTORY OF FERTILIZER PRODUCTS. irreg. $150. British Sulphur Corp. Ltd., Parnell House, 25 Wilton Rd., London SW1V 1NH, England. (reprint service avail. from UMI)

631.8 UK ISSN 0512-2953
WORLD FERTILIZER ATLAS. 1964. irreg., 6th edt. 1979. $180. British Sulphur Corp. Ltd., Parnell House, 25 Wilton Rd., London, SW1V 1NH, England. (reprint service avail. from UMI)

661 UK
WORLD GUIDE TO FERTILIZER PLANT AND EQUIPMENT. irreg. $70. British Sulphur Corp. Ltd., Parnell House, 25 Wilton Rd., London SW1V 1NH, England. (reprint service avail. from UMI)

631.8 UK
WORLD GUIDE TO FERTILIZER PROCESSES AND CONSTRUCTORS. irreg. $130. British Sulphur Corp. Ltd., Parnell House, 25 Wilton Rd., London SW1V 1NH, England. (reprint service avail. from UMI)

614.7 631.8 UK
WORLD GUIDE TO POLLUTION CONTROL IN THE FERTILIZER INDUSTRY. irreg. $60. British Sulphur Corp. Ltd., Parnell House, 25 Wilton Rd., London SW1V 1NH, England. (reprint service avail. from UMI)

631.8 UK
WORLD SURVEY OF PHOSPHATE DEPOSITS. irreg. $450. British Sulphur Corp. Ltd., Parnell House, 25 Wilton Rd., London SW1V 1NH, England. (reprint service avail. from UMI)

631.8 UK
WORLD SURVEY OF SULPHUR RESOURCES. irreg. $192. British Sulphur Corp. Ltd., Parnell House, 25 Wilton Rd., London SW1V 1NH, England. (reprint service aval. from UMI)

WYE COLLEGE (UNIVERSITY OF LONDON). SCHOOL OF RURAL ECONOMICS & RELATED STUDIES. FARM BUSINESS UNIT. OCCASIONAL PAPER. see AGRICULTURE — Agricultural Economics

631.4 ZA
ZAMBIA. MINISTRY OF AGRICULTURE AND WATER DEVELOPMENT. LAND USE BRANCH. SOIL SURVEY REPORT. (Text in English) 1967. irreg. exchange basis. Ministry of Agriculture and Water Development, Land Use Branch, c/o Soil Survey Unit, Mount Makulu Research Station, Box 7, Chilanga, Zambia. circ. controlled.
Formerly: Zambia. Ministry of Lands and Agriculture. Land Use Branch. Soil Survey Report.

633 PL
ZIEMNIAK/KARTOFEL/POTATO. (Text in Polish, English, French, German; summaries in English, Russian) 1969. irreg. free. (Instytut Ziemniaka, Bonin) Panstwowe Wydawnictwo Rolnicze i Lesne, Al. Jerozolimskie 28, Warsaw, Poland.

338.1 RH
ZIMBABWE. CENTRAL STATISTICAL OFFICE. AGRICULTURAL PRODUCTION IN PURCHASE LANDS: NATIONAL AND PROVINCIAL TOTALS. (Text in English) 1969. a. Rhod.$0.50. Central Statistical Office, P.O. Box 8063, Causeway, Salisbury, Zimbabwe. circ. 180.
Formerly: Rhodesia. Central Statistical Office. Agricultural Production in African Purchase Lands. Part 1: National and Provincial Totals.

633.51 RH
ZIMBABWE. COTTON RESEARCH INSTITUE. ANNUAL REPORT. 1969. a. contr.free circ. Cotton Research Institute, Box 530, Gatooma, Zimbabwe. Ed. J. A. Gledhill. circ. controlled.

AGRICULTURE — Dairying And Dairy Products

see also Agriculture—Poultry and Livestock

637.1 US ISSN 0065-7263
AMERICAN ASSOCIATION OF MEDICAL MILK COMMISSIONS. METHODS AND STANDARDS FOR THE PRODUCTION OF CERTIFIED MILK. 1909. a. free. American Association of Medical Milk Commissions, Inc., Box 554, Alpharetta, GA 30201.

637 FR ISSN 0084-6538
ANNUAIRE NATIONAL DU LAIT. 1950. a. 252 F. Editions Comindus, 1, rue Descombes, Paris (17e) France.

AUSTRALIA. BUREAU OF AGRICULTURAL ECONOMICS. DAIRY PRODUCTS: SITUATION AND OUTLOOK. see AGRICULTURE — Agricultural Economics

637 UK ISSN 0069-4932
COATES'S HERD BOOK (DAIRY) 1822. a. £15 members. Shorthorn Society of the United Kingdom of Great Britain and Ireland, 4Th St. National Agricultural Centre, Kenilworth, Warwickshire CV8 2LG, England. Ed. J. Wood Roberts. circ. 400.

637　　　　　JA　ISSN 0388-0028
COLLEGE OF DAIRYING. JOURNAL;
CULTURAL AND SOCIAL SCIENCES/
RAKUNO GAKUEN DAIGAKU KIYO, JINBUN
SHAKAIKAGAKU HEN. (Text mainly in
Japanese; occasionally in English and German;
summaries mainly in English) 1961. a. on exchange
basis. College of Dairying Rakuno-Gakuen, 582
Nishi-Nopporo, Ebetsu, Hokkaido 069-01, Japan.
Ed.Bd. circ. 1,000. Indexed: Chem. Abstr.
　　Supersedes in part: College of Dairy Agriculture,
Hokkaido. Journal.

637　　　　　JA　ISSN 0388-001X
COLLEGE OF DAIRYING. JOURNAL; NATURAL
SCIENCE/RAKUNO GAKUEN DAIGAKU
KIYO, SHIZEN KAGAKU HEN. (Text mainly in
Japanese; occasionally in English and German;
summaries mainly in English) 1961. a. on exchange
basis. College of Dairy Agriculture Rakuno-Gakuen,
582 Nishi-Nopporo, Ebetsu, Hokkaido 069-01,
Japan. Ed.Bd. circ. 1,000. Indexed: Chem.Abstr.
　　Supersedes in part: College of Dairy Agriculture,
Hokkaido. Journal (ISSN 0069-570X)

637　　　　　US
DAIRY HERD IMPROVEMENT LETTER. 1924.
irreg., vol. 54, 1978. free. ‡ U.S. Science and
Education Administration, Animal Improvement
Programs Laboratory, Building 263, BARC-E,
Beltsville, MD 20705. (Co-sponsor: National
Cooperative Dairy Herd Improvement Program) Ed.
Frank N. Dickinson. charts. stat. index. circ.
controlled. Indexed: Dairy Sci.Abstr.
　　Formerly: Dairy Herd Improvement (ISSN 0085-
7580)

DAIRY INDUSTRIES CATALOG. see *FOOD AND
FOOD INDUSTRIES*

637　　　　　CN　ISSN 0707-7904
DAIRY INDUSTRY RESEARCH REPORT. a.
University of Guelph, College of Biological Science,
Guelph, Ont. N1G 2W1, Canada.

637　　　　　US
DAIRY PRODUCER HIGHLIGHTS. 1950. a. free. ‡
National Milk Producers Federation, 30 F Street,
N.W., Washington, DC 20001. charts. stat. circ.
5,000.

637　　　　　US
DAIRY ROUNDUP. 1973. a. free. ‡ Kent Feeds, Inc.,
1600 Oregon St., Muscatine, IA 52761. (tabloid
format)

637　　　　　UK　ISSN 0144-5251
DAIRYMAN'S YEARBOOK. 1978. a. National
Dairymen's Association, 19 Cornwall Terrace,
London NW1 4QP, England. illus.

637　　　　　FR
EUROPE LAITIERE; annuaire international des
produits laitiers - producteurs, negociants,
fournisseurs. a. S. E. P. T., 2 Villa Carman, Boite
Postale 95, 92164 Antony Cedex, France.

637　　　　　UK
FOODNEWS DAIRY PRODUCTS REVIEW.
Variant title: International Dairy Products Review.
(Supplement to: Foodnews) 1976. a. free to
subscribers of Foodnews. Foodnews Co., Montpelier
Vale, Blackheath Village, London SE3 0TJ,
England.

637.1　　　　　US　ISSN 0074-1671
INTERNATIONAL ASSOCIATION OF MILK
CONTROL AGENCIES. PROCEEDINGS OF
ANNUAL MEETINGS. 1937. a. $8. International
Association of Milk Control Agencies, c/o R. C.
Pearce, New York Dept. of Agriculture and
Markets, Albany, NY 12226. circ. c.

637　　　　　BE　ISSN 0074-4484
INTERNATIONAL DAIRY FEDERATION.
ANNUAL BULLETIN/FEDERATION
INTERNATIONALE DE LAITERIE. BULLETIN
ANNUEL. (Text in English and French) 1960. a.,
no. 129, 1980. 1300 Fr. International Dairy
Federation, Square Vergote 41, 1040 Brussels,
Belgium. index. cum. index. circ. 1,500.

637　　　　　BE　ISSN 0538-7078
INTERNATIONAL DAIRY FEDERATION.
ANNUAL MEMENTO/FEDERATION
INTERNATIONALE DE LAITERIE.
MEMENTO ANNUEL. 1968. a. free. International
Dairy Federation, Square Vergote 41, 1040 Brussels,
Belgium. circ. 1,500.

637　　　　　BE　ISSN 0538-7094
INTERNATIONAL DAIRY FEDERATION.
INTERNATIONAL STANDARD/FEDERATION
INTERNATIONALE DE LAITERIE. NORME
INTERNATIONALE. 1955. irreg., no. 99, 1980.
price varies. International Dairy Federation, Square
Vergote 41, 1040 Belgium, Belgium. circ. 3,000.

637　　　　　IE
IRISH CREAMERY MANAGERS' ASSOCIATION.
CREAMERY DIRECTORY AND DIARY.* 1906.
a. £45. Irish Creamery Managers' Association, 33
Kildare St., Dublin, 2, Ireland.
　　Formerly: Irish Creamery Managers' Association.
Creamery Yearbook and Diary (ISSN 0075-0751)

354　　　　　KE　ISSN 0453-5944
KENYA. DAIRY BOARD. ANNUAL REPORT. a.
Dairy Board, Nairobi, Kenya. illus.

637　　　　　IE　ISSN 0303-7002
KERRYGOLD INTERNATIONAL. irreg. Irish Dairy
Board, Dublin, Ireland.

637.1　　　　　US
MILK FACTS. a. free. Milk Industry Foundation, 910
17th St., N.W., Washington, DC 20006.

338.4　　　　　US
MINNESOTA DAIRY PLANTS. a. Agricultural
Department, State Office Bldg., Wabasha St., St.
Paul, MN 55155.

637　　　　　UK　ISSN 0302-0851
NATIONAL INSTITUTE FOR RESEARCH IN
DAIRYING. REPORT. 1971. a. price varies.
(Agricultural Research Council) National Institute
for Research in Dairying, Church Lane, Shinfield,
Reading RG2 9AT, England. Ed. Prof. J.W.G.
Porter. circ. 1,500. Indexed: Dairy Sci.Abstr.
　　Formerly: National Institute for Research in
Dairying. Biennial Report (ISSN 0085-3798)

637　　　　　NE
NETHERLANDS. CENTRAAL BUREAU VOOR
DE STATISTIEK. PRODUCTIE STATISTIEK
VAN DE ZUIVELINDUSTRIE. PRODUCTION
STATISTICS OF THE DAIRY INDUSTRY. (Text
in Dutch and English) 1952. a. Centraal Bureau
voor de Statistiek, Prinses Beatrixlaan 428,
Voorburg, Netherlands (Orders to: Staatsuitgeverij,
Christoffel Plantijnstraat, The Hague, Netherlands)
　　Formerly: Netherlands. Centraal Bureau voor de
Statistiek. Zuivelstatistiek. Dairy Statistics (ISSN
0077-7528)

637　　　　　US
NEW YORK DAIRY STATISTICS. a. free. ‡ New
York Crop Reporting Service, c/o Department of
Agriculture and Markets, State Campus, Albany,
NY 12235. circ. 1,200.
　　Continues: New York Crop Reporting Service.
Statistics Relative to the Dairy Industry in New
York State (ISSN 0077-8974)

354　　　　　NZ
NEW ZEALAND. DAIRY BOARD. ANNUAL
REPORT AND STATEMENT OF ACCOUNTS.
(Includes Statistical Supplements) 1962. a.
NZ.$3.90. Dairy Board, P.O. Box 417, Wellington,
New Zealand. illus. stat. circ. 25,000.
　　Supersedes: New Zealand. Dairy Production and
Marketing Board. Annual Report and Statement of
Accounts (ISSN 0545-7041)

353.9　　　　　US　ISSN 0091-9446
NORTH DAKOTA. MILK STABILIZATION
BOARD. ANNUAL REPORT OF
ADMINISTRATIVE ACTIVITIES. (Report year
ends June 30) 1968. a. North Dakota Milk
Stabilization Board, 2061/2 North 6th St., Room 5,
Bismarck, ND 58501. circ. 300.

338.1　　　　　US
PRODUCTION AND MARKETING:
CALIFORNIA EGGS, CHICKEN AND
TURKEYS. 1973. a. free. Federal-State Market
News Service, 1220 N St., Sacramento, CA 95814.
(Co-Sponsor: California Crop and Livestock
Reporting Service) circ. 1,000.
　　Formed by the merger of: Federal-State Market
News Service. California Egg and Poultry Summary
& California. Livestock and Crop Reporting Service.
Annual Report.

637　　　　　IS
PROFITABILITY OF DAIRY IN ISRAEL/HA-
RIVHIYUT SHEL ANAF HA-REFET. (Issued as
the Institute's Publications. Series D) (Text in
Hebrew; summaries in English) 1964/65. irreg.
I£150($6) Institute of Farm Income Research, 6
Hachashmonaim Blvd., Tel Aviv, Israel.

637　　　　　US　ISSN 0080-1267
REPORT OF MILK UTILIZATION IN
MONTANA. Variant title: Recap of Milk
Utilization in Montana. a. free. Department of
Business Regulation, Milk Control Division, 805
No. Main St., Helena, MT 59601.

637　　　　　JA　ISSN 0082-4763
SNOW BRAND MILK PRODUCTS CO., LTD.
RESEARCH LABORATORY. REPORTS/
YUKIJIRUSHI NYUGYO GIJUTSU
KENKYUSHO HOKOKU. (Text in Japanese;
summaries in English and Japanese) 1950. irreg.,
approx. 1 per year. free. ‡ Snow Brand Milk
Products Co. Ltd. - Yukijirushi Nyugyo K. K.,
Research Laboratory, 1-1-2 Minamidai, Kawagoe,
Saitama 350, Japan. Ed. Kazuo Mino. circ. 400.
Indexed: Chem.Abstr. Dairy Sci.Abstr.

354.68　　　　　SA
SOUTH AFRICA. DAIRY CONTROL BOARD.
ANNUAL REPORT. (Text in Afrikaans and
English) a. Dairy Control Board - Suiwelbeheerraad,
Box 2682, Pretoria 0001, South Africa.
　　Formerly: South Africa. Milk Board. Annual
Report.

637　　　　　SW　ISSN 0039-6869
SVENSKA MEJERIERNAS RIKSFOERENING.
MEDDELANDE. (Text in Swedish; summaries in
English) 1946. irreg. free. Svenska Mejeriernas
Riksfoerening - Swedish Dairies Association,
Postfack, S-101 10 Stockholm 1, Sweden. Ed. Bengt
Salqvist.

WESTERN AUSTRALIA. DEPARTMENT OF
AGRICULTURE. RURAL ECONOMICS AND
MARKETING SECTION. REPORT ON THE
MARKET MILK INDUSTRY IN WESTERN
AUSTRALIA. see *AGRICULTURE — Agricultural
Economics*

AGRICULTURE — Feed, Flour And Grain

633.2　　　　　US
AMERICAN FORAGE AND GRASSLAND
COUNCIL. PROCEEDINGS OF THE
RESEARCH INDUSTRY CONFERENCE. 1968.
a. price varies. American Forage and Grassland
Council, 121 Dantzler Court, Lexington, KY 40503.

633.2　　　　　US
ASSOCIATION OF AMERICAN FEED CONTROL
OFFICIALS. OFFICIAL PUBLICATION. a. $10.
Association of American Feed Control Officials, c/o
West Virginia Department of Agriculture, Rm. E-
111, State Capitol Bldg., Charleston, WV 25305.
circ. 2,000.

AUSTRALIA. BUREAU OF AGRICULTURAL
ECONOMICS. COARSE GRAINS: SITUATION
AND OUTLOOK. see *AGRICULTURE —
Agricultural Economics*

AUSTRALIA. BUREAU OF AGRICULTURAL
ECONOMICS. OILSEEDS: SITUATION AND
OUTLOOK. see *AGRICULTURE — Agricultural
Economics*

AGRICULTURE — FEED, FLOUR AND GRAIN

633.11 338.1   AT
AUSTRALIA. BUREAU OF AGRICULTURAL ECONOMICS. WHEAT: SITUATION AND OUTLOOK. 1951. a. price varies. ‡ Australian Government Publishing Service, P.O. Box 84, Canberra, A.C.T. 2600, Australia. charts, illus, mkt, stat. index.
    Formerly: Wheat Situation (ISSN 0043-4736)

633.1 631   AT
AUSTRALIA. BUREAU OF STATISTICS. WESTERN AUSTRALIAN OFFICE. WESTERN AUSTRALIAN CEREAL CROP FORECAST. 1975. a. Australian Bureau of Statistics, Western Australian Office, 1-3 St. George's Terrace, Perth, W. A. 6000, Australia. Ed. E. Binns. stat.

BAKING DIRECTORY/BUYERS GUIDE. see *BUSINESS AND ECONOMICS — Trade And Industrial Directories*

633   AT
BULK WHEAT. 1967. a. Grain Elevators Board of New South Wales, c/o Charles Reid, 7 Macquarie Place, Sydney, N.S.W. 2000, Australia.

633.11 633.15   MX   ISSN 0304-551X
C I M M Y T INFORMATION BULLETIN. Spanish edition: Folleto de Informacion (ISSN 0304-5498); French edition: Bulletin d'Information (ISSN 0304-5501) no. 27, 1974. irreg. free. Centro Internacional de Mejoramiento de Maiz y Trigo, Londres 40, Apdo. Postal 6-641, Mexico 6, D.F., Mexico. Ed. Steven A. Breth.

633.15   MX   ISSN 0304-548X
C I M M Y T REPORT ON MAIZE IMPROVEMENT. Spanish edition: Informe del C I M M Y T Sobre Mejoramiento de Maiz (ISSN 0304-5471) 1974. a. free. Centro Internacional de Mejoramiento de Maiz y Trigo, Londres 40, Apdo. Postal 66-641, Mexico 6, D.F., Mexico. Ed. Steven A. Breth.
    Supersedes in part: C I M M Y T Annual Report on Maize and Wheat Improvement (ISSN 0007-8441)

633.11   MX   ISSN 0304-5439
C I M M Y T REPORT ON WHEAT IMPROVEMENT. Spanish edition: Informe del C I M M Y T Sobre Mejoramiento de Trigo (ISSN 0304-5420) 1974. a. free. Centro Internacional de Mejoramiento de Maiz y Trigo, Londres 40, Apdo. Postal 6-641, Mexico 6, D.F., Mexico. Ed. Steven A. Breth.
    Supersedes in part: C I M M Y T Annual Report on Maize and Wheat Improvement (ISSN 0007-8441)

633.1 633.15   MX   ISSN 0304-5463
C I M M Y T REVIEW. Spanish edition: Revision de Programas (ISSN 0304-5455) 1975. a. free. Centro Internacional de Mejoramiento de Maiz y Trigo, Londres 40, Apdo. Postal 6-641, Mexico 6, D.F., Mexico. Ed. Steven A. Breth.

633.1   MX   ISSN 0304-5447
C I M M Y T TODAY. Spanish edt.: C I M M Y T hoy (ISSN 0304-5390) 1975. irreg. free. Centro Internacional de Mejoramiento de Maiz y Trigo - International Maize and Wheat Improvement Center, Communications Dept., Londres 40 Apartado Postal 6-641, Mexico 6, D.F., Mexico. illus. circ. 5,500.
    Maize, wheat, barley, triticale

382 633.1   CN
CANADA. GRAIN COMMISSION. ECONOMICS AND STATISTICS DIVISION. CANADIAN GRAIN EXPORTS. a. Grain Commission, Economics and Statistics Division, 747-303 Main St., Winnipeg, Man. R3C 3H5, Canada.
    Continues: Canada. Board of Grain Commissioners. Canadian Grain Exports.

633.1 338.14   CN   ISSN 0380-8718
CANADA. GRAIN COMMISSION. ECONOMICS AND STATISTICS DIVISION. VISIBLE GRAIN SUPPLIES AND DISPOSITION. 1952-53. a. free. Grain Commission, Economics and Statistics Division. 747-303 Main St., Winnipeg, Man. R3C 3H5, Canada. circ. 1,500.
    Continues: Canada. Grain Commission. Marketings, Distribution and Visible Carry-over of Canadian Grain in and Through Licensed Elevators (ISSN 0068-7065)

633   CN   ISSN 0700-2866
CANADA. GRAINS COUNCIL. ANNUAL REPORT. (Text in English and French) 1970. a. free. Grains Council, 760-360 Main St., Winnipeg, Man. R3C 3Z3, Canada. circ. controlled. (tabloid format)

633.1   CN
CANADA. GRAINS COUNCIL. STATISTICAL HANDBOOK. 1974. a. Can.$5. Grains Council, 760-360 Main St., Winnipeg, Man. R3C 2Z3, Canada. circ. 2,000.

633.1   CN
CANADIAN CORN. irreg. free. Grains Council, 760-360 Main St., Winnipeg, Man. R3C 3Z3, Canada.

636   CN
CANADIAN GRAINS FOR BEEF CATTLE. 1976. irreg. Can.$0.50 for multiple copies; one copy free. Grains Council, 760-360 Main St., Winnipeg, Man. R3C 3Z3, Canada. (tabloid format)

636   CN
CANADIAN GRAINS FOR DAIRY CATTLE. 1977. irreg. Can.$0.50 for multiple copies; one copy free. Grains Council, 760-360 Main St., Winnipeg, Man. R3C 3Z3, Canada. circ. 5,000. (tabloid format)

633.1 636.4   CN
CANADIAN GRAINS FOR PIGS. (Text in English and Japanese) 1974. irreg. free for one copy; Can $0.50 for more than 10 copies. Grains Council, 760-360 Main St., Winnipeg, Man. R3C 3Z3, Canada. circ. 5,000. (tabloid format)

633.1 636.5   CN
CANADIAN GRAINS FOR POULTRY. 1974. irreg. free for one copy; Can $0.50 for more than 10 copies. Grains Council, 760-360 Main St., Winnipeg, Man. R3C 3Z3, Canada. circ. 5,000. (tabloid format)

633.1   CN
CANADIAN LIVESTOCK FEED BOARD. ANNUAL REPORT. (Text in English and French) a. Canadian Livestock Feed Board, Box 2250, St. Laurent Sta., Montreal, Que. H4L 4Y7, Canada.

633   AT   ISSN 0069-7680
COMMONWEALTH SCIENTIFIC AND INDUSTRIAL RESEARCH ORGANIZATION. WHEAT RESEARCH UNIT. REPORT. 1960/61. a. free. C. S. I. R. O., Editorial & Publications Service, 314 Albert St., E. Melbourne, Vic. 3002, Australia.

633.2   CU
CUBA. CENTRO DE INFORMACION Y DOCUMENTACION AGROPECUARIO. BOLETIN DE RESENAS. SERIE: PASTOS. 1974. irreg. $5. Centro de Informacion y Documentacion Agropecuario, Calle 11 no. 1057, Gaveta Postal 4149, Havana 4, Cuba.

664.7   CU
CUBA. CENTRO DE INFORMACION Y DOCUMENTACION AGROPECUARIO. BOLETIN DE RESENA. SERIE: VIANDAS, HORTALIZAS Y GRANOS. 1974. irreg. $5. Centro de Informacion y Documentacion Agropecuario, Calle 11 no. 1057, Gaveta Postal 4149, Havana 4, Cuba.

633.2 664.7   US
DISTILLERS FEED CONFERENCE. PROCEEDINGS. 1945. a. free. Distillers Feed Research Council, 1435 Enquirer Bldg., Cincinnati, OH 45202. Indexed: Chem.Abstr.

633.1   US   ISSN 0071-450X
FEED ADDITIVE COMPENDIUM. 1963. a.(with 11 supplements) $10. Miller Publishing Co., 2501 Wayzata Blvd., Box 67, Minneapolis, MN 55440. Ed. Roy Leidahl. adv. circ. 3,000. (reprint service avail. from UMI)

633.1   US   ISSN 0071-4518
FEED INDUSTRY RED BOOK; reference book and buyers' guide for the feed manufacturing industry. 1938. a. Can.$14($12.50) Communications Marketing, Inc., 5100 Edina Industrial Blvd., Edina, MN 55435. Ed. Bruce W. Smith.
    Formerly: Feed Bag Red Book.

338.1   UN   ISSN 0071-710X
FOOD AND AGRICULTURE ORGANIZATION OF THE UNITED NATIONS. NATIONAL GRAIN POLICIES. (Text in English, French and Spanish) 1959. a. price varies. Food and Agriculture Organization of the United Nations, Distribution and Sales Section, Via delle Terme di Caracalla, 00100 Rome, Italy (Dist. in U.S. by: Unipub, 345 Park Ave. S., New York, NY 10010)

GRAIN DIRECTORY/BUYERS GUIDE. see *BUSINESS AND ECONOMICS — Trade And Industrial Directories*

633   PH   ISSN 0074-7793
I R R I ANNUAL REPORT. (Text in English) 1963. a. $28. International Rice Research Institute, Box 933, Manila, Philippines. index. circ. 5,000. (also avail. in microfiche) Indexed: Biol.Abstr. Bibl.Agri. B.R.I. Field Crop Abstr. Plant Breed.Abstr. Rev.Appl.Entomol. Rev. Plant Path. Trop.Abstr. Weed Abstr. World Agri.Econ. & Rural Sociol.Abstr.

633   PH   ISSN 0115-3862
I R R I RESEARCH PAPER SERIES. 1976. irreg. (approx. 20/yr.) $1.85. International Rice Research Institute, Box 933, Manila, Philippines.

633.8   YU   ISSN 0074-6223
INTERNATIONAL HOP GROWERS CONVENTION. REPORT OF CONGRESS. (Issued in Hopfenrundschau, bimonthly periodical of Convention) a. International Hop Growers Convention, Titova 19, Ljubljana, Yugoslavia.
    Held in Wolnzach, West Germany

633   MX   ISSN 0074-6878
INTERNATIONAL MAIZE AND WHEAT IMPROVEMENT CENTER. RESEARCH BULLETIN. Spanish edition: Folleto de Investigacion (ISSN 0304-5536); French edition: Bulletin d'Investigation (ISSN 0304-5528) 1965. irreg. free. Centro Internacional de Mejoramiento de Maiz y Trigo, Londres 40-3er Piso, Ap. Postal 6-641, Mexico 6, D.F., Mexico.

633   PH   ISSN 0115-1142
INTERNATIONAL RICE RESEARCH INSTITUTE. RESEARCH HIGHLIGHTS. 1974. a. $9.80. International Rice Research Institute, Box 933, Manila, Philippines.

633   US
KANSAS CORN PERFORMANCE TESTS. (Subseries of its: Report of Progress) 1939. a. free. ‡ Kansas State University, Agricultural Experiment Station, Manhattan, KS 66506. Ed. Ted L. Walter. stat. circ. 10,000.

633   US
KANSAS SORGHUM PERFORMANCE TESTS. GRAIN & FORAGE. (Subseries of its: Report of Progress) 1958. a. free. ‡ Kansas State University, Agricultural Experiment Station, Manhattan, KS 66506. Ed. Ted L. Walter. stat. circ. 12,000.
    Formerly: Kansas Grain Sorghum Performance Tests.

633   US
KANSAS STATE UNIVERSITY. FOOD AND FEED GRAIN INSTITUTE. TECHNICAL ASSISTANCE IN GRAIN STORAGE, PROCESSING AND MARKETING, AND AGRIBUSINESS DEVELOPMENT. (In 4 subseries: Technical Assistance Reports (US ISSN 0453-2481); Manuals; Special Reports; Research Reports) 1968. irreg. Kansas State University, Food and Feed Grain Institute, Shellenberger Hall, Manhattan, KS 66506. (Co-sponsor: U. S. Agency for International Development) circ. 150.
    Formerly (1968-1974): Kansas State University. Food and Feed Grain Institute. Technical Assistance in Food Grain Drying, Storage, Handling and Transportation (ISSN 0071-7150)

633.2   CN   ISSN 0382-2028
MANITOBA GRASSLAND PROJECTS; provincial report. irreg. Can.$1 per no. Department of Agriculture, Publications Distribution Centre, 411 York Ave., Winnipeg, Man. R3C 3M1, Canada. illus.

MILLING DIRECTORY/BUYERS GUIDE. see *BUSINESS AND ECONOMICS — Trade And Industrial Directories*

633   US   ISSN 0077-5789
NATIONAL SOYBEAN PROCESSORS ASSOCIATION. YEARBOOK. 1936. a. $10. ‡ National Soybean Processors Association, 1800 M St. N. W., Washington, DC 20036. circ. 2,500.

633.7   NE
NETHERLANDS. CENTRAAL BUREAU VOOR DE STATISTIEK. PRODUKTIESTATISTIEKEN: VEEVOEDERINDUSTRIE. a. fl.9. Centraal Bureau voor de Statistiek, Prinses Beatrixlaan 428, Voorburg, Netherlands (Orders to: Staatsuitgeverij, Christoffel Plantijnstraat, The Hague, Netherlands)

633.11   NZ   ISSN 0078-0219
NEW ZEALAND WHEAT REVIEW. a, 1965-67, no. 10. Department of Scientific and Industrial Research, Box 9741, Wellington, New Zealand.

633.1   US
NORTH DAKOTA. STATE WHEAT COMMISSION. BIENNIAL REPORT; report to producers. biennial. State Wheat Commission, 1305 E. Central Ave., Bismarck, ND 58505. charts. illus. stat.

633.1 636.5   CN
OUTLOOK. 1976. a. Can.$1. Grains Council, 760-360 Main St., Winnipeg, Man. R3C 3Z3, Canada.

633.1   BL
REUNIAO GERAL DE CULTURA DO ARROZ. ANAIS. 1976. a. Instituto Rio Grandese do Arroz, Biblioteca, Caixa Postal 1927, Porto Alegre, Brazil.

633.1 338.1   BL
SORGO - UMA ALTERNATIVA ECONOMICA. 1974. a. Cr.$8. Fundacao de Economia e Estatistica, Rua Siqueira Campos 1044, C.P. 2355, Porto Alegre, Brazil. illus.

338.1   SA   ISSN 0300-5747
SOUTH AFRICA. MAIZE BOARD. REPORT ON GRAIN SORGHUM AND BUCKWHEAT FOR THE FINANCIAL YEAR. (Report year ends April 30) (Editions in English and Afrikaans) a. free. ‡ Maize Board - Mielieraad, P.O. Box 669, Pretoria 0001, South Africa. illus. circ. 1,500.

338.1   SA
SOUTH AFRICA. MAIZE BOARD. REPORT ON MAIZE FOR THE FINANCIAL YEAR. (Report year ends April 30) (Editions in English and Afrikaans) a. free. ‡ Maize Board - Mielieraad, P.O. Box 669, Pretoria 0001, South Africa. illus. circ. 4,000 (approx.)
    Formerly: South Africa. Maize Board. Review of the Maize Position.

633.11   SA
SOUTH AFRICA. WHEAT BOARD. ANNUAL REPORT. 1939. a. R.2. ‡ Wheat Board - Koringraad, P.O. Box 908, Pretoria 0001, South Africa. illus. stat. circ. 510 (combined)
    Report year ends Sept. 30

633.1   NR   ISSN 0304-5765
TROPICAL GRAIN LEGUME BULLETIN. 1975. q. free. (International Grain Legume Information Centre) International Institute of Tropical Agriculture, P.M.B. 5320, Ibadan, Nigeria. (Co-sponsor: International Development Research Centre of Canada) Ed. Babs O. Adenaike. adv. bk. rev. abstr. circ. 1,000.

633.1   CN
WHEATS OF THE WORLD. 1978. irreg. free. Grains Council, 760-360 Main St., Winnipeg, Man. R3C 3Z3, Canada.

633.1   UN   ISSN 0084-182X
WORLD GRAIN TRADE STATISTICS. 1950. a. Food and Agriculture Organization of the United Nations, Distribution and Sales Section, Via delle Terme di Caracalla, Rome, Italy (Dist. in U.S. by: Unipub, 345 Park Ave. S., New York, NY 10010)

633.2   GW   ISSN 0170-7809
Z M P BILANZ GETREIDE-FUTTERMITTEL. 1975. a. DM.16. Zentrale Markt- und Preisberichtstelle fuer Erzeugnisse der Land-Forst- und Ernaehrungswirtschaft, Godesberger Allee 142-148, 5300 Bonn-2, W. Germany (B.R.D.)

AGRICULTURE — Poultry And Livestock

see also Agriculture—Dairying and Dairy Products; Leather and Fur Industries; Veterinary Science

636.2   UK
ABERDEEN-ANGUS HERD BOOK. 1884. a. £10. Aberdeen-Angus Cattle Society, Pedigree House, 6 King's Place, Perth, Scotland. circ. 350. (back issues avail.)
    Cattle

636.2   UK   ISSN 0001-317X
ABERDEEN-ANGUS REVIEW. 1919. a. £1.50. Aberdeen-Angus Cattle Society, Pedigree House, 6 Kings Place, Perth, Scotland. Ed. E. J. Gillanders. adv. illus. mkt. circ. 2,600.
    Cattle

636   PL   ISSN 0065-0935
ACTA AGRARIA ET SILVESTRIA. SERIES ZOOTECHNICA. (Text in Polish; summaries in English and Russian) 1961. s-a. price varies. (Polska Akademia Nauk, Oddzial w Krakowie, Komisja Nauk Rolniczych i Lesnych) Panstwowe Wydawnictwo Naukowe, Miodowa 10, Warsaw, Poland (Dist. by Ars Polona-Ruch, Krakoswkie Przedmiescie 7, Warsaw, Poland) Ed. Thomas M. Janowski. bibl. charts.

636   PL
AKADEMIA ROLNICZA, POZNAN. ROCZNIK. ZOOTECHNIKA. (Summaries in English and Russian) 1959. irreg. price varies. Akademia Rolnicza, Poznan, Ul. Wojska Polskiego 28, 60-637 Poznan, Poland. Indexed: Bibl.Agri.

636.4   CN   ISSN 0044-7145
ALBERTA LANDRACE ASSOCIATION. NEWSLETTER. 1959. irreg. Alberta Landrace Swine Association, c/o N. Helfrich, Box 250, Rockford, Alberta, Canada.
    Hogs

636.587   US   ISSN 0065-745X
AMERICAN BANTAM ASSOCIATION. YEARBOOK. 1917. a. membership. American Bantam Association, Box 610, North Amherst, MA 01059. Ed. Fred P. Jeffrey. adv. circ. 3,000.

636.2   US   ISSN 0065-8081
AMERICAN DEXTER CATTLE ASSOCIATION. HERD BOOK. 1920. irreg., vol. 4, 1960. $3. American Dexter Cattle Association, 707 W. Water St., Decorah, IA 52101. Ed. Daisy Moore. cum.index 1960-66.
    Cattle

636.39   US   ISSN 0065-8456
AMERICAN GOAT SOCIETY. YEAR BOOK. Includes: A G S Dairy Goat Yearbook. 1935. a. $2. ‡ American Goat Society, Inc., 1606 Colorado St., Manhattan, KS 66502. Ed. Melinda Overton. adv. index. circ. 400.
    Goats

AMERICAN MEAT SCIENCE ASSOCIATION. RECIPROCAL MEAT CONFERENCE. PROCEEDINGS. see *FOOD AND FOOD INDUSTRIES*

636.3   US   ISSN 0066-0825
AMERICAN SUFFOLK SHEEP SOCIETY. BREEDERS LIST. a. American Suffolk Sheep Society, 52 N. First St., E. Logan, UT 84321.
    Sheep

636   FR   ISSN 0066-3328
ANNUAIRE NATIONAL DE L'AVICULTURE. 1956. a. 132 F. Editions Comindus, 1 rue Descombes, Paris 17e, France.

338.1   AG
ARGENTINA. MERCADO NACIONAL DE HACIENDA. ANUARIO. a. Mercado Nacional de Hacienda, Tellier 2406, Buenos Aires 1440, Argentina. illus. stat.
    Continues: Argentine Republic. Mercado Nacional de Hacienda. Memoria (ISSN 0570-8621)

636   MX
ASOCIACION LATINOAMERICANA DE PRODUCCION ANIMAL. MEMORIA. (Text in Spanish; summaries in English, Spanish, Portuguese) 1966. a. $8. Asociacion Latinoamericana de Produccion Animal, Apartado Postal 41-781, Mexico 10 D.F., Mexico. Ed. Ramon Claveran. abstr. cum.index: vols. 1-10. circ. 1,000. (back issues avail)

AUSTRALIA. BUREAU OF AGRICULTURAL ECONOMICS. EGGS: SITUATION AND OUTLOOK. see *AGRICULTURE — Agricultural Economics*

AUSTRALIA. BUREAU OF AGRICULTURAL ECONOMICS. MEAT: SITUATION AND OUTLOOK. see *AGRICULTURE — Agricultural Economics*

338.4   AT
AUSTRALIA. BUREAU OF STATISTICS. MEAT STATISTICS. a. free. Australian Bureau of Statistics, P.O. Box 10, Belconnen, A.C.T. 2616, Australia. illus. circ. 1,105.
    Formerly: Australia. Bureau of Statistics. Meat Industry.

636   AT
AUSTRALIA. BUREAU OF STATISTICS. SOUTH AUSTRALIAN OFFICE. LIVESTOCK AND LIVESTOCK PRODUCTS. 1908. a. free. Australian Bureau of Statistics, South Australian Office, Box 2272, G.P.O., Adelaide, S.A. 5001, Australia.
    Formerly: Australia. Bureau of Statistics. South Australian Office. Livestock. (ISSN 0067-0944)

AUSTRALIA. BUREAU OF STATISTICS. TASMANIAN OFFICE. WOOL PRODUCTION AND DISPOSAL. see *TEXTILE INDUSTRIES AND FABRICS*

636.2 664.9   AT
AUSTRALIAN MEAT RESEARCH COMMITTEE. ANNUAL REPORT. 1966/67. a. free. (Department of Agriculture) Australian Meat and Livestock Corporation, G.P.O. Box 4129, Sydney 2001, Australia.

636   AT   ISSN 0067-2149
AUSTRALIAN SOCIETY OF ANIMAL PRODUCTION. PROCEEDINGS. 1956. biennial. Aus.$16($18.40) Department of Animal Science and Production, University of Western Australia, Nedlands, W.A. 6009, Australia. Ed.Bd. circ. 2,485. (back issues avail.)

636.4   AT
AUSTRALIAN STUD PIG HERD BOOK. 1911. a. Aus.$3. Australian Pig Breeders' Society, P.O. Box 189, Kiama, N.S.W. 2533, Australia.
    Hogs

636.2   US
BEEF ROUNDUP. 1973. a. free. ‡ Kent Feeds, Inc., 1600 Oregon St., Muscatine, IA 52761. (tabloid format)
    Cattle

636.3   UK
BLACKFACE SHEEP BREEDERS' ASSOCIATION JOURNAL. 1948. a. free. Blackface Sheep Breeders' Association, c/o Ed. & Pub. A. W. Bryson, 4 Alloway Park, Ayr KA7 2AW, Scotland. adv. circ. 1,700(controlled) (processed)
    Sheep

636   UK   ISSN 0067-9224
BLOODSTOCK BREEDERS' REVIEW. 1912. a. £50. Thoroughbred Publishers Ltd., 26 Charing Cross Road, London WC2, England. Ed. Susan Hefferty. circ. 1,400.

636   BL   ISSN 0067-9615
BOLETIM DE INDUSTRIA ANIMAL. (Text in Portuguese; summaries in English) 1929. s-a. Cr.$320($14) Instituto de Zootecnia, Rua Heitor Penteado 56, Caixa Postal 60, 13460 Nova Odessa, Sao Paulo, Brazil. adv. annual index. circ. 1,000. (back issues avail.) Indexed: Biol.Abstr. Chem.Abstr. Nutr.Abstr. Abstr.Trop.Agri. Anim.Breed.Abstr. Dairy Sci.Abstr. Field Crop Abstr. Herb.Abstr. Plant Breed.Abstr.
    Formerly: Revista de Industria Animal.

AGRICULTURE — POULTRY AND LIVESTOCK

636.587   US   ISSN 0068-0117
BOOK OF BANTAMS. 1963. irreg.(quadrennial or quinquennial) $3.50. American Bantam Association, Box 610, North Amherst, MA 01059. Ed. George Fitterer. circ. 10,000.
Poultry

636.3   UK
BORDER LEICESTER FLOCK BOOK. 1890. a. £5.25 to non-members. Society of Border Leicester Sheep Breeders, 4 Alloway Park, Ayr KA7 2AW, Scotland. Ed. A.W. Bryson. circ. 500.
Sheep

630   BL
BRAZIL. CONSELHO NACIONAL DE DESENVOLVIMENTO DE PECUARIA. MERCADO ATACADISTA DE GADO E CARNE: ANALISE DA VARIACAO DOS PRECOS. irreg. Ministerio da Agricultura, Conselho Nacional de Desenvolvimento de Pecuaria, Rio de Janeiro, Brazil. stat.

636.2   UK   ISSN 0068-2012
BRITISH FRIESIAN HERD BOOK. (Supplementary Register avail.) 1909. a. £20. British Friesian Cattle Society of Great-Britain & Ireland, Scotsbridge House, Rickmansworth, Herts, WD3 3BB, England.
Cattle

636.39   UK   ISSN 0068-2039
BRITISH GOAT SOCIETY. HERD BOOK. 1886. a. £5. British Goat Society, Rougham, Bury St. Edmunds, Suffolk, England.
Goats

636.39   UK   ISSN 0068-2047
BRITISH GOAT SOCIETY. YEAR BOOK. 1921. a. £2. British Goat Society, Rougham, Bury St. Edmunds, Suffolk, England.
Goats

636   UV
C E B V. no. 7, 1974. irreg. Communaute Economique du Betail et de la Viande, Secretariat, Ouagadougou, Upper Volta.

619   CN   ISSN 0066-1899
CANADA. AGRICULTURE CANADA. ANIMAL RESEARCH INSTITUTE. RESEARCH REPORT. 1964. a. free. ‡ Agriculture Canada, Animal Research Institute, Ottawa, Ont. K1A OC6, Canada.

636   CN   ISSN 0068-7324
CANADA. AGRICULTURE CANADA. LIVESTOCK MARKET REVIEW. a. free. Agriculture Canada, Ottawa, Canada.

CANADA. MARKETING AND TRADE DIVISION. ANIMAL AND ANIMAL PRODUCTS; OUTLOOK. see *AGRICULTURE — Agricultural Economics*

636.5   CN   ISSN 0068-8134
CANADA WHO'S WHO OF THE POULTRY INDUSTRY. 1955. a. Can.$10. Farm Papers Ltd., 605 Royal Ave., New Westminster, B. C. V3M 1J4, Canada. Ed. Martin Dyck. adv. illus. stat. index.

CANADIAN GRAINS FOR BEEF CATTLE. see *AGRICULTURE — Feed, Flour And Grain*

CANADIAN GRAINS FOR DAIRY CATTLE. see *AGRICULTURE — Feed, Flour And Grain*

CANADIAN GRAINS FOR PIGS. see *AGRICULTURE — Feed, Flour And Grain*

CANADIAN GRAINS FOR POULTRY. see *AGRICULTURE — Feed, Flour And Grain*

636   CN   ISSN 0382-6406
CANADIAN JERSEY HERD RECORD. vol. 38, 1978. irreg. Canadian Jersey Cattle Club, 43 Waterloo Ave., Guelph, Ont. N1H 3K1, Canada.
    Continues: Canadian Jersey Cattle Club. Record (ISSN 0382-6414)

636   CN   ISSN 0068-9696
CANADIAN SOCIETY OF ANIMAL PRODUCTION. PROCEEDINGS.* 1951. a. Canadian Society of Animal Production, No. 907, 151 Slater St., Ottawa 4, Ont., Canada.

636.2   UK   ISSN 0069-4924
COATES'S HERD BOOK (BEEF) 1882. a. £7.50 to members. Beef Shorthorn Cattle Society, 17 York Place, Perth PH2 8EP, Scotland. Ed. T. M. O. Lang.
Cattle

636   CK
COLEGA AGROPECUARIO. 1976. irreg. Sociedad de Ingenieros Agronomos de Antioquia, Calle 54 no. 45-36, Apdo. Aereos 51185, Medellin, Colombia. (Co-sponsors: Colegio de Medicos Veterinarios y Zootecnistas de Antioquia; Association Nacional de Tecnologos Agropecuarios)

COMMISSION OF THE EUROPEAN COMMUNITIES. MARCHES AGRICOLES: SERIE "PRIX". PRODUITS ANIMAUX. see *AGRICULTURE — Agricultural Economics*

636   UK   ISSN 0069-6919
COMMONWEALTH BUREAU OF ANIMAL BREEDING AND GENETICS. TECHNICAL COMMUNICATIONS. 1932. irreg. price varies. Commonwealth Agricultural Bureaux, Farnham Royal, Slough SL2 3BN, England.

COMMONWEALTH SCIENTIFIC AND INDUSTRIAL RESEARCH ORGANIZATION. DIVISION OF ANIMAL PRODUCTION TECHNICAL REPORT. see *BIOLOGY — Physiology*

636   US   ISSN 0084-9146
CONFERENCE ON ARTIFICIAL INSEMINATION OF BEEF CATTLE. PROCEEDINGS. 1967. a. price varies. National Association of Animal Breeders, 401 Bernadette St., Box 1033, Columbia, MO 65205. Ed. Patty Poage.

636.3   NZ
CORRIEDALE. 1962. biennial. NZ.$1. Corriedale Sheep Society (Inc.), Box 13250, Christchurch, New Zealand. Ed. H. M. Studholme. illus.
Sheep

636.5   CU
CUBA. CENTRO DE INFORMACION Y DOCUMENTACION AGROPECUARIO. BOLETIN DE RESENAS. SERIE: AVICULTURA. 1974. irreg. $5. Centro de Informacion y Documentacion Agropecuario, Calle 11 no. 1057, Gaveta Postal 4149, Havana 4, Cuba.

636.4   CU
CUBA. CENTRO DE INFORMACION Y DOCUMENTACION AGROPECUARIO. BOLETIN DE RESENAS. SERIE: GANADO PORCINO. 1974. irreg. $5. Centro de Informacion y Documentacion Agropecuario, Calle 11 no. 1057, Gaveta Postal 4149, Havana 4, Cuba.

636.2   CU
CUBA. CENTRO DE INFORMACION Y DOCUMENTACION AGROPECUARIO. BOLETIN DE RESENAS. SERIE: RUMIANTES. 1974. irreg. Centro de Informacion y Documentacion Agropecuario, Calle 11 no. 1057, Gaveta Postal 4149, Havana 4, Cuba. bibl. charts.
    Supersedes (since 1978): Cuba. Centro de Informacion y Documentacion Agropecuario. Boletin de Resenas. Serie: Ganaderia.

636   BL
D N P A. irreg. Ministerio da Agricultura, Departamento Nacional de Producao Animal, Brasilia, Brazil. stat.

636.2   UK   ISSN 0070-2986
DAVY'S DEVON HERD BOOK. 1884. a. £10. Devon Cattle Breeders' Society, Court House, the Square, Wiveliscombe, Somerset, England. circ. 250.
Cattle

636   DK
DENMARK. STATENS HUSDYRBRUGSUDVALG. BERETNING. (Text in Danish, summaries in English) 1883. irreg. price varies. Statens Husdyrbrugsudvalg - National Committee of Animal Science, Rolighedsvej 25, 1958 Copenhagen V, Denmark. circ. 1,300. Indexed: Nutr.Abstr.
    Supersedes: Denmark. Forsoegslaboratoriet. Beretning (ISSN 0005-8904)

636.3   UK
DORSET DOWN FLOCK BOOK. 1906. a. membership (non-members $2) Dorset Down Sheep Breeders' Association, c/o The Secretary, Brierley House, Summer Lane, Combe Down, Bath, England. Ed. A. S. R. Austin. circ. 150.
Sheep

637.5   US
EGG PRODUCTION TESTS: UNITED STATES AND CANADA. 1959. a. free. U.S. Animal and Plant Health Inspection Service, Bldg 265, BARC-E, Beltsville, MD 20705. Ed. R. D. Schar. circ. 15,000.

636.5   ES
ENCUESTA AVICOLA. irreg. exchange. Direccion General de Economia Agropecuaria, Boulevad de los Heroes, Edificio Latinoamericano, San Salvador, El Salvador. Dir. Rene Aguilar Giron. stat.

636.2   UK   ISSN 0071-0571
ENGLISH GUERNSEY HERD BOOK. 1885. a. £8. English Guernsey Cattle Society, The Bury Farm, Pednor Rd., Chesham, Bucks. HP5 2LA, England. index.
Cattle

636   IT   ISSN 0071-2477
EUROPEAN ASSOCIATION FOR ANIMAL PRODUCTION. PUBLICATIONS. (Each no. available from a different source) (Text in English, French, German) 1950. irreg., 1976 no. 18. price varies. European Association for Animal Production, Corso Trieste 67, 00198 Rome, Italy.

636   IT   ISSN 0071-2485
EUROPEAN ASSOCIATION FOR ANIMAL PRODUCTION. SYMPOSIA ON ENERGY METABOLISM. (Subseries of: European Association for Animal Production. Publications) 1958. triennial; 6th, Stuttgart, 1973. European Association for Animal Production, c/o Dr. K-O v Selle, Sec.-Gen., Corso Trieste 67, 00198 Rome, Italy (Publisher varies with each meeting, 6th Publ. by Juris-Verlag, Darmstadt, W. Germany)

636   UN   ISSN 0532-0623
F A O AFRICAN REGIONAL MEETING ON ANIMAL PRODUCTION AND HEALTH. REPORT OF THE MEETING. (Subseries of Food and Agriculture Organization of the United Nations. Animal Production and Health Division. Meeting Report) 1964. Food and Agriculture Organization of the United Nations, Distribution and Sales Section, Via delle Terme di Caracalla, 00100 Rome, Italy.

636 591   GW   ISSN 0301-2743
FORTSCHRITTE IN DER TIERPHYSIOLOGIE UND TIERERNAEHRUNG/ADVANCES IN ANIMAL PHYSIOLOGY AND ANIMAL NUTRITION. (Supplement to: Zeitschrift fuer Tierphysiologie, Tierernaehrung und Futtermittelkunde) (Text and summaries in English and German) 1972. irreg., no. 12, 1981. price varies. Verlag Paul Parey (Hamburg), Spitalerstr. 12, 2000 Hamburg 1, W. Germany (B.R.D.) Ed. Walter Lenkeit. bibl. illus. index. (reprint service avail. from ISI) Indexed: Biol.Abstr. Ind.Med.

636   UK
GALLOWAY HERD BOOK. 1878. a. £6. Galloway Cattle Society, 131 King St., Castle Douglas, Kirkcudbrightshire DG7 1LZ, Scotland. Ed. Matt Mundell.
Cattle

636.2   UK   ISSN 0430-9928
GALLOWAY JOURNAL. a. free. Galloway Cattle Society, 131 King St., Castle Douglas, Kirkcudbrightshire DG7 1LZ, Scotland. Ed. Matt Mundell. adv. circ. 2,000.
Cattle

636   GW   ISSN 0434-0035
GIESSENER SCHRIFTENREIHE TIERZUCHT UND HAUSTIERGENETIK. 1961. irreg., no. 43, 1980. price varies. Verlag Paul Parey (Hamburg), Spitalerstr. 12, 2000 Hamburg 1, W. Germany (B.R.D.) bibl. illus. index. (reprint service avail. from ISI)

GREAT BRITAIN. MINISTRY OF AGRICULTURE. FISHERIES AND FOOD. FATSTOCK GUARANTEE SCHEME. see *AGRICULTURE — Agricultural Economics*

AGRICULTURE — POULTRY AND LIVESTOCK

636.5 US ISSN 0082-9722
HATCHERIES AND DEALERS PARTICIPATING IN THE NATIONAL POULTRY IMPROVEMENT PLAN. 1937. a. free. U.S. Animal and Plant Health Inspection Service, Animal Physiology and Genetics Institute, Building 265, BARC-E, Beltsville, MD 20705. Ed. R. D. Schar. circ. 6,500.
Formerly: U.S. Department of Agriculture. Animal Science Research Branch. Hatcheries and Dealers Participating in the National Improvement Plan.

636.2 UK ISSN 0073-1943
HERD BOOK OF HEREFORD CATTLE. 1846. a. £9.75. ‡ Hereford Herd Book Society, Hereford House, 3 Offa Street, Hereford HR1 2LL, England.
Cattle

636.2 UK ISSN 0073-1951
HEREFORD BREED JOURNAL. 1932. a. £2. ‡ Hereford Herd Book Society, Hereford House, 3 Offa Street, Hereford HR1 2LL, England. Ed. J. A. Morrison.
Cattle

636 016 US ISSN 0070-1947
INDEX OF CURRENT EQUINE RESEARCH. 1967. irreg., latest issue 1975. free. U.S. Science and Education Administration, Cooperative Research, Washington, DC 20250. Ed. E. I. Pilchard.

INDEX OF CURRENT RESEARCH ON PIGS. see *ABSTRACTING AND INDEXING SERVICES*

636.5 II
INDIAN POULTRY INDUSTRY YEARBOOK. 1974. a. $20. 2C/34 New Rohtak Rd., New Delhi 110005, India. Ed. Bd. adv. bk. rev. circ. 2,000. Indexed: Nutr.Abstr. Anim.Breed.Abstr.
International

636.2 BL
INSEMINACAO ARTIFICIAL. irreg. Ministerio da Agricultura, Departamento Nacional de Producao Animal, Divisao de Fisiopatologia da Inseminacao Artificial, Brasilia, Brazil.

591 636.089 SP
INSTITUTO DE ZOOTECNIA. FACULTAD DE VETERINARIA. CATALOGO DE PUBLICACIONES. irreg. exchange basis. Instituto de Zootecnia, Facultad de Veterinaria, Publicaciones, Av. Medina Azahara 9, Cordoba, Spain. (Affiliate: Consejo Superior de Investigaciones Cientificas) bibl.

636 RM ISSN 0075-3513
INSTITUTUL AGRONOMIC "ION IONESCU DE LA BRAD" LUCRARI STIINTIFICE II ZOOTEHNIE - MEDICINA VETERINARA. irreg. Institutul Agronomic "Ion Ionescu de la Brad", Aleea M. Sadoveanu, Nr. 3, Jassy, Romania.

636 NE
INSTITUUT VOOR VEEVOEDINGSONDERZOEK. REPORT. (Text in Dutch and English) irreg. price varies. Instiuut voor Veevoedingsonderzoek - Institute for Livestock Feeding and Nutrition Research, Runderweg 2, Postbus 160, 8200 AD Lelystad, Netherlands.
Formerly: Instituut voor Veevoedingsonderzoek "Hoorn." Report.

636 NE
INSTITUUT VOOR VEEVOEDINGSONDERZOEK JAARVERSLAG. (Text in Dutch; summaries in English) 1900. a. price varies. Instituut voor Veevoedingsonderzoek - Institute for Livestock Feeding and Nutrition Research, Runderweg 2, Postbus 160, 8200 AD Lelystad, Netherlands.
Formerly: Instituut voor Veevoedingsonderzoek "Hoorn" Jaarverslag (ISSN 0074-0489)

636 NE
INTERNATIONAL CONFERENCE ON PRODUCTION DISEASE IN FARM ANIMALS. PROCEEDINGS. irreg., 3rd, 1976, Wageningen. fl.40. Centre for Agricultural Publishing and Documentation, Box 4, 6700 AA Wageningen, Netherlands.

636.006 ET
INTERNATIONAL LIVESTOCK CENTRE FOR AFRICA. PROGRAMME AND BUDGET. 1974. a. International Livestock Centre for Africa, Box 5689, Addis Ababa, Ethiopia. circ. controlled.
Formerly: International Livestock Centre for Africa. Report on Activities.

636 SP ISSN 0074-6959
INTERNATIONAL MEETING OF ANIMAL NUTRITION EXPERTS. PROCEEDINGS. (Text in English, Italian, French and Spanish) 1958. irreg. $8. Ritena, P.O.B. 466, Barcelona, Spain. Ed. J. Amich-Gali. 6 yr.cum.index. circ. 1,200.

INTERNATIONAL MEETING ON CATTLE DISEASES. REPORTS. see *VETERINARY SCIENCE*

IRELAND (EIRE) CENTRAL STATISTICS OFFICE. CROPS AND PASTURE AND NUMBERS OF LIVESTOCK. see *AGRICULTURE — Crop Production And Soil*

636 IE ISSN 0075-059X
IRELAND (EIRE) CENTRAL STATISTICS OFFICE. LIVESTOCK NUMBERS. a. Central Statistics Office, Earlsfort Terrace, Dublin 2, Ireland.
Stencilled releases

636.5 GW ISSN 0447-2713
JAHRBUCH FUER DIE GEFLUEGELWIRTSCHAFT. a. DM.6. (Zentralverband der Deutschen Gefluegelwirtschaft) Verlag Eugen Ulmer, Wollgrasweg 41, Postfach 700561, 7000 Stuttgart 70, W. Germany (B.R.D.) Ed. Dr. Hermann Vogt, Celle. circ. 4,500.
Poultry

636 UK
JERSEY HERD BOOK AND MEMBERS DIRECTORY. 1958. a. £15. ‡ Jersey Cattle Society of the U.K., Jersey House, 154 Castle Hill, Reading, Berks RG1 7RP, England.
Former titles: Combined Jersey Herd Book, Directory & Elite Register of the U.K; Jersey Herd Book and Directory of the U.K. (ISSN 0075-3629); Jersey Herd Book of the U.K.

JOURNAL OF ANIMAL SCIENCE. SUPPLEMENT. see *VETERINARY SCIENCE*

636.2 636.5 US ISSN 0085-2805
LIVESTOCK AND POULTRY IN LATIN AMERICA. ANNUAL CONFERENCE. (Text in Spanish and English) 1967. a. $5. ‡ University of Florida, Center for Tropical Agriculture, 2001 McCarty Hall, Gainesville, FL 32611. (Co-sponsors: Institute of Food and Agricultural Sciences, Florida Cooperative Extension Service) Ed. Hugh Popenoe. circ. 500.
Cattle and poultry

636 US ISSN 0076-1052
LOUISIANA STATE UNIVERSITY. ANIMAL SCIENCE DEPARTMENT. LIVESTOCK PRODUCERS' DAY REPORT. 1961. a. free. ‡ Louisiana State University, Animal Science Department, Baton Rouge, LA 70803. (Co-Sponsors: Louisiana Agricultural Experiment Station; Louisiana Cooperative Extension Service) circ. 2,000.

636 UK ISSN 0076-5716
MEAT AND LIVESTOCK COMMISSION, BUCKS, ENGLAND. INDEX OF RESEARCH. 1961. a. free. Meat and Livestock Commission, Queensway House, Bletchley, Milton Keynes MK2 2EF, England. Ed. Dr. J. E. Duckworth.
Formerly: Index of Pig Research.

MEAT TRADE YEARBOOK. see *FOOD AND FOOD INDUSTRIES*

636.2 US ISSN 0076-7824
MICHIGAN BEEF CATTLE DAY REPORT. 1965. a. free. Michigan State University, Agricultural Experiment Station, Agriculture Hall, East Lansing, MI 48824. Eds. Dan Fox, Harlan Ritchie. circ. 4,000. (reprint service avail. from UMI,ISI)
Cattle

636 US ISSN 0077-3255
NATIONAL ASSOCIATION OF ANIMAL BREEDERS ANNUAL PROCEEDINGS. 1952. a. price varies. National Association of Animal Breeders, 401 Bernadette St., Box 1033, Columbia, MO 65201. Ed. Wm. M. Durfey.

636 JA
NATIONAL INSTITUTE OF ANIMAL INDUSTRY, CHIBA, JAPAN. ANNUAL REPORT. (Text in Japanese) a. National Institute of Animal Industry - Chikusan Shikenjo, Chiba-shi 280, Japan.

636 JA ISSN 0077-488X
NATIONAL INSTITUTE OF ANIMAL INDUSTRY, CHIBA, JAPAN. BULLETIN/ CHIKUSAN SHIKENJO, CHIBA, JAPAN. CHIKUSAN SHIKENJO KENKYU HOKOKU. (Text in Japanese; summaries in English) 1963. irreg. National Institute of Animal Industry - Chikusan Shikenjo, Chiba-shi 280, Japan. Ed.Bd. abstr. charts. illus. circ. 1,100. Indexed: Biol.Abstr. Chem.Abstr. Nutr.Abstr. Dairy Sci.Abstr. Anim.Breed.Abstr. Bibl.Agri.

636 JA ISSN 0077-4898
NATIONAL INSTITUTE OF ANIMAL INDUSTRY, CHIBA, JAPAN. BULLETIN SUMMARIES. (Summaries in English) 1963. irreg., no. 28, 1974. National Institute of Animal Industry - Chikusan Shikenjo, Chiba-shi 280, Japan. Ed.Bd. circ. 300. Indexed: Biol.Abstr. Chem.Abstr. Nutr.Abstr. Anim.Breed.Abstr. Bibl.Agri. Dairy Sci.Abstr. Bibl.Repro.

636.4 UK ISSN 0077-5312
NATIONAL PIG BREEDERS' ASSOCIATION HERD BOOK. 1885. a. £5 to non-members. National Pig Breeders' Association, 7 Rickmansworth Rd., Watford, Herts, WD1 7HE, England. Ed. A. J. Manchester.
Hogs

636 338.1 NZ ISSN 0078-0138
NEW ZEALAND. MEAT AND WOOL BOARDS' ECONOMIC SERVICE. ANNUAL REVIEW OF THE SHEEP INDUSTRY; review of physical and economic conditions in sheepfarming in New Zealand. 1952. a. free, limited distribution; also available on exchange. Meat and Wool Boards' Economic Service, P.O. Box 5179, Wellington, New Zealand.

NEW ZEALAND POULTRY BOARD. REPORT AND NEW ZEALAND MARKETING AUTHORITY REPORT AND STATEMENT OF ACCOUNTS. see *AGRICULTURE — Agricultural Economics*

OUTLOOK. see *AGRICULTURE — Feed, Flour And Grain*

OXFORD TROPICAL HANDBOOKS. see *AGRICULTURE*

636 PK ISSN 0083-8292
PAKISTAN. DIRECTORATE OF LIVESTOCK FARMS. REPORT. (Text in English) 1962-63. a. Directorate of Livestock Farms, 16 Cooper Rd., Lahore, Pakistan. circ. 100.

636 PN
PANAMA. INSTITUTO DE INVESTIGACION AGROPECUARIA. CARTA INFORMATIVA PECUARIA. irreg. free. Instituto de Investigacion Agropecuaria, Apartado 58, Santiago, Veraguas, Panama. Ed. Elizabeth de Ruiloba. charts. illus.

636.4 US
PORK ROUNDUP. 1973. a. free. ‡ Kent Feeds Inc., 1600 Oregon St., Muscatine, IA 52761. (tabloid format)
Hogs

636.5 US ISSN 0069-4630
POULTRY HEALTH AND MANAGEMENT SHORT COURSE. PROCEEDINGS. 1961. a. $2. Clemson University, Poultry Science Department, Clemson, SC 29631. (Co-Sponsor: South Carolina Poultry Improvement Assn.) Ed. B. Barnett. circ. 150.

636.5 338.1   CN   ISSN 0032-5775
POULTRY MARKET REVIEW. 1967. a. free.
Agriculture Canada, Poultry Division & Markets
Information Section, Ottawa, Ont., Canada.
Poultry

POULTRY MARKET STATISTICS. see
*AGRICULTURE — Abstracting, Bibliographies,
Statistics*

636.2   US
POULTRY ROUNDUP. 1973. a. free. Kent Feeds,
Inc., 1600 Oregon St., Muscatine, IA 52761.

636.5   UK
POULTRY SCIENCE SYMPOSIUM.
PROCEEDINGS. irreg; no. 10, 1975. £6. British
Poultry Science Ltd., London, England. Eds. B. M.
Freeman, K. N. Boorman.

PRODUCTION AND MARKETING:
CALIFORNIA EGGS, CHICKEN AND
TURKEYS. see *AGRICULTURE — Dairying And
Dairy Products*

636.5   IS   ISSN 0079-5968
PROFITABILITY OF POULTRY FARMING IN
ISRAEL/HA-RIVHIYUT SHEL 'ANAF HA-LUL.
(Issued as the Institute's Publications, Series B)
(Text in Hebrew; summaries in English) 1964-65.
irreg. I£150($6) per issue. Institute of Farm Income
Research, 6 Hachashmonaim Blvd., Tel Aviv, Israel.

636 016   PL   ISSN 0079-7162
PRZEGLAD NAUKOWEJ LITERATURY
ZOOTECHNICZNEJ. 1955. a (4 fasc.) price varies.
Panstwowe Wydawnictwo Rolnicze i Lesne, Al.
Jerozolimskie 28, Warsaw, Poland (Dist. by Ars
Polona-Ruch, Krakowskie Przedmiescie 7, Warsaw,
Poland) Ed. Grazyna Znaniecka.

636   GW
RINDERPRODUKTION. ZUCHT,
LEISTUNGSPRUEFUNGEN, BESAMUNG IN
DER BUNDESREPUBLIK DEUTSCHLAND.
(Text in German, summaries in English, French,
Italian) irreg. DM.7.50. (Land- und
Hauswirtschaftlicher Auswertungs- und
Informationsdienst) Landwirtschaftsverlag GmbH,
Marktallee 89, Postfach 480210, 4400 Muenster-
Hiltrup, W. Germany (B.R.D.) stat.

636   PL   ISSN 0080-3669
ROCZNIKI NAUK ROLNICZYCH. SERIA B.
ZOOTECHNICZNA. (Text in Polish; summaries in
English, Polish or Russian) 1903. irreg., 1976, vol.
97, no. 3. price varies. (Polska Akademia Nauk,
Komitet Nauk Zootechnicznych) Panstwowe
Wydawnictwo Naukowe, Miodowa 10, Warsaw,
Poland (Dist. by Ars Polona-Ruch, Krakowskie
Przedmiescie 7, Warsaw, Poland) Ed. Ewa
Potemkowska. bibl. charts.

636.085   US   ISSN 0036-0104
RURAL ROUNDUP. 1950. a. free. ‡ Kent Feeds Inc.,
Muscatine, IA 52761. charts. illus. (tabloid format)

636.2   SA
SANTA GERTRUDES CATTLE JOURNAL. a.
Dreyer Printers & Publishers, 21 Krause St., Box
286, Bloemfontein 9300, South Africa. adv.
Cattle

338.1   AG   ISSN 0081-0630
SOCIEDAD RURAL ARGENTINA. MEMORIA.
(Supplements its Annales) 1887. a. free. ‡ Sociedad
Rural Argentina, Florida 460, Buenos Aires,
Argentina. circ. 15,000.

636   SP
SPAIN. INSTITUTO NACIONAL DE
INVESTIGACIONES AGRARIAS. ANALES.
SERIE: HIGIENE Y SANIDAD ANIMAL. (Text
in Spanish; summaries in English, French, German)
irreg. 300 ptas. per no. Instituto Nacional de
Investigaciones Agrarias., General Sanjurjo 56,
Madrid 3, Spain. bibl, charts, illus.

636   SP
SPAIN. INSTITUTO NACIONAL DE
INVESTIGACIONES AGRARIAS. ANALES.
SERIE: PRODUCCION ANIMAL. (Text in
Spanish; summaries in English, French, German)
1971. irreg (approx 1-2/yr) 300 ptas. per issue.
Instituto Nacional de Investigaciones Agrarias,
General Sanjurjo 56, Madrid 3, Spain. circ. 1,500.
Supersedes in part: Instituto Nacional de
Investigaciones Agronomicas. Anales.

636   SP   ISSN 0210-3303
SPAIN. INSTITUTO NACIONAL DE
INVESTIGACIONES AGRARIAS.
COMUNICACIONES. SERIE: PRODUCCION
ANIMAL. no. 5, 1979. irreg. Instituto Nacional de
Investigaciones Agrarias, General Sanjurjo 56,
Madrid 3, Spain. bibl. charts. stat.

STUDIES IN THE ECONOMICS OF POULTRY
FARMING IN PUNJAB. see *AGRICULTURE —
Agricultural Economics*

636.2   SA   ISSN 0081-9220
SUID-AFRIKAANSE GUERNSEY. Short title: S.A.
Guernsey. (Text in English and Afrikaans) 1960. a.
free. South African Guernsey Cattle Breeders
Society, P.O. Box 248, Humansdorp, South Africa.
Ed. G. M. Smith. circ. 2,000.
Cattle

636.5   US   ISSN 0082-8661
TABLES ON HATCHERY AND FLOCK
PARTICIPATION IN THE NATIONAL
POULTRY IMPROVEMENT PLAN. 1937. a. free.
‡ U.S. Animal and Plant Health Inspection Service,
Bldg. 265, BARC-E, Beltsville, MD 20705. Ed.
R.D. Scher. circ. 4,000.
Incorporating: U. S. Agricultural Research
Service. Animal Science Research Division. Tables
on Hatchery and Flock Participation in the National
Turkey Improvement Plan (ISSN 0082-867X)

636.4   US   ISSN 0082-1608
TAMWORTH ANNUAL. 1965. irreg. single copy
free; additional copies $0.25 ea. Tamworth Swine
Association, 414 Van Deman St., Washington Court
House, OH 43160. Ed. Robert Highfield. bk. rev.
circ. 1,500.
Hogs

636.2 664.9   AT
TASMANIAN MEAT INDUSTRY JOURNAL.
1966. irreg. Aus.$0.20 each. Meat and Allied
Trades' Federation of Australia, Tasmanian
Division, P.O. Box 420, Launceston, Tas. 7250,
Australia. Ed. D. H. H. Bridges.

636   US
TECHNICAL CONFERENCE ON ARTIFICAL
INSEMINATION AND REPRODUCTION. 1978.
biennial. price varies. National Association of
Animal Breeders, 401 Bernadette St., Box 1033,
Columbia, MO 65205. Ed. Patty Poage.

636   CN   ISSN 0084-618X
UNIVERSITY OF ALBERTA. DEPARTMENT OF
ANIMAL SCIENCE. ANNUAL FEEDERS' DAY
REPORT. 1946. a. free. ‡ University of Alberta,
Department of Animal Science, Faculty of
Extension, Edmonton, Alta. T6G 2GA, Canada.
Eds. Dr. R. T. Berg, Dr. C. M. Grieve. circ. 15,000.
(tabloid format; also avail. in microfilm from UMI)
Indexed: Biol.Abstr.

636 382   UY
URUGUAY. INSTITUTO NACIONAL DE
CARNES. DEPARTAMENTO DE
EXPORTACIONES. EXPORTACION DE
CARNES, ESTADISTICAS. a. Instituto Nacional
de Carnes, Departamento de Exportaciones,
Montevideo, Uruguay.

639   VE
VENEZUELA. MINISTERIO DE AGRICULTURA
Y CRIA. DIVISION DE ESTADISTICA.
ENCUESTA AVICOLA NACIONAL. 1962. a.
free. Ministerio de Agricultura y Cria, Direccion de
Planificacion y Estadistica, Division de Estadistica,
Caracas, Venezuela. illus.

639   VE
VENEZUELA. MINISTERIO DE AGRICULTURA
Y CRIA. DIVISION DE ESTADISTICA.
ENCUESTA DA GANADO PORCINO. a.
Ministerio de Agricultura y Cria, Direccion de
Planificacion y Estadistica, Division de Estadistica,
Torre Norte, Centro Simon Bolivar, Caracas,
Venezuela.

636   AT   ISSN 0083-5951
VICTORIA, AUSTRALIA. DEPARTMENT OF
AGRICULTURE. PIG INDUSTRY BRANCH.
PIG FARM MANAGEMENT STUDY. 1962. a.
free. Department of Agriculture, Box 4041, GPO
Melbourne, Victoria 3001, Australia. circ. 1,500.

338.1   AT   ISSN 0083-596X
VICTORIA, AUSTRALIA. DEPARTMENT OF
AGRICULTURE. POULTRY BRANCH.
POULTRY FARM MANAGEMENT STUDY.
1955. a. free. Department of Agriculture, Box 4041,
GPO Melbourne, Victoria 3001, Australia. circ.
1,200.

636   AT
WESTERN AUSTRALIA. DEPARTMENT OF
AGRICULTURE. ANIMAL DIVISION.
ANNUAL REPORT. a. Department of Agriculture,
Animal Division, Perth, W.A., Australia.

636   CN   ISSN 0083-9000
WESTERN THOROUGHBRED. 1964. a. Can.$4.95.
Western Thoroughbred, 727-33A St. N. W.,
Calgary, Alta., Canada. Ed. D. Acton. adv.

WHO'S WHO IN THE EGG AND POULTRY
INDUSTRIES. see *BIOGRAPHY*

636   NZ
WOOL. vol. 6, 1976. a. exchange basis. Massey Wool
Association, Box 421, Palmerston North, New
Zealand.
Sheep

636   UY   ISSN 0084-1552
WORLD CONFERENCE ON ANIMAL
PRODUCTION. PROCEEDINGS. (Text in
English, French, German or Spanish) 1963. irreg.,
1973, 3rd, Melbourne. World Association for
Animal Production, c/o Dr. Hernan Caballero,
Secretary General, Casilla de Correos 1217,
Montevideo, Uruguay.
Proceedings published by organizing committee

636.2   UK   ISSN 0084-1854
WORLD JERSEY CATTLE BUREAU.
CONFERENCE REPORTS. 1954. irreg. free to
members. World Jersey Cattle Bureau, Agricultural
House, Knightsbridge, London S.W.1., England.
Reports published by organizing committee

636.5   US   ISSN 0084-2532
WORLD'S POULTRY SCIENCE ASSOCIATION.
REPORT OF THE PROCEEDINGS OF
INTERNATIONAL CONGRESS. quadrennial.
$20. World's Poultry Science Association, c/o W.
R. Jenkins, Sec.- Treas., USA Branch - W P S A,
ES-USDA, 5509 South Agriculture, Washington,
DC 20250 (For 16th, Inquire: Lauriston von
Schmidt, Rua Aurora, 291-1 Andar-Sala 16, 01209
Sao Paulo, SP, Brazil)
14th, 1974, New Orleans; 15th, 1978, Sao Paulo.
Proceedings published in host country

636   GW   ISSN 0044-3581
ZEITSCHRIFT FUER TIERZUECHTUNG UND
ZUECHTUNGSBIOLOGIE/JOURNAL OF
ANIMAL BREEDING AND GENETICS. (Text in
English, French or German; summaries in English
and German) 1924. 4/yr. DM.358. Verlag Paul
Parey (Hamburg), Spitalerstr. 12, 2000 Hamburg 1,
W. Germany (B.R.D.) Ed. F. Pirchner. bk. rev.
index. (reprint service avail. from ISI) Indexed:
Biol.Abstr. Chem.Abstr. Curr.Cont.

636   RH
ZIMBABWE. CENTRAL STATISTICAL OFFICE.
AGRICULTURAL PRODUCTION IN
EUROPEAN AREAS: LIVESTOCK. NATIONAL
AND PROVINCIAL TOTALS. 1969. a.
Rhod.$0.35. Central Statistical Office, P.O. Box
8063, Causeway, Salisbury, Zimbabwe. circ. 290.
Formerly: Rhodesia. Central Statistical Office.
Agricultural Production in European Areas. Part 1.
Livestock. National and Provincial Totals.

AIR TRANSPORT

see *Transportation—Air Transport*

ALLERGOLOGY AND IMMUNOLOGY

see *Medical Sciences — Allergology and Immunology*

ANAESTHESIOLOGY

see *Medical Sciences — Anaesthesiology*

ANALYTICAL CHEMISTRY

see *Chemistry — Analytical Chemistry*

ANTIQUES

see *Hobbies — Antiques*

ANTHROPOLOGY

see also *Folklore*

A P U PRESS ALASKANA SERIES. (Alaska Pacific University Press) see *HISTORY*

572 UK ISSN 0066-9679
A S A MONOGRAPHS. 1965. irreg., 1974, no. 12. price varies. (Association of Social Anthropologists of the Commonwealth) Academic Press Inc. (London) Ltd., 24 Oval Rd., London N.W.1, England (Dist. in U.S. by: Academic Press Inc., 111 Fifth Ave., New York, NY 10003) index.

309 AT ISSN 0310-9585
A S I F. irreg. Anarcho Surrealist Insurrectionary Feminists Collective, P.O. Box 294, Collingwood, Vic. 3066, Australia.

ACTA ETHNOLOGICA SLOVACA. see *FOLKLORE*

572 GW ISSN 0400-4043
ACTA HUMBOLDTIANA. SERIES GEOGRAPHICA ET ETHNOGRAPHICA. irreg., vol. 8, 1981. price varies. (Deutsche Ibero-Amerika-Stiftung) Franz Steiner Verlag GmbH, Friedrichstr. 24, Postfach 5529, 6200 Wiesbaden, W. Germany (B.R.D.) Ed. Wolfgang Haberland.

572 US ISSN 0065-1850
ADAN E. TREGANZA ANTHROPOLOGY MUSEUM. PAPERS. 1960. irreg., no.16, 1980. price varies. San Francisco State University, Adan E. Treganza Anthropology Museum, 1600 Holloway Ave., San Francisco, CA 94132. Ed. James Dotta. circ. 400-500.
Formerly: California. State College, San Francisco. Department of Anthropology. Occasional Papers in Anthropology.

572 BE
AFRICANA GANDENSIA. 1976. irreg. Rijksuniversiteit te Gent, Seminarie voor Afrikaanse Cultuurgeschiedenis, St. Pietersplein 4, B-9000 Ghent, Belgium.

572 UR
AKADEMIYA NAUK S.S.S.R. INSTITUT ETNOGRAFII. POLEVYE ISSLEDOVANIYA. 1974. irreg. 1.05 Rub. Izdatel'stvo Nauka, Podsosenskii per., 21, Moscow K-62, U. S. S. R. illus.

ALMOGAREN. see *ARCHAEOLOGY*

ALT-THUERINGEN. see *HISTORY — History Of Europe*

ALTERNATE ROUTES; a critical review. see *SOCIAL SCIENCES: COMPREHENSIVE WORKS*

301.2 US
AMERICAN ANTHROPOLOGICAL ASSOCIATION. ABSTRACTS OF MEETINGS. a. price varies. American Anthropological Association, 1703 New Hampshire Ave., N.W., Washington, DC 20009.

572 US ISSN 0065-6933
AMERICAN ANTHROPOLOGICAL ASSOCIATION. ANNUAL REPORT AND DIRECTORY. a. American Anthropological Association, 1703 New Hampshire Ave., N.W., Washington, DC 20009.

572 US ISSN 0065-6941
AMERICAN ANTHROPOLOGIST. SPECIAL PUBLICATION. 1964. irreg. American Anthropological Association, 1703 New Hampshire Ave., N.W., Washington, DC 20009.

572 US ISSN 0065-8200
AMERICAN ETHNOLOGICAL SOCIETY. PROCEEDINGS OF SPRING MEETING. 1957. a. price varies. West Publishing Co., Box 3526, St. Paul, MN 55165. Ed. Robert F. Spenser.

060 301.2 US ISSN 0569-4833
AMERICAN FOUNDATION FOR THE STUDY OF MAN. PUBLICATIONS. irreg. price varies. Johns Hopkins University Press, Baltimore, MD 21218.

572 US ISSN 0065-9452
AMERICAN MUSEUM OF NATURAL HISTORY. ANTHROPOLOGICAL PAPERS. 1907. irreg. price varies. American Museum of Natural History, Central Park W. at 79th St., New York, NY 10024. Ed. Florence Brauner. circ. 2,500. Indexed: Biol.Abstr. Bull.Signal. SSCI. Zoo.Rec.

572 UY
AMERINDIA; revista de prehistoria y etnologia de America. 1962. biennial. Centro de Estudios Arqueologicos y Antropologicos Americanos, Zubillaga 1117, Montevideo, Uruguay. bk. rev.

572 410 FR
AMERINDIA; revue d'ethnolinguistique amerindien. 1976. a. 66 F. Societe d'Etudes Linguistiques et Anthropologiques de France, 5 rue de Marseille, 75010 Paris, France.

ANALES DE ARQUEOLOGIA Y ETNOLOGIA. see *ARCHAEOLOGY*

301.2 930 US
ANCIENT CULTURE AND SOCIETIES. irreg. price varies. W. W. Norton & Company, Inc., 500 Fifth Ave., New York, NY 10036.

301.2 US ISSN 0095-5582
ANNUAL EDITIONS: READINGS IN ANTHROPOLOGY. Short title: Readings in Anthropology. a. $6.25. Dushkin Publishing Group, Sluice Dock, Guilford, CT 06437. illus.

572 US ISSN 0084-6570
ANNUAL REVIEW OF ANTHROPOLOGY. 1972. a. $20. Annual Reviews Inc., 4139 El Camino Way, Palo Alto, CA 94306. Ed. Bernard J. Siegel. bibl. charts. index; cum.index. (back issues avail.; reprint service avail. from ISI) Indexed: Biol.Abstr. Chem.Abstr. SSCI. Lang. & Lang.Behav. M.M.R.I.

301.2 HU
ANTHROPOLOGIA HUNGARICA. (Text in English, French, German, Hungarian) 1961. a. Magyar Termeszettudomanyi Muzeum, Baross u. 13, 1088 Budapest, Hungary. Ed. G. Toth.

572 AT ISSN 0066-4677
ANTHROPOLOGICAL FORUM; an international journal of social and cultural anthropology and comparative sociology. 1963. a. Aus.$3. University of Western Australia, Department of Anthropology, Nedlands, W.A. 6009, Australia. Ed. Ronald M. Berndt. bk. rev. circ. 600-700.

572 US ISSN 0517-3868
ANTHROPOLOGICAL HANDBOOK. 1954. irreg. price varies. (American Museum of Natural History) McGraw-Hill Book Co., 1221 Ave. of the Americas, New York, NY 10020.

572 301.2 US ISSN 0570-2976
ANTHROPOLOGICAL STUDIES. 1969. irreg., no. 8, 1971. price varies. American Anthropological Association, 1703 New Hampshire Ave., N.W., Washington, DC 20009.

572 301.2 GW ISSN 0066-4685
ANTHROPOLOGIE. (Text in German and Czech) 1962/63. irreg., vol. 18, 1980. DM.36. (Moravske Museum, Brno, CS) Rudolf Habelt Verlag, Am Buchenhang 1, 5300 Bonn 1, W. Germany (B.R.D.) Ed. J. Jelinek.

301.2 AU ISSN 0066-4693
ANTHROPOLOGISCHE GESELLSCHAFT, VIENNA. MITTEILUNGEN. 1870. a. S.780. Verlag Ferdinand Berger und Soehne OHG, Wienerstr. 21-23, A-3580 Horn, Austria.

ANTHROPOS; studie z oboru anthropologie, paleoethnologie, paleontologie a kvarterni geologie. see *PALEONTOLOGY*

573 GR
ANTHROPOS. 1974. a. $12. Anthropolghike Eteria Ellados, Daphnomili 5, T.T. 706, Athens, Greece. Ed. Aris N. Poulianos. bk. rev. circ. 1,000.

572 IT ISSN 0391-3163
ANTHROPOS. 1979. irreg., no. 2, 1979. price varies. Liguori Editore s.r.l., Via Mezzocannone 19, 80134 Naples, Italy. Ed. Vittorio Lanternari.

301.2 PL
ANTROPOLOGIA. (Text in Polish; summaries in English) 1971. irreg., no. 4, 1976. price varies. Uniwersytet im. Adama Mickiewicza w Poznaniu, Stalingradzka 1, 61-712 Poznan, Poland (Dist. by: Ars Polona, Krakowskie Przedmiescie 7, 00-068 Warsaw, Poland)
Formerly: Uniwersytet im. Adama Mickiewicza w Poznaniu. Wydzial Biologii i Nauk o Ziemi. Seria Antropologia.

572 PE
ANTROPOLOGIA ANDINA. 1976. a. $10. Centro de Estudios Andinos Cuzco, Apartado 582, Cuzco, Peru. Ed. J. Flores Ochoa. adv. bk. rev. circ. 1,000.

301.2 EC
ANTROPOLOGIA ECUATORIANA. 1978. irreg. S/ 50 per no. Casa de la Cultura Ecuatoriana, Seccion Academica de Antropologia y Arqueologia, Casilla 87, Quito, Ecuador.

573 PE
ANTROPOLOGIA FISICA. 1976. irreg. S/200($4) Museo Nacional de Antropologia y Arqueologia, Plaza Bolivar s/n Pueblo Libre, Lima, Peru.

572 MX ISSN 0570-3697
ANTROPOLOGIA SOCIAL. 1964. irreg. Mex.$60($3) Instituto Indigenista Interamericano - Instituto Indigenista Interamericano, Insurgentes Sur 1690, Col.Florida, Mexico 20, D.F., Mexico.

572 BL
ANUARIO ANTROPOLOGICO. 1976. a. $20. Edicoes Tempo Brasileiro Ltda, Rua Gago Coutinho 61, C.P. 16099, ZC-01 Laranjeiras, Rio de Janeiro, Brazil. Dir. Roberto Cardosa de Oliveira.

572 SP
ANUARIO DE ESTUDIOS AMERICANOS. a; no. 31 forthcoming. 1500 ptas. Consejo Superior de Investigaciones Cientificas, Serrano 117, Madrid, Spain. Ed. Jose Julio Perlado.

301.2 398 SP
ANUARIO DE EUSKO-FOLKLORE; etnografia y paletnografia. 1921. a. Sociedad de Ciencias Aranzadi, Museo San Telmo, Plaza de I. Zuloago, San Sebastian, Spain. circ. 500. (back issues avail)

572 MX
ANUARIO INDIGENISTA/INDIANIST YEARBOOK. (Text in Spanish; summaries in English) 1962. a. Mex.$40($2.50) Instituto Indigenista Interamericano, Insurgentes Sur 1690, Colonia Florida, Mexico 20,D.F., Mexico. bk. rev. circ. controlled. (processed)

ARCHAEOLOGIA AUSTRIACA; Beitraege zur Palaeanthropologie, Ur- und Fruehgeschichte Oesterreichs. see *ARCHAEOLOGY*

ANTHROPOLOGY

572   GW   ISSN 0570-6793
ARCHIV FUER VERGLEICHENDE
KULTURWISSENSCHAFT. 1967. irreg., no. 10,
1974. price varies. Verlag Anton Hain GmbH,
Adelheidstr. 2, Postfach 1220, 6240 Koenigstein, W.
Germany (B.R.D.) Ed. Christian Helfer.

301.2   AU
ARCHIV FUER VOELKERKUNDE. 1946. a. price
varies. (Museum fuer Voelkerkunde) Wilhelm
Braumueller, Universitaets-Verlagsbuchhandlung
GmbH, Servitengasse 5, A-1092 Vienna, Austria.
bk. rev. circ. 800.

572   FR   ISSN 0066-6580
ARCHIVES D'ETHNOLOGIE FRANCAISE. 1970.
irreg. price varies. Musee National des Arts et
Traditions Populaires, 6, Route de Madrid, 75116
Paris, France.

ARCHIWUM ETNOGRAFICZNE. see
SOCIOLOGY

572   AG
ARGENTINA. INSTITUTO ETNICO NACIONAL.
ANALES. 1948. a. Direccion Nacional de
Migraciones, Instituto Etnico Nacional, Buenos
Aires, Argentina. bibl.

ARIZONA STATE UNIVERSITY
ANTHROPOLOGICAL RESEARCH PAPERS.
see *ARCHAEOLOGY*

571 985   PE   ISSN 0066-7803
ARQUEOLOGICAS. (Text in Spanish; occasionally in
language of author) 1957. irreg. latest, no. 15, 1974.
price varies. Museo Nacional de Antropologia y
Arqueologia, Casilla 3640, Lima, Peru. Ed. Ruth
Shady Solis. circ. 1,000-2,000 (approx.)

ASCLEPIO; archivo iberoamericano de historia de la
medicina. see *MEDICAL SCIENCES*

ASSOCIATION FOR GRAVESTONE STUDIES.
NEWSLETTER. see *ART*

570   US   ISSN 0066-9172
ASSOCIATION FOR SOCIAL ANTHROPOLOGY
IN OCEANIA. MONOGRAPH SERIES. 1970.
irreg. price varies. University of Michigan Press,
Box 1104, 839 Greene St., Ann Arbor, MI 48106
(Also avail. from: UMI, 300 N. Zeeb Rd., Ann
Arbor, MI 48106) Ed. Vern Carroll. Indexed:
Sociol.Abstr.

572   UK
ASSOCIATION OF SOCIAL ANTHROPOLOGISTS
OF THE COMMONWEALTH. STUDIES. 1975.
irreg. £6.50. (Association of Social Anthropologists
of the Commonwealth) Malaby Press, Aldine
House, 26 Albemarle St., London W1X 4QY,
England. Ed. Edwin Ardener.

301.2 390   PL   ISSN 0067-0316
ATLAS POLSKICH STROJOW LUDOWYCH. (Text
in Polish; summaries in English, German and
Czech) 1949. irreg. price varies. Polskie
Towarzystwo Ludoznawcze, Ul. Szewska 36, 50-139
Wroclaw, Poland (Dist. by Ars Polona-Ruch,
Krakowskie Przedmiescie 7, Warsaw, Poland) Ed.
Anna Kutrzeba-Pojnarowa. circ. 1,800.

572 301.2   US
BALLENA PRESS ANTHROPOLOGICAL
PAPERS. no. 4, 1975. irreg., no. 18, 1980. price
varies. Ballena Press, Box 1366, Socorro, NM
87801. Eds. Lowell John Bean, Thomas C.
Blackburn.

BALLENA PRESS PUBLICATIONS IN
ARCHAEOLOGY, ETHNOLOGY AND
HISTORY. see *ARCHAEOLOGY*

572 301.2   US
BALLENA PRESS STUDIES IN MESOAMERICAN
ART, ARCHAEOLOGY AND ETHNOHISTORY.
no. 2, 1977. irreg., no. 3, 1978. price varies. Ballena
Press, Box 1366, Socorro, NM 87801. Ed. John A.
Graham.

301.2   US
BASIC ANTHROPOLOGY UNITS. irreg. price
varies. Holt, Rinehart and Winston, 383 Madison
Avenue, New York, NY 10017.

BEITRAEGE ZUR AFRIKAKUNDE. see
HISTORY — History Of Africa

301.2   GW   ISSN 0408-8514
BEITRAEGE ZUR MITTELAMERIKANISCHEN
VOELKERKUNDE. 1953. irreg., no. 14, 1977.
price varies. (Hamburgisches Museum fuer
Voelkerkunde) Klaus Renner Verlag, Am
Sonnenhang 8, 8021 Hohenschaeftlarn, W. Germany
(B.R.D.)

572 500.9   US   ISSN 0067-6160
BERNICE PAUAHI BISHOP MUSEUM,
HONOLULU. OCCASIONAL PAPERS. 1898.
irreg. price varies. Bishop Museum Press, Box
19000-A, Honolulu, HI 96819. index for each vol. is
published when vol. has been closed.

572 500.9   US   ISSN 0067-6179
BERNICE PAUAHI BISHOP MUSEUM,
HONOLULU. SPECIAL PUBLICATIONS. 1892.
irreg. price varies. Bishop Museum Press, Box
19000-A, Honolulu, HI 96819.

BIBLIOGRAFICA FOLCLORICA. see *FOLKLORE*

301.2   PE
BIBLIOTECA DE CULTURA ANDINA.
EDICIONES. 1978. irreg. price varies. G. Herrera
Editores, Plaza San Martin 957-601, Lima, Peru.

572 301.2   PL   ISSN 0067-7760
BIBLIOTEKA POPULARNONAUKOWA. 1958.
irreg. price varies. Polskie Towarzystwo
Ludoznawcze, Szewska 36, 50-139 Wroclaw, Poland
(Dist. by Ars Polona-Ruch, Krakowskie
Przedmiescie 7, Warsaw, Poland) circ. 3,000.

572   NE   ISSN 0067-8023
BIBLIOTHECA INDONESICA. (Text in English)
1968. irreg. price varies. (Koninklijk Instituut voor
Taal-, Land- en Volkenkunde) Martinus Nijhoff
Booksellers, Box 269, The Hague, 2501 AX The
Hague.

570 972   MX   ISSN 0006-6257
BOLETIN DE ESTUDIOS OAXAQUENOS/
BULLETIN OF OAXACA STUDIES. (Text and
summaries in English and Spanish) 1958. irreg.
contr.circ. ‡ Instituto de Estudios Oaxaquenos,
Aptdo. 464, Oaxaca, Oax., Mexico. Ed. John
Paddock. bk. rev. bibl. charts. illus. circ. 1,000
(approx.)

572   PY   ISSN 0560-4168
BOLETIN DE LA SOCIEDAD CIENTIFICA DEL
PARAGUAY Y DEL MUSEO ETNOGRAFICO.
1957. irreg. Museo Etnografico, Espana 395,
Asuncion, Paraguay. (Co-sponsor: Sociedad
Cientifica del Paraguay) bibl.

301.2   BU
BULGARSKA ETNOGRAFIIA. (Text in Bulgarian;
summaries in English and Russian) 1975. irreg. price
varies. (Bulgarska Akademiia na Naukite) Publishing
House of the Bulgarian Academy of Sciences, Ul.
Akad. G. Bonchev, 1113 Sofia, Bulgaria (Dist. by:
Hemus, 6, Rouski Blvd., 1000 Sofia, Bulgaria) Ed.
V. Hadzhinikolov. illus. circ. 1,200.

BY OG BYGD; Norsk Folkemuseums aarbok. see
HISTORY — History Of Europe

CAESARAUGUSTA. see *ARCHAEOLOGY*

951.7   FR
CAHIERS D'ETUDES MONGOLES ET
SIBERIENNES. 1970. a. price varies. Universite de
Paris X (Paris-Nanterre), Laboratoire d'Ethnologie
et de Sociologie Comparative, Laboratoire
d'Ethnologie et de Sociologie Comparative, 200
Ave. de la Republic, 92001 Nanterre, France. Ed.
Roberte Hamoyon. bk. rev. bibl. circ. 500. (back
issues avail.)
Formerly: Etudes Mongoles.

CAHIERS DES EXPLORATEURS. see
GEOGRAPHY

CALGARY ARCHAEOLOGIST. see
ARCHAEOLOGY

572 301   UK   ISSN 0068-6719
CAMBRIDGE PAPERS IN SOCIAL
ANTHROPOLOGY. 1958. irreg., no. 8, 1978.
$32.50 (cloth); $10.95(paper) for latest vol.
Cambridge University Press, Box 110, Cambridge
CB2 3RL, England (and 32 E. 57th St., New York
NY 10022) Eds. Meyer Fortes, J.R. Goody, E.R.
Leach.

572   UK
CAMBRIDGE STUDIES IN CULTURAL
SYSTEMS. 1977. irreg. price varies. Cambridge
University Press, Box 110, Cambridge CB2 3RL,
England (And 32 E. 57th St., New York, NY
10022) Ed. Clifford Geertz.

572   UK   ISSN 0068-6794
CAMBRIDGE STUDIES IN SOCIAL
ANTHROPOLOGY. 1967. irreg., no. 32, 1981.
$19.95 for latest vol. Cambridge University Press,
Box 110, Cambridge CB2 3RL, England (and 32 E.
57 St., New York, NY 10022) Ed. Jack Goody.

301   CN   ISSN 0316-1897
CANADA. NATIONAL MUSEUM OF MAN.
MERCURY SERIES. CANADIAN CENTRE
FOR FOLK CULTURE STUDIES. PAPERS/
CANADA. MUSEE NATIONAL DE L'HOMME.
COLLECTION MERCURE. CENTRE
CANADIEN D'ETUDES SUR LA CULTURE
TRADITIONNELLE. DOSSIERS. (Text in English
or French) 1972. irreg. free. (National Museum of
Man) National Museums of Canada, Ottawa,
Ontario K1A 0M8, Canada.

572   CN   ISSN 0316-1862
CANADA. NATIONAL MUSEUM OF MAN.
MERCURY SERIES. CANADIAN ETHNOLOGY
SERVICE. PAPERS/CANADA. MUSEE
NATIONAL DE L'HOMME. COLLECTION
MERCURE. SERVICE CANADIEN
D'ETHNOLOGIE. DOSSIERS. (Text in English or
French) 1972. irreg. free. (National Museum of
Man) National Museums of Canada, Ottawa,
Ontario K1A 0M8, Canada.

CARNEGIE MUSEUM OF NATURAL HISTORY.
BULLETIN. see *BIOLOGY*

301.2   US
CASE STUDIES IN CULTURAL
ANTHROPOLOGY. irreg. price varies. Holt,
Rinehart and Winston, 383 Madison Ave., New
York, NY 10017.

572   UK   ISSN 0069-0880
CASS LIBRARY OF AFRICAN STUDIES.
AFRICANA MODERN LIBRARY. 1967. irreg.,
no. 18, 1972. price varies. Frank Cass & Co. Ltd.,
Gainsborough House, 11 Gainsborough Rd., London
E11 1RS, England (Dist. in U.S. by: Biblio
Distribution Center, 81 Adams Drive, Totowa, N.J.
07512)

572   ZR   ISSN 0577-1331
CENTRE D'ETUDES ETHNOLOGIQUES.
PUBLICATIONS. SERIE 1: RAPPORTS ET
COMPTES RENDUS. 1966. irreg., no. 7, 1978. C
E E B A Publications, Bandundu, Zaire. bibl.
charts.

572   ZR
CENTRE D'ETUDES ETHNOLOGIQUES.
PUBLICATIONS. SERIE 2: MEMOIRES ET
MONOGRAPHIES. 1972. irreg., no. 46, 1978. C E
E B A Publications, Bandundu, Zaire. bibl. charts.
illus.

CENTRO CAMUNO DI STUDI PREISTORICI.
BOLLETTINO. see *ARCHAEOLOGY*

572 913   US   ISSN 0577-3334
CERAMICA DE CULTURA MAYA. 1961. irreg.,
no. 9, 1976. $4. ‡ Temple University, Laboratory of
Anthropology, c/o Miss Muriel Kirkpatrick,
Coordinator, Laboratory of Anthropology, Temple
University, Philadelphia, PA 19122. Eds. Carol A.
Gifford, Muriel Kirkpatrick. illus. circ. 150. (back
issues avail)

572   FR   ISSN 0578-3917
CIVILISATION MALGACHE. 1964. irreg.
(Universite de Madagascar, Faculte des Lettres et
Sciences Humaines, MG) Editions Cujas, 4,6,8, rue
de la Maison Blanche, 75013 Paris, France.

572   US   ISSN 0069-4487
CLASSICS IN ANTHROPOLOGY. 1964. irreg.,
latest 1978. price varies. University of Chicago
Press, 5801 S. Ellis Ave., Chicago, IL 60637. Ed.
Rodney Needham. (reprint service avail. from
UMI,ISI)

ANTHROPOLOGY

301.2   ES
COLECCION ANTROPOLOGIA E HISTORIA. irreg. Ministerio de Educacion, Administracion del Patrimonio Cultural, Biblioteca del Museo Nacional, Avda. Revolucion, Colonia San Benito, San Salvador, El Salvador. bibl. charts. illus.

572   AG
COLECCION TEMAS DE ANTROPOLOGIA. 1978. irreg. Editorial Huemul S.A., Chacabuco 860, Buenos Aires, Argentina. Eds. Alcira N. Imazio, Guillermo E. Magrassi.

572   913.031   IT
COLLANA DI STUDI PALETNOLOGICI. 1977. irreg. (Universita degli Studi di Pisa, Istituto di Antropologia e Paleontologia Umana) Giardini Editori e Stampatori, Via Santa Bibbiana 28, 56100 Pisa, Italy.

572   SZ
COLLECTANEA INSTITUTI ANTHROPOS. 1967. irreg., no. 15, 1977. price varies. (Anthropos Institut) Editions Saint-Paul, Perolles 36, CH-1700 Fribourg, Switzerland. illus.

301.2   PE
COMUNIDADES Y CULTURAS PERUANAS. 1973. irreg., no. 16, 1979. price varies. Instituto Linguistico de Verano, Departamento de Estudios Etno-Linguisticos, Casilla 2492, Lima 100, Peru. Ed. Mary Ruth Wise. (back issues avail)

572   PO
CONTRIBUICOES PARA O ESTUDO DA ANTROPOLOGIA PORTUGUESA. (Text in Portuguese; summaries in English) vol. 8, 1973. irreg. exchange basis. Universidade de Coimbra, Museu e Laboratorio Antropologico, Rua da Ilha, Coimbra, Portugal. bk. rev. bibl. illus.

572   US   ISSN 0069-9632
CONTRIBUTIONS IN ANTHROPOLOGY. Variant title: Southern Methodist University Contributions in Anthropology. 1965. irreg., no. 12, 1974. price varies. Southern Methodist University, Department of Anthropology, Southern Methodist University, Dallas, TX 75275. Ed. Fred Wendorf.

CROSS CULTURAL RESEARCH AND METHODOLOGY SERIES. see *PSYCHOLOGY*

DAGESTANSKII ETNOGRAFICHESKII SBORNIK. see *SOCIOLOGY*

DANCE RESEARCH ANNUAL. (Congress on Research in Dance) see *DANCE*

DATOS ETNO-LINGUISTICOS. see *LINGUISTICS*

572   PE
DEBATES EN ANTROPOLOGIA. no. 2, 1978. irreg. Pontificia Universidad Catolica del Peru, Departamento de Ciencias Sociales, Fundo Pando s/n, Lima, Peru. Ed. Giovanni Mitrovic. bk. rev.

572   DK
DENMARK. NATIONALMUSEET. PUBLICATIONS: ETHNOGRAPHICAL SERIES. irreg., latest vol. 15, 1975. price varies. Nationalmuseet, Oplysningsafdelingen, Ny Vestergade 10, DK-1471 Copenhagen K, Denmark (Dist. in the U.S. by: Humanities Press, 171 First Ave., Atlantic City, NJ 07716)

301.2   US   ISSN 0077-7951
DESERT RESEARCH INSTITUTE PUBLICATIONS IN THE SOCIAL SCIENCES. 1962. irreg. price varies. University of Nevada, Desert Research Institute, Social Sciences Center, Box 60220, Reno, NV 89506. circ. 700-800. Indexed: Abstr.Anthropol.

301.2   572   UK
DYN; the journal of the Durham University Anthropological Society. 1970. a. or biennial. £0.40. University of Durham, Anthropological Society, South End House, South Rd., Durham DH1 3TG, England. Ed. J. S. Woods. bk. rev. circ. 200. (processed)

572   US   ISSN 0070-8232
EASTERN NEW MEXICO UNIVERSITY. CONTRIBUTIONS IN ANTHROPOLOGY. 1968. irreg., vol. 10, no. 1, 1979. price varies. Eastern New Mexico University, Department of Anthropology, Portales, NM 88130. Ed. Cynthia Irwin-Williams. circ. 1,000.

572   960   FR
ECOLE DES HAUTES ETUDES EN SCIENCES SOCIALES. DOSSIERS AFRICAINS. 1974. irreg., latest 1979. price varies. Editions de l' Ecole des Hautes Etudes en Sciences Sociales, Departement Diffusion, 131 Bd. Saint-Michel, F-75005 Paris, France.

ESTUDIOS ETNOHISTORICOS DEL ECUADOR. see *HISTORY — History Of North And South America*

301.2   GW   ISSN 0071-1837
ETHNOGRAPHICA. (Text in German and Czech) 1959. irreg., no. 5/6, 1966. price varies. (Moravske Museum, Brno, CS) Rudolf Habelt Verlag, Am Buchenhang 1, 5300 Bonn 1, W. Germany (B.R.D.) Ed. L. Kunz.

301.2   SW   ISSN 0081-5632
ETHNOGRAPHICAL MUSEUM OF SWEDEN. MONOGRAPH SERIES. 1953. irreg., 1968, no. 14. price varies. Etnografiska Museet - Ethnographical Museum of Sweden, S-115 27 Stockholm, Sweden. Ed. Karl Erik Larsson.

398   301.2   GW   ISSN 0071-1845
ETHNOLOGIA. 1959. irreg., vol. 8, 1976. price varies. (Gesellschaft fuer Voelkerkunde) E. J. Brill GmbH, Antwerpener Str. 6-12, 5000 Cologne 1, W. Germany (B.R.D.)

572   GW   ISSN 0425-4597
ETHNOLOGIA EUROPAEA; internationale Zeitschrift der europaeischen Ethnologie. irreg. DM.44. Verlag Otto Schwartz und Co., Annastr. 7, 3400 Goettingen, W. Germany (B.R.D.)

572   SW
ETHNOLOGICA SCANDINAVIA; a journal for Nordic ethnology. (Text in English) 1971. a. Kr.50. Folklivsarkivet, Finngatan 8, S-223 62 Lund, Sweden (Subscr. to: Box 1135, S-221 04 Lund, Sweden) Ed. Nils-Arvid Bringeus.

572   YU
ETNOGRAFSKI MUZEJ NA CETINJU. GLASNIK. 1961. irreg. Etnografski Muzej na Cetinju, Trg Revolucije, Cetinje, Yugoslavia.

572   YU
ETNOGRAFSKI MUZEJ U BEOGRADU. GLASNIK. 1926. a. Etnografski Muzej u Beogradu, Studentski trg 13, Belgrade, Yugoslavia.

572   301.2   IT
ETNOLOGIA; antropologia culturale. 1974. irreg. L.6000. Consiglio Nazionale delle Ricerche, Corso Vittorio Emanuele 110, Naples, Italy.
Formerly: Rivista di Etnografia.

572   IT
ETNOLOGIA-ANTROPOLOGIA CULTURALE. 1974. a. L.10000. R.E.A.C., Corso Vitt. Emanuele 110, 80121 Naples, Italy. Ed. Piero Battista. adv. bk. rev. circ. 2,000.

572   SW
ETNOLOGISKA STUDIER. 1933. a. Goeteborgs Etnografiska Museum, N. Harngatan 12, S-411 14 Goeteborg, Sweden. Ed. Kjell Zetterstroem. circ. 1,600.

390   572   YU   ISSN 0423-5509
ETNOLOSKI PREGLED/REVUE D'ETHNOLOGIE. 1962. s-a. (Etnolosko Drustvo Jugoslavije) Etnografski Muzej u Beogradu, Studentski trg 13, Belgrade, Yugoslavia. Ed. Milovan Gavazzi. illus.

572   IV   ISSN 0423-5673
ETUDES EBURNEENNES. 1951. a. Institut Fondamental d'Afrique Noire, Centre de Cote-d'Ivoire, Direction de la Recherche Scientifique, Ministere de l'Education Nationale, Abidjan, Ivory Coast. bibl. illus.

572   BE   ISSN 0071-2035
ETUDES ETHNOLOGIQUES. 1958. irreg. price varies. (Universite Libre de Bruxelles, Institut de Sociologie) Editions de l'Universite de Bruxelles, Parc Leopold, 1040 Brussels, Belgium.

572   960   SG
ETUDES MAURITANIENNES. 1948. irreg. Institut Fondamental d'Afrique Noire, Centre de Mauritanie, Universite de Dakar, B.P. 206, Dakar, Senegal.

572   NG
ETUDES NIGERIENNES. irreg. Institut Fondamental d'Afrique Noire, Centre du Niger, B.P. 48, Niamey, Niger. illus.

572   410   UV
ETUDES VOLTAIQUES. 1950. irreg (approx. 1/yr.) Centre National de la Recherche Scientifique et Technique, B.P. 7047, Ouagadougou, Upper Volta. bibl.

571   AE   ISSN 0071-4712
FICHES TYPOLOGIQUES AFRICAINES. 1961. irreg. Centre de Recherches Anthropologiques Prehistoriques et Ethnographiques, 3 rue Franklin Roosevelt, Algiers, Algeria.

572   US   ISSN 0071-4739
FIELDIANA: ANTHROPOLOGY. 1895. irreg., vol. 69, 1977. price varies. Field Museum of Natural History, E. Roosevelt & S. Lake Shore Dr., Chicago, IL 60605. index. circ. 500. Indexed: Biol.Abstr.

572   US
FLORIDA ANTHROPOLOGICAL SOCIETY PUBLICATIONS. irreg. included in subscr. to Florida Anthropologist. Florida Anthropological Society, Inc., c/o Jeane L. Eyster, Rt. 1, Box 96, Islamorada, FL 33036.

574   970   US
FLORIDA STATE MUSEUM. CONTRIBUTIONS. ANTHROPOLOGY AND HISTORY. 1956. irreg., 1973, no. 18. price varies. ‡ Florida State Museum, University of Florida, Gainesville, FL 32611. Ed. Jerald T. Milanich. bibl. charts, illus. circ. 450. (processed)
Formerly (until 1971): Florida State Museum. Contributions. Social Sciences (ISSN 0071-6162)

572   VE   ISSN 0428-8254
FOLIA ANTROPOLOGICA. 1962. irreg. Museo de Ciencias Naturales, Apartado de Correos 8011, Caracas, Venezuela. abstr.

572   301.2   DK   ISSN 0085-0756
FOLK; DANSK ETNOGRAFISK TIDSSKRIFT. (Text in English, German and French) 1959. a. price varies. Dansk Etnografisk Forening, Nationalmuseet, DK-1471 Copenhagen K, Denmark. Eds. Johannes Nicolaisen, Lise Rishoej Pedersen, Inger Wulff. bibl. illus. circ. 1,000.

572   UK   ISSN 0430-8778
FOLK LIFE; a journal of ethnological studies. 1963. a. £5. (Society for Folk Life Studies) W.S. Maney & Sons Ltd., Hudson Road, Leeds LS9 7DL, England (Subscr. to: Treasurer, Sunnyside Cottage, Halton East, Skipton, Yorkshire, Eng) Ed. J.G. Jenkins. bk. rev. illus. index. circ. 500.

572   SW
FOLKL-LIV; Acta Ethnologica et Folkloristica Europea. (Text in English or Scandinavian language; summaries in English) 1937. a. (Kungliga Gustav Adolfs Akademien) Generalstabens Lithografiske Anstalt, Box 22069, 104 22 Stockholm, Sweden. bk. rev.

572   FI   ISSN 0085-0764
FOLKLIVSSTUDIER. (Subseries of Svenska Litteratursaellsteapet i Finland. Skrifter) (Text in Swedish; summaries in English, German) 1945. irreg., no. 10, 1974. Fmk.50. ‡ Svenska Litteratursaellsakpet i Finland, Snellmansg. 9-11, 00170 Helsinki 17, Finland. Ed. Dr. Phil. Bo Lonnqvist. circ. (controlled)

301.21   GW
FORSCHUNGEN ZUR VOLKSKUNDE. irreg., no. 48, 1976. price varies. Verlag Regensberg, Daimlerweg 58, Postfach 6748/6749, 4400 Muenster, W. Germany (B.R.D.) Eds. B.Koetting, A. Schroeer.

301.2   II
GAUHATI UNIVERSITY. DEPARTMENT OF ANTHROPOLOGY. BULLETIN. 1972. a. Rs.5. Gauhati University, Department of Anthropology, Gauhati 14, Assam, India. Ed. M. C. Goswami. bk. rev. bibl. illus.

572 AT ISSN 0072-1190
GEORGE ERNEST MORRISON LECTURES IN ETHNOLOGY. irreg. Australian National University Press, P.O. Box 4, Canberra, A.C.T. 2600, Australia (Dist. in U.S. by: International Scholarly Book Services, Inc., Box 4347, Portland, OR. 97208)

301.2 SW ISSN 0348-4076
GOTHENBURG STUDIES IN SOCIAL ANTHROPOLOGY. (Subseries of Acta Universitatis Gothoburgensis) 1978. irreg. price varies; also exchange basis. Acta Universitatis Gothoburgensis, Box 5096, S-402 22 Goeteborg 5, Sweden (Dist. in U.S., Canada, and Mexico by: Humanities Press, Inc., 171 First Ave., Atlantic Highlands, NJ 07716) Ed. Goeran Aijmer.

301.2 DK
GREENLAND, MAN AND SOCIETY. 1979. irreg. (Kommissionen for Videnskabelige Undersoegelser i Groenland, GL - Commission for Scientific Research in Greenland) Nyt Nordisk Forlag - Arnold Busck A-S, 49 Koebmagergade 49, DK-1150 Copenhagen K, Denmark. charts. illus.
Supersedes in part (1878-1979): Meddelelser om Groenland (ISSN 0025-6676)

301.2 GW ISSN 0072-9469
HAMBURGISCHES MUSEUM FUER VOELKERKUNDE. MITTEILUNGEN. (Text in German, occasionally in English or French) 1971, N.S. a. price varies. ‡ Hamburgisches Museum fuer Voelkerkunde, Binderstr. 14, 2000 Hamburg 13, W. Germany (B.R.D.) Ed. J. Zwernemann. circ. 200.

572 NZ
HOCKEN LECTURE. 1969. irreg. price varies. ‡ University of Otago, Hocken Library, P.O. Box 56, Dunedin, New Zealand. Ed. M.G. Hitchings. circ. 500.

572 US ISSN 0074-1523
I A A E E MONOGRAPHS. 1965. irreg. price varies. International Association for the Advancement of Ethnology and Eugenics, P.O.B. 3495, Grand Central Station, New York, NY 10017.

572 US ISSN 0074-1515
I A A E E REPRINT. irreg. $0.25-0.50. International Association for the Advancement of Ethnology and Eugenics, P.O.B. 3495, Grand Central Station, New York, NY 10017.

913 301.2 AU
I. C. NACHRICHTEN. 1969. irreg., no.33, 1979. S.25. ‡ Institutum Canarium, Postfach 48, A-5400 Hallein, Austria. Ed. Herbert F. Nowak. bk. rev. charts. illus. circ. 500.

572 SA ISSN 0073-893X
I S M A OCCASIONAL PAPERS. (Text in English) 1964. irreg., latest no. 6, 1969. price varies. ‡ Institute for the Study of Man in Africa, Medical School, Old Medical School, Room C 24, Johannesburg 2001, South Africa. Ed. N.J. Pines. circ. 300.

572 SA ISSN 0073-8921
I S M A PAPERS. (Text in English) 1961. irreg., latest no. 38, 1977. $0.48 per no. for non-members. ‡ Institute for the Study of Man in Africa, Medical School, Old Medical School, Room C 24, Johannesburg 2001, South Africa. Ed. N.J. Pines. circ. 800.

572 323.4 DK ISSN 0105-4503
I W G I A DOCUMENTS; documentation of oppression of ethnic groups in various countries. (Text in English) 1971. irreg. (approx. 6/yr.), no. 34, 1978. $12 to individuals; $24 to institutions. International Work Group for Indigenous Affairs, Frederiksholms Kanal 4A, DK-1220 Copenhagen K, Denmark. Ed.H. Klaivan. cum.index.

572 323.4 DK
I W G I A NEWSLETTER. irreg., no. 19, 1978. International Work Group for Indigenous Affairs, Frederiksholms Kanal 4A, DK-1220 Copenhagen K, Denmark.

572 NR
IGBO PHILOSOPHY.* 1971. a. £N0.2 per no. Igbo Philosophical Association, Bigard Memorial Seminary, P.M.B. 921, Enugu, East Central State, Nigeria. Ed. Rev. Fr. C. E. Ohaeri.

570 BL ISSN 0073-4691
IHERINGIA. SERIE ANTROPOLOGIA. (Text in English, French, German, Latin, Portuguese and Spanish) 1969. irreg., 1972, no. 2. price varies. Fundacao Zoobotanica do Rio Grande do Sul, Museu de Ciencias Naturais, Caixa Postal 1188, 90.000 Porto Alegre, Rio Grande do Sul, Brazil. Ed. Jose Willibaldo Thome. bibl. illus. circ. 1,000. Indexed: Biol.Abstr. Zoo.Rec.

572 US ISSN 0095-2915
ILLINOIS. STATE MUSEUM. RESEARCH SERIES. PAPERS IN ANTHROPOLOGY. 1972. irreg., no. 4, 1979. price varies. Illinois State Museum, Springfield, IL 62706. Key Title: Papers in Anthropology (Springfield)

572 US ISSN 0073-5167
ILLINOIS STUDIES IN ANTHROPOLOGY. 1961. irreg. University of Illinois Press, 54 E. Gregory, Box 5081, Station A, Champaign, IL 61820. (reprint service avail. from UMI)

INDIAN REVIEW OF LIFE SCIENCES. see *AGRICULTURE*

301.2 974 573 GW ISSN 0341-8642
INDIANA; contributions to ethnology and linguistics, archaeology and physical anthropology of Indian America. (Text in English, German or Spanish) 1973. irreg. price varies. (Ibero-Amerikanisches Institut Preussischer Kulturbesitz Berlin) Gebr. Mann Verlag, Lindenstr. 76, Postfach 110303, 1000 Berlin 61, W. Germany (B.R.D.)

570 US ISSN 0073-6899
INDIANA HISTORICAL SOCIETY. PREHISTORY RESEARCH SERIES. 1937. irreg. membership. Indiana Historical Society, 315 W. Ohio St., Indianapolis, IN 46202. Ed. Gayle Thornbrough. circ. 1,000.

572 PE
INSTITUT FRANCAIS D'ETUDES ANDINES. TRAVAUX. (Text in French; summaries in English) 1949. biennial. $6. Institut Francais d'Etudes Andines, Casilla 218, Lima 18, Peru.

INSTITUT FUER DEN WISSENSCHAFTLICHEN FILM. PUBLIKATIONEN ZU WISSENSCHAFTLICHEN FILMEN. SEKTION ETHNOLOGIE. see *MOTION PICTURES*

572 913 CK
INSTITUTO DE ANTROPOLOGIA E HISTORIA DEL ESTADO CARABOBO. BOLETIN. (Text in English, Spanish) a. Instituto de Antropologia e Historia del Estado Carabobo, Caracas, Colombia. Ed. Dr. Henriqueta Penalver. bibl.

572 987 VE
INSTITUTO DE ANTROPOLOGIA E HISTORIA. ANUARIO. 1964. a. Universidad Central de Venezuela, Instituto de Antropologia e Historia, Caracas, Venezuela. bibl. illus.

572 PE
INSTITUTO DE ESTUDIOS ANDINOS. TRABAJO DE CAMPO. 1976. irreg. Instituto de Estudios Andinos, Apartado 289, Huancayo, Peru.

572 PE
INSTITUTO DE ESTUDIOS PERUANOS. PROYECTO DE ESTUDIOS ETNOLOGICOS DEL VALLE DE CHANCAY. MONOGRAFIA. no. 5, 1975. irreg. I E P Ediciones, Horacio Urteaga 694 (Campo de Marte), Lima 11, Peru.

572 MX
INSTITUTO INDIGENISTA INTERAMERICANO SERIE DE EDICIONES ESPECIALES. 1967. irreg. (3-4/yr) Mex.$150($7) Instituto Indigenista Interamericano, Insurgentes Sur 1690, Colonia Florida, Mexico 20, D.F., Mexico. illus. circ. controlled.

972 913 MX ISSN 0076-7557
INSTITUTO NACIONAL DE ANTROPOLOGIA E HISTORIA. ANALES. 1945. irreg. membership. Instituto Nacional de Antropologia e Historia, Cordoba 47, Mexico 7,D.F., Mexico.

572 972 MX ISSN 0076-7573
INSTITUTO NACIONAL DE ANTROPOLOGIA E HISTORIA. INVESTIGACIONES. 1958. irreg., 1970, no. 24. price varies. Instituto Nacional de Antropologia e Historia, Cordoba 47, Mexico 7,D.F., Mexico.

572 972 MX ISSN 0076-7603
INSTITUTO NACIONAL DE ANTROPOLOGIA E HISTORIA. OBRAS VARIAS. 1953. irreg. price varies. Instituto Nacional de Antropologia e Historia, Cordoba 47, Mexico 7,D.F., Mexico.

570 MX ISSN 0076-7611
INSTITUTO NACIONAL DE ANTROPOLOGIA E HISTORIA. SERIE CIENTIFICA. 1967. irreg. price varies. Instituto Nacional de Antropologia e Historia, Cordoba 47, Mexico 7,D.F., Mexico.

572 972 MX ISSN 0076-7549
INSTITUTO NACIONAL DE ANTROPOLOGIA E HISTORIA. SOCIEDAD DE ALUMNOS. (PUBLICACIONES) 1945. irreg. price varies. Instituto Nacional de Antropologia e Historia, Cordoba 45, Mexico 7,D.F., Mexico.

572 301 MX ISSN 0074-0810
INTER-AMERICAN CONFERENCE ON INDIAN LIFE. ACTA/CONGRESOS INDIGENISTAS INTERAMERICANOS. ACTA. every 4 yrs., 7th, 1972, Brasilia, Brazil. Instituto Indigenista Interamericano - Instituto Indigenista Interamericano, Insurgentes Sur 1690, Colonia Florida, Mexico 20,D.F., Mexico. circ. c.

572 AU ISSN 0538-5865
INTERNATIONAL COMMITTEE ON URGENT ANTHROPOLOGICAL AND ETHNOLOGICAL RESEARCH. BULLETIN. (Text in English, French and German) 1958. a. S.90. International Committee on Urgent Anthropological and Ethnological Research, c/o Institut fuer Voelkerkunde, Universitaetsstrasse 7, A-1010 Vienna, Austria. Ed. Dr. Anna Hohenwart-Gerlachstein. charts. illus. stat. circ. 600-800.

572 972.9 CN ISSN 0538-6381
INTERNATIONAL CONGRESS FOR THE STUDY OF PRE-COLUMBIAN CULTURES OF THE LESSER ANTILLES. PROCEEDINGS. 1963. irreg., 7th, 1978. price varies. Universite de Montreal, Centre de Recherches Caraibes, Montreal, Que, H3C 3J7, Canada. Ed. Prof. Ripley P. Bullen.

572 UK ISSN 0074-3496
INTERNATIONAL CONGRESS OF ANTHROPOLOGICAL AND ETHNOLOGICAL SCIENCES. PROCEEDINGS. irreg., 1971, 8th, Copenhagen. International Union of Anthropological and Ethnological Sciences, c/o Prof. Eric Sunderland, Dept. of Anthropology, University of Durham, South End House, South Rd., Durham DH1 3TG, England.
Proceedings published by organizing committee

572 591 US ISSN 0074-3895
INTERNATIONAL CONGRESS OF PRIMATOLOGY. PROCEEDINGS. irreg., 7th, 1979, Bangalore; 8th, 1980, Florence. International Primatological Society, c/o Dr. Allan M. Schrier, Sec.-Gen., Psychology Dept., Brown University, Providence, RI 02912 (Proceedings of 6th Congress avail. from Academic Press, 24 Oval Rd., London N.W. 1, England)
Published in host country: Japan, 1974.

571 YU ISSN 0074-9478
INTERNATIONAL UNION OF PREHISTORIC AND PROTOHISTORIC SCIENCES. PROCEEDINGS OF CONGRESS. irreg; 1-3rd, Belgrade, 1971-1973. ‡ International Union of Prehistoric and Protohistoric Sciences, Institute of Archaeology, Knez Mihajlova 35/2, Belgrade, Yugoslavia.
Proceedings published in host country

572 MX ISSN 0075-0204
INVESTIGACIONES ANTROPOLOGICAS. 1956. irreg. price varies. Instituto Nacional de Antropologia e Historia, Cordoba 47, Mexico 7,D.F., Mexico.

572 PE
INVESTIGACIONES DE CAMPO. 1976. irreg. S/ 200($4) Museo Nacional de Antropologia y Arqueologia, Plaza Bolivar s/n Pueblo Libre, Lima, Peru.

JAHRBUCH FUER OSTDEUTSCHE VOLKSKUNDE. see *FOLKLORE*

JERNAL ANTROPOLOJI DAN SOSIOLOJI. see *SOCIOLOGY*

ANTHROPOLOGY

800   BO
JISUNU. 1974. irreg. Bol.$40($2) (Academia de la Culturas Nativas de Oriente Boliviano) Editorial los Huerfanos, Casilla 2225, Santa Cruz de la Sierra, Bolivia. Ed.Bd. adv. bibl. tr.lit. circ. 1,000.

301.2   II
JOURNAL OF HIMALAYAN STUDIES AND REGIONAL DEVELOPMENT. (Text in English) 1977. a. Rs.20($8) Garhwal University, Institute of Himalayan Studies and Regional Development, Box 12, Srinagar, Garhwal 246174, India. Ed. Tej Vir Singh. adv. bk. rev. circ. 1,000.
    Formerly: Himalaya.

KALULU; bulletin of Malawian oral literature and cultural studies. see *LITERATURE*

KARIBA STUDIES. see *BIOLOGY — Zoology*

572   GW   ISSN 0075-6490
KOELNER ETHNOLOGISCHE MITTEILUNGEN. 1960. irreg., latest no. 4. Bouvier Verlag Herbert Grundmann, Am Hof 32, Postfach 1268, 5300 Bonn 1, W. Germany (B.R.D.)

572   NE   ISSN 0074-0470
KONINKLIJK INSTITUUT VOOR TAAL-, LAND- EN VOLKENKUNDE. TRANSLATION SERIES. (Text in English) 1956. irreg. price varies. Martinus Nijhoff Booksellers, Box 269, 2501 AX the Hague, Netherlands.

572   US   ISSN 0023-4869
KROEBER ANTHROPOLOGICAL SOCIETY. PAPERS. 1950. irreg., approx. s-a. membership. Kroeber Anthropological Society, Dept.of Anthropology, Univ. of California, Berkeley, CA 94720. Ed. Bd. bk. rev. charts. illus. cum.index. circ. 500.

913   UK   ISSN 0075-7349
KUSH. (Text in English; summaries in French, German and other languages) 1953. irreg. price varies. (Antiquities Service of the Sudan) Daniel Greenaway & Sons Ltd., Runnings Rd., Cheltenham GL5 9NT, England.

LANGUE ET CIVILISATION A TRADITION ORALE. see *LINGUISTICS*

572   US
LATIN AMERICAN ANTHROPOLOGY GROUP. CONTRIBUTIONS. a. $5. (Latin American Anthropology Group) American Anthropological Association, 1703 New Hampshire Ave., N.W., Washington, DC 20009.

301.2   GH
LEGON FAMILY RESEARCH PAPERS. 1974. irreg, no. 2, 1975. price varies. University of Ghana, Institute of African Studies, Box 73, Legon, Ghana.

572   US
LIBRARY OF ANTHROPOLOGY. a. price varies. Gordon and Breach Science Publishers, One Park Ave., New York, NY 10016. Ed. Anthony LaRuffa.

LIBYCA; anthropologie, prehistoire, ethnographie. see *ARCHAEOLOGY*

LODZKIE STUDIA ETNOGRAFICZNE. see *FOLKLORE*

572 301   UK   ISSN 0077-1074
LONDON SCHOOL OF ECONOMICS MONOGRAPHS ON SOCIAL ANTHROPOLOGY. 1940. irreg., no. 52, 1975. price varies. Athlone Press, 90-91 Great Russell St., London WC1B 3PY, England (Dist. in U.S by: Humanities Press Inc., 171 First Ave., Atlantic Highlands, NJ 07716)

LOUISIANA STATE UNIVERSITY. SCHOOL OF GEOSCIENCE. MISCELLANEOUS PUBLICATIONS. see *EARTH SCIENCES*

LUD. see *SOCIOLOGY*

572 560 913.031   II
MAN & ENVIRONMENT. (Text in English) 1977. a. Rs.50($10) Indian Society for Prehistoric and Quaternary Studies, c/o Physical Research Laboratory, Ahmedabad 380001, India. Ed. V.N. Misra. bk. rev. circ. 500.

301.29   MY   ISSN 0303-3171
MAN AND SOCIETY/MANUSIA DAN MASYARAKAT. (Text in English or Malay) 1972. a. $4. (University of Malaya, Anthropology and Sociology Department - Universiti Malaya, Jabatan Antropologi dan Sosiologi) University of Malaya Press, c/o University Library, Pantai Valley, Kuala Lumpur, Selangor, Malaysia. Ed. A. Kahar Bador. adv. bk. rev. circ. 1,000.

572 300   AT
MAN IN SOUTHEAST ASIA. 1968. 2-4/yr. Aus.$3. University of Queensland, Department of Anthropology, Sociology and Geography, Brisbane, Qld. 4067, Australia. Eds. Drs. Donald & Elise Tugby. bibl. circ. 600.

301.2   CN
MAN IN THE NORTH PROJECT. TECHNICAL REPORTS. irreg. price varies. Arctic Institute of North America, University Library Tower, 2920 24th Ave. N.W., Calgary, Alta. T2N 1N4, Canada. (reprint service avail. from UMI)

572   US   ISSN 0076-4116
MANKIND MONOGRAPHS. 1961. irreg., unnumbered. price varies. Institute for the Study of Man, Inc., 1629 K St., N.W., Suite 520, Washington, DC 20006. Ed. Dr. R. Gayre. circ. 1,200.

572   US   ISSN 0076-5139
MATERIAL CULTURE MONOGRAPHS (AMERICAN INDIAN) 1969. irreg. price varies. Denver Art Museum, 100 W. 14th Ave. Parkway, Denver, CO 80204. Ed. Richard Conn.

572 301.2   PL   ISSN 0076-521X
MATERIALY I PRACE ANTROPOLOGICZNE. (Text in Polish or English; summaries in English or German) 1938. irreg., 1972, no. 84. price varies. (Polska Akademia Nauk, Zaklad Antropologii) Panstwowe Wydawnictwo Naukowe, Miodowa 10, Warsaw, Poland. Ed. Halina Milicerowa. bibl. illus.

572   US   ISSN 0564-8602
MEMPHIS STATE UNIVERSITY. ANTHROPOLOGICAL RESEARCH CENTER. OCCASIONAL PAPERS. 1967. irreg., no. 8, 1978. $3.50. Memphis State University, Anthropological Research Center, Memphis, TN 38152.

301.2 660   PE
METALURGIA. 1976. irreg. S/200($4) Museo Nacional de Antropologia y Arqueologia, Plaza Bolivar s/n Pueblo Libre, Lima, Peru.

572   US
MICHIGAN STATE UNIVERSITY. MUSEUM PUBLICATIONS. ANTHROPOLOGICAL SERIES. 1971. irreg. price varies. Michigan State University, Museum, East Lansing, MI 48824. Ed. Bd. charts. illus. circ. 1,500.

572   SZ
MICRO-BIBLIOTHECA ANTHROPOS. 1953. irreg. price varies. (Anthropos Institut) Editions Saint-Paul, Perolles 36, CH-1700 Fribourg, Switzerland. (microfilm)

572   US
MISSISSIPPI STATE UNIVERSITY. COLLEGE OF ARTS AND SCIENCES. DEPARTMENT OF ANTHROPOLOGY. OCCASIONAL PAPERS IN ANTHROPOLOGY. 1966. irreg. free. Mississippi State University, Department of Anthropology, Mississippi State, MS 39762. circ. 500.
    Formerly: Mississippi State Unierstiy. College of Arts and Sciences. Department of Sociology and Anthropology. Sociology-Anthropology Reports.

MONTALBAN. see *HUMANITIES: COMPREHENSIVE WORKS*

572   SZ   ISSN 0072-0828
MUSEE D'ETHNOGRAPHIE DE LA VILLE DE GENEVE. BULLETIN ANNUEL. 1958. a. 12 Fr. Musee d'Ethnographie de la Ville de Geneve, 65-67 Bd. Carl-Vogt, 1205 Geneva, Switzerland. Ed. A. Jeanneret. circ. 1,000.

572   BE
MUSEE ROYAL DE L'AFRIQUE CENTRALE. ARCHIVES D'ANTHROPOLOGIE. Short title: Archives d'Anthropologie. 1960. irreg., no. 27, 1980. price varies. Musee Royal de l'Afrique Centrale, 13 Steenweg op Leuven, B-1980 Tervuren, Belgium.
    Continues: Archives d'Ethnographie (ISSN 0563-1742)

572 301.2   DR
MUSEO DE HOMBRE DOMINICANO. PAPELES OCASIONALES. 1973. irreg. price varies. Museo del Hombre Dominicano, Calle Pedro Henriquez Urena, Santo Domingo, Dominican Republic.

MUSEO DEL HOMBRE DOMINICANO. SERIE CATALOGOS Y MEMORIAS. see *MUSEUMS AND ART GALLERIES*

572 301.2   DR
MUSEO DEL HOMBRE DOMINICANO. SERIE CONFERENCIAS. 1974. irreg. price varies. Museo del Hombre Dominicano, Calle Pedro Henriquez Urena, Santo Domingo, Dominican Republic.

301.2   DR
MUSEO DEL HOMBRE DOMINICANO. SERIE ESTUDIO Y ARTE. 1977. irreg. price varies. Museo del Hombre Dominicano, Calle Pedro Henriquez Urena, Plaza de la Cultura, Santo Domingo, Dominican Republic. illus.

301.2   DR
MUSEO DEL HOMBRE DOMINICANO. SERIE INVESTIGACIONES ANTROPOLOGICAS. 1975. irreg. no. 10, 1978. price varies. Museo del Hombre Dominicano, Calle Pedro Henriquez Urena, Plaza de la Cultura, Santo Domingo, Dominican Republic. charts. illus.

MUSEO DEL HOMBRE DOMINICANO. SERIE MESAS REDONDAS. see *MUSEUMS AND ART GALLERIES*

MUSEO NACIONAL DE ANTROPOLOGIA Y ARQUEOLOGIA. SERIE: METALURGIA. see *ARCHAEOLOGY*

573   PE
MUSEO NACIONAL DE ANTROPOLOGIA Y ARQUEOLOGIA. SERIE: ANTROPOLOGIA FISICA. 1976. irreg. Museo Nacional de Antropologia y Arqueologia, Plaza Bolivar, Pueblo Libre, Lima 21, Peru.

572 913   PE
MUSEO NACIONAL DE ANTROPOLOGIA Y ARQUEOLOGIA. SERIE: INVESTIGACIONES DE CAMPO. 1976. irreg. Museo Nacional de Antropologia y Arqueologia, Plaza Bolivar, Pueblo Libre, Lima 21, Peru.

572   UY   ISSN 0077-1244
MUSEO NACIONAL DE HISTORIA NATURAL. COMUNICACIONES ANTROPOLOGICAS. 1956. irreg. free on exchange. Museo Nacional de Historia Natural, Montevideo, Uruguay. Ed. Miguel A. Klappenbach.

572   MX   ISSN 0076-7158
MUSEU NACIONAL DE ANTROPOLOGIA. CUADERNOS. 1963. irreg., 1967, no. 4. price on request. Museu Nacional de Antropologia, Calz. de la Milla y Reforma, Mexico 7, D. F., Mexico.

572   BL   ISSN 0080-3189
MUSEU NACIONAL, RIO DE JANEIRO. BOLETIM. NOVA SERIE. ANTROPOLOGIA. 1942. irreg., no. 31, Jan. 1979. exchange only. Museu Nacional, Quinta da Boa Vista, Rio de Janeiro, GB 08, Brazil. bibl.

572   BL   ISSN 0522-7291
MUSEU PARAENSE EMILIO GOELDI. BOLETIM ANTROPOLOGIA. NOVA SERIE. 1957. irreg. Instituto Nacional de Pesquisas da Amazonia, Museu Paraense Emilio Goeldi, Belem, Para, Brazil.

571   GE   ISSN 0077-2291
MUSEUM FUER UR- UND FRUEHGESCHICHTE THUERINGENS. VEROEFFENTLICHUNGEN. (Text in German; summaries in English, French, Russian) 1958. irreg., vol. 5, 1974. price varies. Hermann Boehlaus Nachfolger, Meyerstr. 50a, 53 Weimar, E. Germany (D.D.R.)

301.2 960   GW   ISSN 0067-5962
MUSEUM FUER VOELKERKUNDE, BERLIN. VEROEFFENTLICHUNGEN. NEUE FOLGE. ABTEILUNG: AFRIKA. 1960. irreg., vol. 8, 1972. price varies. Staatliche Museen Preussischer Kulturbesitz, Museum fuer Voelkerkunde, Berlin, Arnimallee 23/27, 1000 Berlin 33, W. Germany (B.R.D.)

301.2 970 980   GW
MUSEUM FUER VOELKERKUNDE, BERLIN. VEROEFFENTLICHUNGEN. NEUE FOLGE. ABTEILUNG: AMERIKANISCHE NATURVOELKER. 1967. irreg., vol. 5, 1978. price varies. Staatliche Museen Preussischer Kulturbesitz, Museum fuer Voelkerkunde, Berlin, Arnimallee 23/27, 1000 Berlin 33, W. Germany (B.R.D.)

301.2 990   GW   ISSN 0067-5989
MUSEUM FUER VOELKERKUNDE, BERLIN. VEROEFFENTLICHUNGEN. NEUE FOLGE. ABTEILUNG: SUEDSEE. 1961. irreg., vol. 10, 1973. price varies. Staatliche Museen Preussischer Kulturbesitz, Museum fuer Voelkerkunde, Berlin, Arnimallee 23/27, 1000 Berlin 33, W. Germany (B.R.D.)

MUSEUM MEMOIR. see *BIOLOGY — Zoology*

301.2   PL   ISSN 0076-0315
MUZEUM ARCHEOLOGICZNE I ETNOGRAFICZNE, LODZ. PRACE I MATERIALY. SERIA ETNOGRAFICZNA. 1957. irreg., no. 18, 1975. price varies. ‡ Panstwowe Wydawnictwo Naukowe, Miodowa 10, Warsaw, Poland (Dist. by Ars Polona-Ruch, Krakowskie Przedmiescie 7, Warsaw Poland) Ed. Irena Lechowa. circ. 400.

572   PL   ISSN 0084-2796
MUZEUM ETNOGRAFICZNE, WROCLAW. ZESZYTY ETNOGRAFICZNE. (Issued as part of: Rocznik Etnografii Slaskiej) 1963. a. price varies. Muzeum Etnograficzne, Wroclaw, Kazimierza Wielkiego 33, 50-077 Wroclaw, Poland.

301.2   PL   ISSN 0068-4643
MUZEUM GORNOSLASKIE W BYTOMIU. ROCZNIK. SERIA ETNOGRAFIA. 1966. irreg. price varies. Muzeum Gornoslaskie, Pl. Thaelmanna 2, 41-902 Bytom, Poland (Dist. by: Ars Polona-Ruch, Krakowskie Przedmiescie 7, Warsaw, Poland)

572   CN   ISSN 0077-2755
NAPAO: A SASKATCHEWAN ANTHROPOLOGY JOURNAL. 1968. a. Can.$3 to individuals; Can. $4 to institutions. University of Saskatchewan, Department of Anthropology and Archaeology, Senior Anthropology Students, Saskatoon, Sask., Canada. Ed. Urve Linnamae. bk. rev. circ. 400.

301.2 398   CS   ISSN 0554-9256
NAPRSTKOVO MUZEUM ASIJSKYCH, AFRICKYCH A AMERICKYCH KULTUR. ANNALS. (Text in English, French, German, Spanish) 1962. a. exchange basis. Narodni Muzeum, Naprstkovo Muzeum Asijskych, Africkych a Americkych Kultur, Betlemske nam. 1, 110 00 Prague 1, Czechoslovakia. Ed. Libuse Bohackova.

301.2 398   CS
NAPRSTKOVO MUZEUM ASIJSKYCH, AFRICKYCH A AMERICKYCH KULTUR. ANTHROPOLOGICAL PAPERS. (Text in English, French, German, Spanish) 1970. irreg. exchange basis. Narodni Muzeum, Naprstkovo Muzeum Asijskych, Africkych a Americkych Kultur, Betlemske nam. 1, 110 00 Prague 1, Czechoslovakia. Ed. E. Strouhal.

570   PH   ISSN 0076-3772
NATIONAL MUSEUM OF THE PHILIPPINES. MONOGRAPH SERIES. (Text in English) 1970. irreg. $7.50. National Museum of the Philippines, Rizal Park, Manila, Philippines. Ed. Rosario B. Tantoco. circ. controlled.

570   HU   ISSN 0077-6599
NEPRAJZI ERTESITO/ETHNOGRAPHIC REVIEW. (Text in Hungarian; summaries in English, French, German, Russian) 1900. a. exchange basis. Neprajzi Muzeum, Kossuth Lajos ter 12, 1055 Budapest, Hungary.

390   HU   ISSN 0028-2774
NEPRAJZI KOZLEMENYEK. (Text in Hungarian; summaries in English & Russian) 1956. a. exchange basis. Neprajzi Muzeum, Kossuth Lajos ter 12, 1055 Budapest, Hungary. bk. rev.

570 301.2   HU   ISSN 0077-6602
NEPRAJZI TANULMANYOK. 1968. irreg. price varies. (Magyar Tudomanyos Akademia, Neprajzi Kutato Csoport) Akademiai Kiado, Publishing House of the Hungarian Academy of Sciences, P.O. Box 24, H-1363 Budapest, Hungary.

572   US   ISSN 0077-7897
NEVADA. STATE MUSEUM, CARSON CITY. ANTHROPOLOGICAL PAPERS. 1959. irreg., no. 17, 1980. price varies. ‡ Nevada State Museum, Carson City, NV 89701. Indexed: Abstr.Anthropol.

301   NO   ISSN 0489-2089
NORSK ETNOLOGISK GRANSKING. SMAASKRIFTER. 1953. irreg. no. 9, 1974. price varies. Norsk Folkemuseum, Bygdoey, Oslo 2, Norway.

572   NO   ISSN 0029-3601
NORVEG; journal of Nordic ethnology. (Text in Norwegian, English and German) a. Kr.80($16) Universitetsforlaget, Kolstadgt. 1, Box 2959-Toeyen, Oslo 6, Norway (U.S. address: Box 258, Irvington-on-Hudson, NY 10533) Ed. Bjarne Hodne. circ. 700.

572   US   ISSN 0078-2041
NOTES IN ANTHROPOLOGY. 1951. irreg., 1969, vol. XIII. price varies. Florida State University, Department of Anthropology, Tallahassee, FL 32306. Ed. Hale G. Smith.

572   US   ISSN 0078-3005
OCCASIONAL PAPERS IN ANTHROPOLOGY. 1968. irreg., no. 11, 1979. Pennsylvania State University, Department of Anthropology, 409 Social Sciences Bldg., University Park, PA 16802. circ. 500. Indexed: SSCI.

572   AT
OCCASIONAL PAPERS IN ANTHROPOLOGY. 1973. irreg., no. 9, 1980. Aus.$4. University of Queensland, Anthropology Museum, St. Lucia, Qld. 4067, Australia. Ed. Dr. Peter K. Lauer. circ. 300.

301.2   US
OCCASIONAL PUBLICATIONS IN NORTHEASTERN ANTHROPOLOGY. 1976. irreg., latest, no. 7. price varies. Franklin Pierce College, Department of Anthropology, Rindge, NH 03461. Ed. Howard R. Sargent. bibl. illus.

301.2   GH
ODAWURU IN SERIES. 1968. a. price varies. University of Ghana, Institute of African Studies, Box 73, Legon, Ghana.

OESTERREICHISCHE VOLKSKUNDLICHE BIBLIOGRAPHIE. see *FOLKLORE*

OESTERREICHISCHES MUSEUM FUER VOLKSKUNDE: VEROEFFENTLICHUNGEN. see *FOLKLORE*

572   US   ISSN 0078-432X
OKLAHOMA ANTHROPOLOGICAL SOCIETY. BULLETIN. 1953. a. membership. Oklahoma Anthropological Society, c/o Rose King, Corres. Sec., 1000 Horn St., Muskogee, OK 74401. circ. 500. Indexed: Abstr.Anthropol.

572   US   ISSN 0474-0696
OKLAHOMA ANTHROPOLOGICAL SOCIETY. MEMOIR. 1964. irreg. price varies. Oklahoma Anthropological Society, c/o Rose King, Corres. Sec., 1000 Horn St., Muskogee, OK 74401. circ. 500. Indexed: Abstr.Anthropol.

572   NZ   ISSN 0474-8603
OTAGO MUSEUM. RECORDS. ANTHROPOLOGY. 1964. irreg., no. 6, 1972. Otago Museum Trust Board, Great King St., Dunedin, New Zealand. bibl. illus.

301.2
OXFORD MONOGRAPHS ON SOCIAL ANTHROPOLOGY. irreg. price varies. Oxford University Press, 200 Madison Ave., New York, NY 10016 (And Ely House, 37 Dover St., London W1X 4AH, England) Ed. E. Ardener.

P. E. I. COMMUNITY STUDIES. (Prince Edward Island) see *SOCIOLOGY*

572   US   ISSN 0078-740X
PACIFIC ANTHROPOLOGICAL RECORDS. 1968. irreg. price varies. (Bernice Pauahi Bishop Museum, Department of Anthropology) Bishop Museum Press, Box 19000-A, Honolulu, HI 96819.

572   GW   ISSN 0078-7809
PAIDEUMA; Mitteilungen zur Kulturkunde. (Text in English, French, German) 1938. a. DM.48. (Universitaet Frankfurt, Frobenius Institut) Franz Steiner Verlag GmbH, Friedrichstr. 24, Postfach 5529, 6200 Wiesbaden, W. Germany (B.R.D.) Ed. Eike Haberland. adv. illus. circ. 860. (back issues avail.)

573   PE
PALEOBIOLOGIA. 1976. irreg. S/200($4) Museo Nacional de Antropologia y Arqueologia, Plaza Bolivar s/n Pueblo Libre, Lima, Peru.

572 581 410   PH
PANAMIN FOUNDATION RESEARCH SERIES. no. 2, 1976. irreg. Panamin Foundation, Makati, Rizal, Philippines. Ed. D. E. Yen. illus.

572   US   ISSN 0078-9054
PAPERS IN ANTHROPOLOGY. 1958. irreg., no. 15, 1966, no. 17, 1974. price varies. Museum of New Mexico Press, Box 2087, Santa Fe, NM 87503. circ. 1,000-2,000.

570   US
PENNSYLVANIA. HISTORICAL AND MUSEUM COMMISSION. ANTHROPOLOGICAL SERIES. 1971. irreg., latest issue no. 5. Historical and Museum Commission, Box 1026, Harrisburg, PA 17120. Ed. Barry Kent, Harold Myers.

PEOPLES OF EAST AFRICA. see *HISTORY — History Of Africa*

301.2   US
PERGAMON FRONTIERS IN ANTHROPOLOGY SERIES. irreg., vol.4,1976. price varies. Pergamon Press, Inc., Maxwell House, Fairview Park, Elmsford, NY 10523.

572   PE
PERU INDIGENA. (Publ. Suspended 1961-1967) 1948. irreg (aprox. 2/yr) Instituto Indigenista Peruano, Avda. Salaverry, Lima, Peru.

572   BL   ISSN 0553-8467
PESQUISAS: PUBLICACOES DE ANTROPOLOGIA. (Numbering is in continuation of articles published in Pesquisas) no. 6, 1960. irreg. price varies (or exchange) (Universidade do Vale do Rio dos Sinos, Instituto Anchietano de Pesquisas) Unisinos, Praca Tiradentes, 35, Sao Leopoldo RS, Brazil.
Supersedes in Part: Pesquisas.

572   VC
PONTIFICO MUSEO MISSIONARIO ETNOLOGICO. ANNALI. 1937. a. Pontificio Museo Missionario Etnologico, Citta del Vaticano, Rome, Italy. bibl.
Formerly: Annali Lateranensi (1937-1962)

572 301.2   PL
PRACE ETNOLOGICZNE. (Text in Polish; summaries in English and French) 1947. irreg. price varies. Polskie Towarzystwo Ludoznawcze, Szewka 36, 50-139 Wroclaw, Poland (Dist. by Ars Polona-Ruch, Krakowskie Przedmiescie 7, Warsaw, Poland) index. circ. 1,800.

301.2   PL   ISSN 0079-4759
PRACE I MATERIALY ETNOGRAFICZNE. (Text in Polish; summaries in English) 1934. irreg. price varies. Polskie Towarzystwo Ludoznawcze, Szewska 36, 50-139 Wroclaw, Poland (Dist. by Ars Polona-Ruch, Krakowskie Przedmiescie 7, Warsaw, Poland) index. circ. 3,000.

572   AU   ISSN 0032-6534
PRAEHISTORISCHE FORSCHUNGEN. 1950. irreg. price varies. Anthropologische Gesellschaft in Wien, Burgring 7, A-1014 Vienna, Austria. charts. illus. stat. circ. 600.

573 GW ISSN 0343-3528
PRIMATE REPORT. irreg. price varies. Verlag Erich Goltze GmbH und Co. KG, Stresemannstr. 28, 3400 Goettingen, W. Germany (B.R.D.) Ed. A. Spiegel.

572 US
QUEENS COLLEGE PUBLICATIONS IN ANTHROPOLOGY. 1975. a. price varies. Queens College Press, Flushing, NY 11367. Ed. Gloria Levitas. circ. 500. (back issues avail.)

572 573 UN ISSN 0501-3615
RACE QUESTION IN MODERN SCIENCE. 1951. irreg. Unesco Press, 7 Place de Fontenoy, F-75700 Paris, France (Dist. in U.S. by: Unipub, 345 Park Ave. S., New York, NY 10010)

572 SA ISSN 0079-9815
RAYMOND DART LECTURE. 1964. a. price varies. (Institute for the Study of Man in Africa) Witwatersrand University Press, Jan Smuts Ave., Johannesburg 2001, South Africa. (Co-sponsor: Museum of Man and Science, Johannesburg) Ed. N.J. Pines. circ. 1,000.

572 960 UV ISSN 0486-1426
RECHERCHES VOLTAIQUES; collection de travaux de sciences humaines sur la Haute-Volta. 1965. irreg. Centre National de la Recherche Scientifique et Technique, B.P. 7047, Ouagadougou, Upper Volta. (Co-sponsor: Centre National de la Recherche Scientifique, Paris) charts. illus.

330 572 US ISSN 0190-1281
RESEARCH IN ECONOMIC ANTHROPOLOGY; an annual compilation of research. 1978. a. $18.75 to individuals; institutions $37.50. J A I Press, Box 1678, 165 W. Putnam Ave., Greenwich, CT 06830. Ed. George Dalton.

301.2 US
RESOURCES FOR THE STUDY OF ANTHROPOLOGY. irreg. price varies. Houghton Mifflin Co., One Beacon St., Boston, MA 02107.

572 CK
REVISTA COLOMBIANA DE ANTROPOLOGIA. a. exchange basis. Instituto Colombiano de Antropologia, Apdo. Nacional 407, Bogota, Colombia. circ. 2,000.

570 BL ISSN 0034-7701
REVISTA DE ANTROPOLOGIA. 1953. a. $3. (Associacao Brasileira de Antropologia) Universidade de Sao Paulo, Faculdade de Filosofia, Letras e Ciencias Humanas, Caixa Postal 5459, Sao Paulo, Brazil. Ed. Egon Schaden. bk. rev. circ. 800.

572 AG
REVISTA DEL MUSEO AMERICANISTA. 1969. a. Museo Americanista de Antropologia, Historia, Numismatica y Ciencias Naturales, Manuel Castro 254, Lomas de Zamora, Buenos Aires, Argentina.

301.2 NE
RIJKSUNIVERSITEIT TE LEIDEN. INSTITUUT VOOR CULTURELE ANTROPOLOGIE EN SOCIOLOGIE DER NIET-WESTERSE VOLKEN. PUBLICATIE. vol. 11, 1975. irreg. price varies. Rijksuniversiteit te Leiden, Instituut voor Culterele Antropologie en Sociologie der Niet-Westerse Volken, Leiden, Netherlands.

572 975 US ISSN 0271-6925
RIPLEY P. BULLEN MONOGRAPHS IN ANTHROPOLOGY AND HISTORY. 1978. irreg. price varies. (Florida State Museum) University Presses of Florida, 15 N.W. 15th St., Gainesville, FL 32603. Ed. Jerald T. Milanich. (back issues avail.)

572 IT ISSN 0085-5723
RIVISTA DI ANTROPOLOGIA.* (Text in Italian; summaries in English and French) 1893. a. $15. Istituto Italiano di Antropologia, Citta Universitaria, Rome, Italy. Ed. Venerando Correnti. (back issues avail.)

572 CN ISSN 0316-1277
ROYAL ONTARIO MUSEUM. ETHNOGRAPHY MONOGRAPH. 1973. irreg. price varies. Royal Ontario Museum, 100 Queen's Park, Toronto, Ont. M5S 2C6, Canada.

S. I. L. MUSEUM OF ANTHROPOLOGY PUBLICATION. (Summer Institute of Linguistics) see LINGUISTICS

929 948 NO ISSN 0581-4480
SAMISKE SAMLINGER. (Numbers not issued in consecutive order) 1952. irreg., latest 1976. price varies. Norsk Folkemuseum, Bygdoey, Oslo 2, Norway.

572 US ISSN 0080-5890
SAN DIEGO. MUSEUM OF MAN. ETHNIC TECHNOLOGY NOTES. 1967. irreg., no. 15, 1975. $1.50-2. San Diego Museum of Man, Balboa Park, San Diego, CA 92101.

572 US ISSN 0080-5904
SAN DIEGO. MUSEUM OF MAN. PAPERS. 1929. irreg., no. 13, 1977. $2.25-4. San Diego Museum of Man, Balboa Park, San Diego, CA 92101. Ed. Dr. Spencer L. Rogers. index.

301.2 338.1 SW
SCANDINAVIAN INSTITUTE OF AFRICAN STUDIES. RURAL DEVELOPMENT. Short title: Rural Development Series. irreg. (Nordiska Afrikainstitutet - Scandinavian Institute of African Studies) Almqvist and Wiksell International, Box 62, S-101 20 Stockholm, Sweden (Dist. in U.S. by: Africana Publishing Company, 101 Fifth Ave., New York, NY 10003)

SCOTTISH STUDIES. see HISTORY — History Of Europe

572 914.606 SP
SEMANA INTERNACIONAL DE ANTROPOLOGIA VASCA. ACTAS. irreg. Gran Enciclopedia Vasca, Apdo. 1510, Calzadas de Mallona 8, Bilbao 6, Spain. Basque

SERIES ON CONTEMPORARY JAVANESE LIFE. see FOLKLORE

572 JA
SHAKAI-JINRUIGAKU NENPO. (Text in Japanese) 1975. a. (Tokyo Metropolitan University, Shakai-jinruigakkai) Kobundo, 1-7-13 Kanda Surugadai, Chiyoda-ku, Tokyo, Japan.

SLOVACI V ZAHRANICI. see HISTORY — History Of Europe

572 YU
SLOVENSKI ETNOGRAF. (Text in Slovenian; summaries in English, French, German) 1948. a. $15. Slovenski Etnografski Muzej, Presernova cesta 20, Ljubljana, Yugoslavia. bk. rev. circ. 1,000.

572 US ISSN 0081-0223
SMITHSONIAN CONTRIBUTIONS TO ANTHROPOLOGY. 1965. irreg. Smithsonian Institution Press, Washington, DC 20560. Ed. Albert L. Ruffin Jr. circ. 2,100. (reprint service avail. from UMI)

572 911 NE ISSN 0081-0398
SOCIAAL-GEOGRAFISCHE STUDIEN. 1955. irreg., no. 13, 1974. price varies. Van Gorcum, Box 43, Assen, Netherlands. Ed. A. C. De Vooys.

SOCIETE D'ETUDES LINGUISTIQUES ET ANTHROPOLOGIQUES DE FRANCE. NUMERO SPECIAL. see LINGUISTICS

SOCIETE DES EXPLORATEURS ET DES VOYAGEURS FRANCAIS. ANNUAIRE GENERAL. see GEOGRAPHY

301.2 BE
SOCIETE ROYALE BELGE D'ANTHROPOLOGIE ET DE PREHISTOIRE. BULLETIN. (Text in English or French; summaries in English and French) a. 450 Fr. to individuals; 300 Fr. to libraries. Societe Royale Belge d'Anthropologie et de Prehistoire, 31 rue Vautier, 1040 Brussels, Belgium. illus.

SOCIETE SUISSE DES AMERICANISTES.BULLETIN/ SCHWEIZERISCHE AMERIKANISTEN-GESELLSCHAFT. BULLETIN. see HISTORY — History Of North And South America

572 US ISSN 0583-8916
SOCIETY FOR APPLIED ANTHROPOLOGY. MONOGRAPHS. 1959. irreg., no. 11, 1972. price varies. Society for Applied Anthropology, c/o American Anthropological Associaton, 1703 New Hampshire Ave. N.W., Washington, DC 20009.

SOCIOLOGICAL OBSERVATIONS. see SOCIOLOGY

SOLOMON ISLANDS MUSEUM ASSOCIATION. JOURNAL. see MUSEUMS AND ART GALLERIES

572 US ISSN 0081-2994
SOUTHERN ANTHROPOLOGICAL SOCIETY. PROCEEDINGS. 1968. a. price varies. University of Georgia Press, Athens, GA 30602.

572 II
SPECTRA OF ANTHROPOLOGICAL PROGRESS. (Text in English) 1978. irreg. Rs.25($6) University of Delhi, Department of Anthropology, Delhi 110007, India.

572 YU
SRPSKA AKADEMIJA NAUKA I UMETNOSTI. ETNOGRAFSKI INSTITUT. GLASNIK. (Text in Serbocroatian; summaries in Russian, German, English, French) 1894. irreg. Srpska Akademija Nauka i Umetnosti, Etnografski Institut, Vuka Karadzica 5, Belgrade, Yugoslavia. bk. rev. bibl.

572 YU
SRPSKA AKADEMIJA NAUKA I UMETNOSTI. ETNOGRAFSKI INSTITUT. ZBORNIK RADOVA. vol. 6, 1973. irreg. Srpska Akademija Nauka i Umetnosti, Etnografski Institut, Vuka Karadzica 5, Belgrade, Yugoslavia.

572 301.2 YU ISSN 0081-4067
SRPSKI ETNOGRAFSKI ZBORNIK. NASELJA I POREKLO STANOVNISTVA. (Text in Serbo-Croatian; summaries in French, English, Russian or German) 1902. irreg. price varies. Srpska Akademija Nauka i Umetnosti, Knez Mihailova 35, 11001 Belgrade, Yugoslavia (Dist. by: Prosveta, Terazije 16, Belgrade, Yugoslavia) circ. 600.

572 301.2 390 YU ISSN 0081-4075
SRPSKI ETNOGRAFSKI ZBORNIK. RASPRAVE I GRADJA. (Text in Serbo-Croatian; summaries in French, English, Russian or German) 1934. irreg. price varies. Srpska Akademija Nauka i Umetnosti, Knez Mihailova 35, 11001 Belgrade, Yugoslavia (Dist. by: Prosveta, Terazije 16, Belgrade, Yugoslavia) circ. 600.

572 301.2 390 YU ISSN 0081-4083
SRPSKI ETNOGRAFSKI ZBORNIK. SRPSKE NARODNE UMOTVORINE. (Text in Serbo-Croatian; summaries in French, English, Russian or German) 1927. irreg. price varies. Srpska Akademija Nauka i Umetnosti, Knez Mihailova 35, 11001 Belgrade, Yugoslavia (Dist. by: Prosveta, Terazije 16, Belgrade, Yugoslavia) circ. 600.

572 390 YU ISSN 0081-4091
SRPSKI ETNOGRAFSKI ZBORNIK. ZIVOT I OBICAJI NARODNI. (Text in Serbo-Croatian; summaries in French, English, Russian or German) 1894. irreg. price varies. Srpska Akademija Nauka i Umetnosti, Knez Mihailova 35, 11001 Belgrade, Yugoslavia (Dist. by: Prosveta, Terazije 16, Belgrade, Yugoslavia) circ. 600.

STAATLICHES MUSEUM FUER VOELKERKUNDE DRESDEN. ABHANDLUNGEN UND BERICHTE. see MUSEUMS AND ART GALLERIES

572 SW ISSN 0491-2705
STUDIA ETHNOGRAPHICA UPSALIENSIA. 1956. a. (Uppsala Universitet, Institutionen foer Allmaem och Jaemfoerande Etnografi) Almqvist & Wiksell International, Box 62, S-101 20 Stockholm, Sweden.

572 GW
STUDIA ETHNOLOGICA. 1970. irreg., no. 9, 1977. price varies. Verlag Anton Hain GmbH, Adelheidstr. 2, Postfach 1220, 6240 Koenigstein, W. Germany (B.R.D.) Ed. Bd.

572 SW
STUDIA ETHNOLOGICA UPSALIENSIA. 1976. irreg. price varies. (Universitet i Uppsala) Almqvist and Wiksell International, Box 62, S-101 20 Stockholm, Sweden.

572   FI   ISSN 0085-6835
STUDIA FENNICA: REVUE DE LINGUISTIQUE ET D'ETHNOLOGIE FINNOISES. (Text in German, English or French) 1933. irreg., no. 22, 1978. price varies. Suomalaisen Kirjallisuuden Seura - Finnish Literature Society, Hallituskatu 1, 00170 Helsinki 17, Finland. adv. bibl. circ. 1,000. Indexed: M.L.A.

572   SZ
STUDIA INSTITUTI ANTHROPOS. 1950. irreg., no. 34, 1977. price varies. (Anthropos Institut) Editions Saint-Paul, Perolles 36, CH-1700 Fribourg, Switzerland. illus.

572   US   ISSN 0585-5578
STUDIA SUMIRO-HUNGARICA. (Text in English and Hungarian) 1968. irreg., vol. 3, 1974. Gilgamesh Publishing Co., 6050 Boulevard East, 20-A, West New York, NJ 07093. Ed. Miklos Erdy. bibl. charts. illus. circ. 2,000.

572   GW   ISSN 0170-3544
STUDIEN ZUR KULTURKUNDE. (Text in English, French, and German) irreg., vol. 58, 1981. price varies. (Universitaet Frankfurt, Frobenius-Institut) Franz Steiner Verlag GmbH, Friedrichstr. 24, Postfach 5529, 6200 Wiesbaden, W. Germany (B.R.D.) Ed. Eike Haberland.

301.2   US   ISSN 0585-6523
STUDIES IN ANTHROPOLOGICAL METHOD. irreg. price varies. Holt, Rinehart and Winston, 383 Madison Ave., New York, NY 10017.

572   US   ISSN 0085-6843
STUDIES IN ANTHROPOLOGY. irreg, no. 13, 1970. price varies. University Press of Kentucky, Lexington, KY 40506. (also avail. in microform from UMI)

301.2   NE
STUDIES IN ANTHROPOLOGY. 1974. irreg. price varies. Mouton Publishers, Noordeinde 41, 2514 GC The Hague, Netherlands (U.S. addr: Mouton Publishers, c/o Walter de Gruyter, Inc., 200 Saw Mill River Road, Hawthorne, NY 10532)

301.2   US
STUDIES IN ANTHROPOLOGY. 1973. irreg. price varies. Academic Press, Inc., 111 Fifth Ave., New York, NY 10003. Ed. Eugene A. Hammel.

572   NE
STUDIES IN EUROPEAN SOCIETY. 1973. irreg. price varies. Mouton Publishers, Noordeinde 41, 2514 GC The Hague, Netherlands (U.S. addr: Mouton Publishers, c/o Walter de Gruyter, Inc., 200 Saw Mill River Road, Hawthorne, NY 10532) Ed. John Friedl.

398   NE
STUDIES IN FOLKLORE. 1973. irreg. price varies. Mouton Publishers, Noordeinde 41, 2514 GC The Hague, Netherlands (U.S. addr: Mouton Publishers, c/o Walter de Gruyter, Inc., 200 Saw Mill River Road, Hawthorne, NY 10532)

572   NE   ISSN 0081-7953
STUDIES IN GENERAL ANTHROPOLOGY. 1963. irreg. price varies. Mouton Publishers, Noordeinde 41, 2514 GC The Hague, Netherlands (U.S. addr: Mouton Publishers, c/o Walter de Gruyter, Inc., 200 Saw Mill River Road, Hawthorne, NY 10532)

572 301   NE   ISSN 0081-8496
STUDIES IN SOCIAL ANTHROPOLOGY. 1966. irreg. price varies. Mouton Publishers, Noordeinde 41, 2514 GC The Hague, Netherlands (U.S. addr: Mouton Publishers, c/o Walter de Gruyter, Inc., 200 Saw Mill River Road, Hawthorne, NY 10532)

301.2 572   SJ   ISSN 0562-5130
SUDAN SOCIETY/AL-MUJTAMA. (Text in Arabic and English) 1962. a. University of Khartoum, Social Studies Society, Faculty of Economic and Social Studies, Box 321, Khartoum, Sudan.

991.4   PH
SULU STUDIES. (Text and summaries in English) 1972. a. P.18($4) Notre Dame of Jolo College, Jolo, Sulu 7601, Philippines (Orders to: Philippine Social Science Council, Box 655, Greenhills, Rizal 3113, Philippines) Ed. Gerard Rixhon. abstr. charts. illus. circ. 1,000.

SUOMALAIS-UGRILAISEN SEURA. AIKAKAUSKIRJA/SOCIETE FINNO-OUGRIENNE. JOURNAL. see LINGUISTICS

572   UK
SUSSEX ESSAYS IN ANTHROPOLOGY. irreg. £1.20 for 3 nos. c/o Dr. Brian V. Street, University of Sussex, School of Social Studies, Falmer, Brighton, England. Ed.Bd.

TEBIWA MISCELLANEOUS PAPERS. see SCIENCES: COMPREHENSIVE WORKS

572   US
TENNESSEE ANTHROPOLOGICAL ASSOCIATION. MISCELLANEOUS PAPER. 1976. irreg. Tennessee Anthropological Association, Dept. of Anthropology, University of Tennessee, Knoxville, TN 37916.

572   US
THEATA. 1973. a. $2.95. University of Alaska, Student Orientation Services, Fairbanks, AK 99701.

572   RM
TIBISCUS. SERIA ETNOGRAFIE. (Text in Romanian; Summaries in German) a. Muzeul Banatului, Piata Huniade Nr. 1, Timisoara, Romania.

572   NO   ISSN 0332-5997
TRADISJON; tidsskrift for folkeminnevitenskap. 1971. a. Kr.60($12) Universitetsforlaget, Kolstadgt. 1, Box 2959-Toeyen, Oslo 6, Norway (U. S. address: Box 258, Irvington-on-Hudson, NY 10533) Ed. Reimund Kvideland. circ. 800.

911   GW   ISSN 0082-6413
TRIBUS. (Text in German; occasionally in English) 1951. a. DM.39. Linden-Museum Stuttgart-Staatliches Museum fuer Voelkerkunde, Hegelplatz 1, 7000 Stuttgart 1, W. Germany (B.R.D.) Ed. Axel Schulze-Thulin. adv. bk. rev. circ. 600(controlled)

UEBERSEE-MUSEUM, BREMEN. VEROEFFENTLICHUNGEN. REIHE B: VOELKERKUNDE. see FOLKLORE

572   GW   ISSN 0341-9274
UEBERSEE-MUSEUM, BREMEN. VEROEFFENTLICHUNGEN. REIHE D: VOELKERKUNDLICHE MONOGRAPHIEN. 1976. irreg., vol. 6, 1979. price varies. Uebersee-Museum, Bremen, Bahnhofsplatz 13, 2800 Bremen, W. Germany(B.R.D.) Ed. Herbert Ganslmayr.

572 913.031   CU
UNIVERSIDAD DE LA HABANA. CENTRO DE INFORMACION CIENTIFICAS Y TECNICA. CIENCIAS. SERIE 9. ANTROPOLOGIA Y PREHISTORIA. 1972. irreg. exchange. Universidad de la Habana, Centro de Informacion Cientifica y Tecnica, Havana, Cuba. Ed. Ramon Dacal Moure.

572   UY
UNIVERSIDAD DE LA REPUBLICA. FACULTAD DE HUMANIDADES Y CIENCIAS. REVISTA. SERIE CIENCIAS ANTROPOLOGICAS. N.S. 1979. irreg. Universidad de la Republica, Facultad de Humanidades y Ciencias, Seccion Revista, Tristan Narvaja 1674, Montevideo, Uruguay. Dir. Beatriz Martinez Osorio.
   Supersedes in part: Universidad de la Republica. Facultad de Humanidades. Revista.

572   SP   ISSN 0080-9101
UNIVERSIDAD DE SEVILLA. SEMINARIO DE ANTROPOLOGIA AMERICANA. PUBLICACIONES. 1960. irreg. price varies. Universidad de Sevilla, San Fernando 4, Seville, Spain. Ed. Alfredo Jimenez-Nunez.

572   MX   ISSN 0076-7263
UNIVERSIDAD NACIONAL AUTONOMA DE MEXICO. INSTITUTO DE INVESTIGACIONES ANTROPOLOGICAS. CUADERNOS SERIE ANTROPOLOGICA. 1962. irreg. 1969, no. 23. price varies. Universidad Nacional Autonoma de Mexico, Instituto de Investigaciones Antropologicas, Departamento de Distribucion de Libros Universitarias, Insurgentes sur, 299, Mexico 11, D.F., Mexico.

572   MX   ISSN 0076-7298
UNIVERSIDAD NACIONAL AUTONOMA DE MEXICO. INSTITUTO DE INVESTIGACIONES ANTROPOLIGICAS. SERIE ANTROPOLOGICA. 1944. irreg., 1969, no. 11. price varies. Universidad Nacional Autonoma de Mexico, Instituto de Investigaciones Antropologicas, Departamento de Distribucion de Libros Universitarias, Insurgentes sur, 299, Mexico 11, D.F., Mexico.

301.2   PE
UNIVERSIDAD NACIONAL DEL CENTRO DEL PERU. CUADERNOS UNIVERSITARIOS. SERIE: ESTUDIOS ANDINOS DEL CENTRO. (Numbers Not issued consecutively) no. 4, 1978. irreg. Universidad Nacional del Centro del Peru, Departamento de Publicaciones, Calle Puno 635, Huancayo, Peru.

572   BL
UNIVERSIDADE DE SAO PAULO. MUSEU PAULISTA. COLECAO. SERIE DE ETNOLOGIA. 1975. a. Universidade de Sao Paulo, Museu Paulista, Caixa Postal 42.503, Parque da Independencia, 04263 Sao Paulo, Brazil. Ed. Setembrino Petri.
   Supersedes in part (since 1975): Museu Paulista. Colecao (ISSN 0080-6382)

572   BL   ISSN 0080-6390
UNIVERSIDADE DE SAO PAULO. MUSEU PAULISTA. REVISTA. (Text in Portuguese; summaries in English) 1895; N.S. 1947. a. Universidade de Sao Paulo, Museu Paulista, C. P. 42503, 04263 Sao Paulo-SP, Brazil.

572   BL   ISSN 0581-6076
UNIVERSIDADE FEDERAL DE SANTA CATARINA. MUSEU DE ANTROPOLOGIA. ANAIS. 1968. irreg. free or exchange basis. ‡ Universidade Federal de Santa Catarina, Museu de Antropologia, Cx. Postal 476, Campus Universitario, Trindade, 88000 Florianopolis, S.C., Brazil. Ed. Anamaria Beck. bk. rev. bibl. charts. illus. circ. a.

572   GW   ISSN 0170-3099
UNIVERSITAET FRANKFURT. SEMINAR FUER VOELKERKUNDE. ARBEITEN. irreg., vol. 11, 1981. price varies. Franz Steiner Verlag GmbH, Friedrichstr. 24, Postfach 5529, 6200 Wiesbaden, W. Germany (B.R.D.)

301   IV
UNIVERSITE NATIONALE DE COTE D'IVOIRE. ANNALES. SERIE F: ETHNOSOCIOLOGIE. 1969. irreg, vol. 5, 1973. price varies. Universite Nationale de Cote d'Ivoire, Institut d'Ethnosociologie, c/o Bibliotheque Universitaire, B.P. 8859, Abidjan, Ivory Coast. bk. rev. bibl. charts. illus. circ. 1,000.
   Formerly: Universite d'Abidjan. Annales. Serie F: Ethnosociologie.

572   US   ISSN 0066-7501
UNIVERSITY OF ARIZONA. ANTHROPOLOGICAL PAPERS. 1959. irreg., no. 36, 1980. price varies. (University of Arizona, Department of Anthropology) University of Arizona Press, Box 3398, Tucson, AZ 85722.

UNIVERSITY OF CALIFORNIA, BERKELEY. LANGUAGE BEHAVIOR RESEARCH LABORATORY. MONOGRAPH SERIES. see LINGUISTICS

UNIVERSITY OF CALIFORNIA, BERKELEY, LANGUAGE BEHAVIOR RESEARCH LABORATORY, WORKING PAPER SERIES. see LINGUISTICS

572   US   ISSN 0068-6336
UNIVERSITY OF CALIFORNIA PUBLICATIONS. ANTHROPOLOGICAL RECORDS. 1937. irreg. price varies. University of California Press, 2223 Fulton St., Berkeley, CA 94720.

572   US   ISSN 0068-6379
UNIVERSITY OF CALIFORNIA PUBLICATIONS IN ANTHROPOLOGY. 1937. irreg. price varies. University of California Press, 2223 Fulton St., Berkeley, CA 94720.

572 US
UNIVERSITY OF CHICAGO STUDIES IN ANTHROPOLOGY. SERIES IN SOCIAL, CULTURAL, AND LINGUISTIC ANTHROPOLOGY. 1975. irreg. $6. University of Chicago, Department of Anthropology, 1126 E. 59th St., Chicago, IL 60637.

301.2 GH ISSN 0533-8646
UNIVERSITY OF GHANA. INSTITUTE OF AFRICAN STUDIES. LOCAL STUDIES SERIES. irreg. price varies. University of Ghana, Institute of African Studies, Box 73, Legon, Ghana.

572 US
UNIVERSITY OF IDAHO. DEPARTMENT OF SOCIOLOGY/ANTHROPOLOGY. ANTHROPOLOGICAL MONOGRAPHS. 1970. irreg., latest no. 4. price varies. (University of Idaho, Department of Sociology-Anthropology) University Press of Idaho, Moscow, ID 83843. Ed. Roderick Sprague. Indexed: Abstr.Anthropol.

572 US ISSN 0085-2457
UNIVERSITY OF KANSAS. DEPARTMENT OF ANTHROPOLOGY. PUBLICATIONS IN ANTHROPOLOGY. 1969. irreg., no. 11, 1979. price varies. ‡ University of Kansas, Department of Anthropology, c/o Exchange and Gifts Dept., Lawrence, KS 66045. Ed. Robert Jerome Smith. circ. 1,000. Key Title: University of Kansas Publications in Anthropology.

572 913.031 410 CN
UNIVERSITY OF MANITOBA ANTHROPOLOGY PAPERS. 1973. irreg. price varies. University of Manitoba, Department of Anthropology, Winnipeg, Manitoba R3T 2N2, Canada. Ed.Bd. circ. 50-200.

572 US ISSN 0076-5066
UNIVERSITY OF MASSACHUSETTS. DEPARTMENT OF ANTHROPOLOGY. RESEARCH REPORTS. 1968. irreg., no. 17, 1977. price varies. ‡ University of Massachusetts, Department of Anthropology, Amherst, MA 01003. Ed. H. Martin Wobst. adv. circ. 750-1,000.

572 US ISSN 0076-8367
UNIVERSITY OF MICHIGAN. MUSEUM OF ANTHROPOLOGY. ANTHROPOLOGICAL PAPERS. 1949. irreg., no. 65, 1978. price varies. University of Michigan, Museum of Anthropology, University Museums Building, Ann Arbor, MI 48109. (also avail. in microform from UMI)

572 US ISSN 0076-8375
UNIVERSITY OF MICHIGAN. MUSEUM OF ANTHROPOLOGY. MEMOIRS. 1969. irreg., no. 1978. price varies. University of Michigan, Museum of Anthropology, University Museums Building, Ann Arbor, MI 48109.

572 US
UNIVERSITY OF MICHIGAN. MUSEUM OF ANTHROPOLOGY. TECHNICAL REPORTS. 1971. irreg., no. 8, 1978. price varies. University of Michigan, Museum of Anthropology, Univ. Museum Bldg., Rm. 4009, Ann Arbor, MI 48109.

572 US
UNIVERSITY OF MISSOURI, COLUMBIA. MUSEUM OF ANTHROPOLOGY. ANNUAL REPORTS. 1975. a. price varies. University of Missouri-Columbia, Museum of Anthropology, 104 Swallow Hall, Columbia, MO 65211.

572 US ISSN 0580-6976
UNIVERSITY OF MISSOURI, COLUMBIA. MUSEUM OF ANTHROPOLOGY. MUSEUM BRIEFS. 1969. irreg., no. 24, 1978. price varies. ‡ University of Missouri-Columbia, Museum of Anthropology, 104 Swallow Hall, Columbia, MO 65211. Ed. Lawrence H. Feldman. Key Title: Museum Briefs.

572 917 US
UNIVERSITY OF MISSOURI MONOGRAPHS IN ANTHROPOLOGY. 1974. irreg., no. 4, 1978. price varies. University of Missouri-Columbia, Museum of Anthropology, 104 Swallow Hall, Columbia, MO 65201. Ed. Bd.

572 US ISSN 0077-118X
UNIVERSITY OF MONTANA. DEPARTMENT OF ANTHROPOLOGY. CONTRIBUTIONS TO ANTHROPOLOGY. irreg., 1973, nos. 3 & 4. irreg., no. 4, 1974. price varies. University of Montana, Department of Anthropology, Missoula, MT 59801. Ed. Susan R. Sharrock. circ. 300-500. Indexed: Abstr.Anthropol.

572 US ISSN 0085-1205
UNIVERSITY OF NORTHERN COLORADO. MUSEUM OF ANTHROPOLOGY. OCCASIONAL PUBLICATIONS IN ANTHROPOLOGY. ETHNOLOGY SERIES. 1967. irreg. price varies. University of Northern Colorado, Museum of Anthropology, Attn. George E. Fay, Ed., Greeley, CO 80639. circ. 800. (processed)

572 US ISSN 0085-1213
UNIVERSITY OF NORTHERN COLORADO. MUSEUM OF ANTHROPOLOGY. OCCASIONAL PUBLICATIONS IN ANTHROPOLOGY. MISCELLANEOUS SERIES. 1967. irreg. price varies. University of Northern Colorado, Museum of Anthropology, Attn. George E. Fay, Ed., Greeley, CO 80639. circ. 500. (processed)

572 US ISSN 0078-6071
UNIVERSITY OF OREGON ANTHROPOLOGICAL PAPERS. 1971. irreg., vol. 17, 1980. price varies. University of Oregon, Department of Anthropology, Eugene, OR 97403. Ed. C. Melvin Aikens. circ. 500.

UNIVERSITY OF SOUTH CAROLINA. INSTITUTE OF ARCHEOLOGY AND ANTHROPOLOGY. ANNUAL REPORT. see ARCHAEOLOGY

572 JA
UNIVERSITY OF TOKYO. FACULTY OF SCIENCE. JOURNAL. SECTION 5: ANTHROPOLOGY/TOKYO DAIGAKU RIGAKUBU KIYO, DAI-5-RUI, JINRUIGAKU. (Text in English) 1925. a. price varies. University of Tokyo, Faculty of Science - Tokyo Daigaku Rigakubu, 7-3-1 Hongo, Bunkyo-ku, Tokyo 113, Japan (Order from: Maruzen Co., Ltd., 2-3-10 Nihonbashi, Chuo-ku, Tokyo 103, Japan; or their Import and Export Department, Box 5050, Tokyo International, Tokyo 100-31, Japan) circ. 500.

572 US ISSN 0083-4947
UNIVERSITY OF UTAH ANTHROPOLOGICAL PAPERS. 1950. irreg., no. 98, 1978. price varies. University of Utah Press, Salt Lake City, UT 84112. Ed. Jesse D. Jennings.

572 390 301.2 CS ISSN 0083-4106
UNIVERZITA KOMENSKEHO. FILOZOFICKA FAKULTA. ZBORNIK: ETHNOLOGIA SLAVICA; an international review of Slavic ethnology. (Text and summaries in various languages) 1969. a. exchange basis. Univerzita Komenskeho, Filozoficka Fakulta, Gondova 2, 806 01 Bratislava, Czechoslovakia. Ed. Jan Podolak. bk. rev. circ. 1,075.

572 301.2 PL ISSN 0083-4327
UNIWERSYTET JAGIELLONSKI. ZESZYTY NAUKOWE. PRACE ETNOGRAFICZNE. 1963. irreg. price varies. ‡ Panstwowe Wydawnictwo Naukowe, Miodowa 10, Warsaw, Poland (Dist. by Ars Polona-Ruch, Krakowskie Przedmiescie 7, Warsaw, Poland) Ed. Jadwiga Klimazewska. index. circ. 600.

572 US
VANDERBILT UNIVERSITY. DEPARTMENT OF SOCIOLOGY AND ANTHROPOLOGY. PUBLICATIONS IN ANTHROPOLOGY. no. 20, 1978. irreg. price varies. Vanderbilt University, Department of Sociology and Anthropology, Box 1532-Station B, Nashville, TN 37235.

VEREIN FUER VOLKSKUNDE IN WIEN. SONDERSCHRIFTEN. see FOLKLORE

572 918 NE
VICUS CUADERNOS: ARQUEOLOGIA, ANTROPOLOGIA CULTURAL, ETNOLOGIA. (Text and summaries in English and Spanish) 1978. a. fl.60. John Benjamins B.V., Amsteldijk 44, Box 52519, 1007 HA Amsterdam, Netherlands. Ed. M. T. Blache. charts. illus. index. (back issues avail.)

572 CR
VINCULOS. (Text in English, Spanish) 1975. irreg. $4 or exchange basis. Museo Nacional de Costa Rica, Departamento de Antropologia e Historia, Apdo. 749, San Jose, Costa Rica. Ed.Bd. charts. illus.

301.2 GW ISSN 0073-0270
VOELKERKUNDLICHE ABHANDLUNGEN. 1964. irreg. price varies. (Niedersaechsisches Landesmuseum, Hannover) Dietrich Reimer Verlag, Unter den Eichen 57, 1000 Berlin 45, W. Germany (B.R.D.) Ed. Hans Becher. circ. 500.

572 AU
VOELKERKUNDLICHE VEROEFFENTLICHUNGEN. irreg. price varies. (Anthropologische Gesellschaft in Wien) Verlag Ferdinand Berger und Soehne OHG, Wienerstr. 21-23, A-3580 Horn, Austria. Ed. Paul Spindler.

572 US
WADSWORTH SERIES IN ANALYTIC ETHNOGRAPHY. irreg. Wadsworth Publishing Co., 10 Davis Dr., Belmont, CA 94002.

WEIMARER MONOGRAPHIEN ZUR UR- UND FRUEHGESCHICHTE. see ARCHAEOLOGY

572 US ISSN 0083-7997
WENNER-GREN FOUNDATION FOR ANTHROPOLOGICAL RESEARCH. REPORT. 1942. irreg., report for 1976-77 published Dec. 1979. free. ‡ Wenner-Gren Foundation for Anthropological Research, 1865 Broadway, New York, NY 10023. circ. 4,000. (also avail. in microfiche)

WIENER VOELKERKUNDLICHE MITTEILUNGEN. see FOLKLORE

572 US
YALE UNIVERSITY. DEPARTMENT OF ANTHROPOLOGY. PUBLICATIONS IN ANTHROPOLOGY. no. 76, 1976. irreg. Yale University, Department of Anthropology, 2114 Yale Station, CT 06520.

573 US ISSN 0096-848X
YEARBOOK OF PHYSICAL ANTHROPOLOGY (WASHINGTON) vol. 17, 1974. a. $6. American Association of Physical Anthropologists, 1703 New Hampshire Ave., NW., Washington, DC 20009. Ed. John Buettner-Janusch. circ. 2,000.

301.2 572 CN
YEARBOOK OF SYMBOLIC ANTHROPOLOGY. 1975. a. 8p. Universite Laval, Department de l'Anthropologie, Quebec, P.Q. G1K 7P4, Canada (Subscr. to: C. Hurst & Co., Seager Bldg., Brookmill Road, London S.E. 8, England) Ed. Erik Schulmmer.

YMER. see GEOGRAPHY

ZAMBIA. NATIONAL MUSEUMS BOARD. OCCASIONAL PAPER SERIES. see HISTORY — History Of Africa

ZEMALJSKI MUZEJ BOSNE I HERCEGOVINE. GLASNIK. ETNOLOGIJA. see FOLKLORE

ANTHROPOLOGY — Abstracting, Bibliographies, Statistics

572 BE
BIBLIOGRAPHIE ETHNOGRAPHIQUE DE L'AFRIQUE SUD-SAHARIENNE. 1925. a., latest 1980 (covers 1976) 990 Fr. Musee Royal de l'Afrique Centrale, 13 Steenweg op Leuven, B-1980 Tervuren, Belgium.
Formerly (until 1962): Bibliographie Ethnographique du Congo Belge et des Regions Avoisinantes.

291 301.2 GW ISSN 0067-706X
BIBLIOGRAPHIE ZUR SYMBOLIK, IKONOGRAPHIE UND MYTHOLOGIE. 1968. a. DM.40. Verlag Valentin Koerner, H.-Sielcken-Str. 36, Postfach 304, D-7570 Baden-Baden 1, W. Germany (B.R.D.) Eds. Manfred Lurker, Helmut Schneider. adv. bk. rev. circ. 1,000.

573　　　　　　　　US
FILMS: THE VISUALIZATION OF ANTHROPOLOGY. 1972. every 2-3 years. Pennsylvania State University, Audio-Visual Services, University Park, PA 16802. Ed. Lori A. Baldwin.

572 016　　　　　UK　ISSN 0085-2074
INTERNATIONAL BIBLIOGRAPHY OF THE SOCIAL SCIENCES. SOCIAL AND CULTURAL ANTHROPOLOGY. 1955. irreg., vol. 23, 1977. £32.50. Tavistock Publications Ltd., 11 New Fetter Lane, London EC4p 4EE, England (Dist. in U.S. by: Methuen Inc., 733 Third Ave., New York, N.Y. 10017) circ. 2,000.
　　Title page also reads: International Bibliography of Social and Cultural Anthropology.

572 016　　　　　NE　ISSN 0074-0462
KONINKLIJK INSTITUUT VOOR TAAL-, LAND- EN VOLKENKUNDE. BIBLIOGRAPHICAL SERIES. (Text in English) 1965. irreg. price varies. Martinus Nijhoff Booksellers, Box 269, 2501 AX The Hague, Netherlands.

301.2 016　　　　SW
SCANDINAVIAN AFRICANA. 1979. a. Nordiska Afrikainstitutet - Scandinavian Institute of African Studies, Box 2126, S-750 02 Uppsala, Sweden.

ARCHAEOLOGY

see also Paleontology

A A R P MONOGRAPHS. (Art and Archaeology Research Papers) see *ART*

913　　　　　　　NO　ISSN 0332-5202
A M S-SKRIFTER. (Text in Norwegian; summaries in English and German) 1976. irreg. Arkeologisk Museum i Stavanger, Box 478, 4001 Stavanger, Norway. Ed.Bd.
　　Formerly: Arkeologisk Museum i Stavanger.Skrifter.

913　　　　　　　NO　ISSN 0332-6411
A M S-SMAATRYKK. 1978. irreg. Arkeologisk Museum i Stavanger, Box 478, 4001 Stavanger, Norway.

913　　　　　　　NO　ISSN 0332-6306
A M S-VARIA. 1978. irreg. Arkeologisk Museum i Stavanger, Box 478, 4001 Stavanger, Norway. Ed.Bd.

ACADEMIA DE STIINTE SOCIALE SI POLITICE. INSTITUTUL DE ISTORIE SI ARHEOLOGIE CLUJ-NAPOCA. ANUARUL. see *HISTORY — History Of Europe*

ACADEMIE DES INSCRIPTIONS ET BELLES- LETTRES. ETUDES ET COMMENTAIRES. see *LINGUISTICS*

913　　　　　　　IT　ISSN 0065-0900
ACTA AD ARCHAEOLOGIAM ET ARTIUM HISTORIAM PERTINENTIA. (Text in language of contributor) 1962. irreg., vol. 8, 1978. L.150000. (Istituto di Norvegia in Roma) Giorgio Bretschneider, Ed. & Pub., Via Crescenzio 43, 00193. Italy. circ. 700.

913　　　　　　　SW　ISSN 0065-1001
ACTA ARCHAELOGICA LUNDENSIA: MONOGRAPHS OF LUNDS UNIVERSITETS HISTORISKA MUSEUM. SERIES IN 4. (Text in English and German) 1954. irreg., no. 11, 1977. price varies. C.W.K. Gleerup (Subsidiary of: LiberLaeromedel) Box 1205, S-221 05 Lund, Sweden. bk. rev.

571　　　　　　　SW　ISSN 0065-0994
ACTA ARCHAELOGICA LUNDENSIA: MONOGRAPHS OF LUNDS UNIVERSITETS HISTORISKA MUSEUM. SERIES IN 8. (Text in English, German and Swedish) 1957. irreg., no. 11, 1977. price varies. C.W.K. Gleerup (Subsidiary of: LiberLaeromedel) Box 1205, S-221 05 Lund, Sweden. Ed. Berta Stjernquist. bk. rev.

913　　　　　　　DK　ISSN 0065-101X
ACTA ARCHAEOLOGICA. (Text in English and German) a. Kr.240. Munksgaard, 35 Noerre Soegade, DK-1370 Copenhagen K, Denmark. Ed. C. F. Becker. adv. bk. rev. circ. 800. (reprint service avail. from ISI) Indexed: Curr.Cont.

913　　　　　　　PL　ISSN 0001-5229
ACTA ARCHAEOLOGICA CARPATHICA. (Text and summaries in various languages) 1958. a. 60 Zl. (Polska Akademia Nauk, Oddzial w Krakowie, Komisja Archeologiczna) Ossolineum, Publishing House of the Polish Academy of Sciences, Rynek 9, Wroclaw, Poland (Dist. by: Ars Polona-Ruch, Krakowskie Przedmiescie 7, Warsaw, Poland) Ed. Zenon Wozniak. bk. rev.

913　　　　　　　PL　ISSN 0065-0986
ACTA ARCHAEOLOGICA LODZIENSIA. (Text in Polish, summaries in English and French) 1954. a. price varies. (Lodzkie Towarzystwo Naukowe) Ossolineum,Publishing House of the Polish Academy of Sciences, Rynek 9, Wroclaw, Poland (Dist. by: Ars Polona - Ruch, Krakowskie Przedmiescie 7, Warsaw, Poland) Ed. Konrad Jazdzewski. bk. rev.

913　　　　　　　BE
ACTA ARCHAEOLOGICA LOVANIENSIA. 1962. a. price varies. Katholieke Universiteit te Leuven, Departement Archeologie en Kunstwetenschap, Blijde Inkomststraat, 21, B-3000 Louvain, Belgium. Ed. J. Mertens. circ. 450.

913　　　　　　　SZ　ISSN 0065-1052
ACTA BERNENSIA: BEITRAEGE ZUR PRAEHISTORISCHEN, KLASSISCHEN UND JUENGEREN ARCHAEOLOGIE. 1963. irreg. price varies. Staempfli und Cie AG, Postfach 2728, 3001 Berne, Switzerland. Eds. H. G. Bandi, H. Mueller-Beck.

913　　　　　　　GW
ACTA REI CRETARIAE ROMANAE FAUTORUM. SUPPLEMENTA. 1974. irreg. price varies. Rudolf Habelt Verlag, Am Buchenhang 1, 5300 Bonn 1, W. Germany (B.R.D.)

913　　　　　　　PL　ISSN 0137-6616
ACTA UNIVERSITATIS NICOLAI COPERNICI. ARCHEOLOGIA. 1968. irreg. price varies. Uniwersytet Mikolaja Kopernika, Fosa Staromiejska 3, Torun, Poland (Dist. by Osrodek Rozpowszechniania Wydanictw Naukowych PAN, Palac Kultury i Nauki, 00-901 Warsaw, Poland)
　　Formerly: Uniwersytet Mikolaja Kopernika, Torun. Nauki Humanistyczno-Spoleczne. Archeologia (ISSN 0083-4467)

913　　　　　　　US　ISSN 0162-8003
ADVANCES IN ARCHAEOLOGICAL METHOD AND THEORY. 1978. irreg. Academic Press, Inc. (Subsidiary of: Harcourt Brace Jovanovich) 111 Fifth Ave., New York, NY 10003. Ed. Michael B. Schiffer.

913　　　　　　　SZ
AEGYPTICA HELVETICA. (Text in Latin) 1974. irreg., latest no. 6. price varies. (Universitaet Basel, Aegyptologisches Seminar) Editions Belles-Lettres, Case Postale 32, 1211 Geneva 20, Switzerland. (Co- sponsor: Universite de Geneve, Centre d'Etudes Orientales) circ. 600.

AEGYPTOLOGISCHE FORSCHUNGEN. see *HISTORY — History Of The Near East*

913　　　　　　　UR
AKADEMIYA NAUK S.S.S.R. INSTITUT ARKHEOLOGII. KRATKIE SOOBSHCHENIYA. vol. 147, 1976. irreg. price varies. (Akademiya Nauk S.S.S.R., Institut Arkheologii) Izdatel'stvo Nauka, Podsosenskii Per., 21, Moscow K-62, U.S.S.R. Ed. I. Kruglikova. circ. 2,150.

917　　　　　　　US
ALABAMA ARCHAEOLOGICAL SOCIETY. SPECIAL PUBLICATION. 1974. irreg. price varies. Alabama Archaeological Society, 7608 Teal Dr. S.W., Huntsville, AL 35802. Ed. Eugene M. Futato. circ. 500. (also avail. in microform from UMI; reprint service avail. from UMI)

913 400　　　　　AU
ALMOGAREN. (Text in German, English, French, Spanish; summaries in German, English, Spanish) 1970. a. S.350($25) ‡ (Institutum Canarium) Akademische Druck- und Verlagsanstalt, Auerspergasse 12, A-8010 Graz, Austria. (Co- sponsor: Gesellschaft fuer Interdiziplinaere Sahara- Forschung) bk. rev. circ. 1,000.

AMERICAN RESEARCH CENTER IN EGYPT. JOURNAL. see *ART*

913 572　　　　　US　ISSN 0066-0027
AMERICAN SCHOOL OF PREHISTORIC RESEARCH. BULLETINS. 1936. irreg., no. 35, 1979. price varies. Peabody Museum of Archaeology and Ethnology, Harvard University, 11 Divinity Ave., Cambridge, MA 02138.

AMERICAN SCHOOLS OF ORIENTAL RESEARCH. ANNUAL. see *HISTORY — History Of The Near East*

917　　　　　　　US
AMERICAN SOCIETY FOR CONSERVATION ARCHAEOLOGY. PROCEEDINGS. 1976. a. American Society for Conservation Archaeology, c/ o Editor, Department of Anthropology, University of South Carolina, Columbia, SC 29208.

341　　　　　　　SP
AMPURIAS; revista de prehistoria, arqueologia y etnologia. 1939. a. 2000 ptas. (or exchange) Diputacion Provincial de Barcelona, Instituto de Prehistoria y Arqueologia, Palacio del Museo Arqueologico, Parque de Montjuich, Barcelona 4, Spain. bibl. illus. circ. controlled.

913.031　　　　　NE　ISSN 0569-9843
ANALECTA PRAEHISTORICA LEIDENSIA. 1964. irreg. price varies. (Rijksuniversiteit te Leiden, Institute for Prehistory) Leiden University Press, c/ o Martinus Nijhoff, Box 566, 2501 CN The Hague, Netherlands.

918 572　　　　　AG
ANALES DE ARQUEOLOGIA Y ETNOLOGIA. 1940. irreg. Universidad Nacional de Cuyo, Instituto de Arqueologia y Etnologia, Mendoza, Argentina.
　　Former titles (1945-1946): Anales del Instituto de Etnologia Americana; (1940-1944): Anales del Instituto de Etnografica Americana.

913　　　　　　　UK　ISSN 0066-1546
ANATOLIAN STUDIES. 1951. a. £7($18.50) British Institute of Archaeology at Ankara, c/o British Academy, Burlington House, Piccadilly, London W1V 0NS, England. Ed. Prof. O. R. Gurney. circ. 750.

ANATOLICA. see *HISTORY — History Of Asia*

915.49　　　　　　CE
ANCIENT CEYLON. (Text in English) 1971. irreg. Rs.32. Department of Archaeology, Sir Marcus Fernando Rd., Colombo 7, Sri Lanka. illus.

ANCIENT MONUMENTS SOCIETY TRANSACTIONS. see *HISTORY — History Of Europe*

571 954　　　　　II
ANDHRA PRADESH, INDIA. DEPARTMENT OF ARCHAEOLOGY AND MUSEUMS. EPIGRAPHY SERIES. (Text in English) 1967. irreg., no. 11, 1975-76. price varies. Department of Archaeology and Museums, Hyderabad 500001, Andhra Pradesh, India (Or: Publication Bureau, Directorate of Government Printing, Chanchalguda, Hyderabad, Andhra Pradesh, India)
　　Formerly: Andhra Pradesh, India. Department of Archaeology. Epigraphy Series (ISSN 0066-1651)

914　　　　　　　SP　ISSN 0561-3663
ANEJOS DE ARCHIVO ESPANOL DE ARQUEOLOGIA. 1951. irreg. price varies. Consejo Superior de Investigaciones Cientificas, Instituto Espanol de Arqueologia, Medinaceli 4, Madrid 14, Spain. illus.

914.2　　　　　　UK　ISSN 0306-5790
ANGLESEY ANTIQUARIAN SOCIETY TRANSACTIONS. (Text in English and Welsh) 1913. a. £1. ‡ Anglesey Antiquarian Society and Field Club, c/o Hon. Secretary, 22 Lon Ganol, Menai Bridge, Anglesey, Wales. Ed. A. D. Carr. bk. rev. charts. illus. circ. 1,000. (tabloid format)

893 493 UA
ANNUAIRE DE L'EGYPTOLOGIE. 1971. irreg. $9.65. Institut Francais d'Archeologie Orientale du Caire - French Institute of Oriental Archaeology of Cairo, 37 Sharia Sheikh Aly Youssef, Mounira, Cairo, Egypt (Subscr. to: Leila Bookshop, 17 Gawad Hosni St., Cairo, Egypt)

ANTICHITA, ARCHEOLOGIA, STORIA DELL'ARTE. see *ART*

914 IT
ANTICHITA PISANE; rivista di Archeologia e di Topografia Storica. vol. 2, 1975. irreg. (Universita degli Studi di Pisa, Scuola Speciale per Archeologi Preistorici) Pacini Editore, Via della Faggiola 17, 56100 Pisa, Italy.

ANTIKE KUNST. BEIHEFTE. see *ART*

ANTIQUITAS. REIHE 3. ABHANDLUNGEN ZUR VOR- UND FRUEHGESCHICHTE, ZUR KLASSISCHEN UND PROVINZIAL-ROEMISCHEN ARCHAEOLOGIE UND ZUR GESCHICHTE DES ALTERTUMS. see *HISTORY*

ANTIQUITES AFRICAINES. see *HISTORY — History Of Africa*

913 BE
ARCHAELOGIA BELGICA. 1950. irreg. price varies. Service National des Fouilles - Nationale Dienst voor Opgravingen, Parc de Cinquantenaire 1, B-1040 Brussels, Belgium.

913 GW ISSN 0066-5886
ARCHAEO-PHYSIKA. 1965. irreg., vol. 10, 1979. price varies. Rheinland Verlag, Kennedy-Ufer 2, 5000 Cologne 2, W. Germany (B.R.D.) (Distr. by: Rudolf Habelt Verlag, Am Buchenhang 1, 5300 Bonn 1, W. Germany (B.R.D.))

913 UK
ARCHAEOLOGIA. 1770. irreg., vol. 106, 1979. £20. Society of Antiquaries of London, Burlington House, London W1V OHS, England. Ed. F. H. Thompson. circ. 1,700. (also avail. in microfilm from UMI)

913 943.6 571 AU ISSN 0003-8008
ARCHAEOLOGIA AUSTRIACA; Beitraege zur Palaeanthropologie, Ur- und Fruehgeschichte Oesterreichs. (Supplements avail.) 1948. a. price varies. (Universitaet Wien, Institut fuer Ur- und Fruehgeschichte) Franz Deuticke, Helferstorfer Str. 4, A-1010 Vienna, Austria. Ed. Herwig Friesinger. bk. rev. bibl. charts. illus. cum.index. circ. 400. (back issues avail.) Indexed: Chem.Abstr.

571 UK ISSN 0066-5894
ARCHAEOLOGIA CANTIANA. 1844. a. £6($13) ‡ Kent Archaeological Society, c/o R. J. Ansell, Angle-Kin, Sandy Ridge, Borough Green, Kent, England. Ed. A. P. Detsicas. adv. bk. rev. index; cum.index. circ. 1,400.

193 GW ISSN 0066-5908
ARCHAEOLOGIA GEOGRAPHICA. irreg. Flemmings Verlag, Leinpfad 75, 2000 Hamburg 39, W. Germany (B.R.D.)

913 CS
ARCHAEOLOGIA HISTORICA. 1976. irreg. price varies. (Musejni Spolek v Brne) Nakladatelstvi Blok, Rooseveltova 4, 657 00 Brno, Czechoslovakia. (Co-sponsor: Okresni Stredisko Statni Pamatkove Pece a Ochrany Prirody v Olomouci) Ed. Karel Blazek. illus. circ. 1,000.

913 HU ISSN 0066-5916
ARCHAEOLOGIA HUNGARICA. SERIES NOVA. (Text in English, French, German) 1951. irreg., vol. 49, 1975. price varies. (Magyar Tudomanyos Akademia, Regeszeti Intezet) Akademiai Kiado, Publishing House of the Hungarian Academy of Sciences, P.O. Box 24, H-1363 Budapest, Hungary.

560 JA ISSN 0402-852X
ARCHAEOLOGIA JAPONICA. (Text in Japanese; summaries in English) 1948. irreg. 2000 Yen. Japanese Archaeologists Association - Nippon Kokogaku Kyokai, c/o Waseda Daigaku Kokogaku Kenkyushitsu, 647 Totsukamachi 1-chome, Shinjuku-ku, Tokyo 160, Japan.

913 943.8 PL ISSN 0066-5924
ARCHAEOLOGIA POLONA. (Text in various languages) 1958. a. 60. Zl.($13) (Polska Akademia Nauk, Instytut Historii Kultury Materialnej) Ossolineum, Publishing House of the Polish Academy of Sciences, Rynek 9, 50-106 Wroclaw, Poland (Dist. by Ars Polona-Ruch, Krakowskie Przedmiescie 7, Warsaw, Poland) Ed. Witold Hensel.

913 GW ISSN 0066-5932
ARCHAEOLOGICA SLOVACA. CATALOGI. 1968. irreg. price varies. (Instituti Archaeologici Nitriensis Academiae Scientiarum Slovacae, CS) Rudolf Habelt Verlag, Am Buchenhang 1, 5300 Bonn 1, W. Germany (B. R. D.) Ed. A. Tocik.

913 GW ISSN 0066-5940
ARCHAEOLOGICA SLOVACA. FONTES. (Text in German and Czech) 1957. irreg., no. 11, 1972. price varies. (Instituti Archaeologici Nitriensis Academiae Scientiarum Slovacae, CS) Rudolf Habelt Verlag, Am Buchenhang 1, 5300 Bonn 1, W. Germany (B. R. D.) Ed. A. Tocik.

913 016 UK ISSN 0066-5967
ARCHAEOLOGICAL BIBLIOGRAPHY FOR GREAT BRITAIN AND IRELAND. 1950. a. £6.50($13) Council for British Archaeology, 112 Kennington Rd., London SE11 6RE, England. Ed. J. Alcock. author index. circ. 1,000.

ARCHAEOLOGICAL COMPLETION REPORT SERIES. see *HISTORY — History Of North And South America*

913 UK
ARCHAEOLOGICAL EXCAVATIONS. a. price varies. Department of the Environment, 2 Marsham St., London SW1P 3EB, England (Avail. from H.M.S.O., c/o Liaison Officer, Atlantic House, Holborn Viaduct, London EC1P 1BN, England)

913 US ISSN 0066-5975
ARCHAEOLOGICAL EXPLORATION OF SARDIS. MONOGRAPHS. 1971. irreg., vol. 3, 1975. Harvard University Press, 79 Garden St., Cambridge, MA 02138.

571 913 UK ISSN 0066-5983
ARCHAEOLOGICAL JOURNAL. 1844. a. membership. Royal Archaeological Institute, 304, Addison House, Grove End Road, London, NW8 9EL, England. Ed. Dr. Michael Swanton. bk. rev. index; cum.index every 25 years. circ. 2,500. (also avail. in microform from UMI)

913 US ISSN 0003-8067
ARCHAEOLOGICAL SOCIETY OF DELAWARE. BULLETIN. 1933. membership. Archaeological Society of Delaware, Box 301, Wilmington, DE 19899. Ed. Ronald A. Thomas. charts. (also avail. in microform from UMI) Indexed: Abstr.Anthropol.

917 US
ARCHAEOLOGICAL SOCIETY OF DELAWARE. MONOGRAPH. 1976. irreg. Archaeological Society of Delaware, Box 301, Wilmington, DE 19899.

913 BE
ARCHAEOLOGICUM BELGII SPECULUM. (Text in Dutch and French) 1968. irreg., no. 11, 1979. price varies. Service National des Fouilles - Nationale Dienst voor Opgravingen, Parc du Cinquantenaire, B-1040 Brussels, Belgium.

913.031 GW ISSN 0066-6009
ARCHAEOLOGISCHE FUNDE UND DENKMAELER DES RHEINLANDES. 1960. irreg., vol. 4, 1979. price varies. Rheinland-Verlag, Kennedy-Ufer 2, 5000 Cologne 21, W. Germany (B.R.D.) (Distr. by: Rudolf Habelt Verlag, Am Buchenhang 1, 5300 Bonn 1, W. Germany (B.R.D))

913 GW
ARCHAEOLOGISCHE INFORMATIONEN. MITTEILUNGEN ZUR UR- UND FRUEHGESCHICHTE. 1972. irreg. price varies. (Deutsche Gesellschaft fuer Ur- und Fruehgeschichte) Rudolf Habelt Verlag, Am Buchenhang 1, 5300 Bonn 1, W. Germany (B. R. D.)

913.5 GW ISSN 0066-6033
ARCHAEOLOGISCHE MITTEILUNGEN AUS IRAN. NEUE FOLGE. 1968. a. DM.120. (Deutsches Archaeologisches Institut) Dietrich Reimer Verlag, Unter den Eichen 57, 1000 Berlin 45, W. Germany (B.R.D.)

913.363 GW
ARCHAEOLOGISCHES KORRESPONDENZBLATT. 1969. irreg. DM.54. (Roemisch-Germanisches Zentralmuseum, Mainz) Philipp Von Zabern, Welschnonnengasse 11, Postfach 4065, 6500 Mainz, W. Germany (B.R.D.) illus. circ. 1,000.

913 UK
ARCHAEOLOGY ABROAD SERVICE. NEWSHEET. a. Archaeology Abroad Service, 31-34 Garden Square, London W.C.1., England. Formerly: Archaeology Abroad.

913 UK ISSN 0308-8456
ARCHAEOLOGY IN BRITAIN (YEAR) 1976. a. £3.50($8.40) Council for British Archaeology, 112 Kennington Rd., London SE11 6RE, England. circ. 1,150. (back issues avail.)

917 US ISSN 0360-1021
ARCHAEOLOGY OF EASTERN NORTH AMERICA. 1973. a. $12. Eastern States Archeological Federation, Business Office, Box 260, Washington, CT 06793. Ed. Louis A. Brennan. illus.

913 551.46 FR
ARCHAEONAUTICA. 1977. irreg. Centre National de la Recherche Scientifique, 15 Quai Anatole France, 75700 Paris, France (Editorial address: Direction des Recherches Archeologiques Sous-Marines, Fort Saint Jean, 13235 Marseille Cedex 1, France) Ed. Bernard Liou.

913 PL ISSN 0066-605X
ARCHEOLOGIA. (Text in English, French, Polish, German and Russian; summaries in English and Russian) 1950. a. 75 Zl.($15) (Polska Akademia Nauk, Instytut Historii Kultury Materialnej) Ossolineum, Publishing House of the Polish Academy of Sciences, Rynek 9, 50-106 Wroclaw, Poland (Dist. by Ars Polona-Ruch, Krakowskie Przedmiescie 7, Warsaw, Poland) Ed. Kazimierz Majewski.

913 PL
ARCHEOLOGIA. (Text in Polish; summaries in German or English) 1966. irreg., no. 9, 1977. price varies. Uniwersytet im. Adama Mickiewicza w Poznaniu, Stalingradzka 1, 61-712 Poznan, Poland (Dist. by: Ars Polona, Krakowskie Przedmiescie 7, 00-068 Warsaw, Poland)
Formerly: Uniwersytet im Adama Mickiewicza w Poznaniu. Wydzial Filozoficzno-Historyczny. Prace . Seria Archeologia.

913 IT ISSN 0003-8172
ARCHEOLOGIA CLASSICA. 1949. a. (Universita degli Studi di Roma, Istituti di Archeologia e Storia dell'Arte Greca e Romana e di Etruscologia e Antichita Italiche) Erma di "Bretschneider", Via Cassiodoro 19, 00193 Rome, Italy. bk. rev. charts, illus. index.

571 913 FR ISSN 0066-6084
ARCHEOLOGIE MEDITERRANEENNE. 1965. irreg. price varies. Editions Klincksieck, 11 rue de Lille, Paris 7e, France.

913 BE ISSN 0066-6025
ARCHEOLOGISCHE KAARTEN VAN BELGIE/ ARCHAEOLOGISCHE KAARTEN VAN BELGIE. (Text in Dutch and French) 1968. irreg. price varies. Service National des Fouilles - Nationale Dienst voor Opgravingen, Parc du Cinquantenaire 1, B-1040 Brussels, Belgium.

942.8 UK ISSN 0066-6203
ARCHITECTURAL AND ARCHAEOLOGICAL SOCIETY OF DURHAM AND NORTHUMBERLAND. TRANSACTIONS. NEW SERIES. 1968. biennial. £4. ‡ Architectural and Archaeological Society of Durham and Northumberland, c/o University Library, Durham, England. Ed. Peter Scott. circ. 300. (back issues avail.) Indexed: Br.Hum.Ind. Br. Archaeol.Abstr.

ARCHIV FUER PAPYRUSFORSCHUNG UND VERWANDTE GEBIETE. see *HISTORY*

ARHEOLOGIA MOLDOVEI/ARCHEOLOGIE DE LA MOLDAVIE. see *HISTORY — History Of Europe*

913   US   ISSN 0271-0641
ARIZONA STATE UNIVERSITY ANTHROPOLOGICAL RESEARCH PAPERS. 1969. irreg., 2-5/yr. price varies per no. Arizona State University, Department of Anthropology, Tempe, AZ 85281. Ed.G.A.Clark.

917   US
ARKANSAS ARCHAEOLOGICAL SURVEY. PUBLICATIONS ON ARCHAEOLOGY. RESEARCH REPORTS. 1975. price varies. Arkansas Archeological Survey, Coordinating Office, University of Arkansas Museum, Fayetteville, AR 72701.

917   US   ISSN 0587-3533
ARKANSAS ARCHEOLOGICAL SURVEY. PUBLICATIONS ON ARCHEOLOGY. POPULAR SERIES. 1969. irreg. price varies. Arkansas Archeological Survey, Coordinating Office, University of Arkansas Museum, Fayetteville, AR 72701. charts. illus.

917   US
ARKANSAS ARCHAEOLOGICAL SURVEY. PUBLICATIONS ON ARCHAEOLOGY. RESEARCH SERIES. 1967. irreg. price varies. Arkansas Archeological Survey, Coordinating Office, University of Arkansas Museum, Fayetteville, AR 72701. charts. illus.

913   US   ISSN 0004-1718
ARKANSAS ARCHAEOLOGIST. 1960. a. $8 (includes Field Notes) Arkansas Archeological Society, c/o University of Arkansas Museum, Univ. of Arkansas, Fayetteville, AR 72701. Ed. C. R. McGimsey,3rd. illus. maps. Indexed: Hist.Abstr.

913   UR
ARKHEOLOGICHESKIE RABOTY V TADZHIKISTANE. vol. 11, 1971. irreg. 1.45 Rub. (Akademiya Nauk Tadzhikskoi S.S.R., Institut Istcrii) Izdatel'stvo Donish, Ul. Aini 121 Korp. 2, Dushanbe, U.S.S.R. Ed. B. Litvinskii.

913
ARKHEOLOGIYA I ETNOGRAFIYA UDMURTII. 1975. 1 Rub. per issue. Udmurdskii Institut Istorii, Ekonomiki, Literatury, Sovetskaya, 14, 426020 Izhevsk, U.S.S.R. circ. 500.

ART ROMANIC. see *ART*

ARTE Y ARQUEOLOGIA. see *ART*

ARTIBUS ASIAE SUPPLEMENTA. see *ART*

ARTS ZIMBABWE. see *ART*

913   US   ISSN 0066-829X
ASIAN AND PACIFIC ARCHAEOLOGY SERIES. 1967. irreg., no. 8, 1978. price varies. (University of Hawaii, Social Science Research Institute) University Press of Hawaii, 2840 Kolowalu St., Honolulu, HI 96822. (reprint service avail. from UMI,ISI)

913   MX   ISSN 0067-0243
ATLAS ARQUEOLOGICO DE LA REPUBLICA MEXICANA. 1959. irreg. price varies. Instituto Nacional de Antropologia e Historia, Cordoba 45, Mexico 7,D.F.

ATLAS POLSKICH STROJOW LUDOWYCH. see *ANTHROPOLOGY*

220.93   AT   ISSN 0084-747X
AUSTRALIAN JOURNAL OF BIBLICAL ARCHAEOLOGY. 1968. a. Aus.$6. (Australian Society for Biblical Archaeology) University of Sydney, Department of Semitic Studies, Sydney, N.S.W. 2006, Australia. Ed. A. D. Crown. bk. rev. circ. 1,000.

913   AT
AUSTRALIAN SOCIETY FOR HISTORICAL ARCHAEOLOGY. 1973. a. Aus.$3. Australian Society for Historical Archaeology, Department of Archaeology, University of Sydney, Sydney, N.S.W. 2006, Australia. (Co-sponsor: Australian Humanities Research Council) Eds. J. Birmingham, R. I. Jack. circ. 600. (back issues avail.)
Supersedes: Studies in Historical Archaeology.

AZANIA. see *HISTORY — History Of Africa*

913   FR
B E F A R. PUBLICATION. 1877. irreg. (1-2/yr) price varies. (Bibliotheque des Ecoles Francaises d'Athenes et de Rome) Diffusion de Boccard, 11 rue de Medicis, 75006 Paris, France. Ed.Bd. bibl.

572   301.2   900   US
BALLENA PRESS PUBLICATIONS IN ARCHAEOLOGY, ETHNOLOGY AND HISTORY. no. 2, 1974. irreg., no. 15, 1980. price varies. Ballena Press, Box 1366, Socorro, NM 87801. Eds. Philip J Wilke, Albert B. Elasser.

572   US
BALLENA PRESS PUBLICATIONS ON NORTH AMERICAN ROCK ART. 1978. irreg., no. 2, 1978. price varies. Ballena Press, Box 1366, NM 87801. Ed. C. William Clewlow, Jr.

BALLENA PRESS STUDIES IN MESOAMERICAN ART, ARCHAEOLOGY AND ETHNOHISTORY. see *ANTHROPOLOGY*

913   GW   ISSN 0067-5245
BEITRAEGE ZUR UR- UND FRUEHGESCHICHTLICHEN ARCHAEOLOGIE DES MITTELMEERKULTURRAUMES. 1965. irreg., no. 19, 1980. price varies. Rudolf Habelt Verlag, Am Buchenhang 1, 5300 Bonn 1, W. Germany (B.R.D.) Eds. V. Milojcic, W. Schrickel.

BELGIUM. COMMISSION ROYALE DES MONUMENTS ET DES SITES. BULLETIN. see *ARCHITECTURE*

913   UK
BERKSHIRE ARCHAEOLOGICAL COMMITTEE. PUBLICATION. 1975. irreg. price varies. Berkshire Archaeological Committee, Turstins, High St., Upton, Didcott, Berks OX11 9JE, England.

914   UK   ISSN 0309-3093
BERKSHIRE ARCHAEOLOGICAL JOURNAL. 1871. a. £2. Berkshire Archaeological Committee, "Turstins", High St., Upton, Didcot, Berks OX11 9JE, England. Ed. C F. Slade. bk. rev. bibl. illus. index.

913   LE   ISSN 0067-6195
BERYTUS: ARCHAEOLOGICAL STUDIES. (Text in English, French and German) 1934. a. $11. American University of Beirut, Box 1786, Beirut, Lebanon. Ed. William A. Ward. bk. rev. Indexed: Old Test.Abstr.

913   BE
BIBLIOGRAPHIE PAPYROLOGIQUE SUR FICHES. 1941. irreg (6/yr.) 420 Fr. Fondation Egyptologique Reine Elisabeth, Parc du Cinquantenaire 10, B-1040 Brussels, Belgium. Eds. M. Hombert, G. Nachtergael.

BIBLIOGRAPHIE ZUR ARCHAEO-ZOOLOGIE UND GESCHICHTE DER HAUSTIERE. see *BIBLIOGRAPHIES*

913   RM   ISSN 0067-7388
BIBLIOTECA DE ARHEOLOGIE. (Text in Rumanian; summaries in French) 1957. irreg. (Academia de Stiinte Sociale si Politice, Institutul de Arheologie) Editura Academiei Republicii Socialiste Romania, Calea Victoriei 125, Bucharest, Romania (Subscr. to: ILEXIM, Str. 13 Decembrie Nr. 3, P.O. Box 136-137, Bucharest, Romania)

913   SP   ISSN 0067-7507
BIBLIOTECA PRAEHISTORICA HISPANA. 1958. irreg. price varies. Instituto Espanol de Prehistoria, Palacio del Museo Arqueologico Nacional, Serrano, 13, Madrid 1, Spain.

913   PL   ISSN 0067-7639
BIBLIOTEKA ARCHEOLOGICZNA. (Text in Polish; summaries in English or French) 1948. irreg., vol. 25, 1979. price varies. (Polskie Towarzystwo Archeologiczne i Numizmatyczne) Ossolineum, Publishing House of the Polish Academy of Sciences, Rynek 9, Wroclaw, Poland (Dist. by Ars Polona-Ruch, Krakowskie Przedmiescie 7, Warsaw, Poland)

960   090   BE   ISSN 0067-7817
BIBLIOTHECA AEGYPTIACA. 1932. irreg., latest no. 16, 1975. price varies. Fondation Egyptologique Reine Elisabeth, Parc du Cinquantenaire 10, B-1040 Brussels, Belgium.

914   SP   ISSN 0519-9603
BIBLIOTHECA ARCHAEOLOGICA. 1960. irreg. price varies. Consejo Superior de Investigaciones Cientificas, Instituto Espanol de Arqueologia, Medinaceli 4, Madrid 14, Spain. illus.

BIBLIOTHECA LATINA MEDII ET RECENTIORI AEVI. see *HISTORY — History Of Europe*

913   FR   ISSN 0067-8309
BIBLIOTHEQUE DES CAHIERS ARCHEOLOGIQUES. 1966. irreg. price varies. Editions A. et J. Picard, 82 rue Bonaparte, 75006 Paris, France. Ed. Andre Grabar.

913   UK   ISSN 0140-4202
BIRMINGHAM & WARWICKSHIRE ARCHAEOLOGICAL SOCIETY. TRANSACTIONS. 1871. a. £2.50. Birmingham & Warwickshire Archaeological Society, Birmingham & Midland Institute, Margaret Street, Birmingham, England. Eds. Dr. and Mrs. A. Gooder. bk. rev. charts. illus. circ. 450. Indexed: Br.Archaeol.Abstr.

BRACARA AUGUSTA; revista cultural de Regionalismo e historia. see *HISTORY — History Of Europe*

BRADWELL ABBEY FIELD CENTRE FOR THE STUDY OF ARCHAEOLOGY, NATURAL HISTORY & ENVIRONMENTAL STUDIES. OCCASIONAL PAPERS. see *SCIENCES: COMPREHENSIVE WORKS*

913   CS
BRATISLAVA-STUDIA. 1975. irreg. price varies. (Archiv) Obzor, Ceskoslovenskej Armady 29, 893 36 Bratislava, Czechoslovakia.

BREIFNE; journal of Cumann Seanchais Bhreifne. see *HISTORY — History Of Europe*

913   GW   ISSN 0068-0907
BREMER ARCHAEOLOGISCHE BLAETTER. 1960. irreg., no. 7, 1976. price varies. (Bremer Gesellschaft fuer Vorgeschichte) Rudolf Habelt Verlag, Am Buchenhang 1, 5300 Bonn 1, W. Germany (B.R.D.) (Co-sponsor: Focke-Musuem; Vaeterkunde-Museum) Ed. K. H. Brandt.

913   UK   ISSN 0068-1032
BRISTOL AND GLOUCESTERSHIRE ARCHAEOLOGICAL SOCIETY, BRISTOL, ENGLAND. TRANSACTIONS. 1876. a. £3 membership; institutions£6. Bristol and Gloucestershire Archaeological Society, c/o Miss E. Ralph, 9 Pembroke Rd., Bristol BS8 3AU, England. Ed. Dr. N. Herbert. bk. rev. cum.index every 10 years (vol. 79-90 in 1974) circ. 800.

913   709   723   UK
BRITISH ARCHAEOLOGICAL ASSOCIATION. CONFERENCE TRANSACTIONS. irreg. British Archaeological Association, c/o 61 Old Park Ridings, Winchmore Hill, London N21 2ET, England.

571   913   UK   ISSN 0068-1288
BRITISH ARCHAEOLOGICAL ASSOCIATION. JOURNAL. 1843. a. individuals £5; libraries £7. British Archaeological Association, c/o 61 Old Park Ridings, Winchmore Hill, London, N21 2ET, England. Ed. P. Everson. bk. rev. cum. index every 5 years. circ. 1,000.

913   UK   ISSN 0068-2454
BRITISH SCHOOL AT ATHENS. ANNUAL. 1894. a. £30. British School at Athens, 31-34 Gordon Sq., London WC1H 0PY, England. Ed. Prof. R. A. Tomlinson. index. circ. 600.

913   UK   ISSN 0068-2462
BRITISH SCHOOL AT ROME. PAPERS. ARCHAEOLOGY. 1902. a. £14. British School at Rome, 1 Lowther Gardens, Exhibition Rd., London SW7 2AA, England. index.

571   BU   ISSN 0068-3620
BULGARSKA AKADEMIIA NA NAUKITE. ARKHEOLOGICHESKI INSTITUT IZVESTIIA. (Summaries in various languages) 1910. irreg. 4.70 lv. Publishing House of the Bulgarian Academy of Sciences, Ul. Akad. G. Bonchev, 1113 Sofia, Bulgaria (Dist. by: Hemus, 6, Rouski Blvd., 1000 Sofia, Bulgaria) Ed. D. Angelov. circ. 1,000.

913　　　　　　　MR　ISSN 0068-4015
BULLETIN D'ARCHEOLOGIE MAROCAINE.*
1956. a. Division des Antiquites, 23 rue al Brihi, Rabat, Morocco.

914　　　　　　　RM
BULLETIN D'ARCHEOLOGIE SUD-EST EUROPEENNE.* Association Internationale d'Etudes du Sud-Est Europeen, Str. I.C. Frimu Nr. 9, Bucharest, Romania. bibl. illus.

BULLETIN DE CORRESPONDANCE HELLENIQUE. see *CLASSICAL STUDIES*

560　　　　　　　IO
BULLETIN OF PREHISTORY/BERITA PRASEJARAH. (Text in English or Indonesian) 1974. irreg. Rps.500($1.50) National Archaeological Institute of Indonesia, Department of Prehistory - Lembaga Purbakala dan Peninggalan Nasional,Bidang Prasejarah, Jalan Kimia 12, P.O. Box 2533, Jakarta, Indonesia.

913 737　　　　SP　ISSN 0007-9502
CAESARAUGUSTA. 1951, vol. 10, no. 18. a. 400 ptas. (Seminario de Argueologia y Numismatica Aragonesas) Institucion Fernando el Catolico, Pl. de Espana 2, Zaragoza, Spain. bk. rev. bibl. charts. illus. index. cum.index.

913.38　　　　　CN　ISSN 0317-5065
CAHIERS DES ETUDES ANCIENNES. 1972. irreg. price varies. Universite du Quebec a Trois Rivieres, C.P. 500, Trois-Rivieres, Que. G9A 5H7, Canada. Ed. Pierre Senay. illus.

571　　　　　　IT　ISSN 0575-108X
CAHIERS LIGURES DE PREHISTOIRE ET D'ARCHEOLOGIE. (Text in French) 1952. irreg. L.12000($18) Istituto Internazionale di Studi Liguri - International Institute of Ligurian Studies, Museo Bicknell, 39 bis via Romana, 18012 Bordighera, Italy. circ. 1,000.
  Supersedes: Cahiers d'Histoire et d'Archeologie.

913 572　　　　CN　ISSN 0384-191X
CALGARY ARCHAEOLOGIST. 1973. a. free. University of Calgary, Department of Archaeology, Calgary, Alta. T2N 1N4, Canada. Ed. Dr. V. Markotic. bk. rev. circ. 400. (looseleaf format; back issues avail.)

913 979.4　　　US
CALIFORNIA ARCHAEOLOGICAL REPORTS. 1961. irreg., latest no. 18. price varies. ‡ Department of Parks and Recreation, P.O. Box 2390, Sacramento, CA 95811. Ed. John W. Foster. circ. 100-300.
  Formerly: California. Department of Parks and Recreation. Archaeological Report (ISSN 0068-5550)

942　　　　　　UK　ISSN 0068-659X
CAMBRIDGE AIR SURVEYS. 1952. irreg. price varies. Cambridge University Press, Box 110, Cambridge CB2 3RL, England (and 32 E. 57 St., New York NY 10022)

917　　　　　　CN　ISSN 0317-2244
CANADA. NATIONAL MUSEUM OF MAN. MERCURY SERIES. ARCHAEOLOGICAL SURVEY OF CANADA. PAPERS/CANADA. MUSEE NATIONAL DE L'HOMME. COLLECTION MERCURE. COMMISSION ARCHAEOLOGIQUE DU CANADA. DOSSIERS. (Text in English or French) 1972. irreg., no. 83, 1978. free. (National Museum of Man) National Museums of Canada, Ottawa, Ont. K1A OM8, Canada. charts. illus. cum.index.

913 971　　　　CN
CANADIAN HISTORIC SITES; OCCASIONAL PAPERS IN ARCHAEOLOGY AND HISTORY. irreg. price varies. Supply and Services Canada, Publishing Centre, Hull, Que. K1A 0S5, Canada.

971.01　　　　　CN　ISSN 0705-2006
CANADIAN JOURNAL OF ARCHAEOLOGY. (Text in English and French) 1977. a. Canadian Archaeological Association, c/o Archaeological Survey of Canada, National Museum of Man, Ottawa, Ont. K1A OM8, Canada. illus.
  Formerly: Canadian Archaeological Association. Bulletin (ISSN 0315-761X)

913 942　　　　UK　ISSN 0069-0198
CANTERBURY ARCHAEOLOGICAL SOCIETY. OCCASIONAL PAPERS. 1956. irreg., no. 7, 1974. price varies. Canterbury Archaeological Society, c/o L. D. Lyle, 3 Queen's Ave., Canterbury, Kent CT2 8AY, England.

913 655　　　　BE　ISSN 0069-1984
CENTRE NATIONAL D'ARCHEOLOGIE ET D'HISTOIRE DU LIVRE. PUBLICATION. 1965. irreg., 1968, vol. 2. price varies. Centre National d'Archeologie et d'Histoire du Livre, c/o Bibliotheque Royale Albert 1er, 4, Boulevard de l'Empereur, 1000 Brussels, Belgium.

913 016　　　　BE　ISSN 0069-1992
CENTRE NATIONAL DE RECHERCHES ARCHEOLOGIQUES EN BELGIQUE. REPERTOIRES ARCHEOLOGIQUES. SERIE A: REPERTOIRES BIBLIOGRAPHIQUES/ NATIONAAL CENTRUM VOOR OUDHEIDKUNDIGE NAVORSINGEN IN BELGIE. OUDHEIDKUNDIGE REPERTORIA. REEKS A: BIBLIOGRAFISCHE REPERTORIA. (Text in Dutch and French) 1960. irreg. (approx. a) price varies. Centre National de Recherches Archeologiques en Belgique, 1 Parc du Cinquantenaire, 1040 Brussels, Belgium.

913　　　　　　BE　ISSN 0069-200X
CENTRE NATIONAL DE RECHERCHES ARCHEOLOGIQUES EN BELGIQUE. REPERTOIRES ARCHEOLOGIQUES. SERIE B: REPERTOIRES DES COLLECTIONS. (Text in French and Dutch) 1965. irreg. price varies. Centre National de Recherches Archeologiques en Belgique, 1 Parc du Cinquantenaire, 1040 Brussels, Belgium.

913　　　　　　BE　ISSN 0069-2018
CENTRE NATIONAL DE RECHERCHES ARCHEOLOGIQUES EN BELGIQUE. REPERTOIRES ARCHEOLOGIQUES. SERIE C: REPERTOIRES DIVERS. (Text in French and Dutch) 1964. irreg. price varies. Centre National de Recherches Archeologiques en Belgique, 1 Parc du Cinquantenaire, 1040 Brussels, Belgium.

913.031　　　　　IT
CENTRO CAMUNO DI STUDI PREISTORICI. ARCHIVI. 1968. irreg., vol. 7, 1977. $32.50. Centro Camuno di Studi Preistorici, 25044 Capo di Ponte, Brescia, Italy. charts. illus.

913 571　　　　IT　ISSN 0577-2168
CENTRO CAMUNO DI STUDI PREISTORICI. BOLLETTINO. (Text in language of author; summaries in other languages) 1967. a. L.25000($40) Centro Camuno di Studi Preistorici, 25044 Capo di Ponte, Brescia, Italy. Ed. Emmanuel Anati. bk. rev. bibl. charts. illus.

913.031　　　　　IT
CENTRO CAMUNO DI STUDI PREISTORICI. STUDI CAMUNI. irreg; vol. 7, 1977. $6.50. Centro Camuno di Studi Preistorici, 25044 Capo di Ponte, Brescia, Italy.

913　　　　　　IT　ISSN 0069-2204
CENTRO STUDI PER LA MAGNA GRECIA, NAPLES. PUBBLICAZIONI PROPRIE.* 1959. irreg., 1969, no. 6. price varies. Centro Studi per la Magna Grecia, Istituto di Archeologia, Via Giovanni Palladino, 39, 80138 Naples, Italy.

CERAMICA DE CULTURA MAYA. see *ANTHROPOLOGY*

CERCLE D'HISTOIRE ET D'ARCHEOLOGIE DE SAINT-GHISLAIN ET DE LA REGION. ANALES. see *HISTORY — History Of Europe*

913　　　　　　UK　ISSN 0307-6628
CHESHIRE ARCHAEOLOGICAL BULLETIN. no. 4, 1976. irreg. price varies. 11 Wold Court, Hawarden, Clwyd CH5 3LN, Wales. Ed. S. R. Williams.

913　　　　　　GW　ISSN 0069-3715
CHIRON. 1971. a. DM.72. (Deutsches Archaeologisches Institut, Kommission fuer Alte Geschichte und Epigraphik) C. H. Beck'sche Verlagsbuchhandlung, Wilhelmstr. 9, 8000 Munich 40, W. Germany (B.R.D.) circ. 600.

COLLANA DI STUDI PALETNOLOGICI. see *ANTHROPOLOGY*

COLLECTION U. SERIE HISTOIRE ANCIENNE. see *HISTORY*

975 917.55　　　US　ISSN 0069-5971
COLONIAL WILLIAMSBURG ARCHAEOLOGICAL SERIES. 1970. irreg., no. 9, 1978. price varies. ‡ Colonial Williamsburg Foundation, Williamsburg, VA 23185. Ed. Ivor Noel Hume.

913　　　　　　FR　ISSN 0069-8881
CONGRES ARCHEOLOGIQUE DE FRANCE (PUBLICATION.) 1834. a. 170 F. Societe Francaise d'Archeologie, Musee National des Monuments Francais, Palais de Chaillot, 75016 Paris, France. cum.index: 1834-1925; 1926-1954; 1955-1975. circ. 3,000.

913　　　　　　PO　ISSN 0084-9189
CONIMBRIGA. (Text in Portuguese, Spanish, French, English) 1959. a. Esc.300. Universidade de Coimbra, Instituto de Arqueologia, 3000 Coimbra, Portugal (Subscr. to: Casa do Castelo, rua da Sofia, 3000-Coimbra, Portugal) Ed. Jorge de Alarcao. bk. rev. circ. 450.

915.4　　　　　　II
CONSERVATION OF CULTURAL PROPERTY IN INDIA. (Text in English) 1966. a. Rs.15($3) Indian Association for the Study of Conservation of Cultural Property, c/o National Archives of India, Janpath, New Delhi 110001, India. Ed. O. P. Agrawal. adv. bibl.

913　　　　　　UK　ISSN 0307-5087
CONTREBIS. 1974. a. £0.50 per copy. Lancaster Archaeological Society, Lonsdale College, Department of Classics and Archeology, The University, Lancaster, England. Eds. D.C.A. Shotter and A. J. White. bk. rev. bibl, charts, illus. circ. 200.

913　　　　　　IT　ISSN 0069-9748
CONVEGNO DI STUDI SULLA MAGNA GRECIA. ATTI.* 1961. a. Centro Studi per la Magna Grecia, Istituto di Archeologia, Via Giovanni Palladino 39, 80138 Naples, Italy.

913　　　　　　UK　ISSN 0070-024X
CORNISH ARCHAEOLOGY. 1962. a. £3. Cornwall Archaeological Society, c/o Mrs. H. Quinnell, Ed., Dept of Extra-Mural Studies, University, Gandy St., Exeter, England (Subscr. to: Miss D. G. Harris, 25 Park View, Truro, Cornwell England)

913　　　　　　UK　ISSN 0070-0258
CORNWALL ARCHAEOLOGICAL SOCIETY. FIELD GUIDE. irreg. Cornwall Archaeological Society, c/o Mrs. H. Quinnell. Ed., Dept. of Extra-Mural Studies, University, Gandy St., Exeter, England (Subscr. to: Miss D. G. Harris, 25 Park View, Truro, Cornwall, England)

972 913　　　　MX　ISSN 0070-0312
CORPUS ANTIQUITATUM AMERICANENSIUM. 1964. irreg. Instituto Nacional de Antropologia e Historia, Cordoba 45, Mexico 7,D.F., Mexico.

CORSI INTERNAZIONALI DI CULTURA SULL'ARTE RAVENNATE E BIZANTINA. ATTI. see *ART*

913　　　　　　UK　ISSN 0305-5280
COUNCIL FOR BRITISH ARCHAEOLOGY. CURRENT OFFPRINTS AND REPORTS. 1950. a. £1.75($3.50) Council for British Archaeology, 112 Kennington Rd., London SE11 6RE, England. Ed. P. A. Marchant. circ. 1,000.
  Formerly: Current & Forthcoming Offprints on Archaeology in Great Britain & Ireland (ISSN 0526-4375)

913　　　　　　IE
COUNTY KILDARE ARCHAEOLOGICAL SOCIETY. JOURNAL. 1891. a. £3 non-members. County Kildare Archaeological Society, Tullig, Dublin Road Naas, County Kildare, Ireland. Ed. C. Costello. bk. rev. charts. illus. circ. 400. (back issues avail.)

571 913　　　　IE　ISSN 0070-1327
COUNTY LOUTH ARCHAEOLOGICAL AND HISTORICAL JOURNAL. 1904. a. £3. 5, Oliver Plunkett Park, Dundalk, Ireland. Ed. Noel Ross.
  Formerly: County Louth Archaeological Journal.

913　　　　　　　IT　ISSN 0391-1527
CRONACHE POMPEIANE. (Text in English, French, German and Italian) 1975. a. L.30000. (Associazione Internazionale "Amici di Pompei") Gaetano Macchiaroli Editore, Via Carducci 55, Naples 80121, Italy.

913.031　　　　　　SP
CUADERNOS DE PREHISTORIA. 1976. irreg. 500 ptas.($9) Universidad de Granada, Secretariado de Publicaciones, Hospital Real, Granada, Spain. Ed. Soledad Navarrete Enciso.

913 571　　　　　CY　ISSN 0070-2374
CYPRUS. DEPARTMENT OF ANTIQUITIES. ANNUAL REPORT. 1934. a. Mils.1000. Department of Antiquities, Nicosia, Cyprus. circ. 750.

913 571　　　　　CY　ISSN 0070-2366
CYPRUS. DEPARTMENT OF ANTIQUITIES. MONOGRAPHS. 1953. irreg., no. 15, 1977. price varies. Department of Antiquities, Nicosia, Cyprus.

913 571　　　　　CY
CYPRUS. DEPARTMENT OF ANTIQUITIES. REPORT. a. Mils.12000. Department of Antiquities, Nicosia, Cyprus.

913　　　　　RM　ISSN 0070-251X
DACIA; REVUE D'ARCHEOLOGIE ET D'HISTOIRE ANCIENNE. (Text in French, English, German and Russian) a. $20. Editura Academiei Republicii Socialiste Romania, Calea Victoriei 125, Bucharest, Romania (Subscr. to: ILEXIM, Str. 13 Decembrie Nr. 3, P.O. Box 136-137, Bucharest, Romania) Ed. D.M.Pippidi.

913　　　　　　　FR
DELEGATION ARCHEOLOGIQUE FRANCAISE EN IRAN. CAHIERS. 1971. a. 150 F. Association Paleorient, Delegation Archeologique Francaise en Iran, B.P. 5005, 75222 Paris Cedex 05, France. illus.

914　　　　　　　DK
DENMARK. NATIONALMUSEET. PUBLICATIONS: ARCHAEOLOGICAL HISTORICAL SERIES. (Text in Danish, English, French and German) irreg. price varies. Nationalmuseet, Oplysningsafdelingen, Ny Vestergade 10, DK-1471 Copenhagen K, Denmark (Dist. in the U.S. by: Humanities Press, 171 First Ave., Atlantic City, NJ 07716)

571 913　　　　　UK　ISSN 0070-3788
DERBYSHIRE ARCHAEOLOGICAL JOURNAL. 1879. a. £4. Derbyshire Archaeological Society, c/o Trent Valley Archaeological Unit, University of Nottingham, University Park, Nottingham NG7 2RD, England. Ed. D. V. Fowkes. circ. 650.

913　　　　　　UK　ISSN 0305-5795
DEVON ARCHAEOLOGICAL SOCIETY. PROCEEDINGS. 1929. a. £3. Devon Archaeological Society, c/o Dr. V.Maxfield, Dept. of History, University of Exeter, Queen's Drive, Exeter, England. bk. rev. circ. 500. Indexed: Br. Archaeol.Abstr.

913 571　　　　　US　ISSN 0070-668X
DISCOVERIES IN THE JUDAEAN DESERT OF JORDAN. irreg., vol. 6, 1977. price varies. Oxford University Press, 200 Madison Ave., New York, NY 10016 (and Ely House, 37 Dover St., London W1X 4AH, England)

914　　　　　　BE　ISSN 0419-4241
DISSERTATIONES ARCHAEOLOGICAE GANDENSES. 1953. irreg., no. 19, 1980. price varies. Uitgeverij de Tempel, 37 Tempelhof, Bruges, Belgium.

DORSET NATURAL HISTORY AND ARCHAEOLOGICAL SOCIETY. PROCEEDINGS. see *SCIENCES: COMPREHENSIVE WORKS*

913　　　　　　US
DUMBARTON OAKS CONFERENCE PROCEEDINGS. 1968. irreg., latest 1981. price varies. Dumbarton Oaks Center for Pre-Columbian Studies, 1703 32nd St. N.W., Washington, DC 20007. Ed. Elizabeth P. Boone. bibl. charts. illus. circ. 2,000. (back issues avail.)

709　　　　　　US　ISSN 0070-7546
DUMBARTON OAKS PAPERS. 1940. irreg., no. 34, 1980. price varies. (Dumbarton Oaks Center for Byzantine Studies) J. J. Augustin, Inc., Locust Valley, NY 11560.

940　　　　　　US　ISSN 0070-7554
DUMBARTON OAKS STUDIES. 1950. irreg. price varies. (Dumbarton Oaks Center for Byzantine Studies) J. J. Augustin, Inc., Locust Valley, NY 11560.

942.5　　　　　　UK　ISSN 0424-1088
EAST MIDLAND ARCHAEOLOGICAL BULLETIN. a. East Midland Committee of Field Archaaeologists, Trent Valley Archaeological Research Committee, Archaeology Dept., University of Nottingham, University Park, Nottingham, England.

913　　　　　　UK　ISSN 0012-852X
EAST RIDING ARCHAEOLOGIST. 1968. irreg. £2.50 to institutions. East Riding Archaeological Society, 26 Redland Drive, Kirk Ella, Hull HU10 7UZ, England. Ed.Bd. charts. illus. circ. 400.

913　　　　　　FR
ECOLE FRANCAISE DE ROME. COLLECTION. 1-2/yr. price varies. Diffusion de Boccard, 11 rue de Medicis, 75006 Paris, France.
　　Supersedes: Ecole Francaise de Rome. Melanges: Supplement.

913　　　　　　FR
ECOLE FRANCAISE DE ROME. MELANGES: ANTIQUITE. (In two vols.) a. Diffusion de Boccard, 11 rue de Medicis, 75006 Paris, France.

914　　　　　　FR
ECOLE FRANCAISE DE ROME. MELANGES: MOYEN AGES, TEMPS MODERNE. (In two vols.) a. Diffusion de Boccard, 11 rue de Medicis, 75006 Paris, France.

913　　　　　　FR
ECOLES FRANCAISES D'ATHENES ET DE ROME. BIBLIOTHEQUE. PUBLICATIONS. irreg. price varies. Diffusion de Boccard, 11 rue de Medicis, 75006 Paris, France.

962 932　　　　　UA　ISSN 0082-7835
EGYPT. SERVICE DES ANTIQUITES. ANNALES. (Text in language of author) 1900. irreg. price varies. ‡ Egyptian National Museum, Midan-el-Tahir, Kasr el-Nil, Cairo, Egypt. cum.index: vols 1-30.

571　　　　　　US　ISSN 0070-9573
EL PASO ARCHAEOLOGICAL SOCIETY. SPECIAL REPORTS. 1963. a. price varies. El Paso Archaeological Society, Inc., Box 4345, El Paso, TX 79914. Ed. Gerald X. Fitzgerald. circ. 300.

913　　　　　　BE
ELKAB. 1971. irreg., no. 2, 1979. price varies. Fondation Egyptologique Reine Elisabeth, Comite des Fouilles Belges en Egypte, Parc du Cinquantenaire 10, B-1040 Brussels, Belgium.

913　　　　　　II　ISSN 0013-9564
EPIGRAPHIA INDICA. (Text in English) 1888. irreg. Rs.64 per vol.(8 nos. per vol) Archaeological Survey of India, Old University Office Bldg., Mysore 570005, India (Order from: Controller of Publications, Government of India, Civil Lines, Delhi 110054, India) Ed. K.G. Krishnan. bk. rev. charts. illus. index every 2 years. circ. 740.

913 410　　　　　US
EPIGRAPHIC SOCIETY. OCCASIONAL PUBLICATIONS. vol. 7, 1979. irreg. membership. Epigraphic Society, 6 Woodland Street, Arlington, MA 02174. (back issues avail)

913 933　　　　　IS　ISSN 0071-108X
ERETZ-ISRAEL. ARCHAEOLOGICAL, HISTORICAL AND GEOGRAPHICAL STUDIES. (Text in English and Hebrew) 1951. biennial, vol. 14, 1978. $25. Israel Exploration Society, P.O. Box 7041, Jerusalem, Israel. Ed. Menahem Haram. circ. 2,500.

918　　　　　　CL
ESTUDIO ATACAMENOS. 1973. irreg. exchange. Universidad del Norte, Museo de Arqueologia, San Pedro de Atacama, Chile.

913　　　　　　AG
ESTUDIOS DE ARQUEOLOGIA. 1972. irreg., no. 2, 1977. $4. Museo Arqueologico de Cachi, 4417 Cachi, Argentina. Dir. Pio Pablo Diaz. bibl. charts. stat. illus.

ETUDES DE PHILOLOGIE, D'ARCHEOLOGIE ET D'HISTOIRE ANCIENNE. see *PHILOSOPHY*

913　　　　　　MR　ISSN 0071-2027
ETUDES ET TRAVAUX D'ARCHEOLOGIE MAROCAINE.* 1965. irreg. Division des Antiquites, 23, rue al Brihi, Rabat, Morocco.

913.031　　　　　　FR
ETUDES PREHISTORIQUES. 1971. irreg. 35 F. Societe Prehistorique de l'Ardeche, 34 Ave. de Limburg, 69110 Ste. Foy les Lyon, France. Ed. Jean Combier. bibl. illus. circ. 1,000.

913　　　　　　SP　ISSN 0071-3279
EXCAVACIONES ARQUEOLOGICAS EN ESPANA.* 1962. irreg. Comisaria General de Excavaciones Arqueologicas, Serrano 13, Madrid, Spain.

913　　　　　　US　ISSN 0071-3287
EXCAVATIONS AT DURA-EUROPOS. irreg. price varies. (Yale University) J. J. Augustin, Inc., Locust Valley, NY 11560. (Co-sponsor: French Academy of Inscriptions and Letters)

913　　　　　　CS
FONTES. 1972. irreg. price varies. (Slovenske Narodne Muzeum, Archeologicky Ustav) Osveta, Ul, 036 54 Martin, Czechoslovakia. Ed. Jozef Vlachovic. charts. illus. maps.

943.8 913　　　　　PL　ISSN 0071-6863
FONTES ARCHAEOLOGICI POSNANIENSES/ ANNALES MUSEI ARCHAEOLOGICI POSNANIENSIS. (Text in Polish; summaries in English, French and German) 1951. a. price varies. Muzeum Archeologiczne, Poznan, Ul. Wodna 27, Palac Gorkow, 61-781 Poznan, Poland (Dist. by Ars Polona-Ruch, Krakowskie Przedmiescie 7, Warsaw, Poland) Ed. Wlodzimierz Blaszczyk. bk. rev. circ. 600.
　　Formerly: Fontes Praehistorici.

913　　　　　　CS　ISSN 0015-6183
FONTES ARCHAEOLOGICI PRAGENSES. (Text in English, French, German, Russian) 1958. irreg. price varies. Narodni Muzeum, Historicke Muzeum, Vaclavske nam. 1700, 115 79 Prague 1, Czechoslovakia. Ed. Jiri Bren. charts. illus. stat. cum.index. circ. 700. (tabloid format)

FORSCHUNGEN ZUR KUNSTGESCHICHTE UND CHRISTLICHEN ARCHAEOLOGIE. see *ART*

FORSCHUNGEN ZUR RECHTSARCHAEOLOGIE UND RECHTLICHEN VOLKSKUNDE. see *LAW*

913　　　　　　FR
FOUILLES DE DELPHES: COLLECTION. irreg. Diffusion de Boccard, 11 rue de Medicis, 75006 Paris, France.

913　　　　　　FR　ISSN 0071-8394
FRANCE. COMITE DES TRAVAUX HISTORIQUES ET SCIENTIFIQUES. BULLETIN ARCHEOLOGIQUE. (In Two Fascicules: Antiquites Nationales; Afrique du Nord) 1883. a. price varies. Bibliotheque Nationale, 58 rue Richelieu, 75-Paris 2e, France. cum.index: 1883-1940. circ. 750.

913　　　　　　FR　ISSN 0071-8416
FRANCE. COMITE DES TRAVAUX HISTORIQUES ET SCIENTIFIQUES. SECTION D'ARCHEOLOGIE. ACTES DU CONGRES NATIONAL DES SOCIETES SAVANTES. 1957 (congress of 1954) a. price varies. Bibliotheque Nationale, 58 rue de Richelieu, 75084 Paris Cedex 02, 58 rue Richeliue. index. circ. 650.

709　　　　　　GW　ISSN 0071-9757
FUEHRER ZU VOR- UND FRUEGESCHICHTLICHEN DENKMAELERN. 1964. irreg., vol. 32, 1977. dM 12. (Roemisch-Germanisches Zentralmuseum, Mainz) Philipp Von Zabern, Welschnonnengasse 11, Postfach 4065, 6500 Mainz, W. Germany (B.R.D.) index.

ARCHAEOLOGY

913   **GW**
FUNDBERICHTE AUS BADEN-WUERTTEMBERG. 1974. a. price varies. (Landesdenkmalamt Baden-Wuerttemberg) E. Schweizerbart'sche Verlagsbuchhandlung, Johannesstr. 3A, 7000 Stuttgart 1, W. Germany (B.R.D.) Ed. Helga Schach-Doerges. bk. rev. Formerly (1922-1971): Fundberichte aus Schwaben, Neue Folge (ISSN 0071-9897)

913   **GW**   **ISSN 0071-9889**
FUNDBERICHTE AUS HESSEN. 1961. irreg., no. 19/20, 1980. price varies. Rudolf Habelt Verlag, Am Buchenhang 1, 5300 Bonn 1, W. Germany (B.R.D.)

913   **FR**   **ISSN 0072-0119**
GALLIA. SUPPLEMENT. 1943. irreg., 1974, no. 27. price varies. Centre National de la Recherche Scientifique, 15 Quai Anatole-France, 75700 Paris, France.

913   **FR**   **ISSN 0072-0100**
GALLIA PREHISTOIRE. SUPPLEMENT. 1958. Supplements issued from 1963 on- irreg., 1973, no. 7. price varies. Centre National de la Recherche Scientifique, 15 Quai Anatole-France, 75700 Paris, France.

GDANSKIE TOWARZYSTWO NAUKOWE. WYDZIAL I. NAUK SPOLECZNYCH I HUMANISTYCZNYCH. KOMISJA ARCHEOLOGICZNA. PRACE. see *HISTORY — History Of Europe*

913 709   **SZ**   **ISSN 0072-0585**
GENAVA; revue d'archeologie et d'histoire de l'art. 1923. a. 45 Fr. Musee d'Art et d'Histoire, Geneva, Rue Charles Galland, 1211 Geneva 3, Switzerland.

913   **SZ**   **ISSN 0072-4270**
GESELLSCHAFT PRO VINDONISSA. JAHRESBERICHT. 1907. a. price varies. Gesellschaft pro Vindonissa, Vindonissa Museum, 5200 Brugg, Switzerland.

708   **SZ**   **ISSN 0072-4289**
GESELLSCHAFT PRO VINDONISSA. VEROEFFENTLICHUNGEN. 1942. irreg. price varies. Gesellschaft pro Vindonissa, Vindonissa Museum, 5200 Brugg, Switzerland.

913   **UK**   **ISSN 0305-8980**
GLASGOW ARCHAEOLOGICAL JOURNAL. 1969. a. £3. Glasgow Archaeological Society, c/o Hunterian Museum, University of Glasgow, Glasgow G12 8QQ, Scotland. Ed. Dr. Euan W. MacKie. bk. rev. circ. 350. (back issues avail.) Indexed: Br.Archaeol.Abstr.

916   **SA**
GOODWIN SERIES. (Text in English and Afrikaans) 1972. irreg., no. 3, 1979. R.22 (free to subscribers to South African Archaeological Bulletin) South African Archaeological Society, P.O. Box 31, Claremont 7735, South Africa. circ. 1,100.

571 942   **UK**   **ISSN 0072-6842**
GREAT BRITAIN. DEPARTMENT OF THE ENVIRONMENT. ARCHAEOLOGICAL REPORTS. 1956. irreg. price varies. Department of the Environment, 2 Marsham St., London SW1P 3EB, England (Avail. from H.M.S.O., c/o Liaison Officer, Atlantic House, Holborn Viaduct, London EC1P 1BN, England)

GREAT BRITAIN. ROYAL COMMISSION ON THE ANCIENT AND HISTORICAL MONUMENTS AND CONSTRUCTIONS OF ENGLAND. INTERIM REPORT. see *HISTORY — History Of Europe*

GREAT BRITAIN. ROYAL COMMISSION ON THE ANCIENT AND HISTORICAL MONUMENTS AND CONSTRUCTIONS OF WALES AND MONMOUTHSHIRE. INTERIM REPORT. see *HISTORY — History Of Europe*

914   **IT**
GUIDE A I MUSEI E AGLI SCAVI ARCHEOLOGICI DELLA CALABRIA. 1975. irreg. L.2000. Edizioni Parallelo 38, Via 3 Settembre 7, 89100 Reggio Calabria, Italy.

913 580 590   **NO**
GUNNERIA. (Text in Norwegian and English; summaries in English and German) 1971. irreg., no. 29, 1977. Kr.10. Kongelige Norske Videnskabers Selskab, Museet - Royal Norwegian Society of Sciences Museum, Erling Skakkes Gt. 47 C, 7000 Trondheim, Norway. (Co-sponsor: Universitetet i Trondheim) Ed. Bd. circ. controlled. Indexed: Biol.Abstr. Chem.Abstr.
Formerly (until no. 26, 1977): Kongelige Norske Videnskabers Selskab. Museet. Miscellanea.

GWECHALL. see *HISTORY — History Of Europe*

913   **GW**   **ISSN 0072-9183**
HABELTS DISSERTATIONSDRUCKE. REIHE KLASSISCHE ARCHAEOLOGIE. 1969. irreg., no. 12, 1980. price varies. Rudolf Habelt Verlag, Am Buchenhang 1, 5300 Bonn 1, W. Germany (B.R.D.)

913   **GW**   **ISSN 0341-3152**
HAMBURGER BEITRAEGE ZUR ARCHAEOLOGIE. 1971. irreg., vol. 7, 1981. price varies. Verlag Helmut Buske, Schlueterstr. 14, 2000 Hamburg 13, W. Germany (B.R.D.) Eds. Otto-Hermann Frey, Walter Hatto Gross, Erika Sliwa.

940   **UK**   **ISSN 0142-8950**
HAMPSHIRE FIELD CLUB AND ARCHAEOLOGICAL SOCIETY PROCEEDINGS. 1885. a. £8. Hampshire Field Club, c/o P. Stevens, Hon. Sec., County Library Headquarters, 81 North Walls, Winchester, England. Ed. K. Qualmann. bk. rev. charts. illus. circ. 900. (back issues avail.)
Formerly: Hampshire Field. Proceedings.

HISPANIA ANTIQUA EPIGRAPHICA. see *LINGUISTICS*

913 940   **YU**
HISTORIA ARCHAEOLOGICA. (Text in Serbocroatian; summaries in English) 1976. a. Arheoloski Muzej Istre u Puli, M. Balote 3, Pula, Yugoslavia. Ed. Branko Marusic. bibl. charts. illus.

913   **US**   **ISSN 0440-9213**
HISTORICAL ARCHAEOLOGY. 1967. a. $20 includes subscription to Society for Historical Archaeology Newsletter. (Sponsor: Society for the Anthropology of Visual Communication) American Anthropological Association, 1703 New Hampshire Ave., N. W., Washington, Moscow, DC 20009. Ed. Ronald Michael. bk. rev. circ. 1,100. (all back issues avail.) Indexed: Abstr.Anthropol.

913   **US**
I A. (Industrial Archeology) 1976. a. $6. Society for Industrial Archeology, Room 5020, National Museum of History and Technology, Smithsonian Institution, Washington, DC 20560. Ed. Diana Newell. adv. bk. rev. illus. circ. 2,000. (back issues avail.)

I. C. NACHRICHTEN. (Institutum Canarium) see *ANTHROPOLOGY*

570   **US**   **ISSN 0360-0270**
ILLINOIS. STATE MUSEUM. REPORTS OF INVESTIGATIONS. 1948. irreg., no. 37, 181. price varies. Illinois State Museum, Springfield, IL 62706. illus. Key Title: Reports of Investigations - Illinois State Museum.

ILLINOIS. STATE MUSEUM. SCIENTIFIC PAPERS SERIES. see *EARTH SCIENCES — Geology*

INDIANA; contributions to ethnology and linguistics, archaeology and physical anthropology of Indian America. see *ANTHROPOLOGY*

913   **GW**
INFORMATIONSBLAETTER ZU NACHBARWISSENSCHAFTEN DER UR- UND FRUEHGESCHICHTE. 1970. a. price varies. Rudolf Habelt Verlag, Am Buchenhang 1, 5300 Bonn 1, W. Germany (B.R.D.)

913   **PL**   **ISSN 0085-1876**
INFORMATOR ARCHEOLOGICZNY. 1968. a. free. Polska Akademia Nauk, Instytut Historii Kultury Materialnej, Ul. Swierczewskiego 105, Warsaw, Poland. (Co-Publisher: Ministerstwo Kultury i Sztuki) (Co-sponsor: Polskie Towarzystwo Archeologiczne i Numizmatyczne) Ed. Marek Konopka.

913   **GW**
INSCHRIFTEN GRIECHISCHER STAEDTE AUS KLEINASIEN. 1972. irreg., no. 20, 1980. price varies. (Oesterreichische Akademie der Wissenschaften, Kommission fuer die Archaeologische Erforschung, AU) Rudolf Habelt Verlag, Am Buchenhang 1, 5300 Bonn 1, W. Germany (B.R.D.)

913   **BE**
INSTITUT ARCHEOLOGIQUE DU LUXEMBOURG. ANNALES. 1847. a. 550 Fr. (combined price with Bulletin) Institut Archeologique du Luxembourg, Bibliotheque, 13 rue des Martyrs, 6700 Arlon, Belgium.

INSTITUT FRANCAIS D'ARCHEOLOGIE D'ISTANBUL. BIBLIOTHEQUE ARCHEOLOGIQUE ET HISTORIQUE. see *ORIENTAL STUDIES*

INSTITUT HISTORIQUE ET ARCHEOLOGIQUE NEERLANDAIS DE STAMBOULL. PUBLICATIONS. see *HISTORY — History Of Asia*

913 550   **US**
INSTITUTE FOR THE STUDY OF EARTH AND MAN NEWSLETTER. 1974. a. free. Southern Methodist University, Institute for the Study of Earth and Man, c/o Heroy Science Hall, 3225 Daniel Street, Dallas, TX 75203. Ed. Claude C. Albritton, Jr. bibl. illus.

INSTITUTO DE ANTHROPOLOGIA E HISTORIA DEL ESTADO CARABOBO. BOLETIN. see *ANTHROPOLOGY*

913 949.8   **RM**   **ISSN 0074-039X**
INSTITUTUL DE ISTORIE SI ARHEOLOGIE "A. D. XENOPOL". ANUARUL. 1964. a. $10. Editura Academiei Republicii Socialiste Romania, Calea Victoriei 125, Bucharest, Romania (Subscr. to: ILEXIM, Str. 13 Decembrie Nr. 3, P.O. Box 136-137, Bucharest, Romania) Ed. M. Petrescu-Dimbovita.

571 930   **IT**   **ISSN 0074-1469**
INTERNATIONAL ASSOCIATION FOR CLASSICAL ARCHAEOLOGY. PROCEEDINGS OF CONGRESS. (Proceedings published by host country) irreg.; 1978, 11th, London. International Association for Classical Archaeology, 49 Piazza San Marco, 00186 Rome, Italy.

571   **UK**   **ISSN 0074-3429**
INTERNATIONAL CONGRESS FOR PAPYROLOGY. PROCEEDINGS. triennial, 15th Congress 1977, Brussels. DM.120. International Association of Papyrologists, c/o Dr. R. A. Coles, Papyrology Rooms, Ashmolean Museum, Oxford, England.
Proceedings published by organizing committee

INTERNATIONAL UNION OF PREHISTORIC AND PROTOHISTORIC SCIENCES. PROCEEDINGS OF CONGRESS. see *ANTHROPOLOGY*

913   **GW**   **ISSN 0075-0034**
INVENTARIA ARCHAEOLOGICA BELGIQUE. (Text in French) 1956. irreg. DM.20. (International Congress of Prehistoric and Protohistoric Sciences) Rudolf Habelt Verlag, Am Buchenhang 1, 5300 Bonn 1, W. Germany (B.R.D.)

913 943.7   **GW**   **ISSN 0075-0042**
INVENTARIA ARCHAEOLOGICA CESKOSLOVENSKO. (Text in French) 1961. irreg., 1967, no. 4. DM.20. (International Congress of Prehistoric and Protohistoric Sciences) Rudolf Habelt Verlag, Am Buchenhang 1, 5300 Bonn 1, W. Germany (B.R.D.)

913   **GW**   **ISSN 0075-0050**
INVENTARIA ARCHAEOLOGICA DENMARK. (Text in English) 1965. irreg., 1971, no. 8. DM.20. (International Congress of Prehistoric and Protohistoric Sciences) Rudolf Habelt Verlag, Am Buchenhang 1, 5300 Bonn 1, W. Germany (B.R.D.)

913   **GW**   **ISSN 0075-0069**
INVENTARIA ARCHAEOLOGICA DEUTSCHLAND. 1954. irreg., no. 18, 1979. DM.20. (International Congress of Prehistoric and Protohistoric Sciences) Rudolf Habelt Verlag, Am Buchenhang 1, 5300 Bonn 1, W. Germany (B.R.D.)

913   GW   ISSN 0075-0077
INVENTARIA ARCHAEOLOGICA ESPANA. (Text in Spanish) 1958. irreg., 1967, no. 7. price varies. (International Congress of Prehistoric and Protohistoric Sciences) Rudolf Habelt Verlag, Am Buchenhang 1, 5300 Bonn 1, W. Germany (B.R.D.)

913   GW   ISSN 0075-0085
INVENTARIA ARCHAEOLOGICA FRANCE. (Text in French) 1956. irreg., no. 4, 1975. price varies. (International Congress of Prehistoric and Protohistoric Sciences) Rudolf Habelt Verlag, Am Buchenhang 1, 5300 Bonn 1, W. Germany (B.R.D.)

913   GW   ISSN 0075-0093
INVENTARIA ARCHAEOLOGICA GREAT BRITAIN. (Text in English) 1955. irreg., 1968, no. 9. DM.20. (International Congress of Prehistoric and Protohistoric Sciences) Rudolf Habelt Verlag, Am Buchenhang 1, 5300 Bonn 1, W. Germany (B.R.D.)

913   GW   ISSN 0075-0107
INVENTARIA ARCHAEOLOGICA ITALIA. (Text in Italian) 1961. irreg., 1967, no. 4. price varies. (International Congress of Prehistoric and Protohistoric Sciences) Rudolf Habelt Verlag, Am Buchenhang 1, 5300 Bonn 1, W. Germany (B.R.D.)

913   GW   ISSN 0075-0115
INVENTARIA ARCHAEOLOGICA JUGOSLAVIJA. (Text in French) 1957. irreg., no. 24, 1980. DM.20. (International Congress of Prehistoric and Protohistoric Sciences) Rudolf Habelt Verlag, Am Buchenhang 1, 5300 Bonn 1, W. Germany (B.R.D.)

913   GW   ISSN 0075-0123
INVENTARIA ARCHAEOLOGICA NORWAY. (Text in English) 1966. irreg. DM.20. (International Congress of Prehistoric and Protohistoric Sciences) Rudolf Habelt Verlag, Am Buchenhang 1, 5300 Bonn 1, W. Germany (B.R.D.)

913   GW   ISSN 0075-0131
INVENTARIA ARCHAEOLOGICA OESTERREICH. 1956. irreg. DM.20. (International Congress of Prehistoric and Protohistoric Sciences) Rudolf Habelt Verlag, Am Buchenhang 1, 5300 Bonn 1, W. Germany (B.R.D.)

913   GW   ISSN 0075-014X
INVENTARIA ARCHAEOLOGICA POLOGNE. (Text in French) 1958. irreg., no. 44, 1980. DM.20. (International Congress of Prehistoric and Protohistoric Sciences) Rudolf Habelt Verlag, Am Buchenhang 1, 5300 Bonn 1, W. Germany (B.R.D.)

913   GW
INVENTARIA ARCHAEOLOGICA THE NETHERLANDS. 1971. irreg. DM.20. Rudolf Habelt Verlag, Am Buchenhang 1, 5300 Bonn 1, W. Germany (B.R.D.)

913   GW   ISSN 0075-0158
INVENTARIA ARCHAEOLOGICA UNGARN. 1962. irreg., 1971, no. 3. price varies. (International Congress of Prehistoric and Protohistoric Sciences) Rudolf Habelt Verlag, Am Buchenhang 1, 5300 Bonn 1, W. Germany (B.R.D.)

571   US   ISSN 0085-2252
IOWA STATE ARCHAEOLOGIST. REPORT. 1970. a. price varies. University of Iowa, Dept. of Publications, Iowa City, IA 52242. Ed. Duane Anderson. bibl. charts. illus. circ. 500-1,000.

913 390   NE   ISSN 0021-0870
IRANICA ANTIQUA; dealing with archaeology, history, religion, art and literature of ancient Persia. (Text in English, French or German) 1961. irreg., vol. 15, 1980. price varies. E. J. Brill, Oude Rijn 33a-35, Leiden, Netherlands. Eds. R. Ghirsman & L. Vanden Berghe.

571   IS   ISSN 0066-488X
ISRAEL. MINISTRY OF EDUCATION AND CULTURE. DEPARTMENT OF ANTIQUITIES AND MUSEUMS. ATIQOT (ENGLISH SERIES) Title varies: Archaeological Excavation Reports. (Text in English) 1955. irreg., vol. 13, 1978. price varies. Ministry of Education and Culture, Department of Antiquities and Museums, P.O.B. 586, Jerusalem, Israel. Ed. Inna Pommerantz. circ. 1,500.

913   IS   ISSN 0067-0138
ISRAEL. MINISTRY OF EDUCATION AND CULTURE. DEPARTMENT OF ANTIQUITIES AND MUSEUMS. ATIQOT (HEBREW SERIES) (Text in Hebrew; summaries in English) 1955. irreg., vol. 7, 1974. $10. Ministry of Education and Culture, Department of Antiquities and Museums, P.O.B. 586, Jerusalem, Israel. Ed. Inna Pommerantz. circ. 1,500.

571   IT   ISSN 0530-9867
ISTITUTO INTERNAZIONALE DI STUDI LIGURI. COLLEZIONE DI MONOGRAFIE PREISTORICHE ED ARCHEOLOGICHE. (Text in Italian, French and Spanish) 1946. a; latest issue, 1974. price varies. Istituto Internazionale di Studi Liguri, Via Romana, 39 bis, 18012 - Bordighera, Italy. circ. 1,000.

JAARBERICHT "EX ORIENTE LUX; annuaire de la Societe Orientale Neerlandaise "Ex Oriente Lux". see HISTORY — History Of Asia

913   UK   ISSN 0307-5133
JOURNAL OF EGYPTIAN ARCHAEOLOGY. (Text in English; occasionally in French and German) 1914. a. £7.50 tomembers; £10 to non-members. Egypt Exploration Society, 3 Doughty News, London WC1N 2PG, England. Ed. Dr. A. B. Lloyd. bk. rev. cum.index every 5 years. circ. 3,500. (back issues avail.) Indexed: Old Test.Abstr.

JOURNAL OF JURISTIC PAPYROLOGY. see LAW

913   US   ISSN 0147-9024
JOURNAL OF NEW WORLD ARCHAEOLOGY. 1975. irreg. $12. University of California, Los Angeles, Institute of Archaeology, 405 Hilgard Ave., Los Angeles, CA 90024. Ed. C. William Clewlow, Jr. bibl. charts. illus. index. circ. 100. (back issues avail.)

913   IS   ISSN 0075-4501
JUDEAN DESERT STUDIES. (Text in English) 1963. irreg. price varies. Israel Exploration Society, P.O. Box 7041, Jerusalem, Israel.

913   FR   ISSN 0453-3429
KARTHAGO. 1971-72, no. 16. biennial. price varies. (Universite de Paris I (Pantheon-Sorbonne), Centre d'Etudes Archeologiques de la Mediterranee Occidentale) Editions Klincksieck, 11 rue de Lille, Paris (7e), France. (Affiliate: Universite de Paris-Sorbonne) Ed. M.G. Picard. bibl. illus. circ. 750.

913   FR   ISSN 0075-5184
KARTHAGO. COLLECTION EPIGRAPHIQUE. 1968. irreg. price varies. (Universite de Paris I (Pantheon-Sorbonne), Centre d'Etudes Archeologiques de la Mediterranee Occidentale) C.E.A.M.O., 3 rue Michelet, 75006 Paris, France.

913   GW   ISSN 0075-5338
KEILSCHRIFTTEXTE AUS BOGHAZKOI. 1939. irreg., vol. 26, 1978. price varies. (Deutsche Orient-Gesellschaft) Gebr. Mann Verlag, Lindenstr. 76, Postfach 110303, 1000 Berlin 61, W. Germany (B.R.D.) Ed. Heinrich Otten.

KEILSCHRIFTURKUNDEN AUS BOGHAZKOEI. see HISTORY — History Of Asia

941.5   IE   ISSN 0085-2503
KERRY ARCHAEOLOGICAL AND HISTORICAL SOCIETY. JOURNAL. 1968. a. £4 free to members. Kerry Archaeological and Historical Society, County Library, Tralee, Co Kerry, Ireland. Ed. Rev. Kieran o'Shea. circ. 450.

913   GW   ISSN 0075-6512
KOELNER JAHRBUCH FUER VOR- UND FRUEHGESCHICHTE. 1955. irreg., vol. 14, 1977. price varies. (Roemisch-Germanisches Museum) Gebr. Mann Verlag, Lindenstr. 76, Postfach 110303, 1000 Berlin 61, W. Germany (B.R.D.) (Co-sponsor: Archaeologische Gesellschaft, Cologne)

KOELNER ROEMER-ILLUSTRIERTE. see MUSEUMS AND ART GALLERIES

913   GW   ISSN 0075-725X
KUNST UND ALTERTUM AM RHEIN. 1956. irreg., vol. 98, 1980. price varies. Rheinland- Verlag, Kennedy-Ufer 2, 5000 Cologne 21, W. Germany (B.R.D.) (Distr. by: Rudolf Habelt Verlag GmbH, Am Buchenhang 1, 5300 Bonn 1, W. Germany (B.R.D.))

913 940   UK
LEICESTERSHIRE ARCHAEOLOGICAL AND HISTORICAL SOCIETY. TRANSACTIONS. 1866. a. £6. Leicestershire Archaeological and Historical Society, The Guildhall, Guildhall Lane, Leicester LE1 5FQ, England. Ed. Dr. D.T. Williams. adv. bk. rev. circ. 600.

913   UK   ISSN 0075-8914
LEVANT; Journal of the British School of Archaeology in Jerusalem. 1969. a. £4($13) s($6.50) British School of Archaeology in Jerusalem, 2 Hinde Mews, Marylebone Lane, London W1M 5RH, England. Ed. P. R. S. Moorey. circ. 650-700. (back issues avail.)

913 301.2   FR   ISSN 0459-3030
LIBYCA; anthropologie, prehistoire, ethnographie. 1953. a. (Centre de Recherches Anthropologiques, Prehistoriques et Ethnographiques, AE) Flammarion, Service des Periodiques, 26 rue Racine, 75006 Paris, France. illus.

913   UK   ISSN 0459-4487
LINCOLNSHIRE HISTORY AND ARCHAEOLOGY. 1966. a. £5.50 to non-members. Society for Lincolnshire History & Archaeology, 47 Newland, Lincoln LN1 1XZ, England. Ed. Dr. Mary Finch. bk. rev. circ. 865.

571 913   UK   ISSN 0076-0501
LONDON AND MIDDLESEX ARCHAEOLOGICAL SOCIETY. TRANSACTIONS. 1855. a. membership. London and Middlesex Archaeological Society, c/o Museum of London, London Wall, London EC2Y 5HN, England (and Phillimore & Co. Ltd., Shopwyke Hall, Chichester, Sussex, England) Ed. Lawrence S. Snell. bk. rev. circ. 850. Indexed: Br.Hum.Ind. Br.Archaeol.Abstr. Br.Hum.Ind.

913   HU   ISSN 0076-2504
MAGYARORSZAG REGESZETI TOPOGRAFIAJA. 1967. irreg. price varies. (Magyar Tudomanyos Akademia) Akademiai Kiado, Publishing House of the Hungarian Academy of Sciences, P.O. Box 24, H-1363 Budapest, Hungary.

571   II   ISSN 0076-2520
MAHARAJA SAYAJIRAO UNIVERSITY OF BARODA. DEPARTMENT OF ARCHAEOLOGY AND ANCIENT HISTORY. ARCHAEOLOGY SERIES. (Text in English) irreg.(approx. 1 issue per year) price varies. Maharaja Sayajirao University of Baroda, Department of Archaeology and Ancient History, Baroda 390002, Gujarat, India. Ed. R. N. Mehta.

MAINZER ZEITSCHRIFT; Mittelrheinisches jahrbuch fuer Archaeologie, Geschichte und Kunst. see ART

MAN & ENVIRONMENT. see ANTHROPOLOGY

917   US
MARYLAND. GEOLOGICAL SURVEY. ARCHAEOLOGICAL STUDIES. 1973. irreg. Geological Survey, Johns Hopkins University, Merryman Hall, Baltimore, MD 21218. charts. illus. circ. 1,000. (back issues avail.)

913   RM   ISSN 0076-5147
MATERIALE SI CERCETARI ARHEOLOGICE. 1955. irreg. (Academia Republicii Socialiste Romania, Institutul de Arheologie) Editura Academiei Republicii Socialiste Romania, Calea Victoriei 125, Bucharest, Romania (Subscr. to: ILEXIM, Str. 13 Decembrie Nr. 3, P.O. Box 136-137, Bucharest, Romania)

MATERIALIEN ZUR ROEMISCH-GERMANISCHEN KERAMIK. see CERAMICS, GLASS AND POTTERY

MATERIALY ZACHODNIO-POMORSKIE. see HISTORY — History Of Europe

913   UK   ISSN 0076-6097
MEDIEVAL ARCHAEOLOGY. 1957. a. membership. Society for Medieval Archaeology, c/o Harvest House, 62 London Rd., Reading, Berks. RG1 5AS, England.

913　　　　　　　IT　　ISSN 0076-6615
MESOPOTAMIA; rivista di archeologia. (Text in English and Italian) 1966. a. price varies. (Universita degli Studi di Torino) G. Giappichelli Editore, Via Po, 21, Turin, Italy. (Co-sponsor: Centro Ricerche Archeologiche e Scavi di Torino per Il Medio Oriente e l'Asia) Ed. G. Giappichelli.

913　　　　　　　SP　　ISSN 0076-9371
MISION ARQUEOLOGICA ESPANOLA EN NUBIA. MEMORIAS. 1963. irreg. price varies. Museo Arqueologico Nacional, Serrano, 13, Madrid 1, Spain.

913　　　　　　　US　　ISSN 0076-9541
MISSOURI ARCHAEOLOGICAL SOCIETY. MEMOIR SERIES. irreg. Missouri Archaeological Society, P.O. Box 958, Columbia, MO 65201.

913　　　　　　　US　　ISSN 0544-5094
MISSOURI ARCHAEOLOGICAL SOCIETY. RESEARCH SERIES. 1963. irreg. Missouri Archaeological Society, P.O. Box 958, Columbia, MO 65201.

913　　　　　　　US　　ISSN 0076-9576
MISSOURI ARCHAEOLOGIST. 1935. a. $7.50 includes all Society publications. Missouri Archaeological Society, P.O. Box 958, Columbia, MO 65201. Ed. Robert T. Bray.

913　　　　　　　IT　　ISSN 0067-009X
MONGRAFIE DELLA SCUOLA ARCHEOLOGICA DI ATENE E DELLE MISSIONI ITALIANE IN ORIENTE. 1964. irreg., vol. 49, no. 33, N.S., 1971. price varies. (Scuola Archeologica di Atene) Italy. Istituto Poligrafico dello Stato, Piazza Verdi, 10, Rome, Italy. circ. 500.

913　　　　　　　IT　　ISSN 0077-0493
MONOGRAFIE DI ARCHEOLOGIA LIBICA. 1948. irreg.; no. 13, 1976. price varies. Erma di "Bretschneider", Via Cassiodoro 19, 00193 Rome, Italy.

913　　　　　　　BE
MONOGRAPHIES REINE ELISABETH. 1971. irreg., latest vol. 4, 1978. price varies. Fondation Egyptologique Reine Elisabeth, Parc du Cinquantenaire 10, B-1040 Brussels, Belgium.

960 090　　　　BE　　ISSN 0077-1376
MONUMENTA AEGYPTIACA. 1968. irreg., latest no. 2, 1977. price varies. Fondation Egyptologique Reine Elisabeth, Parc du Cinquantenaire 10, B-1040 Brussels, Belgium.

913　　　　　　　GW　　ISSN 0077-1384
MONUMENTA AMERICANA. (Text in German; occasionally also in English or Spanish) 1965. irreg., vol. 9, 1973. price varies. (Ibero-Amerikanisches Institut Preussischer Kulturbesitz Berlin) Gebr. Mann Verlag, Lindenstr. 76, Postfach 110303, 1000 Berlin 61, W. Germany (B.R.D.) Ed. Gerdt Kutscher.

913　　　　　　　HU　　ISSN 0077-1392
MONUMENTA ANTIQUITATIS EXTRA FINES HUNGARIAE REPERTA QUAE IN MUSEO ARTIUM HUNGARICO ALIISQUE MUSEIS ET COLLECTIONIBUS HUNGARICIS CONSERVANTUR. (Text in English) 1968. irreg. price varies. (Magyar Tudomanyos Akademia) Akademiai Kiado, Publishing House of the Hungarian Academy of Sciences, P.O. Box 24, H-1363 Budapest, Hungary.

913　　　　　　　US　　ISSN 0363-7565
MONUMENTA ARCHAEOLOGICA (LOS ANGELES) 1976. irreg. University of California, Los Angeles, Institute of Archaeology, 405 Hilgard Ave., Los Angeles, CA 90024.

913 709　　　　GW　　ISSN 0077-1406
MONUMENTA ARTIS ROMANAE. 1959. irreg., vol. 13, 1977. price varies. Gebr. Mann Verlag, Lindenstr. 76, Postfach 110303, 1000 Berlin 61, W. Germany (B.R.D.) Ed. Heinz Kaehler.

MONUMENTA HISTORICA BUDAPESTINENSIA. see HISTORY — History Of Europe

913 708　　　　US　　ISSN 0077-2194
MUSE. 1967. a. $3. ‡ University of Missouri-Columbia, Museum of Art and Archaeology, One Pickard Hall, Columbia, MO 65211. Eds. Ruth E. Witt, Osmund Overby. circ. 2,500.

MUSEE GUIMET, PARIS. BIBLIOTHEQUE D'ETUDES. see ART

MUSEE GUIMET, PARIS. ETUDE DES COLLECTIONS DU MUSEE. see ART

914　　　　　　　SP
MUSEO ARQUEOLOGICO DE VALLADOLID. MONOGRAFIAS. 1974. irreg. Museo Arqueologico de Valladolid, Palacio de Fabio Nelli, Valladolid, Spain. illus.

913　　　　　　　SP
MUSEO ARQUEOLOGICO NACIONAL. MONOGRAFIAS ARQUEOLOGICAS. no. 5, 1978. irreg. Museo Arqueologico Nacional, Serrano 13, Madrid 1, Spain.

MUSEO NACIONAL DE ANTROPOLOGIA Y ARQUEOLOGIA. SERIE: INVESTIGACIONES DE CAMPO. see ANTHROPOLOGY

913 572　　　　PE
MUSEO NACIONAL DE ANTROPOLOGIA Y ARQUEOLOGIA. SERIE: METALURGIA. 1976. irreg. Museo Nacional de Antropologia y Arqueologia, Plaza Bolivar, Pueblo Libre, Lima 21, Peru. Ed.Ruth Shady Solis.

MUSEUM MEMOIR. see BIOLOGY — Zoology

913　　　　　　　IS　　ISSN 0082-2620
MUSEUM OF ANTIQUITIES OF TEL-AVIV-YAFO. PUBLICATIONS. 1964. irreg. $1. Museum of Antiquites of Tel-Aviv-Yafo, Box 8406, Tel Aviv-Jaffa, Israel.

913 943.8　　　　PL　　ISSN 0458-1520
MUZEUM ARCHEOLOGICZNE I ETNOGRAFICZNE, LODZ. PRACE I MATERIALY. SERIA ARCHEOLOGICZNA. (Summaries in English, French or German) 1956. irreg., 1975, no. 21. price varies. ‡ Panstwowe Wydawnictwo Naukowe, Miodowa 10, Warsaw, Poland (Dist. by Ars Polona-Ruch, Krakowskie Predmiescie 7, Warsaw Poland) Ed. Konrad Jazdzewski. circ. 500.

943.8　　　　　　PL　　ISSN 0075-7039
MUZEUM ARCHEOLOGICZNE, KRAKOW. MATERIALY ARCHEOLOGICZNE. 1959. irreg., 1972, no. 13. Muzeum Archeologiczne, Krakow, Poselska 3, 31-002 Krakow, Poland.

913　　　　　　　PL　　ISSN 0068-4635
MUZEUM GORNOSLASKIE W BYTOMIU. ROCZNIK. SERIA ARCHEOLOGIA. (Text in Polish; summaries in German and Russian) 1962. irreg. price varies. Muzeum Gornoslaskie, Pl. Thaelmanna 2, 41-902 Bytom, Poland (Dist. by Ars Polona-Ruch, Krakowskie Przedmiescie 7, Warsaw, Poland)

NATUR UND MENSCH; JAHRESMITTEILUNGEN DER NATURHISTORISCHEN GESELLSCHAFT NUERNBERG. see BIOLOGY

913 980　　　　US　　ISSN 0077-6297
NAWPA PACHA. (Contributions in English, Inca,, French and Spanish; contributions in other languages accepted) 1963. a. $10 to individuals; institutions $12. Institute of Andean Studies, Box 9307, Berkeley, CA 94709. Eds. John H. Rowe, Patricia J. Lyon. circ. 550.
International series for Andean archaeology

913　　　　　　　PL
NEA PAPHOS. (Text in French and Polish) 1976. irreg. (Polska Akademia Nauk, Zaklad Archeologii Srodziemnomorskiej) Panstwowe Wydawnictwo Naukowe, Miodowa 10, 00-251 Warsaw, Poland. (Dist. by: Ars Polona, Krakowskie Przedmiescie 7, 00-068 Warsaw, Poland) Ed. Kazimierz Michalowski.

913 953　　　　NE
NETHERLANDS INSTITUTE OF ARCHAEOLOGY AND ARABIC STUDIES IN CAIRO. PUBLICATIONS. no. 3, 1979. irreg. price varies. E. J. Brill, Oude Rijn 33a-35, Leiden, Netherlands.

NEVADA. STATE MUSEUM, CARSON CITY. ANTHROPOLOGICAL PAPERS. see ANTHROPOLOGY

913 973　　　　US　　ISSN 0077-8346
NEW HAMPSHIRE ARCHAEOLOGIST. 1950. a. price varies; $0.75 and up. New Hampshire Archeological Society Inc., Averill Rd., Brookline, NH 03033. Ed. Paul E. Holmes. circ. 200.

913　　　　　　　UK
NEW STUDIES IN ARCHAEOLOGY. 1976. irreg. price varies. Cambridge University Press, Box 110, Cambridge CB2 3RL, England (And 32 E. 57th St., New York, NY 10022) Ed.Bd.

913 974.7　　　US　　ISSN 0077-9059
NEW YORK STATE ARCHAEOLOGICAL ASSOCIATION. OCCASIONAL PAPERS. 1958. irreg., 1963, no. 4. price varies. ‡ New York State Archeological Association, c/o Rochester Museum and Science Center, Box 1480, 657 East Ave., Rochester, NY 14603. circ. 750. (back issues avail.)

913 974.7　　　US　　ISSN 0077-9067
NEW YORK STATE ARCHAEOLOGICAL ASSOCIATION. RESEARCHES AND TRANSACTIONS. 1918. irreg., vol. 17, 1977. price varies. ‡ New York State Archeological Association, Rochester Museum, Box 1480, 657 East Ave., Rochester, NY 14607. circ. 750. (back issues avail.)

913　　　　　　　NZ
NEW ZEALAND JOURNAL OF ARCHAEOLOGY. 1979. a. 10. New Zealand Archaeological Association, c/o Anthropology Department, University of Otago, P.O. Box 56, Dunedin, New Zealand. charts. illus.

NOMINA; a newsletter of name studies relating to Great Britain and Ireland. see GENEALOGY AND HERALDRY

NORSK SJOEFARTSMUSEUM. AARSBERETNING. see HISTORY — History Of Europe

913　　　　　　　UK　　ISSN 0305-4659
NORTHAMPTONSHIRE ARCHAEOLOGY. vol. 11, 1976. a. £5. Northamptonshire Archaeological Society, c/o Department of Adult Education, University of Leicester, University Rd., Leicester LE1 7RH, England. Ed. A. E. Brown. bk. rev. illus. circ. 200. Indexed: Br. Archaeol.Abstr.
Formerly: Northamptonshire Federation of Archaeological Societies. Bulletin.

914　　　　　　　SP
NOTICIARIO ARQUEOLOGICO HISPANICO: ARQUEOLOGIA. 1953. a. Comisaria General de Excavaciones Arqueologicas, Palacio del Museo Arquelogico Nacional, Serrano, 13 (1), Madrid, Spain. bibl. illus. circ. 1,200.

913 700　　　　DK　　ISSN 0085-3208
NY CARLSBERG GLYPTOTEK. MEDDELELSER. (Text in Danish; summaries in English, French, and German) 1944. a. Kr.60. Ny Carlsberg Glyptotek, Dantes Plads 1556, Copenhagen V, Denmark. Ed. Flemming Johansen. circ. 1,000.

ODENSE UNIVERSITY CLASSICAL STUDIES. see CLASSICAL STUDIES

913　　　　　　　AU
OESTERREICHISCHES ARCHAEOLOGISCHES INSTITUT. JAHRESHEFTE. 1965. a. S.700. Oesterreichisches Archaeologisches Institut, Universitaet, Dr. Karl Lueger-Ring 1, A-1010 Vienna, Austria. circ. 450.
Supersedes: Oesterreichisches Archaeologisches Institut. Jahreshefte: Grabungen (ISSN 0078-3579)

913　　　　　　　GR　　ISSN 0078-5520
OPUSCULA ATHENIENSIA. (Issued in Svenska Institutet i Athen. Skrifter) (Text in English, German, French) 1951. irreg., no. 13, 1980. price varies. Svenska Institutet i Athen, 9 Mitseon St., Athens 402, Greece (Dist. by: Paul Aastroems Foerlag, Johannebergsgatan 24, S-412 55 Gothenberg, Sweden) Ed. Berit Wells. bk. rev. circ. 1,000.

913　　　　　　　US
OXFORD MONOGRAPHS ON CLASSICAL ARCHAEOLOGY. irreg. price varies. Oxford University Press, 200 Madison Ave., New York, NY 10016 (And Ely House, 37 Dover St., London W1X 4AH, England) Ed.Bd.

913 940   UK   ISSN 0308-5562
OXONIENSIA. 1936. a. £4. Oxfordshire Architectural and Historical Society, Ashmolean Museum, Oxford, England. Ed. Dr. Janet Cooper. bk. rev. bibl. charts. illus. circ. 500.

913   BE
PACT. 1977. a. 1600 Fr. European Study Group on Physical, Chemical and Mathematical Techniques Applied to Archaeology, c/o T. Hackens, 28 Av. Leopold, B-1330 Rixensart, Belgium. Ed. Tony Hackens. circ. 1,000. Indexed: Chem.Abstr.

571   PK   ISSN 0078-7868
PAKISTAN ARCHAEOLOGY. (Text in English) 1964. a. price varies. Department of Archaeology and Museums, 5-B Pakistan Secretariat, Karachi 1, Pakistan.

913   CS
PAMATKY ARCHEOLOGICKE. BIBLIOGRAPHICAL REGISTER. irreg., latest issue (1931-1965), 1974. fl.60 per no. (Ceskoslovenska Akademie Ved, Archeologicky Ustav) Academia Publishing House of the Czechoslovak Academy of Sciences, Vodickova 40, 112 29 Prague 1, Czechoslovakia (Distributor in Western countries: John Benjamins B.V., Amsteldijk 44, Amsterdam (Z.), Netherlands) Ed. Jan Rataj.

PAMYATNIKI KUL'TURY. NOVYE OTKRYTIYA/ MONUMENTS OF CULTURE. NEW DISCOVERIES. see ART

PAN AMERICAN INSTITUTE OF GEOGRAPHY AND HISTORY. COMMISSION ON HISTORY. BIBLIOGRAFIAS. see HISTORY — History Of North And South America

960   BE   ISSN 0078-9402
PAPYROLOGICA BRUXELLENSIA. 1962. irreg., no. 19, 1979. Fondation Egyptologique Reine Elisabeth, Parc du Cinquantenaire 10, B-1040 Brussels, Belgium.

917   US
PEABODY MUSEUM BULLETINS. 1976. irreg., no. 3, 1978. price varies. Peabody Museum of Archaeology and Ethnology, Harvard University, 11 Divinity Ave., Cambridge, MA 02138.

913 572   US   ISSN 0079-029X
PEABODY MUSEUM OF ARCHAEOLOGY AND ETHNOLOGY. MEMOIRS. (Vols. not issued consecutively) 1896. irreg., vol. 19, 1980. price varies. Peabody Museum of Archaeology and Ethnology, Harvard University, 11 Divinity Ave., Cambridge, MA 02138. Ed. Lorna Condon. (also avail. in microfilm from AMS)

913   US
PEABODY MUSEUM OF ARCHAEOLOGY AND ETHNOLOGY. MONOGRAPHS. 1974. irreg., vol. 6, 1981. price varies. Peabody Museum of Archaeology and Ethnology, Harvard University, 11 Divinity Ave., Cambridge, MA 02138.

913 572   US   ISSN 0079-0303
PEABODY MUSEUM OF ARCHAEOLOGY AND ETHNOLOGY. PAPERS. 1891. irreg., vol. 72, 1980. price varies. Peabody Museum of Archaeology and Ethnology, Harvard University, 11 Divinity Ave., Cambridge, MA 02138. Ed. Lorna Condon. (also avail. in microfilm from AMS)

PERSICA. see HISTORY — History Of Asia

943.8 913   PL   ISSN 0079-3256
POLSKA AKADEMIA NAUK. ODDZIAL W KRAKOWIE KOMISJA ARCHEOLOGICZNA. PRACE. (Text in English, German and Polish; summaries in English, German and Russian) 1960. irreg., no. 17, 1979. price varies. Ossolineum, Publishing House of the Polish Academy of Sciences, Rynek 9, 50-106 Wroclaw, Poland (Dist. by Ars Polona-Ruch, Krakowskie Przedmiescie 7, Warsaw, Poland)

913   PL   ISSN 0079-3566
POLSKA AKADEMIA NAUK. ZAKLAD ARCHEOLOGII SRODZIEMNOMORSKIEJ. ETUDES ET TRAVAUX. Title varies: Polska Akademia Nauk. Zaklad Archeologii Srodziemnomorskiej. Prace. (Text in English and French) 1959. irreg., 1975, vol. 16. price varies. Panstwowe Wydawnictwo Naukowe, Ul. Miodowa 10, Warsaw, Poland. Ed. Kazimierz Michalowski. illus.

913   UK   ISSN 0079-4236
POST-MEDIEVAL ARCHAEOLOGY. 1967. a. £8. Society for Post-Medieval Archaeology, c/o J. H. Ashdown, Treas., 53 Bainton Road, Oxford OX2 7AG, England. Ed. D. W. Crossley. bk. rev. cum. index: vols. 1-5, 6-10. circ. 850. (back issues avail.) Indexed: Br.Archaeol.Abstr.

913   PL
POZNANSKIE TOWARZYSTWO PRZYJACIOL NAUK. KOMISJA ARCHEOLOGICZNA. PRACE. (Text in Polish; summaries in German) vol. 9, 1976. irreg. (Poznanskie Towarzystwo Przyjaciol Nauk, Komisja Archeologiczna) Panstwowe Wydawnictwo Naukowe, Miodowa 10, 00-251 Warsaw, Poland (Dist. by Ars Polona, Krakowskie Przedmiescie 7, 00-068 Warsaw, Poland) Ed.Bd. circ. 420.

913   GW   ISSN 0079-4848
PRAEHISTORISCHE ZEITSCHRIFT. 1909. 2/yr. DM.92($46) Walter de Gruyter und Co., Genthiner Str. 13, 1000 Berlin 30, W. Germany (B.R.D.) Eds. H. Jankuhn, V. Milojcic, R. v. Uslar. adv. bk. rev.

913 574.5   US
PREHISTORIC ARCHAEOLOGY AND ECOLOGY. 1973. irreg., latest 1977. price varies. University of Chicago Press, 5801 S. Ellis Ave., Chicago, IL 60637. Eds. Karl W. Butzer, Leslie F. Freeman. adv. bk. rev. (reprint service avail. from UMI,ISI)
Ecology

913   UK   ISSN 0079-497X
PREHISTORIC SOCIETY, LONDON. PROCEEDINGS. 1911. a. membership. Prehistoric Society, Flat 2, 75 Clarendon Rd., London W11 4JF, England. Ed. Dr. J. Coles. bk. rev. circ. 2,000. Indexed: SSCI.

PRINCETON MONOGRAPHS IN ART AND ARCHAEOLOGY. see ART

913   UR
PROBLEMY ARKHEOLOGII I ETNOGRAFII. vol. 1, 1977. irreg. 0.73 Rub. per no. Izdatel'stvo Leningradskii Universitet, Universitetskaya Nab. 7/9, Leningrad B-164, U.S.S.R. circ. 1,185.

913   UR
PROBLEMY ARKHEOLOGII I ETNOGRAFII. 1977. irreg. 0.73 Rub. per issue. Izdatel'stvo Leningradskii Universitet, Universitetskaya Nab. 7/9, Leningrad B-164, U.S.S.R. Ed. R. Its. circ. 1,185.

913   PL   ISSN 0079-7138
PRZEGLAD ARCHEOLOGICZNY. (Text in Polish; summaries in English, French and German) 1919. irreg., vol. 26, 1978. 90 Zl. (Polska Akademia Nauk, Instytut Historii Kultury Materialnej) Ossolineum, Publishing House of the Polish Academy of Sciences, Rynek 9, Wroclaw, Poland (Dist. by Ars Polona-Ruch, Krakowskie Przedmiescie 7, Warsaw, Poland) Ed. Tadeusz Wislanski. bk. rev. circ. 500.

571   SP   ISSN 0079-8215
PYRENAE: CRONICA ARQUEOLOGICA; annual scientific journal. 1965. a. 300 ptas.($6) Universidad de Barcelona, Facultad de Filosofia y Letras, Instituto de Arqueologia, Avenido de Jose Antonio 585, Barcelona 7, Spain. Ed. Juan Maluquer de Motes. bk. rev. circ. 600.

956   IS
QEDEM. (Text in English) 1975. irreg. price varies. Hebrew University of Jerusalem, Institute of Archaeology, Jerusalem, Israel (Israel Exploration Society, P.O.B. 7041, Jerusalem, Israel)

913   IT   ISSN 0079-8258
QUADERNI DI ARCHEOLOGIA DELLA LIBIA. 1950. irreg., no. 11, 1980. price varies. Erma di "Bretschneider", Via Cassiodoro, 19, 00193 Rome, Italy.

913.031   GW   ISSN 0375-7471
QUARTAER; Jahrbuch fuer Erforschung des Eiszeitalters und der Steinzeit. (Text in English, French and German) 1946. a. price varies. (Hugo-Obermaier-Gesellschaft) Verlag Ludwig Roehrscheid GmbH, Am Hof 28, Postfach 2227, D-5300 Bonn 1, W. Germany (B.R.D.) Eds. Dr. Gisela Freund, Dr. E.W. Guenther. bk. rev. illus. circ. 2,000. (reprint service avail. from UMI)

913 930   GW   ISSN 0079-9149
QUELLENSCHRIFTEN ZUR WESTDEUTSCHEN VOR- UND FRUEHGESCHICHTE. 1939. irreg., no. 9, 1974. price varies. Rudolf Habelt Verlag, Am Buchenhang 1, 5300 Bonn 1, W. Germany (B.R.D.) Ed. R. Stampfuss.

RECHERCHES ET DOCUMENTS D'ART ET D'ARCHEOLOGIE. see ART

REPORTS IN MACKINAC HISTORY AND ARCHAEOLOGY. see HISTORY — History Of North And South America

913   IT
REVISTA DI ARCHEOLOGIA. (Text in various languages) 1977. a. Giorgio Bretschneider, Ed. & Pub., Via Crescenzo 43, 00193 Rome, Italy. Ed. Gustavo Traversari. (back issues avail.)

913   FR   ISSN 0557-7705
REVUE ARCHEOLOGIQUE DE NARBONNAISE. 1968. a. price varies. Diffusion de Boccard, 11, rue de Medicis, 75006 Paris, France.

913   BE   ISSN 0035-077X
REVUE BELGE D'ARCHEOLOGIE ET D'HISTOIRE DE L'ART. 1931. a. 650 Fr. Academie Royale d'Archeologie de Belgique, Hotel de Societes Scientifiques, Rue des Champs Elysees, 43, 1050 Brussels, Belgium. illus. Indexed: Art Ind.

REVUE BELGE DE NUMISMATIQUE ET DE SIGILLOGRAPHIE. see HOBBIES — Numismatics

913   FR   ISSN 0035-1849
REVUE D'EGYPTOLOGIE. (Text in English, French & German) 1935. a. price varies. Editions Klincksieck, 11 rue de Lille, Paris (7e), France. Ed. Prof. V. Posener. bk. rev. illus.

REVUE DES ARCHAEOLOGUES ET HISTORIENS D'ART DE LOUVAIN. see ART

REVUE DES ETUDES GRECQUES. see CLASSICAL STUDIES

913 940   FR
REVUE HISTORIQUE ET ARCHEOLOGIQUE DU MAINE.* 1972, vol. 52. irreg. 40. 7 rue de la Reine Berengere 1, Le Mans, France. Ed. Bd. bibl.

913 943   SZ
REVUE HISTORIQUE VAUDOISE. vol. 73, 1975. a. 35 Fr. Societe Vaudoise d'Histoire et d'Archeologie, Rue du Maupas 47, CH-1004 Lausanne, Switzerland. Ed. Laurette Wettstein. charts. illus.

913   GW   ISSN 0557-7853
RHEINISCHE AUSGRABUNGEN. 1968. irreg., no. 21, 1980. price varies. (Landschaftsverband Rheinland) Rheinland-Verlag, Kennedy-Ufer 2, 5000 Cologne 21, W. Germany (B.R.D.) (Distr. by: Rudolf Habelt Verlag, Am Buchenhang 1, 5300 Bonn, W. Germany (B.R.D.))

913   GW   ISSN 0067-9968
RHEINISCHES LANDESMUSEUM, BONN. SCHRIFTEN. 1965. irreg. price varies. Rheinland-Verlag, Kennedy-Ufer 2, 5000 Cologne 21, W. Germany (B. R. D.) (Distr. by: Rudolf Habelt Verlag, Am Buchenhang 1, 5300 Bonn 1, W. Germany (B.R.D.))

913 709   IT   ISSN 0080-3235
RIVISTA ARCHEOLOGICA DELL'ANTICA PROVINCIA E DIOCESI DI COMO; periodico di antichita ed arte. 1872. a. price varies. Societa Archeologica Comense, Piazza Medaglie d'Oro 1, 22100 Como, Italy. bk. rev. circ. 1,200. (back issues avail.)
Formerly: Rivista Archeologica della Provincia di Como.

913   GW   ISSN 0076-2733
ROEMISCH-GERMANISCHES ZENTRALMUSEUM, MAINZ. AUSSTELLUNGSKATALOGE. 1966. irreg., no. 4, 1970. price varies. Rudolf Habelt Verlag, Am Buchenhang 1, 5300 Bonn 1, W. Germany (B.R.D.)

913 709   GW   ISSN 0080-3782
ROEMISCHE BRONZEN AUS DEUTSCHLAND. 1960. irreg. price varies. Philipp Von Zabern, Welschnonnengasse 11, Postfach 4065, 6500 Mainz, W. Germany (B.R.D.) Ed. Heinz Menzel. index.

914.2 820 IE ISSN 0035-8991
ROYAL IRISH ACADEMY. PROCEEDINGS.
SECTION C: ARCHAEOLOGY, CELTIC
STUDIES, HISTORY, LINGUISTICS AND
LITERATURE. 1836. irreg. price varies. Royal Irish
Academy, 19 Dawson St., Dublin 2, Ireland. Ed. B.
Young. charts. illus. Indexed: Br.Archaeol.
Hist.Abstr.

ROYAL ONTARIO MUSEUM. ARCHAEOLOGY
MONOGRAPHS. see *MUSEUMS AND ART GALLERIES*

ROYAL ONTARIO MUSEUM. ART AND
ARCHAEOLOGY. OCCASIONAL PAPERS. see
ART

069 GW ISSN 0080-5157
SAALBURG-JAHRBUCH. a. price varies. (Saalburg-Museum) Walter de Gruyter und Co., Genthiner Str. 13, 1000 Berlin 30, W. Germany (B.R.D.) Ed. D. Baatz.

913 GW ISSN 0080-5866
SAMOS. 1961. irreg. price varies. (Deutsches Archaeologisches Institut) Rudolf Habelt Verlag, Am Buchenhang 1, 5300 Bonn 1, W. Germany (B.R.D.) Ed. Ernst Homann-Wedeking.

913 NE ISSN 0080-6854
SCHOLAE ADRIANI DE BUCK MEMORIAE DICATAE. 1962. irreg., 1970, no. 5 (vol. 6 in prep.) price varies. Nederlands Instituut voor Het Nabije Oosten - Netherlands Institute for the Near East, Noordeindsplein 42, Leiden, Netherlands. Eds. E. van Donzel, A. Klasens. circ. 500.

913 930 GE ISSN 0080-696X
SCHRIFTEN UND QUELLEN DER ALTEN WELT. (Text in German or Latin or Greek) 1959. irreg., vol. 36, 1977. price varies. (Akademie der Wissenschaften der DDR, Zentralinstitut fuer Alte Geschichte und Archaeologie) Akademie-Verlag, Leipziger Str. 3-4, 108 Berlin, E. Germany (D.D.R.)

914 SZ
SCHWEIZER BEITRAEGE ZUR KULTURGESCHICHTE UND ARCHAEOLOGIE DES MITTELALTERS. irreg. Walter Verlag AG, Amthausquai 21, CH-4600 Olten, Switzerland. illus.

387 IS ISSN 0077-5193
SEFUNIM. (Text in English, French and Hebrew) 1966. a. $5. National Maritime Museum, P.O. Box 771, Haifa, Israel. (Co-sponsor: National Maritime Museum Foundation) Ed. Arie Ben-Eli. adv. bk. rev. circ. 2,000.

913 PL ISSN 0080-9594
SILESIA ANTIQUA. (Text in Polish; summaries in English and German) 1959. irreg., vol. 21, 1979. 90 Zl. (Muzeum Archeologiczne, Wroclaw) Ossolineum, Publishing House of the Polish Academy of Sciences, Rynek 9, 50-106 Wroclaw, Poland (Dist. by Ars Polona-Ruch, Krakowskie Przedmiescie 7, Warsaw, Poland)

913 PL ISSN 0080-9993
SLAVIA ANTIQUA; rocznik poswiecony starozytnosciom slowianskim. (Text in Polish; summaries in English and French) 1948. a. $12.50. (Uniwersytet im. Adama Mickiewicza, Katedra Archeologii) Panstwowe Wydawnictwo Naukowe, Miodowa 10, Warsaw, Poland (Dist. by Ars Polona-Ruch, Krakowskie Przedmiescie 7, Warsaw, Poland) (Co-sponsor: Uniwersytet Warszawski. Zaklad Archeologii Slowianskiej. Katedra Archeologii Pradziejowej i Wczesnosredniowiecznej) Ed. Witold Hensel. adv. bk. rev. charts. circ. 500.

914 FR
SOCIETE ARCHEOLOGIQUE DE TARN ET GARONNE. BULLETIN ARCHEOLOGIQUE, HISTORIQUE ET ARTISTIQUE. vol. 103, 1978. a. Societe Archeologique de Tarn et Garonne, Rue des Soubirous-Bas, Tarn et Garonne, Montauban, France. (Co-sponsors: Conseil General du Tarn et Garonne; Caisse d'Epargne de Montauban)

914 FR
SOCIETE ARCHEOLOGIQUE DE TOURAINE. BULLETIN. 1868. a. Musee de l'Hotel Gouin, 25 rue du Commerce, 37000 Tours, France.

913 FR
SOCIETE ARCHEOLOGIQUE DE TOURAINE. MEMOIRES. 1842. irreg. Musee de l'Hotel Gouin, 25 rue du Commerce, 3700 Tours, France. Ed.Bd. charts. illus.

913 UA ISSN 0068-5283
SOCIETE D'ARCHEOLOGIE COPTE. BIBLIOTHEQUE DE MANUSCRITS. 1934; N.S. 1967. irreg., latest issue in print: no. 3, no. 4 in preparation. £E3 per no. Society for Coptic Archaeology, 222 rue Ramses, Cairo, Egypt. bk. rev.

913 UA ISSN 0068-5291
SOCIETE D'ARCHEOLOGIE COPTE. BULLETIN. (Text in French, English, German, Italian) 1935. irreg. £E10 per no. Society for Coptic Archaeology, 222 Avenue Ramses, Cairo, Egypt. bk. rev. cum.index: vols. I-XX in vol. XX.

913 UA ISSN 0068-5305
SOCIETE D'ARCHEOLOGIE COPTE. TEXTES ET DOCUMENTS. 1942. irreg., latest no. 15; nos. 16 & 17 in prep. £E5 per no. Society for Coptic Archaeology, 222 rue Ramses, Cairo, Egypt. bk. rev.

949.33 BE
SOCIETE D'ARCHEOLOGIE, D'HISTOIRE ET DE FOLKLORE DE NIVELLES ET DU BRABANT WALLON. ANNALES. irreg. 300 Fr. Societe d'Archeologie d'Histoire et de Folklore de Nivelles et du Brabant Wallon, Musee de Nivelles, 27 rue de Bruxelles, Brussels, Belgium. illus.

914 FR
SOCIETE D'ARCHEOLOGIE ET D'HISTOIRE DE LA CHARENTE MARITIME. BULLETIN DE LIAISON. 1974. a. 10 F. Societe d'Archeologie et d'Histoire de la Charente Maritime, Musee Archeologique, Esplanade A. Malraux, 17100 Saintes, France.

913 940 SZ ISSN 0081-0959
SOCIETE D'HISTOIRE ET D'ARCHAEOLOGIE DE GENEVE. BULLETIN.* 1892. a. 5 Fr. Societe d'Histoire et d'Archaeologie de Geneve, c/o Bibliotheque Publique et Universitaire de Geneve, Promenade des Bastions, Geneva, Switzerland. index.

SOCIETE D'HISTOIRE ET D'ARCHEOLOGIE DE LA LORRAINE. ANNUAIRE. see *HISTORY — History Of Europe*

913 FR ISSN 0081-0967
SOCIETE D'HISTOIRE ET D'ARCHEOLOGIE DE LA GOELE. BULLETIN D'INFORMATION. 1968. a. 20 F. Societe d'Histoire et d'Archeologie de la Goele, Mairie, Dammartin-en-Goele 77230, France. adv. circ. 1,000.

913 FR ISSN 0081-1181
SOCIETE NATIONALE DES ANTIQUAIRES DE FRANCE. BULLETIN. a. 70 F. Societe Nationale des Antiquaires de France., Pavillon Mollien, Palais du Louvre, Paris 75001, France (Orders to: Editions Klincksieck, 11 rue de Lille, Paris 7E, France)

SOCIETE SUISSE DES AMERICANISTES.BULLETIN/ SCHWEIZERISCHE AMERIKANISTEN-GESELLSCHAFT. BULLETIN. see *HISTORY — History Of North And South America*

913 US ISSN 0081-1300
SOCIETY FOR AMERICAN ARCHAEOLOGY. MEMOIRS. 1941. irreg., no. 31, 1976. Society for American Archaeology, 1703 New Hampshire Ave. N.W., Washington, DC 20009. (Affiliate: American Anthropological Association)

913 US
SOCIETY FOR HISTORICAL ARCHAEOLOGY. SPECIAL PUBLICATION SERIES. 1976. irreg. Society for Historical Archaeology, c/o University of Idaho, Department of Anthropology, Moscow, ID 83843. Ed. John D. Combes. illus.

913 UK ISSN 0306-4859
SOCIETY FOR LINCOLNSHIRE HISTORY AND ARCHAEOLOGY. ANNUAL REPORT AND STATEMENT OF ACCOUNTS. a. Society for Lincolnshire History & Archaeology, 47 Newland, Lincoln LN1 1XZ, England.

913 500.9 UK ISSN 0081-2056
SOMERSET ARCHAEOLOGY AND NATURAL HISTORY. 1849. a. membership. Somerset Archaeological & Natural History Society, Taunton Castle, Taunton, England. Ed. M. B. McDermott. bk. rev. index; cum.index: vols 81-115 (1935-1971) circ. 1,000. Indexed: Br.Hum.Ind. Br.Archeol.Abstr. Formerly: Somersetshire Archaeological and Natural History Society. Proceedings.

SOUTH INDIAN ART AND ARCHAEOLOGICAL SERIES. see *ART*

913 UK ISSN 0457-7817
SOUTH STAFFORDSHIRE ARCHAEOLOGICAL AND HISTORICAL SOCIETY. TRANSACTIONS. 1960. a. £6($9.50) South Staffordshire Archaeological and Historical Society, 58 Wednesbury Rd., Walsall, West Midlands WS1 3RS, England. Ed. J. W. Whiston. illus. circ. 330.

913 US ISSN 0085-6525
SOUTHERN INDIAN STUDIES. 1949. a. $3. Archaeological Society of North Carolina, Univ. of North Carolina, Box 561, Chapel Hill, NC 27514. Ed. Joffre L. Coe. bk. rev. bibl. illus. circ. 300. (also avail. in microfilm from MCA) Indexed: Hist.Abstr.

913 PL ISSN 0081-3834
SPRAWOZDANIA ARCHEOLOGICZNE. (Text in Polish; summaries in English and Russian) 1955. a. 90 Zl. (Polska Akademia Nauk, Instytut Historii Kultury Materialnej) Ossolineum, Publishing House of the Polish Academy of Sciences, Rynek 9, 50-106 Wroclaw, Poland (Dist. by Ars Polona-Ruch, Krakowskie Przedmiescie 7, Warsaw, Poland) Ed. J. Machnik.

SRPSKA AKADEMIJA NAUKA I UMETNOSTI. ODELJENJE DRUSTVENIH NAUKA. SPOMENIK. see *SOCIAL SCIENCES: COMPREHENSIVE WORKS*

913 900 IT ISSN 0585-4911
STUDI GENUENSI. (Text in Italian) 1970; no. 8. a. L.10000($12.50) Istituto Internazionale di Studi Liguri, Via Romana 39 Bis, 18012 Bordighera, Italy. circ. 1,000.

913 HU ISSN 0081-6280
STUDIA ARCHAEOLOGICA. (Text in Italian) 1963. irreg. price varies. (Magyar Tudomanyos Akademia, Regeszeti Intezet) Akademiai Kiado, Publishing House of the Hungarian Academy of Sciences, P.O. Box 24, H-1363 Budapest, Hungary.

913 IT ISSN 0081-6299
STUDIA ARCHAEOLOGICA. 1961. irreg., no. 30, 1979. price varies. Erma di "Bretschneider", Via Cassiodoro, 19, 00193 Rome, Italy.

913 GW
STUDIA ARCHAEOLOGICA. 1969. irreg., no. 64, 1980. price varies. (Universidad, Santiago de Compostela, Seminario de Arqueologia, SP) Rudolf Habelt Verlag, Am Buchenhang 1, 5300 Bonn 1, W. Germany (B.R.D.) (Co-sponsor: Universidad de Valladolid. Departamento de Prehistoria y Arqueologia)

913 PL ISSN 0081-6302
STUDIA ARCHEOLOGICZNE. (Issued as a Subseries of the Acta Universitatis Wratislaviensis) (Text in Polish; summaries in German) 1965. irreg., 1976, vol. 9. price varies. (Uniwersytet Wroclawski) Panstwowe Wydawnictwo Naukowe, Miodowa 10, Warsaw, Poland (Dist. by Ars Polona-Ruch, Krakowskie Przedmiescie 7, Warsaw, Poland) Ed. Jozef Kazmierczyk. charts. illus. circ. 545.

913 220 NE ISSN 0081-6396
STUDIA FRANCISCI SCHOLTEN MEMORIAE DICATA. 1952. irreg., 1973, vol. 4. fl.250($95) Nederlands Instituut voor Het Nabije Oosten - Netherlands Institute for the Near East, Noordeindsplein 42, Leiden, Netherlands. Ed. A.A. Kampmann.

913 PL ISSN 0081-6787
STUDIA PALMYRENSKIE. (Text in Polish; summaries in French) 1966. irreg., 1970, no. 4. price varies. Uniwersytet Warszawski, Katedra Archeologii Srodziemnomorskiej, Krakowskie Przedmiescie 26/28, Warsaw, Poland (Dist. by Ars Polona-Ruch, Krakowskie Przedmiescie 7, Warsaw, Poland) Ed. Kazimierz Michalowski. circ. 500.

ARCHAEOLOGY

913   SW   ISSN 0081-7414
STUDIER I NORDISK ARKEOLGI/STUDIES IN NORTH EUROPEAN ARCHAEOLOGY. (Text in Swedish; some numbers have English summaries) 1953. irreg., no. 13, 1975. price varies. Fornminnesfoereningen i Goeteborg, Skaargaardsgatan 4, S-414 58 Goeteborg, Sweden. (Co-sponsor: Goeteborgs Arkeologiska Museum)

STUDIES IN ANCIENT ART AND ARCHAEOLOGY. see *ART*

913   SW   ISSN 0081-8232
STUDIES IN MEDITERRANEAN ARCHAEOLOGY. MONOGRAPH SERIES. (Text in English, French and German) 1962. irreg., no. 57, 1980. price varies. Paul Aastroems Foerlag, Johannebergsgatan 24, S-412 55 Goeteborg, Sweden. circ. 1,000.

913   SW
STUDIES IN MEDITERRANEAN ARCHAEOLOGY. POCKET-BOOK SERIES. (Text in English, French and German) irreg., no. 11, 1980. Paul Aastroems Foerlag, Johannebergsgatan 24, S-412 55 Goeteborg, Sweden. circ. 3,000.

913   US   ISSN 0585-7023
STUDIES IN PRE-COLUMBIAN ART AND ARCHAEOLOGY. 1966. irreg., no. 24, 1981. price varies. Dumbarton Oaks Center for Pre-Columbian Studies, 1703 32nd St., N.W., Washington, DC 20007. Ed. Elizabeth P. Boone. bibl. charts. illus. circ. 2,000. (back issues avail)

913   IQ   ISSN 0081-9271
SUMER; journal of archaeology in Iraq. (Text in Arabic and other languages) 1945. a. ID.5000($20) State Antiquities Organization, Jamal Abdul Nasr St., Baghdad, Iraq.

913   UK   ISSN 0309-7803
SURREY ARCHAEOLOGICAL COLLECTIONS. 1886. a. membership. Surrey Archaeological Society, Castle Arch, Guildford, Surrey GU1 3SX, England. Ed. Joan M. Harries. bk. rev. cum.index: vols. 1-71. (also avail. in microform from UMI; back issues avail.) Indexed: Br.Archaeol.Abstr.

913   UK   ISSN 0308-342X
SURREY ARCHAEOLOGICAL SOCIETY. RESEARCH VOLUMES. 1974. irreg. membership. Surrey Archaeological Society, Castle Arch, Guildford, Surrey GU1 3SX, England.

913   GR   ISSN 0081-9921
SVENSKA INSTITUTET I ATHEN. SKRIFTER. (Latin title: Acta Instituti Atheniensis Regni Sueciae. Includes Opuscula Atheniensia) 1951. irreg., no. 27, 1980. price varies. Svenska Institutet i Athen - Swedish Institute in Athens, 9 Mitseon St., Athens 402, Greece (Dist. by: Paul Aastroems Foerlag, Johannebergsgatan 24, S-412 55 Gothenberg, Sweden) Ed. Berit Wells. bk. rev. circ. 1,000.

913   IT   ISSN 0081-993X
SVENSKA INSTITUTET I ROM. SKRIFTER. ACTA SERIES PRIMA. (Latin title: Acta Instituti Romani Regni Sueciae. Includes Opuscula Archaeologica and Opuscula Romana) 1932. irreg., no. 36, 1979. price varies. Svenska Institutet i Rom, Via Omero 14, 00197 Rome, Italy (Dist. by: Paul Aastroems Foerlag, Soedra Vaegen 61, S-412 54 Gothenburg, Sweden) Ed. Berit Wells. bk. rev. circ. 1,000.

913   PL   ISSN 0082-044X
SWIATOWIT. (Text in Polish; summaries in English and French) 1899. irreg., 1971, vol. 32. price varies. Uniwersytet Warszawski, Katedra Archeologii Pradziejowaj i Wczesnosredniowiecznej, Krakowskie Przedmiescie 26/28, Warsaw, Poland (Dist. by: Ars Polona-Ruch, Krakowskie Przedmiescie 7, Warsaw, Poland) Ed. Witold Hensel. circ. 500.

913 737   GW   ISSN 0082-061X
SYLLOGE NUMMORUM GRAECORUM DEUTSCHLAND. (1957-1968 (Vol. 1-18) Sammlung v. Aulock; from 1968 issued under new numbering with Staatliche Muenzsammlung Muenchen) 1957, N.S. 1968. irreg., no. 6, 1980. price varies. (Deutsches Archaeologisches Institut) Gebr. Mann Verlag, Lindenstr. 76, Postfach 110303, 1000 Berlin 61, W. Germany (B.R.D.) cum.index (1957-1968 in vol. 19)

TALOHA. see *MUSEUMS AND ART GALLERIES*

TEBIWA MISCELLANEOUS PAPERS. see *SCIENCES: COMPREHENSIVE WORKS*

571   GW   ISSN 0067-4974
TECHNISCHE BEITRAEGE ZUR ARCHAEOLOGIE. Title varies: Beitraege zur Archaeologie. 1959. irreg. price varies. (Roemisch-Germanisches Zentralmuseum, Mainz) Rudolf Habelt Verlag, Am Buchenhang 1, 5300 Bonn 1, W. Germany (B.R.D.) Ed. H. Menzel.

913 976.4   US   ISSN 0082-2930
TEXAS ARCHEOLOGICAL SOCIETY. BULLETIN. 1929. a. $12 includes newsletter. Texas Archeological Society, Center for Archaeological Research, Univ. of Texas at San Antonio, San Antonio, TX 78285. Eds. Eileen Johnson, Carolyn Good. bk. rev. circ. 950. (reprint service avail. from UMI)

917   US   ISSN 0495-2944
TEXAS ARCHEOLOGICAL SOCIETY. SPECIAL PUBLICATION. 1962. irreg., no. 3, 1976. price varies. Texas Archeological Society, Center for Archaeological Research, Univ. of Texas at San Antonio, San Antonio, TX 78285. (reprint service avail. from UMI)

913 976.4   US   ISSN 0082-2949
TEXAS ARCHEOLOGY. 1957. irreg. free with Texas Archeological Society Bulletin. Texas Archeological Society, Center for Archaeological Research, Univ. of Texas at San Antonio, San Antonio, TX 78285. bk. rev. circ. 1,000. (reprint service avail. from UMI)

942   UK   ISSN 0309-9210
THOROTON SOCIETY OF NOTTINGHAMSHIRE. TRANSACTIONS. 1897. a. membership. Thoroton Society of Nottinghamshire, Whip Ridding, Kirklington, Newark, Notts., England. Ed. K.S.S. Train. bk. rev. cum.index: vols. 1-80. circ. 500.

913   GW   ISSN 0082-450X
TIRYNS. (Text in German, English) 1912. irreg., 1971, vol. 5. price varies. (Deutsches Archaeologisches Institut, Athens, GR) Philipp Von Zabern, Welschnonnengasse 11, Postfach 4065, 6500 Mainz, W. Germany (B.R.D.)

913   PL
TOWARZYSTWO NAUKOWE W TORUNIU. PRACE ARCHEOLOGICZNE. irreg., 1974, vol. 7. price varies. Towarzystwo Naukowe w Toruniu, Ul. Slowackiego 8, 87-100 Torun, Poland.

913   SP   ISSN 0082-5638
TRABAJOS DE PREHISTORIA. NUEVA SERIE. 1960-68; n.s. 1969. a. 1500 ptas. Instituto Espanol de Prehistoria, Palacio del Museo Arqueologico Nacional, Serrano 13, Madrid 1, Spain.

913   GW   ISSN 0082-643X
TRIERER GRABUNGEN UND FORSCHUNGEN. (Text in German; summaries in English and French) 1929. irreg, vol. 10, 1977. price varies. (Rheinisches Landesmuseum, Trier) Philipp Von Zabern, Welschnonnengasse 11, Postfach 4065, 6500 Mainz, W. Germany (B.R.D.) index.

913   UK   ISSN 0082-7355
ULSTER JOURNAL OF ARCHAEOLOGY. 1938. a. membership. Ulster Archaeological Society, c/o Archaeology Dept., Queens University, 17 University Square, Belfast BT7 1NN, N. Ireland. Ed. D. M. Waterman. bk. rev. index. circ. 550(approx.)

913   HU
UNGARISCHE AKADEMIE DER WISSENSCHAFTEN. ARCHAELOGISCHES INSTITUT. MITTEILUNGEN. (Text in German) 1970. a. exchange basis. Magyar Tudomanyos Akademia, Regezeti Intezet, Uri utca 49, 1250 Budapest, Hungary.

913   SP   ISSN 0067-4184
UNIVERSIDAD DE BARCELONA. INSTITUTO DE ARQUEOLOGIA Y PREHISTORIA. PUBLICACIONES EVENTUALES. 1960. irreg., 1975, no. 26. price varies. Universidad de Barcelona, Instituto de Arqueologia y Prehistoria, Barcelona 7, Spain.

UNIVERSIDAD DE LA HABANA. CENTRO DE INFORMACION CIENTIFICAS Y TECNICA. CIENCIAS. SERIE 9. ANTROPOLOGIA Y PREHISTORIA. see *ANTHROPOLOGY*

913.031   SP
UNIVERSIDAD DE OVIEDO. DEPARTAMENTO DE PREHISTORIA Y ARQUEOLOGIA. PUBLICACIONES. irreg. Universidad de Oviedo, Departamento de Prehistoria y Arqueologia, Oviedo, Spain.

918   CL
UNIVERSIDAD DEL NORTE. MUSEO DE ARQUEOLOGIA. DOCUMENTOS PARA LA INVESTIGACION. 1974. irreg. exchange. Universidad del Norte, Museo de Arqueologia, San Pedro de Atacama, Chile.

918   PE
UNIVERSIDAD NACIONAL MAYOR DE SAN MARCOS. SEMINARIO DE HISTORIA RURAL ANDINA. SEMINARIO ARQUEOLOGICO. 1977. irreg. Universidad Nacional Mayor de San Marcos, Seminario de Historia Rural, Lima, Peru.

572   BL
UNIVERSIDADE CATOLICA DE GOIAS. GABINETE DE ARQUEOLOGIA. ANUARIO DE DIVULGACAO CIENTIFICA. 1974. a. Universidade Catolica de Goias, Gabinete de Arqueologia, Caixa Postal, 86, Goiania 74000, Brazil. illus.

918   BL
UNIVERSIDADE DE SAO PAULO. MUSEU PAULISTA. COLECAO. SERIE DE ARQUEOLOGIA. 1975. irreg. Universidade de Sao Paulo, Museu Paulista, Caixa Postal 42.503, Parque da Independencia, 04263 Sao Paulo, Brazil. Ed. Setembrino Petri.
   Supersedes in part (since 1975): Museu Paulista. Colecao (ISSN 0080-6382)

913   GW
UNIVERSITAET BONN. SEMINAR FUER ORIENTALISCHE KUNSTGESCHICHTE. VEROEFFENTLICHUNGEN. REIHE A. NIMRUZ. 1974. irreg. price varies. Rudolf Habelt Verlag, Am Buchenhang 1, 5300 Bonn 1, W. Germany (B.R.D.) Ed. Klaus Fischer.

UNIVERSITE DE MADAGASCAR. MUSEE D'ART ET D'ARCHEOLOGIE. TRAVAUX ET DOCUMENTS. see *ART*

UNIVERSITE DE TOULOUSE II (LE MIRAIL). INSTITUT D'ART PREHISTORIQUE. TRAVAUX. see *ART*

016 956   LE
UNIVERSITE SAINT-JOSEPH. MELANGES. (Text in French) 1906. irreg., vol. 47, 1972. ‡ Universite Saint Joseph, B.P. 293, Beirut, Lebanon. R.P. Maurice Tallon, S.J. bk. rev. bibl. illus. cum.index (vols. 1-19) circ. 600.

UNIVERSITY OF ARIZONA. ANTHROPOLOGICAL PAPERS. see *ANTHROPOLOGY*

UNIVERSITY OF CALGARY. ARCHAEOLOGICAL ASSOCIATION. PALEO-ENVIRONMENTAL WORKSHOP. PROCEEDINGS. see *ENVIRONMENTAL STUDIES*

571   US   ISSN 0068-5933
UNIVERSITY OF CALIFORNIA, BERKELEY. ARCHAEOLOGICAL RESEARCH FACILITY. CONTRIBUTIONS. 1965. irreg., no. 38, 1979. price varies. University of California, Berkeley, Archaeological Research Facility, Berkeley, CA 94720. Ed. Robert F. Heizer. circ. 400. (also avail. in microform from UMI)

913   US
UNIVERSITY OF CALIFORNIA, LOS ANGELES. INSTITUTE OF ARCHAEOLOGY. MONOGRAPH SERIES. 1970. irreg., no. 4, 1974. University of California, Los Angeles, Institute of Archaeology, 405 Hilgard Ave, Los Angeles, CA 90024.
   Formerly: University of California, Los Angeles. Institute of Archaeology. Archaeological Survey. Special Monograph Series (ISSN 0068-6204)

913 UK ISSN 0076-0722
UNIVERSITY OF LONDON. INSTITUTE OF ARCHAEOLOGY. BULLETIN. 1958. a. price varies. ‡ University of London, Institute of Archaeology, 31-34 Gordon Square, London WC1H OPY, England. Ed. Prof. J. D. Evans. bk. rev. circ. 800. (also avail. in microfilm from UMI)

913 UK ISSN 0141-8505
UNIVERSITY OF LONDON. INSTITUTE OF ARCHAEOLOGY. OCCASIONAL PUBLICATION. 1977. irreg., no. 5, 1981. University of London, Institute of Archaeology, 31-34 Gordon Square, London WC1H OPY, England.

915 II ISSN 0076-2202
UNIVERSITY OF MADRAS. ARCHAEOLOGICAL SERIES.* 1967. irreg. University of Madras, Chepauk, Triplicane, Madras 600005, Tamil Nadu, India.

UNIVERSITY OF MANITOBA ANTHROPOLOGY PAPERS. see ANTHROPOLOGY

UNIVERSITY OF MISSOURI MONOGRAPHS IN ANTHROPOLOGY. see ANTHROPOLOGY

913 US ISSN 0085-1221
UNIVERSITY OF NORTHERN COLORADO. MUSEUM OF ANTHROPOLOGY. OCCASIONAL PUBLICATIONS IN ANTHROPOLOGY. ARCHAEOLOGY SERIES. 1967. irreg. price varies. University of Northern Colorado, Museum of Anthropology, Attn. George E. Fay, Ed., Greeley, CO 80639. circ. 300. (processed)

913 US ISSN 0160-3078
UNIVERSITY OF OKLAHOMA. ARCHAEOLOGICAL RESEARCH AND MANAGEMENT CENTER. PROJECT REPORT SERIES. 1978. irreg. price varies. University of Oklahoma, Archaeological Research and Management Center, 1808 Newton Dr., Rm. 116, Norman, OK 73019. Ed. Jerry Galm.

913 US ISSN 0160-3086
UNIVERSITY OF OKLAHOMA. ARCHAEOLOGICAL RESEARCH AND MANAGEMENT CENTER. RESEARCH SERIES. 1978. irreg. price varies. University of Oklahoma, Archaeological Research and Management Center, 1808 Newton Drive, Rm. 116, Norman, OK 73019. Ed. Jerry Galm.

913 572 US
UNIVERSITY OF SOUTH CAROLINA. INSTITUTE OF ARCHEOLOGY AND ANTHROPOLOGY. ANNUAL REPORT. 1976. a. University of South Carolina, Institute of Archeology and Anthropology, Columbia, SC 29208.

913 US
UNIVERSITY OF WASHINGTON. OFFICE OF PUBLIC ARCHAEOLOGY. RECONNAISSANCE REPORTS. 1975. irreg., no. 30, 1979. University of Washington, Office of Public Archaeology, Publication Series, 213 Engineering Annex, University of Washington, Seattle, WA 98195.

917 US
UNIVERSITY OF WASHINGTON. OFFICE OF PUBLIC ARCHAEOLOGY. REPORTS IN HIGHWAY ARCHAEOLOGY. 1975. irreg. price varies. University of Washington, Office of Public Archaeology, 213 Engineering Annex, University of Washington, Seattle, WA 98195. circ. 100.

UNIVERZITA KOMENSKEHO. FILOZOFICKA FAKULTA. ZBORNIK: MUSAICA. see ART

913 PL ISSN 0083-4300
UNIWERSYTET JAGIELLONSKI. ZESZYTY NAUKOWE. PRACE ARCHEOLOGICZNE. 1960. irreg., 1972, vol. 14. price varies. ‡ Panstwowe Wydawnictwo Naukowe, Miodowa 10, Warsaw, Poland (Dist. by Ars Polona-Ruch, Krakowskie Przedmiescie 7, Warsaw, Poland) Ed. Janusz K. Kozlowski. circ. 700.

913 GW ISSN 0083-4793
URUK-WARKA: ABHANDLUNGEN DER DEUTSCHEN ORIENT-GESELLSCHAFT. 1913. irreg., vol. 30, 1979. price varies. (Deutsche Orient-Gesellschaft) Gebr. Mann Verlag, Lindenstr. 76, Postfach 110303, 1000 Berlin 61, W. Germany (B.R.D.) (Co-sponsor: Deutsches Archaeologisches Institut)

VICUS CUADERNOS: ARQUEOLOGIA, ANTROPOLOGIA CULTURAL, ETNOLOGIA. see ANTHROPOLOGY

914 NO
VIKING; tidsskrift for Norron arkeologi/journal of Norse archaeology. (Text in Norwegian; summaries in English) 1937. a. Kr.100. Norsk Arkeologisk Selskap, Frederiksgt. 2-3, Oslo 1, Norway. Eds. Sverre Marstrander, Arne Skjoelsvold. charts. illus.

VOORAZIATISCH-EGYPTISCH GENOOTSCHAP "EX ORIENTE LUX". MEDEDELINGEN EN VERHANDELINGEN. see HISTORY — History Of Asia

913 GW
WEGE VOR- UND FRUEHGESCHICHTLICHER FORSCHUNG. 1972. irreg. price varies. Rudolf Habelt Verlag, Am Buchenhang 1, 5300 Bonn 1, W. Germany (B.R.D.) Eds. Rolf Hachmann, Frauke Stein.

913 GE
WEIMARER MONOGRAPHIEN ZUR UR- UND FRUEHGESCHICHTE. 1978. irreg. price varies. Museum fuer Ur- und Fruegeschichte Thueringens, Humboldtstr. 11, 53 Weimar, E. Germany (D.D.R.) Ed. R. Feustel.

913 NR ISSN 0083-8160
WEST AFRICAN JOURNAL OF ARCHAEOLOGY. (Text in English or French) 1971. a. £N6.25. (University of Ibadan, Department of Archaeology) Ibadan University Press, University of Ibadan, Ibadan, Nigeria (Orders to: Department of Archaeology, University of Ibadan, Ibadan, Nigeria) adv. bk. rev. Indexed: SSCI.
Before 1970: West African Archaeological Newsletter.

917 557 US
WEST VIRGINIA REPORTS OF ARCHAEOLOGICAL INVESTIGATIONS. 1969. irreg. ‡ Geological and Economic Survey, Box 879, Morgantown, WV 26505.
Former titles: West Virginia Archaeological Investigations; West Viginia Geological Survey. Archaeological Investigations (ISSN 0083-8535)

WHO'S WHO IN INDIAN RELICS. see HOBBIES

WILBOUR MONOGRAPHS. see HISTORY

913 574.9 UK ISSN 0309-3476
WILTSHIRE ARCHAEOLOGICAL MAGAZINE. 1853. a. membership. ‡ Wiltshire Archaeological and Natural History Society, 41 Long St., Devizes, Wiltshire SN10 1NS, England. adv. bk. rev. circ. 1,000.
Supersedes in part (as of 1975): Wiltshire Archaeological and Natural History Magazine (ISSN 0084-0335)

930 YU
WISSENSCHAFTLICHE MITTEILUNGEN DES BOSNISCH-HERZEGOWINISCHEN LANDESMUSEUMS. ARCHAEOLOGIE. (Text in German) 1976. irreg. Zemaljski Muzej Bosne i Hercegovine, Vojvode Putnika 7, Sarajevo, Yugoslavia. Ed. Vlajko Palavestra.

914.03 UK
WOOLHOPE NATURALISTS' FIELD CLUB, HEREFORDSHIRE. TRANSACTIONS. 1851. a. membership. Woolhope Club, Hereford Library, Hereford, England. Ed. J. W. Tonkin.
Formerly: Woolhope Naturalists' and Archaeologists Field Club, Herefordshire. Transactions (ISSN 0084-1226)

913 US
WORLD ARCHAELOGICAL SOCIETY. SPECIAL PUBLICATION. 1971. irreg. $2 per copy. ‡ World Archaeological Society, c/o Ron Miller, Dir., Star Rt. 140-D, Hollister, MO 65672. bibl. illus.

913 US
WORLD OF ARCHAEOLOGY (BINGHAMTON) irreg., latest 1974. John Day, c/o Conklin Book Center, Inc., Box 5555, Binghamton, NY 13902.

571 913 UK ISSN 0084-4276
YORKSHIRE ARCHAEOLOGICAL JOURNAL. 1869. a. £10 to individuals; £12 to institutions. Yorkshire Archaeological Society, Claremont, Clarendon Road, Leeds LS2 9NZ, England. Ed. R. M. Butler. circ. 1,400.

ZAMBIA MUSEUMS PAPERS SERIES. see HISTORY — History Of Africa

913 GW ISSN 0340-0824
ZEITSCHRIFT FUER ARCHAEOLOGIE DES MITTELALTERS. 1973. a. DM.75. Rheinland-Verlag, Kennedy-Ufer 2, 5000 Cologne 21, W. Germany (B.R.D.) (Distr. by: Rudolf Habelt Verlag, Am Buchenhang 1, 5300 Bonn, W. Germany (B.R.D.)) Eds. Walter Janssen, Heiko Steuer.

913 GW ISSN 0084-5388
ZEITSCHRIFT FUER PAPYROLOGIE UND EPIGRAPHIK. 1967. irreg. DM.98. Rudolf Habelt Verlag, Am Buchenhang 1, 5300 Bonn 1, W. Germany (B.R.D.)

913 YU ISSN 0581-7501
ZEMALJSKI MUZEJ BOSNE I HERCEGOVINE. GLASNIK. ARHEOLOGIJA. (Text chiefly in Serbo-Croatian; summaries in German or Serbo-Croatian) vol. 29, 1974. a. Zemaljski Muzej Bosne i Hercegovine, Vojvode Putnika 7, Sarajevo, Yugoslavia. Ed. Borivoj Covic. bk. rev. bibl. illus.
Continues: Glasnik Zemalskog Muzeja u Sarajevu.

913 SZ
ZUERCHER ARCHAEOLOGISCHE HEFTE. 1976. irreg., no. 4, 1978. 12 Fr. per no. Universitaet Zuerich, Archaeologische Sammlung, Kuenstlergasse 16, 8006 Zurich, Switzerland.

ARCHAEOLOGY — Abstracting, Bibliographies, Statistics

571 060 NE ISSN 0066-3794
ANNUAL BIBLIOGRAPHY OF INDIAN ARCHAEOLOGY. (Text in English) 1928. irreg., 1972, vol. 21. price varies. (Kern Institute of Indology) E. J. Brill, Oude Rijn 332-35, Leiden, Netherlands. bk. rev. index. circ. 800.

016 930 GW
ARCHAEOLOGISCHE BIBLIOGRAPHIE. (Supplement to Deutsches Archaeologisches Institut. Jahrbuch) 1914. irreg. price varies. Walter de Gruyter und Co., Genthiner Str. 13, 1000 Berlin 30, W. Germany (B.R.D.) Ed. Gerhard Reincke. bibl. circ. 800.

913 700 FR ISSN 0080-0953
BULLETIN SIGNALETIQUE. PART 530: REPERTOIRE D'ART ET D'ARCHEOLOGIE. NOUVELLE SERIE. 1973. a. 450 F. Centre National de la Recherche Scientifique, Centre de Documentation Sciences Humaines, 54 Bd. Raspail, 75260 Paris Cedex, France. (Co-sponsor: Comite Francais d'Histoire de l'Art) cum.index.

962 932 UA ISSN 0068-5275
EGYPTIAN NATIONAL MUSEUM. LIBRARY. CATALOGUE. 1966. irreg. price varies. (Service des Antiquites, Museums Sector) Egyptian National Museum, Midan-el-Tahrir, Kasr el-Nil, Cairo, Egypt. Eds. Dia Abou-Ghazi, Abdel-Mohsen El-Khachab. index in preparation.

948 010 DK ISSN 0105-6492
N A A. (Nordic Archaeological Abstracts) (Text in English) 1975. a. Viborg Stiftsmuseum, DK-8800 Viborg, Denmark (Subscr. to: Museumstjenesten, Sjorupvej, Lysgaard, DK-8800 Viborg, Denmark) Ed. Mette Iversen.

913 016 PL ISSN 0137-4885
POLISH ARCHAEOLOGICAL ABSTRACTS. (Text in English) 1972. a. 56 Zl. (Polska Akademia Nauk, Instytut Historii Kultury Materialnej, Zaklad Archeologii Wielkopolski) Ossolineum, Publishing House of the Polish Academy of Sciences, Rynek 9, 50-106 Wroclaw, Poland (Dist. by: Ars Polona - Ruch, Krakowskie Przedmeiscie 7, Warsaw, Poland) Ed. Aleksander Dymaczewski. abstr. bibl. circ. 630.

914 016 SW ISSN 0586-2000
SWEDISH ARCHAEOLOGICAL BIBLIOGRAPHY. 1949. every 5 yrs., latest no. 6, 1978. Kr.120. Svenska Arkeologiska Samfundet - Swedish Archaeological Society, Box 5405, S-114 84 Stockholm, Sweden. Eds. S. Janson, H. Thylander.

ARCHITECTURE

see also Building and Construction; Engineering—Civil Engineering; Housing and Urban Planning; Real Estate

720 US ISSN 0569-5341
A I A EMERGING TECHNIQUES. irreg., latest no. 2. $6. American Institute of Architects, 1735 New York Ave., N.W., Washington, DC 20006.

720 662 US
A I A ENERGY NOTEBOOK. 1976. a. $120. American Institute of Architects, 1735 New York Ave. N. W., Washington, DC 20006.

A R I S. (Art Research in Scandinavia) see *ART*

720 370.58 US
ACCREDITED PROGRAMS IN ARCHITECTURE; and first professional degrees conferred on completion of their curricula in architecture. 1940. a. free. National Architectural Accrediting Board, Inc., 1735 New York Ave. N. W., Washington, DC 20006. Dir. Hugo G. Blasdel. circ. 5,000.
 Formerly (1972-74): Accredited Schools of Architecture; Until 1972: List of Accredited Schools of Architecture (ISSN 0077-3166)

720 US
ACOUSTICAL AND BOARD PRODUCTS. BULLETIN; performance data acoustical materials. Title varies: A B P A Bulletin. 1934. a. $2. ‡ Acoustical and Board Products Association, 205 W. Touhy Ave., Park Ridge, IL 60068. Ed. George Parr. circ. 20,000.
 Formerly: Performance Data on Architectural Acoustical Materials (ISSN 0079-0788)

620 US ISSN 0094-1786
ALASKA. STATE BOARD OF REGISTRATION FOR ARCHITECTS, ENGINEERS AND LAND SURVEYORS. DIRECTORY OF ARCHITECTS, ENGINEERS AND LAND SURVEYORS. irreg. $2. Board of Registration for Architects, Engineers and Land Surveyors, Box 469, Juneau, AK 99801.
 Key Title: Directory of Architects, Engineers and Land Surveyors (Juneau)

920 II ISSN 0587-4793
ALL INDIA ARCHITECTS DIRECTORY. 1969. biennial. Rs.75. Architects Publishing Corp. of India, 51 Sujata, Quarry Rd. Crossing, Malad East, Bombay 400064, India. Ed. Santosh Kumar. adv. circ. 3,000.

726 US ISSN 0363-5694
AMERICAN SOCIETY FOR CHURCH ARCHITECTURE. JOURNAL. irreg. price varies. American Society for Church Architecture, 1200 Architects Bldg., Philadelphia, PA 19103.

720 SP
ANALES DE LA UNIVERSIDAD HISPALENSE. SERIE: ARQUITECTURA. irreg. price varies. Universidad de Sevilla, San Fernando 4, Seville, Spain.

ANDHRA PRADESH, INDIA. DEPARTMENT OF ARCHAEOLOGY AND MUSEUMS. ART AND ARCHITECTURE SERIES. see *ART*

720 FR ISSN 0066-2747
ANNUAIRE DES ARCHITECTES. (Extract from Annuaire du Batiment et des Travaux Publics) 1935. a. (Societe des Architectes Diplomes de l'Ecole Speciale d'Architecture) Saint Lambert Editeur, Boite Postale 72, 13673 Aubagne Cedex, France. adv. circ. 5,000.

724 CK
ANUARIO DE LA ARQUITECTURA EN COLOMBIA. a. (Sociedad Colombiana de Arquitectos) J. Plaza, Ed. & Pub., Calle 98 no. 15-14, Bogota, Colombia. illus.

720 UK ISSN 0066-6092
ARCHIGRAM.* 1961. irreg., 1970, no. 9. price varies. ‡ Archigram Group, 59, Aberdare Gardens, London N.W.6, England. Ed. Peter Cook. adv. bk. rev. circ. 6,000. Indexed: Avery Ind.Archit.Per.

720 UK ISSN 0066-6114
ARCHITECT AND CONTRACTORS YEARBOOK. 1886. a. £5.25. Trade Magazines Ltd., 7 Paddington Street, London, W1, England.

720 FR ISSN 0066-6122
ARCHITECTES. 1968. N.S. 10/yr. 60 F. Ordre des Architectes, Conseil Regional de Paris, 140 Avenue Victor Hugo, 75116 Paris, France. Ed. Marie Dulac.
 Before 1969: Ordre des Architectes. Conseil Regional de Paris. Bulletin.

666.1 US
ARCHITECTS' GUIDE TO GLASS, METAL & GLAZING. 1972. a. $3. U S Glass Publications, Inc., 2701 Union Ave. Extended, Suite 410, Memphis, TN 38112. Ed. John K. Lawo, Jr. adv. bk. rev. charts. illus. stat. circ. 11,000.

720 US ISSN 0066-6173
ARCHITECT'S HANDBOOK OF PROFESSIONAL PRACTICE. irreg., with supplements. $30 for handbook; $12 for supplement. American Institute of Architects, 1735 New York Avenue N.W., Washington, DC 20006.

720 UK ISSN 0066-6181
ARCHITECTS STANDARD CATALOGUES. 1911. a. £25. Standard Catalogue Information Services Ltd., Medway Wharf Rd., Tonbridge, Kent TN9 1QR, England.

720 UK ISSN 0066-619X
ARCHITECTS' YEAR BOOK. 1944. irreg. Elek Books Ltd., 54-58 Caledonian Rd., London N1 9RN, England.

720 HU ISSN 0066-6270
ARCHITECTURA. 1966. irreg. price varies. (Magyar Tudomanyos Akademia) Akademiai Kiado, Publishing House of the Hungarian Academy of Sciences, P.O. Box 24, H-1363 Budapest, Hungary. (Co-sponsor: Magyar Epitomuveszek Szovetsege)

720 US
ARCHITECTURAL HANDBOOK. 1976. a. American Institute of Architects, California Council, 1736 Stockton, San Francisco, CA 94133. Ed. Melton Ferris. adv. circ. 10,000.

720 UK ISSN 0066-622X
ARCHITECTURAL HISTORY; journal of the Society of Architectural Historians of Great Britain. 1958. a. £5. Society of Architectural Historians of Great Britain, 25 Drumsheugh Gardens, Edinburgh EH3 7RN, Scotland. Ed. John A. Newman.

720 US ISSN 0570-6483
ARCHITECTURAL INDEX. 1949. a. price varies. Box 1168, Boulder, CO 80306. Eds. Ervin J. Bell, Mary Ellen Brennan. circ. 4,000. (back issues avail.)

720 UK
ARCHITECTURAL METALWORK ASSOCIATION. MEMBERS SPECIALISED PRODUCTS. 1968. a. free. Architectural Metalwork Association, 18, Croydon Rd., Caterham, Surrey CR3 6YR, England.

720 GR ISSN 0066-6262
ARCHITECTURE IN GREECE/ARCHITECTONIKA THEMATA. (Text in Greek and English) 1967. a. $25. Orestis B. Doumanis, Ed. & Pub., 5 Kleomenous-Loukianou Str., Box 545, Athens 139, Greece (Dist. in U.S. by: Wittenborn and Co., 1018 Madison Ave., New York, NY 10021) adv. bk. rev. index. circ. 5,000. (back issues avail.)

720.7 US ISSN 0092-7856
ARCHITECTURE SCHOOLS IN NORTH AMERICA. 1947. irreg., approx. biennial. $8.95. Association of Collegiate Schools of Architecture, Inc., 1735 New York Ave., N.W., Washington, DC 20006 (And Peterson's Guides, Inc., 228 Alexander St., Princeton, NJ 08540) Eds. Roger L. Schluntz, K. C. Hegener. (reprint service avail. from UMI)
 Incorporating: A C S A Faculty Directory.

720 IT
ARCHITETTURA URBANISTICA: METODI DI PROGRAMMAZIONE E PROGETTI. 1975. irreg; no. 5, 1978. price varies. Giardini Editori e Stampatori, Via Santa Bibbiana 28, 56100 Pisa, Italy. Ed. Giacomo Donato.

ARTS ASIATIQUES. see *ART*

690 AU
AUSTRIA. BUNDESMINISTERIUM FUER BAUTEN UND TECHNIK. WOHNBAUFORSCHUNG. 1971. m. S.250. (Federal Ministry of Construction and Technology) Sparkassenverlag Ges. m.b.H., Grimmelshausengasse 1, A-1030 Vienna, Austria. Ed. Helmut Junker.

720 BB
BARBADOS SOCIETY OF ARCHITECTS. YEARBOOK. a. membership. Barbados Society of Architects, c/o Ferdinand Hart & Leonard, Chartered Quan. Surveyors, Adulo, Rockley, Christ Church, Barbados, W. I.

722 BE ISSN 0522-7496
BELGIUM. COMMISSION ROYALE DES MONUMENTS ET DES SITES. BULLETIN. 1950. N.S. 1970/71. a., vol. 7, 1978. price varies. Commission Royale des Monuments et des Sites, Rue Joseph II, 30, B-1040 Brussels, Belgium.

BIBLIOTECA MARSILIO: ARCHITETTURA E URBANISTICA. see *HOUSING AND URBAN PLANNING*

BRITISH ARCHAEOLOGICAL ASSOCIATION. CONFERENCE TRANSACTIONS. see *ARCHAEOLOGY*

309.2 KE
BUILD KENYA. (Text in English) 1976. m. EAs.95($14) (Architectural Association of Kenya) Peter Moll Africa Ltd., Box 40106, Nairobi, Kenya. Ed. Gavin Bennett. adv. bk. rev. illus. circ. 2,500.
 Supersedes: Plan.

BUILDING PRACTICE. see *BUILDING AND CONSTRUCTION*

721 FI
BYGGARE OCH BYGGNADER I GAMLA MARIEHAMN. (Text in Swedish) 1979. a. Aalands Folkminnesfoerbund, Aalands Museum, Storagatan 9, SF-22101 Mariehamn, Finland.

720 UK
CAMBRIDGE UNIVERSITY. DEPARTMENT OF ARCHITECTURE. AUTONOMOUS HOUSING STUDY WORKING PAPERS. vol. 26, 1975. irreg. price varies. Cambridge University, Department of Architecture, Cambridge CB3 9DT, England.

720 CN
CANADIAN ARCHITECT YEARBOOK. 1964. a. Can.$2. Southam Communications Ltd., 1450 Don Mills Rd., Don Mills,Ont. M3B 2X7, Canada. Ed. Robert Gretton.
 Formerly: Canadian Architecture Yearbook (ISSN 0068-8231)

720 SP
COLECCION ARQUITECTURA/PERSPECTIVAS. irreg. Editorial Gustavo Gili, S.A., Rosellon 87-89, Apdo. de Correos 35.149, Barcelona 29, Spain.

720 SP
COLECCION ARQUITECTURA Y CRITICA. irreg. Editorial Gustavo Gili, S.A., Rosellon 87-89, Apdo. de Correos 35.149, Barcelona 29, Spain.

COLECCION CIENCIA URBANISTICA. see *HOUSING AND URBAN PLANNING*

720 SP ISSN 0071-1632
COLECCION ESTRUCTURAS Y FORMAS. irreg. Editorial Gustavo Gili, S.A., Rosellon 87-89, Barcelona 15, Spain.
 Formerly: Estructuras y Formas.

ARCHITECTURE

720　　　　　　SP　ISSN 0082-2701
COLECCION TEMAS DE ARQUITECTURA ACTUAL. irreg. Editorial Gustavo Gili, S.A., Rosellon 87-89, Barcelona 15, Spain.

712　　　　　　US
COLLOQUIUM ON THE HISTORY OF LANDSCAPE ARCHITECTURE. PAPERS. 1972. irreg., no. 6, 1980. price varies. Dumbarton Oaks Center for Studies in Landscape Architecture, 1703 32nd St. N.W., Washington, DC 20007. circ. 1,150.

720　944　　　　FR
COMMISSION DEPARTEMENTALE DES MONUMENTS HISTORIQUES DU PAS-DE-CALAIS. BULLETIN. 1849; N.S. 1889. a. 45 F. Commission Departementale des Monuments Historiques du Pas-de-Calais, Archives Departementales, Prefecture S.P. 2, 62021 Arras Cedex, France.

CORDELL'S WHO'S WHO IN DESIGN SPECIFYING. see *BUILDING AND CONSTRUCTION*

720　　　　　　US　ISSN 0145-3017
CORPORATE BUYERS OF DESIGN SERVICES/U S A. 1976. biennial. $190. Bids, Inc., Operations Center, Box 3344, Springfield, IL 62708.

720　　　　　　US　ISSN 0070-038X
CORPUS PALLADIANUM. 1968. irreg. $42.50. Pennsylvania State University Press, 215 Wagner Bldg., University Park, PA 16802. (reprint service avail. from UMI)

720　　　　　　US
D M G OCCASIONAL PAPERS. 1972. irreg. (approx. 1-2/yr.) membership. Design Methods Group, University of California, School of Architecture, Berkeley, CA 94720. Ed. Donald P. Grant. abstr. circ. 800. (tabloid format)

720　　　　　　DK
DENMARK. STATENS BYGNINGSFREDNINGSFOND. BERETNING. 1967/68. a. contr. free circ. Statens Bygningsfredningsfond - Government Preservation of Buildings Fund, Amaliegade 13, DK-1256 Copenhagen K, Denmark. illus.

720　745　　　　GR　ISSN 0074-1191
DESIGN IN GREECE/THEMATA CHOROU & TECHNON. (Text in Greek and English) 1970. a. $25. Orestis B. Doumanis, Ed. & Pub., 5 Kleomenous-Loukianou Str., Box 545, Athens 139, Greece (Dist. in U.S. by: Wittenborn and Co., 1018 Madison Ave., New York, NY 10021) adv. index. circ. 5,000. (back issues avail.)

720　155　　　　US
DESIGN RESEARCH INTERACTIONS. Represents: Environmental Design Research Association. International Conference. Proceedings. 1969. a. $25. Environmental Design Research Association, L'Enfant Plaza Sta., Box 23129, Washington, DC 20024. Ed.Bd. circ. 900. (back issues avail.; reprint service avail, from ISI)

720　　　　　　UK
DIRECTORY OF OFFICIAL ARCHITECTURE AND PLANNING. 1956. biennial. £8.25. George Godwin Ltd., 1-3 Pemberton Row, Fleet St., London EC4P 4HL, England.
Formerly: Directory of Official Architects and Planners (ISSN 0070-5977)

720　　　　　　UK　ISSN 0307-1634
E A A REVIEW. 1957. a. £2 to non-members. ‡ (Edinburgh Architectural Association) Edinburgh Pictorial Ltd., Smith's Place House, Edinburgh 6, Scotland. Ed. David Cameron. adv. circ. 1,200.
Formerly: Edinburgh Architectural Association E A A Yearbook.

720　　　　　　UK　ISSN 0140-5039
E. A. R. (Edinburgh Architectural Research) 1973. a. £2. University of Edinburgh, Department of Architecture, 20 Chambers St., Edinburgh EH1 1J2, Scotland. circ. 250.

720　309　　　　US
ENVIRONMENTAL DESIGN PERSPECTIVES; viewpoints on the profession, education and research. (Subseries of: Man-Environment Systems - Focus Series) 1972. Association for the Study of Man-Environment Relations, Box 57, Orangeburg, NY 10962. Ed. Wolfgang F. E. Preiser.

943　　　　　　AU
FUNDBERICHTE AUS OESTERREICH. vol. 12, 1973. a. price varies. Bundesdenkmalamt, Abteilung fuer Bodendenkmalpflege, Saeulenstiege, Hofburg, A-1010 Vienna, Austria. Ed. Horst Adler. charts. illus.

724　　　　　　JA
G A/GLOBAL ARCHITECTURE. irreg. $14.95. A.D.A. Edita Tokyo Co., Ltd, 3-12-14 Sendagaya, Shibuya-ku, Tokyo, Japan. illus. (back issues avail.)

728　352.7　　　JA
GA HOUSES. irreg. $22.50. A. D. A. Edita Tokyo Co., Ltd., 3-12-14 Sendagaya, Shibuya-Ku, Tokyo, Japan. Ed. Yukio Futagawa. illus.

GOTHENBURG STUDIES IN ART AND ARCHITECTURE. see *ART*

720　　　　　　IT
HABITATION SPACE. (Text in 5 languages) 1979. a. $50. Habitation Space(International) S.N.C., Via Vittor Pisani, 16, Casella Postale 10339, 20100 Milan, Italy.

720　　　　　　US　ISSN 0194-3650
HARVARD ARCHITECTURE REVIEW. 1980. a. $20 paper, $30 cloth. M I T Press, 28 Carleton St., Cambridge, MA 02142.

720　　　　　　US
HISTORY OF WORLD ARCHITECTURE. irreg. $45. Harry N. Abrams, Inc., 110 E. 59th St., New York, NY 10022.

720　　　　　　US　ISSN 0161-2336
HOUSE & GARDEN PLANS GUIDE. 1963. s-a. $2 per no. Conde Nast Publications Inc., 350 Madison Ave., New York, NY 10017. Ed. Louis O. Gropp. adv. index. (reprint service avail. from UMI)

720　　　　　　US　ISSN 0073-3571
HOUSE BEAUTIFUL'S HOUSES AND PLANS. 1957. a. $1.50. Hearst Magazines, House Beautiful, 250 W. 55th St., New York, NY 10019. Ed. Richard Beatty. circ. 175,000.

INCHIESTE DI URBANISTICA E ARCHITETTURA; rivista di studi e informazioni. see *HOUSING AND URBAN PLANNING*

721　　　　　　YU
INSTITUT ZA ARHITEKTURU I URBANIZAM SRBIJE. ZBORNIK RADOVA. vol. 7, 1975. a. Institut za Arhitekturu i Urbanizam Srbije, Bulevar Revolucije 73/II, Belgrade, Yugoslavia. Ed. N. Pejovic. charts. illus. tr.lit.

720　309　　　　US　ISSN 0094-4084
INTERNATIONAL DIRECTORY OF BEHAVIOR AND DESIGN RESEARCH. (Subseries of: Man-Environment Systems/Focus Series) 1974. biennial. $12 to non-members; members $6. Association for the Study of Man-Environment Relations, Box 57, Orangeburg, NY 10962. Ed. Dr. Aristide H. Esser.

720　　　　　　FR　ISSN 0075-0018
INVENTAIRE GENERAL DES MONUMENTS ET DES RICHESSES ARTISTIQUES DE LA FRANCE. 1969. irreg. price varies. (Ministere des Affaires Culturelles) Imprimerie Nationale, Service es Ventes, 59128 Flers en Escrebieux, France, France.

720　　　　　　FR
L'IVRE DE PIERRES. 1977. irreg. Aerolande, 3 rue Papin, 75003 Paris, France.

720　　　　　　GW
LANDESKONSERVATOR RHEINLAND. ARBEITSHEFT. 1971. irreg., no. 36, 1980. price varies. (Kultusministerium, Landeskonservator Rheinland) Rheinland-Verlag, Kennedy-Ufer 2, 5000 Cologne 21, W. Germany (B.R.D.) (Distr. by: Rudolf Habelt Verlag GmbH, Am Buchenhang 1, 5300 Bonn, W. Germany (B.R.D.))

712
LANDSCAPE ARCHITECTS REFERENCE MANUAL (ILLUSTRATED FOR DESK & FIELD USE) 1976. biennial. $15.50. Basic Information Services, Inc., 125 N. Cambridge St., Orange, CA 92666. Eds. W. R. Bethard, W. J. Cathcart. adv. bk. rev. charts. illus. circ. 20,000. (back issues avail.)

LANDSCAPE HISTORY. see *HISTORY — History Of Europe*

712　　　　　　UK
LANDSCAPE RESEARCH. 1968. irreg. (approx. 3/yr.) £6.50 for 3 nos. ‡ Landscape Research Group, Dept. of Town and Country Planning, University of Manchester, Manchester M13 9PL, England. Ed. Ian. C. Laurie. bk. rev. circ. 350.
Formerly (until 1976): Landscape Research News (ISSN 0458-7014)

720　690　　　　CN　ISSN 0315-8756
LOG HOUSE. 1974. a. Can.$6. Log House Publishing Co. Ltd., Box 1205, Prince George, B. C. V2L 4V3, Canada. Ed. Mary Mackie. (back issues avail.)
Formerly: Canadian Log House.

720　　　　　　IT　ISSN 0076-101X
LOTUS; A REVIEW OF CONTEMPORARY ARCHITECTURE. (Text in Italian and English) 1968, vol. 5. 4/yr. L.35000. Industrie Grafiche Editoriali, Divisione Periodiche, Via Carlo Goldoni 1, Milan, Italy.

309.2　　　　　US　ISSN 0098-3403
MARYLAND HISTORICAL TRUST. ANNUAL REPORT. a. Maryland Historical Trust, 2525 Riva Rd., Annapolis, MD 21401. Key Title: Annual Report - Maryland Historical Trust.

658　　　　　　UR
MATEMATICHESKIE METODY V EKONOMIKE. vol. 14, 1977. irreg. 0.55 Rub. per no. (Akadamiya Nauk Latviiskoi S.S.R., Institut Ekonomiki) Izdatel'stvo Zinatne, Turgeneva Iela, 19, Riga 226018, U.S.S.R. bibl. charts. circ. 800.

720　　　　　　US
MISSISSIPPI. STATE BOARD OF ARCHITECTURE. ANNUAL REPORT. a. Board of Architecture, Box 16273, Jackson, MS 39206.

720.9　　　　　US　ISSN 0077-474X
NATIONAL INSTITUTE FOR ARCHITECTURAL EDUCATION. YEARBOOK. 1964. a. $15. National Institute for Architectural Education, 139 E. 52nd St., New York, NY 10022. circ. 200.
Formerly: National Institute for Architectural Education. Bulletin.

720　　　　　　AT　ISSN 0077-8656
NEW SOUTH WALES. BOARD OF ARCHITECTS. ARCHITECTS ROLL. 1923. a. Aus.$3. ‡ Government Printer, 196 Miller St., North Sydney, N.S.W. 2001, Australia.

720　　　　　　NO　ISSN 0332-6578
NORSKE ARKITEKTKONKURRANSER. Enclosed in: Arkitektnytt (ISSN 0004-1998) 1953. irreg. Kr.175 includes Arkitektnytt. Norske Arkitekters Landsforbund - Norwegian Architects' League, Josefinesgt. 34, Oslo 3, Norway. Ed. Annemor Meinstad. illus. index.
Competition results.

720　690　　　　SZ
OEFFENTLICHE BAUMAPPE DER OSTSCHWEIZ. a. 12 Fr. Fachpresse Goldach, Hudson & Co., CH-9403 Goldach, Switzerland. Ed. Hans Wittwer. adv. charts.

OLD HOUSE CATALOG; 2500 products, services, and suppliers for restoring, decorating and furnishing the period house. see *INTERIOR DESIGN AND DECORATION — Furniture And House Furnishings*

OLD-HOUSE JOURNAL CATALOG. see *BUILDING AND CONSTRUCTION*

720　　　　　　HU　ISSN 0073-4063
ORSZAGOS MUEMLEKI FELUGYELOSEG. KIADVANYOK. (Text in Hungarian; summaries in German) 1960. irreg., no. 8, 1977. price varies. (Orszagos Muemlekvedelmi Bizottsag) Akademiai Kiado, Publishing House of the Hungarian Academy of Sciences, P.O. Box 24, H-1363 Budapest, Hungary.

OXFORD STUDIES IN THE HISTORY OF ART AND ARCHITECTURE. see *ART*

OXONIENSIA. see *ARCHAEOLOGY*

720　　　　　　US　ISSN 0079-0958
PERSPECTA; THE YALE ARCHITECTURAL JOURNAL. 1951. a. $20 paper, $30 cloth. M I T Press, 28 Carleton St., Cambridge, MA 02142. (reprint service avail. from ISI,UMI)

720 PL
POLITECHNIKA GDANSKA. ZESZYTY NAUKOWE. ARCHITEKTURA. (Text in Polish; summaries in English and Russian) 1958. irreg. price varies. Politechnika Gdanska, Majakowskiego 11/12, 81-952 Gdansk 6, Poland (Dist. by: Osrodek Rozpowszechniania Wydawnictw Naukowych Pan, Palac Kultury i Nauki, 00-901 Warsaw, Poland)

720 700 PL ISSN 0324-9905
POLITECHNIKA WROCLAWSKA. INSTYTUT ARCHITEKTURY I URBANISTYKI. PRACE NAUKOWE. MONOGRAFIE. (Text in Polish; summaries in English and Russian) 1969. irreg., no. 8, 1979. price varies. Politechnika Wroclawska, Wybrzeze Wyspianskiego 27, 50-370 Wroclaw, Poland (Dist. by: Ars Polona-Ruch, Krakowskie Przedmiescie 7, Warsaw, Poland) Ed. Marian Kloza.

720 700 PL ISSN 0324-9891
POLITECHNIKA WROCLAWSKA. INSTYTUT ARCHITEKTURY I URBANISTYKI. PRACE NAUKOWE. STUDIA I MATERIALY. (Text in Polish; summaries in English and Russian) 1971. irreg., no. 5, 1979. price varies. Politechnika Wroclawska, Wybrzeze Wyspianskiego 27, 50-370 Wroclaw, Poland (Dist. by: Ars Polona-Ruch, Krakowskie Przedmiescie 7, Warsaw, Poland) Ed. Marian Kloza.

POLITECHNIKA WROCLAWSKA. INSTYTUT HISTORII ARCHITEKTURY, SZTUKI I TECHNIKI. PRACE NAUKOWE. MONOGRAFIE. see *ART*

POLITECHNIKA WROCLAWSKA. INSTYTUT HISTORII ARCHITEKTURY, SZTUKI I TECHNIKI. PRACE NAUKOWE. STUDIA I MATERIALY. see *ART*

711 720 PL ISSN 0079-3450
POLSKA AKADEMIA NAUK. ODDZIAL W KRAKOWIE. KOMISJA URBANISTYKI I ARCHITEKTURY. TEKA. (Text in Polish; summaries in English and Russian) 1967. a. price varies. Ossolineum, Publishing House of the Polish Academy of Sciences, Rynek 9, 50-106 Wroclaw, Poland (Dist. by Ars Polona-Ruch, Krakowskie Przedmiescie 7, Warsaw, Poland) Ed. Janusz Bogdanowski.

720 PL ISSN 0079-4597
POZNANSKIE TOWARZYSTWO PRZYJACIOL NAUK. KOMISJA BUDOWNICTWA I ARCHITEKTURY. PRACE. (Text in Polish; summaries in English) 1961. irreg., 1972, vol. 2, no. 1. price varies. (Poznan Society of the Friends of Arts and Sciences) Panstwowe Wydawnictwo Naukowe, Ul. Miodowa 10, Warsaw, Poland (Dist. by Ars Polona-Ruch, Krakowskie Przedmiescie 7, Warsaw, Poland) Ed. Wladyslaw Czarnecki. bibl, charts, illus.

720 US
PROFILE; professional file architectural firms. 1978. a. $96 to non-members; members $80. (American Institute of Architects) Archimedia, Inc., 1900 Chestnut St., Philadelphia, PA 19103. Ed. Henry W. Schirmer.

720 AT
R A I A NEWS. irreg. membership. Royal Australian Institute of Architects, National Headquarters, 2A Mugga Way, Red Hill, A.C.T. 2603, Australia. Ed. David Kindon. circ. 6,500.

720.5 CN ISSN 0705-1913
REVIEW OF ARCHITECTURE AND LANDSCAPE ARCHITECTURE. 1977. irreg. c/o University of Toronto, School of Architecture, Department of Landscape Architecture, 230 College St., Toronto, Ont. M5T 1R2, Canada.

720 IT
RICERCHE SULLE DIMORE RURALI IN ITALIA. 1938. irreg., no. 30, 1973. price varies. (Consiglio Nazionale delle Ricerche) Casa Editrice Leo S. Olschki, Casella Postale 66, 50100 Florence, Italy. Eds. Lucio Gambi, Giuseppe Barbieri. circ. 1,000.

720 IE ISSN 0080-4444
ROYAL INSTITUTE OF THE ARCHITECTS OF IRELAND. YEARBOOK. 1909. a. £5. Royal Institute of the Architects of Ireland, 8 Merrion Sq., Dublin 2, Ireland. Ed. J. Owen Lewis. adv. bk. rev. index. circ. 1,000.

720 IE ISSN 0080-472X
ROYAL SOCIETY OF ULSTER ARCHITECTS. YEAR BOOK. 1928. a. free to members. Nicholson and Bass Ltd, 3 Clarence St. W., Belfast BT2 7GP, Ireland. Ed.Bd. adv. circ. 1,000.

720 SI
S I A YEARBOOK. a. membership. Singapore Institute of Architects, Publications Board, 395A/397A Block 23, Outram Park, Singapore 3, Singapore.

720 UK
SCOTLAND'S ARCHITECTURAL HERITAGE. 1975. irreg. 25p. Scottish Tourist Board, 23 Ravelston Terrace, Edinburgh EH4 3EU, Scotland. *History*

720 UK
SCOTTISH GEORGIAN SOCIETY. ANNUAL REPORT. 1972. biennial. £1.50. Scottish Georgian Society, 5B Forres St., Edinburgh EH3 6BJ, Scotland.
Incorporating: Scottish Georgian Society. Bulletin.

SOUTH INDIAN ART AND ARCHAEOLOGICAL SERIES. see *ART*

720 UK ISSN 0081-3567
SPECIFICATION; building methods and products. 1898. a. £45. Architectural Press Ltd., 9 Queen Anne's Gate, Westminster, London SW1H 9BY, England. Ed. David Martin. adv. circ. 6,250.

SPON'S ARCHITECTS' & BUILDERS' PRICE BOOK. see *BUILDING AND CONSTRUCTION*

720 CE
SRI LANKA INSTITUTE OF ARCHITECTS. JOURNAL. a. Sri Lanka Institute of Architects, 50 Rosmead Place, Colombo 7, Sri Lanka.

SRPSKA AKADEMIJA NAUKA I UMETNOSTI. ODELJENJE DRUSTVENIH NAUKA. SPOMENIK. see *SOCIAL SCIENCES: COMPREHENSIVE WORKS*

720 US ISSN 0081-5799
STONES OF PITTSBURGH. 1965. irreg. price varies. Pittsburgh History and Landmarks Foundation, Old Post Office Museum, Pittsburgh, PA 15212. Ed. Arthur P. Ziegler, Jr. circ. 3,000.

720 IT ISSN 0081-6140
STUDI D'ARCHITETTURA ANTICA. 1966. irreg., no. 5, 1974. price varies. Erma di "Bretschneider", Via Cassiodoro, 19, 00193 Rome, Italy.

711 720 PL ISSN 0081-6566
STUDIA I MATERIALY DO TEORII I HISTORII ARCHITEKTURY I URBANISTYKI. (Text in Polish; summaries in English and Russian) 1959. irreg. price varies. (Polska Akademia Nauk) Panstwowe Wydawnictwo Naukowe, Miodowa 10, Warsaw, Poland (Dist. by Ars Polona-Ruch, Krakowskie Przedmiescie 7, Warsaw, Poland) Ed. Jan Zachwatowicz.

720 CN
TECHNICAL UNIVERSITY OF NOVA SCOTIA. SCHOOL OF ARCHITECTURE. REPORT SERIES. 1970. irreg. price varies. ‡ Nova Scotia Technical College, Faculty of Architecture, Box 1000, Halifax, N.S. B3J 2X4, Canada. Ed. Peter Manning. circ. 1,000.
Formerly: Nova Scotia Technical College. School of Architecture. Report Series (ISSN 0078-2491)

774 SI
TECHNOGRAPHICS.* 1972. a. free. Singapore Polytechnic Draughting Society, Singapore Polytechnic, Princess Mary Campus, Dover Rd, Singapore, Singapore. illus. circ. 1,000.

712.025 US ISSN 0092-3745
TEXAS. STATE BOARD OF LANDSCAPE ARCHITECTS. ANNUAL ROSTER. 1970. a. membership. Texas State Board of Landscape Architects, 320 Sam Houston Bldg., Austin, TX 78701. Key Title: Annual Roster - Texas State Board of Landscape Architects.

720 IT ISSN 0082-6006
TRATTATI DI ARCHITETTURA. 1966. irreg. price varies. Edizioni Il Polifilo, Via Borgonuovo 2, 20121 Milan, Italy. Eds. Nino Carboneri & Paolo Portoghesi.

720 SP ISSN 0078-8732
UNIVERSIDAD DE NAVARRA. ESCUELA DE ARQUITECTURA. MANUALES: ARQUITECTURA. 1971. irreg.; 1979, no. 6. price varies. Ediciones Universidad de Navarra, S.A., Plaza de los Sauces, 1 y 2 Baranain, Pamplona, Spain.

720 IT
UNIVERSITA DEGLI STUDI DI GENOVA. ISTITUTO DI PROGETTAZIONE ARCHITETTONICA. QUADERNO.* 1968. irreg. L.10500 per issue. Universita degli Studi di Genova, Istituto di Progettazione Architettonica, Via Opera Pia Cousa 11, Genoa 16145, Italy. illus.

720 UK ISSN 0070-8992
UNIVERSITY OF EDINBURGH. ARCHITECTURE RESEARCH UNIT. REPORT. 1966. irreg. price varies. University of Edinburgh, Architecture Research Unit, 55 George Square, Edinburgh EH8 9JU, Scotland.

720 AT ISSN 0082-0571
UNIVERSITY OF SYDNEY. DEPARTMENT OF ARCHITECTURAL SCIENCE. REPORTS. 1970. irreg. $2. ‡ University of Sydney, Department of Architectural Science, Sydney, N.S.W., Australia. Ed. Prof. H. J. Cowan. Indexed: Aus.Sci.Ind.

720 UK ISSN 0306-0624
UNIVERSITY OF YORK. INSTITUTE OF ADVANCED ARCHITECTURAL STUDIES. RESEARCH PAPERS. no. 7, 1974. irreg. price varies. University of York, Institute of Advanced Architectural Studies, Kings Manor, York YO1 2EP, England. Ed. J. R. B. Taylor. illus. circ. 500.

720 300 US ISSN 0083-4696
URBAN ENVIRONMENT.* 1971. a. $3.95. Macmillan Publishing Co., Inc., 866 Third Ave., New York, NY 10022. Ed. Walter McQuade.

720 US
VIA. a. $20 paper, $30 cloth. M I T Press, 28 Carleton St., Cambridge, MA 02142. (reprint service avail. from ISI,UMI)

940 UK ISSN 0083-6079
VICTORIAN SOCIETY. ANNUAL. 1958. a. price varies. ‡ Victorian Society, 1 Priory Gardens, Bedford Park, London W4 1TT, England. Ed. Ian Sutton. adv. circ. 3,500.

728 GW ISSN 0083-8047
WERKEN UND WOHNEN. 1957. irreg., vol. 13, 1980. price varies. Rheinland-Verlag, Kennedy-Ufer 2, 5000 Cologne 21, W. Germany (B. R. D.) (Distr. by: Rudolf Habelt Verlag, Am Buchenhang 1, 5300 Bonn, W. Germany (B.R.D.)) Ed. Matthias Zender.

720 JA
WORKS OF ARCHITECTS. (Text in Japanese) irreg. Japan Architecture Association, Kansai Branch - Nihon Kenchikuka Kyokai, Kansai Branch, c/o Kensetsu Hosho Bldg., 5 Uemachi, Higashi-ku, Osaka 540, Japan. illus.

WORLD CULTURAL GUIDES. see *TRAVEL AND TOURISM*

YALE PUBLICATIONS IN THE HISTORY OF ART. see *ART*

720 CN
YARDSTICKS FOR COSTING. Variant title: Canadian Architect's Yardsticks for Costing. 1971. a. Can.$48. Southam Communications Ltd., 1450 Don Mills Rd., Don Mills, Ont. M3B 2X7, Canada. Ed. Jas. A. Murray. adv. circ. 2,195.

720.6 UK
YORK GEORGIAN SOCIETY. ANNUAL REPORT. 1943. a. membership. York Georgian Society, Kings, Manor, York YO1 2EW, England. Ed. Jane Hatcher. bk. rev. illus. circ. 600.

720
ZODCHESTVO. 1975. irreg. 2.96 Rub. (Soyuz Arkhitektorov S.S.S.R.) Stroiizdat, Kuznetskii most, 9, Moscow, U.S.S.R.
Formerly: Sovetskaya Arkhitektura.

745.4 US ISSN 0363-9525
37 DESIGN & ENVIRONMENT PROJECTS. 1976. a. $13.95. R C Publications, Inc., 6400 Goldsboro Road, N.W., Washington, DC 20034. illus.

ARCHITECTURE — Abstracting, Bibliographies, Statistics

720 016   US   ISSN 0194-1356
ARCHITECTURE SERIES: BIBLIOGRAPHY. 1978. irreg. Vance Bibliographies, Box 229, Monticello, IL 61856. bibl. index.

ART AND ARCHITECTURE BIBLIOGRAPHIES. see *ART — Abstracting, Bibliographies, Statistics*

720 016   US
AVERY INDEX TO ARCHITECTURAL PERIODICALS. SUPPLEMENT. 1963. irreg. $1235 (15 vol. set); price of supplements varies. (Columbia University, Avery Architectural Library) G. K. Hall & Co., 70 Lincoln Street, Boston, MA 02111.

016.7   US   ISSN 0360-2699
BIBLIOGRAPHIC GUIDE TO ART AND ARCHITECTURE. a. G. K. Hall & Co., 70 Lincoln St., Boston, MA 02111.
     Formerly: Art and Architecture Book Guide (ISSN 0098-2822)

ART

see also *Advertising and Public Relations; Hobbies; Museums and Art Galleries*

700 913   UK
A A R P MONOGRAPHS. (Art and Archaeology Research Papers) 1972. irreg. price varies. A A R P, c/o Dalu Jones & George Michell, Eds., 102 St. Paul's Rd., London N1 2LR, England.

200   GW
A Q. (Text in English, French and German) 1964. irreg. price varies. A Q-Verlag, Erwin Stegentritt, Kantstr. 43, 6602 Dudweiler, W. Germany (B.R.D.) circ. 1,000.
     Formerly: Anti-Quarium.

700   SW   ISSN 0044-5711
A R I S. (Art Research in Scandinavia) (Text in English and Swedish) 1969. a. Kr.50. ‡ Institute of Art History, Kyrkegatan 19, S-221 01 Lund 1, Sweden. Ed. Prof. Sven Sandstroem. bk. rev. illus. circ. 700.

700   US   ISSN 0065-0129
A. W. MELLON LECTURES IN THE FINE ARTS. 1956. irreg., no. 22, 1974. price varies. Princeton University Press, Princeton, NJ 08540. (reprint service avail. from UMI)

700 800 780   GW
ABHANDLUNGEN ZUR KUNST-, MUSIK- UND LITERATURWISSENSCHAFT. no. 3, 1958. irreg., vol. 292, 1979/80. price varies. Bouvier Verlag Herbert Grundmann, Am Hof 32, Postfach 1268, 5300 Bonn 1, W. Germany (B.R.D.)

700   AG
ACADEMIA NACIONAL DE BELLAS ARTES. ANUARIO. a. Academia Nacional de Bellas Artes, Sanchez de Bustamente 2663, Buenos Aires, Argentina. Ed. Bd. illus.

700 800   IT   ISSN 0065-0749
ACCADEMIA LUCCHESE DI SCIENZE, LETTERE ED ARTI. ATTI. NUOVA SERIE. irreg. price varies. Casa Editrice Felice le Monnier, Via Scipione Ammirato 100, C.P. 455, 50136 Florence, Italy.

700 800   IT   ISSN 0065-0714
ACCADEMIA MUSICALE CHIGIANA. QUADERNI. 1942. irreg. price varies. Casa Editrice Leo S. Olschki, Casella Postale 66, 50100 Florence, Italy. circ. 500.

AEGYPTOLOGISCHE FORSCHUNGEN. see *HISTORY — History Of The Near East*

AISTHESIS; revista chilena de investigaciones esteticas. see *PHILOSOPHY*

700   CN   ISSN 0704-9056
ALBERTA ART FOUNDATION. ANNUAL REPORT. 1972. a. Alberta Art Foundation, 11th Floor, CN Tower, Edmonton, Alta., Canada.

700   IT   ISSN 0065-6801
AMERICAN ACADEMY IN ROME. MEMOIRS. 1917. irreg. price varies. American Academy in Rome, Library, Via Angelo Masina, 5, Rome, 00153, Italy.

700 800   US   ISSN 0065-6844
AMERICAN ACADEMY OF ARTS AND SCIENCES. RECORDS OF THE ACADEMY. (Previously issued in the Academy's Proceedings) 1958-59. a. $4. American Academy of Arts and Sciences, 165 Allendale St., Jamaica Plain Sta., Boston, MA 02130. Ed. Stephen Graubard. index.

700 708   US   ISSN 0065-6968
AMERICAN ART DIRECTORY. 1898. biennial. $49.50. (Jaques Cattell Press) R. R. Bowker Company, 1180 Ave. of the Americas, New York, NY 10036 (Orders to P.O. Box 1807, Ann Arbor, Mich. 48106) index. (reprint service avail. from UMI)

707   US   ISSN 0146-9606
AMERICAN ARTIST DIRECTORY OF ART SCHOOLS & WORKSHOPS. 1964. a. $1.50. ‡ American Artist Reprints, (Subsidiary of: Billboard Publications Inc.) 1515 Broadway, New York, NY 10036. Eds. Robert Hudoba, Jon Braude. adv. circ. 120,000.
     Former titles: American Artist Art School Directory; Art School Directory.

AMERICAN ARTS PAMPHLET SERIES. see *LITERATURE*

709   US   ISSN 0065-9991
AMERICAN RESEARCH CENTER IN EGYPT. JOURNAL. 1962. a. $20. J. J. Augustin, Inc., Locust Valley, NY 11560. Ed. Gerald E. Kadish. bk. rev. circ. 800.

AMERICAN SOCIETY OF APPRAISERS. APPRAISAL AND VALUATION MANUAL. see *REAL ESTATE*

AMERICAN SOCIETY OF BOOKPLATE COLLECTORS AND DESIGNERS. YEAR BOOK. see *HOBBIES*

709   TU   ISSN 0066-1333
ANADOLU SANATI ARASTIRMALARI/ RESEARCHES ON ANATOLIAN ART. (Text in English and Turkish; summaries in English) 1968. irreg. TL.35. Technical University of Istanbul, Department of the History of Architecture and Preservation - Istanbul Teknik Universitesi, Gumussuyu Caddesi 87, Beyoglu, Istanbul, Turkey. Ed. Dogan Kuban. circ. 1,000.

700   II
ANDHRA PRADESH, INDIA. DEPARTMENT OF ARCHAEOLOGY AND MUSEUMS. ART AND ARCHITECTURE SERIES. (Text in English) irreg. price varies. Department of Archaeology and Museums, Hyderabad 500001, Andhra Pradesh, India (Or: Publications Bureau, Directorate of Government Printing, Chanchalguda, Hyderabad, Andhra Pradesh, India)

709   GR   ISSN 0066-2119
ANNALES D'ESTHETIQUE/CHRONIKA AISTHETIKES. (Text in Greek, English and French) 1962. a. $10. Societe Hellenique d'Esthetique - Hellenic Society for Aesthetics, Vassilissis Sophias 79, Athens 140, Greece. bk. rev. circ. 1,000.

700   FR
ANNUAIRE DE L'ART INTERNATIONAL. 1961. biennial. 90 F. Patrick Sermadiras Ed.&Pub., 11, rue Arsene Houssaye, 75008 Paris, France. adv. bk. rev. illus.

700   FR   ISSN 0066-3263
ANNUAIRE INTERNATIONAL DES VENTES. (Editions in French and English) 1963. a. 375 F. Librairie Fischbacher, 33 rue de Seine, 75-Paris 6, France. Ed. E. Mayer.

700   FR   ISSN 0066-3352
ANNUAIRE NATIONAL DES BEAUX-ARTS. 1976/77. a. Editions Dany Thibaud, 52 rue Labrouste, 75015 Paris, France.

ART   71

700   US   ISSN 0308-5910
ANNUAL ART SALES INDEX: OIL PAINTINGS, DRAWINGS AND WATERCOLOURS. (Text in English and French; summaries in English) 1968-69. a. $136. ‡ Apollo Book, 391 South Rd., Poughkeepsie, NY 12601. Ed. Richard Hislop. adv. index. circ. 3,000.

700 659.106   US
ANNUAL OF ADVERTISING, EDITORIAL & TELEVISION ART & DESIGN WITH THE ANNUAL COPY AWARDS. 1922. a. $25. Art Directors Club of New York, 488 Madison Ave., New York, NY 10022. (Co-sponsor: Copy Club of New York) Ed. Jennifer Place.
     Formerly (until 1973): Annual of Advertising, Editorial and Television Art and Design (ISSN 0066-4014)

338.4   US   ISSN 0094-0402
ANNUAL REPORT OF THE ARTS ACTIVITIES IN ALABAMA. Cover title: Arts in Alabama. 1967. a. free. Alabama State Council on the Arts and Humanities, 449 S. McDonough St., Montgomery, AL 36130. Ed. Sharon Heflin. illus. circ. 1,500.
     Formerly: Biennial Report of the Arts Activities in Alabama.

709 913   IT
ANTICHITA, ARCHEOLOGIA, STORIA DELL'ARTE. (Text in French and Italian) irreg. Angelo Longo Editore, Via Rocca Ai Fossi 6, Casella Postale 431, 48100 Ravenna, Italy. Ed. Raffaella Farioli.

700   SZ   ISSN 0066-4782
ANTIKE KUNST. BEIHEFTE. (Text in French, English, or German) 1963. irreg., vol. 12, 1980. price varies. ‡ (Vereinigung der Freunde Antiker Kunst) Francke Verlag, Postfach, CH-3000 Berne 26, Switzerland.

700   SP   ISSN 0302-6965
ANUARIO DEL ARTE ESPANOL. 1973. a. Iberico Europea de Ediciones, S.A., Serrano 44, Madrid 1, Spain. illus.

701   US   ISSN 0066-5568
APPRECIATION OF THE ARTS. no. 8, 1973. irreg., latest no. 9. price varies. Oxford University Press, 200 Madison Ave., New York, NY 10016 (and Ely House, 37 Dover St., London W1X 4AH, England) Ed. Harold Osborne.

706   US   ISSN 0066-6637
ARCHIVES OF ASIAN ART. 1945. a. $15. (Friends of Asia House Gallery) Asia Society, 112 East 64 St., New York, NY 10021. Eds. John Rosenfield, Jan Fontein. cum.index: 1945-65. circ. 600(approx.) (back issues avail.)
     Until 1966 Issued As: Chinese Art Society of America. Archives.

950 709   US   ISSN 0571-1371
ARS ORIENTALIS; the arts of Islam and the East. 1954. irreg., no. 11, 1979. price varies. Michigan Publications on East Asia, 104 Lane Hall, University of Michigan, Ann Arbor, MI 48109.
     Supersedes: Ars Islamica.

700   AG
ARS, REVISTA DE ARTE. a. Rodriguez Pena 339, Buenos Aires, Argentina. Ed. I. I. Schlagman.

709   SW   ISSN 0066-7919
ARS SUECICA. (Subseries of Acta Universitatis Upsaliensis) (Text in Swedish; summaries in English or German) 1966. irreg., vol. 4, 1977. price varies. (Uppsala Universitet, Institute of Art History) Almqvist & Wiksell International, Box 62, S-101 20 Stockholm, Sweden. Ed. Rudolf Zeitler.

730   UN   ISSN 0004-5535
ART; the journal of the professional artist/le porte-parole de l'artiste professionnel. (Text in English, French and Spanish) 1953. a. free. Unesco, International Association of Art - Association Internationale des Art Plastiques, 1 rue Miollis, 775015 Paris, France. Ed. Dunbar Marshall-Malagola. circ. 3,000.

700   US   ISSN 0066-7927
ART AND ARTISTS OF THE MONTEREY PENINSULA. 1960. irreg., 3rd issue 1976. $2. Art and Artists of the Monterey Peninsula, Box 1310, Monterey, CA 93940. Ed. Lee C. Harbick. adv. bk. rev. circ. 10,000.

704   II   ISSN 0004-3044
ART AND LIFE. (Text mainly in English; occasionally in English & Bengali) 1967. a. Rs.8($1) Art Study Centre, B 20-185 Bhelupura, Varanasi 1, India. Ed.R. N. Mukerji. adv. bk. rev. charts. illus. circ. 100.

700   II
ART AND THE ARTIST. 1962. irreg. Rs.3 per no. Academy of Fine Arts, 14/2 Old China Bazar St., Calcutta 1, India. Ed.Bd. illus. Indexed: Art Ind.

700   AT   ISSN 0311-0087
ART CRAFT TEACHERS ASSOCIATION MAGAZINE. 1972. irreg. (about 8/yr) Aus.$12.50. Art Craft Teachers Association, Room 12, 350 Victoria St., North Melbourne, Vic. 3051, Australia. Ed. Dorothy Mae Pound. adv. bk. rev. circ. 1,000.

700   IT
ART DIARY. (Text in English, Italian) 1975. a. L.10000($12.95) Giancarlo Politi, Editore, Via Donatello 36, 20131 Milan, Italy. adv.

700   IT   ISSN 0066-7943
ART DIRECTORS CLUB MILANO. 1968. irreg. L.30000. Centro Di, Piazza de Mozzi 1r, Florence 50125, Italy.

704   FR   ISSN 0066-7951
ART ET LES GRANDES CIVILISATIONS. 1968. irreg., 1974, vol. 5. Editions d'Art Lucien Mazenod, 33 rue de Naples, Paris 8, France.

700   AT
ART GALLERY NEWS. 1969? irreg. Aus.$0.05 per no. Benalla Art Gallery Society, Kitson Court, Benalla, Vic. 3672, Australia.

709   US
ART HISTORY SERIES. 1977. irreg. price varies. Decatur House Press, Ltd., 2122 Decatur Pl. N.W., Washington, DC 20008. index.

702.8   US
ART MATERIAL DIRECTORY AND PRODUCT INFORMATION GUIDE. 1952. a. Syndicate Magazines, Inc., 6 E. 43rd St., New York, NY 10017. circ. 10,000.
   Formerly: Art Material Trade News Directory of Art & Craft Materials.

700   US
ART OF THE WORLD LIBRARY. irreg. price varies. Crown Publishers, Inc., One Park Ave., New York, NY 10016.

700   US   ISSN 0193-6867
ART REFERENCE COLLECTION. irreg. price varies. Greenwood Press, 8 Post Rd. W., Westport, CT 06881. Ed. Pamela J. Parry.

700 914   SP
ART ROMANIC. (Contains 2 series, Monografies and Tematica) (Text in Catalan) irreg.; no. 10, 1979. 1000 ptas. Artestudi Edicions, Provença 552, Barcelona 26, Spain. adv. bk. rev. illus.

700   UK
ART WORKERS GUILD. ANNUAL REPORT. 1885. a. membership. Art Workers Guild, 6 Queen Square, London WC1N 3AR, England. Ed. Arthur Llewellyn Smith. bibl. illus. circ. 400(controlled)

709   SA   ISSN 0004-3389
DE ARTE. (Text in Afrikaans and English) 1967. a. R.2.10. University of South Africa, Department of History of Art and Fine Arts, Box 392, Pretoria 0001, South Africa. Ed. Frieda Harmsen. adv. bk. rev. play rev. bibl. illus. circ. 1,220.
   History

700 913   BO   ISSN 0587-5447
ARTE Y ARQUEOLOGIA. 1969. biennial. Universidad Mayor de San Andres, Instituto de Estudios Bolivianos, Casilla Postal 609, La Paz, Bolivia. circ. 500.

709.5   SZ
ARTIBUS ASIAE SUPPLEMENTA. no. 35, 1978. a. price varies. (New York University, Institute of Fine Arts, US) Artibus Asiae Publishers, CH-6612 Ascona, Switzerland (U.S. address: Institute of Fine Arts, New York University, 1 E. 78th St., New York, NY 10021) bibl. illus.

700   EC
ARTISTAS ECUATORIANOS. (Text in English and Spanish) 1976. irreg. $30. Ediciones Paralelo Cero, Box 1135, Av. 12 de Octubre 186, Quito, Ecuador. Dir. Hector Merino Valencia. illus.

708.11   CN
ARTISTS IN CANADA. (Text in French and English) 1970. irreg. Can.$4. National Gallery of Canada, Ottawa, Ont. K1A 0M8, Canada.
   Formerly: National Gallery of Canada. Library. Checklist of Canadian Artists' Files (ISSN 0078-6993)

700   US
ARTISTS IN PERSPECTIVE SERIES. irreg. price varies. Prentice-Hall, Inc., Box 500, Englewood Cliffs, NJ 07632. Ed. H. Janson.

700   US   ISSN 0161-0546
ARTIST'S MARKET(1979) 1979. a. price varies. Writers Digest, 9933 Alliance Rd., Cincinnati, OH 45242.
   Supersedes in part: Art & Crafts Market; Former titles: Artist's & Photographer's Market (ISSN 0146-8294); Artist's Market (ISSN 0361-607X); Which was formerly (until 1973): Cartoonists' Market (ISSN 0147-2461)

700   US
ARTISTS - U S A: GUIDE TO CONTEMPORARY AMERICAN ART. 1970. biennial. price varies. Foundation for the Advancement of Artists, 1315 Walnut St., Philadelphia, PA 19107. Ed. Howard Jeffries.

705 706   AT   ISSN 0066-8095
ARTS. 1958. irreg. Aus.$2 to individuals; Aus. $3 to institutions. University of Sydney, Arts Association, University of Sydney, Sydney, N.S.W., Australia. Ed. T. Herring.

709.5   FR   ISSN 0004-3958
ARTS ASIATIQUES. (Text in French, occasionally in English) 1954. 1-2/yr. price varies. (Ecole Francaise d'Extreme Orient) Editions d'Amerique et d'Orient, 11 rue Saint Sulpice, 75006 Paris, France. Eds. Jean Filliozat & Jeannine Auboyer. bk. rev. charts. illus. circ. 1,500.

700   AT
ARTS COUNCIL OF AUSTRALIA. ANNUAL REPORT. 1948. a. Arts Council of Australia, Suite 605, 6th Floor, Phoenix House, 32-34 Bridge St., Sydney, N.S.W. 2000, Australia. Ed. Jennifer Bott. circ. 1,500.

700   UK   ISSN 0066-8133
ARTS COUNCIL OF GREAT BRITAIN. ANNUAL REPORT AND ACCOUNTS. 1945. a. 80p. Arts Council of Great Britain, 105 Piccadilly, London W1V 0AU, England (Dist. by H.M.S.O., P.O.B. 569, London S.E.1, England)

746 730   FR
ARTS ET OBJETS DU MAROC. Covertitle: Maroc. no.2, 1974. irreg. 50 F. 8, rue Saint-Marc, 75002 Paris, France. Ed. G. J. Malgras. illus.

700   II
ARTS OF HIMACHAL. 1975. irreg. price varies. State Museum, Simla, Department of Languages and Cultural Affairs, Simla, Himachal Pradesh, India.

707.2   US   ISSN 0066-8168
ARTS PATRONAGE SERIES. 1970. irreg., no. 7, 1979. price varies. ‡ Washington International Arts Letter, Box 9005, Washington, DC 20003. Ed. Daniel Millsaps.

700   UK
ARTS REVIEW YEARBOOK. 1973. a. £8. Starcity Ltd., 16 St. James Gardens, London W11, England. Ed. Annabel Terry Engell. adv.

700 792   RH
ARTS ZIMBABWE. 1978. a. Rhod.$3.30($11.54) National Arts Foundation of Zimbabwe, 901-902 Regal Star House, Gordon Ave., Box UA 463, Salisbury, Zimbabwe. index. circ. 3,000.
   Formerly: Arts Rhodesia.

700   AT   ISSN 0311-0095
ARTVIEWS. 1972? irreg. Aus.$0.40 each. Artists' Guild of Australia, 156 Banksia St., Pagewood, NSW 2035, Australia.

709   US   ISSN 0146-5783
ASSOCIATION FOR GRAVESTONE STUDIES. NEWSLETTER. 1977. q. membership. Association for Gravestone Studies, c/o American Antiquarian Society, Worcester, MA 01609 (Subscr. to Sally Thomas, Treas., 82 Hilltop Pl., New London, NH 03257) Ed. Jessie Lie Farber. bk. rev. bibl. illus. circ. 300.

700   US
AUDIOZINE. 1977. irreg. $10 per no. (Mamelle Inc.) Contemporary Arts Press, Box 3123, San Francisco, CA 94119. (audio cassette)

AURORA; Jahrbuch der Eichendorff-Gesellschaft. see *LITERATURE*

AURORA-BUCHREIHE. see *LITERATURE*

700   GW   ISSN 0067-0642
AUS FORSCHUNG UND KUNST. 1968. irreg., no. 21, 1975. price varies. (Geschichtsverein fuer Kaernten, AU) Rudolf Habelt Verlag, Am Buchenhang 1, 5300 Bonn 1, W. Germany (B. R. D.) Ed. Gotbert Moro.

AUSTRIA. BUNDESMINISTERIUM FUER UNTERRICHT UND KUNST. SCHRIFTENREIHE. see *EDUCATION — Teaching Methods And Curriculum*

B. C. MONTHLY. see *LITERATURE*

B L A C. (Black Literature and Arts Congress) see *ETHNIC INTERESTS*

BACK ROADS; an annual magazine of literature and art. see *LITERATURE*

BALLENA PRESS PUBLICATIONS ON NORTH AMERICAN ROCK ART. see *ARCHAEOLOGY*

BAMPTON LECTURES IN AMERICA. see *RELIGIONS AND THEOLOGY*

BARBACANE; revue des pierres et des hommes. see *LITERATURE*

BARBADOS MUSEUM AND HISTORICAL SOCIETY. JOURNAL. see *HISTORY — History Of North And South America*

700   GW
BAYERISCHE STAATSGEMAELDESAMMLUNGEN. JAHRESBERICHT. a. Bayerische Staatsgemaeldesammlungen, Meiserstr. 10, 8000 Munich 2, W. Germany (B.R.D.)

700   CN   ISSN 0315-2359
BEAUX-ARTS. 1972. irreg. price varies. 3625 St. Laurent, Montreal, P.Q. H2X 2V5, Canada. Ed. Tom Dean. circ. 1,000. (back issues avail.)

740 810   US
BEBOP DRAWING CLUB BOOK. 1974. irreg. Artman's Press, 1511 McGee Ave., Berkeley, CA 94703. illus.

700   GW   ISSN 0067-4893
BEIHEFTE DER BONNER JAHRBUECHER. 1950. irreg., no. 41, 1980. price varies. Rheinland-Verlag, Kennedy-Ufer 2, 5000 Cologne 21, W. Germany (B.R.D.) (Distr. by: Rudolf Habelt Verlag, Am Buchenhang 1, 5300 Bonn, W. Germany (B.R.D.))

700   GW   ISSN 0067-5121
BEITRAEGE ZUR KUNST DES CHRISTLICHEN OSTENS. 1964. irreg. price varies. Verlag Aurel Bongers, Hubertusstr. 13, Postfach 220, 4350 Recklinghausen, W. Germany (B. R. D.) illus.

709   GW
BEITRAEGE ZUR KUNSTGESCHICHTE. irreg., vol. 16, 1981. price varies. Walter de Gruyter und Co., Genthiner Str. 13, 1000 Berlin 30, W. Germany (B.R.D.) Ed. Wolfgang Schultz.

BEST EDITORIAL CARTOONS OF THE YEAR. see *LITERARY AND POLITICAL REVIEWS*

BEST IN COVERS AND POSTERS. see *PUBLISHING AND BOOK TRADE*

745.4 US ISSN 0360-8271
BEST IN ENVIRONMENTAL GRAPHICS.
(Subseries of: Print Casebooks) 1975. a. $13.95. R C Publications, Inc., 355 Lexington Ave., New York, NY 10017 (Or 6400 Goldsboro Rd., Washington, DC 20034) illus.

BIBLIOGRAPHY OF APPRAISAL LITERATURE. see *REAL ESTATE — Abstracting, Bibliographies, Statistics*

BIBLIOTECA NAPOLETANA DI STORIA E ARTE. see *HISTORY — History Of Europe*

700 PL ISSN 0067-7698
BIBLIOTEKA KRAKOWSKA. 1897. irreg., vol. 119, 1978. price varies. Towarzystwo Milosnikow Historii i Zabytkow Krakowa, Ul. Sw. Jana 12, 31-018 Krakow, Poland (Dist. by: Ars Polona-Ruch, Krakowskie Przedmiescie 7, Warsaw, Poland) Ed. Janina Bieniarzowna.

929 016 NE ISSN 0067-7930
BIBLIOTHECA EMBLEMATICA. 1962. irreg. price varies. ‡ Haentjens Dekker en Gumbert, Achter Sint Pieter 14, Utrecht, Netherlands. bk. rev.

700 US
BIRTHSTONE. 1975. irreg. $6.50 for 4 nos. Birthstone Magazine, Box 27394, San Francisco, CA 94127 (Or 1319 6th Ave., San Francisco, CA 94122) Ed.Bd. bk. rev. circ. 700.

700 GW ISSN 0068-0036
BONNER BEITRAEGE ZUR KUNSTWISSENSCHAFT. 1950. irreg., 1971, no. 11. price varies. Rheinland-Verlag, Kennedy-Ufer 2, 5000 Cologne 21, W. Germany (B.R.D.) (Distr. by: Rudolf Habelt Verlag, Am Buchenhang 1, 5300 Bonn, W. Germany (B.R.D.)) Eds. Herbert Von Einem, Heinrich Luetzler.

700 US
BOSTON MUSEUM OF FINE ARTS. MUSEUM YEAR. ANNUAL REPORTS. a. price varies. (Boston Museum of Fine Arts) New York Graphic Society, 140 Greenwich Ave., Greenwich, CT 06830.

BRAZIL. DIRETORIA DO PATRIMONIO HISTORICO E ARTISTICO NACIONAL. REVISTA. see *HISTORY — History Of North And South America*

BRITISH ARCHAEOLOGICAL ASSOCIATION. CONFERENCE TRANSACTIONS. see *ARCHAEOLOGY*

BRITISH COLUMBIA ART TEACHERS' ASSOCIATION. JOURNAL. see *EDUCATION — Teaching Methods And Curriculum*

708 GW ISSN 0572-7146
BRUECKE-ARCHIV. 1967. irreg., no. 9/10, 1977/78. price varies. Bruecke-Museum, Bussardsteig 9, 1000 Berlin 33, W. Germany (B.R.D.) Ed. Leopold Reidemeister. illus.

709 NZ
BULLETIN OF NEW ZEALAND ART HISTORY. 1972. a. NZ.$3. University of Auckland, Department of Art History, Private Bag C. 1, Auckland, New Zealand. Ed. Tong Green. circ. 400.

700 US ISSN 0068-4295
BURT FRANKLIN ART HISTORY AND ART REFERENCE SERIES. (Text in various languages) 1968. irreg., 1973, no. 44. price varies. Lenox Hill Publishing and Distributing Corporation, 235 E. 44th St., New York, NY 10017. (back issues avail.)

700 PL ISSN 0067-947X
BYDGOSKIE TOWARZYSTWO NAUKOWE. WYDZIAL NAUK HUMANISTYCZNYCH. PRACE. SERIA D: (SZTUKA) irreg., 1965, no. 3. price varies. Bydgoskie Towarzystwo Naukowe, Jezuicka 4, Bydgoszcz, Poland (Dist. by Ars Polona-Ruch, Krakowskie Przedmiescie 7, Warsaw, Poland)

C Q; poetry and art. (Contemporary Quarterly) see *LITERATURE — Poetry*

CAHIERS DE CIVILISATION MEDIEVALE. SUPPLEMENT. see *HISTORY — History Of Europe*

709 US ISSN 0068-5542
CALIFORNIA DESIGN.* 1962. triennial, 1971, no. 11. $7.50. ‡ Pasadena Art Museum, California Design Program, 411 W. Colorado Blvd., Pasadena, CA 91101. Ed. E. M. Moore.

709 US ISSN 0068-5909
CALIFORNIA STUDIES IN THE HISTORY OF ART. 1962. irreg. price varies. University of California Press, 2223 Fulton St., Berkeley, CA 94720.

917 CN ISSN 0703-6078
CANADA COUNCIL. TOURING OFFICE. BULLETIN. (Text in English and French) 1975. irreg. free. Canada Council, Touring Office, Box 1047, 255 Albert St., Ottawa, Ont. K1P 5V8, Canada. illus.

700 780 792 CN ISSN 0576-4300
CANADA COUNCIL ANNUAL REPORT AND SUPPLEMENT. (Editions in English and French) 1958. a. free. ‡ Canada Council, Communication Service, P.O.B. 1047, 255 Albert St., Ottawa K1P 5V8, Canada. charts. stat. circ. 5,000.

700 CN ISSN 0383-5405
CANADIAN ARTISTS SERIES/COLLECTION: ARTISTES CANADIENS. (Editions in English & French) 1973. irreg. Can.$3.95. National Gallery of Canada, Ottawa, Ont. K1A 0M8, Canada. illus. circ. 5,000.

700 CN ISSN 0068-8487
CANADIAN CONFERENCE OF THE ARTS. MISCELLANEOUS REPORTS. (Text in English and French) 1969. irreg. prices on request. Canadian Conference of the Arts, 141 Laurier Ave. W., Suite 707, Ottawa, Ont. K1P 5J3, Canada.

CANADIAN SOCIETY FOR EDUCATION THROUGH ART. ANNUAL JOURNAL. see *EDUCATION*

CANTO LIBRE; a bilingual trimester of Latin American people's art. see *ETHNIC INTERESTS*

709 FR ISSN 0076-230X
CASA DE VELAQUEZ, MADRID. MELANGES/ CASA DE VELASQUEZ, MADRID. MISCELLANIES. (Text in French and Spanish) 1965. a. price varies. (SP) Diffusion de Boccard, 11 rue de Medicis, 75006 Paris, France.
The Casa is a French institute for research in Madrid

750 IT
CATALOGO BOLAFFI DELLA PITTURA ITALIANA DELL'OTTOCENTO. 1964. irreg., no. 7, 1978. L.60000. Giulio Bolaffi Editore s.p.a., Via Cavour 17F, 10123 Turin, Italy. Ed. Umberto Allemandi. adv. illus. circ. 3,500.

700 IT
CATALOGO NAZIONALE BOLAFFI D'ARTE MODERNA. 1962. a. L.70000. Giulio Bolaffi Editore s.p.a., Via Cavour 17F, 10123 Turin, Italy. Ed. Umberto Allemandi. adv. illus. circ. 6,500.
Former titles (1964-1970): Catalogo Bolaffi d'Arte Moderna (ISSN 0576-8861); (1962-1963): Collezionista d'Arte Moderna.

760 IT
CATALOGO NAZIONALE BOLAFFI DELLA GRAFICA. 1970. a. L.40000. Giulio Bolaffi Editore s.p.a., Via Cavour 17F, 10123 Turin, Italy. Ed. Umberto Allemandi. adv. illus. circ. 3,500.
Formerly (first no. only): Catalogo Bolaffi della Grafica Italiana.

750 UN ISSN 0069-1135
CATALOGUE OF REPRODUCTIONS OF PAINTINGS PRIOR TO 1860. (Text in English, French and Spanish) 1950. irreg., 1972, 9th ed. Unesco, 7-9 Place de Fontenoy, 75700 Paris, France (Dist. in U.S. by: Unipub, 345 Park Ave. S., New York, NY 10010)

750 UN ISSN 0069-1143
CATALOGUE OF REPRODUCTIONS OF PAINTINGS, 1860-1973. (Text in English, French and Spanish) 1950. irreg.; no. 9, 1973. Unesco, 7-9 Place de Fontenoy, Paris, France (Dist. in U.S. by: Unipub, 345 Park Ave. S., New York, NY 10010)

CENACOLO; arte e letteratura. see *LITERATURE*

CENTRE D'HISTOIRE ET D'ART DE LA THUDINIE. PUBLICATIONS. see *HISTORY — History Of Europe*

CHARIOTEER; an annual review of modern Greek culture. see *HISTORY — History Of Europe*

CHOICE (BINGHAMTON); a magazine of poetry and graphics. see *LITERATURE — Poetry*

CINMAY SMRTI PATHAGARA. see *LITERATURE*

700 IT
CIVETTA. no. 2, 1974. irreg.; no. 6, 1977. price varies. Giardini Editori e Stampatori, Via Santa Bibbiana 28, 56100 Pisa, Italy. Ed. Nicola Micieli.

700 945 IT ISSN 0069-4355
CIVILTA VENEZIANA. FONTI E TESTI. SERIE PRIMA: FONTI E TESTI PER LA STORIA DELL'ARTE VENETA. 1959. irreg., 1972, no. 8. price varies. (Fondazione Giorgio Cini) Casa Editrice Leo S. Olschki, Casella Postale 66, 50100 Florence, Italy. circ. 1,000.

700 SP
COLLECCIO DE MATERIALS. (Text in Catalan) 1977. irreg. Artestudi Edicions, Provenca 552, Barcelona 26, Spain.

700 CN ISSN 0530-8836
COLLECTION PANORAMA. irreg. price varies. Editions Lidec, 1083 Ave. van Horne, Montreal 154, Quebec, Canada.

700 US
COLLEGE ART ASSOCIATION MONOGRAPHS. irreg. price varies. (College Art Association of America) New York University Press, Washington Sq., New York, NY 10003.

700 US ISSN 0069-6072
COLORADO SPRINGS FINE ARTS CENTER. REPORT. 1947. a.; latest issue, 1970. free. ‡ Colorado Springs Fine Arts Center, 30 W. Dale St., Colorado Springs, CO 80903.

COMITATUS; A JOURNAL OF MEDIEVAL AND RENAISSANCE STUDIES. see *LITERATURE*

700 AT
CONTEMPORARY ART SOCIETY OF AUSTRALIA. BROADSHEET. 1968? irreg. Contemporary Art Society of Australia, G.P.O. Box 3271, Sydney, NSW 2001, Australia.

700 US
CONTEMPORARY ARTISTS. irreg. $65. Harry N. Abrams, Inc., 110 East 59th St., New York, NY 10022.

150 UK ISSN 0069-973X
CONTROL MAGAZINE. 1965. a. £3. 5 London Mews, London W.2, England. Ed. S. Willats. circ. 700.

700 US ISSN 0363-4574
CORNFIELD REVIEW; an annual of the creative arts. 1976. a. $1. Ohio State University Marion Campus, 1465 Mt. Vernon Ave., Marion, OH 43302. Ed. David Citino. illus. circ. 750.

700 913 IT
CORSI INTERNAZIONALI DI CULTURA SULL'ARTE RAVENNATE E BIZANTINA. ATTI. (Text in English, French, German and Italian) 1953? a. Angelo Longo Editore, Via Rocca Ai Fossi 6, Casella Postale 431, 48100 Ravenna, Italy.

CREATIVITY. see *ADVERTISING AND PUBLIC RELATIONS*

700 US
CRISS-CROSS ART COMMUNICATIONS. no. 5, 1977. irreg. $10 for four issues. Criss-Cross Foundation, Box 2022, Boulder, CO 80306. Ed. Bd. adv. (back issues avail.)

700.5 US ISSN 0090-4112
CRITIQUES. 1970/71. a. Cooper Union for the Advancement of Science and Art, School of Art and Architecture, Cooper Square, New York, NY 10003. Key Title: Critiques (New York)

700 SP
CUADERNOS DE ALHAMBRA. 1965. irreg. price varies. (Patronato de la Alhambra) Universidad de Granada, Secretariado de Publicaciones, Hospital Real, Granada, Spain. Ed. Fray Dario Cabanelas.

700 AG ISSN 0070-1688
CUADERNOS DE HISTORIA DEL ARTE. 1961. a. Arg.$28.50. Instituto de Historia del Arte, Universidad Nacional de Cuyo, Facultad de Filosofia y Letras, Centro Universitario, Parque Gral San Martin, Mendoza, Argentina. Ed.Bd. bk. rev.

709 MX
CUADERNOS DE HISTORIA DEL ARTE. irreg. Universidad Nacional Autonoma de Mexico, Libreria Universitaria, Av. Insurgentes sur 299, Mexico 20, D.F., Mexico.

700 SP
D'ART. (Text Catalan, Spanish) 1972. irreg. 650 ptas.($12.50) Universidad de Barcelona, Departamento de Arte, Av Jose Antonio 585, Barcelona 11, Spain. Ed. Dr. Santiago Alcolea. bk. rev. circ. 1,000. (back issues avail)

700 US
DADAZINE. 1970. 2-3/yr. 1183 Church St., San Francisco, CA 94114. Ed. Bill Gaglione.

706 US
DELAWARE ART MUSEUM. ANNUAL REPORT. 1912. a. free. ‡ Delaware Art Museum, 2301 Kentmere Parkway, Wilmington, DE 19806. Ed. Charles L. Wyrick, Jr. circ. 2,000.
Formerly: Wilmington Society of the Fine Arts. Report (ISSN 0084-0327)

686.3 095 GW ISSN 0341-2474
DENKMAELER DER BUCHKUNST. 1976. irreg., vol. 4, 1981. price varies. Anton Hiersemann Verlag, Rosenbergstr. 113, Postfach 723, 7000 Stuttgart 1, W. Germany (B.R.D.)

DESIGN IN GREECE/THEMATA CHOROU & TECHNON. see *ARCHITECTURE*

741.67 UK ISSN 0084-974X
DESIGNERS IN BRITAIN. 1947. irreg., 1972, vol. 7. price varies. Society of Industrial Artists and Designers, 12 Carlton House Terrace, London SW1Y 5AH, England.

920 830 GW ISSN 0070-4695
DICHTER UND ZEICHNER. 1963. irreg. price varies. Graphikum, Allgaeuerstr. 27, 8000 Munich 71, W. Germany (B.R.D.) Ed. Heinrich Mock.

700 FR ISSN 0070-4776
DICTIONNAIRE DES VALEURS DES MEUBLES ET OBJETS D'ART. 1965. irreg. 100 F. (vol. 1); 117F.(vol. 2) Librairie Fischbacher, 33 rue de Seine, 75-Paris 6, France. Ed. E. Mayer.

709 CN ISSN 0383-4514
DOCUMENTS IN THE HISTORY OF CANADIAN ART/DOCUMENTS D'HISTOIRE DE L'ART CANADIEN. (Text in French or English) 1976. irreg. Can.$10. National Gallery of Canada, Ottawa, Ont., K1A 0M8, Canada. illus. circ. 5,000.

700 US
DOCUMENTS OF MODERN ART. irreg. price varies. Wittenborn and Co., 1018 Madison Ave., New York, NY 10021.

700 US
DOCUMENTS OF 20TH CENTURY ART. irreg. price varies. Viking Press, Inc, 625 Madison Ave, New York, NY 10022.

705 DR
DOMINICAN REPUBLIC. DIRECCION GENERAL DE BELLAS ARTES. CATALOGO DE LA BIENAL DE ARTES PLASTICAS. irreg. Direccion General de Bellas Artes, Santo Domingo, Dominican Republic. illus.

DRAGON. see *LITERATURE*

DUMBARTON OAKS CONFERENCE PROCEEDINGS. see *ARCHAEOLOGY*

ENCYCLIA. see *SCIENCES: COMPREHENSIVE WORKS*

709 MX ISSN 0071-1659
ESTUDIOS DE ARTE Y ESTETICA. 1958. irreg; latest issue, 1972. price varies. ‡ Universidad Nacional Autonoma de Mexico, Instituto de Investigaciones Esteticas, Torre de Humanidades, Ciudad Universitaria, Mexico 20, D.F., Mexico.

709 MX ISSN 0071-1748
ESTUDIOS Y FUENTES DEL ARTE EN MEXICO. 1955. irreg; latest issue, 1978, no. 36. price varies. ‡ Universidad Nacional Autonoma de Mexico, Instituto de Investigaciones Esteticas, Torre de Humanidades, Ciudad Universitaria, Mexico 20, D.F., Mexico.

700 800 PO
ESTUDOS ITALIANOS EM PORTUGAL. (Text in Italian and Portuguese) 1939. irreg., 1968-69, no. 31-32. Esc.150($5.50) (Instituto Italiano di Cultura in Portogallo) Papelaria Fernandes, Largo do Rato 13, Lisbon 2, Portugal. bk. rev. bibl. illus. stat. tr.lit. cum.index. circ. 500. (tabloid format; also avail. in cards)

709 BE ISSN 0071-1969
ETUDES D'HISTOIRE DE L'ART. 1964. irreg. price varies. Institut Historique Belge de Rome, c/o Archives Generales du Royaume, 2-6 rue de Ruysbroeck, B-1000 Brussels, Belgium. circ. controlled.

700 FR ISSN 0071-2426
EUROPEAN ART EXHIBITIONS. CATALOG. 1954. irreg. Council of Europe, Publications Section, F-67006 Strasbourg, France (Dist. in U.S. by Worldwide Books, 37-39 Antwerp St., Boston, MA 02135)

760 GW ISSN 0075-2630
EXLIBRISKUNST UND GEBRAUCHSGRAPHIK. JAHRBUCH. a. DM.50. Deutsche Exlibris-Gesellschaft e.V., Marienstr. 35, 3000 Hannover, W. Germany (B.R.D.) Ed. Norbert H. Ott. adv.

700 US ISSN 0046-3051
FACETS. 1970. 2-3/yr. membership. (Texas Fine Arts Society) Foundation Management Inc., Box 52573, Houston, TX 77052. Ed. Morris R. Edwards. bk. rev. bibl. illus. circ. 3,000.

700 350 US
FEDERAL ART PATRONAGE NOTES. 1974. irreg. $18. Francis V. O'Connor, Ed. & Pub., 250 E. 73rd St., Apt. 11c, New York, NY 10021. adv. bk. rev. illus. circ. 500. (back issues avail.)

700 IT ISSN 0085-0500
FELIX RAVENNA; RIVISTA DI ANTICHITA RAVENNATI, CRISTIANE E BIZANTINE. 1970. a. L.22000. (Universita degli Studi di Bologna, Istituto di Antichita Ravennati e Bizantine) Edizioni del Girasole Ravenna, Via Corrado Rici, 35, 48100 Ravenna, Italy. bk. rev. circ. 500.

709 SW ISSN 0071-481X
FIGURA. NOVA SERIES; Uppsala studies in the history of art. (Subseries of Acta Universitatis Upsaliensis) (Text in English or German) O.S. 1951-59 (no. 1-12); N.S. 1959- irreg., no. 17, 1978. price varies. (Uppsala Universitet, Institute of Art History) Almqvist & Wiksell International, Box 62, S-101 20 Stockholm, Sweden. Ed. Rudolf Zeitler.

700 US
FINE ARTS WORK CENTER IN PROVINCETOWN. NEWSLETTER. irreg. membership. Fine Arts Work Center in Provincetown, Inc., 24 Pearl St., Box 565, Provincetown, MA 02657. illus.

745.5 US
FLORIDA FESTIVAL ARTS DIRECTORY. 1977. a. $2. Department of State, Florida Folklife Program, Box 265, White Springs, FL 32096. Ed. Peggy A. Bulger. circ. 1,000.
Formerly (until 1980): Florida Folk Arts Directory (ISSN 0162-5616)

709 PL ISSN 0071-6723
FOLIA HISTORIAE ARTIUM. (Text in Polish; summaries in French) 1964. irreg., 1974, vol. 10. price varies. (Polska Akademia Nauk, Oddzial w Krakowie, Komisja Teorii i Historii Sztuki) Panstwowe Wydawnictwo Naukowe, Ul. Miodowa 10, Warsaw, Poland (Dist. by Ars Polona-Ruch, Krakowskie Przedmiescie 7, Warsaw, Poland) Ed. Tadeusz Dobrowolski.

745 SP
FOMENTO DE LAS ARTES DECORATIVAS, BARCELONA. AGRUPACION DE DISENO INDUSTRIAL. GUIA DE ASOCIADOS. 1975. irreg. Fomento de las Artes Decorativas, Agrupacion de Diseno Industrial, Barcelona, Spain. illus.

709 900 IT
FONTI E STUDI PER LA STORIA DI BOLOGNA E DELLE PROVINCE EMILIANE E ROMAGNOLE. 1969. irreg., vol. 6, 1977. price varies. ALFA Edizioni, Via Santo Stefano 13, I-40125 Bologna, Italy. circ. 4,000.

709 913 GW ISSN 0532-2189
FORSCHUNGEN ZUR KUNSTGESCHICHTE UND CHRISTLICHEN ARCHAEOLOGIE. irreg., vol. 12, 1981. price varies. Franz Steiner Verlag GmbH, Friedrichstr. 24, Postfach 5529, 6200 Wiesbaden, W. Germany (B.R.D.) Eds. Richard Hamann-Maclean, Otto Feld.

700 UK ISSN 0016-0571
FREEDOM OF VISION. 1964. irreg. £3.15. Ashurstwood Abbey, Sussex RH19 35D, England. Ed. Jean Straker. circ. controlled.

700 US ISSN 0071-9382
FREER GALLERY OF ART, WASHINGTON, D.C. OCCASIONAL PAPERS. 1947. irreg., vol. 4, no. 1, 1971. Smithsonian Institution, 12th St. at Jefferson Dr. S.W., Washington, DC 20560.

FUEHRER ZU VOR- UND FRUEGESCHICHTLICHEN DENKMAELERN. see *ARCHAEOLOGY*

700 JA ISSN 0385-5694
GEIJUTSU SHUNJU. (Text in Japanese) irreg. Geijutsu Shunju Sha, 81 Matsuyamachi, Minami-ku, Osaka 542, Japan. illus.

GENAVA; revue d'archeologie et d'histoire de l'art. see *ARCHAEOLOGY*

700 US ISSN 0147-1902
GEORGIA MUSEUM OF ART BULLETIN. 1974. irreg., formerly q.; last issue vol. 2, no. 2, Fall 1976; 1979 issue in prep. $5. University of Georgia, Georgia Museum of Art, Athens, GA 30602. Ed. Ethel Moore. circ. 1,500. (back issues avail.)

709 720 SW ISSN 0348-4114
GOTHENBURG STUDIES IN ART AND ARCHITECTURE. (Subseries of Acta Universitatis Gothoburgensis) 1978. irreg. price varies. Acta Universitatis Gothoburgensis, Box 5096, S-402 22 Goeteborg 5, Sweden (Dist. in U.S., Canada, and Mexico by: Humanities Press, Inc., 171 First Ave., Atlantic Highlands, NJ 07716) Ed. Maj-Brit Wadell.

760 JA ISSN 0072-548X
GRAPHIC ARTS JAPAN. (Text in English) 1959. a, vol. 21, 1979. $20. Japan Printers' Association, Publicity Bureau, 1-16-8 Shintomi, Chuo-ku, Tokyo, Japan. Ed. Seizo Kimura. adv. bk. rev. (back issues avail.)

659.1 760 SZ ISSN 0072-5528
GRAPHIS ANNUAL; international annual of advertising and editorial graphics. (Text in English, French, German) 1952. a. 105 Fr.($49.50) Walter Herdeg Graphis Press, 107 Dufourstrasse, CH-8008 Zurich, Switzerland (Dist. by Hastings House Publishers, Inc., 10 East 40 St., New York, NY 10016) Ed. Walter Herdeg. index. circ. 19,300.

769.5 SZ
GRAPHIS POSTERS; international annual of poster art. (Text in English, French and German) 1973. a. 92 Fr.($45) Walter Herdeg Graphis Press, 107 Dufourstrasse, 8008 Zurich, Switzerland (Dist. by Hastings House Publishers, Inc., 10 East 40th St., New York, NY 10016) Ed. Walter Herdeg. illus. circ. 8,000.

700 382 UK ISSN 0072-5668
GREAT BRITAIN. DEPARTMENT OF TRADE. EXPORT OF WORKS OF ART. a. H.M.S.O., P.O. Box 569, London SE1 9NH, England.

700　　　　　　　　　UK　ISSN 0309-1945
GREATER LONDON ARTS ASSOCIATION.
ANNUAL REPORT. a. Greater London Arts
Association, 25/31 Tavistock Place, London WC1H
9SG, England. Ed. Barry Jackson. illus. circ. 5,000.
Formerly: Greater London Arts Association.
Annual Report and Yearbook (ISSN 0307-0417)

700　　　　　　　　　FR　ISSN 0066-3069
GUIDE EUROPEEN DE L'AMATEUR D'ART, DE
L'ANTIQUAIRE ET DU BIBLIOPHILE. Short
title: Guide Emer. (Text in English, French,
German, Italian) 1947. biennial. 130 F. Editions
Emer, 50, rue Quai de l'Hotel-de-Ville, 75004 Paris,
France. Ed. Marc Roy. adv. circ. 16,000.

700　600　　　　　　JA　ISSN 0072-9051
GUMMA UNIVERSITY. FACULTY OF
EDUCATION. ANNUAL REPORT: ART AND
TECHNOLOGY SERIES. (Text in Japanese;
summaries in English or Japanese) 1966. a.
exchange basis. Gumma University, Faculty of
Education, Gumma University Library, 1375
Aramaki-cho, Maebashi, Gumma 371, Japan. Ed.Bd.
cum.index. circ. 600.

709.4　　　　　　　　GW　ISSN 0072-9205
HABELTS DISSERTATIONSDRUCKE. REIHE
KUNSTGESCHICHTE. 1953. irreg. price varies.
Rudolf Habelt Verlag, Am Buchenhang 1, 5300
Bonn 1, W. Germany (B.R.D.)

700　　　　　　　　　DK　ISSN 0085-1361
HAFNIA; COPENHAGEN PAPERS IN THE
HISTORY OF ART. (Text in English, French, and
German) 1970. biennial. Kr.100. Koebenhavns
Universitet, Institute of Art History, Esplanaden 34
B, 1263 Copenhagen K, Denmark. Ed. Mirjam
Gelfer-Joergensen. circ. 800.

HAND BOOK. see *LITERATURE*

700　200　　　　　　GW　ISSN 0440-6087
HEILIGE IN BILD UND LEGENDE. irreg., vol. 27,
1974. DM.9.80. Verlag Aurel Bongers, Hubertustr.
13, Postfach 220, 4350 Recklinghausen, W.
Germany (B.R.D.) illus.

HEIRS. see *LITERATURE*

700　　　　　　　　　PL　ISSN 0083-4270
HISTORIA SZTUKI. (Text in Polish: summaries in
German or English) 1959. irreg. price varies.
Uniwersytet im. Adama Mickiewicza w Poznaniu,
Stalingradzka 1, 61-712 Poznan, Poland (Dist. by:
Ars Polona, Krakowskie Przedmiescie 7, 00-068
Warsaw, Poland)
Formerly: Uniwersytet im. Adama Mickiewicza w
Poznaniu. Zeszyty Naukowe. Historia Sztuki.

700　　　　　　　　　GW　ISSN 0341-8448
ICONOGRAPHIA ECCLESIAE ORIENTALIS.
irreg., vol. 12, 1974. DM.9.80. Verlag Aurel
Bongers, Hubertustr. 13, Postfach 220, 4350
Recklinghausen, W. Germany (B.R.D.) Ed. Heinz
Skrobucha. illus.

745　　　　　　　　　VE
IDEAS. a. Bs.20. Instituto de Diseno Fundacion
Neumann, Apartado 61928, Caracas, Venezuela.

700　　　　　　　　　GW
IKONENKALENDER. (Calendar in English and
German) a. DM.26.80. Verlag Aurel Bongers,
Hubertustr. 13, Postfach 220, 4350 Recklinghausen,
W. Germany (B.R.D.) illus.

700　　　　　　　　　US　ISSN 0445-3387
ILLINOIS. STATE MUSEUM. HANDBOOK OF
COLLECTIONS. 1963. irreg., no. 4, 1981. Illinois
State Museum, Springfield, IL 62706.

760　　　　　　　　　JA
ILLUSTRATION IN JAPAN. (Text in Japanese)
1972. a. 5900 Yen. (Daiichi Shuppan Senta)
Kodansha Ltd., 2-12-21 Otowa, Bunkyo-ku, Tokyo
112, Japan (U.S. subscr. address: c/o Harper & Row,
10 E. 53rd St., New York, N.Y. 10022)

741.640　　　　　　　US　ISSN 0073-5477
ILLUSTRATORS; THE ANNUAL OF AMERICAN
ILLUSTRATION. 1959. a. $35. (Society of
Illustrators) Hastings House Publishers, Inc., 10 E.
40th St., New York, NY 10016.

700　　　　　　　　　US　ISSN 0085-1760
INDEX OF ART IN THE PACIFIC NORTHWEST.
1970. irreg., no. 12, 1977. price varies. (University
of Washington, Henry Art Gallery) University of
Washington Press, Seattle, WA 98105.

700　　　　　　　　　BE　ISSN 0085-1892
INSTITUT ROYAL DE PATRIMOINE
ARTISTIQUE. BULLETIN/KONINKLIJK
INSTITUUT VOOR HET
KUNSTPATRIMONIUM. BULLETIN. (Text and
summaries in French and Dutch) 1958. a. 250
Fr.($6) ‡ Institut Royal du Patrimoine Artistique,
Parc du Cinquantenaire, 1, B-1040 Brussels,
Belgium. Indexed: Art & Archeol.Tech.Abstr.

709　　　　　　　　　MX　ISSN 0076-7565
INSTITUTO NACIONAL DE ANTROPOLOGIA E
HISTORIA. COLECCION BREVE. 1968. irreg.
price varies. Instituto Nacional de Antropologia e
Historia, Cordoba 47, Mexico 7,D.F., Mexico.

709　　　　　　　　　MX　ISSN 0076-7506
INSTITUTO NACIONAL DE ANTROPOLOGIA E
HISTORIA. DEPARTAMENTO DE
MONUMENTOS COLONIALES.
(PUBLICACIONES) 1956. irreg. price varies.
Instituto Nacional de Antropologia e Historia,
Departamento de Monumentos Coloniales, Cordoba
47, Mexico 7, D.F., Mexico.

INTERFERENCES, ARTS, LETTRES. see
LITERATURE

700　　　　　　　　　US　ISSN 0074-1922
INTERNATIONAL AUCTION RECORDS. 1967. a.
$85. Editions Publisol, Box 339, Gracie Sta., New
York, NY 10028. Ed. E. Mayer. adv.

760　　　　　　　　　JA　ISSN 0074-2066
INTERNATIONAL BIENNIAL EXHIBITION OF
PRINTS IN TOKYO. (Text in English and
Japanese) 1957. biennial. price varies. National
Museum of Modern Art, Tokyo, 3 Kitanomarukoen,
Chiyoda-ku, Tokyo 102, Japan. circ. 7,000.

709　　　　　　　　　FR　ISSN 0074-4190
INTERNATIONAL CONGRESS ON THE
HISTORY OF ART. PROCEEDINGS. 1873.
quinquennial, 1968, 22nd, Budapest. (International
Committee on the History of Art, SP) Institut
d'Art et d'Archeologie, 3 rue Michelet, Paris 75006,
France.
Proceedings published in host country

740
INTERNATIONAL CRAFT SWAP. 1976. a. $4.
Prairie Press East, 206 Clarke St., Syracuse, NY
13210. Eds. Judy Adams, Juanita Turner.

700　　　　　　　　　GW　ISSN 0074-4565
INTERNATIONAL DIRECTORY OF ARTS. (Text
in English, French, German, Italian, Spanish) 1949.
biennial. DM.165($70) Art Adress Verlag Mueller
KG, Grosse Eschenheimer Str. 16, Postfach 187,
6000 Frankfurt 1, W. Germany (B.R.D.) (US Dist.:
Marquis Who's Who, 200 E. Ohio St., Chicago, IL
60611) adv. index.

700　　　　　　　　　FR　ISSN 0074-7882
INTERNATIONAL SOCIETY FOR PERFORMING
ARTS. LIBRARIES AND MUSEUMS.
CONGRESS PROCEEDINGS. 1957. irreg., 1974.
International Society for Performing Arts, Libraries
and Museums, 1 rue de Sully, 75 Paris 4e, France.
Publisher of proceedings varies

700　920　　　　　　UK
INTERNATIONAL WHO'S WHO IN ART AND
ANTIQUES. 1972. irreg. price varies. Melrose Press
Ltd., 17-21 Churchgate St., Soham, Ely,
Cambridgeshire, England (U.S. subscr. to:
International Biographical Centre, c/o Biblio
Distribution Centre, 81 Adams Drive, Totowa, NJ
07512)

INVENTAIRE GENERAL DES MONUMENTS ET
DES RICHESSES ARTISTIQUES DE LA
FRANCE. see *ARCHITECTURE*

709　　　　　　　　　BU
ISTORIIA NA BULGARSKOTO IZOBRAZITELNO
IZKUSTVO. 1976. irreg. 15 lv. per issue. (Bulgarska
Akademiia na Naukite) Publishing House of the
Bulgarian Academy of Sciences, Ul. Akad. G.
Bonchev, 1113 Sofia, Bulgaria. circ. 10,000.

L'IVRE DE PIERRES. see *ARCHITECTURE*

708　　　　　　　　　US　ISSN 0362-1979
J. PAUL GETTY MUSEUM JOURNAL. 1975. irreg.,
approx. a. price varies. J. Paul Getty Museum,
17985 Pacific Coast Highway, Malibu, CA 90265.
Ed. Burton Fredericksen. illus. (back issues avail.)

700　　　　　　　　　BE　ISSN 0066-3174
JAARBOEK DER SCHONE KUNSTEN/
ALGEMEEN JAARBOEK DER SCHONE
KUNSTEN. (Text in Flemish and French) 1928. a.
450 Fr.($15) Editions ARTO, 85 Avenue Winston
Churchill, 1180 Brussels, Belgium. adv. bk. rev. circ.
4,000.
Formerly: Dessinateurs, Peintres et Sculpteurs de
Belgique (ISSN 0070-3869)

700　616.89　　　　　JA
JAPANESE BULLETIN OF ART THERAPY. (Text
in Japanese and other languages) 1969. a. 3000
Yen($10) Societe Japonaise de Psychopathologie de
l'Expression, c/o Neuropsychiatric Research
Institute, 91 Bentencho, Shinjuku-ku, Tokyo 162,
Japan. Ed. Dr. Yoshihito Tokuda. adv. bk. rev. bibl.
charts. illus. stat. circ. 4,500(controlled) (back
issues avail.)

700　　　　　　　　　US
JAPANESE SWORD SOCIETY OF THE U.S.
BULLETIN. 1959. a. $15. Japanese Sword Society
of the U.S., Inc., 5907 Deerwood Dr., St. Louis,
MO 63123. Ed. Ronald C. Hartmann. circ. 550.

708.9　　　　　　　　SI
JOURNAL OF ASIAN ART. (Text in Chinese and
English) 1972. a. $6. Lee Kong Chian Museum of
Asian Culture, Nanyang University, Upper Jurong
Rd., Singapore 22, Singapore. illus. circ. 2,500.

JOURNAL OF GLASS STUDIES. see *CERAMICS,
GLASS AND POTTERY*

700　　　　　　　　　US　ISSN 0160-208X
JOURNAL OF JEWISH ART. (Text in English,
French) 1974. a. $7. (Spertus College of Judaica)
Abner Schram Enterprises Ltd., 36 Park St.,
Montclair, NJ 07042. Ed. Bezalel Narkiss. bk. rev.
bibl. illus. circ. 2,000. (back issues avail.; reprint
service avail. from UMI)

700　　　　　　　　　FI　ISSN 0075-4633
JYVASKYLA STUDIES IN THE ARTS. 1967. irreg.
price varies; available on exchange. Jyvaskylan
Yliopisto, Kirjasto - University of Jyvaskyla,
Seminaarinkatu 15, 40100 Jyvaskyla 10, Finland.
Ed. Aatos Ojala. circ. 400-500.

708　　　　　　　　　AU　ISSN 0022-7587
KAERNTNER MUSEUMSSCHRIFTEN. 1954. irreg.
price varies. Landesmuseum fuer Kaernten,
Museumgasse 2, A-9010 Klagenfurt, Austria. circ.
200.

KALAVA HA SAHITYAYA. see *LITERATURE*

769.5　　　　　　　　CS
KATALOG SLOVENSKYCH PLAGATOV. 1975.
irreg. price varies. Matica Slovenska, Mudronova
35, 036 52 Martin, Czechoslovakia.

700　　　　　　　　　PL　ISSN 0075-5257
KATALOG ZABYTKOW SZTUKI W POLSCE.
1953. pub'd. by regions; 1976, vol. 8, pt. 2 and vol.
11, pt. 4. price varies. (Polska Akademia Nauk,
Instytut Sztuki) Wydawnictwa Artystyczne i
Filmowe, Pulawska 61, Warsaw, Poland (Dist. by
Ars Polona-Ruch, Krakowskie Przedmiescie,
Warsaw, Poland) Ed. Jerzy Zygmunt Lozinski. circ.
1,500-5,000.

700　　　　　　　　　GW　ISSN 0445-2577
KLEINE IKONENBUECHEREI. irreg., vol. 8, 1974.
DM.9.80. Verlag Aurel Bongers, Hubertustr. 13,
Postfach 220, 4350 Recklinghausen, W. Germany
(B.R.D.) illus.

709　　　　　　　　　GW　ISSN 0075-6563
KOLLOQUIUM UEBER SPAETANTIKE UND
FRUEHMITTELALTERLICHE SKULPTUR.
(Text in German, English, Italian) 1969. biennial.
price varies. Philipp Von Zabern, Welschnonnengass
11, Postfach 4065, 6500 Mainz, W. Germany
(B.R.D.) Ed. Vladimir Milojcic.

709.5   GW   ISSN 0023-5393
KUNST DES ORIENTS/ART OF THE ORIENT. (Text in English and German) 1950. s-a. DM.108. Franz Steiner Verlag GmbH, Friedrichstr. 24, Postfach 5529, 6200 Wiesbaden, W. Germany (B.R.D.) Ed. Klaus Brisch. adv. bk. rev. illus. index. circ. 600. (back issues avail.)

705   AU   ISSN 0075-7241
KUNST-KATALOG: AUKTIONEN. irreg. Dorotheum, Dorotheergasse 11, A 1011 Vienna, Austria.

700   GW
KUNST UND GESELLSCHAFT. 1974. irreg., no. 12, 1977. price varies. Ferdinand Enke Verlag, Herdweg 63, 7000 Stuttgart 1, W. Germany (B.R.D.) Eds. A. Silbermann, R. Koenig, A. Moles.

709   AU   ISSN 0075-2312
KUNSTHISTORISCHE SAMMLUNGEN IN WIEN. JAHRBUCH. 1926. a. S.1100($85) (Kunsthistorisches Museum in Wien) Verlag Anton Schroll und Co., Spengergasse 39, A-1051 Vienna, Austria.

700 900   IT
KUNSTHISTORISCHES INSTITUT IN FLORENZ. MITTEILUNGEN. (Text in German & Italian) 1908. a. DM.90. Kunsthistorisches Institut in Florenz, Via Giusti 44, I-50121 Florence, Italy. Eds. Herbert Keutner, Max Seidel. bibl. illus. index. circ. 1,000(controlled)

700   GW
DAS KUNSTJAHRBUCH. a. DM.64.50. Alexander Baier-Presse, Rheinstr. 33, 6500 Mainz, W. Germany (B.R.D.) Eds.Horst Richter, Karl Ruhrberg, Wieland Schmied.

705   AU
KUNSTJAHRBUCH DER STADT LINZ. 1961. a. S.163. (Stadtmuseum Linz) Anton Schroll und Co., Spengergasse 39, A-1051 Vienna, Austria. Ed. Georg Wacha. bk. rev. circ. 450.
Formerly: Linzer Jahrbuch fuer Kunstgeschichte (ISSN 0075-9732)

706.5   GW   ISSN 0174-3511
KUNSTPREIS-JAHRBUCH. (Includes Vols. A and B) a. DM.75 for vol. A; DM.52 for vol. B. Kunst und Technik Verlagsgesellschaft mbH, Nymphenburgerstr. 86, 8000 Munich 19, W. Germany(B.R.D.) adv. illus.
Formerly: Art-Price Annual.

709   II   ISSN 0458-6506
LALIT KALA. vol. 20, 1981. a. National Academy of Art - Lalit Kala Akademi, Rabindra Bhavan, New Delhi 110001, India.

709   AU   ISSN 0007-280X
LANDESMUSEUM FUER KAERNTEN. BUCHREIHE. 1954. irreg. price varies. Landesmuseum fuer Kaernten, Museumgasse 2, A-9010 Klagenfurt, Austria. circ. 400.

700   US   ISSN 0362-7047
LATVJU MAKSLA. (Text in Latvian) 1975. irreg. $7 per no. American Latvian Association in the U.S., Inc., Box 432, Rockville, MD 20850. Ed. A. Sildegs. adv. illus. circ. 1,000.

700   NE   ISSN 0460-2048
LEIDSE KUNSTHISTORISCHE REEKS. 1966. irreg., vol. 2, 1969. price varies. Leiden University Press, c/o Martinus Nijhoff, Box 566, 2501 CN The Hague, Netherlands.

745   US
LETTERHEADS; the international annual of letterhead design. 1977. a. Century Communications Unlimited, Inc., 1500 Carter Ave., Box 591, Ashland, KY 41101. Ed. David E. Carter.

700   US
LIBRARY OF GREAT PAINTERS. irreg. $40. Harry N. Abrams, Inc., 110 E. 59th St., New York, NY 10022.

LIGHTWORKS. see PHOTOGRAPHY

700 708   US
LOCUS SELECT. 1980. irreg. $25. Filsinger & Company Ltd., 150 Waverly Pl., New York, NY 10014. Ed. Cheryl Filsinger.

708.7   US   ISSN 0024-6557
LOS ANGELES COUNTY MUSEUM OF ART. BULLETIN. 1947. a. $3. Los Angeles County Museum of Art, 5905 Wilshire Blvd., Los Angeles, CA 90036. illus. circ. 27,500. (also avail. in microform) Indexed: Art Ind.
Formerly: Los Angeles County Museum Quarterly.

700   US
LOUISBURG COLLEGE JOURNAL OF ARTS AND SCIENCES. a. Louisburg College, Louisburg, NC 27549. Ed. Humphrey Lee. charts. illus.

700   US
LYLES OFFICIAL ARTS REVIEW. a. $18.95. Apollo Book, 391 South Rd., Poughkeepsie, NY 12601.

MACEDONIAN REVIEW; history, culture, literature, arts. see LITERATURE

709 943   HU   ISSN 0076-2490
MAGYARORSZAG MUEMLEKI TOPOGRAFIAJA. (Text in Hungarian; summaries in English, German, Russian) 1956. irreg. price varies. (Magyar Tudomanyos Akademia) Akademiai Kiado, Publishing House of the Hungarian Academy of Sciences, P.O. Box 24, H-1363 Budapest, Hungary.

MAINFRAENKISCHES JAHRBUCH FUER GESCHICHTE UND KUNST. see HISTORY — History Of Europe

943 913 709   GW   ISSN 0076-2792
MAINZER ZEITSCHRIFT; Mittelrheinisches jahrbuch fuer Archaeologie, Geschichte und Kunst. 1906. a. 60. Mainzer Altertumsverein, Rheinallee 3b, 6500 Mainz, W. Germany (B.R.D.) Ed. Fritz Arens. circ. 770.

705   US   ISSN 0076-4701
MARSYAS. 1941. biennial. $8. New York University, Institute of Fine Arts, 1 E. 78 St., New York, NY 10021 (Dist. by J. J. Augustin, Inc., Locust Valley, N.Y. 11560) Eds. Paul Yule & Andrew Clark. circ. 500. (also avail. in microform from UMI) Indexed: Art Ind.

MASSSTAEBE. see HUMANITIES: COMPREHENSIVE WORKS

708   CN   ISSN 0383-5391
MASTERPIECES IN THE NATIONAL GALLERY OF CANADA/CHEFS-D'OEUVRE DE LA GALERIE NATIONALE DU CANADA. (Text in English and French) 1971. irreg. Can.$2.50. National Gallery of Canada, Ottawa, Ont. K1A 0M8, Canada (Order from: National Museums of Canada, Order Fulfilment, Ottawa, Ont. K1A 0M8, Canada) Eds. Charles Hill, Michael Pantazzi. illus. circ. 5,000.

MEDIAEVALIA. see HISTORY

MEDIEVAL ACADEMY BOOKS. see HISTORY — History Of Europe

MEDIEVAL ACADEMY REPRINTS FOR TEACHING. see HISTORY — History Of Europe

709   US
MICHIGAN STATE UNIVERSITY. MUSEUM PUBLICATIONS. FOLK ART SERIES. irreg. price varies. Michigan State University, Museum, East Lansing, MI 48824.

700   IT
MINIATURA E ARTI MINORI IN CAMPANIA. no. 10, 1975. irreg., no. 13, 1978. price varies. (Banca Sannitica) Societa Editrice Napoletana s.r.l., Corso Umberto I 34, 80138 Naples, Italy. Ed. Mario Rotili.

700   US   ISSN 0076-9096
MINNEAPOLIS INSTITUTE OF ARTS. ANNUAL REPORT. 1961. a. Minneapolis Society of Fine Arts, 2400 Third Ave. South, Minneapolis, MN 55404. circ. 8,000.

708   US   ISSN 0076-910X
MINNEAPOLIS INSTITUTE OF ARTS. BULLETIN. 1914. biennial. $5. Minneapolis Society of Fine Arts, 2400 Third Ave. South, Minneapolis, MN 55404. Ed. Harold Peterson. circ. 12,000. (also avail. in microform from UMI)

700   US
MODERN ARTISTS. irreg. $12.50. Harry N. Abrams, Inc., 110 East 59th St., New York, NY 10022.

700 800   US   ISSN 0161-5866
MONEY BUSINESS: GRANTS AND AWARDS FOR CREATIVE ARTISTS. 1978. irreg. $7. Artists Foundation, Inc., 100 Boylston St., Boston, MA 02116. Ed. Jennifer Dowley.

700   GW   ISSN 0463-1935
MONOGRAPHIEN ZUR RHEINISCH-WESTFAELISCHEN KUNST DER GEGENWART. 1956. irreg., vol. 50, 1976. price varies. Verlag Aurel Bongers, Hubertusstr. 13, Postfach 220, 4350 Recklinghausen, W. Germany (B.R.D.) illus.

700   US   ISSN 0544-845X
MONOGRAPHS ON AMERICAN ART. 1968. irreg., no. 4, 1975. price varies. Sheldon Memorial Art Gallery, 12th & R St., University of Nebraska, Lincoln, NE 68588. illus.

MONUMENTA ARTIS ROMANAE. see ARCHAEOLOGY

700   SP
MONUMENTS DE LA CATALUNYA ROMANICA. (Contains 2 series: Comarques and Museus) (Text in Catalan) 1978. irreg. Artestudi Edicions, Provenca 552, Barcelona 26, Spain. illus.

700   IT
MOSTRE E MUSEI. 1975. irreg., no. 4, 1976. price varies. Societa Editrice Napoletana s.r.l., Corso Umberto I 34, 80138 Naples, Italy. Ed. Raffaello Causa.

709   GW   ISSN 0077-1899
MUENCHNER JAHRBUCH DER BILDENDEN KUNST. 1950. a. price varies. (Staatliche Kunstsammlungen Bayerns) Prestel-Verlag, Mandlstr. 26, 8000 Munich 40, W. Germany (B.R.D.) (Co-sponsor: Zentralinstitut fuer Kunstgeschichte, Munich)

700   GW   ISSN 0580-1583
MUENSTERSCHE STUDIEN ZUR KUNSTGESCHICHTE. 1965. irreg., vol. 5, 1973. DM.24. Verlag Aurel Bongers, Hubertusstr. 13, Postfach 220, 4350 Recklinghausen, W. Germany (B.R.D.) Eds. Werner Hager, Guenther Fiensch. illus.

700   JA
MUSASHINO ART UNIVERSITY. BULLETIN. (Text in Japanese; summaries in English) no. 11, 1978 (published Mar. 1979) a. free. Musashino Art University, 1-736 Ogawa-machi, Kodaira-shi, Tokyo 187, Japan. illus.

700   FR   ISSN 0078-9704
MUSEE GUIMET, PARIS. BIBLIOTHEQUE D'ETUDES. 1892. irreg. price varies. Presses Universitaires de France, 108 Bd. Saint Germaine, 75279 Paris Cedex 6, France (Service des Periodiques, 12 rue Jean de Beauvais, 75005 Paris)

700   FR   ISSN 0078-9712
MUSEE GUIMET, PARIS. ETUDE DES COLLECTIONS DU MUSEE. irreg. Presses Universitaires de France, 108 Bd. Saint Germaine, 75279 Paris Cedex 6, France (Service des Periodiques, 12 rue Jean de Beauvais, 75005 Paris)

MUSEUM FUER VOELKERKUNDE, BERLIN. VEROEFFENTLICHUNGEN. NEUE FOLGE. ABTEILUNG: AMERIKANISCHE NATURVOELKER. see ANTHROPOLOGY

MUSEUM OF FAR EASTERN ANTIQUITIES. BULLETIN. see MUSEUMS AND ART GALLERIES

700   PL   ISSN 0068-4678
MUZEUM GORNOSLASKIE W BYTOMIU. ROCZNIK. SERIA SZTUKA. 1964. irreg. price varies. Muzeum Gornoslaskie, Pl. Thaelmanna 2, 41-902 Bytom, Poland (Dist. by: Ars Polona-Ruch, Krakowskie Przedmiescie 7, Warsaw, Poland)

NATIONAL ART EDUCATION ASSOCIATION. RESEARCH MONOGRAPH. see EDUCATION — Teaching Methods And Curriculum

NATIONAL ASSOCIATION OF SCHOOLS OF ART. DIRECTORY. see EDUCATION — Guides To Schools And Colleges

707.4 US
NATIONAL ASSOCIATION OF WOMEN ARTISTS. ANNUAL EXHIBITION CATALOG. 1889. a. $3. National Association of Women Artists, 41 Union Sq., W., Rm. 906, New York, NY 10003. adv. circ. 1,000 (controlled)

745.1 US
NATIONAL CAROUSEL ASSOCIATION CAROUSEL CENSUS. 1977. a. $15. c/o Donna Lee, 12 Coakley Ave., Harrison, NY 10528. Ed. Barbara Williams. circ. 450.

700 US
NATIONAL DIRECTORY OF ARTS SUPPORT BY BUSINESS CORPORATIONS. (Subseries of: Arts Patronage Series) 1979. every 2 or 3 yrs. $65. Washington International Arts Letter, Box 9005, Washington, DC 20003. Ed. Daniel Millsaps.
Supersedes in part: Arts Support by Private Foundations and Business Corporations.

700 US
NATIONAL DIRECTORY OF ARTS SUPPORT BY PRIVATE FOUNDATIONS. (Subseries of: Arts Patronage Series) 1972. every 2 or 3 yrs., latest 3rd. edt. $55. Washington International Arts Letter, Box 9005, Washington, DC 20003. Ed. Daniel Millsaps.
Formerly: Arts Support by Private Foundations; Supersedes in part: Arts Suppprt by Private Foundations and Business Corporations.

700 US
NATIONAL DIRECTORY OF GRANTS AND AID TO INDIVIDUALS IN THE ARTS, INTERNATIONAL. 1970. every 3 or 4 yrs., latest 4th edt. $15.95. Washington International Arts Letter, Box 9005, Washington, DC 20003. Ed. Daniel Millsaps.
Formerly: Grants and Aid to Individuals in the Arts.

700 US ISSN 0547-6658
NATIONAL ENDOWMENT FOR THE ARTS. GUIDE TO PROGRAMS. 1972. a. $2.05. National Endowment for the Arts, Washington, DC 20506. circ. 70,000.

708.1 069 UK
NATIONAL GALLERY, LONDON. TECHNICAL BULLETIN. vol. 3, 1979. a. National Gallery Publications, Trafalgar Square, London WC2N 5DN, England.

700 US ISSN 0091-7222
NATIONAL GALLERY OF ART. ANNUAL REPORT. 1970. a. $1.25. ‡ National Gallery of Art, Washington, DC 20565. illus. circ. 8,500.

069 708.1 CN ISSN 0319-5864
NATIONAL GALLERY OF CANADA. JOURNAL/ GALERIE NATIONALE DU CANADA. JOURNAL. (Editions in French & English) 1974. irreg. Can.$1 per no. National Gallery of Canada, Ottawa, Ont. K1A 0M8, Canada. illus. circ. 5,000.

708.11 CN ISSN 0078-6985
NATIONAL GALLERY OF CANADA. LIBRARY. CANADIANA IN THE LIBRARY OF THE NATIONAL GALLERY OF CANADA: SUPPLEMENT. (Text in French and English) 1968. irreg. Can.$3. National Gallery of Canada, Library, Ottawa, Ont. K1A 0M8, Canada. index.

730 US ISSN 0363-5937
NATIONAL/INTERNATIONAL SCULPTURE CONFERENCE. PROCEEDINGS. 1960. biennial. University of Kansas, International Sculpture Center, Lawrence, KS 66045. Ed. Elden C. Tefft. illus. circ. 1,000. Key Title: Proceedings of the National/International Sculpture Conference.

730 US ISSN 0098-4817
NATIONAL SCULPTURE SOCIETY, NEW YORK. ANNUAL EXHIBITION. a. $5. National Sculpture Society, 15 E. 26th St., New York, NY 10010. illus. Key Title: Annual Exhibition - National Sculpture Society.

NEW ART REVIEW. see MUSIC

NEW DEPARTURES. see LITERATURE

NEW RENAISSANCE; an internnational magazine of ideas and opinions, emphasizing literature & the arts. see LITERATURE

700 US ISSN 0085-4174
NEWSLETTER ON CONTEMPORARY JAPANESE PRINTS. 1971. irreg. free. Helen & Felix Juda Collection, 644 South June St., Los Angeles, CA 90005. Ed. Irene Drori. illus.

709 GW ISSN 0078-0537
NIEDERDEUTSCHE BEITRAEGE ZUR KUNSTGESCHICHTE. 1961. irreg., vol. 17, 1978. DM.55 (approx.) (Niedersaechsisches Landesmuseum, Hannover) Deutscher Kunstverlag GmbH, Vohburger Str. 1, 8000 Munich 21, W. Germany (B.R.D.) Ed. Hans Werner Grohn. circ. 800.

745 US ISSN 0078-1444
NORTH CAROLINA STATE UNIVERSITY. SCHOOL OF DESIGN. (STUDENT PUBLICATION) 1951. irreg; vol. 25, 1977. $6 per set. North Carolina State University, School of Design, Raleigh, NC 27607.

NY CARLSBERG GLYPTOTEK. MEDDELELSER. see ARCHAEOLOGY

700 DK ISSN 0078-3285
ODENSE UNIVERSITY STUDIES IN ART HISTORY. 1970. irreg. price varies. Odense University Press, 36, Pjentedamsgade, DK-5000 Odense, Denmark.

OESTERREICHISCHE VOLKSKUNDLICHE BIBLIOGRAPHIE. see FOLKLORE

760 AU ISSN 0078-3633
OESTERREICHISCHES JAHRBUCH FUER EXLIBRIS UND GEBRAUCHSGRAPHIK. 1903. a. S.360. Oesterreichische Exlibris-Gesellschaft, Johann Strauss-Gasse 28/18, A-1040 Vienna, Austria. index. circ. 300.

OESTERREICHISCHES MUSEUM FUER VOLKSKUNDE: VEROEFFENTLICHUNGEN. see FOLKLORE

709 US
OHIO ARTS COUNCIL. ANNUAL REPORT. 1965. a. free. Ohio Arts Council, 50 W. Broad St., Suite 2840, Columbus, OH 43215. Ed. Richard A. Jones. illus. stat. circ. 3,000. (tabloid format)

709 US ISSN 0085-4484
OKLAHOMA ART CENTER. ANNUAL EIGHT STATE EXHIBITION OF PAINTING AND SCULPTURE CATALOG. Variant title: Oklahoma Art Center. Annual Eight State Art Exhibition. 1965. a. $1. ‡ Oklahoma Art Center, 3113 Pershing Blvd., Oklahoma City, OK 73107. (Co-Sponsor: State Fair of Oklahoma) illus.

700 US
ON S I T E. 1973. irreg. price varies. (Site, Inc.) Sculpture in the Environment, 60 Greene St., New York, NY 10012. Ed. Alison Sky. illus.

700 CN
ONTARIO ARTS COUNCIL. ANNUAL REPORT. (Text in English and French) 1963. a. Ontario Arts Council, Suite 500, 151 Bloor St. W., Toronto, Ont. M5S 1T6, Canada. Ed. Barbara Sheffield. circ. 3,500. (back issues avail.)

700 NE ISSN 0078-5563
ORBIS ARTIUM; Utrechtse kunsthistorische studien. 1957. irreg., 1970, vol. 12. price varies. ‡ (Rijksuniversiteit te Utrecht, Kunsthistorisch Instituut) Haentjens Dekker en Gumbert, Achter Sint Pieter 14, Utrecht, Netherlands. bk. rev.

700 US ISSN 0078-6551
ORIENTAL STUDIES. irreg., no. 8, 1970. price varies. Freer Gallery of Art, Smithsonian Institution, 12th St. at Jefferson Dr. S.W., Washington, DC 20560.

709 US
OXFORD HISTORY OF ENGLISH ART. irreg. price varies. Oxford University Press, 200 Madison Ave., New York, NY 10016 (And Ely House, 37 Dover St., London W1X 4AH, England) Ed. T.S.R. Boase.

709 720 US
OXFORD STUDIES IN THE HISTORY OF ART AND ARCHITECTURE. irreg. price varies. Oxford University Press, 200 Madison Ave., New York, NY 10016 (And Ely House, 37 Dover St., London W1X 4AH, England) Ed.Bd.

700 913 UR
PAMYATNIKI KUL'TURY. NOVYE OTKRYTIYA/ MONUMENTS OF CULTURE. NEW DISCOVERIES. (Text in Russian; summaries in English) 1974. a. 4.02 Rub. (Akademiya Nauk S.S.S.R., Nauchnyi Sovet po Istorii Mirovoi Kul'tury) Izdatel'stvo Nauka, Podsosenskii Per. 21, Moscow K-62, U. S. S. R. illus.

700 CN ISSN 0319-1214
PANGNIRTUNG. (Text mainly in English; occasionally in French and Inuktitut) 1973. a. Can.$8. Canadian Arctic Producers Co-Operative Ltd., Box 4130, Station E, Ottawa, Ont. K1S 5B2, Canada. circ. 1,500. (back issues avail.)

700 IT
PANORAMICA SUGLI ARTISTI ITALIANI. 1977. irreg. L.25000. Societa Tipografia Editrice Modenese, Via Tabboni 4, 41100 Modena, Italy.

709 US
PHOEBUS; a journal of art history. 1978. a. $3.50. Arizona State University, Department of Art, Tempe, AZ 85281. bk. rev. illus. circ. 1,200.

740 IT ISSN 0079-2055
PIANETA FRESCO. 1967. a. L.2200. ‡ Ettore Sottsass, Ed. & Pub., 14 via Manzoni, Milan 20121, Italy. Ed. Fernanda Pivano Sottsass. circ. 500.

700 IT ISSN 0079-242X
POCKET LIBRARY OF STUDIES OF ART. 1948. irreg., vol. 24, 1979. price varies. Casa Editrice Leo S. Olschki, Casella Postale 66, 50100 Florence, Italy. circ. 1,200.

POLITECHNIKA WROCLAWSKA. INSTYTUT ARCHITEKTURY I URBANISTYKI. PRACE NAUKOWE. MONOGRAFIE. see ARCHITECTURE

POLITECHNIKA WROCLAWSKA. INSTYTUT ARCHITEKTURY I URBANISTYKI. PRACE NAUKOWE. STUDIA I MATERIALY. see ARCHITECTURE

709 720 PL
POLITECHNIKA WROCLAWSKA. INSTYTUT HISTORII ARCHITEKTURY, SZTUKI I TECHNIKI. PRACE NAUKOWE. MONOGRAFIE. (Text in Polish; summaries in English and Russian) 1971. irreg., 1975, no. 7. price varies. Politechnika Wroclawska, Wybrzeze Wyspianskiego 27, 50-370 Wroclaw, Poland (Dist. by: Ars Polona-Ruch, Krakowskie Przedmiescie 7, Warsaw, Poland) Ed. Marian Kloza. circ. 530.

709 720 PL ISSN 0324-9654
POLITECHNIKA WROCLAWSKA. INSTYTUT HISTORII ARCHITEKTURY, SZTUKI I TECHNIKI. PRACE NAUKOWE. STUDIA I MATERIALY. (Text in Polish; summaries in English and Russian) 1972. irreg., 1978, no. 5. price varies. Politechnika Wroclawska, Wybrzeze Wyspianskiego 27, 50-370 Wroclaw, Poland (Dist. by: Ars Polona-Ruch, Krakowskie Przedmiescie 7, Warsaw, Poland) Ed. Marian Kloza. circ. 390.

700 686 PL ISSN 0079-3132
POLONIA TYPOGRAPHICA SAECULI SEDECIMI. (Text in Polish; summaries in French and Russian) 1936. irreg., no. 10, 1975. price varies. (Polska Akademia Nauk, Instytut Badan Literackich) Ossolineum, Publishing House of the Polish Academy of Sciences, Rynek 9, Wroclaw, Poland (Dist. by Ars Polona-Ruch, Krakowskie Przedmiescie 7, Warsaw, Poland) Ed. Alodia Kawecka-Gryczowa. circ. 400.

POLYMERS PAINT AND COLOUR YEAR BOOK. see PAINTS AND PROTECTIVE COATINGS

709 PL ISSN 0079-466X
POZNANSKIE TOWARZYSTWO PRZYJACIOL NAUK. KOMISJA HISTORII SZTUKI. PRACE. 1922. irreg. price varies. Poznanskie Towarzystwo Przyjaciol Nauk, Komisja Historii Sztuki, Mielzynskiego 27/29, Poznan, Poland (Dist by Ars Polona-Ruch, Krakowskie Przedmiescie 7, Warsaw, Poland)

PRENT 190; new circle of collectors of modern graphic art. see *PRINTING*

PRINCETON ESSAYS ON THE ARTS. see *HUMANITIES: COMPREHENSIVE WORKS*

700 913　　　　US　　ISSN 0079-5208
PRINCETON MONOGRAPHS IN ART AND ARCHAEOLOGY. 1932. irreg., latest, no. 43. price varies. Princeton University Press, Princeton, NJ 08540. (reprint service avail. from UMI)

700　　　　　　　FR　　ISSN 0080-0074
RECHERCHES ET DOCUMENTS D'ART ET D'ARCHEOLOGIE. 1937. irreg. price varies. (Musee Guimet. Paris) Presses Universitaires de France, 108 Bd. Saint Germaine, 75279 Paris Cedex 6, France (Service des Periodiques, 12 rue Jean de Beauvais, 75005 Paris)

704.943　　　　　AU　　ISSN 0034-3935
RELIGIOESE GRAPHIK; Blaetter fuer Freunde Christlicher Gebrauchsgraphik. 1946. irreg. (2-3/yr.) S.10($0.50) per no. Stephanus-Verlag, Box 303, A-1071 Vienna, Austria. Ed. Josef Franz Aumann. bk. rev. illus. circ. 2,500.

REVUE BELGE D'ARCHEOLOGIE ET D'HISTOIRE DE L'ART. see *ARCHAEOLOGY*

700　　　　　　　BE　　ISSN 0080-2530
REVUE DES ARCHAEOLOGUES ET HISTORIENS D'ART DE LOUVAIN. 1968. a. 1500 Fr. Universite Catholique de Louvain, Association des Diplomes en Archeologie et Histoire de l'Art, College Erasme, Place B. Pascal, 1, B-1348 Louvain-la-Neuve, Belgium. circ. 850.

709　　　　　　　RM　　ISSN 0080-262X
REVUE ROUMAINE D'HISTOIRE DE L'ART. SERIE BEAUX-ARTS. a. $10. (Academia de Stiinte Sociale si Politice) Editura Academiei Republicii Socialiste Romania, Calea Victoriei 125, Bucharest, Romania (Subscr. to: ILEXIM, Str. 13 Decembrie Nr. 3, P.O. Box 136-137, Bucharest, Romania) Ed. Ion Frunzetti.
　Formerly: Revue Roumaine de l'Histoire de l'Art. Serie Arts Plastiques.

709　　　　　　　RM　　ISSN 0080-2638
REVUE ROUMAINE D'HISTOIRE DE L'ART. SERIE THEATRE, MUSIQUE, CINEMATOGRAPHIE. a. $10. (Academia de Stiinte Sociale si Politice) Editura Academiei Republicii Socialiste Romania, Calea Victoriei 125, Bucharest, Romania (Subscr. to: ILEXIM, Str. 13 Decembrie Nr. 3, P.O. Box 136-137, Bucharest, Romania) Ed. Mihnea Gheorghiu.

700　　　　　　　IT
RIPARTIZONE CULTURA E SPETTACOLO. RASSEGNA DI STUDI E DI NOTIZIE. irreg. Ripartizione Cultura e Spettacolo, Milan, Italy. illus.

709　　　　　　　PL　　ISSN 0080-3472
ROCZNIK HISTORII SZTUKI. (Text in Polish; summaries in English, French and German) 1956. a. 93 Zl. (Polska Akademia Nauk, Instytut Sztuki) Ossolineum, Publishing House of the Polish Academy of Sciences, Rynek 9, Wroclaw, Poland (Dist. by Ars Polona-Ruch, Krakowskie Przedmiescie 7, Warsaw, Poland) circ. 500.

ROEMISCHE BRONZEN AUS DEUTSCHLAND. see *ARCHAEOLOGY*

700　　　　　　　CN　　ISSN 0080-4290
ROYAL CANADIAN ACADEMY OF ARTS. ANNUAL EXHIBITION. CATALOGUE. (Text in English and French) a. Royal Canadian Academy of Arts, 40 University Ave., Suite 1112, Toronto, Ont., Canada.

700 913　　　　CN　　ISSN 0082-5077
ROYAL ONTARIO MUSEUM. ART AND ARCHAEOLOGY. OCCASIONAL PAPERS. 1959. irreg. Royal Ontario Museum, 100 Queen's Park, Toronto, Ont. M5S 2C6, Canada. illus.

ROYAL ONTARIO MUSEUM. HISTORY, TECHNOLOGY AND ART MONOGRAPHS. see *HISTORY*

709　　　　　　　IT　　ISSN 0080-5394
SAGGI E MEMORIE DI STORIA DELL'ARTE. 1957. irreg., 1973, no. 8. price varies. (Fondazione Giorgio Cini) Casa Editrice Leo S. Olschki, Casella Postale 66, 50100 Florence, Italy. circ. 500.

700　　　　　　　NE
SALES RESULTS HOLLAND.* 1973. irreg. Richard Wagner, Ed. & Pub., Box 8077, The Hague, Netherlands.

730　　　　　　　UY
SALON NACIONAL DE ARTES PLASTICAS Y VISUALES. a. Comision Nacional de Artes Plasticas y Visuales, Buenos Aires 668, Montevideo, Uruguay. illus.

354　　　　　　　CN
SASKATCHEWAN CENTRE OF THE ARTS. ANNUAL REPORT. a. Saskatchewan Centre of the Arts, 200 Lakeshore Drive, Regina, Sasketchewan, Canada.

709.9　　　　　　JM　　ISSN 0036-5068
SAVACOU; a journal of the Caribbean artists movement. 1970. irreg; 1-2/yr. $15. (Caribbean Artists Movement) Savacou Publications, Box 170, Mona, Kingston 7, Jamaica, W. Indies. Ed. Edward Kamau Brathwaite. adv. bk. rev. bibl. circ. 2,000.

700　　　　　　　GW　　ISSN 0080-7176
SCHRIFTTUM ZUR DEUTSCHEN KUNST. 1934. N.S. 1962. irreg., vol. 31, 1967. price varies. (Deutscher Verein fur Kunstwissenschaft) Deutscher Verlag fuer Kunstwissenschaft, Lindenstr. 76, 1000 Berlin 61, W. Germany (B.R.D.)

700　　　　　　　UK　　ISSN 0036-911X
SCOTTISH ART REVIEW. 1946. irreg. membership. (Glasgow Art Gallery and Museums Association) Glasgow Art Gallery, Kelvingrove, Glasgow G3 8AG, Scotland. Ed. Patricia L. G. Bascom. adv. bk. rev. illus. circ. 9,000. (also avail. in microform from UMI) Indexed: Art Ind.

700　　　　　　　NE　　ISSN 0080-8350
SCRIPTA ARTIS MONOGRAPHIA. (Text in English, French and German) 1968. irreg. price varies (approx. $25) A P A-Hissink & Co., Box 1850, 1000 BW Amsterdam, Netherlands (Distr. address: Box 122, 3600 AC Maarssen, Netherlands)

746　　　　　　　JA　　ISSN 0583-0664
SHINSHU UNIVERSITY. FACULTY OF TEXTILE SCIENCE AND TECHNOLOGY. JOURNAL. SERIES D: ARTS. (Text in Japanese and European languages; summaries in English) 1956. irreg. exchange basis. Shinshu University, Faculty of Textile Science and Technology - Shinshu Daigaku Sen'i Gakubu, 3-15-1 Tokida, Ueda, Nagano 386, Japan.

SILO. see *LITERATURE*

700　　　　　　　US
SKETCH BOOK. 1937. a. $3. Kappa Pi Internaional Honorary Art Fraternity, Box 7843, Midfield, Birmingham, AL 35228. Ed. Arthur Kennon. circ. 1,000 (controlled)

800 700　　　　UK　　ISSN 0144-6428
SLADE MAGAZINE; murals, poems, drawings, photography, other articles. a. Slade School of Art, University College, London, Gower St., London WC1, England. illus.

SOCIETY FOR RENAISSANCE STUDIES. OCCASIONAL PAPERS. see *LITERATURE*

709　　　　　　　US　　ISSN 0583-9181
SOCIETY FOR THE PRESERVATION OF LONG ISLAND ANTIQUITIES. NEWSLETTER. 1967. a. Society for the Preservation of Long Island Antiquities, 93 North Country Rd., Setauket, NY 11733. Key Title: Newsletter-Society for the Preservation of Long Island Antiquities.

SOFT STONE; an international journal of the arts. see *LITERATURE*

700　　　　　　　CH
SOOCHOW UNIVERSITY JOURNAL OF CHINESE ART HISTORY. (Text in Chinese or English) 1973. irreg. $8 per no. Soochow University, Wai Shuang Hsi, Shih Lin, Taipei, Taiwan, Republic of China. Ed. Bd. illus. circ. 800.

700　　　　　　　US　　ISSN 0081-2684
SOUTH CAROLINA ARTS COMMISSION. ANNUAL REPORT. 1968. a. ‡ Arts Commission, 1800 Gervais St., Columbia, SC 29201. Ed. Karl Allison.

954 913　　　　II
SOUTH INDIAN ART AND ARCHAEOLOGICAL SERIES. (Text in English) 1976. irreg. Equator and Meridian, 8 Selvamnagar, Thanjavur 613001, Tamilnadu, India.

700　　　　　　　US
SOUTH SHORE; an international review of the arts. 1977. irreg. Box 95, AuTrain, MI 49806. Ed. Stephen Chandler.

730　　　　　　　UR
SOVETSKAYA SKUL'PTURA. vol. 74, 1976. irreg. 2.344 Rub. per no. Izdatel'stvo Sovetskii Khudozhnik, Ul.Chernyakhovskogo, 4a, Moscow a-319, U.S.S.R. Ed. V. Tikhanova. bibl. illus. circ. 10,000.

300　　　　　　　NE
SPECIMEN.* (Text in Dutch, English and German; summaries in English) 1972-73. irreg. fl.25 for 3 issues. Exp-Press, P.O. Box 14012, Utrecht, Netherlands. Ed. Marten Hendriks.

SPECULUM ANNIVERSARY MONOGRAPHS. see *HISTORY — History Of Europe*

700 780　　　　YU　　ISSN 0081-4008
SRPSKA AKADEMIJA NAUKA I UMETNOSTI. ODELENJE LIKOVNE I MUZICKE UMETNOSTI. POSEBNA IZDANJA. (Text in Serbo-Croatian; summaries in English, German or Russian) 1954. irreg. price varies. Srpska Akademija Nauka i Umetnosti, Knez Mihailova 35, 11001 Belgrade, Yugoslavia (Dist. by: Prosveta, Terazije 16, Belgrade, Yugoslavia) Ed. Stanojlo Rajicic. circ. 800.

069 700　　　　GE　　ISSN 0067-6004
STAATLICHE MUSEEN ZU BERLIN. JAHRBUCH. FORSCHUNGEN UND BERICHTE. 1957. a. price varies. Akademie-Verlag, Leipziger Str. 3-4, 108 Berlin, E. Germany (D.D.R.)

700　　　　　　　IT　　ISSN 0081-5845
STORIA DELLA MINIATURA. STUDI E DOCUMENTI. 1962. irreg., no. 5, 1980. price varies. Casa Editrice Leo S. Olschki, Casella Postale 66, 50100 Florence, Italy. circ. 1,000.

709 707　　　　CN　　ISSN 0081-6027
STRUCTURIST. 1960. biennial. Can.$10 per no. Eli Bornstein, Ed. & Pub., Box 378, Sub. P.O. 6, University of Saskatchewan, Saskatoon, Sask. S7N 0W0, Canada (Dist. in U.S. by: Wittenborn, 1018 Madison Ave., New York, NY 10021) bk. rev. cum. index for nos. 1-20. circ. 1,200-1,500. (also avail. in microfilm from UMI; back issues avail.)

709 701.18
STUDI E TESTI DI STORIA E CRITICA DELL'ARTE. 1975. irreg., no. 5, 1978. price varies. Societa Editrice Napoletana s.r.l., Corso Umberto I 34, 80138 Naples, Italy.

701　　　　　　　PL　　ISSN 0081-7104
STUDIA Z HISTORII SZTUKI. (Text in Polish; summaries in English, French and German) 1953. irreg., vol. 29, 1979. price varies. (Polska Akademia Nauk, Instytut Sztuki) Ossolineum, Publishing House of the Polish Academy of Sciences, Rynek 9, 50-106 Wroclaw, Poland (Dist. by Ars Polona-Ruch, Krakowskie Przedmiescie 7, Warsaw, Poland)

709　　　　　　　GW　　ISSN 0081-7228
STUDIEN ZUR DEUTSCHEN KUNSTGESCHICHTE. 1894. irreg., no. 358, 1981. price varies. Verlag Valentin Koerner, H.-Sielcken-Str. 36, Postfach 304, D-7570 Baden-Baden 1, W. Germany (B.R.D.) circ. 1,000 (approx.)

700　　　　　　　GW　　ISSN 0081-7325
STUDIEN ZUR KUNST DES NEUNZEHNTEN JAHRHUNDERTS. 1966. irreg. price varies. Prestel-Verlag, Mandlstr. 26, 8000 Munich 40, W. Germany (B.R.D.)

709 950　　　　GW　　ISSN 0170-3684
STUDIEN ZUR OSTASIATISCHEN SCHRIFTKUNST. irreg., vol. 3, 1978. price varies. Franz Steiner Verlag GmbH, Friedrichstr. 24, Postfach 5529, 6200 Wiesbaden, W. Germany (B.R.D.) Ed. Dietrich Seckel.

700 913 US
STUDIES IN ANCIENT ART AND ARCHAEOLOGY. irreg. price varies. Cornell University Press, 124 Roberts Place, Ithaca, NY 14850.

700 US
STUDIES IN BRITISH ART. irreg., latest, 1980. price varies. Yale University Press, 92A Yale Sta., New Haven, CT 06520.

740 US ISSN 0081-8178
STUDIES IN MANUSCRIPT ILLUMINATION. 1954. irreg., no. 8, 1979. Princeton University Press, Princeton, NJ 08540. (reprint service avail. from UMI)

STUDIES IN PRE-COLUMBIAN ART AND ARCHAEOLOGY. see *ARCHAEOLOGY*

708 US ISSN 0091-7338
STUDIES IN THE HISTORY OF ART. 1971. a. $6.50 (approx.) ‡ National Gallery of Art, Washington, DC 20565. charts. illus. circ. 6,000. Formerly: Report and Studies in the History of Art (ISSN 0080-1240)

700 UK ISSN 0039-6168
SURREALIST TRANSFORMACTION. (Text in English & French) 1967. irreg. £4($5) British Surrealist Group, Transformaction, Peeks, Harpford, Sidmouth, Devon EX10 ONH, England. Ed. John Lyle. bk. rev. film rev. illus. circ. 1,000. (tabloid format)

942 UK ISSN 0081-9751
SURVEY OF LONDON. irreg., vol. 39, 1977. price varies. (Greater London Council) Athlone Press, 90-91 Great Russell St., London WC1B 3PY, England (Dist. in U.S. by: Humanities Press Inc., 171 First Ave., Atlantic Highlands, NJ 07716)

701.18 AG
T & C. (Theorie et Critique); theory and criticism, teoria y critica. (Text in English and French) 1979. irreg. International Association of Art Critics, Elpidio Gonzalez 4070, 1407 Buenos Aires, Argentina. Ed.Bd.

TALOHA. see *MUSEUMS AND ART GALLERIES*

750 UK
TEMPERA; year-book of painters in tempera. 1957. a. 60p. ‡ Society of Painters in Tempera, 28 Eldon Rd, London W.8, England. Ed. Rosamund Borradaile. adv. circ. 300.

THORVALDSEN MUSEUM. MEDDELELSER. see *MUSEUMS AND ART GALLERIES*

700 RM
TIBISCUS. SERIA ARTA. (Text in Romanian; summaries in German) Muzeul Banatului, Piata Huniade Nr. 1, Timisoara, Romania.

700 US ISSN 0082-4852
TOLEDO AREA ARTISTS EXHIBITION. 1919. a. price varies. ‡ (Toledo Federation of Art Societies, Inc) Toledo Museum of Art, Box 1013, Toledo, OH 43697.

TOOTHPICK, LISBON & THE ORCAS ISLANDS. see *LITERATURE*

700 PL ISSN 0082-5514
TOWARZYSTWO NAUKOWE W TORUNIU. KOMISJA HISTORII SZTUKI. TEKA. (Subseries of Towarzystwo Naukowe w Toruniu. Wydzial Filologiczno-Filozoficzny. Prace) (Text in Polish; summaries in French) 1959. irreg. price varies. Panstwowe Wydawnictwo Naukowe, Miodowa 10, Warsaw, Poland (Dist. by Ars Polona-Ruch, Krakowskie Przedmiescie 7, Warsaw, Poland) Ed. Artur Hutnikiewicz.

TRAVAUX D'HUMANISME ET RENAISSANCE. see *HISTORY — History Of Europe*

700 US ISSN 0550-0850
UKRAINIAN ART DIGEST/NOTATKI Z MISTETSTBA. (Text in Ukrainian) 1963. a. $5 per issue. Ukrainian Artist's Association in U.S.A., Philadelphia Branch - Obednannya Misttsiv Ukraintsiv v Ameriti. Viddil u Filyadel'fii, 1022 N. Lawrence St., Philadelphia, PA 19123. Ed. Petro Mehyk. bk. rev. illus. circ. 1,000.

700 US ISSN 0083-2103
U. S. NATIONAL ENDOWMENT FOR THE ARTS. ANNUAL REPORT. 1967. a. U. S. National Endowment for the Arts, Washington, DC 20506 (Orders to: Supt. Doc., Washington, DC 20402)

700 AG
UNIVERSIDAD DE BUENOS AIRES. INSTITUTO DE ARTE AMERICANO E INVESTIGACIONES ESTETICAS. ANALES. 1948. a. Universidad de Buenos Aires, Instituto de Arte Americano e Investigaciones Esteticas, Buenos Aires, Argentina. illus.

700 860 MX ISSN 0076-7239
UNIVERSIDAD NACIONAL AUTONOMA DE MEXICO. INSTITUTO DE INVESTIGACIONES ESTETICAS. ANALES. 1937. a. price varies. ‡ Universidad Nacional Autonoma de Mexico, Instituto de Investigaciones Esteticas, Torre de Humanidades, Ciudad Universitaria, Mexico 20, D.F., Mexico. Ed. Xavier Moyssen.

700 MX
UNIVERSIDAD NACIONAL AUTONOMA DE MEXICO. INSTITUTO DE INVESTIGACIONES ESTETICAS. MONOGRAFIAS DE ARTE. 1977. irreg; latest issue, 1979. price varies. Universidad Nacional Autonoma de Mexico, Instituto de Investigaciones Esteticas, Torre I de Humanidades, Ciudad Universitaria, Mexico 20, D.F., Mexico.

UNIVERSIDADE DE SAO PAULO. INSTITUTO DE ESTUDOS BRASILEIROS. REVISTA. see *HISTORY — History Of North And South America*

700 800 IT ISSN 0078-7728
UNIVERSITA DEGLI STUDI DI PADOVA. FACOLTA DI LETTERE E FILOSOFIA. OPUSCOLI ACCADEMICI. 1937. irreg., vol. 13, 1979. price varies. Casa Editrice Leo S. Olschki, Casella Postale 66, 50100 Florence, Italy. circ. 1,000.

700 800 IT ISSN 0078-7736
UNIVERSITA DEGLI STUDI DI PADOVA. FACOLTA DI LETTERE E FILOSOFIA. PUBBLICAZIONI. 1932. irreg., vol. 60, 1979. price varies. Casa Editrice Leo S. Olschki, Casella Postale 66, 50100 Florence, Italy. circ. 1,000.

701.18 IT
UNIVERSITA DEGLI STUDI DI PARMA. ISTITUTO DI STORIA DELL' ARTE. CATALOGHI. (Each issue devoted to an individual artist) 1968. irreg. price varies. Universita degli Studi di Parma, Istituto di Storia dell'Arte, Piazzale della Pace 5, Palazzo Pilotta, 43100 Parma, Italy. bk. rev. bibl. illus. circ. 1,000.

707 IT ISSN 0557-3122
UNIVERSITA DEGLI STUDI DI ROMA. SEMINARIO DI ARCHEOLOGIA E STORIA DELL'ARTE GRECA E ROMANA. STUDI MISCELLANEI. 1961. irreg., no. 25, 1979. price varies. Erma di Bretschneider, Via Cassiodoro, 19, 00193 Rome, Italy.

709 IT ISSN 0564-2477
UNIVERSITA DEGLI STUDI DI TRIESTE. ISTITUTO DI STORIA DELL'ARTE (PUBBLICAZIONI) 1954. irreg. price varies. Edizioni dell' Ateneo S.p.A., P.O. Box 7216, 00100 Rome, Italy. illus. circ. 1,000.

709 GW
UNIVERSITAET BONN. SEMINAR FUER ORIENTALISCHE KUNSTGESCHICHTE. VEROEFFENTLICHUNGEN. REIHE B. ANTIQUITATES ORIENTALES. 1977. irreg. price varies. Rudolf Habelt Verlag, Am Buchenhang 1, 5300 Bonn 1, W. Germany (B.R.D.)

700 AU
UNIVERSITAET INNSBRUCK. KUNSTGESCHICHTLICHE STUDIEN. (Subseries of: Universitaet Innsbruck. Veroeffentlichungen) 1972. irreg. price varies. Oesterreichische Kommissionsbuchhandlung, Maximilianstrasse 17, A-6020 Innsbruck, Austria. Ed. Otto Lutterotti.

709 950 GW ISSN 0170-3692
UNIVERSITAET ZU KOELN. KUNSTHISTORISCHES INSTITUT. ABTEILUNG ASIEN. PUBLIKATIONEN. irreg., vol. 4, 1981. price varies. Franz Steiner Verlag GmbH, Friedrichstr. 24, Postfach 5529, 6200 Wiesbaden, W. Germany (B.R.D.) Eds. R. Goepper, D. Kuhn, U. Wiesner.
History

709 913 MG
UNIVERSITE DE MADAGASCAR. MUSEE D'ART ET D'ARCHEOLOGIE. TRAVAUX ET DOCUMENTS. 1970. irreg., latest no. 18, 1975. Universite de Madagascar, Musee d'Art et d'Archeologie, B.P. 564 Isoraka, Antananarivo, Malagasy Republic.

709 FR ISSN 0563-9794
UNIVERSITE DE TOULOUSE II (LE MIRAIL). INSTITUT D'ART PREHISTORIQUE. TRAVAUX. 1959. a. 69 F. Universite de Toulouse II (le Mirail), 109 bis, rue Vauquelin, 31000 Toulouse, France. (back issues avail)

745 US ISSN 0068-628X
UNIVERSITY OF CALIFORNIA, LOS ANGELES. MUSEUM OF CULTURAL HISTORY. OCCASIONAL PAPERS. 1969. irreg. price varies. ‡ University of California, Los Angeles, Museum of Cultural History, Los Angeles, CA 90024. Ed. Robert Woolard.

700 378 US ISSN 0073-5256
UNIVERSITY OF ILLINOIS AT URBANA-CHAMPAIGN. DEPARTMENT OF ART. NEWSLETTER. 1951. a. free. University of Illinois at Urbana-Champaign, Continuing Education and Public Service-Visual Arts, 123 Fine and Applied Arts Bldg., Champaign, IL 61820. Ed. James R. Shipley.

700 PK ISSN 0080-9616
UNIVERSITY OF SIND. RESEARCH JOURNAL. ARTS SERIES: HUMANITIES AND SOCIAL SCIENCES.* (Text in English) 1961. a. Rs.10. University of Sind, Faculty of Arts, Jamshoro, Hyderabad 6, Pakistan.

700 913 780 CS ISSN 0083-4130
UNIVERZITA KOMENSKEHO. FILOZOFICKA FAKULTA. ZBORNIK: MUSAICA. (Text in Czech or Slovak; summaries in English and German) 1961. irreg. exchange basis. Univerzita Komenskeho, Filozoficka Fakulta, Gondova 2, 806 01 Bratislava, Czechoslovakia. Ed. Bohuslav Novotny. circ. 700.

709 PL ISSN 0083-4424
UNIWERSYTET JAGIELLONSKI. ZESZYTY NAUKOWE. PRACE Z HISTORII SZTUKI. (Text in Polish; summaries in French and Russian) 1962. irreg., 1972, vol. 10. price varies. Panstwowe Wydawnictwo Naukowe, Miodowa 10, Warsaw, Poland (Dist. by Ars Polona-Ruch, Krakowskie Przedmiescie 7, Warsaw, Poland)

700 800 AU ISSN 0083-5463
VER SACRUM; NEUE HEFTE FUER KUNST UND LITERATUR. 1969. irreg. price varies. Jugend und Volk Verlagsgesellschaft, Tiefer Graben 7, A 1014 Vienna, Austria.

VEREIN FUER VOLKSKUNDE IN WIEN. SONDERSCHRIFTEN. see *FOLKLORE*

700 UK ISSN 0083-6028
VICTORIA UNIVERSITY OF MANCHESTER. FACULTY OF ARTS. PUBLICATIONS. 1948. irreg. price varies. ‡ Manchester University Press, Oxford Rd., Manchester M13 9PL, England.

709 BL
VIDA DAS ARTES. irreg. $50. Industrias Graficas Libra, Rua Visconde de Carandai, 19, Jardim Botanico, Rio de Janeiro, Brazil. illus.

700 US
VIDEOZINE. 1977. irreg. $50 per no. (Mamelle Inc.) Contemporary Arts Press, Box 3123, San Francisco, CA 94119. (videotape)

700 UK ISSN 0512-4638
W. A. CARGILL MEMORIAL LECTURES IN FINE ART. irreg. price varies. University of Glasgow Press, Publications Office, Glasgow G12 8QG, Scotland.

ART — ABSTRACTING, BIBLIOGRAPHIES, STATISTICS

709   GW   ISSN 0083-7105
WALLRAF-RICHARTZ-JAHRBUCH; WESTDEUTSCHES JAHRBUCH FUER KUNSTGESCHICHTE. 1924. a. DM.120. Freunde des Wallraf-Richartz-Museums, An der Rechtschule, 5000 Cologne 1, W. Germany (B.R.D.) Ed. Gerhard Bott. circ. 800.

769   US   ISSN 0085-7874
WALTER NEURATH MEMORIAL LECTURES. 1969. a. Transatlantic Arts, Inc., North Village Green, Levittown, NY 11756 (and Thames & Hudson, London, Eng.)

709   US   ISSN 0083-7148
WALTER W. S. COOK ALUMNI LECTURE. 1960. irreg. $5. ‡ (New York University, Institute of Fine Arts) J. J. Augustin, Inc., Locust Valley, NY 11560. index.

705 709   US   ISSN 0083-7156
WALTERS ART GALLERY. JOURNAL. 1938. a. (occasionally biennial) $10. Walters Art Gallery, 600 N. Charles St., Baltimore, MD 21201. Ed. Ann Garside. illus. circ. 1,000. Indexed: Art Ind.

709 069   GE   ISSN 0083-7954
WELTSTAEDTE DER KUNST. EDITION LEIPZIG/GREAT CENTERS OF ART. (English language edition is published by A. S. Barnes &Co., Inc. South Brunswick, N. J. 08512) 1965. irreg. M.49.50. Verlag fuer Kunst und Wissenschaft, Karlstr. 20, 701 Leipzig, E. Germany (D.D.R.)

700   CN   ISSN 0700-2661
WHO DOES WHAT: A GUIDE TO NATIONAL ASSOCIATIONS, SERVICE ORGANIZATIONS AND UNIONS OPERATING IN MOST AREAS OF THE ARTS. Variant title: Who Does What: A Guide to over 800 National Associations, Service Organizations and Unions Operating in Most Areas of the Arts. (Text in English and French) a. Can.$5. Canadian Conference of the Arts, 141 Laurier Ave. W., Suite 707, Ottawa, Ont. K1P 5J3, Canada.

700   CN   ISSN 0384-2355
WHO'S WHO: A GUIDE TO FEDERAL AND PROVINCIAL DEPARTMENTS AND AGENCIES, THEIR FUNDING PROGRAMS, AND THE PEOPLE WHO HEAD THEM. Variant title: Who's Who: A Guide to Federal and Provincial Departments and Agencies and the People Who Head Them. (Text in English and French) a. Can.$5. Canadian Conference of the Arts, 141 Laurier Ave. W., Suite 707, Ottawa, Ont. K1P 5J3, Canada.

700   AU   ISSN 0083-9981
WIENER JAHRBUCH FUER KUNSTGESCHICHTE. (Text in English and German) 1921. a. DM.112. (Institut fuer Oesterreichische Kunstforschung) Hermann Boehlaus Nachf., Schmalzhofgasse 4, Postfach 167, A-1061 Vienna, Austria. (Co-sponsor: Universitaet Wien. Kunsthistorisches Institut) Eds. E. Frodl-Kraft, G. Schmidt. bk. rev. illus. circ. 500.

709 943.6   GW
WIENER RINGSTRASSE-BILD EINER EPOCHE; Die Erweiterung der Inneren Stadt Wien unter Kaiser Franz Joseph. irreg., vol. 11, 1979. price varies. Franz Steiner Verlag GmbH, Friedrichstr.24, Postfach 5529, 6200 Wiesbaden, W. Germany(B.R.D.) Ed.Renate Wagner-Rieger.

WILBOUR MONOGRAPHS. see HISTORY

700   GW   ISSN 0043-5570
DER WILLE ZUR FORM. 1978. irreg. price varies. Paul-Ernst-Gesellschaft, Postfach 279, 4690 Herne 2, W. Germany (B.R.D.) bk. rev. bibl. index. circ. 1,000.

WISCONSIN ACADEMY OF SCIENCES, ARTS AND LETTERS, TRANSACTIONS. see SCIENCES: COMPREHENSIVE WORKS

WITTENBERG REVIEW OF LITERATURE AND ART. see LITERATURE

700 790   NE   ISSN 0084-1498
WORLD COLLECTORS ANNUARY. (Text in English) 1950. a. fl.195($100) World Collectors Publishers, P.O. Box 263, 2270 AG Voorburg, Netherlands. Ed. A.M.E. Van Eijk Van Voorthuijsen. adv. cum.index (1946-1972) circ. 1,000.

745   US   ISSN 0084-1706
WORLD CRAFTS COUNCIL. GENERAL ASSEMBLY. PROCEEDINGS OF THE BIENNIAL MEETING. 1964. biennial; 8th, Kyoto, 1978. $4. World Crafts Council, 29 West 53 St., New York, NY 10019.

WORLD CULTURAL GUIDES. see TRAVEL AND TOURISM

700   PL   ISSN 0084-2982
WROCLAWSKIE TOWARZYSTWO NAUKOWE. KOMISJA HISTORII SZTUKI. ROZPRAWY. (Text in Polish; summaries in English and French) 1960. irreg. price varies. Ossolineum, Publishing House of the Polish Academy of Sciences, Rynek 9, Wroclaw, Poland (Dist. by Ars Polona-Ruch, Krakowskie Przedmiescie 7, Warsaw, Poland) circ. 1,000.

750   PL   ISSN 0084-3032
WSPOLCZESNE MALARSTWO WROCLAWSKIE. 1962. irreg. 6 Zl. ‡ Muzeum Narodowe, Wroclaw, Pl Powstancow Warszawy 5, 50-153 Wroclaw, Poland. circ. 300.

700   US   ISSN 0084-3415
YALE PUBLICATIONS IN THE HISTORY OF ART. 1939. irreg., no. 27, 1978. price varies. Yale University Press, 92A Yale Sta., New Haven, CT 06520.

700 792   KO
YEARBOOK OF CULTURAL & ARTISTIC ACTIVITIES/MUNYEYUNGAM. (Text in Korean) 1977. a. free. Korean Culture & Arts Foundation, 1-130 Dongsoong-dong, Chongro-ku, Seoul 110, S. Korea. circ. 1,500.

709   YU   ISSN 0514-616X
ZBORNIK ZASTITE SPOMENIKA KULTURE/ RECUEIL DES TRAVAUX SUR LA PROTECTION DES MONUMENTS HISTORIQUES. 1950. a. Republicki Zavod za Zastitu Spomenika Kulture, Kalegdan 14, Belgrade, Yugoslavia. Ed. Jovan Sekulic.

741   GW   ISSN 0084-523X
ZEICHENWERK. 1970. irreg. DM.7.80. Georg Kallmeyer Verlag, Grosser Zimmerhof 20, Postfach 1347, 3340 Wolfenbuettel, W. Germany (B.R.D.) (looseleaf format)

700   US
8 X 10 ART PORTFOLIOS. 1972. irreg. Box 363, New York, NY 10013. illus.

ART — Abstracting, Bibliographies, Statistics

016.7   SZ
ART/KUNST; international bibliography of art books/ internationale bibliographie des kunstbuchs/ bibliographie internationale des livres d'art. (Text in English, French, and German) 1972. a. 36 Fr. W. Jaeggi AG, Postfach, CH-4001 Basel, Switzerland. Ed. W. Jaeggi. adv. circ. 7,500.

016 700 720   US
ART AND ARCHITECTURE BIBLIOGRAPHIES. 1973. irreg., no. 4, 1978. price varies. Hennessey & Ingalls, Inc., 8321 Campion Dr., Los Angeles, CA 90045.

709 016   DK
BIBLIOGRAFI OVER DANSK KUNST. 1972. a. free. Kunstakademiet, Bibliotek - Academy of Fine Arts, Library, Kongens Nytorv 1, DK-1050 Copenhagen K, Denmark. Ed. Emma Salling. circ. 500.

097 016   DK
BIBLIOGRAFI OVER EUROPAEISKE KUNSTNERES EX LIBRIS/EUROPAEISCHE EX LIBRIS/EUROPEAN BOOK PLATES/EX LIBRIS D'EUROPE. (Text in Danish, German, French, English) 1967. a, latest combines 1976 and 1977 (pub. 1978) Kr.120. Klaus Roedel, Ed. & Pub., P.O. Box 109, DK-9900 Frederikshavn, Denmark. bibl. circ. 300.

700 016   GE
BIBLIOGRAPHIE BILDENDE KUNST. irreg. Saechsische Landesbibliothek, Marienallee 12, 806 Dresden, E. Germany (D.D.R.)

700 016   GE
BIBLIOGRAPHIE DER ANTIQUARIATS-, AUKTIONS- UND KUNSTKATALOGE. 1975. irreg. Karl-Marx-Universitaet, Universitaetsbibliothek, Beethovenstr. 6, 701 Leipzig, E. Germany (D.D.R.)

BULLETIN SIGNALETIQUE. PART 530: REPERTOIRE D'ART ET D'ARCHEOLOGIE. NOUVELLE SERIE. see ARCHAEOLOGY — Abstracting, Bibliographies, Statistics

700 016   FR
LIVRE D'ART INFORMATION. irreg. free. Union des Editeurs Francais, 117 Bd. Saint Germain, 75279 Paris, France. (Co-sponsor: Syndicat National de l'Edition) bk. rev.

ASTROLOGY

133.5   US   ISSN 0516-9550
AMERICAN ASTROLOGY DIGEST. 1956. a. $1.50. Clancy Publications Inc., 2505 Alvernon Way, Tucson, AZ 85712. Ed. Joanne S. Clancy. adv. charts. illus. tr.lit.

133.5   US
ASTROLOGY REFERENCE BOOK. 1972. a. $5.95. Symbols & Signs, Box 4536, N. Hollywood, CA 91607. Ed. Edith Waldron.
Formerly (until 1980): Astrology Annual Reference Book (ISSN 0363-4140)

133.5 551.6   CE
COLOMBO OBSERVATORY. REPORT. (Text in English) a. Colombo Observatory, Bauddhaloka Mawatha, Colombo 7, Sri Lanka. charts, illus, stat.

133.5   US
DAILY PLANET ALMANAC. 1976. a. $3.95. Daily Planet, Inc., Box 1641, Boulder, CO 80306. Ed. Terry Reim. adv. charts. illus. circ. 27,000. (back issues avail.)

133.5   US
DAILY PLANETARY GUIDE; an encyclopedia of practical astrological applications. 1978. a. $2.50. Llewellyn Publications, Box 43383, St. Paul, MN 55164. Ed. Matt Wood. adv. (reprint service avail. from UMI)

133.5   FR
GUIDE ASTROLOGIQUE. (Supplement to Astre) 1970. a. 6 F. G. Gourdon, Ed. and Pub., 10, rue de Crussol, 75011 Paris, France. adv. illus. circ. 120,000.

133.5   US   ISSN 0085-2384
JOURNAL OF ASTROLOGICAL STUDIES. 1970. irreg. International Society for Astrological Research, Inc., 70 Melrose Place, Montclair, NJ 07042. Ed. Julienne P. Mullette. charts. illus. stat. circ. 2,000.

133   US   ISSN 0145-8868
LLEWELLYN'S ASTROLOGICAL CALENDAR. 1936. a. $3.95. Llewellyn Publications, Box 43383, St. Paul, MN 55164. Ed. Matt Wood. charts. circ. 50,000. (reprint service avail. from UMI)

133   US
LLEWELLYN'S MOON SIGN BOOK. 1906. a. $3.95. Llewellyn Publications, Box 43383, St. Paul, MN 55164. Ed. Matt Wood. adv. charts. tr.lit. circ. 200,000. (also avail. in microform from UMI; back issues avail.; reprint service avail. from UMI)

133.5   US
N A S O JOURNAL. 1972. 1-3/yr. $15. National Astrological Society, 127 Madison Ave, New York, NY 10016. Ed. Henry Weingarten. adv. charts. circ. 1,000 (controlled)

ASTRONOMY

523.8   US   ISSN 0516-9518
A A V S O BULLETIN. a. $10. American Association of Variable Star Observers, 187 Concord Ave., Cambridge, MA 02138. Ed. Janet A. Mattei. Indexed: Astron. & Astrophys.Abstr.

ASTRONOMY

523.8 US
A A V S O REPORT. 1972, no. 29. irreg; 1975, no. 30. $15 per no. American Association of Variable Star Observers, 187 Concord Ave., Cambridge, MA 02138. Ed. Janet A. Mattei. Indexed: Astron. & Astrophys.Abstr.

520 US ISSN 0190-2717
ACADEMY OF SCIENCES OF THE U S S R. CRIMEAN ASTROPHYSICAL OBSERVATORY. BULLETIN. 1977. irreg. $38.50. Allerton Press, Inc., 150 Fifth Ave., New York, NY 10011. Ed. A. B. Severnyi.

520 US ISSN 0190-2709
ACADEMY OF SCIENCES OF THE U S S R. SPECIAL ASTROPHYSICAL OBSERVATORY-NORTH CAUCASUS. BULLETIN. 1977. irreg. $22.50. Allerton Press, Inc., 150 Fifth Ave., New York, NY 10011. Ed. I.M. Kopylov.

523.01 UR
AKADEMIYA NAUK KAZAKHSKOI S.S.R. ASTROFIZICHESKII INSTITUT. TRUDY. vol. 28, 1976. irreg. 2.14 Rub. per no. Izdatel'stvo Nauka Kazakhskoi S.S.R., Ul.Shevchenko 28, 480021 Alma-Ata, U.S.S.R. Ed. T. Omarov. abstr. bibl. illus. circ. 1,000.

520 US
ALMANAC FOR COMPUTERS. 1977. a. U.S. Naval Observatory, Washington, DC 20390.

520 PH ISSN 0569-0838
ALMANAC FOR GEODETIC ENGINEERS. (Text in English) a. P.5($1) Philippine Atmospheric, Geophysical and Astronomical Services Administration, Box 2277, Manila, Philippines. circ. 1,500.

528.6 SP ISSN 0080-5963
ALMANAQUE NAUTICO. 1912. a. 250 ptas.($2.90) approx. Instituo y Observatorio de Marina, San Fernando (Cadiz), Spain. illus. circ. 5,400.

520 523.01 US ISSN 0066-4146
ANNUAL REVIEW OF ASTRONOMY AND ASTROPHYSICS. 1963. a. $20. Annual Reviews Inc., 4139 El Camino Way, Palo Alto, CA 94306. Ed. Geoffrey Burbidge. bibl. index; cum.index. (back issues avail.; reprint service avail. from iSI) Indexed: Chem.Abstr. Sci.Abstr. Int.Aerosp.Abstr. M.M.R.I. Nucl.Sci.Abstr.

ANNUAL REVIEW OF EARTH AND PLANETARY SCIENCES. see *EARTH SCIENCES*

520 UK ISSN 0142-7253
ARCHAEOASTRONOMY. 1979. a. £6($12.50) (£20($50) for combined subscription with Journal for the History of Astronomy) Science History Publications Ltd., Halfpenny Furze, Chalfont St. Giles, Buck. HP8 4NR, England. illus. index.

520 GE
ARCHENHOLD-STERNWARTE. VORTRAEGE UND SCHRIFTEN. 1959. irreg., vol. 6, no. 56, 1978. Archenhold-Sternwarte, Alt-Treptow 1, 1193 Berlin-Treptow, E. Germany (D.D.R.) Ed. D. B. Hermann.

523 US ISSN 0039-2502
ASSOCIATION OF LUNAR AND PLANETARY OBSERVERS. JOURNAL. Varient title: Strolling Astronomer. 1947. irreg. $6 per vol. (6 nos.) Association of Lunar and Planetary Observers, Box 3 AZ University Park, Las Cruces, NM 88003. Ed. Walter H. Haas. adv. bk. rev. charts. illus. stat. index. circ. 880. Indexed: Astron. & Astrophys.Abstr.

522.1 FR
ASSOCIATION POUR LE DEVELOPPEMENT INTERNATIONAL DE L'OBSERVATOIRE DE NICE. BULLETIN. Cover title: A D I O N Bulletin. (Text in English and French) 1964. a. 30 F. Association pour le Developpement International de l'Observatoire, 06300 Nice, France. charts. illus. circ. 400.
Formerly: Association pour le Developpement International de l'Observatoire de Nice. Bulletin d'Information (ISSN 0004-5861)

523 BU
ASTROFIZICHESKIE ISSLEDOVANIIA. (Text in Russian; summaries in English) 1975. irreg. 2 lv. per issue. (Bulgarska Akademiia na Naukite) Publishing House of the Bulgarian Academy of Sciences, Ul. Akad. G. Bonchev, 1113 Sofia, Bulgaria. Ed. N. Nikolov. circ. 800.

520 PL
ASTRONOMIA. (Text in English or Polish; summaries in English) 1964. irreg. price varies. Uniwersytet im. Adama Mickiewicza w Poznaniu, Stalingradzka 1, 61-712 Poznan, Poland (Dist. by: Ars Polona, Krakowskie Przedmiescie 7, 00-068 Warsaw, Poland)
Formerly: Uniwersytet im. Adama Mickiewicza w Poznaniu. Wydzial Matematyki, Fizyki i Chemii. Seria Astronomia.

528 UK
ASTRONOMICAL ALMANAC. 1981. a. price varies. H.M. Nautical Almanac Office, Herstmonceux Castle, Hailsham, Sussex BN27 1RP, England (Avail. from H.M.S.O., c/o Liaison Officer, Atlantic House, Holborn Viaduct, London EC1P 1BN, England) (Co-sponsor: U.S. Naval Observatory, Washington, D.C.)
Supersedes: Astronomical Ephemeris (ISSN 0066-9962) & American Ephemeris and Nautical Almanac (ISSN 0065-8189); Nautical Almanac and Astronomical Ephemeris.

520 II ISSN 0066-9970
ASTRONOMICAL EPHEMERIS OF GEOCENTRIC PLACES OF PLANETS. (Text in English; summaries in Hindi) 1942. a. Rs.5. Shree Jiwaji Observatory, Ujain, Madhya Pradesh, India. Ed. Jyotishastracharya K. K. Joshi.

523 US ISSN 0083-2421
ASTRONOMICAL PHENOMENA. 1951. a. price varies. U. S. Naval Observatory, Department of the Navy, Washington, DC 20390 (Orders to: Supt. of Documents, Washington, DC 20402)

520 AT ISSN 0066-9997
ASTRONOMICAL SOCIETY OF AUSTRALIA. PROCEEDINGS. 1967. irreg., approx. 2/yr. Aus.$10 per no. c/o Division of Radiophysics, C. S. I. R O., Box 76, Epping, N.S.W. 2121, Australia. Ed. R. X. McGee. bk. rev. bibl. charts. stat. circ. 500. Indexed: Astron & Astrophysics Abstr.

520 AT ISSN 0067-0006
ASTRONOMICAL SOCIETY OF VICTORIA. YEARBOOK. 1964. a. Aus.$4. Astronomical Society of Victoria, G.P.O. Box 1059J, Melbourne, Victoria 3001, Australia. Ed. R. J. C. Lawrence. index. circ. 550.

523 HK
ASTRONOMICAL TABLES AND STAR CHARTS FOR HONG KONG. a. price varies. Government Information Services, Beaconsfield House, Queen's Rd., Central, Victoria, Hong Kong, Hong Kong. illus.

520 BU ISSN 0068-3639
ASTRONOMICHESKI KALENDAR NA OBSERVATORIIATA V SOFIA. 1954. a. 1.20 lv. (Bulgarska Akademiia na Naukite, Sektsiia po Astronomiia) Publishing House of the Bulgarian Academy of Sciences, Ul. Akad. G. Bonchev, 1113 Sofia, Bulgaria (Dist. by: Hemus, 6, Rouski Blvd., 1000 Sofia, Bulgaria) Ed. L. Levicharska. circ. 2,500.

520 GW ISSN 0067-0014
ASTRONOMISCHE GRUNDLAGEN FUER DEN KALENDER. 1949. a. DM.46. (Astronomisches Rechen-Institut) Verlag G. Braun GmbH, Karl-Friedrich-Str. 14, Postfach 1709, 7500 Karlsruhe 1, W. Germany (B.R.D.) Ed. T. Lederle. circ. 650.

520 US
ASTRONOMY THROUGH PRACTICAL INVESTIGATION. 1973. base modules plus approx. 1/yr. $0.40 per no. ‡ L. S. W. Associates, Box 82, Mattituck, NY 11952. Ed. Bd. circ. 1,000.

523.01 NO ISSN 0067-0030
ASTROPHYSICA NORVEGICA/NORWEGIAN JOURNAL OF THEORETICAL ASTROPHYSICS. (Text in English) 1950. irreg. price varies. (Universitetet i Oslo, Institutt for Teoretisk Astrofysikk) Universitetsforlaget, Kolstadgt. 1, Box 2959-Toeyen, Oslo 6, Norway (U.S. Address: Box 258, Irvington-on-Hudson, NY 10533) circ. 450. Indexed: Sci.Abstr.

520 523.01 NE ISSN 0067-0057
ASTROPHYSICS AND SPACE SCIENCE LIBRARY; a series of books on the developments of space science and of general geophysics and astrophysics published in connection with the journal Space Science Reviews. 1965. irreg. price varies. D. Reidel Publishing Co., P.O. Box 17, 3300 AA Dordrecht, Netherlands (And Lincoln Building, 160 Old Derby St., Hingham, MA 02043) Ed.Bd. Indexed: Appl.Mech.Rev.

520 SP
ASTRUM. (Text in Spanish; summaries in English and Spanish) 1966. irreg. (2-3/yr) membership. Agrupacion Astronomica de Sabadell, Cardenal Goma 1, Sabadell (Barcelona), Spain. adv. abstr. bibl. illus. stat. circ. 2,000.

523.01 NO ISSN 0373-4854
AURORAL OBSERVATORY. MAGNETIC OBSERVATIONS. (Text in English) 1932. a. free. Auroral Observatory, Box 953, 9001 Tromsoe, Norway.
Formerly (until 1965): Norske Institutt for Kosmisk Fysikk. Magnetic Observations.

523.7 BE ISSN 0524-7780
BELGIUM. INSTITUT ROYAL METEOROLOGIQUE. ANNUAIRE: RAYONNEMENT SOLAIRE/JAARBOEK: ZONNESTRALING. irreg. latest 1977. 500 Fr. Institut Royal Meteorologique, Avenue Circulaire, 3, 1180 Brussels, Belgium. circ. 182.

520 II
BHAGYAVATI PANCHANGA. (Text in Manipuri; summaries in major Indian languages) 1930. a. Rs.5. Bhagyavati Library, Sagolband Road, Meino Lane, Manipur State, Imphal 795001, India. Ed. Shri Utsam Jatra Singh. adv. circ. 5,000.

520 PL ISSN 0067-7558
BIBLIOTEKA KOPERNIKANSKA. (Text in Polish) 1970. irreg. price varies. (Towarzystwo Naukowe w Toruniu) Panstwowe Wydawnictwo Naukowe, Miodowa 10, Warsaw, Poland (Dist. by Ars Polona-Ruch, Krakowskie Przedmiescie 7, Warsaw, Poland)

520 UK ISSN 0068-130X
BRITISH ASTRONOMICAL ASSOCIATION. HANDBOOK. 1932. a. £2.50($6) British Astronomical Association, Burlington House, Piccadilly, London W1V 0NL, England. Ed. Gordon E. Taylor. adv. circ. 6,500.
Formerly: British Astronomical Association. Observer's Handbook.

529 FR ISSN 0068-4236
BUREAU INTERNATIONAL DE L'HEURE. RAPPORT ANNUEL. (Text in French or English) 1967. a. free to qualified personnel. ‡ (International Time Bureau) Observatoire de Paris, 61, Ave. de l'Observatoire, 75014 Paris, France. (Affiliate: International Astronomical Union) Dir. B. Guinot. circ. 4,800. Indexed: Astron. & Astrophys.Abstr.

CALIFORNIA INSTITUTE OF TECHNOLOGY. DIVISION OF GEOLOGICAL AND PLANETARY SCIENCES. REPORT ON GEOLOGICAL AND PLANETARY SCIENCES FOR THE YEAR. see *EARTH SCIENCES — Geology*

523.75 FR
CARTES SYNOPTIQUES DE LA CHROMOSPHERE SOLAIRE ET CATALOGUES DES FILAMENTS ET DES CENTRES D'ACTIVITE. 1919. biennial. free. Observatoire de Paris, Section d'Astrophysique de Meudon, Department Astronomie Solaire et Planetaire, 92190 Meudon, France. Ed. Mme. M. J. Martres. Indexed: Astron.Astrophys.Abstr.
Formerly: Cartes Synoptiques de la Chromosphere Solaire (ISSN 0085-4778)

ASTRONOMY

520   523.013   621.384   BL
CENTRO DE RADIO ASTRONOMIA E
ASTROFISICA MACKENZIE. OBSERVATORIA
NACIONAL. RELATORIO ANUAL. 1965. a.
free. Centro de Radio Astronomia e Astrofisica
Mackenzie, Observatorio Nacional, Rua para 277,
01243 Sao Paulo SP, Brazil. (Affiliate: Brazil.
Conselho Nacional de Desenvolvimento Cientifico e
Tecnologico) circ. 400.
  Formerly: Universidade de Mackenzie. Centro de
Radio Astronomia e Astrofisica. Relatorio Anual.

520   US   ISSN 0582-7094
CERRO TOLOLO INTERAMERICAN
OBSERVATORY (LA SERENA, CHILE).
CONTRIBUTIONS. 1959. irreg. free to qualified
personnel. ‡ Association of Universities for
Research in Astronomy, Library, Kitt Peak National
Observatory, 950 N. Cherry Ave., Box 26732,
Tucson, AZ 85726. (Affiliate: National Science
Foundation) circ. controlled. Indexed: Astron. &
Astrophys.Abstr.

520   CK   ISSN 0120-2758
COLOMBIA. OBSERVATORIO ASTRONOMICO
NACIONAL. ANUARIO. a. $1.50 or exchange.
Universidad Nacional de Colombia, Observatorio
Astronomico Nacional, Aptdo. Aereo 2584, Bogota,
Colombia.

522.1   CK   ISSN 0067-9518
COLOMBIA. OBSERVATORIO ASTRONOMICO
NACIONAL. PUBLICACIONES. (Text in Spanish
or English; summaries in Spanish and English) 1967.
irreg., no. 5, 1971. Universidad Nacional de
Colombia, Observatorio Astronomico Nacional,
Aptdo. Aereo 2584, Bogota, Colombia. circ. 500.

523.01   AT   ISSN 0069-7575
COMMONWEALTH SCIENTIFIC AND
INDUSTRIAL RESEARCH ORGANIZATION.
DIVISION OF RADIOPHYSICS. REPORT. 1952.
irreg. free. C. S. I. R. O., Division of Radiophysics,
P.O. Box 76, Epping 2121. N.S.W., Australia. Ed.
R.X. McGee. circ. 7,000.
  Formerly: Research Activities 1973.

551.6   FR   ISSN 0181-3048
CONNAISSANCE DES TEMPS. 1679. a. price
varies. Bureau des Longitudes, 77 Ave. Denfort-
Rochereau, 75014 Paris, France (Subscr. address:
E.P.S.H.O.M., B.P.426, 29275 Brest Cedex, France)
circ. 1,000.

522.1   UK   ISSN 0143-2028
COSMOS NEWSLETTER. 1977. irreg. free. Royal
Observatory, Blackford Hill, Edinburgh EH9 3HJ,
Scotland.

522.1   US
CRIMEAN ASTROPHYSICAL OBSERVATORY,
NORTH CAUCASUS. BULLETIN. 1978. irreg.
(Crimean Astrophysical Observatory, UR) Allerton
Press, Inc., 150 Fifth Ave., New York, NY 10011.

523.01   CN
DAVID DUNLAP OBSERVATORY
PUBLICATIONS. 1937. irreg. exchange basis.
David Dunlap Observatory, Richmond Hill, Ont.
L4C 4Y6, Canada.

520   629.4   NE
DEVELOPMENTS IN SOLAR SYSTEM AND
SPACE SCIENCE. 1975. irreg., vol. 4, 1979. price
varies. Elsevier Scientific Publishing Co., Box 211,
1000 AE Amsterdam, Netherlands.

DIRECTORY OF PHYSICS & ASTRONOMY
STAFF MEMBERS. see EDUCATION — Higher
Education

520   IE   ISSN 0070-7643
DUNSINK OBSERVATORY. PUBLICATIONS;
communications of the Dublin Institute for
Advanced Studies, Series C. 1960. irreg., vol. 1, no.
7, 1975. price varies. Dublin Institute for Advanced
Studies, 10 Burlington Road, Dublin 4, Ireland.

520   SZ   ISSN 0085-8420
EIDGENOESSISCHE STERNWARTE, ZURICH.
ASTRONOMISCHE MITTEILUNGEN. (Text in
German and English) 1856. irreg., no. 375, 1979.
available on exchange. ‡ Eidgenoessische
Sternwarte, Schmelzbergstr. 25, 8092 Zurich,
Switzerland. Ed. M. Waldmeier. Indexed:
Astron.&Astrophys.Abstr.

520   SZ
EIDGENOESSISCHE STERNWARTE, ZURICH.
TAETIGKEITSBERICHT. 1945. a. 3 F.($1) ‡
Eidgenoessische Sternwarte, Schmelzbergstr. 25,
8092 Zurich, Switzerland. Ed. M. Waldmeier.
Indexed: Astron.&Astropys.Abstr.

528   US   ISSN 0071-0962
EPHEMERIS OF THE SUN, POLARIS AND
OTHER SELECTED STARS WITH
COMPANION DATA AND TABLES. 1910. a. U.
S. Naval Observatory, Dept. of the Navy,
Washington, DC 20390 (Orders to: Supt. of
Documents, Washington, DC 20402)

520   FR   ISSN 0240-8376
EPIDECIDES LUNAIRES/LUNAR EPIDECIS.
1981. a. Service Hydrographique et
Oceanographique de la Marine, 3 Ave. Octave
Greard, 75200 Paris Naval, France.

520   FR   ISSN 0240-8368
EPIMENIDES/EPIMENIS. 1980. a. Service
Hydrographique et Oceanographique de la Marine,
3 Ave. Octave Greard, 75200 Paris Naval, France.

520   GW   ISSN 0531-4496
EUROPEAN SOUTHERN OBSERVATORY.
ANNUAL REPORT. French edition: European
Southern Observatory. Rapport Annuel (ISSN 0343-
4826) 1964. a. free. European Southern
Observatory, Schleissheimer Str. 17, 8046 Garching,
West Germany (B.R.D.) circ. 2,000(combined circ.)

520   FR
FRANCE. BUREAU DES LONGITUDES.
ANNUAIRE: EPHEMERIDES. Cover title:
Ephemerides. (Supplement to: Astronomie) 1967. a.
price varies. (Bureau des Longitudes) Centrale des
Revues, Gauthier-Villars, B.P. 119, 93104 Montreuil
Cedex, France. (Prepared for: Societe Astronomique
de France)
  Supersedes (since 1977): Ephemerides
Astronomiques.

551   523.01   NE
GEOPHYSICS AND ASTROPHYSICS
MONOGRAPHS; an international series of
fundamental textbooks. (Text in English) 1972.
irreg. price varies. D. Reidel Publishing Co., P.O.
Box 17, 3300 AA Dordrecht, Netherlands (And
Lincoln Building, 160 Old Derby St., Hingham, MA
02043) Ed. Billy M. McCormac. charts. illus.

GRADUATE PROGRAMS: PHYSICS,
ASTRONOMY, AND RELATED FIELDS. see
PHYSICS

520   UK   ISSN 0080-4371
GREAT BRITAIN. ROYAL GREENWICH
OBSERVATORY. ANNALS. 1960. irreg. price
varies. ‡ (Science Research Council) Royal
Greenwich Observatory, Herstmonceux Castle,
Hailsham, East Sussex BN27 1RP, England. circ.
300-400.

520   GR   ISSN 0072-7385
GREEK NATIONAL COMMITTEE FOR
ASTRONOMY. ANNUAL REPORTS OF THE
ASTRONOMICAL INSTITUTES OF GREECE.
(Text in English) 1960. a. available on exchange.
Greek National Committee for Astronomy,
Academy of Athens, 14 Anagnostopolou St., Athens
136, Greece.

523.51   US
HANDBOOK OF ELEMENTAL ABUNDANCES
IN METEORITES SERIES:
EXTRATERRESTRIAL CHEMISTRY. 1971. irreg.
$50.50 per no. Gordon and Breach Science
Publishers, 1 Park Ave, New York, NY 10016.

520   551.5   AU
HOERBIGER INSTITUT. MITTEILUNGEN. 1971.
a. (Hoerbiger Institut) Emmerich Selinger, Ed. &
Pub., Postfach 24, A-1234 Vienna, Austria. bk. rev.
charts. illus. circ. 1,000.

528   II
INDIAN ASTRONOMICAL EPHEMERIS. 1958. a.
Rs.25. Meteorological Department, Lodi Rd., New
Delhi 110003, India (Subscr. to: Controller of
Publications, Government of India, Civil Lines,
Delhi 110054, India) index. circ. 800.
  Formerly: Indian Ephemeris and Nautical
Almanac (ISSN 0537-1546)

520   551   BE
INSTITUT D'ASTRONOMIE ET DE
GEOPHYSIQUE GEORGES LEMAITRE.
PUBLICATIONS. (Text in English or French)
1966/67. irreg. Institut d'Astronomie et de
Geophysique Georges Lemaitre, Louvain, Belgium.
illus.

520   MX   ISSN 0303-7584
INSTITUTO DE TONANTZINTLA. BOLETIN.
(Text in English; summaries in Spanish.) 1973. irreg.
Instituto de Tonantzintla, Apartados Postales Nos.
216 y 51, Puebla, Mexico. illus. Indexed:
Chem.Abstr.
  Supersedes: Mexico (City). Universidad Nacional.
Observatorio Astronomico, Tacubaya. Boletin de los
Observatorios Tonantzintla y Tacubaya (ISSN 0539-
6387)

528.6   SP   ISSN 0080-5971
INSTITUTO Y OBSERVATORIO DE MARINA.
EFEMERIDES ASTRONOMICAS. 1971. a; no.
185, 1975. Instituto y Observatorio de Marina, San
Fernando (Cadiz), Spain. circ. 350.

520   NE
INTERNATIONAL ASTRONOMICAL UNION.
GENERAL ASSEMBLY. PROCEEDINGS. irreg.,
16th, 1976, Grenoble. price varies. D. Reidel
Publishing Co., Box 17, 3300 AA Dordrecht,
Netherlands (And Lincoln Building, 160 Old Derby
St., Hingham, MA 02043)

520   NE   ISSN 0074-1809
INTERNATIONAL ASTRONOMICAL UNION.
PROCEEDINGS OF SYMPOSIA. 1955. irreg.,
75th, 1976, Geneva. price varies. D. Reidel
Publishing Co., P.O. Box 17, 3300 AA Dordrecht,
Netherlands (And Lincoln Building, 160 Old Derby
St., Hingham, MA 02043)

520   NE   ISSN 0080-1372
INTERNATIONAL ASTRONOMICAL UNION.
TRANSACTIONS AND HIGHLIGHTS. (Issued in
two parts: Part A: Reports, Part B: Proceedings)
1922. triennial, 15th, 1973, Sydney. price varies. D.
Reidel Publishing Co., P.O. Box 17, 3300 AA
Dordrecht, Netherlands (And Lincoln Building, 160
Old Derby St., Hingham, MA 02043)
  Incorporating: Reports on Astronomy.

525.3   551   JA   ISSN 0074-7432
INTERNATIONAL POLAR MOTION SERVICE.
ANNUAL REPORT/KOKUSAI KYOKU-UNDO
KANSOKU JIGYO NENPO. (Text in English)
1964. a. available on exchange or request. ‡
International Polar Motion Service, Central Bureau
- Kokusai Kyoku-Undo Kansoku Jigyo Chuo-Kyoku,
International Latitude Observatory, Mizusawa 023,
Japan. (Affiliate: Federation of Astronomical and
Geophysical Services) Ed. S. Yumi. circ. 400
(approx.) (also avail. in microform)

INTERSCIENCE MONOGRAPHS AND TEXTS IN
PHYSICS AND ASTRONOMY. see PHYSICS

INTERSCIENCE TRACTS ON PHYSICS AND
ASTRONOMY. see PHYSICS

523.01   US   ISSN 0449-1343
J I L A INFORMATION CENTER. REPORT. irreg.
Joint Institute for Laboratory Astrophysics,
University of Colorado, Boulder, CO 80309.
Indexed: Chem. Abstr.

520   KO
KOREAN ASTRONOMICAL SOCIETY.
JOURNAL. (Text in English and Korean;
Summaries in English) 1967. a. 5000 Won($10)
(free to members) Korean Astronomical Society, c/o
National Astronomical Observatory, Yoksam-Dong,
Kangnam-Ku, Seoul 134-03, S. Korea. circ. 500.

520   US   ISSN 0075-7896
LANDOLT-BOERNSTEIN, ZAHLENWERTE UND
FUNKTIONEN AUS
NATURWISSENSCHAFTEN UND TECHNIK.
NEUE SERIE. GROUP 6: ASTRONOMY. 1965.
irreg., vol. 2, 1981. Springer-Verlag, 175 Fifth Ave.,
New York, NY 10010 (also Berlin, Heidelberg,
Vienna) (reprint service avail. from ISI)

ASTRONOMY

520   US   ISSN 0075-9325
LICK OBSERVATORY. PUBLICATIONS. (At head of title: University of California) 1892. irreg., vol. 22, 1967; latest 1975. price varies. Lick Observatory, Library, University of California, Santa Cruz, Santa Cruz, CA 95064. Indexed: Astron. & Astrophys.Abstr.

520   US
MONOGRAPHS ON ASTRONOMICAL SUBJECTS. irreg. price varies. Oxford University Press, 200 Madison Ave., New York, NY 10016 (And Ely House, 37 Dover St., London W1X 4AH, England) Ed. A. J. Meadows.

MOZAMBIQUE. SERVICO METEOROLOGICO. INFORMACOES DE CARACTER ASTRONOMICO. see EARTH SCIENCES — Geophysics

528   UK   ISSN 0077-619X
NAUTICAL ALMANAC. 1767. a. price varies. H.M. Nautical Almanac Office, Herstmonceux Castle, Hailsham, Sussex BN27 1RP, England (Avail. from H.M.S.O., c/o Liaison Officer, Atlantic House, Holborn Viaduct, London EC1P 1BN, England) (Co-sponsor: U.S. Naval Observatory, Washington, D.C.)

520   GE
NAUTISCHES JAHRBUCH. 1950. a. M.24. Seehydrographischer Dienst, Dierkower Damm 45, 25 Rostock 1, E. Germany (D.D.R.) (Subscr. to: Buchexport, Leninstr. 16, Leipzig, E. Germany) circ. 1,500.

528.3   GW   ISSN 0077-6211
NAUTISCHES JAHRBUCH, ODER EPHEMERIDEN UND TAFELN. a. DM.24. Deutsches Hydrographisches Institut, Bernhard-Nocht-Str. 78, 2000 Hamburg 4, W. Germany (B.R.D.) circ. 5,200.

520   GW   ISSN 0078-2246
NOVA KEPLERIANA. NEUE FOLGE. (Subseries of: Bayerische Akademie der Wissenschaften. Mathematisch-Naturwissenschaftliche Klasse. Abhandlungen. Neue Folge) (Text in German; summaries partly in English) 1969. irreg., no. 6, 1976. price varies. (Kepler-Kommission) C. H. Beck'sche Verlagsbuchhandlung, Wilhelmstr. 9, 8000 Munich 40, W. Germany (B.R.D.)

520   AE   ISSN 0065-6232
OBSERVATOIRE ASTRONOMIQUE D'ALGER. ANNALES. Variant title: Universite d'Alger. Observatoire Astronomique. Annales. irreg., no. 5, 1979. Universite d'Alger, Observatoire Astronomique, Bouzareah, Algeria.

520   SZ   ISSN 0085-0942
OBSERVATOIRE DE GENEVE. PUBLICATIONS. SERIE A. (Text in French and English) 1928. irreg. (approx. a) 5 Fr. Observatoire de Geneve, CH-1290 Sauverny, Switzerland. Indexed: Bull.Signal. Astron.&Astrophys.Abstr.

520   SZ   ISSN 0435-2939
OBSERVATOIRE DE GENEVE. PUBLICATIONS. SERIE B. (Text in English and French) 1967. irreg. price varies. Observatoire de Geneve, CH-1290 Sauverny, Switzerland. Indexed: Bull.Signal. Astron. & Astrophys.Abstr.

520   FR   ISSN 0081-590X
OBSERVATOIRE DE STRASBOURG. PUBLICATION. 1968. irreg. price varies. Observatoire de Strasbourg, 11 rue de l'Universite, 67000 Strasbourg, France. circ. 500.

522.1   SP
OBSERVATORIO ASTRONOMICO DE MADRID. ANUARIO. 1860; n. s. 1907. a. 250 ptas. Observatorio Astronomico Nacional, Alfonso XII No. 3, Madrid 7, Spain.

520   AG   ISSN 0302-2277
OBSERVATORIO ASTRONOMICO MUNICIPAL DE ROSARIO. BOLETIN. (Text in Spanish; summaries in English) irreg. Observatorio Astronomico Municipal de Rosario, Parque Urquiza, Rosario, Argentina. illus.

522.1   BL
OBSERVATORIO NACIONAL RIO DE JANEIRO. EFEMERIDES ASTRONOMICAS. 1885. a. Cr.$100. Observatorio Nacional, Rua General Bruce, 586, Sao Cristovao, Rio de Janeiro, G.B., Brazil.
Formerly (until 1977): Observatorio Nacional Rio de Janeiro. Anuario.

520   551   BL
OBSERVATORIO NACIONAL RIO DE JANEIRO. PUBLICACOES. (Text in English, French, Portuguese) 1977. irreg. free. Observatorio Nacional, Rue General Bruce 586, Sao Cristovao, Rio de Janeiro, Brazil.

522   RM   ISSN 0068-3086
OBSERVATORUL ASTRONOMIC DIN BUCURESTI. ANUARUL. 1940. a. Editura Academiei Republicii Socialiste Romania, Calea Victoriei 125, Bucharest, Romania (Subscr. to: ILEXIM, Str. 13 Decembrie Nr. 3, P.O. Box 136-137, Bucharest, Romania) Ed. C. Dramba. circ. 900. Indexed: Bull.Signal. Ref.Zh. Astron.&Astrophys.Abstr.

520   RM   ISSN 0068-3094
OBSERVATORUL ASTRONOMIC DIN BUCURESTI. OBSERVATIONS SOLAIRES. (Text in French) 1956. a. Editura Academiei Republicii Socialiste Romania, Calea Victoriei 125, Bucharest, Romania (Subscr. to: ILEXIM, Str. 13 Decembrie Nr. 3, P.O. Box 136-137, Bucharest, Romania) Ed. Calin Popovici. bk. rev. circ. 500. Indexed: Bull.Signal. Ref.Zh. Astron.&Astrophys.Abstr.

520   PL   ISSN 0075-7047
OBSERWATORIUM KRAKOWSKI. ROCZNIK ASTRONOMICZNY. DODATEK MIEDZYNARODOWY. (Text in English, Polish and Russian) 1922. irreg., vol. 73, no. 44. price varies. (Polska Akademia Nauk, Komitet Astronomii) Panstwowe Wydawnictwo Naukowe, Ul. Miodowa 10, Warsaw, Poland (Dist. by Ars Polona-Ruch, Krakowskie Przedmiescie 7, Warsaw Poland) Ed. Karol Koziel.

523   SP
OCULTACIONES DE ESTRELLAS POR LA LUNA. 1964. irreg. 1973. no. 39. Instituto y Observatorio de Marina, San Fernando, Cadiz, Spain.

520   AT   ISSN 0079-1067
PERTH OBSERVATORY. COMMUNICATIONS. 1964. irreg., no. 3, 1977. exchange basis. ‡ Perth Observatory, Bickley, W.A. 6076, Australia. circ. 200. Indexed: Astron. & Astrophys.Abstr.

520   PH   ISSN 0115-1207
PHILIPPINE ASTRONOMICAL HANDBOOK. (Text in English) 1950. a. P.5($1) Philippine Atmospheric, Geophysical and Astronomical Services Administration, Box 2277, Manila, Philippines.

522   PH   ISSN 0115-3307
PHILIPPINES. ATMOSPHERE, GEOPHYSICAL AND ASTRONOMICAL SERVICES ADMINISTRATION. TABLE OF SUNRISE, SUNSET, TWILIGHT, MOONRISE AND MOONSET. (Text in English) a. P.5($1) Philippine Atmospheric, Geophysical and Astronomical Services Administration, Box 2277, Manila, Philippines. circ. 300.

PHYSICS AND CHEMISTRY IN SPACE. see CHEMISTRY

520   CS
PRACE ASTRONOMICKEHO OBSERVATORIA NA SKALNATOM PLESE/ACTIVITIES OF THE ASTRONOMICAL OBSERVATORY ON SKALNATE PLESO. (Text in English; summaries in Russian and Slovak) irreg, vol. 8, 1977. price varies. (Slovenska Akademia Vied) Veda, Publishing House of the Slovak Academy of Sciences, Klemensova 19, 895 30 Bratislava, Czechoslovakia.

520   BE   ISSN 0072-4432
RIJKSUNIVERSITEIT TE GENT. STERREKUNDIG OBSERVATORIUM. MEDEDELINGEN: ASTRONOMIE. (Text and summaries in Dutch, English or French) 1939. irreg. free. Rijksuniversiteit te Gent, Sterrekundig Observatorium, Krijgslaan 271, B-9000 Ghent, Belgium.

523   SP
ROTACION DE LA TIERRA. 1970. a. Instituto y Observatorio de Marina, San Fernando, Cadiz, Spain.

522   CN   ISSN 0080-4193
ROYAL ASTRONOMICAL SOCIETY OF CANADA. OBSERVER'S HANDBOOK. 1908. a. Can.$5. Royal Astronomical Society of Canada, 124 Merton St., Toronto, Ont. M4S 2Z2, Canada. Ed. Dr. Roy L. Bishop. index. circ. 16,000.

520   UK   ISSN 0308-5074
ROYAL GREENWICH OBSERVATORY BULLETINS. 1956. irreg.(approx. 3/yr.) price varies. Royal Greenwich Observatory, Herstmonceux Castle, Hailsham, Sussex BN71 1RP, England. (Co-sponsor: Science Research Council) circ. 500-700.

522.1   UK   ISSN 0309-0108
ROYAL OBSERVATORY, EDINBURGH. ANNUAL REPORT. 1974/75. a. exchange basis. Royal Observatory, Blackford Hill, Edinburgh EH9 3HJ, Scotland.

522.1   UK   ISSN 0142-8977
ROYAL OBSERVATORY, EDINBURGH. COMMUNICATIONS. 1949. irreg. exchange basis. Royal Observatory, Blackford Hill, Edinburgh EH9 3HJ, Scotland.

522.1   UK   ISSN 0309-099X
ROYAL OBSERVATORY, EDINBURGH. OCCASIONAL REPORTS. 1976. irreg. exchange basis. Royal Observatory, Blackford Hill, Edinburgh EH9 3HJ, Scotland.

522.1   UK   ISSN 0305-2001
ROYAL OBSERVATORY, EDINBURGH. PUBLICATIONS. 1939. irreg. exchange basis. Royal Observatory, Blackford Hill, Edinburgh EH9 3HJ, Scotland.

523.01   US   ISSN 0085-1965
S T P NOTES. 1968. irreg., approx. 2/yr. International Council of Scientific Unions, Inter-Union Commission of Solar Terrestrial Physics, c/o National Academy of Sciences, 2101 Constitution Ave. N.W., Washington, DC 20418.
Solar physics

520   551.9   US
SERIES ON EXTRATERRESTRIAL CHEMISTRY. 1971. irreg. price varies. Gordon and Breach Science Publishers, 1 Park Ave., New York, NY 10016.

523.01   US   ISSN 0081-0231
SMITHSONIAN CONTRIBUTIONS TO ASTROPHYSICS. 1956. irreg., no. 17, 1974. Smithsonian Institution Press, Washington, DC 20560. Ed. George B. Field. circ. 1,500-2,000. (reprint service avail. from UMI)

520   US   ISSN 0081-0304
SMITHSONIAN INSTITUTION. ASTROPHYSICAL OBSERVATORY. CENTRAL BUREAU FOR ASTRONOMICAL TELEGRAMS. CIRCULAR. 1922. irreg., no. 3437, 1979. price varies. Smithsonian Institution Astrophysical Observatory, 60 Garden St., Cambridge, MA 02138. (Co-sponsor: International Astronomical Union) Ed. B. G. Marsden.

523.01   US   ISSN 0081-0320
SMITHSONIAN INSTITUTION. ASTROPHYSICAL OBSERVATORY. S A O SPECIAL REPORT. (Title varies slightly) (Text in English; summaries in Russian, English, French) 1957. irreg. free. Smithsonian Institution Astrophysical Observatory, 60 Garden St., Cambridge, MA 02138. Ed. George B. Field. cum.index: 1957-1959.

520   FR   ISSN 0081-0738
SOCIETE ASTRONOMIQUE DE BORDEAUX. BULLETIN.* 1961-62. a. price varies. Societe Astronomique de Bordeaux, Hotel des Societes Savantes, 71 rue du Loup, Bordeaux, France.

520 US ISSN 0147-2003
SOUTHWEST REGIONAL CONFERENCE FOR ASTRONOMY AND ASTROPHYSICS. PROCEEDINGS. 1975. a. $7. Southwest Regional Conference for Astronomy and Astrophysics, Department of Physics, Texas Tech University, Lubbock, TX 79409. Eds. Preston F. Gott, Paul S. Riherd. circ. 500. (also avail. in microfiche) Key Title: Proceedings of the Southwest Regional Conference for Astronomy and Astrophysics.

522.19 VC ISSN 0081-3575
SPECOLA ASTRONOMICA VATICANA, CASTEL GANDOLFO, ITALY. ANNUAL REPORT. (Text in English, German, Italian) 1963. a. price varies. ‡ Specola Vaticana, Vatican City. index. circ. 500. Indexed: Astron.&Astrophys.Abstr.

522.1 VC ISSN 0081-3583
SPECOLA ASTRONOMICA VATICANA, CASTEL GANDOLFO, ITALY. MISCELLANEA ASTRONOMICA. (Text in English) 1920. irreg. avail. on exchange basis. ‡ Specola Vaticana, Vatican City. index. circ. 500. Indexed: Astron.&Astrophys.Abstr.

522.1 VC ISSN 0081-3591
SPECOLA ASTRONOMICA VATICANA, CASTEL GANDOLFO, ITALY. RICERCHE ASTRONOMICHE. (Text in English, German, Italian) 1939. irreg. price varies. ‡ Specola Vaticana, Vatican City. cum.index. circ. 500. Indexed: Astron.&Astrophys.Abstr.

522.1 VC ISSN 0081-3605
SPECOLA ASTRONOMICA VATICANA, CASTEL GANDOLFO, ITALY. RICERCHE SPETTROSCOPICHE. (Text in German, English) 1938. irreg. avail. on exchange basis. ‡ Specola Vaticana, Laboratorio Astrofisico, Vatican City. cum.index. circ. 500. Indexed: Chem.Abstr. Curr.Pap.Phys.

528 UK ISSN 0081-4377
STAR ALMANAC FOR LAND SURVEYORS. 1951. a. price varies. H.M. Nautical Almanac Office, Herstmonceux Castle, Hailsham, Sussex BN27 1RP, England (Avail. from: H.M.S.O., c/o Liaison Officer, Atlantic House, London EC1P 1BW, England)

520 PL ISSN 0081-6701
STUDIA COPERNICANA. (Text in English, French, German) 1970. irreg., vol. 19, 1979. $8.15. (Polska Akademia Nauk, Instytut Historii Nauki, Oswiaty i Techniki) Ossolineum, Publishing House of the Polish Academy of Sciences, Rynek 9, Wroclaw, Poland (Dist. by: Ars Polona-Ruch, Krakowskie Przedmiescie 7, Warsaw Poland) Ed. Pawel Czartoryski. illus.

520 PL ISSN 0082-5573
STUDIA SOCIETATIS SCIENTIARUM TORUNENSIS. SECTIO F. (ASTRONOMIA) (Text in English; summaries in Polish) 1956. irreg., 1976, vol. 5, no. 6. price varies. (Towarzystwo Naukowe w Toruniu) Panstwowe Wydawnictwo Naukowe, Miodowa 10, Warsaw, Poland. Ed. Cecylia Iwaniszewska. charts. illus. index. circ. 650.

529 US
STUDY OF TIME. Represents: International Society for the Study of Time. Conference. Proceedings. (Text in English or German) 1971. irreg.; 3rd, Alpbach, 1978. price varies. Springer-Verlag, 175 Fifth Ave., New York, NY 10010 (Also Berlin, Heidelberg, Vienna) Eds. J.T. Fraser, F.C. Haber, G.H. Mueller. bibl. illus. (reprint service avail. from ISI)

520 SZ
SWISS FEDERAL OBSERVATORY, ZURICH. PUBLICATIONS. 1894 (German edt.); 1966 (English edt.) a. 10 Fr. Eidgenoessische Sternwarte, Schmelzberg Str. 25, 8092 Zurich, Switzerland. Ed. M. Waldmeier.

520 AT ISSN 0085-7009
SYDNEY OBSERVATORY PAPERS. 1946. irreg. exchange basis. ‡ Sydney Observatory, c/o Government Astronomer, Observatory Park, Sydney 2000, Australia. Ed. W. H. Robertson. circ. 300. Indexed: Astron.&Astrophys.Abstr.

520 GW
TECHNISCHE UNIVERSITAET HANNOVER. ASTRONOMISCHE STATION. (VEROEFFENTLICHUNGEN) 1958. irreg. price varies. Technische Universitaet Hannover, Institut fuer Theoretische Geodaesie, Nienburger Str. 5, 3000 Hannover 1, W. Germany (B.R.D.) circ. 150. Indexed: Astron.& Astrophys.Abstr.

529 IT
TIME SERVICE. (Text in English) 1972. a. free. Osservatorio Astronomico di Torino, 10025 Pino Torinese (Turin), Italy. charts. stat. index. Indexed: Astron. & Astrophys. Abstr.

520 JA ISSN 0082-4690
TOKYO ASTRONOMICAL BULLETIN. SECOND SERIES. (Text in English and German) 1947. irreg. available on exchange. Tokyo Astronomical Observatory - Tokyo Tenmondai, University of Tokyo, 2-21-1 Osawa, Mitaka, Tokyo 181, Japan.

520 JA ISSN 0082-4704
TOKYO ASTRONOMICAL OBSERVATORY. ANNALS. SECOND SERIES. (Text in English and German) 1937. irreg. available on exchange. Tokyo Astronomical Observatory - Tokyo Tenmondai, University of Tokyo, 2-21-1 Osawa, Mitaka, Tokyo 181, Japan.

520 JA
TOKYO ASTRONOMICAL OBSERVATORY. REPORT. (Text in Japanese) 1932. irreg. available on exchange basis only. Tokyo Astronomical Observatory - Tokyo Tenmondai, University of Tokyo, 2-21-1 Osawa, Mitaka, Tokyo 181, Japan.

520 JA ISSN 0082-4712
TOKYO ASTRONOMICAL OBSERVATORY. REPRINTS. (Text in English and German) 1938. irreg. available on exchange. Tokyo Astronomical Observatory - Tokyo Tenmondai, University of Tokyo, 2-21-1 Osawa, Mitaka, Tokyo 181, Japan.

TOPICS IN ASTROPHYSICS AND SPACE PHYSICS. see AERONAUTICS AND SPACE FLIGHT

520 UK ISSN 0143-0599
U. K. I. R. T. NEWSLETTER. (United Kingdom Infrared Telescope) 1979. irreg., no. 3, 1980. free. Royal Observatory, Blackford Hill, Edinburgh EH9 3HJ, Scotland. Ed. Dr. P.M. Williams. circ. 300. (back issues avail.)

520 UK ISSN 0260-9983
U. K. I. R. T. REPORT. (United Kingdom Infrared Telescope) 1978. irreg., no. 16, 1980. exchange basis. Royal Observatory, Blackford Hill, Edinburgh EH9 3HJ, Scotland.

520 UK ISSN 0143-053X
U K S T U NEWSLETTER. (United Kingdom Schmidt Telescope Unit) 1978. irreg., no. 2, 1979. free. Royal Observatory, Blackford Hill, Edinburgh 4H9 3HJ, Scotland. Ed. Dr. T.G. Hawarden. circ. 300. (back issues avail.)

522.1 US
U.S.S.R. SPECIAL ASTROPHYSICAL OBSERVATORY BULLETIN. 1978. irreg. (UR) Allerton Press, Inc., 150 Fifth Ave., New York, NY 10011.

528 US ISSN 0083-243X
U. S. NAVAL OBSERVATORY. ASTRONOMICAL PAPERS PREPARED FOR USE OF AMERICAN EPHEMERIS AND NAUTICAL ALMANAC. 1882. irreg., vol. 22, 1976. price varies. U. S. Naval Observatory, Washington, DC 20390. index.

520 US ISSN 0083-2448
U. S. NAVAL OBSERVATORY. PUBLICATIONS. SECOND SERIES. irreg. available only on exchange. U. S. Naval Observatory, Department of the Navy, Washington, DC 20390.

520 CL ISSN 0069-3553
UNIVERSIDAD DE CHILE. DEPARTAMENTO DE ASTRONOMIA. PUBLICACIONES. (Text and summaries in Spanish and English) 1967. irreg. free or exchange. ‡ (Universidad de Chile, Departamento de Astronomia) Editorial Universitaria, Av. Maria Luisa Santander 0447, Santiago 9, Chile. Ed. Hugo Moreno. circ. 700. Indexed: Bull.Signal. Astron. & Astrophys. Abstr.

520 BL
UNIVERSIDADE DE SAO PAULO. INSTITUTO ASTRONOMICO E GEOFISICO. ANUARIO ASTRONOMICO. 1930-38; N.S. 1953; N.S. 1974. a. Cr.$130. ‡ Universidade de Sao Paulo, Instituto Astronomico e Geofisico, Caixa Postal 30627, 01000 Sao Paulo, Brazil. Ed. Paulo Benevides Soares. circ. 1,000. Indexed: Bull.Signal. Ref.Zh. Astron. & Astrophys.Abstr.
Formerly: Sao Paulo, Brazil (State) Observatorio. Anuario Astronomico (ISSN 0080-6412)

UNIVERSIDADE DE SAO PAULO. INSTITUTO DE GEOCIENCIAS. BOLETIM. see EARTH SCIENCES

520 IT ISSN 0067-9895
UNIVERSITA DEGLI STUDI DI BOLOGNA. OSSERVATORIO ASTRONOMICO. PUBBLICAZIONI. (Text in Italian and English) 1921. irreg., 1970, vol. 10, no. 7. free to qualified personnel. Universita degli Studi di Bologna, Osservatorio Astronomico, Bologna, Italy. annual index. circ. controlled.

520 GW ISSN 0077-1929
UNIVERSITAET MUENSTER. ASTRONOMISCHES INSTITUT. MITTEILUNGEN. (Text in German; summaries in English) 1951. irreg. free on exchange. Universitaet Muenster, Astronomisches Institut, Domagkstr./Corrensstr., 4400 Muenster, W. Germany (B.R.D.) Indexed: Astron.Jahresber. Astron. & Astrophys.Abstr.

520 GW ISSN 0077-1937
UNIVERSITAET MUENSTER. ASTRONOMISCHES INSTITUT. SONDERDRUCKE. (Text in German; summaries in English) 1971. irreg. free on exchange. Universitaet Muenster, Astronomisches Institut, Domagkstr./Correnstr., 4400 Muenster, W. Germany (B.R.D.) Indexed: Astron.Jahresber. Astron. & Astrophys.Abstr.

520 GW ISSN 0342-4030
UNIVERSITAETSSTERNWARTE ZU WIEN. ANNALEN. (Text in German; summaries in English) 1884. irreg. price varies. (AU) Ferd. Duemmlers Verlag, Postfach 1480-Kaiserstr. 31-37, D-5300 Bonn 1, W. Germany (B.R.D.) Ed. I. Meurers.

520 YU ISSN 0350-3283
UNIVERSITY OF BEOGRAD. FACULTY OF SCIENCES. DEPARTMENT OF ASTRONOMY. PUBLICATIONS. (Text and summaries in English and Russian) 1969. a. free. Univerzitet u Beogradu, Prirodno-Matematicki Fakultet, Katedra za Astronomiju, Studentski trg 16, 11000 Belgrade, Yugoslavia. Ed. Branislav Sevarlic. bibl. charts. illus. circ. 500.

UNIVERSITY OF BRITISH COLUMBIA. DEPARTMENT OF GEOPHYSICS AND ASTRONOMY. ANNUAL REPORT. see EARTH SCIENCES — Geophysics

520 US ISSN 0076-8421
UNIVERSITY OF MICHIGAN OBSERVATORIES. PUBLICATIONS. 1859. irreg., latest, vol. 12, no. 1, 1972. exchange basis. University of Michigan Observatories, Department of Astronomy, Dennison Bldg., Ann Arbor, MI 48109. index. circ. 600.

523.51 US ISSN 0085-3968
UNIVERSITY OF NEW MEXICO. INSTITUTE OF METEORITICS. SPECIAL PUBLICATION. 1970. irreg., 2-3/yr. $5 per no. University of New Mexico, Department of Geology, Institute of Meteoritics, Albuquerque, NM 87131. Ed. Klaus Keil. circ. 1,000. (back issues avail.)

520 US ISSN 0082-3546
UNIVERSITY OF TEXAS MONOGRAPHS IN ASTRONOMY. 1964. irreg., no. 2, 1976. price varies. University of Texas Press, Box 7819, Austin, TX 78712. (reprint service avail. from UMI)

520 US
UNIVERSITY OF TEXAS PUBLICATIONS IN ASTRONOMY. 1969. irreg., no. 10, 1977. price varies. University of Texas at Austin, Department of Astronomy, Physics-Math-Astronomy Bldg, Room 15.212, Austin, TX 78712.

520 CN ISSN 0070-2927
UNIVERSITY OF TORONTO. DAVID DUNLAP OBERVATORY. PUBLICATIONS. 1937. irreg. exchange basis. University of Toronto, David Dunlap Observatory, Richmond Hill, Ontario L4C 4Y6, Canada. illus. circ. 400.

522.1 VC ISSN 0083-5293
VATICAN OBSERVATORY PUBLICATIONS. (Text in English) 1970. irreg. avail on exchange basis. ‡ Specola Vaticana, Vatican City. cum.index in prep. circ. 500. Indexed: Astron. & Astrophys.Abstr.

520 GW ISSN 0340-9821
VEROEFFENTLICHUNGEN DER ASTRONOMISCHEN INSTITUTE DER UNIVERITAET BONN. (Text in German; Summaries in English) 1930. irreg. price varies. (Astronomische Institute der Universitaet Bonn-Sternwarte) Ferd. Duemmlers Verlag, Kaiserstr. 31, D-5300 Bonn 1, W. Germany (B.R.D.)

523.01 CN ISSN 0078-6950
VICTORIA, BRITISH COLUMBIA. DOMINION ASTROPHYSICAL OBSERVATORY. PUBLICATIONS.* 1913. irreg. free. Dominion Astrophysical Observatory, Observatories Branch, Victoria, B.C., Canada.

520 US ISSN 0084-3660
YEARBOOK OF ASTRONOMY. 1965. a. $6.50. W. W. Norton & Company, Inc., 500 Fifth Ave., New York, NY 10036. Ed. Patrick Moore. charts. illus. index.

ASTRONOMY — Abstracting, Bibliographies, Statistics

ASTRONOMY AND ASTROPHYSICS ABSTRACTS. see *PHYSICS — Abstracting, Bibliographies, Statistics*

U S S R REPORT: GEOPHYSICS, ASTRONOMY, AND SPACE. see *EARTH SCIENCES — Abstracting, Bibliographies, Statistics*

AUTOMOBILES

see *Transportation — Automobiles*

BAKERS AND CONFECTIONERS

see *Food and Food Industries — Bakers and Confectioners*

BALL GAMES

see *Sports and Games — Ball Games*

BANKING AND FINANCE

see *Business and Economics — Banking and Finance*

BEAUTY CULTURE

see also *Beauty Culture — Perfumes and Cosmetics*

646.724 FR
ANNUAIRE DES COIFFEURS, DES ESTHETICIENS ET DES PARFUMEURS. a. Societe Francaise d'Edition d'Informations Professionnelles et de Publicite, 1 rue de l'Atalaye, 64200 Biarritz, France. adv.

343.794 US ISSN 0094-4327
CALIFORNIA. STATE BOARD OF COSMETOLOGY. RULES AND REGULATIONS. irreg. $1. State Board of Cosmetology, 1020 N St, Sacramento, CA 95814. Key Title: Rules and Regulations - Board of Cosmetology (Sacramento)

646.7 US
CONFIDENTIAL BEAUTY & BARBER BUYING GUIDE. a. Service Publications, Inc., 100 Park Ave., New York, NY 10017. adv. circ. 2,000.

646.7 UK
INSTITUTE OF ELECTROLYSIS. LIST OF QUALIFIED OPERATORS. 1962. a. Institute of Electrolysis, 251 Seymour Grove, Manchester M16 ODS, Lancs, England.

646 US
MCCALL'S BEAUTY GUIDE. 1979. a. $1.75. McCall Publishing Co., 230 Park Ave., New York, NY 10017.

646.7 US
MODERN STYLES AND HOW-TO'S. 1960. a. Vance Publishing Corporation (Chicago), 300 W. Adams St., Chicago, IL 60606. Ed. Violet Nelson. adv. circ. 110,000.
 Formerly: Modern's How-to Book.

646.7 US ISSN 0544-7178
MODERN'S MARKET GUIDE. 1966. a. $20. Vance Publishing Corporation (Chicago), 300 W. Adams St., Chicago, IL 60606. adv. circ. 6,700.

613 US
PLAYGIRL HEALTH AND BEAUTY GUIDE. 1978. a. $1.95. Playgirl, Inc., 3420ocean Park Blvd., Suite 3000, Santa Monica, CA 90405. adv. circ. 250,000.

646 613 US ISSN 0161-2190
VOGUE BEAUTY & HEALTH GUIDE. 1973. s-a. $2.50 per no. Conde Nast Publications Inc., 350 Madison Ave., New York, NY 10017. adv. illus. (reprint service avail. from UMI)

BEAUTY CULTURE — Perfumes And Cosmetics

646.7 CN ISSN 0084-9324
COSMETICS HANDBOOK/GUIDE DES COSMETIQUES. 1966. a. Can.$3. Drug Merchandising, c/o Robert D. Reid, 481 University Ave., Toronto 2, Ont., Canada. Ed. W.E. Granger. adv. bk. rev. circ. 10,000.

688.54 FR ISSN 0070-475X
DICTIONNAIRE DES PARFUMS DE FRANCE ET DES LIGNES POUR HOMMES. 1964. biennial. (Societe Sebastien Thomas) Editions Sebastien Thomas, 95 Bd. Magenta, Paris 10e, France.

668.55 FR
DICTIONNAIRE DES PRODUITS DE SOINS DE BEAUTE. 1968. biennial. 40 F. (Societe Sebastien Thomas) Editions Sebastien Thomas, 95 Bd. Magenta, Paris 10e, France.
 Formerly: Dictionnaire des Produits de Beaute et de Cosmetologie (ISSN 0070-4768)

615 US ISSN 0417-6383
DIRECTORY OF PROFESSIONAL ELECTROLOGISTS; geographically classified guide to permanent hair removal services. 1956. a. $1.50 (free to qualified personnel) Gordon Blackwell, 30 E. 40 St., New York, NY 10016.

GUIDE DE LA PARFUMERIE. see *BUSINESS AND ECONOMICS — Trade And Industrial Directories*

668.54 668.55 SP
N C P DOCUMENTA. (Noticias de Cosmetica y de Perfumeria) 1977. m. 600 ptas.($8) (or membership) (Sociedad Espanola de Quimicos Cosmeticos) Romargraf S.A., Juventud 55, Hospitalet del Llobregat, Barcelona, Spain. Ed. Bd. charts.

668.5 FR
PARFUMS-BEAUTE. 1978. a. 110 F. Editions Louis Johanet, 68 rue Boursault, 75017 Paris, France.

BEVERAGES

see also *Food and Food Industries; Packaging*

663.2 658.8 IT
AGENDA VINICOLA & DELLE INDUSTRIE ALIMENTARI. 1957? a. Luigi Scialpi Editore, s.r.l., Via Ugo de Carolis 31, 00136 Rome, Italy. adv. circ. 4,000.
 Wine

663.2 US ISSN 0149-6778
AMERICAN WINE SOCIETY. BULLETIN. 1973. irreg. $1. American Wine Society, 4218 Rosewold, Royal Oak, MI 48073. circ. 3,000. (back issues avail.)

663.2 US ISSN 0149-676X
AMERICAN WINE SOCIETY MANUAL. irreg. $2.50. American Wine Society, 4218 Rosewold, Royal Oak, MI 48073. (back issues avail.)

663 FR ISSN 0066-2763
ANNUAIRE DES BOISSONS ET DES LIQUIDES ALIMENTAIRES/JAHRBUCH DES GETRAENKE UND FLUESSIGEN NAHRMITTEL. (Text in French, English, German) 1945. a. Editions du Gonfalon, 29 Route de Dourdan, 91670 Angerville, France.

663.63 FR ISSN 0066-3255
ANNUAIRE INTERNATIONAL DES JUS DE FRUITS.* 1968. a. 60 F. International Federation of Fruit Juice Producers, 10, rue de Liege, 75009 Paris, France.

663 338.47 US ISSN 0066-4367
ANNUAL STATISTICAL REVIEW: THE DISTILLED SPIRITS INDUSTRY. 1942. a. free. Distilled Spirits Council of the United States, Inc., 1300 Pennsylvania Bldg., Washington, DC 20004. circ. 4,000.

663 GT ISSN 0066-8567
ASOCIACION NACIONAL DEL CAFE. DEPARTAMENTO DE ASUNTOS AGRICOLAS. INFORME ANUAL.* a. Asociacion Nacional del Cafe, Departamento de Asuntos Agricolas, Edificio Etisa, Plazuela Espana, Zona 9, Guatemala, Guatemala.

663 US
BEVERAGE INDUSTRY ANNUAL MANUAL. 1967. a. $25. Magazines for Industry, Inc., 747 Third Ave., New York, NY 10017. Ed. Paul Mullins. adv. circ. 8,000.

658.8 US
BEVERAGE INDUSTRY NEWS CALIFORNIA GOLDBOOK. 1961. a. $1 per no. Industry Publications, 703 Market St., San Francisco, CA 94103. Ed. Timothy J. Guiney. adv. circ. 19,000.

663 CK ISSN 0084-7941
BOLETIN DE INFORMACION ESTADISTICA SOBRE CAFE. a. Federacion Nacional de Cafeteros de Colombia, Division de Investigaciones Economicas, Apdo. Aereo 3938, Bogota, Colombia.

663 UK ISSN 0068-0508
BOTTLERS YEAR BOOK. 1932. a. £2($5.20) B. Y. B. Ltd., c/o Jack Adley, 7 Higher Drive, Purley, Surrey CR2 2HP, England. index.

663.3 GW ISSN 0068-0710
BRAUEREIEN UND MAELZEREIEN IN EUROPA. 1900. a. DM.148. Verlag Hoppenstedt und Co., Havelstr. 9, Postfach 4006, 6100 Darmstadt, W. Germany (B.R.D.) adv.
 Brewing

BRAZIL. INSTITUTO DO ACUCAR E DO ALCOOL. CONSELHO DELIBERATIVO. COLETANEA DE RESOLUCOES (E) PRESIDENCIA. COLETANEA DE ATOS. see *AGRICULTURE — Crop Production And Soil*

663.3 US
BREWERS DIGEST ANNUAL BUYERS GUIDE AND BREWERY DIRECTORY. 1947. a. $8. Ammark Publishing Co., Inc., 4049 W. Peterson Ave., Chicago, IL 60646. Ed. Ross Heuer. adv. circ. 3,500.

BEVERAGES — ABSTRACTING, BIBLIOGRAPHIES, STATISTICS

663.3   UK   ISSN 0305-8123
BREWERY MANUAL AND WHO'S WHO IN BRITISH BREWING. 1888. a. £3. ‡ Northwood Publications Ltd, Elm House, 10-16 Elm St., London WC1X OBP, England. Ed. John Roberts.
Formerly: Brewery Manual (ISSN 0068-0931)
Brewing

663.3   CN   ISSN 0068-094X
BREWING AND MALTING BARLEY RESEARCH INSTITUTE. ANNUAL REPORT. a. Brewing and Malting Barley Research Institute, 206 Grain Exchange Bldg., Winnipeg, Manitoba, Canada. circ. controlled.
Brewing

663.3   JA   ISSN 0521-7521
BULLETIN OF BREWING SCIENCE. (Text in European languages) 1955. a. 1200 Yen. Brewing Science Research Institute - Jozo Kagaku Kenkyusho, 1-4-1 Mita, Meguro-ku, Tokyo 153, Japan. Ed. Naoyuki Kunitake. circ. 600. Indexed: Chem.Abstr.
Brewing

663.2   IT
CATALOGO BOLAFFI DEI VINI D'ITALIA. 1969. irreg.; no. 4, 1976. L.25000. Giulio Bolaffi Editore s.p.a., Via Cavour 17F, 10123 Turin, Italy. Ed. Umberto Allemandi. adv. illus. circ. 5,000.
Wine

663   US
COFFEE ANNUAL. a. $2. George Gordon Paton & Co., 182 Front St., New York, NY 10030. adv. charts. illus. stat.

614   US   ISSN 0160-1504
D I S C U S FACTS BOOK. a. free. Distilled Spirits Council of the United States, Inc., 1300 Pennsylvania Bldg., Washington, DC 20004. charts. stat. circ. controlled.
Formerly: Distilled Spirits Council of the United States. Facts Book.

663.3   NE   ISSN 0071-2531
EUROPEAN BREWERY CONVENTION. PROCEEDINGS OF THE INTERNATIONAL CONGRESS. (Text in English, German, French) 1950. biennial. price varies. Box 455, Rotterdam, Netherlands.
Brewing

663   GW   ISSN 0072-422X
GESELLSCHAFT FUER DIE GESCHICHTE UND BIBLIOGRAPHIE DES BRAUWESENS. JAHRBUCH. 1928. a. DM.19.17. Gesellschaft fuer die Geschichte und Bibliographie des Brauwesens, Seestr. 13, 1000 Berlin 65, W. Germany (B.R.D.) Ed. Hans. G. Schultze-Berndt. bk. rev. circ. 800.

663.2   UK
GOOD WINE GUIDE. a. Consumers Association, 14 Buckingham St., London WC2N 6DS, England (Subscr. to: Caxton Hill, Hertford SG13 7LZ, England)
Wine

663.2   UK
HARPERS DIRECTORY OF THE WINE AND SPIRIT TRADE. 1914. a. £23. Harper Trade Journals Ltd., Harling House, 47-51 Great Suffolk St., London SE1 OBS, England. Ed. J. Billington. adv. circ. 6,000.
Formerly: Harpers Directory and Manual of the Wine and Spirit Trade (ISSN 0073-0408)

663.1   US   ISSN 0163-9536
IMPACT: AMERICAN DISTILLED SPIRITS MARKET REVIEW AND FORECAST. 1976. a. $75. Tasco Publishing Corp., 305 E. 53rd St., New York, NY 10022. Ed. Marvin R. Shanken. charts.
Alcoholic

663.2   US   ISSN 0163-9544
IMPACT: THE AMERICAN WINE MARKET REVIEW AND FORECAST. 1975. a. $75. Tasco Publishing Corp., 305 E. 53rd St., New York, NY 10022. Ed. Marvin R. Shanken. charts.
Wine

663.93   BL
INSTITUTO BRASILEIRO DO CAFE. DEPARTAMENTO ECONOMICO. ANUARIO ESTATISTICO DO CAFE. irreg., 1964, no. 1. free. ‡ Instituto Brasileiro do Cafe, Coordenadoria de Estudos da Economia Cafeeira - Brazilian Coffee Institute, Av. Rodrigues Alves, 129, Rio de Janeiro, 20081 Rio de Janeiro. circ. 2,000.
Formerly: Instituto Brasileiro do Cafe. Departamento Economico. Anuario Estatistico do Cafe. (ISSN 0073-988X)

663   BL
INSTITUTO BRASILEIRO DO CAFE. GRUPO EXECUTIVO DE RACIONALIZACAO DE CAFEICULTURA. RELATORIO. 1962. irreg. free. Instituto Brasileiro do Cafe, Grupo Executivo de Racionalizacao de Cafecultura, Av. Rodrigues Alves 129, 3 andar, 20081 Rio de Janeiro, Brazil. illus. circ. 1,000.

663   SZ
INTERNATIONAL BREWERS' DIRECTORY AND SOFT DRINK GUIDE/REGISTRE INTERNATIONAL DES BRASSEURS, EAUX ET LIMONADES. (Text in English, French, German) 1928. every 6 yrs., 8th ed. 1979. 250 Fr. Verlag fuer Internationale Wirtschaftsliteratur GmbH, P.O. Box 108, CH-8047 Zurich, Switzerland. Ed. Walter Hirt.
Formerly: Internationales Firmenregister der Brauindustrie, Malzerien, Mineralwasser und Erfrischungsgetranke (ISSN 0074-9796)

663.63   FR   ISSN 0074-5952
INTERNATIONAL FEDERATION OF FRUIT JUICE PRODUCERS. PROCEEDINGS OF CONGRESS. COMPTE-RENDU DU CONGRES.* 1948. irreg., 1968, 7th, Cannes. International Federation of Fruit Juice Producers, 10, rue de Liege, 75009 Paris, France.

663.2   IT   ISSN 0374-5791
ISTITUTO SPERIMENTALE PER L'ENOLOGIA ASTI. ANNALI. (Text in Italian; summaries in English, German and French) 1970. a. L.5000. Istituto Sperimentale per l'Enologia, Via P. Micca 35, 14100 Asti, Italy. (back issues avail)

663.3   JA   ISSN 0075-6229
KIRIN BREWERY COMPANY, TOKYO. RESEARCH LABORATORY. REPORT/KIRIN BIRU K. K. SOGO KENKYUSHO KENKYU HOKOKU. (Text in English or German) 1958. a. free; available on exchange. Kirin Brewery Co. Ltd., Research Laboratories - Kirin Biru K. K. Sogo Kenkyusho, 3 Miyahara-cho, Gumma 370-12, Japan. Ed. Bd.
Brewing

663   FR   ISSN 0085-221X
MEMENTO DE L'O.I.V. 1928. quinquennial. Office International de la Vigne et du Vin, 11,rue Roquepine, 75008 Paris, France.

663.3   US   ISSN 0076-9932
MODERN BREWERY AGE BLUE BOOK. 1941. a. $50. Business Journals, Inc., 22 S. Smith St., Norwalk, CT 06855. Ed. Debby Kasdan.

663   CN   ISSN 0077-8087
NEW BRUNSWICK. LIQUOR CONTROL COMMISSION. REPORT. (Text in English and French) 1962-63. a. free. Liquor Control Commission, Fredericton, N.B., Canada.

663.2   UK
OFF LICENCE NEWS DIRECTORY. 1961. a. £6. William Reed Ltd., 5 Southwark St., London SE1 1RQ, England. Ed. D. L. Clark.
Formerly: Wine and Spirit Trade Review Directory (ISSN 0084-0343); Incorporating: Directory of Companies and Their Subsidiaries in the Wine, Spirit and Brewing Trades (ISSN 0070-5314) & Trade Directory Wine and Spirit (ISSN 0082-5743)

PLANO DA SAFRA ACUCAR E ALCOOL. see *AGRICULTURE — Crop Production And Soil*

PUBLIC REVENUES FROM ALCOHOL BEVERAGES. see *BUSINESS AND ECONOMICS — Public Finance, Taxation*

663.53   GW   ISSN 0081-3729
SPIRITUOSEN-JAHRBUCH. 1950. a. DM.43.13. Versuchs- und Lehranstalt fuer Spiritusfabrikation und Fermentationstechnologie, Seestr. 13, 1000 Berlin 65, W. Germany (B.R.D.)

663.6   US
STATISTICAL PROFILE OF THE SOFT DRINK INDUSTRY. 1974. $12. National Soft Drink Association, 1101 16th St. N.W., Washington, DC 20036.

663   US   ISSN 0081-931X
SUMMARY OF STATE LAWS AND REGULATIONS RELATING TO DISTILLED SPIRITS. biennial. $8.50. Distilled Spirits Council of the United States, Inc., 1300 Pennsylvania Bldg., Washington, DC 20004.

380.141   II
TEA DIRECTORY. (Text in English) 1960. irreg., latest issue 1976. Rs.20. Tea Board, 14 Brabourne Rd., Calcutta 1, India. Ed. P. R. Sengupta.

663.94   II
TEA RESEARCH ASSOCIATION. ADVISORY BULLETIN. 1971. irreg., no. 8, 1976. Rs.4 per no. Tea Research Association, Tocklai Experimental Station, Jorhat 785008, Assam, India. cum.index every 5 yrs. Indexed: Hort.Abstr. Trop.Abstr.

663   633   II
TEA RESEARCH ASSOCIATION. MEMORANDUM. 1938. irreg. price varies. Tea Research Association, Tocklai Experimental Station, Jorhat 785008, Assam, India. charts. Indexed: Hort.Abstr. Trop.Abstr.

663   633   II
TEA RESEARCH ASSOCIATION. OCCASIONAL SCIENTIFIC PAPERS. (Text in English) irreg., 1970, no. 9. Rs.5 per no. Tea Research Association, Tocklai Experimental Station, Jorhat 785008, Assam, India. bibl. charts. Indexed: Hort.Abstr.

663   630   II   ISSN 0564-6723
TEA RESEARCH ASSOCIATION. SCIENTIFIC ANNUAL REPORT. (Text in English) a. Rs.31. Tea Research Association, Tocklai Experimental Station, Jorhat 785008, Assam, India. Indexed: Hort.Abstr. Trop.Abstr.

663   FR   ISSN 0082-5484
TOUTE LA BOISSON. INTERNATIONAL. a. 125 F. S E P Edition, 194-196 rue Marcadet, 75018 Paris, France.

U. S. BUREAU OF ALCOHOL, TOBACCO AND FIREARMS. ANNUAL REPORT. see *LAW*

WINE HANDBOOK. see *BUSINESS AND ECONOMICS — Marketing And Purchasing*

663.1   US
WINES AND VINES: DIRECTORY OF THE WINE INDUSTRY IN NORTH AMERICA. 1941. a. $12.50. Hiaring Co., 703 Market St., San Francisco, CA 94103. circ. 5,000.
Supersedes: Wines and Vines-Annual Directory of the Wine Industry (ISSN 0084-0351)

BEVERAGES — Abstracting, Bibliographies, Statistics

338.4   CN   ISSN 0527-5024
CANADA. STATISTICS CANADA. DISTILLERIES. (Catalogue 32-206) (Text in English & French) 1918. a. Can.$4.50($5.40) Statistics Canada, Publications Distribution, Ottawa, Ont. K1A 0V7, Canada. (also avail. in microform from MML)

381   663   CN   ISSN 0705-4319
CONTROL AND SALE OF ALCOHOLIC BEVERAGES IN CANADA/CONTROLE ET LA VENTE DES BOISSONS ALCOOLIQUES AU CANADA. (Text and summaries in English and French) 1928. a. Can.$4.50($5.40) Statistics Canada, Publications Distribution, Ottawa, Ont. K1A 0V7, Ottawa K1A 0T6, Canada. (also avail. in microform from MML)

BIBLIOGRAPHIES

011   KE
A B C NEWSLETTER. 1974. irreg., no. 7, 1975. Africa Bibliographic Center, Box 5089, Nairobi, Kenya. bibl.

691.3 620.1 016   US   ISSN 0084-6325
A C I BIBLIOGRAPHY. 1955. irreg., no. 12, 1978. price varies. American Concrete Institute, Box 19150, Redford Station, Detroit, MI 48219.

ABORTION BIBLIOGRAPHY. see *BIRTH CONTROL — Abstracting, Bibliographies, Statistics*

011   SP
ACADEMIA ALFONSO X EL SABIO. CUADERNOS BIBLIOGRAFICOS. 1977. irreg. Academia Alfonso X el Sabio, Murcia, Spain.

013   BE   ISSN 0065-0609
ACADEMIE ROYALE DES SCIENCES, DES LETTRES ET DES BEAUX ARTS DE BELGIQUE. INDEX BIOGRAPHIQUE DES MEMBRES, CORRESPONDANTS ET ASSOCIES. 1948. irreg. 100 Fr. Academie Royale des Sciences, des Lettres et des Beaux Arts de Belgique, 43 Av. des Arts, B-1040 Brussels, Belgium. circ. 350.

016 610   FR
ACTUALITES BIBLIOGRAPHIQUES EN MEDECINE, PHARMACIE ET SCIENCES BIOMEDICALES. 1973. a. free. Sandoz Editions, B.P. 120, 92505 Rueil Malmaisson Cedex, France. Ed. Jacques Archimbaud.

AFRICAN BIBLIOGRAPHIC CENTER, WASHINGTON, D.C. CURRENT READING LIST SERIES. see *HISTORY — Abstracting, Bibliographies, Statistics*

AFRICAN BIBLIOGRAPHY SERIES. see *HISTORY — Abstracting, Bibliographies, Statistics*

015.6   UK   ISSN 0306-9516
AFRICAN BOOKS IN PRINT. 1975. irreg. price varies. Mansell Publishing, 3 Bloomsbury Place, London WC1A 2QA, England. Ed. H. Zell.

630 016   US
AGRICULTURAL COMMODITIES INDEX; ready-reference guide to USDA statistical series. irreg. $95. Oryx Press, 2214 N. Central at Encanto, Suite 103, Phoenix, AZ 85004. Ed. Jane Buzby McFall.

011   JA
AICHI-KEN KYODO SHIRYO SOGO MOKUROKU. 1964. irreg., latest issue, 1973. 1000 Yen. Aichi Library Association - Aichi Toshokan Kyokai, 1-12-1 Higashisakura, Higashi-ku, Nagoya, Aichi, Japan. Ed. Aichi Toshokan Kyokai. bibl.

378.3 011   II
ALUMNI PUBLICATIONS: A CATALOGUE. (First Edition covers 1950-1975) (Text in English) 1976. quinquennial. free. United States Educational Foundation in India, Fulbright House, 12 Hailey Rd., New Delhi 110001, India. Ed. P. D. Sayal.

011   BL   ISSN 0100-0977
AMAZONIA - BIBLIOGRAFIA. 1963. irreg. Cr.$25($7) Instituto Brasileiro de Informacao em Ciencia e Tecnologia, Av. General Justo 171, 4 Andar, 20021 Rio de Janeiro, GB, Brazil.

AMERICAN DISSERTATIONS ON FOREIGN EDUCATION; a bibliography with abstracts. see *EDUCATION — Abstracting, Bibliographies, Statistics*

016 100   US   ISSN 0084-6430
AMERICAN PHILOSOPHICAL SOCIETY. LIBRARY PUBLICATIONS. 1968. irreg.; 1979 no. 8. price varies. American Philosophical Society, Library, 105 S. 5th St., Philadelphia, PA 19106. circ. 100.

AMERICAN REFERENCE BOOKS ANNUAL. see *LIBRARY AND INFORMATION SCIENCES — Abstracting, Bibliographies, Statistics*

080   UN
ANNOTATED ACCESSIONS LIST OF STUDIES AND REPORTS IN THE FIELD OF SCIENCE STATISTICS. (Subseries of its (Document)) 1966. a. Unesco, Division of Statistics on Science and Technology, 7-9 Place de Fontenoy, 75700 Paris, France (Orders to: Unipub, 345 Park Ave., S., New York, NY 10010) abstr. bibl. stat. circ. 1,000.

015   ISSN 0066-2445
ANNOTATED GUIDE TO TAIWAN PERIODICAL LITERATURE. (Text in Chinese and English: summaries in English) 1966. irreg., 3rd edt. 1980-81. $7.25. ‡ Chinese Materials Center, Inc., 809 Taraval St., San Francisco, CA 94116. Ed. Robert L. Irick. bk. rev. circ. 300.

010   FR   ISSN 0066-2720
ANNUAIRE DES ANNUAIRES. 1936. a. Chambre Syndicale des Editeurs d'Annuaires, 28 rue du Docteur-Finlay, 75015 Paris, France.

011   CK   ISSN 0570-393X
ANUARIO BIBLIOGRAFICO COLOMBIANO. 1951. a. Col.300($10) Instituto Caro y Cuervo, Seccion de Publicaciones, Apdo. Aereo 20002, Bogota, Colombia.

015   CR   ISSN 0066-5010
ANUARIO BIBLIOGRAFICO COSTARRICENSE. 1956. irreg. free. ‡ Asociacion Costarricense de Bibliotecarios, Apartado 3308, San Jose, Costa Rica. circ. 500.

011   EC
ANUARIO BIBLIOGRAFICO ECUATORIANO. (Published as the 6th issue each year of Bibliografia Ecuatoriana) 1975. a. Universidad Central del Ecuador, Biblioteca General, Quito, Ecuador.

011   UY
ANUARIO BIBLIOGRAFICO URUGUAYO. (Suspended publication 1949: resumed 1968) 1946. irreg. (Donation or exchange requested) Biblioteca Nacional, Guayabo 1795, Montevideo, Uruguay.

015   UY
ANUARIO - C B A - YEARBOOK. (Text in English & Spanish) 1968. a. Eduardo Darino, Ed. & Pub., Casilla de Correo 1677, Montevideo, Uruguay (U.S. Subscr. to: Darino, Box 1496-GCS, New York, NY 10163) adv. bk. rev. circ. 3,000.
Formerly: Comentarios Bibliograficos Americanos. Anuario (ISSN 0084-893X)

ARCHITECTURE SERIES: BIBLIOGRAPHY. see *ARCHITECTURE — Abstracting, Bibliographies, Statistics*

ASSOCIATION FRANCAISE POUR LA DIFFUSION DU LIVRE SCIENTIFIQUE, TECHNIQUE ET MEDICAL (BULLETINS COLLECTIFS) see *SCIENCES: COMPREHENSIVE WORKS — Abstracting, Bibliographies, Statistics*

526   AT
AUSTRALIA. BUREAU OF MINERAL RESOURCES, GEOLOGY, AND GEOPHYSICS. PUBLICATIONS. (In three parts: Part 1: Publications; Part 2: Maps; Part 3: Index) irreg. price varies. Bureau of Mineral Resources, Geology, and Geophysics, Box 378, Canberra City, A.C.T. 2601, Australia.
Cartography

015   AT   ISSN 0067-1738
AUSTRALIAN BOOKS; SELECT LIST. 1949. a. $2.50. National Library of Australia, Sales & Subscription Unit, Canberra, A.C.T. 2600, Australia.

AUSZUEGE AUS DER LITERATUR DER ZELLSTOFF- UND PAPIER-ERZEUGUNG UND CELLULOSEVERARBEITUNG. see *ENGINEERING — Abstracting, Bibliographies, Statistics*

011   US   ISSN 0145-1642
AYER DIRECTORY OF PUBLICATIONS. 1869. a. $62. Ayer Press, One Bala Ave., Bala Cynwyd, PA 19004. Ed. Betty Gallimore. (also avail. in microfilm from AMS)
Formerly: Ayer Directory of Newspapers, Magazines, and Trade Publications (ISSN 0067-2696)
Listing of newspapers, magazines and trade publications in the U.S., Puerto Rico, Virgin Islands, Canada, Bermuda, Republic of Panama and the Philippines

015   II
B E P I; bibliography of English publications in India. (Text in English) 1970. a. $20. (Indian Bibliographic Centre) Today and Tomorrow's Printers and Publishers, 24-B5 Original Rd., Karol Baugh, New Delhi 110005, India. Eds. H. D. Sharma, L.M.P. Singh, S.P. Mukherji.
Supersedes (1977): Indian Books; Bibliography of Indian Books Published or Reprinted in the English Language (ISSN 0073-6287)

015   II
BANGIYA SAHITYAKOSHA. (Text in Bengali) vol. 9, 1977. a. price varies. Bangla Bhasa Sahitya-o-Samskriti Gabessane Samastha, c/o Pustak Bipani, 27 Beniatola Lane, Calcutta 700009, India. Ed. Asokkumar Kundu. bk. rev. bibl. circ. 1,100.

BANGLADESH DIRECTORY. see *SOCIOLOGY*

011   NE
BESCHREIBENDE BIBLIOGRAPHIEN. (Text in Western languages) 1971. irreg. Editions Rodopi N.V., Keizersgracht 302-304, 1016 EX Amsterdam, Netherlands. Ed. Cola Minis. circ. 500. (back issues avail.)

015   DK   ISSN 0067-6543
BIBLIOGRAFI OVER DANMARKS OFFENTLIGE PUBLIKATIONER. (Text in Danish and English) 1949. a. Kr.60. I.D.E., Danmarks Institut for International Udveksling, Amaliegade 38, 1256 Copenhagen K, Denmark (Sold on commission by: Bibliotekscentralen, Telegrafvej 5, DK-2750 Ballerup, Denmark) Eds. Rita Ejlersen, Gertrud Nielsen. index.
Bibliography of Danish government publications

016 949.8   RM   ISSN 0067-6551
BIBLIOGRAFIA ANALITICA A PERIODICELOR ROMANESTI. 1966. irreg. (Academia Republicii Socialiste Romania) Editura Academiei Republicii Socialiste Romania, Calea Victoriei 125, Bucharest, Romania (Subscr. to: ILEXIM, Str. 13 Decembrie Nr. 3, P.O. Box 136-137, Bucharest, Romania)

BIBLIOGRAFIA BRASILEIRA DE BOTANICA. see *BIOLOGY — Abstracting, Bibliographies, Statistics*

BIBLIOGRAFIA BRASILEIRA DE CIENCIAS SOCIAIS. see *SOCIAL SERVICES AND WELFARE — Abstracting, Bibliographies, Statistics*

BIBLIOGRAFIA BRASILEIRA DE DIREITO. see *LAW — Abstracting, Bibliographies, Statistics*

BIBLIOGRAFIA BRASILEIRA DE ENGENHARIA. see *ENGINEERING — Abstracting, Bibliographies, Statistics*

BIBLIOGRAFIA BRASILEIRA DE FISICA. see *PHYSICS — Abstracting, Bibliographies, Statistics*

BIBLIOGRAFIA BRASILEIRA DE MATEMATICA. see *MATHEMATICS — Abstracting, Bibliographies, Statistics*

BIBLIOGRAFIA BRASILEIRA DE MEDICINA. see *MEDICAL SCIENCES — Abstracting, Bibliographies, Statistics*

BIBLIOGRAFIA BRASILEIRA DE QUIMICA E QUIMICA TECNOLOGICA. see *BUSINESS AND ECONOMICS — Abstracting, Bibliographies, Statistics*

BIBLIOGRAFIA BRASILEIRA DE ZOOLOGIA. see *BIOLOGY — Abstracting, Bibliographies, Statistics*

015.7291   CU   ISSN 0067-6705
BIBLIOGRAFIA CUBANA. 1959. a. exchange basis. (Biblioteca Nacional Jose Marti, Departamento de Coleccion Cubana) Ediciones Cubanas, Vice-Direccion de Exportacion, Apdo. 605, Havana, Cuba. circ. 2,000.

BIBLIOGRAFIA DE LA LITERATURA HISPANICA. see *LITERATURE — Abstracting, Bibliographies, Statistics*

BIBLIOGRAFIA DE RECURSOS NATURALES. see *CONSERVATION — Abstracting, Bibliographies, Statistics*

BIBLIOGRAPHIES

BIBLIOGRAFIA DO ARROZ. see
AGRICULTURE — Abstracting, Bibliographies, Statistics

016 940   RM
BIBLIOGRAFIA DOBROGEI. 1969. a. Biblioteca Judeteana Constanta, B-dul Republicii nr. 7 bis, Constanta, Romania.

015 020   BU
BIBLIOGRAFIA NA BULGARSKATA BIBLIOGRAFIIA/BIBLIOGRAPHY OF BULGARIAN BIBLIOGRAPHIES. 1967. a. 1.25 lv. Narodna Biblioteka Kiril i Metodii, 11, Tolbukhin Blvd., Sofia, Bulgaria. bibl. circ. 500.

200 016   AG
BIBLIOGRAFIA TEOLOGICA COMENTADA DEL AREA IBEROAMERICANA. (Text in Spanish; summaries in English) 1973. a. $25. Instituto Superior Evangelico de Estudios Teologicos, Camacua 282, 1406 Buenos Aires, Argentina. Ed. Eduardo Bierzychudek. bk. rev. bibl. index. circ. 1,000. (back issues avail)

010   CS   ISSN 0067-6780
BIBLIOGRAFICKY ZBORNIK. (Text in Slovak; summaries in English and German) 1957. a. price varies. Matica Slovenska, Mudronova 35, 036 52 Martin, Czechoslovakia. bk. rev.

011   NE   ISSN 0166-9966
BIBLIOGRAFIE VAN NEDERLANDSE PROEFSCHRIFTEN/DUTCH THESES. 1924; 1966 N.S. irreg. price varies. (Rijksuniversiteit te Utrecht, Bibliotheek) Swets Publishing Service (Subsidiary of: Swets en Zeitlinger B.V.) Heereweg 347B, 2126 CA Lisse, Netherlands.
Formerly: Catalogus van Academische Geschriften in Nederland Verschenen.

BIBLIOGRAPHIA CARTOGRAPHICA; international documentation of cartographical literature. see *GEOGRAPHY — Abstracting, Bibliographies, Statistics*

BIBLIOGRAPHIC GUIDE TO ART AND ARCHITECTURE. see *ARCHITECTURE — Abstracting, Bibliographies, Statistics*

BIBLIOGRAPHIC GUIDE TO BLACK STUDIES. see *ETHNIC INTERESTS — Abstracting, Bibliographies, Statistics*

011   US   ISSN 0360-2729
BIBLIOGRAPHIC GUIDE TO CONFERENCE PUBLICATIONS. (Text in various languages) 1974. a. G. K. Hall, & Co., 70 Lincoln St., Boston, MA 02111.
Formerly: Conference Publications Guide (ISSN 0091-7907)

BIBLIOGRAPHIC GUIDE TO DANCE. see *DANCE — Abstracting, Bibliographies, Statistics*

011   US   ISSN 0360-2796
BIBLIOGRAPHIC GUIDE TO GOVERNMENT PUBLICATIONS. (Text in various languages) a. G. K. Hall & Co., 70 Lincoln St., Boston, MA 02111.
Formerly: Government Publications Guide (ISSN 0091-7915)

015   US   ISSN 0360-280X
BIBLIOGRAPHIC GUIDE TO GOVERNMENT PUBLICATIONS-FOREIGN. a. G.K. Hall & Co., 70 Lincoln St., Boston, MA 02111.

BIBLIOGRAPHIC GUIDE TO LAW. see *LAW — Abstracting, Bibliographies, Statistics*

BIBLIOGRAPHIC GUIDE TO MUSIC. see *MUSIC — Abstracting, Bibliographies, Statistics*

BIBLIOGRAPHIC GUIDE TO NORTH AMERICAN HISTORY. see *HISTORY — Abstracting, Bibliographies, Statistics*

BIBLIOGRAPHIC GUIDE TO PSYCHOLOGY. see *PSYCHOLOGY — Abstracting, Bibliographies, Statistics*

010   UN
BIBLIOGRAPHICAL SERVICES THROUGHOUT THE WORLD. quinquennial, 1977, no. 5. price varies. Unesco Press, 7 Place de Fontenoy, F-75700 Paris, France (Dist. in U.S. by: Unipub, 345 Park Ave. S., New York, NY 10010)
Fourth edition covers 1965-69

010   CN   ISSN 0067-6896
BIBLIOGRAPHICAL SOCIETY OF CANADA. PAPERS. (Text in English and French) 1962. a. membership. Bibliographical Society of Canada, Box 1878, Guelph, Ont. N1H 7A1, Canada. Ed. Elizabeth Hulse. bk. rev. circ. 360.
Supersedes: Bibliographical Society of Canada. Newsletter.

015   MG   ISSN 0067-6926
BIBLIOGRAPHIE ANNUELLE DE MADAGASCAR. 1964. a. 500 Fr.($2) ‡ Universite de Madagascar, Bibliotheque Universitaire, B.P. 908, Antananarivo, Malagasy Republic. index. circ. 1,500.

BIBLIOGRAPHIE COURANTE D'ARTICLES DE PERIODIQUES POSTERIEURS A 1944 SUR LES PROBLEMES POLITIQUES, ECONOMIQUES ET SOCIAUX/INDEX TO POST-1944 PERIODICAL ARTICLES ON POLITICAL, ECONOMIC AND SOCIAL PROBLEMS. see *SOCIAL SCIENCES: COMPREHENSIVE WORKS — Abstracting, Bibliographies, Statistics*

BIBLIOGRAPHIE DER BERNER GESCHICHTE/ BIBLIOGRAPHIE DE L'HISTOIRE BERNOISE. see *HISTORY — Abstracting, Bibliographies, Statistics*

011   SZ
BIBLIOGRAPHIE DER SCHWEIZERISCHEN AMTSDRUCKSCRIFTEN/BIBLIOGRAPHIE DES PUBLICATIONS OFFICIELLES SUISSES. (Text and summaries in French, German an Italian) 1946. a. 17 Fr.($9) Bibliotheque Nationale Suisse - Schweizerische Landesbibliothek, Hallwylstrasse 15, CH-3003 Berne, Switzerland. Ed. Ingunn Refenacht. index. circ. 500 (controlled) (back issues avail.)

949.3 011   LU
BIBLIOGRAPHIE LUXEMBOURGEOISE. 1944/45. a. 300 Fr. Bibliotheque Nationale, 37 Boulevard F.-D. Roosevelt, Luxembourg, Luxembourg. (back issues avail.)

913 016.9301   GE
BIBLIOGRAPHIE ZUR ARCHAEO-ZOOLOGIE UND GESCHICHTE DER HAUSTIERE. 1971. a. exchange basis. Akademie der Wissenschaften der DDR, Zentralinstitut fuer Alte Geschichte und Archaeologie, Leipziger Str. 3-4, 108 Berlin, E. Germany (D.D.R.) Ed. Hanns-Hermann Mueller.

BIBLIOGRAPHIES ANALYTIQUES SUR L'AFRIQUE CENTRALE. see *HISTORY — Abstracting, Bibliographies, Statistics*

BIBLIOGRAPHIES ON EDUCATIONAL TOPICS. see *EDUCATION — Abstracting, Bibliographies, Statistics*

011   GW   ISSN 0006-1506
BIBLIOGRAPHISCHE BERICHTE/ BIBLIOGRAPHICAL BULLETIN. (N.F. Bibliographische Beihefte zur Zeitschrift fuer Bibliothekswesen und Bibliographie) (Text in English and German) 1959. irreg., vol. 22, 1980. price varies. (Staatsbibliothek Preussischer Kulturbesitz) Vittorio Klostermann, Frauenlobstr. 22, 6000 Frankfurt 90, W. Germany (B.R.D.) adv. bibl. index. cum.index: 1959-1966; 1966-1970. circ. 1,400.

BIBLIOGRAPHY AND SUBJECT INDEX OF SOUTH AFRICAN GEOLOGY. see *EARTH SCIENCES — Abstracting, Bibliographies, Statistics*

BIBLIOGRAPHY OF AGRICULTURAL BIBLIOGRAPHIES. see *AGRICULTURE — Abstracting, Bibliographies, Statistics*

015   CN   ISSN 0067-7175
BIBLIOGRAPHY OF CANADIAN BIBLIOGRAPHIES. 1960. irreg., 2nd ed. 1972. Can.$20. University of Toronto Press, Front Campus, Toronto, Ont. M5S 1A6, Canada. Ed. P. E. Greig.

BIBLIOGRAPHY OF DOCTORAL DISSERTATIONS; NATURAL AND APPLIED SCIENCES. see *SCIENCES: COMPREHENSIVE WORKS — Abstracting, Bibliographies, Statistics*

BIBLIOGRAPHY OF ECONOMIC AND STATISTICAL PUBLICATIONS ON TANZANIA. see *BUSINESS AND ECONOMICS — Abstracting, Bibliographies, Statistics*

BIBLIOGRAPHY OF ELECTRICAL RECORDINGS IN THE CNS AND RELATED LITERATURE. see *MEDICAL SCIENCES — Abstracting, Bibliographies, Statistics*

BIBLIOGRAPHY OF NOISE. see *ENVIRONMENTAL STUDIES — Abstracting, Bibliographies, Statistics*

015   FJ
BIBLIOGRAPHY OF PERIODICAL ARTICLES RELATING TO THE SOUTH PACIFIC. 1974. a. $12. University of the South Pacific, Library, G.P.O. Box 1168, Suva, Fiji. Ed. Susil Bhan. circ. 170. (back issues avail.)

016   SA   ISSN 0067-7256
BIBLIOGRAPHY OF SOUTH AFRICAN GOVERNMENT PUBLICATIONS. (Text in Afrikaans and English) 1969. irreg. Government Printer, Bosman St., Private Bag X85, Pretoria 0001, South Africa. (Prepared by: Department of National Education, Division of Library Sciences)

016   SY   ISSN 0067-7302
BIBLIOGRAPHY OF THE MIDDLE EAST.* (Subseries of Syrian Documentation Papers) a. $25. Syrian Documentation Papers, P.O. Box 2712, Damascus, Syria.

016   UK   ISSN 0067-7310
BIBLIOGRAPHY OF WORKS BY POLISH SCHOLARS AND SCIENTISTS PUBLISHED OUTSIDE POLAND IN LANGUAGES OTHER THAN POLISH. 1964. irreg. Polish Society of Arts and Sciences Abroad, 20 Princes Gate, London, S.W.7, England.

BIBLIOGRAPHY ON POPULATION AND FAMILY PLANNING IN KOREA. see *BIRTH CONTROL — Abstracting, Bibliographies, Statistics*

070 016   US   ISSN 0067-737X
BIBLIOHRAFICHNYI POKAZHCZYK UKRAINS'KOI PRESY POZA MEZHAMY UKRAINY/BIBLIOGRAPHICAL INDEX OF THE UKRAINIAN PRESS OUTSIDE UKRAINE. (Text in Ukrainian; summaries in English) 1967. triennial. $5. ‡ Ukrainian Museum-Archives, Inc., 1202 Kenilworth Ave., Cleveland, OH 44113. Ed. Alexander Fedynskyj. circ. 700.

015   IT   ISSN 0067-7418
BIBLIOTECA DI BIBLIOGRAFIA ITALIANA. 1923. irreg., vol. 89, 1979. price varies. Casa Editrice Leo S. Olschki, Casella Postale 66, 50100 Florence, Italy. circ. 1,000.

015   SP
BIBLIOTECA UNIVERSITARIA Y PROVINCIAL, BARCELONA. BOLETIN DE NOTICIAS. irreg. free. Universidad de Barcelona, Biblioteca, Avda. Jose Antonio, 585, Barcelona-7, Spain.

010   IT   ISSN 0067-7531
BIBLIOTECONOMIA E BIBLIOGRAFIA. SAGGI E STUDI. 1964. irreg., vol. 11, 1979. price varies. Casa Editrice Leo S. Olschki, Casella Postale 66, 50100 Florence, Italy. Ed. Francesco Barberi. circ. 1,000.

016   GW   ISSN 0067-7884
BIBLIOTHECA BIBLIOGRAPHICA AURELIANA. (Text in English, French, German, Latin) 1959. irreg., vol. 80, 1981. price varies. Verlag Valentin Koerner, H.-Sielcken-Str. 36, Postfach 304, D-7570 Baden-Baden 1, W. Germany (B.R.D.) index.

011   NE
BIBLIOTHECA BIBLIOGRAPHICA NEERLANDICA. 1968. irreg., no. 13, 1980. price varies. De Graaf Publishers, Box 6, 2420 AA Nieuwkoop, Netherlands.

015   UK   ISSN 0067-7914
BIBLIOTHECA CELTICA; A register of publications relating to Wales and the Celtic peoples. 1909. a.(approx.) price varies. National Library of Wales, Aberystwyth, Dyfed SY23 3BU, Wales. index. circ. 450.

BIBLIOGRAPHIES

010   GW   ISSN 0069-5866
BIBLIOTHEKAR-LEHRINSTITUT DES LANDES NORDRHEIN-WESTFALEN. BIBLIOGRAPHISCHE HEFTE. 1957. irreg. price varies. Greven Verlag Koeln, Neue Weyerstr. 1-3, 5000 Cologne 1, W. Germany (B.R.D.)

BIBLIOTHEQUE AFRICAINE. CATALOGUE DES ACQUISITIONS. CATOLOGUS VAN DE AANWINSTEN. see HISTORY — *Abstracting, Bibliographies, Statistics*

011   BE   ISSN 0068-2926
BIBLIOTHEQUE ROYALE ALBERT 1ER. CATALOGUE COLLECTIF DES PERIODIQUES ETRANGERS/KONINKLIJKE BIBLIOTHEEK ALBERT I. CENTRALE CATALOGUS VAN BUITENLANDSE TIDJSCHRIFTEN. (Text in Dutch, French) 1965. irreg. 2400 Fr. Editions "Culture et Civilisation", 115 Av. Gabriel Lebon, 1160 Brussels, Belgium.

015   BO
BIO-BIBLIOGRAFIA BOLIVIANA. 1962. a. Bol.$400($25) Los Amigos del Libro, Casilla 450, La Paz, Cochabamba, Bolivia. Ed. Werner Guttentag. adv. bk. rev. indexes. circ. 1,000.
    Formerly: Bibliografia Boliviana (ISSN 0067-6578)

920   US
BIOGRAPHICAL DICTIONARIES AND RELATED WORKS; an international bibliography of collective biographies. 1967. irreg. $40. Gale Research Company, Book Tower, Detroit, MI 48226. Ed. Robert B. Slocum.

011   IR
BOOKS CATALOGED BY TEHRAN BOOK PROCESSING CENTRE. 1970. a. with quinquennial cum. $10 (quinquennial cum. $20) Institute for Research and Planning in Science and Education, Tehran Book Processing Centre, Box 11-1126, Teheran, Iran. circ. 600.

BOOKS FROM ISRAEL. see PUBLISHING AND BOOK TRADE — *Abstracting, Bibliographies, Statistics*

010   PK   ISSN 0068-0206
BOOKS FROM PAKISTAN. (Text in English) 1967. a. Rs.15. National Book Council of Pakistan, Theosophical Hall, M. A. Jinnah Rd., Karachi, Pakistan.
    Formerly: English Language Publications from Pakistan.

015   US   ISSN 0068-0214
BOOKS IN PRINT. (Vols. 1-2 Authors, Vols. 3-4 Titles) 1947. a. $127. R. R. Bowker Company, 1180 Ave. of the Americas, New York, NY 10036 (Orders to Box 1807, Ann Arbor, MI 48106)

015   US   ISSN 0000-0515
BOOKS IN SERIES IN THE UNITED STATES; original, reprinted, in-print, and out-of-print books, published or distributed in the U.S., in popular, scholarly, and professional series. 1977. biennial. $150. R. R. Bowker Company, 1180 Ave. of the Americas, New York, NY 10036 (Orders to: Box 1807, Ann Arbor, MI 48106)

011   BL
BRAZIL. SERVICO SOCIAL DO COMERCIO. COLECAO BIBLIOGRAFICA. vol. 9, 1978. a. free. Servico Social do Comercio, Rua Voluntarios da Patria 169, 22270 Rio de Janeiro, Brazil. Ed. Bd.

015   UK   ISSN 0068-1350
BRITISH BOOKS IN PRINT. 1874. a. £54. J. Whitaker & Sons Ltd., 12 Dyott St., London WC1A 1DF, England (Dist. in U.S. by: R. R. Bowker Co., P.O. Box 1807, Ann Arbor, MI 48106) (reprint service avail. from UMI)

011   UK   ISSN 0309-0655
BRITISH LIBRARY. LENDING DIVISION. CURRENT SERIALS RECEIVED. 1965. a. £20. British Library, Lending Division, Boston Spa, Wetherby, West Yorkshire LS23 7BQ, England.

016.05   UK
BRITISH RATE & DATA DIRECTORIES AND ANNUALS. a. £4.50. Maclean-Hunter Ltd., 30 Old Burlington St., London W1X 2AE, England. Ed. Jocelyn Redman. adv. circ. 888.

016   GW   ISSN 0068-3043
DAS BUCH DER JUGEND. a. DM.50. (Arbeitskreis fuer Jugendliteratur) Otto Maier Verlag, Marktstr. 22, D-7980 Ravensburg, W. Germany (B.R.D.)

015   940   BU
BULGARIA V CHUZHDATA LITERATURA/ BULGARIA IN FOREIGN LITERATURE. 1966. a. 0.87 lv. Narodna Biblioteka Kiril i Metodii, 11, Tolbukhin Blvd., Sofia, Bulgaria. bibl. circ. 500.

015   BU
BULGARIAN ACADEMIC BOOKS. (Text in English) 1969. a. free. (Bulgarska Akademiia na Naukite) Publishing House of the Bulgarian Academy of Sciences, Ul. Akad. G. Bonchev, 1113 Sofia, Bulgaria. bibl. circ. 2,500

070   015   BU
BULGARSKI PERIODICHEN PECHAT/ BULGARIAN PERIODICALS; vestnitsi, spisaniia, biuletini i periodichni sbornitsi. 1965. a. 1.30 lv. Narodna Biblioteka Kiril i Metodii, 11, Tolbukhin Blvd., Sofia, Bulgaria. Ed. K. Zotova. bibl. circ. 2,100.

010   FR   ISSN 0076-0137
BULLETIN BIBLIOGRAPHIQUE THEMATIQUE; informations bibliographiques,-philosophie, religion, sciences humaines. irreg. price varies. Union des Editeurs Francais, 117 Bld. Saint-Germain, 75279 Paris, France. circ. 35,000.
    Until 1971: Livres d'Aujourd'hui.

010   US   ISSN 0068-4309
BURT FRANKLIN BIBLIOGRAPHY AND REFERENCE SERIES. (Text in various languages) 1949. irreg. price varies. Lenox Hill Publishing and Distributing Corporation, 235 E. 44th St., New York, NY 10017.

011   CN   ISSN 0707-3747
C O N S E R MICROFICHE. (Conversion of Serials); a computer-output-microfiche listing of serial records created in the CONSER project and authenticated by the National Library of Canada and the Library of Congress. (Text in English and French) 1979. a. Can.$55 for base register and supplement. National Library of Canada, Canadiana Editorial Division, Cataloging Branch, 395 Wellington St., Ottawa, Ont. K1A 0N4, Canada (Dist. in U.S. by Library of Congress, Cataloging Distribution Service, Washington, DC 20540) circ. 150. (microfiche)

011   US
CALIFORNIA PERIODICALS ON MICROFILM. 1978. a. $100 price includes California Periodicals Index. Gabriel Micrographics, Box 224, Mankato, MN 56001. Ed. Opal Kissinger. (microfilm)

010   UK   ISSN 0068-6611
CAMBRIDGE BIBLIOGRAPHICAL SOCIETY. TRANSACTIONS. 1949. a. £4 to non-members. Cambridge Bibliographical Society, c/o Cambridge University Library, West Rd., Cambridge CB3 9DR, England. Eds. Brian Jenkins, David McKitterick.

016   UK   ISSN 0068-662X
CAMBRIDGE BIBLIOGRAPHICAL SOCIETY. TRANSACTIONS. MONOGRAPH SUPPLEMENTS. 1951. irreg. membership. Cambridge Bibliographical Society, c/o Cambridge University Library, West Rd., Cambridge CB3 9DR, England.

016   UK
CAMBRIDGE UNIVERSITY LIBRARY. GENIZAH SERIES. irreg. £1 per no. Cambridge University Library, West Rd., Cambridge CB3 9DR, England.

900   016   UK
CAMBRIDGE UNIVERSITY LIBRARY. HISTORICAL BIBLIOGRAPHY SERIES. irreg. £1 per no. Cambridge University Library, West Rd., Cambridge CB3 9DR, England.

016   CN   ISSN 0084-8379
CANADA. DEPARTMENT OF AGRICULTURE. LIBRARY. CURRENT PERIODICALS. PERIODIQUES EN COURS. (Text in English; forward in English and French) 1953. irreg. free. Agriculture Canada, Library, Ottawa, K1A 0C5, Canada. circ. 1,500 (controlled)
    Formerly: Canada. Department of Agriculture. Library. Periodicals Currently Received. Periodiques Couramment Recus.

015   CN   ISSN 0068-8398
CANADIAN BOOKS IN PRINT. 1967. a. price varies. (Canadian Book Publishers' Council) University of Toronto Press, Front Campus, Toronto, Ont. M5S 1A6, Canada. (Co-sponsors: Canadian Booksellers' Association; Canadian Library Association) Ed. Martha Pluscauskas. circ. 2,500.

015.7   CN   ISSN 0318-675X
CANADIAN GOVERNMENT PUBLICATIONS: CATALOGUE/PUBLICATIONS DU GOVERNEMENT CANADIEN: CATALOGUE. (Cumulates monthly catalogue and daily checklist) (Text in English and French) 1954. a. Information Canada, Ottawa, Ont., Canada.

016   378   CN   ISSN 0068-9874
CANADIAN THESES/THESES CANADIENNES. (Text in English and French) 1962. a. price varies. ‡ National Library of Canada, Ottawa, Ont. K1A ON4, Canada (Subscr. to: Supply & Services Canada, Printing and Publishing Division, Ottawa, Ont. K1A 0S9, Canada) Ed. Helena Vesely. index. circ. 1,000. (also avail. in microfilm)

CAREERS (SARATOGA) see OCCUPATIONS AND CAREERS — *Abstracting, Bibliographies, Statistics*

016   US
CARROLL STUDIES. 1975. a. Lewis Carroll Society of North America, 617 Rockford Rd., Silver Spring, MD 20902.

CATALOGO COLECTIVO DE PUBLICACIONES PERIODICAS. see JOURNALISM — *Abstracting, Bibliographies, Statistics*

011   MX
CATALOGO COLECTIVO DE PUBLICACIONES PERIODICAS EXISTENTES EN LAS BIBLIOTECAS DE LA UNIVERSIDAD. 1976. biennial. Mex.$40 (or exchange) Universidad Nacional Autonoma de Mexico, Direccion General de Bibliotecas, Villa Obregon, Ciudad Universitaria, Mexico 20, D.F., Mexico.

CATALOGO DE PUBLICACIONES LATINOAMERICANAS SOBRE FORMACION PROFESIONAL. see OCCUPATIONS AND CAREERS — *Abstracting, Bibliographies, Statistics*

011   JA
CATALOGUE OF BOOKS RECOMMENDED FOR LIBRARIES/SENTEI TOSHO SOMOKUROKU. a. Japan Library Association - Nihon Toshokan Kyokai, 1-1-10 Taishido, Setagaya-ku, Tokyo 154, Japan.

015   UK   ISSN 0591-0986
CATALOGUE OF LITTLE PRESS BOOKS IN PRINT PUBLISHED IN THE UK. 1970. a. 50p. Association of Little Presses of Great Britain, 18 Clairview Rd., London S. W. 16, England (Subscr. National Book League Ltd., 7 Albemarle St. London W1, England) Eds. Bob Cobbing, Lawrence Upton. bibl. circ. 2,000.

944   015   FR
CENTRE INTERNATIONAL DE DOCUMENTATION OCCITANE. SERIE BIBLIOGRAPHIQUE. 1977. irreg. Centre International de Documentation Occitane, Boite Postale 4202, 34325 Beziers Cedex, France.

011   US
CHECKLIST OF SOUTH CAROLINA STATE PUBLICATIONS. 1971. a. free. State Library, P.O. Box 11469, 1500 Senate St., Columbia, SC 29211. Ed. Mary B. Toll. circ. 500 (controlled) (processed)

011   US
CHICOREL INDEX SERIES. 1970. irreg., vol. 17, 1974. $60 per vol. American Library Publishing Co., Inc., 275 Central Park West, New York, NY 10024. Ed. Marietta Chicorel.

011   BL
COLECAO DE ESTUDOS BIBLIOGRAFICOS. 1976. irreg. Fundacao Casa de Rui Barbosa, Rua Sao Clemente 134, Bota Fogo 22260, Rio de Janeiro RJ, Brazil. Dir. Washington Luis Neto.

500 016   BE   ISSN 0080-0937
COMMISSION BELGE DE BIBLIOGRAPHIE,
REPERTOIRE ANNUEL DES COMPTES-
RENDUS DE CONGRES SCIENTIFIQUES.*
(Subseries Of: Bibliographia Belgica) a. Commission
Belge de Bibliographie, Rue des Tanneurs 80-84, B-
1000 Brussels, Belgium.

010   UK   ISSN 0306-1124
COMMONWEALTH BIBLIOGRAPHIES. 1974.
irreg. Commonwealth Institute, Kensington High
St., London W8 6NQ, England.

COMMONWEALTH FORESTRY BUREAU
ANNOTATED BIBLIOGRAPHIES. see *FORESTS
AND FORESTRY — Abstracting, Bibliographies,
Statistics*

013   US   ISSN 0361-6657
COMPREHENSIVE DISSERTATION INDEX.
SUPPLEMENT. (In 5 vols.) 1973. a. $410 or $110
per vol. University Microfilms International, 300 N.
Zeeb Rd., Ann Arbor, MI 48106. (also avail. in
microfiche)

COMPUTER LAW BIBLIOGRAPHY. see
*COMPUTER TECHNOLOGY AND
APPLICATIONS — Abstracting, Bibliographies,
Statistics*

011   US
CORNELL UNIVERSITY. LIBRARIES. GUIDE
SERIES. 1971. irreg. Cornell University Libraries,
Reference Department, John M. Olin Library,
Ithaca, NY 14853. (looseleaf format)

CUMULATIVE BIBLIOGRAPHY OF
LITERATURE EXAMINED BY THE
RADIATION SHIELDING INFORMATION
CENTER. see *PHYSICS — Abstracting,
Bibliographies, Statistics*

016   FR
CURIOSPRESS INTERNATIONAL; annuaire
international des editeurs de publications etranges et
curieuses. (Text in French, English, German,
Spanish & Italian) 1974. biennial. 45 F. c/o Ed.
Pierre Birukoff, INFOS al International, B.P.
127, 75563 Paris 12, France. illus.

015   AT   ISSN 0070-184X
CURRENT AUSTRALIAN SERIALS. 1963. irreg.
Aus.$5. National Library of Australia, Sales and
Subscription Unit, Canberra, A.C.T. 2600, Australia.
index.

CURRENT CHRISTIAN BOOKS. see *RELIGIONS
AND THEOLOGY — Abstracting, Bibliographies,
Statistics*

011   JA
CURRENT CONTENTS OF ACADEMIC
JOURNALS IN JAPAN. (Text in English) 1971. a.
2000 Yen($10) University of Tokyo Press, 7-3-1
Hongo, Bunkyo-ku, Tokyo 113-91, Japan
(Distributed in U.S. & Canada by ISBS, Inc., P.O.
Box 4347, Portland, OR 97208) Ed. Kokusai Bunka
Shinkokai. circ. 1,000.

DANIA POLYGLOTTA; literature on Denmark in
languages other than Danish and books of Danish
interest published abroad. see *LITERATURE —
Abstracting, Bibliographies, Statistics*

015   DK   ISSN 0084-9596
DANSK PERIODICAFORTEGNELSE.
SUPPLEMENT/DANISH NATIONAL
BIBLIOGRAPHY. SERIALS. SUPPLEMENT.
(Text in Danish and English) 1970. a (cumulated)
price varies. (Kongelige Bibliotek)
Bibliotekscentralen, Telegrafvej 5, DK-2750
Ballerup, Denmark.

016   DK   ISSN 0084-9715
DENMARK. RIGSBIBLIOTEKAREMBEDET.
ACCESSIONSKATALOG. (Text in Danish and
English) 1901. a. price varies.
Rigsbibliotekarembedet, Christians Brygge 8, DK-
1219 Copenhagen K, Denmark. Ed. Gerd Borgen
Nielsen. circ. 850.

DEUTSCHER WETTERDIENST.
BIBLIOGRAPHIEN. see *METEOROLOGY —
Abstracting, Bibliographies, Statistics*

053 015   GW   ISSN 0419-005X
DEUTSCHSPRACHIGE ZEITSCHRIFTEN
DEUTSCHLAND - OESTERREICH - SCHWEIZ.
1956. a. DM.57. Verlag der Schillerbuchhandlung
Hans Banger, Alte Neusser Landstr. 302, 5000
Cologne 71, W. Germany (B.R.D.) circ. 8,000.
Formerly: Anschriften Deutschsprachiger
Zeitschriften (ISSN 0066-460X)

500 016   MY
DEVELOPMENT; a selected annotated bibliography.
(Text in English and Malaysian) 1972. irreg.
exchange basis. Malaysian Centre for Development
Studies, Prime Minister's Department, Government
Complex, Block K 11 & K 12, Jalan Duta, Kuala
Lumpur, Malaysia. circ. 1,000.

DIRECTORY OF AUSTRALIAN ASSOCIATIONS.
see *ABSTRACTING AND INDEXING
SERVICES*

DIRECTORY OF CANADIAN PLAYS AND
PLAYWRIGHTS. see *THEATER — Abstracting,
Bibliographies, Statistics*

DIRECTORY OF CONSERVATIVE AND
LIBERTARIAN SERIALS, PUBLISHERS, AND
FREELANCE MARKETS. see *POLITICAL
SCIENCE — Abstracting, Bibliographies, Statistics*

DIRECTORY OF ETHNIC PUBLISHERS AND
RESOURCE ORGANIZATIONS. see *ETHNIC
INTERESTS — Abstracting, Bibliographies,
Statistics*

016 352   CN   ISSN 0084-9944
DIRECTORY OF GOVERNMENTS IN
METROPOLITAN TORONTO. biennial. Can.$4.
Toronto Bureau of Municipal Research, 2 Toronto
St., Suite 306, Toronto, Ont. M5C 2B6, Canada.

015   IR   ISSN 0084-9960
DIRECTORY OF IRANIAN PERIODICALS.
(Subseries of its Reference Book Series) (Editions in
English and Persian) 1970. a. Rs.150($10) Institute
for Research and Planning in Science and
Education, Tehran Book Processing Centre, Box 11-
1126, Teheran, Iran. Eds. Poori Soltani, Zohreh
Alavi. circ. 750 (Persia edt.); 250 (English edt.)

DIRECTORY OF SMALL MAGAZINE/PRESS
EDITORS AND PUBLISHERS. see *PUBLISHING
AND BOOK TRADE — Abstracting,
Bibliographies, Statistics*

010   US   ISSN 0085-0020
DIRECTORY OF THE COLLEGE STUDENT
PRESS IN AMERICA. 1965. triennial. $40.
Oxbridge Communications, Inc., 183 Madison Ave.,
New York, NY 10016. Ed. Georgia Maas. circ.
2,000.

DOCTORAL DISSERTATIONS ON
TRANSPORTATION. see
*TRANSPORTATION — Abstracting,
Bibliographies, Statistics*

016.33   BL
DOCUMENTACAO AMAZONICA; catalogo
coletivo. 1974. irreg. Superintendencia do
Desenvolvimento da Amazonia, Travessa Antonio
Baena 1113, Belem, Brazil. (Prepared by: Rede de
Bibliotecas da Amazonia) stat.
Economic conditions in the Amazon valley

016   IT   ISSN 0070-6906
DOCUMENTI SULLE ARTI DEL LIBRO. 1962.
irreg; latest issue. 1978. price varies. Edizioni Il
Polifilo, Via Borgonuovo 2, 20121 Milan, Italy. Ed.
Alberto Vigevani.

DRUG ABUSE BIBLIOGRAPHY. see *DRUG
ABUSE AND ALCOHOLISM — Abstracting,
Bibliographies, Statistics*

011   UK
DUMBARTON OAKS BIBLIOGRAPHIES; based on
"Byzantinische Zeitschrift". 1973. irreg. price varies.
(Dumbarton Oaks Center for Byzantine Studies, US)
Mansell Publishing, 3 Bloomsbury Place, London
WC1A 2QA, England (Dist. in U.S. by: Mansell,
Merrimack Book Service, 99 Main St., Salem, NH
03079) Ed. Jelisaveta S. Allen. index.

EGYPTIAN NATIONAL MUSEUM. LIBRARY.
CATALOGUE. see *ARCHAEOLOGY —
Abstracting, Bibliographies, Statistics*

015   GW   ISSN 0071-1462
ESSENER BIBLIOGRAPHIE. 1970. a. price varies.
Stadtbibliothek, Hindenburgstr. 25, Essen, W.
Germany (B.R.D.) Ed. Alfred Peter. circ. 1,500.

015   ET   ISSN 0071-1772
ETHIOPIAN PUBLICATIONS: BOOKS,
PAMPHLETS, ANNUALS AND PERIODICAL
ARTICLES. (Name of issuing body varies: Haile
Sellassie I University, University of Addis Ababa,
National University) 1963. a, (latest 1975. $5. Addis
Ababa University, Institute of Ethiopian Studies,
Box 1176, Addis Ababa, Ethiopia. Eds. Degife
Gabre-Tsadik, Mergia Diro. circ. 500.

EUROPEAN ORGANIZATION FOR NUCLEAR
RESEARCH. LISTE DES PUBLICATIONS
SCIENTIFIQUES/LIST OF SCIENTIFIC
PUBLICATIONS. see *PHYSICS — Abstracting,
Bibliographies, Statistics*

010 060   NE   ISSN 0071-3139
EUROPEAN YEARBOOK. 1956. a., except 1964.
price varies. (Council of Europe, FR) Martinus
Nijhoff, Box 566, 2501 CN The Hague,
Netherlands. Ed. A. H. Robertson.

FACHWOERTERBUECHER UND LEXIKA. EIN
INTERNATIONALES VERZEICHNIS/
INTERNATIONAL BIBLIOGRAPHY OF
DICTIONARIES. see *LINGUISTICS —
Abstracting, Bibliographies, Statistics*

FARM AND GARDEN PERIODICALS ON
MICROFILM. see *GARDENING AND
HORTICULTURE — Abstracting, Bibliographies,
Statistics*

016.05   US   ISSN 0146-2660
FAXON LIBRARIANS' GUIDE; to periodicals,
annuals, continuations GPO publications,
monographic series, newspapers, proceedings, serials,
transactions and yearbooks. 1931. a. $10 (or free to
qualified personnel) F. W. Faxon Co., Inc., Faxon
Bldg., 15 Southwest Park, Westwood, MA 02090.
Ed. Beverly D. Heinle. adv. illus. circ. 25,000.
Former titles: Faxon Librarians' Guide to
Periodicals (ISSN 0092-0487); Faxon Indexed
Periodicals.

791.43 016   GE   ISSN 0015-1750
FILMO-BIBLIOGRAFISCHER JAHRESBERICHT.
1965. a. M.8.70. (Hochschule fuer Film und
Fernsehen der DDR) Henschelverlag Kunst und
Gesellschaft, Oranienburger Str. 67/68, 104 Berlin,
E. Germany (D.D.R.) Ed.Bd.

FINDING AIDS TO THE MICROFILMED
MANUSCRIPT COLLECTION OF THE
GENEALOGICAL SOCIETY OF UTAH. see
*GENEALOGY AND HERALDRY — Abstracting,
Bibliographies, Statistics*

010   FI   ISSN 0071-5298
FINLAND. POSTI- JA LENNATINLAITOS.
KOTIMAISTEN SANOMALEHTIEN
HINNASTO. INHEMSK TIDNINGSTAXA. (Text
in Finnish and Swedish) 1855. a. Fmk.14. Posti- ja
Lennatinlaitos - General Direction of Posts and
Telegraphs, Mannerheimintie 11, SF-00100 Helsinki
10, Finland. index.

FOR YOUNGER READERS, BRAILLE AND
TALKING BOOKS. see *BLIND — Abstracting,
Bibliographies, Statistics*

FRANCE. MINISTERE DE LA QUALITE DE LA
VIE. BULLETIN DE DOCUMENTATION. see
*ENVIRONMENTAL STUDIES — Abstracting,
Bibliographies, Statistics*

DIE FRAUENFRAGE IN DEUTSCHLAND.
BIBLIOGRAPHIE. see *WOMEN'S
INTERESTS — Abstracting, Bibliographies,
Statistics*

016.054   US   ISSN 0362-5044
FRENCH PERIODICAL INDEX/REPERTORIEX.
(Text in French) 1976. irreg., latest 1980. price
varies. c/o J.-P. Ponchie, Chitwood Hall, Foreign
Language Department, West Virginia University,
Morgantown, WV 26506.

016 840   US   ISSN 0085-0888
FRENCH XX BIBLIOGRAPHY; CRITICAL AND BIOGRAPHICAL REFERENCES FOR THE STUDY OF FRENCH LITERATURE SINCE 1885. 1969, vol. 5, no. 211. a. $36. French Institute-Alliance Francaise, 22 East 60th St., New York, NY 10022. Co-Sponsor: Camargo Foundation. circ. 1,200.
Continues: French VII Bibliography, Critical and Biographical References for the Study of Contemporary French Literature.

FRENCH 17; an annual descriptive bibliography of French 17th Century studies. see *HISTORY — Abstracting, Bibliographies, Statistics*

GERMANY(FEDERAL REPUBLIC, 1949-). BUNDESANSTALT FUER GEWAESSERKUNDE. HYDROLOGISCHE BIBLIOGRAPHIE. see *EARTH SCIENCES — Abstracting, Bibliographies, Statistics*

015   GW   ISSN 0433-762X
GERMANY (FEDERAL REPUBLIC, 1949-) DEUTSCHER BUNDESTAG. WISSENSCHAFTLICHE DIENSTE. BIBLIOGRAPHIEN. 1961. irreg. free. Deutscher Bundestag, Abteilung Wissenschaftliche Dokumentation, Bundeshaus, 5300 Bonn, W. Germany (B.R.D.)

015   GW   ISSN 0435-7590
GERMANY (FEDERAL REPUBLIC, 1949-) DEUTSCHER BUNDESTAG. WISSENSCHAFTLICHE DIENSTE. MATERIALIEN. 1965. irreg. free. Deutscher Bundestag, Abteilung Wissenschaftliche Dokumentation, Bundeshaus, 5300 Bonn, W. Germany (B. R. D.)

015   GW   ISSN 0302-0657
GESAMTVERZEICHNIS DER ZEITSCHRIFTEN UND SERIEN IN BIBLIOTHEKEN DER BUNDESREPUBLIK DEUTSCHLAND EINSCHLIESSLICH BERLIN (WEST)/UNION LIST OF SERIALS IN LIBRARIES OF THE FEDERAL REPUBLIC OF GERMANY INCLUDING BERLIN (WEST); Neue und geaenderte Titel seit 1971 mit Besitznachweisen/ New and changed titles after 1971 with holdings locations. 1973. a. (Staatsbibliothek Preussischer Kulturbesitz) K.G Saur Verlag KG, Poessenbacherstr. 12 B, Postfach 711009, 8000 Munich 71, W. Germany (B.R.D.)

013   AU   ISSN 0072-4165
GESAMTVERZEICHNIS OESTERREICHISCHER DISSERTATIONEN. 1967. a. S.195. Verband der Wissenschaftlichen Gesellschaften Oesterreichs, Lindengasse 37, A-1070 Vienna, Austria.

015   GH   ISSN 0072-4378
GHANA NATIONAL BIBLIOGRAPHY. 1965. a. $5. Research Library on African Affairs, Box 2970, Accra, Ghana.

016   IT   ISSN 0085-2317
GIUNTA CENTRALE PER GLI STUDI STORICI, ROME. BIBLIOGRAFIA STORICA NAZIONALE. 1939. irreg. L.16000. Giunta Centrale per gli Studi Storici, 50014 Fiesole, Florence, Italy.

015.73   US   ISSN 0072-5188
GOVERNMENT REFERENCE BOOKS; a biennial guide to U.S. Government publications. 1968/69. biennial. $16.65. Libraries Unlimited, Inc., Box 263, Littleton, CO 80160. Ed. Walter L. Newsome.

GREAT BRITAIN. ROYAL COMMISSION ON HISTORICAL MANUSCRIPTS. ACCESSIONS TO REPOSITORIES AND REPORTS ADDED TO THE NATIONAL REGISTER OF ARCHIVES. see *HISTORY — Abstracting, Bibliographies, Statistics*

GREAT BRITAIN. ROYAL COMMISSION ON HISTORICAL MANUSCRIPTS. JOINT PUBLICATION. see *HISTORY — Abstracting, Bibliographies, Statistics*

GREAT BRITAIN. ROYAL HISTORICAL MANUSCRIPTS COMMISSION. COMMISSIONERS' REPORTS TO THE CROWN. see *HISTORY — Abstracting, Bibliographies, Statistics*

050   IT
GUIDA DELLA STAMPA PERIODICA ITALIANA. 1969. irreg., 1977, vol. 5. Unione della Stampa Periodica Italiana, Via Po 102, 00198 Rome, Italy. adv.

016 960   CM
GUIDE BIBLIOGRAPHIQUE DU MONDE NOIR/BIBLIOGRAPHIC GUIDE TO THE NEGRO WORLD. (Text in French and English) 1971. irreg. 6000 Fr.CFA($22.98) Universite de Yaounde, P.O. Box 337, Yaounde, Cameroon (Dist. by: Service Central des Bibliotheques, Services des Publications, B. P. 1312, Yaounde, Cameroon) Eds. Rev. Father Engelbert Mveng & Jean-Roger Fontveille. bibl.

011   US
GUIDE TO ALTERNATIVE PERIODICALS. 1976. a. $3. Sunspark Press, Box 91, Greenleaf, OR 97445. Ed. Don Carnahan. bk. rev. bibl, stat. circ. 2,000.
Formerly: Sunspark.

016 658.8   US   ISSN 0533-5248
GUIDE TO AMERICAN DIRECTORIES. 1954. biennial. $55. B. Klein Publications, Box 8503, Coral Springs, FL 33065. Ed. Bernard Klein.

GUIDE TO AMERICAN EDUCATIONAL DIRECTORIES. see *EDUCATION — Abstracting, Bibliographies, Statistics*

GUIDE TO AMERICAN SCIENTIFIC AND TECHNICAL DIRECTORIES. see *TECHNOLOGY: COMPREHENSIVE WORKS — Abstracting, Bibliographies, Statistics*

GUIDE TO COLLECTIONS OF MANUSCRIPTS RELATING TO AUSTRALIA. see *HISTORY — Abstracting, Bibliographies, Statistics*

020 011   US   ISSN 0164-0747
GUIDE TO MICROFORMS IN PRINT. AUTHOR, TITLE. 1961. a. $84.50. Microform Review, Inc., 520 Riverside Ave., Box 405, Saugatuck Station, Westport, CT 06880. Ed. Ardis V. Carleton. adv.
Supersedes in part: Guide to Microforms in Print (ISSN 0017-5293); Incorporates: International Microforms in Print.

016 070   CN   ISSN 0315-7288
GUIDE TO PERIODICALS AND NEWSPAPERS IN THE PUBLIC LIBRARIES OF METROPOLITAN TORONTO. 1970. a. Can.$20. Metropolitan Toronto Library Board, 789 Yonge St., Toronto, Ontario M4W 2G8, Canada.
Formerly: Toronto. Public Libraries. Guide to Serials Currently Received in the Public Libraries of Metropolitan Toronto.

011.02   US   ISSN 0072-8624
GUIDE TO REFERENCE BOOKS. 1902. irreg., latest 9th ed. price varies. American Library Association, 50 E. Huron St., Chicago, IL 60611. Ed. Eugene Sheehy.

011   UK   ISSN 0072-8640
GUIDE TO REFERENCE MATERIAL. 1959. irreg., 4th ed. 1980. price varies. Library Association Publishing Ltd., 7 Ridgmount St., London WC1E 7AE, England. Ed. A. J. Walford. index.

011   US   ISSN 0072-8667
GUIDE TO REPRINTS. (Text in English, French, German, Italian, Latin and Spanish) 1967. a. $49.50. Guide to Reprints, Inc., Box 249, Kent, CT 06757. Ed. Ann S. Davis. circ. 2,600.

GUIDE TO TRAFFIC SAFETY LITERATURE. see *TRANSPORTATION — Abstracting, Bibliographies, Statistics*

016   IS
HARRY S. TRUMAN RESEARCH INSTITUTE, JERUSALEM. OCCASIONAL PAPERS. (Text in English, Hebrew, and Arabic) 1971. irreg. exchange basis. Hebrew University of Jerusalem, Harry S. Truman Research Institute, Mount Scopus, Jerusalem, Israel. bibl.

026   US
HARVARD-YENCHING LIBRARY BIBLIOGRAPHICAL SERIES. 1970. irreg., approx. triennial. $12 paper; $20 hard bound. Harvard-Yenching Library, 2 Divinity Avenue, Cambridge, MA 02138.

015   GW   ISSN 0170-2408
HIERSEMANNS BIBLIOGRAPHISCHE HANDBUECHER. 1979. irreg., vol. 2, 1981. price varies. Anton Hiersemann Verlag, Rosenbergstr. 113, Postfach 723, 7000 Stuttgart 1, W. Germany(B.R.D.)

011   AG   ISSN 0073-327X
HONTANAR.* irreg. Editorial Universitaria de Buenos Aires, Riva Davia 1571-1573, Buenos Aires, Argentina.

I C S S R UNION CATALOGUE OF SOCIAL SCIENCE PERIODICALS/SERIALS. (Indian Council of Social Science Research) see *SOCIAL SCIENCES: COMPREHENSIVE WORKS — Abstracting, Bibliographies, Statistics*

016   II   ISSN 0073-6627
I N S D O C UNION CATALOGUE SERIES. irreg., no. 16, 1976. Indian National Scientific Documentation Centre, Hillside Rd., New Delhi 110012, India. Ed. S. N. Dutta.

ILLINOIS HEALTH SCIENCES LIBRARIES SERIALS HOLDINGS LIST. see *LIBRARY AND INFORMATION SCIENCES — Abstracting, Bibliographies, Statistics*

297 016   UK   ISSN 0306-9524
INDEX ISLAMICUS. (Cumulates Quarterly Index Islamicus) quinquennial. price varies. (University of London, School of Oriental and African Studies) Mansell Publishing, 3 Bloomsbury Place, London WC1A 2QA, England (Dist. in U.S. by: Mansell, Merrimack Book Service, 99 Main St., Salem, NH 03079)

050 016.5   IO   ISSN 0019-3607
INDEX OF INDONESIAN LEARNED PERIODICALS/INDEKS MADJALAH ILMIAH. (Text in Indonesian with English translations) 1960. a. Rps.750($5) Indonesian Institute of Sciences - Lembaga Ilmu Pengetahuan Indonesia, Jalan Teuku Tjhiki Ditiro 43, Jakarta, Indonesia. index. circ. 1,000.

011   US
INDEX TO REVIEWS OF BIBLIOGRAPHICAL PUBLICATIONS. 1976. a. $14.50. G. K. Hall and Co., 70 Lincoln Street, Boston, MA 02111. Ed. L. Terry Oggel.

950   II   ISSN 0073-6090
INDIA. A REFERENCE ANNUAL. (Text in English) 1953. a. Rs.15($4.50) Ministry of Information and Broadcasting, Research and Reference Division, Publications Division, Patiala House, Tilak Marg, New Delhi 110001, India (U.S. Subscr. Address: M/S Inter Culture Associates, Thompson, CT 06277) circ. 20,000.

INDIAN BOOK REVIEW INDEX. see *PUBLISHING AND BOOK TRADE — Abstracting, Bibliographies, Statistics*

015   II   ISSN 0073-6708
INDIAN STATISTICAL INSTITUTE. LIBRARY. BIBLIOGRAPHIC SERIES.* (Text in English) 1959. irreg. price varies. Indian Statistical Institute, Library, Asutosh Bldg., Calcutta 12, India.

011   AT   ISSN 0310-6659
INDONESIAN ACQUISITIONS LIST/DAFTAR PENGADAAN BAHAN INDONESIA. 1971. irreg. free. National Library of Australia, Canberra, A.C.T. 2600, Australia. circ. 300.

010   FR   ISSN 0073-8034
INITIATION. SERIE TEXTES, BIBLIOGRAPHIES. 1959. irreg. price varies. Editions Cujas, 4,6,8, rue de la Maison-Blanche, 75013 Paris, France.

015   CK   ISSN 0073-991X
INSTITUTO CARO Y CUERVO. SERIE BIBLIOGRAFICA. 1950. irreg., no. 13, 1978. Instituto Caro y Cuervo, Seccion de Publicaciones, Apdo. Aereo 20002, Bogota, Colombia.

378 016   CK
INSTITUTO COLOMBIANO PARA EL FOMENTO DE LA EDUCACION SUPERIOR. BOLETIN BIBLIOGRAFICO. 1975. irreg. Instituto Colombiano para el Fomento de la Educacion Superior, Division de Documentacion y Fomento Bibliotecario, Biblioteca, Bogota, Colombia.

016 MX ISSN 0074-0306
INSTITUTO TECNOLOGICO Y DE ESTUDIOS SUPERIORES. PUBLICACIONES. SERIE: CATALOGOS DE BIBLIOTECA. 1965. irreg., 1969, no. 3. price varies. Instituto Tecnologico y de Estudios Superiores de Monterrey, Sucursal de Correos "J", Monterrey, N.L., Mexico.

INTERNATIONAL BOOKS IN PRINT; English-language titles published outside the USA and Great Britain. see *PUBLISHING AND BOOK TRADE — Abstracting, Bibliographies, Statistics*

INTERNATIONAL DIRECTORY OF LITTLE MAGAZINES AND SMALL PRESSES. see *PUBLISHING AND BOOK TRADE — Abstracting, Bibliographies, Statistics*

011 US
INTERNATIONAL PUBLICATIONS; an annual annotated subject bibliography. 1972. a. $7.50. International Publications Service, 114 E. 32nd St, New York, NY 10016. circ. 10,000.

010 GW ISSN 0074-9672
INTERNATIONALE BIBLIOGRAPHIE DER FACHADRESSBUECHER/INTERNATIONAL BIBLIOGRAPHY OF DIRECTORIES. 1962. irreg., 6th ed., 1978. DM.120($60) K.G. Saur Verlag KG, Poessenbacherstr. 12 B, Postfach 711009, 8000 Munich 71, W. Germany (B.R.D.) (And 175 Fifth Ave., New York, NY 10010) adv.

016 020 GW ISSN 0535-5079
INVENTARE NICHTSTAATLICHER ARCHIVE. 1952. irreg., no. 22, 1979. price varies. (Landschaftsverband Rheinland, Archivberatungsstelle) Rheinland-Verlag, Kennedy-Ufer 2, 5000 Cologne 21, W. Germany (B.R.D.) (Distr. by: Rudolf Habelt Verlag, Am Buchenhang 1, 5300 Bonn, W. Germany (B.R.D.))

010 US ISSN 0000-0043
IRREGULAR SERIALS AND ANNUALS; an international directory. 1967. biennial. $75.00. R.R. Bowker Company, 1180 Ave. of the Americas, New York, NY 10036 (Orders to P.O. Box 1807, Ann Arbor, Mich, 48106)

011 UK
ISIS CUMULATIVE BIBLIOGRAPHY. 1971. price varies. (Smithsonian Institution, History of Science Society, US) Mansell Publishing, 3 Bloomsbury Place, London WC1A 20A, England (Dist. in U.S. by: Mansell, Merrimack Book Service, 99 Main St., Salem, NH 03079) Ed. Magda Whitrow.

ISTITUTO CENTRALE PER LA PATOLOGIA DEL LIBRO "ALFONSO GALLO." BOLLETTINO. see *PUBLISHING AND BOOK TRADE — Abstracting, Bibliographies, Statistics*

JAHRESBIBLIOGRAPHIE MASSENKOMMUNIKATION. see *COMMUNICATIONS — Abstracting, Bibliographies, Statistics*

830 016 GE ISSN 0300-8436
JAHRESVERZEICHNIS DER VERLAGSSCHRIFTEN UND EINER AUSWAHL DER AUSSERHALB DES BUCHHANDELS ERSCHIENENEN VEROEFFENTLICHUNGEN DER DDR, DER BRD UND WESTBERLINS SOWIE DER DEUTSCHSPRACHIGEN WERKE ANDERER LAENDER. 1796. irreg., vol. 172 (for 1969), 1975. price varies. VEB Verlag fuer Buch- und Bibliothekswesen, Gerichtsweg 26, 701 Leipzig, E. Germany (D.D.R.)
Formerly: Jahresverzeichnis des Deutschen Schrifttums (ISSN 0075-2967)

015 JM ISSN 0075-2991
JAMAICAN NATIONAL BIBLIOGRAPHY. (Fourth no. Is an annual cumulation) 1964. a. $13.50. Institute of Jamaica, 12-16 East St., Kingston, Jamaica. Ed. Jacqueline Morgan.
Formerly: Institute of Jamaica, Kingston. West India Reference Library. Jamaican Accessions.

JAMES COOK UNIVERSITY OF NORTH QUEENSLAND. RESEARCH AND PUBLICATIONS REPORT. (0312-9012) see *SCIENCES: COMPREHENSIVE WORKS — Abstracting, Bibliographies, Statistics*

011 JA
JAPAN ENGLISH BOOKS IN PRINT. (Text in English) 1980. triennial. $60. Intercontinental Marketing Corp., I P O Box 5056, Tokyo 100-31, Japan.

015 JA
JAPANESE BOOKS IN PRINT (YEAR) 1977/78. a. 23000 Yen. Japan Book Publishers Association - Nihon Shoseki Shuppan Kyokai, Fukuromachi 6, Shinjuku-ku, Tokyo, Japan.

015.52 JA ISSN 0385-3284
JAPANESE NATIONAL BIBLIOGRAPHY/ZEN NIHON SHUPPANBUTSU SOMOKUROKU. 1948. a. National Diet Library - Kokuritsu Kokkai Toshokan, 1-10-1 Nagata-cho, Chiyoda-ku, Tokyo 100, Japan.

016.3 US ISSN 0075-4951
KANSAS STATE UNIVERSITY. LIBRARY BIBLIOGRAPHY SERIES. 1964. irreg., no. 14, 1974. price varies. Kansas State University, Library Publications, Manhattan, KS 66506.

015 KE
KENYA. GOVERNMENT PRINTING AND STATIONERY DEPARTMENT. CATALOGUE OF GOVERNMENT PUBLICATIONS. a. or biennial. S.5.50($0.80) Government Printing and Stationery Department, P.O. Box 30128, Nairobi, Kenya.

KODALY INSTITUTE OF CANADA. MONOGRAPH; a selected bibliography of the Kodaly concept of music education. see *MUSIC — Abstracting, Bibliographies, Statistics*

010 II ISSN 0075-6970
KOTHARI'S WORLD OF REFERENCE WORKS. 1963. irreg.; latest 1963. $1.50. Kothari Publications, 12 India Exchange Place, Calcutta 700001, India. Ed. H. Kothari. adv.

LAND RESOURCE BIBLIOGRAPHY. see *CONSERVATION — Abstracting, Bibliographies, Statistics*

917.8 UK
LATIN AMERICA REVIEW. 1973. irreg. £1.25. Latin America Review of Books, Ltd., 6-7 New Bridge St., London EC4V 6HR, England. Eds. C. Harding, C. Roper. adv. bk. rev. circ. 5,000.
Formerly: Latin America Review of Books.

LATIN AMERICAN STUDIES IN THE UNIVERSITIES OF THE UNITED KINGDOM. see *HISTORY — Abstracting, Bibliographies, Statistics*

LATIN AMERICAN STUDIES IN THE UNIVERSITIES OF THE UNITED KINGDOM. STAFF RESEARCH IN PROGRESS OR RECENTLY COMPLETED IN THE HUMANITIES AND THE SOCIAL SCIENCES. see *HISTORY — Abstracting, Bibliographies, Statistics*

980 015 SW
LATINOAMERICANA. (Text in Spanish and Swedish) 1978. irreg., no. 4, 1978. free. Latinamerika-Institutet i Stockholm - Institute of Latin American Studies, Stockholm, Odengatan 61, Fack, S-102 30 Stockholm, Sweden.

860 015 CK
LEA. 1976. irreg. Carrera 44 no. 47-61, Apdo. Aereo 4307, Medellin, Colombia. Eds. Luis Amadeo Perez, German Suescun.

LIBRARIANS' GUIDE TO BACK ISSUES OF INTERNATIONAL PERIODICALS; originals & reprints, featuring science, technology, medicine, the humanities. see *JOURNALISM — Abstracting, Bibliographies, Statistics*

011 SP
LIBRORAMA INTERNACIONAL; periodico bibliografico. vol. 2, 1976. irreg. free. Elvira 3, Madrid 28, Spain. Ed. Segundo Martin Macias. adv. bk. rev. circ. 40,000.

011 VE
LIBROS AL DIA. a. Bs.140. Apartado 9324, Caracas, Venezuela. stat.

011 SP ISSN 0377-0974
LIBROS ESPANOLES I S B N. 1973. a. 2200 ptas.($50) Instituto Nacional del Libro Espanol, Agencia Espanola I S B N, Santiago Rusinol 8, Madrid 3, Spain. circ. 20,000.

015 UR
LITERATURA O SAKHALINSKOI OBLASTI. 1968. a. 0.30 Rub. (Sakhalinskaya Oblastnaya Biblioteka) Dalnevostochnoe Knizhnoe Izdatel'stvo, Sakhalinskoe Otdelenie, Ul. Dzerzhinskogo, 34, Yuzhno-Sakhalinsk, U.S.S.R.

016 PL ISSN 0075-9945
LITERATURA PIEKNA. ADNOTOWANY ROCZNIK BIBLIOGRAFICZNY. 1954. a. 120 Zl.($13) (Biblioteka Narodowa, Instytut Bibliograficzny) Stowarzyszenie Bibliotekarzy Polskich, Konopczynskiego 5/7, Warsaw, Poland (Dist. by: Ars Polona-Ruch, Krakowskie Przedmiescie 7, Warsaw, Poland) circ. 5,000.

015 BE
LIVRES BELGES DE LANGUE FRANCAISE. (Text in French) 1960. a. free. ‡ Association Belge des Editeurs de Langue Francaise, 111 avenue du Parc, 1060 Brussels, Belgium. Ed. J. de Raeymaeker. adv. circ. 17,000.
Formerly: Livres Belges.

016 FR
LIVRES DISPONIBLES. 1972. a. 963 F.($200) Cercle de la Librairie, 117 Boulevard Saint-Germain, 75006 Paris, France. (Co-sponsor: Union des Editeurs de Langue Francaise)
Formed by the merger of: Catalogue de l'Edition Francaise (ISSN 0069-1089) & Repertoire des Livres de Langue Francaise Disponibles (ISSN 0080-1003)

M I M C MICROFORMS ANNUAL. (Microforms International Marketing Corporation) see *BUSINESS AND ECONOMICS — Abstracting, Bibliographies, Statistics*

400 800 016 US ISSN 0024-8215
M L A INTERNATIONAL BIBLIOGRAPHY OF BOOKS AND ARTICLES ON THE MODERN LANGUAGES AND LITERATURES. 1922. a. in 3 vols. $60 per vol. (soft cover); hardcover edition $150 for 3 vols. Modern Language Association of America, 62 Fifth Ave., New York, NY 10011. Ed. Eileen M. Mackesy. bibl. index. circ. 32,500.

016 960 CN ISSN 0316-6570
MCGILL UNIVERSITY, MONTREAL. CENTRE FOR DEVELOPING-AREA STUDIES. BIBLIOGRAPHY SERIES. 1972. irreg., no. 10, 1978. price varies. McGill University, Centre for Developing-Area Studies, 815 Sherbrooke St. W., Montreal, Que. H3A 2K6, Canada. Ed. Rosalind E. Boyd. circ. 400.

015 HU
MAGYAR TUDOMANYOS AKADEMIA. KONYVTAR. KEZIRATTAR KATALOGUSAI. (Text in Hungarian; summaries in English, French, German) 1966. irreg., vol. 9, 1976. exchange basis. Magyar Tudomanyos Akademia, Konyvtar, Akademia u. 2, P.O.B. 7, 1361 Budapest 5, Hungary. circ. 800.

MARX KAROLY KOZGAZDASAGTUDOMANYI EGYETEM OKTATOINAK SZAKIRODALMI MUNKASSAGA. see *BUSINESS AND ECONOMICS — Abstracting, Bibliographies, Statistics*

033 GW ISSN 0076-7670
MEYERS GROSSES JAHRESLEXIKON. 1974. a. DM.34. Bibliographisches Institut AG, Dudenstr. 6, Postfach 311, 6800 Mannheim 41, W. Germany (B.R.D.)

011 US ISSN 0092-5349
MICHIGAN. STATE LIBRARY SERVICES. CATALOG OF BOOKS ON MAGNETIC TAPE. 1968. irreg., latest issue 1972. free. ‡ Department of Education, State Library Services, Box 30007, Lansing, MI 48909. Key Title: Catalog of Books on Magnetic Tape (Lansing)

016   US   ISSN 0147-0604
MICHIGAN STATE UNIVERSITY. LIBRARY. AFRICANA: SELECT RECENT ACQUISITIONS. (Text in English, French, Italian, Portuguese, Russian, Spanish and Swahili) 1965. irreg. (approx. 6/yr.) free. ‡ Michigan State University Libraries, International Library, East Lansing, MI 48824. Eds. Dr. Eugene de Benko; Onuma Ezera. circ. 600(controlled) (processed)

600 010   US   ISSN 0076-8316
MICHIGAN TECHNOLOGICAL UNIVERSITY. LIBRARY. SERIAL HOLDINGS LIST. (Subseries of: Library Publication) 1964. irreg. $2. ‡ Michigan Technological University, Library, Houghton, MI 49931.
    Formerly: Michigan. Technological University Houghton. Library. Journal and Serial Holdings.

011   US   ISSN 0164-0739
MICROFORMS IN PRINT. SUPPLEMENT. 1979. a. $35. Microform Review, Inc., 520 Riverside Ave., Box 405, Saugatuck Station, Westport, CT 06880. Ed. Ardis V. Carleton. adv. bibl. circ. 1,000. (back issues avail.)
    Formerly: Microlist (ISSN 0362-1014)

011   US   ISSN 0361-2635
MICROPUBLISHERS' TRADE LIST ANNUAL. Cover title: M T L A, the Micropublishers' Trade List Annual. 1975. a. $98.50. Microform Review Inc., Box 405, Saugatuck Station, Westport, CT 06880. index. (microfiche)

011   US
MINNESOTA PERIODICALS ON MICROFILM. 1972. a. $100 price includes Minnesota Periodicals Index. Minnesota Scholarly Press, Box 224, Mankato, MN 56001. (microfilm; back issues avail.)

015   UR
MOSKOVSKII UNIVERSITET. BIBLIOTEKA. RUKOPISNAYA I PECHATNAYA KNIGA V FONDAKH. 1973. irreg. 0.76 Rub. Moskovskii Universitet, Leninskie Gory, Moscow V-234, U.S.S.R. illus.

016   FR   ISSN 0085-476X
MUSEUM NATIONAL D'HISTOIRE NATURELLE, PARIS. BIBLIOTHEQUE CENTRALE. LISTE DES PERIODIQUES FRANCAIS ET ETRANGERS.SUPPLEMENT. 1971. a. avail. only on exchange. Museum National d'Histoire Naturelle, Bibliotheque Centrale, 38 rue Geoffroy Saint Hilaire, 75005 Paris, France. circ. controlled.

MUSIC & MUSICIANS: BRAILLE SCORES CATALOG - CHORAL. see *BLIND — Abstracting, Bibliographies, Statistics*

MUSIC & MUSICIANS: BRAILLE SCORES CATALOG - ORGAN. see *BLIND — Abstracting, Bibliographies, Statistics*

MUSIC & MUSICIANS: BRAILLE SCORES CATALOG - PIANO. see *BLIND — Abstracting, Bibliographies, Statistics*

MUSIC & MUSICIANS: BRAILLE SCORES CATALOG - VOICE. see *BLIND — Abstracting, Bibliographies, Statistics*

MUSIC & MUSICIANS: INSTRUCTIONAL CASSETTE RECORDINGS CATALOG. see *BLIND — Abstracting, Bibliographies, Statistics*

MUSIC & MUSICIANS: INSTRUCTIONAL DISC RECORDINGS CATALOG. see *BLIND — Abstracting, Bibliographies, Statistics*

MUSIC & MUSICIANS: LARGE-PRINT SCORES AND BOOKS CATALOG. see *BLIND — Abstracting, Bibliographies, Statistics*

011   ZA
NATIONAL BIBLIOGRAPHY OF ZAMBIA. a. 45 n. National Archives, Box R.W. 10, Ridgeway, Lusaka, Zambia. circ. 1,000. (looseleaf format; back issues avail)

NATIONAL INSTITUTE FOR PERSONNEL RESEARCH. LIST OF N I P R PUBLICATIONS. see *BUSINESS AND ECONOMICS — Abstracting, Bibliographies, Statistics*

917.102 015   CN
NATIONAL LIBRARY OF CANADA. NATIONAL CONFERENCE ON THE STATE OF CANADIAN BIBLIOGRAPHY. PROCEEDINGS. 1977. irreg. Can.$7.50. National Library of Canada, 395 Wellington St., Ottawa, Ont. K1A 0N4, Canada (Order from: Supply and Services Canada, Ottawa, Ont. K1A 0S9, Canada) Ed.Bd.

011   CN
NATIONAL LIBRARY OF CANADA: A BIBLIOGRAPHY. 1979. irreg. Can.$9.95. National Library of Canada, 395 Wellington St., Ottawa, Ont. 51A 0N4, Canada (Order from: Supply and Services Canada, Ottawa, Ont. K1A 0S9, Canada)

015   US   ISSN 0090-0044
NATIONAL UNION CATALOG OF MANUSCRIPT COLLECTIONS. 1959/61. a. $90. U.S. Library of Congress, Descriptive Cataloging Division, 10 First St. S.E., Washington, DC 20540 (Subscriptions to: LC Cataloging Distribution Service, Building No. 159, Navy Yard Annex, Washington, DC 20541)

015   PP
NEW GUINEA BIBLIOGRAPHY. 1967. a. K.10 (avail. also on exchange) ‡ University of Papua New Guinea, The Library, Box 4819, University P.O., Papua New Guinea. circ. 300. (processed)

016 978.9   US
NEW MEXICO; AN ANNOTATED DIRECTORY OF INFORMATION SOURCES. 1971. irreg. $15. Southwest Research and Information Center, P.O. Box 4524, Albuquerque, NM 87106. Ed. Peter Montague. circ. 400.

090   CN   ISSN 0085-4166
NEWS FROM THE RARE BOOK ROOM. 1964. irreg. free. ‡ University of Alberta Library, Special Collections Division, Edmonton, Alta. TG6 2J8, Canada. Ed. John W. Charles. circ. 200. (processed offset)

070   US   ISSN 0097-9627
NEWSPAPERS IN MICROFORM. (Supplements Newspapers in Microform: Foreign Countries, 1948-1972; Newspapers in Microform: United States, 1948-1972) 1973. a. price varies. U.S. Library of Congress, Catalog Publication Division, 10 First St. S.E., Washington, DC 20540 (Subscriptions to: LC Cataloging Distribution Service, Building No. 159, Navy Yard Annex, Washington, DC 20541)

016   JA
NIHON HAKUSHIROKU. 1955. irreg. 5800 Yen. Kojunsha, 2-9 Kitakarasuyama, Setagaya-ku, Tokyo, Japan. bibl.

011   US
NOTABLE BOOKS. a. controlled free circ. American Library Association, 50 East Huron St., Chicago, IL 60611.

NOVAYA LITERATURA PO TSENOOBRAZOVANIYU, OPUBLIKOVANNAYA V S.S.S.R; annotirovannyi ukazatel' see *BUSINESS AND ECONOMICS — Abstracting, Bibliographies, Statistics*

011   SP
NOVEDADES; servicio de informacion bibliografica. irreg. Editorial Planeta S.A., Corcega 273-277, Barcelona 8, Spain. illus.

011   YU   ISSN 0350-3577
OBVESTILA REPUBLISKE MATISNE KNJIZNICE. irreg. Narodna in Univerzitetna Knjiznica, Turjaska 1, 61001 Ljubljana, Yugoslavia. Ed. Tomo Martelanc.

010   US   ISSN 0078-5768
OREGON STATE MONOGRAPHS. BIBLIOGRAPHIC SERIES. 1938. irreg., latest no. 18. price varies. Oregon State University Press, 101 Waldo Hall, Corvallis, OR 97331.

330 016   FR   ISSN 0474-5086
ORGANIZATION FOR ECONOMIC COOPERATION AND DEVELOPMENT. CATALOGUE OF PUBLICATIONS. biennial. free. ‡ Organization for Economic Cooperation and Development, 2 rue Andre- Pascal, 75775 Paris 16, France (U. S. orders to: O.E.C.D Publications and Information Center, 1750 Pennsylvania Ave., N.W., Washington, D. C. 20006) (also avail. in microfiche)

BIBLIOGRAPHIES   93

050   FR
ORGANIZATION FOR ECONOMIC COOPERATION AND DEVELOPMENT. LIBRARY. CATALOGUE OF PERIODICALS/ CATALOGUE DES PERIODIQUES. 1966. a. free. ‡ Organization for Economic Cooperation and Development, 2 rue Andre Pascal, 75775 Paris 16, France (U. S. orders to: O.E.C.D. Publications and Information Center, 1750 Pennsylvania Ave., N. W., Washington, D. C. 20006) (also avail. in microfiche)

010   UK   ISSN 0078-7124
OVERSEAS DIRECTORIES, WHO'S WHO, PRESS GUIDES, YEAR BOOKS AND OVERSEAS PERIODICAL SUBSCRIPTIONS. 1947. biennial. £17($30) Publishing and Distributing Co. Ltd., Mitre House, 177 Regent St., London W.1, England. Ed. H. R. Vaughan. adv. circ. 5,000. (also avail. in microfilm from UMI)

016 917.306   US   ISSN 0195-4202
OXBRIDGE DIRECTORY OF ETHNIC PERIODICALS. 1979. biennial. $35. Oxbridge Communications, Inc., 183 Madison Ave., New York, NY 10016. Ed. Patricia Hagood.

011   US   ISSN 0163-7010
OXBRIDGE DIRECTORY OF NEWSLETTERS. 1979. biennial. $45. Oxbridge Communications, Inc., 183 Madison Ave., New York, NY 10016.

016 200   US   ISSN 0191-4502
OXBRIDGE DIRECTORY OF RELIGIOUS PERIODICALS. 1979. triennial. $25. Oxbridge Communications, Inc., 183 Madison Ave., New York, NY 10016.

010   UK   ISSN 0078-7175
OXFORD BIBLIOGRAPHICAL SOCIETY. OCCASIONAL PUBLICATIONS. irreg. price varies. Oxford Bibliographical Society, c/o Bodleian Library, Oxford OX1 3BG, England. Ed.Bd.

010   UK   ISSN 0078-7183
OXFORD BIBLIOGRAPHICAL SOCIETY. PUBLICATIONS. NEW SERIES. 1949. irreg. £5($11) to individuals; £7 ($15) to institutions. Oxford Bibliographical Society, c/o Bodleian Library, Oxford, OX1 3BG, England. Ed.Bd.

PACIFIC ISLANDS STUDIES AND NOTES. see *HISTORY — Abstracting, Bibliographies, Statistics*

956.96 016   JO
PALESTINE-JORDANIAN BIBLIOGRAPHY. (Text in Arabic; summaries in English) a. Jordan Library Association, Box 6289, Amman, Jordan.

015   SP
PANORAMAS BIBLIOGRAFICOS DE ESPANA. no. 2, 1976. irreg. Biblioteca Nacional, Madrid, Spain.

010   KE
PERIODICALS IN EASTERN AFRICAN LIBRARIES: A UNION LIST. 1965. biennial. EAs.80($10) University of Nairobi, Library, Box 30197, Nairobi, Kenya.
    Formerly: Periodicals in East African Libraries: a Union List (ISSN 0079-0877)

500 600 016   US
PERIODICALS THAT PROGRESSIVE SCIENTISTS SHOULD KNOW ABOUT. 1976. biennial. free. Science for the People, Tallahassee Chapter, c/o Progressive Technology, Box 20049, Tallahassee, FL 32304. Ed. Bob Broedel. circ. 5,000.

600 016   BL   ISSN 0100-2767
PERIODICOS BRASILEIROS DE CIENCIAS E TECNOLOGIA. 1956. irreg. Instituto Brasileiro de Informacao em Ciencia e Tecnologia, Av. General Justo 171, 20000 Rio de Janeiro, Brazil.
    Formerly(until 1968): Periodicos Brasileiros de Cultura (ISSN 0100-2716)

015   PE   ISSN 0031-6067
PERU. BIBLIOTECA NACIONAL. BOLETIN. 1943. a. $4. Biblioteca Nacional, Apdo. 2335, Lima, Peru. Ed. Lucila Valderrama. bk. rev. abstr. bibl. illus. circ. 1,000.

BIBLIOGRAPHIES

015   PH
PHILIPPINES. NATIONAL LIBRARY. T N L RESEARCH GUIDE SERIES. Short title: T N L Research Guide Series. 1971. irreg., approx. 2/yr. free; exchange basis. ‡ National Library, Bibliography Division, T. M. Kalaw St., Manila, Philippines. Ed. Lily O. Orbase. circ. 300. (processed)

015   FI
POHJOIS-SUOMEN BIBLIOGRAFIA. (Text in Finnish; summaries in English) 1972. irreg., vol. 3, 1975. $49. Lapin Tutkimusseura, Oulu, Finland.

011   PL   ISSN 0551-651X
POLITECHNIKA POZNANSKA. ZESZYTY NAUKOWE. BIBLIOGRAFIA. 1962. irreg., no. 12, 1977. price varies. Politechnika Poznanska, Pl. Curie-Sklodowskiej 5, Poznan, Poland. Ed. Stanislaw Badon. circ. 150.

PRESS BRAILLE, ADULT. see *BLIND — Abstracting, Bibliographies, Statistics*

070 015   II   ISSN 0445-6653
PRESS IN INDIA. (Issued in two parts) (Text in English) 1957. a. price varies. Ministry of Information and Broadcasting, Registrar of Newspapers for India, Shastri Bhawan, New Delhi, India (Order from: Controller of Publications, Government of India, Civil Lines, Delhi 110054, India) title index. circ. 1,000.
Newpapers and periodicals

013   UK   ISSN 0079-5402
PRIVATE PRESS BOOKS; a checklist of books issued by private presses in the past year. 1960. a. £6($15) to non-members. Private Libraries Association, Ravelston, South View Road, Pinner, Middlesex, England. Ed. David Chambers. adv. index; cum.index. circ. 900(approx.)

PSYCHOLOGY INFORMATION GUIDE SERIES. see *PSYCHOLOGY — Abstracting, Bibliographies, Statistics*

PUBLIC ADMINISTRATION SERIES: BIBLIOGRAPHY. see *PUBLIC ADMINISTRATION — Abstracting, Bibliographies, Statistics*

500 300   FR
PUBLICATIONS DE RECHERCHE SCIENTIFIQUE EN FRANCE/SCHOLARLY BOOKS IN FRANCE. (Text in English and French) irreg. $011. 103 Bd Saint Michel, 75005 Paris, France.

070.5   US   ISSN 0079-7855
PUBLISHERS' TRADE LIST ANNUAL. (In 6 Vols.) 1872. a. $62.50. R.R. Bowker Company, 1180 Ave. of the Americas, New York, NY 10036 (Orders to P.O. Box 1807, Ann Arbor, Mich. 48106) index. (reprint service avail. from UMI)

RAKENNUSALAN JULKAISUHAKEMISTO. see *BUILDING AND CONSTRUCTION — Abstracting, Bibliographies, Statistics*

011   US
READER'S GUIDE SERIES. irreg. price varies. Farrar, Straus & Giroux, Inc., 19 Union Square W., New York, NY 10003.

016   US   ISSN 0079-984X
READEX MICROPRINT PUBLICATIONS. 1960. a. free. Readex Microprint Corp., 101 Fifth Ave., New York, NY 10003. circ. 4,500.

016 200   FR
RECHERCHES INSTITUTIONNELLES. (In 4 Series: Droit et Eglises; Institutions et Histoire; Culture et Religion; Recherche Documentaire) irreg. Universite de Strasbourg II, Centre de Recherche et de Documentation des Institutions Chretiennes, 9 Place de l'Universite, 67084 Strasbourg Cedex, France.

RECHTSBIBLIOGRAPHIE/BIBLIOGRAPHIE JURIDIQUE/LAW BIBLIOGRAPHY. see *LAW — Abstracting, Bibliographies, Statistics*

011   II
REFERENCE CATALOGUE OF INDIAN BOOKS IN PRINT. (Text in English) biennial. $125. Today and Tomorrow's Printers and Publishers, 24-B/5 Original Rd., Karol Bagh, New Delhi 110005, India (Dist. in U.S. by: Indo Americana Literature House, Box 1276, Globe, AZ 85501)

011   US
REFERENCE SOURCES. 1977. a. $65. Pierian Press, 5000 Washtenaw Ave., Ann Arbor, MI 48104. Ed. Linda Mark.

200 016   US   ISSN 0000-0612
RELIGIOUS BOOKS AND SERIALS IN PRINT. 1978. irreg. $42. R.R. Bowker Company, 1180 Ave. of the Americas, New York, NY 10036 (Orders to Box 1807, Ann Arbor, MI 48106)

016   GW   ISSN 0085-5499
REPERTOIRE BIBLIOGRAPHIQUE DES LIVRES IMPRIMES EN FRANCE. 1968. irreg., vol. 30, 1980. price varies. Verlag Valentin Koerner, H.-Sielcken-Str. 36, Postfach 304, D-7570 Baden-Baden 1, W. Germany (B.R.D.)

REPERTOIRE DE L'EDITION AU QUEBEC. see *PUBLISHING AND BOOK TRADE — Abstracting, Bibliographies, Statistics*

015   BE   ISSN 0080-1224
REPERTORIUM VAN WERKEN, IN VLAANDEREN UITGEGEVEN, OF DOOR MONOPOLIEHOUDERS INGEVOERD. 1960. a. 850 Fr. Vereniging ter Bevordering van het Vlaamse Boekwezen - Association of Publishers of Dutch Language Books, Frankrijklei 93, 2000 Antwerp, Belgium.

016.95   US
REVIEW OF ENGLISH BOOKS ON ASIA. irreg. Brigham Young University Press, 205 University Press Bldg., Provo, UT 84602.
Formerly: Annual Review of English Books on Asia (ISSN 0098-7379)

015   CL
REVISTA CHILENA EN VENTA. a. Servicio de Extension de Cultura Chilena, Brasil 9070, La Florida, Santiago, Chile. Dir. Marta Dominguez. (processed)

016   SP   ISSN 0210-0002
REVISTAS ESPANOLAS EN CURSO DE PUBLICACION. 1971. a. 500 ptas. Instituto Bibliografico Hispanico, Calle de Atocha 106, Apdo. 12311, Madrid 12, Spain. bibl. circ. 1,000.

015   UY   ISSN 0085-5642
REVISTERO; el mas completo informe sobre las publicaciones periodicas de America Latina. 1972. a. $35. Eduardo Darino, Ed. & Pub., Casilla de Correo 1677, Montevideo, Uruguay (U.S. Subscr. to: Darino, Box 1496-GCS, New York, NY 10163) circ. 1,000.

REVUE BIBLIOGRAPHIQUE DE SINOLOGIE. see *HISTORY — Abstracting, Bibliographies, Statistics*

015   BL
RIO DE JANEIRO, BRAZIL (STATE). INSTITUTO ESTADUAL DO LIVRO. DIVISAO DE BIBLIOTECAS. BOLETIM BIBLIOGRAFICO. 1977. irreg. Instituto Estadual do Livro, Divisao de Bibliotecas, Av. Presidente Vargas 1261, Rio de Janeiro, Brazil.

RUDOLF STEINER PUBLICATIONS. see *PHILOSOPHY — Abstracting, Bibliographies, Statistics*

015   SA   ISSN 0036-0864
S A N B. (South African National Bibiography) (Text in Afrikaans, Bantu languages and English) 1959. q. with annual cum. R.15($22.50) State Library, Box 397, Pretoria, South Africa. bibl. circ. 560.

011   NE
SAMENSPEL. 1977. irreg. (Nederlandse Organisatie voor Internationale Ontwikkelingssamenwerking - Netherlands Organization for International Development Cooperation) Nederlands Bibliotheek en Lektuur Centrum, Postbus 93054, 2509 AB The Hague, Netherlands. illus.

SCANDINAVIAN AFRICANA. see *ANTHROPOLOGY — Abstracting, Bibliographies, Statistics*

011   US
SCARECROW AUTHOR BIBLIOGRAPHIES. 1969. irreg., no. 44, 1979. price varies. Scarecrow Press, Inc., 52 Liberty St., P.O. Box 656, Metuchen, NJ 08840.

011 310   SZ
SCHWEIZERISCHE BIBLIOGRAPHIE FUER STATISTIK UND VOLKSWIRTSCHAFT/ BIBLIOGRAPHIE SUISSE DE STATISTIQUE ET D'ECONOMIE POLITIQUE. (Text in German and French) biennial. 20 Fr. Statistisches Amt., Hallwylstr. 15, 3003 Berne, Switzerland. (Co-sponsor: Schweizerische Gesellschaft fuer Statistik und Volkswirtschaft)

SCIENTIFIC SERIALS IN THAI LIBRARIES. see *SCIENCES: COMPREHENSIVE WORKS — Abstracting, Bibliographies, Statistics*

011   US
SELECTION GUIDE SERIES. irreg. American Bibliographical Center-Clio Press, Box 4397, 2040 Alameda Padre Serra, Santa Barbara, CA 93103. (Co-publisher: Neal-Schuman Publishers) Ed. Patricia Glass Schuman.

016.05   CN   ISSN 0316-6597
SERIALS HOLDINGS IN THE LIBRARIES OF MEMORIAL UNIVERSITY OF NEWFOUNDLAND, ST. JOHN'S PUBLIC LIBRARY AND COLLEGE OF TRADES AND TECHNOLOGY. 1974. a. free to libraries. Memorial University of Newfoundland, Library, St. John's, Nfld. A1C 5S7, Canada.
Formerly: Memorial University of Newfoundland. Library. Serials Holdings in the Libraries of Memorial University of Newfoundland and St. John's Public Library (ISSN 0316-6600)

016.05   US   ISSN 0095-2702
SERIALS UPDATING SERVICE ANNUAL. 1974. a. $15. F. W. Faxon Co., Inc., Publishing Division, 15 Southwest Park, Westwood, MA 02090. Ed. Mary Jo Sweeney. circ. 200.

011   YU   ISSN 0350-3585
SLOVENSKA BIBLIOGRAFIJA. irreg. Narodna in Univerzitetna Knjiznica, Turjaska 1, 61001 Ljubljana, Yugoslavia. Ed. Tomo Martelanc.

SMALL PRESS RECORD OF BOOKS IN PRINT. see *PUBLISHING AND BOOK TRADE — Abstracting, Bibliographies, Statistics*

016 070.5   US   ISSN 0000-0523
SOURCES OF SERIALS; international serials publishers and their titles with copyright and copy availability information. 1977. irreg. $65. R. R. Bowker Company, 1180 Ave. of the Americas, New York, NY 10036 (Orders to: Box 1807, Ann Arbor, MI 48106)

SOUTH AFRICAN INSTITUTE OF INTERNATIONAL AFFAIRS. BIBLIOGRAPHICAL SERIES/SUID-AFRIKAANSE INSTITUUT VAN INTERNASIONALE AANGELEENTHEDE. BIBLIOGRAFIESE REEKS. see *POLITICAL SCIENCE — Abstracting, Bibliographies, Statistics*

015   AT   ISSN 0311-3078
SOUTH AUSTRALIA. STATE LIBRARY. REFERENCE SERVICES BRANCH. REFERENCE SERVICES BIBLIOGRAPHIES. 1974. irreg. free. Libraries Board of South Australia, Box 419, Adelaide, S.A. 5000, Australia.

010   US   ISSN 0073-4977
SOUTHERN ILLINOIS UNIVERSITY, CARBONDALE. UNIVERSITY LIBRARIES. BIBLIOGRAPHIC CONTRIBUTIONS. 1964. irreg., 1973, no. 8. price varies. Southern Illinois University, Carbondale, Morris Library, Carbondale, IL 62901. Ed. Kenneth G. Peterson.

011   US
SOUTHERN PROGRESSIVE PERIODICALS DIRECTORY UPDATE. 1979. a. $3. Progressive Education, Box 120574, Nashville, TN 37212. Ed. Craig T. Canan. circ. 1,000.

SPORTS DOCUMENTATION CENTRE. LIST OF PERIODICAL HOLDINGS. see *PHYSICAL FITNESS AND HYGIENE — Abstracting, Bibliographies, Statistics*

016   GW ISSN 0075-8728
STAMM LEITFADEN DURCH PRESSE UND
WERBUNG/ANNUAL DIRECTORY OF PRESS
AND ADVERTISING. 1947. a. DM.97. Stamm
Verlag GmbH, Goldammerweg 16, 4300 Essen 1,
W. Germany (B.R.D.) Ed. H. Major. adv. circ.
8,400.

050   US ISSN 0085-6630
STANDARD PERIODICAL DIRECTORY. 1963.
biennial. $120. Oxbridge Communications, Inc., 183
Madison Ave., New York, NY 10016. Ed. Patricia
Hagood. circ. 12,000.

310 015   UK ISSN 0309-5371
STATISTICS - ASIA & AUSTRALASIA: SOURCES
FOR MARKET RESEARCH. 1974. irreg.
£8($26.50) C. B. D. Research Ltd., 154 High St.,
Beckenham, Kent BR3 1EA, England (Dist. in U.S.
by: Gale Research Co., Book Tower, Detroit, MI
48226) Ed. Joan M. Harvey. circ. 2,000.

STORIES: A LIST OF STORIES TO TELL AND TO
READ ALOUD. see *CHILDREN AND
YOUTH* — *Abstracting, Bibliographies, Statistics*

011   UR
STROIIZDAT: THE BEST-DESIGNED BOOKS.
(Text in English) 1978. irreg. (Stroiizdat)
Izdatel'stvo Vneshtorguzdat, Bol'shaya Bronnaya,
6a, Moscow, U.S.S.R.

STUDIES ON THE MORPHOLOGY AND
SYSTEMATICS OF SCALE INSECTS. see
BIOLOGY — *Entomology*

010   RM ISSN 0081-8879
STUDII SI CERCETARI DE BIBLIOLOGIE. SERIE
NOUA. (Text in Romanian; summaries in French)
1955. irreg. (Academia Republicii Socialiste
Romania) Editura Academiei Republicii Socialiste
Romania, Calea Victoriei 125, Bucharest, Romania
(Subscr. to: ILEXIM, Str. 13 Decembrie Nr. 3, P.O.
Box 136-137, Bucharest, Romania)

016   US ISSN 0000-0159
SUBJECT GUIDE TO BOOKS IN PRINT. (Issued in
2 Vols) 1956. a. $87.50. R. R. Bowker Company,
1180 Ave. of the Americas, New York, NY 10036
(Orders to: Box 1807, Ann Arbor, MI 48106)

016   US ISSN 0000-0167
SUBJECT GUIDE TO CHILDREN'S BOOKS IN
PRINT. 1971. a. $38.50. R.R. Bowker Company,
1180 Ave. of the Americas, New York, NY 10036
(Orders to P.O. Box 1807, Ann Arbor, Mich.
48106)

017   US ISSN 0090-290X
SUBJECT GUIDE TO MICROFORMS IN PRINT.
1962-63. a. $89.50. Microform Review, Inc., 520
Riverside Ave., Box 405, Saugatuck Station,
Westport, CT 06880. Ed. Ardis V. Carleton. index.
Incorporates: International Microforms in Print.

011   US ISSN 0149-810X
SUBJECT GUIDE TO REPRINTS. 1979. biennial.
$49.50. Guide to Reprints, Inc., Box 249, Kent, CT
06757. Ed. Ann S. Davis. circ. 800.

016 949.6 GW ISSN 0081-9131
SUEDOSTEUROPA-BIBLIOGRAPHIE. (Text in
European languages) 1956. irreg. price varies.
Suedost-Institut, Guellstr. 7, 8000 Munich 2, W.
Germany (B.R.D.) Ed. Gertrud Krallert-Sattler.

948 015   FI ISSN 0355-0001
SUOMEN KIRJALLISUUS VUOSILUETTELO/
FINNISH NATIONAL BIBLIOGRAPHY
ANNUAL VOLUME/FINLANDS LITTERATUR
AARSKATALOG. Monthly edition (ISSN 0355-
001X) 1972. a. (with m. issues) price varies.
Helsingin Yliopisto, Kirjasto - Helsinki University
Library, Box 312, 00171 Helsinki 17, Finland
(Avail. from: Valtion Painatuskeskus, Annankatu
44,00100 Helsinki 10, Finland) circ. 1,100.

015   SW ISSN 0586-0431
SVENSK TIDSKRIFTSFOERTECKNING/
CURRENT SWEDISH PERIODICALS. 1968.
triennial with a. updates. (Kungliga Biblioteket,
Bibliografiska Institutet) Tidnings AB Svensk
Bokhandel, Sveavaegen 52, S-111 34 Stockholm,
Sweden.

SWAZILAND NATIONAL BIBLIOGRAPHY. see
PUBLISHING AND BOOK TRADE —
Abstracting, Bibliographies, Statistics

TALKING BOOKS, ADULT. see *BLIND* —
Abstracting, Bibliographies, Statistics

029 011   TZ
TANZANIA NATIONAL BIBLIOGRAPHY. 1970. a,
latest 1974/75. EAs.90($11.50) Tanzania Library
Service, Acquisition Department, Box 9283, Dar es
Salaam, Tanzania.
 Formerly: Printed in Tanzania.

TAX FOUNDATION'S RESEARCH
BIBLIOGRAPHY. see *BUSINESS AND
ECONOMICS* — *Abstracting, Bibliographies,
Statistics*

016 315   TH ISSN 0082-3791
THAILAND. NATIONAL STATISTICAL OFFICE.
STATISTICAL BIBLIOGRAPHY. (Text in
English) 1961. irreg. $1.75. National Statistical
Office, Larn Luang Rd., Bangkok, Thailand. circ.
1,000.

THESES AND DISSERTATIONS ACCEPTED IN
PARTIAL FULFILLMENT OF THE
REQUIREMENTS FOR DEGREES GRANTED
BY THE MICHIGAN TECHNOLOGICAL
UNIVERSITY. see *TECHNOLOGY:
COMPREHENSIVE WORKS* — *Abstracting,
Bibliographies, Statistics*

013   DK
THESES AND OTHER PUBLICATIONS OF THE
UNIVERSITY OF COPENHAGEN. (Text in
English) a. exchange basis. I.D.E., Danmarks
Institut for International Udveksling, Amaliegade
38, DK-1256 Copenhagen K, Denmark. circ.
controlled. (processed)

016 980   UK ISSN 0307-109X
THESES IN LATIN AMERICAN STUDIES AT
BRITISH UNIVERSITIES IN PROGRESS AND
COMPLETED. no. 12, 1977/78. irreg. free.
University of London, Institute of Latin American
Studies, 31 Tavistock Square, London WC1H 9HA,
England.

011   US ISSN 0082-4526
TITLES IN SERIES; a handbook for librarians and
students. 1954. irreg., 3rd edt., 1978. $95.
Scarecrow Press, Inc., 52 Liberty St., Metuchen, NJ
08840. Ed. Eleanora A. Baer. circ. 3,500.

TOURISM COMPENDIUM. see *TRAVEL AND
TOURISM* — *Abstracting, Bibliographies, Statistics*

U C L A MUSIC LIBRARY BIBLIOGRAPHY
SERIES. (University of California, Los Angeles) see
MUSIC — *Abstracting, Bibliographies, Statistics*

630 016   US
U S-CANADIAN RANGE MANAGEMENT; a
selected bibliography on ranges, pastures, wildlife,
livestock, and ranching. irreg. $67.50. Oryx Press,
2214 N. Central at Encanto, Suite 103, Phoenix,
AZ 85004.

011   US ISSN 0000-0175
ULRICH'S INTERNATIONAL PERIODICALS
DIRECTORY. (Supplement: Ulrich's Quarterly)
1932. a. starting in 1980; previously biennial. $78.
R. R. Bowker Company, 1180 Ave. of the
Americas, New York, NY 10036 (Orders to P.O.
Box 1807, Ann Arbor, Mich. 48106) index.

016.912   UN
UNESCO. SCIENTIFIC MAPS AND ATLASES
AND OTHER RELATED PUBLICATIONS. irreg.
Unesco, 7-9 Place de Fontenoy, 75700 Paris,
France. bibl. illus.

016   PK
UNION CATALOG OF SCIENTIFIC AND
TECHNICAL PERIODICALS IN THE
LIBRARIES OF PAKISTAN. 1970. irreg., latest
issue, 1975. Rs.5($2.50) Pakistan Scientific and
Technological Information Centre, House No. 6,
Street No. 22, Sector F-7/2, Box No. 1217,
Islamabad, Pakistan. Dir A. R. Mohajir. circ. 500.
(also avail. in microfilm)

013   SA ISSN 0079-4325
UNION CATALOGUE OF THESES AND
DISSERTATIONS OF THE SOUTH AFRICAN
UNIVERSITIES. (Cumulated microfiche edition
covers 1918-1977) (Text in Afrikaans and English)
1918. a. free. Potchefstroom University for Christian
Higher Education, Potchefstroom, South Africa.

015 020   IR
UNION LIST OF LIBRARY AND INFORMATION
SCIENCE PERIODICALS IN THE LIBRARIES
OF IRAN. (Text in Persian and English) 1973.
biennial. Rs.80($6) Institute for Research and
Planning in Science and Education, Tehran Book
Processing Centre, Box 11-1126, Teheran, Iran. Ed.
Farvardin Rastin. circ. 350.

358 016   US ISSN 0082-8696
U. S. AIR FORCE ACADEMY LIBRARY.
SPECIAL BIBLIOGRAPHY SERIES. 1957. irreg.
United States Air Force Academy, Colorado
Springs, CO 80840. circ. 500. (also avail. in
microfiche from NTI)

U. S. DEPARTMENT OF TRANSPORTATION.
BIBLIOGRAPHIC LISTS. see
TRANSPORTATION — *Abstracting,
Bibliographies, Statistics*

016   US ISSN 0083-1581
U. S. LIBRARY OF CONGRESS. HISPANIC
FOUNDATION. BIBLIOGRAPHIC SERIES.
1943. irreg. price varies. U.S. Library of Congress,
Washington, DC 20540.

011   VE
UNIVERSIDAD DE LOS ANDES. INSTITUTO DE
INVESTIGACIONES LITERARIAS. SERIE
BIBLIOGRAFICO. 1971. irreg. Universidad de los
Andes, Instituto de Investigaciones Literarias,
Merida, Venezuela.
 Formerly (until May, 1977): Universidad de los
Andes. Centro de Investigaciones Literarias. Serie
Bibliografico.

020 011   MX ISSN 0006-1719
UNIVERSIDAD NACIONAL AUTONOMA DE
MEXICO. INSTITUTO DE INVESTIGACIONES
BIBLIOGRAFICAS. BOLETIN. 1969. irreg.; latest
1978, representing Jul-Dec. 1973. Mex.$90($4)
Universidad Nacional Autonoma de Mexico,
Instituto de Investigaciones Bibliograficas, Villa
Obregon, Ciudad Universitaria, Mexico 20, D.F.,
Mexico. (Co-sponsor: Biblioteca Nacional) Ed. Jose
Ignacio Mantecon Navasal. bibl. illus.
 Supersedes: Biblioteca Nacional. Boletin.

010   MX ISSN 0076-7468
UNIVERSIDAD NACIONAL AUTONOMA DE
MEXICO. SEMINARIO DE
INVESTIGACIONES BIBLIOTECOLOGICA.
PUBLICACIONES. SERIE B. BIBLIOGRAFIA.
1960. irreg., 1967, no. 4. not for sale. ‡ Universidad
Nacional Autonoma de Mexico, Seminario de
Investigaciones Bibliotecologicas, Torre de Ciencias,
Ciudad Universitaria, Mexico 20, D.F., Mexico. Ed.
Dr. Alicia Perales de Mercado. circ. controlled.
 Theses by alumuni

016   CK
UNIVERSIDAD NACIONAL DE COLOMBIA.
BIBLIOTECA CENTRAL. BOLETIN DE
ADQUISICIONES. 1960. irreg. exchange basis.
Universidad Nacional de Colombia, Biblioteca
Central, Aero 14490, Bogota, Colombia. Ed. Hugo
Parra. circ. 3,000.
 Formerly: Universidad Nacional de Colombia.
Centro de Bibliografia y Documentacion. Boletin
Informativo (ISSN 0069-5920)

025.2   AG ISSN 0076-6399
UNIVERSIDAD NACIONAL DE CUYO.
BIBLIOTECA CENTRAL. BOLETIN
BIBLIOGRAFICO. 1940. irreg.; no. 47, 1975.
available on exchange. ‡ Universidad Nacional de
Cuyo, Biblioteca Central, Centro Universitario-C.C.
420, Mendoza, Argentina.

010   BL
UNIVERSIDADE DE SAO PAULO. FACULDADE
DE ECONOMIA E ADMINISTRACAO.
BIBLIOTECA. BOLETIM. 1965. irreg. exchange.
Universidade de Sao Paulo, Faculdade de Economia
e Administracao, Cidade Universitaria Armando de
Salles Oliveira, C.P. 11498, 01000 Sao Paulo, Brazil.
circ. 250.
 Formerly: Universidade de Sao Paulo. Faculdade
de Ciencias Economicas e Administrativas.
Biblioteca. Boletim.

013   GW ISSN 0080-5173
UNIVERSITAET DES SAARLANDES.
JAHRESBIBLIOGRAPHIE. 1968. a. Universitaet
des Saarlandes, Universitaetsbibliothek, 6600
Saarbruecken 11, W. Germany (B.R.D.) Ed. Otto
Klapp.

016　　　　　　　　NO　ISSN 0085-4247
UNIVERSITETET I TRONDHEIM. NORGES TEKNISKE HOEGSKOLE. BIBLIOTEKET. LITERATURLISTE. 1958. irreg., no. 47, 1975. price varies. Universitetet i Trondheim, Norges Tekniske Hoegskole. Biblioteket, 7034 Trondheim-NTH, Norway. circ. controlled. (tabloid format)

600 015　　　　　　NO　ISSN 0029-1714
UNIVERSITETET I TRONDHEIM. NORGES TEKNISKE HOEGSKOLE. BIBLIOTEKET. MELDINGER OG BOKLISTER. (Text in the language of book title) 1950. 5-6/yr. Universitetet i Trondheim, Norges Tekniske Hoegskole. Biblioteket, 7034 Trondheim-NTH, Norway. circ. 1,600.

027 011　　　　　　US　ISSN 0044-8877
UNIVERSITY OF ARIZONA LIBRARY. BIBLIOGRAPHIC BULLETIN. 1970. irreg. free to libraries. University of Arizona Library, Tucson, AZ 85721. bibl.

010　　　　　　　　NZ　ISSN 0067-0499
UNIVERSITY OF AUCKLAND. LIBRARY. BIBLIOGRAPHICAL BULLETIN. 1964. irreg., no. 10, 1978. exchange basis. ‡ University of Auckland, Library, Auckland, New Zealand.

011　　　　　　　　SA
UNIVERSITY OF CAPE TOWN. LIBRARIES. BIBLIOGRAPHICAL SERIES. (Text in English) 1944. irreg. (unnumbered) University of Cape Town, Libraries, Rondebosch 7700, South Africa.

010　　　　　　　　NR　ISSN 0073-4330
UNIVERSITY OF IBADAN. LIBRARY. BIBLIOGRAPHICAL SERIES. Cover title: Ibadan University Library Bibliographic Series. 1970. irreg. price varies. Ibadan University Press, University of Ibadan, Ibadan, Nigeria.

016 430　　　　　　UK　ISSN 0260-5929
UNIVERSITY OF LONDON. INSTITUTE OF GERMANIC STUDIES. RESEARCH IN GERMANIC STUDIES. 1968. a. £1. ‡ University of London, Institute of Germanic Studies, 29 Russell Square, London WC1B 5DP, England. Formerly(until 1981): University of London. Institute of Germanic Studies. Theses in Progress at British Universities (ISSN 0082-4127)

013　　　　　　　　US　ISSN 0078-1460
UNIVERSITY OF NORTH CAROLINA, GREENSBORO. FACULTY PUBLICATIONS. 1900. a. price varies. ‡ University of North Carolina at Greensboro, Greensboro, NC 27412. circ. 1,000.

011　　　　　　　　CN　ISSN 0384-7411
UNIVERSITY OF OTTAWA. VANIER LIBRARY. LIST OF SERIALS. 1967. irreg. University of Ottawa, Vanier Library, Ottawa, Ont., Canada.

016　　　　　　　　US　ISSN 0564-6855
UNIVERSITY OF TEXAS. HUMANITIES RESEARCH CENTER. BIBLIOGRAPHICAL MONOGRAPH SERIES. 1970. irreg. University of Texas at Austin, Humanities Research Center, Box 7219, Austin, TX 78712.

016　　　　　　　　US　ISSN 0563-2595
UNIVERSITY OF TEXAS. HUMANITIES RESEARCH CENTER. TOWER BIBLIOGRAPHICAL SERIES. 1961. irreg. University of Texas at Austin, Humanities Research Center, Box 7219, Austin, TX 78712.

011　　　　　　　　SA
UNIVERSITY OF THE WITWATERSRAND, JOHANNESBURG. LIBRARY. BIBLIOGRAPHICAL SERIES. 1958. irreg. (unnumbered) University of the Witwatersrand, Johannesburg, Library, Private Bag 31550, Braamfontein 2017, South Africa.

330 016　　　　　　US
UNIVERSITY OF TOLEDO. BUSINESS RESEARCH CENTER. BIBLIOGRAPHIES. 1976. irreg., no.7, 1978. price varies. University of Toledo, College of Business Administration, 2801 W. Bancroft St., Toledo, OH 43606.

016.5　　　　　　　CN　ISSN 0318-174X
UNIVERSITY OF VICTORIA (B.C.) LIBRARY. SERIALS HOLDINGS CATALOGUE. 1971. irreg. University of Victoria, Library, Box 1700, Victoria, B.C. V8W 2Y2, Canada.
　　Formerly: University of Victoria (B.C.) Library. List of Serials.

015　　　　　　　　GW　ISSN 0067-8899
VERZEICHNIS LIEFERBARER BUECHER/ GERMAN BOOKS IN PRINT. Short title: V L B. (Consists of two sections: Authors/Titles/Key-words (in three vols., 8th ed., 1978/79) and Schlagwortverzeichnis/Subject Index (in two vols., 1st ed., 1978/79)) 1971. a. (Buchhaendler-Vereinigung GmbH) K. G. Saur Verlag KG, Poessenbacherstr. 12 B, Postfach 711009, 8000 Munich 71, W. Germany (B.R.D.)

015　　　　　　　　US　ISSN 0507-102X
VIRGINIA STATE PUBLICATIONS IN PRINT. 1965. a. $2. State Library, Historical Publications Division, 11th & Capitol St., Richmond, VA 23219. circ. 700.

VOLHYNIAN BIBLIOGRAPHIC CENTER. PUBLICATIONS. see HISTORY — History Of Europe

011　　　　　　　　UR
VOPROSY BIBLIOGRAFII. 1976. irreg. 0.78 Rub. per issue. Akademiya Nauk S.S.S.R., Biblioteka, Leningrad, U.S.S.R. Ed. A. Moiseeva.

VYBEROVA BIBLIOGRAFIA MUZEOLOGICKEJ LITERATURY. see MUSEUMS AND ART GALLERIES — Abstracting, Bibliographies, Statistics

016　　　　　　　　UK　ISSN 0083-7911
WELSH BIBLIOGRAPHICAL SOCIETY. JOURNAL. 1910. a. £1 individuals; £2 to institutions. Welsh Bibliographical Society, c/o David Jenkins, National Library of Wales, Aberystwyth, Dyfed SY23 3BU, Wales. circ. 200.

WEST AFRICA RICE DEVELOPMENT ASSOCIATION. CURRENT BIBLIOGRAPHY. see AGRICULTURE — Abstracting, Bibliographies, Statistics

010　　　　　　　　US　ISSN 0512-4743
WEST VIRGINIA UNION LIST OF SERIALS. 1962. a. $30. West Virginia University Library, Main Office, Morgantown, WV 26506. Ed. Mildred Moyers.

016　　　　　　　　UK　ISSN 0000-0213
WILLING'S PRESS GUIDE; British European & U.S. edition. 1874. a. $45. ‡ I P C Business Press Ltd., 33-40 Bowling Green Lane, London EC1R 0NE, England. adv. subject index. circ. 7,500.

WINTERGREEN; a directory of progressive periodicals. see LITERARY AND POLITICAL REVIEWS — Abstracting, Bibliographies, Statistics

011　　　　　　　　US
WORLD BIBLIOGRAPHICAL SERIES. 1977. irreg. price varies. American Bibliographical Center-Clio Press, 2040 Alameda Padre Serra, Box 4397, Santa Barbara, CA 93103. Ed. Robert Collison.

Z G A BIBLIOGRAPHIC SERIES. (Zambia Geographical Association) see GEOGRAPHY — Abstracting, Bibliographies, Statistics

011　　　　　　　　CS
ZAHRANICNE PERIODIKA V C S S R. 1972. irreg. Univerzitna Kniznica, Michalska 1, 885 17 Bratislava, Czechoslovakia. (Co-sponsor: Czechoslovakia. Statni Knihovna) Ed. Vincent Kutik. stat. circ. 1,000. (back issues avail.)

011　　　　　　　　ZR
ZAIRE. BIBLIOTHEQUE NATIONALE. BIBLIOGRAPHIE NATIONALE. (Text in French) 1971. irreg., latest 1975. Bibliotheque Nationale, B.P. 3090, Kinshasa/Gombe, Zaire.

ZAMBIA. NATIONAL COUNCIL FOR SCIENTIFIC RESEARCH. N C S R BIBLIOGRAPHY. see SCIENCES: COMPREHENSIVE WORKS — Abstracting, Bibliographies, Statistics

015　　　　　　　　RH
ZIMBABWE NATIONAL BIBLIOGRAPHY. 1961. a. free. ‡ National Archives, Private Bag 7729, Causeway, Salisbury, Zimbabwe. index. circ. 500.
　　Former titles, 1967-1978: Rhodesia National Bibliography (ISSN 0085-5677); 1961-1966: Publications Deposited in the National Archives.

BICYCLES AND MOTORCYCLES

see Sports and Games — Bicycles and Motorcycles

BIOGRAPHY

920　　　　　　　　FR
A LA PREMIERE PERSONNE. 1980. price varies. Editions Syros, 1 rue de Varenne, 75006 Paris, France.

A S C A P BIOGRAPHICAL DICTIONARY. (American Society of Composers, Authors and Publishers) see MUSIC

920 960　　　　　　GW
AFRICAN BIOGRAPHIES. (Text in English) 1967. irreg. DM.15. Friedrich-Ebert-Stiftung, Koelner Str. 149, 5300 Bonn-Bad Godesberg, W. Germany (B.R.D.) Ed. Ruth Erika von Nell. illus. circ. 500.

AGRICULTURAL INSTITUTE OF CANADA. MEMBERSHIP DIRECTORY/INSTITUT AGRICOLE DU CANADA. LISTE DES MEMBRES. see AGRICULTURE

ALL INDIA ARCHITECTS DIRECTORY. see ARCHITECTURE

ALMANACH DU PEUPLE. see ENCYCLOPEDIAS AND GENERAL ALMANACS

925 500　　　　　　US　ISSN 0065-9347
AMERICAN MEN AND WOMEN OF SCIENCE. PHYSICAL AND BIOLOGICAL SCIENCES. 1906. irreg., 14th edt., 1979. $50 per vol.; 8-vol. set $385. (Jaques Cattell Press) R. R. Bowker Company, 1180 Ave. of the Americas, New York, NY 10036 (Orders to P.O. Box 1807, Ann Arbor, Mich. 48106) (reprint service avail. from UMI)

AMERICAN PSYCHIATRIC ASSOCIATION. BIOGRAPHICAL DIRECTORY. see MEDICAL SCIENCES — Psychiatry And Neurology

150 920　　　　　　US　ISSN 0196-6545
AMERICAN PSYCHOLOGICAL ASSOCIATION. DIRECTORY. 1916. biennial. $50 to non-members; members $25. American Psychological Association, 1200-17th St., N.W., Washington, DC 20036. Ed. John A. Lazo. circ. 10,000.
　　Formerly: American Psychological Association. Biographical Directory (ISSN 0090-9076)

920　　　　　　　　US　ISSN 0569-714X
AMERICAN PSYCHOLOGICAL ASSOCIATION. MEMBERSHIP REGISTER. (Supplement to: American Psychological Association Biographical Directory) 1967. biennial. $15 to non-members; members $8. American Psychological Association, 1200 Seventeenth St., N.W., Washington, DC 20036. Ed. John A. Lazo.

920　　　　　　　　FR
ANNUAIRE MONDIAL DES CORSES. biennial. Association Mondiale des Corses, 100, rue Saint-Lazare, 75009 Paris, France. Ed. X. Moreschi. adv. illus.
　　Contains 150,000 addresses of Corsicans, friends of Corsica and Napoleoniens

920　　　　　　　　SZ
ANNUAIRE SUISSE DU MONDE ET DES AFFAIRES/WER IST WER IN DER SCHWEIZ UND IM FUERSTENTUM LIECHTENSTEIN/ SWISS BIOGRAPHICAL INDEX OF PROMINENT PERSONS/CHI E SVIZZERIA E NEL LIECHTENSTEIN? 1972/73. biennial. 120 Fr.($48) Editions International Registry of Who's Who S.A. (Geneva), 23, Ch. du Levant, CH-1005 Lausanne, Switzerland. adv. circ. 500.

ARGENTINA. DEPARTAMENTO DE ESTUDIOS HISTORICOS NAVALES. SERIE C: BIOGRAFIAS NAVALES ARGENTINAS. see MILITARY

AUTHORS IN THE NEWS; compilation of news stories and feature articles from American newspapers and magazines, covering prominent writers in all fields. see LITERATURE

BIOGRAPHY

920   CS   ISSN 0067-8724
BIOGRAFICKE STUDIE. (Text in Slovak; summaries in German and Russian) 1970. approx. a. price varies. Matica Slovenska, Mudronova 35, 036 52 Martin, Czechoslovakia. bk. rev.

BIOGRAPHICAL DICTIONARIES AND RELATED WORKS; an international bibliography of collective biographies. see *BIBLIOGRAPHIES*

920   CN
BIOGRAPHICAL DIRECTORY OF AMERICANS AND CANADIANS OF CROATIAN DESCENT. 1963. quinquennial. Can.$10($10) (Research Center for Canadian Ethnic Studies, US) Western Publishers, Box 30193, Sta. B, Calgary, Alta., Canada. Ed. Vladimir Markotic. bibl. circ. 500(controlled) (back issues avail.)

920 954.7   PK   ISSN 0067-8732
BIOGRAPHICAL ENCYCLOPEDIA OF PAKISTAN. (Text in English) 1955-56. irreg. price varies. Biographical Research Institute, Lahore, Pakistan.

920   UK   ISSN 0067-9240
BLUE BOOK: LEADERS OF THE ENGLISH-SPEAKING WORLD. 1968. a. $30. Gale Research Company, Book Tower, Detroit, MI 48226. circ. 10,000.

920   FR
BOTTIN MONDAIN; Tout Paris-Toute la France. 1903. a. $65. Societe Didot Bottin, 28, rue Docteur Finlay, 75738 Paris Cedex 15, France.

CALIFORNIANS IN CONGRESS. see *POLITICAL SCIENCE*

920   CN   ISSN 0045-4486
CANADIAN BIOGRAPHICAL STUDIES/ETUDES BIOGRAPHIQUES CANADIENNES. 1969. irreg. University of Toronto Press, Front Campus, Toronto, Ont. M5S 1A6, Canada (and 33 E. Tupper St., Buffalo NY 14203) Eds. Alan Wilson, Andre Vachon. (also avail. in microfiche)

920   CN
CANADIAN WHO'S WHO. 1910. a. Can.$75. University of Toronto Press, Front Campus, Toronto, Ont. M5S 1A6, Canada. Ed. Kieran Simpson.
Formerly: Who's Who, The Canadian (ISSN 0068-9963)

CHINA DIRECTORY. see *PUBLIC ADMINISTRATION*

920   VE   ISSN 0069-5033
COLECCION "ANIVERSARIOS CULTURALES".* 1965. irreg., 1968, no. 4. Universidad Central de Venezuela, Direccion de Cultura, Ciudad Universitaria, Caracas, Venezuela.

920   VE
COLECCIONDINA MICA Y SIEMBRA. no. 2, 1976. irreg. Universidad Simon Bolivar, Caracas, Venezuela.

012   US   ISSN 0094-5587
COMMUNITY LEADERS AND NOTEWORTHY AMERICANS. 1967. a. $39.95. American Biographical Institute, 205 W. Martin St., P.O.B. 226, Raleigh, NC 27602. Ed. J.S. Thomson. circ. 5,000.

COMPOSERS OF THE AMERICAS/ COMPOSITORES DE AMERICA. see *MUSIC*

028.1 011   US   ISSN 0010-7468
CONTEMPORARY AUTHORS. 1962. irreg., vols. 85-88, 1979. $48 per 4-vol. unit. Gale Research Company, Book Tower, Detroit, MI 48226. Eds. Frances Carol Locher, Ann Evory. cum.index.

920 944   FR
CONTRIBUTIONS A LA CONNAISSANCE DES ELITES AFRICAINES. 1978. irreg. (Centre de Recherche sur l'Afrique Orientale, Laboratoire Peiresc) Centre National de la Recherche Scientifique, 15 Quai Anatole France, 75700 Paris, France. Dir. Joseph Tubiana. illus.

CREATIVE CANADA. see *THEATER*

930.1   US   ISSN 0361-4735
CURRENT BIOGRAPHIES OF LEADING ARCHAEOLOGISTS. 1975. irreg. $7.95. Chesopiean Archaeological Association, 7507 Pennington Rd., Norfolk, VA 23505.

920   US   ISSN 0084-9499
CURRENT BIOGRAPHY YEARBOOK. 1940. a. $22. ‡ H. W. Wilson Co., 950 University Avenue, Bronx, NY 10452. Ed. Charles Moritz. cum.index (1940-1970)

920   US   ISSN 0147-0965
CURWOOD COLLECTOR. 1972. irreg., approx. 3/yr. $4 for 4 nos. Ivan A. Conger, Ed. & Pub., 1825 Osaukie Rd., Owosso, MI 48867. illus. stat. circ. 200. (processed)
Pertaining to the work of James Oliver Curwood

920   CN   ISSN 0070-4717
DICTIONARY OF CANADIAN BIOGRAPHY. 1966. irreg. University of Toronto Press, Front Campus, Toronto, Ont. M5S 1A6, Canada. Ed. Frances Halpenny. (also avail. in microfiche)

920   UK   ISSN 0419-1137
DICTIONARY OF INTERNATIONAL BIOGRAPHY. 1963. a. price varies. Melrose Press Ltd, 17-21 Churchgate St., Soham, Ely, Cambridgeshire CB7 5DS, England (U.S. subscr. to: International Biographical Centre, c/o Biblio Distribution Centre, 81 Adams Drive, Totowa, NJ 07512) Ed. Ernest Kay.

920   UK   ISSN 0070-4733
DICTIONARY OF LATIN AMERICAN AND CARIBBEAN BIOGRAPHY. 1969. irreg. $20. Melrose Press Ltd., 17-21 Churchgate St., Soham, Ely, Cambridgeshire CB7 5DS, England (U.S. subscr. to: International Biographical Centre, c/o Biblio Distribution Centre, 81 Adams Drive, Totowa, NJ 07512)

920   UK
DICTIONARY OF SCANDINAVIAN BIOGRAPHY. 1972. irreg. price varies. Melrose Press Ltd, 17-21 Churchgate St., Soham, Ely, Cambridgeshire CB7 5DS, England (U.S. subscr. to: International Biographical Centre, c/o Biblio Distribution Centre, 81 Adams Drive, Totowa, NJ 07512) Ed. Ernest Kay.

920   US   ISSN 0070-5101
DIRECTORY OF AMERICAN SCHOLARS. (In 4 vols.: Vol. 1: History; Vol. 2: English, Speech and Drama; Vol. 3: Foreign Languages, Linguistics and Philology; Vol. 4: Philosophy, Religion and Law) 1942. irreg., 7th edt. 1978. $48 per vol.; $175 per set. (Jaques Cattell Press) R. R. Bowker Company, 1180 Ave. of the Americas, New York, NY 10036 (Orders to P.O. Box 1807, Ann Arbor, Mich. 48106) index. (reprint service avail. from UMI)

920 658   II   ISSN 0070-542X
DIRECTORY OF DIRECTORS. (Text in English) 1966. irreg., latest 1982. Rs.100($25) Kothari Publications, 12 India Exchange Place, Calcutta 700001, India. Ed. H. Kothari. adv.

DIRECTORY OF MEDICAL SPECIALISTS. see *MEDICAL SCIENCES*

354.438   US   ISSN 0090-9955
DIRECTORY OF POLISH OFFICIALS. irreg. U.S. Central Intelligence Agency, Washington, DC 20505 (Dist. to Non-U.S. Government users by: Document Expediting (DOCEX) Project, Library of Congress, Washington, DC 20540) circ. controlled.

920 942   UK   ISSN 0070-7120
DORSET WORTHIES. 1962. irreg., no. 13, 1969. 1s.($3) Dorset County Museum, Dorchester, Dorset, England.

FIGURES DE WALLONIE. see *HISTORY — History Of Europe*

809   US   ISSN 0091-4924
FLANNERY O'CONNOR BULLETIN. 1972. a. $3. Georgia College, Box 608, Milledgeville, GA 31061. Ed. Bd. adv. bk. rev. circ. 1,000. (also avail. in microform from UMI; back issues avail.)

920   SA
GRAHAM'S TOWN SERIES. 1971. irreg., no. 4, 1979. price varies. (Rhodes University) A. A. Balkema Ltd., P.O. Box 3117, Cape Town 8000, South Africa (And Box 1675, Rotterdam, Netherlands; in the U.S. and Canada, 99 Main St., Salem, NH 03079)

920   GW   ISSN 0072-7741
GROSSE NATURFORSCHER. 1947. irreg., vol. 42, 1980. price varies. Wissenschaftliche Verlagsgesellschaft mbH, Postfach 40, 7000 Stuttgart 1, W. Germany (B.R.D.) Ed. Heinz Degen.

HAYDN-STUDIEN. see *MUSIC*

HOOVER INSTITUTION BIBLIOGRAPHIES SERIES. see *POLITICAL SCIENCE*

920 954   II   ISSN 0073-6244
INDIA WHO'S WHO. (Text in English) 1969. a. $14. (India News and Feature Alliance) I N F A Publications, Jeevan Deep Bldg., New Delhi 110001, India. adv. circ. 2,000.

509   II
INDIAN NATIONAL SCIENCE ACADEMY. BIOGRAPHICAL MEMOIRS OF FELLOWS. (Text in English) irreg. price varies. Indian National Science Academy, 1 Bahadur Shah Zafar Marg, New Delhi 110002, India. bibl.
Continues: National Institute of Sciences of India. Biographical Memoirs of Fellows (ISSN 0547-7557)

920   UK   ISSN 0143-8263
INTERNATIONAL AUTHOR'S AND WRITER'S WHO'S WHO. 1934. triennial. price varies. Melrose Press Ltd., 17-21 Churchgate St., Soham, Ely, Cambridgeshire CB7 5DS, England (U.S. subscr. to: International Biographical Centre, c/o Biblio Distribution Centre, 81 Adams Drive, Totowa, NJ 07512)
Formerly: Author's and Writer's Who (ISSN 0067-2386)

800   US
INTERNATIONAL AUTHORS AND WRITERS WHO'S WHO. 1934. irreg., 8th edt. 1977. $58. Gale Research Company, Book Tower, Detroit, MI 48226. Ed. Adrian Gaster.

920 610   UK
INTERNATIONAL MEDICAL WHO'S WHO. 1980. irreg. £90. Longman Group Ltd., Longman House, Burnt Mill, Harlow, Essex CM20 2JE, England (Dist. in the U.S. and Canada by: Gale Research Co. Ltd., Book Tower, Detroit, MI 48226)

920   UK   ISSN 0074-9613
INTERNATIONAL WHO'S WHO. 1935. a. $84. Europa Publications Ltd., 18 Bedford Sq., London WC1B 3JN, England.

INTERNATIONAL WHO'S WHO IN ART AND ANTIQUES. see *ART*

INTERNATIONAL WHO'S WHO IN EDUCATION. see *EDUCATION*

520   UK   ISSN 0539-1342
INTERNATIONAL WHO'S WHO IN POETRY. 1958. irreg. price varies. Melrose Press Ltd., 17-21 Churchgate St., Soham, Ely, Cambridgeshire CB7 5DS, England (U.S. subscr. to: International Biographical Centre, c/o Biblio Distribution Centre, 81 Adams Drive, Totowa, NJ 07512)

920   UK   ISSN 0075-6083
KINGS OF TOMORROW SERIES. 1967. irreg. price varies. Monarchist Press Association, 7 Sutherland Rd, West Ealing, London W13 0DX, England. circ. 3,000-4,000.

920   FI
KUKA KUKIN ON/WHO'S WHO IN FINLAND. every 4 yrs. (next ed. Fall 1978) Kustannusosakeyhtio Otava, Uudenmaankatu 10, SF-00120 Helsinki 12, Finland.

920 943   GW
LEBENSBILDER AUS SCHWABEN UND FRANKEN. (Vol. 1-6: Schwaebische Lebensbilder) 1940. irreg. DM.34. (Kommission fuer Geschichtliche Landeskunde) W. Kohlhammer GmbH (Stuttgart), Urbanstr. 12, Postfach 747, 7000 Stuttgart 1, W. Germany (B.R.D.) Ed. Robert Uhland.

BIOGRAPHY

920 574   GE   ISSN 0075-8418
LEBENSDARSTELLUNGEN DEUTSCHER NATURFORSCHER. 1955. irreg., no. 14, 1969. (Deutsche Akademie der Naturforscher Leopoldina) Johann Ambrosius Barth Verlag, Salomonstr. 18b, 701 Leipzig, E. Germany (D.D.R.) Ed. R. Zaunick. (back issues avail.)

LEITENDE MAENNER DER WIRTSCHAFT. see BUSINESS AND ECONOMICS — Management

MEMOIRE DES FEMMES. see WOMEN'S INTERESTS

920   UK
MEN AND WOMEN OF DISTINCTION. 1980. irreg. price varies. Melrose Press Ltd., 17-21 Churchgate St., Soham, Ely, Cambridgeshire CB7 5DS, England.

012   US   ISSN 0461-7398
MEN AND WOMEN OF HAWAII. Variant title: Who's Who in Hawaii. 1918. every 7-10 yrs; 9th edt. 1972. $25. S B Printers, Inc., 420 Ward Ave., Honolulu, HI 96814. Ed. Mrs. Betty Buker. circ. 3,000.

920   UK   ISSN 0306-3666
MEN OF ACHIEVEMENT. 1974. a. price varies. Melrose Press Ltd., 17-21 Churchgate St., Soham, Ely, Cambridgeshire CB7 5DS, England (U.S. subscr. to: International Biographical Centre, c/o Biblio Distribution Centre, 81 Adams Drive, Totowa, NJ 07512) illus.

925 500   US   ISSN 0077-2933
NATIONAL ACADEMY OF SCIENCES. BIOGRAPHICAL MEMOIRS. 1953. irreg. $10 per vol. National Academy of Sciences, 2101 Constitution Ave., N.W., Washington, DC 20418.

920   US   ISSN 0077-5371
NATIONAL REGISTER OF PROMINENT AMERICANS AND INTERNATIONAL NOTABLES. 1966. biennial. $30. National Register of Prominent Americans, Drawer 656, Venice, FL 33595. Ed. William Smith. bk. rev. (also avail. in microform from UMI)

970.3   US   ISSN 0091-6684
NAVAJO HISTORICAL PUBLICATIONS. BIOGRAPHICAL SERIES. 1970. irreg., no. 3, 1970. $1. Navajo Tribal Museum, Box 308, Window Rock, AZ 86515. Ed. J. Lee Correll.

920 803.8   US   ISSN 0077-6475
NEGRO AMERICAN BIOGRAPHIES AND AUTOBIOGRAPHIES. 1969. irreg., no. 7, 1978. price varies. University of Chicago Press, 5801 S. Ellis Ave., Chicago, IL 60637. Ed. John Hope Franklin. (reprint service avail. from UMI,ISI)

NEW ZEALAND BUSINESS WHO'S WHO. see BUSINESS AND ECONOMICS — Trade And Industrial Directories

920   CN   ISSN 0078-0286
NEWFOUNDLAND AND LABRADOR WHO'S WHO.* irreg. E.C. Boone Advertising Ltd., St. John's, N.F., Canada. Ed. J. R. Thoms.
Formerly: Newfoundland Who's Who.

NOUVELLE BIBLIOTHEQUE NERVALIENNE. see LITERATURE

920 659.2   US
O'DWYER'S DIRECTORY OF PUBLIC RELATIONS EXECUTIVES. 1979. biennial. $50. J. R. O'Dwyer Co., Inc., 271 Madison Ave., New York, NY 10016. Ed. Jack O'Dwyer.

OESTERREICHISCHE KOMPONISTEN DES XX. JAHRHUNDERTS. see MUSIC

940 920   UK
OXFORD ENGLISH MEMOIRS AND TRAVELS. irreg. price varies. Oxford University Press, 200 Madison Ave., New York, NY 10016 (And Ely House, 37 Dover St., London W1X 4AH, England) Ed. James Kinsley.

920   UK   ISSN 0079-0729
PEOPLE FROM THE PAST SERIES. 1964. irreg., no. 15, 1977. £4.95. ‡ Dobson Books Ltd., 80 Kensington Church St., London W8 4BZ, England. Ed. Egon Larsen.

920   AG
PERFILES CONTEMPORANEOS. no. 2, 1976. irreg. Editorial Plus Ultra, Viamonte 1755, 1055 Buenos Aires, Argentina. Ed. Jose Isaacson.

PERFIS PARLAMENTARES. see PUBLIC ADMINISTRATION

920 943   GW   ISSN 0080-2670
RHEINISCHE LEBENSBILDER. 1961. irreg., vol. 8, 1980. price varies. Rheinland-Verlag, Kennedy-Ufer 2, 5000 Cologne 21, W. Germany (B.R.D.) (Distr. by: Rudolf Habelt Verlag, Am Buchenhang 1, 5300 Bonn, W. Germany (B.R.D.)) Ed. Bernhard Poll.

920 500   UK   ISSN 0080-4606
ROYAL SOCIETY OF LONDON. BIOGRAPHICAL MEMOIRS OF FELLOWS OF THE ROYAL SOCIETY. (Continues: Obituary Notices of Fellows of the Royal Society, 9 Vols. (1932-54)) 1955. a. price varies. Royal Society of London, 6 Carlton House Terrace, London S.W.1, England. (reprint service avail. from ISI)

920   UK
ST. DAVID'S DAY BILINGUAL SERIES. 1928. a. price varies. University of Wales Press, 6 Gwennyth St., Cathays, Cardiff CF2 4YD, Wales. (reprint service avail. from UMI)

920   BL
SOCIEDADE BRASILEIRA. 1974. a. Livraria Francisco Alves Editora, Rua Sete de Setembro 1177, 20050 Rio de Janeiro RJ, Brazil. adv.
Social register

920 968   SA   ISSN 0085-6363
SOUTH AFRICAN BIOGRAPHICAL AND HISTORICAL STUDIES. 1970. irreg., no. 25, 1979. price varies. A. A. Balkema Ltd., P.O. Box 3117, Cape Town 8000, Cape Town, South Africa (And Box 1675, Rotterdam, Netherlands; in the U.S. and Canada, 99 Main St., Salem, NH 03079)

SOUTH AFRICAN JEWRY AND WHO'S WHO. see ETHNIC INTERESTS

SOUTHERN AFRICAN AND INDIAN OCEAN ISLANDS TRAVEL INDUSTRY'S YEARBOOK, DIRECTORY AND WHO'S WHO. see TRAVEL AND TOURISM

920 778.5   IT
STELLE FILANTI. 1978. irreg. Gremese Editore, Via Cola di Rienzo 136, 00192 Rome, Italy. Eds. Claudio G. Fava, Orio Caldiron.

664 920   II
SUGAR INDUSTRY'S WHO'S WHO AND DIRECTORY. 1976. a. Rs.65($15) V. K. Publications, 36 Todarmal Rd., Bengali Market, New Delhi 110001, India. adv. charts. stat.

SVERIGES FOERFATTARFOERBUND. MEDLEMSFOERTECKNING. see LITERATURE

920   US   ISSN 0083-0011
U. S. DEPARTMENT OF STATE. BIOGRAPHIC REGISTER. (Subseries of its Department and Foreign Service Series) 1860. a. U.S. Department of State, Bureau of Public Affairs, Washington, DC 20250 (Orders to Supt. of Documents, Washington, DC 20402)

920 914.3   NE
VIENNA CIRCLE COLLECTION. 1973. irreg. D. Reidel Publishing Co., Box 17, 3300 AA Dordrecht, Netherlands (And Lincoln Building, 160 Old Derby St.; Hingham, Ma 02043) Eds. H. L. Mulder. R. S. Cohen, B. McGuinness.

920 972   MX   ISSN 0300-208X
WHO'S NOTABLE IN MEXICO; Who's Who in Mexico. (Text in English) 1972. quinquennial. Mex.$300($24) Who's Who in Mexico, Apartado Postal 1311, Mexico 1, D.F., Mexico. Ed. Lucien F. Lajoie.

920   US
WHO'S WHO AMONG AMERICAN HIGH SCHOOL STUDENTS. (In 8 vols., by region) 1967. a. $21.95 per vol. Educational Communications, Inc., 3105 MacArthur Blvd., Northbrook, IL 60062. Ed. Paul C. Krouse. illus. stat.

920   US   ISSN 0362-5753
WHO'S WHO AMONG BLACK AMERICANS. 1976. every 3 yrs. $49.95 to individuals; libraries $39.95. Who's Who Among Black Americans, Inc. (Subsidiary of: Education Communications, Inc.) 3105 MacArther Blvd., Northbrook, IL 60062. Ed. William C. Matney.

780   US   ISSN 0362-3750
WHO'S WHO AMONG MUSIC STUDENTS IN AMERICAN HIGH SCHOOLS; a biographical dictionary of outstanding music students in American high schools. 1975. irreg. Randall Publishing Co., Box 2029, Tuscaloosa, AL 35401.

378 920   US   ISSN 0511-8891
WHO'S WHO AMONG STUDENTS IN AMERICAN JUNIOR COLLEGES. 1966/67. a. $23.80. Randall Publishing Co., Box 2029, Tuscaloosa, AL 35401.

920 379   US
WHO'S WHO AMONG STUDENTS IN AMERICAN UNIVERSITIES AND COLLEGES. a., 41st 1975. $23.80. Randall Publishing Co., Box 2029, Tuscaloosa, AL 35401.

920.01   UK   ISSN 0083-937X
WHO'S WHO; AN ANNUAL BIOGRAPHICAL DICTIONARY. 1849. a. £35. A. & C. Black(Publishers) Ltd., 35 Bedford Row, London WC1R 4JH, England (Dist. in U. S. by: St. Martin's Press, 175 Fifth Ave., New York, NY 10010)

659.1 920   US   ISSN 0511-8905
WHO'S WHO IN ADVERTISING. 1963. biennial. $69.50. Redfield Publishing Co., Inc., Box 325, Monroe, NY 10950.

920   US   ISSN 0083-9396
WHO'S WHO IN AMERICA. 1899. biennial. $89.50. Marquis Who's Who, Inc., 200 E. Ohio St., Chicago, IL 60611 (and 4300 W. 62nd St., Indianapolis, Ind. 46268)

927 700   US   ISSN 0000-0191
WHO'S WHO IN AMERICAN ART. 1936. biennial. $50. (Jaques Cattell Press) R. R. Bowker Company, 1180 Ave. of the Americas, New York, NY 10036 (Orders to P.O. Box 1807, Ann Arbor, Mich. 48106) index. (reprint service avail. from UMI)

920 296   US   ISSN 0196-8009
WHO'S WHO IN AMERICAN JEWRY. irreg. Standard Who's Who, 11980 San Vicente Blvd., Los Angeles, CA 90049. Ed. Harold M. Glass.
Incorporating: Directory of American Jewish Institutions.

WHO'S WHO IN AMERICAN LAW. see LAW

923.2   US   ISSN 0000-0205
WHO'S WHO IN AMERICAN POLITICS. 1967. biennial. $82.50. (Jaques Cattell Press) R. R. Bowker Company, 1180 Ave. of the Americas, New York, NY 10036 (Orders to P.O. Box 1807, Ann Arbor, Mich. 48106) index. (reprint service avail. from UMI)

920 796.357   US
WHO'S WHO IN BASEBALL. 1915. a. $1.50. Who's Who in Baseball Magazine Co. Inc., 250 Hudson St., New York, NY 10013.

920   US   ISSN 0511-8948
WHO'S WHO IN CALIFORNIA. 1928. biennial. $50. Who's Who Historical Society, Box 4240, San Clamente, CA 92672. Ed. Sarah Alice Vitale.
Supersedes (1950-1952): Who's Who in Los Angeles County.

920   US   ISSN 0195-539X
WHO'S WHO IN CALIFORNIA BUSINESS AND FINANCE. 1980. biennial. $60. Who's Who Historical Society, Box 4240, San Clemente, CA 92672. Ed. Sarah Alice Vitale.

920   CN   ISSN 0083-9450
WHO'S WHO IN CANADA. 1911. biennial. price varies. International Press Ltd., 643 Yonge St., Toronto, Ont. M4Y 2A2, Canada. Ed. Jack Kohane.

920   US   ISSN 0147-8265
WHO'S WHO IN CHIROPRACTIC, INTERNATIONAL. 1977. biennial. $49.50. Who's Who in Chiropractic, International Publishing Co., Inc., Box 2615, Littleton, CO 80161. Ed. Fern L. Dzaman.

WHO'S WHO IN COMMUNIST CHINA. see
HISTORY — History Of Asia

WHO'S WHO IN CONSULTING; a reference guide
to professional personnel engaged in consultation for
business, industry and government. see *BUSINESS
AND ECONOMICS — Management*

WHO'S WHO IN DER POLITIK/WHO'S WHO IN
GERMAN POLITICS. see *POLITICAL SCIENCE*

WHO'S WHO IN EDUCATION. see *EDUCATION*

920 332   TH
WHO'S WHO IN FINANCE AND BANKING IN
THAILAND. (Text in English) vol. 2, 1978-79.
biennial. B.300($15) Advance Media Co., Ltd., U
Chuliang Bldg., 968 Rama IV Rd., Bangkok,
Thailand. Ed. Cherachit Vatanavatin. bibl.

920 330   US   ISSN 0083-9523
WHO'S WHO IN FINANCE AND INDUSTRY.
1936. biennial. $57.50. Marquis Who's Who Inc.,
200 E. Ohio St., Chicago, IL 60611 (and 4300 W.
62nd St., Indianapolis, Ind. 46268)
    Formerly: World Who's Who in Commerce and
Industry.

635 920   US   ISSN 0511-8964
WHO'S WHO IN FLORICULTURE. 1955. a. $75 to
non-members. Society of American Florists,
Ornamental Horticulturists, 901 N. Washington St.,
Alexandria, VA 22314. Ed. Edwin A. Pratt. adv.
circ. 8,000.

920   FR   ISSN 0083-9531
WHO'S WHO IN FRANCE/QUI EST QUI EN
FRANCE. 1953. biennial. 390 F. Editions Jacques
Lafitte, 12 rue de l'Arcade, 75008 Paris, France.
adv. circ. 11,000.

920   GH
WHO'S WHO IN GHANA. 1973. biennial, 2nd ed.
1974/76 (pub. 1978) $58. Bartels Publications
(Ghana) Ltd., P.O. Box 4446, Accra, Ghana. Ed.
Charles Bartels. circ. 11,890.

920   US
WHO'S WHO IN GOVERNMENT. 1972. irreg., 3rd
edt., 1977. $55.50. Marquis Who's Who, Inc., 200
E. Ohio St., Chicago, IL 60611 (Subscr. to: 4300 W.
62 St., Indianapolis, IN 46206)

920   II   ISSN 0301-5106
WHO'S WHO IN INDIA. (Text in English) 1973.
irreg., next edt. 1982. Rs.150($40) Kothari
Publications, 12 India Exchange Place, Calcutta
700001, India. Ed. H. Kothari. adv.

920 600   II   ISSN 0083-9558
WHO'S WHO IN INDIAN ENGINEERING AND
INDUSTRY. 1962. irreg.; latest 1962. Rs.30($9)
Kothari Publications, 12 India Exchange Place,
Calcutta 700001, India. Ed. H. Kothari. adv.

500   II   ISSN 0083-9566
WHO'S WHO IN INDIAN SCIENCE. (Text in
English) 1964. irreg., next edt. 1982. Rs.50($15)
Kothari Publications, 12 India Exchange Place,
Calcutta 700001, India. Ed. H. Kothari. adv.

920   IS   ISSN 0083-9590
WHO'S WHO IN ISRAEL. (Beginning 1971/72
issued also in Hebrew, in alternate years, under title
Mi Va-Mi Be-Yisrael) (Text in English) 1950.
biennial. $40. Bronfman & Cohen, Publishers Ltd.,
Box 1109, Tel Aviv, Israel. adv. circ. 3,000.

920   LE   ISSN 0083-9612
WHO'S WHO IN LEBANON. (Text in English)
1963/64. biennial. $40. Publitec Publications,
Gedeon House, 135-137 John Kennedy St., Jisr el
Bacha, Box 5936, Beirut, Lebanon (Dist. in U.S. by:
Unipub, 345 Park Ave. South, New York, NY
10010) Ed. Charles G. Gedeon. adv. circ. 3,000.

920   MY   ISSN 0083-9620
WHO'S WHO IN MALAYSIA AND SINGAPORE.
(Text in English) 1956. biennial. $35. J. Victor
Morais, Ed. & Pub., Box 266, B.P. House, Jalan
Davidson, Kuala Lumpur 0505, Malaysia (Dist. by
International Publications Service, 114 E. 32nd St.,
New York, N.Y. 10016) illus.

WHO'S WHO IN MOVIES. see *MOTION
PICTURES*

920   NZ   ISSN 0083-9655
WHO'S WHO IN NEW ZEALAND. 1907. triennial.
‡ A.H. & A.W. Reed, 68-75 Kingsford Smith St,
Wellington, New Zealand (and Charles E. Tuttle
Co. Inc., Rutland, VT) Ed. J.E. Traue. index 1968-70.

954.7 920   PK   ISSN 0083-9671
WHO'S WHO IN PAKISTAN. (Text in English)
1930. a. Rs.35($30) Barque & Company, Barque
Chambers, Barque Square, 87 Sharah e-Liaquat Ali,
Box 201, Lahore, Pakistan. Ed. A.M. Barque. adv.
circ. 12,000.

659.2 920   US   ISSN 0511-9022
WHO'S WHO IN PUBLIC RELATIONS
(INTERNATIONAL) 1959/60. irreg. P R
Publishing Co., Inc., Box 600, Dudley House,
Exeter, NH 03833.

920 200   US   ISSN 0160-3728
WHO'S WHO IN RELIGION. 1975. irreg. $55.50.
Marquis Who's Who, Inc., 200 E. Ohio St.,
Chicago, IL 60611.

920.053   SU
WHO'S WHO IN SAUDI ARABIA. (Text in English)
1977. a? $45. Tihama, Residential Centre 312, Box
5455, Jeddah, Saudi Arabi.

920 629.1   US   ISSN 0083-9728
WHO'S WHO IN SPACE; international edition. 1966-
67. a. $55. Space Publications, Inc., 1341 G St.,
N.W., Washington, DC 20005. Ed. Norman L.
Baker.

920   SZ   ISSN 0083-9736
WHO'S WHO IN SWITZERLAND. 1951. biennial.
150 Fr. Editions Nagel S.A., 5-7, rue de l'Orangerie,
1211 Geneva 7, Switzerland. circ. 10,000.

920   LE   ISSN 0083-9752
WHO'S WHO IN THE ARAB WORLD. (Text in
English) 1965/66. biennial. $60. Publitec
Publications, Gedeon House, 135-137 John Kennedy
St., Jisr el Bacha, Box 5936, Beirut, Lebanon (Dist.
in U.S. by: Unipub, 345 Park Ave. South, New
York, NY 10010) Ed. Charles G. Gedeon. circ.
5,000.

920   US   ISSN 0083-9760
WHO'S WHO IN THE EAST. 1945. biennial. $57.50.
Marquis Who's Who Inc., 200 E. Ohio St., Chicago,
IL 60611 (and 4300 W. 62nd St., Indianapolis, Ind
46268)

338.1 636 920   US   ISSN 0510-4130
WHO'S WHO IN THE EGG AND POULTRY
INDUSTRIES. 1954. a. $30. Watt Publishing Co.,
Mount Morris, IL 61504. circ. 10,000.

920   US   ISSN 0083-9787
WHO'S WHO IN THE MIDWEST. 1946. biennial.
$57.50. Marquis Who's Who Inc., 200 E. Ohio St.,
Chicago, IL 60611 (and 4300 62nd St.,
Indianiapolis, Ind. 46268)

920   US   ISSN 0083-9809
WHO'S WHO IN THE SOUTH AND SOUTHWEST.
1946. biennial. $57.50. Marquis Who's Who Inc.,
200 E. Ohio St., Chicago, IL 60611 (and 4300 W.
62nd St., Indianapolis, Ind. 46268)

927   US   ISSN 0083-9833
WHO'S WHO IN THE THEATRE. 1912. irreg., 16th
edt., 1977. $64. ‡ Gale Research Company, Book
Tower, Detroit, MI 48226. Ed. Ian Herbert.

920   US   ISSN 0083-9817
WHO'S WHO IN THE WEST. 1946. biennial. $57.50.
Marquis Who's Who Inc., 200 E. Ohio St., Chicago,
IL 60611 (and 4300 W. 62nd St., Indianapolis, Ind.
46268)

920   US   ISSN 0083-9825
WHO'S WHO IN THE WORLD. 1971. biennial; 5th
edt., 1980. $59.50. Marquis Who's Who Inc., 200 E.
Ohio St., Chicago, IL 60611.

WHO'S WHO IN TRAINING AND
DEVELOPMENT. see *BUSINESS AND
ECONOMICS — Management*

920   UK
WHO'S WHO IN WESTERN EUROPE. 1980. irreg.
price varies. Melrose Press Ltd., 17-21 Churchgate
St., Soham, Ely, Cambridgeshire CB7 5DS, England
(U.S. subscr. to: International Biographical Centre,
81 Adams Drive, Totowa, NJ 07512)

920   US   ISSN 0083-9841
WHO'S WHO OF AMERICAN WOMEN. 1958.
biennial. $52.50. Marquis Who's Who Inc., 200 E.
Ohio St., Chicago, IL 60611 (and 4300 W. 62nd St.,
Indianapolis, Ind. 46268)

920   SA
WHO'S WHO OF SOUTHERN AFRICA
INCLUDING MAURITIUS, SOUTH WEST
AFRICA, ZIMBABWE-RHODESIA AND
NEIGHBORING COUNTRIES. (Text in English)
1907. a. $25. Argus Printing & Publishing Co. Ltd.,
Star Bldg., 4th Floor, 47 Sauer St., Johannesburg,
South Africa (Dist. by: International Publications
Service, 114 E. 32nd St., New York, NY 10016)
Ed. T. Binns. adv.
    Former titles: Who's Who of Southern Africa
Including Mauritius, South West Africa, Rhodesia
and Neighboring Countries; Who's Who of Southern
Africa (ISSN 0083-9876); Incorporating: Who's
Who of Rhodesia, Mauritius, Central and East
Africa (ISSN 0083-9868)

920   UK   ISSN 0084-0254
WILLIAM MORRIS SOCIETY. JOURNAL. 1961.
irreg. William Morris Society, Kelmscott House, 26
Upper Mall, London W.6, England. Ed. Geoffrey
Bensusan.

WORLD WHO'S WHO OF WOMEN. see
WOMEN'S INTERESTS

WORLD WHO'S WHO OF WOMEN IN
EDUCATION. see *WOMEN'S INTERESTS*

BIOGRAPHY — Abstracting, Bibliographies, Statistics

BIBLIOGRAPHIA FRANCISCANA. see
*RELIGIONS AND THEOLOGY — Abstracting,
Bibliographies, Statistics*

016   US
BIOGRAPHICAL DICTIONARIES AND
RELATED WORKS. SUPPLEMENT; an
international bibliography of collective biography.
1972. irreg. $40. Gale Research Company, Book
Tower, Detroit, MI 48226. Ed Robert B. Slocum.

920 016   US
BIOGRAPHICAL DICTIONARIES MASTER
INDEX. 1976. irreg. $95 (3 vols.) Gale Research
Company, Book Tower, Detroit, MI 48226. Eds.
Dennis La Beau, Gary C. Tarbert.

920   FR   ISSN 0067-8740
BIOGRAPHIES DE PERSONNALITES
FRANCAISES VIVANTES. (In four parts) 1967. a.
85 F. Documentation Francaise, 29-31 Quai
Voltaire, 75340 Paris 7, France.

920 016   GW
INDEX BIO-BIBLIOGRAPHICUS NOTORIUM
HOMINUM. 1973. irreg., 5-6/yr. DM.340. Biblio
Verlag, Jahnstr. 15, Postfach 1949, 4500
Osnabrueck, W. Germany (B.R.D.) J.P. Lobies.

BIOLOGICAL CHEMISTRY

see *Biology—Biological Chemistry*

BIOLOGY

see also Biology—Biological Chemistry;
Biology—Biophysics; Biology—Botany;
Biology—Cytology and Histology;
Biology—Entomology; Biology—
Genetics; Biology—Microbiology;
Biology—Microscopy; Biology—
Ornithology; Biology—Physiology;
Biology—Zoology; Medical Sciences;
Pharmacy and Pharmacology

574 610   US
A.L.Z.A. CONFERENCE SERIES. 1972. irreg. price varies. Plenum Press, 233 Spring St., New York, NY 10013.

574   PL
ACTA BIOLOGICA. 1975. irreg. 15 Zl. Uniwersytet Slaski w Katowicach, Ul. Bankowa 14, 40-007 Katowice, Poland. Ed. S. M. Klimaszewskiego.

574   GR   ISSN 0065-1095
ACTA BIOLOGICA HELLENICA.* 1965. a. Zoological Laboratory and Museum, Athens, Panepistimiopolis (Kouponia), Athens 621, Greece. (Co-sponsor: University of Salonica, Department of Biological Sciences)

ACTA HUMBOLDTIANA. SERIES GEOLOGICA, PALAEONTOLOGICA ET BIOLOGICA. see EARTH SCIENCES — Geology

574   PL   ISSN 0065-132X
ACTA HYDROBIOLOGICA. (Text and summaries in English and Polish) 1959. irreg., 1975, vol. 17, no. 3. price varies. (Polska Akademia Nauk, Zaklad Biologii Wod) Panstwowe Wydawnictwo Naukowe, Ul. Miodowa 10, Warsaw, Poland (Dist. by Ars Polona-Ruch, Krakowskie Przedmiescie 7, Warsaw, Poland) Ed. Kazimierz Pasternak.

610 576   DK   ISSN 0365-5571
ACTA PATHOLOGICA ET MICROBIOLOGICA SCANDINAVICA. SECTION A: PATHOLOGY. SUPPLEMENTUM. irreg. free to subscribers. Munksgaard, 35 Noerre Soegade, DK-1370 Copenhagen, Denmark. (reprint service avail. from ISI)
Pathology

616.07 576   DK   ISSN 0105-0656
ACTA PATHOLOGICA ET MICROBIOLOGICA SCANDINAVICA. SECTION B: MICROBIOLOGY. SUPPLEMENTUM. irreg. free to subscribers. Munksgaard, 35 Noerre Soegade, DK-1370 Copenhagen K, Denmark. (reprint service avail. from ISI)

575   JA   ISSN 0065-1621
ACTA RADIOBOTANIKA ET GENETIKA/ HOSHASEN IKUSHUJO KENKYU HOKOKU; bulletin of the Institute of Radiation Breeding. (Text in English or Japanese) 1967. irreg., no. 2, 1971. exchange basis. Institute of Radiation Breeding - Norin-sho Nogyo Gijutsu Kenkyusho Hoshasen Ikushujo, Omiya-cho, Naka-gun, Ibaraki 319-22, Japan.

574   CS   ISSN 0001-7124
ACTA UNIVERSITATIS CAROLINAE: BIOLOGICA. (Editions in English, French, German, Russian) 1954. 5-6/yr. 20 Zl.($33) Universita Karlova, Prirodovedecka Fakulta, Katedra Biologie, Vinicna 5, 128 44 Prague 2, Czechoslovakia (Or Exchange Library, Faculty of Natural Science, Vimicina 5, 12844 Prague 2, Czechoslovakia) Ed. Dr. M. Kunst. bibl. charts. illus. stat. index. circ. 800. Indexed: Biol.Abstr. Excerp.Med.

574   PL   ISSN 0208-4449
ACTA UNIVERSITATIS NICOLAI COPERNICI. BIOLOGIA. 1956. irreg. price varies. Uniwersytet Mikolaja Kopernika, Fosa Staromiejska 3, Torun, Poland (Dist. by Osrodek Rozpowszechniania Wydanictw Naukowych PAN, Palac Kultury i Nauki, 00-901 Warsaw, Poland)
Formerly: Uniwersytet Mikolaja Kopernika, Torun. Nauki Matematyczno-Przyrodnicze. Biologia (ISSN 0083-4521)

574.33 574.4 574.8   US   ISSN 0071-1098
ADVANCES IN ANATOMY, EMBRYOLOGY AND CELL BIOLOGY. vol. 39, 1966. irreg., vol. 68, 1981. Springer-Verlag, 175 Fifth Ave., New York, NY 10010 (also Berlin, Heidelberg, Vienna) (reprint service avail. from ISI) Indexed: Ind.Med.

574   US   ISSN 0360-9960
ADVANCES IN BIOENGINEERING. a. $20 to non-members; members $10. American Society of Mechanical Engineers, 345 E. 47th St., New York, NY 10017. Eds. R. C. Eberhart, A. H. Burstein. illus.

574 619   US   ISSN 0065-2598
ADVANCES IN EXPERIMENTAL MEDICINE AND BIOLOGY. 1967. irreg. price varies. Plenum Press, 233 Spring St., New York, NY 10013. Ed.Bd. Indexed: Ind.Med.

574.92   UK   ISSN 0065-2881
ADVANCES IN MARINE BIOLOGY. 1963. irreg., vol. 16, 1978. price varies. Academic Press Inc. (London) Ltd., 24-28 Oval Rd., London N.W.1., England (and 111 Fifth Ave., New York, N.Y. 10022) Eds. F. S. Russell, Maurice Yonge. index.
Marine

574.2   US   ISSN 0099-1147
ADVANCES IN PATHOBIOLOGY. 1975. irreg. price varies. Thieme-Stratton, Inc., 381 Park Avenue South, New York, NY 10016.

ADVANCES IN PSYCHOBIOLOGY. see PSYCHOLOGY

574 610   US   ISSN 0065-3446
ADVANCES IN THE BIOSCIENCES. (Schering Symposium) 1969. 6/yr. $310. Pergamon Press, Inc., Journals Division, Maxwell House, Fairview Park, Elmsford, NY 10523 (And Headington Hill Hall, Oxford OX3 0BW, England) adv. (also avail. in microform from MIM,UMI)

574   US   ISSN 0065-6364
ALLAN HANCOCK MONOGRAPHS IN MARINE BIOLOGY. 1966. irreg., no. 9, 1976. price varies. Allan Hancock Foundation, University of Southern California, Los Angeles, CA 90007. Ed. Mary E. Pippin. circ. 800 (approx.) Indexed: Biol.Abstr. Ocean.Abstr. Aqua.Sci. & Fish.Abstr. Zoo.Rec.
Marine

ALLIANCE FOR ENGINEERING IN MEDICINE AND BIOLOGY. PROCEEDINGS OF THE ANNUAL CONFERENCE. see MEDICAL SCIENCES

574   JA   ISSN 0065-6674
AMAKUSA MARINE BIOLOGICAL LABORATORY. CONTRIBUTIONS. (Collected reprints of papers) (Text and summaries in English or Japanese) 1958. biennial. not for sale; limited controlled circ. Kyushu University, Amakusa Marine Biological Laboratory - Kyushu Daigaku Rigakubu Fuzoku Amakusa Rinkai Jikkensho, 2231 Tomioka, Reihoku-cho, Amakusa-gun, Kumamoto 863-25, Japan. Ed. Taiji Kikuchi. circ. 130(controlled)
Marine

574   JA   ISSN 0065-6682
AMAKUSA MARINE BIOLOGICAL LABORATORY. PUBLICATIONS. (Text and summaries in English) 1966. a. exchange basis. Kyushu University, Amakusa Marine Biological Laboratory - Kyushu Daigaku Rigakubu Fuzoku Amakusa Rinkai Jikkensho, 2231 Tomioka, Reihoku-cho, Amakusa-gun, Kumamoto 863-25, Japan. Ed. Taiji Kikuchi. circ. 450. Indexed: Biol.Abstr.
Marine

551.48 574.5   GW   ISSN 0065-6755
AMAZONIANA; LIMNOLOGIA ET OECOLOGIA REGIONALIS SYSTEMAE FLUMINIS AMAZONAS. (Text and summaries in German and Portuguese) 1965. irreg (4 issues per vol.) DM.16 per issue. Verlag Walter G. Muehlau, Holtenauer Str. 116, 2300 Kiel, W. Germany (B. R. D.) Eds. Djalma Batista (Brazil), Harald Sioli (B.R.D.)

AMERICAN ASSOCIATION OF PATHOLOGISTS AND BACTERIOLOGISTS. SYMPOSIUM. MONOGRAPHS. see MEDICAL SCIENCES

574.4 611   US
AMERICAN LECTURES IN ANATOMY. irreg. price varies. Charles C. Thomas, Publisher, 301-327 E. Lawrence Ave., Springfield, IL 62717.
Anatomy

574   US   ISSN 0065-9436
AMERICAN MIDLAND NATURALIST MONOGRAPH SERIES. 1944. irreg. University of Notre Dame, Notre Dame, IN 46556.

AMERICAN WILDLIFE REGION SERIES. see CONSERVATION

574.4 611   GE   ISSN 0066-1562
ANATOMISCHE GESELLSCHAFT. VERHANDLUNGEN. (Supplement to: Anatomischer Anzeiger) 1887. price varies. VEB Gustav Fischer Verlag, Villengang 2, Postfach 176, 6900 Jena, E. Germany (D.D.R.) Indexed: Ind.Med.
Anatomy

574   PL   ISSN 0066-2232
ANNALES UNIVERSITATIS MARIAE CURIE-SKLODOWSKA. SECTIO C. BIOLOGIA. (Text in Polish or English; summaries in English, French, German, Russian) 1946. a. Uniwersytet Marii Curie-Sklodowskiej, Plac Marii Curie-Sklodowskiej 5, 20-031 Lublin, Poland. Ed. Z. Lorkiewicz. Indexed: Biol.Abstr. Chem.Abstr. Int.Abstr.Biol.Sci.

574   US   ISSN 0090-4384
ANNUAL EDITIONS: READINGS IN BIOLOGY. Variant title: Focus: Biology. 1973/74. a. price varies. Dushkin Publishing Group, Sluice Dock, Guilford, CT 06437. illus.

155.3 306.7   US   ISSN 0163-836X
ANNUAL EDITIONS: READINGS IN HUMAN SEXUALITY. Variant title: Readings in Human Sexuality. Annual Editions. a. $6.55. Dushkin Publishing Group, Sluice Dock, Guilford, CT 06437.
Formerly: Focus: Human Sexuality (ISSN 0147-0655)

ARBEITEN AUS DEM PAUL-EHRLICH-INSTITUT, DEM GEORG-SPEYER-HAUS UND DEM FERDINAND-BLUM-INSTITUT. see MEDICAL SCIENCES

574 619   CL   ISSN 0004-0533
ARCHIVOS DE BIOLOGIA Y MEDICINA EXPERIMENTALES. (Summaries in English) 1964. a. $8. Sociedad de Biologia de Chile, Casilla 16164, Santiago 9, Chile. Ed. Tito Ureta, M.D. adv. bk. rev. circ. 1,000-1,500. (also avail. in microfiche from UMI) Indexed: Biol.Abstr. Chem.Abstr. Curr.Cont. Ind.Med.

574   PR   ISSN 0066-9571
ASSOCIATION OF ISLAND MARINE LABORATORIES OF THE CARIBBEAN. PROCEEDINGS. 1957. irreg., 1973, no. 9. $3. Association of Island Marine Laboratories of the Caribbean, University of Puerto Rico, Dept. of Marine Sciences, Mayaguez, Puerto Rico. Ed. Ernest H. Williams, Jr. circ. 300.

574.05   SP
ASTURNATURA. (Summaries in English) 1973. irreg. Asociacion Asturiana de Amigos de la Naturaleza, Santa Susana, 35, Oviedo, Spain. illus.

574.88   US
ATLAS OF MOLECULAR STRUCTURES IN BIOLOGY. irreg. price varies. Oxford University Press, 200 Madison Ave., New York, NY 10016 (And Ely House, 37 Dover St., London, W1X 4AH, England) Eds. D. C. Phillips, F. M. Richards.
Molecular

574 550   GW   ISSN 0067-2858
BADISCHER LANDESVEREIN FUER NATURKUNDE UND NATURSCHUTZ, FREIBURG. MITTEILUNGEN. NEUE FOLGE. 1919. a. DM.30. Badischer Landesverein fuer Naturkunde und Naturschutz e.V, Albertstr. 5, 7800 Freiburg, W. Germany (B.R.D.) Ed. K. Sauer. bk. rev.

574   US
BANBURY REPORTS. 1979. irreg., no. 3, 1980. $45 for latest issue. Cold Spring Harbor Laboratory, Box 100, Publications Department, Cold Spring Harbor, NY 11724.

574 US ISSN 0090-5542
BASIC LIFE SCIENCES. (Consists of the Proceedings of International Latin American Symposia) 1973. irreg. price varies. Plenum Press, 233 Spring St., New York, NY 10013. Ed. Alexander Hollaender. Indexed: Chem.Abstr. Ind.Med.

BASLER VEROEFFENTLICHUNGEN ZUR GESCHICHTE DER MEDIZIN UND DER BIOLOGIE. see *MEDICAL SCIENCES*

570 550 GW
BEITRAEGE ZUR NATURKUNDE IN OSTHESSEN. 1969. irreg., no. 11-12, 1977. DM.25. (Verein fuer Naturkunde in Osthessen e.V.) Verlag Parzeller und Co., Peterstor 18, Postfach 409, 6400 Fulda, W. Germany (B.R.D.) Ed. Martin Kruepe.

574.9 BE ISSN 0067-5369
BELGIUM. ADMINISTRATION DES EAUX ET FORETS. STATION DE RECHERCHES DES EAUX ET FORETS. TRAVAUX. SERIE D. HYDROBIOLOGIE.* (Text in Flemish, French, and German) 1941. irreg. Administration des Eaux et Forets, Gronendall-Hoilaart, Belgium.

574 US
BENCHMARK PAPERS IN BIOLOGICAL CONCEPTS. 1973. irreg., vol. 3, 1977. price varies. Dowden, Hutchinson & Ross, Inc., 523 Sarah St., Stroudsburg, PA 18360 (Dist. by Academic Press, Inc., 111 Fifth Ave., New York, NY 10003) Ed. P. Gray.

574.5 US
BENCHMARK PAPERS IN ECOLOGY. 1974. irreg., vol. 9, 1979. Dowden, Hutchinson & Ross, Inc., 523 Sarah St., Stroudsburg, PA 18360 (Dist. by Academic Press, Inc., 111 Fifth Ave., New York, NY 10003) Ed. F. B. Golley.

575 574 US
BENCHMARK PAPERS IN SYSTEMATIC AND EVOLUTIONARY BIOLOGY. 1975. irreg., vol. 3, 1976. price varies. Dowden, Hutchinson and Ross, Inc., 523 Sarah St., Stroudsburg, PA 18360 (Dist. by Academic Press, Inc., 111 Fifth Ave., New York, NY 10003) Ed. C. J. Bajema.

BIBLIOTHECA ANATOMICA. see *MEDICAL SCIENCES*

DIE BINNENGEWAESSER; Einzeldarstellungen aus der Limnologie und ihren Grenzgebieten. see *EARTH SCIENCES — Hydrology*

574 FR ISSN 0067-866X
BIO-INFORMATION.* 1969. irreg. price varies. Association en Biologie Appliquee, 50 Rue Gauthier-De-Chatillon, Lille, France.

574 US
BIOENGINEERING SERIES. irreg. price varies. General Technical Services, 8794 W. Chester Pike, Upper Darby, PA 19082.

574.9 JA ISSN 0067-8716
BIOGEOGRAPHICAL SOCIETY OF JAPAN. BULLETIN. (Text in English and Japanese; summaries in English) 1920. irreg.(approx. 12 issues per year) 1000 Yen. (Nippon Seibutsuchiri Gakkai) Academic Press of Japan, 4-5-7 Konan, Minato-ku, Tokyo, Japan. Ed. Yaichiro Okada. index.

574 PL
BIOLOGIA. (Text in Polish; summaries in English) 1961. irreg. price varies. Uniwersytet im Adama Mickiewicza W Poznaniu, Stalingradzka 1, 61-712 Poznan, Poland (Dist. by: Ars Polona, Krakowskie Przedmiescie 7, 00-068 Warsaw, Poland)
Formerly: Uniwersytet im. Adama Mickiewicza w Poznaniu. Wydzial Biologii i Nauk o Ziemi. Seria Biologia.

574 JA ISSN 0520-1810
BIOLOGICAL JOURNAL OF OKAYAMA UNIVERSITY/OKAYAMA DAIGAKU RIGAKUBU SEIBUTSUGAKU KIYO. (Text in English) 1952. irreg. on exchange basis. Okayama University, Department of Biology - Okayama Daigaku Rigakubu Seibutsugaku Kyoshitsu, Faculty of Science, Tsushima, Okayama 700, Japan.

574 FI ISSN 0356-1062
BIOLOGICAL RESEARCH REPORTS FROM THE UNIVERSITY OF JYVASKYLA. 1975. irreg. exchange basis. Jyvaskylan Yliopisto, Kirjasto - University of Jyvaskyla, Seminaarinkatu 15, 40100 Jyvaskyla 10, Finland. Ed. Pertti Eloranta. circ. 400-500.

574 US ISSN 0084-7895
BIOLOGICAL SOCIETY OF NEVADA. OCCASIONAL PAPERS AND MEMOIRS. 1963. irreg. free. ‡ Biological Society of Nevada, Box 167, Verdi, NV 89439. Ed. Ira La Rivers. bk. rev. circ. 300 (controlled) (tabloid format; also avail. in microform from UMI) Indexed: Biol.Abstr. Zoo.Rec.

574 581 591 US ISSN 0006-324X
BIOLOGICAL SOCIETY OF WASHINGTON. PROCEEDINGS. 1880. irreg., approx. 4/yr. $7. Biological Society of Washington, Mail Stop 163, NHB, Smithsonian Institution, Washington, DC 20560. Ed. C.W. Hart. charts. illus. index. cum.ind.: 1881-1922; 1923-1961. circ. 500. Indexed: Biol.Abstr. Key Word Ind.Wildl.Res.

574 UR
BIOLOGICHESKIE NAUKI. 1971. irreg. 1.20 Rub. Kazakhskii Gosudarstvennyi Universitet, Ul. Lenina 18, Alma-Ata, U.S.S.R. bk. rev. bibl. illus. Indexed: Ind.Med.

574 BE
BIOLOGISCH JAARBOEK. 1934. a. Koninklijk Natuurwetenschappelijk Genootschap Dodonaea, Ghent, Belgium. illus.
Supersedes: Botanisch Jaarboek.

574 US
BIOLOGY AND ENVIRONMENT. irreg. price varies. University Park Press (Subsidiary of: American Medical Publishers) Chamber of Commerce Bldg., Baltimore, MD 21202.

574 US
BIOLOGY SERIES (SEATTLE) 1967. irreg., latest 1977. price varies. University of Washington Press, Seattle, WA 98105.

574 US ISSN 0067-8821
BIOMATHEMATICS. (Text in English) 1970. irreg., vol. 10, 1980. price varies. Springer-Verlag, 175 Fifth Ave., New York, NY 10010 (also Berlin, Heidelberg, Vienna) circ. 2,000. (reprint service avail. from ISI) Indexed: Math.R.

BIOMEDICAL MATERIALS RESEARCH SYMPOSIA. see *MEDICAL SCIENCES*

574 NE ISSN 0067-8902
BIOMETEOROLOGY; PROCEEDINGS. Represents: International Biometeorological Congress. Proceedings. triennial, 8th, 1979, Shefayim, Israel. fl.150. (International Society of Biometeorology) Swets Publishing Service, Heereweg 347B, 2161 CA Lisse, Netherlands (Dist. in the U.S. and Canada by: Swets North America, Inc., Box 517 Berwyn, PA 19312) Indexed: Biol.Abstr. Chem.Abstr.

574 SI
BIOSPHERE BULLETIN. (Text in Chinese and English; summaries in English) 1972. irreg. S.$1. ‡ Nanyang University, Biology Society, Jurong Road, Singapore 22, Singapore. Ed. Anne Johnson. adv. bk. rev. charts. illus.

620.2 US ISSN 0572-6565
BIOTECHNOLOGY & BIOENGINEERING SYMPOSIA. 1969. irreg., no. 9, 1979. price varies. John Wiley & Sons, Inc., 605 Third Ave., New York, NY 10016. Indexed: Biol.Abstr. Curr.Cont. Excerp.Med. Sci.Cit.Ind.

574.92 BL ISSN 0067-9593
BOLETIM DE CIENCIAS DO MAR. (Text in English and Portuguese) 1961. irreg.; no. 25, 1974. $90 available on exchange. Universidade Federal do Ceara, Laboratorio de Ciencias do Mar, Av. da Abolicao, 3207, Caixa Postal 1072, Fortaleza, Ceara, Brazil. Ed. Antonio Adauto Fonteles Filho. circ. 1,000.
Formerly: Universidade Federal do Ceara. Estacao de Biologia Marinha. Boletim.

574 BL
BOLETIM DE ZOOLOGIA. (Text in English, French and Portuguese) 1937. a. price varies. Universidade de Sao Paulo, Departamento de Fisiologia Geral de Zoologia, Caixa Postal 11,230, Sao Paulo ZC9, Brazil. (Co-sponsor: Instituto de Biologia Marinha) Supersedes in part (since 1976): Boletim de Zoologia e Biologia Marinha. Nova Serie (ISSN 0067-9623)

BOLETIN DE ESTUDIOS MEDICOS Y BIOLOGICOS. see *MEDICAL SCIENCES*

574 UK ISSN 0068-2306
BRITISH MUSEUM (NATURAL HISTORY) BULLETIN. HISTORICAL. 1949. irreg. price varies. British Museum (Natural History), Cromwell Rd., London SW7 5BD, England. index. circ. 750.

574 US ISSN 0068-2799
BROOKHAVEN SYMPOSIA IN BIOLOGY. 1952, no. 5. irreg., no. 29, 1977. Brookhaven National Laboratory, Upton, NY 11973 (Orders to: National Technical Information Service, 5285 Port Royal Rd., Springfield, VA 22151) Indexed: Ind.Med.

574 AG ISSN 0068-340X
BUENOS AIRES. CENTRO DE INVESTIGACION DE BIOLOGIA MARINA. CONTRIBUCION CIENTIFICIA. (Text in Spanish; summaries in English) 1962. irreg., 1969, no. 42. price varies. Centro de Investigacion de Biologia Marina, Libertad 1235, Buenos Aires, Argentina.

574 BU ISSN 0068-3817
BULGARSKA AKADEMIIA NA NAUKITE. INSTITUT PO MORFOLOGIIA. IZVESTIIA. (Summaries in various languages) 1953. irreg. 2.77 lv. Publishing House of the Bulgarian Academy of Sciences, Ul. Akad. G. Bonchev, 1113 Sofia, Bulgaria (Dist. by: Hemus, 6, Rouski Blvd., 1000 Sofia, Bulgaria) Ed. A. Khadzhiolov. circ. 600.

574.9 US ISSN 0068-5755
CALIFORNIA NATURAL HISTORY GUIDES. 1959. irreg. price varies. University of California Press, 2223 Fulton St., Berkeley, CA 94720. Ed. Arthur Smith.

574 UK ISSN 0068-6697
CAMBRIDGE MONOGRAPHS IN EXPERIMENTAL BIOLOGY. 1954. irreg., no. 19, 1977. $21.50 for latest vol. Cambridge University Press, Box 110, Cambridge CB2 3RL, 200 Euston Rd., London N.W.1, England (and 32 E. 57th St., New York NY 10022)

CANADA. FISHERIES AND MARINE SERVICE. BIOLOGICAL STATION, ST. ANDREWS, NEW BRUNSWICK. GENERAL SERIES CIRCULAR. see *FISH AND FISHERIES*

CANADA. FISHERIES AND MARINE SERVICE. BULLETIN SERIES. see *FISH AND FISHERIES*

CANADA. FISHERIES AND MARINE SERVICE. TECHNICAL REPORT SERIES. see *FISH AND FISHERIES*

574.92 CN ISSN 0068-7995
CANADA. NATIONAL MUSEUMS, OTTAWA. PUBLICATIONS IN BIOLOGICAL OCEANOGRAPHY. French edition: Canada. Musees Nationaux. Publications d'Oceanographie Biologique (ISSN 0381-0151) (Text in English and French) 1970. irreg. price varies, some free. (National Museum of Natural Sciences) National Museums of Canada, Ottawa, Ont. K1A OM8, Canada. Indexed: Biol.Abstr.
Marine

572 CN ISSN 0068-8681
CANADIAN FEDERATION OF BIOLOGICAL SOCIETIES. CANADIAN FEDERATION NEWS OF THE ANNUAL MEETING. (Text in English and French) 1959. a. $1. Canadian Federation of Biological Societies, University of Western Ontario, Department of Pharmacology, London, Ont. N6A 5C1, Canada. Ed. Dr. J. Trevithick.

BIOLOGY

574   **CN**
CANADIAN FEDERATION OF BIOLOGICAL SOCIETIES. PROGRAMME AND PROCEEDINGS OF THE ANNUAL MEETING. (Text in English and French) 1976. a. $2. Canadian Federation of Biological Societies, University of Western Ontario, Department of Pharmacology, London, Ont. N6A 5C1, Canada. author index.
Formed by the merger of: Canadian Federation of Biological Societies. Proceedings (ISSN 0068-869X) & Canadian Federation of Biological Societies. Programme of the Annual Meeting (ISSN 0068-8703)

CANADIAN WILDLIFE SERVICE. REPORT SERIES. see *CONSERVATION*

CARIBBEAN RESEARCH INSTITUTE. REPORT. see *HISTORY — History Of North And South America*

574 572   **US**   **ISSN 0145-9058**
CARNEGIE MUSEUM OF NATURAL HISTORY. BULLETIN. 1976. irreg., no. 3, 1977. price varies. Carnegie Museum of Natural History, 4400 Forbes Ave., Pittsburgh, PA 15213. Ed. Robert E. Porteous. bibl. charts. illus. index. circ. (controlled) (back issues avail.) Indexed: Biol.Abstr.

CENTRE D'ECOLOGIE FORESTIERE ET RURALE. COMMUNICATIONS. see *FORESTS AND FORESTRY*

570   **CE**   **ISSN 0069-2379**
CEYLON JOURNAL OF SCIENCE. BIOLOGICAL SCIENCES. (Text in English) 1957. irreg. Rs.15($8) per no. University of Peradeniya, University Park, Peradeniya, Sri Lanka. Eds. H. Crusz And M. D. Dassanayake. bk. rev. charts. illus. circ. 500.

574.5   **US**   **ISSN 0009-1766**
CHARLES C. ADAMS CENTER FOR ECOLOGICAL STUDIES. OCCASIONAL PAPERS. 1960. irreg. free to qualified personnel. Western Michigan University, Kalamazoo, MI 49001. Ed.Bd. charts. illus. circ. 500. Indexed: Biol.Abstr.
Ecology

574   **CU**
CIENCIAS BIOLOGICAS. (Text in Spanish; summaries in English) 1977. irreg. Academia de Ciencias de Cuba, Industria no. 452, Havana 2, Cuba. Ed.Bd. charts. illus.

574   **SX**   **ISSN 0590-6342**
CIMBEBASIA. SERIES A: NATURAL HISTORY. (Text mainly in English; summaries in German or French) 1962. irreg., vol.5, no.4, 1979. price varies. State Museum, Box 1203, Windhoek, South West Africa. Ed. C. G. Coetzee. index. circ. 1,000.

574.92   **IT**
CIVICA STAZIONE IDROBIOLOGICA DI MILANO. QUADERNI. (Summaries in English) 1970. irreg. Civica Stazione Idrobiologica di Milano, Viale Gadio, 2, 20121 Milan, Italy. bibl, charts, illus.

CLINICAL IMMUNOBIOLOGY. see *MEDICAL SCIENCES — Allergology And Immunology*

574   **US**   **ISSN 0084-8824**
COLD SPRING HARBOR LABORATORY. ABSTRACTS OF PAPERS PRESENTED AT MEETINGS. irreg., 8-10/yr. $5 per no. Cold Spring Harbor Laboratory, Box 100, Publications Department, Cold Spring Harbor, NY 11724. circ. controlled. (processed)

574   **US**   **ISSN 0069-5009**
COLD SPRING HARBOR LABORATORY. ANNUAL REPORT. 1924. a. Cold Spring Harbor Laboratory, P.O. Box 100, Publications Department, Cold Spring Harbor, NY 11724. circ. controlled.

574   **US**   **ISSN 0091-7451**
COLD SPRING HARBOR LABORATORY. SYMPOSIA ON QUANTITATIVE BIOLOGY. 1933. a. $120 for 1979 vols. Cold Spring Harbor Laboratory, Box 100, Publications Department, Cold Spring Harbor, NY 11724. circ. 3,500. Indexed: Biol.Abstr. Curr.Cont. Ind.Med.

574   **US**
COLD SPRING HARBOR MONOGRAPH SERIES. 1970. irreg., vol. 10, 1980. price varies. Cold Spring Harbor Laboratory, Box 100, Publications Department, Cold Spring Harbor, NY 11724.

574   **SP**
COLECCION CIENCIAS BIOLOGICAS. 1974. irreg.; 1979, no. 7. price varies. Ediciones Universidad de Navarra S.A., Plaza de los Sauces 1 y 2, Baranain, Pamplona, Spain.

574   **US**   **ISSN 0069-6285**
COLUMBIA BIOLOGICAL SERIES. 1910. irreg., 1968, no. 24. Columbia University Press, 136 South Broadway, Irvington-On-Hudson, NY 10533.

574.1   **EI**
COMMISSION OF THE EUROPEAN COMMUNITIES. CENTRE FOR INFORMATION AND DOCUMENTATION. ANNUAL REPORT: PROGRAM BIOLOGY-HEALTH PROTECTION. (Text in English, French, German, and Italian) 1972. a. Office for Official Publications of the European Communities, Centre for Information and Documentation, Case Postale 1003, Luxembourg, Luxembourg (Dist. in the U.S. by: European Community Information Service, 2100 M St., NW, Suite 707, Washington, DC 20037)

574   **UK**   **ISSN 0069-7125**
COMMONWEALTH INSTITUTE OF BIOLOGICAL CONTROL. TECHNICAL COMMUNICATIONS. 1960. irreg. price varies. Commonwealth Agricultural Bureaux, Farnham Royal, Bucks, England.

574   **CL**   **ISSN 0069-8784**
CONFERENCIAS DE BIOQUIMICA.* 1967. a. Universidad de Chile, Instituto de Quimica Fisiologica y Patologica, Av. Bernardo O'Higgins 1058, Casilla 10-D, Santiago, Chile.

CONGRESSO NACIONAL DE ANATOMIA PATOLOGICAS. ACTAS. see *MEDICAL SCIENCES*

574   **UK**
CONTEMPORARY BIOLOGY. 1971. irreg. price varies. Edward Arnold (Publishers) Ltd., 41 Bedford Square, London WC1B 3DQ, England.

574.2   **US**   **ISSN 0093-4054**
CONTEMPORARY TOPICS IN IMMUNOBIOLOGY. 1972. irreg. price varies. Plenum Press, 233 Spring St., New York, NY 10013. Ed.Bd. illus. Indexed: Ind.Med.

574.92   **US**
CONTRIBUTIONS IN MARINE SCIENCE. 1945. a. $8. Port Aransas Marine Laboratory, University of Texas, Marine Science Institute, Port Aransas, TX 78373. Ed. Donald Wohlschlag. circ. 1,000. Indexed: Biol.Abstr. Biol. & Agr.Ind. Chem.Abstr. Ocean.Ind.
Former titles: University of Texas. Institute of Marine Science. Contributions (ISSN 0082-3449) & University of Texas. Institute of Marine Science. Publications.
Marine

574 914.106   **UK**
CORNISH BIOLOGICAL RECORDS. 1977. irreg. £0.60 per no. to non-members. Institute of Cornish Studies, Biological Recording Unit, Trevenson House, Pool, Redruth, Cornwall TR15 3RE, England.

574   **US**   **ISSN 0590-7225**
COURS ET DOCUMENTS DE BIOLOGIE. 1969. a. price varies. Gordon and Breach Science Publishers, One Park Ave., New York, NY 10016. Eds. Etienne Wolff, Th. Lender.

574   **US**
CURRENT CONCEPTS IN BIOLOGY. irreg., unnumbered, latest 1973. price varies. Macmillan Publishing Co., Inc., 866 Third Ave., New York, NY 10022.

574   **US**   **ISSN 0070-2137**
CURRENT TOPICS IN CELLULAR REGULATION. 1969. irreg., vol. 18, 1981. price varies. Academic Press Inc., (Subsidiary of: Harcourt Brace Jovanovich) 111 Fifth Ave., New York, NY 10003. Eds. B. L. Horecker, E. R. Stadtman. (also avail. in microfiche) Indexed: Ind.Med.

CURRENT TOPICS IN COMPARATIVE PATHOBIOLOGY. see *MEDICAL SCIENCES*

574   **US**   **ISSN 0070-2153**
CURRENT TOPICS IN DEVELOPMENTAL BIOLOGY. 1966. irreg., vol. 12, 1978. price varies. Academic Press, Inc., 111 Fifth Ave., New York, NY 10003. Eds. Alberto Monroy, A. A. Moscona. Indexed: Ind.Med.

CURRENT TOPICS IN MEMBRANES AND TRANSPORT. see *BIOLOGY — Zoology*

CURRENT TOPICS IN PATHOLOGY. see *MEDICAL SCIENCES*

574   **II**
CURRENT TRENDS IN LIFE SCIENCES. irreg. $25. (University Grants Commission) Today and Tomorrow's Printers and Publishers, 24-B/5 Original Rd., Karol Bagh, New Delhi 110005, India (Dist. in U.S. by: Indo Americana Literature House, Box 1276, Globe, AZ 85501) (Alternate sponsor: Council of Agricultural Research)
Incorporates: Aspects of Plant Science.

DANA-REPORT. see *EARTH SCIENCES — Oceanography*

574   **IT**   **ISSN 0416-928X**
DELPINOA. (Summaries in English.) 1959. irreg. avail. on exchange. Universita degli Studi di Napoli, Istituto e Orto Botanico, Via Foria 223, 80139 Naples, Italy. bibl. charts. illus. circ. 650.

DENMARK. FISKERIMINISTERIET. FORSOEGSLABORATORIUM. AARSBERETINING/ANNUAL REPORT. see *FISH AND FISHERIES*

DESERT TORTOISE COUNCIL. PROCEEDINGS OF SYMPOSIUM. see *EARTH SCIENCES*

DEUTSCHE GESELLSCHAFT FUER PATHOLOGIE. VERHANDLUNGEN. see *MEDICAL SCIENCES*

574   **UK**
DEVELOPMENTAL AND CELL BIOLOGY SERIES. irreg., no. 8, 1981. $34.50 for latest vol. Cambridge University Press, Box 110, Cambridge CB2 3RL, England (And 32 E. 57th St., New York, NY 10022) Eds. D. R. Newth, J. G. Torrey. illus.

574   **NE**
DEVELOPMENTS IN BIOENERGETICS AND BIOMEMBRANES. 1977. irreg., vol. 2, 1979. price varies. Elsevier North-Holland Biomedical Press, Box 211, 1000 AE Amsterdam, Netherlands.

574   **NE**
DEVELOPMENTS IN CELL BIOLOGY. 1977. irreg., vol. 5, 1980. price varies. Elsevier North-Holland Biomedical Press, Box 211, 1000 AE Amsterdam, Netherlands.

574   **NE**
DEVELOPMENTS IN IMMUNOLOGY. 1978. irreg. price varies. Elsevier North-Holland Biomedical Press, Box 211, 1000 AE Amsterdam, Netherlands.

574   **NE**
DEVELOPMENTS IN TOXICOLOGY AND ENVIRONMENTAL SCIENCE. 1977. irreg., vol. 6, 1980. price varies. Elsevier-North Holland Biomedical Press, Box 211, 1000 AE Amsterdam, Netherlands.

DIRECTORY OF PATHOLOGY TRAINING PROGRAMS. see *MEDICAL SCIENCES*

BIOLOGY

574.5 910 FR ISSN 0335-5330
DOCUMENTS DE CARTOGRAPHIE
ECOLOGIQUE. (Text in French, English, German and Italian) 1963. irreg. price varies. Universite de Grenoble I (Universite Scientifique et Medicale de Grenoble), Laboratoire de Biologie Vegetale, Domaine Universitaire de Saint-Martin-d'Heres, B.P. 53 Centre de Tri, 38041 Grenoble Cedex, France. Ed. Paul Ozenda. bk. rev. illus. maps. circ. 900. (back issues avail.) Indexed: Biol.Abstr. Bull.Signal.
Formerly: Documents pour la Carte de la Vegetation des Alpes (ISSN 0419-5728)

574 US
DOCUMENTS IN BIOLOGY. a. price varies. Gordon and Breach Science Publishers, One Park Ave., New York, NY 10016. Eds. Etienne Wolff, Th. Lender.

574 DR
DOMINICAN REPUBLIC. CENTRO NACIONAL DE INVESTIGACIONES AGROPECUARIAS. LABORATORIO. DE SANIDAD VEGETAL. SANIDAD VEGETAL.* irreg. (5-6/yr.) free. Centro Nacional de Investigaciones Agropecuarias, Laboratorio de Sanidad Vegetal, San Cristobal, Dominican Republic. circ. controlled. (processed)

574.5 AT
ECOLOGICAL SOCIETY OF AUSTRALIA. MEMOIRS. 1973. irreg. Aus.$10.50 to non-members. Ecological Society of Australia, Box 1564, Canberra A.C.T. 2601, Australia. Ed. Bd.
Ecology

574.5 AT ISSN 0070-8348
ECOLOGICAL SOCIETY OF AUSTRALIA. PROCEEDINGS. 1966. biennial. price varies. Ecological Society of Australia, Box 1564, Canberra, A.C.T., 2601, Australia.
Ecology

574.5 US ISSN 0070-8356
ECOLOGICAL STUDIES; ANALYSIS AND SYNTHESIS. 1970. irreg., vol. 41, 1981. price varies. Springer-Verlag, 175 Fifth Ave., New York, NY 10010 (also Berlin, Heidelberg, Vienna) (reprint service avail. from ISI)
Ecology

574.5 UN ISSN 0070-8372
ECOLOGY AND CONSERVATION SERIES. (Text in English and French) 1970. irreg; no. 4, 1976. Unesco, 7-9 Place de Fontenoy, 75700 Paris, France (Dist. in U.S. by: Unipub, 345 Park Ave. S., New York, NY 10010)
Ecology

574.5 BU
EKOLOGIIA. (Text in various languages) 1975. irreg. 2 lv. per issue. (Bulgarska Akademiia na Naukite) Publishing House of the Bulgarian Academy of Sciences, Ul. Akad. G. Bonchev, 1113 Sofia, Bulgaria. circ. 800.

574.5 UR
EKOLOGIYA PTITS LITOVSKOI S.S.R. 1977. irreg. Akademiya Nauk Litovskoi S.S.R., Institut Zoologii i Parazitologii, Vil'nius, U.S.S.R. Ed. M. Valyus.

574.9 UK ISSN 0071-1489
ESSEX NATURALIST. 1887.N.S. 1977. a. price varies. Essex Field Club, Passmore Edwards Museum, Romford Road, Stratford, London, E15, England. Ed. David Corke. adv. circ. 100.

574 610 SZ ISSN 0071-3384
EXPERIMENTAL BIOLOGY AND MEDICINE. (Text in English) 1967. irreg. (approx. 1/yr.) 100 Fr.($60) per vol. (1981 price) S. Karger AG, Allschwilerstrasse 10, P.O. Box, CH-4009 Basel, Switzerland. Ed. Bd. (reprint service avail. from ISI) Indexed: Biol.Abstr. Chem.Abstr. Curr.Cont. Ind.Med.

FAUNA ENTOMOLOGICA SCANDINAVICA. see *BIOLOGY — Entomology*

570 US
FLORIDA STATE MUSEUM. BULLETIN. BIOLOGICAL SCIENCES. 1956. irreg. price varies. Florida State Museum, University of Florida, Museum Rd., Gainesville, FL 32611. Ed. Oliver L. Austin, Jr. cum.index. circ. 700.
Formerly: Florida State Museum. Bulletin. Biological Series (ISSN 0071-6154)

FOLIA DENDROLOGICA. see *FORESTS AND FORESTRY*

574 CS
FOLIA FACULTATIS SCIENTIARUM NATURALIUM UNIVERSITATIS PURKYNIANAE BRUNENSIS: BIOLOGIA. irreg (7-12/yr.) price varies. Universita J. E. Purkyne, Prirodovedecka Fakulta, Kotlarska 2, 611 37 Brno, Czechoslovakia.

574 FR ISSN 0080-1038
FRANCE. DELEGATION GENERALE A LA RECHERCHE SCIENTIFIQUE ET TECHNIQUE. REPERTOIRE DES SCIENTIFIQUES FRANCAIS. TOME 3: BIOLOGIE. 1966. irreg. 30 F. Documentation Francaise, 29-31 Quai Voltaire, 75340 Paris 07, France.

574 FR ISSN 0071-8548
FRANCE. DELEGATION GENERALE A LA RECHERCHE SCIENTIFIQUE ET TECHNIQUE. REPERTOIRE NATIONAL DES LABORATOIRES; LA RECHERCHE UNIVERSITAIRE; SCIENCES EXACTES ET NATURELLES. TOME 2: BIOLOGIE. 1966. irreg. 55 F. Documentation Francaise, 29-31 Quai Voltaire, 75340 Paris 07, France.

574 SZ ISSN 0301-0155
FRONTIERS OF MATRIX BIOLOGY. (Text in English) 1973. irreg. (approx. 1/yr.) 120 Fr.($72) per vol. (1981 price) S. Karger AG, Allschwilerstrasse 10, P.O. Box, CH-4009 Basel, Switzerland. Ed. L. Robert. (reprint service avail. from ISI)

574.1 612 GW ISSN 0340-0840
FUNKTIONSANALYSE BIOLOGISCHER SYSTEME. (Text in English and German) irreg. vol. 6, 1979. price varies. (Akademie der Wissenschaften und der Literatur, Mainz) Franz Steiner Verlag GmbH, Friedrichstr. 24, Postfach 5529, 6200 Wiesbaden, W. Germany (B.R.D.) Ed.Gerhard Thews.

570 GW ISSN 0368-2307
GESELLSCHAFT FUER NATURKUNDE IN WUERTTEMBERG. JAHRESHEFTE. 1845. a. price varies. Gesellschaft fuer Naturkunde in Wuerttemberg, Schloss Rosenstein, 7000 Stuttgart 1, W. Germany (B.R.D.) Ed. Horst Janus. circ. 1,100. Indexed: Biol.Abstr.
Formerly: Verein fuer Vaterlaendische Naturkunde in Wuerttemberg. Jahresheft.

574 NE
GIOVANNI LORENZI FOUNDATION. SYMPOSIA. 1978. irreg. price varies. Elsevier North-Holland Biomedical Press, Box 211, 1000 AE Amsterdam, Netherlands.

574 UK
GREAT BRITAIN. INSTITUTE OF TERRESTRIAL ECOLOGY. REPORT. 1975. a. Institute of Terrestrial Ecology, 68 Hills Rd., Cambridge CB2 1LA, England (Avail. from H.M.S.O., c/o Liaison Officer, Atlantic House, Holborn Viaduct, London EC1P 1BN, England)
Incorporating: Merlewood Research Station. Report; Monks Wood Experimental Station. Report (ISSN 0077-0418)

574 DK
GREENLAND BIOSCIENCES. 1979. irreg. (Kommsssionen for Videnskabelige Undersoegelser i Groenland, GL - Commission for Scientific Research in Greenland) Nyt Nordisk Forlag - Arnold Busck A-S, 49 Koebmagergade 49, DK-1150 Copenhagen K, Denmark. charts. illus. Indexed: Biol.Abstr. Chem.Abstr.
Supersedes in part (1878-1979): Meddelelser om Groenland (ISSN 0025-6676)

574 GW ISSN 0085-1299
GRUNDBEGRIFFE DER MODERNEN BIOLOGIE. 1967. irreg. price varies. Gustav Fischer Verlag, Wollgrasweg 49, Postfach 720143, 7000 Stuttgart 70, W. Germany (B.R.D.) adv. bk. rev.

GUIDE TO BIOMEDICAL STANDARDS. see *MEDICAL SCIENCES*

574.88 US
GULF COAST MOLECULAR BIOLOGY CONFERENCE. TRANSACTIONS. 1976. a. $20. Texas Academy of Science, Gulf Coast Molecular Biology Conference, Box 10979-A.S.U., San Angelo, TX 76901. Ed.Bd. circ. 250. Indexed: Curr.Cont.
Molecular

574.92 US
GULF COAST RESEARCH LABORATORY. PUBLICATIONS OF THE MUSEUM. 1969. irreg. price varies. Gulf Coast Research Laboratory, Ocean Springs, MS 39564. Ed. C. E. Dawson. circ. 300. (reprint service avail. from UMI) Indexed: Biol.Abstr. Biol.Abstr.

GUNNERIA. see *ARCHAEOLOGY*

570 US ISSN 0073-0467
HARVARD BOOKS IN BIOLOGY. 1959. irreg., 1971, no. 7. price varies. Harvard University Press, 79 Garden St., Cambridge, MA 02138.

574 US ISSN 0073-1331
HAWAII INSTITUTE OF MARINE BIOLOGY. TECHNICAL REPORTS. 1964. irreg., no. 3, 1973. free to qualified personnel. ‡ Hawaii Institute of Marine Biology, University of Hawaii, Box 1346, Kaneohe, HI 96744. circ. 200. Indexed: Ocean.Abstr.
Marine

HIROSHIMA UNIVERSITY. LABORATORY FOR AMPHIBIAN BIOLOGY. SCIENTIFIC REPORT. see *BIOLOGY — Zoology*

574.9 GW ISSN 0073-2524
HISTORIAE NATURALIS CLASSICA. (Text in English, French, German and Latin) 1958. irreg., no. 102, 1977. price varies. J. Cramer, In den Springaeckern 2, 3300 Braunschweig, W. Germany (B.R.D.) Eds. J. Cramer, K. H. Schwann. circ. 200-500.

574 JA ISSN 0073-294X
HOKKAIDO UNIVERSITY. INSTITUTE OF LOW TEMPERATURE SCIENCE. SERIES B. BIOLOGICAL SCIENCE. (Notes: from No. 1-10 (1952-1956) Series A and B Issued in 1 Vol.) (Text in English) 1954. irreg., no. 11, 1962. exchange basis. Hokkaido University, Institute of Low Temperature Science, North 19, West 8, Kita-ku, Sapporo 060, Japan. Ed. Akira Sakai. Indexed: Biol.Abstr. Chem.Abstr.

574 NE
HORMONES AND CELL REGULATION. 1977. irreg., vol.4, 1980. price varies. Elsevier North-Holland Biomedical Press, Box 211, 1000 AE Amsterdam, Netherlands.

574.92 NO ISSN 0073-4128
HVALRAADETS SKRIFTER/SCIENTIFIC RESULTS OF MARINE BIOLOGICAL RESEARCH. (Text mainly in English) 1931. irreg. price varies. (Norske Videnskaps-Akademi - Norwegian Academy of Science and Letters) Universitetsforlaget, Kolstadgt. 1, Box 2959-Toeyen, Oslo 6, Norway (U.S. address: Box 258, Irvington-on-Hudson, NY 10533)
Marine

574 BU
HYDROBIOLOGY. (Text in Bulgarian, Russian, English and French) 1975. 0.97 lv. single issue. (Bulgarska Akademiia na Naukite) Publishing House of the Bulgarian Academy of Sciences, Ul. Akad. G. Bonchev, Sofia 1113, Bulgaria (Dist. by: Hemus, 6, Rouski Blvd., 1000 Sofia, Bulgaria) bibl. illus.

574.5 MX
I N I R E B INFORMA. 1976. irreg., approx. 8/yr. Mex.$5($.15) Instituto Nacional de Investigaciones sobre Recursos Bioticos, Apartado Postal 63, Xalapa, Veracruz, Mexico.

574.92 UK ISSN 0142-484X
I R C S MEDICAL SCIENCE: KEY REPORTS IN CELL AND MOLECULAR BIOLOGY. 1979. m. £40($110) International Research Communications System (IRCS), St. Leonard's House, St. Leonard's Gate, Lancaster LA1 1PF, England.

ICEFIELD RANGES RESEARCH PROJECT SCIENTIFIC RESULTS. see *EARTH SCIENCES*

574.9 US ISSN 0073-490X
ILLINOIS. NATURAL HISTORY SURVEY. BIOLOGICAL NOTES. 1933. irreg., no. 112, 1979. single copies free. ‡ Illinois Natural History Survey, Natural Resources Bldg., Urbana, IL 61801. Ed. Robert M. Zewadski. Indexed: Biol.Abstr. Wild Life Rev. Zoo.Rec.

ILLINOIS. STATE MUSEUM. SCIENTIFIC PAPERS SERIES. see *EARTH SCIENCES — Geology*

574 US ISSN 0073-4748
ILLINOIS BIOLOGICAL MONOGRAPHS. 1914. irreg. University of Illinois Press, 54 E. Gregory, Box 5081, Station A, Champaign, IL 61820. (also avail. in microform from UMI,JOH; reprint service avail. from UMI)

INDICE DE PROYECTOS EN DESARROLLO EN ECOLOGIA TROPICAL/INDEX OF CURRENT TROPICAL ECOLOGY RESEARCH. see *ABSTRACTING AND INDEXING SERVICES*

574.5 MX
INDICE DE PROYECTOS EN DESARROLLO EN ECOLOGIA DE ZONAS ARIDAS/INDEX OF CURRENT RESEARCH IN ARID ZONES ECOLOGY/INDEX DES PROJECTS EN DEVELOPPMENT SUR L'ECOLOGIE DES ZONES ARIDES. 1978. irreg. Mex.$100($6) per no. Instituto Nacional de Investigaciones sobre Recursos Bioticos, Apartado Postal 63, Xalapa, Veracruz, Mexico.

574 GW ISSN 0344-4430
INFORMATIONSAUFNAHME UND INFORMATIONSVERARBEITUNG IM LEBENDEN ORGANISMUS. 1971. irreg., vol. 3, 1978. price varies. (Akademie der Wissenschaften und der Literatur, Mainz, Mathematisch-Naturwissenschaftliche Klasse) Franz Steiner Verlag GmbH, Friedrichstr. 24, Postfach 5529, 6200 Wiesbaden, W. Germany (B.R.D.) Ed. Martin Lindauer.

INSTITUT FUER DEN WISSENSCHAFTLICHEN FILM. PUBLIKATIONEN ZU WISSENSCHAFTLICHEN FILMEN. SEKTION BIOLOGIE. see *MOTION PICTURES*

INSTITUT FUER MEERESFORSCHUNG, BREMERHAVEN. VEROEFFENTLICHUNGEN. see *EARTH SCIENCES — Oceanography*

INSTITUTE OF ENVIRONMENTAL SCIENCES. ANNUAL MEETING. PROCEEDINGS. see *ENVIRONMENTAL STUDIES*

INSTITUTE OF ENVIRONMENTAL SCIENCES. TUTORIAL SERIES. see *ENVIRONMENTAL STUDIES*

574 BL ISSN 0020-3661
INSTITUTO BIOLOGICO DA BAHIA. BOLETIM. (Summaries in English and Portuguese) 1954. irreg. Instituto Biologico da Bahia, Av. Adhemar de Barros-Ondina, Caixa Postal 553, 40000 Salvador, Bahia, Brazil. Dir. Antonio A.J. da Silva. bibl. charts. illus. Indexed: Biol.Abstr.

INSTITUTO DE LA PATAGONIA. ANALES. see *HISTORY — History Of North And South America*

574 RM
INSTITUTUL PEDAGOGIC ORADEA. LUCRARI STIINTIFICE SERIA BIOLOGIC. (Continues in part its Lucrari Stiintifice: Seria Educatie Fizica, Biologie, Stiinte Medicale (1971-72), its Lucrari Stuntifice: Seria A and Seria B (1969-70), and its Lucrari Stiintifice (1967-68)) (Text in Rumanian, occasionally in English or French; summaries in Rumanian, French, English or German) 1967. a. Institutul Pedagogic Oradea, Calea Armatei Rosii Nr. 5, Oradea, Romania.

INTERNATIONAL ANATOMICAL CONGRESS. PROCEEDINGS. see *MEDICAL SCIENCES*

574 II
INTERNATIONAL BIO-SCIENCES MONOGRAPHS. 1975. a. price varies. Today and Tomorrow's Printers and Publishers, 24-B/5 Original Rd., Karol Bagh, New Delhi 110005, India (Dist. in U.S. by: Indo Americana Literature House, Box 1276, Globe, AZ 85501)

574 NE ISSN 0074-2082
INTERNATIONAL BIOMETEOROLOGICAL CONGRESS. SUMMARIES AND REPORTS PRESENTED TO THE CONGRESS. triennial, 1975, 6th, College Park, MD, U.S.A. price varies. International Society of Biometeorology, Inquire: Dr. S. W. Tromp. Sec. Gen., Hofbrouckerlaan 54, Oegstqueest, Leiden, Netherlands. circ. 1,200. Indexed: Biol.Abstr. Curr.Cont.

574.1 US
INTERNATIONAL CONGRESS ON PHOTOBIOLOGY. PROCEEDINGS. irreg. Plenum Press, 233 Spring St., New York, NY 10013.

574.92 DK ISSN 0106-1003
INTERNATIONAL COUNCIL FOR THE EXPLORATION OF THE SEA. ANNALES BIOLOGIQUES. (Text in English and French) 1943. a. price varies. International Council for the Exploration of the Sea, Palaegade 2, DK-1261 Copenhagen K, Denmark (Subscr. to: C. A. Reitzels Forlag, Noerre Soegade 35, 1370 Copenhagen K, Denmark) index. circ. 500.
Marine

574 II ISSN 0074-7033
INTERNATIONAL MONOGRAPHS ON ADVANCED BIOLOGY AND BIOPHYSICS.* (Text in English) 1969. irreg. $10. Hindustan Publishing Corp., 6-U.B. Jawahar Nagar, Delhi 110007, India.

574 US ISSN 0074-8234
INTERNATIONAL SERIES ON ORAL BIOLOGY. 1960. irreg., 1964, vol. 3. price varies. Pergamon Press, Inc., Maxwell House, Fairview Park, Elmsford, NY 10523. index.
Formerly: International Series of Monographs on Oral Biology.

574 615 US
INTERNATIONAL SYMPOSIUM ON QUANTUM BIOLOGY AND QUANTUM PHARMACOLOGY. PROCEEDINGS. 1974. a. $30. John Wiley & Sons, Inc., 605 Third Ave., New York, NY 10016. Ed. Per-Olov Lowdin.

570 FR
INTERNATIONAL UNION OF BIOLOGICAL SCIENCES. GENERAL ASSEMBLIES. PROCEEDINGS. irreg., 1970, 17th, Washington, D.C. $10. International Union of Biological Sciences, 51 Bd. E. Montmorency, 75016 Paris, France.
Former titles: International Union of Biological Sciences. Reports of General Assemblies (ISSN 0074-9362)

IRAQ NATURAL HISTORY RESEARCH CENTRE AND MUSEUM. PUBLICATION. see *SCIENCES: COMPREHENSIVE WORKS*

574 US
ISOZYMES: CURRENT TOPICS IN BIOLOGICAL AND MEDICINE RESEARCH. 1978. irreg. price varies. Alan R. Liss, Inc., 150 Fifth Ave., New York, NY 10011. Indexed: Biol.Abstr.

574 IS
ISRAEL INSTITUTE FOR BIOLOGICAL RESEARCH. OHOLO BIOLOGICAL CONFERENCE. PROCEEDINGS. (Text in English) a. Israel Institute for Biological Research, Box 19, Ness-Ziona, Israel.

574.92 IT ISSN 0075-1510
ISTITUTO ITALIANO DI IDROBIOLOGIA. MEMORIE. (Text in English, French, German & Italian) 1942. a. (exchange basis only) ‡ Istituto Italiano di Idrobiologia, Verbania Pallanza, Novara, Italy. circ. 800. Indexed: Aqua.Sci. & Fish.Abstr. Water Resour.Abstr.

574 610 US
JOURNAL OF BIOMEDICAL MATERIALS RESEARCH. SYMPOSIA. 1971. irreg., no. 7, 1976. price varies. John Wiley & Sons, Inc., 605 Third Ave., New York, NY 10016.

574 US ISSN 0075-4404
JOURNAL OF ULTRASTRUCTURE RESEARCH. SUPPLEMENT. 1959. irreg., 1973, no. 12. incl. in subscr. to Journal. Academic Press, Inc, 111 Fifth Ave., New York, NY 10003.

574 GW ISSN 0340-5419
KARL-AUGUST-FORSTER-LECTURES; Informationsgesteuerte Synthese / information-directed synthesis. (Subseries(from Vol. 13) of: Research in Molecular Biology) 1971. irreg. price varies. (Akademie der Wissenschaften und der Literatur, Mainz, Mathematisch-Naturwissenschaftliche Klasse) Franz Steiner Verlag GmbH, Friedrichstr. 24, Postfach 5529, 6200 Wiesbaden, W. Germany (B.R.D.) Eds. Rudolf K. Zahn, R. Blasberg.

574 AU ISSN 0075-6547
KOLEOPTEROLOGISCHE RUNDSCHAU. irreg. S.15($6) Zoologisch-Botanische Gesellschaft, Burgring 7, A-1010 Vienna, Austria. circ. 180.

570 DK ISSN 0006-3320
KONGELIGE DANSKE VIDENSKABERNES SELSKAB. BIOLOGISKE SKRIFTER. (Text in English, French, German or Danish) 1941. irreg. (3-4/yr.,), vol. 22, no. 7, 1979. price varies. Kongelige Danske Videnskabernes Selskab - Royal Danish Academy of Sciences and Letters, Dantes Plads 5, DK-1556 Copenhagen V, Denmark (Orders to: Munksgaards Boghandel, Noerregade 6, DK-1165 Copenhagen K, Denmark) bibl. illus. Indexed: Biol.Abstr.

574 JA ISSN 0454-7802
KYOTO UNIVERSITY. FACULTY OF SCIENCE. MEMOIRS. SERIES OF BIOLOGY. (Text in European languages) 1924; N. S. 1967. a. on exchange basis. Kyoto University, Faculty of Science - Kyoto Daigaku Rigakubu, Kitashirakawa Oiwake-cho, Sakyo-ku, Kyoto 606, Japan.

LABORATORY TECHNIQUES IN BIOCHEMISTRY AND MOLECULAR BIOLOGY. see *BIOLOGY — Biological Chemistry*

LEBENSDARSTELLUNGEN DEUTSCHER NATURFORSCHER. see *BIOGRAPHY*

LECTURE NOTES IN BIOMATHEMATICS. see *MATHEMATICS*

LECTURES ON MATHEMATICS IN THE LIFE SCIENCES. see *MATHEMATICS*

580 590 LH
LIECHTENSTEIN. BOTANISCH-ZOOLOGISCHE GESELLSCHAFT SARGANS-WERDENBERG. BERICHT. irreg. $8. Botanisch-Zoologische Gesellschaft Liechtenstein-Sargans-Werdenberg, Heiligkreuz 52, 9490 Vaduz, Liechtenstein. bibl. illus.

570 US ISSN 0459-3774
LIFE SCIENCES. 1964. a. price varies. Gordon and Breach Science Publishers, One Park Ave., New York, NY 10016. Ed. M. Rosenberg.

574.9 UK ISSN 0076-0579
LONDON NATURALIST. 1915. a. £3. London Natural History Society, 110 Meadvale Rd., London W5 1LR, England. Ed. K. H. Hyatt. bk. rev. circ. 2,000. (back issues avail.)

570 US ISSN 0076-1044
LOUISIANA TECH UNIVERSITY. DIVISION OF LIFE SCIENCES RESEARCH. RESEARCH BULLETIN. 1967. a. free. Louisiana Tech University, Division of Life Sciences Research, Box 6158, Tech. Station, Ruston, LA 71272. Ed. John L. Murad.
Formerly: Louisiana. Polytechnic Institute, Ruston. School of Agriculture and Forestry. Research Bulletin.

574.5 910 SW ISSN 0076-1478
LUND STUDIES IN GEOGRAPHY. SERIES B. HUMAN GEOGRAPHY. (Text in English, French and German) 1949. irreg., no. 44, 1977. price varies. (Lunds Universitet, Department of Geography) C.W.K. Gleerup (Subsidiary of: LiberLaeromedel) Box 1205, 221 05 Lund, Sweden. index. cum.index every 4 yrs.

574 US
M B L LECTURES IN BIOLOGY. 1980. irreg. $10. (Marine Biological Laboratory) Alan R. Liss, Inc., 150 Fifth Ave., New York, NY 10011. Eds. Harlyn O. Halvorson, K.L. van Holde.

BIOLOGY

574 US ISSN 0076-4442
MARINE BIOLOGY; PROCEEDINGS OF THE INTERDISCIPLINARY CONFERENCE. 1961. irreg., 1970, vol. 5. $59. (American Institute of Biological Sciences) Gordon & Breach Science Publishers, 1 Park Ave., New York, NY 10016.
Marine

574.92 US
MARINE ECOLOGY; a comprehensive, integrated treatise on life in oceans and coastal waters. 1970. irreg., vol. 4, 1978. price varies. John Wiley & Sons, Inc., 605 Third Ave., New York, NY 10016. Ed. O. Kinne.

574 NZ ISSN 0302-086X
MAURI ORA. 1973. a. NZ.$2.50. University of Canterbury, Department of Zoology, Private Bag, Christchurch, New Zealand. Eds. G. Fenwich and R. Stephenson. bk. rev. circ. 400-500. Indexed: Biol.Abstr. Ref.Zh. Zoo.Rec.

574 610 US ISSN 0076-6356
MEMBRANES: A SERIES OF ADVANCES. 1972. irreg., vol. 3, 1975. price varies. Marcel Dekker, Inc., 270 Madison Ave., New York, NY 10016. Ed. G. Eisenman. Indexed: Ind.Med.

MEMORIAL UNIVERSITY, ST. JOHN'S, NEWFOUNDLAND. MARINE SCIENCES RESEARCH LABORATORY. M.S.R.L. BULLETIN. see *EARTH SCIENCES — Oceanography*

551 540 GW ISSN 0543-5935
"METEOR" FORSCHUNGSERGEBNISSE. REIHE D. BIOLOGIE. (Text in German; summaries in English) 1966. irreg. price varies. (Deutsche Forschungsgemeinschaft) Gebrueder Borntraeger Verlagsbuchhandlung, Johannsstr. 3A, 7000 Stuttgart 1, W. Germany (B.R.D.) Eds. G.Hempel, S.A. Gerlach, O. Kinne. charts. illus.

574 US ISSN 0093-4771
METHODS IN MEMBRANE BIOLOGY. 1974. irreg. price varies. Plenum Press, 233 Spring St., New York, NY 10013. Ed. Edward Korn. Indexed: Chem. Abstr.

570 US ISSN 0076-8227
MICHIGAN STATE UNIVERSITY. MUSEUM PUBLICATIONS. BIOLOGICAL SERIES. (Text in English; summaries occasionally in German) 1957. irreg. (approx. 1-2 per year) price varies. ‡ Michigan State University, Museum, East Lansing, MI 48824. Ed. Rollin H. Baker. circ. 1,850.

574.92 GW ISSN 0342-3247
MIKROFAUNA DES MEERESBODENS. 1970. irreg., vol. 86, 1981. price varies. (Akademie der Wissenschaften und der Literatur, Mainz, Mathematisch-Naturwissenschaftliche Klasse) Franz Steiner Verlag GmbH, Friedrichstr. 24, Postfach 5529, 6200 Wiesbaden, W. Germany (B.R.D.) Ed. Peter Ax.

574 US
MODERN BIOLOGY SERIES. irreg. price varies. Holt, Rinehart and Winston, Inc., 383 Madison Ave., New York, NY 10017.

574 US
MODERN PERSPECTIVES IN BIOLOGY SERIES. irreg. price varies. Harper and Row Publishers, Inc., 10 East 53rd St, New York, NY 10022.

500.9 574 NE ISSN 0077-0639
MONOGRAPHIAE BIOLOGICAE. 1957. irreg., no. 4, 1981. price varies. Dr. W. Junk Publishers, Box 13713, 2501 ES The Hague, Netherlands. Ed. J. Illies.

574 SP ISSN 0077-0647
MONOGRAPHIAE BIOLOGICAE CANARIENSES/BIOLOGICAL MONOGRAPHS OF THE CANARY ISLANDS. (Text and summaries in Spanish and English) 1970. a. price varies; exchange basis. (Cabildo Insular de Gran Canaria, las Palmas) Finca Llano de la Piedra, Santa Lucia de Tirajana, Gran Canaria, Spain. Ed. Guenther Kunkel. circ. 500. Indexed: Excerp.Bot.

574 NE
MONOGRAPHS IN FETAL PHYSIOLOGY. 1976. irreg. price varies. Elsevier North-Holland Biomedical Press, Box 211, 1000 AE Amsterdam, Netherlands.

574.1 US
MONOGRAPHS IN MODERN NEUROBIOLOGY. 1973. irreg., no. 5, 1977. Spectrum Publications, Inc., 175-20 Wexford Terrace, Jamaica, NY 10032. Ed. W. B. Essman.

574 591 US
MOUNT DESERT ISLAND BIOLOGICAL LABORATORY. BULLETIN. 1973, vol. 13. a. $5 to non-members. Mount Desert Island Biological Laboratory, Salsbury Cove, ME 04672. Ed. Dr. William L. Doyle. index. circ. 1,500. Indexed: Curr.Cont.

574.5 AG ISSN 0524-9481
MUSEO ARGENTINO DE CIENCIAS NATURALES "BERNARDINO RIVADAVIA." INSTITUTO NACIONAL DE INVESTIGACION DE LAS CIENCIAS NATURALES. REVISTA. ECOLOGIA. 1963. irreg.; latest issue 1980. Museo Argentino de Ciencias Naturales "Bernardino Rivadavia", Instituto Nacional de Investigacion de las Ciencias Naturales, Avda. Angel Gallardo 470, Casilla de Correo 220-Sucursal 5, Buenos Aires, Argentina.
Ecology

574.92 AG ISSN 0524-9503
MUSEO ARGENTINO DE CIENCIAS NATURALES "BERNARDINO RIVADAVIA." INSTITUTO NACIONAL DE INVESTIGACION DE LAS CIENCIAS NATURALES. REVISTA. HIDROBIOLOGIA. 1963. irreg.; latest issue 1981. Museo Argentino de Ciencias Naturales "Bernardino Rivadavia", Instituto Nacional de Investigacion de las Ciencias Naturales, Avda. Angel Gallardo 470, Casilla de Correo 220-Sucursal 5, Buenos Aires, Argentina.
Marine

574 RM ISSN 0068-3078
MUZEUL DE ISTORIE NATURALA "GR. ANTIPA." TRAVAUX. (Text in English, French, German, Russian; summaries in English, Rumanian, Russian) 1957. irreg. price varies. Muzeul de Istorie Naturala "Gr. Antipa", Soseaua Kiseleff Nr. 1, Bucharest, Romania. Ed. M. Bacescu. bk. rev. index.

570 PL ISSN 0068-466X
MUZEUM GORNOSLASKIE W BYTOMIU. ROCZNIK. SERIA PRZYRODA. (Text in Polish; summaries in English and German) 1962. irreg. price varies. Muzeum Gornoslaskie, Pl. Thaelmanna 2, 41-902 Bytom, Poland (Dist. by Ars Polona-Ruch, Krakowskie Przedmiescie 7, Warsaw, Poland)

574 610 JA ISSN 0386-5541
NATIONAL INSTITUTE OF POLAR RESEARCH. MEMOIRS. SERIES E. BIOLOGY AND MEDICAL SCIENCE. (Text in English) 1959. irreg., No. 32, 1976. exchange basis. National Institute of Polar Research - Kokuritsu Kyokuchi Kenkyujyo, 9-10 Kaga, 1-chome, Itabashi-ku, Tokyo 173, Japan. Ed. Takesi Nagata. circ. 1,000. Indexed: Curr.Antarc.Lit.
Supersedes: Japanese Antarctic Research Expedition, 1956-1962. Scientific Reports. Series E. Biology (ISSN 0075-3394)

574.9 930 GW ISSN 0077-6025
NATUR UND MENSCH; JAHRESMITTEILUNGEN DER NATURHISTORISCHEN GESELLSCHAFT NUERNBERG. 1965. a. price varies. Naturhistorische Gesellschaft Nuernberg, Gewerbemuseumplatz 4, Luitpoldhaus, 8500 Nuernberg, W. Germany (B.R.D.) circ. 2,500.
From 1965-69 issued as: Naturhistorische Gesellschaft Nuernberg. Mitteilungen und Jahresbericht.

574 DK ISSN 0077-6033
NATURA JUTLANDICA. (Text in English or Danish; summaries in English) 1947/48. irreg. free or available on exchange. Naturhistorisk Museum, DK-8000 Aarhus C, Denmark. Ed. H. M. Thamdrup. circ. 350.

574 US
NATURAL HISTORY MISCELLANEA. 1954. irreg., no. 213, 1981. price varies. Chicago Academy of Sciences, 2001 N. Clark St., Chicago, IL 60614. Ed. William J. Beecher. circ. 1,000. (back issues avail.)

574.9 US ISSN 0076-0927
NATURAL HISTORY MUSEUM OF LOS ANGELES COUNTY. CONTRIBUTIONS IN HISTORY. 1968. irreg. price varies. Natural History Museum of Los Angeles County, 900 Exposition Blvd., Los Angeles, CA 90007. circ. 1,000.

570 GW ISSN 0301-2697
NATURWISSENSCHAFTLICHER VEREIN IN HAMBURG. ABHANDLUNGEN UND VERHANDLUNGEN. 1937. a. DM.60 approx. Verlag Paul Parey (Hamburg, Spitalerstr. 12, 2000 Hamburg 1, W. Germany (B.R.D.) Ed. H. J. Muenzing. bk. rev. bibl. illus. index. (reprint service avail. from ISI) Indexed: Chem.Abstr.

574 639.2 US ISSN 0077-8397
NEW HAMPSHIRE. FISH AND GAME DEPARTMENT. MANAGEMENT AND RESEARCH. BIOLOGICAL SURVEY BULLETIN. 1938. no. 3. irreg., 1968, no. 10. Fish and Game Department, Game Management and Research Division, 34 Bridge St., Concord, NH 03301.

574 US ISSN 0077-8370
NEW HAMPSHIRE. FISH AND GAME DEPARTMENT. MANAGEMENT AND RESEARCH. BIOLOGICAL SURVEY SERIES. 1938. irreg., 1970, no. 9. ‡ Fish and Game Department, Game Management and Research Division, 34 Bridge St., Concord, NH 03301. Ed. Hilbert R. Siegler.

574 US ISSN 0077-8389
NEW HAMPSHIRE. FISH AND GAME DEPARTMENT. MANAGEMENT AND RESEARCH. TECHNICAL CIRCULAR SERIES. 1937. irreg., 1968, no. 22a. Fish and Game Department, Game Management and Research Division, 34 Bridge St., Concord, NH 03301.

574.5 AT
NEW SOUTH WALES. NATIONAL PARKS AND WILDLIFE SERVICE. NATIONAL PARKS AND WILDLIFE-A REVIEW. a. Aus.$3. National Parks and Wildlife Service, Box N189, Grosvenor St., Sydney, N.S.W. 2000, Australia.

574 UN ISSN 0077-8877
NEW TRENDS IN BIOLOGY TEACHING. (Text in English and French; summaries in Spanish) 1966. irreg; vol. 4, 1978. 28 F.($1650) Unesco, 7-9 Place de Fontenoy, 75700 Paris, France (Dist. in U.S. by: Unipub, 345 Park Ave. S., New York, NY 10010)

574 JA
NIIGATA UNIVERSITY. FACULTY OF SCIENCE. SCIENCE REPORTS. SERIES D: BIOLOGY. (Text in English; summaries in European languages) 1964. a. exchange basis. Niigata University, Faculty of Science - Niigata Daigaku Rigakubu, 8050 Igarashi Nino-cho, Niigata-shi 950-21, Japan.

574.9 AT ISSN 0078-1630
NORTH QUEENSLAND NATURALIST. 1932. irreg., 1973, vol. 40, no. 1. Aus.$3.50 (membership) North Queensland Naturalists Club, Box 991, Cairns, N. Queensland 4870, Australia. Ed. Miss J. Morris. bk. rev. circ. 220.

NUKADA INSTITUTE FOR MEDICAL AND BIOLOGICAL RESEARCH. REPORTS. see *MEDICAL SCIENCES*

NUTRITION AND THE BRAIN. see *NUTRITION AND DIETETICS*

574 SZ ISSN 0379-220X
O H O L O BIOLOGICAL CONFERENCES (PROCEEDINGS) (Text in English) a, 24th, 1979. 100 Fr.($60) (1981 price) S. Karger AG, Allschwilerstr. 10, P. O. Box, CH-4009 Basel, Switzerland. (reprint service avail. from ISI) Indexed: Biol.Abstr. Curr.Cont. Ind.Med.

OCEANOGRAPHY AND MARINE BIOLOGY: AN ANNUAL REVIEW. see *EARTH SCIENCES — Oceanography*

574 US ISSN 0078-3986
OHIO BIOLOGICAL SURVEY. BIOLOGICAL NOTES. 1964. irreg., no. 11, 1978. price varies. Ohio State University, College of Biological Sciences, 484 W. 12th Ave, Columbus, OH 43210. Ed. Charles C. King. circ. 1,000. Indexed: Biol.Abstr.

574 US ISSN 0078-3994
OHIO BIOLOGICAL SURVEY. BULLETIN. NEW SERIES. 1913; 1959 N.S. irreg., vol. 5, no. 4, 1977. price varies. Ohio State University, College of Biological Sciences, 484 W. 12th Ave, Columbus, OH 43210. Ed. Charles C. King. circ. 1,000. Indexed: Biol.Abstr.

574 US
OHIO BIOLOGICAL SURVEY. INFORMATIVE CIRCULAR. 1973. irreg., no. 10, 1978. price varies. Ohio State University, College of Biological Sciences, 484 W. 12th Ave., Columbus, OH 43210. Ed. Charles C. King. circ. 1,000. Indexed: Biol.Abstr.

574 US
OHIO STATE UNIVERSITY ANNUAL BIOSCIENCES COLLOQUIA. 1975. a. price varies. (Ohio State University, College of Biological Sciences) Ohio State University Press, 2070 Neil Avenue, Columbus, OH 43210.

OKAYAMA UNIVERSITY. OHARA INSTITUTE FUER LANDWIRTSCHAFTLICHE BIOLOGIE. BERICHTE. see *AGRICULTURE — Agricultural Economics*

574 AT
OPERCULUM. 1971. irreg. Aus.$10 (combined subscr. with the Bulletin) Australian Littoral Society, Box 498, Toowang, Qld. 4066, Australia. Ed. E. Hegerl. adv. bk. rev. circ. 2,000. Indexed: Aus.Sci.Ind. Biol.Abstr. Environ.Per.Bibl.
Supersedes: Queensland Littoral Society. Newsletter (ISSN 0048-6353)

ORANGE FREE STATE. NATURE CONSERVATION DIVISION. MISCELLANEOUS PUBLICATIONS SERIES. see *CONSERVATION*

574.082 US ISSN 0078-5857
OREGON STATE UNIVERSITY. ANNUAL BIOLOGY COLLOQUIUM. PROCEEDINGS. 1943. irreg. price varies. Oregon State University Press, 101 Waldo Hall, Corvallis, OR 97731. index.

574 US ISSN 0553-0342
ORGANIZATION OF AMERICAN STATES. DEPARTMENT OF SCIENTIFIC AFFAIRS. SERIE DE BIOLOGIA: MONOGRAFIAS. (Text in Spanish) 1965. irreg., no. 20, 1978. price varies. Organization of American States, Department of Publications, Washington, DC 20006. circ. 3,000.

PALEOBIOLOGIA. see *ANTHROPOLOGY*

PATHOLOGY ANNUAL. see *MEDICAL SCIENCES*

574 US
PERGAMON BIOLOGICAL SCIENCES SERIES. 1973. irreg., vol. 2, 1974. price varies. Pergamon Press, Inc., Maxwell House, Fairview Park, Elmsford, NY 10523.

570 US
PERGAMON STUDIES IN THE LIFE SCIENCES. 1976. irreg. price varies. Pergamon Press, Inc., Maxwell House, Fairview Park, Elmsford, NY 10523.

PETERSON'S GUIDES. ANNUAL GUIDES TO GRADUATE STUDY. BOOK 3: BIOLOGICAL, AGRICULTURAL AND HEALTH SCIENCES. see *EDUCATION — Guides To Schools And Colleges*

PHYSICS AND BIOLOGY. see *PHYSICS*

574 PO ISSN 0032-5147
PORTUGALIAE ACTA BIOLOGICA. (Text in English, French, German & Portuguese) 1944. irreg. price varies. Universidade de Lisboa, Faculdade de Ciencias, Instituto Botanico, Lisbon 2, Portugal. (Co-sponsor: Laboratorio de Patologia Vegetal Verissimo de Almeida) bk. rev. circ. 500. Indexed: Biol.Abstr. Chem.Abstr.

574 PL ISSN 0079-4619
POZNANSKIE TOWARZYSTWO PRZYJACIOL NAUK. KOMISJA BIOLOGICZNA. PRACE. (Text in Polish; summaries in English) 1921. irreg., 1972, vol. 35, no. 5. price varies. Poznanskie Towarzystwo Przyjaciol Nauk, Komisja Biologiczna, Mielzynskiego 27/29, 61-725 Poznan, Poland (Dist. by Ars Polona-Ruch, Krakowskie Przedmiescie 7, Warsaw, Poland) Indexed: Biol.Abstr. Chem.Abstr.

PREHISTORIC ARCHAEOLOGY AND ECOLOGY. see *ARCHAEOLOGY*

574 YU ISSN 0373-2134
PRIRODNJACKI MUZEJ U BEOGRADU. GLASNIK. SERIJA B: BIOLOSKE NAUKE. vol. 30, 1975. irreg. Prirodnjacki Muzej u Beogradu, Njegoseva 51, Belgrade, Yugoslavia. Ed. Zivomir Vasic.

574 CS
PROBLEMY BIOLOGIE KRAJINY/QUESTIONES GEOBIOLOGICAE. irreg, vol. 20, 1977. price varies. (Slovenska Akademia Vied) Veda, Publishing House of the Slovak Academy of Sciences, Klemensova 19, 895 30 Bratislava, Czechoslovakia. Ed. M. Ruzicka.

574 UR
PROBLEMY BIONIKI. vol. 18, 1977. irreg. (Khar'kovskii Institut Radioelektroniki) Izdatel'stvo Vysshaya Shkola-Khar'kov, Universitetskaya 16, 310003 Khar'kov, U.S.S.R. Ed. Yu. Shabanov-Kushnarenko.

PROGRESS IN CLINICAL AND BIOLOGICAL RESEARCH. see *MEDICAL SCIENCES*

574 US ISSN 0301-0082
PROGRESS IN NEUROBIOLOGY. 1973. 8/yr. $165. Pergamon Press,Inc., Journals Division, Maxwell House, Fairview Park, Elmsford, NY 10523 (And Headington Hill Hall, Oxford OX3 0BW, England) Eds. G.A. Kerkut, J.W. Phillis. (also avail. in microform from MIM,UMI) Indexed: Chem.Abstr. Ind.Med.

574.192 574.88 US ISSN 0079-6603
PROGRESS IN NUCLEIC ACID RESEARCH AND MOLECULAR BIOLOGY. (Title Varies. Vol. 1-2, Progress in Nucleic Acid Research) 1963. irreg., latest vol. 22. price varies. Academic Press, Inc 111 Fifth Ave., New York, NY 10003. Eds. J. N. Davidson, W. E. Cohn. (also avail. in microfiche) Indexed: Ind.Med.

574 US ISSN 0079-6859
PROGRESS IN THEORETICAL BIOLOGY. 1967. irreg., vol. 5, 1978. price varies. Academic Press, Inc 111 Fifth Ave., New York, NY 10003. Eds. Robert Rosen, Fred M. Snell.

610 UN
PROSTAGLANDINS IN FERTILITY CONTROL. (Text in English) 1971. a. free. World Health Organization, Research and Training Centre on Human Reproduction, Karolinska Institutet, Fack, S-104 01 Stockholm, Sweden. Ed.Bd.

574 US ISSN 0079-7065
PROTIDES OF THE BIOLOGICAL FLUIDS. 1953. a. $125. Pergamon Press, Inc., Journals Division, Maxwell House, Fairview Park, Elmsford, NY 10523 (U. K. Office: Pergamon Press Ltd., Headington Hill Hall, Oxford OX3 0BW, England) Ed. Dr. H. Peeters. (also avail. in microform from MIM,UMI)

591 ZA ISSN 0079-7901
PUKU. 1963. irreg., no. 7, 1973 (no. 8 in prep.) K.2.50. National Parks and Wildlife Service, Private Bag 1, Chilanga, Zambia (Orders to: Government Printer, Box 136, Lusaka, Zambia) Ed. A. D. H. Ansell. bk. rev. circ. 200 (approx.)

574 371 IT
QUADERNI DI SESSUALITA. (Text in English and Italian) irreg. price varies. Bulzoni Editore, Via dei Liburni 14, 00185 Rome, Italy.

574 610 US
QUANTITATIVE METHODS FOR BIOLOGISTS AND MEDICAL SCIENTISTS. 1964. irreg., latest vol. 1967, unnumbered. price varies. John Wiley & Sons, Inc., 605 Third Ave., New York, NY 10016. Ed. W.J. Dixon.

574.92 639 CN
QUEBEC (PROVINCE) DIRECTION GENERALE DES PECHES MARITIMES CAHIERS D'INFORMATION. (Text in French) 1960. irreg., no. 80, 1977. free; available on exchange. ‡ Ministere de l'Industrie et du Commerce, Direction de la Recherche, 2700 Einstein, Quebec G1P 3W8, Canada. Ed. J. Bergeron. circ. 150. Indexed: Biol.Abstr. Ocean.Ind.
Formerly: Quebec (Province) Marine Biological Station, Grande-Riviere. Cahiers d'Information (ISSN 0079-8762)

574.92 639 CN ISSN 0318-8779
QUEBEC (PROVINCE) DIRECTION GENERALE DES PECHES MARITIMES. DIRECTION DE LA RECHERCHE. RAPPORT ANNUEL. (Text in French) 1953. a. free. ‡ Ministere de l'Industrie et du Commerce, 2700 Einstein, Quebec G1P 3W8, Canada. Ed. J. Bergeron. circ. 400. Indexed: Biol.Abstr. Ocean.Ind.
Supersedes (1969): Quebec (Province) Marine Biological Station, Grande-Riviere. Rapport (ISSN 0079-8754)

574.9 AT ISSN 0079-8843
QUEENSLAND NATURALIST. 1908. irreg. (approx. a) Aus.$4.50. Queensland Naturalists' Club, Box 1220 G.P.O., Brisbane, Qld. 4001, Australia. Ed. Dr. John Pearson.

QUETICO-SUPERIOR WILDERNESS RESEARCH CENTER, ELY, MINNESOTA. ANNUAL REPORT. see *CONSERVATION*

574 554 SP
REAL SOCIEDAD ESPANOLA DE HISTORIA NATURAL. BOLETIN DE GEOLOGIA Y BIOLOGIA. (Text in Spanish; summaries in English, French) 1871. a. free. Real Sociedad Espanola de Historia Natural, Ciudad Universitaria, Madrid 3, Spain.

574 HU ISSN 0079-9955
RECENT DEVELOPMENTS OF NEUROBIOLOGY IN HUNGARY. (Text in English) 1967. irreg. price varies. (Magyar Tudomanyos Akademia) Akademiai Kiado, Publishing House of the Hungarian Academy of Sciences, P.O. Box 24, H-1363 Budapest, Hungary. Ed. K. Lissak.

574.16 301.426 PH
REPRODUCTIONS. (Text in English) 1970. irreg. (15-20/yr.) P.5($4) University of Santo Tomas, Institute for the Study of Human Reproduction, Faculty of Medicine, Espana St., Manila, Philippines. Ed. Vicente J.A. Rosales, M.D. bk. rev. circ. 5,000. (looseleaf format)

RESEARCH IN THE LIFE SCIENCES. see *AGRICULTURE*

574 US ISSN 0569-5376
RESEARCH PROBLEMS IN BIOLOGY. 1963. irreg. price varies. American Institute of Biological Sciences, Biological Sciences Curriculum Study, 1401 Wilson Blvd., Arlington, VA 22209.

RESOURCE AND ENVIRONMENTAL SCIENCE SERIES. see *ENVIRONMENTAL STUDIES*

574 UY ISSN 0304-971X
REVISTA DE BIOLOGIA DEL URUGUAY. (Text in Spanish; summaries in English) 1973. a. $10. c/o Dr. Fernando Mane-Garzon, Ed., Casilla de Correo 157, Montevideo, Uruguay. illus. index. circ. 1,500. (back issues avail.)

574 UY
REVISTA DE BIOLOGIA DEL URUGUAY. 1973. irreg. $10. Fernando Mane-Garzon, Ed. & Pub., Casilla de Correo, 157, Montevideo, Uruguay. illus.

574.92 CL ISSN 0080-2115
REVISTA DE BIOLOGIA MARINA. (Text in Spanish; summaries in Spanish and English) 1948. irreg. vol. 16, no. 3, 1979. $8. Universidad de Chile, Departamento de Oceanologia, Casilla 13 D., Vina del Mar, Chile. Ed. Luis Ramorino Meschi. cum.index. circ. 600. Indexed: Biol.Abstr.

574.92 PE
REVISTA PACIFICA SUR. 1971. a. free. Comision Permanente del Pacifico Sur, Secretaria General, Sinchi Roca 2699, Lima 14, Peru. circ. 1,000. (back issues avail.)
Marine

ROYAL COLLEGE OF PATHOLOGISTS OF AUSTRALIA. BROADSHEETS. see *MEDICAL SCIENCES*

574 590 551   IE   ISSN 0035-8983
ROYAL IRISH ACADEMY. PROCEEDINGS. SECTION B: BIOLOGICAL, GEOLOGICAL AND CHEMICAL SCIENCES. 1836. irreg. price varies. Royal Irish Academy, 19 Dawson St., Dublin 2, Ireland. Ed. B. Young. charts. illus. index. cum.index. circ. 600. Indexed: Biol.Abstr. Chem.Abstr. Curr.Cont. Excerp.Med. Ind.Med. Sci.Abstr. Sci.Cit.Ind. Aqua.Sci. & Fish.Abstr. Phys.Ber.

560 590   CN   ISSN 0384-8159
ROYAL ONTARIO MUSEUM. LIFE SCIENCES. CONTRIBUTIONS. 1928. irreg. price varies. Royal Ontario Museum, 100 Queen's Park, Toronto M5S 2C6, Canada. Ed.Bd. Indexed: Biol.Abstr. Zoo.Rec.

574.9   CN   ISSN 0082-5093
ROYAL ONTARIO MUSEUM. LIFE SCIENCES. MISCELLANEOUS PUBLICATIONS. 1963. irreg. price varies. Royal Ontario Museum, 100 Queen's Park, Toronto, Ontario M5S 2C6, Canada. Indexed: Biol.Abstr. Zoo.Rec.

574   CN   ISSN 0082-5107
ROYAL ONTARIO MUSEUM. LIFE SCIENCES. OCCASIONAL PAPERS. 1935. irreg., no. 32, 1979. price varies. Royal Ontario Museum, 100 Queen's Park, Toronto, Ontario M5S 2C6, Canada. Ed.Bd. Indexed: Biol.Abstr. Zoo.Rec.

574   UK
ROYAL SOCIETY OF EDINBURGH. PROCEEDINGS. (BIOLOGICAL SCIENCES) 1832. a. £17($55) Royal Society of Edinburgh, 22 George Street, Edinburgh, EH2 2PQ, Scotland. Ed. Wm. H. Rutherford. circ. 1,500. Indexed: Biol.Abstr. Chem.Abstr. Ind.Med. Nutr.Abstr.
Former titles: Royal Society of Edinburgh. Proceedings. (Natural Environment) (ISSN 0308-2113); Royal Society of Edinburgh. Proceedings. Section B. Biology (ISSN 0080-455X)

574   UK   ISSN 0080-4622
ROYAL SOCIETY OF LONDON. PHILOSOPHICAL TRANSACTIONS. SERIES B. BIOLOGICAL SCIENCES. 1665. irreg. £57 per vol. Royal Society of London, 6 Carlton House Terrace, London, S.W.1, England. author index every 10 years. (reprint service avail. from ISI) Indexed: Biol.Abstr. Chem.Abstr.

574   UK   ISSN 0080-4649
ROYAL SOCIETY OF LONDON. PROCEEDINGS. SERIES B. BIOLOGICAL SCIENCES. 1832. irreg. £27.50 per vol. Royal Society of London, 6 Carlton House Terrace, London S.W.1, England. author index every 10 yrs. (reprint service avail. from ISI) Indexed: Biol.Abstr. Chem.Abstr. Eng.Ind. Ind.Med. Nutr.Abstr.

574.92   UK   ISSN 0080-8121
S. M. B. A. COLLECTED REPRINTS. (Text in English; occasionally papers in other languages) 1948. a. avail. only on exchange. Scottish Marine Biological Association, Dunstaffage Marine Research Laboratory, P.O.B. 3, OBAN, Argyll, Scotland. circ. 150.
Marine

574   JA
SADO MARINE BIOLOGICAL STATION. ANNUAL REPORT/NIIGATA DAIGAKU RIGAKUBU FUZOKU SADO RINKAI JIKKENJO KENKYU NENPO. (Text and summaries in English) 1971. a. avail. on exchange basis only. Niigata University, Sado Marine Biological Station - Niigata Daigaku Rigakubu Fuzoku Sado Rinkai Jikkenjo, 2-8050 Igarashi, Niigata 950-21, Japan. Ed. Yoshiharu Honma. bibl. circ. controlled.

570   US   ISSN 0080-5467
SAINT BONAVENTURE UNIVERSITY. SCIENCE STUDIES. 1932. a. $1.50. St. Bonaventure University, St. Bonaventure, NY 14778. Ed. Stephen W. Eaton. cum.index: 1932-1942. circ. 600. Indexed: Biol.Abstr.

574   JA   ISSN 0080-6064
SANKYO RESEARCH LABORATORIES. ANNUAL REPORT. (Text in English and Japanese; summaries in English) 1946. a. controlled free circ. Sankyo Co., Ltd., Central Research Laboratories - Sankyo K.K. Chuo Kenkyusho, 1-2-58 Hiro-machi, Shinagawa-ku, Tokyo 140, Japan. Ed. Genshun Sunagawa. abstr.

574   NO   ISSN 0036-4827
SARSIA. (Text in English, French, German) 1961. irreg. price varies. (Universitetet i Bergen) Universitetsforlaget, Kolstadgt. 1, Box 2959-Toeyen, Oslo 6, Norway (U.S. address: Box 258, Irvington-on-Hudson, NY 10533)

591   CN
SASKATCHEWAN. DEPARTMENT OF TOURISM AND RENEWABLE RESOURCES. GAME SURVEYS UNIT. AERIAL ANTELOPE SURVEY REPORT. 1960. a. Department of Tourism and Renewable Resources, Game Surveys Unit, 1825 Lorne St., Regina, Sask. S4P 3N1, Canada. stat. circ. controlled.

333.7   FI   ISSN 0356-3189
SAVONIA. (Text in English) 1972. a. exchange basis. Kuopion Luonnon Ystavain Yhdistys - Kuopio Naturalists' Society, Kuopio Museum, Department of Natural History, Kauppak. 23, SF-70100 Kuopio 10, Finland. Ed. Lauri Karenlampi. charts. illus. stat. (back issues avail.)

574.92 551.46   US
SEARS FOUNDATION FOR MARINE RESEARCH. MEMOIRS. 1948. irreg., no. 1, pt. 6, 1973. Yale University, Sears Foundation for Marine Research, Box 2025 Yale Sta., New Haven, CT 06520.
Marine

SENCKENBERGIANA MARITIMA. ZEITSCHRIFT FUER MEERESGEOLOGIE UND MEERESBIOLOGIE. see *EARTH SCIENCES — Oceanography*

500.9   GW   ISSN 0365-7000
SENCKENBERGISCHE NATURFORSCHENDE GESELLSCHAFT. ABHANDLUNGEN. 1884. irreg. price varies. Senckenbergische Naturforschende Gesellschaft, Senckenberganlage 25, 6000 Frankfurt 1, W. Germany (B.R.D.)

547   KO
SEOUL NATIONAL UNIVERSITY. FACULTY PAPERS. BIOLOGY AND AGRICULTURE SERIES. (Text in English) 1971. a. Seoul National University, Seoul, S. Korea.

574.92   JA   ISSN 0080-9098
SETO MARINE BIOLOGICAL LABORATORY. SPECIAL PUBLICATIONS. (Text in English) 1964. irreg. available on exchange only. Kyoto University, Seto Marine Biological Laboratory - Kyoto Daigaku Rigakubu Fuzoku Seto Rinkai Jikkensho, Shirahama-cho, Nishimuro-gun, Wakayama-ken 649-22, Japan. Ed. Bd. circ. 400.
Marine

SHEVCHENKO SCIENTIFIC SOCIETY. PROCEEDINGS OF THE SECTION OF CHEMISTRY, BIOLOGY AND MEDICINE. see *CHEMISTRY*

574 638   JA   ISSN 0583-0648
SHINSHU UNIVERSITY. FACULTY OF TEXTILE SCIENCE AND TECHNOLOGY. JOURNAL. SERIES A: BIOLOGY. (Text in English) 1951. irreg. exchange basis. Shinshu University, Faculty of Textile Science and Technology - Shinshu Daigaku Sen'i Gakubu, 3-15-1 Tokida, Ueda, Nagano 386, Japan.

574   JA   ISSN 0559-9822
SIEBOLDIA ACTA BIOLOGICA/SHIBORUDIA. (Text in Japanese and English) 1952. irreg. exchange basis. Kyushu University, College of General Education, Biological Laboratory - Kyushu Daigaku Kyoyobu Seibutsugaku Kyoshitsu, 4-2-1 Ropponmatsu, Chuo-ku, Fukuoka 810, Japan.

574   US   ISSN 0270-2614
SKENECTADA. 1979. a. $15. Pine Bush Historic Preservation Project, Inc., Box 22820, 1400 Washington Ave., Albany, NY 12222. Ed. Don Rittner. bk. rev. abstr. charts. illus. circ. 1,000. (back issues avail.)

574   AG   ISSN 0037-8380
SOCIEDAD ARGENTINA DE BIOLOGIA. REVISTA. (Text in Spanish; summaries in English) 1924. irreg. $12. (Sociedad Argentina de Biologia) Instituto de Biologia y Medicina Experimental, Obligado 2490, 1428 Buenos Aires, Argentina. Ed. Enrique J. del Castillo. adv. abstr. charts. illus. index; cum.index. Indexed: Chem.Abstr.

500.9   BO
SOCIEDAD BOLIVIANA DE HISTORIA NATURAL. REVISTA. (Text in Spanish; some summaries in English) 1974. irreg. Sociedad Boliviana de Historia Natural, Casilla de Correo 538, Cochabamba, Bolivia. illus.

574 554   SP   ISSN 0583-7405
SOCIEDAD DE HISTORIA NATURAL DE BALEARES. BOLETIN. (Text in English, French, German, Spanish; sometimes in Italian) 1955. irreg.; 23, 1979. 700 ptas. Sociedad de Historia Natural de Baleares, San Roque, 8, Estudio General Luliano, Palma de Mallorca, Spain. bk. rev.

570 580   PO   ISSN 0081-0665
SOCIEDADE BROTERIANA. MEMORIAS. (Text in European languages; summaries in Portuguese, French and English) 1930. irreg., approx. 1 per year. Esc.600($15) ‡ Sociedade Broteriana, Arcos do Jardim, 3049 Coimbra, Portugal. (Co-sponsor: Universidade de Coimbra. Instituto Botanico) Eds. A. Fernandes & Y. Barros Neves. circ. 1,500. Indexed: Biol.Abstr. Excerp.Bot.

574   PL   ISSN 0079-4570
SOCIETE DES AMIS DES SCIENCES ET DES LETTRES DE POZNAN. BULLETIN. SERIE D: SCIENCES BIOLOGIQUES. (Text in English, French and German) 1960. irreg. price varies. Poznanskie Towarzystwo Przyjaciol Nauk, Mielzynskiego 27/29, 61-725 Poznan, Poland (Dist by Ars Polona-Ruch, Krakowskie Przedmiescie 7, Warsaw, Poland) Ed. Aleksandra Hoffmannowa. bibl. charts. illus. Indexed: Biol.Abstr. Chem.Abstr.

574   US   ISSN 0583-9009
SOCIETY FOR DEVELOPMENTAL BIOLOGY. SYMPOSIUM. (Since 1967: Issued as Supplement to Journal of Developmental Biology) no. 11, 1952. irreg. Academic Press Inc., 111 Fifth Ave., New York, NY 10003. Ed. M. Locke. Indexed: Ind.Med.

574   UK
SOCIETY FOR EXPERIMENTAL BIOLOGY. SEMINAR SERIES. irreg., no. 7, 1981. $45 (cloth); $19.95 (paper) for latest vol. Cambridge University Press, Box 110, Cambridge CB2 3RL, England (And 32 E. 57th St., New York, NY 10022) index.

574   US   ISSN 0081-1386
SOCIETY FOR EXPERIMENTAL BIOLOGY. SYMPOSIA.* 1947. irreg., 1972, vol. 26. price varies. Academic Press, Inc, 630 W. 168th St., New York, NY 10032. index in some numbers. Indexed: Ind.Med.

591   US   ISSN 0361-6525
SOCIOBIOLOGY. 1976. irreg., approx a. $25. California State University, Chico, Department of Biological Sciences, Chico, CA 95929. Ed. David H. Kistner. adv. bk. rev. illus. index. circ. 500. (back issues avail.) Indexed: Biol.Abstr. Bull.Sig. Entomol.Abstr. Zoo.Rec.

574   BU   ISSN 0081-1823
SOFIISKI UNIVERSITET. BIOLOGICHESKI FAKULTET. GODISHNIK. irreg., vol. 63, 1970. 2.33 lv. price varies. Publishing House of the Bulgarian Academy of Sciences, Ul. Akad. G. Bonchev, 1113 Sofia, Bulgaria. circ. 536.

574.92   SA   ISSN 0081-234X
SOUTH AFRICAN ASSOCIATION FOR MARINE BIOLOGICAL RESEARCH. BULLETIN. 1960. a. free. ‡ South African Association for Marine Biological Research, Centenary Aquarium Buildings, 2 West St., Durban 4000, South Africa. Ed. John H. Wallace. circ. controlled. Indexed: Ocean.Abstr. Aqua.Sci.& Fish.Abstr.

SPEZIELLE PATHOLOGISCHE ANATOMIE. see *MEDICAL SCIENCES*

BIOLOGY

570   US
SPRINGER ADVANCED TEXTS IN LIFE SCIENCES. irreg.; 4th, 1979. price varies. Springer Verlag, 175 Fifth Ave., New York, NY 10010 (And Berlin, Heidelberg, Vienna) (reprint service avail. from ISI)

574.5   FR   ISSN 0068-0087
STATION BIOLOGIQUE DE BONNEVAUX (DOUBS). SECTION DE BIOLOGIE ET D'ECOLOGIE ANIMALES. PUBLICATIONS. 1969. irreg(3-4/yr) free. Universite de Besancon, Laboratoire de Biologie et d'Ecologie Animales, Faculte des Sciences, Besancon, France. Ed. P. Real.
Ecology

574   HU   ISSN 0076-244X
STUDIA BIOLOGICA ACADEMIAE SCIENTIARUM HUNGARICAE. (Text in English and German) 1964. irreg., vol. 16, 1978. price varies. (Magyar Tudomanyos Akademia) Akademiai Kiado, Publishing House of the Hungarian Academy of Sciences, P.O. Box 24, H-1363 Budapest, Hungary.

574   610   PL   ISSN 0081-6582
STUDIA I MATERIALY Z DZIEJOW NAUKI POLSKIEJ. SERIA B. HISTORIA NAUK BIOLOGICZNYCH I MEDYCZNYCH. (Text in Polish; summaries in Russian and English) 1957, fasc. 19. irreg., 1972, vol. 23. price varies. (Polska Akademia Nauk, Zaklad Historii Nauki i Techniki) Panstwowe Wydawnictwo Naukowe, Miodowa 10, Warsaw, Poland. Ed. Waldemar Voise.
History

574   RM   ISSN 0039-3398
STUDIA UNIVERSITATIS "BABES-BOLYAI". BIOLOGIA. (Text in Romanian; summaries in English, French, German, Russian) 1958. s-a. exchange basis. Universitatea "Babes-Bolyai", Biblioteca Centrala Universitara, Str. Clinicilor Nr. 2, Cluj-Napoca, Romania. bk. rev. charts. illus. Indexed: Biol.Abstr.

574   US
STUDIES IN BIOLOGY. 1972. irreg. price varies. University Park Press, Chamber of Commerce Bldg., Baltimore, MD 21202.

574   UK   ISSN 0537-9024
STUDIES IN BIOLOGY. 1966. irreg. price varies. Edward Arnold (Publishers) Ltd., 41 Bedford Square, London WC1B 3DQ, England.

574.5
STUDIES IN ECOLOGY. irreg. price varies. University of California Press, 2223 Fulton St., Berkeley, CA 94720.

574.09   US   ISSN 0149-6700
STUDIES IN HISTORY OF BIOLOGY. 1977. a. Johns Hopkins University Press, Baltimore, MD 21218. Eds. W. Coleman, C. Limoges. illus.

SURFACTANT SCIENCE SERIES. see *CHEMISTRY*

574   US   ISSN 0081-9697
SURVEY OF BIOLOGICAL PROGRESS. 1952. irreg., 1962, vol. 4. price varies. Academic Press, Inc, 111 Fifth Ave., New York, NY 10003. Ed. G. S. Avery, Jr. index.

574   US   ISSN 0362-3246
SURVEY OF SOURCES NEWSLETTER. 1975. irreg. free. American Philosophical Society, Survey of Sources for the History of Biochemistry and Molecular Biology, 105 S. Fifth St., Philadelphia, PA 19106. (Co-sponsor: American Academy of Arts and Sciences) Ed. Dr. John T. Edsall. bibl. circ. 500. (back issues avail.)

574   US
SURVEYOR. irreg. free. Ohio State University, College of Biological Sciences, 484 W. 12th Ave., Columbus, OH 43210.

574.92   SW   ISSN 0346-8666
SWEDEN. FISHERY BOARD. INSTITUTE OF MARINE RESEARCH. REPORT. (Text in English, German and Swedish; summaries in English) 1975. irreg., no. 2, 1979. price varies. Fiskeristyrelsen, Institute of Marine Research, S-453 00 Lysekil, Sweden. Ed. A. Lindquist. index. Indexed: Biol.Abstr.
    Formed by the merger of (1950-1972): Sweden Institute of Marine Research. Series Biology. Reports (ISSN 0076-1710) & Sweden. Fisheries Board. Series Hydrography. Reports (ISSN 0562-8490)
Marine

574   HU   ISSN 0082-0695
SYMPOSIA BIOLOGICA HUNGARICA. (Text in English and German) 1960. irreg., vol.19,1979. price varies. (Magyar Tudomanyos Akademia) Akademiai Kiado, Publishing House of the Hungarian Academy of Sciences, P.O. Box 24, H-1363 Budapest, Hungary.

TECHNIQUES OF BIOCHEMICAL AND BIOPHYSICAL MORPHOLOGY. see *BIOLOGY — Biological Chemistry*

574   610   US   ISSN 0040-4675
TEXAS REPORTS ON BIOLOGY AND MEDICINE. 1943. irreg. (approx. 3/yr.) $12. University of Texas at Galveston, Medical Branch, Galveston, TX 77550. Ed. Eleanor Porter. abstr. charts. illus. stat. index. circ. 3,000. (also avail. in microform from UMI) Indexed: Biol.Abstr. Chem.Abstr. Curr.Cont. Excerp.Med. I.P.A. Ind.Med. Sci.Cit.Ind. Int.Abstr.Biol.Sci. JAMA. Nucl.Sci.Abstr.

574   US   ISSN 0082-3945
THEORETICAL AND EXPERIMENTAL BIOLOGY; an international series of monographs. 1961. irreg., 1967, vol. 6. price varies. Academic Press Inc., 111 Fifth Ave., New York, NY 10003. Ed. J. F. Danielli.

574   614.7   NE
TOPICS IN ENVIRONMENTAL HEALTH. 1978. irreg. price varies. Elsevier North-Holland Biomedical Press, Box 211, 1000 AE Amsterdam, Netherlands.

574   NE
TOPICS IN PHOTOSYNTHESIS. 1976. irreg. price varies. Elsevier North-Holland Biomedical Press, Box 211, 1000 AE Amsterdam, Netherlands. Ed. J. Barber.

570   IO   ISSN 0082-6340
TREUBIA; a journal of zoology and hydrobiology of the Indo-Australian archipelago. (Text in English, French or German) 1919. irreg. price varies. Museum Zoologicum Bogoriense - Bogor Zoological Museum, Jalan Ir. H. Juanda 3, Bogor, Indonesia. Ed.Bd. index. cum.index: vols. 1-23. circ. 500. Indexed: Biol.Abstr. Zoo.Rec.

574   510   FI   ISSN 0082-6979
TURUN YLIOPISTO. JULKAISUJA. SARJA A. II. BIOLOGICA- GEOGRAPHICA- GEOLOGICA. (Latin title: Annales Universitatis Turkuensis) (Text in English, German, French, Finnish) 1957. irreg. price varies. Turun Yliopisto - University of Turku, SF-20500 Turku 50, Finland.

UNESCO TECHNICAL PAPERS IN MARINE SCIENCE. see *EARTH SCIENCES — Oceanography*

UNIVERSIDAD DE BOGOTA JORGE TADEO LOZANO. MUSEO DEL MAR. BOLETIN. see *EARTH SCIENCES — Oceanography*

574.92   CK
UNIVERSIDAD DE BOGOTA JORGE TADEO LOZANO. MUSEO DEL MAR. INFORME. (Text in Spanish; summaries in English) 1971. irreg. Col.15. Universidad de Bogota Jorge Tadeo Lozano, Museo del Mar, Calle 23 No. 4-47, Bogota, Colombia. Dir. Jorge Barreto Soulier. bibl.
Marine biology

574   CU
UNIVERSIDAD DE LA HABANA. CENTRO DE INFORMACION CIENTIFICA Y TECNICA. SERIE 4. CIENCIAS BIOLOGICAS. Short title: Catalogo de la Fauna Cubana. (Text in Spanish; summaries in English) irreg. Universidad de la Habana, Centro de Informacion Cientifica y Tecnica, Havana, Cuba.

574   UY
UNIVERSIDAD DE LA REPUBLICA. FACULTAD DE HUMANIDADES Y CIENCIAS. REVISTA. SERIE CIENCIAS. N.S. 1979. irreg. Universidad de la Republica, Facultad de Humanidades y Ciencias, Seccion Revista, Tristan Narvaja 1674, Montivideo, Uruguay. Dir. Beatriz Martinez Osorio.
    Supersedes in part: Universidad de la Republica. Facultad de Humanidades y Ciencias. Revista.

574   MX   ISSN 0076-7174
UNIVERSIDAD NACIONAL AUTONOMA DE MEXICO. INSTITUTO DE BIOLOGIA. ANALES. 1930. a. $12. Universidad Nacional Autonoma de Mexico, Instituto de Biologia, Ciudad Universitaria, Villa Obregon, Mexico 20, D.F., Mexico.

574.92   BL   ISSN 0374-0412
UNIVERSIDADE FEDERAL DE PERNAMBUCO. DEPARTAMENTO DE OCEANOGRAFIA. CENTRO DE TECNOLOGIA. TRABALHOS OCEANOGRAFICAS. (Text in English, French and Portuguese; summaries in English) 1959. irreg. free. Universidade Federal de Pernambuco, Departamento de Oceanografia, Centro de Tecnologia, Av. Bernardo Vieira de Melo 986, Piedade, 5000 Recife, Pernambuco, Brazil. circ. 900(approx.)
    Former titles(1963-1966): Universidade Federal de Pernambuco. Instituto Oceanografico. Trabalhos (ISSN 0080-0236); 1960-1963: Universidade do Recife. Instituto Oceanografico. Trabalhos; 1959-1960: Instituto de Biologia Marinha e Oceanografia. Trabalhos.

574   BL
UNIVERSIDADE FEDERAL DE PERNAMBUCO. INSTITUTO DE BIOCIENCIAS. MEMORIAS. (Text and summaries in English and Portuguese) 1974. irreg. Universidade Federal de Pernambuco, Instituto de Biociencias, Editora Universitaria, Recife, Pernambuco, Brazil.

574   IT   ISSN 0085-0950
UNIVERSITA DEGLI STUDI DI GENOVA. BOLLETINO DEI MUSEI DEGLI ISTITUTI BIOLOGICI. (Text in Italian; summaries in English) a. exchange basis. Universita degli Studi di Genova, Istituto di Zoologia, Via Balbi 5, Genoa, Italy. Ed. Fratelli Pagano.

574   AU
UNIVERSITAET INNSBRUCK. ALPIN-BIOLOGISCHE STUDIEN. (Subseries of: Universitaet Innsbruck. Veroeffentlichungen) 1970. irreg., vol. 6, 1974. price varies. Oesterreichische Kommissionsbuchhandlung, Maximilian Str. 17, A-6020 Innsbruck, Austria. Ed. Heinz Janetschek.

UNIVERSITATEA DIN BRASOV. BULETINUL SERIA C. STIINTE ALE NATURII SI PEDAGOGIE. see *MATHEMATICS*

574.92   US   ISSN 0084-6147
UNIVERSITY OF ALASKA. INSTITUTE OF MARINE SCIENCE. OCCASIONAL PUBLICATION. 1971. irreg., no. 5, 1980. price varies. ‡ University of Alaska, Institute of Marine Science, Fairbanks, AK 99701. Ed. Helen K. Stockholm.
Marine

574.92   US   ISSN 0065-5929
UNIVERSITY OF ALASKA. INSTITUTE OF MARINE SCIENCES. TECHNICAL REPORT. irreg. University of Alaska, Institute of Marine Science, Fairbanks, AK 99701.
Marine

574   IQ   ISSN 0067-2890
UNIVERSITY OF BAGHDAD. BIOLOGICAL RESEARCH CENTRE. BULLETIN.* (Text in English; summaries in Arabic and English) 1965. a. available on exchange. University of Baghdad, Biological Research Centre, Baghdad, Iraq. Ed. Iyad A. Nader. Indexed: Biol.Abstr.

574.2 US ISSN 0068-6131
UNIVERSITY OF CALIFORNIA, IRVINE. CENTER FOR PATHOBIOLOGY. MISCELLANEOUS PUBLICATIONS. 1969. irreg., 1970, no. 2. price varies. University of California, Irvine, Center for Pathobiology, Irvine, CA 92715.
Pathology

574 US ISSN 0068-614X
UNIVERSITY OF CALIFORNIA, IRVINE. MUSEUM OF SYSTEMATIC BIOLOGY. RESEARCH SERIES. 1968. irreg., nos. 4 & 5, 1975. price varies. ‡ University of California, Irvine, Museum of Systematic Biology, Irvine, CA 92664. Ed. Gordon A. Marsh. Indexed: Biol.Abstr.

574.92 US
UNIVERSITY OF CALIFORNIA, SAN DIEGO. INSTITUTE OF MARINE RESOURCES. BIENNIAL REPORT. 1955. biennial. free. ‡ University of California, San Diego, Institute of Marine Resources, Box 1529, La Jolla, CA 92037. Ed. Walter R. Schmitt. circ. 1,000.
Formerly: University of California, San Diego. Institute of Marine Resources. Annual Report (ISSN 0068-6158)
Marine

574.92 SJ
UNIVERSITY OF KHARTOUM. HYDROBIOLOGICAL RESEARCH UNIT. ANNUAL REPORT. (Text in English) a. University of Khartoum, Hydrobiological Research Unit, Box 321, Khartoum, Sudan.

574.92 US ISSN 0090-9750
UNIVERSITY OF MARYLAND. NATURAL RESOURCES INSTITUTE. N. R. I. SPECIAL REPORT. (Subseries of: University of Maryland. Natural Resources Institute. Contribution) irreg. University of Maryland, Natural Resources Institute, Solomons, MD 20688. illus. Key Title: N. R. I. Special Report.
Marine

UNIVERSITY OF OSAKA PREFECTURE. BULLETIN. SERIES B: AGRICULTURE AND BIOLOGY/OSAKA-FURITSU DAIGAKU KIYO, B NOGAKU, SEIBUTSUGAKU. see *AGRICULTURE*

UNIVERSITY OF RHODE ISLAND. GRADUATE SCHOOL OF OCEANOGRAPHY. MARINE TECHNICAL REPORTS. see *EARTH SCIENCES — Oceanography*

574.92 JA ISSN 0493-4334
UNIVERSITY OF TOKYO. FACULTY OF SCIENCE. MISAKI MARINE BIOLOGICAL STATION. CONTRIBUTIONS. (Text in Japanese and English) 1940. a. exchange basis. University of Tokyo, Misaki Marine Biological Station - Tokyo Daigaku Rigakubu Fuzoku Rinkai Jikkensho, 1024 Koajiro Misaki-cho, Miura-shi 238-02, Japan.
Marine

574 CN ISSN 0317-3348
UNIVERSITY OF WATERLOO BIOLOGY SERIES. 1971. irreg. Can.$2.50 per no. University of Waterloo, Department of Biology, Waterloo, Ont. N2L 3G1, Canada.

574.88 PL
UNIWERSYTET JAGIELLONSKI. ZESZYTY NAUKOWE. PRACE Z BIOLOGII MOLEKULARNEJ. (Text in Polish; summaries in English) 1974. irreg. 42 Zl. per issue. (Instytut Biologii Molekularnej) Panstwowe Wydawnictwo Naukowe, Miodowa 10, Warsaw, Poland.

574 SW ISSN 0347-3236
VAEXTSKYDDSRAPPORTER. (Text in Swedish; summaries in English or German) 1977. irreg. price varies. Sveriges Lantbruksuniversitet - Swedish University of Agricultural Sciences, Research Information Centre/Plant Protection, Konsulentavdelningen/Vaextskydd, Box 7044, S-750 07 Uppsala, Sweden. Ed. Goeran Kroeker. charts. illus.

574 FI ISSN 0355-354X
VALTION TEKNILLINEN TUTKIMUSKESKUS. BIOTEKNIIKAN LABBORATORIO. TIEDONANTO/TECHNICAL RESEARCH CENTRE OF FINLAND. BIOTECHNICAL LABORATORY. REPORT. (Text mainly in Finnish, some in English or Swedish) 1970. irreg. price varies. Valtion Teknillinen Tutkimuskeskus - Technical Research Centre of Finland, Vuorimiehentie 5, 02150 Espoo 15, Finland.

574.92 US ISSN 0083-6419
VIRGINIA INSTITUTE OF MARINE SCIENCE, GLOUCESTER POINT. DATA REPORTS. 1965. irreg., no. 14, 1978. $1. Virginia Institute of Marine Science, Gloucester Point, VA 23062. circ. 550. (also avail. in microfiche)
Marine

574.92 US ISSN 0083-6427
VIRGINIA INSTITUTE OF MARINE SCIENCE, GLOUCESTER POINT. EDUCATIONAL SERIES. 1943. irreg., no. 29, 1978. free. Virginia Institute of Marine Science, Gloucester Point, VA 23062. (also avail. in microfiche)
Marine

574.92 US ISSN 0083-6435
VIRGINIA INSTITUTE OF MARINE SCIENCE, GLOUCESTER POINT. MARINE RESOURCES ADVISORY SERIES. 1970. irreg., no. 13, 1977. free. Virginia Institute of Marine Science, Gloucester Point, VA 23062. (also avail. in microfiche)
Marine

574.92 US ISSN 0083-6443
VIRGINIA INSTITUTE OF MARINE SCIENCE, GLOUCESTER POINT. SPECIAL SCIENTIFIC REPORT. 1948. irreg., no. 100, 1979. $1. Virginia Institute of Marine Science, Gloucester Point, VA 23062. (also avail. in microfiche) Indexed: Ocean.Abstr.
Marine

574.92 US ISSN 0083-6397
VIRGINIA INSTITUTE OF MARINE SCIENCE, GLOUCESTER POINT. TRANSLATION SERIES. 1961. irreg; no. 27, 1976. $1. Virginia Institute of Marine Science, Gloucester Point, VA 23062. (also avail. in microfiche)
Marine

VOPROSY RADIOBIOLOGII I BIOLOGICHESKOGO DEISTVIYA TSITOSTATICHESKIKH PREPARATOV. see *MEDICAL SCIENCES — Radiology And Nuclear Medicine*

574 US ISSN 0083-7652
WATER IN BIOLOGICAL SYSTEMS. (Translated from Russian) 1969. irreg., 1971, vol. 3. price varies. Consultants Bureau, Special Research Report (Subsidiary of: Plenum Publishing Corp.) 227 W. 17th St., New York, NY 10011.

574.5 US ISSN 0084-0122
WILDLIFE BEHAVIOR AND ECOLOGY. 1971. irreg., latest 1977. price varies. University of Chicago Press, 5801 S. Ellis Ave., Chicago, IL 60637. Ed. George B. Schaller. (reprint service avail. from UMI,ISI)
Ecology

574 610 GW
WISSENSCHAFTLICHE FORSCHUNGSBERICHTE. REIHE 1. GRUNDLAGENFORSCHUNG UND GRUNDLEGENDE METHODIK. ABT. B. BIOLOGIE UND MEDIZIN/CURRENT TOPICS IN SCIENCE. REIHE 1. BASIC RESEARCH. ABT. B. BIOLOGY AND MEDICINE. 1921. irreg. price varies. Dr. Dietrich Steinkopff Verlag, Saalbaustr. 12, Postfach 11 1008, 6100 Darmstadt 11, W. Germany (B.R.D.) Eds. W. Bruegel, A. W. Holldorf. circ. 2,000.

574 GE ISSN 0084-0963
WISSENSCHAFTLICHE TASCHENBUECHER. REIHE BIOLOGIE. 1963. irreg. price varies. Akademie-Verlag, Leipziger Str. 3-4, 108 Berlin, E. Germany (D.D.R.)

WOOLHOPE NATURALISTS' FIELD CLUB, HEREFORDSHIRE. TRANSACTIONS. see *ARCHAEOLOGY*

BIOLOGY — ABSTRACTING, BIBLIOGRAPHIES, STATISTICS

574.1 612 AG ISSN 0084-1641
WORLD CONGRESS ON FERTILITY AND STERILITY. PROCEEDINGS.* 1923. triennial, 1968, 6th, Tel Aviv. International Fertility Association, c/o Dr. Armando F. Mendizabal, Secretary General, Vincente Lopez 971, Martinez, Buenos Aires, Argentina.
1971, 7th, Tokyo; Format and publisher of proceedings vary

574 JA
YOKOHAMA NATIONAL UNIVERSITY. SCIENCE REPORTS. SECTION II: BIOLOGICAL AND GEOLOGICAL SCIENCES. (Text in Japanese and European languages) 1952. a. exchange basis only. Yokohama National University, Faculty of Education - Yokohama Kokuritsu Daigaku Kyoikugakubu, Tokiwadai 156, Hodogaya-ku, Yokohama 240, Japan. illus.
Formerly: Yokohama National University. Science Reports. Section II: Biological Sciences (ISSN 0513-5613)

574.9 CL ISSN 0084-554X
ZONARIDA.* 1961. irreg. Universidad de Chile-Zona Norte, Departamento de Investigaciones Cientificos, Avda. Universidad de Chile s/n, Casilla 1363, Antofagasta, Chile.

591.5 574.5 US
ZOOPHYSIOLOGY. (Text in English) 1971. irreg., vol. 12, 1980. price varies. Springer-Verlag, 175 Fifth Ave., New York, NY 10010 (also Berlin, Heidelberg, Vienna) Ed. D. S. Farne. (reprint service avail. from ISI)
Formerly (vols. 1-10, 1977): Zoophysiology and Ecology (ISSN 0084-5663)
Ecology

BIOLOGY — Abstracting, Bibliographies, Statistics

581 016 BE ISSN 0066-9784
A.E.T.F.A.T. INDEX; releve des travaux de phanerogamie systematique et des taxons nouveaux concernant l'Afrique au sud du Sahara et Madascar. (Text in English and French) 1953. a. $8.50. Association pour l'Etude Taxonomique de la Flore d'Afrique Tropicale, 19 rue de Decembre, 1200 Brussels, Belgium. cum. index: 1953-1972.

ABSTRACTS OF JAPANESE LITERATURE IN FOREST GENETICS AND RELATED FIELDS. PART A. see *FORESTS AND FORESTRY — Abstracting, Bibliographies, Statistics*

ABSTRACTS OF JAPANESE LITERATURE IN FOREST GENETICS AND RELATED FIELDS. PART B. see *FORESTS AND FORESTRY — Abstracting, Bibliographies, Statistics*

597 016 CN
ATLANTIC SALMON REFERENCES. 1973. irreg. free. Maritimes Regional Library, Box 550, Halifax, N.S. B3J 2S7, Canada. cum.index. circ. 500.

580 015 UK ISSN 0307-2657
B S B I ABSTRACTS; abstracts from literature relating to the Vascular plants of the British Isles. 1971. a. £2. Botanical Society of the British Isles, c/o Dept. of Botany, British Museum (Natural History), London SW7 5BD, England. Ed. D. H. Kent.

581 016 BL ISSN 0067-6586
BIBLIOGRAFIA BRASILEIRA DE BOTANICA. 1955. irreg. Cr.$200($10) Instituto Brasileiro de Informacao em Ciencia e Tecnologia, Rio de Janeiro, Brazil. bk. rev. circ. 300.

590 016 BL ISSN 0067-6691
BIBLIOGRAFIA BRASILEIRA DE ZOOLOGIA. 1950. irreg. Cr.$100($5) Instituto Brasileiro de Informacao em Ciencia e Tecnologia, Av. General Justo 171, Rio de Janeiro, Brazil.

576 016 US
BIBLIOGRAPHY OF GERMFREE RESEARCH. 1962. a. $2.50. University of Notre Dame, Lobund Laboratory, Department of Microbiology, Notre Dame, IN 46556. Ed. B.A. Teah. index. circ. controlled. (tabloid format; back issues avail.)

BIOLOGY — Biological Chemistry

574 100 016 US ISSN 0094-4831
BIBLIOGRAPHY OF SOCIETY, ETHICS AND THE LIFE SCIENCES. 1973. biennial. $5 or with subscr. to bi-m. Hastings Center Report. Institute of Society, Ethics and the Life Sciences, Hastings Center, 360 Broadway, Hastings-on-Hudson, NY 10706. bibl. circ. 9,500.

612.015 016 US
BIOGENIC AMINES IN THE CENTRAL NERVOUS SYSTEM; a bibliography. 1970. a. $10 or with subscr. to Biogenic Amines Bulletin. Brain Information Service-Brain Research Institute, University of California, Los Angeles, Center for Health Sciences, Los Angeles, CA 90024. (Co-sponsor: National Institute of Neurological and Communicative Disorders and Stroke) Ed. James K. Mustain. bibl. circ. 1,000. (processed; back issues avail.)

574 016 US
BIOSIS SEARCH GUIDE; BIOSIS previews edition. 1977. irreg. $75. BioSciences Information Service (BIOSIS), 2100 Arch St., Philadelphia, PA 19103. (looseleaf format)

595 016 FR ISSN 0085-2783
CENTRE INTERNATIONAL DE DOCUMENTATION ARACHNOLOGIQUES. LISTE DES TRAVAUX ARACHNOLOGIQUES. 1968. a. 45 F. ‡ Centre International de Documentation Arachnologique, 61, rue de Buffon, Paris 5e, France. adv. bibl. index. (avail. on records)

311 US
CORNELL UNIVERSITY. NEW YORK STATE COLLEGE OF AGRICULTURE AND LIFE SCIENCES. BIOMETRICS UNIT. ANNUAL REPORT. 1949. a. free. ‡ New York State College of Agriculture and Life Sciences, Cornell University, 337 Warren Hall, Ithaca, NY 14853. Ed. W.T. Federer. abstr. stat. circ. controlled. (processed)

I M B I S; Information fuer medizinisch-biologische Statistik und deren Grenzgebiete. see MEDICAL SCIENCES — Abstracting, Bibliographies, Statistics

574.192 016 NE
INDEX OF BIOCHEMICAL REVIEWS. 1973. a. $5 free to subscribers to FEBS letters. (Federation of European Biochemical Societies) Elsevier North-Holland Biomedical Press, P.O. Box 211, 1000 AE Amsterdam, Netherlands. Ed.Bd. circ. 1,600. Indexed: Chem. Abstr. Curr. Cont.

574.191 016 US
INTERNATIONAL BIOPHYSICS CONGRESS. ABSTRACTS. 1961. irreg. $10. Massachusetts Institute of Technology, Cambridge, MA 02139 (Orders to:, Room 20B-221) Ed. Dr. Walter Rosenelith.

581.133 016 NE
PHOTOSYNTHESIS BIBLIOGRAPHY. (Text in English, German and French) 1974. a. price varies. Dr. W. Junk Publishers, Box 13713, 2501 ES The Hague, Netherlands. Eds. Z. Sestak, J. Catsky. cum.index every 5 yrs. (back issues avail.) Indexed: Biol.Abstr.

581 IS ISSN 0079-225X
PLANT PROTECTION ABSTRACTS. SUPPLEMENT. 1967. irreg. latest issue, 1969. free. Makhteshim Agan, P.O. Box 60, Beersheva, Israel. Ed. J. Y. Rein. circ. 1,700.

581 016 UR
RASTITEL'NYI MIR SIBIRI I DAL'NEGO VOSTOKA; tekushchii ukazatel' literatury. 1975. irreg. 1 Rub. Akademiya Nauk S.S.S.R., Sibirskoe Otdelenie, Prospekt Nauki, 21, Novosibirsk, U.S.S.R.
Formerly: Rastitel'nye Resursy Sibiri i Dal'nego Vostoka.

574 016 US
SERIAL SOURCES FOR THE BIOSIS DATA BASE. 1938. a. $30. BioSciences Information Service (BIOSIS), 2100 Arch St., Philadelphia, PA 19103.
Formerly: Biosis: List of Serials (ISSN 0067-8937)

590 016 UK ISSN 0084-5604
ZOOLOGICAL RECORD. (Includes 27 Separate Sections of Individual Titles) 1864. a. £475 for vol. 113. Zoological Society of London, Regent's Park, London NW1 4RY, England (U.S. subscr. address: c/o M. Juery, S.M.P.F., 14 East 60th St., New York, NY 10022) Eds. H. Gwynne Vevers And Marcia A. Edwards. index. (also avail. in microfilm from UMI; back issues avail)
An international bibliography

BIOLOGY — Biological Chemistry

612.015 US
ADVANCES IN ANTIMICROBIAL AND ANTINEOPLASTIC CHEMOTHERAPY. 1973. irreg. $29.50. University Park Press, American Medical Publishers, Chamber of Commerce Bldg., Baltimore, MD 21202.

ADVANCES IN BIOCHEMICAL ENGINEERING. see ENGINEERING

ADVANCES IN CARBOHYDRATE CHEMISTRY AND BIOCHEMISTRY. see CHEMISTRY — Organic Chemistry

574.19 615 US ISSN 0065-2423
ADVANCES IN CLINICAL CHEMISTRY. 1958. irreg., vol. 20, 1978. price varies. Academic Press, Inc., 111 Fifth Ave., New York, NY 10003. Eds. Harry Sobotka, C. P. Stewart. index. cum.index: vols. 1-5(1958-1962) in vol. 5 (1962) (also avail. in microfiche) Indexed: Ind.Med.

ADVANCES IN COMPARATIVE PHYSIOLOGY AND BIOCHEMISTRY. see BIOLOGY — Physiology

574.192 US ISSN 0084-5930
ADVANCES IN CYCLIC NUCLEOTIDE RESEARCH. 1972. irreg., vol. 11, 1979. price varies. Raven Press, 1140 Ave. of the Americas, New York, NY 10036. Eds. Paul Greengard, G. Alan Robison. Indexed: Biol.Abstr. Chem.Abstr. Curr.Cont. Ind.Med.

574.192 US ISSN 0065-258X
ADVANCES IN ENZYMOLOGY AND RELATED AREAS OF MOLECULAR BIOLOGY. 1942. irreg., vol. 51, 1980. price varies. John Wiley & Sons, Inc., 605 Third Ave., New York, NY 10016. Ed. A. Meister. Indexed: Ind.Med.
Formerly: Advances in Enzymology and Related Subjects of Biochemistry.

574.192 US ISSN 0065-2849
ADVANCES IN LIPID RESEARCH. 1963. irreg., vol. 16, 1978. price varies. Academic Press, Inc., 111 Fifth Ave., New York, NY 10003. Eds. R. Paoletti, D. Kritchevsky. index. (also avail. in microfiche) Indexed: Ind.Med.

612.8 US ISSN 0098-6089
ADVANCES IN NEUROCHEMISTRY. 1975. irreg. price varies. Plenum Press, 233 Spring St., New York, NY 10013. Eds. B. W. Agranoff, M. H. Aprison. Indexed: Chem. Abstr.

612.015 US ISSN 0160-2179
ADVANCES IN POLYAMINE RESEARCH. 1978. irreg., vol. 2, 1978. Raven Press, 1140 Ave. of the Americas, New York, NY 10036. Indexed: Curr.Cont.

574.192 US ISSN 0065-3233
ADVANCES IN PROTEIN CHEMISTRY. 1944. a. price varies. Academic Press, Inc., 111 Fifth Ave., New York, NY 10003. Eds. M.L. Anson, John T. Edsall. index. cum.index: vols. 1-5 (1944-1949) in vol. 6 (1951)vols. 6-10 (1951-1955) in vol. 1 (1956) (also avail. in microfiche) Indexed: Ind.Med.

574.192 615 US
ADVANCES IN STEROID BIOCHEMISTRY AND PHARMACOLOGY (1978) 1970. irreg., vol. 6, 1978. Academic Press Inc., 111 Fifth Ave., New York, NY 10003. Eds. M. H. Briggs, G. A. Christie. Indexed: Ind.Med.
Former titles: Advances in Steroid Biochemistry; Advances in Steroid Biochemistry and Pharmacology (ISSN 0065-339X)

574.192 UK ISSN 0306-0004
AMINO-ACIDS, PEPTIDES AND PROTEINS. vol. 9, 1978. a. price varies. Chemical Society, Burlington House, London W1V OBN, England (Subscr. to: Blackhorse Road, Letchworth, Herts SG6 1HN, Eng.) Ed. Dr. R. C. Sheppard. charts. illus. index. Indexed: Chem.Abstr.

574.192 US ISSN 0066-4154
ANNUAL REVIEW OF BIOCHEMISTRY. 1932. a. $21. Annual Reviews Inc., 4139 El Camino Way, Palo Alto, CA 94306. Ed. Esmond E. Snell. bibl. index; cum.index. (back issues avail.; reprint service avail. from iSI) Indexed: Biol.Abstr. Ind.Med. M.M.R.I.

574 UK
ANNUAL REVIEW OF CLINICAL BIOCHEMISTRY. 1980. a. £12.50. John Wiley & Sons Ltd., Baffins Lane, Chichester, Sussex PO19 1UD, England. Ed. A. M. Goldberg. (reprint service avail. from UMI, ISI)

574.192 AT ISSN 0067-1703
AUSTRALIAN BIOCHEMICAL SOCIETY. PROCEEDINGS. 1968. a. Aus.$8. Australian Biochemical Society, c/o M. K. Gould, Biochemistry Dept., Monash University, Clayton, Victoria 3168, Australia. adv. circ. 1,400. Indexed: Curr.Cont.
Formerly: Australian Biochemical Society. Programme and Abstracts.

574.192 NE ISSN 0067-2734
B B A LIBRARY. (Biochemica & Biophysica Acta) 1963. irreg., vol. 14, 1978. price varies. Elsevier North-Holland Biomedical Press, Box 211, 1000 AE Amsterdam, Netherlands.

574.192 II
BIOCHEMICAL REVIEWS. (Text in English) vol. 43, 1972. a. Society of Biological Chemists, Dept. of Biochemistry, Indian Institute of Science, Bangalore 560012, India.

574.192 UK ISSN 0067-8694
BIOCHEMICAL SOCIETY SYMPOSIA. 1948. a. price varies. Academic Press Inc. (London) Ltd., 24-28 Oval Rd., London N.W. 1, England (And 111 Fifth Ave., New York, NY 10003) Indexed: Ind.Med.

574.192 US ISSN 0067-8678
BIOCHEMISTRY OF DISEASE. 1971. irreg., vol. 7, 1979. price varies. Marcel Dekker, Inc., 270 Madison Ave., New York, NY 10016.
Formerly: Biochemical Pathology.

574.192 541.39 UK ISSN 0301-0708
BIOSYNTHESIS. 1972. a. price varies. Chemical Society, Burlington House, London W1V OBN, England (Subscr. to: Blackhorse Road, Letchworth, Herts SG6 1HN, Eng) Ed. Dr. J. B. Bu'Lock. charts. illus. index. Indexed: Chem.Abstr.

574.192 US ISSN 0069-0732
CAROTENOIDS OTHER THAN VITAMIN A. (Text in English) 1967. irreg., 1972, 3rd. Cluj, Romania; price varies. (International Union of Pure and Applied Chemistry) Pergamon Press, Inc., Maxwell House, Fairview Park, Elmsford, NY 10523 (And Headington Hill Hall, Oxford OX3 OBW, England)

574.192 US ISSN 0069-3111
CHEMISTRY AND BIOCHEMISTRY OF AMINO ACIDS, PEPTIDES, AND PROTEINS. 1971. irreg., vol. 5, 1978. price varies. Marcel Dekker, Inc., 270 Madison Ave., New York, NY 10016. Ed. B. Weinstein.

574.192 612.015 543 US ISSN 0095-4861
CLINICAL AND BIOCHEMICAL ANALYSIS. 1974. irreg., vol. 8, 1978. price varies. Marcel Dekker, Inc., 270 Madison Ave., New York, NY 10016. Ed. M.K. Schwartz.

574.192 NE ISSN 0069-8032
COMPREHENSIVE BIOCHEMISTRY. 1962. irreg., vol. 34, 1979. price varies. Elsevier North-Holland Biomedical Press, Box 211, 1000 AE Amsterdam, Netherlands. Eds. L.L.M. van Deenen, A. Neuberger.

COMPUTERS IN CHEMICAL AND BIOCHEMICAL RESEARCH. see COMPUTER TECHNOLOGY AND APPLICATIONS

CONFERENCIAS DE BIOQUIMICA. see
BIOLOGY

612.015 SZ ISSN 0300-1725
CURRENT PROBLEMS IN CLINICAL
BIOCHEMISTRY. 1968. irreg. price varies. Verlag
Hans Huber, Laenggassstr. 76 und Marktgasse 9,
CH-3000 Berne 9, Switzerland (Dist. by Williams &
Wilkins Company, 428 E. Preston St., Baltimore,
MD 21202) Ed.Bd. Indexed: Ind.Med.
 Formerly: Aktuelle Probleme in der Klinischen
Biochemie (ISSN 0065-5597)

574.192 NE
DEVELOPMENTS IN BIOCHEMISTRY. 1978.
irreg., vol. 8, 1980. price varies. Elsevier North-
Holland Biomedical Press, Box 211, 1000 AE
Amsterdam, Netherlands.

574.192 US
ENZYMOLOGY SERIES. 1975. irreg., vol. 4, 1975.
Marcel Dekker, Inc., 270 Madison Ave., New York,
NY 10016.

574.192 UK ISSN 0071-1365
ESSAYS IN BIOCHEMISTRY. 1965. a. (Biochemical
Society (Book Depot)) Academic Press Inc.
(London) Ltd., 24-28 Oval Rd., London N.W.1,
England (and 111 Fifth Ave., New York, N.Y.
10003) Indexed: Ind.Med.

574.192 US ISSN 0071-4402
FEDERATION OF EUROPEAN BIOCHEMICAL
SOCIETIES. (PROCEEDINGS OF MEETING)
1964. irreg., 12th, 1978. Pergamon Press, Inc.,
Maxwell House, Fairview Park, Elmsford, NY
10523 (And Headington Hill Hall, Oxford OX3
0BW, England)

612.015 610 US
FRANKLIN MCLEAN MEMORIAL RESEARCH
INSTITUTE. ANNUAL REPORT. a. $4.50.
(Energy Research and Development Administration)
Franklin McLean Memorial Research Institute, 950
East 59th Street, Chicago, IL 60637. Ed. Elisabeth
F. Lanzl. bibl. circ. 500. (back issues avail.)
 Formerly: Arch Reports.

574.192 US
GESELLSCHAFT FUER BIOLOGISCHE CHEMIE,
MOSBACH. COLLOQUIUM. (Contributions in
German, English and French) 1951. irreg., no. 31,
1981. price varies. Springer-Verlag, 175 Fifth Ave.,
New York, NY 10010 (also Berlin, Heidelberg,
Vienna) (reprint service avail. from ISI)
 Formerly: Gesellschaft fuer Physiologische
Chemie, Mosbach. Colloquium (ISSN 0072-4246)

612.015 US
HARRY STEENBOCK SYMPOSIA. 1973. a. price
varies. University Park Press, American Medical
Publishers, Chamber of Commerce Bldg., Baltimore,
MD 21202.

574.192 574.191 US ISSN 0096-2708
HORIZONS IN BIOCHEMISTRY AND
BIOPHYSICS. 1974. irreg., vol. 5, 1978. price
varies. Addison-Wesley Publishing Co., Advanced
Book Program, Reading, MA 01867. Ed. Bd.
Indexed: Biol.Abstr. Chem.Abstr. Ind.Med.
Sci.Abstr.

547 619 US
HORMONAL PROTEINS AND PEPTIDES. 1973.
irreg. price varies. Academic Press, Inc., 111 Fifth
Avenue, New York, NY 10003. Ed. C. H. Li.

574.192 541.39 US ISSN 0538-5644
INTERNATIONAL COLLOQUIUM ON RAPID
MIXING AND SAMPLING TECHNIQUES
APPLICABLE TO THE STUDY OF
BIOCHEMICAL REACTIONS.
PROCEEDINGS.* 1964. irreg. Academic Press,
Inc., 111 Fifth Ave., New York, NY 10003.

574 UK
INTERNATIONAL CONFERENCE ON FIBROUS
PROTEINS. PROCEEDINGS. irreg., 4th, 1979,
Palmerston North, New Zealand. Academic Press
Inc.(London) Ltd., 24-28 Oval Rd., London NW1
7DX, England (And 111 Fifth Ave., New York, NY
10003)

574.192 JA ISSN 0074-3534
INTERNATIONAL CONGRESS OF
BIOCHEMISTRY. PROCEEDINGS. 1949.
triennial, 1967, 7th, Tokyo. $5. Japanese
Biochemical Society - Nihon Seikagakkai, c/o Japan
Academic Societies Centre, 2-4-16 Yayoi, Bunkyo-
ku, Tokyo 113, Japan.
 Proceedings published in host country

574.192 574.1 NE ISSN 0074-3690
INTERNATIONAL CONGRESS OF
HISTOCHEMISTRY AND CYTOCHEMISTRY.
PROCEEDINGS. 1960. quadrennial, 5th,
Bucharest. price varies. International Committee for
Histochemistry and Cytochemistry, c/o P. van
Duijn, Sec.-Gen., Dept. of Pathology,
Wassenaarseweg 62, Leiden, Netherlands.

574.192 UK ISSN 0074-4042
INTERNATIONAL CONGRESS ON CLINICAL
CHEMISTRY. ABSTRACTS. triennial, 11th, 1981,
Vienna. International Federation of Clinical
Chemistry, c/o P.M.G. Broughton, Sec., University
Department of Chemical Pathology, General
Infirmary, Leeds LS1 3EX, England. Ed. M. Roth.

574.192 UK ISSN 0074-4069
INTERNATIONAL CONGRESS ON CLINICAL
CHEMISTRY. PAPERS. triennial since 1963, 10th.
1978, Mexico City. International Federation of
Clinical Chemistry, c/o P.M.G. Broughton, Sec.,
University Department of Chemical Pathology,
General Infirmary, Leeds LS1 3EX, England.

574.192 UK ISSN 0074-4050
INTERNATIONAL CONGRESS ON CLINICAL
CHEMISTRY. PROCEEDINGS. triennial, 11th,
1981, Vienna. International Federation of Clinical
Chemistry, c/o P.M.G. Broughton, Sec., University
Department of Chemical Pathology, General
Infirmary, Leeds LS1 3EX, England. Ed. O.
Wieland.

574.192 SW ISSN 0074-7351
INTERNATIONAL PHOTOBIOLOGICAL
CONGRESS. PROCEEDINGS. 1954. quadrennial,
8th, 1980, France. price varies. International
Committee of Photobiology, c/o L. O. Bjorn,
Department of Plant Physiology, Fack, S-220 07
Lund, Sweden. circ. 2,000.

612.015 US ISSN 0147-7366
INTERNATIONAL REVIEW OF BIOCHEMISTRY.
1974. irreg. $29.50 per vol. University Park Press,
American Medical Publishers, Chamber of
Commerce Bldg., Baltimore, MD 21202.

574.192 612 US
INTERNATIONAL SERIES ON PURE AND
APPLIED BIOLOGY. BIOCHEMISTRY
DIVISION. 1959. irreg., 1971, vol. 6. price varies.
Pergamon Press, Inc., Maxwell House, Fairview
Park, Elmsford, NY 10523. index.
 Formerly: International Series of Monographs on
Pure and Applied Biology. Division: Biochemistry
(ISSN 0074-8269)

615.9 US
INTERNATIONAL SYMPOSIUM ON ANIMAL
AND PLANT TOXINS. PROCEEDINGS. irreg.,
2nd, Tel Aviv, 1970. $99 (3 vols.) Gordon and
Breach Science Publishers, 1 Park Ave., New York,
NY 10016. Eds. A. de Vries, E. Kochva. bibl. illus.

574.192 US
INTERNATIONAL SYMPOSIUM ON
ENVIRONMENTAL BIOGEOCHEMISTRY.
PROCEEDINGS. (In 3 vols.) 2nd, 1977. irreg., 3rd,
1978. Ann Arbor Science Publishers, Inc., Box
1425, Ann Arbor, MI 48106. Ed. Wolfgang E.
Krumbein.

574.192 541.28 NE ISSN 0075-3696
JERUSALEM SYMPOSIA ON QUANTUM
CHEMISTRY AND BIOCHEMISTRY. 1969. irreg.
price varies. (Israel Academy of Sciences and
Humanities, Section on Sciences, IS) D. Reidel
Publishing Co., Box 17, 3300 AA Dordrecht,
Netherlands (And Lincoln Building, 160 Old Derby
St., Hingham, MA 02043) Eds. E. D. Bergmann &
B. Pullman.

574.192 574.88 NE ISSN 0075-7535
LABORATORY TECHNIQUES IN
BIOCHEMISTRY AND MOLECULAR
BIOLOGY. (Text in English) 1968. irreg., vol. 8,
1979. price varies. Elsevier North-Holland
Biomedical Press, P.O. Box 211, 1000 AE
Amsterdam, Netherlands. Eds. T.S. Work, E. Work.

574.192 US ISSN 0076-6879
METHODS IN ENZYMOLOGY. 1955. irreg., vol.
62, 1979. price varies. Academic Press Inc., 111
Fifth Ave., New York, NY 10003. Eds. S. P.
Colowick, N. O. Kaplan. Indexed: Biol.Abstr.
Chem.Abstr. Ind. Med.

574.192 543 US ISSN 0076-6941
METHODS OF BIOCHEMICAL ANALYSIS. 1954.
irreg., vol. 26, 1980. price varies. John Wiley &
Sons, Inc., 605 Third Ave, New York, NY 10016.
Ed. David Glick. Indexed: Ind.Med. Math.R.
Comput.Rev.

MOLECULAR BIOLOGY, BIOCHEMISTRY AND
BIOPHYSICS. see *BIOLOGY — Cytology And
Histology*

541 UR
MOLEKULYARNAYA FIZIKA I BIOFIZIKA
VODNYKH SISTEM. 1973. irreg. 1.03 Rub.
Lenizdat, Fontanka, 59, Leningrad, U.S.S.R. illus.
 Supersedes: Struktura i Rol' Vody v Zhivom
Organizme (ISSN 0585-4393)

574.192 PL ISSN 0077-0485
MONOGRAFIE BIOCHEMICZNE. 1962. irreg. price
varies. (Polskie Towarzystwo Biochemiczne)
Panstwowe Wydawnictwo Naukowe, Miodowa 10,
Warsaw, Poland (Dist by Ars Polona-Ruch,
Krakowskie Przedmiescie 7, Warsaw, Poland) Ed.
Konstancja Raczynska-Bojanowska.

574 SZ ISSN 0077-0825
MONOGRAPHS IN DEVELOPMENTAL
BIOLOGY. (Text in English) 1969. irreg. (approx.
1/yr.) 100 Fr.($60) per vol. (1981 price) S. Karger
AG, Allschwilerstrasse 10, P.O. Box, CH-4009
Basel, Switzerland. Ed. A. Wolsky. (reprint service
avail. from ISI) Indexed: Biol.Abstr. Chem.Abstr.
Curr.Cont. Ind.Med.

574.19 612 US ISSN 0094-8950
MONOGRAPHS IN LIPID RESEARCH. 1974. irreg.
price varies. Plenum Press, 233 Spring St., New
York, NY 10013. Ed. David Kritchevsky.

MONOGRAPHS ON PHYSICAL BIOCHEMISTRY.
see *CHEMISTRY — Physical Chemistry*

OSAKA UNIVERSITY. INSTITUTE FOR PROTEIN
RESEARCH. MEMOIRS. see *CHEMISTRY —
Organic Chemistry*

574.192 US ISSN 0364-2801
P A A B S SYMPOSIUM SERIES. 1971. irreg. (Pan-
American Association of Biochemical Societies)
Academic Press, Inc., 111 Fifth Ave., New York,
NY 10003 (And Berkeley Square House, London
W.1, England) Indexed: Chem.Abstr.

PERSPECTIVES IN QUANTUM CHEMISTRY
AND BIOCHEMISTRY. see *CHEMISTRY*

574.192 547 US ISSN 0079-6077
PROGRESS IN BIO-ORGANIC CHEMISTRY.
1971. irreg., vol. 4, 1976. price varies. John Wiley &
Sons, Inc., 605 Third Ave, New York, NY 10016.
Eds. E. T. Kaiser, F. J. Kezdy.

574 GW ISSN 0079-6336
PROGRESS IN HISTOCHEMISTRY AND
CYTOCHEMISTRY. (Text in English, French,
German) 1970. irreg., vol. 13, 1980. price varies.
Gustav Fischer Verlag, Wollgrasweg 49, Postfach
720143, 7000 Stuttgart 70, W. Germany (B.R.D.)
Indexed: Ind.Med.

574.192 541.39 US ISSN 0079-7049
PROTEIN SYNTHESIS: A SERIES OF
ADVANCES. 1971. irreg., vol. 2, 1976. price
varies. Marcel Dekker, Inc., 270 Madison Ave.,
New York, NY 10016. Ed. H. E. McConkey.

591.192 US
RESEARCH METHODS IN NEUROCHEMISTRY.
1972. irreg. price varies. Plenum Press, 233 Spring
St., New York, NY 10013. Eds. Neville Marks,
Richard Rodnight. Indexed: Chem.Abstr.

BIOLOGY — BIOPHYSICS

574.192   US   ISSN 0163-7673
REVIEWS IN BIOCHEMICAL TOXICOLOGY. 1979. irreg., vol.2, 1980. Elsevier North-Holland, Inc., New York, 52 Vanderbilt Ave., New York, NY 10017.

REVIEWS OF PHYSIOLOGY, BIOCHEMISTRY AND EXPERIMENTAL PHARMACOLOGY. see *BIOLOGY — Physiology*

612.015   US
SELECTED PAPERS IN BIOCHEMISTRY. 1972. irreg. $16.50 per vol. University Park Press (Subsidiary of: American Medical Publishers) Chamber of Commerce Bldg., Baltimore, MD 21202.

574.192   II   ISSN 0300-0486
SOCIETY OF BIOLOGICAL CHEMISTS. PROCEEDINGS. (Text in English) a. Society of Biological Chemists, Dept. of Biochemistry, Indian Institute of Science, Bangalore 560012, India.

574.192   US   ISSN 0191-5622
SOLUBILITY DATA SERIES. 1979. irreg. $1200 for 18 vols. (International Union of Pure and Applied Chemistry) Pergamon Press, Inc., Journals Division, Maxwell House, Fairview Park, Elmsford, NY 10523 (And Headington Hill Hall, Oxford OX3 0BW, England) Ed.Prof. A. S. Kertes. (also avail. in microform from MIM,UMI; back issues avail.)

574.192   US
SUB-CELLULAR BIOCHEMISTRY. 1971. a. price varies. Plenum Press, 233 Spring St., New York, NY 10013. Ed. D. B. Roodyn. adv. bk. rev. charts. illus. index. Indexed: Biol.Abstr. Chem.Abstr. Curr.Cont. Ind.Med.

574   US   ISSN 0082-2523
TECHNIQUES OF BIOCHEMICAL AND BIOPHYSICAL MORPHOLOGY. 1972. irreg., vol. 3, 1977. John Wiley & Sons, Inc., 605 Third Ave., New York, NY 10016. Eds. D. Glick, R. M. Rosenbaum.
   Morphology

574.192   US
TOPICS IN BIOELECTROCHEMISTRY AND BIOENERGETICS. 1977. irreg., latest, 1980. price varies. John Wiley & Sons, Inc., 605 Third Ave., New York, NY 10016. Ed. G. Milazzo.

BIOLOGY — Biophysics

574.191 610   US   ISSN 0065-2245
ADVANCES IN BIOLOGICAL AND MEDICAL PHYSICS. 1948. irreg., vol, 16, 1978. price varies. Academic Press, Inc., 111 Fifth Ave., New York, NY 10003. Eds. John H. Lawrence., J. G. Hamilton. index. (also avail. in microfiche) Indexed: Ind.Med.

574.191   JA   ISSN 0065-227X
ADVANCES IN BIOPHYSICS. (Text in English) 1970. a. $14.50. (Biophysical Society of Japan) University of Tokyo Press, 7-3-1 Hongo, Bunkyo-ku, Tokyo 113-91, Japan (Dist. in U.S. by University Park Press, Chamber of Commerce Bldg., Baltimore, MD 21202) Ed. Masao Kotani. cum.index planned. circ. 1,400. Indexed: Ind.Med.

574.191   US   ISSN 0065-3292
ADVANCES IN RADIATION BIOLOGY. 1964. irreg., vol. 8, 1979. price varies. Academic Press, Inc., 111 Fifth Ave., New York, NY 10003. Ed. Bd. index. (also avail. in microfiche)

574.191   US   ISSN 0084-6589
ANNUAL REVIEW OF BIOPHYSICS AND BIOENGINEERING. 1972. a. $20. Annual Reviews Inc., 4139 El Camino Way, Palo Alto, CA 94306. Ed. Lorin J. Mullins. bibl. index: cum.index. (back issues avail.; reprint service avail. from ISI) Indexed: Biol.Abstr. Ind.Med. Sci.Abstr. M.M.R.I. Nucl.Sci.Abstr.

BIOMEKHANIKA/BIOMECHANICS. see *PHYSICS — Mechanics*

574.191 574   US   ISSN 0067-8910
BIOPHYSICAL SOCIETY. ABSTRACTS. 1958. a. included with subscr. to Biophysical Journal. Rockefeller University Press, 1230 York Ave., New York, NY 10021. (reprint service avail. from ISI, UMI)
   Supersedes: Biophysical Society. Symposium Proceedings (ISSN 0520-1985)

574.191   US   ISSN 0070-2129
CURRENT TOPICS IN BIOENERGETICS. 1966. irreg., vol. 8, 1978. price varies. Academic Press, Inc., 111 Fifth Ave., New York, NY 10003. Ed. D. R. Sanadi.
   Bioenergetics

574.191   JA
ELECTROPHYSIOLOGY/DENKI SEIRIGAKU. (Text in English) 1951. irreg. exchange basis. Showa University, School of Medicine, 1-5-8 Hatanodai, Shinagawa-ku, Tokyo 142, Japan.

574.191   US   ISSN 0073-0475
HARVARD BOOKS IN BIOPHYSICS. 1965. irreg., 1965, no. 1. price varies. ‡ (Harvard University Medical School, Department of Biophysics) Harvard University Press, 79 Garden St., Cambridge, MA 02138.

HORIZONS IN BIOCHEMISTRY AND BIOPHYSICS. see *BIOLOGY — Biological Chemistry*

574.191   II
INDIAN BIOPHYSICAL SOCIETY. PROCEEDINGS. irreg. Indian Biophysical Society, c/o Saha Institute of Nuclear Physics, 92 Acharya Prafulla Chandra Rd., Calcutta 700009, India.

INSTYTUT BADAN JADROWYCH. ZAKLAD RADIOBIOLOGII I OCHRONY ZDROWIA. PRACE DOSWIADCZAINE. see *MEDICAL SCIENCES — Radiology And Nuclear Medicine*

INTERNATIONAL CONFERENCE ON FIBROUS PROTEINS. PROCEEDINGS. see *BIOLOGY — Biological Chemistry*

INTERNATIONAL MONOGRAPHS ON ADVANCED BIOLOGY AND BIOPHYSICS. see *BIOLOGY*

574.875   US   ISSN 0160-2462
MEMBRANE TRANSPORT PROCESSES. 1978. irreg., no. 3, 1979. Raven Press, 1140 Ave. of the Americas, New York, NY 10036.

MOLECULAR BIOLOGY, BIOCHEMISTRY AND BIOPHYSICS. see *BIOLOGY — Cytology And Histology*

MOLEKULYARNAYA FIZIKA I BIOFIZIKA VODNYKH SISTEM. see *BIOLOGY — Biological Chemistry*

574.19   US
MONOGRAPHS IN QUANTITATIVE BIOPHYSICS. irreg. price varies. Physical Biological Sciences, Ltd., Publishing Division, Blacksburg, VA 24060.

574.191 574.87   US   ISSN 0301-374X
NEW TECHNIQUES IN BIOPHYSICS AND CELL BIOLOGY. 1973. irreg., latest, 1976. John Wiley & Sons, Inc., 605 Third Ave., New York, NY 10016. Ed. R. H. Pain, B. J. Smith.

NON-IONIZING RADIATION; r.f., microwaves, infra-red, lasers. see *MEDICAL SCIENCES — Radiology And Nuclear Medicine*

574.191   UK
PHOTOBIOLOGY BULLETIN. 1979. irreg. ‡ British Photobiology Society, Department of Zoology and Applied Entomology, Imperial College, London SW7 2BB, England. Ed. Dr. M.B.A. Djamgoz. bk. rev. circ. 300(controlled)

574.191   US   ISSN 0079-6107
PROGRESS IN BIOPHYSICS AND MOLECULAR BIOLOGY. 1950. 6/yr. $110. Pergamon Press, Inc., Journals Division, Maxwell House, Fairview Park, Elmsford, NY 10523 (And Headington Hill Hall, Oxford OX3 0BW, England) Ed. Dr. D. Noble. index. (also avail. in microform from MIM,UMI) Indexed: Appl.Mech.Rev. Ind.Med.

574.191   GE   ISSN 0081-6337
STUDIA BIOPHYSICA; internationale Zeitschrift fuer ausgewaehlte Gebiete der Biophysik. 1966. 8/yr. M.38.80 per no. (Gesellschaft fuer Physikalische und Mathematische Biologie der DDR) Akademie-Verlag, Leipziger Str. 3, 108 Berlin, E. Germany (D.D.R.) (Co-sponsor: Koordinierungszentrum fuer das RGW-Programm Biophysik) Eds. A. Rakow, G. Wangermann, L. P. Kayushin. bk. rev. (also avail. in microfiche) Indexed: Biol.Abstr. Chem.Abstr. Curr.Cont. Excerp.Med. Ref.Zh.

TECHNIQUES OF BIOCHEMICAL AND BIOPHYSICAL MORPHOLOGY. see *BIOLOGY — Biological Chemistry*

BIOLOGY — Botany

see also Agriculture—Crop Production and Soil; Forests and Forestry; Gardening and Horticulture

581   PL   ISSN 0065-0951
ACTA AGROBOTANICA. (Text in Polish and English; summaries in English, French or Polish) 1953. irreg., 1972, vol. 25. price varies. (Polskie Towarzystwo Botaniczne) Panstwowe Wydawnictwo Naukowe, Miodowa 10, Warszaw, Poland. Eds. J. Lekczynska, Z. Starck, A. Gajewska.

581   SP
ACTA BOTANICA BARCINONENSIA. (Text in various languages) 1964. irreg. exchange basis. ‡ Universidad de Barcelona, Facultad de Biologia, Departamento de Botanica, Barcelona, Spain. circ. 1,000.
   Supersedes(since 1978): Acta Geobotanica Barcinonensia (ISSN 0065-1222)

581   CU
ACTA BOTANICA CUBA. irreg. Academia de Ciencias de Cuba, Instituto de Botanica, Industria 452, Havana, Cuba. bibl. illus.

ACTA BOTANICA HORTI BUCURESTIENSIS. see *GARDENING AND HORTICULTURE*

581   CS
ACTA BOTANICA SLOVACA. irreg. price varies. (Slovenska Akademia Vied) Veda, Publishing House of the Slovak Academy of Sciences, Klemensova 19, 895 30 Bratislava, Czechoslovakia.
   Formerly: Acta Botanica; Acta Instituti Botanici.

581   VE   ISSN 0084-5906
ACTA BOTANICA VENEZUELICA. (Text and summaries in Spanish and English) 1965. irreg. price varies. Ministerio de Agricultura y Cria, Instituto Botanico, Apartado 2156, Caracas, Venezuela. Ed. Dr. Tobias Lasser. charts. illus. circ. 1,000. (processed) Indexed: Biol.Abstr.

581.9   SW   ISSN 0084-5914
ACTA PHYTOGEOGRAPHICA SUECICA. (Text and summaries in English, German or Swedish) 1929. irreg., vol.66, 1979. price varies. Svenska Vaextgeografiska Saellskapet - Swedish Society of Plant Geography, c/o Vaextbiologiska Institutionen, Box 559, 751 22 Uppsala, Sweden. Ed. Erik Sjoegren.

581   GW   ISSN 0065-1567
ACTA PHYTOMEDICA; Beihefte zur Phytopathologischen Zeitschrift. (Text in German or English; summaries in English and German) 1973. irreg. price varies. Verlag Paul Parey (Berlin), Lindenstr. 44-47, 1000 Berlin 61, W. Germany (B.R.D.)

581   SW   ISSN 0347-4917
ACTA REGIAE SOCIETATIS SCIENTIARUM ET LITTERARUM GOTHOBURGENSIS. BOTANICA. 1972. irreg. price varies. Goeteborgs Kungliga Vetenskaps- och Vitterhets-Samhaelle, c/o Goeteborgs Universitetsbibliotek, Box 5096, S-402 22 Goeteborg 5, Sweden (Dist. in U.S., Canada, and Mexico by: Humanities Press, Inc., 171 First Ave., Atlantic Highlands, NJ 07716)
   Supersedes in part: Goeteborgs Kungliga Vetenskaps- och Vitterhets-Samhaelle. Handlingar.

BIOLOGY — BOTANY

581	UK	ISSN 0065-2296
ADVANCES IN BOTANICAL RESEARCH. 1963. irreg. price varies. Academic Press Inc. (London) Ltd., 24-28 Oval Rd., London N.W1, England (U.S. Subscr. to: Academic Press Inc., 111 Fifth Ave., New York, NY 10003) Ed. R. D. Preston.

581	II
ADVANCES IN SPORE POLLEN RESEARCH. vol. 3, 1978. a. $16. Today and Tomorrow's Printers and Publishers, 24-B/5 Original Rd., Karol Bagh, New Delhi 110005, India (Dist. in U.S. by: Indo Americana Literature House, Box 1276, Globe, AZ 85501) Ed. P.K.K. Nair.

AGRONOMIA MOCAMBICANA. see *AGRICULTURE*

630	PL	ISSN 0082-1233
AKADEMIA ROLNICZA, SZCZECIN. ZESZYTY NAUKOWE. 1958. irreg., vol. 4, 1975. price varies. Akademia Rolnicza, Szczecin, Janoska 8, 71-424 Szczecin, Poland (Dist. by: Ars Polona-Ruch, Krakowskie Przedmiescie 7, Warsaw, Poland)

581	US	ISSN 0065-6275
ALISO. 1948. a. $7.50. Rancho Santa Ana Botanic Garden, Claremont, CA 91711. Ed. R. K. Benjamin. index published on completion of ea. vol. circ. 550. Indexed: Biol.Abstr.

581	US
ALLERTONIA; a series of occasional papers. 1975. irreg. price varies. Pacific Tropical Botanical Garden, Box 340, Lawai, HI 96765. Ed. Dr. Albert C. Smith.

580	IT	ISSN 0065-6429
ALLIONIA. (Text in Italian; summaries in English) 1952. a. (Istituto Botanico di Torino) Levrotto e Bella, Universita di Torino, Corso Vittorio Emanuele 28, 10125 Turin, Italy. circ. 500. Indexed: Biol.Abstr. Mycol.Abstr.

581 632	US	ISSN 0569-6992
AMERICAN PHYTOPATHOLOGICAL SOCIETY. MONOGRAPHS. 1961. irreg., latest 1980. price varies. American Phytopathological Society, 3340 Pilot Knob Rd., St. Paul, MN 55121.

580	IO	ISSN 0517-8452
ANNALES BOGORIENSES; journal of tropical general botany. (Text in English) 1950. irreg., vol. 7, no. 1, 1979. price varies. Treub Laboratory - Pusat Penelitian Botani, c/o Kebun Raya, Bogor, Indonesia. Eds. S. Saono, S. Sastrapradja, I. Lubis. charts. illus. circ. 315. Indexed: Biol.Abstr. Chem.Abstr. Field Crop Abstr.

581 632	US	ISSN 0066-4286
ANNUAL REVIEW OF PHYTOPATHOLOGY. 1963. a. $20. Annual Reviews Inc., 4139 El Camino Way, Palo Alto, CA 94306. Ed. R.G. Grogan. bibl. index; cum.index. (back issues avail.; reprint service avail. from ISI) Indexed: Biol.Abstr. Chem.Abstr. M.M.R.I. World Agri.Econ. & Rural Sociol.Abstr.

581	US	ISSN 0066-4294
ANNUAL REVIEW OF PLANT PHYSIOLOGY. 1950. a. $20. Annual Reviews Inc., 4139 El Camino Way, Palo Alto, CA 94306. Ed. Dr. Winslow Briggs. bibl. index; cum.index. (back issues avail.; reprint service avail. from ISI) Indexed: Biol.Abstr. Chem.Abstr. M.M.R.I.

582	PL	ISSN 0066-5878
ARBORETUM KORNICKIE. (Text in English and Polish; summaries in English and Russian) 1955. a. price varies. (Polska Akademia Nauk, Zaklad Dendrologii) Panstwowe Wydawnictwo Naukowe, Miodowa 10, Warsaw, Poland (Dist. by Ars Polona-Ruch, Krakowskie Przedmiescie 7, Warsaw, Poland) (Co-sponsor: Arboretum Kornickie) Ed. Stefan Bialobok. bibl. charts. illus.
Formerly: Kornik, Poland. Zaklad Dendrologii i Pomologii. Prace.

581	FR	ISSN 0066-8184
ARVERNIA BIOLOGICA: BOTANIQUE; recueil des travaux des laboratoires de botanique de la Faculte des Sciences de Clermont-Ferrand et de la Station Biologique de Besse. 1930. irreg.(approx. a. since 1964) available only on exchange. Universite de Clermont-Ferrand II, Laboratoire de Biologie Vegetale, 4, rue Ledru, F-63038 Clermont-Ferrand, France. Ed.Bd.

551.5	FI
ATLAS FLORAE EUROPAEAE. (Text in English) 1972. irreg, vol. 3, 1976. Societas Biologica Fennica Vanamo, Snellmaninkatu 9-11, SF-00170 Helsinki 17, Finland (Subscr. to Akateeminen Kirjakauppa (Academic Bookstore), Keskuskatu 1, SF-00100 Helsinki 10, Finland or Tieto Ltd., 5 Elton Rd., Clevedon, Avon BS21 7RA, England) (Co-sponsor: Committee for Mapping the Flora of Europe) Eds. Jaakko Jalas, Juha Suominen.

581	PL	ISSN 0067-0294
ATLAS FLORY POLSKIEJ I ZIEM OSCIENNYCH. (Text in Polish and Latin) 1960. irreg., 1975, vol. 2, no. 4. price varies. (Polska Akademia Nauk, Instytut Botaniki) Panstwowe Wydawnictwo Naukowe, Miodowa 10, Warsaw, Poland. Ed. J. Madalski.

580	PL	ISSN 0067-0324
ATLAS ROZMIESZCZENIA DRZEW I KRZEWOW W POLSCE. (Text in Polish, English and Russian) 1963. irreg., 1976, no. 18. price varies. (Polska Akademia Nauk, Zaklad Dendrologii) Panstwowe Wydawnictwo Naukowe, Ul. Miodowa 10, Warsaw, Poland (Dist. by Ars Polona-Ruch, Krakowskie Przedmiescie 7, Warsaw, Poland) Ed. Kazimierz Browicz.

581	AT	ISSN 0067-1924
AUSTRALIAN JOURNAL OF BOTANY. 1953. bi-m. Aus.$50. C. S. I. R. O., 314 Albert St., E. Melbourne, Victoria 3002, Australia. Ed. L. W. Martinelli. circ. 1,750. (also avail. in microfiche) Indexed: Biol. & Agr.Ind. Curr.Cont.

581	PL	ISSN 0067-2815
BADANIA FIZJOGRAFICZNE NAD POLSKA ZACHODNIA. SERIA B. BIOLOGIA. (Text in Polish; summaries in English, French or German) 1948. irreg., vol. 27, 1974. price varies. (Poznanskie Towarzystwo Przyjaciol Nauk) Panstwowe Wydawnictwo Naukowe, Ul. Miodowa 10, Warsaw, Poland (Dist. by Ars Polona-Ruch, Krakowskie Przedmiescie 7, Warsaw, Poland) Ed. Jan Rafalski.

581 635	US	ISSN 0005-4003
BAILEYA; a journal of horticultural taxonomy. 1953. irreg., latest 1979. $7.50 per vol. or exchange. L. H. Bailey Hortorium, Cornell University, Ithaca, NY 14853. Ed. W. J. Dress. bk. rev. bibl. charts. illus. index. circ. 600. (also avail. in microform from UMI) Indexed: Biol.Abstr.

581	US
BARLEY GENETICS NEWSLETTER; an international communication medium. 1971. a. $5. ‡ Colorado State University, Department of Agronomy, c/o T. Tsuchiya, Ed., Fort Collins, CO 80521. circ. 600(controlled)

581	US	ISSN 0198-7356
BARTONIA. a. price varies. Philadelphia Botanical Club, c/oAcademy of Natural Sciences of Philadelphia, 19tth St. and the Parkway, Philadelphia, PA 19103.

581	SZ	ISSN 0067-4605
BAUHINIA. (Text Mainly in German; occasionally in English, French and Italian) 1955. irreg., vol. 6, 1977. 60 Fr. (Basler Botanische Gesellschaft) Verlag Wepf und Co., Eisengasse 5, 4001 Basel, Switzerland. Ed. R. Leuschner. circ. 500.

581	GW	ISSN 0373-7640
BAYERISCHE BOTANISCHE GESELLSCHAFT. BERICHTE. 1891. a. price varies. ‡ Bayerische Botanische Gesellschaft, Menzinger Str. 67, 8000 Munich 19, W. Germany (B.R.D.) Ed. Wolfgang Lippert. bk. rev. circ. 900. Indexed: Biol.Abstr. Excerp.Bot.

BEITRAEGE ZUR NATURKUNDLICHEN FORSCHUNG IN SUEDWESTDEUTSCHLAND. see *EARTH SCIENCES — Geology*

581.08	NE
BELMONTIA. N.S. 1974. irreg, vol. 9, 1978. exchange basis. Landbouwhogeschool, Laboratory of Plant Taxonomy and Geography - State Agricultural University, Generaal Foulkesweg 37, Wageningen, Netherlands.

581	GW
BIBLIOGRAPHIA PHYTOSOCIOLOGICA SYNTAXONOMICA. 1971. irreg. (2-8 nos./yr.) price varies. J. Cramer, In den Springaeckern 2, 3300 Braunschweig, W. Germany (B.R.D.) Ed. R. Tuexen.

581	GW	ISSN 0067-7892
BIBLIOTHECA BOTANICA; Originalabhandlungen aus dem Gesamtgebiet der Botanik. 1886. irreg., no. 133, 1977. price varies. E. Schweizerbart'sche Verlagsbuchhandlung, Johannesstr. 3A, 7000 Stuttgart 1, W. Germany (B.R.D.) Ed. H. Melchior.

589.2	GW	ISSN 0067-8066
BIBLIOTHECA MYCOLOGICA. 1967. irreg., no. 55, 1977. price varies. J. Cramer, In den Springaeckern 2, 3300 Braunschweig, W. Germany (B.R.D.) circ. 200-400.

581	GW	ISSN 0067-8112
BIBLIOTHECA PHYCOLOGICA. 1967. irreg., no. 29, 1977. price varies. J. Cramer, In den Springaeckern 2, 3300 Braunschweig, W. Germany (B.R.D.) circ. 200-400.

BIOLOGICAL SOCIETY OF WASHINGTON. PROCEEDINGS. see *BIOLOGY*

581	SW	ISSN 0068-0370
BOTANICA GOTHOBURGENSIA. (Subseries of Acta Universitatis Gothoburgensis) (Text in English, German, Norwegian, Swedish) 1963. irreg., no. 7, 1978. price varies; also exchange basis. Acta Universitatis Gothoburgensis, Box 5096, S-402 22 Goeteborg 5, Sweden (Dist. in U. S., Canada, and Mexico by: Humanities Press, Inc., 171 First Ave., Atlantic Highlands, NJ 07716) Eds. Gunnar Harling, Tore Levring, Hemmming Virgin.

580	US
BOTANICAL MONOGRAPHS. irreg. price varies. University of California Press, 2223 Fulton St., Berkeley, CA 94720.

581	US	ISSN 0006-8098
BOTANICAL MUSEUM LEAFLETS. 1932. irreg.(10 nos. to vol.) $20 per vol. ‡ Harvard University, Botanical Museum, Cambridge, MA 02138. Ed. Richard Evans Schultes. illus. index to each vol.(approx. 2 years) circ. 275. Indexed: Biol.Abstr. Chem.Abstr.
Plants useful or hostile to man

581	US
BOTANICAL SOCIETY OF AMERICA. DIRECTORY. biennial. $8. Botanical Society of America Inc., c/o School of Biological Sciences, University of Kentucky, Lexington, KY 40506.
Formerly: Botanical Society of America. Yearbook (ISSN 0068-0400)

581	UK
BOTANICAL SOCIETY OF EDINBURGH TRANSACTIONS. 1836. a. £5 to non-members. Botanical Society of Edinburgh, Royal Botanic Garden, Inverleith Row, Edinburgh EH3 5LR, Scotland. Ed. G. Hadley. bibl. charts. illus. circ. 450. Indexed: Biol.Abstr.
Until vol. 40, 1970: Botanical Society of Edinburgh. Transactions and Proceedings.

581	II
BOTANICAL SURVEY OF INDIA. OCCASIONAL PUBLICATIONS. irreg. price varies. Botanical Survey of India, P.O. Botanic Garden, Howrah 71103, India.

581	SA
BOTANICAL SURVEY OF SOUTH AFRICA. MEMOIRS. 1919. irreg., no. 42, 1978. (Botanical Survey of South Africa) Botanical Research Institute, Department of Agricultural Technical Services, Privage Bag X101, Pretoria 0001, South Africa.

581	SA	ISSN 0006-8241
BOTHALIA. 1924. irreg., vol. 12, no. 3, 1978. R.7.50. Botanical Research Institute, Department of Agricultural Technical Services - Navorsingsinstituut vir Plantkunde, Private Bag X101, Pretoria 0001, South Africa. Ed. Dr. D. J. B. Killick. illus. index. circ. 250. Indexed: Biol.Abstr. Excerp.Bot.

581	US
BOYCE THOMPSON INSTITUTE FOR PLANT RESEARCH. ANNUAL REPORT. 1971, no. 48. a. free. Boyce Thompson Institute for Plant Research, Tower Rd., Cornell University, Ithaca, NY 14853. Ed. D. C. Torgeson. charts. illus. circ. 1,000.

581 BL ISSN 0084-800X
BRADEA. (Text in Latin, Portuguese, English; summaries in English) 1969. irreg. $25. Herbarium Bradeanum, C.P. 15005-ZC-06, 2000 Rio de Janeiro-RJ, Brazil. illus. indexes. circ. 400(controlled) Indexed: Ash.G.Bot.Per.

581 UK ISSN 0068-2292
BRITISH MUSEUM (NATURAL HISTORY) BULLETIN. BOTANY. 1951. irreg. price varies. British Museum (Natural History), Cromwell Rd., London SW7 5BD, England. index. circ. 750. Indexed: Biol.Abstr.

581 UK ISSN 0301-9195
BRITISH PTERIDOLOGICAL SOCIETY. BULLETIN. 1973. a. £3.50 to non-members. British Pteridological Society, 46 Sedley Rise, Loughton, Essex 1G10 1LT, England. Ed. M. H. Rickard. bk. rev. circ. 700.
Supersedes: British Pteridological Society. Newsletter (ISSN 0068-2403)

581 BU ISSN 0068-3655
BULGARSKA AKADEMIIA NA NAUKITE. BOTANICHESKI INSTITUT. IZVESTIIA. (Summaries in various languages) 1950. a. 2.65 lv. Publishing House of the Bulgarian Academy of Sciences, Ul. Akad. G. Bonchev, 1113 Sofia, Bulgaria (Dist. by: Hemus, 6, Rouski Blvd., 1000 Sofia, Bulgaria) Ed. D. Iordanov. circ. 650.

582 AU ISSN 0068-421X
BUNDESANSTALT FUER PFLANZENBAU UND SAMENPRUEFUNG, VIENNA. JAHRBUCH. (Text in German; summaries in German & English) 1948. a. price varies. Bundesanstalt fuer Pflanzenbau und Samenpruefung, Alliierten Str. 1, Postfach 64, A-1201 Vienna, Austria. Ed. R. Meinx. index; cum.index. circ. 750.

581 CN ISSN 0068-7987
CANADA. NATIONAL MUSEUMS, OTTAWA. PUBLICATIONS IN BOTANY/CANADA. MUSEES NATIONAUX. PUBLICATIONS DE BOTANIQUE. (Text in English and French) 1969. irreg. price varies, some free. (National Museum of Natural Sciences) National Museums of Canada, Ottawa, Ont. K1A OM8, Canada. Indexed: Biol.Abstr. Forest.Abstr.

581 CN ISSN 0068-9440
CANADIAN PHYTOPATHOLOGICAL SOCIETY. PROCEEDINGS. 1929. a. Can.$4. ‡ Canadian Phytopathological Society, c/o Dr. R. J. Copeman, Department of Plant Science, University of British Columbia, Vancouver, B.C. V6T 1W5, Canada. Ed. Dr. H. Harding. circ. 700-800. Indexed: Chem.Abstr. Helminthol.Abstr. Rev.Appl.Mycol. Rev.Plant Path.

581 NZ
CANTERBURY BOTANICAL SOCIETY. JOURNAL. 1968. a. price varies. Canterbury Botanical Society, P.O.B. 2443, Christchurch, New Zealand. Ed. John Thompson.

581 US
CAREERS IN BOTANY. 1965. irreg., latest 1978. $0.25. Botanical Society of America Inc., c/o School of Biological Sciences, University of Kentucky, Lexington, KY 40506.
Formerly: Botanical Society of America. Miscellaneous Publications; Formerly: Botany as a Profession (ISSN 0068-0397)

581 CK
CATALOGO ILUSTRADO DE LAS PLANTAS DE CUNDINAMARCA. 1966. irreg. $6 or exchange basis. Universidad Nacional de Colombia, Instituto de Ciencias Naturales, Apdo. 7495, Bogota, Colombia. Ed. Polidoro Pinto-Escobar. bibl. illus. circ. 1,000. Indexed: Biol.Abstr. Bull.Signal.

589 NE
CENTRAALBUREAU VOOR SCHIMMELCULTURES. LIST OF CULTURES. (Text in English) 1909. irreg., 29th ed., 1978. fl.25. Centraalbureau voor Schimmelcultures, Oosterstraat 1, Box 273, 3740 AG Baarn, Netherlands. (also avail. in microfiche)
Mycology

581 CK
CESPEDESIA; boletin cientifico del Departamento del Valle del Cauca. (Text in French, Spanish, summaries in English) irreg. $50. Departamento del Valle del Cauca, Cali, Colombia. illus.

581 US
CHEMIE DER PFLANZENSCHUTZ- UND SCHAEDLINGSBEKAEMPFUNGSMITTEL. 1970. irreg., vol. 6, 1981. price varies. Springer-Verlag, 175 Fifth Ave., New York, NY 10010 (Also Berlin, Heidelberg, Vienna) Ed. R. Wegler. (reprint service avail. from ISI)

581 SP ISSN 0010-0730
COLLECTANEA BOTANICA. (Text in various languages) 1946. irreg. (1-2/yr) Institut Botanic de Barcelona, Parc de Montjuic, Avinguda Dels Muntanyans, Barcelona 4, Spain. bk. rev. bibl.

581 GW
COLLOQUES PHYTOSOCIOLOGIQUES. (Text in French) 1975. irreg., no. 6, 1978. price varies. J. Cramer, In den Springaeckern 2, 3300 Braunschweig, W. Germany (B.R.D.) Ed.J.-M. Gehu. charts. illus. (back issues avail.)

581 UK ISSN 0069-7141
COMMONWEALTH MYCOLOGICAL INSTITUTE. PHYTOPATHOLOGICAL PAPERS. 1956. irreg. price varies. ‡ (Commonwealth Mycological Institute) Commonwealth Agricultural Bureaux, Farnham House, Farnham Royal, Slough SL2 3BN, England.

COMMONWEALTH SCIENTIFIC AND INDUSTRIAL RESEARCH ORGANIZATION. DIVISION OF TROPICAL CROPS AND PASTURES. TECHNICAL PAPER. see *AGRICULTURE — Crop Production And Soil*

581 RM ISSN 0069-9616
CONTRIBUTII BOTANICE. 1958. a. exchange basis only. Universitatea Babes-Bolyai, Gradina Botanica, Str. Republicii nr. 42, Cluj-Napoca, Romania.

581 DK ISSN 0011-6211
DANSK BOTANISK ARKIV. (Text in English) 1913 irreg. Kr.12 per 10 pages; price varies per issue. Dansk Botanisk Forening - Danish Botanical Society, Oe. Farimagsgade 2 D, DK-1353 Copenhagen K, Denmark. Ed. Morten Lange. charts. illus. index. Indexed: Biol.Abstr.

581 GW ISSN 0070-6728
DISSERTATIONES BOTANICAE. 1967. irreg., no. 39, 1977. price varies. J. Cramer, In den Springaeckern 2, 3300 Braunschweig, W. Germany (B.R.D.) Ed. J. Cramer. circ. 500.

581 GW
DOCUMENTS PHYTOSOCIOLOGIQUES. NOUVELLE SERIE. (Text in French) 1977. irreg., no. 3, 1978. price varies. J. Cramer, In den Springaeckern 2, 3300 Braunschweig, W. Germany (B.R.D.) Ed.J.-M. Gehu. illus. (back issues avail.)

581 BE
DUMORTIERA. 1975. irreg., no. 10, 1978. 150 Fr. Jardin Botanique National de Belgique, Domaine de Bouchout, B-1860 Meise, Belgium.

581 UA
EGYPTIAN JOURNAL OF PHYTOPATHOLOGY. (Text in English; summaries in English and Arabic) 1969. a. £E50($3.50) (Egyptian Phytopathological Society, Research Department) National Information and Documentation Centre, 24 Sharia Sherif Pasha, Dokki, Cairo, Egypt. Ed. Abbas F. el-Helaly. circ. 2,000.

581.1 US
ENCYCLOPEDIA OF PLANT PHYSIOLOGY. NEW SERIES. 1975. irreg., vol. 9, 1980. $51.90. Springer Verlag, 175 Fifth Ave., New York, NY 10010 (And Berlin, Heidelberg, Vienna) Eds. A. Pirson, M. H. Zimmermann. (reprint service avail. from ISI)

631.5 581 NE ISSN 0071-2221
EUCARPIA. Represents: European Association for Research on Plant Breeding. Report of the Congress. 1956. triennial, 1974, 7th,Budapest, Hungary. price varies. European Association for Research on Plant Breeding., Secretariat, P.O. Box 128, NL-6140 Wageningen, Netherlands.
1971, 6th, Cambridge, Eng.

581 GW ISSN 0014-4037
EXCERPTA BOTANICA. SECTIO A: TAXONOMICA ET CHOROLOGICA. (Text in English, French and German) 1959. irreg., 7 nos. per vol. DM.178 per vol. Gustav Fischer Verlag, Wollgrasweg 49, Postfach 720143, 7000 Stuttgart 70, W. Germany (B.R.D.) Ed. Frau Follmann-Schrag. adv. bk. rev. cum.index. circ. 550.

581 US ISSN 0071-3392
EXPERIMENTAL BOTANY; AN INTERNATIONAL SERIES OF MONOGRAPHS. 1964. irreg., vol. 13, 1977. price varies. Academic Press Inc., 111 Fifth Ave., New York, NY 10003. Ed. J. F. Sutcliffe.

FAUNA & FLORA. see *CONSERVATION*

581 UK ISSN 0308-0838
FERN GAZETTE. 1909. a. £5 to non-members. British Pteridological Society, 46 Sedley Rise, Loughton, Essex 1G10 1LT, England. Ed. C. N. Page. index. circ. 700.
Formerly (to 1974): British Fern Gazette (ISSN 0524-5826)

500.9 EC ISSN 0015-380X
FLORA. (Text in English and Spanish) 1937. irreg. exchange basis. Instituto Ecuatoriano de Ciencias Naturales, Apartado 408, Quito, Ecuador. Ed. Dr. M. Acosta-Solis. bk. rev. abstr. bibl. charts. illus. circ. 2,000. Indexed: Biol.Abstr.

581 BL ISSN 0071-5751
FLORA ECOLOGICA DE RESTINGAS DO SUDESTE DO BRASIL. 1960. irreg., 1978, no. 23. exchange only. Museu Nacional, Quinta da Boa Vista, 20940 Rio de Janeiro, RJ, Brazil. bibl. illus.

581 GW ISSN 0071-576X
FLORA ET VEGETATIO MUNDI. (Text in English, French and German) 1960. irreg., no. 6, 1977. price varies. J. Cramer, In den Springaeckern 2, 3300 Braunschweig, W. Germany (B.R.D.) Ed. R. Tuexen. circ. 100.

581 NE ISSN 0071-5786
FLORA MALESIANA. SERIES 2: PTERIDOPHYTA. (Text in English) 1959. irreg. price varies. (Foundation Flora Malesiana) Sijthoff & Noordhoff International Publishers b.v., Box 4, 2400 MA Alphen aan den Rijn, Netherlands (Avail. from Foundation at: Schelpenkade 6, Leiden, Netherlands; U.S. Address: 20010 Century Blvd., Germantown, MD 20767) (Co-sponsor: Rijksherbarium) Ed. R. E. Holltum. index. circ. 1,300.

581 US ISSN 0071-5794
FLORA NEOTROPICA. MONOGRAPHS. 1968. irreg., latest no. 25, 1980. price varies. (Organization for Flora Neotropica) New York Botanical Garden, Bronx, NY 10458. (back issues avail.)

581 SW
FLORA OF ECUADOR. (Text in English) 1973. irreg. price varies. Naturvetenskapliga Forskningsraadet, Box 23136, S-104 35 Stockholm, Sweden. (Co-sponsor: Lund Botanical Society) Eds. Gunnar Harling, Benkt Sparre. Indexed: Biol.Abstr.
Formerly: Opera Botanica. Series B. Flora of Ecuador.

581 AT ISSN 0077-8761
FLORA OF NEW SOUTH WALES. 1961. irreg. exchange basis. ‡ National Herbarium, Royal Botanic Gardens, Sydney, N.S.W. 2000, Australia. Ed. D. J. McGillivray. Indexed: Biol.Abstr.
Formerly until 1971: New South Wales. National Herbarium. Contributions.

581 IS
FLORA OF THE U.S.S.R. (Text in English) irreg. Israel Program for Scientific Translations, Box 7145, Jerusalem, Israel (U.S. Distributor: International Scholarly Book Services, Inc., 10300 S.W. Allen Blvd., Beaverton, OR 97005)

581 PL ISSN 0071-5816
FLORA POLSKA; ROSLINY NACZYNIOWE POLSKI I ZIEM OSCIENNYCH. 1927. irreg., 1971, vol. 13. price varies. (Polska Akademia Nauk, Instytut Botaniki) Panstwowe Wydawnictwo Naukowe, Miodowa 10, Warsaw, Poland (Dist. by Ars Polona-Ruch, Krakowskie Przedmiescie 7, Warsaw, Poland)

581   PL   ISSN 0071-5824
FLORA POLSKA: ROSLINY ZARODNIKOWE POLSKI I ZIEM OSCIENNYCH. 1957. irreg., 1970, vol. IV. price varies. Polska Akademia Nauk, Instytut Botaniki, Lubicz 46, Krakow, Poland.

581   PL   ISSN 0071-5840
FLORA SLODKOWODNA POLSKI. 1963. irreg., 1969, vol. 11. price varies. Polska Akademia Nauk, Instytut Botaniki, Lubicz 46, Krakow, Poland. Ed. Karol Starmach.

581   BE
FLORE D'AFRIQUE CENTRALE (ZAIRE-RWANDA-BURUNDI) (Issued in several subseries) irreg. price varies. Jardin Botanique National de Belgique - Nationale Plantentuin van Belgie, Domaine de Bouchout, B-1860 Meise, Belgium. Ed. P. Bamps.
Formerly: Flore du Congo, du Rwanda et du Burundi.

581   FR   ISSN 0430-666X
FLORE DE LA NOUVELLE CALEDONIE ET DEPENDANCES. 1967. irreg., no. 9, 1980. Museum National d'Histoire Naturelle, Laboratoire de Phanerogamie, 16 rue Buffon, 75005 Paris, France. Eds. A. Le Thomas, N. Halle.

581   FR
FLORE DE MADAGASCAR ET DES COMORES. 1937. irreg. Museum National d'Histoire Naturelle, Laboratoire de Phanerogamie, 16 rue de Buffon, 75005 Paris, France. Eds. A. Le Thomas, F. Badre.

581   FR   ISSN 0071-5867
FLORE DU CAMBODGE, DU LAOS ET DU VIETNAM. 1960. irreg., 1977, no. 16. price varies. Museum National d'Histoire Naturelle, Laboratoire de Phanerogamie, 16 rue Buffon, 75005 Paris, France. Eds. J. Raynal & J. Vidal.

581   FR   ISSN 0071-5875
FLORE DU CAMEROUN. 1963. irreg., no. 20, 1977. price varies. Museum National d'Histoire Naturelle, Laboratoire de Phanerogamie, 16 rue Buffon, 75005 Paris, France. Eds. J. Raynal & C. Cusset.

581   FR   ISSN 0071-5883
FLORE DU GABON. 1961. irreg. price varies. Museum National d'Histoire Naturelle, Laboratoire de Phanerogamie, 16 rue Buffon, 75005 Paris, France. Eds. J. Raynal & J. Floret.

581 630   US   ISSN 0071-5948
FLORIDA. DIVISION OF PLANT INDUSTRY. BIENNIAL REPORT. 1916. biennial. one copy free to Florida residents. ‡ Department of Agriculture and Consumer Services, Division of Plant Industry, P.O. Box 1269, Gainesville, FL 32602. circ. 3,000.

581   SA   ISSN 0015-4504
FLOWERING PLANTS OF AFRICA. (Text in Afrikaans and English) 1921. a. R.10. ‡ Botanical Research Institute, Department of Agricultural Technical Services - Navorsingsinstituut vir Plantkunde, Private Bag X101, Pretoria 0001, South Africa. Ed. Dr. D. J. B. Killick. illus. cum.index. circ. 750. Indexed: Biol.Abstr.
Formerly: Flowering Plants of South Africa.

581 595   AG   ISSN 0074-025X
FUNDACION MIGUEL LILLO. MISCELANEA. (Text in Spanish; summaries in English, French, German) 1937. irreg., no. 66, 1978. price varies. ‡ (Fundacion Miguel Lillo) Centro de Informacion Geo-Biologica, N O A, Miguel Lillo 251, Tucuman, Argentina. Ed. Jose Antonio Haedo Rossi. charts. illus. circ. 500. (back issues avail.) Indexed: Biol.Abstr. Ref.Zh.

581   US
FUNDAMENTALS OF BOTANY SERIES. irreg. price varies. Wadsworth Publishing Co., 10 Davis Drive, Belmont, CA 94002.

581   SI   ISSN 0072-0178
GARDENS' BULLETIN, SINGAPORE. (Text in English) 1891. irreg: vol 26, pt. 1, 1972; vol 27, pt. 2, 1975. price varies. Parks & Recreation Department, Botanic Gardens, Cluny Rd., Singapore 1025, Singapore. Ed. Hardial Singh. adv. bk. rev. index. Indexed: Biol.Abstr. Plant.Breed.Abstr.

581   CL   ISSN 0016-5301
GAYANA: BOTANICA. 1961. irreg. Universidad de Concepcion, Instituto Central de Biologia, Casilla 1367, Concepcion, Chile. Ed. Bd. circ. 1,000. Indexed: Biol.Abstr.

581   US   ISSN 0072-0879
GENTES HERBARUM; occasional papers on the kinds of plants. 1920. irreg., 1973, vol. 11. $25 per vol. or exchange. L. H. Bailey Hortorium, Cornell University, Ithaca, NY 14853. Ed. H. E. Moore. index. circ. 200. (also avail. in microform from UMI) Indexed: Biol.Abstr.

581   IE   ISSN 0332-0235
GLASRA. 1976. a. exchange basis. National Botanic Gardens, Glasnevin, Dublin 9, Ireland. circ. 200.
Formerly: National Botanic Gardens. Contributions.

581   US
GRAY HERBARIUM. CONTRIBUTIONS. 1891. irreg. price varies. Harvard University, Gray Herbarium, 22 Divinity Avenue, Cambridge, MA 02138. Ed. Reed C. Rollins. circ. 350.

635   AT
GROWING NATIVE PLANTS. 1971. a. price varies. Department of the Capital Territory, National Botanic Gardens, Canberra, A.C.T. 2601, Australia. Ed. J.W. Wrigley. cum.index.

GUIDE TO GRADUATE STUDY IN BOTANY FOR THE UNITED STATES AND CANADA.
see EDUCATION — Guides To Schools And Colleges

GUNNERIA. see ARCHAEOLOGY

581   JA   ISSN 0073-0912
HATTORI BOTANICAL LABORATORY. JOURNAL/HATTORI SHOKUBUTSU KENKYUSHO HOKOKU; devoted to bryology and lichenology. (Text in European languages) 1947. irreg., (2/yr) 7000-8000 Yen. Hattori Botanical Laboratory - Hattori Shokubutsu Kenkyusho, Obi, Nichinan-shi, Miyazaki-ken 889-25, Japan. Ed. Sinske Hattori.

581   JA   ISSN 0075-4366
HIROSHIMA UNIVERSITY. JOURNAL OF SCIENCE. SERIES B. DIVISION 2. BOTANY/HIROSHIMA DAIGAKU RIKA KIYO, SHOKUBUTSU. (Text in English, French and German) 1930. approx. a. exchange basis. Hiroshima University, Botanical Institute, Higashisenda-cho, Hiroshima 730, Japan. circ. 120 (Japan) 400 (other countries)

581   BL   ISSN 0073-2877
HOEHNEA. (Text in English and Portuguese; summaries in English) 1971. irreg. 1978, vol. 7. price varies. ‡ Instituto de Botanica, Caixa Postal 4005, Sao Paulo, Brazil. Ed. Sonia M.C. Dietrich.
Continues: Arquivos de Botanica do Estado de Sao Paulo.

581   JA
HOKKAIDO UNIVERSITY. FACULTY OF SCIENCE. JOURNAL. SERIES 5: BOTANY. (Text in English) 1930. irreg. exchange basis. Hokkaido University, Faculty of Science - Hokkaido Daigaku Rigakubu, Nishi-8-chome, Kita-10-jo, Kita-ku, Sapporo 060, Japan.

581   JA
HOKKAIDO UNIVERSITY. INSTITUTE OF ALGOLOGICAL RESEARCH. SCIENTIFIC PAPERS/HOKKAIDO DAIGAKU RIGAKUBU KAISO KENKYUSHO OBUN HOKOKU. (Text in English) 1935. irreg. exchange basis. Hokkaido University, Institute of Algological Research, Bokoi, Muroran, Hokkaido 051, Japan.

581   UK
HOOKER'S ICONES PLANETARIUM. (Text in English and Latin) 1837. irreg. price varies. Bentham-Moxon Trust, Royal Botanic Gardens, Kew, Richmond, Surrey TW9 3AB, England. Ed. P. S. Green.

581   SG   ISSN 0073-4403
ICONES PLANTARUM AFRICANARUM. 1953. a. 12 Fr. Institut Fondamental d'Afrique Noire, Boite Postale 206, Dakar, Senegal, Senegal.

581   NE   ISSN 0073-4411
ICONOGRAPHIA MYCOLOGIA. (Supplement to Mycopathologia) (Text in English and Latin) 1959. s-a. fl.218. Dr. W. Junk Publishers (Subsidiary of: Kluwer Academic Publishers Group) Box 13713, 2501 ES The Hague, Netherlands (Orders to: Kluwer Academic Publishers Group, Distribution Center, Box 322, 3300 AH Dordrecht, Netherlands) Ed. D. Verona. circ. 250.

581   BL   ISSN 0073-4705
IHERINGIA. SERIE BOTANICA. (Text in English,French,German,Spanish and Portuguese) 1958. irreg., no. 26, 1981. price varies. Fundacao Zoobotanica do Rio Grande do Sul, Museu de Ciencias Naturais, Caixa Postal 1188, 90.000 Porto Alegre, Rio Grande do Sul, Brazil. Ed. Arno A. Lise. bibl. illus. circ. 600. Indexed: Biol.Abstr. Chem.Abstr.

581   GW   ISSN 0073-5787
INDEX HEPATICARUM. (Text in English) 1962. irreg. price varies. J. Cramer, In den Springaeckern 2, 3300 Braunschweig, W. Germany (B.R.D.) Ed. C. E. B. Bonner. circ. 500.

581   II   ISSN 0073-6376
INDIAN FOREST RECORDS (NEW SERIES) BOTANY. (Text in English) 1937. irreg., 1964, vol. 5, no. 3. price varies. ‡ Forest Research Institute & Colleges, P.O. New Forest, Dehra Dun, India. circ. 500. Indexed: Biol.Abstr. Forest.Abstr. Indian Sci.Abstr.

581.2   II   ISSN 0537-2410
INDIAN PHYTOPATHOLOGICAL SOCIETY. BULLETIN. 1963. irreg. Indian Phytological Society, c/o Indian Agricultural Research Institute, Division of Mycology, New Delhi 110012, India.

581   FR   ISSN 0073-7917
INFORMATIONS ANNUELLES DE CARYOSYSTEMATIQUE ET CYTOGENETIQUE.* 1967. a. price varies. Institut de Botanique, Strasbourg, 8 rue Goethe, Strasbourg, France.

581   GW
INSTITUT FUER ALLGEMEINE BOTANIK UND BOTANISCHER GARTEN. MITTEILUNGEN. (Text in German; summaries in English) 1914. irreg., vol. 15, 1975. exchange basis. ‡ Institut fuer Allgemeine Botanik und Botanischer Garten, Universitaet Hamburg, Jungiusstr. 6, 2000 Hamburg 36, W. Germany (B.R.D.) illus.

581   PO   ISSN 0473-0658
INSTITUTO DE BOTANICA "DR. GONCALO SAMPAIO". PUBLICACOES. 3 SERIE. (Text in English, French and Portuguese) irreg. (approx. 2/yr.) exchange only. Instituto de Botanica "Dr. Goncalo Sampaio", Rua do Camho Alegre, 1191 - Porto, Portugal.

581   MX
INSTITUTO DE INVESTIGACIONES SOBRE RECURSOS BIOTICOS. SERIE: ESTUDIO BOTANICO Y ECOLOGICO DE LA REGION DEL RIO UXPANAPA. 1975. irreg. price varies. Instituto de Investigaciones sobre Recursos Bioticos, Apdo. Postal 63, Xalapa, Veracruz, Mexico.

580   NE   ISSN 0074-7408
INTERNATIONAL ASSOCIATION OF PLANT BREEDERS FOR THE PROTECTION OF PLANT VARIETIES. CONGRESS REPORTS. a, 26th, 1978, W. Germany(B.R.D.) International Association of Plant Breeders for the Protection of Plant Varieties, Rokin 50, 1012 KV Amsterdam, Netherlands.

580   AT   ISSN 0074-2090
INTERNATIONAL BOTANICAL CONGRESS. ABSTRACTS OF PAPERS. every 6 years. price varies. International Botanical Congress, c/o W.J. Cram, Exec. Sec., Australian Academy of Science, Box 783, Canberra, A.C.T. 2601, Australia.

580   AT
INTERNATIONAL BOTANICAL CONGRESS. PROCEEDINGS. every 6 years. price varies. International Botanical Congress, c/o W. J. Cram, Exec. Sec., Australian Academy of Science, Box 783, Canberra, A.C.T. 2601, Australia.

INTERNATIONAL COLLOQUIUM ON PLANT ANALYSIS AND FERTILIZER PROBLEMS. PROCEEDINGS. see *AGRICULTURE — Crop Production And Soil*

589.45   NO   ISSN 0074-7874
INTERNATIONAL SEAWEED SYMPOSIUM. PROCEEDINGS. (Published by host country) 1952. triennial, 9th, 1977, Santa Barbara. International Seaweed Symposium, c/o Dr. A. Jensen, Norwegian Institute of Seaweed Research, 7034 Trondheim NTH, Norway. (Co-sponsor: International Seaweed Association)

581   US
INTERNATIONAL SERIES ON PURE AND APPLIED BIOLOGY. BOTANY DIVISION. 1959. irreg., vol. 9, 1970. price varies. Pergamon Press, Inc., Maxwell House, Fairview Park, Elmsford, NY 10523. index.
Formerly: International Series of Monographs on Pure and Applied Biology. Division: Botany (ISSN 0074-8277)

581.1   632   US
INTERNATIONAL SERIES ON PURE AND APPLIED BIOLOGY. PLANT PHYSIOLOGY DIVISION. 1963. irreg., vol. 5, 1970. price varies. Pergamon Press, Inc., Maxwell House, Fairview Park, Elmsford, NY 10523. index.
Formerly: International Series of Monographs on Pure and Applied Biology. Division: Plant Physiology (ISSN 0074-8293)

581   II   ISSN 0539-0346
INTERNATIONAL SOCIETY OF PLANT MORPHOLOGISTS. YEARBOOK. (Text in English) a. International Society of Plant Morphologists, University of Delhi, Department of Botany, Delhi 110007, India.

581   635   CN   ISSN 0077-1325
JARDIN BOTANIQUE DE MONTREAL. MEMOIRE. (Text in French and English) 1940. irreg. available on exchange. Jardin Botanique de Montreal, 4101 Sherbrooke St. E., Montreal 406, Que., Canada. circ. 800-1,200.

583.47   GW   ISSN 0075-4676
KAKTEEN. GESAMTDARSTELLUNG (MONOGRAPHIE) DER EINGEFUEHRTEN ARTEN NEBST ANZUCHT- UND PFLEGE. 1956. 4/yr. membership. Deutsche Kakteen Gesellschaft, c/o Horst Bork, Marientalstr. 70-72, 4400 Muenster, W. Germany (B.R.D.) index.

589.2   II
KAVAKA/FUNGUS; being transactions of the Mycological Society of India. (Text in English) 1973. a. Rs.25($6) individuals; Rs.50, $12 institutions. Mycological Society of India, 6/A Cunningham Rd., Bangalore 560052, India. Ed. C. V. Subramanian. bibl. illus. Indexed: Biol.Abstr.
Mycology

581   UK   ISSN 0075-5974
KEW BULLETIN. 1946. irreg. price varies. Royal Botanic Gardens, Kew, London, England (Avail. from H.M.S.O., c/o Liaison Officer, Atlantic House, Holborn Viaduct, London EC1P 1BN, England) bk. rev. illus. circ. 550. (also avail. in microform from UMI)

581   UK   ISSN 0075-5982
KEW BULLETIN. ADDITIONAL SERIES. 1958. irreg. Royal Botanic Gardens, Kew, London, England (Avail. from: H.M.S.O., c/o Liaison Officer, Atlantic House, London EC1P 1BW, England) circ. 500.

581   JA
KIHARA INSTITUTE FOR BIOLOGICAL RESEARCH. WHEAT INFORMATION SERVICE. (Text in English) irreg. membership. Kihara Institute for Biological Research - Kihara Seibutsugaku Kenkyusho, 3-122-21 Mutsukawa, Yokohama 232, Japan.

581   RH   ISSN 0451-9930
KIRKIA; the journal of Rhodesian botany. 1960. a. Rhod.$1.50($5) Ministry of Agriculture, Department of Research and Specialist Services, Box 8108, Causeway, Salisbury, Zimbabwe. Eds. H. Wild, R.B. Drummond. bk. rev. circ. 450. (back issues avail.) Indexed: Biol.Abstr. Excerp.Bot.

581   GE   ISSN 0075-7209
KULTURPFLANZE. 1953. irreg., vol. 24, 1976. (Akademie der Wissenschaften der DDR, Zentralinstitut fuer Genetik und Kulturpflanzenforschung Gatersleben) Akademie-Verlag, Leipziger Str. 3-4, 108 Berlin, E. Germany (D.D.R.)

581   AU
LANDESMUSEUM JOANNEUM. ABTEILUNG FUER BOTANIK. MITTEILUNGEN. 1972. irreg. price varies. Landesmuseum Joanneum, Abteilung fuer Botanik, Raubergasse 10, A-8010 Graz, Austria. Ed. Detlef Ernet. bibl. illus. circ. 600.

581   NE
LEIDEN BOTANICAL SERIES. 1975. irreg., vol. 3, 1976. price varies. Leiden University Press, c/o Martinus Nijhoff, Box 566, 2501 CN The Hague, Netherlands.

581   BE   ISSN 0457-4184
LEJEUNIA; revue de botanique. (Text in French; summaries in French and English) N.S. 1961. irreg. price varies. Botanical Society in Liege, Universite de Liege, Departement de Botanique, Sart Tilman, B-4000 Liege, Belgium. (back issues avail) Indexed: Bull.Signal. Agri.Ind.

581   AG   ISSN 0075-9481
LILLOA; revista de botanica. (Text in Latin, Spanish; summaries in English, French, German, Italian) 1937. irreg., vol. 34, 1976. price varies. (Fundacion Miguel Lillo) Centro de Informacion Geo-Biologica N O A, Miguel Lillo 251, 4000 Tucuman, Argentina. Ed. Dr. Jose Antonio Haedo Rossi. charts. illus. bibl. (back issues avail.) Indexed: Biol.Abstr. Bull.Signal. Ref.Zh.

635   580   US
LONGWOOD PROGRAM SEMINARS. 1969. a. free. (Longwood Program in Ornamental Horticulture) University of Delaware, College of Agricultural Sciences, 165 Agricultural Hall, Newark, DE 19711. Ed. Lynn Hershey Chesson. circ. 800(controlled)

581   HU   ISSN 0076-2482
MAGYARORSZAG KULTURFLORAJA. 1956. irreg., no. 6/18, 1979. price varies. (Magyar Tudomanyos Akademia) Akademiai Kiado, Publishing House of the Hungarian Academy of Sciences, Box 24, H-1363 Budapest, Hungary.

581   CS   ISSN 0076-6984
METODICKE PRIRUCKY EXPERIMENTALNI BOTANIKY/METHODS OF EXPERIMENTAL BOTANY. (Text in Czech; contents page also in English and Russian) 1965. irreg., no. 3, 1974. price varies. (Ceskoslovenska Akademie Ved) Academia, Publishing House of the Czechoslovak Academy of Sciences, Vodickova 40, 112 29 Prague 1, Czechoslovakia. Ed. B. Slavik.

581   PL   ISSN 0077-0655
MONOGRAPHIAE BOTANICAE. (Text in Polish, English; summaries in English, German) 1953. irreg., 1972, vol. 37. price varies. (Polskie Towarzystwo Botaniczne) Panstwowe Wydawnictwo Naukowe, Miodowa 10, Warsaw, Poland (Dist. by Ars Polona-Ruch, Krakowskie Przedmiescie 7, Warsaw, Poland) Ed. M. Kostyniuk. bibl, charts.

581   HU   ISSN 0077-0663
MONOGRAPHIE DER FLAUMEICHEN-BUSCHWAELDER. (Text in German) 1961. irreg. price varies. (Magyar Tudomanyos Akademia) Akademiai Kiado, Publishing House of the Hungarian Academy of Sciences, P.O. Box 24, H-1363 Budapest, Hungary.

581   635   US   ISSN 0027-125X
MORTON ARBORETUM QUARTERLY. 1965. q. $4. Morton Arboretum, Lisle, IL 60532. Ed. Joseph P. Larkin. illus. cum. index every 3 yrs. circ. 3,500.

581   AT   ISSN 0077-1813
MUELLERIA. 1955. irreg. available on exchange. ‡ Royal Botanic Gardens and National Herbarium, South Yarra, Victoria 3141, Australia. Ed. H.I. Aston. bk. rev. index. circ. 600. Indexed: Aus.Sci.Ind.

581   AG   ISSN 0376-2793
MUSEO ARGENTINO DE CIENCIAS NATURALES BERNARDINO RIVADAVIA. INSTITUTO NACIONAL DE INVESTIGACION DE LAS CIENCIAS NATURALES. REVISTA. BOTANICA. 1978. irreg.; latest issue 1981. free. Museo Argentino de Ciencias Naturales Bernardino Rivadavia, Avda. Angel Gallardo 470, Casilla de Correo 220-Sucursal 5, Buenos Aires, Argentina. illus.
Continues: Buenos Aires. Museo Argentino de Ciencias Naturales Bernardino Rivadavia. Instituto Nacional de Investigacion de las Ciencias Naturales. Revista. Ciencias Botanicas.

581   BL   ISSN 0080-3197
MUSEU NACIONAL, RIO DE JANEIRO. BOLETIM. NOVA SERIE. BOTANICA. 1944. irreg., no. 53, Mar. 1979. exchange only. Museu Nacional, Quinta da Boa Vista, 20940 Rio de Janeiro RJ, Brazil. illus. Indexed: Biol.Abstr.

581   BL   ISSN 0077-2216
MUSEU PARAENSE EMILIO GOELDI. BOLETIM BOTANICA. NOVA SERIE. 1957. irreg. Instituto Nacional de Pesquisas da Amazonia, Museu Paraense Emilio Goeldi, Belem, Para, Brazil. abstr. cum. index.

581   FR   ISSN 0078-9755
MUSEUM NATIONAL D'HISTOIRE NATURELLE, PARIS. MEMOIRES. NOUVELLE SERIE. SERIE B. BOTANIQUE. 1950. irreg. price varies. Museum National d'Histoire Naturelle, 38, rue Geoffroy-Saint-Hilaire, Paris 5, France.

589.2   UK   ISSN 0077-2364
MUSHROOM SCIENCE. (Text and summaries in English, French, German) 1950. triennial, 1968, 2nd Symposium and 7th Congress, Hamburg. Mushroom Growers' Association, Agriculture House, Knightsbridge, London SW1X 7NJ, England.
Represents: International Congress on Mushroom Science. Proceedings & Scientific Symposium on the Cultivated Mushroom. Proceedings.
Mycology

581   CK   ISSN 0027-5123
MUTISIA; acta botanica Colombiana. (Text in English, French, German & Spanish) 1952. irreg. $5 or exchange basis. Universidad Nacional de Colombia, Instituto de Ciencias Naturales, Apartado Aereo 7495, Bogota, Colombia. Ed. Polidoro Pinto Escobar. bibl.illus. circ. 1,000. Indexed: Biol.Abstr. Bull.Signal.

589.2   UK   ISSN 0027-5522
MYCOLOGICAL PAPERS. 1925. irreg. price varies. (Commonwealth Mycological Institute) Commonwealth Agricultural Bureaux, Farnham House, Farnham Royal, Slough SL2 3BN, England. Ed. A. Johnston.
Mycology

589.2   US   ISSN 0093-4666
MYCOTAXON. 1974. irreg. $32 per vol. Mycotaxon, Ltd., Box 264, Ithaca, NY 14850. Eds. Richard P. Korf, G. L. Hennebert. bk. rev. illus. circ. 600. (also avail. in microform) Indexed: Biol.Abstr. Curr.Cont.
Mycology

581   II   ISSN 0076-1419
NATIONAL BOTANIC GARDENS, LUCKNOW. BULLETIN. (Text in English) 1956. irreg. price varies. ‡ National Botanic Gardens, Lucknow 226001, India. (Affiliate: Council of Scientific and Industrial Research) Indexed: Biol.Abstr. Chem.Abstr.

581   II
NATIONAL BOTANIC GARDENS, LUCKNOW. PROGRESS REPORT. (Text in English) 1966. a. free. ‡ National Botanic Gardens, Lucknow 226001, India. (Affiliate: Council of Scientific and Industrial Research) circ. controlled. Indexed: Biol.Abstr. Chem.Abstr.
Formerly: National Botanic Gardens, Lucknow. Annual Report (ISSN 0076-1400)

BIOLOGY — BOTANY

581.2 595.7   JA   ISSN 0077-4847
NATIONAL INSTITUTE OF AGRICULTURAL SCIENCES, TOKYO. BULLETIN. SERIES C (PLANT PATHOLOGY AND ENTOMOLOGY) (Text in English or Japanese with English summaries) 1952. irreg., no. 31, 1977. avail. on excahnge basis only. National Institute of Agricultural Sciences - Norin-sho Nogyo Gijutsu Kenkyusho, 2-7-1 Nishigahara, Kita-ku, Tokyo 114, Japan. Ed. T. Kono.

581.1 581.15   JA   ISSN 0077-4855
NATIONAL INSTITUTE OF AGRICULTURAL SCIENCES, TOKYO. BULLETIN. SERIES D (PHYSIOLOGY AND GENETICS) (Text in English or Japanese with English summaries) 1952. irreg., no. 28, 1977. avail. on exchange basis only. National Institute of Agricultural Sciences - Norin-sho Nogyo, 2-7-1 Nishigahara, Kita-ku, Tokyo 114, Japan. Ed. K. Sakai.

581   PH   ISSN 0076-3764
NATIONAL MUSEUM OF THE PHILIPPINES. MUSEUM PUBLICATIONS (PAMPHLET SERIES) (Text in English) 1967. irreg. price varies. National Museum of the Philippines, Rizal Park, Manila, Philippines. Ed. Rosario B. Tantoco. circ. controlled. (processed)

581 615.19   NP
NEPAL. DEPARTMENT OF MEDICINAL PLANTS. ANNUAL REPORT. (Text in English) a. Ministry of Forests, Department of Medicinal Plants, Thapathali, Kathmandu, Nepal.

581   US   ISSN 0077-8931
NEW YORK BOTANICAL GARDEN. MEMOIRS. 1900. irreg. price varies. New York Botanical Garden, Bronx, NY 10458. Ed. Clark T. Rogerson. index. (back issues avail.)

581   NR   ISSN 0078-0715
NIGERIAN INSTITUTE FOR OIL PALM RESEARCH. JOURNAL. 1953. irreg. $1.40. Nigerian Institute for Oil Palm Research, P.M.B. 1030, Benin City, Nigeria. adv. bk. rev. indexes. Indexed: Hort.Abstr.

581   US   ISSN 0078-1312
NORTH AMERICAN FLORA. 1905-1949; series II. irreg. price varies. New York Botanical Garden, Bronx, NY 10458. Ed. Clark T. Rogerson. (back issues avail.)

581   US
NORTHERN NUT GROWERS ASSOCIATION. ANNUAL REPORT. 1911. a. $8 membership. Northern Nut Growers Association, Broken Arrow Rd., Hamden, CT 06518. Ed. Richard A. Jaynes. circ. 2,000. Indexed: Hort.Abstr.

581   UK   ISSN 0080-4274
NOTES FROM THE ROYAL BOTANIC GARDEN, EDINBURGH. 1900. irreg., vol. 37, 1978-9. price varies. H.M.S.O. (Scotland), 13a Castle St., Edinburgh EH2 3AR, Scotland. Ed. Dr. J. A. Ratter. bk. rev. illus. circ. 550. Indexed: Biol.Abstr. Excerp.Bot.

581   VE   ISSN 0085-4387
NOTICIERO TUBEROSAS.* (Text in Spanish; summaries in Spanish, occasionally in Portuguese and English) 1971. irreg. free to members. Sociedad Latinoamericana de Tuberosas, Box 97, Maracay, Venezuela. Ed. Alvaro Montaldo. abstr. circ. 250. (processed; also avail. in cards)

581   AT   ISSN 0085-4417
NUYTSIA. 1970. irreg. free. Department of Agriculture, Western Australian Herbarium, Jarrah Rd., South Perth, W.A. 6151, Australia. Ed. A. S. George. circ. 600. Indexed: CALL.

581   DK   ISSN 0078-5237
OPERA BOTANICA. (Text in English) 1953. irreg., no. 63, 1979. price varies. Nordic Journal of Botany, The Secretary, O Farimagsgade 2D, DK-1353 Copehhagen K, Denmark. (Co-sponsor: Lund Botanical Society) Ed. Gunnar Weimarck. index. (back issues avail.) Indexed: Biol.Abstr.

581 591   AG   ISSN 0078-5245
OPERA LILLOANA. (Text in Spanish; summaries in English, French, German, Italian) 1957. irreg. price varies. ‡ (Fundacion Miguel Lillo) Centro de Informacion Geo-Biologica, N O A, Miguel Lillo 205, Tucuman, Argentina. Ed. Jose Antonio Haedo Rossi. index. circ. 500. (back issues avail.) Indexed: Bull. Signal. Biol.Abstr. Ref.Zh.

581   US   ISSN 0078-5776
OREGON STATE MONOGRAPHS. STUDIES IN BOTANY. 1939. irreg., latest no.10. price varies. Oregon State University Press, 101 Waldo Hall, Corvallis, OR 97331.

653.934   MX   ISSN 0300-3701
ORQUIDEA (MEXICO) (Text in English and Spanish) 1971. irreg. Mex.$250($14) ‡ Asociacion Mexicana de Orquideologia AC, Apdo. Postal 53-123, Mexico 17, D.F., Mexico. Ed.Dir. Eric Hagsater. adv. bk. rev. illus. circ. 600. Indexed: Ash.G.Bot.Per. Biol.Abstr. Excerpt.Bot.
Orchids

634.8 587.33   IT   ISSN 0552-9506
OSSERVATORIO REGIONALE PER LE MALATTIE DELLA VITE. OSSERVAZIONI DI METEOROLOGIA, FENOLOGIA E PATOLOGIA DELLA VITE.* 1966. irreg. Osservatorio Regionale per le Malattie della Vite, Palermo, Italy. illus.

PANAMIN FOUNDATION RESEARCH SERIES. see *ANTHROPOLOGY*

581   BL   ISSN 0553-8475
PESQUISAS: PUBLICACOES DE BOTANICA. (Numbering is in continuation of articles published in Pesquisas) no. 8, 1960. irreg. price varies (or exchange) (Universidade do Vale do Rio dos Sinos, Instituto Anchietano de Pesquisas) Unisinos, Praca Tiradentes 35, Sao Leopoldo RS, Brazil.
Supersedes in part: Pesquisas.

581   AU   ISSN 0031-675X
PFLANZENSCHUTZBERICHTE. (Summaries in English) 1947. irreg., vol. 45, 1976. S.165. Bundesanstalt fuer Pflanzenschutz, Trunnerstr. 5, A-1021 Vienna, Austria. Ed. Erich Kahl. adv. bk. rev. charts. illus. index. circ. 600. Indexed: Bibl.Pflanz. Rev.Appl.Entomol. Rev.Plant Path.

581   GW   ISSN 0079-1369
PHANEROGAMARUM MONOGRAPHIAE. 1968. irreg., vol. 8, 1977. price varies. J. Cramer, In den Springaeckern 2, 3300 Braunschweig, W. Germany (B.R.D.) circ. 200.

581   UK
PHYTOCHEMICAL SOCIETY SYMPOSIA SERIES. PROCEEDINGS. 1965. irreg. Academic Press Inc. (London) Ltd., 24-28 Oval Road, London NW1 7DX, England (And 111 Fifth Ave., New York, NY 10003)

581   US   ISSN 0031-9430
PHYTOLOGIA; designed to expedite botanical publication. 1933. irreg., several vols. per year. $9.75 per vol. ‡ H. N. & A. L. Moldenke, Eds. & Pubs., 303 Parkside Rd., Plainfield, NJ 07060. bk. rev. abstr, bibl, charts, illus. index. circ. 400. Indexed: Biol.Abstr. Excerp.Bot.

581   AU   ISSN 0079-2047
PHYTON. ANNALES REI BOTANICAE. 1949. a. S.600 per vol. Verlag Ferdinand Berger und Soehne OHG, Wienerstr. 21-23, 3580 Horn, Austria. Eds. O. Haertel, H. Teppner.

PLANT GENETIC RESOURCES NEWSLETTER. see *CONSERVATION*

581   US   ISSN 0032-0846
PLANT LIFE. (Includes: Amaryllis Yearbook) 1934. a. membership. American Plant Life Society, Box 150, La Jolla, CA 92037. Ed. H. P. Traub. bk. rev. bibl. charts. illus. circ. 500. Indexed: Biol.Abstr.

581   GW   ISSN 0079-2233
PLANT MONOGRAPH: REPRINTS. 1968. irreg., no. 12, 1977. price varies. J. Cramer, In den Springaeckern 2, 3300 Braunschweig, W. Germany (B.R.D.)

581.1   US   ISSN 0079-2241
PLANT PHYSIOLOGY. SUPPLEMENT. 1926(Plant Physiology) a. $5 or with subscr. to Plant Physiology. American Society of Plant Physiologists, Box 1688, Rockville, MD 20850. index. circ. 5,400. (also avail. in microfilm; microfiche; reprint service avail. from UMI) Indexed: Biol.Abstr. Chem.Abstr.
Also Called: American Society of Plant Physiologists. Proceedings of Annual Meeting.

581   PL   ISSN 0080-357X
POLSKIE TOWARZYSTWO BOTANICZNE. SEKCJA DENDROLOGICZNA. ROCZNIK. (Text in Polish, Czech or German; summaries in English, German and Russian) 1926. irreg. price varies. Panstwowe Wydawnictwo Naukowe, Ul. Miodowa 10, Warsaw, Poland (Dist. by Ars Polona-Ruch, Krakowskie Przedmiescie 7, Warsaw, Poland) Ed. Tadeusz Gorczynski.

581   US   ISSN 0340-4773
PROGRESS IN BOTANY. 1949. irreg., vol. 42, 1981. price varies. Springer-Verlag, 175 Fifth Ave., New York, NY 10010 (also Berlin, Heidelberg, Vienna) (reprint service avail. from ISI)
Formerly: Fortschritte der Botanik (ISSN 0071-7878)

581   US   ISSN 0079-6689
PROGRESS IN PHYTOCHEMISTRY. 1968. a. $75. Pergamon Press, Inc., Journals Division, Maxwell House, Fairview Park, Elmsford, NY 10523 (And Headington Hill Hall, Oxford OX3 0BW, England) Ed. L. Reinhold. (also avail. in microform from MIM,UMI)

581   IO   ISSN 0034-365X
REINWARDTIA; a journal on taxonomic botany, plant sociology and ecology. (Text in English, French and German) 1950. irreg. price varies. Herbarium Bogoriense, Jalan Ir. H. Juanda 22-24, Bogor, Indonesia. Ed.Bd. bk. rev. index. circ. 400. Indexed: Biol.Abstr.

582.14   AU   ISSN 0486-4271
REPERTORIUM PLANTARUM SUCCULENTARUM. (Issued as a Subseries of Regnum Vegetabile) 1951. a. $4.25 price varies. International Organization for Succulent Plant Study, c/o Dr. Heimo Friedrich, Osteracker 38, A-6162 Natters, Austria. Eds. G. D. Rowley, L. E. Newton. (reprint service avail. from UMI)

581.87   FR   ISSN 0181-7582
REVUE DE CYTOLOGIE ET DE BIOLOGIE VEGETALES-LA BOTANISTE. 1934. a. (in 4 parts) Laboratoire de Biologie Vegetale Appliquee, 61 rue de Buffon, 75005 Paris, France. Ed. Jean Louis Hamel. bk. rev. charts. illus. index. circ. 11,350. Indexed: Biol.Abstr. Chem.Abstr.
Formed by the merger of: Botaniste (ISSN 0045-2637) & Revue de Cytologie et de Biologie Vegetales (ISSN 0035-1067)

581   BL   ISSN 0080-3014
RICKIA. (Text in English or Portuguese; summaries in English) 1962. irreg.; 1978, vol. 7. Instituto de Botanica, Caixa Postal 4005, Sao Paulo, Brazil. Ed. Oswaldo Fidalgo.
Supersedes in Part: Archivos de Botanica do Estado de Sao Paulo.

581   BL   ISSN 0080-3022
RICKIA. SUPLEMENTO. (Text in English or Portuguese; summaries in English) 1963. irreg., 1971, no 4. price varies; also available on exchange. Instituto de Botanica, Caixa Postal 4005, Sao Paulo, Brazil. Ed. Oswaldo Fidalgo.

ROYAL BOTANICAL GARDENS, HAMILTON, ONT. SPECIAL BULLETIN. see *GARDENING AND HORTICULTURE*

581 635   CN   ISSN 0072-9655
ROYAL BOTANICAL GARDENS, HAMILTON, ONT. TECHNICAL BULLETIN. 1957. irreg. limited distribution; price varies. Royal Botanical Gardens, Box 399, Hamilton, Ont. L8N 3H8, Canada. Ed. Dr. Peter F. Rice. circ. 1,000. (back issues avail.)

BIOLOGY — BOTANY

581.05   SZ   ISSN 0373-2525
SAUSSUREA. 1970. a. 50 F. to libraries and institutions. ‡ Societe Botanique de Geneve, Conservatoire et Jardin Botaniques, Bibliotheque, Case Postale 60, CH-1292 Chambesy/GE, Switzerland. Ed. Herve M. Burdet. adv. illus. circ. 400. Indexed: Biol.Abstr.
    Supersedes: Societe Botanique de Geneve. Travaux (ISSN 0583-8177)

581   GW   ISSN 0085-5960
SCHRIFTENREIHE FUER VEGETATIONSKUNDE. 1966. irreg., no. 12, 1979. price varies. (Bundesforschungsanstalt fuer Naturschutz und Landschaftsoekologie) Landwirtschaftsverlag GmbH, Marktallee 89, Postfach 480210, 4400 Muenster-Hiltrup, W. Germany (B.R.D.). charts. illus. stat.

590   GW   ISSN 0341-3772
SCRIPTA GEOBOTANICA. 1970. irreg. price varies. (Universitaet Goettingen, Lehrstuhl fuer Geobotanik) Verlag Erich Goltze GmbH und Co. KG, Stresemannstr. 28, 3400 Goettingen, W. Germany (B.R.D.) Ed. Hans Heller.

581   US   ISSN 0361-185X
SELBYANA. 1976. irreg., latest no. 5, \$22. Marie Selby Botanical Gardens, 800 S. Palm Ave., Sarasota, FL 33577. Ed. Carlyle A. Luer. illus. circ. 500.

581   US   ISSN 0081-024X
SMITHSONIAN CONTRIBUTIONS TO BOTANY. 1969. irreg. Smithsonian Institution Press, Washington, DC 20560. Ed. Albert L. Ruffin Jr. circ. 1,600. (reprint service avail. from UMI)

581   MX
SOCIEDAD BOTANICA DE MEXICO. BOLETIN. 1941. a. membership. Sociedad Botanica de Mexico, Apartado Postal 70-383, Mexico 20, D.F., Mexico. charts. illus. cum.index: 1941-1975.

581   MX   ISSN 0085-6223
SOCIEDAD MEXICANA DE MICOLOGIA. BOLETIN. (Text in Spanish; summaries in English and French) 1968. a. \$10 (or exchange) Sociedad Mexicana de Micologia, Apdo. Postal 26-378, Mexico 16, D.F., Mexico. Ed. Gaston Guzman. adv. bk. rev. bibl. charts. illus. index; cum. index. circ. 500(controlled) (processed; also avail. in microform from UMI)
    Formerly: Sociedad Mexicana de Micologia. Boletin Informativo.

581   PO
SOCIEDADE BROTERIANA. ANUARIO. (Text in European Languages; summaries in English, French and Portuguese) 1935. a. Esc.120. ‡ Sociedade Broteriana, Arcos do Jardim, 3049 Coimbra, Portugal. (Co-sponsor: Universidade de Coimbra. Instituto Botanico) Eds. A. Fernandes, Rosette Batarda Fernandes. circ. 1,000. Indexed: Biol.Abstr. Excerp.Bot.

581   PO   ISSN 0081-0657
SOCIEDADE BROTERIANA. BOLETIM. (Text in European languages; summaries in English, French, and Portuguese) 1880/81. a. Esc.600(\$15) ‡ Sociedade Broteriana, Arcos do Jardim, 3049 Coimbra, Portugal. (Co-sponsor: Universidade de Coimbra. Instituto Botanico) Eds. A. Fernandes & Firmino Mesquita. circ. 1,500. Indexed: Biol.Abstr. Excerp.Bot.

581   SA   ISSN 0081-251X
SOUTH AFRICAN POLLEN GRAINS AND SPORES. 1953. irreg., latest no. 4, 1970. price varies. (Council for Scientific and Industrial Research) A. A. Balkema Ltd., P.O. Box 3117, Cape Town 8000, South Africa (And Box 1675, Rotterdam, Netherlands; in the U.S. and Canada, 99 Main St., Salem, NH 03079) Ed. E. M. Van Zinderen Bakker.

SPAIN. INSTITUTO NACIONAL DE INVESTIGACIONES AGRARIAS. COMUNICACIONES. SERIE: GENERAL. see *AGRICULTURE*

589   UK   ISSN 0306-2074
SPORE RESEARCH. irreg. Academic Press Inc. (London) Ltd., 24-28 Oval Rd., London NW1 7DX, England (And 111 Fifth Ave., New York, NY 10003) illus.

581   US   ISSN 0584-9144
SPORES. (Represents: International Spore Conference. Proceedings) 1958. triennial. price varies. American Society for Microbiology, 1913 I St., N.W., Washington, DC 20006 (Subscr. to: Box 1192, Birmingham, AL 35201)

580   PL   ISSN 0082-5557
STUDIA SOCIETATIS SCIENTIARUM TORUNENSIS. SECTIO D (BOTANIKA) (Text in Polish; summaries in English) 1951. irreg. price varies. (Towarzystwo Naukowe w Toruniu) Panstwowe Wydawnictwo Naukowe, Ul. Miodowa 10, Warsaw, Poland.

589.2   NE   ISSN 0166-0616
STUDIES IN MYCOLOGY. (Text in English) 1972. irreg. price varies. Centraalbureau voor Schimmelcultures, Oosterstraat 1, Box 273, 3740 AG Baarn, Netherlands.

589.2   AU   ISSN 0082-0598
SYDOWIA: ANNALES MYCOLOGICI; editii in notitiam scientiae mycologicae universalis. (Supplement: Beihefte zur Sydowia: Annales Mycologici, Ser. II) (Text in English, German and Latin) 1947. a. S.600. Verlag Ferdinand Berger und Soehne OHG, Wienerstr. 21-23, 3580 Horn, Austria. Ed. E. Horak.
    Mycology

581   SW   ISSN 0082-0644
SYMBOLAE BOTANICAE UPSALIENSES. (Since vol. 20 issued as part of Acta Universitatis Upsaliensis) (Text and summaries in English, French, German) 1932. irreg., vol. 22, 1975. price varies. (Botaniske Institutionerna, Uppsala - Botanical Institute, Upsala) Almqvist & Wiksell International, Box 62, S-101 20 Stockholm, Sweden. Ed. J. A. Nannfeldt.

TAIWAN AGRICULTURAL RESEARCH INSTITUTE. RESEARCH SUMMARY. see *AGRICULTURE*

TAIWAN AGRICULTURAL RESEARCH INSTITUTE. BULLETIN. see *AGRICULTURE*

581   CH   ISSN 0065-1125
TAIWANIA. Also known as: Acta Botanica Taiwanica. (Text and summaries in English) 1948. a. exchange only. National Taiwan University, College of Science, Taipei, Taiwan 107, Republic of China. Ed.Bd. circ. 350.

581   AT   ISSN 0312-9764
TELOPEA. 1975. irreg. available on exchange; free to qualified personnel. ‡ National Herbarium, Royal Botanic Gardens, Sydney, N.S.W. 2000, Australia. Ed. D. J. McGillivray. illus. Indexed: Biol.Abstr. Excerp.Bot.
    Supersedes: New South Wales National Herbarium. Contributions (ISSN 0077-8753)

632   US
TENNESSEE COOPERATIVE ECONOMIC INSECT SURVEY REPORT: ANNUAL SUMMARY. a. Department of Agriculture, Division of Plant Industries, Insect Survey Comm, Box 40627, Melrose Station, Nashville, TN 37204. illus.

581   US   ISSN 0082-3139
TEXAS RESEARCH FOUNDATION, RENNER. CONTRIBUTIONS. 1950. irreg., 1970, vol. 6. price varies. University of Texas at Dallas, Box 688, Richardson, TX 75080. Ed. Cyrus Longworth Lundell. index in each vol.

TOKYO UNIVERSITY OF EDUCATION. FACULTY OF SCIENCE. SCIENCE REPORTS. SECTION B: ZOOLOGY AND BOTANY/ TOKYO KYOIKU DAIGAKU RIKA KIYO B, DOBUTSUGAKU TO SHOKUBUTSUGU. see *BIOLOGY — Zoology*

581   US   ISSN 0041-2198
TREE-RING BULLETIN. 1935. a. \$5 to individuals. institutions \$10. (Tree-Ring Society) University of Arizona, Laboratory of Tree-Ring Research, Tucson, AZ 85721. Ed. William J. Robinson. charts. illus. maps. cum.index. circ. 350. Indexed: Biol.Abstr.

581   NP
TRIBHUVAN UNIVERSITY. NATURAL HISTORY MUSEUM. JOURNAL. (Text in English) 1977. irreg. Tribhuvan University, Natural History Museum, Swoyambhu, Kathmandu, Nepal.

581   GW   ISSN 0302-9417
TROPISCHE UND SUBTROPISCHE PFLANZENWELT. 1973. irreg., vol. 37, 1981. price varies. (Akademie der Wissenschaften und der Literatur, Mainz, Mathematisch-Naturwissenschaftliche Klasse) Franz Steiner Verlag GmbH, Friedrichstr. 24, Postfach 5529, 6200 Wiesbaden, W. Germany (B.R.D.) Ed. Werner Rauh.

581   MX
UNIVERSIDAD DE GUADALAJARA. INSTITUTO DE BOTANICA. BOLETIN INFORMATIVO. no. 8, 1978. irreg. exchange. Universidad de Guadalajara, Instituto de Botanica, Apdo. Postal 139, Zapopan, Jalisco, Mexico. bibl. illus.

581   SP   ISSN 0580-468X
UNIVERSIDAD DE MADRID. DEPARTAMENTO DE BOTANICA Y FISIOLOGIA VEGETAL. TRABAJOS. 1968. irreg. Universidad Complutense de Madrid, Departmento de Botanica y Fisiologia Vegetal., Ciudad Universitaria, Madrid 3, Spain. bibl. illus.

581   BL   ISSN 0302-2439
UNIVERSIDADE DE SAO PAULO. DEPARTAMENTO DE BOTANICA. BOLETIM DE BOTANICA. (Text in English, Portuguese) 1973. irreg., vol. 6, 1978. Cr.\$100. Universidade de Sao Paulo, Departamento de Botanica, Caixa Postal 11461, 05421 Sao Paulo, Brazil. (Co-sponsor: Instituto de Biociencias) illus. circ. 800. Indexed: Curr.Cont.
    Supersedes (1937-1969): Universidade de Sao Paulo. Faculdade de Filosofia, Ciencias y Letras. Botanica.

581   IT   ISSN 0079-0265
UNIVERSITA DEGLI STUDI DI PAVIA. ISTITUTO BOTANICO. ATTI. 1943. a. price varies. ‡ Universita degli Studi di Pavia, Istituto Botanico, 27100 Pavia, Italy.

581   IT
UNIVERSITA DEGLI STUDI DI ROMA. ISTITUTO BOTANICO. ANNALI DI BOTANICA. (Text in various European languages; summaries in English & Italian) 1903. a. L.9000. Universita degli Studi di Roma, Istituto Botanico, Citta Universitaria, 00100 Rome, Italy. Ed. Gaspare Mazzolani. bk. rev. charts. illus. index. circ. 500. Indexed: Biol.Abstr. Chem.Abstr.

581   FR   ISSN 0069-469X
UNIVERSITE DE CLERMONT-FERRAND II. ANNALES SCIENTIFIQUE. SERIE BIOLOGIE VEGETALE. 1965. irreg. price varies. Universite de Clermont-Ferrand II, Unite d'Enseignement et de Recherche de Sciences Exactes et Naturelles, B.P. 45, 63000 Aubiere, France. circ. 250.

581   CN   ISSN 0041-9168
UNIVERSITE DE MONTREAL. INSTITUTE BOTANIQUE. CONTRIBUTIONS. (Text in English and French) 1922. irreg. Universite de Montreal, Institut Botanique, 4101 rue Sherbrooke E., Montreal 406, Que., Canada. Indexed: Biol.Abstr. Chem.Abstr.

581   US   ISSN 0066-7587
UNIVERSITY OF ARIZONA. LABORATORY OF TREE-RING RESEARCH. PAPERS. 1964. irreg., no. 5, 1975. price varies. University of Arizona Press, Box 3398, Tucson, AZ 85722. bk. rev.

581   UA   ISSN 0068-5313
UNIVERSITY OF CAIRO. HERBARIUM. PUBLICATIONS. (Text in English) 1968. a. free to botanical institutions and interested botanists; not for sale. University of Cairo, Botany Department, Herbarium, Giza, Egypt. Ed. Vivi Taerkholm. circ. 1,500.

581   US   ISSN 0068-6395
UNIVERSITY OF CALIFORNIA PUBLICATIONS IN BOTANY. 1902. irreg. price varies. University of California Press, 2223 Fulton St., Berkeley, CA 94729.

581   TZ
UNIVERSITY OF DAR ES SALAAM. BOTANY DEPARTMENT. DEPARTMENTAL HERBARIUM PUBLICATIONS. 1971. irreg. price varies. ‡ University of Dar es Salaam, Botany Department, P.O. Box 35060, Dar es Salaam, Tanzania.

581   US   ISSN 0580-6097
UNIVERSITY OF MICHIGAN. HERBARIUM. CONTRIBUTIONS. (Text in English and Spanish; summaries in English) 1939. irreg., latest no. 12. price varies. ‡ University of Michigan, University Herbarium, North University Building, Ann Arbor, MI 48109. Eds. Howard Crum, Rogers McVaugh, Robert L. Shaffer. cum.index:1939-1942;1966-1972. circ. 250(approx.)

581   JA
UNIVERSITY OF TOKYO. FACULTY OF SCIENCE. JOURNAL. SECTION 3: BOTANY/ TOKYO DAIGAKU RIGAKUBU KIYO, DAI-3-RUI, SHOKUBUTSUGAKU. (Text in English) 1925. a. price varies. University of Tokyo, Faculty of Science - Tokyo Daigaku Rigakubu, 7-3-1 Hongo, Bunkyo-ku, Tokyo 113, Japan (Order from Maruzen Co. Ltd., 2-3-10 Nihonbashi, Chou-Ku, Tokyo 103, Japan or their Import and Export Dept., Box 5050, Tokyo International, Tokyo 100-31, Japan) circ. 500. (also avail. in microform)

580   YU
UNIVERZITET U BEOGRADU. INSTITUT ZA BOTANIKU I BOTANICKE BASTE. GLASNIK. vol. 10, n.s., 1975. a. Univerzitet u Beogradu, Institut za Botaniku i Botanicke Baste, Takovska 43, Belgrade, Yugoslavia. Ed. Milorad M. Jankovic.

581   PL   ISSN 0302-8585
UNIWERSYTET JAGIELLONSKI. ZESZYTY NAUKOWE. PRACE BOTANICZNE. (Text in Polish summaries in English) 1973. irreg. 33 Zl. per volume. Panstwowe Wydawnictwo Naukowe, Miodowa 10, Warsaw, Poland.

581.9   SW
VAEXTEKOLOGISKA STUDIER. (Text and summaries in English, German, and Swedish) 1972. irreg., no. 11, 1980. price varies. Svenska Vaextgeografiska Saellskapet - Swedish Society of Plant Geography, c/o Vaextbiologiska Institutionen, Box 559, 751 22 Uppsala, Sweden. Ed. Erik Sjoegren.

581   US   ISSN 0083-5269
VASCULAR FLORA OF OHIO. 1967. irreg. price varies. Ohio State University Press, 2070 Neil Ave., Columbus, OH 43210.

581 634.9   HU   ISSN 0083-5323
VEGETATION UNGARISCHER LANDSCHAFTEN. (Text in German) 1957. irreg., vol. 7, 1977. price varies. (Magyar Tudomanyos Akademia) Akademiai Kiado, Publishing House of the Hungarian Academy of Sciences, P.O. Box 24, H-1363 Budapest, Hungary.

581   II
VISTAS IN PLANT SCIENCES. 1975. a. price varies. Today and Tomorrow's Printers and Publishers, 24-B/5 Original Rd., Karol Bagh, New Delhi 110005, India (Dist. in U.S. by: Indo Americana Literature House, Box 1276, Globe, AZ 85501)

581   US
WADSWORTH BOTANY SERIES. irreg. Wadsworth Publishing Co., 10 Davis Dr., Belmont, CA 94002.

581   IT   ISSN 0083-7792
WEBBIA; RACCOLTA DI SCRITTI BOTANICI. (Text in various languages) 1905. a(in 2 pts) L.36000. Universita degli Studi di Firenze, Istituto Botanico, 50121 Florence, Florence, Italy. Ed. Guido Moggi. Indexed: Biol.Abstr. Excerp.Bot.

581.65 632.5   AT   ISSN 0085-803X
WEED SOCIETY OF NEW SOUTH WALES. PROCEEDINGS. 1967. a. price varies. Weed Society of N.S.W., P.O. Box K 287, Haymarket, Sydney, N.S.W. 2000, Australia. circ. 500-1,000.

581   AT
WESTERN AUSTRALIAN HERBARIUM. ANNUAL REPORT. a. Department of Agriculture, Western Australian Herbarium, Tarrah Rd., South Perth, W.A. 6151, Australia.

632 581   US   ISSN 0091-4487
WESTERN SOCIETY OF WEED SCIENCE. PROCEEDINGS. vol. 26, 1973. a. $8. Western Society of Weed Science, c/o J. Lamar Anderson, Department of Plant Science, UMC 48, Utah State University, Logan, UT 84322.

632 581   US   ISSN 0511-8107
WESTERN SOCIETY OF WEED SCIENCE. RESEARCH PROGRESS REPORT. 1952. a. $7. Western Society of Weed Science, c/o J. Lamar Anderson, Department of Plant Science, UMC 48, Utah State University, Logan, UT 83422.

581   US   ISSN 0084-2648
WRIGHTIA; a botanical journal. 1945-1951. irreg., vol. 5, no. 3, 1974. price varies. University of Texas at Dallas, Box 688, Richardson, TX 75080. Ed. Cyrus Longworth Lundell.

580 590   AU   ISSN 0084-5639
ZOOLOGISCH-BOTANISCHE GESELLSCHAFT, VIENNA. ABHANDLUNGEN. irreg. Zoologisch-Botanische Gesellschaft, Burgring 7, A-1010 Vienna, Austria.

580 590   AU   ISSN 0084-5647
ZOOLOGISCH-BOTANISCHE GESELLSCHAFT, VIENNA. VERHANDLUNGEN. 1851. irreg. S.18($10) Zoologisch-Botanische Gesellschaft, Burgring 7, A-1010 Vienna, Austria. bk. rev. circ. 900.

BIOLOGY — Cytology And Histology

574.8 591   US
ACTUALITES PROTOZOOLOGIQUES. (Published in host country) 1974. quadrennial, latest 1978. International Congress of Protozoology, c/o Dr. Hunter, Hawkins Laboratories, Pace University, Pace Plaza, New York, NY 10038.

ADVANCES IN ANATOMY, EMBRYOLOGY AND CELL BIOLOGY. see BIOLOGY

574.8   US   ISSN 0084-5949
ADVANCES IN CYTOPHARMACOLOGY. Vol. I represents: International Symposium on Cell Biology and Cytopharmacology. Proceedings. 1971. irreg., vol. 3, 1979. Raven Press, 1140 Ave. of the Americas, New York, NY 10036. Ed. F. Clementi. Indexed: Biol.Abstr. Chem.Abstr. Curr.Cont. Ind.Med.

574.87   UR   ISSN 0301-2425
BIOFIZIKA ZHIVOI KLETKI. 1970. irreg. 1 Rub. Akademiya Nauk S.S.S.R, Institut Biologicheskoi Fiziki, Akademgorodok, 142292 Pushchino, U. S. S. R. Ed. G. M. Frank. illus. circ. 1,500. Indexed: Ref.Zh.

574.8   US   ISSN 0067-8775
BIOLOGICAL MACROMOLECULES SERIES. 1967. irreg., vol. 7, 1975. price varies. Marcel Dekker, Inc., 270 Madison Ave., New York, NY 10016. Eds. G. D. Fasman and S. N. Timasheff.

574.875   US   ISSN 0067-8864
BIOMEMBRANES. 1971. irreg. price varies. Plenum Press, 233 Spring St., New York, NY 10013. Ed. L. A. Manson. Indexed: Ind.Med.

574.8   US
CELL BIOLOGY; a series of monographs. 1969. irreg. price varies. Academic Press, Inc., 111 Fifth Ave., New York, NY 10003. Ed. D. E. Buetow.

574.8   US
CELL BIOLOGY MONOGRAPHS. 1977. irreg., vol. 7, 1980. Springer-Verlag, 175 Fifth Ave., New York, NY 10010 (also Berlin, Heidelberg, Vienna) (reprint service avail. from ISI)
Supersedes: Protoplasmologia; Handbuch der Protoplasmaforschung (ISSN 0079-7073)

574.8   US
COLD SPRING HARBOR CONFERENCES ON CELL PROLIFERATION. 1974. a. $95 for vol. 6. Cold Spring Harbor Laboratory, Box 100, Publications Department, Cold Spring Harbor, NY 11724.

574.88   US
COLUMBIA SERIES IN MOLECULAR BIOLOGY. irreg., latest 1976. price varies. Columbia University Press, 136 South Broadway, Irvington-on-Hudson, NY 10533.

574.8   US   ISSN 0073-0114
HANDBUCH DER MIKROSKOPISCHEN ANATOMIE DES MENSCHEN. (Numbers not issued consecutively) 1929. irreg.; vol. 7, pt. 6, 1979. Springer-Verlag, 175 Fifth Ave., New York, NY 10010 (also Berlin, Heidelberg, Vienna)

574.8   US
I C N -U C L A SYMPOSIUM ON MOLECULAR BIOLOGY PROCEEDINGS. 1972. irreg., 1st, Squaw Valley, CA, 1972. (International Chemical and Nuclear Corp) Academic Press, Inc., 111 5th Ave., New York, NY 10003. (Co-Sponsor: University of California at Los Angeles, Molecular Biology Institute) Eds. C. Fred Fox, William S. Robinson.

574.87   NE   ISSN 0074-3550
INTERNATIONAL CONGRESS OF CELL BIOLOGY. SUMMARIES OF REPORTS AND COMMUNICATIONS.* irreg., 1968, 12th, Brussels. (International Federation of Cell Biology) Excerpta Medica, P.O. Box 211, Amsterdam, Netherlands (Inquire: Dr. L. A. Franks, Imperial Cancer Research Fund, Lincoln's Inn Fields, London WC2, England)

INTERNATIONAL CONGRESS OF HISTOCHEMISTRY AND CYTOCHEMISTRY. PROCEEDINGS. see BIOLOGY — Biological Chemistry

574.8   US   ISSN 0074-767X
INTERNATIONAL REVIEW OF CONNECTIVE TISSUE RESEARCH. 1963. irreg., vol. 7, 1976. price varies. Academic Press, Inc., 111 Fifth Ave., New York, NY 10003. Eds. David A. Hall, D. S. Jackson. index. Indexed: Ind.Med.

574.8   US   ISSN 0074-7696
INTERNATIONAL REVIEW OF CYTOLOGY. 1952. irreg., vol. 56, 1979. price varies. Academic Press, Inc., 111 Fifth Ave., New York, NY 10003. Eds. G. H. Bourne, J. F. Danielli. index. cum.index: vols. 1-9(1952-1960) in vol. 10(1960) Indexed: Ind.Med.

574.8   US   ISSN 0074-770X
INTERNATIONAL REVIEW OF CYTOLOGY. SUPPLEMENT. 1969. irreg., no. 8, 1978. price varies. Academic Press, Inc., 111 Fifth Ave., New York, NY 10003. Eds. G. H. Bourne, J. F. Danielli. Indexed: Ind.Med.

574.8   US
INTERNATIONAL SYMPOSIUM ON MOLECULAR BIOLOGY. PROCEEDINGS. 1972. irreg., 7th, Baltimore, Maryland and Vienna, Austria, 1974. price varies. Johns Hopkins University Press, Baltimore, MD 21218. bibl. illus.

574.8   UK
MEMBRANE STRUCTURE AND FUNCTION. 1980. irreg. £12.20. John Wiley & Sons Ltd., Baffins Lane, Chichester, Sussex PO19 1UD, England. Ed. E. E. Bittar. (reprint service avail. rom UMI, ISI)

574.8   US   ISSN 0091-679X
METHODS IN CELL BIOLOGY. irreg. Academic Press, Inc, 111 Fifth Ave., New York, NY 10003. Ed. D. M. Prescott. illus. Indexed: Chem.Abstr. Ind.Med.
Continues: Methods in Cell Physiology.

574.88   US
MILES INTERNATIONAL SYMPOSIUM. (Publisher varies) a. $17.50. (Miles Laboratories Inc.) Raven Press, 1140 Ave. of the Americas, New York, NY 10036.
Formerly (until 1971): International Symposium on Molecular Biology Publications.

574   US   ISSN 0077-0221
MOLECULAR BIOLOGY, BIOCHEMISTRY AND BIOPHYSICS. 1967. irreg., no. 32, 1980. Springer-Verlag, 175 Fifth Ave., New York, NY 10010 (also Berlin, Heidelberg, Vienna) (reprint service avail. from ISI) Indexed: Ind.Med.

574.88   US   ISSN 0077-023X
MOLECULAR BIOLOGY; PROCEEDINGS OF THE INTERNATIONAL CONFERENCE. irreg., 1970, 7th, Chania, Crete. $29.50. (International Center for Advanced Studies) Gordon & Breach Science Publishers, 1 Park Avenue, New York, NY 10016.

MONOGRAPHS IN CLINICAL CYTOLOGY. see *MEDICAL SCIENCES*

NEW TECHNIQUES IN BIOPHYSICS AND CELL BIOLOGY. see *BIOLOGY — Biophysics*

PROGRESS IN HISTOCHEMISTRY AND CYTOCHEMISTRY. see *BIOLOGY — Biological Chemistry*

574.8   US   ISSN 0079-6484
PROGRESS IN MOLECULAR AND SUBCELLULAR BIOLOGY. 1969. biennial. price varies. Springer-Verlag, 175 Fifth Ave., New York, NY 10010 (also Berlin, Heidelberg, Vienna) Ed. F. E. Hahn. (reprint service avail. from ISI)

574.8   GW   ISSN 0340-5400
RESEARCH IN MOLECULAR BIOLOGY. 1973. irreg., vol. 11, 1981. price varies. (Akademie der Wissenschaften und der Literatur, Mainz, Mathematisch-Naturwissenschaftliche Klasse) Franz Steiner Verlag GmbH, Friedrichstr. 24, Postfach 5529, 6200 Wiesbaden, W. Germany (B.R.D.) Ed. Rudolf K. Zahn.

574.8   US   ISSN 0080-1844
RESULTS AND PROBLEMS IN CELL DIFFERENTIATION. 1968. irreg., no. 11, 1980. Springer-Verlag, 175 Fifth Ave., New York, NY 10010 (also Berlin, Heidelberg, Vienna) (reprint service avail. from ISI) Indexed: Ind.Med.

BIOLOGY — Entomology

see also Agriculture—Crop Production and Soil; Engineering—Chemical Engineering

595.7   IT   ISSN 0065-0757
ACCADEMIA NAZIONALE ITALIANA DI ENTOMOLOGIA. RENDICONTI. 1951/52. irreg., no. 14, 1971. price varies. Accademia Nazionale Italiana di Entomologia, Istituto di Entomologia Agraria, Borgo XX Giugno, 06100 Perugia, Italy.

595.7   CS
ACTA ENTOMOLOGICA. (Text in English, French and German) 1923. irreg. price varies. Narodni Muzeum, Prirodovedecke Muzeum, Vaclavske nam. 1700, 115 79 Prague 1, Czechoslovakia. Ed. Ludvik Hoberlandt.

595.7   UK   ISSN 0065-2806
ADVANCES IN INSECT PHYSIOLOGY. 1963. irreg., vol. 14, 1979. price varies. Academic Press Inc. (London) Ltd., 24-28 Oval Rd., London NW1 7DX, England (and 111 Fifth Ave., New York, N.Y. 10003) Eds. J. W. L. Beament, J. E. Treherne, V. B. Wigglesworth.

595.7   US   ISSN 0065-6143
ALDRICH ENTOMOLOGY CLUB. NEWSLETTER. 1962. irreg., vol. 10, 1972; vol. 11, 1980. free. ‡ University of Idaho, Department of Entomology, Moscow, ID 83843. Ed. Janet L. Moore. circ. 150.

595.7   US   ISSN 0569-4450
AMERICAN ENTOMOLOGICAL INSTITUTE. CONTRIBUTIONS. 1964. irreg. $30. American Entomological Institute, 5950 Warren Rd., Ann Arbor, MI 48105. Ed. Henry K. Townes. circ. 200. (back vols. avail.)

595.7   US   ISSN 0065-8162
AMERICAN ENTOMOLOGICAL INSTITUTE. MEMOIRS. 1961. irreg. price varies. American Entomological Institute, 5950 Warren Rd., Ann Arbor, MI 48105. Ed. Henry K. Townes. index. circ. 200. (back vols. avail.)

595.7   US   ISSN 0065-8170
AMERICAN ENTOMOLOGICAL SOCIETY. MEMOIRS. 1916. irreg., no. 32, 1979. price varies. American Entomological Society, Academy of Natural Sciences, Philadelphia, PA 19103. Ed. Selwyn S. Roback. index.

595.7   US   ISSN 0066-4170
ANNUAL REVIEW OF ENTOMOLOGY. 1956. a. $20. Annual Reviews Inc., 4139 El Camino Way, Palo Alto, CA 94306. Ed. Thomas E. Mittler. bibl. index; cum.index. (back issues avail.; reprint service avail. from ISI) Indexed: Biol.Abstr. Chem.Abstr. Apic.Abstr. M.M.R.I.

595.2   US   ISSN 0066-8036
ARTHROPODS OF FLORIDA AND NEIGHBORING LAND AREAS. 1965. irreg., vol. 8, 1973. free to Florida residents on request. ‡ Department of Agriculture and Consumer Services, Division of Plant Industry, Box 1269, Gainesville, FL 32602. (back issues avail) Indexed: Biol.Abstr. Bibl.Agri. Zoo.Rec.

595.7   AT
AUSTRALIAN ENTOMOLOGICAL SOCIETY. MISCELLANEOUS PUBLICATIONS. irreg. price varies. Australian Entomological Society, Entomology Branch, Department of Primary Industries, Meiers Rd., Indooroopilly, Qld. 4068, Australia.

595.7   UK   ISSN 0007-1501
BRITISH MUSEUM (NATURAL HISTORY). BULLETIN. ENTOMOLOGY. 1949. irreg. price varies. British Museum (Natural History), Cromwell Rd., London SW7 5BD, England. illus. charts. circ. 750. Indexed: Biol.Abstr.

595.7   US   ISSN 0068-5631
CALIFORNIA INSECT SURVEY. BULLETIN. 1950. irreg. price varies. University of California Press, 2223 Fulton St., Berkeley, CA 94720.

595.1   BE
CATALOGUE DES COLEOPTERES DE BELGIQUE. irreg. 240 Fr. Societe Royale Belge d'Entomologie, 31, rue Vautier, 1040 Brussels, Belgium.

595.7   UK   ISSN 0069-7044
COMMONWEALTH ENTOMOLOGICAL CONFERENCE. REPORT. irreg. price varies. (Commonwealth Institute of Entomology) Commonwealth Agricultural Bureaux, Farnham House, Farnham Royal, Slough SL2 3BN, England. (also avail. in microfilm; back issues avail.)

595.7   AT   ISSN 0069-732X
COMMONWEALTH SCIENTIFIC AND INDUSTRIAL RESEARCH ORGANIZATION. DIVISION OF ENTOMOLOGY. REPORT. 1960/61. a. Aus.$2. C. S. I. R. O., Division of Entomology, Box 1700, Canberra City, A.C.T. 2601, Australia.

595.7   AT   ISSN 0069-7338
COMMONWEALTH SCIENTIFIC AND INDUSTRIAL RESEARCH ORGANIZATION. DIVISION OF ENTOMOLOGY. TECHNICAL PAPER. 1957. irreg. price varies. C.S.I.R.O, Division of Entomology, Box 1700, Canberra City, A.C.T. 2601, Australia.

595.7   US   ISSN 0070-7333
DROSOPHILA INFORMATION SERVICE. 1934. irreg., approx. a. $4. c/o Dr. Philip Hedrick, Division of Biological Sciences, University of Kansas, Lawrence, KS 66045. Ed. E. Novitski.

595.7   GW   ISSN 0171-8177
ENTOMOLOGIA GENERALIS; Zeitschrift fuer wissenschaftliche Entomologie /journal for scientific entomology. (Text in German; summaries in English) 1974. irreg. (4 nos. per vol.) DM.186. Gustav Fischer Verlag, Wollgrasweg 49, Postfach 720143, 7000 Stuttgart 70, W. Germany (B.R.D.) Ed. A. W. Steffan. circ. 450.
Formerly: Entomologica Germanica (ISSN 0340-2266)

959.7   SW   ISSN 0105-3574
ENTOMOLOGICA SCANDINAVICA. SUPPLEMENTUM. irreg., no. 14, 1980. price varies. Naturvetenskapliga Forskningsraadet, Box 23136, S-104 35 Stockholm, Sweden. (Co-sponsor: Scandinavian Society of Entomologists) Ed. Lennart Cederholm.

595.7   CN   ISSN 0071-0709
ENTOMOLOGICAL SOCIETY OF ALBERTA. PROCEEDINGS. 1953. a. membership. ‡ University of Alberta, Department of Entomology, Edmonton, Alta. T6G 2E3, Canada. cum.index every 10 years.

595.7   US   ISSN 0071-0717
ENTOMOLOGICAL SOCIETY OF AMERICA. MISCELLANEOUS PUBLICATIONS. 1959. irreg., vol. 11, 1978. Entomological Society of America, 4603 Calvert Rd., College Park, MD 20740. Ed. Bruce F. Eldridge. cum.index. circ. 200. (also avail. in microform from UMI) Indexed: Biol.Abstr. Chem.Abstr.

595.7   CN   ISSN 0071-075X
ENTOMOLOGICAL SOCIETY OF CANADA. MEMOIRS. (Text in English or French) 1956. irreg.(1-8 per year) included with subscription to Canadian Entomologist. Entomological Society of Canada, 1320 Carling Ave., Ottawa, Ont. K1Z 7K9, Canada. Ed. D.C. Eidt.

595.7   CN   ISSN 0315-2146
ENTOMOLOGICAL SOCIETY OF MANITOBA. PROCEEDINGS. 1945. a. Entomological Society of Manitoba, Inc., 95 Dafoe Rd., Winnipeg. Man. R3T 2M9, Canada.

595.7   CN   ISSN 0071-0768
ENTOMOLOGICAL SOCIETY OF ONTARIO. PROCEEDINGS; annual publication of entomological research in Ontario. 1871. a. Can.$4. ‡ Entomological Society of Ontario, University of Guelph, Dept. of Environmental Biology, Graham Hall, Guelph, Ont., Canada. Ed. W.E. Heming. bk. rev. index. circ. 1,000. Indexed: Biol.Abstr. Chem.Abstr. Rev.Appl.Entomol. Zoo.Rec.

595.7   SA
ENTOMOLOGICAL SOCIETY OF SOUTHERN AFRICA. PROCEEDINGS OF THE CONGRESS. 1974. irreg. Entomological Society of Southern Africa, Box 103, Pretoria, South Africa.

595.7   CS   ISSN 0071-0792
ENTOMOLOGICKE PROBLEMY. (Text in German or Slovak; summaries in English, German, Russian) 1961. irreg. price varies. (Slovenska Akademia Vied, Slovenska Entomologicka Spolocnost) Veda, Publishing House of the Slovak Academy of Sciences, Klemensova 19, 895 30 Bratislava, Czechoslovakia. Ed. Ilja Okali.

595.7   SP   ISSN 0013-9440
EOS; revista espanola de entomologia. (Multilingual Text) 1925. a. 600 ptas. Instituto Espanol de Entomologia, J. Gutierrez Avascal 2, Madrid 6, Spain. Ed. Ramon Agenjo. circ. 550.

595.7   JA   ISSN 0071-1268
ESAKIA. (Text in English, French and German) 1960. irreg. exchange basis only. Kyushu University, Hikosan Biological Laboratory, Entomological Laboratory, Fukuoka 812, Japan. Ed.Bd. charts. illus. Indexed: Biol.Abstr. Entomol.Abstr. Zoo.Rec.

595.7 574   DK
FAUNA ENTOMOLOGICA SCANDINAVICA. (Text in English) 1973. irreg. (2-5/yr.) price varies. Scandinavian Science Press Ltd., Christiansholms Parallelvej 2, DK-2930 Klampenborg, Denmark. Ed. Leif Lyneborg. illus. (back issues avail.) Indexed: Biol.Abstr.

595.7   MX   ISSN 0430-8603
FOLIA ENTOMOLOGICA MEXICANA. (Text and summaries in English and Spanish) 1961. irreg. Mex.$150($12) (or exchange) Sociedad Mexicana de Entomologia, Apdo. Postal 31-312, Mexico 7, D.F., Mexico. Ed. Bd. bibl. charts. cum.index: nos. 138, 1961-1971.

595.7   IT   ISSN 0429-288X
FRAGMENTA ENTOMOLOGICA. (Text in Italian, English, French, German; summaries in Italian, English) 1951. irreg. avail. only on exchange. Istituto Nazionale di Entomologia, Via Catone 34, 00192 Rome, Italy. Ed. Pasquale Pasquini.

FUNDACION MIGUEL LILLO. MISCELANEA. see *BIOLOGY — Botany*

595.7   AT   ISSN 0158-0760
GENERAL AND APPLIED ENTOMOLOGY. 1964. a. Aus.$6. Entomological Society of Australia (N.S.W.), P.O. Box 22, Five Dock, N.S.W. 2046, Australia. Ed. C. E. Chadwick. adv. bk. rev. circ. 210. Indexed: Biol.Abstr. Aus.Sci.Abstr. Rev.Appl.Entomol.
Formerly (until vol. 10, 1978): Entomological Society of Australia (N.S.W.) Journal (ISSN 0071-0725)

BIOLOGY — ENTOMOLOGY

595.7   II   ISSN 0073-6392
INDIAN FOREST RECORDS (NEW SERIES) ENTOMOLOGY. (Text in English) 1935. irreg., vol. 13, no. 1, 1979. price varies. ‡ Forest Research Institute & Colleges, P.O. New Forest, Dehra Dun, India. circ. 500. Indexed: Biol.Abstr. Forest.Abstr. Indian Sci.Abstr.

595.7   JA   ISSN 0020-1804
INSECTA MATSUMURANA. (Text mainly in English) 1926. N.S. 1973. irreg. exchange basis. Hokkaido University, Faculty of Agriculture, Entomological Institute - Hokkaido Daigaku Nogakubu Konchugaku Kyoshitsu, Nishi-9-chome, Kita-9-jo, Kita-ku, Sapporo 060, Japan. charts. illus. Indexed: Biol.Abstr.

595.7   US
INSECTICIDE AND ACARICIDE TESTS. 1976. a. Entomological Society of America, 4603 Calvert Rd., College Park, MD 20740.

595.7   US   ISSN 0073-8115
INSECTS OF MICRONESIA. (Most issues in English only; a few issues in French or German only) 1954. irreg. price varies. Bishop Museum Press, Box 19000-A, Honolulu, HI 96819. vol. indexes will be issued. Indexed: Biol.Abstr.

595.7   US   ISSN 0098-1222
INSECTS OF VIRGINIA. (Subseries of: Virginia Polytechnic Institute and State University. Research Division. Bulletin on Scale Insects) 1969. irreg. exchange basis only. Virginia Polytechnic Institute and State University, Research Division, Blacksburg, VA 24061. illus.

595.7   UK   ISSN 0074-364X
INTERNATIONAL CONGRESS OF ENTOMOLOGY. 1910. quadrennial, 15th. 1976, Washington. price varies. International Congresses of Entomology, Permanent Committee, c/o British Museum (Natural History), Cromwell Rd., London, S.W. 7, England.
    Proceedings published by local committee

595.7   IS   ISSN 0075-1243
ISRAEL JOURNAL OF ENTOMOLOGY. (Text in English) 1966. a. $10. Entomological Society of Israel, Box 6, Bet-Dagan, Israel. Ed.Bd. adv. bk. rev. circ. 200. Indexed: Entomol.Abstr. Rev.Appl.Entomol.

616.968   US
JOURNAL OF MEDICAL ENTOMOLOGY. SUPPLEMENT. 1976. irreg. (Bishop Museum, Department of Entomology) Bishop Museum Press, Box 19000-A, Honolulu, HI 96819.

591   PL   ISSN 0075-6350
KLUCZE DO OZNACZANIA OWADOW POLSKI. 1954. irreg., nos. 69-72, 1974. price varies. (Polskie Towarzystwo Entomologiczne) Panstwowe Wydawnictwo Naukowe, Ul. Miodowa 10, Warsaw, Poland (Dist. by Ars Polona-Ruch, Krakowskie Przedmiescie 7, Warsaw, Poland) index.

595.7   US   ISSN 0075-8795
LEPIDOPTERISTS' SOCIETY. MEMOIRS. 1964. irreg., latest 1971. Lepidopterists' Society, c/o Ron Leuschner, Treas., 1900 John St., Manhattan Beach, CA 90266 (Orders to: Dr. Charles V. Covell, Jr., Department of Biology, University of Louisville, Louisville, KY 40208) Ed. G. L. Godfrey.

595.7   CN   ISSN 0076-3810
MANITOBA ENTOMOLOGIST. 1967. a. Can.$8. Entomological Society of Manitoba, Inc., 195 Dafoe Rd., Winnipeg, Man. R3T 2M9, Canada. Ed. P. H. Westdal. bk. rev. circ. 200. Indexed: Biol.Abstr. Bibl.Agri. Rev.Appl.Entomol. Wild Life Rev.

595.7   US   ISSN 0076-6224
MELANDERIA. 1969. irreg., no. 26, 1976. $2 free to educational institutions. ‡ Washington State Entomological Society, Department of Entomology, Washington State University, Pullman, WA 99163. Eds. Roger D. Akre, Carl Johansen. circ. 950. (back issues avail.) Indexed: Biol.Abstr.

595.7   US   ISSN 0076-6321
MELSHEIMER ENTOMOLOGICAL SERIES. 1967. irreg., approx. 2/yr., latest no. 25. $4 per no. Entomological Society of Pennsylvania, 107 Patterson Bldg., University Park, PA 16802. Ed. Robert Snetsinger. circ. 200.

595.7   GW   ISSN 0077-0698
MONOGRAPHIEN ZUR ANGEWANDTEN ENTOMOLOGIE; Beihefte zur Zeitschrift fuer angewandte Entomologie. (Text in German or English) 1917. irreg., no. 23, 1980. price varies. Verlag Paul Parey (Hamburg), Spitalerstr. 12, 2000 Hamburg 1, W. Germany (B.R.D.) Ed. W. Schwenke. illus. bibl. index. (reprint service avail. from ISI) Indexed: Biol.Abstr. Curr.Cont.

595.7   GW   ISSN 0077-1864
MUENCHNER ENTOMOLOGISCHE GESELLSCHAFT. MITTEILUNGEN. 1910. a. DM.47. Muenchner Entomologische Gesellschaft, Maria-Ward-Str. 1b, 8000 Munich 19, W. Germany (B.R.D.) Ed. Walter Forster.

595.7   AG   ISSN 0524-949X
MUSEO ARGENTINA DE CIENCIAS NATURALES "BERNARDINO RIVADAVIA." INSTITUTO NACIONAL DE INVESTIGACION DE LAS CIENCIAS NATURALES. REVISTA. ENTOMOLOGIA. 1964. irreg.; latest issue 1979. Museo Argentino de Ciencias Naturales "Bernardino Rivadavia", Instituto Nacional de Investigacion de las Ciencias Naturales, Avda. Angel Gallardo 470, Casilla de Correo 220 Sucursal 5, Buenos Aires, Argentina.

NATIONAL INSTITUTE OF AGRICULTURAL SCIENCES, TOKYO. BULLETIN. SERIES C (PLANT PATHOLOGY AND ENTOMOLOGY) see *BIOLOGY — Botany*

595.7   NE   ISSN 0548-1163
NEDERLANDSCHE ENTOMOLOGISCHE VERENIGING. MONOGRAPHS. (Text in Dutch and English) 1964. irreg., no. 8, 1977. price varies. Nederlandse Entomologische Vereniging, Plantage Middenlaan 64, 1018 DH Amsterdam, Netherlands. Ed. Dr. P. van Helsdingen. illus. Indexed: Biol.Abstr.

595.7   US
NEW JERSEY MOSQUITO CONTROL ASSOCIATION. PROCEEDINGS. Variant title: Annual Mosquito Review. 1914. a. $2.50. New Jersey Mosquito Control Association, Inc, c/o Henry R. Rupp, Ed., 1440 Mohawk Rd., North Brunswick, NJ 08902. cum.index:1914-1916. index. (back issues avail.)
    Formerly (until 1975): New Jersey Mosquito Extermination Association. Proceedings.

595.7   NZ   ISSN 0077-9962
NEW ZEALAND ENTOMOLOGIST. 1951. a. NZ.$5.50. Entomological Society of New Zealand, Entomology Division, D.S.I.R., Private Bag, Auckland, New Zealand. Ed. T. K. Crosby. bk. rev. index in vols. 1-4. circ. 700. Indexed: Biol.Abstr. Rev.Appl.Entomol.

595.7   US   ISSN 0362-2622
OCCASIONAL PAPERS IN ENTOMOLOGY. 1959. irreg. exchange basis. Department of Food and Agriculture, Division of Plant Industry, Laboratory Services, 1220 N St., Sacramento, CA 95814. illus. circ. 200. Indexed: Biol.Abstr.
    Continues: California. Bureau of Entomology. Occasional Papers.

OPERA LILLOANA. see *BIOLOGY — Botany*

595.7   US   ISSN 0078-5806
OREGON STATE MONOGRAPHS. STUDIES IN ENTOMOLOGY. 1939. irreg., 1966, no. 4. price varies. Oregon State University Press, 101 Waldo Hall, Corvallis, OR 97331.

595.7   II
ORIENTAL INSECTS MONOGRAPH SERIES. (Text in English) 1972. irreg.; approx. 1/yr. price varies. Association for the Study of Oriental Insects, c/o Department of Zoology, University of Delhi, Delhi 110007, India. (back issues avail.)

595.7   II   ISSN 0300-2713
ORIENTAL INSECTS SUPPLEMENTS SERIES. (Text in English) 1971. irreg.; approx. 1/yr. price varies. Association for the Study of Oriental Insects, c/o Department of Zoology, University of Delhi, Delhi 110007, India. (back issues avail.)

595.7   US   ISSN 0078-7515
PACIFIC INSECTS MONOGRAPHS. 1961. irreg. price varies. (Bishop Museum, Department of Entomology) Bishop Museum Press, Box 19000-A, Honolulu, HI 96819.

595.7   UR
PARAZYTY, PARAZYTOZY TA SHLIAKHYIKH LIKVIDATSII. (Summaries in Russian) 1972. irreg. 1.94 Rub. Akademiya Nauk Ukrainskoi S.S.R., Institut Zoologii, Ul. Lenina, 15, Kiev, U. S. S. R. illus.

595.7   GE   ISSN 0070-7279
REICHENBACHIA; Zeitschrift fuer entomologische Taxonomie. (Text in English, French, German) 1962. irreg. price varies. Staatliches Museum fuer Tierkunde in Dresden, Augustusstr. 2, 8010 Dresden, E. Germany (D.D.R.) Ed. Rainer Emmrich. bk. rev. circ. 500. Indexed: Biol.Abstr. Ber.Biochem.Biol. Zoo.Rec.

595.7   BL   ISSN 0085-5626
REVISTA BRASILEIRA DE ENTOMOLOGIA. (Text in Portuguese and English; summaries in English) 1954. a. $10. Sociedade Brasileira de Entomologia, Caixa Postal 9063, Sao Paulo, Brazil. circ. 200(approx.) Indexed: Biol.Abstr.

595.7   CL   ISSN 0034-740X
REVISTA CHILENA DE ENTOMOLOGIA. (Text in English, German and Spanish) 1951. irreg. $10. Sociedad Chilena de Entomologia, Casilla 2974, Santiago 1, Santiago 1. Ed. Luis E. Pena. bk. rev. bibl. charts. illus. circ. 2,000. Indexed: Biol.Abstr.

595.7   PE   ISSN 0080-2425
REVISTA PERUANA DE ENTOMOLOGIA. (Text in Spanish; summaries in English) 1958. a. S.100($4) Sociedad Entomologica del Peru, Apartado 4796, Lima, Peru. Ed. Pedro G. Aguilar.

595.7   UK   ISSN 0080-4363
ROYAL ENTOMOLOGICAL SOCIETY OF LONDON. SYMPOSIA. 1961. biennial. Royal Entomological Society, 41 Queen's Gate, London SW7 5HU, England (Nos. 5-10 published by: Blackwell Scientific Publications, Ltd., Osney Mead, Oxford, England) Indexed: Zoo.Rec.

595.7   NE   ISSN 0080-8954
SERIES ENTOMOLOGICA. 1966. irreg., vol. 17, 1980. price varies. Dr. W. Junk Publishers, Box 13713, 2501 ES The Hague, Netherlands. Eds. E. Schimitschek, K. A. Spencer. circ. 750.

595.7   UA   ISSN 0081-0983
SOCIETE ENTOMOLOGIQUE D'EGYPTE. BULLETIN/ENTOMOLOGICAL SOCIETY OF EGYPT. BULLETIN. 1908. a, vol. 60, 1976 (in press) £E6($11.66) Entomological Society of Egypt, Box 430, Cairo, Egypt.

595.7   UA   ISSN 0081-0991
SOCIETE ENTOMOLOGIQUE D'EGYPTE. BULLETIN. ECONOMIC SERIES. 1966. a., latest vol. 9, 1975. £E3($5) Entomological Society of Egypt, Box 430, Cairo, Egypt.

595.7   CN   ISSN 0071-0784
SOCIETE ENTOMOLOGIQUE DU QUEBEC. MEMOIRES. (Text in French; summaries in English) 1968. irreg. Societe Entomologique du Quebec, Complex Scientifique, D-1-54, 2700 rue Einstein, Ste.-Foy, Quebec, Que. G1P 3W8, Canada. illus.

595.1   BE
SOCIETE ROYALE BELGE D'ENTOMOLOGIE. MEMOIRES. irreg. price varies. Societe Royale Belge d'Entomologie, 31, rue Vautier, 1040 Brussels, Belgium.

595.7   SA   ISSN 0013-8940
SOUTH AFRICA. DEPARTMENT OF AGRICULTURAL TECHNICAL SERVICES. ENTOMOLOGY MEMOIRS. 1923. 4/yr(approx) price varies. ‡ Department of Agricultural Technical Services, Private Bag X144, Pretoria 0001, South Africa (Orders to: Government Printer, Bosman St., Private Bag X85, Pretoria 0001, South Africa) Ed. P. J. J. Steyn. charts. illus. stat. circ. 700. (reprint service avail. from UMI)

595.7   US
SPRINGER SERIES IN EXPERIMENTAL ENTOMOLOGY. 1979. irreg. Springer Verlag, 175 Fifth Ave., New York, NY 10010 (Also Berlin, Heidelberg, Vienna) Ed. T. A. Miller. (reprint service avail. from ISI)

595.7 GE ISSN 0070-7244
STAATLICHES MUSEUM FUER TIERKUNDE IN DRESDEN. ENTOMOLOGISCHE ABHANDLUNGEN. (Text in English, French and German) 1961. irreg. price varies. Staatliches Museum fuer Tierkunde in Dresden, Augustusstr. 2, 8010 Dresden, E. Germany (D.D.R.) Ed. Rainer Emmrich. bk. rev. circ. 800. Indexed: Biol.Abstr. Ber.Biochem.Biol. Zoo.Rec.

595.7 US
STUDIES ON THE MORPHOLOGY AND SYSTEMATICS OF SCALE INSECTS. (Subseries of: Virginia Polytechnic Institute and State University. Research Division Division. Bulletin on Scale Insects) 1969. irreg. exchange basis only. Virginia Polytechnic Institute and State University, University Research Division, Blacksburg, VA 24051. illus.

595.7 NE ISSN 0040-7496
TIJDSCHRIFT VOOR ENTOMOLOGIE. (Text in Dutch, English, French and German) 1858. a. fl.190. Nederlandse Entomologische Vereniging, Plantage Middenlaan 64, 1018 DH Amsterdam, Netherlands. Ed.Bd. charts. illus. Indexed: Biol.Abstr.

595.7 US ISSN 0082-6391
TRIBOLIUM INFORMATION BULLETIN. 1958. a. $13.50. California State University, San Bernardino, School of Natural Sciences, San Bernardino, CA 92407. Ed. A. Sokoloff. circ. 150. (also avail. in microfilm)

595.7 US ISSN 0068-6417
UNIVERSITY OF CALIFORNIA PUBLICATIONS IN ENTOMOLOGY. 1906. irreg. price varies. University of California Press, 2223 Fulton St., Berkeley, CA 94720.

595.7 US
VIRGINIA POLYTECHNIC INSTITUTE AND STATE UNIVERSITY. RESEARCH DIVISION. BULLETINS ON SCALE INSECTS. no. 3, 1967. irreg. exchange basis only. Virginia Polytechnic Institute and State University, Research Division, Blacksburg, VA 24061. illus.

595.7 US ISSN 0043-0773
WASHINGTON STATE ENTOMOLOGICAL SOCIETY PROCEEDINGS. 1954. irreg., 1-2/yr. $3. ‡ Washington State Entomological Society, Washington State University, Dept. of Entomology, Pullman, WA 99163. Ed. Carl Johansen. bk. rev. charts. illus. circ. 150.

BIOLOGY — Genetics

575.1 591.15 581.15 CS
ACTA MUSEI MORAVIAE. SCIENTIA NATURALES 3: FOLIA MENDELIANA. (Text in Czech, English, German; summaries in English) 1973. a. $2. Moravske Muzeum, Nam.25, Unora 6, 659 37 Brno, Czechoslovakia. Ed. Vitezslav Orel.
 Issued 1966-1972 as: Folia Mendeliana (ISSN 0085-0748)

ACTA RADIOBOTANIKA ET GENETIKA/ HOSHASEN IKUSHUJO KENKYU HOKOKU; bulletin of the Institute of Radiation Breeding. see *BIOLOGY*

573.1 US ISSN 0065-2660
ADVANCES IN GENETICS. 1947. irreg., vol. 20, 1979. price varies. Academic Press, Inc. (Subsidiary of: Harcourt Brace Jovanovich) 111 Fifth Ave., New York, NY 10003. Ed. M. Demerec. index. cum.index: vol. 1-16 (1947-1954) in vol. 7 (1955) Indexed: Ind.Med.

575.1 US ISSN 0065-2679
ADVANCES IN GENETICS. SUPPLEMENT. 1966. irreg., no. 1, 1966 latest. price varies. Academic Press, Inc., 111 Fifth Ave., New York, NY 10003.

573.21 US ISSN 0065-275X
ADVANCES IN HUMAN GENETICS. 1970. a. price varies. Plenum Press, 233 Spring St., New York, NY 10013. Eds. K. Hirschhorn, H. Harris. Indexed: Ind.Med.

591.15 575.1 US ISSN 0066-4197
ANNUAL REVIEW OF GENETICS. 1967. a. $20. Annual Reviews Inc., 4139 El Camino Way, Palo Alto, CA 94306. Ed. Herschel L. Roman. bibl. index; cum.index. (back issues avail.; reprint service avail. from ISI) Indexed: Biol.Abstr. Chem.Abstr. Ind.Med. Anim.Breed.Abstr. M.M.R.I.

575.1 IT ISSN 0066-9830
ASSOCIAZIONE GENETICA ITALIANA. ATTI. (Text and summaries in English or Italian) 1955. a. L.3500($7) Associazione Genetica Italiana, c/o Laboratorio di Mutagenesi e Differenzianento CNR, Via Cisanello 147/B, 56100 - Pisa, Italy.

971 CN ISSN 0067-0200
ATLANTIC PROVINCES STUDIES. 1963. irreg. price varies. (Social Science Research Council of Canada) University of Toronto Press, Front Campus, Toronto, Ont. M5S 1A6, Canada (and 33 East Tupper St., Buffalo, N.Y. 14203) Ed. John F. Graham. (also avail. in microfiche)

575.1 US
BENCHMARK PAPERS IN GENETICS. 1974. irreg., vol. 11, 1979. price varies. Dowden, Hutchinson and Ross, Inc., 523 Sarah St., Stroudsburg, PA 18360 (Dist. by Academic Press, Inc., 111 Fifth Ave., New York, NY 10003) Ed. D. L. Jameson.

BENCHMARK PAPERS IN SYSTEMATIC AND EVOLUTIONARY BIOLOGY. see *BIOLOGY*

591.15 AG ISSN 0067-9720
BOLETIN GENETICO. (Text and summaries in Spanish and English) 1965. irreg.; no. 10, 1979. available on exchange. Instituto Nacional de Tecnologia Agropecuaria, Centro de Investigaciones en Ciencias Agronomicas, Departamento de Genetica, Casilla de Correo No. 25, 1712 Castelar, Argentina.

581 JA ISSN 0574-9549
C I S. (Chromosome Information Service) (Text in English) 1961. s-a. $24. Society of Chromosome Research - Senshokutai Gakkai, c/o International Christian University, 3-10-2 Osawa, Mitaki-shi, Tokyo 181, Japan. Ed. S. Makino.

575.1 US ISSN 0084-876X
CHROMOSOME ATLAS: FISH, AMPHIBIANS, REPTILES AND BIRDS. 1972. irreg., vol. 3, 1975. price varies. Springer Verlag, 175 Fifth Ave., New York, NY 10010 (also Berlin, Heidelberg, Vienna) Eds. K. Benirschke, T.C. Hsu. (reprint service avail. from ISI)

575 SZ ISSN 0376-4230
CONTRIBUTIONS TO VERTEBRATE EVOLUTION. (Text in English) a. 70 Fr.($42) per vol. (1981 price) S. Karger AG, Allschwilerstrasse 10, P.O. Box, CH-4009 Basel, Switzerland. Eds. M.K. Hecht, F.S. Szalay. (reprint service avail. from ISI)

613.9 UK ISSN 0071-223X
EUGENICS SOCIETY SYMPOSIA. 1965. irreg. price varies. Academic Press Inc. (London) Ltd., 24-28 Oval Rd., London NW1 7DX, England (And 111 Fifth Ave., New York, NY 10003) Indexed: Ind.Med.

575.005 US ISSN 0071-3260
EVOLUTIONARY BIOLOGY. 1967. irreg., vol. 11, 1978. Plenum Publishing Corp., 233 Spring St., New York, NY 10013. Ed.Bd.

575 US ISSN 0093-4755
EVOLUTIONARY THEORY; an international journal of fact and interpretation. 1973. irreg. individuals $10; institutions $15. University of Chicago, Biology Department, 1103 E. 57th St., Chicago, IL 60637. Eds. Isidore Nabi, Leigh van Valen. circ. 250. Indexed: Biol.Abstr. Bibl.&Ind.Geol.

GAMMA FIELD SYMPOSIA. see *AGRICULTURE*

575.1 GW ISSN 0170-0561
GENETIK.GRUNDLAGEN UND PERSPEKTIVEN. 1979. irreg. price varies. Dr. Dietrich Steinkopff Verlag, Saalbaustr. 12, Postach 11 1008, 6100 Darmstadt 11, W. Germany (B.R.D.) Eds. K. R. Lewis, B. John. circ. 3,000.

575.1 SZ ISSN 0378-9861
HUMAN GENE MAPPING. (Text in English) a. 200 Fr.($120) (1981 price) (National Foundation-March of Dimes, US) S. Karger AG, Allschwilerstrasse 10, P.O. Box, CH-4009 Basel, Switzerland. Ed. D. Bergsma. abstr. bibl. charts. illus. index. circ. 800. (back issues avail.; reprint service avail. from ISI) Indexed: Biol.Abstr. Chem.Abstr. Curr.Cont. Ind.Med.

573.21 US ISSN 0340-6717
HUMAN GENETICS. SUPPLEMENT. 1979. irreg. price varies. Springer-Verlag, 175 Fifth Ave., New York, NY 10010 (Also Berlin, Heidelberg, Vienna) (reprint service avail. from ISI)

595.7 KE
INTERNATIONAL CENTRE OF INSECT PHYSIOLOGY AND ECOLOGY. ANNUAL REPORT. 1973. a. International Centre of Insect Physiology and Ecology, Box 30772, Nairobi, Kenya. illus.

613.9 NE
INTERNATIONAL CONGRESS OF HUMAN GENETICS. ABSTRACTS. (Abstracts of 4th Congress published in 1971) 1956. quinquennial. fl.49($20-50) Excerpta Medica, P.O.B. 211, 1000 AE Amsterdam, Netherlands.

575 UR
ITOGI NAUKI I TEKHNIKI: GENETIKA CHELOVEKA. 1973. a. 1.13 Rub. Vsesoyuznyi Institut Nauchno-Tekhnicheskoi Informatsii (Viniti), Ul. Baltiiskaya, 14, Moscow, U.S.S.R.

574 575 US
JACKSON LABORATORY ANNUAL REPORT. a. free. Jackson Laboratory, Bar Harbor, ME 04609. Ed. Dr. Charity Waymouth. circ. 1,800.

575.1 II
JOURNAL OF CYTOLOGY AND GENETICS. (Text in English) vol. 12, 1977. a. Rs.50($10) Society of Cytologists and Geneticists, Department of Botany, Karnatak University, Dharwar 580003, India.

575.1 JA ISSN 0080-8539
KIHARA INSTITUTE FOR BIOLOGICAL RESEARCH. REPORT/KIHARA SEIBUTSUGAKU KENKYUSHO. SEIKEN ZIHO. (Text in Japanese and English) 1941. a. 1000 Yen($4) membership. Kihara Institute for Biological Research - Kihara Seibutsugaku Kenkyusho, 3-122-21 Mutsukawa, Yokohama 232, Japan. Ed. Kosuke Yamashita.

KULTURPFLANZE. see *BIOLOGY — Botany*

613.9 SZ ISSN 0077-0876
MONOGRAPHS IN HUMAN GENETICS. (Text in English) 1966. irreg. (approx. 1/yr.) 90 Fr.($54) per vol. (1981 price) S. Karger AG, Allschwilerstrasse 10, P.O. Box, CH-4009 Basel, Switzerland. Ed. L. Beckmann, M. Hauge. (reprint service avail. from ISI) Indexed: Biol.Abstr. Chem.Abstr. Curr.Cont. Ind.Med.

575 US
MONOGRAPHS ON THEORETICAL AND APPLIED GENETICS. 1975. irreg., vol. 5, 1981. price varies. Springer Verlag, 175 Fifth Ave., New York, NY 10010 (And Berlin, Heidelberg, Vienna) Ed.Bd. (reprint service avail. from ISI)

575 JA ISSN 0077-4995
NATIONAL INSTITUTE OF GENETICS, MISHIMA, JAPAN. ANNUAL REPORT/ KOKURITSU IDENGAKU KENKYUSHO, MISHIMA, JAPAN. NENPO. (Text in English) 1949-50. a. free or exchange basis to academic institutions or societies. National Institute of Genetics - Monbu-Sho Kokuritsu Idengaku Kenkyusho, 1111 Yata, Mishima 411, Japan. circ. 600.

OXFORD MONOGRAPHS ON MEDICAL GENETICS. see *MEDICAL SCIENCES*

575.1 SZ ISSN 0301-0139
PIGMENT CELL. (Text in English) 1973. irreg. (approx. 1/yr.) 190 Fr.($114) per vol. (1981 price) S. Karger AG, Allschwilerstrasse 10, P.O. Box, CH-4009 Basel, Switzerland. Ed. V. Riley. (reprint service avail. from ISI)

575.1 US ISSN 0081-4148
STADLER GENETICS SYMPOSIUM.
PROCEEDINGS. 1971. irreg., vol. 9, 1978. price varies. University of Missouri-Columbia, Department of Agronomy, 117 Curtis Hall, Columbia, MO 65201. circ. 1,000. Indexed: Biol.Abstr. Ref.Zh. Ber.Biochem.Biol.

UNIVERSITY OF FLORIDA. SCHOOL OF FOREST RESOURCES & CONSERVATION. COOPERATIVE FOREST GENETICS RESEARCH PROGRAM. PROGRESS REPORT. see FORESTS AND FORESTRY

575.1 CS
UNIVERZITA KOMENSKEHO. PEDAGOGICKA FAKULTA V TRNAVE. PRIRODNE VEDY: BIOLOGIA-GENETIKA. irreg., approx. a. price varies. Slovenske Pedagogicke Nakladatelstvo, Sasinkova 5, 891 12 Bratislava, Czechoslovakia.

BIOLOGY — Microbiology

574.52 PL ISSN 0065-1478
ACTA PARASITOLOGICA POLONICA. (Text in English; summary in Polish) irreg., 1975, vol. 22, fasc. 22-23. price varies. (Polska Akademia Nauk, Zaklad Parazytologii) Panstwowe Wydawnictwo Naukowe, Ul. Miodowa 10, Warsaw, Poland. Ed. Wlodzimierz Michajlow. bibl. illus. Indexed: Key Word Ind.Wildl.Res.

ACTA PATHOLOGICA ET MICROBIOLOGICA SCANDINAVICA. SECTION B: MICROBIOLOGY. SUPPLEMENTUM. see BIOLOGY

576 US ISSN 0065-2164
ADVANCES IN APPLIED MICROBIOLOGY. 1959. irreg., vol. 25, 1979. price varies. Academic Press, Inc., 111 Fifth Ave., New York, NY 10003. Eds. Wayne W. Umbreit. index. Indexed: Ind.Med.

576 US ISSN 0065-2172
ADVANCES IN APPLIED MICROBIOLOGY. SUPPLEMENT. 1968. irreg., no. 1, 1968 latest. price varies. Academic Press, Inc., 111 Fifth Ave., New York, NY 10003.

576 US ISSN 0161-8954
ADVANCES IN AQUATIC MICROBIOLOGY. 1968. irreg., latest vol. 1. price varies. Academic Press, Inc., 111 Fifth Ave., New York, NY 10003. Eds. M. Droop And F. Wood.
Formerly: Advances in Microbiology of the Sea (ISSN 0065-292X)

574.5 US ISSN 0147-4863
ADVANCES IN MICROBIAL ECOLOGY. a. Plenum Publishing Corp., 233 Spring St., New York, NY 10013. Ed. M. Alaxander.

576 US ISSN 0065-2911
ADVANCES IN MICROBIAL PHYSIOLOGY. 1967. irreg., vol.19, 1979. price varies. Academic Press, Inc., 111 Fifth Ave., New York, NY 10003. Eds. A. H. Rose, J. F. Wilkinson. Indexed: Ind.Med.

576.64 574 JA
ADVANCES IN VIROLOGY. (Text in Japanese) 1958. a. Kyoto University, Institute for Virus Research - Kyoto Daigaku Uirusu Kenkyusho, Shogoin Kawahara-cho, Sakyo-ku, Kyoto 606, Japan. Ed. Hisao Uetake. circ. controlled.
Virology

576 616 US ISSN 0065-3527
ADVANCES IN VIRUS RESEARCH. 1953. irreg., vol. 25, 1979. price varies. Academic Press, Inc., 111 Fifth Ave., New York, NY 10003. Eds. Kenneth M. Smith, Max A. Lauffer. index. Indexed: Biol.Abstr. Ind.Med.

AMERICAN ASSOCIATION OF PATHOLOGISTS AND BACTERIOLOGISTS. SYMPOSIUM. MONOGRAPHS. see MEDICAL SCIENCES

616.01 576 US
AMERICAN LECTURES IN CLINICAL MICROBIOLOGY. irreg. price varies. Charles C. Thomas, Publisher, 301-327 E. Lawrence Ave., Springfield, IL 62717.

576 589.9 US ISSN 0067-2777
AMERICAN SOCIETY FOR MICROBIOLOGY. ABSTRACTS OF THE ANNUAL MEETING. 1948. a. $10. American Society for Microbiology, 1913 I St., N.W., Washington, DC 20006 (Subscr. to: Box 1192, Birmingham, AL 35201) index. circ. 7,000. Indexed: Biol.Abstr.
Formerly: Bacteriological Proceedings.

576
AMERICAN SOCIETY FOR MICROBIOLOGY. EASTERN PENNSYLVANIA BRANCH. SYMPOSIA. 1973. a. $16.50. University Park Press, American Medical Publishers, Chamber of Commerce Bldg., Baltimore, MD 21202.

576.64 589.9 US
AMERICAN TYPE CULTURE COLLECTION. CATALOGUE OF CELLS, VIRUSES, RICKETTSIAE, CHLAMYDIAE. biennial. free. American Type Culture Association, 12301 Parklawn Dr., Rockville, MD 20852.
Formerly: American Type Culture Collection. Catalogue of Viruses, Rickettsiae, Chlamydiae (ISSN 0363-2989)

576.64 589.9 US ISSN 0363-2970
AMERICAN TYPE CULTURE COLLECTION. CATALOGUE OF STRAINS OF ALGAE, BACTERIA, BACTERIOPHAGES, FUNGI AND PROTOZOA. biennial. price varies. American Type Culture Association, 12301 Parklawn Dr., Rockville, MD 20852.

576 US ISSN 0066-4227
ANNUAL REVIEW OF MICROBIOLOGY. 1947. a. $20. Annual Reviews Inc., 4139 El Camino Way, Palo Alto, CA 94306. Ed. Mortimer P. Starr. bibl. index; cum.index. (back issues avail.; reprint service avail. from ISI) Indexed: Biol.Abstr. Chem.Abstr. Ind.Med. M.M.R.I.

ANTIBIOTICS. see PHARMACY AND PHARMACOLOGY

BAAS BECKING GEOBIOLOGICAL LABORATORY. ANNUAL REPORT. see EARTH SCIENCES — Geology

576 US
BENCHMARK PAPERS IN MICROBIOLOGY. 1973. irreg., vol. 13, 1979. price varies. Dowden, Hutchinson and Ross, Inc., 523 Sarah St., Stroudsburg, PA 18360 (Dist. by Academic Press, Inc., 111 Fifth Ave., New York, NY 10003) Ed. W. W. Umbreit.

589.9 US
BERGEY'S MANUAL OF DETERMINATIVE BACTERIOLOGY. a. price varies. Williams and Wilkins Co., 428 E. Preston St., Baltimore, MD 21202.

576 BU ISSN 0068-3957
BULGARSKA AKADEMIIA NA NAUKITE. MIKROBIOLOGICHNI INSTITUT. IZVESTIIA. (Text in Bulgarian; summaries in various languages) 1950. irreg. 2.08 lv. Publishing House of the Bulgarian Academy of Sciences, Ul. Akad. G. Bonchev, 1113 Sofia, Bulgaria (Dist. by: Hemus, 6, Rouski Blvd., 1000 Sofia, Bulgaria) Ed. Al. Toschkoff. circ. 600. Indexed: Ind.Med.

BULGARSKA AKADEMIIA NA NAUKITE. TSENTRALNA KHELMINTOLOGICHNA LABORATORIIA. IZVESTIIA. see MEDICAL SCIENCES

COLLEGES AND UNIVERSITIES GRANTING DEGREES IN MICROBIOLOGY. see EDUCATION — Guides To Schools And Colleges

CONTRIBUTIONS TO MICROBIOLOGY AND IMMUNOLOGY. see MEDICAL SCIENCES — Allergology And Immunology

576 US ISSN 0070-217X
CURRENT TOPICS IN MICROBIOLOGY AND IMMUNOLOGY. irreg., vol. 92, 1981. price varies. Springer-Verlag, 175 Fifth Ave., New York, NY 10010 (also Berlin, Heidelberg, Vienna) (reprint service avail. from ISI) Indexed: Ind.Med.
Formerly: Ergebnisse der Mikrobiologie und Immunitaetsforschung.

DENMARK. STATENS HUSDYRBRUGSUDVALG. BERETNING. see AGRICULTURE — Poultry And Livestock

576 US ISSN 0070-4563
DEVELOPMENTS IN INDUSTRIAL MICROBIOLOGY. Represents: Society for Industrial Microbiology. Proceedings of the Annual Meeting. 1960. irreg., 1977, vol 18. $34.95. ‡ (American Institute of Biological Sciences) Society for Industrial Microbiology, 1401 Wilson Blvd., Arlington, VA 22209. Eds. Leland A. Underkofler, Margaret L. Wulf.

INSTITUT PASTEUR D'ALGERIE. ARCHIVES. see MEDICAL SCIENCES — Communicable Diseases

576 FR ISSN 0073-8573
INSTITUT PASTEUR DE LILLE. ANNALES.*
(Some summaries in English) 1948. irreg. Institut Pasteur de Lille, 25-28 rue de Dr. Roux, 75015 Paris, France. Indexed: Ind.Med.

INSTITUT PASTEUR HELLENIQUE. ARCHIVES. see MEDICAL SCIENCES — Communicable Diseases

576 JA ISSN 0073-8751
INSTITUTE FOR FERMENTATION, OSAKA. RESEARCH COMMUNICATIONS/HAKKO KENKYUSHO HOKOKU. (Text and summaries in English) 1963. biennial; 1975, no. 7. 1500 Yen per no. Institute for Fermentation - Hakko Kenkyusho, 2-17-85 Juso-honmachi, Yodogawa-ku, Osaka 532, Japan. Ed. Teiji Iijima. cum.index. (back issues avail.) Indexed: Biol.Abstr.
Until no. 4 (1969) : Institute for Fermentation, Osaka. Annual Report.

576 US
INTERNATIONAL BIODETERIORATION SYMPOSIUM. PROCEEDINGS. BIODETERIORATION OF MATERIALS. irreg. $49.50. Halsted Press (Subsidiary of: John Wiley & Sons, Inc.) 605 Third Ave., New York, NY 10016. Eds. A. Harry Walters, E.H. Hueck-van der Plas. illus.

576 US ISSN 0074-3097
INTERNATIONAL CONFERENCE ON GLOBAL IMPACTS OF APPLIED MICROBIOLOGY. PROCEEDINGS. 1965. irreg., 1970 latest. Halsted Press (Subsidiary of: John Wiley & Sons, Inc.) 605 Third Ave., New York, NY 10016.

576 GW
INTERNATIONAL CONGRESS OF MICROBIOLOGY. PROCEEDINGS. (Supplement to: Zentralblatt Fur Bakteriologie) 12th, 1978. irreg. $118. Gustav Fischer Verlag, Wollgrasweg 49, Postfach 720143, 7000 Stuttgart 70, W. Germany (B.R.D.) Ed. Hans-Jurgen Preusser.

576 CS ISSN 0074-8927
INTERNATIONAL SYMPOSIUM ON THE CONTINUOUS CULTIVATION OF MICROORGANISMS. PROCEEDINGS. biennial, 4th, 1968, Prague. price varies. Academia, Publishing House of the Czechoslovak Academy of Sciences, Vodickova 40, 112 29 Prague 1, Czechoslovakia (Dist. by: Academic Press Inc., 111 Fifth Ave., New York, NY 10003, U.S.A.)

576 615 US
INTERSCIENCE CONFERENCE ON ANTIMICROBIAL AGENTS AND CHEMOTHERAPY. PROGRAM AND ABSTRACTS. Abbreviated title: I C A A C Program and Abstracts. 1961? a. $7. American Society for Microbiology, 1913 I St. N.W., Washington, DC 20006 (Subscr. to: Box 1192, Birmingham, AL 35201)

576.64 574 JA ISSN 0075-7357
KYOTO UNIVERSITY. INSTITUTE FOR VIRUS RESEARCH. ANNUAL REPORT/KYOTO DAIGAKU UIRUSU KENKYUSHO NENKAN KIYO. (Text in English) 1958. a. Kyoto University, Institute for Virus Research - Kyoto Daigaku Uirusu Kenkyusho, Shogoin Kawahara-cho, Kyoto 606, Japan. Ed. Hisao Uetake. circ. controlled. Indexed: Biol.Abstr.
Virology

576   HU   ISSN 0076-2431
MAGYAR TUDOMANYOS AKADEMIA. MIKROBIOLOGIAI KUTATO INTEZET. PROCEEDINGS/HUNGARIAN ACADEMY OF SCIENCES. RESEARCH INSTITUTE FOR MICROBIOLOGY. PROCEEDINGS. 1966. irreg. price varies. Akademiai Kiado, Publishing House of the Hungarian Academy of Sciences, P.O. Box 24, H-1363 Budapest, Hungary. Ed. J. G. Weiszfeiler. Indexed: Biol.Abstr. Chem.Abstr. Excerp.Med.

METHODS IN IMMUNOLOGY AND IMMUNOCHEMISTRY. see MEDICAL SCIENCES — Allergology And Immunology

METHODS IN VIROLOGY. see MEDICAL SCIENCES — Communicable Diseases

576   SP   ISSN 0026-2595
MICROBIOLOGIA ESPANOLA. (Text and summaries in English and Spanish) 1947. irreg. latest no. 29, 1976. 400 ptas. Instituto Jaime Ferran de Microbiologia, Joaquin Costa 32, Madrid 6, Spain. Ed.Bd. bk. rev. bibl. charts. illus. index. Indexed: Biol.Abstr. Bull. Signal. Chem.Abstr. Ind.Med.

576.05   US   ISSN 0098-1540
MICROBIOLOGY (WASHINGTON) 1974. a. $22. American Society for Microbiology, 1913 I St., N.W., Washington, DC 20006 (Subscr. to: Box 1192, Birmingham, AL 35201) Ed. David Schlessinger. Indexed: Chem.Abstr.

576   US
MICROBIOLOGY SERIES. irreg., vol. 4, 1978. price varies. Marcel Dekker, Inc., 270 Madison Ave., New York, NY 10016. Ed. Allan I. Laskin.

576   SZ   ISSN 0077-0965
MONOGRAPHS IN VIROLOGY. (Text in English) 1967. irreg. (approx. 1/yr.) 100 Fr.($60) per vol. (1981 price) S. Karger AG, Allschwilerstrasse 10, P.O. Box, CH-4009 Basel, Switzerland. Ed. J. L. Melnick. (reprint service avail. from ISI) Indexed: Biol.Abstr. Chem.Abstr. Curr.Cont. Ind.Med.

576   US   ISSN 0077-1023
MONOGRAPHS ON IMMUNOLOGY. 1971. irreg., vol. 26, 1978. price varies. Academic Press Inc., 111 Fifth Ave., New York, NY 10003. Eds. F. J. Dixon, Jr., H. G. Kunkel.

PERSPECTIVES IN VIROLOGY. see MEDICAL SCIENCES — Communicable Diseases

576   NE   ISSN 0555-3989
PROGRESS IN INDUSTRIAL MICROBIOLOGY. irreg., vol. 16, 1980. price varies. Elsevier Scientific Publishing Co., Box 211, 1000 AE Amsterdam, Netherlands.

PROGRESS IN MEDICAL VIROLOGY. see MEDICAL SCIENCES — Communicable Diseases

576   MX   ISSN 0034-9771
REVISTA LATINOAMERICANA DE MICROBIOLOGIA. 1958. irreg., latest vol. 19, 1977. Mex.$250($12) Apartado Postal 4-862, Mexico 4, D.F., Mexico.

576   PY   ISSN 0556-6908
REVISTA PARAGUAYA DE MICROBIOLOGIA. (Summaries in English) 1966. a. $10. Universidad Nacional de Asuncion, Facultad de Ciencias Medicas, Catedra de Bacteriologia y Parasitologia, Casilla de Correo 1102, Asuncion, Paraguay. Ed. Arquimedes Canese M.D. illus.

576   FR   ISSN 0081-1068
SOCIETE FRANCAISE DE MICROBIOLOGIE. ANNUAIRE. 1961. triennial. membership. Institut Pasteur, 28 rue du Docteur-Roux, Paris 15e, France.

576   UK   ISSN 0081-1394
SOCIETY FOR GENERAL MICROBIOLOGY. SYMPOSIUM. 1961. irreg., no. 31, 1981. $65 for latest vol. Cambridge University Press, Box 110, Cambridge CB2 3RL, England (and 32 E. 57 St., New York NY 10022) index.

576   US
SPRINGER SERIES IN MICROBIOLOGY. 1978. irreg. price varies. Springer-Verlag, 175 Fifth Ave., New York, NY 10010 (Also Berlin, Heidelberg, Vienna) Ed. M.P. Starr. (reprint service avail. from ISI)

576   US   ISSN 0082-2515
TECHNIQUES IN PURE AND APPLIED MICROBIOLOGY. 1969. irreg., unnumbered, 1979. price varies. John Wiley & Sons, Inc., 605 Third Ave., New York, NY 10016. Ed. Carl-Goeran Heden.

576   JA   ISSN 0082-481X
UNIVERSITY OF TOKYO. INSTITUTE OF APPLIED MICROBIOLOGY. REPORTS. (Text in European languages) 1961. a. controlled free circ. University of Tokyo, Institute of Applied Microbiology - Tokyo Daigaku Oyo Biseibutsu Kenkyusho, 1-1-1 Yayoi, Bunkyo-ku, Tokyo 113, Japan. author index.

576 616   US   ISSN 0083-6591
VIROLOGY MONOGRAPHS/VIRUSFORSCHUNG IN EINZELDARSTELLUNGEN. 1968. irreg., vol. 17, 1980. price varies. Springer-Verlag, 175 Fifth Ave., New York, NY 10010 (also Berlin, Heidelberg, Vienna) (reprint service avail. from ISI) Indexed: Ind.Med.
Formerly: Handbuch der Virusforschung.

ZENTRALBLATT FUER BAKTERIOLOGIE, PARASITENKUNDE, INFEKTIONSKRANKHEITEN UND HYGIENE. ORIGINALE REIHE A: MEDIZINISCHE MIKROBIOLOGIE UND PARASITOLOGIE. see MEDICAL SCIENCES — Communicable Diseases

BIOLOGY — Microscopy

A A F M PROCEEDINGS OF ANNUAL MEETING. (American Association of Feed Microscopists) see MEETINGS AND CONGRESSES

578   UK   ISSN 0065-3012
ADVANCES IN OPTICAL AND ELECTRON MICROSCOPY. 1966. irreg., vol. 7, 1979. price varies. Academic Press Inc. (London) Ltd., 24-28 Oval Rd., London NW1 7DX, England (and 111 Fifth Ave., New York, N.Y. 10003) Eds. V. E. Cosslett, R. Barer.

578.46   GW   ISSN 0070-4687
DIATOMEENSCHALEN IM ELEKTRONENMIKROSKOPSCHEN BILD. (Text in English and German) 1961. a. DM.120. J. Cramer, In den Spingaeckern 2, 3300 Braunschweig, W. Germany (B.R.D.) Ed. J. G. Helmcke. circ. 170.

578   US   ISSN 0424-8201
ELECTRON MICROSCOPY SOCIETY OF AMERICA. PROCEEDINGS. (Proceedings 1-24 (1942-66) Not Published) 1967, 25th. a. $25. Claitor's Publishing Division, 3165 S. Acadian, Box 3333, Baton Rouge, LA 70821. Ed. William Bailey. circ. 700.

578   IS   ISSN 0071-2647
EUROPEAN CONGRESS ON ELECTRON MICROSCOPY. quadrennial; 6th, Jerusalem, 1976. (Israel Society of Electron Microscopy) Tal International, Inquire: Prof. D. Danon, Weizmann Institute of Science, Rehovot, Israel.
Proceedings published in host country

578   GW   ISSN 0076-6771
METHODENSAMMLUNG DER ELEKTRONENMIKROSKOPIE. 1970. irreg., no. 9, 1980. DM.568.50 (DM. 454.80 to members) (Deutsche Gesellschaft fuer Elektronenmikroskopie e.V.) Wissenschaftliche Verlagsgesellschaft mbH, Postfach 40, 7000 Stuttgart 1, W. Germany (B.R.D.) Eds. G. Schimmel, W. Vogell.

578   GW   ISSN 0342-958X
MICROSCOPICA ACTA. SUPPLEMENTA. irreg. price varies. S. Hirzel Verlag, Postfach 347, 7000 Stuttgart 1, W. Germany (B.R.D.)

578   NE
PRACTICAL METHODS IN ELECTRON MICROSCOPY. irreg., vol. 8, 1979. price varies. Elsevier North-Holland Biomedical Press, Box 211, 1000 AE Amsterdam, Netherlands. Ed. A.M. Glauert.

535.3 681.4   US
SCANNING ELECTRON MICROSCOPY; an internaional review of advances in techniques and applications of the scanning electron microscope. 1968. a. price varies. Scanning Electron Microscopy, Inc, Box 66507, AMF O'Hare, IL 60666. Ed. Om Johari. circ. 250. Indexed: Biol.Abstr. Bull.Signal. Chem.Abstr. Excerp.Med. Ind.Med. Met.Abstr. Sci.Abstr. Geo.Abstr.
Formerly: Scanning Electron Microscope Symposium. Proceedings (ISSN 0586-5581)

BIOLOGY — Ornithology

see also Agriculture—Poultry and Livestock; Pets

598.2   PL   ISSN 0001-6454
ACTA ORNITHOLOGICA. (Text in English; summaries in Polish and Russian) irreg., 1975, vol. 14, fasc. 6. price varies. (Polska Akademia Nauk, Instytut Zoologii) Panstwowe Wydawnictwo Naukowe, Miodowa 10, Warsaw, Poland. bibl. charts. index. circ. 1,200. Indexed: Biol.Abstr. Ref.Zh. Key Word Ind.Wildl.Res. Zoo Rec.

598.2   PL
AKADEMIA ROLNICZA, POZNAN. ROCZNIK. ORNITOLOGIA STOSOWANA. (In 1972 Name of Institution Changed from--Wyzsza Szkola Rolnicza) (Summaries in English and Russian) 1966. irreg. price varies. Akademia Rolnicza, Poznan, Ul. Wojska Polskiego 28, 60-637 Poznan, Poland. Indexed: Bibl.Agri.

598.2   US
AMERICAN ORNITHOLOGISTS' UNION. PUBLICATIONS. irreg. price varies. American Ornithologists Union, Dept. of Zoology, Oregon State University, Corvallis, OR 97331 (Or National Museum of Natural History, Smithsonian Institution, Washington, DC 20560)

598.2   GW   ISSN 0003-3154
ANGEWANDTE ORNITHOLOGIE/APPLIED ORNITHOLOGY. (Text mostly in German, occasionally in English, French, Italian) 1961. irreg. DM.16. Biologie-Verlag, Postfach 1449, 6200 Wiesbaden, W. Germany (B.R.D.) Ed. Herbert Bruns.

598.2 152   AT   ISSN 0156-1383
BIRD BEHAVIOUR; an international and multidisciplinary journal. 1977. triennial. Aus.$30($37.75) for institutions; Aus. $15 ($20) for individuals. Bird Behavior Press, c/o Dept. of Psychology, Australian National University, Box 4, Canberra, A.C.T., Australia. Ed. Dr. James J. Counsilman. adv. bk. rev. illus. stat. index. circ. 200. (back issues avail.)
Formerly: Babbler.

598.2   US   ISSN 0067-8945
BIRD CONTROL SEMINAR. PROCEEDINGS. 1962. biennial. $10. Bowling Green State University, Environmental Studies Center, Bowling Green, OH 43403. (Co-sponsors: U.S. Fish & Wildlife Service; National Pest Control Association) Ed. William B. Jackson. circ. 500. Indexed: Wild Life Rev.

598.2   UK
BIRD RESEARCH.* 1937. irreg. World Bird Research Station, Glanton, Northumberland NE66 4AH, England.

598.2 639.9   UK   ISSN 0144-364X
BIRDWATCHER'S YEARBOOK. 1981. a. £4.95($15) Buckingham Press, Rostherne, Hall Close, Maids Moreton, Buckingham MK18 1RH, England. Ed. John E. Pemberton. adv. bk. rev. film rev. bibl. charts. illus. circ. 7,500.

598.2   UK   ISSN 0142-7660
BONNY MOOR HEN. 1978. a. Weardale Field Study Society, c/o J. H. Dingwall, Ling Riggs, Ireshopeburn, Co. Durham DL13 1HN, England. charts. illus.

598.2   UK   ISSN 0068-2675
BRITISH TRUST FOR ORNITHOLOGY. ANNUAL REPORT. 1935. a. membership. British Trust for Ornithology, Beech Grove, Tring, England. Ed. C.W.N. Plant. circ. 7,100.

CANADIAN WILDLIFE SERVICE. MONOGRAPH SERIES. see *CONSERVATION*

598.2 US
CARDINAL. vol. 7, 1977. bi-m. $2. Indiana Audubon Society, Inc., 141 S. Second St., Decatur, IN 46733. Ed. Dr. Charles Wise. circ. 632.

598.2 DK ISSN 0011-6394
DANSK ORNITHOLOGISK FORENINGS TIDSSKRIFT. (Text mainly in Danish; summaries in English) 1906. 2-4/yr. Kr.135. Dansk Ornithologisk Forening, Vesterbrogade 140, DK-1620 Copenhagen V, Denmark. Ed. Bent Pors Nielsen. adv. bk. rev. bibl. illus. index. circ. 7,000. Indexed: Biol.Abstr. Key Word Ind.Wildl.Res. Wildlife Rev. Zoo.Rec.

598.2 CN ISSN 0707-0942
DIRECTORY TO CO-OPERATIVE NATURALISTS' PROJECTS IN ONTARIO. 1976. a. Can.$.50. Long Point Bird Observatory, Box 160, Port Rowan, Ont. N0E 1M0, Canada. Eds. David J. T. Hussell, Erica H. Dunn. circ. 600.

598.2 CN ISSN 0707-7165
ENVOL/FLIGHT. (Text in English and French) 1978. irreg. membership. Club d'Amateurs d'Oiseaux de Montreal, 228 de la Salle, Mont St. Hilaire, Que. J3H 3C2, Canada.

598.2 AG ISSN 0073-3407
HORNERO/OVEN BIRD. (Text in Spanish; occasionally articles in English, French or Portuguese) 1917. a. $7. Asociacion Ornitologica del Plata, 25 de Mayo 749, Buenos Aires, Argentina. bk. rev. index. circ. 800. Indexed: Biol.Abstr.

598.2 UK ISSN 0074-4263
INTERNATIONAL COUNCIL FOR BIRD PRESERVATION. BRITISH SECTION. REPORT. 1937. a. 50p. International Council for Bird Preservation, British Section, c/o Natural History Museum, Cromwell Rd., London SW7 5BD, England.

598.2 UK ISSN 0074-4271
INTERNATIONAL COUNCIL FOR BIRD PRESERVATION. PROCEEDINGS OF CONFERENCES. (Text in English, French, German; occasionally in Japanese and Spanish) irreg., 16th. 1974, Canberra, Australia. International Council for Bird Preservation, c/o British Museum (Natural History), Cromwell Rd., London SW7 5BD, England. Ed. Barclay-Smith.

598.2 IE
IRISH BIRDS. a. Irish Wildbird Conservancy, Dublin, Ireland. Ed. Clive Hutchinson. bk. rev. illus. circ. 200.
Incorporating: Irish Bird Report.

598.2 FR ISSN 0075-4080
JOURNAL DES OISEAUX DU MONDE. (Supersedes: Journal des Oiseaux) irreg. 15 F. 59 rue de Faubourg-Poissonniere, 75009 Paris, France. Ed. Louis Bouille.

598.2 US ISSN 0075-9694
LINNAEAN SOCIETY OF NEW YORK. PROCEEDINGS. 1889. irreg. price varies. Linnaean Society of New York, 15 W. 77th St., New York, NY 10024. Ed. Mark Weinberger. circ. 600.

598.2 US ISSN 0075-9708
LINNAEAN SOCIETY OF NEW YORK. TRANSACTIONS. 1882. irreg. price varies. Linnaean Society of New York, 15 W. 77th St., New York, NY 10024. Ed. Mark Weinberger. circ. 1,000.

598.2 US ISSN 0459-6137
LIVING BIRD. 1962. a. $20 to individuals; $25 to libraries and institutions. Cornell University, Laboratory of Ornithology, 159 Sapsucker Woods Road, Ithaca, NY 14850. Ed. Douglas A. Lancaster. illus. circ. 2,200. (also avail. in microform from UMI) Indexed: Biol.Abstr. Zoo.Rec.

598.2 UK ISSN 0141-4348
LONDON BIRD REPORT. 1936. a. £3. London Natural History Society, 110 Meadvale Rd., London W5 1LR, England. Ed. P. Clement. circ. 2,000. (back issues avail.)

598.207 US
MANOMET BIRD OBSERVATORY RESEARCH REPORT. 1971. irreg. Manomet Bird Observatory, P.O. Box 0, Manomet, MA 02345. Ed.Bd. circ. controlled. (processed)
Bird-banding

598.2 US
NEW HAMPSHIRE AUDUBON ANNUAL. 1921. a. $1. Audubon Society of New Hampshire, 3 Silk Farm Rd., Concord, NH 03301. Ed. Tudor Richards. bk. rev. circ. 3,000.
Formerly: New Hampshire Audubon Quarterly.

598.2 CN ISSN 0383-9567
NOVA SCOTIA BIRD SOCIETY. NEWSLETTER. (Title varies slightly) 1959. irreg. Nova Scotia Bird Society, c/o Nova Scotia Museum, 1747 Summer St., Halifax, N.S. B3H 3A6, Canada. illus. Key Title: Newsletter - Nova Scotia Bird Society.

598.2 US ISSN 0550-4082
NUTTALL ORNITHOLOGICAL CLUB. PUBLICATIONS. 1957. irreg., no. 18, 1979. price varies. Nuttall Ornithological Club, c/o Museum of Comparative Zoology, Harvard Univ., Cambridge, MA 02138. Ed. R. A. Paynter, Jr. bibl. charts. illus. stat. Indexed: Zoo.Rec.

598.2 US ISSN 0078-6594
ORNITHOLOGICAL MONOGRAPHS. 1964. irreg. American Ornithologists' Union, National Museum of Natural History, Smithsonian Institution, Washington, DC 20560. Ed. John William Hardy. circ. 1,000.

598.2 UK ISSN 0307-8698
RINGING AND MIGRATION. 1975. a. $7.20. British Trust for Ornithology, Beech Grove, Tring, Hertfordshire, England.

598.2 CN
SASKATCHEWAN. DEPARTMENT OF TOURISM AND RENEWABLE RESOURCES. GAME SURVEYS UNIT. SEX AND AGE RATIOS OF SHARP-TAILED GROUSE AND GRAY (HUNGARIAN) PARTRIDGE. 1960. a. Department of Tourism and Renewable Resources, Game Surveys Unit, 1825 Lorne St., Regina, Sask. S4P 3N1, Canada. stat. circ. controlled.

598.2 UK ISSN 0080-8415
SEABIRD REPORT. no. 7, 1969. irreg. 50p. Seabird Group, c/o Zoology Department, Tillydrone Ave, Aberdeen AB9 2TN, Scotland. Ed. C. J. Bibby. bk. rev. circ. 350.
Formerly: Seabird Bulletin.

598.2 UK ISSN 0081-2048
SOMERSET BIRDS. 1924. a. 75p. Somerset Ornithological Society, Barnfield, Tower Hill Rd., Crewkerne, Somerset, England. circ. 500.

598.2 US
STUDIES IN AVIAN BIOLOGY. 1978. irreg. price varies. Cooper Ornithological Society, Inc. (Los Angeles), c/o Jane R. Durham, Treas., Box 520, Tempe, Los Angeles, AZ 85281. Ed. Frances S. L. Williamson. index; cum.index every 10 yrs. circ. 2,285.
Supersedes (1900-1974): Pacific Coast Avifauna.

598.2 CN
TCHEBEC. 1970. a. membership. Quebec Society for the Protection of Birds, Box 43, Station B, Montreal, Que., Canada. Ed. Allison Bentley. illus. stat. circ. 750. (back issues avail.)

598.2 US ISSN 0040-4543
TEXAS ORNITHOLOGICAL SOCIETY. BULLETIN. 1967. a. $5 membership. Texas Ornithological Society, Box 19581, Houston, TX 77024. Ed. R. Douglas Slack. bk. rev. abstr. illus. circ. 800. Indexed: Zoo.Rec.

598.2 US
UNIVERSITY OF CALIFORNIA, DAVIS. GAME BIRD WORKSHOP. PROCEEDINGS. 1971. biennial. $1-3 per no. University of California, Davis, Department of Avian Sciences, Davis, CA 95616. Ed. Dr. R. A. Ernst. circ. 175.

639.9 598.2 UK ISSN 0083-8241
WEST MIDLAND BIRD REPORT. a. £1. West Midland Bird Club, c/o J.N. Sears, 81 Alcester Rd., Hollywood, Worcestershire, England.

598.2 UK
WILDFOWL. 1948. a. membership. Wildfowl Trust, Slimbridge, Gloucester GL2 7BT, England.

598.2 ZA
ZAMBIAN ORNITHOLOGICAL SOCIETY OCCASIONAL PAPERS. 1979. irreg., no. 2, 1979. price varies. Zambian Ornithological Society, Box 33944, Lusaka, Zambia.

BIOLOGY — Physiology

see also Medical Sciences

574.1 612 US ISSN 0065-244X
ADVANCES IN COMPARATIVE PHYSIOLOGY AND BIOCHEMISTRY. 1962. irreg., vol. 7, 1978. price varies. Academic Press, Inc., 111 Fifth Ave., New York, NY 10003. Ed. O. E. Lowenstein. index. Indexed: Ind.Med.

ADVANCES IN ENZYME REGULATION. see *MEDICAL SCIENCES*

616.8 US
ADVANCES IN SLEEP RESEARCH. 1974. a. Spectrum Publications, Inc., 175-20 Wexford Terrace, Jamaica, NY 10032. Ed. Dr. Elliot D. Weitzman.

ALFRED BENZON SYMPOSIUM. PROCEEDINGS. see *MEDICAL SCIENCES*

612.6 US ISSN 0090-5348
ANNUAL EDITIONS: READINGS IN HUMAN DEVELOPMENT. 1973/74. a. price varies. Dushkin Publishing Group, Sluice Dock, Guilford, CT 06437. illus.

574.1 US ISSN 0066-4278
ANNUAL REVIEW OF PHYSIOLOGY. 1939. a. $20. Annual Reviews Inc., 4139 El Camino Way, Palo Alto, CA 94306. Ed.I.S. Edelman. bibl. index; cum.index. (microfiche; back issues avail.; reprint service avail. from ISI) Indexed: Biol.Abstr. Chem.Abstr. Ind.Med. Psychol.Abstr. Sci.Cit.Ind. Child Devel.Abstr. M.M.R.I.

612 PO ISSN 0066-7811
ARQUIVO DE ANATOMIA E ANTROPOLOGIA.* (Text in Portuguese; summaries in English, French, German) 1912. a. $10. Universadade de Lisboa, Instituto de Anatomia Normal, Avda. Egas Moniz, Lisbon 4, Portugal.

612 US ISSN 0093-5557
BENCHMARK PAPERS IN HUMAN PHYSIOLOGY. 1973. irreg., vol. 14, 1980. price varies. Dowden, Hutchinson and Ross, Inc., 523 Sarah St., Stroudsburg, PA 18360 (Dist. by Academic Press, Inc., 111 Fifth Ave., New York, NY 10003) Ed. L. L. Langley.

612 UK ISSN 0308-5384
BIOLOGICAL STRUCTURE AND FUNCTION. irreg., no. 8, 1981. $85 for latest vol. Cambridge University Press, Box 110, Cambridge CB2 3RL, England (And 32 E. 57th St., New York NY 10022) Eds. R. J. Harrison, R.M.H. McMinn.

574.1 CH
CHINESE JOURNAL OF PHYSIOLOGY. (Text in English; summaries in English and Chinese) 1927. a. free. Chinese Physiological Society, Department of Biophysics, Box 7432, National Defense Medical Center, Taipei, Taiwan, Republic of China. Ed.Bd. abstr. bibl. charts. illus. circ. 1,000. Indexed: Ind.Med.

591.1 AT ISSN 0155-7742
COMMONWEALTH SCIENTIFIC AND INDUSTRIAL RESEARCH ORGANIZATION. DIVISION OF ANIMAL PRODUCTION REPORT. irreg. C. S. I. R. O., Division of Animal Production, P.O. Box 239, Blacktown 2148, N.S.W., Australia.
Formerly: Commonwealth Scientific and Industrial Research Organization. Division of Animal Physiology. Report. (ISSN 0069-7281)

591.1 AT
COMMONWEALTH SCIENTIFIC AND INDUSTRIAL RESEARCH ORGANIZATION. DIVISION OF ANIMAL PRODUCTION TECHNICAL REPORT. 1969. irreg. free. C.S.I.R.O., Division of Animal Production, Box 239, Blacktown N.S.W. 2148, Australia.
Formerly: Commonwealth Scientific and Industrial Research Organization. Division of Animal Physiology. Technical Report (ISSN 0084-9014)

CONTRIBUTIONS TO HUMAN DEVELOPMENT. see *MEDICAL SCIENCES*

612 US ISSN 0069-9705
CONTRIBUTIONS TO SENSORY PHYSIOLOGY. 1965. irreg., 1971, vol. 5. price varies. Academic Press, Inc., 111 Fifth Ave., New York, NY 10003. Ed. William D. Neff. index. Indexed: Ind.Med.

DENMARK. STATENS HUSDYRBRUGSUDVALG. BERETNING. see *AGRICULTURE — Poultry And Livestock*

FUNKTIONSANALYSE BIOLOGISCHER SYSTEME. see *BIOLOGY*

574.1 US ISSN 0072-9876
HANDBOOK OF PHYSIOLOGY. 1959. irreg. price varies. (American Physiological Society) Williams & Wilkins Co., 428 E. Preston St., Baltimore, MD 21202. Ed. Victor E. Hall.

574.1 US ISSN 0072-9906
HANDBOOK OF SENSORY PHYSIOLOGY. (Text in English) 1971. irreg.; vol. 9, 1978. price varies. Springer-Verlag, 175 Fifth Ave., New York, NY 10010 (also Berlin, Heidelberg, Vienna) Ed.Bd. (reprint service avail. from ISI)

599.01 US
HAROLD C. MACK SYMPOSIUM. PROCEEDINGS. irreg., latest issue, 1972. price varies. (Harper Hospital (Detroit), Department of Gynecology and Obstetrics) Charles C. Thomas, Publisher, 301-327 Lawrence Ave., Springfield, IL 62717. (Co-sponsor: Wayne State University) Eds. Harold C. Mack, Alfred I. Sherman.
Continues: Symposium on the Physiology and Pathology of Human Reproduction (ISSN 0085-7076)

574.191 FR ISSN 0073-8565
INSTITUT MICHEL PACHA. ANNALES. 1968. a. price varies. Institut Michel Pacha, Laboratoire Maritime de Physiologie, Tamaris-sur-Mer, France. bk. rev. Indexed: Biol.Abstr. Bull.Signal.

612 US ISSN 0363-3918
INTERNATIONAL REVIEW OF PHYSIOLOGY. 1974. irreg. price varies. University Park Press, American Medical Publishers, Chamber of Commerce Bldg., Baltimore, MD 21202. Ed. A.C. Guyton.

574.166 SZ ISSN 0074-7920
INTERNATIONAL SEMINAR ON REPRODUCTIVE PHYSIOLOGY AND SEXUAL ENDOCRINOLOGY. PROCEEDINGS. (Text in English) irreg., 6th, 1977, Brussels. 120 Fr.($72) per vol. (1981 price) S. Karger AG, Allschwilerstrasse 10, P.O. Box, CH-4009 Basel, Switzerland. (reprint service avail. from ISI)

574.1 US
INTERNATIONAL SERIES ON PURE AND APPLIED BIOLOGY. MODERN TRENDS IN PHYSIOLOGICAL SCIENCE DIVISION. 1960. irreg., vol. 38, 1973. price varies. Pergamon Press, Inc., Maxwell House, Fairview Park, Elmsford, NY 10523. index.
Formerly: International Series of Monographs on Pure and Applied Biology. Division: Modern Trends in Physiological Sciences (ISSN 0074-8285)

612.4 NE
INTERNATIONAL SYMPOSIUM ON GROWTH HORMONE. ABSTRACTS. (Abstracts of 2nd Symposium published in 1971) 1967. irreg., 1967, 1st, Milan. fl.28($11.75) Excerpta Medica, P.O.B. 211, 1000 AE Amsterdam, Netherlands.

612 HU ISSN 0539-1113
INTERNATIONAL UNION OF PHYSIOLOGICAL SCIENCES. NEWSLETTER. 1964. irreg. $3. (International Union of Physiological Sciences) Akademiai Kiado, Publishing House of the Hungarian Academy of Sciences, P.O. Box 24, H-1363 Budapest, Hungary (c/o A. Kovach, Experimental Research Department, Semmelweis Medical University, Ulloi Ut 78/A, 1082 Budapest, Hungary) circ. 15,000.

574.1 FR ISSN 0074-946X
INTERNATIONAL UNION OF PHYSIOLOGICAL SCIENCES. PROCEEDINGS OF CONGRESS. irreg., 27th, 1977, Paris. International Union of Physiological Sciences, c/o Dr. J. Scherrer, Department of Physiology, U E R Pitie-Salpetriere, 91 Blvd. de l'Hospital, 75634 Paris Cedex 13, France.

612 FR ISSN 0075-4455
JOURNEES DE PHYSIOLOGIE APPLIQUEE AU TRAVAIL HUMAIN. 1959. irreg. 85 F. per no. (Societe d'Ergonomie de la Langue Francaise) N.E.B. Editions Scientifiques, B.P.3, 78350 Jouy-en-Josas, France.

MONOGRAPHS IN PHARMACOLOGY AND PHYSIOLOGY. see *PHARMACY AND PHARMACOLOGY*

574.1 610 NE
NOBEL PRIZE LECTURES-PHYSIOLOGY OF MEDICINE. (Text in English) irreg., approx. every 3 yrs. price varies. Elsevier Scientific Publishing Co., P.O. Box 211, 1000 AE Amsterdam, Netherlands.

574.1 UK ISSN 0079-2020
PHYSIOLOGICAL SOCIETY. MONOGRAPHS. 1953. irreg., no. 35, 1979. $83.50 for latest vol. Cambridge University Press, Box 110, Cambridge CB2 3RL, England (And 32 E. 57th St., New York, NY 10022) Ed.Bd.

574.1 US
PHYSIOLOGICAL SOCIETY OF PHILADELPHIA. MONOGRAPHS. 1976. irreg. Halsted Press (Subsidiary of: John Wiley & Sons, Inc.) 605 Third Ave., New York, NY 10016.

574.1 UK
PHYSIOLOGY, SERIES ONE. (Subseries of: MTP International Review of Science) irreg. Butterworth & Co. (Publishers) Ltd., 88 Kingsway, London WC2B 6AB, England. illus.
Formerly: International Review of Physiology.

574.1 US
PROBLEMS OF HUMAN REPRODUCTION: A WILEY BIOMEDICAL SERIES. 1973. irreg., vol. 2, 1974. price varies. John Wiley & Sons, Inc., 605 Third Ave., New York, NY 10016. Ed. J.B. Josimovich.

PROGRESS IN CLINICAL NEUROPHYSIOLOGY. see *MEDICAL SCIENCES — Psychiatry And Neurology*

574.16 SZ ISSN 0304-4262
PROGRESS IN REPRODUCTIVE BIOLOGY. (Text in English) 1976. irreg. (approx. 1/yr.) 120 Fr.($72) per vol. (1981 price) S. Karger AG, Allschwilerstrasse 10, P.O. Box, CH-4009 Basel, Switzerland. Ed. P.O. Hubinont. illus. circ. 1,000. (reprint service avail. from ISI) Indexed: Biol.Abstr. Curr.Cont.

574.1 619 US
RAVEN PRESS SERIES IN EXPERIMENTAL PHYSIOLOGY. irreg. Raven Press, 1140 Ave. of the Americas, New York, NY 10036.

574.1 540 615 US ISSN 0080-2042
REVIEWS OF PHYSIOLOGY, BIOCHEMISTRY AND EXPERIMENTAL PHARMACOLOGY. irreg., vol. 90, 1981. price varies. Springer-Verlag, 175 Fifth Ave., New York, NY 10010 (also Berlin, Heidelberg, Vienna) (reprint service avail. from ISI) Indexed: Ind.Med.
Continues: Ergebnisse der Physiologie, Biologischen Chemie und Experimentellen Pharmakologie.

612 UK ISSN 0081-153X
SOCIETY FOR THE STUDY OF HUMAN BIOLOGY. SYMPOSIA. 1960. irreg., 1970, vol. 9. price varies. Society for the Study of Human Biology, c/o Dr. A. J. Boyce, Anthropology Laboratory, Dept. of Human Anatomy, S. Park Rd., Oxford OX1 3QX, England.

612 US
SOCIETY FOR THE STUDY OF INBORN ERRORS OF METABOLISM. SYMPOSIA. 1975. a. price varies. University Park Press, American Medical Publishers, Chamber of Commerce Bldg., Baltimore, MD 21202.

574.1 US
SOCIETY OF GENERAL PHYSIOLOGISTS. DISTINGUISHED LECTURE SERIES. 1978. irreg. price varies. Raven Press, 1140 Ave. of the Americas, New York, NY 10036. Indexed: Curr.Cont.

612 US ISSN 0094-7733
SOCIETY OF GENERAL PHYSIOLOGISTS SERIES. 1945? a. price varies. Raven Press, 1140 Ave. of the Americas, New York, NY 10036. Indexed: Curr.Cont. Ind.Med. Sci.Cit.Ind.

574 PL ISSN 0082-5581
STUDIA SOCIETATIS SCIENTIARUM TORUNENSIS. SECTIO G (PHYSIOLOGIA) (Text in Polish; summaries in English) 1961. irreg. price varies. (Towarzystwo Naukowe w Toruniu) Panstwowe Wydawnictwo Naukowe, Miodowa 10, Warsaw, Poland. Ed. Juliusz Narebski. circ. 440.

574 JA ISSN 0564-7630
UNIVERSITY OF TOKYO. RESEARCH INSTITUTE OF LOGOPEDICS AND PHONIATRICS. ANNUAL BULLETIN. (Text in English) a. exchange basis. University of Tokyo Press, 7-3-1 Hongo, Bunkyo-ku, Tokyo 113-91, Japan.

BIOLOGY — Zoology

see also Pets; Veterinary Science

591 CU
ACADEMIA DE CIENCIAS DE CUBA. INSTITUTO DE ZOOLOGIA. INFORME CIENTIFICO-TECNICO. (Text in Spanish; summaries in English) irreg., no. 68, Apr. 1978. Academia de Ciencias de Cuba, Instituto de Zoologia, Industria 452, Havana 2, Cuba.

591 CU
ACADEMIA DE CIENCIAS DE CUBA. INSTITUTO DE ZOOLOGIA. MISCELANEA ZOOLOGICA. irreg. exchange basis. Academia de Ciencias de Cuba, Instituto de Zoologia, Industria 452, Havana 2, Cuba.

ACTA PARASITOLOGICA IUGOSLAVICA. see *MEDICAL SCIENCES — Communicable Diseases*

590 SW ISSN 0072-4807
ACTA REGIAE SOCIETATIS SCIENTIARUM ET LITTERARUM GOTHOBURGENSIS. ZOOLOGICA. (Text in various languages) 1967. irreg., no. 12, 1979. price varies; also exchange basis. Goeteborgs Kungliga Vetenskaps- och Vitterhets-Samhaelle, c/o Goeteborgs Universitetsbibliotek, P.O. Box 5096, S-402 22 Goeteborg 5, Sweden (Dist. in U.S., Canada, and Mexico by: Humanities Press, Inc., 171 First Ave., Atlantic Highlands, NJ 07716)
Supersedes in part: Goeteborgs Kungliga Vetenskaps- och Vitterhets-Samhaelle. Handlingar.

591 BU
ACTA ZOOLOGICA BULGARICA. (Text in various languages) 1975. 2 lv. per issue. (Bulgarska Akademiia na Naukite, Zoologicheski Institut) Publishing House of the Bulgarian Academy of Sciences, Ul. Akad. G. Bonchev, 1113 Sofia, Bulgaria (Dist. by: Hemus, 6, Rouski Blvd., 1000 Sofia, Bulgaria) illus. circ. 800.
Supersedes: Bulgarska Akademiia na Naukite, Sofia. Zoologicheski Institut S Muzei. Izvestiia (ISSN 0068-3981)

BIOLOGY — ZOOLOGY

590   PL   ISSN 0065-1710
ACTA ZOOLOGICA CRACOVIENSIA. (Text in English, French, German, Russian and Polish) 1956. irreg., 1972, vol. 17. price varies. (Polska Akademia Nauk, Zaklad Zoologii Systematycznej) Panstwowe Wydawnictwo Naukowe, Ul. Miodowa 10, Warsaw, Poland. Ed. K. Kowalski. bibl. charts. illus.

590   AG   ISSN 0065-1729
ACTA ZOOLOGICA LILLOANA. (Text in Spanish; summaries in English, French, German, Italian) 1943. irreg.; no. 33, 1978. price varies. (Fundacion Miguel Lillo) Centro de Informacion Geo-Biologica, N O A, Miguel Lillo 251, 4000 Tucuman, Argentina. Ed. Jose Antonio Haedo Rossi. charts. bibl. illus. (also avail. in cards; back issues avail.) Indexed: Biol.Abstr. Bull.Signal. Ref.Zh. Zoo.Rec.

590   MX   ISSN 0065-1737
ACTA ZOOLOGICA MEXICANA.* (Text in English, German and Spanish) 1965. irreg.(6 issues per year) Mex.$30 per year. Museo de Historia Natural de la Ciudad de Mexico, Apartado Postal 18-845, Mexico 18, D.F, Mexico. Ed. Alfredo Barrera. index.

ACTUALITES PROTOZOOLOGIQUES. see *BIOLOGY — Cytology And Histology*

597   551.46   JA
ADVANCES IN FISHERIES OCEANOGRAPHY. (Text in English) 1966. irreg., last published 1973. exchange basis. Japanese Society of Fisheries Oceanography - Suisan Kaiyo Kenkyu-kai, c/o Laboratory of Fisheries Oceanography, Tokyo University of Fisheries, 5-7 Konan 4-chome, Minato-ku, Tokyo 108, Japan.

591   616.9   UK   ISSN 0065-308X
ADVANCES IN PARASITOLOGY. 1963. irreg., vol. 16, 1978. price varies. Academic Press Inc. (London) Ltd., 24-28 Oval Rd., London NW1 7DX, England (and 111 Fifth Ave., New York, N.Y. 10003) Eds. W.H.J. Lumsden, R. Muller. index.

591   PL
AKADEMIA ROLNICZA, WARSAW. ZESZYTY NAUKOWE. ZOOTECHNIKA. (Text in Polish; summaries in English and Russian) irreg., vol. 16, 1980. price varies. Akademia Rolnicza, Warsaw, Rakowiecka 26/30, 02-528 Warsaw, Poland. Formerly: Szkolna Glowna Gospodarstwa Wiejskiego. Zeszyty Naukowe. Zootechnika (ISSN 0509-7134)

590.744   US   ISSN 0090-4473
AMERICAN ASSOCIATION OF ZOOLOGICAL PARKS AND AQUARIUMS. PROCEEDINGS. ANNUAL A A Z P A CONFERENCE. a. $3. American Association of Zoological Parks and Aquariums, Oglebay Park, Wheeling, WV 26003. illus. Key Title: Proceedings. Annual A.A.Z.P.A. Conference.

594   US   ISSN 0065-9169
AMERICAN MALACOLOGICAL UNION. BULLETIN. 1931. a. $13 to non-members. American Malacological Union, Inc., c/o Constance E. Boone, Recording Secretary, 3706 Rice Boulevard, Houston, TX 77005. Ed. Dr. Dolores S. Dundee. index. circ. 700.

591   US   ISSN 0569-8219
AMERICAN SOCIETY OF MAMMALOGISTS. SPECIAL PUBLICATIONS. irreg. American Society of Mammalogists, c/o Dr. Gordon L. Kirkland Jr., Sec.-Treas., Vertebrate Museum, Shippensburg State College, Shippensburg, PA 17257. (reprint service avail. from UMI)

591   US   ISSN 0547-8626
ANIMALS FOR RESEARCH. 1975, vol. 9. biennial. $4.50. National Academy of Sciences, Institute of Laboratory Animal Resources, 2101 Constitution Ave., N.W., Washington, DC 20418.

595   FR   ISSN 0066-2739
ANNUAIRE DES ARACHNOLOGISTES MONDIAUX; acarologistes exceptes. 1968. triennial. 60 F. Centre International de Documentation Arachnologique, 61 rue de Buffon, Paris 5e, France.

594   IS   ISSN 0334-326X
ARGAMON; Israel journal of malacology. (Text in English) 1970. irreg. $6.50. Israel Malacological Society, Netzer Sereni, 70-395, Israel. (Co-sponsor: Nahariya Municipal Malacological Museum) Ed. H. K. Mienis. bk. rev. bibl. charts. illus. index. circ. 525. (back issues avail. from vol. 4) Indexed: Zoo.Rec.

591   BL   ISSN 0066-7870
ARQUIVOS DE ZOOLOGIA. (Text in English, Portuguese and other languages) 1940. irreg. $25. Universidade de Sao Paulo, Museu de Zoologia, Caixa Postal 7172, Sao Paulo, Brazil. Ed. P. E. Vanzolini. circ. 600(approx.) Indexed: Biol.Abstr. Zoo.Rec.

599   AT   ISSN 0310-0049
AUSTRALIAN MAMMALOGY. 1972. a. price varies. Australian Mammal Society, c/o R. Bohringer, School of Anatomy, University of New South Wales, Box 1, Kensington, N.S.W. 2033, Australia. Ed. M. Archer. bk. rev. circ. 2,000. Indexed: Aus.Sci.Ind.

591   AT   ISSN 0067-2238
AUSTRALIAN ZOOLOGIST. 1914. irreg. price varies. Royal Zoological Society of New South Wales, Taronga Zoo, Mosman, N.S.W. 2088, Australia. Ed. E. S. Robinson.

591.15   US
AVIAN CHROMOSOMES NEWSLETTER. 1972. a. free. Cornell University, Department of Poultry Science, Cytogenetics Section, Ithaca, NY 14853. Ed. Dr. Stephen E. Bloom. bibl. circ. 150 (controlled) (looseleaf format; back issues available)

591   PL
BADANIA FIZJOGRAFICZNE NAD POLSKA ZACHODNIA. SERIA C. ZOOLOGIA. (Text in Polish; summaries in English) 1948. irreg. 127 Zl. (Poznanskie Towarzystwo Przyjaciol Nauk) Panstwowe Wydawnictwo Naukowe, Miodowa 10, Warsaw, Poland. illus.

591   639.9   SZ
BEARS-THEIR BIOLOGY AND MANAGEMENT. Represents: International Conference on Bear Research and Management. Papers. no. 3, 1974, Binghamton, New York and Moscow, USSR. irreg. $18. International Union for Conservation of Nature and Natural Resources, 1110 Morges, Switzerland (Dist. in the U.S. by: Unipub, Inc., 345 Park Ave. S., New York, NY 10010)

591   NE   ISSN 0067-4745
BEAUFORTIA; series of miscellaneous publications. (Text in English, French or German) 1951. irreg., vol. 25, 1977. price varies. Universiteit van Amsterdam, Zoologisch Museum, Instituut voor Taxonomische Zoologie, Plantage Middenlaan 53, Amsterdam-C, Netherlands. Indexed: Biol.Abstr. Zoo.Rec.

590   NE   ISSN 0005-7959
BEHAVIOUR; an international journal of comparative ethology. (Text in English and German) 1947. irreg., vol. 79, 1981. fl.72. E. J. Brill, Oude Rijn 33a-35, Leiden, Netherlands. Ed. Dr. G. P. Baerends. bibl. charts. illus. Indexed: Biol.Abstr. Chem.Abstr. Psychol.Abstr. Key Word Ind.Wildl.Res.

BEITRAEGE ZUR NATURKUNDLICHEN FORSCHUNG IN SUEDWESTDEUTSCHLAND. see *EARTH SCIENCES — Geology*

591   US
BENCHMARK PAPERS IN BEHAVIOR. 1974. irreg., latest 1980. price varies. Dowden, Hutchinson & Ross, Inc., 523 Sarah St., Stroudsburg, PA 18360 (Dist. by Academic Press, Inc., 111 Fifth Ave., New York, NY 10003) Eds. M.W. Schein, S.W. Porges. Formerly: Benchmark Papers in Animal Behavior.

591   GE   ISSN 0067-6098
BERLINER TIERPARK-BUCH. 1957. irreg., no. 26, 1974. price varies. Tierpark Berlin, Am Tierpark 125, 1136 Berlin, E. Germany (D.D.R)

591   GE   ISSN 0067-6314
BESTIMMUNGSBUECHER ZUR BODENFAUNA EUROPAS. 1963. irreg., vol. 10, 1977. price varies. Akademie-Verlag, Leipziger Strasse 3-4, 108 Berlin, E. Germany (D.D.R.)

BIOLOGICAL SOCIETY OF WASHINGTON. PROCEEDINGS. see *BIOLOGY*

590   GW   ISSN 0302-671X
BONNER ZOOLOGISCHE MONOGRAPHIEN. 1971. irreg. (1-2/yr.) Zoologisches Forschungsinstitut und Museum A. Koenig, Adenauerallee 150-164, 5300 Bonn, W. Germany (B.R.D.) Ed. H. Ulrich. circ. 400.

591   US   ISSN 0006-9698
BREVIORA. 1952. irreg., no. 448, 1978. price varies. Harvard University, Museum of Comparative Zoology, Cambridge, MA 02138. Ed. Elizabeth Elliott. bibl. illus. circ. 700-900. Indexed: Biol.Abstr.

591   UK   ISSN 0007-1498
BRITISH MUSEUM (NATURAL HISTORY) BULLETIN. ZOOLOGY. 1949. irreg. price varies. British Museum (Natural History), Cromwell Rd., London SW7 5BD, England. charts. illus. circ. 850. Indexed: Biol.Abstr. Zoo.Rec.

591   US   ISSN 0068-2780
BROOKFIELD BANDARLOG. 1967. irreg., 1969, no. 37; latest 1975. membership. Chicago Zoological Society, Zoological Park, Brookfield, IL 60513. Ed. George B. Rabb.

636   BU   ISSN 0068-3841
BULGARSKA AKADEMIIA NA NAUKITE, INSTITUT PO OBSHTA I SRAVNITELNA PATALOGIIA. IZVESTIIA. (Summaries in English and Russian) 1951. irreg. 2.14 lv. per issue. Publishing House of the Bulgarian Academy of Sciences, Ul. Akad. G. Bonchev, 1113 Sofia, Bulgaria (Dist. by: Hemus, 6, Rouski Blvd., 1000 Sofia, Bulgaria) Ed. Z. Mladenov. circ. 500.

590.744   AT   ISSN 0084-8182
BULLETIN OF ZOO MANAGEMENT. 1969. irreg. contr. free circ. Sir Colin MacKenzie Sanctuary, Healesville, Vic. 3777, Australia. bk. rev. circ. 250.

591   CN   ISSN 0068-8037
CANADA. NATIONAL MUSEUMS, OTTAWA. PUBLICATIONS IN ZOOLOGY/CANADA. MUSEES NATIONAUX. PUBLICATIONS DE ZOOLOGIE. (Text in English and French) 1969. irreg. price varies, some free. (National Museum of Natural Sciences) National Museums of Canada, Ottawa, Ont. K1A OM8, Canada.

CANADIAN WILDLIFE SERVICE. MONOGRAPH SERIES. see *CONSERVATION*

594   US   ISSN 0084-862X
CATALOG OF DEALERS' PRICES FOR MARINE SHELLS. (Text in English and Latin) 1965. biennial. $7.50. Of Sea & Shore Publications, Box 219, Port Gamble, WA 98364. Ed. Thomas C. Rice. circ. 2,000. (reprint service avail. from UMI)

591   PO
CIENCIA BIOLOGICA: BIOLOGIA MOLECULAR E CELULAR. (Text in English, French, German, Portuguese; summaries in two languages) 1934. a. $5. Universidade de Coimbra, Departamento de Zoologia, Coimbra, Portugal. Dir. A. P. Carvalho. bk. rev. charts. illus. index. cum.index. circ. 800(controlled)
Former titles: Universidade de Coimbra. Museum Zoologico. Memorias e Estudos (ISSN 0041-8765) & Universidade de Coimbra. Departamento de Zoologia. Ciencia Biologica.

COLORADO COOPERATIVE WILDLIFE RESEARCH UNIT. SPECIAL SCIENTIFIC REPORTS. TECHNICAL PAPERS. see *CONSERVATION*

COMMONWEALTH SCIENTIFIC AND INDUSTRIAL RESEARCH ORGANIZATION. DIVISION OF ANIMAL PRODUCTION REPORT. see *BIOLOGY — Physiology*

591   AT   ISSN 0069-7346
COMMONWEALTH SCIENTIFIC AND INDUSTRIAL RESEARCH ORGANIZATION. DIVISION OF FISHERIES AND OCEANOGRAPHY. FISHERIES SYNOPSIS. 1963. irreg. free. C.S.I.R.O., Division of Fisheries and Oceanography, P.O.B. 21, Cronulla 2230, N.S.W., Australia. Indexed: Biol.Abstr. Ocean.Abstr.

591 636.089　　　SZ　ISSN 0304-5374
COMPARATIVE ANIMAL NUTRITION. (Text in English) 1976. irreg. (approx. 1/yr.) 100 Fr.($60) per vol. (1981 price) S. Karger AG, Allschwilerstrasse 10, P.O. Box, CH-4009 Basel, Switzerland. Ed. M. Rechcigl,Jr. (reprint service avail. from ISI)

572 599.8　　　SZ　ISSN 0301-4231
CONTRIBUTIONS TO PRIMATOLOGY. (Text in English) 1962. irreg. (approx. 2/yr.) 60 Fr.($36) per vol. (1981 price) S. Karger AG, Allschwilerstrasse 10, P.O. Box, CH-4009 Basel, Switzerland. Ed. F. S. Szalay. (reprint service avail. from ISI) Indexed: Biol.Abstr. Chem.Abstr. Curr.Cont.
　　Formerly: Bibliotheca Primatologica (ISSN 0067-8139)

591 639.9　　　SZ
CROCODILES. Represents: Working Meeting of Crocodile Specialists. Proceedings. 1971. irreg., no. 2, 1973. $4.50. International Union for Conservation of Nature and Natural Resources, 1110 Morges, Switzerland (Dist. in the U.S. by: Unipub, Inc., 345 Park Ave. S., New York, NY 10010)

591　　　CU
CUBA. CENTRO DE INFORMACION Y DOCUMENTACION AGROPECUARIO. BOLETIN DE RESENAS. SERIE: GENETICA Y REPRODUCCION. 1974. irreg. $5. Centro de Informacion y Documentacion Agropecuario, Calle 11 no. 1057, Gaveta Postal 4149, Havana 4, Cuba.

591 574　　　US　ISSN 0070-2161
CURRENT TOPICS IN MEMBRANES AND TRANSPORT. 1970. irreg., vol. 11, 1978. price varies. Academic Press Inc., 111 Fifth Ave., New York, NY 10003. Eds. Felix Bronner, Arnest Kleinzeller.

590　　　DK　ISSN 0070-2730
DANISH REVIEW OF GAME BIOLOGY. (Text in English; summaries in Russian and Danish) 1945. irreg. price varies. Vildtbiologisk Station - Game Biology Station, Kaloe, 8410 Roende, Denmark. Ed. Ib Clausager. circ. 2,200. Indexed: Biol.Abstr. Key Word Ind.Wildl.Res. Wildlife Rev. Zoo.Rec.

591　　　NE
DELTA ONDERZOEK HYDROBIOLOGISCH INSTITUUT. COMMUNICATION. (Subseries of: Rijksmuseum van Natuurlijke Historie, Leyden. Zoologische Verhandelingen) irreg. (Delta Onderzoek Hydrobiologisch Instituut) E. J. Brill, Oude Rijn 33a-35, Leiden, Netherlands.

590　　　GW　ISSN 0070-4342
DEUTSCHE ZOOLOGISCHE GESELLSCHAFT. VERHANDLUNGEN. a. price varies. Gustav Fischer Verlag, Wollgrasweg 49, Postfach 720143, 7000 Stuttgart 70, W. Germany (B.R.D.)

591　　　NE
DEVELOPMENT IN MAMMALS. 1977. irreg., vol. 4, 1980. price varies. Elsevier North-Holland Biomedical Press, Box 211, 1000 AE Amsterdam, Netherlands. Ed. M. H. Johnson.

591　　　US　ISSN 0085-0039
DIRECTORY OF THE PUBLIC AQUARIA OF THE WORLD. 1962. irreg; latest issue 1976. free. ‡ Waikik: Aquarium, 2777 Kalakaua Ave., Honolulu, HI 96815. Ed. Charles DeLuca. circ. 1,500.

FAUNA & FLORA. see CONSERVATION

590　　　FI　ISSN 0071-4054
FAUNA FENNICA. (Text in English and German) 1947. irreg.(2/yr.) price varies; available on exchange. Societas Pro Fauna et Flora Fennica, Snellmaninkatu 9-11, 00170 Helsinki, Finland. Ed. Martin Meinander. Indexed: Biol.Abstr. Ref.Zh.

591　　　JA　ISSN 0428-061X
FAUNA JAPONICA. (Text in English) 1960. irreg. (Biogeographical Society of Japan) Keigaku Publishing Co., Ltd., 2-3-1 Sarugaku-cho, Chiyoda-ku, Tokyo 101, Japan.

591　　　IS
FAUNA OF RUSSIA AND ADJACENT COUNTRIES. (Text in English) irreg. Israel Program for Scientific Translations, Box 7145, Jerusalem, Israel (U.S. Distributor: International Scholarly Book Services, Inc., 10300 S. W. Allen Blvd., Beaverton, OR 97005)

591　　　IS
FAUNA OF THE U.S.S.R. (Text in English) irreg. Israel Program for Scientific Translations, Box 7145, Jerusalem, Israel (U.S. Distributor: International Scholarly Book Services, Inc., 10300 S.W. Allen Blvd., Beaverton, OR 97005)

591　　　PL　ISSN 0071-4089
FAUNA SLODKOWODNA POLSKI. (Text in Polish) 1935. irreg. price varies. (Polska Akademia Nauk, Instytut Zoologii, Oddzial w Poznaniu) Panstwowe Wydawnictwo Naukowe, Miodowa 10, Warsaw, Poland (Dist. by Ars Polona-Ruch, Krakowskie Przedmiescie 7, Warsaw, Poland) Ed. Bd.

597　　　US
FISHES OF THE WESTERN NORTH ATLANTIC. vol. 7, 1977. irreg. price varies. Sears Foundation for Marine Research, Box 2025, Yale Station, New Haven, CT 06520. (back issues avail.)

591　　　GW　ISSN 0301-2808
FORTSCHRITTE DER VERHALTENSFORSCHUNG/ADVANCES IN ETHOLOGY. (Supplement to: Zeitschrift fuer Tierpsychologie) (Text and summaries in English, French, German) 1953. irreg. price varies. Verlag Paul Parey (Berlin), Lindenstr. 44-47, 1000 Berlin 61, W. Germany (B.R.D.) Indexed: Biol.Abstr. Curr.Cont. Psychol.Abstr.

591　　　GW　ISSN 0071-7991
FORTSCHRITTE DER ZOOLOGIE/PROGRESS IN ZOOLOGY. (Text in English, French, German) 1935. irreg. price varies. (Deutsche Zoologische Gesellschaft) Gustav Fischer Verlag, Wollgrasweg 49, Postfach 720143, 7000 Stuttgart 70, W. Germany (B.R.D.) Ed. M. Lindauer. Indexed: Biol.Abstr.
　　Supersedes: Ergebnisse und Fortschritte der Zoologie.

FORTSCHRITTE IN DER TIERPHYSIOLOGIE UND TIERERNAEHRUNG/ADVANCES IN ANIMAL PHYSIOLOGY AND ANIMAL NUTRITION. see AGRICULTURE — Poultry And Livestock

591　　　CL　ISSN 0016-531X
GAYANA: ZOOLOGICA. (Text in English and Spanish) 1961. irreg. Universidad de Concepcion, Instituto Central de Biologia, Casilla 1367, Concepcion, Chile. circ. 1,000. Indexed: Biol.Abstr.

591　　　UK　ISSN 0065-4507
GREAT BRITAIN. INSTITUTE OF ANIMAL PHYSIOLOGY. REPORT. 1960-61. biennial. £2. Institute of Animal Physiology, Babraham, Cambridge CB2 4AT, England (Avail. from H.M.S.O., c/o Liaison Officer, Atlantic House, Holborn Viaduct, London EC1P 1BN, England) illus. circ. 700.

595　　　GW　ISSN 0072-9612
HAMBURGISCHES ZOOLOGISCHES MUSEUM UND INSTITUT. MITTEILUNGEN. 1883. a. price varies. Universitaet Hamburg, Zoologisches Institut, Martin-Luther-King-Platz 3, 2000 Hamburg 13, W. Germany (B.R.D.) (Co-sponsor: Zoologisches Museum der Universitaet Hamburg) Ed. Gisela Rack. circ. 600.

591　　　US　ISSN 0027-4100
HARVARD UNIVERSITY. MUSEUM OF COMPARATIVE ZOOLOGY. BULLETIN. 1863. irreg., no. 148, 1978. price varies. Harvard University, Museum of Comparative Zoology, Cambridge, MA 02138. Ed. Elizabeth Elliott. bibl. illus. circ. 800-1,000. Indexed: Biol.Abstr.

594　　　US　ISSN 0073-0807
HARVARD UNIVERSITY. MUSEUM OF COMPARATIVE ZOOLOGY. DEPARTMENT OF MOLLUSKS. OCCASIONAL PAPERS ON MOLLUSKS. 1945. irreg. ‡ Harvard University, Museum of Comparative Zoology, Cambridge, MA 02138. Ed. Kenneth J. Boss.

591　　　JA
HIROSHIMA UNIVERSITY. JOURNAL OF SCIENCE. SERIES B. DIVISION 1: ZOOLOGY/HIROSHIMA DAIGAKU RIKA KIYO, DOBUTSUGAKU. (Text in English and European languages) 1937. a. exchange basis. Hiroshima University, Faculty of Science, Higashisenda-cho, Hiroshima 730, Japan.

590 574　　　JA
HIROSHIMA UNIVERSITY. LABORATORY FOR AMPHIBIAN BIOLOGY. SCIENTIFIC REPORT. (Text in English) 1972. a. exchange basis. Hiroshima University, Laboratory for Amphibian Biology, 1-89 1-chome Higashisenda-cho, Hiroshima 730, Japan.

591　　　JA　ISSN 0368-2188
HOKKAIDO UNIVERSITY. FACULTY OF SCIENCE. JOURNAL. SERIES 6: ZOOLOGY. (Text in English) 1930. irreg. exchange basis. Hokkaido University, Faculty of Science - Hokkaido Daigaku Rigakubu, Nishi-8-chome, Kita-10-jo, Kita-ku, Sapporo 060, Japan.

591　　　BL　ISSN 0073-4721
IHERINGIA. SERIE ZOOLOGIA. (Text in English,French,German,Italian,Latin,Portuguese, and Spanish) 1957. irreg.; no. 58, 1981. price varies. Fundacao Zoobotanica do Rio Grande do Sul, Museu de Ciencias Naturais, Caixa Postal 1188, 90.000 Porto Alegre, Rio Grande do Sul, Brazil. Ed. Arno A. Lise. bibl. illus. circ. 600. Indexed: Biol.Abstr. Zoo.Rec.

591　　　II　ISSN 0537-0744
INDIA. ZOOLOGICAL SURVEY. ANNUAL REPORT. a. Zoological Survey of India, 34 Chittaranjan Ave., Calcutta 12, India.

591　　　II
INDIA. ZOOLOGICAL SURVEY. NEWSLETTER. (Text in English) 197? irreg. Zoological Survey of India, 34 Chittaranjan Ave., Calcutta 12, India.

INDIAN JOURNAL OF FISHERIES. see FISH AND FISHERIES

591 562　　　US　ISSN 0073-7240
INDO-PACIFIC MOLLUSCA. 1959. irreg. price varies. Delaware Museum of Natural History, Box 3937, Greenville, DE 19807. circ. 1,300. Indexed: Biol.Abstr.

590　　　BL　ISSN 0073-9901
INSTITUTO BUTANTAN. MEMORIAS. (Text and summaries in English and Portuguese) 1918. a. ‡ Instituto Butantan, Caixa Postal 65, Sao Paulo, Brazil. Ed.Bd. author index. cum.index: 1918-1969. circ. 1,700. Indexed: Biol.Abstr. Chem.Abstr. Ind.Med. Bull.Inst.Pasteur. Trop.Dis.Bull. Zoo.Rec.

591　　　PO　ISSN 0020-4021
INSTITUTO DE ZOOLOGIA "DR. AUGUSTO NOBRE". PUBLICACOES. (Text in English, French, German & Portuguese; summaries in French) 3-5/yr. exchange basis. Universidade do Porto, Instituto de Zoologia "Dr. Augusto Nobre", Faculdade de Ciencias, Porto, Portugal. bibl. charts. illus. stat. Indexed: Biol.Abstr. Zoo.Rec.

594　　　MX　ISSN 0026-1777
INSTITUTO POLITECNICO NACIONAL. ESCUELA NATIONAL DE CIENCIAS BIOLOGICAS. REVISTA ANALES. (Text in English and Spanish) 1965. a. Mex.$40($4) Instituto Politecnico Nacional, Escuela Nacional de Ciencias Biologicas, Departamento de Publicaciones, Carpio y Plan de Ayaya, Box 42-186, Mexico 17, D.F., Mexico. Ed. Jorge Vargas Chavez.

597.58 333.7　　　SP
INTERNATIONAL COMMISSION FOR THE CONSERVATION OF ATLANTIC TUNAS. REPORT. (Editions in English, French and Spanish) biennial. International Commission for the Conservation of Atlantic Tunas., Calle General Molla 17, Madrid 1, Spain.

595.4　　　CS　ISSN 0074-3445
INTERNATIONAL CONGRESS OF ACAROLOGY. PROCEEDINGS. 1963. quadrennial, 3rd, 1973, Prague. price varies. ‡ Academia, Publishing House of the Czechoslovak Academy of Sciences, Vodickova 40, 112 29 Prague 1, Czechoslovakia (Inquiries to:, K. Samsinak, Sec. of Congress) adv. index. Indexed: Biol.Abstr.

591　　　GW　ISSN 0074-3860
INTERNATIONAL CONGRESS OF PARASITOLOGY. PROCEEDINGS. 1964. quadrennial; 3rd, Munich, 1970. price varies. World Federation of Parasitologists, Institut Fur Medizinische Parasitologie des Univebeidat, D-53 Bonn-Venusber, W. Germany (B.R.D.), 41026 Bologna, Italy.

INTERNATIONAL CONGRESS OF PRIMATOLOGY. PROCEEDINGS. see *ANTHROPOLOGY*

591 US
INTERNATIONAL CONGRESS OF ZOOLOGY. PROCEEDINGS. a. price varies. Natural History Press, c/o Doubleday & Co., 501 Franklin Ave., Garden City, NY 11530.

591 US ISSN 0074-7734
INTERNATIONAL REVIEW OF GENERAL AND EXPERIMENTAL ZOOLOGY. 1964. irreg., 1970, vol. 4. price varies. Academic Press, Inc., 111 Fifth Ave., New York, NY 10003. Eds. William J. L. Felts, Richard J. Harrison. index.

591 US
INTERNATIONAL SERIES ON PURE AND APPLIED BIOLOGY. ZOOLOGY DIVISION. 1966. irreg., vol. 58, 1978. price varies. Pergamon Press, Inc., Maxwell House, Fairview Park, Elmsford, NY 10523. index.
Formerly: International Series of Monographs on Pure and Applied Biology. Division: Zoology (ISSN 0074-8307)

591 UK ISSN 0074-9664
INTERNATIONAL ZOO YEARBOOK. 1960. a. £17 hardcover; £13.50 paperback. Zoological Society of London, Regent's Park, London NW1 4RY, England. Ed. Peter Olney. index. cum.index: vols. 1-11 in vol. 11.

591 SA ISSN 0073-4381
J. L. B.SMITH INSTITUTE OF ICHTHYOLOGY. ICHTHYOLOGICAL BULLETIN. (Continues publication issued under former name of body, Dept. of Ichthyology, Rhodes University) (Text in English) 1956. irreg. price varies. ‡ J. L. B. Smith Institute of Ichthyology, Rhodes University, Grahamstown, South Africa. (Co-Sponsors: South African Council for Scientific and Industrial Research; South Africa Department of National Education) Ed. Margaret M. Smith. cum.index. circ. 1,000 (controlled) Indexed: Zoo.Rec.

591 SA ISSN 0075-2088
J. L. B. SMITH INSTITUTE OF ICHTHYOLOGY. SPECIAL PUBLICATION. (Continues numbering of publication issued under former name of body, Dept. of Ichthyology, Rhodes University) (Text in English) 1967. irreg. price varies. J. L. B. Smith Institute, Rhodes University, Grahamstown 6140, South Africa. (Co-sponsors: South African Council for Scientific and Industrial Research; South Africa Department of National Education) Ed. Margaret M. Smith. index. circ. 1,500(controlled) Indexed: Zoo.Rec.

594 US ISSN 0075-3920
JOHNSONIA; monographs of the marine mollusks of the Western Atlantic. 1941. irreg. price varies. ‡ Harvard University, Museum of Comparative Zoology, Department of Mollusks, Cambridge, MA 02138. Ed. Kenneth J. Boss.

591 572 RH ISSN 0085-249X
KARIBA STUDIES. 1961. irreg., no. 9, 1978. price varies. ‡ National Museums and Monuments Administration, Box 8540, Causeway, Salisbury, Zimbabwe. circ. 60.

591 PL ISSN 0075-5230
KATALOG FAUNY PASOZYTNICZEJ POLSKI. (Text in Polish) 1970. irreg. price varies. (Polskie Towarzystwo Parazytologiczne) Panstwowe Wydawnictwo Naukowe, Miodowa 10, Warsaw, Poland (Dist. by Ars Polona-Ruch, Krakowskie Przedmiescie 7, Warsaw, Poland)

591 PL ISSN 0075-5249
KATALOG FAUNY POLSKI. (Text in Polish) 1960. irreg. price varies. (Polska Akademia Nauk, Instytut Zoologii) Panstwowe Wydawnictwo Naukowe, Ul. Miodowa 10, Warsaw, Poland.

591 AT
KOOLEWONG. 1934. irreg. Aus.$8. Royal Zoological Society of New South Wales, c/o Taronga Zoological Park, Mosman, N.S.W. 2088, Australia. illus.
Formerly (until 1972): Royal Zoological Society of New South Wales. Proceedings (ISSN 0085-5820)

591 AU
LANDESMUSEUM JOANNEUM. ABTEILUNG FUER ZOOLOGIE. MITTEILUNGEN. (Text and summaries in German and English) 1972. irreg; 2-4/yr. price varies. Landesmuseum Joanneum, Abteilung fuer Zoologie, Raubergasse 10, A-8010 Graz, Austria. Ed. Erich Kreissl. bk. rev. illus. tr.lit. index. circ. 600.

591 CK ISSN 0085-2899
LOZANIA; acta zoologica Colombiana. (Text in Spanish; French; German and English) 1952. irreg. $5 or exchange basis. Universidad Nacional de Colombia, Instituto de Ciencias Naturales, Aptdo. Aereo 7495, Bogota, Colombia. Ed. Polidoro Pinto Escobar. bibl. illus. circ. 1,000.

599 NE ISSN 0024-7634
LUTRA. (Summaries in English, French or German) irreg., vol. 14, 1972. fl.10. (Vereniging voor Zoogdierkunde - Society for the Study and Protection of Mammals) E. J. Brill, Oude Rijn 33a-35, Leiden, Netherlands. bk. rev. charts. illus.

599 CS ISSN 0024-7774
LYNX; novitates mammaliologicae. (Text in Czech, English, German, Russian, Slovak) 1962. irreg. 20-30 Kcs. Narodni Muzeum, Prirodovedecke Muzeum, Vaclavske nam. 1700, 115 79 Prague 1, Czechoslovakia. Ed. Ivan Heran. bk. rev. bibl. cum.index. Indexed: Biol.Abstr.

591 HU ISSN 0076-2474
MAGYARORSZAG ALLATVILAGA/FAUNA HUNGARIAE. 1960. irreg. price varies. (Magyar Tudomanyos Akademia) Akademiai Kiado, Publishing House of the Hungarian Academy of Sciences, P.O. Box 24, H-1363 Budapest, Hungary.

591 594 US ISSN 0076-2997
MALACOLOGIA. (Text in English, French, German, Spanish) 1962. irreg., vol. 14, no. 1-2, 1974. $12 individuals; $20 institutions. Institute of Malacology, Institute of Malacology, c/o Academy of Natural Sciences of Philadelphia, 19th St. and the Parkway, Philadelphia, PA 19103. (Co-sponsor: Institute of Malacology) Eds. G. M. Davis, R. Robertson. index. circ. 732.

591 US ISSN 0076-3004
MALACOLOGICAL REVIEW. (Text usually in English; occasionally in French or German) 1968. a. $10 to individuals; institutions $17. Society for Experimental and Descriptive Malacology, Box 420, Whitmore Lake, MI 48189. Ed. J. B. Burch. bk. rev. index. circ. 700. (also avail. in microfilm from UMI) Indexed: Biol.Abstr. Zoo.Rec.

591 GW ISSN 0301-2778
MAMMALIA DEPICTA. (Supplement to: Zeitschrift fuer Saeugetierkunde) (Text and summaries in German, English, French) 1966. irreg., no. 11, 1979. price varies. Verlag Paul Parey (Hamburg), Spitalerstr. 12, 2000 Hamburg 1, W. Germany (B.R.D.) Eds. Wolf Herre, Manfred Roehrs. bibl. illus. index. (reprint service avail, from ISI) Indexed: Biol.Abstr.

591.4 US ISSN 0076-3519
MAMMALIAN SPECIES. 1969. irreg. $10. American Society of Mammalogists, c/o Dr. Gordon L. Kirkland Jr., Sec.-Treas., Vertebrate Museum, Shippensburg State College, Shippensburg, PA 17257. Ed. Sydney Anderson. circ. 1,400. (processed; reprint service avail. from UMI)

597 UK ISSN 0076-4493
MARINE RESEARCH. 1952. irreg. price varies. Marine Research Laboratory, Aberdeen, Scotland.

595.146 CN ISSN 0380-9633
MEGADRILOGICA. (Text in English and French; summaries in English, French, German and Spanish) 1968. irreg. Can.$1.50 per no. University of New Brunswick, Faculty of Forestry, Box 4440, Fredericton, N.B. E3B 5A3, Canada. Ed. Dr. J. W. Reynolds. bibl. illus. circ. 1,000. (back issues avail.) Indexed: Bibl. Agri. Biol. Abstr. Forest Abstr. Zoo Rec.
Earthworms

591 PL ISSN 0076-6372
MEMORABILIA ZOOLOGICA. (Text in Polish; summaries in English, French and Russian) 1958. irreg., (1-2 per yr.), no. 28, 1977. price varies. (Polska Akademia Nauk, Instytut Zoologii) Ossolineum, Publishing House of the Polish Academy of Sciences, Rynek 9, Wroclaw, Poland (Dist. by Ars Polona-Ruch, Krakowskie Przedmiescie 7, Warsaw, Poland) circ. 1,000. Indexed: Biol.Abstr.

591 GE ISSN 0076-8839
MILU; WISSENSCHAFTLICHE UND KULTURELLE MITTEILUNGEN AUS DEM TIERPARK BERLIN. 1960. irreg., vol. 3, 1973. M.15. (Tierpark Berlin) Akademische Verlagsgesellschaft Geest und Portig K.G., Sternwartenstr. 8, 701 Leipzig, E. Germany (D.D.R.) Ed. H. Dathe. index.

591 SP
MISCELLANEA ZOOLOGICA. (Text in Catalan; summaries in English, French and German) 1958. a. 600 ptas. (or exchange) ‡ Museu de Zoologia, Apartado 593, Barcelona 3, Spain. bk. rev. bibl. charts, illus. circ. 1,000. Indexed: Biol.Abstr. Ref.Zh.

591 IT ISSN 0391-1632
MONITORE ZOOLOGICO ITALIANO. MONOGRAFIE/ITALIAN JOURNAL OF ZOOLOGY. MONOGRAPHS. 1975. irreg., no. 2, 1980. L.56000. Universita degli Studi di Firenze, c/o L. Pardi, Ed., Via Romana 17, 50125 Florence, Italy. index; cum.index. (back issues avail.; reprint service avail. from ISI) Indexed: Biol.Abstr. Chem.Abstr. Curr.Cont. Excerp.Med.

591 IT ISSN 0374-9444
MONITORE ZOOLOGICO ITALIANO. SUPPLEMENTO/ITALIAN JOURNAL OF ZOOLOGY. SUPPLEMENT. 1966. irreg. L.17000. Universita degli Studi di Firenze, c/o L. Pardi, Ed., Via Romana 17, 50125 Florence, Italy. index; cum.index. (back issues avail.; reprint service avail. from ISI) Indexed: Biol.Abstr. Chem.Abstr. Curr.Cont. Excerp.Med.

591 PL
MONOGRAFIE FAUNY POLSKI. (Text in Polish, English, French and German; Summaries Also in Russian) 1973. irreg., 1-3/yr. price varies. (Polska Akademia Nauk, Zaklad Zoologii Systematycznej) Panstwowe Wydawnictwo Naukowe, Miodowa 10, 00-251 Warsaw, Poland.

594 US ISSN 0162-8321
MONOGRAPHS OF MARINE MOLLUSCA. 1978. irreg. $17.50. American Malacologists, Inc., Box 2255, Melbourne, FL 32901. Ed. R. Tucker Abbott. circ. 500. Indexed: Biol.Abstr. Zoo.Rec.

591 BE
MUSEE ROYAL DE L'AFRIQUE CENTRALE. ANNALES. SERIE IN 8. SCIENCES ZOOLOGIQUES/KONINKLIJK MUSEUM VOOR MIDDEN-AFRIKA. ANNALEN. REEKS IN 8. ZOOLOGISCHE WETENSCHAPPEN. 1948. irreg., no. 232, 1980. price varies. Musee Royal de l'Afrique Centrale, 13 Steenweg op Leuven, B-1980 Tervuren, Belgium. charts. illus.

591 BE
MUSEE ROYAL DE L'AFRIQUE CENTRALE. DOCUMENTATION ZOOLOGIQUE/ KONINKLIJK MUSEUM VOOR MIDDEN-AFRIKA. ZOOLOGISCHE DOCUMENTATIE. 1961. irreg., latest no. 18, 1974. Musee Royal de l'Afrique Centrale, 13 Steenweg op Leuven, B-1980 Tervuren, Belgium.

591 BL ISSN 0080-312X
MUSEU NACIONAL, RIO DE JANEIRO. BOLETIM. NOVA SERIE. ZOOLOGIA. (Text in Portuguese; summaries mainly in English, occasionally in French and German) 1942. irreg., no. 293, Feb. 1979. exchange only. Museu Nacional, Quinta da Boa Vista, 20940 Rio de Janeiro RJ, Brazil. bibl. charts.

591 BL ISSN 0077-2224
MUSEU PARAENSE EMILIO GOELDI. BOLETIM ZOOLOGIA. NOVA SERIE. 1957. irreg., no. 99, 1980. Instituto Nacional de Pesquisas da Amazonia, Museu Paraense Emilio Goeldi, C.P. 399, Belem, Para, Brazil.

BIOLOGY — ZOOLOGY

591 572 913   RH   ISSN 0304-5323
MUSEUM MEMOIR. 1944. irreg., no. 9, 1979. price varies. National Museums and Monuments Administration, Box 8540, Causeway, Salisbury, Zimbabwe. circ. 35.

590   FR   ISSN 0078-9747
MUSEUM NATIONAL D'HISTOIRE NATURELLE, PARIS. MEMOIRES. NOUVELLE SERIE. SERIE A. ZOOLOGIE. 1950. irreg. price varies. Museum National d'Histoire Naturelle, 38, rue Geoffroy-Saint-Hilaire, Paris 5, France.

594   US   ISSN 0077-5711
NATIONAL SHELLFISHERIES ASSOCIATION. PROCEEDINGS. 1930. a. $8. ‡ National Shellfisheries Association, Biological Laboratory, Oxford, MD 21654. Ed. Sara V. Otto. cum.index: 1930-72. index. circ. 550. Indexed: Biol.Abstr.

590   UK   ISSN 0078-0952
NOMENCLATOR ZOOLOGICUS. 1939. irreg., vol. 7, 1975. £20. Zoological Society of London, Regent's Park, London NW1 4RY, England. Eds. Marcia A. Edwards, H. Gwynne Vevers.
   Contains names of genera and subgenera in zoology from 10th edition of Linnaeus in 1785 to end of 1965, with a bibliographic reference for original description of each

591   US   ISSN 0078-1304
NORTH AMERICAN FAUNA. 1889. irreg., no. 71, 1975. U.S. Fish and Wildlife Service, Department of the Interior, Washington, DC 20240 (Orders to: Supt. Doc., Washington, DC 20402)

599.639   US   ISSN 0078-1622
NORTH PACIFIC FUR SEAL COMMISSION. PROCEEDINGS OF THE ANNUAL MEETING. 1958. a. free. ‡ North Pacific Fur Seal Commission, c/o National Marine Fisheries Service, Washington, DC 20235.

OHIO FISH AND WILDLIFE REPORT. see *CONSERVATION*

OPERA LILLOANA. see *BIOLOGY — Botany*

591   US   ISSN 0078-5830
OREGON STATE MONOGRAPHS. STUDIES IN ZOOLOGY. 1939. irreg., 1968, no. 12. price varies. Oregon State University Press, 101 Waldo Hall, Corvallis, OR 97331.

OSTRACODOLOGIST. see *PALEONTOLOGY*

591   NZ   ISSN 0474-8611
OTAGO MUSEUM. RECORDS. ZOOLOGY. 1964. irreg., no. 2, 1965. Otago Museum Trust Board, Great King St., Dunedin, New Zealand.

591   NZ
OTAGO MUSEUM BULLETIN: ZOOLOGY. 1967. irreg., no. 5, 1979. Otago Museum Trust Board, Great King St., Dunedin, New Zealand.

591   BL   ISSN 0031-1049
PAPEIS AVULSOS DE ZOOLOGIA. (Summaries in English) 1941. irreg. $15 per vol. Universidade de Sao Paulo, Museu de Zoologia, Caixa Postal 7172, Sao Paulo, Brazil. Ed. P. E. Vanzolini. circ. 600(approx.) Indexed: Biol.Abstr. Zoo.Rec.

591   BL   ISSN 0553-8505
PESQUISAS: PUBLICACOES DE ZOOLOGIA. (Numbering Is in continuation of articles published in Pesquisas) no. 6, 1960. irreg. price varies (or exchange) (Universidade do Vale do Rio dos Sinos, Instituto Anchietano de Pesquisas) Unisinos, Praca Tiradentes 35, Sao Leopoldo RS, Brazil.
   Supersedes in Part: Pesquisas.

574   CU
POEYANA. (Published under the title "Poeyana" from January 1964 to August 1970, and again since March 1974.) (Summaries in English) 1964. irreg. free. ‡ Academia de Ciencias de Cuba, Instituto de Zoologia, Industria 452, Havana 2, Cuba. bibl. charts. illus. circ. 2,000. Indexed: Biol.Abstr.
   Formerly: Serie Poeyana (ISSN 0032-2229)

591 639.9   SZ
POLAR BEARS. Represents: Working Meeting of the Polar Bear Specialist Group. Proceedings. no. 5, 1975, St. Prex, Switzerland (pub. 1976) biennial. $4.50. International Union for Conservation of Nature and Natural Resources, 1110 Morges, Switzerland (Dist. in the U.S. by: Unipub, Inc., 345 Park Ave. S., New York, NY 10010)

599   US   ISSN 0079-5100
PRIMATES; comparative anatomy and taxonomy. 1955. irreg., 1970, vol. 8. price varies. Halsted Press (Subsidiary of: John Wiley & Sons, Inc.) 605 Third Ave., New York, NY 10016. Ed. W. C. O. Hill.

R S P B ANNUAL REPORT AND ACCOUNTS. (Royal Society for the Protection of Birds) see *CONSERVATION*

591   US   ISSN 0080-1658
RESEARCH IN PROTOZOOLOGY.* irreg. price varies. Pergamon Press, Inc., Maxwell House, Fairview Park, Elmsford, NY 10523 (And Headington Hill Hall, Oxford OX3 0BW, England) Ed. T. T. Chen.

REVISTA PARAGUAYA DE MICROBIOLOGIA. see *BIOLOGY — Microbiology*

591   IT
RICERCHE DI BIOLOGIA DELLA SELVAGGINA. (Text in Italian; summaries in English, French, German) 1930. irreg., approx. 4/yr. exchange basis. ‡ Istituto Nazionale di Biologia della Selvaggina, Via Stradelli Guelfi 23/A, 40064 Ozzano Emilia(Bo), Italy. circ. 2,000. Indexed: Biol.Abstr. Zoo.Rec.
   Formerly: Ricerche di Zoologia Applicata alla Caccia (ISSN 0044-5061)

591   NE
RIJKSMUSEUM VAN NATUURLIJKE HISTORIE. ZOOLOGISCHE BIJDRAGEN. (Text Mainly in Dutch; occasionally in English, French and German) 1955. irreg. Rijksmuseum van Natuurlijke Historie, Postbus 9517, 2300 RA Leiden, Netherlands (Subscr. addr.: E. J. Brill, Postbus 9000, 2300 RA Leiden Netherlands) circ. 450. Indexed: Zoo.Rec.

591   NE   ISSN 0024-0672
RIJKSMUSEUM VAN NATUURLIJKE HISTORIE. ZOOLOGISCHE MEDEDELINGEN. (Text mainly in English, French or German; occasionally in Dutch) 1915. irreg. price on request. Rijksmuseum van Natuurlijke Historie, Postbus 9517, 2300 RA Leiden, Netherlands (Subscr. addr.: E. J. Brill, Postbus 9000, 2300 RA Leiden Netherlands) charts. illus. circ. 450. Indexed: Biol.Abstr. Zoo.Rec.

ROYAL ONTARIO MUSEUM. LIFE SCIENCES. CONTRIBUTIONS. see *BIOLOGY*

591   UK
ROYAL ZOOLOGICAL SOCIETY OF SCOTLAND. ZOO GUIDE. 1958. irreg. 30p. ‡ Royal Zoological Society of Scotland, Scottish National Zoological Park, Murrayfield, Edinburgh EH12 6TS, Scotland. circ. 100,000. (tabloid format)

591 333.7   CN
SASKATCHEWAN. DEPARTMENT OF TOURISM AND RENEWABLE RESOURCES. GAME SURVEYS UNIT. SPRING SURVEY OF SHARP-TAILED GROUSE AND COCK PHEASANT. 1964. a. Department of Tourism and Renewable Resources, Game Surveys Unit, 1825 Lorne St., Regina, Sask. S4P 3N1, Canada. stat. circ. controlled. (processed)

594   US   ISSN 0085-607X
SHELLER'S DIRECTORY OF CLUBS, BOOKS, PERIODICALS AND DEALERS. 1968. biennial. $2. Of Sea & Shore Publications, Box 219, Port Gamble, WA 98364. Ed. Thomas C. Rice. adv. circ. 2,000. (reprint service avail. from UMI)

590   US   ISSN 0081-0282
SMITHSONIAN CONTRIBUTIONS TO ZOOLOGY. 1969. irreg., no. 266, 1978. Smithsonian Institution Press, Washington, DC 20560. Ed. Albert L. Ruffin Jr. circ. 1,600-2,300. (reprint service avail. from UMI) Indexed: Biol.Abstr. Ocean.Abstr. Pollut.Abstr.

069.7   AT   ISSN 0081-2676
SOUTH AUSTRALIAN MUSEUM, ADELAIDE. RECORDS. 1918. irreg., vol. 17, 1977. Aus.$18. South Australian Museum, North Terrace, Adelaide 5000, S.A., Australia. Ed. Dr. John K. Ling. circ. 650. Indexed: Aus.Sci.Ind. Zoo.Abstr.

591   GE   ISSN 0070-7252
STAATLICHES MUSEUM FUER TIERKUNDE IN DRESDEN. FAUNISTISCHE ABHANDLUNGEN. (Text in English, French, German) 1963. irreg. price varies. Staatliches Museum fuer Tierkunde in Dresden, Augustusstr. 2, 8010 Dresden, E. Germany (D.D.R.) Ed. Rainer Emmrich. bk. rev. circ. 1,000. Indexed: Biol.Abstr. Ber.Biochem.Biol. Zoo.Rec.

594   GE   ISSN 0070-7260
STAATLICHES MUSEUM FUER TIERKUNDE IN DRESDEN. MALAKOLOGISCHE ABHANDLUNGEN. (Text in English, French, German) 1964. irreg. price varies. Staatliches Museum fuer Tierkunde in Dresden, Augustusstr. 2, 8010 Dresden, E. Germany (D.D.R.) Ed. Rainer Emmrich. bk. rev. circ. 500. Indexed: Biol.Abstr. Ber.Biochem.Biol. Zoo.Rec.

591   GE   ISSN 0070-7287
STAATLICHES MUSEUM FUER TIERKUNDE IN DRESDEN. ZOOLOGISCHE ABHANDLUNGEN. (Text in English, French, German) 1961. irreg. price varies. Staatliches Museum fuer Tierkunde in Dresden, Augustusstr. 2, 8010 Dresden, E. Germany (D.D.R.) Ed. Rainer Emmrich. bk. rev. circ. 1,000. Indexed: Biol.Abstr. Ber.Biochem.Biol. Zoo.Rec.

591   PL   ISSN 0082-5565
STUDIA SOCIETATIS SCIENTIARUM TORUNENSIS. SECTIO E (ZOOLOGIA) (Text in Polish; summaries in English) 1948. irreg. price varies. (Towarzystwo Naukowe w Toruniu) Panstwowe Wydawnictwo Naukowe, Ul. Miodowa 10, Warsaw, Poland.

590 591.9   NE   ISSN 0300-5488
STUDIES ON THE FAUNA OF SURINAME AND OTHER GUYANAS. (Subseries of: Natuurwetenschappelijke Studiekring voor Suriname en de Nederlandse Antillen. Uitgaven) 1957. irreg., vol. 16, 1975. Natuurwetenschappelijke Studiekring voor Suriname en de Nederlandse Antillen - Foundation for Scientific Research in Surinam and the Netherlands Antilles, Zoological Laboratory, Plompetorengracht 9, 3512 CA Utrecht, Netherlands. Eds. P. Wagenaar Hummelinck, D. C. Geijskes. illus. circ. 800.

591   US   ISSN 0082-1101
SYNOPSES OF THE BRITISH FAUNA. 1970. irreg., no. 13, 1979. $3.50. (Linnean Society of London, UK) Academic Press Inc., 111 Fifth Ave., New York, NY 10003.

591   GW   ISSN 0040-7305
TIERREICH; eine Zusammenstellung und Kennzeichnung der rezenten Tierformen. (Text in English, French and German) 1897. irreg. price varies. Walter de Gruyter und Co., Genthiner Str. 13, 1000 Berlin 30, W. Germany (B.R.D.) Ed. Bd. adv. bibl. illus. circ. 250(approx.)

590   GE   ISSN 0082-4305
TIERWELT DEUTSCHLANDS. irreg., vol. 66, 1979. price varies. VEB Gustav Fischer Verlag, Villengang 2, Postfach 176, 6900 Jena, E. Germany (D.D.R.) Eds. K. Senglaub, H.-J. Hannemann, H. Schumann.

591 581   JA
TOKYO UNIVERSITY OF EDUCATION. FACULTY OF SCIENCE. SCIENCE REPORTS. SECTION B: ZOOLOGY AND BOTANY/ TOKYO KYOIKU DAIGAKU RIKA KIYO B, DOBUTSUGAKU TO SHOKUBUTSUGU. (Text in English and European languages) 1930. irreg. exchange basis. Tokyo University of Education, Faculty of Science - Tokyo Kyoiku Daigaku Rigakubu, 3-29-1 Otsuka, Bunkyo-ku, Tokyo 112, Japan.

591   FR   ISSN 0069-4681
UNIVERSITE DE CLERMONT-FERRAND II. ANNALES SCIENTIFIQUES. SERIE BIOLOGIE ANIMALE. 1963. irreg. price varies. Universite de Clermont-Ferrand II, Unite d'Enseignement et de Recherche de Sciences Exactes et Naturelles, B.P. 45, 63170 Aubiere, France. circ. 250. (back issues avail)

591.1　　　　　　FR　ISSN 0069-4746
UNIVERSITE DE CLERMONT-FERRAND II.
ANNALES SCIENTIFIQUES. SERIE
PHYSIOLOGIE ANIMALE. 1967. irreg. price
varies. Universite de Clermont-Ferrand II, Unite
d'Enseignement et de Recherche de Sciences
Exactes et Naturelles, B.P. 45, 63170 Aubiere,
France. circ. 250.

591　　　　　　NE　ISSN 0066-1325
UNIVERSITEIT VAN AMSTERDAM.
ZOOLOGISCH MUSEUM. BULLETIN. (Text in
various languages) 1966. irreg., vol. 6, 1977. price
varies. Universiteit van Amsterdam, Zoologisch
Museum, Plantage Middenlaan 53, Amsterdam-C,
Netherlands. Indexed: Biol.Abstr. Zoo.Rec.

590　　　　　　US　ISSN 0068-6506
UNIVERSITY OF CALIFORNIA PUBLICATIONS
IN ZOOLOGY. 1902. irreg. price varies. University
of California Press, 2223 Fulton St., Berkeley, CA
94720.

590　　　　　　US　ISSN 0076-8405
UNIVERSITY OF MICHIGAN. MUSEUM OF
ZOOLOGY. MISCELLANEOUS
PUBLICATIONS. 1916. irreg., no. 156, 1978. price
varies. University of Michigan, Museum of Zoology,
Ann Arbor, MI 48109. Ed. William D. Hamilton.
circ. 1,200.

590　　　　　　US　ISSN 0076-8413
UNIVERSITY OF MICHIGAN. MUSEUM OF
ZOOLOGY. OCCASIONAL PAPERS. 1913. irreg.
price varies. University of Michigan, Museum of
Zoology, Ann Arbor, MI 48109. Ed. William D.
Hamilton. cum.index. circ. 1,200. Key Title:
Occasional Papers of the Museum of Zoology,
University of Michigan.

591　　　　　　PK　ISSN 0079-8045
UNIVERSITY OF THE PUNJAB. DEPARTMENT
OF ZOOLOGY. BULLETIN. NEW SERIES. 1931-
47; 1967 NS. irreg. price varies. University of the
Punjab, Department of Zoology, New Campus,
Lahore, Pakistan. Ed. A. R. Shakoori. circ. 300.
Indexed: Biol.Abstr.

591　　　　　　JA
UNIVERSITY OF TOKYO. FACULTY OF
SCIENCE. JOURNAL. SECTION 4: ZOOLOGY/
TOKYO DAIGAKU RIGAKUBU KIYO DAI-4-
RUI, DOBUTSUGAKU. (Text in English) 1926. a.
price varies. University of Tokyo, Faculty of Science
- Tokyo Daigaku Rigakubu, 7-3-1 Hongo, Bunkyo-
ku, Tokyo 113, Japan (Order from: Maruzen Co.,
Ltd., 2-3-10 Nihonbashi, Chuo-ku, Tokyo 103,
Japan; or their Import and Export Department, Box
5050, Tokyo International, Tokyo 100-31, Japan)
circ. 500. (also avail. in microform)

591　　　　　　PL　ISSN 0083-4416
UNIWERSYTET JAGIELLONSKI. ZESZYTY
NAUKOWE. PRACE ZOOLOGICZNE. (Text in
English and Polish; summaries in English and
Russian) 1957. a. price varies. (Uniwersytet
Jagiellonski) Panstwowe Wydawnictwo Naukowe,
Golebia 24, Krakow, Poland (Dist. by Ars Polona-
Ruch, Krakowskie Przedmiescie 7, Warsaw, Poland)
Ed. Czeslaw Jura.

VERSUCHSTIERKUNDE. see MEDICAL
SCIENCES — Experimental Medicine, Laboratory
Technique

591　　　　　　CS　ISSN 0506-7847
VERTEBRATOLOGICKE ZPRAVY/NOTULAE
VERTEBRATOLOGICAE. (Text in Czech;
summaries in English and German) 1967. a. price
varies. Ceskoslovenska Akademie Ved, Ustav pro
Vyzkum Obratlovcu, Kvetna 8, 603 65 Brno,
Czechoslovakia. Ed. Jiri Havlin. bk. rev. bibl. circ.
1,000. (back issues avail)

591　　　　　　NZ　ISSN 0083-6060
VICTORIA UNIVERSITY OF WELLINGTON
ZOOLOGY PUBLICATIONS. 1949. irreg., nos.
68-70, 1978. available on exchange. Victoria
University of Wellington, Zoology Department,
Private Bag, Wellington, New Zealand. Ed. Prof. J.
A. F. Garrick. cum.index. circ. 800. Indexed:
Biol.Abstr.

594　　　　　　US　ISSN 0361-1175
WESTERN SOCIETY OF MALACOLOGISTS.
ANNUAL REPORT. 1968. a. $7.50. Western
Society of Malacologists, c/o Kay Webb, Treas., 501
Anita St., No. 186, Chula Vista, CA 92011. Ed.
Hans Bertsch. illus. circ. 250. Key Title: Annual
Report - Western Society of Malacologists.
　　Continues: Western Society of Malacologists.
Echo; Abstracts and Proceedings of the Annual
Meeting.

599　　　　　　JA　ISSN 0083-9086
WHALES RESEARCH INSTITUTE, TOKYO,
JAPAN. SCIENTIFIC REPORTS/GEIRUI
KENKYUSHO EIBUN HOKOKU. (Text in
English) 1948. a. price varies. Whales Research
Institute - Geirui Kenkyusho, 1-3-1 Etchujima,
Kota-ku, Tokyo 135, Japan. Ed. Hideo Omura.
index. circ. 500. Indexed: Ocean.Abstr.
Pollut.Abstr.

WILDLIFE - A REVIEW. see CONSERVATION

591　　　　　　PL
WYZSZA SZKOLA PEDAGOGICZNA, KRAKOW.
PRACE ZOOLOGICZNE. (Summaries in English
and Russian) 1967. irreg. 112.00 Zl. Wyzsza Szkola
Pedagogiczna, Krakow, Podchorazych 2, 30-084
Krakow, Poland. bibl. illus.

598.1　　　　　　US　ISSN 0098-2644
YEARBOOK OF HERPETOLOGY. Cover title: H I
S S Yearbook of Herpetology. 1974. irreg., 2nd edt.
in prep. (Herpetological Information Search
Systems) American Museum of Natural History,
Central Park West at 79th St., New York, NY
10024. bibl. illus.

591　　　　　　PL
ZOOLOGIA. (Text in Polish; summaries in English)
1962. irreg. price varies. Uniwersytet im. Adama
Mickiewicza w Poznaniu, Stalingradzka 1, 61-712
Poznan, Poland (Dist. by: Ars Polona, Krakowskie
Przedmiescie 7, 00-068 Warsaw, Poland)
　　Formerly: Uniwersytet im. Adama Mickiewicza w
Poznaniu. Wydzial Biologii i Nauk o Ziemi. Seria
Zoologia.

591　　　　　　US
ZOOLOGICAL PARKS & AQUARIUMS IN THE
AMERICAS. 1930. biennial. $15 libraries; $50 non-
members; $8 members. American Association of
Zoological Parks & Aquariums, Oglebay Park,
Wheeling, WV 26003. Ed. Conne Dillon. adv. stat.
index. circ. 3,000.
　　Formerly: Zoos & Aquariums in the Americas
(ISSN 0090-1628)

591　　　　　　UK　ISSN 0084-5612
ZOOLOGICAL SOCIETY OF LONDON.
SYMPOSIA. 1960. irreg. price varies. Academic
Press Inc. (London) Ltd., 24-28 Oval Rd, London
NW1 7DX, England (And 111 Fifth Ave., New
York, NY 10003)

591　　　　　　UK　ISSN 0084-5620
ZOOLOGICAL SOCIETY OF LONDON.
TRANSACTIONS. 1833. irreg. price varies.
Zoological Society of London, Regent's Park,
London NW1 4RY, England. Ed. Dr. H. Gwynne
Vevers. Indexed: Biol.Abstr. Zoo.Rec.

591　　　　　　SA
ZOOLOGICAL SOCIETY OF SOUTHERN
AFRICA. NEWSLETTER. 1959. irreg.
membership. Zoological Society of Southern Africa,
c/o P. R. Condy, Treas., Department of Zoology,
University of Pretoria, Pretoria 0002, South Africa.
Ed. A. E. Louw. bk. rev. abstr. charts. illus. circ.
500(approx.)
　　Former titles: Zoological Society of Southern
Africa. Occasional Bulletin; Zoological Society of
Southern Africa. News Bulletin (ISSN 0044-5126)

591 574　　　　　　II
ZOOLOGICAL SURVEY OF INDIA. MEMOIRS.
(Text in English) 1907. irreg. price varies.
Zoological Survey of India, 34, Chittaranjan Ave.,
Calcutta 700012, India. circ. 450. (back issues
avail.)

591　　　　　　CS
ZOOLOGICKA ZAHRADA V PRAZE. VYROCNI
ZPRAVA/ANNUAL REPORT. (Text and
summaries in Czech and English) 1963. a.
Zoologicka Zahrada v Praze - Zoological Garden of
Prague, Troja 120, 171 00 Prague 7,
Czechoslovakia. Ed. Jiri Volf.

ZOOLOGISCH-BOTANISCHE GESELLSCHAFT,
VIENNA. ABHANDLUNGEN. see BIOLOGY —
Botany

ZOOLOGISCH-BOTANISCHE GESELLSCHAFT,
VIENNA. VERHANDLUNGEN. see
BIOLOGY — Botany

590　　　　　　GW　ISSN 0077-2135
ZOOLOGISCHE STAATSSAMMLUNG,
MUENCHEN. VEROEFFENTLICHUNGEN.
1950. irreg., latest, vol. 18. price varies. Zoologische
Staatssammlung Muenchen, Maria-Ward-Str. 1b,
8000 Munich 19, W. Germany (B.R.D.) Ed. Walter
Forster.

591　　　　　　DK　ISSN 0084-5655
ZOOLOGY OF ICELAND. (Text in English) 1938.
irreg. price varies. Munksgaard, 35 Noerre Soegade,
DK-1370 Copenhagen K, Denmark. Eds. A.
Fridriksson, S. L. Tuxen. index. circ. 400. (reprint
service avail. from ISI) Indexed: Curr.Cont.

591　　　　　　SA　ISSN 0044-5274
ZOON. (Editions in Afrikaans & English) 1964. irreg.
free. National Zoological Gardens of South Africa,
Box 754, Pretoria, South Africa. Ed. Johan Booyens.

BIOPHYSICS

see Biology—Biophysics

BIRTH CONTROL

see also Population Studies

613.7　　　　　　BG
BANGLADESH ASSOCIATION FOR
VOLUNTARY STERILIZATION. ANNUAL
REPORT. (Text in English) Tk.25. Bangladesh
Association for Voluntary Sterilization, 526
Dhanmondi Residential Area, Rd. No. 8, Dacca,
Bangladesh.

301.4　　　　　　PK
F P A P BIENNIAL REPORT. (Text in English)
1964. biennial. Family Planning Association of
Pakistan, 3-A Temple Rd., Lahore, Pakistan. circ.
1,500.
　　Formerly: Family Planning Association of
Pakistan. Annual Report (ISSN 0071-3759)

301.42　　　　　　II
FAMILY PLANNING ASSOCIATION OF INDIA.
REPORT. (Text in English) a. Family Planning
Association of India, 1 Jeevan Udyog, Dadabhai
Naoroji Rd., Bombay 400001, India. illus.

301.42　　　　　　KE
FAMILY PLANNING ASSOCIATION OF KENYA.
ANNUAL REPORT. 1971. a. free. Family Planning
Association of Kenya, Phoenix House, Kenyatta
Ave., Box 30581, Nairobi, Kenya. Ed. J. K.
Chumba. illus. Key Title: Annual Report - Family
Planning Association of Kenya.

301.4　　　　　　UK　ISSN 0538-9089
FAMILY PLANNING IN FIVE CONTINENTS.
1967. irreg. £1.25($2.75) International Planned
Parenthood Federation, 18-20 Lower Regent St.,
London SW1Y 4PW, England. stat. circ.
9,000(controlled) (processed)

362.8　　　　　　US　ISSN 0095-3121
FAMILY PLANNING PROGRAMS IN
OKLAHOMA; annual statistical report. 1971. a.
Maternal and Child Health Service, Oklahoma City,
OK 73105. illus. circ. 450.

301.4　　　　　　UK
I P P F IN ACTION. 1974. a. free. International
Planned Parenthood Federation, 18-20 Lower
Regent St., London SW1Y 4PW, England. illus.
　　Formerly: International Planned Parenthood
Federation. Annual Report (ISSN 0307-6857)

I U S S P PAPERS. see POPULATION STUDIES

BIRTH CONTROL

613.9 US ISSN 0163-8262
IMPACT (SYRACUSE) 1978. a. free. Syracuse University, Institute for Family Research and Education, 760 Ostrom Ave., Syracuse, NY 13210. Ed. Craig W. Snyder. adv. bk. rev. circ. 50,000. (tabloid format)

613.94 EC
INFORME ANUAL DE LAS ACTIVIDADES DE LAS UNIDADES OPERATIVAS DE SALUD EN EL PROGRAMA DE PLANIFICACION FAMILIAR DEL MINISTERIO DE SALUD. a. Ministerio de Salud Publica, Departamento Nacional de Poblacion, Quito, Ecuador.

301.426 II
INSTITUTE OF ECONOMIC RESEARCH. PUBLICATIONS ON FAMILY PLANNING. (Text in English) irreg. price varies. Institute of Economic Research, Deputy Director, Vidyagiri, Dharwar 580004, Karnataka, India.

301.4 UK ISSN 0308-213X
INTERNATIONAL PLANNED PARENTHOOD FEDERATION. REPORT TO DONORS, PROGRAMME DEVELOPMENT & FINANCIAL STATEMENTS. 1971. a. International Planned Parenthood Federation, 18-20 Lower Regent St., London SW1Y 4PW, England. circ. 1,000(controlled)

INTERNATIONAL POPULATION CONFERENCE. PROCEEDINGS. see *POPULATION STUDIES*

INTERNATIONAL UNION FOR THE SCIENTIFIC STUDY OF POPULATION. NEWSLETTER. see *POPULATION STUDIES*

301.426 618 US ISSN 0097-9074
JOHNS HOPKINS UNIVERSITY. POPULATION INFORMATION PROGRAM. POPULATION REPORT. SERIES A. ORAL CONTRACEPTIVES. (Text in Arabic, English, French, Spanish, Portuguese) 1972. irreg. free to qualified personnel. Johns Hopkins University, Population Information Program, 624 N. Broadway, Baltimore, MD 21205. Dirs. Helen K. Kolbe, Phyllis T. Piotrow. bibl. illus. charts. stat. index. circ. controlled. (looseleaf format; back issues avail.)
Formerly: George Washington University. Population Information Program. Population Report. Series A. Oral Contraceptives.
Contraceptives

301.426 618 US ISSN 0092-9344
JOHNS HOPKINS UNIVERSITY. POPULATION INFORMATION PROGRAM. POPULATION REPORT. SERIES B. INTRAUTERINE DEVICES. (Text in Arabic, English, French, Spanish, Portuguese) 1972. irreg. free to qualified personnel. Johns Hopkins University, Population Information Program, 624 N. Broadway, Baltimore, MD 21205. Dirs. Helen K. Kolbe, Phyllis T. Piotrow. bibl.illus. charts. stat. index. circ. controlled. (looseleaf format; back issues avail.)
Formerly: George Washington University. Population Information Program. Population Report. Series B. Intrauterine Devices.
Contraceptives

301.426 US ISSN 0091-9268
JOHNS HOPKINS UNIVERSITY. POPULATION INFORMATION PROGRAM. POPULATION REPORT. SERIES C. STERILIZATION (FEMALE) (Text in Arabic, English, French, Spanish, Portuguese) 1972. irreg. free to qualified personnel. Johns Hopkins University, Population Information Program, 624 N. Broadway, Baltimore, MD 21205. Dirs. Helen K. Kolbe,Phyllis T. Piotrow. bibl. illus. charts. stat. index. circ. controlled. (looseleaf format; back issues avail.)
Formerly: George Washington University. Population Information Program. Population Report. Series C. Sterilization (Female)
Sterilization

613.94 610 US ISSN 0093-4488
JOHNS HOPKINS UNIVERSITY. POPULATION INFORMATION PROGRAM. POPULATION REPORT. SERIES D. STERILIZATION (MALE) 1973. irreg. free to qualified personnel. ‡ Johns Hopkins University, Population Information Program, 624 N. Broadway, Baltimore, MD 21205. Dirs. Helen K. Kolbe, Phyllis T. Piotrow. illus. charts. bibl. stat. index. circ. controlled. (looseleaf format; back issues avail.)
Formerly: George Washington University. Population Information Program. Population Report. Series D. Sterilization (Male)
Sterilization

301.426 618 US ISSN 0097-9082
JOHNS HOPKINS UNIVERSITY. POPULATION INFORMATION PROGRAM. POPULATION REPORT. SERIES E. LAW AND POLICY. (Text in Arabic, English, French, Spanish, Portuguese) 1972. irreg. free to qualified personnel. Johns Hopkins University, Population Information Program, 624 N. Broadway, Baltimore, MD 21205. Dirs. Helen K. Kolbe, Phyllis T. Piotrow. bibl. illus. charts. stat. index. circ. controlled. (looseleaf format; back issues avail.)
Formerly: George Washington University. Population Information Program. Populaton Report. Series E. Law and Policy.

301.426 618 US ISSN 0091-9284
JOHNS HOPKINS UNIVERSITY. POPULATION INFORMATION PROGRAM. POPULATION REPORT. SERIES F. PREGNANCY TERMINATION. (Text in Arabic, English, French, Spanish, Portuguese) 1972. irreg. free to qualified personnel. Johns Hopkins University, Population Information Program, 624 N. Broadway, Baltimore, MD 21205. Dirs. Helen K. Kolbe, Phyllis T. Piotrow. bibl. illus. charts. stat. index. circ. controlled. (looseleaf format; back issues avail.)
Formerly: George Washington University. Population Information Program. Population Report. Series F. Pregnancy Termination.

301.426 618 US ISSN 0091-9276
JOHNS HOPKINS UNIVERSITY. POPULATION INFORMATION PROGRAM. POPULATION REPORT. SERIES G. PROSTAGLANDINS. (Text in Arabic, English, French, Spanish and Portuguese) 1972. irreg. free to qualified personnel. Johns Hopkins University, Population Information Program, 624 N. Broadway, Baltimore, MD 21205. Dirs. Helen K. Kolbe, Phyllis T. Piotrow. bibl. illus. charts. stat. index. circ. controlled. (looseleaf format; back issues avail.)
Formerly: George Washington University. Population Information Program. Population Report. Series G. Prostaglandins.

301.426 618 US ISSN 0093-4496
JOHNS HOPKINS UNIVERSITY. POPULATION INFORMATION PROGRAM. POPULATION REPORTS. SERIES H. BARRIER METHODS. (Text in Arabic, English, French, Spanish and Portuguese) 1972. irreg. free to qualified personnel. Johns Hopkins University, Population Information Program, 624 N. Broadway, Baltimore, MD 21205. Dirs. Helen K. Kolbe, Phyllis T. Piotrow. bibl. illus. charts. stat. index. circ. controlled. (looseleaf format; back issues avail.)
Formerly: George Washington University. Population Information Program. Population Report. Series H. Barrier Methods.

613.94 610 US ISSN 0097-9090
JOHNS HOPKINS UNIVERSITY. POPULATION INFORMATION PROGRAM. POPULATION REPORT. SERIES I. PERIODIC ABSTINENCE. 1973. irreg. free to qualified personnel. ‡ Johns Hopkins University, Population Information Program, 624 N. Broadway, Baltimore, Washington, MD 21205. Dirs.Helen K. Kolbe, Phyllis T. Piotrow. bibl. charts. illus. stat. circ. controlled. (looseleaf format; back issues avail.)
Formerly: George Washington University. Population Information Program. Population Report. Series I. Periodic Abstinence.

301.426 618 US
JOHNS HOPKINS UNIVERSITY. POPULATION INFORMATION PROGRAM. POPULATION REPORT. SERIES J. FAMILY PLANNING PROGRAMS. (Text in Arabic, English, French, Spanish, Portuguese) 1972. irreg. free to qualified personnel. Johns Hopkins University, Population Information Program, 624 N. Broadway, Baltimore, MD 21205. Dirs. Helen K.Kolbe, Phyllis T. Piotrow. bibl. illus. charts. stat. index. circ. controlled. (looseleaf format; back issues avail.)
Formerly: George Washington University. Population Information Program. Population Report. Series J. Family Planning Programs.

613.94 US ISSN 0097-9104
JOHNS HOPKINS UNIVERSITY. POPULATION INFORMATION PROGRAM. POPULATION REPORT. SERIES K. INJECTABLES AND IMPLANTS. (Text in Arabic, English, French, Spanish, Portuguese) 1975. irreg. free to qualified personnel. Johns Hopkins University, Population Information Program, 624 N. Broadway, Baltimore, MD 21205. Dirs. Helen K. Kolbe, Phyllis T. Piotrow. bibl. charts. illus. stat. index. circ. controlled. (looseleaf format; back issues avail.)
Formerly: George Washington University. Population Information Program. Population Report. Series K. Injectables and Implants.

613.9 KO
JOURNAL OF POPULATION STUDIES. (Text in English and Korean) no. 19, 1975. a. $3. Institute of Population Problems, Sahak Bldg. Rm. 305, 147-21 Kye-Dong, Chongro-ku, Seoul, S. Korea. charts, illus. stat.

301.426 KO
KOREAN INSTITUTE FOR FAMILY PLANNING. ANNUAL REPORT. 1971. a. free. Korean Institute for Family Planning, 115, Nokbun-Dong, Sudaemun-Ku, Seoul 122, S. Korea.

301.42 II ISSN 0077-4944
N I F P GENERAL SERIES. 1965. irreg., 1970, no. 22. free; available on exchange. National Institute of Family Planning, L-17 Green Park, New Delhi 1100016, India. Ed. S. Pramanik. circ. 3,000.

301.42 II ISSN 0077-4952
N I F P MANUAL SERIES. 1966. irreg. free; available on exchange. National Institute of Family Planning, L-17 Green Park, New Delhi 1100016, India. Ed. S. Pramanik. circ. 3,000.

301.42 II ISSN 0077-4960
N I F P MONOGRAPH SERIES. 1966. irreg., 1973, no. 19. free; available on exchange. National Institute of Family Planning, L-17 Green Park, New Delhi 1100016, India. Ed. S. Pramanik. circ. 3,000.

301.42 II ISSN 0077-4979
N I F P REPORT SERIES. 1966. irreg., 1973, no. 12. free; available on exchange. National Institute of Family Planning, L-17 Green Park, New Delhi 1100016, India. Ed. S. Pramanik. circ. 3,000.

301.42 II ISSN 0077-4987
N I F P TECHNICAL PAPER SERIES. 1966. irreg., 1973, no. 17. free; available on exchange. National Institute of Family Planning, L-17 Green Park, New Delhi 1100016, India. Ed. S. Pramanik. circ. 3,000.

362.8 NP
NEPAL FAMILY PLANNING AND MATERNAL CHILD HEALTH BOARD. ANNUAL REPORT. (Text in English) a. Family Planning Association of Nepal, Box 486, Kathmandu, Nepal. stat.

312 618.2 US
NORTH CAROLINA REPORTED ABORTIONS. biennial. Department of Human Resources, Division of Health Services, Public Health Statistics Branch, Box 2091, Raleigh, NC 27602.
Abortion

POPULATION AND FAMILY PLANNING PROGRAMS. see *POPULATION STUDIES*

PROSTAGLANDINS IN FERTILITY CONTROL. see *BIOLOGY*

312 301.426 SI
REPORT OF NATIONAL SURVEY ON FAMILY PLANNING IN SINGAPORE. 1974. a. $25. Family Planning and Population Board, Singapore, Singapore. charts. stat.

362   US   ISSN 0085-7408
TRUE TO LIFE. 1970. irreg. price varies. Reproductive Health Resources, Inc., 1507 21st St., Suite 100, Sacramento, CA 95814 (And 238 N. Colonial Homes Circle, N.W., Atlanta, GA 30309) circ. 160,000.

618 614   US   ISSN 0094-0933
U.S. CENTER FOR DISEASE CONTROL. ABORTION SURVEILLANCE. ANNUAL SUMMARY. a. free. U.S. Center for Disease Control, 1600 Clifton Rd., N.E., Atlanta, GA 30333.
Abortion

362.8   US   ISSN 0094-4424
U.S. CENTER FOR DISEASE CONTROL. FAMILY PLANNING SERVICES: ANNUAL SUMMARY. a. U.S. Center for Disease Control, Atlanta, GA 30333. stat. Key Title: Family Planning Services; Annual Survey.

301.4   UK   ISSN 0535-1774
WORLD LIST OF FAMILY PLANNING AGENCIES. irreg. free. International Planned Parenthood Federation, 18-20 Lower Regent St., London SW1Y 4PW, England.

BIRTH CONTROL — Abstracting, Bibliographies, Statistics

618 016   US   ISSN 0092-9522
ABORTION BIBLIOGRAPHY. 1970. a. price varies. Whitston Publishing Co. Inc., Box 958, Troy, NY 12181. Ed. Mary K. Floyd.
Abortion

301.426 016 613.9   UN
BIBLIOGRAPHY ON HUMAN REPRODUCTION, FAMILY PLANNING, AND POPULATION DYNAMICS. (Text in English) 1972. biennial (with quarterly supplements) free. ‡ World Health Organization, Regional Office for South-East Asia, Regional Centre for Documentation on Human Reproduction, Family Planning, and Populaton Dynamics, Indraprastha Estate, Ring Road, New Delhi, India. circ. 1,500.

301.426 312 016   KO
BIBLIOGRAPHY ON POPULATION AND FAMILY PLANNING IN KOREA. (Text in English) 1977. a. Korean Institute for Family Planning, 115 Nokbun-Dong, Sudaemun-ku, Seoul, S. Korea. bibl.
Formerly: Korean Population and Family Planning. Bibliography Series.

614 618   CN   ISSN 0700-138X
CANADA. STATISTICS CANADA. THERAPEUTIC ABORTIONS/AVORTEMENTS THERAPEUTIQUES. (Catalog 82-211) (Text in English and French) 1972. a. Can.$8($9.60) Statistics Canada, Publications Distribution, Ottawa, Ont. K1A 0V7, Canada. (also avail. in microform from MML)

301   US   ISSN 0095-3105
NEBRASKA STATISTICAL REPORT OF ABORTIONS. a. free. Bureau of Vital Statistics, Lincoln, NE 68500.
Abortion

BLIND

see also *Social Services and Welfare*

362   CN   ISSN 0068-9378
CANADIAN NATIONAL INSTITUTE FOR THE BLIND. NATIONAL ANNUAL REPORT. 1919. a. ‡ Canadian National Institute for the Blind, 1929 Bayview Ave, Toronto, Ont. M4G 3E8, Canada. Ed. R. F. Mercer. circ. 6,000.

027.663   US   ISSN 0363-9029
CASSETTE BOOKS. biennial. free. U. S. Library of Congress, National Library Service for the Blind and Physically Handicapped, 1291 Taylor St., N.W., Washington, DC 20542. bk. rev. index. (also avail. in Braille; record)

808.068   US
EXPECTATIONS. 1948. a. free to blind who qualify. ‡ Braille Institute of America, Inc., 741 North Vermont Ave., Los Angeles, CA 90029. Ed. Betty Kalagian. illus. index. circ. 3,000. (Braille)

011   GE
HOERBUCHVERZEICHNIS. a. Zentralbuecherei fuer Blinde, Gustav-Adolf-Str. 7, 701 Leipzig, E. Germany (D.D.R.) bibl.

647.9   US   ISSN 0018-9812
I H B REPORTER. 1942. irreg. free. Industrial Home for the Blind, 57 Willoughby St., Brooklyn, NY 11201 (Braille ed. avail. from: I H B Braille Library, 320 Fulton Ave., Hempstead, NY 11550) Ed. Stuart P. Leffler. illus. circ. 2,700. (looseleaf format)

LIBRARY RESOURCES FOR THE BLIND AND PHYSICALLY HANDICAPPED. see *LIBRARY AND INFORMATION SCIENCES*

647.9654   II
NATIONAL ASSOCIATION FOR THE BLIND. ANNUAL REPORT. (Text in English) a. National Association for the Blind, Jehangir Wadia Bldg., 51, Mahatma Gandhi Rd., Bombay 400023, India. stat.

371   US   ISSN 0270-4234
NATIONAL SOCIETY TO PREVENT BLINDNESS. REPORT. a. National Society to Prevent Blindness, 79 Madison Ave., New York, NY 10016.
Formerly: National Society for the Prevention of Blindness. Report.

371.9   GW
REHA-RUNDBRIEF. irreg. free. Deutsche Blindenstudienanstalt, Mobilitaetszentrum, Am Schlag 8, 3550 Marburg, W. Germany (B.R.D.) Ed. Jochen Fischer. circ. 100.

REHABILITATION GAZETTE; international journal of independent living for the disabled. see *EDUCATION — Special Education And Rehabilitation*

362   UK   ISSN 0080-4479
ROYAL NATIONAL INSTITUTE FOR THE BLIND. INFORMATION LEAFLETS. irreg. free. Royal National Institute for the Blind, Braille House, 338-346 Goswell Rd., London EC1V 7JE, England.

362.61   UK
ST. DUNSTAN'S ANNUAL REPORT. 1916. a. free. St. Dunstan's for Men and Women Blinded on War Service, 191, Old Marylebone Rd., London NW1 5QN, England. illus. circ. controlled. (back issues avail.)

362.41   US
SEEING EYE ANNUAL REPORT. 1939. a. free. ‡ Seeing Eye Inc., Box 375, Morristown, NJ 07960. charts. illus. circ. 18,500.

362.41   SA
SOUTH AFRICAN NATIONAL COUNCIL OF THE BLIND. BIENNIAL REPORT. (Text in English and Afrikaans) 1932. biennial. ‡ South African National Council for the Blind, P.O. Box 26211, Arcadia 0007, South Africa.

TALKING BOOKS IN THE PUBLIC LIBRARY SYSTEMS OF METROPOLITAN TORONTO. see *LIBRARY AND INFORMATION SCIENCES*

BLIND — Abstracting, Bibliographies, Statistics

371.911   US   ISSN 0071-7266
FOR YOUNGER READERS, BRAILLE AND TALKING BOOKS. 1967. biennial. free. U.S. Library of Congress, National Library Service for the Blind and Physically Handicapped, 1291 Taylor St., N.W., Washington, DC 20542. bk. rev. index. (also avail. in Braille; talking book)

027.663 016 780   US   ISSN 0145-3173
MUSIC & MUSICIANS: BRAILLE SCORES CATALOG - CHORAL. irreg. free. U.S. Library of Congress, National Library Service for the Blind and Physically Handicapped, 1291 Taylor St., N.W., Washington, DC 20542. (also avail. in Braille; talking book; record; video cassette)

027.663 016 780   US   ISSN 0145-3149
MUSIC & MUSICIANS: BRAILLE SCORES CATALOG - ORGAN. irreg. free. U.S. Library of Congress, National Library Service for the Blind and Physically Handicapped, 1291 Taylor St., N.W., Washington, DC 20542. (also avail. in Braille; talking book; record; video cassette)

027.663 016 780   US   ISSN 0145-3130
MUSIC & MUSICIANS: BRAILLE SCORES CATALOG - PIANO. irreg. free. U.S. Library of Congress, National Library Service for the Blind and Physically Handicapped, 291 Taylor St., N.W., Washington, DC 20542. (also avail. in Braille; talking book; record; video cassette; also avail. in large type)

027.663 016 780   US   ISSN 0145-3157
MUSIC & MUSICIANS: BRAILLE SCORES CATALOG - VOICE. irreg. free. U.S. Library of Congress, National Library Service for the Blind and Physically Handicapped, 1291 Taylor St., N.W., Washington, DC 20542. (also avail. in Braille; talking book; record; video cassette)

027.663 016 780   US   ISSN 0145-2525
MUSIC & MUSICIANS: INSTRUCTIONAL CASSETTE RECORDINGS CATALOG. irreg. free. U.S. Library of Congress, National Library Service for the Blind and Physically Handicapped, 291 Taylor St., N.W., Washington, DC 20542. (also avail. in Braille; talking book; record; video cassette)

027.663 016 780   US   ISSN 0145-2517
MUSIC & MUSICIANS: INSTRUCTIONAL DISC RECORDINGS CATALOG. irreg. free. U.S. Library of Congress, National Library Service for the Blind and Physically Handicapped, 1291 Taylor St., N.W., Washington, DC 20542. (also avail. in Braille; talking book; record; video cassette)

027.663 016 780   US   ISSN 0363-8472
MUSIC & MUSICIANS: LARGE-PRINT SCORES AND BOOKS CATALOG. 1977. irreg. free. U.S. Library of Congress, National Library Service for the Blind and Physically Handicapped, 291 Taylor St., N.W., Washington, DC 20542. (also avail. in Braille; talking book; record; video cassette)

371.911   US   ISSN 0079-502X
PRESS BRAILLE, ADULT. 1966. biennial. free. U.S. Library of Congress, National Library Service for the Blind and Physically Handicapped, 1291 Taylor St., N.W., Washington, DC 20542. bk. rev. index. (also avail. in talking book; Braille)

027.6 016 362.4   US   ISSN 0484-1506
RECORDING FOR THE BLIND. CATALOG OF RECORDED BOOKS. 1960. biennial. price varies. Recording for the Blind, 215 East 58th St., New York, NY 10028.

026   US   ISSN 0082-1519
TALKING BOOKS, ADULT. 1935. biennial. free. U.S. Library of Congress, National Library Service for the Blind and Physically Handicapped, 1291 Taylor St., N.W., Washington, DC 20542. bk. rev. index. (also avail. in talking book; Braille)

BOATS AND BOATING

see *Sports and Games — Boats and Boating*

BOTANY

see *Biology — Botany*

BUILDING AND CONSTRUCTION

see also *Building and Construction — Carpentry and Woodwork; Building and Construction — Hardware; Architecture; Engineering — Civil Engineering; Heating, Plumbing and Refrigeration; Housing and Urban Planning*

BUILDING AND CONSTRUCTION

690 US ISSN 0065-0021
A B C DIRECTORY. 1949. a. $35. A B C Directory, 4126 College Ave., Des Moines, IA 50311. Ed. Claire E. Scoltock. adv. circ. 4,000.

691.3 US ISSN 0065-7875
A C I MANUAL OF CONCRETE PRACTICE. (In 3 vols.) 1967. a. $88 per set. American Concrete Institute, Box 19150, Redford Station, Detroit, MI 48219.

691.3 US ISSN 0065-7883
A C I MONOGRAPH. 1964. irreg., no. 10, 1977. price varies. (American Concrete Institute) Iowa State University Press, S. State Ave., Ames, IA 50010.

A E M S SEMINAR (PAPERS) (American Engineering Model Society) see ENGINEERING

ACTA POLYTECHNICA SCANDINAVICA. CIVIL ENGINEERING AND BUILDING CONSTRUCTION SERIES. see ENGINEERING — Civil Engineering

690 338 CN ISSN 0381-9663
ALBERTA CONSTRUCTION INDUSTRY DIRECTORY. PURCHASING GUIDE. 1976. a. Sanford Evans Publishing Ltd., Box 6900, Winipeg, Man. R3C 3B1, Canada. adv. illus. circ. 9,859.

691.3 US ISSN 0065-7646
AMERICAN CEMENT DIRECTORY; directory of companies and personnel, North, Central, and South America. 1910. a. $30. Bradley Pulverizer Co., 123 S. Third St., Allentown, PA 18105. Ed. Samuel R. Wolf. adv. index. circ. 2,000.

625.84 691 US ISSN 0517-0745
AMERICAN CONCRETE INSTITUTE. COMPILATION. 1962. irreg. price varies. American Concrete Institute, Box 19150, Redford Sta., Detroit, MI 48219.

691 US ISSN 0097-4145
AMERICAN CONCRETE INSTITUTE. PROCEEDINGS. Published in American Concrete Institute Journal. 1905. a. price varies. American Concrete Institute, Box 19150, Redford Sta., Detroit, MI 48219. (also avail. in microform from UMI)

691 US ISSN 0065-7891
AMERICAN CONCRETE INSTITUTE. SPECIAL PUBLICATION. 1962. irreg, latest 1976. price varies. American Concrete Institute, P. O. Box 19150, Redford Sta., Detroit, MI 48219.

690 US ISSN 0065-9940
AMERICAN RAILWAY BRIDGE AND BUILDING ASSOCIATION. PROCEEDINGS. a. 1969, vol. 74. membership. American Railway Bridge and Building Association, Cary Bldg., 18154 Harwood Ave., Homewood, IL 60430. Ed. Richard B. Cross. adv. circ. 800.

AMERICAN SOCIETY FOR TESTING AND MATERIALS. COMPILATION OF A S T M STANDARDS IN BUILDING CODES. see ENGINEERING — Engineering Mechanics And Materials

ANCIENT MONUMENTS SOCIETY TRANSACTIONS. see HISTORY — History Of Europe

690 624 FR
ANNUAIRE BATIMENT ET TRAVAUX PUBLICS. a. Saint Lambert Editeur, B.P.72, 13673 Aubagne Cedex, France.

ANNUAL BOOK OF A S T M STANDARDS. PART 13. CEMENT; LIME; CEILINGS AND WALLS (INCLUDING MANUAL OF CEMENT TESTING) see ENGINEERING — Engineering Mechanics And Materials

ANNUAL BOOK OF A S T M STANDARDS. PART 14. CONCRETE AND MINERAL AGGREGATES (INCLUDING MANUAL OF CONCRETE TESTING) see ENGINEERING — Engineering Mechanics And Materials

ANNUAL BOOK OF A S T M STANDARDS. PART 16. CHEMICAL-RESISTANT NONMETALLIC MATERIALS. VITRIFIED CLAY AND CONCRETE PIPE AND TILE; MASONRY MORTARS AND UNITS; ASBESTOS-CEMENT PRODUCTS. see ENGINEERING — Engineering Mechanics And Materials

ANNUAL BOOK OF A S T M STANDARDS. PART 18. THERMAL AND CRYOGENIC INSULATING MATERIALS; BUILDING SEALS AND SEALANTS; FIRE TESTS; BUILDING CONSTRUCTIONS; ENVIRONMENTAL ACOUSTICS. see ENGINEERING — Engineering Mechanics And Materials

ANNUAL BOOK OF A S T M STANDARDS. PART 19. NATURAL BUILDING STONES; SOIL AND ROCK; PEATS, MOSSES, AND HUMUS. see ENGINEERING — Engineering Mechanics And Materials

ANNUAL BOOK OF A S T M STANDARDS. PART 34. PLASTIC PIPE. see ENGINEERING — Engineering Mechanics And Materials

692 US ISSN 0066-6157
ARCHITECTS, CONTRACTORS & ENGINEERS GUIDE TO CONSTRUCTION COSTS. 1968. a. $10. A.C. and E. Publishing Co., 4820 Pleasant Ave., Minneapolis, MN 55409. Ed. D. Roth.

666.95 CN ISSN 0478-4049
ASBESTOS PRODUCER/PRODUCTEUR D'AMIANTE. (Text in English and French) 1954. irreg. Quebec Asbestos Mining Association, Box 1643, Sta. B, Montreal, Que. H3B 3L3, Canada. illus.

621.9 US ISSN 0164-0593
ASSOCIATED EQUIPMENT DISTRIBUTORS. RENTAL RATES COMPILATION; nationally averaged rental rates for construction equipment including complete model specifications. 1949? a. $20. Associated Equipment Distributors, 615 W. 22nd St., Oak Brook, IL 60521. Ed. David Loftus. illus. circ. 20,000.
Formerly: Associated Equipment Distributors. Rental Compilation (ISSN 0364-8893)

690 AU
AUSTRIA. BUNDESMINISTERIUM FUER BAUTEN UND TECHNIK. ABTEILUNG BAUKOORDINIERUNG. VORSCHAU. 1969. a. S.350. Bundesministerium fuer Bauten und Technik, Beirat fuer Bauwirtschaft, Stubenring 1, A-1011 Vienna, Austria. Ed. Hermann Lebeda. stat. index. circ. controlled.

690 UK ISSN 0068-3507
B AND C J DIRECTORY. 1963. a. price varies. I P C Building and Contract Journals Ltd., Surrey House, 1 Throwley Way, Sutton, Surrey, England. Ed. I. Biscoe. adv.
Incorporating: B and C J Building Directory & B and C J Public Works Directory.

691 US ISSN 0161-6293
B P C. (Building Products Catalog) 1978. a. $30. Hutton Publishing Co. Inc., 333 Broadway, Jericho, NY 11753. circ. 11,000.

690 JA
B R I RESEARCH PAPERS/KENCHIKU KENKYUSHO CHOSA SHIKEN KENKYU GAIYO HOKOKU. (Text in English) 1960. irreg. exchange basis. Building Research Institute - Kensetsu-sho Kenchiku Kenkyusho, Ministry of Construction, 8-28 3-chome Hyakunin-cho, Shinjuku-ku, Tokyo 160, Japan.

691 GW
BAUEN MIT ALUMINIUM. 1965. a. DM.15. (Aluminium-Zentrale e.V.) Aluminium-Verlag GmbH, Koenigsallee 30, Postfach 1207, 4000 Duesseldorf 1, W. Germany (B.R.D) adv. circ. 22,000.

690 GW ISSN 0522-4950
BAUINGENIEUR-PRAXIS. 1965. irreg. price varies. Wilhelm Ernst und Sohn, Hohenzollerndamm 170, 1000 Berlin 31, W. Germany (B. R. D.) Ed. Robert von Halasz. illus.

690 GW ISSN 0067-4664
BAUWELT KATALOG. 1929. a. DM.29.40 plus postage. Bertelsmann Fachzeitschriften GmbH, Kreuzstr. 14-16, Postfach 200421, 8000 Munich 2, W. Germany (B.R.D) Ed. Katrin Barleben. adv.

332.3 UK
BELLMAN LECTURE. biennial. free. Abbey National Building Society, Abbey House, Baker St., London N.W.1, England.
Continues: Bellman Memorial Lecture (ISSN 0522-8670)

620.135 GW
BETON-KALENDER. 1906. a. DM.82. Wilhelm Ernst und Sohn, Hohenzollerndamm 170, 1000 Berlin 31, W. Germany (B. R. D.) Ed. Gotthard Franz.

691.3 GW ISSN 0409-2740
BETONTECHNISCHE BERICHTE. (Text in German; summaries English and French) 1960. a. DM.39.80. (Verein Deutscher Zementwerke e.V.) Beton-Verlag GmbH, Duesseldorfer Str. 8, Postfach 110134, 4000 Duesseldorf 11, W. Germany (B.R.D). Ed. Kurt Walz. index. cum.index. circ. 1,500. Indexed: Ref.Zh.
Concrete

690 CN ISSN 0067-642X
BETTER BUILDING BULLETIN. 1949. irreg. $0.10. National Research Council of Canada, Ottawa, Ontario K1A 0R6, Canada. Ed. M.A. Gerard.

692.8 US
BIG BOOK; building industry guide. 1974. a. price varies. Slater Publications, Inc., 679 Highland Ave., Needham Heights, MA 02194. Ed. Robert T. Slater. adv. circ. 10,000. (also avail. in magnetic tape; back issues avail.)

690 US ISSN 0195-8461
BLUE BOOK OF MAJOR HOME BUILDERS. 1965. a. $125. C M R Associates, Inc., 11A Village Green, Crofton, MD 21114. Ed. Donald F. Spear. circ. 900.

690 720 UK ISSN 0084-8026
BRITISH BUILDING PRODUCTS CATALOGUE; a catalogue of British building products available to architects overseas. 1950. a. £2.2. Standard Catalogue Information Services Ltd., Medway Wharf Rd., Tonbridge, Kent TN9 1QR, England. Ed. B.D. Dottridge. index.

338.4 SA
BUILDING AND ALLIED INDUSTRIES OFFICIAL HANDBOOK. a. (Building Industries Federation (South Africa)) South African Builder (Pty) Ltd., Federated Insurance House, 1 de Villiers St., Box 11359, Johannesburg 2000, South Africa.
Formerly: Building and Allied Trades Official Handbook (ISSN 0407-7202)

690 UK ISSN 0084-814X
BUILDING AND ENGINEERING REVIEW.* 1965. a. 50p. c/o J. Woods, 10 Kingsberry Park, Rosetta, Belfast BT6 0HT, Northern Ireland.

690.24 SI
BUILDING AND ESTATE MANAGEMENT SOCIETY. PROCEEDINGS OF THE ANNUAL SEMINAR. 1974. a. Building and Estate Management Society, Ladyhill Campus, 3 Ladyhill Rd., Singapore, Singapore.

691 UK ISSN 0068-3523
BUILDING BOARD DIRECTORY. 1959. biennial. £14. Benn Publications Ltd., 25 New Street Square, London EC4A 3JA, England (Orders to: Directories Dept., Sovereign Way, Tonbridge, Kent TN9 1RW, England) Ed. John Topham. adv. circ. 3,000.

692 US ISSN 0068-3531
BUILDING CONSTRUCTION COST DATA. 1942. a. $22.50. Robert S. Means Co., Inc., 100 Construction Plaza, Kingston, MA 02364. Ed. Robert S. Godfrey. index.

692 US ISSN 0091-3499
BUILDING COST FILE. (Avail. in four regional editions: New York, Atlanta, Chicago, Los Angeles) 1972. a. $19.95. Litton Educational Publishing, 680 Kinderkamack Rd., Oradell, NJ 07675.

BUILDING AND CONSTRUCTION

690 II ISSN 0007-3571
BUILDING PRACTICE. 1970. a. Rs.40($5) M. N. Gogate, Ed. & Pub., Tardeo Airconditioned Market, 4th Floor, Bombay 400034, India. adv. bk. rev. abstr. illus. circ. 2,000.

690 DK
BYGGE- OG BOLIGPOLITISKE UDVIKLING. 1971. a. free. Boligministeriet - Ministry of Housing, Slotsholmsgade 12, 1216 Copenhagen K, Denmark. circ. 300.

624 DK ISSN 0106-3715
BYGNINGSSTATISKE MEDDELELSER. (Text in Danish and English) 1929. irreg.(approx. 4/yr.) Kr.120. Dansk Selskab for Bygningsstatik, Bygning 118, Lundtoftevej 100, 2800 Lyngby, Denmark. Ed. L. Pilegaard Hansen. bibl. charts. illus. circ. 950. Indexed: Appl.Mech.Rev.

C A L U S RESEARCH REPORTS. (Centre for Advanced Land Use Studies) see *REAL ESTATE*

691 SW
C B I AARSBERAETTELSE/REPORT OF ACTIVITIES. (Text in Swedish and English) 1972/73. a. free. Cement- och Betonginstitutet - Swedish Cement and Concrete Research Institute, S-100 44 Stockholm, Sweden.
Cement and concrete

691 SW ISSN 0346-6906
C B I FORSKNING/RESEARCH. 1974. irreg. (approx. 8/yr.) Cement- och Betonginstitutet - Swedish Cement and Concrete Research Institute, S-100 44 Stockholm, Sweden.
Cement and concrete

691 SW ISSN 0346-8240
C B I RAPPORTER/REPORTS. (Text in English and Swedish; summaries in English) 1974. irreg. (approx. 6/yr.) Cement och Betonginstitutet - Swedish Cement and Concrete Research Institute, S-100 44 Stockholm, Sweden.
Cement and concrete

691 SW ISSN 0348-2790
C B I REKOMMENDATIONER/ RECOMMENDATIONS. 1974. irreg. (approx. 3/yr.) Cement- och Betonginstitutet - Swedish Cement and Concrete Research Institute, S-100 44 Stockholm, Sweden.
Cement and concrete

690 FR ISSN 0419-2281
C I B DIRECTORY OF BUILDING RESEARCH INFORMATION AND DEVELOPMENT ORGANIZATIONS. 1959. irreg., latest issue 1978. 40 Fr. International Council for Building Research, Studies and Documentation, 4 Av. du Recteur Poincare, 75782 Paris Cedex 16, France.

690 UK ISSN 0305-408X
C I R I A REPORT. 1965. irreg., approx 6/yr. price varies per no. Construction Industry Research and Information Association, 6 Storey's Gate, London SW1P 3AU, England. circ. controlled.

690 CN ISSN 0068-841X
CANADIAN BUILDING SERIES. 1967. irreg., 1970, no. 4. price varies. (National Research Council of Canada, Division of Building Research) University of Toronto Press, Front Campus, Toronto, Ont. M5S 1A6, Canada. Ed. Robert F. Legget. (also avail. in microfiche)

380 690 683.8 CN ISSN 0456-3867
CANADIAN HARDWARE, ELECTRICAL & BUILDING SUPPLY DIRECTORY. 1949. a. Can.$20($30) Lloyd Publications of Canada, Box 262, West Hill, Ont. M1E 4R5, Canada. Ed. J. Lloyd. adv. index. circ. 8,500.

690 CN ISSN 0068-984X
CANADIAN TECHNICAL ASPHALT ASSOCIATION. PROCEEDINGS OF THE ANNUAL CONFERENCE. 1956. a. membership. Canadian Technical Asphalt Association, P.O. Box 1387, Victoria, B.C., Canada. Ed. J. L. M. Scott. circ. 600.

690 AT
CARPENTER AND JOINER. 1960. irreg. (Building Workers' Industrial Union of Australia, Victorian Branch) Industrial Printing and Publicity Co. Ltd., 122 Dover St., Richmond, Vic. 3121, Australia. Ed. A. Zeeno.

CATALOG OF MODEL SERVICES AND SUPPLIES. see *ENGINEERING*

693 JA
CEMENT ASSOCIATION OF JAPAN. REVIEW OF THE GENERAL MEETING. (Text in English) 1947. a. 3,000 Yen. Cement Association of Japan, c/o Hattori Bldg., 1-1 Kyobashi, Chuo-ku, Tokyo 104, Japan. abstr.

620.1 JA
CEMENT ASSOCIATION OF JAPAN. REVIEW OF THE GENERAL MEETING. TECHNICAL SESSION. (Text in English) 1973. a. 3,500 Yen. Cement Association of Japan, c/o Hattori Bldg., 1-1 Kyobashi, Chuo-ku, Tokyo 104, Japan. abstr.

690 US ISSN 0069-1402
CEMENT INDUSTRY TECHNICAL CONFERENCE. RECORD. a. price varies. Institute of Electrical and Electronics Engineers, Inc., Industry Applications Society, 445 Hoes Lane, Piscataway, NJ 08854.

666.8 II
CEMENT RESEARCH INSTITUTE OF INDIA. ANNUAL REPORT. (Text in English) a. Cement Research Institute of India, M-10 South Extension II, Ring Rd., New Delhi 110049, India. illus.

691 AG ISSN 0008-8927
CEMENTO PORTLAND. 1944. a. contr. circ. Instituto del Cemento Portland Argentino, Calle San Martin 1137, Buenos Aires, Argentina. Ed. Carlos E. Duvoy. bk. rev. bibl. charts. illus. circ. 30,000.
Cement and concrete

690 II ISSN 0557-319X
CENTRAL BUILDING RESEARCH INSTITUTE. BUILDING DIGESTS. (Text in English) 1963. irreg. Rs.5 for 5 issues. Central Building Research Institute, Roorkee, Uttar Pradesh, India. cum. index no. 23-55 in no. 57; no. 56-89 in no. 90. (back issues avail)

016 690 II ISSN 0557-322X
CENTRAL BUILDING RESEARCH INSTITUTE. LIST OF PUBLICATIONS. (Text in English) irreg. free. Central Building Research Institute, Roorkee, Uttar Pradesh, India.

690 CN
CENTRAL ONTARIO CONSTRUCTION INDUSTRY DIRECTORY AND PURCHASING GUIDE. 1977. a. Can.$4. Sanford Evans Publishing Co. Ltd., Box 6900, 1077 St. James St., Winnipeg, Man. R3C 3B1, Canada. adv. circ. 4,984.

690 AT ISSN 0311-1903
CHARTERED BUILDER. 1972. irreg. Aus.$1. (Australian Institute of Building) Magazine Art Pty. Ltd., 35 Willis St., Hampton, Vic. 3188, Australia. Ed. Peter Williams.

690 NE
COBOUW MAGAZINE. 1973. fortn. fl.230. Ten Hagen B.V., Box 34, 2501 AG the Hague, Netherlands. Ed. J. Raven. adv. bk. rev. illus. circ. 7,000.
Formerly: C M.

691 FR
COMITE EURO-INTERNATIONAL DU BETON. BULLETIN D'INFORMATION. 1957. irreg. membership. ‡ Euro-International Committee for Concrete - Comite Euro-International du Beton, Secretariat Permanent, 6 rue Lauriston, 75116 Paris, France. circ. controlled.
Formerly: Comite Europeen du Beton. Bulletin d'Information (ISSN 0071-2574)
Cement and concrete

690 AT
COMMONWEALTH SCIENTIFIC AND INDUSTRIAL RESEARCH ORGANIZATION. DIVISION OF BUILDING RESEARCH. TECHNICAL PAPER. 1954. irreg. price varies. C. S. I. R. O., Division of Building Research, Graham Rd., Highett, Vic. 3190, Australia.

691.3 US ISSN 0069-827X
CONCRETE INDUSTRIES YEARBOOK. 1938. a. $40. Pit and Quarry Publications, Inc., 105 West Adams St., Chicago, IL 60603. Ed. Buron C. Herod. adv. circ. 8,500.

693 AT ISSN 0311-1180
CONCRETE MASONRY ASSOCIATION OF AUSTRALIA. PROJECT REVIEW. 1971. irreg. price varies. Concrete Masonry Association of Australia, 147 Walker St., North Sydney, N.S.W. 2060, Australia. Eds. C. F. Morrish and N. J. R. Christie.

691.3 UK
CONCRETE SOCIETY. TECHNICAL REPORT. no. 13, 1977. irreg. Concrete Society, Terminal House, Grosvenor Gardens, London SW1W OAJ, England (Dist. in U.S. by: Scholium International, Inc., 130-30 31st Ave., Flushing, NY 11354)
Concrete

691.3 UK ISSN 0069-8288
CONCRETE YEAR BOOK. 1924. a. £10($25) Cement and Concrete Association, Wexham Springs, Slough, Bucks. SL3 6PL, England. Ed. Paul Maxwell-Cook. adv. circ. 5,000. (reprint service avail. from UMI)

690 BE ISSN 0045-8023
CONFEDERATION NATIONALE DE LA CONSTRUCTION. ANNUAIRE. (Text in Dutch and French) 1948. a. 1300 Fr. Confederation Nationale de la Construction, Lombardstraat 34-42, 1000 Brussels, Belgium.

338.4 US ISSN 0069-9187
CONSTRUCTION IN HAWAII. 1967. a. free. Bank of Hawaii, Economics Division, Box 2900, Honolulu, HI 96846. Ed. Wesley H. Hillendahl. (back issues avail.)
Formerly: Housing Activity in Hawaii.

690 II
CONSTRUCTION INDUSTRIES AND TRADE ANNUAL. a. Praveen Corp., Sayajiganj, Baroda 390005, India. Ed. C. M. Pandit.
Formerly: Construction Industries and Trade Journal (ISSN 0010-6828)

690 UK
CONSTRUCTION INDUSTRY EUROPE. 1974. biennial. £18. House Information Services Ltd., 1 Cresswell Park, London SE3 9RG, England.

690 US ISSN 0069-9217
CONSTRUCTION WRITERS ASSOCIATION. NEWSLETTER. 1953. irreg., 1975. Construction Writers Association, 601 13 St. N.W., Rm. 202, Washington, DC 20005. Ed. E. E. Halmos, Jr. circ. 100.

690 US
CONSTRUCTIONEER DIRECTORY. a. $10. Reports Corp., 323 Main St., Chatham, NJ 07928. Ed. Kenneth A. Hanan. adv. illus.

690 AT
CORDELL'S WHO'S WHO IN BUILDING: HOUSING. a. (plus quarterly updates) Aus.$195. Cordell Building Publications, 160 Sailors Bay Rd., Northbridge, N.S.W. 2063, Australia.

690 AT
CORDELL'S WHO'S WHO IN BUILDING: NON-HOUSING. a. (plus quarterly updates) Aus.$195. Cordell Building Publications, 160 Sailors Bay Rd, Northbridge, N.S.W. 2063, Australia.

690 721 AT
CORDELL'S WHO'S WHO IN DESIGN SPECIFYING. a. Aus.$195. Cordell Building Publications, 160 Sailors Bay Rd., Northbridge, N.S.W. 2063, Australia.

CORPORATE BUYERS OF DESIGN SERVICES/U S A. see *ARCHITECTURE*

692.8 US ISSN 0161-7257
CURRENT CONSTRUCTION COSTS. a. $18.95. Lee Saylor, Inc., 1855 Olympic Blvd., Walnut Creek, CA 94596.

CURRENT CONSTRUCTION REPORTS: HOUSING UNITS AUTHORIZED FOR DEMOLITION IN PERMIT-ISSUING PLACES. see *HOUSING AND URBAN PLANNING*

690 CY
CYPRUS. DEPARTMENT OF STATISTICS AND RESEARCH. CONSTRUCTION AND HOUSING REPORT. a. Mils.400. Department of Statistics and Research, Ministry of Finance, Nicosia, Cyprus.

BUILDING AND CONSTRUCTION

690   SZ   ISSN 0070-6868
DOCUMENTATION DU BATIMENT. (Published in Bulletin Technique de la Suisse Romande) 1952. a. membership. (Societe Suisse des Ingenieurs et des Architectes) Imprimerie la Concorde, Case Postale 330, CH-1010 Lausanne, Switzerland.

690   747   UK
DOORS & WINDOWS. (Architects & Specifiers Guide Series) a. £3.50. Builder Group, 3 Pemberton Row, London W.C.3, England.

692.8   US   ISSN 0098-6453
E N R DIRECTORY OF CONTRACTORS. (Engineering News-Record) Cover title: Contractors. 1974. a. McGraw-Hill Publications Co., 1221 Ave. of the Americas, New York. Ed. Jim Webber. illus. circ. 11,000.

690   330   FR
ECONOMIE FRANCAISE EN PERSPECTIVES SECTORIELLES: FILIERE BATIMENT, GENIE CIVIL, MATERIAUX DE CONSTRUCTION. (Vol. 5 of 5) a. 3500 F. (for all 5 vols.) Bureau d'Informations et de Previsions Economiques, 122 Av Charles de Gaulle, 92522 Neuilly sur Seine, France.
    Formerly: Prevision a Un An de la Filiere Construction; Supersedes in part: Prevision a Un An de l'Economie Francaise.

692   US
ENGELSMAN'S GENERAL CONSTRUCTION COST GUIDE. 1966. a. with s-a. supplements. $15. Van Nostrand Reinhold Co., 135 W. 50th St., New York, NY 10020 (Orders to 7625 Empire Dr., Florence, KY 41042) Ed. Coert Engelsman.
    Formerly: C E Cost Guide (ISSN 0068-4716)

624   621.9   AU   ISSN 0013-998X
ERDBAU. 1964. m. free. Eisner Baumaschinen Ges. m.b.H., Industriezentrum N-S, Str. Nr. 1, Object 27, A-2351 Wiener Neudorf, Austria. Ed. Hermann Gruss. charts. illus.
    Construction equipment

690   FR
EUROPEAN CEMENT ASSOCIATION. ANNUAL EUROPEAN REVIEW. no. 2, 1980. a. 100 F. (European Cement Association) Cembureau, 2, rue St. Charles, 75740 Paris, France. stat.
    Formerly: Cement Market and Outlook.

690   UK   ISSN 0307-0107
EXTERNAL WALLS. (Architects & Specifiers Guide Series) a. £3.50. Builder Group, 23 Pemberton Row, London W.C.3, England. Ed. Christopher Sykes.

690   UK
FACULTY OF BUILDING. REGISTER OF MEMBERS. 1972. irreg. £5 per no. (Faculty of Building) Millbank Publications Ltd., 48 Crawford St., London W1H 1HA, England. adv. circ. 5,500.

690   GW   ISSN 0071-4585
DER FERTIGHAUS-KATALOG. 1965. a. DM.19.80. Fachschriften-Verlag GmbH, Hoehenstr. 17, Postfach 1329, 7012 Fellbach, W. Germany (B.R.D.)

690   FI   ISSN 0071-531X
FINLAND. RAKENNUSHALLITUS. TUTKIMUS-JA KEHITYSTOIMINNAN. TIEDOTE. 1966. irreg. free. ‡ Rakennushallitus, Tutkimus-ja Kehitystoiminnan - National Board of Building, Siltasaarenkatu 18A, Helsinki 53, Finland. Ed. P. Routio.
    Formerly: Finland. Rakennushallitus. Tiedotuksia.

690   UK
FLOORING. (Architects & Specifiers Guide Series) a. £3.50. Builder Group, 23 Pemberton Row, London W.C.3, England.

622.3   US   ISSN 0533-005X
FOUNDRY CATALOG FILE. 1970/71. biennial. $20. Penton-IPC, 614 Superior Ave., W., Cleveland, OH 44113. adv. circ. 7,420. (reprint service avail. from UMI)

690   CN   ISSN 0318-0344
FRASER'S CONSTRUCTION & BUILDING DIRECTORY. a. Can.$35. Maclean-Hunter Ltd., 481 University Ave., Toronto, Ont. M5W 1A7, Canada.

690   US   ISSN 0195-847X
GOLD BOOK OF MULTI HOUSING. 1979. a. $115. C M R Associates, Inc., 11A Village Green, Crofton, MD 21114. Ed. Donald F. Spear. circ. 450.

691   YU   ISSN 0350-1701
GRADJEVINSKI FAKULTET. INSTITUT ZA MATERIJALE I KONSTRUKCIJE. ZBORNIK ISTRAZIVACKIH RADOVA. 1972. a. 400 din. Univerzitet u Sarajevu, Gradjevinski Fakultet, Institut za Materijale i Konstrukcije, Stjepana Tomica 5, Sarajevo, Yugoslavia. Ed. Nadezda Knezevic Vuksanovic. circ. 500-1,000.

GREAT BRITAIN. BUILDING RESEARCH ESTABLISHMENT. REPORTS. see *FIRE PREVENTION*

690   UK   ISSN 0068-354X
GREAT BRITAIN. BUILDING RESEARCH ESTABLISHMENT. ANNUAL REPORT. Variant title: Building Research Establishment. Annual Report. a. price varies. Building Research Establishment, Garston, Watford WD2 7JR, England.
    Former titles: Forest Products Research; Fire Research Annual Reports (ISSN 0071-5433)

GREAT BRITAIN. DEPARTMENT OF THE ENVIRONMENT. METRICATION IN THE CONSTRUCTION INDUSTRY. see *METROLOGY AND STANDARDIZATION*

690   UK
GREAT BRITAIN. H.M.S.O. GOVERNMENT PUBLICATIONS SECTIONAL LISTS. irreg. free. H.M.S.O., P.O. Box 569, London SE1 9NH, England.

690   US   ISSN 0194-083X
GREEN BOOK OF HOME IMPROVEMENT CONTRACTORS. 1978. a. $125. C M R Associates, Inc., 11A Village Green, Crofton, MD 21114. Ed. Donald F. Spear. circ. 300.

690   US   ISSN 0160-7340
GUIDE TO MANUFACTURED HOMES. 1978. irreg. $4. National Association of Home Manufacturers, 6521 Arlington Blvd., Falls Church, VA 22042. adv. circ. 10,000.

690   US
GUIDE TO QUALITY CONSTRUCTION PRODUCTS. 1973. a. free. Producers' Council, Inc., 1717 Massachusetts Ave. N.W., Washington, DC 20036. Ed. D. Lynn Forlidas. circ. 35,000.

683   CN
HARDWARE MERCHANDISING'S CANADIAN HARDWARE HANDBOOK. 1957. a. Can.$15. Maclean-Hunter Ltd., 481 University Ave., Toronto, Ont. M5W 1A7, Canada. Ed. Norm Rosen.
    Formerly: Hardware Merchandising's Hardware Handbook (ISSN 0073-036X)

690   US
HEAVY CONSTRUCTION COST FILE. a. $22.50. Van Nostrand Reinhold Co., 135 W. 50th St., New York, NY 10020 (Orders to 7625 Empire Dr., Florence, KY 41042)

338.4   HK
HONG KONG BUILDER DIRECTORY. (Text in English) a. HK.$85. Far East Trade Press Ltd., Room 1913, Hanglung Centre, 2-20 Patterson St., Causeway Bay, Hong Kong, Hong Kong. illus.

690   UK
HOUSE'S GUIDE TO THE CONSTRUCTION INDUSTRY (1979) 1968. a. £14. House Information Services Ltd., 1 Cresswell Park, London SE3 9RG, England. Ed. D. S. Parlett.
    Former titles: Construction Industry U.K; House's Guide to the Construction Industry; House's Guide to the Building Industry (ISSN 0073-361X)

331.83   690   US
HOUSING UNITS IN CONNECTICUT. ANNUAL SUMMARY. a. Department of Community Affairs, Box 786, 1179 Main St., Hartford, CT 06103.
    Formerly: Connecticut. Department of Community Affairs. Division of Research and Program Evaluation. Construction Activity Authorized by Building Permits. Summary (ISSN 0069-9020)

691   US
ILLINOIS DEALER DIRECTORY AND BUYER'S GUIDE. 1932. a. $17.50. Illinois Lumber and Material Dealers Association, 400 Leland Building, Springfield, IL 62701. adv. circ. 750.
    Formerly: Illinois Directory and Suppliers Listing (ISSN 0073-4799)

INCOME-EXPENSE ANALYSIS: APARTMENTS. see *REAL ESTATE*

691   BE
INDUSTRIE CIMENTIERE BELGE/BELGISCHE CEMENTNIJVERHEID. (Text and summaries in Dutch and French) 1977. a. Federation de l'Industrie Cimentiere - Verbond der Cementrijverheid, 46 rue Cesar Franck, 1050 Brussels, Belgium. stat. circ. 400-550.

690   MX
INFORMACIONES TECNICAS PARA LA CONSTRUCCION. 1971. a. Informaciones Tecnicas, S.A., Av. Insurgentes Sur 730, Mexico 12, D.F., Mexico. adv. circ. 6,000.

690   UK   ISSN 0073-9014
INSTITUTE OF BUILDING. YEAR BOOK AND DIRECTORY OF MEMBERS. 1967/68. a. $30. Chartered Institute of Building, Englemere, Kings Ride, Ascot, Berks, SL5 8BJ, England. adv. circ. 3,000. (reprint service avail. from UMI)

690   UK   ISSN 0073-9073
INSTITUTE OF CLERK OF WORKS' OF GREAT BRITAIN INCORPORATED. YEAR BOOK.* 1930. a. 52.5p. G. W. Harris, 43 Leopold Road, Willesden, London, NW10, England.

692   UK   ISSN 0073-9669
INSTITUTE OF QUANTITY SURVEYORS. YEAR BOOK. 1941. biennial. £10. Institute of Quantity Surveyors, 98 Gloucester Place, London W1H 4AT, England. Ed. B. R. Peck. adv. index. circ. 8,500.

690   UK
INSULATION HANDBOOK. a. £8. Comprint Ltd., 177 Hagden Lane, Watford, Herts WD1 8LW, England.

690   US
INTERNATIONAL CONFERENCE OF BUILDING OFFICIALS. ACCUMULATIVE SUPPLEMENTS TO THE CODES. a. price varies. International Conference of Building Officials, 5360 South Workman Mill Rd., Whittier, CA 90601.

690   US
INTERNATIONAL CONFERENCE OF BUILDING OFFICIALS. ANALYSIS OF REVISIONS TO THE UNIFORM BUILDING CODE. triennial. $4.50 to non-members; members $3.70. International Conference of Building Officials, 5360 South Workman Mill Rd., Whittier, CA 90601.

690   US
INTERNATIONAL CONFERENCE OF BUILDING OFFICIALS. BUILDING DEPARTMENT ADMINISTRATION. 1973. irreg. $28 to non-members; members $25. International Conference of Building Officials, 5360 South Workman Mill Rd., Whittier, CA 90601.

690   US
INTERNATIONAL CONFERENCE OF BUILDING OFFICIALS. DWELLING CONSTRUCTION UNDER THE UNIFORM BUILDING CODE. triennial. to non-members; members $4.50. International Conference of Building Officials, 5360 South Workman Mill Rd., Whittier, CA 90601.

690   US
INTERNATIONAL CONFERENCE OF BUILDING OFFICIALS. ONE AND TWO FAMILY DWELLING CODE. (Includes supplements) irreg. price varies. International Conference of Building Officials, 5360 South Workman Mill Rd., Whittier, CA 90601.

690   US
INTERNATIONAL CONFERENCE OF BUILDING OFFICIALS. PLAN REVIEW MANUAL. irreg. $15.90 to non-members; members $14.60. International Conference of Building Officials, 5360 South Workman Mill Rd., Whittier, CA 90601.

690 US
INTERNATIONAL CONFERENCE OF BUILDING OFFICIALS. UNIFORM CODE FOR THE ABATEMENT OF DANGEROUS BUILDINGS. triennial. $4.50 to non-members; members $3.70. International Conference of Building Officials, 5360 South Workman Mill Rd., Whittier, CA 90601.

690 US
INTERNATIONAL CONFERENCE OF BUILDING OFFICIALS. UNIFORM FIRE CODE. triennial. price varies. International Conference of Building Officials, 5360 South Workman Mill Rd., Whittier, CA 90601.

690 692 US ISSN 0501-1213
INTERNATIONAL CONFERENCE OF BUILDING OFFICIALS. UNIFORM HOUSING CODE. 1955. triennial. $4.50 to non-members; members $3.70. International Conference of Building Officials, 5360 South Workman Mill Rd., Whittier, CA 90601.

690 US
INTERNATIONAL CONFERENCE OF BUILDING OFFICIALS. UNIFORM MECHANICAL CODE. triennial. price varies. International Conference of Building Officials, 5360 South Workman Mill Rd., Whittier, CA 90601.

690 FR ISSN 0074-428X
INTERNATIONAL COUNCIL FOR BUILDING RESEARCH, STUDIES AND DOCUMENTATION. CONGRESS REPORTS. 1959. triennial. latest issue 1977. price varies. International Council for Building Research, Studies and Documentation, 4 Av. du Recteur Poincare, 75782 Paris Cedex 16, France.

690 PH ISSN 0074-588X
INTERNATIONAL FEDERATION OF ASIAN AND WESTERN PACIFIC CONTRACTORS' ASSOCIATIONS. PROCEEDINGS OF THE ANNUAL CONVENTION. (Proceedings published by organizing committee) biennial, 16th, 1978, Jakarta. International Federation of Asian and Western Pacific Contractors Associations, Padilla Building, 3rd Fl., Ortigas Commercial Center, Emerald Ave., Pasig, Metro Manila, Philippines.

691 FI
INTERNATIONAL TRADE CONFERENCE OF WORKERS OF THE BUILDING, WOOD AND BUILDING MATERIALS INDUSTRIES. (BROCHURE) irreg, 7th, 1975. Trade Unions International of Workers of the Building, Wood and Building Materials Industries, Box 281, 00101 Helsinki 10, Finland.

690 IE
IRISH CONSTRUCTION MATERIALS REVIEW SERIES. Each issue titled separately: Irish Timber Review. Irish Roofing and Cladding Review. Irish Concrete Review. Irish Construction Metals Review. 1973. irreg. £1.50($6) Regional & Technical Publications, 36 Morehampton Rd., Dublin 4, Ireland. Ed. Denis Bergin. adv. bk. rev. circ. 3,000.

690 IS ISSN 0069-9195
ISRAEL. CENTRAL BUREAU OF STATISTICS. CONSTRUCTION IN ISRAEL/HA-BINUI BE-YISRAEL. (Subseries of the Bureau's Special Series) (Text in Hebrew and English) 1960-63. a. I£90. Central Bureau of Statistics, Box 13015, Jerusalem, Israel.

690 314 JM
JAMAICA. DEPARTMENT OF STATISTICS. ABSTRACT OF BUILDING AND CONSTRUCTION STATISTICS. 1977. irreg. Department of Statistics, 9 Swallowfield Rd., Kingston 5, Jamaica. Dir.Mrs. C.P. McFarlane.

K B S-RAPPORTER. see *HOUSING AND URBAN PLANNING*

690 US ISSN 0075-6768
KONSTRUKTIONSBUECHER. 1955. irreg., vol. 31, 1978. price varies. Springer-Verlag, 175 Fifth Ave., New York, NY 10010 (also Berlin, Heidelberg, Vienna) (reprint service avail. from ISI)

690 SW ISSN 0075-6776
KONTROLLRAADET FOER BETONGVAROR. MEDDELANDE. 1950. a. free. Kontrollraadet foer Betongvaror - Swedish Council for Precast Concrete Control, S: T Eriksgatan 58, 112 34 Stockholm, Sweden. circ. 9,500.

692 331 US ISSN 0098-3608
LABOR RATES FOR THE CONSTRUCTION INDUSTRY. 1974. a. $24.75. Robert S. Means Co., Inc., 100 Construction Plaza, Kingston, MA 02364. Ed. Robert S. Godfrey.

691 IT
LATOMISTICA. (Text in English and Italian) irreg. Angelo Longo Editore, Via Rocca Ai Fossi 6, Casella Postale 431, 48100 Ravenna, Italy. Ed. Giordano Gamberini.
History

691 UK ISSN 0305-6589
LAXTON'S BUILDING PRICE BOOK. a. £15. Kelly's Directories, Ltd., Windsor Court, East Grinstead, West Sussex RH19 1XB, England. Ed. N.R. Wheatley. adv. stat. circ. 15,000.

338.7 691 CN ISSN 0318-1340
LIAISON. 1971. irreg. free contr. circ. Ciments Canada Lafarge Ltd., Sales Promotion and Advertising Dept., 606 rue Cathcart, Montreal, Que. H3B 7K9, Canada. illus.
Cement and concrete

LOG HOUSE. see *ARCHITECTURE*

690 NE
MACHINEPARK. 1966. m. fl.195. Ten Hagen B.V., Box 34, 2501 AG the Hague, Netherlands. Ed. F. Oremus. adv. bk. rev. illus. circ. 3,750.

647.9 UK
MAINTENANCE BUYERS GUIDE. 1953. a. £9. Turret Press Ltd., 4 Local Board Rd., Watford, Herts WD1 2JS, England. adv. charts. illus. stat. index.
Former titles: Manual of Building Maintenance; Manual of Maintenance (ISSN 0009-8639)
Maintenance

690 620 CN
MANITOBA CONSTRUCTION INDUSTRY DIRECTORY. PURCHASING GUIDE. 1966. a. Sanford Evans Publishing Ltd., 1077 St. James St., Box 6900, Winnipeg, Man. R3C 3B1, Canada. adv. circ. 5,285.

690 US
MECHANICAL & ELECTRICAL COST DATA. 1978. a. $27.50. Robert S. Means Co., Inc., 100 Construction Plaza, Duxbury, MA 02332. Ed. Melville J. Mossman.

MECHANIKA I BUDOWNICTWO LADOWE/ MECHANICS AND BUILDING ENGINEERING. see *ENGINEERING — Mechanical Engineering*

690 658 SA
MERKELS' BUILDERS' PRICING AND MANAGEMENT MANUAL. 1948. a. R.25. Thomson Publications S. A. (Pty) Ltd., Box 8308, Johannesburg 2000, South Africa. Ed. H. Merkel. adv.

MERKEL'S ELECTRICIAN'S MANUAL. see *ELECTRICITY AND ELECTRICAL ENGINEERING*

692 US ISSN 0076-700X
METRO BUILDING INDUSTRY DIRECTORY. 1968. a. $10. A.C. and E. Publishing Co., 4820 Pleasant Ave., Minneapolis, MN 55409.

690 CN ISSN 0380-8599
N B C /N F C NEWS. (National Building Code / National Fire Code) (Text in English and French) 1976. irreg. free. (Associate Committee on the National Building Code) National Research Council of Canada, Ottawa, Ont. K1A 0R6, Canada. (Co-sponsor: Associate Committee on the National Fire Code) Ed. M. A. Burton. circ. 22,000.
Formerly: N B C News (ISSN 0027-612X)

695 UK
N F R C YEARBOOK. a. £8. National Federation of Roofing Contractors, 15 Soho Square, London W1V 5FB, England.
Roofing

690 FI ISSN 0078-1126
N K B SKRIFTSERIE/N K B PUBLICATION SERIES. (Text in Danish, English, Norwegian, and Swedish) 1964. irreg., no. 36, 1978. free. Nordiske Komite for Bygningsbestemmelsei, Sodra Esplanaden 10, Helsinki 13, Finland. (Co-sponsor: Finish Ministeriet for Inrikesarendena)

691.3 US ISSN 0077-5355
N R M C A PUBLICATION. 1931. irreg., 1973, no. 144. price varies. National Ready Mixed Concrete Association, 900 Spring St., Silver Spring, MD 20910. Ed. R.D. Gaynor. circ. 2,000. Indexed: Concr.Abstr.

691 UK ISSN 0077-4480
NATIONAL FEDERATION OF PLASTERING CONTRACTORS. YEAR BOOK. 1958. a. free. Comprint Ltd., 177 Hagden Lane, Watford, Herts WD1 8LW, England. Ed. K. Williams. adv. circ. 2,500.

690 CN ISSN 0701-5216
NATIONAL RESEARCH COUNCIL, CANADA. DIVISION OF BUILDING RESEARCH. BUILDING PRACTICE NOTE. 1976. irreg. free. National Research Council of Canada, Division of Building Research, Ottawa, Ont., K1A 0R6, Canada. Ed. J. C. Nurski.

690 CN ISSN 0077-5460
NATIONAL RESEARCH COUNCIL, CANADA. DIVISION OF BUILDING RESEARCH. BUILDING RESEARCH NOTE. 1950. irreg. free. National Research Council of Canada, Division of Building Research, Ottawa K1A 0R6, Canada. Ed. J. C. Nurski.

690 CN ISSN 0077-5479
NATIONAL RESEARCH COUNCIL, CANADA. DIVISION OF BUILDING RESEARCH. COMPUTER PROGRAM. 1960. irreg. free. National Research Council of Canada, Division of Building Research, Ottawa K1A 0R6, Ont., Canada. Ed. M. E. Wimberley.

690 CN ISSN 0381-4319
NATIONAL RESEARCH COUNCIL, CANADA. DIVISION OF BUILDING RESEARCH. D B R PAPER. 1975. irreg. price varies. National Research Council of Canada, Division of Building Research, Ottawa, Ont. K1A 0R6, Canada. Ed. M. E. Wimberley.

690 CN
NATIONAL RESEARCH COUNCIL, CANADA. DIVISION OF BUILDING RESEARCH. PROCEEDINGS. 1976. irreg. price varies. National Research Council of Canada, Division of Building Research, Ottawa, Ont. K1A 0R6, Canada. Ed. M. A. Gerard.

690 CN ISSN 0077-5517
NATIONAL RESEARCH COUNCIL, CANADA. DIVISION OF BUILDING RESEARCH. RESEARCH PROGRAM. a. National Research Council of Canada, Division of Building Research, Montreal Rd., Ottawa, Ont. K1A 0R6, Canada. Ed. M.A. Gerard.

690 CN ISSN 0701-5208
NATIONAL RESEARCH COUNCIL, CANADA. DIVISION OF BUILDING RESEARCH. SPECIAL TECHNICAL PUBLICATION. 1973. irreg. price varies. National Research Council of Canada, Division of Building Research, Ottawa, Ont. K1A 0R6, Canada. Ed. M. A. Gerard.

690 CN ISSN 0708-1375
NEW BRUNSWICK CONSTRUCTION PRODUCTS DIRECTORY. 1976. biennial. Department of Commerce and Development, Fredericton, N.B., Canada.

NEW ZEALAND. DEPARTMENT OF STATISTICS. POPULATION AND MIGRATION PART A: POPULATION. see *POPULATION STUDIES*

NEW ZEALAND. DEPARTMENT OF STATISTICS. POPULATION AND MIGRATION. PART B: EXTERNAL MIGRATION. see *POPULATION STUDIES*

BUILDING AND CONSTRUCTION

690 NO ISSN 0065-0226
NORGES LANDBRUKSHOEGSKOLE. INSTITUTT FOR BYGNINGSTEKNIKK. AARSMELDING/ ANNUAL REPORT. (Text in Norwegian; summaries in English) 1964. a. free. Norges Landbrukshoegskole, Institutt for Bygningsteknikk, Box 15, N-1432 Aas-NLH, Norway.

NORGES LANDBRUKSHOEGSKOLE. INSTITUTT FOR BYGNINGSTEKNIKK. BYGGEKOSTNADSINDEKS FOR DRIFTSBYGNINGER I JORDBRUKET. PRISUTVIKLINGEN. see *AGRICULTURE*

690 NO ISSN 0065-0234
NORGES LANDBRUKSHOEGSKOLE. INSTITUTT FOR BYGNINGSTEKNIKK. MELDING. (Text in Norwegian; summaries in English) 1951. irreg., no. 104, 1981. free. Norges Landbrukshoegskole, Institutt for Bygningsteknikk, Box 15, N-1432 Aas-NLH, Norway.

691 674 US ISSN 0078-1800
NORTHWESTERN-IOWA DEALER REFERENCE MANUAL; retail lumber and building material dealer directory and buyers' guide. a. $35. ‡ Northwestern Lumbermen, Inc., 1111 Douglas Dr., No., Minneapolis, MN 55422. (Co-sponsor: Iowa Lumbermens Association) Ed. Beth J. Bairnson. index.

690 620 CN
NORTHWESTERN ONTARIO CONSTRUCTION INDUSTRY DIRECTORY. PURCHASING GUIDE. 1976. a. Sanford Evans Publishing Ltd., 1077 St. James St., Box 6900, Winnipeg, Man. R3C 3B1, Canada. circ. 2,438.

OEFFENTLICHE BAUMAPPE DER OSTSCHWEIZ. see *ARCHITECTURE*

729 691 US
OLD-HOUSE JOURNAL CATALOG. 1976. a. $10.95. Old-House Journal Corporation, 69A Seventh Ave., Brooklyn, NY 11217. Ed. Clem Labine. adv. illus. circ. 25,000.
Formerly: Old-House Journal Buyers' Guide.

690 620 CN
ONTARIO GOLDEN HORSESHOE CONSTRUCTION INDUSTRY DIRECTORY. PURCHASING GUIDE. 1976. a. Sanford Evans Publishing Ltd., 1077 St. James St., Box 6900, Winnipeg, Man. R3C 3B1, Canada. adv. circ. 6,651.

338.47 666 FR ISSN 0474-5493
ORGANIZATION FOR ECONOMIC COOPERATION AND DEVELOPMENT. CEMENT INDUSTRY. INDUSTRIE DU CIMENT. (Text in English and French) 1954. irreg. $3. Organization for Economic Cooperation and Development, 2 rue Andre Pascal, 75775 Paris 16, France (U.S. orders to: O.E.C.D. Publications and Information Center, 1750 Pennsylvania Ave., N. W., Washington, D. C. 20006) (also avail. in microfiche)

POLITECHNIKA GDANSKA. ZESZYTY NAUKOWE. BUDOWNICTWO LADOWE. see *ENGINEERING — Civil Engineering*

POLITECHNIKA LODZKA. ZESZYTY NAUKOWE. BUDOWNICTWO. see *ENGINEERING — Civil Engineering*

691 PL
POLITECHNIKA WARSZAWSKA. INSTYTUT TECHNOLOGII I ORGANIZACJI PRODUKCJI BUDOWLANEJ. PRACE. (Text in Polish; summaries in English and Russian) 1971. irreg. price varies. Politechnika Warszawska, Plac Jednosci Robotniczej 1, 00-661 Warsaw, Poland. illus. circ. 360-560.

690 PL ISSN 0324-9883
POLITECHNIKA WROCLAWSKA. INSTYTUT BUDOWNICTWA. PRACE NAUKOWE. KONFERENCJE. (Text in Polish and English; summaries in Russian) 1974. irreg., no. 5, 1978. price varies. Politechnika Wroclawska, Wybrzeze Wyspianskiego 27, 50-370 Wroclaw, Poland (Dist. by: Ars Polona-Ruch, Krakowskie Przedmiescie 7, Warsaw, Poland) Ed. Marian Kloza. circ. 475.

690 PL ISSN 0324-9875
POLITECHNIKA WROCLAWSKA. INSTYTUT BUDOWNICTWA. PRACE NAUKOWE. MONOGRAFIE. (Text in Polish; summaries in English and Russian) 1969. irreg., 1978, no. 10. price varies. Politechnika Wroclawska, Wybrzeze Wyspianskiego 27, 50-370 Wroclaw, Poland (Dist. by: Ars Polona-Ruch, Krakowskie Przedmiescie 7, Warsaw, Poland) Ed. Marian Kloza.

690 PL ISSN 0137-6241
POLITECHNIKA WROCLAWSKA. INSTYTUT BUDOWNICTWA. PRACE NAUKOWE. STUDIA I MATERIALY. (Text in Polish; summaries in English and Russian) 1971. irreg., no. 13, 1979. price varies. Politechnika Wroclawska, Wybrzeze Wyspianskiego 27, 50-370 Wroclaw, Poland (Dist. by: Ars Polona-Ruch, Krakowskie Przedmiescie 7, Warsaw, Poland) Ed. Marian Kloza.

POLITECHNIKA WROCLAWSKA. INSTYTUT INZYNIERII CHEMICZNEJ I URZADZEN CIEPLNYCH. PRACE NAUKOWE. STUDIA I MATERIALY. see *ENGINEERING — Chemical Engineering*

POZNANSKIE TOWARZYSTWO PRZYJACIOL NAUK. KOMISJA BUDOWNICTWA I ARCHITEKTURY. PRACE. see *ARCHITECTURE*

690 GW ISSN 0085-5154
PRIVATES BAUSPARWESEN. 1950. a. DM.17.60. Domus-Verlag GmbH, Dottendorfer Str. 82, Postfach 150137, 5300 Bonn 5, W. Germany (B.R.D.)

338.2 UK
PRODUCTION OF AGGREGATES IN GREAT BRITAIN. 1958. a. price varies. Department of the Environment, 2 Marsham St., London SW1P 3EB, England (Avail. from H.M.S.O., c/o Liaison Officer, Atlantic House, Holborn Viaduct, London EC1P 1BN, England) circ. 1,000.
Formerly: Great Britain. Department of the Environment. Sand and Gravel Production.

690 SI
QUANTIBUILD. (Text in English) 1968. a. Singapore Polytechnic Building Society, Prince Edward Rd., Singapore 2, Singapore. Ed. Bd. adv. bibl. charts. illus. circ. 3,000-3,500.

690 FI ISSN 0355-550X
RAKENTAJAIN KALENTERI. 1917. a. Fmk.105. Rakennusmestarien Keskusliitto - Central Association of Construction Engineers, Lapinlahdenkatu 14, 00180 Helsinki 18, Finland. Ed. Lauri Seppanen. adv. circ. 14,000.

692.5 US ISSN 0098-9568
REAL ESTATE VALUATION COST FILE. 1975. a. Construction Publishing Co., Inc. (Subsidiary of: Van Nostrand Reinhold) 450 W. 33rd St., New York, NY 10001.

691 US ISSN 0149-7642
RED BOOK OF HOUSING MANUFACTURERS. 1974. a. $125. C M R Associates, Inc., 11A Village Green, Crofton, MD 21114. Ed. Donald F. Spear. circ. 400.

691 US ISSN 0569-8057
REINFORCED CONCRETE RESEARCH COUNCIL. BULLETINS. 1950. irreg., no. 20, 1979. price varies; some free. ‡ American Society of Civil Engineers, Portland Cement Association, Reinforced Concrete Research Council, c/o Dr. A. E. Fiorata, 5420 Old Orchard Road, Skokie, IL 60077. circ. 500. (back issues avail.)
Cement and concrete

690 NE
RENOVATIE EN ONDERHOUD; maandblad voor stadsvernieuwing, vernieuwbouw, bedrijfsrenovatie, onderhoud en beheer. 1976. m. fl.185. Ten Hagen B.V., Box 34, 2501 AG the Hague, Netherlands. Ed. F. Oremus. adv. illus. circ. 4,800.

REPERTOIRE DE MATERIAUX ET ELEMENTS CONTROLES DU BATIMENT. see *METROLOGY AND STANDARDIZATION*

690 US
RESIDENTIAL COST MANUAL; new construction, remodeling, and valuation. a. Van Nostrand Reinhold Co., 135 W. 50th St., New York, NY 10020 (Orders to: 7625 Empire Dr., Florence, KY 41042)

690 US
RESTON SERIES IN CONSTRUCTION TECHNOLOGY. irreg. price varies. Reston Publishing Company, Inc., 11480 Sunset Hills Rd., Reston, VA 22090.

690 UK ISSN 0080-4037
ROOFING. (Architects & Specifiers Guide Series) a. £3.50. Builder Group, 23 Pemberton Row, London W.C.3, England. Ed. Christopher Sykes. adv. circ. 5,000.

690 AT ISSN 0310-4257
RYDGE'S CCEM INDUSTRY REPORT AND BUYERS GUIDE. (Construction, Civil Engineering and Mining) 1973. a. Rydge Publications Pty. Ltd., G.P.O. Box 3337, Sydney, NSW 2001, Australia.

690 FR
SAGERET; ANNUAIRE GENERAL DU BATIMENT ET DES TRAVAUX PUBLICS. (In 5 Vols.) 1809. a. 270 F. Sageret, 5 et 7 rue Plumet, 75015 Paris, France.

690 620 CN
SASKATCHEWAN CONSTRUCTION INDUSTRY DIRECTORY. PURCHASING GUIDE. 1975. a. Sanford Evans Publishing Ltd., 1077 St. James St., Box 6900, Winnipeg, Man. R3C 3B1, Canada. adv. circ. 5,183.

690 DK ISSN 0581-9423
SCANDINAVIAN BUILDING RESEARCH. (Issued in 2 Parts) 1964. biennial. Scandinavian Building Research Congress, c/o Danish Building Research Institute, Box 119, DK-2970 Hoersholm, Denmark.

690 624 UK ISSN 0085-6002
SCOTTISH BUILDING & CIVIL ENGINEERING YEAR BOOK. 1960. a. £5($5) ‡ Edinburgh Pictorial Ltd., Smiths Place House, Edinburgh 6, Scotland. Ed. C.C. Cumming. adv. circ. 3,000. (processed)

690 683 UK ISSN 0080-8059
SCOTTISH HARDWARE AND DRYSALTERS ASSOCIATION. YEARBOOK. 1967. a. membership. Scottish Hardware and Drysalters Association, 16 Royal Terrace, Glasgow, C3, Scotland.

690 UK ISSN 0080-8717
SELL'S BUILDING INDEX. 1923. a. £15. Sell's Publications Ltd., Sell's House, 39 East St., Epsom KT17 1BQ, Surrey, England. adv. bk. rev. circ. 4,000.

690 620 CN ISSN 0704-6790
SOUTH CENTRAL ONTARIO CONSTRUCTION INDUSTRY DIRECTORY. PURCHASING GUIDE. 1976. a. Sanford Evans Publishing Ltd., 1077 St. James St., Box 6900, Winnipeg, Man. R3C 3B1, Canada. circ. 4,982.

690 620 CN
SOUTHWESTERN ONTARIO CONSTRUCTION INDUSTRY DIRECTORY. PURCHASING GUIDE. 1976. a. Sanford Evans Publishing Ltd., 1077 St. James St., Box 6900, Winnipeg, Man. R3C 3B1, Canada. adv. circ. 6,293.

690 UK ISSN 0306-3046
SPON'S ARCHITECTS' & BUILDERS' PRICE BOOK. 1873. a. £10.50. E. & F. N. Spon Ltd., 11 New Fetter Lane, London EC4P 4EE, England. Ed. Bd. adv. stat. circ. 13,000.

690 UK ISSN 0144-8404
SPON'S LANDSCAPE PRICEBOOK. 1972. biennial. £12.50. E. & F. N. Spon Ltd., 11 New Fetter Lane, London EC4P 4EE, England. Ed. Derek Lovejoy & Partners. illus. circ. 2,500.
Formerly: Spon's Landscape Handbook (ISSN 0306-3054)

338.4   US   ISSN 0083-0852
STEAM-ELECTRIC PLANT CONSTRUCTION COST AND ANNUAL PRODUCTION EXPENSES.* (Former name of issuing body: U. S. Federal Power Commission) a. U. S. Energy Information Administration, 1726 M St., N.W., Rm. 200, Washington, DC 20461 (Orders to: Supt. Doc., Washington, DC 20402)

STEEL FABRICATIONS. see *METALLURGY*

STUDIES IN CONSTRUCTION ECONOMY. see *REAL ESTATE*

690   FI
SUOMEN BETONITEOLLISUUDEN KESKUSJARJESTO. JULKAISU/ASSOCIATION OF THE CONCRETE INDUSTRY IN FINLAND. PUBLICATION. irreg. price varies. Suomen Betoniteollisuuden Keskusjarjesto, Lapinlahdenkatu 1a A 8, 00180 Helsinki 18, Finland.

690   SW   ISSN 0068-0613
SVENSKA RIKSBYGGEN. BYGGTEKNISK INFORMATION. 1960. q. Kr.40. AB Svensk Byggtjaenst, Box 7853, S-103-99 Stockholm, Sweden. Ed. Ulla Zacharski. circ. 1,700.

690   SW
SWEDEN. STATENS RAAD FOER BYGGNADSFORSKNING. CURRENT PROJECTS. (Text in English) a. free. Statens Raad Foer Byggnadsforskning - Swedish Council for Building Research, Sankt Goeransgatan 66, S-112 33 Stockholm, Sweden.

690   SW   ISSN 0586-6766
SWEDEN. STATENS RAAD FOER BYGGNADSFORSKNING. DOCUMENT. (Text in English; summaries in English and Swedish) irreg. Statens Raad Foer Byggnadsforskning - Swedish Council for Building Research, Sankt Goeransgatan 66, S-112 33 Stockholm, Sweden (Orders to: Svensk Byggtjaenst, Box 7853, S-103 99 Stockholm, Sweden)

690   SW   ISSN 0585-3400
SWEDEN. STATENS RAAD FOER BYGGNADSFORSKNING. INFORMATIONSBLAD. irreg. Statens Raad foer Byggnadsforskning - Swedish Council for Building Research, Sankt Goeransgatan 66, S-112 33 Stockholm, Sweden (Orders to: Svensk Byggtjaenst, Box 7853, S-103 99 Stockholm, Sweden)

690   SW
SWEDEN. STATENS RAAD FOER BYGGNADSFORSKNING. RAPPORT. (Text in Swedish; summaries in English and Swedish) irreg. Statens Raad foer Byggnadsforskning - Swedish Council for Building Research, Sankt Goeransgatan 66, S-112 33 Stockholm, Sweden (Orders to: Svensk Byggtjaenst, Box 7853, S-103 99 Stockholm, Sweden)

690   SW
SWEDEN. STATENS RAAD FOER BYGGNADSFORSKNING. SYNOPSES. (Text in English) 1977. irreg. (8-10/yr.) free. Statens Raad Foer Byggnadsforskning - Swedish Council for Building Research, Sankt Goeransgatan 66, S-112 33 Stockholm, Sweden.

690   SW
SWEDEN. STATENS RAAD FOER BYGGNADSFORSKNING. VERKSAMHETSPLAN. a. Statens Raad Foer Byggnadsforskning - Swedish Council for Building Research, Sankt Goeransgatan 66, S-112 33 Stockholm, Sweden.

690   SW
SWEDISH BUILDING RESEARCH NEWS. (Text in English) 1976. irreg. (3-4/yr.) free. Statens Raad Foer Byggnadsforskning - Swedish Council for Building Research, Sankt Goeransgatan 66, S-112 33 Stockholm, Sweden.

690   CN   ISSN 0082-0431
SWEET'S CANADIAN CONSTRUCTION CATALOGUE FILE. (Text in English and French) 1966. a. limited distribution. ‡ McGraw-Hill Information Systems Company of Canada Ltd., 330 Progress Ave., Scarborough, Ont. M1P 2Z5, Canada. Ed. Frank A. Spangenberg. circ. 7,000.

338.4   US   ISSN 0361-1388
SWEET'S ENGINEERING CATALOG FILE. SUMMARY EDITION: MECHANICAL, SANITARY AND RELATED PRODUCTS. 1976. a. McGraw-Hill Information Systems Co., Sweet's Division, 1221 Ave. of the Americas, New York, NY 10020.

690   US   ISSN 0094-825X
SWEET'S INDUSTRIAL CONSTRUCTION & RENOVATION FILE WITH PLANT ENGINEERING EXTENSION MARKET LIST. 1974. a. McGraw-Hill Information Systems Co., Sweet's Division, 1221 Ave. of the Americas, New York, NY 10020.

690   US   ISSN 0197-6753
T M R TRAVEL MARKETING REPORT. 1981. biennial. $500. Travel Marketing Report, Box 66323, O'Hare International Airport, Chicago, IL 60666.

TECHNOGRAPHICS. see *ARCHITECTURE*

690 620   CN
TORONTO & AREA CONSTRUCTION INDUSTRY DIRECTORY. PURCHASING GUIDE. 1977. a. Sanford Evans Publishing Ltd., 1077 St. James St., Box 6900, Winnipeg, Man. R3C 3B1, Canada. adv. circ. 19,517.

TREATED WOOD PERSPECTIVES/ PERSPECTIVES DES BOIS TRAITES. see *FORESTS AND FORESTRY — Lumber And Wood*

693.71   UK   ISSN 0041-3909
TUBULAR STRUCTURES. 1963. irreg. (2-3/yr.) free to qualified personnel. ‡ British Steel Corp., Tubes Division, Corby Works, Corby, Northants, England. Ed. James Wilson. charts. illus. stat. circ. 12,000.

691   FR
U.N.I.C.E.M. ANNUAIRE OFFICIEL. 1945. a. 168 F. Union Nationale des Industries de Carrieres et Materiaux de Construction, 3, rue Alfred-Roll, 75001 Paris, France. Dirs. Jean Lhespitau, Patrick Jenoudet. adv. circ. 5,000.

690   US   ISSN 0082-7584
UNIFORM BUILDING CODE. 1927. triennial. price varies. International Conference of Building Officials, 5360 S. Workman Mill Road, Whittier, CA 90601. Ed. Charlotte H. Cooper.

690   UN
U. N. ANNUAL BULLETIN OF HOUSING AND BUILDING STATISTICS FOR EUROPE. (Supplements) (Text in English, French, and Russian) 1958. a; latest 1979. $7. United Nations Economic Commission for Europe, Palais des Nations, 1200 Geneva 10, Switzerland (Or United Nations Publications, Room LX-2300, New York, NY 10017) charts. stat. (processed)
Formerly: U. N. Quarterly Housing Construction Summary for Europe (ISSN 0041-7424)

690   US   ISSN 0082-934X
U. S. BUREAU OF THE CENSUS. CENSUS OF CONSTRUCTION INDUSTRIES. (Issued in Area, Industry and Special Report Series) 1930. quinquennial; irreg. until 1967. price varies. U.S. Bureau of the Census, Dept. of Commerce, Washington, DC 20233 (Orders to: Supt. of Documents, Washington DC 20402)

690   US   ISSN 0083-1794
U. S. NATIONAL BUREAU OF STANDARDS. BUILDING SCIENCE SERIES. irreg. price varies. U. S. National Bureau of Standards, Washington, DC 20234 (Orders to: Supt. of Documents, Washington, DC 20402)

690   US
UNIVERSITY OF ILLINOIS. SMALL HOMES COUNCIL. BUILDING RESEARCH COUNCIL. COUNCIL NOTES. 1945. irreg. $2. ‡ University of Illinois at Urbana-Champaign, Small Homes Council - Building Research Council, 1 E. St. Mary's Rd., Champaign, IL 61820. Ed. H. R. Spies. circ. 3,900.
Formerly: University of Illinois. Small Homes Council. Building Research Council. Circulars (ISSN 0073-5396)

690   US   ISSN 0073-540X
UNIVERSITY OF ILLINOIS. SMALL HOMES COUNCIL. BUILDING RESEARCH COUNCIL. RESEARCH REPORT. 1948. irreg. ‡ University of Illinois at Urbana-Champaign, Small Homes Council, Building Research Council, 1 E. St. Mary's Rd., Champaign, IL 61820. Ed. H. R. Spies.

690   US   ISSN 0073-5426
UNIVERSITY OF ILLINOIS. SMALL HOMES COUNCIL. BUILDING RESEARCH COUNCIL. TECHNICAL NOTES. 1966. irreg., no. 14, 1979. University of Illinois at Urbana-Champaign, Small Homes Council, Building Research Council, 1 E. St. Mary's Rd., Champaign, IL 61820. Ed. H. R. Spies.

691.3   FI   ISSN 0357-3737
VALTION TEKNILLINEN TUTKIMUSKESKUS. BETONI- JA SILIKAATTITEKNIIKAN LABORATORIO. TIEDONANTO/TECHNICAL RESEARCH CENTRE OF FINLAND. CONCRETE LABORATORY. REPORT. (Text mainly in Finnish, some in English or Swedish) 1970. irreg. price varies. Valtion Teknillinen Tutkimuskeskus - Technical Research Centre of Finland, Vuorimiehentie 5, 02150 Espoo 15, Finland.
Concrete

VALTION TEKNILLINEN TUTKIMUSKESKUS. RAKENNETEKNIIKAN LABORATORIO. TIEDONANTO/TECHNICAL RESEARCH CENTRE OF FINLAND. LABORATORY OF STRUCTURAL ENGINEERING. REPORT. see *ENGINEERING*

690   GW   ISSN 0507-6714
VEREIN DEUTSCHER ZEMENTWERKE. FORSCHUNGSINSTITUT DER ZEMENTINDUSTRIE. TAETIGKEITSBERICHT. 1948. triennial. free. Verein Deutscher Zementwerke e.V., Tannenstr. 2, 4000 Duesseldorf 30, W. Germany (B.R.D.) circ. 2,000.

VIRGINIA POLYTECHNIC INSTITUTE AND STATE UNIVERSITY. WOOD RESEARCH AND WOOD CONSTRUCTION LABORATORY. SPECIAL REPORT. see *FORESTS AND FORESTRY — Lumber And Wood*

690 620   CN
WEST COAST BRITISH COLUMBIA CONSTRUCTION INDUSTRY DIRECTORY. PURCHASING GUIDE. 1977. a. Sanford Evans Publishing Ltd., 1077 St. James St., Box 6900, Winnipeg, Man. R3C 3B1, Canada. adv. circ. 7,692.

690   GW
WIR BAUEN UNSER HAUS SELBST. 1973. a. DM.14.80. Fachschriften-Verlag GmbH, Hoehenstr. 17, Postfach 1329, 7012 Fellbach, W. Germany (B.R.D.)

690   GW
WOCHENEND-, FERIEN- UND ZWEITHAUS-KATALOG. 1971. every other year. DM.14.80. Fachschriften-Verlag GmbH, Hoehenstrasse 17, Postfach 1329, 7012 Fellbach, W. Germany (B.R.D.) Ed. Eberhard Wolf.

690   NE   ISSN 0084-1072
WONINGBOUWSTUDIES. 1969. irreg., 1971, no. 13. price varies. Staatsuitgeverij, Christoffel Plantijnstr., The Hague, Netherlands. (Prepared by: Stichting Research Instituut voor de Woningbouw)

693   FR
WORLD CEMENT DIRECTORY. irreg. Cembureau, 2 rue Saint Charles, 75740 Paris Cedex 15, France. illus.
Cement and concrete

690 620   CN   ISSN 0704-8785
YORK-SIMCOE ONTARIO CONSTRUCTION INDUSTRY DIRECTORY. PURCHASING GUIDE. 1977. a. Sanford Evans Publishing Ltd., 1077 St. James St., Box 6900, Winnipeg, Man. R3C 3B1, Canada. adv. circ. 5,014.

691   GW   ISSN 0514-2938
ZEMENT-TASCHENBUCH. 1950. biennial. DM.12. (Verein Deutscher Zementwerke e.V.) Bauverlag GmbH, Wittelsbacherstr. 10, 6200 Wiesbaden, W. Germany (B.R.D.) adv. index. circ. 50,000 (approx.)

690　　　　　　　　　AU
ZEMENT UND BETON. 1955. irreg. (4-6/yr.) S.300. Verein der Oesterreichischen Zementfabrikanten, Mentergasse 3, A-1070 Vienna, Austria. (Co-sponsor: Oesterreichischer Betonverein) Ed. Alfred Boehm. bk. rev. abstr. illus. circ. 1,700.
Cement and concrete

BUILDING AND CONSTRUCTION — Abstracting, Bibliographies, Statistics

AMERICAN IRON AND STEEL INSTITUTE. ANNUAL STATISTICAL REPORT. see *ENGINEERING — Abstracting, Bibliographies, Statistics*

690　　　　　　　AT　ISSN 0067-1010
AUSTRALIA. BUREAU OF STATISTICS. TASMANIAN OFFICE. BUILDING INDUSTRY. 1968-69. a. free. Australian Bureau of Statistics, Tasmanian Office, Box 66A, G.P.O., Hobart, Tasmania 7001, Australia. circ. 450. (processed)

331　314　　　　AU　ISSN 0067-2300
AUSTRIA. STATISTISCHES ZENTRALAMT. DIE WOHNBAUTAETIGKEIT. (Subseries of: Beitraege zur Oesterreichischen Statistik) 1956. a. S.100. ‡ Oesterreichische Staatsdruckerei, Vienna, Austria. circ. 400.

690　314　　　　GW　ISSN 0084-7739
BAUSTATISTISCHES JAHRBUCH. 1960. a. DM.20. Hauptverband der Deutschen Bauindustrie, Abraham-Lincoln-Str. 30, Postfach 2966, 6200 Wiesbaden, W. Germany (B.R.D.)

690　331.83　　　　BE
BELGIUM. INSTITUT NATIONAL DE STATISTIQUE. STATISTIQUES DE LA CONSTRUCTION ET DU LOGEMENT. (Text in Dutch and French) irreg. (1-2/yr.) 300 Fr. per no. Institut National de Statistique, 44 rue de Louvain, 1000 Brussels, Belgium.
Formerly: Belgium. Institut National de Statistique. Batiments et Logements (ISSN 0067-544X)

690　016　　　　CS　ISSN 0007-3326
BUILDING ABSTRACTS SERVICE C I B.* 1959. 2-4/yr. free. Vyzkumny Ustav Vystavby a Architektury, Letenska 3, 118 45 Prague 1, Czechoslovakia. bibl. circ. 100. (looseleaf format)

690　016　　　　SW　ISSN 0348-9221
BYGGNORMINDEX/SWEDISH BUILDING CODES AND STANDARDS INDEX. (Text in Swedish; summaries in English) 1979. a. Kr.50. Institutet foer Byggdokumentation - Swedish Institute of Building Documentation, Haelsingegatan 49, S-113 31 Stockholm, Sweden.

338.4　　　　CN　ISSN 0575-7975
CANADA. STATISTICS CANADA. BUILDING PERMITS. ANNUAL SUMMARY/PERMIS DE BATIR. (Catalog 64-203) (Text in French, English) 1966. a. Can.$7($8.40) Statistics Canada, Publications Distribution, Ottawa, Ont. K1A 0V7, Ontario 51A 0V7, Canada. (also avail. in microform from MML)

338.4　　　　CN　ISSN 0382-0971
CANADA. STATISTICS CANADA. CONCRETE PRODUCTS MANUFACTURERS/FABRICANTS DE PRODUITS EN BETON. (Catalog 44-205) (Text in English and French) 1927. a. Can.$4.50($5.40) Statistics Canada, Publications Distribution, Ottawa, Ont. K1A 0V7, Canada. (also avail. in microform from MML)

CANADA. STATISTICS CANADA. ELECTRICAL CONTRACTING INDUSTRY/ ENTREPRENEURS D'INSTALLATIONS ELECTRIQUES. see *ELECTRICITY AND ELECTRICAL ENGINEERING — Abstracting, Bibliographies, Statistics*

CANADA. STATISTICS CANADA. MECHANICAL CONTRACTING INDUSTRY/ LES ENTREPRENEURS D'INSTALLATIONS MECANIQUES. see *ENGINEERING — Abstracting, Bibliographies, Statistics*

690　　　　CN　ISSN 0703-7295
CANADA. STATISTICS CANADA. NON-RESIDENTIAL GENERAL BUILDING CONTRACTING INDUSTRY/INDUSTRIE DES ENTREPRISES GENERALES EN CONSTRUCTION NON DOMICILIAIRE. (Catalog 64-207) (Text in English and French) 1971. a. Can.$6($7.20) Statistics Canada, Publications Distribution, Ottawa, Ont. K1A 0V7, Canada. (also avail. in microform from MML)

690　016　　　　CN　ISSN 0008-3089
CANADIAN BUILDING ABSTRACTS. (Text in English and French) 1960. a. free. National Research Council of Canada, Division of Building Research, Ottawa K1A 0R6, Canada. Ed. G. P. Williams. abstr. author index in each issue. circ. 4,000.

690　　　　CN　ISSN 0527-4974
CONSTRUCTION IN CANADA/CONSTRUCTION AU CANADA. (Catalogue 64-201) 1951. a. Can.$7($8.40) Statistics Canada, Ottawa, Ont. K1A 0V7, Ottawa, Ont. K1A 0T6, Canada. (also avail. in microform from MML)

338　690　　　　FR
EUROPEAN CEMENT ASSOCIATION. WORLD STATISTICAL REVIEW. no. 2, 1980. a. 100 F. (European Cement Association) Cemburea u, 2, rue St. Charles, 75240 Paris, France.
Formerly: European Cement Association, Statistical Review.

690　314　　　　GW　ISSN 0072-1719
GERMANY (FEDERAL REPUBLIC, 1949-) STATISTISCHES BUNDESAMT. AUSGEWAEHLTE ZAHLEN FUER DIE BAUWIRTSCHAFT. m. DM.103.20. W. Kohlhammer-Verlag GmbH, Abt. Veroeffentlichungen des Statistischen Bundesamtes, Philipp-Reis-Str. 3, Postfach 421120, 6500 Mainz 42, W. Germany (B.R.D.)

690　314　　　　GW
GERMANY(FEDERAL REPUBLIC, 1949-) STATISTISCHES BUNDESAMT. FACHSERIE 4, REIHE 5. (Consists of two subseries: Reihe 5.1: Beschaeftigung, Umsatz und Geraetebestand der Betriebe im Baugewerbe; and Reihe 5.2: Beschaeftigung, Umsatz und Investitionen der Unternehmen im Baugewerbe) a. price varies. W. Kohlhammer-Verlag GmbH, Abt. Veroeffentlichungen des Statistischen Bundesamtes, Philipp-Reis-Str. 3, Postfach 421120, 6500 Mainz 42, W. Germany (B.R.D.)
Formerly: Germany(Federal Republic, 1949-) Statistiches Bundesamt. Fachserie 4, Reihe 5: Beschaeftigung, Umsatz, Investitionen und Kosten Struktur in Baugewerbe (ISSN 0072-1727)

690　314　　　　GW　ISSN 0072-1735
GERMANY (FEDERAL REPUBLIC, 1949-) STATISTISCHES BUNDESAMT. FACHSERIE 5, REIHE 1: BAUTAETIGKEIT. a. DM.8.10. W. Kohlhammer-Verlag GmbH, Abt. Veroeffentlichungen des Statistischen Bundesamtes, Philipp-Reis-Str. 3, Postfach 421120, 6500 Mainz 42, W. Germany (B.R.D.)

690　314　　　　GW　ISSN 0072-1743
GERMANY (FEDERAL REPUBLIC, 1949-) STATISTISCHES BUNDESAMT. FACHSERIE 5, REIHE 2: BEWILLIGUNGEN IM SOZIALEN WOHNUNGSBAU. a. DM.7. W. Kohlhammer-Verlag GmbH, Abt. Veroeffentlichungen des Statistischen Bundesamtes, Philipp-Reis-Str. 3, Postfach 421120, 6500 Mainz 42, W. Germany (B.R.D.)

690　314　　　　GW　ISSN 0072-1751
GERMANY (FEDERAL REPUBLIC, 1949-) STATISTISCHES BUNDESAMT. FACHSERIE 5, REIHE 3: BESTAND AN WOHNUNGEN. a. DM.6. W. Kohlhammer-Verlag GmbH, Abt. Veroeffentlichungen des Statistischen Bundesamtes, Philipp-Reis-Str. 3, Postfach 421120, 6500 Mainz 42, W. Germany (B.R.D.)

692　314　　　　GW
GERMANY (FEDERAL REPUBLIC, 1949-) STATISTISCHES BUNDESAMT. FACHSERIE 17, REIHE 5: KAUFWERTE FUER BAULAND. q. price varies. W. Kohlhammer-Verlag GmbH, Abt. Veroeffentlichungen des Statistischen Bundesamtes, Philipp-Reis-Str. 3, Postfach 421120, 6500 Mainz 42, W. Germany (B.R.D.)
Supersedes: Germany(Federal Republic, 1949-) Statistisches Bundesamt. Preise, Loehne, Wirtschaftsrechnungen. Reihe 5: Preise und Preisindices fuer Bauwerke und Bauland (ISSN 0072-3908)

690　　　　HU
HUNGARY. KOZPONTI STATISZTIKAI HIVATAL. BERUHAZASI, EPITOIPARI, LAKASEPITESI ZSEBKONYV-/-POCKETBOOK OF INVESTMENTS, BUILDING INDUSTRY AND HOME-BUILDING. a. Statisztikai Kiado Vallalat, Kaszas u 10-12, 1033 Budapest 3, Hungary.

338.47　　　　HU
HUNGARY. KOZPONTI STATISZTIKAI HIVATAL. EPITOIPARI ARAK ALAKULASA. (Subseries of Hungary. Kozponti Statisztikai Hivatal. Statisztikai Idoszaki Kozlemenyek) 1970. irreg. 90 Ft. Statisztikai Kiado Vallalat, Kaszas U.10-12, P.O.B.99, 1300 Budapest, Hungary. stat.

690　　　　LY　ISSN 0075-9279
LIBYA. CENSUS AND STATISTICAL OFFICE. REPORT OF THE SURVEY OF LICENSED CONSTRUCTION UNITS. (Text in Arabic and English) 1967. a. free. Census and Statistical Department, Ministry of Planning, Tripoli, Libya.

690　315　　　　MY　ISSN 0085-3046
MALAYSIA. DEPARTMENT OF STATISTICS. SURVEY OF CONSTRUCTION INDUSTRIES: PENINSULAR MALAYSIA. (Text in English and Malay) 1963. a, latest 1974. M.$5. Department of Statistics - Jabatan Perangkaan, Jalan Young, Kuala Lumpur 10-01, Malaysia. stat. circ. 400.

690　016　　　　SA　ISSN 0077-3581
NATIONAL BUILDING RESEARCH INSTITUTE. COMPLETE LIST OF N B R I PUBLICATIONS. a. free. National Building Research Institute, Box 395, Pretoria 0001, South Africa.

690　016　　　　CN　ISSN 0085-3828
NATIONAL RESEARCH COUNCIL, CANADA. DIVISION OF BUILDING RESEARCH. BIBLIOGRAPHY. 1951. irreg. free. National Research Council of Canada, Division of Building Research, Ottawa K1A 0R6, Canada. Ed. M. E. Wimberley. bk. rev.

338.4　　　　NZ
NEW ZEALAND. DEPARTMENT OF STATISTICS. BUILDING STATISTICS. a. NZ.$1.10. Department of Statistics, Wellington, New Zealand (Subscr. to: Government Printing Office, Publications, Publications, Private Bag, Wellington, New Zealand) illus. stat.

690　　　　NZ
NEW ZEALAND. DEPARTMENT OF STATISTICS. CENSUS OF BUILDING AND CONSTRUCTION. quinquennial. NZ.$1. Department of Statistics, Private Bag, Wellington, New Zealand (Subscr. to: Government Printing Office, Publications, Private Bag, Wellington, New Zealand)

314　690　　　　PL　ISSN 0079-2632
POLAND. GLOWNY URZAD STATYSTYCZNY. ROCZNIK STATYSTYCZNY BUDOWNICTWA. YEARBOOK OF CONSTRUCTION STATISTICS.* (Issued in its Seria Roczniki Branzowe. Branch Yearbooks) irreg. Glowny Urzad Statystyczny, Al. Niepodleglosci 208, 00-925 Warsaw, Poland.

690　016　　　　FI
RAKENNUSALAN JULKAISUHAKEMISTO. biennial. Rakennuskirja Oy, Bulevardi 3 B, 00120 Helsinki 12, Finland.

690　310　　　　SA
SOUTH AFRICA. DEPARTMENT OF STATISTICS. BUILDING PLANS PASSED AND BUILDINGS COMPLETED. (Report No. 05-44) a., latest 1975. R.5. Department of Statistics, Private Bag X44, Pretoria 0001, South Africa (Orders to: Government Printer, Bosman St., Private Bag X85, Pretoria 0001,South Africa)

690 310   SP   ISSN 0561-4902
SPAIN. MINISTERIO DE LA VIVIENDA. ESTADISTICA DE LA INDUSTRIA DE LA CONSTRUCCION. (Subseries of Spain. Ministerio de la Vivienda. Documentos Informativos) a. Ministerio de la Vivienda, Secretaria General Tecnica, Madrid, Spain.

690 314   SW   ISSN 0085-6991
SWEDEN. STATISTISKA CENTRALBYRAAN. STATISTISKA MEDDELANDEN. SUBGROUP BO (HOUSING AND CONSTRUCTION) (Text in Swedish; tables heads and summaries in English) 1963 N.S. irreg. Kr.100. Liber Foerlag, Fack, S-162 89 Vaellingby, Sweden. circ. 1,375.

BUILDING AND CONSTRUCTION —
Carpentry And Woodwork

694   PL
AKADEMIA ROLNICZA, WARSAW. ZESZYTY NAUKOWE. TECHNOLOGIA DREWNA. (Summaries in Russian and English) irreg., no. 11, 1979. price varies. Akademia Rolnicza, Warsaw, Rakowiecka 26/30, 02-528 Warsaw, Poland. illus.

694   US   ISSN 0361-7238
MODERN PLYWOOD TECHNIQUES; proceedings. 1975. a. price varies. (Plywood Clinic) Miller Freeman Publications, Inc., 500 Howard St., San Francisco, CA 94105. illus.

698.3   NE
NEDERLANDSE HOUTBOND. JAARVERSLAG. irreg. Nederlandse Houtbond, Keizersgracht 298, Amsterdam, Netherlands.

694 674   US
WHERE TO BUY HARDWOOD PLYWOOD AND VENEER. 1960. a. free. Hardwood Plywood Manufacturers Association, Box 2789, Reston, VA 22090. Dir. Clark E. McDonald. circ. 5,000.
Formerly: Where to Buy Hardwood Plywood.

694   US
WOODWORKER HANDBOOKS. irreg. Drake Publishers, Inc., 381 Park Ave., New York, NY 10016.

694   US
WORLD DIRECTORY OF WOOD-BASED PANEL PRODUCERS. 1977. biennial. Miller Freeman Publications, Inc., 500 Howard St., San Francisco, CA 94105. Ed. H. R. Fraser.

BUILDING AND CONSTRUCTION —
Hardware

683   GW   ISSN 0067-4583
BAUBESCHLAG-TASCHENBUCH. 1952. a. DM.17.50. Gert Wohlfarth GmbH Verlag Fachtechnik und Mercator-Verlag, Koehnenstr. 5-11, 4100 Duisburg 1, W. Germany (B.R.D.) adv. bk. rev. circ. 5,000.

683   UK   ISSN 0067-5725
BENN'S HARDWARE DIRECTORY; the year book of the Hardware Trade Journal. 1913. a. £17. ‡ Benn Publications Ltd., 25 New Street Square, London EC4A 3JA, England. index. circ. 3,500.

683   UK
BENN'S INTERNATIONAL HARDWARE EXPORTER. (Supplement to "Hardware Trade Journal") a. Benn Publications Ltd., 25 New Street Square, London EC4A 3JA, England. Ed. Allen Barrett. adv. illus. stat. circ. 8,000.

683   US
LOCKSMITH LEDGER/SECURITY GUIDE & DIRECTORY. 1969. a. $5. Nickerson & Collins Co., 1800 Oakton, Des Plaines, IL 60018. adv. circ. 24,552. (reprint service avail. from UMI)

683   FR   ISSN 0025-9055
MEMENTO GENERAL TEQUI QUINCAILLERIE. 1965. a. 110 F. Union Francaise d'Annuaires Professionnels, 13 Av. Vladimir Komarov, B.P. 36, 78190 Trappes, France.
Incorporating: Memento General de la Quincaillerie & Repertoire Tequi Quincaillerie.

338.7   US
NATIONAL HARDWARE WHOLESALERS' GUIDE. a. $5. W. R. C. Smith Publishing Co., 1760 Peachtree Rd. N.W., Atlanta, GA 30357. Ed. Diane D. Burrell. adv.
Formerly: Southern Wholesalers' Guide (ISSN 0586-8491)

SCOTTISH HARDWARE AND DRYSALTERS ASSOCIATION. YEARBOOK. see *BUILDING AND CONSTRUCTION*

683   UK
SHOP EQUIPMENT & MATERIALS GUIDE. 1958. a. £4. Westbourne Journals Ltd., Crown House, Morden, Surrey, England. Ed. Colin Bousfield. adv.
Formerly: Shop Equipment & Shopfitting Directory (ISSN 0080-9381)

BUSINESS AND ECONOMICS

also specific industries

330   FI
AABO AKADEMI. EKONOMISK-GEOGRAFISKA INSTITUTIONEN. MEDDELANDEN. (Text in English and Swedish; summaries in English and Finnish) 1961. irreg., no. 13, 1979. price varies. ‡ Aabo Akademi, Ekonomisk-Geografiska Institutionen - Aabo Swedish University School of Economics, Institute of Commercial Geography, Henriksgatan 7, 20500 Aabo 50, Finland.
Formerly: Handelshoegeskolan vid Aabo Akademi. Ekonomisk-Geografiska Institutionen. Meddelanden (ISSN 0564-5409)

330   FI
AABO AKADEMI. EKONOMISK-GEOGRAFISKA INSTITUTIONEN. MEMORANDA. (Text in English and Swedish; summaries in English and Finnish) 1967. irreg., no. 25, 1979. price varies. Aabo Akademi, Ekonomisk-Geografiska Institutionen - Aabo Swedish University School of Economics, Institute of Commercial Geography, Henriksgatan 7, 20500 Aabo 50, Finland. Ed. Goesta A. Eriksson. circ. controlled.
Formerly: Handelshoegeskolan vid Aabo Akademi. Ekonomisk-Geografiska Institutionen. Memoranda (ISSN 0564-5409)

330   HU   ISSN 0324-6957
ACTA MARXISTICA LENINISTICA. POLITIKAI GAZDASAGTAN TANULMANYOK. (Text in Hungarian, occasionally German, Russian) vol. 24, 1978. irreg. Kossuth Lajos Tudomanyegyetem, Egyetem Ter 1, 4010 Debrecen, Hungary. Ed. Jozsef Darai.

330   NE
ADVANCED TEXTBOOKS IN ECONOMICS. 1971. irreg., vol. 16, 1980. price varies. North-Holland Publishing Co., Box 211, 1000 AE Amsterdam, Netherlands. Eds. C.J. Bliss, M.D. Intriligator.

330   US
ADVANCES IN ECONOMETRICS. 1980. a. $18.75 to individuals; institutions $37.50. J A I Press, Box 1678, 165 W. Putnam Ave., Greenwich, CT 06830. Ed. R. L. Basmann.

AFRICA GUIDE. see *POLITICAL SCIENCE*

330   IT   ISSN 0065-4264
AGENDA DEL DIRIGENTE DI AZIENDA.* a. Editoriale Emme Elle s.r.l., Via Reno, 30, Rome, Italy.

330 070   SP
AGRUPACION DE PERIODISTAS DE INFORMACION ECONOMICA. INFORME. 1975. a. 200 ptas. Agrupacion de Periodistas de Informacion Economica, Plaza del Callao 4, Madrid 13, Spain.

330   PL
AKADEMIA EKONOMICZNA, KRAKOW. ZESZYTY NAUKOWE. (Text in Polish; summaries in English and Russian) 1955. irreg., no. 65, 1975. 10 Zl. per no. Akademia Ekonomiczna, Krakow, Ul. Rakowicka 27, 35-510 Krakow, Poland.
Formerly: Wyzsza Szkola Ekonomiczna. Zeszyty Naukowe (ISSN 0075-5125)

330   PL   ISSN 0079-4546
AKADEMIA EKONOMICZNA, POZNAN. ZESZYTY NAUKOWE .SERIA 1. (Former name of issuing body Wyzsza Szkola Ekonomiczna) 1961. irreg. price varies. Akademia Ekonomiczna, Poznan, Marchlewskiego 146, 60-967 Poznan, Poland. circ. 300.

330   PL   ISSN 0079-4554
AKADEMIA EKONOMICZNA, POZNAN. ZESZYTY NAUKOWE. SERIA 2. PRACE HABILITACYJNE I DOKTORSKIE. (Former name of issuing body Wyzsza Szkola Ekonomiczna) irreg. price varies. Akademia Ekonomiczna, Poznan, Marchlewskiego 146, 60-967 Poznan, Poland. circ. 200.

330   PL
AKADEMIA EKONOMICZNA WE WROCLAWIU. PRACE NAUKOWE. irreg. 9 Zl. Akademia Ekonomiczna, Wroclaw, Komandorska 118-120, 50-950 Wroclaw, Poland. illus.
Formerly: Wyzsza Szkola Ekonomiczna we Wroclawiv. Prace Naukowe.

330   GE   ISSN 0065-5279
AKADEMIE DER WISSENSCHAFTEN DER DDR. ZENTRALINSTITUT FUER WIRTSCHAFTSWISSENSCHAFTEN. SCHRIFTEN. 1955. irreg.,no. 15,1976. price varies. Akademie-Verlag, Leipziger Str. 3-4, 108 Berlin, E. Germany (D.D.R.) bibl. charts. illus.

330   US
ALFRED A. KNOPF BOOKS IN ECONOMICS. irreg. price varies. Alfred A. Knopf (Subsidiary of: Random House) 201 E. 50 St., New York, NY 10022.

650 378   US
AMERICAN ASSEMBLY OF COLLEGIATE SCHOOLS OF BUSINESS. MEMBERSHIP DIRECTORY. a. $2.50. American Assembly of Collegiate Schools of Business, 11500 Olive St. Rd., Suite 142, St. Louis, MO 63141. Ed. Audrey S. Easton.
Formerly: American Assembly of Collegiate Schools of Business. Accredited Schools, Officers, Committees (ISSN 0065-7131)

330 650   SP
ANALES DE LA UNIVERSIDAD HISPALENSE. SERIE: EMPRESARIALES. vol. 2, 1976. irreg. price varies (or exchange) Universidad de Sevilla, San Fernando 4, Seville, Spain.
Formerly: Anales de la Universidad Hispalense. Serie: Ciencias Economicas y Empresariales.

330.9   BL
ANALISE. (Text in English, Portuguese) a. Publicacoes Executivas Brasileiras Ltda, Rua dos Ingleses 150, Caixa Postal 30837, CEP 01329 Sao Paulo, Brazil. illus.

330   FR
ANNALES ECONOMIQUES DE CLERMONT-FERRAND. 1971. irreg. price varies. Editions Cujas, 4,6, 8 rue de la Maison Blanche, 75013 Paris, France.

330   PL   ISSN 0459-9586
ANNALES UNIVERSITATIS MARIAE CURIE-SKLODOWSKA. SECTIO H. OECONOMIA. (Text in Polish; summaries in Polish and Russian) 1967. a. price varies. Uniwersytet Marii Curie-Sklodowskiej, Plac Marii Curie-Sklodowskiej 5, 20-031 Lublin, Poland. Ed. R. Orlowski.

330   GW
ANNALES UNIVERSITATIS SARAVIENSIS. WIRTSCHAFTSWISSENSCHAFTLICHE ABTEILUNG. SCHRIFTENREIHE. 1962. irreg., vol. 88, 1977. price varies. (Universitaet des Saarlandes, Wirtschaftswissenschaftliche Fakultaet) Carl Heymanns Verlag KG, Gereonstr. 18-32, 5000 Cologne 1, W. Germany (B.R.D.)

330   FR
ANNUAIRE DESFOSSES. vol. 62, 1978. a. 665 F. Societe de Documentation et d'Analyses Financieres, 7 rue Bergere, 75009 Paris, France.

330   FR
ANNUAIRE ECONOMIQUE. a. Euro-Publi Marcel Puget, 9 Bd des Italiens, 75002 Paris, France.

BUSINESS AND ECONOMICS

330 US ISSN 0090-4309
ANNUAL EDITIONS: READINGS IN BUSINESS. 1973/74. a. price varies. Dushkin Publishing Group, Sluice Dock, Guilford, CT 06437. illus.

330 US ISSN 0090-4430
ANNUAL EDITIONS: READINGS IN ECONOMICS. 1973/74. a. price varies. Dushkin Publishing Group, Sluice Dock, Guilford, CT 06437. illus. Key Title: Economics. Text.

330 NE
ASEPELT SERIES. 1962. irreg., vol. 5, 1976. price varies. North-Holland Publishing Co., Box 211, 1000 AE Amsterdam, Netherlands.

330 HK
ASIA YEARBOOK. 1960. a. $8.95. Far Eastern Economic Review Ltd., Box 160, Hong Kong, Hong Kong. Ed. Donald Wise. adv.
Formerly: Far Eastern Economic Review. Yearbook (ISSN 0071-3821)

330 AG
ASOCIACION DE ECONOMISTAS ARGENTINOS. COLECCION INSTITUTO SUPERIOR. irreg, no. 3, 1976. Editorial el Coloquio, Junin 735, Buenos Aires, Argentina. charts, stat.

330 CN ISSN 0319-003X
ATLANTIC CANADA ECONOMICS ASSOCIATION. ANNUAL CONFERENCE: A C E A PAPERS. no. 4, 1975. a. Can.$10. Atlantic Canada Economics Association, c/o Prof. Ralph Winter, Ed., Department of Economics, Acadia University, Wolfville, N.S. B0P 1X0, Canada. charts. stat.

330 BG
BAMLADESA ARTHANAITIKA JARIPA. (Text in Bengali) 1971. a. Ministry of Finance, Economic Adviser's Wing, Bangladesh Secretariat, Shed No. 27, Dacca 2, Bangladesh.
Formerly (until 1974/75): Bangladesh Economic Survey (ISSN 0070-8704)

330 UK ISSN 0306-9338
BANGOR OCCASIONAL PAPERS IN ECONOMICS. 1973. irreg. price varies. University of Wales Press, 6 Gwennyth St., Cathays, Cardiff CF2 4YD, Wales. Ed. Jack Revell. (reprint service avail. from UMI)

330 300 AU
BEIRAT FUER WIRTSCHAFTS UND SOZIALFRAGEN. a. S.26. Alser Str. 24, A-1095 Vienna 9, Austria. Eds. Klaus Hecke, Hans Reithofer.

330 CN ISSN 0706-7852
BENEFITS FOR SASKATCHEWAN INDUSTRY FROM RESOURCE DEVELOPMENT. 1979. irreg. Department of Industry and Commerce, S.P.C. Bldg., 7th Floor, Regina, Sask. S4P 2Y9, Canada.

330 SZ ISSN 0067-6128
BERNER BEITRAEGE ZUR NATIONALOEKONOMIE. 1965. irreg., vol. 34, 1978. price varies. Paul Haupt AG, Falkenplatz 14, CH-3001 Berne, Switzerland. Ed.Bd.

BERNER STUDIEN ZUM FREMDENVERKEHR. see *TRAVEL AND TOURISM*

338 310 SZ
BIBLIOGRAPHIE SUISSE DE STATISTIQUE ET D'ECONOMIE POLITIQUE. biennial. Schweizerische Gesellschaft fuer Statistik und Volkswirtschaft - Societe Suisse de Statistique et d'Economie Politique, Hallwylstr. 15, CH-3003 Berne, Switzerland.

330 RM ISSN 0067-8082
BIBLIOTHECA OECONOMICA. (Text in Rumanian; summaries in English, French and Russian) irreg. (Institutul Central de Cercetari Economice) Editura Academiei Republicii Socialiste Romania, Calea Victoriei 125, Bucharest, Romania (Subscr. to: ILEXIM, Str. 13 Decembrie Nr. 3, P.O. Box 136-137, Bucharest, Romania)

BLACK ECONOMIC RESEARCH CENTER. OCCASIONAL PAPER. see *ETHNIC INTERESTS*

650 SA
BLUE-BOOK OF S.A. BUSINESS. (Text in English) 1949. a. R.44($55) Communications Group, Business Press Division, White-Ray House, 51 Wale St., Box 335, Cape Town 8000, South Africa. Ed. F. M. Botha. adv.
Formerly: Business Blue-Book of Southern Africa (ISSN 0068-4406)

330 332.6 GW ISSN 0067-9496
BOERSEN- UND WIRTSCHAFTSHANDBUCH. 1865. a. DM.29.50. Societaets-Verlag, Frankenallee 71, Postfach 2929, 6000 Frankfurt 1, W. Germany (B.R.D.) adv. index. circ. 10,000.

330 EC
BOLETIN TRIMESTRAL DE INFORMACION ECONOMICA. 1946. irreg. Universidad Central del Ecuador, Instituto de Investigaciones Economicas, Casilla 1088, Quito, Ecuador.

330 US ISSN 0068-0354
BOSTWICK PAPER. 1968. irreg., 1978, no. 3. $4. Bostwick Press, Box 15, University of Richmond, VA 23173. Ed. Thomas S. Berry. circ. 500. Indexed: Vert.File Ind.

338.9 BL
BRAZILIAN ECONOMIC STUDIES. 1975. irreg. price varies. Instituto de Planejamento Economico e Social, Rua Melvin Jones 5, ZC-00 Centro, Rio de Janeiro, Brazil.

330 CN
BRITISH COLUMBIA INSTITUTE FOR ECONOMIC POLICY ANALYSIS SERIES. 1976. irreg. price varies. University of British Columbia Press, 303-6344 Memorial Rd., Vancouver, B.C. V6T 1W5, Canada.

330 300 MR ISSN 0007-4586
BULLETIN ECONOMIQUE ET SOCIAL DU MAROC. (Editions in Arabic and English) 1936. irreg. (4 nos. per subscr.) DH.50 for 4 numbers. Societe d'Etudes Economiques Sociales et Statistiques du Maroc, B.P. 535, Rabat-Chellah, Morocco. Ed. Abdelkhebir Khatibi. bk. rev. cum.index. circ. 1,300.

BURT FRANKLIN ESSAYS IN HISTORY, ECONOMICS, AND SOCIAL SCIENCES. see *HISTORY*

330 US ISSN 0146-4744
BUSINESS ASSISTANCE MONOGRAPH SERIES. irreg. Federal Reserve Bank of Boston, Urban Affairs Section, Boston, MA 02106.

330 US ISSN 0145-7071
BUSINESS PEOPLE IN THE NEWS; a compilation of news stories and feature articles from American newspapers and magazines covering people in industry, finance and labor. 1976. irreg. $32. Gale Research Company, Book Tower, Detroit, MI 48226. Ed. Barbara Nykoruk. illus. index.

650 US ISSN 0362-823X
BUSINESS RESEARCH BULLETIN. vol. 73, 1972. irreg. University of Nebraska-Lincoln, College of Business Administration, Bureau of Business Research, Lincoln, NE 68508. illus, bibl, stat.

650 US ISSN 0068-449X
BUSINESS SCIENCE MONOGRAPHS.* 1965. irreg. Southern Illinois University, Carbondale, Business Research Bureau, Carbondale, IL 62901.

330 IE
BUSINESS STUDIES SERIES. 1979. irreg. price varies. Confederation of Irish Industry, Confederation House, Kildare St., Dublin 2, Ireland. Ed. Gerald O'Brien.

338 UK
C B I ANNUAL REPORT. a. Confederation of British Industry, 103 New Oxford St., London WC1A 1DU, England.

330 CN
C. D. HOWE RESEARCH INSTITUTE. POLICY REVIEW AND OUTLOOK. (Text in English and French) 1974. a. C. D. Howe Research Institute, Suite 2064, 1155 Metcalfe St., Montreal, Que. H3B 2X7, Canada. (also avail. in microform from MML)

330 CK
C.E.D.E. DOCUMENTOS DE TRABAJO. 1973. irreg. Universidad de los Andes, Centro de Estudios sobre Desarrollo Economico, Calle 18A Carrera 1e, Apdo. Aereo 4976, Bogota, Colombia. Ed.Bd. bibl. charts. stat.

330 UK
CAMBRIDGE ECONOMIC HANDBOOKS. NEW SERIES. irreg. price varies. Cambridge University Press, Box 110, Cambridge CB2 3RL, England (And 32 E. 57th St., New York NY 10022) Ed. F. H. Hahn.

330 UK ISSN 0068-6832
CAMBRIDGE UNIVERSITY. DEPARTMENT OF APPLIED ECONOMICS. MONOGRAPHS. 1948. irreg., no. 27, 1980. $47.50 for latest vol. Cambridge University Press, Box 110, Cambridge CB2 3RL, England (And 32 E. 57th St., New York, NY 10022)

330 UK ISSN 0068-6840
CAMBRIDGE UNIVERSITY. DEPARTMENT OF APPLIED ECONOMICS. OCCASIONAL PAPERS. 1964. irreg., no. 52, 1980. $24.95 (cloth); $13.95(paper) for latest vol. Cambridge University Press, Box 110, Cambridge CB2 3RL, England (and 32 E. 57 St., New York, NY 10022)

330 382 CN ISSN 0068-7677
CANADA IN THE ATLANTIC ECONOMY. 1968. irreg. University of Toronto Press, Front Campus, Toronto, Ont. M5S 1A6, Canada.

336 CN ISSN 0384-8744
CANADIAN JOURNAL OF PUBLIC AND COOPERATIVE ECONOMY/REVUE CANADIENNE D'ECONOMIE PUBLIQUE ET COOPERATIVE. (Text in French and English) 1968. a. Can.$5.($5.50) CIRIEC Canada, Dept. of Economics, Sir George Williams Univ., 1455 Boul de Maisonneuve, Montreal 107, Canada. Ed. G. Davidovic. (also avail. in microfiche from MML)
Formerly: Centre Canadien International de Recherches et d'Information sur l'Economie Publique et Cooperative. Revue du Canadien (ISSN 0045-6063)

330 US ISSN 0162-6353
CAROLINAS COMPANIES. 1971. a. $12. Interstate Securities Corporation, c/o Research Dept., 2700 NCNB Plaza, Charlotte, NC 28280. Ed. Kay Norwood. index. circ. 10,000.
Formerly: North Carolina Companies.

330 UK ISSN 0069-0937
CASS LIBRARY OF INDUSTRIAL CLASSICS. 1966. irreg., no. 28, 1969. price varies. Frank Cass & Co. Ltd., Gainsborough House, 11 Gainsborough Rd., London E11 1RS, England (Dist. in U.S. by: Biblio Distribution Center, 81 Adams Drive, Totowa, N.J. 07512)

330 614.7 FR
CENTRE ECONOMIE, ESPACE, ENVIRONNEMENT. CAHIERS. irreg. Economica, 49 rue Hericart, 75015 Paris, France.

330 FR ISSN 0071-8343
CENTRE NATIONAL DE LA RECHERCHE SCIENTIFIQUE. SEMINAIRE D'ECONOMETRIE. CAHIERS. 1951. irreg. price varies. Centre National de la Recherche Scientifique, Seminaire d'Econometrie, 15 Quai Anatole-France, 75700 Paris, France.

330 FR ISSN 0071-8270
CENTRE NATIONAL DE LA RECHERCHE SCIENTIFIQUE. SEMINAIRE D'ECONOMETRIE. MONOGRAPHIES. 1960. irreg. price varies. Centre National de la Recherche Scientifique, Seminaire d'Econometrie, 15 Quai Anatole-France, 75700 Paris, France.

650 US ISSN 0084-8727
CHARLES C. MOSKOWITZ LECTURES. 1961. a. price varies. (New York University, School of Commerce) Macmillan Publishing Co., Inc., Washington Sq., New York, NY 10012. Ed. Abraham Gitlow. circ. 2,000.

330 US
CHICAGO M B A; a journal of selected papers. 1977. a. $3. University of Chicago, Graduate School of Business, 583 Greenwood Ave., Chicago, IL 60637. Ed. Charles R. Overfelt.

BUSINESS AND ECONOMICS

330   BE   ISSN 0069-3952
CHRONOLOGIE DES COMMUNAUTES EUROPEENNES. 1970. irreg. price varies. (Universite Libre de Bruxelles, Institut d'Etudes Europeennes) Editions de l'Universite de Bruxelles, Parc Leopold, 1040 Brussels, Belgium.

330   BL
CIENCIAS ECONOMICAS. irreg. Ordem dos Economistas de Sao Paulo, Viaduto 9 de Julho, 26, Sao Paulo, Brazil. illus.
Continues: Revista de Ciencias Economicas; Economia, Financas, Administracao, Estatistica (ISSN 0484-6796)

330   SZ
COLLOQUES ECONOMIQUES. (Text in French or German) 1974. irreg. 12 Fr. Editions Universitaires de Fribourg, 36 Bd. de Perolles, CH-1700 Fribourg, Switzerland.

330 368   CK
COLOMBIA. SUPERINTENDENCIA BANCARIA. SEGUROS Y CAPITALIZACION. 1969. a. free. Superintendencia Bancaria, Bogota, Colombia. circ. 1,200.

330   US   ISSN 0069-6331
COLUMBIA STUDIES IN ECONOMICS. 1968. irreg., no. 10, 1979. Columbia University Press, 136 South Broadway, Irvington-On-Hudson, NY 10533.

650   US
COLUMBIA UNIVERSITY GRADUATE SCHOOL OF BUSINESS. DISSERTATIONS SERIES. irreg. price varies. (Columbia University, Graduate School of Business) Free Press, c/o Macmillan, 866 Third Ave., New York, NY 10022.

330   EI   ISSN 0531-3023
COMMISSION OF THE EUROPEAN COMMUNITIES. COLLECTION D'ECONOMIE ET POLITIQUE REGIONALE. (Some editions also in German, Italian and Dutch) irreg. price varies. Office for Official Publications of the European Communities, C.P. 1003, Luxembourg 1, Luxembourg (Dist. in U.S. by European Community Information Service, 2100 M. St., N.W. Suite 707, Washington D.C. 20037)

330   EI   ISSN 0069-6773
COMMISSION OF THE EUROPEAN COMMUNITIES. STUDIES: ECONOMIC AND FINANCIAL SERIES. (Text in Dutch, English, French, German and Italian) 1962. irreg. Office for Official Publications of the European Communities, Case Postale 1003, Luxembourg 1, Luxembourg (Dist. in the U.S. by European Community Information Service, 2100 M St. N.W., Suite 707, Washington, DC 20037)

338   US
CONFERENCE BOARD. ANNUAL SURVEY OF CORPORATE CONTRIBUTIONS. (Subseries of: Conference Board. Report) a. $15 to non-members; members $5. ‡ Conference Board, Inc., 845 Third Ave, New York, NY 10022. Indexed: B.P.I. P.A.I.S.
Formerly: Conference Board. Report on Company Contributions (ISSN 0069-8369)

650 330   US   ISSN 0069-8350
CONFERENCE BOARD. CUMULATIVE INDEX. 1963. a. free. Conference Board, Inc., 845 Third Ave., New York, NY 10022. Ed. Ellen Ackerman. circ. 50,000.

CONFERENCE BOARD IN CANADA. EXECUTIVE BULLETIN. see *BUSINESS AND ECONOMICS — Management*

330   CN
CONFERENCE BOARD IN CANADA. OCCASIONAL PAPERS. irreg. Conference Board in Canada, Suite 100, 25 McArthur Rd., Ottawa, Ont. K1L 6R3, Canada.

330   CN   ISSN 0384-9988
CONFERENCE BOARD IN CANADA. TECHNICAL PAPERS. 1977. irreg. Can.$3 to members; Can. $15 to non-members. Conference Board in Canada, Suite 100, 25 McArthur Rd., Ottawa, Ont. K1L 6R3, Canada.

330   ES
CONGRESO NACIONAL DE PROFESIONALES EN CIENCIAS ECONOMICAS. MEMORIA. 1972. irreg. Congreso Nacional de Profesionales en Ciencias Economicas, San Salvador, El Salvador.

330 332   US
CONTEMPORARY STUDIES IN ECONOMIC AND FINANCIAL ANALYSIS. 1976. irreg. price varies. J A I Press, Box 1678, 165 W. Putnam Ave., Greenwich, CT 06830. Eds. Edward Altman, Ingo Walter. charts. stat.

330   BL
CONTRIBUICOES EM ECONOMIA. 1977. irreg. Editora Campus Ltda. (Subsidiary of: Elsevier North-Holland, Inc.) Rua Japeri 35, 20000 Rio de Janeiro RJ, Brazil. Ed. Claudio M. Rothmuller. illus.

330   CK
CORPORACION FINANCIERA COLOMBIANA. EJERCICIO. a. Corporacion Financiera Colombiana, Carrera nos. 26-45, Apdo Aereo 11843, Bogota, Colombia.

330 332.6   US   ISSN 0145-692X
CORPORATE PROFILES FOR EXECUTIVES & INVESTORS. a. $14.50. Rand McNally & Co., 8225 N. Central Pk., Skokie, IL 60076. charts.

330   US
COWLES FOUNDATION MONOGRAPHS. 1970. irreg.,no. 25, 1975. price varies. Yale University Press, 92A Yale Sta., New Haven, CT 06520.
Formerly: Cowles Foundation for Research in Economics at Yale University. Monographs (ISSN 0084-9413)

330   CS   ISSN 0590-5001
CZECHOSLOVAK ECONOMIC PAPERS. (Text in English) 1959. irreg. price varies. (Ceskoslovenska Akademie Ved, Ekonomicky Ustav) Academia, Publishing House of the Czechoslovak Academy of Sciences, Vodickova 40, 112 29 Prague 1, Czechoslovakia. bk. rev. bibl.

338   DK   ISSN 0106-4967
DENMARK. JORDBRUGSOEKONOMISK INSTITUT. AARSBERETNING. 1979. a. free. Jordbrugsoekonomisk Institut, Valby Langgade 19, DK-2500 Valby, Denmark.

338   DK   ISSN 0106-1291
DENMARK. JORDBRUGSOEKONOMISK INSTITUT. LANDBRUGETS OEKONOMI. 1979. a. free. Jordbrugsoekonomisk Institut, Valby Langgade 19, DK-2500 Valby, Denmark.

338   DK   ISSN 0106-2689
DENMARK. JORDBRUGSOEKONOMISK INSTITUT. MEDDELELSE. 1967. irreg. (2-4/yr.) free. Jordbrugsoekonomisk Institut, Valby Langgade 19, 2500 Valby, Denmark.
Formerly: Denmark. Landoekonomiske Driftsbureau. Meddelelse (ISSN 0460-1424)

338   DK   ISSN 0106-3642
DENMARK. JORDBRUGSOEKONOMISK INSTITUT. MEMORANDUM. irreg. free. Jordbrugsoekonomisk Institut, Valby Langgade 19, 2500 Valby, Denmark.
Formerly: Denmark. Landoekonomiske Driftsbureau. Memorandum.

338   DK   ISSN 0106-0864
DENMARK. JORDBRUGSOEKONOMISK INSTITUT. UNDERSOEGELSE. irreg. (1-3/yr.) free. Jordbrugsoekonomisk Institut, Valby Langgade 19, 2500 Valby, Denmark.
Formerly: Denmark. Landoekonomiske Driftsbureau. Undersoegelse.

650 370.58   US
DIRECTORY OF ACCREDITED INSTITUTIONS. 1962/63. a. $0.75. Association of Independent Colleges and Schools, Accrediting Commission, Suite 600, 1730 M St. N.W., Washington, DC 20036. Ed. James M. Phillips. circ. 4,500.
Formerly: Directory of Business Schools (ISSN 0070-5187)

330   II
DIRECTORY OF ECONOMIC RESEARCH CENTRES IN INDIA. (Supplements issued annually) 1972. irreg., 2nd edition, 1975. Rs.85($13.20) Information Research Academy, Box 10250, Calcutta 700019, India. Ed. Partha Subir Guha. adv. circ. 2,500.

330   US
DIRECTORY OF JAPANESE FIRMS, OFFICES AND OTHER ORGANIZATIONS IN THE UNITED STATES. 1969. triennial. $16.90. Japan External Trade Organization (JETRO), 232 N. Michigan Ave., Chicago, IL 60601 (Dist. by California Business Corporation, 900 Wilshire Blvd., Suite 414, Los Angeles, CA 90017)
Formerly: Directory of Japanese Firms, Offices and Subsidiaries in the United States.

650   US   ISSN 0070-640X
DIRECTORY OF STATE AND FEDERAL FUNDS AVAILABLE FOR BUSINESS DEVELOPMENT. 1966. irreg., latest edt. 1977. $5. Pilot Books, 347 Fifth Ave., New York, NY 10016.

330   US   ISSN 0146-6534
DOW JONES-IRWIN BUSINESS ALMANAC. 1977. a. $14. Dow Jones-Irwin, Homewood, IL 60430. Eds. Sumner N. Levine, Caroline Levine.

330   NE
DYNAMIC ECONOMICS SERIES. 1976. irreg., vol. 3, 1979. price varies. North-Holland Publishing Co., P.O. Box 211, 1000 AE Amsterdam, Netherlands. Ed. Maurice Wilkinson.

330 650   SA
DYNAMICA. (Text in Afrikaans and English) 1964. a. R.1.05. University of South Africa, Department of Business Economics, Box 392, Pretoria 0001, South Africa. adv. circ. 3,170.

338   US   ISSN 0163-3457
E D A RESEARCH REVIEW. 1967. irreg. free to qualified personnel. U.S. Economic Development Administration, Office of Economic Research, Department of Commerce, Rm. 6018, Washington, DC 20230. Ed. Barbara L. Newlen. abstr. circ. controlled. (processed)

330   CN
E.S. WOODWARD LECTURES IN ECONOMICS. irreg. University of British Columbia, Department of Economics, 1873 East Mall, Suite 997, University Campus, Vancouver, B.C. V6T 1Y2, Canada.

330   US
EAST WEST EUROPEAN ECONOMIC INTERACTION. 1976. irreg., no. 4, 1978. Springer-Verlag, 175 Fifth Ave., New York, NY 10010 (Also Berlin, Heidelberg, Vienna) (reprint service avail. from ISI)

330   CK
ECONOMIA. 1959. irreg. Compania Editoria Continente, Edificio Morulanda, Carrera 6a, 14-74, Bogota, Colombia. Dir. E. Fierro Forero. bibl. illus.
Formerly: Economia Gran Colombiana (1959-1963)

330   PE
ECONOMIA. 1978. irreg. Pontificia Universidad Catolica, Departamento de Economia, Apartado 12514, Lima 21, Peru. bk. rev.

330   PO
ECONOMIA E FINANCAS. 1933. a. Universidade Tecnica de Lisboa, Instituto Superior de Ciencias Economicas e Financeiras, Lisbon, Portugal.

330   HO   ISSN 0424-2483
ECONOMIA POLITICA. 1962. irreg.; no. 6, 1973. £1 per no. Universidad Nacional Autonoma de Honduras, Instituto de Investigaciones Economicas y Sociales, Ciudad Universitaria, Tegucigalpa, Honduras. Ed. Victor Meza. bk. rev. circ. 1,000.

ECONOMIC ANALYSIS OF NORTH AMERICAN SKI AREAS. see *SPORTS AND GAMES — Outdoor Life*

330.1   II   ISSN 0070-8437
ECONOMIC AND SCIENTIFIC RESEARCH FOUNDATION, NEW DELHI. ANNUAL REPORT. 1967/68. a. Economic and Scientific Research Foundation, Federation House, New Delhi 110001, India. circ. 1,000.

330   IE
ECONOMIC AND SOCIAL RESEARCH INSTITUTE. POLICY SERIES. 2. Economic and Social Research Institute, 4 Burlington Rd., Dublin 4, Ireland.

BUSINESS AND ECONOMICS

330   IE   ISSN 0070-8755
ECONOMIC AND SOCIAL RESEARCH INSTITUTE. PUBLICATIONS SERIES. PAPER. (Notes: No. 1-35 Issued by the Institute Under an Earlier Name; Economic Research Institute) 1961. irreg. price varies. Economic and Social Research Institute, 4 Burlington Rd., Dublin 4, Ireland.

330   CN   ISSN 0225-8013
ECONOMIC COUNCIL OF CANADA. DISCUSSION PAPER. (Text in English and French) 1973. irreg. Economic Council of Canada, Box 527, Ottawa, Ont. K1P 5V6, Canada. bibl.

330   US
ECONOMIC DEVELOPMENT SERIES. irreg. price varies. Oxford University Press, 200 Madison Ave., New York, NY 10016 (And Ely House, 37 Dover St., London W1X 4AH, England) Ed. Gerald M. Meier.

330   US
ECONOMIC OUTLOOK FOR NEW JERSEY. a. free. Office of Economic Policy, 142 W. State St., Trenton, NJ 08625.

330.9   TZ
ECONOMIC REFLECTIONS. 1972. irreg. University of Dar es Salaam, Economics Association, Box 35184, Dar es Salaam, Tanzania.

330   SW
ECONOMIC RESEARCH REPORTS. SERIES A. no. 17, 1975. irreg. Kr.19. Swedish Industrial Publications, Box 5501, Stockholm, Sweden.

330   BG   ISSN 0070-8631
ECONOMIC REVIEW.* (Text in English) 1964-65. a. University of Dacca, Economics Association, c/o Dept. of Economics, Ramna, Dacca 2, Bangladesh.

330   JA
ECONOMIC STUDIES QUARTERLY. (Text in English or Japanese) irreg. Japanese Association of Theoretical Economics - Toyo Keizai Shinposha, 1-4 Hongokucho, Nihonbashi, Chuo-ku, Tokyo 103, Japan.

330   US   ISSN 0013-0397
ECONOMIC TOPICS SERIES. 1970. irreg., approx 2/yr. $1.50 per no. Joint Council on Economic Education, 1212 Ave. of the Americas, New York, NY 10036. charts. illus. stat.

330   US   ISSN 0090-4422
ECONOMICS: ENCYCLOPEDIA. 1973/74. a. price varies. Dushkin Publishing Group, Sluice Dock, Guilford, CT 06437. illus.

330   BE   ISSN 0070-8771
ECONOMIE BELGE ET INTERNATIONALE/ BELGISCHE EN INTERNATIONALE ECONOMIE. a. Editions de l'Universite de Bruxelles, Parc Leopold, B-1040 Brussels, Belgium.

330.1   FR   ISSN 0070-8801
ECONOMIE ET SOCIETE. 1970. irreg. price varies. Editions du Seuil, 27 rue Jacob, 75261 Paris Cedex 06, France. Ed. Edmond Blanc.

ECONOMIE FRANCAISE EN PERSPECTIVES SECTORIELLES: FILIERE BATIMENT, GENIE CIVIL, MATERIAUX DE CONSTRUCTION. see *BUILDING AND CONSTRUCTION*

331   FR   ISSN 0068-4821
ECONOMIES ET SOCIETES. SERIE AB. ECONOMIE DU TRAVAIL. 1960. irreg., 1969, latest issue. 42 F. Institut de Sciences Mathematiques et Economiques Appliquees, Paris, Institut Henri Poincare, 11 rue Pierre et Marie Curie, 75005 Paris, France. Dir. H. Bartoli. circ. 1,600.

330   FR   ISSN 0068-483X
ECONOMIES ET SOCIETES. SERIE G. ECONOMIE PLANIFIEE. 1956. irreg. 42 F. Institut de Sciences Mathematiques et Economiques Appliquees, Paris, Institut Henri Poincare, 11 rue Henri et Marie Curie, 75005 Paris, France. Ed. Henri Chambre.

330.1   FR   ISSN 0068-4880
ECONOMIES ET SOCIETES. SERIE M. PHILOSOPHIE - SCIENCES SOCIALES ECONOMIE. irreg. 42 F. Institut de Sciences Mathematiques et Economiques Appliquees, Paris, Institut Henri Poincare, 11 rue Pierre et Marie Curie, 75005 Paris, France. Dir. Jean Lacroix. circ. 1,600.

330.1   FR   ISSN 0068-4872
ECONOMIES ET SOCIETES. SERIE T. INFORMATION - RECHERCHE INNOVATION. 1959. irreg. 42 F. Institut de Sciences Mathematiques et Economiques Appliquees, Paris, Institut Henri Poincare, 11 rue Pierre et Marie Curie, 75005 Paris, France. Dir. F. Russo. circ. 1,600.

330   EC   ISSN 0070-8925
ECUADOR ECONOMICO.* a. Universidad Central del Ecuador, Instituto de Investigaciones Economicas, Casilla 1088, Quito, Ecuador.

330   CN   ISSN 0319-034X
EDUCATIONAL ABC OF CANADIAN INDUSTRY. (Editions in French & English) 1976? a. Educational ABC's of Canadian Industry Ltd., Suite 203, 696 Yonge St., Toronto, Ont. M4Y 2A7, Canada. adv.
Formerly: A B C's of Canadian Industry.

330   US
ELIOT JANEWAY LECTURES ON HISTORICAL ECONOMICS. 1978. irreg. price varies. Princeton University Press, Princeton, NJ 08540. (reprint service avail. from UMI)

330   US   ISSN 0014-0864
ESSAYS IN ECONOMICS. 1955. irreg. University of South Carolina, College of Business Administration, Division of Research, Columbia, SC 29208. Ed. Hugh S. Norton. bibl. charts. stat. circ. 1,900(controlled)

330   BL
ESTUDO DE DEFLATORES PARA A ECONOMIA DO RIO GRANDE DO SUL. 1974. irreg. Cr.$30. Fundacao de Economia e Estatistica, Rua Sigueira Campos 1044- 4 Andar, Box 2355, 90000 Porto Alegre, Brazil. stat. (also avail. in microfilm; microfiche)

382   FR   ISSN 0302-0622
EURO COOPERATION; ECONOMIC STUDIES ON EUROPE. irreg. free. Banco di Roma, 5, Avenue du Coq, F-750009 Paris, France. (Co-Sponsors: Commerzbank; Credit Lyonnais) stat.

330   UK   ISSN 0260-1508
EXHIBITOR'S HANDBOOK. 1980. a. £12. Kogan Page Ltd., 120 Pentonville Rd., London N1 9JN, England. Ed. Michael Edwards. adv. index.

330   GW   ISSN 0071-769X
F I W - SCHRIFTENREIHE. 1962. irreg., vol. 84, 1979. price varies. (Forschunginstitut fuer Wirtschaftsverfassung und Wettbewerb e.V.) Carl Heymanns Verlag KG, Gereonstr. 18-32, 5000 Cologne 1, W. Germany (B.R.D.) adv. bk. rev.

330   US
FEDERAL RESERVE BANK OF ATLANTA. WORKING PAPER SERIES. 1976. irreg. free. Federal Reserve Bank of Atlanta, Box 1731, Atlanta, GA 30301. (back issues avail.)

FEDERATION FRANCAISE ET EUROPEENNE DU COMMERCE, DE L'INDUSTRIE ET DE L'EPARGNE. REVUE. see *BUSINESS AND ECONOMICS — International Commerce*

330   CN
FINANCIAL POST SURVEY OF PREDECESSOR AND DEFUNCT COMPANIES. 1981. biennial. Can.$20. Maclean-Hunter Ltd., 481 University Ave., Toronto, Ont. M5W 1A7, Canada. Ed. Peigi Alcorn. circ. 10,000.
Aids in tracing mergers, amalgamations, name changes or charter cancellations of Canadian companies

330   PL   ISSN 0071-674X
FOLIA OECONOMICA CRACOVIENSIA. (Text in Polish; summaries in English and Russian) 1960. a. 40 Zl. (Polska Akademia Nauk, Oddzial w Krakowie, Komisja Nauk Ekonomicznych) Ossolineum, Publishing House of the Polish Academy of Sciences, Rynek 9, Wroclaw, Poland (Dist. by Ars Polona-Ruch, Krakowskie Przedmiescie 7, Warsaw, Poland) Ed. Aleksander Zelias. circ. 530.

330 650   IT
FONDAZIONE GIOVANNI AGNELLI. PROGETTO POLITICA INDUSTRIALE. QUADERNO DI RICERCA. no. 2, 1975. irreg. (Fondazione Giovanni Agnelli) Editorale Valentino, Via G. Giacosa 38, Turin 10125, Italy.

330   MX
FONDO DE CULTURA. SERIE DE LECTURAS. 1973. irreg. Fondo de Cultura Economica, Av. Universidad 975, Mexico 12, D.F., Mexico. Ed. Oscar Soberon Martinez. adv. bk. rev. bibl. circ. 5,000.

650   UK
FOUNDATION FOR BUSINESS RESPONSIBILITIES. DIALOGUES. irreg; 1972, no. 2. ‡ Foundation for Business Responsibilities, 40 Doughty St., London WC1N 2LF, England.
Formerly: Industrial Educational and Research Foundation. Dialogues.

650   UK   ISSN 0073-7410
FOUNDATION FOR BUSINESS RESPONSIBILITIES. DISCUSSION PAPER. 1965. irreg. price varies. Foundation for Business Responsibilities, 40 Doughty St., London WC1N 2LF, England. bk. rev.

650   UK   ISSN 0073-7429
FOUNDATION FOR BUSINESS RESPONSIBILITIES. OCCASIONAL PAPERS. 1965. irreg. price varies. Foundation for Business Responsibilities, 40 Doughty St., London WC1N 2LF, England. bk. rev.

658   UK   ISSN 0073-7437
FOUNDATION FOR BUSINESS RESPONSIBILITIES. RESEARCH PAPER. 1965. irreg. price varies. Foundation for Business Responsibilities, 40 Doughty St., London WC1N 2LF, England. bk. rev.

330   GW   ISSN 0067-5938
FREIE UNIVERSITAET BERLIN. OSTEUROPA-INSTITUT. WIRTSCHAFTSWISSENSCHAFTLICHE VEROEFFENTLICHUNGEN. 1954. irreg. price varies. Freie Universitaet Berlin, Osteuropa-Institut, Garystr. 55, 1000 Berlin 33 (Dahlem), W. Germany (B.R.D.) Ed.Bd. circ. 500.

FUNDACAO CENTRO DE PESQUISAS ECONOMICAS E SOCIAIS DO PIAUI. RELATORIO DE ATIVIDADES. see *SOCIOLOGY*

665.7   FR   ISSN 0072-0046
G; DOCUMENTATION TECHNIQUE ET COMMERCIALE DES VENDEURS DE GAZ. 1970. irreg. Gaz de France, Direction Commerciale, 23 rue Philibert-Delorme, 75840 Paris Cedex 17, France.
Replaces: Gaz et L'Industrie.
House organ

330   GW   ISSN 0072-0534
GEGENWARTSFRAGEN DER OST-WIRTSCHAFT. 1966. irreg. price varies. (Osteuropa-Institut, Munich) Guenter Olzog Verlag, Thierschstr. 11, 8000 Munich 22, W. Germany (B.R.D.) Eds. Hans Raupach, Werner Gumpel. bk. rev. circ. 1,000.

330   GH
GHANA ECONOMIC REVIEW. a. $2.47. Editorial and Publishing Services, Box 5743, Accra, Ghana. Ed. Moses Danquah. adv. charts, illus, stat.

GOKHALE INSTITUTE MIMEOGRAPH SERIES. see *POLITICAL SCIENCE*

GOKHALE INSTITUTE OF POLITICS AND ECONOMICS. STUDIES. see *POLITICAL SCIENCE*

BUSINESS AND ECONOMICS

330　　　　　　　GW　ISSN 0072-9566
HAMBURGER JAHRBUCH FUER
WIRTSCHAFTS- UND
GESELLSCHAFTSPOLITIK. 1956. a. price varies.
Verlag J. C. B. Mohr (Paul Siebeck), Wilhelmstr.
18, Postfach 2040, 7400 Tuebingen, W. Germany
(B.R.D.) Ed.Bd.

330　　　　　　　US　ISSN 0073-0505
HARVARD ECONOMIC STUDIES. irreg., no. 144,
1974. price varies. Harvard University Press, 79
Garden St., Cambridge, MA 02138.

330　　　　　　　US　ISSN 0073-0777
HARVARD UNIVERSITY. GRADUATE SCHOOL
OF BUSINESS ADMINISTRATION. BAKER
LIBRARY. KRESS LIBRARY OF BUSINESS
AND ECONOMICS. PUBLICATIONS. 1939.
irreg., no. 23, 1977. price varies. Harvard
University, Graduate School of Business
Administration. Baker Library, Soldiers Field Rd.,
Boston, MA 02159. (back issues avail.)

330　　　　　　　UK　ISSN 0073-2818
HOBART PAPERS. 1960. irreg. $55 (combined
subscription for all series) Institute of Economic
Affairs, 2 Lord North St., London S.W.1, England
(Dist. in North America by: Transatlantic Arts, Inc.,
88 Bridge St., Central Islip, NY 11722) (also avail.
in microfiche)

650　　　　　　　US　ISSN 0073-2907
HOFSTRA UNIVERSITY YEARBOOK OF
BUSINESS. (Each number has also a distinctive
title) 1964. irreg., latest 1980. $18. Hofstra
University, School of Business, Hempstead, NY
11550.

330.08　　　　　　　JA
HOKKAIDO ECONOMIC PAPERS. (Text in
English) 1969. irreg. Hokkaido University, Faculty
of Economics and Business Administration -
Hokkaido Daigaku Keizaigakubu, North 9, West 7,
Kitaku, Sapporo 060, Japan.

330　　　　　　　HK　ISSN 0018-4578
HONG KONG ECONOMIC PAPERS. 1961. a. $5.
Hong Kong Economic Association, Box 14004,
Hong Kong, Hong Kong (Subscr. to: United
Publishers Services (Hong Kong) Ltd., Stanhope
House, 734 Kings Rd., Hong Kong, Hong Kong)
Ed. Ronald Hsia. adv. bk. rev. circ. 1,000.

330　　　　　　　II　ISSN 0419-0432
HUKERIKAR MEMORIAL LECTURE SERIES.
(Text in English) 1964. irreg. price varies. Institute
of Economic Research, Deputy Director, Vidyagiri,
Dharwar 580004, Karnataka, India.

330　　　　　　　US　ISSN 0068-6069
I B E R SPECIAL PUBLICATIONS. 1962. irreg. $2-
$6.50. University of California, Berkeley, Institute of
Business and Economic Research, 156 Barrows Hall,
Berkeley, CA 94720. Ed. Nancy Blumenstock.

330　　　　　　　GW　ISSN 0170-5695
I F O INSTITUT FUER
WIRTSCHAFTSFORSCHUNG. STUDIEN ZU
HANDELS- UND
DIENSTLEISTUNGSFRAGEN. 1962. irreg., no.
20, 1976. price varies. I F O Institut fuer
Wirtschaftsforschung, Poschingerstr. 5, 8000
Munich 80, W. Germany (B.R.D.) circ. 500.
Formerly: I F O Institut fuer
Wirtschaftsforschung. Studien zu Handelsfragen
(ISSN 0073-4268)

330　　　　　　　US
I S E R RESEARCH NOTES. 1968. irreg., latest
issue, 1975. free. University of Alaska, Institute of
Social and Economic Research, 707 A St., Suite
206, Anchorage, AK 99501. Ed. Ronald Crowe.
Formerly: I S E G R Research Notes (ISSN
0065-5945)

338　　　　　　　II
INDIA. MINISTRY OF HEAVY INDUSTRY.
REPORT. (Text in English) 1973. irreg. Ministry of
Heavy Industry, New Delhi, India.

330　　　　　　　US
INDUSTRIAL DEVELOPMENT AND THE
SOCIAL FABRIC. 1978. irreg. price varies. J A I
Press, Box 1678, 165 W. Putnam Ave., Greenwich,
CT 06830. Ed. Glenn Porter.

330　　　　　　　UK　ISSN 0073-909X
INSTITUTE OF ECONOMIC AFFAIRS.
OCCASIONAL PAPERS. 1963. irreg. $55
(combined subscription for all series) Institute of
Economic Affairs, 2 Lord North St., London SW1,
England (Dist. in North America by: Transatlantic
Ants. Inc., 88 Bridge St., Central Islip, NY 11722)
(also avail. in microfiche)

330　　　　　　　UK　ISSN 0073-9103
INSTITUTE OF ECONOMIC AFFAIRS.
RESEARCH MONOGRAPHS. 1966. irreg. $55
(combined subscription for all series) Institute of
Economic Affairs, 2 Lord North St., London S.W.1,
England (Dist. in North America by: Transatlantic
Arts, Inc., 88 Bridge St., Central Islip, NY 11722)
(also avail. in microfiche)

330　　　　　　　II
INSTITUTE OF ECONOMIC RESEARCH.
PUBLICATIONS ON ECONOMICS. (Text in
English) irreg. price varies. Institute of Economic
Research, Deputy Director, Vidyagiri, Dharwar
580004, Karnataka, India.

330　　　　　　　US
INSTITUTE OF SOCIAL AND ECONOMIC
RESEARCH. REPORTS. 1963. irreg., no. 45, 1977.
price varies. University of Alaska, Institute of Social
and Economic Research, 707 A St., Suite 206,
Anchorage, AK 99501. Ed. Ronald Crowe.
Formerly: Institute of Social, Economic and
Government Research. Reports (ISSN 0065-5937)

330　　　　　　　AG　ISSN 0074-0349
INSTITUTO TORCUATO DI TELLA. CENTRO DE
INVESTIGACIONES ECONOMICAS.
DOCUMENTOS DE TRABAJO. 1966. irreg.,
1969, no. 45. price varies. Instituto Torcuato di
Tella, Conde 1717, Buenos Aires, Argentina. circ.
200.

330　　　　　　　CN　ISSN 0704-7584
INTERNATIONAL DEVELOPMENT RESEARCH
CENTRE. ANNUAL REPORT/CENTRE DE
RECHERCHES POUR LE DEVELOPPEMENT
INTERNATIONAL. RAPPORT ANNUEL. (Text
in English and French) 1971. a. International
Development Research Centre, Box 8500, Ottawa,
Ont. K1G 3H9, Canada. illus.

650　378　　　　　　　US　ISSN 0074-4611
INTERNATIONAL DIRECTORY OF PROGRAMS
IN BUSINESS AND COMMERCE. 1966. irreg.
American Assembly of Collegiate Schools of
Business, 11500 Olive St. Rd., Suite 142, St. Louis,
MO 63141.

330　　　　　　　UK　ISSN 0074-4646
INTERNATIONAL ECONOMIC ASSOCIATION.
PROCEEDINGS OF THE CONFERENCES AND
CONGRESSES. 1956. irreg. Macmillan Press Ltd.
(Subsidiary of: Macmillan Publishers Ltd.) 4 Little
Essex St., London WC2R 3LF, England.

330　　　　　　　US
INTERNATIONAL ECONOMIC STUDIES
INSTITUTE. CONTEMPORARY ISSUES. 1975.
irreg. International Economic Studies Institute, 1625
Eye St. N.W., Suite 907, Washington, DC 20006.

330　　　　　　　II　ISSN 0074-7068
INTERNATIONAL MONOGRAPHS ON STUDIES
IN INDIAN ECONOMICS.* (Text in English)
1969. irreg., 1970, no. 2. price varies. Hindustan
Publishing Corp., 6-U.B. Jawahar Nagar, Delhi
110007, India.

330　　　　　　　NE
INTERNATIONAL STUDIES IN ECONOMICS
AND ECONOMETRICS. (Text in English) 1969.
irreg. price varies. D. Reidel Publishing Co., P.O.
Box 17, 3300 AA Dordrecht, Netherlands (And
Lincoln Building, 160 Old Derby St., Hingham, MA
02043) (back issues avail.)

332　338　　　　　　　FR
INVENTAIRES ECONOMIQUES ET
INDUSTRIELS REGIONAUX. (Separate volumes
for each region) (Text and summaries in English,
French, German and Spanish) 1976. a. price varies
per regional volume. Société Nouvelle d'Editions
pour l'Industrie, 22, Avenue Franklin D. Roosevelt,
75008 Paris, France. charts. stat.

330　　　　　　　CN
INVENTORY OF INDUSTRIAL PARKS IN
QUEBEC. 1977. a. Department of Industry and
Commerce, Industrial Infrastructure Division, 1
Place Ville-Maria, 23rd Floor, Montreal, Que. H3B
3M6, Canada. circ. 2,500.

330　　　　　　　IT　ISSN 0075-1529
ISTITUTO MOBILIARE ITALIANO. ANNUAL
REPORT. (Editions in English & Italian) 1932. a. ‡
Istituto Mobiliare Italiano, 25 Viale dell' Arte,
00144 Rome, Italy. circ. 2,400.

330　　　　　　　US　ISSN 0075-2045
J. ANDERSON FITZGERALD LECTURE. 1959.
irreg., 1969, no. 5. price varies. University of Texas
at Austin, Bureau of Business Research, Austin, TX
78712.

330　340　336.2　　　　　　　GW　ISSN 0075-2886
JAHRESFACHKATALOG RECHT-WIRTSCHAFT-
STEUERN. 1949. a. DM.31.30. Werbegemeinschaft
Elwert und Meurer, Hauptstr. 101, 1000 Berlin 62,
W. Germany (B.R.D.) adv. bk. rev.

JEWISH AGENCY FOR ISRAEL. OFFICE FOR
ECONOMIC AND SOCIAL RESEARCH.
ANNUAL. see SOCIAL SCIENCES:
COMPREHENSIVE WORKS

330　　　　　　　US　ISSN 0361-6576
JOURNAL OF ECONOMICS. 1975. a. $9. Missouri
Valley Economic Association, c/o J. F. Schwier,
Ed., 4378 Lindell Blvd., St. Louis, MO 63108
(Orders to: c/o Dr. Donald Schilling, 217
Middlebush, UM-C, Columbia, MO 65201) bk. rev.
circ. 350.

JYVASKYLA STUDIES IN COMPUTER SCIENCE,
ECONOMICS AND STATISTICS. see
COMPUTER TECHNOLOGY AND
APPLICATIONS

320　330　　　　　　　US
KAPITALISTATE. 1973. irreg., approx 1/yr. $12 for
4 nos. to individuals; institutions $24. Box 5138,
Palo Alto, CA 94705. adv. bk. rev. bibl. circ. 5,000.
(back issues avail.)
Formerly: Working Papers on the Kapitalistate.

650　　　　　　　JA　ISSN 0453-4557
KEIO BUSINESS REVIEW. (Text in English) vol. 15,
1978. a. price varies. Keio University Society of
Business and Commerce, c/o Faculty of Business
and Commerce, Mita Minato-ku, Tokyo 108, Japan
(Dist. by: Japan Publications Trading Co., Ltd., P.O.
Box 5030 Tokyo International, Tokyo, Japan) Ed.
Tadahiro Yamamasu. charts. stat.

650　　　　　　　JA　ISSN 0075-5346
KEIO MONOGRAPHS OF BUSINESS AND
COMMERCE. 1967. irreg., 1971, no. 3. price
varies. (Keio University Society of Business and
Commerce) Japan Publications Trading Co. Ltd.,
Box 5030, Tokyo International, Tokyo 100-31,
Japan (Or 1255 Howard St., San Francisco, CA
94103)

650　330　　　　　　　US　ISSN 0078-4184
KENT STATE UNIVERSITY. CENTER FOR
BUSINESS AND ECONOMIC RESEARCH.
COMPARATIVE ADMINISTRATION
RESEARCH INSTITUTE SERIES. 1968. irreg.,
1970, no. 2. price varies. Kent State University,
Center for Business and Economic Research, Kent,
OH 44242. circ. 1,000.

330　650　　　　　　　US　ISSN 0078-4206
KENT STATE UNIVERSITY. CENTER FOR
BUSINESS AND ECONOMIC RESEARCH.
PRINTED SERIES. 1962. irreg., 1968, no. 9. price
varies. Kent State University, Center for Business
and Economic Research, Kent, OH 44242. circ.
1,000.

330　650　　　　　　　US　ISSN 0078-4214
KENT STATE UNIVERSITY. CENTER FOR
BUSINESS AND ECONOMIC RESEARCH.
RESEARCH PAPERS. 1964. irreg., 1968, no. 6.
price varies. Kent State University, Center for
Business and Economic Research, Kent, OH 44242.
circ. 500.

330　380　　　　　　　KE
KENYA ENTERPRISE; incorporating trade directory.
a. EAs.100. Translinkers Publishing Co., Box 44169,
Nairobi, Kenya.

330 JA ISSN 0075-6415
KOBE ECONOMIC AND BUSINESS RESEARCH SERIES. (Text in English) 1962. irreg. exchange basis. Kobe University, Research Institute for Economics and Business Administration, Rokkaido-cho, Nada-ku, Kobe, Japan. Eds. K. Itow, H. Yamamoto. circ. 500.

330 JA ISSN 0075-6407
KOBE ECONOMIC AND BUSINESS REVIEW. (Text in English) 1953. a. exchange basis. Kobe University, Research Institute for Economics and Business Administration, Rokkaido-cho, Nada-ku, Kobe. Japan. Eds. K. Itow, H. Yamamoto. circ. 450.

330 JA ISSN 0454-1111
KOBE UNIVERSITY ECONOMIC REVIEW. (Text in English) 1955. a. Kobe University, Faculty of Economics, Rokkodai-cho, Nadu-ku, Kobe, Japan.

330 HU ISSN 0075-6989
KOZGAZDASAGI ERTEKEZESEK. 1962. irreg. price varies. (Magyar Tudomanyos Akademia) Akademiai Kiado, Publishing House of the Hungarian Academy of Sciences, P.O. Box 24, H-1363 Budapest, Hungary.

338 NO ISSN 0452-7208
KRISTOFER LEHMKUHL FORELESNING. 1958. a. free. Norges Handelshoeyskole - Norwegian School of Economics and Business Administration, Helleveien 30, 5000 Bergen, Norway. circ. 500.

330 UK ISSN 0076-0668
L S E RESEARCH MONOGRAPHS.* irreg., 1969, no. 4. (London School of Economics and Political Science) Weidenfeld and Nicolson Ltd., 5 Winsley St., Oxford Circus, London W.1, England (Dist. in U.S. by: Humanities Press, Inc., 303 Park Ave. S., New York, NY 10010)

LECTURE NOTES IN ECONOMICS AND MATHEMATICAL SYSTEMS; Operations Research, Computer Science, Social Science. see *MATHEMATICS*

LEGAL CONNECTION: CORPORATIONS AND LAW FIRMS; a directory of publicly-held corporations and their law firms. see *LAW*

338 FI
LIIKEARKISTOYHDISTYS. JULKAISUJA. 1963. irreg., no. 5, 1979. price varies. Liikearkistoyhistys r.y. - Finnish Business Archives Association, Box 271, SF-00101 Helsinki 10, Finland. Ed. Ossi Jokimies. adv.

338 UK
LONDON SCHOOL OF BUSINESS. CENTRE FOR ECONOMIC FORECASTING. ECONOMIC OUTLOOK. irreg. London School of Business, Centre for Economic Forecasting, Sussex Place, Regent's Park, London NW1 4SA, England.

330 UK
LOUGHBOROUGH OCCASIONAL PAPERS IN ECONOMICS. irreg. free. Loughborough University of Technology, Department of Economics, Loughborough, Leics. LE11 3TU, England. circ. 50(controlled) (back issues avail.)

330 US
LOUISIANA TECH UNIVERSITY. RESEARCH MONOGRAPH SERIES. 1958. irreg. $2. Louisiana Tech University, Division of Administration and Business Research, Box 5796, Ruston, LA 71270. Dir. Dr. James R. Michael. circ. controlled. (tabloid format)

330 JM
M D C BUSINESS JOURNAL. 1976. irreg. Management Development Centre, Salvatori Building, P.O. Box 1301, Port of Spain, Trinidad.

330 650 MH
MACAU INDUSTRY. 1977. a. Macau Business Centre. Edificio Ribeiro, P.O. Box 138, Macao. stat.

330 IS ISSN 0076-5473
MAURICE FALK INSTITUTE FOR ECONOMIC RESEARCH IN ISRAEL. REPORT. (Editions in English and Hebrew) 1964-66. triennial. Maurice Falk Institute for Economic Research in Israel, 17 Keren Hayesod St., Jerusalem, Israel.

650 CN
MEETINGS, CONFERENCES & CONVENTIONS: A FINANCIAL POST GUIDE. 1969. a. Maclean-Hunter Ltd., 481 University Ave., Toronto, Ont. M5W 1A7, Canada. Ed. Ann Rhodes. adv. charts. illus. circ. controlled.
Formerly: Financial Post Report on Conventions, Conferences and Business Meetings.

338.7 II ISSN 0376-5423
MEGHALAYA INDUSTRIAL DEVELOPMENT CORPORATION. ANNUAL REPORT. (Text in English) 1972. a. Meghalaya Industrial Development Corporation, Additional Civil Secretariat Bldg., Shillong 1, India. Key Title: Annual Report--Meghalaya Industrial Development Corporation.

650 US ISSN 0076-7832
MICHIGAN BUSINESS CASES. 1964. irreg. price varies. University of Michigan, Graduate School of Business Administration, Division of Research, Tappan and Monroe Sts., Ann Arbor, MI 48109. Ed.Bd. (reprint service avail. from UMI)

650 US ISSN 0076-7840
MICHIGAN BUSINESS PAPERS. 1937. irreg., no. 62, 1977. price varies. University of Michigan, Graduate School of Business Administration, Division of Research, Ann Arbor, MI 48109. Ed. Bd. (reprint service avail. from UMI)

650 US ISSN 0076-7859
MICHIGAN BUSINESS REPORTS. 1938. irreg., no. 60, 1977. price varies. University of Michigan, Graduate School of Business Administration, Division of Research, Ann Arbor, MI 48109. Ed. Bd. (reprint service avail. from UMI)

650 US ISSN 0076-7867
MICHIGAN BUSINESS STUDIES. 1926; N.S. 1975. irreg., N.S. no. 3, 1977. price varies. University of Michigan, Graduate School of Business Administration, Division of Research, Ann Arbor, MI 48109. Ed. Bd. (reprint service avail. from UMI)

650 US ISSN 0076-7972
MICHIGAN INTERNATIONAL BUSINESS STUDIES. 1963. irreg. price varies. University of Michigan, Graduate School of Business Administration, Division of Research, Ann Arbor, MI 48109. Ed. Bd. (reprint service avail. from UMI)

MIDDLE EAST YEARBOOK. see *POLITICAL SCIENCE*

338.9 AG
MIRADOR; panorama de la civilizacion industrial. (Text in Spanish, summaries in English, French, Portuguese) 1958. irreg. Editorial Mirador, Santiago del Estero 315, Buenos Aires, Argentina. Ed. C. Levin. bk. rev. illus.

650 AT ISSN 0311-2780
MITCHELL BUSINESS REVIEW. 1974. a. Aus.$2. Mitchell College of Advanced Education, Business and Administration Society, Bathurst, NSW 2795, Australia. Ed. John Priest.

330 MY
MONOGRAPH SERIES ON MALAYSIAN ECONOMIC AFFAIRS. 1971. irreg., no. 4, 1977. University of Malaya, Faculty of Economics & Administration, Lembah Pantai, Kuala Lumpur 22-11, Malaysia. Ed. Mrs. Khoo Siew Mun. bibl. circ. 1,000.

330 BE
MUSEE ROYAL DE L'AFRIQUE CENTRALE. DOCUMENTATION ECONOMIQUE/ KONINKLIJK MUSEUM VOOR MIDDEN-AFRIKA. ECONOMISCHE DOCUMENTATIE. 1961. irreg., no. 3, 1973. price varies. Musee Royal de l'Afrique Centrale, 13 Steenweg op Leuven, B-1980 Tervuren, Belgium.

MUSZAKI ES GAZDASAGI FEJLODES FO IRANYAI/MAIN TRENDS OF TECHNICAL AND ECONOMIC DEVELOPMENT. see *TECHNOLOGY: COMPREHENSIVE WORKS*

N A B T E REVIEW. (National Association for Business Teacher Education) see *EDUCATION — Higher Education*

330.72 US ISSN 0077-3611
NATIONAL BUREAU OF ECONOMIC RESEARCH. ANNUAL REPORT. 1920. a. free. National Bureau of Economic Research, 1050 Massachusetts Ave, Cambridge, MA 02138.

330 US ISSN 0077-3638
NATIONAL BUREAU OF ECONOMIC RESEARCH. GENERAL SERIES. 1921. irreg., no. 101, 1974. price varies. National Bureau of Economic Research, 1050 Massachusetts Ave, Cambridge, MA 02138 (Since 1964 Dist. by: Columbia University Press, 136 South Broadway, Irvington-on-Hudson, N.Y. 10533) Indexed: SSCI.

338.9 US
NATIONAL BUREAU OF ECONOMIC RESEARCH. URBAN AND REGIONAL STUDIES. 1972. irreg., no. 4, 1976. $17.50. National Bureau of Economic Research, 1050 Massachusetts Ave, Cambridge, MA 02138.

330.72 US
NATIONAL BUREAU OF ECONOMIC RESEARCH. WORKING PAPER. no. 329, 1979. irreg. National Bureau of Economic Research, 1050 Massachusetts Ave., Cambridge, MA 02138.

330 301 UK ISSN 0070-8453
NATIONAL INSTITUTE OF ECONOMIC AND SOCIAL RESEARCH, LONDON. ECONOMIC AND SOCIAL STUDIES. 1946. irreg., no. 32, 1980. $39.50 for latest vol. Cambridge University Press, Box 110, Cambridge CB2 3RL, England (and 32 E. 57 St., New York, NY 10022) index.

330 UK ISSN 0077-4928
NATIONAL INSTITUTE OF ECONOMIC AND SOCIAL RESEARCH, LONDON. OCCASIONAL PAPERS. 1946. irreg., no. 32, 1980. $29.50 for latest vol. Cambridge University Press, Box 110, Cambridge CB2 3RL, England (and 32 E. 57 St., New York NY 10022)

330.1 UK
NATIONAL INSTITUTE OF ECONOMIC AND SOCIAL RESEARCH, LONDON. REGIONAL PAPERS. 1970. irreg., no. 3, 1974. $13.95 for latest vol. Cambridge University Press, Box 110, Cambridge CB2 3RL, England (and 32 E. 57 St., New York NY 10022)
Formerly: National Institute of Economic and Social Research, London. Regional Studies (ISSN 0077-4936)

NEW AFRICAN YEARBOOK. see *POLITICAL SCIENCE*

330 NZ ISSN 0077-9954
NEW ZEALAND ECONOMIC PAPERS. 1967. a; biennial until 1971. $4. ‡ New Zealand Association of Economists, P.O. Box 568, Wellington, New Zealand. Ed. G.R. Hawke. bk. rev. circ. 450.

330 NZ ISSN 0078-0049
NEW ZEALAND INSTITUTE OF ECONOMIC RESEARCH. DISCUSSION PAPER. 1961. irreg. price varies. New Zealand Institute of Economic Research, P.O. Box 3479, Wellington 1, New Zealand. Ed. S.M. Usher.

330 NZ ISSN 0078-0057
NEW ZEALAND INSTITUTE OF ECONOMIC RESEARCH. REPORT. 1960. a. NZ.$3. New Zealand Institute of Economic Research, P.O. Box 3479, Wellington, New Zealand. Ed. S.M. Usher.

330 NZ ISSN 0078-0065
NEW ZEALAND INSTITUTE OF ECONOMIC RESEARCH. RESEARCH PAPER. 1961. irreg., no. 25, 1979. price varies. New Zealand Institute of Economic Research, Box 3479, Wellington, New Zealand. Ed. S.M Usher.

330 NZ ISSN 0078-0073
NEW ZEALAND INSTITUTE OF ECONOMIC RESEARCH. TECHNICAL MEMORANDUM. 1961. irreg, no. 19, 1978. price varies. New Zealand Institute of Economic Research, P.O. Box 3479, Wellington 1, New Zealand. Ed. S.M. Usher.

338.1 NR ISSN 0331-0361
NIGERIAN ECONOMIC SOCIETY. PROCEEDINGS OF THE ANNUAL CONFERENCE. a. Nigerian Economic Society, c/o Dept. of Economics, University of Ibadan, Ibadan, Nigeria.

NIGERIAN INSTITUTE OF SOCIAL AND
ECONOMIC RESEARCH. ANNUAL REPORT.
see *SOCIAL SCIENCES: COMPREHENSIVE
WORKS*

338   NE
NIJENRODE STUDIES IN BUSINESS. 1977. irreg.
price varies. Martinus Nijhoff, Box 566, 2501 CN
The Hague, Netherlands.

330.1   NO   ISSN 0078-1029
NORD-NORGE NAERINGSLIV OG OEKONOMI.
1948. irreg. price varies. Studieselskapet for Nord-
Norsk Naeringsliv, Sjoegaten 15, 8001 Bodoe,
Norway. cum. index nos. 1-41 in vol. 41.

330   CN
OBSERVATIONS. 1974. irreg. Can.$5. C. D. Howe
Research Institute, Suite 2064, 1155 Metcalfe St.,
Montreal, Que. H3B 2X7, Canada. (also avail. in
microform from MML) Indexed: Can. B.P.I.
    Formerly (until 1980): H R I Observations (ISSN
0381-5250)

330   US   ISSN 0149-1091
O'DWYER'S DIRECTORY OF CORPORATE
COMMUNICATIONS. 1975. a. $60. J. R.
O'Dwyer Co., Inc., 271 Madison Ave., New York,
NY 10016. Ed. Jack O'Dwyer. adv. stat. index.

330   US   ISSN 0078-3390
OEKONOMETRIE UND
UNTERNEHMENSFORSCHUNG/
ECONOMETRICS AND OPERATIONS
RESEARCH. (Text in German; occasionally in
English) 1962. irreg., no. 21, 1976. price varies.
Springer-Verlag, 175 Fifth Ave., New York, NY
10010 (also Berlin, Heidelberg, Vienna) (reprint
service avail. from ISI)

330   GE   ISSN 0078-3404
OEKONOMISCHE STUDIENTEXTE. 1959. irreg.
price varies. (Akademie der Wissenschaften der
DDR, Zentralinstitut fuer
Wirtschaftswissenschaften) Akademie-Verlag,
Leipziger Str. 3-4, 108 Berlin, E. Germany (D.D.R.)

330   AU   ISSN 0078-3595
OESTERREICHISCHES WIRTSCHAFTSINSTITUT
FUER STRUKTURFORSCHUNG UND
STRUKTURPOLITIK. SCHRIFTENREIHE. 1968.
irreg. free. Oesterreichisches Wirtschaftsinstitut fuer
Strukturforschung und Strukturpolitik, Hessenplatz,
A-4020 Linz, Austria. Ed. Albert Leibenfrost. circ.
2,000.
    Formerly: Oesterreichisches Institut fuer
Mittelstandspolitik. Schriftenreihe.

333   JA
OITA UNIVERSITY. RESEARCH INSTITUTE OF
ECONOMICS. BULLETIN. (Text in Japanese)
1967. a. Oita University, Research Institute of
Economics, Oita, Japan.

330   US
OKLAHOMA COUNCIL ON ECONOMIC
EDUCATION NEWSLETTER. 1961. a.
membership. Oklahoma Council on Economic
Education, Oklahoma State Univ., Rm. 112 Business
Bldg., Stillwater, OK 74074. Ed. Clayton
Millington. circ. 5,000.

330   650   US
OKLAHOMA STATE UNIVERSITY. COLLEGE
OF BUSINESS ADMINISTRATION. WORKING
PAPERS. 1966. irreg., no. 77-25, latest. free.
Oklahoma State University, College of Business
Administration, Office of Business and Economic
Research, Stillwater, OK 74074.
    Supersedes: Oklahoma State University. College
of Business Administration. Extension Service.
Business Papers (ISSN 0078-4427)

330   CN
ONTARIO ECONOMIC COUNCIL. RESEARCH
STUDIES. no. 3, 1976. irreg. Can.$5.75. University
of Toronto Press, Toronto, Ont., Canada.

658   CN   ISSN 0078-5083
ONTARIO RESEARCH FOUNDATION. ANNUAL
REPORT. 1928. a. free. Ontario Research
Foundation, Dept. of Marketing Services, Sheridan
Park, Ont. L5K 1B3, Canada.

330   PL   ISSN 0474-2893
OPOLSKIE ROCZNIKI EKONOMICZNE. 1968. a.
price varies. (Polskie Towarzystwo Ekonomiczne,
Oddzial w Opolu) Panstwowe Wydawnictwo
Naukowe, Miodowa 10, Warsaw, Poland.

330   US   ISSN 0078-5784
OREGON STATE MONOGRAPHS. STUDIES IN
ECONOMICS. 1939. irreg., latest no.6. price varies.
Oregon State University Press, 101 Waldo Hall,
Corvallis, OR 97331.

330   JA   ISSN 0078-6640
OSAKA CITY UNIVERSITY ECONOMIC
REVIEW.* (Text in English, French, German and
other languages) 1965. a. 1000 Yen. Osaka City
University, Faculty of Economics, 459 Sugimoto-
cho, Sumiyoshi-ku, Osaka 558, Japan.

OSTEUROPASTUDIEN DER HOCHSCHULEN
DES LANDES HESSEN. REIHE 1. GIESSENER
ABHANDLUNGEN ZUR AGRAR- UND
WIRTSCHAFTSFORSCHUNG DES
EUROPAEISCHEN OSTENS. see
AGRICULTURE — Agricultural Economics

330   US
PACIFIC NORTHWEST METALS AND
MINERALS CONFERENCE. PROCEEDINGS
OF GOLD AND MONEY SESSION AND
GOLD TECHNICAL SESSION. 1960. irreg., 5th,
1975, Portland, Oregon. price varies. Department of
Geology and Mineral Industries, 1069 State Office
Bldg., Portland, OR 97201.

338.9   PK   ISSN 0078-821X
PAKISTAN INSTITUTE OF DEVELOPMENT
ECONOMICS. REPORT. (Text in English) 1962.
irreg., latest issue, 1969. Pakistan Institute of
Development Economics, Box No. 1091, Islamabad,
Pakistan. circ. 1,000.

338.9   PK   ISSN 0078-8228
PAKISTAN INSTITUTE OF DEVELOPMENT
ECONOMICS. RESEARCH REPORT. (Text in
English) 1963. irreg. price varies. Pakistan Institute
of Development Economics, P.O. Box 1091,
Islamabad, Pakistan. circ. controlled.

330   US
PENNSYLVANIA CONFERENCE OF
ECONOMISTS. PROCEEDINGS OF THE
ANNUAL MEETING. 1951. a. $15. Pennsylvania
Conference of Economists, c/o Alexander Garvin,
Economics Dept., Indiana University of
Pennsylvania, Indiana, PA 15701. Ed. Joseph
Horton. charts. circ. 500. (back issues avail.)

650   US   ISSN 0079-0540
PENNSYLVANIA STATE UNIVERSITY.
COLLEGE OF BUSINESS ADMINISTRATION.
CENTER FOR RESEARCH. OCCASIONAL
PAPERS. 1964. irreg. price varies. Pennsylvania
State University, College of Business
Administration, Center for Research, 801 Business
Administration Building, University Park, PA
16802.

PERGAMON MANAGEMENT AND BUSINESS
SERIES. see *BUSINESS AND ECONOMICS —
Management*

330   FR
PERSPECTIVES DE L'ECONOMIQUE. SERIE 2.
ECONOMIE CONTEMPORAINE. 1969. irreg.
price varies. Editions Calmann-Levy, 3 rue Auber,
Paris 9e, France. Ed. Christian Schmidt.

330   FR
PERSPECTIVES DE L'ECONOMIQUE. SERIE 3.
CRITIQUE. 1969. irreg. price varies. Editions
Calmann-Levy, 3 rue Auber, Paris 9e, France. Ed.
Christian Schmidt.

330   PL
POLITECHNIKA GDANSKA. ZESZYTY
NAUKOWE. EKONOMIA. (Text in Polish;
summaries in English and Russian) 1967. irreg. price
varies. Politechnika Gdanska, Majakowskiego 11/12,
81-952 Gdansk 6, Poland (Dist. by: Osrodek
Rozpowszechniania Wydawnictw Naukowych Pan,
Palac Kultury i Nauki, 00-901 Warsaw, Poland)

330   PL   ISSN 0137-6306
POLITECHNIKA WROCLAWSKA. OSRODEK
BADAN PROGNOSTYCZNYCH. PRACE
NAUKOWE. KONFERENCJE. (Text in Polish;
summaries in English and Russian) 1975. irreg.,
1977, no. 6. price varies. Politechnika Wroclawska,
Wybrzeze Wyspianskiego 27, 50-370 Wroclaw,
Poland (Dist. by: Ars Polona-Ruch, Krakowskie
Przedmiescie 7, Warsaw, Poland) Ed. Marian Kloza.

330   CN   ISSN 0381-1603
POLITICAL ECONOMY SERIES. 1938. irreg.
University of Toronto Press, Front Campus,
Toronto, Ont. M5S 1A6, Canada.

330   PL   ISSN 0079-3353
POLSKA AKADEMIA NAUK. ODDZIAL W
KRAKOWIE. KOMISJA NAUK
EKONOMICZNYCH. PRACE. (Text in Polish;
summaries in English) 1960. irreg. price varies.
Ossolineum, Publishing House of the Polish
Academy of Sciences, Rynek 9, 50-106 Wroclaw,
Poland (Dist. by Ars Polona-Ruch, Krakowskie
Przedmiescie 7, Warsaw, Poland)

330   FR
PREVISIONS GLISSANTES DETAILLEES 1979-
1984. a. Bureau d'Informations et de Previsions
Economiques, 122 Av Charles de Gaulle, 92522
Neuilly sur Seine, France.
    Former titles: Previson a Moyen Terme de
l'Economie Francaise & Prevision Glissante a Cinq
Ans.

330   510   US   ISSN 0079-5240
PRINCETON STUDIES IN MATHEMATICAL
ECONOMICS. 1964. irreg., latest, no. 7. price
varies. Princeton University Press, Princeton, NJ
08540. Ed.Bd. (reprint service avail. from UMI)

330   US   ISSN 0079-5291
PRINCETON UNIVERSITY. ECONOMETRIC
RESEARCH PROGRAM. RESEARCH
MEMORANDUM. 1957. irreg., no. 221, 1977. $1-
3. Princeton University, Econometric Research
Program, Department of Economics, 207 Dickinson
Hall, Princeton, NJ 08540. (back issues avail.)

PROBLEMS IN A BUSINESS SOCIETY. see
SOCIOLOGY

330   US
PROBLEMS OF THE MODERN ECONOMY
SERIES. irreg. price varies. W. W. Norton &
Company, Inc., 500 Fifth Avenue, New York, NY
10036.

330.1   FR   ISSN 0079-5984
PROFITS. 1970. irreg. price varies. Tchou Editeur, 6
rue du Mail, Paris 2e, France.

330   US
PROGRAMME FOR GROWTH SERIES. 1964.
irreg., vol. 12, 1974. price varies. Halsted Press
(Subsidiary of: John Wiley & Sons, Inc.) 605 Third
Ave, New York, NY 10016. Ed. R. Stone.

330   CN   ISSN 0316-5078
QUEEN'S UNIVERSITY. INSTITUTE FOR
ECONOMIC RESEARCH. DISCUSSION PAPER.
1969. irreg. Can.$200. Queen's University, Institute
for Economic Research, Kingston. Ont. K7L 3N6,
Canada. bibl. circ. 200.

330   US
R & D ECONOMIC COMMENT. 1974. irreg. free.
Mississippi Research and Development Center,
Drawer 2470, Jackson, MS 39205. charts. stat. circ.
6,000.

R.B.R.R. KALE MEMORIAL LECTURES. see
POLITICAL SCIENCE

330   UK   ISSN 0305-814X
READING IN POLITICAL ECONOMY. 1967.
irreg., no. 25, 1980. $55 (combined subscription for
all series) Institute of Economic Affairs, 2 Lord
North St., London S.W.1, England (Dist. in North
America by: Transatlantic Arts, Inc., 88 Bridge St.,
Central Islip, NY 11722) adv. bk. rev. (also avail. in
microfiche)
    Formerly: Readings in Political Economy (ISSN
0079-9874)

330   GW
REDEN ZUR WIRTSCHAFTSPOLITIK. 1973. irreg.
Bundesministerium fuer Wirtschaft, 5300 Bonn, W.
Germany (B.R.D.) illus.

330 US ISSN 0080-0627
REGIONAL SCIENCE RESEARCH INSTITUTE, PHILADELPHIA. MONOGRAPH SERIES. 1965. irreg. price varies. Regional Science Research Institute, 256 N. Pleasant St., Wentworth Bldg., Amherst, MA 01002. Ed. Benjamin H. Stevens. (reprint service avail. from UMI)

330 US
RESEARCH IN CORPORATE SOCIAL PERFORMANCE AND POLICY; an annual compilation of research. 1978. a. $17.25 to individuals; institutions $34.50. J A I Press, Box 1678, 165 W. Putnam Ave., Greenwich, CT 06830. Ed. Lee Preston.

330 650 US ISSN 0080-1631
RESEARCH IN ECONOMICS/BUSINESS ADMINISTRATION. 1959. irreg., 1975, no. 21. price varies. University of North Carolina at Chapel Hill, Graduate School of Business Administration, Chapel Hill, NC 27514. Ed.Bd. circ. 400-1,400. Indexed: J. of Econ.Lit.

330 340 US ISSN 0193-5895
RESEARCH IN LAW AND ECONOMICS. 1979. a. $16.25 to individuals; institutions $32.50. J A I Press, Box 1678, 165 W. Putnam Ave., Greenwich, CT 06830. Ed. Richard O. Zerbe.

330 II
REVIEW OF COMMERCE STUDIES. 1972. a. Rs.10($2.50) University of Delhi, School of Economics, Department of Commerce, Delhi 110007, India. Ed. A. B. Ghosh. (back issues avail)

330 JA ISSN 0302-6574
REVIEW OF ECONOMICS AND BUSINESS. (Text in English) 1972. (Kansai University) Kansai University Press, 3-3-35 Yamate-cho, Suita-shi 564, Osaka, Japan. Ed. Ikutu Ueno. stat.

330 VE
REVISTA DE ECONOMIA. 1961. a. Universidad de Los Andes, Facultad de Economia, Merida, Venezuela.
Formerly: Economia (ISSN 0070-8399)

330 US ISSN 0080-2972
RICHARD J. GONZALEZ LECTURE. Title varies: Gonzalez Lecture Series. 1966. irreg., no. 5, 1974. price varies. University of Texas at Austin, Bureau of Business Research, Austin, TX 78712.

330 BE
RIJKSUNIVERSITEIT TE GENT. FACULTEIT VAN DE ECONOMISCHE WETENSCHAPPEN. WERKEN. irreg. Rijksuniversiteit te Gent, Faculteit van de Economische Wetenschappen, Hoveniersberg 4, B-9000 Ghent, Belgium. Ed. E. de Lembre, W. Georges.

330 PL ISSN 0080-343X
ROCZNIK EKONOMICZNY. 1961. a. price varies. Panstwowe Wydawnictwo Naukowe, Ul. Miodowa 10, Warsaw, Poland. Ed.Bd. adv. bk. rev. circ. 600-700.

330 650 US ISSN 0068-5836
SAN DIEGO STATE UNIVERSITY. BUREAU OF BUSINESS AND ECONOMIC RESEARCH. MONOGRAPHS. irreg. price varies. San Diego State University, Bureau of Business and Economic Research, School of Business Administration, San Diego, CA 92182.

330 650 US ISSN 0068-5844
SAN DIEGO STATE UNIVERSITY. BUREAU OF BUSINESS AND ECONOMIC RESEARCH. RESEARCH STUDIES AND POSITION PAPERS. 1965. no. 2. irreg., 1968, no. 18. price varies. San Diego State University, Bureau of Business and Economic Research, School of Business Administration, San Diego, CA 92182.

330.1 GW
SCHRIFTEN ZUR WIRTSCHAFTSWISSENSCHAFTLICHEN FORSCHUNG. 1962. irreg., no. 134, 1979. price varies. Verlag Anton Hain GmbH, Adelheidstr. 2, Postfach 1220, 6240 Koenigstein, W. Germany (B.R.D.) Ed. Bd.

380 US ISSN 0275-7443
SECOND 1,500 COMPANIES. 1980. a. $100. Economic Information Systems, 310 Madison Ave., New York, NY 10017.

330 KO
SEOUL NATIONAL UNIVERSITY. ECONOMIC REVIEW.* (Text in English, French and German) 1967. a. free. Seoul National University, College of Commerce, Institute of Economic Research, 19 Jongam-Dong Sungbuk-Gu, Seoul, S. Korea (Subscr. to: Publishing Center of Seoul National University, 199 Dongsung-Dong Jongro-Gu, Seoul, S. Korea) bk. rev. charts. illus. stat.

330 CK
SERIE ECONOMIA COLOMBIANA. 1975. irreg. $2.50. Ediciones Tiempo Presente, Bogota, Colombia. charts. stat.

330 BL
SERIE PENSAMENTO ECONOMICO BRASILEIRO. 1975. irreg. price varis. Instituto de Planejamento Economico e Social, Caixa Postal 2672, Rio de Janeiro, Brazil. Ed. A.F. Vilar de Queiroz.

650 UK
SIR FREDERIC HOOPER AWARD ESSAY. 1969. a. membership. Foundation for Business Responsibilities, 40 Doughty St., London WC1N 2LF, England.

338 320 UK ISSN 0080-9780
SIR GEORGE EARLE MEMORIAL LECTURE ON INDUSTRY AND GOVERNMENT. 1966. a. price varies. Foundation for Business Responsibilities, 40 Doughty St., London WC1N 2LF, England. bk. rev.

SOCIAAL-ECONOMISCHE RAAD. VERSLAG. see SOCIOLOGY

340 BL
SOCIEDADES POR ACOES. 1977. irreg. Editora Resenha Universitaria, Rua Quatinga 12, 04140 Sao Paulo, Brazil.

330 US ISSN 0073-4942
SOUTHERN ILLINOIS UNIVERSITY, CARBONDALE. BUSINESS RESEARCH BUREAU. REGIONAL STUDIES IN BUSINESS AND ECONOMICS. MONOGRAPHS.* 1965. irreg. Southern Illinois University, Carbondale, Business Research Bureau, Carbondale, IL 62901.

330 SP
SPAIN. INSTITUTO NACIONAL DE INDUSTRIA. MEMORIA I N I (YEAR) a. Instituto Nacional de Industria, Plaza de Salamanca 8, Madrid, Spain. charts. stat.

330 SP
SPAIN. INSTITUTO NACIONAL DE INDUSTRIA. PROGRAMA DE INVESTIGACIONES ECONOMICAS: SERIE E. no. 8, 1977. irreg. Instituto Nacional de Industria, Programa de Investigaciones Economicas, Plaza del Marque de Salamanca 8-30, Madrid 6, Spain.

332.1 US ISSN 0081-3559
SPECIAL PAPERS IN INTERNATIONAL ECONOMICS. 1955. irreg., no. 14, 1980. $25 (includes Essays in International Finance; Reprints in International Finance; Studies in International Finance) ‡ Princeton University, International Finance Section, Dept. of Economics, Dickinson Hall, Princeton, NJ 08544. Dir. Peter B. Kenen. circ. 2,000. (also avail. in microfilm from UMI; back issues avail.; reprint service avail. from UMI)

330 GW ISSN 0531-9323
STATISTISCHE STUDIEN. irreg. price varies. (Universitaet Erlangen-Nuernberg, Institut fuer Statistik) Franz Steiner Verlag GmbH, Friedrichstr. 24, Postfach 5529, 6200 Wiesbaden, W. Germany (B.R.D.) Ed. Ingeborg Esenwein-Rothe.

330 PL ISSN 0081-6930
STUDIA SPOLECZNO-EKONOMICZNE. 1968. irreg., latest issue 1979, no. 9. 35 Zl. Instytut Slaski, Instytut Naukowo-Badawczy, Luboszycka 3, Opole, Poland.

330 RM ISSN 0578-5472
STUDIA UNIVERSITATIS "BABES-BOLYAI." OECONOMICA. (Text in Romanian; summaries in English, French, German, Russian) 1960. s-a. exchange basis. Universitatea "Babes-Bolyai", Biblioteca Centrala Universitara, Str. Clinicilor nr. 2, Cluj-Napoca, Romania.

330 NE
STUDIES IN BAYESIAN ECONOMETRICS. 1979. irreg., vol. 3, 1979. price varies. North-Holland Publishing Co., Box 211, 1000 AE Amsterdam, Netherlands.

650 US ISSN 0081-7635
STUDIES IN BUSINESS AND SOCIETY. 1965. irreg., latest 1977. price varies. (University of Chicago, Graduate School of Business) University of Chicago Press, 5801 S. Ellis Ave., Chicago, IL 60637. (reprint service avail. from UMI,ISI)

STUDIES IN DEVELOPMENT AND PLANNING. see BUSINESS AND ECONOMICS — International Development And Assistance

330 UK ISSN 0081-7856
STUDIES IN ECONOMICS. 1970. irreg., no. 11, 1976. price varies. George Allen & Unwin (Publishers) Ltd., 40 Museum St., London W.C.1, England.

330 US ISSN 0148-6535
STUDIES IN ECONOMICS. 1966. irreg. $1 per no. Institute for Humane Studies, 1177 University Drive, Menlo Park, CA 94025. bibl. circ. 5,000. (back issues avail.)

330 US ISSN 0081-8062
STUDIES IN INTERNATIONAL ECONOMIC RELATIONS. 1963. irreg., no. 8, 1974. $10. National Bureau of Economic Research, 1050 Massachusetts Ave, Cambridge, MA 02138 (Since 1968 Dist. by: Columbia University Press, 136 South Broadway, Irvington-on-Hudson, N.Y. 10533)

330 NE
STUDIES IN INTERNATIONAL ECONOMICS. 1974. irreg., vol. 5, 1979. price varies. North-Holland Publishing Co., Box 211, 1000 AE Amsterdam, Netherlands.

330 NE
STUDIES IN PUBLIC ECONOMICS. 1979. irreg., vol. 2, 1979. price varies. North-Holland Publishing Co., Box 211, 1000 AE Amsterdam, Netherlands.

330 301 US
STUDIES IN SOCIAL ECONOMICS. 1967. irreg., no. 19, 1979. price varies. Brookings Institution, 1775 Massachusetts Ave. N.W., Washington, DC 20036.

330 US
STUDIES IN WAGE-PRICE POLICY. 1967. irreg., no. 4, 1975. price varies. Brookings Institution, 1775 Massachusetts Ave. N.W., Washington, DC 20036.

STUDIES ON THE MORPHOLOGY AND SYSTEMATICS OF SCALE INSECTS. see BIOLOGY — Entomology

330 FI ISSN 0355-6034
SUOMEN PANKKI. JULKAISUJA. SERIE A/ BANK OF FINLAND. PUBLICATIONS. SERIES A/FINLANDS BANK. PUBLIKATIONER. SERIE A. (Vols. 1-35, in Finnish and Swedish, were pub. annually) (Text in Finnish, Swedish or English) 1942. irreg., no. 52, 1981. price varies. Suomen Pankki - Bank of Finland, Information Department, Box 160, SF-00101 Helsinki 10, Finland. Ed. Annikki Leukkunen. circ. 1,200.
Formerly: Suomen Pankki Taloustieteellinen Tutkimuslaitos. Julkaisuja. Series A: Taloudellisia Selvityksia (ISSN 0081-9476)

330 FI ISSN 0357-4776
SUOMEN PANKKI. JULKAISUJA. SERIE B/BANK OF FINLAND. PUBLICATIONS. SERIES B/ FINLANDS BANK. PUBLIKATIONER. SERIE B. (Text in Finnish or Swedish; summaries in English) 1943. irreg., no. 35, 1980. price varies. Suomen Pankki - Bank of Finland, Information Department, Box 160, SF-00101 Helsinki 10, Finland. Ed. Annikki Leukkunen. circ. 800.
Formerly (until no. 31, 1969): Finlands Bank. Institut foer Ekonomisk Forskning. Publikationer (ISSN 0081-9484)

330　　　　　　　FI　　ISSN 0081-9492
SUOMEN PANKKI. JULKAISUJA. SERIE C/
BANK OF FINLAND. PUBLICATIONS. SERIES
C/FINLANDS BANK. PUBLIKATIONER. SERIE
C. (Text mainly in Finnish, occasionally in Swedish)
1962. irreg., no. 6, 1969. price varies. Suomen
Pankki - Bank of Finland, Information Department,
Box 160, SF-00101 Helsinki 10, Finland. Ed.
Annikki Leukkunen. circ. 300.

330　　　　　　　FI　　ISSN 0355-6042
SUOMEN PANKKI. JULKAISUJA. SERIE D/
BANK OF FINLAND. PUBLICATIONS. SERIES
D/FINLANDS BANK. PUBLIKATIONER.
SERIE D. (Text in Finnish, Swedish or English)
1963. irreg., no. 48, 1981. price varies. Suomen
Pankki - Bank of Finland, Information Department,
Box 160, SF-00101 Helsinki 10, Finland. Ed.
Annikki Leukkunen. circ. 500.
Formerly: Suomen Pankki Series D.
Mimeographed Series (ISSN 0081-9506)

330　　　　　　　UK　　ISSN 0081-9670
SURREY PAPERS IN ECONOMICS. 1967. irreg.
50p. per no. University of Surrey, Bookshop,
Guildford, Surrey GU2 5XH, England. Eds. R. P.
Troeller, S. F. Frowen.
Formerly: International Economics.

339　　　　　　　US
SURVEYS OF APPLIED ECONOMICS. 1973. irreg.
price varies. Saint Martins Press, 175 Fifth Avenue,
New York, NY 10010.

330　　　　　　　SW　　ISSN 0082-0067
SWEDEN. KONJUNKTURINSTITUTET.
OCCASIONAL PAPER. (Text in English) 1964.
irreg., no. 9, 1976. price varies.
(Konjunkturinstitutet - National Institute of
Economic Research) Liber Foerlag, Fack, S-162 89
Vaellingby, Sweden.

330　　　　　　　SW
SWEDISH NATURAL SCIENCE RESEARCH
COUNCIL. SWEDISH COMMITTEE ON
RESEARCH ECONOMICS. FEK REPORTS.
(Text in English) 1972. irreg. (2-3/yr.)
Naturvetenskapliga Forskningsraadet, Editorial
Service, Box 23136, S-104 35 Stockholm, Sweden.
Ed. Goeran Friborg.

330　　　　　　　SZ
SWITZERLAND. KOMMISSION FUER
KONJUNKTURFRAGEN. ALLFAELLIGE
STUDIEN. French edition: Switzerland.
Commission de Recherches Economiques. Etudes
Occasionnelles. (Supplement to: Switzerland.
Eidgenoessisches Volkswirtschaftsdepartement.
Volkswirtschaft and to Schweizerische
Nationalbank. Monatsbericht) irreg.
Eidgenoessisches Volkswirtschaftsdepartement,
Kommission fuer Konjunkturfragen, Belpstr. 53,
3003 Berne, Switzerland.

330　　　　　　　TZ
TANZANIA INDUSTRIAL STUDIES AND
CONSULTING ORGANISATION. ANNUAL
REPORT AND ACCOUNTS. 1978. a. Tanzania
Industrial Studies and Consulting Organisation, Box
2650, Dar es Salaam, Tanzania. (back issues avail.)

TEMADOKUMENTACIOS KIADVANYOK/
THEMATICAL REVIEWS. see TECHNOLOGY:
COMPREHENSIVE WORKS

650　　　　　　　US　　ISSN 0082-3066
TEXAS INDUSTRY SERIES. 1951. irreg., 1968, no.
11. price varies. University of Texas at Austin,
Bureau of Business Research, Austin, TX 78712.

330.1　　　　　　　FR　　ISSN 0082-3988
THEORIE DE LA PRODUCTION. 1970. irreg., 2-3/
yr. price varies. (Institut de Recherches en
Economie de la Production) Editions Cujas, 4,6,8,
rue de la Maison-Blanche, 75013 Paris, France. Dir.
Jacques De Bandt.

TOLL FREE BUSINESS. see
COMMUNICATIONS — Telephone And
Telegraph

380　　　　　　　US　　ISSN 0275-7435
TOP 1,500 COMPANIES. 1980. a. $100. Economic
Information Systems, 310 Madison Ave., New
York, NY 10017.

380　　　　　　　US　　ISSN 0275-7427
TOP 1,500 PRIVATE COMPANIES. 1980. a. $100.
Economic Information Systems, 310 Madison Ave.,
New York, NY 10017.

330　　　　　　　US
TRADESHOW/CONVENTION GUIDE. 1964. a.
$55. Budd Publications, Inc., Box 7, New York, NY
10004. Ed. Kitty Huffer. adv. circ. 11,183.

330　　　　　　　HU　　ISSN 0133-7769
TRENDS IN WORLD ECONOMY. (Text in English,
French, German, Hungarian, Russian, Spanish)
1971. irreg (4-6/yr) price varies. Vilaggazdasagi
Tudomanyos Tanacs, Kallo esperes u. 15, P.O.B. 36,
1531 Budapest, Hungary. Ed. Peter Mandi. circ.
1,000. (processed)

650　　　　　　　US
TRY US; national minority business directory. 1969. a.
$15. National Minority Business Campaign, 1201
12th Ave. North, Minneapolis, MN 55411. circ.
10,000.
Formerly: National Minority Business Directory
(ISSN 0077-5231)

338 650　　　　　　　US　　ISSN 0082-7126
U C L A BUSINESS FORECAST FOR THE
NATION AND CALIFORNIA. 1960. a. $35.
University of California, Los Angeles, Graduate
School of Management, U.C.L.A. Business
Forecasting Project, 405 Hilgard Ave., Los Angeles,
CA 90024. Ed. Robert M. Williams. circ. 2,000.

330 650 330.9　　　　　　　US
U S S R REPORT: ECONOMIC AFFAIRS. 1969.
irreg (approx. 48/yr.) $144. U.S. Joint Publications
Research Service, 1000 N. Glebe Rd., Arlington,
VA 22201 (Orders to: NTIS, Springfield, VA
22161)
Formerly: Translations on U S S R Economic
Affairs.

330　　　　　　　CL
UNIVERSIDAD DE CHILE. FACULTAD DE
CIENCIAS ECONOMICAS Y
ADMINISTRATIVAS. DESARROLLO. irreg.
Universidad de Chile, Facultad de Ciencias
Economicas y Administrativas, Santiago, Chile.

330　　　　　　　SP
UNIVERSIDAD DE DEUSTO. PUBLICACIONES.
ECONOMIA. 1972. irreg., no. 4, 1976. Universidad
Comercial de Deusto, Bilbao, Spain.

330　　　　　　　UY
UNIVERSIDAD DE LA REPUBLICA. FACULTAD
DE CIENCIAS ECONOMICAS Y DE
ADMINISTRACION. REVISTA. 1940; N. S. 1950.
irreg. Universidad de la Republica, Facultad de
Ciencias Economicas y de Administracion,
Montivideo, Uruguay. bibl. charts.

330　　　　　　　SP
UNIVERSIDAD DE SEVILLA. INSTITUTO
GARCIA OVIEDO. CUADERNOS. irreg. price
varies. Universidad de Sevilla, Instituto Garcia
Oviedo, San Fernando 4, Seville, Spain.

330　　　　　　　PE
UNIVERSIDAD DEL PACIFICO. CENTRO DE
INVESTIGACION. SERIE: COYUNTURA
ECONOMICA. irreg. Universidad del Pacifico,
Centro de Investigacion, Lima, Peru.

330　　　　　　　AG
UNIVERSIDAD NACIONAL DEL LITORAL.
FACULTAD DE CIENCIAS ECONOMICAS
COMERCIALES Y POLITICAS. 1926. irreg.
Universidad Nacional del Litoral, Facultad de
Ciencias Economicas Comerciales y Politicas, Santa
Fe, Argentina.

330　　　　　　　PE
UNIVERSIDAD NACIONAL MAYOR DE SAN
MARCOS. FACULTAD DE CIENCIAS
ECONOMICAS Y COMERCIALES. REVISTA.
1929. irreg. Universidad Nacional Mayor de San
Marcos, Facultad de Ciencias Economicas y
Comerciales, Casilla 2631, Lima, Peru. bibl.
Formerly: Revista Economica y Financiera.

330　　　　　　　BL
UNIVERSIDADE DE SAO PAULO. INSTITUTO
DE PESQUISAS ECONOMICAS. TRABALHO
PARA DISCUSSAO. no. 16, 1975. irreg.
Universidade de Sao Paulo, Instituto de Pesquisas
Economicas, Sao Paulo, Brazil.

330　　　　　　　IT
UNIVERSITA DEGLI STUDI DI PARMA.
FACOLTA DI ECONOMIA E COMMERCIO.
STUDI E RICERCHE. 1964. a. Universita degli
Studi di Parma, Facolta di Economia e Commercio,
Parma, Italy.

330　　　　　　　IT　　ISSN 0080-4010
UNIVERSITA DEGLI STUDI DI ROMA.
ISTITUTO DI ECONOMIA POLITICA.
COLLANA DI STUDI. 1969. irreg., no. 7, 1971.
price varies. Edizioni dell' Ateneo & Bizzarri, P.O.
Box 7216, 00100 Rome, Italy. circ. 1,000.

330　　　　　　　GW　　ISSN 0531-0318
UNIVERSITAET ZU KOELN. INSTITUT FUER
HANDELSFORSCHUNG. MITTEILUNGEN.
SONDERHEFTE. 168. irreg., no. 26, 1980. price
varies. Verlag Otto Schwartz und Co., Annastr. 7,
3400 Goettingen, W. Germany (B.R.D.) Ed.
Edmund Sundhoff.

330　　　　　　　RM
UNIVERSITATEA "AL. I. CUZA" DIN IASI.
ANALELE STIINTIFICE. SECTIUNEA 3C:
STIINTE ECONOMICE. (Text in Romanian;
summaries in foreign languages) a. $10.
Universitatea "Al. I. Cuza" din Iasi, Calea 23
August Nr.11, Jassy, Romania (Subscr. to: ILEXIM,
Str. 13 Decembrie Nr. 3, P.O. Box 136-137,
Bucharest, Romania) bk. rev. abstr. charts. illus.

338.9　　　　　　　BE　　ISSN 0068-2993
UNIVERSITE LIBRE DE BRUXELLES. INSTITUT
D'ETUDES EUROPEENNES. ENSEIGNEMENT
COMPLEMENTAIRE. NOUVELLE SERIE. 1965-
68 Premiere Serie, 1968 Nouvelle Serie. irreg., latest
1971. price varies. Editions de l'Universite de
Bruxelles, Parc Leopold, 1040 Brussels, Belgium.

338.9　　　　　　　BE　　ISSN 0068-3000
UNIVERSITE LIBRE DE BRUXELLES. INSTITUT
D'ETUDES EUROPEENNES. THESES ET
TRAVAUX ECONOMIQUES. 1967. irreg. price
varies. Editions de l'Universite de Bruxelles, Parc
Leopold, 1040 Brussels, Belgium.

330　　　　　　　US　　ISSN 0083-3940
UNIVERSITIES-NATIONAL BUREAU
CONFERENCE SERIES. 1949. irreg., no. 28,
1976. $17.50. National Bureau of Economic
Research, 1050 Massachusetts Ave, Cambridge, MA
02138.

330　　　　　　　US
UNIVERSITY OF ALABAMA. CENTER FOR
BUSINESS AND ECONOMIC RESEARCH
MONOGRAPH SERIES. 1973. irreg. price varies.
University of Alabama, College of Commerce and
Business Administration, P.O. Box AK, University,
AL 35486. Ed. James Southern.

UNIVERSITY OF ALASKA. INSTITUTE OF
SOCIAL AND ECONOMIC RESEARCH.
RESEARCH SUMMARY. see SOCIOLOGY

650　　　　　　　CN　　ISSN 0065-6070
UNIVERSITY OF ALBERTA. FACULTY OF
BUSINESS ADMINISTRATION AND
COMMERCE. RESEARCH STUDIES IN
BUSINESS.* irreg. University of Alberta, Faculty of
Business Administration and Commerce, Edmonton
7, Alberta, Canada.

330　　　　　　　CN
UNIVERSITY OF BRITISH COLUMBIA.
DEPARTMENT OF ECONOMICS.
DISCUSSION PAPER. 1968. irreg. University of
British Columbia, Department of Economics, 1873
East Mall, Suite 997, University Campus,
Vancouver, B.C. V6T 1Y2, Canada.

330　　　　　　　CN　　ISSN 0381-0410
UNIVERSITY OF BRITISH COLUMBIA.
DEPARTMENT OF ECONOMICS. RESOURCES
PAPER. 1976. irreg. University of British Columbia,
Department of Economics, 1873 East Mall, Suite
997, University Campus, Vancouver, B.C. V6T 1Y2,
Canada.

330 338　　　　　　　US　　ISSN 0068-6077
UNIVERSITY OF CALIFORNIA. INSTITUTE OF
BUSINESS AND ECONOMIC RESEARCH.
PUBLICATIONS. 1948. irreg. price varies.
University of California Press, 2223 Fulton St.,
Berkeley, CA 94720.

BUSINESS AND ECONOMICS

650 US ISSN 0069-3359
UNIVERSITY OF CHICAGO. GRADUATE SCHOOL OF BUSINESS. SELECTED PAPERS. 1962. irreg. University of Chicago, Graduate School of Business, Chicago, IL 60637. Dir. Betty E. McGuire. circ. 10,000.

330 TZ
UNIVERSITY OF DAR ES SALAAM. ECONOMIC RESEARCH BUREAU. OCCASIONAL PAPER. Short title: E R B Occasional Paper Series. 1966. irreg. price varies. University of Dar es Salaam, Economic Research Bureau, Box 35096, Dar es Salaam, Tanzania. circ. 100.

330 TZ ISSN 0418-3746
UNIVERSITY OF DAR ES SALAAM. ECONOMIC RESEARCH BUREAU. PAPERS. Short title: E R B Papers. 1966. irreg. price varies. University of Dar es Salaam, Economic Research Bureau, Box 35096, Dar es Salaam, Tanzania.

650 US ISSN 0070-3761
UNIVERSITY OF DENVER. COLLEGE OF BUSINESS ADMINISTRATION. OCCASIONAL STUDIES. 1969. irreg. free. University of Denver, College of Business Administration, Div. of Research, 2020 S. Race St., Denver, CO 80210.

650 US ISSN 0070-377X
UNIVERSITY OF DENVER. COLLEGE OF BUSINESS ADMINISTRATION. SPECIAL PUBLICATION. 1970. irreg. free. University of Denver, College of Business Administration, Div. of Research, 2020 S. Race St., Denver, CO 80210.

330 US ISSN 0085-1051
UNIVERSITY OF GEORGIA. COLLEGE OF BUSINESS ADMINISTRATION. RESEARCH MONOGRAPH SERIES. 1964. irreg., 1971, no. 5. $5. University of Georgia, College of Business Administration, Division of Research, Athens, GA 30602. Ed. Lorena Akioka. circ. controlled.

330 US ISSN 0072-1263
UNIVERSITY OF GEORGIA. COLLEGE OF BUSINESS ADMINISTRATION. TRAVEL RESEARCH SERIES. 1962. irreg.,1973,nos. 1-15. free. University of Georgia, College of Business Administration, Athens, GA 30602. circ. controlled.

UNIVERSITY OF GLASGOW. SOCIAL AND ECONOMIC RESEARCH STUDIES. see *SOCIAL SCIENCES: COMPREHENSIVE WORKS*

UNIVERSITY OF GLASGOW. SOCIAL AND ECONOMIC STUDIES. OCCASIONAL PAPERS. see *SOCIAL SCIENCES: COMPREHENSIVE WORKS*

UNIVERSITY OF MELBOURNE. INSTITUTE OF APPLIED ECONOMIC AND SOCIAL RESEARCH. MONOGRAPHS. see *SOCIAL SERVICES AND WELFARE*

UNIVERSITY OF MELBOURNE. INSTITUTE OF APPLIED ECONOMIC AND SOCIAL RESEARCH. TECHNICAL PAPERS. see *SOCIAL SCIENCES: COMPREHENSIVE WORKS*

650 US ISSN 0076-8332
UNIVERSITY OF MICHIGAN. GRADUATE SCHOOL OF BUSINESS ADMINISTRATION. LEADERSHIP AWARD LECTURE. 1968. a. University of Michigan, Graduate School of Business Administration, Division of Research, Tappan and Monroe Sts., Ann Arbor, MI 48109. (reprint service avail. from UMI)

650 US ISSN 0077-7943
UNIVERSITY OF NEVADA. BUREAU OF BUSINESS AND ECONOMIC RESEARCH. RESEARCH REPORT. 1961. irreg. price varies. University of Nevada, Bureau of Business and Economic Research, Reno, NV 89557.

650 658 US ISSN 0068-4430
UNIVERSITY OF NEW MEXICO. BUREAU OF BUSINESS AND ECONOMIC RESEARCH. BUSINESS INFORMATION SERIES. 1951. irreg. free. University of New Mexico, Bureau of Business and Economic Research, Albuquerque, NM 87131. Ed. Betsie Kasner.

650 US ISSN 0078-1452
UNIVERSITY OF NORTH CAROLINA, CHAPEL HILL. GRADUATE SCHOOL OF BUSINESS ADMINISTRATION. TECHNICAL PAPERS. 1961. irreg., 1968, no. 9. $1.-$2. University of North Carolina at Chapel Hill, Graduate School of Business Administration, Chapel Hill, NC 27514. Ed.Bd. circ. 400-800.

330 382 346 JA ISSN 0473-4637
UNIVERSITY OF OSAKA PREFECTURE. BULLETIN. SERIES D: SCIENCES OF ECONOMY, COMMERCE AND LAW. 1957. a. exchange basis. University of Osaka Prefecture - Osaka-furitsu Daigaku, 4-804 Mozuume-machi, Sakai-shi, Osaka 591, Japan.

330 US ISSN 0081-8437
UNIVERSITY OF PENNSYLVANIA. WHARTON SCHOOL OF FINANCE AND COMMERCE. STUDIES IN QUANTITATIVE ECONOMICS. 1966. irreg. price varies. University of Pennsylvania Wharton School of Finance and Commerce, Economics Research Unit, 3718 Locust Walk, Philadelphia, PA 19104.

338 SI
UNIVERSITY OF SINGAPORE. ECONOMIC RESEARCH CENTRE. OCCASIONAL PAPERS. 1977. irreg. Chopmen Enterprises, 428-429 Katong Shopping Centre, Singapore 1543, Singapore.

330 US
UNIVERSITY OF SOUTH CAROLINA. BUREAU OF BUSINESS AND ECONOMIC RESEARCH. OCCASIONAL STUDIES. 1972. irreg., no. 10, 1976. University of South Carolina, College of Business Administration, Division of Research, Columbia, SC 29208. Ed.Hugh S. Norton. charts. illus. circ. 1,900(controlled)

338.9 330 SA ISSN 0081-5454
UNIVERSITY OF STELLENBOSCH. BUREAU FOR ECONOMIC RESEARCH. SURVEY OF CONTEMPORARY ECONOMIC CONDITIONS AND PROSPECTS. (Supplement avail.) 1957. a. R.25 (supplement R.15) University of Stellenbosch, Bureau for Economic Research, Private Bag 5050, Stellenbosch 7600, South Africa. Ed. A. J. M. de Vries. circ. 3,000. (tabloid format)
Incorporates: University of Stellenbosch. Bureau for Economic Research. Prospects.

330 UK ISSN 0306-7408
UNIVERSITY OF STRATHCLYDE, FRASER OF ALLANDER INSTITUTE FOR RESEARCH ON THE SCOTTISH ECONOMY. RESEARCH MONOGRAPH. 1975. irreg. price varies. University of Strathclyde, Fraser of Allander Institute for Research on the Scottish Economy, 100 Montrose St., Glasgow G4 OLZ, Scotland. bibl.

330 AT ISSN 0085-7025
UNIVERSITY OF SYDNEY ECONOMICS SOCIETY. ECONOMIC REVIEW. 1955. 3/yr. Aus.$2. University of Sydney, Economics Society, Box 35, Wentworth Bldg., Sydney, N.S.W. 2006, Australia.

650 US ISSN 0082-3244
UNIVERSITY OF TEXAS, AUSTIN. BUREAU OF BUSINESS RESEARCH. BUSINESS GUIDE. 1950. irreg., latest, 1978. price varies. University of Texas at Austin, Bureau of Business Research, Austin, TX 78712.

650 US ISSN 0495-2634
UNIVERSITY OF TEXAS, AUSTIN. BUREAU OF BUSINESS RESEARCH. PUBLICATIONS. a. University of Texas at Austin, Bureau of Business Research, Austin, TX 78712. Key Title: Publications-Bureau of Business Research, the University of Texas at Austin.

650 US
UNIVERSITY OF TEXAS, AUSTIN. BUREAU OF BUSINESS RESEARCH. RESEARCH REPORT SERIES. 1928. irreg., latest, 1980. price varies. University of Texas at Austin, Bureau of Business Research, Austin, TX 78712.
Formerly: University of Texas, Austin. Bureau of Business Research. Research Monograph (ISSN 0082-3279)

330 382 US ISSN 0081-8135
UNIVERSITY OF TEXAS, AUSTIN. BUREAU OF BUSINESS RESEARCH. STUDIES IN LATIN AMERICAN BUSINESS. 1959. irreg., latest, 1979. price varies. University of Texas at Austin, Bureau of Business Research, Austin, TX 78712.

UNIVERSITY OF THE WEST INDIES. INSTITUTE OF SOCIAL AND ECONOMIC RESEARCH. WORKING PAPERS. see *SOCIOLOGY*

UNIVERSITY OF TOLEDO. BUSINESS RESEARCH CENTER. BIBLIOGRAPHIES. see *BIBLIOGRAPHIES*

330 US
UNIVERSITY OF TOLEDO. BUSINESS RESEARCH CENTER. HODGE MEMORIAL GRADUATE LECTURES. 1968. irreg., no.6, 1977. free. University of Toledo, College of Business Administration, 2801 W. Bancroft St., Toledo, OH 43606.

650 US
UNIVERSITY OF TOLEDO. BUSINESS RESEARCH CENTER. MISCELLANEOUS PAPERS. 1968. irreg., no. 10, 1976. price varies. University of Toledo, College of Business Administration, 2801 W. Bancroft St., Toledo, OH 43606. Dir. Thomas A. Klein.

650 US
UNIVERSITY OF TOLEDO. BUSINESS RESEARCH CENTER. OCCASIONAL PAPERS. (Subseries of Toledo Business Report) 1963. irreg., no. 24, 1977. price varies. University of Toledo, College of Business Administration, 2801 W. Bancroft St., Toledo, OH 43606. Dir. Thomas A. Klein. circ. 800.

650 US
UNIVERSITY OF TOLEDO. BUSINESS RESEARCH CENTER. REGIONAL RESEARCH REPORTS. (Subseries of Toledo Business Report) 1962. irreg., no. 11, 1976. price varies. University of Toledo, College of Business Administration, 2801 W. Bancroft. St, Toledo, OH 43606. Dir. Thomas A. Klein. circ. 800.

301 330 CN
UNIVERSITY OF TORONTO. INSTITUTE FOR POLICY ANALYSIS. ANNUAL REPORT. 1976. irreg. ‡ University of Toronto, Institute for Policy Analysis, 150 St. George St., Toronto, Ont. M5S 1A1, Canada.
Supersedes: University of Toronto. Institute for the Quantitative Analysis of Social and Economic Policy. News Letter (ISSN 0082-5271)

301 330 CN
UNIVERSITY OF TORONTO. INSTITUTE FOR POLICY ANALYSIS. REPRINT SERIES. 1967. irreg. free. ‡ University of Toronto, Institute for Policy Analysis, 150 St. George St., Toronto, Ont. M5S 1A1, Canada.
Formerly: University of Toronto. Institute for the Quantitative Analysis of Social and Economic Policy. Reprint Series (ISSN 0082-5298)

301 330 CN
UNIVERSITY OF TORONTO. INSTITUTE FOR POLICY ANALYSIS. WORKING PAPER SERIES. irreg. free. ‡ University of Toronto, Institute for Policy Analysis, 150 St. George St., Toronto, Ont. M5S 1A1, Canada.
Formerly: University of Toronto. Institute for the Quantitative Analysis of Social and Economic Policy. Working Paper Series (ISSN 0082-5301)

330 YU
UNIVERZITET VO SKOPLJE. EKONOMSKIOT FAKULTET. GODISNIK/UNIVERSITE DE SKOPJE. FACULTE DES SCIENCES ECONOMIQUE. ANNUAIRE. (Text in Macedonian; summaries in English, French, German and Russian) 1956. a. Univerzitet vo Skoplje, Ekonomskiot Fakultet, Skopje, Yugoslavia. circ. 500.

330 335 PL
UNIWERSYTET GDANSKI. WYDZIAL EKONOMIKI TRANSPORTU. ZESZYTY NAUKOWE. INSTYTUT EKONOMII POLITYCZNEJ. PRACE I MATERIALY. (Text in Polish; summaries in English and Russian) 1971. irreg. price varies. Uniwersytet Gdanski, Ul. Czerwonej Armii 110, 81-824 Sopot, Poland.

330 PL ISSN 0083-4289
UNIWERSYTET JAGIELLONSKI. ZESZYTY NAUKOWE. PRACE GEOGRAFICZNE. PRACE Z GEOGRAFII EKONOMICZNEJ. 1960. irreg. price varies. ‡ (Instytut Geografii) Panstwowe Wydawnictwo Naukowe, Miodowa 10, Warsaw, Poland (Dist. by Ars Polona-Ruch, Krakowskie Przedmiescie 7, Warsaw, Poland) circ. 680. (also avail. in microfilm) Indexed: Ref.Zh.

330 UR
VOPROSY EKONOMIKI NARODNOGO KHOZYAISTVA MURMANSKOI OBLASTI. irreg. 0.48 Rub. Akademiya Nauk S.S.S.R., Kol'skii Filial, Otdel Ekonomicheskikh Issledovanii, Apatity, Akademgorodok, U. S. S. R. illus.

650 US
W. H. IRONS MEMORIAL LECTURE SERIES. 1971. irreg. University of Texas at Austin, Bureau of Business Research, Austin, TX 78712.

330 UK ISSN 0083-7350
WARWICK ECONOMIC RESEARCH PAPERS. 1968. irreg., 1971, no. 14. free. ‡ University of Warwick, Department of Economics, Coventry CV4 7AL, England. circ. 250. (also avail. in microfilm)

650 UK
WARWICK INDUSTRIAL ECONOMIC AND BUSINESS RESEARCH PAPERS. 1969. irreg. 50p. ‡ University of Warwick, Centre for Industrial Economic & Business Research, Coventry, Warwickshire CV4 7AL, England. Ed. Prof. J.R. Perrin. circ. 300. (also avail. in microfilm)
Formerly: Warwick Research Industrial and Business Studies (ISSN 0083-7369)

330 JA
WASEDA BUSINESS AND ECONOMIC STUDIES. (Text in English) 1965. a. free. Waseda University, Graduate Division of Commerce, 1-6-1 Nishi-Waseda, Shinjuku-ku, Tokyo 160, Japan. charts. illus. circ. 500.

650 US ISSN 0083-7504
WASHINGTON STATE UNIVERSITY. BUREAU OF ECONOMIC AND BUSINESS RESEARCH. STUDY. irreg., no. 49, 1972. ‡ Washington State University Press, Pullman, WA 99164. (reprint service avail. from UMI)

330 US ISSN 0068-4392
WEST VIRGINIA UNIVERSITY. BUSINESS AND ECONOMIC STUDIES. 1949. irreg., vol. 13, 1976. $3.50. West Virginia University, Bureau of Business Research, Morgantown, WV 26506. index; cum.index: 1949-1975. Indexed: P.A.I.S. Vert.File Ind.

WHO'S WHO IN CALIFORNIA BUSINESS AND FINANCE. see *BIOGRAPHY*

WHO'S WHO IN FINANCE AND INDUSTRY. see *BIOGRAPHY*

330 US ISSN 0084-0246
WILLIAM K. MCINALLY LECTURE. 1966. irreg. University of Michigan, Graduate School of Business Administration, Division of Research, Tappan and Monroe Sts., Ann Arbor, MI 48109. (reprint service avail. from UMI)

330 AU ISSN 0507-7206
WIRTSCHAFTSUNIVERSITAET WIEN. DISSERTATIONEN. 1969. irreg., no. 26, 1978. price varies. Verband der Wissenschaftlichen Gesellschaften Oesterreichs, Lindengasse 37, A-1010 Vienna, Austria.
Formerly: Hochschule fuer Welthandel in Wien. Dissertationen.

330.1 GW
WIRTSCHAFTSWISSENSCHAFTLICHE SCHRIFTEN. 1953. irreg., no. 11, 1976. price varies. Verlag Anton Hain GmbH, Adelheidstr. 2, Postfach 1220, 6240 Koenigstein, W. Germany (B.R.D.) Ed. Bd.

330 GW ISSN 0083-7113
WIRTSCHAFTSWISSENSCHAFTLICHE UND WIRTSCHAFTSRECHTLICHE UNTERSUCHUNGEN. 1962. irreg. price varies. (Walter Eucken Institut) Verlag J.C.B. Mohr (Paul Siebeck), Wilhelmstr. 18, Postfach 2040, 7400 Tuebingen, W. Germany (B.R.D.)

650 US ISSN 0084-0513
WISCONSIN BUSINESS MONOGRAPHS. 1968. irreg., no. 11, 1980. price varies. ‡ University of Wisconsin-Madison, Bureau of Business Research and Service, 110 Commerce Building, 1155 Observatory Dr., Madison, WI 53706.
Formerly: University of Wisconsin. Bureau of Business Research and Service. Monographs (ISSN 0512-0918)

330 US ISSN 0084-0599
WISCONSIN ECONOMY STUDIES. 1967. irreg., 1973, no. 14. price varies. ‡ University of Wisconsin-Madison, Bureau of Business Research and Service, 110 Commerce Building, 1155 Observatory Dr., Madison, WI 53706.
Formerly: Wisconsin Commerce Studies.

330 PL ISSN 0084-2974
WROCLAWSKI ROCZNIK EKONOMICZNY. 1968. a. price varies. (Polskie Towarzystwo Ekonomiczne) Panstwowe Wydawnictwo Naukowe, Oddzial we Wroclawiu, Ul. Pretficza 9/11, 53-328 Wroclaw, Poland (Dist. by: Ars Polona, Krakowskie Przedmiescie 7, 00-068 Warsaw, Poland) Ed.Bd. circ. 750.

330 US
YALE UNIVERSITY. ECONOMIC GROWTH CENTER. DISCUSSION PAPERS. nos. 249-263, 1976-77. irreg. $25. Yale University, Economic Growth Center, Box 1987 Yale Sta., New Haven, CT 06520.

330 ZA
ZAMBIA. CENTRAL STATISTICAL OFFICE. INDUSTRY MONOGRAPHS. irreg., latest no. 8. K.4. Central Statistical Office, Box 1908, Lusaka, Zambia.

330 US
ZEROWORK. 1975. irreg., no. 3, 1980. Social Science Division, State University of New York, Purchase, NY 10577. Ed. Bd. adv. bk. rev. film rev. bibl. cum. index. circ. 300. (back issues avail.)

BUSINESS AND ECONOMICS — Abstracting, Bibliographies, Statistics

657 US
ACCOUNTANTS' INDEX. 1950? q. with a. cum. $135. American Institute of Certified Public Accountants, 1211 Ave.of the Americas, New York, NY 10036.

330 317 US ISSN 0066-0736
AMERICAN STATISTICAL ASSOCIATION. BUSINESS AND ECONOMIC STATISTICS SECTION. PROCEEDINGS. 1954. a. American Statistical Association, 806 15th St., N.W., Suite 640, Washington, DC 20005. (also avail. in microform from UMI)

650 016 UK ISSN 0261-0108
ANBAR MANAGEMENT PUBLICATIONS BIBLIOGRAPHY. 1961. a. £5. Anbar Publications Ltd., Box 23, Wembley HA9 8DJ, England. Ed. A. C. Ede. bk. rev.
Formerly: Anbar Management Services Bibliography (ISSN 0003-2808)

382 316 AO ISSN 0066-1848
ANGOLA. DIRECCAO DOS SERVICOS DE ESTATISTICA. ESTATISTICAS DO COMERCIO EXTERNO. (Text in Portuguese) 1938. irreg. Direccao dos Servicos de Estatistica, Caixa Postal 1215, Luanda, Angola. stat. circ. 750.

382 316 TG
ANNUAIRE DES STATISTIQUES DU COMMERCE EXTERIEUR DU TOGO. a, latest 1976(pub. 1979) 2000 Fr.CFA. Direction de la Statistique, Boite Postale 118, Lome, Togo.

315 BG ISSN 0071-7371
ANNUAL FOREIGN TRADE STATISTICS OF BANGLADESH. (Text in English) 1961-63. a. Bureau of Statistics, Secretariat, Dacca 2, Bangladesh.

317 650 US ISSN 0066-4375
ANNUAL SUMMARY OF BUSINESS STATISTICS, NEW YORK STATE. 1948. a. free. Department of Commerce, 99 Washington Ave., Albany, NY 12245. Ed. Peter A. Ansell. circ. 1,500.

382 318 GT ISSN 0570-426X
ANUARIO ESTADISTICO CENTROAMERICANO DE COMERCIO EXTERIOR. 1964. a. $10. General Treaty on Central American Economic Integration, Permanent Secretariat, 4 Avenida No. 10-25, Zona 14, Guatemala City, Guatemala.

382 318 MX
ANUARIO ESTADISTICO DE COMERCIO EXTERIOR DE LOS ESTADOS UNIDOS MEXICANOS. a. free. Secretaria de Industria y Comercio, Direccion General de Estadistica, Ave Cuauhtemoc 80, Mexico D.F., Mexico.

330 318 VE ISSN 0066-5185
ANUARIO ESTADISTICO DE LOS ANDES; VENEZUELA.* 1966. a. Universidad de Los Andes, Instituto de Investigaciones Economicas, Facultad de Economia, Merida, Venezuela.

338 318 AG
ARGENTINA. INSTITUTO NACIONAL DE ESTADISTICA Y CENSOS. INDICADORES INDUSTRIALES. SERIE I. 1974. a. Instituto Nacional de Estadistica y Censos, Hipolito Yrigoyen 250, Buenos Aires, Argentina.

330 317 US ISSN 0518-6242
ARIZONA STATISTICAL REVIEW. a. Valley National Bank of Arizona, Economic Research Department, 241 N. Central Ave., Box 71, Phoenix, AZ 85001. stat.
Formerly: Statistical Review of Arizona.

382.6 319 AT
AUSTRALIA. BUREAU OF STATISTICS. AUSTRALIAN EXPORTS, COUNTRY BY COMMODITY. 1958/59. a. Aus.$7.20. Australian Bureau of Statistics, P.O. Box 10, Belconnen, A.C.T. 2616, Australia. circ. 1,422.
Formerly: Australia. Bureau of Statistics. Australian Exports Bulletin (ISSN 0067-186X)

382 319 AT
AUSTRALIA. BUREAU OF STATISTICS. AUSTRALIAN IMPORTS, COUNTRY BY COMMODITY. 1966/67. a. Aus.$3. Australian Bureau of Statistics, P.O. Box 10, Belconnen, A.C.T. 2616, Australia. circ. 1,553.
Formerly: Australia. Bureau of Statistics. Australian Imports Bulletin (ISSN 0067-1916)

339.394 AT ISSN 0312-6250
AUSTRALIA. BUREAU OF STATISTICS. AUSTRALIAN NATIONAL ACCOUNTS - NATIONAL INCOME AND EXPENDITURE. a. Aus.$4.75. Australian Bureau of Statistics, P.O. Box 10, Belconnen, A.C.T. 2616, Australia. illus. stat. circ. 3,985.

336 AT ISSN 0045-0111
AUSTRALIA. BUREAU OF STATISTICS. BALANCE OF PAYMENTS. 1957/58. a. free. Australian Bureau of Statistics, P.O. Box 10, Belconnen, A.C.T. 2616, Australia. circ. 2,500.

331.2 319 AT
AUSTRALIA. BUREAU OF STATISTICS. EARNINGS AND HOURS OF EMPLOYEES. a. free. Australian Bureau of Statistics, P.O. Box 10, Belconnen, A.C.T. 2616, Australia. circ. 2,500.

338 AT
AUSTRALIA. BUREAU OF STATISTICS. ESTIMATES OF GROSS PRODUCT BY INDUSTRY AT CURRENT AND CONSTANT PRICES. 1965-66. a. free. Australian Bureau of Statistics, P.O. Box 10, Belconnen, A.C.T. 2616, Australia. circ. 2,800.

382.5 319 AT ISSN 0067-0804
AUSTRALIA. BUREAU OF STATISTICS. IMPORTS CLEARED FOR HOME CONSUMPTION. 1959-60. a. Aus.$12 for part 1; Aus. $15 for part 2. Australian Bureau of Statistics, P.O. Box 10, Belconnen, A.C.T. 2616, Australia. circ. 1,100 (part 1); 1,140 (part 2)

339 319 AT
AUSTRALIA. BUREAU OF STATISTICS. INCOME DISTRIBUTION. (In three parts) 1968-69; N. S. 1973. irreg. free. Australian Bureau of Statistics, P.O. Box 10, Belconnen, A.C.T. 2616, Australia. stat. circ. 6,100.

338 310   AT
AUSTRALIA. BUREAU OF STATISTICS.
INDEXES OF MANUFACTURING
PRODUCTION. a. free. Australian Bureau of
Statistics, Box 10, Belconnen, A.C.T. 2616,
Australia. circ. 3,700.
 Formerly: Australian. Bureau of Statistics,
Indexes of Factory Production.

331 319.4   AT
AUSTRALIA. BUREAU OF STATISTICS. LABOUR
MOBILITY. 1972. irreg., latest Feb. 1976. free.
Australian Bureau of Statistics, P.O. Box 10,
Belconnen, A.C.T. 2616, Australia. circ. 1,883.

331 319   AT
AUSTRALIA. BUREAU OF STATISTICS. LABOUR
STATISTICS. 1912. a. Aus.$2.75. Australian Bureau
of Statistics, P.O. Box 10, Belconnen, A.C.T. 2616,
Australia. circ. 1,820.
 Continues: Australia. Bureau of Statistics. Labour
Report (ISSN 0067-0812)

319 380   AT
AUSTRALIA. BUREAU OF STATISTICS. NEW
SOUTH WALES OFFICE. TRANSPORT AND
COMMUNICATION. 1972; N. S. 1975. a.
Australian Bureau of Statistics, N. S. W. Office, St.
Andrews House, Sydney Square, George St.,
Sydney, N. S. W. 2000, Australia. stat.
 Formerly: Australia. Bureau of Statistics. New
South Wales Office. Trade, Transport and
Communication.

387.5 319   AT
AUSTRALIA. BUREAU OF STATISTICS.
OUTWARD OVERSEAS CARGO. a. free.
Australian Bureau of Statistics, P.O. Box 10,
Belconnen, A.C.T. 2616, Australia. circ. 1,500.
 Formerly: Australia. Bureau of Statistics. Sea and
Air Cargo, Outward Overseas.

AUSTRALIA. BUREAU OF STATISTICS.
OVERSEAS AND COASTAL SHIPPING. see
TRANSPORTATION — Abstracting,
Bibliographies, Statistics

382 319   AT   ISSN 0067-0863
AUSTRALIA. BUREAU OF STATISTICS.
OVERSEAS TRADE BULLETIN. 1904. a.
Aus.$19.75 for part 1; Aus. $3.70 for part 2.
Australian Bureau of Statistics, P.O. Box 10,
Belconnen, A.C.T. 2616, Australia. circ. 1,702(part
1); 1.679 (part 2)

AUSTRALIA. BUREAU OF STATISTICS. PUBLIC
AUTHORITY FINANCE. STATE AND LOCAL
AUTHORITIES. see BUSINESS AND
ECONOMICS — Public Finance, Taxation

336 319.4   AT
AUSTRALIA. BUREAU OF STATISTICS.
QUEENSLAND OFFICE. GOVERNMENT
FINANCE. a. Australian Bureau of Statistics,
Queensland Office, 345 Ann St., Brisbane, Qld.
4000, Australia.
 Formerly: Australia. Bureau of Statistics.
Queensland Office. Public Finance: Government
Authorities.

332 319   AT
AUSTRALIA. BUREAU OF STATISTICS.
QUEENSLAND OFFICE. PRIVATE FINANCE.
a. Australian Bureau of Statistics, Queensland
Office, 345 Ann St., Brisbane, Qld. 4000, Australia.

330.9 319   AT
AUSTRALIA. BUREAU OF STATISTICS.
SEASONALLY ADJUSTED INDICATORS. a.
Aus.$6.60. Australian Bureau of Statistics, P.O. Box
10, Belconnen, A.C.T. 2616, Australia. circ. 1,965.

338 319   AT   ISSN 0310-0871
AUSTRALIA. BUREAU OF STATISTICS. SOUTH
AUSTRALIAN OFFICE. MANUFACTURING
ESTABLISHMENTS. a. free. Australian Bureau of
Statistics, South Australian Office, Box 2272, G. P.
O., Adelaide, S. A. 5001, Australia.
 Formerly: Australia. Bureau of Census and
Statistics. South Australian Office. Factories (ISSN
0067-0928)

338 319   AT   ISSN 0067-0987
AUSTRALIA. BUREAU OF STATISTICS. SOUTH
AUSTRALIAN OFFICE. RURAL
PRODUCTION. 1947/48. a. free. Australian
Bureau of Statistics, South Australian Office, Box
2772, G.P.O., Adelaide, S.A. 5001, Australia.

658.8   AT
AUSTRALIA. BUREAU OF STATISTICS. SURVEY
OF RETAIL ESTABLISHMENTS AND
SELECTED SERVICE ESTABLISHMENTS:
AUSTRALIAN CAPITAL TERRITORY. 1972-73.
a. free. Australian Bureau of Statistics, P.O. Box 10,
Belconnen, A.C.T. 2616, Australia. circ. 1,200.
 Formerly: Australia. Bureau of Statistics. Survey
of Retail Establishments: Australian Capital
Territory.

AUSTRALIA. BUREAU OF STATISTICS.
TASMANIAN OFFICE. INDUSTRIAL
ACCIDENT STATISTICS. see INDUSTRIAL
HEALTH AND SAFETY — Abstracting,
Bibliographies, Statistics

331.2 319   AT   ISSN 0067-1045
AUSTRALIA. BUREAU OF STATISTICS.
TASMANIAN OFFICE. LABOUR, WAGES AND
PRICES. 1969. a. free. Australian Bureau of
Statistics, Tasmanian Office, Box 66A, G.P.O.,
Hobart, Tasmania 4001, Australia. index. circ. 560.

336 319   AT   ISSN 0312-7850
AUSTRALIA. BUREAU OF STATISTICS.
TASMANIAN OFFICE. LOCAL
GOVERNMENT FINANCE. 1974. a. free.
Australian Bureau of Statistics, Tasmanian Office,
Box 66A, G.P.O., Hobart, Tasmania 7001,
Australia. circ. 460. (processed)
 Supersedes: Australia. Bureau of Statistics.
Tasmanian Office. Finance (ISSN 0067-1037)

380 387 319   AT   ISSN 0067-107X
AUSTRALIA. BUREAU OF STATISTICS.
TASMANIAN OFFICE. TRADE AND
SHIPPING. 1924-25. a. free. Australian Bureau of
Statistics, Tasmanian Office, Box 66A, G.P.O.,
Hobart, Tasmania 7001, Australia. circ. 470.
(processed)

331.88   AT   ISSN 0312-1437
AUSTRALIA. BUREAU OF STATISTICS. TRADE
UNION STATISTICS: AUSTRALIA. a. free.
Australian Bureau of Statistics, P.O. Box 10,
Belconnen, A.C.T. 2616, Australia. illus. circ. 2,000.

658   AT
AUSTRALIA. BUREAU OF STATISTICS.
VICTORIAN OFFICE. MANUFACTURING
ESTABLISHMENTS: DETAIL OF
OPERATIONS. 1968. a. free. Australian Bureau of
Statistics, Victorian Office, Box 2796Y, G.P.O.,
Melbourne Vic. 3001, Australia. charts. stat. circ.
650.

338.4 319   AT
AUSTRALIA.BUREAU OF STATISTICS.
WESTERN AUSTRALIAN OFFICE. CENSUS
OF MANUFACTURING ESTABLISHMENTS.
SUMMARY OF OPERATIONS BY INDUSTRY
CLASS. a. Australian Bureau of Statistics, Western
Australian Office, 1-3 St. George's Terrace, Perth,
W.A. 6000, Australia. Ed. E. Binns. circ. 500.
 Formerly: Australia. Bureau of Statistics. Western
Australian Office. Economic Censuses:
Manufacturing Establishments: Summary of
Operations by Industry Class.

614.85 319   AT
AUSTRALIA. BUREAU OF STATISTICS.
WESTERN AUSTRALIAN OFFICE.
INDUSTRIAL ACCIDENTS. SERIES A:
ABSENCE FROM WORK FOR ONE DAY OR
MORE. 1961/62. a. free. Australian Bureau of
Statistics, Western Australian Office, 1-3 St George
Terrace, Perth, W.A. 6000, Australia. Ed. E. Binns.
circ. 200. (processed)
 Supersedes in part: Australian Bureau of
Statistics. Western Australian Office. Industrial
Accidents (ISSN 0067-1266)

614.85 319   AT
AUSTRALIA. BUREAU OF STATISTICS.
WESTERN AUSTRALIAN OFFICE.
INDUSTRIAL ACCIDENTS. SERIES B:
ABSENCE FROM WORK FOR ONE WEEK OR
MORE. 1962-63. a. free. Australian Bureau of
Statistics, Western Australian Office, 1-3 St.
George's Terrace, Perth, W.A. 6000, Australia. Ed.
E. Binns. circ. 2,000. (processed)
 Supersedes in part: Australia. Bureau of Statistics.
Western Australian Office. Industrial Accidents.

336.2 319   AT   ISSN 0067-1444
AUSTRALIA. DEPARTMENT OF THE
TREASURY. INCOME TAX STATISTICS. (Title
Varies: Commonwealth Income Tax Statistics) 1963-
64. a. price varies. Australian Government
Publishing Service, Box 84, Canberra, A.C.T. 2600,
Australia.

330.9 319   AT   ISSN 0310-4230
AUSTRALIA. DEPARTMENT OF THE
TREASURY. ROUND-UP OF ECONOMIC
STATISTICS. irreg. Department of the Treasury,
Publishing Branch, P.O. Box 84, Canberra, A.C.T.
2600, Australia. stat.

336.2 319   AT   ISSN 0519-6035
AUSTRALIA. DEPARTMENT OF THE
TREASURY. TAXATION BRANCH. TAXATION
STATISTICS.* 1959/60. a. Department of the
Treasury, Box 84, Canberra, A.C.T. 2600, Australia.
stat.

314.3 331.7   AU
AUSTRIA. STATISTISCHES ZENTRALAMT.
ERHEBUNG DER LAND-UND
FORSTWIRTSCHAFTLICHEN
ARBEITSKRAEFTE. irreg. Kommissionsverlag der
Oesterreichischen Staatsdruckerei, Rennweg 12a,
1037 Vienna, Austria.

338 314   AU
AUSTRIA. STATISTISCHES ZENTRALAMT.
GEWERBESTATISTIK. (Subseries of its Beitraege
zur Oesterreichischen Statistik) 1965. a.
Oesterreichisches Statistisches Zentralamt, Nene
Hofburg, Heldenplatz, 1014 Vienna, Austria. circ.
450.

338 314   AU
AUSTRIA. STATISTISCHES ZENTRALAMT.
INDUSTRIE STATISTIK. (Subseries of its
Beitraege zur Oesterreichischen Statistik) 1954. a.
Oesterreichisches Statistisches Zentralamt, Nene
Hofburg, Heldenplatz, 1014 Vienna, Austria.

338.7 314   AU   ISSN 0081-5233
AUSTRIA. STATISTISCHES ZENTRALAMT.
STATISTIK DER AKTIENGESELLSCHAFTEN
IN OESTERREICH. 1962. a. S.350.
(Oesterreichisches Statistisches Zentralamt) Carl
Ueberreuter, Alserstr. 24, 1095 Vienna, Austria.

318 382   BF
BAHAMAS. DEPARTMENT OF STATISTICS.
EXTERNAL TRADE. a. $6. Department of
Statistics, P.O. Box N 3904, Nassau, Bahamas.

331.1 339 318   BF
BAHAMAS. DEPARTMENT OF STATISTICS.
HOUSEHOLD INCOME REPORT. 1973. irreg.
$5. Department of Statistics, P.O. Box N 3904,
Nassau, Bahamas. illus.
 Incorporating(since 1975): Bahamas. Department
of Statistics. Labour Force and Income Distribution.

330.9 310   CR   ISSN 0522-098X
BANCO CENTRAL DE COSTA RICA.
ESTADISTICAS ECONOMICAS. 1974. a. free.
Banco Central de Costa Rica, Avda. Central, Calles
2 y 4, Apdo. 10058, San Jose, Costa Rica. charts.
circ. 300.

BANCO CENTRAL DE HONDURAS. SECCION
DE SEGUROS. BOLETIN DE ESTADISTICAS
DE SEGUROS. see INSURANCE — Abstracting,
Bibliographies, Statistics

330.9 318   VE   ISSN 0522-1153
BANCO CENTRAL DE VENEZUELA. SECCION
A.L.A.L.C. ALGUNAS ESTADISTICAS DE LOS
PAISES DE A.L.A.L.C. 1966. irreg. Banco Central
de Venezuela, Seccion Asociacion Latinoamericana de
Libre Comercio, Departamento de Investigaciones
Economicas, Caracas, Venezuela.

382 316   BG
BANGLADESH BANK. STATISTICS
DEPARTMENT. ANNUAL IMPORT
PAYMENTS. (Text in English) 1973/74. a.
unpriced. Bangladesh Bank, Department of Public
Relations and Publications, Motijheel Commercial
Area, Dacca 2, Bangladesh. stat.

330 315   JA   ISSN 0070-8666
BANK OF JAPAN. ECONOMIC STATISTICS
ANNUAL. Title varies: Economic Statistics of
Japan. (Text and Title in Japanese and English) a.
price varies. Bank of Japan, Statistics Department -
Nihon Ginko, 2-2-1 Hongok-cho, Nihonbashi,
Chuo-ku, Toyko 103, Japan (Order from: Japan
Publications Trading Co., Ltd., Box 5030, Tokyo
International, Tokyo, Japan; or 1255 Howard St.,
San Francisco, CA 94103)

382 316   SJ   ISSN 0522-246X
BANK OF SUDAN. FOREIGN TRADE
STATISTICAL DIGEST. (Text in English) 1968. a.
Bank of Sudan, Statistics Department, Box 313,
Khartoum, Sudan.

319   BB
BARBADOS. STATISTICAL SERVICE.
FINANCIAL STATISTICS. a. Statistical Service,
National Insurance Building, Fairchild St.,
Bridgetown, Barbados, W. Indies.

319   BB   ISSN 0067-4125
BARBADOS. STATISTICAL SERVICE. OVERSEAS
TRADE REPORT. 1957. a. Statistical Service,
National Insurance Building, Fairchild St.,
Bridgetown, Barbados, W. Indies.

332 314   BE
BELGIUM. INSTITUT NATIONAL DE
STATISTIQUE. STATISTIQUES FINANCIERES.
(Text in Dutch and French) 1972. irreg. (3-4/yr.)
300 Fr. Institut National de Statistique, Rue de
Louvain 44, 1000 Brussels, Belgium. charts. stat.

016.331   BE
BELGIUM. OFFICE NATIONAL DE L'EMPLOI.
LISTE DES INFORMATIONS STATISTIQUES
ET DES PUBLICATIONS DE L'O N E M.
(Subseries of: Belgium. Office National de l'Emploi.
Collection "Notes Documentaires") irreg. Office
National de l'Emploi, Boulevard de l'Empereur 7,
1000 Brussels, Belgium.

540 016   BL   ISSN 0100-0756
BIBLIOGRAFIA BRASILEIRA DE QUIMICA E
QUIMICA TECNOLOGICA. 1970. irreg.
Cr.$100($5) Instituto Brasileiro de Informacao em
Ciencia e Tecnologia, Av. General Justo 171, 4
Andar, 20000 Rio de Janeiro, Brazil. bk. rev.
    Supersedes: Bibliografia Brasileira de Quimica
(ISSN 0067-6683) & Bibliografia Brasileira de
Quimica Tecnologia (ISSN 0405-721X)

330 016   PO   ISSN 0067-6764
BIBLIOGRAFIA SOBRE A ECONOMIA
PORTUGUESA. (Text in Portuguese; summaries in
French) 1948/49. irreg. 100 esc. Instituto Nacional
de Estatistica, Av. Antonio Jose de Almeida, Lisbon
1, Portugal (Orders to: Imprensa Nacional, Casa da
Moeda, Direccao Comercial, rua D. Francisco
Manuel de Melo 5, Lisbon 1, Portugal)

338   US   ISSN 0360-2702
BIBLIOGRAPHIC GUIDE TO BUSINESS AND
ECONOMICS. 1974. a. $225. G. K. Hall & Co., 70
Lincoln St., Boston, MA 02111. bibl.
    Formerly (until 1975): Business & Economics
Book Guide.

330 016.3309   TZ
BIBLIOGRAPHY OF ECONOMIC AND
STATISTICAL PUBLICATIONS ON
TANZANIA. 1967. irreg. Bureau of Statistics, Box
796, Dar es Salaam, Tanzania.

330 315   II
BIBLIOGRAPHY OF PUBLICATIONS FROM
ECONOMIC RESEARCH CENTRES IN INDIA.
(Supplements issued annually) 1973. irreg., latest
edition, 1974. Rs.85($13.20) Information Research
Academy, Box 10250, Calcutta 700019, India. Ed.
Partha Subir Guha. adv. circ. 1,700.

330 016   US   ISSN 0066-8761
BIBLIOGRAPHY OF PUBLICATIONS OF
UNIVERSITY BUREAUS OF BUSINESS AND
ECONOMIC RESEARCH. Variant title: A U B E
R Bibliography. 1957. a. $12.50 per volume.
(Association for University Business and Economic
Research) West Virginia University, Bureau of
Business Research, Morgantown, WV 26506. Eds.
Stanley J. Kloc and Joan Vannorsdall Schroeder.
adv. cum.index: 1957-75. (also avail. in microfiche)

331.1 316   BS
BOTSWANA. CENTRAL STATISTICS OFFICE.
EMPLOYMENT SURVEY. (Text in English) a,
latest 1975. Central Statistics Office, Ministry of
Finance and Development Planning, Gaborone,
Botswana (Orders to: Government Printer, Box 87,
Gaborone, Botswana)

338 318   BL
BRAZIL. COMISSAO DE FINANCIAMENTO DA
PRODUCAO. ANUARIO ESTATISTICO. 1973. a.
free. Comissao de Financiamento da Producao,
Avda. W-3 Norte Quadra 514, Bloco "B" Lote 7,
70000 Brasilia, D.F., Brazil.

381 318   BL
BRAZIL. FUNDACAO INSTITUTO BRASILEIRO
DE GEOGRAFIA E ESTATISTICA.
DEPARTAMENTO DE ESTATISTICAS
INDUSTRIAIS, COMERCIAIS E DE SERVICOS.
COMERCIO INTERESTADUAL, ESPORTACAO
POR VIAS INTERNAS. 1968. a. $5. Fundacao
Instituto Brasileiro de Geografia e Estatistica,
Departamento de Estatisticas Industriais, Comerciais
e de Servicos, Centro de Servicos Graficos, Av.
Brasil 15671, ZC 91 Rio de Janeiro RJ, Brazil. stat.

338.9 314   UK   ISSN 0068-1210
BRITISH AID STATISTICS; STATISTICS OF
ECONOMIC AID TO DEVELOPING
COUNTRIES. a. £9.50. Overseas Development
Administration, Stag Place, London SW1E 5DH,
England.

331 314   UK
BRITISH LABOUR STATISTICS. YEAR BOOK.
1969. £20. Department of Employment, 12 St.
James's Square, London SW1Y 4LL, England
(Avail. from H.M.S.O., c/o Liaison Officer, Atlantic
House, Holborn Viaduct, London EC1P 1BN,
England) charts. stat.

338 317   CN   ISSN 0317-7882
CANADA. STATISTICS CANADA. AGGREGATE
PRODUCTIVITY MEASURES/MESURES
GLOBALES DE PRODUCTIVITE. (Catalog 14-
201) (Text in English and French) 1946. a.
Can.$6($7.20) Statistics Canada, Publications
Distribution, Ottawa, Ont. K1A 0V7, Canada. (also
avail. in microform from MML)
    Former titles: Canada. Statistics Canada.
Aggregate Productivity Trends/Tendances de la
Productivite des Agregats (ISSN 0068-7073);
Indexes of Output per Person Employed and per
Man-Hour in Canada, Commercial Industries (ISSN
0073-6082)

236 317   CN   ISSN 0575-8254
CANADA. STATISTICS CANADA.
CONSOLIDATED GOVERNMENT FINANCE/
FINANCES PUBLIQUES CONSOLIDEES.
(Catalogue 68-202) (Text in English and French)
1954. a. Can.$6($7.20) Statistics Canada,
Publications Distribution, Ottawa, Ont. K1A 0V7,
Canada. (also avail. in microform from MML)

658.8 317   CN   ISSN 0590-5702
CANADA. STATISTICS CANADA. DIRECT
SELLING IN CANADA/VENTE DIRECTE AU
CANADA. (Catologue 63-218) (Text in English
and French) 1966. a. Can.$4.50($5.40) Statistics
Canada, Publications Distribution, Ottawa, Ont.
K1A 0V7, Canada. (also avail. in microform from
MML)

331.1 317   CN   ISSN 0703-4873
CANADA. STATISTICS CANADA.
EMPLOYMENT, EARNINGS AND HOURS.
SEASONALLY-ADJUSTED SERIES/EMPLOI,
REMUNERATIONS ET HEURES; SERIES
DESAISONNALISEES. (Catalogue 72-206) (Text
in English and French) 1961. a. Can.$15($18)
Statistics Canada, Publications Distribution, Ottawa,
Ont. K1A 0V7, Canada. (also avail. in microform
from MML)

382   CN   ISSN 0317-5375
CANADA. STATISTICS CANADA. EXPORTS-
MERCHANDISE TRADE/EXPORTATIONS-
COMMERCE DE MERCHANDISES. (Catalogue
65-202) (Text in English and French) 1939. a.
Can.$30($36) Statistics Canada, Publications
Distribution, Ottawa, Ont. K1A 0V7, Canada. (also
avail. in microform from MML)

312   CN   ISSN 0703-7368
CANADA. STATISTICS CANADA. FAMILY
INCOMES(CENSUS FAMILIES)/REVENUS
DES FAMILLE (FAMILLES DE
RECENSEMENT) (Catalogue 13-208) (Text in
English and French) 1971. a. Can.$4.50($5.40)
Statistics Canada, Publications Distribution, Ottawa,
Ont. K1A 0V7, Canada. (also avail. in microform
from MML)

CANADA. STATISTICS CANADA. FEDERAL
GOVERNMENT EMPLOYMENT IN
METROPOLITAN AREAS/EMPLOI DANS
L'ADMINISTRATION FEDERALE REGIONS
METROPOLITAINES. see PUBLIC
ADMINISTRATION — Abstracting,
Bibliographies, Statistics

336 317   CN   ISSN 0575-8521
CANADA. STATISTICS CANADA. FEDERAL
GOVERNMENT FINANCE/FINANCES
PUBLIQUES FEDERALES. (Catalogue 68-211)
(Text in English and French) 1953. a. Can.$6($7.20)
Statistics Canada, Publications Distribution, Ottawa,
Ont. K1A 0V7, Canada. (also avail. in microform
from MML)

331.11 317   CN   ISSN 0703-2684
CANADA. STATISTICS CANADA. HISTORICAL
LABOUR FORCE STATISTICS, ACTUAL
DATA, SEASONAL FACTORS, SEASONALLY
ADJUSTED DATA/STATISTIQUES
CHRONOLOGIQUES SUR LA POPULATION
ACTIVE, CHIFFRES REELS, FACTEURS
SAISONNIERS ET DONNEES
DESAISONNALISEES. (Catalogue 71-201) (Text
in English and French) 1953. a. Can.$10($12)
Statistics Canada, Publications Distribution, Ottawa,
Ont., K1A 0V7, Canada. (also avail. in microform
from MML)

382   CN   ISSN 0380-1349
CANADA. STATISTICS CANADA. IMPORTS-
MERCHANDISE TRADE/IMPORTATIONS-
COMMERCE DE MARCHANDISES. (Catalogue
65-203) (Text in English and French) 1939. a.
Can.$30($36) Statistics Canada, Publications
Distribution, Ottawa, Ont. K1A 0V7, Canada. (also
avail. in microform from MML)

332.6 317   CN   ISSN 0380-7053
CANADA. STATISTICS CANADA. INVESTMENT
STATISTICS SERVICE BULLETIN/
BULLETIN DE SERVICE SUR LA
STATISTIQUE DES INVESTISSEMENTS.
(Catalogue 61-007) (Text in English and French)
1975. irreg.(service bulletin) Can.$15($18) Statistics
Canada, Publications Distribution, Ottawa, Ont.
K1A 0V7, Canada. (also avail. in microform from
MML)

331 317   CN   ISSN 0380-2108
CANADA. STATISTICS CANADA. LABOUR
COSTS IN CANADA: EDUCATION,
LIBRARIES AND MUSEUMS/COUTS DE LA
MAIN D'OEUVRE AU CANADA.
ENSEIGNEMENT, BIBLIOTHEQUES ET
MUSEES. (Catalogue 72-616) (Text in English and
French) 1974. irreg. Can.$1.05($1.40) Statistics
Canada, Publications Distribution, Ottawa, Ont.
K1A 0V7, Canada. (also avail. in microform from
MML)

331 317   CN   ISSN 0319-4930
CANADA. STATISTICS CANADA. LABOUR
COSTS IN CANADA: FINANCE, INSURANCE
AND REAL ESTATE/COUTS DE LA MAIN-
D'OEUVRE AU CANADA: FINANCES,
ASSURANCES, ET IMMEUBLE. (Catalog 72-610)
(Text in English and French) 1970. irreg.
Can.$1($1.20) Statistics Canada, Publications
Distribution, Ottawa, Ont. K1A 0V7, Canada. (also
avail. in microform from MML)

338   CN   ISSN 0575-9021
CANADA. STATISTICS CANADA.
MISCELLANEOUS MANUFACTURING
INDUSTRIES/INDUSTRIES
MANUFACTURIERES DIVERSES. (Catalogue
47-205) (Text in English and French) 1930. a.
Can.$6($7.20) Statistics Canada, Publications
Distribution, Ottawa, Ont, K1A 0V7, Canada. (also
avail. in microform from MML)

BUSINESS AND ECONOMICS — ABSTRACTING, BIBLIOGRAPHIES, STATISTICS

339 317   CN   ISSN 0707-9559
CANADA. STATISTICS CANADA. PRIVATE AND PUBLIC INVESTMENT IN CANADA, MID-YEAR REVIEW/INVESTISSEMENTS PRIVES ET PUBLICS AU CANADA. REVUE DE LA MI-ANNEE. (Catalogue 61-206) (Text in English and French) 1968. a. Can.$6($7.20) Statistics Canada, Publications Distribution, Ottawa, Ont. K1A 0V7, Canada. (also avail. in microform from MML)

339 317   CN   ISSN 0318-2274
CANADA. STATISTICS CANADA. PRIVATE AND PUBLIC INVESTMENT IN CANADA. OUTLOOK/INVESTISSEMENTS PRIVES ET PUBLICS AU CANADA. PERSPECTIVES. (Catalogue 61-205) (Text in English and French) 1968. a. Can.$6($7.20) Statistics Canada, Publications Distribution, Ottawa, Ont. K1A 0V7, Canada. (also avail. in microform from MML)

338.4 317   CN   ISSN 0575-9455
CANADA. STATISTICS CANADA. PRODUCTS SHIPPED BY CANADIAN MANUFACTURERS/PRODUITS LIVRES PAR LES FABRICANTS CANADIENS. (Catalogue 31-211) (Text in English and French) 1961. a. Can.$8($9.60) Statistics Canada, Publications Distribution, Ottawa, Ont. K1A 0V7, Canada. (also avail. in microform from MML)

336   CN   ISSN 0575-9463
CANADA. STATISTICS CANADA. PROVINCIAL GOVERNMENT ENTERPRISE FINANCE/FINANCES DES ENTREPRISES PUBLIQUES PROVINCIALES. (Catalog 61-204) (Text in English and French) 1958. a. Can.$7($8.40) Statistics Canada, Publications Distribution, Ottawa, Ont. K1A 0V7, Canada. (also avail. in microform from MML)

336 317   CN   ISSN 0318-8876
CANADA. STATISTICS CANADA. PROVINCIAL GOVERNMENT FINANCE, ASSETS, LIABILITIES, SOURCES AND USES OF FUNDS/FINANCES PUBLIQUES PROVINCIALES, ACTIF, PASSIF, SOURCES ET UTILISATIONS DES FONDS. (Catalogue 68-209) (Text in English and French) 1950. a. Can.$8($9.60) Statistics Canada, Publications Distribution, Ottawa, Ont. K1A 0V7, Canada. (also avail. in microform from MML)

336   CN   ISSN 0575-9501
CANADA. STATISTICS CANADA. PROVINCIAL GOVERNMENT FINANCE, REVENUE AND EXPENDITURE (ESTIMATES) /FINANCES PUBLIQUES PROVINCIALES, REVENUS ET DEFENSES (PREVISIONS) (Catalog 68-205) (Text in English and French) 1951. a. Can.$7($8.40) Statistics Canada, Publications Distribution, Ottawa, Ont. K1A 0V7, Canada. (also avail. in microform from MML)

658.8 317   CN   ISSN 0380-7878
CANADA. STATISTICS CANADA. RETAIL CHAIN STORES/MAGASINS DE DETAIL A SUCCURSALES. (Catalogue 63-210) (Text in English and French) 1933. a. Can.$7($8.40) Statistics Canada, Publications Distribution, Ottawa, Ont. K1A 0V7, Canada. (also avail. in microform from MML)

338 317   CN   ISSN 0068-7227
CANADA. STATISTICS CANADA. SURVEY OF PRODUCTION/RELEVE DE LA PRODUCTION. (Catalog 61-202) (Text in English and French) 1920. a. Can.$6($7.20) Statistics Canada, Publications Distribution, Ottawa, Ont. K1A 0V7, Canada. (also avail. in microform from MML)

331 317   CN   ISSN 0575-9978
CANADA. STATISTICS CANADA. TRUSTEED PENSION PLANS-FINANCIAL STATISTICS/REGIMES DE PENSIONS EN FIDUCIE STATISTIQUE FINANCIERE. (Catalog 74-201) (Text in English and French) 1957. a. Can.$6($7.20) Statistics Canada, Publications Distribution, Ottawa, Ont. K1A 0V7, Canada. (also avail. in microform from MML)

658.8 317   CN   ISSN 0527-6411
CANADA. STATISTICS CANADA. VENDING MACHINE OPERATORS/EXPLOITANTS DE DISTRIBUTEURS AUTOMATIQUES. (Catalog 63-213) (Text in English and French) 1958. a. Can.$4.50($5.40) Statistics Canada, Publications Distribution, Ottawa, Ont. K1A 0V7, Canada. (also avail. in microform from MML)

332.6 317   CN   ISSN 0318-8868
CANADA'S INTERNATIONAL INVESTMENT POSITION/BILAN CANADIEN DES INVESTISSEMENTS INTERNATIONAUX. (Catalogue 67-202) (Text in English and French) 1926. a. Can.$8($9.60) Statistics Canada, Publications Distribution, Ottawa, Ont. K1A 0V7, Canada. (also avail. in microform from MML)

338 316   ZA   ISSN 0069-1429
CENSUS OF INDUSTRIAL PRODUCTION IN ZAMBIA. 1962. a, latest 1973. K.1. Central Statistical Office, P.O. Box 1908, Lusaka, Zambia.

310   FJ
CENSUS OF PRIVATE NON-PROFIT MAKING INSTITUTIONS IN FIJI. A REPORT. irreg., latest 1976. Bureau of Statistics, Box 2221, Suva, Fiji.

319   BB
CENTRAL BANK OF BARBADOS. BALANCE OF PAYMENTS. (Formerly Issued by Barbados Statistical Service) a. Statistical Service, National Insurance Building, Fairchild St., Bridgetown, Barbados, W. Indies.

332 310   UK   ISSN 0141-5468
CHARTERED INSTITUTE OF PUBLIC FINANCE AND ACCOUNTANCY. FINANCIAL GENERAL & RATING STATISTICS. 1978. a. £10. Chartered Institute of Public Finance and Accountancy, 1 Buckingham Place, London SW1E 6HS, England. (back issues avail.)

336.2 310   UK   ISSN 0260-5546
CHARTERED INSTITUTE OF PUBLIC FINANCE AND ACCOUNTANCY. RATE COLLECTION STATISTICS. ACTUALS. 1935. a. £10. Chartered Institute of Public Finance and Accountancy, 1 Buckingham Place, London SW1E 6HS, England. (back issues avail.)

382 318   CL
CHILE. INSTITUTO NACIONAL DE ESTADISTICAS. COMERCIO EXTERIOR. 1967. a. Instituto Nacional de Estadisticas, Casilla 6177-Correo 22, Santiago, Chile.

339 318   CL
CHILE. INSTITUTO NACIONAL DE ESTADISTICAS. INDICE DE PRECIOS AL CONSUMIDOR. 1968. irreg. Instituto Nacional de Estadisticas, Casilla 6177-Correo 22, Santiago, Chile.

336.2 315   CH
CHINA (REPUBLIC). DEPARTMENT OF STATISTICS. YEARBOOK OF TAX STATISTICS. (Text in Chinese and English) 1974. a. Department of Statistics, Taipei, Taiwan, Republic of China.

332 336 318   CK
COLOMBIA. DEPARTAMENTO ADMINISTRATIVO NACIONAL DE ESTADISTICA. ANUARIO DE ESTADISTICAS FISCALES Y FINANCIERAS. 1960. a. $5. Departamento Administrativo Nacional de Estadistica, Banco Nacional de Datos, Avenida Eldorado, Centro Administrativo Nacional, Apartado Aereo 80043, Bogota, Colombia. Ed. Dr. Saul Ojeda Gomez. adv. bk. rev.

382 314   GR
COMMERCE EXTERIEUR DE LA GRECE. (Text in French and Greek) a., latest 1975/1976. $7. National Statistical Service, Publications and Information Division, 14-16 Lycourgou St., Athens 112, Greece.
Formerly (until 1965): Foreign Trade of Greece (ISSN 0071-738X)

330   GP
COMPTES ECONOMIQUES DE LA GUADELOUPE. 1968. a. 5 F. Institut National de la Statistique et des Etudes Economiques, B.P.96, 97102 Basse Terre, Guadeloupe. stat. circ. 530.

330 318   MQ
COMPTES ECONOMIQUES DE LA MARTINIQUE. 1968. irreg.; latest, 1973. 5 F. Institut National de la Statistique et des Etudes Economiques, 18, Bd A. Pinard, Route de Schoelcher, B.P.605, 97261 Fort de France Cedex, Martinique adv. stat. circ. 600.

330 316   FR
COMPTES ECONOMIQUES DU TERRITOIRE FRANCAIS DES AFARS ET DES ISSAS. irreg. £5. Institut National de la Statistique et des Etudes Economiques, 18, Bd A. Pinard, F 75675 Paris 14, France. stat. circ. 600.

339 314   BE   ISSN 0069-8075
COMPTES NATIONAUX DE LA BELGIQUE. (Text in Dutch and French) a. Institut National de Statistique, 44 rue de Louvain, 1000 Brussels, Belgium.

330 016   UK   ISSN 0045-8368
CONTENTS OF RECENT ECONOMICS JOURNALS. 1971. a. £39.25. H.M.S.O., P.O. Box 569, London SE1 9NH, England. circ. 1,000.

338.9 318   BO
CORPORACION BOLIVIANA DE FOMENTO. MARCHA DE LA ECONOMIA NACIONAL. RESUMEN ESTADISTICO. 1975. a. Corporacion Boliviana de Fomento, La Paz, Bolivia. charts. stat.

318 331.11   CR
COSTA RICA. DIRECCION GENERAL DE ESTADISTICA Y CENSOS. ENCUESTA DE HOGARES, EMPLEO Y DESEMPLEO: AREA METROPOLITANA DE SAN JOSE. 1976. irreg, latest 1978. Direccion General de Estadistica y Censos, Apartado 10163, San Jose, Costa Rica.

382   UK   ISSN 0309-5460
CURRENT AFRICAN DIRECTORIES. 1972. irreg. £10($30) ‡ C B D Research Ltd., 154 High St., Beckenham, Kent BR3 1EA, England (Dist. in U.S. by: Gale Research Co., Book Tower, Detroit, MI 48226) Ed. I.G. Anderson. circ. 1,500.
Incorporating: African Companies.

011   UK
CURRENT ASIAN & AUSTRALASIAN DIRECTORIES; a guide to directories published in or relating to all countries in Asia, Australasia & Oceania. 1978. irreg. £27($85) C B D Research Ltd., 154 High St., Beckenham, Kent BR3 1EA, England. Ed. I. G. Anderson.

016   UK   ISSN 0070-1858
CURRENT BRITISH DIRECTORIES. 1953. irreg., 9th, 1979. £33($105) ‡ C. B. D. Research Ltd., 154 High St., Beckenham, Kent BR3 1EA, England (Dist. in U.S. by: Gale Research Co., Book Tower, Detroit, MI 48226) Eds. G. P. Henderson and I. G. Anderson. adv. index. circ. 2,000.

011   UK   ISSN 0070-1955
CURRENT EUROPEAN DIRECTORIES. 1969. irreg., 2nd, 1981. ‡ C. B. D. Research Ltd., 154 High St., Beckenham, Kent BR3 1EA, England (Dist. in U.S. by: Gale Research Co., Book Tower, Detroit, MI 48226) Ed. G. P. Henderson. adv. index. circ. 2,000.

331.1   US   ISSN 0091-9209
CURRENT GOVERNMENTS REPORTS: CITY EMPLOYMENT. (Series GE-2) 1948. a. price varies. U.S. Bureau of the Census, Washington, DC 20233. Ed. Alan V. Stevens. Key Title: City Employment.

CURRENT GOVERNMENTS REPORTS: LOCAL GOVERNMENT EMPLOYMENT IN SELECTED METROPOLITAN AREAS AND LARGE COUNTIES. see *PUBLIC ADMINISTRATION — Abstracting, Bibliographies, Statistics*

336.73 317   US   ISSN 0090-5895
CURRENT GOVERNMENTS REPORTS: STATE GOVERNMENT FINANCES. (Series GF-3) a. price varies. U.S. Bureau of the Census, Subscriber Services Section, Washington, DC 20233. Ed. Vance Kane. Key Title: State Government Finances.
Continues: U.S. Bureau of the Census. State Finances.

BUSINESS AND ECONOMICS — ABSTRACTING, BIBLIOGRAPHIES, STATISTICS

381 CY
CYPRUS. DEPARTMENT OF STATISTICS AND RESEARCH. ANALYSIS OF WHOLESALE AND RETAIL TRADE. a. Mils.250. Department of Statistics and Research, Ministry of Finance, Nicosia, Cyprus.

331.11 CY
CYPRUS. DEPARTMENT OF STATISTICS AND RESEARCH. ANNUAL REPORT OF VACANCIES. (Text in English and Greek) 1970. a. Mils.300. Department of Statistics and Research, Ministry of Finance, Nicosia, Cyprus.

331.11 CY
CYPRUS. DEPARTMENT OF STATISTICS AND RESEARCH. ANNUAL REPORT ON UNEMPLOYMENT. (Text in English and Greek) 1973. a. Mils.400. Department of Statistics and Research, Ministry of Finance, Nicosia, Cyprus.

330 314 CY ISSN 0070-2412
CYPRUS. DEPARTMENT OF STATISTICS AND RESEARCH. ECONOMIC REPORT. (Title varies, 1955-62, Economic Review) 1954. a. Mils.750($2.20) Department of Statistics and Research, Ministry of Finance, Nicosia, Cyprus.

331.11 CY
CYPRUS. DEPARTMENT OF STATISTICS AND RESEARCH. MANPOWER SURVEY. (Text in English) 1966. a. Mils.500. Department of Statistics and Research, Ministry of Finance, Nicosia, Cyprus.

331.2 312 CY
CYPRUS. DEPARTMENT OF STATISTICS AND RESEARCH. WAGES, SALARIES AND HOURS OF WORK. a. Mils.350. Department of Statistics and Research, Ministry of Finance, Nicosia, Cyprus.

382 314 DK ISSN 0070-2781
DANMARKS VAREINDFOERSEL OG-UDFOERSEL/FOREIGN TRADE OF DENMARK. (Subseries of its Statistisk Tabel Vaerk) 1883. a. Kr.12.80. Danmarks Statistik, Sejroegade 11, 2100 Copenhagen OE, Denmark.

331.11 314 DK ISSN 0070-346X
DENMARK. DANMARKS STATISTIK. ARBEJDSLOESHEDEN/UNEMPLOYMENT. (Subseries of its Statistiske Meddelelser) (Text in Danish; notes in English) 1910-14. a. Kr.9.13. Danmarks Statistik, Sejroegade 11, 2100 Copenhagen OE, Denmark.

336.2 314 DK
DENMARK. DANMARKS STATISTIK. EJENDOMS- OG SELSKABSBESKATNINGEN I SKATTEAARET. (Subseries of its Statistiske Meddelelser) (Text in Danish; notes in English) 1938. a. Kr.8.40. Danmarks Statistik, Sejroegade 11, 2100 Copenhagen OE, Denmark.
Supersedes in part: Denmark. Danmarks Statistik. Ejendoms- og Personbeskatingen i Skattearet (ISSN 0070-3494)

336.2 314 DK
DENMARK. DANMARKS STATISTIK. INDKOMSTER OG FORMVER VED SLUTLIGNINGEN. (Subseries of its Statistisk Tabelvaerk) 1970. a. Kr.16 plus tax. Danmarks Statistik, Sejroegade 11, 2100 Copenhagen OE, Denmark.
Supersedes: Denmark. Danmarks Statistik. Indkomstansaettelser Til Staten (ISSN 0070-3493)

338 314 DK ISSN 0070-3532
DENMARK. DANMARKS STATISTIK. INDUSTRISTATISTIK/INDUSTRIAL STATISTICS. (Subseries of its Statistiske Meddelelser) (Text in Danish; notes in English) 1905. a. Kr.12. Danmarks Statistik, Sejroegade 11, 2100 Copenhagen OE, Denmark.

330 314 DK
DENMARK. DANMARKS STATISTIK. KONJUNKTURO. VERSIGT/ECONOMIC TRENDS. (Text in: Danish and English) irreg. Danmarks Statistik, Sejroegade 11, 2100 Copenhagen OE, Denmark. illus.

330 CN
DEVINDEX; index to literature on third world economic and social development. (Text in English & French) 1976. a. free or on exchange. International Development Research Centre, Box 8500, Ottawa, Ont. K1G 3H9, Canada. Ed. Gisele Morin-Labatut. circ. 2,000. (also avail. in microfiche)
Formerly: Devindex Canada.

339 314 YU ISSN 0300-2527
DRUSTVENI PROIZVOD I NARODNI DOHODAK. (Subseries of Statisticki Bilten) 1969/70. a. 30 din.($1.67) Savezni Zavod za Statistiku, Uzun Mirkova 1, Belgrade, Yugoslavia. stat.

330 016 SW
E F I NYTT/E F I NEWS. (Text in Swedish; summaries in English) 1973. irreg. free. Handelshoegskolan i Stockholm, Ekonomiska Forskningsinstitutet - Economic Research Institute at the Stockholm School of Economics, Box 6501, 113 83 Stockholm, Sweden.

338 318 EC ISSN 0302-5233
ECUADOR. INSTITUTO NACIONAL DE ESTADISTICA Y CENSOS. ENCUESTA ANUAL DE MANUFACTURA Y MINERIA. irreg. Instituto Nacional de Estadistica y Censos, Av. 10 de Agosto 229, Quito, Ecuador. charts. stat.

331.11 318 EC ISSN 0070-8917
ECUADOR. INSTITUTO NACIONAL DE ESTADISTICA Y CENSOS. ESTADISTICA DEL TRABAJO; indice de empleo y remuneraciones. irreg. Instituto Nacional de Estadistica y Censos, Junta Nacional de Planificacion y Coordinacion Economica, 10 de Agosto No. 229, Quito, Ecuador.

331.2 US
EMPLOYMENT AND EARNINGS: UNITED STATES. a. price varies. U. S. Bureau of Labor Statistics, Dept. of Labor, 441 G St. N.W., Washington, DC 20212 (Orders to: Supt. of Documents, Washington, DC 20402) (also avail. in microform from UMI)
Formerly: Employment and Earnings Statistics for the United States (ISSN 0071-013X)

338 318 VE
ENCUESTA INDUSTRIAL: RESULTADOS NACIONALES. 1974. irreg. Direccion General de Estadistica y Censos Nacionales, Centro Simon Bolivar, Edificio sur, Caracas, Venezuela. stat.

332.6 318 PN
ESTADISTICA PANAMENA. INVERSIONES DIRECTAS EXTRANJERAS EN PANAMA. 1960. irreg. Bol.$.30. Direccion de Estadistica y Censo, Apartado 5213, Panama 5, Panama. stat. circ. 1,000.

330 318 PN
ESTADISTICA PANAMENA. SITUACION ECONOMICA. SECCION 321 Y 325. INDUSTRIA ENCUESTA. 1957. a. Direccion de Estadistica y Censo, Contraloria General, Apdo. 5213, Panama 5, Panama. circ. 1,600.

338 318 PN
ESTADISTICA PANAMENA. SITUACION SOCIAL. SECCION 441-TRABAJO Y SALARIOS. ESTADISTICAS DEL TRABAJO. 1968. a. Bol.$.30. Direccion de Estadistica y Censo, Contraloria General, Apartado 5213, Panama 5, Panama. circ. 1,500.
Incorporating: Panama. Direccion de Estadistica y Censo. Estadistica Panamena Serie M: Empleo (ISSN 0078-8961)

338.09 314 SP
ESTADISTICAS DE PRODUCCION INDUSTRIAL; analisis y resultados. a. Servicio Sindical de Estadisticas, Huertas 73, Madrid, Spain.

382.09 318 VE
ESTADISTICAS DEL COMERCIO EXTERIOR DE VENEZUELA. BOLETIN. irreg. Direccion General de Estadistica y Censos Nacionales, Caracas, Venezuela.

382 316 ET ISSN 0425-4309
ETHIOPIA. CUSTOMS HEAD OFFICE. EXTERNAL TRADE STATISTICS. (Text in English) 1946. a. Eth.$6($2.90) Customs Head Office, P.O. Box 3248, Addis Ababa, Ethiopia. charts. stat. index.

338 016 UK ISSN 0071-2582
EUROPEAN COMPANIES; a guide to sources of information. 1961. irreg., 4th, 1982. ‡ C.B.D. Research Ltd., 154 High St., Beckenham, Kent BR3 1EA, England (Dist. in U.S. by: Gale Research Co., Book Tower, Detroit, MI 48226) Ed. G. P. Henderson. adv. circ. 2,000.

310 AF
EXPORT STATISTICS OF AFGHANISTAN/IHSA'IYAH-I AMUAL-I SADIRATI-I AFGHANISTAN. (Text in Persian or English) no. 1354, 1975. a. $20. Central Statistical Office, Nader Shah Minah, Block No. 4, Box 2002, Kabul, Afghanistan. stat.

382 316 GM
EXTERNAL TRADE STATISTICS OF GAMBIA. Variant title: Gambia. Central Statistics Department. Annual Report of External Trade Statistics. (Formerly issued by Central Statistics Division) 1973. a., latest 1975/1976. d. 25. Central Statistics Department, Wellington St., Banjul, Gambia.

338 016 US
F & S INDEX EUROPE. ANNUAL. 1979. a. $195. Predicasts, Inc., 200 University Circle Research Center, 11001 Cedar Ave., Cleveland, OH 44106. Ed. Georgiana Eckles. abstr. bibl. stat. tr.lit. index.

338 016 US
F & S INDEX INTERNATIONAL ANNUAL. 1969. a. $195. Predicasts, Inc., 200 University Circle Research Center, 11001 Cedar Ave., Cleveland, OH 44106.

331 US
FEDERAL CIVILIAN WORK FORCE STATISTICS. OCCUPATIONS OF FEDERAL BLUE-COLLAR WORKERS. 1957. a. free. U.S. Office of Personnel Management, Agency Compliance and Evaluation, Work Force Analysis and Statistics Branch, 1900 E St. N.W., Washington, DC 20415. circ. 500. Indexed: C.I.S.Ind.
Formerly: Occupations of Federal Blue-Collar Workers.

317 US
FEDERAL CIVILIAN WORK FORCE STATISTICS. WORK YEARS AND PERSONNEL COSTS. EXECUTIVE BRANCH, UNITED STATES GOVERNMENT. 1970. a. free. U.S. Office of Personnel Management, Agency Compliance and Evaluation, Work Force Analysis and Statistics Branch, 1900 E St., N.W., Washington, DC 20415. circ. 500.
Former titles: Work-Years and Personnel Costs. Executive Branch of the United States Government; Work-Years and Personnel Costs. Executive Branch, U.S. Government; Man-Years and Personnel Costs. Executive Branch, U.S. Government.

315 339 FJ
FIJI. BUREAU OF STATISTICS. FIJI HOUSEHOLD INCOME AND EXPENDITURE SURVEY. 1973. a. Bureau of Statistics, Box 2221, Suva, Fiji. stat.

336 314 FI ISSN 0430-5566
FINLAND. TILASTOKESKUS. KUNTIEN FINANSSITILASTO/FINLAND. STATISTIKCENTRALEN. KOMMUNAL FINANSSTATISTIK/FINLAND. CENTRAL STATISTICAL OFFICE. COMMUNAL FINANCES. (Section XXXI of Official Statistics of Finland) (Text in Finnish and Swedish; summaries in English) 1927. a. Fmk.35. Tilastokeskus, Annankatu 44, SF-00100 Helsinki 10, Finland (Subscr. to: Government Printing Centre, Box 516, SF-00100 Helsinki 10, Finland)

312.2 FI ISSN 0355-2144
FINLAND. TILASTOKESKUS. KUOLEMANSYYT/FINLAND. STATISTIKCENTRALEN. DOEDSORSAKER/FINLAND. CENTRAL STATISTICAL OFFICE. CAUSES OF DEATH IN FINLAND. (Section VI B of Official Statistics of Finland) (Text in Finnish, Swedish and English) 1939. a. Fmk.22. Tilastokeskus, Annankatu 44, SF-00100 Helsinki 10, Finland (Subscr. to: Government Printing Centre, Box 516, SF-00100 Helsinki 10, Finland)

314 332   FI   ISSN 0355-2454
FINLAND. TILASTOKESKUS. PANKIT/
FINLAND. STATISTIKCENTRALEN.
BANKERNA/FINALND. CENTRAL
STATISTICAL OFFICE. BANKS. (Section VII C
of Official Statistics of Finland) (Text in Finnish,
Swedish and English) 1974. a. Fmk.17.
Tilastokeskus, Annankatu 44, SF-00100 Helsinki 10,
Finland (Subscr. to: Government Printing Centre,
Box 516, SF-00100 Helsinki 10, Finland)
  Formed by the merger of: Finland. Tilastokeskus.
Osuuspankkitilasto & Finland. Tilastokeskus.
Saastopankkitilasto & Finland. Tilastokeskus.
Liikepankit Ja Kiinnitys Luottolaitokset.

338 314   FI   ISSN 0071-5344
FINLAND. TILASTOKESKUS.
TEOLLISUUSTILASTO/FINLAND.
STATISTISKA CENTRALBYRAAN/FINLAND.
CENTRAL STATISTICAL OFFICE.
INDUSTRIAL STATISTICS. (Section XVIII A of
Official Statistics of Finland) (Text in Finnish and
Swedish; Summaries in English) 1884. a. price
varies. Tilastokeskus, Annankatu 44, SF-00101
Helsinki 10, Finland (Subscr. to: Government
Printing Centre, Box 516, SF-00100 Helsinki 10,
Finland)

314 339   FI   ISSN 0355-211X
FINLAND. TILASTOKESKUS. TULO- JA
OMAISUUSTILASTO/FINLAND.
STATISTIKCENTRALEN. INKOMST- OCH
FOERMOEGENHETSTATISTIK/FINLAND.
CENTRAL STATISTICAL OFFICE. STATISTICS
OF INCOME AND PROPERTY. (Section IV B of
Official Statistics of Finland) (Text in Finnish,
Swedish and English) 1926. a. Fmk.19.
Tilastokeskus, Annanakatu 44, SF-00100 Helsinki
10, Finland (Subscr. to: Government Printing
Centre, Box 516, SF-00100 Helsinki 10, Finland)

314 338   FI   ISSN 0355-2071
FINLAND. TILASTOKESKUS. TUTKIMUKSIA/
FINLAND. STATISTIKCENTRALEN.
UNDERSOEKNINGAR/FINLAND. CENTRAL
STATISTICAL OFFICE. STUDIES. 1966. irreg.
price varies. Tilastokeskus, Annankatu 44, SF-00100
Helsinki 10, Finlamd (Subscr. to: Government
Printing Centre, Box 516, SF-00100 Helsinki 10,
Finland)

382 316   UN   ISSN 0071-7398
FOREIGN TRADE STATISTICS OF AFRICA.
SERIES A: DIRECTION OF TRADE. (Text in
English and French) irreg.; no. 22, 1974. price
varies. United Nations Economic Commission for
Africa - Commission Economique pour l'Afrique,
Box 3001, Addis Ababa, Ethiopia (Dist. by: United
Nations Publications, Room LX-2300, New York,
NY 10017; or Distribution and Sales Section, Palais
des Nations, CH-1211 Geneva 10, Switzerland)

382 316   UN   ISSN 0071-7401
FOREIGN TRADE STATISTICS OF AFRICA.
SERIES B: TRADE BY COMMODITY. (Text in
English and French) irreg.; no. 25, 1974. price
varies. United Nations Economic Commission for
Africa - Commission Economique pour l'Afrique,
Box 3001, Addis Ababa, Ethiopia (Dist. by: United
Nations Publications, Room LX-2300, New York,
NY 10017; or Distirbution and Sales Section, Palais
des Nations, CH-1211 Geneva 10, Switzerland)

382 315   IR   ISSN 0075-0492
FOREIGN TRADE STATISTICS OF IRAN.
YEARBOOK.* (Text in English and Arabic) a.
Ministry of Finance and Economic Affairs, Teheran,
Iran.

382 315   PH
FOREIGN TRADE STATISTICS OF THE
PHILIPPINES. a. P.60($20) National Census and
Statistics Office, Ramon Magsaysay Blvd., Box 779,
Manila, Philippines.

382 315   YE
FOREIGN TRADE STATISTICS OF YEMEN
ARAB REPUBLIC. (Text in English) a. Central
Bank of Yemen, Research Department, Box 59,
Sana'a, Yemen. stat.

382 314   FR   ISSN 0071-8688
FRANCE. DIRECTION GENERALE DES
DOUANES ET DROITS INDIRECTS.
STATISTIQUES DU COMMERCE EXTERIEUR:
IMPORTATIONS- EXPORTATIONS.
NOMENCLATURE: N.G.P. (NOMENCLATURE
GENERALE DES PRODUITS) a. 135 F.
Imprimerie Nationale, Service des Ventes, 59128
Flers en Escrebieux, France.

330 310   FR
FRANCE. INSTITUT NATIONAL DE LA
STATISTIQUE ET DES ETUDES
ECONOMIQUES. COLLECTIONS. SERIE C,
COMPTES ET PLANIFICATION. (Text in
French; summaries in English and Spanish) 1969.
irreg. 175 F. for 8 nos. Institut National de la
Statistique et des Etudes Economiques, 18, Bd. A.
Pinard, 75675 Paris 14, France. circ. 3,000.

330 314   FR
FRANCE. INSTITUT NATIONAL DE LA
STATISTIQUE ET DES ETUDES
ECONOMIQUES. COLLECTIONS. SERIE E,
ENTREPRISES. irreg. 175 F. for 8 nos. Institut
National de la Statistique et des Etudes
Economiques, 18, Bd. A. Pinard, F 75675 Paris 14,
France. stat. circ. 3,000.

330 310   FR
FRANCE. INSTITUT NATIONAL DE LA
STATISTIQUE ET DES ETUDES
ECONOMIQUES. COLLECTIONS. SERIE M,
MENAGES. (Text in French; Summaries in English
and Spanish) 1969. irreg. 220 F. for 10 nos. Institut
National de la Statistique et des Etudes
Economiques, 18, Bd. A. Pinard, 75675 Paris 14,
France. circ. 3,000.

334   FR   ISSN 0336-6979
FRANCE. INSTITUT NATIONAL DE LA
STATISTIQUE ET DES ETUDES
ECONOMIQUES. DOCUMENTS DIVERS. irreg.
Institut National de la Statistique et des Etudes
Economiques, 118 Bd. A. Pinard, 75675 Paris
Cedex 14, France.

338 314   FR   ISSN 0071-8211
FRANCE. SERVICE DU TRAITEMENT DE
L'INFORMATION ET DES STATISTIQUES
INDUSTRIELLES. ANNUAIRE DE
STATISTIQUE INDUSTRIELLE. 1947. a. 110 F.
Service du Traitement de l'Information et des
Statistiques Industrielles, 85 Bd. du Montparnasse,
75270 Paris 6, France.
  Formerly: France. Bureau Central de Statistique
Industrielle. Annuaire de Statistique Industrielle.

338 311   FR
FRANCE. SERVICE DU TRAITEMENT DE
L'INFORMATION ET DES STATISTIQUES
INDUSTRIELLES. RECUEIL STATISTIQUES.
1974. irreg; no. 14, 1977. price varies. Service du
Traitement de l'Information et des Statistiques
Industrielles, 85 Bd. du Montparnasse, 75006 Paris,
France.

331.11 314   GW
GERMANY (FEDERAL REPUBLIC, 1949-)
BUNDESANSTALT FUER ARBEIT.
BERUFSBERATUNG. ERGEBNISSE DER
BERUFSBERATUNGSSTATISTIK. (Beilage Zu
den Amtlichen Nachrichten der Bundesanstalt fuer
Arbeit) 1953. a. DM.9. ‡ Bundesanstalt fuer Arbeit,
Regensburger Str. 104, 8500 Nuernberg 1, W.
Germany (B.R.D.) index.

331 314   GW   ISSN 0072-1557
GERMANY (FEDERAL REPUBLIC,1949-)
BUNDESMINISTERIUM FUER ARBEIT UND
SOZIALORDNUNG. HAUPTERGEBNISSE DER
ARBEITS-UND SOZIALSTATISTIK. 1952. a.
DM.12. Bundesministerium fuer Arbeit und
Sozialordnung, Postfach 140280, 5300 Bonn 1, W.
Germany (B.R.D.)

382 314   GW   ISSN 0072-1638
GERMANY (FEDERAL REPUBLIC, 1949-)
STATISTISCHES BUNDESAMT.
ALPHABETISCHES LAENDERVERZEICHNIS
FUER DIE AUSSENHANDELSSTATISTIK. irreg.
DM.6 each. W. Kohlhammer-Verlag GmbH, Abt.
Veroeffentlichungen des Statistischen Bundesamtes,
Philipp-Reis-Str. 3, Postfach 421120, 6500 Mainz
42, W. Germany (B.R.D.)

382 314   GW
GERMANY(FEDERAL REPUBLIC, 1949-)
STATISTISCHES BUNDESAMT.
AUSLANDSSTATISTIK NR. 6370010: FOREIGN
TRADE ACCORDING TO THE STANDARD
INTERNATIONAL TRADE CLASSIFICATION
(SITC) - SPECIAL TRADE. q. with a. cumulation.
DM.72.80. W. Kohlhammer-Verlag GmbH, Abt.
Veroeffentlichungen des Statistischen Bundesamtes,
Philipp-Reis-Str. 3, Postfach 421120, 6500 Mainz
42, W. Germany (B.R.D.)

382 314   GW   ISSN 0072-1700
GERMANY (FEDERAL REPUBLIC, 1949-)
STATISTISCHES BUNDESAMT.
AUSSENHANDEL. REIHE 7:
SONDERBEITRAEGE. irreg. price varies. W.
Kohlhammer-Verlag GmbH, Abt.
Veroeffentlichungen des Statistischen Bundesamtes,
Philipp-Reis-Str. 3, Postfach 421120, 6500 Mainz
42, W. Germany (B.R.D.)

338 314   GW
GERMANY (FEDERAL REPUBLIC, 1949-)
STATISTISCHES BUNDESAMT. FACHSERIE
AUSLANDSSTATISTIK, REIHE 2:
PRODUZIERENDE GEWERBE IM AUSLAND.
(Consists of several subseries) irreg. price varies. W.
Kohlhammer-Verlag GmbH, Abt.
Veroeffentlichungen des Statistischen Bundesamtes,
Philipp-Reis-Str. 3, Postfach 421120, 6500 Mainz
42, W. Germany (B.R.D.)

331.2 310   GW
GERMANY (FEDERAL REPUBLIC, 1949-)
STATISTISCHES BUNDESAMT. FACHSERIE
AUSLANDSSTATISTIK, REIHE 4: LOEHNE
UND GEHAELTER IM AUSLAND. 1950/51. a.
price varies. W. Kohlhammer-Verlag GmbH, Abt.
Veroeffentlichungen des Statistischen Bundesamtes,
Philipp-Reis-Str. 3, Postfach 421120, 6500 Mainz
42, W. Germany (B.R.D.)

382 310   GW   ISSN 0072-3940
GERMANY (FEDERAL REPUBLIC, 1949-)
STATISTISCHES BUNDESAMT. FACHSERIE
AUSLANDSSTATISTIK, REIHE 5: PREISE UND
PREISINDIZES IM AUSLAND. m. DM.44.40. W.
Kohlhammer-Verlag GmbH, Abt.
Veroeffentlichungen des Statistischen Bundesamtes,
Philipp-Reis-Str 3, Postfach 421120, 6500 Mainz 42,
W. Germany (B.R.D.)

331 314   GW   ISSN 0072-1832
GERMANY (FEDERAL REPUBLIC, 1949-)
STATISTISCHES BUNDESAMT. FACHSERIE 1,
REIHE 4: ERWERBETAETIGKEIT. irreg. price
varies. W. Kohlhammer-Verlag GmbH, Abt.
Veroeffentlichungen des Statistischen Bundesamtes,
Philipp-Reis-Str. 3, Postfach 421120, 6500 Mainz
42, W. Germany (B.R.D.)

338 314   GW
GERMANY (FEDERAL REPUBLIC, 1949-)
STATISTISCHES BUNDESAMT. FACHSERIE 2,
REIHE 2.1: ABSCHLUESSE DER
KAPITALGESELLSCHAFTEN. 1971. a.
DM.11.70. W. Kohlhammer-Verlag GmbH, Abt.
Veroeffentlichungen des Statistischen Bundesamtes,
Philipp-Reis-Str. 3, Postfach 421120, 6500 Mainz
42, W. Germany (B.R.D.)

338 314   GW
GERMANY (FEDERAL REPUBLIC, 1949-)
STATISTISCHES BUNDESAMT. FACHSERIE 2,
REIHE 3: ABSCHLUESSE DER
OEFFENTLICHEN VERSORGUNGS- UND
VERKEHRSUNTERNEHMEN. 1959. a. DM.8.30.
W. Kohlhammer-Verlag GmbH, Abt.
Veroeffentlichungen des Statistischen Bundesamtes,
Philipp-Reis-Str. 3, Postfach 421120, 6500 Mainz
42, W. Germany (B.R.D.)

332.1 314   GW   ISSN 0072-2030
GERMANY (FEDERAL REPUBLIC, 1949-)
STATISTISCHES BUNDESAMT. FACHSERIE 2,
4: ZAHLUNGSSCHWIERIGKEITEN. (Consists of
two subseries) q. price varies. W. Kohlhammer-
Verlag GmbH, Abt. Veroeffentlichungen des
Statistischen Bundesamtes, Philipp-Reis-Str. 3,
Postfach 421120, 6500 Mainz 42, W. Germany
(B.R.D.)

338 314   GW ISSN 0072-2073
GERMANY (FEDERAL REPUBLIC, 1949-)
STATISTISCHES BUNDESAMT. FACHSERIE 4,
REIHE S: SONDERBEITRAEGE. 1951. irreg.
price varies. W. Kohlhammer-Verlag GmbH, Abt.
Veroeffentlichungen des Statistischen Bundesamtes,
Philipp-Reis-Str. 3, Postfach 421120, 6500 Mainz
42, W. Germany (B.R.D.)

338 314   GW
GERMANY (FEDERAL REPUBLIC, 1949-)
STATISTISCHES BUNDESAMT. FACHSERIE 4,
REIHE 1: ZUSAMMENFASSENDE DATEN
FUER DAS PRODUZIERENDE GEWERBE.
irreg. price varies. W. Kohlhammer-Verlag GmbH,
Abt. Veroeffentlichungen des Statistischen
Bundesamtes, Philipp-Reis-Str. 3, Postfach 421120,
6500 Mainz 42, W. Germany (B.R.D.)

338 314   GW
GERMANY (FEDERAL REPUBLIC, 1949-)
STATISTISCHES BUNDESAMT. FACHSERIE 4,
REIHE 2: INDIZES FUER DAS
PRODUZIERENDE GEWERBE. (Consists of
several subseries) 1951. m. price varies. W.
Kohlhammer-Verlag GmbH, Abt.
Veroeffentlichungen des Statistischen Bundesamtes,
Philipp-Reis-Str. 3, Postfach 421120, 6500 Mainz
42, W. Germany (B.R.D.)

338 314   GW
GERMANY (FEDERAL REPUBLIC, 1949-)
STATISTISCHES BUNDESAMT. FACHSERIE 4,
REIHE 2.2: INDICES DES
AUFTRAGSEINGANGS, DES UMSATZES UND
DES AUFTRAGSBESTANDS FUER DAS
VERARBEITENDE GEWERBE UND FUER
DAS BAUHAUPT GEWERBE. m. DM.74.70. W.
Kohlhammer-Verlag GmbH, Abt.
Veroeffentlichungen des Statistischen Bundesamtes,
Philipp-Reis-Str. 3, Postfach 421120, 6500 Mainz
42, W. Germany (B.R.D.)
   Supersedes: Germany (Federal Republic, 1949-)
Statistisches Bundesamt. Fachserie 4, Reihe 2:
Indices des Auftragseingangs in Ausgewaehlten
Industriezweigen und im Bauhauptgewerbe (ISSN
0072-209X)

338 314   GW
GERMANY (FEDERAL REPUBLIC, 1949-)
STATISTISCHES BUNDESAMT. FACHSERIE 4,
REIHE 3.1: PRODUKTION IM
PRODUZIERENDEN GEWERBE. (Consists of
several subseris) 1951. q. DM.53.60. W.
Kohlhammer-Verlag GmbH, Abt.
Veroeffentlichungen des Statistischen Bundesamtes,
Philipp-Reis-Str. 3, Postfach 421120, 6500 Mainz
42, W. Germany (B.R.D.)

338 314   GW ISSN 0072-2103
GERMANY (FEDERAL REPUBLIC, 1949-)
STATISTISCHES BUNDESAMT. FACHSERIE 4,
REIHE 7: HANDWERK. irreg. price varies. W.
Kohlhammer-Verlag GmbH, Abt.
Veroeffentlichungen des Statistischen Bundesamtes,
Philipp-Reis-Str. 3, Postfach 421120, 6500 Mainz
42, W. Germany (B.R.D.)

380 314   GW ISSN 0072-1964
GERMANY (FEDERAL REPUBLIC, 1949-)
STATISTISCHES BUNDESAMT. FACHSERIE 6,
REIHE 1: GROSSHANDEL. a. price varies. W.
Kohlhammer-Verlag GmbH, Abt.
Veroeffentlichungen des Statistischen Bundesamtes,
Philipp-Reis-Str. 3, Postfach 421120, 6500 Mainz
42, W. Germany (B.R.D.)

380 314   GW ISSN 0072-1972
GERMANY (FEDERAL REPUBLIC, 1949-)
STATISTISCHES BUNDESAMT. FACHSERIE 6,
REIHE 3: EINZELHANDEL. (Consists of several
subseries) a. price varies. W. Kohlhammer-Verlag
GmbH, Abt. Veroeffentlichungen des Statistischen
Bundesamtes, Philipp-Reis-Str. 3, Postfach 421120,
6500 Mainz 42, W. Germany (B.R.D.)

381 314   GW
GERMANY (FEDERAL REPUBLIC, 1949-)
STATISTISCHES BUNDESAMT. FACHSERIE 6,
REIHE 5: WAHRENVERKEHR MIT BERLIN
(WEST) m. DM.28.80. W. Kohlhammer-Verlag
GmbH, Abt. Veroeffentlichungen des Statistischen
Bundesamtes, Philipp-Reis-Str. 3, Postfach 421120,
6500 Mainz 42, W. Germany (B.R.D.)

382 314   GW ISSN 0072-1980
GERMANY (FEDERAL REPUBLIC, 1949-)
STATISTISCHES BUNDESAMT. FACHSERIE 6,
REIHE 6: WAHRENVERKEHR MIT DER
DEUTSCHEN DEMOKRATISCHEN REPUBLIK
UND BERLIN (OST) m. DM.86.40. W.
Kohlhammer-Verlag GmbH, Abt.
Veroeffentlichungen des Statistischen Bundesamtes,
Philipp-Reis-Str. 3, Postfach 421120, 6500 Mainz
42, W. Germany (B.R.D.)

382 314   GW ISSN 0072-1646
GERMANY (FEDERAL REPUBLIC, 1949-)
STATISTISCHES BUNDESAMT. FACHSERIE 7,
REIHE 1: ZUSAMMENFASSENDE
UEBERSICHTEN FUER DEN
AUSSENHANDEL. m. DM.86.40. W.
Kohlhammer-Verlag GmbH, Abt.
Veroeffentlichungen des Statistischen Bundesamtes,
Philipp-Reis-Str. 3, Postfach 421120, 6500 Mainz
42, W. Germany (B.R.D.)

382 314   GW ISSN 0072-1654
GERMANY (FEDERAL REPUBLIC, 1949-)
STATISTISCHES BUNDESAMT. FACHSERIE 7,
REIHE 2: AUSSENHANDEL NACH WAREN
UND LAENDERN (SPEZIALHANDEL) m. with
a. cumulation. DM.248.40. W. Kohlhammer-Verlag
GmbH, Abt. Veroeffentlichungen des Statistischen
Bundesamtes, Philipp-Reis-Str. 3, Postfach 421120,
6500 Mainz 42, W. Germany (B.R.D.)

382 314   GW ISSN 0072-1662
GERMANY (FEDERAL REPUBLIC, 1949-)
STATISTISCHES BUNDESAMT. FACHSERIE 7,
REIHE 3: AUSSENHANDEL NACH
LAENDERN UND WARENGRUPPEN
(SPEZIALHANDEL) q. with a. cumulation.
DM.72.80. W. Kohlhammer-Verlag GmbH, Abt.
Veroeffentlichungen des Statistischen Bundesamtes,
Philipp-Reis-Str. 3, Postfach 421120, 6500 Mainz
42, W. Germany (B.R.D.)

382 314   GW
GERMANY (FEDERAL REPUBLIC, 1949-)
STATISTISCHES BUNDESAMT. FACHSERIE 7,
REIHE 4. AUSSENHANDEL MIT
AUSGEWAEHLTEN WAREN; Reihe 4.1: Ein-
und Ausfuhr von Mineraloel (Generalhandel) m.
with a. cumulation. DM.74.40. W. Kohlhammer-
Verlag GmbH, Abt. Veroeffentlichungen des
Statistischen Bundesamtes, Philipp-Reis-Str. 3,
Postfach 421120, 6500 Mainz 42, W. Germany
(B.R.D.)

382 314   GW ISSN 0072-1697
GERMANY (FEDERAL REPUBLIC, 1949-)
STATISTISCHES BUNDESAMT. FACHSERIE 7,
REIHE 6: DURCHFUHR IM SEEVERKEHR
UND SEEUMSCHLAG. a. DM.7. W.
Kohlhammer-Verlag GmbH, Abt.
Veroeffentlichungen des Statistischen Bundesamtes,
Philipp-Reis-Str. 3, Postfach 421120, 6500 Mainz
42, W. Germany (B.R.D.)

332.6 314   GW
GERMANY (FEDERAL REPUBLIC, 1949-)
STATISTISCHES BUNDESAMT. FACHSERIE 9,
REIHE 2: AKTIENMAERKTE. m. DM.28.80. W.
Kohlhammer-Verlag GmbH, Abt.
Veroeffentlichungen des Statistischen Bundesamtes,
Philipp-Reis-Str.3, Postfach 421120, 6500 Mainz 42,
W. Germany (B.R.D.)
   Formerly: Germany (Federal Republic, 1949-)
Statistisches Bundesamt. Geld und Kredit. Reihe 2:
Aktienkurse (ISSN 0072-2022)

336 314   GW
GERMANY (FEDERAL REPUBLIC, 1949-)
STATISTISCHES BUNDESAMT. FACHSERIE
14: FINANZEN UND STEUERN. (Consists of
several subseries) 1959. irreg. price varies. W.
Kohlhammer-Verlag GmbH, Abt.
Veroeffentlichungen des Statistischen Bundesamtes,
Philipp-Reis-Str. 3, Postfach 421120, 6500 Mainz
42, W. Germany (B.R.D.)

339.42 314   GW
GERMANY (FEDERAL REPUBLIC, 1949-)
STATISTISCHES BUNDESAMT. FACHSERIE
15, REIHE 1: EINNAHMEN UND AUSGABEN
AUSGEWAEHLTER PRIVATER HAUSHALTE.
1954. m. DM.28.80. W. Kohlhammer-Verlag
GmbH, Abt. Veroeffentlichungen des Statistischen
Bundesamtes, Philipp-Reis-Str. 3, Postfach 421120,
6500 Mainz 42, W. Germany (B.R.D.)
   Supersedes: Germany(Federal Republic, 1949-)
Statistiches Bundesamt. Fachserie 15, Reihe 1:
Wirtschaftsrechnungen (ISSN 0072-386X)

331.2 338.1 314   GW
GERMANY (FEDERAL REPUBLIC, 1949-)
STATISTISCHES BUNDESAMT. FACHSERIE
16, REIHE 1: ARBEITERVERDIENSTE IN DER
LANDWIRTSCHAFT. a. DM.1.30. W.
Kohlhammer-Verlag GmbH, Abt.
Veroeffentlichungen des Statistischen Bundesamtes,
Philipp-Reis-Str. 3, Postfach 421120, 6500 Mainz
42, W. Germany (B.R.D.)
   Supersedes: Germany(Federal Republic, 1949-)
Statistisches Bundesamt. Preise, Loehne,
Wirtschaftsrechnungen. Reihe 14: Arbeiterverdienste
in der Landwirtschaft.

331.2 314   GW ISSN 0072-3789
GERMANY (FEDERAL REPUBLIC, 1949-)
STATISTISCHES BUNDESAMT. FACHSERIE
16, REIHE 2: ARBEITNEHMERVERDIENSTE
IN INDUSTRIE UND HANDEL. q. price varies.
W. Kohlhammer-Verlag GmbH, Abt.
Veroeffentlichungen des Statistischen Bundesamtes,
Philipp-Reis-Str. 3, Postfach 421120, 6500 Mainz
42, W. Germany (B.R.D.)

331.2 314   GW ISSN 0072-3797
GERMANY (FEDERAL REPUBLIC, 1949-)
STATISTISCHES BUNDESAMT. FACHSERIE
16, REIHE 3: ARBEITERVERDIENSTE IM
HANDWERK. 1957. s-a. DM.4.80. W.
Kohlhammer-Verlag GmbH, Abt.
Veroeffentlichungen des Statistischen Bundesamtes,
Philipp-Reis-Str. 3, Postfach 421120, 6500 Mainz
42, W. Germany (B.R.D.)

336 314   GW ISSN 0072-3843
GERMANY (FEDERAL REPUBLIC, 1949-)
STATISTISCHES BUNDESAMT. FACHSERIE
16, REIHE 4: TARIFLOEHNE UND
TARIFGEHAELTER. s-a. price varies. W.
Kohlhammer-Verlag GmbH, Abt.
Veroeffentlichungen des Statistischen Bundesamtes,
Philipp-Reis-Str. 3, Postfach 421120, 6500 Mainz
42, W. Germany (B.R.D.)

338.5 314   GW
GERMANY (FEDERAL REPUBLIC, 1949-)
STATISTISCHES BUNDESAMT. FACHSERIE
17, REIHE 2: PREISE UND PREISINDIZES
FUER GEWERBLICHE PRODUKTE.
ERZEUGERPREISE. m. DM.44.40. W.
Kohlhammer-Verlag GmbH, Abt.
Veroeffentlichungen des Statistischen Bundesamtes,
Philipp-Reis-Str. 3, Postfach 421120, 6500 Mainz
42, W. Germany (B.R.D.)
   Formerly: Germany (Federal Republic, 1949-)
Statistisches Bundesamt. Fachserie 17, Reihe 2:
Preise und Preisindizes fuer Industrielle Produkte.
Erzeugerpreise (ISSN 0072-3886)

338.5 314   GW ISSN 0072-3878
GERMANY (FEDERAL REPUBLIC, 1949-)
STATISTISCHES BUNDESAMT. FACHSERIE
17, REIHE 3: INDEX DER
GRUNDSTOFFRPREISE. 1955. m. DM.28.80. W.
Kohlhammer-Verlag GmbH, Abt.
Veroeffentlichungen des Statistischen Bundesamtes,
Philipp-Reis-Str. 3, Postfach 421120, 6500 Mainz
42, W. Germany (B.R.D.)

380 314   GW
GERMANY (FEDERAL REPUBLIC, 1949-)
STATISTISCHES BUNDESAMT. FACHSERIE
17, REIHE 4: MESSZAHLEN FUER
BAULEISTUNGSPREISE UND PREISINDIZES
FUER BAUWERKE. m. DM.24.80. W.
Kohlhammer-Verlag GmbH, Abt.
Veroeffentlichungen des Statistischen Bundesamtes,
Philipp-Reis-Str. 3, Postfach 421120, 6500 Mainz
42, W. Germany (B.R.D.)

339 314 GW ISSN 0072-3916
GERMANY (FEDERAL REPUBLIC, 1949-) STATISTISCHES BUNDESAMT. FACHSERIE 17, REIHE 7: PREISE UND PREISINDIZES DER LEBENSERHALTUNG. m. price varies. W. Kohlhammer-Verlag GmbH, Abt. Veroeffentlichungen des Statistischen Bundesamtes, Philipp-Reis-Str. 3, Postfach 421120, 6500 Mainz 42, W. Germany (B.R.D.)

382 314 GW
GERMANY (FEDERAL REPUBLIC, 1949-) STATISTISCHES BUNDESAMT. FACHSERIE 17, REIHE 8: PREISE UND PREISINDIZES FUER DEN EIN- UND AUSFUHR. 1955. m. DM.44.40. W. Kohlhammer-Verlag GmbH, Abt. Veroeffentlichungen des Statistischen Bundesamtes, Philipp-Reis-Str. 3, Postfach 421120, 6500 Mainz 42, W. Germany (B.R.D.)

339 310 GW ISSN 0072-3827
GERMANY (FEDERAL REPUBLIC, 1949-) STATISTISCHES BUNDESAMT. FACHSERIE 17, REIHE 10: INTERNATIONALER VERGLEICH DER PREISE FUER DIE LEBENSERHALTUNG. 1960. m. DM.28.80. W. Kohlhammer-Verlag GmbH, Abt. Veroeffentlichungen des Statistischen Bundesamtes, Philipp-Reis-Str. 3, Postfach 421120, 6500 Mainz 42, W. Germany (B.R.D.)

330 314 GW ISSN 0072-4009
GERMANY (FEDERAL REPUBLIC, 1949-) STATISTISCHES BUNDESAMT. FACHSERIE 18, REIHE 1: KONTEN UND STANDARDTABELLEN. a. price varies. W. Kohlhammer-Verlag GmbH, Abt. Veroeffentlichungen des Statistischen Bundesamtes, Philipp-Reis-Str. 3, Postfach 421120, 6500 Mainz 42, W. Germany (B.R.D.)

314 GW ISSN 0072-4106
GERMANY (FEDERAL REPUBLIC, 1949-) STATISTISCHES BUNDESAMT. WARENVERZEICHNIS FUER DIE AUSSENHANDELSSTATISTIK. a. DM.37. W. Kohlhammer-Verlag GmbH, Abt. Veroeffentlichungen des Statistischen Bundesamtes, Philipp-Reis-Str. 3, Postfach 421120, 6500 Mainz 42, W. Germany (B.R.D.)

382 016 GW
GERMANY, FEDERAL REPUBLIC. BUNDESSTELLE FUER AUSSENHANDELSINFORMATION. PUBLIKATIONS-SPIEGEL. 1972. a. free. Bundesstelle fuer Aussenhandelsinformation, Blaubach 13, 5000 Cologne 1, W. Germany (B.R.D.) bibl.

330 316 GH ISSN 0072-4335
GHANA. CENTRAL BUREAU OF STATISTICS. ECONOMIC SURVEY. 1951. a, latest 1972-74. Central Bureau of Statistics, Box 1098, Accra, Ghana (Avail. from: Ministry of Information, Box 745, Accra, Ghana)

331.2 314 UK
GREAT BRITAIN. DEPARTMENT OF EMPLOYMENT. STATISTICS DIVISION. TIME RATES OF WAGES AND HOURS OF WORK. a. Department of Employment, 8 St. James's Square, London SW1Y 4JB, England.

338 314 UK
GREAT BRITAIN. DEPARTMENT OF INDUSTRY. BUSINESS STATISTICS OFFICE REPORT ON THE CENSUS OF PRODUCTION. (Issued in parts. Subseries of the Business Monitor) 1970. a. Department of Industry, Business Statistics Office, Cardiff Road, Newport, Gwent NPT 1XG, England (Avail. from H.M.S.O., c/o Liaison Officer, Atlantic House, Holborn Viaduct, London EC1P 1BN, England) stat.
Formerly: Great Britain. Department of Trade and Industry. Business Statistics Office. Report on the Census of Production.

338 314 GR ISSN 0072-7393
GREECE. NATIONAL STATISTICAL SERVICE. ANNUAL INDUSTRIAL SURVEY. (Text in Greek and English) 1958. a, latest 1973. $2.50. National Statistical Service, Publications and Information Division, 14-16 Lycourgou St., Athens 112, Greece.
Formerly: Greece. National Statistical Service. Results of the Annual Industrial Survey.

331.1 GR
GREECE. NATIONAL STATISTICAL SERVICE. EMPLOYMENT SURVEY CONDUCTED IN URBAN AND SEMI-URBAN AREAS. a., latest 1977. $1. National Statistical Service, Publications and Information Division, 14-16 Lycourgou St., Athens 112, Greece.

336 314 GR
GREECE. NATIONAL STATISTICAL SERVICE. PUBLIC FINANCE STATISTICS. (Text in Greek and English) 1962. a., latest 1975. $2. National Statistical Service, Publications and Information Division, 14-16 Lycourgou St., Athens 112, Greece.
Formerly (until 1972): Greece. National Statistical Service. Statistical Yearbook of Public Finance (ISSN 0072-7431)

336 GR
GREECE. NATIONAL STATISTICAL SERVICE. STATISTICS ON THE DECLARED INCOME OF LEGAL ENTITIES AND ITS TAXATION. (Text in Greek) 1959. a., latest 1975. $1. National Statistical Service, Publications and Information Division, 14-16 Lycourgou St., Athens 112, Greece.

336 GR
GREECE. NATIONAL STATISTICAL SERVICE. STATISTICS ON THE DECLARED INCOME OF PHYSICAL PERSONS AND ITS TAXATION. 1960. a., latest 1976. $2.50. National Statistical Service, Publications and Information Division, 14-16 Lycourgou St., Athens 112, Greece.

381 319 GU
GUAM. DEPARTMENT OF COMMERCE. STATISTICAL ABSTRACT. Variant title: Guam Statistical Abstract. (Text in English) 1970. a. free contr. circ. in Guam; $1 in the U.S. Department of Commerce, Economic Research Center, Box 682, Agana, GU 96910. (tabloid format)

338 317 GT
GUATEMALA. DIRECCION GENERAL DE ESTADISTICA. DIRECTORIA NACIONAL DE ESTABLECIMIENTOS INDUSTRIALES. a. Direccion General de Estadistica, Ministerio de Economia, 8A Calle no. 9-55, Zona 1, Guatemala, Guatemala.

331 317 US
HANDBOOK OF OKLAHOMA EMPLOYMENT STATISTICS. 1952. a.(in 2 vols.) free. ‡ Employment Security Commission, Research & Planning Division, 310 Will Rogers Bldg., Oklahoma City, OK 73105. Ed. David Breedlove. stat. circ. 750.

650 016 US
HARVARD UNIVERSITY. GRADUATE SCHOOL OF BUSINESS ADMINISTRATION. BAKER LIBRARY. CORE COLLECTION, AN AUTHOR AND SUBJECT GUIDE. 1969/70. a. $15. Harvard University, Graduate School of Business Administration. Baker Library, Soldiers Field, Boston, MA 02163.

016 650 US
HARVARD UNIVERSITY. GRADUATE SCHOOL OF BUSINESS ADMINISTRATION. BAKER LIBRARY. CURRENT PERIODICAL PUBLICATIONS IN BAKER LIBRARY. 1971/72. a. $26. ‡ Harvard University, Graduate School of Business Administration. Baker Library, Soldiers Field Rd., Boston, MA 02163.

331 317 US
HAWAII. DEPARTMENT OF LABOR AND INDUSTRIAL RELATIONS. LABOR FORCE STATISTICS. 1974. a. free. Department of Labor and Industrial Relations, Research and Statistics Office, 825 Mililani St., Honolulu, HI 96813.

330 016 FI
HELSINGEN KAUPPAKORKEAKOULU. JULKAISUSARJA D. (Text in English and Finnish) 1975. irreg., D-28, 1978. price varies. Helsingen Kauppakorkeakoulu, Kirjasto - Helsinki School of Economics, Library, Runeberginkatu 22-24, 00100 Helsinki 10, Finland. Ed. Bd. bibl.
Supersedes: Helsingen Kauppakorkeakoulu. Kirjasto. Julkaisusarja.

338 318 HO
HONDURAS. DIRECCION GENERAL DE ESTADISTICA Y CENSOS. INVESTIGACION INDUSTRIAL. irreg. Direccion General de Estadistica y Censos, Tegucigalpa, Honduras.

339 315 HK
HONG KONG. ESTIMATES OF GROSS DOMESTIC PRODUCT. (Text in English) 1973. a. HK.$7. Census and Statistics Department, Kai Tak Commercial Bldg., 317 Des Voeux Rd., Central, Hong Kong, Hong Kong (Subscr. to: Government Information Services, Beaconsfield House, Queen's Rd., Central, Victoria, Hong Kong)

381 314 HU ISSN 0134-1138
HUNGARY. KOZPONTI STATISZTIKAI HIVATAL. BELKERESKEDELMI EVKONYV. a. 96 Ft. Statisztikai Kiado Vallalat, Kaszas U.10-12, P.O.B.99, 1300 Budapest 3, Hungary.

314 338 HU ISSN 0133-8684
HUNGARY. KOZPONTI STATISZTIKAI HIVATAL. IPARI ZSEBKONYV. a. 23 Ft. Statisztikai Kiado Vallalat, Kaszas U.10-12, P.O.B.99, 1300 Budapest 3, Hungary.

331.2 314 HU
HUNGARY. KOZPONTI STATISZTIKAI HIVATAL. KEPZETTSEG-KERESET. (Subseries of: Hungary Kozponti Statisztikai Hivatal. Statisztikai Idoszaki Kozlemenyek) 1966. irreg. price varies. Statisztikai Kiado Vallalat, Kaszas U.10-12, P.O.B.99, 1300 Budapest 3, Hungary.

382 314 HU ISSN 0133-9133
HUNGARY. KOZPONTI STATISZTIKAI HIVATAL. KULKERESKEDELMI STATISZTIKAI EVKONYV. 1971. irreg. 174 Ft. (Kozponti Statisztikai Hivatal) Statisztikai Kiado Vallalat, Kaszas U.10-12, P.O.B.99, 1300 Budapest 3, Hungary.

310 AF
IMPORTS STATISTICS OF AFGHANISTAN/ IHSA'IYAH-I AMUAL-I VARIDATI-I AFGHANISTAN. (Text in Persian or English) no. 1354, 1975. a. $20. Central Statistical Office, Nader Shah Minah, Block No. 4, Box 2002, Kabul, Afghanistan. stat.

330 016 US
INDEX OF ECONOMIC ARTICLES IN JOURNALS AND COLLECTIVE VOLUMES. 1961. irreg., vol. 15, 1976. $100. ‡ American Economic Association, 1313 21st. Ave. So., Nashville, TN 37212 (Order from: Richard D. Irwin, Inc., 1818 Ridge Rd., Homewood, IL 60430) (back issues avail.)

338 315 II ISSN 0073-6139
INDIA. CENTRAL STATISTICAL ORGANIZATION. ANNUAL SURVEY OF INDUSTRIES/UDYOGEN KA VARSHIKA SARVEKSHANA.* (Text in English and Hindi) 1973-74. a. Rs.5.70($2.06) Central Statistical Organization, Sardar Patel Bhavan, Parliament St., New Delhi 110001, India. circ. 500.

331 315 II
INDIA. LABOUR BUREAU. POCKET BOOK OF LABOUR STATISTICS. 1959. a. Rs.15($5.40) Labour Bureau, Simla 171004, India (Order from: Controller of Publications, Government of India, Civil Lines, Delhi 110054, India) stat. circ. 2,700.

INDICADORES SOCIOECONOMICOS Y DE COYUNTURA. see *SOCIOLOGY — Abstracting, Bibliographies, Statistics*

339 318 BO
INDICE DE PRECIOS AL CONSUMIDOR, CIUDAD DE LA PAZ (ANUAL) 1974. a. $2.20. Instituto Nacional de Estadistica, Ministerio de Planeamiento y Coordinacion, La Paz, Bolivia.

330 016 CK ISSN 0019-7033
INDICE ECONOMICO COLOMBIANO; literatura economica colombiana. 1951. a. Col.$200($8) Universidad de Antioquia, Escuela Interamericana de Bibliotecologia, Apartado Aereo 1226, Medellin, Colombia. Ed. M. A. Cristina Suaza. bibl. index. circ. 500.

315.98 IO ISSN 0376-9984
INDONESIA STATISTICS. (Text in English) a. First National City Bank, Jl. Thamrin 45, Box 2463, Jakarta, Indonesia.

BUSINESS AND ECONOMICS — ABSTRACTING, BIBLIOGRAPHIES, STATISTICS

331 016   US   ISSN 0070-0142
INDUSTRIAL AND LABOR RELATIONS BIBLIOGRAPHY SERIES. 1952. irreg.; no. 15, 1978. price varies. New York State School of Industrial and Labor Relations, Cornell University, Ithaca, NY 14853.

338 314   YU
INDUSTRIJSKI PROIZVODI. (Subseries of Statisticki Bilten) a. 30 din.($1.67) Savezni Zavod za Statistiku, Uzun Mirkova 1, Belgrade, Yugoslavia. stat. circ. 1,000.

INSTITUTE OF INTERNATIONAL POLITICS AND ECONOMICS. DOCUMENTATION BULLETIN. see *POLITICAL SCIENCE — Abstracting, Bibliographies, Statistics*

658 016   US   ISSN 0095-490X
INTERCOLLEGIATE BIBLIOGRAPHY. NEW CASES IN ADMINISTRATION. 1975. irreg. price varies. (American Assembly of Collegiate Schools of Business) Intercollegiate Case Clearing House, Soldiers Field Post Office, Boston, MA 02163. (Cosponsor: Harvard University Graduate School of Business Administration) Ed. Christopher H. Lovelock. bibl. (back issues avail.)

330 016   UK   ISSN 0085-204X
INTERNATIONAL BIBLIOGRAPHY OF THE SOCIAL SCIENCES. ECONOMICS. 1952. irreg., vol. 28, 1979. price varies. (Unesco, UN) Tavistock Publications Ltd., 11 New Fetter La., London EC4P 4EE, England (Dist. in U.S. by: Methuen Inc., 733 Third Ave., New York, N.Y. 10017) circ. 2,000.
    Title Page Also Reads: International Bibliography of Economics.

331 016   UN   ISSN 0074-641X
INTERNATIONAL INSTITUTE FOR LABOUR STUDIES. INTERNATIONAL EDUCATIONAL MATERIALS EXCHANGE. LIST OF AVAILABLE MATERIALS. 1968. irreg., no. 10, 1978. price varies. International Institute for Labour Studies, C.P.6, CH-1211 Geneva 22, Switzerland.

310 658   UK   ISSN 0308-2938
INTERNATIONAL MARKETING DATA AND STATISTICS. 1975. a. $150. Euromonitor Publications Ltd., Box 26, 18 Doughty St., London WC1N 2PN, England.

332.1 310   UN
INTERNATIONAL MONETARY FUND. GOVERNMENT FINANCE STATISTICS YEARBOOK. 1977. a. $10. International Monetary Fund, 700 19th St., N.W., Washington, DC 20431. Ed. Werner Dannemann. charts. stat. circ. 3,000. (also avail. in magnetic tape)

332.67 314   YU
INVESTICIJE.* (Subseries of Statisticki Bilten) 1966. a. 60 din.($3.24) Savezni Zavod za Statistiku, Uzun Mirkova 1, Belgrade, Yugoslavia. stat. circ. 1,000.

331   US
IOWA. BUREAU OF LABOR. RESEARCH AND STATISTICS DIVISION. BIENNIAL REPORT. 1885. biennial. free. Bureau of Labor, Research and Statistics Division, East 7th & Court Avenue, Des Moines, IA 50319. stat. circ. 300. (processed)

330 315   IR
IRAN. MINISTRY OF ECONOMY. BUREAU OF STATISTICS. SERIES.* 1969, no. 49. Ministry of Finance and Economic Affairs, Bureau of Statistics, Director General of Statistics, Main Palace, Tehran, Iran. Ed. A. Sh. Shaheen. charts. stat.

381 315   IR
IRAN. MINISTRY OF ECONOMY. INTERNAL WHOLESALE TRADE STATISTICS.* (Text in English) a. free. Ministry of Finance and Economic Affairs, Teheran, Iran. stat. circ. controlled. (also avail. in record)

382 315   IR
IRAN. MINISTRY OF ECONOMY. INTERNATIONAL TRADE STATISTICS.* (Text in English) irreg (approx 1/yr) free. Ministry of Finance and Economic Affairs, Teheran, Iran. stat. circ. controlled. (also avail. in record)

338 315   IR   ISSN 0075-0506
IRANIAN INDUSTRIAL STATISTICS.* (Text in English and Persian) 1962. a. free. Ministry of Finance and Economic Affairs, Bureau of Statistics, Tehran, Iran.

338 315   IQ
IRAQ. CENTRAL STATISTICAL ORGANIZATION. RESULTS OF THE INDUSTRIAL SURVEY OF LARGE ESTABLISHMENTS IN IRAQ. (Edition in Arabic and English) 1957. a. ID.1500. Central Statistical Organization, Baghdad, Iraq.

382 315   IQ   ISSN 0021-0900
IRAQ. CENTRAL STATISTICAL ORGANIZATION. SUMMARY OF FOREIGN TRADE STATISTICS. (Text and title in Arabic and English) 1960. a. ID.250. Central Statistical Organization, Baghdad, Iraq. circ. 500.

331 314   IE   ISSN 0075-0638
IRELAND (EIRE) CENTRAL STATISTICS OFFICE. TREND OF EMPLOYMENT AND UNEMPLOYMENT. 1935. a. 45p. Central Statistics Office, Earlsfort Terrace, Dublin 2, Ireland.

382 315   IS
ISRAEL. CENTRAL BUREAU OF STATISTICS. ANNUAL FOREIGN TRADE STATISTICS. (Part 1-Imports; Part 2-Exports; by Commodity and Country) (Text in English and Hebrew) 1975. a. price varies. Central Bureau of Statistics, P.O.B. 13015, Jerusalem, Israel. stat.
    Supersedes: Israel. Central Bureau of Statistics. Foreign Trade Statistics Quarterly (ISSN 0021-1990); Israel. Central Bureau of Statistics. Monthly Foreign Trade Statistics.

382 315   IS   ISSN 0075-1421
ISRAEL. CENTRAL BUREAU OF STATISTICS. ISRAEL'S FOREIGN TRADE/SEHAR HUTS SHEL YISRAEL. (Subseries of Israel. Central Bureau of Statistics. Special Series) (Text in English and Hebrew) 1951. irreg., latest issue, no. 498, 1974. I£70. Central Bureau of Statistics, Box 13015, Jerusalem, Israel.

331 315   IS   ISSN 0075-1049
ISRAEL. CENTRAL BUREAU OF STATISTICS. LABOUR FORCE SURVEYS. (Subseries of its Special Series) (Text in Hebrew and English) 1954. irreg., latest issue, no. 611, 1977. I£160. Central Bureau of Statistics, Box 13015, Jerusalem, Israel.

331 315   IS   ISSN 0075-1073
ISRAEL. CENTRAL BUREAU OF STATISTICS. STRIKES AND LOCK-OUTS. (Subseries of its Special Series) (Text in Hebrew and English) 1965-67. irreg., latest issue, no. 257, 1967. price varies. Central Bureau of Statistics, Box 13015, Jerusalem, Israel.

381 315   IS   ISSN 0075-1103
ISRAEL. CENTRAL BUREAU OF STATISTICS. TRADE SURVEY. (Subseries of the Bureau's Special Series) (Text in Hebrew and English) 1965-66. a (latest 1976/77) I£110. Central Bureau of Statistics, Box 13015, Jerusalem, Israel. stat. (back issues avail.)

330 314   IT   ISSN 0075-1723
ITALY. ISTITUTO CENTRALE DI STATISTICA. ANNUARIO DI STATISTICHE INDUSTRIALI. a. L.8000. Istituto Centrale di Statistica, Via Cesare Balbo 16, 00100 Rome, Italy.

382 314   IT   ISSN 0075-1782
ITALY. ISTITUTO CENTRALE DI STATISTICA. ANNUARIO STATISTICO DEL COMMERCIO INTERNO. a. L.13000. Istituto Centrale di Statistica, Via Cesare Balbo 16, 00100 Rome, Italy.

382 314   IT   ISSN 0390-6558
ITALY. ISTITUTO CENTRALE DI STATISTICA. STATISTICA ANNUALE DEL COMMERCIO CON L'ESTERO. TOMO I. a. L.11000. Istituto Centrale di Statistica, Via Cesare Balbo 16, 00100 Rome, Italy.
    Supersedes in part: Italy. Istituto Centrale di Statistica. Statistica Annuale del Commercio con l'Estero (ISSN 0075-1871)

382 314   IT   ISSN 0390-6566
ITALY. ISTITUTO CENTRALE DI STATISTICA. STATISTICA ANNUALE DEL COMMERCIO CON L'ESTERO. TOMO II. a. L.22000. Istituto Centrale di Statistica, Via Cesare Balbo 16, 00100 Rome, Italy.
    Supersedes in part: Italy. Istituto Centrale di Statistica. Statistica Annuale del Commercio con l'Estero (ISSN 0075-1871)

382 318   NA   ISSN 0077-6653
JAARSTATISTIEK VAN DE IN-EN UITVOER PER GOEDERENSOORT VAN DE NEDERLANDSE ANTILLEN.* a. fl.20. Bureau voor de Statistiek, Fort Amsterdam, Netherlands Antilles.

382 318   NA   ISSN 0077-6645
JAARSTATISTIEK VAN DE IN-EN UITVOER PER LAND VAN DE NEDERLANDSE ANTILLEN.* a. fl.20. Bureau voor de Statistiek, Fort Amsterdam, Netherlands Antilles.

382 318   JM
JAMAICA. DEPARTMENT OF STATISTICS. EXTERNAL TRADE ANNUAL REVIEW. 1970. a. Jam.$2.50. Department of Statistics, 9 Swallowfield Rd., Kingston 5, Jamaica. stat.

331.11 315   JA   ISSN 0075-3181
JAPAN. BUREAU OF STATISTICS. EMPLOYMENT STATUS SURVEY/JAPAN. SORIFU. TOKEIKYOKU. SHUGYOKOZO KIHON CHOSA. (Includes: Employment Statistics) 1956. triennial. price varies. Bureau of Statistics - Japan. Tokeikyoku, Office of the Prime Minister, 95 Wakamatsu-cho, Shinjuku-ku, Tokyo 162, Japan (Subscribe to: Government Publications Service Center, 1-2-1 Kasumigaseki, Chiyoda-Ku, Tokyo 100, Japan)

331 315   JA
JAPAN. MINISTRY OF LABOUR. YEARBOOK OF LABOUR STATISTICS. (Text in Japanese and English) 1948. a. 3500 Yen. Ministry of Labour, Statistics and Information Department - Nihon Rodosho, Minister's Secretariat, Tokyo 100, Japan. charts. stat. circ. 800.
    Includes some foreign labor statistics

330 016   JA   ISSN 0448-8709
JAPAN SCIENCE REVIEW: ECONOMIC SCIENCES. (Text in Japanese and English) 1953. a. (Japan Union of Associations of Economic Sciences) Japan Society for the Promotion of Science, 2-1-2 Hitotsubashi, Chiyoda-ku, Tokyo 101, Japan. stat. author index.
    Bibliographical notices of Japanese periodicals abstracts

330 016   JA
JAPANESE ANNUAL BIBLIOGRAPHY OF ECONOMICS. (Text in English) a. Science Council of Japan - Nihon Gakujutsu Kaigi, 7-22-34 Roppongi, Minato-ku, Tokyo 106, Japan.

382 315   JO   ISSN 0075-4021
JORDAN. DEPARTMENT OF STATISTICS. EXTERNAL TRADE STATISTICS. 1965. a. $15 incl. its Annual Statistical Yearbook. Department of Statistics, Amman, Jordan.

330.9 317   US   ISSN 0361-591X
KENTUCKY DESKBOOK OF ECONOMIC STATISTICS. irreg. Department of Commerce, Division of Research and Planning, Capitol Plaza Tower, Frankfort, KY 40601.
    Formerly: Deskbook of Kentucky Economic Statistics.

338 316   KE
KENYA. CENTRAL BUREAU OF STATISTICS. REGISTER OF MANUFACTURING FIRMS. 1970. irreg. EAs.10. Central Bureau of Statistics, Box 30266, Nairobi, Kenya (Orders to: Government Printing and Stationery Department, Box 30128, Nairobi, Kenya)
    Formerly: Kenya. Ministry of Finance and Economic Planning. Statistics Division. Register of Manufacturing Firms.

316.76 338   KE
KENYA. CENTRAL BUREAU OF STATISTICS. STATISTICAL ABSTRACT. 1961. a. Central Bureau of Statistics, Box 30266, Nairobi, Kenya (Orders to: Government Printing and Stationery Department, Box 30128, Nairobi, Kenya)
    Formerly: Kenya. Ministry of Economic Planning and Development. Statistics Division. Statistical Abstract (ISSN 0075-5850)

338.9 315   KO   ISSN 0075-6830
KOREA (REPUBLIC) BUREAU OF STATISTICS. ANNUAL REPORT OF THE PRICE SURVEY/ MULGA YONBO. (Text in Korean and English) 1969. a. 1000 Won. Bureau of Statistics, Economic Planning Board, Gyeongun-Dong, Jongro-Gu, Seoul, S. Korea. Ed. Heung-Koo Kang. circ. 800.

BUSINESS AND ECONOMICS — ABSTRACTING, BIBLIOGRAPHIES, STATISTICS

339 315   KO   ISSN 0075-6822
KOREA (REPUBLIC) BUREAU OF STATISTICS. ANNUAL REPORT ON THE FAMILY INCOME AND EXPENDITURE SURVEY/TOSI GAGYE YONBO. (Text in Korean and English) 1966. a. 1500 Won. Bureau of Statistics, Economic Planning Board, Gyeongun-Dong, Jongro-Gu, Seoul, S. Korea. Ed. Heung-Koo Kang. circ. 1,000.

KOREA (REPUBLIC) BUREAU OF STATISTICS. REPORT ON MINING AND MANUFACTURING SURVEY/ KWANGGONGUP TONGGYE ZO SA BOGO SEO. see *MINES AND MINING INDUSTRY — Abstracting, Bibliographies, Statistics*

380 315   KO   ISSN 0075-6857
KOREA (REPUBLIC) BUREAU OF STATISTICS. WHOLESALE AND RETAIL TRADE CENSUS REPORT/TOSOMAEUP CENSUS BOGO SEO. (Text in Korean and English) 1968. triennial. 1935 Won. Bureau of Statistics, Economic Planning Board, Gyeongun-Dong, Jongro-Gu, Seoul, S. Korea. Ed. Heung-Koo Kang. circ. 700.

331.88   IO
LABOUR FORCE SITUATION IN INDONESIA: PRELIMINARY FIGURES/KEADAAN ANGKATAN KERJA DI INDONESIA: ANGKA SEMENTARA. (Text in English and Indonesian) 1977. irreg. 2 per no. Central Bureau of Statistics - Biro Pusat Statistik, Jalan Dr. Sutomo 8, Box 3, Jakarta, Indonesia.

331.1 016   II   ISSN 0075-756X
LABOUR LITERATURE: A BIBLIOGRAPHY. (Text in English) 1957. N.S. 1971. a. free. ‡ Ministry of Labour, Library, Sharam Shakti Bhavan, Rafi Marg, New Delhi, India. Ed. S. P. Kulshresth. circ. 250. (processed)

330 315   LE   ISSN 0075-837X
LEBANON. DIRECTION CENTRALE DE LA STATISTIQUE. COMPTES ECONOMIQUES.* (Text in Arabic and French) a. Direction Centrale de la Statistique, Ministere du Plan, Beirut, Lebanon.

338 316   LY   ISSN 0075-9244
LIBYA CENSUS AND STATISTICAL OFFICE. INDUSTRIAL CENSUS. (Text in Arabic and English) 1964. decennial. free. Census and Statistical Department, Ministry of Planning, Tripoli, Libya.

338 316   LY   ISSN 0075-9252
LIBYA. CENSUS AND STATISTICAL OFFICE. REPORT OF THE ANNUAL SURVEY OF LARGE MANUFACTURING ESTABLISHMENTS. (Text in Arabic and English) 1965. a. free. Census and Statistical Department, Ministry of Planning, Tripoli, Libya.

331.2 314   YU   ISSN 0300-2535
LICNI DOHOCI. (Subseries of Statisticki Bilten) a. 30 din.($1.67) Savezni Zavod za Statistiku, Uzun Mirkova 1, Belgrade, Yugoslavia. stat. circ. 1,000.

331 016   GW
LITERATURDOKUMENTATION ZUR ARBEITSMARKT- UND BERUFSFORSCHUNG. 1972. a. DM.20. Bundesanstalt fuer Arbeit, Institut fuer Arbeitsmarkt- und Berufsforschung, Regensburger Str. 104, 8500 Nuernberg, W. Germany (B.R.D.) index,cum. index: 1972-1974.

330 314   LU   ISSN 0076-1583
LUXEMBOURG. SERVICE CENTRAL DE LA STATISTIQUE ET DES ETUDES ECONOMIQUES. BULLETIN DU STATEC. 1955. irreg. (8-10/yr.) 500 Fr. Service Central de la Statistique et des Etudes Economiques, B.P. 304, Luxembourg, Luxembourg.

330 314   LU   ISSN 0070-881X
LUXEMBOURG. SERVICE CENTRAL DE LA STATISTIQUE ET DES ETUDES ECONOMIQUES. CAHIERS ECONOMIQUES. SERIE A: ECONOMIE LUXEMBOURGEOISE. 1950. biennial. price varies. Service Central de la Statistique et des Etudes Economiques, B.P. 304, Luxembourg, Luxembourg.

330 314   LU
LUXEMBOURG. SERVICE CENTRAL DE LA STATISTIQUE ET DES ETUDES ECONOMIQUES. CAHIERS ECONOMIQUES. SERIE B: COMPTES NATIONAUX. a. price varies. Service Central de la Statistique et des Etudes Economiques, B.P. 304, Luxembourg, Luxembourg.

338 314   LU
LUXEMBOURG. SERVICE CENTRAL DE LA STATISTIQUE ET DES ETUDES ECONOMIQUES. CAHIERS ECONOMIQUES. SERIE C: APERCUS SUR L'INDUSTRIE. irreg., latest 1980. price varies. Service Central de la Statistique et des Etudes Economiques, B.P. 304, Luxembourg, Luxembourg.

330 314   LU
LUXEMBOURG. SERVICE CENTRAL DE LA STATISTIQUE ET DES ETUDES ECONOMIQUES. CAHIERS ECONOMIQUES. SERIE D: ETUDES DIVERSES. irreg. price varies. Service Central de la Statistique et des Etudes Economiques, B.P. 304, Luxembourg, Luxembourg.

380.1   US   ISSN 0362-4552
M I M C MICROFORMS ANNUAL. biennial. Microforms International Marketing Corporation (Subsidiary of: Pergamon Press, Inc.) Fairview Park, Elmsford, NY 10523.

330   HU   ISSN 0133-0152
MAGYAR KOZGAZDASAGI IRODALOM/ HUNGARIAN ECONOMIC LITERATURE. 1972. a. price varies or exchange basis. Marx Karoly Kozgazdasagtudomanyi Egyetem, Dimitrov Ter 8, Budapest 9, Hungary. Ed. Peter Hegedus. index. circ. 500.

382 316   MW   ISSN 0076-325X
MALAWI. NATIONAL STATISTICAL OFFICE. ANNUAL STATEMENT OF EXTERNAL TRADE. 1964. a. K.9. ‡ National Statistical Office, P.O. Box 333, Zomba, Malawi.

330 316   MW   ISSN 0076-3241
MALAWI. NATIONAL STATISTICAL OFFICE. ANNUAL SURVEY OF ECONOMIC ACTIVITIES. (Issued in 1966 as: Census of Industrial Production) 1966. a. K.3.50($3.90) ‡ National Statistical Office, P.O. Box 333, Zomba, Malawi.

331 316   MW
MALAWI. NATIONAL STATISTICAL OFFICE. REPORTED EMPLOYMENT AND EARNINGS: ANNUAL REPORT. a. K.2.50. National Statistical Office, Box 333, Zomba, Malawi. stat.

330 316   ML   ISSN 0076-3411
MALI. SERVICE DE LA STATISTIQUE GENERALE, DE LA COMPTABILITE NATIONALE ET DE LA MECANOGRAPHIE. ANNUAIRE STATISTIQUE.* 1962. a. price varies. Service de la Statistique Generale, de la Comptabilite Nationale et de la Mecanographie, Bamako, Mali. index.
Before 1962 issued as: Chambre de Commerce d'Agriculture et d'Industrie de Bamako, Mali. Annuaire Statistique (ISSN 0069-2522)

336 316   ML
MALI. SERVICE DE LA STATISTIQUE GENERALE, DE LA COMPTABILITE NATIONALE ET DE LA MECANOGRAPHIE. STATISTIQUES DOUANIERES DU COMMERCE EXTERIEUR.* Service de la Statistique Generale, de la Comptabilite Nationale et de la Mecanographie, Bamako, Mali.

338 314   MM   ISSN 0076-3462
MALTA. CENTRAL OFFICE OF STATISTICS. CENSUS OF PRODUCTION REPORT. a. £0.25. Central Office of Statistics, Auberge de Castille, Valletta, Malta (Subscr. to: Department of Information, Auberge de Castille, Valletta, Malta)

338 317   CN   ISSN 0382-4012
MANUFACTURING INDUSTRIES OF CANADA: SUB-PROVINCIAL AREAS/INDUSTRIES MANUFACTURIERES DU CANADA: NIVEAU INFRAPROVINCIAL. (Catalog 31-209) (Text in English and French) 1946. a. Can.$20($24) Statistics Canada, Publications Distribution, Ottawa, Ont. K1A 0V7, Canada. (also avail. in microform from MML)

658   CN   ISSN 0590-9325
MARKET RESEARCH HANDBOOK. (Catalogue 63-224) (Text in English and French) 1975. a. Can.$25($30) Statistics Canada, Publications Distribution, Ottawa, Ont. K1A 0V7, Canada. (also avail. in microform from MML)

382   US
MARKET SHARE REPORTS. irreg. country reports $4.75 each. $418 set: commodity reports $3.25 each. $3025 set. U.S. National Technical Information Service, 5285 Port Royal Road, Springfield, VA 22161. Dir. William T. Knox. stat.

330   HU   ISSN 0521-4211
MARX KAROLY KOZGAZDASAGTUDOMANYI EGYETEM: DOKTORI ERTEKEZESEK. 1969. biennial. exchange basis. Marx Karoly Kozgazdasagtudomanyi Egyetem, Dimitrov Ter 8, Budapest 9, Hungary. Ed. Eva Csonka. index. circ. 300.

330   HU
MARX KAROLY KOZGAZDASAGTUDOMANYI EGYETEM OKTATOINAK SZAKIRODALMI MUNKASSAGA. 1968. biennial. exchange basis. Marx Karoly Kozgazdasagtudomanyi Egyetem, Dimitrov Ter 8, Budapest 9, Hungary. Ed. Zsuzsa Mosolygo. index. circ. 1,000.

338 016   US
MERGERS & ACQUISITIONS. A COMPREHENSIVE WORLD BIBLIOGRAPHY. 1972. quinquennial. Mergers & Acquisitions Inc., P.O. Box 36, McLean, VA 22101. Ed. Stanley Foster Reed. circ. 10,000.

338 318   MX
MEXICO. DIRECCION DE ESTADISTICA. ESTADISTICA INDUSTRIAL MENSUAL. a. free. Secretaria de Programacion y Presupuesto, Articulo 123 no. 88, Mexico 1, D.F., Mexico, Mexico 1, D. F., Mexico (Orders to: Direccion General de Estudios del Territorio Nacional, Balderas 71, Col. Centro, Mexico 1, D.F., Mexico) charts. stat. circ. controlled.

338 318   MX   ISSN 0071-1543
MEXICO. DIRECCION GENERAL DE ESTADISTICA. ESTADISTICA INDUSTRIAL ANUAL. 1963. irreg.; latest 1974. free. Secretaria de Programacion y Presupuesto, Articulo 123 no. 88, Mexico 1, D.F., Mexico (Orders to: Direccion General de Estudios del Territcrio Nacional, Balderas 71, Col. Centro, Mexico 1, D.F., Mexico)

331 318   MX   ISSN 0076-7492
MEXICO. SECRETARIA DE PROGRAMACION Y PRESUPUESTO. 1938. free. Secretaria de Programacion y Presupuesto, Departamento de Estadisticas Industriales, Articulo 123 no. 88, Mexico 1, D.F., Mexico (Orders to: Direccion General de Estudios del Territorio Nacional, Balderas 71, Col. Centro, Mexico 1, D.F., Mexico)

330 016   US   ISSN 0091-9047
MICHIGAN BUSINESS AND ECONOMIC RESEARCH BIBLIOGRAPHY. irreg. free. University of Michigan, Institute of Science & Technology, Division of Research, Ann Arbor, MI 48109. Ed. A. W. Swinyard.

336 315   PH
N E D A STATISTICAL YEARBOOK OF THE PHILIPPINES. (Text in English) 1974. a. National Economic and Development Authority, Box 1116, Manila, Philippines.

339.373   US   ISSN 0361-3895
NATIONAL INCOME AND PRODUCT ACCOUNTS OF THE UNITED STATES: STATISTICAL TABLES. 1965. irreg. $12.50. U.S. Department of Commerce, Office of Business Economics, Washington, DC 20203 (Order from: NTIS, 5285 Port Royal Rd., Springfield, Va 22161)

339 315   TH   ISSN 0077-4723
NATIONAL INCOME STATISTICS OF THAILAND.* (Text in Thai and English) 1964. a. free. National Economic Development Board, Secretary-General, Krung Kasem Rd., Bangkok, Thailand.

658.3 016   SA   ISSN 0077-4766
NATIONAL INSTITUTE FOR PERSONNEL RESEARCH. LIST OF N I P R PUBLICATIONS. 1970. a. free. ‡ National Institute for Personnel Research, Box 10319, Johannesburg 2000, South Africa. circ. 900.

338 314   YU   ISSN 0300-2497
NEKI POKAZATELJI TEHNICKOG RAZVOJA PRIVREDE JUGOSLAVIJE. (Subseries of Statisticki Bilten. Continues Statistika Nove Tehniki. Issued also in English) a. 20 din.($1.11) Savezni Zavod za Statistiku, Uzun Mirkova 1, Belgrade, Yugoslavia. circ. 1,000.

016 338.9   NP
NEPAL DOCUMENTATION; occasional bibliography. (Text in English and Nepali) 1972. irreg. Rs.10($4) Centre for Economic Development and Administration, Box 797, Kirtipur Campus, Kathmandu, Nepal. index. (back issues avail.)

338.9 315   NP   ISSN 0077-6564
NEPAL INDUSTRIAL DEVELOPMENT CORPORATION. STATISTICAL ABSTRACTS.* (Text in English) irreg. Nepal Industrial Development Corporation, N.I.D.C. Bldg., Durbar Marg, Box 10, Kathmandu, Nepal.

332.75 314   NE   ISSN 0077-6793
NETHERLANDS. CENTRAAL BUREAU VOOR DE STATISTIEK. FAILLISSEMENTSSTATISTIEK. BANKRUPTCIES. (Text in Dutch and English) 1951. a. fl.6.30. Centraal Bureau voor de Statistiek, Prinses Beatrixlaan 428, Voorburg, Netherlands (Orders to: Staatsuitgeverij, Christoffel Plantijnstraat, The Hague, Netherlands)

332 314   NE
NETHERLANDS. CENTRAAL BUREAU VOOR DE STATISTIEK. HYPOTHEKEN. STATISTICS OF MORTGAGES. (Text in Dutch and English) 1965. a. fl.10.85. Centraal Bureau voor de Statistiek, Prinses Beatrixlaan 428, Voorburg, Netherlands (Orders to: Staatsuitgeverij, Christoffel Plantijnstraat, The Hague, Netherlands)
Formerly: Netherlands. Centraal Bureau voor de Statistiek. Hypotheken en Hypotheekbanken. Statistics of Mortgages (ISSN 0077-6823)

382 314   NE   ISSN 0077-6882
NETHERLANDS. CENTRAAL BUREAU VOOR DE STATISTIEK. NAAMLIJSTEN VOOR DE STATISTIEK VAN DE BUITENLANDSE HANDEL. LIST OF GOODS FOR THE STATISTICS OF FOREIGN TRADE. 1969. a. fl.45. Centraal Bureau voor de Statistiek, Prinses Beatrixlaan 428, Voorburg, Netherlands (Orders to: Staatsuitgeverij, Christoffel Plantijnstraat, The Hague, Netherlands)

382 314   NE   ISSN 0077-6890
NETHERLANDS. CENTRAAL BUREAU VOOR DE STATISTIEK. NAAMLIJSTEN VOOR DE STATISTIEK VAN DE BUITENLANDSE HANDEL. SUPPLEMENT. LIST OF GOODS FOR THE STATISTICS OF FOREIGN TRADE. SUPPLEMENT. 1962. a. fl.27.50. Centraal Bureau voor de Statistiek, Prinses Beatrixlaan 428, Voorburg, Netherlands (Orders to: Staatsuitgeverij, Christoffel Plantijnstraat, The Hague, Netherlands)

663   NE
NETHERLANDS. CENTRAAL BUREAU VOOR DE STATISTIEK. PRODUKTIESTATISTIEKEN: BIERBROUWERIJEN EN MOUTERIJEN, ALCOHOLFABRIEKEN, DISTILEERDERIJEN EN FRISDRANKENINDUSTRIE. a. fl.11.25. Centraal Bureau voor de Statistiek, Prinses Beatrixlaan 428, Voorburg, Netherlands (Orders to: Staatsuitgeverij, Christoffel Plantijnstraat, The Hague, Netherlands)
Fomer titles: Netherlands. Centraal Bureau voor de Statistiek. Produktiestatistieken: Bierbrouwerijen en Mouterijen, Distileerderijen en Likeurstokerijen; Netherlands. Centraal Bureau voor de Statistiek. Produktiestatistieken: Distilleerderijen en Likeurstokerijen.

331 338.1 314   NE   ISSN 0077-6963
NETHERLANDS. CENTRAAL BUREAU VOOR DE STATISTIEK. STATISTIEK DER LONEN IN DE LANDBOUW. STATISTICS OF WAGES IN AGRICULTURE. (Text in Dutch and English) 1958/59. irreg. fl.4. Centraal Bureau voor de Statistiek, Prinses Beatrixlaan 428, Voorburg, Netherlands (Orders to: Staatsuitgeverij, Christoffel Plantijnstraat, The Hague, Netherlands)

332   NE
NETHERLANDS. CENTRAAL BUREAU VOOR DE STATISTIEK. STATISTIEK VAN DE INVESTERINGEN IN VASTE ACTIVA IN DE NIJVERHEID. STATISTICS ON FIXED CAPITAL FORMATION IN INDUSTRY. (Text in Dutch and English) 1951-52. a. fl.11.75. Centraal Bureau voor de Statistiek, Prinses Beatrixlaan 428, Voorburg, Netherlands (Orders to: Staatsuitgeverij, Christoffel Plantijnstraat, The Hague, Netherlands)
Formerly: Netherlands. Centraal Bureau voor de Statistiek. Statistiek van de Investeringen in Vaste Activa in de Industrie (ISSN 0077-7110)

332 314   NE
NETHERLANDS. CENTRAAL BUREAU VOOR DE STATISTIEK. STATISTIEK VAN DE SPAARGELDEN. STATISTICS OF SAVINGS. (Text in Dutch and English) 1965. a. price varies. Centraal Bureau voor de Statistiek, Prinses Beatrixlaan 428, Voorburg, Netherlands (Orders to: Staatsuitgeverij, Christoffel Plantijnstraat, The Hague, Netherlands)

382 314   NE   ISSN 0077-7293
NETHERLANDS. CENTRAAL BUREAU VOOR DE STATISTIEK. STATISTIEK VAN HET INTERNATIONAAL GOEDERENVERVOER. STATISTICS OF THE INTERNATIONAL GOODS TRAFFIC. (Text in Dutch and English) 1963. a. fl.24.25. Centraal Bureau voor de Statistiek, Prinses Beatrixlaan 428, Voorburg, Netherlands (Orders to: Staatsuitgeverij, Christoffel Plantijnstraat, The Hague, Netherlands)

331 314   NE
NETHERLANDS. CENTRAAL BUREAU VOOR DE STATISTIEK. STATISTIEK WERKZAME PERSONEN. a. fl.14.75. Centraal Bureau voor de Statistiek, Prinses Beatrixlaan 428, Voorburg, Netherlands (Orders to: Staatsuitgeverij, Christoffel Plantijnstraat, The Hague, Netherlands)

330 310   NE
NETHERLANDS. CENTRAAL BUREAU VOOR DE STATISTIEK. STATISTISCHE ONDERZOEKINGEN. (Text in Dutch and English) 1947. irreg. price varies. Centraal Bureau voor de Statistiek, Prinses Beatrixlaan 428, Voorburg, Netherlands (Orders to: Staatsuitgeverij, Christoffel Plantijnstraat, The Hague, Netherlands)
Formerly: Netherlands. Centraal Bureau voor de Statistiek. Statistische en Econometrische Onderzoekingen. Statistical and Econometric Studies (ISSN 0077-7048)

339 314   NE   ISSN 0077-7498
NETHERLANDS. CENTRAAL BUREAU VOOR DE STATISTIEK. VERMOGENSVERDELING. REGIONALE GEGEVENS. DISTRIBUTION OF PERSONAL WEALTH. REGIONAL DATA. (Text in Dutch and English) 1951. irreg. fl.18.10. Centraal Bureau voor de Statistiek, Prinses Beatrixlaan 428, Voorburg, Netherlands (Orders to: Staatsuitgeverij, Christoffel Plantijnstraat, The Hague, Netherlands)

338 314   NE   ISSN 0077-751X
NETHERLANDS. CENTRAAL BUREAU VOOR DE STATISTIEK. WINSTSTATISTIEK DER GROTERE NAAMLOZE VENNOOTSCHAPPEN. PROFIT-STATISTICS OF THE LIMITED LIABILITY COMPANIES. (Text in Dutch and English) 1939-51. a. fl.7. Centraal Bureau voor de Statistiek, Prinses Beatrixlaan 428, Voorburg, Netherlands (Orders to: Staatsuitgeverij, Christoffel Plantijnstraat, The Hague, Netherlands)

331.11 317   US   ISSN 0091-0767
NEW YORK (STATE) DEPARTMENT OF LABOR. DIVISION OF RESEARCH AND STATISTICS. EMPLOYMENT STATISTICS. vol. 10, 1973. irreg., vol. 11, 1975. free. Department of Labor, Division of Research and Statistics, 2 World Trade Center, Rm. 6804, New York, NY 10047 (Dist. by: Office of Public Information, State Campus, Albany, N.Y. 12240) stat. circ. controlled.

331.1 317   US   ISSN 0550-6638
NEW YORK (STATE). DEPARTMENT OF LABOR. STATISTICS ON OPERATIONS. a. Department of Labor, Division of Research and Statistics, Two World Trade Center, New York, NY 10047 (Dist. by: Office of Public Information, State Campus, Albany, N.Y. 12240) illus. stat.

382 339 319   NZ   ISSN 0110-4616
NEW ZEALAND. DEPARTMENT OF STATISTICS. BALANCE OF PAYMENTS. a. NZ.$1.20. Department of Statistics, Private Bag, Wellington, New Zealand (Subscr. to: Government Printing Office, Publications, Private Bag, Wellington, New Zealand)

382 319   NZ   ISSN 0077-9660
NEW ZEALAND. DEPARTMENT OF STATISTICS. EXPORTS. a. NZ.$7.50. Department of Statistics, Private Bag, Wellington, New Zealand (Subscr. to: Government Printing Office, Publications, Private Bag, Wellington, New Zealand)

382.5 319   NZ   ISSN 0077-9679
NEW ZEALAND. DEPARTMENT OF STATISTICS. IMPORTS. 1962. a. NZ.$7.50. Department of Statistics, Wellington, New Zealand (Subscr. to: Government Printing Office, Publications, Private Bag, Wellington, New Zealand)

336   NZ   ISSN 0110-3776
NEW ZEALAND. DEPARTMENT OF STATISTICS. INCOMES AND INCOME TAX STATISTICS. a. NZ.$3.75. Department of Statistics, Private Bag, Wellington, New Zealand (Subscr. to: Government Printing Office, Publications, Private Bag, Wellington, New Zealand)

331 319   NZ   ISSN 0110-5019
NEW ZEALAND. DEPARTMENT OF STATISTICS. PART A: PRICES. a. NZ.$1.85. Department of Statistics, Private Bag, Wellington, New Zealand (Subscr. to: Government Printing Office, Publications, Private Bag, Wellington, New Zealand)
Supersedes in part: New Zealand. Department of Statistics. Price, Wages and Labour (ISSN 0077-9911)

382 319   NZ   ISSN 0077-9806
NEW ZEALAND. DEPARTMENT OF STATISTICS. REPORT AND ANALYSIS OF EXTERNAL TRADE. a. NZ.$1.85. Department of Statistics, Private Bag, Wellington, New Zealand (Subscr. to: Government Printing Office, Publications, Private Bag, Wellington, New Zealand)

339.3 319   NZ   ISSN 0110-344X
NEW ZEALAND. DEPARTMENT OF STATISTICS. SYSTEM OF NATIONAL ACCOUNTS. a. NZ.$1. Department of Statistics, Private Bag, Wellington, New Zealand (Subscr. to: Government Printing Office, Publications, Private Bag, Wellington, New Zealand)
Formerly: New Zealand. Department of Statistics. National Income and Expenditure (ISSN 0077-989X)

319 339   NZ   ISSN 0110-392X
NEW ZEALAND HOUSEHOLD SURVEY. 1974. a. NZ.$2.20. Department of Statistics, Wellington, New Zealand (Subscr. to: Government Printing Office, Publications, Private Bag, Wellington, New Zealand) stat.
Formerly: New Zealand. Department of Statistics. Household Sample Survey.

316 382   NR   ISSN 0078-0634
NIGERIA. FEDERAL OFFICE OF STATISTICS. REVIEW OF EXTERNAL TRADE.* (Text in English) 1964. a. 5s. Federal Office of Statistics, Lagos, Nigeria.

316 381   NR   ISSN 0078-0642
NIGERIA. FEDERAL OFFICE OF STATISTICS. TRADE REPORT.* (Text in English) a. 22s. 6d. Federal Office of Statistics, Lagos, Nigeria.

331 310   US   ISSN 0074-9974
NORTH AMERICAN CONFERENCE ON LABOR STATISTICS. SELECTED PAPERS. 1959. irreg., latest issue, 1978. U.S. Bureau of Labor Statistics, 441 G St. N.W., Washington, DC 20212 (Orders to: Supt. of Documents, Washington, DC 20402) Ed. Henry R. Traubitz. circ. 700.
Formerly: Interstate Conference on Labor Statistics. Proceedings.

BUSINESS AND ECONOMICS — ABSTRACTING, BIBLIOGRAPHIES, STATISTICS

331 314   NO   ISSN 0078-1878
NORWAY. STATISTISK SENTRALBYRAA. ARBEIDSMARKEDSTATISTIKK/LABOUR MARKET STATISTICS. (Subseries of its Norges Offisielle Statistikk) (Text in Norwegian and English) 1967. a. Kr.1600. Statistisk Sentralbyraa, Box 8131 Dep., Oslo 1, Norway. circ. 2,100.

314.81   NO
NORWAY. STATISTISK SENTRALBYRAA. FORRETNINGS- OG SPAREBANKER/COMMERCIAL AND SAVINGS BANKS. (Subseries of Norges Offisielle Statistikk) biennial? Statistisk Sentralbyraa, Box 81311-Dep., Oslo 1, Norway.

338 314   NO   ISSN 0078-1886
NORWAY. STATISTISK SENTRALBYRAA. INDUSTRISTATISTIKK/INDUSTRIAL STATISTICS. (Subseries of its Norges Offisielle Statistikk) (Text in Norwegian and English) 1961. a. Kr.15. Statistisk Sentralbyraa, Box 8131 Dep., Oslo 1, Norway. circ. 2,800.

332.1 314   NO   ISSN 0078-1908
NORWAY. STATISTISK SENTRALBYRAA. KREDITTMARKED STATISTIKK/CREDIT MARKET STATISTICS. (Subseries of its Norges Offisielle Statistikk) (Text in Norwegian and English) 1955. a. Kr.20. Statistisk Sentralbyraa, Box 8131 Dep., Oslo 1, Norway.

331 314   NO   ISSN 0078-1916
NORWAY. STATISTISK SENTRALBYRAA. LOENNSSTATISTIKK/WAGE STATISTICS. (Subseries of its Norges Offisielle Statistikk) (Text in Norwegian and English) 1950. a. Kr.15. Statistisk Sentralbyraa, Box 8131 Dep., Oslo 1, Norway. circ. 1,700.

314   NO
NORWAY. STATISTISK SENTRALBYRAA. NASJONALREGNSKAPL/NATIONAL ACCOUNTS. (Subseries of its Norges Offisielle Statistikk) 1865. a. price varies. Statistisk Sentralbyraa, Box 8131 Dep., Oslo 1, Norway. circ. 2,400.

330 314   NO   ISSN 0078-1924
NORWAY. STATISTISK SENTRALBYRAA. OEKONOMISK UTSYN/ECONOMIC SURVEY. (Subseries of its Norges Offisielle Statistikk) (Text in Norwegian; summaries in English) 1936. a. Kr.25. Statistisk Sentralbyraa, Box 8131 Dep., Oslo 1, Norway. circ. 5,000.

382 314   NO   ISSN 0078-1940
NORWAY. STATISTISK SENTRALBYRAA. UTENRIKSHANDEL/EXTERNAL TRADE. (Subseries of its Norges Offisielle Statistikk) (Text in Norwegian and English) 1961. a. price varies. Statistisk Sentralbyraa, Box 8131 Dep., Oslo 1, Norway. circ. 2,000.

381 314   NO   ISSN 0078-1959
NORWAY. STATISTISK SENTRALBYRAA. VAREHANDELSSTATISTIKK/WHOLESALE AND RETAIL TRADE STATISTICS. (Subseries of its Norges Offisielle Statistikk) (Text in Norwegian and English) 1966. irreg. Kr.15. Statistisk Sentralbyraa, Box 8131 Dep., Oslo 1, Norway. circ. 1,600.

330 016   UR
NOVAYA LITERATURA PO TSENOOBRAZOVANIYU, OPUBLIKOVANNAYA V S.S.S.R; annotirovannyi ukazatel' 1970. irreg. 0.42 Rub. Nauchno-Issledovatel'skii Institut po Tsenoobrazovaniyu, Vtoraya Yaroslavskaya ul., 3, Moscow, U.S.S.R.

332 310   FR   ISSN 0304-3371
O E C D FINANCIAL STATISTICS/STATISTIQUES FINANCIERES DE L'OCDE. (Text in English and French) 1971. a. with 5 updating supplements and monthly supplements on interest rates. 380 F.($95) Organization for Economic Cooperation and Development, 2 rue Andre-Pascal, 75775 Paris Cedex 16, France (U.S. orders to: O.E.C.D. Publications and Information Center, 1750 Pennsylvania Ave., N.W., Washington, DC 20006) (also avail. in microfiche)

339 314   AU   ISSN 0085-4433
OESTERREICHS VOLKSEINKOMMEN. 1952. a. price varies. Oesterreichisches Statistisches Zentralamt, Nene Hofburg, Heldenplatz 1014, Austria. circ. 3,000.

331 317   US
OKLAHOMA. EMPLOYMENT SECURITY COMMISSION. ACTUARIAL DIVISION. HANDBOOK OF EMPLOYMENT SECURITY PROGRAM STATISTICS. 1952. a. free. Employment Security Commission, Actuarial Division, Will Rogers Bldg., Oklahoma City, OK 73105. Ed. Dennis O. Martin. stat. circ. 500.

331   US
OKLAHOMA. EMPLOYMENT SECURITY COMMISSION. RESEARCH AND PLANNING DIVISION. COUNTY EMPLOYMENT AND WAGE DATA. 1952. a. free. Employment Security Commission, Research & Planning Division, 310 Will Rogers Bldg., Oklahoma City, OK 73105. Ed. Dennis Martin. stat. circ. 800.

381 317   CN   ISSN 0317-8161
ONTARIO. MINISTRY OF CONSUMER AND COMMERCIAL RELATIONS. STATISTICAL REVIEW. irreg. Ministry of Consumer and Commercial Relations, Toronto, Canada.

338.9 310   FR   ISSN 0474-5442
ORGANIZATION FOR ECONOMIC COOPERATION AND DEVELOPMENT. HISTORICAL STATISTICS. STATISTIQUES RETROSPECTIVES. (Text in English and French) 1966. irreg. Organization for Economic Cooperation and Development, 2 rue Andre Pascal, 75775 Paris 16, France (U.S. orders to: O.E.C.D. Publications and Information Center, 1750 Pennsylvania Ave., N.W., Washington, DC 20006) (also avail. in microfiche)

338 314   FR   ISSN 0474-5469
ORGANIZATION FOR ECONOMIC COOPERATION AND DEVELOPMENT. INDUSTRIAL STATISTICS. STATISTIQUES INDUSTRIELLES. (Text in English and French) 1955. irreg. Organization for Economic Cooperation and Development, 2 rue Andre Pascal, 75775 Paris 16, France (U.S. orders to: O.E.C.D. Publications and Information Center, 1750 Pennsylvania Ave., N.W., Washington, DC 20006) (also avail. in microfiche)

382   FR
ORGANIZATION FOR ECONOMIC COOPERATION AND DEVELOPMENT. INTER-REGIONAL DRY CARGO MOVEMENTS/MOUVEMENTS INTERREGIONAUX DE CARGAISONS SECHES. irreg. Organization for Economic Cooperation and Development, 2, rue Andre-Pascal, 75775 Paris 16, France (U. S. Orders to: O.E.C.D. Publications Center, 1750 Pennsylvania Ave., N. W., Washington, D. C. 20006) (also avail. in microfiche)

311.11 310   FR   ISSN 0474-5515
ORGANIZATION FOR ECONOMIC COOPERATION AND DEVELOPMENT. LABOUR FORCE STATISTICS (YEARBOOK) / STATISTIQUES DE LA POPULATION ACTIVE. (Text in English and French) 1950. a (with q. supplements) $20. Organization for Economic Cooperation and Development, Chateau de la Muette, 2 rue Andre Pascal, 75775 Paris 16, France (U.S. orders to: O.E.C.D. Publications and Information Center, 1750 Pennsylvania Ave., N.W., Washington, D.C. 20006) (also avail. in microfiche)

336.2   FR
ORGANIZATION FOR ECONOMIC COOPERATION AND DEVELOPMENT. REVENUE STATISTICS OF OECD MEMBER COUNTRIES. (Text in English and French) 1965. a. $10. Organization for Economic Cooperation and Development, 2 rue Andre - Pascal, 75775 Paris Cedex 16, France (U.S. orders to: O.E.C.D. Publications and Information Center, 1750 Pennsylvania Ave., N.W., Washington, DC 20006) (also avail. in microfiche)

382   FR
ORGANIZATION FOR ECONOMIC COOPERATION AND DEVELOPMENT. STATISTICS OF FOREIGN TRADE. SERIES C: TABLES BY COMMODITIES. IMPORTS AND EXPORTS/STATISTIQUES DU COMMERCE EXTERIEUR. SERIE C: TABLEAUX PAR PRODUITS. (Editions in English and French) 1975. a. 120 F.($30) Organization for Economic Cooperation and Development, 2 rue Andre-Pascal, 75775 Paris Cedex 16, France (U.S. orders to: O.E.C.D. Publications and Information Center, 1750 Pennsylvania Ave., N.W., Washington, DC 20006) (also avail. in microfiche)
Former titles: Organization for Economic Cooperation and Development. Statistics of Foreign Trade. Series C: Trade by Commodities. Market Summaries. Imports and Exports/Statistiques du Commerce Exterieur. Serie C: Exchange Par Produits. Resume Par Marches. Importations et Exportations & O E C D Foreign Trade Statistics. Serie C.

336   PK
PAKISTAN. FINANCE DIVISION. PUBLIC FINANCE STATISTICS. (Text in English) 1975/76. a. Finance Division, Islamabad, Pakistan.

339 315   PK   ISSN 0078-7981
PAKISTAN. STATISTICS DIVISION. CONSUMER PRICE INDEX: SCOPE AND LIMITATIONS.* (Text in English) a. Statistics Division, 63 Muslim Abab, Karachi 5, Pakistan (Order from: Manager of Publications, Government of Pakistan, 2nd Floor, Ahmad Chamber, Tariq Rd., P.E.C.H.S., Karachi 29, Pakistan)

339.4 315   PK
PAKISTAN. STATISTICS DIVISION. HOUSEHOLD INCOME & EXPENDITURE SURVEY.* (Text in English) a. Rs.6. Statistics Division, 63 Muslim Abab, Karachi 5, Pakistan (Order from: Manager of Publications, Government of Pakistan, 2nd Floor, Ahmad Chamber, Tariq Rd., P.E.C.H.S., Karachi 29, Pakistan) stat.

338.9 315   PK
PAKISTAN INSTITUTE OF DEVELOPMENT ECONOMICS. STATISTICAL PAPERS. 1967. irreg. price varies. Pakistan Institute of Development Economics, Box 1091, Islamabad, Pakistan. Ed. Bd. stat. circ. 1,000.

382 319   PP
PAPUA NEW GUINEA. BUREAU OF STATISTICS. INTERNATIONAL TRADE STATISTICS. 1972/1973. a. Bureau of Statistics, P. O. Wards Strip, Papua New Guinea. Ed. J. J. Shadlow. circ. 901.
Supersedes: Papua New Guinea. Bureau of Statistics. Overseas Trade Statistics (ISSN 0078-9291)

338 315   PP   ISSN 0078-7701
PAPUA NEW GUINEA. BUREAU OF STATISTICS. RURAL INDUSTRIES. 1959. a. free. Bureau of Statistics, P.O. Wards Strip, Papua New Guinea. Ed. J. J. Shadlow. circ. 884.

338 315   PP   ISSN 0078-9321
PAPUA NEW GUINEA. BUREAU OF STATISTICS. RURAL INDUSTRIES. PRELIMINARY STATEMENT. 1968. a. free. Bureau of Statistics, P.O. Wards Strip, Papua New Guinea. Ed. J. J. Shadlow. circ. 884.

338 319   PP   ISSN 0078-9259
PAPUA NEW GUINEA. BUREAU OF STATISTICS. STATISTICAL BULLETIN: CAPITAL EXPENDITURE BY PRIVATE BUSINESSES. 1968. a. free. Bureau of Statistics, P.O. Wards Strip, Papua New Guinea. Ed. J.J. Shadlow. circ. 652.

381 319   PP
PAPUA NEW GUINEA. BUREAU OF STATISTICS. STATISTICAL BULLETIN: SURVEY OF RETAIL SALES AND SELECTED SERVICES. (Text in English) 1967/68. a. Bureau of Statistics, P.O. Wards Strip, Papua New Guinea. circ. 612.

338 315   PP   ISSN 0078-933X
PAPUA NEW GUINEA. BUREAU OF STATISTICS. SECONDARY INDUSTRIES. 1959. a. free. Bureau of Statistics, P.O. Wards Strip, Papua New Guinea. Ed. J. J. Shadlow. circ. 758.

338 315   PP   ISSN 0078-9313
PAPUA NEW GUINEA. BUREAU OF
STATISTICS. SECONDARY INDUSTRIES
(FACTORIES AND WORKS). PRELIMINARY
STATEMENT. 1966/67. a. free. Bureau of
Statistics, P.O. Wards Strip, Papua New Guinea.
Ed. J. J. Shadlow. circ. 758.

336.2 319   PP   ISSN 0078-9372
PAPUA NEW GUINEA. BUREAU OF
STATISTICS. TAXATION STATISTICS.
PRELIMINARY BULLETIN. 1966/67. a. free.
Bureau of Statistics, P.O. Wards Strip, Papua New
Guinea. Ed. J. J. Shadlow. circ. 590.

338 318   PY   ISSN 0085-4743
PARAGUAY. MINISTERIO DE INDUSTRIA Y
COMERCIO. DIVISION DE REGISTRO Y
ESTADISTICA INDUSTRIAL. ENCUESTA
INDUSTRIAL.* irreg. free. Ministerio de Industria
y Comercio, Division de Registro y Estadistica
Industrial, Av. Espana 475, Asuncion, Paraguay.
stat. (processed)

330.9 318   BL
PARANA, BRAZIL. SECRETARIA DE ESTADO
PARA OS NEGOCIOS DA FAZENDA; estatistica
economico-financeira. irreg. Secretaria de Estado
para os Negocios da Fazenda, Curitiba, Brazil. illus.

338.4 317   US   ISSN 0556-3615
PENNSYLVANIA. DEPARTMENT OF
COMMERCE. BUREAU OF STATISTICS,
RESEARCH AND PLANNING. STATISTICS
FOR MANUFACTURING INDUSTRIES. a.
Department of Commerce, Bureau of Statistics,
Research and Planning, 630B Health and Welfare
Bldg., Harrisburg, PA 17101. Key Title: Statistics
for Manufacturing Industries. (Harrisburg)

331.1 315   PH
PHILIPPINES. LABOR STATISTICS SERVICE.
YEAR BOOK OF LABOR STATISTICS. (Text in
English) 1973. irreg., latest 1977. Labor Statistics
Service, Phoenix Building, Intramuros, Manila,
Philippines. stat.

381   PH
PHILIPPINES. NATIONAL CENSUS AND
STATISTICS OFFICE. ANNUAL SURVEY OF
ESTABLISHMENTS. (In 8 parts) 1973. a, latest
1974. National Census and Statistics Office, Ramon
Magsaysay Blvd., Box 779, Manila, Philippines.

381 315   PH
PHILIPPINES. NATIONAL CENSUS AND
STATISTICS OFFICE. ANNUAL SURVEY OF
WHOLESALE AND RETAIL
ESTABLISHMENTS. a, latest 1969. P.9($3)
National Census and Statistics Office, Ramon
Magsaysay Blvd., Box 779, Manila, Philippines.

382 315   PH
PHILIPPINES. NATIONAL CENSUS AND
STATISTICS OFFICE. COASTWISE TRADE
REPORT. a, latest 1974. P.50($14) National Census
and Statistics Office, Ramon Magsaysay Blvd., Box
779, Manila, Philippines.

381 315   PH
PHILIPPINES. NATIONAL CENSUS AND
STATISTICS OFFICE. DIRECTORY OF LARGE
ESTABLISHMENTS. irreg., latest 1975. P.45($13)
National Census and Statistics Office, Ramon
Magsaysay Blvd., Box 779, Manila, Philippines.

332.1 314   PL   ISSN 0079-2640
POLAND. GLOWNY URZAD STATYSTYCZNY.
ROCZNIK STATYSTYCZNY FINANSOW.
YEARBOOK OF FINANCE STATISTICS.
(Subseries of its: Statystyka Polski) 1968. irreg.
Glowny Urzad Statystyczny, Al. Niepodleglosci
208, 00-925 Warsaw, Poland.

382 314   PL   ISSN 0079-2683
POLAND. GLOWNY URZAD STATYSTYCZNY.
ROCZNIK STATYSTYCZNY HANDLU
WEWNETRZNEGO/YEARBOOK OF
INTERNATIONAL TRADE STATISTICS.
(Subseries of its: Statystyka Polski) 1969. irreg. 55
Zl. Glowny Urzad Statystyczny., Al. Niepodleglosci
208, 00-925 Warsaw, Poland.

338 314   PL   ISSN 0079-2705
POLAND. GLOWNY URZAD STATYSTYCZNY.
ROCZNIK STATYSTYCZNY INWESTYCJI I
SRODKOW TRWALYCH. YEARBOOK OF
INVESTMENT AND FIXED ASSETS
STATISTICS.* (Issued in its Seria Roczniki
Branzowe. Branch Yearbooks) a. Glowny Urzad
Statystyczny, Al. Niepodleglosci 208, 00-925
Warsaw, Poland.

331 314   PL   ISSN 0079-2772
POLAND. GLOWNY URZAD STATYSTYCZNY.
ROCZNIK STATYSTYCZNY PRACY.
YEARBOOK OF LABOUR STATISTICS.* (Issued
in its Seria Roczniki Branzowe. Branch Yearbooks)
irreg. Glowny Urzad Statystyczny, Al.
Niepodleglosci 208, 00-925 Warsaw, Poland.

338 314   PL   ISSN 0079-2764
POLAND. GLOWNY URZAD STATYSTYCZNY.
ROCZNIK STATYSTYCZNY PRZEMYSLU.
YEARBOOK OF INDUSTRY STATISTICS.*
(Issued in its Seria Roczniki Branzowe. Branch
Yearbooks) a. Glowny Urzad Statystyczny, Al.
Niepodleglosci 208, 00-925 Warsaw, Poland.

382 314   PL   ISSN 0079-2691
POLAND. GLOWNY URZAD STATYSTYCZNY.
ROCZNIK STATYSTYKI HANDLU
ZAGRANICZNEGO. (Subseries of its: Statystyka
Polski) (Text in Polish with English translation)
1966. 56 Zl. Glowny Urzad Statystyczny, Al.
Niepodleglosci 208, Warsaw, Poland.

331 314   PL   ISSN 0079-2896
POLAND. GLOWNY URZAD STATYSTYCZNY.
ZATRUDNIENIE W GOSPODARCE
NARODOWEJ. (Subseries of its: Statystyka Polski)
1969. a. 24 Zl. Glowny Urzad Statystyczny, Al.
Niepodleglosci 208, 00-925 Warsaw, Poland.

338 314   PO
PORTUGAL. ESTATISTICAS INDUSTRIAIS:
CONTINENTE E ILHAS ADJACENTES. 1943. a.
$60. Instituto Nacional de Estatistica, Av. Antonio
Jose de Almeida, Lisbon 1, Portugal (Orders to:
Imprensa Nacional, Casa da Moeda, Direccao
Comercial, rua D. Francisco Manuel de Melo 5,
Lisbon 1, Portugal)
 Formerly: Portugal. Instituto Nacional de
Estatistica. Estatistica Industrial (ISSN 0079-418X)

336 314   PO   ISSN 0079-4171
PORTUGAL. INSTITUTO NACIONAL DE
ESTATISTICA. ESTATISTICAS DAS
FINANCAS PUBLICAS. 1968. a. $50. Instituto
Nacional de Estatistica, Av. Antonio Jose de
Almeida, Lisbon 1, Portugal (Orders to: Imprensa
Nacional, Casa da Moeda, Direccao Comercial, rua
D. Francisco Manuel de Melo 5, Lisbon 1, Portugal)

382 314   PO   ISSN 0079-4147
PORTUGAL. INSTITUTO NACIONAL DE
ESTATISTICA. ESTATISTICAS DO COMERCIO
EXTERNO. (Text in Portuguese and French) a.
price varies. Instituto Nacional de Estatistica, Av.
Antonio Jose de Almeida, Lisbon, Portugal (Orders
to: Imprensa Nacional, Casa da Moeda, Direccao
Comercial, rua D. Francisco Manuel de Melo 5,
Lisbon 1, Portugal)

336.2 314   PO   ISSN 0079-4120
PORTUGAL. INSTITUTO NACIONAL DE
ESTATISTICA. ESTATISTISTICAS DAS
CONTRIBUCOES E IMPOSTOS. 1878. a. $110.
Instituto Nacional de Estatistica, Av. Antonio Jose
de Almeida, Lisbon 1, Portugal (Orders to:
Imprensa Nacional, Casa da Moeda, Direccao
Comercial, rua D. Francisco Manuel de Melo 5,
Lisbon 1, Portugal)

331.11 314   PO
PORTUGAL. MINISTERIO DO TRABALHO.
SERVICO DE ESTATISTICAS. ESTATISTICAS
DO TRABALHO. (Text in Portuguese; summaries
in English, French) 1975. irreg. Ministerio do
Trabalho, Servico de Estatisticas, Servico de
Informacao Cientifica e Tecnica, Rua D. Filipa de
Vilhena 17, Lisbon 1, Portugal.

338 016   US   ISSN 0092-7767
PREDICASTS. SOURCE DIRECTORY. 1973. a.
$110 with 3 quarterly supplements. Predicasts, Inc.,
200 University Circle Research Center, 11001
Cedar Ave., Cleveland, OH 44106. Ed.Nellie
Connor. bibl. Key Title: Source Directory of
Predicasts, Inc.

338 016   US
PREDICASTS F & S INDEX UNITED STATES.
1962. a. $195. Predicasts, Inc., 200 University
Circle Research Center, 11001 Cedar Ave,
Cleveland, OH 44106.
 Formerly: F & S Index of Corporations and
Industries. Annual.

331.1 016   CN   ISSN 0075-613X
QUEEN'S UNIVERSITY AT KINGSTON.
INDUSTRIAL RELATIONS CENTRE.
BIBLIOGRAPHY SERIES. 1965. irreg., no. 6,
1975. price varies. ‡ Queen's University, Industrial
Relations Centre, Kingston, Ont. K7L 3N6, Canada.

332.1 319 330.9   AT   ISSN 0080-1798
RESERVE BANK OF AUSTRALIA. STATISTICAL
BULLETIN. SUPPLEMENT. 1937. issued
irregularly as supplements to monthly bulletin. free.
Reserve Bank of Australia, 65 Martin Place, Box
3947 G.P.O., Sydney, N.S.W. 2001, Australia. circ.
11,000.

381 310   US   ISSN 0361-0020
RETAILING IN TENNESSEE. irreg. Department of
Revenue, Sales and Use Tax Division, Nashville,
TN 37219. stat.

332.6 650 016   US   ISSN 0361-3917
S I E GUIDE TO BUSINESS AND INVESTMENT
BOOKS. 1970. irreg.(approx. every 4-5 years)
$12.95. Select Information Exchange, 2095
Broadway, New York, NY 10023. Ed. George H.
Wein. bk. rev. circ. 10,000.
 Formerly: Guide to Business & Investment Books
(ISSN 0072-8276)

658.8 310   US
SALES & MARKETING MANAGEMENT SURVEY
OF BUYING POWER (PART I) 1929. a. $50. Bill
Communications, Inc., 633 Third Avenue, New
York, NY 10017. Ed. Robert H. Albert. adv. charts.
stat. circ. 46,000. (reprint service avail. from UMI)
 Formerly: Sales Management Survey of Buying
Power (Part I)

658.8 310   US
SALES & MARKETING MANAGEMENT SURVEY
OF BUYING POWER (PART II) 1973. a. $20. Bill
Communications, Inc., 633 Third Avenue, New
York, NY 10017. Ed. Robert H. Albert. adv. charts.
stat. circ. 46,000. (reprint service avail. from UMI)
 Formerly: Sales Management Survey of Buying
Power (Part II)

658.8 310   US
SALES & MARKETING MANAGEMENT SURVEY
OF INDUSTRIAL PUCHASING POWER. 1974.
a. $20. Bill Communications, Inc., 633 Third Ave.,
New York, NY 10017. Ed. Robert H. Albert. adv.
charts. stat. circ. 46,000. (reprint service avail. from
UMI)
 Formerly: Sales Management Survey of Industrial
Purchasing Power.

658.8 310   US
SALES & MARKETING MANAGEMENT SURVEY
OF SELLING COSTS. 1973. a. $20. Bill
Communications, Inc., 633 Third Avenue, New
York, NY 10017. Ed. Robert H. Albert. adv. charts.
stat. circ. 46,000. (reprint service avail. from UMI)
 Formerly: Sales Management Survey of Selling
Costs.

330.95   UN
SAMPLE SURVEYS IN THE ESCAP REGION. a.
United Nations Economic and Social Commission
for Asia and the Pacific, The United Nations
Building, Rajadamnern Ave., Bangkok 2, Thailand.
stat.
 Formerly: United Nations. Economic
Commission for Asia and the Far East. Sample
Surveys in the ECAFE Region.

382 315   MY   ISSN 0080-6455
SARAWAK EXTERNAL TRADE STATISTICS.
(Text in English) 1954. a. M.$20. ‡ Department of
Statistics, Federal Complex, Jalan Simpang Tiga,
Kuching, Sarawak, Malaysia.

382 319   SU
SAUDI ARABIA. CENTRAL DEPARTMENT OF
STATISTICS. FOREIGN TRADE STATISTICS. a.
s.R.100. Central Department of Statistics, Box 3735,
Riyadh, Saudi Arabia.

BUSINESS AND ECONOMICS — ABSTRACTING, BIBLIOGRAPHIES, STATISTICS

330 315.6   SU
SAUDI ARABIA. CENTRAL DEPARTMENT OF STATISTICS. STATISTICAL INDICATOR. (Text in Arabic and English) 1976. a. free. Central Department of Statistics, P. O. Box 3735, Riyadh, Saudi Arabia. charts. stat.

332 016   US   ISSN 0077-4014
SELECTED AND ANNOTATED BIBLIOGRAPHY OF REFERENCE MATERIALS IN CONSUMER CREDIT. irreg., latest 1973. $1. National Consumer Finance Association, 1000 16th St., Washington, DC 20036.

016 330.9   US
SELECTED BIBLIOGRAPHY OF RECENT ECONOMIC DEVELOPMENT PUBLICATIONS. irreg., latest 1975-76. Vanderbilt University, Graduate Program in Economic Development, Nashville, TN 37235.

338 315   SI   ISSN 0080-9675
SINGAPORE. DEPARTMENT OF STATISTICS. REPORT ON THE CENSUS OF INDUSTRIAL PRODUCTION. a. S.$7. Department of Statistics, Box 3010, Singapore 1, Singapore.

315 331   SI
SINGAPORE. NATIONAL STATISTICAL COMMISSION. SINGAPORE STANDARD INDUSTRIAL CLASSIFICATION. irreg. National Statistical Commission, P.O. Box 3010, Singapore 9050, Singapore.

330 016   AG   ISSN 0080-9772
SINTESIS BIBLIOGRAFICA.* 1964. irreg., 1972, no. 9. free. Universidad Nacional de la Plata, Biblioteca Publica, Plaza Rocha 137, La Plata, Argentina. Formerly: Boletin Hemerografico.

382 316   SA   ISSN 0081-2196
SOUTH AFRICA. DEPARTMENT OF CUSTOMS AND EXCISE. FOREIGN TRADE STATISTICS. a. (2 vols.) R.12.25 per vol. Department of Customs and Excise, Private Bag X47, Pretoria 0001, South Africa (Orders to: Government Printer, Private Bag X85, Pretoria 0001, South Africa)

331.1   SA
SOUTH AFRICA. DEPARTMENT OF STATISTICS. LABOUR STATISTICS: WAGE RATES, EARNINGS AND AVERAGE HOURS WORKED IN THE PRINTING AND NEWSPAPER INDUSTRY, ENGINEERING INDUSTRY, BUILDING INDUSTRY AND COMMERCE. (Report No. 01-20) a., latest 1977. R.5. Department of Statistics, Private Bag X44, Pretoria 0001, South Africa (Orders to: Government Printer, Bosman St., Private Bag X85, Pretoria 0001, South Africa)

339   SA
SOUTH AFRICA. DEPARTMENT OF STATISTICS. REPORT ON PRICES. (Report No. 11-01) a., latest 1977. R.3.50. Department of Statistics, Private Bag X44, Pretoria 0001, South Africa (Orders to: Government Printer, Bosman St., Private Bag X85, Pretoria 0001, South Africa)

338.23   SA
SOUTH AFRICA. DEPARTMENT OF STATISTICS. SURVEY OF THE ACCOUNTS OF COMPANIES IN SECONDARY AND TERTIARY INDUSTRIES. (Report No. 09-01) a., latest 1976/77. R.5.60. Department of Statistics, Private Bag X44, Pretoria 0001, South Africa (Orders to: Government Printer, Bosman St., Private Bag X85, Pretoria 0001,South Africa)

331.1 317   US   ISSN 0094-2200
SOUTH DAKOTA. DEPARTMENT OF LABOR. RESEARCH AND STATISTICS. ANNUAL REPORT ON STATE AND AREA OCCUPATIONAL REQUIREMENTS FOR VOCATIONAL EDUCATION. a. Department of Labor, 607 N. 4th St., Box 1730, Aberdeen, SD 57401. Key Title: Annual Report on State and Area Occupational Requirements for Vocational Education (Aberdeen)

336.2 317   US   ISSN 0085-6460
SOUTH DAKOTA. DEPARTMENT OF REVENUE. ANNUAL STATISTICAL REPORT. 1952. a. Department of Revenue, Division of Property Tax, Capitol Lake Plaza Bldg., Pierre, SD 57501. charts. circ. 450. (processed)
    Formerly: South Dakota Department of Revenue. Annual Report.

338 314   SP   ISSN 0081-3354
SPAIN. INSTITUTO NACIONAL DE ESTADISTICA. ESTADISTICA INDUSTRIAL. a. 800 ptas. Instituto Nacional de Estadistica, Avda. Generalisimo 91, Madrid 16, Spain.

331 314   SP   ISSN 0081-3389
SPAIN. INSTITUTO NACIONAL DE ESTADISTICA. POBLACION ACTIVA. a. Instituto Nacional de Estadistica, Avda. Generalisimo 91, Madrid 16, Spain.

336 314   SP   ISSN 0081-3435
SPAIN. MINISTERIO DE HACIENDA. INFORMACION ESTADISTICA.* a. Ministerio de Hacienda, Madrid, Spain.

350 336   II
STATE DOMESTIC PRODUCT OF HIMACHAL PRADESH. (Text in English) 1963. a. Directorate of Economics and Statistics, Simla, Himachal Pradesh, India. circ. 700.
    Supersedes: State Income of Himachal Pradesh.

330 317   US   ISSN 0081-4695
STATISTICAL ABSTRACT OF LOUISIANA. 1965. triennial; 6th ed. 1977. $5. Louisiana State University, College of Business Administration, Division of Business and Economic Research, New Orleans, LA 70122. Ed. James R. Bobo.

317 650   US   ISSN 0191-0310
STATISTICAL ABSTRACT OF OKLAHOMA. 1956. biennial. $10. University of Oklahoma, Center for Economic and Management Research, College of Business Administration, 307 W. Brooks St., Rm. 4, Norman, OK 73019. circ. 1,000.

332.1 315   TH
STATISTICAL DATA ON COMMERCIAL BANKS IN THAILAND. (Text in English) 1964. a. free. Bangkok Bank Ltd., Economic Research Division, 9 Suapa Rd., Bangkok, Thailand. illus.

382 314   EI   ISSN 0081-4857
STATISTICAL OFFICE OF THE EUROPEAN COMMUNITIES. ASSOCIES STATISTIQUE DU COMMERCE EXTERIEUR. ANNUAIRE. (Text in French; summaries in French, German, Dutch, Italian and English) 1968. a. B.P. 1907, Luxembourg, Luxembourg (Dist. in the U.S. by: European Community Information Service, 2100 M St., NW, Suite 707, Washington, DC 20037)

382.094 314   EI   ISSN 0586-4925
STATISTICAL OFFICE OF THE EUROPEAN COMMUNITIES. AUSSENHANDEL: ANALITISCHE UBERSICHTEN. FOREIGN TRADE: ANALYTICAL TABLES. (Text in French and German) a. B.P. 1907, Luxembourg, Luxembourg (Dist. in the U.S. by: European Community Information Service, 2100 M St., NW, Suite 707, Washington, DC 20037)

314   EI   ISSN 0081-4873
STATISTICAL OFFICE OF THE EUROPEAN COMMUNITIES. BASIC STATISTICS. (Text in German, French, Italian, Dutch, English) 1961. a. $30.20. B.P. 1907, Luxembourg, Luxembourg (Dist. in the U.S. by: European Community Information Service, 2100 M St., NW, Suite 707, Washington, DC 20037)

382 314   EI   ISSN 0081-4881
STATISTICAL OFFICE OF THE EUROPEAN COMMUNITIES. COMMERCE EXTERIEUR: PRODUCTS C E C A. (Text in French, German, Italian, Dutch) irreg. B.P. 1907, Luxembourg, Luxembourg (Dist. in the U.S. by: European Community Information Service, 2100 M St., NW, Suite 707, Washington, DC 20037)

382 314   EI   ISSN 0081-4903
STATISTICAL OFFICE OF THE EUROPEAN COMMUNITIES. FOREIGN TRADE: STANDARD COUNTRY CLASSIFICATION. (Text in German, French, Italian, Dutch, English) a. B.P. 1907, Luxembourg, Luxembourg (Dist. in the U.S. by: European Community Information Service, 2100 M St., NW, Suite 707, Washington, DC 20037)

339 314   EI   ISSN 0081-4911
STATISTICAL OFFICE OF THE EUROPEAN COMMUNITIES. NATIONAL ACCOUNTS. YEARBOOK. (Text in German, French, Italian, Dutch, English) a. B.P. 1907, Luxembourg, Luxembourg (Dist. in the U.S. by: European Community Information Service, 2100 M St., NW, Suite 707, Washington, DC 20037)

330 316   EI   ISSN 0081-492X
STATISTICAL OFFICE OF THE EUROPEAN COMMUNITIES. OVERSEAS ASSOCIATES. ANNUAIRE STATISTIQUES DES ETATS AFRICAINS ET MALGACHE. (Text in French) a. B.P. 1907, Luxembourg, Luxembourg (Dist. in the U.S. by: European Community Information Service, 2100 M St., NW, Suite 707, Washington, DC 20037)

336 314   EI   ISSN 0081-4938
STATISTICAL OFFICE OF THE EUROPEAN COMMUNITIES. RECETTES FISCALES. ANNUAIRE. (Text in French and German) a. B.P. 1907, Luxembourg, Luxembourg (Dist. in the U.S. by: European Community Information Service, 2100 M St., NW, Suite 707, Washington, DC 20037)

338.4 314   EI   ISSN 0081-4970
STATISTICAL OFFICE OF THE EUROPEAN COMMUNITIES. STATISTIQUES INDUSTRIELLES ANNUAIRE. (Text in French, German, Italian, Dutch) a. 600 Fr.($14.50) B.P. 1907, Luxembourg, Luxembourg (Dist. in the U.S. by: European Community Information Service, 2100 M St., NW, Suite 707, Washington, DC 20037)

330 314   EI   ISSN 0081-4997
STATISTICAL OFFICE OF THE EUROPEAN COMMUNITIES. YEARBOOK REGIONAL STATISTICS. (Text in German, French, Italian, Dutch, English) a. B.P. 1907, Luxembourg, Luxembourg (Dist. in the U.S. by: European Community Information Service, 2100 M St., NW, Suite 707, Washington, DC 20037)

330 315   JA   ISSN 0081-5047
STATISTICAL SURVEY OF ECONOMY OF JAPAN.* 1955. a. 1400 Yen. Ministry of Foreign Affairs, Economic Affairs Bureau, Minister's Secretariat, Tokyo, Japan.

338.9 316   KE
STATISTICAL SURVEY OF THE EAST AFRICAN COMMUNITY INSTITUTIONS. 1973. a; latest vol. 1974/75. EAs.7.50. East African Community, Statistical Department, Box 30462, Nairobi, Kenya.

336 315   CH
STATISTICAL YEARBOOK OF THE REPUBLIC OF CHINA. 1975. a. Directorate-General of Budget, Accounting, and Statistics, Executive Yuan, Taipei, Taiwan, Republic of China. stat.

314   UK   ISSN 0081-5098
STATISTICS - AFRICA; sources for market research. 1970. irreg., 2nd, 1978. £25($80) ‡ C.B.D. Research Ltd., 154 High St., Beckenham, Kent BR3 1EA, England (Dist. in U.S. by: Gale Research Co., Book Tower, Detroit, MI 48226) Ed. Joan M. Harvey. index. circ. 2,000.

317 318   UK   ISSN 0309-5452
STATISTICS - AMERICA; sources for market research (North, Central & South America) 1973. irreg., 2nd, 1980. £43.50($135) ‡ C.B.D. Research Ltd., 154 High St., Beckenham, Kent BR3 1EA, England (Dist. in U.S. by: Gale Research Co., Book Tower, Detroit, MI 48226) Ed. Joan M. Harvey. circ. 2,000.

314   UK   ISSN 0081-5101
STATISTICS - EUROPE; sources for market research. 1968. irreg., 4th, 1981. ‡ C.B.D. Research Ltd., 154 High St., Beckenham, Kent BR3 1EA, England (Dist. in U.S. by: Gale Research Co., Book Tower, Detroit, MI 48226) Ed. Joan M. Harvey. index. circ. 2,000.

382 315   SY   ISSN 0081-5136
STATISTICS OF FOREIGN TRADE OF SYRIA; classified according to United Nations standard international trade classification. (Text in Arabic and English) 1964. a. $10. Central Bureau of Statistics, Damascus, Syria.

338 315 JA ISSN 0081-5209
STATISTICS ON JAPANESE INDUSTRIES. (Text in English) 1965. a. 1500 Yen. Ministry of International Trade and Industry, Research and Statistics Division - Tsusho Sangyo Chosakai, Minister's Secretariat, 6-15-1 Ginza, Chuo-ku, Tokyo 104, Japan. circ. 1,000.

330.9 310 MX
STATISTICS ON THE MEXICAN ECONOMY. (Text in English) 1977. a. Nacional Financiera S.A., Isabel la Catolica 51, Mexico 1, D.F., Mexico.

382 314 YU ISSN 0084-4373
STATISTIKA SPOLJNE TRGOVINE SFR JUGOSLAVIJE. 1946-49. a. 400 din.($22.22) Savezni Zavod za Statistiku, Uzun Mirkova 1, Belgrade, Yugoslavia. circ. 1,500.

382.5 316 IV ISSN 0081-5276
STATISTIQUES DU COMMERCE EXTERIEUR DE COTE D'IVOIRE. 1961. a. Service des Statistiques Douanieres, Abidjan, Ivory Coast.

382 316 AE
STATISTIQUES DU COMMERCE EXTERIEUR DE L'ALGERIE. (Text in French) 1963. m., q., & a. 120-150 din. Direction des Douanes, 19, rue du Docteur Saadane, Algiers, Algeria.

382 316 TI ISSN 0081-5292
STATISTIQUES DU COMMERCE EXTERIEUR DE LA TUNISIE. a, latest 1976. Institut National de la Statistique, 27 rue de Liban, Tunis, Tunisia.

382 316 MG ISSN 0081-5306
STATISTIQUES DU COMMERCE EXTERIEUR DE MADAGASCAR. 1965. a. FMG.1310. Institut National de la Statistique et de la Recherche Economique, Ministere des Finances et du Plan, B.P. 485, Antananarivo, Malagasy Republic.

318.8 388 SR
SURINAM. ALGEMEEN BUREAU VOOR DE STATISTIEK. KWARTAAL STATISTIEK VAN DE INDUSTRIELE PRODUKTIE. (Text in Dutch) irreg. Algemeen Bureau voor de Statistiek, Paramaribo, Surinam.

339.4 SZ
SURVEY OF LIVING COSTS IN MAJOR CITIES WORLDWIDE. irreg. Business International S.A., 7 rue Versonnex, Geneva, Switzerland. stat.

331.1 314 SW
SWEDEN. STATISTISKA CENTRALBYRAAN. ARBETSKRAFTUNDERSOEKNINGEN. ARSMEDELTAL. (At head of title: Statistiska Tabeller) 1963. irreg. Liber Foerlag, Fack, S-162 89 Vaellingby, Sweden. illus. stat.

338 314 SW ISSN 0082-0172
SWEDEN. STATISTISKA CENTRALBYRAAN. INDUSTRI. (Text in Swedish; summaries in English) 1911. a. price varies. Liber Foerlag, Fack, S-162 89 Vaellingby, Sweden. circ. 1,500.

314 331 SW ISSN 0082-0180
SWEDEN. STATISTISKA CENTRALBYRAAN. INFORMATION I PROGNOSFRAGOR/FORECASTING INFORMATION. (Text in Swedish, occasionally in English; summaries in English) 1965. irreg. Kr.60. Liber Foerlag, Fack, S-162 89 Vaellingby, Sweden. circ. 1,500-5,500.
Estimation of future manpower resources and of demand for selected professional and educational categories

658.3 314 SW ISSN 0082-0202
SWEDEN. STATISTISKA CENTRALBYRAAN. KOMMUNAL PERSONAL. (In 2 parts: Del 1, Landstingspersonal; del 2, Primarkommunal Personal) (Text in Swedish; title heads in English) 1968. a. price varies. Liber Foerlag, Fack, S-162 89 Vaellingby, Sweden. circ. 600.

331.2 314 SW ISSN 0082-0210
SWEDEN. STATISTISKA CENTRALBYRAAN. LOENER. 1929. a. Kr.29. Liber Foerlag, Fack, S-162 89 Vaellingby, Sweden. circ. 900.
Wages

314 331 SW ISSN 0082-0237
SWEDEN. STATISTISKA CENTRALBYRAAN. STATISTISKA MEDDELANDEN. SUBGROUP AM (LABOR MARKET) (Text in Swedish; table heads and summaries in English) 1963 N.S. irreg. Kr.160. Liber Foerlag, Fack, S-162 89 Vaellingby, Sweden. circ. 1,250.

338 381 314 SW ISSN 0082-0261
SWEDEN. STATISTISKA CENTRALBYRAAN. STATISTISKA MEDDELANDEN. SUBGROUP H (TRADE) (Text in Swedish; table heads and summaries in English) 1963 N.S. irreg. Kr.40. Liber Foerlag, Fack, S-162 89 Vaellingby, Sweden. circ. 2,000.

338 314 SW ISSN 0082-027X
SWEDEN. STATISTISKA CENTRALBYRAAN. STATISTISKA MEDDELANDEN. SUBGROUP I (MANUFACTURING) (Text in Swedish; table heads and summaries in English) 1963 N.S. irreg. Kr.120. Liber Foerlag, Fack, S-162 89 Vaellingby, Sweden. circ. 1,300.

336 314 SW ISSN 0082-0296
SWEDEN. STATISTISKA CENTRALBYRAAN. STATISTISKA MEDDELANDEN. SUBGROUP N (NATIONAL ACCOUNTS AND FINANCE) (Text in Swedish; table heads and summaries in English) 1963 N.S. irreg. Kr.160. Liber Foerlag, Fack, S-162 89 Vaellingby, Sweden. circ. 1,500.

330 314 SW ISSN 0082-030X
SWEDEN. STATISTISKA CENTRALBYRAAN. STATISTISKA MEDDELANDEN. SUBGROUP P (PRICES AND PRICE INDICES) (Text in Swedish; table heads and summaries in English) 1963 N.S. irreg. Kr.100. Liber Foerlag, Fack, S-162 89 Vaellingby, Sweden. circ. 2,150.

382 314 SW ISSN 0082-0369
SWEDEN. STATISTISKA CENTRALBYRAAN. UTRIKESHANDEL/FOREIGN TRADE. (Text in Swedish; summaries in English) 1911. m. Kr.75. Liber Foerlag, Fack, S-162 89 Vaellingby, Sweden. circ. 1,500.

382 314 SZ
SWITZERLAND. DIRECTORATE GENERAL OF CUSTOMS. ANNUAL REPORT. (2 parts) (Text in French and German) a. (includes Part 1 and Part 2. Eidgenoessische Oberzolldirektion, Abetilung Handelsstatistik, Monbijourstr. 40, 3003 Berne, Switzerland.

382 314 SZ ISSN 0081-525X
SWITZERLAND: DIRECTORATE GENERAL OF CUSTOMS. ANNUAL STATISTICS. (3 volumes) (Text in French and German) a. 43 Fr. (vols. 1 and 2); 35 Fr. (vol. 3) Eidgenoessische Oberzolldirektion, Abetilung Handelsstatistik - Directorate General of Customs, Trade Statistics Division, Monbijourstr. 40, 3003 Berne, Switzerland.

338 316 TZ
TANZANIA. BUREAU OF STATISTICS. SURVEY OF INDUSTRIAL PRODUCTION. 1965. a. Bureau of Statistics, Box 796, Dar es Salaam, Tanzania (Orders to: Government Publications Agency, Box 1801, Dar es Salaam, Tanzania)
Formerly: Tanzania.Central Statistical Bureau. Survey of Industrial Production (ISSN 0564-6545)

016 336.2 US ISSN 0496-974X
TAX FOUNDATION'S RESEARCH BIBLIOGRAPHY. 1959. irreg. Tax Foundation, Inc., 1875 Connecticut Ave., N.W., Washington, DC 20009.

330 US
TEXAS FACT BOOK. a. price varies. University of Texas at Austin, Bureau of Business Research, Austin, TX 78712. stat.

315 338 TH
THAILAND. NATIONAL STATISTICAL OFFICE, REPORT OF INDUSTRIAL SURVEY IN NORTHEAST REGION/THAILAND. SAMNAKNGAN SATHITI HAENG CHAT. (Text in English and Thai) 1972. irreg. National Statistical Office, Lan Luang Rd., Bangkok, Thailand. charts. stat.

382 TH
THAILAND'S FOREIGN TRADE STATISTICS. (Text mainly in English and Thai; some Chinese) irreg. B.250. Interstate Publications, Box 5-85, Pathumwan, Bangkok 5, Thailand.

TOPICATOR; classified article guide to the advertising/communications/marketing periodical press. see *ADVERTISING AND PUBLIC RELATIONS — Abstracting, Bibliographies, Statistics*

332 318 TR ISSN 0082-6529
TRINIDAD AND TOBAGO. CENTRAL STATISTICAL OFFICE. FINANCIAL STATISTICS. 1966. a; latest issue, 1974-75. T.T.$1. Central Statistical Office, Textel Building, 1, Edward Street, Port of Spain, Trinidad (Subscr. to: Government Printery, 2 Victoria Ave, Port of Spain, Trinidad)

317.29 331.1 TR
TRINIDAD AND TOBAGO. CENTRAL STATISTICAL OFFICE. LABOUR FORCE BY SEX. (Subseries of: Its Continuous Sample Survey of Population) irreg.; latest issue, 1973. T.T.$0.75. Central Statistical Office, Textel Building, 1, Edward Street, Port of Spain, Trinidad (Orders to: Government Printing Office, 2 Victoria Ave., Port of Spain, Trinidad) illus. stat.

382 318 TR ISSN 0082-6545
TRINIDAD AND TOBAGO. CENTRAL STATISTICAL OFFICE. OVERSEAS TRADE. ANNUAL REPORT. (Issued in two parts) 1951. a. $3.50 (pt. A), $ 2 (pt. B) Central Statistical Office, Textel Building, 1, Edward Street, Port of Spain, Trinidad (Subscr. to: Government Printery, 2 Victoria Ave., Port of Spain, Trinidad)

338.5 314 BU
TSENI. 1969. a. 1.45 lv. Ministerstvo na Informatsiiata i Suobshteniiata, 18, Ul. Graf Ignatiev, Sofia, Bulgaria. (Co-sponsor: Tsentralno Statistichesko Upravlenie) stat. circ. 280.

338 316 TI
TUNISIA. INSTITUT NATIONAL DE LA STATISTIQUE. RECENSEMENT DES ACTIVITES INDUSTRIELLES. a, latest 1976. Institut National de la Statistique, 27 rue de Liban, Tunis, Tunisia.
Formerly: Tunisia. Institut National de la Statistique. Statistiques Industrielles (ISSN 0082-6839)

382 318 TU ISSN 0082-6901
TURKEY. DEVLET ISTATISTIK ENSTITUSU. DIS TICARET YILLIK ISTATISTIK/STATISTIQUE ANNUELLE DU COMMERCE EXTERIEUR/ANNUAL FOREIGN TRADE STATISTICS. 1964. a. free or on exchange basis. State Institute of Statistics, Necatibey Caddesi 114, Ankara, Turkey.

382 339 016 UN ISSN 0041-5227
U N C T A D GUIDE TO PUBLICATIONS. (Text in English, French, and Spanish) a. free. United Nations Conference on Trade and Development, Information Service, Palais des Nations, CH-1211 Geneva 10, Switzerland.

338 016 UN
UNITED NATIONS INDUSTRIAL DEVELOPMENT ORGANIZATION. GUIDES TO INFORMATION SOURCES. 1972. irreg., no. 32, 1979. $4. United Nations Industrial Development Organization, Lerchenfelderstrasse 1, Box 707, A-1011 Vienna, Austria (Orders from Europe, Africa and Middle East to: Distribution and Sales Section, Palais des Nations, 1211 Geneva 10 Switzerland. Orders from Asia, the Pacific and North and South America to: United Nations Publications, Room LX-2300, New York, NY 10017)

331.2 317 US
U.S. BUREAU OF LABOR STATISTICS. AREA WAGE SURVEYS. irreg. throughout the year for individual areas. price varies. U. S. Bureau of Labor Statistics, 441 G St. N.W., Washington, DC 20212 (Orders to: Supt. of Documents, Washington, DC 20402)

BUSINESS AND ECONOMICS — ABSTRACTING, BIBLIOGRAPHIES, STATISTICS

331.2 317 US
U.S. BUREAU OF LABOR STATISTICS. DIGEST OF SELECTED PENSION PLANS. 1971. irreg., approx. 2 supplements per yr. price varies. U. S. Bureau of Labor Statistics, 441 G St. N.W., Washington, DC 20212 (Orders to: Supt. of Documents, Washington, DC 20402) (looseleaf format)

331.2 317 US ISSN 0091-8261
U.S. BUREAU OF LABOR STATISTICS. EMPLOYEE COMPENSATION IN THE PRIVATE NONFARM ECONOMY. 1970. a. price varies. U. S. Bureau of Labor Statistics, 441 G St. N.W., Washington, DC 20212 (Orders to: Supt. of Documents, Washington, DC 20402) (also avail. in microform) Key Title: Employee Compensaton in the Private Nonfarm Economy.

331.1 317 US ISSN 0082-9056
U. S. BUREAU OF LABOR STATISTICS. HANDBOOK OF LABOR STATISTICS. (Subseries of its Bulletins) 1924/26. a. price varies. U.S. Bureau of Labor Statistics, 441 G St., N.W., Washington, DC 20210 (Orders to: Supt. of Documents, Washington, DC 20402)

331 317 US
U. S. BUREAU OF LABOR STATISTICS. MAJOR PROGRAMS. a. free. U. S. Bureau of Labor Statistics, 441 G St., Washington, DC 20212 (Orders to: Supt. of Documents, Washington, DC 20402)

331.2 317 US ISSN 0501-7041
U.S. BUREAU OF LABOR STATISTICS. NATIONAL SURVEY OF PROFESSIONAL, ADMINISTRATIVE, TECHNICAL AND CLERICAL PAY. a. price varies. U. S. Bureau of Labor Statistics, 441 G. Street, N.W., Washington, DC 20212 (Orders to: Supt. of Documents, Washington, DC 20402) (also avail. in microform)

331.11 317 US
U.S. BUREAU OF LABOR STATISTICS. PRODUCTIVITY INDEXES FOR SELECTED INDUSTRIES. a. price varies. U.S. Bureau of Labor Statistics, 441 G Street, N.W., Washington, DC 20212 (Orders to: Supt. of Documents, Washington, DC 20402) (also avail. in microform)
  Formerly: U.S. Bureau of Labor Statistics. Indexes of Output per Man-Hour; Selected Industries.

330 016 US ISSN 0091-9039
U. S. DEPARTMENT OF COMMERCE. PUBLICATIONS; A CATALOG AND INDEX. 1950. a. $5.50. U. S. Department of Commerce, Office of Publications, Washington, DC 20230 (Orders to: Supt. of Documents, Washington, DC 20402) Eds. E. Neil Sawyer & Doris H. Gerhoff. bibl. Key Title: United States Department of Commerce Publications.
  Continues: U.S. Department of Commerce. Library. United States Department of Commerce Publications. Supplement (ISSN 0499-0994)

332.1 317 US ISSN 0083-0666
U. S. FEDERAL DEPOSIT INSURANCE CORPORATION. BANK OPERATING STATISTICS. 1967. a. single copy free. U.S. Federal Deposit Insurance Corporation., 550 17th St., N.W., Washington, DC 20429.

U.S. FOREIGN AGRICULTURAL TRADE STATISTICAL REPORT, CALENDAR YEAR. see *AGRICULTURE — Abstracting, Bibliographies, Statistics*

U.S. FOREIGN AGRICULTURAL TRADE STATISTICAL REPORT, FISCAL YEAR. see *AGRICULTURE — Abstracting, Bibliographies, Statistics*

330 016 CK
UNIVERSIDAD DE ANTIOQUIA. CENTRO DE INVESTIGACIONES ECONOMICAS. BOLETIN BIBLIOGRAFICO. 1969. irreg. free. Universidad de Antioquia, Centro de Investigaciones Economicas, Medellin, Colombia.

330.9 016 AG
UNIVERSIDAD DE BUENOS AIRES. INSTITUTO DE ECONOMIA. BIBLIOGRAFIA SOBRE ECONOMIA NACIONAL. 1950. Universidad de Buenos Aires, Instituto de Economia, Buenos Aires, Argentina. Ed. J. Broide.

330 310 GH
UNIVERSITY OF GHANA. INSTITUTE OF STATISTICAL, SOCIAL AND ECONOMIC RESEARCH. TECHNICAL PUBLICATION SERIES. 1966. irreg.; no. 35, 1975. University of Ghana, Institute of Statistical, Social and Economic Research, Box 74, Legon, Ghana.
  Formerly: University of Ghana. Institute of Statistical, Social and Economic Research. Technical Research Monographs (ISSN 0072-4416)

330 016 US ISSN 0082-3236
UNIVERSITY OF TEXAS, AUSTIN. BUREAU OF BUSINESS RESEARCH. BIBLIOGRAPHY. 1947. irreg; no. 18, 1976. price varies. University of Texas at Austin, Bureau of Business Research, Austin, TX 78712.

330.9 316 UV
UPPER VOLTA. INSTITUT NATIONAL DE LA STATISTIQUE ET DE LA DEMOGRAPHIE. BULLETIN ANNUAIRE D'INFORMATION STATISTIQUE ET ECONOMIQUE. no. 16, 1975. a. Institut National de la Statistique et de la Demographie, Ouagadougou, Upper Volta.
  Supersedes: Upper Volta. Direction de la Statistique et de la Mecanographie. Bulletin Mensuel d'Information Statistique et Economique; Upper Volta. Direction de la Statistique et de la Mecanographie. Bulletin Annuaire Statistique et Economiques.

331.1 317 US ISSN 0095-1382
VERMONT. DEPARTMENT OF EMPLOYMENT SECURITY. STATISTICAL TABLES. irreg. Department of Employment Security, Box 488, Montpelier, VT 05602. Key Title: Statistical Tables - Department of Employment Security.

382 315 MY ISSN 0085-8080
WEST MALAYSIA ANNUAL STATISTICS OF EXTERNAL TRADE. (Text in English & Malay) 1962. a. M.$12. Department of Statistics - Jabatan Perangkaan, Jalan Young, Kuala Lumpur 10-01, Malaysia. circ. 1,400.

314 330.9 AU ISSN 0510-5609
WIRTSCHAFTSZAHL. 1961. irreg. (1-2/yr) Handelskammer Niederoesterreich, Herrengasse 10, A-1014 Vienna, Austria. Ed. Walter Wiltschegg. charts. circ. 1,000.

338.9
WORLD BANK RESEARCH PROGRAM: ABSTRACTS OF CURRENT STUDIES. 1974. a. World Bank, 1818 H St., N.W., Washington, DC 20433.

332.1 310 UK
WORLD BANKING SURVEY. Variant title: World Banking Statistical Annual Survey. a. £15($39.50) Financial Times Business Publishing Ltd., Box 118, Bracken House, 10 Cannon St., London EC4P 4BY, England. Ed. D.W. Webster. charts. illus. stat. circ. 12,000.

382 310 UN ISSN 0084-3822
YEARBOOK OF INTERNATIONAL TRADE STATISTICS. 1951. a. price varies. (United Nations Statistical Office) United Nations Publications, LX 2300, New York, NY 10017 (Or Distribution and Sales Section, CH-1211 Geneva 10, Switzerland)

331 310 UN ISSN 0084-3857
YEAR BOOK OF LABOUR STATISTICS. (Text in English, French and Spanish) 1935-36. a. 95 Fr.($47.50) International Labour Office - Bureau International du Travail, Publications Sales Service, CH 1211 Geneva 22, Switzerland (U.S. Distributor: I L O Branch Office, 1750 New York Ave. N.W., Washington, DC 20006) circ. 6,000. (also avail. in microfiche)

339 UN ISSN 0084-3881
YEARBOOK OF NATIONAL ACCOUNTS STATISTICS. (Text in French) 1958. a. price varies. United Nations Publications, LX 2300, New York, NY 10017 (Or Distribution and Sales Section, CH-1211 Geneva 10, Swittzerland)

331.1 314 YU
YUGOSLAVIA. SAVEZNI ZAVOD ZA STATISTIKU. ANKETA O OSTVARIVANJU PRAVA RADNIKA IZ RADNOG ODNOSA. irreg. 10 din.($0.60) Savezni Zavod za Statistiku, Uzun Mirkova 1, Belgrade, Yugoslavia. stat.

339.4 314 YU
YUGOSLAVIA. SAVEZNI ZAVOD ZA STATISTIKU. ANKETA O PORODICNIM BUDZETIMA RADNICKIH DOMACINSTAVA. (Subseries of: Yugoslavia. Savezni Zavod Statistiku. Statisticki Bilten) (Issued also in English) irreg. 4 din. Savezni Zavod za Statistiku, Uzun Mirkova 1, Belgrade, Yugoslavia. stat.

314 338 YU
YUGOSLAVIA. SAVEZNI ZAVOD ZA STATISTIKU. INDUSTRIJSKE ORGANIZACIJE. (Subseries of: Yugoslavia. Savezni Zavod za Statistiku. Statisticki Bilten) irreg. 5 din. Savezni Zavod za Statistiku, Uzun Mirkova 1, Belgrade, Yugoslavia. stat.

331 314 YU
YUGOSLAVIA. SAVEZNI ZAVOD ZA STATISTIKU. SAMOUPRAVLJANJE U PRIVREDI. (Subseries of its Statisticki Bilten) irreg. 20 din.($1.11) Savezni Zavod za Statistiku, Uzun Mirkova 1, Belgrade, Yugoslavia. stat. circ. 1,000.

658 331 314 YU
YUGOSLAVIA. SAVEZNI ZAVOD ZA STATISTIKU. SAMOUPRAVLJANJE U USTANOVAMA DRUSTVENIH SLUZBI. (Subseries of: Yugoslavia. Savezni Zavod za Statistiku. Statisticki Bilten) irreg. 10 din. Savezni Zavod za Statistiku, Uzun Mirkova 1, Belgrade, Yugoslavia. stat.

331 314 YU ISSN 0513-0883
YUGOSLAVIA. SAVEZNI ZAVOD ZA STATISTIKU. ZAPOSLENO OSOBLJE. (Subseries of its Statisticki Bilten) 20 din.($1.11) Savezni Zavod za Statistiku, Uzun Mirkova 1, Belgrade, Yugoslavia. circ. 1,000.

382 316 ZR ISSN 0304-5692
ZAIRE. INSTITUT NATIONAL DE LA STATISTIQUE. ANNUAIRE DES STATISTIQUES DU COMMERCE EXTERIEUR. a. Institut National de la Statistique, Kinshasa, Zaire.
  Formerly: Zaire. Direction de la Statistique et des Etudes Economiques. Annuaire des Statistiques du Commerce Exterieur (ISSN 0069-8830)

382 316 ZA ISSN 0084-4489
ZAMBIA. CENTRAL STATISTICAL OFFICE. ANNUAL STATEMENT OF EXTERNAL TRADE. (Published in 2 vols: Vol. 1, Imports, Exports and Re-Exports by S.I.T.C. Grouping; Vol. 2, Major Country Analysis) 1964. a, latest 1976. K.4 per vol. Central Statistical Office, P.O. Box 1908, Lusaka, Zambia.

382.1 336 ZA
ZAMBIA. CENTRAL STATISTICAL OFFICE. BALANCE OF PAYMENTS STATISTICS. a, latest 1975. K.1. Central Statistical Office, Box 1908, Lusaka, Zambia.

316 331 ZA ISSN 0084-4500
ZAMBIA. CENTRAL STATISTICAL OFFICE. EMPLOYMENT AND EARNINGS. 1969. irreg., latest 1974/76. K.1. Central Statistical Office, P.O. Box 1908, Lusaka, Zambia.

316 650 ZA ISSN 0084-4519
ZAMBIA. CENTRAL STATISTICAL OFFICE. FINANCIAL STATISTICS OF PUBLIC CORPORATIONS. 1965. a, latest 1969. K.0.30. Central Statistical Office, P.O. Box 1908, Lusaka, Zambia.

539.7 016 GE
ZIDIS. (Text in English) 1979. irreg. Akademie der Wissenschaften der DDR, Zentralinstitut fuer Isotopen- und Strahlenforschung, Permoserstr. 15, 705 Leipzig, E. Germany (D.D.R.) (Subscr. to: Buchexport, P.F. 160, 701 Leipzig, E. Germany (D.D.R.)) Ed. R. Schroeter. bibl. circ. 450. (also avail. in microfiche)
  Formed by the merger of: Isotype Titles (ISSN 0047-1550) & Zidis-Information (ISSN 0323-4290)

336 RH
ZIMBABWE. CENTRAL STATISTICAL OFFICE. INCOME TAX STATISTICS; analysis of assessments and loss statements. a. Rhod.$0.50. Central Statistical Office, Box 8063, Causeway, Salisbury, Zimbabwe. circ. 250.

BUSINESS AND ECONOMICS —
Accounting

657   US
A I C P A PROFESSIONAL STANDARDS. (A subscription service consisting of 3 periodically updated volumes; Vol 1: Auditing, Management Advisory Services, Tax Practices; Vol. 2: Professional Ethics; Vol. 3: Accounting) 1974. $323 to non-members. (American Institute of Certified Public Accountants) Commerce Clearing House, Inc., 4025 W. Peterson Ave., Chicago, IL 60646. (looseleaf format)

657   US
ACCOUNTANTS INTERNATIONAL STUDIES. irreg. price varies. American Institute of Certified Public Accountants, 1211 Avenue of the Americas, New York, NY 10036.

657   MY   ISSN 0126-625X
ACCOUNTING JOURNAL. (Text in English) 1971. a. M.$4. University of Malaya Accounting Club, Faculty of Economics and Administration, University of Malaya, Lembah Pantai, Kuala Lumpur 22-11, Malaysia. Ed.Bd. adv. bibl. charts. circ. 500-1,000.

657   NZ   ISSN 0065-2075
ADVANCED ACCOUNTANCY SEMINAR. PROCEEDINGS. 1951. a. price varies. ‡ Victoria University of Wellington, Dept. of Accountancy, Private Bag, Wellington, New Zealand. circ. 200.

657   CN   ISSN 0226-0808
ADVANCED FINANCIAL ACCOUNTING NOTES. 1980. a. Can.$12.50. Clarence Byrd Inc., Suite 13, 2190 South Bay Rd., Sudbury, Ont. P3E 4S8, Canada.

657   US   ISSN 0360-8840
AMERICAN ACCOUNTING ASSOCIATION. SOUTHEAST REGIONAL GROUP. COLLECTED PAPERS OF THE ANNUAL MEETING. a. American Accounting Association, c/o Paul Gerhardt, Admin.Sec., 5717 Bessie Dr., Sarasota, FL 33583. illus. Key Title: Collected Papers of the Annual Meeting, Southeast Regional Group, American Accounting Association.

657   336.2   US   ISSN 0065-874X
AMERICAN INSTITUTE OF CERTIFIED PUBLIC ACCOUNTANTS. DIVISION OF FEDERAL TAXATION. STATEMENTS ON RESPONSIBILITIES IN TAX PRACTICE. 1964. irreg. membership. American Institute of Certified Public Accountants, Division of Federal Taxation, 1211 Avenue of the Americas, New York, NY 10036. circ. 160,000.

657   US   ISSN 0065-8766
AMERICAN INSTITUTE OF CERTIFIED PUBLIC ACCOUNTANTS. MANAGEMENT ADVISORY SERVICES. GUIDELINE SERIES. 1968. irreg., no. 7, 1977. price varies. American Institute of Certified Public Accountants, 1211 Ave. of the Americas, New York, NY 10036.

657   US
AUDITING RESEARCH MONOGRAPH. 1972. irreg., no. 2, 1976. price varies. American Institute of Certified Public Accountants, 1211 Ave. of the Americas, New York, NY 10036.

657   AT
AUSTRALIAN ACCOUNTING RESEARCH FOUNDATION. RESEARCH STUDIES. 1970. irreg. price varies. ‡ Australian Accounting Research Foundation, 49 Exhibition St., Melbourne, Vic. 3000, Australia. (Co-sponsors: Australian Society of Accountants; Institute of Chartered Accountants in Australia)
Formerly: Accountancy Research Foundation, Melbourne. Accounting and Auditing Research Committee. Research Studies (ISSN 0084-5884)

657   AT   ISSN 0005-0261
AUSTRALIAN SOCIETY OF ACCOUNTANTS. BULLETIN. 1956. irreg. price varies. ‡ Australian Society of Accountants, 170 Queen St., Melbourne 3000, Australia. charts. illus. circ. 3,000.
Formerly: A.S.A. Bulletin and A.I.C.A. Bulletin.

657   SA   ISSN 0067-6349
BESTUURLIKE INFORMASIE/MANAGERIAL INFORMATION. (Text in English and Afrikaans) 1969. a. Potchefstroom University for Christian Higher Education, Department Kosteberekening, Posbus 368, Bedryfsrekeningkunde, Potchetstroom, South Africa. Ed. J. E. Sorgorager D'Econ.

657   AG
BOLETIN INTERAMERICANO DE CONTABILIDAD. irreg. $10. Asociacion Interamericana de Contabilidad, Av. Cordoba 1261, Buenos Aires, Argentina. (Co-sponsor: Federacion Argentina de Colegios de Graduados en Ciencias Economicas) circ. 15,000.

657   CN   ISSN 0068-8983
C I C A HANDBOOK. (Editions in English and French) 1968. irreg. Can.$15 (base vol.) Can.$10 (supplements) ‡ Canadian Institute of Chartered Accountants, 250 Bloor St. E., Toronto, Ont. M4W 1G5, Canada. circ. 51,000.

657   CN
CANADIAN INSTITUTE OF CHARTERED ACCOUNTANTS. UNIFORM FINAL EXAMINATION HANDBOOK; contains life questions and approaches to answering the uniform final examination. (Editions in English and French) a. price varies. ‡ Canadian Institute of Chartered Accountants, 250 Bloor St. East, Toronto, Ont. M4W 1G5, Canada. circ. 9,000.
Formerly: Canadian Institute of Chartered Accountants. Intermediate and Final Examinations.

657.6   UK
CIRCULATION AUDITING AROUND THE WORLD; memorandum report by the secretary-general. 1962. a. $2. International Federation of Audit Bureaus of Circulations, 19 Dunraven Street, Park Lane, London W1Y 3FE, England. Ed. K. Derbyshire. circ. controlled.

657   US
CONTEMPORARY ISSUES IN INTERNATIONAL ACCOUNTING: OCCASIONAL PAPER. 1978. irreg. University of Illinois at Urbana-Champaign, Center for International Education & Research in Accounting, 320 Commerce West, Box 109, Urbana, IL 61801. Ed. H. M. Schoenfeld.

657.025   CN   ISSN 0527-9275
DIRECTORY OF CANADIAN CHARTERED ACCOUNTANTS. a. price varies. Canadian Institute of Chartered Accountants, 250 Bloor St. E., Toronto, Ont. M4W 1G5, Canada. circ. 4,000.

657   CN   ISSN 0226-6822
FINANCIAL ACCOUNTING PROBLEMS WITH DETAILED SOLUTIONS. 1980. a. Can.$12.50. Clarence Byrd Inc., Site 13, Box 6, S.S.1, Sudbury, Ont. P3E 4S8, Canada.

657   CN   ISSN 0071-5115
FINANCIAL REPORTING IN CANADA. 1953. biennial. price varies. Canadian Institute of Chartered Accountants, 250 Bloor St. East, Toronto, Ont. M4W 1G5, Canada. Ed. G. Lew. circ. 3,500.

FINANCIAL REPORTING TRENDS: LIFE INSURANCE. see *INSURANCE*

FINANCIAL REPORTING TRENDS: PROPERTY/CASUALTY INSURANCE. see *INSURANCE*

FINANCIAL REPORTING TRENDS: SAVINGS AND LOAN. see *BUSINESS AND ECONOMICS — Banking And Finance*

658.1   US   ISSN 0440-4122
HASKINS & SELLS. SELECTED PAPERS. 1955. a. Haskins & Sells, 1114 Ave. of the Americas, New York, NY 10036. illus. Key Title: Selected Papers - Haskins & Sells.

657   AU
HOCHSCHULE FUER WELTHANDEL, WIEN. INSTITUT FUER ORGANISATION UND REVISIONSWESEN. VERHANDLUNGEN. 1953. irreg. price varies. Manzsche Verlags- und Universitaetsbuchhandlung, Kohlmarkt 16, A-1014 Vienna, Austria. Ed. L. Illetschko.

657   FR
INSTITUT FRANCAIS DES EXPERTS COMPTABLES. CAHIERS. 1970. irreg., approx 2/yr. included in subscr. to Economie et Comptabilite. Institut Francais des Experts Comptables, 139 rue du Faubourg Saint-Honore, 75008 Paris, France. circ. 5,000.

657   AT
INSTITUTE OF CHARTERED ACCOUNTANTS IN AUSTRALIA. ANNUAL REPORT AND ACCOUNTS. a. Institute of Chartered Accountants in Australia, Box 3921, Sydney, N.S.W. 2001, Australia.

657   UK   ISSN 0073-9030
INSTITUTE OF CHARTERED ACCOUNTANTS IN ENGLAND AND WALES. MANAGEMENT INFORMATION SERIES. 1968. irreg. price varies. Institute of Chartered Accountants in England and Wales, Chartered Accountants' Hall, Moorgate Pl., London EC2P 2BJ, England.

657   UK   ISSN 0073-9049
INSTITUTE OF CHARTERED ACCOUNTANTS IN ENGLAND AND WALES. PRACTICE ADMINISTRATION SERIES, EXPOSURE DRAFTS AND STATEMENTS OF STANDARD ACCOUNTING PRACTICE. irreg. price varies. Institute of Chartered Accountants in England and Wales, Chartered Accountants' Hall, Moorgate Pl., London EC2P 2BJ, England.

657   GY   ISSN 0380-4011
INSTITUTE OF CHARTERED ACCOUNTANTS OF GUYANA. NEWSLETTER. irreg. Institute of Chartered Accountants of Guyana, 10 Water St., Kingston, Guyana.

657   UK   ISSN 0073-9057
INSTITUTE OF CHARTERED ACCOUNTANTS OF SCOTLAND. OFFICIAL DIRECTORY. 1896. a. £8. Institute of Chartered Accountants of Scotland, 27 Queen Street, Edinburgh, EH2 1LA, Scotland.

657   US
INTERNATIONAL CONGRESS OF ACCOUNTANTS. PROCEEDINGS. every five years. price varies. Accounting Corporation of America, Box 81147, San Diego, CA 92138.

657   IS
ISRAEL C P A. (Text in English) 1971. irreg., no.3, 1975. price varies. Institute of Certified Public Accountants in Israel, P. O. Box 29281, 1 Montefiore St., Tel Aviv, Israel.

657   GW
JAHRBUCH FUER PRAKTIKER DES RECHNUNGSWESENS. 1956. a. DM.19.80. Taylorix-Fachverlag Schegler & Co., Rotebuehlstr. 72, Postfach 829, 7000 Stuttgart 1, W. Germany (B.R.D.) Eds. W. Alt, W. Kresse. circ. 6,000.
Formerly: Taschenbuch fuer den Buchhalter (ISSN 0082-1853)

657   IS
JERUSALEM CONFERENCE ON ACCOUNTANCY. (Text in English) 1971. triennial. price varies. Institute of Certified Public Accountants in Israel, P. O. Box 29281, 1 Montefiore St., Tel Aviv, Israel.

657   US
JOURNAL OF ACCOUNTING RESEARCH. SUPPLEMENT. 1972. a. $3. University of Chicago, Graduate School of Business, Institute of Professional Accounting, Chicago, IL 60637. Ed. Nicholas Dopuch. charts.
Formerly (until 1974): Empirical Research in Accounting; Selected Studies (ISSN 0424-9283)

657   AT
LAW AND ACCOUNTING PRACTICE MANAGEMENT MANUAL. 1981. 3-4/yr. Aus.$100. C C H Australia Ltd., P.O. Box 230, North Ryde, N.S.W. 2113, Australia. (looseleaf format)

MAIN HURDMAN & CRANSTOUN NEWS SUMMARY. see *BUSINESS AND ECONOMICS — Public Finance, Taxation*

BUSINESS AND ECONOMICS — BANKING AND FINANCE

657 336   MY
MALAYSIA. PERBENDAHARAAN. ANGGARAN BELANJAWAN. (Text in Malaysian) irreg. Treasury, Jalan Chan Sow Lin, Kuala Lumpur, Malaysia. stat.

657   US
MODERN ACCOUNTING AND AUDITING CHECKLISTS (SUPPLEMENT) supplements issued periodically to update base volume. $37.50 for base volume. Warren, Gorham and Lamont, Inc., 210 South St., Boston, MA 02111.

657   US   ISSN 0077-3360
N A M F ACCOUNTING MANUAL; a uniform accounting system for metal finishers. 1968. irreg. $100 to non-members; members $15. National Association of Metal Finishers, 111 E. Wacker Dr., Chicago, IL 60601. Ed. J. D. Carey.

657   US   ISSN 0077-5770
NATIONAL SOCIETY OF PUBLIC ACCOUNTANTS. PROCEEDINGS OF THE ANNUAL PROFESSIONAL INSTITUTE. 1969. a. $6. ‡ National Society of Public Accountants, 1717 Pennsylvania Ave., N.W., Washington, DC 20006. Ed. Elsie D. Weigel. circ. 1,100.

657   AT
NEW ENGLAND ACCOUNTING PRACTICE REPORT. 1972. irreg. Aus.$6. University of New England, Department of Accounting & Financial Management, Accounting Systems Research Centre, Armidale, N.S.W. 2351, Australia. Ed. Prof. G. O. Meredith. bk. rev. circ. 500.

657   NZ
NEW ZEALAND SOCIETY OF ACCOUNTANTS. COST AND MANAGEMENT ACCOUNTING DIVISION. C M A BULLETIN. 1969. irreg., no. 11, 1974. price varies. New Zealand Society of Accountants, Willbank House, 57 Willis St., Wellington, New Zealand. Ed. Bd. bibl. charts. circ. 1,300.

657   US   ISSN 0090-6735
OREGON. STATE BOARD OF ACCOUNTANCY. CERTIFIED PUBLIC ACCOUNTANTS, PUBLIC ACCOUNTANTS, PROFESSIONAL CORPORATIONS, AND ACCOUNTANTS AUTHORIZED TO CONDUCT MUNICIPAL AUDITS IN OREGON. Cover title: Combined Rosters of Certified Public Accountants, Public Accountants and Accountants Authorized to Conduct Municipal Audits Registered to Practice in Oregon. a. $2.50. Department of Commerce, Board of Accountancy, Labor & Industries Bldg., Salem, OR 97310. circ. 3,000. Key Title: Certified Public Accountants, Public Accountants, Professional Corporations, and Accountants Authorized to Conduct Municipal Audits in Oregon.
   Continues: Oregon. State Board of Accountancy. Roster of Accountants Authorized to Conduct Municipal Audits (ISSN 0471-8356)

PLUNKETT FOUNDATION FOR CO-OPERATIVE STUDIES. STUDY SERIES. see
AGRICULTURE — Agricultural Economics

RAILWAY ACCOUNTING RULES. see
TRANSPORTATION — Railroads

657   SI   ISSN 0080-9640
SINGAPORE ACCOUNTANT. (Text and summaries in English) 1966. a. S.$2 to non-members. ‡ Singapore Society of Accountants, Rooms 3 & 8, 15-B Amber Mansions, Orchard Rd., Singapore 9, Singapore. Ed. Han Kang Hong.

657   US   ISSN 0586-5050
STUDIES IN ACCOUNTING RESEARCH. 1969. irreg. price varies. American Accounting Association, c/o Paul A. Gerhardt, Admin.Sec., 5717 Bessie Dr., Sarasota, FL 33583.

657   US   ISSN 0073-5191
UNIVERSITY OF ILLINOIS AT URBANA-CHAMPAIGN. CENTER FOR INTERNATIONAL EDUCATION AND RESEARCH IN ACCOUNTING. MONOGRAPH. 1964. irreg. price varies. University of Illinois at Urbana-Champaign, Center for International Education and Research in Accounting, 320 Commerce West, Box 109, Urbana, IL 61801. Ed. V. K. Zimmerman. adv. circ. 600-800.

657   US   ISSN 0081-7465
UNIVERSITY OF TEXAS, AUSTIN. BUREAU OF BUSINESS RESEARCH. STUDIES IN ACCOUNTING. 1966. irreg; no. 7, 1977. price varies. University of Texas at Austin, Bureau of Business Research, Austin, TX 78712.

657   US
WADSWORTH ACCOUNTING SERIES. irreg. Wadsworth Publishing Co., 10 Davis Dr., Belmont, CA 94002.

BUSINESS AND ECONOMICS — Banking And Finance

see also Business and Economics — Economic Situation and Conditions; Business and Economics — Investments; Insurance

332.1   US   ISSN 0084-5833
A D C A; AMERICAN DIRECTORY COLLECTIONS AGENCIES. 1918. a. $10. Service Publishing Co., Washington Building 639, 15th and New York Ave. N.W., Washington, DC 20005.

AFFAIRES ET GENS D'AFFAIRES. see
HISTORY — History Of Europe

AGRICULTURAL DEVELOPMENT BANK OF PAKISTAN. ANNUAL REPORT AND STATEMENT OF ACCOUNTS. see
AGRICULTURE — Agricultural Economics

332   SP
AGRUPACION SINDICAL NACIONAL DE EMPRESAS DE FINANCIACION. CENSO. irreg. Agrupacion Sindical Nacional de Empresa de Financiacion, Paseo del Prado 18 y 20, Madrid, Spain.

332   KU
ALAHLI BANK OF KUWAIT K.S.C. ANNUAL REPORT AND BALANCE SHEET. a. Alahli Bank of Kuwait K.S.C., Commercial Centre 5, Box 1387, Kuwait. charts. illus. stat.

332   CN   ISSN 0318-3971
ALBERTA OPPORTUNITY COMPANY. ANNUAL REPORT. 1974. a. Alberta Opportunity Co., 14th Floor, Capitol Square, 10065 Jasper Ave., Edmonton, Alta. T5J 0H4, Canada.

332.1   NE   ISSN 0065-6224
ALGEMENE BANK NEDERLAND. ANNUAL REPORT. (Text in English) 1964. a. free. Algemene Bank Nederland, Vijzelstraat 32, Amsterdam, Netherlands.

332   US
ALMANAC OF BUSINESS AND INDUSTRIAL FINANCIAL RATIOS. 1971. a. $16. Prentice-Hall, Inc., Englewood Cliffs, NJ 07632. Ed. Dr. Leo Troy. charts. stat. index. circ. 5,000.

332.1 651.8   US   ISSN 0095-5396
AMERICAN BANKERS ASSOCIATION. NATIONAL OPERATIONS & AUTOMATION CONFERENCE. PROCEEDINGS. 1963. a. $17.50. ‡ American Bankers Association, Operations and Automation Division, 1120 Connecticut Avenue, N.W., Washington, DC 20036.
   Formerly: American Bankers Association. National Automation Conference. Proceedings (ISSN 0065-7441)

332.1 651.8   US   ISSN 0363-2539
AMERICAN BANKERS ASSOCIATION. OPERATIONS AND AUTOMATION DIVISION. RESULTS OF THE NATIONAL OPERATIONS & AUTOMATION SURVEY. 1975. triennial. American Bankers Association, 1120 Connecticut Ave., N.W., Washington, DC 20036. Key Title: Results of the National Operations & Automation Survey.
   Continues: American Bankers Association. Operations and Automation Division.Results of the National Automation Survey.

332.1   US
AMERICAN BANKERS ASSOCIATION KEY TO ROUTING NUMBERS. 1911. a. $25. Rand McNally & Co., Bank Publications Division, 8255 N. Central Park, Skokie, IL 60076 (Orders to: Box 7600, Chicago, IL 60680) circ. 12,000. (also avail. in magnetic tape)

332.1   NE   ISSN 0066-1309
AMSTERDAM-ROTTERDAM BANK. ANNUAL REPORT. 1964. a. Amsterdam-Rotterdam Bank N.V., Herengracht 595, Amsterdam, Netherlands.

332   US   ISSN 0421-9910
ANALYSIS OF PUBLIC UTILITY FINANCING. 1950. w., q., and a. $145 for all issues; $95 for q., a., $65 for annual only. ‡ Ebasco Services Incorporated, 100 Church St., New York, NY 10007. Ed. H. Genzale.

332   FR   ISSN 0066-278X
ANNUAIRE DES CAISSES D'EPARGNE; FRANCE ET OUTRE-MER. biennial. price varies. Editions de l' Epargne, 174 Bld. Saint-Germain, Paris 6e, France.

332   US
ANNUAL FINANCING DIRECTORY. 1973. a. $25. Institutional Investor Systems, Inc., 488 Madison Ave., Circulation Dept., New York, NY 10022. Ed. Peter Landau.

ANUARIO FINANCIERO Y DE SOCIEDADES ANONIMAS DE ESPANA. see *BUSINESS AND ECONOMICS — Production Of Goods And Services*

338.91 330   SJ
ARAB BANK FOR ECONOMIC DEVELOPMENT IN AFRICA. ANNUAL REPORT. a. Arab Bank for Economic Development in Africa, Box 2640, Khartoum, Sudan. charts. illus. stat.

332.1 338.9   PH   ISSN 0066-8370
ASIAN DEVELOPMENT BANK. ANNUAL REPORT. (Text in English) 1967. a. ‡ Asian Development Bank, Box 789, Manila 2800, Philippines. circ. 11,000.

ASIAN DEVELOPMENT BANK. BOARD OF GOVERNORS. SUMMARY OF PROCEEDINGS (OF THE) ANNUAL MEETING. see *BUSINESS AND ECONOMICS — International Development And Assistance*

332 338.9   PH   ISSN 0066-8397
ASIAN DEVELOPMENT BANK. OCCASIONAL PAPERS. 1969. irreg., 1972, no. 6. contr. free circ. Asian Development Bank, P.O. Box 789, Manila 2800, Philippines.

332   CK
ASOCIACION NACIONAL DE INSTITUCIONES FINANCIERAS. SIMPOSIO SOBRE MERCADO DE CAPITALES. no. 3, 1974. a. Banco de la Republica, Carrera 7a no. 14-78, Apdo. Postal 402, Bogota, Colombia.

332.1   LE
ASSOCIATION DES BANQUES DU LIBAN. BILANS DES BANQUES.* irreg. Association of Banks in Lebanon, Rue de l'Armee, Box 967, Beirut, Lebanon. stat.

332.1   US   ISSN 0363-910X
B A I INDEX OF BANK PERFORMANCE. irreg. Bank Administration Institute, 303 S. Northwest Hwy., Park Ridge, IL 60068.

332.1   BL
B N H RELATORIO DE ATIVIDADES. a. Banco Nacional da Habitacao, Secretaria de Divulgacao, Rio de Janeiro, Brazil. charts. illus. stat.

332.1   IT   ISSN 0067-3161
BANCA D'ITALIA. ASSEMBLEA GENERALE ORDINARIA DEI PARTECIPANTI. 1894. a. free. ‡ Banca d'Italia, Servizio Studi, Via Nazionale, 91, Rome, Italy. circ. 6,000.

382 332   RM
BANCA ROMANA DE COMERT EXTERIOR. ANNUAL BULLETIN. (Text in English) a. Banca de Comert Exterior, Calea Victoriei Nr.22-24, Bucharest, Romania.

BUSINESS AND ECONOMICS — BANKING AND FINANCE

332.1 330.9 CL ISSN 0067-3196
BANCO CENTRAL DE CHILE, SANTIAGO. MEMORIA ANUAL. 1926. a. $9. Banco Central de Chile, Departamento de Informaciones Economicas y Estadisticas, Casilla 967, Santiago, Chile. circ. 1,500.

332.1 CR ISSN 0067-320X
BANCO CENTRAL DE COSTA RICA. MEMORIA ANUAL. 1950. a. free. Banco Central de Costa Rica, San Jose, Costa Rica. charts. stat.

332.1 AG
BANCO CENTRAL DE LA REPUBLICA ARGENTINA. CENTRO DE ESTUDIOS MONETARIOS Y BANCARIOS. DISCUSSION PAPER. (Text in English and Spanish) 1976. irreg.; no. 7, Sep., 1979. Banco Central de la Republica Argentina, Centro de Estudios Monetarios y Bancarios, Reconquista 266-78, Buenos Aires, Argentina. circ. 250.

332.1 AG
BANCO CENTRAL DE LA REPUBLICA ARGENTINA. CENTRO DE ESTUDIOS MONETARIOS Y BANCARIOS. SERIE DE COMPUTACION. 1975. irreg., no. 4, May 1977. Banco Central de la Republica Argentina, Centro de Estudios Monetarios y Bancarios, Reconquista 266-78, Buenos Aires, Argentina.

332.1 AG
BANCO CENTRAL DE LA REPUBLICA ARGENTINA. CENTRO DE ESTUDIOS MONETARIOS Y BANCARIOS. SERIE DE ESTUDIOS TECNICOS. 1975. irreg.; no. 33, Jun. 1978. Banco Central de la Republica Argentina, Centro de Estudios Monetarios y Bancarios, Reconquista 266-78, Buenos Aires, Argentina.

332.1 AG
BANCO CENTRAL DE LA REPUBLICA ARGENTINA. CENTRO DE ESTUDIOS MONETARIOS Y BANCARIOS. SERIE DE INFORMACION PUBLICA. 1976. irreg., no. 9, Sep., 1979. Banco Central de la Republica Argentina, Centro de Estudios Monetarios y Bancarios, Reconquista 266-78, Buenos Aires, Argentina.

332 NQ
BANCO CENTRAL DE NICARAGUA. BOLETIN ANUAL. 1936. a. free. Banco Central de Nicaragua, Biblioteca y Servicios de Informacion, Managua, Nicaragua. bk. rev. charts. stat. circ. 2,500.
Former titles: Banco Central de Nicaragua. Boletin Semestral & Banco Central de Nicaragua. Boletin Trimestral (ISSN 0005-4690)

332.1 NQ ISSN 0067-3226
BANCO CENTRAL DE NICARAGUA. INFORME ANUAL. 1961. a. Banco Central de Nicaragua, Apartado 2252, Managua, Nicaragua. Dir. Noel Lacayo Baretto.

332.1 ES
BANCO CENTRAL DE RESERVA DE EL SALVADOR. MEMORIA. 1934. a. Banco Central de Reserva de el Salvador, Apdo. Postal (06) 106, San Salvador, El Salvador. Dir. Guillermo Hidalgo Quehl. charts. stat. circ. 3,100.

332 PE
BANCO CENTRAL DE RESERVA DEL PERU. MEMORIA. irreg. Banco Central de Reserva del Peru, Apartado 1958, Lima, Peru. charts. stat.

332.1 VE ISSN 0067-3269
BANCO CENTRAL DE VENEZUELA. MEMORIA. 1940. a. free. ‡ Banco Central de Venezuela, Esquina de las Carmelitas, Caracas, Venezuela. circ. 2,000.

332.1 EC ISSN 0067-3277
BANCO CENTRAL DEL ECUADOR. MEMORIA DEL GERENTE GENERAL. 1948. irreg. free. Banco Central del Ecuador, Quito, Ecuador. charts, illus. stat.

332.1 PY ISSN 0067-3285
BANCO CENTRAL DEL PARAGUAY. MEMORIA.* (Title varies) 1952. a. free. Banco Central del Paraguay, Independencia Nacional y 25 de Mayo, Paraguay.

332.1 UY
BANCO CENTRAL DEL URUGUAY. RESENA DE LA ACTIVIDAD ECONOMICO-FINANCIERA. irreg. Banco Central del Uruguay, Departamento de Investigaciones Economicas, Cerrito 351, Montevideo, Uruguay. stat.

332.1 SP
BANCO DE BILBAO. AGENDA FINANCIERA. vol. 14, 1975. a. Banco de Bilbao, Gran Via 12, Bilbao 1, Spain.

332 SP
BANCO DE BILBAO. INFORME - MEMORIA. a. Banco de Bilbao, Servicio de Estudios, Gran via 12, Bilbao, Spain. charts. illus. stat.
Formerly: Banco de Bilbao. Memoria.

332.1 SP ISSN 0067-3315
BANCO DE ESPANA. INFORME ANUAL. 1962. a. free to qualified personnel. ‡ Banco de Espana, Seccion de Publicaciones, Alcala 50, Madrid 14, Spain. circ. 8,000.

332 SP
BANCO DE FINANCIACION INDUSTRIAL. LA BANCA PRIVADA. irreg. Banco de Financiacion Industrial, Servicio de Estudios, P. de la Castellano 112, Madrid 6, Spain. illus. stat.

332 GT
BANCO DE GUATEMALA. ESTUDIO ECONOMICO Y MEMORIA DE LABORES. 1945. a. Banco de Guatemala, Seccion de Servicios Auxiliares, 7 Avda. no. 22-01, Zona 1, Guatemala City, Guatemala.
Continues (after 1967): Banco de Guatemala. Memoria.

332 CK
BANCO DE LA REPUBLICA. FINANCIAMIENTO EXTERNO. 1977. a. $20. Banco de la Republica, Carrera 7a No. 14-78, Apdo. Postal 402, Bogota, Colombia. (Co-sponsor: Asociacion Bancaria de Colombia) Ed. Daniel Schlesinger Ricaurte.

332.1 330.9 MX ISSN 0067-3374
BANCO DE MEXICO. INFORME ANUAL. a. Banco de Mexico, Subdireccion de Investigacion Economica y Bancaria, Apdo. 98 bis, Mexico 1, D.F., Mexico. charts. (also avail. in microfiche)

332.1 BL
BANCO DO BRASIL. ANNUAL REPORT. (Text in English) a. Banco do Brasil S.A., Setor Bancario Sul, Bloco A, Edificio Sede do Banco do Brasil, 70000 Brasilia, Brazil. Ed.Bd. charts. illus. stat.

332.1 BL
BANCO DO ESTADO DE PERNAMBUCO. BANDEPE RELATORIO. (Summary in English) 1969. a. free. Banco do Estado de Pernambuco, Cais do Apolo, 222, Recife, Brazil. illus, stat. circ. 3,000.

332 MX
BANCO NACIONAL DE COMERCIO EXTERIOR, S.A., MEXICO. ANNUAL REPORT. Spanish edition: Informe Anual. 1938. irreg., latest ed., 1978. free. ‡ Banco Nacional de Comercio Exterior S.A., Departamento de Publicaciones, Chapultepec 230-20, piso, Mexico 7, D.F., Mexico. illus. stat.

332.1 HO ISSN 0067-3390
BANCO NACIONAL DE FOMENTO, TEGUCIGALPA. MEMORIA ANUAL. 1950. irreg; latest issue 1976. free. Banco National de Fomento, Tegucigalpa, Honduras. circ. 2,000.

332.1 PN
BANCO NACIONAL DE PANAMA. ASESORIA ECONOMICA. MEMORIA ANUAL. 1906. a. free. Banco Nacional de Panama, Asesoria Economica, Apdo 5220, Panama 5, Panama. circ. 1,500.

332 PN
BANCO NACIONAL DE PANAMA. INFORME DEL GERENTE GENERAL. 1975. Banco Nacional de Panama, Apdo. 5220, Panama City, Panama.

332 BL
BANCO NACIONAL DO DESENVOLVIMENTO ECONOMICO. ANNUAL REPORT. (Portuguese edition available) (Text in English) a. Banco Nacional do Desenvolvmento Economico, Av. Rio Branco 53, Rio de Janeiro RJ, Brazil. charts. illus. stat.

332.1 AG
BANCO SINDICAL. MEMORIA Y BALANCE GENERAL. no. 10. 1978. a. Banco Sindical, Reconquista 319-27, Buenos Aires, Argentina.

332.1 EC
BANCOS CENTRALES DE LOS PAISES DEL ACUERDO DE CARTAGENA. BOLETIN ESTADISTICO. a. Bancos Centrales de los Paises del Acuerdo de Cartagena, Quito, Ecuador.

332.1 BG
BANGLADESH BANK. ANNUAL REPORT. (Text in English) a. Bangladesh Bank, Department of Public Relations and Publications, Motijheel Commercial Area, Dacca 2, Bangladesh.

332.1 US ISSN 0067-3501
BANK ADMINISTRATION INSTITUTE. ACCOUNTING BULLETINS. 1965. irreg. $1. Bank Administration Institute, 303 South Northwest Highway, Box 500, Park Ridge, IL 60068.

332.1 US ISSN 0067-351X
BANK ADMINISTRATION INSTITUTE. ANNUAL REPORT. 1964. a. free. Bank Administration Institute, 303 South Northwest Highway, Box 500, Park Ridge, IL 60068.

BANK ADMINISTRATION INSTITUTE. PERSONNEL ADMINISTRATION COMMISSION. BIENNIAL SURVEY OF BANK OFFICER SALARIES. see BUSINESS AND ECONOMICS — Personnel Management

332.1 US ISSN 0067-3544
BANK ADMINISTRATION INSTITUTE. SECURITY BULLETINS. 1969. irreg. price varies. Bank Administration Institute, 303 South Northwest Highway, Park Ridge, IL 60068. (reprint service avail. from UMI)

332 US
BANK DIRECTORY OF NEW ENGLAND. 1913. a. $10. Shawmut Bank of Boston, N.A., Correspondent Banking Group, One Federal St., Boston, MA 02211. circ. controlled.

330.9 IO ISSN 0302-6795
BANK EKSPOR IMPOR INDONESIA. ANNUAL REPORT/LAPORAN TAHUNAN. (Text in English and Indonesian) a. Bank Ekspor Impor Indonesia, Jl. Lapagan Setasium 1, Box 32, Jakarta, Indonesia. illus. stat.

332.1 SZ ISSN 0067-3560
BANK FOR INTERNATIONAL SETTLEMENTS. ANNUAL REPORT. (Text in French, German and Italian) a. not for sale; avail. to limited qualified personnel. Bank for International Settlements, 7 Centralbahnstrasse, Case Postale 262, CH-4002 Basel, Switzerland. charts. stat. index. circ. controlled.

332 SZ ISSN 0408-4284
BANK FOR INTERNATIONAL SETTLEMENTS. MONETARY AND ECONOMIC DEPARTMENT. INTERNATIONAL COMMODITY POSITION. GENERAL SURVEY. irreg. not for sale; avail. to limited qualified personnel. Bank for International Settlements, 7 Centralbahnstrasse, Case Postale 262, 4002 Basel, Switzerland. circ. controlled.

332 PK
BANK GUIDE. (Text in English) 1977. a. Barque & Company, Barque Chambers, Barque Square, 87 Sharah e-Liquat Ali, Box 201, Lahore, Pakistan.

338.8 US ISSN 0519-1572
BANK HOLDING COMPANY FACTS. irreg., latest 1979. Association of Bank Holding Companies, 730 15th St. N.W., Washington, DC 20005. stat.

332.1 CN ISSN 0067-3587
BANK OF CANADA. ANNUAL REPORT. 1935. a. free. Bank of Canada, Distribution Section, Secretary's Dept., Ottawa K1A 0G9, Canada.

332.1 CN ISSN 0067-3595
BANK OF CANADA. STAFF RESEARCH STUDIES. 1969. irreg. free. Bank of Canada, Distribution Section, Secretary's Dept., Ottawa K1A 0G9, Canada.

BUSINESS AND ECONOMICS — BANKING AND FINANCE

330.9   CE
BANK OF CEYLON. ANNUAL REPORT AND ACCOUNTS. (Text in English) a. Bank of Ceylon, 41 Bristol St., Colombo 1, Sri Lanka. illus.
    Former titles: Bank of Ceylon. Annual Report & Bank of Ceylon. Report and Accounts (ISSN 0067-3617)

332.1   UK   ISSN 0308-5279
BANK OF ENGLAND. REPORT AND ACCOUNTS. a. Bank of England, Economics Division, Threadneedle St., London E.C. 2., England. (reprint service avail. from UMI)
    Formerly: Bank of England. Report (ISSN 0067-3625)

332   FI   ISSN 0081-945X
BANK OF FINLAND. ANNUAL STATEMENT. Finnish Edition (ISSN 0355-595X); Swedish Edition (ISSN 0585-9573) 1866. a. Fmk.1.40. Suomen Pankki - Bank of Finland, Information Department, Box 160, SF-00101 Helsinki 10, Finland. Ed. Tellervo Aurikko. circ. 4,100 (all edts.)

332   FI   ISSN 0081-9468
BANK OF FINLAND. YEARBOOK. Finnish edition: Suomen Pankki. Vuosikirja (ISSN 0355-5925); Swedish edition: Finlands Bank. Aarsbok (ISSN 0355-5933) (Editions in Finnish, Swedish and English) 1914. a. Fmk.17.50. Suomen Pankki - Bank of Finland, Information Department, Box 160, SF-00101 Helsinki 10, Finland. Ed. Annikki Leukkunen. circ. 2,900 (all edts.)

332.1   IS   ISSN 0067-365X
BANK OF ISRAEL. ANNUAL REPORT. (Editions in English and Hebrew) a. Bank of Israel, Mizpeh Building, 29 Jaffa Rd., Box 780, Jerusalem, Israel.

332.1   IS   ISSN 0067-3641
BANK OF ISRAEL. MAIN POINTS OF THE ANNUAL REPORT. a. Bank of Israel, Mizpeh Building, 29 Jaffa Rd., Box 780, Jerusalem, Israel.

332   JM   ISSN 0067-3668
BANK OF JAMAICA. REPORT AND STATEMENT OF ACCOUNTS. a. free. Bank of Jamaica, P.O. Box 621, King St., Kingston, Jamaica.

332.1   JA   ISSN 0067-3676
BANK OF JAPAN. ANNUAL REPORT OF THE POLICY BOARD. (Text in English) a. free. Bank of Japan, Foreign Department - Nihon Ginko, C.P.O. Box 203, Tokyo 100-91, Japan. charts. stat.

332.1   KO   ISSN 0067-3706
BANK OF KOREA. ANNUAL REPORT. a. not for sale. Bank of Korea, Research Dept., Seoul, S. Korea.

332.1   MF   ISSN 0067-3722
BANK OF MAURITIUS. ANNUAL REPORT. (Text in English) 1968. a. free. ‡ Bank of Mauritius, P.O. Box 29, Port Louis, Mauritius. circ. 1,000.

332.1   PP
BANK OF PAPUA NEW GUINEA. REPORT AND FINANCIAL STATEMENTS. (Text in English) a. free. Bank of Papua New Guinea, Douglas St., Port Moresby, Papua New Guinea. illus. stat.

332   KO
BANK OF SEOUL AND TRUST COMPANY. ECONOMIC REVIEW. no. 5, 6, 1977. irreg. Bank of Seoul and Trust Company, Seoul, S. Korea.

332.1   SL
BANK OF SIERRA LEONE. ANNUAL REPORT AND ACCOUNTS. a. free. Bank of Sierra Leone, P.O. Box 30, Freetown, Sierra Leone.
    Formerly: Bank of Sierra Leone. Annual Report (ISSN 0067-3730)

332.1   SJ   ISSN 0067-3749
BANK OF SUDAN. REPORT. a. free. Bank of Sudan, Box 313, Khartoum, Sudan.

BANK OF TANZANIA. ECONOMIC AND OPERATIONS REPORT. see *BUSINESS AND ECONOMICS — Economic Situation And Conditions*

332   IO   ISSN 0408-4632
BANK PEMBANGUNAN INDONESIA. ANNUAL REPORT. (Text in English) 1960. a. free. Bank Pembangunan Indonesia - Development Bank of Indonesia, Box 140, Jakarta, Indonesia. Ed. Bd. charts. illus. stat.

332.1   UK
BANK SORTING CODE NUMBERS. 1967. a. £1.40. (Association of London Clearing Banks) I P C Business Press Ltd., 33-40 Bowling Green Lane, London EC1R 0NE, England. circ. 100,000.

332   331.8   GW   ISSN 0067-3781
DER BANKANGESTELLTE. a. DM.48.50. (Deutsche Angestellten-Gewerkschaft) Walhalla- und Praetoria-Verlag Georg Zwichenpflug, Dolomitenstr. 1, Postfach 301, 8400 Regensburg 1, W. Germany (B.R.D.) Ed. Juergen Haker. bk. rev.

332.1   UK   ISSN 0067-379X
BANKERS ALMANAC AND YEAR BOOK. 1886. a. $100. I P C Business Press Ltd., 33-40 Bowling Green Lane, London EC1R 0NE, England. adv. circ. 16,500.

332.1   US
BANKERS' ASSOCIATION FOR FOREIGN TRADE. PROCEEDINGS. 55th, 1977. a. Bankers Association for Foreign Trade, 1101 Sixteenth Street, N.W., Washington, DC 20036.

332.1   US
BANKERS DIARY AND GUIDE. a. $22.85. Warren, Gorham and Lamont, Inc., 210 South St., Boston, MA 02111.

332   HK
BANKERS HANDBOOK FOR ASIA. 1976. a. HK.$150($30) Asian Finance Publications Ltd., Suite D, 9th Floor, Hyde Centre, 223 Gloucester Rd., Hong Kong, Hong Kong. Ed. T. K. Seshadri. adv. charts. illus. circ. 10,000.

332   II   ISSN 0067-3803
BANKERS' WHO'S WHO. (Text in English) 1962/63. irreg. £15. Business Publications International, United India Life Building, Box 548, F-Block, Connaught Place, New Delhi 1, India. Ed. K. L. Sahgal. adv. bk. rev. circ. 10,000. (back issues avail.)

332   US
BANKING BUYING GUIDE. 1977. a. Simmons-Boardman Publishing Corporation, 508 Birch St., Bristol, CT 06010. adv. circ. 25,340(controlled)

332.1   US
BANKING GUIDES - ASIA, AUSTRALIA, NEW ZEALAND WITH PRINCIPAL HOTELS AND BANK HOLIDAYS. Cover title: Asian Banking Guide. a. Manufacturers Hanover Trust Co., International Division, 350 Park Ave., New York, NY 10022.

332.1   PK   ISSN 0067-3811
BANKING STATISTICS OF PAKISTAN. (Text in English) 1948-57. a. Rs.20($5) State Bank of Pakistan, Central Directorate, Public Relations Department, I.I. Chundrigar Rd., Box 4456, Karachi, Pakistan. circ. 500.

332.1   SZ   ISSN 0067-382X
BANKWIRTSCHAFTLICHE FORSCHUNGEN. 1969. irreg., no. 50, 1978. price varies. (Universitaet Zuerich, Institut fuer Schweizerisches Bankwesen) Paul Haupt AG, Falkenplatz 14, CH-3001 Berne, Switzerland. (Co-sponsor: Hochschule St. Gallen fuer Wirtschafts- und Sozialwissenschaften, Institut fuer Bankwirtschaft)

332.1   GW   ISSN 0067-3838
BANKWIRTSCHAFTLICHE STUDIEN. 1970. irreg., vol. 12, 1981. price varies. Physica-Verlag Rudolf Liebing GmbH und Co., Werner-von-Siemens-Str. 5, Postfach 5840, 8700 Wuerzburg 1, W. Germany (B.R.D.) Ed. Werner Vollrodt.

332   MG
BANQUE CENTRALE DE LA REPUBLIQUE MALGACHE. RAPPORT D'ACTIVITE. a, latest 1972 (1973-1976 in prep.) free. Banque Centrale de la Republique Malgache, B.P. 550, Antananarivo, Malagasy Republic.
    Formerly: Institut d'Emission Malgache. Rapport d'Activite (ISSN 0073-8255)

332.1   TI   ISSN 0067-3854
BANQUE CENTRALE DE TUNISIE. BULLETIN.* 1959. irreg. Banque Centrale de Tunisie, 7 Place de la Monnaie, Tunis, Tunisia.

332.1   TI   ISSN 0067-3862
BANQUE CENTRALE DE TUNISIE. RAPPORT D'ACTIVITE.* (Title varies: Rapport Annuel) 1958/59. a. Banque Centrale de Tunisie, 7 Place de la Monnaie, Tunis, Tunisia.

332   SG   ISSN 0067-3889
BANQUE CENTRALE DES ETATS DE L'AFRIQUE DE L'OUEST. RAPPORT ANNUEL. 1962. a. free. Banque Centrale des Etats de l'Afrique de l'Ouest, 3 Ave. W. Ponty, B.P. 1398, Dakar, Senegal (Provisional address: 29 rue de Colisee, Paris (8e), France) circ. 2,000.

332.1   SG   ISSN 0067-3897
BANQUE CENTRALE DES ETATS DE L'AFRIQUE DE L'OUEST. RAPPORT D'ACTIVITE. 1963. a. Banque Centrale des Etats de l'Afrique de l'Ouest, 3 Ave. W. Ponty, B.P. 1398, Senegal, France (Provisional address: 29 rue de Colisee, Paris (8e), France)

332.1   ZR
BANQUE COMMERCIALE ZAIROISE. REPORTS AND BALANCE SHEETS. a. Banque Commerciale Zairoise, B.P. 2798, Kinshasa, Zaire.

332.1   BE   ISSN 0067-3919
BANQUE DE BRUXELLES. RAPPORT ANNUEL. 1935. a. free. Banque de Bruxelles, Rue de la Regence, 2, 1000 Brussels, Belgium.

332.1   FR   ISSN 0067-3927
BANQUE DE FRANCE. COMPTE- RENDU. a. free. Banque de France, Service de l'Information, 43 rue de Valois, 75049 Paris Cedex 1, France.

332.1   BD   ISSN 0067-3935
BANQUE DE LA REPUBLIQUE DU BURUNDI. RAPPORT ANNUEL. (Text in French) 1964. a. 11 Fr.CFA. ‡ Banque de la Republique du Burundi, B.P. 705, Bujumbura, Burundi. circ. 1,000(approx.)

332.1   FR   ISSN 0067-3900
BANQUE DES ETATS DE L'AFRIQUE CENTRALE. RAPPORT D'ACTIVITE. a. Banque des Etats de l'Afrique Centrale, 29 rue du Colisee, Paris 8e, France.

332.1   MR   ISSN 0067-396X
BANQUE DU MAROC. RAPPORT ANNUEL. a. free. Banque du Maroc, 277 Ave. Mohammed V, Rabat, Morocco.

332.1   ZR   ISSN 0300-1172
BANQUE DU ZAIRE. RAPPORT ANNUEL. a. Banque du Zaire, B.P. 2697, Kinshasa, Zaire.
    Formerly: Banque Nationale du Congo. Rapport Annuel (ISSN 0067-4001)

332.1   MR
BANQUE MAROCAINE DU COMMERCE EXTERIEUR. ANNUAL REPORT. a. Banque Marocaine du Commerce Exterieur, 241 Bd. Mohammed V, Casablanca, Morocco.

332.1   BE   ISSN 0067-3978
BANQUE NATIONALE DE BELGIQUE. RAPPORT SUR LES OPERATIONS. (Editions in Dutch, English and French) a. Banque Nationale de Belgique, 5 Bd. de Berlaimont, B-1000 Brussels, Belgium.

332.1   RW
BANQUE NATIONALE DE RWANDA. RAPPORT ANNUEL. a. Banque Nationale de Rwanda, B.P. 531, Kigali, Rwanda. stat.

332.1   MG   ISSN 0067-401X
BANQUE NATIONALE MALAGASY DE DEVELOPPEMENT. RAPPORT D'ACTIVITE. 1964. free. Banque Nationale Malagasy de Developpement, B.P. 365, Antananarivo, Malagasy Republic.

332.1   SZ   ISSN 0067-4028
BANQUE POPULAIRE SUISSE. INFORMATION. (Editions in French, German & sometimes English) irreg., no. 66, 1977. free. ‡ Banque Populaire Suisse, Bundesgasse 26, Case Postale 2620, 3001 Berne, Switzerland. circ. 30,000.

BUSINESS AND ECONOMICS — BANKING AND FINANCE

332.1   TG
BANQUE TOGOLAISE DE DEVELOPPEMENT. RAPPORT D'ACTIVITES. (Text in French) a, latest 1975-1976. Banque Togolaise de Developpement, B.P. 65, Lome, Togo.
    Formerly: Banque Togolaise de Developpement. Rapport Annuel (ISSN 0067-4036)

332.7   NE   ISSN 0005-9110
BERICHTEN VAN DE AFDELING VOLKSKREDIETWEZEN. 1964. irreg., no. 26, 1976. free. Ministerie van Cultuur Recreatie en Maatschappelijk Werk, Steenvoordelaan 370, Rijswijk (Z.H.), Netherlands. charts. stat.

BIENNIAL SURVEY OF BANK PERSONNEL POLICIES AND PRACTICES. see *BUSINESS AND ECONOMICS — Personnel Management*

332   UY
BOLSA DE VALORES DE MONTEVIDEO. ESTUDIOS ESTADISTICOS. 1976. irreg. Bolsa de Valores de Montevideo, Misiones 1400, Montevideo, Uruguay.

332   UK   ISSN 0068-3566
BUILDING SOCIETIES. YEAR BOOK. 1927. a. £15.50. Franey and Co. Ltd., Burgon Street, London, EC4, England. Ed. Eric Holmes. adv.

330.9   KU
BURGAN BANK. ANNUAL REPORT. 1977. a. Burgan Bank, Abdulla al-Salem St., Box 5389 Safat, Kuwait.

332   UK   ISSN 0068-4457
BUSINESS MONITOR: MISCELLANEOUS SERIES. M3 COMPANY FINANCE. a. price varies. Department of Industry, 1 Victoria St., London S.W.1., England (Avail. from H.M.S.O., c/o Liaison Officer, Atlantic House, Holborn Viaduct, London EC1P 1BW, England)

332   US
C M R E MONOGRAPHS. 1971. irreg., latest no. 33. $2 per no. Committee for Monetary Research and Education, Inc., Box 1630, Greenwich, CT 06830.
    Former titles: C M R E Monetary Tracts; C M R E Money Tracts.

332.1   EC
C O F I E C. INFORME ANUAL. a. Compania Financiera Ecuatoriana de Desarrollo, Av. 10 de Agosto No. 1564, P.O. Box 411, Quito, Ecuador. illus. stat.

332.1   LU
CAISSE D'EPARGNE DE L'ETAT DU GRANDE-DUCHE DE LUXEMBOURG. RAPPORTS ET BILANS. 1901. a. free. Caisse d'Epargne de l'Etat du Grande-Duche de Luxembourg, 1, Place de Metz, Luxembourg, Luxembourg.

332   SP   ISSN 0409-9192
CAJA DE AHORROS Y MONTE DE PIEDAD DE LAS BALEARES. MEMORIA. irreg. Caja de Ahorros y Monte de Piedad de las Baleares, C. Ramon Llull 2, Palma de Mallorca, Spain. Dir. Carlos Blanes Nouvilas. illus. charts. stat.

332.3   US   ISSN 0084-828X
CALIFORNIA SAVINGS AND LOAN DATA BOOK. 1956. a. free to individual requests. ‡ California Savings and Loan League, 9800 S. Sepulveda Blvd., Suite 500, Los Angeles, CA 90045. Ed. Robert L. Kocher. circ. 15,000.

CANADA. DEPARTMENT OF INSURANCE. REPORT. CO-OPERATIVE CREDIT ASSOCIATIONS. see *INSURANCE*

CANADA. DEPARTMENT OF INSURANCE. REPORT. SMALL LOANS COMPANIES AND MONEY-LENDERS. see *INSURANCE*

CANADA. DEPARTMENT OF INSURANCE. REPORT. TRUST AND LOAN COMPANIES. see *INSURANCE*

332   CN
CANADA. TREASURY BOARD. INDEX OF FEDERAL INFORMATION BANKS. a. price varies. Treasury Board, 160 Elgin St., Ottawa, Ont. K1A 0G5, Canada (Subscr. to: Supply and Services Canada, Publications Division, Ottawa, Ont. K1A 0S9, Canada)

332.1   CN   ISSN 0068-8347
CANADIAN BANKRUPTCY REPORTS. 1921. N.S. 1960. m (2 vols per year) Can.$55 per vol. Carswell Co. Ltd., 2330 Midland Ave., Agincourt, Ont. M1S 1P7, Canada. Ed. Bd. circ. 675.

332.413   CN   ISSN 0068-8649
CANADIAN DEPRECIATION GUIDE. 1950. irreg., 15th ed., 1980. Can.$9. C C H Canadian Ltd., 6 Garamond Ct., Don Mills, Ont. M3C 1Z5, Canada. index.

332.1   BB
CARIBBEAN DEVELOPMENT BANK. BOARD OF GOVERNORS. ANNUAL MEETING OF THE BOARD OF GOVERNORS: SUMMARY OF PROCEEDINGS. (Text in English) 1971. a. Caribbean Development Bank, Board of Governors, Wildey, St. Michael, Barbados, W. Indies. circ. 300.

332   BB
CENTRAL BANK OF BARBADOS. ANNUAL STATISTICAL DIGEST. 1975. a. Central Bank of Barbados, Box 1016, Treasury Bldg., Bridgetown, Barbados. charts. stat.

332.1   CE   ISSN 0069-1496
CENTRAL BANK OF CEYLON. ANNUAL REPORT. (Text in English,Sinhalese and Tamil) 1950. a. $3. ‡ Central Bank of Ceylon, Janadhipathi Mawatha, Colombo 1, Sri Lanka.

332.1   CH   ISSN 0069-150X
CENTRAL BANK OF CHINA, T'AI-PEI. ANNUAL REPORT. (Editions in Chinese and English) 1962. a. not for sale. Central Bank of China, Taipei, Taiwan, Republic of China. circ. 3,500 (Chinese edt.); 2,000 (English edt.)

332.1   CY   ISSN 0069-1518
CENTRAL BANK OF CYPRUS. ANNUAL REPORT. (Text in English) 1965. a. free. Central Bank of Cyprus, Box 1087, Nicosia, Cyprus.

332.1   UA
CENTRAL BANK OF EGYPT. ANNUAL REPORT. 1961. a. free. Central Bank of Egypt, 31 Sharia Kasr-el Nil, Cairo, Egypt.
    Formerly: Central Bank of Egypt. Board of Directors. Report (ISSN 0069-1526)

332   IQ   ISSN 0069-1534
CENTRAL BANK OF IRAQ, BAGHDAD. REPORT. (Text in Arabic and English) 1951. a. free. ‡ Central Bank of Iraq, Statistics and Research Department, P.O. Box 64, Baghdad, Iraq. circ. 2,000.

332.1   IE   ISSN 0069-1542
CENTRAL BANK OF IRELAND. REPORT. (Includes Spring Quarterly Bulletin) 1943. a. free. Central Bank of Ireland, Box 559, Dame St, Dublin 2, Ireland. circ. 4,000.

332   JO   ISSN 0069-1550
CENTRAL BANK OF JORDAN. ANNUAL REPORT/BANK AL-MARKAZI AL-URDUNI. ANNUAL REPORT. a. Central Bank of Jordan, Department of Research and Studies, Box 37, Amman, Jordan.

332.1   KE   ISSN 0069-1569
CENTRAL BANK OF KENYA. ANNUAL REPORT. 1966/67. a. Central Bank of Kenya, Box 30463, Nairobi, Kenya.

332   KU
CENTRAL BANK OF KUWAIT. ANNUAL REPORT. (Editions in Arabic and English) a. free. Central Bank of Kuwait, Box 526, Kuwait.

332   MM   ISSN 0577-0653
CENTRAL BANK OF MALTA. ANNUAL REPORT. 1968. free. Central Bank of Malta, Castille Square, Valletta, Malta. circ. 1,400.

332.1   NR   ISSN 0069-1577
CENTRAL BANK OF NIGERIA. ANNUAL REPORT AND STATEMENT OF ACCOUNTS. 1960. a. Central Bank of Nigeria, P.M.B. 12194, Tinubu Square, Lagos, Nigeria. circ. 4,000.

332.1   SO
CENTRAL BANK OF SOMALI. ANNUAL REPORT AND STATEMENT OF ACCOUNTS. (Text in English) 1961. a. free. Central Bank of Somali, Economic Research and Statistics Department, Box 11, Mogadishu, Somalia.
    Former titles (until no. 14, 1974): Somali National Bank. Annual Report and Statement of Accounts; Somali National Bank. Report and Balance Sheet (ISSN 0067-3188)

354   BF
CENTRAL BANK OF THE BAHAMAS. ANNUAL REPORT AND STATEMENT OF ACCOUNTS. 1974. a. Central Bank of the Bahamas, P.O. Box N4868, Nassau, Bahamas. illus. stat.

332.1   GM
CENTRAL BANK OF THE GAMBIA. ANNUAL REPORT. 1971. a. Central Bank of the Gambia, Economic Research Department, 1-2 Buckle St., Banjul, Gambia.

332.1   PH   ISSN 0069-1585
CENTRAL BANK OF THE PHILIPPINES. ANNUAL REPORT. (Statistical Appendix avail.) a. P.10($5) Central Bank of the Philippines, Department of Economic Research, A. Mabini corner Vito Cruz Streets, Manila, Philippines.

332   TU
CENTRAL BANK OF THE REPUBLIC OF TURKEY. ANNUAL REPORT. a. Central Bank of the Republic of Turkey - Turkiye Cumhuriyet Merkez Bankasi, Bankalar Caddesi 48, Ankara, Turkey.

332.1   TR   ISSN 0069-1593
CENTRAL BANK OF TRINIDAD AND TOBAGO. REPORT. 1965. a. free. ‡ Central Bank of Trinidad and Tobago, P.O.B. 1250, Independence Sq., Port-Of-Spain, Trinidad. circ. 1,000.

332   YE   ISSN 0301-6625
CENTRAL BANK OF YEMEN. ANNUAL REPORT. (Text in Arabic and English) 1971/72. a. free. Central Bank of Yemen, Box 59, San'a, Yemen.

332.1   MX   ISSN 0577-2451
CENTRO DE ESTUDIOS MONETARIOS LATINOAMERICANOS. ENSAYOS. 1963. irreg. price varies. Centro de Estudios Monetarios Latinoamericanos, Durango 54, Mexico 7 D.F., Mexico. circ. 1,000.

332   CH
CHIAO T'UNG YIN HANG. ANNUAL REPORT.* (Text in English) a. Bank of Communications, 91 Heng Yang Road, Taipei, Taiwan, Republic of China.

332   FR
COLLECTION RADIOGRAPHIE DU CAPITAL - LES LIAISONS FINANCIERES. (In 2 vols.: Tome I - Societes Francaises; Tome II - Societes Francaises a Participations Etrangeres) 1966. a. 1234 F. DAFSA Documentation, 7 rue Bergere, 75009 Paris, France. adv.
    Formerly: Liaisons Financieres en France (ISSN 0075-8957)

332   CK
COLOMBIA. SUPERINTENDENCIA BANCARIA. INFORME DE LABORES. 1924. a. free. Superintendencia Bancaria, Bogota, Colombia. circ. 1,200.

332   ET   ISSN 0588-6694
COMMERCIAL BANK OF ETHIOPIA. ANNUAL REPORT. a. free. Commercial Bank of Ethiopia, Box 255, Addis Ababa, Ethiopia. charts. illus. stat.

332.1   GR   ISSN 0424-9402
COMMERCIAL BANK OF GREECE. REPORT OF THE CHAIRMAN OF THE BOARD OF DIRECTORS. (Text in English) a. free. Commercial Bank of Greece, Public Relations Department, 11 Sofokleous St., Athens 122, Greece. illus. stat.

332   KU
COMMERCIAL BANK OF KUWAIT. ANNUAL REPORT OF THE BOARD OF DIRECTORS AND ACCOUNTS. a. Commercial Bank of Kuwait, Box 2861, Mubarak al-Kabir St., Safat, Kuwait.

BUSINESS AND ECONOMICS — BANKING AND FINANCE

332   US
COMMERCIAL WEST BANK DIRECTORY. a. $26 to individuals; Commercial West subscribers $20. Financial Communications Inc, 5100 Edina Industrial Blvd, Edina, MN 55435. adv. circ. 5,600.

332.1   FR
COMMISSION DE CONTROLE DES BANQUES. RAPPORT ANNUEL. a. price varies. (Commission de Controle des Banques) Banque de France, Service de l'Information, 43 rue de Valois, 75001 Paris, France (Or Commission de Controle des Banques, 73 rue de Richelieu, 75002 Paris)

334.2   US
COMPARATIVE DIGEST OF CREDIT UNION ACTS. 1959. a. $10. Credit Union National Association, Box 431-B, Madison, WI 53701. Ed. Robert W. Davis.

332.1   US   ISSN 0084-9154
CONFERENCE ON BANK STRUCTURE AND COMPETITION. PROCEEDINGS. 1964. a. free. ‡ Federal Reserve Bank of Chicago, Public Information Center, Research Dept., Box 834, Chicago, IL 60690.

332   658.8   UK
CONSUMER CREDIT ASSOCIATION OF THE UNITED KINGDOM. MEMBERSHIP DIRECTORY. 1912. a. £2.25. Consumer Credit Association of the United Kingdom, 192A Nantwich Road, Crewe, Cheshire CW2 6BP, England. adv. circ. 1,500.
    Formerly: Retail Credit Federation Membership Directory (ISSN 0080-1852)

CONTEMPORARY STUDIES IN ECONOMIC AND FINANCIAL ANALYSIS. see *BUSINESS AND ECONOMICS*

332.1   CH
COOPERATIVE BANK OF TAIWAN. ANNUAL REPORT/TAI-WAN SHENA HO TSO CHIN KU. ANNUAL REPORT. 1957. a. free. Cooperative Bank of Taiwan, 75-1 Kuan Chien Rd., Taipei, Taiwan, Republic of China. illus. stat.

332.1   DK
COPENHAGEN HANDELSBANK. ANNUAL REPORT. a. Copenhagen Handelsbank, Holmens Kanal 2, DK-1091 Copenhagen, Denmark. charts. stat.

332   US
CORPORATE FUND RAISING DIRECTORY. a. $27.50. Public Service Materials Center, 415 Lexington Ave., New York, NY 10017.

332.1   US   ISSN 0091-3855
COST OF PERSONAL BORROWING IN THE UNITED STATES. 1971. a. $32. ‡ Financial Publishing Co., 82 Brookline Ave, Boston, MA 02215. Ed. Charles H. Gushee. charts. (back issues avail.)

658.15   US   ISSN 0070-1467
CREDIT MANUAL OF COMMERCIAL LAWS. a. $32. National Association of Credit Management, 475 Park Ave. South, New York, NY 10016. Ed. James J. Andover. (reprint service avail. from UMI)

334.2   US   ISSN 0092-4954
CREDIT UNION DIRECTORY AND BUYERS' GUIDE. 1973. a. $39 or in subscr. to complete Credit Union Information Service, $96. National Institute for Public Services, Credit Union Information Service, 7315 Wisconsin Ave., Suite 210W, Washington, DC 20014. Ed. Richard M. Guilderson Jr. adv. circ. 6,000.
    Formerly: C U I S Credit Union Directory and Buyers' Guide.
    Credit unions

334.2   US   ISSN 0074-4468
CREDIT UNION YEARBOOK. 1954. a. free. Credit Union National Association, Inc., Box 431, Madison, WI 53701. circ. 50,000.
    Formerly: International Credit Union Yearbook.
    Credit unions

332.3   AU
CREDITANSTALT-BANKVEREIN. ANNUAL REPORT. (Text in English) a. Creditanstalt-Bankverein, Schottengasse 6, A-1010 Vienna, Austria.
    Continues: Creditanstalt-Bankverein. Report.

332   CY
CYPRUS DEVELOPMENT BANK. ANNUAL REPORT. a. Cyprus Development Bank, Nicosia, Cyprus.

332.1   DK
DANSKE BANK AF 1871. ANNUAL REPORT. (Text in English) a. Danske Bank af 1871, 12, Holmens Kanal, DK-1092 Copenhagen K, Denmark.
    Formerly (until 1976): Danske Landmandsbank. Annual Report (ISSN 0070-2838)

332   UK   ISSN 0482-1319
DAY'S REGISTER OF REGISTRARS. a., plus periodic updates. £10 includes supplements. Extel Statistical Services Ltd., 37-45 Paul St., London EC2A 4PB, England. circ. 1,300.

332.1   GW   ISSN 0070-394X
DEUTSCHE BUNDESBANK. GESCHAEFTSBERICHT. (Editions in German and English) 1948. a. Deutsche Bundesbank, Postfach 2633, 6000 Frankfurt 1, W. Germany (B.R.D.). circ. 50,000(German edt.); 6,000(English edt.)

332.1   GW
DEUTSCHE GENOSSENSCHAFTSBANK. BERICHT. English edition: Deutsche Genossenschaftsbank. Annual Report. a. Deutsche Genossenschaftsbank, Wiesenhuettenstr. 10, Postfach 2628, 6000 Frankfurt 1, W. Germany (B.R.D.) charts. stat.

332   CK
DIRECTORIO DE INSTITUCIONES FINANCIERAS. a. Col.300($10) Editores y Distribuidores Asociados Ltda., Avda. Jimenez 4-49, Apartado 14965, Bogota 1, Colombia.

332.3   US   ISSN 0070-5098
DIRECTORY OF AMERICAN SAVINGS AND LOAN ASSOCIATIONS. 1955. a. $40. T. K. Sanderson Organization, 200 E. 25 St., Baltimore, MD 21218. Ed. T. K. Sanderson.

332.1   378   US   ISSN 0084-9855
DIRECTORY OF BANKERS SCHOOLS. biennial. $8. ‡ American Bankers Association, 1120 Connecticut Ave. N.W., Washington, DC 20036.

332.1   CN   ISSN 0070-5225
DIRECTORY OF CANADIAN TRUST COMPANIES. 1953. a. ‡ Trust Companies Association of Canada, Suite 400, Board of Trade Bldg., 11 Adelaide St., W., Toronto, Ont. M5H 1L9, Canada.

332   UI
DIRECTORY OF FINANCIAL DIRECTORIES. irreg. 90 Fr. F. H. Books Ltd., Box 74, Guernsey, Channel Islands.

332.2   US   ISSN 0092-6132
DIRECTORY OF THE MUTUAL SAVINGS BANKS OF THE UNITED STATES. 1924. a. $30 to non-members; $12 to members, govt. agencies and libraries. National Association of Mutual Savings Banks, 200 Park Ave., New York, NY 10166. Ed. Iris Chekenian.
    Continues: Directory and Guide to the Mutual Savings Banks of the United States.

332.1   US   ISSN 0093-951X
DIRECTORY OF TRUST INSTITUTIONS. a. Communication Channels, Inc., 6285 Barfield Rd., Atlanta, GA 30328. illus.
    Continues: Directory of Trust Institutions of United States and Canada.

332.1   DR
DOMINICAN REPUBLIC. SUPERINTENDENCIA DE BANCOS. ANUARIO ESTADISTICO. a. Superintendencia de Bancos, Santo Domingo, Dominican Republic.

332   US   ISSN 0163-6855
EASTERN FINANCE ASSOCIATION. PROCEEDINGS OF THE ANNUAL MEETING. 1973. a. $10. Eastern Finance Association, c/o Prof. John Clark, College of Business Administration, Drexel University, Philadelphia, PA 19104. circ. 700.

332   FR
ECONOMIES ET SOCIETES. SERIE MO. ECONOMIE MONETAIRE. 1978. irreg. 42 F. Institut de Sciences Mathematiques et Economiques Appliquees, Paris, Institut Henri Poincare, 11 rue Pierre et Marie Curie, 75005 Paris, France. Ed.C. de Bossieu.

332.1   EC
ECUADOR. SUPERINTENDENCIA DE BANCOS. CONFERENCIA BANCARIA NACIONAL. MEMORIA. no. 5, 1975. irreg. Superintendencia de Bancos, Av. 10 de Agosto 277, Apdo 424, Quito, Ecuador.

332   EC
ECUADOR. SUPERINTENDENCIA DE BANCOS. DOCUMENTOS. irreg., no. 7, 1978. Superintendencia de Bancos, 10 de Agosto 251, Casilla 424, Quito, Ecuador. charts, stat.

332   EC
ECUADOR. SUPERINTENDENCIA DE BANCOS. INVERSIONES EXTRANJERAS EN EL ECUADOR. irreg., no. 5, 1977. Superintendencia de Bancos, Avda. 10 de Agosto 251, Apartado 424, Quito, Ecuador.

332   EC
ECUADOR. SUPERINTENDENCIA DE BANCOS. MEMORIA. a. Superintendencia de Bancos, Avda 10 de Agosto no. 251, Casilla 424, Quito, Ecuador. charts. stat.

EL SALVADOR. SUPERINTENDENCIA DE BANCOS Y OTRAS INSTITUCIONES FINANCIERAS. ESTADISTICAS: SEGUROS, FIANZAS, BANCOS. see *INSURANCE*

332   US
EQUAL CREDIT OPPORTUNITY MANUAL (SUPPLEMENT) supplements issued periodically to update base volume. $48.50 for base volume. Warren, Gorham and Lamont, Inc., 210 South St., Boston, MA 02111.

332   US   ISSN 0071-142X
ESSAYS IN INTERNATIONAL FINANCE. 1943. irreg., no. 141, 1980. $8 (includes Reprints in International Finance) Princeton University, International Finance Section, Dept. of Economics, Dickinson Hall, Princeton, NJ 08544. Dir. Peter B. Kenen. circ. 3,000. (also avail. in microfilm from UMI; back issues avail.; reprint service avail. from UMI)

332.4   CL
ESTUDIOS MONETARIOS. 1968. irreg. Banco de Chile, Gerencia de Estudios, Ahumada 251, Casilla 151D, Santiago, Chile. Ed. Maria Elena Ovalle. circ. 2,000.

332.2   EI
EUROPEAN ECONOMIC COMMUNITY SAVINGS BANK GROUP. REPORT. (Edts. in English, French and German) 1966. biennial. 200 Fr. European Economic Community Savings Banks Group, 92-94 Square E. Plasky, Bte. 1, 1040 Brussels, Belgium. Eds. K. Meyer-Horn, M. Focan. circ. 3,000.

332.1   BE   ISSN 0071-2787
EUROPEAN FEDERATION OF FINANCE HOUSE ASSOCIATIONS. ANNUAL REPORT. (Text in English, French, German) 1963. a. 1500 Fr. for non-members (includes Newsletters and Conference Proceedings) European Federation of Finance House Associations, Ave. de Tervuren 267, 1150 Brussels, Belgium. Ed. Florent J. de Cuyper.

332.1   BE   ISSN 0071-2795
EUROPEAN FEDERATION OF FINANCE HOUSE ASSOCIATIONS. CONFERENCE PROCEEDINGS. (Text in English, French, German) 1961. a. 1500 Fr. for non-members (includes Annual Report and Newsletters) European Federation of Finance House Associations, 267 Av. de Tervuren, 1150 Brussels, Belgium. Ed. Florent J. DeCuyper.

332.6   EI   ISSN 0071-2868
EUROPEAN INVESTMENT BANK. ANNUAL REPORT. (Text in Danish, Dutch, English, French, German and Italian) 1958. a. free. European Investment Bank, 2 Place de Metz, Luxembourg, Luxembourg (Dist. in U.S. by: European Community Information Service, 2100 M St., NW, Suite 707, Washington, DC 20037)

BUSINESS AND ECONOMICS — BANKING AND FINANCE

EXPORT-IMPORT BANK OF JAPAN. ANNUAL REPORT. see *BUSINESS AND ECONOMICS — International Commerce*

332.1   US   ISSN 0071-3511
EXPORT-IMPORT BANK OF THE UNITED STATES. SUMMARY OF OPERATIONS. Title varies: Export-Import Bank of the United States. Annual Report. 1945. a. free. Export-Import Bank of the United States, 811 Vermont Ave., N.W., Washington, DC 20571. circ. 20,000.

332.1   CN
FACTBOOK: CHARTERED BANKS OF CANADA. (Editions in English and French) 1968. a. free. ‡ Canadian Bankers' Association, Box 282, Toronto Dominion Centre, Toronto M5K 1K2, Ontario, Canada. circ. 64,000.

332.7   US
FAIR CREDIT REPORTING MANUAL. 1971. irreg., 2nd edt. 1977; supplements issued periodically to update base vol. $47.25 for base volume. Warren, Gorham and Lamont, Inc., 210 South St., Boston, MA 02111. Ed. Ralph C. Clontz, Jr.

332   CN   ISSN 0071-3864
FARM CREDIT CORPORATION. ANNUAL REPORT. 1929. a. free. Farm Credit Corporation, Box 6309, Postal Station -J, Ottawa, Ont. K2A 3W9, Canada.

332.1   CN   ISSN 0071-3872
FARM CREDIT CORPORATION. FEDERAL FARM CREDIT STATISTICS/STATISTIQUES DU CREDIT AGRICOLE FEDERAL. a. Farm Credit Corporation, Box 6309, Postal Station-J, Ottawa, Ont. K2A 3W9, Canada.

332   CN
FEDERAL BUSINESS DEVELOPMENT BANK. ANNUAL REPORT. a. Federal Business Development Bank, 901 Victoria Square, Montreal, Que. H2Z 1R1, Canada.

332.1   US
FEDERAL HOME LOAN BANK OF ATLANTA. ANNUAL REPORT. a. Federal Home Loan Bank of Atlanta, Atlanta, GA 30304. illus. stat.

332.3   US   ISSN 0098-2830
FEDERAL HOME LOAN BANK OF SAN FRANCISCO. ANNUAL REPORT. a. free. Federal Home Loan Bank of San Francisco, Box 7948, 600 California St., San Francisco, CA 94120. illus. Key Title: Annual Report - Federal Home Loan Bank of San Francisco.

332.1   US
FEDERAL HOME LOAN BANK OF SAN FRANCISCO. PROCEEDINGS OF THE ANNUAL CONFERENCE. 1975. a. $6. Federal Home Loan Bank of San Francisco, 600 California St., Box 7948, San Francisco, CA 94120.

332.1   US   ISSN 0094-7156
FEDERAL HOME LOAN MORTGAGE CORPORATION. REPORT. a. Federal Home Loan Mortgage Corporation, 311 First St., N.W., Washington, DC 20001. illus. stat. Key Title: Report of the Federal Home Loan Mortgage Corporation.

FEDERAL INCOME TAXATION OF BANKS AND FINANCIAL INSTITUTIONS (SUPPLEMENT) see *BUSINESS AND ECONOMICS — Public Finance, Taxation*

332.4   US   ISSN 0361-8013
FEDERAL RESERVE BANK OF MINNEAPOLIS. ANNUAL REPORT. a. Federal Reserve Bank of Minneapolis, 250 Marquette Ave., Minneapolis, MN 55480.

332   334   SW
FEDERATION OF SWEDISH CO-OPERATIVE BANKS. ANNUAL REPORT. a. Sveriges Foereningsbankers Foerbund, Fack, S-102 40 Stockholm, Sweden. (Co-sponsor: Foereningsbankernas Bank)

332   US
FINANCIAL ANALYSTS RESEARCH FOUNDATION. OCCASIONAL PAPER. 1975. irreg. $5 per no. Financial Analysts Research Foundation, University of Virginia, Box 6550, Charlottesville, VA 22906.

332   NE
FINANCIAL AND MONETARY STUDIES. no.4, 1979. irreg. price varies. Sijthoff & Noordhoff International Publishers b.v., Box 4, 2400 MA Alphen aan den Rijn, Netherlands (And 6 Winchester Terrace, Winchester, MA 01890)

332.1   US   ISSN 0362-1405
FINANCIAL INDUSTRY NUMBER STANDARD DIRECTORY. 1976. irreg. Depository Trust Company, 55 Water St., New York, NY 10041.

332   657   US   ISSN 0160-8827
FINANCIAL REPORTING TRENDS: SAVINGS AND LOAN. 1974. a. free. Ernst & Whinney, 2000 National City Center, Cleveland, OH 44114. charts. stat. circ. 4,000.

332   US   ISSN 0066-5363
FINANCIAL REVIEW. 1966. a. $5. Eastern Finance Association, c/o Geoffrey Booth, Ed., College of Business Administration, University of Rhode Island, Kingston, RI 02881. Ed. Geoffrey Booth. adv. bk. rev. circ. 1,100. Indexed: J. of Econ.Lit.
Formerly: Appalachian Financial Review.

332.1   US   ISSN 0363-8987
FINANCIAL STUDIES OF THE SMALL BUSINESS. 1976. a. $31 (expanded edt. $39) Financial Research Associates, 1629 K St. N.W., Suite 520, Washington, DC 20006.

332   CS   ISSN 0322-9653
FINANCNI ZPRAVODAJ. 1956. irreg., 15/yr. 15 Kcs. for 5 nos. Ministerstvo Financi CSR, Letenska 15, Prague 1, Czechoslovakia. Ed. Anna Mrazova. charts. index.
Formerly: Federalni Ministerstvo Financi. Vestnik (ISSN 0042-4641)

332.1   LB
FIRST NATIONAL CITY BANK, LIBERIA. ANNUAL REPORT. a. First National City Bank, P.O. Box 280, Monrovia, Liberia. illus. stat.

332   US   ISSN 0094-8535
FLORIDA BANK MONITOR; selected financial data for Florida banks. a. $40. Monitor Publications (Miami), P.O. Box 1055, Miami, FL 33133. Ed. Charity H. Johnson. stat. (back issues avail.)

332.1   CH
FLOW OF FUNDS IN TAIWAN DISTRICT, REPUBLIC OF CHINA. (Text in Chinese an English) 1968. a. Central Bank of China, Taipei, Taiwan, Republic of China. circ. 1,200.

332.31   FR   ISSN 0071-8254
FRANCE. CAISSE NATIONALE DE CREDIT AGRICOLE. RAPPORT SUR LE CREDIT AGRICOLE MUTUEL. English edition: Credit Agricole Annual Report. 1975. a. free. Caisse Nationale de Credit Agricole, 91-93 Boulevard Pasteur, 75015 Paris, France. circ. 4,000 (French edt.); 1,710 (English edt.)

332.7   FR
FRANCE. CONSEIL NATIONAL DU CREDIT. RAPPORT ANNUEL. a. (Conseil National du Credit) Banque de France, Service de l'Information, 43 rue de Valois, 75001 Paris, France (Dist. by: Imprimerie de Montligeon, La Chapelle Montligeon, 61400 Montagne au Perche, France)

332.2   FR
FRANCE. MINISTERE DE L'ECONOMIE ET DES FINANCES. CAISSES D'EPARGNE ORDINAIRE. irreg. Ministere de l'Economie et des Finances, Service d'Edition et de Vente des Publications Officielles, 39 rue de la Convention, 75015 Paris, France.

332   UK   ISSN 0072-5633
GREAT BRITAIN. DEPARTMENT OF TRADE. BANKRUPTCY: GENERAL ANNUAL REPORT. a. H.M.S.O., P.O. Box 569, London SE1 9NH, England (Avail. from H.M.S.O., c/o Liaison Officer, Atlantic House, Holborn Viaduct, London EC1P 1BN, England)

332   UK   ISSN 0072-7105
GREAT BRITAIN. ROYAL MINT. ANNUAL REPORT. a. 80p. Royal Mint, Tower Hill, London EC3N 4DR, England (Avail. from H.M.S.O., c/o Liaison Officer, Atlantic House, Holborn Viaduct, London EC1P 1BN, England) illus.

332   FR   ISSN 0066-2933
GROUPEMENT DES SOCIETES IMMOBILIERES D'INVESTISSEMENT. ANNUAIRE. 1966. a. 75 F. Groupement des Societes Immobilieres d'Investissement, 18, rue de Vienne, 75008 Paris, France. charts. stat.

322   GW
GRUNDLAGEN UND PRAXIS DES BANK- UND BOERSENWESENS. 1976. irreg. price varies. Erich Schmidt Verlag(Bielefeld), Viktoriastr. 44A, 4800 Bielefeld, W. Germany (B.R.D.)

332.4   UK   ISSN 0306-3933
HAMBRO EUROMONEY DIRECTORY. a. $25. Euromoney Publications Ltd., Nestor House, Playhouse Yard, London E.C.4, England.

332.1   AU
HAUPTVERBAND DER OESTERREICHISCHEN SPARKASSEN. JAHRESBERICHT. (Text in German; summaries in English, French and German) 1912. a. Hauptverband der Oesterreichischen Sparkassen, P.O. Box 256, A-1011 Vienna, Austria. charts. stat. circ. 4,000.

332.1   US   ISSN 0070-7082
HEWITT-DONLON CATALOG OF UNITED STATES SMALL SIZE PAPER MONEY. 1964. a. $2.50. Hewitt Bros., 7320 Milwaukee Ave., Chicago, IL 60648. Eds. Nathan Goldstein, Lee F. Hewitt. circ. 1,500,0000.

332.1   US
HISTORICAL CHART BOOK. a. $1.25 (or included in subcr. to Federal Reserve Chart Book) U.S. Federal Reserve System, Board of Governors, Publications Services, Rm. MP-510, Washington, DC 20551.

332.7   HK
HONG KONG EXPORT CREDIT INSURANCE CORPORATION. ANNUAL REPORT. a. Hong Kong Export Credit Insurance Corporation, Box 939, G.P.O., Hong Kong, Hong Kong.

HOUSING FINANCE COMPANY OF KENYA. ANNUAL REPORT AND ACCOUNTS. see *HOUSING AND URBAN PLANNING*

330.1   US   ISSN 0085-1620
HOW TO AVOID FINANCIAL TANGLES: SECTION A. ELEMENTARY PROPERTY PROBLEMS AND FINANCIAL RELATIONSHIPS. 1969. irreg., 1976, vol. 16, no. 12. $2. ‡ American Institute for Economic Research, Great Barrington, MA 01230. Ed. Bruce H. French.

330.1   US   ISSN 0085-1639
HOW TO AVOID FINANCIAL TANGLES: SECTION B. WILLS AND TRUSTS, TAXES, AND HELP FOR THE WIDOW. 1969. irreg., vol. 19, 1979. $2. American Institute for Economic Research, Great Barrington, MA 01230. Ed. Bruce H. French.

332.3   KU
INDUSTRIAL BANK OF KUWAIT. ANNUAL REPORT. (Text in English) 1975. a. Industrial Bank of Kuwait - Bank al-Kuwayt al-Sinai, Box 3146, Safat, Kuwait.

332.1   SJ   ISSN 0073-7356
INDUSTRIAL BANK OF SUDAN. BOARD OF DIRECTORS. ANNUAL REPORT. (Text in English and Arabic) 1962. a. free. Industrial Bank of Sudan, United Nations Sq., P.O. Box 1722, Khartoum, Sudan.

332.1   JO
INDUSTRIAL DEVELOPMENT BANK. ANNUAL REPORT AND BALANCE SHEET/BANK AL-INMA AL-SINAI. ANNUAL REPORT AND BALANCE SHEET. 1964. a. Industrial Development Bank, Majlis al-Ommah St., Box 1982, Amman, Jordan. charts. illus.

332.1   KE
INDUSTRIAL DEVELOPMENT BANK LIMITED. ANNUAL REPORT AND ACCOUNTS. a; latest 1975. Industrial Development Bank Limited, Bima House, P.O. Box 44036, Nairobi, Kenya. illus. stat.

BUSINESS AND ECONOMICS — BANKING AND FINANCE

332.1   II   ISSN 0073-7372
INDUSTRIAL DEVELOPMENT BANK OF INDIA. ANNUAL REPORT. (Text in English; occasionally in Hindi) 1964/65. a. free. Industrial Development Bank of India, Jolly Maker Chambers No. 1, 227 Backbay Reclamation Scheme, Bombay 400021, India.

332.1   IS   ISSN 0073-7380
INDUSTRIAL DEVELOPMENT BANK OF ISRAEL LIMITED. REPORT. (Text in English & Hebrew) a. Industrial Development Bank of Israel Limited, Tel Aviv, Israel.

332.1   PK   ISSN 0073-7399
INDUSTRIAL DEVELOPMENT BANK OF PAKISTAN. REPORT. (Text in English) 1961-62. a. Industrial Development Bank of Pakistan, State Life Bldg., Wallace Rd., Karachi, Pakistan.

332.1   TU   ISSN 0073-7402
INDUSTRIAL DEVELOPMENT BANK OF TURKEY. ANNUAL STATEMENT. (Text in English) a. Industrial Development Bank of Turkey - Turkiye Sinai Kalkinma Bankasi, Meclisi Mebusan Cad. 137, Box 59, Findikli, Istanbul, Turkey.

332   336.1   GW   ISSN 0067-9941
INSTITUT "FINANZEN UND STEUERN." GRUENE BRIEFE. 1954. irreg., no. 184, 1979. price varies. Institut "Finanzen und Steuern." e.V., Markt 10, Postfach 1808, 5300 Bonn, W. Germany (B.R.D.) index, cum.index. (back issues avail.)

332   336.1   GW   ISSN 0067-995X
INSTITUT "FINANZEN UND STEUERN." SCHRIFTENREIHE. 1950. irreg., no. 115, 1979. price varies. Institut "Finanzen und Steuern." e.V., Markt 10, Postfach 1808, 5300 Bonn, W. Germany (B.R.D.) index, cum.index. (back issues avail.)

332   US   ISSN 0073-8778
INSTITUTE FOR MONETARY RESEARCH. MONOGRAPHS. 1962. irreg. price varies. ‡ Institute for Monetary Research, 1200 15th St. N.W., Washington, DC 20005. Ed. Elgin Groseclose. index.

332.1   PK   ISSN 0073-8999
INSTITUTE OF BANKERS IN PAKISTAN. COUNCIL. REPORT AND ACCOUNTS. (Text in English) s-a. Institute of Bankers in Pakistan, Karachi, Pakistan.

332.1   CN   ISSN 0318-4315
INSTITUTE OF CANADIAN BANKERS. EDUCATIONAL PROGRAMS. French edition: Institut des Banquiers Canadiens. Programmes d'Education (ISSN 0318-4323) (Editions in English and French) 1968. a. Institute of Canadian Bankers, 1801 McGill College Ave., Suite 720, Montreal, Que. H3A 2N4, Canada.

332.1   338.9   US   ISSN 0074-087X
INTER-AMERICAN DEVELOPMENT BANK. ANNUAL REPORT. Spanish edition: Inter-American Development Bank. Informe Anual (ISSN 0074-087X) (Editions also in French & Portuguese) 1960. a. Inter-American Development Bank, 808 17th St., N.W., Washington, DC 20577.
Incorporating: Inter-American Development Bank. Statement of Loans.

332.1   338.9   US   ISSN 0074-0861
INTER-AMERICAN DEVELOPMENT BANK. BOARD OF GOVERNORS. PROCEEDINGS OF THE MEETING. Spanish edt.: Inter-American Development Bank. Board of Governors. Anals (de la) Reunion (ISSN 0538-3102) (Edts. in Spanish, English, and Portuguese) 1960. a. Inter-American Development Bank, 808 17th St., N.W., Washington, DC 20577.

332.1   CH
INTERNATIONAL COMMERCIAL BANK OF CHINA. ANNUAL REPORT. (Text in English) a. International Commercial Bank of China, 100 Chi Lin Rd., Taipei 104, Taiwan, Republic of China. stat.
Continues: Chung-Kuo Yin Hang. Annual Report.

332   UN   ISSN 0074-6061
INTERNATIONAL FINANCE CORPORATION. REPORT. 1956/57. a. International Finance Corporation, 1818 H St., N.W., Washington, DC 20433.

332   UN
INTERNATIONAL MONETARY FUND. ANNUAL REPORT OF THE EXECUTIVE BOARD. (Editions in English, French, German and Spanish) 1947. a. (September) free. International Monetary Fund, 700 19th St., N.W., Washington, DC 20431. Ed. Norman K. Humphreys. (also avail. in microform from UMI; reprint service avail. from UMI)
Formerly: International Monetary Fund. Annual Report of the Executive Directors (ISSN 0085-2171)

332   UN
INTERNATIONAL MONETARY FUND. ANNUAL REPORT ON EXCHANGE ARRANGEMENTS AND EXCHANGE RESTRICTIONS. (Text in English) 1950. a. (August) free ($5 per additional copy) International Monetary Fund, 700 19th St., N.W., Washington, DC 20431. (also avail. in microform from UMI; reprint service avail. from UMI)
Formerly: International Monetary Fund. Annual Report on Exchange Restrictions (ISSN 0085-2163)

332   UN   ISSN 0538-8759
INTERNATIONAL MONETARY FUND. PAMPHLET SERIES. 1964. irreg. free. International Monetary Fund, 700 19th St., N.W., Washington, DC 20431. Ed. Norman K. Humphreys. (reprint service avail. from UMI)

332   UN   ISSN 0094-1735
INTERNATIONAL MONETARY FUND. SELECTED DECISIONS OF THE INTERNATIONAL MONETARY FUND AND SELECTED DOCUMENTS. (Text in English, French and Spanish) 1972. irreg. free. International Monetary Fund, 700 19th St., N.W., Washington, DC 20431. index. (reprint service avail. from UMI)
Continues: International Monetary Fund. Selected Decisions of the Executive Directors and Selected Documents.

330   UN   ISSN 0074-7025
INTERNATIONAL MONETARY FUND. SUMMARY PROCEEDINGS OF THE ANNUAL MEETING OF THE BOARD OF GOVERNORS. (Includes list of members of delegations) 1946. a. free. International Monetary Fund, 700 19th St., N.W., Washington, DC 20431. (reprint service avail. from UMI)

332   US
INTERNATIONAL MONETARY MARKET YEARBOOK. 1972. a. $6. Chicago Mercantile Exchange, 444 W. Jackson Blvd., Chicago, IL 60606. circ. 4,000.

332   SZ
INTERNATIONAL SAVINGS BANKS INSTITUTE. REPORT. biennial. International Savings Banks Institute, 1-3 rue Albert-Gos, 1206 Geneva, Switzerland.

332   US   ISSN 0074-9370
INTERNATIONAL UNION OF BUILDING SOCIETIES AND SAVINGS ASSOCIATIONS. CONGRESS PROCEEDINGS. (Text in French, German, English, Spanish) 1914. triennial, 1977, 14th, San Francisco. International Union of Building Societies and Savings Associations, c/o Don F. Geyer, Sec.-Gen., 111 E. Wacker Dr., 25th Fl., Chicago, IL 60601.

332.1   IR
IRAN BANKING ALMANAC. a. $22. Iranian Bankers' Association, 21 Jabbarzadegan St., Takht Tavous Ave., Teheran, Iran. stat.

658.8   332   IE   ISSN 0075-0573
IRELAND (EIRE) CENTRAL STATISTICS OFFICE. HIRE-PURCHASE AND CREDIT SALES. a. Central Statistics Office, Earlsfort Terrace, Dublin 2, Ireland.
Stencilled releases

332   SU
ISLAMIC DEVELOPMENT BANK. ANNUAL REPORT. 1975. a. Islamic Development Bank, Box 5925, Jeddah, Saudi Arabia.

332.1   IS   ISSN 0075-1146
ISRAEL DISCOUNT BANK. REPORT. (Text in English) 1955. a. free. Israel Discount Bank Limited, 27-29 Yehuda Halevy St., Tel Aviv, Israel.

332   378   US   ISSN 0093-3961
JOURNAL OF FINANCIAL EDUCATION. 1972. a. $6. San Jose State University, School of Business, San Jose, CA 95192. Ed. G. R. Sanderson. adv. circ. 800.
Formerly: Financial Education (ISSN 0190-7654)

332   YU   ISSN 0075-4536
JUGOSLOVENSKA INVESTICIONA BANKA. ANNUAL REPORT. 1956. a. free. Jugoslovenska Investiciona Banka, Terazije 9, Box 152, 11001 Belgrade, Yugoslavia. Ed. Ljubisa K. Plavsic. circ. 1,700.

332.1   KE
KENYA COMMERCIAL BANK. DIRECTOR'S REPORT AND ACCOUNTS AND EXECUTIVE CHAIRMAN'S STATEMENT. a. Kenya Commercial Bank, Box 48400, Nairobi, Kenya.

332.1   KO   ISSN 0075-6806
KOREA DEVELOPMENT BANK; ITS FUNCTIONS AND ACTIVITIES. (Text in English) 1965. a. free. Korea Development Bank, Research Department, Box 28, Seoul, S. Korea. Ed. Min Beoung Yun.

332   KU
KUWAIT INVESTMENT COMPANY. (REPORT) a. Kuwait Investment Company, Box 1005, Safat, Kuwait.

332   PH
LAND BANK OF THE PHILIPPINES. ANNUAL REPORT. 1974. a. Land Bank of the Philippines, B.F. Condominium, 6th Fl., Aduana St., Manila, Philippines. Ed. Danilo R. Cueto. charts. illus. stat. circ. 6,000.

332.1   LO
LESOTHO BANK. REPORT AND ACCOUNTS. Cover title: Lesotho Bank. Annual Report. a. Lesotho Bank, Box 999, Kingsway, Maseru, Lesotho.

332.2   BL
LINHAS DE FINANCIAMENTO DO B N H. vol. 3, 1978. a. Banco Nacional da Habitacao, Secretaria de Divulgacao, Assessoria de Planejamento e Coordenacao, Av. Republica do Chile 230, Rio de Janeiro RJ, Brazil. Dir. Luiz Sande. charts. stat.

LUZ. see *AGRICULTURE*

332.1   II   ISSN 0076-2563
MAHARASHTRA STATE FINANCIAL CORPORATION. ANNUAL REPORT. (Text in English) 1963. a. free. Maharashtra State Financial Corporation, New Excelsior Building, 7, 8 & 9th Floors, Amrit Keshav Nayak Marg, Fort, Bombay 400001, India. charts. stat.

332.1   MW   ISSN 0076-3322
MALAWI. POST OFFICE SAVINGS BANK. ANNUAL REPORT. 1964. a. Post Office Savings Bank, Box 521, Blantyre, Malawi. circ. 300.

332   CN
MANITOBA. CO-OPERATIVE LOANS AND LOANS GUARANTEE BOARD. ANNUAL REPORT. 1971. a. Co-Operative Loans and Loans Guarantee Board, Mall Centre, 8th Floor, 491 Portage Ave., Winnipeg, Man. R3B 2E7, Canada.

334   CN
MANITOBA. DEPARTMENT OF CO-OPERATIVE DEVELOPMENT. REPORT. RAPPORT. (Text in English and French) 1972. a. Department of Co-Operative Development, Winnipeg, Man., Canada. illus.
Continues: Manitoba Credit Unions: Annual Report.

332.1   IS   ISSN 0076-4515
MARITIME BANK OF ISRAEL. ANNUAL REPORT/BANK HA-SAPANUT LE-YISRAEL. ANNUAL REPORT. (Text in English and Hebrew) a. free. Maritime Bank of Israel, Ltd, P.O. Box 1529, Tel Aviv 61000, Israel.

332   US
MONEY MASTERS ANNUAL. a. $10. I. M. Systems, Box 686, Montclair, NJ 07042. charts. stat.

BUSINESS AND ECONOMICS — BANKING AND FINANCE

332   FR
LA MONNAIE EN (YEAR) 1970. a. free. Banque de France, Service de l'information, 43 rue de Valois, 75001 Paris, France. (Co-sponsor: France.Conseil National du Credit)

MONNAIES, PRIX, CONJONCTURE. see *HISTORY*

332.3   US   ISSN 0077-1546
MORTGAGE BANKING: FINANCIAL STATEMENTS AND OPERATING RATIOS. 1963. a. $25. Mortgage Bankers Association of America, Economics and Research Department, 1125 15th Str., N.W., Washington, DC 20005.
Formerly: Mortgage Banking: Trends, Financial Statements and Operating Ratios.

332.3   US
MORTGAGE BANKING: LOANS CLOSED AND SERVICING VOLUME. 1971. a. $20. Mortgage Bankers Association of America, Economics and Research Department, 1125 15th St., N.W., Washington, DC 20005.

332.3   US
MORTGAGE BANKING: SURVEY OF SINGLE-FAMILY LOAN OPERATIONS (COST STUDY) 1969. irreg. $20. Mortgage Bankers Association of America, 1125 15th St., N.W., Washington, DC 20005.

332.7   US   ISSN 0094-1522
N. C. F. A. OFFICE MANUAL. biennial. $45 to nonmembers. National Consumer Finance Association, 1000-16th St. N.W., Washington, DC 20036.
Formerly: Consumer Finance Roster.

332.1   GR   ISSN 0077-3514
NATIONAL BANK OF GREECE. ANNUAL REPORT/ETHNIKE TRAPEZA TES HELLADOS. APOLOGISMOS. (Editions in English & Greek) 1843. a. free. National Bank of Greece, Economic Research Department, 86 Eolou St., Athens 121, Greece. circ. 10,000(Greek edt.); 7,000(English edt.)

332   KU
NATIONAL BANK OF KUWAIT S.A.K. ANNUAL REPORT OF THE BOARD OF DIRECTORS AND ACCOUNTS. a. National Bank of Kuwait S.A.K., Abdullah al-Salim St., Box 95, Kuwait.

332.1   LB
NATIONAL BANK OF LIBERIA. ANNUAL REPORT. 1974. a. National Bank of Liberia, Box 2048, E. G. King Plaza, Broad St., Monrovia, Liberia. stat.

332   PK
NATIONAL BANK OF PAKISTAN. ANNUAL REPORT. (Text in English) a. National Bank of Pakistan, I.I. Chundrigar Rd., Karachi 2, Pakistan.

332.1   PK   ISSN 0077-3522
NATIONAL BANK OF PAKISTAN. REPORT AND STATEMENT OF ACCOUNTS. (Text in English) a. National Bank of Pakistan, I. I. Chundrigar Rd., Karachi 2, Pakistan.

NATIONAL BANK OF YUGOSLAVIA. ANNUAL REPORT. see *BUSINESS AND ECONOMICS — Economic Situation And Conditions*

332.3   DQ
NATIONAL COMMERCIAL & DEVELOPMENT BANK. ANNUAL REPORT AND FINANCIAL STATEMENTS. a. National Commercial & Development Bank, 64 Hillsborough Street, P.O. Box 215, Roseau, Dominica, West Indies. (Affiliate: A I D Bank) illus.
Formerly: Dominica Agricultural and Industrial Development Bank. Annual Report and Financial Statements.

332.1   SL
NATIONAL DEVELOPMENT BANK. ANNUAL REPORT AND ACCOUNTS. (Text in English) 1969. a. free. ‡ National Development Bank, Leone House, 21/23 Siaka Stevens St., Freetown, Sierra Leone. stat. circ. 450.

332.1   GH
NATIONAL INVESTMENT BANK, GHANA. ANNUAL REPORT. Short title: N I B Annual Report. 1963. a, latest 1976. ‡ National Investment Bank, 37 Liberty Ave., P.O. Box 3726, Accra, Ghana. illus. stat. circ. controlled.
Formerly: National Investment Bank, Ghana. Report of the Directors (ISSN 0077-5061)

332   NP
NEPAL BANK LIMITED. ANNUAL REPORT AND BALANCE SHEET. (Text in English) a. Nepal Bank Limited, Dharma Path, Kathmandu, Nepal. charts. stat.

332.1   NP
NEPAL RASTRA BANK. ANNUAL REPORT. (Text in English) a. free. Nepal Rastra Bank, Research Department, Baluwatar, Kathmandu, Nepal.
Formerly: Nepal Rastra Bank. Report of the Board of Directors (ISSN 0077-6580)

332   NE
NETHERLANDS BANKING DIGEST. 1976. irreg. free. Nederlands Instituut voor het Bank- en Effectenbedrijf, Herengracht 136, 1015 BV Amsterdam, Netherlands. circ. 3,000.

332   NE
NETHERLANDS INSTITUTE OF BANKERS AND STOCK BROKERS. PUBLICATIONS. vol. 31, 1977. irreg. price varies. Martinus Nijhoff, Box 566, 2501 CN The Hague, Netherlands.

332.1   338.9   NE   ISSN 0077-7560
NETHERLANDS INVESTMENT BANK FOR DEVELOPING COUNTRIES. ANNUAL REPORT. (Text in English) a. Netherlands Investment Bank for Developing Countries - Nederlandse Investeringsbank voor Ontwikkelingslanden N.V., The Hague, Netherlands.

332.1   US
NEW JERSEY. DEPARTMENT OF BANKING. ANNUAL REPORT. a. $6. Department of Banking, Box CN040, Trenton, NJ 08625. circ. 1,300.
Formed by the merger of: New Jersey. Division of Savings and Loan Associations. Annual Report (ISSN 0098-8073) & New Jersey. Division of Banking. Annual Report (ISSN 0098-7409)

332   US
NEW YORK UNIVERSITY. SALOMON BROTHERS CENTER FOR THE STUDY OF FINANCIAL INSTITUTIONS. MONOGRAPH SERIES IN FINANCE AND ECONOMICS. irreg. $6 to qualified personnel; others $12. New York University, Salomon Brothers Center for the Study of Financial Institutions, Graduate School of Business Administration, 90 Trinity Pl., New York, NY 10006.

332.1   NR   ISSN 0549-2734
NIGERIAN INDUSTRIAL DEVELOPMENT BANK. ANNUAL REPORT AND ACCOUNTS. 1971. a. free. Nigerian Industrial Development Bank, Mandilar House, Yabuku Gowon St., Box 2357, Lagos, Nigeria. illus. circ. 2,000.

332   JA
NIHON KAIHATSU GINKO. CHOSABU. CHOSA GEPPO. 1973. irreg. free. Japan Development Bank - Nihon Kaihatsu Ginko, 1-9-1- Otemachi, Chiyoda-ku, Tokyo, Japan. circ. 2,300.

332.1   NO   ISSN 0078-1185
NORGES BANK. REPORT AND ACCOUNTS. Cover title: Norges Bank. Annual Report. (Text in English) a. Norges Bank, Box 336, Oslo 1, Norway.

332.1   NO
NORSKE CREDITBANK. Caption title: Norske Creditbank. Report of the Board of Directors. a. Norske Creditbank, Kirkegaten 21, Oslo 1, Norway.
Formerly: Norske Creditbank. Annual Report.

332.3   US   ISSN 0091-2093
NORTH DAKOTA. CONSUMER CREDIT DIVISION. CONSOLIDATED ANNUAL REPORT OF LICENSEES. a. Consumer Credit Division, Bismarck, ND 58501. illus. stat. Key Title: Consolidated Annual Report of Licensees (Bismarck)

332   US
OCCASIONAL PAPERS IN METROPOLITAN BUSINESS AND FINANCE. irreg. $5 per no. New York University, Salomon Brothers Center for the Study of Financial Institutions, Graduate School of Business Administration, 90 Trinity Pl., New York, NY 10006.

332.1   AU
OESTERREICHISCHE BANKWISSENSCHAFTLICHE GESELLSCHAFT. SCHRIFTENREIHE. 1953. irreg., vol. 57, 1979. price varies. Manzsche Verlags- und Universitaetsbuchhandlung, Kohlmarkt 16, A-1014 Vienna, Austria. Ed. Hans Krasensky.

332.1   AU   ISSN 0078-3528
OESTERREICHISCHE NATIONALBANK. BERICHT UEBER DAS GESCHAEFTSJAHR MIT RECHNUNGSABSCHLUSS. (Editions in English and German) 1956. a. free. Oesterreichische Nationalbank, Otto-Wagner-Platz 3, A-1090 Vienna, Austria.

382   332   FR   ISSN 0474-5655
ORGANIZATION FOR ECONOMIC COOPERATION AND DEVELOPMENT. COUNCIL. CODE DE LA LIBERATION DES MOUVEMENTS DE CAPITAUX. CODE OF LIBERALISATION OF CAPITAL MOVEMENTS. (Editions in English and French) irreg. $7.50. Organization for Economic Cooperation and Development, 2 rue Andre Pascal, 75775 Paris 16, France (U.S. orders to: O.E.C.D. Publications and Information Center, 1750 Pennsylvania Ave., N.W., Washington, DC 20006) (also avail. in microfiche)

332.1   PK   ISSN 0078-7884
PAKISTAN BANKING DIRECTORY.* (Text in English) 1966-67. a. Sanaullah Publications, Box 4186, Karachi, Pakistan.

332   US   ISSN 0079-0761
PER JACOBSSON FOUNDATION. PROCEEDINGS. (Editions in English, French, Spanish) 1964. a. free. Per Jacobsson Foundation, International Monetary Fund Bldg., Washington, DC 20431. (Affiliate: International Monetary Fund) Ed. Gordon Williams. circ. 20,000 (Eng. edt.); 2,500 (Fr. edt.); 1,500 (Span. edt.)
Formerly: Per Jacobsson Memorial Lecture (ISSN 0079-077X)

332   US   ISSN 0079-2063
PICK'S CURRENCY YEARBOOK. 1955. a. $180. Pick Publishing Corp., 21 West St., New York, NY 10006. Ed. George T. Steve. charts. stat. index. circ. 1,000.

332.1   US   ISSN 0085-4999
POLK'S WORLD BANK DIRECTORY. INTERNATIONAL EDITION. 1894. a. $40.50. R.L. Polk & Co., 2001 Elm Hill Pike, Box 1340, Nashville, TN 37202. adv. bk. rev. charts. stat. circ. 17,500.

332.7   FR
PRINCIPAUX MECANISMES DE DISTRIBUTION DE CREDIT. irreg., vol. 6, 1978. 5 F. Banque de France, Service de l'Information, 43 rue de Valois, 75001 Paris, France.

332   PR
PUERTO RICO. GOVERNMENT DEVELOPMENT BANK. ANNUAL REPORT. a. Banco Gubernamental de Fomento, Centro Gubernamental Minillas, Av. de Diego 22, San Juan, PR 00911.
Formerly: Puerto Rico. Government Development Bank. Report of Activities.

BUSINESS AND ECONOMICS — BANKING AND FINANCE

332.1　　　　II　　ISSN 0304-8101
PUNJAB NATIONAL BANK. ANNUAL REPORT.
(Text in English) a. Punjab National Bank, Ltd., 5
Parliament St., New Delhi 10001, India. Key Title:
Annual Report - Punjab National Bank.

332　　　　　　QA
QATAR NATIONAL BANK (S.A.Q.). REPORT OF
THE DIRECTORS AND BALANCE SHEET. a.
Qatar National Bank (S.A.Q.), Box 1000, Doha,
Qatar.

332 650　　　　US　　ISSN 0080-3340
R M A ANNUAL STATEMENT STUDIES. 1923. a.
$22.20 to non-members. ‡ Robert Morris
Associates, 1616 Philadelphia National Bank Bldg.,
Philadelphia, PA 19107. index. circ. 25,000.

RAND MCNALLY LIST OF BANK-
RECOMMENDED ATTORNEYS. see *LAW*

332 364　　　UK　　ISSN 0080-0538
REGENCY INTERNATIONAL DIRECTORY; of
enquiry agents, private detectives & debt collecting
agencies. 1967. a. $22.50. Regency International
Publications Ltd., Newstone House, 127 Sandgate
Rd., Folkestone, Kent CT20 2BL, England. Ed.
Alan L. Valle.

332　　　　　　US
REPORT ON DOMESTIC AND
INTERNATIONAL COMMERCIAL LOAN
CHARGE-OFFS. 1972. a. $11 to non-members;
members $7.50. Robert Morris Associates, 1616
Philadelphia National Bank Bldg., Philadelphia, PA
19107.
　　Former titles: Domestic and International
Commercial Loan Charge-Offs (ISSN 0192-7639);
Commercial Loan Charge-Offs.

332　　　　US　　ISSN 0080-1380
REPRINTS IN INTERNATIONAL FINANCE.
1965. irreg., no. 20, 1980. $8 (includes Essays in
International Finance) ‡ Princeton University,
International Finance Section, Dept. of Economics,
Dickinson Hall, Princeton, NJ 08544. Ed. Peter B.
Kenen. circ. 3,000. (also avail. in microfilm from
UMI; back issues avail.; reprint service avail. from
UMI)

332　　　　US　　ISSN 0196-3821
RESEARCH IN FINANCE. 1979. a. $17.25 to
individuals; institutions $34.50. J A I Press, Box
1678, 165 W. Putnam Ave., Greenwich, CT 06830.
Ed. Haim Levy.

332.1　　　　AT　　ISSN 0080-1771
RESERVE BANK OF AUSTRALIA. ANNUAL
REPORT. 1960. a. free. Reserve Bank of Australia,
65 Martin Place, Box 3947 G.P.O., Sydney, N.S.W.
2001, Australia. circ. 27,000.

332.1 330.9　　AT　　ISSN 0080-178X
RESERVE BANK OF AUSTRALIA. OCCASIONAL
PAPERS. 1970. irreg. free. Reserve Bank of
Australia, 65 Martin Place, Box 3947 G.P.O.,
Sydney, N.S.W. 2001, Australia. circ. 6,000.

332　　　　　II　　ISSN 0080-1801
RESERVE BANK OF INDIA. ANNUAL REPORT.
(Text in English) a. price varies. Reserve Bank of
India, Box 1036, Bombay 400001, India.

332　　　　MW　　ISSN 0486-5383
RESERVE BANK OF MALAWI. REPORT AND
ACCOUNTS. a. free. Reserve Bank of Malawi,
Research Department, Box 565, Blantyre, Malawi.

REVISTA A P I C E/A P I C E JOURNAL.
(Asociacion Panamericana de Instituciones de
Credito Educativo) see *EDUCATION*

332　　　　　　BL
REVISTA DO B I N D E. English edition: B I N D E
Annual Report. 1963. a. Banco Nacional do
Desenvolvimento Economico, Av. Rio Branco, 53,
Rio de Janeiro, Brazil. bibl. charts. stat.
　　Former title: Banco Nacional do
Desenvolvimento Economico. Relatorio Anual.

332.1　　　　BL　　ISSN 0556-6916
REVISTA PARANAENSE DE
DESENVOLVIMENTO. q. Banco de
Desenvolvimento do Parana, S.A., Av. Vicente
Machado, 445, Caixa Postal 6042, Curitiba, Parana,
Brazil. Dir. Andre Zacharow. charts. stat.

332.1　　　　SZ　　ISSN 0080-2611
REVUE INTERNATIONALE D'HISTOIRE DE LA
BANQUE. 1968. a. price varies. (Banco di Napoli,
IT) Librarie Droz, 11 rue Massot, 1211 Geneva 12,
Switzerland. bk. rev.

332　　　　　　SZ
S B C BOOKLET. (Text in English) irreg.
Schweizerischer Bankverein - Swiss Bank
Corporation, 1 Aeschenvorstadt, CH-4002 Basel,
Switzerland.

S B I C DIRECTORY AND HANDBOOK OF
SMALL BUSINESS FINANCE. see *BUSINESS
AND ECONOMICS — Small Business*

332　　　　　SU　　ISSN 0581-8672
SAUDI ARABIAN MONETARY AGENCY.
STATISTICAL SUMMARY. a. Saudi Arabian
Monetary Agency, Research and Statistics
Department, Box 2992, Riyadh, Saudi Arabia.
charts. stat.

332.2　　　　US　　ISSN 0581-8761
SAVINGS AND LOAN FACT BOOK. 1954. a. price
varies. United States League of Savings
Associations, 111 E. Wacker Drive, Chicago, IL
60601.

332.2　　　　US　　ISSN 0163-6782
SAVINGS AND LOAN MARKET STUDY. a.
United States League of Savings Associations, 111
E. Wacker Dr., Chicago, IL 60601.

332 346.066　　SZ
SCHRIFTENREIHE FINANZWIRTSCHAFT UND
FINANZRECHT. 1970. irreg., no. 24, 1978. price
varies. Paul Haupt AG, Falkenplatz 14, CH-3001
Berne, Switzerland.

332.1　　　　　SZ
SCHWEIZERISCHE BANKWESEN. (Text in
German) a. (Schweizerische Nationalbank) Orell
Fuessli Graphische Betriebe AG, Dietzingerstr. 3,
CH-8036 Zurich, Switzerland. stat.

332 340　　　US　　ISSN 0080-8474
SECURITIES LAW REVIEW. 1969. a. $52.50. ‡
Clark Boardman Co., Ltd., 435 Hudson St., New
York, NY 10014. Ed. Harold S. Bloomenthal. circ.
1,500.

332.4　　　　　SI
SINGAPORE. BOARD OF COMMISSIONERS OF
CURRENCY, ANNUAL REPORT. a. Board of
Commissions of Currency, Empress Place,
Singapore 6, Singapore.

335 368　　　　SI
SINGAPORE BANKING, FINANCE &
INSURANCE. 1979. a. S.$4. Times Directories
Private Ltd., 530 Cuppage Centre, 55 Cuppage Rd.,
Singapore 0922, Singapore.

332.1　　　　　KO
SMALL AND MEDIUM INDUSTRY BANK,
SEOUL. ANNUAL REPORT. 1962. a. free. Small
and Medium Industry Bank, Seoul, S. Korea. Ed.
Kwan-Heng Chough. circ. 1,000.
　　Formerly: Medium Industry Bank, Seoul. Report
(ISSN 0076-6143)

332.1　　　　　BE
SOCIETE GENERALE DE BANQUE. RAPPORT.
a. Societe Generale de Banque, Montagne du Parc
3, B-1000 Brussels, Belgium.

332　　　　BE　　ISSN 0081-1114
SOCIETE GENERALE DE BELGIQUE.
RAPPORT/REPORT. (Editions in English and
French) 1822. a. free. Societe Generale de Belgique,
External Relations Department, 30 rue Royale, B-
1000 Brussels, Belgium.

332.1　　　　　SA
SOUTH AFRICAN RESERVE BANK. REPORT OF
THE ORDINARY GENERAL MEETING.
(Editions in Afrikaans and English) 1922. a. free.
South African Reserve Bank, P.O. Box 427, Pretoria
0001, South Africa. circ. 4,000(controlled) (tabloid
format)

SPECIAL PAPERS IN INTERNATIONAL
ECONOMICS. see *BUSINESS AND
ECONOMICS*

332　　　　　II　　ISSN 0585-0991
STATE BANK OF INDIA. REPORT OF THE
CENTRAL BOARD OF DIRECTORS. (Text in
English) 1955. a. International Book House, Ltd., 9
Ash Lane, Mahatma Gandhi Rd., Bombay 1, India.
　　Supersedes: Report for the Half Year of the
Imperial Bank of India.

332.1　　　　CS　　ISSN 0081-539X
STATNI BANKA CESKOSLOVENSKA.
BULLETIN. 1967. a. free. Statni Banka
Ceskoslovenska, Na prikope 28, 110 03 Prague 1,
Czechoslovakia.

332　　　　GW　　ISSN 0081-7279
STUDIEN ZUR FINANZPOLITIK. 1964. irreg., no.
26, 1980. price varies. I F O Institut fuer
Wirtschaftsforschung, Poschingerstr. 5, 8000
Munich 80, W. Germany (B.R.D.) circ. 500.

332　　　　US　　ISSN 0081-766X
STUDIES IN CAPITAL FORMATION AND
FINANCING. 1956. irreg., 1973, no. 13. $15.
National Bureau of Economic Research, 1050
Massachusetts Ave, Cambridge, MA 02138. Ed.
Raymond W. Goldsmith.

332　　　　US　　ISSN 0081-7791
STUDIES IN CONSUMER INSTALMENT
FINANCING. 1940. irreg., 1967, no. 13. $12.50.
National Bureau of Economic Research, 1050
Massachusetts Ave, Cambridge, MA 02138.

332　　　　US　　ISSN 0081-7805
STUDIES IN CORPORATE BOND FINANCING.
1953. irreg., 1967, no. 4. $7.50. National Bureau of
Economic Research, 1050 Massachusetts Ave,
Cambridge, MA 02138.

332　　　　US　　ISSN 0081-8070
STUDIES IN INTERNATIONAL FINANCE. 1950.
irreg., no. 46, 1980. $25 (includes Essays in
International Finance; Reprints in International
Finance; Special Papers in International Economics)
‡ Princeton University, International Finance
Section, Dept. of Economics, Dickinson Hall,
Princeton, NJ 08544. Dir. Peter B. Kenen. circ.
2,000. (also avail. in microfilm from UMI; back
issues avail.; reprint service avail. from UMI)

332　　　　　　SJ
SUDAN COMMERCIAL BANK. REPORT OF THE
BOARD OF DIRECTORS. irreg. Sudan
Commercial Bank, Box 1116, Khartoum, Sudan.

332　　　　　　SW
SVENSK OBLIGATIONSBOK. 1913. a. Kr.200.
Svenska Bankfoereningen - Swedish Bankers
Association, Box 7603, S-103 94 Stockholm,
Sweden. Ed. Gudrun Edman.

332.1　　　　SW　　ISSN 0081-9913
SVENSKA HANDELSBANKEN. ANNUAL
REPORT. Variant title: Svenska Handelsbanken.
Annual Report and Auditors' Report. a. free.
Svenska Handelsbanken, Kungstraedgaardsgatan 2,
S-103 23 Stockholm, Sweden.

332.1　　　　　SW
SVERIGES RIKSBANK.
FOERVALTNINGSBERAETTELSE. English
edition: Central Bank of Sweden. Annual Report
(ISSN 0347-5042) a. Sveriges Riksbank, Box 16283,
S-103 25 Stockholm, Sweden.

332.1　　　　SW　　ISSN 0348-7342
SVERIGES RIKSBANK. STATISTISK AARSBOK/
CENTRAL BANK OF SWEDEN. STATISTICAL
YEARBOOK. (Tables in English and Swedish)
1908. a. Kr.5. Sveriges Riksbank, Box 16283, S-103
25 Stockholm, Sweden.
　　Formerly (until 1979): Sveriges Riksbank.
Aarsbok (ISSN 0039-6702)

332　　　　　　SQ
SWAZILAND. CENTRAL STATISTICAL OFFICE.
CAPITAL FUND ESTIMATES. a. Central
Statistical Office, Box 456, Mbabane, Swaziland.

332.1　　　　SW　　ISSN 0082-0091
SWEDEN. RIKSGAELDSKONTORET. AARSBOK.
1920. a. Riksgaeldskontoret - National Debt Office,
Box 16306, 103 26 Stockholm, Sweden (Orders to:
Liber Foerlag, Fack, S-162 89 Vaellingby, Sweden)
Ed. Lars Kalderen. circ. 1,000.

BUSINESS AND ECONOMICS — BANKING AND FINANCE

332 SZ
SWISS BANK CORPORATION. REPORT OF THE BOARD OF DIRECTORS TO THE ANNUAL GENERAL MEETING OF SHAREHOLDERS. a. Schweizerischer Bankverein - Swiss Bank Corporation, 1 Aeschenvorstadt, CH-4002 Basel, Switzerland.

332.1 US
TEXAS BANKING RED BOOK. 1946. a. $12.50. Bankers Digest, Inc., 1908 Mercantile Commerce Bldg., Dallas, TX 75201. Ed. Bonnie Blackman. adv. circ. 15,000. (looseleaf format)

332 US
THORNDIKE ENCYCLOPEDIA OF BANKING AND FINANCIAL TABLES (SUPPLEMENT) annual supplements update base volume. $47.50 for base volume. Warren, Gorham and Lamont, Inc., 210 South St., Boston, MA 02111.

332 SZ
U B S PUBLICATIONS ON BUSINESS, BANKING AND MONETARY PROBLEMS. irreg., no. 53, 1978. Union de Banques Suisses - Union Bank of Switzerland, Bahnhofstrasse 45, 8000 Zurich, Switzerland.

332 MR
UNION BANCARIA HISPANO MARROQUI. ASSEMBLEE GENERALE ORDINAIRE DES ACTIONNAIRES. RAPPORT. a. Union Bancaria Hispano Marroqui, Assemblee Generale Ordinaire des Actionnaires, 69 rue du Prince Moulay Abdallah, Casablanca, Morocco.

332 FI ISSN 0355-0133
UNION BANK OF FINLAND. ANNUAL REPORT. 1952. a. Union Bank of Finland, P.B. 868, 00101 Helsinki 10, Finland.
Formerly: Pohjoismaiden Yhdyspankki. Report.

332 UK ISSN 0503-2628
UNIT TRUST YEARBOOK. 1964. a. £7.75. (Association of Unit Trust Managers) Fundex Ltd., Minster House, Arthur St., London EC4R 9AX, England. adv. circ. 3,500. (tabloid format)
Supersedes: Directory of Unit Trusts.

U. S. FEDERAL DEPOSIT INSURANCE CORPORATION. ANNUAL REPORT. see *INSURANCE*

332.1 US ISSN 0083-0674
U. S. FEDERAL DEPOSIT INSURANCE CORPORATION. CHANGES AMONG OPERATING BANKS AND BRANCHES. a. single copy free. U.S. Federal Deposit Insurance Corporation., 550 17th St., N.W., Washington, DC 20429.

332 US
U.S. FEDERAL DEPOSIT INSURANCE CORPORATION. OPERATING BANK OFFICES. a. U.S. Federal Deposit Insurance Corporation, 550 17th St. N.W., Washington, DC 20429.

332 US
U.S. FEDERAL DEPOSIT INSURANCE CORPORATION. TRUST. ASSETS OF INSURED COMMERCIAL BANKS. a. U.S. Federal Deposit Insurance Corporation, 550 17th St. N.W., Washington, DC 20429.

332.7 US ISSN 0083-0720
U. S. FEDERAL HOME LOAN BANK BOARD. REPORT. (Included in the April issue of the Federal Home Loan Bank Board Journal from 1971) 1947. a. free. U. S. Federal Home Loan Bank Board, Office of Communications, 1700 G St., N.W., Washington, DC 20552. circ. 10,600.

332.7 US ISSN 0083-0747
U. S. FEDERAL HOME LOAN BANK BOARD. TRENDS IN THE SAVINGS AND LOAN FIELD. a. U. S. Federal Home Loan Bank Board, Office of Communications, 1700 G St., N.W., Washington, DC 20552. Ed. Elizabeth Miller. circ. 600.

332.1 US ISSN 0083-0887
U. S. FEDERAL RESERVE SYSTEM. ANNUAL REPORT. 1914. a. free. U. S. Federal Reserve System, Board of Governors, 20th St. and Constitution Ave. N.W., Publications Services, Washington, DC 20551. circ. 10,000.

332.1 US
U.S. FEDERAL RESERVE SYSTEM. ANNUAL STATISTICAL DIGEST. a. approx. $10. U.S. Federal Reserve System, Board of Governors, Publications Services, Rm. MP-510, Washington, DC 20551.

334.2 US
U.S. NATIONAL CREDIT UNION ADMINISTRATION. ANNUAL REPORT. a. free. U.S. National Credit Union Administration, 1776 G. St., N.W., Washington, DC 20456.
Credit unions

334.2 US ISSN 0564-9498
U. S. NATIONAL CREDIT UNION ADMINISTRATION. RESEARCH REPORT. 1969. irreg., June 1976, no. 10. U. S. National Credit Union Administration, 1776 G. St., N.W., Washington, DC 20456. illus.
Credit unions

334.2 US
U.S. NATIONAL CREDIT UNION ADMINISTRATION. WORKING PAPERS. 1975. irreg. price varies. U.S. National Credit Union Administration, 1776 G. St., N.W., Washington, DC 20456.
Credit unions

332.4 US
U.S. TREASURY DEPARTMENT. BUREAU OF GOVERNMENT FINANCIAL OPERATIONS. ANNUAL REPORT OF THE SECRETARY OF THE TREASURY ON THE STATE OF THE FINANCES. a. U.S. Department of the Treasury, Bureau of Government Financial Operations, Pennsylvania Ave. & Madison Pl., N.W., Washington, DC 20226 (Orders to: Superintendent of Documents, Washington, DC 20402)

332.4 US
U. S. TREASURY DEPARTMENT. BUREAU OF GOVERNMENT FINANCIAL OPERATIONS. FEDERAL AID TO STATES. a. free. U.S. Department of the Treasury, Bureau of Government Financial Operations, Pennsylvania Ave. & Madison Pl., N.W., Washington, DC 20226.

332.4 US ISSN 0098-3896
U. S. TREASURY DEPARTMENT. BUREAU OF GOVERNMENT FINANCIAL OPERATIONS. REPORT ON FOREIGN CURRENCIES HELD BY THE U. S. GOVERNMENT. s-a (Aug. and Feb.) U. S. Department of the Treasury, Bureau of Government Financial Operations, Washington, DC 20226. stat. Key Title: Report on Foreign Currencies Held by the U. S. Government.
Formerly: U. S. Treasury Department. Bureau of Accounts. Report on Foreign Currencies in the Custody of the United States.

332.4 US
U.S. TREASURY DEPARTMENT. BUREAU OF THE MINT, ANNUAL REPORT OF THE DIRECTOR OF THE MINT. 1800? a. $5. U.S. Department of the Treasury, Bureau of the Mint, 15th & Pennsylvania Ave., N.W., Washington, DC 20220 (Orders to: Superintendent of Documents, Washington, DC 20402)

332.4 US
U.S. TREASURY DEPARTMENT. OFFICE OF REVENUE SHARING. ANNUAL REPORT. a. U.S. Department of the Treasury, Office of Revenue Sharing, 2401 E St., N.W., Washington, DC 20226.

332.3 US ISSN 0098-8944
UNITED STATES LEAGUE OF SAVINGS ASSOCIATIONS. ANNALS. a. $5. United States League of Savings Associations, 111 E. Wacker Dr., Chicago, IL 60601. Key Title: Savings Association Annals.

332 AU
UNIVERSITAET INNSBRUCK. FINANZWISSENSCHAFTLICHE STUDIEN. (Subseries of: Universitaet Innsbruck. Veroeffentlichungen) 1969. irreg. price varies. Oesterreichische Kommissionsbuchhandlung, Maximilianstr. 17, A-6020 Innsbruck, Austria. Ed. Clemens August Andreae.

332 US ISSN 0081-7570
UNIVERSITY OF TEXAS, AUSTIN. BUREAU OF BUSINESS RESEARCH. STUDIES IN BANKING AND FINANCE. 1958. irreg., no. 11, 1978. price varies. University of Texas at Austin, Bureau of Business Research, Austin, TX 78712.

332 US
UNIVERSITY OF TOLEDO. BUSINESS RESEARCH CENTER. STUDIES IN FINANCIAL INSTITUTIONS. 1971. irreg.,no. 12, 1977. price varies. University of Toledo, College of Business Administration, 2801 W. Bancroft St., Toledo, OH 43606. Dir. Thomas A. Klein.

332 FR
V.I.P. DE LA FINANCE ET DE LA BANQUE. 1978. biennial. 447 F. Societe d'Etudes et de Publications Industrielles, 15 Square de Vergennes, 75015 Paris, France. (Affiliate: France Expansion)

332 VE
VENEZUELA. MINISTERIO DE HACIENDA. MEMORIA. a. Ministerio de Hacienda, Edificio Norte, Caracas, Venezuela. Ed.Bd. stat.

332.1 US ISSN 0083-5730
VERMONT. COMMISSIONER OF BANKING AND INSURANCE. ANNUAL REPORT OF THE BANK COMMISSIONER. 1880. a. free. ‡ Department of Banking and Insurance, Division of Banking, 120 State St., Montpelier, VT 05602. circ. 700.

332 US
WADSWORTH SERIES IN FINANCE. irreg. Wadsworth Publishing Co., 10 Davis Dr., Belmont, CA 94002.

WALL STREET JOURNAL INDEX. see *BUSINESS AND ECONOMICS — Investments*

332.1 US ISSN 0272-5371
WESTERN BANK DIRECTORY. a. $14. Western Banker Publications, Inc., 58 Sutter St., San Francisco, CA 94104.

332.1 GW ISSN 0077-2119
WESTFAELISCHE WILHELMS-UNIVERSITAET MUENSTER. INSTITUT FUER KREDITWESEN. SCHRIFTENREIHE. irreg. price varies. Betriebswirtschaftlicher Verlag Dr. Th. Gabler KG, Taunusstr. 54, Postfach 1546, 6200 Wiesbaden 1, W. Germany (B.R.D.) Ed. L. Muelhaupt. circ. 500-600.

332 UI
WHO'S WHO IN BANKING IN EUROPE. irreg. 100 Fr. F. H. Books Ltd., Box 74, Guernsey, Channel Islands.

332 UK ISSN 0307-6032
WHO'S WHO IN FINANCE. irreg., vol. 2, 1975. £17.50($40.50) Teakfield Ltd., 1 Westmead, Farnborough, Hants. GU14 7RU, England.

WHO'S WHO IN FINANCE AND BANKING IN THAILAND. see *BIOGRAPHY*

332 UK
WORKING ABROAD. 1977. irreg. £6.50. Money Management, Minster House, Arthur St., London EC4R 9AX, England.

332.1 UK
WORLD BANKING. a. $15. Investors Chronicle Publication, 30 Finsbury Square, London EC2A 1PJ, England. illus.

332 US
WORLD COUNCIL OF CREDIT UNIONS. INTERNATIONAL ANNUAL REPORT. a. World Council of Credit Unions, 5910 Mineral Pt. Rd., Box 391, Madison, WI 53701. charts. illus. stat. circ. 25,000.
Formerly: World Council of Credit Unions. Yearbook.

332.4 US ISSN 0090-2810
WORLD CURRENCY CHARTS. 1963. irreg., latest, 8th edt. price varies. ‡ American International Investment Corporation, 351 California St., San Francisco, CA 94104. charts. circ. 2,000.

BUSINESS AND ECONOMICS — CHAMBER OF COMMERCE PUBLICATIONS

332.1　　　　　　　TU
YAPI VE KREDI BANKASI. ANNUAL REPORT.
(Text in English) a. Yapi ve Kredi Bankasi, Istiklal
Caddesi, Korsan Cikmazi 1, Box 250, Beyoglu,
Istanbul, Turkey.

332.4　　　　　　　FR
LA ZONE FRANC. 1957. a. 35 F. Comite Monetaire
de la Zone Franc, Banque de France. Service de
l'Information, 43 rue de Valois, 75049 Paris, France.
　　Continues: France. Comite Monetaire de la Zone
Franc. Rapport.

332.1　　　　　　　SZ
100 EUROPEAN BANKS; a comparative analysis of
100 leading European banks. 1974. a. (St. Gall
Institute of Banking Studies) Paul Haupt AG,
Falkenplatz 14, CH-3001 Berne, Switzerland.

BUSINESS AND ECONOMICS —
Chamber Of Commerce Publications

330　　　　　　FR　　ISSN 0065-1788
ACTIVITE ECONOMIQUE DE LA HAUTE-
NORMANDIE. 1970. a. 35 F. Chambre Regionale
de Commerce et d'Industrie de Haute-Normandie,
Palais des Consuls, Quai de la Bourse, Rouen,
France. adv. circ. 1,000.

338　　　　　　US　　ISSN 0145-4048
ALABAMA DIRECTORY OF MINING AND
MANUFACTURING. a. $20. Development Office,
c/o State Capitol, Montgomery, AL 36130. Ed.
Richard W. McLaney. adv. index. circ. 5,000.
　　Supersedes (as of 1976): Industrial Alabama
(ISSN 0073-7321)

382　　　　　　MR　　ISSN 0065-7689
AMCHAM MOROCCO. Cover title: American
Chamber of Commerce in Morocco. Annual
Review. (Text in English and French) 1966. a. free.
American Chamber of Commerce in Morocco, 53
rue Allal Ben Abdallah, Casablanca, Morocco. adv.

382　　　　　　BL　　ISSN 0065-7662
AMERICAN CHAMBER OF COMMERCE FOR
BRAZIL. ANNUAL DIRECTORY. 1917. a.
membership. American Chamber of Commerce for
Brazil, Praca Pio X no. 15, Caixa Postal 916-ZC-00,
20.000 Rio de Janeiro, Brazil. circ. 1,500.

382　　　　　　FR　　ISSN 0065-7670
AMERICAN CHAMBER OF COMMERCE IN
FRANCE. DIRECTORY. 1948. a. 180 F.($37)
American Chamber of Commerce in France, 21 Av.
George V, 75008 Paris, France. Ed. Jacqueline R.
Gauthey. adv. circ. 1,800.

382　　　　　　IT　　ISSN 0569-3667
AMERICAN CHAMBER OF COMMERCE IN
ITALY. DIRECTORY. 1964. a. L.25000($40)
American Chamber of Commerce in Italy, Via
Agnello 12, 20121 Milan, Italy. Ed. Gabriella
Gabet. adv. circ. 4,500.

382　　　　　　TH
AMERICAN CHAMBER OF COMMERCE IN
THAILAND. HANDBOOK DIRECTORY.
biennial. $5. American Chamber of Commerce in
Thailand, 140 Wireless Rd., Bangkok, Thailand.

338　　　　　　US
AMERICAN SUBSIDIARIES OF GERMAN
FIRMS. 1968. a. $40 to non-members; members
$20. German American Chamber of Commerce, 666
Fifth Ave., New York, NY 10019. circ. 1,200.

381　　　　　　FR　　ISSN 0066-2798
ANNUAIRE DES CHAMBRES DE COMMERCE
ET D'INDUSTRIE. 1963. a. (approx.) 20 F. ‡
Assemblee Permanente des Chambres de Commerce
et d'Industrie, 45, Ave. d'Iena, 75116 Paris, France.
adv.

330　　　　　　ML　　ISSN 0080-0988
ANNUAIRE DES ENTREPRISES DU MALI. Title
varies: Repertoire des Entreprises Financieres,
Commerciales Industrielles Exercant en Republique
du Mali. 1964. irreg. 150 FM. ‡ Chambre de
Commerce et d'Industrie du Mali, B.P. 46, Bamako,
Mali. circ. 150.

382　　　　　　IT　　ISSN 0069-6625
ANNUAIRE DU COMMERCE FRANCO-
ITALIEN. 1968/69. a. L.9000. Chambre de
Commerce Francaise et d'Industrie en Italie, Via
Meravigli, 12, I-20123-Milan, Italy.
　　Formerly: Commerce Franco-Italien; Annuaire de
Societes.

382　　　　　　FR　　ISSN 0066-3115
ANNUAIRE FRANCO-ITALIEN. 1963/64. biennial.
150 F. Chambre de Commerce Italienne de Paris,
134 rue du Faubourg Saint-Honore, Paris 8e,
France. adv. circ. 2,000.

382　　　　　　FR　　ISSN 0066-3123
ANNUAIRE FRANCO-SUISSE. 1951/52. biennial.
Chambre de Commerce Suisse en France, 16 Av. de
l'Opera, 75001 Paris, France.

650　　　　　　FR　　ISSN 0066-3743
ANNUAIRES FRANCAIS ET LISTES
D'ADRESSES SUSCEPTIBLES D'INTERESSER
LE COMMERCE ET L'INDUSTRIE. 1974, 3rd
ed. irreg. 60 F. Chambre de Commerce et
d'Industrie de Paris, 27 Av. de Friedland, 75008
Paris, France.

382　　　　　　US
ASIAN AMERICAN TRADE DIRECTORY. 1964.
irreg. $15. (Association of Asian-American
Chambers of Commerce) Kayward Publications
(Subsidiary of: International Press Service) Box
1933, Washington, DC 20013. Ed. Dr. Edward de
R - Panthen. adv. bk. rev. film rev. illus. pat. stat.
tr.lit. index. circ. 10,000.

330　　　　　　ZR
ASSOCIATION NATIONALE DES ENTREPRISES
ZAIROISES. CIRCULAIRE D'INFORMATION.
1932. irreg. Association Nationale des Entreprises
Zairoises, B. P. 7247, Kinshasa, Zaire.
　　Formerly: Federation Nationale des Chambres de
Commerce, d'Industrie et d'Agriculture de la
Republique du Zaire. Circulaire d'Information (ISSN
0085-0497)

381　　　　　　AT　　ISSN 0310-3811
AUSTRALIA. CHAMBER OF INDUSTRIES,
NORTHERN TERRITORY. NORTHERN
TERRITORY BUSINESS JOURNAL. 1972. irreg.
Aus.$20. Chamber of Industries, Northern Territory,
Director, P.O. Box 1409, Darwin, NT 5794,
Australia.

338　　　　　　UK
AVAILABLE FROM WALES. a. $45. (Federation of
Welsh Chambers of Commerce) Kemps Group
(Printers & Publishers) Ltd., 1-5 Bath St., London
EC1V 9QA, England.

380　　　　　　AG
BOLSA. (Supplements avail.) vol.56,1960. irreg. $3 per
no. Bolsa de Comercio de Buenos Aires, Sarmiento
299, Buenos Aires, Argentina. adv. illus. mkt. stat.
　　Formerly: Bolsa de Comercio de Buenos Aires.
Boletin (ISSN 0006-6923)

380　　　　　　AG　　ISSN 0006-6931
BOLSA DE COMERCIO DE ROSARIO. REVISTA.
1913. a. free. Bolsa de Comercio de Rosario,
Rosario, Santa Fe, Argentina. adv. mkt. stat.

382　　　　　　FR　　ISSN 0068-1415
BRITISH CHAMBER OF COMMERCE IN
FRANCE. YEAR BOOK. 1939. a. British Chamber
of Commerce, 6 rue Halevy, 75009 Paris, France.

960　　　　　　SA
C C I YEAR BOOK & DIRECTORY. a. R.1.50. Cape
Chamber of Industries, Broadway Industries Centre,
Heerengracht, Box 1536, Cape Town 8000, South
Africa. Ed. J. F. Roos. adv.

381　　　　　　VE　　ISSN 0008-1876
CAMARA DE COMERCIO DE LA GUAIRA.
BOLETIN ESTADISTICO. 1946. a. free. Camara
de Comercio de la Guaira, Frente a la Plaza el
Consul, Edificio "Camera de Comercio", Maiquetia,
Apartado 150 la Guaira Departamento Vargas,
Venezuela. adv. charts. illus. stat.

382　　　　　　VE
CAMARA VENEZOLANO BRITANICA DE
COMERCIO E INDUSTRIA. ANUARIO. (Text in
English and Spanish) 1972. a. Bs.35. ‡ Camara
Venezolano Britanica de Comercio e Industria,
Edificio Blandin, Chacaito, Apdo. 5713, Caracas
101, Venezuela. Dir. Charles R. Neville. adv. circ.
2,000.
　　Formerly: Asociacion Venezolano Britanica de
Comercio e Industria. Anuario (ISSN 0084-6848)

381　　　　　　IT
CAMERA DI COMMERCIO INDUSTRIA
ARTIGIANATO E AGRICOLTURA DI
MILANO. SCAMBI COMMERCIALI CON
L'ESTERO. a (in 2 vols.) L.10000 (per vol.)
Camera di Commercio Industria Artigianato e
Agricoltura di Milano, Via Meravigli, 20123 Milan,
Italy.

381　　　　　　IT
CAMERA DI COMMERCIO, INDUSTRIA,
ARTIGIANATO E AGRICOLTURA DI
PADOVA. NOTIZIARIO ESTERO. irreg. free.
Camera di Commercio, Industria, Artigianato e
Agricoltura di Padova, Via E. Filiberto 34, Padua,
Italy.

382　　　　　　UK　　ISSN 0309-0329
CANADA-U.K. YEAR BOOK. a. £2.50. Canada-
United Kingdom Chamber of Commerce, British
Columbia House, 1-3 Lower Regent St., London
SW1Y 4NZ, England.

382　　　　　　SP　　ISSN 0069-1178
CATALUNA EXPORTA. 1964. a. 1000 ptas. Camara
Oficial de Comercio, Industria y Navegacion de
Barcelona, General Primo de Rivera, 11-13,
Barcelona 2, Spain. circ. 1,000.

381　　　　　　CE
CEYLON CHAMBER OF COMMERCE. ANNUAL
REVIEW OF BUSINESS AND TRADE. (Text in
English) 1839. a. $15. Ceylon Chamber of
Commerce, Box 274, 127, Lower Chatham St.,
Colombo 1, Sri Lanka. Ed.Bd. charts. stat.

380.1　　　　　　IO
CHAMBER OF COMMERCE AND INDUSTRY IN
WEST JAVA. MEMBER LIST/KAMAR
DAGANG DAN INDUSTRI DI JAWA BARAT.
DAFTAR ANGGOTA. (Text in English and
Indonesia) a. Chamber of Commerce and Industry
in West Java, Jl. Sunaiaraja 3, Bandung, West Java,
Indonesia.

381　　　　　　SL　　ISSN 0080-9527
CHAMBER OF COMMERCE OF SIERRA LEONE.
JOURNAL. (Text in English) 1965. a. Le.1.50.
Chamber of Commerce of Sierra Leone, P.O. Box
502, Freetown, Sierra Leone. Ed. (Mrs.) F.
Iscandari. adv. circ. 1,000.

380.1　　　　　　PH
CHAMBER OF COMMERCE OF THE
PHILLIPPINES. TRADE DIRECTORY. a.
Chamber of Commerce of the Philippines,
Magallanes Drive, Manila 2801, Philippines. illus.

380.1　　　　　　CM
CHAMBRE DE COMMERCE, D'INDUSTRIE ET
DES MINES DU CAMEROUN. COMPTE-
RENDU D'ACTIVITES. irreg. Chambre de
Commerce, d'Industrie et des Mines du Cameroun,
B.P. 4011, Douala, Cameroon.

381 330　　　　　ML　　ISSN 0067-3110
CHAMBRE DE COMMERCE ET D'INDUSTRIE
DU MALI. PRECIS FISCAL, COMMERCIAL,
DES CHANGES ET DES ECHANGES. 1964. a.
price varies. ‡ Chambre de Commerce et d'Industrie
du Mali, B.P. 46, Bamako, Mali. circ. 200.

382　　　　　　FR　　ISSN 0069-2557
CHAMBRE DE COMMERCE FRANCO-
ASIATIQUE. ANNUAIRE DES MEMBRES.
(Special number of: Asie Nouvelle) 1968. a.
Chambre de Commerce Franco-Asiatique, 94 rue St.
Lazare, 75009 Paris, France.

382　　　　　　FR　　ISSN 0069-2573
CHAMBRE DE COMMERCE SUEDOISE EN
FRANCE. ANNUAIRE. 1931/32. a. 55 F.
Chambre de Commerce Suedoise en France, 106
rue la Fayette, Paris 8e, France.

BUSINESS AND ECONOMICS — CHAMBER OF COMMERCE PUBLICATIONS

382 FR ISSN 0069-2581
CHAMBRE OFFICIELLE FRANCO ALLEMANDE DE COMMERCE ET D'INDUSTRIE. LISTE DES MEMBRES/OFFIZIELLE DEUTSCH-FRANZOESISCHE INDUSTRIE- UND HANDELSKAMMER. MITGLIDERLISTE. 1966. a. 60 Fr. Chambre Officielle Franco Allemande de Commerce et d'Industrie, 18 rue Balard, 75015 Paris, France.

381 FR
CHAMBRE REGIONALE DE COMMERCE ET D'INDUSTRIE D'ALSACE. RAPPORT SUR LES ACTIVITES. a. Chambre Regionale de Commerce et d'Industrie d'Alsace, 10, Place Gutenberg, 67081 Strasbourg, France.

382 FR
COMMERCE EXTERIEUR DES REGIONS PROVENCE, COTE D'AZUR ET CORSE. 1968. a. 10 F. per no. Chambre de Commerce et d'Industrie de Marseille, Palais de la Bourse, 13231 Marseille Cedex 1, France. illus. circ. 2,000.

380 NR ISSN 0069-6633
COMMERCE IN NIGERIA. 1950. a. Lagos Chamber of Commerce and Industry, Lagos, Nigeria.

381 CK
CONFEDERACION COLOMBIANA DE CAMARAS DE COMERCIO. ASAMBLEA GENERAL. INFORME FINAL. irreg. Confederacion Colombiana de Camaras de Comercio, Carrera 9a No.16-21, Bogota, Colombia.

338 UK ISSN 0140-8186
COVENTRY CHAMBER OF COMMERCE & INDUSTRY DIRECTORY. a. Kemp's Group (Printers & Publishers) Ltd., 1-5 Bath St., London EC1V 9QA, England. adv.

338 UK
CROYDON CHAMBER OF COMMERCE AND INDUSTRY DIRECTORY. a. Kemp's Group (Printers & Publishers) Ltd., 1-5 Bath St., London EC1V 9QA, England.

381 CE
DIRECTORY OF EXPORTERS. (Text in English) 1975. a. $9. Ceylon Chamber of Commerce, Export Section, Chamber of Commerce Bldg., Box 274, Colombo 1, Sri Lanka. adv.

338 US ISSN 0190-3047
DIRECTORY OF MANUFACTURERS, STATE OF HAWAII. 1969. biennial. $17. ‡ Chamber of Commerce of Hawaii, Dillingham Building, 735 Bishop St., Honolulu, HI 96813. Ed. Tatsuko Honjo. index.

330 US
DIRECTORY OF WESTERN NEW YORK BUSINESS AND CIVIC ORGANIZATIONS. a. $12. Buffalo Area Chamber of Commerce, 107 Delaware Ave., Buffalo, NY 14202.

381 UK
DUNDEE AND TAYSIDE CHAMBER OF COMMERCE AND INDUSTRY. BUYER'S GUIDE & TRADE DIRECTORY. 1958. a. £3. Dundee and Tayside Chamber of Commerce and Industry, Panmure St., Dundee DD1 1ED, Scotland. Ed. W.D. Shaw. adv. circ. controlled.
Formerly: Dundee Chamber of Commerce. Buyer's Gudie & Trade Directory.

330.9 SP
ECONOMIA ALAVESA. a. 300 ptas. Camara Oficial de Comercio e Industria de Alava, General Alava 22, Vitoria, Spain.

330 IT
ECONOMIA DE PUGLIA. 1971. irreg. (Unione Regionale della Camera di Commercio, Industria, Artigianato ed Agricoltura della Puglia, Centro Studi e Ricerche Economico-Sociali) Adriatica Editrice, Bari, Italy.

330 ML ISSN 0071-0008
ELEMENTS DU BILAN ECONOMIQUE. 1961. irreg., latest issue, 1965. ‡ Chambre de Commerce et d'Industrie du Mali, B.P. 46, Bamako, Mali. circ. 200.

338 915.4 CE
ENTERPRISE NEWSLETTER. (Text in English) 1974. irreg. Ceylon Chamber of Commerce, Chamber of Commerce Bldg., Box 274, Colombo 1, Sri Lanka. adv. illus.
Formerly: Enterprise Magazine.

960 IV
L'ENTREPRISE IVOIRIENNE. a. Chambre d'Industrie de Cote d'Ivoire, B.P. 1758, Abidjan, Ivory Coast.

963 ET
ETHIOPIAN CHAMBER OF COMMERCE. STATISTICAL DIGEST. 1967. a. $2.45. Ethiopian Chamber of Commerce, Box 517, Addis Ababa, Ethiopia. (reprint service avail. from ISI)

381 PK ISSN 0071-4429
FEDERATION OF PAKISTAN CHAMBERS OF COMMERCE INDUSTRY. BRIEF REPORT OF ACTIVITIES. (Text in English) a. Rs.100. Federation of Pakistan Chambers of Commerce and Industry, St-28, Block 5, Scheme-V, Share-Firdousi Kehkashan, Clifton, Karachi, Pakistan.

382 UK ISSN 0071-917X
FRANCO BRITISH TRADE DIRECTORY.* 1883. a. £15. French Chamber of Commerce in Great Britain, 54 Conduit St., London W.1., England.

382 UA ISSN 0072-1433
GERMAN ARAB TRADE. irreg. membership. Deutsch-Arabische Handelskammer - German-Arab Chamber of Commerce, 2 Sheif Str., Cairo, Egypt.

382 TH
GERMAN-THAI CHAMBER OF COMMERCE HANDBOOK. a. $6. German-Thai Chamber of Commerce, 699 Silom Rd., Kongboonma Bldg., Bangkok, Thailand. Ed. Wayne Morrison.

380 UK
GLASGOW CHAMBER OF COMMERCE. REGIONAL DIRECTORY. a. £15. Glasgow Chamber of Commerce, 30 George Square, Glasgow G2 1EQ, Scotland. adv. index. circ. 5,000.
Formerly: Glasgow Chamber of Commerce. Industrial Index to Glasgow & West of Scotland.

381 US ISSN 0035-5100
GREATER RICHMOND CHAMBER OF COMMERCE. RESEARCH BULLETIN. irreg. free. Richmond Chamber of Commerce, 201 E. Franklin St., Richmond, VA 23219. charts. stat. (processed)
Formerly: Richmond Chamber of Commerce. Research Bulletin.

380 SP
GUIA DEL COMERCIO Y DE LA INDUSTRIA DE MADRID. 1960. biennial. $31. Camara Oficial de Comercio e Industria de Madrid., Huertas, 13, Madrid-12, Spain. adv. circ. 2,000.
Continues: Catalogo de la Industria de Madrid (ISSN 0528-2438)

382 FR ISSN 0072-7962
GUIDE ANNUAIRE DU COMMERCE FRANCO-ALLEMAND/JAHRBUCH FUER DEN DEUTSCH-FRANZOESISCHEN HANDEL.* (Text in French and German) 1961/62. irreg., 1965, 2nd ed. Chambre Officielle Franco Allemande de Commerce et d'Industrie, 18 rue Balard, 75015 Paris, France.

381 US
HERE IS YOUR INDIANA GOVERNMENT. 1944. biennial. $2. Indiana State Chamber of Commerce, Board of Trade Building, Indianapolis, IN 64204. Ed. Carl Henn. circ. 40,000.

380.1 HK
HONG KONG JUNIOR CHAMBER. ANNUAL REVIEW.* a. Hong Kong Junior Chamber, 23. Ice House St., Hong Kong, Hong Kong. illus.

338 380 GW
INDUSTRIE- UND HANDELSKAMMER HANNOVER-HILDESHEIM. INFORMATION - KOMMENTAIRE. 1949. a. free. Industrie- und Handelskammer Hannover-Hildesheim, Berliner Allee 25, 3000 Hannover, W. Germany (B.R.D.) Eds. Dr. H.G. Hess, W. Krause. stat. tr.lit. index. circ. 13,000.

380.1 FR
INTERNATIONAL CHAMBER OF COMMERCE. HANDBOOK. irreg. International Chamber of Commerce, 38 Cours Albert 1, 75008 Paris, France.

381 IR
INTERNATIONAL CHAMBER OF COMMERCE. IRANIAN COMMITTEE. PUBLICATION/KOMITE-YE IRANI-YE OTAQ-E BAZARGANI-YE BEYNOLMELALI. NASHRIYEH. (Text in Persian, English & French) 1962. irreg. free. International Chamber of Commerce, Iranian Committee, 254 Takht-e Jamshid Ave., Teheran, Iran. Ed. Mansur Sadri.

380 US ISSN 0538-5466
INTERNATIONAL CHAMBER OF COMMERCE. UNITED STATES COUNCIL. REPORT. irreg. International Chamber of Commerce, United States Council, 1212 Ave. of the Americas, New York, NY 10036.

382 IR
IRAN CHAMBER OF COMMERCE, INDUSTRIES AND MINES. DIRECTORY. biennial. Iran Chamber of Commerce, Industries and Mines, 254 Takht Jamshid Ave., Teheran, Iran.

338 PK ISSN 0075-5079
KARACHI. CHAMBER OF COMMERCE AND INDUSTRY. REPORT. (Text in English) a. free. Chamber of Commerce and Industry, Aiwan-e-Tijarat, Box 4158, Nicol Rd., Karachi 2, Pakistan.

380.1 KE
KENYA NATIONAL CHAMBER OF COMMERCE AND INDUSTRY. ANNUAL REPORT. a. Kenya National Chamber of Commerce and Industry, Nairobi, Kenya. stat.

382 FR
LIST OF AMERICAN FIRMS IN FRANCE. (Text in English) 1967. a. 190 F.($40) for non-members. American Chamber of Commerce in France, 21 Av. George V, 75008 Paris, France. Ed. Jacqueline R. Gauthey. circ. 1,000.

381 UK
LONDON CHAMBER OF COMMERCE & INDUSTRY. DIRECTORY. 1882. a. £15. London Chamber of Commerce and Industry, 69 Cannon St., London EC4N 5AB, England. adv. circ. 9,000.
Formerly: London Chamber of Commerce & Industry. Annual Report & Annual Directory (ISSN 0076-0528)

381 UK
MANCHESTER CHAMBER OF COMMERCE AND INDUSTRY. REGIONAL DIRECTORY. (Text in English,French and German) a. $45. (Manchester Chamber of Commerce and Industry) Kemp's Group (Printers & Publishers) Ltd., 1-5 Bath St., London EC1V 9QA, England. adv. illus. tr.lit.

380.1 UK ISSN 0306-5758
MANCHESTER CHAMBER OF COMMERCE AND INDUSTRY. YEARBOOK. (Text in: English, French, and German) a. Manchester Chamber of Commerce and Industry, Ship Canal House, King St., Manchester M6O 2HB, England. illus.

380.1 UK ISSN 0302-4148
MERSEYSIDE CHAMBER OF COMMERCE AND INDUSTRY. DIRECTORY. a. Industrial Newspapers Ltd., Queensway House, Queensway, Redhill, Surrey RH1 1QS, England.

382 NE
NETHERLANDS-AMERICAN TRADE DIRECTORY. (Text in English) vol. 3, 1976. a. fl.40($16) to members; non-members fl. 75 ($40) American Chamber of Commerce in the Netherlands, Carnegieplein 5, The Hague, Netherlands.

BUSINESS AND ECONOMICS — COOPERATIVES

382   UK   ISSN 0308-1273
NETHERLANDS-BRITISH TRADE DIRECTORY. 1961. a. £15 to non-members. Netherlands-British Chamber of Commerce, The Dutch House, 307/308 High Holborn, London WC1V 7LS, England. Ed. Jim H. Van de Worp. adv. circ. 2,500.

338   UK
NORTH WEST ENGLAND INDUSTRIAL CLASSIFIED DIRECTORY. irreg. £9. (North West Industrial Development Association) Kemps Publications Ltd., Federation House, 2309 Coventry Rd., Sheldon, Birmingham B26 3PG, England. adv. illus. tr.lit.

382   UK   ISSN 0305-0998
NORWEGIAN CHAMBER OF COMMERCE. YEAR BOOK AND DIRECTORY OF MEMBERS. (Text in English) 1908. a. free to members. ‡ Norwegian Chamber of Commerce (London) Inc., 21-24 Cockspur St., London S.W.1, England. Ed. Anders D. Hald. adv. circ. 1,800.

330   GW
OSTSEEJAHRBUCH. 1934. a. price varies. Industrie- und Handelskammer zu Luebeck, Breite Strasse 6-8, 2400 Luebeck, W. Germany (B.R.D.) Ed. Hans-Jochen Arndt. circ. 1,200.
Former title: Wirtschaft im Ostseeraum (ISSN 0084-0483)

338   PK
PAKISTAN DIRECTORY OF TRADE AND INDUSTRY. (Text in English) 1976. a. Rs.25. Lahore Chamber of Commerce and Industry, Box 597, 11 Race Course Rd., Lahore, Pakistan.

381   US   ISSN 0098-5368
PENNSYLVANIA CHAMBER OF COMMERCE. DIRECTORY OF STATE, REGIONAL AND COMMERCIAL ORGANIZATIONS. a. $7. Pennsylvania Chamber of Commerce, 222 N. Third St., Harrisburg, PA 17101. Ed. Alice M. Hoffer. circ. 650. Key Title: Directory of State, Regional and Commercial Organizations.

330.9   SP
PROVINCIA DE ZARAGOZA. INFORME ECONOMICO. a. price varies. Camara Oficial de Comercio e Industria de Zaragoza, D. Jaime I No. 18, Zaragoza 1, Spain. circ. 1,000.
Formerly(until 1976): Desarrollo Industrial y Mercantil en la Provincia de Zaragoza.

381   CN
REPERTOIRE DES ASSOCIATIONS. 1963. a. Can.$10. Chambre de Commerce du District de Montreal, 1080 Cote du Beaver Hall, Montreal, Que. H2Z 1T1, Canada. Ed. Marie-Paule Durocher. adv. stat. tr.lit. circ. 5,500.

381 330   ML   ISSN 0080-1011
REPERTOIRE DES PRINCIPAUX TEXTES LEGISLATIFS ET REGLEMENTAIRES PROMULGUES EN REPUBLIQUE DU MALI. 1959. a. ‡ Chambre de Commerce et d'Industrie du Mali, B.P. 46, Bamako, Mali. circ. 100.

338.9   FR   ISSN 0080-2506
REVUE FRANCAISE DE COOPERATION ECONOMIQUE AVEC ISRAEL. 1969. bi-m. 10 F. per issue. Chambre de Commerce France-Israel, 47 Faubourg Saint-Honore, 75008 Paris, France. Dir. W. Mimouni. adv. bk. rev. circ. 5,000.
Before 1969: Revue Economique France-Israel.

650   US   ISSN 0080-5882
SAN DIEGO BUSINESS SURVEY. a. $1.25 to non-members. San Diego Chamber of Commerce, 110 West C St., Suite 6199, San Diego, CA 92101.

382   BL
SAO PAULO YEARBOOK. 1946. a. membership. American Chamber of Commerce for Brazil, Sao Paulo Branch, Rua Formosa 367, 01049 Sao Paulo SP, Brazil. circ. 3,000.

338.9   UK
SCOTLINK. 1959. a. free. Junior Chamber Scotland, 34 Hunter St., Kirkaldy, Fife KY1 1ED, Scotland. (Affiliate: Jaycees International) adv. circ. 2,000.
Formerly: Scotland Tomorrow (ISSN 0080-7923)

330   BE   ISSN 0080-8792
SEMINAIRE BELGE DE PERFECTIONNEMENT AUX AFFAIRES. EXPOSES.* a. price varies. Chambre de Commerce de Bruxelles, Rue de Treves 112, 1040 Brussels, Belgium.

382   SI
SINGAPORE INTERNATIONAL CHAMBER OF COMMERCE. INVESTOR'S GUIDE. a. Singapore International Chamber of Commerce, Denmark House, Singapore 0104, Singapore. charts. stat.

382   SI   ISSN 0583-3736
SINGAPORE INTERNATIONAL CHAMBER OF COMMERCE. REPORT. 1837. a. S.$20 per no. ‡ Singapore International Chamber of Commerce, Denmark House, Singapore 0104, Singapore. Ed. Roderick Maclean. stat. circ. 1,000.

338   UK
SOUTHAMPTON CHAMBER OF COMMERCE REGIONAL DIRECTORY. a. $45. Kemp's Group (Printers & Publishers) Ltd., 1-5 Bath St., London EC1V 9QA, England.

381   CE
SRI LANKA IN BRIEF. (Text in English) 1977. a. Ceylon Chamber of Commerce, Chamber of Commerce Bldg., Box 274, Colombo 1, Sri Lanka.

650 380   JA   ISSN 0585-0444
STANDARD TRADE INDEX OF JAPAN. Title varies: Japan Register of Merchants, Manufacturers and Shippers. (Text in English) 1950. a. $64. Japan Chamber of Commerce and Industry, Room 505, World Trade Center Bldg., 2-4-1 Hamamatsu-cho, Minato-ku, Tokyo 105, Japan.

382.5   II   ISSN 0537-1120
SURVEY OF INDIA'S EXPORTS. (Text in English) a. Rs.20. Indian Chamber of Commerce, Calcutta, World Trade Department, India Exchange Place, Calcutta 700001, India.

380   US   ISSN 0069-2441
SURVEY OF LOCAL CHAMBERS OF COMMERCE. biennial. $15. Chamber of Commerce of the U. S., 1615 H St., N.W., Washington, DC 20062.

380.1   SW
TRADE DIRECTORY OF WESTERN SWEDEN. 1953. irreg., latest 1976 (next 1980) free. Gothenburg Chamber of Commerce, Storgatan 26, S-411 38 Goeteborg, Sweden. circ. 5,000.

382   US   ISSN 0502-5842
UNITED STATES-ITALY TRADE DIRECTORY. 12th edt. 1977. biennial. $30. Italy-America Chamber of Commerce, Inc., 350 Fifth Ave., New York, NY 10001. adv. circ. 4,000.

380.14   AT   ISSN 0311-127X
V. C. M. FILE. 1973. w. Aus.$10 membership. Victorian Chamber of Manufacturers, Industry House, 370 St. Kilda Rd., Melbourne, Vic. 3004, Australia. Ed. H. Leek. adv.

382   VE
VENEZUELAN-AMERICAN CHAMBER OF COMMERCE AND INDUSTRY. YEARBOOK AND MEMBERSHIP DIRECTORY. 1961. a. Bs.100($25) Venezuelan-American Chamber of Commerce and Industry, Apartado 5181, Caracas 1010, Venezuela. Ed. Dr. Frank J. Amador. adv. circ. 2,000. (reprint service avail. from UMI)
Formerly: American Chamber of Commerce of Venezuela. Yearbook and Membership Directory (ISSN 0065-7697)

650   US   ISSN 0083-839X
WEST VIRGINIA BUSINESS INDEX. ANNUAL REVIEW NUMBER. 1940. a. $50. West Virginia Chamber of Commerce, 1101 Kanawha Valley Bldg., Charleston, WV 25301 (Orders to Box 2787, Charleston, WV 25330) Ed. Margaret A. Poling.
Before 1970: West Virginia Business Index.

382   US
WHO'S WHO IN THE MOBILE AREA. a. $20 to non-members. ‡ Mobile Area Chamber of Commerce, Box 2187, Mobile, AL 36601. Ed. Roy E. Hannah. circ. 2,000.

381   AT
WHO'S WHO IN U.S. BUSINESS IN AUSTRALIA. 1974. a. Aus.$30. American Chamber of Commerce in Australia, 50 Pitt St., Third Floor, Sydney, N.S.W. 2000, Australia. Ed. K. Bannon. circ. 2,000.

380   US   ISSN 0084-2478
WORLD WIDE CHAMBER OF COMMERCE DIRECTORY. 1967. a. $12.50. Johnson Publishing Co. (Loveland), P.O. Box 455, Loveland, CO 80537. circ. 7,500.

BUSINESS AND ECONOMICS —
Cooperatives

334   US   ISSN 0065-793X
AMERICAN COOPERATION YEARBOOK. 1925. a. $9.50. ‡ American Institute of Cooperation, 1800 Massachusetts Ave., Washington, DC 20036. Ed. Beryle Stanton. index. circ. 5,000.

334   FR   ISSN 0071-4356
ANNUAIRE DE LA COOPERATION F.N.C.C. 1914. biennial. 55 F. ‡ (Federation Nationale des Cooperatives de Consommation) Societe Cooperative d'Edition et de Librairie, 27-33 Quai Le Gallo, 92100 Boulogne sur Seine, France. circ. 1,000.

334   BS
BOTSWANA. MINISTRY OF AGRICULTURE. DIVISION OF CO-OPERATIVE DEVELOPMENT. ANNUAL REPORT. a. Ministry of Agriculture, Division of Co-Operative Development, Gaborone, Botswana. illus. stat.

334   FR
CAISSE CENTRALE DE COOPERATION ECONOMIQUE. RAPPORT ANNUEL. a. Caisse Centrale de Cooperation Economique, 233 Bd. St. Germain, 75007 Paris, France. illus.
Formerly: Caisse Centrale de Cooperation Economique. Rapport d'Activite (ISSN 0575-1632)

334   UK
CO-OPERATIVE STATISTICS. 1879. a. £4. Co-Operative Union Ltd., Holyoake House, Hanover St., Manchester, England. circ. 1,000.

334   II   ISSN 0069-9837
COOPERATIVE TRADE DIRECTORY FOR SOUTHEAST ASIA. (Text in English) 1964. irreg., 1970, 3rd ed. supplement. Rs.20($3) per set. International Co-Operative Alliance, Regional Office and Education Centre for South-East Asia, Box 3312, 43 Friends Colony, New Delhi 110014, India. Ed. M. V. Madane. circ. 300.

334   US
COOPERATIVES & THE LAW; annual proceedings. 1974. a. $3. University of Wisconsin-Extension, University Center for Cooperatives, Lowell Hall, 610 Langdon St., Madison, WI 53706. Ed. R. Wayne Robinson. circ. 200.

CREDIT UNION DIRECTORY AND BUYERS' GUIDE. see *BUSINESS AND ECONOMICS — Banking And Finance*

CREDIT UNION YEARBOOK. see *BUSINESS AND ECONOMICS — Banking And Finance*

334   CS
CZECHOSLOVAK COOPERATIVE MOVEMENT IN FIGURES. irreg. free. Ustredni Rada Druzstev, Tesnov 5, 110 06 Prague 1, Czechoslovakia. charts. stat.

334   CK
DIRECTORIO NACIONAL DE ENTIDADES COOPERATIVOS. irreg. Departamento Administrativo Nacional de Estadistica, Division de Edicion, Avda. Eldovado, Bogota, Colombia.

334 658.8   SZ   ISSN 0071-4410
FEDERATION OF MIGROS COOPERATIVES. ABRIDGED REPORT; summary of the report of the Board of Directors to the Assembly of Delegates. Variant title: Federation of Migros Cooperatives. Annual Report. (Editions in English, French, and German) 1941 French and German eds., 1956 English ed. a. free. ‡ Federation of Migros Cooperatives, Limmatstrasse 152, Box 266, CH-8031 Zurich, Switzerland. circ. 5,000. (tabloid format)

FEDERATION OF SWEDISH CO-OPERATIVE BANKS. ANNUAL REPORT. see *BUSINESS AND ECONOMICS — Banking And Finance*

334 GW
DIE GENOSSENSCHAFTEN IN DER
BUNDESREPUBLIK DEUTSCHLAND. 1965.
biennial. free. Deutsche Genossenschaftsbank,
Wiesenhuettenstr. 10, 6000 Frankfurt, W. Germany
(B.R.D.) Ed. Gunther Aschhoff. illus. stat. circ.
5,000.

AL-GHAD. see *LITERARY AND POLITICAL REVIEWS*

334 BL
INSTITUTO NACIONAL DE COLONIZACAO E
REFORMA AGRARIA. COORDENADORIA
REGIONAL DO PARANA. SINOPSE DO
COOPERATIVISMO NO PARANA. 1970. irreg.
Instituto Nacional de Colonizacao e Reforma
Agraria, Coordenadoria Regional do Parana,
Curitiba, Brazil. illus.

334 UK ISSN 0074-4247
INTERNATIONAL COOPERATIVE ALLIANCE.
CONGRESS REPORT. 1895. quadrennial; 26th,
1976, paris. £5.50. International Co-Operative
Alliance, 11 Upper Grosvenor St., London W1X
9PA, England.

334 II ISSN 0074-4255
INTERNATIONAL COOPERATIVE ALLIANCE.
COOPERATIVE SERIES. (Text in English) 1965.
irreg. International Co-Operative Alliance, Regional
Office and Education Centre for South-East Asia,
Box 3312, 43 Friends Colony, New Delhi 110014,
India.

334 IS ISSN 0080-1313
ISRAEL. MINISTRY OF LABOUR. REGISTRAR
OF COOPERATIVE SOCIETIES. REPORT ON
THE COOPERATIVE MOVEMENT IN ISRAEL.
(Text in English) 1964. a. I£0.50. Ministry of
Labour and Social Affairs, Registrar of Cooperative
Societies, 10 Yad Harutzim St., Talpiot, Box 1260,
Jerusalem, Israel. circ. 1,200.

MANITOBA. DEPARTMENT OF CO-OPERATIVE
DEVELOPMENT. REPORT. RAPPORT. see
BUSINESS AND ECONOMICS — Banking And Finance

334.099 AT ISSN 0481-3375
QUEENSLAND. REGISTRAR OF CO-OPERATIVE
AND OTHER SOCIETIES. REPORT.* a.
Government Printer, Brisbane, Australia. illus.

334 CN ISSN 0080-097X
REPERTOIRE DES COOPERATIVES DU
QUEBEC. 1969. a. free. Editeur Officiel du Quebec,
1283 Bd. Charest ouest, Quebec G1N 2C9, Canada.
circ. 1,500.

334 IS
REVIEW OF PUBLIC AND CO-OPERATIVE
ECONOMY IN ISRAEL. 1973. irreg. I£10.
(International Centre of Research and Information
on Public and Cooperative Economy, Israeli
Section.) Jerusalem Academic Press., Box 3640,
Jerusalem, Israel. stat.

334 II
SAHYOG. a. Cooperative Training College, Vallabh
Vidyanagar, Gujarat, India.

334 GW ISSN 0080-7028
SCHRIFTEN ZUR KOOPERATIONSFORSCHUNG.
BERICHTE. 1968. irreg. price varies.
(Forschungsgesellschaft fuer Genossenschaftswesen,
Muenster) Verlag J.C.B. Mohr (Paul Siebeck),
Wilhelmstr. 18, Postfach 2040, 7400 Tuebingen, W.
Germany (B.R.D.)

334 GW ISSN 0080-7036
SCHRIFTEN ZUR KOOPERATIONSFORSCHUNG.
STUDIEN. 1951. irreg. price varies.
(Forschungsgesellschaft fuer Genossenschaftswesen,
Muenster) Verlag J.C.B. Mohr (Paul Siebeck),
Wilhelmstr. 18, Postfach 2040, 7400 Tuebingen, W.
Germany (B.R.D.)
Formerly: Quellen und Studien.

334 GW ISSN 0080-7044
SCHRIFTEN ZUR KOOPERATIONSFORSCHUNG.
VORTRAEGE. 1950. irreg. price varies.
(Forschungsgesellschaft fuer Genossenschaftswesen,
Muenster) Verlag J.C.B. Mohr (Paul Siebeck),
Wilhelmstr. 18, Postfach 2040, 7400 Tuebingen, W.
Germany (B.R.D.)
Formerly: Vortraege und Aufsaetze.

U.S. FARM CREDIT ADMINISTRATION.
ANNUAL REPORT OF THE FARM CREDIT
ADMINISTRATION AND THE COOPERATIVE
FARM CREDIT SYSTEM. see
AGRICULTURE — Agricultural Economics

U.S. NATIONAL CREDIT UNION
ADMINISTRATION. ANNUAL REPORT. see
BUSINESS AND ECONOMICS — Banking And Finance

U. S. NATIONAL CREDIT UNION
ADMINISTRATION. RESEARCH REPORT. see
BUSINESS AND ECONOMICS — Banking And Finance

U.S. NATIONAL CREDIT UNION
ADMINISTRATION. WORKING PAPERS. see
BUSINESS AND ECONOMICS — Banking And Finance

330 CN
UNIVERSITE DE SHERBROOKE.
DEPARTEMENT D'ECONOMIQUE. DOSSIERS
SUR LES COOPERATIVES. 1973. irreg. price
varies. Universite de Sherbrooke, Departement
d'Economique, Sherbrooke, Que. J1K 2R1, Canada.

334 FI ISSN 0356-1364
UNIVERSITY OF HELSINKI. DEPARTMENT OF
COOPERATIVE STUDIES. PUBLICATIONS.
(Text in English and Finnish) 1967. irreg.
(unnumbered) price varies. Helsingin Yliopisto,
Department of Cooperative Studies, Franzeninkatu
13, 00500 Helsinki 50, Finland. circ. 100-200.

VAIKUNTH MEHTA NATIONAL INSTITUTE OF
COOPERATIVE MANAGEMENT.
PUBLICATIONS. see *BUSINESS AND ECONOMICS — Management*

334 334 ZA ISSN 0514-5430
ZAMBIA. DEPARTMENT OF COOPERATIVES.
ANNUAL REPORT. a. 20 n. Government Printer,
Box 136, Lusaka, Zambia. stat.

BUSINESS AND ECONOMICS — Domestic Commerce

381 FR ISSN 0066-3182
ANNUAIRE GENERAL DES COOPERATIVES
FRANCAISES ET DE LEURS FOURNISSEURS;
FRANCE, AFRIQUE ET MARCHE COMMUN.
1956. a. 26 F. Office des Cooperatives et des
Collectivites, 49 rue de Richelieu, 75001 Paris,
France. adv.

380.1 II
ANNUAL REPORT ON THE WORKING AND
AFFAIRS OF MYSORE SALES
INTERNATIONAL LIMITED. (Text in English) a.
Mysore Sales International Limited, Bangalore,
India.
Government business enterprises

381 IT ISSN 0084-6627
ANNUARIO GENERALE ITALIANO. a. Guida
Monaci, Via Francesco Crispi 10, 00187 Rome,
Italy.

658.87 BL
ANUARIO BRASILEIRO DE SUPERMERCADOS.
1971. a. $17.50. (Associacao Brasileira dos
Supermercados) Publicacoes Informativas Ltda., Rua
Caetes 139, 05016 Sao Paulo, Brazil. Ed. J.C. Salles
Neto. adv. illus. circ. 18,000.

CAMARA DE COMERCIANTES EN
ARTEFACTOS PARA EL HOGAR. REVISTA.
see *INTERIOR DESIGN AND DECORATION — Furniture And House Furnishings*

381 FR ISSN 0069-1100
CATALOGUE DES PRODUITS AGREES PAR
QUALITE-FRANCE. 1963, 2nd ed. irreg. 3 F.
Association Nationale pour la Promotion et le
Controle de la Qualite, 18 rue Volney, 75002 Paris,
France.

380 SP
COLECCION TEMAS DE AHORRO Y CREDITO.
no. 9, 1975. irreg. Confederacion Espanola de Cajas
de Ahorros, Fondo para la Investigacion Economica
y Social, Juan Hurtado de Mendoza 14, Madrid 16,
Spain.

381 CN
COMMERCE. LE POINT; une revue annuel de
l'economie du Quebec. a. Can.$14($21) included in
subscr. to Commerce. Revue Commerce, Maison du
Commerce, 1080 Cote du Beaver Hall, Montreal,
Que. H2Z 1T1, Canada. Ed. Maurice Chartrand.
adv. circ. 42,004.

381 CN ISSN 0383-9737
COMMERCE JOURNAL. 1933. N.S. 1941. a.
University of Toronto, Commerce Club, Toronto,
Ont., Canada.

381 II ISSN 0591-1710
COMMERCE YEARBOOK OF PUBLIC SECTOR.
(Text in English) 1970. a. Rs.125. Commerce
Publications Limited, Manek Mahal, 90 Veer
Nariman Rd., Churchgate, Bombay 400020, India.
Ed. Vadilal Dagli.

381 US ISSN 0275-746X
CONGRESSIONAL DISTRICT BUSINESS
PATTERNS. 1981. a. $125. Economic Information
Systems, 310 Madison Ave, New York, NY 10017.

DOMESTIC WATERBORNE TRADE OF THE
UNITED STATES. see *TRANSPORTATION — Ships And Shipping*

381 EC
ECUADOR. MINISTERIO DE INDUSTRIAS,
COMERCIO E INTEGRACION.DOCUMENTO.
1975. a. Ministerio de Industrias, Comercio e
Integracion, Quito, Ecuador.

381 EC
ECUADOR. MINISTERIO DE INDUSTRIAS,
COMERCIO E INTEGRACION. INFORME A
LA NACION. 1974. a. Ministerio de Industrias,
Comercio e Integracion, Quito, Ecuador. illus.

380.1 TG
ENQUETE SUR LES ENTERPRISES
INDUSTRIELLES ET COMMERCIALES DU
TOGO. a, latest 1971(pub. 1975) 3000 Fr.CFA.
Direction de la Statistique, Boite Postale 118, Lome,
Togo. stat.

381 AT ISSN 0085-0268
ENTERPRISE.* 1963. a. free. University of New
South Wales, Commerce Society, Box 81, The
Union, Univ. of N.S.W., Kensington, N.S.W. 2033,
Australia.

381 658 US ISSN 0547-8804
FINANCIAL AND OPERATING RESULTS OF
DEPARTMENT AND SPECIALTY STORES. a.
$45 to non-members: members $30. National Retail
Merchants Association, Financial Executives
Division, 100 W 31st St., New York, NY 10001.

381 FR ISSN 0071-8483
FRANCE. COMMISSION CENTRALE DES
MARCHES. GUIDE DU FOURNISSEUR DE
L'ETAT ET DES COLLECTIVITES LOCALES.
1964. irreg., latest issue, 1972. 26 Fr. (Ministere de
l'Economie et des Finances, Commission Centrale
des Marches) Moniteur des Travaux Publics et du
Batiment, 17 rue d'Uzes, 75065 Paris, France. circ.
12,000.
Formerly: France. Commission Centrale des
Marches. Guide du Fournisseur de l'Etat.

381 658 FR ISSN 0071-8386
FRANCE-COLLECTIVITES: GUIDE NATIONAL
DES CHEFS DES SERVICES D'ACHATS ET
DES FOURNISSEURS DE COLLECTIVITES.
1962-63. a. 140 F. Office des Cooperatives et des
Collectivites, 49 rue de Richelieu, 75001 Paris,
France.

381 GU
GUAM. DEPARTMENT OF COMMERCE.
ANNUAL ECONOMIC REPORT. (Text in
English) 1969. a. free contr. circ. in Guam; $1 in
the U.S. Department of Commerce, Economic
Research Center, Box 682, Agana, GU 96910.
(tabloid format)

182 BUSINESS AND ECONOMICS — ECONOMIC SITUATION AND CONDITIONS

380.1   GU
GUAM. DEPARTMENT OF COMMERCE. OCCASIONAL PAPER. irreg., latest issue 1976. Department of Commerce, Box 682, Agana, GU 96910.

380.1   GU
GUAM. DEPARTMENT OF COMMERCE. PROCEEDINGS FROM ECONOMIC CONFERENCE. 1970. a. $1. Department of Commerce, Box 682, Agana, GU 96910. (Co-sponsor: Guam Chamber of Commerce) Ed. R. Raymond Castro. circ. 300.

338   FI   ISSN 0356-5092
HINNAT JA KILPAILU/PRISER OCH KONKURRENS. (Text in Finnish and Swedish) 1959. irreg. (3-4/yr.) free. Elinkeinohallitus - National Board of Trade and Consumer Interests, Haapaniemenkatu 4 A, 00531 Helsinki 53, Finland. Ed. Mirja Kekki. index. circ. 1,500.
    Formerly(until 1977): Kilpailunvapauslehti (ISSN 0023-1401)

380   SZ   ISSN 0080-603X
HOCHSCHULE ST. GALLEN FUER WIRTSCHAFTS- UND SOZIALWISSENSCHAFTEN. FORSCHUNGSINSTITUT FUER ABSATZ UND HANDEL. SCHRIFTENREIHE. 1960. irreg., vol. 16, 1976. price varies. Paul Haupt AG, Falkenplatz 14, CH-3001 Berne, Switzerland.

381   IR   ISSN 0074-1213
INTERNAL TRADE OF IRAN.* (Text in English and Persian) 1965. a. free. Ministry of Finance and Economic Affairs, Bureau of Statistics, Tehran, Iran.

380   JA
JAPANESE GENERAL TRADING COMPANIES YEARBOOK/SOGO-SHOSHA. (Text in English) 1976. a. 3300 Yen. Tokyo Economic Information Service Co., Taiso Bldg., 1-9-1 Takaracho, Chuo-ku, Tokyo 104, Japan.

381   MY
MALAYSIA. DEPARTMENT OF INLAND REVENUE. ANNUAL REPORT/MALAYSIA. JABATAN HASIL DALAM NEGERI. LAPURAN TAHUNAN. (Text in Malay) 1972. a. Department of Inland Revenue, Kuala Lumpur, Malaysia.

MARKETING CALIFORNIA DRIED FRUITS: PRUNES, RAISINS, DRIED APRICOTS & PEACHES. see AGRICULTURE — Agricultural Economics

380   BL
MERCADO COMUM BRASILEIRO. irreg. Editora de Guias Ltda, Av. Paulista 1776, 01098 Sao Paulo, Brazil. illus.

353.9   US   ISSN 0094-3479
MICHIGAN. DEPARTMENT OF COMMERCE. ANNUAL REPORT SUMMARY. a. Department of Commerce, Lansing, MI 48913. illus. stat. Key Title: Annual Report Summary - Michigan Department of Commerce.

MONOGRAPHIES DE L'INDUSTRIE ET DU COMMERCE EN FRANCE. see BUSINESS AND ECONOMICS — Production Of Goods And Services

381.41   SA
NATIONAL FRESH PRODUCE MARKET, JOHANNESBURG. ANNUAL REPORT OF THE DIRECTOR. (Report year ends June 30) 1913. a. free. National Fresh Produce Market, Box 577, Johannesburg 2000, South Africa. circ. 350. (processed)

381   SA   ISSN 0077-5894
NATIONAL TRADE-INDEX OF SOUTHERN AFRICA. 1928. a. R.36. C. T. Directories, Box 760, Durban, South Africa. adv.

381   NQ   ISSN 0078-0510
NICARAGUA. DIRECCION GENERAL DE ADUANAS. MEMORIA. 1918. a. $7. Direccion General de Aduanas, Managua, Nicaragua. stat. circ. 200.

381   GW
NORDFRIESLAND; Chronik in Wort und Bild; Handbuch fuer den Kreis Nordfriesland. a. DM.5. Flensburger Zeitungsverlag GmbH, Nikolaistr. 7, 2390 Flensburg, W. Germany (B.R.D.) illus.

380   NO
NORWAY. MINISTRY OF INDUSTRY AND HANDICRAFT. REPORTS TO THE STORTING. irreg. price varies. Ministry of Industry and Handicraft, Akersgaten 42, Box 8014-Dep., Oslo 1, Norway.

381.3   FR
ORGANIZATION FOR ECONOMIC COOPERATION AND DEVELOPMENT. ANNUAL REPORTS ON CONSUMER POLICY IN O E C D MEMBER COUNTRIES. (Text in English) a. $6.25. Organization for Economic Cooperation and Development, 2 rue Andre-Pascal, 75775 Paris Cedex 16, France (U.S. orders to: O.E.C.D. Publications and Information Center, 1750 Pennsylvania Ave., N.W. Washington, DC 20006) (also avail. in microfiche)

PHILIPPINES. MINISTRY OF TRADE. ANNUAL REPORT. see BUSINESS AND ECONOMICS — International Commerce

381 332.6   II
PONDICHERRY INDUSTRIAL PROMOTION, DEVELOPMENT AND INVESTMENT CORPORATION. ANNUAL REPORTS AND ACCOUNTS. (Text in English) a. Pondicherry Industrial Promotion, Development and Investment Corporation Ltd., 38 Romain Rolland St, Pondicherry 605001, India. circ. controlled.

380.1   CN   ISSN 0383-4352
SASKATCHEWAN TRADING CORPORATION. ANNUAL REPORT. 1974. a. Saskatchewan Trading Corporation, 315 Legislative Bldg., Regina, Sask., Canada.

380   GW   ISSN 0080-7001
SCHRIFTEN ZUR HANDELSFORSCHUNG. 1951 N.S. irreg., no. 63, 1981. price varies. (Universitaet zu Koeln, Institut fuer Handelsforschung) Verlag Otto Schwartz und Co., Annastr. 7, 3400 Goettingen, W. Germany (B.R.D.)

381   SJ
SUDAN. DEPARTMENT OF STATISTICS. INTERNAL TRADE AND OTHER STATISTICS. (Text in English) a. Department of Statistics, Box 700, Khartoum, Sudan.

380   BL
TODO. irreg. Editora de Guias Ltda, Caixa Postal 4724, 01407 Sao Paulo, Brazil (And Av. Paulista 1776, 01098 Sao Paulo, Brazil) illus.

380   US   ISSN 0082-5956
TRANSPORTATION STATISTICS IN THE UNITED STATES. 1954. irreg. price varies. U.S. Interstate Commerce Commission., 12th St. and Constitution Ave., N.W., Washington, DC 20423 (Orders to: Supt. Doc., Washington, DC 20402)

381   US   ISSN 0083-0917
U. S. FEDERAL TRADE COMMISSION. ANNUAL REPORT. 1915. a. price varies. U.S. Federal Trade Commission., Pennsylvania Ave. at Sixth St. N.W., Washington, DC 20580 (Orders to: Supt. of Documents, Washington, DC 20402) Key Title: Annual Report of the Federal Trade Commission.

381   US
U. S. FEDERAL TRADE COMMISSION. COURT DECISIONS PERTAINING TO THE FEDERAL TRADE COMMISSION. a. price varies. U.S. Federal Trade Commission., Washington, DC 20580 (Orders to: Supt. of Documents, Washington, DC 20402)
    Formerly: U.S. Federal Trade Commission. Statutes and Court Decisions Pertaining to the Federal Trade Commission. Supplements (ISSN 0083-0933)

381   US   ISSN 0083-0925
U. S. FEDERAL TRADE COMMISSION. FEDERAL TRADE COMMISSION DECISIONS, FINDINGS, ORDERS AND STIPULATIONS. 1915. a. price varies. U.S. Federal Trade Commission., Washington, DC 20580 (Orders to: Supt. of Documents, Washington, DC 20402)

381   US   ISSN 0083-1514
U. S. INTERSTATE COMMERCE COMMISSION. ANNUAL REPORT. 1887. a. price varies. U.S. Interstate Commerce Commission., 12th St. and Constitution Ave., N.W., Washington, DC 20423 (Orders to: Supt. Doc., Washington, DC 20402)

381   US   ISSN 0083-1522
U. S. INTERSTATE COMMERCE COMMISSION. INTERSTATE COMMERCE ACTS ANNOTATED. 1930, vols. 1-5. irreg. price varies. U.S. Interstate Commerce Commission., 12th St. and Constitution Ave., N.W., Washington, DC 20423 (Orders to: Supt. Doc., Washington, DC 20402)

381   US   ISSN 0083-1530
U. S. INTERSTATE COMMERCE COMMISSION. INTERSTATE COMMERCE COMMISSION REPORTS. DECISIONS OF THE INTERSTATE COMMERCE COMMISSION OF THE UNITED STATES. 1887. irreg. price varies. U.S. Interstate Commerce Commission., 12th St. and Constitution Ave., N.W., Washington, DC 20423 (Orders to: Supt. Doc., Washington, DC 20402)

UNIVERSITY OF OSAKA PREFECTURE. BULLETIN. SERIES D: SCIENCES OF ECONOMY, COMMERCE AND LAW. see BUSINESS AND ECONOMICS

381   CN   ISSN 0083-517X
VANCOUVER. BOARD OF TRADE. ANNUAL REPORT. 1887. a. Board of Trade, 1177 W. Hastings, Vancouver, B.C., Canada. Ed. Richard G. Cross. circ. 3,500.

381   US   ISSN 0083-8454
WEST VIRGINIA. DEPARTMENT OF COMMERCE. ANNUAL REPORT. 1961. a. free. Department of Commerce, State Capitol, Charleston, WV 25305. Ed. Sheri A. O'Dell. circ. 5,000.

BUSINESS AND ECONOMICS — Economic Situation And Conditions

AFRICA INSTITUTE. COMMUNICATIONS. see HISTORY — History Of Africa

AFRICA INSTITUTE. OCCASIONAL PUBLICATIONS. see HISTORY — History Of Africa

AFRICA SOUTH OF THE SAHARA. see HISTORY — History Of Africa

330.9   US
ALABAMA ECONOMIC OUTLOOK. 1978. biennial. $2.50. Development Office, c/o State Capitol, Montgomery, AL 36130.

ALBANIA REPORT. see POLITICAL SCIENCE

338.9   CN   ISSN 0080-1534
ALBERTA RESEARCH COUNCIL. CONTRIBUTION SERIES. 1942. irreg. free. Alberta Research Council, 11315-87 Avenue, Edmonton, Alta. T6G 2C2, Canada.

330   IT   ISSN 0065-6151
ALESSANDRIA, ITALY. CENTRO DOCUMENTAZIONE E RICERCHE ECONOMICO-SOCIALI. QUADERNO. 1963. irreg., no. 108, 1979. free. Amministrazione Provinciale, Alessandria, Italy. Dir. Carlo Beltrame. circ. 1,000.

330.9   FR
AMENAGEMENT DU TERRITOIRE ET DEVELOPPEMENT REGIONAL; les faits, les idees, les institutions. 1968. a. (Institut d'Etudes Politiques de Grenoble, Centre d'Etude et de Recherche sur l'Administration Economique et l'Amenagement du Territoire) Documentation Francaise, 29-31 Quai Voltaire, 75007 Paris, France. bibl. charts. index.

330   TI   ISSN 0066-3042
ANNUAIRE ECONOMIQUE DE LA TUNISIE. English edition: Economic Yearbook of Tunisia (ISSN 0070-8747) 1964. biennial. $20. Union Tunisienne de l'Industrie, du Commerce et de l'Artisanat, 32 rue Charles de Gaulle, Tunis, Tunisia. adv. circ. 5,000.

BUSINESS AND ECONOMICS — ECONOMIC SITUATION AND CONDITIONS

330.9   SP
ANUARIO ECONOMICO Y SOCIAL DE ESPANA. 1975. a. Editorial Planeta S.A., Corcega 273-277, Barcelona 8, Spain. illus.

330.9   AG
ARGENTINE ECONOMIC DEVELOPMENT. (Text in English & French) biennial. Ministerio de Economia, Balcarce 136, Buenos Aires, Argentina.

330.9   320   UK
ASIA & PACIFIC. 1980. a. £12.50($30) World of Information, 21 Gold St., Saffron Walden, Essex CB10 1EJ, England. Ed. Graham Hancock.
   Formerly (until 1981): Asia and Pacific Annual Review.

330.9   320.253   US
ASIA SERIALS: VIETNAM REPORT. 1966. irreg. (approx 86/yr.) $344. U.S. Joint Publications Research Service, 1000 N. Glebe Rd., Arlington, VA 22201 (Orders to: NTIS, Springfield, VA 22161)
   Former titles: Translations on Vietnam; Translations on North Vietnam.

330.9   LE
ASSOCIATION DES BANQUES DU LIBAN. RAPPORT DU CONSEIL. Cover title: Association des Banques du Liban. Rapport Annuel. (Text in French) irreg. Association of Banks in Lebanon, Rue de l'Armee, Box 967, Beirut, Lebanon. stat.

330.1   CN   ISSN 0067-0162
ATLANTIC PROVINCES ECONOMIC COUNCIL. ANNUAL REPORT. 1966. a. membership. Atlantic Provinces Economic Council, One Sackville Place, Halifax, N.S. B3J 1K1, Canada. circ. 1,500. (reprint service avail. from UMI)

330.9   BF   ISSN 0067-2912
BAHAMAS HANDBOOK AND BUSINESSMAN'S ANNUAL. 1960. a. $12.90. Etienne Dupuch Jr., P.O. Box N7513, Nassau, Bahamas. Ed. S.P. Dupuch. index.

330.9   BB
BALANCE OF PAYMENTS OF BARBADOS. 1976. a. Central Bank of Barbados, P.O. Box 1016, Bridgetown, Barbados.

330.9   IT
BANCA D'ITALIA. CONTRIBUTI ALLA RICERCA ECONOMICA. English edition: Banca d'Italia. Economic Papers. 1971. a. free. Banca d'Italia, Servizio Studi, Via Nazionale 91, Rome, Italy.

BANCO CENTRAL DE CHILE, SANTIAGO. MEMORIA ANUAL. see *BUSINESS AND ECONOMICS — Banking And Finance*

330.9   CR
BANCO CENTRAL DE COSTA RICA. BALANZA DE PAGOS. 1950. a. free. Banco Central de Costa Rica, Avda.Central, Calles 2 y 4, Apdo. 10058, San Jose, Costa Rica. circ. 1,200.

330.9   CR
BANCO CENTRAL DE COSTA RICA. SERIE "COMENTARIOS SOBRE ASUNTOS ECONOMICOS". 1972. irreg. free. Banco Central de Costa Rica, Avda.Central, Calles 2 y 4, San Jose, Costa Rica (And: Apdo. 10058, San Jose, Costa Rica) circ. 300.

330   HO
BANCO CENTRAL DE HONDURAS. INFORME ECONOMICO. 1956. irreg. Banco Central de Honduras, Departamento de Estudios Economicos, Tegucigalpa, Honduras. charts. stat.

330.9   HO   ISSN 0067-3218
BANCO CENTRAL DE HONDURAS. MEMORIA. 1950. a. Banco Central de Honduras, Departamento de Estudios Economicos, Tegucigalpa, Honduras. charts. stat.

330.9   NQ
BANCO CENTRAL DE NICARAGUA. DEPARTMENTO DE ESTUDIOS ECONOMICOS. INDICADORES ECONOMICOS. 1976. irreg. Banco Central de Nicaragua, Departamento de Estudios Economicos, Managua, Nicaragua. charts. stat.

330   VE   ISSN 0067-3250
BANCO CENTRAL DE VENEZUELA. INFORME ECONOMICO. 1962. a. Banco Central de Venezuela, Esquina de las Carmelitas, Caracas, Venezuela.

330   EC
BANCO CENTRAL DEL ECUADOR. BOLETIN - ANUARIO. 1978. a. free or exchange basis. Banco Central del Ecuador, Av. 10 de Agosto (Plaza Bolivar), La Alameda, Quito, Ecuador. Ed. Aurelio Salas. charts. stat.
   Incorporating: Banco Central de Ecuador. Memoria Anual de Actividades.

330   UY
BANCO CENTRAL DEL URUGUAY. INDICADORES DE LA ACTIVIDAD ECONOMICA-FINANCIERA. irreg. Banco Central del Uruguay, Montevideo, Uruguay. stat.

330.9   SP
BANCO DE BILBAO. ECONOMIC REPORT. (Text in English) a. Banco de Bilbao, Economic Research Department, Bilbao, Spain. charts. stat.

330.9   SP   ISSN 0522-1315
BANCO DE BILBAO. INFORME ECONOMICO. 1950. a. Banco de Bilbao, Servicio de Estudios, Apartado 21, Bilbao, Spain. charts. stat.

330.9   GT
BANCO DE GUATEMALA. ESTADISTICAS DEL SECTOR EXTERNO. no. 3, 1975. irreg. Banco de Guatemala, Departamento de Estudios Economicos, 7 Av. No. 22-01, Zona 1, Guatemala City, Guatemala. stat.

BANCO DE MEXICO. INFORME ANUAL. see *BUSINESS AND ECONOMICS — Banking And Finance*

338.9   BL
BANCO DO NORDESTE DO BRASIL. SERIE ESTUDOS ECONOMICOS E SOCIAIS. 1975. irreg. $3. Banco do Nordeste do Brasil, Rua Senador Pompeu 834, Galeria Pedro Jorge, 60000 Fortaleza - Ceara, Brazil.

330.9   EC
BANCO NACIONAL DE FOMENTO. INFORME DE LABORES. a. Banco Nacional de Fomento, Departamento de Relaciones Publicas, Apdo. 685, Quito, Ecuador. charts. illus. stat.

330   PN
BANCO NACIONAL DE PANAMA. ASESORIA ECONOMICA Y PLANIFICACION. CARTA ECONOMICA. 0971. 2-4/yr. free. Banco Nacional de Panama, Asesoria Economica y Planificacion, Apdo. 5220, Panama 5, Panama. bk. rev. charts. illus. stat. circ. 1,000.

330.9   BL
BANCO NACIONAL DO DESENVOLVIMENTO ECONOMICO. RELATORIO DAS ATIVIDADES. English edition: Banco Nacional do Desenvolvimento Economico. Annual Report. a. Banco Nacional do Desenvolvimento Economico, Av. Rio Branco 53, Rio de Janeiro RJ, Brazil. charts. illus. stat.

330.9   BL   ISSN 0522-2079
BANCO REGIONAL DE DESENVOLVIMENTO DO EXTREMO SUL. RELATORIO DA DIRECTORIA. 1965. a. Banco Regional de Desenvolvimento do Extremo sul, Caixa Postal 139, 90,000 Porto Alegre RS, Brazil. illus. circ. 1,000.

338.9   BG
BANGLADESH. PLANNING COMMISSION. ANNUAL DEVELOPMENT PROGRAMME. Bengali edition: Barshika Unnayana Karmasuci. (Text in English) a. Planning Commission, Dacca, Bangladesh.

330   JA   ISSN 0067-3684
BANK OF JAPAN. BUSINESS REPORT. (Text in English) s-a. free. Bank of Japan, Foreign Department - Nihon Ginko, C.P.O. Box 203, Tokyo 100-91, Japan.

330   JA   ISSN 0067-3692
BANK OF JAPAN. ECONOMIC RESEARCH DEPARTMENT. B O J SPECIAL PAPER.* 1961. irreg. Bank of Japan - Nihon Ginko, C.P.O. Box 203, Tokyo 100-91, Japan.

330.9   LY   ISSN 0067-3714
BANK OF LIBYA. ANNUAL REPORT OF THE BOARD OF DIRECTORS.* (Editions in Arabic and English) 1957. a. free. Bank of Libya, Economic Research Division, Box 1103, Tripoli, Libya.

330.9   332   TZ   ISSN 0067-3757
BANK OF TANZANIA. ECONOMIC AND OPERATIONS REPORT. a. free. Bank of Tanzania, Research and Statistics Department, Box 2939, Dar es Salaam, Tanzania. circ. 3,000.
   Formerly: Bank of Tanzania. Economic Report (ISSN 0067-3765)

330   TH   ISSN 0067-3773
BANK OF THAILAND. ANNUAL ECONOMIC REPORT. a. $5. Bank of Thailand, Department of Economic Research, Bang Khunprom, Bangkok, Thailand.

330.9   TH
BANK OF THAILAND. PAPER. 1974/75. irreg. Bank of Thailand, Department of Economic Research, Bangkok, Thailand.

330   TH
BANK OF THAILAND: ECONOMIC HIGHLIGHTS. 1976. a. free. Bank of Thailand, Department of Economic Research, Bangkok, Thailand.

330.9   CN   ISSN 0382-4756
BANQUE DE COMMERCE CANADIENNE IMPERIALE. LETTRE COMMERCIALE. (Text in French) no. 5, 1976. irreg. Banque de Commerce Canadienne Imperiale, Bureau Regional, Montreal, Que. H3C 3B2, Montreal, Que., Canada. charts. stat.

330.9   FR
BANQUE DE FRANCE. COMITE MONETAIRE DE LA ZONE FRANC. SECRETARIAT. RAPPORT. a. Banque de France, Comite Monetaire de la Zone Franc, Service de l'Information, 43 rue de Valois, 75049 Paris Cedex 1, France.

338.9   FR   ISSN 0522-3199
BANQUE DE FRANCE. DIRECTION DE LA CONJONCTURE. STRUCTURE ET EVOLUTION FINANCIERE DES REGIONS DE PROVINCE. 1966. a. free. Banque de France, Service de l'Information, 43 rue de Valois, 75049 Paris Cedex 1, France. stat.

332   LU
BANQUE INTERNATIONALE A LUXEMBOURG. CAHIERS ECONOMIQUES. 1975. irreg. free. Banque Internationale a Luxembourg, 2 Boulevard Royal, Luxembourg, Luxembourg. circ. 5,000.

330.9   FR
BANQUE INTERNATIONALE POUR L'AFRIQUE OCCIDENTALE. CONSEIL D'ADMINISTRATION. RAPPORT ET RESOLUTIONS, RAPPORT DES COMMISSAIRES AUX COMPTES. irreg. Banque Internationale pour l'Afrique Occidentale, Conseil d'Administration, 9 Ave. de Messine, 75008 Paris, France. illus.

330   UK   ISSN 0307-4552
BARCLAYS COUNTRY REPORTS. irreg. free. Barclays Bank Group, Economic Intelligence Unit, 54 Lombard St., London EC3P 3AA, Eng. (looseleaf format)

330.9   US   ISSN 0094-1115
BASIC ECONOMIC DATA FOR IDAHO. irreg. Department of Employment, Planning, Research and Evaluation Bureau, Box 35, Boise, ID 83735. stat.

330.943   GW
BERLINER WIRTSCHAFTSDATEN. 1973. irreg. Senator fuer Wirtschaft, Martin Luther Str. 105, 1000 Berlin 62, W. Germany (B.R.D.) (looseleaf format)

330.9   BL
BIBLIOTECA DE ECONOMIA. 1977. irreg. Edicoes Graal, 33 rua Sao Salvador, Laranjeiras, ZC 01, 20.000, Rio de Janeiro, Brazil.

330.9   NP
BIKASA EKA VIHANGAM DRSHTI. (Text in English) q. Rs.10. Keshav Babu Tiwari, Kathmandu, Nepal.

BUSINESS AND ECONOMICS — ECONOMIC SITUATION AND CONDITIONS

330.9   CN   ISSN 0381-7245
BLUE BOOK OF CANADIAN BUSINESS. a. Can.$49.50. Canadian Newspaper Services International Ltd., 96 Eglinton Ave. E., Toronto, Ont. M4P 1C5, Canada. Ed. Bd. illus.

330.9   BL   ISSN 0100-4271
BRASIL(YEAR); how, why and what to import from Brazil. (Text in English) 1973. a. free. Associacao de Exportadores Brasileiros, Av. Marechal Camara 210, 20020 Castelo, Rio de Janeiro RJ, Brazil. adv. illus. circ. 500.

330.9   BL
BRAZIL. SECRETARIA DE PLANEJAMENTO. INSTITUTO DE PLANEJAMENTO ECONOMICO E SOCIAL. SERIE DOCUMENTOS. 1976. irreg. Instituto de Planejamento Economico e Social, Caixa Postal 2672, Rio de Janeiro, Brazil.

330.9   BL
BRAZIL. SUPERINTENDENCIA DO DESENVOLVIMENTO DO NORDESTE. RELATORIO ANUAL. irreg. exchange basis. Superintendencia do Desenvolvimento do Nordeste, Av. Prof. Moraes Rego s/n, Edificio SUDENE, Cidade Universitaria, 50000 Recife,, Pernambuco, Brazil. charts. stat.

330.9   CN   ISSN 0701-757X
BRITISH COLUMBIA ECONOMIC ACTIVITY. 1945. a. free. Ministry of Economic Development, Victoria, B.C. V8V 1X4, Canada. Ed. G.R. Knight. circ. 5,000.
    Formerly: British Columbia Economic Outlook Survey (ISSN 0319-0412)

338.9   EI   ISSN 0068-4120
BULLETIN OF THE EUROPEAN COMMUNITIES. SUPPLEMENT. (Text in Danish, Dutch, English, French, German and Italian) 1968. irreg. (Commission of the European Communities) Office for Official Publications of the European Communities, Boite Postale 1003, Luxembourg, Luxembourg (Dist. in U.S. by: European Community Information Service, 2100 M St., NW, Suite 707, Washington, DC 20037)

330.9   SP
BUSINESS OPPORTUNITIES IN SPAIN. (Edts. in English, French, Spanish) a. Banco de Santander, Publicidad y Estudios, Paseo de Pereda, 9/12, Santander 2, Spain.

330.9   US   ISSN 0360-3938
BUSINESS OUTLOOK. (Subseries of: Conference Board. Report) 1947. a. $15 to non-members, $5 to members. Conference Board, Inc., 845 Third Ave., New York, NY 10022. illus. stat.
    Continues: National Industrial Conference Board. Business Outlook: an Evening with the Economic Forum.

330.9   MY
BUSINESS TRENDS ASIA REPORT. 1979. irreg. M.$60. M P R C (Asia) Sdn. Berhad, 7 Jalan Baiduri, Box 706, Kuala Lumpur 01-02, Malaysia. Ed. Paul Markandan. bk. rev. stat. circ. controlled.

330.9   BL
C D E. 1974. irreg. Conselho de Desenvolvimento Economico, Brasilia, Brazil. illus.

330.9   CK
C.E.D.E. MONOGRAFIAS. 1959. irreg. price varies. Universidad de los Andes, Centro de Estudios sobre Desarrollo Economico, Apdo. Aereo 4976, Bogota, Colombia.

330.9   US
CALIFORNIA DATA BRIEF. 1977. irreg. free. University of California, Berkeley, Institute of Governmental Studies, Berkeley, CA 94720. Ed. Ted K. Bradshaw. circ. 1,950. (processed)

330.9   CN
CANADA. DEPARTMENT OF CONSUMER AND CORPORATE AFFAIRS. DIRECTORY OF INVESTIGATIONS AND RESEARCH REPORT. (Text in English and French) a. free. Department of Consumer and Corporate Affairs, Ottawa, Ont. K1A 0C9, Canada.

354   CN
CANADA. DEPARTMENT OF INDUSTRY, TRADE AND COMMERCE. REVUE ANNUELLE-INDUSTRIE ET COMMERCE. a. Department of Industry, Trade, and Commerce, Ottawa, Ont. K1A 0H5, Canada. illus.

330   TR   ISSN 0069-0481
CARIBBEAN ECONOMIC ALMANAC; a collection of economic and statistical data covering the Caribbean area. 1962. irreg. Economic and Business Research Information and Advisory Service, P.O. Box 780, Port of Spain, Trinidad. Ed. Max B. Ifill.

330.9   BB
CENTRAL BANK OF BARBADOS . ANNUAL REPORT. a. Central Bank of Barbados, Box 1016, Treasury Building, Bridgetown, Barbados. charts, stat.

330.9   CE
CENTRAL BANK OF CEYLON. REVIEW OF THE ECONOMY/ARTHIKA VIVARANAYA. (Text in English) 1975. a. Rs.10($6) Central Bank of Ceylon Department of Economic Research, Deputy Director of Information, Janadhipathi Mawathi, Colombo 1, Sri Lanka.

330.9   KU
CENTRAL BANK OF KUWAIT. ECONOMIC REPORT. (Editions in Arabic and English) a. free. Central Bank of Kuwait, Research Department - Bank al-Kuwayt al-Markazi, Box 526, Kuwait. charts. stat.

330.9   NR   ISSN 0008-9281
CENTRAL BANK OF NIGERIA. ECONOMIC AND FINANCIAL REVIEW. 1963. irreg., vol. 16, no. 2, 1978. free. Central Bank of Nigeria, P.M.B. 12194, Tinubu Square, Lagos, Nigeria. charts. stat. circ. 4,000.

330.9   BO
CENTRO DE INVESTIGACION Y PROMOCION DEL CAMPESINADO. CUADERNOS DE INVESTIGACION. 1973. irreg. Centro de Investigacion y Promocion del Campesinado, Sagarnaga 479, Casilla 5854, La Paz, Bolivia.

330.9   CE   ISSN 0528-757X
CEYLON ECONOMIST. (Text in English) 1952. irreg. Ceylon Economic Research Association, P.O. Box 175, Colombo, Sri Lanka. charts. illus.

330.9   CL
CHILE. OFICINA DE PLANIFICACION NACIONAL. INFORME ECONOMICO ANUAL. 1974. a. $10. Oficina de Planificacion Nacional, Biblioteca, Seccion Publicaciones, Ahumada 48, Casilla 9140, Santiago, Chile.

330.9   BL
COLECAO ECONOMIA. irreg. Editora Paz e Terra, Rua Andre Cavalcanti 80, 20231 Fatima, Rio de Janeiro, Brazil. Ed. Bd.

330.9   CK
COLOMBIA ECONOMICA. irreg. Publicaciones Contextos Ltda, Calle 18 no. 7-18, Apartado 12382, Bogota, Colombia. Ed. Jose M. Espinosa.

330.9   SP
COMENTARIO SOCIOLOGICO. no. 17, 1977. irreg. Confederacion Espanola de Cajas de Ahorros, Servicio de Estudios Sociologicos, Alcala 27, Madrid, 14, Spain.

334   GW
COMMONWEAL ECONOMY SERIES. (Text in English) 1970. irreg. free. Bank fuer Gemeinwirtschaft Aktiengesellschaft, Postfach 2244, 6000 Frankfurt, W. Germany (B.R.D.) Ed.Bd. stat.

330   CN   ISSN 0069-7842
COMMUNITY IMPROVEMENT CORPORATION. ANNUAL REPORT/SOCIETE D'AMENAGEMENT REGIONAL. RAPPORT ANNUEL. (Text in English and French) 1967. a. free contr. circ. Community Improvement Corporation, 377 York St., Fredericton, N.B., Canada. circ. 1,000.

330   CN   ISSN 0381-0100
CONFERENCE BOARD IN CANADA. QUARTERLY PROVINCIAL FORECAST. 1976. irreg. Conference Board in Canada, Suite 100, 25 McArthur Rd., Ottawa, Ont. K1L 6R3, Canada.

341.7   EI
COUNCIL OF THE EUROPEAN COMMUNITIES. REVIEW OF THE COUNCIL'S WORK. a. Office for Official Publications of the European Communities, Boite Postale 1003, Luxembourg, Luxembourg (Dist. in the U.S. by: European Community Information Service, 2100 M St., NW, Suite 707, Washington, DC 20037)

336   SZ
COUNTRY STUDIES; Union Bank of Switzerland reports. (Editions in English, French, German, Italian and Spanish) irreg. free. Union de Banques Suisses, Bahnhofstrasse 45, 8000 Zurich, Switzerland. circ. 11,200 (English edt.); 58,500 (all edts.)

650   US
CURRENT BUSINESS REPORTS. U.S. Bureau of the Census, Washington, DC 20233 (Subscriptions to Monthly Retail and Wholesale Trade Reports to: Supt. of Documents, Washington, DC 20402, Other reports in the series available from Bureau's Subscriber Services Section)

330.9   US   ISSN 0362-4730
D R I EUROPEAN REVIEW. irreg. Data Resources, Inc., 29 Hartwell Ave., Lexington, MA 02173.

338.9   CN   ISSN 0381-7024
DALHOUSIE UNIVERSITY. INSTITUTE OF PUBLIC AFFAIRS. OCCASIONAL PAPERS. 1977. irreg. Dalhousie University, Institute of Public Affairs, Halifax, N.S. B3H 3J5, Canada.

330.9   CR
DATOS SOCIO-ECONOMICOS DE COSTA RICA. 1974. a. free. Banco Central de Costa Rica, Avda.Central, Calles 2 y 4, San Jose, Costa Rica (And: Apdo. 10058, San Jose, Costa Rica) charts. stat. circ. 1,500.

330   DK   ISSN 0106-2891
DENMARK. MINISTERIET FOR GROENLAND. STATISTISK KONTOR. MEDDELELSER. irreg. free. Ministeriet for Groenland, Statistisk Kontor, Hausergade 3, 1128 Copenhagen K, Denmark. circ. 700.
    Formerly: Denmark. Ministeriet for Groenland. Oekonomisk-Statistisk Kontor. Meddelelser.

330.9   BL
DIAGNOSTICOS APEC. (Text in English, Portuguese) irreg. APEC Editora S.A., Rua Sorocaba 295, Rio de Janeiro, Brazil. Ed. Victor da Silva Alves Filho.

330.9   DQ
DOMINICA. MINISTRY OF FINANCE AND DEVELOPMENT. STATISTICAL DIGEST. quinquennial. Ministry of Finance and Development, Roseau, Dominica, West Indies.

330.9   DQ
DOMINICA. MINISTRY OF FINANCE AND DEVELOPMENT. VITAL STATISTICS REPORT. quinquennial. e.c. $2. Ministry of Finance and Development, Roseau, Dominica, West Indies.

330.9 330.1   US
EASTERN EUROPE REPORT: ECONOMIC AND INDUSTRIAL AFFAIRS. 1968. irreg. (approx 121/yr.) $544. U.S. Joint Publications Research Service, 1000 N. Glebe Rd., Arlington, VA 22201 (Orders to: NTIS, Springfield, VA 22161)
    Formerly: Translations on Eastern Europe. Economic and Industrial Affairs.

338.9   BL
ECONOMIA BRASILEIRA E SUAS PERSPECTIVAS-APECAO. (Text in English, Portuguese) 1962. a. $75. APEC Editora, S.A., Rua Sorocaba 295, Botafogo, Rio de Janeiro, Brazil. Eds. Victor da Silva, Mircea Buescu. circ. 10,000.

330.9   CK   ISSN 0422-2733
ECONOMIA COLOMBIANA. no. 115, 1976. irreg. Contraloria General, Edificio de los Ministerios, Apdo. Nacional 9020, Bogota, Colombia.

330.9   CU
ECONOMIA CUBANA. English edition: Cuban Economy. a. Comite Estatal de Estadisticas, Centro de Informacion Cientifico-Tecnico, Av. Tercera no. 4410, Municipio de Playa, Havana, Cuba. stat.

BUSINESS AND ECONOMICS — ECONOMIC SITUATION AND CONDITIONS

330.9   IT
ECONOMIA MARCHE. irreg., no. 7, 1980. Societa Editrice il Mulino, Via S. Stefano 6, 40125 Bologna, Italy. Ed. Bd.

330.9   US   ISSN 0095-2850
ECONOMIC AND SOCIAL PROGRESS IN LATIN AMERICA; ANNUAL REPORT. Spanish edition: Progreso Economico y Social en America Latina. Informe. (Editions also in Portuguese and French) 1961. a. Inter-American Development Bank, 808 17th St. N.W., Washington, DC 20577. stat. Key Title: Economic and Social Progress in Latin America.
    Continues: Socio-Economic Progress in Latin America; Annual Report (ISSN 0074-0888)

338.9   UN
ECONOMIC AND SOCIAL SURVEY OF ASIA AND THE PACIFIC. (Text in English and French) 1948. irreg. $8. United Nations Economic and Social Commission for Asia and the Pacific, United Nations Bldg., Rajadamnern Ave., Bangkok 2, Thailand (Dist. by: United Nations Publications, Room LX-2300, New York, NY 10017; or Distribution and Sales Section, Palais des Nations, CH-1211 Geneva 10, Switzerland)
    Formerly: Economic Survey of Asia and the Far East (ISSN 0070-8690)

330   TH
ECONOMIC CONDITIONS IN/AND OUTLOOK FOR THAILAND. 1978. a. free. Bank of Thailand, Department of Economic Research, Bangkok, Thailand.

330   CN   ISSN 0070-847X
ECONOMIC COUNCIL OF CANADA. ANNUAL REPORT. (Text in English and French) 1964. a. free. Supply and Services Canada, Publishing Centre, Hull,Que. K1A 0S9, Canada.

330   CN   ISSN 0070-8488
ECONOMIC COUNCIL OF CANADA. ANNUAL REVIEW. (Text in English and French) 1964. a. price varies. Supply and Services Canada, Publishing Centre, Hull. Que. K1a 0S9, Canada.

330.9   MW
ECONOMIC DEVELOPMENT OF MALAWI SINCE INDEPENDENCE. (Text in English) 1970. a. free. Department of Information, Box 494, Blantyre, Malawi.

338.9   UN   ISSN 0070-8712
ECONOMIC SURVEY OF EUROPE. (Text in English and French) 1948. a.; latest, 1974 (pub. 1974) price varies. United Nations Economic Commission for Europe, Palais des Nations, 1200 Geneva 10, Switzerland (Or United Nations Publications, Room LX-2300, New York, NY 10017)

330   II
ECONOMIC SURVEY OF INDIA. (Text in English and Marathi) 1962. a. free. Directorate of Economics and Statistics, D.D. Building, Old Custom House, Bombay 400023, India. Ed. S. M. Vidwans.
    Formerly: Maharashtra: an Economic Review (ISSN 0076-2539)

330   JA   ISSN 0021-4833
ECONOMIC SURVEY OF JAPAN. English edition of: Annual Economic White Paper of Economic Planning Agency, Japan. (Text in English) 1969. a. 3900 Yen($23) (Economic Planning Agency) Japan Times, Ltd., 4-5-4 Shibaura, Minato-ku, Tokyo 108, Japan. charts. mkt. stat. (processed)
    Supersedes: Japanese Economic Statistics.

338.9   UN   ISSN 0070-8720
ECONOMIC SURVEY OF LATIN AMERICA. (Editions in English and Spanish) 1949. a. $22 price varies. United Nations Economic Commission for Latin America - Comision Economica de las Naciones Unidas para America Latina, Casilla 179-D, Santiago, Chile (Or United Nations Sales Section, Room A-315, New York, NY 10017; or Distribution and Sales Section, Palais des Nations, CH-1211 Geneva 10, Switzerland) stat. index.

330.9   LB
ECONOMIC SURVEY OF LIBERIA. (Text in English) a, latest 1976. $5. Ministry of Planning and Economic Affairs, Box 9016, Monrovia, Liberia. stat.

330   RH   ISSN 0070-8739
ECONOMIC SURVEY OF RHODESIA. 1965. a. $0.50. Government Printer, Box 8062, Causeway, Zimbabwe.
    Formerly: Review of the Economy of Rhodesia (ISSN 0080-1992)

330.9   SI
ECONOMIC SURVEY OF SINGAPORE. (Text in English) 1974. a. S.$10. Ministry of Trade and Industry, CPF Bldg., 39th Fl., 79 Robinson Rd., Singapore 0106, Singapore (Orders to: Singapore National Printers, Box 485, Singapore, Singapore) circ. 4,500.

330   TI   ISSN 0070-8747
ECONOMIC YEARBOOK OF TUNISIA. (Text in Arabic, French, English) 1964. biennial. $6. Union Tunisienne de l'Industrie, du Commerce et de l'Artisanat, 32 rue Charles de Gaulle, Tunis, Tunisia. adv. circ. 5,000.

330   TI   ISSN 0070-878X
ECONOMIE DE LA TUNISIE EN CHIFFRES. (Text in French) 1960. a, latest 1974/75. Institut National de la Statistique, 27 rue de Liban, Tunis, Tunisia.

330.9   FR
ECONOMIE FRANCAISE EN DONNES D'ENCADREMENT. (Volume 1 of 5) a. 3500 F. (for all 5 vols.) Bureau d'Informations et de Previsions Economiques, 122 Av. Charles de Gaulle, 92522 Neuilly sur Seine, France.
    Supersedes in part: Prevision a Un an de l'Economie Francaise.

ECONOMIE FRANCAISE EN PERSPECTIVES SECTORIELLES: FILIERE BATIMENT, GENIE CIVIL, MATERIAUX DE CONSTRUCTION. see *BUILDING AND CONSTRUCTION*

338   FR
ECONOMIE FRANCAISE EN PERSPECTIVES SECTORIELLES: INDUSTRIES DE BIENS DE CONSOMMATION. (Volume 2 of 5) a. 3500 F. (for all 5 vols.) Bureau d'Informations et de Previsions Economiques, 122 Av. Charles de Gaulle, 92522 Neuilly sur Seine Cedex, France. stat.
    Supersedes in part: Prevision a Un a de l'Economie Francaise.

338   FR
ECONOMIE FRANCAISE EN PERSPECTIVES SECTORIELLES: INDUSTRIES DE BIENS D'EQUIPEMENT. (Volume 3 of 5) a. 3500 F. (for all 5 volumes) Bureau d'Informations et de Previsions Economiques, 122 Av. Charles de Gaulle, 92522 Neuilly sur Seine Cedex, France. stat.
    Supersedes in part: Prevision a Un de l'Economie Francaise.

338   FR
ECONOMIE FRANCAISE EN PERSPECTIVES SECTORIELLES: INDUSTRIES DE BIENS INTERMEDIARIES. (Volume 4 of 5) a. 3500 F. (for all 5 vols.) Bureau d'Informations et de Previsions Economiques, 122 Av Charles de Gaulle, 92522 Neuilly sur Seine Cedex, France. stat.
    Supersedes in part: Prevision a Un An de l'Economie.

330.9   FR
ECONOMIE IVOIRIENNE. (Numero special du Bulletin de l'Afrique Noire) 1970. a. 470 F. Ediafric - la Documentation Africaine, 57 Avenue d'Iena, 75783 Paris Cedex 16, France. illus.

330.9   US
ECONOMIES OF THE WORLD. irreg. price varies. Oxford University Press, 200 Madison Ave., New York, NY 10016 (And Ely House, 37 Dover St., London W1X 4AH England) Ed. Nita Watts.

330   UK   ISSN 0424-3331
ECONOMIST INTELLIGENCE UNIT. E I U WORLD OUTLOOK. 1969. a. $50. Economist Intelligence Unit, Ltd, Spencer House, St. James's Place, London SW1A 1NI, England.

330.9   EC
ECUADOR. CORPORACION FINANCIERA NACIONAL. BOLETIN ESTADISTICO. no. 6, 1978. irreg. Corporacion Financiera Nacional, Robles 731 y Amazonas, Apartado de Correos 163, Quito, Ecuador. charts.

334   IO
EDISI CHUSUS BULLETIN KOPERASI.* 1971. irreg. Rps.350 per no. Department of Manpower, Transmigration and Cooperatives - Departemen Tenaga Kerja, Transmigrasi dan Koperasi, Jl. H.A. Salim 58, Box 45, Jakarta, Indonesia. charts. stat.

330.9   ES
EL SALVADOR. MINISTERIO DE PLANIFICACION Y COORDINACION DEL DESARROLLO ECONOMICO Y SOCIAL. MEMORIA DE LABORES. 1976. irreg. Ministerio de Planificacion y Coordinacion del Desarrollo Economico y Social, San Salvador, El Salvador.

330.9   ES
EL SALVADOR, INFORME ECONOMICO Y SOCIAL. 1975. a. free. Ministerio de Planificacion y Coordinacion del Desarrollo Economico y Social, San Salvador, Salvador. stat. circ. 75-100. (processed)
    Continues: Economia Salvodorena.
    Includes comparative data for previous years

330.9   GW
EMPIRICA. 1974. s-a. DM.70. (Oesterreichisches Institut fuer Wirtschaftsforschung, AU) Gustav Fischer Verlag, Postfach 720143, 7000 Stuttgart 70, W.Germany (B.R.D.) Eds. H. Seidel, K. Aiginger. adv. circ. 800.

330.9   BL
ENSAYOS E C I E L. (Text and summaries in English, Spanish & Portuguese) 1974. irreg., vol. 5, 1978. free. (Organization of American States, US) Programa de Estudios Conjuntos sobre Integracion Economica Latinoamericano, Caixa Postal 740, Rio de Janeiro, Brazil. Ed. Eduardo Albertal. circ. 2,000.

330.9   SP
ESPANA AL DIA. 1972. irreg. Consorcio Americano de Ediciones, Victor de la Serna 5, Madrid, Spain. illus.

330.9   300   SJ
ESSAYS ON THE ECONOMY AND SOCIETY OF THE SUDAN. 1977. irreg. Economic and Social Research Council, Box 1166, Khartoum, Sudan. Ed. Ali Mohamed el Hassan. bibl.

330.9   CL
ESTUDIOS CIEPLAN. 1976. irreg. (10-12/yr) Corporacion de Investigaciones Economicas para Latinoamericano, Casilla 16496, Correo 9, Santiago, Chile.

332   SP
ESTUDIOS ECONOMICOS. 1972. irreg. 100 ptas. Banco de Espana, Seccion de Publicaciones, Alcala 50, Madrid 14, Spain. stat.

330.9   BL
ESTUDOS SOBRE O NORDESTE. irreg. Editora Paz e Terra, Rua Andre Cavalcanti, Bairro de Fatima, Rio de Janeiro, Brazil. Ed. Bd.

330.9   FR
ETUDE SUR LA SITUATION FINANCIERE DES REGIONS. a. (Conseil National du Credit) Banque de France, Service de l'Information, 43 rue de Valois, 75001 Paris, France.

330   FR   ISSN 0071-3252
EVOLUTION DE L'ECONOMIE DES PAYS SUD-AMERICAINS.* a. Banque Francaise et Italienne, Paris, France.

381   GU
FACTS ABOUT DOING BUSINESS IN GUAM U.S.A. 1964. irreg., latest issue 1973. free in Guam; $1 in the U.S. Department of Commerce, Agana, GU 96910. (tabloid format)

338.9   BE
FAITS ET LES DECISIONS DE LA COMMUNAUTE ECONOMIQUE EUROPEENNE. (Text in French) 1969. irreg. (Universite Libre de Bruxelles, Institut d'Etudes Europeennes) Editions de l'Universite de Bruxelles, Institut d'Etudes Europeennes, B-1040 Brussels, Belgium.

FAR EAST AND AUSTRALASIA. see *HISTORY — History Of Australasia And Other Areas*

BUSINESS AND ECONOMICS — ECONOMIC SITUATION AND CONDITIONS

330.9   US
FEDERAL RESERVE BANK OF ATLANTA. RESEARCH PAPER SERIES. 1976. irreg., no.6, 1979. free. Federal Reserve Bank of Atlanta, Atlanta, GA 30303. circ. 2,000.

330   FI   ISSN 0071-5271
FINLAND. KANSANTALOUSOSASTO. TALOUDELLINEN KATSAUS. ECONOMIC SURVEY. (Supplement to the Budget) (Text in Finnish, Swedish, English) 1948. a, latest 1976. Fmk.14. Valtion Painatuskeskus - Government Printing Centre; Ministry of Finance, Annankatu 44, 00100 Helsinki 10, Finland.

338.5   JA
FIVE YEAR ECONOMIC FORECAST/GOKANEN KEIZAI YOSOKU. (Text in English and Japanese) 1975. a. Japan Economic Research Center, Research Divisions - Nihon Keizai Kenkyu Senta, 1-9-5 Otemachi, Chiyoda-ku, Tokyo 100, Japan. Ed. Nobuyoshi Namiki. circ. controlled.

338.9   US   ISSN 0071-7282
FORECAST. 1964. a. free. United California Bank, Research and Planning Division, Box 3666 Terminal Annex, Los Angeles, CA 90051. circ. 40,000.

330.9   US   ISSN 0090-9467
FOREIGN ECONOMIC TRENDS AND THEIR IMPLICATIONS FOR THE UNITED STATES. irreg. $37.50. U.S. Industry and Trade Administration, Bureau of International Commerce, Washington, DC 20203 (Orders to: Supt. of Documents, Washington, DC 20402) illus. stat. (also avail. in microform from UMI) Indexed: Ind.U.S.Gov.Per.
    Continues: Economic Trends and Their Implications for the United States.

330   FR   ISSN 0071-8505
FRANCE. COMMISSION TECHNIQUE DES ENTENTES. ECONOMIQUES RAPPORTS. 1954. a. Commission Technique des Ententes, 41 Quai Branly, Paris, France. circ. controlled.

330.9   FR   ISSN 0339-2945
FRANCE. DEPARTEMENT D'ECONOMIE ET DE SOCIOLOGIE RURALES. BULLETIN D'INFORMATION. 1974. irreg. free. Institut National de la Recherche Agronomique, Departement d'Economie et de Sociologie Rurales, 6 Passage Tenaille, 75014 Paris, France. circ. 2,400.

338.9   DR
FUNDACION DOMINICANA DE DESARROLLO. INFORME ANUAL. a. Fundacion Dominicana de Desarrollo, Calle Mercedes 4, Santo Domingo, Z. P. No. 1, Dominican Republic. Ed. Enrique Armenteros. charts. illus.

330   EI   ISSN 0069-6749
GENERAL REPORT ON THE ACTIVITIES OF THE EUROPEAN COMMUNITIES. (Supersedes the General Report on the Activities of the Community published individually by the European Coal and Steel Community. High Authority; European Economic Community. Commission; European Atomic Energy Community. Commission) (Text in Dutch, English, French, German, Italian) 1968. a. price varies. Commission of the European Communities, Service des Renseignements, 200 rue de la Loi, Brussels 4, Belgium (Dist. in U.S. by: European Community Information Service, 2100 M St., NW, Suite 707, Washington, DC 20037)

330.9   GH
GHANA. (Text in English) irreg. Information Services Department, Box 745, Accra, Ghana. illus.

330.9   GH   ISSN 0435-9348
GHANA COMMERCIAL BANK. ANNUAL REPORT. a. free. Ghana Commercial Bank, Box 134, Accra, Ghana.

330.9   II
GOA, DAMAN, AND DIU. BUREAU OF ECONOMICS, STATISTICS, AND EVALUATION. EVALUATION REPORT. 1969. irreg. Bureau of Economics, Statistics, and Evaluation, Panaji, Goa, India. stat. circ. 150.

330   CH
GRAPHICAL SURVEY OF THE ECONOMY OF TAIWAN DISTRICT, REPUBLIC OF CHINA. (Text in Chinese and English) 1972. a. not for sale. Central Bank of China, Taipei, Taiwan, Republic of China. circ. 2,000.

380.1   GU
GUAM ECONOMIC ANNUAL REVIEW. 1963. a. Department of Commerce, Box 682, Agana, GU 96910.
    Formerly: Guam. Department of Commerce. Quarterly Review of Business Conditions.

330   BL
GUANABARA: O BALANCO ECONOMICO. 1972. a. free. Instituto de Desenvolvimento da Guanabara, Av. Calogeras, 15 - 3. andar, Rio de Janeiro, Brazil. illus. stat. circ. 1,000.

GUATEMALA. BANCO NACIONAL DE DESARROLLO AGRICOLA. MEMORIA. see AGRICULTURE — Agricultural Economics

338   BO
GUIA BOLIVIA; Industria, Comercio, Ganaderia. 1976. irreg. Editora Nacional, Bolivar 3235, Cochabamba, Bolivia.

330   UY
GUIA PARA INVERSIONES EN EL URUGUAY. 1976. irreg. Comision Coordinadora para el Desarrollo Economico, Av. Rondeau 1908, Montevideo, Uruguay.

330.9   KE
GUIDELINES FOR INDUSTRIAL INVESTORS IN KENYA. Cover title: Kenya. Ministry of Commerce and Industry. Industrial Investment Guidelnes. 1967. irreg. Ministry of Commerce and Industry, Industrial Survey and Promotion Centre, Uchumi, Nkrumah Ave., Box 30430, Nairobi, Kenya. illus.

330.9   US   ISSN 0067-3633
HAWAII ANNUAL ECONOMIC REVIEW. 1950. a. single copies free. Bank of Hawaii, Economics Division, P.O. Box 2900, Honolulu, HI 96846. Ed. Wesley H. Hillendahl. stat. circ. 15,000. (back issues avail.) Indexed: B.P.I. P.A.I.S.
    Formerly: Economy of Hawaii.

330.9   HK
HONG KONG ANNUAL REPORT. a. price varies. Government Information Services, Beaconsfield House, Queen's Rd., Central, Victoria, Hong Kong.

330.9   HK
HONG KONG SOCIAL AND ECONOMIC TRENDS. (Text in English) 1973. triennial. HK.$42. Census and Statistics Department, Kai Tak Commercial Bldg., 317 Des Voeux Rd., Central, Hong Kong, Hong Kong (Subscr. to: Government Information Services, Beaconsfield House, Queen's Rd., Central, Victoria, Hong Kong)

330   II
I S E C MONOGRAPH. no. 4, 1976. irreg. Rs.20($4.50) (Institute for Social and Economic Change) World Press Ltd., 37A College St., Calcutta 700073, India. Ed. F.K.R.V. Rao.

330   US   ISSN 0093-9552
ILLINOIS STATE AND REGIONAL ECONOMIC DATA BOOK. 1970. a. free. Department of Business and Economic Development, 222 S. College, Springfield, IL 62706. stat. circ. 2,000(controlled)

330.9 318   BL
INDICE DO BRASIL/BRAZILIAN INDEX YEARBOOK. irreg. Indice - o Banco de Dados, Rua Alcindo Guanabara 24, Rio de Janeiro, Brazil. illus.

INDUSTRIAL REVIEW OF JAPAN; an annual in-depth report on the state of the Japanese economy. see BUSINESS AND ECONOMICS — Production Of Goods And Services

330.9   SP
INFORMACION COMERCIAL ESPANOL. CUADERNOS ECONOMICOS. (Supplement to Informacion Comercial Espanola. Revista Mensual) 1977. irreg. Informacion Comercial Espanol, Almagro 34, Madrid, Spain (Subcr. to: Goya 73, Madrid, Spain)

INFORMATION ABOUT INVESTMENT IN TASMANIA. see BUSINESS AND ECONOMICS — Investments

330.9   BL
INFORMATION ON PARANA. Portuguese ed.: Parana Informacoes. 1973. irreg. free. ‡ Banco de Desenvolvimento do Parana, S.A., Av. Vicente Machado, 445, Cx. Postal 6042, Curitiba, Parana, Brazil. Ed. Luiz Fernando Osti Magalhaes. illus.

330.9   MX
INGRESOS Y EGRESOS DE LA FAMILIAS EN LA REPUBLICA MEXICANA. 1953. irreg. Direccion General de Muestreo, Mexico D.F., Mexico.
    Formerly (until 1956): Ingresos y Egresos de la Poblacion de Mexico.

330.9   FR
INSTITUT D'ECONOMIE REGIONALE BOURGOGNE-FRANCHE-COMTE. CAHIERS. irreg. no. 24, 1977. 30 F. Institut d'Economie Regionale Bourgogne-Franche-Comte, 14 Bd Gabriel, 21000 Dijon, France.

330.9   VE
INSTITUTO DE CREDITO AGRICOLA Y PECUARIO. INFORME ANNUAL. 1975. a. Instituto de Credito Agricola y Pecuario, Barquisimeto, Venezuela.
    Continues: Banco Agricola y Pecuario. Informe.

338.9   PE
INSTITUTO DE ESTUDIOS PERUANOS. ANALISIS ECONOMICO. 1970. irreg. price varies. I E P Ediciones, Horacio Urteaga 694 (Campo de Marte), Lima 11, Peru.

330   AG
INSTITUTO TORCUATO DI TELLA. CENTRO DE INVESTIGACIONES ECONOMICAS. INFORMES DE INVESTIGACION. 1966. irreg. price varies. Instituto Torcuato di Tella, Conde 1717, Buenos Aires, Argentina.

330   UN
INTERNATIONAL LABOUR OFFICE. P R E A L C. INVESTIGACIONES SOBRE EMPLEO. 1978. irreg. $5 per no. International Labour Office, Programa Regional del Empleo para America Latina y el Caribe (P R E A L C) - Oficina Internacional del Trabajo, Box 618, Santiago, Chile. circ. 1,000.

382   IS
ISRAEL EXPORT AND TRADE JOURNAL. (Text in English) 1941. a. $30. Israel Periodicals Company Ltd., Box 11586, Tel Aviv, Israel. Ed. Judy Levy. adv. bk. rev. illus. stat. circ. 18,500.
    Formerly: Israel Export Annual.

330   IT   ISSN 0075-1995
ITALY. MINISTERO DEL BILANCIO E DELLA PROGRAMMAZIONE ECONOMICA. RELAZIONE GENERALE SULLA SITUAZIONE ECONOMICA DEL PAESE. 1951. a. Ministero del Bilancio, Rome, Italy.

330   US   ISSN 0075-1642
ITALY: AN ECONOMIC PROFILE. 1959. a. free. Italian Embassy in the United States, Commercial Office, 2600 Virginia Ave. N.W. (Suite 200), 1601 Fuller St., N.W., DC 20009. circ. 10,000. (back issues avail.)

330   AU
JAHRBUCH DER OESTERREICHISCHEN WIRTSCHAFT. 1975. a. Bundeskammer der Gewerblichen Wirtschaft, Stubenring 12, A-1010 Vienna, Austria. Ed. Franz Geibler.

330   GW   ISSN 0449-5225
JAHRBUCH DER WIRTSCHAFT OSTEUROPAS/ YEARBOOK OF EAST-EUROPEAN ECONOMICS. (Editions in English and German) 1970. a. DM.96. (Osteuropa-Institut, Munich) Guenter Olzog Verlag, Thierschstr. 11/15, 8000 Munich 22, W. Germany (B.R.D.) Ed. Hans Raupach. bk. rev. circ. 800.

330   JA   ISSN 0075-3238
JAPAN ECONOMIC RESEARCH CENTER. CENTER PAPER SERIES. (Text in English) 1965. irreg. Japan Economic Research Center, General Administration Division - Nihon Keizai Kenkyu Senta, 1-9-5 Otemachi, Chiyoda-ku, Tokyo 100, Japan. (back issues avail.)

BUSINESS AND ECONOMICS — ECONOMIC SITUATION AND CONDITIONS

330 JA ISSN 0075-3246
JAPAN ECONOMIC YEAR BOOK. (Text in English) 1954. a. $32. Oriental Economist - Toyo Keizai Shinposha, 1-4 Hongokucho, Nihonbashi, Chuo-ku, Tokyo 103, Japan. Ed. Atsuo Tsuruoka.

330.9 320 US
JAPAN REPORT. 1975. irreg. (approx. 27/yr.) $135. U.S. Joint Publications Research Service, 1000 N. Glebe Rd., Arlington, VA 22201 (Orders to: NTIS, Springfield, VA 22161)
Formerly: Translations on Japan.

330 JA
KEIDANREN KEIZAI SHIRYO. (Text in Japanese) 1947. irreg. $2. Japan Federation of Economic Organizations - Keizai Dantai Rengokai (KEIDANREN), 1-9-4 Otemachi, Chiyoda-ku, Tokyo 100, Japan. charts. illus. stat. circ. 3,500.

330 JA
KEIDANREN PAMPHLET. (Text in Japanese) 1950. irreg. $2.50. Japan Federation of Economic Organizations - Keizai Dantai Rengokai (KEIDANREN), 1-9-4 Otemachi, Chiyoda-ku, Tokyo 100, Japan. charts. illus. stat. circ. 3,500.

330 JA
KEIDANREN POCKET SERIES. (Text in Japanese) 1975. irreg. free. Japan Federation of Economic Organizations - Keizai Dantai Rengokai (KEIDANREN), 1-9-4 Otemachi, Chiyoda-ku, Tokyo 100, Japan. circ. 10,000.

330.9 US
KENTUCKY. COUNCIL OF ECONOMIC ADVISORS. POLICY PAPERS SERIES. 1977. irreg., 4-5/yr. $10. Kentucky Council of Economic Advisors, College of Business and Economics, University of Kentucky, Lexington, KY 40506. Ed. Dr. Charles G. Renfro. circ. 600. Indexed: P.A.I.S.

330.9 KE
KENYA. CENTRAL BUREAU OF STATISTICS. ECONOMIC SURVEY. 1960. a. EAs.10. Central Bureau of Statistics, Box 30266, Nairobi, Kenya (Orders to: Government Printing and Stationery Department, Box 30128, Nairobi, Kenya)
Formerly: Kenya. Ministry of Economic Planning and Development. Economic Survey (ISSN 0075-5842)

330.9 UK
KENYA YEARBOOK. a. £10($30) Publishing and Distributing Co. Ltd., 177 Regent St., London W.1., England. adv. charts. illus.

330.9 II ISSN 0453-7440
KERALA; AN ECONOMIC REVIEW. (Text in English) 1959. a. price varies. Kerala State Planning Board, Trivandrum 4, India. circ. 2,000.

KOREA POLICY SERIES. see *POLITICAL SCIENCE*

330.9 320.253 US
KOREAN AFFAIRS REPORT. 1966. irreg. (approx. 75/yr.) $225. U.S. Joint Publications Research Service, 1000 N. Glebe Rd., Arlington, VA 22201 (Orders to: NTIS, Springfield, VA 22161)
Formerly: Translations on North Korea.

330 GW
LATEINAMERIKA: WIRTSCHAFTLICHE DATEN. 1968. a. Deutsche Ueberseeische Bank, Ballindamm 7, 2000 Hamburg 1, W. Germany (B.R.D.) charts. stat. circ. 10,000.

330.9 320 UK
LATIN AMERICA & CARIBBEAN. (Editions in English and Spanish) 1979. a. £12.50($30) World of Information, 21 Gold St., Saffron Walden, Essex CB10 1EJ, England. Ed. Graham Hancock. adv. illus. stat.
Formerly (until 1981): Latin America Annual Review & the Caribbean.

330.9 320 US
LATIN AMERICA REPORT. 1967. irreg. (approx. 241/yr.) $723. U.S. Joint Publications Research Service, 1000 N. Glebe Rd., Arlington, VA 22201 (Orders to: NTIS, Springfield, VA 22161)
Formerly: Translations on Latin America.

330.9 LO
LESOTHO NATIONAL DEVELOPMENT CORPORATION. NEWSLETTER. irreg. Lesotho National Development Corporation, Box 666, Maseru, Lesotho.

382 330 LH
LIECHTENSTEIN. PRESS AND INFORMATION OFFICE. PRESS FOLDER. (Text in German, English, French) 1968. triennial. free. Press and Information Office, Government Palace, FL-9490 Vaduz, Liechtenstein. circ. 5,000.

330 LH
LIECHTENSTEIN ECONOMY. (Text in German, English, French) 1962. triennial. 6 Fr. Press and Information Office, Government Palace, FL-9490 Vaduz, Liechtenstein. circ. 6,000.

330.9 916 MW
LIVING IN MALAWI. (Text in English) 1964. biennial. free. Department of Information, Box 494, Blantyre, Malawi. circ. 6,000.

338 UA
M E O BULLETIN. irreg. (approx. 32/yr.) Le.4.50 per no. Middle East Observer, 8 Chawarby St., Cairo, Egypt.

330.9 MY
M P R C REPORT ON FINANCE, COMMERCE, INDUSTRY: INDONESIA. 1972. irreg. M.$100. ‡ M P R C (Asia) Sdn. Berhad, 7 Jalan Baiduri, Box 706, Kuala Lumpur 01-02, Malaysia. Ed. Paul Markandan. bk. rev. stat. circ. controlled.

330.9 MY
M P R C REPORT ON FINANCE, COMMERCE, INDUSTRY: INDONESIA. SUPPLEMENT. 1974. irreg. M.$40. M P R C (Asia) Sdn. Berhad, 7 Jalan Baiduri, Box 706, Kuala Lumpur 01-02, Malaysia. Ed. Paul Markandan. bk. rev. stat.

330.9 MY
M P R C REPORT ON FINANCE, COMMERCE, INDUSTRY: SINGAPORE. 1972. irreg. M.$30. ‡ M P R C (Asia) Sdn. Berhad, 7 Jalan Baiduri, Box 706, Kuala Lumpur 01-02, Malaysia. Ed. Paul Markandan. bk. rev. stat. circ. controlled.

330.9 MY
M P R C REPORT ON FINANCE, COMMERCE, INDUSTRY: SOUTH EAST ASIA. 1977. irreg. M.$150. M P R C (Asia) Sdn. Berhad, 7 Jalan Baiduri, Box 706, Kuala Lumpur 01-02, Malaysia. Ed. Paul Markandan. bk. rev. stat. circ. (controlled)

330.9 MY
M P R C REPORT ON FINANCE, COMMERCE, INDUSTRY: THAILAND. 1973. irreg. M.$100. ‡ M P R C (Asia) Sdn. Berhad, 7 Jalan Baiduri, Box 706, Kuala Lumpur 01-02, Malaysia. Ed. Paul Markandan. bk. rev. stat. circ. controlled.

330.1 MW ISSN 0076-3101
MALAWI ECONOMIC REPORT. a. K.2.75. Government Printer, P.O. Box 37, Zomba, Malawi.

330 MY
MALAYSIA. TREASURY. ECONOMIC REPORT. (Editions in English and Malay) 1972. a. M.$5($2.04) Treasury - Perbendaharaan, Jalan Chan Sow Lin, Kuala Lumpur, Malaysia. charts. stat. circ. 3,122 English ed.; 1,100 Malay ed.

330.9 MM
MALTA. CENTRAL OFFICE OF STATISTICS. ECONOMIC SURVEY. a. Central Office of Statistics, Valletta, Malta (Subscr. to: Department of Information, Auberge de Castille, Valletta, Malta)

330 AT
MANAGEMENT REPORTS ON THE AUSTRALIAN ECONOMY. (Title Varies: Management Guide to the Economies of Australia and New Zealand) 1965. a. Aus.$30. W. D. Scott & Co., 100 Pacific Highway, North Sydney, N.S.W. 2060, Australia.
Formerly: Australian Economy; Business Forecast (ISSN 0084-7348)

330 CN ISSN 0318-6415
MANITOBA COMMUNITY REPORTS. 1959. a. free. ‡ Department of Economic Development, 602-155 Carlton St., Winnipeg, Man. R3C OV8, Canada. stat. circ. controlled.

MEMO FROM BELGIUM. see *POLITICAL SCIENCE*

977 US
METROPOLITAN MILWAUKEE ECONOMIC FACT BOOK. Title varies: Economic Fact Book on Metropolitan Milwaukee. 1965. a. $20. Metropolitan Milwaukee Association of Commerce, 756 N. Milwaukee St., Milwaukee, WI 53202.
Formerly: Metropolitan Milwaukee Association of Commerce. Economic Studies (ISSN 0076-7077)

972 MX ISSN 0543-7741
MEXICO; facts, figures, trends. Spanish edition: Mexico; Hechos, Cifras, Tendencias. 1960. irreg; latest issue 1976. $8 spanish edition; $12 English edition. ‡ Banco Nacional de Comercio Exterior, S.A., Departamento de Publicaciones, Ave. Chapultepec 230 (2 piso), Mexico 7, D.F., Mexico.

330.9 UK ISSN 0305-3210
MIDDLE EAST REVIEW. (Editions in English, German and Arabic) 1974. a. £12.50($30) World of Information, 21 Gold St., Saffron Walden, Essex CB10 1EJ, England. Ed. Graham Hancock. adv. illus. stat.
Formerly (until 1981): Middle East Annual Review.

330.9 US
MINNESOTA PROFILE. a. free. Department of Economic Development, 480 Cedar St., St. Paul, MN 55101. circ. 4,000.

330.9 US
MISSOURI ECONOMIC INDICATORS. vol. 1, no. 4, 1976. irreg. University of Missouri-Columbia, Public Affairs Information Service, Middlebush Hall, Columbia, MO 65201. (Co-sponsor: Missouri Office of Administration. Division of Budget and Planning)

330.9 320 US
MONGOLIA REPORT. irreg. (approx. 8/yr.) $24. U.S. Joint Publications Research Service, 1000 N. Glebe Rd., Arlington, VA 22201 (Orders to: NTIS, Springfield, VA 22161)
Formerly: Translations on Mongolia.

330.9 ET ISSN 0077-3506
NATIONAL BANK OF ETHIOPIA. LOCAL PRICES. 1963. irreg. $5 per no. National Bank of Ethiopia, Economic Research and Planning Division, c/o Research Library, Box 5550, Addis Ababa, Ethiopia.

330 YU ISSN 0077-2798
NATIONAL BANK OF YUGOSLAVIA. ANNUAL REPORT. (Text in English) 1958. a. Narodna Banka Jugoslavije, Bulevar Revolucije 15, Box 1010, 11001 Belgrade, Yugoslavia. circ. 1,200.

330.9 IR ISSN 0572-5941
NATIONAL INCOME OF IRAN. 1974. irreg., latest 1977. free. Bank Markazi Iran, Economic Statistics Department - Central Bank of Iran, Ave. Ferdowsi, Teheran, Iran.

330.9 US ISSN 0145-9317
NEAR EAST AND NORTH AFRICA REPORT. irreg. (approx. 144/yr.) $576. U.S. Joint Publications Research Service, 1000 N. Glebe Rd., Arlington, VA 22201 (Orders to: NTIS, Springfield, VA 22161)
Former titles: Translations on Near East and North Africa; Translations on Near East.

330.9 US ISSN 0362-1138
NEBRASKA. DEPARTMENT OF ECONOMIC DEVELOPMENT. ANNUAL ECONOMIC REPORT. irreg. Department of Economic Development, Division of Research, Box 94666, State Capitol, Lincoln, NE 68509. illus. Key Title: Annual Economic Report, Nebraska.

309.2 US
NEBRASKA COMMUNITY IMPROVEMENT PROGRAM. a. $10. Department of Economic Development, Division of Community Affairs, Box 94666, Lincoln, NE 68509. (Co-Sponsor: University of Nebraska Extension Division) illus.

330.9 NP
NEPAL. RASHTRIYA PANCAYATA. ARTHIKA SAMITI. (Text in Nepali) a. Rashtriya Panchayat Sachivalaya, Rashtriya Panchayat Bhavan, Singhdarbar, Kathmandu, Napal.

BUSINESS AND ECONOMICS — ECONOMIC SITUATION AND CONDITIONS

650   US   ISSN 0077-9083
NEW YORK STATE BUSINESS FACT BOOK. PART 1: BUSINESS AND MANUFACTURING. (Issued as State Book and 12 Economic Area books) 1947. approx. every 5 years. free. Department of Commerce, 99 Washington Ave., Albany, NY 12245. Ed. Peter A. Ansell. circ. 5,000.

650   US   ISSN 0077-9091
NEW YORK STATE BUSINESS FACT BOOK. PART 2: POPULATION AND HOUSING. (Issued as State Book and 12 Economic Area books) 1947. every 10 years. free. Department of Commerce, 99 Washington Ave., Albany, NY 12245. Ed. Peter A. Ansell. circ. 5,000.

650   US   ISSN 0077-9105
NEW YORK STATE BUSINESS FACT BOOK. SUPPLEMENT. 1961. a. free. Department of Commerce, 99 Washington Ave., Albany, NY 12245. Ed. Peter A. Ansell. circ. 4,000.

330   AG   ISSN 0078-0863
NIVEL DE LA ECONOMIA ARGENTINA. 1962. a. free. Oficina de Estudios para la Colaboracion Economica Internacional, Buenos Aires, Argentina. circ. 3,000.

330.9   NO
NORGES BANK. SKRIFTSERIE. (Text in English or Norwegian) 1973. irreg., no.9, 1980. Norges Bank, Economic Intelligence Department, Box 336, Oslo 1, Norway.

338   US   ISSN 0549-8368
NORTH DAKOTA GROWTH INDICATORS. 1959. irreg. free. Business and Industrial Development Department, 523 E. Bismark Ave., Bismarck, ND 58505.

330.9   FR
NOTES DE CONJONCTURE REGIONALE. (Covers each of the twenty-two regions of France) irreg. (3-4/yr from each of the 22 regions) Banque de France, Service de l'Information, 43 rue de Valois, 75049 Paris Cedex 1, France. stat.

330.9   VE
NUEVA CIENCIA. 1975. irreg. $10. Universidad Central de Venezuela, Instituto de Investigaciones Economicas y Sociales, Apdo. 40-545, Caracas, Venezuela.

338   US   ISSN 0362-9716
OHIO INVENTORY OF BUSINESS AND INDUSTRIAL CHANGE. irreg. Department of Economic and Community Development, Bureau of Business Research, 65 South Front St., Columbus, OH 43215. stat.

330.9   CN
OPPORTUNITY IN NORTHERN CANADA. 1974. q. Can.$4 single issue. Fleet Publications Canada Ltd., Box 1679, Winnipeg, Manitoba R3C 2Z6, Canada. illus.

330   US
OREGON, AN ECONOMIC PROFILE. biennial. free. Department of Economic Development, 155 Cottage St. N.E., Salem, OR 97310. charts.

330.9   FR
ORGANIZATION FOR ECONOMIC COOPERATION AND DEVELOPMENT. ECONOMIC SURVEYS: AUSTRALIA. irreg. $3. Organization for Economic Cooperation and Development, 2, rue Andre-Pascal, 75775 Paris 16, France (U.S. orders to: O.E.C.D. Publications and Information Center, 1750 Pennsylvania Ave., N.W., Washington, D. C. 20006) illus. stat. (also avail. in microfiche)

330   FR   ISSN 0474-5124
ORGANIZATION FOR ECONOMIC COOPERATION AND DEVELOPMENT. ECONOMIC SURVEYS: AUSTRIA. 1959. irreg. Organization for Economic Cooperation and Development, 2 rue Andre Pascal, 75775 Paris 16, France (U.S. orders to: O.E.C.D. Publications and Information Center, 1750 Pennsylvania Ave., N.W., Washington, DC 20006) (also avail. in microfiche)
Supersedes in part: Organization for Economic Cooperation and Development. Economic Conditions in Austria and Switzerland.

330   FR   ISSN 0474-5132
ORGANIZATION FOR ECONOMIC COOPERATION AND DEVELOPMENT. ECONOMIC SURVEYS: BELGIUM-LUXEMBOURG ECONOMIC UNION. 1960. irreg. Organization for Economic Cooperation and Development, 2 rue Andre Pascal, 75775 Paris 16, France (U.S. orders to: O.E.C.D. Publications and Information Center, 1750 Pennsylvania Ave., N.W., Washington, DC 20006) (also avail. in microfiche)

330   FR   ISSN 0474-5140
ORGANIZATION FOR ECONOMIC COOPERATION AND DEVELOPMENT. ECONOMIC SURVEYS: CANADA. 1959. irreg. Organization for Economic Cooperation and Development, 2, rue Andre Pascal, 75775 Paris 16, France (U. S. orders to: O.E.C.D. Publications and Information Center, 1750 Pennsylvania Ave., N. W., Washington, D. C. 20006) (also avail. in microfiche)

330.9   FR   ISSN 0474-5159
ORGANIZATION FOR ECONOMIC COOPERATION AND DEVELOPMENT. ECONOMIC SURVEYS: DENMARK. 1960. irreg. Organization for Economic Cooperation and Development, 2, rue Andre Pascal, 75775 Paris 16, France (U. S. orders to: O.E.C.D. Publications and Information Center, 1750 Pennsylvania Ave., N. W., Washington, D. C. 20006) (also avail. in microfiche)

330.9   FR
ORGANIZATION FOR ECONOMIC COOPERATION AND DEVELOPMENT. ECONOMIC SURVEYS: FINLAND. irreg. 200 F.($50) Organization for Economic Cooperation and Development, 2 rue Andre Pascal, 75775 Paris 16, France (U.S. orders to: O.E.C.D. Publications and Information Center, 1750 Pennsylvania Ave. N.W., Washington, DC 20006) (also avail. in microfiche)

330   FR   ISSN 0474-5167
ORGANIZATION FOR ECONOMIC COOPERATION AND DEVELOPMENT. ECONOMIC SURVEYS: FRANCE. 1953. irreg. Organization for Economic Cooperation and Development, 2, rue Andre Pascal, 75775 Paris 16, France (U. S. orders to: O.E.C.D. Publications and Information Center, 1750 Pennsylvania Ave., N. W., Washington, D. C. 20006) (also avail. in microfiche)

330   FR   ISSN 0474-5175
ORGANIZATION FOR ECONOMIC COOPERATION AND DEVELOPMENT. ECONOMIC SURVEYS: GERMANY. 1953. Organization for Economic Cooperation and Development, 2 rue Andre Pascal, 75775 Paris 16, France (U. S. orders to: O.E.C.D. Publications and Information Center, 1750 Pennsylvania Ave. N.W., Washington, D.C. 20006) (also avail. in microfiche)

330   FR   ISSN 0474-5183
ORGANIZATION FOR ECONOMIC COOPERATION AND DEVELOPMENT. ECONOMIC SURVEYS: GREECE. 1954. irreg. Organization for Economic Cooperation and Development, 2 rue Andre Pascal, 75775 Paris 16, France (U.S. orders to: O.E.C.D. Publications and Information Center, 1750 Pennsylvania Ave., N.W., Washington, D. C. 20006) (also avail. in microfiche)

330.9   FR   ISSN 0474-5191
ORGANIZATION FOR ECONOMIC COOPERATION AND DEVELOPMENT. ECONOMIC SURVEYS: ICELAND. 1960. a. Organization for Economic Cooperation and Development, 2 rue Andre Pascal, 75775 Paris 16, France (U. S. orders to: O.E.C.D. Publications and Information Center, 1750 Pennsylvania Ave., N. W., Washington, D. C. 20006) (also avail. in microfiche)

330   FR   ISSN 0474-5205
ORGANIZATION FOR ECONOMIC COOPERATION AND DEVELOPMENT. ECONOMIC SURVEYS: IRELAND. 1960. irreg. Organization for Economic Cooperation and Development, 2 rue Andre Pascal, 75775 Paris 16, France (U. S. orders to: O.E.C.D. Publications and Information Center, 1750 Pennsylvania Ave., N. W., Washington, D. C. 20006) (also avail. in microfiche)

330   FR   ISSN 0474-5213
ORGANIZATION FOR ECONOMIC COOPERATION AND DEVELOPMENT. ECONOMIC SURVEYS: ITALY. (Not published in 1978) 1953. irreg. Organization for Economic Cooperation and Development, 2 rue Andre Pascal, 75775 Paris 16, France (U.S. orders to: O.E.C.D Publications and Information Center Pennsylvania Ave. N.W., Washington, D.C. 20006) (also avail. in microfiche)

330   FR   ISSN 0474-5221
ORGANIZATION FOR ECONOMIC COOPERATION AND DEVELOPMENT. ECONOMIC SURVEYS: JAPAN. 1964. irreg. Organization for Economic Cooperation and Development, 2, rue Andre Pascal, 75775 Paris 16, France (U.S. orders to: O.E.C.D. Publications and Information Center, 1750 Pennsylvania Ave., N.W., Washington, DC 20006) (also avail. in microfiche)

330   FR   ISSN 0474-523X
ORGANIZATION FOR ECONOMIC COOPERATION AND DEVELOPMENT. ECONOMIC SURVEYS: NETHERLANDS. 1954. irreg. Organization for Economic Cooperation and Development, 2, rue Andre Pascal, 75775 Paris 16, France (U. S. orders to: O.E.C.D. Publications and Information Center, 1750 Pennsylvania Ave., N. W., Washington, D. C. 20006) (also avail. in microfiche)

330   FR   ISSN 0376-6438
ORGANIZATION FOR ECONOMIC COOPERATION AND DEVELOPMENT. ECONOMIC SURVEYS: NEW ZEALAND. irreg. 200 F.($50) Organization for Economic Cooperation and Development, 2 rue Andre Pascal, 75775 Paris 16, France (U.S. orders to: O.E.C.D. Publications and Information Center, 1750 Pennsylvania Ave. N.W., Washington, DC 20006) (also avail. in microfiche)

330   FR   ISSN 0474-5248
ORGANIZATION FOR ECONOMIC COOPERATION AND DEVELOPMENT. ECONOMIC SURVEYS: NORWAY. 1960. irreg. Organization for Economic Cooperation and Development, 2, rue Andre Pascal, 75775 Paris 16, France (U. S. orders to: O.E.C.D. Publications and Information Center, 1750 Pennsylvania Ave., N. W., Washington, D. C. 20006) (also avail. in microfiche)

330   FR   ISSN 0474-5256
ORGANIZATION FOR ECONOMIC COOPERATION AND DEVELOPMENT. ECONOMIC SURVEYS: PORTUGAL. 1960. irreg. Organization for Economic Cooperation and Development, 2, rue Andre Pascal, 75775 Paris 16, France (U. S. orders to: O.E.C.D. Publications and Information Center, 1750 Pennsylvania Ave., N. W., Washington, D. C. 20006) (also avail. in microfiche)

330   FR   ISSN 0474-5272
ORGANIZATION FOR ECONOMIC COOPERATION AND DEVELOPMENT. ECONOMIC SURVEYS: SPAIN. 1958. irreg. Organization for Economic Cooperation and Development, 2, rue Andre Pascal, 75775 Paris 16, France (U. S. orders to: O.E.C.D. Publications and Information Center, 1750 Pennsylvania Ave., N. W., Washington, D. C. 20006) (also avail. in microfiche)

330   FR   ISSN 0474-5280
ORGANIZATION FOR ECONOMIC COOPERATION AND DEVELOPMENT. ECONOMIC SURVEYS: SWEDEN. 1954. irreg. Organization for Economic Cooperation and Development, 2 rue Andre Pascal, 75775 Paris 16, France (U. S. orders to: O.E.C.D. Publications and Information Center, 1750 Pennsylvania Ave., N. W., Washington, D. C. 20006) (also avail. in microfiche)

330   FR   ISSN 0474-5299
ORGANIZATION FOR ECONOMIC COOPERATION AND DEVELOPMENT. ECONOMIC SURVEYS: SWITZERLAND. 1959. irreg. Organization for Economic Cooperation and Development, 2 rue Andre Pascal, 75775 Paris 16, France (U.S. orders to: O.E.C.D. Publications and Information Center, 1750 Pennsylvania Ave. N.W., Washington, D. C. 20006) (also avail. in microfiche)

330 FR ISSN 0474-5302
ORGANIZATION FOR ECONOMIC
COOPERATION AND DEVELOPMENT.
ECONOMIC SURVEYS: TURKEY. (Not
published in 1978) 1954. irreg. Organization for
Economic Cooperation and Development, 2 rue
Andre Pascal, 75775 Paris 16, France (U. S. orders
to: O.E.C.D. Publications and Information Center,
1750 Pennsylvania Ave., N. W., Washington, D. C.
20006) (also avail. in microfiche)

330 FR ISSN 0474-5310
ORGANIZATION FOR ECONOMIC
COOPERATION AND DEVELOPMENT.
ECONOMIC SURVEYS: UNITED KINGDOM.
1953. irreg. Organization for Economic Cooperation
and Development, 2 rue Andre Pascal, 75775 Paris
16, France (U. S. orders to: O.E.C.D. Publications
and Information Center, 1750 Pennsylvania Ave.,
N. W., Washington, D. C. 20006) (also avail. in
microfiche)

330 FR ISSN 0474-5329
ORGANIZATION FOR ECONOMIC
COOPERATION AND DEVELOPMENT.
ECONOMIC SURVEYS: UNITED STATES. 1953.
irreg. Organization for Economic Cooperation and
Development, 2 rue Andre Pascal, 75775 Paris 16
(U.S. orders to: O.E.C.D. Publications and
Information Center, 1750 Pennsylvania Ave., N.W.,
Washington, DC 20006) (also avail. in microfiche)

330 949.7 FR ISSN 0474-5264
ORGANIZATION FOR ECONOMIC
COOPERATION AND DEVELOPMENT.
ECONOMIC SURVEYS: SOCIALIST FEDERAL
REPUBLIC OF YUGOSLAVIA. 1962. irreg.
Organization for Economic Cooperation and
Development, 2 rue Andre Pascal, 75775 Paris 16,
France (U. S. orders to: O.E.C.D. Publications and
Information Center, 1750 Pennsylvania Ave., N.
W., Washington, D. C. 20006) (also avail. in
microfiche)

330.9 II
ORISSA, INDIA. FINANCE DEPARTMENT.
WHITE PAPER ON THE ECONOMIC
CONDITIONS AND THE DEVELOPMENTAL
ACTIVITIES IN ORISSA. (Text in English) a.
(Finance Department) Orissa Government Press,
Cuttack, Orissa, India.
    Continues: Orissa, India. Finance Department.
White Paper on Departmental Activities,
Government of Orissa (ISSN 0472-0989)

330.9 GW
OSTINFORMATION. irreg. DM.3. Bundesstelle fuer
Aussenhandelsinformation, Blaubach 13, 5000
Cologne 1, W. Germany (B.R.D.)

338.9 US ISSN 0079-0486
P. E. L. STATE BULLETIN; a report to League
members on significant government developments.
1958. irreg., 1969, vol. XII, no. 2. free. ‡
Pennsylvania Economy League, P.O.B. 105,
Harrisburg, PA 17108. circ. controlled

330 PK ISSN 0078-8082
PAKISTAN ECONOMIC SURVEY. (Text in
English) 1962. a. price varies. Finance Division,
Islamabad, Pakistan (Order from: Manager of
Publications, Government of Pakistan, 2nd Floor,
Ahmad Chamber, Tariq Rd., P.E.C.H.S., Karachi
29, Pakistan) index.

330.9 PN
PANAMA. MINISTERIO DE PLANIFICACION Y
POLITICA ECONOMICA. INFORME
ECONOMICO. a. Ministerio de Planificacion y
Politica Economica, Direccion de Planificacion
Economica y Social, Panama, Panama. stat.

PENNSYLVANIA JOURNAL OF URBAN
ECONOMIC DEVELOPMENT. see *HOUSING
AND URBAN PLANNING*

330.9 US
PERFORMANCE REPORT OF THE ALASKA
ECONOMY. Cover title: Alaska Economy; Year-
End Performance Report. 1972. a. Department of
Commerce and Economic Development, Division of
Economic Enterprise, Pouch EE, Juneau, AK
99801. illus. stat.

338.9 PE ISSN 0085-4840
PERU. OFICINA REGIONAL DE DESARROLLO
DEL NORTE. ANALISIS GENERAL DE
SITUACION DE LA REGION NORTE.* 1969.
irreg. Oficina Regional de Desarrollo del Norte, Av.
Luis Gonzalez No 1915, Chiclayo, Peru.

330.9 PH
PHILIPPINE DEVELOPMENT REPORT. (Text in
English) a. National Economic and Development
Authority, Box 1116, Manila, Philippines. stat.
Formerly (until 1977): Philippines. National
Economic and Development Authority. Report on
the Economy.

330.9 ZR
PORTEFEUILLE; revue des entreprises. 1971. irreg.
10 40 Z. Department du Portefeuille, B.P. 3473,
Kinhasa/Gombe, Zaire. Ed. Atunaku Adunagow.
Indexed: P.A.I.S.

330.9 PO
PORTUGAL. MINISTERIO DO PLANO E DA
COORDENACAO ECONOMICA.
DEPARTAMENTO CENTRAL DE
PLANEAMENTO. PLANO. irreg. Ministerio do
Plano e da Coordenacao Economica, Departamento
Central de Planeamento, Rua Professor Gomes
Teixeira, Lisbon 2, Portugal.

330 PO
PORTUGUESE ECONOMIC SITUATION FROM
AN EXTERNAL RELATIONSHIP POINT OF
VIEW. 1976. irreg. Ministerio do Plano e da
Coordenacao Economica, Departamento Central de
Planeamento, Lisbon, Portugal.

330 IT ISSN 0033-1902
PROVINCIA DI FORLI IN CIFRE. (Supplement to
Rassegna Economica) 1959. irreg. L.15000 includes
Rassegna Economica. Camera di Commercio,
Industria, Artigianato e Agricoltura di Forli, Corso
della Repubblica 5, 47100 Forli, Italy. Ed. Luciano
Castrucci.

330.9 US
PRUDENTIAL INSURANCE COMPANY OF
AMERICA. ECONOMIC FORECAST. vol. 27,
1978. a. Prudential Insurance Co. of America,
Economic & Investment Research Dept., 5 Plaza,
Newark, NJ 07101. charts.

330 PR ISSN 0079-7871
PUERTO RICO. DEPARTMENT OF THE
TREASURY. ECONOMY & FINANCES. 1955. a.
free. Department of the Treasury, Economics
Division, Box 4515, San Juan, PR 00905. Ed. Ting
Chen Hsu. charts. stat. circ. 1,500.

330.9 US ISSN 0091-5696
QUALITY OF LIFE IN IOWA; an economic and
social report to the Governor. 1970. a. Office for
Planning and Programming, Capitol Hill Annex, 523
E. 12 St., Des Moines, IA 50319. Ed. Ronald
Sagraves. illus. stat.

330 SY ISSN 0079-9688
RAPPORT ANNUEL SUR L'ECONOMIE ARABE.
(Text in French) 1964/1965. a. $43. Office Arabe
de Presse et de Documentation, 67 Place
Chahbander, P.O. Box 3550, Damascus, Syria.

330 SY ISSN 0079-9696
RAPPORT ANNUEL SUR L'ECONOMIE
SYRIENNE. (Text in French) 1963/64. a. $75.
Office Arabe de Presse et de Documentation, P.O.
Box 3550, 67 Place Chanbandar, Damascus, Syria.

338.9 PE
REALIDAD PERUANA. no. 3, 1975. irreg. price
varies. Editorial Horizonte, Camana 878, Lima,
Peru. charts. stat.

388 US ISSN 0080-0449
REFERENCE BOOK - ARGENTINA. (Issued in 2
vols) (Text in Spanish) a. Dun & Bradstreet, Inc., 99
Church St., New York, NY 10007 (And Florida
234, Buenos Aires, Argentina)

380 US ISSN 0080-0457
REFERENCE BOOK - REPUBLIC OF SOUTH
AFRICA. (Published in 4 provincial editions: Sec. 1:
Orange Free State, Sec. 2: Cape Province, Sec. 3:
Natal, Sec. 4: Transvaal) a. not available to libraries.
Dun & Bradstreet, Inc., 99 Church St., New York,
NY 10007 (And 91 Kerk St., Johannesburg, South
Africa)

338 BG
REPORT ON THE BACKGROUND, CURRENT
PROGRAMMES AND PLANNED
DEVELOPMENT OF THE BANGLADESH
INSTITUTE OF DEVELOPMENT STUDIES.
(Text in English) 1975. a. Bangladesh Institute of
Development Studies, Adamjee Court, Motijheel
Commercial Area, Dacca 2, Bangladesh.

RESERVE BANK OF AUSTRALIA. OCCASIONAL
PAPERS. see *BUSINESS AND ECONOMICS —
Banking And Finance*

330.9 NZ
RESERVE BANK OF NEW ZEALAND.
RESEARCH PAPERS. 1971. irreg. free. Reserve
Bank of New Zealand, Economic Dept., Box 2498,
Wellington, New Zealand. bibl. stat. circ. 2,000.

330.9 RH
RHODESIA, A FIELD FOR INVESTMENT. 1961.
a; latest issue, 1974. ‡ c/o H.C.P. Anderson, Box
1566, Salisbury, Zimbabwe. adv. illus. stat. circ.
3,000(controlled)

330.9 RW
RWANDA. DIRECTION GENERALE DE LA
STATISTIQUE. SITUATION ECONOMIQUE DE
LA REPUBLIQUE RWANDAISE AU 31
DECEMBRE. 1973 (N.S.) $7. Direction Generale
de la Statistique, B.P. 46, Kigali, Rwanda.
    Formerly: Rwanda. Direction Generale de la
Documentation et de la Statistique Generale.
Situation Economique de la Republique Rwandaise
au 31 Decembre.

330.9 CE
SAMVARDHANA. (Text in English or Sinhalese)
irreg. Rs.3.75 per no. 27/3 M Housing Scheme,
Kiribathgoda, Kelaniya, Sri Lanka.
    Economic and developmental studies of Sri
Lanka

330.5 US
SAN JOAQUIN VALLEY BUSINESS
PERSPECTIVES. irreg., approx. 3/yr. $8. California
State University, Fresno, School of Business and
Administrative Sciences, Fresno, CA 93740.

330.9 CN ISSN 0558-6976
SASKATCHEWAN ECONOMIC REVIEW. 1951. a.
Bureau of Statistics, T.C. Douglas Bldg., 3475
Albert St., Regina, Sask. S4S 6X6, Canada. circ.
4,000.

338.9 CN ISSN 0080-6676
SASKATCHEWAN'S FINANCIAL AND
ECONOMIC POSITION. 1954. biennial. free.
Department of Finance, 119 Legislative Bldg.,
Regina, Saskatchewan, Canada. circ. 4,500.

336 SZ
SCHWEIZERISCHE KONJUNKTUR UND IHRE
AUSSICHTEN. French edition: Situation
Economique Suisse et ses Perspectives. (Supplement
to: Switzerland. Eidgenoessisches Volkswirtschafts
Departement. Volkswirtschaft and to Schweizerische
Nationalbank. Monatsbericht) a. Eidgenoessisches
Volkswirtschaftsdepartement, Kommission fuer
Konjunkturfragen, Belpstr. 53, 3003 Berne,
Switzerland.

330.9 FR
SERIE EO/INTERNATIONAL. irreg. Editions d'
Organisation, 5, rue Rousselet, 75007 Paris, France.
Eds. Gerard le Pan de Ligny, Luc Boyer.

338.9 DK
SETTING UP IN DENMARK; a survey of economic,
legal and financial aspects of foreign investment in
Denmark. 1972. biennial. free. Copenhagen
Handelsbank - Kjoebenhavns Handelsbank, Holmens
Kanal 2, DK-1091 Copenhagen K, Denmark. charts.
illus. stat.

388 US ISSN 0080-9756
SINOPSIS DUN - BRAZIL. (Text in Portuguese) a.
not available to libraries. Dun & Bradstreet, Inc., 99
Church St., New York, NY 10007 (And Avenida
Sao Joao 473, 1st Fl., Sao Paulo, Brazil)

330.1 IV ISSN 0080-9829
SITUATION ECONOMIQUE DE COTE
D'IVOIRE.* 1960. irreg. Service de la Statistique,
B.P. 222, Abidjan, Ivory Coast.

330 MR ISSN 0080-9845
SITUATION ECONOMIQUE DU MAROC. a.
DH.20. Direction de la Statistique, B.P. 178, Rabat, Morocco.

330 SG ISSN 0080-9853
SITUATION ECONOMIQUE DU SENEGAL. 1962. a, latest 1976. 2500 Fr.CFA. Direction de la Statistique, B.P. 116, Dakar, Senegal.

330.9 FR
SITUATION ECONOMIQUE ET PERSPECTIVES D'AVENIR. irreg. Chambre de Commerce et d'Industrie de Pau, 21 rue Louis Barthou, Pau, France.

330.9 FR ISSN 0151-8720
SOCIETE GENERALE POUR FAVORISER DE DEVELOPPEMENT DU COMMERCE ET DE L'INDUSTRIE EN FRANCE. BULLETIN. (Text in English) no. 7, Feb. 1978. irreg. Societe Generale pour Favoriser de Developpement du Commerce et de l'Industre en France, c/o Y. Laulan, 29 Bd. Haussmann, 75009 Paris, France. illus.

315.4 330.9 II
SOCIO-ECONOMIC REVIEW OF PUNJAB. (Subseries of the Organisation's Publication) a. Economic and Statistical Organisation, Chandigarh, Punjab, India. stat.

332 SA ISSN 0081-2528
SOUTH AFRICAN RESERVE BANK. ANNUAL ECONOMIC REPORT/SUID-AFRIKOANSE RESERWEBANK. JAARLIKSE EKONOMIESE VERSLAG. (Editions in English and Afrikaans) 1961. a. R.2. South African Reserve Bank, Box 427, Pretoria 0001, South Africa. circ. 3,000 (English edt.) ;1,050 (Afrikaans edt.)

330.9 320 US
SOUTH AND EAST ASIA REPORT. irreg. (approx/ 39/yr.) $156. U.S. Joint Publications Research Service, 1000 N. Glebe Rd., Arlington, VA 22201 (Orders to: NTIS, Springfield, VA 22161)
Formerly: Translations on South and East Asia.

330.9 CE
SRI LANKA. MINISTRY OF PLANNING AND ECONOMIC AFFAIRS. DIVISION OF EXTERNAL RESOURCES. ECONOMIC INDICATORS. a. Ministry of Planning and Economic Affairs, Division of External Resources, Box 277, Ceylingo House, 2nd Floor, Colombo 1, Sri Lanka. charts. stat.

338.9 US ISSN 0073-1080
STATE OF HAWAII DATA BOOK. 1962. a. $10. Department of Planning and Economic Development, P.O. Box 2359, Honolulu, HI 96804. Ed. Robert C. Schmitt. circ. 3,000.

330.9 IT ISSN 0391-6103
STUDI D'ECONOMIA. 1976. irreg., no. 12, 1979. price varies. Liguori Editore s.r.l., Via Mezzocannone 19, 80134 Naples, Italy. Ed. D. W. Pearce.

330.9 NE
STUDIES IN REGIONAL SCIENCE AND URBAN ECONOMICS. 1977. irreg., vol. 5, 1980. price varies. North-Holland Publishing Co., Box 211, Amsterdam, Netherlands. Eds. Ake Andersson, Walter Isard.

330.9 320 US
SUBSAHARAN AFRICA REPORT. irreg. (approx. 189/yr.) $567. U.S. Joint Publications Research Service, 1000 N. Glebe Rd., Arlington, VA 22201 (Orders to: NTIS, Springfield, VA 22161)
Former titles: Translations on Subsaharan Africa; Translations on Africa.

SUDAN. ECONOMIC AND SOCIAL RESEARCH COUNCIL. BULLETIN. see SOCIAL SCIENCES: COMPREHENSIVE WORKS

SUDAN. ECONOMIC AND SOCIAL RESEARCH COUNCIL. RESEARCH REPORT. see SOCIAL SCIENCES: COMPREHENSIVE WORKS

330 SJ
SUDAN. MINISTRY OF FINANCE AND NATIONAL ECONOMY. ECONOMIC AND FINANCIAL RESEARCH SECTION. ECONOMIC SURVEY. a. Ministry of Finance and National Economy, Economic and Financial Research Section, Box 2092, Khartoum, Sudan.
Supersedes: Sudan. National Planning Commission. Economic Survey (ISSN 0081-9050)

SUDAN ECONOMIC AND SOCIAL RESEARCH COUNCIL. OCCASIONAL PAPER. see SOCIAL SCIENCES: COMPREHENSIVE WORKS

330.9 SQ
SWAZILAND. ECONOMIC PLANNING OFFICE. ECONOMIC REVIEW.* a. Economic Planning Office, Mbabane, Swaziland. illus.

330.9 SZ
SWISS FINANCIAL YEAR BOOK. 1977. a. 75 Fr. Elvetica Edizioni S.A., Via Odescalchi 18, Casella Postale 694, CH-6830 Chiasso, Switzerland. Ed. M. G. Grosso. circ. 5,000.

330.9 NE
TILBURG STUDIES IN ECONOMETRICS. 1977. irreg. price varies. Martinus Nijhoff, Box 566, 2501 CN The Hague, Netherlands.

330.9 NE ISSN 0564-6278
TILBURG STUDIES IN ECONOMICS. 1969. irreg., vol. 18, 1977. fl.60($25) per no. Martinus Nijhoff, Box 566, 2501 CN The Hague, Netherlands.

318 330.9 TR
TRINIDAD AND TOBAGO. CENTRAL STATISTICAL OFFICE. BUSINESS SURVEYS. irreg. Central Statistical Office, Textel Bldg., 1 Edward St., Port of Spain, Trinidad.

U S S R REPORT: ECONOMIC AFFAIRS. see BUSINESS AND ECONOMICS

U S S R REPORT: INDUSTRIAL AFFAIRS. see BUSINESS AND ECONOMICS — Production Of Goods And Services

U S S R REPORT: PROBLEMS OF THE FAR EAST. see POLITICAL SCIENCE — International Relations

U S S R REPORT: TRADE AND SERVICES. see BUSINESS AND ECONOMICS — Production Of Goods And Services

UNITED NATIONS. ECONOMIC AND SOCIAL COUNCIL. OFFICIAL RECORDS. see POLITICAL SCIENCE — International Relations

650 US
U.S. BUREAU OF THE CENSUS. CENSUS OF RETAIL TRADE, WHOLESALE TRADE AND SELECTED SERVICE INDUSTRIES. 1929. quinquennial. price varies. U.S. Bureau of the Census, Dept. of Commerce, Washington, DC 20233 (Orders to: Supt. Doc., Washington, DC 20402)
Continues: U.S. Bureau of the Census. Census of Business (ISSN 0082-9323)
Individual reports prepared for each census

650 US ISSN 0082-9463
U. S. BUREAU OF THE CENSUS. COUNTY BUSINESS PATTERNS. (Since 1964, individual volumes bound and issued annually as Final Reports) 1946. a. price varies. U.S. Bureau of the Census, Dept. of Commerce, Washington, DC 20233 (Orders to: Supt. Doc., Washington, DC 20402)

330 US
U. S. EXECUTIVE OFFICE OF THE PRESIDENT. ECONOMIC REPORT OF THE PRESIDENT. a. $3.60. U. S. Executive Office of the President, 1600 Pennsylvania Ave., N.W., Washington, DC 20500 (Orders to: Supt. of Documents, Washington, DC 20402)

330.9 SP
UNIVERSIDAD DE SEVILLA. INSTITUTO DE DESARROLLO REGIONAL. EDICIONES. irreg. price varies. Universidad de Sevilla, Instituto de Desarrollo, San Fernando 4, Seville, Spain. charts. illus.

UNIVERSITY OF NAIROBI. INSTITUTE FOR DEVELOPMENT STUDIES. DISCUSSION PAPERS. see HISTORY — History Of Africa

UNIVERSITY OF NAIROBI. INSTITUTE FOR DEVELOPMENT STUDIES. WORKING PAPERS. see HISTORY — History Of Africa

330.9 SA
UNIVERSITY OF PORT ELIZABETH. INSTITUTE FOR PLANNING RESEARCH. FACT PAPER SERIES/UNIVERSITEIT VAN PORT ELIZABETH. INSTITUUT VIR BEPLANNINGSNAVORSING. FEITESTUK REEKS. 1971. irreg., no. 21, 1977. University of Port Elizabeth, Institute for Planning Research, Box 1600, Port Elizabeth 6000, South Africa.

330.9 SA
UNIVERSITY OF PORT ELIZABETH. INSTITUTE FOR PLANNING RESEARCH. INFORMATION BULLETIN SERIES/UNIVERSITEIT VAN PORT ELIZABETH. INSTITUUT VIR BEPLANNINGSNAVORSING. INLIGTINGSBULLETIN REEKS. 1971. irreg., no. 10, 1976. University of Port Elizabeth, Institute for Planning Research, Box 1600, Port Elizabeth 6000, South Africa.

330 US ISSN 0082-3228
UNIVERSITY OF TEXAS, AUSTIN. BUREAU OF BUSINESS RESEARCH. AREA ECONOMIC SURVEY. 1955. irreg., no. 34, 1973. price varies. University of Texas at Austin, Bureau of Business Research, Austin, TX 78712.

330 US ISSN 0083-4610
UPPER MIDWEST ECONOMIC STUDY. PROGRESS REPORT. 1960. irreg. free. Upper Midwest Council, 250 Marquette Ave., Minneapolis, MN 55480.

330 US ISSN 0083-4637
UPPER MIDWEST ECONOMIC STUDY. TECHNICAL PAPER. 1961. irreg., 1964, no. 11. free. Upper Midwest Council, 250 Marquette Ave., Minneapolis, MN 55480.

330 US ISSN 0083-4645
UPPER MIDWEST ECONOMIC STUDY. URBAN REPORT. 1961. irreg., 1964, no. 8. free. Upper Midwest Council, 250 Marquette Ave., Minneapolis, MN 55480.

330.1 GW ISSN 0085-7661
VERBAENDE, BEHOERDEN, ORGANISATIONEN DER WIRTSCHAFT. a. DM.81. Verlag Hoppenstedt und Co., Havelstr. 9, Postfach 4006, 6100 Darmstadt, W. Germany (B. R. D.)

330.9 US ISSN 0095-3075
VIRGINIA. EMPLOYMENT COMMISSION. MANPOWER RESEARCH DIVISION. ECONOMIC ASSUMPTIONS. a. Employment Commission, Manpower Research Division, 703 E. Main St., Richmond, VA 23219. stat. Key Title: Economic Assumptions.

330.9 US
WAYNE STATE UNIVERSITY. CENTER FOR ECONOMIC STUDIES. MONOGRAPHS. irreg. price varies. Wayne State University Press, 5959 Woodward Ave., Detroit, MI 48202. (back issues avail.)

330.9 US ISSN 0097-7675
WEST VIRGINIA ECONOMIC PROFILE. irreg., latest 1977. Department of Commerce, Industrial Development Division, Charleston, WV 25311.

WESTERN AUSTRALIAN POCKET YEARBOOK. see HISTORY — History Of Australasia And Other Areas

WESTERN AUSTRALIAN YEARBOOK. NEW SERIES. see HISTORY — History Of Australasia And Other Areas

330.9 320 US
WESTERN EUROPE REPORT. 1968. irreg. (approx. 165/yr.) $495. U.S. Joint Publications Research Service, 1000 N. Glebe Rd., Arlington, VA 22201 (Orders to: NTIS, Springfield, VA 22161)
Formerly: Translations on Western Europe.

330   JA
WHITE PAPER ON JAPANESE ECONOMY. (Text in English) 1970. a. $39. (Economic Planning Agency) Business Intercommunication, Inc., C.P.O. Box 587, Tokyo 100-02, Japan.

330   UN   ISSN 0084-1714
WORLD ECONOMIC SURVEY. (Text in English, French and Spanish) 1948. a. price varies. United Nations Publications, LX 2300, New York, NY 10017 (Or Distribution and Sales Section, CH-1211 Geneva 10, Switzerland)

330.9   ZA
ZAMBIA. NATIONAL COMMISSION FOR DEVELOPMENT PLANNING. ECONOMIC REPORT. irreg. National Commission for Development Planning, Lusaka, Zambia.

BUSINESS AND ECONOMICS — Economic Systems And Theories, Economic History

330.9   YU
ACTA HISTORICO-OECONOMICA IUGOSLAVIAE; casopis za ekonomsku istoriju jugoslavije. (Text in Serbocroatian; summaries in German, English) 1974. a. 42 din.($5.40) Komisija za Ekonomsku Historiju Jugoslavije, Strossmayerov trg 2, Zagreb, Yugoslavia. Ed. Ivan Erceg. bk. rev. circ. 1,000.

330.1   FI   ISSN 0355-2667
ACTA WASAENSIA. (Text and summaries in English) 1971. irreg., no. 13, 1980. price varies. Vaasan Korkeakoulu - Univeristy of Vaasa, Raastuvankatu 31, 65100 Vaasa 10, Finland. Ed. Kauko Mikkonen. circ. 200.

330.1   BL
ANUARIO ECONOMICO-FISCAL. 1970. irreg; latest 1977, vol. 8. free. Coordenacao de Sistema de Informacoes Economico-Fiscais, Esplanada dos Ministerios, Bloco 5, 70079 Brasilia D.F., Brazil. illus. stat.

330.1   II
ASSAM ECONOMIC JOURNAL. (Text in English) vol. 3, 1977. a. Rs.10($2) Dibrugarh University, Department of Economics, Dibrugarh 786001, India.

330.1   SZ   ISSN 0522-7216
BEITRAEGE ZUR WIRTSCHAFTSPOLITIK. 1965. irreg., no. 30, 1978. price varies. Paul Haupt AG, Falkenplatz 14, CH-3001 Berne, Switzerland.

330 331   UK
BUSINESS ARCHIVES COUNCIL. BROADSHEET. no. 3, 1976. irreg. Business Archives Council, Dominion House, 37-45 Tooley St., London S.E. 1., England.

330.1   FR
CAHIERS D'ECONOMIE POLITIQUE. 1974. irreg., no. 5, 1979. (Universite de Picardie) Presses Universitaires de France, 108 Bd. St. Germaine, 75279 Paris Cedex 6, France (Orders to: Service des Periodiques, 12 rue Jean de Beauvais, 75005 Paris)

330   UK
CAMBRIDGE STUDIES IN ECONOMIC HISTORY. irreg. price varies. Cambridge University Press, Box 110, Cambridge CB2 3RL, England (And 32 E. 57th St., New York NY 10022) Ed.Bd.

CAPITALISMO E SOCIALISMO. see *POLITICAL SCIENCE*

330.1   SP
COLECCION DE ECONOMIA. 1976. irreg.; 1979, no. 4. price varies. Ediciones Universidad de Navarra S.A, Plaza de los Sauces 1 y 2, Baranain, Pamplona, Spain.

330   US   ISSN 0069-6323
COLUMBIA ESSAYS ON THE GREAT ECONOMISTS. 1971. irreg., 1976, no. 6. Columbia University Press, 136 South Broadway, Irvington-On-Hudson, NY 10533.

330.1 320   US
COMPARATIVE POLITICAL ECONOMY AND PUBLIC POLICY SERIES. 1975. irreg., vol. 3, 1978. price varies. Sage Publications, Inc., 275 S. Beverly Dr., Beverly Hills, CA 90212 (And Sage Publications, Ltd., 28 Banner St., London EC1Y 8QE, England) Ed.Bd.

330.1   US   ISSN 0084-9235
CONTRIBUTIONS IN ECONOMICS AND ECONOMIC HISTORY. 1970. irreg. price varies. Greenwood Press, 88 Post Rd. W., Westport, CT 06881. Ed. Robert Sobel.

330   NE   ISSN 0573-8555
CONTRIBUTIONS TO ECONOMIC ANALYSIS. 1952. irreg., vol. 127, 1980. price varies. North-Holland Publishing Co., Box 211, 1000 AE Amsterdam, Netherlands. Eds. J. Tinbergen, D.W. Jorgenson, J. Waelbroeck.

330.1   FR   ISSN 0070-1572
CROISSANCE URBAINE ET PROGRES DES NATIONS. 1969. irreg. price varies. Editions Cujas, 4,6,8 rue de la Maison-Blanche, 75013 Paris, France. Dir. Andre Piatter.

EASTERN EUROPE REPORT: ECONOMIC AND INDUSTRIAL AFFAIRS. see *BUSINESS AND ECONOMICS — Economic Situation And Conditions*

330   IT   ISSN 0070-8402
ECONOMIA E STORIA. (Contributions in Italian, English, French and German) vol. 5, 1803. irreg. price varies. Edizione Bizzari, 11B via Ruggero Bonghi, 00184 Rome, Italy. Ed. Oscar Nuccio. circ. 1,000.
    Reprints

330.1   BG
ECONOMICUS. (Text in English) vol. 2, Apr. 1976. irreg. Tk.2. Chittagong University, Department of Economics, Chittagong, Bangladesh.

330   FR   ISSN 0068-4864
ECONOMIES ET SOCIETES. SERIE AF. HISTOIRE QUANTITATIVE DE L'ECONOMIE FRANCAISE. 1961. irreg. 42 F. Institut de Sciences Mathematiques et Economiques Appliquees, Paris, Institut Henri Poincare, 11 rue Pierre et Marie Curie, 75005 Paris, France. Ed. J. Marczewski. circ. 1,600.

335   FR   ISSN 0068-4856
ECONOMIES ET SOCIETES. SERIE S. ETUDES DE MARXOLOGIE. 1959. irreg. 42 F. Institut de Sciences Mathematiques et Economiques Appliquees, Paris, Institut Henri Poincare, 11 rue Pierre et Marie Curie, 75005 Paris, France. Dir. M. Rubel. bk. rev. circ. 1,600.

949 330.1   NE
ECONOMISCH- EN SOCIAAL-HISTORISCH JAARBOEK. 1916. a. price varies. (Nederlandsch Economisch-Historisch Archief) Martinus Nijhoff, Box 566, 2501 CN The Hague, Netherlands.
    Supersedes: Economisch-Historisch Jaarboek.

330   UR
EKONOMIKO-MATEMATICHESKIE METODY V PLANIROVANII NARODNOGO KHOZYAISTVA. irreg. 0.97 Rub. Akademiya Nauk Tadzhikskoi S.S.R., Institut Ekonomiki, Prospekt Lenina 37, Dushanbe, U.S.S.R. illus.

330   BE   ISSN 0071-1977
ETUDES D'HISTOIRE ECONOMIQUE ET SOCIALE. 1941. irreg. price varies. Institut Historique Belge de Rome, c/oArchives Generales du Royaume, 2-6 Rue de Ruysbroeck, B-1000 Brussels, Belgium. circ. controlled.

330.1   SZ
FINANZWISSENSCHAFTLICHE SCHRIFTEN. irreg., no. 2, 1976. Verlag Peter Lang AG, Muenzgraben 2, Postfach, CH-3000 Berne 7, Switzerland.

330   US   ISSN 0071-8106
FOUNDATION FOR THE STUDY OF CYCLES. RESEARCH BULLETIN. 1950. irreg. price varies.
‡ Foundation for the Study of Cycles, 124 South Highland Ave., Pittsburgh, PA 15206. Ed. G. Shirk.

330   HU   ISSN 0072-033X
GAZDASAGTORTENETI ERTEKEZESEK. (Text in Hungarian; occasional summaries in German or Russian) 1958. irreg. price varies. (Magyar Tudomanyos Akademia) Akademiai Kiado, Publishing House of the Hungarian Academy of Sciences, P.O. Box 24, H-1363 Budapest, Hungary.

330   SW   ISSN 0072-5080
GOETEBORGS UNIVERSITET. ECONOMISK-HISTORISKA INSTITUTIONEN. MEDDELANDEN. (Text in Swedish; usually summaries in English or French) 1958. irreg., no. 46, 1980. price varies; also available on exchange from University of Gothenburg Library. Goeteborgs Universitet, Ekonomisk-Historiska Institutionen, Stora Nygatan 23-25, S-411 08 Goeteborg, Sweden. circ. 400.

330.1   SW
GOETEBORGS UNIVERSITET. NATIONALEKONOMISKA INSTITUTIONEN. EKONOMISKA STUDIER. irreg., no. 5, 1978. Goeteborgs Universitet, Nationalekonomiska Institutionen, Vasaparken, 411 24 Goeteborg, Sweden.

330.1   HT
HAITI. CONSEIL NATIONAL DE DEVELOPPEMENT ET DE PLANIFICATION. PLAN ANNUEL ET BUDGET DE DEVELOPPEMENT. a. (Conseil National de Developpement et de Planification) Haiti. Secretaire d'Etat du Plan, Port-au-Prince, Haiti.

650   US   ISSN 0073-067X
HARVARD STUDIES IN BUSINESS HISTORY. 1931. irreg., no. 28, 1975. price varies. (Harvard University Graduate School of Business Administration) Harvard University Press, 79 Garden St., Cambridge, MA 02138. Ed. Alfred D. Chandler, Jr.

330   UK   ISSN 0309-1783
HOBART PAPERBACKS; studies in the translation of economic ideas into practical policy and the economics of government. 1971. irreg. $55 (combined subscription for all series) Institute of Economic Affairs, 2 Lord North St., London SW1P 3LB, England (Dist. in North America by: Transatlantic Arts, Inc., 88 Bridge St., Central Islip, NY 11722)

330.07   SW
INDUSTRIAL INSTITUTE FOR ECONOMIC AND SOCIAL RESEARCH. CURRENT RESEARCH PROJECTS. (Text in English) irreg. Industriens Utredningsinstitut, Grevgatan 34, Box 5037, S-102 41 Stockholm, Sweden.

INTERNATIONAL LABOUR OFFICE. P R E A L C. INVESTIGACIONES SOBRE EMPLEO. see *BUSINESS AND ECONOMICS — Economic Situation And Conditions*

330   GE   ISSN 0075-2800
JAHRBUCH FUER WIRTSCHAFTSGESCHICHTE. 1960. a (in two parts) M.56. (Akademie der Wissenschaften der DDR, Institut fuer Wirtschaftsgeschichte) Akademie-Verlag, Leipziger Str. 3-4, 108 Berlin, E. Germany (D.D.R.)

330.1   SA   ISSN 0379-6205
JOURNAL FOR STUDIES IN ECONOMICS AND ECONOMETRICS/TYDSKRYF VIR STUDIES IN EKONOMIE EN EKONOMETRIE. Short title: S E E. 1977. irreg.(2-4/yr.) R.2 per no. University of Stellenbosch, Bureau for Economic Research, Private Bag 5050, University, Stellenbosch 7600, South Africa. Eds. J.L. Sadie, A.J.M. de Vries. circ. 500.

330.1   US
KENTUCKY. COUNCIL OF ECONOMIC ADVISORS. STUDIES IN APPLIED ECONOMICS. 1980. irreg., 4-5/yr. $10. Kentucky Council of Economic Advisors, University of Kentucky, College of Business & Economics, Lexington, KY 40506. Ed. Dr. Charles G. Renfro. circ. 400.

330 510   GW
MATHEMATICAL SYSTEMS IN ECONOMICS. 1972. irreg., vol. 64, 1981. price varies. Verlag Anton Hain GmbH, Adelheidstr. 2, Postfach 1220, 6240 Koenigstein, W. Germany (B. R. D.)

BUSINESS AND ECONOMICS — INTERNATIONAL COMMERCE

330.1   BE
MUSEE ROYAL DE L'AFRIQUE CENTRALE. ANNALES. SERIE IN 8. SCIENCES ECONOMIQUES/KONINKLIJK MUSEUM VOOR MIDDEN-AFRIKA. ANNALEN. REEKS IN 8. ECONOMISCHE WETENSCHAPPEN. 1947. irreg., no. 11, 1980. price varies. Musee Royal de l'Afrique Centrale, 13 Steenweg op Leuven, B-1980 Tervuren, Belgium. charts. illus.

330.1   NO   ISSN 0085-431X
NORWAY. STATISTISK SENTRALBYRAA. ARTIKLER/ARTICLES. (Text in Norwegian; summaries in English) 1957. irreg. price varies. Statistisk Sentralbyraa, Box 8131 Dep., Oslo 1, Norway. circ. 1,800.

330   300   UK   ISSN 0078-3013
OCCASIONAL PAPERS IN ECONOMIC AND SOCIAL HISTORY. 1969. irreg. individually priced. University of Hull Publications Committee, Hull HU6 7RX, England. Ed. John Saville. Indexed: SSCI.

330   FR   ISSN 0079-0982
PERSPECTIVES DE L'ECONOMIQUE. SERIE 1. LES FONDATEURS DE L'ECONOMIE. 1969. irreg. price varies. Editions Calmann-Levy, 3 rue Auber, Paris 9e, France. Ed. Christian Schmidt.

330.1   320   US
POLITICAL ECONOMY OF WORLD-SYSTEMS ANNUALS. 1978. a. $18.50 for hardcover; softcover $8.95. Sage Publications, Inc., 275 S. Beverly Dr., Beverly Hills, CA 90212 (And Sage Publications, Ltd., 28 Banner St., London EC1Y 8QE, England) Ed. Immanuel Wallerstein. (back issues avail.)

330   UK
READINGS IN ECONOMIC HISTORY AND THEORY. 1974. irreg. £2.50-2.90 per no. J. M. Dent & Sons Ltd., 26 Albemarle St., London W1X 4OY, England.

330   US   ISSN 0363-3268
RESEARCH IN ECONOMIC HISTORY; an annual compilation of research. 1976. a. $17.25 to individuals; institutions $34.50. J A I Press, Box 1678, 165 W. Putnam Ave., Greenwich, CT 06830. Ed. Paul Uselding. bibl. charts. stat.

330.1   US
RESEARCH IN EXPERIMENTAL ECONOMICS. 1979. a. $18.75 to individuals; institutions $37.50. J A I Press, Box 1678, 165 W. Putnam Ave., Greenwich, CT 06830. Ed. Vernon L. Smith.

330.1   320   US   ISSN 0161-7230
RESEARCH IN POLITICAL ECONOMY; an annual compilation of research. 1978. a. $16.25 to individuals; institutions $32.50. J A I Press, Box 1678, 165 W. Putnam Ave., Greenwich, CT 06830. Ed. Paul Zarembka.

330.1   AU
SOZIAL- UND WIRTSCHAFTSHISTORISCHE STUDIEN. 1972. irreg. price varies. Verlag fuer Geschichte und Politik, Neulinggasse 26, A-1030 Vienna, Austria. Eds. A. Hoffmann, M. Mitterauer.

330.1   PL   ISSN 0081-6485
STUDIA HISTORIAE OECONOMICA. (Text in English, German and French) 1966. irreg., 1976, vol. 11. price varies. Uniwersytet im. Adama Mickiewicza w Poznaniu, Stalingradzka 1, 61-712 Poznan, Poland (Dist. by: Ars Polona, Krakowskie Przedmiescie 7, 00-068 Warsaw, Poland) Ed. Jerzy Topolski. circ. 1,500.

330.1   US
STUDIEN UEBER WIRTSCHAFT-UND SYSTEMVERGLEICHE. (Text in English or German) 1971. irreg.; vol. 9, 1978. price varies. Springer-Verlag, 175 Fifth Ave., New York, NY 10010 (Also Berlin, Heidelberg, Vienna) Ed. F. Nemschak. (reprint service avail. from ISI)

STUDIEN ZUR RECHTS-, WIRTSCHAFTS- UND KULTURGESCHICHTE. see *LAW*

330   US   ISSN 0081-7643
STUDIES IN BUSINESS CYCLES. 1927. irreg., no. 23, 1974. price varies; no. 23 $15. National Bureau of Economic Research, 1050 Massachusetts Ave, Cambridge, MA 02138 (Since 1965 Dist. by: Columbia University Press, 136 South Broadway, Irvington-on-Hudson, N.Y. 10533)

330   US
STUDIES IN ECONOMIC HISTORY. irreg. price varies. Harvard University Press, 79 Garden St., Cambridge, MA 02138.

330   FR   ISSN 0082-2477
TECHNIQUES ECONOMIQUES MODERNES. ANALYSE ECONOMIQUE. 1964. irreg. price varies. Ecole Pratique des Hautes Etudes, Centre d'Etudes des Techniques Economiques Modernes, 1 rue Therese, 75001 Paris, France.

330.1   IT   ISSN 0391-3295
TEORIE ECONOMICHE. 1977. irreg., no. 10, 1980. price varies. Liguori Editore s.r.l., Via Mezzocannone 19, 80134 Naples, Italy. Eds. Bruno Jossa, Salvatore Vinci.

330.1   CM
UNIVERSITE DE YAOUNDE. FACULTE DE DROIT ET DES SCIENCES ECONOMIQUES. ECONOMIE GENERALE. irreg. Universite de Yaounde, Faculte de Droit et des Sciences Economiques, B.P. 337, Yaounde, Cameroon.

330.07   LE
UNIVERSITE SAINT-JOSEPH. FACULTE DE DROIT ET DES SCIENCES ECONOMIQUES. ANNUAIRE. (Text in Arabic, English and French) a. Universite Saint-Joseph, Faculte de Droit et des Sciences Economiques, Box 293, Beirut, Lebanon.

330.1   FI
UNIVERSITY OF VAASA. PROCEEDINGS. DISCUSSION PAPERS. 1979. irreg., no. 27, 1980. Vaasan Korkeakoulu - University of Vaasa, Raastuvank. 31, 65100 Vaasa 10, Finland. Ed. Kauko Mikkonen.
Formerly (until 1981): Vaasa School of Economics. Proceedings. Discussion Papers (ISSN 0357-3486)

330.1   FI
VAASAN KORKEAKOULU. JULKAISUJA. OPETUSMONISTEITA. 1972. irreg., no. 20, 1980. Vaasan Korkeakoulu - University of Vaasa, Raastuvankatu 31, 65100 Vaasa 10, Finland. Ed. Kauko Mikkonen.
Formerly (until 1981): Vaasan Kauppakorkeakoulu. Julkaisuja. Opetusmonisteita (ISSN 0355-2624)

330.1   FI
VAASAN KORKEAKOULU. JULKAISUJA. TUTKIMUKSIA. 1970. irreg., no. 74, 1980. price varies. Vaasan Korkeakoulu - University of Vaasa, Raastuvankatu 31, 65100 Vaasa 10, Finland. Ed. Kauko Mikkonen.
Formerly (unitl 1981): Vaasan Kauppakorkeakoulu. Julkaisuja. Tutkimuksia (ISSN 0355-2632)

VIERTELJAHRSCHRIFT FUER SOZIAL-UND WIRTSCHAFTSGESCHICHTE. BEIHEFTE. see *SOCIAL SCIENCES: COMPREHENSIVE WORKS*

330.1   US
WIRTSCHAFTSPOLITISCHE STUDIEN. 1976. irreg.; no. 4, 1978. price varies. Springer-Verlag, 175 Fifth Ave., New York, NY 10010 (Also Berlin, Heidelberg, Vienna) (reprint serivce avail. from ISI)

330.1   309   GW   ISSN 0170-3579
WISSENSCHAFTLICHE PAPERBACKS; Sozial- und Wirtschaftsgeschichte. irreg., vol. 16, 1981. price varies. Franz Steiner Verlag GmbH, Friedrichstr. 24, Postfach 5529, 6200 Wiesbaden, W. Germany (B.R.D.) Ed.Hans Pohl.
History

330   US
WORLD ECONOMIC HISTORY. irreg. Cornell University Press, 124 Roberts Place, Ithaca, NY 14850.

330.9   US
YALE SERIES IN ECONOMIC HISTORY. irreg., latest, 1976. Yale University Press, 92A Yale Sta., New Haven, CT 06520.

330.1   GW   ISSN 0342-3956
ZEITSCHRIFT FUER UNTERNEHMENSGESCHICHTE. BEIHEFTE. irreg., vol. 19, 1981. price varies. (Gesellschaft fuer Unternehmensgeschichte e.V., Koeln) Franz Steiner Verlag GmbH, Friedrichstr. 24, Postfach 5529, 6200 Wiesbaden, W. Germany (B.R.D.) Eds. W. Treue, H. Pohl.

BUSINESS AND ECONOMICS — International Commerce

382   UA
A B C - ARAB TRADE REFERENCE: ARAB & MIDDLE EAST COUNTRIES. (Text in Arabic, English, French, German, and Italian) 1973. irreg. 99 Shari Ramsis, Al-Qahirah, Egypt. illus.

382   GW   ISSN 0065-003X
A B C EUROP PRODUCTION. (Text in German; indexed in English, French, German, Italian, Portuguese, Spanish) 1960. a. prices on request. A B C-Verlagshaus Darmstadt, Berliner Allee 8, 6100 Darmstadt, W. Germany (B.R.D.) (Dist. by: International Publications Service, 114 E. 32nd St., New York, NY 10016) adv. circ. 18,000.

382   UY
A L A L C CARTA INFORMATIVA. (Text in Portuguese) 1976. bi-m. free. Asociacion Latinoamericana de Libre Comercio, Oficina de Ventas, Cebollati 1461, Casilla de Correo 577, Montevideo, Uruguay. abstr. stat.

382   AE
ALGERIA. INSTITUT NATIONAL ALGERIEN DU COMMERCE EXTERIEUR. ANNUAIRE DES EXPORTATEURS. (Text in Arabic, English and French) 1976. a. 80 din. Institut National Algerien du Commerce Exterieur - Algerian National Institute for Foreign Trade, 6 Bd. Anatole France, Algiers, Algeria.

382   US
AMERICAN EXPORT REGISTER. (Index in English, French, German and Spanish) 1945. a. $50. Thomas Publishing Co., One Penn Plaza, New York, NY 10001. index.
Formerly: American Register of Exporters and Importers (ISSN 0065-9967)

382   CY   ISSN 0526-5053
ANALYSIS OF CYPRUS FOREIGN TRADE. a. Mils.250. Department of Statistics and Research, Ministry of Finance, Nicosia, Cyprus.

382   FR
ANNUAIRE BLEU/BLUE DIRECTORY FOR INTERNATIONAL TRADE. (Editions in English, French, German, Spanish) 1928. a. 588 F. Centre d'Expansion Francaise, 8 rue Saint-Marc, 75002 Paris, France. (Co-sponsor: Centre d'Expansion Europeenne) adv.

382   FR
ANNUAIRE DES AGENTS COMMERCIAUX COURTIERS ET REPRESENTANTS DE COMMERCE-FRANCE ET MARCHE COMMUN. 1972. irreg. 65 rue de Rivoli, 75001 Paris, France. adv.

382   FR
ANNUAIRE DES ENTREPRISES ET ORGANISMES D'OUTRE-MER. 1910. a. 368 Fr. Rene Moreux et Cie, 190 Boulevard Haussmann, 75008 Paris, France.
Formerly: Annuaire des Entreprises d'Outre-Mer, des Organismes Officiels et Professionels d'Outre-Mer, des Organismes de Cooperation Francais, Entrangers et Internationaux (ISSN 0066-2828)

382   HT
ANNUAIRE DU COMMERCE EXTERIEUR D'HAITI: IMPORTATIONS, EXPORTATIONS. a. Administration Generale des Douanes, Port-au-Prince, Haiti. stat.

607.34   658.84   FR
ANNUAIRE INTERNATIONAL DES FOIRES, EXPOSITIONS ET SALONS SPECIALISES. (Includes calendrier mural) 1970. a. 180 F. Editions Gozlan, 94 rue St. Lazare, 75442 Paris Cedex 09, France.

BUSINESS AND ECONOMICS — INTERNATIONAL COMMERCE

382   UK   ISSN 0072-5846
ANNUAL STATEMENT OF THE OVERSEAS TRADE OF THE UNITED KINGDOM. a. price varies. Customs and Excise Department, King's Beam House, 39-41 Mark Lane, London EC1R 7HE, England (Avail. from H.M.S.O., c/o Liaison Officer, Atlantic House, Holborn Viaduct, London EC1P 1BN, England)

382   SP   ISSN 0570-3980
ANUARIO COMERCIAL IBEROAMERICANO. Added title: Trade Directory of Spanish-Lusitanian and Latin American Countries and the U.S.A. (Text in English, French, German and Spanish) 1953. a. Oficina Informativa de Comercio Exterior, Madrid, Spain. illus.

382   MX
ANUARIO DE COMERCIO EXTERIOR DE MEXICO. 1939. irreg., latest, 1972-73. Mex.$6. ‡ Banco Nacional de Comercio Exterior, S.A., Departamento de Publicaciones, Av. Chapultepec 230, Mexico 7, D.F., Mexico.

382   AG   ISSN 0066-5118
ANUARIO DEL COMERCIO EXTERIOR LATINO-AMERICANO; guide to the industry and foreign trade of Latin America. 1966. a. $30 free to advertisers. ‡ (Latin American Free Trade Association) E.P.I.S.A., Rivadavia 825, 2 Piso, Buenos Aires, Argentina. Ed. E.F. Cappagli. index.
Formerly: Anuario de los Paises de A L A L C (ISSN 0571-3846)

382   MX
ANUARIO DEL EXPORTADOR. a. Instituto Mexicano de Comercio Exterior, Av. Alfonso Reyes 30, Mexico, D.F., Mexico.

382   UK   ISSN 0140-1874
ARAB BUSINESS YEARBOOK. 1976. a. £17. Graham & Trotman Ltd., 14 Clifford St., London W1X 1RD, England. Ed. S.M.A. Barrow.

382   II   ISSN 0066-8230
ASIA-AFRICA WORLD TRADE REGISTER. (Text in English; classified headings in English, French, Spanish and German) 1970. irreg. £7. Business Publications International, United India Life Building, Box 548, F-Block, Connaught Place, New Delhi 1, India. Ed. K. L. Sahgal. adv. circ. 10,000.
Classified business directory on countries of Asia-Africa with international section

382   UK
ASIAN LIVING COSTS. 1970. a. £18. Confederation of British Industry, 103 New Oxford St., London WC1A 1DU, England.

382   UY
ASOCIACION LATINOAMERICANA DE LIBRE COMERCIO. ESTADISTICAS DE COMERCIO EXTERIOR--SERIE A-EXPORTACIONES. (Separate volume for each member country) 1972. a. Asociacion Latinoamericana de Libre Comercio, Cebollati 1461, Casilla de Correo 577, Montevideo, Uruguay.
Formerly: Asociacion Latinoamericana de Libre Comercio. Comercio Exterior. Argentina. Exportacion (ISSN 0571-3870)

382   UY
ASOCIACION LATINOAMERICANA DE LIBRE COMERCIO. ESTADISTICAS DE COMERCIO EXTERIOR-SERIE B-IMPORTACIONES. (Separate volume for each member country) 1973. a. Asociacion Latinoamericana de Libre Comercio, Cebollati 1461, Casilla de Correo 577, Montevideo, Uruguay.
Formerly: Asociacion Latinoamericana de Libre Comercio. Comercio Exterior Argentina. Importacion (ISSN 0571-3889)

382   UY
ASOCIACION LATINOAMERICANA DE LIBRE COMERCIO. ESTADISTICAS DE COMERCIO EXTERIOR - SERIE C - IMPORTACIONES ZONALES. (Separate volume for each member country) 1974. a. Asociacion Latinoamericana de Libre Comercio, Cebollati 1461, Casilla de Correo 577, Montevideo, Uruguay.
Formerly: Asociacion Latinoamericana de Libre Comercio. Comercio Exterior Brasil. Importacion (ISSN 0571-3897)

382   UY   ISSN 0571-3935
ASOCIACION LATINOAMERICANA DE LIBRE COMERCIO. LISTA CONSOLIDADA DE CONCESIONES. a. Asociacion Latinoamericana de Libre Comercio, Cebollati 1461, Casilla de Correo 577, Montevideo, Uruguay.

382   UY
ASOCIACION LATINOAMERICANA DE LIBRE COMERCIO. LISTA NACIONAL DE ARGENTINA. a. Asociacion Latinoamericana de Libre Comercio, Cebollati 1461, Casilla de Correo 577, Montevideo, Uruguay.
Formerly: Asociacion Latinoamericana de Libre Comercio. Lista Nacional de la Republica Argentina (ISSN 0571-4001)

382   UY
ASOCIACION LATINOAMERICANA DE LIBRE COMERCIO. LISTA NACIONAL DE BOLIVIA. a. Asociacion Latinoamericana de Libre Comercio, Cebollati 1461, Casilla de Correo 577, Montevideo, Uruguay.

382   UY   ISSN 0571-396X
ASOCIACION LATINOAMERICANA DE LIBRE COMERCIO. LISTA NACIONAL DE BRASIL. a. Asociacion Latinoamericana de Libre Comercio, Cebollati 1461, Casilla de Correo 577, Montevideo, Uruguay.

382   UY   ISSN 0571-3978
ASOCIACION LATINOAMERICANA DE LIBRE COMERCIO. LISTA NACIONAL DE CHILE. a. Asociacion Latinoamericana de Libre Comercio, Cebollati 1461, Casilla de Correo 577, Montevideo, Uruguay.

382   UY   ISSN 0571-3986
ASOCIACION LATINOAMERICANA DE LIBRE COMERCIO. LISTA NACIONAL DE COLOMBIA. a. Asociacion Latinoamericana de Libre Comercio, Cebollati 1461, Casilla de Correo 577, Montevideo, Uruguay.

382   UY   ISSN 0571-3994
ASOCIACION LATINOAMERICANA DE LIBRE COMERCIO. LISTA NACIONAL DE ECUADOR. a. Asociacion Latinoamericana de Libre Comercio, Cebollati 1461, Casilla de Correo 577, Montevideo, Uruguay.

382   UY   ISSN 0571-401X
ASOCIACION LATINOAMERICANA DE LIBRE COMERCIO. LISTA NACIONAL DE MEXICO. a. Asociacion Latinoamericana de Libre Comercio, Cebollati 1461, Casilla de Correo 577, Montevideo, Uruguay.

382   UY   ISSN 0571-4028
ASOCIACION LATINOAMERICANA DE LIBRE COMERCIO. LISTA NACIONAL DE PARAGUAY. a. Asociacion Latinoamericana de Libre Comercio, Cebollati 1461, Casilla de Correo 577, Montevideo, Uruguay.

382   UY   ISSN 0571-4036
ASOCIACION LATINOAMERICANA DE LIBRE COMERCIO. LISTA NACIONAL DE PERU. a. Asociacion Latinoamericana de Libre Comercio, Cebollati 1461, Casilla de Correo 577, Montevideo, Uruguay.

382   UY   ISSN 0571-4044
ASOCIACION LATINOAMERICANA DE LIBRE COMERCIO. LISTA NACIONAL DE URUGUAY. a. Asociacion Latinoamericana de Libre Comercio, Cebollati 1461, Casilla de Correo 577, Montevideo, Uruguay.

382   UY
ASOCIACION LATINOAMERICANA DE LIBRE COMERCIO. LISTA NACIONAL DE VENEZUELA. a. Asociacion Latinoamericana de Libre Comercio, Cebollati 1461, Casilla de Correo 577, Montividero, Uruguay.

382   UY   ISSN 0571-4087
ASOCIACION LATINOAMERICANA DE LIBRE COMERCIO. SERIE INSTRUMENTOS. 1963. irreg. Asociacion Latinoamericana de Libre Comercio, Cebollati 1461, Casilla de Correo 577, Montevideo, Uruguay.

ASPIS; the classified Greek commercial directory. see *BUSINESS AND ECONOMICS — Trade And Industrial Directories*

382   AT
AUSTRALIAN EXPORTS. 1964. a. Aus.$35. Peter Isaacson Publications, 46-49 Porter St., Prahran, Vic. 3181, Australia. Ed. Les Griffiths.
Formerly: Australian Directory of Exports (ISSN 0084-7305)

382   GW   ISSN 0415-7508
B D I DEUTSCHLAND LIEFERT/B D I GERMANY SUPPLIES/B D I L'ALLEMAGNE FOURNIT/B D I ALEMANIA SUMINISTRA; official export register of the Federation of German Industries. (Text in English, French, German and Spanish) 1952. a. DM.80. (Bundesverband der Deutschen Industrie) Gemeinschaftsverlag GmbH, Spreestr. 9, 6100 Darmstadt, W. Germany (B.R.D.) adv. circ. 11,000.

382   341   US
B N A'S LAW REPRINTS: TRADE REGULATION. 1967. irreg. $215 per yr. Bureau of National Affairs, Inc., 1231 25th St. N.W., Washington, DC 20037. Ed. Mildred Mason. index.
Formerly: Law Reprints. Trade Regulation Series (ISSN 0075-8256)

382.1   JM
BALANCE OF PAYMENTS OF JAMAICA. a. free. Bank of Jamaica, Research Dept., Box 621, Kingston, Jamaica. illus. stat.

BALANCE OF PAYMENTS OF SIERRA LEONE. see *BUSINESS AND ECONOMICS — Public Finance, Taxation*

BALANCE OF PAYMENTS OF TRINIDAD AND TOBAGO. see *BUSINESS AND ECONOMICS — Public Finance, Taxation*

BALANZA DE PAGOS DE ESPANA. see *BUSINESS AND ECONOMICS — Public Finance, Taxation*

BANCA ROMANA DE COMERT EXTERIOR. ANNUAL BULLETIN. see *BUSINESS AND ECONOMICS — Banking And Finance*

380   NQ
BANCO CENTRAL DE NICARAGUA. COMERCIO EXTERIOR DE NICARAGUA POR PRODUCTOS Y PAISES. a. Banco Central de Nicaragua, Departamento de Estudios Economicos, Division de Economia Internacional, Aptos. 2252-2253, Managua, Nicaragua. stat. circ. 3,000.

382   CK   ISSN 0302-9611
BANCO DE LA REPUBLICA. REGISTROS DE EXPORTACION E IMPORTACION. a. free. Banco de la Republica, Departamento de Investigaciones Economicas, Carrera 7A No. 14-78, Apdo. Postal 402, Bogota, Colombia.
Formerly: Banco de la Republica. Bogota. Registros de Importaciones.

382   JA
BANK OF JAPAN. PRICE INDEXES ANNUAL. (Text in Japanese and English) a. price varies. Bank of Japan, Statistics Department - Nihon Ginko, 2-2-1 Hongoku-cho, Nihonbashi, Chuo-ku, Tokyo 103, Japan (Order from: Japan Publications Trading Co., Ltd., Box 5030, Tokyo International, Tokyo, Japan; or 1255 Howard St., San Francisco, CA 94103)
Formerly: Bank of Japan. Export and Import Price Indexes Annual.

BANK OF LIBYA. BALANCE OF PAYMENTS. see *BUSINESS AND ECONOMICS — Public Finance, Taxation*

382   BE   ISSN 0067-561X
BELGIUM. OFFICE BELGE DU COMMERCE EXTERIEUR. BIJVOEGSEL B B H. REEKS B. irreg. Office Belge du Commerce Exterieur, 162 Boulevard Emile Jacqmain, 1000 Brussels, Belgium.

382   BL
BOLETIM DO COMERCIO EXTERIOR DA BAHIA/BAHIA'S FOREIGN TRADE BULLETIN.* irreg. Departamento Estadual de Estatistica, Rua Carlos Gomes, 111 - 20. andar, Salvador, Bahia, Brazil. stat.

382   UY
BOLETIN DE INFORMACION COMERCIAL. 1972. m. $12. Asociacion Latinoamericana de Libre Comercio, Oficina de Informacion Comercial, Casilla 577, Montevideo, Uruguay.

BUSINESS AND ECONOMICS — INTERNATIONAL COMMERCE

310 382   BO
BOLIVIA. INSTITUTO NACIONAL DE ESTADISTICA. ANUARIO DE COMERCIO EXTERIOR. 1968. a. $20.60. Instituto Nacional de Estadistica, Av. 6 de Agosto no. 2507, La Paz, Bolivia.

382   FR   ISSN 0068-0494
BOTTIN INTERNATIONAL. (Text in English, French, German and Spanish) 1895. a. $80. Societe Didot Bottin, 28, rue Docteur Finlay, 75738 Paris Cedex 15, France.

382   UK   ISSN 0140-5772
BRITISH EXPORTERS. 1916. a. £12. Sell's Publications Ltd., Sell's House, 39 East St., Epsom KT17 1BQ, Surrey, England. adv. bk. rev. circ. 3,500.
    Formerly: Sell's British Exporters (ISSN 0080-8709)

382   UK
BRITISH EXPORTS/EXPORTATIONS BRITANNIQUES/BRITISCHER EXPORT/EXPORTACIONES BRITANICAS. (Text in English; indexes in French, German, Spanish) 1969. a. £25. Kompass Publishers Ltd., Windsor Court, East Grinstead House, East Grinstead, West Sussex RH19 1XD, England. adv. circ. 12,000.
    Former titles: British Exports. Export Services. (ISSN 0305-7682); British Exports (ISSN 0068-1970)

382   UK   ISSN 0068-4465
BUSINESS MONITOR: MISCELLANEOUS SERIES. M4 OVERSEAS TRANSACTIONS. a. price varies. Department of Industry, 1 Victoria St., London S.W.1., England (Avail. from H.M.S.O., c/o Liaison Officer, Atlantic House, Holborn Viaduct, London EC1P 1BW, England)

382   UK
BUSINESS YEARBOOK OF BRAZIL, MEXICO & VENEZUELA. 1980. a. £17. Graham & Trotman Ltd., 14 Clifford St., London W1X 1RD, England. Ed. S. Andrade.

CALIFORNIA INTERNATIONAL TRADE REGISTER. see *BUSINESS AND ECONOMICS — Trade And Industrial Directories*

CANADA. GRAIN COMMISSION. ECONOMICS AND STATISTICS DIVISION. CANADIAN GRAIN EXPORTS. see *AGRICULTURE — Feed, Flour And Grain*

CANADA IN THE ATLANTIC ECONOMY. see *BUSINESS AND ECONOMICS*

382.097   CN   ISSN 0702-0333
CANADA-JAPAN, THE EXPORT-IMPORT PICTURE. 1964. biennial. Canada-Japan Trade Council, Fuller Bldg., Suite 903, 75 Albert St., Ottawa, Ont. K1P 5E7, Canada. charts, stat.

382   FR   ISSN 0071-836X
CENTRE NATIONAL DU COMMERCE EXTERIEUR. ANNUAIRE.* 1966. a. Centre National du Commerce Exterieur, 10 Av. d'Iena, Paris 16e, France.

382   FR   ISSN 0071-8378
CHAMBRE SYNDICALE DES COMMISSIONAIRES POUR LE COMMERCE EXTERIEUR. ANNUAIRE OFFICIEL.* 1962. a. Editions Slog, 20 rue de Leningrad, Paris 8e, France.

382   US
CHASE WORLD GUIDE FOR EXPORTERS. (Includes supplementary bulletins) a. $195. Chase World Information Corporation, One World Trade Center, Suite 4627, New York, NY 10048.

382 660   II   ISSN 0531-5980
CHEMICALS AND ALLIED PRODUCTS EXPORT PROMOTION COUNCIL. EXPORTERS DIRECTORY. (Text in English) a. Chemicals and Allied Products Export Promotion Council, World Trade Centre, 14/1B Ezra St, Calcutta 700001, India.

380   US   ISSN 0577-7259
CHICAGO MERCANTILE EXCHANGE YEARBOOK. a. $4.50. Chicago Mercantile Exchange, Market News Department, 444 W. Jackson Blvd., Chicago, IL 60606.

382   CH
CHINA, REPUBLIC. EXPORT PROCESSING ZONE ADMINISTRATION. EXPORTS OF EPZ. (Text in Chinese and English) a. Export Processing Zone Administration, Kaohsiung, Taiwan, Republic of China.

382   BL
COMERCIO EXTERIOR DO BRASIL; importacao. 1972. a. free. Secretaria da Receita Federal, Coordenacao do Sistema de Informacoes Economico-Fiscais, Esplanada dos Ministerios, Bloco 5, 70079 Brasilia D.F., Brazil. stat.

382   BE
COMMERCE EXTERIEUR DE L'U.E.B.L. AVEC LES PAYS D'AFRIQUE. (Text in French and Dutch) 1967. a. Office Belge du Commerce Exterieur, 162 Boulevard Emile Jacqmain, 1000 Brussels, Belgium.
    Each issue includes comparative figures for previous two years on commerce of the Union Economique Belgo-Luxemburgeoise

382   BE
COMMERCE EXTERIEUR DE L'U.E.B.L. AVEC LES PAYS D'AMERIQUE LATINE/BUITENLANDSE HANDEL VAN DE B.L.E.U. MET DE LANDEN VAN LATIJNS AMERIKA BRUXELLES. a. Office Belge du Commerce Exterieur, 162 Boulevard Emile Jacqmain, 1000 Brussels, Belgium. stat.
    Each issue includes comparative figures for previous two years on commerce of the Union Economique Belgo-Luxemburgeoise

382   BE
COMMERCE EXTERIEUR DE L'U.E.B.L. AVEC LES PAYS D'ASIE/BUITENLANDSE HANDEL VAN DE B.L.E.U. MET DE LANDEN VAN AZIE BRUXELLES. a. Office Belge du Commerce Exterieur, 162 Boulevard Emile Jacqmain, 1000 Brussels, Belgium. stat.
    Each issue includes comparative figures for previous two years on commerce of the Union Economique Belgo-Luxembourgeoise

382   BE
COMMERCE EXTERIEUR DE L'U.E.B.L. AVEC LES PAYS DE L'EST/BUITENLANDSE HANDEL VAN DE B.L.E.U. MET DE OOSTLANDEN BRUXELLES. a. Office Belge du Commerce Exterieur, 162 Boulevard Emile Jacqmain, 1000 Brussels, Belgium. stat.
    Each issue includes comparative figures for previous two years on commerce of the Union Economique Belgo-Luxembourgeoise

382   BE
COMMERCE EXTERIEUR DE L'U.E.B.L. AVEC LES PAYS DE LA C.E.E/BUITLANDSE HANDEL VAN DE B.L.E.U. MET DE E.E.G.-LIDSTATEN BRUXELLES. a. Office Belge du Commerce Exterieur, 162 Boulevard Emile Jacqmain, 1000 Brussels, Belgium. stat.
    Each issue includes comparative figures for previous two years on commerce between the European Economic Community and the Union Economique Belgo-Luxembourgeoise

382   BE
COMMERCE EXTERIEUR DE L'U.E.B.L. AVEC LES PAYS INDUSTRIALISES (AUTRE QUE LES PAYS DE LA C.E.E. ET L'A.E.L.E.)/BUITENLANDSE HANDEL VAN DE B.L.E.U. MET DE INDUSTRIELANDEN (NIET E.E.G.-EN E.V.A.-LIDSTATEN BRUXELLES) a. Office Belge du Commerce Exterieur, 162 Boulevard Emile Jacqmain, 1000 Brussels, Belgium. stat.
    Each issue includes comparative figures for previous two years on commerce between the Union Economique Belgo-Luxembourgeoise and the European Economic community and European Free Trade Association

382   IV
COMMERCE EXTERIEUR DE LA COTE D'IVOIRE: RESULTATS ET EVOLUTION. irreg. Direction des Affaires Economiques et des Relations Economiques Exterieures, Abidjan, Ivory Coast. stat.

382   SG
COMMERCE EXTERIEUR DU SENEGAL. 1975. a. Direction de la Statistique, B.P. 116, Dakar, Senegal.

COMMISSION OF THE EUROPEAN COMMUNITIES. REPORT ON COMPETITION POLICY/RAPPORT SUR LA POLITIQUE DE CONCURRENCE. see *BUSINESS AND ECONOMICS — Production Of Goods And Services*

382   UK   ISSN 0308-4892
COMMITTEE ON INVISIBLE EXPORTS. ANNUAL REPORT. a. free. Committee on Invisible Exports, The Stock Exchange, 7th Floor, London EC2N 1HH, England. illus. stat.

382   JA   ISSN 0546-0786
COMMODITY CLASSIFICATION FOR FOREIGN TRADE STATISTICS: JAPAN. (Text in Japanese and English) a. 3400 Yen($36) Japan Tariff Association, c/o Jibiki Daini Bldg., 4-7-8 Kojimachi, Chiyoda-ku, Tokyo, Japan.

382   BE
COMPAGNIE FINANCIERE EUROPEENNE ET D'OUTRE-MER. RAPPORT ANNUEL. 1972. a. free. Compagnie Financiere Europeene et d'Outre-Mer, 13, rue de Brederode, 1000 Brussels, Belgium.
    Former titles: Compagnie Europeenne et d'Outre-Mer. Rapports; Compagnie du Congo pour le Commerce et l'Industrie. Assemblee Generale. Rapports.

CONTEMPORARY ISSUES IN INTERNATIONAL ACCOUNTING: OCCASIONAL PAPER. see *BUSINESS AND ECONOMICS — Accounting*

382   US   ISSN 0070-2250
CUSTOM HOUSE GUIDE. 1862. a. fee (includes subscr. to American Import/Export Bulletin) North American Publishing Co., 401 N. Broad St., Philadelphia, PA 19108. Ed. Edward Kiernan. index.

382   AT
CUSTOMS OFFICER'S ASSOCIATION OF AUSTRALIA. FOURTH DIVISION. FOURTH DIVISION CUSTOMS OFFICER. 1968. irreg. Aus.$0.05 per no. Percival Publishing Co. Pty. Ltd., 862-870 Elizabeth St., Sydney, N.S.W. 2000, Australia.

382   CY   ISSN 0070-2420
CYPRUS. DEPARTMENT OF STATISTICS AND RESEARCH. STATISTICS OF IMPORTS AND EXPORTS. 1961. a. Mils.2000($5.80) Department of Statistics and Research, Ministry of Finance, Nicosia, Cyprus.
    Supersedes in part: Cyprus. Department of Statistics and Research. Statistics of Imports, Exports and Shipping.

CYPRUS. TOURISM ORGANISATION. ANNUAL REPORT. see *TRAVEL AND TOURISM*

382   DK
DANMARKS EKSPORTMARKEDER. 1971. irreg. Udenrigsministeriet, Handelsafdelingen - Ministry of Foreign Affairs, Loengangstraede 21, DK-1468 Copenhagen K, Denmark.

DIGEST OF COMMERCIAL LAWS OF THE WORLD. see *LAW*

382   PH
DIMENSIONS OF PHILIPPINE EXPORTS. (Text in English) 1974. a. Ministry of Trade, Information Division, Filcapital Building, Ayala Ave., Makati, Metro Manila, Philippines. Ed. Socorro B. Ramos. stat.

382   US   ISSN 0070-5071
DIRECTORY OF AMERICAN FIRMS OPERATING IN FOREIGN COUNTRIES. 1955/56. irreg., 9th edt., 1979. $125. World Trade Academy Press, Inc., 50 E. 42nd St., New York, NY 10017. Ed. J. L. Angel. circ. 4,500.

DIRECTORY OF EXPORT BUYERS IN THE U.K. see *BUSINESS AND ECONOMICS — Trade And Industrial Directories*

382   PK
DIRECTORY OF EXPORTERS AND MANUFACTURERS. (Text in English) vol. 8, 1978. a. Rs.150($19) Publishers International, Bandukwala Bldg., No. 4, I.I. Chundrigar Rd, Karachi, Pakistan.
    Formerly: Directory of Pakistan Exporters.

382 II
DIRECTORY OF INDIAN EXPORTERS.
(Continues: Directory of Exporters of Indian Produce and Manufactures) (Text in English) 1919. triennial. R.8.46. ‡ Department of Commercial Intelligence and Statistics, 1 Council House St., Calcutta 700001, India (Order from: Controller of Publications, Civil Lines, New Delhi 110054, India) adv. circ. 4,600.
Formerly: Indian Export Directory.

382 US ISSN 0070-5799
DIRECTORY OF MARYLAND EXPORTERS-IMPORTERS; an international handbook. 1970. triennial. $6. Department of Economic and Community Development, 2525 Riva Rd., Annapolis, MD 21401. Ed. Fred E. Ziegenhorn. adv.

382 US
DIRECTORY OF MIDDLE EAST IMPORTS. 2nd ed. 1981. irreg. $65. Inter-Crescent Publishing Co., Inc., Box 8481, Dallas, TX 75205.

382 US ISSN 0070-6531
DIRECTORY OF UNITED STATES IMPORTERS. 1966. biennial. $175. Twin Coast Newspapers, Inc., 110 Wall St., New York, NY 10005. Ed. E. S. Boccia. adv. index.

382 DQ ISSN 0417-9382
DOMINICA. MINISTRY OF FINANCE AND DEVELOPMENT. ANNUAL OVERSEAS TRADE REPORT. (Former Name of Issuing Body: Treasury Department) a. $3. Ministry of Finance and Development, Roseau, Dominica, West Indies.

382.6 US ISSN 0149-8118
DUN & BRADSTREET EXPORTERS' ENCYCLOPAEDIA-WORLD MARKETING GUIDE. 1904. a. (including supplementary bi-m bulletins) $230. Dun & Bradstreet International, Box 3224, Church Street Station, New York, NY 10008. Ed. Peter F. Greene. adv. index. circ. 4,500.
Formerly: Exporters' Encyclopaedia-World Marketing Guide (ISSN 0071-3546)

382 SZ ISSN 0531-4119
E F T A TRADE. a. free. European Free Trade Association, 9-11 rue de Varembe, 1211 Geneva 20, Switzerland.

382 BE
EAST-WEST TRADE YEARBOOK. 1978. a. 5000 Fr. East-West S.P.R.L., 10, Bd. Saint Lazare, 1030 Brussels, Belgium. stat.

382 UY
ENDEUDAMIENTO EXTERNO DEL URUGUAY. irreg. Banco Central del Uruguay, Division Asesoria Economica y Estudios, Cerrito 351, Montevideo, Uruguay. stat.

ESTADISTICA PANAMENA. SITUACION ECONOMICA. SECCION 341. BALANZA DE PAGOS. see *BUSINESS AND ECONOMICS — Public Finance, Taxation*

382 SZ ISSN 0531-4127
EUROPEAN FREE TRADE ASSOCIATION. ANNUAL REPORT. German edition: European Free Trade Association. Jahresbericht (ISSN 0531-7428) (Editions in English, French and German) 1960/61. a. free. European Free Trade Association, 9-11 rue de Varembe, 1211 Geneva 20, Switzerland.

382.6 CN ISSN 0708-1332
EXPORT CANADA. 1978. a. 20. Continental Export Promotions Ltd., Box 1048, Sta. A., Surrey, B.C. V3S, Canada. illus.

382.6 UK ISSN 0071-3554
EXPORT DATA; export document requirements of all countries. 1917. a. £20. Benn Publications Ltd., 25 New Street Square, London EC4A 3JA, England. Ed. Cynthia Patey. adv. index. circ. 3,000.
Formerly: Export Data Exporters Year Book (ISSN 0071-3554)

382 DK
EXPORT DIRECTORY OF DENMARK. (Text in English, French, German and Spanish; summaries in English) 1927. a. free. Kraks Legat, Nytorv 17, DK-1450 Copenhagen K, Denmark. circ. 20,000.

382 US
EXPORT DIRECTORY/U.S. BUYING GUIDE. biennial. $175. Journal of Commerce, 110 Wall St., New York, NY 10005 (Subscr. addr.: Journal of Commerce, 445 Marshall St., Phillipsburg, NJ 08865)

382 US
EXPORT GRAFICAS U S A. (Text in Spanish) 1980. a. $15. Graphic Arts Trade Journals International, Inc., 399 Conklin St., Suite 306, Box 81, Farmingdale, NY 11735. adv. circ. 16,000.

382 US ISSN 0147-409X
EXPORT GRAFICS U S A. (Text in English) 1977. a. $15. Graphic Arts Trade Journals International, Inc., 399 Conklin St., Suite 306, Box 81, Farmingdale, L.I., NY 11735. Eds. Lydia Miura, George Humphrey. adv. circ. 16,000.

382 332.1 JA ISSN 0071-3503
EXPORT-IMPORT BANK OF JAPAN. ANNUAL REPORT.* 1951. a. free. Export-Import Bank of Japan, 1-4-1 Otemachi, Chiyoda-ku, Tokyo, Japan. circ. 3,500.

332.1 KO
EXPORT-IMPORT BANK OF KOREA. ANNUAL REPORT. (Text in English) a. Export-Import Bank of Korea, Box 4009, Seoul 100, S. Korea. charts. illus. stat.

382.7 PR
EXPORT-IMPORT MARKETS; Caribbean-Latin America. (Text & summaries in English) 1978. a. $50. Witcom Group, El Caribe Bldg., 210 Ponce de Leon, San Juan, PR 00901 (U.S. dist.: Dun & Bradstreet International, Box 3224, Church St. Station, New York, NY 10008) Ed. Hugo Miranda. adv. stat. (back issues avail)
Formerly: Exporter Guide - Caribbean and Latin America.

382 SA
EXPORT PROFILE OF SOUTH AFRICA. a. R.5. Da Gama Publishers (Pty) Ltd., 311 Locarno House, 20 Loveday St., Box 61464, Marshalltown 2107, South Africa. Ed. D. de Freitas. adv.

382 US ISSN 0556-3585
EXPORTS BY PENNSYLVANIA MANUFACTURERS. 1972. a. free. ‡ Department of Commerce, Bureau of Statistics, Research & Planning, 630B Health and Welfare Bldg., Harrisburg, PA 17120. Ed. W. R. Kresge.

382 CH ISSN 0301-9217
EXPORTS OF THE REPUBLIC OF CHINA. 1970-71. a. $25. ‡ Taipei World Trade Center, Sungshan Airport, 390 Tun Hwa N. Road, Taipei 105, Taiwan, Republic of China. circ. 5,000.

382.5 LB
EXTERNAL TRADE OF LIBERIA: IMPORT AND EXPORT. (Text in English) a, latest 1975. $5. Ministry of Planning and Economic Affairs, Box 9016, Monrovia, Liberia.

382 FR ISSN 0071-4240
FEDERATION FRANCAISE ET EUROPEENNE DU COMMERCE, DE L'INDUSTRIE ET DE L'EPARGNE. REVUE.* irreg. price varies. Federation Francaise et Europeenne du Commerce de l'Industrie et de l'Epargne, 44 rue de Reuilly, Paris (12e), France.

382 FR ISSN 0071-4704
FICHES ANALYTIQUES DE LA PRESSE TECHNIQUE FRANCAISE. 1965. irreg. price varies. Centre National du Commerce Exterieur, 10 Av. d'Iena, Paris 16e, France.

382 CK
FONDO DE PROMOCION DE EXPORTACIONES. DIRECTORIO DE EXPORTADORES/EXPORT DIRECTORY. (Text in English, Spanish) 1976. a. Fondo de Promocion de Exportaciones, Apartado Aereo 17966, Bogota, Colombia. adv. illus.

FOOD AND AGRICULTURE ORGANIZATION OF THE UNITED NATIONS. TRADE YEARBOOK. see *AGRICULTURE — Agricultural Economics*

382 BL
FOREIGN INVESTMENTS IN BRAZIL. irreg. Banco Central do Brasil, Departamento de Fiscalizcao e Registro de Capitais Estrangeiros, Edificio Vera Cruz, Setor Comercial Sul, 7000 Brasilia, D.F., Brazil.

382 US
FOREIGN MARKET AIRGRAMS. irreg. $2 per no. (U.S. Industry and Trade Administration, Bureau of International Commerce) U.S. National Technical Information Service, 5285 Port Royal Rd., Springfield, VA 22161.

382 US
FOREIGN MARKETS REPORTS. irreg. $10 per no. (U.S. Industry and Trade Administration, Bureau of International Commerce) U.S. National Technical Information Service, 5285 Port Royal Rd., Springfield, VA 22161.

382 US
FOREIGN TRADE MARKETPLACE. 1977. irreg. $48. Gale Research Company, Book Tower, Detroit, MI 48226. Ed. George J. Schulz.

382 BL
FOREIGN TRADE OF BRAZIL. (Text in Protuguese) 1969. a. free. Coordenacao de Sistema de Informacoes Economico-Fiscais, Esplanada dos Ministerios, 70079 Brasilia, Brazil.

382 665 US ISSN 0363-6798
FOREIGN TRADE REPORTS. BUNKER FUELS. 1948. monthly and annual. $3.25. U.S. Bureau of the Census, Washington, DC 20233.

382 US ISSN 0361-0047
FOREIGN TRADE REPORTS. SUMMARY OF U.S. EXPORT AND IMPORT MERCHANDISE TRADE. 1945. m. $14.90 including FT 975, 985, 986. U. S. Bureau of the Census, Washington, Springfield, DC 20233.

382 US ISSN 0095-7771
FOREIGN TRADE REPORTS. U.S. AIRBORNE EXPORTS AND GENERAL IMPORTS. m. $14.90 including FT-900, 975, 985. U. S. Bureau of the Census, Washington, DC 20233.

382 US ISSN 0095-0890
FOREIGN TRADE REPORTS. U.S. WATERBORNE EXPORTS AND GENERAL IMPORTS; trade area, district, port, type service and U.S. flag. 1952. monthly and annual. $14.50 includes subscriptions to FT 900, 975, 986. U.S. Bureau of the Census, c/o Subscriber Services Section (Publications), Washington, DC 20233. Key Title: U.S. Waterborne Exports and General Imports.

382 US
FOREIGN TRADE REPORTS. VESSEL ENTRANCES AND CLEARANCES. 1945-1951 issued monthly. a. $14.90 includes subscr. to the monthly FT 900, 985, 986. U. S. Bureau of the Census, Washington, DC 20233.

382 FR ISSN 0071-8645
FRANCE. DIRECTION GENERALE DES DOUANES ET DROITS INDIRECTS. COMMENTAIRES ANNUELS DES STATISTIQUES DU COMMERCE EXTERIEUR. irreg. Imprimerie Nationale, Service des Ventes, 59128 Flers en Escrebieux, 75732 Paris Cedex 15.

382 FR ISSN 0071-8726
FRANCE. DIRECTION NATIONALE DES DOUANES ET DROITS INDIRECTS. TABLEAU GENERAL DES TRANSPORTS. 1964. a. price varies. Imprimerie Nationale, Service des Ventes, 59128 Flers en Escrebieux, France, France.

382 FR ISSN 0071-8718
FRANCE. DIRECTION NATIONALE DES DOUANES ET DROITS INDIRECTS. TRANSPORT DU COMMERCE EXTERIEUR. a. price varies. Imprimerie Nationale, Service des Ventes, 59128 Flers en Escrebieux, France.

FRANCE. MINISTERE DE L'ECONOMIE ET DES FINANCES. BALANCE DES PAIEMENTS ENTRE LA FRANCE ET L'EXTERIEUR. see *BUSINESS AND ECONOMICS — Public Finance, Taxation*

BUSINESS AND ECONOMICS — INTERNATIONAL COMMERCE

FRANCO BRITISH TRADE DIRECTORY. see BUSINESS AND ECONOMICS — Chamber Of Commerce Publications

382   UN
G A T T STUDIES IN INTERNATIONAL TRADE. (Editions in English, French and Spanish) 1971. irreg.,no. 7, 1978. price varies. General Agreement on Tariffs and Trade, Centre William Rappard, 154 rue de Lausanne, 1211 Geneva 21, Switzerland (Dist. in U.S. by: Unipub, 345 Park Ave. S., New York, NY 10010) circ. 9,000 (comb. circ.)

382   UN   ISSN 0072-0615
GENERAL AGREEMENT ON TARIFFS AND TRADE. G A T T ACTIVITIES IN (YEAR) (Edts. in English, French and Spanish) 1959/60. a. price varies. General Agreement on Tariffs and Trade, Centre William Rappard, 154 rue de Lausanne, 1211 Geneva 21, Switzerland (Dist. in U.S. by: Unipub, 345 Park Ave. S., New York, NY 10010) circ. 9,000 comb. circ.

382   UN   ISSN 0072-0623
GENERAL AGREEMENT ON TARIFFS AND TRADE. BASIC INSTRUMENTS AND SELECTED DOCUMENTS SERIES. SUPPLEMENT. (Edts. in English, French and Spanish) 1952. a. price varies. General Agreement on Tariffs and Trade, Centre William Rappard, 154 rue de Lausanne, 1211 Geneva 21, Switzerland (Dist. in U.S. by: Unipub, 345 Park Ave. S., New York, NY 10010) cum.index. circ. 4,400 (comb. circ.)

382   UN   ISSN 0072-064X
GENERAL AGREEMENT ON TARIFFS AND TRADE. INTERNATIONAL TRADE. (Editions in English, French and Spanish) 1953. a. price varies. General Agreement on Tariffs and Trade, Centre William Rappard, 154 rue de Lausanne, 1211 Geneva 21, Switzerland (Dist. in U.S. by: Unipub, 345 Park Ave. S., New York, NY 10010) circ. 5,800 (comb. circ.)

GREAT BRITAIN. DEPARTMENT OF TRADE. EXPORT OF WORKS OF ART. see ART

382   UK   ISSN 0072-5676
GREAT BRITAIN. DEPARTMENT OF TRADE. IMPORT DUTIES ACT 1958. ANNUAL REPORT. a. H.M.S.O., P.O. Box 569, London SE1 9NH, England.

382   UV
GUIDE DE L'HOMME D'AFFAIRES VOLTAIQUE. a. Office National du Commerce Exterieur, B.P. 389, Ouagadougou, Upper Volta.

382   GY   ISSN 0533-991X
GUYANA. STATISTICAL BUREAU. ANNUAL ACCOUNT RELATING TO EXTERNAL TRADE. 1954. a. $3. Statistical Bureau, Georgetown, Guyana.

383   DK   ISSN 0069-9888
HANDELSHOEJSKOLEN I KOEBENHAVN. INSTITUTTET FOR UDENRIGSHANDEL. SMAASKRIFTER. 1963. irreg., no. 11, 1975. price varies. Handelshoejskolen i Koebenhavn, Instituttet for Udenrigshandel, 1925 Copenhagen, Denmark. Ed. Lauge Stetting.

382   NE   ISSN 0073-3032
HOLLAND EXPORTS. (Text in English, French, German and Spanish) 1952. a. price varies. A B C voor Handel en Industrie C. V., Koningin Wilhelminalaan 16, P.O. Box 190, Haarlem, Netherlands. adv.

382   HK
HONG KONG REVIEW OF OVERSEAS TRADE. (Text in English) 1964. a. HK.$30. Census and Statistics Department, Kai Tak Commercial Bldg., 317 Des Voeux Rd., Central, Hong Kong, Hong Kong (Subscr. to: Government Information Services, Beaconsfield House, Queen's Rd, Central, Victoria, Hong Kong) charts. stat.

382   BE   ISSN 0067-5628
I C E SUPPLEMENT. SERIE C. irreg. Office Belge du Commerce Exterieur, 132 Boulevard Emile Jacqmain, 1000 Brussels, Belgium.

382   JA
I D E SPECIAL PAPERS. (Text in English) no. 3, 1976. irreg. Institute for Developing Economics, 42 Ichigaya-Hommura-Cho, Shinjuku-Ku, Tokyo 162, Japan. charts, stat.

382   II   ISSN 0073-6546
I I T C DIRECTORY. (Text in English) 1969. a. free; selected distribution. Indian International Trade Center, 59 Jolly Maker Chambers I, Nariman Point, Bombay 400020, India.

IMPORT/EXPORT WOOD PURCHASING GUIDE. see FORESTS AND FORESTRY — Lumber And Wood

382   II   ISSN 0536-9983
IMPORT TRADE CONTROL: HANDBOOK OF RULES AND PROCEDURES. (Text in English) a. Ministry of Commerce, New Delhi, India (Order from: Controller of Publications, Government of India, Civil Lines, Delhi 110054, India)

382   II   ISSN 0536-9061
IMPORT TRADE CONTROL POLICY. (Issued in two volumes) (Text in English) a. price varies. Ministry of Commerce, New Delhi, India (Order from: Controller of Publications, Government of India, Civil Lines, Delhi 110054, India)

382   US   ISSN 0073-5604
IMPORTERS AND EXPORTERS TRADE PROMOTION GUIDE. 1967. biennial. $5. World Wide Trade Service, Box 283, Medina, WA 98039. Ed. George Lucas.

382   CH
IMPORTS OF THE REPUBLIC OF CHINA. 1973-74. a. $25. Taipei World Trade Center, Sungshan Airport, 390 Tun Hwa N. Road, Taipei 105, Taiwan, Republic of China. circ. 8,000.

382   II   ISSN 0073-6473
INDIAN INSTITUTE OF FOREIGN TRADE. REPORT. (Text in English) a. price varies. Indian Institute of Foreign Trade, Ashok Bhawan, 93 Nehru Pl., New Delhi 110024, India.

382   US
INDIANA INTERNATIONAL TRADE DIRECTORY. a. Department of Commerce, International Trade Division, State House, Indianapolis, IN 46204.

382   II
INDIA'S PRODUCTION, EXPORTS, AND INTERNAL CONSUMPTION OF COIR. (Text and summaries in English) 1967. a. Rs.30. ‡ Coir Board, Cochin 682016, Kerala, Kerala, India. stat. circ. 500.
Formerly: India's Exports and Internal Consumption of Coir and Coir Goods.

387   UK   ISSN 0534-7793
INTERNATIONAL CARGO HANDLING COORDINATION ASSOCIATION. RAPPORTS DES COMITES NATIONAUX. a. membership only. International Cargo Handling Coordination Association, Abford House, 15 Wilton Road, London SW1V ILX, England. circ. 1,800 (c.)

INTERNATIONAL COAL. see MINES AND MINING INDUSTRY

INTERNATIONAL CUSTOMS JOURNAL/ BULLETIN INTERNATIONAL DES DOUANES. see BUSINESS AND ECONOMICS — Public Finance, Taxation

INTERNATIONAL MONETARY FUND. BALANCE OF PAYMENTS YEARBOOK. see BUSINESS AND ECONOMICS — Macroeconomics

382   SI
INTERNATIONAL TRADE AND SINGAPORE. (Text in English) 1974. irreg. S.$36. Sima Publishers, 76F/78F, Boon Keng Road, Block 4, 12, Singapore, Singapore. illus.

ITALY. ISTITUTO CENTRALE DI STATISTICA. ANNUARIO STATISTICO DEL COMMERCIO INTERNO. see BUSINESS AND ECONOMICS — Abstracting, Bibliographies, Statistics

ITALY. ISTITUTO CENTRALE DI STATISTICA. STATISTICA ANNUALE DEL COMMERCIO CON L'ESTERO. TOMO I. see BUSINESS AND ECONOMICS — Abstracting, Bibliographies, Statistics

ITALY. ISTITUTO CENTRALE DI STATISTICA. STATISTICA ANNUALE DEL COMMERCIO CON L'ESTERO. TOMO II. see BUSINESS AND ECONOMICS — Abstracting, Bibliographies, Statistics

382   GW   ISSN 0075-224X
JAHRBUCH DER EXPORT- UND VERSANDTLEITER. 1952. a. DM.46. K. O. Storck and Co., Verlag und Druckerei GmbH, Stahltwiete 7, 2000 Hamburg 50, W. Germany (B.R.D.) adv.

382   US
JAPAN'S ECONOMY AND TRADE. 1974. irreg. (Ministry of Foreign Affairs, JA) Japan Information Service, c/o Consulate General of Japan, 1737 Post St., San Francisco, CA 94115.

382   KE
KENYA. COMMISSIONER OF CUSTOMS AND EXCISE. ANNUAL TRADE REPORT. a. EAs.60. Commissioner of Customs and Excise, Box 40160, Nairobi, Kenya.
Supersedes in part: Annual Trade Report of Tanzania, Uganda and Kenya.

382   GW
KIELER STUDIEN. irreg., vol. 164, 1980. price varies. (Universitaet Kiel, Institut fuer Weltwirtschaft) Verlag J.C.B. Mohr (Paul Siebeck), Wilhelmstr. 18, Postfach 2040, 7400 Tuebingen, W. Germany (B.R.D.) Ed. Herbert Giersen.

382   UK   ISSN 0309-1961
LECTURES IN COMMERCIAL DIPLOMACY. 1976. irreg. Trade Policy Research Centre, 1 Gough Sq., London EC4A 3DE, England.

M T I A N E G'S EXPORT NOTE PAD. (Metal Trades Industry Association National Export Group) see METALLURGY

382 336   CN   ISSN 0076-1990
MCGOLDRICK'S HANDBOOK OF CANADIAN CUSTOMS TARIFF AND EXCISE DUTIES. a. Can.$21. McMullin Publishers Ltd., 417 St. Pierre St., Montreal, Que. H2Y 2M4, Canada. adv.

382   BL
MADE IN BRAZIL; Brazilian export market. no, 6, 1977. a. Assessoria de Promocao e Cultura Editora Ltda., Avda Brigadeiro Luis Antonio 402, P.O. Box 5390, 01318 Sao Paulo, Brazil. (Co-sponsors: Ministerio da Industria; Banco do Brasil) Ed. Jose L. Ribeiro Leite. adv. charts, illus. stat.

382   GW   ISSN 0085-2937
MADE IN EUROPE BUYERS' GUIDE. (Text in English) 1954. a. free to subscribers of Made in Europe. Made in Europe Marketing Organization GmbH & Co. KG, Unterlindau 21-29, 6000 Frankfurt 1, W. Germany (B.R.D.) (U.S. Subscr. to: Made in Europe, 150 Green St., Brooklyn, NY 11222) Ed. H. E. Reisner. adv. circ. 16,000. (also avail. in microfilm from UMI; reprint service avail. from ISI)

MALAWI. NATIONAL STATISTICAL OFFICE. BALANCE OF PAYMENTS. see BUSINESS AND ECONOMICS — Public Finance, Taxation

382   UK   ISSN 0076-3713
MANCHESTER GUARDIAN SOCIETY FOR THE PROTECTION OF TRADE. ANNUAL REPORT. 1826. a. Manchester Guardian Society for the Protection of Trade, 47 Mosley St., Manchester, M6O 8AA, England.

382 679   II
MARINE PRODUCTS EXPORT REVIEW. (Text in English) 1973. irreg. Marine Products Export Development Authority, World Trade Centre, M. G. Rd., P.B. 1708, Cochin 682016, India.

382   MR   ISSN 0076-4655
MAROC EN CHIFFRE. 1961. a. DH.20. Direction de la Statistique, B.P. 178, Rabat, Morocco. (Co-sponsor: Banque Marocaine du Commerce Exterieur, Direction du Developpement)

BUSINESS AND ECONOMICS — INTERNATIONAL COMMERCE

382   GW   ISSN 0076-6208
MEIER-DUDY/MEIER'S DIRECTORY OF EXPORTERS AND IMPORTERS; Meier's Addressbuch der Exporteure und Importeure. (Text in English, French, Spanish) 1903. a. DM.55. Verlag von Meier's Adressbuch der Exporteure Rudolf Dudy KG, Feldweg 9, 6394 Graevenwiesbach 5, W. Germany (B.R.D.) (Dist. by Intl. Publications Service, 114 E. 32nd St., New York, N.Y. 10016) Ed. Christa Reichel. adv. bk. rev. circ. 3,500.

382   FR
MICROTABLES IMPORTS-EXPORTS OF O E C D COUNTRIES. irreg. 1000 F.($250) Organization for Economic Cooperation and Development, 2 rue Andre Pascal, 75775 Paris Cedex 16, France (U.S. orders to: O E C D Publications Center, 1750 Pennsylvania Ave. N.W., Washington, DC 20006) (microfiche)

382   UK   ISSN 0140-7953
MIDDLE EAST LIVING COSTS. 1977. a. £18. Confederation of British Industry, 103 New Oxford St., London WC1A 1DU, England.

382   US
MINNESOTA EXPORT SURVEY SUMMARY. biennial. free. Department of Economic Development, 480 Cedar St., St. Paul, MN 55101. circ. 500.

382   US
MINNESOTA EXPORTER'S ASSISTANCE GUIDE. a. free. Department of Economic Development, 480 Cedar St., St. Paul, MN 55101. circ. 2,000.

382   US
MINNESOTA'S ROLE IN INTERNATIONAL TRADE. irreg. free. Department of Economic Development, 480 Cedar St., St. Paul, MN 55101. circ. 1,000.

382   AT   ISSN 0311-0273
MITSUI NEWS. 1973. irreg. Mitsui and Co. Australia, Ltd., Royal Exchange Building, 56 Pitt St., Sydney, N.S.W. 2000, Australia.

382   US
MULTINATIONAL CORPORATION: STUDIES ON U.S. FOREIGN INVESTMENT. 1972. irreg., only vol. 1 issued to date. price varies. U.S. Industry and Trade Administration, Bureau of International Economic Policy and Research, Office of International Investment, 14th St. & Constitution Ave., N.W., Washington, DC 20230.

382   910.202   US   ISSN 0093-7487
MULTINATIONAL EXECUTIVE TRAVEL COMPANION. 1970. a. $20 ($12.95 foreign) Guides to Multinational Business, Inc., Harvard Sq., Box 92, Cambridge, MA 02138. adv. charts. stat. tr.lit. circ. 515,000(controlled) (back issues avail.)

NATIONAL ACCOUNTS OF RHODESIA. see BUSINESS AND ECONOMICS — Public Finance, Taxation

382   NN
NEW HEBRIDES. BUREAU OF STATISTICS. OVERSEAS TRADE/COMMERCE EXTERIEUR. (Text in English, French) 1971. a. Bureau of Statistics, Port Vila, New Hebrides. stat. circ. 400.

382   US
NEW YORK (STATE) DEPARTMENT OF COMMERCE. EXPORTS OF NEW YORK MANUFACTURES. (Subseries of its Research Bulletin) 1965. irreg., latest issue 1975. free. Department of Commerce, 99 Washington Ave, Albany, NY 12245. Ed. Peter A. Ansell. circ. 1,000.

382.7   NZ
NEW ZEALAND. DEPARTMENT OF TRADE AND INDUSTRY. IMPORT LICENSING SCHEDULE. 1938. irreg. price varies. Department of Trade and Industry, Wellington, New Zealand. circ. 6,000.

382   NZ
NEW ZEALAND EXPORT-IMPORT CORPORATION. REPORT. 1975. a. New Zealand Export-Import Corporation, Wellington, New Zealand.

382   BE
NORTH ATLANTIC TREATY ORGANIZATION. DIRECTORATE OF ECONOMIC AFFAIRS. COLLOQUIUM. SERIES. a., no. 6, 1978. North Atlantic Treaty Organization, Directorate of Economic Affairs, Box 2146, Brussels, Belgium.

382   NO   ISSN 0029-3628
NORWAY. (Editions in Arabic, English, French, German, and Spanish) 1977. a. free. Norges Eksportraad - Export Council of Norway, Drammensveien 40, Oslo 2, Norway. Ed. Gunnar Jerman. adv. illus. circ. 35,000.

382   JA
NOW IN JAPAN. no. 22, 1976. irreg. Japan External Trade Organization, 2 Akasaka Aoicho, Minato-ku, Tokyo 107, Japan. (processed)

OFFICE EQUIPMENT EXPORTER. see BUSINESS AND ECONOMICS — Office Equipment And Services

ORGANIZATION FOR ECONOMIC COOPERATION AND DEVELOPMENT. COUNCIL. CODE DE LA LIBERATION DES MOUVEMENTS DE CAPITAUX. CODE OF LIBERALISATION OF CAPITAL MOVEMENTS. see BUSINESS AND ECONOMICS — Banking And Finance

382   FR   ISSN 0304-3282
ORGANIZATION FOR ECONOMIC COOPERATION AND DEVELOPMENT. GUIDE TO LEGISLATION ON RESTRICTIVE BUSINESS PRACTICES. SUPPLEMENTS. (Editions in English and French) 1976, 11th series of supplements. 2/yr. 150 F.($37.50) Organization for Economic Cooperation and Development, 2 rue Andre - Pascal, 75775 Paris Cedex 16, France (U.S. orders to: O.E.C.D. Publications and Information Center, 1750 Pennsylvania Ave., N.W., Washington, DC 20006) (also avail. in microfiche)

382   UK   ISSN 0078-7167
OWEN'S COMMERCE AND TRAVEL AND INTERNATIONAL REGISTER. 1953. a. £6($43) Owen's Commerce and Travel Ltd., 100 Belsize Lane, London NW3 5BB, England. Ed. M.F. Owen. adv.

PACIFIC COAST COUNCIL ON LATIN AMERICAN STUDIES. PROCEEDINGS. see HISTORY — History Of North And South America

382   PK   ISSN 0078-8104
PAKISTAN. EXPORT PROMOTION BUREAU. EXPORT GUIDE SERIES. irreg. Export Promotion Bureau, National Assembly Bldg., Court Rd., Karachi, Pakistan.

338.1   382   PK   ISSN 0078-8112
PAKISTAN. EXPORT PROMOTION BUREAU. FRESH FRUITS.* (Text in English) a. Export Promotion Bureau, National Assembly Bldg., Court Rd., Karachi, Pakistan.

332   382   PK   ISSN 0078-8058
PAKISTAN CUSTOMS TARIFF. (Text in English) 1960. irreg. price varies. Central Board of Revenue, Karachi, Pakistan (Order from: Manager of Publications, Government of Pakistan, 2nd Floor, Ahmad Chamber, Tariq Rd., P.E.C.H.S., Karachi 29, Pakistan)

382   PK   ISSN 0078-8090
PAKISTAN EXPORT DIRECTORY. (Text in English) 1966-67. a. (Export Promotion Bureau) Trade and Industry Publications Limited, Trade and Industry House, 14 West Wharf Road, Box 4611, Karachi 2, Pakistan. Ed. G. Naseeruddin.

PAKISTAN'S BALANCE OF PAYMENTS. see BUSINESS AND ECONOMICS — Public Finance, Taxation

382   PP   ISSN 0078-9283
PAPUA NEW GUINEA. BUREAU OF STATISTICS. PRIVATE OVERSEAS INVESTMENT. 1967/68. a. free. Bureau of Statistics, P.O. Wards Strip, Papua New Guinea. Ed. J. J. Shadlow. circ. 683.

382   PH
PHILIPPINE EXPORT DIRECTORY. 1975. a. $5. Institute of Export Development, P.O. Box 181 Greenhills, San Juan, Rizal, Philippines. Ed. Asuncion B. Kalalo. circ. 800-1,000.

382   381   PH
PHILIPPINES. MINISTRY OF TRADE. ANNUAL REPORT. (Text in English) 1948. a. free. Ministry of Trade, Information Division, Filcapital Building, Ayala Ave., Makati, Metro Manila, Philippines. Formerly: Philippines. Department of Commerce and Industry. Annual Report (ISSN 0079-1539)

382   PH
PHILIPPINES. MINISTRY OF TRADE. TREND ANALYSIS OF THE TWENTY LEADING EXPORTS AND PROSPECTS IN THE YEAR AHEAD. (Text in English) 1974. irreg. Ministry of Trade, Information Division, Filcapital Building, Ayala Ave., Makati, Metro Manila, Philippines. Ed. Socorro B. Ramos.

382   PH
PHILIPPINES. MINISTRY OF TRADE. TWENTY LEADING IMPORTS. (Text in English) 1974. irreg. Ministry of Trade, Information Division, Filcapital Building, Ayala Ave., Makati, Metro Manila, Philippines. Ed. Socorro B. Ramos.

382.7   EI
PRACTICAL GUIDE TO THE USE OF THE EUROPEAN COMMUNITIES' SCHEME OF GENERALIZED TARIFF PREFERENCES. (Text in Danish, Dutch, English, French, German and Italian) a. $14. (Commission of the European Communities, Directorate-General for External Relations) Office for Official Publications of the European Communities, C.P. 1003, Luxembourg 1, Luxembourg. charts. stat.

PRINCIPAL INTERNATIONAL BUSINESSES; the world marketing directory. see BUSINESS AND ECONOMICS — Marketing And Purchasing

382   PL
PROBLEMY HANDLU ZAGRANICZNEGO. (Text in Polish; summaries in English and Russian) 1971. irreg. price varies. (Instytut Koniunktur i Cen Handlu Zagranicznego) Panstwowe Wydawnictwo Ekonomiczne, Ul. Niecala 4A, Warsaw, Poland. stat.

650   FR   ISSN 0079-9262
QUI REPRESENTE QUI. (Text and summaries in English, French, German, Spanish) 1956. a. 250 F. Societe Nouvelle d'Editions pour l'Industrie, 22 Avenue F. D. Roosevelt, 75008 Paris, France. adv. illus.
   Lists 13000 branches or foreign representatives of importers in France

382   FR   ISSN 0080-1070
REPERTOIRE DES SOCIETES DE COMMERCE EXTERIEUR FRANCAISES. 1969. irreg. 75 F. (Federation Nationale des Syndicats de Societes de Commerce Exterieur) E. T. P., 31 Ave. Pierre I de Serbie, 75784 Paris Cedex 16, France. circ. 3,000.

330   US
RESEARCH IN INTERNATIONAL BUSINESS AND FINANCE; an annual compilation of research. 1979. a. $18.75 to individuals; institutions $37.50. J A I Press, Box 1678, 165 W. Putnam Ave., Greenwich, CT 06830. Ed. Robert G. Hawkins.

382   SA   ISSN 0081-2552
S A F T O ANNUAL REPORT/SUID-AFRIKAANSE BUITELANDSE HANDELSORGONISASIE JAARVERSLAG. (Text in Afrikaans and English) a. free. South African Foreign Trade Organization, Box 9039, Johannesburg 2000, South Africa.

382   SE
SEYCHELLES TRADE REPORT. a, latest 1977 (pub. 1979) Rs.60. President's Office, Statistics Division, Box 206, Mahe, Seychelles (Subcr. to: Government Printer, Box 205, Union Vale, Mahe, Seychelles)

382   US
SINO-UNITED STATES TRADE STATISTICS. (Subseries of its Special Report) 1974. a. $10. National Council for U.S.-China Trade, 1050 17th St., N.W., Suite 350, Washington, DC 20036. (back issues avail.)

BUSINESS AND ECONOMICS — INTERNATIONAL COMMERCE

382   SP   ISSN 0080-9985
SLAM: TRADE YEAR BOOK OF AFRICA. (Text in English and French; summaries in English, French, Italian, Spanish) 1962. irreg.; no. 8, 1980. $60. Editorial Ofice, German Perez Carasco 63, Madrid 27, Spain. Ed. Arsenio Pardo Rodriguez. adv. circ. 15,000.
    Formerly: Spanish, Lusitanian, American Trade Directory.

382   FR   ISSN 0081-1289
SOCIETES ET FOURNISSEURS D'AFRIQUE NOIRE ET DE MADAGASCAR. GUIDE ECONOMIQUE NOIRE. (1962, no. 1, as Annuaire Economique des Etats d'Afrique Noire; title varies) a. 310 F. Ediafric-la Documentation Africaine, 57 Av. d'Iena, 75783 Paris Cedex 16, France.

382   CE   ISSN 0069-2360
SRI LANKA EXPORT DIRECTORY. a. Ministry of Trade and Shipping, Colombo 3, Sri Lanka.

382   EI
STATISTICAL OFFICE OF THE EUROPEAN COMMUNITIES. COMMERCE EXTERIEUR: NOMENCLATURE DES PAYS. (Multilingual Text) irreg. B.P. 1907, Luxembourg, Luxembourg (Dist. in the U.S. by: European Community Information Service, 2100 M St., NW, Suite 707, Washington, DC 20037).

382   US   ISSN 0553-0237
STUDIES IN EXPORT PROMOTION. 1966. irreg. Organization of American States, Department of Publications, Washington, DC 20006.

STUDIES IN INTERNATIONAL ECONOMIC RELATIONS. see BUSINESS AND ECONOMICS

380.5   FR
SYSTEME D'INFORMATION SUR LES TRANSPORTS DE MARCHANDISES: RESULTATS GENERAUX, TRAFIC INTERIEUR ET INTERNATIONAL. a. Departement des Statistiques de Transport, Ministere des Transports, 55-57 rue Brillat-Savarin, 75658 Paris Cedex 13, France.
    Formerly: Systeme d'Information sur les Transports de Marchandises: Resultats Generaux, Trafic International.

382.6   CH   ISSN 0494-5336
TAIWAN EXPORTS. (Text Mainly in English) 1957. irreg. Board of Foreign Trade, 1 Hu Kou St., Taipei, Taiwan, Republic of China. illus.

382   TZ
TANZANIA IMPORT AND EXPORT DIRECTORY. 1975. irreg. National Bank of Commerce, International Banking Department, Box 1255, Dar es Salaam, Tanzania. illus.

TASMANIA. DEPARTMENT OF THE TREASURY. COMMONWEALTH GRANTS TO TASMANIA. see BUSINESS AND ECONOMICS — Public Finance, Taxation

382   FI
TECHNIK UND FORM AUS FINNLAND. (Text in German) 1936. a. Fmk.22. Finnish Foreign Trade Association, Arkadiankatu 4-6B, 00100 Helsinki 10, Finland. illus. circ. 12,000.
    Formerly (until 1981): Finnische Handelsrundschau (ISSN 0015-2420)

382   TH
THAILAND TRADE INDEX. (Text in English and Thai) 1976. a. Interstate Publications, Box 5-85, Pathumwan, Bangkok 5, Thailand. adv. illus. stat.

382 387   UK
TOWARDS A SHIPPING POLICY FOR THE EEC. 1978. irreg. £40. Seatrade Publications Ltd., Fairfax House, Colchester CO1 1RJ, England.

382   IR   ISSN 0082-5751
TRADE INDEX OF IRAN. (Text in English) a. $9. Iran Marketing Co., P.O. Box 12-1499, Nadershah 140, Teheran, Iran. Eds. Kamran M. Naghdi, D. Neyestani.

382   CH   ISSN 0082-5778
TRADE OF CHINA. (Subseries of Its Maritime Customs. I. Statistical Series) (Text in English and Chinese) 1950. a. $30. Inspectorate General of Customs, Statistical Department, 85, Hsin-Sheng S. Rd. Sec., 1, Taipei, Taiwan, Republic of China. circ. 550.

UNITED NATIONS. COMMISSION ON INTERNATIONAL TRADE LAW. YEARBOOK. see LAW — International Law

382   US   ISSN 0082-9846
U.S. BUREAU OF DOMESTIC AND INTERNATIONAL BUSINESS ADMINISTRATION. OVERSEAS BUSINESS REPORTS. irreg. $36.50. U.S. Industry and Trade Administration, Bureau of Domestic Commerce, U.S. Department of Commerce, Washington, DC 20230 (Orders to: Supt. of Documents, Washington, DC 20402)
    Continues the Same Title Issued by the U.S. Bureau of International Commerce.

382   US   ISSN 0094-8411
U.S. BUREAU OF EAST-WEST TRADE. EXPORT ADMINISTRATION REGULATIONS. 1941. a. $30 including updating Export Administration Bulletins. U.S. Industry and Trade Administration, Bureau of East-West Trade, U.S. Dept. of Commerce, Washington, DC 20203 (Subscr. to: Supt. of Documents, Washington, DC 20402) (looseleaf format)
    Formerly: Export Control Regulations (ISSN 0082-8947)

382   US   ISSN 0082-8939
U. S. BUREAU OF INTERNATIONAL COMMERCE. ANNUAL REPORTS. a. U.S. Industry and Trade Administration, Bureau of International Commerce, Washington, DC 20203 (Orders to: Supt. Doc., Washington, DC 20402)

382   US   ISSN 0082-8963
U. S. BUREAU OF INTERNATIONAL COMMERCE. TRADE LISTS. irreg. $1. U.S. Industry and Trade Administration, Bureau of International Commerce, DIB, Main Commerce Bldg., Washington, DC 20230.

382   US   ISSN 0565-0933
U. S. BUREAU OF THE CENSUS. GUIDE TO FOREIGN TRADE STATISTICS. irreg. $4.05. U.S. Bureau of the Census, Foreign Trade Division, Washington, DC 20233 (Orders to: Supt. of Documents, Washington, DC 20402) (also avail. in microform)

353.1 382   US   ISSN 0083-002X
U. S. DEPARTMENT OF STATE. COMMERCIAL POLICY SERIES. (Subseries of its Departmental Series) 1934. irreg. price varies. U.S. Department of State, Bureau of Public Affairs, Washington, DC 20250 (Orders to Supt. of Documents, Washington, DC 20402)

382   US   ISSN 0091-2492
U.S. EXECUTIVE OFFICE OF THE PRESIDENT. INTERNATIONAL ECONOMIC REPORT OF THE PRESIDENT. (Vols. for 1973- include the Annual Report of the Council in International Economic Policy) 1973. a. U.S. Executive Office of the President, Executive Office Building, Washington, DC 20500 (For sale by the Supt. of Docs., G.P.O., Washington, D.C. 20402) stat. Key Title: International Economic Report of the President.

U. S. FOREIGN AGRICULTURAL SERVICE. FOOD AND AGRICULTURAL EXPORT DIRECTORY. see AGRICULTURE — Agricultural Economics

382   US   ISSN 0565-1190
U. S. IMPORTS FOR CONSUMPTION AND GENERAL IMPORTS; TARIFF SCHEDULES ANNOTATED BY COUNTRY. 1965. a. U. S. Bureau of the Census, Dept. of Commerce, Washington, DC 20233 (Orders to: Supt. Doc., Washington, DC 20402)

382   US
U.S. INTERNATIONAL TRADE COMMISSION. ANNUAL REPORT. 1917. a. U.S. International Trade Commission, 701 E St., N.W., Washington, DC 20436. circ. 3,000.
    Formerly: U.S. Tariff Commission. Annual Report (ISSN 0083-3428)

382   US   ISSN 0083-3436
U.S. INTERNATIONAL TRADE COMMISSION. IMPORTS OF BENZENOID CHEMICALS AND PRODUCTS. 1945. a. U.S. International Trade Commission, 701 E St., N.W., Washington, DC 20436.

350.827   US   ISSN 0083-3444
U.S. INTERNATIONAL TRADE COMMISSION. OPERATION OF THE TRADE AGREEMENTS PROGRAM. 1934/48. a. U.S. International Trade Commission, 701 E St. N.W., Washington, DC 20436.

382   US   ISSN 0083-1263
UNITED STATES IMPORT DUTIES ANNOTATED. irreg. $4. U. S. Bureau of the Census, Dept. of Commerce, Washington, DC 20233 (Orders to: Supt. of Documents, Washington, DC 20402)

382   PL
UNIWERSYTET GDANSKI. WYDZIAL EKONOMIKI TRANSPORTU. ZESZYTY NAUKOWE. INSTYTUT HANDLU ZAGRANICZNEGO. PRACE I MATERIALY. (Text in Polish; summaries in English and Russian) 1971. irreg. price varies. Uniwersytet Gdanski, Ul. Czerwonej Armii 110, 81-824 Sopot, Poland. circ. 300.

382   UY
URUGUAY. DIRECCION GENERAL DE COMERCIO EXTERIOR. ESTADISTICAS DE COMERCIO EXTERIOR. 1977. a. Direccion General de Comercio Exterior, Montevideo, Uruguay. circ. 1,000.

382 387   US   ISSN 0083-6532
VIRGINIA PORT AUTHORITY. BOARD OF COMMISSIONERS. ANNUAL REPORT. 1953. a. free. Port Authority, 1600 Maritime Tower, Norfolk, VA 23510. charts. stat. cum.index 1953.

382 387   US   ISSN 0083-6516
VIRGINIA PORT AUTHORITY. FOREIGN TRADE ANNUAL REPORT: THE PORTS OF VIRGINIA. 1970. a. free. Port Authority, 1600 Maritime Tower, Norfolk, VA 23510. charts. stat. cum.index 1969.

382   GW   ISSN 0042-966X
W G A GESCHAEFTSBERICHT. 1947. a. free. Wirtschaftsvereinigung Gross- und Aussenhandel, Gotenstr. 21, 2000 Hamburg 1, W. Germany (B.R.D.) adv. bk. rev. illus. circ. 2,000.

380.1   IS   ISSN 0302-5489
WE REPRESENT IN ISRAEL AND ABROAD. (Text in English) irreg. Tanne Advertising Ltd., 19 Gruzenberg St., P.O.B. 29322, Tel Aviv, Israel.

382   UK   ISSN 0142-646X
WEST EUROPEAN LIVING COSTS. 1972. a. £18. Confederation of British Industry, 103 New Oxford St., London WC1A 1DU, England.

382   JA
WHITE PAPER ON INTERNATIONAL TRADE: JAPAN. (Abridged version of the same title published by the Ministry of International Trade and Industry) (Text in English) a. $30. Japan External Trade Organization, 2 Akasaka Aoicho, Tokyo 107, Japan. circ. 5,000.

382   II   ISSN 0084-1501
WORLD COMMERCE ANNUAL. (Text in English) 1967. a. £9. Business Publications International, United India Life Building, Box 548, F-Block, Connaught Place, New Delhi 1, India. Ed. K. L. Saghal. adv. circ. 10,000. (back issues avail.)

382   US   ISSN 0512-3739
WORLD TRADE ANNUAL. 1963. a. price varies. (United Nations Statistical Office, UN) Walker & Co., 720 Fifth Ave., New York, NY 10019.

382   US   ISSN 0512-3747
WORLD TRADE ANNUAL SUPPLEMENT. 1964. a. $75.90 per vol. (United Nations Statistical Office, UN) Walker & Co., 720 Fifth Ave., New York, NY 10019.

382 387   IS   ISSN 0084-3830
YEARBOOK OF ISRAEL PORTS STATISTICS/ SHENATON STATISTI: LE NEMLEI ISRAEL. (Absorbed its English edition Yearbook of Israel Ports Statistics with no. 3, 1965-66) (Text in English and Hebrew) 1963-64. a. Israel Ports Authority, P.O. Box 20121, Tel-Aviv, Israel.

382   YU   ISSN 0084-4349
YUGOSLAV EXPORT-IMPORT DIRECTORY. (Not issued in 1977) (Text in English and German) 1956. irreg. $5. (Privredna Komora) Yugoslaviapublic, Knez Mihailova 10, Box 447, 11001 Belgrade, Yugoslavia. adv. circ. 5,000.

BUSINESS AND ECONOMICS — International Development And Assistance

A P O ANNUAL REPORT. (Asian Productivity Organization) see *BUSINESS AND ECONOMICS — Production Of Goods And Services*

338.9   IV   ISSN 0568-1308
AFRICAN DEVELOPMENT BANK. REPORT BY THE BOARD OF DIRECTORS/BANQUE AFRICAINE DE DEVELOPPEMENT. RAPPORT DU CONSEIL D'ADMINISTRATION. Cover title: African Development Bank. Annual Report. French cover title: Banque Africaine de Developpement. Rapport Annuel. 1966. a. African Development Bank, B.P. No. 1387, Abidjan 01, Ivory Coast.

338.91   IV
AFRICAN DEVELOPMENT FUND. ANNUAL REPORT/FONDS AFRICAIN DE DEVELOPPEMENT. RAPPORT ANNUEL. 1974. a. free. African Development Fund, B.P. 1387, Abidjan, Ivory Coast. circ. 5,000.

338.9   SG
AFRICAN DEVELOPMENT RESEARCH ANNUAL/ANNUAIRE DES RECHERCHES AFRICAINES SUR LES PROBLEMES DE DEVELOPPEMENT. (Text in English & French) 1973. a. $20. Council for the Development of Economic and Social Research in Africa, B.P. 3304, Dakar, Senegal. Ed. M. Bujra. bibl.

338.9   SG
AFRICAN INSTITUTE FOR ECONOMIC DEVELOPMENT AND PLANNING. PROGRAMME.* (Text in English and French) 1972. a. Nouvelles Editions Africaines, Dakar, Senegal.

330.9   SG
AFRICAN INSTITUTE FOR ECONOMIC DEVELOPMENT AND PLANNING. SERIES IN ECONOMIC AND SOCIAL DEVELOPMENT/ INSTITUT AFRICAIN DE DEVELOPPEMENT ECONOMIQUE ET DE PLANIFICATION. COLLECTION D'ETUDES SUR LE DEVELOPPEMENT ECONOMIQUE ET SOCIAL. irreg. 500 Fr. Nouvelles Editions Africaines, Dakar, Senegal. illus.

338.9   FR
ANNUAIRE DU TIERS MONDE. a. $40.95. Imprimerie et Librairie Berger-Levrault, 5 rue Auguste-Compte, Paris 6e, France.

338.91   NZ
ANNUAL AID REVIEW, MEMORANDUM OF NEW ZEALAND. Cover title: Review of the New Zealand Aid Programme. 1974. a. Ministry of Foreign Affairs, Wellington, New Zealand.

ARAB BANK FOR ECONOMIC DEVELOPMENT IN AFRICA. ANNUAL REPORT. see *BUSINESS AND ECONOMICS — Banking And Finance*

338.9   KU   ISSN 0304-6729
ARAB FUND FOR ECONOMIC AND SOCIAL DEVELOPMENT. ANNUAL REPORT. (Text in Arabic and English) 1973. a. free. Arab Fund for Economic and Social Development, P.O. Box 21923, Kuwait. illus.

ASIAN DEVELOPMENT BANK. ANNUAL REPORT. see *BUSINESS AND ECONOMICS — Banking And Finance*

332.1   PH   ISSN 0066-8389
ASIAN DEVELOPMENT BANK. BOARD OF GOVERNORS. SUMMARY OF PROCEEDINGS (OF THE) ANNUAL MEETING. 1968. a. non-priced. ‡ Asian Development Bank, P.O. Box 789, Manila 2800, Philippines. circ. 1,000.

ASIAN DEVELOPMENT BANK. OCCASIONAL PAPERS. see *BUSINESS AND ECONOMICS — Banking And Finance*

ASIAN PRODUCTIVITY ORGANIZATION. REVIEW OF ACTIVITIES OF NATIONAL PRODUCTIVITY. see *BUSINESS AND ECONOMICS — Production Of Goods And Services*

338.91   AT
AUSTRALIA. DEPARTMENT OF FOREIGN AFFAIRS. DEVELOPMENT ASSISTANCE BUREAU. ANNUAL REVIEW. a. Department of Foreign Affairs, Development Assistance Bureau, Canberra, A.C.T. 2600, Australia.

BOCHUMER MATERIALEN ZUR ENTWICKLUNGSFORSCHUNG UND ENTWICKLUNGSPOLITIK. see *POLITICAL SCIENCE — International Relations*

BOCHUMER SCHRIFTEN ZUR ENTWICKLUNGSFORSCHUNG UND ENTWICKLUNGSPOLITIK. see *POLITICAL SCIENCE — International Relations*

338.9   US   ISSN 0069-682X
C E D NEWSLETTER. 1966. s-a. free. Committee for Economic Development, 477 Madison Ave., New York, NY 10022. (reprint service avail. from UMI)

338.9   CN
C I D A ANNUAL REVIEW. (Text in English and French) 1969. a. Canadian International Development Agency, Information Division, 200 rue Principale, Hull, Que. K1A OG4, Ottawa, Ontario K1A OG4, Canada. Ed. Charles Morrow. charts. illus. stat. circ. controlled.

338.9   UK
C M E A STATISTICAL YEARBOOK. 1977. a. $55. (Council for Mutual Economic Assistance) I P C Business Press, Ltd., 40 Bowling Green Lane, London EC1R ONE, England.

338.9   CN
CANADIAN INTERNATIONAL DEVELOPMENT AGENCY. THOUGHTS ON INTERNATIONAL DEVELOPMENT/CANADA. AGENCE CANADIENNE DE DEVELOPPEMENT INTERNATIONAL. REFLEXIONS SUR LE DEVELOPPEMENT INTERNATIONAL. (Text in French and English) 1971. irreg (2/yr) Canadian International Development Agency, Information Division, 200 rue Principale, Hull, Que. K1A OG4, Ottawa, Ontario K1A OG4, Canada. Ed. Paul Gerin-Lajoie. circ. controlled.

332.1 016   UN
CATALOG OF WORLD BANK PUBLICATIONS. Variant title: World Bank Catalog of Publications. 1973. a. free. World Bank, 1818 H St., N.W., Washington, DC 20433. index.
    Issued 1973-1974 as: World Bank Catalog. Accession List.

338   CE   ISSN 0069-5947
COLOMBO PLAN BUREAU. TECHNICAL COOPERATION UNDER THE COLOMBO PLAN. REPORT. (Supersedes same title issued by the Council for Technical Co-Operation in South and South-East Asia) (Text in English) 1952. a. free. Colombo Plan Bureau, 12 Melbourne Ave., Box 596, Colombo 4, Sri Lanka. circ. 1,600.

338.9   CE
COLOMBO PLAN FOR CO-OPERATIVE ECONOMIC AND SOCIAL DEVELOPMENT IN ASIA AND THE PACIFIC. CONSULTATIVE COMMITTEE. REPORT. (Text in English) 1952. irreg. free. Colombo Plan Bureau, 112 Melbourne Ave., Box 596, Colombo 4, Sri Lanka. index; cum.index, 1952-1972. circ. 1,600.
    Formerly: Colombo Plan for Co-Operative Economic Development in South and South-East Asia; Report of the Consultative Committee. (ISSN 0069-5963)

330   EI   ISSN 0069-6692
COMMISSION OF THE EUROPEAN COMMUNITIES. ETUDES: SERIE AIDE AU DEVELOPPEMENT. (Editions also in German Italian and Dutch) 1967. irreg.; 1969, no. 3. price varies. Office for Official Publications of the European Communities, C.P. 1003, Luxembourg, Luxembourg (Dist. in U.S. by: European Community Information Service, 2100 M St., NW, Suite 707, Washington, DC 20037)

338.9   GT   ISSN 0553-6863
CONVENIOS CENTROAMERICANOS DE INTEGRATION ECONOMICA. (Text in English and Spanish) 1963. irreg., latest, vol. 11. $2.13. General Treaty on Central American Economic Integration, Permanent Secretariat, 4-a Avenida 10-25, Zone 14, Guatemala City, Guatemala.

338.91   DK
DENMARKS DELTAGELSE I DET INTERNATIONALE UDVIKLINGSSAMARBEJDE. a. Danida - Danish International Development Agency, Amaliegade 7, DK-1256 Copenhagen K, Denmark.

338.91   DK
DENMARK'S DEVELOPMENT ASSISTANCE. ANNUAL REPORT. 1974. a. free. Danida - Danish International Development Agency, Amaliegade 7, DK-1256 Copenhagen K, Denmark. illus. stat.

338.9   SG
ECONOMIE AFRICAINE. a. 9000 Fr.CFA. Societe Africaine d'Edition, 16 bis, rue de Thiong, Dakar, Senegal (And 32 rue de l'Echiquier, Paris, France)

338.9   FR   ISSN 0068-4813
ECONOMIES ET SOCIETES. SERIE F. DEVELOPPEMENT, CROISSANCE, PROGRES DES PAYS EN VOIE DE DEVELOPPEMENT. 1955. irreg. 42 F. Institut de Sciences Mathematiques et Economiques Appliquees, Paris, Institut Henri Poincare, 11 rue Henri et Marie Curie, 75005 Paris, France. Ed. Pierre Pascallon. circ. 1,600.

338.9   EI
EUROPEAN COAL AND STEEL COMMUNITY. CONSULTATIVE COMMITTEE. HANDBOOK. French edt: Communaute Europeene du Charbon et de l'Acier. Commission des Communautes Europeennes. Comite Consultatif. Manuel. 1953. a.; 16th edt., 1971. free. European Coal and Steel Community, Consultative Committee, Secretariat, B.-P. 1907, Luxembourg, Luxembourg. circ. controlled.

338.9   EI   ISSN 0423-6831
EUROPEAN COAL AND STEEL COMMUNITY. CONSULTATIVE COMMITTEE. YEARBOOK. French edt.: Communaute Europeene du Charbon et de l'Acier. Comite Consultatif. Annuaire. German edt.: Europaeische Gemeinschaft fuer Kohle und Stahl. Beratender Ausschuss. Jahrbuch. 1954. a. free. European Coal and Steel Community, Consultative Committee, Secretariat, B.P. 1907, Luxembourg, Luxembourg. circ. controlled.

338.9   BE   ISSN 0071-2884
EUROPEAN LEAGUE FOR ECONOMIC COOPERATION. PUBLICATIONS. (Text in English or French) 1949. irreg. free. ‡ European League for Economic Cooperation, Ave. de la Toison d'Or 1-Bte. 11, 1060 Brussels, Belgium.

336   BE   ISSN 0531-7436
EUROPEAN LEAGUE FOR ECONOMIC COOPERATION. REPORT OF THE SECRETARY GENERAL ON THE ACTIVITIES OF E. L. E. C. a. free. European League for Economic Cooperation, Ave. de la Toison d'Or 1-Bte. 11, 1060 Brussels, Belgium.

338.9   BE   ISSN 0071-2892
EUROPEAN LEAGUE FOR ECONOMIC COOPERATION. REPORTS OF THE INTERNATIONAL CONGRESS. (Issued in the League's Publications) irreg., 1969, 6th, Brussels. free. European League for Economic Cooperation, Ave. de la Toison, B-1060 Brussels, Belgium.

338.91   IT
FINAFRICA BULLETIN. no. 4, 1976. irreg. Cassa di Risparmio delle Provincie Lombarde, Via San Vigilio 10, I-20142 Milan, Italy. Ed. Arnaldo Mauri. bk. rev.

BUSINESS AND ECONOMICS — INTERNATIONAL DEVELOPMENT AND ASSISTANCE

338.9 FR
FRANCE. SECRETARIAT D'ETAT AUX AFFAIRES ETRANGERES CHARGE DE LA COOPERATION. DIRECTION DE L'AIDE AU DEVELOPPEMENT. MALI. DOSSIER D'INFORMATION ECONOMIQUE. 1971. irreg. free. Secretariat d'Etat aux Affaires Etrangeres Charge de la Cooperation, Direction de l'Aide au Developpement, 37 Quai d'Orsay, 75700 - Paris, France. circ. 500. (processed)

338.9 FR
FRANCE. SECRETARIAT D'ETAT AUX AFFAIRES ETRANGERES CHARGE DE LA COOPERATION. DIRECTION DE L'AIDE AU DEVELOPPEMENT. NIGER. DOSSIER D'INFORMATION ECONOMIQUE. 1970. irreg. free. Secretariat d'Etat aux Affaires Etrangeres Charge de la Cooperation, Direction de l'Aide au Developpement, 37 Quai d'Orsay, 75700 - Paris, France. abstr. charts. stat. circ. 500. (processed)

338.9 FR
FRANCE. SECRETARIAT D'ETAT AUX AFFAIRES ETRANGERES CHARGE DE LA COOPERATION. DIRECTION DE L'AIDE AU DEVELOPPEMENT. COTE D'IVOIRE. DOSSIER D'INFORMATION ECONOMIQUE. 1969. irreg. free. Secretariat d'Etat aux Affaires Etrangeres Charge de la Cooperation, Direction de l'Aide au Developpement, 37 Quai d'Orsay, 757000 - Paris, France. circ. 500. (processed)

FREEDOM FROM HUNGER CAMPAIGN. F F H C REPORT. see *AGRICULTURE — Agricultural Economics*

338.9 GT ISSN 0553-6898
GENERAL TREATY FOR CENTRAL AMERICAN ECONOMIC INTEGRATION. PERMANENT SECRETARIAT. NEWSLETTER. 1963. irreg. General Treaty on Central American Economic Integration, Permanent Secretariat, 4-a Avenida 10-25, Zone 14, Guatemala City, Guatemala.

338.9 FR ISSN 0474-5434
GEOGRAPHICAL DISTRIBUTION OF FINANCIAL FLOWS TO LESS DEVELOPED COUNTRIES. (DISBURSEMENTS) 1956. irreg. $17.50. Organization for Economic Cooperation and Development, 2 rue Andre Pascal, 75775 Paris 16, France (U. S. orders to: O.E.C.D. Publications and Information Center, 1750 Pennsylvania Ave., N. W., Washington, D. C. 20006) (also avail. in microfiche)
   Supersedes: Organization for Economic Cooperation and Development. Flow of Financial Resources to Less Developed Countries.

338.91 US ISSN 0161-6684
HUMAN RIGHTS AND THE U.S. FOREIGN ASSISTANCE PROGRAM. 1978. a. Center for International Policy, 120 Maryland Ave., Washington, DC 20002.

338 UK ISSN 0141-1314
I D S RESEARCH REPORT. 1978. irreg. University of Sussex, Institute of Development Studies, Brighton, Sussex BN1 9RE, England.

338.9 UN ISSN 0073-7577
INDUSTRIAL PLANNING AND PROGRAMMING SERIES. 1968. irreg., vol. 4, 1974. $1. United Nations Industrial Development Organization, Lerchenfelderstrasse 1, Box 707, A-1011 Vienna, Austria (Orders from Europe, Africa and Middle East to: Distribution and Sales Section, Palais des Nations, 1211 Geneva 10 Switzerland. Orders from Asia, the Pacific and North and South America to: United Nations Publications, Room LX-2300, New York, NY 10017)

330 FR
INFORMATION, COMPUTER AND COMMUNICATIONS POLICY. (Editions in English and French) 1971. irreg., no. 12, 1978. $20. Organization for Economic Cooperation and Development, Working Party on Information, Computers and Communications Policy, 2 rue Andre-Pascal, 75775 Paris 16, France (U. S. orders to: O.E.C.D. Publications and Information Center, 1750 Pennsylvania Ave., N. W., Washington, D. C. 20006) (also avail. in microfiche)
   Supersedes (since 1979): O E C D Informatics Studies Series.

330 FR ISSN 0073-8247
INSTITUT D'EMISSION D'OUTRE MER, PARIS. RAPPORT D'ACTIVITE. 1967. a. free. ‡ Institut d'Emission d'Outre Mer, Paris., 233 Boulevard St.-Germain, Paris 7e, France.

338.9 FR
INSTITUT D'ETUDES DU DEVELOPPEMENT. CAHIERS. 1975. irreg. price varies. (Institut d'Etudes du Developpement, SZ) Presses Universitaires de France, 108 Bd. Saint Germaine, 75279 Paris Cedex 6, France (Service des Periodiques, 12 rue Jean de Beauvais, 75005 Paris)

INSTITUT FUER IBEROAMERIKA-KUNDE. SCHRIFTENREIHE. see *POLITICAL SCIENCE — International Relations*

INSTITUT PANAFRICAIN POUR LE DEVELOPPEMENT. TRAVAUX MANUSCRITS. see *AGRICULTURE — Agricultural Economics*

338.91 658 CM
INSTITUT PANAFRICAIN POUR LE DEVELOPPEMENT. CENTRE D'ETUDES ET DE RECHERCHES APPLIQUEES. EVALUATION DU SEMINAIRE SUR LA METHODOLOGIE DU MANAGEMENT DES PROJETS. a? Pan-African Institute for Development, Center of Applied Research, Box 4056, Douala, Cameroon.

338.91 658 CM
INSTITUT PANAFRICAIN POUR LE DEVELOPPEMENT. CENTRE DE FORMATION AU MANAGEMENT DES PROJETS. BILAN DES ACTIVITIES. Pan-African Institute for Development, Training Centre for Project Management, Box 556, Douala, Cameroon.

330.06 JA
INSTITUTE OF DEVELOPING ECONOMIES. ANNUAL REPORT. (Text in English) a. Institute of Developing Economies, 42 Ichigaya-Hommura-cho, Shinjuku-ku, Tokyo 162, Japan.

INSTITUTE OF DEVELOPMENT STUDIES. ANNUAL REPORT. see *BUSINESS AND ECONOMICS — Production Of Goods And Services*

380 338 UY ISSN 0538-3048
INTER-AMERICAN COUNCIL OF COMMERCE AND PRODUCTION. URUGUAYAN SECTION. PUBLICACIONES. 1951. irreg. Inter-American Council of Commerce and Production, Misiones 1400, Montevideo, Uruguay.

INTER-AMERICAN DEVELOPMENT BANK. ANNUAL REPORT. see *BUSINESS AND ECONOMICS — Banking And Finance*

INTER-AMERICAN DEVELOPMENT BANK. BOARD OF GOVERNORS. PROCEEDINGS OF THE MEETING. see *BUSINESS AND ECONOMICS — Banking And Finance*

338.9 AG ISSN 0538-3110
INTER-AMERICAN DEVELOPMENT BANK. INSTITUTE FOR LATIN AMERICAN INTEGRATION. ANNUAL REPORT. (English Edition) 1965. a. $20. Banco Interamericano de Desarrollo, Instituto para la Integracion de America Latina, Cerrito 264, Buenos Aires. circ. controlled.

338.9 UN ISSN 0085-2392
JOURNAL OF DEVELOPMENT PLANNING. (Editions in English, French, Spanish) 1969. irreg. price varies. United Nations Publications, LX 2300, New York, NY 10017 (Or Distribution and Sales Section, Palais des Nations, CH-1211 Geneva 10, Switzerland)

338.9 PK ISSN 0544-8433
MONOGRAPHS IN THE ECONOMICS OF DEVELOPMENT. 1972, no. 17. irreg. price varies. Pakistan Institute of Development Economics, Box 1091, Islamabad, Pakistan. Ed. Bd. circ. 1,500.

338.91 US ISSN 0077-6319
NEAR EAST FOUNDATION. ANNUAL REPORT. 1935. a., publication suspended between 1950 and 1960. free. ‡ Near East Foundation, 29 Broadway, Suite 1125, New York, NY 10006. Ed. John M. Sutton. circ. 20,000.

338.91 NE
NETHERLANDS. MINISTERIE VAN BUITENLANDSE ZAKEN. VOORLICHTINGSDIENST ONTWIKKELINGSSAMENWERKING/ IMPLEMENTATION AND VINDICATION OF POLICY. (Text in English) 2/yr. Ministerie van Buitenlandse Zaken, Voorlichtingsdienst Ontwikkelingssamenwerking - Ministry of Foreign Affairs. Information Service for Development Cooperation, Herengracht 3a, The Hague, Netherlands. illus.

NETHERLANDS INVESTMENT BANK FOR DEVELOPING COUNTRIES. ANNUAL REPORT. see *BUSINESS AND ECONOMICS — Banking And Finance*

338.9 NO
NORGES SAMARBEID MED UTVIKLINGSLANDENE. a. Direktoratet for Utviklingshjelp - Norwegian Agency for International Development, Box 8142, Oslo 1, Norway. illus.

338.9 AU ISSN 0078-3536
OESTERREICHISCHE SCHRIFTEN ZUR ENTWICKLUNGSHILFE. 1963. irreg. price varies. Verlag Ferdinand Berger und Soehne OHG, Wienerstr. 21-23, A-3580 Horn, Austria. Ed. Leopold Scheidl.

ORGANIZATION FOR ECONOMIC COOPERATION AND DEVELOPMENT. COUNCIL. CODE DE LA LIBERATION DES MOUVEMENTS DE CAPITAUX. CODE OF LIBERALISATION OF CAPITAL MOVEMENTS. see *BUSINESS AND ECONOMICS — Banking And Finance*

330 FR
ORGANIZATION FOR ECONOMIC COOPERATION AND DEVELOPMENT. ACTIVITIES OF O E C D: REPORT BY THE SECRETARY GENERAL. 1971. a. $9. Organization for Economic Cooperation and Development, 2 rue Andre-Pascal, 75775 Paris 16, France (U.S. orders to: O.E.C.D Publication and Information Center 1750 Pennsylvania Ave., N.W., Washington, D.C. 20006) (also avail. in microfiche)

338.9 FR ISSN 0474-5663
ORGANIZATION FOR ECONOMIC COOPERATION AND DEVELOPMENT. DEVELOPMENT ASSISTANCE COMMITTEE. REPORT BY THE CHAIRMAN ON THE ANNUAL REVIEW. 1961. a. $19. Organization for Economic Cooperation and Development, 2 rue Andre Pascal, 75775 Paris 16, France (U.S. orders to: O.E.C.D. Publications and Information Center, 1750 Pennsylvania Ave., N. W., Washington, D. C. 20006) (also avail. in microfiche)

338.9 FR
ORGANIZATION FOR ECONOMIC COOPERATION AND DEVELOPMENT. DEVELOPMENT COOPERATION; efforts and policies of the members of the Development Assistance Committee. (Editions in English and French) a. Organization for Economic Cooperation and Development, 2 rue Andre - Pascal, 75775 Paris Cedex 16, France (U.S. orders to: O.E.C.D. Publications and Information Center, 1750 Pennsylvania Ave., N.W., Washington, DC 20006) (also avail. in microfiche)

338.9 FR
ORGANIZATION FOR ECONOMIC COOPERATION AND DEVELOPMENT. LIAISON BULLETIN BETWEEN DEVELOPMENT RESEARCH AND TRAINING INSTITUTES. q. $6.50. Organization for Economic Cooperation and Development, Development Centre, 2 rue Andre Pascal, 75775 Paris Cedex 16, France (U. S. orders to: O.E.C.D. Publications and Informatin Center, 1750 Pennsylvania Ave., N. W., Washington, D. C. 20006) (also avail. in microfiche)

338.91 US ISSN 0092-7643
OVERSEAS DEVELOPMENT COUNCIL. ANNUAL REPORT. 1971. a. free. Overseas Development Council, 1717 Massachusetts Ave., N.W., Suite 501, Washington, DC 20036. Ed. Valeriana Kallab. illus. Key Title: Annual Report - Overseas Development Council.

338.91 US
OVERSEAS DEVELOPMENT COUNCIL. COMMUNIQUE. 1971. irreg. $0.25 per no. Overseas Development Council, 1717 Massachusetts Ave. N.W., Washington, DC 20036. Ed. Rosemarie Philips.

338.9 US
OVERSEAS DEVELOPMENT COUNCIL. DEVELOPMENT PAPERS. 1970. irreg., no. 30, 1981. price varies. Overseas Development Council, 1717 Massachusetts Ave. N.W., Washington, DC 20036. Ed. Valeriana Kallab. charts. illus.

338.9 US ISSN 0078-7108
OVERSEAS DEVELOPMENT COUNCIL. MONOGRAPH SERIES. 1970. irreg., no. 14, 1980. price varies. Overseas Development Council, 1717 Massachusetts Ave. N.W., Washington, DC 20036. Ed. Valeriana Kallab.

338.91 US
OVERSEAS DEVELOPMENT COUNCIL. OCCASIONAL PAPERS. 1971. irreg., no. 11, 1978. price varies. Overseas Development Council, 1717 Massachusetts Ave. N.W., Washington, DC 20036. Ed. Valeriana Kallab.

338.9 JA
OVERSEAS ECONOMIC COOPERATION FUND. ANNUAL REPORT/KAGAI KEIZAI KYORYOKU KIKIN NENPO. (Text in English) 1972. a. Overseas Economic Cooperation Fund - Kagai Keizai Kyoryoku Kikin, Takebashi Godo Bldg, 4-1, Ohtemachi 1-chome, Chiyoda-ku, Tokyo 100, Japan.

PAKISTAN INSTITUTE OF DEVELOPMENT ECONOMICS. REPORT. see *BUSINESS AND ECONOMICS*

PAKISTAN INSTITUTE OF DEVELOPMENT ECONOMICS. RESEARCH REPORT. see *BUSINESS AND ECONOMICS*

980 US ISSN 0552-9913
PAN AMERICAN DEVELOPMENT FOUNDATION. ANNUAL REPORT. 1964. a. free. Pan-American Development Foundation, 1625 I St. N.W., Room 622, Washington, DC 20006. circ. 2,500.

630 338.91 UK ISSN 0143-8484
PLUNKETT DEVELOPMENT SERIES. 1980. irreg. price varies. Plunkett Foundation for Co-Operative Studies, 31 St. Giles St., Oxford OX1 3LF, England.

338.9 US
PROBLEMS AND PROGRESS IN DEVELOPMENT. 1968. irreg. price varies. Pergamon Press, Inc., Maxwell House, Fairview Park, Elmsford, NY 10523.

PROFILES OF THE NATIONAL PRODUCTIVITY ORGANIZATIONS IN A P O MEMBER COUNTRIES. (Asian Productivity Organization) see *BUSINESS AND ECONOMICS — Production Of Goods And Services*

338.9 AU
R G W IN ZAHLEN/C M E A DATA. (Council for Mutual Economic Assistance); Statistisches taschenbuch. (Text in German; with English key and index) 1968. a. 428. Wiener Institut fuer die Internationale Wirtschaftsvergleiche, Postfach 87, A-1103 Vienna, Austria.

338.9 PK ISSN 0557-8280
READINGS IN DEVELOPMENT ECONOMICS. 1970. irreg. price varies. Pakistan Institute of Development Economics, Box 1091, Islamabad, Pakistan. bibl. charts. stat. circ. 1,000.

338 HO
REVISTA DE LA INTEGRACION Y EL DESARROLLO DE CENTROAMERICA. 1976. irreg. Banco Centroamericano de Integracion Economica, Apartado Postal 772, Teguciagalpa, Honduras.
Formerly: Revista de la Integracion Centroamericana.

338.91 320 960 US
SAGE SERIES ON AFRICAN MODERNIZATION AND DEVELOPMENT. (Not published in 1977) 1976. a. $18.50 for hardcover; $8.95 for softcover. Sage Publications, Inc., 275 S. Beverly Dr., Beverly Hills, CA 90212 (And Sage Publications, Ltd., 28 Banner St., London EC1Y 8QE, England) Ed. Peter C. W. Gutkind. (back issues avail.)

327 338.9 IT ISSN 0081-1416
SOCIETY FOR INTERNATIONAL DEVELOPMENT. WORLD CONFERENCE PROCEEDINGS. 1964, 6th, first published proceedings. irreg., (approx. biennial) Society for International Development, Palazzo Civilta del Lavoro, 00144 Rome, Italy.

338.9 MY
SOUTHEAST ASIA DEVELOPMENT CORPORATION BERHAD. REPORTS AND ACCOUNTS. a. Southeast Asia Development Corporation Berhad, G.P.O. Box 2171, Kuala Lumpur 01-20, Malaysia. charts. stat.

338.9 US
STUDIES IN DEVELOPMENT AND PLANNING. (Text in English) 1973. irreg., vol. 7, 1977. price varies. (Nederlandse Economische Hogeschool - Netherlands School of Economics) Martinus Nijhoff, Social Sciences Division, 160 Old Derby St., Hingham, MA 02043.

STUDIES IN INTERNATIONAL ECONOMIC RELATIONS. see *BUSINESS AND ECONOMICS*

338.9 UN ISSN 0085-6908
STUDIES ON SELECTED DEVELOPMENT PROBLEMS IN VARIOUS COUNTRIES IN THE MIDDLE EAST. 1967. a.; latest 1973. price varies. United Nations Economic Commission for Western Asia, United Nations Building, Box 4656, Bir Hassan, Beirut, Lebanon (Dist. by: Distribution and Sales Section, Palais des Nations, CH-1211 Geneva 10, Switzerland)

338.9 US
T A I C H COUNTRY REPORTS: DEVELOPMENT ASSISTANCE PROGRAMS OF U.S. NON-PROFIT ORGANZATIONS ABROAD. 1973. irreg. free to qualified personnel. ‡ (American Council of Voluntary Agencies for Foreign Service, Inc) Technical Assistance Information Clearing House, 200 Park Ave. S., New York, NY 10003. index. circ. 1,500.

338.9 US
T A I C H COUNTRY REPORTS: DEVELOPMENT ASSISTANCE PROGRAMS OF U.S. NON-PROFIT ORGANIZATIONS ABROAD. 1973. irreg. (American Council of Voluntary Agencies for Foreign Service, Inc.) Technical Assistance Information Clearing House, 200 Park Ave. S., New York, NY 10003. index. circ. 800.

338.9 CN
THOUGHTS ON INTERNATIONAL DEVELOPMENT. (Text in English and French) irreg., no. 11, 1976. Canadian International Development Agency, Information Division, Communications Branch, 200 rue Principale, Hull, Que. K1A OG4, Canada.

338.9 FR
TIERS-MONDE EN MARCHE. 1976. irreg. 160 F. Imprimerie et Librairie Berger-Levrault, 5, rue Auguste-Compte, Paris 6e, France. Ed. Pierre-Francois Gonidec, Edmond Jouve. bibl. illus.

338 PH
TRENDS IN DEVELOPING ASIA. 1970. a. unpriced. Asian Development Bank, Economic Office, P.O. Box 789, Manila 2800, Philippines. Ed. Burton T. Onate.

338.91 US
U S AND WORLD DEVELOPMENT: AGENDA. 1973. a. $6.95 paperback; $23.95 hardcover. Overseas Development Council, 1717 Massachusetts Ave. N.W., Washington, DC 20036. Ed. Valeriana Kallab.
Formerly: U S and the Developing World: Agenda for Action.

338.9 UN ISSN 0082-8475
UNITED NATIONS. TRADE AND DEVELOPMENT BOARD. OFFICIAL RECORDS. (Supplements avail.) irreg., 11th session, 1971. price varies. United Nations Trade and Development Board, Palais des Nations, 1211 Geneva 10, Switzerland (Or United Nations Publications, Room LX-2300, New York, NY 10017)

338.9 UN ISSN 0082-8106
UNITED NATIONS ECONOMIC AND SOCIAL COMMISSION FOR ASIA AND THE PACIFIC. DEVELOPMENT PROGRAMMING TECHNIQUES SERIES. 1961. irreg; no. 9, vol. 3, 1973. price varies. United Nations Economic and Social Commission for Asia and the Pacific, United Nations Bldg., Rajadamnern Ave., Bangkok 2, Thailand, NY 10017 (Dist. by: United Nations Publications, Room LX-2300, New York, NY 10017; or Distribution and Sales Section, Palais des Nations, CH-1211 Geneva 10, Switzerland)

338.9 UN ISSN 0082-8122
UNITED NATIONS ECONOMIC AND SOCIAL COMMISSION FOR ASIA AND THE PACIFIC. REGIONAL ECONOMIC COOPERATION SERIES. 1965. irreg; no. 9, 1974. price varies. United Nations Economic and Social Commission for Asia and the Pacific, The United Nations Building, Rajamnern Ave., Bangkok 2, Thailand (Dist. by: United Nations Publications, Room LX-2300, New York, NY 10017; or Distribution and Sales Section, Palais des Nations, CH-1211 Geneva 10, Switzerland)

338.9 US ISSN 0083-0062
U. S. DEPARTMENT OF STATE. ECONOMIC COOPERATION SERIES. 1948. irreg. price varies. U.S. Department of State, Bureau of Public Affairs, Washington, DC 20250 (Orders to Supt. of Documents, Washington, DC 20402)

U.S. EXECUTIVE OFFICE OF THE PRESIDENT. INTERNATIONAL ECONOMIC REPORT OF THE PRESIDENT. see *BUSINESS AND ECONOMICS — International Commerce*

338.91 UK ISSN 0144-9486
UNIVERSITY COLLEGE OF SWANSEA. CENTRE FOR DEVELOPMENT STUDIES. MONOGRAPH SERIES. 1977. irreg(3-4/yr) price varies. Geo Books, c/o Geo Abstracts Ltd., University of East Anglia, Norwich NR4 7TJ, England.

338.91 UK ISSN 0144-9494
UNIVERSITY COLLEGE OF SWANSEA. CENTRE FOR DEVELOPMENT STUDIES. OCCASIONAL PAPERS SERIES. 1977. irreg (3-4/yr.) price varies. Geo Books, c/o Geo Abstracts Ltd., University of East Anglia, Norwich NR4 TTJ, England.

338.91 SJ
UNIVERSITY OF KHARTOUM. DEVELOPMENT STUDIES AND RESEARCH CENTRE. DISCUSSION PAPERS. irreg. University of Khartoum, Development Studies and Research Centre, Box 321, Khartoum, Sudan.

338.91 SJ
UNIVERSITY OF KHARTOUM. DEVELOPMENT STUDIES AND RESEARCH CENTRE. MONOGRAPH SERIES. irreg. University of Khartoum, Development Studies and Research Centre, Box 321, Khartoum, Sudan. Ed. Sadig Rasheed.

338.91 SJ
UNIVERSITY OF KHARTOUM. DEVELOPMENT STUDIES AND RESEARCH CENTRE. OCCASIONAL PAPERS. 1979. irreg. University of Khartoum, Development Studies and Research Centre, Box 321, Khartoum, Sudan. Ed. Sadig Rasheed.

309.2 KE
UNIVERSITY OF NAIROBI. INSTITUTE FOR DEVELOPMENT STUDIES. OCCASIONAL PAPER. 1967. irreg., no. 31, 1979. price varies. ‡ University of Nairobi, Institute for Development Studies, Box 30197, Nairobi, Kenya. bibl. illus. stat. circ. 200 (approx.)
Continues: University College, Nairobi. Institute for Development Studies. Occasional Papers (ISSN 0547-1796)

338.9 AU
WIENER INSTITUT FUER INTERNATIONALE WIRTSCHAFTSVERGLEICHE. FORSCHUNGSBERICHTE. 1972. irreg. S.450($38) Wiener Institut fuer Internationale Wirtschaftsvergleiche, Postfach 87, A-1103 Vienna, Austria. Ed. Friedrich Levcik. circ. 700.

338.9 AU
WIENER INSTITUT FUER INTERNATIONALE WIRTSCHAFTSVERGLEICHE. REPRINT SERIE. irreg., no. 16, 1972. S.450($38) ‡ Wiener Institut fuer Internationale Wirtschaftsvergleiche, Postfach 87, A-1103 Vienna, Austria. Ed. Friedrich Levcik. charts, stat. circ. 400.

338.9 UN
WORLD BANK. ANNUAL REPORT. (Text in English, French, German, Japanese, Spanish and Arabic) 1947. a. free. World Bank, 1818 H St., N.W., Washington, DC 20433. charts. stat.

338.9 UN
WORLD BANK. COMMODITY TRADE AND PRICE TRENDS. (Text in English, French and Spanish) 1968. a. free. World Bank, 1818 H St., N.W., Washington, DC 20433. Ed. Shamsher Singh.

338.9 UN
WORLD BANK. ECONOMIC DEVELOPMENT INSTITUTE. E D I SEMINAR PAPERS. 1972. irreg. price varies. ‡ World Bank, Economic Development Institute, 1818 H. St., N.W., Washington, DC 20433. bibl.

332.1 912 UN ISSN 0512-2457
WORLD BANK ATLAS. 1967. a. unpriced. ‡ World Bank, 1818 H St., N.W., Washington, DC 20433.

332.1 338.9 UN ISSN 0074-199X
WORLD BANK STAFF OCCASIONAL PAPERS. 1967. irreg.; no. 19, 1975. free. World Bank, 1818 H St., Washington, DC 20433 (Dist. by: Johns Hopkins University Press, Baltimore, Md. 21218)

BUSINESS AND ECONOMICS — Investments

AGRI-BUSINESS BUYERS REFERENCE. see *AGRICULTURE — Agricultural Economics*

332.6 350 US ISSN 0092-6736
ALASKA. DEPARTMENT OF REVENUE. STATE INVESTMENT PORTFOLIO. (Report year ends June 30) a. Department of Revenue, Box SB, Juneau, AK 99811. stat. Key Title: State Investment Portfolio. (Juneau)

ALMANAC OF BUSINESS AND INDUSTRIAL FINANCIAL RATIOS. see *BUSINESS AND ECONOMICS — Banking And Finance*

332.6 US ISSN 0569-2954
AMERICAN BANKERS ASSOCIATION. COMMITTEE ON UNIFORM SECURITY IDENTIFICATION PROCEDURES. C U S I P DIRECTORY. 1969. a. $650. Standard & Poor's Corporation, 25 Broadway, New York, NY 10004. Key Title: C.U.S.I.P. Directory.

332.6 US ISSN 0091-3804
AMERICAN BANKERS ASSOCIATION. COMMITTEE ON UNIFORM SECURITY IDENTIFICATION PROCEDURES. C U S I P DIRECTORY: CORPORATE DIRECTORY. a. $440. Standard & Poor's Corporation, 25 Broadway, New York, NY 10004. Key Title: C.U.S.I.P. Directory. Corporate Directory.

332.6 368.32 US ISSN 0459-3650
AMERICAN COUNCIL OF LIFE INSURANCE. ECONOMIC AND INVESTMENT REPORT. 1972. a. American Council of Life Insurance, 1850 K St. N.W., Washington, DC 20006. Key Title: Economic and Investment Report.
Former titles: American Life Insurance Association. Economic and Investment Report; Life Insurance Association of America. Economic and Investment Report.

AMERICAN SOCIETY OF APPRAISERS. APPRAISAL AND VALUATION MANUAL. see *REAL ESTATE*

332.6 US ISSN 0066-0760
AMERICAN STOCK EXCHANGE. AMEX DATABOOK. 1968. irreg., latest issue 1976. $1. ‡ American Stock Exchange, Inc, 86 Trinity Place, New York, NY 10006. Dir. of Pub. Vincent A. Green.

332.6 US ISSN 0066-0779
AMERICAN STOCK EXCHANGE. ANNUAL REPORT. a. American Stock Exchange Inc., 86 Trinity Place, New York, NY 10006.

332.6 US
ANALYSTS HANDBOOK. 1964. a. $335. Standard & Poor's Corporation, 25 Broadway, New York, NY 10004. Ed. Roy Anderson. stat.

332.6 US ISSN 0161-4002
ANNUAL INSTITUTE ON SECURITIES LAW AND REGULATIONS. PROCEEDINGS. 1977. a. (Institute on Securities Laws and Regulations) Matthew Bender & Co., Inc., 235 E. 45th St., New York, NY 10017.

332.6 UK
ANNUAL INVESTMENT FILE. 1979. a. $4.50. Urban Publishing Co., 17 The Green, Richman, London TW9 1PX, England. circ. 52,000.

332.6 FR ISSN 0066-9008
ASSOCIATION DES SOCIETES ET FONDS FRANCAIS D'INVESTISSEMENT. ANNUAIRE. 1963. biennial. 18,35 1st copy free. ‡ Association des Societes et Fonds Francais d'Investissement, 1 rue d'Astorg, 75008 Paris, France. abstr.stat. cum.index. circ. 20,000.

338.01 US ISSN 0067-1959
AUSTRALIAN MARKET GUIDE. biennial. not available for sale to libraries. Dun & Bradstreet, Inc., 99 Church St., New York, NY 10007 (And 24 Albert Rd., Melbourne South 3205, Australia)

332.6 SZ
BASLER EFFEKTENBOERSE. JAHRESBERICHT/ RAPPORT ANNUEL/ANNUAL REPORT. (Text in German, French, and English) 1961. a. Basler Effektenboerse - Basel Stock Exchange, Freie Str. 3, Postfach 244, 4001 Basel, Switzerland. charts.

332.6 SZ
BERNER BOERSENVEREIN. JAHRESBERICHT. (Text in German) a. membership. Berner Boersenverein - Berne Stock Exchange, Aarbergergasse 30, 3011 Berne, Switzerland.

332.6 US ISSN 0362-8701
BEST'S INSURANCE SECURITIES RESEARCH SERVICE. 1968. irreg. A.M. Best Co., Oldwick, NJ 08858. illus. (looseleaf format)

BIBLIOGRAPHY OF APPRAISAL LITERATURE. see *REAL ESTATE — Abstracting, Bibliographies, Statistics*

BOERSEN- UND WIRTSCHAFTSHANDBUCH. see *BUSINESS AND ECONOMICS*

332.64 SP
BOLSA DE BARCELONA. MEMORIA. a. Colegio de Agentes de Cambio y Bolsa de Barcelona, Servicio de Estudios e Informacion, Paseo Isabel II s/n, Barcelona, Spain. charts.
Formerly: Bolsa de Barcelona. Estadisticas.

332.64 PE
BOLSA DE VALORES DE LIMA. MEMORIA. 1975. a. Bolsa de Valores de Lima, Lima, Peru.

332.64 EC
BOLSA DE VALORES DE QUITO. INFORMES Y MEMORIA ANUAL. a. Bolsa de Valores de Quito, Av. 6 de Diciembre y Pazmino 245, Apartado 3272, Quito, Ecuador.

332.6 BL
BOLSA DE VALORES DE SAO PAULO. RELATORIO. (Text in English and Portuguese) a. free. Bolsa de Valores de Sao Paulo, Rua Alvares Penteado 151, Sao Paulo, Brazil. stat.

332.6 BL ISSN 0034-7558
BOLSA DE VALORES DE SAO PAULO. REVISTA. irreg. free. Bolsa de Valores de Sao Paulo, Rua Alvares Penteado 151, Sao Paulo, Brazil. adv. charts. illus.

332.6 BL ISSN 0557-0506
BOLSA DE VALORES DO RIO DE JANEIRO. RESUMO ANUAL. 1964. a. Cr.$7($2) Bolsa de Valores do Rio de Janeiro - Rio de Janeiro Stock Exchange, Praca 15 de Novembro, 20, Rio de Janeiro, Brazil. circ. 500.

332.6 CN ISSN 0317-607X
BOND RECORD. 1972. a. Can.$11 includes supplements. ‡ Canadian Daily Quotation Service Ltd., Box 518, Station K, Toronto, Ont. M4P 2G9, Canada. circ. 4,000.
Formerly: Investment Dealers' Association of Canada. Canada and Canadian Provinces: Funded Debts Outstanding (ISSN 0075-028X)

332.6 CN ISSN 0068-161X
BRITISH COLUMBIA MUNICIPAL YEARBOOK. 1949. a. Can.$8.50. (British Columbia Bond Dealers Association) JSB Productions Ltd., Box 46475, Station G, Vancouver, B.C. V6R 4G7, Canada. Ed. Joan Stewart. adv. circ. 2,500.

332.63 US ISSN 0195-3591
C F T C DATABOOK. a. U.S. Commodity Futures Trading Commission, 2033 K St., N.W., Washington, DC 20581.

332.6 CN
CANADA. FOREIGN INVESTMENT REVIEW AGENCY. ANNUAL REPORT. 1975/76. a. Foreign Investment Review Agency, Box 2800 Station D, Ottawa, Ont. K1P 6A5, Canada.

332.6 CN ISSN 0380-2221
CANADIAN FINANCIAL E-Z DIRECTORY. 1964. a. 12.50. Canadian Daily Quotation Service Ltd., Box 518, Station K, Toronto, Ont. M4P 2G9, Canada.

332.65 US ISSN 0577-571X
CAPITAL INVESTMENTS OF THE WORLD PETROLEUM INDUSTRY. 1946. a. free. Chase Manhattan Bank, Energy Economics Division, One Chase Manhattan Plaza, New York, NY 10015. Ed. Richard Dobias. circ. 30,000.

332.6 AT ISSN 0311-3655
CHART BOOK OF THE MELBOURNE SHARE PRICE INDEX. 1965. a. Aus.$5.50. Stock Exchange of Melbourne Ltd., 351 Collins St., Melbourne, Vic. 3000, Australia.

CHEMICAL NEW PRODUCT DIRECTORY. see *BUSINESS AND ECONOMICS — Marketing And Purchasing*

332.6 CH
CHINA, REPUBLIC. MINISTRY OF ECONOMIC AFFAIRS. MAIN STATISTICS OF SECURITIES. vol. 7, 1977. irreg. Ministry of Economic Affairs, Securities and Exchange Commission, 15th Floor, 7 Roosevelt Rd., Taipei, Taiwan, Republic of China.

332.6 US
COMMODITIES MAGAZINE REFERENCE GUIDE TO FUTURES MARKETS. 1973. a. $6. Commodities Magazine, Inc., 219 Parkade, Cedar Falls, IA 50613. Ed. Darrell Jobman. adv. stat, tr. lit. circ. 50,000. (also avail. in microfiche; back issues avail.)

332.6 US
COMMODITY PRICES. 1974. irreg. $18. Gale Research Company, Book Tower, Detroit, MI 48226. Ed. Paul Wasserman.

338 US ISSN 0069-6862
COMMODITY YEAR BOOK. 1939. a. $22.95. Commodity Research Bureau, Inc., One Liberty Plaza, New York, NY 10006. Ed. Harry Jiler. index.

346 332.6 US ISSN 0093-7800
COMPLIANCE AND LEGAL SEMINAR. PROCEEDINGS. a. Securities Industry Association, Inc. (Washington), 490 L'Enfant Plaza East S.W., Washington, DC 20024. Key Title: Proceedings - Compliance and Legal Seminar.

CORPORATE PROFILES FOR EXECUTIVES & INVESTORS. see *BUSINESS AND ECONOMICS*

BUSINESS AND ECONOMICS — INVESTMENTS

332.6 US
CREDIT AND CAPITAL MARKETS; sources and uses of funds. 1948. a. free. ‡ Bankers Trust Company, Economics Division, P.O. Box 318, New York, NY 10015. Ed. Donald E. Woolley. stat. circ. 30,000. (processed) Indexed: Vert.File Ind.
Formerly: Investment Outlook (ISSN 0522-2974)

332.6 JA
DIAMOND, STOCK INVESTMENT EDITION/ DAIYAMONDO KABUSHIKI-TOSHI-BAN. (Text in Japanese) 1977. bi-m. 5700 Yen. Diamond Inc., 4-2, 1-chome, Kasumigaseki, Chiyoda-ku, Tokyo 100, Japan. Ed. Toshikazu Yatsu.

332.6 US ISSN 0149-6581
DIRECTORY OF COMPANIES REQUIRED TO FILE ANNUAL REPORTS WITH THE SECURITIES AND EXCHANGE COMMISSION UNDER THE SECURITIES EXCHANGE ACT OF 1934; alphabetically and by industry groups. 1950. a. $4.75. U.S. Securities and Exchange Commission, Office of Economic Research, 500 N. Capitol St., Washington, DC 20549 (Orders to: Supt. of Documents, Washington, DC 20402) Ed. N. B. Marshall. index. circ. 5,000. (reprint service avail. from UMI)
From 1976, continues: Directory of Companies Filing Annual Reports with the Securities and Exchange Commission Under the Securities Exchange Act of 1934.

332.67 AT
DIRECTORY OF PROPERTY INVESTORS AND DEVELOPERS. irreg. Davies and Dalziel Investment Service, G.P.O. Box 1392m, Melbourne, Vic. 3001, Australia.

332.6 US
DIRECTORY OF SECURITIES RESEARCH. 1976. a. $75. W. R. Nelson & Company, 551 Fifth Ave., New York, NY 10017. Ed. Vicki J. Epstein.

332.6 US ISSN 0362-0689
DOW JONES COMMODITIES HANDBOOK. 1976. a. $3.95. Dow Jones & Co. Inc., Dow Jones Books, Box 300, Princeton, NJ 08540. illus.

332.6 US ISSN 0093-9528
DUN & BRADSTREET REFERENCE BOOK OF TRANSPORTATION. Title varies: Reference Book of Transportation. biennial. Trinc Transportation Consultants, 475 l'Enfant Plaza, S.W., Suite 4200, Washington, DC 20024.
Supersedes: Dun's Reference Book of Transportation, Inc.

332.6 US ISSN 0098-2466
DUN & BRADSTREET'S GUIDE TO YOUR INVESTMENTS. 1973, 17th ed. a. $8.95 paperback; $14.95 hardcover. Thomas Y. Crowell Co. (Subsidiary of: Dun- Donnelley Publishing Corp.) 10 E. 53rd St., New York, NY 10022.
Continues: Your Investments; How to Increase Your Capital and Income.

332.66 EI
E I B-INFORMATION. (Text in Danish, Dutch, English, French, German and Italian) no. 19, 1979. irreg. European Investment Bank, 2 Place de Metz, Boite Postal 2005, Luxembourg, Luxembourg. charts.

ELECTRONICS NEW PRODUCT DIRECTORY. see BUSINESS AND ECONOMICS — Marketing And Purchasing

332.6 778.5 US
FILM ANGELS. a. $65. Leo Shull Publications, 134 W. 44th St., New York, NY 10036.

332.65 US
FINANCIAL ANALYSIS OF A GROUP OF PETROLEUM COMPANIES. 1945. a. free. Chase Manhattan Bank, Energy Economics Division, One Chase Manhattan Plaza, New York, NY 10015. Ed. Colin Carter. circ. 30,000.

332.6 US ISSN 0360-5825
FINANCIAL CORPORATE BOND TRANSFER SERVICE. 1972. a. with m. supplements. $238. Financial Information, Inc., 30 Montgomery St., Jersey City, NJ 07302.

332.6 CN ISSN 0071-5050
FINANCIAL POST SURVEY OF INDUSTRIALS. 1927. a. Can.$27. Maclean-Hunter Ltd., 481 University Ave., Toronto M5W 1A7, Canada. Ed. John Byrne. adv. circ. 13,000.
Investment and statistical data on public Canadian industrial securities

332.678 US ISSN 0364-0752
FINANCIAL STOCK GUIDE SERVICE. DIRECTORY OF ACTIVE STOCKS. a (m. supplements) $347 includes Directory of Obsolete Securities. Financial Information, Inc., 30 Montgomery St., Jersey City, NJ 07302.

332.6 US ISSN 0085-0551
FINANCIAL STOCK GUIDE SERVICE. DIRECTORY OF OBSOLETE SECURITIES. 1927. a. $100 to qualified personnel. Financial Information, Inc., 30 Montgomery St., Jersey City, NJ 07302.

332.6 FR
FRANCE. COMMISSION DES OPERATIONS DE BOURSE. RAPPORT AU PRESIDENT DE LA REPUBLIQUE. irreg. France. Direction des Journaux Officiels, 26, rue Desaix, 75732 Paris Cedex 15, France.

332.6 NE ISSN 0072-4467
GIDS BIJ DE PRIJSCOURANT. 1894. a. fl.125. J. H. de Bussy, Keizersgracht 810, Amsterdam, Netherlands. circ. 2,000.
A concise guide to all securities that have quotations on the official list of the Amsterdam Stock Exchange

332.6 CN
GRAPHOSCOPE'S HISTORICAL PERFORMANCE REVIEW. a. Can.$8.50. Canadian Analyst Ltd., 32 Front St. W., Suite 237, Toronto, Ont. M5J 1C5, Canada.

332.6 UK ISSN 0072-5692
GREAT BRITAIN. DEPARTMENT OF TRADE. PARTICULARS OF DEALERS IN SECURITIES AND OF TRUST UNITS. a. H.M.S.O., P.O. Box 569, London SE1 9NH, England.

GREECE AS LINK BETWEEN ARAB COUNTRIES AND THE WEST; handbook for the businessman and investor. see TRAVEL AND TOURISM

GRUNDLAGEN UND PRAXIS DES BANK- UND BOERSENWESENS. see BUSINESS AND ECONOMICS — Banking And Finance

332.6 US ISSN 0072-9892
HANDBOOK OF SECURITIES OF THE UNITED STATES GOVERNMENT AND FEDERAL AGENCIES AND RELATED MONEY MARKET INSTRUMENTS. 1922. biennial. $3 (free to qualified institutions) First Boston Corp., 20 Exchange Place, New York, NY 10005. circ. 60,000.

332.64 GR
HELLENIC INDUSTRIAL DEVELOPMENT BANK. INVESTMENT GUIDE. Spine title: E T B A Investment Guide. (Text in English, French, Greek and German) 1969. irreg. (every 2-3 yrs.) Dr.150($6.60) Hellenic Industrial Development Bank, 18 El. Venizelos St., Athens 135, Greece. circ. 5,000 (Greek edt.); 5,000 (English edt.); 3,000 (French edt.); 30,000 (German edt.)

332.6 GW ISSN 0073-3342
HOPPENSTEDT VADEMECUM DER INVESTMENTFONDS. 1961. irreg. DM.120. Verlag Hoppenstedt und Co., Havelstr. 9, Postfach 4006, 6100 Darmstadt, W. Germany (B.R.D.) adv. bk. rev.

332.6 BL
HOW TO INVEST IN BRAZIL. (Text in English) a (with q supplements) $100. ESTEPE, Publishing Department, Rua Senador Dantas 19 Grupo 707, ZC-06 20000 Rio de Janeiro, Brazil.

332.6 US ISSN 0075-0255
I B A OCCASIONAL PAPER. (Former name of issuing body: Investment Bankers Association of America) irreg. Securities Industry Association, Inc., 20 Broad St., New York, NY 10005.

332.6 US ISSN 0095-3148
ILLINOIS. STATE BOARD OF INVESTMENT. INVESTMENT TRANSACTIONS. a. State Board of Investment, Springfield, IL 62706. Key Title: Investment Transactions.

332.6 HK
INDUSTRIAL INVESTMENT HONG KONG. 1968. a. free to qualified personnel. Commerce & Industry Department, Fire Brigade, Hong Kong, Hong Kong, Hong Kong. Ed. Robert Sun. illus. stat. circ. 15,000.

332.6 330.9 AT ISSN 0082-1985
INFORMATION ABOUT INVESTMENT IN TASMANIA. Cover title: Tasmania; a Businessman's Handbook. 1960. irreg. free. Directorate of Industrial Development & Trade, 152 Macquarie St., Hobart, Tas. 7000, Australia. Ed. G. M. Burejeff. circ. 5,000.

332.6 341 US ISSN 0074-2163
INTERNATIONAL CENTRE FOR SETTLEMENT OF INVESTMENT DISPUTES. ANNUAL REPORT. (Editions also in French and Spanish) 1966/67. a. free. International Centre for the Settlement of Investment Disputes, 1818 H St. N.W., Washington, DC 20433. circ. 20,000.

338 332.6 US ISSN 0074-6908
INTERNATIONAL MARKET GUIDE - CONTINENTAL EUROPE. a. not available to libraries in U. S. Dun & Bradstreet International, Box 3224, Church Street Station, New York, NY 10008.

332.67 PN
INVEST IN PANAMA. (Text in English) vol. 3, 1979. irreg. Banco Nacional de Panama, Via Espana - Torre B.N.P., P.O. Box 5220, Panama 5, Panama.

332.6 BE ISSN 0075-0247
INVESTISSEMENTS ETRANGERS EN BELGIQUE. a. Ministere des Affaires Economiques, 6 rue de l'Industrie, 1040 Brussels, Belgium.

332.6 UK
INVESTMENT TRUST YEAR BOOK. 1978. a. £8.45. (Association of Investment Trust Companies) Money Management, Minster House, Arthur St., London EC4R 9AX, England. circ. 3,000. (tabloid format)

332.67 US
INVESTOR RESPONSIBILITY RESEARCH CENTER. ANNUAL REPORT. 1973. a. Investor Responsibility Research Center, Inc., 1522 K St., N.W., Washington, DC 20005. Ed. Margaret Carroll.

380 JA
INVESTORS GUIDE OF JAPAN. (Text in English) vol. 2, 1973. a. 5000 Yen($16) Ariyama Trade Service, Inc., C.P.O. Box 1078, Osaka, Japan. Ed. Keiichi Ariyama. adv. charts.

332.6 NP
INVESTORS' GUIDE TO NEPAL. (Text in English) 1975. Industrial Services Centre, Box 1318, Kathmandu, Nepal.

332.6 AT ISSN 0075-3785
JOBSON'S YEAR BOOK OF PUBLIC COMPANIES OF AUSTRALIA AND NEW ZEALAND. 1927. a. Aus.$85. Jobson's Publications (Subsidiary of: Dun & Bradstreet (Australia) Pty. Ltd.) G.P.O. Box 425G, Melbourne, Vic. 3001, Australia. Ed. H.J. Rijnhart. adv.

332.67 US
JOHNSON'S INVESTMENT COMPANY CHARTS. 1949. a. $125 includes q. performance reports. Johnson's Charts, Inc., 545 Elmwood Ave., Buffalo, NY 14222. Eds. Hugh A. Johnson and Fred C. Cohn. film rev. charts. illus. stat. circ. 1,000-2,000.

332.6 DK
KOEBENHAVNS FONDSBOERS. AARSRAPPORT/COPENHAGEN STOCK EXCHANGE. ANNUAL REPORT. a. Koebenhavns Fondsboers, Nikolaj Plads 6, 1067 Copenhagen K, Denmark. stat.

BUSINESS AND ECONOMICS — INVESTMENTS

338   332.6   II
KOTHARI'S ECONOMIC AND INDUSTRIAL GUIDE OF INDIA. (Text in English) 1936. irreg., 33 edt., 1980. price varies. Kothari & Sons, 114 Nungambakkam High Rd., Madras 600034, India. Ed. C. B. Gihanshyamdas. adv. circ. 5,000.
Continues: Kothari's Economic Guide and Investor's Handbook of India.

332.6   MY   ISSN 0126-7558
KUALA LUMPUR STOCK EXCHANGE. COMPANIES HANDBOOK. (Text in English) 1974. a. $20. Kuala Lumpur Stock Exchange, Damansara Centre, 4th Fl., Block C, Damansara Heights, Kuala Lumpur 23-04, Malaysia. adv. stat. circ. 2,500.

332.6   US   ISSN 0098-0005
LIST OF LEGAL INVESTMENTS FOR SAVINGS BANKS IN CONNECTICUT. a. $3.50. Office of the Bank Commissioner, State Office Building, 165 Capitol Ave., Hartford, CT 06115.

332.6   UK
MANAGED AND PROPERTY BONDS. 1971. a. £4.75 Fundex Ltd., Minster House, Arthur St., London EC4R 9AX, England. adv. circ. 3,000.
Formerly: Property and Managed Bonds.

332   JA
MANUAL OF FOREIGN EXCHANGE CONTROL IN JAPAN. irreg. free. Bank of Japan, Foreign Department - Nihon Ginko, C.P.O. Box 203, Tokyo 100-91, Japan.

332.6   JA
MANUAL OF FOREIGN INVESTMENT IN JAPAN. irreg. free. Bank of Japan, Foreign Department - Nihon Ginko, C.P.O. Box 203, Tokyo 100-91, Japan.

353.9   332.6   US   ISSN 0090-9912
MONTANA. OFFICE OF THE LEGISLATIVE AUDITOR. STATE OF MONTANA BOARD OF INVESTMENTS. REPORT ON EXAMINATION OF FINANCIAL STATEMENTS. (Report year ends June 30) a. free. Office of the Legislative Auditor, State Capitol, Helena, MT 59601. stat. Key Title: State of Montana Investment Program. Report on Audit.

332.6   US   ISSN 0027-0814
MOODY'S BANK & FINANCE MANUAL. a. $525 (includes s-w. Moody's Bank & Finance News Reports) Moody's Investors Service, Inc., 99 Church St., New York, NY 10007.

332.6   US   ISSN 0545-0217
MOODY'S INDUSTRIAL MANUAL. 1900. a. $525 price includes semi-weekly news reports. Moody's Investors Service, Inc., 99 Church St., New York, NY 10007. stat. index.

332.6   US
MOODY'S INVESTORS FACT SHEETS. 1977. irreg.(with q. cum.) $800. Moody's Investors Service, Inc., 99 Church St., New York, NY 10007. (looseleaf format)

332.6   US   ISSN 0545-0233
MOODY'S MUNICIPAL & GOVERNMENT MANUAL. a. $675 price includes semi-weekly news reports. Moody's Investors Service, Inc., 99 Church St., New York, NY 10007. stat. index.

332.6   US
MOODY'S O T C INDUSTRIAL MANUAL. a. $450 (includes weekly Moody's O T C News Reports) Moody's Investors Service, Inc., 99 Church St., New York, NY 10007.

332.6   US   ISSN 0545-0241
MOODY'S PUBLIC UTILITY MANUAL. a. $425 (includes s-w. Moody's Public Utility News Reports) Moody's Investors Service, Inc., 99 Church St., New York, NY 10007.

332.6   US
MOODY'S TRANSPORTATION MANUAL. a. $425 (includes s-w. Moody's Transportation News Reports) Moody's Investors Service, Inc., 99 Church St., New York, NY 10007.

332.6   US   ISSN 0076-4175
MUTUAL FUNDS ALMANAC. 1969. a. $20 soft cover Hirsch Organization, Inc., 6 Deer Trail, Old Tappan, NJ 07675. Ed. Yale Hirsch. circ. 10,000.
Formerly: Manual of Mutual Funds.

332.6   US
NATIONAL INVESTOR RELATIONS INSTITUTE. EXECUTIVE SUMMARY OF THE ANNUAL NATIONAL CONFERENCE. 1976. a. $10 to non-members. National Investor Relations Institute, 1629 K St., N.W., Washington, DC 20006. illus.
Formerly: National Investor Relations Institute. Proceedings of the Annual National Conference (ISSN 0094-1204)

332.6   US   ISSN 0077-5703
NATIONAL SECURITIES AND RESEARCH CORPORATION. ANNUAL FORECAST. Variant title: National's Forecast For...(Year) 1948. a. free. ‡ National Securities & Research Corp., 605 Third Ave., New York, NY 10016.

332.6   US   ISSN 0092-4679
NATIONAL SECURITY TRADERS ASSOCIATION. TRADERS' ANNUAL. 1961. a. $5. Investment Dealers' Digest (IDD) Inc., 150 Broadway, New York, NY 10038. illus. circ. 5,000.

332.6   314   NE   ISSN 0077-6718
NETHERLANDS. CENTRAAL BUREAU VOOR DE STATISTIEK. BELEGGINGEN VAN INSTITUTIONELE BELEGGERS. INVESTMENTS OF INSTITUTIONAL INVESTORS. (Text in Dutch and English) 1966. a. fl.10.25. Centraal Bureau voor de Statistiek, Prinses Beatrixlaan 428, Voorburg, Netherlands (Orders to: Staatsuitgeverij, Christoffel Plantijnstraat, The Hague, Netherlands)

NETHERLANDS INSTITUTE OF BANKERS AND STOCK BROKERS. PUBLICATIONS. see BUSINESS AND ECONOMICS — Banking And Finance

332.6   US
OPTIONEER. 46/yr. $89. Worden & Worden, Inc., Worden Building, 1915 Floranada Rd., Fort Lauderdale, FL 33308.

332.6   NO   ISSN 0085-4565
OSLO BOERS. BERETNING. 1896. a. free. Oslo Boers - Oslo Stock Exchange, Tollbugt. 2, Oslo 1, Norway. circ. 1,600.

332.6   US   ISSN 0196-1276
OVERSEAS PRIVATE INVESTMENT CORPORATION. ANNUAL REPORT. 1971. a. Overseas Private Investment Corporation, 1129 20th St., N.W., Washington, DC 20527. Key Title: Annual Report - Overseas Private Investment Corporation.

332.6   US
PACIFIC STOCK EXCHANGE. ANNUAL REPORT. a. Pacific Stock Exchange, 301 Pine St., San Francisco, CA 94104.

332.6   PK   ISSN 0078-8198
PAKISTAN INDUSTRIAL CREDIT AND INVESTMENT CORPORATION. REPORT. (Text in English) 1958. a. Pakistan Industrial Credit and Investment Corporation, P.O. Box 5080, Karachi, Pakistan. charts. stat.

332.63   PH
PHILIPPINE STANDARD COMMUNITY CLASSIFICATION. a. National Economic and Development Authority, Box 1116, Manila, Philippines.

332.6   PH   ISSN 0079-1504
PHILIPPINES. BOARD OF INVESTMENTS. ANNUAL REPORT. 1968. a. free. ‡ Board of Investments, Ortigas Building, Ortigas Avenue, Box 676, Rizal, Philippines. circ. 3,000.

PONDICHERRY INDUSTRIAL PROMOTION, DEVELOPMENT AND INVESTMENT CORPORATION. ANNUAL REPORTS AND ACCOUNTS. see BUSINESS AND ECONOMICS — Domestic Commerce

332.67   341   US   ISSN 0090-9742
PRIVATE INVESTORS ABROAD; problems and solutions in international business. 1967. a. $28.50. (Southwestern Legal Foundation, International and Comparative Law Center) Matthew Bender & Co., Inc., 235 E. 45 St., New York, NY 10017.

R.E.I.T. FACT BOOK. (National Association of Real Estate Investment Trusts) see REAL ESTATE

332.6   US
S I E SOPHISTICATED INVESTOR. (Includes Guide to Business & Investment Services) 1967. irreg. $1. Select Information Exchange, 2095 Broadway, New York, NY 10023. Ed. George H. Wein. adv. bk. rev. bibl. circ. 100,000.
Former titles: Investment Sources and Ideas (ISSN 0085-6355); Sources and Ideas; Incorporating: Sophisticated Investor.

332.6   GW   ISSN 0080-5572
SALING AKTIENFUEHRER. 1872. a. DM.82. Verlag Hoppenstedt und Co., Havelstr. 9, Postfach 4006, 6100 Darmstadt, W. Germany (B.R.D.) adv.

332.6   TH
SECURITIES EXCHANGE OF THAILAND. HANDBOOK. 1975. irreg. Securities Exchange of Thailand, Siam Center, 4th Floor (Rm. 412), 965 Ram I Rd., Bangkok, Thailand.

332.6   US   ISSN 0075-0263
SECURITIES INDUSTRY ASSOCIATION. STATE AND LOCAL PENSION FUNDS. 1968. biennial. Securities Industry Association, Inc. (Washington), 490 L'Enfant Plaza East S.W., Washington, DC 20024.
Formerly: Investment Bankers Association of America. State and Local Pension Funds; Supersedes: Investment Bankers Association. State Pension Fund.

338.7   US   ISSN 0094-467X
SECURITIES INVESTOR PROTECTION CORPORATION. ANNUAL REPORT. 1971. a. free. Securities Investor Protection Corp., 900 17th St. N.W., Suite 800, Washington, DC 20006. Ed. Jeffrey R. McCord. stat. circ. 15,000. Key Title: Annual Report - Securities Investor Protection Corporation.

332.6   JA
SECURITIES MARKET IN JAPAN. (Text in English) biennial. Japan Securities Research Institute, Shokenkaikan, 1-14 Nihonbashi, Kabaya-cho, Chuo-ku, Tokyo, Japan. illus. stat.

332.6   US
SECURITY INDUSTRY YEARBOOK. 1981. a. $55. Securities Industry Association, Inc., Research Dept., 19th Fl., 20 Broad, New York, NY 10005.

332.6   AT   ISSN 0037-3311
SHAREHOLDER. 1966. irreg. membership. Australian Shareholders Association, N.S.W. Branch, 51 Pitt St., Sydney, N.S.W. 2000, Australia. adv. charts. illus.

332.678   SA
SOUTH AFRICA: A GUIDE TO FOREIGN INVESTORS. a. Erudita Publications(Pty) Ltd., Box 25111, Ferreirasdorp, Johannesburg 2048, South Africa.

332.6   US
STANDARD AND POOR'S DIRECTORY OF BOND AGENTS. Short title: Directory of Bond Agents. (Includes bimonthly cum. supplement) 1975. irreg. $337. Standard & Poor's Corporation, 25 Broadway, New York, NY 10004. Ed. Vito Calbi.

332.6   PK   ISSN 0081-4466
STATE BANK OF PAKISTAN. INDEX NUMBERS OF STOCK EXCHANGE SECURITIES. (Text in English) 1963. a. State Bank of Pakistan, Central Directorate, Public Relations Department, I.I. Chundrigar Rd., Box 4456, Karachi, Pakistan.

332.6   UK   ISSN 0305-1129
STOCK EXCHANGE, LONDON. MEMBERS AND FIRMS OF THE STOCK EXCHANGE. Cover title: Members of the Stock Exchange. 1802. a. £1.50. ‡ Council of the Stock Exchange, London EC2N 1HP, England. circ. 8,000.

332.6   UK   ISSN 0076-0684
STOCK EXCHANGE, LONDON. STOCK EXCHANGE OFFICIAL YEAR BOOK. 1875. a. $110. I P C Business Press Ltd., 33-40 Bowling Green Lane, London EC1R 0NE, England. adv. circ. 6,750.

BUSINESS AND ECONOMICS — LABOR AND INDUSTRIAL RELATIONS

332.6   SI   ISSN 0583-3981
STOCK EXCHANGE OF SINGAPORE. HANDBOOK. (Text in English) 1966. a. S.$18. Stock Exchange of Singapore Ltd., Honk Leong Bldg., Rm. 1403, Raffles Quay, Singapore 0104, Singapore. adv. circ. 6,000.

332.6   US
STOCK TRADER'S ALMANAC. 1968. a. $15.75 soft cover. ‡ Hirsch Organization, Inc., 6 Deer Trail, Old Tappan, NJ 07605. Ed. Yale Hirsch. circ. 25,000.

336.2 332.6   US   ISSN 0081-5624
STOCK VALUES AND DIVIDENDS FOR TAX PURPOSES. a. $6. Commerce Clearing House, Inc., 4025 W. Peterson Ave., Chicago, IL 60646.

332.6   SW
STOCKHOLMS FONDBOERS. BERAETTELSE/ STOCKHOLM STOCK EXCHANGE. REPORT. a. Stockholms Fondboers, Kaellargraend, S-111 29 Stockholm, Sweden.

332.6   FI   ISSN 0585-9581
SUOMEN OBLIGAATIOKIRJA/FINNISH BOND ISSUES/OBLIGATIONSBOK FOER FINLAND. (Text in English, Finnish and Swedish) a. Fmk.8.40. Suomen Pankki - Bank of Finland, Information Department, Box 160, Sf-00101 Helsinki 10, Finland. Ed. Eevi Mattila. circ. 530.

332.6   AT
SYDNEY STOCK EXCHANGE. RESEARCH DEPARTMENT, COMPANY REVIEW SERVICE. (Text and Summaries in English) 1938. a. Aus.$750($500) ‡ Sydney Stock Exchange, Research Department, 20 Bond St, Sydney, N.S.W., Australia. stat. index. circ. 980. (looseleaf format)
Former titles: Sydney Stock Exchange. Research and Statistical Department. Company Review Service; Sydney Stock Exchange. Research and Statistical Department. Company Statistical Service.

332.6   IT   ISSN 0082-1446
TACCUINO DELL'AZIONISTA. 1935. a. L.40000. Edizioni S A S I P, Via S. Vittore al Teatro 1, 20123 Milan, Italy. Eds. Mrs. Enrico Colombi, Carlo Colombi. index. circ. 5,000.

332.6 792   US
THEATRE ANGELS. a. $55. Leo Shull Publications, 134 W. 44th St., New York, NY 10036.

332.6   US   ISSN 0082-7916
UNITED GRAPHIC GUIDE. a. $12. ‡ United Business Service Company, 210 Newbury St., Boston, MA 02116. charts.

331 332.6   US
U.S. RAILROAD RETIREMENT BOARD. ANNUAL REPORT. 1936. a. price varies. U.S. Railroad Retirement Board, 844 Rush St., Chicago, IL 60611 (Order from: Supt. of Documents, Washington, DC 20402) circ. 1,200.

332.63   US   ISSN 0083-3215
U. S. SECURITIES AND EXCHANGE COMMISSION. ANNUAL REPORT. 1935. a. price varies. U. S. Securities and Exchange Commission, 500 N. Capitol St., Washington, DC 20549 (Orders to: Supt. of Documents, Washington, DC 20402) (reprint service avail. from UMI)

332.63   US   ISSN 0083-3223
U. S. SECURITIES AND EXCHANGE COMMISSION. DECISIONS AND REPORTS. 1934. irreg. price varies. U. S. Securities and Exchange Commission, 500 N. Capitol St., Washington, DC 20549 (Orders to: Supt. of Documents, Washington, DC 20402) (also avail. in microform from UMI; reprint service avail. from UMI)

332.63   US   ISSN 0083-3231
U. S. SECURITIES AND EXCHANGE COMMISSION. JUDICIAL DECISIONS. 1934/ 39. irreg. price varies. U.S. Securities and Exchange Commission, 500 N. Capitol St., Washington, DC 20549 (Orders to: Supt. of Documents, Washington, DC 20402) (also avail. in microform from UMI; reprint service avail. from UMI)

332.6   CN   ISSN 0083-520X
VANCOUVER STOCK EXCHANGE. ANNUAL REPORT. a. Vancouver Stock Exchange, 536 Howe St., Vancouver, B.C. V6C 2E1, Canada.

332.6   US   ISSN 0092-749X
WALKER'S MANUAL OF WESTERN CORPORATIONS. 1909. a. $158. Walker's Manual Incorporated, 5855 Naples Plaza, Suite 101, Long Beach, CA 90803. Ed. Carol T. Honey. adv. index. (back issues avail.)
Formerly: Walker's Manual of Western Corporations & Securities.

332.6   US   ISSN 0083-7075
WALL STREET JOURNAL INDEX. 1958. a. and m. $150 for annual; $325 for m. plus a. Dow Jones & Co., Inc., P.O. Box 300, Princeton, NJ 08540. (also avail. in microfilm; microfiche)

332.6   US
WHITE'S TAX EXEMPT BOND MARKET RATINGS. 1954. a. $300. Interactive Data Services, Inc., 22 Cortlandt St., New York, NY 10007. Ed. Wilson White, Jr.

332.6   US   ISSN 0090-418X
WHO'S WHO IN THE SECURITIES INDUSTRY. (Published for the annual convention of the Securities Industry Association as a part of the Economist SIA convention editions. Issued formerly as part of Economist I. B. A. convention editions) 1912. a. $6. ‡ Economist Publishing Co., 12 East Grand Ave., Chicago, IL 60611. Ed. George R. Stearns. adv. illus. circ. 6,000.

332.6   US
WISCONSIN. COMMISSIONER OF SECURITIES. BIENNIAL REPORT. 1937. biennial since 1967. free. ‡ Commissioner of Securities, P.O. Box 1768, Madison, WI 53701. circ. 1,000.
Formerly: Wisconsin. Commissioner of Securities. Annual Report (ISSN 0084-0548)

332.6   LE   ISSN 0075-8361
YEAR-BOOK OF THE LEBANESE JOINT-STOCK COMPANIES/ANNUAIRE DES SOCIETES LIBANAISES PAR ACTION. (Text in French; index in Arabic, English and French) 1964. a. latest 1977. $45. Middle East Commercial Information Center, P.O. Box 6466, Beirut, Lebanon (Dist. by UNIPUB, 345 Park Ave. South, New York, NY 10010) Ed. Charles G. Gedeon. adv. circ. 2,000.

332.6   LE
YEAR-BOOK OF THE LEBANESE LIMITED LIABILITY COMPANIES/ANNUAIRE DER SOCIETES LIBANAISES A RESPONSIBILITE LIMITEE. (Text in French; indices in Arabic, English and French) 1973. a, latest 1977. $35. Middle East Commercial Information Center, Box 6466, Beirut, Lebanon (Dist. by: Unipub, 345 Park Ave. South, New York, NY 10010) Ed. Charles C. Gadeon. adv. circ. 2,000.

332.6   SZ
ZUERCHER BOERSE. JAHRESBERICHT. a. (Zurich Stock Exchange) Effektenboersenverein Zuerich, Bleicherweg 5, 8001 Zurich, Switzerland. charts. illus. stat.

332.6   SZ
ZURICH STOCK EXCHANGE. HANDBOOK. no. 3, 1974. a. (Zuercher Boerse) J. Vontobel & Co., Bankers, Bahnhofstrasse 3, CH-8022 Zurich, Switzerland. illus.

BUSINESS AND ECONOMICS — Labor And Industrial Relations

see also Labor Unions

A I I E. INDUSTRIAL AND LABOR RELATIONS MONOGRAPH SERIES. (American Institute of Industrial Engineers, Inc.) see *ENGINEERING*

331.2   US
A M S DIRECTORY OF OFFICE SALARIES. 1946. a. $75 for non-members. Administrative Management Society, Maryland Rd., Willow Grove, PA 19090. Ed. Doris M. Graff.

331.2   US
A M S GUIDE TO MANAGEMENT COMPENSATION. 1973. a. $50 to members; $75 to non-members. Administrative Management Society, Maryland Rd., Willow Grove, PA 19090.

AGRICULTURAL WAGES IN INDIA. see *AGRICULTURE — Agricultural Economics*

331.1   US
ALABAMA. DEPARTMENT OF INDUSTRIAL RELATIONS. ANNUAL PLANNING INFORMATION. a. free. Department of Industrial Relations, Research and Statistics Division, Montgomery, AL 36130. illus. stat.
Formerly: Alabama. Department of Industrial Relations. Annual Manpower Planning Report (ISSN 0361-297X)

331.88   US   ISSN 0362-4196
ALASKA. EMPLOYMENT SECURITY DIVISION. LABOR FORCE ESTIMATES BY INDUSTRY AND AREA. 1961; N.S. 1970. a. free. ‡ Department of Labor, Commissioner's Office, Research and Analysis Section, Box 149, Juneau, AK 99811. circ. 400.
Formerly: Alaska. Employment Security Division. Workforce Estimates, by Industry and Area (ISSN 0065-5805)

331.1   US   ISSN 0091-9535
ALASKA. OFFICE OF THE GOVERNOR. GOVERNOR'S MANPOWER PLAN. 1965. a. ‡ Office of the Governor, Juneau, AK 99801. illus. circ. controlled.

AMERICAN ASSOCIATION OF ENGINEERING SOCIETIES. ENGINEERING MANPOWER COMMISSION. ENGINEERING ENROLLMENT DATA. see *ENGINEERING*

AMERICAN ASSOCIATION OF ENGINEERING SOCIETIES. ENGINEERING MANPOWER COMMISSION. ENGINEERS' SALARIES: SPECIAL INDUSTRY REPORT. see *ENGINEERING*

AMERICAN ASSOCIATION OF ENGINEERING SOCIETIES. ENGINEERING MANPOWER COMMISSION. PROFESSIONAL INCOME OF ENGINEERS. see *ENGINEERING*

AMERICAN ASSOCIATION OF ENGINEERING SOCIETIES. ENGINEERING MANPOWER COMMISSION. PLACEMENT OF ENGINEERING AND TECHNOLOGY GRADUATES. see *ENGINEERING*

AMERICAN ASSOCIATION OF ENGINEERING SOCIETIES. ENGINEERING MANPOWER COMMISSION. SALARIES OF ENGINEERING TECHNICIANS AND TECHNOLOGISTS. see *ENGINEERING*

AMERICAN BAR ASSOCIATION. SECTION OF LABOR RELATIONS LAW. PROCEEDINGS. see *LAW*

331.1 340   US
AMERICAN BAR ASSOCIATION. SECTION OF LABOR RELATIONS LAW. COMMITTEE REPORTS. 1969. a. in 2 vols. $4.90 per vol. American Bar Association, Section of Labor Relations Law, 1155 E. 60 St., Chicago, IL 60637. circ. 8,300.
Formerly: American Bar Association. Section of Labor-Relations Law. Report (ISSN 0065-7492)

AMERICAN SOCIETY OF PENSION ACTUARIES. TRANSCRIBINGS. ANNUAL CONFERENCE. see *INSURANCE*

331   US
ANNUAL CONFERENCE ON LABOR AT NEW YORK UNIVERSITY. PROCEEDINGS. 1948. a. $28.50 for 1976 vol. (New York University, Institute of Labor Relations) Matthew Bender & Co., Inc., 235 E. 45 St, New York, NY 10017. Ed. Richard Adelman.

331.1   SP
ANUARIO DE LAS RELACIONES LABORALES EN ESPANA. 1975. a. Ediciones de la Torre, Calle Espronceda 20, Madrid 3, Spain. adv. bk. rev. circ. 2,000.

331   GW
ARBEITERBEWEGUNG- THEORIE UND GESCHICHTE. JAHRBUECHER. 1973. a. DM.13.80. Fischer Taschenbuch Verlag, Geleitsstr. 25, 6000 Frankfurt, W. Germany (B.R.D.) Ed. Claudio Pozzoli. bk. rev. bibl.

BUSINESS AND ECONOMICS — LABOR AND INDUSTRIAL RELATIONS

331.2   AU
ARBEITSKOSTEN IN DER INDUSTRIE OESTERREICHS. 1960. triennial. free. Bundeskammer der Gewerblichen Wirtschaft, Abteilung fuer Statistik und Dokumentation, Stubenring 12, A-1010 Vienna, Austria. Ed. Guenther Herget. stat. circ. 2,000.

331   AU   ISSN 0587-1689
ARBEITSMARKT POLITIK. 1969. irreg. price varies. Hochschule fuer Sozial- und Wirtschaftswissenschaften, Linz, Oesterreichisches Institut fuer Arbeitsmarkt Politik, 4045 Auhof, A-4045 Linz/Donau.

331.15 340   GW   ISSN 0066-586X
ARBEITSRECHT DER GEGENWART. 1963. a. price varies. Erich Schmidt Verlag (Bielefeld), Viktoriastr. 44A, Postfach 7330, 4800 Bielefeld 1, W. Germany (B.R.D.) Ed. Gerhard Mueller. adv. bk. rev.

331   SZ   ISSN 0003-777X
ARBEITSRECHT UND ARBEITSLOSENVERSICHERUNG. (Text in French and German) 1953. irreg. (3-4/yr.) 18 Fr. (Bundesamt fuer Industrie, Gewerbe und Arbeit) Schulthess Polygraphischer Verlag AG, Zwingliplatz 2, 8001 Zurich, Switzerland. adv. index. circ. 1,677.

331   US
ARCHIVES OF LABOR AND URBAN AFFAIRS NEWSLETTER. 1971. irreg., formerly q. free. Wayne State University, Archives of Labor and Urban Affairs, Walter Reuther Library, 5401 Cass Ave., Detroit, MI 48202. Ed. George Tselos. bibl. circ. 3,000. (back issues avail.)
    Formerly: Archives of Labor History and Urban Affairs Newsletter (ISSN 0044-8729)

331   AG
ARGENTINA. DIVISION DE ESTADISTICAS SOCIALES. CONFLICTOS DEL TRABAJO. 1961. a. Division de Estadisticas Sociales, Buenos Aires, Argentina. stat.

331.1   US   ISSN 0092-2889
ARKANSAS AVERAGE COVERED EMPLOYMENT AND EARNINGS BY COUNTY AND INDUSTRY. 1948. irreg. free. Employment Security Division, Research and Analysis Section, Little Rock, AR 72201. circ. 300.

331   CN   ISSN 0703-0878
B. C. LABOUR DIRECTORY. 1973. a. free. Ministry of Labour, Research and Planning Branch, Parliament Bldg., Victoria, B.C. V8V 1X4, Canada. Ed. Jerry Meadows. circ. 1,500.

331.2   US   ISSN 0093-4267
BATTELLE MEMORIAL INSTITUTE. COLUMBUS LABORATORIES. REPORT ON NATIONAL SURVEY OF COMPENSATION PAID SCIENTISTS AND ENGINEERS ENGAGED IN RESEARCH AND DEVELOPMENT ACTIVITIES. 1968. a. $3.85. ‡ Battelle Memorial Institute, Columbus Laboratories, 505 King Ave, Columbus, OH 43201 (Order from: Supt. of Documents, U.S. Govt. Printing Office, Washington, DC 20402) stat. circ. 2,000. Key Title: Report on National Survey of Compensation Paid Scientists and Engineers Engaged in Research and Development Activities.

331   BE   ISSN 0067-5385
BELGIUM. CONSEIL NATIONAL DU TRAVAIL. RAPPORT DU SECRETARIAT SUR L'ACTIVITE DU CONSEIL/BELGIUM. NATIONALE ARBEIDSRAAD. VERSLAG VAN DE SECRETARIS OVER DE ACTIVITEIT VAN DE RAAD. 1958. a. Conseil National du Travail, Ave. de la Joyeuse Entree 17-21, 1040 Brussels, Belgium.

331   BE   ISSN 0067-5644
BELGIUM. OFFICE NATIONAL DE L'EMPLOI. RAPPORT ANNUEL. 1935. a. 300 Fr. Office National de l'Emploi, Boulevard de l'Empereur, 7, 1000 Brussels, Belgium. circ. 3,000.

331   II   ISSN 0067-9917
BOMBAY LABOUR JOURNAL.* (Text in English) 1960. a. free. Bombay Labour Institute, Dadabhai Chamarbaugwala Rd., Parel, Bombay 12, India. Ed. Mrs. S. A. Vaidya.

331   BL
BRAZIL. MINISTERIO DO TRABALHO E PREVIDENCIA SOCIAL. CENTRO DE DOCUMENTACAO E INFORMATICA. MERCADO DE TRABALHO: FLUTUACAO. 1972. irreg. Ministerio do Trabalho e Previdencia Social, Centro de Documentacao e Informatica, Rio de Janeiro, Brazil.

331.2   CN
BRITISH COLUMBIA. DEPARTMENT OF LABOUR. NEGOTIATED WORKING CONDITIONS. a. Department of Labour, Research Branch, Victoria, B.C., Canada. illus.
    Formerly: Working Conditions in British Columbia Industry.

331   CN   ISSN 0319-0404
BRITISH COLUMBIA. LABOUR RELATIONS BOARD. ANNUAL REPORT. 1974. a. Labour Relations Board, 1620 W. 8th Ave., Vancouver, B.C., Canada.

331.2   CN   ISSN 0705-9698
BRITISH COLUMBIA. MINISTRY OF LABOUR. ANNUAL REPORT. 1918. a. Ministry of Labour, Victoria, B.C., Canada. Ed. Jack E. Nugent. illus. circ. 3,000.
    Formerly: British Columbia. Department of Labour. Annual Report (ISSN 0381-2898)

331   CN   ISSN 0703-0665
BRITISH COLUMBIA. MINISTRY OF LABOUR. RESEARCH AND PLANNING BRANCH. NEGOTIATED WORKING CONDITIONS. 1976. a. Ministry of Labour, Research and Planning Branch, Parliament Bldgs., Victoria, B.C. V8V 1X4, Canada.

331   NE
BULLETIN OF COMPARATIVE LABOUR RELATIONS. (Text in English) irreg (1-2/yr.) price varies. (Rijksuniversiteit Te Leuven, Institute for Labour Relations, BE) Kluwer B.V., Postbus 23, 7400 GA Deventer, Netherlands. Ed. R. Blanpain.

BUSINESS ARCHIVES COUNCIL. BROADSHEET. see BUSINESS AND ECONOMICS — Economic Systems And Theories, Economic History

331.1   US   ISSN 0362-4129
CALIFORNIA. DEPARTMENT OF INDUSTRIAL RELATIONS. ANNUAL REPORT. a. Department of Industrial Relations, Box 603, San Francisco, CA 94101. illus. Key Title: Annual Report for the Department of Industrial Relations.

331.2   US   ISSN 0098-8332
CALIFORNIA. EMPLOYMENT DATA AND RESEARCH DIVISION. TAXABLE AND TOTAL WAGES, REGULAR BENEFITS PAID, EMPLOYER CONTRIBUTIONS EARNED, AND AVERAGE COVERED EMPLOYMENT, BY INDUSTRY. (Subseries of: Employment Data Reports) a. free. Employment Development Department, Employment Data and Research Division, 800 Capitol Mall, Sacramento, CA 95814.

331.1   US   ISSN 0008-1191
CALIFORNIA INDUSTRIAL RELATIONS REPORTS. 1953. 1-2/yr. free. ‡ Department of Industrial Relations, Division of Labor Statistics and Research, Box 603, San Francisco, CA 94101. charts. stat.

330   UK
CAMBRIDGE UNIVERSITY DEPARTMENT OF APPLIED ECONOMICS. PAPERS IN INDUSTRIAL RELATIONS AND LABOUR. 1975. irreg., no. 4, 1979. $35.50 (cloth); $15.50(paper) for latest vol. Cambridge University Press, Box 110, Cambridge CB2 3RL, England (And 32 E. 57th St., New York, NY 10022)

331   CN
CANADA. LABOUR CANADA. ANNUAL REVIEW. a. free. Labour Canada, Ottawa, Ont. K1A 0J2, Canada. (reprint service avail. from MML)

331   CN   ISSN 0068-743X
CANADA. LABOUR CANADA. WAGE RATES, SALARIES AND HOURS OF LABOUR. (Text in English and French) 1916. a. Can.$7.25($8.70) ‡ Labour Canada, Ottawa, Ont. K1A 0J2, Canada. (reprint service avail. from MML)

331   CN   ISSN 0068-7448
CANADA. WOMEN'S BUREAU. WOMEN IN THE LABOUR FORCE: FACTS AND FIGURES. (Text in English and French) a. free. Women's Bureau, Ottawa K1A 0J2, Ont., Canada. Ed. Sylva Gelber. circ. 10,000.

331   CN   ISSN 0068-905X
CANADIAN LABOUR TERMS. irreg., 7th ed., 1978. Can.$3. C C H Canadian Ltd., 6 Garamond Ct., Don Mills, Ont. M3C 1Z5, Canada.

331.2   CN   ISSN 0705-6680
CANADIAN PERSPECTIVE. 1976. irreg. $25 (free to members) Association of Canadian Pension Management, 49 Gloucester St., Toronto, Ont. M4Y 1L8, Canada.

331 368.4   CK
COLOMBIA. MINISTERIO DE TRABAJO Y SEGURIDAD SOCIAL. MEMORIA. 1967. a. Ministerio de Trabajo y Seguridad Social, Bogota, Colombia.
    Supersedes: Colombia. Ministerio de Trabajo, Higiene y Prevision Social. Memoria.

331 340   EI   ISSN 0423-6955
COMMISSION OF THE EUROPEAN COMMUNITIES. COLLECTION DU DROIT DU TRAVAIL. (Editions also in German, Italian and Dutch) 1958. irreg. price varies. Office for Official Publications of the European Communities, C.P. 1003, Luxembourg 1, Luxembourg (Dist. in U.S. by European Community Information Service, 2100 M. St., N.W., Suite 707, Washington DC 20037)
    Series opened by the ECSC

158.7 331   EI   ISSN 0425-4937
COMMISSION OF THE EUROPEAN COMMUNITIES. COLLECTION PHYSIOLOGIE ET PSYCHOLOGIE DU TRAVAIL. (Editions also available in German, Italian and Dutch) 1967. irreg. 1969, no. 6. price varies. Office for Official Publications of the European Communities, C.P. 1003, Luxembourg 1, Luxembourg (Dist. in the U.S. by: European Community Information Service, 2100 M St., NW, Suite 707, Washington, DC 20037)

331   EI   ISSN 0591-0110
COMMISSION OF THE EUROPEAN COMMUNITIES. EXPOSE ANNUEL SUR LES ACTIVITIES DES SERVICES DE MAIN-D'OUVRE DES ETATS MEMBRES DE LA COMMUNAUTE. (Editions also in German, Italian and Dutch) 1969. a. 5.60 F. Office for Official Publications of the European Communities, C.P. 1003, Luxembourg 1, Luxembourg (Dist. in the U.S. by: European Community Information Service, 2100 M St., NW, Suite 707, Washington, DC 20037)

331.2   IT   ISSN 0069-794X
COMPARAZIONE DEI SALARI E DEL COSTO DEL LAVORO IN EUROPA. (Editions in English and Italian) 1957. irreg., latest issue, 1969. Associazione Industriale Lombarda, Via Pantano 9, 20122 Milan, Italy.

CONDITION OF FARMWORKERS AND SMALL FARMERS. see AGRICULTURE

331.2   CN
CONDITIONS DE TRAVAIL AU QUEBEC DES ACTIVITES ECONOMIQUES CHOISIES. 1968. a. Bureau of Statistics, Service du Travail et de la Main d'Oeuvre, Hotel du Gouvernement, Quebec, P.Q., Canada. stat. circ. controlled.

331.1   II   ISSN 0069-8555
CONFERENCE ON HUMAN RELATIONS IN INDUSTRY. PROCEEDINGS. (Text in English) 1959. a. $4. ‡ South India Textile Research Association, Coimbatore 641014, India. Ed. P. V. Veeraraghavan. bk. rev. circ. 600.

331.4   US   ISSN 0146-3608
CONTRIBUTIONS IN LABOR HISTORY. 1977. irreg. Greenwood Press, 88 Post Rd. W., Westport, CT 06881.

331   IT   ISSN 0069-9772
CONVEGNO NAZIONALE PER LA CIVILTA DEL LAVORO. ATTI. 1958. a. free. ‡ Federazione Nazionale dei Cavalieri del Lavoro, Palazzo della Civilta del Lavoro, Quadrato della Concordia 9, 00144 Rome, Italy. Ed. Giorgio Gicca-Palli. circ. 600.

331.1　　　　　US　ISSN 0070-0029
CORNELL INTERNATIONAL INDUSTRIAL AND LABOR RELATIONS REPORTS. 1954. irreg.; no. 10, 1980. price varies. New York State School of Industrial and Labor Relations, Cornell University, Ithaca, NY 14853.

331.1　　　　　US　ISSN 0070-0053
CORNELL STUDIES IN INDUSTRIAL AND LABOR RELATIONS. 1951. irreg.; no. 19, 1977. price varies. New York State School of Industrial and Labor Relations, Cornell University, Ithaca, NY 14853.

CORPORATE PENSION FUND SEMINAR. PROCEEDINGS. see INSURANCE

331　　　　　MX
CUADERNOS OBREROS. irreg. Mex.$15. Centro de Estudios Historicos del Movimiento Obrero Mexicano, Avda. Jose M. Vertiz No. 96, Mexico 7, D.F., Mexico.

CURRENT GOVERNMENTS REPORTS: COUNTY EMPLOYMENT. see PUBLIC ADMINISTRATION

CURRENT GOVERNMENTS REPORTS: FINANCES OF EMPLOYEE RETIREMENT SYSTEMS OF STATE AND LOCAL GOVERNMENTS. see BUSINESS AND ECONOMICS — Public Finance, Taxation

CURRENT GOVERNMENTS REPORTS, GE-GOVERNMENT EMPLOYMENT. see PUBLIC ADMINISTRATION

CURRENT GOVERNMENTS REPORTS, GR FINANCES OF SELECTED PUBLIC EMPLOYEE RETIREMENT SYSTEMS. see BUSINESS AND ECONOMICS — Public Finance, Taxation

331　　　　　US
CURRENT GOVERNMENTS REPORTS: PUBLIC EMPLOYMENT. (Series GE-1) 1940. a. price varies. U. S. Bureau of the Census, Dept. of Commerce, Washington, DC 20233. Ed. Alan V. Stevens.

331.1　　　　　CN　ISSN 0318-952X
CURRENT INDUSTRIAL RELATIONS SCENE IN CANADA. 1973. a. Can.$40. Queen's University, Industrial Relations Centre, Kingston, Ont. K7L 3N6, Canada.

368.4 331　　　　　CY　ISSN 0070-2390
CYPRUS. MINISTRY OF LABOUR AND SOCIAL INSURANCE. ANNUAL REPORT. (Text in Greek; summary in English available) 1943. a. free. Ministry of Labour and Social Insurance, Nicosia, Cyprus.

331.12　　　　　CY
CYPRUS. MINISTRY OF LABOUR AND SOCIAL INSURANCE. LABOUR RESEARCH AND STATISTICS SECTION. REPORT ON THE ISLAND-WIDE MANPOWER SURVEY. (Subseries of its Manpower Research Series) (Text in English) a, 8th, 1973. Ministry of Labour and Social Insurance, Labor Research and Statistics Section, Nicosia, Cyprus. stat.

331　　　　　GW　ISSN 0415-6552
DEUTSCHER ARBEITSAMTSKALENDER. 1959. a. DM.55. Walhalla- und Praetoria-Verlag Georg Zwichenpflug, Dolomitenstr. 1, Postfach 301, 8400 Regensburg 1, W. Germany (B.R.D.)

331　　　　　EI
DOCUMENTATION EUROPEENNE - SERIE SYNDICALE ET OUVRIERE. (Editions also in German, Italian and Dutch) 1968. irreg. free. ‡ Commission of the European Communities, Direction Generale de la Presse et Information, Rue de la Loi 200, 1049 Brussels, Belgium (Dist. in U.S. by European Community Information Service, 2100 M St. N.W., Suite 707, Washington, DC 20037) circ. controlled.

331.1　　　　　US
E E O C COMPLIANCE MANUAL. 1975. irreg. $81. Bureau of National Affairs, Inc., 1231 25th St., N.W., Washington, DC 20037. Ed. Michael Levin-Epstein. (looseleaf format)

ECONOMIES ET SOCIETES. SERIE AB. ECONOMIE DU TRAVAIL. see BUSINESS AND ECONOMICS

331.1　　　　　PR　ISSN 0555-6635
EMPLEO Y DESEMPLEO EN PUERTO RICO/EMPLOYMENT AND UNEMPLOYMENT IN PUERTO RICO: CALENDAR YEARS. (Text in English and Spanish) 1967. free. Department of Labor, Hato Rey, PR 00917.

331.2　　　　　CN　ISSN 0701-1539
EMPLOYEE BENEFIT COSTS IN CANADA. 1953. biennial. Can.$90. Thorne Riddell Associates Ltd., Royal Trust Tower, Toronto Dominion Center, Box 260, Toronto, Ont. M5K 1J9, Canada. Ed. S. G. Ilk. circ. 500.
　Formerly: Fringe Benefit Costs in Canada (ISSN 0071-9625)

331.2　　　　　US　ISSN 0093-5735
ENGINEERING, SCIENTIFIC AND TECHNICAL SALARY SURVEY. irreg. Merchants and Manufacturers Association, 2300 Occidental Center, 1150 S. Olive St., Los Angeles, CA 90015. illus.

331　　　　　CN　ISSN 0709-5597
EXECUTIVE COMPENSATION SERVICE. PROFESSIONAL, SCIENTIFIC, TECHNICAL REMUNERATION, CANADA. 1978. a. Can.$225. Canadian Management Centres, 40 University Ave., Suite 1110, Toronto, Ont. M5J 1T1, Canada.

EXECUTIVE COMPENSATION SERVICE. REPORTS ON INTERNATIONAL COMPENSATION. BRAZIL. see BUSINESS AND ECONOMICS — Management

EXECUTIVE COMPENSATION SERVICE. TECHNICIAN REPORT. see BUSINESS AND ECONOMICS — Management

331.2　　　　　US
FEDERAL CIVILIAN WORK FORCE STATISTICS. PAY STRUCTURE OF THE FEDERAL CIVIL SERVICE. 1947. a. U.S. Office of Personnel Management, Agency Compliance and Evaluation, Work Force Analysis and Statistics Branch, Washington, DC 20415 (Subcr. to Supt. Docs., Govt. Printing Off., Washington, DC 20402) charts. stat. circ. 900(controlled) Indexed: C.I.S.Ind.
　Former titles: Federal Civilian Manpower Statistics. Pay Structure of the Federal Civil Service; Pay Structure of the Federal Civil Service.

331　　　　　US
FEDERAL CIVILIAN WORK FORCE STATISTICS. OCCUPATIONS OF FEDERAL WHITE-COLLAR WORKERS. 1951. a. ‡ U.S. Office of Personnel Management, Agency Compliance and Evaluation, Work Force Analysis and Statistics Branch, 1900 E St. N.W., Washington, DC 20415 (Subscr. to Supt. of Docs., Washington, DC 20402) circ. 1,000. (also avail. in microfilm) Indexed: C.I.S.Ind.
　Former titles: Occuaptions of Federal White-Collar Workers; Federal White-Collar Workers. Their Occupations and Salaries.

331.11　　　　　US
FEDERAL CIVILIAN WORK FORCE STATISTICS. EQUAL EMPLOYMENT OPPORTUNITY STATISTICS. 1965. a. price varies. ‡ U.S. Office of Personnel Management, Agency Compliance and Evaluation, Work Force Analysis and Statistics Branch, Washington, DC 20415 (Subscr. to Supt. of Docs., Govt. Printing Off., Washington, DC 20402) circ. 3,200. (also avail. in microfilm) Indexed: C.I.S.Ind.
　Former titles: Federal Civilian Workforce Statistics. Minority Group Employment in the Federal Government; Federal Civilian Manpower Statistics. Minority Group Employment in the Federal Government; Minority Group Employment in the Federal Government; Study of Minority Group Employment in the Federal Government.

331　　　　　FI　ISSN 0430-5280
FINLAND. TYOVIOMAMINISTERIO. TYOVOIMAKATSAUS/FINLAND. MINISTRY OF LABOUR. LABOUR REPORTS.* (Text in English or Finnish) irreg. Tyovoimaministerio, Suunnittelusasto - Ministry of Labour, Planning Division, Helsinki, Finland (Orders to: Valtion Painatuskeskus, Annakatu 44, 00100 Helsinki 10, Finland) illus.

331.11　　　　　FR
FRANCE. INSTITUT NATIONAL D'ETUDES DEMOGRAPHIQUES. CENTRE D'ETUDES DE L'EMPLOI. CAHIERS. 1972. irreg., no. 15, 1978. price varies. Institut National d'Etudes Demographiques, Centre d'Etudes de l'Emploi, 27 rue du Commandeur, 75675 Paris Cedex 14, France.

FRANCE. INSTITUT NATIONAL DE LA STATISTIQUE ET DES ETUDES ECONOMIQUES. COLLECTIONS. SERIE D, DEMOGRAPHIE ET EMPLOI. see POPULATION STUDIES

331 340　　　　　GW　ISSN 0071-9900
FUNDHEFT FUER ARBEITSRECHT. 1945. a. price varies. C. H. Beck'sche Verlagsbuchhandlung, Wilhelmstr. 9, 8000 Munich 40, W. Germany (B.R.D.) Ed. Wolfgang Blomeyer. circ. 1,500.

G.A.I.U. HANDBOOK OF WAGES, HOURS AND FRINGE BENEFITS. (Graphic Arts International Union) see PRINTING

331.1　　　　　UK　ISSN 0306-5413
GREAT BRITAIN. COMMISSION ON INDUSTRIAL RELATIONS. ANNUAL REPORT. (Subseries of its Report) 1972. a. price varies. Commission on Industrial Relations, GKN House, 22 Kingsway, London W.C.2, England (Avail. from H.M.S.O., c/o Liaison Officer, Atlantic House, Holborn Viaduct, London EC1P 1BN, England)

331.1　　　　　UK
GREAT BRITAIN. DEPARTMENT OF EMPLOYMENT. RESEARCH. 1972/73. a. £3. Dept. of Employment, 49 High Holborn, London WC1V 6HB, England (Avail. from H.M.S.O., c/o Liaison Officer, Atlantic House, Holborn Viaduct, London EC1P 1BN, England)

331.2　　　　　UK　ISSN 0308-1419
GREAT BRITAIN. DEPARTMENT OF EMPLOYMENT. NEW EARNINGS SURVEY. 1970. a. £40.02. Department of Employment, Information Section 3, 12 St. James's Sq., London SW1Y 4LL, England (Avail. from H.M.S.O., c/o Liaison Officer, Atlantic House, Holborn Viaduct, London EC1P 1BN, England)

331.11　　　　　UK　ISSN 0072-6532
GREAT BRITAIN. MANPOWER RESEARCH UNIT. MANPOWER STUDIES. 1964. irreg. price varies. H.M.S.O., P.O.B. 569, London SE1 9NH, England.

331.1　　　　　US　ISSN 0072-8853
GUIDEBOOK TO LABOR RELATIONS. a. $9.50. Commerce Clearing House, Inc., 4025 W. Peterson Ave., Chicago, IL 60646.

331　　　　　US
HANDBOOK OF LABOR FORCE DATA FOR SELECTED AREAS OF OKLAHOMA. 1966. a. Employment Security Commission, Research & Planning Division, 310 Will Rogers Bldg., Oklahoma City, OK 73105. Ed. Wayne Hugus. stat. circ. 300.

331.4　　　　　US　ISSN 0083-3622
HANDBOOK ON WOMEN WORKERS. (Subseries of Women's Bureau Bulletin) 1948. biennial. price varies. U.S. Department of Labor, Women's Bureau, 200 Constitution Ave. N.W., Washington, DC 20210 (Orders to: Supt. Doc., Washington, DC 20402)

331　　　　　US
HANDICAPPED REQUIREMENTS HANDBOOK. base vol. plus m.updates. $65. Federal Programs Advisory Service, 2120 L St. N.W., Suite 210, Washington, DC 20037.

331.11　　　　　US
HAWAII. DEPARTMENT OF LABOR AND INDUSTRIAL RELATIONS. SUB-AREA REVIEW. a. Department of Labor and Industrial Relations, Research and Statistics Office, 825 Mililani St., Honolulu, HI 96815.
　Former titles: Hawaii Labor Trends; Area Manpower Review Hawaii-Honolulu; Honolulu's Annual Area Manpower Review (ISSN 0441-7895)

BUSINESS AND ECONOMICS — LABOR AND INDUSTRIAL RELATIONS

331 II ISSN 0418-5633
I.A.M.R. REPORTS. (Text in English) 1963. irreg. price varies. Institute of Applied Manpower Research, Indrapastha Estate, Mahatma Gandhi Marg, New Delhi 110002, India. Ed. Bd.

331.1 US ISSN 0070-0177
I L R PAPERBACKS. 1967. irreg., no. 17, 1979. price varies. New York State School of Industrial and Labor Relations, Cornell University, Ithaca, NY 14853.

353.9 US ISSN 0362-3912
IDAHO. DEPARTMENT OF LABOR AND INDUSTRIAL SERVICES. ANNUAL REPORT. 1974. a. Department of Labor and Industrial Services, 317 Main St., Rm. 400, Boise, ID 83720. stat. Key Title: Annual Report of the Idaho Department of Labor and Industrial Services.

331 US ISSN 0085-1728
ILLINOIS LABOR HISTORY SOCIETY REPORTER. 1970. irreg., approx. 3/yr. $5. ‡ Illinois Labor History Society, 600 S. Michigan Ave., Chicago, IL 60605. Ed. Leslie F. Orear. circ. 2,500.

331 II
INDIA. MINISTRY OF LABOUR. ANNUAL REPORT. (Text in English) a. Ministry of Labour, New Delhi, India.
Supersedes (1974): India. Department of Labour and Employment. Annual Report (ISSN 0579-3238)

614.85 CN ISSN 0073-7313
INDUSTRIAL ACCIDENT PREVENTION ASSOCIATION. GUIDE TO SAFETY. 1965. a. Can.$0.50 ; free to member firms. Industrial Accident Prevention Association, 2 Bloor St. E., Toronto, Ont. M4W 3C2, Canada. circ. 50,000.

331.1 US ISSN 0019-7912
INDUSTRIAL AND LABOR RELATIONS FORUM. 1964. s-a. $5. New York State School of Industrial and Labor Relations, Cornell University, Ithaca, NY 14853. adv. bk. rev. bibl. charts. index. cum.index: vol. 1-8 (1964-1972. circ. 300. (also avail. in microform from UMI; back issues avail) Indexed: P.A.I.S. Work Rel.Abstr.

331 AT ISSN 0155-2589
INDUSTRIAL ARBITRATION REPORTS, NEW SOUTH WALES. 1900. irreg. Aus.$20. Department of Industrial Relations & Technology, 50 Philip St, Sydney, NSW 2000, Australia (Subscr. to: Government Printing Office, 390-422 Harris St., Ultimo, N.S.W. 2007, Australia) Ed. M.C.E. Coleman.

331 US
INDUSTRIAL RELATIONS CHRONOLOGIES. vol. 2, 1976. a. University of Massachusetts, Labor Relations and Research Center, Amherst, MA 01002.

331 US
INDUSTRIAL RELATIONS RESEARCH ASSOCIATION. PROCEEDINGS OF THE ANNUAL SPRING MEETING. a. membership. Industrial Relations Research Association, 7226 Social Science Bldg., University of Wisconsin, Madison, WI 53706.

331 US
INDUSTRIAL RELATIONS RESEARCH ASSOCIATION. PROCEEDINGS OF THE ANNUAL WINTER MEETING. a. membership. Industrial Relations Research Association, 7226 Social Science Bldg., University of Wisconsin, Madison, WI 53706.

331.1 CN ISSN 0073-7593
INDUSTRIAL RELATIONS RESEARCH IN CANADA. (Text in English and French) 1969. a. free. Labour Canada, Ottawa, Ont. K1A 0J2, Canada. circ. 1,500. (reprint service avail. from MML)
Formerly: Canada. Department of Labor. Labour and Industrial Relations Research in Canada. Progress Report.

331.2 ZR
INSTITUT NATIONAL DE PREPARATION PROFESSIONNELLE. CAHIER.* irreg. 1. Institut National de Preparation Professionnelle, B. P. 7248, Kinshasa 1, Zaire. illus.

331.1 US ISSN 0073-9421
INSTITUTE OF LABOR AND INDUSTRIAL RELATIONS. POLICY PAPERS IN HUMAN RESOURCES AND INDUSTRIAL RELATIONS. 1967. irreg., no. 23, 1975. price varies. ‡ Institute of Labor and Industrial Relations, 401 Fourth St., Ann Arbor, MI 48103. (Co-Sponsors: University of Michigan; Wayne State University) Ed. Louis A. Ferman. (reprint service avail. from UMI)

331 US ISSN 0073-943X
INSTITUTE OF LABOR AND INDUSTRIAL RELATIONS. REPRINT SERIES. 1957. irreg., no. 65, 1975. free. ‡ Institute of Labor and Industrial Relations, 401 Fourth St., Ann Arbor, MI 48103. (Co-Sponsors: University of Michigan; Wayne State University) Eds. Charles M. Rehmus, Ronald W. Haughton. (reprint service avail. from UMI)

331 CN
INTERNATIONAL CONFERENCE ON TRENDS IN INDUSTRIAL AND LABOUR RELATIONS. no. 2, 1976. irreg. McGill University, Industrial Relations Centre, Montreal, Que. H3A 1G5, Canada. Ed. Prof. Frances Bairstow.

331 UN
INTERNATIONAL INSTITUTE FOR LABOUR STUDIES. PUBLIC LECTURE SERIES. 1975. irreg. 5 Fr. International Institute for Labour Studies, C.P. 6, CH-1211 Geneva 22, Switzerland.

331 UK ISSN 0074-6509
INTERNATIONAL INSTITUTE FOR LABOUR STUDIES. PUBLICATIONS. 1966. irreg. (UN) Macmillan Press Ltd. (Subsidiary of: Macmillan Publishers Ltd.) Little Essex St., London WC2R 3LF, England.

331 UN
INTERNATIONAL INSTITUTE FOR LABOUR STUDIES. RESEARCH SERIES. 1976. irreg. price varies. International Institute for Labour Studies, C.P.6, CH-1211 Geneva 22, Switzerland.

331 UN ISSN 0074-6673
INTERNATIONAL LABOUR CONFERENCE. REPORTS TO THE CONFERENCE AND RECORD OF PROCEEDINGS. (Editions in English, French, Spanish, German and Russian) 1919. a. 265 Fr.($132.50) covering 14 to 18 vols. per conference. International Labour Office - Bureau International du Travail, Publications Sales Service, CH-1211 Geneva 22, Switzerland (Dist. in U.S. by: I L O Branch Office, 1750 New York Ave., N.W., Washington, DC 20006) (back vols. avail in microform)

INTERNATIONAL LABOUR LAW REPORTS. see *LAW*

331.1 US ISSN 0149-449X
IOWA. DEPARTMENT OF JOB SERVICE. ANNUAL REPORT. 1938. a. contr.free circ. Department of Job Service, 1000 East Grand Avenue, Des Moines, IA 50319. Ed. Walt Crede. circ. 2,000.
Formerly: Iowa. Employment Security Commission. Annual Report.

331.1 US ISSN 0091-262X
IOWA. DEPARTMENT OF JOB SERVICE. RESEARCH AND STATISTICS DIVISION. ANNUAL MANPOWER PLANNING REPORT. 1969. a. contr.free circ. Department of Job Service, 1000 East Grand Ave., Des Moines, IA 50319. Ed. Clay Seaton. stat. Key Title: Annual Iowa Manpower Planning Report.

331 JA
JAPAN INSTITUTE OF LABOUR. PROCEEDINGS. (Text in English) 1965. biennial. price varies. Japan Institute of Labour - Nihon Rodo Kyokai, Chutaikin Bldg, 7-6 Shibakoen 1-chome, Minato-ku, Tokyo 105, Japan. circ. 600.

331.2 US
JOINT GOVERNMENTAL SALARY SURVEY : ARIZONA. 1975. a. free. ‡ Department of Administration, Personnel Division, 1831 West Jefferson, Phoenix, AZ 85007. charts. stat. circ. controlled. (tabloid format)
Supersedes: Survey of Salaries and Employee Benefits of Private and Public Employers in Arizona. (ISSN 0091-5599)

331 US ISSN 0078-4192
KENT STATE UNIVERSITY. CENTER FOR BUSINESS AND ECONOMIC RESEARCH. LABOR AND INDUSTRIAL RELATIONS SERIES. 1968. irreg., no. 3, 1975. price varies. Kent State University, Center for Business and Economic Research, Kent, OH 44242. circ. 500.

331 KO ISSN 0454-7543
KOREA (REPUBLIC) ECONOMIC PLANNING BOARD. ANNUAL REPORT ON THE ECONOMICALLY ACTIVE POPULATION. (Text in Korean & English) 1963. a. 870 Won. Bureau of Statistics, Economic Planning Board, Gyeongun-Dung, Jongro-Gu, Seoul, S. Korea. Ed. Heung-Koo Kang. circ. 1,000.

331 US
LABOR FORCE IN IDAHO. a. free. Department of Employment, Bureau of Research and Analysis, Box 35, Boise, ID 83735. stat.

331.1 US ISSN 0362-3793
LABOR FORCE STATUS OF INDIANA RESIDENTS. a. Employment Security Division, Indianapolis, IN 46204.

LABOR RATES FOR THE CONSTRUCTION INDUSTRY. see *BUILDING AND CONSTRUCTION*

331.1 US ISSN 0075-7489
LABOR RELATIONS YEARBOOK. 1966. a. $18. Bureau of National Affairs, Inc., 1231 25th St., N.W., Washington, DC 20037.

331 CN ISSN 0700-3862
LABOUR/TRAVAILLEUR; journal of Canadian labour studies/revue d'etudes ouvrieres Canadiennes. (Text in English and French) 1976. s-a. Can.$10. Committee on Canadian Labour History, Department of History, Dalhousie University, Halifax, N.S., Canada. Ed. Gregory S. Kealey. adv. bk. rev. bibl. circ. 850. (also avail. in microfilm from MML; back issues avail.) Indexed: Hist.Abstr. Alt.Press Ind. Amer.Hist & Life.

331.88 CN ISSN 0706-8441
LABOUR HISTORY. 1977. irreg. membership. (Provincial Specialists Association) B. C. Teachers' Federation, 2235 Burrard St., Vancouver, B.C. V6J 3H9, Canada. illus.

331 II
LABOUR IN THE PUBLIC SECTOR UNDERTAKINGS: BASIC INFORMATION. 1968. irreg. price varies. Ministry of Labour, Implementation and Evaluation Division, New Delhi, India (Order from: Controller of Publications, Government of India, Civil Lines, Delhi 110054, India) stat.

331 340 PK
LABOUR LAW CASES. (Text in English) 1947. a. Rs.100. Bureau of Labour Publications, Zam Zam Chambers, Dunolly Rd., P.O. Box 5833, Karachi-2, Pakistan. Ed. M. Shafi. abstr. (back issues avail.)

331 CN ISSN 0075-7586
LABOUR STANDARDS IN CANADA. NORMES DU TRAVAIL AU CANADA. (Text in English and French) 1951. a. Can.$6.25($7.50) Labour Canada, Ottawa, Ont., Canada. circ. 1,500. (reprint service avail. from MML)

331 UK ISSN 0306-0837
LLAFUR. 1972. a. membership. Society for the Study of Welsh Labour History, c/o Deian Hopkin, Editor, Department of History, University College, Aberystwyth, Wales. circ. 1,500. (back issues avail.) Indexed: Hist.Abstr.

331 LU
LUXEMBOURG. ADMINISTRATION DE L'EMPLOI. RAPPORT ANNUEL. a. free. Administration de l'Emploi, 32, Ave. de la Porte-Neuve, B. P. 23, Luxembourg, Luxembourg.
Formerly: Luxembourg. Office National du Travail. Rapport Annuel (ISSN 0076-1567)

331 669 AT ISSN 0085-3321
M. T. I. A. ANNUAL REPORT. a. Aus.$5. Metal Trades Industry Association of Australia, 105 Walker Street, North Sydney, N.S.W. 2060, Australia. Ed. L.R. Davies.

BUSINESS AND ECONOMICS — LABOR AND INDUSTRIAL RELATIONS

331.1   CN   ISSN 0076-194X
MCGILL UNIVERSITY, MONTREAL.
INDUSTRIAL RELATIONS CENTRE. ANNUAL
CONFERENCE PROCEEDINGS. no. 12, 1976. a.
price varies. McGill University, Industrial Relations
Centre, 1001 Sherbrooke St. W., Montreal 110 P.Q.,
Canada.

331.11   US   ISSN 0093-7886
MAINE. BUREAU OF LABOR AND INDUSTRY.
OCCUPATIONAL WAGE SURVEY. a. Bureau of
Labor and Industry, Department of Commerce and
Industry, State Office Building, Augusta, ME 04330.
stat. Indexed: Vert.File Ind.

350.1   CN   ISSN 0706-3792
MANITOBA. MUNICIPAL EMPLOYEES
BENEFITS BOARD. ANNUAL REPORT. 1977.
a. Municipal Employees Benefits Board, 200-400
Tache Ave, Winnipeg, Man. R2H 3C3, Canada.

331.1   CN   ISSN 0076-3853
MANITOBA LABOUR-MANAGEMENT REVIEW
COMMITTEE. ANNUAL REPORT. 1965. a. free.
Department of Labour, Room 608, Norquay Bldg.,
Winnipeg, Man. R3C 0V8, Canada. Ed. H. D.
Woods.

MASSACHUSETTS. DIVISION OF
EMPLOYMENT SECURITY. SURVEY OF
UNFILLED JOB OPENINGS - BOSTON. see
OCCUPATIONS AND CAREERS

331   US   ISSN 0076-4930
MASSACHUSETTS. DIVISION OF
EMPLOYMENT SECURITY. ANNUAL
PLANNING REPORT. a. Division of Employment
Security, Labor Area Research Department, Charles
F. Hurley Bldg., Government Center, Boston, MA
02114.

331   US   ISSN 0076-4922
MASSACHUSETTS. DIVISION OF
EMPLOYMENT SECURITY. EMPLOYMENT
AND WAGES IN ESTABLISHMENTS SUBJECT
TO THE MASSACHUSETTS EMPLOYMENT
SECURITY LAW. STATE SUMMARY. 1970. a.
free. Division of Employment Security, Charles F.
Hurley Bldg., Government Center, Boston, MA
02114.

331   US   ISSN 0076-4949
MASSACHUSETTS. DIVISION OF
EMPLOYMENT SECURITY. STATISTICAL
DIGEST. (Supplements its Annual Report) 1968. a.
free. Division of Employment Security, Charles F.
Hurley Bldg., Government Center, Boston, MA
02114. Ed. Catharine M. Carney. circ. 1,000.

331   MX   ISSN 0302-4822
MEXICO. COMISON NACIONAL DE LOS
SALARIOS MINIMOS. INFORME DE
LABORES. a. Comision Nacional de los Salarios
Minimos, Mexico, Mexico. stat.

331.1   US   ISSN 0090-8401
MICHIGAN. EMPLOYMENT SECURITY
COMMISSION. ANNUAL PLANNING
REPORT. 1972. a. free. Employment Security
Commission, 7310 Woodward Avenue, Detroit, MI
48202. illus. stat. circ. 500. Key Title: Annual
Manpower Planning Report. Detroit Labor Market
Area.
    Formerly: Michigan. Employment Security
Commission. Labor Market Analysis Section.
Annual Manpower Planning Report: Detroit Labor
Market Area (ISSN 0090-8401)

331   US   ISSN 0076-7999
MICHIGAN INTERNATIONAL LABOR STUDIES.
1968. irreg., vol. 5, 1972. University of Michigan,
Graduate School of Business Administration,
Division of Research, Tappan and Monroe Sts., Ann
Arbor, MI 48109. (reprint service avail. from UMI)

353.9   US   ISSN 0092-9212
MICHIGAN STATE EMPLOYEES' RETIREMENT
SYSTEM FINANCIAL AND STATISTICAL
REPORT. 1953. a. free. ‡ Department of
Management and Budget, Stevens T. Mason
Building, 2Nd Floor, West Wing, Lansing, MI
48913. stat. Key Title: Michigan State Employees'
Retirement System.

MICHIGAN STATE UNIVERSITY. CENTER FOR
RURAL MANPOWER & PUBLIC AFFAIRS.
REPORT. see *AGRICULTURE — Agricultural
Economics*

331   US
MINNESOTA. DEPARTMENT OF ECONOMIC
SECURITY. ANNUAL REPORT. 1936. a. free.
Department of Economic Security, 390 N. Robert
St., St. Paul, MN 55101. Ed. Richard A. Williams.
circ. 3,500.
    Former titles (until 1979): Minnesota.
Department of Employment Services. Annual
Report (ISSN 0364-717X); (1969-1974): Minnesota.
Department of Manpower Services. Annual Report
(ISSN 0076-9126); Before 1969: Minnesota.
Department of Employment Security. Annual
Report.

331.2   US   ISSN 0092-5950
N M R I COMPENSATION IN MASS
RETAILING, SALARIES AND INCENTIVES.
1972. biennial. $60 to non-members; members $40.
‡ National Mass Retailing Institute, 570 Seventh
Avenue, New York, NY 10018. illus.
    Formerly: M R I Compensation in Mass
Retailing, Salaries and Incentives.

331.2   US
NEVADA WAGE SURVEY. Variant title: Nevada
Statewide Wage Survey. 1973. a. Employment
Security Department, 500 E. Third St., Carson City,
NV 89713. circ. 2,500.
    Formerly: State of Nevada Wage Report (ISSN
0081-4563)

331   CN   ISSN 0077-8052
NEW BRUNSWICK. DEPARTMENT OF LABOUR
AND MANPOWER. ANNUAL REPORT. (Text
in English and French) 1944. a. free. Department of
Labour and Manpower, Fredericton, New
Brunswick, Canada. Ed. Linda Fallon. circ. 400.
    Formerly: New Brunswick. Department of
Labour. Annual Report (ISSN 0077-8052)

331.7   US   ISSN 0094-7687
NEW HAMPSHIRE ANNUAL RURAL
MANPOWER REPORT. a. free. Department of
Employment Security, 32 South Main St., Concord,
NH 03301. stat.

331.1   US   ISSN 0095-1102
NEW HAMPSHIRE OCCUPATIONAL OUTLOOK.
irreg. Department of Employment Security,
Concord, NH 03301.

331   US   ISSN 0092-1459
NEW JERSEY COVERED EMPLOYMENT
TRENDS BY GEOGRAPHICAL AREAS OF
THE STATE. 1944. a. free. ‡ Department of Labor
and Industry, Division of Planning and Research,
Office of Labor Statistics, P.O. Box 359, Trenton,
NJ 08625. circ. 1,100.

331   US   ISSN 0077-8508
NEW JERSEY PUBLIC EMPLOYER-EMPLOYEE
RELATIONS. 1970. irreg., no. 29, 1977. free. ‡
Rutgers University, Institute of Management and
Labor Relations, New Brunswick, NJ 08903. circ.
1,500.

331   US
NEW YORK (CITY). OFFICE OF LABOR
RELATIONS. INTERPRETIVE
MEMORANDUM. vol. 22, 1976. irreg. Office of
Labor Relations, 250 Broadway, New York, NY
10007.

331.1   US   ISSN 0093-5034
NEW YORK (STATE) DEPARTMENT OF LABOR.
DIVISION OF RESEARCH AND STATISTICS.
LABOR RESEARCH REPORT. irreg. Department
of Labor, Division of Research and Statistics, Two
World Trade Center, Rm. 6804, New York, NY
10047 (Dist. by: Office of Public Information, State
Campus, Albany, N.Y. 12240) stat. Key Title: Labor
Research Report (Albany)
    Continues: New York (State) Division of
Employment. Research and Statistics Office.
Research Bulletin.

331   US   ISSN 0070-0134
NEW YORK STATE SCHOOL OF INDUSTRIAL
AND LABOR RELATIONS. BULLETIN.
(Supersedes Its Extension Bulletin and Research
Bulletin) 1951. irreg.; no. 65, 1976. price varies.
New York State School of Industrial and Labor
Relations, Cornell University, Ithaca, NY 14853.

331   US
NEW YORK STATE SCHOOL OF INDUSTRIAL
AND LABOR RELATIONS. INSTITUTE OF
PUBLIC EMPLOYMENT. MONOGRAPH. 1973.
irreg.; no. 9, 1978. price varies. New York State
School of Industrial and Labor Relations, Institute
of Public Employment, Cornell University, Box
1000, Ithaca, NY 14853.

331   US
NEW YORK STATE SCHOOL OF INDUSTRIAL
AND LABOR RELATIONS. INSTITUTE OF
PUBLIC EMPLOYMENT. OCCASIONAL
PAPERS. 1973. irreg., no. 13, 1977. $1.50 per no.
New York State School of Industrial and Labor
Relations, Institute of Public Employment, Box
1000, Cornell University, Ithaca, NY 14853.

331   US   ISSN 0070-0185
NEW YORK STATE SCHOOL OF INDUSTRIAL
AND LABOR RELATIONS. KEY ISSUES
SERIES. 1967. irreg.; no. 24, 1979. price varies.
New York State School of Industrial and Labor
Relations, Cornell University, Ithaca, NY 14853.
Ed. Jozetta H. Srb.

331 319   NZ   ISSN 0110-5027
NEW ZEALAND. DEPARTMENT OF
STATISTICS. PART B: WAGES AND LABOUR.
a. NZ.$1.85. Department of Statistics, Private Bag,
Wellington, New Zealand (Subscr. to: Government
Printing Office, Publications, Private Bag,
Wellington, New Zealand)
    Supersedes in part: New Zealand. Department of
Statistics. Prices, Wages and Labour.

331.11   NR
NIGERIA. NATIONAL MANPOWER BOARD.
MANPOWER STUDIES. 1963. irreg (1-2/yr) price
varies. National Manpower Board, 5 Oil Mills St.,
Lagos, Nigeria. stat. circ. 500.

331   JA
NIHON NO ROSHI KANKEI. 1973. a. 3000 Yen.
Japan Institute of Labour - Nihon Rodo Kyokai,
Chutaikin Bldg., 1-7-6 Shibakoen, Minato-ku,
Tokyo, Japan.
    Continues: Nempo Nihon no Roshi Kankei.

331.11   US   ISSN 0078-155X
NORTH DAKOTA. EMPLOYMENT SECURITY
BUREAU. ANNUAL REPORT. 1937. a. free.
Employment Security Bureau, Box 1537, 1000 E.
Divide Ave., Bismarck, ND 58505. Ed. Tom
Pederson. circ. 200.

331.11   US   ISSN 0078-1568
NORTH DAKOTA. EMPLOYMENT SECURITY
BUREAU. BIENNIAL REPORT TO THE
GOVERNOR. 1964. biennial. free. Employment
Security Bureau, Box 1537, 1000 E. Divide Ave.,
Bismarck, ND 58505. Ed. Tom Pederson. circ. 75.

331.868   US   ISSN 0078-169X
NORTHEASTERN UNIVERSITY STUDIES IN
REHABILITATION. irreg., 1970, no. 10. $10. D.C.
Heath & Company, 125 Spring St., Lexington, MA
02173. Indexed: Psychol.Abstr.

331   NO   ISSN 0078-1835
NORWAY. ARBEIDSDIREKTORATET.
AARSMELDING. (Text in Norwegian, summary in
English) a. Arbeidsdirektoratet, Postboks 8127, Oslo
1, Norway.

331.1 340   PR   ISSN 0029-4195
NOTICIAS DEL TRABAJO. vol.31, 1970. irreg. free.
‡ Department of Labor, Bureau of Labor Statistics,
Avenida Barbosa 414, Hato Rey, PR 00917. charts.
stat. circ. 15,000.

331.2   CN   ISSN 0380-5689
NOVA SCOTIA. DEPARTMENT OF LABOUR.
ANNUAL REPORT. 1935. a. Department of
Labour, Box 697, Halifax, N.S., Canada.

331.2   CN   ISSN 0550-1741
NOVA SCOTIA. DEPARTMENT OF LABOUR.
ECONOMICS AND RESEARCH DIVISION.
WAGE RATES, SALARIES AND HOURS OF
LABOUR IN NOVA SCOTIA. 1967. a. free.
Department of Labour, Economics and Research
Division, P.O. Box 697, Halifax, Nova Scotia,
Canada. charts. (processed)

BUSINESS AND ECONOMICS — LABOR AND INDUSTRIAL RELATIONS

331   CN   ISSN 0550-9955
NOVA SCOTIA LABOUR-MANAGEMENT STUDY CONFERENCE. PROCEEDINGS. no. 12, 1976. irreg. Can.$3. Dalhousie University, Institute of Public Affairs, Halifax, N.S. B3H 3J5, Canada.

331   NZ   ISSN 0078-3064
OCCASIONAL PAPERS IN INDUSTRIAL RELATIONS. 1966. irreg. price varies. Victoria University of Wellington, Industrial Relations Centre, Private Bag, Wellington, New Zealand.

331   US
OKLAHOMA. EMPLOYMENT SECURITY COMMISSION. RESEARCH AND PLANNING DIVISION. ANNUAL REPORT TO THE GOVERNOR. 1939. a. free. ‡ Employment Security Commission, Research and Planning Division, 310 Will Rogers Bldg., Oklahoma City, OK 73105. Ed. Wesley Wilson. charts. stat. circ. 600.

331.4   BE   ISSN 0078-5164
OPEN DOOR INTERNATIONAL FOR THE EMANCIPATION OF THE WOMAN WORKER. REPORT OF CONGRESS. 1929. irreg., 1966, 13th. London. free. ‡ Open Door International, 16 rue Americain, B-1050 Brussels, Belgium. Ed. Adele Hauwel.

ORGANIZATION FOR ECONOMIC COOPERATION AND DEVELOPMENT. SOCIAL AFFAIRS DIVISION. DEVELOPING JOB OPPORTUNITIES. see OCCUPATIONS AND CAREERS

331.11   FR
ORGANIZATION FOR ECONOMIC COOPERATION AND DEVELOPMENT. DEVELOPMENT CENTRE. EMPLOYMENT SERIES. (Editions in English and French) 1971. irreg. Organization for Economic Cooperation and Development, 2 rue Andre-Pascal, 75775 Paris 16, France (U.S. orders to: O.E.C.D. Publications and Information Center, 1750 Pennsylvania Ave., N. W., Washington, D. C. 20006) (also avail. in microfiche)

331.11   FR   ISSN 0474-5337
ORGANIZATION FOR ECONOMIC COOPERATION AND DEVELOPMENT. EMPLOYMENT OF SPECIAL GROUPS. 1965. irreg. Organization for Economic Cooperation and Development, 2 rue Andre Pascal, 75775 Paris 16, France (U. S. orders to: O.E.C.D. Publications and Information Center, 1750 Pennsylvania Ave., N. W., Washington, D. C. 20006) (also avail. in microfiche)

331.11   FR   ISSN 0473-6788
ORGANIZATION FOR ECONOMIC COOPERATION AND DEVELOPMENT. REVIEWS OF MANPOWER AND SOCIAL POLICIES. 1963. irreg. Organization for Economic Cooperation and Development, 2 rue Andre Pascal, 75775 Paris 16, France (U. S. orders to: O.E.C.D. Publications and Information Center, 1750 Pennsylvania Ave., N. W., Washington, D. C. 20006) (also avail. in microfiche)

331.11   FR   ISSN 0474-5922
ORGANIZATION FOR ECONOMIC COOPERATION AND DEVELOPMENT. SOCIAL AFFAIRS DIVISION. EMPLOYMENT OF SPECIAL GROUPS. 1965. irreg. Organization for Economic Cooperation and Development, 2, rue Andre Pascal, 75775 Paris 16, France (U.S. orders to: O.E.C.D. Publications and Information Center, 1750 Pennsylvania Ave., N.W., Washington, DC 20006) (also avail. in microfiche)

331   FR
PARTICIPATION. (Supplement to France.Ministere du Travail. Bulletin Mensuel des Statistiques du Travail) irreg. Ministere du Travail, 127 rue de Grenelle, 75700 Paris, France.

331   US
PENNSYLVANIA. LABOR RELATIONS BOARD. REPORT. 1937. a. free. Department of Labor and Industry, 1617 Labor & Industry Bldg., 7Th & Forster Sts., Harrisburg, PA 17120. Ed. Robert E. Trump, Jr. charts. stat.

331.11   PO
PORTUGAL. MINISTERIO DO TRABALHO. SERVICO DE INFORMACAO CIENTIFICA E TECNICA. BOLETIM DO TRABALHO E EMPREGO. irreg. Esc.600. Ministerio do Trabalho, Servico de Informacao Cientifica e Tecnica, Praca de Londres 2, Lisbon, Portugal.

331   CN   ISSN 0085-512X
PRINCE EDWARD ISLAND. DEPARTMENT OF LABOUR. ANNUAL REPORT. 1967. a. free. ‡ Department of Labour, Box 2000, Charlottetown, P.E.I. C1A 7N8, Canada.

331.1   US   ISSN 0079-5305
PRINCETON UNIVERSITY. INDUSTRIAL RELATIONS SECTION. RESEARCH REPORT. 1926(as Report series) irreg., 1969, no. 113. price varies. ‡ Princeton University, Industrial Relations Section, Box 248, Princeton, NJ 08540. circ. 1,000.

331.11   US   ISSN 0079-8134
PURDUE UNIVERSITY. OFFICE OF MANPOWER STUDIES. MANPOWER REPORT. 1965. irreg. $2.50. Purdue University, Office of Manpower Studies, West Lafayette, IN 47907. Ed. J. P. Lisack.

331.1   CN   ISSN 0317-2546
QUEEN'S UNIVERSITY. INDUSTRIAL RELATIONS CENTRE. RESEARCH AND CURRENT ISSUES SERIES. 1964. irreg., no. 40, 1981. price varies. ‡ Queen's University, Industrial Relations Centre, Kingston, Ont. K7L 3N6, Canada. circ. 500-1,500.
Formerly: Queen's University. Industrial Relations Centre. Research Series (ISSN 0075-6164)

331.1   CN   ISSN 0075-6148
QUEEN'S UNIVERSITY AT KINGSTON. INDUSTRIAL RELATIONS CENTRE. REPORT OF ACTIVITIES. a. free. ‡ Queen's University, Industrial Relations Centre, Kingston, Ont. K7L 3N6, Canada.

331.1   CN   ISSN 0075-6156
QUEEN'S UNIVERSITY AT KINGSTON. INDUSTRIAL RELATIONS CENTRE. REPRINT SERIES. 1961. irreg., no. 48, 1980. price varies. ‡ Queen's University, Industrial Relations Centre, Kingston, Ont. K7L 3N6, Canada.

331.86   UK
RECRUITMENT AND TRAINING SERVICES HANDBOOK. irreg. $50. Kemp's Group(Printers & Publishers) Ltd., 1-5 Bath St., London EC1V 9QA, England. adv.

331   US
RESEARCH IN LABOR ECONOMICS. 1977. a. $18.75 to individuals; institutions $37.50. J A I Press, Box 1678, 165 W. Putnam Ave., Greenwich, CT 06830. Ed. Ronald G. Ehrenberg.

331.2   CN   ISSN 0080-1860
RETAIL WAGES AND SALARIES IN CANADA. a. Can.$3.50. Retail Council of Canada, 74 Victoria St., Toronto, Ont. M5C 2A5, Canada.

331   361.3   HT   ISSN 0482-8062
REVUE DU TRAVAIL. 1951. a. Departement du Travail et du Bien-Etre Social, Port-au-Prince, Haiti. stat.

331.1   CN   ISSN 0706-4926
SASKATCHEWAN. DEPARTMENT OF LABOUR. WAGES AND WORKING CONDITIONS BY OCCUPATION. 1974. a. Department of Labour, Policy Planning and Research Division, 1914 Hamilton St., Regina, Sask. S4P 4V4, Canada.

331.1   CN   ISSN 0317-7335
SASKATCHEWAN LABOUR REPORT. 1950. m. free. Department of Labour, Policy Planning and Research Division, 1914 Hamilton St., Regina, Sask. S4P 4V4, Canada. stat. circ. 8,000.

331   CN   ISSN 0702-9888
SELECTED LABOUR STATISTICS FOR NOVA SCOTIA. a. free. Department of Labour and Manpower, Research Division, Box 697, Halifax, N. S. B3J 2T8, Canada.

331.11   338   PE
SERIE PRAXIS. 1973. irreg. $5. Centro de Estudios y Promocion del Desarrollo (DESCO), Av. Salaverry 1945, Lima 14, Peru. circ. 3,000.

331.1   US   ISSN 0080-8997
SERIES ON COMPANY APPROACHES TO INDUSTRIAL RELATIONS. 1962. irreg., no. 5, 1969. $2 per no. ‡ Machinery and Allied Products Institute, 1200 18 St. N.W., Washington, DC 20036. (Co-Sponsor: Council for Technological Advancement) Ed. Richard R. MacNabb.

331   SI
SINGAPORE. MINISTRY OF LABOUR. ANNUAL REPORT. (Text in English) 1946. a. price varies. Ministry of Labour, Havelock Rd., Singapore 1, Singapore. charts. stat.

SINGAPORE. MINISTRY OF SCIENCE AND TECHNOLOGY. NATIONAL SURVEY OF SCIENTIFIC MANPOWER. see SCIENCES: COMPREHENSIVE WORKS

SOUTH AFRICA. UNEMPLOYMENT INSURANCE FUND. REPORT/SOUTH AFRICA. WERKLOOSHEIDVERSEKERINGSFONDS. VERSLAG. see INSURANCE

331.096   SA
SOUTH AFRICAN LABOUR BULLETIN. 1974. irreg (8-10/yr.) R.10 individuals; R. 20 institutions. Institute for Industrial Education, Box 18109, Dalbridge, Durban, South Africa. Ed. J. R. Mawbey. bk. rev. circ. 500.

331   AT   ISSN 0311-0702
SOUTH AUSTRALIA. DEPARTMENT OF LABOUR AND INDUSTRY. GUIDE TO LEGISLATION. 1972. irreg. free. Department of Labour and Industry, G.P.O. Box 297 A, Adelaide, SA 5001, Australia.

310   331   US
SOUTH CAROLINA. DEPARTMENT OF LABOR. ANNUAL REPORT. 1936. a. free. Department of Labor, Box 11329, 3600 Forest Dr., Columbia, SC 29211. Ed. George R. Burnett.

331.1   US   ISSN 0095-4799
SOUTH CAROLINA'S MANPOWER IN INDUSTRY; labor force estimates and nonagricultural wage and salary employment by major industry division and selected industry groups; annual averages. 1973. Employment Security Commission, Research and Statistics Section, Columbia, SC 29201.

331   US
SOUTH DAKOTA. DEPARTMENT OF LABOR. ANNUAL PLANNING REPORT SOUTH DAKOTA. a. free. Department of Labor, Office of Administrative Services, Box 1730, Aberdeen, SD 57401. stat.

331.1   US
SOUTH DAKOTA. DEPARTMENT OF LABOR. OFFICE OF ADMINISTRATIVE SERVICES. ANNUAL REPORT VOCATIONAL EDUCATION REPORT. a. free. Department of Labor, Office of Administrative Services, Research and Statistics, Box 1730, Aberdeen, SD 57401. stat.

STAT A PRAVO. see LAW

331.1   US   ISSN 0095-6430
STATE OF FLORIDA COMPREHENSIVE MANPOWER PLAN. irreg. State Manpower Planning Council, Caldwell Bldg., Tallahassee, FL 32304.

331.8   US
STATISTICS ON WORK STOPPAGES, NEW YORK STATE. (Subseries of: Labor Research Report) 1946. a. free. Department of Labor, Division of Research and Statistics, Two World Trade Center, Rm. 6804, New York, NY 10047.

331.8   CN   ISSN 0081-5985
STRIKES AND LOCKOUTS IN CANADA/ GREVES ET LOCK-OUT AU CANADA. (Text in English and French) 1913. a. Can.$4($4.80) Labour Canada, Ottawa, Ont. K1A 0J2, Canada. circ. 1,700. (reprint service avail. from MML)

371.42   331   US
STUDIES IN HUMAN RESOURCES DEVELOPMENT. 1974. irreg. price varies. University of Texas at Austin, Bureau of Business Research, Center for the Study of Human Resources, Austin, TX 78712. Ed. Bd. bibl.

331 UK
STUDIES IN LABOR AND SOCIAL LAW. 1977. irreg. price varies. Mansell Publishing, 3 Bloomsbury Place, London WC1A 2QA, England (Dist. in U.S. by: Mansell, Merrimack Book Service, 99 Main St., Salem, NH 03079) Eds. B. A. Hepple, Paul O'Higgins.

331 UK
STUDIES IN LABOUR HISTORY. 1976. a. £8($20) to libraries;£3($8) to individuals. John L. Noyce, Ed. & Pub., P.O. Box 450, Brighton, Sussex BN1 8GR, England. bk. rev. bibl. circ. 500-1,000.
History

331.63 US ISSN 0081-878X
STUDIES OF NEGRO EMPLOYMENT. (Subseries of: Wharton. School of Finance and Commerce. Industrial Research Unit. Industrial Research Unit Studies) 1970. irreg. price varies. University of Pennsylvania Wharton School of Finance and Commerce, Industrial Research Unit, Philadelphia, PA 19104. adv. (also avail. in microfilm)

331 US ISSN 0190-1133
SURVEY OF RETIREMENT, THRIFT AND PROFIT SHARING PLANS COVERING SALARIED EMPLOYEES OF THE 50 LARGEST U. S. INDUSTRIAL COMPANIES. a. Wyatt Co., 65 William St., Boston (Wellesley Hills), MA 02181.

331.2 SQ
SWAZILAND. CENTRAL STATISTICAL OFFICE. EMPLOYMENT AND WAGES. 1969. a. Central Statistical Office, Box 456, Mbabane, Swaziland.

331.116 SW
SWEDEN. STATENS ARBETSGIVARVERK. ARBETSGIVARVERKET INFORMERAR. 1965. irreg. (4-6/yr.) free. Statens Arbetsgivarverk - National Swedish Agency for Government Employers, Fack, 103 10 Stockholm, Sweden. Ed. Bertil Drougge.
Former titles (until 1979): Sweden. Statens Avtalsverk. Information Fraan S A V (ISSN 0036-0996); Sweden. Statens Avtalsverk. Aktuellt.

331 US
TENNESSEE ANNUAL AVERAGE LABOR FORCE ESTIMATES. 1970. a. free. Department of Employment Security, Research and Statistics Section, 519 Cordell Hull Building, Nashville, TN 37219. stat. circ. controlled.
Formed by the merger of: Tennessee Civilian Work Force Estimates (ISSN 0085-7165) & Tennessee Annual Average Work Force Estimates.

331 US
TENNESSEE LABOR MARKET INFORMATION DIRECTORY. a. Department of Employment Security, Research & Statistics Section, 519 Cordell Hull Bldg., Nashville, TN 37219.

331 TH
THAILAND STANDARD INDUSTRIAL CLASSIFICATION. (Text in English and Thai) 1972. irreg. Department of Labour, Bangkok, Thailand.

331 SW ISSN 0082-4542
TJAENSTEMAENNENS CENTRALORGANISATION. AARET. a. Tjaenstemaennens Centralorganisation - Swedish Central Organization of Salaried Employees, Linnegatan 14, Box 5252, 102 45 Stockholm, Sweden.

331.2 US
TOP EXECUTIVE COMPENSATION. (Subseries of: Conference Board. Report) 1960. biennial. $45 to non-members; members $15. Conference Board, Inc., 845 Third Ave., New York, NY 10022. illus. stat.

331 CK
TRABAJO. 1950. irreg. Ministerio del Trabajo, Oficina No. 42, Bogota, Colombia. Ed. I. Reyes Rosada.

658.31 US ISSN 0098-5619
TRAINING RESOURCES; buyer's guide & consultant directory. a. American Society for Training and Development, Box 5307, Madison, WI 53705.
Continues: A S T D Consultant Directory.

331.2 CN ISSN 0381-3258
TRENDS IN COLLECTIVE BARGAINING SETTLEMENTS IN NOVA SCOTIA. 1975. a. Department of Labour, Economics and Research Division, Box 697, Halifax, N.S., Canada.

350 UN ISSN 0049-5395
U N I T A R NEWS. (Editions in English and French) vol. 5, 1973. irreg. free. ‡ United Nations Institute for Training and Research, 801 U.N. Plaza, 801 United Nations Plaza, NY 10017. Ed. Christina McDougall. bk. rev. bibl. charts. illus. circ. 3,000.

331.11 UG ISSN 0082-724X
UGANDA. MINISTRY OF PLANNING AND ECONOMIC DEVELOPMENT. STATISTICS DIVISION. ENUMERATION OF EMPLOYEES. 1959. a. price varies. ‡ Ministry of Planning and Economic Development, Statistics Division, P.O. Box 13, Entebbe, Uganda (Subscr. to: Government Printer, Box 33, Entebbe, Uganda)

331 US
U. S. BUREAU OF INTERNATIONAL LABOR AFFAIRS. MONOGRAPH. no. 2, 1979. irreg. U.S. Bureau of International Labor Affairs, Foreign Publications Group, Room S5015, Washington, DC 20210. Ed. Joan W. Leslie.

331.89 US ISSN 0082-9013
U. S. BUREAU OF LABOR STATISTICS. ANALYSIS OF WORK STOPPAGES. (Subseries of its Bulletins Series) 1941. m. and a. U.S. Bureau of Labor Statistics., 411 G. St. N.W., Washington, DC 20212 (Orders to: Supt. of Documents, Washington, DC 20402)

331 US ISSN 0082-903X
U. S. BUREAU OF LABOR STATISTICS. B L S STAFF PAPER. 1967. irreg. price varies. U. S. Bureau of Labor Statistics, 441 G. St. N.W., Washington, DC 20212 (Orders to: Supt. of Documents, Washington, DC 20402)

331 US ISSN 0082-9021
U. S. BUREAU OF LABOR STATISTICS. BULLETINS. 1913. irreg. price varies. U.S. Bureau of Labor Statistics, 441 G St. N.W., Washington, DC 20212 (Orders to: Supt. of Documents, Washington, DC 20402)

331.1 US
U. S. BUREAU OF LABOR STATISTICS. EMPLOYMENT AND EARNINGS: STATES AND AREAS. (Subseries of its Bulletin Series) 1939. a. U.S. Bureau of Labor Statistics., 441 G St., N.W., Washington, DC 20212 (Orders to: Supt. of Documents, Washington, DC 20402)
Formerly: U.S. Bureau of Labor Statistics. Employment and Earnings Statistics for States and Areas (ISSN 0082-9048)

331.1 US ISSN 0082-9064
U. S. BUREAU OF LABOR STATISTICS. INDUSTRY WAGE SURVEYS. (Subseries of its Bulletin Series) issued irreg. throughout the year by regional offices. U.S. Bureau of Labor Statistics, 441 G St., N.W., Washington, DC 20212 (Orders to: Supt. of Documents, Washington, DC 20402)

331.1 US ISSN 0082-9099
U.S. BUREAU OF LABOR STATISTICS. UNION WAGES AND HOURS SURVEYS. (Subseries of its Bulletins Series) 1936. irreg. U.S. Bureau of Labor Statistics., 441 G St., N.W., Washington, DC 20210 (Orders to: Supt. of Documents, Washington, DC 20402)
Issued in parts: Building Trades; Grocery Store Employees; Local Transit Operating Employees; Motortruck Drivers and Helpers; Printing Trades

331.1 US ISSN 0082-9102
U.S. BUREAU OF LABOR STATISTICS. WAGE CHRONOLOGIES. (Subseries of its Bulletin Series) irreg. U.S. Bureau of Labor Statistics, 441 G St., N.W., Washington, DC 20212 (Orders to: Supt. of Documents, Washington, DC 20402)
Chronological records of amounts and characteristics of changes in wages and related benefits achieved in collective bargaining agreements

331.11 US
U.S. DEPARTMENT OF LABOR. EMPLOYMENT AND TRAINING ADMINISTRATION. MANPOWER RESEARCH AND DEVELOPMENT PROJECTS. 1963. a. free. U.S. Employment and Training Administration, 14th and Constitution Ave., N.W., Washington, DC 20210.
Formerly: Manpower Research Projects (ISSN 0082-9994)

331 US
U.S. DEPARTMENT OF LABOR. REGISTER OF REPORTING LABOR ORGANIZATION. irreg. U.S. Labor Management Services Administration, New Department of Labor Building, 200 Constitution Ave., Washington, DC 20216 (Orders to: Supt. of Documents, U.S. Government Printing Office, Washington, DC 20402)

331 US ISSN 0083-0526
U.S. EQUAL EMPLOYMENT OPPORTUNITY COMMISSION. ANNUAL REPORT. Title varies: Equal Employment Opportunity Report. 1968. a. U.S. Equal Employment Opportunity Commission., 2401 E St., N.W., Washington, DC 20506 (Orders to: Supt. Doc., Washington, DC 20402)

331.15 US ISSN 0083-0771
U. S. FEDERAL MEDIATION AND CONCILIATION SERVICE. ANNUAL REPORT. 1948. a. price varies. U.S. Federal Mediation and Conciliation Service., 2100 K St. N.W., Washington, DC 20427 (Available from: Supt. of Documents, Washington, DC 20402)

331 US
U. S. NATIONAL CENTER FOR PRODUCTIVITY AND QUALITY OF WORKING LIFE. ANNUAL REPORT TO THE PRESIDENT AND CONGRESS. a. U.S. National Center for Productivity and Quality of Working Life, Washington, DC 20036 (Order from: Supt. of Documents, Washington, DC 20402)

331.1 US ISSN 0361-7440
U.S. NATIONAL COMMISSION FOR MANPOWER POLICY. ANNUAL REPORT TO THE PRESIDENT AND THE CONGRESS. (Subseries of: U.S. National Commission for Manpower Policy. Report) 1975. a. U.S. National Commission for Manpower Policy, 1522 K St. N.W., Suite 300, Washington, DC 20005. Key Title: Annual Report to the President and the Congress of the National Commission for Manpower Policty.

331.155 US ISSN 0083-2200
U. S. NATIONAL LABOR RELATIONS BOARD. ANNUAL REPORT. 1936. a. price varies. U. S. National Labor Relations Board, 1717 Pennsylvania Ave. N.W., Washington, DC 20572 (Orders to: Supt. of Documents, Washington, DC 20402)

331.156 US ISSN 0083-2219
U. S. NATIONAL LABOR RELATIONS BOARD. COURT DECISIONS RELATING TO THE NATIONAL LABOR RELATIONS ACT. 1939. irreg., vol. 22 latest. $12.20. U. S. National Labor Relations Board, 1717 Pennsylvania Ave. N.W., Washington, DC 20570 (Orders to: Supt. of Documents, Washington, DC 20402)

331.154 US ISSN 0083-2286
U. S. NATIONAL MEDIATION BOARD. ANNUAL REPORT. 1935. a. $10.00 subscription includes Annual Reports, Emergeny Board Reports, Certifications and Dismissals, Determinations of Craft or Class, Findings upon Investigation, other NMB information releases. U. S. National Mediation Board, 1425 K St. N.W., Washington, DC 20572.

331 US ISSN 0083-2278
U. S. NATIONAL MEDIATION BOARD. (REPORTS OF EMERGENCY BOARDS) 3-4/yr. $10.00 subscription includes Annual Reports, Emergency Board Reports, Certifications and Dismissals, Determinations of Craft or Class, Findings upon Investigation, other NMB information releases. U. S. National Mediation Board, 1425 K St. N.W., Washington, DC 20572.

U.S. RAILROAD RETIREMENT BOARD. ANNUAL REPORT. see *BUSINESS AND ECONOMICS — Investments*

331 US ISSN 0068-6255
UNIVERSITY OF CALIFORNIA, LOS ANGELES. INSTITUTE OF INDUSTRIAL RELATIONS. MONOGRAPH SERIES. 1953. irreg., no. 25, 1979. University of California, Los Angeles, Institute of Industrial Relations, Los Angeles, CA 90024.

331 US ISSN 0073-1226
UNIVERSITY OF HAWAII. INDUSTRIAL RELATIONS CENTER. OCCASIONAL PUBLICATIONS. 1948. irreg., no. 131, 1979. price varies. University of Hawaii, Industrial Relations Center, 2404 Maile Way, Honolulu, HI 96822.

331.1 US ISSN 0073-5353
UNIVERSITY OF ILLINOIS AT URBANA-CHAMPAIGN. INSTITUTE OF LABOR AND INDUSTRIAL RELATIONS. REPRINT SERIES. 1950. irreg. free to qualified personnel. University of Illinois at Urbana-Champaign, Institute of Labor and Industrial Relations, 504 E. Armory Ave., Champaign, IL 61820. Ed. Alice Vernon.

331 US ISSN 0578-6371
UNIVERSITY OF IOWA. CENTER FOR LABOR AND MANAGEMENT. RESEARCH SERIES. irreg. price varies. University of Iowa, College of Business Administration, Center for Labor and Management, Phillips Hall, Iowa City, IA 52240.
    Supersedes: University of Iowa. Center for Labor and Management. Monograph Series (ISSN 0075-045X)

331.8 US ISSN 0078-2076
UNIVERSITY OF NOTRE DAME. DEPARTMENT OF ECONOMICS. UNION-MANAGEMENT CONFERENCE. PROCEEDING. 1953. a. $2. University of Notre Dame, Department of Economics, Box 476, Notre Dame, IN 46556. Eds. Rev. Mark J. Fitzgerald and John J. Broderick. circ. 500-600.

331.1 US
UNIVERSITY OF NOTRE DAME. SAINT MARY'S COLLEGE. LAW SCHOOL. DEPARTMENT OF ECONOMICS. CONFERENCE ON CHANGING FACTORS IN COLLECTIVE BARGAINING. PROCEEDINGS. 1953. a. $2. University of Notre Dame, Department of Economics, IN 46556 (Rev. Mark J. Fitzgerald, Box 476, Notre Dame, Indiana 46556) Eds. Rev. Mark J. Fitzgerald, C.S.C. and Dr. John J. Broderick. circ. 700-1,000 (approx.) (back issues from 1958 avail.)

331.1 US ISSN 0075-7470
UNIVERSITY OF PENNSYLVANIA. WHARTON SCHOOL OF FINANCE AND COMMERCE. LABOR RELATIONS AND PUBLIC POLICY SERIES. REPORTS. 1968. irreg. University of Pennsylvania Wharton School of Finance and Commerce, Industrial Research Unit, Philadelphia, PA 19104.

331 TR
UNIVERSITY OF THE WEST INDIES, TRINIDAD. INSTITUTE OF SOCIAL & ECONOMIC RESEARCH. OCCASIONAL PAPERS: HUMAN RESOURCES SERIES. 1977. irreg. price varies. University of the West Indies, Institute of Social & Economic Research, St. Augustine, Trinidad, West Indies. Eds. Jack Harewood, Marianne Ramesar. charts. stat. circ. 220. (back issues avail.)

331.1 US ISSN 0083-4912
UNIVERSITY OF UTAH. INSTITUTE OF INDUSTRIAL RELATIONS. BULLETIN.* 1960. irreg. price varies. University of Utah, Institute of Industrial Relations, 227 College of Business, Salt Lake City, UT 84112.

331.3 NE ISSN 0083-534X
VEILIGHEIDSJAARBOEK. 1959. a. fl.46.50. Veiligheidsinstituut, Hobbemastraat 22, 1007 AR Amsterdam, Netherlands. adv. circ. 5,000.

331 NE
VERENIGING VOOR ARBEIDSRECHT. GESCHRIFTEN. 1979. irreg. Samsom Uitgeverij B.V., Postbus 4, 2400 MA Alphen aan den Rijn, Netherlands.

331 US
VIRGINIA. EMPLOYMENT COMMISSION. ANNUAL PLANNING REPORT. a. Employment Commission, Richmond, VA 23219.

331 US
VIRGINIA. EMPLOYMENT COMMISSION. ANNUAL REPORT. a. Employment Commission, Richmond, VA 23219. stat.

331 US
VIRGINIA. EMPLOYMENT COMMISSION. ANNUAL RURAL MANPOWER REPORT. a. Employment Commission, Richmonnd, VA 23219. stat.

331 US
VIRGINIA. EMPLOYMENT COMMISSION. LABOR MARKET TRENDS. irreg. Employment Commission, Richmond, VA 23219. charts.

331 US
WADSWORTH SERIES IN LABOR ECONOMICS AND INDUSTRIAL RELATIONS. irreg. Wadsworth Publishing Co., 10 Davis Dr., Belmont, CA 94002.

331 SW
WAGES AND TOTAL LABOUR COSTS FOR WORKERS: INTERNATIONAL SURVEY. a. Kr.50. Svenska Arbetsgivarefoereningen - Swedish Employers' Confederation, 103 30 Stockholm, Sweden.

WASHINGTON (STATE). INDIAN ASSISTANCE DIVISION.INDIAN ECONOMIC EMPLOYMENT ASSISTANCE PROGRAM. ANNUAL REPORT. see *ETHNIC INTERESTS*

380 GW
WERBE-MITTEL KATALOG. a. DM.24.05. Goeller Verlag, Hauptstr. 4, Postfach 240, 7570 Baden-Baden, W. Germany (B.R.D.) Ed. H.-J. Goeller. adv. circ. 10,000.

331 US
WERTHEIM PUBLICATIONS IN INDUSTRIAL RELATIONS. irreg. Harvard University Press, 79 Garden St., Cambridge, MA 02138.

331 II ISSN 0043-3071
WEST BENGAL LABOUR GAZETTE. (Text in English) 1957. irreg. (Department of Labour) West Bengal Government Press, Publication Branch, 38 Gopal Nagar Rd., Alipore, Calcutta 27, India. stat.

331.11 US
WEST VIRGINIA EMPLOYMENT AND EARNINGS TRENDS: ANNUAL SUMMARY. 1968. a. free. Department of Employment Security, Research and Statistics Division, 112 California Avenue, Charleston, WV 25305. Ed. Lowell Witters. circ. 800-1,000.

344.73 US ISSN 0097-9171
WISCONSIN. EMPLOYMENT RELATIONS COMMISSION. REPORTER.* irreg. Industrial Relations Service Bureau, 3420 Heritage Dr., Minneapolis, MN 55435. Key Title: Industrial Relations Service Bureau's Wisconsin Employment Relations Commission, Reporter.

331.4 US
WOMEN IN THE WORKING WORLD. 1975. biennial. Department of Economic Security, Bureau of Statistical Information-Research and Analysis, Box 6123, Phoenix, AZ 85005.

331 CN ISSN 0084-1307
WORKING CONDITIONS IN CANADIAN INDUSTRY/CONDITIONS DE TRAVAIL DANS L'INDUSTRIE CANADIENNE. (Text in English and French) 1957. a. Can.$5($6) Labour Canada, Ottawa, Ont. K1A 0J2, Canada. circ. 1,800. (reprint service avail. from MML)

331 US
WYOMING. EMPLOYMENT SECURITY COMMISSION. RESEARCH & ANALYSIS SECTION. ANNUAL PLANNING REPORT. a. Employment Security Commission, Research & Analysis Section, Box 2760, Casper, WY 82601.

331.7 US ISSN 0095-389X
WYOMING. EMPLOYMENT SECURITY COMMISSION. RESEARCH AND ANALYSIS SECTION. FARM LABOR REPORT. a. free. Employment Security Commission, Research and Analysis Section, Box 2760, Casper, WY 82601. Key Title: Farm Labor Report (Casper)

331 US
WYOMING. EMPLOYMENT SECURITY COMMISSION. ANNUAL REPORT. Employment Security Commission, Box 2760, Casper, WY 82601.

331.1 US ISSN 0097-739X
WYOMING AREA MANPOWER REVIEW. a. free. Employment Security Commission, Research and Analysis Section, Casper, WY 82601. stat.

331 US ISSN 0512-4395
WYOMING STATISTICAL REVIEW. a. Employment Security Commission, Research & Analysis Section, Box 2760, Casper, WY 82601. stat.

331 ZA ISSN 0084-4632
ZAMBIA. DEPARTMENT OF LABOUR. REPORT. a. 60 n. Government Printer, P.O. Box 136, Lusaka, Zambia.

331.1 YU
ZAPOSLENI PO OBCINAH. irreg. 20 din. Zavod SR Slovenije za Statistiko, Vozarski Pot 12, Ljubljana, Yugoslavia. Ed. Mlinar Branko.

BUSINESS AND ECONOMICS — Macroeconomics

339 UY
BANCO CENTRAL DEL URUGUAY. DIVISION ASESORIA ECONOMICA Y ESTUDIOS. PRODUCTO E INGRESO NACIONALES. ACTUALIZACION DE LAS PRINCIPALES VARIABLES. irreg. Banco Central del Uruguay, Division Asesoria Economica y Estudios, Montevideo, Uruguay.

338.9 CJ
CAYMAN ISLANDS. DEPARTMENT OF FINANCE AND DEVELOPMENT. ESTIMATES OF GROSS DOMESTIC PRODUCT AND RELATED AGGREGATES. 1972. a. Department of Finance and Development, Grand Cayman Island, Cayman Islands, B.W.I. Dir. Thomas C. Jefferson.

339 CH
CHINA, REPUBLIC. DIRECTORATE-GENERAL OF BUDGET, ACCOUNTING AND STATISTICS. REPORT ON THE SURVEY OF PERSONAL INCOME DISTRIBUTION IN TAIWAN AREA. (Text in English and Chinese) 1974. a. Directorate-General of Budget, Accounting and Statistics, Executive Yuan, Taipei, Taiwan, Republic of China. charts. illus. stat.

339 CK
COLOMBIAN ECONOMY. (Text in English) 1978. $25. Camara de Comercio Colombo-Americana, Apdo. Aereo 8008, Bogota, Colombia. Ed. Oscar A. Bradford. adv. charts. circ. 1,000.

339.2 US ISSN 0069-8652
CONFERENCE ON RESEARCH IN INCOME AND WEALTH. 1937. irreg., no. 41, 1976. $20. National Bureau of Economic Research, 1050 Massachusetts Ave, Cambridge, MA 02138.

CURRENT POPULATION REPORTS: CONSUMER BUYING INDICATORS. see *POPULATION STUDIES*

CURRENT POPULATION REPORTS: CONSUMER INCOME. see *POPULATION STUDIES*

339 US
CURRENT POPULATION REPORTS: CONSUMER INCOME. INCOME IN (YEAR) OF FAMILIES AND PERSONS IN THE UNITED STATES. (Series P-60) 1967. a. price varies. U. S. Bureau of the Census, Subscribers Services, Washington, DC 20233 (Orders to: Supt. of Documents, Washington, DC 20402)
    Formerly: U. S. Bureau of the Census. Income (in Year) of Families in the United States (ISSN 0073-568X)

BUSINESS AND ECONOMICS — MANAGEMENT

339 US
CURRENT POPULATION REPORTS: CONSUMER INCOME. MONEY INCOME (IN YEAR) OF FAMILIES AND PERSONS IN THE UNITED STATES. (Series P-60) a. price varies. U. S. Bureau of the Census, Washington, DC 20233 (Orders to: Supt. of Documents, Washington, DC 20402)
Formerly: Money Income (in Year) of Families, Unrelated Individuals and Persons in the United States (ISSN 0073-5698)

339 TU
ECONOMIC INDICATORS OF TURKEY. (Editions in English and Turkish) a. Turkiye Is Bankasi, Economic Research Department, Ataturk Bulvari 191, Kavaklidere, Ankara, Turkey. stat. circ. 2,500 (English edt.); 5,000 (Turkish edt.)

339 SZ ISSN 0070-9514
EIDGENOESSISCHE ZUKUNFT: BAUSTEINE FUER DIE KOMMENDE SCHWEIZ. 1963. irreg., no. 14, 1976. price varies. Paul Haupt AG, Falkenplatz 14, CH-3001 Berne, Switzerland. Ed. Friedrich Salzmann.

GREAT BRITAIN. BOARD OF INLAND REVENUE. THE SURVEY OF PERSONAL INCOMES. see *BUSINESS AND ECONOMICS — Public Finance, Taxation*

339 UK ISSN 0072-5927
GREAT BRITAIN. DEPARTMENT OF EMPLOYMENT. FAMILY EXPENDITURE SURVEY. 1957. a. £6.50. Department of Employment, St. James's Square, London SW1Y 4JB, England (Avail. from H.M.S.O., c/o Liaison Officer, Atlantic House, Holborn Viaduct, London EC1P 1BN, England)

339 GU
GUAM. DEPARTMENT OF COMMERCE. PERSONAL INCOME STUDY. 1973. a. free. Department of Commerce, Box 682, Agana, GU 96910. (tabloid format)

330 II
INDIA. CENTRAL STATISTICAL ORGANIZATION. NATIONAL ACCOUNTS STATISTICS. 1948/49-51/52. a. Rs.33($11.88) Central Statistical Organization, Sardar Patel Bhavan, Sansad Marg, New Delhi 110001, India.
Formerly: India. Central Statistical Organization. Estimates of National Income (ISSN 0073-6147)

332 UN
INTERNATIONAL MONETARY FUND. BALANCE OF PAYMENTS YEARBOOK. 1949. m (plus annual issue) $20 ($8 to university libraries, faculty, and students) International Monetary Fund, 700 19th St. N.W., Washington, DC 20431. Ed. Werner Dannemann. stat. circ. 3,000. (also avail. in microform from UMI; magnetic tape; reprint service avail. from UMI)

IRELAND (EIRE) CENTRAL STATISTICS OFFICE. NATIONAL INCOME AND EXPENDITURE. see *BUSINESS AND ECONOMICS — Public Finance, Taxation*

336 JO ISSN 0449-1513
JORDAN. DEPARTMENT OF STATISTICS. NATIONAL ACCOUNTS. (Text in English) 1960. a. $5. Department of Statistics, Amman, Jordan.

339 US
KENTUCKY PERSONAL INCOME REPORT. 1970. a. $5 outside Kentucky. University of Kentucky, Center for Applied Economic Research, Rm. 451 Commerce Bldg., College of Business and Economics, Lexington, KY 40506. circ. 500.
Formerly: Kentucky Personal Income (ISSN 0075-5532)

339 KU
KUWAIT. CENTRAL STATISTICAL OFFICE. YEARLY BULLETIN OF PRICE INDEX NUMBERS. (Text in English) a. Central Statistical Office, Box 15, Kuwait.

339.368 BS ISSN 0302-2056
NATIONAL ACCOUNTS OF BOTSWANA. a., latest 1976/1977. Central Statistics Office, Ministry of Finance and Development Planning, Gaborone, Botswana (Orders to: Government Printer, Box 87, Gaborone, Botswana) stat.

339 336 US ISSN 0071-5484
NATIONAL BUREAU OF ECONOMIC RESEARCH. FISCAL STUDIES. 1942. irreg., 1971, no. 14. $10. National Bureau of Economic Research, 1050 Massachusetts Ave, Cambridge, MA 02138.

330 US
NATIONAL PLANNING ASSOCIATION REPORTS. 1974,no.135. irreg. $20. National Planning Association, 1606 New Hampshire Ave. N.W., Washington, DC 20009. Ed. Martha L. Benz. bibl. charts. stat. circ. 2,000.

339.2 US ISSN 0079-0907
PERSONAL INCOME IN COUNTIES OF NEW YORK STATE. (Subseries of the Department's Research Bulletin) 1961. a. free. Department of Commerce, 99 Washington Ave., Albany, NY 12245. Ed. Peter A. Ansell. circ. 1,500.

339 PH
PHILIPPINES. NATIONAL ECONOMIC AND DEVELOPMENT AUTHORITY. NATIONAL INCOME SERIES. (Text in English) irreg., latest no. 3. price varies. National Economic and Development Authority, Box 1116, Padre Faura St., Manila, Philippines. illus.

339 SZ
PRICES AND EARNINGS AROUND THE GLOBE. (Editions in English, French, German, Italian and Spanish) 1970. irreg, 3rd edt., 1976. free. Union de Banques Suisses, Bahnhofstrasse 45, 8000 Zurich, Switzerland. circ. 34,500 (English edt.); 181,000 (all edts.)

339 US ISSN 0194-3960
RESEARCH IN HUMAN CAPITAL AND DEVELOPMENT. 1979. a. $17.25 to individuals; institutions $34.50. J A I Press, Box 1678, 165 W. Putnam Ave., Greenwich, CT 06830. Ed. Ismail Sirageldin.

339 RE
REUNION. SECRETARIAT GENERAL POUR LES AFFAIRES ECONOMIQUES. STATISTIQUES ET INDICATEURS ECONOMIQUES. a. Secretariat General pour les Affaires Economiques, 97405 Saint-Denis, Reunion.

STATISTICAL OFFICE OF THE EUROPEAN COMMUNITIES. BALANCES OF PAYMENTS YEARBOOK. see *BUSINESS AND ECONOMICS — Public Finance, Taxation*

339 UK ISSN 0081-864X
STUDIES IN THE NATIONAL INCOME AND EXPENDITURE OF THE UNITED KINGDOM. 1966. irreg., no. 6, 1979. $21.50 for latest vol. (National Institute of Economic and Social Research) Cambridge University Press, Box 110, Cambridge CB2 3RL, England (and 32 E. 57 St., New York NY 10022) (Co-sponsor: Cambridge University, Department of Applied Economics) Ed. Richard Stone.

STUDIES IN WAGE-PRICE POLICY. see *BUSINESS AND ECONOMICS*

339.2 SJ
SUDAN. DEPARTMENT OF STATISTICS. NATIONAL INCOME ACCOUNTS AND SUPPORTING TABLES. (Text in Arabic and English) a. Department of Statistics, National Income Division, Box 700, Khartoum, Sudan. illus. stat.

SURVEY OF BUYING POWER. see *BUSINESS AND ECONOMICS — Marketing And Purchasing*

339 US ISSN 0085-3410
SURVEYS OF CONSUMERS; contributions to behavioral economics. 1972. irreg. $14. ‡ University of Michigan, Institute for Social Research, Box 1248, Ann Arbor, MI 48106.
Formerly (1960-1970): Survey of Consumer Finances (ISSN 0081-9727)

339 GW
TECHNISCHER FORTSCHRITT (BERLIN) 1978. irreg. price varies. Duncker und Humblot, Dietrich-Schaefer-Weg 9, 1000 Berlin 41, W. Germany (B.R.D.)

309.2 SA
UNIVERSITY OF PORT ELIZABETH. INSTITUTE FOR PLANNING RESEARCH. ANNUAL REPORT/UNIVERSITEIT VAN PORT ELIZABETH. INSTITUUT VIR BEPLANNINGSNAVORSING. JAARVERSLAG. (Text in Afrikaans and English) 1970. a. free. University of Port Elizabeth, Institute for Planning Research, Box 1600, Port Elizabeth 6000, South Africa. circ. 400 (controlled) (back issues avail)

339 VE
VENEZUELA. MINISTERIO DE HACIENDA. CUENTA GENERAL DE INGRESOS Y GASTOS PUBLICOS, BIENES NACIONALES, INCLUSIVE MATERIAS: INGRESOS Y GASTOS.* a. Ministerio de Hacienda, Caracas, Venezuela.

BUSINESS AND ECONOMICS — Management

650 US
A M A MANAGEMENT BRIEFINGS. 1971. irreg., approx. 12/yr. $5 per no. to members; others $7.50. American Management Associations, 135 W. 50th St., New York, NY 10020 (Subscr. to: Box 319, Saranac Lake, N.Y. 12983) charts. illus. circ. controlled.

650 US
A M A SURVEY REPORTS. 1973. irreg., approx. 3/yr. $10 per no. to non-members; members $7.50. American Management Associations, 135 W. 50th St., New York, NY 10020 (Subscr. to: Box 319, Saranac Lake, N.Y. 12983) charts. illus. stat.

A M S DIRECTORY OF OFFICE SALARIES. (Administrative Management Society) see *BUSINESS AND ECONOMICS — Labor And Industrial Relations*

A M S GUIDE TO MANAGEMENT COMPENSATION. (Administrative Management Society) see *BUSINESS AND ECONOMICS — Labor And Industrial Relations*

650 US
A S M BOOKSHELF SERIES. irreg. price varies. Association for Systems Management, 24587 Bagley Rd., Cleveland, OH 44138.

658.01 UK ISSN 0066-9709
A T M OCCASIONAL PAPERS. 1965. irreg. price varies. Association of Teachers of Management, c/o M. Greatorex, Polytechnic of Central London, 35 Marylebone Road, London NW1 5LS, England.

658 US ISSN 0065-0668
ACADEMY OF MANAGEMENT. PROCEEDINGS. 1938. a. $11.50. Academy of Management, Box KZ, Mississippi State University, MS 39762. Ed. Bd. illus. index. circ. 1,800. (also avail. in microform from UMI; back issues avail.)

658 CN
ADMINISTRATIVE DIGEST BUSINESS DIRECTORY. a. Southam Communications Ltd., 1450 Don Mills Rd., Don Mills, Ont. M3B 2X7, Canada. adv.

658 IT
AGENDA EDIZIONE GUIDA MONACI. S.P.A. a. L.10000. Guida Monaci, Via F. Crispi 10, 00187 Rome, Italy. adv.

330 GW ISSN 0065-5384
AKADEMIE FUER FUEHRUNGSKRAEFTE DER WIRTSCHAFT. TASCHENBUECHER ZUR BETRIEBSPRAXIS. irreg. price varies. Verlag fuer Wissenschaft, Wirtschaft und Technik GmbH und Co., An den Weiden 15, Postfach 242, 3388 Bad Harzburg, W. Germany (B.R.D.)

658 SP
ALTA DIRECCION. MONOGRAFIAS. irreg. 550 ptas. Ediciones Nauta, S.A., Loreto 16, Barcelona 15, Spain. Ed. Juan L. Gutierrez Ducons.

658 US
AMERICAN INSTITUTE FOR DECISION SCIENCES. NATIONAL CONFERENCE PROCEEDINGS. a. $12. American Institute for Decision Sciences, University Plaza, Atlanta, GA 30303.

BUSINESS AND ECONOMICS — MANAGEMENT

658   US   ISSN 0360-7100
AMERICAN INSTITUTE FOR DECISION SCIENCES. SOUTHEAST SECTION. PROCEEDINGS. 1971. a. $10. American Institute for Decision Sciences, Southeast Section, Department of Business Administration, Virginia Polytechnic Institute and State University, Blacksburg, VA 24061. Ed. Bernard W. Taylor, III. abstr. charts. pat. index. circ. 400.

658   US   ISSN 0065-9185
AMERICAN MANAGEMENT ASSOCIATION. RESEARCH STUDIES. irreg. $13.50 to non-members; members $10. American Management Associations, 135 W. 50 St., New York, NY 10020 (Subscr. to: Box 319, Saranac Lake, N.Y. 12983)

658   US   ISSN 0065-9193
AMERICAN MANAGEMENT ASSOCIATION. SEMINAR PROGRAM. 1963. irreg. American Management Associations, 135 W. 50th St., New York, NY 10020 (Subscr. to: Box 319, Saranac Lake, N.Y. 12983)

658   US   ISSN 0191-1783
AMERICAN PRODUCTION AND INVENTORY CONTROL SOCIETY. ANNUAL CONFERENCE PROCEEDINGS. 1960. a. $20. American Production and Inventory Control Society, Inc., Watergate Bldg., Suite 504, 2600 Virginia Ave., N.W., Washington, DC 20037. Ed. Henry F. Sander. circ. 18,000.
Former titles: A P I C S Annual Conference Proceedings (ISSN 0065-9819); A P I C S International Technical Conference Proceedings (ISSN 0190-8340)

658   UK   ISSN 0307-0409
ANBAR YEARBOOK; the compleat Anbar. 1972. a. £60. Anbar Publications Ltd., P.O. Box 23, Wembley HA9 8DJ, England. Ed. J.W. Goodman. abstr. bibl. index.

658   US
APPLICATIONS OF MANAGEMENT SCIENCE. 1979. a. $19.75 to individuals; institutions $39.50. J A I Press, Box 1678, 165 W. Putnam Ave., Greenwich, CT 06830. Ed. Randall L. Schultz.

658   SW   ISSN 0571-0731
ARKIVINFORMATION. 1957. irreg. (3/yr.) Kr.30. Naeringslivets Arkivraad, Klubbacken 16, 126 56 Haegersten, Sweden. Ed. Karl Erik Thelin. bk. rev. circ. 10,000.

650   US
AUBURN UNIVERSITY. PROJECT THEMIS RESEARCH. ANNUAL REPORT. irreg. price varies. Management Information Service, Box 5129, Detroit, MI 48326.

658   US
BASIC MANAGEMENT SERIES. irreg. price varies. Holt, Rinehart and Winston, 383 Madison Ave., New York, NY 10017.

BEITRAEGE ZUR DATENVERARBEITUNG UND UNTERNEHMENSFORSCHUNG. see *COMPUTER TECHNOLOGY AND APPLICATIONS*

658.1   US   ISSN 0360-8743
BEST IN ANNUAL REPORTS. (Subseries of: Print Casebooks) 1975. a. $13.95. R C Publications, Inc., 355 Lexington Ave., New York, NY 10017 (Or 6400 Goldsboro Rd., Washington, DC 20034) illus.

658   SZ   ISSN 0067-639X
BETRIEBSWIRTSCHAFTLICHE MITTEILUNGEN. 1958. irreg. price varies. (Hochschule St. Gallen fuer Wirtschafts- und Sozialwissenschaften, Institut fuer Betriebswirtschaft) Paul Haupt AG, Falkenplatz 14, CH-3001 Berne, Switzerland.

658   378   US   ISSN 0361-1108
BRICKER'S INTERNATIONAL DIRECTORY OF UNIVERSITY-SPONSORED EXECUTIVE DEVELOPMENT PROGRAMS. 1970. a. $75. Bricker Publications, Box 188, South Chatham, MA 02659. Ed. George W. Bricker. circ. 1,000. (back issues avail.)

658   FR   ISSN 0078-950X
BUREAU UNIVERSITAIRE DE RECHERCHE OPERATIONNELLE.CAHIERS. 1957. irreg. 80 F. for 4 numbers. Bureau Universitaire de Recherche Operationnelle, 4 Place Jussieu, 75230 Paris, France. circ. 1,000.

658   US   ISSN 0068-4384
BUSINESS ALMANAC SERIES. 1966. irreg., 1973, no. 22. $4.95. Oceana Publications Inc., Dobbs Ferry, NY 10522.

658   UK   ISSN 0308-0455
BUSINESS GRADUATES ASSOCIATION ADDRESS BOOK. 1969. a. £20 to non-members. Business Graduates Association Ltd., 9 Courtleigh Gardens, London NW11 9JX, England. Ed. Alan Philipp. adv. bk. rev. circ. 2,500. Indexed: Anbar. Anbar.

658   II   ISSN 0068-5356
CALCUTTA MANAGEMENT ASSOCIATION. ANNUAL REPORT. (Text in English) 1959. a. membership. Calcutta Management Association, 1 Shakespeare Sarani, Calcutta 700071, India.

658.4   CN   ISSN 0318-5036
CANADIAN ASSOCIATION OF ADMINISTRATIVE SCIENCES. PROCEEDINGS, ANNUAL CONFERENCE/ RAPPORT, LA CONFERENCE ANNUELLE. 1973. irreg. Canadian Association of Administrative Sciences, School of Business, Queen's University at Kingston, Kingston, Ont., Canada. illus.
Formerly: Association of Canadian Schools of Business. Proceedings of the Annual Conference (ISSN 0066-9490)

658   CN   ISSN 0068-8320
CANADIAN ASSOCIATION OF MANAGEMENT CONSULTANTS. ANNUAL REPORT. 1963. a. free. Canadian Association of Management Consultants, Box 6329, Sta. a, Toronto, Ont. M5W 1P7, Canada. circ. 1,800.

658   FR
CENTRE D'ETUDES ET DE GESTION FINANCIERES. NOTICE CIRCULAIRE. a. Institut de Technologie Previsionnelle Appliquee, 2 Bd. Longchamp, 13001 Marseille, France. Ed. Michel Helmer. charts. stat.

658   US   ISSN 0009-8434
CLASSIFICATION MANAGEMENT. 1965. a. $10. ‡ National Classification Management Society, P.O. Box 7453, Alexandria, VA 22307. Ed. Lorimer F. McConnell. circ. 300.

658   FR
COLLECTION E F G. (Economie-Formation-Gestion) irreg. Editions d' Organisation, 5 rue Rousselet, 75007 Paris, France. Ed. Michel Bernard.

658   FR   ISSN 0069-651X
COMITE NATIONAL DE L'ORGANISATION FRANCAISE. ANNUAIRE. 1950. a. Association Francaise de Management, 119 rue de Lille, F-75007 Paris, France.

CONFERENCE BOARD IN CANADA. CANADIAN STUDIES. see *BUSINESS AND ECONOMICS — Production Of Goods And Services*

658   330   CN   ISSN 0704-0601
CONFERENCE BOARD IN CANADA. EXECUTIVE BULLETIN. 1977. irreg. membership. (Compensation Research Centre) Conference Board in Canada, Suite 100, 25 McArthur Rd., Ottawa, Ont. K1L 6R3, Canada.

658   FR
CONSEIL NATIONAL DU PATRONAT FRANCAIS. ANNUAIRE. a. 132 F. Union Francaise d'Annuaires Professionnels, 13 Avenue Vladimir Komarov, B.P. 36, 78190 Trappes, France. index.

658   US
CONSULTANTS AND CONSULTING ORGANIZATIONS DIRECTORY; a reference guide to concerns and individuals engaged in consultation for business, industry and government. irreg., 4th edt., 1979. $95. Gale Research Company, Book Tower, Detroit, MI 48226. Ed. Paul Wasserman. index.

658   GW
CONTROLLER MAGAZIN. 1976. 6/yr. DM.92. (Controller Verein e.V., Muenchen) Management Service Verlag, Untertaxeweg 76, 8035 Gauting 2, W. Germany (B.R.D.) Ed. Albrecht Deyhle. bk. rev. charts. illus. stat. circ. 2,500.

658.4   US   ISSN 0307-3025
CORPORATE PLANNER'S YEARBOOK. 1974. a. (Society for Long Range Planning) Pergamon Press, Inc., Maxwell House, Fairview Park, Elmsford, NY 10523.

658   658.8   SP
CUADERNOS UNIVERSITARIOS DE PLANIFICACION EMPRESARIAL Y MARKETING. 1975. q. 1500 ptas.($26) (Universidad Autonoma de Madrid, Fundacion Universidad Empresa) Editorial Macrometrica, Paseo Calvo Sotelo 29, Madrid 4, Spain. Ed. Bd. bibl. charts.

658.4   II
DECISION. (Text in English) 1974. s-a. Rs.15. Indian Institute of Management, 56-A B.T. Rd., Calcutta, India.

658   SP
DIRECCION DE EMPRESAS Y ORGANIZACIONES. 1976. irreg.; 1979, no. 7. price varies. Ediciones Universidad de Navarra S.A., Plaza de los Sauces 1 y 2, Baranain, Pamplona, Spain.

650   US   ISSN 0419-2052
DIRECTORS GUILD OF AMERICA. DIRECTORY OF MEMBERS. 1967-68. a. $7. Directors Guild of America, Inc., 7950 Sunset Blvd., Hollywood, CA 90046.

658   II   ISSN 0070-5322
DIRECTORY OF COMPANY SECRETARIES. (Text in English) 1969. irreg.; Rs.30($9) Kothari Publications, 12 India Exchange Place, Calcutta 700001, India. Ed. H. Kothari. adv.

DIRECTORY OF DIRECTORS. see *BIOGRAPHY*

658   UK   ISSN 0070-5438
DIRECTORY OF DIRECTORS. 1878. a. $50. I P C Business Press Ltd., 33-40 Bowling Green Lane, London EC1R 0NE, England. adv. circ. 6,500.
Alphabetical list of directors of principal business concerns with their directorships covering the United Kingdom

658.31   US   ISSN 0090-6484
DIRECTORY OF EXECUTIVE RECRUITERS. 1971. a. $10 (single issue) ‡ Consultants News, Templeton Road, Fitzwilliam, NH 03447. Ed. James H. Kennedy.

658.3   US
DIRECTORY OF MANAGEMENT CONSULTANTS. 1976. irreg., 2nd edt. 1979. $37.50. Consultants News, Templeton Rd., Fitzwilliam, NH 03447. Ed. James H. Kennedy.

658   US   ISSN 0070-7627
DUN AND BRADSTREET REFERENCE BOOK OF CORPORATE MANAGEMENTS. 1967. a. ‡ Dun & Bradstreet, Inc., 99 Church St., New York, NY 10007. circ. 3,500.
Formerly: Moody's Handbook of Corporate Managements (ISSN 0545-0209)

658
ECONOMIES ET SOCIETES. SERIE GS. SCIENCE DE GESTION. irreg. 42 F. Institut de Sciences Mathematiques et Economiques Appliquees, Paris, Institut Henri Poincare, 11 rue Pierre et Marie Curie, 75005 Paris, France. Ed. Henri Savall.

338   658.5   UR
EKONOMIKO-MATEMATICHESKIE METODY PLANIROVANIYA I UPRAVLENIYA. 1972. irreg. 0.72 Rub. Akademiya Nauk S. S. S. R., Dal'nevostochnyi Nauchnyi Tsentr, Ul. Leninskaya 50, Vladivostok, U.S.S.R.

658   SP
EMPRESA Y SU ENTORNO. SERIE AC. 1967. irreg.; 1979, no. 7. price varies. Ediciones Universidad de Navarra, S.A., Plaza de los Sauces, 1 y 2 Baranain, Pamplona, Spain.
Formerly: Universidad de Navarra. Instituto de Estudios Superiores de la Empresas. Coleccion I E S E. Serie AC (ISSN 0078-8716)

BUSINESS AND ECONOMICS — MANAGEMENT

658 SP
EMPRESA Y SU ENTORNO. SERIE L. 1970. irreg.; 1979, no. 12. price varies. Ediciones Universidad de Navarra, S.A., Plaza de los Sauces, 1 y 2 Baranain, Pamplona, Spain.
Formerly: Universidad de Navarra. Instituto de Estudios Superiores de la Empresas. Coleccion I E S E. Serie L (ISSN 0078-8708)

650 US ISSN 0071-0210
ENCYCLOPEDIA OF BUSINESS INFORMATION SOURCES. irreg., 4th edt.; 1980. $48. Gale Research Company, Book Tower, Detroit, MI 48226. Ed. Paul Wasserman.
Formerly: Executives Guide to Information Sources.

658 PK
EXECUTIVE. (Text in English) 1975. a. Institute of Business Administration, Karachi, Pakistan. illus.

658 US
EXECUTIVE COMPENSATION; biennial survey. 12th, 1978. biennial. Dartnell Corp., 4660 Ravenswood Ave., Chicago, IL 60640.

658 US ISSN 0095-4144
EXECUTIVE COMPENSATION SERVICE. REPORTS ON INTERNATIONAL COMPENSATION. ARGENTINA. a. American Management Associations, Executive Compensation Service, 135 W. 50th St., New York, NY 10020 (Subscr. to: Box 319, Saranac Lake, N.Y. 12983) illus. stat. Key Title: Reports on International Compensation. Argentina.

331.2 US
EXECUTIVE COMPENSATION SERVICE. REPORTS ON INTERNATIONAL COMPENSATION. BRAZIL. irreg. American Management Associations, Executive Compensation Service, 135 W. 50th St., New York, NY 10020 (Subscr. to: Box 319, Saranac Lake, NY 12983)

331.2 US ISSN 0090-9971
EXECUTIVE COMPENSATION SERVICE. REPORTS ON INTERNATIONAL COMPENSATION. PUERTO RICO. irreg. American Management Associations, Executive Compensation Service, 135 West 50th St., New York, NY 10020 (Subscr. to: Box 319, Saranac Lake, N.Y. 12983) stat. Key Title: Reports on International Compensation. Puerto Rico.

330 US ISSN 0093-8750
EXECUTIVE COMPENSATION SERVICE. TECHNICIAN REPORT. 1973. a. American Management Associations, Executive Compensation Service, 135 W. 50th St., New York, NY 10020 (Subscr. to: Box 319, Saranac Lake, NY 12983) Ed. Michael D. Marvin.

658 FR
FICHES E O-FORMATION PERMANENTE. irreg. price varies. Editions Organisation, 5 rue Rousselet, 75007 Paris, France. Ed. Armand Dayan. bibl. (cards)

658 CN ISSN 0071-5042
FINANCIAL POST DIRECTORY OF DIRECTORS. 1931. a. Can.$45. Maclean-Hunter Ltd., 481 University Ave., Toronto M5W 1A7, Canada. Ed. Jean Graham. adv. circ. 5,000.

658 NO ISSN 0071-7630
FORRETNINGS- OG BEDRIFTSLEDEREN. 1959. a. Kr.105. Forlaget Tanum-Norli A-S, Kr. Augustsgt. 7A, Oslo 1, Norway. Ed. Nil M. Apeland. circ. 3,900.

658 SZ ISSN 0071-9765
FUEHRUNG UND ORGANISATION DER UNTERNEHMUNG. 1961. irreg. price varies. (Hochschule St. Gallen fuer Wirtschafts- und Sozialwissenschaften, Institut fuer Betriebswirtschaft) Paul Haupt AG, Falkenplatz 14, CH-3001 Berne, Switzerland.

658 IT
GESTIONE INFORMATA. no. 2, 1978. irreg., no. 3, 1979. price varies. Liguori Editore s.r.l., Via Mezzocannone 19, 80134 Naples, Italy. Ed. Lucio Potito.

658 FR ISSN 0072-7792
GROUPEMENT DES DIRECTEURS PUBLICITAIRES DE FRANCE. ANNUAIRE. 1968. a. 250 F. membership. Nouvelles Editions de la Publicite, 9 rue Leo-Delibes, 75116 Paris, France. adv.
Formerly: Annuaire General des Publicitaires de France.

GUIDE TO GRADUATE MANAGEMENT EDUCATION; a guide for prospective students. see EDUCATION — Guides To Schools And Colleges

658 GW ISSN 0073-0122
HANDBUCH DER RATIONALISIERUNG. 1958. irreg. DM.390. (Rationalisierungskuratorium der Deutschen Wirtschaft) Industrie-Verlag Carlheinz Gehlsen, Dechenstr. 7, Postfach 287, 5300 Bonn, W. Germany (B.R.D.)

650 658.01 US ISSN 0073-0785
HARVARD UNIVERSITY. GRADUATE SCHOOL OF BUSINESS ADMINISTRATION. PROGRAM FOR MANAGEMENT DEVELOPMENT. PUBLICATION. 1960. a. price varies. Harvard University, Graduate School of Business Administration, Boston, MA 02163.

380 658 JA ISSN 0018-2796
HITOTSUBASHI JOURNAL OF COMMERCE AND MANAGEMENT. 1961. s-a. 1500 Yen. Hitotsubashi University, Hitotsubashi Academy, 2-1 Naka, Kunitachi, Tokyo 186, Japan. Ed. K. Okamoto. charts. illus. stat. cum.index in prep. circ. 940.

658 SZ
HOCHSCHULE ST. GALLEN FUER WIRTSCHAFTS- UND SOZIALWISSENSCHAFTEN. VEROEFFENTLICHUNGEN. SCHRIFTENREIHE BETRIEBSWIRTSCHAFT. 1973. irreg., no. 5, 1979. price varies. Paul Haupt AG, Falkenplatz 14, CH-3001 Berne, Switzerland.

658 HK ISSN 0018-4594
HONG KONG MANAGER. (Text in Chinese and English) 1965. m. membership. ‡ Hong Kong Management Association, Management House, 26 Canal Road West, Happy Valley, Hong Kong, Hong Kong. Ed. J. R. Hung. adv. bk. rev. abstr. charts. illus. stat. tr.lit. index. circ. 3,500.

658 II
I F M R PUBLICATIONS. no. 12, 1975. irreg. Institute for Financial Management and Research, Madras, Madras 600034, India (Dist. by: Vora & Co., Publishers, 3 Round Bldg., Kalbadevi, Bombay 400002, India)

658.01 US ISSN 0073-4624
IDEAS FOR MANAGEMENT; proceedings of the annual conference. 1948. a. $12. Association for Systems Management, 24587 Bagley Rd., Cleveland, OH 44138. Ed. R. B. MacCaffrey.

658 UK ISSN 0304-4270
INSEAD ADDRESS BOOK/I N S E A D ADDRESS BOOK. 1959/60. a. £200($65) to non-members. ‡ (INSEAD Alumni Association) A P Books, 9 Courtleigh Gardens, London NW11 9JX, England. Ed. Alan Phillip. adv. circ. 3,750.

658 FR
INSTITUT FRANCAIS DES SCIENCES ADMINISTRATIVES. (PUBLICATIONS) 1967. irreg. price varies. Editions Cujas, 4,6,8 rue de la Maison Blanche, 75013 Paris, France.

INSTITUT PANAFRICAIN POUR LE DEVELOPPEMENT. CENTRE D'ETUDES ET DE RECHERCHES APPLIQUEES. EVALUATION DU SEMINAIRE SUR LA METHODOLOGIE DU MANAGEMENT DES PROJETS. see BUSINESS AND ECONOMICS — International Development And Assistance

INSTITUT PANAFRICAIN POUR LE DEVELOPPEMENT. CENTRE DE FORMATION AU MANAGEMENT DES PROJETS. BILAN DES ACTIVITIES. see BUSINESS AND ECONOMICS — International Development And Assistance

658.007 IO
INSTITUTE FOR MANAGEMENT EDUCATION AND DEVELOPMENT. REPORT. (Text in English) a. Institute for Management Education and Development - Lembaga Pendidikan dan Pembinaan Management, Jalan Mentang Raya 9, Jakarta, Indonesia.

309.2 TZ
INSTITUTE OF DEVELOPMENT MANAGEMENT. REPORT OF THE ACTIVITIES OF THE INSTITUTE. 1973. a. Institute of Development Management, Box 604, Morogoro, Mzumbe, Tanzania.

338.9 US ISSN 0082-0911
INSTITUTE OF MANAGEMENT SCIENCES. SYMPOSIUM ON PLANNING. PROCEEDINGS. irreg., 1968, 11th. Institute of Management Sciences, Time Planning College, 146 Westminster St., Providence, RI 02903. Eds. Gene E. Talbert, Hasan Ozbekhan.

658 AG
INSTITUTO PARA EL DESARROLLO DE EJECUTIVOS EN LA ARGENTINA. NOTICIAS. no. 8, Dec., 1977. Instituto para el Desarrollo de Ejectivos en la Argentina, Sistema de Actualizacion Empresaria, Moreno 1850, Buenos Aires, Argentina. Ed. Silvia Fittipaldi.

658 JA ISSN 0085-2120
INTERNATIONAL COUNCIL FOR SCIENTIFIC MANAGEMENT. PROCEEDINGS OF WORLD CONGRESS. 1924, Prague. triennial since 1951; 1969, 15th, Tokyo. price varies; $18 for 15th. International Management Association of Japan, 28 Shiba-Nishikuho-Sakuragawa-cho, Minato-ku, Tokyo, Japan (Inquire: World Council of Management, Box 20, 1211 Geneva 20, Switzerland)
Proceedings published by organizing committee

150 US ISSN 0160-7146
JACOB MARSCHAK INTERDISCIPLINARY COLLOQUIUM ON MATHEMATICS IN THE BEHAVIORAL SCIENCES. 1959. a. $5.50. (Western Management Sciences Institute) University of California, Los Angeles, Graduate School of Management, 405 Hilgard Ave., Los Angeles, CA 90024. circ. 100.

658 II
JODHPUR MANAGEMENT JOURNAL. 1971. a. Rs.15($5) University of Jodhpur, Faculty of Commerce, Jodhpur 342001, Rajasthan, India. Ed. K. Agarwala. adv. bk. rev. circ. 1,000.

658.2 JA
JOURNAL OF INDUSTRY AND MANAGEMENT/SANGYO KEIEI KENKYUSHOHO. (Text in Japanese) irreg. Kyushu Sangyo University - Kyushu Sangyo Daigaku, 2-327 Shokadai, Higashi-ku, Tokyo, Japan.

658 CE
KALAMANAKARANAYA; management. (Text in Sinhalese) 1977. Rs.1.50. University of Sri Lanka, Vidyodaya Campus, Management Studies Society, Gangodawila, Nugegoda, Sri Lanka.

KENT STATE UNIVERSITY. CENTER FOR BUSINESS AND ECONOMIC RESEARCH. COMPARATIVE ADMINISTRATION RESEARCH INSTITUTE SERIES. see BUSINESS AND ECONOMICS

658 JA ISSN 0085-2570
KOBE UNIVERSITY. SCHOOL OF BUSINESS ADMINISTRATION. ANNALS. (Text in English) 1957. a. exchange basis. ‡ Kobe University, School of Business Administration, Rokkodai-cho, Nada-ku, Kobe 657, Japan. Ed. Susumu Kaido. bibl. charts. circ. controlled.

658 US
L R I GUIDES TO MANAGEMENT. MONOGRAPHS. 1965. irreg.; latest issue no. 7. price varies. Leadership Resources Inc., One First Virginia Plaza, Suite 344, 6400 Arlington Blvd., Falls Church, VA 22042. Ed. David S. Brown.
Formerly: Management Monographs (ISSN 0076-3640)

BUSINESS AND ECONOMICS — MANAGEMENT

920 650   GW   ISSN 0075-871X
LEITENDE MAENNER DER WIRTSCHAFT. 1940. a. DM.245. Verlag Hoppenstedt und Co., Havelstr. 9, Postfach 4006, 6100 Darmstadt, W. Germany (B.R.D.) adv.

658   629.13   US   ISSN 0565-7199
MANAGEMENT (BALTIMORE); a continuing literature survey with indexes. 1968. a. $6.50. U.S. National Aeronautics and Space Administration, Scientific and Technical Information Facility, Box 8757, Baltimore/Washington International Airport, MD 21240 (Order from: N T I S, Springfield, VA 22161) index.

629.8   US   ISSN 0076-3624
MANAGEMENT GUIDE TO N C.* 1964. irreg., 1971, no. 2. $11.50. Numerical Control Society, 1201 Waukegan Rd., Glenview, IL 60025. Ed. M De Vries.

658   PP
MANAGEMENT IN PAPUA NEW GUINEA. triennial. Papua New Guinea Institute of Management, Box 1010, Lae, Papua New Guinea. Ed.Bd.

658 4   UG   ISSN 0300-2144
MANAGEMENT JOURNAL. Short title: Management. 1968. a. S.2. ‡ Management Training and Advisory Centre, P.O. Box 4655, Kampala, Uganda. adv. illus. circ. 2,500.
   Formerly: M T A C Journal.

658   US   ISSN 0085-3054
MANAGEMENT MONOGRAPHS (NEW YORK) irreg., latest issue 1976. $20-50. Business International Corp., One Dag Hammarskjold Plaza, New York, NY 10017.

658   GW
MANAGEMENT WISSEN JAHRBUCH. 1974. a. DM.28. Vogel-Verlag KG, Postfach 6740, Max-Planck-Str. 7-9, 8700 Wuerzburg 1, W. Germany (B.R.D.) adv.

658   ET   ISSN 0580-8898
MANAGER AND ENTREPRENEUR.* 1972. irreg, latest 1974, vol. 3. Centre for Entrepreneurship and Management, Box 3246, Addis Ababa, Ethiopia. Ed. R. J. Richardson. adv. charts. illus.

658   BG
MANEGGIARE. (Text in English or Bengali) 1977. irreg. Tk.10. University of Chittagong, Department of Management, Chittagong, Bangladesh.

MEDICAL GROUP MANAGEMENT ASSOCIATION. INTERNATIONAL DIRECTORY. see *MEDICAL SCIENCES*

658 381   FR   ISSN 0076-8812
MILLESIME. 1953. a. 25 F.($5) Association des Anciens Eleves de l'Ecole Superieur de Commerce de Paris, 79 Avenue de la Republique, Paris 11, France. adv. bk. rev. circ. 8,000.

658.4   MY
NATIONAL PRODUCTIVITY CENTRE, MALAYSIA. ANNUAL REPORT/PUSAT DAYA PENGELUARAN NEGARA. LAPURAN TAHUNAN. (Text in English and Malay) a. National Productivity Centre, Petaling Jaya, Malaysia.

OEKONOMETRIE UND UNTERNEHMENSFORSCHUNG/ ECONOMETRICS AND OPERATIONS RESEARCH. see *BUSINESS AND ECONOMICS*

001.4 658   GW   ISSN 0078-5318
OPERATIONS RESEARCH-VERFAHREN/METHODS OF OPERATIONS RESEARCH. (Text in English and German) 1963. irreg., vol. 36, 1980. price varies. Verlag Anton Hain GmbH, Adelheid Str. 2, Postfach 1220, 6240 Koenigstein, W. Germany (B. R. D.) Ed. Rudolf Henn. circ. 300-700.

658   GW   ISSN 0048-2129
ORDO; Jahrbuch fuer die Ordnung von Wirtschaft und Gesellschaft. 1948. a. price varies. Gustav Fischer Verlag, Wollgrasweg 49, 7000 Stuttgart 70, W. Germany (B.R.D.)

658   US
ORGANIZATIONAL COMMUNICATIONS ABSTRACTS. a. (American Business Communication Association) Sage Publications, Inc, 275 S. Beverly Dr., Beverly Hills, CA 90212. (Co-sponsor: International Communication Association, Austin, Texas.) (also avail. in microform from UMI; reprint service avail. from UMI)

658   UR
ORGANIZATSIYA UPRAVLENIYA. 1971. irreg. 0.81 Rub. Izdetel'stvo Ekonomika, Berezhkovskaya nab., 6, 121864 Moscow, U.S.S.R.

658   US
PERGAMON MANAGEMENT AND BUSINESS SERIES. 1972. irreg., vol. 5, 1974. price varies. Pergamon Press, Inc., Maxwell House, Fairview Park, Elmsford, NY 10523.

658   SZ   ISSN 0079-2276
PLANUNG UND KONTROLLE IN DER UNTERNEHMUNG. 1966. irreg., vol. 6, 1976. price varies. (Hochschule St. Gallen fuer Wirtschafts- und Sozialwissenschaften, Institut fuer Betriebswirtschaft) Paul Haupt AG, Falkenplatz 14, CH-3001 Berne, Switzerland.

PLUNKETT FOUNDATION FOR CO-OPERATIVE STUDIES. STUDY SERIES. see *AGRICULTURE — Agricultural Economics*

658   PL   ISSN 0324-9484
POLITECHNIKA WROCLAWSKA. INSTYTUT ORGANIZACJI I ZARZADZANIA. PRACE NAUKOWE. KONFERENCJE. (Text in Polish; summaries in English and Russian) 1973. irreg., no. 10, 1979. price varies. Politechnika Wroclawska, Wybrzeze Wyspianskiego 27, 50-370 Wroclaw, Poland (Dist. by: Ars Polona-Ruch, Krakowskie Przedmiescie 7, Warsaw, Poland) Ed. Marian Kloza.

658   PL   ISSN 0324-9492
POLITECHNIKA WROCLAWSKA. INSTYTUT ORGANIZACJI I ZARZADZANIA. PRACE NAUKOWE. MONOGRAFIE. (Text in Polish; summaries in English and Russian) 1970. irreg., no. 6, 1979. price varies. Politechnika Wroclawska, Wybrzeze Wyspianskiego 27, 50-370 Wroclaw, Poland (Dist. by: Ars Polona-Ruch, Krakowskie Przedmiescie 7, Warsaw, Poland) Ed. Marian Kloza.

658   PL   ISSN 0324-9468
POLITECHNIKA WROCLAWSKA. INSTYTUT ORGANIZACJI I ZARZADZANIA. PRACE NAUKOWE. STUDIA I MATERIALY. (Text in Polish; summaries in English and Russian) 1970. irreg., no. 11, 1979. price varies. Politechnika Wroclawska, Wybrzeze Wyspianskiego 27, 50-370 Wroclaw, Poland (Dist. by: Ars Polona-Ruch, Krakowskie Przedmiescie 7, Warsaw, Poland) Ed. Marian Kloza.

658 338   US   ISSN 0079-3825
POOR'S REGISTER OF CORPORATIONS, DIRECTORS AND EXECUTIVES. 1928. a. with 3 supplements. $215. Standard & Poor's Corporation, 25 Broadway, New York, NY 10004. Ed. T. Lupo. (also avail. in magnetic tape)

650 658   SZ   ISSN 0079-4880
PRAKTISCHE BETRIEBSWIRTSCHAFT. 1958. irreg., vol. 8, 1978. price varies. (Hochschule St. Gallen fuer Wirtschafts- und Sozialwissenschaften, Institut fuer Betriebswirtschaft) Paul Haupt AG, Falkenplatz 14, CH-3001 Berne, Switzerland.

658   SZ   ISSN 0079-7111
PRUEFEN UND ENTSCHEIDEN. 1958. irreg., no. 8, 1978. price varies. (Universitaet Bern, Institut fuer Betriebswirtschaft) Paul Haupt AG, Falkenplatz 14, CH-3001 Berne, Switzerland.

658   GW
QUANTITATIVE METHODEN DER UNTERNEHMUNGSPLANUNG. 1975. irreg., no.16, 1980. price varies. Verlag Anton Hain GmbH, Adelheidstr. 2, Postfach 1220, 6240 Koenigstein, W. Germany (B.R.D.) Eds. H. Goeppl, D. Opitz.

QUI REPRESENTE QUI. see *BUSINESS AND ECONOMICS — International Commerce*

RESEARCH IN ECONOMICS/BUSINESS ADMINISTRATION. see *BUSINESS AND ECONOMICS*

RESEARCH IN PUBLIC POLICY AND MANAGEMENT. see *PUBLIC ADMINISTRATION*

658   FR
REVUE INTERNATIONALE DES CADRES.* 1972. a. 30 rue de Gramont, Paris 2e, France. Ed. Bd.

658   GW   ISSN 0067-6381
SCHRIFTENREIHE BETRIEBSWIRTSCHAFTICHE BEITRAEGE ZUR ORGANISATION UND AUTOMATION. 1966. irreg., vol. 26, 1977. price varies. Betriebswirtschaftlicher Verlag Dr. Th. Gabler KG, Taunusstr. 54, Postfach 1546, 6200 Wiesbaden 1, W. Germany (B.R.D.) Eds. E. Grochla, N. Szyperski.

658   GW   ISSN 0080-7087
SCHRIFTENREIHE ZUR THEORETISCHEN UND ANGEWANDTEN BETRIEBSWIRTSCHLAFTSLEHRE. 1966. irreg. price varies. Betriebswirtschaftlicher Verlag Dr. Th. Gabler KG, Taunusstr. 54, Postfach 1546, 6200 Wiesbaden 1, W. Germany (B.R.D.) Eds. L. Pack, H. Wagner.

SELBSTBEDIENUNG--DYNAMIK IM HANDEL. see *FOOD AND FOOD INDUSTRIES — Grocery Trade*

650   US
SERIES IN ADMINISTRATION. irreg. price varies. Harper and Row Publishers, Inc., 10 East 53rd St., New York, NY 10022.

658   US   ISSN 0193-4201
SIGNIFICANT ISSUES FACING DIRECTORS. 1976. a. $21. Directors Publications, Inc., Pine Tree Drive, Box 5198, Westport, CT 06881. Ed. Abraham Nad. (back issues avail.)

SIR FREDERIC HOOPER AWARD ESSAY. see *BUSINESS AND ECONOMICS*

658   NE
STUDIES IN MANAGEMENT SCIENCE AND SYSTEMS. 1975. irreg., vol. 6, 1978. price varies. North-Holland Publishing Co., Box 211, 1000 AE Amsterdam, Netherlands. Ed. B. V. Dean.

658   NE   ISSN 0081-8194
STUDIES IN MATHEMATICAL AND MANAGERIAL ECONOMICS. 1964. irreg., vol. 27, 1979. price varies. North Holland Publishing Co., Box 211, 1000 AE Amsterdam, Netherlands. Ed. H. Theil.

658   US
STUDIES IN MEDIA MANAGEMENT. irreg. price varies. Communication Arts Books, 10 East 40th St., New York, NY 10016.

TOP EXECUTIVE COMPENSATION. see *BUSINESS AND ECONOMICS — Labor And Industrial Relations*

658   US
TRAINING AND DEVELOPMENT ORGANIZATIONS DIRECTORY; a reference work describing firms, institutes, and other agencies offering training programs for business, industry and government. 1978. irreg., 2nd edt. 1980. $90. Gale Research Company, Book Tower, Detroit, MI 48226. Ed. Paul Wasserman.

658 650   UY
UNIVERSIDAD DE LA REPUBLICA. INSTITUTO DE ADMINISTRACION. BOLETIN. 1976. irreg.; no. 80, 1979. Universidad de la Republica, Instituto de Administracion, Montevideo, Uruguay.

658   UY   ISSN 0077-1287
UNIVERSIDAD DE LA REPUBLICA. INSTITUTO DE ADMINISTRACION. CUADERNO. 1956. irreg.; no. 80, 1979. price varies. Universidad de la Republica, Instituto de Administracion, 18 de Julio 1953 4p, Montevideo, Uruguay.

UNIVERSIDAD DE SEVILLA. INSTITUTO GARCIA OVIEDO. PUBLICACIONES. see *LAW*

658   SZ
UNIVERSITAET ZUERICH. INSTITUT FUER BETRIEBSWIRTSCHAFTLICHE FORSCHUNG. SCHRIFTENREIHE. 1970. irreg., no. 30, 1979. price varies. Paul Haupt AG, Falkenplatz 14, CH-3001 Berne, Switzerland.

658 US ISSN 0146-2571
UNIVERSITY OF CALIFORNIA, LOS ANGELES. GRADUATE SCHOOL OF MANAGEMENT. ANNUAL REPORT. 1972. a. free. University of California, Los Angeles, Graduate School of Management, 405 Hilgard Ave., Los Angeles, CA 90024. Ed. Rebecca Novelli. circ. 16,000.

658 US ISSN 0094-1565
UNIVERSITY OF TOLEDO. BUSINESS RESEARCH CENTER. WORKING PAPERS IN OPERATIONS ANALYSIS. 1969. irreg., latest edition, 1978. price varies. University of Toledo, College of Business Administration, 2801 W. Bancroft St., Toledo, OH 43606. Dir. Thomas A. Klein.

658 CN
UNIVERSITY OF TORONTO. FACULTY OF MANAGEMENT STUDIES. WORKING PAPER SERIES. 1971. irreg. Can.$5 or on exchange basis. University of Toronto, Faculty of Management Studies, 246 Bloor St. W., Toronto, Ont. M5S 1V4, Canada. Ed. Frank Mathewson.

658 SZ ISSN 0083-4548
UNTERNEHMUNG UND UNTERNEHMUNGSFUEHRUNG. 1968. irreg. price varies. (Hochschule St. Gallen fuer Wirtschafts- und Sozialwissenschaften, Institut fuer Betriebswirtschaft) Paul Haupt AG, Falkenplatz 14, 3001 Berne, Switzerland.

658 FR
V.I.P. DU CONSEIL. 1978. biennial. 447 F. Societe d'Etudes et de Publications Industrielles, 15 Square de Vergennes, 75015 Paris, France. (Affiliate: France Expansion) Ed. Zina Avril. circ. 1,000.

658 II ISSN 0083-5102
VAIKUNTH MEHTA NATIONAL INSTITUTE OF COOPERATIVE MANAGEMENT. PUBLICATIONS.* irreg. price varies. Vaikunth Mehta National Institute of Cooperative Management, Reserve Bank of India Bldg., Ganeshkhind Rd., Poona 411016, India.

330 658 FR ISSN 0083-6095
VIE DES AFFAIRES;* bulletin consacre a l'analyse des avis emis par les dirigeants d'entreprise a l'egard du droit economique et des politiques gouvernementales. 1970. irreg. price varies. Agence Legislative, 22 rue de Chateaudun, Paris 11e, France.

658.562 US ISSN 0083-8217
WEST COAST RELIABILITY SYMPOSIUM. 5th, 1964. irreg., 12th, 1971. (American Society for Quality Control, Los Angeles Section) Western Periodicals Co., 13000 Raymer St., North Hollywood, CA 91605.

658 US
WHAT IT COSTS TO RUN AN AGENCY. biennial, 15th 1973. Rough Notes Co., Inc., 1200 N. Meridian St., Indianapolis, IN 46204.

658 338 US ISSN 0083-9302
WHO OWNS WHOM. CONTINENTAL EUROPE. (Text in English, French and German) 1961. a. $194. Dun & Bradstreet Ltd., Publications Division, 6-8 Bonhill St., London EC2A 4BU, England. index.

658 920 US ISSN 0083-9485
WHO'S WHO IN CONSULTING; a reference guide to professional personnel engaged in consultation for business, industry and government. 1968. irreg.; 2nd edt., 1973. $58. Gale Research Company, Book Tower, Detroit, MI 48226.

658.31 920 US ISSN 0092-4598
WHO'S WHO IN TRAINING AND DEVELOPMENT. 1970. a. $25 to non-members. American Society for Training and Development, P.O. Box 5307, Madison, WI 53705. Ed. Michael H. Cook. adv. illus. circ. 12,000.
Continues: American Society for Training and Development. Membership Directory (ISSN 0569-776X)

650 US
WILEY SERIES ON SYSTEMS AND CONTROLS FOR FINANCIAL MANAGEMENT. 1971. irreg., unnumbered, latest, 1980. price varies. John Wiley & Sons, Inc., 605 Third Ave., New York, NY 10016. Eds. Robert L. Shultis, Frank M. Mastromano.

658 US
YEAR-END REGULATORY REVIEW. 1976. a. $10. Directors Publications, Inc., Pine Tree Dr., Box 5198, Westport, CT 06881. Ed. Abraham Nad.

BUSINESS AND ECONOMICS — Marketing And Purchasing

see also Advertising and Public Relations

ALBERTA PETROLEUM MARKETING COMMISSION. ANNUAL REPORT. see *PETROLEUM AND GAS*

658.8 US ISSN 0065-8103
AMERICAN DROP-SHIPPERS DIRECTORY. 1964. a. $5 postpaid. World Wide Trade Service, P.O. Box 283, Medina, WA 98039. Ed. George Lucas. adv. bk. rev.

658.8 US
AMERICAN MARKETING ASSOCIATION. COMMITTEE ON ATTITUDE RESEARCH. PAPERS PRESENTED AT THE ANNUAL CONFERENCE. 1973, 5th. a. price varies. American Marketing Association, Committee on Attitude Research, 222 S. Riverside Plaza, Chicago, IL 60606.

658.8 US ISSN 0093-1454
AMERICAN MARKETING ASSOCIATION. DIRECTORY OF MARKETING SERVICES AND MEMBERSHIP ROSTER. biennial. price varies. American Marketing Association, 222 S. Riverside Plaza, Chicago, IL 60606.

658.8 US ISSN 0065-9231
AMERICAN MARKETING ASSOCIATION. PROCEEDINGS. 1921. irreg. American Marketing Association, 222 S. Riverside Plaza, Chicago, IL 60606. index.
Incorporating: A M A Combined Proceedings Series & A M A Papers of the Conferences; Formerly: A M A Abstracts of Papers of the Conferences (ISSN 0065-9215)

380.1 II ISSN 0376-5512
ANDHRA PRADESH STATE TRADING CORPORATION LIMITED. ANNUAL REPORT. (Text in English) a. Andhra Pradesh State Trading Corporation Limited, 5-10-174 Fatchmaiden Rd., Hyderabad 500004, India. Key Title: Annual Report-Andhra Pradesh State Trading Corporation Limited.

658.8 FR ISSN 0066-300X
ANNUAIRE DU MARKETING. 1964-65. a. 195 F. Association Nationale pour le Developpment des Techniques de Marketing, 30 rue d'Astorg, 75008 Paris, France. adv. bk. rev. circ. 3,000.

658.8 FR ISSN 0066-3077
ANNUAIRE EUROPEEN DES DIRECTEURS COMMERCIAUX ET DE MARKETING. 1958. a. 150 F. Dirigeants Commerciaux de France, 30 rue d'Astorg, 75008 Paris, France. adv.

658.8 US
ANNUAL EDITIONS: READINGS IN MARKETING. Short title: Readings in Marketing. a. $6.25. Dushkin Publishing Group, Sluice Dock, Guilford, CT 06437. illus.

ANUARIO BRASILEIRO DE SUPERMERCADOS. see *BUSINESS AND ECONOMICS — Domestic Commerce*

658.8 US ISSN 0068-063X
BRADFORD'S DIRECTORY OF MARKETING RESEARCH AGENCIES AND MANAGEMENT CONSULTANTS IN THE UNITED STATES AND THE WORLD. 1943. irreg.; 13th ed. 1971; biennial Addenda. $25.50. Bradford's Directory, Box 276, Dept. B-X, Fairfax, VA 22030.

658 AT
BUSINESS WHO'S WHO AUSTRALIAN BUYING REFERENCE. 1967. a. Aus.$81.50. R.G. Riddell Pty.Ltd., 2 Dist St, Milsons Point, N.S.W. 2061, Australia (Dist. in U.S. by: International Publications Service, 114 E. 32nd St., New York, NY 10016) Ed. R. G. Riddell. adv. circ. 3,000.
Formerly: Riddell's Australian Purchasing Yearbook (ISSN 0085-5715)

381 US ISSN 0098-3047
C S A SPECS BUYING GUIDE FOR STORE PLANNERS. (Chain Store Age) irreg. Lebhar-Friedman, Inc., 425 Park Ave., New York, NY 10016. illus.

CADEAU ET L'ENTREPRISE; les techniques de stimulation des ventes. see *ADVERTISING AND PUBLIC RELATIONS*

658.7 US
CALIFORNIA. DEPARTMENT OF CONSUMER AFFAIRS. ANNUAL REPORT. a. Department of Consumer Affairs, 1020 N St., Sacramento, CA 95814.

658.7 CN
CANADIAN DIRECTORY OF SHOPPING CENTRES. 1975. a. 165. Maclean-Hunter Ltd., 481 University Ave., Toronto, Ont. M5W 1A7, Canada. Ed. Barbara Lewiecki. (looseleaf format)

658.182 US ISSN 0069-2395
CHAIN STORE AGE SUPERMARKET SALES MANUAL. (Part of July issue of Chain Store Age: Supermarket Edition) 1934. a. Lebhar-Friedman, Inc., 425 Park Ave., New York, NY 10022. Ed. Kenneth P. Partch. index.

658.8 332.6 US ISSN 0160-6360
CHEMICAL NEW PRODUCT DIRECTORY. 1973. a. $300. Marketing Development, 402 Border Rd., Concord, MA 01742. Ed. Bud Anderson. charts. (back issues avail.)
Supersedes in part (as of 1977): Survey of New Products Introduced by N.Y.S.E. Listed Companies; Formerly (until 1974): New Product Directory of N.Y.S.E. Listed Companies.

658.8 US
CHILDREN'S MEDIA MARKET PLACE. 1978. biennial. $16.95. Gaylord Bros. Inc., Box 4901, Syracuse, NY 13221. (Co-Publisher: Neal-Schuman Publications, Inc.) Eds. Deirdre Boyle, Stephen Calvert. circ. 2,000.

658.8 BL
COLECAO DOCUMENTA/CRESO. 1976. irreg. Editora Documentario, Rua Muniz Barreto 12, Rio de Janeiro, Brazil. illus.

CONSUMER CREDIT ASSOCIATION OF THE UNITED KINGDOM. MEMBERSHIP DIRECTORY. see *BUSINESS AND ECONOMICS — Banking And Finance*

658.8 UK ISSN 0308-4353
CONSUMER EUROPE. 1977. biennial. $115. Euromonitor Publications Ltd., Box 26, 18 Doughty St., London WC1N 2PN, England.

CREDIT MANUAL OF COMMERCIAL LAWS. see *BUSINESS AND ECONOMICS — Banking And Finance*

CUADERNOS UNIVERSITARIOS DE PLANIFICACION EMPRESARIAL Y MARKETING. see *BUSINESS AND ECONOMICS — Management*

383 US
D M M A IN DEPTH. 1976. irreg. Direct Mail-Marketing Association, 6 E. 43rd St., New York, NY 10017. bk. rev.

658 GW ISSN 0084-9766
DEUTSCHE MESSEN UND AUSSTELLUNGEN - EIN ZAHLENSPIEGEL. 1967. a. Ausstellungs- und Messe-Ausschuss der Deutschen Wirtschaft E.V., Lindenstr. 8, 5000 Cologne 1, W. Germany (B.R.D.)

658.8 US ISSN 0070-4970
DIRECT SELLING;* association membership roster listing major companies and commodities. a. Direct Selling Association, 1730 M St., N.W., Washington, DC 20036.

650 658.8 US ISSN 0070-556X
DIRECTORY OF FRANCHISING ORGANIZATIONS. 1959. a. $3.50. Pilot Books, 347 Fifth Ave., New York, NY 10016. Ed. S. Small.

BUSINESS AND ECONOMICS — MARKETING AND PURCHASING

658.8 US
DIRECTORY OF PREMIUM, INCENTIVE AND TRAVEL BUYERS. 1970. a. with quarterly supplements. $110. Salesmans Guide Inc., 1140 Broadway, New York, NY 10001.
Formerly: Directory of Premium and Incentive Buyers (ISSN 0070-6124)

658.7 US
DIRECTORY OF SHOP-BY-MAIL BARGAIN SOURCES. 1978. irreg. $2.95. Pilot Books, 347 Fifth Ave., New York, NY 10016. Eds. Margaret A. Boyd, Sue Scott-Martin.
Purchasing

658.3 US ISSN 0364-8966
DIRECTORY OF U.S. AND CANADIAN MARKETING SURVEYS AND SERVICES. 1976. biennial. $125. Charles H. Kline & Co., Inc., 330 Passaic Ave., Fairfield, NJ 07006. Ed. Joan Huber.

658.8 US ISSN 0070-704X
DOLLARS AND CENTS OF SHOPPING CENTERS. 1961. triennial. $49.25 to non-members; members $36.50. ‡ Urban Land Institute, 1200 18 St. N.W., Washington, DC 20036. (reprint service avail. from UMI)

658.8 US
DROP SHIP BUYERS GUIDE. 1958. irreg., latest 1973. $3 per copy. Rutward Mail Order Publications, Box 471, Georgetown, CT 06829. Ed. William E. O'Brien. circ. 5,000.

DROP SHIPPING SOURCE DIRECTORY OF MAJOR CONSUMER PRODUCT LINES. see *BUSINESS AND ECONOMICS — Trade And Industrial Directories*

DRUG STORE MARKET GUIDE; a detailed distribution analysis. see *PHARMACY AND PHARMACOLOGY*

658.8 US ISSN 0070-7619
DUN AND BRADSTREET MILLION DOLLAR DIRECTORY. VOL. 1. 1959. a. Dun's Marketing Services (Subsidiary of: Dun and Bradstreet, Inc.) Three Century Dr., Parsippany, NJ 07054. (also avail. in magnetic tape)

658.8 US
DUN AND BRADSTREET MILLION DOLLAR DIRECTORY. VOL. 2. 1964. a. $150. ‡ Dun's Marketing Services (Subsidiary of: Dun and Bradstreet, Inc.) Three Century, Parsippany, NJ 07054. (also avail. in magnetic tape)
Formerly: Dun & Bradstreet Middle Market Directory (ISSN 0070-7600)

658.8 US ISSN 0070-7821
E I A GUIDE. 1946. a. $10. Directories of Industry, Inc., 9371 Kramer, Unit 1, Westminster, CA 92683. Ed. Billa Wann. adv. circ. 25,000.
Formerly: Western Industrial Purchasing Guide and Electronic/Sources.

070.5 US
EDITOR AND PUBLISHER MARKET GUIDE. 1924. a. $35. Editor & Publisher Co., Inc., 575 Lexington Ave., New York, NY 10022. circ. 7,000.

658.8 332.6 US
ELECTRONICS NEW PRODUCT DIRECTORY. 1976. a. $450. Marketing Development, 402 Border Rd., Concord, MA 01742. Ed. Sally Cancelmo.
Supersedes in part: Survey of New Products Introduced by N.Y.S.E. Listed Companies.

658.8 US ISSN 0071-0695
ENTERTAINMENT INDUSTRY SERIES. 1961. irreg.(approx. 1/yr.) price varies. Seven Arts Press, Inc., 6605 Hollywood Blvd., Suite 215, Hollywood, CA 90028. Ed. Walter E. Hurst. bk. rev. cum.index: 1961-1971 (for vols. 1-6) circ. 3,000.

658.8 UK ISSN 0071-2930
EUROPEAN MARKETING DATA AND STATISTICS. 1962. a. $150. Euromonitor Publications Ltd., Box 26, 18 Doughty St., London WC1N 2PN, England.

658 BE ISSN 0423-8044
EUROPEAN PURCHASING CONFERENCE. (PROCEEDINGS)* (Text in English, French or German) irreg. European Federation of Purchasing, c/o J. Hyde, Secretary-General, 1, rue aux Laines, 1000 Brussels, Belgium.

658 US ISSN 0071-3716
FAIRCHILD'S FINANCIAL MANUAL OF RETAIL STORES. 1923. a. $50. Fairchild Books (Subsidiary of: Fairchild Publications Inc.) 7 East 12th St., New York, NY 10003. Ed. Robin Feldman. stat. circ. 2,000. (back issues avail.)

658.8 CN
FINANCIAL POST CANADIAN MARKETS. 1925. a. Can.$29. Maclean-Hunter Ltd., 481 University Ave., Toronto M5W IA7, Ont., Canada. Ed. Anne Hipwell. adv. circ. 7,000. (also avail. in microfiche)
Formerly: Financial Post Survey of Markets (ISSN 0071-5077)
Marketing facts on 400 Canadian geographical locations

658.8 US
FINDEX; directory of market research reports, studies and surveys. a.(with mid-year suppl.) $79.50. Find-SVP, 500 Fifth Ave., New York, NY 10036. Eds. Diana Degen, Thomas E. Miller.

FRASER'S CANADIAN TRADE DIRECTORY. see *BUSINESS AND ECONOMICS — Trade And Industrial Directories*

GALLAGHER PRESIDENTS' REPORT. see *ADVERTISING AND PUBLIC RELATIONS*

658.8 US
GIFTWARE NEWS MANAGEMENT/MERCHANDISING GUIDE AND TABLEWARE DIRECTORY. 1977. a. Talcott Communications Corp., 5461 N. East River Rd., Chicago, IL 60656. Ed. Cholm Houghton. adv. circ. 39,800.

HANDBOOK OF ADVERTISING AND MARKETING SERVICES. see *ADVERTISING AND PUBLIC RELATIONS*

658.871 IT
I.R.D.S. (International Register of Department Stores) (Text in English, French, German, Italian, Spanish) 1962. a. L.250000($250) ‡ Consulente Immobiliare, Via Vittor Pisani 16, Casella Postale 10339, 20100 Milan, Italy. Ed. F. Tamborrino.
Formerly: Department Store Suppliers (ISSN 0011-8907)

658.8 UK ISSN 0073-9650
INSTITUTE OF PURCHASING AND SUPPLY. YEARBOOK. 1963. a. £5. Institute of Purchasing and Supply, I.P.S. House, High St., Ascot, Berks, England. Ed. Robert Brookes. adv. circ. 800.

658.8 FR ISSN 0074-1582
INTERNATIONAL ASSOCIATION OF CHAIN STORES. REPORT OF PLENARY SESSION. 1952. irreg., 1976. 19th, Rio de Janeiro. membership. International Association of Chain Stores, Dr. Gen. Frederic C. Treidell, 61 Quai d'Orsay, 75007 Paris, France.

658.8 UK
INTERNATIONAL DIRECTORY OF PUBLISHED MARKET RESEARCH. 1976. a. $40. British Overseas Trade Board, 50 Ludgate Hill, London EC4M 7HU, England.

658.8 US
INTERNATIONAL VENDING BUYER'S GUIDE AND DIRECTORY. a. $7.50. Vending Times, Inc., 211 E. 43 St., New York, NY 10017.
Absorbed: Vending Buyer's Guide.

658 GW
INTERNATIONALE BEITRAEGE ZUR MARKT-, MEINUNGS- UND ZUKUNFTSFORSCHUNG. irreg. price varies. Wickert Institute Tuebingen, 7919 Illereichen, W. Germany (B.R.D.)

IRELAND (EIRE) CENTRAL STATISTICS OFFICE. HIRE-PURCHASE AND CREDIT SALES. see *BUSINESS AND ECONOMICS — Banking And Finance*

380.4 NE
KALENDER VAN INTERNATIONALE JAAR- EN VAKBEURZEN. a. free. Ministerie van Economische Zaken, Economische Voorlichtingsdienst, Bezuidenhoutseweg 151, The Hague, Netherlands.

658 GW
LAGERTECHNIK. a. Europa Fachpresse-Verlag GmbH (Subsidiary of: Sueddeutsche Verlag) Leopoldstr. 175, 8000 Munich 40, W. Germany (B.R.D.) adv. circ. 10,200.

658.8 US ISSN 0092-4857
M E I MARKETING ECONOMICS GUIDE. 1973. a. $16.50. Marketing Economics Institute, Ltd., 441 Lexington Ave., New York, NY 10017. Ed. Alfred Hong. illus. stat. (also avail. in magnetic tape)

658 US
M R A RESEARCH SERVICE DIRECTORY. 1973. biennial. $35. Marketing Research Association, Inc., 221 N. LaSalle St., Chicago, IL 60601 (Subscr. c/o Callahan Research, Inc., 31 E. 28th St., New York, NY 10016) Ed. William J. Callahan. circ. 950.

658.8 US ISSN 0085-2953
MAIL ORDER BUSINESS DIRECTORY. 1955. biennial. $55. B. Klein Publications, Box 8503, Coral Springs, FL 33065.

382 II
MARKET INFORMATION SERIES. (Text in English) 1971. irreg., latest issue, 1974. Rs.7.50 per no. Trade Development Authority, 16 Parliament St., New Delhi 110001, India (Subscr. to: M/S Central News Agency, 23-90 Connaught Circus, New Delhi 110001, India) Ed. A. C. Banerjee. circ. 750.

658.8 UK ISSN 0076-4523
MARKET RESEARCH SOCIETY. YEARBOOK. 1968. a. £10. Market Research Society, 15 Belgrave Sq., London SW1X 8PF, England. Ed. Phyllis Vangelder. adv. circ. 3,500.

658.8 US ISSN 0098-1397
MARKETING ECONOMICS KEY PLANTS; guide to industrial purchasing power. 1960. biennial. $80. Marketing Economics Institute, Ltd., 441 Lexington Ave., New York, NY 10017. Ed. Alfred Hong. stat. (also avail. in magnetic tape)
Formerly: Market Statistics Key Plant Directory (ISSN 0076-4531)

381 615 US ISSN 0093-125X
MARKETING GUIDE. Variant title: Drug Topics Marketing Guide. 1973. a. $10. Medical Economics Co., 680 Kinderkamack Rd., Oradell, NJ 07649. Ed. Ralph Thurlow. circ. 1,000.
Consumer spending patterns for over 300 product lines sold in drugstores

658.8 FR
MARKETING INDUSTRIEL; bulletin de marketing industriel. English edition: Industrial Marketing. 1970. irreg. free. METRA, 16/20 rue Barbes, 92128 Montrouge, France. Ed. Michel Laury. circ. 6,000.
Formerly: Marketing et Developpement Industriel (ISSN 0076-4566)

658.8 UK ISSN 0076-4647
MARKETS YEAR BOOK. 1955. a. £2.90. ‡ World's Fair Ltd., 2 Daltry St., Oldham, Lancs, England. circ. 2,500.

658.7 UK ISSN 0076-4167
MATERIALS HANDLING BUYERS GUIDE. 1963. a. £8.50. Turret Press Ltd., 4 Local Board Rd., Watford, Herts WD1 2JS, England. Ed. Peter de Lacey. adv. index.
Formerly: Manual of Materials Handling and Ancilliary Equipment (ISSN 0076-4167)

658.8 US
MERCHANDISE & OPERATING RESULTS OF DEPARTMENT AND SPECIALITY STORES. a. $45 to non-members; members $30. National Retail Merchants Association, Financial Executives Division, 100 W. 31st St., New York, NY 10001.

338.4 US ISSN 0092-8410
N. A. C. D. S. LILLY DIGEST. a. free. (National Association of Chain Drug Stores) Eli Lilly & Co., General Offices and Principal Laboratories, Indianapolis, IN 46206. Ed. David J. Carter. illus. stat.

658.8 US
NATIONAL COUNCIL OF PHYSICAL DISTRIBUTION MANAGEMENT. ANNUAL MEETING. PROCEEDINGS. vol. 13, 1975. a. $20. National Council of Physical Distribution Management, 222 W. Adams St., Chicago, IL 60606. charts.

658.8 US
NATIONAL ICE CREAM RETAILERS ASSOCIATION. YEARBOOK. a. National Ice Cream Retailers Association, 325 W. Adams St., Muncie, IN 47305. adv. illus.

658.8 US
PERSPECTIVES ON MARKETING SERIES. irreg. price varies. Harper and Row Publishers, Inc., 10 East 53rd St, New York, NY 10022.

658.8 US ISSN 0032-5619
POTENTIALS IN MARKETING. 1968. irreg. free. Lakewood Publications, Inc, 731 Hennepin Ave, Minneapolis, MN 55403. Ed. R. W. Anderson. adv. illus. circ. 67,000.

PREVIEW/ENGINEERING; technical information, new products, ideas, literature. see *ENGINEERING*

658.8 382 US
PRINCIPAL INTERNATIONAL BUSINESSES; the world marketing directory. 1974. a. $395. Dun & Bradstreet International, Box 3224, Church Street Station, New York, NY 10008.

910 658.8 US
RAND MCNALLY COMMERCIAL ATLAS AND MARKETING GUIDE. 1876. a. $135. Rand McNally & Co., 8255 N. Central Park, Skokie, IL 60076 (Orders to: Box 7600, Chicago, IL 60680) Ed. Patricia Healy. charts. stat. index. circ. 5,000.

658.8 US ISSN 0191-3026
RESEARCH IN MARKETING; an annual compilation of research. 1978. a. $17.25 to individuals; institutions $34.50. J A I Press, Box 1678, 165 W. Putnam Ave., Greenwich, CT 06830. Ed. Jagdish N. Sheth.

658.83 UK
RETAIL TRADE INTERNATIONAL. 1975. biennial. $385. Euromonitor Publications Ltd., Box 26, 18 Doughty St., London WC1N 2PN, England.
Formerly: Retail Trade Europe.

658.8 GW
SCHRIFTENREIHE UNTERNEHMENSFUEHRUNG UND MARKETING. 1972. irreg. price varies. Betriebswirtschaftlicher Verlag Dr. Th. Gabler KG, Taunusstr. 54, Postfach 1546, 6200 Wiesbaden 1, W. Germany (B.R.D.) Ed. H. Meffert.

658.8 SZ ISSN 0302-2048
SCHWEIZERISCHE GESELLSCHAFT FUER MARKTFORSCHUNG. GESCHAEFTSBERICHT. (Text in German) irreg., no. 37, 1977. Schweizerische Gesellschaft fuer Marktforschung, Bleicherweg 21, 8022 Zurich, Switzerland. stat.

658.8 BL
SHOPPING: OPCOES DE COMPRA PARA A GRANDE SAO PAULO. (Text in Portuguese) 1975. irreg. Editora de Guias Ltda, Rua Cincinato Braga 388, 01333sao Paulo, Brazil. illus.

SPORTS MANAGEMENT REVIEW. see *SPORTS AND GAMES*

658.8 UK ISSN 0081-5810
STORES AND SHOPS RETAIL DIRECTORY. 1939. a. £23. Newman Publishing Ltd., 48 Poland St., London W1V 4PP, England.

658.8 UK ISSN 0081-5829
STORES OF THE WORLD DIRECTORY. 1953. biennial. £24. Newman Publishing Ltd., 48 Poland St., London W1V 4PP, England.

658.8 US ISSN 0081-9662
SURPLUS DEALERS DIRECTORY. 1950. a. $12.50 includes monthly bulletin. Institute of Surplus Dealers, 51-41 59 Pl., Woodside, NY 11377. Ed. Fred D. Reder.

658 330 US
SURVEY OF BUYING POWER. a. price varies. Bill Communications, Inc., 633 Third Ave., New York, NY 10017. (reprint service avail. from UMI)

380.14 SW
SWEDEN. STATENS KONSUMENTRAAD. VERKSAMHETSBERAETTELSE. (Vol. for 1969/70 covers period July 1969-Dec. 1970.) irreg. Statens Konsumentraad - National Council for Consumer Goods Research and Consumer Information, Lund, Sweden.

658 II
TEA TRADING CORPORATION OF INDIA. ANNUAL REPORT. (Text in English) a. Tea Trading Corporation of India Ltd., 225-F Acharya Jagadish Bose Rd., Calcutta 700020, India.

658.8 US
THOMAS REGISTER OF AMERICAN MANUFACTURERS AND THOMAS REGISTER CATALOG FILE. (14 Vol. Set) 1905. a. $85. Thomas Publishing Co., One Penn Plaza, New York, NY 10001. Ed. Walter E. Willets. index.
Formerly: Thomas Register of American Manufacturers (ISSN 0082-4216)

658.8 US
U.S. DEPARTMENT OF COMMERCE. CONSUMER GOODS AND SERVICES DIVISION. FRANCHISE OPPORTUNITIES HANDBOOK. 1965. a. price varies. U. S. Department of Commerce, Room 1104, Washington, DC 20230 (Orders to Supt. of Documents, U.S. Government Printing Office, Washington, DC 20402)

658.8 US ISSN 0081-8186
UNIVERSITY OF TEXAS, AUSTIN. BUREAU OF BUSINESS RESEARCH. STUDIES IN MARKETING. 1953. irreg; no. 23, 1976. price varies. University of Texas at Austin, Bureau of Business Research, Austin, TX 78712.

658 659.1 FR
V.I.P. DU MARKETING ET DE LA PUBLICITE. 1976. biennial. 447 F. Societe d'Etudes et de Publications Industrielles, 15 Square de Vergennes, 75015 Paris, France. (Affiliate: France Expansion)

658.8 UK ISSN 0143-4381
VENDING INTERNATIONAL MANUAL; the handbook of British vending. 1969. a. £5.75($15) Weald of Kent Publications (Tonbridge) Ltd., 47 High St., Tonbridge, Kent, England. Ed. G. E. Roy Pearl.
Vending machines

658.8 UK ISSN 0083-9175
WHERE TO BUY. (Composed of 4 Volumes: Chemicals; Building; Electrical; Agricultural and Horticultural) 1930. a. £4 plus postage for each vol. Industrial Newspapers Ltd., Queensway House, 2 Queensway, Redhill, Surrey RH1 1QS, England. Ed. F. Loader.

658.8 UK ISSN 0083-9310
WHO OWNS WHOM, NORTH AMERICA. 1969. a. $113. Dun & Bradstreet Ltd., Publications Division, 6-8 Bonhill St., London EC2A 4BU, England. index.

658.8 US
WINE HANDBOOK. Variant title: Wine Marketing Handbook. a. Gavin-Jobson Associates, 488 Madison Ave., New York, NY 10022.

YEAR BOOK OF AGRICULTURAL CO-OPERATION. see *AGRICULTURE — Agricultural Economics*

658 US ISSN 0275-7451
ZIP CODE BUSINESS PATTERNS. 1981. a. $125. Economic Information Systems, 310 Madison Ave., New York, NY 10017.

BUSINESS AND ECONOMICS — Office Equipment And Services

651 FR
ANNUAIRE DE LA MECANOGRAPHIE, MATERIEL DE BUREAU, INFORMATIQUE. 1978. a. 135 F. Editions Louis Johanet, 68 rue Boursault, 75017 Paris, France.

651 CN ISSN 0319-2148
CANADIAN OFFICE REDBOOK. a. Whitsed Publishing Ltd., 2 Bloor St. W., Suite 2504, Toronto, Ont. M4W 3E2, Canada. adv. circ. 32,000.

651 US ISSN 0072-4327
GEYER'S WHO MAKES IT DIRECTORY. 1877. a. avail. only with subscription to Geyer's Dealer Topics. Geyer-McAllister Publications, 51 Madison Ave., New York, NY 10010. Ed. C. Edwin Shade. adv. circ. 15,700.

651.07 II ISSN 0304-7083
INSTITUTE OF SECRETARIAT TRAINING AND MANAGEMENT. ANNUAL REPORT. (Text in English) a. Institute of Secretariat Training and Management, West Block 1, Wing 5, R. K. Puram, New Delhi 110022, India. Key Title: Annual Report-Institute of Secretariat Training and Management.

651 IT
MOBILI PER UFFICIO. a. L.10000. Compagnia Pubblicazioni Internazionali, Viale Stelvio 21, 20159 Milan, Italy. Ed. Giuseppe Vallardi. adv. circ. 25,000.

NATIONAL BUSINESS EDUCATION YEARBOOK. see *EDUCATION — Teaching Methods And Curriculum*

380.1 NR
NIGERIAN OFFICE AND RESIDENTIAL DIRECTORY. 1971/72. a. I C I C (Directory Publishers) Ltd., P.M.B. 3204, Surulere, Lagos, Nigeria. Ed. Olu Adeyemi.
Formerly: Nigerian Office and Quarters Directory (ISSN 0085-4190)

651.2 382 US ISSN 0471-1424
OFFICE EQUIPMENT EXPORTER. 1946. a. Office Publications, Inc., 1200 Summer St., Stamford, CT 06904. Ed. James Gorman. adv. circ. 11,500(controlled)

651 US ISSN 0085-445X
OFICINA; REVISTA DE EQUIPOS PARA OFICINAS. (Text and summaries in Spanish) 1940. a. Office Publications, Inc., 1200 Summer St., Stamford, CT 06904. Ed. William Schulhof. circ. 13,000.

651 AT ISSN 0078-3749
RYDGE'S OFFICE EQUIPMENT BUYERS GUIDE. 1965. a. Aus.$20($7) Rydge Publications Pty. Ltd., Box 3337, G. P. O., Sydney, N.S.W. 2000, Australia. adv. circ. 10,000.

338 UK ISSN 0081-461X
STATIONERY TRADE REFERENCE BOOK AND BUYER GUIDE. 1954. a. £15. Whitehall Press Ltd., Earl House, 27 Earl St., Maidstone, Kent ME14 1PE, England.

BUSINESS AND ECONOMICS — Personnel Management

658.3 US ISSN 0095-2826
AMERICAN SOCIETY FOR PERSONNEL ADMINISTRATION. PERSONNEL AND INDUSTRIAL RELATIONS COLLEGES. 1974. irreg. American Society for Personnel Administration, 30 Park Dr., Berea, OH 44017. (reprint service avail. from BLH, UMI) Key Title: Personnel and Industrial Relations Colleges, an A.S.P.A. Directory.

658.3 BL
BANCO DA AMAZONIA. CENTRO DE DOCUMENTACAO E BIBLIOTECA. CONTEXTO BOLETIM. (Text in Portuguese; summaries in English) 1974. irreg. Banco da Amazonia, Centro de Documentacao e Biblioteca, Av. Presidente Vargas, 800 - 16. Andar, Belem, Brazil. bibl. illus.

331.2 US ISSN 0525-4620
BANK ADMINISTRATION INSTITUTE. PERSONNEL ADMINISTRATION COMMISSION. BIENNIAL SURVEY OF BANK OFFICER SALARIES. $16. Bank Administration Institute, Personnel Administration Commission, 303 S. Northwest Hwy., Box 500, Park Ridge, IL 60068. illus. stat. Key Title: Biennial Survey of Bank Officer Salaries.
Formerly: Bank Officer Salary Survey (ISSN 0067-3528)

332.1 658.3 US
BIENNIAL SURVEY OF BANK PERSONNEL
POLICIES AND PRACTICES. 1962. biennial. $8.
Bank Administration Institute, Personnel
Administration Commission, 303 South Northwest
Highway, Park Ridge, IL 60068.
  Formerly: Bank Administration Institute.
Personnel Policies and Practices (ISSN 0067-3536)

658.3 US ISSN 0093-1942
CONFERENCE OF STATE EMPLOYMENT
SECURITY PERSONNEL OFFICERS. REPORT.
1970. a. free. ‡ U.S. Employment and Training
Administration, 601 D St. N.W., Washington, DC
20213. circ. controlled. Key Title: Report of the
Annual Conference of State Employment Security
Personnel Officers.

658.3 FR ISSN 0071-2493
EUROPEAN ASSOCIATION FOR PERSONNEL
MANAGEMENT. CONGRESS REPORTS. 1963.
irreg., 1977, Madrid. European Association for
Personnel Management, 20, rue des Fosses St.
Jacques, 75005 Paris, France.

658.4 US ISSN 0092-4989
INTERNATIONAL DIRECTORY OF EXECUTIVE
RECRUITERS. 1973. irreg. $11. ‡ Consultants
News, Templeton Road, Fitzwilliam, NH 03447.
Ed. James H. Kennedy.

651 JA
KEIEI ROMU NO SHISHIN. 1972. a. 2300 Yen.
Nihon Keieisha Dantai Remmei Kohobu, 1-2-1
Marunouchi, Chiyoda-ku, Tokyo, Japan. Ed. Hoshin
Matzuzaki. illus. circ. 2,500.

658.3 UK
KNOW YOUR TRAINING FILMS. 1975. a (3 up-
dating supplements) £11.75. Quest Research
Publications Ltd., P.O. Box 168, London SE26 6PR,
England. Ed. Alec Hughes.

658.311 US ISSN 0076-0889
LOOKING INTO LEADERSHIP SERIES.* 1961.
irreg. price varies. ‡ Leadership Resources, Inc.,
One First Virginia Plaza, Suite 344, 6400 Arlington
Blvd., Falls Church, VA 22042.

658.3 US
MODERN PERSONNEL FORMS (SUPPLEMENT)
supplements issued periodically to update base
volume. $44 for base volume. Warren, Gorham and
Lamont, Inc., 210 South St., Boston, MA 02111.

658.3 US ISSN 0077-3441
NATIONAL ASSOCIATION OF SUGGESTION
SYSTEMS. STATISTICAL REPORT. 1943. a. $5
to members only. National Association of
Suggestion Systems, 435 N. Michigan, Chicago, IL
60611.

658.3 SA ISSN 0077-4758
NATIONAL INSTITUTE FOR PERSONNEL
RESEARCH. ANNUAL REPORT. 1946. a. free.
National Institute for Personnel Research -
Nasionale Instituut vir Personeelnavorsing, P.O. Box
10319, Johannesburg 2000, South Africa. Ed. G. K.
Nelson. circ. 600.

658.3 US ISSN 0077-7889
NEVADA. DIVISION OF PERSONNEL.
BIENNIAL REPORT.* biennial. Division of
Personnel, Carson City, NV 89701.

658.3 US ISSN 0078-4001
OHIO. DIVISION OF STATE PERSONNEL.
ANNUAL REPORT. 1960/61. a. free. Division of
State Personnel, Department of Administrative
Services, 30 E. Broad St, Columbus, OH 43215.

658.3 UK ISSN 0306-6673
PERSONNEL AND TRAINING MANAGEMENT
YEARBOOK. 1970. a. £12.95. Kogan Page Ltd.,
120 Pentonville Rd., London N1 9JN, England.

658.3 US
PERSONNEL POLICIES AND BENEFITS FOR
THE APPAREL INDUSTRY. biennial. $15 to non-
members; members $8. American Apparel
Manufacturers Association, 1611 N. Kent St., Suite
800, Arlington, VA 22209.
  Supersedes in part: Apparel Plant Wages and
Personnel Policies (ISSN 0084-6678)

331 PO
PORTUGAL. MINISTERIO DAS CORPORACOES
E PREVIDENCIA SOCIAL. GABINETE DE
PLANEAMENTO. INGUERITO EMPREGO.
(Subseries of its Serie Estatistica) (Summaries in
English and French) irreg. Ministerio das
Corporacoes e Previdencia Social, Gabinete de
Planeamento, Lisbon, Portugal. stat.

PSYCHOLOGIA AFRICANA. see *PSYCHOLOGY*

658.3 BL
R I: REVISTA DOS RECURSOS HUMANOS NA
EMPRESA. irreg. Associacao Brasileira de
Administracao de Pessoal, Servicos Editoriais, Rua
Cardoso de Almeida 163, Sao Paulo, Brazil. illus.

TRAINING RESOURCES; buyer's guide & consultant
directory. see *BUSINESS AND ECONOMICS —
Labor And Industrial Relations*

658.3 US ISSN 0361-6797
U.S. CIVIL SERVICE COMMISSION. BUREAU OF
PERSONNEL MANAGEMENT EVALUATION.
EVALUATION METHODS SERIES. 1975. irreg.
U.S. Office of Personnel Management, Washington,
DC 20415. stat. Key Title: Evaluation Methods
Series.

353.001 658.3 US ISSN 0093-366X
U. S. CIVIL SERVICE COMMISSION.
PERSONNEL RESEARCH AND
DEVELOPMENT CENTER. TECHNICAL
STUDY. 1974. irreg. free. ‡ U.S. Office of
Personnel Management, 1900 E. St., N.W.,
Washington, DC 20415. Key Title: Technical Study
- U.S. Civil Service Commission. Personnel
Research and Development Center.

658.3 US ISSN 0081-8348
UNIVERSITY OF TEXAS, AUSTIN. BUREAU OF
BUSINESS RESEARCH. STUDIES IN
PERSONNEL AND MANAGEMENT. 1951.
irreg., no. 23, 1971. price varies. University of Texas
at Austin, Bureau of Business Research, Austin, TX
78712.

BUSINESS AND ECONOMICS —
Production Of Goods And Services

338.9 JA ISSN 0066-846X
A P O ANNUAL REPORT. (Text in English) 1962.
a. free. Asian Productivity Organization, Aoyama
Dai-Ichi Mansions, 8-4-14 Akasaka, Minato-ku,
Tokyo 107, Japan. circ. 5,000.

338 NE
ADRESLIJST VAN DE ZUID-HOLLANDSE
INDUSTRIE. 1951. biennial. fl.104. Economisch
Technologisch Instituut voor Zuid-Holland,
Beursgebouw, Meent 110, 3001 DA Rotterdam,
Netherlands. circ. 450.
  Formerly: Industrie-Adresboek voor Zuid-Holland
(ISSN 0073-7704)

338 UK
AIDS FOR INDUSTRY-NORTH WEST
ENGLAND. 1981. a. North West Industrial
Development Association, Brazennose House (West
Door), Brazennose St., Manchester M2 5AZ,
England. Ed. Chris J. Koral. circ. 2,000.

338 PK
ALL PAKISTAN TEXTILE MILLS ASSOCIATION.
ANNUAL REPORT. (Text in English) a. All
Pakistan Textile Mills Association, Muhammadi
House, 3rd Floor, I. I. Chundrigar Rd., Karachi 2,
Pakistan.

650 FR ISSN 0066-3379
ANNUAIRE NATIONAL DES FOURNISSEURS
DES ADMINISTRATIONS FRANCAISES. 1962,
2nd ed. a. Edition et Publicite Jean Vanvert, 32 rue
Yves-Toudic, Paris 10e, France.

338.9 II ISSN 0066-3891
ANNUAL DEVELOPMENT PLAN OF MADHYA
PRADESH. (Text in English) 1959/60. a. price
varies. Planning and Development Department,
Bhopal, Madhya Pradesh, India.

338.6 FR ISSN 0300-1547
ANNUAL REPORTS ON COMPETITION POLICY
IN O E C D MEMBER COUNTRIES. (Text in
English) 1972. irreg. price varies. Organization for
Economic Cooperation and Development, 2 rue
Andre-Pascal, 75775 Paris 16, France (U.S. orders
to: O.E.C.D. Publications and Information Center,
1750 Pennsylvania Ave. N.W., Washington, DC
20006) (also avail. in microfiche)

338 IT
ANNUARIO OTTICO ITALIANO. biennial. Edizioni
Ariminum, Via Negroli 51, Milan 20133, Italy.

338 BL
ANUARIO DAS INDUSTRIAS DO ESTADO DO
RIO GRANDE DO SUL. 1976. a. Secretaria da
Industria e Comercio, Porto Alegre, Brazil. (Co-
sponsor: Federacao das Industrias do Estado do Rio
Grande do Sul)

330 SP ISSN 0301-7443
ANUARIO FINANCIERO Y DE SOCIEDADES
ANONIMAS DE ESPANA. 1916. a. 4000 ptas.
Editorial S O P E C S.A., Mauricio Legendre 27,
Madrid 16, Spain. circ. 3,500.

338 US ISSN 0146-2997
ARIZONA MINING AND MANUFACTURING. a.
Department of Economic Security, Box 6123,
Phoenix, AZ 85005. stat.
  Formerly: Industrial Development in Arizona:
Manufacturing (ISSN 0537-5126)

338 JA ISSN 0571-3005
ASIAN PRODUCTIVITY ORGANIZATION.
REVIEW OF ACTIVITIES OF NATIONAL
PRODUCTIVITY. 1962. a. Asian Productivity
Organization, Aoyama Dai-Ichi Mansions, 8-4-14
Akasaka, Minato-ku, Tokyo 107, Japan.

338 AT
AUSTRALIA. DEPARTMENT OF INDUSTRY
AND COMMERCE. BULLETIN. 1973. irreg. free.
Department of Industry and Commerce, Canberra,
A.C.T. 2600, Australia (Dist. by: Australian
Government Publishing Service, Box 84, Canberra,
A.C.T. 2600, Australia) Ed. Tom Muir.
  Formerly: Australia. Department of
Manufacturing Industry. Bulletin (ISSN 0311-2209)

338.994 AT
AUSTRALIA. INDUSTRIES ASSISTANCE
COMMISSION. ANNUAL REPORT. 1974. a.
price varies. Australian Government Publishing
Service, Box 84, Canberra, A.C.T. 2600, Australia.
illus.

338 AU ISSN 0067-2254
AUSTRIA. BUNDESKAMMER FUER DIE
GEWERBLICHE WIRTSCHAFT.* a.
Bundeskammer der Gewerblichen Wirtschaft,
Vienna, Austria.

338 US
B A R-B R I BAR REVIEW. TRUSTS. a. B A R-B R
I Bar Review, 11801 W. Olympic Blvd., Los
Angeles, CA 90064.

338 GW
B D I-ORGANISATIONSPLAN. 1950. biennial. free.
Bundesverband der Deutschen Industrie,
Oberlaender Ufer 84-88, 5000 Cologne 51, W.
Germany (B. R. D.) circ. controlled.

338.9 BE
B E N E L U X ECONOMIC UNION. CONSEIL
CENTRAL DE L'ECONOMIE. RAPPORT DU
SECRETARAIRE SUR L'ACTIVITE DU
CONSEIL. 1950. biennial. free. B E N E L U X
Economic Union, Central Economic Council, Rue
de la Regence 39, 1000 Brussels, Belgium.
  Formerly: Benelux Economic Union. Conseil
Consultatif Economique et Social Rapport du
Secretaire Concernant les Activites du Conseil
(ISSN 0522-8948)

338 BL
BANCO NACIONAL DO DESENVOLVIMENTO
ECONOMICO. PLANO DE ACAO/BANCO
NACIONAL DO DESENVOLVIMENTO
ECONOMICO. PLAN OF ACTION. (Editions in
Spanish and English) triennial. Banco Nacional do
Desenvolvimento Economico, Ave. Rio Branco 53,
Rio de Janeiro, Brazil.

BUSINESS AND ECONOMICS — PRODUCTION OF GOODS AND SERVICES

330.9 MR
BANQUE NATIONALE POUR LE DEVELOPPEMENT ECONOMIQUE. RAPPORT ANNUEL. (Text in French, Arabic) a. Banque Nationale pour le Developpement Economique, B.P. 407, Place des Alaouites, Rabat, Morocco. illus. stat.

338 SA
BANTU INVESTMENT CORPORATION OF SOUTH AFRICA. ANNUAL REPORT/BANTOE BELEGGINGSKORPORASIE VAN SUID-AFRIKA. JAARVERSLAG. (Text in Afrikaans and English) a. Bantu Investment Corporation of South Africa, 179A Skinner St., Karel Schoeman Building, Pretoria 0002, South Africa.

338 US ISSN 0093-8025
BASEBOOK. Title varies: Predicasts Basebook. 1973. a. $325. Predicasts, Inc., 200 University Circle Research Center, 11001 Cedar Ave., Cleveland, OH 44106.

310 338 BO
BOLIVIA. INSTITUTO NACIONAL DE ESTADISTICA. ANUARIO DE ESTADISTICAS INDUSTRIALES. 1965. a. $10.30. Instituto Nacional de Estadistica, Av. 6 de Agosto no. 2507, La Paz, Bolivia.

338.7 BS
BOTSWANA DEVELOPMENT CORPORATION. ANNUAL REPORT. a. Botswana Development Corporation, Gaborone, Botswana.

338 BL ISSN 0045-2742
BRAZIL. SUPERINTENDENCIA DO DESENVOLVIMENTO DA AMAZONIA. S U D A M DOCUMENTA. (Text in Portugese; summaries in Portuguese & English) 1970. irreg. free. Superintendencia do Desenvolvimento da Amazonia, Travessa Antonio Baena 1113, Caixa Postal 874, Belem-Para, Brazil. adv.

338.981 BL
BRAZIL DEVELOPMENT SERIES/SERIES DESENVOLVIMENTO BRASILEIRO. (Text in English and Portuguese) 1971. a. $20. (Brazilian Institute of Economic Studies) TELEPRESS Servicos de Imprensa, Ltda., Rua Albuquergque Lins, 1315, 01230 Sao Paulo, S.P., Brazil. Ed. Olavo G. Otero. illus. circ. 10,000.

338.9 UK
BRITISH-NORTH AMERICAN RESEARCH ASSOCIATION. COMMITTEE PUBLICATIONS. 1970. irreg. price varies. ‡ British-North American Research Association, 1 Gough Square, London E.C.4., England. Ed. Bd. bibl. charts.

338.9 UK
BRITISH-NORTH AMERICAN RESEARCH ASSOCIATION. OCCASIONAL PAPERS. 1972. irreg. 60p. per no. British-North American Research Association, 1 Gough Square, London E.C.4., England. bibl. charts.

330 PH
BUSINESS PROSPECTS. Represents: Business Prospects Conference. Proceedings. 1971. a. $25. Vision Publishing Corporation, Box 4314, Manila, Philippines. Ed. Alfredo T. Sevilla. adv. charts. illus. stat. circ. 5,000.

330 MY
BUSINESSCOPE. (Text in English or Malay) 1971. a. $3.50. University of Malaya Business Club, Kuala Lumpur, Malaysia. Ed. Lim Beo Leong. adv. bibl. stat. circ. 1,000.

C E D NEWSLETTER. (Committee for Economic Development) see *BUSINESS AND ECONOMICS — International Development And Assistance*

338 BL
CADASTRO INDUSTRIAL DA BAHIA. 1973. free. Federacao das Industrias do Estado da Bahia, Rua Miguel Calmon 39, Salvador, Bahia, Brazil. circ. controlled.

338 BL
CADASTRO INDUSTRIAL DO PARA. irreg. Federacao das Industrias, Av. Nazare, 759, Belem, Para, Brazil.

338.7 CM
CAMEROON DEVELOPMENT CORPORATION. ANNUAL REPORT AND ACCOUNTS/RAPPORT ANNUEL ET COMPTE-RENDU FINANCIER. (Text in English and French) a. free. Cameroon Development Corporation, Bota, Victoria, Cameroon. illus. circ. 5,000. Key Title: Annual Report and Accounts-Cameroon Development Corporation.

CANADIAN ENGINEERING & INDUSTRIAL YEAR BOOK. see *ENGINEERING*

338 US ISSN 0090-7111
CENSUS OF MAINE MANUFACTURES. (Subseries of: Maine. Bureau of Labor. B L Bulletin) 1948. a. free. Department of Manpower Affairs, State Office Bldg., Code 45, Augusta, ME 04333. stat. circ. 600. Indexed: Vert.File Ind.

338.47 PR ISSN 0552-5276
CENSUS OF MANUFACTURING INDUSTRIES OF PUERTO RICO. (Text in English and Spanish) a. free. Department of Labor, Bureau of Labor Statistics, 414 Barbosa Ave., Hato Rey, PR 00917. stat. circ. 1,000. (tabloid format)

338.9 US ISSN 0069-1674
CENTRAL NAUGATUCK VALLEY REGIONAL PLANNING AGENCY. ANNUAL REPORT. 1960. a. $5 contribution. ‡ Central Naugatuck Valley Regional Planning Agency, 20 E. Main St., Waterbury, CT 06702. circ. 500. (processed)

338.9 EC
CENTRO DE DESARROLLO INDUSTRIAL DEL ECUADOR. NOTICIAS TECNICAS. 1973. a (with m bulletins) free. Ministry of Industry, Centro de Desarrollo Industrial, Box 5833, Guayaquil, Ecuador. circ. 1,200.

338 CH
CHINA DEVELOPMENT CORPORATION. ANNUAL REPORT.* (Vols. for 1959-72 issued by the body under its English form of name) 1959. a. China Development Corporation, 131 Nanking East Road, Section 5, Taipei, Taiwan, Republic of China. illus. stat.

338 CR
CIFRAS SOBRE PRODUCCION INDUSTRIAL. 1977. a. Banco Central de Costa Rica, Avda. Central, Calles 2 y 4, Apdo. 10058, San Jose, Costa Rica. charts. stat. circ. 300.

338 CK
COLOMBIA. DEPARTAMENTO ADMINISTRATIVO NACIONAL DE ESTADISTICA. ANUARIO DE ESTADISTICAS INDUSTRIALES. 1972. a. Departamento Administrativo Nacional de Estadistica, Banco Nacional de Datos, Apdo. Nacional 80043, Bogota D.E., Colombia.
Supersedes: Colombia. Departamento Administrativo Nacional de Estadistica. Industria Manufacturera Nacional.

COMMISSION OF THE EUROPEAN COMMUNITIES. ETUDES: SERIE AIDE AU DEVELOPPEMENT. see *BUSINESS AND ECONOMICS — International Development And Assistance*

338 EI
COMMISSION OF THE EUROPEAN COMMUNITIES. CAHIERS DE RECONVERSION INDUSTRIELLE. (Editions also in English, German, Italian and Dutch) 1963. irreg., 1971, no. 17. Office for Official Publications of the European Communities, C.P. 1003, Luxembourg 1, Luxembourg (Dist. in U.S. by European Communities Information Service, 2100 M. St., N.W., Suite 707, Washington DC 20037) circ. controlled.

338.6 EI
COMMISSION OF THE EUROPEAN COMMUNITIES. REPORT ON COMPETITION POLICY/RAPPORT SUR LA POLITIQUE DE CONCURRENCE. (Text in English, French, German, Italian and Dutch) 1972. a. 100 Fr. Office for Official Publications of the European Communities, C.P. 1003, Luxembourg 1, Luxembourg (Dist. in the U.S. by: European Community Information Service, 2100 M St., NW, Suite 707, Washington, DC 20037)

338.4 EI ISSN 0531-3015
COMMISSION OF THE EUROPEAN COMMUNITIES. COLLECTION D'ECONOMIE DU TRAVAIL. (Editions also in German, Italian and Dutch) 1962. irreg. 1968, vol. III. price varies. Office for Official Publications of the European Communities, C.P. 1003, Luxembourg 1, Luxembourg (Dist. in the U.S. by: European Community Information Service, 2100 M St., NW, Suite 707, Washington, DC 20037)

338.5 EI ISSN 0069-6706
COMMISSION OF THE EUROPEAN COMMUNITIES. ETUDES: SERIE CONCURRENCE- RAPPROCHEMENT DES LEGISLATIONS. (Editions also in English, German, Italian and Dutch) 1966. irreg.; no. 18 in prep. Office for Official Publications of the European Communities, C.P. 1003, Luxembourg 1, Luxembourg (Dist. in U.S. by European Community Information Service, 2100 M St., N.W., Suite 707, Washington, D.C 20037)

338 EI ISSN 0591-1737
COMMISSION OF THE EUROPEAN COMMUNITIES. ETUDES: SERIE INDUSTRIE. (Editions in French, German, Italian, Dutch and occasionally English) irreg.; 1971, no. 6. price varies. Office for Official Publications of the European Communities, C.P. 1003, Luxembourg 1, Luxembourg (Dist. in U.S. by European Community Information Service, 2100 M St., N.W., Suite 707, Washington, D.C. 20037)

338.9 AT
COMMITTEE FOR ECONOMIC DEVELOPMENT OF AUSTRALIA. C E D A INFORMATION PAPERS (IP SERIES) 1979. irreg. price varies. Committee for Economic Development of Australia, 186 Exhibition St., Melbourne, Vic. 3000, Australia.

338.9 AT
COMMITTEE FOR ECONOMIC DEVELOPMENT OF AUSTRALIA. C E D A "M" SERIES. 1961. irreg. price varies. Committee for Economic Development of Australia, 186 Exhibition St., Melbourne, Vic. 3000, Australia. Ed. Bd.

338 AT
COMMITTEE FOR ECONOMIC DEVELOPMENT OF AUSTRALIA. C E D A "P" SERIES; policy statements. 1965. irreg. price varies. Committee for Economic Development of Australia, 186 Exhibition St, Melbourne, Vic. 3000, Australia. Ed.Bd.

COMMONWEALTH SCIENTIFIC AND INDUSTRIAL RESEARCH ORGANIZATION. DIVISION OF LAND USE RESEARCH. TECHNICAL PAPER. see *AGRICULTURE — Agricultural Economics*

COMMONWEALTH SCIENTIFIC AND INDUSTRIAL RESEARCH ORGANIZATION. LAND RESEARCH SERIES. see *AGRICULTURE — Agricultural Economics*

338 AG
CONFEDERACION GENERAL DE LA INDUSTRIA. COMISION DIRECTIVA. INFORME DE LAS ACTUACIONES CUMPLIDAS. irreg. Confederacion General de la Industria., Comision Directiva, Rivadavia 1115, Buenos Aires, Argentina.

338 AG ISSN 0301-9349
CONFEDERACION GENERAL DE LA INDUSTRIA. MEMORIA Y BALANCE GENERAL. irreg. Confederacion General de la Industria, Rivadavia 1115, Argentina.
Continues: Confederacion de la Industria. Memoria y Balance General.

338 CN ISSN 0069-8342
CONFERENCE BOARD IN CANADA. CANADIAN STUDIES. 1959. irreg. price varies. ‡ Conference Board in Canada, Suite 100, 25 McArthur Rd., Ottawa, Ont. K1L 6R3, Canada.

CONNAISSANCE DE L'OUEST. see *GEOGRAPHY*

338 CR
CORPORACION COSTARRICENSE DE FINANCIAMIENTO INDUSTRIAL. MEMORIA ANUAL. a. Corporacion Costarricense de Financiamiento Industrial, Apartado 10067, San Jose, Costa Rica.

338   US   ISSN 0498-8477
CURRENT INDUSTRIAL REPORTS. (Series of over 100 reports covering vast range of industrial activities) m.,q., and annual reports. U.S. Bureau of the Census, Industry Division, Department of Commerce, Washington, DC 20233 (Request complete listing of titles in the series from the Bureau's Subscriber Services Section)

338   CY   ISSN 0590-4854
CYPRUS. DEPARTMENT OF STATISTICS AND RESEARCH. ANNUAL INDUSTRIAL PRODUCTION SURVEY. a. Mils.250. Department of Statistics and Research, Ministry of Finance, Nicosia, Cyprus.

338   CY
CYPRUS. DEPARTMENT OF STATISTICS AND RESEARCH. INDEX NUMBERS OF INDUSTRIAL PRODUCTION. a. Mils.250. Department of Statistics and Research, Ministry of Finance, Nicosia, Cyprus.

338   CY
CYPRUS. DEPARTMENT OF STATISTICS AND RESEARCH. SERVICES SURVEY. a. Mils.250. Department of Statistics and Research, Ministry of Finance, Nicosia, Cyprus.

338   DK
DANMARKS 2000 STOERSTE VIRKSOMHEDER/2000 LARGEST COMPANIES IN DENMARK. (Text in Danish and English) 1967. a. Kr.270.55. Teknisk Forlag A-S, Skelbaekgade 4, DK-1717 Copenhagen V, Denmark. Ed. Peter Hoeg-Brask. adv. circ. 3,000.
     Former titles: Danmarks 1000 Stoerste Virkomheder; Danmarks 500 Stoerste Virksomheder (ISSN 0419-9472)

309.2   US
DELAWARE VALLEY REGIONAL PLANNING COMMISSION. ANNUAL REPORT. Cover title: D.V.R.P.C. Annual Report. a. free. Delaware Valley Regional Planning Commission, Penn Towers Bldg., 1819 J. F. Kennedy Blvd., Philadelphia, PA 19103. illus.
     Formerly: Delaware Valley Regional Planning Commission. Biennial Report (ISSN 0098-6232)

338   PH
DEVELOPMENT ACADEMY OF THE PHILIPPINES. ANNUAL REPORT. (Text in English) 1974. a. Development Academy of the Philippines, Office of Special Services, Box 5160 MCC, Makati, Metro Manila, Philippines. illus.

338   US
DIRECTORY OF INTER-CORPORATE OWNERSHIP. Variant title: Who Owns Whom in America. 1970/71. irreg., latest 1974. $75. World Trade Academy Press, Inc., 50 E. 42nd St., New York, NY 10017. Ed. J. L. Angel.
     Formerly: American Register of Inter-Corporate Ownership (ISSN 0065-9975)

309.2   US
DIRECTORY OF MISSOURI'S REGIONAL PLANNING COMMISSIONS. (Vols. for 1972/73 prepared by the Department of Community Affairs) Office of Administration, Division of Budget and Planning, Capitol Bldg., Rm. B-9, Box 809, Jefferson City, MO 65101. illus.
     Formerly: Directory of Missouri's Regional Planning System (ISSN 0090-7812)

338.7   II
DIRECTORY OF PUBLIC ENTERPRISES IN INDIA. (Text in English) 1974. a. National Forum of Public Enterprises, C-40 South Extension II, New Delhi 49, India. illus.

338   AO
DIVULGACAO. 1969. a. Camara Municipal du Lobito, Caixa Postal Tres, Lobito, Angola. charts. illus.

338.9   SA   ISSN 0070-8518
ECONOMIC DEVELOPMENT PROGRAMME FOR THE REPUBLIC OF SOUTH AFRICA. 1964. irreg. Government Printer, Bosman St., Private Bag X85, Pretoria 0001, South Africa. (Prepared by: Department of Planning)

ECONOMIE FRANCAISE EN PERSPECTIVES SECTORIELLES: INDUSTRIES DE BIENS DE CONSOMMATION. see BUSINESS AND ECONOMICS — Economic Situation And Conditions

ECONOMIE FRANCAISE EN PERSPECTIVES SECTORIELLES: INDUSTRIES DE BIENS D'EQUIPEMENT. see BUSINESS AND ECONOMICS — Economic Situation And Conditions

ECONOMIE FRANCAISE EN PERSPECTIVES SECTORIELLES: INDUSTRIES DE BIENS INTERMEDIARIES. see BUSINESS AND ECONOMICS — Economic Situation And Conditions

338   EC   ISSN 0070-8887
ECUADOR. CENTRO DE DESARROLLO INDUSTRIAL. INFORME DE LABORES. 1959. a; latest issue, 1973. free. Centro de Desarrollo Industrial, Av. Orellana 1297, Box 2321, Quito, Ecuador. circ. 600.

338   EC
ECUADOR. MINISTERIO DE INDUSTRIAS, COMERCIO E INTEGRACION. BOLETIN DE INFORMACION DE LAS EMPRESAS ACOGIDAS A LA LEY DE FOMENTO INDUSTRIAL. 1974. a. Ministerio de Industrias, Comercio e Integracion, Quito, Ecuador.

338   UR
EKONOMIKA I ORGANIZATSIYA PROMYSHLENNOGO PROIZVODSTVA. (Subseries of Respublikanskie Mezhvedomstvennye Sborniki) 1972. irreg. 1.50 Rub. (Belorusskii Gosudarstvennyi Institut Narodnogo Khozyaistva) Izdatel'stvo Vysshaya Shkola B. S. S. R., Minsk, U.S.S.R.

338.3   UR
EKONOMIKA PROMYSLOVOSTI. (Subseries of: Kharkivskyi Politekhnichnyi Instytut. Vestnik) irreg. 0.53 Rub. Kharkivskyi Politekhnichnyi Instytut, Ul. Frunze, 21, Kharkov, U.S.S.R. illus.

338.4   FR
ENGINEERING INDUSTRIES IN O E C D MEMBER COUNTRIES: NEW BASIC STATISTICS. (Vols. for 1963/70- issued in pts.) (Text in English and French) a. $7. Organization for Economic Cooperation and Development, 2 rue Andre-Pascal, 75775 Paris, France (U.S. orders to: O.E.C.D. Publications and Information Center, 1750 Pennsylvania Ave. N.W., Washington, D.C. 20006) (also avail. in microfiche)

ENQUETE SUR LES ENTERPRISES INDUSTRIELLES ET COMMERCIALES DU TOGO. see BUSINESS AND ECONOMICS — Domestic Commerce

338.9   SP   ISSN 0084-5132
ESCUELA DE GERENTES DE COOPERATIVAS. CARTILLAS DE COOPERACION. 1971. irreg.; latest issue, 1978. 25 ptas. (Escuela de Gerentes de Cooperativas) Centro Nacional de Educacion Cooperativa, Palacio de la Cooperacion, Apdo. de Correos 15, San Felix 9, Zaragoza, Spain. (Affiliate: Federacion Nacional de Cooperativas de Espana) Ed. Joaquin Mateo.

338.9   SP   ISSN 0084-5159
ESCUELA DE GERENTES DE COOPERATIVAS. COLECCION TEXTOS. irreg. price varies. Escuela de Gerentes de Cooperativas, Palacio de la Cooperacion, Apdo. de Correos 15, San Felix 9, Zaragoza, Spain. (Co-sponsor: Centro Nacional de Educacion Cooperativa) Ed. Joaquin Mateo.

338.9   SP   ISSN 0084-5167
ESCUELA DE GERENTES DE COOPERATIVAS. CUADERNOS DE PRACTICAS. irreg. 100 ptas. Escuela de Gerentes de Cooperativas, Palacio de la Cooperacion, Apdo. de Correos 15, San Felix 9, Zaragoza, Spain. (Co-sponsor: Centro Nacional de Educacion Cooperativa) Ed. Joaquin Mateo.

338.9   SP   ISSN 0084-5175
ESCUELA DE GERENTES DE COOPERATIVAS. SERIE ESPECIAL. irreg. 200 ptas. Escuela de Gerentes de Cooperativas, Palacio de la Cooperacion, Apdo. de Correos 15, San Felix 9, Zaragoza, Spain. (Co-sponsor: Centro Nacional de Educacion Cooperativa)

338   NO
EUROPE'S 5000 LARGEST COMPANIES. a. $60. A-S Oekonomisk Literatur, Ebbellsgate 3, Oslo 1, Norway (Dist. in the U.S. by: Dun and Bradstreet International, Box 3224, Church St. Station, New York, NY 10008)

338   BE
FEDERATION DES ENTREPRISES DE BELGIQUE. RAPPORT ANNUEL. a. Federation des Entreprises de Belgique, Rue Ravenstein 4, 1000 Brussels, Belgium.
     Formerly: Federation des Industries Belges. Rapport Annuel (ISSN 0071-4178)

338   US
FERTIGUNG UND BETRIEB. 1974. irreg., vol. 12, 1979. price varies. Springer-Verlag, 175 Fifth Ave., New York, NY 10010 (Also Berlin, Heidelberg, Vienna) (reprint service avail. from ISI)
     Supersedes: Werkstattbuecher fuer Betriebsfachleute Konstrukteure und Studenten (ISSN 0083-8055)

338.9   FI   ISSN 0355-8878
FINLAND. VALTIONEUVOSTON KANSLIAN. JULKAISUJA. 1972. irreg. price varies. Valtion Painatuskeskus - Government Printing Centre; Council of State, Annankatu 44, 00100 Helsinki 10, Finland.
     Formerly (1960-1971): Finland. Valtakunnansuunnittelutoimisto. Julkaisuja. Sarja A (ISSN 0071-5360)

330   FR   ISSN 0071-6847
FONDS DE DEVELOPPMENT ECONOMIQUE ET SOCIAL. CONSEIL DE DIRECTION. RAPPORT. a. (Ministere de l'Economie et des Finances) Imprimerie Nationale, Service des Ventes, 59128 Flers en Escrebieux, France.

338   PH   ISSN 0085-0802
FOREIGN INVESTMENT OPPORTUNITIES IN THE PHILIPPINES. (Text and summaries in English) 1968. a. free. ‡ Board of Investments, Ortigas Building, Ortigas Avenue, Box 676, Rizal, Philippines. circ. 3,000.

338   US
FORTUNE DOUBLE 500 DIRECTORY. 1955; expanded 1970. a. $5. ‡ Time, Inc., Fortune Division, Time & Life Bldg., Rm. 1828, Rockefeller Center, New York, NY 10020. stat.

338   FR   ISSN 0071-870X
FRANCE. DIRECTION GENERALE DE LA CONCURRENCE ET DES PRIX. BULLETIN OFFICIEL DES SERVICES DES PRIX. 1941. irreg. 6.50 F. (Direction General de la Concurrence et des Prix) France. Direction des Journaux Officiels, 26, rue Desaix, 75732 Paris, France.

330   FR   ISSN 0071-8920
FRANCE. MINISTERE DE L'ECONOMIE. RAPPORT DU CONSEIL DE DIRECTION DU FONDS DE DEVELOPPEMENT ECONOMIQUE ET SOCIAL. a. 45 F. £47. Ministere de l'Economie, Service de l'Information, 93 rue de Rivoli, 75056 Paris, France.
     Formerly: France. Ministere de l'Economie et des Finances. Rapport du Conseil de Direcion du Fonds de Developpement Economique et Social.

338   US
GENERAL MOTORS PUBLIC INTEREST REPORT. a. General Motors Corporation, Detroit, MI 48202.

330   GW   ISSN 0072-159X
GERMANY (FEDERAL REPUBLIC, 1949-) SACHVERSTAENDIGENRAT ZUR BEGUTACHTUNG DER GESAMTWIRTSCHAFTLICHEN ENTWICKLUNG. JAHRESGUTACHTEN; unter Anpassungszwang. 1964. a. DM.29. (Sachverstaendigenrat zur Begutachtung der Gesamtwirtschaftlichen Entwicklung) W. Kohlhammer Verlag GmbH, Abt. Veroeffentlichungen des Statistischen Bundesamtes, Philipp-Reis-Str. 3, Postfach 421120, 6500 Mainz 42, W. Germany (B. R. D.) circ. 3,300.

BUSINESS AND ECONOMICS — PRODUCTION OF GOODS AND SERVICES

338.9 BE ISSN 0304-5978
GEWESTELIJKE ECONOMISCHE RAAD VOOR VLAANDEREN. ACTIVITEITSVERSLAG. (Subseries of: G.E.R.V. Berichten) 1972. irreg. Gewestelijke Economische Raad voor Vlaanderen, Antwerp Tower, De Keyserlei 5, Bus 15, 2000 Antwerp, Belgium.

338 UK ISSN 0072-565X
GREAT BRITAIN. DEPARTMENT OF TRADE. COMPANIES: GENERAL ANNUAL REPORT. a. H.M.S.O., P.O. Box 569, London SE1 9NH, England.

GREAT BRITAIN. DOMESTIC COAL CONSUMERS' COUNCIL. ANNUAL REPORT. see *MINES AND MINING INDUSTRY*

338.9 UK ISSN 0072-694X
GREAT BRITAIN. NATIONAL ECONOMIC DEVELOPMENT OFFICE. MONOGRAPHS. 1970. irreg. National Economic Development Office, Millbank Tower, Millbank St., London S.W.1, England (Avail. from H.M.S.O., c/o Liaison Officer, Atlantic House, Holborn Viaduct, London EC1P 1BN, England)

338 AT ISSN 0085-1280
GROWTH. 1961. irreg. Aus.$6. Committee for Economic Development of Australia, 186 Exhibition St., Melbourne, Vic 3000, Australia. Indexed: Aus.P.A.I.S.

330.9 SG
GUIDE DE L'INVESTISSEUR INDUSTRIEL AU SENEGAL. irreg. 3000 Fr.CFA. Societe Nationale d'Etude et de Promotion Industrielle, 14, rue Maunoury, B.P. 100, Dakar, Senegal. illus.

338 II
GUJARAT INDUSTRIAL DEVELOPMENT CORPORATION. ANNUAL REPORT. (Text in English) a. Gujarat Industrial Development Corporation, Ashram Rd., Ahmedabad 9, India. illus. stat.

338 GW ISSN 0073-0068
HANDBUCH DER GROSSUNTERNEHMEN. 1940. a. DM.361. Verlag Hoppenstedt und Co., Havelstr. 9, Postfach 4006, 6100 Darmstadt, W. Germany (B.R.D.) adv.

338.9 US ISSN 0073-1072
HAWAII. DEPARTMENT OF PLANNING AND ECONOMIC DEVELOPMENT. ANNUAL REPORT. 1962. a. free. Department of Planning and Economic Development, P.O. Box 2359, Honolulu, HI 96804. Ed. Hideto Kono. circ. 1,500.

339 BL
I P E A SERIE MONOGRAFICA. 1971. irreg. price varies. Instituto de Planejamento Economico e Social, Caixa Postal 2672, Rio de Janeiro, Brazil. Ed. Manoel Augusto Costa.

338 US ISSN 0095-1870
INDUSTRIAL CONTACT LIST FOR NORTH CAROLINA COMMUNITIES. Cover title: North Carolina Industrial Contact List. irreg. free to qualified personnel. Department of Commerce, Industrial Development Division, 430 N. Salisbury St., Raleigh, NC 27611.

338 US ISSN 0495-145X
INDUSTRIAL DEVELOPMENT IN THE T.V.A. AREA. 1959. a. Tennessee Valley Authority, Division of Power Utilization, 815 Power Building, Chattanooga, TN 37401. illus. stat.

338.7 CN
INDUSTRIAL ENTERPRISES INCORPORATED. ANNUAL REPORT. 1966. a. ‡ Industrial Enterprises Inc., Charlottetown, P.E.I. C1E 1B0, Canada.

338 US ISSN 0099-1872
INDUSTRIAL GROWTH IN TENNESSEE, ANNUAL REPORT. a. free. Department of Economic and Community Development, 10th Floor, Andrew Jackson Bldg., Nashville, TN 37219. stat.

338 JA
INDUSTRIAL LOCATION HANDBOOK/KOGYO RITCHI HANDOBUKKU. (Text in Japanese) 1966. triennial. Japan Industrial Location Center - Nihon Kogyo Ritchi Senta, 2-1 Shiba-Kotohiramachi, Minato-ku, Tokyo, Japan. charts, illus.

338 CN ISSN 0073-7569
INDUSTRIAL LOCATIONS IN CANADA. 1966. a. free to subscribers of the Financial Times of Canada. Financial Times of Canada, Suite 500, 920 Yonge St., Toronto, Ont. M4W 3L5, Canada. Ed. David Tafler. adv. circ. 100,000.

338 UK
INDUSTRIAL POLICY GROUP. PAPERS.* 1971, no. 9. irreg. 50p. per no. Industrial Policy Group, 21 Tothill St., London SW01, England. Ed. Bd.

338 FR
INDUSTRIAL PRODUCTION: HISTORICAL STATISTICS. (Text in English, French) 1966. irreg. Organization for Economic Cooperation and Development, 2 rue Andre Pascal, 75016 Paris, France (U.S. orders to: O.E.C.D. Publications and Information Center, 1750 Pennsylvania Ave., N.W., Washington, DC 20006) (also avail. in microfiche)

338 UK ISSN 0073-7615
INDUSTRIAL RESEARCH IN UNITED KINGDOM. 1946. irreg., 9th edt., 1980. ‡ Longman Group Ltd., Longman House, Burnt Mill, Harlow, Essex, England (Dist. in U.S. and Canada by: Gale Research Co. Ltd., Book Tower, Detroit, MI 48226) index.

600 330 JA ISSN 0537-5452
INDUSTRIAL REVIEW OF JAPAN; an annual in-depth report on the state of the Japanese economy. (Text in English) 1962. a. 3500 Yen($19.50) Japan Economic Journal - Nihon Keizai Shinbunsha, 1-9-5 Otemachi, Chiyoda-ku, Tokyo 100, Japan.

658 UK
INDUSTRIAL SOCIETY. HANDBOOK AND DIARY. 1960. a. £1.50. Industrial Society, Box 1BQ, 48 Bryanston Square, London W1A 1BQ, England. bibl. stat. circ. 30,000.

338 SA ISSN 0073-7658
INDUSTRIAL SOUTH AFRICA. 1956. every 4 yrs. R.10.00. Seal Publishing Co. (Pty) Ltd., P.O. Box 4960, Johannesburg, South Africa. Ed. Martin Spring.

338 II ISSN 0073-7666
INDUSTRIAL STRUCTURE OF RAJASTHAN. (Text in English) 1958. a. Rs.5. Directorate of Economics and Statistics, Krishi Bhawan, Jaipur, Rajasthan, India.

338 NE
INDUSTRIE ADRESBOEK VAN NOORD-HOLLAND. irreg. fl.60. Economisch-Technologische Dienst voor Noord-Holland, Stolbergstraat 9, Haarlem, Netherlands.

338 CM
INDUSTRIE CAMEROUNAISE. a. Syndicat des Industries du Cameroun, B. P. 673, Douala, Cameroon.

338 JA ISSN 0446-1266
INDUSTRIES OF JAPAN. (Text in English) 1958. a. 800 Yen. (Mainichi Daily News) Mainichi Newspapers, 1-1-1 Hitotsubashi, Chiyoda-ku, Tokyo 100, Japan. stat.

338 916.76 KE ISSN 0073-781X
INDUSTRY IN EAST AFRICA. 1962/63. a. $10. United Africa Press Ltd., Box 1237, Nairobi, Kenya. Ed. C. N. Bhatt.

338 DK ISSN 0446-2491
INGENIOEREN INDKOEBSBOG. 1960. a. Kr.177.95. Teknisk Forlag A-S, Skelbaekgade 4, DK-1717 Copenhagen V, Denmark. adv. circ. 5,000.

338 AU ISSN 0073-8468
INSTITUT FUER GEWERBEFORSCHUNG, VIENNA. TAETIGKEITSBERICHT. a. free. Institut fuer Gewerbeforschung, Tuerkenschanzstr. 18, A-1180 Vienna, Austria. Ed. Inge Froehlich.

338.9 UK
INSTITUTE OF DEVELOPMENT STUDIES. ANNUAL REPORT. a. University of Sussex, Institute of Development Studies, Brighton BN1 9RE, England.

338.9 BL
INSTITUTO DE PLANEJAMENTO ECONOMICO E SOCIAL. ESTUDOS PARA O PLANEJAMENTO. 1972. irreg. price varies. Instituto de Planejamento Economico e Social, Rua Melvin Jones 5, Z C-00 Centro, Rio de Janeiro, Brazil.

338 IS ISSN 0081-9743
ISRAEL. MINISTRY OF COMMERCE AND INDUSTRY. SURVEYS AND DEVELOPMENT PLANS OF INDUSTRY IN ISRAEL/HA-TA'ASIYAH HA-YISRE'ELIT. (Hebrew and English Editions) 1964. a. free. Ministry of Commerce and Industry, Jerusalem, Israel. Ed. A. Shaliv. circ. 1,000.
Formerly: Survey of Industry in Israel.

338 IT ISSN 0075-1987
ITALY. ISTITUTO NAZIONALE PER LO STUDIO DELLA CONGIUNTURA. QUADERNI ANALITICI. irreg. L.3500 per no. Istituto Nazionale per Lo Studio della Congiuntura, Rome, Italy. circ. 360.

338.4 IV
IVORY COAST. BUREAU DE DEVELOPPEMENT INDUSTRIEL. COUTS DES FACTEURS EN COTE D'IVOIRE. irreg. Bureau de Developpement Industriel, B.P. 4196, Abidjan, Ivory Coast. illus.

338 IV
IVORY COAST. BUREAU DE DEVELOPPEMENT INDUSTRIEL. PROGRAMME D'ACTIVITE. irreg. Bureau de Developpement Industriel, B.P. 4196, Abidjan, Ivory Coast.

338 IV
IVORY COAST. BUREAU DE DEVELOPPEMENT INDUSTRIEL. PROGRAMME TRIENNIAL DES ACTIVITES. triennial. Bureau de Developpement Industriel, B.P. 4196, Abidjan, Ivory Coast.

338 IV
IVORY COAST. BUREAU DE DEVELOPPEMENT INDUSTRIEL. RAPPORT D'ACTIVITES. irreg. Bureau de Developpement Industriel, B.P. 4196, Abidjan, Ivory Coast.

338 IV
IVORY COAST. BUREAU DU DEVELOPPEMENT INDUSTRIEL. SITUATION DE L'INDUSTRIE IVOIRIENNE. irreg. Bureau de Developpement Industriel, B.P. 4196, Abidjan, Ivory Coast. illus. stat.

338 JA
JAPAN. GOVERNMENT INDUSTRIAL DEVELOPMENT LABORATORY, HOKKAIDO. ANNUAL REPORT/HOKKAIDO KOGYO KAIHATSU SHIKENJO NEMPO. 1961. a. Government Industrial Development Laboratory, Hokkaido - Hokkaido Kogyo Kaihatsu Shikenjo, 41-2 Higashi-tsukisamu, Toyohira-ku, Sapporo 061-01, Hokkaido, Japan. abstr.

338 JA
JAPAN. GOVERNMENT INDUSTRIAL RESEARCH INSTITUTE, KYUSHU ANNUAL REPORT/KYUSHU KOGYO GIJUTSU SHIKENJO NEMPO. (Text in Japanese) a. Government Industrial Research Institute, Kyushu, 807-1 Shukumachi, Tosu-Kyushu 841, Japan. abstr.

338 JA ISSN 0075-3289
JAPAN CENSUS OF MANUFACTURES: REPORT BY COMMODITIES. 1909. a. 4600 Yen. Ministry of International Trade and Industry, Research and Statistics Division - Tsusho Sangyo Chosakai, Minister's Secretariat, 6-15-1 Ginza, Chuo-ku, Tokyo 104, Japan. circ. 800.

338.9 KE
KENYA. CENTRAL BUREAU OF STATISTICS. DEVELOPMENT ESTIMATES. a. EAs.50. Central Bureau of Statistics, Box 30266, Nairobi, Kenya (Orders to: Government Printing and Stationery Department, Box 30128, Nairobi, Kenya)
Formerly: Kenya. Ministry of Economic Planning and Development. Statistics Division. Development Estimates (ISSN 0075-5818)

BUSINESS AND ECONOMICS — PRODUCTION OF GOODS AND SERVICES

338.9   KE
KENYA. CENTRAL BUREAU OF STATISTICS. ESTIMATES OF RECURRENT EXPENDITURES. 1959. a. EAs.15. Central Bureau of Statistics, Box 30266, Nairobi, Kenya (Orders to: Government Printing and Stationery Department, Box 30128, Nairobi, Kenya)
   Formerly: Kenya. Ministry of Economic Planning and Development. Statistics Division. Estimates of Recurrent Expenditures (ISSN 0075-5834)

338.9   KE
KENYA. CENTRAL BUREAU OF STATISTICS. ESTIMATES OF REVENUE EXPENDITURES. 1959. a. EAs.3. Central Bureau of Statistics, Box 30266, Nairobi, Kenya (Orders to: Government Printing and Stationery Department, Box 30128, Nairobi, Kenya)
   Formerly: Kenya. Ministry of Economic Planning and Development. Estimates of Revenue Expenditures (ISSN 0075-5826)

330.9   GW   ISSN 0341-0978
DIE KONJUNKTUR IM HANDWERK. 1954. a. price varies. (Rheinisch-Westfaelisches Institut fuer Wirtschaftsforschung, Essen) Duncker und Humblot, Dietrich-Schaefer-Weg 9, Postfach 410329, 1000 Berlin 41, W. Germany (B.R.D.) Ed. Th. Beckermann.
   Formerly: Konjunkturberichte ueber das Handwerk (ISSN 0075-675X)

338.9   KO
KOREA (REPUBLIC) ECONOMIC PLANNING BOARD. ANNUAL REPORT ON CURRENT INDUSTRIAL PRODUCTION SURVEY. (Text in Korean & English) 1970. a. 3040 Won. Bureau of Statistics, Economic Planning Board, Gyeongun-Dung, Jongro-Gu, Seoul, S. Korea. Ed. Heung-Koo Kang. circ. 800.

KOTHARI'S ECONOMIC AND INDUSTRIAL GUIDE OF INDIA. see *BUSINESS AND ECONOMICS — Investments*

338   380.5   LB
LIBERIA. MINISTRY OF COMMERCE, INDUSTRY AND TRANSPORTATION. ANNUAL REPORT. a. Ministry of Commerce, Industry and Transportation, Box 9041, Monrovia, Liberia.

338   LB
LIBERIA. MINISTRY OF PLANNING AND ECONOMIC AFFAIRS. ACTIVITY REPORT. irreg. Ministry of Planning and Economic Affairs, Box 9016, Monrovia, Liberia.

338   LB   ISSN 0459-2182
LIBERIA. MINISTRY OF PLANNING AND ECONOMIC AFFAIRS. ANNUAL REPORT TO THE SESSION OF THE LEGISLATURE OF THE REPUBLIC OF LIBERIA. 1965/66. a, latest 1977. $5. Ministry of Planning and Economic Affairs, Box 9016, Monrovia, Liberia.
   Continues: Liberia. Department of Planning and Economic Affairs. Annual Report.

338   II   ISSN 0076-0269
LOCATIONS OF INDUSTRIES IN GUJARAT STATE. (Text in English) 1956. irreg. Rs.7.30. Bureau of Economics and Statistics, Sector No. 18, Gandhinagar, India.

338   II   ISSN 0541-5357
M B I'S INDIAN INDUSTRIES ANNUAL. (Text in English) 1963. a. Rs.20. Chary Publications, 14 Sidh Prasad, Ghatkopar Mahul Rd., Tilak Nagar, Bombay 400089, India.
   Survey of Indian economy, industry and engineering

338   US
MIDEAST BUSINESS GUIDE. 1977. a. $12. News Circle Publishing Co., c/o Joseph Haiek, Ed., Box 74637, Los Angeles, CA 90004. adv.

338   US
MINNESOTA NEW & EXPANDING INDUSTRY. a. free. Department of Economic Development, 480 Cedar St., St. Paul, MN 55101. circ. 2,000.

338   US   ISSN 0540-4193
MISSOURI'S NEW AND EXPANDING INDUSTRIES. 1952. a. free. Division of Commerce and Industrial Development, P.O. Box 118, Jefferson City, MO 65101. circ. 2,900.

338   US   ISSN 0077-040X
MONITOR; the voice of industry in New York State. 1914. irreg. free to qualified personnel. Associated Industries of New York State, Inc., 150 State St., Albany, NY 12207. Ed. Lavina Finin.

338   380   FR   ISSN 0077-0701
MONOGRAPHIES DE L'INDUSTRIE ET DU COMMERCE EN FRANCE.* 1970. irreg. price varies. 24 Place Malesherbes, Paris 17e, France.

338.9   NP   ISSN 0077-6548
NEPAL INDUSTRIAL DEVELOPMENT CORPORATION. ANNUAL REPORT. (Text in English) 1959-60. a. free. Nepal Industrial Development Corporation, N.I.D.C. Bldg., Durbar Marg, Box 10, Kathmandu, Nepal.

338.9   NP   ISSN 0077-6556
NEPAL INDUSTRIAL DEVELOPMENT CORPORATION. INDUSTRIAL DIGEST. (Text in English) 1966. a. Rs.30($0.50) Nepal Industrial Development Corporation, N.I.D.C. Bldg., Durbar Marg, Box 10, Kathmandu, Nepal. Ed. Ramesh Nath Dhungel.

330   NE   ISSN 0077-7536
NETHERLANDS. CENTRAAL PLANBUREAU. CENTRAL ECONOMIC PLAN. (Includes the National Budget) a. fl.19.50. Staatsuitgeverij, Chr. Plantijnstr., The Hague, Netherlands. (Prepared by: Centraal Planbureau)

338   US
NEW AND EXPANDING INDUSTRIES REPORT FOR ALABAMA. 1962. a. free. Development Office, c/o State Capitol, Montgomery, AL 36130. Ed. Fred Denton. index.

338.9   CN   ISSN 0077-8117
NEW BRUNSWICK. RESEARCH AND PRODUCTIVITY COUNCIL. REPORT. 1962. a. Research and Productivity Council, Frederiction, New Brunswick, Canada.

338.9   US   ISSN 0077-8478
NEW JERSEY. ECONOMIC POLICY COUNCIL. ANNUAL REPORT OF ECONOMIC POLICY COUNCIL AND OFFICE OF ECONOMIC POLICY. 1968. a. free. ‡ Office of Economic Policy, 142 W. State St., Trenton, NJ 08625. Ed. Peter Bearse. circ. 2,000.

338   NR
NEW NIGERIA DEVELOPMENT COMPANY LIMITED. ANNUAL REPORT AND ACCOUNTS. a. free. New Nigeria Development Company Ltd., P.M.B. 2120, Kaduna, Nigeria.
   Supersedes: Northern Nigeria Development Corporation. Report.

338   NZ
NEW ZEALAND. DEPARTMENT OF TRADE & INDUSTRY. REPORT. a. price varies. Government Printing Office, Private Bag, Wellington, New Zealand.

338.9   NZ
NEW ZEALAND. INDUSTRIAL RESEARCH AND DEVELOPMENT GRANTS ADVISORY COMMITTEE. REPORT. 1970/71. a. price varies. Government Printing Office, Private Bag, Wellington, New Zealand.

338.9   NR
NIGERIA. ANTI-INFLATION TASK FORCE. REPORT. 1975. a. NC.1. Anti-Inflation Task Force, Lagos, Nigeria. charts. stat.

338   FR   ISSN 0078-0960
NOMENCLATURE DES ENTREPRISES NATIONALES A CARACTERE INDUSTRIEL OU COMMERCIAL ET DES SOCIETES D'ECONOMIE MIXTE D'INTERET NATIONAL. irreg. price varies; 1975, two volumes 77F. (Ministere de l'Economie et des Finances) Imprimerie Nationale, Service des Ventes, 59128 Flers en Escrebieux, France.

338   US
NORTH CAROLINA. DEPARTMENT OF HUMAN RESOURCES. ANNUAL REPORT. a. Department of Human Resources, 325 N. Salisbury St., Raleigh, NC 27611.

338   UK
NORTH WEST INDUSTRIAL DEVELOPMENT ASSOCIATION. ANNUAL REPORT. a. membership. ‡ North West Industrial Development Association, Brazennose House (West Door), Brazennose St., Manchester M2 5AZ, England. Ed. Clifford F. Chapman.

338   FR   ISSN 0474-5450
ORGANIZATION FOR ECONOMIC COOPERATION AND DEVELOPMENT. INDUSTRIAL PRODUCTION. PRODUCTION INDUSTRIELLE. (Text in English and French) irreg. $5. Organization for Economic Cooperation and Development, 2 rue Andre Pascal, 75775 Paris 16, France (U. S. orders to: O.E.C.D. Publications and Information Center, 1750 Pennsylvania Ave., N. W., Washington, D. C. 20006) (also avail. in microfiche)

341.1   FR   ISSN 0029-7038
ORGANIZATION FOR ECONOMIC COOPERATION AND DEVELOPMENT. LIAISON BULLETIN BETWEEN RESEARCH AND TRAINING INSTITUTES. (Editions in English and French) irreg. 26($8) Organization for Economic Cooperation and Development, 2 rue Andre-Pascal, 75775 Paris Cedex 16, France (U. S. orders to: O.E.C.D. Publications and Information Center, 1750 Pennsylvania Ave., N.W., Washington, DC 20006) (also avail. in microfiche; back issues avail.)

338   NR
OYO STATE. MINISTRY OF ECONOMIC PLANNING AND COMMUNITY DEVELOPMENT. ANNUAL REPORT.* a. Ministry of Economic Planning and Community Development, Ibadan, Nigeria (Orders to: Oyo State Government Printer, Ibadan, Nigeria)
   Formerly: Western State. Ministry of Economic Planning and Community Development. Annual Report.

338   PK   ISSN 0078-8392
PAKISTAN. OFFICE OF THE ECONOMIC ADVISER. GOVERNMENT SPONSORED CORPORATIONS AND OTHER INSTITUTIONS. (Text in English) 1965. a. free; limited distribution. Office of the Economic Adviser, Islamabad, Pakistan.

338.9   PK   ISSN 0078-8414
PAKISTAN. PLANNING AND DEVELOPMENT DIVISION. DEVELOPMENT PROGRAMME. (Text in English) a. Planning and Development Division, P Block, Islamabad, Pakistan.

338.9   PK   ISSN 0078-8201
PAKISTAN INDUSTRIAL DEVELOPMENT CORPORATION. REPORT. (Text in English) 1952-53. a. Pakistan Industrial Development Corporation, PIDC House, Dr. Ziauddin Ahmad Rd., Karachi 4, Pakistan.

338.9   JA
PEOPLE AND NATIONAL LAND POLICY/HITO TO KOKUDO. (Text in Japanese.) 1975. irreg. 450 Yen. Kokudo Keikaku Kyokai, 21 Kotohiracho, Minato-ku, Tokyo 105, Japan. illus.

338   US   ISSN 0554-2731
PLANT LOCATION; the industrial & economic development workbook. 1959. a. $12. Simmons-Boardman Publishing Corporation, 508 Birch St., Bristol, CT 06010. Ed. Fredric Good. adv. bibl. stat. circ. 41,000(controlled) (also avail. in microform from UMI)

338.9   GW   ISSN 0079-2284
PLANUNGSSTUDIEN. 1969. irreg., vol.16, 1977. price varies. Alfred Metzner Verlag GmbH, Zeppelinallee 43, Postfach 970148, 6000 Frankfurt 97, W. Germany (B.R.D.) Ed. Joseph H. Kaiser.

338   PL   ISSN 0137-690X
POLITECHNIKA POZNANSKA. ZESZYTY NAUKOWE. EKONOMIKA I ORGANIZACJA PRZEMYSLU. 1969. irreg. price varies. Politechnika Poznanska, Pl. Curie Sklodowskiej 5, Poznan, Poland. Ed. Teobald Olejnik. circ. 250.

POOR'S REGISTER OF CORPORATIONS, DIRECTORS AND EXECUTIVES. see *BUSINESS AND ECONOMICS — Management*

BUSINESS AND ECONOMICS — PRODUCTION OF GOODS AND SERVICES

338 314 PO
PORTUGAL. INSTITUTO NACIONAL DE ESTATISTICA. SERVICOS CENTRAIS. ESTATISTICAS DAS SOCIEDADES: CONTINENTE E ILHAS ADJACENTES. (Text in French, Portuguese) a. Esc.120. Instituto Nacional de Estatistica, Servicos Centrais, Av. Antonio Jose de Almeida, Lisbon, Portugal.

338 IV
PRINCIPALES INDUSTRIES INSTALLEES EN COTE D'IVOIRE. 1968. a. free. Chambre d'Industrie de Cote d'Ivoire, B.P. 1758, Abidjan, Ivory Coast.
Formerly: Principales Industries Ivoiriennes.

338 PL ISSN 0079-581X
PROBLEMY REJONOW UPRZEMYSLAWIANYCH. (Text in Polish, English, German, Russian) 1968. irreg. price varies. (Polska Akademia Nauk) Panstwowe Wydawnictwo Naukowe, Miodowa 10, Warsaw, Poland (Dist. by Ars Polona-Ruch, Krakowskie Przedmiescie 7, Warsaw, Poland) Ed. Zygmunt Lachert.

658.2 US
PRODUCTION'S MANUFACTURING PLANBOOK. 1973. a. $5. Bramson Publishing Co., Box 101, Bloomfield Hills, MI 48013. adv. circ. 80,000. (reprint service avail. from UMI)

338 PE ISSN 0032-9908
PRODUCTIVIDAD. 1961. a. free. Centro Nacional de Productividad, Jiron Zepita 423, P. O. Box 5442, Edificio Ferrand, 5 Piso, Lima, Peru. Dir. Alfredo Massa Galvez. adv. abstr. charts. illus. circ. 2,500.

338 JA
PROFILES OF THE NATIONAL PRODUCTIVITY ORGANIZATIONS IN A P O MEMBER COUNTRIES. (Text in English) a. Asian Productivity Organization, Aoyama Dai-Ichi Mansions, 8-4-14 Akasaka, Minato-ku, Tokyo 107, Japan.

338 IT ISSN 0555-4810
PROSPETTIVE DELL'INDUSTRIA ITALIANA. (Subseries of Collana de Studi e Documentazione) 1964. a. L.5000. Servizio Italiano Pubblicazioni Internazionali s.r.l., Viale dell'Astronomia 30, 00144 Rome, Italy.

333.7 US ISSN 0079-7634
PUBLIC POLICY ISSUES IN RESOURCE MANAGEMENT. 1965. irreg., vol. 5, 1973. price varies. (University of Washington, Graduate School of Public Affairs) University of Washington Press, Seattle, WA 98105.

338.7 II
PUNJAB STATE INDUSTRIAL DEVELOPMENT CORPORATION. ANNUAL REPORT.* (Text in English) a. Punjab State Industrial Development Corporation, United Commercial Bank Bldg., 3rd Floor, Sector 17-B, Chandigarh, India. illus. stat.

338 IT
QUADERNI DI FABBRICA E STATO. 1977. irreg. Rosenberg & Sellier, Via Andrea Doria 14, 10123 Turin, Italy. stat.

354 AT
QUEENSLAND. DEPARTMENT OF COMMERCIAL AND INDUSTRIAL DEVELOPMENT. ANNUAL REPORT. 1972. a. free. Department of Commercial and Industrial Development, Box 183 P.O., North Quay, Brisbane, Qld. 4000, Australia. illus. circ. 7,000.

338.7 II
RAJASTHAN STATE WAREHOUSING CORPORATION. ANNUAL REPORT AND ACCOUNTS. (Text in English) a. Rajasthan State Warehousing Corporation, Govind Bhavan, Subhash Marg, C-Scheme, Jaipur 1, India. stat.

338.9 UR
REGIONAL'NAYA NAUKA O RAZMESHCHENII PROIZVODITEL'NYKH SIL; sbornik referativnykh rabot. irreg. 0.67 Rub. Akademiya Nauk S. S. S. R., Sibirskoe Otdelenie, Institut Ekonomiki i Organizatsii Promyshlennogo Proizvodstva, Novosibirsk, Akademgorodok, U.S.S.R. illus.

REHABILITATION INDUSTRIES CORPORATION. ANNUAL REPORT. see
EDUCATION — Special Education And Rehabilitation

338 650 FR ISSN 0080-1089
REPERTOIRE DICTIONNAIRE INDUSTRIEL.* 1956. a. Service de Renseignements du Repertoire Industriel, 13 rue de Marivaux, Paris 2e, France.

338.767 II
REPUBLIC FORGE COMPANY. ANNUAL REPORT. (Text in English) 14th, 1971/72. a. Republic Forge Company, Maula Ali, Hyderabad 40, India. stat. Key Title: Annual Report-Republic Forge Company.

338 SP
RESUMEN DE ACTIVIDADES I N I (YEAR) irreg. Instituto Nacional de Industria, Plaza de Salamanca, 8, Madrid, Spain. illus.
Formerly: Spain. Instituto Nacional de Industria. Resumen de Actividades.

338 CK ISSN 0034-8686
REVISTA DE PLANEACION Y DESARROLLO. 1969. irreg. $5. (Departamento Nacional de Planeacion) Colombiana de Impresos, Carrera 13 no. 26-45, Bogota, Colombia. circ. 2,000.

330 US
RICE UNIVERSITY. PROGRAM OF DEVELOPMENT STUDIES. DISCUSSION PAPERS. 1970. irreg. (approx 12-16/yr) free to qualified personnel. ‡ Rice University, Program of Development Studies, 121 Sewall Hall, Houston, TX 77001. Ed. Ronald Soligo. stat. circ. controlled.

338.9 MY
SARAWAK ECONOMIC DEVELOPMENT CORPORATION. ANNUAL REPORT AND STATEMENT OF ACCOUNTS. (Text in English) 1972. a. free. Sarawak Economic Development Corporation, Electra House, 2nd Fl., Box 400, Kuching, Sarawak, Malaysia.

338.7 GW
SCHRIFTEN DES WERKSARCHIVS. 1969. irreg. Henkel KGaA, Postfach 1100, 4000 Duesseldorf 1, W. Germany (B.R.D.) Ed. Manfred Schoene. illus.

338 ZR ISSN 0377-5135
SCIENCES, TECHNIQUES, INFORMATIONS C R I A C. irreg. Centre de Recherches Industrielles en Afrique Centrale, B. P. 54, Lubumbashi, Zaire. illus.
Formerly: Centre de Recherche Industrielles en Afrique Centrale. Bulletin d'Information.

338 380 BL
SEMINARIO NACIONAL DE CONTROLE DE QUALIDADE. ANAIS. 1973. irreg. Federacao das Industrias do Estado do Rio Grande do Sul, Porto Alegre, Brazil.

SERIE PRAXIS. see BUSINESS AND
ECONOMICS — Labor And Industrial Relations

338 US
SHAVINGS FROM THE CHRONICLE OF THE EARLY AMERICAN INDUSTRIES ASSOCIATION. 1971. irreg., no. 26, 1976. $12 includes Chronicle. Early American Industries Association, 2 Winding Lane, Scarsdale, NY 10583. Ed. John S. Kebabian. bk. rev. circ. 2,500.
History

338.9 SI ISSN 0080-9683
SINGAPORE. ECONOMIC DEVELOPMENT BOARD. ANNUAL REPORT. (Text in English) 1962. a. price varies. ‡ Economic Development Board, P.O. Box 2692, Singapore, Singapore. circ. 7,000.

338 CK
SOCIEDAD COLOMBIANA DE PLANIFICACION. CUADERNOS.* irreg. Sociedad Colombiana de Planificacion, Apartado Aereo 12029, Bogota, Colombia.

338 SP
SPAIN. MINISTERIO DE INDUSTRIA. RESULTADOS DE LA ENCUESTA DE COYUNTURA INDUSTRIAL: SECTOR INDUSTRIAL. 1963. irreg. included with the review Economia Industrial. Ministerio de Industria, Claudio Coells 44, Madrid-1, Spain. bk. rev. circ. 10,000.

338 GR ISSN 0072-7458
STATE OF GREEK INDUSTRY IN (YEAR) (Text in English) 1940. a. free. Federation of Greek Industries, 5 Xenophontos Str., Athens 118, Greece. circ. 4,000.

338 SW
STATSFOERETAG. AARSREDOVISNING/ SWEDISH STATE COMPANY. ANNUAL REPORT. a. free. Statsfoeretag AB, Fack, S-103 40 Stockholm, Sweden. illus.

338.9 320 US
STUDIES IN EAST EUROPEAN AND SOVIET PLANNING, DEVELOPMENT AND TRADE. 1963. irreg. price varies. Indiana University, International Development Institute, 1005 E. Tenth St., Bloomington, IN 47401.

STUDIES ON TAXATION AND ECONOMIC DEVELOPMENT. see BUSINESS AND
ECONOMICS — Public Finance, Taxation

338.9 FI ISSN 0355-6050
SUOMEN PANKKI. JULKAISUJA. KASVUTUTKIMUKSIA/BANK OF FINLAND. PUBLICATIONS. STUDIES ON FINLAND'S ECONOMIC GROWTH. Short English title: Studies on Finland's Economic Growth. (Text in Finnish; summaries in English) 1966. irreg., no. 10, 1979. price varies. Suomen Pankki - Bank of Finland, Information Department, Box 160, SF-00101 Helsinki 10, Finland. Ed. Annikki Leukkunen. circ. 750.
Formerly: Suomen Pankki. Taloustieteellinen Tutkimuslaitos. Julkaisuja. Series Kasvututkimuksia (ISSN 0081-9514)

338 SW
SVERIGES 1000 STOERSTA FOERETAG/1000 LARGEST COMPANIES IN SWEDEN. (Supplement to: Veckans Affaerer) (Text in Swedish and English) a. Kr.104.50. Specialtidningsfoerlaget AB, Sveavaegen 53, 105 44 Stockholm, Sweden. charts. stat.

338 II
TAMIL NADU INDUSTRIAL DEVELOPMENT CORPORATION. ANNUAL REPORT. (Report year ends Mar. 31) (Text in English) 7th, 1972. a. Tamil Nadu Industrial Development Corporation, Local Library Authority Building, 3rd Floor, 150-A Anna Salai, Madras, India. illus. stat.

TAMIL NADU TOURISM DEVELOPMENT CORPORATION. ANNUAL REPORT. see
TRAVEL AND TOURISM

338 TZ
TANZANIA. MINISTRY OF ECONOMIC AFFAIRS AND DEVELOPMENT PLANNING. HALI YA UCHUMI WA TAIFA. 1973. a. ‡ Ministry of Economic Affairs and Development Planning, P.O. Box 9242, Dar es Salaam, Tanzania (Subscr. to: Government Publications Agency, P.O. Box 1801, Dar es Salaam, Tanzania) stat.
Formerly: Tanzania. Ministry of Economic Affairs and Development Planning. Annual Economic Survey.

TECHNO-TIP. see TECHNOLOGY:
COMPREHENSIVE WORKS

338 US ISSN 0361-2597
TEXAS. INDUSTRIAL COMMISSION. ANNUAL REPORT. 1962. a. free. Industrial Commission, Box 12728, Capital Sta., Austin, TX 78711. illus. stat. circ. 750.

650 UK ISSN 0082-4429
TIMES 1000; lists leading companies in Britain and Overseas. 1966. a. £13. Times Books Ltd., 16 Golden Square, London W1R 4BN, England. Ed. Margaret Allen. adv. circ. 9,000.

338 SA ISSN 0563-8895
TOP COMPANIES. (Supplement to: Financial Mail) 1967. a. (South African Associated Newspapers) Financial Mail (Pty) Ltd., Box 9959, Johannesburg, South Africa. illus.

338.9 TU ISSN 0082-6944
TURKEY. DEVLET PLANAMA TESKILATI. YILI PROGRAMI UCUNCU BES YIL/ANNUAL PROGRAM OF THE FIVE YEAR DEVELOPMENT PLAN. 1963. a. State Planning Organization - Devlet Planlama Teskilati, Ankara, Turkey.

338 330.9 US
U S S R REPORT: INDUSTRIAL AFFAIRS. 1969. irreg. (approx. 41/yr.) $143.50. U.S. Joint Publications Research Service, 1000 N. Glebe Rd., Arlington, VA 22201 (Orders to: NTIS, Springfield, VA 22161)
  Formerly: Translations on U S S R Industrial Affairs.

338 330.9 US
U S S R REPORT: TRADE AND SERVICES. 1973. irreg. (approx. 74/yr.) $259. U.S. Joint Publications Research Service, 1000 N. Glebe Rd., Arlington, VA 22201 (Orders to: NTIS, Springfield, VA 22161)
  Formerly: Translations on U S S R Trade and Services.

354 UG
UGANDA ESTIMATES OF DEVELOPMENT EXPENDITURES. a, latest 1977/78. EAs.20 price varies. Government Printer, Box 33, Entebbe, Uganda.

338 US ISSN 0082-9307
U.S. BUREAU OF THE CENSUS. ANNUAL SURVEY OF MANUFACTURES. 1949. a; exemption for the years covered by Census of Manufactures. price varies. U.S. Bureau of the Census, Subscriber Services Section (Publications), Washington, DC 20233.

338 US ISSN 0082-9374
U. S. BUREAU OF THE CENSUS. CENSUS OF MANUFACTURES. (Issued in Subject, Index and Special Reports Series) 1810. quinquennial; 1972 census reports issued periodically. price varies. U.S. Bureau of the Census, Dept. of Commerce, Washington, DC 20233 (Order forms and announcements available from the Bureau; publication orders to: Supt. of Documents, Washington, DC 20402)

650 US ISSN 0083-1344
U. S. INDUSTRIAL OUTLOOK. 1960. a. $5.85. U.S. Industry and Trade Administration, Bureau of Domestic Commerce, Dept. of Commerce, Washington, DC 20230 (Orders to: Supt. of Documents, Washington, DC 20402) Eds. Wesley H. Long, John J. Bistay. charts, illus, stat. index. circ. 35,000. (also avail. in microfiche)

U.S. OFFICE OF MINORITY BUSINESS ENTERPRISE. MINORITY ENTERPRISE PROGRESS REPORT. see *ETHNIC INTERESTS*

338 AG ISSN 0457-1673
UNIVERSIDAD NACIONAL DE LA PLATA. INSTITUTO DE LA PRODUCCION. SERIE CONTRIBUCIONES. 1960. irreg. Universidad Nacional de la Plata, Instituto de la Produccion, Calle 53, No. 419, La Plata, Argentina. Ed. Servando R. M. Dozo. charts. stat.

338 US ISSN 0518-6544
UNIVERSITY OF ARKANSAS. INDUSTRIAL RESEARCH AND EXTENSION CENTER. ANNUAL REPORT. 1956. a. free. University of Arkansas, Industrial Research and Extension Center, Box 3017, Little Rock, AR 72203. Ed. William G. Conley. circ. 1,200.

338
UNIVERSITY OF ARKANSAS. INDUSTRIAL RESEARCH AND EXTENSION CENTER. RESEARCH MEMORANDUM. no. 64, 1975. irreg. University of Arkansas, Industrial Research and Extension Center, Box 3017, Little Rock, AR 72203.

UNIVERSITY OF NAIROBI. INSTITUTE FOR DEVELOPMENT STUDIES. OCCASIONAL PAPER. see *BUSINESS AND ECONOMICS — International Development And Assistance*

338 US ISSN 0083-9094
UNIVERSITY OF PENNSYLVANIA. WHARTON SCHOOL OF FINANCE AND COMMERCE. INDUSTRIAL RESEARCH UNIT. STUDIES. irreg., 1969, no. 45. University of Pennsylvania Wharton School of Finance and Commerce, Industrial Research Unit, Philadelphia, PA 19104.

338.9 352 PH ISSN 0079-9246
UNIVERSITY OF THE PHILIPPINES. COMMUNITY DEVELOPMENT RESEARCH COUNCIL. STUDY SERIES. irreg., 1969, no. 27. $3.50. University of the Philippines, Community Development Research Council, Rm. 207, Education Bldg., Diliman, Quezon City, Philippines.

338 PL
UNIWERSYTET GDANSKI. WYDZIAL EKONOMIKI PRODUKCJI. ZESZYTY NAUKOWE. ZAGADNIENIA EKONOMIKI PRZEMYSLU. (Text in Polish; summaries in English and Russian) irreg. 10 Zl. Uniwersytet Gdanski, Ul. Czerwonej Armii 110, 81-824 Sopot, Poland. illus.

338 FI ISSN 0356-8091
VALTIONYHTIOT. a. Fmk.22.50. Valtionyhtioiden Toimisto, Aleksanterinkatu 10, Helsinki 17, Finland.

338 US ISSN 0363-2067
VERMONT INDUSTRIAL DEVELOPMENT AUTHORITY. ANNUAL REPORT. 1975. a. Vermont Industrial Development Authority, Pavilion Office Building, Montpelier, VT 05602. circ. 100. Key Title: Annual Report - Vermont Industrial Development Authority.

338.9 US
WEST VIRGINIA UNIVERSITY. CENTER FOR EXTENSION AND CONTINUING EDUCATION. RESEARCH SERIES. 1968. irreg., no. 19, 1976. price varies. West Virginia University, Center for Extension and Continuing Education, Office of Research and Development, 17 Grant Ave., Morgantown, WV 26506.
  Formerly: West Virginia University. Center for Appalachian Studies and Development. Research Series (ISSN 0083-8411)

338.9 AT ISSN 0511-6910
WESTERN AUSTRALIA. MAJOR INVESTMENT PROJECTS, PUBLIC AND PRIVATE, CURRENT AND PROPOSED. 1963. a. Department of Industrial Development, 32 St. George's Terrace, Perth, W.A. 6000, Australia. circ. 4,000.

330.9 WS
WESTERN SAMOA. DEPARTMENT OF ECONOMIC DEVELOPMENT. DEVELOPMENT OF WESTERN SAMOA.* a. Department of Economic Development, Apia, Western Samoa. stat.

WHO OWNS WHOM. CONTINENTAL EUROPE. see *BUSINESS AND ECONOMICS — Management*

338.9689 ZA
ZAMBIA. MINISTRY OF PLANNING AND FINANCE. ANNUAL REPORT. 1971. a. 20 n. Ministry of Planning and Finance, Box RW 62, Lusaka, Zambia (Orders to: Government Printer, Box 136, Lusaka, Zambia)
  Formed by the merger of: Zambia. Ministry of Development and National Guidance. Annual Report & Zambia. Ministry of Finance. Annual Report (ISSN 0084-4896)

338 RH
ZIMBABWE. CENTRAL STATISTICAL OFFICE. CENSUS OF PRODUCTION. 1962. a. Rhod.$0.85. Central Statistical Office, Box 8063, Causeway, Salisbury, Zimbabwe. circ. 220.

338 SP
132 EXPRES. 1973. a. free. Subdireccion de Estudios Economicos y Marketing, Avenida Generalisimo, 146, Madrid-16, Spain. charts. illus. stat. tr.lit. (tabloid format)

BUSINESS AND ECONOMICS — Public Finance, Taxation

336 US ISSN 0163-1241
ABINGDON CLERGY INCOME TAX GUIDE. 1972. a. $2.95. Abingdon, 201 Eighth Ave. S., Nashville, TN 37203.
  Formerly (until 1978?): Clergy's Federal Income Tax Guide (ISSN 0090-9866)

ALASKA. DEPARTMENT OF REVENUE. STATE INVESTMENT PORTFOLIO. see *BUSINESS AND ECONOMICS — Investments*

AMERICAN INSTITUTE OF CERTIFIED PUBLIC ACCOUNTANTS. DIVISION OF FEDERAL TAXATION. STATEMENTS ON RESPONSIBILITIES IN TAX PRACTICE. see *BUSINESS AND ECONOMICS — Accounting*

336 II
ANDHRA PRADESH STATE FINANCIAL CORPORATION. REPORT AND ACCOUNTS. (Text in English) 1956. a. Andhra Pradesh State Financial Corporation, 5-9-194 Chirag Ali Lane, Hyderabad 500001, India. stat.
  Continues: Andhra Pradesh State Financial Corporation. Report.

336 TZ ISSN 0496-8492
APPROPRIATION ACCOUNTS, REVENUE STATEMENTS, ACCOUNTS OF THE FUNDS AND OTHER PUBLIC ACCOUNTS OF TANZANIA. 1965. irreg., latest 1972-73. Government Publications Agency, Box 1801, Dar es Salaam, Tanzania.

336 AG
ARGENTINA. SECRETARIA DE ESTADO DE HACIENDA. MEMORIA. 1860. a. Secretaria de Estado de Hacienda, Buenos Aires, Argentina.

336 BL
ARRECADACAO DOS TRIBUTOS FEDERAIS. 1974. a. Coordenacao de Sistema de Informacoes Economico-Fiscais, Esplanada dos Ministerios, Bloco 5, 70000 Brasilia D.F., Brazil. illus.

336 AT
AUSTRALIA. BUREAU OF STATISTICS. PUBLIC AUTHORITY FINANCE. STATE AND LOCAL AUTHORITIES. (Text in English) 1971. a. Aus.$1.50. Australian Bureau of Statistics, P.O. Box 10, Belconnen, A.C.T. 2616, Australia. stat. circ. 1,150.

336 AT
AUSTRALIA. BUREAU OF STATISTICS. VICTORIAN OFFICE. LOCAL GOVERNMENT FINANCE. 1958. a. free. Australian Bureau of Statistics, Victorian Office, Box 2796Y, G.P.O. Melbourne, Victoria 3001, Australia. circ. 1,100.
  Formerly: Australia. Bureau of Statistics. Victorian Office. Government Finance (ISSN 0067-1142)

336.2 AT
AUSTRALIA. DEPARTMENT OF POLICE AND CUSTOMS. REVIEW OF ACTIVITIES. 1954. a. free. Department of Police and Customs, Public Relations Section, Barton, A.C.T. 2600, Australia. Ed. W. McNanara. circ. 8,000.
  Formerly: Australia. Department of Customs and Excise. Review of Activities (ISSN 0067-1347)

336 AT
AUSTRALIA. DEPARTMENT OF THE TREASURY. TREASURY ECONOMIC PAPER. 1972. a. Department of the Treasury, Box 84, Canberra, A.C.T. 2600, Australia. charts, stat.

336.1 AT
AUSTRALIA. GRANTS COMMISSION. GRANTS COMMISSION REPORT ON FINANCIAL ASSISTANCE FOR LOCAL GOVERNMENT. 1974. irreg. price varies. Australian Government Publishing Service, Box 84, Canberra, A.C.T. 2600, Australia. illus. stat.
  Formerly: Australia. Grants Commission. Grants Commission Report on Special Assistance for States.

336.2 AT
AUSTRALIAN INCOME TAX ASSESSMENT ACT; including regulations, rates and international agreements. 1969. a. Aus.$13.50. C C H Australia Ltd., P.O. Box 230, North Ryde, NSW 2113, Australia.

336.2 AT
AUSTRALIAN MASTER TAX GUIDE. a. Aus.$13.50. C C H Australia Ltd., Box 230, North Ryde, N. S. W. 2113, Australia.

336.2 AT
AUSTRALIAN SALES TAX GUIDE. 1973. irreg.(approx. 6/yr) Aus.$185. C C H Australia Ltd., Box 230, P. O., North Ryde, N.S.W. 2113, Australia. index.

BUSINESS AND ECONOMICS — PUBLIC FINANCE, TAXATION

336 340 AT
AUSTRALIAN TAX CASES. 1969. fortn. Aus.$175. C C H Australia Ltd., P.O. Box 230, North Ryde, NSW 2113, Australia. Indexed: Curr.Aus.N.Z.Leg.Lit.Ind.

336.2 AT
AUSTRALIAN TAXPAYER'S ASSOCIATION. ANNUAL TAXATION SUMMARY. 1919. a. Aus.$5. ‡ Australian Taxpayer's Association, 343 Little Collins St., Melbourne, Australia. Ed. Eric Risstrom. circ. 40,000.
Formerly: Federated Taxpayer's Association of Australia. Annual Taxation Summary.

336.2 US ISSN 0092-6876
AUTOMATIC TAXFINDER AND TAX PREPARER'S HANDBOOK. irreg. Recordkeeper Tax Publications, Inc., 48 West 21st. St., New York, NY 10010.

336 BA
BAHRAIN. MONETARY AGENCY. ANNUAL REPORT. a. Monetary Agency, Box 27, Manama, Bahrain. charts. stat.

336 382 SL ISSN 0067-2998
BALANCE OF PAYMENTS OF SIERRA LEONE. a. free. Bank of Sierra Leone, P.O. Box 30, Freetown, Sierra Leone.

336 382 TR ISSN 0067-3005
BALANCE OF PAYMENTS OF TRINIDAD AND TOBAGO. a; latest issue, 1975. T.T.$1. Central Statistical Office, Textel Building, 1, Edward Street, Port of Spain, Trinidad (Orders to: Government Printing Office, 2 Victoria Ave., Port of Spain, Trinidad)

336 382 SP ISSN 0067-3021
BALANZA DE PAGOS DE ESPANA. a. Ministerio de Comercio, Servicio de Estudios, Madrid, Spain.

336 382 LY ISSN 0075-921X
BANK OF LIBYA. BALANCE OF PAYMENTS. (Text in Arabic and English) 1954. a. free. Bank of Libya, Box 1103, Tripoli, Libya.

336.2 NE ISSN 0077-670X
BELASTINGDRUK IN NEDERLAND/BURDEN OF TAXES IN THE NETHERLANDS. (Text in Dutch and English) 1943. a. fl.18.65. Centraal Bureau voor de Statistiek, Prinses Beatrixlaan 428, Voorburg, Netherlands (Orders to: Staatsuitgeverij, Christoffel Plantijnstraat, The Hague, Netherlands)

353 US
BITTKER AND EUSTICE'S FEDERAL INCOME TAXATION OF CORPORATIONS AND SHAREHOLDERS (SUPPLEMENT) supplements issued periodically to update base volume. $42.50 for base volume. Warren, Gorham and Lamont, Inc., 210 South St., Boston, MA 02111.

350 US
BITTKER FORMS BOOK (SUPPLEMENT) supplements issued periodically to update base volume. $47.25 for base volume. Warren, Gorham and Lamont, Inc., 210 South St., Boston, MA 02111.

336 BS ISSN 0068-0451
BOTSWANA. ANNUAL STATEMENTS OF ACCOUNTS. a., latest 1977/1978. R.4. Government Printer, Box 87, Gaborone, Botswana.

336.2 BS
BOTSWANA. DEPARTMENT OF INCOME TAX. ANNUAL REPORT. 1972. a. Department of Income Tax, Gaborone, Botswana.

336.68 BS ISSN 0524-1448
BOTSWANA. ESTIMATES OF REVENUE AND EXPENDITURE. (Continues the publication with the same title issued by Beuchanaland (Protectorate)) a., latest 1975/1976. R.2. Government Printer, Box 87, Gaborone, Botswana. stat.

336.2 BL
BRAZIL. COORDENACAO DO SISTEMA DE INFORMACOES ECONOMICO-FISCAIS. IMPOSTO SOBRE PRODUTOS INDUSTRIALIZADOS; ARRECADACAO SETORIAL. a. free. Secretaria da Receita Federal, Coordenacao do Sistema de Informacoes Economico-Fiscais, Esplanada dos Ministerios, Bloco 5, 70079 Brasilia, D.F., Brazil.
Formerly: Brazil. Centro de Informacoes Economico-Fiscais. Imposto sobre Produtos Industrializados; Arrecadacao Setorial.

382.7 BL
BRAZIL. SECRETARIA DA RECEITA FEDERAL. CENTRO DE INFORMACOES ECONOMICO-FISCAIS. RENDAS ADUANEIRAS. 1973. a. Secretaria da Receita Federal, Coordenacao do Sistema de Informacoes Economico-Fiscais, Esplanada dos Ministerios, Bloco 5, 70079 Brasilia D.F., Brazil.

336 PK
BUDGET OF THE GOVERNMENT OF PAKISTAN. DEMANDS FOR GRANTS AND APPROPRIATIONS. (Text in English) a. free to qualified personnel. Finance Division, Islamabad, Pakistan.
Supersedes: Pakistan. Ministry of Finance. Budget of the Central Government (ISSN 0078-8317)

336.2 UK ISSN 0525-3063
BUTTERWORTHS BUDGET TAX TABLES. 1966. a. price varies. ‡ Butterworth & Co. (Publishers) Ltd., 88 Kingsway, London WC2B 6AB, England. circ. 13,000.

336.2 UK
BUTTERWORTHS ORANGE TAX HANDBOOK. 1976. a. Butterworth & Co. (Publishers) Ltd., 88 Kingsway, London WC2B 6AB, England. Ed. Moiz Sadikali. circ. 9,500.

336.2 UK
BUTTERWORTHS YELLOW TAX HANDBOOK. 1962. a. Butterworth & Co. (Publishers) Ltd., 88 Kingsway, London, WC2B 6AB, England. Ed. David Roberts. circ. 19,000.
Formerly: Butterworths Tax Handbook (ISSN 0068-452X)

336 US ISSN 0068-5801
CALIFORNIA. STATE BOARD OF EQUALIZATION. ANNUAL REPORT. 1879. a. free. State Board of Equalization, 1020 N St., Room 130, Sacramento, CA 95814. Ed. Sidney A. Mandel. circ. 3,500.

336 CN
CANADA. DEPARTMENT OF FINANCE. ECONOMIC REVIEW. (Editions in English and French) a. Can.$3.50($4.20) Department of Finance, 160 Elgin St., Ottawa, Ont. K1A 0G5, Canada. Ed. Scott Hatfield. charts. illus. stat. circ. 10,000 (English edt.); 2,500 (French edt.)
Formerly: Canada Department of Finance. Budget Papers.

336.02 CN
CANADA. DEPARTMENT OF NATIONAL REVENUE. REPORT: CUSTOMS, EXCISE AND TAXATION. (Text in English and French) a. Department of National Revenue, Customs and Excise Branch, 48 Besserer St, Ottawa, Ont., Canada.

336.2 CN
CANADA. TAX REVIEW BOARD. ANNUAL REPORT/RAPPORT ANNUEL. 1973. a. free contr. circ. Tax Review Board, Ottawa, Ont., Canada.

336.2 CN ISSN 0317-946X
CANADIAN TAX FOUNDATION. PROVINCIAL AND MUNICIPAL FINANCES. 1963. biennial. price varies. Canadian Tax Foundation, Box 6, 130 Adelaide St. W., Toronto, Ont. M5H 3Ps, Canada.
Until 1969: Canadian Tax Foundation. Provincial Finances (ISSN 0068-9823)

336.2 CN ISSN 0316-3571
CANADIAN TAX FOUNDATION. TAX CONFERENCE. REPORT OF PROCEEDINGS. 1947. a. Canadian Tax Foundation, Box 6, 130 Adelaide St. W., Toronto, Ont. M5H 3P5, Canada.

336.2 CN ISSN 0008-512X
CANADIAN TAX PAPERS. irreg. price varies. Canadian Tax Foundation, Box 6, 130 Adelaide St. W., Toronto, Ont. M5H 3P5, Canada.

336 CJ
CAYMAN ISLANDS. CURRENCY BOARD. REPORT. a. Currency Board, Grand Cayman, Cayman Islands, B.W.I. illus.

336 CL
CHILE. DIRECCION DE PRESUPUESTOS. CALCULO DE ENTRADAS DE LA NACION.* a. Direccion de Presupuestos, Piso 12, Of. 27, Teatinos 120, Santiago, Chile. charts.

336 CL
CHILE. DIRECCION DE PRESUPUESTOS. DEPARTAMENTO DE ESTUDIOS FINANCIEROS. FINANZAS PUBLICAS.* 1957. a. contr.circ. Direccion de Presupuestos, Departamento de Estudios Financieros, Teatinos 120, Piso 12, Of. 27, Santiago, Chile. bibl. charts. stat.

336 CL
CHILE. DIRECCION DE PRESUPUESTOS. EXPOSICION SOBRE EL ESTADO DE LA HACIENDA PUBLICA.* 1914. a. not for sale. Direccion de Presupuestos, Piso 12, Of. 27, Teatinos 120, Santiago, Chile. charts. stat.

336 CL
CHILE. DIRECCION DE PRESUPUESTOS. INSTRUCCIONES PARA LA EJECUCION DE LA LEY DE PRESUPUESTOS.* a. Direccion de Presupuestos, Piso 12, Of. 27, Teatinos 120, Santiago, Chile. charts.

336 CL
CHILE. DIRECCION DE PRESUPUESTOS. LEY DE PRESUPUESTOS.* 1884. a. Direccion de Presupuestos, Piso 12, Of. 27, Teatinos 120, Santiago, Chile. charts.

336 CL ISSN 0577-8131
CHILE. SERVICIO DE IMPUESTOS INTERNOS. MEMORIA. 1965. a. Servicio de Impuestos Internos, Santiago, Chile.

336 CK
COLOMBIA. DIRECCION GENERAL DEL PRESUPUESTO. PROYECTO DE PRESUPUESTO. a. Direccion General del Presupuesto, Bogota, Colombia.
Formerly: Colombia. Direccion General del Presupuesto. Proyecto de Presupuesto (ISSN 0588-3598)

336 EI ISSN 0590-6571
COMMISSION OF THE EUROPEAN COMMUNITIES. FINANCIAL REPORT. (Editions also in French, German, Italian and Dutch) 1956. a. Commission of the European Communities, Services de Renseignement et de Diffusion des Documents, Rue de la Loi 200, 1049 Brussels, Belgium (Dist. in the U.S. by: European Community Information Service, 2100 M St., NW, Suite 707, Washington, DC 20037) circ. controlled.

336.2 EI
COMMISSION OF THE EUROPEAN COMMUNITIES. DIRECTORATE OF TAXATION. INVENTORY OF TAXES. (Text in English; some also in Dutch, Flemish, French, German, or Italian) irreg. Office for Official Publications of the European Communities, C.P. 1003, Luxembourg, Luxembourg (Dist. in the U.S. by: European Community Information Service, 2100 M St., NW, Suite 707, Washington, DC 20037)

354.67 CM
COMPTES NATIONAUX DU CAMEROUN. a., latest 1976/1977. 3000 Fr.CFA. Direction de la Statistique et de la Comptabilite Nationale - Department of Statistics and National Accounts, Boite Postale 660, Yaounde, Cameroon.

CONGRESS OF MICRONESIA. JOINT COMMITTEE ON PROGRAM AND BUDGET PLANNING. PUBLIC HEARINGS ON HIGH COMMISSIONER'S PRELIMINARY BUDGET. see *PUBLIC ADMINISTRATION*

BUSINESS AND ECONOMICS — PUBLIC FINANCE, TAXATION

353.9   US   ISSN 0099-0108
CONNECTICUT. TREASURY DEPARTMENT. ANNUAL REPORT. a. Treasury Department, Hartford, CT 06115. illus. Key Title: Annual Report of the Treasurer, State of Connecticut.

350   US
CONSOLIDATED TAX RETURN (SUPPLEMENT) supplements issued periodically to update base volume. $37.50 for base volume. Warren, Gorham and Lamont, Inc., 210 South St., Boston, MA 02111.

336   SP   ISSN 0069-9292
CONTABILIDAD NACIONAL DE ESPANA. irreg. Instituto Nacional de Estadistica, Avda. Generalisimo 91, Madrid 16, Spain.

336.2   BL
COORDENACAO DO SISTEMA DE TRIBUTACAO, BRAZIL. PARECERES NORMATIVOS. (Subseries of Biblioteca Mapa Fiscal) 1970. irreg. Bol.$2200. Mapa Fiscal Editora S.A., Rua Miguel Teles Jr., 382 a 394, Sao Paulo, Brazil. Eds. J. Goncalves, J. Vallim. bk. rev. index. circ. 15,000.

336.2   CN   ISSN 0070-0282
CORPORATE MANAGEMENT TAX CONFERENCE. 1959-60. a. price varies. Canadian Tax Foundation, Box 6, 130 Adelaide St. W., Toronto, Ont. M5H 3P5, Canada.

336   CR
COSTA RICA. DIRECCION GENERAL DE LA TRIBUTACION DIRECTA. ESTADISTICA DEMOGRAFIA FISCAL DEL IMPUESTO SOBRE LA RENTA. PERIODOS. no. 71, 1974. irreg. Direccion General de Tributacion Directa, San Jose, Costa Rica.

336   CR   ISSN 0070-0576
COSTA RICA. MINISTERIO DE HACIENDA OFICINA DEL PRESUPESTO. INFORME.* a. Ministerio de Hacienda, Oficina del Presupuesto, San Jose, Costa Rica.

336   NR
CROSS RIVER STATE. MINISTRY OF ECONOMIC DEVELOPMENT AND RECONSTRUCTION. STATE DEVELOPMENT PLAN.* 1970/74. irreg. 5p. Ministry of Economic Development and Reconstruction, Calabar, Nigeria (Dist. by: Cross River State Government Printer, Calabar, Nigeria) illus. stat.
    Formerly: South-Eastern State. Ministry of Economic Development and Reconstruction. State Development Plan.

336   MX
CUENTA DE LA HACIENDA PUBLICA FEDERAL. (Each edition published in 2 or more vols.) 1977. irreg. Direccion General de Contabilidad Gubernamental, Articulo 123 no. 88, Mexico 1, D.F., Mexico.

336   US
CURRENT GOVERNMENT REPORTS: STATE TAX COLLECTIONS. (Series GF-1) annual. U.S. Bureau of the Census, Subscriber Services Section, Washington, DC 20233.

336   US   ISSN 0360-2508
CURRENT GOVERNMENTS REPORTS: CHART BOOK ON GOVERNMENT DATA. ORGANIZATION, FINANCES AND EMPLOYMENT. (Series GF-7) 1966. a. price varies. U.S. Bureau of the Census, U.S. Dept. of Commerce, Washington, DC 20233.
    Formerly: U.S. Bureau of the Census. Recurrent Reports on Governments (Series G F-7) Chart Book on Government Finances and Employment (ISSN 0082-9420)

336.73   US   ISSN 0082-9439
CURRENT GOVERNMENTS REPORTS: CITY GOVERNMENT FINANCES. (Series GF-4) 1965. irreg. price varies. U.S. Bureau of the Census, U.S. Department of Commerce, Washington, DC 20233. Key Title: City Government Finances.
    National totals for cities and towns that had population of 50,000 or more in 1970

336   US   ISSN 0098-678X
CURRENT GOVERNMENTS REPORTS: COUNTY GOVERNMENT FINANCES. (Series GF-8) annual. U.S. Bureau of the Census, Subscriber Services Section, Washington, DC 20233.

336 331 350   US
CURRENT GOVERNMENTS REPORTS: FINANCES OF EMPLOYEE RETIREMENT SYSTEMS OF STATE AND LOCAL GOVERNMENTS. (Series GF-2) annual. U.S. Bureau of the Census, Subscriber Services Section, Washington, DC 20233.

336   US   ISSN 0090-5259
CURRENT GOVERNMENTS REPORTS, GF - GOVERNMENT FINANCE. a. $20.50 annual subscription for GE, GF, GR, GT series. U.S. Bureau of the Census, Subscriber Services Section, Washington, DC 20233.

336   US   ISSN 0095-3741
CURRENT GOVERNMENTS REPORTS: GOVERNMENTAL FINANCES. (Series GF-5) annual. U.S. Bureau of the Census, Subscriber Services Section, Washington, DC 20233. Key Title: Governmental Finances (Washington)

336 331 350   US
CURRENT GOVERNMENTS REPORTS, GR FINANCES OF SELECTED PUBLIC EMPLOYEE RETIREMENT SYSTEMS. q. U.S. Bureau of the Census, Subscriber Services Section, Washington, DC 20233.

336.2   US
CURRENT GOVERNMENTS REPORTS, GSS STATE AND LOCAL GOVERNMENT SPECIAL STUDIES. irreg. U.S. Bureau of the Census, Dept. of Commerce, Washington, DC 20233 (Orders to: Supt. Doc., Washington, D.C. 20402)

336   US   ISSN 0501-7718
CURRENT GOVERNMENTS REPORTS, GT QUARTERLY SUMMARY OF STATE AND LOCAL TAX REVENUE. q. U.S. Bureau of the Census, Subscriber Services Section, Washington, DC 20233.

336   US
CURRENT GOVERNMENTS REPORTS: LOCAL GOVERNMENT FINANCES IN SELECTED METROPOLITAN AREAS AND LARGE COUNTIES. (Series GF-6) annual. U.S. Bureau of the Census, Subscriber Services Section, Washington, DC 20233.

336   CY   ISSN 0070-2323
CYPRUS. BUDGET: ESTIMATES OF REVENUE AND EXPENDITURE. (Text in English) a. Mils.1000($2.20) Government Printing Office, Nicosia, Cyprus.

336   CY   ISSN 0084-9510
CYPRUS. DEVELOPMENT ESTIMATES. a. Mils.750($1.50) Government Printing Office, Nicosia, Cyprus.

336   CY   ISSN 0574-8305
CYPRUS. LOAN COMMISSIONERS. ACCOUNTS AND STATISTICS FOR THE YEAR. 1954. a. £0.25. Loan Commissioners, Nicosia, Cyprus. circ. 350.

336   US   ISSN 0084-9685
DELAWARE. STATE TREASURER. ANNUAL REPORT. a. free. State Treasurer, Thomas Collins Building, Dover, DE 19901. circ. controlled.

336.2   DK
DENMARK. DIREKTORATET FOR TOLDVAESENET. TOLDVAESENETS AKTIVITETER. 1971. a. Direktoratet for Toldvaesenet, Amaliegade 44, DK-1256 Copenhagen K, Denmark. illus.
    Formerly (until 1977): Denmark. Direktoratet for Toldvaesenet. Toldvaesenet.

336.2   US   ISSN 0093-8823
DIRECT LEVIES ON GAMING IN NEVADA; analysis of the rates and structure by all levels of government. a. Gaming Control Board, Economic Research Unit, 1150 E. William St., Carson City, NV 89710.

336   EC
ECUADOR. CORPORACION FINANCIERA NACIONAL. MEMORIA. a. free. Corporacion Financiera Nacional, Robles 731 y Amazona, Apdo. de Correos 163, Quito, Ecuador. charts. illus. stat.
    Formerly (until 1977): Ecuador. Comision de Valores. Corporacion Financiera Nacional. Memoria (ISSN 0589-7688)

336   EC
ECUADOR. DIRECCION GENERAL DE RECAUDACIONES. BOLETIN. irreg. Direccion General de Recaudaciones, Quito, Ecuador. charts. stat.

336   SZ
ERTRAGSBILANZ DER SCHWEIZ. French edition: Balance Suisse des Revenus. (Supplement to Switzerland. Eidgenoessisches Volkswirtschaftsdepartement. Volkswirtschaft and Schweizerische Nationalbank. Monatsbericht) a. Eidgenoessisches Volkswirtschaftsdepartement, Kommission fuer Konjunkturfragen, Belpstr. 53, 3003 Berne, Switzerland.

336 382   PN   ISSN 0378-7397
ESTADISTICA PANAMENA. SITUACION ECONOMICA. SECCION 341. BALANZA DE PAGOS. 1954-58. a. Bl..30. Direccion de Estadistica y Censo, Contraloria General, Apartado 5213, Panama 5, Panama. circ. 1,700.

336   LO
ESTIMATES OF THE REVENUE AND EXPENDITURE OF THE KINGDOM OF LESOTHO. a. Government Printer, Maseru, Lesotho.

336.73   US   ISSN 0071-3678
FACTS AND FIGURES ON GOVERNMENT FINANCE. 1941. biennial. ‡ Tax Foundation, Inc., 1875 Connecticut Ave., N.W., Washington, DC 20009. Ed. Elsie Watters.

336.2   US   ISSN 0092-6531
FEDERAL ESTATE AND GIFT TAXES EXPLAINED, INCLUDING ESTATE PLANNING. irreg., latest 1979. $9. Commerce Clearing House, Inc., 4025 W. Peterson Ave., Chicago, IL 60646. Key Title: Federal Estate and Gift Taxes Explained.

FEDERAL FUNDING GUIDE FOR ELEMENTARY AND SECONDARY EDUCATION. see *EDUCATION — School Organization And Administration*

336.1   US   ISSN 0362-4285
FEDERAL FUNDING GUIDE FOR LOCAL GOVERNMENTS. 1976. a. $57.95. Government Information Services, 752 National Press Building, N.W., Washington, DC 20045. Ed. Jan Balhin.

336.2   US   ISSN 0071-4135
FEDERAL GRADUATED WITHHOLDING TAX TABLES. a. $3.75 pap. Commerce Clearing House, Inc., 4025 W. Peterson Ave., Chicago, IL 60646.

336.1   US   ISSN 0361-1582
FEDERAL GRANT-IN-AID ACTIVITY IN FLORIDA: A SUMMARY REPORT. 1974. a. $2.22 free. Department of Administration, Division of State Planning, Bureau of Intergovernmental Relations, 660 Apalachee Pkwy., Tallahassee, FL 32304. stat.

353 332   US
FEDERAL INCOME TAXATION OF BANKS AND FINANCIAL INSTITUTIONS (SUPPLEMENT) supplements issued periodically to update base volume. $47.50 for base volume. Warren, Gorham and Lamont, Inc., 210 South St., Boston, MA 02111.

336.1   US   ISSN 0363-7166
FEDERAL PROGRAMS, STATE OF ARIZONA. a. Department of Administration, Finance Division, Phoenix, AZ 85007.

336.2   US   ISSN 0071-4143
FEDERAL TAX RETURN MANUAL. 1960. a. $57. Commerce Clearing House, Inc., 4025 W. Peterson Ave., Chicago, IL 60646. (looseleaf format)

336   FR   ISSN 0071-4348
FEDERATION NATIONALE DES CONSEILS JURIDIQUES ET FISCAUX. CAHIERS.* (Supersedes its Actualites Federales, discontinued in 1963) 1967, N.S. irreg. price varies. Federation Nationale des Conseils Juridiques et Fiscaux, 16 Pl. de la Madeleine, Paris 8e, France.

336.2   NE
FED'S FISCALE BROCHURES. 1964. irreg. approx. 6/yr. price varies. Uitgeverij FED B. V., Polstraat 10, Deventer, Netherlands. Eds. D. Bruell, J. E. A. M. van Dijck.

BUSINESS AND ECONOMICS — PUBLIC FINANCE, TAXATION

336 FJ
FIJI. CENTRAL MONETARY AUTHORITY. ANNUAL REPORT. 1975. a. Central Monetary Authority, Minister of Finance, YMCA Building, Stinson Parade, Suva, Fiji. charts. stat.

336 FI ISSN 0071-5255
FINLAND. KANSANTALOUSOSASTO. KANSANTALOUDEN KEHITYSARVIO. SUMMARY: NATIONAL BUDGET FOR FINLAND. (Text in Finnish; summaries in English) 1966. a. Fmk.10. Valtion Painatuskeskus - Government Printing Centre; Ministry of Finance, Annankatu 44, 00100 Helsinki 10, Finland.

353.9 US ISSN 0094-8551
FLORIDA. BUREAU OF LOCAL GOVERNMENT FINANCE. ANNUAL LOCAL GOVERNMENT FINANCIAL REPORT. a. free. Bureau of Local Government Finance, 111 Carlton Bldg., Tallahassee, FL 32304. Key Title: Annual Local Government Financial Report, State of Florida.

336.2 FR
FRANCE. CONSEIL DES IMPOTS. RAPPORT AU PRESIDENT DE LA REPUBLIQUE. irreg. price varies. France. Direction des Journaux Officiels, 26 rue Desaix, 75732 Paris Cedex 15, France. (Co-sponsor: Ministere de l'Environnement et du Cadre de Vie) (also avail. in microfiche)

336 FR ISSN 0071-8637
FRANCE. DIRECTION GENERALE DES DOUANES ET DROITS INDIRECTS. ANNUAIRE ABREGE DE STATISTIQUES. irreg. Imprimerie Nationale, Service des Ventes, 59128 Flers en Escrebieux, 75732 Paris Cedex 15.

336 FR ISSN 0071-8742
FRANCE. INSPECTION GENERALE DES FINANCES. ANNUAIRE. 1952. a. Imprimerie Nationale, S.E.V.P.O., 39 rue de la Convention, 75732 Paris Cedex 15, France.

336 382.1 FR ISSN 0071-8890
FRANCE. MINISTERE DE L'ECONOMIE ET DES FINANCES. BALANCE DES PAIEMENTS ENTRE LA FRANCE ET L'EXTERIEUR. a. Ministere de l'Economie et des Finances, Direction du Tresor, 93 rue de Rivoli, 75056 Paris, France. circ. controlled.

336 FR ISSN 0071-8904
FRANCE. MINISTERE DU BUDGET. BUDGET. 1952. a. price varies. Ministere du Budget, Service de l'Information, 93 rue de Rivoli, 75056 Paris, France (Dist. by: Documentation Francaise, 29-31 Quai Voltaire, Paris Cedex 07, France)
 Formerly: France. Ministere de l'Economie et des Finances. Budget.

350 US
FREEMAN AND FREEMAN'S TAX PRACTICE DESKBOOK (SUPPLEMENT) supplements issued periodically to update base volume. $32.50 for base volume. Warren, Gorham and Lamont, Inc., 210 South St., Boston, MA 02111.

354.67 GO
GABON. DIRECTION GENERALE DES FINANCES ET DU BUDGET. PROJET DU BUDGET GENERAL. irreg. Direction Generale des Finances et du Budget, Ministere de l'Economie et des Finances, Libreville, Gabon. stat.

354.667 GH
GHANA. SUPREME MILITARY COUNCIL. BUDGET PROPOSALS. a. NC.1. Supreme Military Council, Ministry of Finance, Accra, Ghana. stat.

336 US ISSN 0072-5161
GOVERNMENT FINANCE BRIEF. NEW SERIES. 1965. irreg., 1980, no. 30. $1. ‡ Tax Foundation, Inc., 1875 Connecticut Ave., N.W., Washington, DC 20009. Ed. Elsie Watters.

339.4 UK
GREAT BRITAIN. BOARD OF INLAND REVENUE. THE SURVEY OF PERSONAL INCOMES. irreg. £1.50. Board of Inland Revenue, Somerset House, London W.C.2., England (Avail. from H.M.S.O., c/o Liaison Officer, Atlantic House, Holborn Viaduct, London EC1P 1BN, England) stat.

GREAT BRITAIN. DEPARTMENT OF THE ENVIRONMENT. LOCAL GOVERNMENT FINANCIAL STATISTICS: ENGLAND AND WALES. see PUBLIC ADMINISTRATION — Municipal Government

336.1 UK
GREAT BRITAIN. DEPARTMENT OF THE ENVIRONMENT. RATE REBATES IN ENGLAND AND WALES. (Joint publication with the Welsh Office) a. price varies. Department of the Environment, 2 Marsham St., London SW1P 3EB, England (Avail. from H.M.S.O., c/o Liaison Officer, Atlantic House, Holborn Viaduct, London EC1P 1BN, England)

336.1 UK
GREAT BRITAIN. DEPARTMENT OF THE ENVIRONMENT. RATES AND RATEABLE VALUES IN ENGLAND AND WALES. (Joint publication with the Welsh Office) 1970/1971. irreg. £0.95. Department of the Environment, 2 Marsham St., London SW1P 3EB, England (Avail. from H. M. S. O., c/o Liason Officer, Atlantic House, London EC1P 1BN, England)

336 UK
GREAT BRITAIN. TREASURY. SUPPLY ESTIMATES. 1850. a. price varies. H.M. Treasury, Parliament St., London SW1P 3AG, England (Avail. from H.M.S.O., c/o Liaison Officer, Atlantic House, Holborn Viaduct, London EC1P 1BN, England) stat. index.

336.2 GU ISSN 0072-7873
GUAM. DEPARTMENT OF REVENUE AND TAXATION. REPORT. 1969. a. $2. Department of Revenue and Taxation, P.O. Box 2796, Agana, GU 96910.

336 382 FR ISSN 0072-8187
GUIDE NATIONAL DES DOUANES ET DROITS INDIRECTS. 1961. biennial. 300 F. Syndicat National Unifie des Douanes et Droits Indirects, 5 rue Geoffroy Marie, 75009 Paris, France. adv. circ. 10,000.

336.2 JA ISSN 0072-8551
GUIDE TO JAPANESE TAXES. (Text in English) 1965. a. $20. Zaikei Shoho Sha, 1-2-14 Higashi Shimbashi, Minato-ku, Tokyo, Japan (Dist. in U.S. by: Fred B. Rothman & Co., 10368 W. Centennial Rd., Littleton, CO 80123) Ed. Yuji Gomi. circ. 6,000.

336.2 NZ ISSN 0072-8616
GUIDE TO NEW ZEALAND INCOME TAX PRACTICE. 1964. a. NZ.$20. Sweet & Maxwell (N.Z.) Ltd., Private Bag, Auckland, New Zealand (Dist. by Carswell Co. Ltd., 2330 Midland Avenue, Agincourt 742, Ont., Canada) Ed. Charles A. Staples. adv. circ. 8,750.

336.2 US ISSN 0072-8837
GUIDEBOOK TO CALIFORNIA TAXES. 1950. a. $9 pap. Commerce Clearing House, Inc., 4025 W. Peterson Ave., Chicago, IL 60646.

336.2 US ISSN 0093-8637
GUIDEBOOK TO FLORIDA TAXES. $8. Commerce Clearing House, Inc., 4025 W. Peterson Ave., Chicago, IL 60646.

336.2 US ISSN 0072-8845
GUIDEBOOK TO ILLINOIS TAXES. 1971. a. $9. Commerce Clearing House, Inc., 4025 W. Peterson Ave., Chicago, IL 60646.

336.2 US ISSN 0072-8861
GUIDEBOOK TO MASSACHUSETTS TAXES. 1967. a. $9 pap. Commerce Clearing House, Inc., 4025 W. Peterson Ave., Chicago, IL 60646.

336.2 US ISSN 0072-887X
GUIDEBOOK TO MICHIGAN TAXES. 1968. a. $9. Commerce Clearing House, Inc., 4025 W. Peterson Ave., Chicago, IL 60646.

336.2 US ISSN 0072-8888
GUIDEBOOK TO NEW JERSEY TAXES. 1969. a. $9. Commerce Clearing House, Inc., 4025 W. Peterson Ave., Chicago, IL 60646.

336.2 US ISSN 0072-8896
GUIDEBOOK TO NEW YORK TAXES. 1965. a. $9. Commerce Clearing House, Inc., 4025 W.

336.2 US ISSN 0091-1186
GUIDEBOOK TO NORTH CAROLINA TAXES. 1972. a. $9. Commerce Clearing House, Inc., 4025 W. Peterson Ave., Chicago, IL 60646.

336.2 US ISSN 0091-4010
GUIDEBOOK TO OHIO TAXES. 1972. a. $9. Commerce Clearing House, Inc., 4025 W. Peterson Ave., Chicago, IL 60646.

336.2 US ISSN 0072-890X
GUIDEBOOK TO PENNSYLVANIA TAXES. 1965. a. $9. Commerce Clearing House, Inc., 4025 W. Peterson Ave., Chicago, IL 60646.

336.2 US ISSN 0093-8645
GUIDEBOOK TO WISCONSIN TAXES. irreg. $9. Commerce Clearing House, Inc., 4025 W. Peterson Ave., Chicago, IL 60646.

336 II ISSN 0533-649X
GUJARAT STATE FINANCIAL CORPORATION. ANNUAL REPORT. (Text in English) a. Gujarat State Financial Corporation, Jaladarshan Bldg., Ashram Rd., Navrangpura, Box 4030, Ahmedabad 380009, India. illus. stat.

336.2 NE
HANDBOOK ON THE U.S.-GERMAN TAX CONVENTION. (Text in English and German) 1966. irreg. fl.580 incl. base vol. International Bureau of Fiscal Documentation, Box 20237, 1000 HE Amsterdam, Netherlands. (looseleaf format)

336 GW
HANDBUCH DER STEUERVERANLAGUNGEN: EINKOMMENSTEUER, KOERPERSCHAFTSTEUER, GEWERBESTEUER, UMSATZSTEUER. (Subseries of the institute's Schriften) 1964. a. DM.89. (Deutsches Wissenschaftliches Steuerinstitut der Steuerberater und Steuerbevollmaechtigten e.V.) C.H. Beck'sche Verlagsbuchhandlung, Wilhelmstr. 9, 8000 Munich 40, W. Germany(B.R.D.)

HAWAII. LEGISLATIVE AUDITOR. SPECIAL REPORTS. see PUBLIC ADMINISTRATION

336 HK
HONG KONG. CENSUS AND STATISTICS DEPARTMENT. THE BUDGET: ECONOMIC BACKGROUND. (Text in English) 1973. a. HK.$6. Economic Services Branch, Central Government Offices, Lower Albert Rd., Hong Kong, Hong Kong (Subscr. to: Government Information Services, Beaconsfield House, Queen's Rd., Central, Victoria, Hong Kong)

336 HU
HUNGARY. KOZPONTI STATISZTIKAI HIVATAL, NEPGAZDASAGI MERLEGEK. 1970. irreg. Statisztikai Kiado Vallalat, Kaszas U.10-12., P.O.B.99, 1300 Budapest 3, Hungary.

336.2 US ISSN 0073-5027
ILLINOIS STATE BAR ASSOCIATION. FEDERAL TAX SECTION NEWSLETTER. 1954. irreg., 1970, vol. 17, no. 2. membership. ‡ Illinois State Bar Association, Illinois Bar Center, Springfield, IL 62701. Ed. John G. Campbell. circ. 1,500(controlled) (back issues avail.)

336.2 US ISSN 0073-5671
INCOME, ESTATE AND GIFT TAX PROVISIONS: INTERNAL REVENUE CODE. a. $12 pap. Commerce Clearing House, Inc., 4025 W. Peterson Ave., Chicago, IL 60646.

336.2 335 US ISSN 0098-1729
INCOME TAX GUIDE FOR MILITARY PERSONNEL. irreg. $1.95. A F T A C Enterprises, 4902 La Barranca, San Antonio, TX 78233.

336.2 II ISSN 0073-6120
INDIA. CENTRAL BOARD OF REVENUE. CENTRAL EXCISE MANUAL.* (Text in English) a. Rs.6.25($2.85) Central Board of Revenue, Ministry of Finance, New Delhi, India.

336 II
INDIA. FINANCE DEPARTMENT. BUDGET OF THE CENTRAL GOVERNMENT. a. Finance Department, New Delhi, India. charts. stat.
 Supersedes: India. Ministry of Finance. Budget (ISSN 0536-9290)

BUSINESS AND ECONOMICS — PUBLIC FINANCE, TAXATION

INSTITUT "FINANZEN UND STEUERN."
GRUENE BRIEFE. see *BUSINESS AND ECONOMICS — Banking And Finance*

INSTITUT "FINANZEN UND STEUERN."
SCHRIFTENREIHE. see *BUSINESS AND ECONOMICS — Banking And Finance*

336   US
INTERNAL REVENUE CODE. Cover title: Complete Internal Revenue Code. a. Research Institute of America, Inc., 589 Fifth Ave., New York, NY 10017.

336.24   US   ISSN 0074-1205
INTERNAL REVENUE GUIDE TO YOUR FEDERAL INCOME TAX. 1962. a. $1.25. (U.S. Internal Revenue Service) Arco Publishing Co. Inc., 219 Park Ave. S., New York, NY 10003. bk. rev.

336   SZ   ISSN 0074-1744
INTERNATIONAL ASSOCIATION OF STATE LOTTERIES. (REPORTS OF CONGRESS) 1974. biennial, 12th, 1976, Nairobi. 8 Fr.($300) International Association of State Lotteries, Hirschengraben 62, Box 644, 8021 Zurich, Switzerland. adv. bk. rev. circ. 1,000.
    Reports published in host country

336   NE   ISSN 0074-2104
INTERNATIONAL BUREAU OF FISCAL DOCUMENTATION. ANNUAL REPORT. (Text in English) 1953. a. free. International Bureau of Fiscal Documentation, Box 20237, 1000 HE Amsterdam, Netherlands. Ed. Dir. J. van Hoorn, Jr.

336   NE   ISSN 0074-2112
INTERNATIONAL BUREAU OF FISCAL DOCUMENTATION. PUBLICATION. irreg., no. 26, 1979. price varies. International Bureau of Fiscal Documentation, Box 20237, 1000 HE Amsterdam, Netherlands.

336.2   BE   ISSN 0074-4476
INTERNATIONAL CUSTOMS JOURNAL/ BULLETIN INTERNATIONAL DES DOUANES. (Text in English, French, German, Italian, Spanish) 1891. irreg. International Customs Tariffs Bureau - Bureau International des Tariffs Douaniers, Rue de l'Association 38, B-1000 Brussels, Belgium (Dist. in the U.S. by: National Technical Information Service, U.S. Department of Commerce, Springfield, VA 22161)

332   NE
INTERNATIONAL FISCAL HARMONIZATION SERIES. 1969. irreg., no. 3, 1975. price varies. International Bureau of Fiscal Documentation, Box 20237, 1000 HE Amsterdam, Netherlands.

336   GW   ISSN 0074-6533
INTERNATIONAL INSTITUTE OF PUBLIC FINANCE. PAPERS AND PROCEEDINGS. (Text in English, French, German) 1938. a. $14.20 price varies. ‡ International Institute of Public Finance, Universitaet, 6600 Saarbruecken 11, W. Germany (B.R.D.) circ. 600.

336   IE   ISSN 0075-0603
IRELAND (EIRE) CENTRAL STATISTICS OFFICE. NATIONAL INCOME AND EXPENDITURE. 1958. a. 90p. Central Statistics Office, Earlsfort Terrace, Dublin 2, Ireland. circ. 2,000.
    Supersedes in part: Irish Statistical Survey.

336   IE   ISSN 0075-0670
IRELAND (EIRE) DEPARTMENT OF FINANCE. FINANCIAL STATEMENT OF THE MINISTER FOR FINANCE. a. Department of Finance, Dublin, Ireland.

336   IS
ISRAEL. KNESSET. VA'ADAT HA-KESAFIM MISPARIM AL VA'ADAT HA-KESAFIM/ ISRAEL. KNESSET. FINANCE COMMITTEE. DATA ON ACTIVITIES. 1972/73. a. ‡ Knesset, Finance Committee, Jerusalem, Israel. Ed. Ivor Kershner. circ. controlled. (processed)

336   IV
IVORY COAST. MINISTERE DE L'ECONOMIE, ES FINANCES ET DU PLAN. COMPTES DE LA NATION. 1966. a. $20. Ministere de l'Economie, des Finances et du Plan, B. P. 5-65, Abidjan, Ivory Coast.
    Formerly: Ivory Coast. Ministere du Plan. Comptes de la Nation.

336.24   US   ISSN 0084-4314
J. K. LASSER'S YOUR INCOME TAX. 1937. a. $2.95. (J. K. Lasser Institute) Simon and Schuster, Inc., 630 Fifth Ave., New York, NY 10020 (Orders to: 1 W. 39th St., New York, N.Y. 10018) Ed. J. K. Lasser.

336.2   US   ISSN 0075-2061
J. K. LASSER'S YOUR INCOME TAX, PROFESSIONAL ED. 1962. a. $12.95. (J. K. Lasser Institute) Simon and Schuster, Inc., 630 Fifth Ave., New York, NY 10020.

JAHRESFACHKATALOG RECHT-WIRTSCHAFT-STEUERN. see *BUSINESS AND ECONOMICS*

336   II
KARNATAKA. FINANCE DEPARTMENT. ANNUAL REPORT. (Text in English) a. Finance Department, Bangalore, Karnataka, India.
    Supersedes: Mysore. Finance Department. Annual Report.

336.3   US   ISSN 0095-1498
KENTUCKY LOCAL DEBT REPORT. a. Office for Local Government, New Capitol Annex Bldg., Frankfort, KY 40601.

336   LO   ISSN 0075-8817
LESOTHO. TREASURY. REPORT ON THE FINANCES AND ACCOUNTS. a. R.4. Treasury, P.O. Box 401, Maseru, Lesotho.

354   LB
LIBERIA. GENERAL AUDITING OFFICE. ANNUAL REPORT ON THE OPERATION OF THE GENERAL AUDITING OFFICE. a. General Auditing Office, Monrovia, Liberia.

336   LB   ISSN 0304-727X
LIBERIA. MINISTRY OF FINANCE. ANNUAL REPORT. 1972. a. Ministry of Finance, Broad St., Monrovia, Liberia. charts. stat.

336   US   ISSN 0085-2821
LOCAL GOVERNMENT FINANCES IN MARYLAND. 1948. a. Department of Fiscal Services, Division of Fiscal Research, 90 State Circle, Annapolis, MD 21401. stat. circ. controlled. (processed)

336.2   CN   ISSN 0076-048X
LOI DE L'IMPOT SUR LE REVENU, CANADIENNE. 10th ed., 1979. a. Can.$27. C.C.H. Canadian Ltd., 6 Garamond Ct., Don Mills, Ont. M3C 1Z5, Canada. index.

336.17   CN
LOTO-QUEBEC. RAPPORT ANNUEL. (Editions in English and French) 1973. a. Societe d'Exploitation des Loteries et Courses du Quebec, 2000 Berri St., Montreal, Que. H2L 4N5, Canada. illus.

336   LU   ISSN 0076-1559
LUXEMBOURG. MINISTERE DES FINANCES. BUDGET DE L'ETAT. a. contr. free circ. Ministere des Finances, Luxembourg, Luxembourg.

336   LU
LUXEMBOURG. MINISTERE DES FINANCES. PROJET DE LOI CONCERNANT LE BUDGET DES RECETTES ET DES DEPENSES DE L'ETAT. a. contr. free circ. Ministere des Finances, Luxembourg, Luxembourg.

MCGOLDRICK'S HANDBOOK OF CANADIAN CUSTOMS TARIFF AND EXCISE DUTIES. see *BUSINESS AND ECONOMICS — International Commerce*

336   II   ISSN 0076-2555
MAHARASHTRA STATE BUDGET IN BRIEF. (Text in English and Marathi) 1960/61. a. free. Directorate of Economics and Statistics, D.D. Bldg., Old Custom House, Bombay 400023, India. Ed. S. M. Vidwans. circ. controlled.

657.46 336.2   US
MAIN HURDMAN & CRANSTOUN NEWS SUMMARY. irreg? Main Hurdman & Cranstoun (Certified Public Accountants), 140 Broadway, New York, NY 10005.

336.2   US
MAIN HURDMAN & CRANSTOUN TAX NEWSLETTER. irreg? Main Hurdman & Cranstoun (Certified Public Accountants), 140 Broadway, New York, NY 10005.

336.2   US   ISSN 0361-3550
MAINE. BUREAU OF PROPERTY TAXATION. BIENNIAL REPORT. 1974. biennial. Bureau of Property Taxation, Room 202, State Office Building, Augusta, ME 04330. stat. Key Title: Biennial Report of the Bureau of Property Taxation.

336   MW   ISSN 0076-3020
MALAWI. ACCOUNTANT GENERAL. REPORT. a, latest 1975. K.4.75. Government Printer, P.O. Box 37, Zomba, Malawi.

336   MW   ISSN 0076-3195
MALAWI. MINISTRY OF FINANCE. BUDGET STATEMENT.* a. Government Printer, P.O. Box 37, Zomba, Malawi.

336   MW
MALAWI. MINISTRY OF FINANCE. FINANCIAL STATEMENT. (Subseries of its Budget Document) a. Government Printer, Box 37, Zomba, Malawi.

336 382   MW   ISSN 0085-3003
MALAWI. NATIONAL STATISTICAL OFFICE. BALANCE OF PAYMENTS. 1964. a. K.2.50($2.80) ‡ National Statistical Office, Box 333, Zomba, Malawi.

336   MW   ISSN 0076-3314
MALAWI. OFFICE OF THE AUDITOR GENERAL. REPORT. a. K.2. Government Printer, P.O. Box 37, Zomba, Malawi.

MALAYSIA. PERBENDAHARAAN. ANGGARAN BELANJAWAN. see *BUSINESS AND ECONOMICS — Accounting*

336   US
MASTER FEDERAL TAX MANUAL. Cover title: Research Institute Master Federal Tax Manual. 1975. a. Research Institute of America, Inc., 589 Fifth Ave., New York, NY 10017. Ed.Bd.

336   MF   ISSN 0076-549X
MAURITIUS. CUSTOMS AND EXCISE DEPARTMENT. ANNUAL REPORT. a, latest 1975. Rs.175. Customs and Excise Department, Port Louis, Mauritius (Orders to: Government Printing Office, Elizabeth II Ave., Port Louis, Mauritius)

336   MF   ISSN 0076-5562
MAURITIUS. PUBLIC ACCOUNTS COMMITTEE. REPORT.* a. price varies. Government Printing Office, Elizabeth II Ave., Port Louis, Mauritius.

336.776   US   ISSN 0095-0645
MINNESOTA. DEPARTMENT OF REVENUE. BIENNIAL REPORT. 1972. biennial. Department of Revenue, Centennial Office Bldg., St. Paul, MN 55145. stat. Key Title: Biennial Report - State of Minnesota, Department of Revenue.
    Continues: Minnesota. Department of Taxation. Biennial Report.

366.778   US
MISSOURI. DEPARTMENT OF REVENUE. ANNUAL COMBINED FINANCIAL REPORT. 1919. a. Department of Revenue, Jefferson City, MO 65101. (Co-Sponsor: Missouri State Treasurer) stat. circ. 500.

MONTANA. GOVERNOR'S ANNUAL REPORT. see *PUBLIC ADMINISTRATION*

336 382   RH
NATIONAL ACCOUNTS OF RHODESIA. 1946. a. Rhod.$1. ‡ Central Statistical Office, P.O. Box 8063, Causeway, Salisbury, Zimbabwe. circ. 300.
    Formerly: National Accounts and Balance of Payments of Rhodesia (ISSN 0077-2941)

336   MM   ISSN 0077-295X
NATIONAL ACCOUNTS OF THE MALTESE ISLANDS. a. Central Office of Statistics, Auberge de Castille, Valletta, Malta (Subscr. to: Department of Information, Auberge de Castille, Valletta, Malta)

336.2   US
NATIONAL ASSOCIATION OF MANUFACTURERS. FISCAL & ECONOMIC POLICY DEPARTMENT. TAXATION REPORT. irreg. National Association of Manufacturers., Fiscal & Economic Policy Department, 1776 F St. N.W., Washington, DC 20006.

336 NO ISSN 0077-3573
NATIONAL BUDGET OF NORWAY. (Text in English) 1959. a. free. Ministry of Finance, Oslo - Dep., Oslo 11, Norway.

NATIONAL BUREAU OF ECONOMIC RESEARCH. FISCAL STUDIES. see *BUSINESS AND ECONOMICS — Macroeconomics*

336 CN ISSN 0077-4529
NATIONAL FINANCES; AN ANALYSIS OF THE REVENUES AND EXPENDITURES OF THE GOVERNMENT OF CANADA. 1954-55. a. Can.$10. Canadian Tax Foundation, Box 6, 130 Adelaide St. W., Toronto, Ont. M5H 3P5, Canada.

336.2 US ISSN 0069-8687
NATIONAL TAX ASSOCIATION-TAX INSTITUTE OF AMERICA. PROCEEDINGS OF THE ANNUAL CONFERENCE. 1907. a. $20 (or membership) National Tax Association-Tax Institute of America, 21 E. State St., Columbus, OH 43215. Ed. Stanley J. Bowers. index. circ. 2,500. (reprint service avail. from UMI)
Formerly: Conference on Taxation. Proceedings.

336 NE ISSN 0077-6866
NETHERLANDS. CENTRAAL BUREAU VOOR DE STATISTIEK. NATIONALE REKENINGEN. NATIONAL ACCOUNTS. (Text in Dutch and English) 1948-50. a. fl.26. Centraal Bureau voor de Statistiek, Prinses Beatrixlaan 428, Voorburg, Netherlands (Orders to: Staatsuitgeverij, Christoffel Plantijnstraat, The Hague, Netherlands)

336 US
NEW ENGLAND WAR TAX RESISTANCE NEWSLETTER. 1968. a. free. New England War Tax Resistance, Box 174, MIT Branch P.O., Cambridge, MA 02139. Ed.Bd. circ. 350.

336 NZ
NEW ZEALAND. INLAND REVENUE DEPARTMENT. REPORT. a. Government Printing Office, Private Bag, Wellington, New Zealand.

336.2 AT
NEW ZEALAND INCOME TAX LAW AND PRACTICE. 1973. irreg.(approx. every 3 weeks) Aus.$428. C C H Australia Ltd., Box 230, P.O., North Ryde, N.S.W. 2113, Australia. Indexed: Curr.Aus.N.Z.Leg.Lit.Ind.

336 NZ
NEW ZEALAND LOTTERY BOARD. REPORT. (Title varies slightly) 1963. a. NZ.$0.10. Lottery Board of Control, c/o Dept. of Internal Affairs, Wellington, New Zealand. stat.
Formerly (until 1977): New Zealand. Lottery Board of Control. Report (ISSN 0545-7297)

336 AT
NEW ZEALAND MASTER TAX GUIDE. 1973. a. Aus.$16. C C H Australia Ltd, P.O. Box 230, North Ryde, N.S.W. 2113, Australia.

336.2 US ISSN 0078-138X
NORTH CAROLINA. DEPARTMENT OF REVENUE. FRANCHISE TAX AND CORPORATE INCOME TAX BULLETINS FOR TAXABLE YEARS. 1964. biennial. free. Department of Revenue, Raleigh, NC 27611.

O E C D STUDIES IN RESOURCE ALLOCATION. see *PUBLIC ADMINISTRATION*

336 GW
DER OEFFENTLICHE HAUSHALT; Archiv fuer das oeffentliche Haushaltswesen. 1960. irreg. DM.64. Verlag Otto Schwarz und Co., Annastr. 7, 3400 Goettingen, W. Germany (B.R.D.) Ed. H. Karehnke.

336 SZ
OFFENTLICHE FINANZEN DER SCHWEIZ/ FINANCES PUBLIQUES EN SUISSE. (Subseries of Statistische Quellenwerke der Schweiz) (Text in French and German) 1972. a. Statistisches Amt., Hallwylstr. 15, CH-3003 Berne, Switzerland.

336.2 US
OKLAHOMA. AD VALOREM TAX DIVISION. PROGRESS REPORT TO THE LEGISLATURE ON PROPERTY REVALUATION. 1968. a. free. ‡ Tax Commission, Ad Valorem Tax Division, 2501 Lincoln Blvd., Oklahoma City, OK 73194. Ed. Lewis H. Bohr. stat. circ. 500. (processed)

336.2 US
OREGON PROPERTY TAX STATISTICS. 1970. a. $4. Department of Revenue, State Office Bldg., Salem, OR 97310.
Formerly: Oregon. Department of Revenue. Summary of Levies and Statistics.

336.2 US
OREGON RATIO AND ASSESSMENT DATA ROLL. 1971. a. $5. Department of Revenue, State Office Bldg., Salem, OR 97310.
Formerly: Oregon. Department of Revenue. Sales Ratio Study.

336.2 JA ISSN 0078-7094
OUTLINE OF JAPANESE TAX. 1953. a. 3500 Yen. National Tax Agency, 3-1-1 Kasumigaseki, Chiyoda-ku, Tokyo 100, Japan. Ed. Oookura Zaimukyokai.

336 PK
PAKISTAN. FINANCE DIVISION. ANNUAL BUDGET STATEMENT (FINAL) (Text in English) a. Finance Division, Islamabad, Pakistan. stat.

336 PK
PAKISTAN. FINANCE DIVISION. BUDGET IN BRIEF. (Text in English) 1964-65. a. free to qualified personnel. Finance Division, Islamabad, Pakistan.
Formerly: Pakistan. Ministry of Finance. Budget in Brief (ISSN 0078-8309)

336 PK
PAKISTAN. FINANCE DIVISION. ECONOMIC ANALYSIS OF THE BUDGET. (Text in English) a. free to qualified personnel. Finance Division, Islamabad, Pakistan.
Continues: Pakistan. Ministry of Finance. Economic Analysis of the Central Government (ISSN 0078-8325)

338.9 PK
PAKISTAN. FINANCE DIVISION. ESTIMATES OF FOREIGN ASSISTANCE. (Text in English) irreg. Finance Division, Islamabad, Pakistan.
Supersedes (1976-1977): Pakistan. Ministry of Finance Estimates of Foreign Assistance (ISSN 0555-8786)

336 PK
PAKISTAN. FINANCE DIVISION. SUPPLEMENTARY DEMANDS FOR GRANTS AND APPROPRIATIONS. (Text in English) 1973/74. irreg. free to qualified personnel. Finance Division, Islamabad, Pakistan. charts. stat. circ. controlled.

336 PK ISSN 0078-7892
PAKISTAN BASIC FACTS. (Text in English) a. Rs.5. Office of the Economic Adviser, Islamabad, Pakistan.
Formerly: Pakistan. Ministry of Finance. Basic Facts About the Budget (ISSN 0078-8295)

PAKISTAN CUSTOMS TARIFF. see *BUSINESS AND ECONOMICS — International Commerce*

336 382 PK ISSN 0078-852X
PAKISTAN'S BALANCE OF PAYMENTS. (Text in English) 1948-50. a. Rs.10. State Bank of Pakistan, Central Directorate, Public Relations Department, I.I. Chundrigar Rd., Box 4456, Karachi, Pakistan.

336 AT
PAPUA NEW GUINEA INCOME TAX LEGISLATION. 1976. irreg. Aus.$188. C C H Australia Ltd., P.O. Box 230, North Ryde, N.S.W. 2113, Australia.

336 US
PENNSYLVANIA. STATE TAX EQUALIZATION BOARD. ANNUAL CERTIFICATION. vol. 28, 1975. a. State Tax Equalization Board, Harrisburg, PA 17126.

336.2 US ISSN 0092-6655
PERSONAL INCOME TAX ANALYSIS. 1969. a. $4. Department of Revenue, State Office Bldg., Salem, OR 97310.
Formerly: Analysis of Oregon's Personal Income Tax Returns.

336.2 PH ISSN 0079-1547
PHILIPPINES. NATIONAL TAX RESEARCH CENTER. REPORT. 1960. a. National Tax Research Center, First BF Condominium, Aduana St., Intramuros, Manila, Philippines. circ. 1,000.
Formerly: Philippines. Joint Legislature Executive Tax Commission. Report.

336 US ISSN 0079-2217
PLANNING, PROGRAMMING, BUDGETING FOR CITY, STATE, COUNTY OBJECTIVES. P P B NOTE SERIES. (Notes 1-8 are combined in single vol.; not available separately) 1967. irreg., 1971-1972 notes 12, 13, 14. $1.50. Public Services Laboratory, Georgetown University, Washington, DC 20007. Ed. Selma J. Mushkin.

336 PL ISSN 0079-2594
POLAND. GLOWNY URZAD STATYSTYCZNY. BUDZET PANSTWA. STATE BUDGET.* a. Glowny Urzad Statystyczny, Al. Niepodleglosci 208, 00-925 Warsaw, Poland.

336 PO ISSN 0079-4201
PORTUGAL. MINISTERIO DAS FINANCAS. RELATORIO DO ORCAMENTO GERAL DO ESTADO.* a. price varies. Ministerio das Financas, Lisbon 2, Portugal.

POSTBUECHL. see *COMMUNICATIONS — Postal Affairs*

336 US
PROPERTY TAX BULLETIN. no. 21, 1960. irreg., no. 46, 1976. $0.50 per no. University of North Carolina at Chapel Hill, Institute of Government, Box 990, Chapel Hill, NC 27514.

336.2 US
PUBLIC REVENUES FROM ALCOHOL BEVERAGES. a. free. Distilled Spirits Council of the United States, Inc., 1300 Pennsylvania Bldg., Washington, DC 20004.

336 PR ISSN 0079-7863
PUERTO RICO. NEGOCIADO DEL PRESUPUESTO. RESOLUCIONES CONJUNTAS DEL PRESUPUESTO GENERAL Y DE PRESUPUESTOS ESPECIALES. a. free; limited distribution. Negociado del Presupuesto - Puerto Rico. Bureau of the Budget, Box 3228, San Juan, PR 00904.

R W P STEUERRECHT. AUSGABE A. (Rechts- und Wirtschafts-Praxis.) see *LAW*

R W P STEUERRECHT. AUSGABE B. (Rechts- und Wirtschafts-Praxis) see *LAW*

336 II ISSN 0079-9556
RAJASTHAN, INDIA. DIRECTORATE OF ECONOMICS AND STATISTICS. BUDGET STUDY. (Text in English and Hindi) 1959. a. free. Directorate of Economics and Statistics, Krishi Bhawan, Jaipur, Rajasthan, India.

336 SY ISSN 0080-0309
RECUEIL COMPLET DES BUDGETS DE LA SYRIE. a. $35. Office Arabe de Presse et de Documentation, P.O. Box 3550, 67 Place Chahbandar, Damascus, Syria.

336.2 AT ISSN 0080-0414
REDUCING YOUR INCOME TAX. 1970. a. $3.50. A. H. & A. W. Reed, 53 Myoora Rd., Terrey Hills, N.S.W. 2084, Australia. Ed. Jon Clinton. circ. 20,000.

336 FR ISSN 0080-0945
REPERTOIRE COMPLEMENTAIRE ALPHABETIQUE DES VALEURS MOBILIERES FRANCAISES ET ETRANGERES NON COTEES EN FRANCE. a. 993,72 F. Editions Financieres Alphabetiques, 3 Av. Trudaine, 75009 Paris, France.

336 FR ISSN 0080-1127
REPERTOIRE GENERAL ALPHABETIQUE DES VALEURS COTEES EN FRANCE ET DES VALEURS NON COTEES. (Suppl. available: la Vie des Societes) 1953, 36th ed. a. 958,44 F. Editions Financieres Alphabetiques, 3 Av. Trudaine, 75009 Paris, France.

BUSINESS AND ECONOMICS — PUBLIC FINANCE, TAXATION

336   LO   ISSN 0085-2740
REPORT BY THE AUDITOR GENERAL ON THE ACCOUNTS OF LESOTHO. 1966. a; latest issue, 1972-73. $0.50. ‡ Auditor General, Box 502, Maseru, Lesotho.

336   TR
REPORT OF THE AUDITOR GENERAL ON THE ACCOUNTS OF TRINIDAD AND TOBAGO. a; latest issue, 1973. $1.80. (Auditor General of Trinidad and Tobago) Trinidad and Tobago. Government Printer, Tragarete Rd., Port-of-Spain, Trinidad. stat.

336.1   US   ISSN 0091-8695
REPORT ON FEDERAL FUNDS RECEIVED IN IOWA. 1971. a. free. Office for Planning and Programming, 523 E. 12th St., Des Moines, IA 50319 Ed. A. Thomas Wallace.
    Continues its Report on Federal Grants-in-Aid in Iowa.

336.2   UK   ISSN 0143-280X
ROWLAND'S TAX GUIDE. 1978. a. Butterworth & Co. (Publishers) Ltd., 88 Kingsway, London WC2B 6AB, England. Eds. Nigel Eastaway, David Trill.

332.1   SU   ISSN 0558-7220
SAUDI ARABIAN MONETARY AGENCY. ANNUAL REPORT. 1961. a. Saudi Arabian Monetary Agency, Research and Statistics Departments, Box 2992, Riyadh, Saudi Arabia.

336.2   NE
SELECTED MONOGRAPHS ON TAXATION. (Text in English) 1974. irreg. fl.45 per vol. International Bureau of Fiscal Documentation, Box 20237, 1000 HE Amsterdam, Netherlands. (Co-sponsor: Harvard Law School International Tax Program)

336   SE
SEYCHELLES. OFFICE OF THE PRESIDENT. BUDGET ADDRESS. (Text in Creole, English and French) a. President's Office, Victoria, Mahe, Seychelles.

336   SL
SIERRA LEONE. MINISTRY OF FINANCE. BUDGET SPEECH. a. Ministry of Finance, Freetown, Sierra Leone.

332   SI
SINGAPORE TRADE CLASSIFICATION & CUSTOMS DUTIES. (Text in English) 1967. irreg. S.$10($8.86) per no. Customs and Excise Department, Custom House, Maxwell Rd, Singapore 0106, Singapore. circ. 6,000.

336   US   ISSN 0494-8203
SOURCE REFERENCES FOR FACTS AND FIGURES ON GOVERNMENT FINANCE. biennial. Tax Foundation, Inc., 1875 Connecticut Ave., N.W., Washington, DC 20009.

336 370   US   ISSN 0090-8649
SOUTHERN REGIONAL EDUCATION BOARD. STATE AND LOCAL REVENUE POTENTIAL. 1968. a. Southern Regional Education Board, 130 Sixth St. N.W., Atlanta, GA 30031. Ed. Kenneth E. Quindry. charts. stat. circ. controlled.

336   SP   ISSN 0081-3451
SPAIN. INSTITUTO DE CREDITO OFICIAL. MEMORIA DEL CREDITO OFICIAL. 1963. a. free. ‡ Instituto de Credito Oficial, Paseo del Prado, 4, Madrid-14, Spain. charts. stat. circ. 3,000.

336   SP
SPAIN. MINISTERIO DE HACIENDA. DIRECCION GENERAL DE SEGUROS. BALANCES Y CUENTAS; seguros privados. a. free. Ministerio de Hacienda, Direccion General de Seguros, Madrid, Spain. charts.
    Formerly: Spain. Ministerio de Hacienda. Memoria (ISSN 0081-3443)

353   US
STANLEY AND KILCULLEN'S FEDERAL INCOME TAX LAW (SUPPLEMENT) supplements issued periodically to update base volume. $24.50 for base volume. Warren, Gorham and Lamont, Inc., 210 South St., Boston, MA 02111.

336.2   US   ISSN 0081-4598
STATE TAX HANDBOOK. 1964. a. $8.50 pap. Commerce Clearing House, Inc., 4025 W. Peterson Ave., Chicago, IL 60646.

336   EI   ISSN 0081-4865
STATISTICAL OFFICE OF THE EUROPEAN COMMUNITIES. BALANCES OF PAYMENTS YEARBOOK. (Text in German, French, Italian, Dutch, English) a. B.P. 1907, Luxembourg, Luxembourg (Dist. in the U.S. by: European Community Information Service, 2100 M St., NW, Suite 707, Washington, DC 20037)

336   NE   ISSN 0077-6998
STATISTIEK DER RIJKSFINANCIEN/ STATISTICS OF THE STATE FINANCES OF THE NETHERLANDS. (Text in Dutch and English) 1943-44. irreg. fl.7.50. Centraal Bureau voor de Statistiek, Prinses Beatrixlaan 428, Voorburg, Netherlands (Orders to: Staatsuitgeverij, Christoffel Plantijnstraat, The Hague, Netherlands)

353   US
STEPHENS, MAXFIELD AND LIND'S FEDERAL ESTATE AND GIFT TAXATION (SUPPLEMENT) supplements issued periodically to update base volume. $37.50 for base volume. Warren, Gorham and Lamont, Inc., 210 South St., Boston, MA 02111.

336.2 331.8   GW
STEUER-GEWERKSCHAFTS-HANDBUCH. a. DM.24.95. (Bund Deutscher Steuerbeamten) Walhalla- und Praetoria-Verlag Georg Zwichenpflug, Dolomitenstr. 1, Postfach 301, 8400 Regensburg 1, W. Germany (B.R.D.) (Co-sponsor: Deutsche Steuer-Gewerkschaft)

336.2   SZ
STEUERBELASTUNG IN DER SCHWEIZ/ CHARGE FISCALE EN SUISSE. (Subseries of Statistische Quellenwerke der Schweiz) (Text in French and German) irreg. Statistisches Amt., Hallwylstrasse 15, 3003 Berne, Switzerland.

336.2   GW   ISSN 0081-5519
STEUERBERATER-JAHRBUCH; zugleich Bericht ueber den jaehrlich stattfindenden Fachkongress der Steuerberater der B R D. 1950. a. DM.105. (Fachinstitut der Steuerberater) Verlag Dr. Otto Schmidt KG, Ulmenallee 96-98, 5000 Cologne 51, W. Germany (B. R. D.)

STOCK VALUES AND DIVIDENDS FOR TAX PURPOSES. see *BUSINESS AND ECONOMICS — Investments*

336   US   ISSN 0081-7929
STUDIES IN FEDERAL TAXATION. TAX STUDY. 1969. irreg., no. 5, 1976. price varies. ‡ American Institute of Certified Public Accountants, 1211 Avenue of the Americas, New York, NY 10036.

336   US
STUDIES OF GOVERNMENT FINANCE: SECOND SERIES. 1975. irreg., no. 6, 1977. price varies. Brookings Institution, 1775 Massachusetts Ave. N.W., Washington, DC 20036.

336.2   PN
STUDIES ON TAX ADMINISTRATION SERIES. (Text in English, Spanish) no. 18, 1977. irreg. $2. Inter-American Center of Tax Administrators, Apdo. 215, Panama 1, Panama.

336.2 338   NE   ISSN 0071-2191
STUDIES ON TAXATION AND ECONOMIC DEVELOPMENT. (Text in English) 1961. irreg., no. 5, 1978. price varies. International Bureau of Fiscal Documentation, Box 20237, 1000 HE Amsterdam, Netherlands.

353   SQ
SWAZILAND. MONETARY AUTHORITY. ANNUAL REPORT. a, latest 1974/75. free. Monetary Authority, Box 546, Mbabane, Swaziland.

336   SW
SWEDEN. FINANSDEPARTMENTET. REGERINGENS BUDGETFOERSLAG. (Text in Swedish or English) a. Kr.8. (Ministry of Finance) Liber Foerlag, Fack, S-162 89 Vaellingby, Sweden.

336   SW   ISSN 0079-7561
SWEDEN. RIKSREVISIONSVERKET. STATENS FINANSER; Riksrevisionsverkets aarsbok. 1970. a. Kr.19. (National Audit Bureau) Liber Foerlag, Fack, S-162 89 Vaellingby, Sweden. circ. 5,200.

336   SW   ISSN 0082-0393
SWEDISH BUDGET. (Text in English) 1962/63. a. Kr.13.60. Ministry of the Budget, Fack, S-103 10 Stockholm, Sweden. (Co-sponsor: Ministry of Economic Affairs)

336.2   FR
SYNDICAT GENERAL DES IMPOTS. GUIDE FONCIERS. 1957. a. Euro-Publi Marcel Puget, 9 Bld. des Italiens, Paris 2e, France.
    Formerly: Syndicat General des Impots. Guide National de l'Enregistrement et des Domaines (ISSN 0082-1055)

336   FR   ISSN 0082-1209
SYSTEMES-DECISIONS. SECTION II. GESTION FINANCIERE ET COMPTABILITE. 1970. irreg. price varies. Presses Universitaires de France, 108 Bd. Saint Germaine, 75279 Paris Cedex 6, France (Service des Periodiques, 12 rue Jean de Beauvais, 75005 Paris)

336   FR
TABLEAUX FISCAUX EUROPEENS. irreg. price varies. Cahiers Fiscaux Europeens, 51 Avenue Victoria, 06000 Nice, France. Ed. Pierre Fontaneau. (looseleaf format)

350.827   US   ISSN 0082-173X
TARIFF SCHEDULES OF THE UNITED STATES ANNOTATED. irreg. $23. U.S. International Trade Commission, E St. between 7th & 8th Sts., N.W., Washington, DC 20436 (Order from: U.S. Govt. Printing Office, Washington, DC 20402)

336.1   AT
TASMANIA. DEPARTMENT OF THE TREASURY. COMMONWEALTH GRANTS TO TASMANIA. (At head of title, 1972- : Parliament of Tasmania) irreg. Tasmanian Government Printer, c/o T. J. Hughes, Hobart, Tas., Australia. stat.

336.946   AT
TASMANIA. DEPARTMENT OF THE TREASURY. CONSOLIDATED REVENUE FUND; summary of estimated expenditure (including expenditure reserved by law) and estimated revenue. Tasmanian Government Printer, Hobart, Tasmania, Australia. stat.

TAX BURDEN ON TOBACCO. see *TOBACCO — Abstracting, Bibliographies, Statistics*

350 347   US
TAX COURT PRACTICE (SUPPLEMENT) supplements issued periodically to update base volume. $37.50 for base volume. Warren, Gorham and Lamont, Inc., 210 South St., Boston, MA 02111.

336.2   US   ISSN 0082-2159
TAX FOUNDATION, NEW YORK. RESEARCH PUBLICATIONS. NEW SERIES. 1965. irreg., 1980, no. 34. ‡ Tax Foundation, Inc., 1875 Connecticut Ave., N.W., Washington, DC 20009. Ed. Elsie Watters.

350   US
TAX FRAUD AND EVASION (SUPPLEMENT) supplements issued periodically to update base volume. $56 for base volume. Warren, Gorham and Lamont, Inc., 210 South St., Boston, MA 02111.

336.2   CN
TAX MEMO. vol 54, 1974. irreg. price varies. Canadian Tax Foundation, Box 6, 130 Adelaide St. W., Toronto, Ont. M5H 3P5, Canada. charts. stat.

336.2   UK
TAX PLANNING REVIEW. a. Butterworth & Co. (Publishers) Ltd., 88 Kingsway, London WC2B 6AB, England.

336.2   UK
TAX PRACTITIONER'S DIARY. a. Butterworth & Co. (Publishers) Ltd., 88 Kingsway, London WC2B 6AB, England.

336.2   CN   ISSN 0227-1265
TAX PRINCIPLES TO REMEMBER. French edition: Elements Fondamentaux de l'Impot (ISSN 0227-1273) (Editions in English and French) 1972. a. membership. Canadian Institute of Chartered Accountants, 250 Bloor St. E., Toronto, Ont. M4W 1G5, Canada.

336   US
TAX YEAR IN REVIEW. 1978. a. Research Institute of America, Inc., 589 Fifth Ave., New York, NY 10017. Ed.Bd.

336.2   US   ISSN 0068-581X
TAXABLE SALES IN CALIFORNIA (SALES AND USE TAX) 1960. q. and a. free. State Board of Equalization, 1020 N St., Room 130, Sacramento, CA 95808. Ed. Jeff Reynolds. circ. 5,000.
    Formerly: Trade Outlets and Taxable Retail Sales in California.

336.2   UK
TAXATION IN MIDDLE EAST, AFRICA & ASIA. 1977. irreg. £12.50. Confederation of British Industry, 103 New Oxford St., London WC1A 1DU, England.

336.2   UK   ISSN 0082-2167
TAXATION IN WESTERN EUROPE; a guide for industrialists. 1959. irreg. £7.50. ‡ Confederation of British Industry, 103 New Oxford St., London WC1A 1DU, England.

350   US
TAXATION OF CLOSELY HELD CORPORATIONS (SUPPLEMENT) supplements issued periodically to update base volume. $42.25 for base volume. Warren, Gorham and Lamont, Inc., 210 South St., Boston, MA 02111.

350   608.7
TAXATION OF PATENTS, TRADEMARKS, COPYRIGHTS AND KNOW-HOW (SUPPLEMENT) supplements issued periodically to update base volume. $49.50 for base volume. Warren, Gorham and Lamont, Inc., 210 South St., Boston, MA 02111.

336.2   PK
TAXATION STRUCTURE OF PAKISTAN. (Text in English) 1974-75. a. Finance Division, Islamabad, Pakistan.

336.2   NZ   ISSN 0082-2175
TAXATION TABLES. 1936. a. NZ.$6. Sweet and Maxwell (N.Z.) Ltd., Private Bag, Auckland, New Zealand (Dist. by: Carswell Co. Ltd., 2330 Midland Ave., Agincourt, Ont. M1S, 1P7, Canada) circ. 4,500.

336   TH
THAILAND'S BUDGET IN BRIEF. (Text in English) irreg. Bureau of the Budget, Bangkok, Thailand.

TIMBER TAX JOURNAL. see *FORESTS AND FORESTRY*

336.2   UK
TOLLEY'S CORPORATION TAX. a. £2.50. Tolley Publishing Co. (Subsidiary of: Benn Bros. Ltd.) 102-104 High St., Croydon, Surrey CR0 1ND, England. Ed. G. L. Harvey. (back issues avail.)

336.2   UK   ISSN 0305-8921
TOLLEY'S INCOME TAX. a. £4.75. Tolley Publishing Co., 102-104 High St., Croydon, Surrey CR0 1ND, England.

336.2   UK   ISSN 0307-6687
TOLLEY'S TAX TABLES. a. £1. Tolley Publishing Co., 102-104 High St., Croydon, Surrey CR0 1ND, England. stat.

TRUCK TAXES BY STATES. see *TRANSPORTATION — Trucks And Trucking*

336.2   US   ISSN 0564-4402
TULANE TAX INSTITUTE. 1951. a. $30. Claitors Publishing Division, 3165 S. Acadian at Interstate 10, Box 3333, Baton Rouge, LA 70821.

336   TI   ISSN 0082-6820
TUNISIA. MINISTERE DU PLAN. BUDGET ECONOMIQUE. a. free. Ministere du Plan, Tunis, Tunisia.

336   UG   ISSN 0082-7231
UGANDA. MINISTRY OF PLANNING AND ECONOMIC DEVELOPMENT. STATISTICS DIVISION. BACKGROUND TO THE BUDGET. (Years 1971-72, 1972-73, 1973-74, not published) 1957-58. a; latest issue, 1970. price varies. ‡ Ministry of Planning and Economic Development, Statistics Division, P.O. Box 13, Entebbe, Uganda (Subscr. to: Government Printer, Box 33, Entebbe, Uganda)

330.9   TS
UNITED ARAB EMIRATES. CURRENCY BOARD. ANNUAL REPORT. (Text in Arabic and English) a. Currency Board, Box 854, Abu Dhabi Town, Abu Dhabi, United Arab Emirates.

330.9   TS
UNITED ARAB EMIRATES. CURRENCY BOARD. BULLETIN. (Text in English) 1974. irreg., vol. 2, 1976. Currency Board, Box 854, Abu Dhabi Town, Abu Dhabi, United Arab Emirates. charts. stat.

336.3   US   ISSN 0091-3553
U. S. COMMUNITY SERVICES ADMINISTRATION. FEDERAL OUTLAYS IN SUMMARY. 1967. a. U.S. Community Services Administration, 1200 Nineteenth St., N.W., Washington, DC 20506 (Orders to: National Technical Information Service, Springfield, VA 22151) stat. (also avail. in microfiche from NTI) Key Title: Federal Outlays in Summary.
    Formerly: U.S. Office of Economic Opportunity. Federal Outlays in Summary.

U. S. DEPARTMENT OF AGRICULTURE, ECONOMICS, STATISTICS, AND COOPERATIVES SERVICE. FARM REAL ESTATE TAXES, RECENT TRENDS AND DEVELOPMENTS. see *AGRICULTURE — Agricultural Economics*

336.2   US   ISSN 0083-0534
U. S. EXCISE TAX GUIDE. a. $6 pap. Commerce Clearing House, Inc., 4025 W. Peterson Ave., Chicago, IL 60646.

336   US   ISSN 0083-1476
U. S. INTERNAL REVENUE SERVICE. ANNUAL REPORT. 1863. a. U.S. Internal Revenue Service., 1111 Constitution Ave., N.W., Washington, DC 20224 (Orders to: Supt. Doc., Washington, DC 20402)

336.2   US   ISSN 0083-1484
U. S. INTERNAL REVENUE SERVICE. TAX GUIDE FOR SMALL BUSINESS. 1956. a. U.S. Internal Revenue Service, 1111 Constitution Ave., N.W., Washington, DC 20224 (Orders to: Supt. Doc., Washington, DC 20402)

336.2   US   ISSN 0083-1700
U. S. MASTER TAX GUIDE. a. $9 pap. Commerce Clearing House, Inc., 4025 W. Peterson Ave., Chicago, IL 60646.

336   US   ISSN 0362-9163
U.S. OFFICE OF MANAGEMENT AND BUDGET. SPECIAL ANALYSIS: BUDGET OF THE UNITED STATES GOVERNMENT. 1976/77. a. U.S. Office of Management and Budget, Washington, DC 20503. Key Title: Special Analysis: Budget of the United States Government.

336   US
U.S. TREASURY DEPARTMENT. COMBINED STATEMENT OF RECEIPTS; EXPENDITURES; AND BALANCE OF THE UNITED STATES, GOVERNMENT. a. $7. U.S. Department of the Treasury, Bureau of Government Financial Operations, Pennsylvania Ave. & Madison Pl., N.W., Washington, DC 20226 (Orders to: Supt. of Documents, Washington, DC 20402) (back issues available)

UNIVERSITY OF OREGON. BUREAU OF GOVERNMENTAL RESEARCH AND SERVICE. LOCAL GOVERNMENT FINANCE. see *PUBLIC ADMINISTRATION — Municipal Government*

336.2   US
WASHINGTON (STATE). DEPARTMENT OF REVENUE. RESEARCH AND INFORMATION DIVISION. COMPARATIVE STATE/LOCAL TAXES. 1967. a. Department of Revenue, General Administration Bldg., Olympia, WA 98504. stat. circ. controlled.

336.2   US
WASHINGTON (STATE). DEPARTMENT OF REVENUE. RESEARCH AND INFORMATION DIVISION. PROPERTY TAX LEVY AND COLLECTION STATISTICS. 1970. a. Department of Revenue, General Administration Bldg., Olympia, WA 98504. stat. circ. controlled. (tabloid format)

336.2   634.9   US   ISSN 0362-7462
WASHINGTON (STATE). DEPARTMENT OF REVENUE. FOREST TAX REPORT. irreg. Department of Revenue, Olympia, WA 98504. Key Title: Forest Tax Report.

336   US   ISSN 0091-6102
WEST VIRGINIA RESEARCH LEAGUE. STATISTICAL HANDBOOK; a digest of selected data on state and local government in West Virginia. 1970. a. free. West Virginia Research League Inc., 1107 Charleston National Plaza, Charleston, WV 25301. Ed. Patrick J. Lamb. charts. stat. circ. controlled.

336   US
WEST VIRGINIA TAX CALENDAR. a. $25. West Virginia Chamber of Commerce, Box 2789, Charleston, WV 25330.

336.2   PR   ISSN 0083-9132
WHAT YOU SHOULD KNOW ABOUT TAXES IN PUERTO RICO. (Was Not published for 1977; publication will resume for 1978 edition) 1956. a. free. Department of the Treasury, Office of Economic Research, Box S-4515, San Juan, PR 00915. circ. 1,600.

336.2   UK
WHILLANS'S TAX TABLES. 1948. a. ‡ Butterworth & Co. (Publishers) Ltd., 88 Kingsway, London WC2B 6AB, England. Ed. Leslie Livens. circ. 24,000.
    Formerly: Whillan's Tax Tables and Tax Reckoner (ISSN 0308-7948)

336.3   US   ISSN 0363-4795
WORLD MILITARY AND SOCIAL EXPENDITURES. 1974. a. $3.50. World Priorities, Inc., Box 1003, Leesburg, VA 22075. Ed. Ruth Lecer Sivard. circ. 10,000.

336.2   US   ISSN 0094-9019
WYOMING. DEPARTMENT OF REVENUE AND TAXATION. ANNUAL REPORT. 1973. a. free. Department of Revenue and Taxation, Barrett Building, Cheyenne, WY 82002. stat. Key Title: Annual Report of the Department of Revenue and Taxation of the State of Wyoming.

336   ZA
ZAMBIA. CENTRAL STATISTICAL OFFICE. NATIONAL ACCOUNTS. 1965. a, latest 1973. K.0.20. Central Statistical Office, P.O. Box 1908, Lusaka, Zambia.

336.2   ZA   ISSN 0084-4675
ZAMBIA. DEPARTMENT OF TAXES. ANNUAL REPORT OF THE COMMISSIONER OF TAXES. 1964-65. a. 10 n. Government Printer, P.O. Box 136, Lusaka, Zambia.

336   ZA   ISSN 0084-4683
ZAMBIA. DEPARTMENT OF THE ADMINISTRATOR-GENERAL AND OFFICIAL RECEIVER. REPORT. 1964. a. 10 n. Government Printer, P.O. Box 136, Lusaka, Zambia.

336   ZA   ISSN 0084-4497
ZAMBIA. OFFICE OF THE AUDITOR-GENERAL. REPORT OF THE AUDITOR-GENERAL. 1963. a. 30 n. Government Printer, P.O. Box 136, Lusaka, Zambia.

336.2   JA
ZEIMU TOKEI KARA MITA HOJIN KIGYO NO JITTAI. Short title: Hojin Kigyo No Jittai. (Text in Japanese) 1963. a. National Tax Agency, Income Tax Section - Kokuzeicho Somuka, 3-1-1 Kasumigaseki, Chiyoda-ku, Tokyo 100, Japan.

ZIMBABWE. CENTRAL STATISTICAL OFFICE. INCOME TAX STATISTICS; analysis of assessments and loss statements. see *BUSINESS AND ECONOMICS — Abstracting, Bibliographies, Statistics*

336 RH
ZIMBABWE. ESTIMATES OF EXPENDITURE. a. Rhod.$2.10. Government Printer, Box 8062, Causeway, Zimbabwe.

336 RH
ZIMBABWE. MINISTRY OF FINANCE. FINANCIAL STATEMENT. 1940. a. Rhod.$0.50 per no. Ministry of Finance, Private Bag 7705, Causeway, Zimbabwe (Subscr. to: Government Printer, Box 8062, Causeway, Zimbabwe) circ. 1,200.
Formerly: Rhodesia. Ministry of Finance. Budget Statement.

336 GW
ZOLLKALENDER. a. DM.49.95. (Bund der Deutschen Zollbeamten) Walhalla- und Praetoria-Verlag Georg Zwichenpflug, Dolomitenstr. 1, Postfach 301, 8400 Regensburg 1, W. Germany (B.R.D.)

336.2 US
1040 PREPARATION. a. $16.50. Commerce Clearing House, Inc., 14025 W. Peterson Ave., Chicago, IL 60646. illus.
Formerly: Practical Guide to Individual Income Tax Return Preparation (ISSN 0098-1575)

BUSINESS AND ECONOMICS — Small Business

338 II ISSN 0376-804X
ANDHRA PRADESH SMALL SCALE INDUSTRIAL DEVELOPMENT CORPORATION. ANNUAL REPORT. (Text in English) a. Andhra Pradesh Small Scale Industrial Development Corporation, 5-10-174 Nizam Sugar Factory Bldg., Hyderabad 500004, India. Key Title: Annual Report-Andhra Pradesh Small Scale Industrial Development Corporation.

338.6 BE ISSN 0067-5393
BELGIUM. CONSEIL SUPERIEUR DES CLASSES MOYENNES. RAPPORT ANNUEL DU SECRETAIRE GENERAL. Dutch edition: Belgium. Hoge Raad voor de Middenstand. Jaarverslag van de Secretaris Generaal. (Editions in French and Dutch) 1951. a. free. Conseil Superieur des Classes Moyennes, 24 rue de la Charite, 1040 Brussels, Belgium.

338.9 CK
CAJA DE CREDITO AGRARIO, INDUSTRIAL Y MINERO. FINANCIAMIENTO DE LA PEQUENA Y MEDIANA INDUSTRIA. 1973. a. Caja de Credito Agrario, Industrial y Minero, Bogota, Colombia. charts. stat.

338.7 NE ISSN 0070-8836
ECONOMISCH INSTITUUT VOOR HET MIDDEN- EN KLEINBEDRIJF. VERSLAG. 1961. a. free. Economisch Instituut voor het Midden- en Kleinbedrijf, Neuhuyskade 94, Postbus 96818, 2509 JE The Hague, Netherlands.

381 JA
INFORMATION AND INVESTIGATION REPORT/JOHO CHOSA REPORT. irreg. Small Business Information Centre - Chusho Kigyo Joho Senta, c/o Small Business Promotion Corporation, Sankaido Bldg., 1-9-13 Akasaka, Minato-ku, Tokyo, Japan.

658 650 US ISSN 0190-3225
MANAGEMENT AIDS FOR SMALL BUSINESS ANNUAL. a. free. U. S. Small Business Administration, 1441 L St., N.W., Washington, DC 20416 (Orders to: Supt. Doc., Washington, DC 20402)
Formerly: Management Aids for Small Manufacturers (ISSN 0076-3578)

338 US
S B I C DIRECTORY AND HANDBOOK OF SMALL BUSINESS FINANCE. 1970. a. $15. International Wealth Success, Inc., 24 Canterbury Rd., Rockville Center, NY 11570. Ed. Tyler G. Hicks.

650 US ISSN 0081-0118
SMALL BUSINESS MANAGEMENT SERIES. 1952. irreg. price varies. U. S. Small Business Administration, 1441 L St., N.W., Washington, DC 20416 (Orders to: Supt. Doc., Washington, DC 20402).

338 CN ISSN 0708-3041
SMALL BUSINESS NEWS. 1976. irreg. Federal Business Development Bank, 901 Victoria Square, Montreal, Que. H2Z 1R1, Canada. illus.

330.9 US
SMALL BUSINESS REPORTER. 4-6/yr. $2 per no. Bank of America, Box 37000, San Francisco, CA 94137.

338 II
SMALL INDUSTRIES GUIDE.* irreg.; 1969, no. 2. Rs.02 per issue. Ministry of Industrial Development, Development Commissioner-Small Scale Industries, Internal Trade and Company Affairs, New Delhi, India. charts. stat.

338 NR
SMALL-SCALE INDUSTRIES: SOUTH EASTERN AND BENUE PLATEAU STATES OF NIGERIA. a. University of Nigeria, Department of Economics, Nsukka, Nigeria. Eds. E. C. Iwuji, A. E. Okorafor.

U. S. INTERNAL REVENUE SERVICE. TAX GUIDE FOR SMALL BUSINESS. see BUSINESS AND ECONOMICS — Public Finance, Taxation

338 US ISSN 0083-3274
U. S. SMALL BUSINESS ADMINISTRATION. ANNUAL REPORT. (Supersedes its Report to the President and Congress) 1953. a. free. U.S. Small Business Administration, 1441 L St., N.W., Washington, DC 20416.

650 US
U.S. SMALL BUSINESS ADMINISTRATION. SBIC DIGEST. m. U.S. Small Business Administration, Investment Division, Washington, DC 20416.
From Feb. 1976, incorporating (in February issue): S B I C Industry Review (ISSN 0083-3282)

BUSINESS AND ECONOMICS — Trade And Industrial Directories

380.1 HK ISSN 0532-9175
A.A.'S FAR EAST BUSINESSMAN'S DIRECTORY. Title varies: Far East Businessman's Directory. (Text in English) a. Artists Associates, G.P.O. Box 1623, Hong Kong, Hong Kong. illus.

380 GW
A B C DER DEUTSCHEN WIRTSCHAFT; Quellenwerk fuer Einkauf-Verkauf. a. prices on request. A B C-Verlagshaus Darmstadt, Berliner Allee 8, 6100 Darmstadt, W. Germany (B.R.D.) circ. 23,000.

380 YU
A B C PRIVREDE JUGOSLAVIJE. 1973. a. Privredni Vjesnik, Roosveltov Trg 2, Box 631, Zagreb, Yugoslavia. Ed. Ante Gavranovic.

380 US ISSN 0161-8563
ALABAMA STATE INDUSTRIAL DIRECTORY. a. $55. State Industrial Directories Corp., Two Penn Plaza, New York, NY 10001.

380.1 US ISSN 0095-1269
ALABAMA WORLD TRADE DIRECTORY. irreg., latest 1974. $7.50. Development Office, Rm. 547 State Office Bldg., 500 Dexter Ave., Montgomery, AL 36104.

380 US
ALASKA STATE INDUSTRIAL DIRECTORY. biennial. $42. State Industrial Directories Corp., Two Penn Plaza, New York, NY 10001.

ALBERTA CONSTRUCTION INDUSTRY DIRECTORY. PURCHASING GUIDE. see BUILDING AND CONSTRUCTION

380 CN
ALMANACH MODERNE. (Text in French) 1956. a. Can.$3. Bert-Hold Inc., 9393 Edison Ave., Montreal, Que. H1J 1T5, Canada. Ed. Paul Rochon. adv.

338 AG
AMERICAN BUSINESS IN ARGENTINA. 1974. a. $70. American Chamber of Commerce in Argentina, Avda. Roque Saenza Pena 567, Buenos Aires, Argentina. adv. illus.
Formerly: Directory of American Business in Argentina.

AMERICAN DROP-SHIPPERS DIRECTORY. see BUSINESS AND ECONOMICS — Marketing And Purchasing

382 GR ISSN 0065-8537
AMERICAN-HELLENIC CHAMBER OF COMMERCE. BUSINESS DIRECTORY. SPECIAL ISSUE. (Text in English) 1970. biennial. $25. American-Hellenic Chamber of Commerce, 17 Valaoritou St., Athens 134, Greece. Ed. D. Georgiopoulos. adv. circ. 5,000.
Supplement to: American-Hellenic Chamber of Commerce. Business Directory (ISSN 0065-8529)

AMERICAN MARKETING ASSOCIATION. DIRECTORY OF MARKETING SERVICES AND MEMBERSHIP ROSTER. see BUSINESS AND ECONOMICS — Marketing And Purchasing

380 FR
ANNUAIRE DES CENTRALES ET GROUPEMENTS D'ACHATS; le livre d'or de la distribution francaise. 1969. biennial. 330 F. Societe d'Edition et de Promotion Agricoles, Industrielles et Commerciales, 42 rue du Louvre, 75001 Paris, France. bk. rev. bibl. circ. 5,000. (tabloid format)

382 FR
ANNUAIRE DES EXPORTATEURS FRANCAIS COMMERCANT AVEC L'U.R.S.S. 1976. a. 300 F. non-members; 100 F. to members. Chambre de Commerce Franco-Sovietique, 22 Av. F. D. Roosevelt, 75008 Paris, France. adv.

380 FR
ANNUAIRE DES HYPERMARCHES. 1973. biennial. 220 F. Societe d'Edition et de Promotion Agricoles, Industrielles et Commerciales, 42 rue du Louvre, 75001 Paris, France. adv. circ. 5,000.
Formerly: Hyperguide des Hypermarches.

670 FR
ANNUAIRE DESECHALIERS. (Text in French; table of contents and subtitles in English and German) 1975. a. 140 F. Periodiques Parisiens, 150 Champs Elysees, 75008 Paris, France.

380 AT
ANNUAIRE FRANCAIS D'AUSTRALIE.* (Text in English and French) 1957. biennial. Aus.$5. Courrier Australien, 389 George St., Sydney, N.S.W. 2000, Australia. Ed. Albert Sourdin.

670 IT ISSN 0066-4510
ANNUARIO POLITECNICO ITALIANO. (Text in Italian; classifications in English, French, German, Spanish) 1916. a. L.74000($125) Unites s.r.l., 12 via Silvio Pellico, 20121 Milan, Italy. Ed. Maria Magni Santi. adv. index. circ. 10,000.
Directory of Italian manufacturers

380.1 SP
ANUARIO DE EMPRESAS EXPORTADORAS. 1974. a. Organizacion Sindical Espanola, Servicio de Accion Exterior Empresarial, Casa Sindical, Paseo del Prado 18, Madrid, Spain.

338 CK
ANUARIO EMPRESARIAL DE COLOMBIA; registro nacional de comerciantes. 1972. a. Col.500($30) (Confederacion Colombiana de Camaras de Comercio) Editorial Prensa Moderna, Carrera 9a no. 16-21, Bogota, Colombia. Ed. Olga Vasquez Lebolo. circ. 15,000.

338 BL
ANUARIO INDUSTRIAL DO ESPIRITO SANTO. 1973. irreg. Cr.$50($15) ‡ (Instituto de Desenvolvimento Industrial do Espirito Santo) Federacao das Industrias do Estado do Espirito Santo, Av. Princesa Isabel 54, Vitoria, Espirito Santo, Brazil. circ. 3,000.

677 NZ
APPAREL BUYERS GUIDE YEAR BOOK. a. NZ.$6. Apparel Publishing Ltd., Box 56-071, Dominion Rd., Auckland 3, New Zealand.

BUSINESS AND ECONOMICS — TRADE AND INDUSTRIAL DIRECTORIES

382　　　　　　　　　FR　ISSN 0066-5398
APPEL SERVICE; REPERTOIRE D'ADRESSES UTILES POUR LE COMMERCE ET L'INDUSTRIE.* 1968. irreg. price varies. Editions Publiplast, 55 rue du Faubourg-Montmartre, Paris 9e, France.

380　　　　　　　　　　　　　　　UK
ARAB TRADE DIRECTORY. (Text in Arabic, English and French) biennial. $120. Publishing and Distributing Co. Ltd., 177 Regent St., London W.1., England. adv.

380　　　　　　　　　　　　　　　US
ARAB TRADE GUIDE. irreg., latest issue 1978. $75. Inter-Crescent Publishing Co., Inc., Box 8481, Dallas, TX 75205.

380　　　　　　　　　　　　　　　UK
ARABIAN YEARBOOK. 1978. a. $90. Publishing and Distributing Co. Ltd., 177 Regent St., London W.1., England.

380　　　　　　　　US　ISSN 0195-7082
ARIZONA STATE INDUSTRIAL DIRECTORY. a. $35. State Industrial Directories Corp., Two Penn Plaza, New York, NY 10001.

380　　　　　　　　　　　　　　　US
ARKANSAS STATE INDUSTRIAL DIRECTORY. a. $40. State Industrial Directories Corp., Two Penn Plaza, New York, NY 10001.

ASIAN AMERICAN TRADE DIRECTORY. see *BUSINESS AND ECONOMICS — Chamber Of Commerce Publications*

382　　　　　　　　UK　ISSN 0260-2474
ASPIS; the classified Greek commercial directory. (Text in English and Greek) 1980. a. Aspis Publicatons, 89 Tottenham Lane, London N8 9BE, England. illus.

338　　　　　　　　AT　ISSN 0311-2667
AUSTRALIAN KEY BUSINESS DIRECTORY. 1973. a. Aus.$115. Dun and Bradstreet (Australia) Pty. Ltd., 24 Albert St., South Melbourne, Vic. 3205, Australia. Ed. H. Rijnhart.

AUSTRALIAN MARKET GUIDE. see *BUSINESS AND ECONOMICS — Investments*

AUTORIDADES E EXECUTIVOS. see *COMMUNICATIONS*

380　　　　　　　　BA　ISSN 0408-215X
BAHRAIN TRADE DIRECTORY. (Text in Arabic and English) a. Box 524, Manama, Bahrain. Ed. A. E. Ashir.

664.752　　　　　　　　　　　　　US
BAKING DIRECTORY/BUYERS GUIDE. a. $15. Sosland Publishing Co., 4800 Main St., Kansas City, MO 64112. Ed. Morton I. Sosland.

380　　　　　　　　　　　　　　　II
BANGLADESH DIRECTORY AND YEAR BOOK. (Text in English) 1976. a. Rs.75($15) Associated Book Promoters, 9/2A Ekbalpur Lane, Calcutta 700023, India.

381　　　　　　　　PK　ISSN 0067-4230
BARQUE'S PAKISTAN TRADE DIRECTORY AND WHO'S WHO. (Text in English) 1949-50. a. $65.40. Barque & Company, Barque Chambers, Barque Square, 87 Shahrah e-Liaquat Ali, Box 201, Lahore, Pakistan. Ed. A.M. Barque. adv. circ. 15,000.

650 382　　　　　　　GW　ISSN 0067-6063
BERLINER HANDELSREGISTER VERZEICHNIS. a. DM.76. Addressbuch-Gesellschaft Berlin mbH, Friedrichstr. 210, 1000 Berlin 61, W. Germany (B.R.D.) index.

BOAT EQUIPMENT BUYERS' GUIDE. see *SPORTS AND GAMES — Boats And Boating*

BOTTIN AUTO-CYCLE-MOTO. see *TRANSPORTATION — Automobiles*

338　　　　　　　　　　　　　　　FR
BOTTIN PROFESSIONS. 1895. a. (6 vols.) $265. Societe Didot Bottin, 28 rue du Docteur Finlay, 75738 Paris Cedex 15, France. index.

BREWERS DIGEST ANNUAL BUYERS GUIDE AND BREWERY DIRECTORY. see *BEVERAGES*

380　　　　　　　　　　　　　　　UK
BRITAIN'S TOP 1000 PRIVATE COMPANIES. a. £12. Jordan & Sons (Surveys) Ltd., Jordan House, 47 Brunswick Place, London N1 6EE, England. adv. bk. rev. charts. stat. circ. 2,000.

BRITISH ALTERNATIVE THEATRE DIRECTORY. see *THEATER*

BRITISH THEATRE DIRECTORY. see *THEATER*

382　　　　　　　　FI　ISSN 0355-0346
BUSINESS CONTACTS IN FINLAND. 1974. irreg. Yritystieto Oy, Box 148, 00181 Helsinki 18, Finland. Ed. Borje Thilman. adv. circ. 10,000.

338.4　　　　　　　　　　　　　　HK
BUSINESS DIRECTORY OF HONG KONG. (Text in English) 1977. a. Current Publications Co., 12 Kau U Fong, 2nd Floor, Box 9848, Hong Kong, Hong Kong. Ed. Charles Lau. adv.

338　　　　　　　　　　　　　　　IO
BUSINESS GUIDE BOOK TO JAKARTA. (Text in English) 1969. a. $7.50. ‡ GINSI - National Importers Association of Indonesia, Wisma Nusantara Building, Jalan Majapahit No. 1, Jakarta, Indonesia (Foreign correspondence to: EKON Advertising Agency, Box 2744, Jakartta, Indonesia) Ed.Bd. adv. illus. circ. 10,000.
Continues: Djakarta Business Guide Book.

658.8　　　　　　　　AT　ISSN 0068-4503
BUSINESS WHO'S WHO OF AUSTRALIA. 1964. a. Aus.$123.50. R.G. Riddell Pty. Ltd., 2 Dind St, Milsons Point, N.S.W. 2061, Australia (Dist. by Intl. Publications Service, 114 E. 32nd St., New York, N.Y. 10016) adv. circ. 8,000.
Formerly: Business Who's Who of Australia and Australian Purchasing Yearbook.

382 910　　　　　　　　　　　　　CH
BUSINESSMAN'S DIRECTORY OF R.O.C. (Text in English) 1971. a. $25. Taiwan Enterprise Press, Box 73-74, Taipei, Taiwan, Republic of China. Ed. Henry K. C. Lee. adv. bk. rev. circ. 50,000.
Formerly: World Buyers Guide.

380.1　　　　　　　　　　　　　　CH
BUSINESSMAN'S DIRECTORY, THE REPUBLIC OF CHINA. (Text in English and Chinese) 1971. a. $15. Tong-Hsing Culture Press, P.O. Box 73-4, Taipei, Republic of China. Ed. Henry K. C. Lee. adv. bk. rev. circ. 30,000.

382　　　　　　　　　　　　　　　II
BUY FROM INDIA; Indian exporters directory. (Text in English) 1974. a. Rs.75($18) Industrocom International, 10 Mangal Baugh, Pushpa Park, Malad, Bombay 400064, India. adv. illus.

380.1 382　　　　　　　　　　　　US
CALIFORNIA INTERNATIONAL TRADE REGISTER. 1980. biennial. $59.95. Times Mirror Press, 1115 So. Boyle Ave., Los Angeles, CA 90023. Ed. Phyllis Newman. circ. 1,500.

380　　　　　　　　　　　　　　　US
CALIFORNIA STATE INDUSTRIAL DIRECTORY. a. $77.50. State Industrial Directories Corp., Two Penn Plaza, New York, NY 10001.

770　　　　　　　　　　　　　　　JA
CAMERART PHOTO TRADE DIRECTORY. 1958. a. $21. CamerArt, Inc., C.P.O. Box 620, Tokyo, Japan. illus.

CAMP DIRECTORS PURCHASING GUIDE. see *SPORTS AND GAMES — Outdoor Life*

796.51　　　　　　　　UK　ISSN 0068-6948
CAMPING CARAVANNING AND SPORTS EQUIPMENT TRADES DIRECTORY. 1966. a. £12.50. Camping and Sports Equipment Ltd., 4 Spring Street, London W2 3RA, England. Ed. P. Moloney. adv. circ. 3,500.
Formerly: Camping and Sports Equipment Trades Directory.

330 658　　　　　　　　　　　　　CN
CANADIAN AUTOMOTIVE AFTERMARKET DIRECTORY/MARKETING GUIDE. a. Can.$30. Wadham Publications, Ltd., 109 Vanderhoof Ave., Toronto, Ont. M4G 2J2, Canada. Ed. Sam S. Dixon. adv. circ. 3,512.

338　　　　　　　　US　ISSN 0315-0879
CANADIAN KEY BUSINESS DIRECTORY. a. $120. Dun & Bradstreet Inc., 99 Church St., New York, NY 10007.

372　　　　　　　　　　　　　　　TR
CARIBBEAN FREE TRADE ASSOCIATION. DIRECTORY. (Text in English) 1974. a. International Publications Ltd., Queen's Park West, Port-of-Spain, Trinidad. illus.

380　　　　　　　　UK　ISSN 0069-0996
CASTLE'S TOWN AND COUNTY TRADES DIRECTORY. 1948. a. £7. United Publicity Services Ltd., Gray's Inn Road, London, WC1, England.

380　　　　　　　　　　　　　　　MX
CATALOGO PRODUCTOS Y SERVICIOS DEL ESTADO DE MEXICO. 1973. a. Asociacion de Industriales del Estado de Mexico, Diagonal Jose T. Cuellar 99 A, Mexico 8, D.F., Mexico.

338　　　　　　　　　　　　　　　CJ
CAYMAN ISLANDS HANDBOOK AND BUSINESSMAN'S GUIDE. 1973. a. $10. Northwester Company Ltd., P.O. Box 243, George Town, Grand Cayman, B.W.I. Ed. Jim Graves. adv. illus. circ. 5,000.

338 670　　　　　　　　　　　　　MW
CHAMBER OF COMMERCE AND INDUSTRY OF MALAWI. INDUSTRIAL AND TRADE DIRECTORY. biennial, 5th, 1978. Chamber of Commerce and Industry of Malawi, Box 258, Blantyre, Malawi.
Formerly: Industrial Directory and Brand Names Index of Malawi.

380　　　　　　　　　　　　　　　PK
CHAMBER'S TRADE DIRECTORY. (Text in English) irreg. Rs.20. Chamber of Commerce and Industry, Aiwan-e-Tijarat, Box 4158, Nicol Rd., Karachi 2, Pakistan.

660　　　　　　　　US　ISSN 0094-3681
CHEM SOURCES - EUROPE. a. $70. Directories Publishing Co., Box 422, Flemington, NJ 08822 (Outside U.S. and Canada Dist. by Chemical Sources Europe, Box 178, Mountain Lakes, NJ 07046; or Box 87846, 2508 The Hague, Netherlands)

660　　　　　　　　　　　　　　　US
CHEM SOURCES - U.S.A. 1958. a. $100 initial subscription. Directories Publishing Co., Box 422, Flemington, NJ 08822.

380　　　　　　　　　　　　　　　KO
CHONGUK KIOPCHE CHONGNAM/ DIRECTORY OF KOREAN BUSINESS.* (Text in Korean) irreg. Taehan Sanggong Hoeuiso, Korea Chamber of Commerce & Industry, Seoul, S. Korea.

338　　　　　　　　UK　ISSN 0142-5072
CITY OF LONDON DIRECTORY & LIVERY COMPANIES GUIDE. 1863. a. £11.50. City Press Ltd., Fairfax House, Colchester, Essex CO1 1RJ, England. Ed. Patricia M. Hetherington. circ. 1,500.

670　　　　　　　　US　ISSN 0069-4525
CLASSIFIED DIRECTORY OF WISCONSIN MANUFACTURERS. 1921. a. $50. Wisconsin Association of Manufacturers & Commerce, 111 E. Wisconsin Ave., Milwaukee, WI 53202. Ed. Jean C. Peterson. adv. index. circ. 4,500.

338　　　　　　　　　　　　　　　IT
COLLANA DI STUDI E DOCUMENTAZIONE. 1962. irreg.; no. 40, 1978. price varies. Servizio Italiano Pubblicazioni Internazionali s.r.l., Viale dell'Astronomia, 30, 00144 Rome, Italy.

380　　　　　　　　　　　　　　　US
COLORADO STATE INDUSTRIAL DIRECTORY. biennial. $40. State Industrial Directories Corp., Two Penn Plaza, New York, NY 10001.

BUSINESS AND ECONOMICS — TRADE AND INDUSTRIAL DIRECTORIES

380.1   ET
COMMERCIAL BANK OF ETHIOPIA. TRADE DIRECTORY. irreg. free. Commercial Bank of Ethiopia, P.O. Box 255, Addis Ababa, Ethiopia.

670   US
CONNECTICUT AND RHODE ISLAND DIRECTORY OF MANUFACTURERS. 1981? biennial? Commerce Register, Inc., 213 First St., Ho-Ho-Kus, NJ 07423.

338   US   ISSN 0098-6186
CONNECTICUT STATE INDUSTRIAL DIRECTORY. 1972. a. $50. State Industrial Directories Corp., 2 Penn Plaza, New York, NY 10001. Ed. Allan Appel.

CONSULTANTS AND CONSULTING ORGANIZATIONS DIRECTORY; a reference guide to concerns and individuals engaged in consultation for business, industry and government. see BUSINESS AND ECONOMICS — Management

CONTAINER CONTACTS. see TRANSPORTATION

380   UK   ISSN 0309-2143
CONVERTER DIRECTORY; suppliers and services to the U.K. converting industry. a. Embankment Press Ltd., Bldg. 59, G.E.C. Estate, East Lane, Wembley, Middlesex, England. (reprint service avail. from UMI)

COOPERATIVE TRADE DIRECTORY FOR SOUTHEAST ASIA. see BUSINESS AND ECONOMICS — Cooperatives

338.4   660   US   ISSN 0574-1181
CORPORATE DIAGRAMS AND ADMINISTRATIVE PERSONNEL OF THE CHEMICAL INDUSTRY. 1958. irreg. $150 for 14th edt. Chemical Economic Services, Box 468, Palmer Square P.O., Princeton, NJ 08540. Ed. Kenneth R. Kern. index. (back issues avail.)

380   US   ISSN 0589-7920
CORPORATE REPORT FACT BOOK; a directory of publicly held companies in the Ninth Federal Reserve District. 1968. a. plus supplement. $44. Dorn Communications, Inc., 7101 York Ave. S., Minneapolis, MN 55435.

381   CY   ISSN 0070-2331
CYPRUS CHAMBER OF COMMERCE AND INDUSTRY DIRECTORY;* guide to commerce, industry, tourism and agriculture. (Text in English) 1967. irreg., 1970, 2nd ed. $25. D. Couvas & Sons Ltd., P.O. Box 35, Limasol, Cyprus (Dist. by: International Publications Service, 114 E. 32nd St., New York, NY 10016)

670   621.381   AT
D P INDEX. 1977. a. Aus.$35. Peter Isaacson Publications, 46-49 Porter St., Prahran, Vic. 3181, Australia. adv.
    Computer equipment

380   US   ISSN 0148-5652
DELAWARE STATE INDUSTRIAL DIRECTORY. a. $15. State Industrial Directories Corp., Two Penn Plaza, New York, NY 10001.

338.4   US   ISSN 0098-6755
DELAWARE STATE MINORITY BUSINESS DIRECTORY. irreg. Office of Minority Business Enterprises, 630 State College Rd., Dover, DE 19901.

659.1   US   ISSN 0195-4326
DESIGN DIRECTORY; a listing of firm and consultants in industrial, graphic, interior and environmental design. 1979. a. $39. Wefler & Associates, Inc., 2 N. Riverside Plaza, Chicago, IL 60606. Ed. W. Daniel Wefler. (back issues avail.)

338   380   GW   ISSN 0418-8381
DAS DEUTSCHE FIRMEN-ALPHABET; Industrie, Handel, Verkehr, Organisationen. a. DM.65. Deutscher Adressbuch-Verlag, Holzhofallee 38, Postfach 110320, 6100 Darmstadt, W. Germany (B.R.D.) circ. 7,000.

338   GW
DEUTSCHES BUNDES-ADRESSBUCH: INDUSTRIE, GROSS- UND AUSSENHANDEL, DIENSTLEISTUNGEN, ORGANISATIONEN. a. DM.100. Deutscher Adressbuch-Verlag, Holzhofallee 38, Postfach 110320, 6100 Darmstadt, W. Germany (B.R.D.) illus.
    Continues: Deutsches Bundes-Adressbuch der Firmen aus Industrie, Handel und Verkehr.

338   JA
DIAMOND'S JAPAN BUSINESS DIRECTORY. (Text in English) 1970. a. 47000($230) Diamond Lead Co., Ltd., 4-2 Kasumigaseki 1-chome, Chiyoda-ku, Tokyo 100, Japan. Ed. Hiroshi Matsumura. circ. 45,000. (back issues avail)

338   UY
DICCIONARIO DE LA PRODUCCION Y DE LA INDUSTRIA. 1975. a. $25. Centro de Estudios y Publicaciones de la Industria y la Produccion, Vazquez 1429, Montevideo, Uruguay. Ed. Carlos Pacheco. adv. illus.

380   CR
DIRECTORIO DE LA INDUSTRIA Y COMERCIO DE CENTROAMERICA Y PANAMA. irreg. Servicios de Anuario Telefonico Internacional, Apartado 5272, San Jose, Costa Rica. illus.

338   GT
DIRECTORIO INDUSTRIAL, CENTROAMERICA-PANAMA. 1973. irreg. General Treaty on Central American Economic Integration, Permanent Secretariat, Guatemala City, Guatemala.

380.1   LB
DIRECTORY AND WHO'S WHO IN LIBERIA. 1971. irreg. A & A Enterprises Inc., Box 103, Monrovia, Liberia. adv. illus.

DIRECTORY OF AMERICAN FIRMS OPERATING IN FOREIGN COUNTRIES. see BUSINESS AND ECONOMICS — International Commerce

DIRECTORY OF CARDAMOM PLANTERS. see AGRICULTURE — Crop Production And Soil

670   US   ISSN 0070-5241
DIRECTORY OF CENTRAL ATLANTIC STATES MANUFACTURERS. MARYLAND, DELAWARE, VIRGINIA, WEST VIRGINIA, NORTH CAROLINA, SOUTH CAROLINA. Variant title: Central Atlantic States Manufacturers Directory. 1950. a. $50. Seaboard Publishing Co., 714 E. Pratt St., Baltimore, MD 21202. Ed. T. K. Sanderson.

338   US   ISSN 0084-9898
DIRECTORY OF COLORADO MANUFACTURERS. 1948. a. $25. University of Colorado, Graduate School of Business Administration, Boulder, CO 80309. Ed. Gerald L. Allen. circ. 1,500.

338   US
DIRECTORY OF DEPARTMENT STORES. a. $115. Business Guides, Inc., 425 Park Ave., New York, NY 10022.

338   US
DIRECTORY OF DRUG STORE CHAINS; includes wholesale druggists. a. $119. Business Guides, Inc., 425 Park Ave., New York, NY 10022.

DIRECTORY OF ELECTRIC LIGHT AND POWER COMPANIES. see ELECTRICITY AND ELECTRICAL ENGINEERING

338   UK
DIRECTORY OF ENGINEERING CAPACITY. vol. 17, 1975. a. £2($5) Coventry Chamber of Commerce & Industry, 123 St. Nicholas St., Coventry CV1 4FD, England. Ed. Norman Lissaman. adv. circ. 550.

011   UK   ISSN 0070-5500
DIRECTORY OF EUROPEAN ASSOCIATIONS. PART 1: NATIONAL INDUSTRIAL TRADE & PROFESSIONAL ASSOCIATIONS. 1971. irreg., 3rd, 1981. £50($150) C.B.D. Research Ltd., 154 High St., Beckenham, Kent BR3 1EA, England (Dist. in U.S. by: Gale Research Co., Book Tower, Detroit, MI 48226) Ed. I. G. Anderson. circ. 4,000.

382   UK   ISSN 0142-4769
DIRECTORY OF EXPORT BUYERS IN THE U.K. 1978. a. Trade Research Publications, 6 Beech Hill Court, Berkhamsted, Herts. HP4 2PR, England.

650   US   ISSN 0070-5543
DIRECTORY OF FOREIGN FIRMS OPERATING IN THE UNITED STATES. 1970. irreg., 4th edt., 1979. $85. World Trade Academy Press, Inc., 50 E. 42nd St., New York, NY 10017. Ed. J. L. Angel. circ. 400.

DIRECTORY OF GAS UTILITY COMPANIES. see PETROLEUM AND GAS

338   US
DIRECTORY OF GENERAL MERCHANDISE, MAIL ORDER FIRMS AND FAMILY CENTERS. a. $109. Business Guides, Inc., 425 Park Ave., New York, NY 10022.

DIRECTORY OF GEOPHYSICAL AND OIL COMPANIES WHO USE GEOPHYSICAL SERVICE. see PETROLEUM AND GAS

338.4   HK
DIRECTORY OF HONG KONG INDUSTRIES. (Text in English) 1976. a. Hong Kong Productivity Centre, Box 6123, G.P.O., Hong Kong, Hong Kong. adv.

650   NR   ISSN 0084-9952
DIRECTORY OF INCORPORATED (REGISTERED) COMPANIES IN NIGERIA. 1970. a. £N15($30) I C I C (Directory Publishers) Ltd., P.M.B. 3204, Surulere, Lagos, Nigeria. Ed. Olu Adeyemi.

382.45   621   II   ISSN 0417-5964
DIRECTORY OF INDIAN ENGINEERING EXPORTERS. 1957. irreg., 8th edition, 1977. price varies. Engineering Export Promotion Council, World Trade Centre, 3rd Floor, 14/1B Ezra St., Calcutta 700001, India. adv. illus. circ. 5,000.

382   US
DIRECTORY OF INDONESIAN IMPORTERS. a. $140. Croner Publications, Inc., 211-03 Jamaica Ave., Queens Village, NY 11428.

338   PK
DIRECTORY OF INDUSTRIAL ESTABLISHMENTS IN PUNJAB. (Text in English) 1975. a. Rs.40. Directorate of Industries and Mineral Development, Lahore, Punjab, Pakistan.

330   IS
DIRECTORY OF ISRAEL. (Text in English) 1953. a. $45. N.A. Etrogy Publishing Company, Box 815, Tel-Aviv, Israel (Dist. by International Publications Service, 303 Park Ave. S., New York, N.Y. 10010) Ed. A. Etrogy. adv. bk. rev.
    Formerly: Directory of Israeli Merchants and Manufacturers (ISSN 0070-5705)

659.1   US   ISSN 0419-2923
DIRECTORY OF MAILING LIST HOUSES. 1955. biennial. $30. B. Klein Publications, Box 8503, Coral Springs, FL 33065. Ed. Bernard Klein.

670   US
DIRECTORY OF MANUFACTURERS-MINNESOTA. biennial. $20. Department of Economic Development, 480 Cedar St., St. Paul, MN 55101. circ. 3,500.

DIRECTORY OF MARYLAND EXPORTERS-IMPORTERS; an international handbook. see BUSINESS AND ECONOMICS — International Commerce

670   US
DIRECTORY OF MASSACHUSETTS MANUFACTURERS. a. $21. Associated Industries of Massachusetts, 4005 Prudential Tower, Boston, MA 02199.

670   US   ISSN 0070-5845
DIRECTORY OF MICHIGAN MANUFACTURERS. 1937. a. $95. Pick Publications, Inc., 8543 Puritan Ave., Detroit, MI 48238. Ed. N.S. Hendricks. adv. circ. 15,000.

DIRECTORY OF OIL WELL DRILLING CONTRACTORS. see PETROLEUM AND GAS

DIRECTORY OF OIL WELL SUPPLY COMPANIES. see PETROLEUM AND GAS

380.1   PH
DIRECTORY OF PHILIPPINE EXPORTERS AND IMPORTERS. a. Directory of Philippine Industries, Box 2653, Manila, Philippines.

670   PH
DIRECTORY OF PHILIPPINE MANUFACTURERS AND PRODUCERS. a. Directory of Philippine Industries, Box 2653, Manila, Philippines.

DIRECTORY OF PREMIUM, INCENTIVE AND TRAVEL BUYERS. see BUSINESS AND ECONOMICS — Marketing And Purchasing

380.1   US   ISSN 0419-3512
DIRECTORY OF SHOPPING CENTERS. 1957. a. $168. National Research Bureau, Inc., 424 N. 3rd St., Burlington, IA 52601. Ed. Milton Paule. circ. 4,000.
    Formerly: Shopping Center Directory (ISSN 0037-4210)

670   SI   ISSN 0070-6337
DIRECTORY OF SINGAPORE MANUFACTURERS. (Text in English) 1960. a. S.$15($4) Singapore Manufacturers' Association, P.O. Box No. 213, Colombo Court Post Office, North Bridge Road, Singapore, 6, Singapore. Ed. E. A. Clark. adv. circ. 5,000.

380   CE
DIRECTORY OF STATE CORPORATIONS. (Text in English) a. Rs.10. Sri Lanka Institute for the Study of State Corporations, 380 Bauddhaloka Mawatha, Colombo 7, Sri Lanka.

338   672   US   ISSN 0070-6426
DIRECTORY OF STEEL FOUNDRIES IN THE UNITED STATES, CANADA AND MEXICO. 1930. biennial. $15. Steel Founders' Society of America, 20611 Center Ridge Rd., Rocky River, OH 44116. Ed. Cheryl Hallstrom. circ. 1,500.

670   US   ISSN 0070-6450
DIRECTORY OF TEXAS MANUFACTURERS. 1933. a. $60. University of Texas at Austin, Bureau of Business Research, Austin, TX 78712.

664   US
DIRECTORY OF THE CANNING, FREEZING, PRESERVING INDUSTIRES. 1966. biennial. $60. James J.Judge, Inc., Box550, Westminster, MD 21157. Ed. James J. Judge. circ. 3,000. (back issues avail.)

380.1   530   US
DIRECTORY OF THE SOLAR INDUSTRY. 1976. a. $20. Solar Data, 13 Evergreen Rd., Hampton, NH 03842. Ed. Richard N. Livingstone.

DIRECTORY OF U.S. AND CANADIAN MARKETING SURVEYS AND SERVICES. see BUSINESS AND ECONOMICS — Marketing And Purchasing

DIRECTORY OF UNITED STATES IMPORTERS. see BUSINESS AND ECONOMICS — International Commerce

DIRECTORY OF WOOL, HOSIERY & FABRICS. see TEXTILE INDUSTRIES AND FABRICS

540   US   ISSN 0196-0555
DIRECTORY OF WORLD CHEMICAL PRODUCERS. a. Chemical Information Services, Box 61, Oceanside, NY 11572.

DROP SHIP BUYERS GUIDE. see BUSINESS AND ECONOMICS — Marketing And Purchasing

380   658.8   US
DROP SHIPPING SOURCE DIRECTORY OF MAJOR CONSUMER PRODUCT LINES. 1977. a. $5. Consolidated Marketing Services, Inc., 507-Fifth Ave., New York, NY 10017. Ed. Nicholas T. Scheel.

DUN AND BRADSTREET METALWORKING DIRECTORY. see METALLURGY

338   US
DUN & BRADSTREET STANDARD REGISTER. Variant title: Dun & Bradstreet/Seyd's Register. (Published in 5 volumes: Vol. 1, Northern Counties, Vol. 2. Midlands, Vol. 3. London, Vol. 4. Southern Counties and Wales, Vol. 5. Scotland and North Ireland) 1965. a. L.1.24 not available to libraries. Dun & Bradstreet, Inc., 99 Church St., New York, NY 10007 (And 26-32 Clifton St., London EC2P 2LY, England)
    Former titles: Dun & Bradstreet Register (ISSN 0070-7635); Bradstreet's Register; Incorporating: Seyd's Commercial Lists (ISSN 0080-911X)

DUNDEE AND TAYSIDE CHAMBER OF COMMERCE AND INDUSTRY. BUYER'S GUIDE & TRADE DIRECTORY. see BUSINESS AND ECONOMICS — Chamber Of Commerce Publications

E B G. (Electronics Buyers Guide) see ELECTRICITY AND ELECTRICAL ENGINEERING

E C A YEAR BOOK DESK DIARY. (Electrical Contractors' Association) see ELECTRICITY AND ELECTRICAL ENGINEERING

380   MG
L'ECONOMIE. 1970. a. B.P. 777, Antananarivo, Malagasy Republic. Ed. Romuald Bigaignon. adv. illus. stat.
    Supersedes: Economie Malgache & Annuaire National de l'Industrie et du Commerce.

380   EC
ECUADOR. MINISTERIO DE INDUSTRIAS, COMERCIO E INTEGRACION. EMPRESAS ACOGIDAS A LA LEY DE FOMENTO INDUSTRIAL. DIRECTORIO INDUSTRIAL. 1957. irreg. Ministerio de Industrias, Comercio e Integracion, Quito, Ecuador.

338   380   GW
EINKAUFS 1X1 DER DEUTSCHEN INDUSTRIE. 1961. a. DM.65. Deutscher Adressbuch-Verlag, Holzhofallee 38, Postfach 110320, 6100 Darmstadt, W. Germany (B.R.D.) adv. index in English and French. circ. 8,000.
    Sources of supply in Germany

ELECTRICAL BUYER'S GUIDE. see ELECTRICITY AND ELECTRICAL ENGINEERING

537   US
ELECTRONIC DESIGN'S GOLD BOOK. 1974. a. $30. Hayden Publishing Co., Inc., 50 Essex St., Rochelle Park, NJ 07662. Ed. George Weingarten. adv.

338   621.3   US   ISSN 0422-9053
ELECTRONIC INDUSTRY TELEPHONE DIRECTORY. 1963. a. $29.95 (foreign $40) Harris Publishing Co.(Twinsburg), 2057-2 Aurora Rd., Twinsburg, OH 44087. Eds. Beatrice Harris, Lonetta Witt. adv. circ. 95,000.

338   621.3   US
ELECTRONIC REPRESENTATIVES DIRECTORY. 1956. a. $15 (foreign $20) Harris Publishing Co. (Twinsburg), 2057-2 Aurora Rd., Twinsburg, OH 44087. Ed. Jeanne Ring. adv. circ. 10,000.

ELEKTRONIKINDUSTRIENS INDKOEBSBOG. see ELECTRICITY AND ELECTRICAL ENGINEERING

EMBROIDERY DIRECTORY. see TEXTILE INDUSTRIES AND FABRICS

ENCYCLOPEDIA OF INFORMATION SYSTEMS AND SERVICES. see COMPUTER TECHNOLOGY AND APPLICATIONS

ENGINEER BUYERS GUIDE. see ENGINEERING

ENGINEERING INDUSTRIES ASSOCIATION. CLASSIFIED DIRECTORY AND BUYERS GUIDE. see ENGINEERING

791.4   US   ISSN 0271-8014
ENTERTAINMENT INDUSTRY DIRECTORY. a. $11.95. Star Maker Informative Listing Enterprises, 6255 Sunset Blvd., Hollywood, CA 90028.

EUROPEAN ELECTRONIC COMPONENT DISTRIBUTOR DIRECTORY. see ELECTRICITY AND ELECTRICAL ENGINEERING

EUROPEAN RIG- AND SUPPLY SHIP OWNERS. see TRANSPORTATION — Ships And Shipping

615   US   ISSN 0071-3309
EXECUTIVE DIRECTORY OF THE U.S. PHARMACEUTICAL INDUSTRY. 1966. irreg. $65 for 3rd edt. (1976) Chemical Economic Services, Box 468, Palmer Square P.O., Princeton, NJ 08540. Ed. Kenneth R. Kern. index.

382   BL
EXPORT DIRECTORY OF BRAZIL/GUIA BRASILEIRO DE EXPORTACAO. (Text in English, French, German, Portuguese, Spanish) 1964. a. Editora de Guias Ltda, Rua Desembargador Viriato 2, 20000 Rio de Janeiro GB, Brazil. (Co-sponsor: Banco do Brasil) illus.
    Formerly: G B E: Export Directory of Brazil.

380   IC
F I S FRETTABREF. 1969, no. 1, vol. 5. irreg. (approx. 6/yr.) membership. Felag Islenzkra Storkaupmanna - Association of Icelandic Wholesalers and Importers, Tjarnargata 14, Box 476, Reykjavik, Iceland. Ed. Julius S. Olafsson. circ. 250 (controlled)

382   PK
FEDERATION OF PAKISTAN CHAMBERS OF COMMERCE AND INDUSTRY. DIRECTORY OF EXPORTERS. (Text in English) 1977. a. Rs.50. Federation of Pakistan Chambers of Commerce and Industry, St-28, Block 5, Scheme-V, Share-Firdousi Kehkashan, Clifton, Karachi, Pakistan.

FEED INDUSTRY RED BOOK; reference book and buyers' guide for the feed manufacturing industry. see AGRICULTURE — Feed, Flour And Grain

380   CE
FERGUSON'S CEYLON DIRECTORY. (Text in English) 1859. a. Rs.100($7.85) Associated Newspapers of Ceylon Ltd., Box 1195, Lake House, Colombo 10, Sri Lanka. Ed. P. S. Perera. adv. stat. circ. 5,000.

670   FR
FICHIERS INDUSTRIELS DU SUD OUEST. 1974. a. S.E.C.I., 214 Av. Raymond Naves, 31500 Toulouse, France. Ed. Patrick le Martin. adv.

380   US   ISSN 0163-4712
FLORIDA STATE INDUSTRIAL DIRECTORY. a. $65. State Industrial Directories Corp., Two Penn Plaza, New York, NY 10001.

380   JA
FOOD ECONOMICS YEARBOOK/SHOKURYO KEIZAI NENKAN.* a. 2500 Yen. Shokuryo Keizai Shimbun Sha, 35-12 Ishigatsujimachi, Tennoji-ku, Osaka 543, Japan. illus.
    Continues: Sogo Keizai Nenkan.

670   PH
FOREIGN BUYERS OF PHILIPPINE COTTAGE INDUSTRY PRODUCTS. a. Directory of Philippine Industries, Box 2653, Manila, Philippines.

338.4   US
FORTUNE WORLD BUSINESS DIRECTORY; the 500 largest industrials and the 50 largest banks outside the U.S. 1957; expanded 1976. a. $4. Time Inc., Fortune Division, Rm. 1828, Time & Life Building, Rockefeller Center, New York, NY 10020. charts. stat.

338   US   ISSN 0318-8752
FRANCHISE ANNUAL; complete handbook and directory. 1969. a. $14.95. (International Franchise Opportunities) Info Press, Inc., 736 Center St., Lewiston, NY 14092. Ed. E.L. Dixon. index. circ. 10,000.

380.1   658   CN   ISSN 0071-9277
FRASER'S CANADIAN TRADE DIRECTORY. 1913. a. Can.$75. Maclean-Hunter Ltd., 481 University Ave., Toronto, Ont. M5W 1A7, Canada.

380.1　　　　　　　GM
GAMBIA. CENTRAL STATISTICS
DEPARTMENT. DIRECTORY OF
ESTABLISHMENTS. (Formerly issued by Central
Statistics Division) a, latest 1974. d.3. Central
Statistics Department, Wellington St., Banjul,
Gambia.

GEFAHRGUT KONTAKTE/DANGEROUS
CARGO CONTACTS. see
TRANSPORTATION — Ships And Shipping

330　　　　　US　　ISSN 0435-5482
GEORGIA MANUFACTURING DIRECTORY.
biennial. $20. Department of Industry and Trade,
1400 N. Omni International, Box 1776, Atlanta,
GA 30301. Ed. Susan Barnett. circ. 4-6,000.

380　　　　　US　　ISSN 0161-8571
GEORGIA STATE INDUSTRIAL DIRECTORY. a.
$50. State Industrial Directories Corp., Two Penn
Plaza, New York, NY 10001.

664.752　　　　　US
GRAIN DIRECTORY/BUYERS GUIDE. a. $15.
Sosland Publishing Co., 4800 Main St., Kansas City,
MO 64112. Ed. Morton I. Sosland.

338　　　　　GU　　ISSN 0072-7865
GUAM BUSINESS DIRECTORY. (Text in English)
1954. irreg. free contr. circ. in Guam; $1 in the U.S.
Department of Commerce, Economic Research
Center, Box 682, Agana, GU 96910.

GUIA DAS EDITORAS BRASILEIRAS. see
PUBLISHING AND BOOK TRADE

382　　　　　IT　　ISSN 0432-9120
GUIDA NAZIONALE DEL COMMERCIO CON
L'ESTERO; annuario di consultazione per
importatori ed exportatori. 1947. a. L.20000. Istituto
Editoriale Pubblicazioni Internazionali, Piazza
Ruggero di Sicilia 1, 00162 Rome, Italy. adv.

380　668.55　　　FR　　ISSN 0072-7989
GUIDE DE LA PARFUMERIE. (Text in French;
summaries in English, French, German) 1948.
biennial. 100 F. Editions Publi-Guid, 195 Quai de la
Gourdine, 77400 Lagny, France. Ed. Charles
Hieblot. index in English, French, German.

338.0961　　　　TI
GUIDE ECONOMIQUE DE LA TUNISIE. 1976. a.
Societe I E A, 16 rue de Rome, Tunis, Tunisia. illus.

380　　　　　US
GUIDE TO KEY BRITISH ENTERPRISES I AND
II. a. Dun & Bradstreet, Inc., 99 Church St., New
York, NY 10007 (And 26-32 Clifton St., London
EC2P 2LY, England)
Formerly: British Middle Market Directory
(ISSN 0068-2268)

GUIDOR. (Guide Annuaire Officiel du Complexe de
Rungis) see FOOD AND FOOD INDUSTRIES —
Grocery Trade

338　　　　　AG
GUIPREX. (Guia de Productores y Exportadores
Latinoamericanos) (Text in English and Spanish)
1975. a. Zona s.r.l, Bartolome Mitre 1225, Buenos
Aires, Argentina. illus.

380　　　　　AU
HANDELSREGISTER OESTERREICH; mit dem
genauen Wortlaut der amtlichen Protokollierung.
1947. a. S.900. Jupiter Verlag GmbH, Robertgasse
2, A-1020 Vienna, Austria.

HARPERS GUIDE TO SPORTS TRADE. see
SPORTS AND GAMES

380　　　　　US
HAWAII STATE INDUSTRIAL DIRECTORY.
biennial. $26. State Industrial Directories Corp.,
Two Penn Plaza, New York, NY 10001.

380　338　　　　AU　　ISSN 0531-5824
HEROLD EXPORT-ADRESSBUCH VON
OESTERREICH/AUSTRIAN EXPORT
DIRECTORY/ANNUAIRE D'EXPORTATION
DE L'AUTRICHE/ANUARIO DE
EXPORTACION DE AUSTRIA. (Text in English,
German, French and Spanish) 1950. a. S.390($20)
Herold Vereinigte Anzeigen-Gesellschaft M.B.H.,
Wipplingerstr. 14, A-1013 Vienna, Austria.

382　　　　　HK　　ISSN 0073-3245
HONG KONG MANUFACTURERS AND
EXPORTERS REGISTER. 1963. irreg., 1975, 8th
edt. $18. Oriental Publicity Service, P.O. Box 4366,
N.P., Hong Kong, Hong Kong. Ed. Anthony Leung.
adv. circ. 5,000.

382　　　　　UK　　ISSN 0073-3261
HONG KONG TRADE DIRECTORY. 1964-65. a.
£1.75. Diplomatic Press and Publishing Co., 44-46
South Ealing Rd., London W.5, England. Ed. Harry
Richter.

380　　　　　US
IDAHO STATE INDUSTRIAL DIRECTORY.
biennial. $35. State Industrial Directories Corp.,
Two Penn Plaza, New York, NY 10001.

380　　　　　US
ILLINOIS STATE INDUSTRIAL DIRECTORY. a.
$95. State Industrial Directories Corp., Two Penn
Plaza, New York, NY 10001.

INDIAN HOSIERY DIRECTORY. see CLOTHING
TRADE

380　　　　　US　　ISSN 0190-1362
INDIANA STATE INDUSTRIAL DIRECTORY. a.
$70. State Industrial Directories Corp., Two Penn
Plaza, New York, NY 10001.

INDONESIAN SHIPPING DIRECTORY. see
TRANSPORTATION — Ships And Shipping

382　　　　　US
INDUSTRIAL DIRECTORY OF THE
COMMONWEALTH OF PENNSYLVANIA.
1913. irreg., 27th edt., 1980. $15. Department of
Commerce, Bureau of Statistics, Research and
Planning, 630B Health & Welfare Bldg., Harrisburg,
PA 17120 (Orders to: Bureau of Management
Services, State Book Store, Box 1365, Harrisburg,
PA 17125)

338.7　　　　　UK
INDUSTRIAL DIRECTORY OF WALES. irreg. £4.
Development Corp. for Wales, 15 Park Place,
Cardiff CF1 3DQ, Wales.

670　　　　　AU　　ISSN 0073-7712
INDUSTRIE COMPASS OESTERREICH. 1869. a.
S.800. (Austrian Chamber of Commerce) Compass-
Verlagsgesellschaft Rudolf Hanel & Sohn,
Wipplingerstrasse 32, A-1013 Vienna, Austria. adv.

381　　　　　II　　ISSN 0073-7763
INDUSTRIES DIRECTORY, CAPITALS.* irreg.
Rs.30. J.K. Publications, 16 Park Area, Delhi 5,
India. Ed. J.K. Jain.

381　　　　　II　　ISSN 0073-7771
INDUSTRIES DIRECTORY, DELHI.* irreg. Rs.5.
J.K. Publications, 16 Park Area, Delhi 5, India. Ed.
J.K. Jain.

381　　　　　II　　ISSN 0073-7798
INDUSTRIES DIRECTORY, NORTHERN INDIA.*
irreg. Rs.15. J.K. Publications, 16 Park Area, Delhi
5, India. Ed. J.K. Jain.

380　　　　　US
INFORMATION SOURCES. 1976. a. $21.
Information Industry Association, 316 Pennysylvania
Ave., S.E., Washington, DC 20003. Ed. Faye
Henderson.

INGENIOEREN INDKOEBSBOG. see BUSINESS
AND ECONOMICS — Production Of Goods And
Services

771　　　　　US　　ISSN 0148-5121
INTERNATIONAL FILE OF MICROGRAPHICS
EQUIPMENT & ACCESSORIES. 1977. biennial.
$250. Microform Review, Inc., 520 Riverside Ave.,
Box 405, Saugatuck Station, Westport, CT 06880.
(hardcopy index, microfiche catalog)

338.1　　　　　US　　ISSN 0074-6193
INTERNATIONAL GREEN BOOK; directory of
U.S. and Latin American processors of cottonseed,
soybean, linseed and peanuts. 1910. a. $20. Cotton
Gin and Oil Mill Press, P.O. Box 18092, Dallas, TX
75218. adv. circ. 500. (also avail. in microform from
UMI)

INTERNATIONAL MARKET GUIDE -
CONTINENTAL EUROPE. see BUSINESS AND
ECONOMICS — Investments

INTERNATIONAL PULP & PAPER DIRECTORY.
see PAPER AND PULP

INTERNATIONAL REFRACTORIES HANDBOOK
& DIRECTORY. see CERAMICS, GLASS AND
POTTERY

380.1　　　　　GW　　ISSN 0094-1611
INTERNATIONALES VERZEICHNIS DER
WIRTSCHAFTSVERBAENDE/WORLD GUIDE
TO TRADE ASSOCIATIONS. irreg. $74. K.G.
Saur Verlag KG, Poessenbacherstr. 12 B, Postfach
711009, 8000 Munich 71, W. Germany (B.R.D.)
(And 175 Fifth Ave., New York, NY 10010)

338　　　　　NR
INVESTMENTS AND CREDIT CORPORATION
OF OYO STATE. INDUSTRIAL DIRECTORY.
1970. irreg. Investments and Credit Corporation of
Oyo State, P.M.B. 5085, Ibadan, Nigeria.
Formerly: Western Nigeria Development
Corporation. Industrial Directory.

INVESTORS GUIDE OF JAPAN. see BUSINESS
AND ECONOMICS — Investments

380.1　　　　　US
IOWA INTERNATIONAL DIRECTORY. biennial.
free. Iowa Development Commission, 250 Jewett
Building, Des Moines, IA 50309.
Former titles: Iowa Manufacturer's Export
Directory; Iowa Directory of Exporting Companies;
Iowa International Directory.

380　　　　　US
IOWA STATE INDUSTRIAL DIRECTORY.
biennial. $26. State Industrial Directories Corp.,
Two Penn Plaza, New York, NY 10001.

338.0962　　　　UA
ITTIHAD AL-SINAAT AL-MISRIYAH.
YEARBOOK. Vols. for 1971-72 issued by the body
under its English form of name: Federation of
Egyptian Industries. Yearbook. (Text in English)
1961. a. £E5. Federation of Egyptian Industries,
26a, Sherif Pasha St., Cairo, Egypt. Ed. Gamil el
Sabban. adv. stat. circ. 900.
Continues: Ittihad al-Sinaat Bi-al-Jumhuriyah al-
Arabiyah al-Muttahidah. Yearbook.

338.7　　　　　IO
JAKARTA BUSINESS DIRECTORY. (Text in
English or Indonesian) 1974. irreg. Kamar Dagang
dan Industri Jakarta, Jalan W. Jakarta Fair, Tromol
Post 3077, Jakarta, Indonesia. illus.

380.1　　　　　IO
JAKARTA BUYER'S GUIDE. (Text in English and
Indonesian) 1977. a. B.P. Jakarta Buyer's Guide,
Jalan Gunung Sahari 64, Jakarta, Indonesia.

380.1　　　　　IO
JAKARTA METROPOLITAN BUYERS' GUIDE.
(Text in English) a. C.V. Taro & Co., Jalan
Samanhudi ZB, Box 3472, Jakarta, Indonesia.

338　　　　　JA　　ISSN 0075-322X
JAPAN DIRECTORY. (Text in English) 1931. a.
2800 Yen($140) Japan Press, Ltd., C.P.O. Box 6,
Tokyo, Japan (Or 2-12-8 Kita Aoyama, Minato-ku,
Tokyo 107, Japan) Ed. Yoshio Wada. adv. circ.
25,000.

382　　　　　JA
JAPAN TIMES DIRECTORY. a. 4000 Yen. Japan
Times, Ltd., 4-5-4 Shibaura, Minato-ku, Tokyo 108,
Japan.
Names, addresses, phone numbers of foreign
residents in Japan, and leading enterprises, foreign
and Japanese

380　　　　　US
JIDDAH CHAMBER OF COMMERCE &
INDUSTRY ANNUAL TRADE DIRECTORY. a.
$90. Inter-Crescent Publishing Co., Inc., Box 8481,
Dallas, TX 75205.

380　　　　　US
KANSAS STATE INDUSTRIAL DIRECTORY.
biennial. $35. State Industrial Directories Corp.,
Two Penn Plaza, New York, NY 10001.

338　　　　　UK
KELLY'S BRITISH INDUSTRY AND SERVICES
IN THE COMMON MARKET. a. £20. Kelly's
Directories Ltd., Windsor Court, East Grinstead
House, East Grinstead, West Sussex RH19 1XB,
England.

BUSINESS AND ECONOMICS — TRADE AND INDUSTRIAL DIRECTORIES

670 338   UK   ISSN 0075-5370
KELLY'S MANUFACTURERS AND MERCHANTS DIRECTORY; list of manufacturers and merchants (alphabetical and classified) 1877. a. £35. Kelly's Directories, Ltd., Windsor Court, East Grinstead House, East Grinstead, West Sussex RH19 1XB, England. adv. circ. 15,000.

910.2   UK   ISSN 0075-5389
KELLY'S POST OFFICE LONDON DIRECTORY; comprehensive list of trades in London (classified and alphabetical) 1799. a. £30. Kelly's Directories, Ltd., Windsor Court, East Grinstead Hous, East Grinstead, West Sussex RH19 1XB, England. adv. circ. 8,000.

670   UK   ISSN 0075-5419
KEMPS DIRECTORY. a. $70. Kemp's Group (Printers & Publishers) Ltd., 1-5 Bath St, London EC1V 9QA, England. adv.

KEMPS PROPERTY INDUSTRY YEARBOOK. see *REAL ESTATE*

380   US   ISSN 0190-1354
KENTUCKY STATE INDUSTRIAL DIRECTORY. a. $40. State Industrial Directories Corp., Two Penn Plaza, New York, NY 10001.

338.4   KE
KENYA. CENTRAL BUREAU OF STATISTICS. DIRECTORY OF INDUSTRIES. irreg., latest 1974. EAs.15. Central Bureau of Statistics, Ministry of Finance and Planning, Nairobi, Kenya (Orders to: Government Printing and Stationery Office, Box 30128, Nairobi, Kenya)
Continues: Kenya. Ministry of Finance and Economic Planning. Statistics Division. Register of Manufacturing Firms.

KENYA ENTERPRISE; incorporating trade directory. see *BUSINESS AND ECONOMICS*

380.1   KE
KENYA, UGANDA, TANZANIA, EAST AFRICAN COMMUNITY DIRECTORY; TRADE COMMERCE INDEX. 1959/60. irreg. East African Directory Company, P.O. Box 41237, Nairobi, Kenya. illus.
Continues: Kenya, Uganda, Tanzania, Zambia, Malawi and Ethiopia Directory; Trade and Commercial Index (ISSN 0453-6525)

668.4   US
KLINE GUIDE TO THE PLASTICS INDUSTRY. 1978. triennial. $100. Charles H. Kline & Co., Inc., 330 Passaic Ave., Fairfield, NJ 07006. Ed. James A. Rauch.

670   DK   ISSN 0075-661X
KOMPAS DANMARK; indeks over Danmarks industri og Naegringsliv. (Text in Danish; classifications in Danish, German, French, English, Spanish; summaries in Danish, English, German) 1961. a. Kr.260($78) (Foundation for Promoting International Economic Information, SZ) Forlaget Kompas-Denmark, Landskornagade 70, DK-2100 Copenhagen, Denmark (Dist. in the U.S. by: Croner Publications, Inc., 211-03 Jamaica Ave., Queens Village, NY 11428) Ed. C. Kjaergaard-Hansen. adv. bk. rev. circ. 6,000.

670 664   FR
KOMPASS ALIMENTATION. (Text and Summaries in English, French, German and Spanish) 1974. a. 250 F. Societe Nouvelle d'Editions pour l'Industrie, 22 Avenue F.D. Roosevelt, 75008-Paris, France. adv. illus.

670   AT   ISSN 0075-6628
KOMPASS AUSTRALIA; register of Australian industry and commerce. 1970. a. Aus.$85. (Associated Chambers of Manufacturers of Australia) Peter Isaacson Publications, 46-49 Porter St., Prahran Victoria 3181, Australia.

670   BE   ISSN 0075-6636
KOMPASS BELGIUM/LUXEMBOURG; repertoire de l'economie de la Belgique et du Luxembourg. (Text in French and Flemish; classifications in French, Flemish, German, English, Italian, Spanish; summaries in French, Flemish, German, English, Spanish) 1961. a. 2385 Fr.($78) (Foundation for Promoting International Economic Information, SZ) Kompass Belgium S.A., Office International de Librairie, Avenue Marnix 30, B-1050 Brussels, Belgium (Dist. in the U.S. and Canada by: Croner Publications, Inc., 211-03 Jamaica Ave., Queens Village, NY 11428)

670   GW
KOMPASS DEUTSCHLAND; informationswerk ueber ausgewaehlte Deutsche firmen/register of selected German industry and commerce. (Text in German with some Dutch, English, French, Italian or Spanish) a. $156. (Foundation for Promoting International Economic Information, SZ) Kompass Deutschland Verlag, Kaiser-Joseph-Str. 180, 7800 Freiburg, W. Germany (B.R.D.) (Dist. in U.S. and Canada by: Croner Publications, Inc., 211-03 Jamaica Ave., Queens Village, NY 11428)

670   SP   ISSN 0075-6644
KOMPASS ESPANA; repertorio general de la economia espanola. (Text in Spanish; classifications in Spanish, German, French, English, Italian; summaries in Spanish, French, German, English) 1960. a. $60. (Foundation for Promoting International Economic Information, SZ) Kompass Espana SA, Av. del General Peron 26, Madrid, 20, Spain (Croner Publications Inc., 211-03 Jamaica Ave., Queens Village, NY 11428)

670   NE   ISSN 0075-6660
KOMPASS HOLLAND; informatiewerk over het Nederlandse Bedrijfsleven. (Text in Dutch; classifications and summaries in Dutch, German, French, English, Spanish, Italian) 1964. a. fl.180. (Foundation for Promoting International Economic Information, SZ) Kompass Nederland N.V., Van Stolkweg 6, The Hague, Netherlands (Subscr. to Croner Publications, Inc., 211-03 Jamaica Ave., Queens Village, NY 11428) adv. bk. rev. circ. 20,000.

670   HK   ISSN 0075-6679
KOMPASS HONG KONG; register of Hong Kong industry and commerce. (Text in English; titles in English, French, German, Chinese, Japanese; summaries in English, French, German) 1970. a. HK.$120. (Foundation for Promoting International Economic Information, SZ) Kompass Hong Kong, c/o Commerce and Industry Dept., 46 Connaught Rd., Hong Kong, Hong Kong.

670   IT   ISSN 0075-6687
KOMPASS ITALIA; repertorio generale dell'economia Italiana. (Text in Italian; classifications and summaries in Italian, French, English and German, Spanish) 1962. a. L.125000. (Foundation for Promoting International Economic Information, SZ) Etas Kompass Periodici Tecnici S.p.A., Via A. Mantegna N. 6, I-20154 Milan, Italy (Distr. in U.S. & Canada by: Croner Publications, 211-05 Jamaica Ave., Queens Village, NY 11428)

670   MR   ISSN 0075-6695
KOMPASS MAROC; register of Moroccan industry and commerce. (Text and classifications in French; summaries in English and French) 1970. a. $39. (Foundation for Promoting International Economic Information, SZ) Kompass Maroc-Veto, Boite Postale 11100, MA Casablanca, Morocco (Dist. in U.S. and Canada by: Croner Publications, 211-03 Jamaica Ave., Queens Village, NY 11428) (Affiliate: Kompass International AG, Zurich) adv. circ. 6,000.

380   NO   ISSN 0075-6709
KOMPASS NORGE; indeks over Norges industri og Naeringsliv. (Text in Norwegian, German, French, English, Spanish; summaries in Norwegian, English, German) 1970. a. Kr.260. (Foundation for Promoting International Economic Information, SZ) Kompass Norge A-S, Steinkargt. 10, N-4000 Stavanger, Norway (Dist. in the U.S. by: Croner Publications, Inc. 211-03 Jamaica Ave., Queens Village, NY 11428) adv. circ. 5,000.

670   SZ   ISSN 0075-6717
KOMPASS SCHWEIZ/LIECHTENSTEIN; informationswerk der Schweizerischen. Wirtschaft. (Text in French, German, Italian; classifications in German, French, English, Spanish, Italian; summaries in Germar, French, and English) 1947. a. $78. (Foundation for Promoting International Economic Information) Kompass International AG, Neuhausstrasse 4, CH-8044 Zurich, Switzerland (Dist. in the U.S. and Canada by: Croner Publications, Inc., 211-03 Jamaica Ave., Queens Village, NY 11428) adv. circ. 7,800.

380   FR
KOMPASS SPECIAL SERVICES. 1934? a. Societe Nouvelle d'Editions pour l'Industrie, 22 Ave. F.D. Roosevelt, 75008 Paris, France.

670   SW   ISSN 0075-6725
KOMPASS SVERIGE; handbok oever Sveriges industri og Naeringsliv. (Text in Swedish; classifications in Swedish, English, French, German, Spanish; summaries in Swedish, English, German) 1958. a. Kr.110($78) (Foundation for Promoting International Economic Information, SZ) Kompass Sweden, Malmvaegen 80, S-191 04 Sollentuna, Sweden (Dist. in U.S. and Canada by: Croner Publications, Inc., 211-03 Jamaica Ave., Queens Village, NY 11428)

670 687   FR
KOMPASS TEXTILE ET HABILLEMENT. (Text and Summaries in English, French, German and Spanish) 1974. a. 250 F. Societe Nouvelle d'Editions pour l'Industrie, 22 Ave. F.D. Roosevelt, 75008 Paris, France. adv. illus.

670   UK
KOMPASS UNITED KINGDOM; register of British industry and commerce. (Text in English; classifications in English, French, German, Italian, Spanish) 1962. a. £60. Kompass Publishers Ltd., Windsor Court, East Grinstead House, East Grinstead, West Sussex RH19 1XD, England. (Co-publisher: Confederation of British Industry) adv. circ. 9,000.
Formerly: Kompass United Kingdom/CBI (ISSN 0075-6733)

380   DK   ISSN 0302-5403
KONGERIGET DANMARKS HANDELS-KALENDER. 1883. a. Kr.95. Postbox 240, Moellergade 19, 5700 Svendborg, Denmark.

338   PH
KONTAKS. (Supplement to Philippines Business Directory) a. P.60($10) Philippines Business Directory, Box 3199, Manila, Philippines. adv.

380 659   KO
KOREA ANNUAL. Korean edition: Hapdong Yongam (ISSN 0073-0335) (Text in Korean) 1958. a. $12. Hapdong News Agency, 108-4, Soosong-Dong, Chongro-Ku, Box Kwangwhamoon 145, Seoul, S. Korea. Ed. Park Yong-kon. circ. 16,000.

380 659   KO   ISSN 0075-6814
KOREA DIRECTORY. 1958. a. Korea Directory Co., P.O. Box 242 Kwanghwamoon, Seoul, S. Korea.

338   DK
KRAK; industrial and trade directory for Denmark. (Issued in 5 vols.) 1790. a. Kr.405. Kraks Legat, Nytorv 17, DK-1450 Copenhagen K, Denmark. Ed. M. Handest. adv. circ. 15,000.

670   LE   ISSN 0075-8353
LEBANESE INDUSTRIAL AND COMMERCIAL DIRECTORY/ANNUAIRE DES PROFESSIONS AU LIBAN. (Text in French; index in Arabic, English and French) 1953. biennial. $15, Middle East Commercial Information Center, P.O. Box 6466, Beirut, Lebanon (Dist. by UNIPUB, 345 Park Ave. South, New York, NY 10010) Ed. Charles G. Gedeon. adv. circ. 10,000.

382.025   LB
LIBERIAN TRADE DIRECTORY; basic trade information, exporters & importers. irreg. Ministry of Commerce, Industry and Transportation, Director of Foreign Trade, Box 9041, Monrovia, Liberia.

666   US
LITTLE BLACK BOOK; annual directory of ceramic mold manufacturers in the United States. 1973. a. $1.95. Daisy Publishing Co. , Inc, 429 Boren Ave. N., Seattle, WA 98109. Ed. Dale Swant. adv. circ. 9,000.

670   UK
LONDON DIRECTORY OF INDUSTRY AND COMMERCE. a. $45. Kemp's Group (Printers & Publishers) Ltd., 1-5 Bath St., London EC1V 9QA, England. adv.
    Former titles: London Directory; Trades Register of London (ISSN 0082-5808)

380   UK
LONDON DIRECTORY OF INDUSTRY & COMMERCE. a. Publishing and Distributing Co. Ltd., 177 Regent St., London W.1., England.

LONDON SHIPPING CONTACTS. see *TRANSPORTATION — Ships And Shipping*

380   US   ISSN 0190-129X
LOUISIANA STATE INDUSTRIAL DIRECTORY. a. $25. State Industrial Directories Corp., Two Penn Plaza, New York, NY 10001.

380   AU   ISSN 0076-2105
MADE IN AUSTRIA. (Text in German, French, and English) 1966. a. S.400. Jupiter Verlag GmbH, Robertgasse 2, A-1020 Vienna, Austria. index.

670   TI
MADE IN TUNISIA; guide des industries tunisiennes. 1974. biennial. $30. Ceres Productions, 6 Ave Montplaisir, Tunis, Tunisia. adv. circ. 10,000.

338   FR
MAFOGRA. 1963. a. 156.10 F. Societe des Editions de l' Imprimerie Nouvelle, 89, rue Barrault, 75013 Paris, France. Ed. M. Mauduit. circ. 6,000.

MAGAZINE INDUSTRY MARKET PLACE; the directory of American periodical publishing. see *PUBLISHING AND BOOK TRADE*

338   US   ISSN 0145-9007
MAINE MARKETING DIRECTORY. 1965. a. $5. State Development Office, Desk MMD, State House, Augusta, ME 04333.
    Formerly: Directory of Maine Manufacturers.

338   US   ISSN 0098-6194
MAINE STATE INDUSTRIAL DIRECTORY. 1974. biennial. $20. State Industrial Directories Corp., 2 Penn Plaza, New York, NY 10001.

670   US
MAINE, VERMONT AND NEW HAMPSHIRE DIRECTORY OF MANUFACTURERS. 1979? biennial? Commerce Register, Inc., 213 First St., Ho-Ho-Kus, NJ 07423.

382   UK
MAJOR COMPANIES OF BRAZIL, MEXICO AND VENEZUELA. 1979/80. a. £52. Graham & Trotman Ltd., 14 Clifford St., London W1X 1RD, England. Ed. S. J. Longrigg.

382   UK
MAJOR COMPANIES OF NIGERIA. 1979. a. £30. Graham & Trotman Ltd., 14 Clifford St., London W1X 1RD, England. Ed. M. Lawn.

382   UK
MAJOR COMPANIES OF THE ARAB WORLD. 1977. a. £52. Graham & Trotman Ltd., 14 Clifford St., London W1X 1RD, England. Ed. G. C. Bricault.

381 060   MM
MALTA CHAMBER OF COMMERCE. TRADE DIRECTORY. a. $4.20. Malta Chamber of Commerce, The Exchange, Republic St., Valletta, Malta. Ed. Joseph G. Vassallo. adv. circ. 1,500.
    Former titles: Malta Trade Directory (ISSN 0076-3446); Malta Chamber of Commerce Classified Directory.

650   US   ISSN 0076-4213
MANUFACTURERS' AGENTS' GUIDE. 1956. biennial. $29.95. ‡ Manufacturers' Agent Publishing Co., Inc., 663 Fifth Ave., New York, NY 10022. Ed. E.K. Sharp.

670   US
MANUFACTURING DIRECTORY OF IDAHO. 1972. biennial. $30. University of Idaho, Center for Business Development and Research, College of Business and Economics, Moscow, ID 83843. Ed. George M. Armstrong. circ. 1,275. (also avail. in microfiche)

384   US   ISSN 0076-4418
MARCONI'S INTERNATIONAL REGISTER; international cable address directory. 1898. a. $55. Telegraphic Cable & Radio Registrations, Inc., 1600 Harrison Ave., Mamaroneck, NY 10543. Ed. L.G. Smith, Jr. adv. index. circ. controlled.

380   US   ISSN 0148-5660
MARYLAND STATE INDUSTRIAL DIRECTORY. a. $35. State Industrial Directories Corp., Two Penn Plaza, New York, NY 10001.

670   US
MASSACHUSETTS DIRECTORY OF MANUFACTURERS. 1981? biennial? Commerce Register, Inc., 213 First St., Ho-Ho-Kus, NJ 07423.

380   US   ISSN 0148-7558
MASSACHUSETTS STATE INDUSTRIAL DIRECTORY. a. $57. State Industrial Directories Corp., Two Penn Plaza, New York, NY 10001.

MEDICAL PRODUCT OF JAPAN; directory of medical equipment. see *MEDICAL SCIENCES*

960   MR
MEMENTO THERAPEUTIQUE DU MAROC. a. $8. Johanny Peillon, B.P. 5054, Dakar-Fann, Morocco.

960   MR
MEMENTO THERAPEUTIQUE DU TUNISIE. a. $8. Johanny Peillon, B.P. 5054, Dakar-Fann, Morocco.

960   MR
MEMENTO THERAPEUTIQUE POUR L'AFRIQUE NOIRE FRANCOPHONE. a. Johanny Peillon, B.P. 5054, Dakar-Fann, Morocco.

METAL & ENGINEERING INDUSTRY YEAR BOOK. see *ENGINEERING*

380   US   ISSN 0190-1338
MICHIGAN STATE INDUSTRIAL DIRECTORY. a. $70. State Industrial Directories Corp., Two Penn Plaza, New York, NY 10001.

382   JA
MIDDLE EAST TRADER & COMPANY DIRECTORY. 1977. a. Johnan Co. Ltd., No. 2 1-chome, Kyobashi, Chuo-ku, Tokyo, Japan.

633   US
MILLING DIRECTORY/BUYERS GUIDE. 1973. a. $15. Sosland Publishing Co., 4800 Main St., Kansas City, MO 64112. Ed. Morton I. Sosland. stat. circ. 9,200.
    Former titles: Milling and Grain Directory; Directory of Mills and Milling Executives.

380   US   ISSN 0195-7112
MINNESOTA STATE INDUSTRIAL DIRECTORY. a. $50. State Industrial Directories Corp., Two Penn Plaza, New York, NY 10001.

380.1   US
MINORITY SUPPLIES REPORT & DIRECTORY; industrial reference guide of minority businesses in the U.S. 1971. a. Project Magazine Inc., P.O. Box 8214, Philadelphia, PA 19101. Ed. Emory Washington.

380   US   ISSN 0190-1346
MISSISSIPPI STATE INDUSTRIAL DIRECTORY. a. $25. State Industrial Directories Corp., Two Penn Plaza, New York, NY 10001.

380   US
MISSOURI STATE INDUSTRIAL DIRECTORY. a. $47. State Industrial Directories Corp., Two Penn Plaza, New York, NY 10001.

380   US   ISSN 0195-7120
MONTANA STATE INDUSTRIAL DIRECTORY. biennial. $25. State Industrial Directories Corp., Two Penn Plaza, New York, NY 10001.

380   UK
MOTOR TRADER DIRECTORY. 1975. biennial. £5($13) I P C Transport Press Ltd., Dorset House, Stamford Street, London, SE1, England. Ed. C. Goffey. adv. circ. 5,000. (also avail. in microfilm)
    Supersedes: Trader Handbook (ISSN 0082-5794)

338.8   US   ISSN 0363-4426
MULTINATIONAL MARKETING & EMPLOYMENT DIRECTORY. 7th edt., 1977. irreg. $150. World Trade Academy Press, Inc., 50 East 42nd St., New York, NY 10017.
    Formed by the Merger of Angel's National Directory of Personnel Managers & Multinational Corporations Operating Overseas & National & International Employment Handbook for Specialized Personnel.

380   US
N A S C O CAMPUS CO-OP DIRECTORY. 1974. biennial. $1.50. North American Students of Cooperation, Box 7293, Ann Arbor, MI 48107. Ed. Margaret Lamb. adv. circ. 5,000.
    Formerly: Cooperatives in Campus Areas of North America.

959.5   MY
N S T DIRECTORY OF MALAYSIA. (Text in English) 1974. a. M.$36. New Straits Times Press (Malaysia) Berhad, 31 Jalan Riong, Kuala Lumpur 22-03, Malaysia. adv. bk. rev. circ. 3,000.
    Formerly: Straits Times Directory of Malaysia; Supersedes in part: Straits Times Directory of Malaysia and Singapore (ISSN 0585-3931)

NATIONAL APPAREL SUPPLIERS AND CONTRACTORS DIRECTORY. see *CLOTHING TRADE*

NATIONAL ASSOCIATION OF WASTE DISPOSAL CONTRACTORS. TRADE DIRECTORY. see *PUBLIC HEALTH AND SAFETY*

320   US   ISSN 0095-3113
NATIONAL DIRECTORY OF STATE AGENCIES. biennial. $65.15. Information Resources Press, 1700 N. Moore St., Ste. 700, Arlington, VA 22209.

NATIONAL METALWORKING BLUE BOOK. see *METALLURGY*

380   US
NEBRASKA STATE INDUSTRIAL DIRECTORY. biennial. $20. State Industrial Directories Corp., Two Penn Plaza, New York, NY 10001.

380   US   ISSN 0195-7139
NEVADA STATE INDUSTRIAL DIRECTORY. a. $15. State Industrial Directories Corp., Two Penn Plaza, New York, NY 10001.

NEW BRUNSWICK CONSTRUCTION PRODUCTS DIRECTORY. see *BUILDING AND CONSTRUCTION*

338   US   ISSN 0098-6216
NEW HAMPSHIRE STATE INDUSTRIAL DIRECTORY. 1972. biennial. $20. State Industrial Directories Corp., 2 Penn Plaza, New York, NY 10001.

670   US
NEW JERSEY DIRECTORY OF MANUFACTURERS. 1979. a. $60. Commerce Register, Inc, 213 First St., Ho-Ho-Kus, NY 07423. circ. 2,000.

338   US   ISSN 0098-6224
NEW JERSEY STATE INDUSTRIAL DIRECTORY. 1901. a. $90. State Industrial Directories Corp., 2 Penn Plaza, New York, NY 10001. Ed. J.E. Smith. stat. circ. 10,000.

380   US
NEW MEXICO STATE INDUSTRIAL DIRECTORY. biennial. $25. State Industrial Directories Corp., Two Penn Plaza, New York, NY 10001.

NEW YORK PRODUCTION MANUAL; for motion pictures, television commercials and videotape industries. see *MOTION PICTURES*

NEW YORK STATE BUSINESS FACT BOOK. PART 1: BUSINESS AND MANUFACTURING. see *BUSINESS AND ECONOMICS — Economic Situation And Conditions*

NEW YORK STATE BUSINESS FACT BOOK. SUPPLEMENT. see *BUSINESS AND ECONOMICS — Economic Situation And Conditions*

BUSINESS AND ECONOMICS — TRADE AND INDUSTRIAL DIRECTORIES

338   US   ISSN 0548-9067
NEW YORK STATE INDUSTRIAL DIRECTORY. 1963? a. $95. State Industrial Directories Corp., 2 Penn Plaza, New York, NY 10001. stat.

650   NZ   ISSN 0077-9571
NEW ZEALAND BUSINESS WHO'S WHO. 1935. a. NZ.$35. F E P Productions Ltd., Box 9143, Wellington, New Zealand.

381.45   NZ
NEW ZEALAND WHOLE EARTH CATALOGUE. 1972. a. NZ.$5.95. ‡ Alister Taylor, Ed. & Pub., Whole Earth Mail Order Dept., Box 87, Martinborough, New Zealand. bk. rev. illus. circ. 20,000.

330   CN
NEWFOUNDLAND & LABRADOR BUSINESS DIRECTORY. 1936. a. Maritime Directories Inc., Box 2039, St. Johns, Nfld., Canada. Ed. Eric MacEwan. adv.

381   NR   ISSN 0078-057X
NIGERIA ANNUAL AND TRADING DIRECTORY.* a. O A B Press Service Ltd., P.O. Box 802, Lagos, Nigeria.

381   NR   ISSN 0078-0596
NIGERIA BUSINESS DIRECTORY.* 1967. a. 7 Coates Street, Ebute-Metta, Lagos, Nigeria.

380.1   338   NO   ISSN 0078-1215
NORGES HANDELS-KALENDER/NORWEGIAN DIRECTORY OF COMMERCE/ANNUAIRE DU COMMERCE DU NORVEGE/NORWEGISCHE HANDELS-ADRESSBUCH; adressbok for handel, handverk og industri. (Text in Norwegian; explanations and headings in English, French and German) 1878. a. Kr.400($80) S.M. Bryde Forlag, Tordenskjoldsgate 4, Oslo 1, Norway (Dist. in U.S. by: International Publications Service, 114 E. 32nd St., New York, NY 10016) adv. circ. 8,000.

670   US
NORTH AMERICAN MANUFACTURERS & SUPPLIERS DIRECTORY. 1978. a. $35. Comtrade Corp., 4897 Chateau Dr., Box 178406, San Diego, CA 92117. Ed. Bernard L. Haas. adv. circ. 5,000.

338   US
NORTH CAROLINA METALWORKING DIRECTORY. 1975. triennial. $10. North Carolina State University, Industrial Extension Service, Box 5506, Raleigh, NC 27650. Ed. Robert L. Edwards. circ. 1,000.

380   US   ISSN 0161-4738
NORTH CAROLINA STATE INDUSTRIAL DIRECTORY. a. $60. State Industrial Directories Corp., Two Penn Plaza, New York, NY 10001.

380   US
NORTH DAKOTA STATE INDUSTRIAL DIRECTORY. biennial. $15. State Industrial Directories Corp., Two Penn Plaza, New York, NY 10001.

O'DWYERS DIRECTORY OF PUBLIC RELATIONS FIRMS. see *ADVERTISING AND PUBLIC RELATIONS*

380   US
OHIO STATE INDUSTRIAL DIRECTORY. a. $70. State Industrial Directories Corp., Two Penn Plaza, New York, NY 10001.

OIL DIRECTORY OF ALASKA. see *PETROLEUM AND GAS*

OIL DIRECTORY OF CANADA. see *PETROLEUM AND GAS*

OIL DIRECTORY OF COMPANIES OUTSIDE THE U.S. AND CANADA. see *PETROLEUM AND GAS*

OIL DIRECTORY OF HOUSTON, TEXAS. see *PETROLEUM AND GAS*

338   US
OKLAHOMA DIRECTORY OF MANUFACTURERS AND PRODUCTS. Cover title: Oklahoma Directory of Manufacturers. 1957. biennial. $20. Department of Industrial Development, Box 53424, Oklahoma City, OK 73152. Ed. Lee Zimmerman. circ. 3,500.

380   US
OKLAHOMA STATE INDUSTRIAL DIRECTORY. a. $35. State Industrial Directories Corp., Two Penn Plaza, New York, NY 10001.

380   US   ISSN 0195-7147
OREGON STATE INDUSTRIAL DIRECTORY. a. $30. State Industrial Directories Corp., Two Penn Plaza, New York, NY 10001.

380   UK
OVERSEAS TRADE DIRECTORIES. 1947. approx. biennial or triennial. £17($10) Publishing and Distributing Co. Ltd., Mitre House, 177 Regent St., London W.1., England. Ed. H.R. Vaughan. adv. circ. 5,000. (also avail. in microfilm from UMI)

380.1   PK
PAKISTAN BUSINESS AND SHOPPING GUIDE. (Text in English) 1973. a. Rs.25($5) Maulai Enterprise, J-6/2 al-Naseer, Federal B Area, Block No. 1, Off Sir Shah Sulaiman Rd., Karachi 19, Pakistan. Ed. Syed Wali Ahmad Maulai. adv. stat. circ. 5,000. (back issues avail.)

670   US
PENNSYLVANIA DIRECTORY OF MANUFACTURERS. 1980? biennial? Commerce Register, Inc., 213 First St., Ho-Ho-Kus, NJ 07423.

382   US   ISSN 0360-8859
PENNSYLVANIA EXPORTERS DIRECTORY. Cover title: Pennsylvania Exporters. 1966. a. free. ‡ Department of Commerce, Bureau of Statistics, Research and Planning, 630B Health & Welfare Bldg., Harrisburg, PA 17120. Ed. W. Ronald Kresge. circ. 1,000.
Formerly: Pennsylvania Manufacturing Exporters (ISSN 0091-6129)

338   US   ISSN 0553-6065
PENNSYLVANIA STATE INDUSTRIAL DIRECTORY. 1969. a. $90. State Industrial Directories Corp., 2 Penn Plaza, New York, NY 10001. stat. tr.lit.

PHILIPPINE EXPORT DIRECTORY. see *BUSINESS AND ECONOMICS — International Commerce*

338   PH
PHILIPPINES BUSINESS DIRECTORY. a. P.150($30) Philippines Business Directory, Box 3199, Manila, Philippines. adv.

380.1   US
POOL & SPA NEWS DIRECTORY. 1968. a. $9.50. Leisure Publications, Inc., 3923 W. 6 St., Los Angeles, CA 90020. Ed. Irene F. Coupe. circ. 10,000.
Formerly: Pool News Directory.

382   US
PORTUGUESE-AMERICAN BUSINESS REVIEW/ DIRECTORY. 1979. a. $25. (Portugal-U.S. Chamber of Commerce, Inc.) Motivational Communications, Inc., 175 Fifth Ave., New York, NY 10010. Ed. Barry V. Conforte. adv. stat. circ. 50,000.

PROCESS ENGINEERING DIRECTORY. see *ENGINEERING — Chemical Engineering*

382   670   SP   ISSN 0079-5836
PRODEI; catalogue of Spanish Manufacturers, Exporters and Importers. (Text and summaries in Spanish, English, French and German) 1945. biennial. $63. Almirante 21, Madrid 4, Spain. Ed. Jose Capel Alvarez. adv. circ. 10,000.

650   338   II   ISSN 0079-5925
PROFESSIONAL AND TRADE ORGANISATIONS IN INDIA. 1963. irreg., latest 1982. Rs.30($10) Kothari Publications, 12 India Exchange Place, Calcutta 700001, India. Ed. H. Kothari. adv.

070.5   US   ISSN 0000-0671
PUBLISHERS, DISTRIBUTORS AND WHOLESALERS OF THE UNITED STATES. 1979. a. R.R. Bowker Company, 1180 Ave. of the Americas, New York, NY 10036 (Orders to Box 1807, Ann Arbor, MI 48106).
Formerly: Publishers and Distributors of the United States (ISSN 0000-0620)

338   PR   ISSN 0090-3612
PUERTO RICO OFFICIAL INDUSTRIAL DIRECTORY. 1966. a. $60. (Economic Development Administration) Witcom Group, 210 Ponce de Leon Ave., San Juan, PR 00901 (U.S. Distrib: Dun & Bradstreet International, Box 3224 Church St. Sta., New York, NY 10008) adv. stat.

PULP & PAPER BUYERS GUIDE. see *PAPER AND PULP*

650   FR   ISSN 0079-9270
QUI VEND ET ACHETE QUOI; annuaire economique de Haute Normandie. 1970. a. 120 F. Chambre Regionale de Commerce et d'Industrie de Haute-Normandie, Palais des Consuls, Quai de la Bourse, Rouen, France. circ. 3,000.

382   SP
QUIEN VENDE EN ESPANA LOS PRODUCTOS EXTRANJEROS/WHO SELLS FOREIGN PRODUCTS IN SPAIN. 1966. biennial. 1500 ptas. Prointer-Ediciones, Puerta del Sol 11, Madrid, Spain.

629.04   US   ISSN 0098-9215
RADIO CONTROL BUYERS GUIDE. Title varies: R C Buyers Guide. 1975. a. $7.50. Boynton & Associates, Clifton House, Clifton, VA 22024.

338   UK
REGISTER OF DEFUNCT & OTHER COMPANIES. a. £5. I P C Business Press Ltd., 33-40 Bowling Green Lane, London EC1R 0NE, England. adv. circ. 1,200.

670   FR   ISSN 0337-5714
REPERTOIRE GENERAL DE LA PRODUCTION FRANCAISE. Variant title: Kompass France. (Text in French; classifications and summaries in French, English, German, Spanish) 1923. a. 1000 F. Societe Nouvelle d'Editions pour l'Industrie, 22 Avenue Franklin D. Roosevelt, 75008 Paris, France. adv. illus. circ. 10,000. (also avail. in magnetic tape)
Formerly: Annuaire Industriel. Repertoire Generale de la Production Francaise (ISSN 0075-6652)
General economic and financial information on 55,000 French firms and 14,000 foreign. Includes trademarks

380   US   ISSN 0148-5679
RHODE ISLAND STATE INDUSTRIAL DIRECTORY. biennial. $20. State Industrial Directories Corp., Two Penn Plaza, New York, NY 10001.

ROUTES; directory of International Freighting Services. see *TRANSPORTATION*

650   SW
S T C MATRIKEL. 1941. a. Kr.5.90. Sveriges Trae- och Byggvaruhandlares Centralfoerbund - Federation of Swedish Timber- and Buildings Material Merchants, Box 14019, 104 40 Stockholm 14, Sweden. Ed. Roland Kindblom. adv. circ. 1,400.

380.1   US
SAUDI ARABIA TRADE DIRECTORY. irreg. $125. Inter-Crescent Publishing Co., Inc., Box 8481, Dallas, TX 75205.

380   UK   ISSN 0080-8148
SCOTTISH NATIONAL REGISTER OF CLASSIFIED TRADES. 1938. a. £12. Sell's Publications Ltd., 39 East St., Epsom KT17 1BQ, Surrey, England. bk. rev. circ. 3,000.

380   CN
SCOTT'S TRADE DIRECTORY OF METROPOLITAN TORONTO. 1980. irreg. Can.$99. Scott's Industrial Directories, 75 Thomas St., Oakville, Ont. L6J 3A3, Canada.

SECURITY PRODUCTS AND SERVICES INDEX. see *CRIMINOLOGY AND LAW ENFORCEMENT*

338   UK
SELL'S DIRECTORY. 1885. a. £20. Sell's Publications Ltd., Sell's House, 39 East St., Epsom KT17 1BQ, Surrey, England. adv. bk. rev. circ. 7,000.
Former titles: Sell's Directory of Products & Services (ISSN 0080-8725); Sell's Directory of British Industry and Commerce.

BUSINESS AND ECONOMICS — TRADE AND INDUSTRIAL DIRECTORIES

338 UK
SIGN MAKERS AND SUPPLIERS YEAR BOOK AND DIRECTORY. 1971. a. £2.80. A. E. Morgan Publications Ltd., 172 Kingston Rd., Ewell, Epsom, Surrey KT19 0SB, England. adv. illus. index.

330 SI
SINGAPORE BUSINESS YEARBOOK. (Text in English) 1972. a. S.$6. Times Periodicals Private Ltd., 422 Thomson Rd., Singapore 1129, Singapore. adv. circ. 6,500.
Formerly: Singapore Trade & Industry Yearbook.

382 SI
SINGAPORE INDIAN CHAMBER OF COMMERCE. DIRECTORY. (Text in English) a. S.$7. Singapore Indian Chamber of Commerce, 55-a, Robinson Road, Box 1038, Singapore, Singapore.

SKANDINAVISKE SKIPSREDERIER/YEARBOOK OF SCANDINAVIAN SHIPOWNERS. see TRANSPORTATION — Ships And Shipping

338 PK
SMAR'S INDUSTRIAL DIRECTORY OF PAKISTAN. (Text in English) 1971. a. Rs.25($20) Smar International, 6 Afshan Chambers, Tariq Rd., P.E.C.H.S., Karachi 29, Pakistan. Ed. Mahmud-Ul-Hassan. adv. circ. 5,000.

SOCIALIST SHIPPING CONTACTS. see TRANSPORTATION — Ships And Shipping

380 US ISSN 0162-0878
SOUTH CAROLINA STATE INDUSTRIAL DIRECTORY. a. $30. State Industrial Directories Corp., Two Penn Plaza, New York, NY 10001.

380 US
SOUTH DAKOTA STATE INDUSTRIAL DIRECTORY. biennial. $15. State Industrial Directories Corp., Two Penn Plaza, New York, NY 10001.

SPORTSGUIDE FOR INDIVIDUAL SPORTS; the master reference for individual sports marketing. see SPORTS AND GAMES

SPORTSGUIDE FOR TEAM SPORTS; the master reference for team sports marketing. see SPORTS AND GAMES

STANDARD DIRECTORY OF ADVERTISERS. see ADVERTISING AND PUBLIC RELATIONS

380 US
STATE INDUSTRIAL DIRECTORIES. CHICAGO GEOGRAPHIC EDITION. biennial. $55. State Industrial Directories Corp., Two Penn Plaza, New York, NY 10001.

STORES AND SHOPS RETAIL DIRECTORY. see BUSINESS AND ECONOMICS — Marketing And Purchasing

STORES OF THE WORLD DIRECTORY. see BUSINESS AND ECONOMICS — Marketing And Purchasing

STOWAGE AND SEGREGATION TO I M D G CODE. see TRANSPORTATION — Ships And Shipping

959.5 SI
STRAITS TIMES DIRECTORY OF SINGAPORE. Variant title: S T Directory of Singapore. (Text in English) a. S.$40. Times Periodicals Private Ltd., 422 Thomson Rd., Singapore 1129, Singapore. adv. bk. rev. circ. 3,000.
Supersedes in part: Straits Times Directory of Malaysia and Singapore (ISSN 0585-3931)

380 UK
STUBBS DIRECTORY; professional and commercial products and services. 1879. a. £27.50. Dun & Bradstreet Ltd., 6-8 Bonhill St., London EC2A 4BU, England. adv. circ. 3,500. (also avail. in magnetic tape)
Formerly (until 1979): Stubbs Buyers Guide (ISSN 0081-6043)

670 FI
SUOMEN TEOLLISUUSLIITTO. JASENLUETTELO/FINLANDS INDUSTRIFOERBUND. MEDLEMSFOERTECKNING/FEDERATION OF FINNISH INDUSTRIES. LIST OF MEMBERS. (Text in English, Finnish and Swedish) irreg. Suomen Teollisuusliitto, Etelaranta 10, PL 220, 00131 Helsinki 13, Finland.

SURPLUS DEALERS DIRECTORY. see BUSINESS AND ECONOMICS — Marketing And Purchasing

678.2 668.4 FR ISSN 0224-2435
SYNDICAT GENERAL DES COMMERCES ET INDUSTRIES DU CAOUTCHOUC ET DES PLASTIQUES. GUIDE. 1978. biennial. 80 F. Syndicat General du Caoutchouc et des Plastiques, 112 Bd. Hausmann, 75008 Paris, France. Ed. P. Mercier. circ. 3,000.

338 670 CH ISSN 0082-1470
TAIWAN BUYERS' GUIDE; alphabetical and classified lists of 12000 Taiwan manufacturers, importers, exporters and services. (Editions in Chinese and English) 1958. a. China Productivity Center, P.O. Box 769, 62 Sining South Road, Taipei, Taiwan, Republic of China. Ed. Chauncey Bee. adv. bk. rev. circ. 20,000.

328 CH
TAIWAN EXPORTERS GUIDE. (Text in Chinese, English and Spanish) 1977. a. $30. Taiwan Enterprise Press, Box 73-74, Taipei, Taiwan, Republic of China. Ed. Henry K. C. Lee. adv. bk. rev. circ. 20,000.

382 CH
TAIWAN TRADE DIRECTORY. (Text in Chinese and English) 1963. a. Importers & Exporters Association of Taipei, Box 598, Taipei 104, Taiwan, Republic of China.

338 670 TZ
TANZANIA. BUREAU OF STATISTICS. DIRECTORY OF INDUSTRIES. (Not published 1972-1974) 1968. irreg., latest 1975. Bureau of Statistics, Box 796, Dar es Salaam, Tanzania (Orders to: Government Publications Agency, Box 1801, Dar es Salaam, Tanzania)

338 TZ ISSN 0564-724X
TANZANIA DIRECTORY OF TRADES. 1969. irreg. Shamrock Agencies, Box 977, Moshi, Tanzania.

670 AT
TASMANIAN MANUFACTURERS DIRECTORY. 1978. irreg. Department of Industrial Development, Box 1336n, Hobart, Tas. 7001, Australia.

380 UK
TELEKOMPASS. 1969. a. £8. Kompass Publishers Ltd., Windsor Court, East Grinstead House, East Grinstead, West Sussex RH19 1XD, England.
Formerly: Dial Industry.

380 US ISSN 0190-1311
TENNESSEE STATE INDUSTRIAL DIRECTORY. a. $30. State Industrial Directories Corp., Two Penn Plaza, New York, NY 10001.

380 US
TEXAS STATE INDUSTRIAL DIRECTORY. biennial. $70. State Industrial Directories Corp., Two Penn Plaza, New York, NY 10001.

650 US
TEXAS TRADE AND PROFESSIONAL ASSOCIATIONS AND OTHER SELECTED ORGANIZATIONS. 1951. a. $4.50. University of Texas at Austin, Bureau of Business Research, Austin, TX 78712. Ed. Rita Wright.
Formerly: Selected Trade and Professional Associations in Texas (ISSN 0080-8644)

380 II
THACKER'S CALCUTTA DIRECTORY; including Calcutta's Who's Who. (Text in English) 43rd ed., 1975. a. Rs.30($4) Thacker's Press & Directories, 6B Bentinck St., Calcutta 700001, India.
Business, commercial, educational, legal, government and legislative information pertaining to Calcutta and West Bengal

380.1 TH ISSN 0563-3400
THAI CHAMBER OF COMMERCE. BUSINESS DIRECTORY. (Text in English) irreg. $13. Thai Chamber of Commerce., 150 Rajbopitre Road, Bangkok, Thailand. Ed. Phensri Hiraniri. illus.

380.1 II
THAPAR'S INDIAN INDUSTRIAL DIRECTORY AND IMPORT AND EXPORT DIRECTORY OF THE WORLD. (Text in English) a. $60. Thapar International Industrial Information Services, Giriraj Bldg., 1st Floor, Flat E, 11, Altamount Rd, Cumballa Hill, Bombay 400026, India. Ed. Yash Pal Thapar. adv. circ. 50,000.
Formerly: Calcutta Market.

THOMAS REGISTER OF AMERICAN MANUFACTURERS AND THOMAS REGISTER CATALOG FILE. see BUSINESS AND ECONOMICS — Marketing And Purchasing

381 IE ISSN 0082-4224
THOM'S COMMERCIAL DIRECTORY. 1844. a. $40. Thom's Directories Ltd., 38 Merrion Square, Dublin 2, Ireland. Ed. J. L. Wootton, Snr.

380.1 674 UK ISSN 0082-4372
TIMBER TRADES DIRECTORY. 1890. irreg. £28. Benn Publications Ltd., 25 New Street Square, London EC4A 3JA, England. Ed. John Topham. adv. index. circ. 2,000.
Classified lists of firms engaged in timber and allied trades throughout the world

338 NR
TIMES TRADE AND INDUSTRIAL DIRECTORY. 1972. irreg. £N2.10. Daily Times of Nigeria Ltd., Box 139, Lagos, Nigeria. illus.

380.1 NP
TRADE AND INDUSTRIAL DIRECTORY OF NEPAL. (Text in English) 1972-1973. a. Adri Trade Link, 355 Gucha Tole, Kathmandu, Nepal. illus.

650 US ISSN 0082-5689
TRADE ASSOCIATIONS AND PROFESSIONAL BODIES OF THE UNITED KINGDOM. 1962. irreg., 6th edt. 1976. price varies. Pergamon Press, Inc., Maxwell House, Fairview Park, Elmsford, NY 10523.

382 UK
TRADE DIRECTORY OF GUYANA. 1974. a. £1.50. Diplomatic Press & Publishing Co., 44-46 South Ealing Rd., London W.5, England.

382 UK ISSN 0082-5697
TRADE DIRECTORY OF MALTA. 1965. a. £1($1.50) Diplomatic Press & Publishing Co., 44-46 South Ealing Rd., London W.5, England. Ed. Harry Richter.

382 UK
TRADE DIRECTORY OF PAPUA NEW GUINEA. a. £1.50. Diplomatic Press & Publishing Co., 44-46 South Ealing Rd., London W.5, England.

380.1 SE
TRADE DIRECTORY OF SEYCHELLES. 1976. a. $7.25. Express Transport Company Ltd., Box 239, Mahe, Seychelles. charts. illus. stat.

382 UK ISSN 0082-5735
TRADE DIRECTORY OF THE REPUBLIC OF THE SUDAN. 1957-58. a. £2.50. Diplomatic Press & Publishing Co., 44-46 South Ealing Rd., London W.5, England. Ed. Arthur H. Thrower.

382.6 II ISSN 0082-5824
TRADO; ASIAN-AFRICAN DIRECTORY OF EXPORTERS, IMPORTERS AND MANUFACTURERS. (Text in English) 1956. a. $50. Trado Publications Pvt. Ltd., C-6 Safdarjung Development Area, Community Center, New Delhi 110016, India (Dist. by International Publications Service, 114 E. 32nd St., New York, N.Y. 10016) Ed. R. K. Chug. adv. index. circ. 10,000.

380.1 TR
TRINIDAD AND TOBAGO DIRECTORY OF COMMERCE, INDUSTRY & TOURISM. 1972. irreg. International Publications Ltd., 17 Queen's Park West, Port-of-Spain, Trinidad and Tobago. illus.

382   UK   ISSN 0082-657X
TRINIDAD AND TOBAGO TRADE DIRECTORY.
1963-64. a. £1.50. Diplomatic Press & Publishing Co., 44-46 South Ealing Rd., London W.5, England. Ed. Harry Richter. index.

TRY US; national minority business directory. see *BUSINESS AND ECONOMICS*

338   TU   ISSN 0082-6952
TURKISH TRADE DIRECTORY & TELEX INDEX/TURK TICARET REHBERI VE TELEKS INDEKS. (Text in Turkish and English) 1963. irreg., 7th edt., 1978. $45. Constante Basin Ajansi, Peykhane Caddesi No. 14, Cemberlitas, Istanbul, Turkey.

670   UK   ISSN 0082-7142
U K TRADE NAMES. 1966. biennial. £35. Kompass Publishers Ltd., Windsor Court, East Grinstead House, East Grinstead, West Sussex RH19 1XD, England. circ. 2,500.

650 338   AT
UNIVERSAL BUSINESS DIRECTORIES, ADELAIDE BUSINESS AND STREET DIRECTORY. 1942. a. Aus.$14.50. Universal Business Directories Pty.Ltd., 64 Talavera Rd., North Ryde, N.S.W. 2113, Australia. adv.
   Formerly: Universal Business Directories, Adelaide and South Australia Country Trade and Business Directory (ISSN 0083-3797)

650 338   AT
UNIVERSAL BUSINESS DIRECTORIES, BRISBANE AND SUBURBAN BUSINESS AND STREET DIRECTORY. 1934. a. Aus.$15. Universal Business Directories Pty.Ltd., 64 Talavera Rd., North Ryde, N.S.W. 2113, Australia. adv.
   Formerly: Universal Business Directories, Brisbane and Suburban Business and Trade Directory (ISSN 0083-369X)

650 338   AT   ISSN 0083-3746
UNIVERSAL BUSINESS DIRECTORIES MELBOURNE AND SUBURBAN BUSINESS AND TRADE DIRECTORY. 1948. a. Aus.$18. Universal Business Directories Pty. Ltd., 64 Talavera Rd., North Ryde, N.S.W. 2113, Australia. adv.

650 338   AT
UNIVERSAL BUSINESS DIRECTORIES, NEW SOUTH WALES BUSINESS AND STREET DIRECTORY. 1949. a. Aus.$50. Universal Business Directories Pty.Ltd., 64 Talavera Rd., North Ryde, N.S.W. 2113, Australia. adv.
   Formerly: Universal Business Directories, Combined New England, North and North West New South Wales Business and Trade Directory (ISSN 0083-3711)

650 338   AT
UNIVERSAL BUSINESS DIRECTORIES, NORTHERN QUEENSLAND BUSINESS AND STREET DIRECTORY. 1934. a. Aus.$20. Universal Business Directories Pty.Ltd., 64 Talavera Rd., North Ryde, N.S.W. 2113, Australia. adv.
   Formerly: Universal Business Directories, Northern Queensland Business and Trade Directory (ISSN 0083-3762)

650 338   AT   ISSN 0083-3789
UNIVERSAL BUSINESS DIRECTORIES PERTH AND FREMANTLE AND SUBURBS BUSINESS AND TRADE DIRECTORY.* 1960. a. Aus.$12.50. Universal Business Directories (WA) Pty. Ltd., 20 Milford St., East Victoria Park, W. Australia, Australia.

650 338   AT
UNIVERSAL BUSINESS DIRECTORIES, SOUTHERN QUEENSLAND BUSINESS AND STREET DIRECTORY. 1934. a. Aus.$12.50. Universal Business Directories Pty.Ltd., 64 Talavera Rd., North Ryde, N.S.W. 2113, Australia. adv.
   Formerly: Universal Business Directories, Southern Queensland Business and Trade Directory (ISSN 0083-3800)

338 650   AT
UNIVERSAL BUSINESS DIRECTORIES, SYDNEY AND SUBURBAN BUSINESS AND STREET DIRECTORY. 1948. a. Aus.$20. Universal Business Directories Pty.Ltd., 64 Talavera Rd., North Ryde, N.S.W. 2113, Australia. adv.
   Formerly: Universal Business Directories, Sydney and Suburban Business and Trade Directory (ISSN 0083-3819)

338 650   AT
UNIVERSAL BUSINESS DIRECTORIES, TASMANIA BUSINESS AND STREET DIRECTORY. 1950. a. Aus.$5. Universal Business Directories Pty.Ltd., 64 Talavera Rd., North Ryde, N.S.W. 2113, Australia. adv.
   Formerly: Universal Business Directories, Tasmania Business and Trade Directory (ISSN 0083-3827)

650 338   AT
UNIVERSAL BUSINESS DIRECTORIES, VICTORIA COUNTRY TRADE DIRECTORY. 1940. a. Aus.$33. Universal Business Directories Pty.Ltd., 64 Talavera Rd., North Ryde, N.S.W. 2113, Australia. adv.
   Formerly: Universal Business Directories. East Victoria Country Trade Directory (ISSN 0083-372X)

650 338   AT   ISSN 0083-3843
UNIVERSAL BUSINESS DIRECTORIES WESTERN AUSTRALIA COUNTRY BUSINESS AND TRADE DIRECTORY.* 1940. a. Aus.$12.50. Universal Business Directories (WA) Pty. Ltd., 20 Milford St., East Victoria Park, W. Australia, Australia.

382.6   US   ISSN 0092-2374
UTAH EXPORT DIRECTORY. 1970. irreg., latest, 1980. $15 per no. ‡ University of Utah, Bureau of Economic and Business Research, Salt Lake City, UT 84112. (Co-Sponsor: University of Utah Center for Economic and Community Development) Ed. Mari Lou Wood. illus. circ. controlled.

V K G JAHRBUCH. (Verband der Kraftfahrzeugteile- und Zweiradgrosshaendler e.V.) see *TRANSPORTATION — Automobiles*

VACUUM TECHNOLOGY DIRECTORY & BUYERS GUIDE. see *TECHNOLOGY: COMPREHENSIVE WORKS*

338   US   ISSN 0083-5692
VERIFIED DIRECTORY OF MANUFACTURERS' REPRESENTATIVES. 1957. biennial. $43.80. ‡ Manufacturers' Agent Publishing Co. Inc., 663 Fifth Ave., New York, NY 10022. Ed. E.K. Sharp.

670   US
VERMONT DIRECTORY OF MANUFACTURERS. biennial. $5. Agency of Development and Community Affairs, Pavilion Office Bldg., Montpelier, VT 05602. Ed. George A. Donovan. circ. 8,000.

338   US   ISSN 0098-6208
VERMONT STATE INDUSTRIAL DIRECTORY. 1974. biennial. $20. State Industrial Directories Corp., 2 Penn Plaza, New York, NY 10001.

971.3   CN   ISSN 0317-2961
VERNON'S CITY OF GUELPH (ONTARIO) DIRECTORY. a. Vernon Directories, Hamilton, Ont., Canada.

778.55   US
VIDEO REGISTER. 1979. a. $34.95. Knowledge Industry Publications, Inc., 701 Westchester Ave., White Plains, NY 10604. Ed. Eileen Gardner.

380   US
WASHINGTON STATE INDUSTRIAL DIRECTORY. biennial. $44.50. State Industrial Directories Corp., Two Penn Plaza, New York, NY 10001.

338   AT
WESTERN AUSTRALIAN MANUFACTURERS DIRECTORY. 1971. a. Department of Industrial Development, 32 St. George's Terrace, Perth, W.A. 6000, Australia. circ. 8,500.

WHERE TO BUILD-WHERE TO REPAIR. see *TRANSPORTATION — Ships And Shipping*

WHERE TO BUY. see *BUSINESS AND ECONOMICS — Marketing And Purchasing*

659.1   US   ISSN 0511-8794
WHITMARK DIRECTORY; source book of talent, fashion and audio visual services for the Southwest. 1967/68. a. $37.50. Whitmark Associates, 4120 Main St., Suite 100, Dallas, TX 75226. Ed. Margaret F. Murrell. adv. circ. 2,000. (back issues avail)

658   UK   ISSN 0140-4040
WHO OWNS WHOM. UNITED KINGDOM AND REPUBLIC OF IRELAND. 1958. a. $148. Dun & Bradstreet Ltd., Publications Division, 6-8 Bonhill St., London EC2A 4BU, England. Ed. I. M. Fyfe. index.
   Formerly: Who Owns Whom. United Kingdom (ISSN 0083-9329)

WIE ERREICHE ICH WEN? see *TRANSPORTATION — Ships And Shipping*

WORLD DIRECTORY OF PHARMACEUTICAL MANUFACTURERS. see *PHARMACY AND PHARMACOLOGY*

382   II
WORLD REGISTER OF TRADES. (Text in English) 1975. biennial. Rs.300($40) Amalgamated Press, Narang House, 41 Ambalal Doshi Marg, Bombay 400023, India. Ed. N. J. da Silva. circ. 5,000.
   Formerly: World Register of Chambers of Commerce/Associations & Trades.

338 540   UK
WORLDWIDE CHEMICAL DIRECTORY. vol. 2, 1977. a. £40. I P C Industrial Press Ltd., 33-40 Bowling Green Lane, London EC1B ONE, England.

677 620   II
WORRALL'S TEXTILE & ENGINEERING DIRECTORY. (Text in English) a. Rs.100. Commerce Publications Limited, Manek Mahal, 90 Veer Nariman Rd., Churchgate, Bombay 400020, India. Ed. Vadilal Dagli.
   Formerly: Textile & Engineering Directory for India & Pakistan.

YUGOSLAV EXPORT-IMPORT DIRECTORY. see *BUSINESS AND ECONOMICS — International Commerce*

916.89   ZA
ZAMBIA DIRECTORY. a?, 15th, 1979. K.10. Directory Publishers of Zambia Ltd., Box 1659, Ndola, Zambia.

380.1   ZA   ISSN 0084-5116
ZAMBIAN INDUSTRIAL DIRECTORY. irreg. K.1. Associated Reviews Ltd., Lufunsa Avenue, Box 717, Ndola, Zambia. illus.

CANCER

see *Medical Sciences—Cancer*

CARDIOVASCULAR DISEASES

see *Medical Sciences—Cardiovascular Diseases*

CARPENTRY AND WOODWORK

see *Building and Construction—Carpentry and Woodwork*

CERAMICS, GLASS AND POTTERY

see also *Art*

CERAMICS, GLASS AND POTTERY

666   IT
ADVANCES IN CERAMICS PROCESSING. (Text in English) 1942. triennial. Ceramurgica S.p.A., Casella Postale 174, 48018 Faenza, Italy. Ed. Pietro Vincenzini.
Ceramics

666   PL
AKADEMIA GORNICZO-HUTNICZA IM. STANISLAWA STASZICA. INSTYTUT CERAMIKI SPECJALNEJ I OGNIOTRWALEJ. PRACE NAUKOWE.* 1973. irreg. 2 Zl. (Instiutut Ceramiki Specjalnej i Ogniotrwalej) Panstwowe Wydawnictwo Naukowe, Miodowa 10, Warsaw, Poland. abstr. bibl.

666   US   ISSN 0065-7654
AMERICAN CERAMIC SOCIETY. SPECIAL PUBLICATIONS. 1969, no. 1-5. irreg. price varies. ‡ American Ceramic Society, Inc., 65 Ceramic Drive, Columbus, OH 43214. Indexed: Ceram.Abstr.
Ceramics

666   IT   ISSN 0003-2891
ANDAR PER CERAMICHE. (Text in Italian; summaries in English, French and German) 1969. a. L.2500. Via C. Cavour 24, 42013 Casalgrande, Reggio Emilia, Italy. Ed. Mirko A. Montanari. adv. index. cum.index. circ. 8,000(controlled)
Ceramics

666.1   FR   ISSN 0066-3557
ANNUAIRE NATIONAL DU VERRE. 1966. irreg; every 3/4 years. 40 F. Federation des Chambres Syndicales de l'Industrie du Verre, Office d'Etudes Publicitaires, 23 rue Galvani, Paris 7e, France. (Co-sponsor: Federation des Cristalleries Verreries a la Main et Mixtes)
Glass

ANNUAL BOOK OF A S T M STANDARDS. PART 17. REFRACTORIES, GLASS AND OTHER CERAMIC MATERIALS; MANUFACTURED CARBON AND GRAPHITE PRODUCTS. see *ENGINEERING — Engineering Mechanics And Materials*

666   IT   ISSN 0066-4472
ANNUARIO CERAMICA. 1970. a. L.6000. Casa Editrice Palazzo Vecchio, Via Vittorio Emanuele, 155, 50134 Florence, Italy. adv.
Ceramics

ARCHITECTS' GUIDE TO GLASS, METAL & GLAZING. see *ARCHITECTURE*

666   BE   ISSN 0447-9823
ASSOCIATION INTERNATIONALE POUR L'HISTOIRE DU VERRE. BULLETIN. (Text in English, French and German) 1962. irreg. price varies. International Association for the History of Glass, Musee du Verre, 13 Quai de Maastricht, 4000 Liege, Belgium. bk. rev. circ. 200.

666   UK
BRITISH CERAMIC RESEARCH ASSOCIATION. SPECIAL PUBLICATIONS. 1948. irreg.(2-3/yr.) no. 98, 1979. British Ceramic Research Association, Queen's Road, Penkhull, Stoke-on-Trent ST4 7LQ, England. bibl. charts. illus. circ. 500-2,000.
Ceramics

666   UK   ISSN 0524-5141
BRITISH CERAMIC SOCIETY. PROCEEDINGS. irreg. price varies. British Ceramic Society, Shelton House, Stoke Rd., Shelton, Stoke- on- Trent ST4 2DR, England.
Ceramics

666.1   UK   ISSN 0068-2020
BRITISH GLASS INDUSTRY RESEARCH ASSOCIATION. ANNUAL REPORT. 1955. a. membership or on exchange. ‡ British Glass Industry Research Association, Northumberland Rd., Sheffield S10 2UA, England. Ed. P. J. Doyle. circ. 1,000.
Glass

666   CN   ISSN 0068-8444
CANADIAN CERAMIC SOCIETY. JOURNAL. 1928. a. $10. Canadian Ceramic Society, 2175 Sheppard Ave. E., Suite 110, Willowdale, Ont, Canada. Ed. K. Bell. circ. 800.
Ceramics

748   US   ISSN 0069-0708
CARNIVAL GLASS PRICE GUIDE. biennial. $3. Marion T. Hartung, 814 Constitution St., Emporia, KS 66801.

666   US
CERAMIC DATA BOOK. 1922. a. $4. Cahners Publishing Co. (Chicago), Division of Reed Holdings, Inc., 5 S. Wabash Ave., Chicago, IL 60603 (Subscr. address: 270 St. Paul St., Denver, CO 80206) Ed. J.J. Svec. adv. charts. circ. 11,072.
Ceramics

666   CN   ISSN 0069-2220
CERAMIC PLANTS IN CANADA. a. price varies. Department of Energy, Mines and Resources, Mineral Policy Sector, Ottawa, Ontario K1A OE4, Canada (Oders to: Supply and Services Canada, Publishing Centre, Hull, Que. K1A 0S5, Canada)

666 666.1   US   ISSN 0069-2239
CERAMICS AND GLASS SERIES. 1970. irreg., vol. 4, 1974. price varies. Marcel Dekker, Inc., 270 Madison Ave., New York, NY 10016. Ed. J. B. Wachtman, Jr.
Ceramics and glass

666 658.8   US   ISSN 0069-3677
CHINA GLASS AND TABLEWARE RED BOOK DIRECTORY. (13th issue of monthly magazine China Glass and Tableware) 1906. a. included in subscr. to monthly. Ebel-Doctorow Publications, Inc., 1115 Clifton Ave, Clifton, NJ 07013. Ed. Susan Sievers Grisham. adv. circ. 6,000.

666   FR   ISSN 0069-830X
CONFEDERATION DES INDUSTRIES CERAMIQUES DE FRANCE. ANNUAIRE. 1953/54. biennial. 100 F. (Confederation des Industries Ceramiques de France) Septima, 14 rue Falguiere, 75015 Paris, France. adv.
Ceramics

666   GW   ISSN 0070-4199
DEUTSCHE KERAMISCHE GESELLSCHAFT. FACHAUSSCHUSSBERICHTE. 1953. irreg., no. 19, 1974. price varies. Deutsche Keramische Gesellschaft e.V., Menzenberger Str. 47, Postfach 1226, 5340 Bad Honnef 1, W. Germany (B.R.D.)
Ceramics

666.1   GW
DEUTSCHER GLASERKALENDER; Ratgeber und Helfer fuer Glaser und Fensterbauer. 1950. a. price varies. Verlag Karl Hofmann, Steinwasenstr. 6-8, Postfach 1360, 7060 Schorndorf, W. Germany (B.R.D.) adv. stat. circ. 5,500.
Glass

666   UK   ISSN 0071-0547
ENGLISH CERAMIC CIRCLE. TRANSACTIONS. 1927. a. price varies. ‡ W. & J. Mackey Ltd., Lordswood, Chatham, Kent, England. Ed. Donald C Towner. index every 3 years. cum.index: 1927-1970.
Ceramics

GIFT AND DECORATIVE ACCESSORIES BUYERS DIRECTORY. see *GIFTWARE AND TOYS*

666   II
GLASS, POTTERIES AND CERAMIC ANNUAL. (Text in English) 1970. a. $15. Praveen Corp., Sayajiganj, Baroda 390005, India. Ed. C. M. Pandit. Formerly: Glass, Potteries and Ceramic Journal (ISSN 0017-1042)

666   UA
GROUPE INTERNATIONAL D'ETUDE DE LA CERAMIQUE EGYPTIENNE. BULLETIN DE LIAISON. (Text in English, French and German) 1975. a. Institut Francais d'Archeologie Orientale du Caire, 37 Sharia Sheikh Aly Youssef, Mounira, Cairo, Egypt. Ed. Helen Jacquet-Gordon. circ. 200. (back issues avail)
Ceramics

666   FR   ISSN 0074-218X
INTERNATIONAL CERAMIC CONGRESS. PROCEEDINGS. (Proceedings published by host country) irreg., 1974, 13th, Amsterdam. European Ceramic Association, 44, rue Copernic, 75 Paris 16e, France.
Ceramics

666   IS   ISSN 0074-2597
INTERNATIONAL CLAY CONFERENCE. PROCEEDINGS. (4th conference, Spain, 1972, was not published) triennial, 1969, 3rd, Tokyo. Israel Program for Scientific Translations, P.O. Box 7145, Jerusalem, Israel.

666 669   US   ISSN 0147-300X
INTERNATIONAL GLASS/METAL CATALOG. 1958. a. $30. (Artlee Catalog, Inc.) Ashlee Publishing Co., Inc., 110 E. 42nd St., New York, NY 10017. Ed. Oscar S. Glasberg. adv. circ. 11,000. Former titles, until 1973: Glass/Metal Catalog (ISSN 0072-4645); Glass/Metal Directory.

666 382   UK
INTERNATIONAL REFRACTORIES HANDBOOK & DIRECTORY. 1976. quadrennial. £15. London and Sheffield Publishing Co. Ltd., 5 Pond St., Hampstead, London NW3 2PN, England.

666.1 748   US   ISSN 0075-4250
JOURNAL OF GLASS STUDIES. 1959. a. $15. Corning Museum of Glass, Corning Glass Center, Corning, NY 14831. Ed. John H. Martin. cum.index (vol.1-15) circ. 1,150. (also avail. in microform from UMI; reprint service avail. from UMI) Indexed: Bull.Signal. Chem.Abstr. Br.Archeol.Abstr.
Glass

LITTLE BLACK BOOK; annual directory of ceramic mold manufacturers in the United States. see *BUSINESS AND ECONOMICS — Trade And Industrial Directories*

666 913   GW   ISSN 0076-5171
MATERIALIEN ZUR ROEMISCH-GERMANISCHEN KERAMIK. 1914. irreg., no. 10, 1981. price varies. (Deutsches Archaeologisches Institut, Roemisch-Germanische Kommission) Rudolf Habelt Verlag, Am Buchenhang 1, 5300 Bonn 1, W. Germany (B.R.D.)

666   NZ   ISSN 0078-0189
NEW ZEALAND POTTERY AND CERAMICS RESEARCH ASSOCIATION. TECHNICAL REPORT. 1947. irreg., no. 26, 1974. free. New Zealand Pottery and Ceramics Research Association (Inc.), Private Bag, Lower Hutt, New Zealand. circ. 200.

666   PL   ISSN 0079-3264
POLSKA AKADEMIA NAUK. ODDZIAL W KRAKOWIE. KOMISJA CERAMICZNA. PRACE: CERAMIKA. (Text in English and Polish; summaries in English and Russian) 1964. irreg., no. 29, 1978. price varies. Ossolineum, Publishing House of the Polish Academy of Sciences, Rynek 9, Wroclaw, Poland (Dist. by Ars Polona-Ruch, Krakowskie Przedmiescie 7, Warsaw, Poland) Ed. Roman Pampuch. circ. 520. Indexed: Chem.Abstr. Eng.Ind.

666 738.1   UK   ISSN 0032-5678
POTTERY QUARTERLY; a review of craft pottery. 1954. irreg. £5.50 for 4 nos. Murray Fieldhouse, Northfields Studio, Northfields, Tring, Herts, England. adv. bk. rev. illus. index. circ. 2,500. (also avail. in microfilm from UMI)

666.7   US   ISSN 0080-049X
REFRACTORY MATERIALS; a series of monographs. 1966. irreg., 1971, vol. 7. price varies. Academic Press Inc., 111 Fifth Ave., New York, NY 10003. Ed. John L. Margrave.

666   UK   ISSN 0080-7575
SCIENCE OF CERAMICS. 1962. irreg. price varies. Academic Press Inc (London) Ltd., 24-28 Oval Rd, London NW1 7DX, England (and 111 Fifth Ave., New York, N.Y. 10003) Ed. G. H. Stewart.
Ceramics

748   ISSN 0081-1602
SOCIETY OF GLASS DECORATORS. PAPERS PRESENTED AT ANNUAL SEMINAR. a. $25 to non-members; members $10. Society of Glass Decorators, 207 Grant St., Port Jefferson, NY 11777. Ed. Frank S. Child.

666.1   US   ISSN 0081-6000
STRUCTURE OF GLASS. (Represents: Proceedings of All-Union Symposia on the Glassy State) (Text in English; translation of original Russian text) 1958. irreg., 1973, vol. 8. price varies. Consultants Bureau, 233 Spring St., New York, NY 10013. Ed. E. A. Porai-Koshits.
Glass

666 US ISSN 0082-0954
SYMPOSIUM ON SPECIAL CERAMICS, STOKE-ON-TRENT, ENGLAND. SPECIAL CERAMICS, PROCEEDINGS. 1959. irreg. (British Ceramic Research Association, UK) Academic Press, Inc, 111 Fifth Ave., New York, NY 10003.
Ceramics

666.122 US ISSN 0569-7468
SYMPOSIUM ON THE ART OF GLASSBLOWING PROCEEDINGS. 1956. a. American Scientific Glassblowers Society, 1507 Hagley Rd., Toledo, OH 43612. bibl. illus.
Glass

666 738 UK
TABLEWARE REFERENCE BOOK. 1971. a. $15. International Trade Publications Ltd., Queensway House, 2 Queensway, Redhill, Surrey RH1 1QS, England. adv.
Formerly: Tableware and Pottery Gazette Reference Book (ISSN 0082-1438)

999.1 943 GW ISSN 0170-3447
VEROEFFENTLICHUNGEN ZUR GESCHICHTE DES GLASES UND DER GLASHUETTER IN DEUTSCHLAND; Historische Topographie. irreg., vol. 4, 1978. price varies. Franz Steiner Verlag GmbH, Friedrichstr. 24, Postfach 5529, 6200 Wiesbaden, W. Germany (B.R.D.) Ed. Axel von Saldern.

666 UK ISSN 0511-4063
WEDGWOOD SOCIETY OF LONDON. PROCEEDINGS. 1956. biennial. price varies. Wedgwood Society, c/o Mrs. T.B. Jarvis, Roman Villa, Rockbourne, Fordingbridge, Hants. SP6 EPG, England. Ed. Alison Kelly. illus. circ. 20.

666.3 CN ISSN 0049-7495
WESTERN POTTER. irreg. Potters Guild of British Columbia, c/o Community Arts Council, 315 West Cordova St., Vancouver, B.C. V6B 1E5, Canada. illus.
Pottery

666.7 GW ISSN 0084-5485
ZIEGELEITECHNISCHES JAHRBUCH. 1950. a. DM.22. Bauverlag GmbH, Wittelsbacherstr. 10, 6200 Wiesbaden, W. Germany (B.R.D.)

CERAMICS, GLASS AND POTTERY — Abstracting, Bibliographies, Statistics

338.4 CN ISSN 0575-8661
CANADA. STATISTICS CANADA. GLASS AND GLASS PRODUCTS MANUFACTURERS/FABRICANTS DE VERRE ET D'ARTICLES EN VERRE. (Catalog 44-207) (Text in English and French) 1927. a. Can.$4.50($5.40) Statistics Canada, Publications Distribution, Ottawa, Ont. K1A 0V7, Canada. (also avail. in microform from MML)

CHAMBER OF COMMERCE PUBLICATIONS

see Business and Economics—Chamber of Commerce Publications

CHEMICAL ENGINEERING

see Engineering—Chemical Engineering

CHEMISTRY

see also Chemistry—Analytical Chemistry; Chemistry—Crystallography; Chemistry—Electrochemistry; Chemistry—Inorganic Chemistry; Chemistry—Organic Chemistry; Chemistry—Physical Chemistry

540 US ISSN 0065-7719
A C S MONOGRAPHS. 1924. irreg., 1974, no. 169. American Chemical Society, 1155 16th St., N.W., Washington, DC 20036. Ed. Marjorie Caserio.

540 US ISSN 0097-6156
A C S SYMPOSIUM SERIES. 1974. irreg. price varies. American Chemical Society, 1155 16th St. N.W., Washington, DC 20036. Ed. M. Joan Comstock. circ. 1,500. Indexed: Chem.Abstr.

540 CH ISSN 0001-3927
ACADEMIA SINICA. INSTITUTE OF CHEMISTRY. BULLETIN. 1959. a. NT.$60($4) Academia Sinica, Institute of Chemistry, Taipei, Taiwan, Republic of China. Ed.Bd. charts. illus. circ. 1,000. Indexed: Chem.Abstr.

ACTA PHYSICA ET CHIMICA DEBRECINA. see *PHYSICS*

669 540 FI ISSN 0001-6853
ACTA POLYTECHNICA SCANDINAVICA. CHEMISTRY INCLUDING METALLURGY SERIES. (Text and summaries in English, German, and French) irreg (2-3/yr.) Fmk.60. Teknillisten Tieteiden Akatemia - Finnish Academy of Technical Sciences, Kansakoulukatu 10 A, SF-00100 Helsinki 10, Finland. Ed. Pekka Kivalo. index; cum index (1958-1979) circ. 250. (also avail. in microfilm from UMI; back issues avail.; reprint service avail. from UMI)

540 US ISSN 0065-2393
ADVANCES IN CHEMISTRY SERIES. 1950. irreg. price varies. American Chemical Society, 1155 16 St. N.W., Washington, DC 20036. Ed. M. Joan Comstock. circ. 1,500. (also avail. in microfiche) Indexed: Chem.Abstr.

ADVANCES IN INORGANIC CHEMISTRY AND RADIOCHEMISTRY. see *CHEMISTRY — Inorganic Chemistry*

541.28 US ISSN 0065-3276
ADVANCES IN QUANTUM CHEMISTRY. 1964. irreg., vol. 11, 1978. price varies. Academic Press, Inc., 111 Fifth Ave., New York, NY 10003. Ed. Per-Olav Lowdin. index.

540 US ISSN 0065-7727
AMERICAN CHEMICAL SOCIETY. ABSTRACTS OF PAPERS (AT THE NATIONAL MEETING) 1937. biannual. $15 per no.; division member $13. American Chemical Society, Special Issues Sales, 1155 16 St., N.W., Washington, DC 20036. Ed. Colleen Sundstrom. circ. 4,000. (processed)

540 US ISSN 0065-7735
AMERICAN CHEMICAL SOCIETY. ABSTRACTS OF PAPERS (AT THE REGIONAL MEETINGS) irreg. American Chemical Society, Special Issues Sales, 1155 16 St., N.W., Washington, DC 20036. circ. controlled. (processed)

AMERICAN CHEMICAL SOCIETY. DIRECTORY OF GRADUATE RESEARCH. see *EDUCATION — Guides To Schools And Colleges*

540 US ISSN 0084-6376
AMERICAN INSTITUTE OF CHEMISTS. MEMBERSHIP DIRECTORY. 1969. biennial. $10. ‡ American Institute of Chemists, Inc., 7315 Wisconsin Ave., Washington, DC 20014. Ed. David A. H. Roethel. adv. circ. 7,000.

542 US ISSN 0066-1910
ANLEITUNG FUER DIE CHEMISCHE LABORATORIUMSPRAXIS. 1970. irreg., vol. 16, 1981. price varies. Springer-Verlag, 175 Fifth Ave., New York, NY 10010 (also Berlin, Heidelberg, Vienna) Ed. H. Mayer-Kaupp. (reprint service avail. from ISI)

540 FI ISSN 0066-1961
ANNALES ACADEMIAE SCIENTIARUM FENNICAE. SERIES A, 2: CHEMICA. (Text in English, French, German) 1944. irreg. price varies. Suomalainen Tiedeakatemia - Academia Scientiarum Fennica, Snellmanink. 9-11, SF-00170 Helsinki 17, Finland. Ed. Reino Nasanen. circ. 500-550. (also avail. in microform; back issues avail.; reprint service avail. from UMI) Indexed: Biol.Abstr. Bull.Signal. Chem.Abstr. Excerp.Med. Ind.Med. Ref.Zh. Anal.Abstr. Bibl.Agri. Hort.Abstr. Phys.Abstr.

660.2 US ISSN 0140-9115
ANNUAL REPORTS ON FERMENTATION PROCESSES. 1977. a. Academic Press, Inc., 111 Fifth Ave., New York, NY 10003. Ed. D. Perlman. Indexed: Chem. Abstr.

540 US
BAKER SERIES IN CHEMISTRY. irreg. price varies. Cornell University Press, 124 Roberts Place, Ithaca, NY 14850.

540 US
BENCHMARK PAPERS IN POLYMER CHEMISTRY. 1978. irreg. Dowden, Hutchinson & Ross, Inc., 523 Sarah St., Stroudsburg, PA 18360 (Dist by Academic Press, Inc., 111 Fifth Ave., New York, NY 10003) Ed. E.S. Proskauer.

540 660 II ISSN 0067-9925
BOMBAY TECHNOLOGIST. (Text in English) 1951. a. Rs.4.($0.50) approx.) Technological Association, University of Bombay, Department of Chemical Technology, Matunga, Bombay 19, India. Indexed: Biol.Abstr. Chem.Abstr.

540 UK
CAMBRIDGE TEXTS IN CHEMISTRY AND BIOCHEMISTRY. irreg. price varies. Cambridge University Press, Box 110, Cambridge CB2 3RL, England (And 32 E. 57th St., New York NY 10022) Ed.Bd.
Formerly: Cambridge Chemistry Texts.

338.4 CN ISSN 0315-985X
CANADIAN CHEMICAL REGISTER. 1971. a. $2.50. Department of Industry, Trade and Commerce, Chemicals Branch, Ottawa, Ont. K1A OH5, Canada.

660 US
CATALYSIS: SCIENCE AND TECHNOLOGY. 1981. irreg. Springer-Verlag, 175 Fifth Ave., New York, NY 10010 (Also Berlin, Heidelberg, Vienna) Eds. J. R. Anderson, M. Boudart. (reprint service avail. from ISI)

CHEM SOURCES - EUROPE. see *BUSINESS AND ECONOMICS — Trade And Industrial Directories*

CHEM SOURCES - U.S.A. see *BUSINESS AND ECONOMICS — Trade And Industrial Directories*

540 PL
CHEMIA. (Text in Polish; summaries in English) 1960. irreg. Uniwersytet im. Adama Mickiewicza w Poznaniu, Stalingradzka 1, 61-712 Poznan, Poland (Dist. by: Ars Polona, Krakowskie Przedmiescie 7, 00-068 Warsaw, Poland)
Formerly: Uniwersytet im. Adama Mickiewicza w Poznaniu. Wydzial Matematyki, Fizyki i Chemii. Seria Chemia.

380.1 SA
CHEMICAL INDUSTRIES YEARBOOK AND BUYERS' GUIDE. 1972. biennial. R.30. Thomson Publications S.A. (Pty) Ltd., Box 8308, Johannesburg 2000, South Africa. adv.
Formerly: Chemical Industry Buyers' Guide for S.A.

CHEMICAL NEW PRODUCT DIRECTORY. see *BUSINESS AND ECONOMICS — Marketing And Purchasing*

540 US
CHEMICAL PURCHASING CHEMICALS DIRECTORY. 1964. a. Myers Publishing Co., Inc., 2135 Summer St., Stamford, CT 06905. Ed. Ting Gough. adv. circ. 14,800.

540 US ISSN 0094-6249
CHEMICAL REFERENCE MANUAL. 1973. irreg. Matheson Coleman & Bell Manufacturing Chemists, 2909 Highland Ave., Norwood, OH 45212. illus.

540 UK ISSN 0306-4875
CHEMICAL SOCIETY, LONDON, ANNUAL REPORT OF COUNCIL AND ACCOUNTS. a. Chemical Society, Burlington House, London W1V PBN, England. illus.

CHEMISTRY

540   UK   ISSN 0080-4428
CHEMICAL SOCIETY, LONDON,
MONOGRAPHS FOR TEACHERS. 1959.
irreg.(approx. 3 nos. per year) price varies. Chemical
Society, Burlington House, London W1V 0BN,
England. Ed. Lynette K. Hamblin. Indexed:
Chem.Abstr.
    Formerly: Royal Institue of Chemistry.
Monographs for Teachers.

540   UK
CHEMICALS. (Text in English; introduction in
French, German, Spanish) 1920. biennial. £8. ‡
Chemical Industries Association Ltd., Alembic
House, 93 Albert Embankment, London SE1 7TU,
England. Eds. A. G. Wyatt, M. T. Damer. circ.
13,000.
    Formerly: British Chemicals & Their
Manufacturers.

CHEMICALS AND ALLIED PRODUCTS EXPORT
PROMOTION COUNCIL. EXPORTERS
DIRECTORY. see BUSINESS AND
ECONOMICS — International Commerce

540   AT
CHEMIST CATALOGUE. a. Aus.$118. Permail Pty.
Ltd, Box 56, Artarmon, N. S. W. 2064, Australia.

540   UK   ISSN 0069-312X
CHEMISTRY AND INDUSTRY BUYERS' GUIDE.
Title varies: Buyers' Guide of Chemicals.
(Supplement to Chemistry and Industry) 1936. a.
£3. Society of Chemical Industry, 14 Belgrave
Square, London, SW1, England.

540   US   ISSN 0069-3146
CHEMISTRY OF FUNCTIONAL GROUPS. 1965.
irreg., unnumbered, latest, 1980. price varies. John
Wiley & Sons, Inc., 605 Third Ave., New York, NY
10016. Ed. Saul Patai.

COMPUTERS IN CHEMICAL AND
BIOCHEMICAL RESEARCH. see COMPUTER
TECHNOLOGY AND APPLICATIONS

540   651.8   US
COMPUTERS IN CHEMISTRY AND
INSTRUMENTATION. 1973. irreg., vol. 7, 1977.
Marcel Dekker, Inc., 270 Madison Ave., New York,
NY 10016. Ed.Bd.

540   US
CONCEPTS IN CHEMISTRY. irreg. price varies.
Houghton Mifflin Co., One Beacon St., Boston, MA
02107.

540   CS
CONFERENCE ON COORDINATION
CHEMISTRY PROCEEDINGS. irreg., 6th, 1976,
Bratislava. price varies. Slovenska Vysoka Skola
Technicka, Janska 1, 880 37 Bratislava,
Czechoslovakia.

541.224   US   ISSN 0069-9845
COORDINATION CHEMISTRY. (Text in English;
occasionally French or German) 1968, 9th. irreg.,
15th 1973, Moscow; 16th 1974, Dublin. price
varies. (International Union of Pure and Applied
Chemistry) Pergamon Press, Inc., Maxwell House,
Fairview Park, Elmsford, NY 10523 (And
Headington Hill Hall, Oxford OX3 0BW, England)

540   US
COURS ET DOCUMENTS DE CHIMIE. a. price
varies. Gordon and Breach Science Publishers, One
Park Ave., New York, NY 10016. Eds. A.
Casadevall, M. Magat.

540   US
CURRENT CHEMICAL CONCEPTS. irreg. price
varies. Academic Press, Inc., 111 Fifth Avenue,
New York, NY 10003. Ed. Louis Meites.

540   615.9   US
CURRENT TOPICS IN ENVIRONMENTAL AND
TOXICOLOGICAL CHEMISTRY. a. price varies.
Gordon and Breach Science Publishers, One Park
Ave., New York, NY 10016.

660   US   ISSN 0012-3277
DIRECTORY OF CHEMICAL PRODUCERS-U.S.A.
1961. a, with semi-annual supplements. $595. S R I
International, Chemical Industries Division, Menlo
Park, CA 94025. Ed. E. M. Klapproth. charts. stat.

660   US
DIRECTORY OF CHEMICAL PRODUCERS-
WESTERN EUROPE. 1978. a. with semi-annual
supplements. $790. S R I International, Chemical
Industries Division, Menlo Park, CA 94025. Ed.
E.M. Klapproth. charts. stat.

DIRECTORY OF WORLD CHEMICAL
PRODUCERS. see BUSINESS AND
ECONOMICS — Trade And Industrial Directories

540   US
DOCUMENTS IN CHEMISTRY. a. price varies.
Gordon and Breach Science Publishers, One Park
Ave., New York, NY 10016. Eds. A. Casadavell,
M. Magat.

614.7   UK   ISSN 0305-7712
ENVIRONMENTAL CHEMISTRY; specialist
periodical reports. 1975. biennial. price varies.
Chemical Society, Burlington House, London W1v
0BN, England (Subscr. Address: Blackhorse Rd.,
Letchworth, Herts SG6 1HN, England) Ed. G.
Eglinton. charts. illus. index. Indexed: Chem.Abstr.

540   US   ISSN 0071-1373
ESSAYS IN CHEMISTRY. 1970. a. price varies.
Academic Press Inc., 111 Fifth Ave., New York,
NY 10003. Eds. J. N. Bradley, R. Gillard, R. F.
Hudson.

540   UK
EUROPEAN CHEMICAL BUYER'S GUIDE. 1975.
a. £20. I. P. C. Business Press Ltd., 33-40 Bowling
Green Lane, London EC1R 0NE, England. adv.
circ. 5,000.

541.2   US   ISSN 0093-1713
EXCITED STATES. 1974. irreg. Academic Press,
Inc., 111 Fifth Ave., New York, NY 10003. Ed. E.
L. Lim. illus. (also avail. in microfiche)

540   CS
FOLIA FACULTATIS SCIENTIARUM
NATURALIUM UNIVERSITATIS
PURKYNIANAE BRUNENSIS: CHEMIA. irreg
(7-12/yr.). price varies. Universita J. E. Purkyne,
Prirodovedecka Fakulta, Kotlarska 2, 611 37 Brno,
Czechoslovakia.

540   FR   ISSN 0080-1046
FRANCE. DELEGATION GENERALE A LA
RECHERCHE SCIENTIFIQUE ET TECHNIQUE.
REPERTOIRE DES SCIENTIFIQUES
FRANCAIS. TOME 4: CHIMIE. 1966. irreg. 26 F.
Documentation Francaise, 29-31 Quai Voltaire,
75340 Paris 07, France.

540   FR   ISSN 0071-8556
FRANCE. DELEGATION GENERALE A LA
RECHERCHE SCIENTIFIQUE ET TECHNIQUE.
REPERTOIRE NATIONAL DES
LABORATOIRES; LA RECHERCHE
UNIVERSITAIRE; SCIENCES EXACTES ET
NATURELLES. TOME 3: CHIMIE. 1966. irreg.
26 F. Documentation Francaise, 29-31 Quai
Voltaire, 75340 Paris 07, France.

540   660   YU   ISSN 0367-4444
GLASNIK HEMICARA I TEHNOLOGA BOSNE I
HERCEGOVINE. (Subseries of: Documenta
Chemica Yugoslavica) irreg. 100 din. Akademija
Nauka i Umjetnosti Bosne i Hercegovine, Hemijski
Institut, Vojvode Putnika 43, Sarajevo, Yugoslavia.
Ed. Franjo Krleza.

540   UK   ISSN 0072-6524
GREAT BRITAIN. LABORATORY OF THE
GOVERNMENT CHEMIST. ANNUAL REPORT
OF THE GOVERNMENT CHEMIST. 1959. a.
price varies. H.M.S.O., P.O.B. 569, London SE1
9NH, England.

540   FR
GUIDE DE LA CHIMIE INTERNATIONAL. a.
255,19 F. per no. S.E.P Edition, 194-196 rue
Marcadet, 75018 Paris, France.

GUIDE TO FLUORESCENCE LITERATURE. see
PHYSICS

HINDUSTAN LATEX. VARSHIKA RIPORTA/
HINDUSTAN LATEX. ANNUAL REPORTS. see
PLASTICS

HUNGARIAN ACADEMY OF SCIENCES.
CENTRAL RESEARCH INSTITUTE FOR
PHYSICS. YEARBOOK/MAGYAR
TUDOMANYOS AKADEMIA.KOZPONTI
FIZIKAI KUTATO INTEZET. EVKONYV. see
PHYSICS

540   SP
I.Q.S; trabajos de fin de carrera. 1971. a. $10. Instituto
Quimico de Sarria, Barcelona 17, Spain. circ.
controlled. (back issues avail.) Indexed: Chem.Abstr.

540   FR
IMAGES DE LA CHIMIE. 1973. irreg. Centre
National de la Recherche Scientifique, 15 Quai
Anatole France, 75700 Paris, France.

INDIAN CHEMICAL DIRECTORY. see
ENGINEERING — Chemical Engineering

540   RM
INSTITUTUL PEDAGOGIC ORADEA. LUCRARI
STIINTIFICE SERIA CHIMIE. (Text in
Rumanian, occasionally in English or French;
summaries in Rumanian, French, English or
German) 1967. a. Institutul Pedagogic Oradea,
Calea Armatei Rosii Nr. 5, Oradea, Romania.
    Continues in part its Lucrari Stiintifice: Seria
Matematica, Fizica, Chimie (1971-72); its Lucrari
Stiintifice: Seria A and Seria B (1969-70) and its
Lucrari Stiintifice (1967-68)

540   660   US   ISSN 0074-3925
INTERNATIONAL CONGRESS OF PURE AND
APPLIED CHEMISTRY. (LECTURES) (Text in
English; occasionally French or German) 1960.
biennial, 1973, 24th Hamburg; 1975, 25th,
Jerusalem. price varies. (International Union of Pure
and Applied Chemistry) Pergamon Press, Inc.,
Maxwell House, Fairview Park, Elmsford, NY
10523 (And Headington Hill Hall, Oxford OX3
0BW, England) Ed. Prof. B. C. L. Weedon.
    1973, 24th, Hamburg

540   II   ISSN 0074-7041
INTERNATIONAL MONOGRAPHS ON
ADVANCED CHEMISTRY.* (Text in English)
1965. irreg. $7.50. Hindustan Publishing Corp., 6-
U.B. Jawahar Nagar, Delhi 110007, India.

540   US
INTERNATIONAL SERIES OF MONOGRAPHS
ON CHEMISTRY. irreg. price varies. Oxford
University Press, 200 Madison Ave., New York,
NY 10016 (And Ely House, 37 Dover St., London
W1X 4AH, England) Eds. J. S. Rowlinson, J. E.
Baldwin.

541.28   US
INTERNATIONAL SYMPOSIUM ON ATOMIC,
MOLECULAR AND SOLID-STATE THEORY,
COLLISION PHENOMENA AND
COMPUTATIONAL METHODS.
PROCEEDINGS. Represents: International Journal
of Quantum Chemistry. Symposium. Variant title:
Lowdin Symposia. 1967. irreg. $30. John Wiley &
Sons, Inc., 605 Third Ave., New York, NY 10016.
Ed. Per-Olov Lowdin.
    Former titles (1974-1977): International
Symposium on Atomic, Molecular and Solid-State
Theory and Quantum Statistics. Proceedings (ISSN
0360-8832); (1969-1973): International Symposium
on Atomic, Molecular and Solid-State Theory and
Quantum Biology. Proceedings (ISSN 0076-1370);
(1967): International Symposium on Atomic,
Molecular and Solid-State Theory. Proceedings.

540   US
INTERNATIONAL SYMPOSIUM ON NITROGEN
FIXATION. PROCEEDINGS. 1976. irreg. $25.
Washington State University Press, Pullman, WA
99163. (reprint service avail. from UMI)

540   US
INTERNATIONAL UNION OF PURE AND
APPLIED CHEMISTRY. CHEMICAL DATA
SERIES. no. 14, 1977. irreg. Pergamon Press, Inc.,
Maxwell House, Fairview Park, Elmsford, NY
10523 (And Headington Hill Hall, Oxford OX3
0BW, England)

JERUSALEM SYMPOSIA ON QUANTUM
CHEMISTRY AND BIOCHEMISTRY. see
BIOLOGY — Biological Chemistry

540   HU   ISSN 0075-5397
KEMIA UJABB EREDMENYEI. 1970. irreg. price varies. (Magyar Tudomanyos Akademia) Akademiai Kiado, Publishing House of the Hungarian Academy of Sciences, P.O. Box 24, H-1363 Budapest, Hungary. Ed. Bela Csakvari.

540   HU
KEMIAI KOZLEMENYEK. (Summaries in English and Hungarian) 1952. 2 vols./yr. (4 parts each) $9 per vol. (Magyar Tudomanyos Akademia, Kemiai Tudomanyok Osztalya) Akademiai Kiado, Publishing House of the Hungarian Academy of Sciences, Box 24, H-1363 Budapest, Hungary. Ed. M. Beck. bk. rev. bibl. charts. index for each vol. cum.index. Indexed: Chem.Abstr. Curr.Cont.
    Formerly: Magyar Tudomanyos Akademia. Tudomanyok Osztalya. Kozlemenyek.

540   FI   ISSN 0356-7818
KEMISTIN KALENTERI. (Text in Finnish and Swedish) 1947. a. Suomen Kemistiliitto - Finnish Union of Chemists, Rautatielaisenkatu 6, 00520 Helsinki 52, Finland. Ed. Kirsti Viljakainen. adv. circ. 3,000.

540   MY
KIMIA. 1970. a. free to qualified personnel. ‡ Malaysian Institute of Chemistry, c/o Rubber Research Institute of Malaysia, Jalan Ampang, Box 150, Kuala Lumpur, Malaysia. Ed. M. M. Singh. adv. illus. circ. 1,500.

540   JA   ISSN 0085-2635
KYUSHU UNIVERSITY. FACULTY OF SCIENCE. MEMOIRS. SERIES C: CHEMISTRY/KYUSHU DAIGAKU RIGAKUBU KIYO, C. KAGAKU. (Text in English) 1948. a. exchange basis. Kyushu University, Faculty of Science, Department of Chemistry - Kyushu Daigaku Rigakubu, 6-10-1 Hakozaki, Higashi-ku, Fukuoka 812, Japan. circ. 600.

542   US   ISSN 0458-595X
LABORATORY GUIDE TO INSTRUMENTS, EQUIPMENT AND CHEMICALS. (Special issue of Analytical Chemistry) 1955. a. $5. American Chemical Society, 1155 16th St. N.W., Washington, DC 20036. Ed. Arthur Poulos. adv. bk. rev. circ. 72,000.
    Former titles, until 1966: A C S Laboratory Guide (ISSN 0065-7700); Analytical Chemistry Buyers Guide.

540   US
LECTURE NOTES IN CHEMISTRY. 1976. irreg., vol. 23, 1981. price varies. Springer-Verlag, 175 Fifth Ave., New York, NY 10010 (Also Berlin, Heidelberg, Vienna) Ed. Bd. (reprint service avail. from ISI)

541.24   US   ISSN 0076-1370
LOEWDIN SYMPOSIA; PROCEEDINGS OF THE INTERNATIONAL SYMPOSIUM ON ATOMIC, MOLECULAR, AND SOLID-STATE THEORY AND QUANTUM BIOLOGY. 1967. irreg., no. 13, 1979. price varies. John Wiley & Sons, Inc., 605 Third Ave, New York, NY 10016. Ed. Per-Olov Loewdin.
    Reprints of articles from the International Journal of Quantum Chemistry

543   UK   ISSN 0305-9987
MASS SPECTROMETRY. 1971. biennial. price varies. Chemical Society, Burlington House, London W1V 0BN, England. Ed. Dr. R.A.W. Johnstone. charts. illus. Indexed: Chem.Abstr.

540 510   GW   ISSN 0340-6253
MATCH; informal communications in mathematical chemistry. (Text mostly in English, occasionally in French and German) 1975. irreg. DM.35 for 4 issues. Max-Planck-Institut fuer Kohlenforschung, Institut fuer Strahlenchemie, Stiftstr. 34-36, 4330 Muelheim, W. Germany (B.R.D.) Eds. O. E. Polansky, H. J. Kuehn. bk. rev. adv. bibl. charts. index. Indexed: Chem.Abstr. Math.R.

MONOGRAPHS ON THE PHYSICS AND CHEMISTRY OF MATERIALS. see *PHYSICS*

MUSEUM NATIONAL D'HISTOIRE NATURELLE, PARIS. MEMOIRES. NOUVELLE SERIE. SERIE D. SCIENCES PHYSICO-CHIMIQUES. see *PHYSICS*

540   UN   ISSN 0077-8885
NEW TRENDS IN CHEMISTRY TEACHING. (Text in English and French) 1967. irreg; vol. 4 forthcoming. Unesco, 7-9 Place de Fontenoy, 75700 Paris, France (Dist. in U.S. by: Unipub, 345 Park Ave. S., New York, NY 10010) Ed. P. Farago.

540   JA
NIIGATA UNIVERSITY. FACULTY OF SCIENCE. SCIENCE REPORTS. SERIES C: CHEMISTRY. (Text in European languages) 1964. irreg. exchange basis. Niigata University, Faculty of Science - Niigata Daigaku Rigakubu, 8050 Igarashi Nino-cho, Niigata-shi 950-21, Japan.

540   NE
NOBEL PRIZE LECTURES - CHEMISTRY. (Text in English) irreg., approx. every 3 yrs. price varies. Elsevier Scientific Publishing Co., P.O. Box 211, 1000 AE Amsterdam, Netherlands.

540   NE
NUCLEAR METHODS MONOGRAPHS. 1978. irreg. price varies. Elsevier Scientific Publishing Co., Box 211, 1000 AE Amsterdam, Netherlands.

540   US   ISSN 0553-0377
ORGANIZATION OF AMERICAN STATES. DEPARTMENT OF SCIENTIFIC AFFAIRS. SERIE DE QUIMICA: MONOGRAFIAS. 1965. irreg., no. 21, 1979. price varies. Organization of American States, Department of Publications, Washington, DC 20006. circ. 3,000.

540   US   ISSN 0302-4199
OXFORD CHEMISTRY SERIES. 1972. irreg. price varies. Oxford University Press, 200 Madison Ave., New York, NY 10016 (And Ely House, 37 Dover St., London W1X 4AH, England) Ed.Bd. bibl. charts.

540   SW
P K L KEMIKALIER. biennial. Kr.75. Plast- och Kemikalieleverantoerers Foerening - Swedish Plastics and Chemicals Suppliers Association, Box 5512, S-114 85 Stockholm, Sweden.

540   CS
PEDAGOGICKA FAKULTA V USTI NAD LABEM. SBORNIK: RADA CHEMICKA. (Text in Czech or German; summaries in Czech, English, German, Russian) irreg. 22 Kcs. Statni Pedagogicke Nakladatelstvi, Ostrovni 30, 113 01 Prague 1, Czechoslovakia. illus.

540 574.192   US
PERSPECTIVES IN QUANTUM CHEMISTRY AND BIOCHEMISTRY. irreg., vol. 2, 1978. John Wiley & Sons, Inc., 605 Third Ave., New York, NY 10016. Ed. Bernard Pullman.

540   NE
PHASE TRANSITION PHENOMENA. 1979. irreg. price varies. Elsevier Scientific Publishing Co., Box 211, 1000 AE Amsterdam, Netherlands.

540   UK   ISSN 0556-3860
PHOTOCHEMISTRY. 1970. a. price varies. Chemical Society, Burlington House, London W1V 0BN, England (Subscr. to: Blackhorse Rd., Letchworth, Herts. SG6 1HN, England) Ed. Prof. D. Bryce-Smith. charts. index. Indexed: Chem.Abstr.

540 530   US   ISSN 0079-1938
PHYSICS AND CHEMISTRY IN SPACE. 1970. irreg., no. 10, 1978. price varies. Springer-Verlag, 175 Fifth Ave., New York, NY 10010 (also Berlin, Heidelberg, Vienna) Ed. F. Roederes. (reprint service avail. from ISI)

PHYSICS AND CHEMISTRY OF MATERIALS WITH LAYERED STRUCTURES. see *PHYSICS — Mechanics*

540   PL   ISSN 0416-7309
POLITECHNIKA GDANSKA. ZESZYTY NAUKOWE. CHEMIA. (Text in Polish; summaries in English and Russian) 1955. irreg. price varies. Politechnika Gdanska, Majakowskiego 11/12, 81-952 Gdansk 6, Poland (Dist. by: Osrodek Rozpowszechniania Wydawnictw Naukowych Pan, Palac Kultury i Nauki, 00-901 Warsaw, Poland)

540   PL   ISSN 0075-7055
POLITECHNIKA KRAKOWSKA. ZESZYTY NAUKOWE. CHEMIA. irreg. price varies. Politechnika Krakowska, Warszawska 24, Krakow, Poland (Dist. by Ars Polona-Ruch, Krakowskie Przedmiescie 7, Warsaw, Poland)

540   PL   ISSN 0458-1555
POLITECHNIKA LODZKA. ZESZYTY NAUKOWE. CHEMIA. (Text in Polish; summaries in English and Russian) 1954. irreg. price varies. Politechnika Lodzka, Ul. Zwirki 36, 90-924 Lodz, Poland (Dist. by: Ars Polona-Ruch, Krakowskie Przedmiescie 7, Warsaw, Poland) Ed. Boleslaw Bochwic. circ. 383. Indexed: Chem.Abstr.

540   PL   ISSN 0137-6896
POLITECHNIKA POZNANSKA. ZESZYTY NAUKOWE. CHEMIA TECHNIKI ZASTOSOWAN. (Text in Polish; summaries in English and Russian) 1962. irreg., 1972, no. 11. price varies. Politechnika Poznanska, Pl. Curie-Sklodowskiej 5, Poznan, Poland. Ed. Zbigniew Kurzawa. circ. 150.
    Former titles: Politechnika Poznanska. Zeszyty Naukowe. Chemia Techniki Zastosowan (ISSN 0079-4473); Politechnika Poznanska. Zeszyty Naukowe. Chemia.

540 660   PL   ISSN 0372-9494
POLITECHNIKA SLASKA. ZESZYTY NAUKOWE. CHEMIA. (Text in Polish; summaries in English and Russian) 1957. irreg. price varies. Politechnika Slaska, W. Pstrowskiego 7, 44-100 Gliwice, Poland (Dist. by: Ars Polona, Krakowskie Przedmiescie 7, 00-068 Warsaw, Poland) Ed. Genowefa Bienkiewicz. circ. 250.

540   NE
POLYMER SCIENCE LIBRARY. 1979. irreg. price varies. Elsevier Scientific Publishing Co., Box 211, 1000 AE Amsterdam, Netherlands.

540   US
PROCESS EQUIPMENT SERIES. 1979. irreg. Technomic Publishing Co., Inc., 265 Post Rd. W., Westport, CT 06880. Eds. Paul N. Cheremisinoff, Mahesh V. Bhatia. charts.

540   NE
PROGRESS IN FILTRATION AND SEPARATION. 1979. irreg. price varies. Elsevier Scientific Publishing Co., Box 211, 1000 AE Amsterdam, Netherlands. Ed. R.J. Wakeman.

540 510   NE   ISSN 0079-6468
PROGRESS IN MEDICINAL CHEMISTRY. 1961. irreg., vol. 16, 1979. price varies. Elsevier North-Holland Biomedical Press, Box 211, 1000 AE Amsterdam, Netherlands. Eds. G.P. Ellis, G.B. West.

540 539   US   ISSN 0149-1970
PROGRESS IN NUCLEAR ENERGY(NEW SERIES) 1977. 6/yr. (2 vols./yr.) $165. Pergamon Press, Inc., Journals Division, Maxwell House, Fairview Park, Elmsford, NY 10523 (And Headington Hill Hall, Oxford, Eng) Eds. R. Sher, M.M.R. Williams. (also avail. in microform from MIM,UMI)
    Supersedes (as of 1977): Progress in Nuclear Energy. Series 3-Process Chemistry (ISSN 0079-6514) & Progress in Nuclear Energy. Series 9-Analytical Chemistry (ISSN 0079-6530); Supersedes(1956-1977): Progress in Nuclear Energy. Series 3-Process Chemistry (ISSN 0079-6557)

540   IT
QUADERNI DI CHIMICA APPLICATA. irreg. Casa Editrice Ambrosiana, Via G. Frua 6, 20146 Milan, Italy. Ed. E. Mariani.

540   US   ISSN 0080-181X
RESIDUE REVIEWS. (Text in English; occasionally in German or French) 1962. irreg., no. 80, 1981. Springer-Verlag, 175 Fifth Ave., New York, NY 10010 (also Berlin, Heidelberg, Vienna) (reprint service avail. from ISI)

ROYAL IRISH ACADEMY. PROCEEDINGS. SECTION B: BIOLOGICAL, GEOLOGICAL AND CHEMICAL SCIENCES. see *BIOLOGY*

540 SI
S N I C BULLETIN. (Text in English) 1972. a. membership. Singapore National Institute of Chemistry, c/o Dept. of Chemistry, University of Singapore, Singapore 10, Singapore. charts. circ. 1,000.
Formerly: Singapore National Institute of Chemistry. Bulletin.

SAITAMA UNIVERSITY. SCIENCE REPORTS. SERIES A: MATHEMATICS. see *MATHEMATICS*

540 530 IT ISSN 0391-3244
SCIENZE DELLA MATERIA. 1977. irreg., no. 3, 1979. price varies. Liguori Editore s.r.l., Via Mezzocannone 19, 80134 Naples, Italy. Ed. Giuseppe del Re.

SERIES ON EXTRATERRESTRIAL CHEMISTRY. see *ASTRONOMY*

540 574 610 US
SHEVCHENKO SCIENTIFIC SOCIETY. PROCEEDINGS OF THE SECTION OF CHEMISTRY, BIOLOGY AND MEDICINE. (Text in English and Ukrainian) 1973, vol. 7. irreg. $2. Shevchenko Scientific Society, 302 W. 13th St., New York, NY 10014.
Supersedes in part its: Proceedings of the Section of Mathematics, Natural Sciences and Medicine (ISSN 0470-5017)

540 PL ISSN 0081-0711
SOCIETATIS SCIENTIARUM LODZIENSIS. ACTA CHIMICA. (Text in English; summaries in Polish) 1955. irreg., 1972, vol. 17. price varies. (Lodzkie Towarzystwo Naukowe) Panstwowe Wydawnictwo Naukowe, Ul. Miodowa 10, Warsaw, Poland (Dist. by Ars Polona-Ruch, Krakowskie Przedmiescie 7, Warsaw, Poland) Ed. Anna Chrzaszczewska. bibl. charts.

540 FR
SOCIETE CHIMIQUE DE FRANCE. ANNUAIRE. a. 150 F. Societe Chimique de France, 250, rue Saint-Jacques, France.

540 UK ISSN 0584-8555
SPECTROSCOPIC PROPERTIES OF INORGANIC & ORGANOMETALLIC COMPOUNDS; specialist periodical reports. 1972, vol. 5. a. price varies. Chemical Society, Burlington House, London W1V 0BN, England. Ed. Prof. N. N. Greenwood. charts. illus. index. Indexed: Chem.Abstr.

SPRINGER SERIES IN CHEMICAL PHYSICS. see *PHYSICS*

541 US ISSN 0081-5993
STRUCTURE AND BONDING. (Text in English) 1966. irreg., vol. 46, 1981. $25-35. Springer-Verlag, 175 Fifth Ave., New York, NY 10010 (also Berlin, Heidelberg, Vienna) circ. 1,500. (reprint service avail. from ISI)

540 PL ISSN 0082-5530
STUDIA SOCIETATIS SCIENTIARUM TORUNENSIS. SECTIO B (CHEMIA) (Text in Polish; summaries in English) 1954. irreg. price varies. (Towarzystwo Naukowe w Toruniu) Panstwowe Wydawnictwo Naukowe, Ul, Miodowa 10, Warsaw, Poland.

540 RM ISSN 0039-3401
STUDIA UNIVERSITATIS "BABES-BOLYAI". CHEMIA. (Text in Romanian; summaries in English, French, German or Russian) 1958. s-a. exchange basis. Universitatea "Babes-Bolyai", Biblioteca Centrala Universitara, Str. Clinicilor Nr. 2, Cluj-Napoca, Rumania. abstr. charts. illus. index. Indexed: Chem.Abstr. Psychol.Abstr.

546.723 US ISSN 0196-1772
SULFUR REPORTS. 1980. irreg. $73 per vol. Harwood Academic Publishers GmbH, Box 786, Cooper Statin, New York, Ny 10276. Ed. Alexander Senning.

540 574 US ISSN 0081-9603
SURFACTANT SCIENCE SERIES. 1966. irreg., vol. 8, 1977. price varies. Marcel Dekker, Inc., 270 Madison Ave., New York, NY 10016. Eds. M. J. Schick, F. M. Fowkes.

540 US ISSN 0081-976X
SURVEY OF PROGRESS IN CHEMISTRY. 1963. irreg., vol. 8, 1977. price varies. Academic Press, Inc, 111 Fifth Ave., New York, NY 10003. Ed. Arthur F. Scott. index.

540 US ISSN 0082-2531
TECHNIQUES OF CHEMISTRY. 1971. irreg., vol. 15, 1980. price varies. John Wiley & Sons, Inc., 605 Third Ave., New York, NY 10016. Ed. A. Weissberger.
Incorporating: Technique of Inorganic Chemistry & Technique of Organic Chemistry (ISSN 0082-240X)

541 UK ISSN 0305-9995
THEORETICAL CHEMISTRY. 1973. biennial. Chemical Society, Burlington House, London W1V 0BN, England (Subscr. to: Blackhorse Rd., Letchworth, Herts. SG6 1HN, Eng.) Eds. Prof. R.N. Dixon, Dr. C. Thomson. charts. illus. index.
Formerly: Quantum Chemistry.

541 US ISSN 0082-3961
THEORETICAL CHEMISTRY; a series of monographs. 1965. irreg., vol. 5, 1976. price varies. Academic Press Inc., 111 Fifth Ave., New York, NY 10003. Ed. D. P. Craig.

541.2 US ISSN 0361-0551
THEORETICAL CHEMISTRY: ADVANCES AND PERSPECTIVES. 1975. irreg. Academic Press, Inc., 111 Fifth Ave., New York, NY 10003. (also avail. in microfiche)

540 US
TOPICS IN CURRENT CHEMISTRY. 1965. irreg., vol. 98, 1981. price varies. Springer-Verlag, 175 Fifth Ave., New York, NY 10010 (also Berlin, Heidelberg, Vienna) (reprint service avail. from ISI)
Formerly: Fortschritte der Chemischen Forschung (ISSN 0071-7894)

TOPICS IN INORGANIC AND GENERAL CHEMISTRY. see *CHEMISTRY — Inorganic Chemistry*

541.223 US ISSN 0082-500X
TOPICS IN STEREOCHEMISTRY. 1967. irreg., vol. 10, 1979. price varies. John Wiley & Sons, Inc., 605 Third Ave., New York, NY 10016. Eds. N. L. Allinger, E. L. Eliel.

660 UK ISSN 0309-2356
U K CHEMICAL INDUSTRY STATISTICS HANDBOOK. 1969. a. £10. ‡ Chemical Industries Association Ltd., Alembic House, 93 Albert Embankment, London SE1 7TU, England. Ed. L. S. Adler. stat. index. circ. 1,000.

540 US ISSN 0146-5031
U V CURING BUYER'S GUIDE. 1977. a. $22. Technology Marketing Corp., 17 Park St., Norwalk, CT 06851. Ed.Bd.

UNIVERSITATEA DIN TIMISOARA. ANALELE. STIINTE FIZICO-CHIMICE. see *PHYSICS*

540 FR ISSN 0069-4703
UNIVERSITE DE CLERMONT-FERRAND II. ANNALES SCIENTIFIQUE. SERIE CHEMIE. 1960. irreg. price varies. Universite de Clermont-Ferrand II, Unite d'Enseignement et de Recherche de Sciences Exactes et Naturelles, B.P. 45, 63170 Aubiere, France. circ. 250.

UNIVERSITE LAVAL. CENTRE DE RECHERCHES SUR LES ATOMES ET LES MOLECULES. RAPPORT ANNUEL; physics and chemistry of atoms and molecules. see *PHYSICS — Nuclear Energy*

540 PL
UNIWERSYTET GDANSKI. WYDZIAL MATEMATYKI, FIZYKI, CHEMII. ZESZYTY NAUKOWE. CHEMIA. (Text in Polish; summaries in English) 1972. irreg. price varies. Uniwersytet Gdanski, Ul. Czerwonej Armii 110, 81-824 Sopot, Poland.

540 PL ISSN 0083-4319
UNIWERSYTET JAGIELLONSKI. ZESZYTY NAUKOWE. PRACE CHEMICZNE. (Text in Polish; summaries in English, French, Russian) 1959, no. 5. irreg., 1972, vol. 17. price varies. Panstwowe Wydawnictwo Naukowe, Miodowa 10, Warsaw, Poland (Dist. by Ars Polona-Ruch, Krakowskie Przedmiescie 7, Warsaw, Poland) Indexed: Chem.Abstr.

540 PL
UNIWERSYTET SLASKI W KATOWICACH. PRACE CHEMICZNE. irreg., 1975, vol. 5. 8 Zl. Uniwersytet Slaski w Katowicach, Ul. Bankowa 14, 40-007 Katowice, Poland. Ed. Jozefa Sliwioka. charts.

VOM WASSER; ein Fachbuch fuer Wasserchemie und Wasserreinigungstechnik. see *WATER RESOURCES*

540 US
WADSWORTH SERIES IN CHEMISTRY. irreg. Wadsworth Publishing Co., 10 Davis Dr., Belmont, CA 94002.

540 AT ISSN 0085-8153
WESTERN AUSTRALIA. GOVERNMENT CHEMICAL LABORATORIES. REPORT OF INVESTIGATIONS. 1968. irreg. free to qualified personnel. Government Chemical Laboratories, 30 Plain Street, Perth, W.A. 6000, Australia. circ. 50.

540 530 GW
WISSENSCHAFTLICHE FORSCHUNGSBERICHTE. REIHE 1. GRUNDLAGENFORSCHUNG UND GRUNDLEGENDE METHODIK. ABT. A. CHEMIE UND PHYSIK/CURRENT TOPICS IN SCIENCE. REIHE 1. BASIC RESEARCH. ABT. A. CHEMISTRY AND PHYSICS. 1921. irreg. price varies. Dr. Dietrich Steinkopff Verlag, Saalbaustr. 12, Postfach 11 1008, 6100 Darmstadt 11, W. Germany (B.R.D.) Eds. W. Bruegel, A. W. Holldorf. circ. 2,000.

540 GE ISSN 0084-0971
WISSENSCHAFTLICHE TASCHENBUECHER. REIHE CHEMIE. 1962. irreg. price varies. Akademie-Verlag, Leipziger Str. 3-4, 108 Berlin, E. Germany (D.D.R.) Eds. H. Klare, E. Leibnitz.

540 US
WORLD AROMATICS AND DERIVATIVES. 1973. a., with on-line access. price on request. S R I International, World Petrochemicals Program, Menlo Park, CA 94025. Ed. J.L. Blackford. charts. stat.
Formerly: Benzene-Toluene-Xylenes and Derivatives.

540 US
WORLD C4 HYDROCARBONS AND DERIVATIVES. 1974. a., with on-line access. price on request. S R I International, World Petrochemicals Program, Menlo Park, CA 94025. Ed. J.L. Blackford. charts. stat.
Formerly: C4 Hydrocarbons and Derivatives.

540 US
WORLD ETHYLENE AND DERIVATIVES. 1973. a., with on-line access. price on request. S R I International, World Petrochemicals Program, Menlo Park, CA 94025. Ed. J.L. Blackford. charts. stat.
Formerly: Ethylene and Derivatives.

540 US
WORLD PROPYLENE AND DERIVATIVES. 1973. a., with s-a. supplements and on-line access. price on request. S R I International, World Petrochemicals Program, Menlo Park, CA 94025. Ed. J.L. Blackford. charts. stat.
Formerly: Propylene and Derivatives.

WORLDWIDE CHEMICAL DIRECTORY. see *BUSINESS AND ECONOMICS — Trade And Industrial Directories*

CHEMISTRY — Abstracting, Bibliographies, Statistics

541.36 016 US ISSN 0149-2268
BULLETIN OF CHEMICAL THERMODYNAMICS (1977) 1950. a. $20 individuals; institutions $30. (International Union of Pure and Applied Chemistry, Commission on Thermodynamics) Thermochemistry, Inc., Oklahoma State University, Department of Chemistry, Stillwater, OK 74074. Ed. Robert D. Freeman. adv. bk. rev. circ. 500. Indexed: Chem.Abstr. Phys.Ber.
Former titles, vol. 5-19, 1962-1976: Bulletin of Thermodynamics and Thermochemistry (ISSN 0068-4139); Vol. 1-4, 1958-1961: Bulletin of Chemical Thermodynamics; Supersedes: Thermochemical Bulletin and Bulletin of Unpublished Thermal Material.

EIGHT PEAK INDEX OF MASS SPECTRA. see *PHYSICS — Abstracting, Bibliographies, Statistics*

544.92 016 US ISSN 0072-8446
GUIDE TO GAS CHROMATOGRAPHY LITERATURE. 1964. irreg., 1974, vol. 3. price varies. Plenum Publishing Corp., I.F.I.--Plenum Data Co., 233 Spring St., New York, NY 10013.

547 016 UK ISSN 0536-6518
INDEX OF REVIEWS IN ORGANIC CHEMISTRY. 1971. a., with triennial cumulations. price varies. Chemical Society, Burlington House, London W1V 0BN OBN, England. Ed. Dr. D.A. Lewis. index.

540 US
U S S R REPORTS: CHEMISTRY. 1973. irreg. (approx. 5/yr.) $20. U.S. Joint Publications Research Service, 1000 N. Glebe Rd., Arlington, VA 22201 (Orders to: NTIS, Springfield, VA 22161)
Formerly: U S S R and Eastern Europe Scientific Abstracts: Chemistry; Which was formed by the merger of: U S S R Scientific Abstracts: Chemistry; East European Scientific Abstracts: Chemistry.

CHEMISTRY — Analytical Chemistry

545.822 US ISSN 0065-2091
ADVANCES IN ACTIVATION ANALYSIS. 1969. irreg., 1972, vol. 2. $35.50 1972. Academic Press, Inc., (Subsidiary of: Harcourt Brace Jovanovich) 111 Fifth Ave., New York, NY 10003. Eds. J. M. A. Lenihan, S. J. Thomson.

543 US ISSN 0065-2148
ADVANCES IN ANALYTICAL CHEMISTRY AND INSTRUMENTATION. 1960. irreg., 1973, vol. 11. price varies. John Wiley & Sons, Inc., 605 Third Ave., New York, NY 10016. Eds. C.N. Reilley & F. McLafferty.

544.92 US ISSN 0065-2415
ADVANCES IN CHROMATOGRAPHY. 1966. irreg., 1979, vol. 17. price varies. Marcel Dekker, Inc., 270 Madison Ave., New York, NY 10016. Eds. J. Calvin Giddings And Roy A. Keller.

543 US
ANALYTICAL CHEMISTRY OF THE ELEMENTS SERIES. 1963. irreg., unnumbered, 1975 latest. price varies. Halsted Press (Subsidiary of: John Wiley & Sons, Inc.) 605 Third Ave., New York, NY 10016.

544.92 NE
ANALYTICAL CHEMISTRY SYMPOSIA SERIES. 1979. irreg., vol. 6, 1980. price varies. Elsevier Scientific Publishing Co., Box 211, 1000 AE Amsterdam, Netherlands.
Formerly: Chromatography Symposia Series.

543 UK ISSN 0583-8894
ANALYTICAL SCIENCES MONOGRAPHS. 1973. irreg., no. 5, 1978. price varies. Chemical Society, Burlington House, London W1V 0BN, England. bibl. charts. illus.

ANNUAL BOOK OF A S T M STANDARDS. PART 12. CHEMICAL ANALYSIS OF METALS; SAMPLING AND ANALYSIS OF METAL BEARING ORES. see *ENGINEERING — Engineering Mechanics And Materials*

ANNUAL BOOK OF A S T M STANDARDS. PART 42. EMISSION, MOLECULAR, AND MASS SPECTROSCOPY; CHROMATOGRAPHY; RESINOGRAPHY; MICROSCOPY. see *ENGINEERING — Engineering Mechanics And Materials*

543 US ISSN 0066-961X
ASSOCIATION OF OFFICIAL ANALYTICAL CHEMISTS. OFFICIAL METHODS OF ANALYSIS. 1920. quinquennial. $75. Association of Official Analytical Chemists, 111 N. 19th St., Suite 210, Arlington, VA 22209. Ed. William Horwitz. index. circ. 17,000. Indexed: Chem.Abstr.

543 US ISSN 0145-5338
BENCHMARK PAPERS IN ANALYTICAL CHEMISTRY. 1976. irreg., vol. 2, 1976. Dowden, Hutchinson & Ross, Inc., 523 Sarah St., Stroudsburg, PA 18360 (Dist. by Academic Press, Inc., 111 Fifth Ave., New York, NY 10003)

543 US ISSN 0069-2867
CHELATES IN ANALYTICAL CHEMISTRY: A COLLECTION OF MONOGRAPHS. 1967. irreg., vol. 5, 1976. price varies. Marcel Dekker, Inc., 270 Madison Ave., New York, NY 10016. Eds. H. A. Flaschka, A. J. Barnard, Jr. Indexed: Chem.Abstr.

543 US ISSN 0069-2883
CHEMICAL ANALYSIS; a series of monographs on analytical chemistry and its applications. 1949. irreg., vol. 55, 1980. price varies. John Wiley & Sons, Inc., 605 Third Ave., New York, NY 10016. Eds. P.J. Elving, J.D. Winefordner. index.

543 GW ISSN 0340-8221
CHEMISCHE ANALYSE. 1907. irreg., no. 5, 1962. price varies. Ferdinand Enke Verlag, Herdweg 63, 7000 Stuttgart 1, W. Germany (B.R.D.) Ed. W. Koch.

544.92 US ISSN 0095-2214
CHROMATOGRAPHY NEWSLETTER. 1972. irreg. free. ‡ Perkin-Elmer Corp., Main Ave., Norwalk, CT 06856. Ed. L.S. Ettre. circ. 8,000(controlled) (back issues available) Indexed: Chem.Abstr.

CLINICAL AND BIOCHEMICAL ANALYSIS. see *BIOLOGY — Biological Chemistry*

542 US ISSN 0070-315X
DECHEMA MONOGRAPHIEN. irreg., vol. 89, 1980. price varies. (Deutsche Gesellschaft fuer Chemisches Apparatewesen e.V. - DECHEMA, GW) Verlag Chemie International, Inc., Plaza Center, Ste. E, 1020 N.W. 6th St., Deerfield Beach, FL 33441 (And Pappellalee 3, Postfach 1260, 6940 Weinheim, W. Germany (B.R.D.)) index. (reprint service avail. from ISI)

543 US ISSN 0070-9778
ELECTROANALYTICAL CHEMISTRY: A SERIES OF ADVANCES. (Subseries of Monographs in Electroanalytical Chemistry and Electrochemistry) 1966. irreg., vol. 11, 1979. price varies. Marcel Dekker, Inc., 270 Madison Ave., New York, NY 10016. Ed. A. J. Bard.

543.085 US
EUROPEAN CONGRESS ON MOLECULAR SPECTROSCOPY. PROCEEDINGS. vol. 12, 1975. a. Elsevier North-Holland, Inc., New York, 52 Vanderbilt Ave., New York, NY 10017.

543 US ISSN 0074-8099
INTERNATIONAL SERIES ON ANALYTICAL CHEMISTRY. 1961. irreg., vol. 58, 1975. price varies. Pergamon Press, Inc., Maxwell House, Fairview Park, Elmsford, NY 10523. index.
Formerly: International Series of Monographs on Analytical Chemistry.

544.92 US ISSN 0021-9665
JOURNAL OF CHROMATOGRAPHIC SCIENCE. Includes annual no.: International Chromatography Guide. 1963. m. $48. Preston Publications, Inc., 6366 Gross Point Rd., Box 48312, Niles, IL 60648. Ed. R. P. W. Scott. adv. bk. rev. charts. illus. index. circ. 6,000. (also avail. in microfilm) Indexed: Biol.Abstr. Curr.Cont. Anal.Abstr. Chem.Titles.
Formerly: Journal of Gas Chromatography.

544.92 NE
JOURNAL OF CHROMATOGRAPHY LIBRARY. 1973. irreg., vol. 19, 1981. price varies. Elsevier Scientific Publishing Co., Box 211, 1000 AE Amsterdam, Netherlands.

METHODS OF BIOCHEMICAL ANALYSIS. see *BIOLOGY — Biological Chemistry*

543 US ISSN 0076-8642
MIKROCHIMICA ACTA. SUPPLEMENT. 1966. irreg., no. 7, 1977. Springer-Verlag, 175 Fifth Ave., New York, NY 10010 (also Berlin, Heidelberg, Vienna) (reprint service avail. from ISI)

543 UK ISSN 0305-9782
MOLECULAR SPECTROSCOPY. 1973. a. price varies. Chemical Society, Burlington House, London W1V 0BN, England (Subscr. to: Blackhorse Road, Letchworth, Herts SG6 1HN, Eng) Eds. Prof. D. A. Long, Prof. J. Sheridan, Dr. R. F. Barrow. charts. illus. index. Indexed: Chem.Abstr.

543 UK ISSN 0305-9790
MOLECULAR STRUCTURE BY DIFFRACTION METHODS. 1973. a. price varies. Chemical Society, Burlington House, London W1V 0BN, England (Subscr. to: Blackhorse Road, Letchworth, Herts SG6 1HN, Eng) Eds. Prof. M. R. Truter, Dr. L. E. Sutton. charts. illus. index. Indexed: Chem.Abstr.

MONOGRAPHS IN ELECTROANALYTICAL CHEMISTRY AND ELECTROCHEMISTRY. see *CHEMISTRY — Electrochemistry*

543 547 US ISSN 0078-6136
ORGANIC ELECTRONIC SPECTRAL DATA. 1960. irreg., vol. 15, 1979. price varies. (Organic Electronic Spectral Data, Inc.) John Wiley & Sons, Inc., 605 Third Ave., New York, NY 10016. Ed.Bd.

544.66 US ISSN 0092-0509
POWDER DIFFRACTION FILE SEARCH MANUAL. ALPHABETICAL LISTING. INORGANIC. (Subseries of the Committee's Publication SMA) a. ‡ Joint Committee on Powder Diffraction Standards., International Center for Diffraction Data, 1601 Park Lane, Swarthmore, PA 19081. index.

544.66 US ISSN 0092-1300
POWDER DIFFRACTION FILE SEARCH MANUAL. FINK METHOD. INORGANIC. (Subseries of the Committee's Publication SMF) a. ‡ Joint Committee on Powder Diffraction Standards., International Center for Diffraction Data, 1601 Park Lane, Swarthmore, PA 19081. index.

544.66 US ISSN 0092-1319
POWDER DIFFRACTION FILE SEARCH MANUAL. HANAWALT METHOD. INORGANIC. (Subseries of the Committee's Publication SMH) a. ‡ Joint Committee on Powder Diffraction Standards., International Center for Diffraction Data, 1601 Park Lane, Swarthmore, PA 19081. index.

543 US ISSN 0079-6042
PROGRESS IN ANALYTICAL CHEMISTRY. (Represents: Proceedings of the Eastern Analytical Symposia.) 1968. irreg. price varies. Plenum Press, 233 Spring Ave., New York, NY 10013. Eds. Ivor L. Simmons, Galen W. Ewing.

PROGRESS IN NUCLEAR MAGNETIC RESONANCE SPECTROSCOPY. see *PHYSICS — Nuclear Energy*

543 US
REAGENT CHEMICALS. every 4 yrs. price varies. American Chemical Society, Committee on Analytical Reagents, 1155 16th St., N.W., Washington, DC 20036.

543 UK ISSN 0300-9963
SELECTED ANNUAL REVIEWS OF THE ANALYTICAL SCIENCES. 1971. a. price varies. Chemical Society, Burlington House, London W1V 0BN, England. Ed. L. S. Bark. Indexed: Chem.Abstr.

543.085 UK ISSN 0306-1353
SOCIETY FOR ANALYTICAL CHEMISTRY. ANNUAL REPORTS ON ANALYTICAL ATOMIC SPECTROSCOPY. a. price varies. Society for Analytical Chemistry, 9/10 Savile Row, London W1X 1AF, England.

545.3 SZ
SURFACE TECHNOLOGY. (Text and summaries in English) 1972. m. 360 Fr. Elsevier Sequoia S.A., Box 851, 1001 Lausanne 1, Switzerland. Ed. J.P.G. Farr. adv. bk. rev. illus. index. (also avail. in microfilm; back issues avail.) Indexed: Chem. Abstr. Curr.Cont. Eng.Ind. Met.Abstr. Sci.Cit.Ind. INSPEC. Met.Finish.Abstr. Phys.Ber.
Formerly (until Dec. 1975): Electrodeposition and Surface Treatment.

543 NE
TECHNIQUES AND INSTRUMENTATION IN ANALYTICAL CHEMISTRY. 1978. irreg. price varies. Elsevier Scientific Publishing Co., Box 211, 1000 AE Amsterdam, Netherlands.

544.63 US
THERMODYNAMICS RESEARCH CENTER. HYDROCARBON PROJECT. SELECTED VALUES OF PROPERTIES OF HYDROCARBONS AND RELATED COMPOUNDS. CATEGORY B: SELECTED INFRARED SPECTRAL DATA. 1943. irreg., supplement B-79, 1977. $1 per sheet. (Texas Engineering Experiment Station) Thermodynamics Research Center, Texas A & M University, College Station, TX 77843. Ed. Kenneth R. Hall. circ. 500. (looseleaf format)
Formerly: Thermodynamics Research Center. A P I 44. Hydrocarbon Project. Selected Values of Properties of Hydrocarbons and Related Compounds. Category B: Selected Infrared Spectral Data (ISSN 0065-9649)

547.3 543.085 US
THERMODYNAMICS RESEARCH CENTER. HYDROCARBON PROJECT. SELECTED VALUES OF PROPERTIES OF HYDROCARBONS AND RELATED COMPOUNDS. CATEGORY C: SELECTED ULTRAVIOLET SPECTRAL DATA. 1945. irreg., supplement c-47, 1980. $1 per sheet. (Texas Engineering Experiment Station) Thermodynamics Research Center, Texas A & M University, College Station, TX 77843. Ed. Kenneth R. Hall. circ. 400. (looseleaf format)
Formerly: Thermodynamics Research Center. A P I 44. Hydrocarbon Project. Selected Values of Properties of Hydrocarbons and Related Compounds. Category C: Selected Ultraviolet Spectral Data (ISSN 0065-9657); Incorporating: Thermodynamics Research Center Data Project. Selected Values of Properties of Chemical Compounds. Category C. Selected Ultraviolet Spectral Data.

547.3 543.085 US
THERMODYNAMICS RESEARCH CENTER. HYDROCARBON PROJECT. SELECTED VALUES OF PROPERTIES OF HYDROCARBONS AND RELATED COMPOUNDS. CATEGORY D: SELECTED RAMAN SPECTRAL DATA. 1948. irreg., supplement D-23, 1978. $1 per sheet. (Texas Engineering Experiment Station) Thermodynamics Research Center, Texas A & M University, College Station, TX 77843. Ed. Kenneth R. Hall. circ. 300.
Formerly: Thermodynamics Research Center. A P I 44. Hydrocarbon Project. Selected Values of Properties of Hydrocarbons and Related Compounds. Category D: Selected Raman Spectral Data (ISSN 0082-4038)

547.3 543.085 US
THERMODYNAMICS RESEARCH CENTER. HYDROCARBON PROJECT. SELECTED VALUES OF PROPERTIES OF HYDROCARBONS AND RELATED COMPOUNDS. CATEGORY E: SELECTED MASS SPECTRAL DATA. 1947. irreg., supplement E-56, 1979. $1 per sheet. (Texas Engineering Experiment Station) Thermodynamics Research Center, Texas A & M University, College Station, TX 77843. Ed. Kenneth R. Hall. circ. 500. (looseleaf format)
Formerly: Thermodynamics Research Center. A P I 44. Hydrocarbon Project. Selected Values of Properties of Hydrocarbons and Related Compounds. Category E: Selected Mass Spectral Data (ISSN 0065-9673); Incorporating: Thermodynamics Research Center Data Project. Selected Values of Properties of Chemical Compounds. Category E. Selected Mass Spectral Data.

547.3 US
THERMODYNAMICS RESEARCH CENTER. HYDROCARBON PROJECT. SELECTED VALUES OF PROPERTIES OF HYDROCARBONS AND RELATED COMPOUNDS. CATEGORY F: SELECTED NUCLEAR MAGNETIC RESONANCE DATA. 1959. irreg., supplement F-25, 1979. $1 per sheet. (Texas Engineering Experiment Station) Thermodynamics Research Center, Texas A & M University, College Station, TX 77843. Ed. Kenneth R. Hall. circ. 350. (looseleaf format)
Formerly: Thermodynamics Research Center. A P I 44. Hydrocarbon Project. Selected Values of Properties of Hydrocarbons and Related Compounds. Category F: Selected Nuclear Magnetic Resonance Data (ISSN 0065-9681)

541.36 541.3 US ISSN 0082-4046
THERMODYNAMICS RESEARCH CENTER DATA PROJECT. SELECTED VALUES OF PROPERTIES OF CHEMICAL COMPOUNDS. CATEGORY A. TABLES OF SELECTED VALUES OF PHYSICAL AND THERMODYNAMIC PROPERTIES OF CHEMICAL COMPOUNDS. 1955. irreg., supplement a-44, 1980. $1.50 per sheet. Thermodynamics Research Center, Texas A & M University, College Station, TX 77843. Ed. Kenneth R. Hall. circ. 400. (looseleaf format)

544.63 US ISSN 0082-402X
THERMODYNAMICS RESEARCH CENTER DATA PROJECT. SELECTED VALUES OF PROPERTIES OF CHEMICAL COMPOUNDS. CATEGORY B. SELECTED INFRARED SPECTRAL DATA. 1959. irreg., supplement B-20, 1976. $1 per sheet. Thermodynamics Research Center, Texas A & M University, College Station, TX 77843. Ed. Kenneth R. Hall. circ. 300. (looseleaf format)

547.128 US ISSN 0082-4070
THERMODYNAMICS RESEARCH CENTER DATA PROJECT. SELECTED VALUES OF PROPERTIES OF CHEMICAL COMPOUNDS. CATEGORY F. SELECTED NUCLEAR MAGNETIC RESONANCE SPECTRAL DATA. 1960. irreg., f-29, 1980. $1. Thermodynamics Research Center, Texas A & M University, College Station, TX 77843. Ed. Kenneth R. Hall. circ. 250. (looseleaf format)

547.3 543.085 US
THERMODYNAMICS RESEARCH CENTER HYDROCARBON PROJECT. SELECTED VALUES OF PROPERTIES OF HYDROCARBONS AND RELATED COMPOUNDS. CATEGORY G: SELECTED C-13 NUCLEAR MAGNETIC RESONANCE SPECTRAL DATA. 1975. irreg., supplement G-9, 1979. $1 per sheet. (Texas Engineering Experiment Station) Thermodynamics Research Center, Texas A & M University, College Station, TX 77843. Ed. Kenneth R. Hall. circ. 350.
Former titles: Thermodynamics Research Center. Hydrocarbon Project. Selected Values of Properties of Hydrocarbons and Related Compounds. Catagory G: Selected 130 Nuclear Magnetic Resonance Spectral Data; Thermodynamics research center A p I 44. hydrocarbon project. selected values of properties of hydrocarbons and related compounds. category g: Selected 130 Nuclear Magnetic Resonance Spectral Data.

543 US ISSN 0082-626X
TREATISE ON ANALYTICAL CHEMISTRY. PART 3: ANALYTICAL CHEMISTRY IN INDUSTRY. 1967. irreg., vol. 4, 1977. price varies. John Wiley & Sons, Inc., 605 Third Ave., New York, NY 10016. Eds. I.M. Kolthoff and P.J. Elving.

543 US ISSN 0082-6251
TREATISE ON ANALYTICAL CHEMISTRY. PART 2: ANALYTICAL CHEMISTRY OF THE ELEMENTS; ANALYTICAL CHEMISTRY OF ORGANIC AND INORGANIC COMPOUNDS. 1961. irreg., vol. 17, 1980. price varies. John Wiley & Sons, Inc., 605 Third Ave., New York, NY 10016. Eds. I.M. Kolthoff and P.J. Elving.

543 US ISSN 0082-6243
TREATISE ON ANALYTICAL CHEMISTRY. PART 1: THEORY AND PRACTICE OF ANALYTICAL CHEMISTRY. 1959. irreg., vol. 12. price varies. John Wiley & Sons, Inc., 605 Third Ave, New York, NY 10016. Eds. I.M. Kolthoff and P.J. Elving.

643 NE ISSN 0167-2940
TRENDS IN ANALYTICAL CHEMISTRY. 1981. irreg. $120.93. Associated Scientific Publishers, Journals Division, Box 211, 1000AE Amsterdam, Netherlands. Ed. P.T. Shepherd. charts.

543 NE ISSN 0069-8024
WILSON & WILSON'S COMPREHENSIVE ANALYTICAL CHEMISTRY. 1959. irreg., vol. 9, 1979. price varies. Elsevier Scientific Publishing Co., Box 211, 1000 AE Amsterdam, Netherlands. Ed. G. Svehla.

CHEMISTRY — Crystallography

548.9 US
ADVANCES IN LIQUID CRYSTALS. 1975. irreg., vol. 3, 1978. price varies. Academic Press, Inc., 111 Fifth Ave., New York, NY 10003. Ed. G. H. Brown. (also avail. in microfiche)

548 US ISSN 0514-8863
AMERICAN CRYSTALLOGRAPHIC ASSOCIATION. MONOGRAPHS. 1944. irreg.,no. 8, 1979. price varies. American Crystallographic Association, 335 East 45th St., New York, NY 10017 (Orders to: Polycrystal Book Service, Box 11567, Pittsburgh, PA 15238) Ed. S.C. Abrahams. circ. 500-2,000. Indexed: Bull.Signal. Chem.Abstr. Phys.Abstr.

548 US ISSN 0569-4221
AMERICAN CRYSTALLOGRAPHIC ASSOCIATION. PROGRAM & ABSTRACTS. 1950. biennial. $2.50. American Crystallographic Association, 335 E. 45th St., New York, NY 10017 (Orders to Polycrystal Book Service, Box 11567, Pittsburgh, PA 15238) Ed. S. C. Abrahams. circ. 2,500. Indexed: Bull.Signal. Chem.Abstr. Phys.Abstr.

548 US ISSN 0065-8006
AMERICAN CRYSTALLOGRAPHIC ASSOCIATION. TRANSACTIONS. 1965. a. $7.50. American Crystallographic Association, 335 East 45th St., New York, NY 10017 (Orders to: Polycrystal Book Service, Box 11567, PA 15238) Ed. S.C. Abrahams. circ. 2,300. Indexed: Chem.Abstr.

548 US
CRYSTALS: GROWTH, PROPERTIES AND APPLICATIONS. 1978. irreg., vol. 4, 1980. price varies. Springer-Verlag, 175 Fifth Ave., New York, NY 10010 (Also Berlin, Heidelberg, Vienna) (reprint service avail. from ISI)

DEFECTS IN SOLIDS. see *PHYSICS*

548.3 US ISSN 0072-7814
GROWTH OF CRYSTALS. (All-Union Conferences on Crystal Growth, plus collections of papers issued between Conferences) 1958. irreg., vol. 10, 1975. price varies. Consultants Bureau (Subsidiary of: Plenum Publishing Corp.) 233 Spring St., New York, NY 10013. Eds. A. V. Shubnikov, N. N. Sheftal'

548 DK ISSN 0074-9389
INTERNATIONAL UNION OF
CRYSTALLOGRAPHY. ABSTRACTS OF THE
TRIENNIAL CONGRESS. (Supplement to: Acta
Crystallographica. Section A) (Text in English,
French or German) triennial since 1960; 1975, 10th
General Assembly, Amsterdam. Munksgaard,
Noerre Soegade 35, DK-1370 Copenhagen K,
Denmark. (reprint service avail. from ISI)

548 NE ISSN 0074-9397
INTERNATIONAL UNION OF
CRYSTALLOGRAPHY. STRUCTURE REPORTS.
1940-41. a. price varies. Bohn, Scheltema en
Holkema, Box 10697, Amsterdam, Netherlands. Ed.
W. B. Pearson. index. cum.index: 1940-1950 in vol.
14; 1951-60 in vol. 25.

LANDOLT-BOERNSTEIN, ZAHLENWERTE UND
FUNKTIONEN AUS
NATURWISSENSCHAFTEN UND TECHNIK.
NEUE SERIE. GROUP 3: CRYSTAL PHYSICS.
see *PHYSICS*

548 US
WILEY MONOGRAPHS IN
CRYSTALLOGRAPHY. irreg., latest 1976. John
Wiley & Sons, Inc., 605 Third Ave., New York, NY
10016. Ed. M. J. Buerger.

CHEMISTRY — Electrochemistry

541.37 660 US ISSN 0567-9907
ADVANCES IN ELECTROCHEMISTRY AND
ELECTROCHEMICAL ENGINEERING. 1961.
irreg., vol. 11, 1978. price varies. John Wiley &
Sons, Inc., 605 Third Ave., New York, NY 10016.
Ed. H. Gerischer.

541.37 UR
AKADEMIYA NAUK KAZAKHSKOI S.S.R.
INSTITUT ORGANICHESKOGO KATALIZA I
ELEKTROKHIMII. TRUDY. vol. 15, 1977. irreg.
1.34 Rub. per no. Izdatel'stvo Nauka Kazakhskoi
S.S.R., Ul.Shevchenko 28, 480021 Alma-Ata,
U.S.S.R. Ed. L. Kozin. abstr. bibl. illus. circ. 1,000.
Indexed: Chem.Abstr.

541.37 UR ISSN 0568-6776
AKADEMIYA NAUK S. S. S. R. SIBIRSKOE
OTDELENIE URALSKII NAUCHNYI TSENTR.
INSTITUT ELEKTRKHIMII. TRUDY. 1960. irreg.
1.36 Rub. (single issue) Akademiya Nauk S.S.S.R.,
Uralskii Nauchnyi Tsentr, Ul. Pervomaiskaya, 91,
Sverdlovsk, U.S.S.R. illus. circ. 1,000. (also avail. in
microfilm)

541.37 US
ELECTROCHEMICAL SOCIETY SERIES. 1948.
irreg., unnumbered, latest, 1978. price varies.
(Electrochemical Society, Inc.) John Wiley &
Sons, Inc., 605 Third Ave., New York, NY 10016.

541.37 UK ISSN 0305-9979
ELECTROCHEMISTRY. 1970. a. price varies.
Chemical Society, Burlington House, London W1V
OBN, England (Subscr. to: Blackhorse Road,
Letchworth, Herts. SG6 1HN, Eng.) Ed. H. R.
Thirsk. Indexed: Chem.Abstr.

541.37 US ISSN 0076-9924
MODERN ASPECTS OF ELECTROCHEMISTRY.
no. 3, 1964. irreg. price varies. Plenum Press, 233
Spring St., New York, NY 10013. Eds. B. E.
Conway, J. Bockris.

543 541.37 US ISSN 0077-0833
MONOGRAPHS IN ELECTROANALYTICAL
CHEMISTRY AND ELECTROCHEMISTRY.
1969. irreg., unnumbered, latest 1973. price varies.
Marcel Dekker, Inc., 270 Madison Ave., New York,
NY 10016. Ed. A. J. Bard.

541.37 US ISSN 0082-254X
TECHNIQUES OF ELECTROCHEMISTRY. 1972.
irreg., 1973, vol. 2. John Wiley & Sons, Inc., 605
Third Ave., New York, NY 10016. Ed. Ernest
Yeager, Alvin J. Salkind.

CHEMISTRY — Inorganic Chemistry

546 541.38 US ISSN 0065-2792
ADVANCES IN INORGANIC CHEMISTRY AND
RADIOCHEMISTRY. 1959. irreg., vol. 22, 1979.
price varies. Academic Press, Inc., 111 Fifth Ave.,
New York, NY 10003. Eds. H. J. Emeleus, A. G.
Sharpe. index. (also avail. in microfiche)

546.34 US ISSN 0065-2954
ADVANCES IN MOLTEN SALT CHEMISTRY.
1971. irreg. price varies. Plenum Press, 233 Spring
St., New York, NY 10013. Eds. J. Braunstein, G.
Mamantov, G. P. Smith.

ANNUAL REPORTS IN INORGANIC AND
GENERAL SYNTHESES. see *CHEMISTRY —
Physical Chemistry*

546 US
BENCHMARK PAPERS IN INORGANIC
CHEMISTRY. (Each vol. has distinctive title) 1972.
irreg., vol. 6, 1977. price varies. Dowden,
Hutchinson & Ross, Inc., 523 Sarah St.,
Stroudsburg, PA 18360 (Dist. by Academic Press,
Inc., 111 Fifth Ave., New York, NY 10003) Ed. H.
H. Sisler.

CHEMICAL SOCIETY, LONDON. ANNUAL
REPORTS ON THE PROGRESS OF
CHEMISTRY. SECTION A: PHYSICAL AND
INORGANIC CHEMISTRY. see *CHEMISTRY —
Physical Chemistry*

546 US
INORGANIC CHEMISTRY CONCEPTS. 1977.
irreg., vol. 6, 1981. price varies. Springer-Verlag,
175 Fifth Ave., New York, NY 10010 (also Berlin,
Heidelberg, Vienna) Ed.Bd. (reprint service avail.
from ISI)
Supersedes (1949-1969): Anorganische und
Allgemeine Chemie in Einzeldarstellungen (ISSN
0066-4553)

546 UK ISSN 0305-697X
INORGANIC CHEMISTRY OF THE MAIN
GROUP ELEMENTS. 1973. a. price varies.
Chemical Society, Burlington House, London W1V
OBN, England (Subscr. to: Blackhorse Road,
Letchworth, Herts SG6 1HH, Eng.) Ed. C.C.
Addison. charts. illus. index. Indexed: Chem.Abstr.

546 UK ISSN 0305-9774
INORGANIC CHEMISTRY OF THE TRANSITION
ELEMENTS. 1972. a. price varies. Chemical
Society, Burlington House, London W1V OBN,
England (Subscr to: Blackhorse Road, Letchworth,
Herts SG6 1HN, Eng.) Ed. Dr. B.F.G. Johnson.
charts. illus. index. Indexed: Chem.Abstr.

INORGANIC REACTION MECHANISMS. see
CHEMISTRY — Physical Chemistry

546.4 US
INTERNATIONAL CONFERENCE ON
PLUTONIUM AND OTHER ACTINIDES.
PROCEEDINGS. vol. 5, 1975. irreg. Elsevier
North-Holland, Inc., New York, 52 Vanderbilt Ave.,
New York, NY 10017. Eds. H. Blank, R. Lindner.
charts.

546.44 US
INTERNATIONAL TRANSPLUTONIUM
ELEMENT SYMPOSIUM. PROCEEDINGS. vol.
4, 1975. irreg. Elsevier North-Holland, Inc., New
York, 52 Vanderbilt Ave., New York, NY 10017.
Eds. W. Mueller, R. Lindner.

ISSLEDOVANIYA V OBLASTI KHIMII
REDKOZEMEL'NYKH ELEMENTOV. see
EARTH SCIENCES

546 US ISSN 0076-1753
M T P INTERNATIONAL REVIEW OF SCIENCE.
INORGANIC CHEMISTRY, SERIES 1. 1972.
irreg. $24.50 $21.50 by subscription; Index $12.50;
$11.50 by subscription. University Park Press,
Chamber of Commerce Bldg., Baltimore, MD
21202. Ed. H. J. Emeleus.

546 US
METAL IONS IN BIOLOGICAL SYSTEMS. vol. 7,
1978. irreg. price varies. Marcel Dekker, Inc., 270
Madison Ave., New York, NY 10016. Ed. Helmut
Siegel.

546 US
MONOGRAPHS IN INORGANIC CHEMISTRY.
1966. irreg. price varies. Plenum Press, 233 Spring
St., New York, NY 10013. Ed. Eugene G. Rochow.

546.536 JA
NIPPON TUNGSTEN REVIEW. (Text in English)
1968. a. exchange basis. Nippon Tungsten Co., Ltd.
- Nippon Tangusuten K. K., 460 Sanno, Shiobaru,
Minami-ku, Fukuoka-shi 815, Japan.

546 PL ISSN 0324-9832
POLITECHNIKA WROCLAWSKA. INSTYTUT
CHEMII NIEORGANICZNEJ I METALURGII
PIERWIASTKOW RZADKICH. PRACE
NAUKOWE. KONFERENCJE. (Text in Polish;
summaries in English and Russian) 1973. irreg., no.
9, 1975. price varies. Politechnika Wroclawska,
Wybrzeze Wyspianskiego 27, 50-370 Wroclaw,
Poland (Dist. by: Ars Polona-Ruch, Krakowskie
Przedmiescie 7, Warsaw, Poland) Ed. Marian Kloza.
Indexed: Chem.Abstr.

546 PL ISSN 0324-9840
POLITECHNIKA WROCLAWSKA. INSTYTUT
CHEMII NIEORGANICZNEJ I METALURGII
PIERWIASTKOW RZADKICH. PRACE
NAUKOWE. MONOGRAFIE. (Text in Polish;
summaries in English and Russian) 1970. irreg., no.
19, 1979. price varies. Politechnika Wroclawska,
Wybrzeze Wyspianskiego 27, 50-370 Wroclaw,
Poland (Dist. by: Ars Polona-Ruch, Krakowskie
Przedmiescie 7, Warsaw, Poland) Ed. Marian Kloza.

546 PL ISSN 0370-0755
POLITECHNIKA WROCLAWSKA. INSTYTUT
CHEMII NIEORGANICZNEJ I METALURGII
PIERWIASTKOW RZADKICH. PRACE
NAUKOWE. STUDIA I MATERIALY. (Text in
Polish; summaries in English and Russian) 1970.
irreg., no. 17, 1979. price varies. Politechnika
Wroclawska, Wybrzeze Wyspianskiego 27, 50-370
Wroclaw, Poland (Dist. by: Ars Polona-Ruch,
Krakowskie Przedmiescie 7, Warsaw, Poland) Ed.
Marian Kloza.

POWDER DIFFRACTION FILE SEARCH
MANUAL. ALPHABETICAL LISTING.
INORGANIC. see *CHEMISTRY — Analytical
Chemistry*

POWDER DIFFRACTION FILE SEARCH
MANUAL. FINK METHOD. INORGANIC. see
CHEMISTRY — Analytical Chemistry

POWDER DIFFRACTION FILE SEARCH
MANUAL. HANAWALT METHOD.
INORGANIC. see *CHEMISTRY — Analytical
Chemistry*

546 US ISSN 0079-6379
PROGRESS IN INORGANIC CHEMISTRY. 1959.
irreg., vol. 27, 1980. price varies. John Wiley &
Sons, Inc., 605 Third Ave., New York, NY 10016.
Ed. S.J. Lippard.

546 GW ISSN 0340-2509
SPEZIELLE ANORGANISCHE CHEMIE. (Text in
English and German) 1976. price varies. Dr.
Dietrich Steinkopff Verlag, Saalbaustr. 12, Postfach
11 1008, 6100 Darmstadt 11, W. Germany (B.R.D.)
Ed. A. Schneider.

546 NE
STUDIES IN INORGANIC CHEMISTRY. 1978.
irreg. price varies. Elsevier Scientific Publishing Co.,
Box 211, 1000 AE Amsterdam, Netherlands.

536 HU ISSN 0082-1306
SZILIKATKEMIAI MONOGRAFIAK. 1960. irreg.
price varies. (Magyar Tudomanyos Akademia)
Akademiai Kiado, Publishing House of the
Hungarian Academy of Sciences, P.O. Box 24, H-
1363 Budapest, Hungary.

546 540 NE ISSN 0082-495X
TOPICS IN INORGANIC AND GENERAL
CHEMISTRY. (Text in English) 1964. irreg., vol.
18, 1980. price varies. Elsevier Scientific Publishing
Co., P.O. Box 211, 1000 AE Amsterdam,
Netherlands. Ed. R. J. H. Clark.

546.712 US ISSN 0082-4992
TOPICS IN PHOSPHOROUS CHEMISTRY. 1964.
irreg., vol. 10, 1980. price varies. John Wiley &
Sons, Inc., 605 Third Ave., New York, NY 10016.
Eds. M. Grayson & E.J. Griffith.

546.6 540 US ISSN 0082-5921
TRANSITION METAL CHEMISTRY: A SERIES OF ADVANCES. 1966. irreg., vol. 7, 1972. price varies. Marcel Dekker, Inc., 270 Madison Ave., New York, NY 10016. Ed. R. L. Carlin.

546 NO
UNIVERSITETET I TRONDHEIM. NORGES TEKNISKE HOEGSKOLE. INSTITUTT FOR UORGANISK KJEMI. AVHANDLING. 1976. irreg., no. 36, 1979. Universitetet i Trondheim, Norges Tekniske Hoegskole. Institutt for Uorganisk Kjemi, 7034 Trondheim-NTH, Norway. circ. 250.

CHEMISTRY — Organic Chemistry

547.5 US ISSN 0065-2121
ADVANCES IN ALICYCLIC CHEMISTRY. 1966. irreg., 1971, vol. 3. price varies. Academic Press, Inc., 111 Fifth Ave., New Yor, NY 10003. Eds. Harold Hart, Gerasimos J. Karabatsos.

547.78 574.192 US ISSN 0065-2318
ADVANCES IN CARBOHYDRATE CHEMISTRY AND BIOCHEMISTRY. 1945. irreg., vol. 36, 1979. price varies. Academic Press, Inc., 111 Fifth Ave., New York, NY 10003. Eds. Melville L. Wolfrom, R. Stuart Tipson. index. cum.index: vols. 1-19 (1954-1964)in vol. 19(1964) (also avail. in microfiche) Indexed: Ind.Med.
Formerly(1945-1968): Advances in Carbohydrate Chemistry (ISSN 0096-5332)

547.59 US ISSN 0065-2725
ADVANCES IN HETEROCYCLIC CHEMISTRY. (Supplements avail.) 1963. irreg., no. 24, 1979. price varies. Academic Press, Inc., 111 Fifth Ave., New York, NY 10003. Ed. A.R. Katritzky. index. (also avail. in microfiche)

547 US ISSN 0065-3047
ADVANCES IN ORGANIC CHEMISTRY; methods and results. 1960. irreg., vol. 9, pt. 2, 1979. price varies. John Wiley & Sons, Inc., 605 Third Ave., New York, NY 10016. Eds. R. A. Raphael, E. C. Taylor, H. Wynberg. index.

547 US
ADVANCES IN ORGANIC COATINGS SCIENCE AND TECHNOLOGY. 1979. irreg. price varies. Technomic Publishing Co., Inc., 265 Post Rd. W., Westport, CT 06880. Eds. Geoffrey D. Parfitt, Angelos V. Patsis.

547.05 US ISSN 0065-3055
ADVANCES IN ORGANOMETALIC CHEMISTRY. 1964. irreg., vol. 17, 1979. price varies. Academic Press, Inc., 111 Fifth Ave., New York, NY 10003. Eds. F. G. A. Stone, Robert West. index. (also avail. in microfiche)

547 US ISSN 0065-3195
ADVANCES IN POLYMER SCIENCE/ FORTSCHRITTE DER HOCHPOLYMEREN-FORSCHUNG. (Contributions in German, English and French) 1958. irreg., vol. 41, 1981. price varies. Springer-Verlag, 175 Fifth Ave., New York, NY 10010 (also Berlin, Heidelberg, Vienna) (repring service avail. from ISI)
Polymers

547 UR
AKADEMIYA NAUK KAZAKHSKOI S.S.R. INSTITUT KHIMICHESKIKH NAUK. TRUDY. vol. 46, 1977. irreg. 1.88 Rub. per no. Izdatel'stvo Nauka Kazakhskoi S.S.R., Ul.Shevchenko 28, 480021 Alma-Ata, U.S.S.R. Ed. M. Goryaev. abstr. bibl. illus. circ. 1,000. Indexed: Chem.Abstr.

547 GW ISSN 0340-210X
AKTUELLE PROBLEME DER POLYMER-PHYSIK. (Text in English, German) 1970. a. price varies. Dr. Dietrich Steinkopff Verlag, Saalbaustr. 12, Postfach 11 1008, 6100 Darmstadt 11, W. Germany (B.R.D.) Eds. E. W. Fischer, F. H. Mueller.
Polymers

547.72 UK ISSN 0305-9707
ALKALOIDS. vol. 8, 1978. a. price varies. Chemical Society, Burlington House, London W1V OBN, England (Subscr. to: Blackhorse Road, Letchworth, Herts SG6 1HN, England) Ed. Prof. M. F. Grundon. charts. illus. index. Indexed: Chem.Abstr.

547 US
AMERICAN LECTURES IN LIVING CHEMISTRY. irreg. price varies. Charles C. Thomas, Publisher, 301-327 E. Lawrence Ave., Springfield, IL 62717.

547 US
ANALYSIS OF ORGANIC MATERIALS: AN INTERNATIONAL SERIES OF MONOGRAPHS. irreg., latest 1977. price varies. Academic Press Inc., 111 5th Ave., New York, NY 10021 (and Maxwell House, Fairview Pk., Elmsford, N.Y. 10523) Eds. R. Belcher, S. Anderson.
Formerly: Monographs in Organic Functional Group Analysis (ISSN 0077-0906)

547.6 UK ISSN 0305-9715
AROMATIC AND HETEROAROMATIC CHEMISTRY. 1973. a. price varies. Chemical Society, Burlington House, London W1V OBN, England (Subscr. to: Blackhorse Road, Letchworth, Herts SG6 1HN, Eng.) Eds. Proj. H. Suschitzky, Dr. O. Meth-Cohn. charts. illus. index. Indexed: Chem.Abstr.

547 US ISSN 0067-4915
BEILSTEINS HANDBUCH DER ORGANISCHEN CHEMIE. FOURTH SUPPLEMENT. (The main work was published: 1918-1937; First Supplement: 1928-1938; Second Supplement: 1941-1957; Third Supplement: 1958-1974. as of vol. 17, the Third and Fourth Supplements are combined.) 1972. irreg., vol. 23, 1980. price varies. Springer-Verlag, 175 Fifth Ave., New York, NY 10010 (also Berlin, Heidelberg, Vienna) (reprint service avail. from ISI)

547 US
BENCHMARK PAPERS IN ORGANIC CHEMISTRY. 1974. irreg., vol. 6, 1977. price varies. Dowden, Hutchinson and Ross, Inc., 523 Sarah St., Stroudsburg, PA 18360 (Dist. by Academic Press, Inc., 111 Fifth Ave., New York, NY 10003) Ed. C. A. Vanderwerf.

547 UK ISSN 0576-7172
CARBOHYDRATE CHEMISTRY. 1972. vol. 5. a. price varies. Chemical Society, Burlington House', London W1V OBN, England. Ed. Prof. J. S. Brimacombe. charts. illus. index. Indexed: Chem.Abstr.

547 UK ISSN 0069-3030
CHEMICAL SOCIETY, LONDON. ANNUAL REPORTS ON THE PROGRESS OF CHEMISTRY. SECTION B: ORGANIC CHEMISTRY. 1904. a. £23. Chemical Society, Burlington House, Piccadilly, London W1V OBN, England. Eds. M. F. Ansell, P. G. Sammes. index. cum.index: vols. 1-46.

547 US ISSN 0069-3138
CHEMISTRY AND PHYSICS OF CARBON: A SERIES OF ADVANCES. 1966. irreg., vol. 14, 1978. price varies. Marcel Dekker, Inc., 270 Madison Ave., New York, NY 10016. Eds. P.L. Walker, Jr., P.A. Thrower.

547.59 US ISSN 0069-3154
CHEMISTRY OF HETEROCYCLIC COMPOUNDS; a series of monographs. 1950. irreg., vol. 40, 1980. John Wiley & Sons, Inc., 605 Third Ave., New York, NY 10016. Eds. Arnold Weissburger, Edward C. Taylor. index.

547 US ISSN 0069-3162
CHEMISTRY OF NATURAL PRODUCTS. (Text in English; occasionally French or German) 1961. irreg., 1974, 9th Ottawa, pub. 1979. price varies. (International Union of Pure and Applied Chemistry) Pergamon Press, Inc., Maxwell House, Fairview Park, Elmsford, NY 10523 (And Headington Hill Hall, Oxford OX3 0BW, England)

547.05 US
CHEMISTRY OF ORGANOMETALLIC COMPOUNDS. 1965. irreg., 1973, latest vol. unnumbered. John Wiley & Sons, Inc., 605 Third Ave., New York, NY 10016. Ed. D. Seyferth.

547 US
CREATION AND DETECTION OF THE EXCITED STATE. 1971. irreg., vol. 4, 1976. Marcel Dekker, Inc., 270 Madison Ave., New York, NY 10016. Ed. W. R. Ware.

664 NE
DEVELOPMENTS IN FOOD SCIENCE. 1978. irreg. price varies. Elsevier Scientific Publishing Co., Box 211, 1000 AE Amsterdam, Netherlands.

547 UK ISSN 0301-8938
FLUOROCARBON AND RELATED CHEMISTRY. 1971. biennial. price varies. Chemical Society, Burlington House, London W1V OBN, England (Subscr. to: Blackhorse Road, Letchworth, Herts SG6 1HN, Eng) Eds. R.E. Banks, M.G. Barlow. charts. illus. index. Indexed: Chem.Abstr.

547 UK ISSN 0300-3493
FOREIGN COMPOUND METABOLISM IN MAMMALS. 1971. biennial. price varies. Chemical Society, Burlington House, London W1V OBN, England (Subscr. to: Blackhorse Road, Letchworth, Herts SG6 1HN, Eng) Ed. D.E. Hathway. charts. illus. index. Indexed: Chem.Abstr.

547 US ISSN 0071-7886
FORTSCHRITTE DER CHEMIE ORGANISCHER NATURSTOFFE/PROGRESS IN THE CHEMISTRY OF ORGANIC NATURAL PRODUCTS. 1938. irreg., vol. 40, 1981. Springer-Verlag, 175 Fifth Ave., New York, NY 10010 (also Berlin, Heidelberg, Vienna) cum.index: vols. 1-20 (1938-62) available separately. (reprint service avail. from ISI)

547 UK
GENERAL AND SYNTHETIC METHODS; a specialist periodical report. 1978. irreg. Chemical Society, Burlington House, London W1V OBN, England.

547.84 660.284 US ISSN 0073-2109
HIGH POLYMERS; a series of monographs on the chemistry, physics and technology of high polymeric substances. 1940. irreg., vol. 29, 1977. price varies. John Wiley & Sons, Inc., 605 Third Ave, New York, NY 10016. Ed.Bd. index.
Polymers

547.633 US
INTERNATIONAL CATECHOLAMINE SYMPOSIUM. PROCEEDINGS. irreg. price varies. Pergamon Press, Inc., Maxwell House, Fairview Park, Elmsford, NY 10523.

547 US ISSN 0074-8242
INTERNATIONAL SERIES ON ORGANIC CHEMISTRY. 1959. irreg., vol. 10, 1970. price varies. Pergamon Press, Inc., Maxwell House, Fairview Park, Elmsford, NY 10523. index.
Formerly: International Series of Monographs on Organic Chemistry.

547 NE
ISOTOPES IN ORGANIC CHEMISTRY. 1975. irreg. Elsevier Scientific Publishing Co., Box 211, 1000 AE Amsterdam, Netherlands. Eds. E. Buncel, C. L. Lee.

547 UR ISSN 0303-2361
ITOGI NAUKI I TEKHNIKI: TEKHNOLOGIIA ORGANICHESKIKH VESHCHESTV. 1971. a. 0.61 Rub. Vsesoyuznyi Institut Nauchno-Tekhnicheskoi Informatsii (Viniti), Ul. Baltiiskaya, 14, Moscow, U.S.S.R. illus.
Continues: Itogi Nauki: Tekhnologiya Organicheskikh Veshchestv (ISSN 0579-1766)

540 547 JA ISSN 0075-2010
ITSUU LABORATORY, TOKYO. ANNUAL REPORT/ITSUU KENKYUSHO NENPO. (Text in English and German; summaries in Japanese) 1950. irreg.(a. or biennial) available on exchange. Itsuu Laboratory - Itsuu Kenkyusho, 2-28-10 Tamagawa, Setagaya-ku, Tokyo 173, Japan. Ed. M. Natsume.

547.84 US ISSN 0360-8905
JOURNAL OF POLYMER SCIENCE. POLYMER SYMPOSIA EDITION. 1963. irreg., no. 66, 1979. price varies. John Wiley & Sons, Inc., 605 Third Ave., New York, NY 10016. illus. (also avail. in microform from UMI)
Supersedes: Journal of Polymer Science. Part C: Polymer Symposia (ISSN 0449-2994)
Polymers

CHEMISTRY — ORGANIC CHEMISTRY

547.59   US   ISSN 0090-2268
LECTURES IN HETEROCYCLIC CHEMISTRY. (Suppl. issue of Journal of Heterocyclic Chemistry) 1971. biennial. $12 per no. HeteroCorporation, Box 16000 MH, Tampa, FL 33687. Indexed: Chem. Abstr.

547   US   ISSN 0076-1761
M T P INTERNATIONAL REVIEW OF SCIENCE. ORGANIC CHEMISTRY. 1972. irreg. $24.50 $21.50 by subscription; Index $12.50; $11.50 by subscription. University Park Press, Chamber of Commerce Bldg., Baltimore, MD 21202. Ed. D. H. Hey.

665.4   GW   ISSN 0076-891X
M W V /A E V JAHRESBERICHT. (Arbeitsgemeinschaft Erdoel-Gewinnung und-Verarbeitung) a. Mineraloelwirtschafts Verband e.V., Steindamm 71, 2000 Hamburg 1, W. Germany (B.R.D.)
Oils and fats

547   US   ISSN 0076-2075
MACROMOLECULAR CHEMISTRY. (Text in English; occasionally in French or German) 1962. irreg., 1969, 4th, 5th, 6th, Prague. price varies. (International Union of Pure and Applied Chemistry) Pergamon Press, Inc., Maxwell House, Fairview Park, Elmsford, NY 10523 (And Headington Hill Hall, Oxford OX3 0BW, England) Ed. Prof. B. C. L. Weedon.
1972, 8th, Helsinki

547   US   ISSN 0076-2083
MACROMOLECULAR REVIEWS. (Subseries of: Journal of Polymer Science) 1967. irreg., vol. 15, 1979. price varies. John Wiley & Sons, Inc., 605 Third Ave, New York, NY 10016. Ed. A. Peterlin.

547 541.39   US   ISSN 0076-2091
MACROMOLECULAR SYNTHESES. 1963. irreg., vol. 7, 1980. price varies. John Wiley & Sons, Inc., 605 Third Ave, New York, NY 10016.

547   SZ
MAKROMOLEKULARE CHEMIE. RAPID COMMUNICATIONS. irreg. $45. Huethig und Wepf Verlag, Eisengasse 5, CH-4001 Berne, Switzerland. Ed. Werner Kern.
Formerly: Makromolekulare Chemie. Short Communications.

547   US   ISSN 0077-0884
MONOGRAPHS IN MACROMOLECULAR CHEMISTRY. 1968. irreg., unnumbered, latest 1970. price varies. Marcel Dekker, Inc., 270 Madison Ave., New York, NY 10016. Ed. G. E. Ham.

665   SP
OLEO; anuario espanol de aceites y grasas e industrias auxiliares. no. 6, 1976. biennial. 750 ptas. Julian Yebenes Guerrero, Fernando VI, 27, Madrid 4, Spain. adv. stat.

547   US   ISSN 0078-611X
ORGANIC CHEMISTRY; a series of monographs. 1964. irreg., latest 1978. price varies. Academic Press Inc., 111 Fifth Ave., New York, NY 10003. Ed. Alfred T. Blomquist.

547   UK
ORGANIC CHEMISTRY. SERIES TWO. vol. 8, 1976. irreg. Butterworth & Co. (Publishers) Ltd., 88 Kingsway, London WC2B 6AB, England. Ed. D. H. Hey. bibl, charts, illus. index.

547   UK   ISSN 0305-9812
ORGANIC COMPOUNDS OF SULPHUR, SELENIUM AND TELLURIUM. 1971. biennial. price varies. Chemical Society, Burlington House, London W1V OBN, England (Subscr. to: Blackhorse Road, Letchworth, Herts SG6 1HN, Eng) Ed. D. Hogg. charts. illus. index. Indexed: Chem.Abstr.

ORGANIC ELECTRONIC SPECTRAL DATA. see *CHEMISTRY — Analytical Chemistry*

547 541.39   US   ISSN 0078-6144
ORGANIC PHOTOCHEMICAL SYNTHESES. 1971. irreg., vol. 2, 1977. price varies. John Wiley & Sons, Inc., 605 Third Ave, New York, NY 10016. Ed.Bd.

547 541.35   US   ISSN 0078-6152
ORGANIC PHOTOCHEMISTRY: A SERIES OF ADVANCES. 1967. irreg., vol. 3, 1973. price varies. Marcel Dekker, Inc., 270 Madison Ave., New York, NY 10016. Ed. O. L. Chapman. Indexed: Chem.Abstr.

547 541.39   US   ISSN 0078-6160
ORGANIC REACTION MECHANISMS. ANNUAL SURVEY. 1966. irreg., vol. 10, 1976. price varies. John Wiley & Sons, Inc., 605 Third Ave, New York, NY 10016. Ed.Bd.

547 541.39   US   ISSN 0078-6179
ORGANIC REACTIONS. 1942. irreg., vol. 26, 1980. price varies. John Wiley & Sons, Inc., 605 Third Ave, New York, NY 10016. Ed. W.G. Dauben.

547   US   ISSN 0078-6187
ORGANIC SUBSTANCES OF NATURAL ORIGIN. 1967. irreg., 1969, vol.2. price varies. Marcel Dekker, Inc., 270 Madison Ave., New York, NY 10016. Eds. W. I. Taylor, A. R. Battersby.

547 541.39   US   ISSN 0078-6209
ORGANIC SYNTHESES. (Vols. 1-49 avail. only in: Organic Syntheses Collective Volumes) vol. 1-9, 1941. a. price varies. John Wiley & Sons, Inc., 605 Third Ave, New York, NY 10016.

547 541.39   US   ISSN 0078-6217
ORGANIC SYNTHESES COLLECTIVE VOLUMES. 1941. irreg., 1973, vol. 5. price varies. John Wiley & Sons, Inc., 605 Third Ave, New York, NY 10016. cum.index vols. 1-5, 1976.

547   US   ISSN 0078-6225
ORGANISCHE CHEMIE IN EINZELDARSTELLUNGEN. 1950. irreg., no. 15, 1974. price varies. Springer-Verlag, 175 Fifth Ave., New York, NY 10010 (also Berlin, Heidelberg, Vienna) (reprint service avail. from ISI)

547.05   UK   ISSN 0301-0074
ORGANOMETALLIC CHEMISTRY. 1972. a. price varies. Chemical Society, Burlington House, London W1V OBN, England (Subscr. to: Blackhorse Road, Letchworth, Herts SG6 1HN, Eng) Eds. Prof. E. W. Abel, Prof. F. G. Stone. charts. illus. index. Indexed: Chem.Abstr.

547   US   ISSN 0078-6489
ORGANOMETALLIC COMPOUNDS OF THE GROUP IV ELEMENTS. 1968. irreg., vol. 2, 1972. price varies. Marcel Dekker, Inc., 270 Madison Ave., New York, NY 10016. Ed. A. G. MacDiarmid.

547.05 541.39   US
ORGANOMETALLIC REACTIONS AND SYNTHESES. 1971. irreg. price varies. Plenum Press, 233 Spring St., New York, NY 10013. Eds. E.I. Becker and M. Tsutsui.
Formerly(until vol. 6, 1977): Organometallic Reactions Series (ISSN 0078-6497)

547   UK   ISSN 0475-1582
ORGANOPHOSPHORUS CHEMISTRY. vol. 9, 1978. a. price varies. Chemical Society, Burlington House, London W1V 0BN, England (Subscr. to: Blackhorse Rd. Letchworth, Herts SG6 1HN England) Ed. Prof. S. Trippett. charts. illus. index. Indexed: Chem.Abstr.

547.75   JA   ISSN 0078-6705
OSAKA UNIVERSITY. INSTITUTE FOR PROTEIN RESEARCH. MEMOIRS. (Text in English) 1959. a. on exchange basis. ‡ Osaka University, Institute for Protein Research - Osaka Daigaku Tanpakushitsu Kenkyusho, 5311 Yamadakami, Suita, Osaka 565, Japan. Ed. Kozo Narita.

541 547   PL   ISSN 0324-9824
POLITECHNIKA WROCLAWSKA. INSTYTUT CHEMII ORGANICZNEJ I FIZYCZNEJ. PRACE NAUKOWE. KONFERENCJE. (Text in Polish and English) 1974. irreg., no. 6, 1979. price varies. Politechnika Wroclawska, Wybrzeze Wyspianskiego 27, 50-370 Wroclaw, Poland (Dist. by: Ars Polona-Ruch, Krakowskie Przedmiescie 7, Warsaw, Poland) Ed. Marian Kloza. circ. 325.

541 547   PL   ISSN 0324-9816
POLITECHNIKA WROCLAWSKA. INSTYTUT CHEMII ORGANICZNEJ I FIZYCZNEJ. PRACE NAUKOWE. MONOGRAFIE. (Text in Polish; summaries in English and Russian) 1969. irreg., no. 4, 1979. price varies. Politechnika Wroclawska, Wybrzeze Wyspianskiego 27, 50-370 Wroclaw, Poland (Dist. by: Ars Polona-Ruch, Krakowskie Przedmiescie 7, Warsaw, Poland) Ed. Marian Kloza.

541 547   PL   ISSN 0370-081X
POLITECHNIKA WROCLAWSKA. INSTYTUT CHEMII ORGANICZNEJ I FIZYCZNEJ. PRACE NAUKOWE. STUDIA I MATERIALY. (Text in Polish; summaries in English and Russian) 1970. irreg., no. 8, 1978. price varies. Politechnika Wroclawska, Wybrzeze Wyspianskiego 27, 50-370 Wroclaw, Poland (Dist. by: Ars Polona-Ruch, Krakowskie Przedmiescie 7, Warsaw, Poland) Ed. Marian Kloza.

541.393   US
POLYMER MONOGRAPHS. a. price varies. Gordon and Breach Science Publishers, One Park Ave., New York, NY 10016. Ed. Herbert Morawetz.
Polymers

547   US   ISSN 0079-3736
POLYMER REVIEWS. 1958. irreg., 1971, vol.18. price varies. John Wiley & Sons, Inc., 605 Third Ave, New York, NY 10016. Eds. H. Mark and E.H. Immergut.
Polymers

547.3466   US   ISSN 0092-0576
POWDER DIFFRACTION FILE SEARCH MANUAL. ORGANIC. (Subseries of the Committee's Publication SMO) a. ‡ Joint Committee on Powder Diffraction Standards., International Center for Diffraction Data, 1601 Park Lane, Swarthmore, PA 19081. index.

PROGRESS IN BIO-ORGANIC CHEMISTRY. see *BIOLOGY — Biological Chemistry*

PROGRESS IN COLLOID AND POLYMER SCIENCE/FORTSCHRITTSBERICHTE UEBER KOLLOIDE UND POLYMERE. see *CHEMISTRY — Physical Chemistry*

547   US   ISSN 0163-7827
PROGRESS IN LIPID RESEARCH. 1952. 4/yr. $60. Pergamon Press, Inc., Journals Division, Maxwell House, Fairview Park, Elmsford, NY 10523 (And Headington Hill Hall, Oxford OX3 0BW, England) Ed. Dr. Ralph T. Holman. (also avail. in microform from MIM,UMI)
Formerly: Progress in the Chemistry of Fats and Other Lipids (ISSN 0079-6832)
Oils and fats

PROGRESS IN PHYSICAL ORGANIC CHEMISTRY. see *CHEMISTRY — Physical Chemistry*

547   US   ISSN 0079-6700
PROGRESS IN POLYMER SCIENCE. 1967. 4/yr. $70. Pergamon Press, Inc., Journals Division, Maxwell House, Fairview Park, Elmsford, NY 10523 (And Headington Hill Hall, Oxford OX3 0BW, England) Ed. A. D. Jenkins. index. (also avail. in microform from MIM,UMI) Indexed: Chem.Abstr.
Polymers

547   UR   ISSN 0079-6883
PROGRESS POLIMERNOI KHIMII. 1965. irreg. Akademiya Nauk S.S.S.R., Institut Elementoorganicheskikh Soedinenii, Ul. Vavilova, 14, Moscow, U. S. S. R.

547 541.39   NE   ISSN 0079-9823
REACTION MECHANISMS IN ORGANIC CHEMISTRY. (Text in English) 1963. irreg., vol. 10, 1975. price varies. Elsevier Scientific Publishing Co., P.O. Box 211, 1000 AE Amsterdam, Netherlands.

547 541.39   US   ISSN 0486-0748
REACTIVE INTERMEDIATES IN ORGANIC CHEMISTRY. 1968. irreg,, latest, 1977. price varies. John Wiley & Sons, Inc., 605 Third Ave., New York, NY 10016. Ed. G.A. Olah.

CHEMISTRY — PHYSICAL CHEMISTRY

547 US
REACTIVITY AND STRUCTURE: CONCEPTS OF ORGANIC CHEMISTRY. 1975. irreg., vol. 12, 1980. price varies. Springer-Verlag, 175 Fifth Ave., New York, NY 10010 (Also Berlin, Heidelberg, Vienna) Ed.Bd. (reprint service avail. from ISI)

547 HU ISSN 0079-9947
RECENT DEVELOPMENTS IN THE CHEMISTRY OF NATURAL CARBON COMPOUNDS. (Text in English) 1965. irreg., vol. 8, 1977. price varies. (Magyar Tudomanyos Akademia) Akademiai Kiado, Publishing House of the Hungarian Academy of Sciences, P.O. Box 24, H-1363 Budapest, Hungary.

547 US ISSN 0080-309X
RING INDEX: A LIST OF RING SYSTEMS USED IN ORGANIC CHEMISTRY. SUPPLEMENT. 1960. irreg. $15. (American Chemical Society) Chemical Abstracts Service, Box 3012, Columbus, OH 43210. Indexed: Chem.Abstr.

547 NE ISSN 0080-3758
RODD'S CHEMISTRY OF CARBON COMPOUNDS. 1964. irreg. price varies. Elsevier Scientific Publishing Co., Box 211, 1000 AE Amsterdam, Netherlands. Ed. S. Coffey.

547 UK ISSN 0305-6198
SATURATED HETEROCYCLIC CHEMISTRY. 1971. a. price varies. Chemical Society, Burlington House, London W1V 0BN, England (Subscr. to: Blackhorse Rd., Letchworth, Herts SG6 1HN, England) Ed. Dr. G. Pattenden. charts. illus. index. Indexed: Chem.Abstr.

547 US
STUDIES IN ORGANIC CHEMISTRY. 1973. irreg., vol. 9, 1980. price varies. Marcel Dekker, Inc., 270 Madison Ave., New York, NY 10016. Ed. P. Gassman.

SULFUR REPORTS. see CHEMISTRY

547 541.39 SZ ISSN 0082-1136
SYNTHETIC METHODS OF ORGANIC CHEMISTRY. (Text in English) 1946. irreg (approx. 1/yr.) 400 Fr.($240) per vol. (1981 price) S. Karger AG, Allschwilerstrasse 10, P.O. Box, CH-4009 Basel, Switzerland. Ed. W. Theilheimer. (reprint service avail. from ISI) Indexed: Biol.Abstr. Chem.Abstr. Curr.Cont. Ind.Med.

547 541.39 US ISSN 0082-2418
TECHNIQUES AND APPLICATIONS IN ORGANIC SYNTHESIS. 1965. irreg., unnumbered, latest 1979. price varies. Marcel Dekker, Inc., 270 Madison Ave., New York, NY 10016. Ed. R. L. Augustine.

547 US ISSN 0082-2434
TECHNIQUES AND METHODS OF POLYMER EVALUATION. 1966. irreg., vol. 4, 1975. price varies. Marcel Dekker, Inc., 270 Madison Ave., New York, NY 10016. Eds. P. E. Slade, Jr. and L. T. Jenkins.

547 UK ISSN 0300-5992
TERPENOIDS AND STEROIDS. 1972, vol. 2. a. price varies. Chemical Society, Burlington House, London W1V 0BN, England (Subscr. to: Blackhorse Road, Letchworth, Herts SG6 1HN, Eng) Ed. Dr. J. R. Hanson. charts. illus. index. Indexed: Chem. Abstr.

THERMODYNAMICS RESEARCH CENTER. INTERNATIONAL DATA SERIES. SELECTED DATA ON MIXTURES. SERIES A. THERMODYNAMIC PROPERTIES OF NON-REACTING BINARY SYSTEMS OF ORGANIC SUBSTANCES. see CHEMISTRY — Physical Chemistry

CHEMISTRY — Physical Chemistry

ABSORPTION SPECTRA IN THE ULTRAVIOLET AND VISIBLE REGION. see PHYSICS — Optics

541.395 US ISSN 0360-0564
ADVANCES IN CATALYSIS. 1948. irreg., no. 28, 1979. price varies. Academic Press, Inc., 111 Fifth Ave., New York, NY 10003. Ed. W. G. Frankenburg. index. cum.index: vols. 1-5 (1948-1953) in vol. 6 (1964) (also avail. in microfiche)
Formerly: Advances in Catalysis and Related Subjects (ISSN 0065-2342)

ADVANCES IN CHEMICAL PHYSICS. see PHYSICS

541.39 US ISSN 0065-2741
ADVANCES IN HIGH TEMPERATURE CHEMISTRY. 1967. irreg., 1972, vol. 4. price varies. Academic Press, Inc., 111 Fifth Ave., New York, NY 10003. Ed. Leroy Eyring.

543 541.35 US ISSN 0065-3152
ADVANCES IN PHOTOCHEMISTRY. 1963. irreg., vol. 12, 1980. price varies. John Wiley & Sons, Inc., 605 Third Ave., New York, NY 10016. Eds. W. A. Noyes, Jr., G. S. Hammond, J. N. Pitts. index.

547.1 UK ISSN 0065-3160
ADVANCES IN PHYSICAL ORGANIC CHEMISTRY. 1963. irreg., vol. 16, 1978. price varies. Academic Press Inc. (London) Ltd., 24-28 Oval Rd., London NW1 7DX, England (and 111 Fifth Ave., New York, N.Y. 10003) Ed. V. Gold.

541.39 546.1 US ISSN 0092-1335
ANNUAL REPORTS IN INORGANIC AND GENERAL SYNTHESES. 1972. irreg., vol. 5, 1978. Academic Press, Inc., 111 Fifth Ave., New York, NY 10003. Ed. Kurt Niedenzu, Hans Zimmer. illus.

547.1 541.39 US ISSN 0066-409X
ANNUAL REPORTS IN ORGANIC SYNTHESIS. 1971. a. price varies. Academic Press, Inc., 111 Fifth Avenue, New York, NY 10003. Eds. John McMurray, R. Bryan Miller.

541.3 US ISSN 0066-426X
ANNUAL REVIEW OF PHYSICAL CHEMISTRY. 1950. a. $20. Annual Reviews Inc., 4139 El Camino Way, Palo Alto, CA 94306. Ed. B.S. Rabinovitch. bibl. index. cum.index. (back issues avail.; reprint service avail. from ISI) Indexed: Chem.Abstr. Sci.Abstr. M.M.R.I. Nucl.Sci.Abstr.

541.395 NE
ASPECTS OF HOMOGENEOUS CATALYSIS: A SERIES OF ADVANCES. (Text in English) 1970. biennial. price varies. D. Reidel Publishing Co., P.O. Box 17, 3300 AA Dordrecht, Netherlands (And Lincoln Building, 160 Old Derby St., Hingham, MA 02043) Ed. Renate Ugo.

541.3 US
BENCHMARK PAPERS IN PHYSICAL CHEMISTRY AND CHEMICAL PHYSICS. 1978. irreg., vol. 3, 1979. Dowden, Hutchinson & Ross, Inc., 523 Sarah St., Stroudsburg, PA 18360 (Dist. by Academic Press, Inc., 111 Fifth Ave., New York, NY 10003) Eds. J. Kaufman, W. Koski.

541.3 BL
BIOMASSA. 1979. a. Revista Brasileira de Tecnologia, c/o G. Massarani, COPPE UFRJ, Caixa Postal 1191, 20000 Rio de Janeiro, RJ, Brazil. Ed.Bd.

BIOSYNTHESIS. see BIOLOGY — Biological Chemistry

541.36 US ISSN 0572-6921
BRIGHAM YOUNG UNIVERSITY. CENTER FOR THERMOCHEMICAL STUDIES. CONTRIBUTIONS.* irreg., no. 66, 1975. price varies. Brigham Young University, Center for Thermochemical Studies, Provo, UT 84602.

541.395 NE
CATALYSIS BY METAL COMPLEXES. 1976. irreg. D. Reidel Publishing Co., Box 17, 3300 AA Dordrecht, Netherlands (And Lincoln Building, 160 Old Derby St., Hingham, MA 02043)
Formerly: Homogeneous Catalysis in Organic and Inorganic Chemistry.

541.3 UK
CHEMICAL PHYSICS OF SOLIDS AND THEIR SURFACES. 1972. a. price varies. Chemical Society, Burlington House, London W1V OBN, England (Subscr. to: Blackhorse Road, Letchworth, Herts. SG6 1HN, Eng) Eds. Prof. M.W. Roberts, Prof. J.M. Thomas. charts. illus. index. Indexed: Chem.Abstr.
Formerly: Surface and Defect Properties of Solids (ISSN 0305-3873)

541.3 546 UK ISSN 0308-6003
CHEMICAL SOCIETY, LONDON. ANNUAL REPORTS ON THE PROGRESS OF CHEMISTRY. SECTION A: PHYSICAL AND INORGANIC CHEMISTRY. 1904. a. £21. Chemical Society, Burlington House, Piccadilly, London W1V OBN, England. Eds. R. P. Bell, M. F. Lappert. index. cum.index: vols. 1-46.
Formerly: Chemical Society, London. Annual Reports on the Progress of Chemistry. Section A: General, Physical and Inorganic Chemistry (ISSN 0069-3022)

541.36 UK ISSN 0305-9731
CHEMICAL THERMODYNAMICS. 1973. a. price varies. Chemical Society, Burlington House, London W1V OBN, England (Subscr. to: Blackhorse Road, Letchworth, Herts SG6 1HN, Eng.) Ed. Prof. D. H. Everett. charts. illus. index. Indexed: Chem.Abstr.

541.3 UK ISSN 0305-9723
COLLOID SCIENCE. 1973. a. price varies. Chemical Society, Burlington House, London W1V OBN, England (Subscr. address: Blackhorse Road, Letchworth, Herts SG6 1HN, England) Ed. D.H. Everett. charts. illus. index. Indexed: Chem.Abstr.

541.3 NE ISSN 0069-8040
COMPREHENSIVE CHEMICAL KINETICS. (Text in English) 1969. irreg., vol. 22, 1980. price varies. Elsevier Scientific Publishing Co., P.O. Box 211, 1000 AE Amsterdam, Netherlands. Eds. C. H. Bamford, C. F. H. Tipper.

541.3 UK ISSN 0305-974X
DIELECTRIC AND RELATED MOLECULAR PROCESSES. 1972. biennial. price varies. Chemical Society, Burlington House, London W1V OBN, England (Subscr. to: Blackhorse Road, Letchworth, Herts SG6 1HN, Eng) Ed. Mansel Davies. charts. illus. index. Indexed: Chem.Abstr.

541.3 UK ISSN 0305-9758
ELECTRON SPIN RESONANCE; specialist periodical reports. 1973. a. price varies. Chemical Society, Burlington House, London W1V OBN, England (Subscr. address: Blackhorse Rd., Letchworth, Herts SG6 1HN, England) Ed. Prof. P. B. Ayscough. charts. illus. index. Indexed: Chem.Abstr.

546.1 UK ISSN 0305-9766
ELECTRONIC STRUCTURE & MAGNETISM OF INORGANIC COMPOUNDS. 1972. a. price varies. Chemical Society, Burlington House, London W1V OBN, England (Subscr. address: Blackhorse Rd., Letchworth, Herts SG6 1HN, England) Ed. Dr.P. Day. charts. illus. index. Indexed: Chem.Abstr.

541.3 UK ISSN 0301-5696
FARADAY SYMPOSIA. 1968. a. price varies. Chemical Society, Burlington House, London W1V OBN, England. charts. illus. index. Indexed: Chem.Abstr.
Formerly: Symposia of the Faraday Society.

541 BU
FIZIKO-KHIMICHESKA MEKHANIKA/PHYSICO-CHEMICAL MECHANICS. (Text in Bulgarian, German, Russian; summaries in English, Russian) 1975. irreg. 1.50 lv. per no. (Bulgarska Akademiia na Naukite) Publishing House of the Bulgarian Academy of Sciences, Ul. Akad. G. Bonchev, 1113 Sofia, Bulgaria (Dist. by: Hemus, 6, Rouski Blvd., 1000 Sofia, Bulgaria). illus. circ. 600.

541.3 GW ISSN 0071-7924
FORTSCHRITTE DER PHYSIKALISCHEN CHEMIE/CURRENT TOPICS IN PHYSICAL CHEMISTRY. (Text in English and German) 1957. irreg., vol. 10, 1976. price varies. Dr. Dietrich Steinkopff Verlag, Saalbaustr. 12, Postfach 11 1008, 6100 Darmstadt 11, W. Germany (B.R.D.) Ed. Wilhelm Jost. index. circ. 1,500.

CHEMISTRY — PHYSICAL CHEMISTRY

541.39 UK ISSN 0309-6890
GAS KINETICS AND ENERGY TRANSFER; specialist periodical reports. 1975. biennial. price varies. Chemical Society, Burlington House, W1V 0BN, England (Subscr. Address: Blackhorse Rd., Letchworth, Herts SG6 1HN, England) Eds. P. G. Ashmore, R. J. Donovan. charts; illus. index. Indexed: Chem.Abstr.
Formerly: Reaction Kinetics.

546 541.39 UK ISSN 0305-8255
INORGANIC REACTION MECHANISMS. 1972, vol. 2. irreg. (every 18 mos) price varies. Chemical Society, Burlington House, London W1V 0BN, England (Subscr. to: Blackhorse Road, Letchworth, Herts SG6 1HN, Eng.) Ed. A. McAuley. charts. illus. index. Indexed: Chem.Abstr.

547.1 541.39 US ISSN 0073-8077
INORGANIC SYNTHESES SERIES. 1939. a., vol. 16, 1974. $19.95. (Inorganic Syntheses, Inc.) McGraw-Hill Book Co., 1221 Ave. of the Americas, New York, NY 10020. Ed. Robert Parry. adv. bk. rev. index, cum.index vols. 1-10 in vol. 10.

INTERNATIONAL COLLOQUIUM ON RAPID MIXING AND SAMPLING TECHNIQUES APPLICABLE TO THE STUDY OF BIOCHEMICAL REACTIONS. PROCEEDINGS. see BIOLOGY — Biological Chemistry

541.3 JA
INTERNATIONAL CONFERENCE ON HIGH PRESSURE. PROCEEDINGS. no. 4, 1975. irreg. Physico-Chemical Society of Japan - Nihon Butsuri Kagaku Kenkyukai, c/o Kyoto University, Faculty of Science, Kitashirakawa Oiwake-cho, Kyoto 606, Japan.

541.395 US ISSN 0538-6640
INTERNATIONAL CONGRESS ON CATALYSIS. PROCEEDINGS. (Text in English, French or German) 1960. irreg., 5th, 1973. price varies. Elsevier North-Holland, Inc., New York, 52 Vanderbilt Ave., New York, NY 10017.

541.3 US
INTERNATIONAL JOURNAL OF CHEMICAL KINETICS. SYMPOSIUM. 1975. irreg. $30. John Wiley & Sons, Inc., 605 Third Ave., New York, NY 10016. Ed. Sidney W. Benson.

541.345 US
INTERNATIONAL SYMPOSIUM ON ADSORPTION-DESORPTION PHENOMENA. PROCEEDINGS. irreg., Florence, 1971. $20.50. Academic Press, Inc, 111 5th Ave., New York, NY 10003. Ed. F. Ricca.

541.372 US ISSN 0092-0193
ION EXCHANGE AND SOLVENT EXTRACTION; a series of advances. 1966. irreg., vol. 7, 1977. Marcel Dekker, Inc., 270 Madison Ave., New York, NY 10016. Eds. J.A. Marinsky, Y. Marcus. illus.
Formed by the 1973 merger of: Ion Exchange; a Series of Advances (ISSN 0075-0328) & Solvent Extraction Reviews.

541.345 GW ISSN 0075-6555
KOLLOID-GESELLSCHAFT. VERHANDLUNGSBERICHTE. (Text in English, French, German) 1922. biennial. price varies. Dr. Dietrich Steinkopff Verlag, Saalbaustr. 12, Postfach 11 1008, 6100 Darmstadt 11, W. Germany (B.R.D.) Eds. H. G. Kilian, A. Weiss. index. circ. 2,000.

LASER FOCUS BUYERS' GUIDE. see PHYSICS — Optics

541.3 US ISSN 0076-177X
M T P INTERNATIONAL REVIEW OF SCIENCE. PHYSICAL CHEMISTRY. 1972. irreg. $21.50. University Park Press, Chamber of Commerce Bldg., Baltimore, MD 21202. Ed. A. D. Buckingham. index.

MACROMOLECULAR SYNTHESES. see CHEMISTRY — Organic Chemistry

541.3 UK
MODERN PHYSICS IN CHEMISTRY. 1976. irreg. Academic Press Inc. (London) Ltd., 24 Oval Rd., London NW1 7DX, England (Dist. in U.S. by: Academic Press Inc., 111 Fifth Ave., New York, NY 10003)

541.372 US ISSN 0077-0795
MONOGRAPHS IN CHEMISTRY IN NON-AQUEOUS IONIZING SOLVENTS.* irreg. price varies. Pergamon Press, Inc., Maxwell House, Fairview Park, Elmsford, NY 10523 (And Headington Hill Hall, Oxford OX3 0BW, England) Eds. G. Jander, H. Spandau, C. C. Addison.

574.192 541.3 US
MONOGRAPHS ON PHYSICAL BIOCHEMISTRY. irreg. price varies. Oxford University Press, 200 Madison Ave., New York, NY 10016 (And Ely House, 37 Dover St., London W1X 4AH, England) Eds. W.F. Harrington, A.R. Peacocke.

541.3 UK ISSN 0305-9804
NUCLEAR MAGNETIC RESONANCE. 1972. a. price varies. Chemical Society, Burlington House, London W1V 0BN, England (Subscr. to: Blackhorse Road, Letchworth, Herts SG6 1HN, Eng) Ed. Prof. R. S. Abraham. charts. illus. index. Indexed: Chem.Abstr.

541.3 JA ISSN 0078-429X
OKAYAMA UNIVERSITY. RESEARCH LABORATORY FOR SURFACE SCIENCE. REPORTS. (Text in European languages) 1954. irreg. free or exchange. Okayama University, Research Laboratory for Surface Science - Okayama Daigaku Rigakubu Kaimen-kagaku Kenkyu Shisetsu, Faculty of Science, Tsushima, Okayama 700, Japan.

ORGANIC PHOTOCHEMICAL SYNTHESES. see CHEMISTRY — Organic Chemistry

ORGANIC PHOTOCHEMISTRY: A SERIES OF ADVANCES. see CHEMISTRY — Organic Chemistry

ORGANIC REACTION MECHANISMS. ANNUAL SURVEY. see CHEMISTRY — Organic Chemistry

ORGANIC REACTIONS. see CHEMISTRY — Organic Chemistry

ORGANIC SYNTHESES. see CHEMISTRY — Organic Chemistry

ORGANIC SYNTHESES COLLECTIVE VOLUMES. see CHEMISTRY — Organic Chemistry

ORGANOMETALLIC REACTIONS AND SYNTHESES. see CHEMISTRY — Organic Chemistry

541 JA
OSAKA (PREFECTURE). RADIATION CENTER, ANNUAL REPORT/OSAKA-FURITSU HOSHASEN CHUO KENKYUSHO NENPO. (Text in English) 1961. a. exchange basis. Radiaton Center - Osaka-furitsu Hoshasen Chuo Kenkyusho, 704 Shinke-cho, Sakai 593, Japan.

541.35 US ISSN 0079-1806
PHOTOCHEMISTRY. (Text in English: occasionally in French or German) 1964. irreg., 1972, 4th, Baden-Baden, W. Germany; 1974, 5th, Enschede, Netherlands. price varies. (International Union of Pure and Applied Chemistry) Pergamon Press, Inc., Maxwell House, Fairview Park, Elmsford, NY 10523 (And Headington Hill Hall, Oxford OX3 0BW, England)

541.3 US ISSN 0079-1881
PHYSICAL CHEMISTRY; a series of monographs. 1952. irreg., vol. 37, 1978. price varies. Academic Press Inc., 111 Fifth Ave., New York, NY 10003. Ed. Ernest M. Loebl.

541.3 UK
PHYSICAL CHEMISTRY. SERIES TWO. vol. 6, 1976. Butterworth & Co. (Publishers) Ltd., 88 Kingsway, London W.C. 2, England. Ed. A. D. Buckingham. bibl. charts. illus. index.

546.1 NE
PHYSICAL INORGANIC CHEMISTRY. 1968. irreg., no. 2, 1973 Elsevier Scientific Publishing Co., Box 211, 1000 AE Amsterdam, Netherlands. Ed. M. F. Lappert.

541.3 NE
PHYSICAL SCIENCES DATA. 1978. irreg., vol. 8, 1980. price varies. Elsevier Scientific Publishing Co., Box 211, 1000 AE Amsterdam, Netherlands.

PHYSICS AND CHEMISTRY OF THE ORGANIC SOLID STATE. see PHYSICS

PLASTICHEM. see ENGINEERING — Chemical Engineering

POLITECHNIKA WROCLAWSKA. INSTYTUT CHEMII ORGANICZNEJ I FIZYCZNEJ. PRACE NAUKOWE. KONFERENCJE. see CHEMISTRY — Organic Chemistry

POLITECHNIKA WROCLAWSKA. INSTYTUT CHEMII ORGANICZNEJ I FIZYCZNEJ. PRACE NAUKOWE. MONOGRAFIE. see CHEMISTRY — Organic Chemistry

POLITECHNIKA WROCLAWSKA. INSTYTUT CHEMII ORGANICZNEJ I FIZYCZNEJ. PRACE NAUKOWE. STUDIA I MATERIALY. see CHEMISTRY — Organic Chemistry

539 US ISSN 0081-1939
PREPARATION AND PROPERTIES OF SOLID STATE MATERIALS. 1971. irreg., vol. 4, 1978. free. Marcel Dekker, Inc., 270 Madison Ave., New York, NY 10016. Ed. W.R. Wilcox. bibl. charts. illus.

541.3 547 GW ISSN 0071-8017
PROGRESS IN COLLOID AND POLYMER SCIENCE/FORTSCHRITTSBERICHTE UEBER KOLLOIDE UND POLYMERE. (Supplement To: Kolloid- Zeitschrift & Zeitschrift fuer Polymere) 1909. irreg., vol. 65, 1978. price varies. Dr. Dietrich Steinkopff Verlag, Saalbaustr. 12, Postfach 11 1008, 6100 Darmstadt 11, W. Germany (B.R.D.) Eds. H. G. Kilian, A. Weiss. adv. circ. 2,000. Indexed: Curr.Cont.

547.1 US ISSN 0079-6662
PROGRESS IN PHYSICAL ORGANIC CHEMISTRY. 1963. irreg., vol. 12, 1976. price varies. John Wiley & Sons, Inc., 605 Third Ave., New York, NY 10016. Eds. A. Streitwieser, Jr. & R.W. Taft.

541.39 US ISSN 0079-6743
PROGRESS IN REACTION KINETICS. 1961. 4/yr. $66. Pergamon Press, Inc., Journals Division, Maxwell House, Fairview Park, Elmsford, NY 10523 (And Headington Hill Hall, Oxford OX3 0BW, England) Eds. Prof. K. R. Jennings, Prof. R. B. Cundall. index. (also avail. in microform from MIM,UMI) Indexed: Chem.Abstr.

541 US ISSN 0079-6786
PROGRESS IN SOLID STATE CHEMISTRY. 1964. 4/yr. $70. Pergamon Press, Inc., Journals Division, Maxwell House, Fairview Park, Elmsford, NY 10523 (And Headington Hill Hall, Oxford OX3 0BW, England) Eds. Prof. Gerd M. Rosenblatt, Prof. Wayne L. Worrell. index. (also avail. in microform from MIM,UMI) Indexed: Chem.Abstr.

541 US
PROGRESS IN SURFACE AND MEMBRANE SCIENCE. vol. 9, 1975. irreg., latest vol. 12. Academic Press Inc., 111 Fifth Avenue, New York, NY 10003. (also avail. in microfiche)

PROTEIN SYNTHESIS: A SERIES OF ADVANCES. see BIOLOGY — Biological Chemistry

541 JA ISSN 0441-2516
RADIOACTIVITY SURVEY DATA IN JAPAN. (Text in English) 1963. a. exchange basis. National Institute of Radiological Sciences - Hohasen Igaku Sogo Kenkyusho, 4-9-1 Anagawa, Chiba 280, Japan.

541 UK ISSN 0301-0716
RADIOCHEMISTRY. 1972. biennial. price varies. Chemical Society, Burlington House, London W1V 0BN, England (Subscr. to: Blackhorse Rd., Letchworth, Herts SG6 1HN, Eng) Ed. Dr. G. W. A. Newton. charts. illus. Indexed: Chem.Abstr.

REACTION MECHANISMS IN ORGANIC CHEMISTRY. see CHEMISTRY — Organic Chemistry

REACTIVE INTERMEDIATES IN ORGANIC CHEMISTRY. see CHEMISTRY — Organic Chemistry

541 US ISSN 0079-9971
RECENT PROGRESS IN SURFACE SCIENCE. 1964. irreg., 1970, vol. 3. price varies. Academic Press, Inc, 111 Fifth Ave., New York, NY 10003. Ed. Bd. index.

541.3 530 US ISSN 0080-1666
RESEARCH IN SURFACE FORCES. (Papers from Lab. of Surface Phenomena, Institute of Physical Chemistry, Academy of Sciences, U.S.S.R) (English translation of original Russian) 1963. irreg., 1974, vol. 4. price varies. Consultants Bureau, Special Research Report (Subsidiary of: Plenum Publishing Corp.) 117 W. 17th St., New York, NY 10011. Ed. B. V. Deryagin.

541.36 NE
STUDIES IN MODERN THERMODYNAMICS. 1979. irreg. price varies. Elsevier Scientific Publishing Co., Box 211, 1000 AE Amsterdam, Netherlands.

541.3 NE
STUDIES IN PHYSICAL AND THEORETICAL CHEMISTRY. 1978. irreg. price varies. Elsevier Scientific Publishing Co., Box 211, 1000 AE Amsterdam, Netherlands.

SYMPOSIA ON THE PHARMACOLOGY OF THERMOREGULATION. see *PHARMACY AND PHARMACOLOGY*

541.36 536 US ISSN 0082-0784
SYMPOSIUM (INTERNATIONAL) ON COMBUSTION. Variant title: International Symposium on Combustion. Proceedings. (Research papers) 1928/37. biennial, 18th, 1980, Waterloo, Ont. $66. Combustion Institute, 986 Union Trust Bldg., Pittsburgh, PA 15219. cum.index in 10th issue. circ. 3,500(approx.)

541.3 US ISSN 0082-0989
SYMPOSIUM ON THERMOPHYSICAL PROPERTIES. PROCEEDINGS. 1959. irreg., 6th, 1973; 7th, 1978. price varies. American Society of Mechanical Engineers, Heat Transfer Division, Standing Committee on Thermophysical Properties, 345 E. 47 St., New York, NY 10017. Ed. P. E. Liley. (also avail. in microfiche; microfilm)

SYNTHETIC METHODS OF ORGANIC CHEMISTRY. see *CHEMISTRY — Organic Chemistry*

TECHNIQUES AND APPLICATIONS IN ORGANIC SYNTHESIS. see *CHEMISTRY — Organic Chemistry*

547.1 US
THERMODYNAMICS RESEARCH CENTER. HYDROCARBON PROJECT. SELECTED VALUES OF PROPERTIES OF HYDROCARBONS AND RELATED COMPOUNDS. CATEGORY A: TABLES OF SELECTED VALUES OF PHYSICAL AND THERMODYNAMIC PROPERTIES OF HYDROCARBONS. 1942. irreg., supplement A-79, 1979. $1.50 per sheet. (Texas Engineering Experiment Station) Thermodynamics Research Center, Texas A & M University, College Station, TX 77843. Ed. Kenneth R. Hall. circ. 500. (looseleaf format)
Formerly: Thermodynamics Research Center. A P I 44. Hydrocarbon Project. Selected Values of Properties of Hydrocarbons and Related Compounds. Category A: Tables of Selected Values of Physical and Thermodynamic Properties of Hydrocarbons (ISSN 0065-9630)

541.3 547.1 US ISSN 0147-1503
THERMODYNAMICS RESEARCH CENTER. INTERNATIONAL DATA SERIES. SELECTED DATA ON MIXTURES. SERIES A. THERMODYNAMIC PROPERTIES OF NON-REACTING BINARY SYSTEMS OF ORGANIC SUBSTANCES. 1973. irreg. $1.75 per sheet. Thermodynamics Research Center, Texas A & M University, College Station, TX 77843. Ed. Henry V. Kehiaian. circ. 200. Indexed: Chem.Abstr.

THERMODYNAMICS RESEARCH CENTER DATA PROJECT. SELECTED VALUES OF PROPERTIES OF CHEMICAL COMPOUNDS. CATEGORY A. TABLES OF SELECTED VALUES OF PHYSICAL AND THERMODYNAMIC PROPERTIES OF CHEMICAL COMPOUNDS. see *CHEMISTRY — Analytical Chemistry*

541.3 CN ISSN 0041-9370
UNIVERSITY OF ALBERTA. DEPARTMENT OF CHEMISTRY. DIVISION OF THEORETICAL CHEMISTRY. TECHNICAL REPORT. 1966. irreg. (5-10/yr.) free. ‡ University of Alberta, Department of Chemistry, Edmonton, Alta. T6G 2G2, Canada. Ed. Prof. Serafin Fraga. circ. 150. (processed) Indexed: Bull.Signal. Chem.Abstr.

530 NE ISSN 0090-1911
VIBRATIONAL SPECTRA AND STRUCTURE. 1972. irreg., vol. 17, 1979. price varies. Elsevier Scientific Publishing Co., Box 211, 1000 AE Amsterdam, Netherlands. Ed. J. Durig. charts. illus. index.

541 UR
VOPROSY KHIMII I KHIMICHESKOI TEKHNOLOGII. vol. 42, 1976. irreg. price varies. (Dnepropetrovskii Khimiko-Tekhnologicheskii Institut) Izdatel'stvo Vysshaya Shkola Khar'kovskogo Universiteta, Ul.Universitetskaya 16, Khar'kov 310003, U.S.S.R. Ed. M. Loshkarev. abstr. bibl. charts. illus. circ. 1,000. Indexed: Chem.Abstr.

541.3 US
WILEY MONOGRAPHS IN CHEMICAL PHYSICS. 1970. irreg., latest vol. 1974, unnumbered. price varies. (Wiley-Interscience) John Wiley & Sons, Inc., 605 Third Ave., New York, NY 10016. Eds. J.B. Birks, S.P. McGlynn.

WORLD PLASTICS. see *PLASTICS*

CHILDREN AND YOUTH — About

see also Education; Medical Sciences — Pediatrics

ALBERTA. DEPARTMENT OF EDUCATION. EARLY CHILDHOOD SERVICES PROGRAM HIGHLIGHTS. see *EDUCATION*

370 649.1 FR ISSN 0069-7761
ANNUAIRE DES COMMUNAUTES D'ENFANTS. 1954. a. 15 F. Association Nationale des Communautes d'Enfants, 145 Bd. Magenta, 75010 Paris, France.

028.5 US
BEST BOOKS FOR CHILDREN; preschool through the middle grades. irreg. $35. R.R. Bowker Company, 1180 Ave. of the Americas, New York, NY 10036 (Orders to Box 1807, Ann Arbor, MI 48106)

649 618.92 US
BOSTON CHILDREN'S MEDICAL CENTER. PUBLICATIONS FOR PARENTS. irreg. price varies. Delacorte Press (Subsidiary of: Dial Press) 1 Dag Hammarskjold Plaza, 245 E. 47 St., New York, NY 10017.

369.4 CN ISSN 0045-334X
BUFFALO. irreg. free. ‡ Girl Guides of Canada, Manitoba Council, 200-267 Edmonton St., Winnipeg, Man. R3C 1S2, Canada. Ed.Bd. circ. 1,800.

369.4 CK
CHASQUI. vol. 2, 1976. irreg. Asociacion Guias Scouts de Colombia, Apdo. Aereo 5774, Medellin, Colombia. Ed. Maria E. Botero.
Scouting

649 US
CHILD CARE; a comprehensive guide series. 1975. irreg., vol. 3, 1978. Human Sciences Press, 72 Fifth Ave., New York, NY 10011. Ed. Stevanne Auerbach. (reprint service avail. from ISI,UMI)

649 US
CHILD CARE HANDBOOK. 1973. irreg. $6. American Home Economics Association, 2010 Massachusetts Ave. N.W., Washington, DC 20036.
Care and hygiene

CHILDHOOD CITY NEWSLETTER. see *PSYCHOLOGY*

364.36 US
CHILDREN IN CUSTODY; a report on juvenile detention and correctional facility census. 1971. a. free. U.S. Department of Justice, Bureau of Justice Statistics, 633 Indiana Ave. N.W., Washington, DC 20531 (Orders to: Box 6000, Rockville, MD 20850) circ. 12,000.
Supersedes: U. S. Department of Health, Education and Welfare. Statistics on Public Institutions for Delinquent Children (ISSN 0082-9935)

028.5 UK
CITY SPARROWS. 1872. a. 10p. ‡ Scottish Children's League of Pity, 41 Polwarth Terrace, Edinburgh EH11 1NU, Scotland. Ed. Mrs. Forbes. adv. circ. 1,500.

155.4 US ISSN 0147-1082
CONTEMPORARY PROBLEMS OF CHILDHOOD; a bibliographic series. 1977. irreg. Greenwood Press, 88 Post Rd. W., Westport, CT 06881. Ed. Carol Ann Winchell.

362.7 NE
DIRECTIE KINDERBESCHERMING. biennial. ‡ Ministerie van Justitie, Raamweg 47, The Hague, Netherlands. stat. circ. 2,000.

362.7 US ISSN 0092-7368
EARLY CHILDHOOD DEVELOPMENT IN TEXAS. 1971. biennial. Department of Community Affairs, Office of Early Childhood Development, P.O. Box 13166, Austin, TX 78701. charts. stat.

649 155.4 FR
ENFANT DU PREMIER AGE. a. Comite Francais pour la Sante, 143 rue Leon Maurice Nordmand, 75013 Paris, France. (Co-sponsor: Caisse Nationale d'Assurance Maladie)

364 UK ISSN 0072-6443
GREAT BRITAIN. HOME OFFICE. STUDIES IN THE CAUSES OF DELINQUENCY AND THE TREATMENT OF OFFENDERS. 1955. irreg. price varies. H.M.S.O., P.O. Box 569, London SE1 9NH, England.

362.7 649 FR
GUIDE DE LA JEUNE MAMAN. a. 17 rue Viete, 75017 Paris, France.

HAWAII. DEPARTMENT OF HEALTH. MENTAL HEALTH SERVICES FOR CHILDREN AND YOUTH; children's MH services branch. see *SOCIAL SERVICES AND WELFARE*

INTERNATIONAL CHILDREN'S CENTRE. PARIS. REPORT OF THE DIRECTOR-GENERAL TO THE EXECUTIVE BOARD. see *SOCIOLOGY*

INTERNATIONAL CHILDREN'S CENTRE. PARIS. TRAVAUX ET DOCUMENTS. see *SOCIOLOGY*

649 US
INTERNATIONAL MONOGRAPH SERIES ON EARLY CHILD CARE. a. price varies. Gordon and Breach Science Publishers, One Park Ave., New York, NY 10016. Eds. Halbert B. Robinson, Nancy M. Robinson.

364.36 IS ISSN 0075-1022
ISRAEL. CENTRAL BUREAU OF STATISTICS. JUVENILE DELINQUENCY. (Subseries of its Special Series) (Text in Hebrew and English) 1960-61. irreg., latest issue, no. 408, 1970. I£70. Central Bureau of Statistics, Box 13015, Jerusalem, Israel.

027.62 BE
J E B-POINTS. Variant title: Points. irreg (approx. 2/yr.) Direction Generale de la Jeunesse et des Loisirs, Galerie Ravenstein 78, 1000 Brussels, Belgium.
Supersedes in part: J E B Cahiers (ISSN 0008-0292)

JAMAICA CHILDREN'S SERVICE SOCIETY. ANNUAL REPORT. see *SOCIAL SERVICES AND WELFARE*

649 AT
KNOWING CHILDREN. 1970. irreg. Aus.$0.12 each. Creche and Kindergarten Association of Queensland, 14 Edmondstone St, Newmarket, Qld. 4051, Australia. Ed. Grace Young. adv. bk. rev. circ. 10,000.

LIBERIA. MINISTRY OF LABOUR, YOUTH & SPORTS. ANNUAL REPORT. see *SOCIAL SERVICES AND WELFARE*

649.1 614   FR   ISSN 0076-2814
MAISONS D'ENFANTS ET D'ADOLESCENTS DE FRANCE. ALBUM-ANNUAIRE NATIONAL; publication documentaire illustree des establissements de vacances, de repos, de soins, de cure et de prevention pour enfants et adolescents. a; latest edition 28th, 1976. 120 F. Editions Gaston Gorde, 45 Av. Paul Doumer, Roguebrune, France.

362.7   US
MARYLAND. JUVENILE SERVICES ADMINISTRATION. ANNUAL STATISTICAL REPORT. 1967. a. free. Department of Health and Mental Hygiene, Juvenile Services Administration, 201 W. Preston St., Baltimore, MD 21201.
Formerly: Maryland. Department of Juvenile Services. Annual Statistical Report (ISSN 0076-4744)

NATIONAL ASSOCIATION FOR DEAF/BLIND AND RUBELLA HANDICAPPED. NEWSLETTER. see *SOCIAL SERVICES AND WELFARE*

362   UK   ISSN 0302-1998
NATIONAL CHILDREN'S BUREAU. ANNUAL REVIEW. a. membership. National Children's Bureau, 8 Wakley St., Islington, London EC1V 7QE, England. Ed. G. A. Clark. (back issues avail.)

364.36   NE
NETHERLANDS. CENTRAAL BUREAU VOOR DE STATISTIEK. JUSTICIELE KINDERBESCHERMING. (Text in Dutch and English) 1950-51. a. fl.8.50. Centraal Bureau voor de Statistiek, Hoofdafdeling Statistieken van Criminaliteit en Rechtspleging, Prinses Beatrixlaan 428, Voorburg, Netherlands (Orders to: Staatsuitgeverij, Christoffel Plantijnstraat, The Hague, Netherlands)
Formerly: Netherlands. Centraal Bureau voor de Statistiek. Toepassing der Kinderwetten. Application of Juvenile Law (ISSN 0077-7471)

649   UK
NEW BABY. 1972. a. $2 free in U.K. ‡ (Health Visitors Association) B. Edsall & Co. Ltd., 36 Eccleston Square, London SW1V 1PF, England. Ed. P. Scowen. adv. illus. pat. circ. 550,000(controlled)

NEW BRUNSWICK. DEPARTMENT OF YOUTH. REPORT. see *CHILDREN AND YOUTH — For*

PAPERS AND REPORTS ON CHILD LANGUAGE DEVELOPMENT. see *LINGUISTICS*

649   US
REDBOOK'S YOUNG MOTHER. 1969. a. free. ‡ Redbook Publishing Co. (Subsidiary of: Chartcom, Inc.) 230 Park Ave., New York, NY 10017. Ed. Kay Sullivan. adv. illus. circ. 3,595,000 (reg. edt. 2,995,000; pre-natal edt. 600,000)

155.4 370   US   ISSN 0091-3065
REVIEW OF CHILD DEVELOPMENT RESEARCH. (Vols. 1 & 2 published by Russell Sage Foundation) irreg., vol. 5, 1976. price varies. (Society for Research in Child Development, Inc.) University of Chicago Press, 5801 S. Ellis Ave., Chicago, IL 60637. adv. bk. rev. (reprint service avail. from UMI,ISI)

354   CN   ISSN 0317-4344
SASKATCHEWAN. DEPARTMENT OF CULTURE AND YOUTH. ANNUAL REPORT. a. free. Department of Culture and Youth, Regina, Sask., Canada. illus.

369.4   SZ
SCOUTING 'ROUND THE WORLD/SCOUTISME A TRAVERS LE MONDE; facts and figures on world scouting and on national scout organizations which are members of the World Organization of the Scout Movement. biennial. 10 Fr. (World Organization of the Scout Movement) World Scout Bureau, Case Postale 78, 1211 Geneva 4, Switzerland.
Scouts

155.4   US   ISSN 0037-976X
SOCIETY FOR RESEARCH IN CHILD DEVELOPMENT. MONOGRAPHS. vol. 42, 1977. irreg., 4-6 per yr. $25. Univ. of Chicago Press, 5801 S. Ellis Ave., Chicago, IL 60637 (Orders to: 11030 Langley Ave., Chicago, IL 60628) Ed. Frances D. Horowitz. (also avail. in microform from UMI; reprint service avail. from UMI,ISI) Indexed: Biol.Abstr. Curr.Cont. Ind.Med. SSCI. Sci.Cit.Ind. Lang.& Lang.Behav.Abstr.

STUDIECENTRUM VOOR JEUGDMISDADIGHEID. PUBLIKATIE/CENTRE D'ETUDE DE LA DELINQUANCE JUVENILE. PUBLICATION. see *CRIMINOLOGY AND LAW ENFORCEMENT*

345   US   ISSN 0566-4152
UTAH. JUVENILE COURT. ANNUAL REPORT. a. Juvenile Court, 339 South 6th East, Salt Lake City, UT 84102. illus. Key Title: Annual Report - Utah Juvenile Court.
Formerly: Utah. Juvenile Court. Annual Administrative Report.

362.7   US   ISSN 0091-8482
WORKSHOP FOR CHILD CARE STAFF OF FLORIDA'S CHILD CARING FACILITIES. REPORT. a. $1 per no. Florida Group Childcare Association, Box 2050, Jacksonville, FL 32203. Key Title: Report - Workshop for Child Care Staff of Florida's Child Caring Facilities.

WORLD ALLIANCE OF Y M C A'S DIRECTORY. see *CLUBS*

369.433   UK   ISSN 0084-1412
WORLD ASSOCIATION OF GIRL GUIDES AND GIRL SCOUTS. REPORT OF CONFERENCE. triennial, 22nd 1981. World Association of Girl Guides and Girl Scouts, 132 Ebury St., London SW1W 9QQ, England.

369.43   SZ
WORLD SCOUT BUREAU. BIENNIAL REPORT. 1922. biennial. $3. (World Organization of the Scout Movement) World Scout Bureau, Case Postale 78, 1211 Geneva 4, Switzerland. circ. 1,200.
Formerly: Boy Scouts World Bureau. Biennial Report.
Scouts

Y CANADA. see *CLUBS*

Y M C A'S OF THE WORLD. see *CLUBS*

365   US   ISSN 0092-4539
YOUTH CORRECTIONAL INSTITUTION, BORDENTOWN, N.J. ANNUAL REPORT.* a. Youth Correctional Institution, Bordentown, NJ 08505. Key Title: Annual Report - Youth Correctional Institution (Bordentown)

CHILDREN AND YOUTH — Abstracting, Bibliographies, Statistics

649   AT
AUSTRALIA. BUREAU OF STATISTICS. CHILD CARE. irreg., latest May 1977. free. Australian Bureau of Statistics, P.O. Box 10, Belconnen, A.C.T. 2616, Australia. stat. circ. 3,000. (back issues avail.)

028.5 010   US   ISSN 0067-9070
BLACK EXPERIENCE IN CHILDREN'S BOOKS. 1946. irreg., latest issue 1979. $3 handling charge. New York Public Library, Office of Branch Libraries, 8 E. 40th St., New York, NY 10016. Ed. Barbara Rollock. index.
Formerly: Books About Negro Life for Children.

028.1   US
CHILDREN'S BOOK REVIEW INDEX. 1976. a. $28. Gale Research Company, Book Tower, Detroit, MI 48226. Ed. Gary C. Tarbert.

649   US
CHILDREN'S CATALOG. 1909. quinquennial, with a. supplements. $40. ‡ H. W. Wilson Co., 950 University Ave., Bronx, New York, NY 10452. Ed. Estelle A. Fidell. bk. rev.

CHILDREN'S LITERARY ALMANAC. see *PUBLISHING AND BOOK TRADE — Abstracting, Bibliographies, Statistics*

GERMANY (FEDERAL REPUBLIC, 1949-) STATISTISCHES BUNDESAMT. FACHSERIE 13, REIHE 6: OEFFENTLICHE JUGENDHILFE. see *SOCIAL SERVICES AND WELFARE — Abstracting, Bibliographies, Statistics*

345   US
NORTH DAKOTA. SOCIAL SERVICE BOARD. JUVENILE COURT AND STATE YOUTH AUTHORITY. DELINQUENCY, DEPENDENCY AND NEGLECT. SPECIAL PROCEEDINGS. irreg. Social Service Board, Bismarck, ND 58501.
Formerly(until 1975): North Dakota. Social Service Board Statistics, Juvenile Court and State Youth Authority (ISSN 0098-8782)

345   US   ISSN 0094-2677
OHIO JUVENILE COURT STATISTICS. a. Department of Mental Health and Mental Retardation, Bureau of Statistics, 65 S. Front St., Columbus, OH 43215. stat.

028.5 016   AT   ISSN 0081-2641
SOUTH AUSTRALIA. LIBRARIES BOARD. BOOKS FOR YOUNG PEOPLE; an annotated list. 1959. irreg. Aus.$0.50. Libraries Board of South Australia, Box 419, G.P.O., Adelaide, S. A. 5001, Australia. Indexed: Aus.P.A.I.S.

028.5   US
STORIES: A LIST OF STORIES TO TELL AND TO READ ALOUD. 7th edt., 1977. irreg. $3. New York Public Library, Office of Branch Libraries, 8 E. 40th St., New York, NY 10016. Ed. Marilyn Berg Iarusso.

028.5 011   US   ISSN 0039-4351
SUBJECT INDEX TO CHILDREN'S MAGAZINES. 1948. m. (semi-annual cumulations in Feb. & Aug) $5. 2020 University Ave., Suite 6, Madison, WI 53705. Ed. Gladys Cavanagh. circ. 6,500.

364.36   US   ISSN 0082-9900
U.S. SOCIAL AND REHABILITATION SERVICE. JUVENILE COURT STATISTICS. a. free. U.S. Social and Rehabilitation Service, 330 C St. S.W., Washington, DC 20201.

CHILDREN AND YOUTH — For

A A U JUNIOR OLYMPIC HANDBOOK. (Amateur Athletic Union of the United States) see *SPORTS AND GAMES*

028.5   UK   ISSN 0144-574X
ABOUT BOOKS FOR CHILDREN. a. Federation of Children's Book Groups, c/o Mrs. B. Marriott, 6 Cavendish Court Park Rd., Eccleshill, Bradford, W. Yorks.BD10 8AW, England. illus.
Formerly: Federation of Children's Book Groups. Yearbook (ISSN 0307-6091)

028.5   GW
ARBEITSKREIS FUER JUGENDLITERATUR. JAHRBUCH. 1972. a. DM.14. Verlag Julius Klinkhardt, Ramsauer Weg 5, 8173 Bad Heilbrunn, W. Germany (B.R.D.) Ed. K. E. Maier.

DIE BARKE; Lehrer-Jahrbuch. see *LITERATURE*

028.5   UK
BIG ENID BLYTON STORY ANNUAL. a. £1.75. Purnell Books, Berkshire House, Queen St., Maidenhead, Berkshire SL6 1NF, England.

900   US
BOOKS FOR YOUNG EXPLORERS SERIES. a. National Geographic Society, 17th & M Sts. N.W., Washington, DC 20036.

301.58   UK   ISSN 0068-0605
BOYS' BRIGADE, LONDON. ANNUAL REPORT. 1883. a. £1. Boys' Brigade, Inc., Brigade House, Parsons Green, London SW6 4TH, England. Ed. Brigade Secretary. circ. 4,000.

051   CN   ISSN 0316-8484
CANADIAN CHILDREN'S ANNUAL. 1975. a. Potlatch Publications, 35 Dalewood Cresc., Hamilton, Ont. L8S 4B5, Canada.

CHIROPRACTICS, HOMEOPATHY, OSTEOPATHY

028.5   US   ISSN 0069-3464
CHILDREN'S BOOKS; A LIST OF BOOKS FOR PRESCHOOL THROUGH JUNIOR HIGH SCHOOL AGE. 1964. a. price varies. U. S. Library of Congress, Washington, DC 20540 (Orders to: Supt. of Documents, Washington, DC 20402)

CHILDREN'S BOOKS OF THE YEAR. see *PUBLISHING AND BOOK TRADE*

CHILDREN'S LITERATURE SERIES. see *LITERATURE*

028.5   FR
COLLECTION KNOWLEDGE & TECHNIQUE: YOUTH. (Text in English) 1977. irreg. Editions Denoel, 19 rue de l'Universite, Paris 7e, France. Dir. Philippe Lorin.

EXPECTATIONS. see *BLIND*

028.52   US   ISSN 0361-9729
GIRLS & BOYS TOGETHER; a bibliography/catalog of non-sexist children's literature. irreg. $1. Feminist Book Mart, 162-11 Ninth Ave., Whitestone, NY 11357.

INDIAN COUNCIL FOR CHILD WELFARE. ANNUAL REPORT. see *SOCIAL SERVICES AND WELFARE*

028.5   AU
INITIATIVE. 1966. irreg. (4-6/yr.) membership. Junge Generation in der Volkspartei, Jugendklub Innere Stadt, Wollzeile 24, 1010 Vienna, Austria. Ed. Guenter Zillich. adv. illus. circ. 1,000.
    Formerly (until 1972): Magazin Vier und Zwanzig (ISSN 0024-9785)

INTERAMERICAN CHILDREN'S INSTITUTE. REPORT OF THE GENERAL DIRECTOR. see *SOCIAL SERVICES AND WELFARE*

369.4   AU   ISSN 0074-5790
INTERNATIONAL FALCON MOVEMENT. CONFERENCE REPORTS.* (Reports published in its monthly paper, the IFM-Bulletin) (Text in English, German, French, Swedish and Spanish) irreg., 1970, 11th, Germany. International Falcon Movement, Rauhensteingasse 5, P. O. Box 583, 1011 Vienna, Austria.

362.7   UK   ISSN 0074-7416
INTERNATIONAL PLAYGROUND ASSOCIATION. CONFERENCE REPORT. (Text in English, French or German) 1961. approx. triennial; 6th, Milan, 1976. membership. ‡ International Playground Association, 12 Cherry Tree Dr., Sheffield S11 9AE, England. Ed. Miss M. E. Otter.

J'AIME LIRE. see *RELIGIONS AND THEOLOGY*

JUNIOR AGE YEAR BOOK AND DIARY. see *CLOTHING TRADE*

361   CN   ISSN 0077-8079
NEW BRUNSWICK. DEPARTMENT OF YOUTH. REPORT. a. Department of Youth, Fredericton, N.B., Canada.
    Formerly: New Brunswick. Department of Youth and Welfare. Report.

028.5   AU   ISSN 0078-3560
OESTERREICHISCHER BUCHKLUB DER JUGEND. JAHRBUCH. 1949. a. membership; no subscriptions. Oesterreichischer Buchklub der Jugend, Mayerhofgasse 6, A-1040 Vienna, Austria. Eds. R. Bamberger, W. Jambor.

OUT OF SCHOOL SCIENTIFIC AND TECHNICAL EDUCATION. see *SCIENCES: COMPREHENSIVE WORKS*

PISTIS. see *RELIGIONS AND THEOLOGY*

028.5   NE
FRIMO. 1975. m. fl.5.10. L. C. G. Malmberg B.V., Leeghwaterlaan 16, S-Hertogenbosch, Netherlands. Ed. P. Arnoldussey. circ. 60,000.
    Ages 3-6

362.7   AU   ISSN 0080-701X
SCHRIFTEN ZUR JUGENDLEKTUERE. irreg. price varies. Oesterreichischer Buchklub der Jugend, Mayerhofgasse 6, A-1040 Vienna, Austria.

362.7   AU   ISSN 0080-7117
SCHRIFTENREIHE DES BUCHKLUBS DER JUGEND. irreg. price varies. Oesterreichischer Buchklub der Jugend, Mayerhofgasse 6, A-1040 Vienna, Austria.

SCHWANN CHILDREN'S & CHRISTMAS RECORD & TAPE GUIDE. see *MUSIC*

028.5   SZ
SCHWEIZERISCHER BUND FUER JUGENDLITERATUR. JAHRESBERICHT/ LIGUE SUISSE POUR LA LITTERATURE DE LA JEUNESSE. RAPPORT ANNUEL. a. Schweizerischer Bund fuer Jugendliteratur, Zentralsekretariat, Herzogstr. 5, 3014 Berne, Switzerland.

028.5   US
SILVER LINING. a. World Pen Pals, 1690 Como Ave., St. Paul, MN 55108.

028.5   UR
SPUTNIK SEL'SKOI MOLODEZHI. a. 0.35 Rub. Izdatel'stvo Molodaya Gvardiya, Ul. Sushevskaya, 21, Moscow a-55, U.S.S.R. illus.

790.1   CN   ISSN 0226-7004
SUMMER BREEZES. 1980. a. United Church of Canada, Division of Communication, 85 St. Clair Ave. E., Toronto, Ont. M4T 1M8, Canada. illus.

808.068 028.5   SW
SVENSKA BARNBOKSINSTITUTET. SKRIFTER/ SWEDISH INSTITUTE FOR CHILDREN'S BOOKS. STUDIES. 1971. irreg., no. 9, 1977. Svenska Barnboksinstitutet, Trajaerhovsgatan 36, S-116 21 Stockholm, Sweden.

028.5   US
VERMONT CHILDREN'S MAGAZINE. 1975. irreg., approx. 4/yr. $5. Vermont Children's Magazine, Inc., Box 941, Burlington, VT 05402. Ed. Edward H. Osborn. bk. rev. circ. 5,000.

745.59   US   ISSN 0512-5901
WOMAN'S DAY CHRISTMAS IDEAS FOR CHILDREN. a. $1.10. Fawcett Publications, Inc., 1515 Broadway, New York, NY 10036. Ed. Dan Blue. illus. Key Title: Christmas Ideas for Children.

020   US
YOUNG ADULT ALTERNATIVE NEWSLETTER. 1973. 5/yr. $4. c/o Carol Starr, Ed., 37167 Mission Blvd., Fremont, CA 94536. bk. rev. circ. 700. (processed) Indexed: CALL.

028.5   US
YOUTH INFO DIGEST. 1971. a. $6. Washington Workshops, 1329 E St. N.W., Suite 1111, Washington, DC 20004. Ed. Leo S. Tonkin. circ. 5,000.

371.4   US   ISSN 0163-1640
18 ALMANAC; a handbook for leaving high school. 1973. a. $2. 13-30 Corporation, 505 Market St., Knoxville, TN 37902. Ed. Phillip W. Moffitt. adv. circ. 500,000.

CHIROPRACTICS, HOMEOPATHY, OSTEOPATHY

see *Medical Sciences—Chiropractics, Homeopathy, Osteopathy*

CIVIL DEFENSE

see also *Military*

350.755   FR
FRANCE. SERVICE INTERDEPARTEMENTAL DE LA PROTECTION CIVILE. BULLETIN. irreg; latest Mar. 1980. free. Service Interdepartemental de la Protection Civile, 12 Quai de Gesvres, Paris 4, France. bibl. charts. illus.
    Formerly: Bulletin de la Protection Civile de la Prefecture de Police.

363.35 614   CN   ISSN 0078-2378
NOVA SCOTIA. EMERGENCY MEASURES ORGANIZATION. REPORT. 1963. a. Emergency Measures Organization, Box 1502, Halifax, N.S. B3J 2Y3, Canada.

CIVIL ENGINEERING

see *Engineering—Civil Engineering*

CIVIL RIGHTS

see *Political Science—Civil Rights*

CLASSICAL STUDIES

see also *Archaeology; History; Linguistics; Literature; Museums and Art Galleries*

700   IT   ISSN 0065-681X
AMERICAN ACADEMY IN ROME. PAPERS AND MONOGRAPHS. 1919. irreg. price varies. American Academy in Rome, Via Angelo Masina 5, 00153 Rome, Italy.

AMERICAN PHILOLOGICAL ASSOCIATION. SPECIAL PUBLICATIONS. see *LINGUISTICS*

880   AT   ISSN 0066-4774
ANTICHTHON; journal of the Australian Society for Classical Studies. 1967. a. Aus.$10($12.25) University of Sydney, Australian Society for Classical Studies, Dept. of Greek, Sydney N.S.W. 2006, Australia. Eds. K. J. McKay, P. R. C. Weaver. adv. circ. 400.

ARCHEOLOGIA CLASSICA. see *ARCHAEOLOGY*

470 480   PL   ISSN 0066-6866
ARCHIWUM FILOLOGICZNE. (Vols. are not issued in chronological order) (Text in Polish, Latin, German and French; summaries in French) 1958. irreg., vol. 40, 1979. price varies. (Polska Akademia Nauk, Komitet Nauk o Kulturze Antycznej) Ossolineum, Publishing House of the Polish Academy of Sciences, Rynek 9, Wroclaw, Poland (Dist. by Ars Polona-Ruch, Krakowskie Przedmiescie 7, Warsaw, Poland) Ed. Kazimierz Kumaniecki, Bronislaw Bilinski. circ. 500-1,000.

489   FI   ISSN 0570-734X
ARCTOS; ACTA PHILOLOGICA FENNICA. (Text in English, French, German, Italian and Latin) 1954. a. Fmk.47($12) Klassilis - Filologinen Yhdistys, Hallituskatu 11-13, SF-00100 Helsinki 10, Finland (Dist. by: Academic Bookstore,SF-00100 Helsinki 10, Finland)

BERLINER BYZANTINISTISCHE ARBEITEN. see *HISTORY — History Of Europe*

800   FR
BIBLIOTECA CLASICA GREDOS. 1976. irreg. Editorial Gredos, Sanchez Pacheco 81, Madrid 2, Spain.

800 950   IT
BIBLIOTECA DEGLI STUDI CLASSICI E ORIENTALI. 1974. irreg.; no. 12, 1978. price varies. Giardini Editori e Stampatori, Via Santa Bibbiana 28, 56100 Pisa, Italy.

800   SZ   ISSN 0067-7965
BIBLIOTHECA HELVETICA ROMANA. 1954. irreg., 1973, no. 12. price varies. (Institut Suisse de Rome, IT) Librarie Droz, 11, rue Massot, 1211 Geneva 12, Switzerland.

880 GW ISSN 0340-7853
BIBLIOTHEK DER GRIECHISCHEN LITERATUR.
Abbreviated title: B G L. 1971. irreg., vol. 14, 1981.
price varies. Anton Hiersemann Verlag,
Rosenbergstr. 113, Postfach 723, 7000 Stuttgart 1,
W. Germany (B.R.D.) Eds. P. Wirth, W. Gessel.

880 FR ISSN 0007-4217
BULLETIN DE CORRESPONDANCE
HELLENIQUE. 1877. a (in two fascicules) price
varies. (Ecole Francaise d'Athenes, GR) Diffusion
de Boccard, 11 rue de Medicis, 75006 Paris, France.
charts. illus.

480 880 US ISSN 0068-5895
CALIFORNIA STUDIES IN CLASSICAL
ANTIQUITY. 1968. irreg. price varies. University
of California Press, 2223 Fulton St., Berkeley, CA
94720.

870 UK
CAMBRIDGE CLASSICAL STUDIES. irreg., no. 26,
1981. $35 for latest vol. Cambridge University
Press, Box 110, Cambridge CB2 3RL, England
(And 32 E. 57th St., New York NY 10022) Ed. Bd.

880 870 UK ISSN 0068-6638
CAMBRIDGE CLASSICAL TEXTS AND
COMMENTARIES. 1965. irreg., no. 22, 1981.
$49.50 for latest vol. Cambridge University Press,
Box 110, Cambridge CB2 3RL, England (and 32 E.
57 St., New York, NY 10022) Ed.Bd. index.

400 UK ISSN 0068-6735
CAMBRIDGE PHILOLOGICAL SOCIETY.
PROCEEDINGS. 1882. a. £5. Cambridge
Philological Society, Museum of Classical
Archaeology, Little St. Mary's Lane, Cambridge
CB2 1RR, England. Eds. E. J. Kenney, J. Diggle.
circ. 700.

400 UK ISSN 0068-6743
CAMBRIDGE PHILOLOGICAL SOCIETY.
PROCEEDINGS. SUPPLEMENT. 1965. irreg., vol.
6, 1980. £3.50. Cambridge Philological Society,
Museum of Classical Archaeology, Little St. Mary's
Lane, Cambridge CB2 1RR, England. Eds. E. J.
Kenney, J. Diggle.

800 NE
CINCINNATI CLASSICAL STUDIES. NEW
SERIES. 1977. irreg., vol. 3, 1978. price varies. E.J.
Brill, Oude Rijn 33a-35, Leiden, Netherlands.

800 DK
CLASSICA ET MEDIAEVALIA; revue Danoise de
philologie et d'histoire. (Text in English, French,
German) 1938. a. Kr.195.65. (Dansk Selskab for
Oldtids og Middelalderforskning) Gyldendalske
Boghandel-Nordisk Forlag A-S, Klareboderne 3,
DK-1001 Copenhagen K, Denmark. Ed. Franz
Blatt.

800 UK ISSN 0069-4460
CLASSICAL ASSOCIATION. PROCEEDINGS.
1903. a. £1. ‡ Classical Association, c/o G. R.
Watson, Dept. of Classics and Archaeology,
University of Nottingham, Nottingham, England.
Ed. C. Collard. adv. circ. 4,500. (also avail. in
microform from UMI)

800 US
CLASSICAL ASSOCIATION OF NEW ENGLAND.
ANNUAL BULLETIN. 1906. a. membership only.
‡ Classical Association of New England, c/o Gilbert
Lawall, Ed., 71 Sand Hill Rd., Amherst, MA 01002.
bibl. illus. circ. 700.

870 880 IT ISSN 0069-4479
CLASSICI GRECI E LATINI. 1967, no.2. irreg. price
varies. Casa Editrice Felice le Monnier, Via
Scipione Ammirato, 100, C.P.455, 50136 Florence,
Italy.

745 091 GW
CORPUS DER BYZANTINISCHEN
MINIATURENHANDSCHRIFTEN (C B M)
1977. irreg., vol. 3, 1981. price varies.
(Oesterreichische Akademie der Wissenschaften,
Kommission fuer Byzantinistik, AU) Anton
Hiersemann Verlag, Rosenbergstr. 113, Postfach
723, 7000 Stuttgart 1, W. Germany (B.R.D.) Eds.
Otto Demus, Irmgard Hutter.

954.82 II
DAMILICA. (Text in English or Tamil) 1970. irreg.
Rs.18.50. Department of Archaeology, Madras,
Tamil Nadu, India. bibl. illus.

489 BE ISSN 0070-4792
DIDACTICA CLASSICA GANDENSIA. 1962. a.
300 Fr. ‡ Rijksuniversiteit te Gent, Blandijnberg 2,
B-9000 Ghent, Belgium (Orders to: Mrs. Verbeken-
de Pauw, St.-Pietersnieuwstraat 109, B-9000 Ghent,
Belgium) Eds. J. Veremans, F. Decreus.

489 BE ISSN 0070-685X
DOCUMENTATIO DIDACTICA CLASSICA. (Text
in Latin) 1963. a. 200 Fr. Rijksuniversiteit te Gent,
Blandijnberg 2, B-9000 Ghent, Belgium (Orders to:
Mrs. Verbeken-de Pauw, St.-Pietersnieuwstraat 109,
B-9000 Ghent, Belgium) Eds. J. Veremans, F.
Decreus.
   Classical philology

800 SZ ISSN 0071-0822
ENTRETIENS SUR L'ANTIQUITE CLASSIQUE.
1958, no.3. irreg., vol. 22, 1976. price varies.
(Fondation Hardt pour l'Etude de l'Antiquite
Classique) Librarie Droz, 11 rue Massot, 1211
Geneva 12, Switzerland.

FILOLOGIA KLASYCZNA. see LINGUISTICS

470 480 HU ISSN 0072-5021
GOROG ES LATIN IROK TARA/SCRIPTORES
GRAECI ET LATINI. (Text in Latin or Greek, and
Hungarian) 1954. irreg. price varies. (Magyar
Tudomanyos Akademia) Akademiai Kiado,
Publishing House of the Hungarian Academy of
Sciences, P.O. Box 24, H-1363 Budapest, Hungary.

870 UK
GREEK AND LATIN STUDIES SERIES. 1965.
irreg. price varies. ‡ Routledge & Kegan Paul Ltd.,
Broadway House, Newtown Rd., Henley-on-
Thames, Oxon. RG9 1EN, England (U.S. orders to:
Routledge Journals, 9 Park St., Boston, MA 02108)
Eds. T. A. Dorey, D. R. Dudley.
   Formerly: Studies in Latin Literature and Its
Influence (ISSN 0081-8143)

930 940 US ISSN 0072-7474
GREEK, ROMAN AND BYZANTINE
MONOGRAPHS. 1959. irreg.,no. 8, 1978. price
varies. Duke University, Department of Classical
Studies, Box 4715, Duke Sta., Durham, NC 27706.
Ed.Kent J. Rigsby. circ. 500.

930 940 US ISSN 0072-7482
GREEK, ROMAN AND BYZANTINE STUDIES.
SCHOLARLY AIDS. (Supplement to quarterly
journal Greek, Roman and Byzantine Studies) 1961.
irreg., 1969, no. 2. price varies. Duke University,
Dept. of Classical Studies, Box 4715, Duke Sta.,
Durham, NC 27706. Ed.Kent J. Rigsby.

800 SP
HABIS. (Text in English, French, German, Spanish)
1970. a. Universidad de Sevilla, Secretariado de
Publicaciones, Seville, Spain. charts, illus.

HARVARD STUDIES IN CLASSICAL
PHILOLOGY. see LINGUISTICS

930 410 SZ ISSN 0073-0939
HAUTES ETUDES DU MONDE GRECO-
ROMAIN. 1964. irreg., 1966, no. 2. price varies.
(Ecole Pratique des Hautes Etudes, Centre de
Recherches d'Histoire et de Philologie, FR)
Librarie Droz, 11 rue Massot, 1211 Geneva 12,
Switzerland. circ. 1,000.

480 IT ISSN 0017-9981
HELIKON; revista di tradizione e cultura classica.
1961. irreg., vol. 16, 1976. Universita degli Studi di
Messina, Messina, Italy (Dist. by: Erma di
Bretschneider, Via Cassiodor 19, 00193 Rome,
Italy)

HERMES-EINZELSCHRIFTEN. see LINGUISTICS

930 BE
HUMANISTICA LOVANIENSIA; journal of Neo-
Latin studies. 1968. a. price varies. (Katholieke
Universiteit te Leuven, Seminarium Philologiae
Humanisticae) Leuven University Press,
Krakenstraat 3, 3000 Louvain, Belgium. bk. rev.
circ. 750. (back issues avail.)

930 BE
HUMANISTICA LOVANIENSIA. SUPPLEMENTA.
1978. irreg., vol. 2, 1979. Leuven University Press,
Krakerstraat 3, B-3000 Louvain, Belgium.

480 880 GW ISSN 0085-1671
HYPOMNEMATA; Untersuchungen zur Antike und
zu ihrem Nachleben. 1962. irreg., no. 65, 1980.
price varies. Vandenhoeck und Ruprecht, Theaterstr.
13, Postfach 77, 3400 Goettingen, W. Germany
(B.R.D.)

800 US ISSN 0363-1923
ILLINOIS CLASSICAL STUDIES. 1976. a.
(University of Illinois at Urbana-Champaign,
Classics Department) Scholars Press, University of
Montana, Missoula, MT 59812. Ed. Miroslav
Marcovich.

480 880 IT ISSN 0073-5752
INCUNABULA GRAECA. 1961. irreg., no. 76, 1981.
price varies. Edizioni dell' Ateneo S.p.A., P.O. Box
7216, 00100 Rome, Italy. circ. 1,500.

INTERNATIONAL ASSOCIATION FOR
CLASSICAL ARCHAEOLOGY. PROCEEDINGS
OF CONGRESS. see ARCHAEOLOGY

950 IT
ISTITUTO UNIVERSITARIO ORIENTALE DI
NAPOLI. SEMINARIO DI STUDI DEL MONDO
CLASSICO. ANNALI. SEZIONE LINGUISTICA.
1978. a. Giardini Editori e Stampatori, Via Santa
Bibbiana 28, 56100 Pisa, Italy. Ed.Bd.

930 880 JA ISSN 0582-4524
JOURNAL OF CLASSICAL STUDIES/SEIYO
KOTENGAKU KENKYU. (Extracts in English)
1928. a. (Classical Society of Japan) Iwanami
Shoten Publishers, 2-5-5 Hitotsubashi, Chiyoda-ku,
Tokyo 101, Japan.

880 UK ISSN 0075-4269
JOURNAL OF HELLENIC STUDIES. 1880. a. £15
to non-members. Society for the Promotion of
Hellenic Studies, 31-34 Gordon Square, London
WC1H OPP, England. Ed. E. L. Bowie. adv. bk.
rev. circ. 3,000.

870 UK ISSN 0075-4358
JOURNAL OF ROMAN STUDIES. (Text in English,
Latin, French, German, and Greek) 1911. a.
membership. Society for the Promotion of Roman
Studies, 31-34 Gordon Sq., London WC1H 0PP,
England. Ed. M. H. Crawford. adv. bk. rev.
cum.index vols. I-XL. circ. 2,800. Indexed:
Hum.Ind.

KTEMA; civilisations de l 'Orient, de la Grece et de
Rome Antiques. see HISTORY — History Of Asia

909 SW
KULTUREN. a. Kr.40. Kulturhistoriska Foereningen
foer Soedra Sverige, 221 01 Lund, Sweden. illus.

480 880 GW ISSN 0024-7421
LUSTRUM; Internationale Forschungsberichte aus
dem Bereich des Klassischen Altertums. 1956. irreg.,
no. 22, 1979-80. price varies. Vandenhoeck und
Ruprecht, Theaterstr. 13, Postfach 77, 3400
Goettingen, W. Germany (B.R.D.) Eds. Hans-
Joachim Mette & Andreas Thierfelder. adv. circ.
1,000.

880 930 GR ISSN 0076-289X
MAKEDONIKA. (Text and summaries in English,
French, and German) 1940. a. Dr.300. Society for
Macedonian Studies, Vas. Sophias 4, Thessaloniki,
Greece.

870 880 US ISSN 0076-471X
MARTIN CLASSICAL LECTURES. (A series of
lectures delivered annually at Oberlin College)
1931. irreg., 1970, no.24. price varies. (Oberlin
College) Harvard University Press, 79 Garden St.,
Cambridge, MA 02138.

913 NR
MUSEUM AFRICUM; West African journal of
classical and related studies. 1972. a.; vol. 3, 1974.
£N3. West African Classical Association,
Department of Classics, University of Ibadan,
Ibadan, Nigeria (Dist. by: Rudolf Habelt Verlag
GmbH, Am Buchenhang 1, 53 Bonn 5, West
Germany (B.R.D.)) Ed. L. A. Thompson. adv. bk.
rev.
   Supersedes: Nigeria and the Classics (ISSN 0549-
2629)

930 AU
MYKENISCHE STUDIEN. (Subseries of
Oesterreichische Akademie der Wissenschaften.
Philosophisch-Historische Klasse. Sitzungsberichte)
1972. irreg. price varies. (Oesterreichische
Akademie der Wissenschaften, Kommission fuer
Mykenische Forschung) Verlag der
Oesterreichischen Akademie der Wissenschaften,
Ignaz Seipel-Platz 2, A-1010 Vienna, Austria. illus.
 Subseries of Akademie der Wissenschaften,
Vienna. Philosophisch-Historische Klasse.
Sitzungsberichte.

480 US ISSN 0077-6521
NEO-HELLENIKA. (Text in English, French,
German, Italian and Spanish) 1970. irreg., no. 3,
1978. $20. University of Texas at Austin, Center for
Neo-Hellenic Studies, 1010 W. 22nd St., Austin, TX
78712. adv. bk. rev.

800 UK
NEW SURVEYS IN THE CLASSICS. 1966. a.
membership; free to subscribers of "Greece and
Rome". (Classical Association) Oxford University
Press, Press Rd, Neasden, London NW10 0DD,
England. Ed. Bd. bibl.

870 SZ ISSN 0078-0936
NOCTES ROMANAE; Forschungen ueber die Kultur
der Antike. 1949. irreg., vol. 15, 1977. price varies.
Paul Haupt AG, Falkenplatz 14, CH-3001 Berne,
Switzerland. Eds. Walter Wilit, Georg Luck.

913 DK
ODENSE UNIVERSITY CLASSICAL STUDIES.
(Text in French and English) 1971. irreg., no. 10,
1977. price varies. Odense University Press, 36,
Pjentedamsgade, DK-5000 Odense, Denmark. (back
issues avail.)

OPUSCULA ATHENIENSIA. see *ARCHAEOLOGY*

930 GW ISSN 0078-5555
ORBIS ANTIQUUS. 1960. irreg. price varies.
Aschendorffsche Verlagsbuchhandlung, Soester Str.
13, 4400 Muenster, W. Germany (B.R.D.) Ed. Max
Wegner.

480 880 BE ISSN 0030-6584
OTIA. (Text in French) 1953. a. 300 Fr. Universite de
Liege, Association des Classiques, 110 Blvd. de la
Sauveniere, B-4000 Liege, Belgium. circ. 650.
Formerly: Universite de Liege. Association de
Classiques Bulletin Semestriel.

OXFORD MONOGRAPHS ON CLASSICAL
ARCHAEOLOGY. see *ARCHAEOLOGY*

800 GW ISSN 0552-9638
PALINGENESIA. (Text in English and German)
irreg., vol. 16, 1981. price varies. Franz Steiner
Verlag GmbH, Friedrichstr. 24, Postfach 5529, 6200
Wiesbaden, W. Germany (B.R.D) Eds. P. Steinmetz,
O. Lendle.

870 880 IT ISSN 0078-9240
PAPIRI GRECI E LATINI. irreg. price varies.
(Societa Italiana per la Ricerca dei Papiri Greci e
Latini) Casa Editrice Felice le Monnier, Via
Scipione Ammirato 100, C.P.455, 50136 Florence,
Italy.

PHILOSOPHIA ANTIQUA. see *PHILOSOPHY*

800 FR ISSN 0035-2004
REVUE DES ETUDES ANCIENNES. 1929. irreg.
150 F. Universite de Bordeaux III, Domaine
Universitaire, 33405 Talence Cedex, France. bk. rev.
abstr. bibl. charts. illus. index.

880 480 FR ISSN 0035-2039
REVUE DES ETUDES GRECQUES. 1888. irreg.;
vol. 93, 1980. 235 F. Societe d'Edition les Belles
Lettres, 95 Bd. Raspail, 75006 Paris, France. Ed.
Prof. Plassart. bk. rev. abstr. bibl. illus. index. circ.
2,000.

930 400 FR
REVUE DES ETUDES LATINES. 1928. a. 200 F.
(Societe des Etudes Latines) Societe d'Edition les
Belles Lettres, 95, Boulevard Raspail, 75006 Paris,
France. Ed. Marcel Durry. bk. rev. bibl. cum.index
every 5 yrs. circ. 2,000.

880 IT ISSN 0080-3251
RIVISTA DI CULTURA CLASSICA E
MEDIOEVALE. QUADERNI. 1960. irreg., no. 15,
1975. price varies. Edizioni dell' Ateneo S.p.A.,
P.O. Box 7216, 00100 Rome, Italy. circ. 2,000.

ROEMISCHE HISTORISCHE MITTEILUNGEN.
see *HISTORY — History Of Europe*

480 GW ISSN 0341-3209
ROMANISTIK IN GESCHICHTE UND
GEGENWART. 1975. irreg., no. 10, 1981. price
varies. Verlag Helmut Buske, Schlueterstr. 14, 2000
Hamburg 13, W. Germany (B.R.D.) Eds. H.
Haarmann, H.J. Niederehe, Dieter Kremer.

870 930 IT
ROMANOBARBARICA. 1976. a. L.25000.
(Universita degli Studi di Roma, Istituto di Lingua e
Letteratura Latina) Herder Editrice e Libreria s.r.l.,
Piazza Montecitorio 120, 00186 Rome, Italy. Ed.
Bruno Luiselli, Manlio Simonetti.

800 US ISSN 0080-6684
SATHER CLASSICAL LECTURES. 1924. irreg.
price varies. University of California Press, 2223
Fulton St., Berkeley, CA 94720.

400 IS
SCRIPTA CLASSICA ISRAELICA. (Text in English,
German or Latin) 1974. a. $10. (Israel Society for
the Promotion of Classical Studies) Jerusalem
Academic Press, Box 3640, Jerusalem, Israel. illus.

870 IT ISSN 0080-8393
SCRIPTORES LATINI; COLLANA DI SCRITTORI
LATINI AD USO ACCADEMICO. 1965. irreg.,
no. 18, 1981. price varies. Edizioni dell' Ateneo
S.p.A., P.O. Box 7216, 00100 Rome, Italy. circ.
1,000.

800 IT
SCRITTURA E CIVILTA. 1977. a. L.27000.
(Universita degli Studi di Roma, Istituto di
Paleografia) Bottega d'Erasmo, Via G. Ferrari 9,
10124 Turin, Italy. Ed. Armando Petrucci.

880 IT ISSN 0081-6159
STUDI DI METRICA CLASSICA. 1962. irreg., no. 7,
1981. price varies. Edizioni dell' Ateneo S.p.A.,
P.O. Box 7216, 00100 Rome, Italy. circ. 1,500.

480 470 SW ISSN 0081-6450
STUDIA GRAECA ET LATINA
GOTHOBURGENSIA. (Subseries of Acta
Universitatis Gothoburgensis) (Text in various
languages) 1955. irreg., no. 41, 1979. price varies;
also exchange basis. (Goeteborgs Universitet,
Institute of Classical Studies) Acta Universitatis
Gothoburgensis, Box 5096, S-402 22 Goeteborg 5,
Sweden (Dist. in U. S., Canada, and Mexico by:
Humanities Press, Inc., 171 First Ave., Atlantic
Highlands, NJ 07716) Eds. Cajus Fabricius, Aake
Fridh.

880 BE
STUDIA HELLENISTICA. irreg. price varies.
Eikenboslaan 19, B-3200 Kessel 10, Belgium.

932 GW ISSN 0340-2215
STUDIEN ZUR ALTAEGYPTISCHEN KULTUR.
1974. irreg., no. 7, 1979. price varies. Verlag
Helmut Buske, Schlueterstr. 14, 2000 Hamburg 13,
W. Germany (B.R.D.) Eds. Hartwig Altenmueller,
Dietrich Wildung.

800 NE ISSN 0081-7724
STUDIES IN CLASSICAL LITERATURE. 1966.
irreg. price varies. Mouton Publishers, Noordeinde
41, 2514 GC The Hague, Netherlands (U.S. addr:
Mouton Publishers, c/o Walter de Gruyter, Inc.,
200 Saw Mill River Road, Hawthorne, NY 10532)

STUDIES IN MEDITERRANEAN
ARCHAEOLOGY. MONOGRAPH SERIES. see
ARCHAEOLOGY

STUDIES IN MEDITERRANEAN
ARCHAEOLOGY. POCKET-BOOK SERIES. see
ARCHAEOLOGY

STUDIES IN MYCENAEAN INSCRIPTIONS AND
DIALECT. see *LINGUISTICS*

489 890 RM ISSN 0081-8844
STUDII CLASICE. (Text in Rumanian, French,
English, German, Italian and Russian) 1959. a. $15.
(Societatea de Studii Clasice din Republica
Socialista Romania) Editura Academiei Republicii
Socialiste Romania, Calea Victoriei 125, Bucharest,
Romania (Subscr. to: ILEXIM, Str. 13 Decembrie
Nr. 3, P.O. Box 136-137, Bucharest, Romania) Eds.
Al Graur and D.M. Pippidi. bk. rev. circ. 900.

800 AT ISSN 0311-2233
STUDIUM. 1972. irreg. Aus.$1 for non-members.
Sydney Medieval and Renaissance Group, History
Department, University of Sydney, Sydney, NSW
2006, Australia. Eds. J. O. Ward and L. S.
Davidson. bk. rev. circ. 200.

880 NE
SUPPLEMENTUM EPIGRAPHICUM GRAECUM.
1923. irreg., vol. 26, 1976-77. Sijthoff & Noordhoff
International Publishers B.V., Box 4, 2400 MA
Alphen aan den Rijn, Netherlands. Eds. H.W.
Pleket, R.S. Stroud.

SVENSKA INSTITUTET I ATHEN. SKRIFTER. see
ARCHAEOLOGY

SVENSKA INSTITUTET I ROM. SKRIFTER.
ACTA SERIES PRIMA. see *ARCHAEOLOGY*

870 BE
SYMBOLAE. SERIES A. 1976. irreg., vol. 8, 1979.
Leuven University Press, Krankenstraat 3, B-3000
Louvain, Belgium.

800 400 NO ISSN 0039-7679
SYMBOLAE OSLOENSES. (Text in Ancient Greek,
English, French, German and Latin) 1922. a.
Kr.115($23) (Societatis Graeco-Latinae)
Universitetsforlaget, Kolstadgt. 1, Box 2959-Toeyen,
Oslo 6, Norway (U.S. address: Box 258, Irvington-
on-Hudson, NY 10533) Ed. Eiliv Skard. illus.
cum.index pub. in 1959 covering first 35 vols. circ.
300.

480 880 PL
SYMBOLAE PHILOLOGORUM
POSNANIENSIUM. (Text in Latin, Polish, English;
summaries in Latin) 1973. irreg. price varies.
Uniwersytet im. Adama Mickiewicza w Poznaniu,
Stalingradzka 1, 61-712 Poznan, Poland (Dist. by:
Ars Polona, Krakowskie Przedmiescie 7, 00-068
Warsaw, Poland) Eds. Ioannes Wikarjak, Georgius
Danielewicz.

TIRYNS. see *ARCHAEOLOGY*

489 FI ISSN 0082-7029
TURUN YLIOPISTO. KLASSILLISEN
FILOLOGIAN LAITOS. OPERA EX INSTITUTO
PHILOLOGIAE CLASSICAE UNIVERSITATIS
TURKUENSIS EDITA. (Subseries of Turun
Yliopisto. Julkaisuja. Sarja B. Humaniora) (Text in
English, German, French, Italian) 1969. irreg., no.
6, 1976. price varies. Turun Yliopisto, Klassillisen
Filologian Laitos - University of Turku, Department
of Classical Philology, SF-20500 Turku 50, Finland.
Ed. Heikki Koskenniemi. circ. 300.

UNIVERSITA DEGLI STUDI DI GENOVA.
ISTITUTO DI FILOLOGIA CLASSICA E
MEDIEVALE. PUBBLICAZIONI. see
LINGUISTICS

880 US ISSN 0068-6344
UNIVERSITY OF CALIFORNIA PUBLICATIONS.
CLASSICAL STUDIES. 1965. irreg. price varies.
University of California Press, 2223 Fulton St.,
Berkeley, CA 94720.

489 UK ISSN 0076-0730
UNIVERSITY OF LONDON. INSTITUTE OF
CLASSICAL STUDIES. BULLETIN. 1954. a. £9.
University of London, Institute of Classical Studies,
31-34 Gordon Square, London WC1H 0PY,
England. Ed. E. W. Handley.

489 UK ISSN 0076-0749
UNIVERSITY OF LONDON. INSTITUTE OF
CLASSICAL STUDIES. BULLETIN
SUPPLEMENT. 1957. irreg., no. 40, 1979. price
varies. University of London, Institute of Classical
Studies, 31-34 Gordon Sq., London WC1H 0PY,
England. Ed. E. W. Handley.

800 UK ISSN 0459-7354
UNIVERSITY OF LONDON CLASSICAL
STUDIES. 1960. irreg., no. 8, 1976. price varies.
Athlone Press, 90-91 Great Russell St., London
WC1B 3PY, England (Dist in U.S. by: Humanities
Press Inc., 171 First Ave., Atlantic Highlands, NJ
07716)

930 913 480 880 CS ISSN 0083-4114
UNIVERZITA KOMENSKEHO. FILOZOFICKA
FAKULTA. ZBORNIK: GRAECOLATINA ET
ORIENTALIA. (Text in English, French, German,
Latin; summaries in Slovak) 1969. a. exchange basis.
(Univerzita Komenskeho, Filozoficka Fakulta)
Slovenske Pedagogicke Nakladatelstvo, Sasinkova 5,
89112 Bratislava, Czechoslovakia. Eds. Miloslaus
Okal, Ladislaus Drozdik. circ. 824.

VERBA SENIORUM. see *RELIGIONS AND THEOLOGY*

870 US
VERGILIAN SOCIETY NEWSLETTER. a.
membership. Vergilian Society of America, Inc., c/o
R. Den Adel, Ed., Rockford College, 5050 E. State
St., Rockford, IL 61101. circ. 1,500.

809 016 US ISSN 0506-7294
VERGILIUS. 1956. a. $2. Vergilian Society, c/o C. P.
Twichell, The Choate School, Wallingford, CT
06492. Ed. Janice M. Bernario.

800 CN ISSN 0316-2508
VEXILLUM. 1972. irreg. (B.C. Association of
Teachers of Classics) B.C. Teachers' Federation,
105-2235 Burrard St., Vancouver, B.C. V6J 3H9,
Canada. circ. 200.
Formerly: B. C. Association of Teachers of
Classics. Newsletter (ISSN 0045-2912)

880 UK ISSN 0083-629X
VIRGIL SOCIETY. PROCEEDINGS. 1961-62. a.
price varies. Virgil Society, c/o F. Robertson,
Faculty of Letters, Reading University, Reading,
England. Ed. H. MacL. Currie. bk. rev.

WIENER STUDIEN. ZEITSCHRIFT FUER
KLASSISCHE PHILOLOGIE UND PATRISTIK.
see *LINGUISTICS*

800 UK ISSN 0084-330X
YALE CLASSICAL STUDIES. irreg., no. 26, 1981.
$35 for latest vol. Yale University, Department of
Classics, Box 110, Cambridge CB2 3RL, England
(And 32 E. 57th St., New York NY 10022)

CLASSICAL STUDIES — Abstracting, Bibliographies, Statistics

800 016 FR
ANNEE PHILOLOGIQUE; bibliographie critique et
analytique de l'antiquite greco-latine. (Text in all
Occidental languages; summaries in English, French
and German) 1924; N.S. 1928. a. 250 F.
International Society of Classical Bibliography, 11
Ave. Rene Coty, 75014 Paris, France (Distr. by:
Societe d'Edition les Belles Lettres, 95 Bd. Raspail,
75006 Paris, France) Ed. Juliette Ernst.

CLEANING AND DYEING

see also *Textile Industries and Fabrics*

667.3 CS ISSN 0009-0727
CESKOSLOVENSKY KOLORISTA.* 1960. 3-4/yr.
free. Sdruzeni pro Odbyt Dehtovych Barviv, Na
Porici 24, Prague 2, Czechoslovakia. charts. circ.
1,500.

667.12 FR
FEDERATION DES ENTREPRENEURS DE
NETTOYAGE DE FRANCE. ANNUAIRE
OFFICIEL. a. Federation des Entrepreneurs de
Nettoyage de France, 23 rue Tronchet, 75008 Paris,
France. adv.

INTERNATIONAL FEDERATION OF
ASSOCIATIONS OF TEXTILE CHEMISTS AND
COLORISTS. REPORTS OF CONGRESS. see
TEXTILE INDUSTRIES AND FABRICS

CLEANING AND DYEING — Abstracting, Bibliographies, Statistics

338.4 CN ISSN 0384-3912
CANADA. STATISTICS CANADA.
MANUFACTURERS OF SOAP AND
CLEANING COMPOUNDS/FABRICANTS DE
SAVON ET DE PRODUITS DE NETTOYAGE.
(Catalog 46-214) (Text in English and French)
1918. a. Can.$4.50($5.40) Statistics Canada,
Publications Distribution, Ottawa, Ont. K1A 0V7,
Canada. (also avail. in microform from MML)

CLOTHING TRADE

see also *Clothing Trade—Fashions; Leather and Fur Industries; Shoes and Boots; Textile Industries and Fabrics*

687 FR
ANNUAIRE DE LA MERCERIE, NOUVEAUTES,
BONNETERIE, LINGERIE, CONFECTIONS.
1923. a. 50 F. Editions Duc, 10 rue de Lancry,
75010 Paris, France. adv.

APPAREL PLANT WAGES SURVEY. see *TEXTILE INDUSTRIES AND FABRICS*

687.2 US ISSN 0362-2452
BODY FASHIONS-INTIMATE APPAREL
DIRECTORY. 1922. a. $5. Harcourt Brace
Jovanovich, Inc., 757 Third Avenue, New York,
NY 10017. Ed. Deane L. Moskowitz. adv. index.
Former titles: Body Fashions Directory and
Source of Supply; Corset and Underwear Review
Directory.

687 685.31 UK
CLOTHING AND FOOTWEAR INSTITUTE YEAR
BOOK AND MEMBERSHIP REGISTER. 1956. a.
£10. Clothing and Footwear Institute, Albert Road,
Hendon, London NW4 2JS, England. adv. circ.
6,700.
Formerly: Clothing Institute Year Book and
Membership Register (ISSN 0307-8515)

687 US ISSN 0070-5195
DIRECTORY OF BUYING OFFICES AND
ACCOUNTS. a. $35. Salesman's Guide, Inc., 1140
Broadway, New York, NY 10001. circ. 5,000.
Resident buying offices, corporate buying offices
and merchandise brokers: New York, Chicago, Los
Angeles

FAIRCHILD'S TEXTILE & APPAREL FINANCIAL
DIRECTORY. see *TEXTILE INDUSTRIES AND FABRICS*

687 US
FOCUS, AN ECONOMIC PROFILE OF THE
APPAREL INDUSTRY. biennial. $30 to non-
members; members $18. American Apparel
Manufacturers Association, Suite 800, 1611 N. Kent
St., Arlington, VA 22209.

687 US
GARMENT MANUFACTURER'S INDEX. 1937. a.
$3. Klevens Publications, Inc., 7600 Ave. V,
Littlerock, CA 93543. Ed. H. B. Schwartz. adv. circ.
18,684.

685.4 US ISSN 0072-4777
GLOVE NEWS. irreg. membership. National
Association of Glove Manufacturers, 52 S. Main St.,
Gloversville, NY 12078.

687 IT
GUIDA ALL'ABBIGLIAMENTO ITALIANO. 1978.
biennial. L.30000. Gesto s.r.l., Via Cesare Battisti
21, 20122 Milan, Italy. adv. circ. 15,000.

687.4 US
HAT LIFE YEAR BOOK & DIRECTORY; directory
of men's hat and cap industry. 1933. a. $4. Peter
Annunziata, 551 Summit Ave., Jersey City, NJ
07306. adv. circ. 7,000.
Formerly: Hat Life Year Book (ISSN 0073-0904)

687.3 US
HOSIERY STATISTICS. 1935. a. $35. National
Association of Hosiery Manufacturers, 516
Charlottetown Mall, Box 4098, Charlotte, NC
28204. Ed. Sid Smith. charts. stat. circ. 1,000
(controlled) (back issues avail)

687 II
INDIAN HOSIERY DIRECTORY. (Text in English)
1950. a. Rs.15. Journal's Publication, Samrala Rd,
Ludhiana 141008, India. Ed. G. Lal Tussavuv.

687.13 UK
JUNIOR AGE YEAR BOOK AND DIARY. 1950. a.
£1.95. Blandford Business Press, Pembrook House,
Wellesley Rd., Croydon CB9 2BX, England. Ed.
Sue Pearce. adv.

KOMPASS TEXTILE ET HABILLEMENT. see
BUSINESS AND ECONOMICS — Trade And Industrial Directories

658 US
MAJOR MASS MARKET MERCHANDISERS.
1965. a. $65. Salesman's Guide, Inc., 1140
Broadway, New York, NY 10001. Ed. Edward R.
Blank. circ. 700. (reprint service avail. from UMI)

687 US
NATIONAL APPAREL SUPPLIERS AND
CONTRACTORS DIRECTORY. (Separate
Western Southern, Eastern and National editions)
1971. a. $12.95 for National edition; $4.95 each for
others. Denyse and Co. Inc., 6226 Vineland Ave.,
North Hollywood, CA 91606. Ed. Denyse C.
Selesnick. adv. circ. 16,000.
Supersedes in part: Western Apparel Industry
National Suppliers and Contractors Directory (ISSN
0083-8667)

687 US ISSN 0077-5983
NATIONWIDE DIRECTORY OF MEN'S AND
BOYS WEAR BUYERS (EXCLUSIVE OF NEW
YORK METROPOLITAN AREA) 1958. a.(with
quarterly supplements) $60. Salesman's Guide, Inc.,
1140 Broadway, New York, NY 10001.

687 US
NATIONWIDE DIRECTORY OF SPORTING
GOODS BUYERS. a. $75 (includes semi-annual
supplement) Salesman's Guide, Inc., 1140
Broadway, New York, NY 10001. index.

658.8 687 US ISSN 0077-5991
NATIONWIDE DIRECTORY OF WOMEN'S AND
CHILDREN'S WEAR BUYERS (EXCLUSIVE OF
NEW YORK METROPOLITAN AREA) 1963.
a.(with quarterly supplements) $60. Salesman's
Guide, Inc., 1140 Broadway, New York, NY 10001.

658.8 US ISSN 0077-6009
NATIONWIDE MAJOR MASS MARKET
MERCHANDISERS (EXCLUSIVE OF NEW
YORK METROPOLITAN AREA) 1964. a. $55.
Salesman's Guide, Inc., 1140 Broadway, New York,
NY 10001. index.

687 746 US
NECKWEAR INDUSTRY DIRECTORY. biennial.
$7 per no. Neckwear Association of America, 432
Park Ave. S., New York, NY 10016. Ed. Gerald
Andersen. circ. 25,000.

687 FR
REVUE DE LA MERCERIE, NOUVEAUTES,
BONNETERIE, LINGERIE; CONFECTIONS;
publication d'information des commerces du textile,
de l'habillement et industries annexes. irreg. 100 F.
Editions Duc, 10 rue de Lancry, 75010 Paris,
France. illus.

687 677 GW
TASCHENBUCH FUER DIE BEKLEIDUNGS-
INDUSTRIE. a. DM.32. Fachverlag Schiele und
Schoen GmbH, Markgrafenstr. 11, 1000 Berlin 61,
W. Germany (B.R.D.) Eds. W. Rieser, W.
Schierbaum. charts. illus. stat.

687 US ISSN 0084-1056
WOMEN'S ACCESSORIES DIRECTORY; NEW
YORK METROPOLITAN AREA. 1951. a. $10.
Salesman's Guide, Inc., 1140 Broadway, New York,
NY 10001. index.

687.12 US ISSN 0084-1064
WOMEN'S COATS AND SUITS DIRECTORY;
NEW YORK METROPOLITAN AREA. 1951. a.
$10. Salesman's Guide, Inc., 1140 Broadway, New
York, NY 10001. index.

CLOTHING TRADE — Abstracting, Bibliographies, Statistics

687.2 CN ISSN 0384-2967
CANADA. STATISTICS CANADA.
FOUNDATION GARMENT INDUSTRY/
INDUSTRIE DES CORSETS ET SOUTIENS-
GORGE. (Catalogue 34-212) (Text in English &
French) 1920. a. Can.$4.50($5.40) Statistics Canada,
Publications Distribution, Ottawa, Ont. K1A 0V7,
Canada. (also avail. in microform from MML)

687.3 CN ISSN 0384-3343
CANADA. STATISTICS CANADA. KNITTING
MILLS/BONNETERIE. (Catalogue 34-215) (Text
in English & French) 1918. a. Can.$6($7.20)
Statistics Canada, Publications Distribution, Ottawa,
Ont. K1A 0V7, Canada. (also avail. in microform
from MML)

338.4 CN ISSN 0527-5679
CANADA. STATISTICS CANADA. MEN'S
CLOTHING INDUSTRIES/INDUSTRIE DES
VETEMENTS POUR HOMMES. (Catalogue 34-
216) (Text in English & French) 1918. a.
Can.$4.50($5.40) Statistics Canada, Publications
Distribution, Ottawa, Ont. K1A 0V7, Canada. (also
avail. in microform from MML)

687 CN ISSN 0384-3769
CANADA. STATISTICS CANADA.
MISCELLANEOUS CLOTHING INDUSTRIES/
INDUSTRIES DIVERSES DE L'HABILLEMENT.
(Catalogue 34-218) (Text in English and French)
1949. a. Can.$6($7.20) Statistics Canada,
Publications Distribution, Ottawa, Ont. K1A 0V7,
Canada. (also avail. in microform from MML)

338.4 CN ISSN 0384-4498
CANADA. STATISTICS CANADA. WOMEN'S
AND CHILDREN'S CLOTHING INDUSTRIES/
INDUSTRIES DES VETEMENTS POUR DAMES
ET POUR ENFANTS. (Catalogue 34-217) (Text in
English and French) 1918. a. Can.$6($7.20)
Statistics Canada, Publications Distribution, Ottawa,
Ont. K1A 0V7, Canada. (also avail. in microform
from MML)

CLOTHING TRADE — Fashions

687.4 741.672 FR ISSN 0066-2518
ANNUAIRE DE LA CHAPELLERIE ET DE LA
MODE. 1909. a. 50 F. Editions Louis Johanet, 68
rue Boursault, Paris 17, France.

BETTER HOMES AND GARDENS BRIDES
BOOK. see *WOMEN'S INTERESTS*

659.152 GE ISSN 0068-0532
BOUTIQUE. 1967. a. $1.50. Verlag Fuer die Frau,
Friedrich-Ebert-Str. 76-78, 701 Leipzig, E. Germany
(D.D.R.)

CANADIAN FUR TRADE DIRECTORY. see
LEATHER AND FUR INDUSTRIES

746.92 UK ISSN 0590-8876
COSTUME. 1967. a. membership. Costume Society, 3
Corringway, London NW11 7ED, England. Ed. Dr.
Ann Saunders. bk. rev. bibl. charts. illus. circ.
1,000.

746.92 390 CN ISSN 0383-4239
COSTUME SOCIETY OF ONTARIO.
NEWSLETTER. 1971. irreg. membership. Costume
Society of Ontario, c/o A. Suddon, 209 Brunswick
Ave., Toronto, Ont. M5S 2M4, Canada. bk. rev.
circ. 150-175.

391 US ISSN 0361-2112
DRESS. 1975. a. membership. Costume Society of
America, Costume Institute, Metropolitan Museum
of Art, 5Th Avenue at 82nd St., New York, NY
10028 (Orders to: Helene von Rosenstiel, 88
Prospect Park West, No. 3B, Brooklyn, NY 11215)
Ed. Robert Riley. illus.

646.4 US
HOMESEWING RESOURCE DIRECTORY OF
BRANDED LINE MERCHANDISE IN THE
HOMESEWING INDUSTRY. 1963. a. $4 per no.;
or with subscr. to Homesewing Trade News.
Homesewing Trade News, 330 Sunrise Hwy,
Rockville Centre, NY 11570. Ed. Nat Danas. adv.
circ. 13,590.
Formerly: Resource Directory of Branded Line
Merchandise in the Homesewing Industry.

646.4 US
MCCALL'S CREATIVE CLOTHES. 1975. biennial.
$150. McCall Pattern Co., 230 Park Ave., New
York, NY 10017. Ed. Margaret Gilman. adv. bk.
rev. illus.

659.152 UK ISSN 0076-6437
MEN'S WEAR YEAR BOOK AND DIARY. 1926. a.
£2.55. Men's Wear Publishing Co. Ltd., Knightway
House, 20 Soho Square, London, W1V 6DT,
England.

659.1 US
MODELS MART DIRECTORY OF MODELING
SCHOOLS AND AGENCIES USA AND
CANADA. 1973. biennial. $15. Peter Glenn
Publications, Inc., 17 E. 48th St., New York, NY
10017. Ed. Rose Marie Taylor.

NECKWEAR INDUSTRY DIRECTORY. see
CLOTHING TRADE

646.4 GW
SCHNITTMUSTER MODEBLATT. 1975. s-a.
DM.2.90 per no. Sonnenverlag GmbH, Bismarckstr.
4, Postfach 720, 7570 Baden-Baden, W. Germany
(B.R.D.) Ed.P. Kulig. adv.

659.152 GE ISSN 0081-3672
SPEZIAL. 1966. a. Verlag Fuer die Frau, Friedrich-
Ebert-Str. 76-78, 701 Leipzig, D.D.R.
Blouses, skirts, combinations

646.4 GW
STRICK UND HAEKELMODE. 1975. 6/yr.
DM.1.80 per no. Sonnenverlag GmbH, Bismarckstr.
4, Postfach 720, 7570 Baden-Baden, W. Germany
(B.R.D.) Ed.P. Kulig. adv.

741.672 GE ISSN 0083-6893
VOLLSCHLANK. 1967. s-a. $1.95. Verlag Fuer die
Frau, Friedrich-Ebert-Str. 76-78, 701 Leipzig, E.
Germany (D.D.R.)

CLUBS

see also College and Alumni

ANNEE SPORTIVE U.S.M.T. (Union Sportive
Metropolitaine des Transports) see *SPORTS AND
GAMES*

366.1 UK ISSN 0066-7900
ARS QUATUOR CORONATORUM; transaction of
the Quatuor Coronati Lodge of Research. 1888. a.
membership. Q. C. Correspondence Circle Ltd., 27
Great Queen St., London WC2B 5BB, England. Ed.
C. N. Batham. index. circ. 13,500.

367 VE ISSN 0004-4792
ASOCIACION CULTURAL HUMBOLDT.
BOLETIN. 1965. a. free. Asociacion Cultural
Humboldt, Apdo. 60.501 Chacao, Caracas,
Venezuela. Ed.Bd. circ. 1,000.

366 FR ISSN 0339-705X
ASSOCIATION FRANCE-MALTE. no. 15, 1975.
irreg. Association France-Malte, 9 rue du Quatre-
Septembre, 75002 Paris, France. Ed. Pierre Dimech.
Continues: Association France-Malte. Bulletin
(ISSN 0339-7068)

658 AT
AUSTRALIAN JAYCEES NATIONAL
DIRECTORY. 1970. a. Australian Jaycees, 6
Thesiger Court, Deakin A.C.T. 2600, Australia.

366 BE
BIBLIOTHEQUE INTERNATIONALE D'ETUDES
MACONNIQUES. 1975. irreg. Editions du
Baucens, Rue Hector Denis 13, 7490 Braine -le-
Compte, Belgium.

BRASIER. see *RELIGIONS AND THEOLOGY —
Roman Catholic*

367 UK ISSN 0524-5168
BRITISH CLUB YEAR BOOK. 1961. biennial. £7.35.
British Club Year Book & Directory Ltd., 8
Cavendish Place, London W.1., England. Ed. A.
Jefferson. circ. 2,000. (back issues avail.)

367 SP
BROTS DE COLLCEROLA. (Text in Catalan) 1970.
Delegacion Vallvidrera del C. E. A., Mont d'Orsa
17, Barcelona 17, Spain. Ed. Vigens Fonolleda. play
rev. abstr. illus. pat. circ. 150(controlled)

BUFFALO. see *CHILDREN AND YOUTH —
About*

366 CN ISSN 0382-6031
CANADIAN MANHOOD. 191? irreg. Young Men's
Christian Association of Canada, National Council,
Toronto, Ont., Canada. illus.
Continues: Ideal Men.

367 US
CIRCLES OF FRIENDS: 200 NEW WAYS TO
MAKE FRIENDS IN WASHINGTON DC. 1976.
biennial. $3. Mail Order USA, Box 19083,
Washington, DC 20036. Ed. Dorothy O'Callaghan.
illus. circ. 5,000.

367 US ISSN 0362-5168
KNICKERBOCKER CLUB. CLUB BOOK. a.
Knickerbocker Club, New York, 2 E. 62nd St., New
York, NY 10022. Key Title: Club Book of the
Knickerbocker Club.

LAST MONTH'S NEWSLETTER. see
HUMANITIES: COMPREHENSIVE WORKS

790.132 US ISSN 0363-3284
NEW COLLECTOR'S DIRECTORY. 1976. irreg.,
approx. triennial. $5.95. Padre Productions, Box
1275, San Luis Obispo, CA 93406. Ed. Robert D.
Connolly. bk. rev. bibl. index. circ. 5,000.

810 366 US
OZIANA. 1971. a. $1. International Wizard of Oz
Club, Inc., 220 N. 11th St., Escanaba, MI 49829.
circ. 800.

369.4 AT ISSN 0310-818X
SCOUT ASSOCIATION OF AUSTRALIA. REVIEW
OF PROGRESS. 1971. a. free. Scout Association of
Australia, Brigadier R. Fullford, National
Headquarters, Churchill House, 218 Northbourne
Avenue, Braddon, A. C. T. 2601, Australia.

369.4 UK
WELSH ASSOCIATION OF YOUTH CLUBS.
YEARBOOK OF ACTIVITIES; leaders handbook.
1965. a. £1. Welsh Association of Youth Clubs,
Andrews Buildings, 67 Queen Street, Cardiff, Wales.
Ed. D.G. Frost. adv. index. circ. 1,000. (tabloid
format)

369 SZ
WORLD ALLIANCE OF Y M C AS. ANNUAL
REPORT. 1979. a. 3 Fr.($2) World Alliance of
Young Men's Christian Associations, 37 Quai
Wilson, 1201 Geneva, Switzerland. Ed. Erika
Tysoe-Duelken. circ. 2,000.

369.4 SZ ISSN 0513-6032
WORLD ALLIANCE OF Y M C A'S DIRECTORY.
1920. biennial. 5 Fr. World Alliance of Young
Men's Christian Associations, 37 Quai Wilson, 1201
Geneva, Switzerland. circ. 7,500.

367 267 CN ISSN 0315-095X
Y CANADA. (Text in English and French) 1971.
irreg. Young Men's Christian Association of
Canada, National Council, 2160 Yonge St., Toronto,
Ont. M4S 2A9, Canada. illus.

267 SZ
Y M C A'S OF THE WORLD. 1958. irreg., latest
issue 1977. 9 Fr. World Alliance of Young Men's
Christian Associations, 37 Quai Wilson, 1201
Geneva, Switzerland.

369.5 US
YOUNG WOMEN'S CHRISTIAN ASSOCIATION
OF THE UNITED STATES OF AMERICA.
NATIONAL BOARD. ANNUAL REPORT. a.
Young Women's Christian Association of the
United States of America, National Board, 600
Lexington Ave., New York, NY 10022.

COLLEGE AND ALUMNI

see also Literary and Political Reviews; Literature

ADMINISTRATOR. see *PUBLIC ADMINISTRATION*

ALPHA PSI OMEGA: PLAYBILL. see *THEATER*

AMOEBA. see *MEDICAL SCIENCES*

378   US
ASSOCIATION OF COLLEGE HONOR SOCIETIES, BOOKLET OF INFORMATION. 1945. biennial, latest issue 1974. free. Association of College Honor Societies, c/o Dorothy I. Mitsifer, Sec.-Treas., 1411 Lafayette Pkwy, Williamsport, PA 17701. Ed. Dion W. J. Shea. circ. 5,000.

378.1   UK   ISSN 0007-0157
BRIGHTONIAN. 1870. a. £1. ‡ Brighton College, Brighton BN2 2AL, Sussex, England. Ed. P.H.L. Chasseaud. adv. bibl. charts. illus. play rev. circ. 2,600.

378.1   CN   ISSN 0383-2406
CANADIAN CAMPUS CAREER DIRECTORY. 1968. a. Can.$3.75. Whitsed Publishing Ltd., 2 Bloor St. W., Suite 250, Toronto, Ont. M4W 3E2, Canada. Ed. Arlene Gould. adv. circ. 13,000.
Former titles: Canadian Campus; Campus (Toronto) (ISSN 0045-4133)

378.599   PH
CENTRALITE. irreg. $4.50. Central Philippine University, Box 231, Iloilo City, Philippines. illus.

CHIMES. see *LITERATURE*

378.1   HK   ISSN 0009-6261
CHUNG CHI BULLETIN. (Text in Chinese and English) 1951. a. not for sale. Chinese University of Hong Kong, Chung Chi College, Shatin N.T., Hong Kong. Ed. Patrick Yin. bibl. charts. illus. circ. 3,800.
Formerly: Chung Chi College Bulletin.

378.1   US   ISSN 0010-0293
COGWHEEL.* 1949. a. $5. ‡ Alpha Pi Mu, Industrial Engineering Honor Society, Box 19747 UTA Sta., Arlington, TX 76019. illus. circ. controlled.

378.1   UK   ISSN 0010-0676
COLFEIAN. 1900. a. £1. ‡ Old Colfeians Association, Horn Park, Eltham Rd., London S.E. 12, England. Ed.Bd. adv. illus. circ. 1,750.

378.1   UK   ISSN 0012-8643
EASTBOURNIAN. 1870. a. £1.50. ‡ Eastbourne College, Eastbourne, Sussex, England. Ed. H. B. Harral. adv. illus. circ. 1,200(controlled)

378.1   UK   ISSN 0046-3701
FETTESIAN. 1878. a. 75p. Fettes College, Edinburgh, Scotland. Ed. M. C. Leslie. adv. circ. 1,200. (tabloid format)

378.1   SA   ISSN 0015-8054
FORT HARE PAPERS. (Text in Afrikaans & English; summaries in English) 1945. irreg., latest vol. 7, no. 1. R.0.50 per no. Fort Hare University Press, Private Bag 1322, Alice, Cape Province 5700, South Africa. Ed. J. A. Lamprecht. charts. illus. circ. 1,500. (tabloid format) Indexed: Chem.Abstr. Curr.Cont.

378   US   ISSN 0098-3284
GRADUATE; a handbook for leaving school. 1971. a. 13-30 Corporation, 505 Market St., Knoxville, TN 37902. Ed. Phillip W. Moffitt. adv. circ. 360,000.

GREEN SHEET; University of Hawaii newsletter. see *EDUCATION — Higher Education*

378   CL
IMAGEN U.C.V. 1977. a. free. (Universidad Catolica de Valparaiso, Oficina de Planificacion y Estudios) Ediciones Universitarias de Valparaiso, Casilla 1414, Valparaiso, Chile. illus. circ. 1,000.

378   US   ISSN 0093-5220
INSIDERS' GUIDE TO THE COLLEGES. 1971. biennial. Berkley Publishing Corp., 200 Madison Ave., New York, NY 10016.

378   CN
KEYSTONE. a. Waterloo Lutheran University, Student Board of Publications, Waterloo, Ont., Canada. Ed. Michael Burch. adv.

378.1   US
MARSHALL NEWS. 1959. a. membership. Association of Marshall Scholars and Alumnae i, c/o Patrick Henry, Sec.-Gen., Swarthmore College, Swarthmore, PA 19081. circ. 550.
Formerly: Association of Marshall Scholars and Alumni. Newsletter (ISSN 0004-573X)

378   US
NUTSHELL; a handbook for college. 1969. a. 13-30 Corporation, 505 Market St., Knoxville, TN 37902. Ed. Phillip W. Moffitt. adv. circ. 1,000,000.

378   CN
PHAROS. a. Can.$15. Dalhousie University, Student Union, Halifax, N.S. B3H 4J2, Canada.

081   US   ISSN 0092-4318
PLATTE VALLEY REVIEW. 1973. a. $3. Kearney State College, Kearney, NE 68847. Ed. Bd. illus. circ. 1,000.

378   EC
PONTIFICIA UNIVERSIDAD CATOLICA DEL ECUADOR. REVISTA. Cover title: Revista de la Universidad Catolica. vol. 5, 1977. irreg. S/30 per no. or exchange. Pontificia Universidad Catolica de Ecuador, Avda. 12 de Octubre 1076 y Carrion, Apdo. 2184, Quito, Ecuador. Ed. Ernesto Proano.

378   CN
QUAD. a. Can.$7. Bishop's University, Students' Association, Lennoxville, Que. J1M 1Z7, Canada. Eds. Greg Stace, Raymond Deiy. adv.

371.83   UK   ISSN 0048-6809
RATCLIFFIAN. 1870. a. £2.50. Ratcliffe College, Leicester, England. Ed. Rev. Michael Waters. adv. illus. index. circ. 800.

378.1   SA
RHODES REVIEW. (Text mainly in English; occasionally in Afrikaans) 1975. a. free. ‡ Rhodes University, Box 94, Grahamstown, South Africa. Ed. A. Temple. adv. bk. rev. circ. 12,000.
Incorporating: Rhodes Newsletter (ISSN 0035-4678)

378.1   US   ISSN 0036-5076
SAVANNAH STATE COLLEGE BULLETIN. (Alumni Issue; Homecoming Issue; General Information Issue) 1947. a. Savannah State College, State College Branch, c/o Office of Public Relations, Savannah, GA 31404. Ed. Wilton C. Scott. bk. rev. bibl. illus. circ. 4,000. (avail. on records)

378   US
TALLADEGAN. vol. 93, 1975. a. free. Talladega College, Talladega, Alabama. Ed. Juliette Bowles. illus.

378   UK
THUNDERER. 1961. a. 50p. Royal Naval Engineering College, Manadon, Plymouth, England. Eds. Stuart Brooks, Gerry Thwaites. adv. illus. circ. 400 (controlled)

378   IE
U. C. C. RECORD. (Text in English and Gaelic) 1944. a. 25p. (University College, Cork) Cork University Press, Cork, Ireland. Ed. Mary F. Conroy. index. circ. 500. (back issues available)

081   US   ISSN 0098-9525
UNION (CRANFORD) 1975. irreg. Union College, 1033 Springfield Ave., Cranford, NJ 07016. (Affiliate: Co-Sponsor: Union County Technical Institute)

278   US
U.S. NAVAL ACADEMY ALUMNI ASSOCIATION. REGISTER OF ALUMNI. 1938. a. $15. U S Naval Academy Alumni Association, Inc., Alumni House, Annapolis, MD 21402. Ed. Capt. Roy C. Smith III. adv. index. circ. 2,800. (processed)

UNIVERSITY OF CHICAGO RECORD. see *EDUCATION — Higher Education*

378   PH
UNIVERSITY OF THE PHILIPPINES. OFFICE OF ALUMNI RELATIONS. ALUMNI DIRECTORY. 1970. a. $15.35. University of the Philippines, Office of Alumni Relations, Diliman, Quezon City, Philippines.

378   AT   ISSN 0313-6906
UNIVERSITY OF WOLLONGONG. ANNUAL REPORT. a. free cont. circ. University of Wollongong, Box 1144, Wollongong, N.S.W. 2500, Australia.

378   AT   ISSN 0312-0007
UNIVERSITY OF WOLLONGONG. CALENDAR. a. Aus.$1. University of Wollongong, Box 1144, Wollongong, N. S. W. 2500, Australia.

378.1   US   ISSN 0043-3136
WEST GEORGIA COLLEGE REVIEW. (Not published in 1976) 1968. a. West Georgia College, Learning Resources Committee, Carrollton, GA 30118. Ed. Jimmy C. Stokes. bk. rev. bibl. circ. 600.

COLLEGE AND ALUMNI — Abstracting, Bibliographies, Statistics

378   US
MISSISSIPPI. BOARD OF TRUSTEES OF STATE INSTITUTIONS OF HIGHER LEARNING. ANNUAL REPORT. 1945. a. free. Mississippi Board of Trustees of State Institutions of Higher Learning, P.O. Box 2336, Jackson, MS 39205. Ed. Dr. E. E. Thrash. charts. stat. circ. controlled. (processed)

COMMUNICABLE DISEASES

see Medical Sciences — Communicable Diseases

COMMUNICATIONS

see also Communications — Postal Affairs; Communications — Radio and Television; Communications — Telephone and Telegraph; Journalism

A I A A COMMUNICATIONS SATELLITE SYSTEMS CONFERENCE. TECHNICAL PAPERS. (American Institute of Aeronautics and Astronautics) see *AERONAUTICS AND SPACE FLIGHT*

371.33   FR
A.V.C.D. - ANNUAIRE DE L'AUDIOVISUEL; guide de l'equipement et des fournisseurs. a. 80 F. Groupe Tests, 41 rue de la Grange aux Belles, 75010 Paris, France (Service Abonnement, 71 Bd. Richard Lenoir, 75011 Paris, France) Ed. Clement Pillerault.

384   FR   ISSN 0066-2976
ANNUAIRE DU CORPS INTERMINISTERIEL DES INGENIEURS DES TELECOMMUNICATIONS.* 1959. a. Association des Ingenieurs des Postes et Telecommunications, M. Delhaye, 20 Av. de Segur, Paris 7e, France.

301.16   BL
ANUARIO BRASILEIRO DE MEDIA. 1967. a. Cr.$1500. Publicacoes Informativas Ltda., Rua Caetes 139, 05016 Sao Paulo, Brazil. Ed. J.C. Salles Neto. adv. circ. 7,500.

301.16   GW   ISSN 0570-751X
AREOPAG; Jahrbuch fuer Kultur and Kommunikation. 1980. a. DM.26. Verlag Gunther Neske, Postfach 7240, D-7417 Pfullingen, Kloster, W. Germany (B.R.D.) Ed. Bd.

ASSOCIATION FOR EDUCATIONAL COMMUNICATIONS AND TECHNOLOGY. MONOGRAPHS. see *EDUCATION*

COMMUNICATIONS

301.16   VE
ASUNTO. 1975. irreg. Universidad del Zulia, Escuela de Comunicacion Social, Maracaibo, Venezuela.

621.38   338   BL
AUTORIDADES E EXECUTIVOS. irreg. Associacao Brasileira de Telecomunicacoes, Rua da Quitanda, 191, Rio de Janeiro, Brazil. illus.

301.16   070.43   SZ
BEITRAEGE ZUR KOMMUNIKATIONSWISSENSCHAFT UND MEDIENFORSCHUNG. 1975. irreg. Verlag Peter Lang AG, Muenzgraben 2, Postfach, CH-3000 Berne 7, Switzerland.

301   US
BURRELLE'S NEW JERSEY MEDIA DIRECTORY. 1980. a. $25. Burrelle's Media Directories, 75 E. Northfield Ave., Livingston, NJ 07039.

301   US
BURRELLE'S NEW YORK STATE MEDIA DIRECTORY. 1980. a. $30. Burrelle's Media Directories, 75 E. Northfield Ave., Livingston, NJ 07039.

301   US
BURRELLE'S PENNSYLVANIA MEDIA DIRECTORY. 1980. a. $28. Burrelle's Media Directories, 75 E. Northfield Ave., Livingston, NJ 07039.

384   US
C R C REPORT SERIES. (Communication Research Center) irreg. Boston University, School of Public Communication, 128 Bay State Rd., Boston, MA 02215.

621.38   US
CABLE/BROADBAND COMMUNICATIONS BOOK; a guide to cable and new communications technologies. 1975. a. $15.50. Communications Press, 1346 Connecticut Ave. N.W, Washington, DC 20036. Ed. Mary Louise Hollowell.
Formerly (until 1978): Cable Handbook.

301.16   CN   ISSN 0317-2716
CANADA. NATIONAL MUSEUM OF MAN. MERCURY SERIES. COMMUNICATIONS DIVISION. PAPERS/CANADA. MUSEE NATIONAL DE L'HOMME. COLLECTION MERCURE. DIVISION DES COMMUNICATIONS. DOSSIERS. (Text in English or French) 1973. irreg. price varies; some free. (National Museum of Man) National Museums of Canada, Ottawa, Ontario K1A 0M8, Canada.

301.16   CN
CANADIAN SPEECH COMMUNICATION JOURNAL. 1967. a. $5. Canadian Speech Association, Centralia College, Huron Park, Ont. N0M 1Y0, Canada. Ed. Donald Cameron. bk. rev. circ. 200. Indexed: ERIC.

659   US   ISSN 0009-9384
CLIO: DEVOTED TO COMMERCIALS; mass communications. 1969. a. $4. CLIO Awards Enterprises, Inc., 30 E. 60th St., New York, NY 10022. Ed. Michael E. Levy. adv. bk. rev. film rev. play rev. charts. illus. circ. 6,000.

301.16   SP
COLECCION COMUNICACION VISUAL. irreg. price varies. Editorial Gustavo Gili S.A., Rosellon 87-89, Apdo. de Correos 35.149, Barcelona 29, Spain. illus.

301.16   SZ
COMMUNICATIO PUBLICA. 1974. irreg., no. 7, 1978. price varies. Paul Haupt AG, Falkenplatz 14, CH-3001 Berne, Switzerland.

001.5   US   ISSN 0094-2588
COMMUNICATION DIRECTORY. 1970. irreg.; 2nd edt., 1973-74. $4 prepaid; $8 invoiced. ‡ Council of Communication Societies, P.O. Box 1074, Silver Spring, MD 20910. Ed. Vernon M. Root. index. indexes. circ. 1,500-2,000.
Formerly: Directory of Communication Organizations (ISSN 0070-5292)

301.16   US
COMMUNICATION RESEARCH NOTES. irreg.? University of Texas at Austin, Center for Communication Research, Austin, TX 78712. Ed. Alfred G. Smith.

301.16   001.53   US   ISSN 0162-8216
COMMUNICATION THEORY IN THE CAUSE OF MAN; notes on the application of theory to the strengthening of democratic institutions. 1970. irreg., approx. 2/yr. $6 for 4 nos. 2346 Lansford Ave., Box 5095, San Jose, CA 95150. Ed. Frederick B. Wood. circ. 150. (back issues avail.)

380   JA   ISSN 0084-9081
COMMUNICATIONS. (Text in English) 1970. decennial. Movie-TV Marketing, Box 30, Central Post Office, Tokyo 100-91, Japan. Ed. Glenn F. Ireton. adv.

001.5   US   ISSN 0069-777X
COMMUNICATIONS HANDBOOK. 1963. a. $1.50. Ziff-Davis Publishing Co., One Park Ave., New York, NY 10016. Ed. Arthur P. Salsberg. adv. circ. 100,000.

301.16   US   ISSN 0095-4063
COMMUNICATIONS WORLD. (Including the Complete White's Radio Log) a. $1.95. Davis Publications, Inc., 380 Lexington Ave., New York, NY 10017. Ed. Julian Martin. adv. illus.

301.16   VE
COMUNICACION. irreg. Apartado 20133, Caracas, Venezuela.

CONFEDERACAO NACIONAL DOS TRABALHADORES EM COMUNICACOES E PUBLICIDADE. RELATORIO ANUAL. see *LABOR UNIONS*

621.38   383   PO
CORREIOS E TELECOMUNICACOES DE PORTUGAL. ANUARIO ESTATISTICO. a. Correios e Telecomunicacoes de Portugal, Rua Alexandre Herculano 100, Lisbon, Portugal. illus.

DIRECTORY OF U. S. GOVERNMENT AUDIOVISUAL PERSONNEL. see *EDUCATION — Teaching Methods And Curriculum*

301.16   US
DISORDERS OF HUMAN COMMUNICATION. 1980. irreg., vol. 4, 1981. price varies. Springer-Verlag, 175 Fifth Ave., New York, NY 10010 (Also Berlin, Heidelberg, Vienna) Ed. Bd. (reprint service avail. from ISI)

070.172   US   ISSN 0424-4923
EDITOR & PUBLISHER INTERNATIONAL YEAR BOOK; encyclopedia of the newspaper industry. 1921. a. $35. Editor & Publisher Co., Inc., 575 Lexington Ave., New York, NY 10022. Ed. Robert U. Brown. circ. 15,000. (also avail. in microform)

621.38   BL
EMPRESA BRASILEIRA DE TELECOMUNICACOES. RELATORIO. 1974. a. Empresa Brasileira de Telecomunicacoes, Assessoria de Comunicacao Social, Av. Presidente Vargas 1012, Rio de Janeiro, Brazil. circ. 5,000.

ESTADISTICA PANAMENA. SITUACION ECONOMICA. SECCIONES 333 Y 334. TRANSPORTES Y COMUNICACIONES. see *TRANSPORTATION*

621.38   UK   ISSN 0046-5593
G E C TELECOMMUNICATIONS JOURNAL. 1930. irreg. free. ‡ (General Electric Co. Ltd. of England) G E C Telecommunications Ltd., Box 53, Coventry CV3 1HJ, England. Ed. A. B. Rettie. charts. illus. circ. 4,000 (controlled)
Formerly: G E C-A E I Telecommunications. *Telecommunications*

301.16   US   ISSN 0097-8175
GEBBIE PRESS ALL-IN-ONE DIRECTORY. Title varies: All-in-One Directory. 1972. a. $40. Gebbie Press, Box 1000, New Paltz, NY 12561. Ed. Amalia Gebbie. illus.

380.1   BL
GUIA DE COMUNICACAO A DISTANCIA. irreg. Editora de Guias Ltda., Av. Paulista 1776, Sao Paulo 01098, Brazil. illus.

301.16   US
HUMANISTIC STUDIES IN THE COMMUNICATIONS ARTS. irreg. price varies. Hastings House Publishers, Inc., 10 E. 40th St., New York, NY 10016.

621.38   US   ISSN 0536-1486
I E E E INTERNATIONAL CONFERENCE ON COMMUNICATIONS. CONFERENCE RECORD. 1965. irreg., approx. biennial. $33. Institute of Electrical and Electronics Engineers, Inc, 445 Hoes Lane, Piscataway, NJ 08854. bibl. illus.

384   621.38   UK
I E E TELECOMMUNICATIONS SERIES. 1976. irreg. (Institution of Electrical Engineers) Peter Peregrinus Ltd., Box 26, Hitchin, Herts. SG5 1SA, England (U.S. address: IEEE Service Center, 445 Hoes Lane, Piscataway, NJ 08854) Ed. J. E. Flood. charts. stat.

380   II   ISSN 0536-7506
INDIA. OFFICE OF THE COMPTROLLER AND AUDITOR-GENERAL. REPORT: UNION GOVERNMENT (POSTS AND TELEGRAPHS) 1970/71. a. $1.71. Office of the Comptroller and Auditor-General, Controller of Publications, Civil Lines, Delhi 110054, India. stat.

301.16   II
INDIAN INSTITUTE OF MASS COMMUNICATION. ANNUAL REPORT. (Text in English) a. Indian Institute of Mass Communications, D-13, South Extension, Part II, New Delhi 110049, India.

301.16   US   ISSN 0000-0450
INFORMATION INDUSTRY MARKET PLACE; an international directory of information products and services. Short title: I I M P. Published outside North and South America as: Information Trade Directory (ISSN 0142-0208) a. $32.50. R.R. Bowker Company, 1180 Ave. of the Americas, New York, NY 10036 (Orders to Box 1807, Ann Arbor, MI 48106) (Co-publisher: Learned Information (Europe) Ltd.)
Formerly: Information Market Place.

621.38   PL   ISSN 0020-451X
INSTYTUT LACZNOSCI. PRACE. (Text in Polish; summaries in English, French, German and Russian) 1954. irreg. price varies. Wydawnictwa Komunikacji i Lacznosci, Kazimierzowska 52, Warsaw, Poland. Ed. Prof. L. Kedzierski. (also avail. in microfilm) Indexed: Sci.Abstr. INSPEC.

384   UK   ISSN 0579-3742
INTERNATIONAL ASSOCIATION FOR MASS COMMUNICATION RESEARCH. LETTER FROM THE PRESIDENT. 1968. irreg. International Association for Mass Communications Research, c/o James D. Halloran, Centre for Mass Communications Research, University of Leicester, 104 Regent Rd., Leicester, England.

384   UK
INTERNATIONAL ASSOCIATION FOR MASS COMMUNICATIONS RESEARCH. MONOGRAPHS. biennial. International Association for Mass Communications Research, c/o Prof. James D. Halloran, Centre for Mass Communications Research, University of Leicester, 104 Regent Rd, Leicester, England.

621.38   US
INTERNATIONAL CONFERENCE ON DIGITAL SATELLITE COMMUNICATIONS. PROCEEDINGS. irreg., 4th 1979. $20. Institute of Electrical and Electronics Engineers, Inc., 445 Hoes Lane, Piscataway, NJ 08854 (Avail. from Teleglobe Canada, 680 Sherbrooke St. W., Montreal H3A 2S4, Canada) (also avail. in microfiche)

380.3   IE
IRELAND'S COMMUNICATION DIRECTORY. 1973. a. £6. Higgins P.R. Services, Ballymount Ind. Estate, Dublin 12, Ireland. Ed. Denis Bergin. adv. circ. 1,000.
Formerly: Communications Directory & Yearbook.

621.38   LB
LIBERIA MINISTRY OF POSTS AND TELECOMMUNICATIONS. ANNUAL REPORT. a. Ministry of Posts and Telecommunications, Monrovia, Liberia.

621.38 026 016 US
LIBRARY TELECOMMUNICATIONS
DIRECTORY: CANADA - UNITED STATES.
1968. a. $2. ‡ Duke University Medical Center
Library, Library Systems and Communications
Division, Durham, NC 27710. Ed. Warren Bird.
circ. 1,200. (processed)

301.16 US ISSN 0196-8017
MASS COMMUNICATION REVIEW YEARBOOK.
1980. a. Sage Publications, Inc., 275 S. Beverly Dr.,
Beverly Hills, CA 90212 (And Sage Publications,
Ltd., 28 Banner St., London EC1Y 8QE, England)
Ed. G. Cleveland Wilhoit.

384 AT
MASS MEDIA REVIEW. irreg. Australian Society for
Education in Film and Television, G.P.O. Box
252C, Hobart, Tas. 7001, Australia.

MASSACHUSETTS INSTITUTE OF
TECHNOLOGY. RESEARCH LABORATORY
OF ELECTRONICS. R L E PROGRESS
REPORT. see *ELECTRICITY AND
ELECTRICAL ENGINEERING*

384 US
MIDWEST MEDIA. 1958. a. $45. Midwest Newsclip,
360 N. Michigan Ave., Chicago, IL 60601. Ed.
Jeffrey Hill. stat. index. circ. 1,000.

808 US
MISSOURI SPEECH JOURNAL. 1970. a. $4.
(Speech and Theatre Association of Missouri)
Central Missouri State University, Warrensburg,
MO 64093. Ed. Tom Harte. circ. 175.

NATIONAL CENTER FOR AUDIO TAPES.
CATALOG. see *EDUCATION — Teaching
Methods And Curriculum*

621.38 US
NATIONAL TELECOMMUNICATION FORUM.
CONFERENCE RECORD. a. Institute of
Electrical and Electronics Engineers, Inc., 445 Hoes
Lane, Piscataway, NJ 08854.
Formerly: National Telemetering Conference.
Record; Supersedes: National Telecommunication
Conference. Record.
Telecommunications

NEW NIPPON ELECTRIC TECHNICAL REVIEW/
SHIN NIPPON DENKI GIHO. see
*ELECTRICITY AND ELECTRICAL
ENGINEERING*

384 CN ISSN 0078-3722
OFFICE DES COMMUNICATIONS SOCIALES,
MONTREAL. CAHIERS D'ETUDES ET DE
RECHERCHES. 1965. irreg. price varies. ‡ Office
des Communications Sociales, 4005 rue de
Bellechasse, Montreal, Que. H1X 1J6, Canada. circ.
500-1,000.

301.16 US
PEOPLE AND COMMUNICATION. 1977. irreg.,
vol. 4, 1978. price varies. Sage Publications, Inc.,
275 S. Beverly Dr., Beverly Hills, CA 90212 (And
Sage Publications, Ltd., 28 Banner St., London
EC1Y 8QE, England) Ed. F. Gerald Kline, Peter
Clarke. (back issues avail.)

PORTUGAL. INSTITUTO NACIONAL DE
ESTATISTICA. SERVICOS CENTRAIS.
ESTATISTICAS DOS TRANSPORTES E
COMMUNICACOES: CONTINENTE, ACORES
E MADEIRA. see *TRANSPORTATION*

020 US ISSN 0163-5689
PROGRESS IN COMMUNICATION SCIENCES.
1979. every 18 mos. $18.50. Ablex Publishing
Corporation, 355 Chestnut St., Norwood, NJ 07648.
Ed.Bd.

354 CN
QUEBEC (PROVINCE) MINISTERE DES
COMMUNICATIONS. RAPPORT ANNUEL.
1972. a. free. Ministere des Communications,
Quebec, Canada. illus. stat.

001.5 UN ISSN 0080-1356
REPORTS AND PAPERS ON MASS
COMMUNICATIONS. (Text in English and
French) 1953. irreg.; no. 71, 1974. price varies.
Unesco, 7-9 Place de Fontenoy, 75700 Paris, France
(Dist. in U.S. by: Unipub, 345 Park Ave. S., New
York NY 10010)

621.38 001.5 GE
ROBOTRON TECHNISCHE MITTELUNGEN.
(Text in German; summaries in English, French,
Russian) irreg. Robotron-Elektronik Radeberg,
Wilhelm-Pick-Str. 70, 8142 Radeberg, E. Germany
(D.D.R.) illus. charts.

384 US
SAGE ANNUAL REVIEWS OF
COMMUNICATION RESEARCH. 1972. a. $8.95
for softcover; hardcover $18.50. Sage Publications,
Inc., 275 S. Beverly Drive, Beverly Hills, CA 90212
(And Sage Publications, Ltd., 28 Banner St.,
London EC1Y 8QE, England) Eds. F. Gerald Kline,
Peter Clarke. (back issues avail.)

301.16 CE
SANNIVEDANA. (Text in Sinhalese or English) a.
Rs.3.50. University of Sri Lanka, Vidyalankara
Campus, Department of Mass Communications,
Kelaniya, Sri Lanka.

001.5 US ISSN 0081-5179
STATISTICS OF THE COMMUNICATIONS
INDUSTRY IN THE UNITED STATES. 1939. a.
price varies. U.S. Federal Communications
Commission., 1919 M St., N.W., Washington, DC
20554 (Orders to: Supt. of Documents, Washington,
DC 20402)

001.5 US ISSN 0585-7031
STUDIES IN PUBLIC COMMUNICATION. irreg.
price varies. Communication Arts Books, 10 East
40th St., New York, NY 10016.

621.38 GW ISSN 0082-1764
TASCHENBUCH DER FERNMELDE-PRAXIS.
1963. a. DM.29.20. Fachverlag Schiele und Schoen
GmbH, Markgrafenstr. 11, 1000 Berlin 61, W.
Germany (B.R.D.) Ed. H. Pooch. adv. circ. 7,500.

537 JA
TOHOKU UNIVERSITY. RESEARCH INSTITUTE
OF ELECTRICAL COMMUNICATION.
TECHNICAL REPORT. (Text in English) 1964.
irreg. exchange basis. Tohoku University, Research
Institute of Electrical Communication - Tohoku
Daigaku Denki Tsushin Kenkyusho, 2-1-1 Katahira,
Sendai 980, Japan.

621.38 JA
TOYO'S TECHNICAL BULLETIN/TOYO
TSUSHINKI GIHO. (Text in Japanese) 1963. a.
exchange basis. Toyo Communication Equipment
Company - Toyo Tsushinki K. K., 3-484
Tsukagoshi, Saiwai-ku, Kawasaki-shi 210, Japan.

TRANSPORT & COMMUNICATIONS BULLETIN
FOR ASIA & THE FAR EAST. see
TRANSPORTATION

U.S. ADMINISTRATIVE OFFICE OF THE
UNITED STATES COURTS. REPORT ON
APPLICATIONS FOR ORDERS AUTHORIZING
OR APPROVING THE INTERCEPTION OF
WIRE OR ORAL COMMUNICATIONS. see
LAW

001.5 US ISSN 0083-0585
U. S. FEDERAL COMMUNICATIONS
COMMISSION. ANNUAL REPORT. 1935. a.
price varies. U.S. Federal Communications
Commission., 1919 M St., N.W., Washington, DC
20554 (Orders to: Supt. Doc., Washington, DC
20402)

001.5 US ISSN 0083-0607
U. S. FEDERAL COMMUNICATIONS
COMMISSION. I N F BULLETINS. 1949. irreg.,
latest issue, 1976. free. ‡ U. S. Federal
Communications Commission, 1919 M St., N.W.,
Washington, DC 20554.

001.5 US ISSN 0083-0615
U. S. FEDERAL COMMUNICATIONS
COMMISSION. RULES AND REGULATION.
(Issued in 10 vols. covering different subjects) irreg.
price varies. U.S. Federal Communications
Commission., 1919 M St., N.W., Washington, DC
20554 (Orders to: Supt. of Documents, Washington,
DC 20402)

001.5 GW ISSN 0341-3136
UNIVERSITAET BONN. INSTITUT FUER
KOMMUNIKATIONSFORSCHUNG UND
PHONETIK. FORSCHUNGSBERICHTE. 1966.
irreg., vol. 74, 1981. price varies. Verlag Helmut
Buske, Schluetersr. 14, 2000 Hamburg 13, W.
Germany (B.R.D.) Ed. Gerold Ungeheuer.

621.3 JA
UNIVERSITY OF TELECOMMUNICATIONS.
RESEARCH LABORATORY OF
COMMUNICATION SCIENCES. ANNUAL
REPORT/DENKI TSUSHIN DAIGAKU DENKI
TSUSHIN KENKYU SHISETSU NENPO. (Text in
Japanese) 1961. a. University of
Telecommunications, Research Laboratory of
Communication Sciences, 1-5-1 Chofugaoka, Chofu-
shi, Tokyo 181, Japan. illus.

621.38 UY
URUGUAY. ADMINISTRACION NACIONAL DE
TELECOMUNICACIONES. MEMORIA
ANUAL. a. Administracion Nacional de
Telecomunicaciones, Paraguay 2431, Casilla Correo
909, Montevideo, Uruguay.
Telecommunication

621.38 FI ISSN 0355-368X
VALTION TEKNILLINEN TUTKIMUSKESKUS.
TELETEKNIIKAN LABORATORIO.
TIEDONANTO/TECHNICAL RESEARCH
CENTRE OF FINLAND.
TELECOMMUNICATIONS LABORATORY.
REPORT. (Text mainly in Finnish, some in English
or Swedish) 1970. irreg. price varies. Valtion
Teknillinen Tutkimuskeskus - Technical Research
Centre of Finland, Vuorimiehentie 5, 02150 Espoo
15, Finland.
Telecommunication

301.16 II ISSN 0043-7948
WORD. (Text in English) 1963. a. Rs.5($1) Bharatiya
Vidya Bhavan, Kulapati K. M. Munshi Marg,
Bombay 400007, India. Ed. G. S. Pohekar. adv. bk.
rev. circ. 1,000.

621.38 US
WORLDWIDE REPORT:
TELECOMMUNICATIONS POLICY.
RESEARCH AND DEVELOPMENT. irreg.
(approx. 31/yr.) $155. U.S. Joint Publications
Research Service, 1000 N. Glebe Rd., Arlington,
VA 22201 (Orders to: NTIS, Springfield, VA
22161)
Formerly: Telecommunications Policy. Research
and Development.

621.38 US
YANKEE INGENUITY. irreg. Yankee Group,
Harvard Square, Box 43, Cambridge, MA 02138.

384.6 UN
YEARBOOK OF COMMON CARRIER
TELECOMMUNICATION STATISTICS/
ANNUAIRE STATISTIQUE DES
TELECOMMUNICATIONS DU SECTEUR
PUBLIC. (Each Vol. Cumulative over 10 Yrs.)
(Text in English, French and Spanish) a.
International Telecommunication Union - Union
Internationale des Telecommunications, Place de
Nations, 1211 Geneva 20, Switzerland.
Incorporating: Telecommunication Statistics.

COMMUNICATIONS — Abstracting, Bibliographies, Statistics

384.5 US
AMERICAN RADIO. 1976. s-a. $44 for Spring
Report, $36 for Fall Report. c/o James H. Duncan,
Jr., Gilmore Advertising, 200 Michigan Bldg.,
Kalamazoo, MI 49006.

AUSTRALIA. BUREAU OF STATISTICS. NEW
SOUTH WALES OFFICE. TRANSPORT AND
COMMUNICATION. see *BUSINESS AND
ECONOMICS — Abstracting, Bibliographies,
Statistics*

266 COMMUNICATIONS — POSTAL AFFAIRS

384   CN   ISSN 0703-7244
CANADA. STATISTICS CANADA. CABLE TELEVISION/TELEDISTRIBUTION. (Catalogue 56-205) (Text in English and French) 1967. a. Can.$6($7.20) Statistics Canada, Publications Distribution, Ottawa, Ont. K1A 0V7, Canada. (also avail. in microform from MML)
    Formerly: Canada. Statistics Canada. Community Antenna Television/Services de Television a Antenne Collective.

338.4   CN   ISSN 0527-494X
CANADA. STATISTICS CANADA. COMMUNICATIONS EQUIPMENT MANUFACTURERS/FABRICANTS D'EQUIPEMENT DE TELECOMMUNICATION. (Catalog 43-206) (Text in English and French) 1960. a. Can.$4.50($5.40) Statistics Canada, Publications Distribution, Ottawa, Ont. K1A 0V7, Canada. (also avail. in microform from MML)

384.54   CN   ISSN 0575-9560
CANADA. STATISTICS CANADA. RADIO AND TELEVISION BROADCASTING/ RADIODIFFUSION ET TELEVISION. (Catalog 56-204) (Text in English and French) 1961. a. Can.$6($7.20) Statistics Canada, Publications Distribution, Ottawa, Ont. K1A 0V7, Canada. (also avail. in microform from MML)

384   CN   ISSN 0703-7252
CANADA. STATISTICS CANADA. TELECOMMUNICATIONS STATISTICS/ STATISTIQUE DES TELECOMMUNICATIONS. (Catalog 56-201) (Text in English and French) 1917. a. Can.$4.50($5.40) Statistics Canada, Publications Distribution, Ottawa, Ont. K1A 0V7, Canada. (also avail. in microform from MML)

334.097   CN   ISSN 0380-0334
CANADA. STATISTICS CANADA. TRANSPORTATION AND COMMUNICATIONS DIVISION. COMMUNICATIONS SERVICE BULLETIN/ COMMUNICATIONS-BULLETIN DE SERVICE. (Catalogue 56-001) (Text in English and French) 1971. irreg(service bulletin) Can.$15($18) Statistics Canada, Publications Distribution, Ottawa, Ont. K1A 0V7, Canada. (also avail. in microform from MML)

GREECE. NATIONAL STATISTICAL SERVICE. TRANSPORT AND COMMUNICATION STATISTICS. see *TRANSPORTATION — Abstracting, Bibliographies, Statistics*

314   380.3   HU
HUNGARY. KOZPONTI STATISZTIKAI HIVATAL. KOZLEKEDESI ES HIRKOZLESI EVKONYV. a. 69 Ft. Statisztikai Kiado Vallalat, Kaszas U.10-12, P.O.B.99, 1300 Budapest 3, Hungary.

621.8 016   UN
INTERNATIONAL TELECOMMUNICATION UNION. CENTRAL LIBRARY. LISTE DES PERIODIQUES. LIST OF PERIODICALS. LISTA DE REVISTAS. (Text in English, French, Spanish) 1967. a. International Telecommunication Union, Central Library - Union Internationale des Telecommunications, Place des Nations, 1211 Geneva 20, Switzerland. Ed. A. G. el-Zanati.

621.38 016   UN
INTERNATIONAL TELECOMMUNICATION UNION. CENTRAL LIBRARY. LISTES DES PUBLICATIONS ANNUELLES. LIST OF ANNUALS. LISTA DE PUBLICACIONES ANUALES. (Text in French, English and Spanish) 1972. a. International Telecommunication Union, Central Library - Union Internationale des Telecommunications, Place des Nations, 1211 Geneva 20, Switzerland. Ed. A. G. el-Zanati. circ. 1,000.

301.16 016   GW
JAHRESBIBLIOGRAPHIE MASSENKOMMUNIKATION. (Text in Various Languages) 1974. a. DM.2. Universitaet Bremen Bibliothek, Postfach 330160, D-2800, Bremen 33, W. Germany (B.R.D.) Ed. Wilbert Ubbens. bibl. index. circ. 500. (back issues avail.)

NORWAY. STATISTISK SENTRALBYRAA. SAMFERDSELSSTATISTIKK/TRANSPORT AND COMMUNICATION STATISTICS. see *TRANSPORTATION — Abstracting, Bibliographies, Statistics*

384   314   NO
NORWAY. TELEVERKET. STATISTIKK. 1970. a. Kr.12.50. Teledirektoratet, Box 6701, Oslo 1, Norway.
    Continues: Norway. Televerket. Statistisk Arbok.

SWEDEN. STATISTISKA CENTRALBYRAAN. STATISTISKA MEDDELANDEN. SUBGROUP T (TRANSPORT AND OTHER FORMS OF COMMUNICATION) see *TRANSPORTATION — Abstracting, Bibliographies, Statistics*

791.45 016   CS
VYBEROVA ANOTOVANA BIBLIOGRAFIE STUDIJNICH MATERIALU. 1960/64. a. Ceskoslovenska Televize, Studijni Odbor, Oddeleni Dokumentace a Odborne Informace, Jindrisska 16, 111 50 Prague 1, Czechoslovakia. Ed. Milena Medova. bibl. circ. 300.

384.6   US
WORLD'S TELEPHONES. 1912. a. American Telephone and Telegraph Company, Long Lines Department, 201 Littleton Rd., Rm. 220, Morris Plains, Bedminster, NJ 07950. stat. circ. 40,000.
    Supersedes (1973-1974): Calling the World (ISSN 0360-3539)

COMMUNICATIONS — Postal Affairs

see also Hobbies — Philately

383   BE
BELGIUM. REGIE DES POSTES. RAPPORT D'ACTIVITE. a. Regie des Postes, Centre Monnaie, 1000 Brussels, Belgium. illus.

381   US   ISSN 0068-4201
BULLINGER'S POSTAL AND SHIPPERS GUIDE FOR THE UNITED STATES AND CANADA. 1871. a. $91 yearly rental. ‡ Bullinger's Guides, Inc., 63 Woodland Ave., Box 501, Westwood, NJ 07675. Ed. John H. Stork. circ. 3,500.

CORREIOS E TELECOMUNICACOES DE PORTUGAL. ANUARIO ESTATISTICO. see *COMMUNICATIONS*

383   US
DIRECTORY OF MAIL DROPS IN THE UNITED STATES AND CANADA. 1976. a. $4. Loompanics Unlimited, Box 264, Mason, MI 48854. Ed. Michael Hov. circ. 2,000.

383   GW   ISSN 0435-7329
GERMANY (FEDERAL REPUBLIC, 1949-) BUNDESMINISTERIUM FUER DAS POST-UND FERNMELDEWESEN. JAHRESRECHNUNG, NACHWEISUNG UEBER DIE EINNAHMEN UND AUSGABEN DER DEUTSCHEN BUNDESPOST. 1959. a. Bundesministerium fuer das Post-und Fernmeldewesen, Adenauerallee 81, 5300 Bonn, W. Germany (B.R.D.)
    Continues: Germany (Federal Republic). Bundesministerium fuer das Post- und Fernmeldewesen. Jahresnachweisung ueber die Einnahmen und Ausgaben der Deutschen Bundespost.

383   IS   ISSN 0075-1308
ISRAEL. MINISTRY OF COMMUNICATIONS. STATISTICS/ISRAEL. MISRAD HA-TIKSHORET. STATISTIKAH. (Editions in Hebrew and English) 1955. a. Ministry of Communications, Jaffa Rd. 23, Jerusalem, Israel. circ. 300.

383   US   ISSN 0191-6971
NATIONAL ZIP CODE & POST OFFICE DIRECTORY. a. $7.50. U.S. Postal Service, Washington, DC 20260 (Orders to: Supt. of Documents, Washington, DC 20402)
    Formed by the 1979 merger of: National Zip Code Directory (ISSN 0160-6476) & Directory of Post Offices.

383   336   AU
POSTBUECHL. a. free. Steiger-Werbung Verlags- und Werbegesellschaft mbH, Hermanngasse 25, A-1070 Vienna, Austria. circ. 100,000.

SCOTTISH POSTMARK GROUP. HANDBOOK. see *HOBBIES — Philately*

383   UN   ISSN 0083-3878
UNION POSTALE UNIVERSELLE. 1874. irreg.; 17th, Lausanne, 1974. 90 Fr. ‡ Universal Postal Union - Union Postale Universelle, Welpostrasse 4, CH-3000 Berne 15, Switzerland. circ. 950.

383   UN   ISSN 0085-7602
UNION POSTALE UNIVERSELLE. STATISTIQUE DES SERVICES POSTAUX. (Text in French) 1966. a, latest 1976. 56 Fr. ‡ Universal Postal Union - Union Postale Universelle, Welpostrasse 4, CH-3000 Berne 15, Switzerland. circ. 700.

383.2   US   ISSN 0092-2765
U. S. POSTAL SERVICE. SUPPORT GROUP. REVENUE AND COST ANALYSIS. 1970/71. a. U. S. Postal Service, Rates and Classification Department, Washington, DC 20260. stat. Key Title: Revenue and Cost Analysis-Support Group (Washington)

383   ZA
ZAMBIA. POSTS AND TELECOMMUNICATIONS CORPORATION. ANNUAL REPORT. 1963/64. a. 50 n. Government Printer, P.O. Box 136, Lusaka, Zambia.
    Formerly (1963/64-1974/75): Zambia. General Post Office. Annual Report of the Postmaster-General (ISSN 0084-5019)

383   384.6   US
ZIP/AREA CODE DIRECTORY. 1979. irreg. $2.95. Pilot Books, 347 Fifth Ave., New York, NY 10016.

COMMUNICATIONS — Radio And Television

384   GW   ISSN 0066-5746
A R D - JAHRBUCH. 1969. a. DM.11.80. Hans-Bredow-Institut, Heimhuder Str. 21, 2000 Hamburg 13, W. Germany (B.R.D.) Ed. Hans Bausch. circ. 13,000.

621.38   UK   ISSN 0065-3314
ADVANCES IN RADIO RESEARCH. 1964. irreg. price varies. Academic Press Inc. (London) Ltd., 24-28 Oval Rd., London N.W.1, England (and 111 Fith Ave., New York, N.Y. 10003) Ed. J. A. Saxton. index.

384.54   FR   ISSN 0066-247X
ANNUAIRE BIOGRAPHIQUE DU CINEMA ET DE LA TELEVISION EN FRANCE ET EN BELGIQUE.* 1953/54. irreg. Contact-Editions, 5 rue Robert-Estienne, Paris 8e, France.

384.554   FR   ISSN 0066-3565
ANNUAIRE O. G. M. (Partie 1: Radio-Television - Electronique - Electroacoustique; Partie 2: Musique) a. 140 F. per vol. (Office General de la Musique) Editions Louis Johanet, 68 rue Boursault, 75017 Paris, France. adv.

621.388   US
ANNUAL CONFERENCE ON C A T V RELIABILITY. (PROCEEDINGS) 1977. a. Institute of Electrical and Electronics Engineers, Inc., Broadcast, Cable, and Consumer Electronics Society, 445 Hoes Lane, Piscataway, NJ 08854.

384.5   SW   ISSN 0044-9989
AUDIENCE AND PROGRAMME RESEARCH. (Text in English) 1969. irreg. (4-6/yr.) free. ‡ Sveriges Radio, Audience and Program Research Department, S-105 10 Stockholm, Sweden. Ed. Christina Bergvall. circ. 500.

BACKSTAGE TV FILM/TAPE & SYNDICATION DIRECTORY. see *MOTION PICTURES*

384.12   GW   ISSN 0067-4966
BEITRAEGE ZUM RUNDFUNKRECHT. 1965. irreg., vol.21, 1977. price varies. (Arbeitsgemeinschaft der Oeffentlich-rechtlichen Rundfunkanstalten der Bundesrepublik Deutschland) Alfred Metzner Verlag GmbH, Zeppelinallee 43, Postfach 970148, 6000 Frankfurt 97, W. Germany (B.R.D.)

384.5   UK
BERNARDS AND BABANI PRESS RADIO & ELECTRONICS BOOKS. 1971. irreg; no. 5, 1972. Babani Press, Shepherds Bush Rd., London W6 7NF, England.

COMMUNICATIONS — RADIO AND TELEVISION

384.55 YU
BIT INTERNATIONAL; television today. (Text in Croatian and English) 1968. irreg. $7. Galerije Grada Zagreba, Katarinin trg 2, 41000 Zagreb, Yugoslavia. Ed. Bozo Bek. illus. circ. 5,000.

384 US
BLUE SKY. 1973. irreg. $5. Communications Institute of Boulder, Box 1773, Boulder, CO 80302. Ed. Thomas B. Cross. adv. bk. rev. circ. 2,000.

621.38 UK ISSN 0068-1377
BRITISH BROADCASTING CORPORATION. B B C HANDBOOK. 1928. a. £3. British Broadcasting Corp., 35 Marylebone High St., London W1M 4AA, England. index.

621.384 UK ISSN 0005-2817
BRITISH BROADCASTING CORPORATION. B B C ENGINEERING. 1955. irreg.(approx. 4 per year) $8. British Broadcasting Corp., 35 Marylebone High St., London W1M 4AA, England. Indexed: INSPEC.
Formerly: British Broadcasting Corporation. Engineering Division. Monograph.

384.54 US
BROADCAST MONOGRAPHS. 174. irreg. Broadcast Education Association, 1771 N. St. N.W., Washington, DC 20036.

384 UK
BROADCAST YEARBOOK AND DIARY. 1961. a. £17.25. Broadcast Magazine, 111a Wardour St., London W1V 3TD, England. Ed. Patricia Williams. adv. circ. 4,000.

791.4 US
BROADCASTING/CABLE YEARBOOK. 1933. a. $60. Broadcasting Publications, Inc., 1735 DeSales St., Washington, DC 20036. Ed. Sol Taishoff. adv. circ. 30,000. (also avail. in microfilm)
Formed by the merger of: Broadcasting Cable Sourcebook; Formerly: Broadcasting Yearbook (ISSN 0068-2713)

384.54 NZ
BROADCASTING CORPORATION OF NEW ZEALAND. REPORT. 1974. a. Government Printing Office, Private Bag, Wellington, New Zealand.
Formerly (until 1976): New Zealand. Broadcasting Council. Report.

384.5 US
BUSINESS RADIO BUYERS GUIDE. 1971. a. $8.95. ‡ Cardiff Publishing Company, 3900 S. Wadsworth, Suite 560, Denver, CO 80235. Ed. Judy S. Lockwood. adv. circ. 10,000.

C T V D: CINEMA-TV-DIGEST; a quarterly review of the serious, foreign-language cinema-TV-press. see *MOTION PICTURES*

791 US
CABLE AND STATION COVERAGE ATLAS AND 35-MILE ZONE MAPS. 1966. a. $89.50. Television Digest, Inc., 1836 Jefferson Place, N.W., Washington, DC 20036. Ed. Albert Warren. index.
Formerly: C A T V and Station Coverage Atlas and 35-Mile Zone Maps (ISSN 0068-4694)

384.55 US ISSN 0363-1915
CABLE FILE. 1976. a. $69.95. Titsch Publishing Co., Box 5400TA, Denver, CO 80217. Ed. Kate Hampford. stat. circ. 4,000.

384 CN
CANADA. CANADIAN RADIO-TELEVISION AND TELECOMMUNICATIONS COMMISSION. ANNUAL REPORT. (Editions in English and French) 1968/69. a. free. Canadian Radio-Television and Telecommunications Commission, Ottawa, Ont. K1A ON2, Canada (Orders to: Supply and Services Canada, Publishing Centre, Hull, Que. K1A 0S5, Canada)
Formerly: Canada. Radio-Television Commission. Annual Report (ISSN 0068-9556)

621.38 CN
CANADIAN AMATEUR ADVANCED STUDY GUIDE. 1976. a. Can.$8. Canadian Amateur Radio Federation Inc., Box 356, Kingston, Ont. K7L 4W2, Canada. circ. 10,000.
Amateur

621.38 CN
CANADIAN AMATEUR RADIO REGULATIONS HANDBOOK. 1970. a. Can.$8. ‡ Canadian Amateur Radio Federation Inc., Box 356, Kingston, Ont. K7L 4W2, Canada. Ed. A. P. Stark. circ. 10,000.
Amateur

384 UK
CASE STUDIES ON BROADCASTING SYSTEMS. irreg. price varies. Routledge & Kegan Paul Ltd., Broadway House, Newtown Rd., Henley-on-Thames, Oxon. RG9 1EN, England (U.S. address: Routledge Journals, 9 Park St., Boston, MA 02108)

791 FR ISSN 0069-1119
CATALOGUE GENERAL. RADIO, TELEVISION, ELECTROPHONES, MAGNETOPHONES, HAUTE-FIDELITE, STEREOPHONIE, AUDIO-VISUEL; guide officiel de l'acheteur. 1957. a. 8. Documentation Professionnelle, 12 rue Richer, 75009 Paris, France. adv.

791 BE ISSN 0528-4759
CENTRE INTERNATIONAL DE LIAISON DES ECOLES DE CINEMA ET DE TELEVISION. BULLETIN D'INFORMATIONS. irreg. International Liason Centre for Cinema and Television Schools - Centre International de Liaison des Ecoles de Cinema et de Television, c/o Raymond Ravar, 8 rue Theresienne, B-1000 Brussels, Belgium.

CENTRO DE RADIO ASTRONOMIA E ASTROFISICA MACKENZIE. OBSERVATORIA NACIONAL. RELATORIO ANUAL. see *ASTRONOMY*

621.38 GW
COMMUNICATION RESEARCH AND BROADCASTING. (Text in English) 1979. irreg. price varies. (Internationales Zentralinstitut fuer das Jugend- und Bildungsfernsehen) K. G. Saur Verlag KG, Peossenbacherstr. 2, 8000 Munich 71, W. Germany (B.R.D.)

COMMUNICATOR; a TV technicians newsletter. (Radio Corporation of America) see *ELECTRICITY AND ELECTRICAL ENGINEERING*

384 GW ISSN 0084-9790
DEUTSCHLANDFUNK. JAHRBUCH. 1962. biennial. Deutschlandfunk, Raderbergguertel 40, 5000 Cologne 51, W. Germany (B.R.D.)

384.5 SG
DISOO. no. 25, 1973. irreg. Office de Radiodiffusion-Television, 58 Blvd. de la Republique, Dakar, Senegal.

384 SZ
E B U MONOGRAPHS, LEGAL AND ADMINISTRATIVE SERIES. (Editions in English and French) 1964. irreg. price varies. European Broadcasting Union, Case Postale 193, CH-1211 Geneva 20, Switzerland.

384 SZ
E B U SEMINARS FOR PRODUCERS AND DIRECTORS OF EDUCATIONAL TELEVISION FOR SCHOOLS AND ADULTS. (Editions in English and French) 1962. a. 5 Fr. European Broadcasting Union, Case Postale 193, CH-1211 Geneva 20, Switzerland.

384 SZ
E B U WORKSHOPS FOR PRODUCERS AND DIRECTORS OF TELEVISION PROGRAMMES FOR CHILDREN AND YOUNG PEOPLE. (Editions in English and French) 1968. biennial. 8 Fr. European Broadcasting Union, Case Postale 193, CH-1211 Geneva 20, Switzerland.

384.55 PE
EMPRESA NACIONAL DE TELECOMMUNICACIONES DEL PERU. MEMORIA ANUAL. a. free. Empresa Nacional de Telecomunicaciones, Las Begonias 475, San Isidro 27, Lima, Peru. illus. stat. circ. 3,000. (back issues avail)

ENTERTAINMENT INDUSTRY DIRECTORY. see *BUSINESS AND ECONOMICS — Trade And Industrial Directories*

384.12 FI ISSN 0084-4225
FINNISH BROADCASTING COMPANY. SECTION FOR LONG-RANGE PLANNING. RESEARCH REPORTS. (Text in English) irreg., no. 18, 1977. free. Finnish Broadcasting Company, Section for Long-Range Planning, Kesakatu 2, 00260 Helsinki 26, Finland.

621.384 US ISSN 0015-7260
FOREIGN RADIO AMATEUR CALLBOOK MAGAZINE. 1920. a. $12.95 (with update Service Editions) Radio Amateur Callbook, Inc., 925 Sherwood Drive, Lake Bluff, IL 60044. adv.
Amateur

GADNEY'S GUIDE TO 1800 INTERNATIONAL CONTESTS, FESTIVALS & GRANTS IN FILM & VIDEO, PHOTOGRAPHY, TV-RADIO BROADCASTING, WRITING, POETRY, PLAYWRITING & JOURNALISM. see *MOTION PICTURES*

GREATER BOSTON MEDIA DIRECTORY. see *JOURNALISM*

384 UK ISSN 0508-850X
GUIDE TO BROADCASTING. 1946. irreg., 18th edt., 1980. £3.50. Butterworth & Co (Publishers) Ltd., Borough Green, Sevenoaks, Kent, England.

791.45 US ISSN 0073-3601
HOUSEHOLDS WITH TELEVISION SETS IN THE UNITED STATES. (Subseries of Current Housing Reports, H-121: Housing Characteristics) 1955. irreg. free. U. S. Bureau of the Census, Washington, DC 20233 (Orders to: Supt. Doc., Washington, DC 20402)

384 UK ISSN 0308-423X
I B A TECHNICAL REVIEW. 1972. irreg., no. 13, 1980. Independent Broadcasting Authority, 70 Brompton Rd., London SW3 1EY, England. charts. illus.

384.54 US ISSN 0093-1926
I.R.C.A. FOREIGN LOG.* 1972. a. price varies. ‡ International Radio Club of America, Box 21074, Seattle, WA 98111. Ed. Bruce Portzer. circ. 300.

791.4 US ISSN 0074-7564
I R T S GOLD MEDAL ANNUAL. 1964. a. membership. International Radio and Television Society, Inc., 420 Lexington Ave., New York, NY 10017. adv.

384.54 UK ISSN 0309-0175
INDEPENDENT BROADCASTING AUTHORITY. ANNUAL REPORT AND ACCOUNTS. 1954-1955. a. £2.50. Independent Broadcasting Authority, 70 Brompton Road, London SW3 1EY, England (Dist. by: H.M.S.O., 49 High Holborn, London WC1V 6HB, England)

384 US
INTERNATIONAL AND COMPARATIVE BROADCASTING. irreg. price varies. Temple University Press, Philadelphia, PA 19122.

384 SZ
INTERNATIONAL FORUM OF LIGHT MUSIC IN RADIO. (Editions in English and French) 1973. biennial. 5 Fr. European Broadcasting Union, Case Postale 193, CH-1211 Geneva 20, Switzerland.

384.55 US ISSN 0539-0761
INTERNATIONAL TELEVISION ALMANAC. 1956. a. $35. Quigley Publishing Co., 159 W. 53 St., New York, NY 10019. Ed. Richard Gertner. adv. charts. stat.

791 SZ ISSN 0082-0776
INTERNATIONAL TELEVISION SYMPOSIUM AND TECHNICAL EXHIBIT, MONTREUX. (PAPERS) 1961. biennial. 250 Fr. ‡ International Television Symposium and Technical Exhibit, Case Postale 122, 1820 Montreaux, Switzerland. adv. circ. 4,000.

621.38 BE ISSN 0074-9516
INTERNATIONAL UNION OF RADIO SCIENCE. PROCEEDINGS OF GENERAL ASSEMBLIES. (Text in English and French) 1928. triennial, 19th, 1978, Helsinki. $3. International Union of Radio Science, c/o C. M. Minnis, Rue de Nieuwenhove 18, B-1180 Brussels, Belgium. circ. 1,200.
Formerly: International Scientific Radio Union. Proceedings of General Assemblies.

COMMUNICATIONS — RADIO AND TELEVISION

384 621.38 GW ISSN 0535-4358
INTERNATIONALES HANDBUCH FUER RUNDFUNK UND FERNSEHEN. 1957. biennial. DM.74. Hans-Bredow-Institut, Heimhuder Str. 21, 2000 Hamburg 13, W. Germany (B.R.D.) adv. circ. 2,500.

384 US
LIVE WIRE; the Twin Cities newsletter on telecommunications. 1975. irreg. free. University of Minnesota, University Student Telecommunications Corp., University/Community Video Center, 506A Rarig Center, Minneapolis, MN 55455. Ed. Arthur C. Sturm.

621.38 II
MASS MEDIA IN INDIA. (Text in English) 1978. a. Rs.15. Ministry of Information and Broadcasting, Publications Division, Patiala House, Tilak Marg, New Delhi 110001, India.

MEDIA ENCYCLOPEDIA; working press of the nation. see *JOURNALISM*

384.54 US
MOBILE RADIO HANDBOOK. 1977. a. $24.95. Titsch Publishing Co., Box 5400TA, Denver, CO 80217. Ed. Mike McCready. adv. index. circ. 6,000.

MOVIE/TV MARKETING GLOBAL MOTION PICTURE YEAR BOOK. see *MOTION PICTURES*

621.38 JA ISSN 0077-2631
N H K TECHNICAL MONOGRAPH/N H K GIJUTSU KENKYOJO. (Nippon Hoso Kyokai) (Text in English) 1963. a. exchange basis. Japan Broadcasting Corp., Technical Research Laboratories, Research and Information Division, 1-10-11 Kinuta, Setagaya-ku, Tokyo 157, Japan. circ. 1,100. Indexed: Chem.Abstr. Elec.Eng.Abstr.
Broadcast engineering

621.38 NZ
N. Z. A. R. T. AMATEUR RADIO CALLBOOK. 1928. a. NZ.$15 includes monthly Break-In. ‡ New Zealand Association of Radio Transmitters, Inc., Box 1459, Christchurch, New Zealand. Ed. B. D. Jensen. adv. bk. rev. circ. 4,600.
Amateur

384.5 US
NATIONAL RADIO PUBLICITY DIRECTORY. 1972. a (with s-a. supplements) $85. Peter Glenn Publications, Inc., 17 E. 48th St., New York, NY 10017. Ed. Ronald T. Robinson. adv. (looseleaf format)

NEDERLANDS THEATER- EN TELEVISIE JAARBOEK. see *THEATER*

384.54 US ISSN 0078-1347
NORTH AMERICAN RADIO-T V GUIDE. 1963. a. $5.95. Howard W. Sams & Co. Inc., 4300 W. 62nd St., Indianapolis, IN 46268. Ed. Vane A. Jones.

OFFICE DES COMMUNICATIONS SOCIALES, MONTREAL. CAHIERS D'ETUDES ET DE RECHERCHES. see *COMMUNICATIONS*

621.38 US
OFFICIAL REGISTRY OF C B OPERATORS. 1976. a. $5. Today Publications and News Service, Inc., 621 National Press Bldg., Washington, DC 20045. index.

384.5 US ISSN 0556-5006
PHOTOFACT ANNUAL INDEX. 1946. a.(with q. supplements) $0.50. Howard W. Sams & Co. Inc., 4300 W. 62nd St., Indianapolis, IN 46268. Ed. Joe Groves. adv. index. cum.index. circ. controlled.

384 PL
POLSKI ZWIAZEK KROTKOFALOWCOW. BIULETYN. irreg. 178 Zl. Polski Zwiazek Krotkofalowcow, Ul. Nowy Zjazd 1, Warsaw, Poland. illus.

PRESS RADIO AND T.V. GUIDE. see *JOURNALISM*

384.5 UK ISSN 0079-9475
R S G B AMATEUR RADIO CALL BOOK. a. £3.21. Radio Society of Great Britain, 35 Doughty St., London WC1N 2AE, England. Ed. A.W. Hutchinson. circ. 8,000.

621.38 US ISSN 0033-7706
RADIO AMATEUR CALLBOOK MAGAZINE; United States listings. 1920. a. $13.95. Radio Amateur Callbook, Inc., 925 Sherwood Drive, Lake Bluff, IL 60044. adv.
Amateur

621.384 US ISSN 0079-9440
RADIO AMATEUR'S HANDBOOK. (Editions in English and Spanish) 1926 English ed., 1938 Spanish ed. a. $15.75 hardcover; $10 paper. ‡ American Radio Relay League, Inc., 225 Main St., Newington, CT 06111. Ed. D. De Maw. illus. index. circ. 110,000.
Amateur

621.38 US
RADIO AMATEUR'S LICENSE MANUAL. irreg., approx. biennial. $4. American Radio Relay League, Inc., 225 Main St., Newington, CT 06111.
Amateur

384 AT
RADIO FACTS AND FIGURES. 1959. a. free. Federation of Australian Commercial Broadcasters, Research and Promotion Division, Australian Radio Advertising Bureau, 8 Glen St., Milson's Point, N.S.W. 2061, Australia.

621.384 US ISSN 0079-9467
RADIO HANDBOOK. 1935. irreg., 21st edt., 1978. $21.50. (Editors and Engineers Ltd.) Howard W. Sams & Co., Inc., 4300 W. 62nd St., Indianapolis, IN 46268. Ed. William I. Orr.

629.135 US
RADIO TECHNICAL COMMISSION FOR AERONAUTICS. PROCEEDINGS OF THE ANNUAL ASSEMBLY MEETING. 1955. a. $16. Radio Technical Commission for Aeronautics, Suite 655, 1717 H St., N.W., Washington, DC 20006. Ed. Jodie Alcorn. circ. 750.

621.38 384.5 US
REFERNCE DATA FOR RADIO ENGINEERS. irreg. price varies. Howard W. Sams & Co., Inc., 4300 West 62nd St., Indianapolis, IN 46268.

370 BL
REVISTA BRASILEIRA DE TELEDUCACAO. irreg. Associacao Brasileira de Teleducacao, C.P. 56008, Rio de Janeiro, Brazil.

384.55 BL
REVISTA TELEBRAS. 1976. irreg. free. Telecomunicacoes Brasileiras S.A., S.A.S. Quadro 6, Bloco H, Lotes 5 a 8, Caixa Postal 11,1218, CEP 70,313 Brasilia, DF, Brazil. Ed. A. Eduardo Diniz Schlaepfer. circ. 12,000.

RHODE ISLAND MEDIA DIRECTORY. see *JOURNALISM*

SCREEN INTERNATIONAL FILM AND T.V. YEARBOOK. see *MOTION PICTURES*

791.45 US
SERIES, SERIALS, AND PACKAGES. 1949. a. $179. Broadcast Information Bureau, Inc., 100 Lafayette Dr., Syosset, NY 11791. Ed. Avra Leah Fliegelman. adv. index.
Formerly: T V Film Source Book. Series, Serials and Packages (ISSN 0082-1373)

791.44 US
SPARKS. 1968. a. membership; selective distribution. ‡ Society of Wireless Pioneers, P.O. Box 530, Santa Rosa, CA 95402. Ed. William A. Breniman. circ. 3,500.
Formerly (until 1976): Wireless Pioneer (ISSN 0084-0440)
Directory, roster, biographical information for those in field of wireless radio

301.16 JA
STUDIES OF BROADCASTING; an international annual of broadcasting science. (None published 1970-71) (Text in English) 1963. a. on exchange basis. Japan Broadcasting Corp., Radio & TV Culture Research Institute, Theoretical Research Center - Nippon Hoso Kyohai, 2-1-1 Atago, Minato-ku, Tokyo 105, Japan. Eds. G. Kurono, K. Sata. illus. circ. 900.

384.554 US
T V BASICS. a. free. Television Bureau of Advertising, 1345 Avenue of the Americas, New York, NY 10019.

384.55 IT
T V COLOR. 1978. a. L.3800($7) Gruppo Editoriale Suono, Via del Casaletto 380, 00151 Rome, Italy. adv. illus. circ. 80,000.

791 371.3 US ISSN 0082-1357
T V FEATURE FILM SOURCE BOOK. 1949. a.; includes 2 supplements. $199. Broadcast Information Bureau, Inc., 100 Lafayette Dr., Syosset, NY 11791. Ed. Avra Leah Fliegelman. adv. index.

791.45 CN ISSN 0082-1365
T V-FILM FILEBOOK; information on Canadian TV-film industry. 1960. a. Can.$4. 2533 Gerrard St. E., Scarborough, Ont., Canada. Ed. A. C. Benson. adv. circ. 2,500.

384.55 UK
TELEVISION & RADIO. 1963. a. £2.95. Independent Broadcasting Authority, 70 Brompton Rd., London SW3 1EY, England (Dist. by: Independent Television Publications, 247 Tottenham Court Rd., London W1P 0AU, England) Ed. Eric Croston.
Former titles: Guide to Independent Television and Independent Local Radio; I T V Guide to Independent Television (ISSN 0536-2121)

384.55 US
TELEVISION CONTACTS. (Mid-Year Update) 1976, 5th edition. a.; monthly updates. $90. Larimi Communications, Inc., 151 E. 50 St., New York, NY 10022. Ed. Michael McMahon.

791 US ISSN 0082-268X
TELEVISION FACTBOOK. (Vol. 1. Stations; Vol. 2. Services) 1945. a. $127.50. Television Digest, Inc., 1836 Jefferson Place N.W., Washington, DC 20036. Ed. Albert Warren. index.

791.45 778.5 US
TELEVISION NETWORK MOVIES. a. $75. Television Index, Inc., 150 Fifth Ave., New York, NY 10011.

791.45 US
TELEVISION TRADE-IN BLUE BOOK. 1953. a. $8. Dealerscope, 23868 Hawthorne Blvd., Suite 100, Torrance, CA 90505. adv. (also avail. in microform from UMI)
Formerly: Television Blue Book (ISSN 0085-7149)

621.384 CN ISSN 0076-0587
UNIVERSITY OF WESTERN ONTARIO. CENTRE FOR RADIO SCIENCE. ANNUAL REPORT. 1968. a. ‡ University of Western Ontario, Centre for Radio Science, London, Ont. N6A 5C2, Canada. circ. 100.

VERMONT MEDIA DIRECTORY. see *JOURNALISM*

384 CN
VIDEO EXCHANGE DIRECTORY. vol. 4, 1976. a. Satellite Video Exchange Society, 261 Powell St., Vancouver, B.C. V6A 1G3, Canada. bibl.

621.388 US
VIDEOLOG: PROGRAMS FOR BUSINESS AND INDUSTRY. irreg. Esselte Video, Inc., 127 W. 56th St., New York, NY 10019. Ed. Lawrence Eidelberg.
Formerly: Video Directory: Programs for Business and Industry; Supersedes in part: Video Bluebook.

621.388 US
VIDEOLOG: PROGRAMS FOR GENERAL INTEREST AND ENTERTAINMENT. irreg. Esselte Video, Inc., 127 W. 56th St., New York, NY 10019.
Formerly: Video Directory: Programs for General Interest and Entertainment; Supersedes in part: Video Bluebook.

621.388 US
VIDEOLOG: PROGRAMS FOR THE HEALTH SCIENCES. irreg. Esselte Video, Inc., 127 W. 56th St., New York, NY 10019. Ed. Lawrence Eidelberg.
Former titles: Video Directory: Programs for Health Sciences; Until 1978: Health Sciences Video Directory.

791.4 US
VIDEOPLAY PROGRAM SOURCE GUIDE. a. C. S. Tepfer Publishing Co., Inc., 51 Sugar Hollow Rd., Danbury, CT 06810.

VIDEORECORDINGS AVAILABLE IN THE PUBLIC LIBRARIES OF METROPOLITAN TORONTO. see *LIBRARY AND INFORMATION SCIENCES*

384 US
W E S T TELEMEMO.* 1970. irreg. membership. ‡ Western Educational Society for Telecommunications, 2001 Associated Rd., Fullerton, CA 92631. Ed. Susan Franko. circ. 5-7,000.
Formerly: W E S T Newsletter.

792 US ISSN 0508-6795
WHO'S WHERE; who's where in show business. biennial. $4. Leo Shull Publications, 134 W. 44th St., New York, NY 10036. Ed. Leo Shull. circ. 15,000.
Title varies: Show Business Who's Where (ISSN 0488-7115)

791.44 UK ISSN 0084-0459
WIRELESS WORLD DIARY. 1918. a. 60-97p. I.P.C. Business Press Ltd., 33-40 Bowling Green Lane, London EC1R 0NE, England. Ed. D. R. Bray. circ. 8,000.

384 US
WORLD RADIO & T.V. HANDBOOK. 29th, 1975. a. Watson-Guptill Publications, Inc., One Astor Plaza, New York, NY 10036.

COMMUNICATIONS — Telephone And Telegraph

384.6 AT
AUSTRALIA. POSTMASTER GENERAL'S DEPARTMENT. RESEARCH LABORATORIES. REPORT. 1925. irreg. Postmaster General's Department, Research Laboratories, 59 Collins St., Melbourne, Vic. 3000, Australia. Ed. A. O'Rourke.

384 AT ISSN 0067-2181
AUSTRALIAN TELECOMMUNICATION MONOGRAPHS. 1963. irreg. Aus.$4 to non-members. Telecommunication Society of Australia, Box 1802Q, Melbourne, Vic. 3001, Australia. Ed. V. J. White.

384.1 US
DIRECTORY OF UNITED STATES ELECTRONIC MAIL DROPS. 1978. a. $7.85. Tahoe Information & Business Services, Box 4031, Stateline, NV 89449. Ed. Laurance J. Foley. charts. illus. (back issues avail.)

384 UK ISSN 0579-6903
I. P. T. C. NEWSLETTER. 1965. 3/yr. International Press Telecommunications Council - Comite International des Telecommunications de Presse, Studio House, Hen and Chickens Ct., 184 Fleet St., London EC4A 2dU, England. Dir. Oliver G. Robinson. adv. circ. 1,600.

384.6 US
INDEPENDENT PHONEFACTS. a. United States Independent Telephone Association, 1801 K St. N.W., Suite 1201, Washington, DC 20006. charts. illus. stat.

384.1 UN ISSN 0074-9044
INTERNATIONAL TELECOMMUNICATION UNION. LIST OF TELEGRAPH OFFICES OPEN FOR INTERNATIONAL SERVICE. (Preface in English, French and Spanish) 1869. every 5 years. 66 Fr. International Telecommunication Union - Union Internationale des Telecommunications, Distribution and Sales Section, Place des Nations, CH-1211 Geneva 20, Switzerland.

384.1 UN ISSN 0085-2201
INTERNATIONAL TELECOMMUNICATION UNION. REPORT ON THE ACTIVITIES. (Editions in English, French, Spanish) 1948. a. price varies. International Telecommunication Union - Union Internationale des Telecommunications, Place des Nations, 1211 Geneva 20, Switzerland.

INTERNATIONAL TELEPHONE DIRECTORY OF THE DEAF. see *DEAF*

384 AT ISSN 0310-8031
INTERNATIONAL TELEX DIRECTORY. INTERNATIONAL SERVICE. 1972. a. Playfair Publishing Group, P.O. Box 52, Northbridge, N.S.W. 2063, Australia.

384.55 GW
JAEGER AND WALDMANN INTERNATIONAL TELEX DIRECTORY. 1952. a. $110 includes Touring Telex Tourist Guide and Telex-Post updating supplements. Telex-Verlag Jaeger und Waldmann, Holzfoallee 38, Postfach 111060, 6100 Darmstadt 2, W. Germany (B.R.D.) (Dist. by: Universal Media Co., Div. of Shamgar, Inc.,212 Broadway, Box 45, Bethpage, NY 11714) Ed. W. Lucius. adv.
Formerly: Jaeger and Waldmann World Telex Directory.

384.1 UN ISSN 0074-9001
LIST OF CABLES FORMING THE WORLD SUBMARINE NETWORK. (Text in English, French and Spanish) 1877. irreg., 1972, 18th ed. 16 Fr. International Telecommunication Union - Union Internationale des Telecommunications, Place des Nations, 1211 Geneva 20, Switzerland.

384.1 UN ISSN 0074-901X
LIST OF DESTINATION INDICATORS AND TELEX IDENTIFICATION CODES. (Text in English, French and Spanish) 1966. triennial; 3rd edt., 1973. price varies. International Telecommunication Union - Union Internationale des Telecommunications, Place des Nations, 1211 Geneva 20, Switzerland.

384.1 UN ISSN 0074-9028
LIST OF INTERNATIONAL TELEPHONE ROUTES. (Text in English, French and Spanish) 1961. a.; 16th edt., 1976. price varies. International Telecommunication Union - Union Internationale des Telecommunications, Place des Nations, 1211 Geneva 20, Switzerland.

MARCONI'S INTERNATIONAL REGISTER; international cable address directory. see *BUSINESS AND ECONOMICS — Trade And Industrial Directories*

384.6 NG
NIGER. OFFICE DES POSTES ET TELECOMMUNICATIONS. ANNUAIRE OFFICIEL DES TELEPHONES. a. Office des Postes et Telecommunications, Niamey, Niger.

POLITEKNIKA WROCLAWSKA. INSTYTUT TELEKOMUNIKACJI I AKUSTYKI. PRACE NAUKOWE. KONFERENCJE. see *ELECTRICITY AND ELECTRICAL ENGINEERING*

POLITEKNIKA WROCLAWSKA. INSTYTUT TELEKOMUNIKACJI I AKUSTYKI. PRACE NAUKOWE. MONOGRAFIE. see *ELECTRICITY AND ELECTRICAL ENGINEERING*

POLITEKNIKA WROCLAWSKA. INSTYTUT TELEKOMUNIKACJI I AKUSTYKI. PRACE NAUKOWE. STUDIA I MATERIALY. see *ELECTRICITY AND ELECTRICAL ENGINEERING*

384 CN ISSN 0080-6633
SASKATCHEWAN TELECOMMUNICATIONS. ANNUAL REPORT. 1947. a. ‡ Saskatchewan Telecommunications, 2350 Albert St., Regina, Sask. S4P 2Y4, Canada. circ. 2,000.

384.5 US ISSN 0098-5910
SOCIETY OF WIRELESS PIONEERS. YEARBOOK. biennial. Society of Wireless Pioneers, Box 530, Santa Rosa, CA 95402. illus. Key Title: Yearbook- Society of Wireless Pioneers.

384.1 UN ISSN 0074-9052
TABLE OF INTERNATIONAL TELEX RELATIONS AND TRAFFIC. (Text in English, French and Spanish) 1964. a. price varies. International Telecommunication Union - Union Internationale des Telecommunications, Place des Nations, 1211 Geneva 20, Switzerland.

384 GW ISSN 0082-190X
TASCHENBUCH DER POST- UND FERNMELDE-VERWALTUNG. 1970. a. DM.29.20. Fachverlag Schiele und Schoen GmbH, Markgrafenstr. 11, 1000 Berlin 61, W. Germany (B.R.D.) Ed. H. Bonson. adv. circ. 45,000.
Formerly: Taschenbuch fuer Fernmelde-Verwaltung.

TASCHENBUCH FUER DEN FERNMELDEDIENST. see *MILITARY*

621.38 HU
TAVKOZLESI KUTATO INTEZET. ANNUAL. (Text in English) irreg., last issue in 1975. free on request. Tavkozlesi Kutato Intezet - Research Institute for Telecommunication, Budapest, Hungary. illus.

621.38 SI
TELECOMMUNICATION AUTHORITY OF SINGAPORE. TELECOMS ANNUAL REPORT. 1974. a. price varies. Telecommunication Authority of Singapore, Telecoms Headquarters, Comcentre, 31 Exeter Rd., Singapore 0923, Singapore. circ. controlled.
Formed by the 1974 merger of: Telecommunication Authority of Singapore. T A S Annual Report & Singapore Telephone Board Annual Report.

384 621.385 US ISSN 0082-2655
TELEPHONE ENGINEER AND MANAGEMENT DIRECTORY. 1937. a. $30. Harcourt Brace Jovanovich, Inc. (Wheaton), 402 W. Liberty Dr., Wheaton, IL 60187. Ed. Raymond H. Smith. adv. circ. 9,600.

384 US
TELEPHONY'S DIRECTORY & BUYER'S GUIDE FOR THE TELEPHONE INDUSTRY. 1895. a. $14. Telephony Publishing Corp., 55 E. Jackson Blvd., Chicago, IL 60604. Ed. Gerry Barrett. circ. 11,000. (reprint service avail. from UMI)
Formerly: Telphony's Directory of the Telephone Industry (ISSN 0082-2671)

384.6 330 US ISSN 0146-6801
TOLL FREE BUSINESS. a. $11.95. Toll Free Planning Services, Inc., Box 102, Minneapolis, MN 55440.

384.6 US ISSN 0363-2962
TOLL FREE DIGEST; a directory of toll free telephone numbers. a. $2. Toll Free Digest Co., Box 800, Claverack, NY 12513.

384 FR ISSN 0082-5980
TRANSTELEL; TRANSMISSIONS, TELECOMMUNICATIONS, ELECTRONIQUE EN FRANCE.* 1962. biennial. Bureau des Relations Exterieures et Sociales, 30 rue Bergere, Paris 9e, France.

384 US ISSN 0083-1298
UNITED STATES INDEPENDENT TELEPHONE ASSOCIATION. ANNUAL STATISTICAL VOLUME. Cover title: Independent Telephone Statistics. (In 2 vols.) 1954. a. $25 to non-members. United States Independent Telephone Association, 1801 K. Street N.W. Suite 1201, Washington, DC 20006. index. circ. 1,000.

384.6 US
UNITED STATES INDEPENDENT TELEPHONE ASSOCIATION. HOLDING COMPANY REPORT. a. United States Independent Telephone Association, 1801 K St., N.W., Suite 1201, Washington, DC 20006.

ZIP/AREA CODE DIRECTORY. see *COMMUNICATIONS — Postal Affairs*

COMPUTER TECHNOLOGY AND APPLICATIONS

see also Library and Information Sciences

A C M ADMINISTRATIVE DIRECTORY OF COLLEGE AND UNIVERSITY COMPUTER SCIENCE/DATA PROCESSING PROGRAMS AND COMPUTER FACILITIES. (Association for Computing Machinery, Inc.) see *EDUCATION — Guides To Schools And Colleges*

001.642   US   ISSN 0361-2163
A C M ANNUAL WORKSHOP ON
MICROPROGRAMMING. CONFERENCE
RECORD. Variant title: SI. 1974, no. 7. a. price
varies. ‡ Association for Computing Machinery,
Special Interest Group on Microprogramming, 1133
Ave of the Americas, New York, NY 10036
(Orders to A C M Order Dept., Box 64645,
Baltimore, MD 21264) bibl. charts. Key Title:
Micro Proceedings.

621.381   US
A C M MONOGRAPH SERIES. irreg., unnumbered,
latest 1979. price varies. (Association for Computing
Machinery) Academic Press, Inc. (Subsidiary of:
Harcourt Brace Jovanovich) 111 Fifth Ave., New
York, NY 10003. Ed. Thomas A. Standish.

621.381   US
A C M SYMPOSIUM ON THE THEORY OF
COMPUTING. 1972, no. 4. a. $10. ‡ Association
for Computing Machinery, Special Interest Group
on Automata and Compatability Theory, 1133 Ave.
of the Americas, New York, NY 10036. bibl.
charts.

ACTA POLYTECHNICA SCANDINAVICA.
MATHEMATICS AND COMPUTER SCIENCE
SERIES. see MATHEMATICS

001.64   US   ISSN 0065-2458
ADVANCES IN COMPUTERS. 1960. irreg., vol. 18,
1979. price varies. Academic Press, Inc., 111 Fifth
Ave., New York, NY 10003. Ed. Franz L. Alt. index.
(also avail. in microfiche)

001.642   UK   ISSN 0084-6198
ALGOL BULLETIN. (Text in English) 1959. irreg.
(approx. 3/yr.) $7 per 3 issues. International
Federation for Information Processing, c/o Dr. C.
H. Lindsey, Dept. of Computer Science, University
of Manchester, Manchester MI3 9PL, England. bk.
rev. circ. 500. (looseleaf format; back issues avail.)
Indexed: Comput.Rev.

625.7 651.8   US   ISSN 0091-5122
AMERICAN ASSOCIATION OF STATE
HIGHWAY AND TRANSPORTATION
OFFICIALS. SUB-COMMITTEE ON
COMPUTER TECHNOLOGY. PROCEEDINGS.
NATIONAL CONFERENCE. 1970. a. free.
American Association of State Highway and
Transportation Officials, U.S. Department of
Transportation, 444 N. Capitol St. N.W., Suite 225,
Washington, DC 20001. Ed. Keith F. Kohler. circ.
controlled. Key Title: Proceedings - Committee on
Computer Technology.

AMERICAN BANKERS ASSOCIATION.
NATIONAL OPERATIONS & AUTOMATION
CONFERENCE. PROCEEDINGS. see BUSINESS
AND ECONOMICS — Banking And Finance

AMERICAN BANKERS ASSOCIATION.
OPERATIONS AND AUTOMATION DIVISION.
RESULTS OF THE NATIONAL OPERATIONS
& AUTOMATION SURVEY. see BUSINESS AND
ECONOMICS — Banking And Finance

651.8 001.6   US
AMERICAN INSTITUTE OF INDUSTRIAL
ENGINEERS. COMPUTER AND
INFORMATION SYSTEMS DIVISION.
MONOGRAPHS. irreg., latest no.9. price varies.
American Institute of Industrial Engineers, Inc., 25
Technology Park/Atlanta, Norcross, GA 30092.
(reprint service avail. from UMI)

621.38   UR
ANALOGO-DISKRETNYE PREOBRAZOVANIYA
SIGNALOV. 1975. irreg. 0.50 Rub. (Akademiya
Nauk Latviiskoi S.S.R., Institut Elektroniki i
Vychislitel'noi Tekhniki) Izdevnieciba Zinatne,
Turgeneva iela, 19, Riga, U. S. S. R.

ANNALES SOCIETATIS MATHEMATICAE
POLONAE. SERIES 4: FUNDAMENTA
INFORMATICAE. see MATHEMATICS

001.642   US   ISSN 0066-4138
ANNUAL REVIEW IN AUTOMATIC
PROGRAMMING. 1960. 4/yr. $50. Pergamon
Press, Inc., Journals Division, Maxwell House,
Fairview Park, Elmsford, NY 10523 (And
Headington Hill Hall, Oxford OX3 0BW, England)
Ed. M. I. Halpern. (also avail. in microform from
MIM,UMI).

001.6   US
ANNUAL SIMULATION
SYMPOSIUM.(PROCEEDINGS) 8th, 1975. a. $22.
(Annual Simulation Symposium, Inc.) Institute of
Electrical and Electronics Engineers, Inc., Computer
Society, 5855 Naples Plaza, No. 301, Long Beach,
CA 90803. (Co-sponsor: Society for Computer
Simulation)

001.6   JA
ANNUAL SURVEY OF COMPUTER USERS. 1966.
a. 8000 Yen. (Information Processing Society of
Japan) Japan Management Science Institute, 4-28-26
Minami-Aoyama, Minato-ku, Tokyo 107, Japan.

001.6   US
ANNUAL SYMPOSIUM ON FOUNDATIONS OF
COMPUTER SCIENCE. PROCEEDINGS. 1959?
a. $22 to non-members; members $16.50. Institute
of Electrical and Electronics Engineers, Inc.,
Computer Society, 5855 Naples Plaza, Suite 301,
Long Beach, CA 90803.
Formerly(until 1974): Annual Symposium on
Switching and Automata Theory. Proceedings.

003   US
APPLIED SYSTEMS SCIENCE. a. price varies.
Gordon and Breach Science Publishers, One Park
Ave, New York, NY 10016. Ed. George Klir.

001.6   HK
ASIAN COMPUTER YEARBOOK. 1976. a. $25.
Computer Publications Ltd., Seabird House, Seventh
Floor, 22-28 Wyndham St., Hong Kong, Hong
Kong. Ed. Euan Barty. adv. bk. rev. circ. 8,000.

621.381   US   ISSN 0066-9091
ASSOCIATION FOR COMPUTING MACHINERY.
PROCEEDINGS OF NATIONAL
CONFERENCE. (Suspended 1953-63) 1946. a. $38
to non-members; members $28. Association for
Computing Machinery, 1133 Ave. of the Americas,
New York, NY 10036.

370.28   US   ISSN 0147-9296
ASSOCIATION FOR EDUCATIONAL DATA
SYSTEMS. ANNUAL CONVENTION
PROCEEDINGS. 1973. a. $15. Association for
Educational Data Systems, 1201 16th St., N.W.,
Washington, DC 20036. Eds. Robert Nelson, Sue
Talley. (reprint service avail. from UMI)

370.28   US   ISSN 0092-6280
ASSOCIATION FOR EDUCATIONAL DATA
SYSTEMS. HANDBOOK AND DIRECTORY.
1967. irreg., latest issue 1973. membership. National
Computer Systems, 1201 16th St., N. W.,
Washington, DC 20036. adv. circ. 2,000. Key Title:
Handbook and Directory - Association for
Educational Data Systems.

001.53   FR
ASSOCIATION FRANCAISE POUR LA
CYBERNETIQUE ECONOMIQUE ET
TECHNIQUE. ANNUAIRE. 1965. irreg.
Association Francaise pour la Cybernetique
Economique et Technique, 156, Boulevard Pereire,
75017 Paris, France.
Formerly: Association Francaise d'Informatique
et de Recherche Operationnelle. Annuaire (ISSN
0066-9296); Formed by the merger of: Societe
Francaise de Recherche Operationelle. Annuaire &
Association Francaise de Calcul et de Traitement
d'Information. Annuaire.
Cybernetics

ASSOCIATION OF AMERICAN RAILROADS.
DATA SYSTEMS DIVISION. PAPERS. see
TRANSPORTATION — Railroads

001.642   US
ASSOCIATION OF COMPUTER PROGRAMMERS
AND ANALYSTS. PROCEEDINGS OF THE
FOUNDERS CONFERENCE. a. price varies.
Association of Computer Programmers and
Analysts, P.O. Box 95, Kensington, MD 20795.

621.381   AT   ISSN 0313-3311
AUSTRALIAN COMPUTER SOCIETY.
CONFERENCE PROCEEDINGS. no. 8, 1978.
biennial. Aus.$50. Australian Computer Society,
Box 640, Crows Nest, N.S.W. 2065, Australia. circ.
1,600.

621.381   AT   ISSN 0067-1819
AUSTRALIAN COMPUTER SOCIETY. COUNCIL.
REPORT.* 1967. a. free upon request. Australian
Computer Society, 28 Chippen St, Chippendale,
N.S.W 2008, Australia.

621.381 001.6   AT
AUSTRALIAN COMPUTER SOCIETY.
QUEENSLAND BRANCH. NEWSLETTER. 1969.
irreg. Australian Computer Society, Inc.,
Queensland Branch, 288 Queen St., Brisbane, Qld.
4000, Australia. Ed. J. W. Lubke.

AUSTRALIAN NATIONAL UNIVERSITY,
CANBERRA. DEPARTMENT OF
ENGINEERING PHYSICS. PUBLICATION EP-
RR. see ENGINEERING

651.8   SZ   ISSN 0379-0258
AUTOMATIC DATA PROCESSING
INFORMATION BULLETIN. (Editions in English,
French, German, Spanish) 1967. 3/yr. free.
International Social Security Association, Box 1,
1211 Geneva 22, Switzerland.

621.38   UR
AVTOMATIZIROVANNYE SISTEMY
UPRAVLENIYA. 1974. irreg. 1.10 Rub.
(Ministerstvo Vysshego i Srednego Spetsial'nogo
Obrazovaniya) Izdatel'stvo Leningradskii
Universitet, Universitetskaya nab. 7/9, Leningrad B-
164, U.S.S.R.

001.6   SZ
BASIC SOFTWARE. 1977. irreg. price varies. Paul
Haupt AG, Falkenplatz 14, CH-3001 Berne,
Switzerland.

001.6 658   GW
BEITRAEGE ZUR DATENVERARBEITUNG UND
UNTERNEHMENSFORSCHUNG. 1972. irreg.,
vol. 25, 1981. price varies. Verlag Anton Hain
GmbH, Adelheidstr. 2, Postfach 1220, 6240
Koenigstein, W. Germany (B.R.D.) Ed. A.
Angermann.

BENCHMARK PAPERS IN ELECTRICAL
ENGINEERING & COMPUTER SCIENCE. see
ELECTRICITY AND ELECTRICAL
ENGINEERING

001   US   ISSN 0271-8189
BEST OF MICRO. 1978. a. price varies. Micro Ink,
Inc., 34 Chelmsford Ave., Chelmsford, MA 01824
(Subscr. to: Box 6502, Chelmsford, MA 01824) Ed.
Robert M. Tripp.

BIBLIOGRAFIA BRASILEIRA DE
DOCUMENTACAO. see LIBRARY AND
INFORMATION SCIENCES

001.64 621.381   UK
BRITISH COMPUTER SOCIETY. MICROFORM
SPECIALIST GROUP. ANNUAL
PROCEEDINGS. 1976. a. British Computer
Society, Microform Specialist Group, 29 Portland
Place, London W1N 4HU, England.

001.53   BU   ISSN 0068-385X
BULGARSKA AKADEMIIA NA NAUKITE.
INSTITUT PO TEKHNICHESKA
KIBERNETIKA. IZVESTIIA. (Summaries in
English and Russian) 1964. irreg. 1.42 lv. (Institut
po Tekhnicheska Kibernetika) Publishing House of
the Bulgarian Academy of Sciences, Ul. Akad. G.
Bonchev, 1113 Sofia, Bulgaria (Dist. by: Hemus, 6,
Rouski Blvd., 1000 Sofia, Bulgaria) circ. 600.

651.8   US
BUSINESS DATA PROCESSING: A WILEY
SERIES. 1971. irreg., unnumbered, latest, 1979.
price varies. John Wiley & Sons, Inc., 605 Third
Ave., New York, NY 10016.

621.381   CN
BUYERS' GUIDE TO PROCESS EQUIPMENT,
CONTROLS & INSTRUMENTATION. 1917. a.
Can.$10. Southam Communications Ltd., 1450 Don
Mills Rd., Don Mills, Ont. M3B 2X7, Canada. Ed.
Bob Orchard. adv. circ. 14,200.

001.6   US   ISSN 0360-1617
C.A.C. DOCUMENT. irreg. University of Illinois at
Urbana-Champaign, Center for Advanced
Computation, Dept. of Computer Science, Urbana,
IL 61801.

620.0042 001.64   GW
C A D/G D V- REPORT. (Computer Aided Design-Geometrische Daten Verarbeitung-EDV- Zeichnen) 1978. bi-m. DM.29. Verlag Zeichentechnik, Schulstr. 4-6, 6277 Camberg, W. Germany (B.R.D.) (Co-publisher: Camberger Verlag Ulrich Lange) Ed. Ulrich Lange. adv. bk. rev. bibl. circ. 15,000.

C E R N SCHOOL OF COMPUTING. PROCEEDINGS. (European Organization for Nuclear Research) see PHYSICS

621.381   UK
CAMBRIDGE COMPUTER SCIENCE TEXTS. 1972. irreg., no. 12, 1980. $38.50 (cloth); $15.95(paper) for latest vol. Cambridge University Press, Box 110, Cambridge CB2 3RL, England (And 32 E. 57th St., New York NY 10022) Ed.Bd.

001.6   CN   ISSN 0383-7319
CANADIAN DATA PROCESSING DIRECTORY. 1975. a. Can.$25. Whitsed Publishing Ltd., 2 Bloor St. W., Suite 2504, Toronto, Ont. M4W 3E2, Canada. Ed. Beverley Bleackely. adv. circ. 21,000.

112 331   CN   ISSN 0318-1944
CANADIAN INFORMATION PROCESSING SOCIETY. CANADIAN SALARY SURVEY. a. Can.$25. Canadian Information Processing Society, Ste. 214, 212 King St. W., Toronto, Ont. M5H 1K5, Canada. adv. charts. stat.

001.64   CN   ISSN 0316-8956
CANADIAN INFORMATION PROCESSING SOCIETY. COMPUTER CENSUS. a. Can.$50. Canadian Information Processing Society, Ste. 214, 212 King St. W., Toronto, Ont. M5H 1K5, Canada. adv. charts. stat.

001.642   CN
CANADIAN INFORMATION PROCESSING SOCIETY. SOFTWARE SURVEY. a. Can.$25. Canadian Information Processing Society, Ste. 214, 212 King St. W., Toronto, Ont. M5H 1K5, Canada.

001.53   US   ISSN 0340-0034
COMMUNICATION AND CYBERNETICS. 1966. irreg., vol. 17, 1977. price varies. Springer-Verlag, 175 Fifth Ave., New York, NY 10010 (also Berlin, Heidelburg, Vienna) (reprint service avail. from ISI)
Formerly: Kommunikation und Kybernetik in Einzeldarstellungen (ISSN 0075-6601)
Cybernetics

COMMUNICATION THEORY IN THE CAUSE OF MAN; notes on the application of theory to the strengthening of democratic institutions. see COMMUNICATIONS

COMPUTATIONAL LINGUISTICS AND COMPUTER LANGUAGES. see LINGUISTICS

621.381   NE
COMPUTER-AIDED DESIGN OF ELECTRONIC CIRCUITS. 1978. irreg. price varies. Elsevier Scientific Publishing Co., Box 211, 1000 AE Amsterdam, Netherlands.

001.6 001.5   US
COMPUTER AND INFORMATION SCIENCES SYMPOSIUM. PROCEEDINGS. 4th, 1974. irreg. price varies. Plenum Publishing Corp., 233 Spring St., New York, NY 10013. bibl.

621.381
COMPUTER DESIGN AND ARCHITECTURE SERIES. 1976. irreg. Elsevier North-Holland, Inc., New York, 52 Vanderbilt Ave., New York, NY 10017. Ed. Edward McCluskey.

001.6   US
COMPUTER DIRECTORY AND BUYER'S GUIDE. (Supplement to: Computers and People) a. $14.50 with Computers and People, $23.50. Berkeley Enterprises, Inc., 815 Washington St., Newtonville, MA 02160. Ed. E. C. Berkeley. adv. illus.

001.64 001.6   US
COMPUTER GRAPHICS AND ART. 1976. a. $18. Berkeley Enterprises, Inc., 815 Washington Street, Newtonville, MA 02160. Ed. Grace C. Hertlein. bk. rev. charts. illus. circ. 350. Indexed: Comput.Rev.

001.6   US   ISSN 0194-4134
COMPUTER LAW MONOGRAPH SERIES. 1979. irreg. Center for Computer-Law, 3500 S. Figueroa, Suite 211, Los Angeles, CA 90007. Ed. Michael D. Scott. circ. 200.

001.64   US
COMPUTER MONOGRAPHS. 1968. irreg., no. 23, 1975. price varies. Elsevier North-Holland, Inc., New York, 52 Vanderbilt Ave., New York, NY 10017. Ed. S. Gill.

001.6   US
COMPUTER NETWORKING SYMPOSIUM. PROCEEDINGS. a. $14 to non-members; members $10.50. Institute of Electrical and Electronics Engineers, Inc., Computer Society, 5855 Naples Plaza, No. 301, Long Beach, CA 90803. (Co-sponsor: U.S. National Bureau of Standards)

001.6   US
COMPUTER-READABLE DATA BASES: A DIRECTORY AND DATA SOURCEBOOK. biennial. $95. (American Society for Information Science) Knowledge Industry Publications, Inc., 701 Westchester Ave., White Plains, NY 10604. Ed. Martha E. Williams.

651.8 510   US
COMPUTER SCIENCE AND APPLIED MATHEMATICS. irreg. Academic Press, Inc., 111 Fifth Ave., New York, NY 10003. Ed. Werner Reinboldt.

001.6 340   SZ
COMPUTER UND RECHT. 1976. irreg. price varies. Schulthess Polygraphischer Verlag AG, Zwingliplatz 2, 8001 Zurich, Switzerland.

651.8   UK
COMPUTER USERS' YEAR BOOK. 1969. a. £24.95. Computer Users' Year Book, 430 Holdenhurst Rd., Bournemouth BH8 9XD, England. Ed. R. Grant. adv. bk. rev. circ. 800.

001.64 621.381   US   ISSN 0069-8180
COMPUTER YEARBOOK. 1952. a. $39. Computer Yearbook Co., Box 2658, Detroit, MI 48231. Ed. Frank H. Gille.
Former titles: Data Processing Yearbook & Computer Yearbook and Directory.

621.3 616   US
COMPUTERS IN CARDIOLOGY. Represents: International Conference on Computers in Cardiology. Proceedings. 1974. a. $25 to non-members; members $18.75. Institute of Electrical and Electronics Engineers, Inc., Computer Society, 5855 Naples Plaza No. 301, Long Beach, CA 90803. (Co-sponsors: U.S. National Institutes of Health; European Society of Cardiology)

651.8 540 574.192   US
COMPUTERS IN CHEMICAL AND BIOCHEMICAL RESEARCH. vol. 2, 1974. irreg. Academic Press Inc., 111 Fifth Ave., New York, NY 10003. Eds. Charles E. Klapfenstein, Charles L. Wilkins.

COMPUTERS IN CHEMISTRY AND INSTRUMENTATION. see CHEMISTRY

CONFERENCE ON COMPUTERS IN RADIOLOGY. PROCEEDINGS. see MEDICAL SCIENCES — Radiology And Nuclear Medicine

001.642   US   ISSN 0090-7383
CONFERENCE ON DATA SYSTEMS LANGUAGES. DATA BASE TASK GROUP. REPORT. 1969. irreg.; latest issue, 1971. $8. ‡ Association for Computing Machinery, Programming Language Committee, Order Dept., 1133 Avenue of the Americas, New York, NY 10036 (And British Computer Society, 29 Portland Pl., London WIN 4AP, England) illus. Key Title: Report - C.O.D.A.S.Y.L. Data Base Task Group.

001.642   US
CURRENT TRENDS IN PROGRAMMING METHODOLOGY. 1977. irreg. $21.95. Prentice-Hall, Inc., Box 500, Englewood Cliffs, NJ 07632.

001.53   BE
CYBERNETICS: WORKS IN PROGRESS/CYBERNETICS: DOCUMENTS DE TRAVAIL. irreg., latest no. 3. 800 Fr.($32) International Association for Cybernetics, Palais des Expositions, Place Andre Rijckmans, 5000 Namur, Belgium.
Cybernetics

D P INDEX. see BUSINESS AND ECONOMICS — Trade And Industrial Directories

651.8   UK   ISSN 0143-1102
D P INTERNATIONAL. 1980. a. £18 to non-members. (Institute of Data Processing Management) Sterling Professional Publications Ltd., 86-88 Edgware Rd., London W2 2YW, England.

001.6   CN   ISSN 0384-8116
DALHOUSIE UNIVERSITY. COMPUTER CENTRE. NEWSLETTER. vol. 13, 1980. irreg. Dalhousie University, Computer Centre, Halifax, N.S. B3H 4H8, Canada. Ed. Katherine Fraser. adv. circ. 650. (looseleaf format)

DALHOUSIE UNIVERSITY. SCHOOL OF LIBRARY SERVICE. OCCASIONAL PAPERS. see LIBRARY AND INFORMATION SCIENCES

001.6   US
DATA BASE MONOGRAPH SERIES. no. 6, 1978. irreg. $15 per no. Q E D Information Sciences, Inc., Box 181, 141 Lind, Wellesley, MA 02181. Ed. Robert M. Curtice.

001.6   US
DATA COMMUNICATIONS BUYERS' GUIDE. 1978. a. $25. McGraw Hill, Inc., 1221 Ave. of the Americas, New York, NY 10020. Ed. George R. Davis. adv.

001.6   US
DATA USE AND ACCESS LABORATORIES. ANNUAL REPORT. a. Data Use and Access Laboratories, 1601 N. Kent St., Suite 900, Arlington, VA 22209.

001.6   US
DESIGN AUTOMATION CONFERENCE.(PROCEEDINGS) 1963? a. $25 to non-members; members $18.75. Institute of Electrical and Electronics Engineers, Inc., Computer Society, 5855 Naples Plaza, Suite 301, Long Beach, CA 90803. (Co-sponsor: Association for Computing Machinery, Special Interest Group on Design Automation)
Formerly(until 1974): Design Automation Workshop. Proceedings (ISSN 0420-0098)

DIRECTORY OF AUTOMATED CRIMINAL JUSTICE INFORMATION SYSTEMS. see CRIMINOLOGY AND LAW ENFORCEMENT

651.26   UK
DIRECTORY OF INSTRUMENTS, ELECTRONICS, AUTOMATION. 1965. a. £15. Morgan-Grampian Book Publishing Co., Morgan-Grampian House, 30 Calderwood St., London, SE18 6QH, England. Ed. Jane Doyle. adv. circ. 2,500.
Formerly: Instruments, Electronics and Automation Purchasing Directory (ISSN 0074-0578)

001.6   US   ISSN 0271-0129
DISCONTINUED INTEGRATED CIRCUIT D.A.T.A. BOOK. 8th edt., 1978/79. a. $28. D. A. T. A. Inc., 45 U.S. Hwy. 46, Box 602, Pine Brook, NJ 07058.
Formerly: D.A.T.A. Book of Discontinued Integrated Circuits (ISSN 0146-4825)

001.6   US
ENCYCLOPEDIA OF INFORMATION SYSTEMS AND SERVICES. irreg., latest, 3rd edt. Gale Research Company, Book Tower, Detroit, MI 48226. Ed. Anthony T. Kruzas.

001.6   FR
ENQUETE ECONOMIQUE DES SOCIETES DE SERVICE ET CONSEIL EN INFORMATIQUE. a. (Delegation a l'Informatique) Documentation Francaise, 29-31 Quai Voltaire, 75340 Paris, France. stat.

001.6   FR
EUROPAUTOMATION. 1964. a. 83-85 Avenue d'Italie, 75013 Paris, France. Ed. R. J. Giffrain. adv. illus. circ. 3,500.

F.I.D./C.R. REPORT SERIES. (International Federation for Documentation) see LIBRARY AND INFORMATION SCIENCES

FORMAL LINGUISTICS. see MATHEMATICS

001.6   US
FOURTH QUADRANT. 1979. irreg. free. Digicomp Research Corp., Terrace Hill, Ithaca, NY 14850. Ed. Jeffrey Cox. circ. 400.

001.6　　　　　US　ISSN 0190-5848
FRONTIERS IN EDUCATION CONFERENCE.
PROCEEDINGS. 1971. a. $25. Institute of
Electrical and Electronics Engineers, Inc., 345 E.
47th St., New York, NY 10017.

001.64　621.381　　　NE
FUNDAMENTAL STUDIES IN COMPUTER
SCIENCE. irreg., vol. 8, 1979. price varies. North-
Holland Publishing Co., Box 211, 1000 AE
Amsterdam, Netherlands.

510.78
GRADUATE ASSISTANT DIRECTORY IN
COMPUTER SCIENCES. a. $5. Association for
Computing Machinery, 1133 Ave. of the Americas,
New York, NY 10036.

001.642　　　　　UK
GREAT BRITAIN. CIVIL SERVICE
DEPARTMENT. CENTRAL COMPUTER
AGENCY. GUIDE. 1973. irreg. £1.50. Civil
Service Department, Central Computer Agency,
Whitehall, London SW1A 2AZ, England (Avail.
from H.M.S.O., c/o Liaison Officer, Atlantic House,
London EC1P 1BW, England) illus.

001.64　651.8　　UK　ISSN 0072-582X
GREAT BRITAIN. DEPARTMENT OF
EDUCATION AND SCIENCE. COMPUTER
BOARD FOR UNIVERSITIES AND RESEARCH
COUNCILS. REPORT. 1968. irreg. Department of
Education and Science, Computer Board for
Universities and Research Councils, Elizabeth
House, York Rd., London SE1 7PH, England
(Avail. from H.M.S.O., c/o Liaison Officer, Atlantic
House, Holborn Viaduct, London EC1P 1BN,
England)

003　　　　　US　ISSN 0073-1129
HAWAII INTERNATIONAL CONFERENCE ON
SYSTEM SCIENCES. PROCEEDINGS. 1968. a.
$42. (University of Hawaii, Department of Electrical
Engineering) Western Periodicals Co., 13000
Raymer St., North Hollywood, CA 91605. (Co-
sponsor: Information Sciences Program)

651.8　　　　　US
I E E E COMPUTER SOCIETY CONFERENCE
ON PATTERN RECOGNITION AND IMAGE
PROCESSING. PROCEEDINGS. a. Institute of
Electrical and Electronics Engineers, Inc., Computer
Society, 5855 Naples Plaza, Suite 301, Long Beach,
CA 90803.

001.5　　　　　US
I E E E INTERNATIONAL SYMPOSIUM ON
INFORMATION THEORY. ABSTRACTS OF
PAPERS. 1974? a. Institute of Electrical and
Electronics Engineers, Inc., 445 Hoes Lane,
Piscataway, NJ 08854.

003　　　　　AU
I I A S A ANNUAL REPORT. (Text in English)
1973. a. International Institute for Applied Systems
Analysis, Laxenburg, Austria. illus. circ. 2,500.

001.6　　　　　IS
I L T A M TECHNICAL REPORTS. (Text in
English) irreg. I.L.T.A.M. Corporation for Planning
and Research, 78 Yirmeyahu St., Romema, P.O.B.
13080, Jerusalem 91130, Israel.

001.6　　　　　GW
INFORMATIK. irreg., vol. 31, 1980. price varies.
Bibliographisches Institut AG, Dudenstr. 6, Postfach
311, 6800 Mannheim 1, W. Germany (B.R.D.) Eds.
K.-H. Boehling, U. Kulisch, H. Maurer.

001.6　　　　　US
INFORMATIK-FACHBERICHTE. (Text in English
or German) 1976. irreg., vol. 36, 1981. price varies.
Springer-Verlag, 175 Fifth Ave., New York, NY
10010 (Also Berlin, Heidelberg, Vienna) Ed. W.
Brauer. (reprint service avail. from ISI)

001.6　003　　US　ISSN 0537-6149
INFORMATION AND SYSTEMS THEORY. 1969.
a. price varies. Gordon and Breach Science
Publishers, One Park Ave., New York, NY 10016.
Ed.Bd.

INFORMATION PROCESSING ASSOCIATION
OF ISRAEL. NATIONAL CONFERENCE ON
DATA PROCESSING. PROCEEDINGS. see
LIBRARY AND INFORMATION SCIENCES

001.6　350　　　FR
INFORMATIQUE DANS LES
ADMINISTRATIONS FRANCAISES. 1975. a. 15
F. (Commission Interministerielle de l'Informatique)
Documentation Francaise, 29-30 Quai Voltaire,
75340 Paris, France.

INSPEC REPORTS. see *LIBRARY AND INFORMATION SCIENCES*

001.6　　　　　SP　ISSN 0085-1981
INTERGOVERNMENTAL COUNCIL FOR
AUTOMATIC DATA PROCESSING.
PROCEEDINGS OF CONFERENCE.
(Proceedings of 3rd to 5th Conferences published in
"ICA-Information") 1968. irreg.; 1972, 6th West
Germany. Intergovernmental Council for Automatic
Data Processing, c/o Manuel Heredero, Servicio
Central de Informatica, Paseo de Calvo Sotelo 16,
Madrid 1, Spain.

651.8　　　　　US
INTERNATIONAL CONFERENCE ON
COMPUTER
COMMUNICATIONS.(PROCEEDINGS) 2nd,
1972. irreg., 3rd 1976. Institute of Electrical and
Electronics Engineers, Inc., Computer Society, 5855
Naples Plaza, Suite 301, Long Beach, CA 90803.

001.53　　　US　ISSN 0360-8913
INTERNATIONAL CONFERENCE ON
CYBERNETICS AND SOCIETY.
PROCEEDINGS. irreg. Institute of Electrical and
Electronics Engineers, Inc., 445 Hoes Lane,
Piscataway, NJ 08854. illus.
　Former titles (1974): International Conference on
Systems , Man and Cybernetics. Record; I E E E
Systems, Man, and Cybernetics Group. Annual
Conference Record.
Cybernetics

621.381　　　　　US
INTERNATIONAL CONFERENCE ON
PARALLEL PROCESSING. PROCEEDINGS.
1973. a. price varies. Institute of Electrical and
Electronics Engineers, Inc., Computer Society, 5855
Naples Plaza, Suite 301, Long Beach, CA 90808.
Ed. Oscar N. Garcia.

001.642　　　　　US
INTERNATIONAL CONFERENCE ON
RELIABLE SOFTWARE.(PROCEEDINGS) 1973.
irreg., latest 1975. $12. Institute of Electrical and
Electronics Engineers, Inc., Computer Society, 445
Hoes Lane, Piscataway, New York, NJ 08854.
　Former titles (1973): I E E E Symposium on
Computer Software Reliability. Record (ISSN 0091-
469X); Symposium on Computer Software
Engineering--Reliability, Management, Design.

001.6　　　　　US
INTERNATIONAL CONFERENCE ON
SOFTWARE ENGINEERING. PROCEEDINGS.
1975. a. Institute of Electrical and Electronics
Engineers, Inc., Computer Society, 5855 Naples
Plaza, Suite 301, Long Beach, CA 90803.

001.6　　　　　US
INTERNATIONAL CONFERENCE ON VERY
LARGE DATA BASES. PROCEEDINGS. 1974?
a. Institute of Electrical and Electronics Engineers,
Inc., Computer Society, 5855 Naples Plaza, No.
301, Long Beach, CA 90803.

001.53　　　BE　ISSN 0074-3380
INTERNATIONAL CONGRESS FOR
CYBERNETICS. PROCEEDINGS. ACTES. 1956.
triennial, 8th, 1976, Namur. 3000 Fr.($120)
International Association for Cybernetics -
Association Internationale de Cybernetique, Palais
des Expositions, Place Andre Rijckmans, 5000
Namur, Belgium.
Cybernetics

629.8　　　　GW　ISSN 0074-3526
INTERNATIONAL CONGRESS OF AUTOMATIC
CONTROL. PROCEEDINGS. 1960. triennial,
1975, 6th, Boston. International Federation of
Automatic Control, c/o M. A. Kaaz, Graf-Recke
Str. 84, Postfach 1139, 4000 Duesseldorf 1, W.
Germany (B.R.D.)
　Proceedings published in host country

INTERNATIONAL CONGRESS OF CYBERNETIC
MEDICINE. PROCEEDINGS. see *MEDICAL SCIENCES*

651.8　001.6　　　　US
INTERNATIONAL DATA PROCESSING
CONFERENCE. PROCEEDINGS. (Published as
Sept. issue of Data Management) 1970. a. Data
Processing Management Association, 505 Busse
Highway, Park Ridge, IL 60068. (reprint service
avail. from UMI)

001.6　　　　　US
INTERNATIONAL DIRECTORY OF SOFTWARE.
1977. a. $140. C U Y B Publications Ltd., 633
Third Ave., New York, NY 10017. Ed. Robert
Grant. adv. circ. 10,000.
　Formerly: C U Y B Directory of Software.

001.6　　　　　US
INTERNATIONAL JOINT CONFERENCE ON
ARTIFICIAL INTELLIGENCE. ADVANCE
PAPERS OF THE CONFERENCE. irreg., 4th,
1975, Tbilisi, Georgia, USSR. $17.50. International
Joint Conference on Artificial Intelligence, c/o Dr.
Bruce Buchanon, Artificial Intelligence Laboratory,
Stanford University, Stanford, CA 94305.

001.5　651.8　　　　US
INTERNATIONAL JOINT CONFERENCE ON
PATTERN RECOGNITION. CONFERENCE
RECORD. 1974. biennial? $25. Institute of
Electrical and Electronics Engineers, Inc., 445 Hoes
Lane, Piscataway, NJ 08854.

001.6　　　　　GW
INTERNATIONAL ONLINE INFORMATION
MEETING (PROCEEDINGS) 2nd, 1978. irreg.
$58.70. K.G. Saur KG, Poessenbacherstr. 12 B,
Postfach 71109, 8000 Munich 71, W. Germany
(B.R.D.)

621.38　510.8　　　US
INTERNATIONAL OPTICAL COMPUTING
CONFERENCE. DIGEST OF PAPERS. irreg.,
approx. a. Institute of Electrical and Electronics
Engineers, Inc., Computer Society, 5855 Naples
Plaza, No. 301, Long Beach, CA 90803. (Co-
sponsor: Society of Photo-Optical Instrumentation
Engineers)
　Supersedes (as of 1974): Optical Computing
Symposium. Digest of Papers.

629.8　　　　US　ISSN 0074-8080
INTERNATIONAL SERIES ON AUTOMATION
AND AUTOMATIC CONTROL. 1964. irreg.,
1965, vol. 7. price varies. Pergamon Press, Inc.,
Maxwell House, Fairview Park, Elmsford, NY
10523. index.
　Formerly: International Series of Monographs on
Automation and Automatic Control.

621.3　　　　US　ISSN 0363-8928
INTERNATIONAL SYMPOSIUM ON FAULT-
TOLERANT COMPUTING. PROCEEDINGS. a.
$25 to non-members; $18.75 for members. Institute
of Electrical and Electronics Engineers, Inc.,
Computer Society, 5855 Naples Plaza, No. 301,
Long Beach, CA 90803. Key Title: Proceedings -
International Symposium on Fault-Tolerant
Computing.
　Supersedes: International Symposium on Fault-
Tolerant Computing. Digest (ISSN 0074-882X)

621.3　　　　　US
INTERNATIONAL SYMPOSIUM ON MINI AND
MICROCOMPUTERS. PROCEEDINGS. Short
title: MIMI. 1976? a. $20 to non-members; members
$15. Institute of Electrical and Electronics
Engineers, Inc., Computer Society, 5855 Naples
Plaza, Suite 301, Long Beach, CA 90803.

001.6　　　　　UI
INTERNATIONAL TRACTS IN COMPUTER
STUDIES. 1976. a. price varies. Advance
Publications, Block D, Hirzell Court, St. Peter Port,
Guernsey, Channel Islands. Eds. D. Evans, S.
Chomet. circ. 1,000.

001.6　　　　　US
INTERNATIONAL ZURICH SEMINAR ON
DIGITAL
COMMUNICATIONS.(PROCEEDINGS) 1970.
biennial. $20 to non-members; members $15.
Institute of Electrical and Electronics Engineers,
Inc., Computer Society, 5855 Naples Plaza, No.
301, Long Beach, CA 90803.

001.6 US
JOINT COLLEGE CURRICULA WORKSHOP IN COMPUTER SCIENCE, ENGINEERING AND DATA PROCESSING.(PAPERS) irreg., 4th, 1978. Institute of Electrical and Electronics Engineers, Inc., Computer Society, 5855 Naples Plaza, No. 301, Long Beach, CA 90803.

001.6 UK ISSN 0308-9541
JOURNAL OF APPLIED SYSTEMS ANALYSIS. 1969. a. £6($12) to individuals; £10 ($19) to institutions. University of Lancaster, Department of Systems, Bailrigg, Lancaster LA1 4YR, England. Ed. P. B. Checkland. bk. rev. charts. stat. circ. 750. (also avail. in microfilm from UMI) Indexed: Chem.Abstr. Anbar. Exec.Sci.Inst.
Formerly (until vol. 5, no. 1, Nov. 1976): Journal of Systems Engineering (ISSN 0022-4820)

001.6 350 310 FI ISSN 0357-9921
JYVASKYLA STUDIES IN COMPUTER SCIENCE, ECONOMICS AND STATISTICS. (Text in English) 1980. irreg. price varies. Jyaskylan Yliopisto, Kirjasto - University of Jyvaskyla, Seminaarink. 15, 40100 Jyvaskyla 10, Finland. Ed. Lauri Saretsalo. circ. 450.

001.53 GW
KYBERNETIK JAHRESKATALOG; Datenverarbeitung, Automation, Bildungstechnologie, Grenzgebiete. 1967. a. DM.21.40. Werbegemeinschaft Elwert und Meurer, Hauptstr. 101, 1000 Berlin 62, W. Germany (B.R.D.) Ed. Dagulf D. Mueller. adv.
Supersedes in part: Jahreskatalog Kybernetik, Automation, Informatik (ISSN 0075-2908)

001.6 651.8 JA
KYOTO UNIVERSITY. DATA PROCESSING CENTER. REPORT/KYOTO DAIGAKU OGATA KEISANKI SENTA EIBUN REPOTO. (Text in English) irreg. exchange basis. Kyoto University, Data Processing Center - Kyoto Daigaku Ogata Keisanki Senta, Yoshida Hon-cho, Sakyo-ku, Kyoto-shi 606, Japan.

001.6 US
LECTURE NOTES IN COMPUTER SCIENCE. 1973. irreg., vol. 102, 1981. price varies. Springer-Verlag, 175 Fifth Ave., New York, NY 10010 (Also Berlin, Heidelberg, Vienna) Eds. G. Goos, J. Hartmanis. (reprint service avail. from ISI)

651.8 CS
LORMATIC; informacni bulletin. irreg. price varies. Institute for Application of Computing Technique in Control, Revolucni 24, Prague 1, Czechoslovakia.

651.8 US ISSN 0361-5421
M P, THE MICROPROCESSOR; annual study of the market and applications for the microprocessor and microcomputers by E D N Magazine. a. $400. Cahners Publishing Co., Inc. (Boston), 221 Columbus Ave., Boston, MA 02116. illus.

001.53 US ISSN 0076-2032
MACHINE INTELLIGENCE WORKSHOP. 1967. a. price varies. Halsted Press (Subsidiary of: John Wiley & Sons, Inc.) 605 Third Ave., New York, NY 10016. Eds. D. Michie, B. Meltzer.

MATEMATICHESKIE PROBLEMY GEOFIZIKI. see EARTH SCIENCES — Geophysics

001.6 US
MICRO-DELCON DELAWARE BAY MICROCOMPUTER CONFERENCE. PROCEEDINGS. a. Institute of Electrical and Electronics Engineers, Inc., Computer Society, 5855 Naples Plaza, No. 301, Long Beach, CA 90803.

621.381 US
MODELING AND SIMULATION. 1969. a. $75. Instrument Society of America, 400 Stanwix Street, Pittsburgh, PA 15222.

510.78 621 BL ISSN 0077-0817
MONOGRAPHS IN COMPUTER SCIENCE AND COMPUTER APPLICATIONS. (Text in English) 1969. irreg. free. ‡ Pontificia Universidade Catolica do Rio de Janeiro, Departamento de Informatica, Rua Marques de Sao Vicente 225, ZC-19 Rio de Janeiro, Brazil. Ed. Sueli Mendes dos Santos.

629.8 JA
NAGOYA UNIVERSITY. FACULTY OF ENGINEERING. AUTOMATIC CONTROL LABORATORY. RESEARCH REPORTS/ NAGOYA DAIGAKU KOGAKUBU JIDO SEIGYO. (Text in English since 1969) 1955. a. free. Nagoya University, Faculty of Engineering, Automatic Control Laboratory - Nagoya Daigaku Kogakubu Fuzoku Jido Seigyo, Furo-cho, Chikusa-ku, Nagoya 464, Japan. abstr. charts. circ. controlled. (back issues avail)

001.64 621.381 US ISSN 0095-6880
NATIONAL COMPUTER CONFERENCE AND EXPOSITION. (PROCEEDINGS) (Subseries of: A F I P S Conference Proceedings) a. American Federation of Information Processing Societies, 210 Summit Ave., Montvale, NJ 07645. illus. Key Title: National Computer Conference and Exposition.

NATIONAL INSTITUTE FOR TRANSPORT AND ROAD RESEARCH. USER MANUALS FOR COMPUTER PROGRAMS/NASIONALE INSTITUUT VIR VERVOER- EN PADNAVORSING. GEBRUIKERSHANDBOEKE VIR REKENAARPROGRAMME. see TRANSPORTATION — Roads And Traffic

621.381 001.642 CN
NATIONAL RESEARCH COUNCIL, CANADA. MAN-COMPUTER COMMUNICATIONS CONFERENCE. PROCEEDINGS. (Text in French and English) vol. 4; 1975. irreg. Can.$5. National Research Council of Canada, Montreal Rd., Ottawa, Ont. K1A 0R6, Canada. charts. stat.

NETWORK PLANNING PAPER. see LIBRARY AND INFORMATION SCIENCES

001.6 UR
OBRABOTKA SIMVOL'NOI INFORMATSII. 1973. irreg. 0.47 Rub. Akademiya Nauk S. S. S. R., Vychislitel'nyi Tsentr, Ul. Vavilova, 40, Moscow V-333, U.S.S.R. illus.

510 PL
POLISH ACADEMY OF SCIENCES. INSTITUTE OF COMPUTER SCIENCE. REPORTS. (Text in Polish, English, Russian) 1969. irreg., no. 380, 1977. free. Polska Akademia Nauk, Institute of Computer Science, PKiN, Box 22, 00-901 Warsaw, Poland. Ed. Andrzej Blikle. circ. 450-700. Indexed: Math.R.Ref.Zh.
Formerly: Polska Akademia Nauk. Centrum Obliczeniowe. Prace (ISSN 0079-3175)

629 621 PL ISSN 0434-0760
POLITECHNIKA SLASKA. ZESZYTY NAUKOWE. AUTOMATYKA. (Text in Polish; summaries in English and Russian) 1961. irreg. price varies. Politechnika Slaska, W. Pstrowskiego 7, 44-100 Gliwice, Poland (Dist. by: Ars Polona, Krakowskie Przedmiescie 7, 00-068 Warsaw, Poland) Ed. Anna Skrzywan-Kosek. circ. 270.

001.53 621.38 PL ISSN 0324-9794
POLITECHNIKA WROCLAWSKA. INSTYTUT CYBERNETYKI TECHNICZNEJ. PRACE NAUKOWE. KONFERENCJE. (Text in Polish; summaries in English and Russsian) 1973. irreg., no. 21, 1979. price varies. Politechnika Wroclawska, Wybrzeze Wyspianskiego 27, 50-370 Wroclaw, Poland (Dist. by: Ars Polona-Ruch, Krakowskie Przedmiescie 7, Warsaw, Poland) Ed. Marian Kloza.

621 PL ISSN 0324-9786
POLITECHNIKA WROCLAWSKA. INSTYTUT CYBERNETYKI TECHNICZNEJ. PRACE NAUKOWE. MONOGRAFIE. (Text in Polish; summaries in English and Russian) 1974. irreg., no. 9, 1979. price varies. Politechnika Wroclawska, Wybrzeze Wyspianskiego 27, 50-370 Wroclaw, Poland (Dist. by Ars Polona, Krakowskie Przedmiescie 7, 00-068 Warsaw, Poland) Ed. Marian Kloza. circ. 675.

001.53 621.38 PL ISSN 0324-9808
POLITECHNIKA WROCLAWSKA. INSTYTUT CYBERNETYKI TECHNICZNEJ. PRACE NAUKOWE. STUDIA I MATERIALY. (Text in Polish; summaries in English and Russian) 1972. irreg., no. 28, 1979. price varies. Politechnika Wroclawska, Wybrzeze Wyspianskiego 27, 50-370 Wroclaw, Poland (Dist. by: Ars Polona-Ruch, Krakowskie Przedmiescie 7, Warsaw, Poland) Ed. Marian Kloza.

001.4 PL ISSN 0137-3595
POSTEPY CYBERNETYKI. 1965. q. 30 Zl. per no. (Polskie Towarzystwo Cybernetyczne) Ossolineum, Publishing House of the Polish Academy of Sciences, Rynek 9, Wroclaw, Poland (Dist. by: Ars Polona-Ruch, Krakowskie Przedmiescie 7, Warsaw, Poland) Ed. Robert Staniszewski.
Formerly: Polskie Towarzystwo Cybernetyczne. Biuletyn (ISSN 0079-3655)

363.6 651.8 US ISSN 0079-4430
POWER INDUSTRY COMPUTER APPLICATIONS CONFERENCE. RECORD.* biennial. Institute of Electrical and Electronics Engineers, Inc., 445 Hoes Lane, Piscataway, NJ 08854.

001.64 621.381 US ISSN 0079-5283
PRINCETON UNIVERSITY. COMPUTER SCIENCES LABORATORY. TECHNICAL REPORT. 1960. irreg. ‡ Princeton University, Department of Electrical Engineering, Computer Sciences Laboratory, Princeton, NJ 08540.

001.53 BU
PROBLEMI NA TEKHNICHESKATA KIBERNETIKA. (Text in various languages) 1975. irreg. 2 lv. per issue. (Bulgarska Akademiia na Naukite) Publishing House of the Bulgarian Academy of Sciences, Ul. Akad. G. Bonchev, 1113 Sofia, Bulgaria. circ. 800.

001.64 621.381 US ISSN 0095-1951
PROCEDURES IN COMPUTER SCIENCES. 1972. irreg. Smithsonian Institution, Information Systems Division, Washington, DC 20560.

001.53 US ISSN 0275-8717
PROGRESS IN CYBERNETICS AND SYSTEMS RESEARCH. 1975. irreg., vol. 7, 1981. price varies. Hemisphere Publishing Corporation, 1025 Vermont Ave., N.W., Washington, DC 20005 (Orders to: 19 W. 44th St., New York, Ny 10036) charts. illus. (back issues avail.) Indexed: Curr.Cont.

RANDGEBIEDEN; een interdisciplinaire serie. see LINGUISTICS

001.6 US
ROCKY MOUNTAIN SYMPOSIUM ON MICROCOMPUTERS: SYSTEMS, SOFTWARE, ARCHITECTURE. 1977. irreg., no. 2, 1978. $16 to non-members; members $12. Institute of Electrical and Electronics Engineers, Inc., Computer Society, 5855 Naples Plaza, No. 301, Long Beach, CA 90803.

621.381 SA
S.A. COMPUTER GUIDE. 1979. a. R.55. Thomson Publications S. A. (Pty) Ltd., Box 8308, Johannesburg 2000, South Africa. Ed. Wren Mast-Ingle. adv.

SEMICONDUCTOR TEST SYMPOSIUM. DIGEST OF PAPERS. see ELECTRICITY AND ELECTRICAL ENGINEERING

621.381
SILICON GULCH GAZETTE. 1977. irreg., vol. 4, 1979. free. Computer Faire Inc., 333 Swett Rd., Woodside, CA 94062. Ed. Jim C. Warren Jr. adv. bk. rev. circ. 50,000.

001.6 US
SIMULATION. Represents: International Associations of Science and Technology for Development. Proceedings. 1975. irreg., latest, Montreux, 1977. $50. (International Associations of Science and Technology for Development) Acta Press, Box 2481, Anaheim, CA 92804. Ed. M.H. Hamza.

001.6 SI
SINGAPORE COMPUTER SOCIETY. JOURNAL. 1971. irreg. $2 single issue. ‡ Singapore Computer Society, P.O. Box 2570, Singapore, Singapore. adv. illus. circ. 500.

003 US ISSN 0094-2898
SOUTHEASTERN SYMPOSIUM ON SYSTEM THEORY. PROCEEDINGS. 5th, 1973. a. North Carolina State University, Department of Computer Science, Raleigh, NC 27600. (Co-sponsors: Duke University; University of North Carolina at Chapel Hill; Institute of Electrical and Electronics Engineers Computer Society) Key Title: Proceedings of the Annual Southeastern Symposium on System Theory.

651.8 410   GW   ISSN 0343-5202
SPRACHE UND DATENVERARBEITUNG. (Text in English and German) 1977. 2/yr. DM.58. Max Niemeyer Verlag, Pfrondorfer Str. 4, 7400 Tuebingen, W. Germany (B.R.D.) Eds. Wilfried Lenders, Harald Zimmermann.

629.8 301.2   PL
STUDIA Z AUTOMATYKI. (Text in Polish; summaries in English) 1969. irreg., 1970, vol. 1, no. 2. price varies. (Poznanskie Towarzystwo Przyjaciol Nauk, Komisja Automatyki) Panstwowe Wydawnictwo Naukowe, Ul. Miodowa 10, Warsaw, Poland (Dist. by Ars Polona-Ruch, Krakowskie Przedmiescie 7, Warsaw, Poland) Ed. Tadeusz Puchalka.
  Formerly: Poznanskie Towarzystwo Przyjaciol Nauk. Komisja Automatyki. Prace (ISSN 0079-4589)

621.381   NE
STUDIES IN AUTOMATION AND CONTROL. 1978. irreg., vol. 3, 1980. price varies. Elsevier Scientific Publishing Co., Box 211, 1000 AE Amsterdam, Netherlands.

001.424   US   ISSN 0141-1004
STUDIES IN OPERATIONS RESEARCH. a. price varies. Gordon and Breach Science Publishers, One Park Ave., New York, NY 10016. Ed. A. Ghosal.

001.64   US   ISSN 0094-7474
SUMMER COMPUTER SIMULATION CONFERENCE. PROCEEDINGS; simulation of continuous systems. (Winter Simulation Conference. Proceedings also published annually; sponsoring body and publisher vary) 1970. a. price varies. (Society for Computer Simulation) American Federation of Information Processing Societies, 210 Summit Ave., Montvale, NJ 07645. bk. rev. illus. index; cum index. (back issues avail)

001.6   US
SYMPOSIUM ON COMPUTER APPLICATIONS IN MEDICAL CARE. 1977. a. Institute of Electrical and Electronics Engineers, Inc., Computer Society, 5855 Naples Plaza, Suite 301, Long Beach, CA 90803.

621.3   US
SYMPOSIUM ON COMPUTER ARCHITECTURE. CONFERENCE PROCEEDINGS. 1973? a. Institute of Electrical and Electronics Engineers, Inc., Computer Society, 5855 Naples Plaza, Suite 301, Long Beach, CA 90803. (Co-sponsor: Association for Computing Machinery)

001.6   US
SYMPOSIUM ON MACHINE PROCESSING OF REMOTELY SENSED DATA.(PAPERS) irreg., latest 1979. $25 to non-members; members $18.75. (Purdue University, Laboratory for Applications of Remote Sensing) Institute of Electrical and Electronics Engineers, Inc., Computer Society, 5855 Naples Plaza, No. 301, Long Beach, CA 90803.

SYMPOSIUM ON THE USE OF CYBERNETICS ON THE RAILWAY. see TRANSPORTATION — Railroads

001.6   NE
T R W SERIES OF SOFTWARE TECHNOLOGY. 1978. irreg., vol. 3, 1980. price varies. North-Holland Publishing Co., Box 211, 1000 AE Amsterdam, Netherlands.

621.38 001.6   UR
TECHNINE KIBERNETIKA/TEKHNICHESKAYA KIBERNETIKA. (Text in Russian; summaries in English and Lithuanian) 1974. irreg. price varies. (Akademiya Nauk Litovskoi S.S.R., Institut Fiziko-Tekhnicheskikh Problem Energetiki) Izdatel'stvo Mintis, Lenino Prosp. 3, Vilnius, U.S.S.R. (Subscr. to: Mezhdunarodnaya Kniga, Moscow, G-200, U. S. S. R.) Ed. A. Nemura. circ. 1,500.

621.386   US
TEXAS CONFERENCE ON COMPUTING SYSTEMS. PROCEEDINGS. 1972. a. (University of Texas at Austin) Institute of Electrical and Electronics Engineers, Inc., Computer Society, 5855 Naples Plaza, Suite 301, Long Beach, CA 90803.

001.6 621.381   US
TEXTS AND MONOGRAPHS IN COMPUTER SCIENCE. 1975. irreg. price varies. Springer-Verlag, 175 Fifth Ave., New York, NY 10010 (Also Berlin, Heidelberg, Vienna) Eds. F. L. Bauer, D. Gries.

THEATER COMPUTER USERS GROUP NOTES. see THEATER

629.8   GW
THEORETISCHE UND EXPERIMENTELLE METHODEN DER REGELUNSTECHNIK. irreg., vol. 13, 1977. price varies. Bibliographisches Institut AG, Dudenstr. 6, 6800 Mannheim 41, W. Germany (B.R.D.)

003   US   ISSN 0563-4407
THEORIE DES SYSTEMES. 1968. a. price varies. Gordon and Breach Science Publishers, One Park Ave., New York, NY 10016. Eds. J. Richalet, P. Vidal.

001.64 621.381   US
U S A-JAPAN COMPUTER CONFERENCE. PROCEEDINGS. 2nd, 1975. a. $32. American Federation of Information Processing Societies, 210 Summit Ave., Montvale, NJ 07645. (Co-sponsor: Information Processing Society of Japan)

U. S. NATIONAL CENTER FOR HEALTH STATISTICS. STANDARDIZED MICRO-DATA TAPE TRANSCRIPTS. see SOCIAL SERVICES AND WELFARE

001.64 621.381   CN   ISSN 0316-4683
UNIVERSITY OF ALBERTA. DEPARTMENT OF COMPUTING SCIENCE. TECHNICAL REPORTS. 1965. irreg. Can.$2.50 or on exchange. ‡ University of Alberta, Department of Computing Science, Edmonton, Alta. T6G 2H1, Canada. circ. 60.
  Formerly: Alberta. University, Edmonton. Department of Computing Science. Publication (ISSN 0065-6062)

001.64 621.381   UK
UNIVERSITY OF NEWCASTLE-UPON-TYNE. COMPUTING LABORATORY. TECHNICAL REPORT. irreg. £15($35) University of Newcastle-Upon-Tyne, Computing Laboratory, Claremont Tower, Newcastle-Upon-Tyne NE1 7RU, England. Ed. B. Shaw. bibl. charts.

001.64 621.381   AT   ISSN 0079-886X
UNIVERSITY OF QUEENSLAND. COMPUTER CENTRE. PAPERS. 1968. irreg. price varies. ‡ University of Queensland Press, P.O. Box 42, St. Lucia, Queensland 4067, Australia.

001.64 621.381   AT   ISSN 0082-0547
UNIVERSITY OF SYDNEY. BASSER DEPARTMENT OF COMPUTER SCIENCE. TECHNICAL REPORT. 1957. irreg., no. 127, 1978. free. ‡ University of Sydney, Basser Department of Computer Science, Sydney 2006, N.S.W., Australia. circ. 150.

621.381 001.64   JA   ISSN 0564-8742
UNIVERSITY OF TOKYO. COMPUTER CENTER. REPORT. (Text in English) 1962. a. exchange basis. University of Tokyo, Computer Center - Tokyo Daigaku Ogata Keisanki Senta, 2-11-6 Yayoi, Bunkyo-ku, Tokyo 113, Japan.

001.6   FI   ISSN 0356-004X
VALTION TEKNILLINEN TUTKIMUSKESKUS. A T K-PALVELUTOIMISTO. TIEDONANTO/TECHNICAL RESEARCH CENTRE OF FINLAND. COMPUTING SERVICE. REPORT. (Text mainly in Finnish, some in English or Swedish) 1977. irreg. price varies. Valtion Teknillinen Tutkimuskeskus - Technical Research Centre of Finland, Vuorimiehentie 5, 02150 Espoo 15, Finland.

001   US
VIEWPOINTS (CHICAGO); the journal of data collection. biennial. $10. Marketing Research Association, Inc., 221 N. LaSalle St., Chicago, IL 60601.

629 621.38   UR
VOPROSY TEORII SISTEM AVTOMATICHESKOGO UPRAVLENIYA. 1974. irreg. 1 Rub. Izdatel'stvo Leningradskii Universitet, Universitetskaya nab. 7/9, Leningrad B-164, U.S.S.R.

001.64   US
WILEY SERIES IN COMPUTING. 1972. irreg., unnumbered, latest, 1980. price varies. John Wiley & Sons, Inc., 605 Third Ave., New York, NY 10016. Ed. C. A. Lang.

651.8   US
WORLDWIDE DIRECTORY OF COMPUTER COMPANIES. irreg., 2nd edt., 1973. $44.50. Marquis Academic Media, 200 East Ohio Street, Chicago, IL 60611.
  Formerly: Directory of North American Computer Companies.

YANKEE INGENUITY. see COMMUNICATIONS

COMPUTER TECHNOLOGY AND APPLICATIONS — Abstracting, Bibliographies, Statistics

001.64 016   US   ISSN 0149-1199
A C M GUIDE TO COMPUTING LITERATURE. 1964. a. $50 to non-members; members $25. Association for Computing Machinery, 1133 Ave. of the Americas, New York, NY 10036. Ed. A. R. Blum. circ. 2,500. (back issues avail.)
  Formerly: Bibliography and Subject Index of Current Computing Literature (ISSN 0149-1202)

001.3   US   ISSN 0195-3567
COMPUTER LAW BIBLIOGRAPHY. 1979. a. $18.50. Center for Computer-Law, 3500 S. Figueroa, Suite 211, Los Angeles, CA 90017. Eds. Michael D. Scott, David S. Yen. circ. 1,000.

651.8 016   NE   ISSN 0074-283X
INTERNATIONAL COMPUTER BIBLIOGRAPHY; a guide to books on the use, application and effect of computers in scientific, commercial, industrial and social environments. (Text in English; summaries in English, French and German) 1968. irreg. price varies. Netherlands A D P Research Centre, Stadhouderskade 6, Amsterdam, Netherlands. (Co-sponsor: National Computing Center, England)

629.8 016   FR   ISSN 0474-5868
ORGANIZATION FOR ECONOMIC COOPERATION AND DEVELOPMENT. LIBRARY. SPECIAL ANNOTATED BIBLIOGRAPHY; AUTOMATION. BIBLIOGRAPHIE SPECIALE ANALYTIQUE. (Text in English and French) 1964. irreg. Organization for Economic Cooperation and Development, 2 rue Andre Pascal, 75775 Paris 16, France (U. S. orders to: O.E.C.D. Publications and Information Center, 1750 Pennsylvania Ave., N. W., Washington, D. C. 20006) (also avail. in microfiche)

001.53 001.6   US
U S S R REPORT: CYBERNETICS, COMPUTERS, AND AUTOMATION TECHNOLOGY. 1973. irreg. (approx. 9/yr.) $27. U.S. Joint Publications Research Service, 1000 N. Glebe Rd., Arlington, VA 22201 (Orders to: NTIS, Springfield, VA 22161)
  Formerly: U S S R and Eastern Europe Scientific Abstracts: Cybernetics, Computers, and Automation Technology; Which was formed by the merger of: U S S R Scientific Abstracts: Cybernetics, Computers, and Automation Technology; East European Scientific Abstracts: Cybernetics, Computers, and Automation Technology.

CONSERVATION

see also Environmental Studies; Forests and Forestry; Water Resources

A.C.A. REVIEW. (Anglers Cooperative Association) see FISH AND FISHERIES

333.78   US   ISSN 0065-5708
ALASKA. DEPARTMENT OF FISH AND GAME. ANNUAL REPORT. 1949. a. Department of Fish and Game, Subport Building, Juneau, AK 99801.

CONSERVATION

639 US ISSN 0516-4303
ALASKA. DEPARTMENT OF FISH AND GAME. INFORMATIONAL LEAFLET. no. 170, 1976. irreg. Department of Fish and Game, Subport Bldg., Juneau, AK 99801.

333.7 US ISSN 0084-0130
ALASKA. DEPARTMENT OF FISH AND GAME. WILDLIFE BOOKLET SERIES. irreg. Department of Fish and Game, Subport Building, Juneau, AK 99801.

333.7 US ISSN 0149-6646
ALASKA. DEPARTMENT OF NATURAL RESOURCES. ANNUAL REPORT. a. Department of Natural Resources, Pouch M, Juneau, AK 99811.

ALASKA'S LAND. see *ENVIRONMENTAL STUDIES*

ALBERTA. ENERGY RESOURCES CONSERVATION BOARD. OPERATIONS REPORT. see *ENERGY*

639.9 US ISSN 0065-9150
AMERICAN LITTORAL SOCIETY. SPECIAL PUBLICATIONS. irreg. $1. American Littoral Society, Sandy Hook, Highlands, NJ 07732. (reprint service avail. from UMI)

574 US ISSN 0569-9096
AMERICAN WILDLIFE REGION SERIES. 1957. irreg. price varies. Naturegraph Publishers, Box 1075, Happy Camp, CA 96039. Ed. David L. Moore.

ARID ZONE RESEARCH. see *EARTH SCIENCES*

333.78 US
ASSOCIATION OF MIDWEST FISH AND WILDLIFE COMMISSIONERS. PROCEEDINGS. 1934. a. with membership or attendance at meeting. Association of Midwest Fish and Wildlife Commissioners, Gary Boushelle, Secretary, Dept. of Natural Resources, 408 Kalamazoo Plaza, Lansing, MI 48914.
Formerly: Association of Midwest Fish and Game Commissioners Proceedings (ISSN 0066-9601)

AUSTRALIA. DEPARTMENT OF THE ENVIRONMENT AND CONSERVATION. REPORT. see *ENVIRONMENTAL STUDIES*

333.7 AT ISSN 0587-5846
AUSTRALIAN CONSERVATION FOUNDATION. ANNUAL REPORT. 1968. a. Australian Conservation Foundation, 672B Glenferrie Rd, Hawthorn, Vic. 3122, Australia. illus.

BEARS-THEIR BIOLOGY AND MANAGEMENT. see *BIOLOGY — Zoology*

333.7 GW ISSN 0525-4736
BEITRAEGE ZUR LANDESENTWICKLUNG. 1966. irreg., no. 40, 1980. price varies. (Landschaftsverband Rheinland, Referat Landschaftspflege) Rheinland-Verlag, Kennedy-Ufer 2, 5000 Cologne 21, W. Germany (B.R.D.) (Distr. by: Rudolf Habelt Verlag, Am Buchenhang 1, 5300 Bonn, W. Germany (B.R.D.))

BIRDWATCHER'S YEARBOOK. see *BIOLOGY — Ornithology*

333.7 MX
BOLETIN INFORMATIVO - CEDOCLA. 1972. irreg. Centro Regional Latinoamericano de Estudios para la Conservacion y Restauracion de Bienes Culturales, Antiguo Convento de Churubusco, Mexico, D.F., Mexico. illus.

333.7 BL
BRAZIL. SUPERINTENDENCIA DO DESENVOLVIMENTO DO NORDESTE. DEPARTAMENTO DE RECURSOS NATURAIS. BOLETIM DE RECURSOS NATURAIS. a. Superintendencia do Desenvolvimento do Nordeste, Departamento de Recursos Naturais, Recife, Pernambuco, Brazil. illus. stat.

333.7 CN ISSN 0068-1458
BRITISH COLUMBIA. DEPARTMENT OF RECREATION AND CONSERVATION. ANNUAL REPORT. 1957. a. Department of Recreation and Conservation, Parliament Buildings, Victoria, B.C. V8W 1E6, Canada.

333.7 069 CN ISSN 0380-9854
C C I JOURNAL. (Text in English and French) 1976. a. free. Canadian Conservation Institute, 1030 Innes Rd., Ottawa, Ont. K1A 0M8, Canada. (Affiliate: National Museums of Canada) illus. circ. 8,000. (back issues avail.)

333.7 CN ISSN 0706-4152
C C I TECHNICAL BULLETINS. (Text in English and French) 1975. irreg. free. Canadian Conservation Institute, 1030 Innes Rd., Ottawa, Ont. K1A 0M8, Canada. (Affiliate: National Museums of Canada) bibl. illus. (back issues avail.)

639.9 US ISSN 0095-3601
CAL-NEVA WILDLIFE; TRANSACTIONS. a. (Wildlife Society, Western Section) Cal-Neva Wildlife, c/o Wendell Miller, 4606 San Marino Dr., Davis, CA 95616. Ed. Jim Yoakum. illus. (back issues avail.) Key Title: Cal-Neva Wildlife.

333.7 US
CALIFORNIA. DEPARTMENT OF FISH AND GAME. FISH AND GAME CODE. biennial with alternate supplements. $4.05. Department of Fish and Game, 1416 Ninth St., Sacramento, CA 95814 (Subscr. to: Office of Procurement, Publications Section, Box 1015, North Highlands, CA 95660) Ed. Leslie F. Edgerton. index. circ. 1,550.

333.7 US
CALIFORNIA. DEPARTMENT OF FISH AND GAME. FISH AND GAME CODE. SUPPLEMENT. biennial. Department of Fish and Game, 1416 Ninth St., Sacramento, CA 95814 (Subscr. to: Office of Procurement, Publications Section, Box 1015, North Highlands, CA 95660) Ed. Leslie F. Edgerton. index.

333.91 CN
CANADA. FISHERIES AND ENVIRONMENT CANADA. REPORT OF OPERATIONS UNDER THE CANADA WATER ACT. (Text in English and French) 1973. a. Fisheries and Environment Canada, Ottawa, Ont. K1A 0H3, Canada.

333.78 CN
CANADA. PARKS CANADA. C O R D STUDY TECHNICAL NOTE. Cover title: C O R D Technical Note. 1972. irreg. Parks Canada, Information Division, Ottawa, Ont. K1A 0H4, Hull, P.Q. K1A 1G2.

333.7 CN ISSN 0068-7693
CANADA LAND INVENTORY. REPORT. 1965. irreg. Lands Directorate, 20th Floor P.V.M., Ottawa, Ont. K1A 0E7, Canada. circ. 1,500.

333.7 CN ISSN 0318-2789
CANADIAN CONSERVATION DIRECTORY. irreg. Canadian Nature Federation, 75 Albert St., Suite 203, Ottawa, Ont. K1P 6G1, Canada.

590 CN ISSN 0069-0015
CANADIAN WILDLIFE SERVICE. MONOGRAPH SERIES. 1961. irreg.,no. 5, 1972. price varies. Canadian Wildlife Service, Ottawa, Ont. K1A 0E7, Canada (Dist. by: Dept. of Supply and Services, Ottawa, Ont. K1A 0S6, Canada) Indexed: Biol.Abstr.

639.9 CN
CANADIAN WILDLIFE SERVICE. OCCASIONAL PAPERS. 1966. irreg; no. 29, 1976. free. ‡ Canadian Wildlife Service, Ottawa, Ont. K1A 0E7, Canada. circ. 2,000. Indexed: Key Word Ind.Wildl.Res.

639.9 CN ISSN 0069-0023
CANADIAN WILDLIFE SERVICE. PROGRESS NOTES/SERVICE CANADIEN DE LA FAUNE. CAHIERS DE BIOLOGIE. (Text in English and French) 1967. irreg., no. 69, 1976. free. ‡ Canadian Wildlife Service, Ottawa, Ont. K1A 0E7, Canada. circ. 2,000. Indexed: Key Word Ind.Wildl.Res.

333.7 574 CN ISSN 0069-0031
CANADIAN WILDLIFE SERVICE. REPORT SERIES. 1966. irreg., no. 39, 1976. price varies. ‡ Canadian Wildlife Service, Ottawa, Ont. K1A 0E7, Canada (Dist. by: Dept. of Supply and Services, Ottawa, Ont. K1A 0S6, Canada) circ. 3,000. Indexed: Biol.Abstr. Key Word Ind.Wildl.Res.

333.7 SA
CAPE OF GOOD HOPE. DEPARTMENT OF NATURE CONSERVATION AND MUSEUM SERVICES. ANNUAL REPORT. (Text in Afrikaans and English) 1965. a. free. Department of Nature Conservation, Wale St., Cape Town, South Africa. charts. illus. circ. 2,000. (processed)
Former titles: Cape of Good Hope. Department of Nature Conservation. Annual Report; Cape of Good Hope. Department of Nature Conservation. Newsletter (ISSN 0008-5804)

CARIBBEAN RESEARCH INSTITUTE. REPORT. see *HISTORY — History Of North And South America*

CLOVER LEAFLET. see *FORESTS AND FORESTRY*

340 US
COLORADO. DIVISION OF WILDLIFE. GAME RESEARCH REVIEW. 1964. biennial. $1.50. Division of Wildlife, 6060 Broadway, Denver, CO 80216. Ed. Oliver B. Cope. bibl. charts. illus. circ. 600. Indexed: Biores. Ind. Wild Life Rev.

333.7 US ISSN 0084-8875
COLORADO. DIVISION OF WILDLIFE. SPECIAL REPORT. 1962. irreg., no. 39, 1976. $1. ‡ Division of Wildlife, 6060 Broadway, Denver, CO 80216. Ed. Oliver B. Cope. circ. 600. Indexed: Biol.Abstr. Key Word Ind.Wildl.Res. Wild Life Rev.

333.7 639.9 US ISSN 0084-8883
COLORADO. DIVISION OF WILDLIFE. TECHNICAL PUBLICATION. 1955. irreg., no. 31, 1975. price varies. Division of Wildlife, 6060 Broadway, Denver, CO 80216. Ed. Oliver B. Cope. bibl. charts. illus. stat. circ. 600. Indexed: Biol.Abstr. Wild Life Rev.

639.9 591 US ISSN 0069-6005
COLORADO COOPERATIVE WILDLIFE RESEARCH UNIT. SPECIAL SCIENTIFIC REPORTS. TECHNICAL PAPERS. 1964. irreg. (Division of Wildlife) Colorado State University, Cooperative Wildlife Research Unit, 103 Coop Units Bldg., Fort Collins, CO 80523. (Co-sponsor: U.S. Fish and Wildlife Service)

COMMONS, OPEN SPACES AND FOOTPATHS PRESERVATION SOCIETY. ANNUAL REPORT. see *SPORTS AND GAMES — Outdoor Life*

639.9 AT ISSN 0084-9073
COMMONWEALTH SCIENTIFIC AND INDUSTRIAL RESEARCH ORGANIZATION. DIVISION OF WILDLIFE RESEARCH. TECHNICAL MEMORANDUM. 1969. irreg. C.S.I.R.O., Division of Wildlife Research, Box 84, Lyneham, A.C.T. 2602, Australia.

639.9 AT ISSN 0069-763X
COMMONWEALTH SCIENTIFIC AND INDUSTRIAL RESEARCH ORGANIZATION. DIVISION OF WILDLIFE RESEARCH. TECHNICAL PAPER. 1958. irreg. C. S. I. R. O., Division of Wildlife Research, P.O. Box 84, Lyneham 2602, A.C.T., Australia. index.

333.7 CN
CONSERVATION COUNCIL OF ONTARIO. CONFERENCE PROCEEDINGS. irreg. price varies. Conservation Council of Ontario, 45 Charles St., 6th Floor, Toronto, Ont. M4Y 1S2, Canada.

333.7 CN
CONSERVATION COUNCIL OF ONTARIO. REPORTS. irreg. price varies. Conservation Council of Ontario, 45 Charles St., 6th Floor, Toronto, Ont. M4Y 1S2, Canada.

333.7 US ISSN 0069-911X
CONSERVATION DIRECTORY; a listing of organizations, agencies and officials concerned with natural resource use and management. 1955. a. $6. ‡ National Wildlife Federation, Inc., 1412 16th St. N.W., Washington, DC 20036. Ed. Jeanette Bryant. circ. 10,000. (back issues avail.)

333.7 CN ISSN 0380-4496
CONSERVATION IN ALBERTA. a. free. Energy Resources Conservation Board, 603 Sixth Ave. S.W., Calgary, Alta. T2P 0T4, Canada.

CONSERVATION

333.72   US   ISSN 0094-1670
CONSERVATION IN KANSAS. 1972. a. State Conservation Commission, Topeka, KS 66612. illus. stat.
    Continues: Kansas. State Soil Conservation Committee. Soil Conservation in Kansas (ISSN 0453-2384)

333.75   CN   ISSN 0573-715X
CONSERVATION TOPICS. 1951. irreg. Canadian Forestry Association of British Columbia, Vancouver, B.C., Canada. illus.

COORDINATION DIRECTORY OF STATE AND FEDERAL AGENCY WATER AND LAND RESOURCES OFFICIALS. see *WATER RESOURCES*

333.7   FR
COUNCIL OF EUROPE. EUROPEAN INFORMATION CENTRE FOR NATURE CONSERVATION. DOCUMENTATION SERIES. 1976. irreg. free. Council of Europe, European Information Centre for Nature Conservation, B.P. 431. 67006 Strasbourg Cedex, France. bibl.

CROCODILES. see *BIOLOGY — Zoology*

339.49   UK   ISSN 0070-3001
DAWN SONG AND ALL DAY.* 1949. irreg. 17. sp. World Bird Research Station, Glanton, Northumberland, England.
    Formerly: Dawn Song.

DELAWARE. DEPARTMENT OF NATURAL RESOURCES AND ENVIRONMENTAL CONTROL. ANNUAL REPORT. see *ENVIRONMENTAL STUDIES*

639.9   US   ISSN 0418-7598
DESERT BIGHORN COUNCIL. TRANSACTIONS. 1957. a. $5. Desert Bighorn Council, Death Valley National Monument, Death Valley, CA 92328. Ed. Dr. Charles L. Douglas. cum. index. circ. 300. (back issues avail.)

339.49   US   ISSN 0070-5497
DIRECTORY OF NATURE CENTERS AND RELATED ENVIRONMENTAL EDUCATION FACILITIES. Title varies: Directory of Environmental Education Facilities. 3rd edt., 1971. irreg., approx. triennial. $3. National Audubon Society, Environmental Information and Education Division, 950 Third Ave., New York, NY 10022.
    Formerly: Nature Centers and Outdoor Education Facilities.

DIRECTORY OF WATER POLLUTION RESEARCH LABORATORIES. see *ENVIRONMENTAL STUDIES*

DIRECTORY TO CO-OPERATIVE NATURALISTS' PROJECTS IN ONTARIO. see *BIOLOGY — Ornithology*

333.7   EC
ECUADOR. MINISTERIO DE RECURSOS NATURALES Y ENERGETICOS. INFORME DE LABORES. irreg. Ministerio de Recursos Naturales y Energeticos, Quito, Ecuador. illus.

333.7   ES
EL SALVADOR. MINISTERIO DE AGRICULTURA Y GANADERIA. DIRECCION GENERAL DE RECURSOS NATURALES RENOVABLES. PLAN ANUAL OPERATIVO. a. Direccion General de Recursos Naturales Renovables, Final la Avda. Norte, Santa Tecla, El Salvador.

ENVIRONMENTAL HOTLINE. see *ENVIRONMENTAL STUDIES*

ENVIRONMENTAL LEGISLATIVE BULLETIN. see *ENVIRONMENTAL STUDIES*

639.9   SA   ISSN 0046-3388
FAUNA & FLORA. (Text in Afrikaans and English) 1950. irreg. free. ‡ Nature Conservation Division, Private Bag X209, Pretoria, South Africa. Ed. Dr. S. M. Hirst. illus. circ. 10,000. Indexed: Biol.Abstr. Wild Life Rev. Zoo.Rec.

639.9   FI   ISSN 0015-2447
FINNISH GAME RESEARCH/ RIISTATIETEELLISIA JULKAISUJA. (Text mainly in English) 1948. irreg. free. Finnish Game and Fisheries Research Institute, Game Division, Unioninkatu 45 B, 00170 Helsinki 17, Finland. Ed. Teppo Lampio. circ. 1,200. Indexed: Biol.Abstr. Key Word Ind.Wildl.Res. Wild Life Rev. Zoo.Rec.
    Formerly (1948-1964): Papers on Game Research.

339.49   US   ISSN 0069-9128
FISH AND WILDLIFE FACTS.* irreg. free. U. S. Fish and Wildlife Service, U.S. Dept. of the Interior, Washington, DC 20240.
    Formerly: Conservation Notes.

FISHERIES AND WILDLIFE PAPER. VICTORIA. see *FISH AND FISHERIES*

333.7   US
FOCUS (MOSCOW); on renewable natural resources. a. free. University of Idaho, Forest, Wildlife and Range Experiment Station, Moscow, ID 83843. Ed. Susan R. Hieb.

333.7   UK
GREAT BRITAIN. INSTITUTE OF TERRESTRIAL ECOLOGY. SYMPOSIA. 1965. irreg. price varies. Institute of Terrestrial Ecology, 68 Hills Rd., Cambridge CB2 1LA, England. (also avail. in microfiche)
    Formerly (until no. 7, 1975): Great Britain. Monks Wood Experimental Station. Symposia (ISSN 0077-0426)

333.7   AT
GREEN PAGES: DIRECTORY OF NON-GOVERNMENT ENVIRONMENTAL GROUPS IN AUSTRALIA. 1970. irreg. Aus.$10. Australian Conservation Foundation, 672 B Glenferrie Rd., Hawthorn, Vic. 3122, Australia.
    Formerly: Australian Conservation Foundation. Conservation Directory.

HISTORICAL SOCIETY OF PRINCETON, NEW JERSEY. NEWS & NOTES. see *HISTORY — History Of North And South America*

333.7   634.9   US   ISSN 0073-3369
HORACE M. ALBRIGHT CONSERVATION LECTURESHIP. 1961. a. free. University of California, Berkeley, Department of Forestry and Conservation, 145 Mulford Hall, Berkeley, CA 94720.

333.7   AT   ISSN 0085-1663
HUNTER VALLEY RESEARCH FOUNDATION. MONOGRAPHS. 1959. irreg. price varies. Hunter Valley Research Foundation, Box 23, Tighes Hill, N.S.W. 2297, Australia. Indexed: Aus.Sci.Ind.

333.7   SZ
I U C N ANNUAL REPORT. (Text in English) 1970. a. International Union for Conservation of Nature and Natural Resources, 1110 Morges, Switzerland. Ed. Robert I. Standish. circ. 2,000.
    Formerly (until 1975/1976): I U C N Yearbook (ISSN 0074-9265)

639   US   ISSN 0073-4527
IDAHO. DEPARTMENT OF FISH AND GAME. FEDERAL AID INVESTIGATION PROJECTS. PROGRESS REPORTS AND PUBLICATIONS. a. and irreg. free; limited distribution. Department of Fish and Game, Box 25, Boise, ID 83707. circ. controlled.

333.7   US   ISSN 0073-6872
INDIANA. DIVISION OF FISH AND WILDLIFE. ANNUAL REPORT. 1949. a. free. Division of Fish and Wildlife, 607 State Office Bldg., Indianapolis, IN 46204.

639.9   US   ISSN 0095-1676
INDIANA. DIVISION OF FISH AND WILDLIFE. MANAGEMENT SERIES. 1974. irreg. Division of Fish and Wildlife, 607 State Office Bldg., Indianapolis, IN 46204. illus. Key Title: Management Series (Indianapolis)

INDIANA UNIVERSITY. SCHOOL OF PUBLIC AND ENVIRONMENTAL AFFAIRS. OCCASIONAL PAPERS. see *ENVIRONMENTAL STUDIES*

333.9   RE
INFO-NATURE. 1974. irreg. 20 Fr.CFA. (Societe Reunionnaise pour l'Etude et la Protection de la Nature) Museum d'Histoire Naturelle, B.P. 1012, 5 rue Labourdonnais, 97400 Saint-Denis, Reunion. illus.

333.7   CL   ISSN 0538-0898
INSTITUTO DE INVESTIGACION DE RECURSOS NATURALES. PUBLICACION. no. 7, 1973. irreg. Instituto de Investigacion de Recursos Naturales, Santiago, Chile. bibl. charts. illus.

333.7   639.9   US   ISSN 0161-3332
INTERNATIONAL ASSOCIATION OF FISH AND WILDLIFE AGENCIES. PROCEEDINGS OF THE CONVENTION. 1946. a. International Association of Fish and Wildlife Agencies, 1412 16th St. N.W., Washington, DC 20036. circ. 1,250. (back issues avail.)

INTERNATIONAL ATLANTIC SALMON FOUNDATION. SPECIAL PUBLICATION SERIES. see *FISH AND FISHERIES*

INTERNATIONAL CENTRE OF INSECT PHYSIOLOGY AND ECOLOGY. ANNUAL REPORT. see *BIOLOGY — Genetics*

INTERNATIONAL COMMISSION FOR THE CONSERVATION OF ATLANTIC TUNAS. REPORT. see *BIOLOGY — Zoology*

333.7   SZ   ISSN 0074-9281
INTERNATIONAL UNION FOR CONSERVATION OF NATURE AND NATURAL RESOURCES. PROCEEDINGS AND PAPERS OF THE TECHNICAL MEETING. 1949. triennial; 12th meeting with 11th general assembly, 1972, Banff, Canada. $7.50. International Union for Conservation of Nature and Natural Resources, 1110 Morges, Switzerland (Dist. in the U.S. by: Unipub, Inc., 345 Park Ave. S., New York, NY 10010) Ed. Sir Hugh Elliott.

333.7   SZ   ISSN 0074-929X
INTERNATIONAL UNION FOR CONSERVATION OF NATURE AND NATURAL RESOURCES. PROCEEDINGS OF THE GENERAL ASSEMBLY. 1948. triennial; 11th, Banff, Canada, 1972. International Union for Conservation of Nature and Natural Resources, 1110 Morges, Switzerland. Ed. Sir Hugh Elliott.

639.9   US   ISSN 0090-4856
IOWA WILDLIFE RESEARCH BULLETIN. 1972. irreg., no. 19, 1975. State Conservation Commission, Wildlife Section, 300 4th St., Des Moines, IA 50319.

333.7   II   ISSN 0022-457X
JOURNAL OF SOIL AND WATER CONSERVATION IN INDIA. (Text in English) 1952. a. Rs.12($2) Soil Conservation Society of India, DVC Campus, Hazaribagh, Bihar, India. Ed. K. S. V. Raman. adv. charts. illus. circ. 600. (back issues avail.) Indexed: Biol.Abstr. Chem.Abstr.

500.9   SA   ISSN 0075-6458
KOEDOE; research journal for National Parks in the Republic of South Africa. (Text in English and Afrikaans; summaries in English) 1958. a, latest no. 22, 1979. R.5.30. National Parks Board - Nasionale Parkeraad, P.O. Box 787, Pretoria 0001, South Africa. Eds. G. de Graaff, P. T. van der Walt. cum.index: vols. 1-10 in vol. 11(1968) circ. 1,500. Indexed: Zoo.Rec.

500.9   SA   ISSN 0075-6466
KOEDOE. MONOGRAPHS. 1966. irreg. R.5.20. National Parks Board - Nasionale Parkeraad, P.O. Box 787, Pretoria 0001, South Africa. Eds. G. de Graaff, P. T. van der Walt. circ. 2,000. Indexed: Zoo.Rec.

333.7   SA   ISSN 0075-7780
LAMMERGEYER. 1960. irreg. R.1. Parks, Game & Fish Preservation Board, P.O. Box 662, Pietermaritzburg 3200, South Africa. Ed. D.T. Rowe-Rowe. circ. 700. Indexed: Biol.Abstr. Curr.Cont. Wilf Life Rev. Zoo.Rec.

LUDWIG BOLTZMANN-INSTITUT FUER UMWELTWISSENSCHAFTEN UND NATURSCHUTZ. MITTEILUNGEN. see *ENVIRONMENTAL STUDIES*

MALAWI. DEPARTMENT OF FORESTRY AND GAME. REPORT. see *FORESTS AND FORESTRY*

333.7   US
MAN, HIS COMMUNITY AND NATURAL RESOURCES SERIES. vol. 3, 1976. irreg. Ann Arbor Science Publishers, Inc., Box 1425, Ann Arbor, MI 48106. Ed. Donald Field.

340   639.9   US   ISSN 0196-4690
MARINE MAMMAL PROTECTION ACT OF 1972 ANNUAL REPORT. a. U.S. National Marine Fisheries Service, National Oceanic and Atmospheric Administration, Washington, DC 20235.
     Formerly: Administration of the Marine Mammal Protection Act of 1972 (ISSN 0148-186X)

353.9   US
MARYLAND. DEPARTMENT OF NATURAL RESOURCES. ANNUAL ACTIVITIES REPORT. 1971. a. free. Department of Natural Resources, Tawes State Office Building, 580 Taylor Ave., Annapolis, MD 21401. Ed. S. Murphy. illus. circ. 1,500.

333.78   US   ISSN 0076-4957
MASSACHUSETTS. DIVISION OF FISHERIES AND GAME. ANNUAL REPORT. 1866. a. Division of Fisheries and Wildlife, 100 Cambridge St., Boston, MA 02202.

333.9   US   ISSN 0076-8057
MICHIGAN NATURAL RESOURCES COUNCIL. SCIENTIFIC ADVISORY COMMITTEE. ANNUAL REPORT. 1968. a. $1. Department of Natural Resources, Natural Resources Council, Scientific Advisory Committee, Lansing, MI 48926.

333.7   US   ISSN 0090-8177
MINNESOTA. DEPARTMENT OF NATURAL RESOURCES. BIENNIAL REPORT. 1968. biennial. free. ‡ Department of Natural Resources, 350 Centennial Office Bldg., St. Paul, MN 55155. Ed. Brendan J. Connelly. charts. illus.

353.9   US
MINNESOTA. DEPARTMENT OF NATURAL RESOURCES. PROPOSED PROGRAM BUDGET, DETAILED ESTIMATES. 1973. biennial. ‡ Department of Natural Resources, Centennial Office Bldg., St. Paul, MN 55155. illus.

639.97   US   ISSN 0363-5341
MINNESOTA. DIVISION OF FISH AND WILDLIFE, ENVIRONMENT SECTION. SPECIAL PUBLICATION. irreg. Department of Natural Resources, Division of Fish and Wildlife, St. Paul, MN 55155. illus. Key Title: Special Publication - Minnesota Department of Natural Resources, Division of Fish and Wildlife, Environment Section.

639.9   US
MINNESOTA. DIVISION OF FISH & WILDLIFE. TECHNICAL BULLETIN. 1944. irreg. free. ‡ Department of Natural Resources, Division of Fish & Wildlife, St. Paul, MN 55155.
     Formerly: Minnesota. Division of Game and Fish. Technical Bulletin (ISSN 0076-9134)

333.7   US
MINNESOTA. STATE PLANNING AGENCY. ENVIRONMENTAL PLANNING DIVISION. LAND USE PLANNING REPORT. 1975. irreg. State Planning Agency, Environmental Planning Section, Capitol Square Bldg., 550 Cedar St., St. Paul, MN 55155. charts.

MISSISSIPPI. STATE GAME AND FISH COMMISSION. ANNUAL REPORT TO THE REGULAR SESSION OF THE MISSISSIPPI LEGISLATURE. see *FISH AND FISHERIES*

333.7   US   ISSN 0085-3496
MISSOURI. DEPARTMENT OF CONSERVATION. ANNUAL REPORT. 1937. a. $1. Department of Conservation, Box 180, Jefferson City, MO 65102. Ed. June Hunzeker. circ. 800. (processed)

MOUNTAINEER; to explore, study, preserve and enjoy the natural beauty of Northwest America. see *SPORTS AND GAMES — Outdoor Life*

333   790.13   US
NATIONAL OUTDOOR LIVING DIRECTORY. 1973. irreg (with annual supplements) $2.50. Live Free Inc., Box 743, Harvey, IL 60426. Ed. James Jones. adv. circ. 600.

333.7   UK   ISSN 0077-5916
NATIONAL TRUST FOR SCOTLAND YEARBOOK. 1961. a. membership. ‡ National Trust for Scotland, 5 Charlotte Sq., Edinburgh EH2 4DU, Scotland. circ. 50,000.

NATURAL RESOURCES RESEARCH. see *EARTH SCIENCES*

339.49   FR
NATURE AND ENVIRONMENT SERIES. (Editions in English and French) 1967. irreg. price varies. Council of Europe, European Information Centre for Nature Conservation, Publications Section, 67006 Strasbourg, France (Dist. in U.S. by Manhattan Publishing Co., 225 Lafayette St., New York, N.Y. 10012)
     Formerly: Conservation of Nature and Natural Resources (ISSN 0069-9144)

333.7   614.7   AT   ISSN 0311-0745
NATURE CONSERVATION COUNCIL OF N. S. W. BULLETIN. 1972. irreg. free. Nature Conservation Council of New South Wales, 230 Scenic Rd., Killcare Heights (via Hardy's Bay), NSW 2256, Australia. Ed. Allen A. Strom.

333.7   UK   ISSN 0466-6046
NATURE IN CAMBRIDGESHIRE. vol. 18, 1975. a. 50p. Cambridgeshire & Isle of Ely Naturalists Trust, 1 Brookside, Cambridge CB2 1JF, England. Ed. P. H. Oswald. circ. 2,000. (tabloid format)

333.7   CN
NEW BRUNSWICK. FIELD SERVICES BRANCH. PROVINCIAL PARK STATISTICS. irreg. free. Field Services Branch, Box 1030, Fredericton, N.B. E3B 5C3, Canada. illus.

333.7   US   ISSN 0077-8362
NEW HAMPSHIRE. FISH AND GAME DEPARTMENT. BIENNIAL REPORT. 1865. biennial. free. Fish and Game Department, 34 Bridge St., Concord, NH 03301. circ. 1,000.

333.7   AT   ISSN 0310-6756
NEW SOUTH WALES. NATIONAL PARKS AND WILDLIFE SERVICE. PARKS AND WILDLIFE. 1971. a. Aus.$10. National Parks and Wildlife Service, Adc Building, 189-193 Kent St., Sydney, NSW 2000, Australia.

353.9   US
NEW YORK (STATE). DEPARTMENT OF ENVIRONMENTAL CONSERVATION. ANNUAL REPORT. Cover title: State of New York's Environment. a. Department of Environmental Conservation, 50 Wolf Rd., Albany, NY 12205. illus.

NEW ZEALAND. MINISTRY OF ENERGY. REPORT. see *ENERGY*

333.7   NZ
NEW ZEALAND. SOIL BUREAU. SOIL SURVEY REPORTS. 1973. irreg. price varies. Soil Bureau, Private Bag, Lower Hutt, New Zealand.

712.5   CN   ISSN 0078-0502
NIAGARA PARKS COMMISSION. ANNUAL REPORT. 1886. a. free. Niagara Parks Commission, Niagara Falls, Ont. L2E 6T2, Canada. circ. 500.

333.7   US   ISSN 0078-1355
NORTH AMERICAN WILDLIFE AND NATURAL RESOURCES CONFERENCE. TRANSACTIONS. 1915. a. $12. Wildlife Management Institute, 709 Wire Bldg., Washington, DC 20005. Ed. K. J. Sabol. cum.index. circ. 1,200. (reprint service avail. from ISI)

333.7   US   ISSN 0097-7268
NORTH CAL - NEVA RESOURCE CONSERVATION AND DEVELOPMENT PROJECT. ANNUAL WORK PLAN. a. North Cal-Neva Resource Conservation and Development Project, Box 888, Alturas, CA 96101. illus. Key Title: Annual Work Plan - North Cal-Neva Resource Conservation and Development Project.

339.49   PL   ISSN 0078-3250
OCHRONA PRZYRODY. (Text in Polish; summaries in English and French) 1920. a, price varies. (Polska Akademia Nauk, Zaklad Ochrony Przyrody) Panstwowe Wydawnictwo Naukowe, Ul. Miodowa 10, Warsaw, Poland (Dist by Ars Polona-Ruch, Krakowskie Przedmiescie 7, Warsaw, Poland) Ed. Kazimierz Zarzycki. bibl, charts, illus. Indexed: Biol.Abstr.

333.7   591   US   ISSN 0085-4468
OHIO FISH AND WILDLIFE REPORT. 1971. irreg., no. 6, 1977. free. ‡ Department of Natural Resources, Division of Wildlife, Fountain Square, Bldg. C, Columbus, OH 43224. Ed. Kenneth W. Laub. circ. 1,000. Indexed: Biol.Abstr. Wildlife Rev.
     Supersedes: Ohio Fish Monographs (ISSN 0078-4028) & Ohio Game Monographs (ISSN 0078-4036)

333.9   US   ISSN 0095-442X
OKLAHOMA. CONSERVATION COMMISSION. BIENNIAL REPORT. biennial. contr. free circ. Conservation Commission, 20 State Capital Bldg., Oklahoma City, OK 73105. stat.

OLD-HOUSE JOURNAL CATALOG. see *BUILDING AND CONSTRUCTION*

333.7   CN   ISSN 0381-3924
ONTARIO. MINISTRY OF NATURAL RESOURCES. FOREST RESEARCH REPORT. 1952. irreg. free. Ministry of Natural Resources, Parliament Bldgs., Toronto, Ont., Canada. circ. 800.
     Former titles: Ontario. Division of Forests. Research Library. Research Report (ISSN 0078-4753); Ontario. Department of Lands and Forests. Research Branch. Research Report.

ONTARIO. MINISTRY OF THE ENVIRONMENT. ANNUAL REPORT. see *ENVIRONMENTAL STUDIES*

OPERCULUM. see *BIOLOGY*

333.7   SA
ORANGE FREE STATE. NATURE CONSERVATION DIVISION. ANNUAL REPORT. (Text in Afrikaans and English) 1971. a. free. ‡ Nature Conservation Division, Box 266, Bloemfontein 9300, South Africa. circ. 500.

574   SA
ORANGE FREE STATE. NATURE CONSERVATION DIVISION. MISCELLANEOUS PUBLICATIONS SERIES. (Text in English and Afrikaans) 1970. irreg., latest no. 5. free. ‡ Nature Conservation Division, P.O. Box 517, Bloemfontein 9300, South Africa.

333   PN
PANAMA. DIRECCION GENERAL DE RECURSOS NATURALES RENOVABLES. MEMORIA. irreg. Direccion General de Recursos Naturales Renovables, Ministerio de Desarrollo Agropecuario, Panama, Panama. illus.

333.7   US   ISSN 0079-0621
PENNSYLVANIA STATE UNIVERSITY. INSTITUTE FOR RESEARCH ON LAND AND WATER RESOURCES. INFORMATION REPORTS. 1967. irreg., no. 109, 1979. ‡ Pennsylvania State University, Institute for Research on Land and Water Resources, University Park, PA 16802. Ed. Sophia Tsong.

333.7   US   ISSN 0079-063X
PENNSYLVANIA STATE UNIVERSITY. INSTITUTE FOR RESEARCH ON LAND AND WATER RESOURCES. RESEARCH PUBLICATION. 1964. irreg., no. 101, 1978. ‡ Pennsylvania State University, Institute for Research on Land and Water Resources, University Park, PA 16802. Ed. Sophia Tsong.

PHILIPPINES. BUREAU OF MINES. ANNUAL REPORT. see *MINES AND MINING INDUSTRY*

PHILIPPINES. DEPARTMENT OF NATURAL RESOURCES. ANNUAL REPORT. see *ENVIRONMENTAL STUDIES*

333.7   614.7   PH
PHILIPPINES. DEPARTMENT OF NATURAL RESOURCES. PLANS AND PROGRAMS. 1976. a. Department of Natural Resources, Diliman, Quezon City, Philippines. charts. stat.

631　　　　　　　UN　ISSN 0048-4334
PLANT GENETIC RESOURCES NEWSLETTER.
(Text in English, French, Spanish) 1957. irreg., latest: no. 37, 1979. Food and Agriculture Organization of the United Nations, Crop Ecology and Genetic Resources Unit, Distribution and Sales Section, Via delle Termi di Caracalla, 00100 Rome, Italy. Ed. Erna Bennett. bk. rev. abstr. bibl. charts. illus. circ. 2,000. (processed)
　　Formerly: Plant Introduction Newsletter.

POLAR BEARS. see BIOLOGY — Zoology

719.32　　　　　　US
PUBLICATIONS IN ARCHAELOGY. 1951. irreg. U.S. National Park Service, Interior Bldg., Washington, DC 20240 (Orders to: Supt. Doc., Washington, DC 20402)
　　Formerly: U.S. National Park Service. Archaeological Research Series (ISSN 0083-2308)

333.7　　　　　　CN
QUEBEC (PROVINCE) MINISTERE DES RICHESSES NATURELLES. RAPPORT. English edition: Quebec (Province). Department of Natural Resources. Report. a. Ministere des Richesses Naturelles, Distribution et Documentation, 1620 Bd. l'Entente, Quebec G1S 4N6, Canada. illus. stat.

QUEBEC (PROVINCE) MINISTERE DES TERRES ET FORETS. CONSEIL CONSULTATIF DES RESERVES ECOLOGIQUES. RAPPORT ANNUEL. see FORESTS AND FORESTRY

333.7 574　　　US　ISSN 0079-9211
QUETICO-SUPERIOR WILDERNESS RESEARCH CENTER, ELY, MINNESOTA. ANNUAL REPORT. 1949. a. free. Wilderness Research Foundation, 3100 Prudential Plaza, Chicago, IL 60601. Ed. Clifford E. Ahlgren.

333.7　　　　　　US　ISSN 0079-922X
QUETICO-SUPERIOR WILDERNESS RESEARCH CENTER, ELY, MINNESOTA. TECHNICAL NOTES. 1952. irreg., 1968, no. 5. Wilderness Research Foundation, 3100 Prudential Plaza, Chicago, IL 60601. Ed. Clifford E. Ahlgren.

639.9　　　　　　UK　ISSN 0080-4509
R S P B ANNUAL REPORT AND ACCOUNTS. 1890. a. 75p. ‡ Royal Society for the Protection of Birds, The Lodge, Sandy, Bedfordshire SG19 2DL, England. Ed. Nicholas Hammond. circ. 280,000.

333.7　　　　　　BL
ROESSLERIA. 1977. irreg. Instituto de Pesquisas de Recursos Naturais Renovaveis, Rua Goncalves Dias 570, Porto Alegre 90000, Brazil. illus.

333.7 796.5 799　　US　ISSN 0094-8845
ST. LAWRENCE UNIVERSITY. CONFERENCE ON ECOLOGY OF THE ADIRONDACK PARK (PROCEEDINGS) 1972. a. $3. St. Lawrence University, 123 Vilas Hall, Canton, NY 13617. Ed. Allen P. Splete.

333.7　　　　　　US　ISSN 0085-5898
SAN FRANCISCO BAY CONSERVATION AND DEVELOPMENT COMMISSION. ANNUAL REPORT. 1971. a. free. ‡ San Francisco Bay Conservation and Development Commission, 30 Van Ness Ave., San Francisco, CA 94102. illus.

SASKATCHEWAN. DEPARTMENT OF TOURISM AND RENEWABLE RESOURCES. GAME SURVEYS UNIT. SPRING SURVEY OF SHARP-TAILED GROUSE AND COCK PHEASANT. see BIOLOGY — Zoology

354　　　　　　CN　ISSN 0318-4684
SASKATCHEWAN. DEPARTMENT OF TOURISM AND RENEWABLE RESOURCES. ANNUAL REPORT. 1974. a. Department of Tourism and Renewable Resources, 1825 Lorne St., Regina, Sask. S4P 3V7, Canada. stat.

591　　　　　　CN
SASKATCHEWAN. DEPARTMENT OF TOURISM AND RENEWABLE RESOURCES. GAME SURVEYS UNIT. WINTER MULE DEER SURVEY IN SOUTHWESTERN SASKATCHEWAN. Cover title: Mule Deer Aerial Survey Report. 1969. a. Department of Tourism and Renewable Resources, Game Surveys Unit, Administration Bldg., Regina, Sask. 54S 0B1, Canada. stat. circ. controlled.

SAVONIA. see BIOLOGY

333.7　　　　　　GW
SCHRIFTENREIHE AUS DEN NATURSCHUTZGEBIETEN BAYERNS. 1978. irreg. price varies. (Landesamt fuer Umweltschutz) R. Oldenbourg Verlag GmbH, Rosenheimer Str. 145, 8000 Munich 80, W. Germany (B.R.D.)

333.7　　　　　　GW
SCHRIFTENREIHE NATURSCHUTZ UND LANDSCHAFTSPFLEGE. irreg. price varies. (Landesamt fuer Umweltschutz) R. Oldenbourg Verlag GmbH, Rosenheimer Str. 145, 8000 Munich 80, W. Germany (B.R.D.)

333　　　　　　AT
SCOPE. 1967. irreg. free. Department of Lands, G.P.O. Box 39, Sydney, NSW 2001, Australia. Ed. J. Markey.

333.7　　　　　　UK　ISSN 0080-7850
SCOTLAND. DEPARTMENT OF AGRICULTURE AND FISHERIES. RED DEER COMMISSION. ANNUAL REPORT. 1959. a. price varies. Department of Agriculture and Fisheries, Red Deer Commission, Chesser House, 500 Gorgie Rd., Edinburgh EH1 3DA, Scotland (Avail. from H.M.S.O., 13a Castle St., Edinburgh EH2 3AR, Scotland) illus.

639.9　　　　　　TZ
SERENGETI RESEARCH INSTITUTE. ANNUAL REPORT. 1966. a, latest 1974/76. price varies. Serengeti Research Institute, P.O. Seronera, via Arusha, Arusha, Tanzania. illus. circ. 200.

333.7 917　　　US　ISSN 0080-9519
SIERRA CLUB EXHIBIT FORMAT SERIES. 1960. irreg., 1968, vol. 25. ‡ Sierra Club, 530 Bush St., San Francisco, CA 94108.

333.78　　　　　　UK
SOCIETY FOR THE PROMOTION OF NATURE CONSERVATION. TECHNICAL PUBLICATIONS. 1969. irreg. price varies. Society for the Promotion of Nature Conservation, c/o T.S. Sands (Ass. Sec.), The Green, Nettleham, Lincoln LN2 2NR, England. bk. rev. circ. 80,000.
　　Formerly: Society for the Promotion of Nature Reserves. Technical Publications (ISSN 0081-1513)

333.7　　　　　　SA
SOUTH AFRICA, NATIONAL PARKS BOARD. a. R.2. National Parks Board - Nasionale Parkeraad, Devenish St. Extension, Muckleneuk, Box 787, Pretoria 0001, South Africa. illus. stat.

SPEAK. see SOCIOLOGY

639.9 333.95　　　PL
STUDIA NATURAE. SERIA A. WYDAWNICTWA NAUKOWE. (Text in Polish and English; summaries in English) 1967. irreg. price varies. (Polska Akademia Nauk) Panstwowe Wydawnictwo Naukowe, Miodowa 10, Warsaw, Poland (Dist. by: Ars Polona-Ruch, Krakowskie Przedmiescie 7, Warsaw, Poland)
　　Formerly: Studia Naturae (ISSN 0081-6760)

639.9 333.95　　　PL
STUDIA NATURAE. SERIA B. WYDAWNICTWA POPULARNO-NAUKOWE. (Text in Polish and English; summaries in English) 1952. irreg. price varies. (Polska Akademia Nauk) Panstwowe Wydawnictwo Naukowe, Miodowa 10, Warsaw, Poland (Dist. by: Ars Polona-Ruch, Krakowskie Przedmiescie 7, Warsaw, Poland)
　　Formerly: Studia Naturae (ISSN 0081-6760)

333　　　　　　SW　ISSN 0347-8173
SWEDEN. STATENS NATURVAARDSVERK. NATURVAARDSVERKETS AARSBOK. (Subseries of: Sweden. Statens Naturvaardsverk. Publikationer) a. Kr.43. (National Environment Protection Board) Liber Foerlag, Fack, S-162 89 Vaellingby, Sweden.

639.9　　　　　　US　ISSN 0070-833X
TALL TIMBERS CONFERENCE ON ECOLOGICAL ANIMAL CONTROL BY HABITAT MANAGEMENT. PROCEEDINGS. 1969. irreg. Tallahassee Tall Timbers Research Station, Route 1, Box 160, Tallahassee, FL 32303. Ed. Roy Komarek.

333.7　　　　　　US　ISSN 0082-2787
TENNESSEE VALLEY AUTHORITY. ANNUAL REPORT. 1934. a. free. Tennessee Valley Authority, Knoxville, TN 37902. circ. 300.

333.7　　　　　　US　ISSN 0096-1248
TENNESSEE VALLEY AUTHORITY. DIVISION OF LAND AND FOREST RESOURCES. TECHNICAL NOTE. irreg. Tennessee Valley Authority, Division of Land and Forest Resources, Norris, TN 37828. bibl. stat.

U S-CANADIAN RANGE MANAGEMENT; a selected bibliography on ranges, pastures, wildlife, livestock, and ranching. see BIBLIOGRAPHIES

333.7　　　　　　UG
UGANDA. GAME DEPARTMENT ANNUAL REPORT. 1925. a. EAs.51. Game Department, Box 4, Entebbe, Uganda (Orders to Uganda Government Printer, Box 33, Entebbe, Uganda)

333.7　　　　　　US　ISSN 0092-9433
U.S. ENVIRONMENTAL PROTECTION AGENCY. CLEAN WATER; REPORT TO CONGRESS. a. U.S. Environmental Protection Agency, 401 M St. S.W, Washington, DC 20460. circ. 15,000.

U. S. FISH AND WILDLIFE SERVICE. RESEARCH REPORTS. see FISH AND FISHERIES

U.S. FISH AND WILDLIFE SERVICE. SELECTED LIST OF FEDERAL LAWS AND TREATIES RELATING TO SPORT FISH AND WILDLIFE. see LAW

339.49　　　　　　US　ISSN 0084-0165
U. S. FISH AND WILDLIFE SERVICE. WILDLIFE LEAFLETS.* 1939. irreg. U. S. Fish and Wildlife Service, Washington, DC 20240.

333.7　　　　　　US　ISSN 0361-9737
U.S. NATIONAL PARK SERVICE. PUBLIC USE OF THE NATIONAL PARK SYSTEM; CALENDAR YEAR REPORT. 1972. a. free. National Park Service, Interior Bldg., Washington, DC 20240. circ. 2,000.

333.7　　　　　　US　ISSN 0093-3074
U. S. NATIONAL PARK SERVICE. PUBLIC USE OF THE NATIONAL PARK SYSTEM; FISCAL YEAR REPORT. 1972/73. a. ‡ National Park Service, Interior Bldg., Washington, DC 20240. illus. stat. circ. 2,000. Key Title: Public Use of the National Park System (Washington)

333.7　　　　　　US
U.S. WATER AND POWER RESOURCES SERVICE. ANNUAL REPORT. 1949. a. free. U.S. Water and Power Resources Service, Engineering and Research Center, Box 25007, Denver Federal Center, Denver, CO 80225.
　　Formerly: Federal Reclamation Projects: Water and Land Resource Accomplishments.

333.7　　　　　　US
UNIVERSITY OF IDAHO. COLLEGE OF FORESTRY, WILDLIFE AND RANGE SCIENCES.LIBRARY ADDITIONS. 1975. irreg., vol. 4, 1978. free. University of Idaho, Forest, Wildlife and Range Experiment Station, Moscow, ID 83843. Ed. Susan R. Hieb. circ. 3,000.

333.7　　　　　　US　ISSN 0073-4586
UNIVERSITY OF IDAHO. FOREST, WILDLIFE AND RANGE EXPERIMENT STATION, MOSCOW. STATION BULLETIN. 1965. irreg., 1977, no. 19. free. ‡ University of Idaho, Forest, Wildlife and Range Experiment Station, Moscow, ID 83843. circ. 1,000. Indexed: Biol.Abstr.

333.7　　　　　　US　ISSN 0073-4594
UNIVERSITY OF IDAHO. FOREST, WILDLIFE AND RANGE EXPERIMENT STATION, MOSCOW. STATION NOTE. 1965. irreg., 1977, no. 28. free. ‡ University of Idaho, Forest, Wildlife and Range Experiment Station, Moscow, ID 83843. circ. 1,000. Indexed: Biol.Abstr.

639.9　　　　　　US　ISSN 0360-800X
UTAH. DIVISION OF WILDLIFE RESOURCES. BIENNIAL REPORT. 1893. biennial. Division of Wildlife Resources, 1596 W. North Temple, Salt Lake City, UT 84116. illus. (also avail. in microfiche) Key Title: Biennial Report-State of Utah, Division of Wildlife Resources.
　　Continues: Utah. State Department of Fish and Game. Biennial Report.

333.7 628   GW   ISSN 0300-8665
VEREIN FUER WASSER-, BODEN- UND
LUFTHYGIENE. SCHRIFTENREIHE. irreg. price
varies. Gustav Fischer Verlag, Wollgrasweg 49,
Postfach 720143, 7000 Stuttgart 70, W. Germany
(B.R.D.) Ed. F. Meinck. Indexed: Ind.Med.

339.49   GW
VEREIN ZUM SCHUTZ DER BERGWELT.
JAHRBUCH. 1900. a. DM.27.50. Verein zum
Schutz der Bergwelt e.V., Praterinsel 5, 8000
Munich 22, W. Germany. Ed. Dr. Meister. circ.
4,800.
  Former title: Verein zum Schutze der
Alpenpflanzen und Tiere. Jahrbuch (ISSN 0083-
5625)

VIZGAZDALKODAS ES KORNYEZETVEDELEM.
see WATER RESOURCES

574 333.7   ET   ISSN 0083-7059
WALIA. (Not published in 1973) (Text in English)
1969. a. Eth.$3. ‡ Ethiopian Wildlife and Natural
History Society, P.O. Box 1160, Addis Ababa,
Ethiopia. Ed.Bd. adv. circ. 450.

333.9   US   ISSN 0362-8906
WASHINGTON (STATE). NATURAL AREAS
ADVISORY COMMITTEE. BIENNIAL REPORT.
1974. biennial. Department of Natural Resources,
Olympia, WA 98504. illus. Key Title: Biennial
Report - Natural Areas Advisory Committee.

790   US   ISSN 0090-2497
WASHINGTON (STATE) NATURAL RESOURCES
AND RECREATION AGENCIES. ANNUAL
REPORT. 1971. biennial. free. State Office of
Financial Management, Forecasting and Support
Division, House Office Bldg., Olympia, WA 98504
(Dist. by: State Library, Olympia WA 98504)
  Incorporating: Washington (State) Parks and
Recreation Commission. Annual Report (ISSN
0083-7490)

WEST MIDLAND BIRD REPORT. see
BIOLOGY — Ornithology

333.7   US
WESTERN ASSOCIATION OF FISH AND
WILDLIFE AGENCIES. PROCEEDINGS. 1940.
a. $5.00. Western Association of Fish and Wildlife
Agencies, c/o Robert L. Salter, Box 25, 600 S.
Walnut St., Boise, ID 83707. cum.index 1940-1969.
circ. 500. (processed)
  Formerly: Western Association of State Game
and Fish Commissioners. Proceedings (ISSN 0085-
8102)

333.7 614.7   AT
WESTERN AUSTRALIA. CONSERVATION AND
ENVIRONMENT COUNCIL. ANNUAL
REPORT. 1972. a. free. ‡ Department of
Conservation and Environment, 1 Mount St., Perth,
W.A. 6000, Australia.
  Formerly: Western Australia. Environmental
Protection Council. Annual Report.

WESTERN AUSTRALIA. DEPARTMENT OF
FISHERIES & WILDLIFE. REPORT. see FISH
AND FISHERIES

639.9   AT
WESTERN AUSTRALIA. DEPARTMENT OF
FISHERIES AND WILDLIFE. WILDLIFE
RESEARCH BULLETIN. 1956. irreg. not for sale;
free to government and conservation agencies.
Department of Fisheries and Wildlife, 108 Adelaide
Terrace, Perth, W.A. 6000, Australia. circ. 1,000.

333.7   US   ISSN 0083-8934
WESTERN LANDS AND WATERS SERIES. 1959.
irreg. price varies. Arthur H. Clark Co., 1264 S.
Central Ave., Glendale, CA 91204. index.

333.7 591   NZ   ISSN 0110-604X
WILDLIFE - A REVIEW. 1970. a. free. Department
of Internal Affairs, Wildlife Service, Wellington,
New Zealand. Ed. P. Morrison. charts, illus. index.
circ. 2,000. (processed) Indexed: Biol.Abstr.

333.7 799   US   ISSN 0084-0173
WILDLIFE MONOGRAPHS. 1958. irreg., no. 70,
1979. included with subscr. to Journal of Wildlife
Management. Wildlife Society, 7101 Wisconsin
Ave., N.W., Suite 611, Washington, DC 20014. Ed.
Louis A. Krumholz. (reprint service avail. from
UMI)

333.7   AT
WILDLIFE PRESERVATION SOCIETY OF
QUEENSLAND. NEWSLETTER. 1968. irreg.
Aus.$0.25 each. Wildlife Preservation Society of
Queensland, G.P.O. Box 2030, Brisbane, Qld 4001,
Australia.

333.7   US   ISSN 0084-0564
WISCONSIN. DEPARTMENT OF NATURAL
RESOURCES. TECHNICAL BULLETIN. 1950.
irreg. free. Department of Natural Resources, Box
7721, Madison, WI 53707. Ed. Ruth L. Hine. circ.
1,500. Indexed: Biol.Abstr. Ocean.Abstr.
Pollut.Abstr. Key Title: Technical Bulletin -
Department of Natural Resources (Madison)

WORLD DIRECTORY OF ENVIRONMENTAL
ORGANIZATIONS. see ENVIRONMENTAL
STUDIES

354.689   ZA   ISSN 0084-4586
ZAMBIA. COMMISSION FOR THE
PRESERVATION OF NATURAL AND
HISTORICAL MONUMENTS AND RELICS.
ANNUAL REPORT. 1948. a. 25 n. ‡ Commission
for the Preservation of Natural and Historical
Monuments and Relics, P. O. Box 124, Livingstone,
Zambia.

333.7   ZA
ZAMBIA. NATURAL RESOURCES
DEPARTMENT. ANNUAL REPORT. (Not
published 1973-1975) 1964. a. 30 n. Government
Printer, P.O. Box 136, Lusaka, Zambia.
  Former titles: Zambia. Natural Resources
Advisory Board. Annual Report; Zambia. Office of
the Conservateur of Natural Resources. Annual
Report; Zambia. Natural Resources Board. Annual
Report (ISSN 0084-4993)

333.7   RH
ZIMBABWE. MINISTRY OF LANDS AND
NATURAL RESOURCES. REPORT OF THE
SECRETARY FOR LANDS AND NATURAL
RESOURCES. (Subseries of: Rhodesia. Parliament.
C.S.R.) 1968. a. Rhod.$1.05. ‡ Government Printer,
Box 8062, Causeway, Zimbabwe. stat. circ. 400.
  Supersedes in part: Rhodesia. Ministry of Mines
and Lands. Report of the Secretary for Mines and
Lands.

CONSERVATION — Abstracting, Bibliographies, Statistics

333.7 016   CL
BIBLIOGRAFIA DE RECURSOS NATURALES.
1965. irreg. Instituto de Investigacion de Recursos
Naturales, Santiago, Chile.

333.7 016   UK   ISSN 0460-1408
LAND RESOURCE BIBLIOGRAPHY. 1968. irreg.
Ministry of Overseas Development, Land Resources
Division, Tolworth Tower, Surbiton, Surrey KT6
7DY, England.

333.7 016   CN
QUEBEC (PROVINCE) MINISTERE DES
RICHESSES NATURELLES. REPERTOIRE DES
PUBLICATIONS. (Text in French) irreg. free.
Ministere des Richesses Naturelles, Distribution et
Documentation, 1620 Bd. l'Entente, Quebec G1S
4N6, Canada. bibl.

CONSUMER EDUCATION AND PROTECTION

640.73   US   ISSN 0275-1356
AMERICAN COUNCIL ON CONSUMER
INTERESTS. PROCEEDINGS OF THE
ANNUAL CONFERENCE. 1955. a. price varies.
American Council on Consumer Interests, c/o Mel
Zelenak, Exec.Dir., 162 Stanley Hall, University of
Missouri, Columbia, MO 65201.

640.73   FR   ISSN 0220-5424
BULLETIN DES CONSOMMATEURS. irreg. Union
des Consommateurs, 74 rue Alexandre Guilmant,
92190 Meudon, France.

640.73   BB
CARIBBEAN NEWSLETTER. 1975. a. Caribbean
Consumers Documentation Centre, Gibson House,
Spry Street, St. Michael, Barbados, W. I. Ed.
Doreen Devonish. (processed)

640   US   ISSN 0084-8654
CENTER FOR CONSUMER EDUCATION
SERVICES. MONOGRAPHS. 1972. irreg. $1.
Department of Education, Division of Vocational
Education, Center for Consumer Education
Services, Building 871, Plainfield Ave., Edison, NJ
08817.

CONSUMER BULLETIN/BULLETIN AUX
CONSOMMATEURS. see
TRANSPORTATION — Automobiles

640.73   US   ISSN 0193-9297
CONSUMER COMPLAINT CONTACT SYSTEM,
ANNUAL REPORT. 1978. a. U.S. Consumer
Product Safety Commission, Directorate for
Communications, Washington, DC 20207.

640.73   US
CONSUMER GUIDE: BEST BUYS & DISCOUNT
PRICES. a. $3.50. Consumer Guide Magazine, 3841
W. Oakton, Skokie, IL 60076.
  Formerly: Consumer Guide: Consumer Buying
Guide.

640.73   US
CONSUMER PROTECTION DIRECTORY. 1973.
irreg., 2nd edt., 1975. $44.50. Marquis Academic
Media (Subsidiary of: Marquis Who's Who, Inc.)
200 E. Ohio St., Chicago, IL 60611.
  Supersedes in part: Directory of Consumer
Protection and Environmental Agencies.

640.73   US
CONSUMER SOURCEBOOK. 1974. irreg; 1977, 2nd
edt. $58. Gale Research Company, Book Tower,
Detroit, MI 48226. Eds. Paul Wasserman, Jean
Morgan.

640.73   AT
CONSUMERS AFFAIRS COUNCIL OF
TASMANIA. ANNUAL REPORT. 1971. a. free.
Consumers Affairs Council of Tasmania, Box
1320N, Hobart, Tas., Australia. charts. stat. circ.
750. (back issues avail.)
  Formerly: Consumers Protection Council of
Tasmania. Annual Report.

640.73   US
CONSUMERS DIGEST GUIDE TO DISCOUNT
BUYING. Title varies: Guide to Discount Buying.
Discount Buying Guide. a. $4.95. Consumers
Digest, Inc., 5705 N. Lincoln Ave., Chicago, IL
60659.

641   NE   ISSN 0069-9284
CONSUMERS DIRECTORY. (Text in English) 1960.
biennial. fl.50. International Organization of
Consumers Unions, Emmastraat 9, 2595 EG The
Hague, Netherlands. circ. 1,200.

640.73   US
CONTACTS IN CONSUMERISM. 3rd ed., 1980/81.
a. $25. Fraser Associates, 1800 K St., N.W. Suite
1006, Washington, DC 20006. Ed. Ann P. Harvey.

381   US   ISSN 0094-8853
COUNCIL OF BETTER BUSINESS BUREAUS.
ANNUAL REPORT. 1972. a. Council of Better
Business Bureaus, 1150 17th St. N.W., Washington,
DC 20036. circ. 5,000(controlled)

640.73   US
DISCLOSURE. 1974. 9/yr. $10. National Training
and Information Center, 1123 W. Washington Blvd.,
Chicago, IL 60607. Ed. Ted Wysocki. charts. stat.
circ. 5,000. (tabloid format; back issues avail.)

640.73   US   ISSN 0363-2083
E M COMPLAINT DIRECTORY FOR
CONSUMERS. 1970. a. $2.50. Credit Union
National Association, Box 431-B, Madison, WI
53701. Ed. S. Stark.

640.73   US
FACTORY OUTLET SHOPPING GUIDE FOR
NEW ENGLAND. 1973. a. $3.95. Factory Outlet
Shopping Guide Publications, Box 239, Oradell, NJ
07649. Ed. Jean D. Bird. adv. bk. rev. circ. 25,000.

640.73　　　US　ISSN 0146-1125
FACTORY OUTLET SHOPPING GUIDE FOR
NEW JERSEY AND ROCKLAND COUNTY.
1971. a. $3.95. Factory Outlet Shopping Guide
Publications, Box 239, Oradell, NJ 07649. Ed. Jean
D. Bird. adv. bk. rev. circ. 40,000.

640.73　　　US　ISSN 0146-2865
FACTORY OUTLET SHOPPING GUIDE FOR
NEW YORK, LONG ISLAND, WESTCHESTER.
1972. a. $3.95. Factory Outlet Shopping Guide
Publications, Box 239, Oradell, NJ 07649. Ed. Jean
D. Bird. adv. bk. rev. circ. 40,000.

640.73　　　US　ISSN 0146-2881
FACTORY OUTLET SHOPPING GUIDE FOR
NORTH AND SOUTH CAROLINA. 1977. a.
$3.95. Factory Outlet Shopping Guide Publications,
Box 239, Oradell, NJ 07649. Ed. Jean D. Bird.

640.73　　　US　ISSN 0146-2903
FACTORY OUTLET SHOPPING GUIDE FOR
PENNSYLVANIA. 1973. a. $3.95. Factory Outlet
Shopping Guide Publications, Box 239, Oradell, NJ
07649. Ed. Jean D. Bird. adv. bk. rev. circ. 35,000.
Formerly: Factory Outlet Shopping Guide for
Eastern Pennsylvania.

640.73　　　US　ISSN 0146-2873
FACTORY OUTLET SHOPPING GUIDE FOR
WASHINGTON D.C., MARYLAND,
DELAWARE, VIRGINIA. 1975. a. $3.95. Factory
Outlet Shopping Guide Publications, Box 239,
Oradell, NJ 07649. Ed. Jean D. Bird. adv. bk. rev.
circ. 20,000.

640.73　　　US　ISSN 0363-9185
HELP (WASHINGTON); the useful almanac. 1977.
irreg. $4.95. Consumer News, Inc., 813 National
Press Bldg., Washington, DC 20009.

640　　　NE　ISSN 0538-8988
INTERNATIONAL ORGANIZATION OF
CONSUMERS UNIONS. PROCEEDINGS. (Each
proceeding has a distinctive title) 1960. irreg., 9th,
1978, London. fl.25. International Organization of
Consumers Unions, Emmastraat 9, 2595 EG The
Hague, Netherlands. Ed. Bd. bibl.

640.73　　　US　ISSN 0095-5590
NEW YORK (STATE) CONSUMER PROTECTION
BOARD. ANNUAL REPORT. a. Consumer
Protection Board, Albany, NY 12207. illus. Key
Title: Annual Report - State Consumer Protection
Board.

640.73　　　UK　ISSN 0144-4379
PAPER BAG. 1979. a. National Federation of
Consumer Groups, 70 Alcester Rd. S., Birmingham
B14 7PT, England.

640.73　　　US
PUBLIC CITIZEN PLATFORM. Box 19404,
Washington, DC 20036.

640.73　　　CN
QUEBEC (PROVINCE) OFFICE DE LA
PROTECTION DU CONSOMMATEUR.
RAPPORT D'ACTIVITES. 1972. a. free. Office de
la Protection du Consommateur, 800 Carré
d'Youville, Quebec G1R 4Y5, Canada. circ. 700.

381　　　US　ISSN 0092-8003
S.O.S. DIRECTORY. (Save on Shopping, Shop Outlet
Stores) 1972. a. $6.95. Save on Shopping Directory,
Box 10482, Jacksonville, FL 32207. Ed. Iris Ellis.
circ. 150,000.

640.73　　　US　ISSN 0190-2210
STATE CONSUMER ACTION. a. $1.05. U.S. Office
of Consumer Affairs, Washington, DC 20201
(Orders to: Supt. Doc., Washington, DC 20402)

640　　　SW　ISSN 0082-0121
SWEDEN. STATENS INSTITUT FOER
KONSUMENTFRAAGOR. MEDDELAR.* 1957.
irreg. price varies. Statens Institut foer
Konsumentfraagor - National Consumer Institute,
Raalambsvaegen 8, 112 59 Stockholm, Sweden.

640.73　　　CN
TRUFAX DIRECTORY & CONSUMER GUIDE.
1979. a. Better Business Publishing Ltd., 321 Bloor
St. E., Suite 901, Toronto, Ont. M4W 3K6, Canada.
Ed. Gail Muir. adv.

640　　　US　ISSN 0069-9276
U.S. NATIONAL BUREAU OF STANDARDS.
CONSUMER INFORMATION SERIES. irreg.
price varies. U. S. National Bureau of Standards,
U.S. Dept. of Commerce, Washington, DC 20234
(Orders to: Supt. of Documents, Washington, DC
20402)

352　　　US　ISSN 0190-2962
U. S. OFFICE OF CONSUMER AFFAIRS.
DIRECTORY: FEDERAL, STATE, AND LOCAL
GOVERNMENT CONSUMER OFFICES. 1973. a.
$0.95. U.S. Office of Consumer Affairs, 621
Reporters Bldg., Washington, DC 20201 (Orders to:
Supt. of Documents, Washington, DC 20402) Ed.
Betty Bay. Key Title: Directory, Federal, State and
Local Government Consumer Offices.
Formerly: U. S. Office of Consumer Affairs.
Directory: Federal, State, County, and City
Government Consumer Offices (ISSN 0190-2954)

CONSUMER EDUCATION AND PROTECTION — Abstracting, Bibliographies, Statistics

640.73　016　　US　ISSN 0094-0534
CONSUMERS INDEX TO PRODUCT
EVALUATIONS AND INFORMATION
SOURCES. 1973. q. with annual cum. $59.50.
Pierian Press, 5000 Washetnaw Ave., Ann Arbor,
MI 48104. Ed. Linda Mark. adv. bk. rev.

COOPERATIVES

see Business and Economics—Cooperatives

CRIMINOLOGY AND LAW ENFORCEMENT

see also Education—Special Education and
Rehabilitation; Medical Sciences—
Forensic Sciences

353.9　　　US　ISSN 0362-7284
ALASKA. CRIMINAL INVESTIGATION BUREAU.
ANNUAL REPORT. a. Criminal Investigation
Bureau, Box 6188, Anchorage, AK 99502. Key
Title: Annual Report - Criminal Investigation
Bureau.

353.9　　　US　ISSN 0095-3415
ALASKA. VIOLENT CRIMES COMPENSATION
BOARD. ANNUAL REPORT. 1973. a. Violent
Crimes Compensation Board, Pouch N, Juneau, AK
99811. illus. Key Title: Annual Report - State of
Alaska. Violent Crimes Compensation Board.

364　　　II　ISSN 0065-6283
ALL INDIA CRIME PREVENTION SOCIETY.
ANNUAL REPORT AND AUDITED
STATEMENT OF ACCOUNTS. 1962. a. free. All
India Crime Prevention Society, Pragati Ashram,
Balaganj, Lucknow, India. Ed. Paripurnanand
Varma. bk. rev.

364　　　US　ISSN 0065-7948
AMERICAN CORRECTIONAL ASSOCIATION.
ANNUAL CONGRESS OF CORRECTION.
PROCEEDINGS. 1870. a. $14 for 1980
Proceedings. American Correctional Association,
4321 Hartwick Rd., L208, College Park, MD 20740.
circ. 800. (also avail. in microfiche)

364　　　US　ISSN 0002-8126
AMERICAN CRIMINOLOGIST. 1953. irreg.
membership. ‡ American Association of
Criminology, Box 1115, North Marshfield, MA
02059. Ed. Wayne A. Forester. bk. rev. circ. 2,500.
(looseleaf format)
Former titles: American Criminologist's
Newsletter; Registered Criminologist's Newsletter.

365　　　US　ISSN 0066-0051
AMERICAN SERIES OF FOREIGN PENAL
CODES. 1960. irreg., no. 21, 1977. price varies.
New York University, Criminal Law Education and
Research Center, 40 Washington Square So., Room
434, New York, NY 10012 (Dist. by Fred B.
Rothman, 57 Leuning St., S. Hackensack, N.J.
07606) Ed. John Delaney.

340　　　US
ANNUAL CRIMINAL JUSTICE PLAN FOR
ILLINOIS. 1969. a. Law Enforcement Commission,
120 S. Riverside Plaza, Chicago, IL 60606.

364　　　PL　ISSN 0066-6890
ARCHIWUM KRYMINOLOGII. (Text in Polish;
summaries in English) 1960. irreg., 1976, vol. 7. 80
Zl. per volume. (Polska Akademia Nauk, Instytut
Nauk Prawnych) Ossolineum, Publishing House of
the Polish Academy of Sciences, Rynek 9, Wroclaw,
Poland. Ed. Stanislaw Batawia.

353.979　364　　US　ISSN 0066-7382
ARIZONA. DEPARTMENT OF PUBLIC SAFETY.
ANNUAL REPORT. 1969. a. free. ‡ Department
of Public Safety, P.O. Box 6638, Phoenix, AZ
85005. illus. stat.
Incorporating: Arizona. Department of Public
Safety. Statistical Reviews (ISSN 0066-7390)

364　　　AT
AUSTRALIAN CRIME PREVENTION COUNCIL.
NATIONAL CONFERENCE. PROCEEDINGS.
1960. biennial. price varies. Australian Crime
Prevention Council, No. 1 Carmel Court, Rio Vista,
Qld. 4217, Australia.

364.4　　　AT
AUSTRALIAN CRIME PREVENTION COUNCIL.
NATIONAL NEWSLETTER. irreg. Australian
Crime Prevention Council, No. 1 Carmel Court, Rio
Vista, Qld. 4217, Australia. Ed. J. H. Purcell.

345.73　　　US　ISSN 0098-8049
B A R-B R I BAR REVIEW. CRIMINAL LAW. a. B
A R-B R I Bar Review, 11801 W. Olympic Blvd.,
Los Angeles, CA 90064. Key Title: Criminal Law.

346　　　US　ISSN 0098-7611
B A R-B R I BAR REVIEW. TORTS. a. B A R-B R I
Bar Review, 11801 W. Olympic Blvd., Los Angeles,
CA 90064. Key Title: Torts.

364　　　SZ
BEITRAEGE ZUR EMPIRISCHEN
KRIMINOLOGIE. 1976. irreg. Verlag Peter Lang
AG, Muenzgraben 2, Postfach, CH-3000 Berne 7,
Switzerland.

365　　　GW　ISSN 0067-5237
BEITRAEGE ZUR
STRAFVOLLZUGSWISSENSCHAFT. 1967. irreg.,
no. 15, 1976. price varies. C. F. Mueller Juristischer
Verlag GmbH, Im Weiher 10, Postfach 102640,
6900 Heidelberg 1, W. Germany (B.R.D.) Eds. Th.
Wuertenberger, H. Mueller-Dietz.

364　　　SZ　ISSN 0067-6144
BERNER KRIMINOLOGISCHE
UNTERSUCHUNGEN. 1962. irreg., 1973, vol. 8.
price varies. Paul Haupt AG, Falkenplatz 14, CH-
3001 Berne, Switzerland.

351.74　　　BS　ISSN 0068-046X
BOTSWANA. COMMISSIONER OF THE POLICE.
ANNUAL REPORT. a. R.1. Commissioner of the
Police, Gaborone, Botswana.

364　　　VE
C E N I P E C REVISTA. 1976. a. Universidad de los
Andes, Centro de Investigaciones Penales y
Criminologicas, Calle 23, Edif. Canizales Aapto. 3
Piso 2, Merida, Venezuela (Subscr. to: Av. Andes,
Via la Parroqquia, Merida, Venezuela) Ed. Hector
Febres Cordero. bk. rev.

364　　　US　ISSN 0093-8912
CALIFORNIA. COUNCIL ON CRIMINAL
JUSTICE. COMPREHENSIVE PLAN FOR
CRIMINAL JUSTICE. a. Office of Criminal Justice
Planning, 7171 Bowling Drive, Sacramento, CA
95823. illus. stat. Key Title: Comprehensive Plan
for Criminal Justice (Sacramento)

CRIMINOLOGY AND LAW ENFORCEMENT

364   UK
CAMBRIDGE UNIVERSITY. INSTITUTE OF CRIMINOLOGY. OCCASIONAL PAPERS. 1974. irreg., no. 6, 1980. price varies. Cambridge University, Institute of Criminology, Cambridge CB3 9DT, England.

354.71   CN   ISSN 0383-4379
CANADA. CORRECTIONAL INVESTIGATOR. ANNUAL REPORT. (Text in English and French) 1974. a. Correctional Investigator, Box 950, Sta. B, Ottawa, Ont. K1P 5R1, Canada. illus. circ. 2,500.

364   CN   ISSN 0068-9777
CANADIAN STUDIES IN CRIMINOLOGY. 1971. irreg. (University of Toronto, Centre of Criminology) University of Toronto Press, Front Campus, Toronto, Ont. M5S 1A6, Canada. Ed. J. Edwards. (also avail. in microfiche)

362.8
CAPITAL PUNISHMENT. (Subseries of: National Prisoner Statistics) 1971. a. free. U.S. Department of Justice, Bureau of Justice Statistics, 633 Indiana Ave., N.W., Washington, DC 20531 (Orders to: Box 6000, Rockville, MD 20850) circ. 12,000.

364   343   VE
CAPITULO CRIMINOLOGICO. 1973. a. Bs.15. Universidad del Zulia, Facultad de Derecho, Maracaibo, Venezuela.

364   US
CARNAHAN CONFERENCE ON ELECTRONIC CRIME COUNTERMEASURES. PROCEEDINGS. a. University of Kentucky, College of Engineering, Office of Research and Engineering Services, Lexington, KY 40506. (back issues avail.)

363.2   US   ISSN 0091-8806
CINCINNATI. DIVISION OF POLICE. ANNUAL REPORT. At head of title, 1971-: Police Statistics of Cincinnati. a. $4. Division of Police, Dept. of Safety, Records Section, Cincinnati, OH 45200. stat. Key Title: Annual Report of the Division of Police (Cincinnati)

364   US   ISSN 0090-2756
CONNECTICUT. DEPARTMENT OF CORRECTION. PUBLICATIONS. 1970. irreg. Department of Corrections, Research Section, 340 Capitol Ave., Hartford, CT 06115. Ed. James Harris. stat. circ. 200 (controlled) (processed)

364.36   US
CRIME AND DELINQUENCY IN CALIFORNIA. 1965. a. free. Department of Justice, Bureau of Criminal Statistics and Special Services, P.O. Box 13427, Sacramento, CA 95813.
    Formerly: California. Bureau of Criminal Statistics. Crime and Delinquency. Incorporating: Adult Criminal Detention Reference Tables (ISSN 0092-2080); Adult Probation Program Report, which was formerly called Adult Probation Reference Report; Adult Prosecution; Crimes and Arrests; Juvenile Probation; Reference Tables Adult and Juvenile Probation (ISSN 0094-7717)

364   US
CRIME AND DELINQUENCY TOPICS, MONOGRAPH SERIES. irreg. U. S. National Institute of Mental Health, Center for Studies of Crime and Delinquency, 5600 Fishers Lane, Rockville, MD 20852 (Orders to: Supt. of Documents, Washington, DC 20402)
    Formerly: Crime and Delinquency Issues, Monographic Series (ISSN 0070-1505)

365   US
CRIME AND JUSTICE. 1972. irreg. price varies. A M S Press, Inc., 56 E. 13th St., New York, NY 10003. Ed. Jackwell Susman. bibl. charts. stat. cum.index 1970-1972.

364   US   ISSN 0146-5759
CRIME IN VIRGINIA. a. Department of State Police, Uniform Crime Reporting Section, 7700 Midlothian Turnpike, U.S. Route 60, Richmond, VA 23211.

364   UK   ISSN 0070-1521
CRIMINAL APPEAL REPORTS. 1908. irreg. £30. Sweet & Maxwell Stevens Journals, 11 New Fetter Lane, London, EC4, England (Dist. in U. S. & Canada by: Carswell Co. Ltd., 233 Midland Ave., Agincourt, Ont., Canada) Ed. Percy Metcalfe.

364   US   ISSN 0362-8353
CRIMINAL JUSTICE PLAN (RICHMOND) 1969. irreg. Division of Justice and Crime Prevention, 8501 Mayland Dr., Richmond, VA 23229. Ed. Martin B. Matt. circ. 2,500.

364   US   ISSN 0092-4652
CRIMINAL JUSTICE PLAN FOR NEW JERSEY. 1972. a. free. State Law Enforcement Planning Agency, 3535 Quaker Bridge Rd., Trenton, NJ 08625. illus.
    Continues: New Jersey Plan for Criminal Justice.

362.8   US   ISSN 0095-5833
CRIMINAL VICTIMIZATION IN THE UNITED STATES. (Subseries of: National Crime Panel Survey Report) 1973. a. free. U.S. Department of Justice, Bureau of Justice Statistics, 633 Indiana Ave. N.W., Washington, DC 20531 (Orders to: Box 6000, Rockville, MD 20850) circ. 12,000.

364   342   FR
CRIMINOLOGY, CRIMINAL LAW, PENOLOGY. (Part of these studies Are reports presented to the European conferences of directors of criminological research institutes) 1960. a. price varies. Council of Europe, European Committee on Crime Problems, Publications Section, Strasbourg, France (Dist. in U.S. by Manhattan Publishing Co., 225 Lafayette St., New York, N.Y. 10012) adv. bk. rev.
    Formerly: Collected Studies in Criminological Research (ISSN 0069-5300)

364   US
CRIMINOLOGY REVIEW YEARBOOK. 1979. a. $32.50. Sage Publications, Inc., 275 S. Beverly Dr., Beverly Hills, CA 90212 (And Sage Publications, Ltd., 28 Banner St., London EC1Y 8QE, England) Ed.Bd.

364   UK
CROPWOOD ROUND-TABLE CONFERENCE PAPERS. 1968. irreg., no. 9, 1977. price varies. Cambridge University, Institute of Criminology, Cambridge CB3 9DT, England.

345   DK
DENMARK. DIREKTORATET FOR KRIMINALFORSORGEN. KRIMINALFORSORGEN. (Text in Danish; summaries in English) a. Direktoratet for Kriminalforsorgen, Justitsministeriet, Klareboderne 1, DK-1115 Copenhagen K, Denmark. illus.

364   US
DIMENSIONS. vol. 3, 1977. a. Department of Corrections, Office of Public Information, Stevens T. Mason Bldg., Box 30003, Lansing, MI 48909. Ed. Gail R. Light.
    Formerly: Michigan. Department of Corrections. Criminal Statistics.

364   US   ISSN 0362-9287
DIRECTORY - JUVENILE AND ADULT CORRECTIONAL DEPARTMENTS, INSTITUTIONS, AGENCIES, AND PAROLING AUTHORITIES OF THE UNITED STATES AND CANADA. 1955. a. $25. American Correctional Association, 4321 Hartwick Rd., College Park, MD 20740. Ed. Diana Travisono. adv. circ. 4,000.
    Former titles (until 1976): Directory - Juvenile and Adult Correctional Institutions and Agencies of the United States and Canada; (1972-1973): Directory - Juvenile Adult Correctional Institutions and Agencies of the United States of America, Canada, and Great Britain (ISSN 0090-4872); Directory of Correctional Institutions and Agencies of the United States of America, Canada, and Great Britain (ISSN 0070-5373); American Correctional Association Directory: State and Federal Correctional Institutions (ISSN 0065-7956)

364   US
DIRECTORY OF AUTOMATED CRIMINAL JUSTICE INFORMATION SYSTEMS. 1972. biennial. free. U.S. Law Enforcement Assistance Administration, National Criminal Justice Reference Service, Washington, DC 20531. circ. 5,000. (also avail. in microfiche)

364.6   US   ISSN 0361-7327
DIRECTORY OF CALIFORNIA JUSTICE AGENCIES SERVING JUVENILES AND ADULTS. 1968. a. Department of the Youth Authority, 4241 Williamsbourgh Dr., Sacramento, CA 95823 (Orders to: Documents Section, Box 1015, North Highlands, CA 95660)
    Formerly: Directory of California Services for Juvenile and Adult Offenders (ISSN 0419-229X)

365   FR
EUROPEAN COMMITTEE ON CRIME PROBLEMS. BULLETIN ON LEGISLATIVE ACTIVITIES. 1965. a. free. Council of Europe, European Committee on Crime Problems, Publications Section, 67006 Strasbourg, France (Dist. in U. S. by Manhattan Publishing Co., 225 Lafayette St., New York, N. Y. 10012) cum. index (1965-1972)
    Formerly: Council of Europe. European Committee on Crime Problems. International Exchange of Information Bills and Draft Regulations on Penal Matters. (ISSN 0590-7136)

362.8   US
EXPENDITURE AND EMPLOYMENT DATA FOR THE CRIMINAL JUSTICE SYSTEM. 1969. a. free. U.S. Department of Justice, Bureau of Justice Statistics, 633 Indiana Ave., N.W., Washington, DC 20531 (Orders to: Box 6000, Rockville, MD 20850) circ. 6,000.

364   UK   ISSN 0072-6435
GREAT BRITAIN. HOME OFFICE. RESEARCH STUDIES. irreg. H.M.S.O., P.O. Box 569, London SE1 9NH, England.

GREAT BRITAIN. HOME OFFICE. STUDIES IN THE CAUSES OF DELINQUENCY AND THE TREATMENT OF OFFENDERS. see CHILDREN AND YOUTH — About

353.9   US   ISSN 0098-5708
HAWAII. CRIMINAL INJURIES COMPENSATION COMMISSION. ANNUAL REPORT. a. Criminal Injuries Compensation Commission, Box 339, Honolulu, HI 96809. Key Title: Annual Report - Criminal Injuries Compensation Commission.

364   US   ISSN 0095-4209
HAWAII. STATE LAW ENFORCEMENT AND JUVENILE DELINQUENCY PLANNING AGENCY. ANNUAL ACTION PROGRAM. a. State Law Enforcement and Juvenile Delinquency Planning Agency, Honolulu, HI 96813. circ. contr. circ. Key Title: Annual Action Program - State Law Enforcement Agency.

312.276   US   ISSN 0098-8537
HOMICIDE IN CALIFORNIA. 1963. irreg. free. Department of Justice, Bureau of Criminal Statistics and Special Services, 3301 C St, Box 13427, Sacramento, CA 95813. illus. stat.

HUBER LAW SURVEY. see SOCIAL SERVICES AND WELFARE

364   US   ISSN 0093-7134
IDAHO'S COMPREHENSIVE PLAN FOR CRIMINAL JUSTICE. 1972. irreg. Law Enforcement Planning Commission, Boise, ID 83702. illus. stat.
    Continues: Idaho. Law Enforcement Planning Commission. Comprehensive Plan for Law Enforcement and Criminal Justice.

340   US   ISSN 0073-487X
ILLINOIS LAW ENFORCEMENT COMMISSION. ANNUAL REPORT. (Not issued in 1972) 1969. a. ‡ Law Enforcement Commission, 120 S. Riverside Plaza, Chicago, IL 60606. circ. 7,000.

364.4   301   YU
INSTITUT ZA KRIMINOLOSKA I SOCIOLOSKA ISTRAZIVANJA. ZBORNIK. (Summaries in English, French and Russian) 1972. a. $4. Institut za Kriminoloska i Socioloska Istrazivanja, Gracanicka 18, 11000 Belgrade, Yugoslavia. bk. rev.

364   US   ISSN 0538-7191
INTERNATIONAL DIRECTORY OF PRISONERS' AID AGENCIES. irreg. $1. International Prisoners' Aid Association, c/o Badr-El-Din Ali, Executive Dir., Department of Sociology, University of Louisville, Louisville, KY 40208.

CRIMINOLOGY AND LAW ENFORCEMENT

351.74 UK ISSN 0579-5567
INTERNATIONAL POLICE ASSOCIATION. MEETING OF THE INTERNATIONAL EXECUTIVE COUNCIL. (Text in English, French and German) 1950. a; latest edition, 1976. £2. International Police Association, County Police Hqtrs., Sutton Rd., Maidstone, Kent, England. Ed. H. V. D. Hallett. index.

351.74 UK ISSN 0579-6881
INTERNATIONAL POLICE ASSOCIATION. TRAVEL SCHOLARSHIPS. 1970. a; latest edition, 1976. £2. International Police Association, County Police Hqtrs., Sutton Rd., Maidstone, Kent., England. Ed. H. V. D. Hallett. index. circ. controlled.

364 UN ISSN 0074-7688
INTERNATIONAL REVIEW OF CRIMINAL POLICY. (Text in English, French and Spanish) 1955. a.; no. 31, 1974. $2. United Nations, Department of Economic and Social Affairs, Secretariat, New York, NY 10017 (Dist. by: United Nations Publications, Room LX-2300, New York, NY 10017; or Distribution and Sales Section, Palais des Nations, CH-1211 Geneva 10, Switzerland)

364 FR ISSN 0539-032X
INTERNATIONAL SOCIETY OF CRIMINOLOGY. BULLETIN.* irreg. International Society of Criminology, 4 rue de Mondovi, 75001 Paris, France.

364 SW
INTERNATIONAL SYMPOSIUM ON WOUND BALLISTICS. PROCEEDINGS. (Supplement to: Acta Chirurgica Scandinavica) 3rd, 1978. irreg. $42. Almqvist & Wiksell International, Box 62, S-101 20 Stockholm, Sweden. Ed. T. Seeman. illus.

364 IS ISSN 0075-1006
ISRAEL. CENTRAL BUREAU OF STATISTICS. CRIMINAL STATISTICS. (Subseries of its Special Series) (Text in Hebrew and English) 1948-49. irreg., latest issue, no. 569, 1975. I£160. Central Bureau of Statistics, Box 13015, Jerusalem, Israel.

364 IS ISSN 0075-1391
ISRAEL STUDIES IN CRIMINOLOGY. (Text in English) 1970. irreg. $11. (Tel Aviv University, Institute of Criminology and Criminal Law) Bezalel Tcherikover, Pubs., Ltd., 12 Ha'sharon St., Tel Aviv, Israel. Ed. Shlomo Shoham.

364 US
JOHN JAY COLLEGE OF CRIMINAL JUSTICE. CRIMINAL JUSTICE CENTER. MONOGRAPH. 1976. irreg., no. 13, 1981. John Jay Press, 444 W. 56th St., New York, NY 10019.

JUSTICE IN AMERICA SERIES. see LAW

JUVENILE LAW LITIGATION DIRECTORY. see LAW

353.9 US ISSN 0095-6384
KENTUCKY LAW ENFORCEMENT COUNCIL. ANNUAL REPORT. a. free. Law Enforcement Council, Eastern Kentucky University, Box 608, Richmond, KY 40475. Key Title: Annual Report - Kentucky Law Enforcement Council.

364 GW
KRIMINALITAET UND IHRE VERWALTER. 1972. irreg., no. 7, 1980. price varies. Ferdinand Enke Verlag, Herdweg 63, 7000 Stuttgart 1, W. Germany (B.R.D.) Eds. D. Peters, H. Peters.

354 GW ISSN 0454-5265
KRIMINALWISSENSCHAFTLICHE ABHANDLUNGEN. 1967. irreg., vol. 10, 1978. price varies. Max Schmidt-Roemhild Verlag, Mengstr. 16, 2400 Luebeck 1, W. Germany (B.R.D.) Ed.Friedrich Geerds.

364 GW ISSN 0075-7144
KRIMINOLOGIE. ABHANDLUNGEN UEBER ABWEGIGES SOZIALVERHALTEN. 1964. irreg., no. 17, 1980. price varies. Ferdinand Enke Verlag, Herdweg 63, 7000 Stuttgart 1, W. Germany (B.R.D.) Ed. T. Wuertenberger.

364 US ISSN 0075-7152
KRIMINOLOGISCHE ABHANDLUNGEN. 1946. irreg., no. 11, 1975. price varies. Springer-Verlag, 175 Fifth Ave., New York, NY 10010 (also Berlin, Heidelberg, Vienna) (reprint service avail. from ISI)

364 NE
KRIMINOLOGISCHE CAHIERS. 1977. irreg. price varies. Samsom Uitgeverij B.V., Postbus 4, Alphen aan den Rijn, Netherlands.

364 GW ISSN 0075-7136
KRIMINOLOGISCHE GEGENWARTSFRAGEN. 1953. irreg., no. 14, 1980. price varies. Ferdinand Enke Verlag, Herdweg 63, 7000 Stuttgart 1, W. Germany (B.R.D.)
Formerly: Kriminalbiologische Gegenwartsfragen.

364 GW
KRIMINOLOGISCHE SCHRIFTENREIHE. 1961. irreg. price varies. (Deutsche Kriminologische Gesellschaft) Verlag fuer Kriminalistische Fachliteratur, Im Weiher 10, Postfach 102640, 6900 Heidelberg 1, W. Germany (B.R.D.)

364 US
LAW ENFORCEMENT AND CRIMINAL JUSTICE EDUCATION DIRECTORY. irreg. $9.75. International Association of Chiefs of Police, Inc., Professional Development Division, 11 Firstfield Rd., Gaithersburg, MD 20760.

363.2 US ISSN 0090-9386
MAINE. CRIMINAL JUSTICE PLANNING & ASSISTANCE AGENCY. CRIMINAL JUSTICE INTERNSHIP PROGRAM. REPORT AND EVALUATION. 1970. irreg., latest 1974. Criminal Justice Planning & Assistance Agency, 11 Parkwood Dr., Augusta, ME 04330. illus. circ. 1,600(controlled)
Formerly: Maine. Law Enforcement Planning & Assistance Agency. Maine Criminal Justice Internship Program; Report and Evaluation.

353.9 US
MAINE. CRIMINAL JUSTICE PLANNING & ASSISTANCE AGENCY. PROGRESS REPORT. 1972. a. Criminal Justice Planning & Assistance Agency, 11 Parkwood Dr., Augusta, ME 04330. illus. circ. 1,600.
Formerly: Maine. Law Enforcement Planning & Assistance Agency. Progress Report (ISSN 0090-6107)

345 US ISSN 0098-079X
MAINE PROSECUTOR, CRIMINAL LEGISLATION MANUAL. Short title: Criminal Legislation Manual. irreg. free only to qualified personnel in Maine. Department of the Attorney General, Law Enforcement Education Section, State House, Augusta, ME 04330. circ. controlled.

364 MW ISSN 0076-308X
MALAWI. POLICE FORCE. ANNUAL REPORT. a, latest 1971/72. K.0.60. Government Printer, P.O. Box 37, Zomba, Malawi.

353.9 US ISSN 0362-9198
MARYLAND. DIVISION OF CORRECTION. REPORT. a. Division of Correction, 920 Greenmount Ave., Baltimore, MD 21202. Key Title: Report - Maryland Division of Correction.

364 US
MARYLAND. GOVERNOR'S COMMISSION ON LAW ENFORCEMENT AND THE ADMINISTRATION OF JUSTICE. COMPREHENSIVE PLAN. (Published in 2 vols.) a. $37.50. Governor's Commission on Law Enforcement and the Administration of Justice, Investment Pl., Suite 700, Towson, MD 21204 (Order from: National Technical Information Service, Port Royal Rd., Springfield, VA 22151) illus. stat.

353.9 US
MARYLAND. POLICE AND CORRECTIONAL TRAINING COMMISSIONS. REPORT TO THE GOVERNOR, THE SECRETARY OF PUBLIC SAFETY AND CORRECTIONAL SERVICES, AND MEMBERS OF THE GENERAL ASSEMBLY. (Report year ends June 30.) 1971/72. a. free. Correctional Training Commission, Room 16, 7 Church Lane, Pikesville, MD 21208. circ. 700.
Formed by the merger of: Maryland. Police Training Commission. Annual Report (ISSN 0085-3135) & Maryland. Correctional Training Commission. Annual Report (ISSN 0090-9963)

365 US ISSN 0076-4884
MASSACHUSETTS. ADVISORY COMMITTEE ON CORRECTION. ANNUAL REPORT.* 1953. a. Department of Correction, 100 Cambridge St., Boston, MA 02202.

364 US
MASSACHUSETTS. DEPARTMENT OF CORRECTION. COMMISSIONER OF CORRECTION. STATISTICAL REPORTS. 1922. a. $1. Department of Correction, State Office Bldg, 100 Cambridge St, Boston, MA 02202 (Order from: Bureau of Public Documents, Room 116, State House, Boston, MA 02133) Ed. Daniel LeClair. charts. stat. circ. 800.

364 US ISSN 0085-3143
MASSACHUSETTS CORRECTIONAL INSTITUTION, NORFOLK, NORFOLK COLONY SCHOOL. REPORT. 1934. a. ‡ Massachusetts Department of Correction, 100 Cambridge St., Boston, MA 02202 (And 43 Main St., Norfolk, MA 02056) circ. 1,500 (controlled) (tabloid format)

353.9 US
MICHIGAN. DEPARTMENT OF STATE POLICE. ANNUAL REPORT. 1919. a. ‡ Department of State Police, 714 S. Harrison Rd., East Lansing, MI 48823. illus. circ. controlled.
Continues: Michigan. State Police. Annual Report.

345 US ISSN 0093-9390
MICHIGAN. OFFICE OF CRIMINAL JUSTICE. COMPREHENSIVE LAW ENFORCEMENT AND CRIMINAL JUSTICE PLAN. a. Office of Criminal Justice, Lansing, MI 48933. illus. Key Title: Comprehensive Law Enforcement and Criminal Justice Plan (Lansing)

364 US ISSN 0085-3380
MICHIGAN POLICE JOURNAL. bi-m. $20. Michigan Association of Chiefs of Police, 2248 E. Mt. Hope, Suite H, Okemos, MI 48864. Ed. Nancy L. Brent. adv. circ. 817.

364 US
MINNESOTA. CRIME CONTROL PLANNING BOARD. COMPREHENSIVE PLAN. 1969. a. Crime Control Planning Board, 444 Lafayette Rd., St. Paul, MN 55101. illus. stat. circ. 500.
Formerly: Minnesota. Governor's Commission on Crime Prevention and Control. Comprehensive Plan (ISSN 0094-2073)

365.6 US
MINNESOTA. DEPARTMENT. OF CORRECTIONS. CHARACTERISTICS ON INSTITUTIONAL POPULATIONS. 1965. a. Department of Corrections, 430 Metro Square Bldg., State Office Bldg., St. Paul, MN 55101.
Formerly: Minnesota. Department of Corrections. Research, Information and Data Systems Unit. Characteristics of Populations Under Supervision of the Institutions and Field Services. (ISSN 0092-1033)

353.9 US ISSN 0094-1409
MINNESOTA. OFFICE OF OMBUDSMAN FOR CORRECTIONS. ANNUAL REPORT. 1973. a. Office of Ombudsman for Corrections, 333 Sibley St., Ste. 102, St. Paul, MN 55101. Ed. Theartrice Williams. illus. circ. 500-600. Key Title: Annual Report - Ombudsman for Corrections (St. Paul)

364.36 371.93 US ISSN 0077-3476
NATIONAL ASSOCIATION OF TRAINING SCHOOLS AND JUVENILE AGENCIES. PROCEEDINGS. 1904. a. $3. National Association of Training Schools and Juvenile Agencies, 5256 N. Central Ave., Indianapolis, IN 46220. circ. 1,000.

365 US
NATIONAL DIRECTORY OF LAW ENFORCEMENT ADMINISTRATORS AND CORRECTIONAL AGENCIES; including police chiefs, sheriffs, state and federal criminal investigation divisions, correctional institutions, county and regional criminal prosecutors, and related agencies. 1962. a. $22.50 price varies; vol. 10-$14.50. ‡ National Police Chiefs & Sheriffs Information Bureau, Box 92007, Milwaukee, WI 53202. Ed. M. E. Wyrick.

350 US ISSN 0194-1704
NATIONAL EMPLOYMENT LISTING SERVICE FOR THE CRIMINAL JUSTICE SYSTEM. FEDERAL EMPLOYMENT INFORMATION DIRECTORY. 1978. a. $5. Sam Houston State University, National Employment Listing Service, Texas Criminal Justice Center, Huntsville, TX 77341. Ed. Daniel J. Miller. circ. 1,600.

363.2 US ISSN 0194-0813
NATIONAL EMPLOYMENT LISTING SERVICE FOR THE CRIMINAL JUSTICE SYSTEM. POLICE EMPLOYMENT GUIDE. 1978. a. $9.95. Sam Houston State University, National Employment Listing Service, Texas Criminal Justice Center, Huntsville, TX 77341. Ed. Daniel J. Miller. circ. 1,000.

371.42 US ISSN 0194-0805
NATIONAL EMPLOYMENT LISTING SERVICE FOR THE CRIMINAL JUSTICE SYSTEM. SPECIAL EDITION: EDUCATION OPPORTUNITIES. 1978. a. $4.50. Sam Houston State University, National Employment Listing Service, Texas Criminal Justice Center, Huntsville, TX 77341. Ed. Daniel J. Miller. circ. 2,000.

365 US
NATIONAL JAIL AND ADULT DETENTION DIRECTORY. a. $25. American Correctional Association, 4321 Hartwick Rd., Suite L-208, College Park, Md 20740. Ed. Diana Travisono. adv. circ. 4,000.

364 JA ISSN 0453-0667
NATIONAL RESEARCH INSTITUTE OF POLICE SCIENCE. ANNUAL REPORT/KAGAKU KEISATSU KENKYUSHO NENPO. (Text in Japanese) 1956. a. National Research Institute of Police Science - Kagaku Keisatsu Kenkyusho, 6 Sanban-cho, Chiyoda-ku, Tokyo 102, Japan.

NATIONAL RESEARCH INSTITUTE OF POLICE SCIENCE. DATA/KAGAKU KEISATSU KENKYUSHO SHIRYO. see PUBLIC ADMINISTRATION

353.9 US ISSN 0094-1247
NEBRASKA. STATE PATROL. ANNUAL REPORT. a. free. State Patrol, State House, Box 94637, Lincoln, NE 68509. illus. Key Title: Annual Report - Nebraska State Patrol.

363.2 US
NEBRASKA LAW ENFORCEMENT TRAINING CENTER. ANNUAL REPORT. a. Nebraska Law Enforcement Training Center, Rt. 3, Box 50, Grand Island, NE 68801. illus. stat.

364 NE ISSN 0077-6734
NETHERLANDS. CENTRAAL BUREAU VOOR DE STATISTIEK. CRIMINELE STATISTIEK. CRIMINAL STATISTICS. (Text in Dutch and English) 1950-51. a. fl.17.75. Centraal Bureau voor de Statistiek, Prinses Beatrixlaan 428, Voorburg, Netherlands (Orders to: Staatsuitgeverij, Christoffel Plantijnstraat, The Hague, Netherlands)

365 NE ISSN 0077-6815
NETHERLANDS. CENTRAAL BUREAU VOOR DE STATISTIEK. GEVANGENISSTATISTIEK. STATISTICS OF PRISONS. (Text in Dutch and English) 1950-51. a. fl.7.85. Centraal Bureau voor de Statistiek, Prinses Beatrixlaan 428, Voorburg, Netherlands (Orders to: Staatsuitgeverij, Christoffel Plantijnstraat, The Hague, Netherlands)

363.2 US ISSN 0092-1084
NEVADA. COMMISSION ON CRIME, DELINQUENCY AND CORRECTIONS. COMPREHENSIVE LAW ENFORCEMENT PLAN. Spine title: Nevada Law Enforcement Plan. 1970. irreg. Commission on Crime, Delinquency, and Corrections, Carson City, NV 89701. stat. illus. Key Title: Comprehensive Law Enforcement Plan (Carson City)

364 US
NEW HAMPSHIRE COMPREHENSIVE CRIMINAL JUSTICE PLAN. 1972. a. $30. Crime Commission, 169 Manchester St., Concord, NH 03301.
Formerly: New Hampshire Comprehensive Law Enforcement Plan (ISSN 0094-7628)

364 US
NEW MEXICO. GOVERNOR'S COUNCIL ON CRIMINAL JUSTICE PLANNING. COMPREHENSIVE CRIMINAL JUSTICE PLAN. a. Governor's Council on Criminal Justice Planning, 425 Old Sante Fe Trail, Sante Fe, NM 87501. stat.

364 AT ISSN 0310-3684
NEW SOUTH WALES. ATTORNEY-GENERAL. BUREAU OF CRIME STATISTICS AND RESEARCH. STATISTICAL REPORT. 1972. irreg. free. Attorney-General, Bureau of Crime Statistics and Research, G.P.O. Box 6, Sydney, N.S.W. 2001, Australia. Ed. Dr. T. Vinson.

364 US ISSN 0077-9148
NEW YORK (STATE) CRIME VICTIMS COMPENSATION BOARD. REPORT. (Subseries of New York (State) Legislature. Legislative Document) 1967. a. Crime Victims Compensation Board, 875 Central Ave., Albany, NY 12206.

353.9 US ISSN 0095-4047
NEW YORK (STATE). DIVISION OF CRIMINAL JUSTICE SERVICE. ANNUAL REPORT. 1973. a. Division of Criminal Justice Services, Executive Park Tower, Stuyvesant Plaza, Albany, NY 12203. Key Title: Annual Report - State of New York, Division of Criminal Justice Services.

364 US ISSN 0077-944X
NEW YORK UNIVERSITY. COMPARATIVE CRIMINAL LAW PROJECT. PUBLICATIONS. 1960. irreg., no. 6, 1968. price varies. New York University, Criminal Law Education and Research Center, 40 Washington Square South, Room 434, New York, NY 10012 (Dist. by Fred B. Rothman, 57 Leuning St., S. Hackensack, N.J. 07606) Ed. John Delaney. circ. 1,000.

364 US ISSN 0077-9458
NEW YORK UNIVERSITY. CRIMINAL LAW EDUCATION AND RESEARCH CENTER. MONOGRAPH SERIES. 1969. irreg., no. 9, 1969. price varies. New York University, Criminal Law Education and Research Center, Room 434, 40 Washington Sq. S., New York, NY 10012 (Dist. by Fred B. Rothman, 57 Leuning St., S. Hackensack, N.J. 07606) Ed. John Delaney.

364 US ISSN 0094-0984
OHIO'S COMPREHENSIVE CRIMINAL JUSTICE PLAN. 1972. a. Administration of Justice Division, Columbus, OH 43215. illus.

364 US
OKLAHOMA. CRIME COMMISSION. ANNUAL REPORT. 1976. a. Crime Commission, 3033 N. Walnut, Oklahoma City, OK 73105. Ed. Billie Dempewolf. circ. 300.

362.8 US
PAROLE IN THE UNITED STATES. (Subseries of: Uniform Parole Reports) 1976. a. free. U.S. Department of Justice, Bureau of Justice Statistics, 633 Indiana Ave., N.W., Washington, DC 20531 (Orders to: Box 6000, Rockville, MD 20850) circ. 5,000.

364 US ISSN 0079-0222
PATTERSON SMITH SERIES IN CRIMINOLOGY, LAW ENFORCEMENT AND SOCIAL PROBLEMS. 1967. irreg. price varies. Patterson Smith Publishing Corporation, 23 Prospect Terrace, Montclair, NJ 07042. adv. bk. rev.
Formerly: Patterson Smith Reprint Series in Criminology. Law Enforcement and Social Problems.

364 US ISSN 0091-4118
PENNSYLVANIA. CRIME COMMISSION. REPORT. 1970. biennial. free. ‡ Crime Commission, 523 E. Lancaster Ave., St. Davids, PA 19087.

364 US
PETER W. RODINO INSTITUTE OF CRIMINAL JUSTICE. ANNUAL JOURNAL. Short title: Rodino Institute Journal. 1979. a. free. Jersey City State College, Peter W. Rodino Institute of Criminal Justice, 2039 Kennedy Blvd., Jersey City, NJ 07305. Ed. William R. Reopell. (back issues avail.)

345 US ISSN 0092-8933
POLICE AND LAW ENFORCEMENT. 1973. irreg. price varies. A M S Press Inc., 56 E. 13th St., New York, NY 10003. Eds. James T. Curran, Austin Fowler, Richard H. Ward. bibl. stat.

364 US
POLICE CHIEF; professional voice of law enforcement. 1934. m. $12. International Association of Chiefs of Police, Inc., 11 Firstfield Rd., Gaithersburg, MD 20760. Ed. Alice C. Pitcher. adv. bk. rev. film rev. index. circ. 20,000. (back issues avail) Indexed: CJPI.

351.74 US ISSN 0079-2950
POLICE YEARBOOK. 1961. a. $7. Davis Publishing Co., 250 Potrero St., Santa Cruz, CA 95060. Eds. Robert A. Davis, Sr., Robert E. Ford.
Civil Service questions

PRESIDIO. see LITERATURE

365 US
PRISONERS YELLOW PAGES. 1976. irreg., latest issue 1980. $3.95 (free to prisoners) (Universal Fellowship of Metropolitan Community Churches, Board of Institutional Ministry) Universal Fellowship Press, 5300 Santa Monica Blvd., Suite 304, Los Angeles, CA 90029. Ed. Rev. Bob Arthur.

364.6 US ISSN 0079-5615
PROBATION AND PAROLE. 1969. a. $4. New York State Probation and Parole Officers Association, Box 114, Canal St. Sta., New York, NY 10013. circ. 1,200. Indexed: CJPI.

364 PL
PRZESTEPCZOSC NA SWIECIE. irreg., t. 9, 1977. (Instytut Problematyki Przestepczosci) Panstwowe Wydawnictwo Naukowe, Miodowa 10, 00-251 Warsaw, Poland. bibl.

362.7 UK
RAINER FOUNDATION. ANNUAL REPORT. 1976. a. Rainer Foundation, 89a Blackheath Hill, London SE10 8TJ, England.
Continues: London Police Court Mission. Annual Report.

REGENCY INTERNATIONAL DIRECTORY; of enquiry agents, private detectives & debt collecting agencies. see BUSINESS AND ECONOMICS — Banking And Finance

364.6 US ISSN 0362-7489
REPORT OF PROBATION SUPERVISION WORKLOAD. a. Department of Corrections, Bureau of Management Information, 22 E. Cary, Richmond, VA 23219.

364 US
SAGE RESEARCH PROGRESS SERIES IN CRIMINOLOGY. 1977. irreg.(4-6/yr.) $12 for hardcover; softcover $5.95. (American Society for Criminology) Sage Publications, Inc., 275 S. Beverly Dr., Beverly Hills, CA 90212 (And Sage Publications, Ltd., 28 Banner St., London EC1Y 8QE, England) Ed. James A. Inciardi. (back issues avail.)

363.2 US
SAINT LOUIS POLICE JOURNAL. 1912. 6-10/yr. free to qualified organizations. Metropolitan Police Department, Public Information Division, 1200 Clark Ave., St. Louis, MO 63103. Ed. John Thieman. charts. illus. circ. 5,400.

364 US
SAM HOUSTON STATE UNIVERSITY. INSTITUTE OF CONTEMPORARY CORRECTIONS AND THE BEHAVIORAL SCIENCES. PROCEEDINGS INTERAGENCY WORKSHOP. 1970. a. Sam Houston State University, Institute of Contemporary Corrections and the Behavioral Sciences, Huntsville, TX 77340. circ. controlled. (processed)

364 NO ISSN 0085-5936
SCANDINAVIAN STUDIES IN CRIMINOLOGY. 1965. irreg. price varies. Universitetsforlaget, Kolstadgt. 1, Box 2959-Toeyen, Oslo 6, Norway (U. S. address: Box 258, Irvington-on-Hudson, NY 10533) Ed. Nils Christie.

364.4 UK ISSN 0307-7780
SECURITECH; the international guide to security equipment. (Text in Arabic, English, French, German, Spanish & other languages) 1972. a. $16. Unisaf Publications Ltd., Unisaf House, 32-36 Dudley Rd, Tunbridge Wells, Kent TN1 1LH, England. Ed. H. Klopper. circ. 13,000.

SECURITY AND PROTECTION MANUAL. see FIRE PREVENTION

364.4 380.1   SA
SECURITY PRODUCTS AND SERVICES INDEX. 1978. a. R.14.95. Thomson Publications S.A. (Pty) Ltd., Box 8308, Johannesburg 2000, South Africa. Ed. Beth Flood. adv.

365   BL
SERIE ESTUDOS PENITENCIAROS. irreg. Cortez e Moraes Ltda, Rua Ministro Godoy 1002, 05015 Sao Paulo, Brazil. bibl.

362.8   US
SOURCEBOOK OF CRIMINAL JUSTICE STATISTICS. 1973. a. free. U.S. Department of Justice, Bureau of Justice Statistics, 633 Indiana Ave., N.W., Washington, DC 20531 (Orders to: Box 6000, Rockville, MD 250850) circ. 8,000.

365.6   SA
SOUTH AFRICA. PRISONS DEPARTMENT. ANNUAL STATISTICS BY THE COMMISSIONER OF PRISONS/JAARLIKSE STATISTIEKE DEUR DIE KOMMISSARIS VAN GEVANGENISSE. (Report year ending June 30) (Text in English and Afrikaans) a. Government Printer, Bosman St., Private Bag X85, Pretoria 0001, South Africa.

364.4   SA   ISSN 0300-1555
SOUTH AFRICA. PRISONS DEPARTMENT. REPORT OF THE COMMISSIONER OF PRISONS/VERSLAG VAN DIE KOMMISSARIS VAN GEVANGENISSE.* Cover title: Prisons. (Order and language of titles varies) a. Government Printer, Bosman St., Private Bag X85, Pretoria 0001, South Africa. illus. stat.
  Continues its Annual Report of the Director of Prisons.

362.8   US
STATE COURT CASELOAD STATISTICS. 1975. a. free. U.S. Department of Justice, Bureau of Justice Statistics, 633 Indiana Ave., N.W., Washington, DC 20531 (Orders to: Box 6000, Rockville, MD 20850) circ. 5,000.

364   US   ISSN 0090-3221
STATE OF NEBRASKA UNIFORM CRIME REPORT. Cover title: Crime in Nebraska. 1972. a. free. Commission on Law Enforcement and Criminal Justice, Box 94946, Lincoln, NE 68509. Ed. Marilyn Kumm. charts. stat. circ. 1,500.

364   US
STATE OF NEVADA COMPREHENSIVE CRIMINAL JUSTICE PLAN. irreg. Commission on Crime, Delinquency, and Corrections, Carson City, NV 89701. illus. stat.

364   US   ISSN 0363-5643
STATE OF WASHINGTON COMPREHENSIVE PLAN FOR CRIME CONTROL AND THE ADMINISTRATION OF JUSTICE. irreg. Law and Justice Planning Office, Olympia, WA 98504.

364.36   BE   ISSN 0585-5721
STUDIECENTRUM VOOR JEUGDMISDADIGHEID. PUBLIKATIE/ CENTRE D'ETUDE DE LA DELINQUANCE JUVENILE. PUBLICATION. 1958. irreg., no. 49, 1979. price varies. Studiecentrum voor Jeugdmisdadigheid - Centre d'Etude de la Delinquance Juvenile, Avenue Jeanne 44, 1050 Brussels, Belgium.

364   US
STUDIES IN CRIME AND JUSTICE. 1972. irreg., latest 1977. price varies. University of Chicago Press, 5801 S. Ellis Ave., Chicago, IL 60637. Ed.3d. adv. bk. rev. (reprint service avail. from UMI,ISI)

SUPREME COURT HISTORICAL SOCIETY. YEARBOOK. see *LAW*

364   GW   ISSN 0082-1934
TASCHENBUCH FUER KRIMINALISTEN. 1951. a. DM.11.80. Verlagsanstalt Deutsche Polizei GmbH, Forststr. 3a, 4010 Hilden, W. Germany (B.R.D.) Ed. Waldemar Burghard. adv. bk. rev. circ. 1,500.

364.6   US   ISSN 0095-1900
TEXAS. DEPARTMENT OF CORRECTIONS. RESEARCH AND DEVELOPMENT DIVISION. RESEARCH REPORT. 1971. irreg., no. 27, 1975. Department of Corrections, Research and Development Division, Huntsville, TX 77340. Key Title: Research Report - Texas Department of Corrections; Treatment Directorate, Research and Development Division.

362.8   US
TRENDS IN EXPENDITURE AND EMPLOYMENT DATA FOR THE CRIMINAL JUSTICE SYSTEM. 1974. a. free. U.S. Department of Justice, Bureau of Justice Statistics, 633 Indiana Ave., N.W., Washington, DC 20531 (Orders to: Box 6000, Rockville, MD 20850) circ. 7,000.

364   US   ISSN 0082-7592
UNIFORM CRIME REPORTS FOR THE UNITED STATES. Cover title: Crime in the United States. each edition kept up-to-date with quarterly and annual supplements. price varies. U.S. Federal Bureau of Investigation, Ninth St. and Pennsylvania Ave., Constitution Ave. & 10th St., N.W., Washington, DC 20535.

364   UN   ISSN 0082-8025
UNITED NATIONS CONGRESS ON THE PREVENTION OF CRIME AND THE TREATMENT OF OFFENDERS. REPORT. irreg.; no. 4, 1971. price varies. United Nations Publications, Room LX-2300, New York, NY 10017 (Or Distribution and Sales Section, CH-1211 Geneva 10, Switzerland)

364.1   US   ISSN 0360-3245
U.S. FEDERAL BUREAU OF INVESTIGATION. BOMB SUMMARY. a. U.S. Federal Bureau of Investigation, Pennsylvania Ave., N.W. & 9th St., Washington, DC 20535. (Co-sponsor: National Bomb Data Center) Key Title: Bomb Summary.

353.007   US   ISSN 0565-6567
U. S. LAW ENFORCEMENT ASSISTANCE ADMINISTRATION. ANNUAL REPORT. 1968/ 69. a. $2.50. U.S. Law Enforcement Assistance Administration, 633 Indiana Ave., N.W., Washington, DC 20531 (Orders to: Supt. of Documents, G.P.O., Washington DC 20402) circ. 2,500.

353.007   US
U.S. PARK POLICE. ANNUAL REPORT. a. U.S. National Park Service, United States Park Police, 1100 Ohio Drive S.W., Washington, DC 20242 (Orders to: Supt. Docs., Washington, DC 20402) illus. stat.

364   VE   ISSN 0507-570X
UNIVERSIDAD CENTRAL DE VENEZUELA. INSTITUTO DE CIENCIAS PENALES Y CRIMINOLOGICAS. ANUARIO. 1967. irreg; no. 5, 1971. price varies. Universidad Central de Venezuela, Facultad de Derecho, Instituto de Ciencias Penales y Criminologicas, Caracas, Venezuela. Ed. Tulio Chiossone. bk. rev. bibl. charts.

364   US   ISSN 0068-6174
UNIVERSITY OF CALIFORNIA, BERKELEY. SCHOOL OF CRIMINOLOGY. SAN FRANCISCO PROJECT. RESEARCH REPORT. 1965. irreg., 1969, no. 14. price varies. University of California, Berkeley, School of Criminology, Berkeley, CA 94720. Ed. Robert M. Carter.

364   AT   ISSN 0085-7033
UNIVERSITY OF SYDNEY. INSTITUTE OF CRIMINOLOGY. PROCEEDINGS. 1967. irreg. price varies. University of Sydney, Institute of Criminology, Publications Officer, 173-175 Phillip St., Sydney, N.S.W. 2000, Australia (Orders to: Government Printer. Box 75, Pyrmont, N.S.W. 2009, Australia) circ. 2,000.

VIRGINIA. CRIMINAL JUSTICE SERVICES COMMISSION. ANNUAL REPORT. see *LAW*

354.941   AT
WESTERN AUSTRALIA. DEPARTMENT OF CORRECTIONS. ANNUAL REPORT. 1957. a. ‡ Western Australia Government Printing Office, Station St., Wembley, W.A. 6014, Australia.

364.6   US   ISSN 0095-4306
WISCONSIN. DIVISION OF CORRECTIONS. OFFICE OF INFORMATIOM MANAGEMENT. JUVENILE PROBATION ADMISSIONS. (Subseries of its Statistical Bulletin C) irreg. Division of Corrections, Office of Information Management, Box 7925, Madison, WI 53707. Key Title: Juvenile Probation Admissions.
  Formerly: Wisconsin. Division of Corrections. Bureau of Planning, Development and Research. Juvenile Probation Admissions.

364.6   US
WISCONSIN. DIVISION OF CORRECTIONS. OFFICE OF INFORMATION MANAGEMENT. WORK RELEASE-STUDY RELEASE PROGRAM. (Subseries of: Wisconsin. Division of Corrections. Bureau of Planning, Development, and Research. Statistical Bulletin, C.) 1970. irreg. Division of Corrections, Office of Information Management, Box 7925, Madison, WI 53707. Key Title: Work Release-Study Release Program.
  Formerly: Wisconsin. Division of Corrections. Bureau of Planning, Development and Research. Work Release-Study Release Program (ISSN 0095-0564)

364   US
WISCONSIN CRIMINAL JUSTICE INFORMATION, CRIME AND ARRESTS. 1969. a. free. Wisconsin Crime Information Bureau, P.O. Box 2718, Madison, WI 53701. index. (tabloid format)

345.54   II
YEARLY ALL INDIA CRIMINAL DIGEST. (Supplement to Shree Krishan Agarwal's All India Criminal Digest, 1961-1970) (Text in English) 1971. a. Rs.65. Law Book Co., Sardar Patel Marg, Box 4, Allahabad 1, India. Ed. S. K. Agarwal. circ. 2,600.

365   ZA   ISSN 0084-4659
ZAMBIA. PRISONS DEPARTMENT. REPORT. 1964. a. 35 n. Government Printer, P.O. Box 136, Lusaka, Zambia.

CRIMINOLOGY AND LAW ENFORCEMENT — Abstracting, Bibliographies, Statistics

364.4 319   AT
AUSTRALIA. BUREAU OF STATISTICS. QUEENSLAND OFFICE. LAW AND ORDER. a. Australian Bureau of Statistics, Queensland Office, 345 Ann St., Brisbane, Qld. 4000, Australia.

364 016   UK   ISSN 0068-6883
CAMBRIDGE UNIVERSITY. INSTITUTE OF CRIMINOLOGY. BIBLIOGRAPHICAL SERIES. 1966. irreg., no. 9, 1979. price varies. Cambridge University, Institute of Criminology, Cambridge CB3 9DT, England. Ed. R. Perry. arranged by subject with subject and author indexes. circ. 1,000. Indexed: Abstr.Crim. & Pen.

364.1   CN   ISSN 0706-2788
CANADA. STATISTICS CANADA. HOMICIDE STATISTICS/STATISTIQUE DE L'HOMICIDE. (Catalog 85-209) (Text in English and French) 1961. a. Can.$8($9.60) Statistics Canada, Publications Distribution, Ottawa, Ont. K1A 0V7, Canada. stat. (also avail. in microform from MML)
  Formerly: Canada. Statistics Canada. Murder Statistics/Statistique de l'Homicide (ISSN 0575-917X)

362.2   UK
CHARTERED INSTITUTE OF PUBLIC FINANCE AND ACCOUNTANCY. POLICE STATISTICS. ACTUALS. 1949. a. £5. Chartered Institute of Public Finance and Accountancy, 1 Buckingham Place, London SW1E 6HS, England. (back issues avail.)

362.2   UK   ISSN 0144-9915
CHARTERED INSTITUTE OF PUBLIC FINANCE AND ACCOUNTANCY. POLICE STATISTICS. ESTIMATES. 1974. a. £5. Chartered Institute of Public Finance and Accountancy, 1 Buckingham Place, London SW1E 6HS, England. (back issues avail.)
  Formerly: Chartered Institute of Public Finance and Accountancy. Police Estimates Statistics. Actuals (ISSN 0307-1294)

364 314   CY
CYPRUS. DEPARTMENT OF STATISTICS AND RESEARCH. CRIMINAL STATISTICS. (Text in English and Greek) 1974. a. Mils.500. Department of Statistics and Research, Ministry of Finance, Nicosia, Cyprus.

364 314   DK   ISSN 0070-3540
DENMARK. DANMARKS STATISTIK. KRIMINALSTATISTIK. (Subseries of its Statistiske Meddelser) 1933-37. a. Kr.8.40. Danmarks Statistik, Sejroegade 11, 2100 Copenhagen OE, Denmark.

364 318   CK
ESTADISTICA DE CRIMINALIDAD. 1963. a. Policia Nacional, Carrera 15, No. 10-41, Bogota, Colombia. illus. stat.
    Formerly: Criminalidad (1963-1973)

314 364   FI   ISSN 0355-2187
FINLAND. TILASTOKESKUS. TUOMIOISTUINTEN TOIMINTA/FINLAND. STATISTIKCENTRALEN. DOMSTOLARNAS VERKSAMHET/FINLAND. CENTRAL STATISTICAL OFFICE. FUNCTION OF COURTS. (Section 23 C of Official Statistics of Finland) (Text in Finnish, Swedish and English) 1929. a. Fmk.18. Tilastokeskus, Annankatu 44, SF-00100 Helsinki 10, Finland (Subscr. to: Government Printing Centre, Box 516, SF-00100 Helsinki 10, Finland)

364   GR
GREECE. NATIONAL STATISTICAL SERVICE. STATISTICS ON CIVIL, CRIMINAL AND REFORMATORY JUSTICE. a., latest 1976. $2.50. National Statistical Service, Publications and Information Division, 14-16 Lycourgou St., Athens 112, Greece.

363.2 016   UK
INTERNATIONAL BIBLIOGRAPHY OF SELECTED POLICE LITERATURE. 1968. a. £1.50. International Police Association, 1 Fox Rd., West Bridgford, Nottingham NG2 6AJ, England. Ed. H.V.D. Hallett.

NORTH DAKOTA. SOCIAL SERVICE BOARD. JUVENILE COURT AND STATE YOUTH AUTHORITY. DELINQUENCY, DEPENDENCY AND NEGLECT. SPECIAL PROCEEDINGS. see CHILDREN AND YOUTH — *Abstracting, Bibliographies, Statistics*

365   NO
NORWAY. STATISTISK SENTRALBYRAA. KRIMINALSTATISTIKK/CRIMINAL STATISTICS: PRISONERS. (Subseries of its Norges Offisielle Statistikk) (Text in Norwegian and English) 1966. a. price varies. Statistisk Sentralbyraa, Box 8131-Dep., Oslo 1, Norway. circ. 1,200.

364.4   NO
NORWAY. STATISTISK SENTRALBYRAA. SIVILRETTSSTATISTIKK/CIVIL JUDICIAL STATISTICS. (Subseries of its Norges Offisielle Statistikk) (Text in Norwegian and English) 1886. a. Statistisk Sentralbyraa, Box 8131-Dep., Oslo 1, Norway. illus. stat. circ. 1,200.

315 364   SI
SINGAPORE. NATIONAL STATISTICAL COMMISSION. SINGAPORE STANDARD CRIME CLASSIFICATION. irreg. National Statistical Commission, P.O. Box 3010, Singapore 9050, Singapore.

364   BE   ISSN 0081-5268
STATISTIQUE CRIMINELLE DE LA BELGIQUE. (Text in Dutch and French) 1944. a. 120 Fr. Institut National de Statistique, 44 rue de Louvain, 1000 Brussels, Belgium.
    Formerly (until 1944): Statistique Judiciare de la Belgique.

364   US   ISSN 0360-9146
UNIFORM CRIME REPORT FOR THE STATE OF MICHIGAN. 1973. a. Department of State Police, 714 S. Harrison Rd., East Lansing, MI 48823. illus.
    Continues: Michigan Law Enforcement Officials Report on Crime.

364   US
WISCONSIN. DIVISION OF CORRECTIONS. OFFICE OF INFORMATION MANAGEMENT. PROBATION AND PAROLE TERMINATIONS. (Subseries of its Statistical Bulletin) 1972. a. Division of Corrections, Office of Information Management, Box 7925, Madison, WI 53707. stat. (processed)
    Formerly: Wisconsin. Division of Corrections. Bureau of Planning, Development and Research. Probation and Parole Terminations (ISSN 0095-4306)

365   US
WISCONSIN. DIVISION OF CORRECTIONS. OFFICE OF INFORMATION MANAGEMENT. RELEASES FROM JUVENILE INSTITUTIONS. (Statistical Bulletin C-52) 1972. a. Division of Corrections, Office of Information Management, Box 7925, Madison, WI 53707. stat. (processed)
    Formerly: Wisconsin. Division of Corrections. Bureau of Planning, Development and Research. Releases from Juvenile Institutions (ISSN 0362-7470)

CROP PRODUCTION AND SOIL

see *Agriculture—Crop Production and Soil*

CRYSTALLOGRAPHY

see *Chemistry—Crystallography*

CYTOLOGY AND HISTOLOGY

see *Biology—Cytology and Histology*

DAIRYING AND DAIRY PRODUCTS

see *Agriculture—Dairying and Dairy Products*

DANCE

see also *Music; Theater*

793.33   GW   ISSN 0001-0979
A D T V - NACHRICHTEN. 1950. a. membership. Allgemeiner Deutscher Tanzlehrer Verband, Oberheidter Str. 34 B, 5600 Wuppertal 12, W. Germany (B.R.D.)
    Ballroom dancing

ANNEE DE L'OPERA ET DE LA DANSE. see *MUSIC*

792   US
ARCHIVES NEWS. 1976. irreg., approx. 4/yr. membership. San Francisco Archives for the Performing Arts, 3150 Sacramento St., San Francisco, CA 94115. Ed. Judith Solomon. circ. 1,500.

ARTS ZIMBABWE. see *ART*

793.33   UK   ISSN 0404-6919
BALLROOM DANCING YEAR BOOK. a. £1.20. ‡ International Dance Teachers Association Ltd, 76 Bennett Road, Brighton BN2 5JL, England. Ed. Lyndon B. Wainwright. adv. bibl. index;cum.index. circ. 5,300.

BRISTOL FOLK NEWS. see *MUSIC*

CONTACTS & FACILITIES; in the entertainment industry. see *THEATER*

793.3   US   ISSN 0070-2676
DANCE DIRECTORY; programs of professional preparation in American colleges and universities. irreg., 10th edt., 1978. price varies. American Alliance for Health, Physical Education, Recreation, and Dance, 1900 Association Dr., Reston, VA 22091. circ. 2,000,000. (reprint service avail. from ISI,UMI) Indexed: ERIC.

792.8   UK   ISSN 0306-0128
DANCE GAZETTE. 1930. 3/yr. £3. Royal Academy of Dancing, 48 Vicarage Crescent, London SW11 3LT, England (U.S. Orders to: Elaine Keller, 8 College Ave., Upper Montclair, NJ 07043.) Ed. Lois Hainsworth. adv. bk. rev. circ. 15,000. (also avail. in microform from UMI)

793.3   US
DANCE LIFE. 1975. irreg., approx. 3/yr. $5.50 for 3 issues. 158 E. 7th St., New York, NY 10009. Ed. D. Lindner. adv. illus. circ. 3,000.
    Formerly: Dance Life in New York (ISSN 0361-5685)

793.3   US   ISSN 0070-2684
DANCE MAGAZINE ANNUAL; catalogue of dance artists and attractions, programs, resources and services. 1967. a. $15. Danad Publishing Co., 1180 Ave. of the Americas, New York, NY 10036. Ed. Heidi van Obenauer. adv. index. circ. 4,000.

792.8 378.0025   US
DANCE MAGAZINE DIRECTORY OF COLLEGE AND UNIVERSITY DANCE. biennial. $7.50. Danad Publishing Co., 1180 Ave. of the Americas, New York, NY 10036. Ed. Heidi von Obenauer. adv. illus.

793 792   US
DANCE RESEARCH ANNUAL. 1968. a. Congress on Research in Dance, Dance Dept., Education 675D, New York University, 35 W. 4th St., New York, NY 10003.
    Formerly: C O R D Research Annual.

793.32   US   ISSN 0070-2692
DANCE WORLD. 1966. a. $15.95. Crown Publishers, Inc., One Park Ave., New York, NY 10016.

792 780   US
ENJOYING THE ARTS. 1975. irreg. $7.97 per issue. Richards Rosen Press, 29 E. 21 St., New York, NY 10010. Ed. Ruth C. Rosen. illus.
    Young adult

ESSAYS ON ASIAN THEATER, MUSIC AND DANCE. see *THEATER*

793.3   US   ISSN 0071-6294
FOCUS ON DANCE. Variant title: Dance Heritage-Focus on Dance. 1960. irreg., no. 8, 1977. price varies. American Alliance for Health, Physical Education, Recreation, and Dance, 1900 Association Dr., Reston, VA 22091. (reprint service avail. from ISI,UMI)

793.31   US   ISSN 0163-528X
FOLK DANCE DIRECTORY. a. $0.60. Folk Dance Association, Box 500, Midwood Station, Brooklyn, NY 11230.

793.31   UK
FOLK DIRECTORY. 1977? a. £2 to non-members. English Folk Dance and Song Society, Cecil Sharp House, 2 Regents Park Rd., London NW1 7AY, England.

FOLK MUSIC JOURNAL. see *MUSIC*

793.31   US
FORWARD AND BACK. 1979. irreg. $1 per no. Jacob Bloom, Ed. & Pub., 34 Andrew St., Newton, MA 02161. circ. 100.

793.3   PL   ISSN 0076-2989
MALA BIBLIOTEKA BALETOWA. 1957. irreg. price varies. Polskie Wydawnictwo Muzyczne, Al. Krasinskiego 11, Krakow, Poland (Dist. by: Ars Polona-Ruch, Krakowskie Przedmiescie 7, Warsaw, Poland)

780 792   US
MONOGRAPHS ON MUSIC, DANCE AND THEATER IN ASIA. 1974. a. $4.50. Asia Society, Performing Arts Program, 133 E. 58th St., New York, NY 10022. Ed. Beate Gordon.

DANCE —
Abstracting, Bibliographies, Statistics

792 016   US   ISSN 0360-2737
BIBLIOGRAPHIC GUIDE TO DANCE.
(Supplement to New York Public Library.
Performing Arts Research Center. Dictionary
Catalog of the Dance Collection) 1975. a. G.K. Hall
& Co., 70 Lincoln St., Boston, MA 02111.

DEAF

see also Education—Special Education and
Rehabilitation; Social Services and
Welfare

617.8   US   ISSN 0095-3474
A.C.A. INDUSTRY GUIDE TO HEARING AIDS.
INTERNATIONAL EDITION. 1975. a. Acoustic
Corporation of America, 145 Tremont St., Boston,
MA 02111. illus.
Hearing aids

A S H A DIRECTORY. (American Speech-Language-
Hearing Association) see *MEDICAL
SCIENCES — Otorhinolaryngology*

A S H A REPORTS. (American Speech-Language-
Hearing Association) see *MEDICAL
SCIENCES — Otorhinolaryngology*

AMERICAN LECTURES IN SPEECH AND
HEARING. see *MEDICAL SCIENCES —
Otorhinolaryngology*

617.8   GW   ISSN 0571-8678
AUDIO-TECHNIK. (Text in German; summaries in
French and German) 1958. irreg., no. 30, 1979.
free. Robert Bosch GmbH, Geschaeftsbereich
Elektronik, Forckenbeckstr. 9-13, 1000 Berlin 33,
W. Germany (B.R.D.) circ. 3,000.

371.912   AT   ISSN 0005-0334
AUSTRALIAN TEACHER OF THE DEAF. 1956. a.
Aus.$11. Australian Association of Teachers of the
Deaf, Box 100, Croydon Park. N.S.W. 2133.,
Australia. Ed. Dr. L. E. Yang. adv. bk. rev. stat.
cum.index. circ. 500. Indexed: Aus.Educ.Ind. DSH
Abstr.
Study and teaching

391.912   US   ISSN 0045-8430
C A I D NEWSLETTER. 1971. irreg. (2-3/yr.)
membership. Convention of American Instructors of
the Deaf, 814 Thayer Ave., Silver Spring, MD
20910. Ed.Bd. bibl. circ. 4,000.

371.912   US
CONFERENCE OF EXECUTIVES OF AMERICAN
SCHOOLS FOR THE DEAF. PROCEEDINGS.
1948. biennial. $3. Conference of Executives of
American Schools for the Deaf, 5034 Wisconsin
Ave. N.W., Washington, DC 20016. circ. 600.

362.4   US
CONNECTICUT. COMMISSION ON THE DEAF
AND HEARING-IMPAIRED. ANNUAL
REPORT. 1974. a. free. Commission on the Deaf
and Hearing-Impaired, 40 Woodland St., Hartford,
CT 06105.
Formerly: Connecticut. Commission to Study and
Investigate the Problems of Deaf and Hearing-
Impaired Persons. Annual Report (ISSN 0094-
727X)

CONTRIBUTIONS TO THE STUDY OF MUSIC
AND DANCE. see *MUSIC*

371.912   US
CONVENTION OF AMERICAN INSTRUCTORS
OF THE DEAF. PROCEEDINGS AND
SELECTED PAPERS. a. price varies. Convention
of American Instructors of the Deaf, 814 Thayer
Ave., Silver Spring, MD 20910. (also avail. in
microform from UMI; back issues avail.)
Formerly: Convention of American Instructors of
the Deaf. Proceedings.

362.42 384.6   US   ISSN 0160-7472
INTERNATIONAL TELEPHONE DIRECTORY OF
THE DEAF. a. Teletypewriters for the Deaf, Inc.,
Box 28332, Washington, DC 20005.

362.42 371.912   US   ISSN 0024-8398
M S H A. 1965. a. $15 per no. Michigan Speech and
Hearing Association, 855 Grove St., East Lansing,
MI 48823. Eds. William A. Ahroon, D. Omar
Robinson. adv. circ. 1,500.

155.4512   US
MENTAL HEALTH IN DEAFNESS. 1977. irreg. (2-
4/yr.) Saint Elizabeths Hospital, Associate
Superintendent for Psychiatry, Washington, DC
20032. Ed. Dr. Luther D. Robinson. circ. 3,000.
(back issues avail.)

REHABILITATION GAZETTE; international journal
of independent living for the disabled. see
*EDUCATION — Special Education And
Rehabilitation*

362.42   SA
SOUTH AFRICAN NATIONAL COUNCIL FOR
THE DEAF. ANNUAL DIARY. a. R.5.50. South
African National Council for the Deaf, Box 31663,
Braamfontein, Transvaal, South Africa.

371.9 362.42   GW
STATISTISCHE NACHRICHTEN UEBER
BILDUNGS- UND SOZIALEINRICHTUNGEN
FUER HOERGESCHAEDIGTE IM
DEUTSCHPRACHIGEN RAUM. 1971. triennial.
DM.14. Bund Deutscher Taubstummenlehrer,
Franz-Arens-Str. 1, 4300 Essen 1, W. Germany
(B.R.D.) Ed. Werner Netsch.

362   IT   ISSN 0510-8292
WORLD CONGRESS OF THE DEAF.
PROCEEDINGS.* irreg. World Federation of the
Deaf, c/o C. Magarotto, Secretary, Via Gregorio
VII, N. 120, 00165 Rome, Italy.

DENTISTRY

see *Medical Sciences—Dentistry*

DERMATOLOGY AND VENEREOLOGY

see *Medical Sciences—Dermatology and
Venereology*

DOMESTIC COMMERCE

see *Business and Economics—Domestic
Commerce*

DRUG ABUSE AND ALCOHOLISM

see also *Pharmacy and Pharmacology*

616.861   US
A D P A SELECTED PAPERS OF ANNUAL
MEETINGS. 1950. a. $10. Alcohol and Drug
Problems Association of North America, 1101 15th
St. N.W., Washington, DC 20005. Ed. Ruth Brock.
circ. 2,500.
Formerly: North American Association of
Alcoholism Programs. Meeting. Selected Papers
(ISSN 0078-1274)

362.2   HK
ACTION COMMITTEE AGAINST NARCOTICS.
ANNUAL REPORT. 1965/66. irreg. free. Action
Committee Against Narcotics, c/o Narcotics
Division, Government Secretariat, Central
Government Offices (East Wing), Lower Albert Rd,
Hong Kong, Hong Kong. illus. circ. 10,000.
Formerly: Narcotics Progress Report.

616.86 157.63   CN   ISSN 0065-6119
ADDICTION RESEARCH FOUNDATION OF
ONTARIO. ANNUAL REPORT. 1951. a.
contr.free circ. ‡ Addiction Research Foundation of
Ontario, 33 Russell St., Toronto, Ontario M5S 2S1,
Canada. circ. 2,000.
Formerly: Alcoholism and Drug Addiction
Research Foundation. Annual Report (ISSN 0065-
6119)

353.9   US   ISSN 0095-3318
ALASKA. OFFICE OF ALCOHOLISM. REPORT. a.
Department of Health and Social Services, Office of
Alcoholism, Juneau, AK 99801. illus. Key Title:
Report - Office of Alcoholism, Department of
Health and Social Services, State of Alaska.

616.861 362.292   CN   ISSN 0319-423X
ALBERTA. ALCOHOLISM AND DRUG ABUSE
COMMISSION. ANNUAL REPORT. 1970. a.
Alcoholism and Drug Abuse Commission, 10050
112th St., Edmonton, Alta. T5K 1L9, Canada.

610   US
ALCOHOL IN OUR SOCIETY. 1965. irreg. price
varies. Department of Health, Division of
Alcoholism and Drug Abuse, 909 Basin Ave.,
Bismarck, ND 58505. Auths. Bernard Larsen, Levi
N. Larsen. circ. 38,000.

362.2 616.8   US   ISSN 0093-3279
ALCOHOLISM DIGEST ANNUAL. 1973. a.
Information Planning Associates, Inc., 656 Quince
Orchard Blvd., Gaithersburg, MD 20760. illus.

616.863   CN   ISSN 0002-5038
ALCOHOLISM REVIEW. 1955 (Suspended
publication June 1958-Oct. 1973) irreg. Alcoholism
Foundation of British Columbia, Vancouver, B.C.,
Canada. illus.

616.863 157.63   AT   ISSN 0157-8200
AUSTRALIA. NATIONAL INFORMATION
SERVICE ON DRUG ABUSE. TECHNICAL
INFORMATION BULLETIN. 1971. irreg. free.
(Department of Health, Drugs of Dependence
Section) Australian Government Publishing Service,
P.O. Box 84, Canberra, A.C.T. 2600, Australia. circ.
1,793.
Formerly: Australia. National Drug Information
Service. Technical Information Bulletin (ISSN 0310-
6012)

616.863   US   ISSN 0520-1802
BIOLOGICAL COUNCIL. COORDINATING
COMMITTEE FOR SYMPOSIA ON DRUG
ACTION. SYMPOSIUM PROCEEDINGS. irreg.
price varies. University Park Press, Chamber of
Commerce Bldg., Baltimore, MD 21202.

354.711   CN
BRITISH COLUMBIA. ALCOHOL AND DRUG
COMMISSION. ANNUAL REPORT. 1973. a.
Alcohol and Drug Commission, Box 21, 805 W.
Broadway, Vancouver, B.C. V52 1K1, Canada.

616.861   CN   ISSN 0068-2853
BROOKSIDE MONOGRAPHS. 1953. irreg. price
varies. (Addiction Research Foundation of Ontario)
University of Toronto Press, Front Campus,
Toronto, Ont. M5S 1A6, Canada (and 33 East
Tupper St., Buffalo, N. Y. 14203) (also avail. in
microfiche)

362.2   CN   ISSN 0705-5587
CANADA ADDICTIONS FOUNDATION.
DIRECTORY/FONDATION CANADIENNE
DES TOXICOMANIES. REPERTOIRE. (Text in
English and French) 1977. irreg. Fondation
Canadienne des Toxicomanies, 251 Laurier W.,
Suite 1100, Ottawa, Ont. K1P 5J6, Canada. circ.
1,000.

616.86   YU   ISSN 0033-8567
CENTAR ZA PROUCANANJE I SUZBIJANJE
ALKOHOLIZMA I DRUGIH OVISNOSTI.
RADOVI. (Text in Croatian, summaries in English)
1966. irreg. $3 per issue. Centar za Proucavanje i
Suzbijanje Alkoholizma i Drugih Ovisnosti - Centre
for Study and Control of Alcoholism and Other
Addictions, Vinogradska 29, 41000 Zagreb,
Yugoslavia. Ed. Dr. Vladimir Hudolin. adv. illus.
stat. circ. 1,000.

616.86 157.6   US
COPING CATALOG; a guide to resources in the greater Washington area for alcohol and drug addiction problems. 1974. a. $12.50. Washington Area Council on Alcoholism & Drug Abuse, Inc., 1221 Massachusetts Ave., N.W., Washington, DC 20005. Ed. Eleanor R. Edelstein. index. circ. 2,000. (processed)
   Formerly: Directory of Resources for Alcoholics.

616.865   US   ISSN 0361-1612
COUNCIL FOR TOBACCO RESEARCH--U.S.A. REPORT. a. Council for Tobacco Research--U.S.A. Inc., 110 E. 59th St., New York, NY 10022. Key Title: Report of the Council for Tobacco Research-U.S.A., Inc.

157.63 616.86   CN   ISSN 0228-863X
DIRECTORY OF ALCOHOL AND DRUG TREATMENT SOURCES IN ONTARIO. 1981. a. Can.$24.95. Addiction Research Foundation of Ontario, 33 Russell St., Toronto, Ont. M5S 2S1, Canada. Ed. Carol McDermott.

360   US
DIRECTORY OF COMMUNITY SERVICES FOR DRUG ABUSE IN CALIFORNIA. 1974. a. free. Department of Alcohol and Drug Abuse, Division of Drug Abuse, 111 Capitol Mall, Sacramento, CA 95814. Ed. Mark Whisler. circ. 6,500.
   Formerly: Drug Abuse: Directory of Community Services in California.

157.63   US   ISSN 0364-0671
DRUG ABUSE; a directory of training resources in California. Variant title: Drug Abuse Training Resource Directory. irreg. State Office of Narcotics and Drug Abuse, Sacramento, CA 95814.

613.83   US   ISSN 0070-735X
DRUG ABUSE PAPERS. 1969. irreg. $5.50. University of California, Berkeley, University Extension, Berkeley, CA 94720.

618   US   ISSN 0361-4344
F D A DRUG BULLETIN. vol. 5, 1975. irreg., approx. m. U.S. Food and Drug Administration, 5600 Fisher's Lane, Rockville, MD 20857. Indexed: I.P.A.

616.863 610   US   ISSN 0098-311X
HEALTH CONSEQUENCES OF SMOKING. 1967. a. price varies. U.S. Office on Smoking and Health, Technical Information Center, Park Bldg., Rm. 116, 5600 Fisheries Lane, Rockville, MD 20857. Ed. Bd. bibl. index.

362.2   US   ISSN 0093-7819
ILLINOIS. DEPARTMENT OF MENTAL HEALTH. DRUG ABUSE PROGRAM. PROGRESS REPORT. irreg. Department of Mental Health and Developmental Disabilities, Drug Abuse Program, State Office Bldg., 160 N. La Salle, Chicago, IL 60601. illus. Key Title: Progress Report - State of Illinois. Department of Mental Health. Drug Abuse Program.

613.81   SZ
INTERNATIONAL CONGRESS ON ALCOHOLISM AND DRUG DEPENDENCE. PROCEEDINGS. triennial, 32nd, 1978, Warsaw. price varies. International Council on Alcohol and Addictions, C.P. 140, 1001 Lausanne, Switzerland.

613.81   SZ   ISSN 0074-6622
INTERNATIONAL INSTITUTE ON THE PREVENTION AND TREATMENT OF ALCOHOLISM. SELECTED PAPERS. 1964. a, 24th, 1978, Zurich. price varies. International Council on Alcohol and Addictions, C.P. 140, 1001 Lausanne, Switzerland. Eds. Archer and Eva Tongue. circ. 1,000-2,000.
   Formerly: European Institute on the Prevention and Treatment of Alcoholism. Selected Papers.

613.81   SZ
INTERNATIONAL INSTITUTE ON THE PREVENTION AND TREATMENT OF DRUG DEPENDENCE. SELECTED PAPERS. 1970. a. price varies. International Council on Alcohol and Addictions, C.P. 140, 1001 Lausanne, Switzerland. circ. 1,000(approx.)

613.8   US   ISSN 0074-7114
INTERNATIONAL NARCOTIC CONFERENCE. REPORT: PROCEEDINGS OF ANNUAL CONFERENCE. 1960. a. $25. International Narcotic Enforcement Officers Association, Suite 1310, 112 State St., Albany, NY 12207. Ed. Celeste Morga. adv. bk. rev. circ. 10,000.

300   UN
INTERNATIONAL NARCOTICS CONTROL BOARD. COMPARATIVE STATEMENT OF ESTIMATES AND STATISTICS ON NARCOTIC DRUGS FURNISHED BY GOVERNMENTS IN ACCORDANCE WITH THE INTERNATIONAL TREATIES. (Text in English and French) a. $1. International Narcotics Control Board - Organe Internationale de Controle des Stupefiants, Distribution and Sales Section, Palais des Nations, CH-1200 Geneva 10, Switzerland (Or United Nations Publications, Room LX-2300, New York, NY 10017)

362.2   US   ISSN 0363-4507
IOWA COMPREHENSIVE STATE PLAN FOR DRUG ABUSE PREVENTION: ANNUAL PERFORMANCE REPORT. a. Drug Abuse Authority, 615 East 14th St., Suite D, Des Moines, IA 50319.

616.8   GW
JAHRBUCH ZUR FRAGE DER SUCHTGEFAHREN. 1958. a. DM.4.75. Neuland-Verlagsgesellschaft mbH, Adenauerallee 48, 2000 Hamburg 1, W. Germany (B.R.D.) Ed. Wilhelm Biel. circ. 3,800.
   Formerly: Jahrbuch zur Alkohol- und Tabakfrage (ISSN 0075-2827)

616.861   US   ISSN 0363-468X
JOURNAL OF STUDIES ON ALCOHOL. SUPPLEMENT. 1961. irreg., no. 8, 1979. price varies. Rutgers Center of Alcohol Studies, Publications Division, New Brunswick, NJ 08903. Ed. Timothy G. Coffey. index. (also avail. in microfilm from UMI) Indexed: Ind.Med. SSCI.
   Formerly (until 1975): Quarterly Journal of Studies on Alcohol. Supplement (ISSN 0079-8312)

362.2   US   ISSN 0362-7098
LOUISIANA. DIVISION OF MENTAL HEALTH. ANNUAL PERFORMANCE REPORT AND CONTINUATION OF THE STATE PLAN FOR DRUG ABUSE PREVENTION. a. Division of Mental Health, Box 42215, Baton Rouge, LA 70804. Key Title: Annual Performance Report and Continuation of the State Plan for Drug Abuse Prevention.

616.8   US
MARIHUANA AND HEALTH; ANNUAL REPORT TO THE U.S. CONGRESS FROM THE SECRETARY OF HEALTH, EDUCATION AND WELFARE. a. U.S. National Institute on Drug Abuse, 5600 Fishers Lane, Rockville, MD 20852.

362.2   US   ISSN 0090-3809
MONTANA STATE PLAN FOR ALCOHOL ABUSE AND ALCOHOLISM PREVENTION, TREATMENT AND REHABILITATION.* a. Department of Health and Environmental Services, Cogswell Building, Helena, MT 59601.
   Report year ends June 30

616.861   US   ISSN 0147-0515
N.I.A.A.A.-R.U.C.A.S. ALCOHOLISM TREATMENT SERIES. 1978. irreg. price varies. Rutgers Center of Alcohol Studies, Publications Division, New Brunswick, NJ 08903. index.
   Formerly: N.I.A.A.A.-R.U.C.A.S. Alcoholism Treatment Monographs.

616.863   US   ISSN 0360-9642
N I D A SUPPORTED DRUG TREATMENT PROGRAMS. U.S. National Institute on Drug Abuse, 5600 Fishers Lane, Rockville, MD 20852.

616.86   HK
NARCOTICS REPORT, HONG KONG. 1978. a. $20. Government Information Services, Beaconsfield House, Queens Rd., Central, Victoria, Hong Kong, Hong Kong.

157.63   US
NEW YORK (CITY). COMPREHENSIVE PLAN FOR DRUG ABUSE PREVENTION AND TREATMENT. 1970. a.; latest issue, 1972. free. ‡ Addiction Services Agency, 65 Worth St., New York, NY 10013.

616.861   NO   ISSN 0078-673X
NORWAY. STATENS INSTITUTT FOR ALKOHOLFORSKNING. SKRIFTER. (Text in English or Norwegian) 1962. irreg. price varies. (Statens Institutt for Alkoholforskning) Universitetsforlaget, Kolstadgt. 1, Box 2959-Toeyen, Oslo 6, Norway (U.S. address: Box 258, Irvington-on-Hudson, NY 10533) Ed. Sverre Brun-Gulbrandsen. (back issues avail.)

616.86   CN   ISSN 0707-9834
NOVA SCOTIA. COMMISSION ON DRUG DEPENDENCY. ANNUAL REPORT. 1972. a. Commission on Drug Dependency, Halifax, N. S., Canada.

353.9   US
OKLAHOMA. DRUG ABUSE DIVISION. ANNUAL REPORT. Variant title: Oklahoma. Office of Drug Abuse. Annual Performance Report, Drug Abuse Treatment Programs and Continuation Plan. a. Department of Mental Health, Drug Abuse Division, Box 53277, Capitol Sta., Oklahoma City, OK 73105. charts, stat.

616.8   US   ISSN 0093-9714
RESEARCH ADVANCES IN ALCOHOL & DRUG PROBLEMS. 1974. a. John Wiley & Sons, Inc., 605 Third Ave., New York, NY 10016. Ed. J. R. Gibbons.

616.8   US   ISSN 0080-4983
RUTGERS UNIVERSITY. CENTER OF ALCOHOL STUDIES. MONOGRAPH. 1958. irreg., no. 13, 1978. price varies. Rutgers Center of Alcohol Studies, Publications Division, New Brunswick, NJ 08903. index.

157.6   US
SAGE ANNUAL REVIEWS OF DRUG AND ALCOHOL ABUSE. 1977. a. $8.95 for softcover; hardcover $18.50. Sage Publications, Inc., 275 S. Beverly Dr., Beverly Hills, CA 90212 (And Sage Publications, Ltd., 28 Banner St., London EC1Y 8QE, England) Ed. James A. Inciardi. (back issues avail.)

354   CN   ISSN 0381-2278
SASKATCHEWAN. ALCOHOLISM COMMISSION. ANNUAL REPORT. 1969. a. free. Alcoholism Commission, 2134 Hamilton Street, Regina, Saskatchewan, Canada. illus. stat. circ. 1,000.

616.86   CN
SOCIETE DES ALCOOLS DU QUEBEC. RAPPORT ANNUEL. (Vols. for 1967/68-1969/70 issued by the Board under its French form of name: Regie des Alcools du Quebec) 1971. a. Societe des Alcools du Quebec, C. P. 1058, Place d'Armes, Montreal, P. Q., Canada.
   Formerly: Quebec (Province). Liquor Board. Rapport Annuel (ISSN 0481-2875)

157.63 616.86   CN   ISSN 0228-8648
SUBSTANCE ABUSE BOOK REVIEW INDEX. 1980. a. Can.$5.95. Addiction Research Foundation of Ontario, 33 Russell St., Toronto,Ont. M5S 2S1, Canada. Ed. Jane Bemko.

616.8   US   ISSN 0093-8599
U. S. NATIONAL CLEARINGHOUSE FOR DRUG ABUSE INFORMATION. REPORT SERIES. irreg. U. S. National Clearinghouse for Drug Abuse Information, P.O. Box 1635, Rockville, MD 20850. bibl. (looseleaf format)

157.63 616.863   US
U. S. NATIONAL INSTITUTE ON DRUG ABUSE. RESEARCH MONOGRAPH SERIES. Variant title: N I D A Research Monograph. 1974. irreg., no. 23, 1979. free. U.S. National Institute on Drug Abuse, Division of Research, 5600 Fishers Lane, Rockville, MD 20857. Ed.Bd. bibl. charts. (back issues avail.) Indexed: Chem.Abstr. Ind.Med. Psychol.Abstr. Psychopharmacol.Abstr.

362.2   US   ISSN 0090-662X
YEARBOOK OF DRUG ABUSE. (Subseries of Drug Abuse Series) 1973. a. price varies. Human Sciences Press, 72 Fifth Ave., NY 10011. (reprint service avail. from ISI,UMI)

DRUG ABUSE AND ALCOHOLISM —
Abstracting, Bibliographies, Statistics

016 616.861   CN   ISSN 0065-1885
ADDICTION RESEARCH FOUNDATION OF ONTARIO. BIBLIOGRAPHIC SERIES. 1967. irreg. price varies. Addiction Research Foundation of Ontario, 33 Russell St., Toronto, Ont. M5S 2S1, Canada. Ed. R. J. Hall.

616.86 016   US   ISSN 0093-2515
DRUG ABUSE BIBLIOGRAPHY. (Supplement to: Drugs of Addiction and Non-Addiction, Their Use and Abuse. a Comprehensive Bibliography 1960-1969) 1970. a. price varies. Whitston Publishing Co. Inc., Box 958, Troy, NY 12181.

616.861 016   US   ISSN 0074-204X
INTERNATIONAL BIBLIOGRAPHY OF STUDIES ON ALCOHOL. 1966. irreg. price varies. Rutgers Center of Alcohol Studies, Publications Division, New Brunswick, NJ 08903. Ed. Mark Keller. index.

614 310   NO
NORWAY. STATISTISK SENTRALBYRAA. ALKOHOL OG ANDRE RUSMIDLER/ ALCOHOL AND DRUGS. (Subseries of its Norges Offisielle Statistikk) (Text in English and Norwegian) a. Kr.10. Statistisk Sentralbyraa, Box 8131 Dep., Oslo 1, Norway.

EARTH SCIENCES

see also Earth Sciences—Geology; Earth Sciences—Geophysics; Earth Sciences—Hydrology; Earth Sciences—Oceanography

550 620   TH
A G E DIGEST. (Printed version of AGE Data Base) a. membership. Asian Information Center for Geotechnical Engineering, c/o Asian Institute of Technology, Box 2754, Bangkok, Thailand.

550 600   NO   ISSN 0065-1109
ACTA BOREALIA A. SCIENTIA. (Text in English and Norwegian) 1951. irreg. price varies. Tromsoe Museum, 9000 Tromsoe, Norway.

550 577   YU
ACTA CARSOLOGICA/KRASOSLOVNI ZBORNIK. vol.7, 1976. a. (Slovenska Akademija Znanosti in Umetnosti, Razred za Prirodoslovne Vede) Institut za Raziskovanje Krasa, Novi trg 3, Ljubljana, Yugoslavia. Ed. Svetozar Ilesic.

551   UR
AKADEMIYA NAUK CSSR. VOSTOCHNO-SIBIRSKII FILIAL, IRKUTSK. INSTITUT GEOKHIMII. GEOKHIMYA ENDOGENNYCH PROTSESSOV. 1977. irreg. 1.19 Rub. per issue. Institut Geokhimii, Ul. Favorskogo, 1, 664033 Irkutsk, U.S.S.R. Ed. L. Tauson. circ. 700.

551   UR
AKADEMIYA NAUK CSSR. VOSTOCHNO-SIBIRSKII FILIAL, IRKUTSK. INSTITUT GEOKHIMII. GEOKHIMICHESKIE METODY POISKOV, METODY ANALIZA. 1977. irreg. 1.40 Rub. per issue. Institut Geokhimii, Ul. Favorskogo, 1, 664033 Irkutsk, U.S.S.R. Ed. L. Tauson. circ. 700.

550   CN
ALBERTA RESEARCH COUNCIL. EARTH SCIENCE REPORTS. 1955. irreg. price varies. Alberta Research Council, 11315 87th Ave., Edmonton, Alta T6G 2C2, Canada.

550   US   ISSN 0569-2393
AMERICAN ASSOCIATION FOR THE ADVANCEMENT OF SCIENCE. COMMITTEE ON DESERT AND ARID ZONE RESEARCH. CONTRIBUTIONS. irreg. free. American Association for the Advancement of Science, Southwestern and Rocky Mountain Division, Box 3AF, Las Cruces, NM 88001. Ed. Donald D. MacPhail.

550   US   ISSN 0084-6597
ANNUAL REVIEW OF EARTH AND PLANETARY SCIENCES. 1973. a. $20. Annual Reviews Inc., 4139 El Camino Way, Palo Alto, CA 94306. Ed. G. W. Wetherill. bibl. cum.ind. (back issues avail.; reprint service avail. from ISI) Indexed: Chem.Abstr. Int.Aerosp.Abstr. M.M.R.I.

550   UN   ISSN 0066-7366
ARID ZONE RESEARCH. (Text in English and French) 1953. irreg., 1970, vol. 30. price varies. Unesco, 7-9 Place de Fontenoy, 75700 Paris, France (Dist. in U.S. by: Unipub, 345 Park Ave. S., New York, NY 10010)

550   UK   ISSN 0066-8044
ARTHUR HOLMES SOCIETY. JOURNAL. 1958-59. a. 25p. ‡ Arthur Holmes Society, University of Durham, Department of Geological Sciences, South Road, Durham DH1 3LE, England. circ. 300.
Until 1966: Durham University Geological Society. Journal.

551.9   CN
ASSOCIATION OF EXPLORATION GEOCHEMISTS. SPECIAL PUBLICATIONS. irreg. price varies. Association of Exploration Geochemists, Box 523, Rexdale, Ont. M9W 5L4, Canada.

AUSTRALIA. BUREAU OF MINERAL RESOURCES, GEOLOGY, AND GEOPHYSICS. 1: 250000 GEOLOGICAL MAPS AND EXPLANATORY NOTES SERIES. see *EARTH SCIENCES — Geology*

550   AT   ISSN 0084-7089
AUSTRALIA. BUREAU OF MINERAL RESOURCES, GEOLOGY AND GEOPHYSICS. BULLETIN. 1932. irreg. price varies. Bureau of Mineral Resources, Geology & Geophysics, Box 378, Canberra City, A.C.T. 2601, Australia. Indexed: Aus.Sci.Ind.

550   AT   ISSN 0084-7100
AUSTRALIA. BUREAU OF MINERAL RESOURCES, GEOLOGY AND GEOPHYSICS. REPORTS. 1948. irreg. price varies. Bureau of Mineral Resources, Geology & Geophysics, Box 378, Canberra City, A.C.T. 2601, Australia.

BIOGEOGRAPHICA. see *ENVIRONMENTAL STUDIES*

550   BO   ISSN 0067-9828
BOLIVIA. SERVICIO GEOLOGICO. BOLETIN. 1961. irreg. price varies. Servicio Geologico, Casilla 2729, La Paz, Bolivia.

550   BO   ISSN 0067-9836
BOLIVIA. SERVICIO GEOLOGICO. CIRCULARE. 1964. irreg. P.2($0.20) Servicio Geologico, Casilla 2729, La Paz, Bolivia.

550   BO   ISSN 0067-9844
BOLIVIA. SERVICIO GEOLOGICO. INFORME. a. P.240($0.35) Servicio Geologico, Casilla 2729, La Paz, Bolivia.

BOLIVIA. SERVICIO GEOLOGICO. SERIE MINERALOGICA. CONTRIBUCIONE. see *MINES AND MINING INDUSTRY*

550.5   II
BULLETIN OF EARTH SCIENCES. (Text in English) 1972. a. Rs.15($3) Indian Society of Earth Scientists, c/o Dept. of Geology, Poona University, Poona 411007, India. Ed. G. G. Deshpande. adv. illus. circ. 300.

550   UK
CAMBRIDGE EARTH SCIENCE SERIES. irreg. price varies. Cambridge University Press, Box 110, Cambridge CB2 3RL, England (And 32 E. 57th St., New York NY 10022) Ed.Bd.

550 020   CN   ISSN 0226-3343
CANADA. EARTH PHYSICS BRANCH. LIBRARY. LIBRARY NEWS. (Text in English and French) 1970. irreg. Earth Physics Branch, Library, Carling Ave., Ottawa, Ont., Canada.

550   JA
COLLECTED PAPERS ON EARTH SCIENCES. (Text in English) a. exchange basis. Nagoya University, Department of Earth Sciences - Nagoya Daigaku Rigakubu Chikyu Kagaku Kyoshitsu, Faculty of Science, Chikusa-ku, Nagoya 464, Japan.

628 550   JA   ISSN 0547-1435
COLLECTED PAPERS ON SCIENCES OF ATMOSPHERE AND HYDROSPHERE. (Text in Japanese and English) 1964. a. exchange basis. Nagoya University, Water Research Institute - Nagoya Daigaku Suishitsu Kagaku Kenkyu Shisetsu, Furo-cho, Chikusa-ku, Nagoya 464, Japan.

550   CN   ISSN 0074-9427
COMMISSION FOR THE GEOLOGICAL MAP OF THE WORLD. BULLETIN. (Text in English and French) 1962. irreg.; (approx 2 per year); no. 18, 1974. Commission for the Geological Map of the World, c/o R. D. Russell, Department of Geophysics, University of British Columbia, 2075 Wesbrook Place, Vancouver V6T 1W5, Canada. Ed. F. Delany. circ. 200.

COMMONWEALTH SCIENTIFIC AND INDUSTRIAL RESEARCH ORGANIZATION. DIVISION OF APPLIED GEOMECHANICS. TECHNICAL PAPER. see *MINES AND MINING INDUSTRY*

COMMONWEALTH SCIENTIFIC AND INDUSTRIAL RESEARCH ORGANIZATION. DIVISION OF APPLIED GEOMECHANICS. TECHNICAL REPORT. see *MINES AND MINING INDUSTRY*

COMMONWEALTH SCIENTIFIC AND INDUSTRIAL RESEARCH ORGANIZATION. INSTITUTE OF EARTH RESOURCES. ANNUAL REPORT. see *ENGINEERING — Civil Engineering*

553   CY   ISSN 0574-8267
CYPRUS. GEOLOGICAL SURVEY DEPARTMENT. ANNUAL REPORT. 1956. a. free to institutions. Geological Survey Department, Nicosia, Cyprus. charts. illus. stat. index. (processed)

550   CY
CYPRUS. GEOLOGICAL SURVEY DEPARTMENT. BULLETIN. 1963. irreg., no. 7, 1977. price varies. Geological Survey Department, Nicosia, Cyprus.

550   CY   ISSN 0574-8259
CYPRUS. GEOLOGICAL SURVEY DEPARTMENT. MEMOIRS. (Text and summaries in English) 1959. irreg.,latest no. 8. Mils.3500. Geological Survey Department, Nicosia, Cyprus. charts. illus.

550 598.1   US   ISSN 0191-3875
DESERT TORTOISE COUNCIL. PROCEEDINGS OF SYMPOSIUM. 1976. a. $5. Desert Tortoise Council, 1835 Klauber Ave., San Diego, CA 92114.

550 020   US
DIRECTORY OF GEOSCIENCE LIBRARIES, U.S. AND CANADA. 1968. irreg., 2nd edt. 1974. Geoscience Information Society, American Geological Institute, 5205 Leesburg Pike, Falls Church, VA 22041. Eds. Richard D. Walker, Diane Parker.

550   UN   ISSN 0070-7910
EARTH SCIENCES SERIES. (Text in English and French) 1969. irreg; no. 12, 1974. Unesco, 7-9 Place de Fontenoy, 75700 Paris, France (Dist. in U.S. by: Unipub, 345 Park Ave. S., New York, NY 10010)

550   GW   ISSN 0170-3188
ERDWISSENSCHAFTLICHE FORSCHUNG. (Text in English and German) irreg., vol. 16, 1981. price varies. (Akademie der Wissenschaften und der Literatur, Mainz, Kommission fuer Erdwissenschaftliche Forschung) Franz Steiner Verlag GmbH, Friedrichstr. 24, Postfach 5529, 6200 Wiesbaden, W. Germany (B.R.D.) Ed.Wilhelm Lauer.

550   GE   ISSN 0071-9404
FREIBERGER FORSCHUNGSHEFTE. MONTANWISSENSCHAFTEN: REIHE C. GEOWISSENSCHAFTEN. irreg. price varies. (Bergakademie Freiberg) VEB Deutscher Verlag fuer Grundstoffindustrie, Karl-Heine-Str. 27, 7031 Leipzig, E. Germany (D.D.R.)

526 BU
GEODESY. (Text in Bulgarian, English, French, German, Russian; summaries in various languages) 1975. a. 1 lv. (Bulgarska Akademiia na Naukite, Tsentralna Laboratoriia po Geodeziia) Publishing House of the Bulgarian Academy of Sciences, Ul. Akad. G. Bonchev, 1113 Sofia, Bulgaria (Dist. by: Hemus, 6, Rouski Blvd., 1000 Sofia, Bulgaria) adv. circ. 600.
Supersedes: Bulgarska Akademiia na Naukite, Sofia, Tsentralnata Laboratoriia po Geodeziia. Izvestiia (ISSN 0068-3701)

550 GW ISSN 0170-3250
GEOECOLOGICAL RESEARCH. (Text in English) irreg., vol. 4, 1980. price varies. Franz Steiner Verlag GmbH, Friedrichstr. 24, Postfach 5529, 6200 Wiesbaden, W. Germany (B.R.D.) Ed.Ulrich Schweinfurth.

550 GW ISSN 0343-2521
GEOJOURNAL; international journal for physical, biological and human geosciences. (Text in English) 1977. 6/yr. DM.248. Akademische Verlagsgesellschaft, Bahnhofstr. 39, Postfach 1107, 6200 Wiesbaden, W. Germany (B.R.D) Ed.Wolf Tietze. adv. bk. rev. abstr. bibl. charts. illus. index. circ. 1,500. (back issues avail.)

550 US ISSN 0094-7091
GEOKHIMIYA TRANSLATIONS. 1973. irreg., approx. a. American Geological Institute, 5205 Leesburg Pike, Falls Church, VA 22041.

550 SZ ISSN 0171-1687
GEOMETHODICA. Represents: Basler Geomethodisches Colloquium. Veroeffentlichungen/ Basel Geomethodological Meeting. Proceedings. (Proceedings for 1st and 2nd meetings published in Basler Afrika Bibliographies. Mitteilungen, vol. 15 (1976) and vol. 19 (1977)) (Text in German; summaries in English, French and German) 1978. a. 26 Fr. Basler Afrika Bibliographien, Postfach 2037, CH-4001 Basel, Switzerland. Ed. Hartmut Leser. illus. circ. 300.

550 US ISSN 0072-1409
GEOSCIENCE INFORMATION SOCIETY. PROCEEDINGS. (Contains papers presented at symposia held with annual meetings) 1969. a. $15 to non-members. ‡ Geoscience Information Society, c/o American Geological Institute, 5205 Leesburg Pike, Falls Church, VA 22041. circ. 250(ap.)

550 UK
GEOSOURCES. 1969. irreg. price varies. Geosystems, P.O. Box 1024, Westminster, London S.W.1, England. adv.
Formerly: Geoserials (ISSN 0072-1417)

550 BL ISSN 0072-4998
GONDWANA NEWSLETTER. (Text in English) 1969. irreg. available on exchange. Universidade Federal do Rio Grande do Sul, Instituto de Geociencias, Centro de Investigacao do Gondwana, Rua Gen. Vitorino 255, 90,000 Porto Alegre, Rio Grande do Sul, Brazil. Eds. Maria E. Pacheco, Hedy L. Hofmann. adv. bibl.

550 UK
GREAT BRITAIN. INSTITUTE OF GEOLOGICAL SCIENCES. METRIC WELL INVENTORY. 1980. irreg. Institute of Geological Sciences, Exhibition Rd., South Kensington, London SW7 2DE, England. illus. circ. 350.
Supersedes: Great Britain. Institute of Geological Sciences. Well Inventory Series. Metric Units (ISSN 0308-5368)

550 570 551.6 US ISSN 0073-4373
ICEFIELD RANGES RESEARCH PROJECT SCIENTIFIC RESULTS. 1969. irreg. price varies. ‡ American Geographical Society, Broadway at 156th St., New York, NY 10032. (Co-Sponsor: Arctic Institute of North America) Ed. Vivian C. Bushnell. circ. 800. Indexed: Geo.Abstr. Meteor. & Geoastrophys.Abstr.

555.4 II
INDIAN ACADEMY OF GEOSCIENCE. JOURNAL. (Text in English) vol. 14, 1972. a. $24. Indian Academy of Geoscience, Osmania University, Department of Geology, Hyderabad 500007, Andhra Pradesh, India (Subscr. to: Prints India, 11 Darya Ganj, New Delhi 110002, India) illus.
Continues: Indian Geoscience Association. Journal.

INSTITUTE FOR THE STUDY OF EARTH AND MAN NEWSLETTER. see ARCHAEOLOGY

INTERNATIONAL ASSOCIATION OF VOLCANOLOGY AND CHEMISTRY OF THE EARTH'S INTERIOR. NEWSLETTER. see EARTH SCIENCES — Geophysics

550 US ISSN 0538-9984
INTERNATIONAL SERIES ON EARTH SCIENCES. 1958. irreg., vol. 34, 1979. price varies. Pergamon Press, Inc., Maxwell House, Fairview Park, Elmsford, NY 10523. index.
Formerly: International Series of Monographs on Earth Sciences.

550 540 UR
ISSLEDOVANIYA V OBLASTI KHIMII REDKOZEMEL'NYKH ELEMENTOV. 1969. irreg. 0.55 Rub. Saratovskii Universitet, Saratov, U.S.S.R.

550 JA ISSN 0075-3343
JAPANESE ANTARCTIC RESEARCH EXPEDITION DATA REPORTS. (Text in English) 1968. irreg., no. 54, 1980. exchage basis. National Institute of Polar Research - Kokuritsu Kyokuchi Kenkyujyo, 9-10 Kaga, 1-chome, Itabashi-ku, Tokyo 173, Japan. Ed. Takesi Nagata. circ. 500. Indexed: Curr.Antarc.Lit.

550 JA ISSN 0022-0442
JOURNAL OF EARTH SCIENCES. 1953. a. exchange basis. Nagoya University, Department of Earth Sciences - Nagoya Daigaku Rigakubu Chikyu Kagaku Kyoshitsu, Faculty of Science, Chikusa-ku, Nagoya 464, Japan. Ed.Bd. circ. 376. Indexed: Chem.Abstr.

550 JA ISSN 0449-2560
JOURNAL OF GEOSCIENCES/OSAKA-SHIRITSU DAIGAKU RIGAKUBU CHIGAKU KIYO. (Text in English) 1957. a. exchange basis. Osaka City University, Department of Geosciences - Osaka-shiritsu Daigaku Rigakubu Chigaku Kyoshitsu, Faculty of Sciences, 459 Sugimoto-cho, Sumiyoshi-ku, Osaka 558, Japan.

KANSAS GEOLOGICAL SURVEY. ENERGY RESOURCES SERIES. see ENERGY

550 UR
LITOLOGIYA I PALEOGEOGRAFIYA. 1972. triennial. 1 Rub. (Leningradskii Universitet, Kafedra Litologii i Morskoi Geologii) Izdatel'stvo Leningradskii Universitet, Universitetskaya nab. 7/9, Leningrad B-164, U.S.S.R. (Subscr. to: Mezhdunarodnaya Kniga, Moscow, G-200, U. S. S. R.) Ed. N. V. Logvinenko. bibl, illus. circ. 600. Indexed: Ref.Zh.

550 AG ISSN 0076-0897
LORENTZIA. 1970. irreg. $1. ‡ Universidad Nacional de Cordoba, Facultad de Ciencias Exactas, Fisicas y Naturales, Museo Botanico, 5000 Cordoba, Argentina. circ. 1,000. Indexed: Biol.Abstr. Sci.Abstr. Excerp.Bot.

550 US
LOUISIANA STATE UNIVERSITY. MUSEUM OF GEOSCIENCE. MELANGES. 1971. irreg., (approx. 1/yr) $1. ‡ Louisiana State University, School of Geoscience, Geology Building, Baton Rouge, LA 70803. Ed. R.E. Ferrell. illus. (back issues avail.)

550 572 US
LOUISIANA STATE UNIVERSITY. SCHOOL OF GEOSCIENCE. MISCELLANEOUS PUBLICATIONS. 1967. irreg.; latest issue 1977. price varies. Louisiana State University, School of Geoscience, Geology Building, Baton Rouge, LA 70803. Ed. R.E. Ferrell.

550 CN ISSN 0076-1850
MCGILL UNIVERSITY, MONTREAL. AXEL HEIBERG ISLAND RESEARCH REPORTS. 1961. irreg. Can.$3 per no. McGill University, P.O. Box 6070, Montreal, 101, Canada. Indexed: Chem.Abstr. Arct.Bibl.

550 574 CN ISSN 0541-6299
MCGILL UNIVERSITY, MONTREAL. MARINE SCIENCES CENTRE. ANNUAL REPORT. 1965. a. Can.$3. ‡ McGill University, Marine Sciences Centre, 3620 University St., Montreal, P.Q. H3A 2B2, Canada. circ. controlled. Indexed: Ocean.Abstr.

551.9 551 NE ISSN 0076-6895
METHODS IN GEOCHEMISTRY AND GEOPHYSICS. 1964. irreg., vol. 15, 1980. price varies. Elsevier Scientific Publishing Co., Box 211, 1000 AE Amsterdam, Netherlands.

550 US
MONOGRAPHS IN GEOSCIENCE. 1967. irreg. price varies. Plenum Press, 233 Spring St., New York, NY 10013. Ed. Rhodes W. Fairbridge.

550 574 FR ISSN 0078-9763
MUSEUM NATIONAL D'HISTOIRE NATURELLE, PARIS. MEMOIRES. NOUVELLE SERIE. SERIE C. SCIENCES DE LA TERRE. 1950. irreg. price varies. Museum National d'Histoire Naturelle, 38, Rue Geoffroy-Saint-Hilaire, Paris 5, France. Indexed: Ocean.Abstr. Pollut.Abstr.

550 559 JA ISSN 0386-5533
NATIONAL INSTITUTE OF POLAR RESEARCH. MEMOIRS. SERIES C: EARTH SCIENCES. (Text and summaries in English) 1964. irreg., no. 12, 1977. exchange basis. National Institute of Polar Research - Kokuritsu Kyokuchi Kenkyujyo, 9-10 Kaga, 1-chome, Itabashi-ku, Tokyo 173, Japan. Ed. Takesi Nagata. circ. 1,000. Indexed: Curr.Antarc.Lit.
Supersedes: Japanese Antarctic Research Expedition, 1956-1962. Scientific Reports. Series C: Earth Sciences. (ISSN 0075-3378)

NATIONAL RESEARCH COUNCIL, CANADA. ASSOCIATE COMMITTEE ON GEOTECHNICAL RESEARCH. TECHNICAL MEMORANDUM. see ENGINEERING

550 333.7 UN ISSN 0077-6092
NATURAL RESOURCES RESEARCH. (Text in English and French) 1963. irreg; vol. 12, 1974. price varies. Unesco, 7-9 Place de Fontenoy, 75700 Paris, France (Dist. in U.S. by: Unipub, 345 Park Ave. S., New York, NY 10010)

NAUKA O ZEMI. SERIA GEOGRAPHICA. see GEOGRAPHY

550 AU ISSN 0078-351X
OESTERREICHISCHE MOORFORSCHUNG.* irreg. Neydharting Verlag, Pfarrplatz 3-4, A-4020 Linz, Austria.

550 PL ISSN 0370-0836
POLITECHNIKA WROCLAWSKA. INSTYTUT GEOTECHNIKI. PRACE NAUKOWE. KONFERENCJE. (Text in Polish; summaries in English and Russian) 1972. irreg., 1978, no. 11. price varies. Politechnika Wroclawska, Wybrzeze Wyspianskiego 27, 50-370 Wroclaw, Poland (Dist. by: Ars Polona-Ruch, Krakowskie Przedmiescie 7, Warsaw, Poland) Ed. Marian Kloza.

550 PL ISSN 0084-2834
POLITECHNIKA WROCLAWSKA. INSTYTUT GEOTECHNIKI. PRACE NAUKOWE. MONOGRAFIE. (Text in Polish; summaries in English, French and Russian) 1971. irreg., no. 9, 1979. price varies. Politechnika Wroclawska, Wybrzeze Wyspianskiego 27, 50-370 Wroclaw, Poland (Dist. by: Ars Polona-Ruch, Krakowskie Przedmiescie 7, Warsaw, Poland) Ed. Marian Kloza.

550 PL ISSN 0084-2842
POLITECHNIKA WROCLAWSKA. INSTYTUT GEOTECHNIKI. PRACE NAUKOWE. STUDIA I MATERIALY. (Text in Polish; summaries in English, French and Russian) 1969. irreg., 1977, no. 10. price varies. Politechnika Wroclawska, Wybrzeze Wyspianskiego 27, 50-370 Wroclaw, Poland (Dist. by: Ars Polona-Ruch, Krakowskie Przedmiescie 7, Warsaw, Poland) Ed. Marian Kloza.

550 FR
REUNION ANNUELLE DES SCIENCES DE LA TERRE; resumes des communications. 1973. a. Societe Geologique de France, 77 rue Claude Bernard, 75005 Paris, France. (Co-sponsors: Societe Francaise de Mineralogie; Union Francaise de Geologues) illus.

550 GW ISSN 0080-2689
RHEINISCHE SCHRIFTEN. 1963. irreg. price varies. Rheinland-Verlag, Kennedy-Ufer 2, 5000 Cologne 21, W. Germany (B.R.D.) (Distr. by: Rudolf Habelt Verlag, Am Buchenhang 1, 5300 Bonn, W. Germany (B.R.D.))

620 550   US   ISSN 0080-9004
SERIES ON ROCK AND SOIL MECHANICS. 1971. irreg (4-6/yr) price varies. ‡ Trans Tech Publications, 16 Bearskin Neck, Rockport, MA 01966. Ed. Dr. R. H. Wohlbier.

550   US   ISSN 0081-0274
SMITHSONIAN CONTRIBUTIONS TO THE EARTH SCIENCES. 1969. irreg. Smithsonian Institution Press, Washington, DC 20560. Ed. Albert L. Ruffin Jr. circ. 1,850. (reprint service avail. from UMI)

550   US   ISSN 0085-6142
SMITHSONIAN INSTITUTION. CENTER FOR SHORT LIVED PHENOMENA. ANNUAL REPORT. 1971. a. $25. Smithsonian Institution, Center for Short Lived Phenomena, 60 Garden St., Cambridge, MA 02138 (Subscr. to: Unipub, Box 433, Murray Hill Station, New York, NY 10016) Ed.Bd. bibl. charts. illus.

550   CL   ISSN 0069-3561
UNIVERSIDAD DE CHILE. DEPARTAMENTO DE GEOLOGIA. SERIE APARTADO. (Text in Spanish and English) 1947. irreg., 1969, no. 22. Esc.15. Universidad de Chile, Facultad de Ciencias Fisicas y Matematicas, Departamento de Geologia, Santiago, Chile.

550   UY
UNIVERSIDAD DE LA REPUBLICA. FACULTAD DE HUMANIDADES Y CIENCIAS. REVISTA. SERIE CIENCIAS DE LA TIERRA. N.S. 1979. irreg. Universidad de la Republica, Facultad de Humanidades y Ciencias, Seccion Revista, Tristan Narvaja 1674, Montevideo, Uruguay. Dir. Beatriz Martinez Osorio.
Supersedes in part: Universidad de la Republica. Facultad de Humanidades y Ciencias. Revista.

550   BL   ISSN 0080-0244
UNIVERSIDAD FEDERAL DE PERNAMBUCO. INSTITUTO DE GEOSCIENCIAS. SERIE B: ESTUDOS E PESQUISAS.* (Incorporates Its series: Mineralogia, Paleontologia, Petrologia and Geologia) (Text in Portuguese; summaries in English, French or German) 1971. irreg. not for sale. Universidade Federal de Pernambuco, Centtro de Tecnologia, Recife, PE, Brazil. circ. 1,000.

550 520   BL
UNIVERSIDADE DE SAO PAULO. INSTITUTO DE GEOCIENCIAS. BOLETIM. (Includes some summaries in English) 1970. irreg. Universidade de Sao Paulo, Instituto de Geociencias, Cidade Universitaria "Armando de Salles Oliveira", Bloco, 19, Sao Paulo, Brazil. illus.
Formerly: Universidade de Sao Paulo. Instituto de Geociencias y Astronomia. Boletim. Supersedes Mineralogia, and Geologia, issued by the university's Faculdade de Filosofia, Ciencias e Letras.

550   BL
UNIVERSIDADE FEDERAL DO RIO GRANDE DO SUL. INSTITUTO DE GEOCIENCIAS. PESQUISAS. (Text in Portuguese; summaries in English) 1972. irreg. $7. Universidade Federal do Rio Grande do Sul, Instituto de Geociencias, Rua Gen. Vitorino 255, Porto Alegre, Brazil. Indexed: Geosci.Doc.

550 560   GW   ISSN 0585-7856
UNIVERSITAET STUTTGART. INSTITUT FUER GEOLOGIE UND PALAEONTOLOGIE ARBEITEN NEUE FOLGE. (Text in German; summaries in English and French) 1954. irreg., vol. 72, 1978. price varies. Universitaet Stuttgart, Institut fuer Geologie und Palaeontologie, Boeblinger Str. 72, 7000 Stuttgart 1, W. Germany (B.R.D.) Ed. K. Hinkelbein. illus. circ. 400.

550   US   ISSN 0068-645X
UNIVERSITY OF CALIFORNIA PUBLICATIONS IN GEOLOGICAL SCIENCES. 1893. irreg. price varies. University of California Press, 2223 Fulton St., Berkeley, CA 94720.

550 919.8   US   ISSN 0069-6145
UNIVERSITY OF COLORADO. INSTITUTE OF ARCTIC AND ALPINE RESEARCH. OCCASIONAL PAPERS. 1971. irreg. price varies. ‡ University of Colorado, Institute of Arctic and Alpine Research, Boulder, CO 80309. (also avail. in microfiche from NTI; reprint service avail. from UMI) Indexed: Geo.Abstr.

550   JA   ISSN 0040-8999
UNIVERSITY OF TOKYO. FACULTY OF SCIENCE. JOURNAL. SECTION 2: GEOLOGY, MINERALOGY, GEOGRAPHY, GEOPHYSICS/ TOKYO DAIGAKU RIGAKUBU KIYO, DAI-2-RUI, CHISHITSUGAKU, KOBUTSUGAKU, CHIRIGAKU, CHIYU BUTSURIGAKU. (Text in English) 1912. a. University of Tokyo, Faculty of Science - Tokyo Daigaku Rigakubu, 7-3-1 Hongo, Bunkyo-ku, Tokyo 113, Japan (Order from: Maruzen Co., Ltd., 2-3-10 Nihonbashi, Chuo-ku, Tokyo 103, Japan; or their Import and Export Department, Box 5050, Tokyo International, Tokyo 100-31, Japan) Ed. N. Watanabe. bibl. charts. illus. Indexed: Biol.Abstr. Chem.Abstr. Met.Abstr.

WEST CANADIAN RESEARCH PUBLICATIONS OF GEOLOGY AND RELATED SCIENCES. see EARTH SCIENCES — Geology

EARTH SCIENCES — Abstracting, Bibliographies, Statistics

016 554   BE   ISSN 0065-0420
ABSTRACTS OF BELGIAN GEOLOGY AND PHYSICAL GEOGRAPHY. (Text in English) 1967. a. 150 Fr.($10) Rijksuniversiteit te Gent, Geologisch Instituut, Krijgslaan 271, B-9000 Ghent, Belgium. Ed. L. Walschot. adv. bk. rev. circ. 150.

551.7 560   US   ISSN 0192-7272
AMERICAN ASSOCIATION OF STRATIGRAPHIC PALYNOLOGISTS. ABSTRACTS OF PAPERS PRESENTED AT THE ANNUAL MEETINGS. a. free. American Association of Stratigraphic Palynologists Foundation., c/o Robert T. Clarke, Mobil R & D Corp. Field Research Laboratory, Box 900, Dallas, TX 75221.

AUSTRALIA. BUREAU OF MINERAL RESOURCES, GEOLOGY AND GEOPHYSICS. OPEN FILE CIRCULAR. see MINES AND MINING INDUSTRY — Abstracting, Bibliographies, Statistics

551.46 016   BE
BIBLIO-MER.* irreg. 480 Fr.($10) Editions Biblio-Mer, Ankerstraat 10, 8400 Oostende, Belgium. Ed. R. Roze. bk. rev. bibl.

551 016   SA   ISSN 0584-2360
BIBLIOGRAPHY AND SUBJECT INDEX OF SOUTH AFRICAN GEOLOGY. 1957. a, latest 1976. R.3.60. Geological Survey, Private Bag X112, Pretoria 0001, South Africa (Orders to: Government Printer, Bosman St., Private Bag X85, Pretoria 0001, South Africa)

557 016   US   ISSN 0067-7272
BIBLIOGRAPHY OF THE GEOLOGY OF MISSOURI. 1956. a. $0.25 per issue. Department of Natural Resources, Division of Geology and Land Survey, Box 250, Rolla, MO 65401. Ed. Jerry D. Vineyard.

557 016   CN
CANADA. GEOLOGICAL SURVEY. ABSTRACTS OF PUBLICATIONS. 1966. a. price varies. Geological Survey of Canada, 601 Booth St., Ottawa, Ont. K1A OE8, Canada (Dist. by: Supply and Services Canada, Ottawa, Ont. K1A 0S9, Canada) abstr. circ. 1,500. (processed)

557 016   CN   ISSN 0707-2996
CANADA. GEOLOGICAL SURVEY. INDEX OF PUBLICATIONS OF THE GEOLOGICAL SURVEY OF CANADA. 1900. a. price varies. Geological Survey of Canada, 601 Booth St., Ottawa K1A OE8, Canada (Dist. by: Supply and Services Canada, Ottawa, Ont. K1A 0S9, Canada) index. cum.index (1959-69)

551.4 015   GW   ISSN 0340-4242
GERMANY(FEDERAL REPUBLIC, 1949-). BUNDESANSTALT FUER GEWAESSERKUNDE. HYDROLOGISCHE BIBLIOGRAPHIE. 1936. a. price varies. Bundesanstalt fuer Gewaesserkunde, Kaiserin-Augusta-Anlagen 15-17, 5400 Koblenz, W. Germany(B.R.D.) (Co-sponsors: International Union for Geodesy and Geophysics; International Association for Hydrological Sciences)

551 016   II
INDIAN GEOLOGICAL INDEX. Alternate title: I. G. I. (Text in English) 1971. a. Rs.50. D-42 Vivek Vihar, Delhi 32, India.
Geological literature of India

551.46 016   US
SEA GRANT PUBLICATIONS INDEX. 1968. a. $5. National Sea Grant Depository, Pell Library Building, University of Rhode Island, Narragansett Bay Campus, Narragansett, RI 02882. Ed.Bd. bibl. index; cum. index. circ. 13,000.

551 016   SP
SPAIN. INSTITUTO GEOLOGICO Y MINERO. CATALOGO DE EDICIONES. irreg. (Instituto Geologico y Minero) Spain. Ministerio de Industria, Claudio Coello, 44, Madrid, Spain. bibl. illus.

551 520   US
U S S R REPORT: GEOPHYSICS, ASTRONOMY, AND SPACE. 1961. irreg. (approx. 24/yr.) $120. U.S. Joint Publications Research Service, 1000 N. Glebe Rd., Arlington, VA 22201 (Orders to: NTIS, Springfield, VA 22161)
Former titles: U S S R and Eastern Europe Scientific Abstracts: Geophysics, Astronomy, and Space (ISSN 0363-7220); Soviet-Bloc Research in Geophysics, Astronomy, and Space (ISSN 0038-5336)

551.46 016   VE   ISSN 0590-3343
UNIVERSIDAD DE ORIENTE. INSTITUTO OCEANOGRAFICO BIBLIOTECA. BOLETIN BIBLIOGRAFICO. 1964. a; no. 11, 1974. free. Universidad de Oriente, Instituto Oceanografico, Cumana, Venezuela. Ed. Mario G. Revollo. bibl. circ. 1,000 controlled.

551 016   US   ISSN 0065-5856
UNIVERSITY OF ALASKA. GEOPHYSICAL INSTITUTE. BIBLIOGRAPHY OF PUBLICATIONS. 1960. irreg. free. University of Alaska, Geophysical Institute, Library, Fairbanks, AK 99701.

EARTH SCIENCES — Geology

see also Mines and Mining Industry

549   AT   ISSN 0045-0707
A M D E L BULLETIN. 1966. a. free. Australia Mineral Development Laboratories, Flemington St., Frewville, S.A. 5063, Australia. Ed. K. J. Henley. circ. 800. Indexed: Chem.Abstr. Eng.Ind. Mineral.Abstr.

A. P. E. A. JOURNAL. (Australian Petroleum Exploration Association) see PETROLEUM AND GAS

550   CU
ACADEMIA DE CIENCIAS DE CUBA. INSTITUTO DE GEOLOGIA. RESUMENES, COMMUNICACIONES Y NOTAS DEL CONSEJO CIENTIFICO. irreg. Academia de Ciencias de Cuba, Instituto de Geologia, Finca El Caney Capdevila, Havana, Cuba. illus.
Formerly: Academia de Ciencias de Cuba. Instituto de Geologia. Resumenes del Consejo Cientifico.

557   CU
ACADEMIA DE CIENCIAS DE CUBA. INSTITUTO DE GEOLOGIA. SERIE GEOLOGICA.* (Summaries in English) 1968. 3-4/yr. exchange basis. Academia de Ciencias de Cuba, Instituto de Geologia, Finca El Caney Capdevila, Havana, Cuba. bibl. charts. illus. stat. circ. controlled.

ACTA GEOGRAPHICA DEDRECINA. see GEOGRAPHY

550   AG   ISSN 0567-7513
ACTA GEOLOGICA LILLOANA. (Text in Spanish; summaries in English, French, German, Italian) 1957. irreg.; no. 15, 1978. ‡ (Fundacion Miguel Lillo) Centro de Informacion Geo-Biologica, N O A, Miguel Lillo 251, 4000 Tucuman, Argentina. Ed. Dr. Jose A. Haedo Rossi. bibl. charts. illus. stat. index. circ. 500. (back issues avail.) Indexed: Bull.Signal. Ref.Zh.

550.1 CH ISSN 0065-1265
ACTA GEOLOGICA TAIWANICA. (Text and summaries in English) 1947. a. avail. on exchange basis only. National Taiwan University, Department of Geology, Taipei, Taiwan, Republic of China. circ. 600.

551 GW ISSN 0375-5452
ACTA HUMBOLDTIANA. SERIES GEOLOGICA, PALAEONTOLOGICA ET BIOLOGICA. (Text in French and German) irreg., vol. 2, 1978. price varies. (Deutsche Ibero-Amerika-Stiftung) Franz Steiner Verlag GmbH, Friedrichstr. 24, Postfach 5529, 6200 Wiesbaden, W. Germany (B.R.D.) Ed. Wolfgang Haberland.

551.9 US
ADVANCES IN PHYSICAL GEOCHEMISTRY. 1981. irreg. Springer-Verlag, 175 Fifth Ave., New York, NY 10010 (Also Berlin, Heidelberg, Vienna) Ed. S. Saxena. (reprint service avail. from ISI)

551 UR
AKADEMIYA NAUK S. S. S. R. SIBIRSKOE OTDELENIE. VOSTOCHNO- SIBIRSKII FILIAL. INSTITUT GEOKHIMII. EZHEGODNIK.* (Summaries in English) 1969. irreg. 1 Rub. Akademiya Nauk S.S.S.R., Vostochno- Sibirskii Filial, Institut Geokhimii, Ul. Favorskogo, 1, 664033 Irkutsk, U.S.S.R. Ed. L.V. Tauson. bibl.

557 US ISSN 0065-5635
ALABAMA GEOLOGICAL SOCIETY. GUIDEBOOK FOR THE ANNUAL FIELD TRIP. (Title Varies: Vol. 1, Field Trip Guidebook) 1964. a.(two books appeared in 1964) price varies. ‡ Alabama Geological Society, Box 6184, University, AL 35486. circ. 100-150.

557 US ISSN 0065-5724
ALASKA. DIVISION OF GEOLOGICAL AND GEOPHYSICAL SURVEYS. ANNUAL REPORT. 1912. a. free on request. Department of Natural Resources, Division of Geological and Geophysical Surveys, Box 80007, College, AK 99708.

557 US ISSN 0065-5759
ALASKA. DIVISION OF GEOLOGICAL AND GEOPHYSICAL SURVEYS. INFORMATION CIRCULAR. irreg. free. Department of Natural Resources, Division of Geological and Geophysical Surveys, Box 80007, College, AK 99708.

551 US ISSN 0065-5767
ALASKA. DIVISION OF GEOLOGICAL AND GEOPHYSICAL SURVEYS. LABORATORY NOTE. irreg. free. Department of Natural Resources, Division of Geological and Geophysical Surveys, Box 80007, College, AK 99708.

551 US ISSN 0065-5775
ALASKA. DIVISION OF GEOLOGICAL AND GEOPHYSICAL SURVEYS. LABORATORY REPORT. 1969. irreg. free. Department of Natural Resources, Division of Geological and Geophysical Surveys, Box 80007, College, AK 99708.

551 US ISSN 0360-3881
ALASKA. DIVISION OF GEOLOGICAL AND GEOPHYSICAL SURVEYS. SPECIAL REPORT. 1967. irreg. price varies. Department of Natural Resources, Division of Geological and Geophysical Surveys, Box 80007, College, AK 99708.

550 CN ISSN 0034-5172
ALBERTA RESEARCH COUNCIL. BULLETINS. 1958. irreg. price varies. Alberta Research Council, Publications Dept., 11315-87th Ave., Edmonton T6G 2C2, Alta., Canada. bibl. charts. illus. stat.

556 AE ISSN 0401-345X
ALGERIA. SERVICE GEOLOGIQUE. BULLETIN. irreg., approx. 2/yr. price varies. Service Geologique, Ministere de l'Industrie et de l'Energie, Direction des Mines et de la Geologie, Immeuble Mauretania, Blvd. Colonel Amirouche, Agha, Algeria (Subscr. address: Librairie Science et Culture, 37 rue Didouche Mourad, Algiers, Algeria) Indexed: Bull.Signal.

AMERICAN ASSOCIATION OF PETROLEUM GEOLOGISTS. MEMOIR. see PETROLEUM AND GAS

551 US ISSN 0160-8843
AMERICAN ASSOCIATION OF STRATIGRAPHIC PALYNOLOGISTS. CONTRIBUTIONS SERIES. irreg. American Association of Stratigraphic Palynologists Foundation, c/o Robert T. Clarke, Mobil R & D Corp. Field Research Laboratory, Box 900, Dalas, TX 75221.

550 AO ISSN 0003-3456
ANGOLA. DIRECCAO PROVINCIAL DOS SERVICOS DE GEOLOGIA E MINAS. BOLETIM. (Text in English,French and Portuguese) 1960. irreg. Esc.50. Direccao Provincial dos Servicos de Geologia e Minas, C. P. 1260-C, Luanda, Angola. charts. illus. maps. stat.

550.1 FI ISSN 0066-197X
ANNALES ACADEMIAE SCIENTIARUM FENNICAE. SERIES A, 3: GEOLOGICA-GEOGRAPHICA. (Text in English, French, German) 1942. irreg. price varies. Suomalainen Tiedeakatemia - Academia Scientiarum Fennica, Snellmanink, 9-11, 00120 Helsinki 17, Finland. Ed. Toive Aartolahti. circ. 600. (also avail. in microform; back issues avail.; reprint service avail. from UMI) Indexed: Biol.Abstr. Bull.Signal. Psychol.Abstr. Ref.Zh. Doc.Geogr. Geo.Abstr.

ANNALES UNIVERSITATIS MARIAE CURIE-SKLODOWSKA. SECTIO B. GEOGRAPHIA, GEOLOGIA, MINERALOGIA ET PETROGRAPHIA. see GEOGRAPHY

551.31 UK ISSN 0260-3055
ANNALS OF GLACIOLOGY. 1980. a. price varies. International Glaciological Society, Cambridge CB2 1ER, England. Ed.Bd. illus. circ. 800.
Glaciology

556 016 ZA ISSN 0066-2410
ANNOTATED BIBLIOGRAPHY AND INDEX OF THE GEOLOGY OF ZAMBIA. 1959. irreg., latest issue 1972-1973. K.1. Geological Survey, P.O. Box R.W. 135, Lusaka, Zambia.

ANUARIOS DE GEOMAGNETISMO - ANO... see EARTH SCIENCES — Geophysics

558 622 AG ISSN 0066-7145
ARGENTINA. SERVICIO NACIONAL MINERO GEOLOGICO. ANALES. 1904; n.s. 1947. irreg; no. 17, 1976. price varies. Servicio Nacional Minero Geologico, Biblioteca, Avenida Santa Fe 1548, Buenos Aires, Argentina.
Formerly: Argentine Republic. Direccion Nacional de Geologia y Mineria. Anales.

558 622 AG ISSN 0066-7153
ARGENTINA. SERVICIO NACIONAL MINERO GEOLOGICO. BOLETIN. 1914; n.s. 1932. irreg. price varies. Servicio Nacional Minero Geologico, Biblioteca, Av. Santa Fe 1548, Buenos Aires, Argentina.
Formerly: Argentine Republic. Direccion Nacional de Geologia y Mineria. Boletin.

551 AG
ARGENTINA. SERVICIO NACIONAL MINERO GEOLOGICO. INFORMES TECNICOS. 1957. irreg; latest no. 153, 1970. Servicio Nacional Minero Geologico, Biblioteca, Av. Santa Fe 1548, Buenos Aires, Argentina.

553 AG ISSN 0066-717X
ARGENTINA. SERVICIO NACIONAL MINERO GEOLOGICO. REVISTA. 1965. irreg. free. Servicio Nacional Minero Geologico, Julio a Roca 651, 9 Piso, Buenos Aires, Argentina.
Formerly: Argentina. Instituto Nacional de Geologia y Mineria. Revista.

557 US ISSN 0066-7412
ARIZONA GEOLOGICAL SOCIETY DIGEST.* 1958. irreg. price varies. Arizona Geological Society, P.O. Box 4503, University Station, Tucson, AZ 85717. Ed. Judith P. Jenney. adv. circ. 1,000.

557 US
ARKANSAS. GEOLOGICAL COMMISSION. INFORMATION CIRCULARS. 1956. irreg., no. 23, 1975. price varies. Geological Commission, Vardell Parham Geology Center, 3815 West Roosevelt Rd., Little Rock, AR 72204. illus. (back issues avail.)

557 US
ARKANSAS. GEOLOGICAL COMMISSION. MISCELLANEOUS PUBLICATIONS. 1940. irreg., latest 1975. price varies. (Geological Commission) Vardell Parham Geology Center, 3815 West Roosevelt Rd., Little Rock, AR 72204. illus. (back issues avail.)

526 AT
AUSTRALIA. BUREAU OF MINERAL RESOURCES, GEOLOGY, AND GEOPHYSICS. 1: 250000 GEOLOGICAL MAPS AND EXPLANATORY NOTES SERIES. irreg. Aus.$3 per sheet. Bureau of Mineral Resources, Geology, and Geophysics, Box 378, Canberra City, A.C.T. 2601, Australia.
Cartography

AUSTRALIAN INSTITUTE OF PETROLEUM. ANNUAL REPORT. see PETROLEUM AND GAS

551 AT ISSN 0084-750X
AUSTRALIAN NATIONAL UNIVERSITY, CANBERRA. GEOLOGY DEPARTMENT. PUBLICATION. 1962. irreg. price varies. ‡ Australian National University, Geology Department, Box 4, Canberra, A.C.T. 2600, Australia. circ. 500.

796.525 AT
AUSTRALIAN SPELEO ABSTRACTS. 1970. a. price varies. ‡ Sydney Speleological Society, P.O. Box 198, Broadway, N.S.W. 2007, Australia. Ed. Gregory J. Middleton. index; cum. index. circ. 50-200. Indexed: Aus.Speleo Abstr.
Speleology

550.5 AT ISSN 0572-5860
BAAS BECKING GEOBIOLOGICAL LABORATORY. ANNUAL REPORT. a. free. Baas Becking Geobiological Laboratory, c/o Bureau of Mineral Resources, P.O. Box 378, Canberra City A.C.T., 2601, Australia. illus.

BADISCHER LANDESVEREIN FUER NATURKUNDE UND NATURSCHUTZ, FREIBURG. MITTEILUNGEN. NEUE FOLGE. see BIOLOGY

554 UR ISSN 0067-3064
BALTICA. (International Yearbook for Quaternary Geology and Palaeogeography, Coastal Morphology and Shore Processes, Marine Geology and Recent Tectonics of the Baltic Sea Area) (Text in English, French, German and Russian; summaries in English, German and Russian) 1963. biennial. price varies. Akademiya Nauk Litovskoi S. S. R., Lenino Prospektas 3, Vilnius, U.S.S.R. Ed. Vytautas Gudelis.

BAYERISCHE STAATSSAMMLUNG FUER PALAEONTOLOGIE UND HISTORISCHE GEOLOGIE. MITTEILUNGEN. see PALEONTOLOGY

554 GW ISSN 0067-5008
BEITRAEGE ZUR GEOLOGIE VON THUERINGEN. 1926. irreg. (Thueringer Geologischer Verein e.V.) Verlag Dr. Hans Werner Rothe, Kasselerstr. 53, 6368 Bad Vilbel, W. Germany (B. R. D.)

BEITRAEGE ZUR NATURKUNDE IN OSTHESSEN. see BIOLOGY

551 581 591 GW ISSN 0005-8122
BEITRAEGE ZUR NATURKUNDLICHEN FORSCHUNG IN SUEDWESTDEUTSCHLAND. 1864. a. DM.50. Landessammlungen fuer Naturkunde, Erbprinzenstr. 13, 7500 Karlsruhe 1, W. Germany (B.R.D.) bk. rev. charts. illus. circ. 700.

538.7 BE ISSN 0524-7764
BELGIUM. INSTITUT ROYAL METEOROLOGIQUE. ANNUAIRE: MAGNETISME TERRESTRE/JAARBOEK: AARDMAGNETISME. (Text in Flemish and French) a. 500 Fr. Institut Royal Meteorologique, Avenue Circulaire, 3, 1180 Brussels, Belgium. circ. 150.

EARTH SCIENCES — GEOLOGY

551 US
BENCHMARK PAPERS IN GEOLOGY. 1972. irreg., vol. 56,1980. price varies. Dowden, Hutchinson and Ross, Inc., 523 Sarah St., Stroudsburg, PA 18360 (Dist. by Academic Press, Inc., 111 Fifth Ave., New York, NY 10003) Ed. R.W. Fairbridge.

550 PL ISSN 0067-9003
BIULETYN GEOLOGICZNY. (Text in Polish; summaries in English and Russian) 1961. irreg. price varies. Uniwersytet Warszawski, Katedra Geologii, Krakowskie Przedmiescie 26/28, Warsaw, Poland. Ed. Witold C. Kowalski. circ. 500.

558 BL ISSN 0067-964X
BOLETIM PARANAENSE DE GEOCIENCIAS. (Text in English and Portuguese) 1960. irreg.; nos. 28-29, 1970/71. available on exchange. Universidade Federal do Parana, Setor de Tecnologia, 80000 Curitiba, Parana, Brazil. Ed. Riad Salamuni. circ. 1,200. Indexed: Bibl. & Ind.Geol.
Until 1966: Boletim Paranaense de Geografia.

550 VE ISSN 0006-6281
BOLETIN DE GEOLOGIA. (Summaries in English and Spanish) 1951. irreg. price varies. Ministerio de Energia y Minas, Direccion de Geologia, Torre Norte, Centro Simon Bolivar, Piso 19, Caracas, Venezuela. Ed.Bd.

354 BS
BOTSWANA. GEOLOGICAL SURVEY AND MINES DEPARTMENT. ANNUAL REPORTS. irreg. $0.50. Geological Survey and Mines Department, Gaborone, Botswana. illus.

551.44 UK ISSN 0305-859X
BRITISH CAVE RESEARCH ASSOCIATION. TRANSACTIONS. 1974. irreg. (approx 4/yr) £12.50 to non-members. British Cave Research Association, c/o Bryan Ellis, 30 Main Rd., Westonzoyland, Bridgwater, Somerset TA7 0EB, England. Ed. T. D. Ford. adv. index. circ. 1,000.
Former titles: Cave Research Group of Great Britain. Transactions. (ISSN 0069-1305); Cave Science; British Hypogean Fauna and Biological Records.
Speleology

622 557 CN ISSN 0068-144X
BRITISH COLUMBIA. MINISTRY OF ENERGY, MINES AND PETROLEUM RESOURCES. BULLETIN. 1940, N.S. irreg. price varies. Ministry of Energy, Mines and Petroleum Resources, Parliament Bldgs, Victoria, B.C. V8V 1X4, Canada. Indexed: Eng.Ind.

551.4 UK ISSN 0306-3380
BRITISH GEOMORPHOLOGICAL RESEARCH GROUP. TECHNICAL BULLETIN. irregg; (2-3/yr) price varies. Geo Books, c/o Geo Abstracts Ltd., University of East Anglia, Norwich NR4 7TJ, England. (back issues avail.)

551 UK ISSN 0007-1471
BRITISH MUSEUM (NATURAL HISTORY) BULLETIN. GEOLOGY. 1949. irreg. price varies. British Museum (Natural History), Cromwell Rd., London SW7 5BD, England. charts. illus. circ. 850. Indexed: Biol.Abstr. Chem.Abstr.
Incorporating: British Museum (Natural History) Bulletin. Mineralogy (ISSN 0007-148X)

554 UK
BRITISH REGIONAL GEOLOGY. 1935. irreg. price varies. Institute of Geological Sciences, Exhibition Rd., London SW7 2DE, England (Avail. from H.M.S.O., c/o Liaison Officer, Atlantic House, Holborn Viaduct, London EC1P 1BN, England) illus. circ. 15,000.

C S P G MEMOIRS. (Canadian Society of Petroleum Geologists) see *PETROLEUM AND GAS*

551 FR ISSN 0008-0241
CAHIERS GEOLOGIQUES. (Summaries in English and French) 1950. 1-2/yr. 40 F.($9) 70 F. for institutions. Association des Amis et Ancien Eleves du Laboratoire de Geologie, I, Faculte des Science, Tour 14-15-16, 4 Etage, 9 Quai St. Bernard, Paris (5e), France. Ed. J. P. Michel. adv. bk. rev. abstr. bibl. illus. stat. index. circ. 1,000. Indexed: Biol.Abstr. Chem.Abstr.

551 US ISSN 0008-1000
CALIFORNIA. DIVISION OF MINES AND GEOLOGY. BULLETIN. 1888. 2-3/yr. ‡ Division of Mines and Geology, 1416 Ninth St., Room 1341, Sacramento, CA 95814. index.

551 520 US ISSN 0045-3943
CALIFORNIA INSTITUTE OF TECHNOLOGY. DIVISION OF GEOLOGICAL AND PLANETARY SCIENCES. REPORT ON GEOLOGICAL AND PLANETARY SCIENCES FOR THE YEAR. 1971-1973; resumed 1978. a. California Institute of Technology, Division of Geological and Planetary Sciences, Pasadena, CA 91125. Ed. Shari McKee. circ. 1,600.

551.34 CN ISSN 0068-7758
CANADA. ATMOSPHERIC ENVIRONMENT SERVICE. ICE SUMMARY AND ANALYSIS, CANADIAN ARCTIC. 1964. a. Can.$1.50. Atmospheric Environment Service, 4905 Dufferin St., Downsview, Ont., M3H 5T4, Canada. Ed. W. E. Markham.

551.34 CN ISSN 0068-7766
CANADA. ATMOSPHERIC ENVIRONMENT SERVICE. ICE SUMMARY AND ANALYSIS, EASTERN CANADIAN SEABOARD. 1964. a. Can.$1.50. Atmospheric Environment Service, 4905 Dufferin St., Downsview, Ont., M3H 5T4, Canada.

551.34 CN ISSN 0068-7774
CANADA. ATMOSPHERIC ENVIRONMENT SERVICE. ICE SUMMARY AND ANALYSIS, HUDSON BAY AND APPROACHES. 1964. a. Can.$1.50. Atmospheric Environment Service, 4905 Dufferin St., Downsview, Ont., M3H 5T4, Canada.

552 CN
CANADA. DEPARTMENT OF INDIAN AND NORTHERN AFFAIRS. SCHEDULE OF WELLS, OIL AND GAS NORTH OF 60. 1960. a. price varies. Department of Indian and Northern Affairs, Oil and Minerals Division, 400 Laurier Ave. W., Ottawa, Ont. K1A OH4, Canada. bibl. stat. index; cum.index. circ. 2,000.

557 CN ISSN 0068-7626
CANADA. GEOLOGICAL SURVEY. BULLETIN. (Text in English and French) 1945. irreg. price varies. Geological Survey of Canada, 601 Booth St., Ottawa, Canada (Dist. by: Supply and Services Canada, Ottawa, Ont. K1A 0S9, Canada) index. cum.index 1845-1969. circ. 1,500.

557 CN
CANADA. GEOLOGICAL SURVEY. ECONOMIC GEOLOGY REPORT. 1963. irreg. Geological Survey of Canada, 601 Booth St., Ottawa, Ont. K1A 0S9, Canada. bibl. illus.

557 CN ISSN 0068-7634
CANADA. GEOLOGICAL SURVEY. MEMOIR. (Text in English and French) 1910. irreg. price varies. Geological Survey of Canada, 601 Booth St., Ottawa, Canada (Dist. by: Supply and Services Canada, Ottawa, Ont. K1A 0S9, Canada) index. cum.index 1845-1969. circ. 1,500.

557 CN ISSN 0068-7642
CANADA. GEOLOGICAL SURVEY. MISCELLANEOUS REPORT. 1960. irreg. price varies. Geological Survey of Canada, 601 Booth St., Ottawa, Canada (Dist. by: Supply and Services Canada, Ottawa, Ont. K1A 0S9, Canada) circ. 2,000.

557 CN ISSN 0068-7650
CANADA. GEOLOGICAL SURVEY. PAPER. (Text in English and French) 1935. irreg. price varies. Geological Survey of Canada, 601 Booth St., Ottawa, Canada (Dist. by: Supply and Services Canada, Ottawa, Ont. K1A 0S9, Canada) index. cum.index 1845-1969. circ. 1,500.

557 CN ISSN 0069-0619
CARLETON UNIVERSITY, OTTAWA. DEPARTMENT OF GEOLOGY. GEOLOGICAL PAPERS. 1958. irreg. Can.$5 or on exchange basis. ‡ Carleton University, Department of Geology, Ottawa, Ont. K1S 5B6, Canada. Ed. K. Hooper. Indexed: Chem.Abstr.

551 CL
CARTA GEOLOGICA DE CHILE. (Text in Spanish; summaries in English) 1959. irreg. $6 per no. Instituto de Investigaciones Geologicas, Augustinas 785, Casilla 10465, Santiago, Chile. Ed. Manuel Suarez. circ. 1,000.

558 BL
CARTA GEOLOGICA DO BRASIL AO MILIONESIMO. 1974. irreg. Cr.$100. Departamento Nacional da Producao Mineral, Setor Autarcuia Norte, Quadra 1, Bloco B, Brasilia, D.F., Brazil. charts.

551.44 US ISSN 0069-1313
CAVE STUDIES.* (No. 1-5 originally published as Activity Reports of the Western Speleological Institute) 1953. irreg., no. 13, 1972. no. 1-11 in one vol., $3.; no. 12, $2.; no. 13, $6.75. Cave Research Associates, 3842 Brookdale Blvd., Castro Valley, CA 94546. Ed. Raymond DeSaussure. index. cum.index: 1953-59.
Speleology

551.4 FR ISSN 0068-4791
CENTRE DE GEOMORPHOLOGIE, CAEN. BULLETIN. 1967. irreg. by exchange. Centre National de la Recherche Scientifique, Centre de Geomorphologie, Rue des Tilleuls, 14000 Caen, France.

551 556 FR
CENTRE GEOLOGIQUE ET GEOPHYSIQUE DE MONTPELLIER. PUBLICATIONS. SERIE GEOLOGIE. 1961. irreg. price varies. Centre National de la Recherche Scientifique, 15 Quai Anatole-France, 75700 Paris, France.
Formerly: France. Centre de Recherches sur les Zones Arides. Publications. Serie Geologie (ISSN 0069-1798)

796.525 UK ISSN 0309-409X
CHELSEA SPELEOLOGICAL SOCIETY. RECORDS. irreg. ‡ Chelsea Speleological Society, Chelsea Community Centre, Worlds End Estate, Kings Rd., London, England. Ed. Harry Pearman. circ. 250. (processed)

558 CK
COLOMBIA. MINISTERIO DE MINAS Y ENERGIA. MEMORIA AL CONGRESO DE LA REPUBLICA. irreg. Ministerio de Minas y Energia, Bogota, Colombia.
Continues: Colombia. Ministerio de Minas y Petroleos. Informe.

553 UK ISSN 0588-7720
COMMONWEALTH GEOLOGICAL LIAISON OFFICE. LIAISON REPORT. 1952. irreg. free. Commonwealth Committee on Mineral Resources and Geology, Geological Liaison Office, Marlborough House, Pall Mall, London SW1Y 5HX, England. circ. 600.

551 UK ISSN 0588-7763
COMMONWEALTH GEOLOGICAL LIAISON OFFICE. SPECIAL PUBLICATION. irreg. Commonwealth Committee on Mineral Resources and Geology, Geological Liaison Office, Marlborough House, Pall Mall, London SW1Y-5HX, England. circ. 500.

551.44 SZ ISSN 0069-8911
CONGRES NATIONAL DE SPELEOLOGIE. ACTES. (Text in French and German) 1969. irreg. price varies. Societe Suisse de Speleologie, c/o Institut de Geologie, Universite de Neuchatel, 11 rue Emile-Argand, CH-2000 Neuchatel, Switzerland. Ed. R. Gigon.
Speleology

551 US
CONTRIBUTION TO PRECAMBRIAN GEOLOGY. 1969. irreg., no. 6, 1976. Department of Natural Resources, Division of Geology and Land Survey, Box 250, Rolla, MO 65401. bibl. charts. illus. circ. 1,500.

551.3 GW ISSN 0343-4125
CONTRIBUTIONS TO SEDIMENTOLOGY. (Text in English and German) 1973. irreg. (1-2/yr.) price varies. E. Schweizerbart'sche Verlagsbuchhandlung, Johanesstr. 3A, 7000 Stuttgart 1, W. Germany (B.R.D.) Ed.Bd.

554   SP
CUADERNOS DE GEOLOGIA IBERICA. (Text in Spanish and French; summaries in Spanish, French, English and German) 1969. a; latest issue, 1974. price varies. ‡ Universidad Complutense de Madrid, Facultad de Ciencias, Departamento de Economicas Geologicas, Pabellon, Madrid-3, Spain. Ed. Carmina Virgili. charts. illus. circ. 1,000. (tabloid format)

557 551   US   ISSN 0092-9565
CURRENT GEOLOGICAL AND GEOPHYSICAL STUDIES IN MONTANA. (Subseries of: Montana. State Bureau of Mines and Geology. Special Publications) 1969. a. ‡ Bureau of Mines and Geology, Montana College of Mineral Science and Technology, Room 203-B, Main Hall, Butte, MT 59701. Comp. Richard B. Berg. stat. circ. 700.

551   DK
DANMARKS GEOLOGISKE UNDERSOEGELSE. SERIE A/GEOLOGICAL SURVEY OF DENMARK. SERIES A. 1976. irreg. Denmarks Geologiske Undersoegelse, 31 Thoravej, DK-2400 Copenhagen, Denmark.

551   DK
DANSK GEOLOGISK FORENING. AARSSKRIFT. (Text in Danish or English) a. Dansk Geologisk Forening - Geological Society of Denmark, Oester Voldgade 5-7, 1350 Copenhagen K, Denmark. illus.

557   US   ISSN 0070-3273
DELAWARE GEOLOGICAL SURVEY BULLETINS. 1953. irreg., no. 15, 1977. ‡ Geological Survey, University of Delaware, Newark, DE 19711. Indexed: Abstr.N.Amer.Geol.

557   US   ISSN 0011-7749
DELAWARE GEOLOGICAL SURVEY REPORTS OF INVESTIGATIONS. 1957. irreg., no. 32, 1979. ‡ Geological Survey, Univ. of Delaware, Newark, DE 19711. Indexed: Chem.Abstr. Abstr.N.Amer.Geol.

551   US
DESITTER REGIONAL GEOLOGY SERIES. 1964. irreg., latest vol. 1974, unnumbered. price varies. John Wiley & Sons, Inc., 605 Third Ave., New York, NY 10016. Ed. L.V. de Sitter.

551   NE
DEVELOPMENTS IN ECONOMIC GEOLOGY. 1975. irreg., vol. 13, 1980. price varies. Elsevier Scientific Publishing Co., Box 211, 1000 AE Amsterdam, Netherlands.

551   NE
DEVELOPMENTS IN GEOCHEMISTRY. 1978. irreg. price varies. Elsevier Scientific Publishing Co., Box 211, 1000 AE Amsterdam, Netherlands.

551.8   NE   ISSN 0419-0254
DEVELOPMENTS IN GEOTECTONICS. 1965. irreg., vol. 15, 1980. price varies. Elsevier Scientific Publishing Co., Box 211, 1000 AE Amsterdam, Netherlands.

552   NE
DEVELOPMENTS IN PETROLOGY. 1971. irreg., vol. 6, 1979. Elsevier Scientific Publishing Co., Box 211, 1000 AE Amsterdam, Netherlands.

551   NE
DEVELOPMENTS IN PRECAMBRIAN GEOLOGY. 1978. irreg., vol. 5, 1981. price varies. Elsevier Scientific Publishing Co., Box 211, 1000 AE Amsterdam, Netherlands.

551.3   NE   ISSN 0070-4571
DEVELOPMENTS IN SEDIMENTOLOGY. 1964. irreg., vol. 28, 1980. price varies. Elsevier Scientific Publishing Co., Box 211, 1000 AE Amsterdam, Netherlands.

557   US   ISSN 0071-0857
ENVIRONMENTAL GEOLOGY. 1971. irreg. $8 per no. Geological Survey, Montpelier, VT 05602 (Order from: Vermont Dept. of Libraries, 111 State St., Montpelier VT 05602)

554   GW   ISSN 0071-1160
ERLANGER GEOLOGISCHE ABHANDLUNGEN. 1952. irreg. price varies. Universitaet Erlangen, Geologisches Institut, Schlossgarten 5, 8520 Erlangen, W. Germany (B.R.D.) Ed. Bruno von Freyberg.

557 622   CN
EXPLORATION IN BRITISH COLUMBIA. 1969. a. price varies. Ministry of Energy, Mines and Petroleum Resources, Parliament Bldgs., Victoria, B.C. V8V 1X4, Canada.
  Former titles: Geology, Exploration, and Mining in British Columbia (ISSN 0085-1027); Lode Metals in British Columbia.

551   US   ISSN 0096-2651
FIELDIANA: GEOLOGY. 1895. irreg. price varies. Field Museum of Natural History, Roosevelt Rd. and Lake Shore Dr., Chicago, IL 60605. charts. illus. circ. 500. Indexed: Biol.Abstr. Chem.Abstr.

551   FJ
FIJI. MINERAL RESOURCES DIVISION. MEMOIR. (Text in English) 1964. irreg., latest issue, no. 3. price varies. ‡ Ministry of Lands and Mineral Resources, Mineral Resources Division, P.M. Bag, Suva, Fiji.
  Formerly: Geological Survey of Fiji Memoir.

557   US   ISSN 0085-0608
FLORIDA. BUREAU OF GEOLOGY. GEOLOGICAL BULLETINS. 1908. irreg., no. 56, 1973. price varies. ‡ Department of Natural Resources, Division of Resource Management, Bureau of Geology, 903 W. Tennessee St., Tallahassee, FL 32304. circ. 500.

557   US   ISSN 0085-0616
FLORIDA. BUREAU OF GEOLOGY. INFORMATION CIRCULARS. 1948. irreg., no.92, 1979. price varies. ‡ Department of Natural Resources, Division of Resource Management, Bureau of Geology, 903 W. Tennessee St., Tallahassee, FL 32304. circ. 500.

557   US   ISSN 0085-0624
FLORIDA. BUREAU OF GEOLOGY. MAP SERIES. 1952. irreg., no. 91, 1979. price varies. ‡ Department of Natural Resources, Division of Resource Management, Bureau of Geology, 903 W. Tennessee St., Tallahassee, FL 32304. circ. 500.

557   US   ISSN 0085-0632
FLORIDA. BUREAU OF GEOLOGY. REPORT OF INVESTIGATIONS. 1934. irreg., no. 86, 1978. price varies. ‡ Department of Natural Resources, Division of Resource Management, Bureau of Geology, 903 W. Tennessee St., Tallahassee, FL 32304. circ. 500.

557   US   ISSN 0085-0640
FLORIDA. BUREAU OF GEOLOGY. SPECIAL PUBLICATIONS. 1956. irreg., no. 22, 1979. price varies. ‡ Department of Natural Resources, Division of Resource Management, Bureau of Geology, 903 W. Tennessee St., Tallahassee, FL 32304. circ. 500.

551.44   US   ISSN 0071-6006
FLORIDA SPELEOLOGICAL SOCIETY. SPECIAL PAPERS.* 1961. irreg. $0.50. Florida Speleological Society, Box 12581, University Station, Gainesville, FL 32601. Ed. Robert A. Smith.
  Speleology

550   CS
FOLIA FACULTATIS SCIENTIARUM NATURALIUM UNIVERSITATIS PURKYNIANAE BRUNENSIS: GEOLOGIA. irreg (7-12/yr.) price varies. Universita J. E. Purkyne, Prirodovedecka Fakulta, Kotlarska 2, 611 37 Brno, Czechoslovakia.

FOLIA GEOGRAPHICA. GEOGRAPHICA-PHYSICA. see *GEOGRAPHY*

554   GW   ISSN 0071-8009
FORTSCHRITTE IN DER GEOLOGIE VON RHEINLAND UND WESTFALEN. (Text in German; summaries in English and French) 1958. irreg., no. 29, 1980. price varies. Geologisches Landesamt, De Greiff-Str. 195, 4150 Krefeld, W. Germany (B.R.D.)

554 622   FR   ISSN 0071-8246
FRANCE. BUREAU DE RECHERCHES GEOLOGIQUES ET MINIERES. MEMOIRES. (Text in French; summaries in English, French and German) 1960. irreg., no. 100, 1979. price varies. Bureau de Recherches Geologiques et Minieres, Division Edition et Vente, B.P. 6009, 45060 Orleans Cedex, France. Ed. C. Megnien. Indexed: Bull.Signal. Chem.Abstr. Ref.Zh. Geo.Abstr.

554   FR
FRANCE. BUREAU DE RECHERCHES GEOLOGIQUES ET MINIERES. RESUME DES PRINCIPAUX RESULTATS SCIENTIFIQUES ET TECHNIQUES. a. free. Bureau de Recherches Geologiques et Minieres, Division Edition et Vente, Boite Postale 6009, 45060 Orleans Cedex, France. illus.

550 622   GE   ISSN 0071-9390
FREIBERGER FORSCHUNGSHEFTE. MONTANWISSENSCHAFTEN: REIHE A. BERGBAU UND GEOTECHNIK, ARBEITSSCHUTZ UND SICHERHEITSTECHNIK, GRUNDSTOFF-VERFAHRENSTECHNIK, MASCHINEN- UND ENERGIETECHNIK. irreg. price varies. (Bergakademie Freiberg) VEB Deutscher Verlag fuer Grundstoffindustrie, Karl-Heine-Str. 27, 7031 Leipzig, E. Germany (D.D.R.)

FUNDACION MIGUEL LILLO. MISCELANEA. see *BIOLOGY — Botany*

551   II   ISSN 0368-2323
GEOCHEMICAL SOCIETY OF INDIA. JOURNAL. (Text in English) 1965. a. Rs.35($8) Geochemical Society of India, Patna 5, India. Ed. R. C. Sinha. bk. rev. bibl. charts. illus. Indexed: Chem.Abstr.

GEOGRAFIJA IR GEOLOGIJA. see *GEOGRAPHY*

558   CK   ISSN 0072-0992
GEOLOGIA COLOMBIANA. (Text in Spanish; summaries in English, French, German and Italian) 1962. irreg. exchange basis. ‡ Universidad Nacional de Colombia, Departamento de Geologia, Apdo. Aereo 14490, Bogota, D.E., Columbia. Ed.Bd. bk. rev. circ. 5,000.

550   PL   ISSN 0072-100X
GEOLOGIA SUDETICA. (Text in Polish, English, French; summaries in English and Polish) 1964. a. 150 Zl. (Polska Akademia Nauk, Zaklad Nauk Geologicznych) Ossolineum, Publishing House of the Polish Academy of Sciences, Rynek 9, 50-106 Wroclaw, Poland (Dist. by: Ars Polona-Ruch, Krakowskie Przedmiescie 7, Warsaw, Poland) Ed. K. Smulikowski.

016 557   US   ISSN 0533-7356
GEOLOGIC FIELD TRIP GUIDEBOOKS OF NORTH AMERICA; A UNION LIST INCORPORATING MONOGRAPHIC TITLES. irreg. 2nd, 1971. price varies. Phil Wilson Publishing Company, 1939 W. Gray, Houston, TX 77019.

554   GW   ISSN 0016-755X
GEOLOGICA BAVARICA. 1949. irreg. price varies. Bayerisches Geologisches Landesamt, Prinzregentenstrasse 28, 8000 Munich 22, W. Germany (B.R.D.) charts. illus. maps. circ. 800. Indexed: Biol.Abstr. Chem.Abstr.

551 560   GW   ISSN 0072-1018
GEOLOGICA ET PALAEONTOLOGICA. (Text in German and English) 1967. a. price varies. N.G. Elwert Verlag, Reitgasse 7/9, Postfach 1128, 3550 Marburg, W. Germany (B.R.D.) Eds. M. Lindstroem, W. Schmidt. circ. 500.

554   NE   ISSN 0072-1026
GEOLOGICA ULTRAIECTINA. (Text in English) 1957. irreg., no. 23, 1980. price varies. Rijksuniversiteit te Utrecht, Geologisch Instituut, Oude Gracht 320, Utrecht, Netherlands.

557   CN   ISSN 0072-1042
GEOLOGICAL ASSOCIATION OF CANADA. SPECIAL PAPER. 1956. a. price varies. Geological Association of Canada, 111 Peter St. Suite 509, Toronto, Ont. M5U 2H1, Canada.

551 560   US   ISSN 0072-1069
GEOLOGICAL SOCIETY OF AMERICA. MEMOIRS. (Each vol. has distinctive title) 1934. irreg., no. 150, 1977. price varies. Geological Society of America, 3300 Penrose Pl., Boulder, CO 80301. index. Indexed: Biol.Abstr. Chem.Abstr.

551   US   ISSN 0091-5041
GEOLOGICAL SOCIETY OF AMERICA. MEMORIALS. 1973. irreg. price varies. Geological Society of America, 3300 Penrose Place, Boulder, CO 80301. bibl. illus. Key Title: Memorials - Geological Society of America.

551 560　　　US　ISSN 0072-1077
GEOLOGICAL SOCIETY OF AMERICA.
SPECIAL PAPERS. (Each vol. has distinctive title) 1934. irreg., no. 178, 1977. price varies. Geological Society of America, 3300 Penrose Pl., Boulder, CO 80301. index.

551　　　US　ISSN 0095-3547
GEOLOGICAL SOCIETY OF AMERICA.
YEARBOOK. a. Geological Society of America, Boulder, CO 80301. Key Title: Yearbook - Geological Society of America.

559.4　　　AT　ISSN 0072-1085
GEOLOGICAL SOCIETY OF AUSTRALIA.
SPECIAL PUBLICATION. 1967. irreg., no. 8, 1980. price varies. Geological Society of Australia, 10 Martin Pl., Sydney, N.S.W. 2000, Australia.

555　　　CH
GEOLOGICAL SOCIETY OF CHINA. MEMOIRS. (Text in English) no. 2, 1977. irreg. Geological Society of China, 245, Section 3, Chilung Rd, Taipei, Taiwan, Republic of China.

551　　　UA　ISSN 0446-4648
GEOLOGICAL SOCIETY OF EGYPT. ANNUAL MEETING. ABSTRACTS OF PAPERS. (Summaries in English) 1963. a. free. National Information and Documentation Centre, 24 Sharia Sherif Pasha, Dokki, Cairo, Egypt. Ed. E. M. el-Shazly.

551　　　IQ　ISSN 0533-8301
GEOLOGICAL SOCIETY OF IRAQ. JOURNAL. (Text in Arabic and English) 1968. a. $15. ‡ Geological Society of Iraq, P.O. Box 547, Baghdad, Iraq. charts. illus. circ. 500.

551　　　JM　ISSN 0435-401X
GEOLOGICAL SOCIETY OF JAMAICA
JOURNAL. 1958. a (plus special issues) Jam.$2.50. Geological Society of Jamaica, University of the West Indies, Geology Department, Mona, Kingston 7, Jamaica. Ed. R. M. Wright. bk. rev. charts. illus. circ. 500.

555　　　MY　ISSN 0072-1093
GEOLOGICAL SOCIETY OF MALAYSIA.
BULLETIN. (Text and summaries in English) 1968. irreg., no. 10, 1978. price varies. Geological Society of Malaysia, c/o Department of Geology, University of Malaya, Kuala Lumpur, Malaysia. Ed. Ahmad Jantan. circ. 600. (back issues avail.)

556　　　SA
GEOLOGICAL SOCIETY OF SOUTH AFRICA.
SPECIAL PUBLICATION. 1970. irreg; latest issue, 1976. price varies. Geological Society of South Africa, P.O. Box 61019, Marshalltown, Transvaal, South Africa. circ. 2,000.

554　　　IE　ISSN 0085-0985
GEOLOGICAL SURVEY OF IRELAND.
BULLETIN. 1970. irreg., vol. 2, pt. 2, 1976. £1.50. Geological Survey of Ireland, Department of Industry and Commerce, 14, Hume Street, Dublin 2, Ireland. cum.index. circ. 6-700. Indexed: Geo.Abstr.

554　　　IE　ISSN 0085-0993
GEOLOGICAL SURVEY OF IRELAND.
INFORMATION CIRCULARS. 1970. irreg. free. Geological Survey of Ireland, Department of Industry and Commerce, 14 Hume St., Dublin 2, Ireland. circ. 500.

554　　　IE　ISSN 0085-1000
GEOLOGICAL SURVEY OF IRELAND.
MEMOIRS. 1856. irreg. price varies. Geological Survey of Ireland, Department of Industry and Commerce, 14 Hume St., Dublin 2, Ireland. circ. 1,000.

554　　　IE　ISSN 0085-1019
GEOLOGICAL SURVEY OF IRELAND. SPECIAL PAPERS. 1971. irreg. price varies. Geological Survey of Ireland, Department of Industry and Commerce, 14 Hume St., Dublin 2, Ireland. circ. 600.

559.4　　　AT　ISSN 0079-8819
GEOLOGICAL SURVEY OF QUEENSLAND.
REPORT. 1963-1979 (vol. 100) irreg. exchange basis. Geological Survey of Queensland, Mineral House, 41 George St., B, Brisbane, Queensland 4000, Australia. Ed. J. T. Woods. Indexed: Aus.Sci.Ind. Bibl. & Ind.Geol.

551　　　AU
GEOLOGISCHE BUNDESANSTALT, VIENNA.
ABHANDLUNGEN. (Text mainly in German; occasionally in other languages) 1852. irreg. price varies. Geologische Bundesanstalt, Rasumofskygasse 23, Postfach 154, A-1031 Vienna, Austria. Ed. Franz Bauer. circ. 1,000-1,500(approx.) (also avail. in microfilm) Indexed: Ref.Zh.

551　　　GW　ISSN 0341-6445
GEOLOGISCHES JAHRBUCH. REIHE F:
BODENKUNDE. (Text in English and German; summaries in English, French, German, Russian) 1973. irreg. price varies. (Bundesanstalt fuer Geowissenschaften und Rohstoffe) E. Schweizerbart'sche Verlagsbuchhandlung, Johannesstr. 3A, 7000 Stuttgart 1, W. Germany (B.R.D.)

551　　　UK
GEOLOGISTS' YEAR BOOK. 1977. a. Dolphin Press, Link House, West St., Poole, Dorset BH15 1LL, England.

555　　　JA
GEOLOGY AND MINERAL RESOURCES OF JAPAN/NIHON CHISHITSU KOSANSHI. (Text in English) 1956. irreg. exchange basis. Geological Survey of Japan - Tsusho Sangyo-sho Kogyo Gijutsu-in Chishitus Chosasho, 135 Hisamoto, Takatsu-ku, Kawasaki 213, Japan.

555　　　PK　ISSN 0435-4311
GEONEWS. (Text in English) 1968. irreg., vol. 2, 1972. Geological Survey of Pakistan, c/o Chief Librarian, Box 15, Quetta, Pakistan.

557　　　US
GEORGIA. GEOLOGICAL SURVEY. BULLETIN. 1894. irreg. price varies. ‡ Department of Natural Resources, Geologic and Water Resources Division, 19 Hunter St., Rm. 400, Atlanta, GA 30334. Ed. L.P. Stafford.

557　　　US
GEOSCIENCE WISCONSIN. 1977. irreg. $4. Geological and Natural History Survey, University of Wisconsin-Extension, 1815 University Ave., Madison, WI 53706.

091　　　FR
GEOSTANDARDS NEWSLETTER. 1977. Association Nationale de la Recherche Technique, Working Group "Analytical Standards of Minerals, Ores, and Rocks", 101 Ave. Raymond Poincare, 75116 Paris, France.

551　　　YU
GEOTEHNIKA; informativno glasilo radne zajednice Geotehnika. 1965. irreg. Geotehnika, Kupska 2, Zagreb, Yugoslavia. Ed. Zvonko Jelic.

551　　　US　ISSN 0094-9779
GEOTHERMAL WORLD DIRECTORY. 1972. a. $50. ‡ Geothermal World-Publishers, 5762 Firebird Ct., Mission Oaks, CA 93010. adv. bk. rev. bibl. charts. illus. tr. lit. circ. 8,000.

551　　　IT　ISSN 0017-0291
GIORNALE DI GEOLOGIA; annali del Museo Geologico di Bologna. (Text in English, French, German & Italian; summaries in English & Italian) irreg. price varies. Via Zamboni, 63, 40127 Bologna, Italy. (back issues avail) Indexed: Biol.Abstr. Chem.Abstr.

551.31　　　US　ISSN 0149-1776
GLACIOLOGICAL DATA. 1977. irreg. free. U.S. Environmental Data and Information Service, World Data Center A for Glaciology (Snow and Ice), Institute of Arctic and Alpine Research, University of Colorado, Boulder, CO 80309. (Co-Sponsor: National Academy of Sciences) bk. rev. index. circ. 900.
Supersedes the quarterly issued from 1960-1976: Glaciological Notes (ISSN 0017-0712)
Glaciology

551.44　　　SP
GOURS. 1973. a. 100 ptas.($1.50) Fomento Martinense, Grupo Espeleologico, Calle Provenza 593-595, Barcelona 26, Spain. Ed. Francisco Rubinat Aumedes. adv. circ. 500.

551　　　UK　ISSN 0073-9308
GREAT BRITAIN. INSTITUTE OF GEOLOGICAL SCIENCES. ANNUAL REPORT. 1965. biennial; latest 1981. price varies. Institute of Geological Sciences, Exhibition Rd., South Kensington, London SW7 2DE, England (Avail. from H.M.S.O., c/o Liaison Officer, Atlantic House, Holborn Viaduct, London EC1P 1BN, England) illus. circ. 1,000.
Issued 1906-64 as: Great Britain. Geological Survey. Summary of Progress.

551 557　　　UK
GREAT BRITAIN. INSTITUTE OF GEOLOGICAL SCIENCES. CLASSICAL AREAS OF BRITISH GEOLOGY. 1977. irreg. Institute of Geological Sciences, Exhibition Rd., South Kensington, London SW7 2DE, England. circ. 2,500.

554 560　　　UK　ISSN 0072-6494
GREAT BRITAIN. INSTITUTE OF GEOLOGICAL SCIENCES. MEMOIRS OF THE GEOLOGICAL SURVEY OF GREAT BRITAIN. 1846. irreg. price varies. Institute of Geological Sciences, Exhibition Rd., London SW7 2DE, England (Avail. from H.M.S.O., c/o Liaison Officer, Atlantic House, Holborn Viaduct, London EC1P 1BN, England) illus. circ. 1,000.

553 622　　　UK　ISSN 0308-5333
GREAT BRITAIN. INSTITUTE OF GEOLOGICAL SCIENCES. MINERAL ASSESSMENT REPORT. irreg. price varies. Institute of Geological Sciences, Exhibition Rd., London SW7 2DE, England (Avail. from H.M.S.O., c/o Liaison Officer, Atlantic House, Holborn Viaduct, London EC1P 1BN, England) illus. circ. 500.

551　　　UK　ISSN 0073-9332
GREAT BRITAIN. INSTITUTE OF GEOLOGICAL SCIENCES. OVERSEAS GEOLOGY AND MINERAL RESOURCES. 1950. irreg. price varies. Institute of Geological Sciences, Exhibition Rd., South Kensington, London SW7 2DE, England (Avail. from H.M.S.O., c/o Liaison Officer, Atlantic House, Holborn Viaduct, London EC1P 1BN, England) illus. circ. 1,000.

551　　　UK　ISSN 0308-5325
GREAT BRITAIN. INSTITUTE OF GEOLOGICAL SCIENCES. OVERSEAS MEMOIRS. 1975. irreg. price varies. Institute of Geological Sciences, Exhibition Rd., South Kensington, London SW7 2DE, England (Avail. from H.M.S.O., c/o Liaison Officer, Atlantic House, Holborn Viaduct, London EC1P 1BN, England) illus. circ. 1,000.

551　　　UK　ISSN 0073-9359
GREAT BRITAIN.INSTITUTE OF GEOLOGICAL SCIENCES. REPORT. 1969. irreg. price varies. Institute of Geological Sciences, Exhibition Rd., South Kensington, London SW7 2DE, England (Avail. from H.M.S.O., c/o Liaison Officer, Atlantic House, Holborn Viaduct, London EC1P 1BN, England) circ. 1,000.

551 581　　　DK
GREENLAND GEOSCIENCE. (Text mainly in English, occasionally in Danish, French or German) 1979. irreg. (Kommissionen for Videnskabelige Undersoegelser i Groenland, GL - Commission for Scientific Research in Greenland) Nyt Nordisk Forlag - Arnold Busck A-S, 49 Koebmagergade, DK-1150 Copenhagen K, Denmark. Ed. Valdemar Poulsen. charts. illus. maps. Indexed: Biol.Abstr. Chem.Abstr.
Supersedes in part (1878-1979): Meddelelser om Groenland (ISSN 0025-6676)

551　　　DK　ISSN 0105-3507
GROENLANDS GEOLOGISKE UNDERSOEGELSE. BULLETIN/GEOLOGICAL SURVEY OF GREENLAND. BULLETIN. (Nos.1-114 also published in Meddelelser Om Groenland) (Text mainly in English) 1948. irreg. price varies. Groenlands Geologiske Undersoegelse, Oester Voldgade 10, DK-1350 Copenhagen K, Denmark.

551　　　DK　ISSN 0418-6559
GROENLANDS GEOLOGISKE UNDERSOEGELSE. RAPPORT/GEOLOGICAL SURVEY OF GREENLAND. REPORT. (Text mainly in English) 1964. irreg. (6-10/yr.) price varies. Groenlands Geologiske Undersoegelse, Oester Voldgade 10, DK-1350 Copenhagen K, Denmark. bibl. charts. illus.

557　　　　　　GY
GUYANA. GEOLOGY & MINES COMMISSION.
ANNUAL REPORT. a. $5. Geology and Mines
Commission, P.O. Box 1028, Georgetown, Guyana.
Formerly: Guyana. Geological Survey
Department.Annual Reports (ISSN 0072-9108)

557　　　　　　GY
GUYANA. GEOLOGY & MINES COMMISSION.
MINERAL RESOURCES PAMPHLET. 1953.
irreg., 1971, no. 14. $5. Geology & Mines
Commission, P.O. Box 1028, Georgetown, Guyana.
Formerly: Guyana. Geological Survey
Department. Mineral Resources Pamphlet (ISSN
0072-9124)

551.7　　　　　GW　ISSN 0073-0130
HANDBUCH DER STRATIGRAPHISCHEN
GEOLOGIE. 1959. irreg. price varies. Ferdinand
Enke Verlag, Herdweg 63, 7000 Stuttgart 1, W.
Germany (B.R.D.) Eds. F. Lotze, H. Murawski.

555　　　　　　II
HIMALAYAN GEOLOGY. (Text in English) 1971.
a. price varies. Hindustan Publishing Corp., 6-U.B.
Jawahar Nagar, Delhi 110007, India.

555　　　　　　JA　ISSN 0073-2303
HIROSHIMA UNIVERSITY. DEPARTMENT OF
GEOLOGY. GEOLOGICAL REPORT. (Text in
Japanese; summaries in English) 1951. irreg., no. 19,
1974. not for sale. Hiroshima University,
Department of Geology and Mineralogy, 1-89 1-
chome Higashisenda-cho, Hiroshima 730, Japan.

551 549　　　　JA　ISSN 0075-4374
HIROSHIMA UNIVERSITY. JOURNAL OF
SCIENCE. SERIES C. GEOLOGY AND
MINERALOGY. (Text in English, French and
German) 1951. irreg., vol. 7, no. 2, 1974. not for
sale. Hiroshima University, Department of Geology
and Mineralogy, 1-89 1-chome Higashisenda-cho,
Hiroshima 730, Japan. title index.

IDAHO. BUREAU OF MINES AND GEOLOGY.
BULLETIN. see MINES AND MINING
INDUSTRY

IDAHO. BUREAU OF MINES AND GEOLOGY.
INFORMATION CIRCULAR. see MINES AND
MINING INDUSTRY

558　　　　　　BL　ISSN 0073-4713
IHERINGIA. SERIE GEOLOGIA. (Text in English,
French, German, Italian, Latin, Portuguese and
Spanish) 1967. irreg.; no. 5, 1978. price varies.
Fundacao Zoobotanica do Rio Grande do Sul,
Museu de Ciencias Naturais, Caixa Postal 1188,
90.000 Porto Alegre, Rio Grande do Sul, Brazil. Ed.
Arno A. Lise. bibl. illus. circ. 1,000. Indexed:
Biol.Abstr.

557　　　　　　US　ISSN 0073-5051
ILLINOIS. STATE GEOLOGICAL SURVEY.
BULLETINS. 1906. irreg., no. 95, 1975. free. ‡
State Geological Survey, Natural Resources Bldg.,
615 E. Peabody Dr., Champaign, IL 61820. circ.
5,000.

557　　　　　　US　ISSN 0073-506X
ILLINOIS. STATE GEOLOGICAL SURVEY.
CIRCULARS. 1932. irreg., no. 514, 1980. free. ‡
State Geological Survey, Natural Resources Bldg.,
615 E. Peabody Dr., Campaign, IL 61820. circ.
2,000-6,000.

557　　　　　　US　ISSN 0073-5078
ILLINOIS. STATE GEOLOGICAL SURVEY.
EDUCATIONAL SERIES. 1931. irreg., no. 12,
1980. free. ‡ State Geological Survey, Natural
Resources Bldg., 615 E. Peabody Dr., Champaign,
IL 61820. circ. 16,000-40,000.

557　　　　　　US　ISSN 0073-5086
ILLINOIS. STATE GEOLOGICAL SURVEY.
ENVIRONMENTAL GEOLOGY NOTES. 1965.
irreg., no. 89, 1980. free. ‡ State Geological Survey,
Natural Resources Bldg., 615 E. Peabody Dr.,
Champaign, IL 61820. circ. 2,000-6,000.

557　　　　　　US　ISSN 0073-5094
ILLINOIS. STATE GEOLOGICAL SURVEY.
GUIDEBOOK SERIES. 1950. irreg., no. 15, 1979.
free. ‡ State Geological Survey, Natural Resources
Bldg., 615 E. Peabody Dr., Champaign, IL 61820.
circ. 2,000.

557 970 570　　US　ISSN 0445-3395
ILLINOIS. STATE MUSEUM. SCIENTIFIC
PAPERS SERIES. 1940. irreg., vol. 17, 1981. price
varies. Illinois State Museum, Springfield, IL 62706.
illus.

ILLINOIS MINERALS NOTES. see MINES AND
MINING INDUSTRY

ILLINOIS PETROLEUM. see PETROLEUM AND
GAS

551.3　　　　　II
INDIAN STRATIGRAPHY. (Text in English) 1973.
irreg. price varies. Hindustan Publishing Corp., 6-
U.B. Jawahar Nagar, Delhi 110007, India.

353.9　　　　　US　ISSN 0362-3513
INDIANA. GEOLOGICAL SURVEY. ANNUAL
REPORT OF THE STATE GEOLOGIST. a.
Geological Survey, Department of Natural
Resources, Indianapolis, IN 46204.

553　　　　　　GT　ISSN 0073-9936
INSTITUTO CENTRO AMERICANO DE
INVESTIGACION Y TECNOLOGIA
INDUSTRIAL. PUBLICACIONES
GEOLOGICAS. (Text in English or Spanish) 1966.
irreg.; no. 5, 1977. price varies. Instituto Centro
Americano de Investigacion y Tecnologia Industrial,
Avenida la Reforma 4-47, Zona 10, Apartado Postal
1552, Guatemala, Guatemala. Ed. Dr. Gabriel
Dengo. circ. 1,000. (back issues avail.)

550　　　　　　CL　ISSN 0020-3939
INSTITUTO DE INVESTIGACIONES
GEOLOGICAS. BOLETIN. (Text in Spanish;
summaries in English) 1958. irreg. $6 per no.
Instituto de Investigaciones Geologicas, Augustinas
785, Casilla de Correo 10465, Santiago, Chile. Ed.
Manuel Suarez. charts. illus. circ. 1,000.

558　　　　　　CK
INSTITUTO NACIONAL DE INVESTIGACIONES
GEOLOGICO MINERAS. PUBLICACIONES
GEOLOGICAS ESPECIALES DEL
INGEOMINAS. 1978. irreg., no. 5, 1979. Instituto
Nacional de Investigaciones Geologico Mineras,
Carrera 30 No. 5l-59, Bogota D.E., Colombia.

550　　　　　　RM
INSTITUTUL DE GEOLOGIE SI GEOFIZICA.
ANUARUL. (Text in English and Romanian;
summaries in English) 1908. a. price varies.
Institutul de Geologie si Geofizica, Str. Caransebes,
Nr. 1, Bucharest, Romania. circ. 950. Indexed:
Bull.Signal. Ref.Zh.

550　　　　　　RM
INSTITUTUL DE GEOLOGIE SI GEOFIZICA.
STUDII TEHNICE SI ECONOMICE. (Text in
English and Romanian; summaries in English,
French, German) 1933. irreg. price varies. Institutul
de Geologie si Geofizica, Str. Caransebes, Nr. 1,
Bucharest, Romania. circ. 900. Indexed: Ref.Zh.

553　　　　　　RM
INSTITUTUL DE MINE PETROSANI. LUCRARI
STIINTIFICE. (Text in Romanian; summaries in
English, French, German) irreg. Institutul de Mine
Petrosani, Str. Institutului Nr. 20, Petrosani,
Romania. illus.

557　　　　　　GY　ISSN 0074-1027
INTER-GUIANA GEOLOGICAL CONFERENCE.
PROCEEDINGS. 1950. irreg. 9th, 1972, Venezuela.
G.$30. Guyana Geology & Mines Commission, Box
1028, Georgetown, Guyana. Ed. Dr. M. A. Lee.

551　　　　　　AT
INTERNATIONAL GONDWANA SYMPOSIUM.
PAPERS. no. 3, 1973. irreg. Aus.$37.50($92)
Australian National University Press, Box 4,
Canberra, A.C.T. 2600, Australia. Ed. K.S.W.
Campbell. bibl. index.

551.3　　　　　GW　ISSN 0074-7904
INTERNATIONAL SEDIMENTOLOGICAL
CONGRESS. GUIDEBOOK. (Represents
International Sedimentological Congress.
Proceedings) 1946. quadrennial, 1971, 8th,
Heidelberg. DM.48. Institut fuer Sediment
Forschung, Postfach 103020, 6900 Heidelberg, W.
Germany (B.R.D.)
Proceedings published in host country

551　　　　　　NZ　ISSN 0074-932X
INTERNATIONAL UNION FOR QUATERNARY
RESEARCH. CONGRESS PROCEEDINGS. (Text
and summaries in English, French, German,
Russian) 1936. quadrennial, 1973, 9th, Christchurch,
New Zealand. Royal Society of New Zealand, Box
12249, Wellington, New Zealand.

551　　　　　　US　ISSN 0361-7629
IOWA. GEOLOGICAL SURVEY. ANNUAL
REPORT OF THE STATE GEOLOGIST TO THE
GEOLOGICAL BOARD. a. Geological Survey,
123 N. Capitol St., Iowa City, IA 52242. illus. Key
Title: Annual Report of the State Geologist to the
Geological Board.

557　　　　　　US
IOWA GEOLOGICAL SURVEY. REPORTS OF
INVESTIGATIONS. 1964. irreg., approx. biennial.
price varies. Geological Survey, 123 North Capitol
St., Iowa City, IA 52242. Ed. Donald Koch.

555　　　　　　IR　ISSN 0075-0484
IRAN. GEOLOGICAL SURVEY. REPORT. 1964.
irreg., no. 24, 1972. price varies. ‡ Geological
Survey, Box 1555, Teheran, Iran. circ. 2,000.

555　　　　　　IS　ISSN 0075-1200
ISRAEL. GEOLOGICAL SURVEY. BULLETIN.
(Text in English; summaries in Hebrew) 1956. irreg.,
no. 73, 1979. $5. ‡ Geological Survey, 30 Malkhe
Israel St., Jerusalem, Israel. Ed.Bd. circ. 1,200.

IVORY COAST. DIRECTION DES MINES ET DE
LA GEOLOGIE. RAPPORT PROVISOIRE SUR
LES ACTIVITIES DU SECTEUR. see MINES
AND MINING INDUSTRY

551　　　　　　GE
JAHRBUCH FUER GEOLOGIE. a, vol. 11/12,
1975/76 (pub. 1978) M.90. (Zentrales Geologisches
Institut) Akademie-Verlag, Leipziger Strasse 3-4,
108 Berlin, E. Germany (D.D.R.)

551.44　　　　　GW　ISSN 0075-2894
JAHRESHEFTE FUER KARST- UND
HOEHLENKUNDE. a. (Verband Deutscher
Hoehlen- und Karstfoerscher e.V.) Fr. Mangold'sche
Buchhandlung, Karlstr. 6, 7902 Blaubeueren, W.
Germany (B.R.D.)
Speleology

551　　　　　　JA
JAPAN. GEOLOGICAL SURVEY. CRUISE
REPORT. (Text in English) 1974. irreg. Geological
Survey of Japan - Tsusho Sangyo-sho Kogyo
Gijutsu-in Chishitsu Chosasho, 135 Hisamato,
Takatsu-ku, Kawasaki 213, Japan. Ed. Hideo
Takeda. charts. illus.
Deep sea mineral resources

551　　　　　　US　ISSN 0075-3890
JOHNS HOPKINS UNIVERSITY STUDIES IN
GEOLOGY. 1922. irreg., 1973. no. 21. price varies.
‡ (Johns Hopkins University, Department of Earth
and Planetary Sciences) Johns Hopkins University
Press, Baltimore, MD 21218.

551　　　　　　IC　ISSN 0449-0576
JOKULL. (Text in English & Icelandic) 1950? a. $12.
Joklarannsoknafelag Islands - Iceland Glaciological
Society, Science Institute, Dunhaga 3, 107
Reykjavik, Iceland (Subscr. to: Box 94, Reykjavik,
Iceland) (Co-sponsor: Jarofroeoafelag Islands -
Geoscience Society of Iceland) Ed. Sigurdur
Thorarinsson.

557　　　　　　US
KANSAS GEOLOGICAL SURVEY. BULLETIN.
1913. irreg. $4 per no. Geological Survey, 1930
Ave. "A", Campus West, University of Kansas,
Lawrence, KS 66044. illus. maps.

557　　　　　　US
KANSAS GEOLOGICAL SURVEY. CHEMICAL
QUALITY SERIES. 1975. irreg. $2.50. Geological
Survey, 1930 Ave. "A", Campus West, University of
Kansas, Lawrence, KS 66044.

557　　　　　　US　ISSN 0075-4927
KANSAS GEOLOGICAL SURVEY. COMPUTER
CONTRIBUTION. 1966. irreg., 1970, no. 50. price
varies: $0.50-$1.50 ea. Geological Survey,
University of Kansas, Lawrence, KS 66044. Ed. D.
F. Merriam.

557 US
KANSAS GEOLOGICAL SURVEY.
EDUCATIONAL SERIES. 1973. irreg. price varies.
Geological Survey, 1930 Ave. "A", Campus West,
University of Kansas, Lawrence, KS 66044.

557 US
KANSAS GEOLOGICAL SURVEY. GEOLOGY
SERIES. 1975. irreg. $3 per no. Geological Survey,
1930 Ave. "A", Campus West, University of Kansas,
Lawrence, KS 66044.

557 US ISSN 0075-4935
KANSAS GEOLOGICAL SURVEY. SHORT
PAPERS IN RESEARCH. (Included with Bulletins)
1967. a. ‡ Geological Survey, Unviersity of Kansas,
Lawrence, KS 66044. Ed. Gary Alan Waldron.

557 US
KANSAS GEOLOGICAL SURVEY. SUBSURFACE
GEOLOGY SERIES. 1974. irreg. $3 per no.
Geological Survey, 1930 Ave. "A", Campus West,
University of Kansas, Lawrence, KS 66044.

KENYA. MINES AND GEOLOGICAL
DEPARTMENT. ANNUAL REPORT. see MINES
AND MINING INDUSTRY

551.44 SP
KOBIE. (Text in Spanish, Basque; summaries in
English, French) 1969. a. 700 ptas. (Grupo
Espeleologico Vizcaino) Diputacion de Vizcaya, c/o
Sr. Ugalde, Biblioteca Provincial, Astarloa St.,
Bilbao, Spain.
Speleology

551 DK
KOEBENHAVNS UNIVERSITET. GEOLOGISK
CENTRALINSTITUT. AARSBERETNING. a.
contr. free circ. Koebenhavns Universitet, Geologisk
Centralinstitut, Oester Voldgade 10, 1350
Copenhagen K, Denmark. circ. 525(controlled)

551 622 NE ISSN 0075-6741
KONINKLIJK NEDERLANDS GEOLOGISCH
MIJNBOUWKUNDIG GENOOTSCHAP.
VERHANDELINGEN. (Before 1969 published in 2
series: Geologische Serie, and Mijnbouwkundige
Serie) (Text in English) 1912. irreg., no. 32, 1980.
price varies. Koninklijk Nederlands Geologisch
Mijnbouwkundig Genootschap - Royal Geological
and Mining Society of the Netherlands, Postbus
490, 2501 CL The Hague, Netherlands. circ. 2,000-
2,500.

549 UR ISSN 0454-3343
KONSTITUTSIYA I SVOISTA MINERALOV. (Text
in Russian; summaries in English) 1967. a. price
varies. (Akademiya Nauk Ukrainskoi S.S.R.)
Izdatel'stvo Naukova Dumka, Ul. Repina 3, Kiev,
U.S.S.R. Ed. A. S. Povarennykh.

552 CS
KRYSTALINIKUM; contributions to the geology and
petrology of crystalline complexes. (Text in English)
vol. 11, 1975. a. price varies. Academia, Publishing
House of the Czechoslovak Academy of Sciences,
Vodickova 40, 112 29 Prague 1, Czechoslovakia.
bibl. charts. illus.

555 JA
KUMAMOTO UNIVERSITY. DEPARTMENT OF
GEOLOGY. JOURNAL. (Text in English) 1952.
irreg. on exchange basis. Kumamoto University,
Department of Geology - Kumamoto Daigaku
Rigakubu Chigaku Kyoshitsu, Faculty of Science, 2-
39-1 Kurokami, Kumamoto 860, Japan.

555 JA ISSN 0023-6179
KYUSHU UNIVERSITY. FACULTY OF SCIENCE.
MEMOIRS. SERIES D: GEOLOGY/KYUSHU
DAIGAKU RIGAKUBU KIYO, D,
CHISHITSUGAKU. (Text in English) 1940. a.
exchange basis. Kyushu University, Faculty of
Science, Department of Geology - Kyushu Daigaku
Rigakubu, 6-10-1 Hakozaki, Higashi-ku, Fukuoka
812, Japan. circ. 1,050.

LANDESMUSEUM JOANNEUM. ABTEILUNG
FUER GEOLOGIE, PALAEONTOLOGIE UND
BERGBAU. MITTEILUNGEN. see
PALEONTOLOGY

551 NE ISSN 0075-8639
LEIDSE GEOLOGISCHE MEDEDELINGEN. (Text
in English) 1925. irreg. price varies; also avail. on
exchange. ‡ Rijksuniversiteit te Leiden, Geologisch
en Mineralogisch Instituut, Garenmarkt 1b, Leiden,
Netherlands.

554 UR ISSN 0459-0805
LENINGRADSKII UNIVERSITET. UCHENYE
ZAPISKI. SERIYA GEOLOGICHESKIKH
NAUK. 1950. irreg. 1 Rub. (Geologicheskii
Fakultet) Izdatel'stvo Leningradskii Universitet,
Universitetskaya nab. 7/9, Leningrad B-164,
U.S.S.R. illus.

557 US ISSN 0459-8474
LOUISIANA. GEOLOGICAL SURVEY. WATER
RESOURCES BULLETIN. 1960. irreg., no. 20,
1975. $3 per no. Geological Survey, Box G,
University Station, Baton Rouge, LA 70893. illus.
(back issues avail.)

538.7 SW ISSN 0076-1354
LOVOE GEOMAGNETIC OBSERVATORY
YEARBOOK. (Text in English) 1930. a. Kr.25.
Sveriges Geologiska Undersoekning - Geological
Survey of Sweden, Box 670, S-751 28 Uppsala,
Sweden. Ed. Folke Eleman.

557 US
MAINE GEOLOGICAL SURVEY. BULLETINS.
1944. irreg., latest, no. 24, 1973. price varies.
Geological Survey, Department of Conservation,
State House Sta. No. 22, Augusta, ME 04330.

556 MW ISSN 0076-311X
MALAWI. GEOLOGICAL SURVEY. ANNUAL
REPORT. a. price varies. Geological Survey, Box
27, Zomba, Malawi (Orders to: Government Printer,
Box 37, Zomba, Malawi)

556 MW ISSN 0076-3128
MALAWI. GEOLOGICAL SURVEY. BULLETIN.
irreg. price varies. Geological Survey, Box 27,
Zomba, Malawi (Orders to: Government Printer,
Box 37, Zomba, Malawi)

556 MW ISSN 0076-3136
MALAWI. GEOLOGICAL SURVEY. MEMOIR.
1958. irreg. price varies. Geological Survey, Box 27,
Zomba, Malawi (Orders to: Government Printer,
Box 37, Zomba, Malawi)

556 MW ISSN 0076-3144
MALAWI. GEOLOGICAL SURVEY. RECORDS.
1959. irreg., no. 8, 1975. price varies. Geological
Survey, Box 27, Zomba, Malawi (Orders to:
Government Printer, Box 37, Zomba, Malawi)

559 MY ISSN 0126-5628
MALAYSIA. GEOLOGICAL SURVEY. ANNUAL
REPORT. (Text in English) 1949. a. M.$20.
Geological Survey, c/o Library, Kuching, Sarawak,
Malaysia. circ. 500.

MANITOBA. MINERAL RESOURCES DIVISION.
GEOLOGICAL PAPER. see MINES AND
MINING INDUSTRY

557 CN
MANITOBA. MINERAL RESOURCES DIVISION.
PUBLICATION. irreg. Mineral Resources Division,
Box 12, 989 Century St., Winnipeg, Man. R3H
0W4, Canada.
Formerly: Manitoba. Mining Engineering
Division. Publication (ISSN 0085-3070)

557 CN
MANITOBA. MINERAL RESOURCES DIVISION.
REPORT OF FIELD ACTIVITIES. irreg. Mineral
Resources Division, Box 12, 989 Century St.,
Winnipeg, Man. R3H 0W4, Canada.
Formerly: Manitoba. Mining Engineering
Division. Report of Field Activities.

557 US ISSN 0076-4779
MARYLAND. GEOLOGICAL SURVEY.
BULLETIN. 1944. irreg., no. 32, 1977. price varies.
Geological Survey, Merryman Hall, Johns Hopkins
University, Baltimore, MD 21218. index. Indexed:
Chem.Abstr.

557 US ISSN 0076-4787
MARYLAND. GEOLOGICAL SURVEY.
EDUCATIONAL SERIES. 1964. irreg., no. 33,
1980. price varies. Geological Survey, Merryman
Hall, Johns Hopkins University, Baltimore, MD
21218.

557 US ISSN 0076-4795
MARYLAND. GEOLOGICAL SURVEY.
INFORMATION CIRCULAR. 1963. irreg., no. 33,
1980. price varies. Geological Survey, Merryman
Hall, Johns Hopkins University, Baltimore, MD
21218.

557 US ISSN 0076-4809
MARYLAND. GEOLOGICAL SURVEY. REPORT
OF INVESTIGATIONS. 1965. irreg., no. 33, 1980.
price varies. Geological Survey, Merryman Hall,
Johns Hopkins University, Baltimore, MD 21218.

554 BE
MEMOIRES POUR SERVIR A L'EXPLICATION
DES CARTES GEOLOGIQUES ET MINIERES
DE LA BELGIQUE. (Text in French and Flemish;
summaries in English) irreg. Service Geologiquede
Belgique, 13, rue Jenner, 1040 Brussels, Belgium.
Ed.Bd. charts.

551 GW ISSN 0076-7689
MEYNIANA; Veroeffentlichungen aus dem
Geologischen Institut der Universitaet Kiel. 1952. a.
price varies. Universitaet Kiel, Geologisch-
Paläontologisches Institut, Olshausenstr. 40/60, D-
2300 Kiel, W. Germany (B.R.D.) (Co-sponsor:
Museum der Universitaet Kiel) Ed. Werner Prange.
Indexed: Bibl. & Ind.Geol.

557 US ISSN 0543-8497
MICHIGAN. GEOLOGICAL SURVEY DIVISION.
BULLETIN. 1964. irreg. Department of Natural
Resources, Geological Survey Division, Box 30028,
Lansing, MI 48909. Eds. B.L. Champion, S.E.
Wilson.

557 US
MICHIGAN. GEOLOGICAL SURVEY DIVISION.
REPORT OF INVESTIGATION. 1967. irreg., no.
23, 1979. price varies. Department of Natural
Resources, Geological Survey Division, Box 30028,
Lansing, MI 48909. Eds. B. L. Champion, S. E.
Wilson. illus.

662 US ISSN 0026-4547
MINERAL INDUSTRIES NEWSLETTER. 1960. s-a.
free. South Dakota School of Mines and
Technology, Geology, Mining & Metallurgy Depts.,
Rapid City, SD 57701. Ed. Dr. Perry H. Rahn. bk.
rev. illus. circ. 1,800. (processed)

551 549
MINERALS AND ROCKS; monograph series of
theoretical and experimental studies. 1968. irreg.,
vol. 16, 1981. price varies. Springer-Verlag, 175
Fifth Ave., New York, NY 10010 (also Berlin,
Heidelberg, Vienna) Ed. P. J. Wyllie. (reprint
service avail. from ISI)
Former titles: Mineralogie und Petrographie in
Einzel Darstellungen; Minerals, Rocks and
Inorganic Materials (ISSN 0076-8944)

557 US ISSN 0544-3105
MINNESOTA. GEOLOGICAL SURVEY.
INFORMATION CIRCULARS. 1962. irreg., no.
17, 1979. price varies. Geological Survey, 1633
Eustis St., St. Paul, MN 55108. (back issues avail.)

557 US ISSN 0076-9177
MINNESOTA. GEOLOGICAL SURVEY. REPORT
OF INVESTIGATIONS. 1963. irreg., vol. 23, 1979.
price varies. Geological Survey, 1633 Eustis St., St.
Paul, MN 55108. (back issues avail.)

551 560 US ISSN 0077-085X
MONOGRAPHS IN GEOLOGY AND
PALEONTOLOGY. 1967. irreg. price varies.
Princeton University Press, Princeton, NJ 08540.
(reprint service avail. from UMI)

526.9
MONOGRAPHS ON SOIL SURVEY. irreg. price
varies. Oxford University Press, 200 Madison Ave.,
New York, NY 10016 (And Ely House, 37 Dover
St., London W1X 4AH, England) Ed.Bd.

557 US ISSN 0077-1090
MONTANA. BUREAU OF MINES AND
GEOLOGY. BULLETIN. 1919. irreg., B107, 1978.
price varies. Bureau of Mines and Geology,
Montana College of Mineral Science and
Technology, Butte, MT 59701.
Incorporating(after 1959): Montana. Bureau of
Mines and Geology. Ground Water Reports (ISSN
0077-1112)

557 622　　　　　US　ISSN 0077-1120
MONTANA. BUREAU OF MINES AND
GEOLOGY. MEMOIR. 1928. irreg., M44, 1977.
Bureau of Mines and Geology, Montana College of
Mineral Science and Technology, Butte, MT 59701.

557　　　　　　　US　ISSN 0077-1139
MONTANA. BUREAU OF MINES AND
GEOLOGY. SPECIAL PUBLICATIONS.
(Continues numbering of Miscellaneous
Contributions, 1932-1957) 1957. irreg., SP 79, 1978.
price varies. Bureau of Mines and Geology,
Montana College of Mineral Science and
Technology, Butte, MT 59701.

557　　　　　　　US　ISSN 0163-2825
MOUNTAIN STATE GEOLOGY. 1961. a. free.
Geological and Economic Survey, Box 879,
Morgantown, WV 26505. circ. 1,500.
　　Formerly: West Virginia Geological Survey.
Newsletter (ISSN 0083-8470)

551　　　　　　　　BE
MUSEE ROYAL DE L'AFRIQUE CENTRALE.
ANNALES. SERIE IN 8. SCIENCES
GEOLOGIQUES/KONINKLIJK MUSEUM
VOOR MIDDEN-AFRIKA. ANNALEN. REEKS
IN 8. GEOLOGISCHE WETENSCHAPPEN.
1948. irreg., no. 86, 1979. price varies. Musee Royal
de l'Afrique Centrale, 13 Steenweg op Leuven, B-
1980 Tervuren, Belgium. charts. illus.

551　　　　　　　　BE
MUSEE ROYAL DE L'AFRIQUE CENTRALE.
DEPARTEMENT DE GEOLOGIE ET DE
MINERALOGIE. RAPPORT ANNUEL. 1957. a.
400 Fr. Musee Royal de l'Afrique Centrale,
Departement de Geologie et de Mineralogie, 13
Steenweg op Leuven, B-1980 Tervuren, Belgium.
charts.

550　　　　　　　　AG
MUSEO ARGENTINO DE CIENCIAS
NATURALES BERNARDINO RIVADAVIA.
INSTITUTO NACIONAL DE INVESTIGACION
DE LAS CIENCIAS NATURALES. REVISTA.
GEOLOGIA. 1949. irreg.; latest issue 1980. free.
Museo Argentino de Ciencias Naturales Bernardino
Rivadavia, Avda. Angel Gallardo 470, Casilla de
Correo-Sucursal 5, Buenos Aires, Argentina. illus.
　　Continues: Buenos Aires. Museo Argentino de
Ciencias Naturales Bernardino Rivadavia. Instituto
Nacional de Investigacion de las Ciencias Naturales.
Revista. Ciencias Geologicas.

500.907　　　　　　AG
MUSEO DE HISTORIA NATURAL DE SAN
RAFAEL. INSTITUTO DE CIENCIAS
NATURALES. NOTAS. 1957. irreg. Museo de
Historia Natural, Instituto de Ciencias Naturales,
Avda. San Martin y Francis, 5600 San Rafael,
Argentina. Ed. Humberto A. Lagiglia. circ. 1,000.

550　　　　　BL　ISSN 0080-3200
MUSEU NACIONAL, RIO DE JANEIRO.
BOLETIM. NOVA SERIE. GEOLOGIA. 1943.
irreg. exchange only. Museu Nacional, Quinta da
Boa Vista, Rio de Janeiro, GB 08, Brazil.

500.9 915　　　　　FR
MUSEUM NATIONAL D'HISTOIRE
NATURELLE, PARIS. NOTES ET MEMOIRES
SUR LE MOYEN-ORIENT. 1933. irreg. price
varies. Museum National d'Histoire Naturelle, 38
rue Geoffroy Saint-Hillaire, 75005 Paris, France.
Dir. Louis Dubertret. illus.
　　Formerly (vol. I-IV): Museum National d'Histoire
Naturelle, Paris. Notes et Memoires de la Section
d'Etudes Geologiques du Haut-Commissariat
Francais en Syrie et au Liban.

554　　　　　　　　NO
N G U BULLETIN. (Text in English) irreg., no. 322,
1977. price varies. (Norges Geologiske
Undersoekelse - Geological Survey of Norway)
Universitetsforlaget, Kolstadgt. 1, Box 2959-Toeyen,
Oslo 6, Norway (U. S. address: Box 258, Irvington-
on-Hudson, NY 10533) Ed. David Roberts. bibl.
charts. illus.

551　　　　　　　　NO
N G U SKRIFTER. (Text in Norwegian; summaries in
English) irreg., no. 331, 1977. price varies. (Norges
Geologiske Undersoekelse - Geological Survey of
Norway) Universitetsforlaget, Kolstadgt. 1, Box
2959-Toeyen, Oslo 6, Norway (U.S. address: Box
258, Irvington-on-Hudson, NY 10533) Ed. David
Roberts.

553.53　　　　　US　ISSN 0077-5673
N S G A CIRCULAR. 1928. irreg., 1973, no. 120.
price varies. National Sand and Gravel Association,
900 Spring St., Silver Spring, MD 20910. Ed. R.D.
Gaynor. circ. 1,000.

551.44　　　　　　AT
NARGUN. 1967. 10/yr. Aus.$6. Victorian
Speleological Association, G.P.O. Box 5425cc,
Melbourne, Vic.3001, Australia. Ed. S. White. circ.
170. Indexed: Aus.Speleo.Abstr.

559　　　　　JA　ISSN 0386-5517
NATIONAL INSTITUTE OF POLAR RESEARCH.
MEMOIRS. SERIES A: AERONOMY. (Text and
summaries in English) 1963. irreg., no. 16, 1979.
exchange basis. National Institute of Polar Research
- Kokuritsu Kyokuchi Kenkyujyo, 9-10 Kaga, 1-
chome, Itabashi-ku, Tokyo 173, Japan. Ed. Takesi
Nagata. circ. 1,000. Indexed: Curr.Antarc.Lit.
　　Supersedes: Japanese Antarctic Research
Expedition, 1956-1962. Scientific Reports. Series A:
Aeronomy (ISSN 0075-3351)

NATUR UND MENSCH;
JAHRESMITTEILUNGEN DER
NATURHISTORISCHEN GESELLSCHAFT
NUERNBERG. see *BIOLOGY*

526　　　　　　　　UR
NAUCHNO-ISSLEDOVATEL'SKII INSTITUT
PRIKLADNOI GEODEZII. TRUDY. 1976. irreg.
0.80 Rub. per issue. Izdatel'stvo Tsniigaik, Ul.
Onezhskaya, 26, Moscow A-Y13, U.S.S.R. Ed. V.
Chernikov. abstr, charts. circ. 500.

554　　　　　　　　BU
NEFTENA I VUGLISHTNA GEOLOGIIA/
PETROLEUM AND COAL GEOLOGY. (Text in
Bulgarian or Russian; summaries in English, French,
German) 1975. irreg. 0.61 lv. (Bulgarska Akademiia
na Naukite) Publishing House of the Bulgarian
Academy of Sciences, Ul. Akad. G. Bonchev, 1113
Sofia, Bulgaria (Dist. by: Hemus, 6, Rouski Blvd.,
1000 Sofia, Bulgaria) illus. circ. 500.
　　Formerly: Bulgarska Akademiia na Naukite.
Geologicheski Institut. Izvestiia. Seriie Neftena i
Vuglishtna Geologiia.

554　　　　　NE　ISSN 0077-7617
NETHERLANDS. RIJKS GEOLOGISCHE DIENST.
JAARVERSLAG/NETHERLANDS
GEOLOGICAL SURVEY. ANNUAL REPORT.
(Text in Dutch; summaries in English) 1972. a. free.
Rijks Geologische Dienst, Spaarne 17, P.O. Box
157, 2000 AD Haarlem, Netherlands. circ. 800.

551 560　　　　GW　ISSN 0077-7749
NEUES JAHRBUCH FUER GEOLOGIE UND
PALAEONTOLOGIE. ABHANDLUNGEN. 1807.
3 nos./vol.,2-3 vols./yr. price varies. E.
Schweizerbart'sche Verlagsbuchhandlung,
Johannesstr. 3A, 7000 Stuttgart 1, W. Germany
(B.R.D.) Ed.Bd. adv. index. Indexed: Biol.Abstr.
Chem.Abstr.
　　Supersedes in part and continues volume
numbering of: Neues Jahrbuch fuer Mineralogie,
Geologie und Palaeontologie. Abhandlungen.

557 622　　　　　US
NEVADA. BUREAU OF MINES AND GEOLOGY.
BULLETIN. 1904. irreg. no. 33, 1978. price varies.
Bureau of Mines and Geology, University of
Nevada, Reno, NV 89557.

557 622　　　　　US　ISSN 0095-5264
NEVADA. BUREAU OF MINES AND GEOLOGY.
REPORT. 1962. irreg., no. 33, 1977. Bureau of
Mines and Geology, University of Nevada, Reno,
NV 89557. illus. Key Title: Report - Nevada Bureau
of Mines and Geology.
　　Continues: Nevada. Bureau of Mines. Report.

NEW CALDEONIA. SERVICE DES MINES ET DE
LA GEOLOGIA. RAPPORT ANNUEL. see
MINES AND MINING INDUSTRY

559　　　　　NN　ISSN 0077-8443
NEW HEBRIDES. CONDOMINIUM
GEOLOGICAL SURVEY. REPORTS. (Numbering
of reports has been discontinued) 1966. irreg. price
varies. Condominium Geological Survey, British
Residency, Port Vila, New Hebrides.

559　　　　　　　　NN
NEW HERBRIDES. CONDOMINIUM
GEOLOGICAL SURVEY. ANNUAL REPORTS.
1964. a. price varies. Condominium Geological
Survey, British Residency, Port Vila, New Hebrides.
Ed. Senior Geologist.
　　Formerly: New Hebrides. Anglo-French
Condominium Geological Survey. Annual Reports.
(ISSN 0077-8435)

557　　　　　　　　US
NEW JERSEY. BUREAU OF GEOLOGY AND
TOPOGRAPHY. BULLETIN. no. 47, 1940. irreg.,
no. 75, 1976. price varies. Bureau of Geology and
Topography, Box 1390, Trenton, NJ 08625.

557　　　　　　　　US
NEW JERSEY. BUREAU OF GEOLOGY AND
TOPOGRAPHY. GEOLOGIC REPORT SERIES.
1959. irreg., no. 11, 1976. price varies. Bureau of
Geology and Topography, Box 1390, Trenton, NJ
08625.

557　　　　　　US　ISSN 0077-8567
NEW MEXICO GEOLOGICAL SOCIETY.
GUIDEBOOK, FIELD CONFERENCE. 1950. a.
$25 hardcover; $20 softcover. New Mexico
Geological Society, Campus Station, Socorro, NM
87801. adv. circ. 2,500.

559.4　　　　　AT　ISSN 0155-5561
NEW SOUTH WALES. GEOLOGICAL SURVEY.
BULLETIN. 1922. irreg., no. 24, 1973. price varies.
Department of Mineral Resources and
Development, G.P.O. Box 5288, Sydney, N.S.W.
2001, Australia. Ed. H. Basden. index. circ. 400.
Indexed: Bibl.&Ind.Geol.

559.4　　　　　AT　ISSN 0077-8710
NEW SOUTH WALES. GEOLOGICAL SURVEY.
MEMOIRS: GEOLOGY. 1887. irreg., no. 11, 1971.
price varies. Department of Mineral Resources &
Development, Box 5288, Sydney, N.S.W. 2001,
Australia. Ed. H. Basden. index. circ. 400. Indexed:
Bibl.&Ind.Geol.

NEW SOUTH WALES. GEOLOGICAL SURVEY.
MINERAL INDUSTRY SERIES. see *MINES
AND MINING INDUSTRY*

NEW SOUTH WALES. GEOLOGICAL SURVEY.
MINERAL RESOURCES SERIES. see *MINES
AND MINING INDUSTRY*

559.4　　　　　AT　ISSN 0155-3372
NEW SOUTH WALES. GEOLOGICAL SURVEY.
RECORDS. 1889. irreg., no. 17, 1976. price varies.
Department of Mineral Resources and
Development, G.P.O. Box 5288, Sydney, N.S.W.
2001, Australia. Ed. H. Basden. circ. 400. Indexed:
Bibl.&Ind.Geol.

559　　　　　NZ　ISSN 0077-9628
NEW ZEALAND. DEPARTMENT OF
SCIENTIFIC AND INDUSTRIAL RESEARCH.
GEOLOGICAL SURVEY. BULLETIN. 1906.
irreg., no. 91, 1975. price varies. Department of
Scientific and Industrial Research, P.O. Box 30368,
Lower Hutt, New Zealand. circ. 1,100.

557　　　　　CN　ISSN 0078-0308
NEWFOUNDLAND. MINERAL DEVELOPMENT
DIVISION. GEOLOGICAL SURVEY.
BULLETIN. irreg. price varies. Mineral
Development Division, St. John's, Newfoundland,
Canada.

557　　　　　CN　ISSN 0078-0375
NEWFOUNDLAND. MINES BRANCH.
GEOLOGICAL SURVEY OF
NEWFOUNDLAND. BULLETIN SERIES. 1934.
irreg. price varies. Mineral Development Division,
Confederation Bldg., St. John's, Newfoundland,
Canada.

557　　　　　CN　ISSN 0078-0383
NEWFOUNDLAND. MINES BRANCH.
GEOLOGICAL SURVEY OF
NEWFOUNDLAND. REPORT SERIES. 1953.
irreg. price varies. Mineral Development Division,
Confederation Bldg., St. John's. Newfoundland,
Canada.

557　　　　　　　　CN
NEWFOUNDLAND AND LABRADOR.
GEOLOGICAL REPORT. irreg. price varies.
Mineral Development Division, St. Johns, Nfld.,
Canada. bibl. charts. circ. controlled.

EARTH SCIENCES — GEOLOGY

551.7 GW ISSN 0078-0421
NEWSLETTERS ON STRATIGRAPHY.* (Text in English or German) 1970. 3/yr. DM.98. Gebrueder Borntraeger Verlagsbuchhandlung, Johannesstr. 3A, 7000 Stuttgart 1, W. Germany (B.R.D.) Ed. G. Luettig. adv. abstr. charts. illus.

555 549 JA
NIIGATA UNIVERSITY. FACULTY OF SCIENCE. SCIENCE REPORTS. SERIES E: GEOLOGY AND MINERALOGY. (Text in English) 1967. a. exchange basis. Niigata University, Faculty of Science - Niigata Daigaku Rigakubu, 8050 Igarashi Nino-cho, Niigata-shi 950-21, Japan.

551 NO
NORGES GEOLOGISKE UNDERSOEKELSE. ARMELDING. a. Norges Geologiske Undersoekelse - Geological Survey of Norway, Leiv Erikssons vei 39, Trondheim 7000, Norway. illus.

551 NO ISSN 0085-4271
NORSK POLARINSTITUTT. AARBOK. (Text in English and Norwegian; summaries in English and Russian) 1960. a, latest 1977 (pub. 1978) price varies. Norsk Polarinstitutt, Postboks 158, 1330 Oslo Lufthavn, Norway. Ed. Tore Gjelsvik.

551 NO
NORSK POLARINSTITUTT. MEDDELELSER. 1926. irreg., no. 106, 1976. Norsk Polarinstitutt, Postboks 158, 1330 Oslo Lufthavn, Norway.
Formerly: Norges Svalbard- og Ishavs- Undersoekelser.

551 NO ISSN 0474-8042
NORSK POLARINSTITUTT. POLARHAANDBOK. Short title: Polarhaandbok. 1964. irreg., latest 1979. Norsk Polarinstitutt, Postboks 158, 1330 Oslo Lufthavn, Norway.

551 NO
NORSK POLARINSTITUTT. SKRIFTER. 1929. irreg., no. 169, 1978 (not pub. consecutively) Norsk Polarinstitutt, Postboks 158, 1330 Oslo Lufthavn, Norway.
Former titles: Norges Svalbard- og Ishavs- Undersoekelser. Skrifter; Skrifter om Svalbard og Ishavet; Skrifter om Svalbard og Nordishavet; Norske Statsunder Stoettede Spitsbergenekspedisjoner. Resultater.

557 US
NORTH DAKOTA. GEOLOGICAL SURVEY. BULLETIN. 1920. irreg., no. 70, 1979. price varies. Geological Survey, University Station, Grand Forks, ND 58202. (back issues avail.)

557 US ISSN 0091-9004
NORTH DAKOTA. GEOLOGICAL SURVEY. EDUCATIONAL SERIES. 1972. irreg., no. 12, 1979. price varies. Geological Survey, Grand Forks, ND 58202. (Co-sponsor: North Dakota Department of Public Instruction) illus. Indexed: Bibl. & Ind.Geol. Key Title: Educational Series - North Dakota Geological Survey.

557 US ISSN 0078-1576
NORTH DAKOTA. GEOLOGICAL SURVEY. MISCELLANEOUS SERIES. 1957. irreg., no. 57, 1979. price varies. Geological Survey, Grand Forks, ND 58202. Indexed: Bibl. & Ind.Geol.

557 US
NORTH DAKOTA. GEOLOGICAL SURVEY. REPORT OF INVESTIGATIONS. 1949. irreg., no. 66, 1979. price varies. Geological Survey, University Station, Grand Forks, ND 58202. (back issues avail.)

557 US
NORTHWEST GEOLOGY. 1972. a. $2. ‡ University of Montana, Department of Geology, Missoula, MT 59812. Ed. Sheila Fountain. bibl. charts. illus. circ. 400. (back issues avail.) Indexed: Bibl.&Ind.Geol.

O. R. S. T. O. M. RECUEIL DE TRAVAUX. OCEANOGRAPHIE. (Office de la Recherche Scientifique et Technique Outre-Mer) see EARTH SCIENCES — Oceanography

554 GW ISSN 0078-2939
OBERRHEINISCHE GEOLOGISCHE ABHANDLUNGEN. 1929. a. price varies. Verlag C. F. Mueller GmbH (Karlsruhe), Rheinstr. 122, Postfach 210949, 7500 Karlsruhe 21, W. Germany (B. R. D.) Ed. H. Illies. circ. 450.

551 GW ISSN 0078-2947
OBERRHEINISCHER GEOLOGISCHER VEREIN. JAHRESBERICHTE UND MITTEILUNGEN. 1911. a. price varies. E. Schweizerbart'sche Verlagsbuchhandlung, Johannesstr. 3a, 7000 Stuttgart 1, W. Germany (B.R.D.) Ed. K. Hinkelbein.

557 US
OHIO. DIVISION OF GEOLOGICAL SURVEY. BULLETIN. 1903. irreg., no. 67, 1979. price varies. Department of Natural Resources, Division of Geological Survey, Fountain Square, Bldg. B, Columbus, OH 43224. illus. (back issues avail.)

557 US ISSN 0472-6685
OHIO. DIVISION OF GEOLOGICAL SURVEY. EDUCATIONAL LEAFLET. 1952. irreg. no. 11, 1979. free. Department of Natural Resources, Division of Geological Survey, Fountain Square, Bldg. B, Columbus, OH 43224. (back issues avail.)

557 US
OHIO. DIVISION OF GEOLOGICAL SURVEY. GEOLOGICAL NOTE. 1975. irreg., no. 6, 1979. price varies. Department of Natural Resources, Division of Geological Survey, Fountain Square, Bldg. B, Columbus, OH 43224. illus. (back issues avail)

557 US ISSN 0097-9473
OHIO. DIVISION OF GEOLOGICAL SURVEY. GUIDEBOOK. 1973. irreg., no. 4, 1975. price varies. Department of Natural Resources, Division of Geological Survey, Fountain Sq., Columbus, OH 43224. illus. Key Title: Guidebook - State of Ohio, Department of Natural Resources, Division of Geological Survey.

557 US
OHIO. DIVISION OF GEOLOGICAL SURVEY. INFORMATION CIRCULAR. 1946. irreg., no. 49, 1980. price varies. Department of Natural Resources, Division of Geological Survey, Fountain Square, Bldg. B, Columbus, OH 43224. illus. (back issues avail.)

557 US ISSN 0361-0519
OHIO. DIVISION OF GEOLOGICAL SURVEY. MISCELLANEOUS REPORT. 1974. irreg. Department of Natural Resources, Division of Geological Survey, Columbus, OH 43224. Indexed: Chem.Abstr. Key Title: Miscellaneous Report - State of Ohio, Department of Natural Resources, Division of Geological Survey.

557 US
OHIO. DIVISION OF GEOLOGICAL SURVEY. REPORT OF INVESTIGATIONS. 1947. irreg., no. 118, 1980. price varies. Department of Natural Resources, Division of Geological Survey, Fountain Square, Bldg. B, Columbus, OH 43224. illus. (back issues avail.)

557 US ISSN 0078-4389
OKLAHOMA. GEOLOGICAL SURVEY. BULLETIN. 1908. irreg., no. 130, 1981. price varies. Geological Survey, The University of Oklahoma, 830 Van Vleet Oval, Room 163, Norman, OK 73019. Ed. Wm. Rose. circ. 1,000. (reprint service avail. from UMI)

557 US ISSN 0078-4397
OKLAHOMA. GEOLOGICAL SURVEY. CIRCULAR. 1908. irreg., no. 80, 1980. price varies. Geological Survey, University of Oklahoma, 830 van Vleet Oval, Rm. 163, Norman, OK 73019. Ed. William Rose. circ. 1,000. (reprint service avail. from UMI)

557 US
OKLAHOMA. GEOLOGICAL SURVEY. EDUCATIONAL PUBLICATION. 1971. irreg. price varies. Oklahoma Geological Survey, University of Oklahoma, 830 van Fleet Oval, Room 163, Norman, OK 73019. Ed. William D. Rose. circ. 500-2,000.

557 US ISSN 0078-4400
OKLAHOMA. GEOLOGICAL SURVEY. GUIDEBOOK. 1953. irreg., no. 19, 1979. price varies. Geological Survey, University of Oklahoma, 830 van Vleet Oval, Rm. 163, Norman, OK 73019. Ed. William Rose. circ. 500. (reprint service avail. from UMI)

ONTARIO. GEOLOGICAL SURVEY. ANNUAL REPORT OF THE REGIONAL AND RESIDENT GEOLOGIST. see MINES AND MINING INDUSTRY

557 622 CN
ONTARIO. GEOLOGICAL SURVEY. GUIDE BOOKS. 1968. irreg., 1-2/yr. price varies. Geological Survey, 77 Grenville St., Parliament Bldgs., Toronto, Ont., Canada.
Formerly: Ontario. Division of Mines. Guide Books.

ONTARIO. GEOLOGICAL SURVEY. REPORT. see MINES AND MINING INDUSTRY

551 CN ISSN 0704-2590
ONTARIO GEOLOGICAL SURVEY STUDY. 1977. irreg. Ministry of Natural Resources, Parliament Bldgs., Toronto,Ont. M7A 1W3, Canada. bibl. charts. illus. index.

ONTARIO INSTITUTE OF PEDOLOGY. DEPARTMENT OF LAND RESOURCE SCIENCE. PROGRESS REPORT. see AGRICULTURE — Crop Production And Soil

OPERA LILLOANA. see BIOLOGY — Botany

557 622 US ISSN 0078-5709
OREGON. STATE DEPARTMENT OF GEOLOGY AND MINERAL INDUSTRIES. BULLETIN. 1938. irreg., no. 97, 1978. price varies. Department of Geology and Mineral Industries, 1069 State Office Building, Portland, OR 97201.

557 622 US ISSN 0078-5717
OREGON. STATE DEPARTMENT OF GEOLOGY AND MINERAL INDUSTRIES. G M I SHORT PAPERS. 1939. irreg., no. 97, 1978. price varies. Department of Geology and Mineral Industries, 1069 State Office Building, Portland, OR 97201.

557 622 US ISSN 0078-5725
OREGON. STATE DEPARTMENT OF GEOLOGY AND MINERAL INDUSTRIES. MISCELLANEOUS PAPERS. 1950. irreg., no. 20, 1978. price varies. Department of Geology and Mineral Industries, 1069 State Office Building, Portland, OR 97201.

557 622 US ISSN 0078-5733
OREGON. STATE DEPARTMENT OF GEOLOGY AND MINERAL INDUSTRIES. MISCELLANEOUS PUBLICATIONS. 1950. irreg., latest issue, 1975. Department of Geology and Mineral Industries, 1069 State Office Building, Portland, OR 97201.

OREGON. STATE DEPARTMENT OF GEOLOGY AND MINERAL INDUSTRIES. OIL AND GAS INVESTIGATIONS. see PETROLEUM AND GAS

557 US ISSN 0078-5814
OREGON STATE MONOGRAPHS. STUDIES IN GEOLOGY. 1940. irreg., 1971, no. 10. price varies. Oregon State University Press, 101 Waldo Hall, Corvallis, OR 97331.

555 PK ISSN 0078-8163
PAKISTAN. GEOLOGICAL SURVEY. RECORDS. (Text in English) 1949. irreg. price varies. ‡ Geological Survey of Pakistan, c/o Chief Librarian, Box 15, Quetta, Pakistan. circ. 1,500.

PALEONTOLOGY AND GEOLOGY OF THE BADWATER CREEK AREA, CENTRAL WYOMING. see PALEONTOLOGY

561 US ISSN 0191-6122
PALYNOLOGY. 1970. a. $15. American Association of Stratigraphic Palynologists Foundation, c/o Robert T. Clarke, Mobil R & D Corp. Field Research Laboratory, Box 900, Dallas, TX 75221. Ed. Vaughn M. Bryant. circ. 800. Indexed: Biol.Abstr. Petrol.Abstr.
Supersedes(as of 1977): Geoscience and Man (ISSN 0072-1395); Incorporating: American Association of Stratigraphic Palynologists. Proceedings of the Annual Meeting (ISSN 0084- 6309)

PEGG/PROFESSIONAL ENGINEER, GEOLOGIST, GEOPHYSICIST. see ENGINEERING

PETROLEUM GEOLOGY OF TAIWAN/T'AIWAN SHIH YU TI CHIH. see *PETROLEUM AND GAS*

550   PL   ISSN 0079-3396
POLSKA AKADEMIA NAUK. ODDZIAL W KRAKOWIE. KOMISJA NAUK MINERALOGICZNYCH. PRACE MINERALOGICZNE. (Text in English or Polish; summaries in English or Russian) 1965. irreg., no. 62, 1979. price varies. Ossolineum, Publishing House of the Polish Academy of Sciences, Rynek 9, 50-106 Wroclaw, Poland (Dist. by: Ars Polona - Ruch, Krakowskie Przedmiescie 7, Warsaw, Poland) Ed. Andrzej Bolewski.

551   PL   ISSN 0079-3663
POLSKIE TOWARZYSTWO GEOLOGICZNE. ROCZNIK/SOCIETE GEOLOGIQUE DE POLOGNE. ANNALES. (Text in English, French, Polish and Russian; summaries in the same languages) 1923. q. 100 Zl. (Geological Society of Poland) Panstwowe Wydawnictwo Naukowe, Miodowa 10, Warsaw, Poland. Ed. Tadeusz Wieser. bibl, charts, illus, index. circ. 1,800.

550 910   PL   ISSN 0079-4643
POZNANSKIE TOWARZYSTWO PRZYJACIOL NAUK. KOMISJA GEOGRAFICZNO-GEOLOGICZNA. PRACE. (Text in Polish; summaries in English) 1936. irreg., 1976, vol. 16. price varies. Panstwowe Wydawnictwo Naukowe, Miodowa 10, Warsaw, Poland (Dist by Ars Polona-Ruch, Krakowskie Przedmiescie 7, Warsaw, Poland) Ed. Andrzej Karczewski. circ. 400.

550   PL   ISSN 0079-3361
PRACE GEOLOGICZNE. (Text in Polish; summaries in English and Russian) 1960. irreg., no. 119, 1979. price varies. (Polska Akademia Nauk, Oddzial w Krakowie, Komista Nauk Geologicznych) Ossolineum, Publishing House of the Polish Academy of Sciences, Rynek 9, Wroclaw, Poland (Dist. by Ars Polona-Ruch, Krakowskie Przedmiescie 7, Warsaw, Poland) index.

549 550 560   YU   ISSN 0367-4983
PRIRODNJACKI MUZEJ U BEOGRADU. GLASNIK. SERIJA A: MINERALOGIJA, GEOLOGIJA, PALEONTOLOGIJA. 1948. irreg. Prirodnjacki Muzej u Beogradu, Njegoseva 51, Belgrade, Yugoslavia. Ed. Zivomir Vasic.

QUATERNARIA. see *PALEONTOLOGY*

557   CN   ISSN 0079-8738
QUEBEC (PROVINCE) DEPARTMENT OF NATURAL RESOURCES. GEOLOGICAL REPORTS. (Text in English and French) 1930. irreg. price varies. ‡ Ministere des Richesses Naturelles, Distribution et Documentation, 1620 Bd. de l'Entente, Quebec G1S 4N6, Canada. Ed. R. Gagnon. circ. 800. (also avail. in microfiche)

557   CN   ISSN 0079-8746
QUEBEC (PROVINCE) MINISTERE DES RICHESSES NATURELLES. TRAVAUX SUR LE TERRAIN. 1927. a. price varies. Ministere des Richesses Naturelles, Distribution et Documentation, 1620 Bd. de l'Entente, Quebec G1S 4N6, Canada.

559.4   AT   ISSN 0079-8800
QUEENSLAND. GEOLOGICAL SURVEY. PUBLICATIONS. 1879. irreg. exchange basis. Department of Mines, Mineral House, 41 George St., Brisbane, Qld. 4000, Australia. cum. index. Indexed: Aus.Sci.Ind. Bibl.&Ind.Geol.

551   SW
QUFO. (Text in Swedish) 1979. irreg. price varies. Societas Upsaliensis pro Geologia Quaternia, Department of Quaternary Geology, Box 555, S-751 22 Uppsala, Sweden.

REAL SOCIEDAD ESPANOLA DE HISTORIA NATURAL. BOLETIN DE GEOLOGIA Y BIOLOGIA. see *BIOLOGY*

551   II
RECENT RESEARCHES IN GEOLOGY. (Text in English) 1973. irreg. price varies. Hindustan Publishing Corp., 6-U.B. Jawahar Nagar, Delhi 110007, India.

558   CL
REVISTA GEOLOGICA DE CHILE. (Text in Spanish; summaries in English) 1974. irreg. $6. Instituto de Investigaciones Geologicas, Agustinas 785, Casilla 10465, Santiago, Chile. Ed. Manuel Suarez. circ. 1,000.

551   RM   ISSN 0556-8102
REVUE ROUMAINE DE GEOLOGIE, GEOPHYSIQUE ET GEOGRAPHIE. GEOLOGIE. (Text in English, French, German and Russian) 1957. a. $12. (Academia Republicii Socialiste Romania) Editura Academiei Republicii Socialiste Romania, Calea Victoriei 125, Bucharest, Romania (Subscr. to: ILEXIM, Str. 13 Decembrie Nr. 3, P.O. Box 136-137, Bucharest, Romania) Ed.Bd. bk. rev. charts. illus. index. Indexed: Chem.Abstr. Geotimes.
    Supersedes in Part: Revue de Geologie et de Geographie.

ROYAL IRISH ACADEMY. PROCEEDINGS. SECTION B: BIOLOGICAL, GEOLOGICAL AND CHEMICAL SCIENCES. see *BIOLOGY*

550   CS   ISSN 0036-5270
SBORNIK GEOLOGICKYCH VED: ANTROPOZOIKUM/JOURNAL OF GEOLOGICAL SCIENCES: ANTHROPOZOIC. (Text and summaries in Czech, English, French, German) 1951. irreg. 25-35 Kcs. per no. Ustredni Ustav Geologicky, Malostranske nam. 19, 118 21 Prague 1, Czechoslovakia (Subscr. to: Artia, Ve Smeckach 30, 111 27 Prague 1) Ed. Karel Zebera. charts. illus. circ. 600. (back issues avail.) Indexed: Bull.Signal. Ref.Zh. Bibl. & Ind.Geol.

551   CS   ISSN 0581-9172
SBORNIK GEOLOGICKYCH VED: GEOLOGIE/JOURNAL OF GEOLOGICAL SCIENCES: GEOLOGY. (Text in Czech, English or German; summaries also in French and Russian) 1921. 1-3/yr. 25-40 Kcs. per no. Ustredni Ustav Geologicky, Malostranske nam. 19, 118 21 Prague 1, Czechoslovakia (Subscr. to: Artia, Ve Smeckach 30, 111 27 Prague 1) Ed. Josef Svoboda. charts. illus. maps. circ. 700. Indexed: Bull.Signal. Ref.Zh. Bibl.& Ind.Geol.

551   CS   ISSN 0581-9180
SBORNIK GEOLOGICKYCH VED: LOZISKOVA GEOLOGIE, MINERALOGIE/JOURNAL OF GEOLOGICAL SCIENCES: ECONOMIC GEOLOGY, MINERALOGY. (Text in Czech, English or German; summaries also in French and Russian) 1963. irreg. 25-40 Kcs. per no. Ustredni Ustav Geologicky, Malostranske nam. 19, 118 21 Prague 1, Czechoslovakia (Subscr. to: Artia, Ve Smeckach 30, 111 27 Prague 1) Ed. Joel Pokorny. charts. illus. circ. 600. (back issues avail.) Indexed: Bull.Signal. Ref.Zh. Bibl.& Ind.Geol.

550   CS   ISSN 0036-5300
SBORNIK GEOLOGICKYCH VED: TECHNOLOGIE, GEOCHEMIE/JOURNAL OF GEOLOGICAL SCIENCES: TECHNOLOGY, GEOCHEMISTRY. (Text in Czech, English or German; summaries in Czech and Russian) 1962. irreg. 25-35 Kcs. per no. Ustredni Ustav Geologicky, Malostranske nam. 19, 118 21 Prague 1, Czechoslovakia (Subscr. to: Artia, Ve Smeckach 30, 111 27 Prague 1) (Co-sponsor: Ustav Nerostnych Surovin, Kutna Hora) Ed. Jiri Vtelensky. charts. illus. circ. 600. (back issues avail.) Indexed: Bull.Signal. Ref.Zh. Bibl.& Ind.Geol.

551   FR
SCIENCES DE LA TERRE: SERIE INFORMATIQUE GEOLOGIQUE. Cover title: Sciences de la Terre: Informatique Geologique. irreg. Fondation Scientifique de la Geologie et des ses Applications, 94 Ave. de Lattre de Tassigny, 54000 Nancy, France.

554   FR   ISSN 0302-2684
SCIENCES GEOLOGIQUES - MEMOIRES. 1927. irreg. price varies. Universite de Strasbourg I (Universite Louis Pasteur), Institut de Geologie, Bibliotheque, 1 rue Blessig, 67084 Strasbourg Cedex, France. Ed. Georges Millot. circ. 1,000. Indexed: Chem.Abstr.
    Formerly: Service de la Carte Geologique d'Alsace et de Lorraine. Memoires (ISSN 0080-9020)

551   NE   ISSN 0375-7587
SCRIPTA GEOLOGICA. (Text in English; Occasionally in French, German or Spanish) 1971. irreg. price varies. Rijksmuseum van Geologie en Mineralogie - Netherlands National Museum of Geology and Mineralogy, Hooglandse Kerkgracht 17, 2312 HS Leiden, Netherlands. Ed. Bd. bibl. charts. illus. circ. 350. Indexed: Mineral.Abstr.

551.3   CN   ISSN 0080-8482
SEDIMENT DATA FOR SELECTED CANADIAN RIVERS. 1965. a. free. Inland Waters Directorate, Ottawa, Ont. K1A OE7, Canada. Indexed: Eng.Ind.

551   BL
SEMINARIO BRASILEIRO SOBRE TECNICAS EXPLORATORIAS EM GEOLOGIA. ANAIS. 1976. irreg. Departamento Nacional da Producao Mineral, Av. Pasteur 404, Rio de Janeiro, Brazil.

SENCKENBERGISCHE NATURFORSCHENDE GESELLSCHAFT. ABHANDLUNGEN. see *BIOLOGY*

550   CS   ISSN 0036-1372
SLOVENSKA AKADEMIA VIED. GEOLOGICKY USTAV D. STURA: ZBORNIK: ZAPADNE KARPATY. (Text in English, German or Slovak; summaries in English or German) 1-2/yr. 20 Kcs.($3.50) per no. Veda, Publishing House of the Slovak Academy of Sciences, Klemensova 19, 895 30 Bratislava, Czechoslovakia. Ed. Ondrej Samuel. charts. illus. index. Indexed: Chem.Abstr.
    Supersedes: Slovenska Akademia Vied. Geologicky Ustav D. Stura. Geologicke Prace.

SOCIEDAD DE HISTORIA NATURAL DE BALEARES. BOLETIN. see *BIOLOGY*

558   PE   ISSN 0079-1091
SOCIEDAD GEOLOGICA DEL PERU. BOLETIN. (Text in Spanish; summaries in English and French) 1925. irreg. S.3.50($8.50) Sociedad Geologica del Peru, Apartado 2559, Lima, Peru. Ed. C. Canepa. adv. bk. rev. circ. 1,000.

554   FR
SOCIETE GEOLOGIQUE DE FRANCE. MEMOIRES. irreg (1-4 nos. per yr.) 415 F. Societe Geologique de France, 77, rue Claude-Bernard, 75005 Paris, France.

551   BU
SOFIISKI UNIVERSITET. GEOLOGO-GEOGRAFSKI FAKULTET. GEOLOGIIA. GODISHNIK. (Summaries in English, French and German) 1905. irreg. 2.74 lv. per issue. Izdatelstvo Nauka i Izkustvo, 6, Rouski Blvd., Sofia, Bulgaria. Ed. N. Nikolova. circ. 580.

SOUTH AFRICA. DEPARTMENT OF MINES. ANNUAL REPORT. see *MINES AND MINING INDUSTRY*

551   SA   ISSN 0584-2352
SOUTH AFRICA. GEOLOGICAL SURVEY. ANNALS. 1962. a., latest vol. 12, 1977/1978. price varies. Geological Survey, Private Bag X112, Pretoria 0001, South Africa (Orders to: Government Printer, Bosman St., Private Bag X85, Pretoria 0001, South Africa)

551   SA
SOUTH AFRICA. GEOLOGICAL SURVEY. BULLETIN. 1934. irreg., latest no. 66. price varies. Geological Survey, Private Bag X112, Pretoria 0001, South Africa (Orders to: Government Printer, Bosman St., Private Bag X85, Pretoria 0001, South Africa)

550   SA   ISSN 0560-9208
SOUTH AFRICA. GEOLOGICAL SURVEY. HANDBOOK. 1959. irreg., latest no. 7. price varies. Geological Survey, Private Bag X112, Pretoria 0001, South Africa (Orders to: Government Printer, Bosman St., Private Bag X85, Pretoria 0001, South Africa)

551   SA
SOUTH AFRICA. GEOLOGICAL SURVEY. MEMOIRS. irreg., latest no. 69, 1976. price varies. Geological Survey, Private Bag X112, Pretoria 0001, South Africa (Orders to: Government Printer, Bosman St., Private Bag X85, Pretoria 0001, South Africa)

551 SA
SOUTH AFRICA. GEOLOGICAL SURVEY.
SEISMOLOGIC SERIES. 1972. irreg., latest no.
10, 1980. price varies. Geological Survey, Private
Bag X112, Pretoria 0001, South Africa (Orders to:
Government Printer, Bosman St., Private Bag X85,
Pretoria 0001, South Africa)

551 SA
SOUTH AFRICA. GEOLOGICAL SURVEY.
SPECIAL PUBLICATIONS. 1910. irreg., latest no.
20, 1977. price varies. Geological Survey, Private
Bag X112, Pretoria 0001, South Africa (Orders to:
Government Printer, Bosman St., Private Bag X85,
Pretoria 0001, South Africa)

559.4 AT ISSN 0016-7673
SOUTH AUSTRALIA. GEOLOGICAL SURVEY.
BULLETIN. 1912. irreg. price varies. ‡ Geological
Survey of South Australia, Box 151, Eastwood, S.
A. 5063, Australia. charts. illus. index; cum.index:
v.1-38 (1912-1963) circ. 700.

559.4 AT ISSN 0016-7681
SOUTH AUSTRALIA. GEOLOGICAL SURVEY.
REPORT OF INVESTIGATIONS. 1954. irreg.
price varies. Geological Survey of South Australia,
Box 151, Eastwood, S. A. 5063, Australia. Ed. W.A.
Fairburn. charts. illus. circ. 700.

557 US
SOUTH DAKOTA. GEOLOGICAL SURVEY.
BIENNIAL REPORTS OF THE STATE
GEOLOGIST. 1914. biennial. $0.75. Geological
Survey, Science Center University, Vermillion, SD
57401. (back issues avail.)

557 US ISSN 0085-6479
SOUTH DAKOTA GEOLOGICAL SURVEY.
BULLETIN. 1894. irreg., no. 25, 1976. price varies.
Geological Survey, Science Center University,
Vermillion, SD 57069. circ. controlled.

557 US ISSN 0085-6487
SOUTH DAKOTA GEOLOGICAL SURVEY.
CIRCULAR. 1917. irreg.; no. 43, 1976. price varies.
Geological Survey, Science Center University,
Vermillion, SD 57069. circ. controlled.

557 US ISSN 0085-6495
SOUTH DAKOTA GEOLOGICAL SURVEY.
REPORTS OF INVESTIGATION. 1929. irreg.,
latest issue 1974. price varies. Geological Survey,
Science Center University, Vermillion, SD 57069.
circ. controlled.

556 SA
SOUTH WEST AFRICA SERIES. MEMOIRS. (Text
in English; summaries in Afrikaans) irreg., no. 6,
1980. price varies. Geological Survey, Private Bag
X112, Pretoria 0001, South Africa (Orders to:
Government Printer, Bosman St., Private Bag X85,
Pretoria 0001, South Africa)

551 SP
SPAIN. INSTITUTO GEOLOGICO Y MINERO.
INFORMES. irreg. 300 ptas. (Instituto Geologico y
Minero) Spain. Ministerio de Industria, Servicio de
Publicaciones, Claudio Coello 44, Madrid 1, Spain.

551 UK ISSN 0435-3951
SPECIAL ISSUES. 1965. irreg. price varies. John
Wiley & Sons Ltd., Baffins Lane, Chichester, Sussex
P019 1UD, England. Ed. Dr. G. Newall. bk. rev.
circ. 850. (reprint service avail. from UMI,ISI)

551 US ISSN 0081-4350
STANFORD UNIVERSITY. PUBLICATIONS.
GEOLOGICAL SCIENCES. vol. 4, 1954. irreg.,
vol. 17, 1979. price varies. Stanford University,
School of Earth Sciences, Stanford, CA 94305.

551 US ISSN 0039-0089
STATE GEOLOGISTS JOURNAL. 1949. a. $5.
Association of American State Geologists, c/o E. A.
Noble, Ed., North Dakota Geological Survey,
University Station, Grand Forks, ND 58202. circ.
200.

551 SW ISSN 0345-0074
STRIAE; a monograph series for quaternary studies.
(Text in English, French and German) 1975. irreg.,
no. 12, 1979. price varies. Societas Upsaliensis pro
Geologia Quaternia, Department of Quaternary
Geology, Box 555, S-751 22 Uppsala, Sweden. Ed.
Lars-Koenig Koenigsson.

551 SW ISSN 0348-4386
STRIOLAE. (Text in English, French and German)
1979. irreg., no. 6, 1979. price varies. Societas
Upsaliensis pro Geologia Quaternia, Department of
Quaternary Geology, Box 555, S-751 22 Uppsala,
Sweden.

554 914 PL ISSN 0081-6418
STUDIA GEOGRAFICZNO-FIZYCZNE Z
OBSZARU OPOLSZCZYZNY. 1968. irreg. 20 Zl.
Instytut Slaski, Instytut Naukowo-Badawczy,
Luboszycka 3, Opole, Poland.

550 PL ISSN 0081-6426
STUDIA GEOLOGICA POLONICA.* (Text in
English and Polish) 1958. irreg. price varies. (Polska
Akademia Nauk, Oddzial w Krakowie, Komisja
Nauk Geologicznych) Wydawnictwa Geologiczne,
Rakowiecka 4, Warsaw, Poland (Dist. by Ars
Polona-Ruch, Krakowskie Przedmiescie 7, Warsaw,
Poland)

STUDIA SOCIETATIS SCIENTIARUM
TORUNENSIS. SECTIO C (GEOGRAFIA ET
GEOLOGIA) see GEOGRAPHY

550 910 RM ISSN 0039-341X
STUDIA UNIVERSITATIS "BABES-BOLYAI".
GEOLOGIA. GEOGRAPHIA. (Text in Romanian;
summaries in English, French, German, Russian)
1958. s-a. exchange basis. Universitatea "Babes-
Bolyai", Biblioteca Centrala Universitara,
Str.Clinicilor. Nr. 2, Cluj-Napoca, Romania. charts.
illus. maps. index. Indexed: Chem.Abstr.

551.44 UK ISSN 0585-718X
STUDIES IN SPELEOLOGY. 1964. a. £2 to non-
members. William Pengelly Cave Studies Trust Ltd.,
16 New Road, Kingston Upon Thames, Surrey,
England. Ed. A.J. Sutcliffe. adv. bk. rev. index. circ.
600.
Speleology

557 US ISSN 0081-8747
STUDIES IN VERMONT GEOLOGY. 1970. irreg.
$4 per no. Geological Survey, Montpelier, VT
05602 (Order from: Vermont Dept. of Libraries, 111
State St., Montpelier, VT 05602)

556 622 SQ ISSN 0081-9999
SWAZILAND. GEOLOGICAL SURVEY AND
MINES DEPARTMENT. ANNUAL REPORT.
1958. a. R.0.50 ‡ Geological Survey and Mines
Department, P.O. Box 9, Mbabane, Swaziland. circ.
500.

556 622 SQ ISSN 0082-0008
SWAZILAND. GEOLOGICAL SURVEY AND
MINES DEPARTMENT. BULLETIN. 1961. a.
price varies. ‡ Geological Survey and Mines
Department, P.O. Box 9, Mbabane, Swaziland. circ.
500.

538.7 SW ISSN 0075-403X
SWEDEN. SVERIGES GEOLOGISKA
UNDERSOEKNING. JORDMAGNETISKA
PUBLIKATIONER/GEOMAGNETIC
PUBLICATIONS. (Text in English) 1919. irreg.,
no. 21, 1975. Kr.50. Sveriges Geologiska
Undersoekning - Geological Survey of Sweden, Box
670, S-751 28 Uppsala, Sweden. Ed. Folke Eleman.

554 SW ISSN 0082-0024
SWEDEN. SVERIGES GEOLOGISKA
UNDERSOEKNING. SERIE C.
AVHANDLINGAR OCH UPPSATSER/
MEMOIRS AND NOTICES. (Text in Swedish,
English, German; summaries in English) 1868.
irreg., no. 713, 1975. price varies. Sveriges
Geologiska Undersoekning - Geological Survey of
Sweden, Box 670, S-751 28 Uppsala, Sweden.
cum.index: 1858-1958.

554 SW ISSN 0082-0016
SWEDEN. SVERIGES GEOLOGISKA
UNDERSOEKNING.SERIE CA.
AVHANDLINGAR OCH UPPSATSER I
KVARTO/NOTICES IN QUARTO AND FOLIO.
1900. irreg., no. 48, 1974. price varies. Sveriges
Geologiska Undersoekning - Geological Survey of
Sweden, Box 670, S-751 28 Uppsala, Sweden.

551.44 AT
SYDNEY SPELEOLOGICAL SOCIETY.
OCCASIONAL PAPER. 1965. irreg. price varies. ‡
Sydney Speleological Society, P.O. Box 198,
Broadway, Sydney, N.S.W. 2007, Australia. Ed.
Ross Ellis. circ. 200-5,000. Indexed: Aus.Speleo
Abstr.
Formerly: Sydney Speleological Society.
Communications (ISSN 0085-7017)
Speleology

559.4 AT ISSN 0082-2043
TASMANIA. DEPARTMENT OF MINES.
GEOLOGICAL SURVEY BULLETINS. 1907.
irreg., 1973, no. 54. Aus.$1.50($5) Department of
Mines, Box 124B, G.P.O., Hobart, Tasmania,
Australia 7001. Ed. E. L. Martin. circ. 300.
Indexed: Bibl.&Ind.Geol.

551 AT ISSN 0082-2078
TASMANIA. DEPARTMENT OF MINES.
TECHNICAL REPORTS. 1957. irreg., no. 19,
1975. Aus.$1($2) Department of Mines, Box 124B,
G.P.O., Hobart, Tasmania, Australia 7001. Ed. E. L.
Martin. circ. 300. Indexed: Bibl.&Ind.Geol.

549 UR
TEKTONIKA I STRATIGRAFIYA. 1972. irreg., vol.
11, 1976. Akademiya Nauk Ukrainskoi S.S.R.,
Institut Geologicheskikh Nauk Izdatel'stvo /
Naukova Dumka, Ul.Repina 3, Kiev, U.S.S.R.

551 560 NE ISSN 0308-7506
TERTIARY RESEARCH GROUP. SPECIAL
PAPERS. irreg (1-2/yr) (Tertiary Research Group,
UK) Dr. W. Backhuys, Publisher, Oudorpweg 12,
3062 RC Rotterdam, Netherlands.

551 560 JA ISSN 0082-4658
TOHOKU UNIVERSITY. INSTITUTE OF
GEOLOGY AND PALEONTOLOGY.
CONTRIBUTIONS/TOHOKU DAIGAKU
RIGAKUBU CHISHITSUGAKU
KOSEIBUTSUGAKU KYOSHITSU KENKYU
HOBUN HOKOKU. (Text in Japanese; summaries
in English) 1921. irreg., no. 75, 1975. available on
exchange. Tohoku University, Institute of Geology
and Paleontology - Tohoku Daigaku Rigakubu
Chishitsugaku Koseibutsugaku Kyoshitsu,
Aobayama, Sendai 980, Japan. Eds. N. Kitamura, T.
Kotaka and Y. Takayanagi. circ. 750. (also avail. in
microfilm; microfiche)

551 560 JA ISSN 0082-464X
TOHOKU UNIVERSITY. INSTITUTE OF
GEOLOGY AND PALEONTOLOGY. SCIENCE
REPORTS. SECOND SERIES. (Text in English)
1912. irreg., vol. 45, no. 2, 1975. available on
exchange. Tohoku University, Institute of Geology
and Paleontology - Tohoku Daigaku Rigakubu
Chishitsugaku Koseibutsugaku Kyoshitsu,
Aobayama, Sendai 980, Japan. Eds. N. Kitamura, T.
Kotaka and Y. Takayanagi. circ. 750. (also avail. in
microfilm; microfiche)

555 549 915 JA
TOKYO UNIVERSITY OF EDUCATION.
FACULTY OF SCIENCE. SCIENCE REPORTS.
SECTION C: GEOGRAPHY, GEOLOGY AND
MINERALOGY. (Text in European languages)
1936. irreg. exchange basis. Tokyo University of
Education, Faculty of Science - Tokyo Kyoiku
Daigaku, 3-29-1 Otsuka, Bunkyo-ku, Tokyo 112,
Japan.

TURUN YLIOPISTO. JULKAISUJA. SARJA A. II.
BIOLOGICA- GEOGRAPHICA- GEOLOGICA.
see BIOLOGY

556 UG ISSN 0082-7215
UGANDA. GEOLOGICAL SURVEY AND MINES
DEPARTMENT. ANNUAL REPORT. a,latest
1973. price varies. Geological Survey and Mines
Department, P.O. Box 9, Entebbe, Uganda.

557 US ISSN 0083-1093
U. S. GEOLOGICAL SURVEY. BULLETIN. 1883.
irreg. U.S. Geological Survey, 12201 Sunrise Valley
Dr., Reston, VA 22092 (Orders to: 604 S. Pickett
St., Alexandria, VA 22304)

557 US ISSN 0083-1107
U. S. GEOLOGICAL SURVEY. CIRCULAR. 1933.
irreg. free. U. S. Geological Survey, 12201 Sunrise
Valley Dr., Reston, VA 22092 (Orders to: 604 S.
Pickett St., Alexandria, VA 22304)

EARTH SCIENCES — GEOLOGY

557 US
U.S. GEOLOGICAL SURVEY. PROFESSIONAL PAPERS. irreg. U.S. Geological Survey, 12201 Sunrise Valley Drive, Reston, VA 22092 (Orders to: 604 S. Pickett St., Alexandria, VA 22304)

557 US ISSN 0162-9484
U. S. GEOLOGICAL SURVEY. YEARBOOK. a. U.S. Geological Survey, 2201 Sunrise Valley Dr., Reston, VA 22092 (Orders to: 604 S. Pickett St., Alexandria, VA 22304)
Formerly: U.S. Geological Survey. Annual Report (ISSN 0147-8478)

550 CK ISSN 0120-0283
UNIVERSIDAD INDUSTRIAL DE SANTANDER. BOLETIN DE GEOLOGIA. (Text in Spanish, occasionally in English and French) 1962? irreg. $3 or exchange basis. Universidad Industrial de Santander, Biblioteca, Apdo. Aereo 678, Bucaramanga, Santander, Colombia. abstr. charts. illus. circ. 1,200. Indexed: Chem.Abstr.

557 MX
UNIVERSIDAD NACIONAL AUTONOMA DE MEXICO. INSTITUTO DE GEOLOGIA. REVISTA. 1975. a. Universidad Nacional Autonoma de Mexico, Instituto de Geologia, Apdo. 70-296, Ciudad Universitaria, Mexico 20, D.F., Mexico. charts.

UNIVERSIDAD NACIONAL DE ROSARIO. FACULTAD DE CIENCIAS, INGENIERIA Y ARQUITECTURA. INSTITUTO DE FISIOGRAFIA Y GEOLOGIA. PUBLICACIONES. see *GEOGRAPHY*

558 BL
UNIVERSIDADE DE SAO PAULO. INSTITUTO DE GEOGRAFIA, SEDIMENTOLOGIA E PEDOLOGIA.* (Summaries in English and French) 1971. irreg; (approx. 2-3/yr) Universidade de Sao Paulo, Instituto de Geografia, Sedimentologia e Pedologia, Cidade Universitaria, C.P. 20715, 05508 Sao Paulo-SP, Brazil.

551 560 IT
UNIVERSITA DEGLI STUDI DI FERRARA. ISTITUTO DI GEOLOGIA. ANNALI. SEZIONE 9. SCIENZE GEOLOGICHE. (Text in Italian, French or English) 1951. irreg., vol. 5, no. 13, 1978. exchange basis. Universita degli Studi di Ferrara, Istuto di Geologia, C.So Ercole 1 d'Este 32, Ferrara, Italy. index. circ. 450.
Formerly: Universite degli Studi di Ferrara. Istituto di Geologia, Paleontologia e Paleontologia Umana. Annali. Sezione 9. Scienze Geologiche (ISSN 0071-4550)

554 560 IT
UNIVERSITA DEGLI STUDI DI FERRARA. ISTITUTO DI GEOLOGIA. PUBBLICAZIONI. (Text in Italian, French or English) 1950. a. available on exchange. Universita degli Studi di Ferrara, Istituto di Geologia, C.So Ercole 1 d' Este, 32, Ferrara, Italy. index. circ. 450.
Formerly: Universita degli Studi di Ferrara. Istituto di Geologia, Paleontologia e Paleontologia Umana. Pubblicazioni (ISSN 0071-4577)

554 IT
UNIVERSITA DEGLI STUDI DI NAPOLI. ISTITUTO DI GEOLOGIA APPLICATA. MEMORIE E NOTE. 1948. irreg. free. Universita degli Studi di Napoli, Istituto di Geologia Applicata, Naples, Italy. illus.

554 560 GW ISSN 0072-1115
UNIVERSITAET HAMBURG. GEOLOGISCH-PALAEONTOLOGISCHES INSTITUT. MITTEILUNGEN. (Text in German and English) 1948. a. DM.20($5) Universitaet Hamburg, Geologisch-Palaeontologisches Institut, Von Melle Park 11, 2000 Hamburg 13, W. Germany (B.R.D.) Ed. Gero Hillmer.

554 AU
UNIVERSITAET INNSBRUCK. ALPENKUNDLICHE STUDIEN. (Subseries of: Universitaet Innsbruck. Veroeffentlichungen) 1968. irreg., vol. 10, 1972. price varies. Oesterreichische Kommissionsbuchhandlung, Maximilianstrasse 17, A-6020 Innsbruck, Austria. Ed. Franz Fliri.

554 GW ISSN 0069-5874
UNIVERSITAET ZU KOELN. GEOLOGICHES INSTITUT. SONDERVEROEFFENTLICHUNGEN. (Text in German; summaries in English) 1956. irreg., 1973, no. 22. DM.6. Universitaet zu Koeln, Geologisches Institut, Zuelpicher Str. 49, 5000 Cologne 41, W. Germany (B.R.D.)

550 RM ISSN 0075-3521
UNIVERSITATEA "AL. I. CUZA" DIN IASI. ANALELE STIINTIFICE. SECTIUNEA 2B: GEOLOGIE. (Text in Romanian; Summaries in Foreign Languages) 1955. a. Universitatea "Al. I. Cuza" din Iasi, Calea 23 August Nr. 11, Jassy, Romania (Subscr. to: ILEXIM, Str. 13 Decembrie Nr. 3, P.O. Box 136-137, Bucharest, Romania)

554 549 FR ISSN 0069-4711
UNIVERSITE DE CLERMONT-FERRAND II. ANNALES SCIENTIFIQUES. SERIE GEOLOGIE ET MINERALOGIE. 1959. irreg. price varies. Universite de Clermont-Ferrand II, Unite d'Enseignement et de Recherche de Sciences Exactes et Naturelles, B.P. 45, 63170 Aubiere, France. circ. 250. (back issues avail)

557 CN
UNIVERSITY OF BRITISH COLUMBIA. DEPARTMENT OF GEOLOGICAL SCIENCES. REPORT. 1962. irreg., no. 17, 1976. Can.$3 per no. or on exchange basis. ‡ University of British Columbia, Department of Geological Sciences, Vancouver, B. C. V6T 1W5, Canada. Ed. W. R. Danner. circ. 400.
Formerly: University of British Columbia. Department of Geology. Report (ISSN 0068-1733)

556 SA
UNIVERSITY OF CAPE TOWN. DEPARTMENT OF GEOLOGY. PRECAMBRIAN RESEARCH UNIT. ANNUAL REPORT. 1963. a. University of Cape Town, Department of Geology. Precambrian Research Unit, Rondebosch 7700, South Africa.

556 SA ISSN 0250-216X
UNIVERSITY OF CAPE TOWN. DEPARTMENT OF GEOLOGY. PRECAMBRIAN RESEARCH UNIT. BULLETIN. 1965. irreg., no. 23, 1978. exchange basis only. University of Cape Town, Department of Geology. Precambrian Research Unit, Rondebosch 7700, South Africa. (Affiliate: Chamber of Mines of South Africa) Ed. P. Joubert. bibl. charts. circ. 350-400.

UNIVERSITY OF GUELPH. DEPARTMENT OF GEOGRAPHY. GEOGRAPHICAL PUBLICATION. see *GEOGRAPHY*

557 US ISSN 0075-5575
UNIVERSITY OF KENTUCKY. GEOLOGICAL SURVEY. GUIDEBOOK TO GEOLOGICAL FIELD TRIPS. 1952. irreg. price varies. Kentucky Geological Survey, 311 Breckinridge Hall, University of Kentucky, Lexington, KY 40506. Ed. Donald W. Hutcheson.

557 US ISSN 0075-5605
UNIVERSITY OF KENTUCKY. GEOLOGICAL SURVEY. REPRINTS. 1925. irreg., Series 11, no. 8, 1980. price varies: $0.25-$1. Kentucky Geological Survey, 311 Breckinridge Hall, University of Kentucky, Lexington, KY 40506. Ed. Donald W. Hutcheson.

557 US ISSN 0075-5559
UNIVERSITY OF KENTUCKY. GEOLOGICAL SURVEY. SERIES X. BULLETIN. 1879. irreg., 1969, no. 5. price varies. Kentucky Geological Survey, 311 Breckinridge Hall, University of Kentucky, Lexington, KY 40506. Ed. Donald W. Hutcheson.

557 US ISSN 0075-5591
UNIVERSITY OF KENTUCKY. GEOLOGICAL SURVEY. SERIES X. REPORT OF INVESTIGATIONS. 1949. irreg., no. 21, 1978. price varies. Kentucky Geological Survey, 311 Breckinridge Hall, University of Kentucky, Lexington, KY 40506. Ed. Donald W. Hutcheson.

557 US ISSN 0075-5567
UNIVERSITY OF KENTUCKY. GEOLOGICAL SURVEY. SERIES XI. COUNTY REPORT. 1912. irreg., no. 1, 1979. price varies. Kentucky Geological Survey, 311 Breckinridge Hall, University of Kentucky, Lexington, KY 40506. Ed. Donald W. Hutcheson.

557 US ISSN 0075-5583
UNIVERSITY OF KENTUCKY. GEOLOGICAL SURVEY. SERIES XI. INFORMATION CIRCULAR. 1951. irreg. no. 4, 1980. price varies. Kentucky Geological Survey, 311 Breckinridge Hall, University of Kentucky, Lexington, KY 40506. Ed. Donald W. Hutcheson.

557 US ISSN 0075-5613
UNIVERSITY OF KENTUCKY. GEOLOGICAL SURVEY. SERIES XI. SPECIAL PUBLICATION. 1953. irreg., no. 2, 1980. price varies. Kentucky Geological Survey, 311 Breckinridge Hall, University of Kentucky, Lexington, KY 40506. Ed. Donald W. Hutcheson.
Issued Also in This Series: Kentucky Oil and Gas Association. Technical Session. Proceedings.

557 US ISSN 0075-5621
UNIVERSITY OF KENTUCKY. GEOLOGICAL SURVEY. SERIES XI. THESIS SERIES. 1966. irreg., no. 1, 1980. price varies. Kentucky Geological Survey, 311 Breckinridge Hall, University of Kentucky, Lexington, KY 40506. Ed. Donald W. Hutcheson.

556 UK ISSN 0075-8558
UNIVERSITY OF LEEDS. RESEARCH INSTITUTE OF AFRICAN GEOLOGY. ANNUAL REPORT. 1955-56. a. £1.50. ‡ University of Leeds, Department of Earth Sciences, Research Institute of African Geology, Leeds, England. Ed. M. P. Coward. circ. 500.

550 PK
UNIVERSITY OF PUNJAB. INSTITUTE OF GEOLOGY. GEOLOGICAL BULLETIN. (Text in English) 1961. irreg., no. 15, 1978. Rs.15($1.50) University of the Punjab, Institute of Geology, New Campus, Lahore, Pakistan. circ. controlled. Indexed: Biol.Abstr.

553 557 US ISSN 0082-3287
UNIVERSITY OF TEXAS, AUSTIN. BUREAU OF ECONOMIC GEOLOGY. ANNUAL REPORT. 1960. a. free. University of Texas at Austin, Bureau of Economic Geology, University Station, Box X, Austin, TX 78712. (reprint service avail. from UMI)

557 US ISSN 0082-3309
UNIVERSITY OF TEXAS, AUSTIN. BUREAU OF ECONOMIC GEOLOGY. GEOLOGICAL CIRCULAR. 1965. irreg., no. 79-4, 1979. price varies. University of Texas at Austin, Bureau of Economic Geology, University Station, Box X, Austin, TX 78712. (reprint service avail. from UMI)

557 US ISSN 0363-4132
UNIVERSITY OF TEXAS, AUSTIN. BUREAU OF ECONOMIC GEOLOGY. GUIDEBOOK. 1958. irreg., no. 19, 1979. price varies. University of Texas at Austin, Bureau of Economic Geology, University Station, Box X, Austin, TX 78712. (reprint service avail. from UMI)

553 US ISSN 0082-3333
UNIVERSITY OF TEXAS, AUSTIN. BUREAU OF ECONOMIC GEOLOGY. MINERAL RESOURCE CIRCULARS. 1930. irreg., no. 62, 1979. price varies. University of Texas at Austin, Bureau of Economic Geology, University Station, Box X, Austin, TX 78712. (back issues avail.; reprint service avail. from UMI)

557 US ISSN 0082-335X
UNIVERSITY OF TEXAS, AUSTIN. BUREAU OF ECONOMIC GEOLOGY. REPORT OF INVESTIGATIONS. 1946. irreg., no. 97, 1979. price varies. University of Texas at Austin, Bureau of Economic Geology, University Station, Box X, Austin, TX 78712. (reprint service avail. from UMI)

559.8 NZ
UNIVERSITY OF WAIKATO. ANTARCTIC RESEARCH UNIT. REPORT. 1972. irreg. free. University of Waikato, Antarctic Research Unit, Hamilton, New Zealand. circ. 250.

550 PL ISSN 0083-4238
UNIWERSYTET IM. ADAMA MICKIEWICZA W POZNANIU. WYDZIAL BIOLOGII I NAUK O ZIEMI. PRACE. SERIA GEOLOGIA. 1961. irreg. price varies. Uniwersytet im. Adama Mickiewicza w Poznaniu, Stalingradzka 1, 61-712 Poznan, Poland.

551　　　　　　　　SW
UPPSALA UNIVERSITET. GEOLOGICAL
INSTITUTION. BULLETIN. (Subseries of Acta
Universitatis Upsaliensis) (Text in English) N.S.
1970. irreg. price varies. Almqvist & Wiksell
International, Box 62, S-101 20 Stockholm, Sweden.
Eds. Bengt Collini, Richard A. Reyment. bibl.
charts. illus.

550　　　　　　　　CS
USTREDNI USTAV GEOLOGICKY. VYZKUMNE
PRACE. irreg. free to qualified personnel. Ustredni
Ustav Geologicky, Malostranske nam. 19, 118 21
Prague 1, Czechoslovakia (Subscr. to: Artia, Ve
Smeckach 30, 111 27 Prague 1)

557 553　　　US　　ISSN 0098-4825
UTAH GEOLOGICAL AND MINERAL SURVEY.
BULLETIN. no. 35, 1948. irreg., no. 113, 1978.
price varies. Geological and Mineral Survey, 606
Black Hawk Way, Salt Lake City, UT 84108. illus.
Key Title: Bulletin - Utah Geological and Mineral
Survey.

557　　　　　US　　ISSN 0083-484X
UTAH GEOLOGICAL ASSOCIATION. ANNUAL
GUIDEBOOK. (Association formed by merger of
Utah Geological Society and Intermountain
Association of Geologists. Title varies: Symposium)
1971. a. (not pub. 1978) price varies. Utah
Geological Association, P.O. Box 11334, Salt Lake
City, UT 84111 (Dist. by: Utah Geological and
Mineral Survey, 606 Black Hawk Way, Salt Lake
City, UT 84108) Ed. Lowell Hilpert.

551　　　　　FI　　ISSN 0355-3450
VALTION TEKNILLINEN TUTKIMUSKESKUS.
GEOTEKNIIKAN LABORATORIO.
TIEDONANTO/TECHNICAL RESEARCH
CENTRE OF FINLAND. GEOTECHNICAL
LABORATORY. REPORT. (Text mainly in
Finnish, some in English or Swedish) 1971. irreg.
price varies. Valtion Teknillinen Tutkimuskeskus -
Technical Research Laboratory of Finland,
Vuorimiehentie 5, 02150 Espoo 15, Finland.

557　　　　　US　　ISSN 0083-5757
VERMONT. GEOLOGICAL SURVEY. BULLETIN.
1950. irreg. Geological Survey, Montpelier, VT
05602 (Order from: Vermont Dept. of Libraries, 111
State St., Montpelier VT 05602)

557　　　　　US　　ISSN 0083-5765
VERMONT. GEOLOGICAL SURVEY. SPECIAL
PUBLICATION. 1962. irreg. $5 per no. Geological
Survey, Montpelier, VT 05602 (Order from:
Vermont Dept. of Libraries, 111 State St.,
Montpelier VT 05602)

559.4　　　　AT　　ISSN 0085-7750
VICTORIA, AUSTRALIA. GEOLOGICAL
SURVEY. BULLETIN. 1903. irreg. price varies. ‡
Geological Survey of Victoria, Dept. of Minerals &
Energy, 140 Bourke St., Melbourne, Vic. 3000,
Australia. Eds. Dr. C. Abele, P. Fishley. circ. 750.

559.4　　　　AT　　ISSN 0085-7769
VICTORIA, AUSTRALIA. GEOLOGICAL
SURVEY. MEMOIRS. 1903. irreg. price varies. ‡
Geological Survey of Victoria, Dept. of Minerals &
Energy, 140 Bourke St., Melbourne, Vic. 3000,
Australia. Eds. Dr. C. Abele, P. Fishley. circ. 750.

559.4　　　　AT
VICTORIA, AUSTRALIA. GEOLOGICAL
SURVEY. REPORTS. 1968. irreg. price varies.
Geological Survey of Victoria, Dept. of Minerals &
Energy, 140 Bourke St., Melbourne, Vic. 3000,
Australia. Eds. Dr. C. Abele, P. Fishley.

VIRGINIA. DIVISION OF MINERAL
RESOURCES. PUBLICATIONS. see *MINES
AND MINING INDUSTRY*

557　　　　　US　　ISSN 0507-1259
VIRGINIA POLYTECHNIC INSTITUTE AND
STATE UNIVERSITY. DEPARTMENT OF
GEOLOGICAL SCIENCES. GEOLOGICAL
GUIDEBOOKS. irreg., no. 5, 1971. price varies.
Virginia Polytechnic Institute and State University,
Department of Geological Sciences, Blacksburg, VA
24060. circ. controlled. (back issues available)
Continues: Virginia Polytechnic Institute,
Blacksburg, Engineering Extension Division.
Geological Guidebook.

526　　　　　BU
VISSHA GEODEZIIA. (Text in various languages)
1975. irreg. 1.50 lv. per issue. (Bulgarska Akademiia
na Naukite) Publishing House of the Bulgarian
Academy of Sciences, Ul. Akad. G. Bonchev, 1113
Sofia, Bulgaria. circ. 800.

557　　　　　US
WASHINGTON (STATE). DIVISION OF
GEOLOGY AND EARTH RESOURCES.
BULLETIN. 1910. irreg., no. 71, 1978. price varies.
Department of Natural Resources, Division of
Geology and Earth Resources, Olympia, WA 98501.
(back issues avail.)

WASHINGTON (STATE) DIVISION OF
GEOLOGY AND EARTH RESOURCES.
INFORMATION CIRCULAR. see *MINES AND
MINING INDUSTRY*

551.44　　　　UK　　ISSN 0083-811X
WESSEX CAVE CLUB OCCASIONAL
PUBLICATION. 1967. irreg.(approx. 1 issue per
year) price varies. ‡ Wessex Cave Club, Priddy,
Wells, Somerset BA5 3AX, England. bk. rev. index.
circ. 300.
Speleology

550 016　　CN　　ISSN 0083-8195
WEST CANADIAN RESEARCH PUBLICATIONS
OF GEOLOGY AND RELATED SCIENCES.
1961. irreg., ser. 4, no. 1, 1975. price varies;
available on exchange. (Stereogrammetry Ltd.) West
Canadian Research Publications, P.O. Box 997,
Calgary, Alta. T2P 2K4, Canada. Ed. Dr. P. J.
Haman. bk. rev.

557　　　　　US
WEST TEXAS GEOLOGICAL SOCIETY.
PUBLICATIONS. no. 73-62, 1973. irreg. West
Texas Geological Society, Box 1595, Midland, TX
79702.

557 553.2　　US
WEST VIRGINIA COAL-GEOLOGY BULLETINS.
1973. irreg. Geological and Economic Survey, Box
879, Morgantown, WV 26505.
Formerly: West Virginia Geological Survey. Coal-
Geology Bulletin.

WEST VIRGINIA ENVIRONMENTAL GEOLOGY
BULLETINS. see *ENVIRONMENTAL STUDIES*

551.4　　　　　US
WEST VIRGINIA FIELD TRIP GUIDES. 1952.
irreg. Geological and Economic Survey, Box 879,
Morgantown, WV 26505.
Formerly: West Virginia Geological Survey. Field
Trip Guide.

551.4　　　　　US
WEST VIRGINIA GEOLOGIC EDUCATION
SERIES. 1957. irreg. Geological and Economic
Survey, Box 879, Morgantown, WV 26505.
Formerly: West Virginia Geological Survey.
Educational Series (ISSN 0510-1492)

557　　　　　US
WEST VIRGINIA REPORTS OF GEOLOGIC
INVESTIGATIONS. 1947. irreg. ‡ Geological and
Economic Survey, Box 879, Morgantown, WV
26505.
Former titles: West Virginia Geologic
Investigations; West Virginia Geological Survey.
Reports of Investigations (ISSN 0083-8543)

557　　　　　US
WEST VIRGINIA RIVER BASIN BASIC DATA
REPORTS. 1968. irreg. ‡ Geological and Economic
Survey, Box 879, Morgantown, WV 26505.
Former titles: West Virginia Geological Survey.
River Basin Basic Data Reports; West Virginia
Geological Survey. Basic Data Reports (ISSN 0083-
8497)

557 551.48　　US
WEST VIRGINIA RIVER BASIN BULLETINS.
1968. irreg. ‡ Geological and Economic Survey, Box
879, Morgantown, WV 26505.
Formerly: West Virginia Geological Survey. River
Basin Bulletins (ISSN 0083-856X)

557　　　　　US
WEST VIRGINIA STATE PARK GEOLOGY
BULLETINS. 1951. irreg. ‡ Geological and
Economic Survey, Box 879, Morgantown, WV
26505.
Formerly: West Virginia Geological Survey. State
Park Bulletins (ISSN 0083-8578)

559.4　　　　AT　　ISSN 0511-6996
WESTERN AUSTRALIA. GEOLOGICAL SURVEY.
ANNUAL REPORT. 1940. a. Aus.$4. Geological
Survey, 66 Adelaide Terrace, East Perth, W.A.
6000, Australia.

559.4　　　　AT　　ISSN 0085-8137
WESTERN AUSTRALIA. GEOLOGICAL SURVEY.
BULLETIN. 1898. irreg. price varies. Geological
Survey, Rm. 501, 66 Adelaide Tce., East Perth,
W.A. 6000, Australia.

559.4　　　　AT　　ISSN 0085-8145
WESTERN AUSTRALIA. GEOLOGICAL SURVEY.
REPORT. 1969. irreg. $1 ea. Geological Survey, 66
Adelaide Tce., East Perth, W.A. 6000, Australia.

557　　　　　US
WISCONSIN. GEOLOGICAL AND NATURAL
HISTORY SURVEY. BULLETIN. 1898. irreg., no.
87, 1976. price varies. Geological and Natural
History Survey, University of Wisconsin-Extension,
1815 University Ave., Madison, WI 53706.

557　　　　　US
WISCONSIN. GEOLOGICAL AND NATURAL
HISTORY SURVEY. GEOSCIENCE
INFORMATION SERIES. 1953? irreg., no. 12,
1976. price varies. Geological and Natural History
Survey, University of Wisconsin-Extension, 1815
University Ave., Madison, WI 53706.

557　　　　　US　　ISSN 0512-0640
WISCONSIN. GEOLOGICAL AND NATURAL
HISTORY SURVEY. INFORMATION
CIRCULARS. 1955. irreg., no. 35, 1977. Geological
and Natural History Survey, University of Wisonsin-
Extension, 1815 University Ave., Madison, WI
53706.

557　　　　　US　　ISSN 0512-0659
WISCONSIN. GEOLOGICAL AND NATURAL
HISTORY SURVEY. SPECIAL REPORT. 1967.
irreg., no. 6, 1976. price varies. Geological and
Natural History Survey, University of Wisconsin-
Extension, 1815 University Ave., Madison, WI
53706.

557　　　　　US
WYOMING. GEOLOGICAL SURVEY. BULLETIN.
no. 5, 1974. irreg. Geological Survey, University of
Wyoming, Box 3008, University Sta., Laramie, WY
82071.

557　　　　　US
WYOMING. GEOLOGICAL SURVEY. REPORT
OF INVESTIGATIONS. 1951. irreg., no. 12, 1976.
price varies. Geological Survey, University of
Wyoming, Box 3008, University Sta., Laramie, WY
82070.

557　　　　　US
WYOMING GEOLOGICAL ASSOCIATION.
GUIDEBOOK, ANNUAL FIELD
CONFERENCE. 25th, 1973. a. Wyoming
Geological Association, Box 2454, Casper, WY
82601.

557　　　　　US
WYOMING GEOLOGICAL ASSOCIATION.
PUBLICATIONS. irreg. Wyoming Geological
Association, Box 2454, Casper, WY 82601.

551　　　　　US
WYOMING MINERAL YEARBOOK. 1971. a. free.
Department of Economic Planning and
Development, Mineral Division, Barrett Bldg.,
Cheyenne, WY 82002. circ. 1,000.

556　　　　　ZA　　ISSN 0084-473X
ZAMBIA. GEOLOGICAL SURVEY. ANNUAL
REPORTS. 1961. a, latest issue 1974. K.1.
Geological Survey, P.O. Box R.W. 135, Lusaka,
Zambia (Avail. from: Government Printer, Box 136,
Lusaka, Zambia)

556 ZA ISSN 0084-4748
ZAMBIA. GEOLOGICAL SURVEY. ECONOMIC REPORTS. 1963. irreg., latest no. 50. price varies. Geological Survey, P.O. Box R.W. 135, Lusaka, Zambia. Indexed: Bibl.&Ind.Geol.

556 ZA ISSN 0084-4756
ZAMBIA. GEOLOGICAL SURVEY. OCCASIONAL PAPERS. irreg., latest no. 70. price varies. ‡ Geological Survey, P.O. Box R.W. 135, Lusaka, Zambia.

556 ZA ISSN 0084-4764
ZAMBIA. GEOLOGICAL SURVEY. REPORTS. 1954. irreg., latest 41, 1978. price varies. Geological Survey, P.O. Box R.W. 135, Lusaka, Zambia. Indexed: Bibl.&Ind.Geol.
Accounts of regional mapping

556 ZA
ZAMBIA. GEOLOGICAL SURVEY. TECHNICAL REPORTS. irreg., latest no. 79. price varies. Geological Survey, Box R.W. 135, Lusaka, Zambia.

ZIMBABWE. MINISTRY OF WATER DEVELOPMENT. HYDROLOGICAL SUMMARIES. see ENGINEERING — Hydraulic Engineering

ZIMBABWE. MINISTRY OF WATER DEVELOPMENT. HYDROLOGICAL YEAR BOOK. see ENGINEERING — Hydraulic Engineering

ZITTELIANA; Abhandlungen der Bayerischen Staatssammlung fuer Palaeontologie und Historische Geologie. see PALEONTOLOGY

EARTH SCIENCES — Geophysics

551 UR ISSN 0065-0080
A. I. VOEIKOV MAIN GEOPHYSICAL OBSERVATORY, LENINGRAD. DATA OF MEASUREMENTS OF ELECTRIC FIELD STRENGTH OF THE ATMOSPHERE AT VARIOUS ALTITUDES BY THE RESULTS OF SOUNDINGS. (Text and tables in English and Russian) irreg. Glavnaya Geofizicheskaya Observatoriya im. A. I. Voeikova, Karbysheva, 7, Leningrad K-18, U.S.S.R.

551 UR ISSN 0065-0099
A. I. VOEIKOV MAIN GEOPHYSICAL OBSERVATORY, LENINGRAD. RESULTS OF GROUND OBSERVATIONS OF ATMOSPHERIC ELECTRICITY. ADDITIONAL ISSUE. (Text and tables in English and Russian) a. Glavnaya Geofizicheskaya Observatoriya im. A. I. Voeikova, Karbysheva, 7, Leningrad K-18, U.S.S.R.

551 SW ISSN 0072-4815
ACTA REGIAE SOCIETATIS SCIENTIARUM ET LITTERARUM GOTHOBURGENSIS. GEOPHYSICA. (Text in various languages) 1968. irreg., latest no. 2, 1969. price varies; also exchange basis. Goeteborgs Kungliga Vetenskaps- och Vitterhets- Samhaelle, c/o Goeteborgs Universitetsbibliotek, P.O. Box 5096, S-402 22 Goeteborg 5, Sweden (Dist. in U.S., Canada and Mexico by: Humanities Press, Inc., 171 First Ave., Atlantic Highlands, NJ 07716)
Supersedes in part: Goeteborgs Kungliga Vetenskaps- och Vitterhets-Samhaelle. Handlingar.

551 ET ISSN 0072-9345
ADDIS ABABA UNIVERSITY. GEOPHYSICAL OBSERVATORY. CONTRIBUTIONS. (Name of issuing body varies: Haile Sellassie I University, University of Addis Ababa, National University) (Text in English and French summaries in English, occasionally in Amharic) 1958. irreg. available on exchange. Addis Ababa University, Geophysical Observatory, Box 1176, Addis Ababa, Ethiopia. Ed. Pierre Gouin. circ. 400.

551 US ISSN 0065-2687
ADVANCES IN GEOPHYSICS. 1952. irreg., vol. 21, 1979. price varies. Academic Press, Inc., 111 Fifth Ave., New York, NY 10003. Ed. H. E. Landsberg. index. (also avail. in microfiche)

551 US ISSN 0065-2695
ADVANCES IN GEOPHYSICS. SUPPLEMENT. 1966. irreg., no. 1, 1966 latest. price varies. Academic Press, Inc., 111 Fifth Ave., New York, NY 10003. Ed. H. E. Landsberg.

ALASKA. DIVISION OF GEOLOGICAL AND GEOPHYSICAL SURVEYS. ANNUAL REPORT. see EARTH SCIENCES — Geology

ALASKA. DIVISION OF GEOLOGICAL AND GEOPHYSICAL SURVEYS. INFORMATION CIRCULAR. see EARTH SCIENCES — Geology

ALASKA. DIVISION OF GEOLOGICAL AND GEOPHYSICAL SURVEYS. LABORATORY NOTE. see EARTH SCIENCES — Geology

ALASKA. DIVISION OF GEOLOGICAL AND GEOPHYSICAL SURVEYS. LABORATORY REPORT. see EARTH SCIENCES — Geology

ALASKA. DIVISION OF GEOLOGICAL AND GEOPHYSICAL SURVEYS. SPECIAL REPORT. see EARTH SCIENCES — Geology

551 US ISSN 0065-8448
AMERICAN GEOPHYSICAL UNION. GEOPHYSICAL MONOGRAPH SERIES. 1956. irreg., no. 20, 1977. price varies. American Geophysical Union, 2000 Florida Ave. N.W., Washington, DC 20009. Ed.Bd. (reprint service avail. from ISI)

550 UN ISSN 0066-4383
ANNUAL SUMMARY OF INFORMATION ON NATURAL DISASTERS. French edt.: Resume Annuel d'Informations sur les Catastrophes Naturelles. 1966. irreg; no. 7, 1972. Unesco, 7-9 Place de Fontenoy, 75700 Paris, France (Dist. in U.S. by: Unipub, 345 Park Ave. S., New York, NY 10010)

538.7 SP
ANUARIOS DE GEOMAGNETISMO - ANO... 1962. a. free to geophysical centers. Instituto Geografico Nacional, Seccion de Geomagnetismo y Aeronomia, General Ibanez de Ibero 3, Apdo. 3007, Madrid 3, Spain. circ. 200 (controlled)
Formerly(until 1975): Anuarios del Servicio de Geomagnetismo y Aeronomia.

ARCHIV FUER METEOROLOGIE, GEOPHYSIK UND BIOKLIMATOLOGIE. SERIES A. METEOROLOGY AND GEOPHYSICS. SUPPLEMENT. see METEOROLOGY

551 559.8 AT
AUSTRALIAN ACADEMY OF SCIENCE. NATIONAL COMMITTEE FOR ANTARCTIC RESEARCH. AUSTRALIAN ANTARCTIC AND SUB-ANTARCTIC RESEARCH PROGRAMMES. irreg. Australian Academy of Science, National Committee for Antarctic Research, Box 216, Canberra City, Canberra, A.C.T. 2601, Australia. Ed. P.D. O'Connor.

AUSTRIA. ZENTRALANSTALT FUER METEOROLOGIE UND GEODYNAMIK. JAHRBUCH. see METEOROLOGY

BELGIUM. INSTITUT ROYAL METEOROLOGIQUE. PUBLICATIONS. see METEOROLOGY

551 PL ISSN 0067-9038
BIULETYN PERYGLACJALNY. (Text in English, French, German, Polish, and Russian) 1954. irreg., no. 27, 1978. price varies. (Lodzkie Towarzystwo Naukowe) Ossolineum, Publishing House of the Polish Academy of Sciences, Rynek 9, Wroclaw, Poland (Dist. by: Ars Polona - Ruch, Krakowskie Przedmiescie 7, Warsaw, Poland) (Co-sponsor: Polska Akademia Nauk) Ed. A. Dylikowa.

551 PO
BOLETIM MICROSSISMICO. irreg. exchange basis. Universidade do Porto, Instituto Geofisico, Sierra do Pilar, Villa Nova de Gaia, Portugal. charts.

551.22 PO ISSN 0006-6109
BOLETIM SISMICO. 1958. a. exchange basis. Universidade do Porto, Instituto Geofisico, Sierra do Pilar, Vila Nova de Gaia, Portugal.
Seismology

551 BU ISSN 0068-3736
BULGARSKA AKADEMIIA NA NAUKITE. GEOFIZICHNI INSTITUT. IZVESTIIA. (Summaries in various languages) 1960. a. 1.55 lv. Publishing House of the Bulgarian Academy of Sciences, Ul. Akad. G. Bonchev, 1113 Sofia, Bulgaria (Dist. by: Hemus, 6, Rouski Blvd., 1000 Sofia, Bulgaria) Ed. L. Krustanov. circ. 550.

551 CS
BULLETIN OF THE SLOVAK SEISMOGRAPHIC STATIONS: BRATISLAVA, SROBAROVA, HURBANOVO AND SKALNATE PLESO. (Text and summaries in English) 1972. a. 17($2.85) (Slovenska Akademia Vied, Geofyzikalny Ustav) Veda, Publishing House of the Slovak Academy of Sciences, Klemensova 19, 895 30 Bratislava, Czechoslovakia. Ed. Klara Mrazova. abstr. circ. 500. (tabloid format)

551.21 JA ISSN 0525-1524
BULLETIN OF VOLCANIC ERUPTIONS. (Issued with "Bulletin Volcanologique," published by the co-sponsor) (Text in English) 1961. irreg., no. 13, 1975. Volcanological Society of Japan - Nihon Kazan Gakkai, c/o Earthquake Research Institute, University of Tokyo, 1-1-1 Yayoi, Bunkyo-ku, Tokyo 113, Japan. (Co-sponsor: International Association of Volcanology and Chemistry of the Earth's Interior)

551.21 IT
BULLETIN VOLCANOLOGIQUE. 1942. irreg., 4 nos./vol. $22 to individuals; institutions $30(includes Newsletter) International Association of Volcanology and Chemistry of the Earth's Interior, c/o Dr. F. Esu Cugusi, Ed., Instituto di Geologia Applicata, Via Eudossiana 18, 00184 Rome, Italy.

551.22 CN
CANADA. EARTH PHYSICS BRANCH. GEODYNAMIC SERIES. 1974. a. Earth Physics Branch, 1 Observatory Cresc., Ottawa, Ont. K1A 0Y3, Canada.

651.22 CN
CANADA. EARTH PHYSICS BRANCH. GEOMAGNETIC SERIES. 1975. a. Earth Physics Branch, 1 Observatory Cresc., Ottawa, Ont. K1A 0Y3, Canada.

551.22 CN
CANADA. EARTH PHYSICS BRANCH. GEOTHERMAL SERIES. 1974. a. Earth Physics Branch, 1 Observatory Cresc., Ottawa, Ont. K1A 0Y3, Canada.

551.22 CN
CANADA. EARTH PHYSICS BRANCH. GRAVITY MAP SERIES. 1961. a. Earth Physics Branch, 1 Observatory Cresc., Ottawa, Ont. K1A 0Y3, Canada.

551.22 CN ISSN 0084-8387
CANADA. EARTH PHYSICS BRANCH. SEISMOLOGICAL SERIES. 1954. a. Earth Physics Branch, 1 Observatory Cresc., Ottawa, Ont., Canada. (processed)
Formerly: Ottawa. Dominion Observatory. Seismological Series.
Seismology

551 CN ISSN 0068-8819
CANADIAN GEOPHYSICAL BULLETIN. 1947. a. free. National Research Council of Canada, Canadian National Committee for the I.U.G.G., Ottawa, Ont. K1A OR6, Canada. Ed. M. E. Evans. circ. 1,200.

CANADIAN ROCK MECHANICS SYMPOSIUM. PROCEEDINGS. see MINES AND MINING INDUSTRY

551 526 FR ISSN 0069-6528
COMITE NATIONAL FRANCAIS DE GEODESIE ET GEOPHYSIQUE. COMPTES-RENDUS. 1921. a. price varies. Comite National Francais de Geodesie et Geophysique, c/o M. Georges Laclavere, 53, Avenue de Breteuil, 75007 Paris, France. circ. 600.

EARTH SCIENCES — GEOPHYSICS

551 526   FR   ISSN 0069-6536
COMITE NATIONAL FRANCAIS DE GEODESIE ET GEOPHYSIQUE. RAPPORT NATIONAL FRANCAIS A L'U G G I. 1972. quadrennial. price varies. Comite National Francais de Geodesie et Geophysique, c/o M. Georges Laclavere, 53, Avenue de Breteuil, 75007 Paris, France. circ. 600.

551   SZ
CONTRIBUTIONS TO CURRENT RESEARCH IN GEOPHYSICS. 1975. irreg. price varies. Birkhaeuser Verlag, Elisabethenstr. 19, CH-4010 Basel, Switzerland.

551   US
CRUSTAL AND UPPER MANTLE STRUCTURE IN EUROPE. MONOGRAPHS. 1976. irreg. (European Seismological Commission) Springer Verlag, 175 Fifth Ave., New York, NY 10010 (Also Berlin, Heidelberg, Vienna) (reprint service avail. from ISI)

CURRENT GEOLOGICAL AND GEOPHYSICAL STUDIES IN MONTANA. see *EARTH SCIENCES — Geology*

551 510   NE
DEVELOPMENTS IN GEOMATHEMATICS. 1974. irreg.. vol. 4, 1979. price varies. Elsevier Scientific Publishing Co., Box 211, 1000 AE Amsterdam, Netherlands.

551   NE   ISSN 0070-458X
DEVELOPMENTS IN SOLID EARTH GEOPHYSICS. 1964. irreg., vol. 12, 1980. price varies. Elsevier Scientific Publishing Co., Box 211, 1000 AE Amsterdam, Netherlands.

551   IE   ISSN 0070-7422
DUBLIN INSTITUTE FOR ADVANCED STUDIES. SCHOOL OF COSMIC PHYSICS. GEOPHYSICAL BULLETIN. 1950. irreg., no. 33, 1975. price varies. Dublin Institute for Advanced Studies, 10 Burlington Rd., Dublin 4, Ireland.
Issued also as: Dublin Institute for Advanced Studies. Communications. Series D.

551.22   US
EARTHQUAKE HISTORY OF THE UNITED STATES. 1928. quinquennial. price varies; rev.ed. through 1970, $5. U.S. National Geophysical and Solar-Terrestrial Data Center, 325 Broadway, Boulder, CO 80303 (Orders to National Technical Information Service, Springfield, VA 22161) Eds. Jerry L. Coffman, Carl A. von Hake. stat. (also avail. in microfiche from NTI)
Seismology

551   SZ   ISSN 0084-5779
EIDGENOESSISCHE TECHNISCHE HOCHSCHULE ZUERICH. INSTITUT FUER GEOPHYSIK.SCHWEIZERISCHE ERDBEBENDIENST. JAHRESBERICHT. 1913. a. contr. free circ. Eidgenoessische Technische Hochschule Zuerich, Institut fuer Geophysik, E.T.H. Horngerberg, CH-8093 Zurich, Switzerland. circ. controlled.

913   GW
ERDSTALL. 1975. a. DM.15. Arbeitskreis fuer Erdstallforschung, Schorndorferstr. 31, 8495 Roding, W. Germany (B.R.D.)

551   NE   ISSN 0531-2728
EUROPEAN ASSOCIATION OF EXPLORATION GEOPHYSICISTS. CONSTITUTION AND BY-LAWS, MEMBERSHIP LIST. a. fl.24. European Association of Exploration Geophysicists, Box 162, 2501 AN The Hague, Netherlands. circ. 3,000.

622.15   US   ISSN 0071-3473
EXPLORATION GEOPHYSICS. irreg., 1969, vol. 51. price varies. Consultants Bureau, Special Research Report, 227 W. 17th St., New York, NY 10011. Ed. M. K. Polshkov.

551.22   UK
FELT AND DAMAGING EARTHQUAKES. 1976. a. £3. International Seismological Centre, Newbury, Berks. RG13 1LZ, England.

551.5   FI   ISSN 0081-783X
FINNISH METEOROLOGICAL INSTITUTE. STUDIES ON EARTH MAGNETISM. (Text in English) 1911. irreg., no. 25, 1976. price varies. ‡ Ilmatieteen Laitos - Finnish Meteorological Institute, Box 503, SF-00101 Helsinki 10, Finland.

551   US
GEODYNAMICS INTERNATIONAL. (Text in English) no. 12, 1978. irreg. $1.67. ‡ U.S. Environmental Data and Information Service, World Data Center A for Solid Earth Geophysics, Boulder, CO 80303. (Co-sponsor: International Council of Scientific Unions, Inter-Union Commission on Geodynamics) circ. 2,500.
Supersedes: Inter-Union Commission on Geodynamics Report & Geodynamics Highlights.

551   UR   ISSN 0072-1182
GEOFIZICHESKII BYULLETEN/GEOPHYSICAL BULLETIN. (Text in Russian; summaries in English) 1956. irreg., approx. 2/yr. free on exchange. (Akademiya Nauk S.S.S.R., Mezhduvedomstvennyi Geofizicheskii Komitet) Izdatel'stvo Nauka, Podsosenskii per., 21, Moscow K-62, U. S. S. R. Ed. A. Kh. Khrgian. bk. rev. circ. 1,200.

551   HU   ISSN 0016-7177
GEOFIZIKAI KOZLEMENYEK/GEOPHYSICAL TRANSACTIONS. (Text in English, German, Hungarian, Russian) 1952. a. $20.50. Eotvos Lorand Tudomanyegyetem Geofizikai Intezet, Columbus u. 17-23, 1145 Budapest 14, Hungary (Subscr. to: Kultura, Box 149, H-1389 Budapest, Hungary) Ed. Eva Kilenyi. charts. illus. maps. circ. 1,400. Indexed: Appl. Mech. Rev. Chem.Abstr. Ref.Zh.

551   NO   ISSN 0072-1174
GEOPHYSICA NORVEGICA/NORWEGIAN JOURNAL OF GEOPHYSICS. (Text in English) 1934. irreg. price varies. Universitetsforlaget, Kolstadgt. 1, Box 2959-Toeyen, Oslo 6, Norway (U.S. address: Box 258, Irvington-on-Hudson, NY 10533) Ed. Eigil Hesstveldt. (back issues avail.) Indexed: Chem.Abstr. Sci.Abstr. Meteor. & Geoastrophys.Abstr.

551   US
GEOPHYSICAL DIRECTORY. 1948. a. $12. ‡ Geophysical Directory, Inc., 2200 Welch Ave., Houston, TX 77019 (Subscr. to P.O. Box 13508, Houston, TX 77019) Ed. Claudia La Calli. adv. circ. 8,500.

GEOPHYSICS AND ASTROPHYSICS MONOGRAPHS; an international series of fundamental textbooks. see *ASTRONOMY*

551   GE
GEOPHYSIK UND GEOLOGIE; Geophsikalische Veroeffentlichungen der Karl-Marx-Universitaet Leipzig. Dritte Serie. 1974. irreg. price varies. (Karl-Marx-Universitaet) Akademie-Verlag, Leipziger Str. 3-4, 108 Berlin, E. Germany (D.D.R.) Ed. R. Lauterbach.
Formerly: Leipzig. Universitaet. Geophysikalisches Institut. Veroeffentlichungen. Zweite Serie (ISSN 0016-8041)

551   FR   ISSN 0398-3218
GEOPHYSIQUE. 1957. irreg. Office de la Recherche Scientifique et Technique Outre-Mer, 70-74, Route d'Aulnay, 93140 Bondy, France.
Supersedes: Cahiers O.R.S.T.O.M. Serie Geophysique.

551   DK   ISSN 0069-987X
GEOTEKNISK INSTITUT, COPENHAGEN. BULLETIN. (Text in English; some earlier issues in Danish) 1956. irreg., no. 30, 1977. price varies. Geoteknisk Institut - Danish Geotechnical Institute, 1 Maglebjergvej, DK-2800 Lyngby, Denmark.

551.4   UR   ISSN 0568-6245
GLYATSIOLOGIYA/GLACIOLOGY. Variant title: Glyatsiologicheskie Issledovaniya. 1959. irreg. exchange basis. Akademiya Nauk S.S.S.R., Mezhduvedomstvennyi Geofizicheskii Komitet, Molodezhnaya ul., 3, Moscow, U. S. S. R. Eds. G. A. Avsyuk, V. M. Kotlyakov. circ. 1,000. Indexed: Ref.Zh.

538.7   UK   ISSN 0073-9316
GREAT BRITAIN.INSTITUTE OF GEOLOGICAL SCIENCES. GEOMAGNETIC BULLETINS. 1969. irreg. price varies. Institute of Geological Sciences, Exhibition Rd., London SW7 2DE, England (Avail. from H.M.S.O., c/o Liaison Officer, Atlantic House, Holborn Viaduct, London EC1P 1BN, England) circ. 600.

551.22   UK   ISSN 0308-5082
GREAT BRITAIN. INSTITUTE OF GEOLOGICAL SCIENCES. SEISMOLOGICAL BULLETINS. 1972. irreg. price varies. Institute of Geological Sciences, Exhibition Rd., London SW7 2DE, England (Avail. from H.M.S.O., c/o Liaison Officer, Atlantic House, Holborn Viaduct, London EC1P 1BN, England) circ. 500.
Seismology

551   UK   ISSN 0072-6613
GREAT BRITAIN. METEOROLOGICAL OFFICE. GEOPHYSICAL MEMOIRS. 1912. irreg. price varies. H. M. S. O., P. O. Box 569, London SE1 9NH, England.

551   US
HAWAII INSTITUTE OF GEOPHYSICS. BIENNIAL REPORT. 1965. biennial. free. Hawaii Institute of Geophysics, 2525 Correa Rd., Honolulu, HI 96822. Ed. Rita Pujalet. circ. 320.

551   US
HAWAII INSTITUTE OF GEOPHYSICS. CONTRIBUTIONS. a. Hawaii Institute of Geophysics, 2525 Correa Rd., Honolulu, HI 96822.

551   US
HAWAII INSTITUTE OF GEOPHYSICS. TECHNICAL REPORTS. irreg. Hawaii Institute of Geophysics, 2525 Correa Rd., Honolulu, HI 96822.

551   JA   ISSN 0441-067X
HOKKAIDO UNIVERSITY. FACULTY OF SCIENCE. JOURNAL. SERIES 7: GEOPHYSICS. (Text in English) 1957. irreg. on exchange basis. Hokkaido University, Faculty of Science - Hokkaido Daigaku Rigakubu, Nishi-8-chome, Kita-10-jo, Kita-ku, Sapporo 060, Japan.

538.7   JA   ISSN 0536-1095
I A G A NEWS. 1963. irreg. International Association of Geomagnetism and Aeronomy - Association Internationale de Geomagnetisme et d'Aeronomie, c/o Prof. Fukushima, Secretary, Geophysical Institute, University of Tokyo, Bunkyo-ku, Tokyo 113, Japan. Ed. N. Fukushima. circ. 2,400.

551   II
INDIAN GEOPHYSICAL UNION BULLETIN. 1964. a. Indian Geophysical Union, Hyderabad 7, India. Ed. Bd. bibl. charts.

INSTITUT D'ASTRONOMIE ET DE GEOPHYSIQUE GEORGES LEMAITRE. PUBLICATIONS. see *ASTRONOMY*

INSTITUTE FOR PETROLEUM RESEARCH AND GEOPHYSICS, HOLON, ISRAEL. REPORT. see *PETROLEUM AND GAS*

551   JA
INSTITUTE OF GEOSCIENCE. ANNUAL REPORT. (Text in English) no. 3, 1976. a. University of Tsukuba, Institute of Geoscience, Ibaraki-Prefecture 300-31, Japan. Ed. Bd.

551   SP   ISSN 0080-5955
INSTITUTO Y OBSERVATORIO DE MARINA. OBSERVACIONES METEOROLOGICAS, MAGNETICAS Y SISMICAS. ANALES. 1870. a. Instituto y Observatorio de Marina, Seccion de Geofisica, San Fernando (Cadiz), Spain. circ. 400.

551   RM   ISSN 0068-306X
INSTITUTUL DE GEOLOGIE SI GEOFIZICA. DARI DE SEAMA ALE SEDINTELOR. (Text in Romanian; summaries in English; contains page in French) 1907. 5/yr. price varies. Institutul de Geologie si Geofizica, Str. Caransebes Nr. 1, Bucharest, Romania. bk. rev. circ. 950. Indexed: Bull.Signal. Ref.Zh.

551.44   RM   ISSN 0065-0498
INSTITUTUL DE SPEOLOGIE EMIL RACOVITZA. TRAVAUX. (Text in French) 1962. a. 60 lei($12) Editura Academiei Republicii Socialiste Romania, Calea Victoriei 125, Bucharest, Romania (Subscr. to: ILEXIM, Str. 13 Decembrie Nr. 3, P.O. Box 136-137, Bucharest, Romania) Ed. Tr. Orghidan. bk. rev. circ. 450. Indexed: Biol.Abstr. Ref.Zh. Zoo.Rec.
Formerly: Academia Republicii Socialiste Romania. Institutul de Speologie Emil Racovitza. Travaux.

EARTH SCIENCES — GEOPHYSICS

551.2 551.9   IT   ISSN 0579-5362
INTERNATIONAL ASSOCIATION OF VOLCANOLOGY AND CHEMISTRY OF THE EARTH'S INTERIOR. NEWSLETTER. 1968. irreg. $22 to individuals; institutions $30(includes Bulletin Volcanologique) International Association of Volcanology and Chemistry of the Earth's Interior, c/o Dr. F. Esu Cugusi, Instituto di Geologia Applicata, 18 via Eudossiana, Rome 00184, Italy. circ. controlled.

551   US   ISSN 0074-6142
INTERNATIONAL GEOPHYSICS SERIES. 1959. irreg., vol. 19, 1975. price varies. Academic Press Inc., 111 Fifth Ave., New York, NY 10003. Ed. J. Van Mieghem.

531.14   FR
INTERNATIONAL GRAVIMETRIC BUREAU. BULLETIN D'INFORMATION. (Text in English or French) 1960. s-a. 60 F. International Gravimetric Bureau, 4 Pl. Jussieu, Tour 14, 75230 Paris Cedex 5, France. circ. 350.

551.22 624.151   JA   ISSN 0074-655X
INTERNATIONAL INSTITUTE OF SEISMOLOGY AND EARTHQUAKE ENGINEERING. BULLETIN. 1964. a. International Institute of Seismology and Earthquake Engineering - Kensetsu-sho Kenchiku Kenkyusho Kokusai Jishin Kogakubu, Building Research Institute-Ministry of Construction, 1 Tatehara, Oho-machi, Tsukuba-gun, Ibaraki Prefecture, Japan. Ed. Michio Otsuka. circ. 850 (controlled)
Seismology

551.22   JA   ISSN 0074-6568
INTERNATIONAL INSTITUTE OF SEISMOLOGY AND EARTHQUAKE ENGINEERING. EARTHQUAKE REPORT. 1965. irreg. International Institute of Seismology and Earthquake Engineering - Kensetsu-sho Kenchiku Kenkyusho Kokusai Jishin Kogakubu, Building Research Institute-Ministry of Construction, 1 Tatehara, Oho-machi, Tsukuba-gun, Ibaraki Prefecture, Japan. Ed. Michio Otsuka. circ. 1,000 (controlled)
Seismology

551.22   JA   ISSN 0074-6584
INTERNATIONAL INSTITUTE OF SEISMOLOGY AND EARTHQUAKE ENGINEERING. LECTURE NOTE. 1966. irreg; latest issue, 1972. International Institute of Seismology and Earthquake Engineering - Kensetsu-sho Kenchiku Kenkyusho Kokusai Jishin Kogakubu, Building Research Institute-Ministry of Construction, 1 Tatehara, Oho-machi, Tsukuba-gun, Ibaraki Prefecture, Japan. Ed. Michio Otsuka. circ. 700 (controlled)
Seismology

551.22   JA   ISSN 0074-6592
INTERNATIONAL INSTITUTE OF SEISMOLOGY AND EARTHQUAKE ENGINEERING. PROGRESS REPORT. 1966. irreg. International Institute of Seismology and Earthquake Engineering - Kensetsu-sho Kenchiku Kenkyusho Kokusai Jishin Kogakubu, Building Research Institute-Ministry of Construction, 1 Tatehara, Oho-machi, Tsukuba-gun, Ibaraki Prefecture, Japan. Ed. Michio Otsuka. circ. 550 (controlled)
Seismology

551.22   JA   ISSN 0074-6606
INTERNATIONAL INSTITUTE OF SEISMOLOGY AND EARTHQUAKE ENGINEERING. REPORT OF INDIVIDUAL STUDY BY PARTICIPANTS TO I I S E E. 1965. a. International Institute of Seismology and Earthquake Engineering - Kensetsu-sho Kenchiku Kenkyusho Kokusai Jishin Kogakubu, Building Research Institute-Ministry of Construction, 1 Tatehara, Oho-machi, Tsukuba-gun, Ibaraki Prefecture, Japan. Ed. Michio Otsuka. circ. 600.
Seismology

551.22   JA   ISSN 0074-6614
INTERNATIONAL INSTITUTE OF SEISMOLOGY AND EARTHQUAKE ENGINEERING. YEAR BOOK. 1963. a. International Institute of Seismology and Earthquake Engineering - Kensetsu-sho Kenchiku Kenkyusho Kokusai Jishin Kogakubu, Building Research Institute-Ministry of Construction, 1 Tatehare, Oho-machi, Tsukuba-gun, Ibaraki Prefecture, Japan. Ed. Michio Otsuka. circ. 500.
Seismology

551   NE   ISSN 0538-9771
INTERNATIONAL SEDIMENTARY PETROGRAPHICAL SERIES. 1955. irreg., no. 16, 1977. price varies. E. J. Brill, Oude Rijn 33a-35, Leiden, Netherlands. Eds. W. J. Clarke, B. H. Purser, C. W. Wagner. (back issues avail.)

INTERNATIONAL UNION OF GEODESY AND GEOPHYSICS. MONOGRAPH. see *GEOGRAPHY*

INTERNATIONAL UNION OF GEODESY AND GEOPHYSICS. PROCEEDINGS OF THE GENERAL ASSEMBLY. see *GEOGRAPHY*

551   IT
ISTITUTO NAZIONALE DE GEOFISICA. ANALI DI GEOFISICA. (Text in English, French & Italian) 1948. a. $45. Istitutto Nazionale di Geofisica, Via Ruggero Bonghi, 11/B, 00184 Rome, Italy. Ed. Michele Caputo. bk. rev. abstr. bibl. illus. index. circ. 600 (controlled) (looseleaf format; back issues avail)

538   UR
ITOGI NAUKI I TEKHNIKI: GEOMAGNETIZM I VYSOKIE SLOI ATMOSFERY. 1972. a. 1.87 Rub. Vsesoyuznyi Institut Nauchno-Tekhnicheskoi Informatsii (Viniti), Ul. Baltiiskaya, 14, Moscow, U.S.S.R. illus.

551   SW
KIRUNA GEOPHYSICAL INSTITUTE. PREPRINT. Short title: K G I Preprint. (Text and summaries in English) 1969. irreg. price varies; free to qualified institutions. Kiruna Geophysical Institute, P.O. Box 704, S-981 01 Kiruna, Sweden. charts. circ. 300. (back issues avail.)

551   SW
KIRUNA GEOPHYSICAL INSTITUTE. REPORT. Short title: K G I Report. (Text in English) 1973. irreg., no. 79:3, 1979. Kiruna Geophysical Institute, P.O. Box 704, S-981 01 Kiruna, Sweden. charts. circ. 300. (back issues avail.)

551   SW
KIRUNA GEOPHYSICAL INSTITUTE. SOFTWARE REPORT. Short title: K G I Software Report. (Text in English) 1977. irreg. price varies; free to qualified institutions. Kiruna Geophysical Institute, P.O.Box 704, S-981 01 Kiruna, Sweden. (back issues avail.)

551   SW
KIRUNA GEOPHYSICAL INSTITUTE. TECHNICAL REPORT. Short title: K G I Technical Report. Swedish short title: K G I Teknisk Rapport. (Text and summaries in English and Swedish) 1969. irreg. price varies; free to qualified institutions. Kiruna Geophysical Institute, P.O. Box 704, S-981 01 Kiruna, Sweden. (back issues avail.)

551   US   ISSN 0075-790X
LANDOLT-BOERNSTEIN, ZAHLENWERTE UND FUNKTIONEN AUS NATURWISSENSCHAFTEN UND TECHNIK. NEUE SERIE. GROUP 5: GEOPHYSICS. 1981. irreg. Springer-Verlag, 175 Fifth Ave., New York, NY 10010 (also Berlin, Heidelberg, Vienna) (reprint service avail. from ISI)

550.38   FI   ISSN 0071-5212
MAGNETIC RESULTS FROM NURMIJARVI GEOPHYSICAL OBSERVATORY. (Text in English) 1958. a. price varies. ‡ Ilmatieteen Laitos - Finnish Meteorological Institute, Box 503, SF-00101 Helsinki 10, Finland.

551   HU   ISSN 0524-8655
MAGYAR ALLAMI EOTVOS LORAND GEOFIZIKAI INTEZET. EVI JELENTES/ LORAND EOTVOS HUNGARIAN GEOPHYSICAL INSTITUTE. ANNUAL REPORT. (Text in Hungarian, English, Russian) 1966. a. Eotvos Lorand Tudomanyegyetem Geofizikai Intezet, Columbus u. 17-23, 1145 Budapest 14, Hungary. Ed. Eva Kilenyi. charts. illus. maps. circ. 1,250.

550 001.6   UR   ISSN 0301-6897
MATEMATICHESKIE PROBLEMY GEOFIZIKI. 1969. irreg. 1.41 Rub. Akademiya Nauk S.S.S.R., Vychislitel'nyi Tsentr, Ul. Vavilova, 40, Moscow V-333, U.S.S.R. illus.

"METEOR" FORSCHUNGSERGEBNISSE. REIHE B. METEOROLOGIE UND AERONOMIE. see *METEOROLOGY*

551   GW   ISSN 0543-5919
"METEOR" FORSCHUNGSERGEBNISSE. REIHE C. GEOLOGIE UND GEOPHYSIK. (Text in German; summaries in English) 1968. irreg., no. 23, 1975. price varies. (Deutsche Forschungsgemeinschaft) Gebrueder Borntraeger Verlagsbuchhandlung, Johannesstr. 3A, 7000 Stuttgart 1, W. Germany (B.R.D.) Eds. E. Seibold, H.J. Duerbaum. charts. illus.

METHODS IN GEOCHEMISTRY AND GEOPHYSICS. see *EARTH SCIENCES*

551.5   MZ
MOZAMBIQUE. SERVICO METEOROLOGICO. ANUARIO DE OBSERVACOES. PARTE I: OBSERVACOES DE SUPERFICIE. 1909. a. free. Servico Meteorologico, C.P. 256, Maputo, Mozambique. stat.

551.5   MZ
MOZAMBIQUE. SERVICO METEOROLOGICO. ANUARIO DE OBSERVACOES. PARTE II: OBSERVACOES DE ALTITUDE. 1909. a. free. Servico Meteorologico, C.P. 236, Maputo, Mozambique. stat.

551.5 520   MZ
MOZAMBIQUE. SERVICO METEOROLOGICO. INFORMACOES DE CARACTER ASTRONOMICO. 1955. a. free. Servico Meteorologico, C. P. 256, Maputo, Mozambique. stat.

551   CN   ISSN 0541-4393
MUSKEG RESEARCH CONFERENCE. PROCEEDINGS. irreg., latest 18th, Aug., 1979. price varies. National Research Council of Canada, Associate Committee on Geotechnical Research, Ottawa, Ont. K1A OA6, Canada.

551   II   ISSN 0073-4144
NATIONAL GEOPHYSICAL RESEARCH INSTITUTE. PUBLICATIONS. 1953. a. price varies. National Geophysical Research Institute, Uppal Rd., Hyderabad 500007, India. (Affiliate: Council of Scientific and Industrial Research) bk. rev.

551.22   JA
NATIONAL RESEARCH CENTER FOR DISASTER PREVENTION. SEISMOLOGICAL BULLETIN. (Text in English) 1970. irreg. on exchange basis. National Research Center for Disaster Prevention - Kokuritsu Bosai Kagaku Gijutsu Senta, 3-chome, Tennodai, Sakura-mura, Ibaraki-ken 300-32, Japan.
Seismology

551   NZ   ISSN 0110-6112
NEW ZEALAND. DEPARTMENT OF SCIENTIFIC AND INDUSTRIAL RESEARCH. GEOPHYSICS DIVISION. REPORT. 1952. irreg. NZ.$2.50. Department of Scientific and Industrial Research, Geophysics Division, Wellington, New Zealand. circ. 200.

551   NZ   ISSN 0110-7089
NEW ZEALAND. DEPARTMENT OF SCIENTIFIC AND INDUSTRIAL RESEARCH. GEOPHYSICS DIVISION. TECHNICAL NOTE. 1952. irreg. NZ.$2.50. Department of Scientific and Industrial Research, Geophysics Division, Wellington, New Zealand.

551   NO   ISSN 0078-1193
NORGES GEOTEKNISKE INSTITUTT. PUBLIKASJON/NORWEGIAN GEOTECHNICAL INSTITUTE. PUBLICATIONS. (Text in English and Norwegian; summaries in English) 1953. irreg., no. 134, 1981. price varies. Norges Geotekniske Institutt - Norwegian Geotechnical Institute, P.O. Box 40 Taasen, Oslo 8, Norway. Ed. Finn A. Joerstad. cum.index: no. 1-30. Indexed: Geotech.Abstr.

551   NO   ISSN 0078-1207
NORWEGIAN GEOTECHNICAL INSTITUTE. TECHNICAL REPORT. (Text in English) 1962. irreg. $4.50. Norges Geotekniske Institutt - Norwegian Geotechnical Institute, P.O. Box 40 Taasen, Oslo 8, Norway. Ed. Finn A. Joerstad. Indexed: Geotech.Abstr.

EARTH SCIENCES — GEOPHYSICS

551　　　　　　　　　　PO
OBSERVACOES MAGNETICAS (ACORES) 1975. a. Esc.150. Instituto Nacional de Meteorologia e Geofisica, Rua C do Aeroporto, 1700 Lisbon, Portugal. stat.

551　　　　　　　　　　BL
OBSERVATORIO NACIONAL RIO DE JANEIRO. CONTRIBUICOES CIENTIFICAS. (Text in English, French, Portuguese) 1977. irreg. Observatorio Nacional, Rua General Bruce 586, Sao Cristovao, Rio de Janeiro, Brazil.

OBSERVATORIO NACIONAL RIO DE JANIERO. PUBLICACOES. see *ASTRONOMY*

551.05　　　　　　　　BO
PAN AMERICAN INSTITUTE OF GEOGRAPHY AND HISTORY. COMMISSION ON GEOPHYSICS. BOLETIN. irreg. Instituto Panamericano de Geografia e Historia, Casilla 6003, La Paz, Bolivia.

551　　　PL　　ISSN 0079-3574
POLSKA AKADEMIA NAUK. INSTYTUT GEOFIZYKI. MATERIALY I PRACE. (Text in English and Polish; summaries in English) 1963. irreg., 1973, no. 71. price varies. Panstwowe Wydawnictwo Naukowe, Ul. Miodowa 10, 00-246 Warsaw, Poland (Dist. by: Ars Polona-Ruch, Krakowskie Przedmiescie 7, Warsaw, Poland) Ed. Roman Teisseyre.

PORTUGAL. INSTITUTO NACIONAL DE METEOROLOGIA E GEOFISICA. REVISTA. see *METEOROLOGY*

551　　　　　　　　　　UR
PRIKLADNAYA GEOFIZIKA. vol. 85, 1977. irreg. 1.00 Rub. per no. (Vsesoyuznyi Nauchno-Issledovatel'skii Institut Geofizicheskikh Metodov Razvedki) Izdatel'stvo Nedra, Tret'yakovskii Proezd 1/19, Moscow K-12, U.S.S.R. Ed. M. Polshkov. abstr. circ. 25,000.

551　　　II　　ISSN 0079-628X
PROGRESS IN GEOPHYSICS; annual report on the geophysical activities in the Republic of India. (Subseries of the National Geophysical Research Institute's Publications) (Text in English) 1966. a. $47. National Geophysical Research Institute, Uppal Rd., Hyderabad 500007, India. (Affiliate of Council of Scientific and Industrial Research) bk. rev.

551.22　　　FI　　ISSN 0079-774X
PUBLICATIONS IN SEISMOLOGY.* (Text in English; occasionally in Finnish) 1960. irreg. available on exchange. Helsingin Yliopisto, Seismologian Laitos - University of Helsinki, Institute of Seismology, Et. Hesperiankatu 4, Helsinki 10, Finland. Ed. Ekjo Vesanen.

551　　　RM　　ISSN 0556-8110
REVUE ROUMAINE DE GEOLOGIE, GEOPHYSIQUE ET GEOGRAPHIE. GEOPHYSIQUE. (Text in English, French, German and Russian) 1957. a. $12. (Academia Republicii Socialiste Romania) Editura Academiei Republicii Socialiste Romania, Calea Victoriei 125, Bucharest, Romania (Subscr. to: ILEXIM, Str. 13 Decembrie Nr. 3, P.O. Box 136-137, Bucharest, Romania) Ed. Bd. bk. rev. charts. illus. index.
Supersedes in part: Revue de Geologie et de Geographie.

RIJKSUNIVERSITEIT TE GENT. STERRENKUNDIG OBSERVATORIUM. MEDEDELINGEN: METEOROLOGIE EN GEOFYSICA. see *METEOROLOGY*

552.06 551　　　　　　JA
ROCK MAGNETISM AND PALEOGEOPHYSICS. (Text in English) 1973. a. controlled free circ. Rock Magnetism and Paleogeophysics Research Group in Japan, c/o University of Tokyo, Faculty of Science, Geophysical Institute, 7-3-1 Hongo, Bunkyo-ku, Tokyo 113, Japan. Ed. Masaru Kono. circ. 500.

551 538.7　　　PL　　ISSN 0082-0458
ROCZNIK MAGNETYCZNY/ANNUAIRE MAGNETIQUE. (Text in French and Polish; summaries in French) 1949. irreg. price varies. (Polska Akademia Nauk, Instytut Geofizyki) Panstwowe Wydawnictwo Naukowe, Miodowa 10, Warsaw, Poland (Dist. by Ars Polona-Ruch, Krakowskie Przedmiescie 7, Warsaw, Poland) Ed. Roman Teisseyre.

526　　　　　　　　　　YU
SAVEZ GEODETSKIH INZENJERA I GEOMETARA HRVATSKE. GEODET. (Text in Serbocroatian) 1958. 2-3/yr. free to members. Savez Geodetskih Inzenjera i Geometara SR Hrvatske, Berislaviceva 6, Zagreb, Yugoslavia. Ed. Miljenko Solaric.
Formerly: Savez Geodetskih Inzenjera i Geometara Hrvatske. Obavijesti (ISSN 0029-7461)

551　　　CS　　ISSN 0036-5319
SBORNIK GEOLOGICKYCH VED: UZITA GEOFYZIKA/JOURNAL OF GEOLOGICAL SCIENCES: APPLIED GEOPHYSICS. (Text in Czech, English, German, Russian) 1963. irreg. 25-40 Kcs. per no. Ustredni Ustav Geologicky, Malostranske nam. 19, 118 21 Prague 1, Czechoslovakia (Subscr. to: Artia, Ve Smeckach 30, 111 27 Prague 1) (Co-sponsor: Geofyzika, n.p. Brno) Ed. Bretislav Beranek. charts. illus. circ. 600. (back issues avail.) Indexed: Bull.Signal. Ref.Zh. Bibl.& Ind.Geol.

551　　　CS　　ISSN 0586-4607
SLOVENSKA AKADEMIA VIED. GEOFYZIKALNY USTAV. CONTRIBUTIONS. (Text and summaries in English and Russian) 1971. irreg. price varies. Veda, Publishing House of the Slovak Academy of Sciences, Klemensova 19, 895 30 Bratislava, Czechoslovakia. Ed. Petronela Ochabova. circ. 500.

622.15　　　　　　　　　US
SOCIETY OF EXPLORATION GEOPHYSICISTS. SPECIAL PUBLICATIONS (SYMPOSIA) SERIES. 1947. irreg. price varies. Society of Exploration Geophysicists, P.O.B. 3098, Tulsa, OK 74101.

538.767　　　　　　　　JA
SOLAR TERRESTRIAL ENVIRONMENTAL RESEARCH IN JAPAN. (Text in English) 1977. irreg. (3-4/yr.) University of Tokyo, Institute of Space and Aeronautical Science, 4-6-1 Komaba, Meguro-ku, Tokyo 153, Japan. Ed. Bd. abstr. circ. 1,200. (also avail. in microfilm) Indexed: Appl.Mech.Rev. Chem.Abstr.
Supersedes (1950-1976): Report of Ionosphere and Space Research in Japan (ISSN 0034-4672)

551　　　　　　　　　　UR
SOLNECHNAYA RADIATSIYA I RADIATSIONNYI BALANS MIROVAYA SET' (Text in English or Russian) 1978. irreg. 0.50 Rub. per issue. Glavnaya Geofizicheskaya Observatoriya Im. Voeikova, Karbysheva, 7, 194018 Leningrad, U.S.S.R.

551.22　　　　　US
SOVIET SEISMOLOGICAL RESEARCH. (Includes 2 subseries: Computational Seismology & Seismic Instruments) 1979. irreg. approx. 1 vol. per yr. Allerton Press, Inc., 150 Fifth Ave., New York, NY 10011.
Seismology

551　　　　　　　　　　SW
STATENS GEOTEKNISKA INSTITUT. RAPPORTS/SWEDISH GEOTECHNICAL INSTITUTE. REPORTS. (Text in English or Swedish) 1977. irreg. price varies. Statens Geotekniska Institut, Fack, 581 01 Linkoeping, Sweden. Indexed: Geotech.Abstr.
Supersedes: Statens Goetekniska Institut. Meddelander & Statens Goetekniska Institut. Saertryck och Preliminaera Rapporter (ISSN 0562-0953) & Statens Geotekniska Institut. Proceedings (ISSN 0081-5705)

551.4　　　PL　　ISSN 0081-6434
STUDIA GEOMORPHOLOGICA CARPATHO-BALCANICA. (Text in Polish, English, French and Russian; summaries in English, French, Russian and Polish) 1967. a. 45 Zl. per volume. (Polska Akademia Nauk, Oddzial w Krakowie, Komisja Nauk Geograficznych) Ossolineum, Publishing House of the Polish Academy of Sciences, Rynek 9, Wroclaw, Poland (Dist. by Ars Polona-Ruch, Krakowskie Przedmiescie 7, Warsaw, Poland) Ed. Leszek Starkel.

526　　　FI　　ISSN 0085-6932
SUOMEN GEODEETTISEN LAITOKSEN. JULKAISUJA/FINNISH GEODETIC INSTITUTE. PUBLICATIONS/FINNISCHE GEODAETISCHE INSTITUT. VEROEFFENTLICHUNGEN. (Text and summaries in English, French and German) 1923. irreg., no. 89, 1979. price varies. Suomen Geodeettinen Laitos - Finnish Geodetic Institute, Pasilankatu 43 A, SF-00240 Helsinki 24, Finland. circ. 800.

551.22　　　UN　　ISSN 0082-7479
UNESCO EARTHQUAKE STUDY MISSIONS. (Text in English and French) irreg. price varies. Unesco, 7-9 Place de Fontenoy, 75700 Paris, France (Dist. in U.S. by: Unipub, 345 Park Ave. S., New York NY 10010)
Seismology

U.S. AIR FORCE GEOPHYSICS LABORATORY. AFGL (SERIES) see *MILITARY*

551.22　　　US　　ISSN 0091-1429
UNITED STATES EARTHQUAKES. a. price varies. U.S. National Geophysical and Solar-Terrestrial Data Center, 325 Broadway, Boulder, CO 80303 (Available from Supt. of Documents, U.S. Government Printing Office, Washington, D.C. 20402) illus.
Seismology

551　　　MX　　ISSN 0076-7182
UNIVERSIDAD NACIONAL AUTONOMA DE MEXICO. INSTITUTO DE GEOFISICA. ANALES. 1955. irreg. vol. 21, 1975. $4. Universidad Nacional Autonoma de Mexico, Instituto de Geofisica, Circuito Exterior, Ciudad Universitaria, Mexico 20, D.F., Mexico. Ed. Jorge Bouton. bibl. charts. circ. 850. (back issues avail.)

551　　　MX　　ISSN 0076-7204
UNIVERSIDAD NACIONAL AUTONOMA DE MEXICO. INSTITUTO DE GEOFISICA. MONOGRAFIAS. 1959. irreg. $4. Universidad Nacional Autonoma de Mexico, Instituto de Geofisica, Circuito Exterior, Ciudad Universitaria, Mexico 20, D.F., Mexico. Ed. Jorge Bouton.

551　　　　　　　　　　GW
UNIVERSITAET MUENCHEN. GEOPHYSIKALISCHES OBSERVATORIUM, FUERSTENFELDBRUCK. VEROEFFENTLICHUNGEN. SERIE A. 1959. a. exchange basis. Universitaet Muenchen, Geophysikalisches Observatorium, Ludwigshoehe 8, 8080 Fuerstenfeldbruck, W. Germany (B.R.D.)

551　　　GW　　ISSN 0077-2100
UNIVERSITAET MUENCHEN. GEOPHYSIKALISCHES OBSERVATORIUM, FUERSTENFELDBRUCK. VEROEFFENTLICHUNGEN. SERIE B. 1960. irreg., no. 5, 1974. exchange basis. Universitaet Muenchen, Geophysikalisches Observatorium, Ludwigshoehe 8, 8080 Fuerstenfeldbruck, W. Germany (B.R.D.)

551 551.5　　　GW　　ISSN 0069-5882
UNIVERSITAET ZU KOELN. INSTITUT FUER GEOPHYSIK UND METEOROLOGIE. MITTEILUNGEN. (Text in German and English) 1965. irreg., no. 22, 1975. Universitaet zu Koeln, Institut fuer Geophysik und Meteorologie, Albertus Magnus Platz, 5000 Cologne, W. Germany (B.R.D.)

551　　　US　　ISSN 0041-9362
UNIVERSITY OF ALASKA. GEOPHYSICAL INSTITUTE. REPORT SERIES. 1948. irreg. price varies. University of Alaska, Geophysical Institute, Fairbanks, AK 99701.

551 520　　　CN　　ISSN 0068-1725
UNIVERSITY OF BRITISH COLUMBIA. DEPARTMENT OF GEOPHYSICS AND ASTRONOMY. ANNUAL REPORT. 1958. a. free. ‡ University of British Columbia, Department of Geophysics and Astronomy, 2075 Wesbrook Mall, Vancouver, B.C. V6T 1W5, Canada. Ed. T. K. Menon. circ. 700.

EARTH SCIENCES — Hydrology

551.22   US   ISSN 0092-4288
UNIVERSITY OF NEVADA. SEISMOLOGICAL LABORATORY. BULLETIN. 1970. irreg., latest 1976 (for 1974) ‡ University of Nevada, Seismological Laboratory, Reno, NV 89507. Ed. Alan Ryall. illus. circ. 100. Key Title: Bulletin of the Seismological Laboratory (Reno)
Seismology

538.7   NE   ISSN 0077-7587
YEARBOOK GEOMAGNETISM: PARAMARIBO, SURINAM. (Subseries of: Publikatienummer) 1958. a. fl.10. Royal Netherlands Meterological Institute, De Bilt, Netherlands. (Co-sponsors: Surinam Department of Public Works and Traffic; Surinam Department of Development) circ. 235.

551   GE   ISSN 0065-5023
ZENTRALINSTITUT FUER PHYSIK DER ERDE. SEISMOLOGISCHER DIENST JENA. SEISMOLOGISCHE BULLETIN. 1965. irreg. price varies. (Akademie der Wissenschaften der DDR, Zentralinstitut fuer Physik der Erde, Seismologischer Dienst Jena) Akademie-Verlag, Leipziger Str. 3-4, 108 Berlin, E. Germany (D.D.R.)

EARTH SCIENCES — Hydrology

551.4   US   ISSN 0065-2768
ADVANCES IN HYDROSCIENCE. 1964. irreg., vol. 11, 1978. price varies. Academic Press, Inc., 111 Fifth Ave., New York, NY 10003. Ed. Ven Te Chow. index. (also avail. in microfiche)
   Formerly: Methods in Hydroscience (ISSN 0076-6909)

551.48   UR
AKADEMIYA NAUK S.S.S.R. SIBIRSKOE OTDELENIE. LIMNOLOGICHESKU INSTITUT. TRUDY. vol. 25, 1976. irreg. $7.95. (Sibirskoe Otdelenie an SSSR, Limnologicheskii Institut) Izdatel'stvo Nauka, Prospekt Naukt, 21, Novosibirsk, U.S.S.R. Ed. B. Zonov.

ALBERTA RESEARCH COUNCIL. RIVER ENGINEERING AND SURFACE HYDROLOGY REPORTS. see *ENGINEERING — Civil Engineering*

551.4   NE
AMSTERDAM HYDROLOGY SERIES. 1977. irreg. price varies. Editions Rodopi N.V., Keizersgracht 302-304, 1016 EX Amsterdam, Netherlands. Ed. J. J. de Vries. circ. 500.

070 551.4   FR   ISSN 0373-3629
ANNALES HYDROGRAPHIQUES. 1848. 2-3 yr. price varies. Service Hydrographique et Oceanographique de la Marine, 3, Avenue Octave Greard, 75200 Paris Naval, France (Subscr. address: EPSHOM, B.P. 426, 29275 Brest Cedex, France) charts, illus. index, cum. index. circ. 400.

551.4   UN
ANUARIO HIDROLOGICO DEL ISTMO CENTROAMERICANO. 1966-67. a. free. ‡ United Nations Central American Hydrometeorological Project, Regional Committee for Water Resources, Apdo. 4328, Managua, Nicaragua. Ed. Eduardo Basso. circ. 300. (back issues avail)

ARCHIVIO DI OCEANOGRAFIA E LIMNOLOGIA. see *EARTH SCIENCES — Oceanography*

551.4   AT   ISSN 0067-219X
AUSTRALIAN WATER RESOURCES COUNCIL. HYDROLOGICAL SERIES. 1966. a. irreg. price varies. ‡ Australian Government Publishing Service, Box 84, Canberra, A.C.T. 2600, Australia. Indexed: Sel.Water Res.Abstr.

551.48   GW   ISSN 0067-8643
DIE BINNENGEWAESSER; Einzeldarstellungen aus der Limnologie und ihren Grenzgebieten. (Text in German and English) 1926. irreg., vol. 26/2, 1978. price varies. E. Schweizerbart'sche Verlagsbuchhandlung, Johannesstr. 3A, 7000 Stuttgart 1, W. Germany (B.R.D.) Eds. H. J. Elster, W. Ohle. Indexed: Ber.Biochem.Biol.

551.48   CR   ISSN 0067-9747
BOLETIN HIDROLOGICO. 1958. a. limited distribution. Instituto Costarricense de Electricidad, Apto. 10032, San Jose, Costa Rica. charts. illus. stat. index. circ. controlled.

551.48   CN   ISSN 0068-7669
CANADA. HYDROGRAPHIC SERVICE. WATER LEVELS. 1962. a. $1. Fisheries and Marine Service, Ottawa, Ontario K1A 0E6, Canada. circ. 700.

551.4   CN
CANADA. INLAND WATERS DIRECTORATE. HISTORICAL STREAMFLOW SUMMARY: ALBERTA. (On cover, 1970- : Water Survey of Canada) 1970. triennial. free. ‡ Inland Waters Directorate, Ottawa, Ont. K1A 0E7, Ottawa. circ. 400.

551.4   CN
CANADA. INLAND WATERS DIRECTORATE. HISTORICAL STREAMFLOW SUMMARY: ATLANTIC PROVINCES. triennial. free. ‡ Inland Waters Directorate, Ottawa, Ont. K1A 0E7, Canada. stat. circ. 400.

551.4   CN
CANADA. INLAND WATERS DIRECTORATE. HISTORICAL STREAMFLOW SUMMARY: BRITISH COLUMBIA. (On cover, 1970- : Water Survey of Canada) 1970. triennial. free. ‡ Inland Waters Directorate, Ottawa, Ont. K1A 0E7, Canada. circ. 400.

551.4   CN
CANADA. INLAND WATERS DIRECTORATE. HISTORICAL STREAMFLOW SUMMARY: MANITOBA. (On cover, 1970- : Water Survey of Canada) 1970. triennial. free. ‡ Inland Waters Directorate, Ottawa, Ont. K1A 0S9, Canada. circ. 400.

551.4   CN
CANADA. INLAND WATERS DIRECTORATE. HISTORICAL STREAMFLOW SUMMARY: ONTARIO. (On cover, 1970- : Water Survey of Canada) 1970. triennial. free. ‡ Inland Waters Directorate, Ottawa, Ont. K1A 0S9, Canada. circ. 400.

551.4   CN
CANADA. INLAND WATERS DIRECTORATE. HISTORICAL STREAMFLOW SUMMARY: SASKATCHEWAN. 1970. triennial. free. ‡ Inland Waters Directorate, Ottawa, Ont. K1A 0E7, Canada. circ. 400.

551.4   CN
CANADA. INLAND WATERS DIRECTORATE. HISTORICAL STREAMFLOW SUMMARY: YUKON TERRITORY AND NORTHWEST TERRITORIES. (On cover, 1970- : Water Survey of Canada) 1970. triennial. free. ‡ Inland Waters Directorate, Ottawa, Ont. K1A 0S9, Canada. circ. 400.

551.4   CN
CANADA.INLAND WATERS DIRECTORATE. WATER RESOURCES RESEARCH SUPPORT PROGRAM /PROGRAMME DE SUBVENTION A LA RECHERCHE SUR LES RESOURCES EN EAU. (Text in: English and French) irreg. Inland Waters Directorate, Ottawa, Ont. K1A 0S9, Canada.

551.49   CN
CANADA. MARINE ENVIRONMENTAL DATA SERVICE. MONTHLY AND YEARLY MEAN WATER LEVELS/MOYENNES MENSUELLES ET ANNUELLES DES NIVEAUX D'EAU. (Text in English and French) irreg. Marine Environmental Data Service, 7Th Floor. W., 240 Sparks St., Ottawa, Ont. K1A 0E6, Canada. circ. 100.

553   CN
CANADA. WATER SURVEY. SURFACE WATER DATA: BRITISH COLUMBIA. a. Inland Waters Directorate, Ottawa, Ont. K1A 0S9, Canada.

551.48   US   ISSN 0069-6110
COLORADO STATE UNIVERSITY. HYDROLOGY PAPERS. 1963. irreg., nos. 95-100, 1978. $3. ea. Colorado State University, College of Engineering, Fort Collins, CO 80521.

553.79   US   ISSN 0094-9671
CONFERENCE ON GROUND WATER. PROCEEDINGS. biennial. $4. University of California, Davis, Water Resources Center, Davis, CA 95616. (Co-Sponsor: California Department of Water Resources) Key Title: Proceedings - Conference on Ground Water.

551.48   US   ISSN 0589-400X
CONNECTICUT WATER RESOURCES BULLETIN. irreg. Department of Environmental Protection, Hartford, CT 06115. illus.

DEUTSCHES GEWAESSERKUNDLICHES JAHRBUCH. DONAUGEBIET. see *WATER RESOURCES*

DEUTSCHES GEWAESSERKUNDLICHES JAHRBUCH. KUESTENGEBIET DER NORT- UND OSTSEE. see *WATER RESOURCES*

DEUTSCHES GEWAESSERKUNDLICHES JAHRBUCH. RHEINGEBIET: ABSCHNITT MAIN. see *WATER RESOURCES*

551.48   NE
DEVELOPMENTS IN WATER SCIENCE. 1974. irreg. price varies. Elsevier Scientific Publishing Co., Box 211, 1000 AE Amsterdam, Netherlands.

551.48   EC
ECUADOR.INSTITUTO NACIONAL DE METEOROLOGIA E HIDROLOGIA. ANUARIO HIDROLOGICO. 1963. a. available on exchange. Instituto Nacional de Meteorologia e Hidrologia, Daniel Hidalgo No. 132 y 10 de Agosto, Quito, Ecuador. index.
   Supersedes: Ecuador. Servicio Nacional de Meteorologia e Hidrologia. Anuario Hidrologico (ISSN 0070-8933)

551.4   SZ
EIDGENOESSISCHE TECHNISCHE HOCHSCHULE ZUERICH. VERSUCHSANSTALT FUER WASSERBAU, HYDROLOGIE UND GLAZIOLOGIE. JAHRESBERICHT. 1971. a. free. Eidgenoessische Technische Hochschule Zuerich, Versuchsanstalt fuer Wasserbau, Hydrologie und Glaziologie, ETH-Zentrum, CH-8092 Zurich, Switzerland. Ed. D. Vischer. illus.

551.4 627   SZ
EIDGENOESSISCHE TECHNISCHE HOCHSCHULE ZUERICH. VERSUCHSANSTALT FUER WASSERBAU, HYDROLOGIE UND GLAZIOLOGIE. MITTEILUNGEN. 1971. a. free. Eidgenoessische Technische Hochschule Zuerich, Versuchsanstalt fuer Wasserbau, Hydrologie und Glaziologie, ETH-Zentrum, CH-8092 Zurich, Switzerland. Ed. D. Vischer. illus.

551.48   GW   ISSN 0071-1128
ERGEBNISSE DER LIMNOLOGIE. (Supplement to Archiv fuer Hydrobiologie) (Text in German and English) 1964. irreg., no. 11, 1978. price varies. (Internationale Vereinigung fuer Theoretische und Angewandte Limnologie) E. Schweizerbart'sche Verlagsbuchhandlung, Johannesstr. 3A, 7000 Stuttgart 1, W. Germany (B.R.D.) Eds. H. J. Elster, W. Ohle. adv.

551.48   DK
FOLIO LIMNOLOGICA SCANDINAVICA. (Text in English) 1943. irreg., no. 17, 1977. Koebenhavns Universitet, Freshwater Biological Laboratory, 51 Helsingoersgade, DK-3400 Hilleroed, Denmark. Ed.Bd.

551.49   US   ISSN 0468-5067
GROUNDWATER BULLETIN. irreg. Department of Natural and Economic Resources, Groundwater Section, Raleigh, NC 27611. illus.
   Continues: North Carolina. Division of Ground Water. Ground Water Bulletin.

551.48   IS   ISSN 0073-4217
HYDROLOGICAL YEARBOOK OF ISRAEL/ SHENATON HIDROLOGI LE-YISRAEL. (Text in Hebrew and English) 1946/47. a. I£25. Ministry of Agriculture Water Commission, Hydrological Service, Box 6381, Jerusalem, Israel. circ. 450.

353.9   US   ISSN 0362-3289
IDAHO. DEPARTMENT OF WATER
RESOURCES. ANNUAL REPORT. a. Department
of Water Resources, 1365 N. Orchard St., Boise, ID
83720. Key Title: Annual Report of the Idaho
Department of Water Resources.

INDEX DE REFERENCES: INVENTAIRE DES
STATIONS HYDROMETRIQUES. see *WATER RESOURCES*

551.48   SW   ISSN 0082-0032
INSTITUTE OF FRESHWATER RESEARCH,
DROTTNINGHOLM. REPORT. (Text in English)
1933. irreg., no. 54, 1975. exchange basis. Institute
of Freshwater Research, S-170 11 Drottningholm,
Sweden.

INSTYTUT METEOROLOGII I GOSPODARKI
WODNEJ. PRACE. see *METEOROLOGY*

551.4   FR   ISSN 0579-6733
INTERNATIONAL ASSOCIATION OF
HYDROGEOLOGISTS. MEMOIRES. irreg.
International Association of Hydrogeologists, 6-8
rue Chasseloup Laubat, 75737 Paris de Cedex 15,
France.

551.48   GW   ISSN 0538-4680
INTERNATIONAL ASSOCIATION OF
THEORETICAL AND APPLIED LIMNOLOGY.
COMMUNICATIONS. (Text in English and
German) 1953. irreg. (approx. 1/yr.) price varies. ‡
(International Association of Theoretical and
Applied Limnology) E. Schweizerbart'sche
Verlagsbuchhandlung, Johannesstr. 3A, 7000
Stuttgart 1, W. Germany (B.R.D.) Ed. V. Sladecek.
circ. 4,000 (approx.) Indexed: Biol.Abstr.

551.48   GW   ISSN 0368-0770
INTERNATIONAL ASSOCIATION OF
THEORETICAL AND APPLIED LIMNOLOGY.
PROCEEDINGS/INTERNATIONALE
VEREINIGUNG FUER THEORETISCHE UND
ANGEWANDTE LIMNOLOGIE.
VERHANDLUNGEN. (Text in English, French
and German) 1922. triennial. E. Schweizerbart'sche
Verlagsbuchhandlung, Johannesstr. 3, 7000 Stuttgart
1, W. Germany (B.R.D.) Ed.V. Sladecek. index.

INTERNATIONAL HYDROGRAPHIC
CONFERENCE. REPORTS OF PROCEEDINGS.
see *EARTH SCIENCES — Oceanography*

INTERNATIONAL HYDROGRAPHIC
ORGANIZATION. YEARBOOK. see *EARTH SCIENCES — Oceanography*

551.4 627   US
INTERNATIONAL SYMPOSIUM ON URBAN
HYDROLOGY, HYDRAULICS AND
SEDIMENT CONTROL. PROCEEDINGS. 1974.
a. $33.50. (University of Kentucky, College of
Engineering, Office of Continuing Education and
Extension) ORES Publications, College of
Engineering, Univ. of Kentucky, Lexington, KY
40506. Ed.Bd. (also avail. in microfiche; back issues
avail.)
Formerly (until 1978): International Symposium
on Urban Storm Water Management. Proceedings.

551.4   GW   ISSN 0538-7779
INTERNATIONALE HYDROLOGISCHE
DEKADE: JAHRBUCH DER
BUNDESREPUBLIK DEUTSCHLAND/
INTERNATIONAL HYDROLOGICAL
DECADE: YEARBOOK OF THE FEDERAL
REPUBLIC OF GERMANY. (Text in English and
German) 1965. a. free. Bundesanstalt fuer
Gewaesserkunde, Kaisern-Augusta-Anlagen 15-17,
5400 Koblenz, W. Germany (B.R.D.) (Co-sponsor:
Deutsche Forschungsgemeinschaft)

551.4   JA
JAPAN. MARITIME SAFETY AGENCY.
HYDROGRAPHIC DEPARTMENT. REPORT
OF HYDROGRAPHIC RESEARCH. no. 14, 1979.
irreg. Maritime Safety Agency, Hydrographic
Department, 5-3-1 Tsukiji, Chuo-ku, Tokyo 104,
Japan.

JOURNAL OF GREAT LAKES RESEARCH. see *ENVIRONMENTAL STUDIES*

551.48   US
KANSAS GEOLOGICAL SURVEY. BASIC DATA
SERIES. GROUND-WATER RELEASES. 1973.
irreg. price varies. Geological Survey, 1930 Ave.
"A", Campus West, University of Kansas, Lawrence,
KS 66044.

551.48   US
KANSAS GEOLOGICAL SURVEY. GROUND
WATER SERIES. 1974. irreg. $3 per no.
Geological Survey, 1930 Ave. "A", Campus West,
University of Kansas, Lawrence, KS 66044.

LAKE MICHIGAN WATER QUALITY REPORT.
see *ENVIRONMENTAL STUDIES*

551.48   GE   ISSN 0075-9511
LIMNOLOGICA. 1962. irreg., vol. 11, 1976. price
varies. Akademie-Verlag, Leipziger Str. 3-4, 108
Berlin, E. Germany (D.D.R.) Ed. Theodor
Schraeder.

551   US
LONG ISLAND WATER RESOURCES BULLETIN.
1971. irreg (approx. 2 per year) free. ‡ U.S.
Geological Survey, Water Resources Division (New
York), 5 Aerial Way, Syosset, NY 11791.
(Published with: Nassau or Suffolk County)

LOUISIANA WATER RESOURCES RESEARCH
INSTITUTE. ANNUAL REPORT. see *WATER RESOURCES*

MISSOURI. DIVISION OF GEOLOGICAL
SURVEY AND WATER RESOURCES. WATER
RESOURCES REPORT. see *WATER RESOURCES*

553   US   ISSN 0092-1602
NEW JERSEY. DIVISION OF WATER
RESOURCES. SPECIAL REPORT. no. 5, 1936.
irreg., no. 38, 1974. Department of Environmental
Protection, Division of Water Resources, Trenton,
NJ 08625 (Order from: Bureau of Geology and
Topography, Box 2809, Trenton NJ 08625) illus.

553   US   ISSN 0545-2252
NEW JERSEY. DIVISION OF WATER
RESOURCES. WATER RESOURCES
CIRCULARS. no. 3, 1961. irreg, latest issue no. 23.
price varies. Department of Environmental
Protection, Division of Water Resources, Trenton,
NJ 08625.

551.48   US
NEW MEXICO. BUREAU OF MINES AND
MINERAL RESOURCES. HYDROLOGIC
REPORT. 1971. irreg., no. 4, 1976. price varies.
Bureau of Mines and Mineral Resources, Socorro,
NM 87801. illus. (also avail. in microfiche)
Supersedes: Ground-Water Reports (1948-1970)

551   NO
NORSK INSTITUTT FOR VANNFORSKNING.
AARBOK. 1958/67. a. free. Norsk Institutt for
Vannforskning - Norwegian Institute for Water
Research, Postboks 333, Blindern, Oslo 3, Norway.
Ed. Knut Pedersen. illus.

551   NO
NORSK INSTITUTT FOR VANNFORSKNING.
TEMARAPPORT. irreg., latest no. 4, 1979. Norsk
Institutt for Vannforskning - Norwegian Institute for
Water Research, Postboks 333, Blindern, Oslo 3,
Norway. charts. illus.

551.48 627   FR   ISSN 0071-8998
O.R.S.T.O.M. ANNALES HYDROLOGIQUES.
(Formerly its Annuaire Hydrologique) first series
from 1949-59. Second series from 1959. a. price
varies. Office de la Recherche Scientifique et
Technique Outre-Mer, 70-74 Route d'Aulnay,
93140 Bondy, France. circ. 600.

551.48   UN
OPERATIONAL HYDROLOGY REPORTS. irreg.
price varies. World Meteorological Organization, 41
Ave. Giuseppe Motta, CH-1211 Geneva 20,
Switzerland (Dist. in U.S. by: Unipub, 345 Park
Ave. S., New York, NY 10010)

551.48 623.82   UK
PROGRESS IN UNDERWATER SCIENCE.
(Contains papers submitted at annual and regional
symposia of the Underwater Association) vol. 5,
1979(N.S.) a. (Underwater Association) Pentech
Press Ltd., 4 Graham Lodge, Graham Rd., London,
NW4, England. Eds. K. Hiscock, A. D. Baume.

551.4   CS   ISSN 0036-5289
SBORNIK GEOLOGICKYCH VED:
HYDROGEOLOGIE, INZENYRSKA
GEOLOGIE/JOURNAL OF GEOLOGICAL
SCIENCES: HYDROGEOLOGY,
ENGINEERING GEOLOGY. (Text and
summaries in Czech, English, French, German,
Russian) 1964. irreg. 25-35 Kcs. per no. Ustredni
Ustav Geologicky, Malostranske nam. 19, 118 21
Prague 1, Czechoslovakia (Subscr. to: Artia, Ve
Smeckach 30, 111 27 Prague 1) Ed. Jan Jetel.
charts. illus. circ. 600. (back issues avail.) Indexed:
Bull.Signal. Ref.Z.H. Bibl.& Ind.Geol.

551.4   CN
SELECTED STREAMFLOW DATA FOR
ONTARIO. 1969. a. Ministry of the Environment,
Water Resources Branch, 135 St. Clair Avenue
West, Toronto, Ontario M4V 1P5, Canada.

551.4   CE
SRI LANKA. IRRIGATION DEPARTMENT.
HYDROLOGY DIVISION. HYDROLOGICAL
ANNUAL. a. Irrigation Department, Hydrology
Division, Bauddhaloka Mawatha, Colombo 7, Sri
Lanka. illus.

551.48   US   ISSN 0376-4826
STEIRISCHE BEITRAEGE ZUR
HYDROGEOLOGIE. a. $34. Springer-Verlag, 175
Fifth Ave., New York, NY 10010 (Also Berlin,
Heidelberg, Vienna) Ed. Josef Zoetl. (reprint service
avail. from ISI)

551.48   UN   ISSN 0081-7449
STUDIES AND REPORTS IN HYDROLOGY
SERIES. (Text in English and French) 1969. irreg.;
no. 18, 1974. Unesco, 7-9 Place de Fontenoy, 75700
Paris, France (Dist. in U.S. by: Unipub, 345 Park
Ave. S., New York NY 10010)

627   RM
STUDII DE HIDRAULICA. (Text in Romanian;
summaries in English and French) a. Academia de
Stiinte Agricole si Silvice, Institutul de Cercetari
Pentru Imbunatatiri Funciare, B-dul Marasti Nr. 61,
Bucharest, Romania (Subscr. to: ILEXIM, Str. 13
Decembrie Nr. 3, P.O. Box 136-137, Bucharest,
Romania)

551.48   UN   ISSN 0082-2310
TECHNICAL PAPERS IN HYDROLOGY SERIES.
1970. irreg.; no. 13, 1974. Unesco, 7-9 Place de
Fontenoy, 75700 Paris, France (Dist. in U.S. by:
Unipub, 345 Park Ave. S., New York NY 10010)

553.7   US   ISSN 0092-332X
U. S. GEOLOGICAL SURVEY. WATER
RESOURCES INVESTIGATIONS. U.S. Geological
Survey, 12201 Sunrise Valley Drive, Reston, VA
22092 (Most reports avail. only in microfiche from:
NTIS, 5285 Port Royal Rd., Springfield, VA 22161)
Key Title: Water-Resources Investigations.

333.91   US   ISSN 0083-1131
U. S. GEOLOGICAL SURVEY. WATER SUPPLY
PAPERS. 1896. irreg. U.S. Geological Survey,
12201 Sunrise Valley Drive, Reston, VA 22092
(Orders to: 604 S. Pickett St., Alexandria, VA
22304)

551.4   MX
UNIVERSIDAD NACIONAL AUTONOMA DE
MEXICO. INSTITUTO DE GEOFISICA. DATOS
GEOFISICOS A TABLAS DE PREDICCION DE
MAREAS, PUERTOS DEL GOLFO DE MEXICO
Y MAR CARIBE. 1963. a. $3. Universidad
Nacional Autonoma de Mexico, Instituto de
Geofisica, Circuito Exterior, Ciudad Universitaria,
Mexico 20, D.F., Mexico. Ed. Jorge Bouton.

551.4   MX
UNIVERSIDAD NACIONAL AUTONOMA DE
MEXICO. INSTITUTO DE GEOFISICA. DATOS
GEOFISICOS A TABLAS DE PREDICCION DE
MAREAS, PUERTOS DEL OCEANO
PACIFICO. 1963. a. $3. Universidad Nacional
Autonoma de Mexico, Instituto de Geofisica,
Circuito Exterior, Ciudad Universitaria, Mexico 20,
D.F., Mexico. Ed. Jorge Bouton.

551.4   SZ
UNIVERSITE DE NEUCHATEL. CENTRE
D'HYDROGEOLOGIE. BULLETIN. (Text in
French, German) 1976. biennial. Universite de
Neuchatel, Centre d'Hydrogeologie, 11 rue Emile
Argand, CH-2000 Neuchatel, Switzerland. circ. 500.

WATER RESOURCES DATA FOR PUERTO RICO. see *WATER RESOURCES*

WATER RESOURCES RESEARCH IN VIRGINIA, ANNUAL REPORT. see *WATER RESOURCES*

WATER RESOURCES SUMMARY. see *WATER RESOURCES*

WEST VIRGINIA RIVER BASIN BULLETINS. see *EARTH SCIENCES — Geology*

EARTH SCIENCES — Oceanography

551.46 AT
A I M S MONOGRAPH SERIES. irreg. Aus.$4.70 or on exchange. Australian Institute of Marine Science, Private Mail Bag No. 3, Townsville M.S.O., Queensland 4810, Australia.

551.46 CU
ACADEMIA DE CIENCIAS DE CUBA. INSTITUTO DE OCEANOLOGIA. INFORMES CIENTIFICOS TECNICOS. (Text in Spanish; summaries in English) irreg. Academia de Ciencias de Cuba, Instituto de Oceanologia, Avda. 1ra. no. 18406, Havana, Cuba. Dir. Argelia Fernandez. illus.

551.46 CU ISSN 0567-5782
ACADEMIA DE CIENCIAS DE CUBA. INSTITUTO DE OCEANOLOGIA. SERIE OCEANOLOGICA. (Text in Spanish; summaries in English) 1968. irreg. free on exchange. Academia de Ciencias de Cuba, Instituto de Oceanologia, Avda. 1ra. no. 18406, Havana 16, Cuba. Dir. Argelia Fernandez. Indexed: Biol.Abstr. Deep Sea Res. & Oceanogr.Abstr.

550 CU
ACADEMIA DE CIENCIAS DE CUBA. INSTITUTO DE OCEANOLOGIA. TABLAS DE MAREAS. Cover title: Tablas de Mareas: Costas de Cuba. a. Academia de Ciencias de Cuba, Instituto de Oceanologia, Avda. 1ra. no. 18406, Havana, Cuba. illus.

551.46 YU ISSN 0001-5113
ACTA ADRIATICA. 1938. a. exchange basis. Institut za Oceanografiju i Ribarstvo, Mose Pijade 63, Box 114, 58001 Split, Yugoslavia. Ed. Mira Zore Armanda. circ. 650. Indexed: Biol.Abstr. Chem.Abstr. Ocean.Abstr. Pollut.Abstr.

551.4 CH
ACTA OCEANOGRAPHICA TAIWANICA. 1971. a. $20. National Taiwan University, Institute of Oceanography, Box 23-13, Taipei, Taiwan, Republic of China. Ed.Bd. bk. rev. circ. 600-1,000.

ADVANCES IN FISHERIES OCEANOGRAPHY. see *BIOLOGY — Zoology*

ADVANCES IN MARINE BIOLOGY. see *BIOLOGY*

551.46 UY
ALMANAQUE. a. Servicio de Oceanografia e Hidrografia, Capurro 980, Casilla de Correo 1381, Montevideo, Uruguay.

551.46 II ISSN 0066-1686
ANDHRA UNIVERSITY MEMOIRS IN OCEANOGRAPHY. (Text in English) 1954. irreg. price varies. Andhra University Press and Publications, Waltair, Visakhapatnam 530003, Andhra Pradesh, India. Ed. E. C. la Fond.

551.46 FR ISSN 0180-989X
ANNUAIRE DES MAREES POUR L'AN... TOME 1. PORTS DE FRANCE. 1839. a. price varies. ‡ Service Hydrographique et Oceanographique de la Marine, 3, Avenue Octave Greard, 75200 Paris Naval, France (Subscr. address: Epshom., B.P. 426, 29275 Brest Cedex, France) index. circ. 10,000. (tabloid format)

551.46 CL
APUNTES OCEANOLOGICOS. 1966. irreg. exchange. Universidad de Chile, Instituto de Investigaciones Oceanologicas, Casilla 1240, Antofagasta, Chile.

ARCHAEONAUTICA. see *ARCHAEOLOGY*

551.46 551.48 IT ISSN 0066-667X
ARCHIVIO DI OCEANOGRAFIA E LIMNOLOGIA. (Text in Italian or congress languages; summaries in English and Italian) 1941. irreg., latest, vol. 19, no. 2. L.5000 per no. Istituto di Biologia del Mare, Riva 7 Martiri 1364-A, 30122 Venice, Italy. Ed. B. Battaglia. bk. rev. circ. 500. Indexed: Biol.Abstr. Ocean.Abstr. Pollut.Abstr. Ocean.Ind.

551.4 AG ISSN 0004-1076
ARGENTINA. SERVICIO DE HIDROGRAFIA NAVAL. BOLETIN. 1964. irreg; latest, vol. 13, nos. 1/2, 1976. exchange basis. Servicio de Hidrografia Naval, Montes de Oca 2124, Codigo Postal 1271, Buenos Aires, Argentina. bk. rev. circ. 300.

551.46 CN ISSN 0381-4831
BEDFORD INSTITUTE OF OCEANOGRAPHY. COMPUTER NOTE. 1966. irreg. free. Bedford Institute of Oceanography, Dartmouth, N.S. B2Y 4A2, Canada. Ed. M. P. Latremouille. circ. 50. (microfiche)

551.46 CN
BEDFORD INSTITUTE OF OCEANOGRAPHY. DATA REPORT. 1965. irreg. free. Bedford Institute of Oceanography, Dartmouth, N.S., Canada. Ed. M. P. Latremouille. cum. index (1962-78) circ. 150. (microfiche) Indexed: Ocean.Abstr.
Formerly: Bedford Institute of Oceanography. A O L Data Series (ISSN 0067-4788)

551.46 CN
BEDFORD INSTITUTE OF OCEANOGRAPHY. REPORT. 1962. irreg. free. ‡ Bedford Institute of Oceanography, Dartmouth, N.S., Canada. Ed. M. P. Latremouille. circ. 400. Indexed: Ocean.Abstr.
Formerly: Atlantic Oceanographic Laboratory. A O L Report (ISSN 0067-4796)

551.46 CN
BEDFORD INSTITUTE OF OCEANOGRAPHY REVIEW. 1968. a. free. ‡ Bedford Institute of Oceanography, Dartmouth, N.S. B2Y 4A2, Canada. Ed. M. P. Latremouille. circ. 5,000(controlled)
Formerly: Bedford Institute of Oceanography. Biennial Review (ISSN 0067-480X)

551.46 GE ISSN 0067-5148
BEITRAEGE ZUR MEERESKUNDE. 1961. irreg., no. 39, 1977. price varies. (Akademie der Wissenschaften der DDR, Institut fuer Meereskunde, Warnemuende) Akademie-Verlag, Leipziger Strasse 3-4, 108 Berlin, E. Germany (D.D.R.) Ed. Erich Bruns. Indexed: Ocean.Abstr. Pollut.Abstr.

551.46 US
C G O U TECHNICAL REPORT. 1964. irreg. U.S. Coast Guard, Oceanographic Unit, 400 Seventh St., S.W., Washington, DC 20590 (Order from: N T I S, Springfield, VA 22151) circ. 300.

551.46 US
C R C HANDBOOK OF MARINE SCIENCE. 1976. irreg. price varies. (Chemical Rubber Company) C R C Press, Inc., 2000 N.W. 24th St., Boca Raton, FL 33431. bibl.

551.46 CN
CANADA. MARINE SCIENCES DIRECTORATE. PACIFIC REGION. PACIFIC MARINE SCIENCE REPORT. irreg. free. Marine Sciences Directorate, Pacific Region, 1230 Government St., Victoria, B.C, Canada. illus.

623.894 CN ISSN 0068-9882
CANADIAN TIDE AND CURRENT TABLES. 1967. a. Can.$0.50. Department of Energy, Mines and Resources, Ottawa, Ont. K1A 0G1, Canada.

CENTRAL MARINE FISHERIES RESEARCH INSTITUTE. BULLETIN. see *FISH AND FISHERIES*

551.46 JA
CHOI NENPO/YEARBOOK OF TIDAL RECORDS. (Text in Japanese) 1966. a. Geographical Survey Institute, Kitazato-1, Yatabe-Machi, Tsukuba-Gun, Ibaraki-Ken 300-21, Japan. circ. 400.

COMMONWEALTH SCIENTIFIC AND INDUSTRIAL RESEARCH ORGANIZATION. DIVISION OF FISHERIES AND OCEANOGRAPHY. ANNUAL REPORT. see *FISH AND FISHERIES*

551.46 AT ISSN 0519-5659
COMMONWEALTH SCIENTIFIC AND INDUSTRIAL RESEARCH ORGANIZATION. DIVISION OF FISHERIES AND OCEANOGRAPHY. CIRCULAR. 1940. irreg., 1971, latest. free. C. S. I. R. O., Division of Fisheries and Oceanography, Box 21, Cronulla, N.S.W. 2230, Australia.

COMMONWEALTH SCIENTIFIC AND INDUSTRIAL RESEARCH ORGANIZATION. DIVISION OF FISHERIES AND OCEANOGRAPHY. REPORT. see *FISH AND FISHERIES*

551.2 551 UK ISSN 0069-9691
CONTRIBUTIONS TO MARINE SCIENCE. 1957. a. available on exchange. University College of North Wales., Marine Science Laboratories, Menai Bridge, Anglesey, Wales. circ. 140.

551.46 DK ISSN 0070-2668
DANA-REPORT. (Carlsberg Foundation's oceanographical expedition round the world 1928-30 and previous Dana expeditions) (Text in English; occasionally French or German) 1934. irreg. price varies. (Carlsberg Foundation) Scandinavian Science Press Ltd., Christiansholms Parallelvej 2, DK-2930 Klampenborg, Denmark. Ed. E. Bertelsen. cum.index: 1934-1969.

551.46 IS ISSN 0070-3095
DEAD SEA WORKS, BEERSHEBA, ISRAEL. REPORT OF THE DIRECTORS. (English translation of Hebrew text) 1963-64. a. ‡ Dead Sea Works, Ltd., Beersheba, Israel. circ. 1,000.

551.46 GW ISSN 0070-4164
DEUTSCHE HYDROGRAPHISCHE ZEITSCHRIFT. ERGAENZUNGSHEFT. REIHE A. 1952. irreg., no. 15, 1978. Deutsches Hydrographisches Institut, Bernhard-Nocht-Str. 78, 2000 Hamburg 4, W. Germany (B.R.D.) Eds. G. Heise, H. Walden.

551.46 GW ISSN 0070-4172
DEUTSCHE HYDROGRAPHISCHE ZEITSCHRIFT. ERGAENZUNGSHEFT. REIHE B. 1956. irreg., no. 15, 1980. Deutsches Hydrographisches Institut, Bernhard-Nocht-Str. 78, 000 Hamburg 4, W. Germany (B.R.D.) Eds. G. Heise, H. Walden.

551.46 GW ISSN 0070-4458
DEUTSCHES HYDROGRAPHISCHES INSTITUT. JAHRESBERICHT. 1947. a. DM.6.50. Deutsches Hydrographisches Institut, Bernhard-Nocht-Str. 78, 2000 Hamburg 4, W. Germany (B.R.D.) circ. 2,300.

551.46 US
DIRECTORY OF MARINE SCIENTISTS IN THE UNITED STATES. 1950. irreg., latest issue 1975. $6.50. National Academy of Sciences, Ocean Affairs Board, 2101 Constitution Ave., Washington, DC 20018. Ed. Richard C. Vetter.
Until 1975: Directory of Oceanographers in the United States (ISSN 0070-5969); Until 1964: International Directory of Oceanographers.

551.46 UK ISSN 0070-6698
DISCOVERY REPORTS. 1929. irreg. price varies. Institute of Oceanographic Sciences, Wormley, Godalming, Surrey GU8 5UB, England. Ed. P. M. David. Indexed: Biol.Abstr. Aqua.Sci.&Fish.Abstr.

551.46 574 US ISSN 0070-7481
DUKE UNIVERSITY. COOPERATIVE OCEANOGRAPHIC PROGRAM. PROGRESS REPORT. 1965. a. free. Duke University Marine Laboratory, Cooperative Oceanographic Program, Beaufort, NC 28516. circ. 500.

551.46 NE ISSN 0078-3226
ELSEVIER OCEANOGRAPHY SERIES. 1964. irreg., vol. 30, 1980. price varies. Elsevier Scientific Publishing Co., Box 211, 1000 AE Amsterdam, Netherlands.

EPIMENIDES/EPIMENIS. see *ASTRONOMY*

551.4 FI ISSN 0357-1076
FINNISH MARINE RESEARCH. (Text mainly in English) 1920. irreg., no. 246, 1979. price varies. Merentutkimuslaitos - Institute of Marine Research, Box 14 166, SF-00141 Helsinki 14, Finland (Orders to: Government Printing Centre, Box 516, SF-00101 Helsinki 10, Finland) Ed. Paavo Tulkki. (back issues avail) Indexed: Biol. Abstr. Ocean.Abstr. Pcllut.Abstr.
Formerly (until 1978): Finland. Merentutkimuslaitos. Julkaisu (ISSN 0025-9985)

FLINDERS INSTITUTE FOR ATMOSPHERIC AND MARINE SCIENCES. COMPUTING REPORTS. see *METEOROLOGY*

FLINDERS INSTITUTE FOR ATMOSPHERIC AND MARINE SCIENCES. RESEARCH REPORTS. see *METEOROLOGY*

FLINDERS INSTITUTE FOR ATMOSPHERIC AND MARINE SCIENCES. TECHNICAL REPORTS. see *METEOROLOGY*

551.5 AT
FLINDERS INSTITUTE FOR ATMOSPHERIC AND MARINE SCIENCES. CRUISE REPORTS. 1972. irreg., no. 7, 1978. Flinders Institute for Atmospheric and Marine Sciences, Bedford Park, S.A. 5042, Australia. Ed. Peter Schwerdtfeger. circ. 150.

551.2 US ISSN 0095-0157
FLORIDA MARINE RESEARCH PUBLICATIONS. 1973. irreg., approx. 5/yr. free. Department of Natural Resources, Marine Research Laboratory, 100 8th Ave. S.E., St. Petersburg, FL 33701. Ed. Dr. K.A. Steidinger. charts. illus. circ. 1,000. Indexed: Biol.Abstr. Ocean.Abstr. Aqua.Sci. & Fish.Abstr. Commer.Fish.Abstr. Deep Sea Res. & Oceanogr.Abstr. Zoo.Rec.
Supersedes its Educational Series, Leaflet Series, Professional Papers, Saltwater Fishery Leaflets, Special Scientific Report, and Technical Series.

551.46 FR ISSN 0336-3112
FRANCE. CENTRE NATIONAL POUR L'EXPLOITATION DES OCEANS. CENTRE OCEANOLOGIQUE DE BRETAGNE. RECUEIL DES TRAVAUX. 1972. irreg; 1978, no. 6. Centre National pour l'Exploitation des Oceans, Centre Oceanologique de Bretagne, 29 N - Plouzane, France (Subscr. to: Centre Oceanologique de Bretagne, Section Documentation, B.P. 337, 29273 Brest Cedex, France) Ed. Raoul Piboubes. Indexed: Biol.Abstr. Bull.Signal. Chem.Abstr. Ocean.Abstr. Poll.Abstr. Bibl.Geogr.Int. Ocean.Abstr.Bibl.

551.46 FR ISSN 0335-8259
FRANCE. CENTRE NATIONAL POUR L'EXPLOITATION DES OCEANS. COLLOQUES. ACTES. 1971. irreg; 1979, no. 7. Centre National pour l'Exploitation des Oceans, Centre Oceanologique de Bretagne, 29 N - Plouzane, France (Subscr. to: Centre Oceanologique de Bretagne, Section Documentation, B.P. 337, 29273 Brest Cedex, France) Ed. Raoul Piboubes. Indexed: Biol.Abstr. Bull.Signal. Chem.Abstr. Ocean.Abstr. Poll.Abstr. Bibl.Geogr.Int. Ocean.Abstr.Bibl.

551.46 347.75 FR ISSN 0339-2910
FRANCE. CENTRE NATIONAL POUR L'EXPLOITATION DES OCEANS. PUBLICATIONS. SERIE: RAPPORTS ECONOMIQUES ET JURIDIQUES. 1973. irreg; 1978, no. 5. Centre National pour l'Exploitation des Oceans, Centre Oceanologique de Bretagne, 29 N - Plouzane, France (Subscr. to: Centre Oceanologique de Bretagne, Section Documentation, B.P. 337, 29273 Brest Cedex, France) Ed. Raoul Piboubes. Indexed: Biol.Abstr. Bull.Signal. Chem.Abstr. Ocean.Abstr. Poll.Abstr. Bibl.Geogr.Int. Ocean.Abstr.Bibl. Zoo.Rec.

551.46 FR ISSN 0339-2899
FRANCE. CENTRE NATIONAL POUR L'EXPLOITATION DES OCEANS. PUBLICATIONS. SERIE: RAPPORTS SCIENTIFIQUES ET TECHNIQUES. 1971. irreg; 1978, no. 38. Centre National pour l'Exploitation des Oceans, Centre Oceanologique de Bretagne, 29 N - Plouzane, France (Subscr. to: Centre Oceanologique de Bretagne, Section Documentation, B.P. 337, 29273 Brest Cedex, France) Ed. Raoul Piboubes. Indexed: Biol.Abstr. Bull.Signal. Chem.Abstr. Ocean.Abstr. Poll.Abstr. Bibl.Geogr.Int. Ocean.Abstr.Bibl. Zoo.Rec.

551.46 FR ISSN 0339-2902
FRANCE. CENTRE NATIONAL POUR L'EXPLOITATION DES OCEANS. PUBLICATIONS. SERIE: RESULTATS DES CAMPAGNES A LA MER. 1971. irreg. Centre National pour l'Exploitation des Oceans, Centre Oceanologique de Bretagne, 29 N - Plouzane, France (Subscr. to: Centre Oceanologique de Bretagne, Section Documentation, B.P. 337, 29273 Brest Cedex) Ed. Raoul Piboubes. charts. stat. Indexed: Biol.Abstr. Bull.Signal. Chem.Abstr. Ocean.Abstr. Poll.Abstr. Bibl.Geogr.Int. Ocean Abstr.Bibl. Zoo.Rec.

551.4 GW ISSN 0084-9774
GEZEITENTAFELN. 1879. a. DM.24. Deutsches Hydrographisches Institut, Bernhard-Nocht-Str. 78, 2000 Hamburg 4, W. Germany (B.R.D.) circ. 1,600. (tabloid format)

551.46 SW
GOETEBORGS UNIVERSITET. OCEANOGRAFISKA INSTITUTIONEN. REPORTS. (Text in English and Swedish) 1969. irreg., no. 34, 1979. free. Goeteborgs Universitet, Oceanografiska Institutionen, Box 4038, 400 40 Goeteborg, Sweden. circ. 100.
Supersedes: Oceanografiska Institutet, Goeteborg. Meddelanden (ISSN 0072-5072)

551.46 US ISSN 0072-9027
GULF RESEARCH REPORTS. 1961. a. price varies; free to qualified personnel. Gulf Coast Research Laboratory, Ocean Springs, MS 39564. Ed. Harold D. Howse. circ. 725. (reprint service avail. from UMI) Indexed: Aqua.Sci. & Fish Abstr. Curr.Cont. Mar.Sci.Cont.Tab.

551.46 639.2 JA ISSN 0439-3511
HOKKAIDO UNIVERSITY. FACULTY OF FISHERIES. DATA RECORD OF OCEANOGRAPHIC OBSERVATIONS AND EXPLORATORY FISHING/KAIYO CHOSA GYOGYO SHIKEN YOHO. (Text in Japanese and European languages) 1957. a. exchange basis. Hokkaido University, Faculty of Fisheries, 3-1-1 Minato-machi, Hakodate, Hokkaido 040, Hokkaido 041, Japan. circ. 600.

551.46 DK
I C E S OCEANOGRAPHIC DATA LISTS AND INVENTORIES. (Text in English) 1971. irreg. price varies. International Council for the Exploration of the Sea, Palaegade 2, DK-1261 Copenhagen K, Denmark (Subscr. to: C. A. Reitzels Forlag, Noerre Soegade 35, 1370 Copenhagen K, Denmark) circ. 300.
Supersedes: I C E S Oceanographic Data Lists (ISSN 0074-4328) & International Council for the Exploration of the Sea. Bulletin Hydrographique.

551.46 SP
INMERSION Y CIENCIA. nos. 8-9, Jun. 1975. irreg. Federacion Espanola de Actividades Subacuaticas, Departamento de Actividades Cientificas, Santalo 15, Barcelona 16, Spain. Ed. Antonio Ballester. bibl. charts. illus.

551.46 574.92 GW ISSN 0068-0915
INSTITUT FUER MEERESFORSCHUNG, BREMERHAVEN. VEROEFFENTLICHUNGEN. (Text in German; summaries in English) 1952. irreg., vol. 14, 1974. DM.20($10) (approx.) per issue. Institut fuer Meeresforschung, Am Handelshafen 12, Bremerhaven, W. Germany (B.R.D.) (Co-sponsor: Bremen Senator fuer Wissenschaft und Kunst) Eds. S. A. Gerlach, A. Gaertner. Indexed: Biol.Abstr. Chem.Abstr. Aqua.Sci. & Fish.Abstr. Mar.Sci.Cont.Tab.

551.46 MC ISSN 0304-5714
INSTITUT OCEANOGRAPHIQUE. MEMOIRES. (Text in French; summaries in English and French) 1904. irreg., no. 9,1975. price varies. Musee Oceanographique de Monaco, Ave. Saint-Martin, Monte Carlo, Monaco. illus. (back issues avail) Indexed: Biol. Abstr. Ref. Zh.

551.46 JA
INSTITUTE FOR SEA TRAINING. JOURNAL. (Text in Japanese, summaries in English) 1951. irreg. Institute for Sea Training, 2-1-3 Kasumigaseki, Chiyoda-ku, Tokyo 100, Japan. Ed.Bd.

551.46 UK ISSN 0309-4472
INSTITUTE OF OCEANOGRAPHIC SCIENCES. ANNUAL REPORT. 1973. a. £3. Institute of Oceanographic Sciences, Wormley, Godalming, Surrey GU8 5UB, England.

551.46 UK ISSN 0309-7463
INSTITUTE OF OCEANOGRAPHIC SCIENCES. COLLECTED REPRINTS. 1953. a. available on exchange. ‡ Institute of Oceanographic Sciences, Wormley, Godalming, Surrey GU8 5UB, England. Ed. D. W. Privett.
Formerly: Wormley, England (Surrey) National Institute of Oceanography. Collected Reprints (ISSN 0084-2605)

551.46 SP ISSN 0074-0195
INSTITUTO ESPANOL DE OCEANOGRAFIA. BOLETIN. (Text in Spanish; summaries in English and French) 1948. irreg., 1969, no. 171. Instituto Espanol de Oceanografia, Alcala 27, Madrid 14, Spain.

551.46 SP ISSN 0074-0209
INSTITUTO ESPANOL DE OCEANOGRAFIA. TRABAJOS. (Text in Spanish; summaries in French) 1929. irreg. Instituto Espanol de Oceanografia, Alcala 27, Madrid 14, Spain.

551 AG ISSN 0325-6790
INSTITUTO NACIONAL DE INVESTIGACION Y DESARROLLO PESQUERO. SERIE CONTRIBUCIONES. (Text in Spanish or English; summaries in Spanish, English and French) 1961. irreg. available on exchange. ‡ Instituto Nacional de Investigacion y Desarrollo Pesquero, Casilla de Correo 175, 7600 Mar del Plata, Argentina. index. Indexed: Ocean.Abstr. Aqua.Sci.& Fish. Abstr.
Formerly: Instituto di Biologia Marina. Serie Contribuciones (ISSN 0076-4302)

551.46 IT ISSN 0082-6456
INSTITUTO SPERIMENTALE TALASSOGRAFICO, TRIESTE. PUBBLICAZIONE. 1919. irreg.; no. 528, 1976. price varies. Istituto Sperimentale Talassografico, Viale R. Gessi, 2, 34123 Trieste, Italy. Indexed: Ocean.Abstr. Pollut.Abstr.

551.46 UN ISSN 0074-1175
INTERGOVERNMENTAL OCEANOGRAPHIC COMMISSION. TECHNICAL SERIES. (Text in English, French, Russian and Spanish) 1965. irreg., 1972, no. 10. price varies. Unesco, 7-9 Place de Fontenoy, 75700 Paris, France (Dist. in U.S. by: Unipub, 345 Park Ave. S., New York, NY 10010)

551.46 FR
INTERNATIONAL ASSOCIATION FOR THE PHYSICAL SCIENCE OF OCEANOGRAPHY. PROCES-VERBAUX. (Text in French or English) 1934. irreg. price varies. International Association for the Physical Science of Oceanography, Publications Office, 39 rue Gay Lussac, Paris, France. circ. 600. (back issues avail.)

INTERNATIONAL ASSOCIATION OF THEORETICAL AND APPLIED LIMNOLOGY. PROCEEDINGS/INTERNATIONALE VEREINIGUNG FUER THEORETISCHE UND ANGEWANDTE LIMNOLOGIE. VERHANDLUNGEN. see *EARTH SCIENCES — Hydrology*

551.46 DK ISSN 0373-2045
INTERNATIONAL COUNCIL FOR THE EXPLORATION OF THE SEA. BULLETIN STATISTIQUE. 1906. a. price varies. International Council for the Exploration of the Sea, Palaegade 2, DK-1261 Copenhagen K, Denmark (Subscr. to: C. A. Reitzels Forlag, Noerre Soegade 35, DK-1370 Copenhagen K, Denmark) circ. 450 (approx.)

551.46 DK ISSN 0074-431X
INTERNATIONAL COUNCIL FOR THE
EXPLORATION OF THE SEA. COOPERATIVE
RESEARCH REPORTS. (Series A and B merged
into one series in 1972) 1962. irreg. price varies.
International Council for the Exploration of the Sea,
Palaegade 2, DK-1261 Copenhagen K, Denmark
(Subscr. to: C. A. Reitzels Forlag, Noerre Soegade
35, DK-1370 Copenhagen K, Denmark) circ. 400.

551.46 DK ISSN 0020-6466
INTERNATIONAL COUNCIL FOR THE
EXPLORATION OF THE SEA. JOURNAL DU
CONSEIL. (Text in English and French) 1926.
irreg. Kr.120. International Council for the
Exploration of the Sea, Palaegade 2, DK-1261
Copenhagen K, Denmark (Subscr. to: C. A. Reitzels
Forlag, Noerre Soegade 35, DK-1370 Copenhagen
K, Denmark) Ed. F. R. Harden Jones. bk. rev.
cum.index (vols. 1-25) circ. 950. Indexed:
Chem.Abstr. Biol.Abstr. Ocean.Abstr.
Pollut.Abstr.

551.46 DK ISSN 0074-4336
INTERNATIONAL COUNCIL FOR THE
EXPLORATION OF THE SEA. RAPPORTS ET
PROCES-VERBAUX DES REUNIONS. 1903.
irreg., no. 175, 1980. price varies. International
Council for the Exploration of the Sea, Palaegade 2,
DK-1261 Copenhagen K, Denmark (Subscr. to: C.
A. Reitzels Forlag, Noerre Soegade 35, DK-1370
Copenhagen K, Denmark) circ. 500(approx.)
Indexed: Biol.Abstr.

551.48 MC ISSN 0074-6274
INTERNATIONAL HYDROGRAPHIC
CONFERENCE. REPORTS OF PROCEEDINGS.
(Editions in English and French) 1919.
quinquennial, 11th, 1977, Monte Carlo. 65 F.
International Hydrographic Organization, 7 Ave.
President J. F. Kennedy, Monte Carlo, Monaco.
(reprint service avail. from ISI,UMI)

551.46 MC
INTERNATIONAL HYDROGRAPHIC
ORGANIZATION. YEARBOOK. (Text in French
and English) 1928. a. 40 F. International
Hydrographic Organization, 7 Ave. President J.F.
Kennedy, Monte Carlo, Monaco. circ. 240. (reprint
service avail. from ISI, UMI)
Formerly: International Hydrographic Bureau.
Yearbook (ISSN 0074-6282)

551.467 UN ISSN 0074-6320
INTERNATIONAL INDIAN OCEAN
EXPEDITION. COLLECTED REPRINTS. (Text
in original language of reprints) 1962. irreg.; vol. 8,
1970. distrib. only to libraries, foundations, etc.
Unesco, 7-9 Place de Fontenoy, 75700 Paris,
France. index.

551.46 UN ISSN 0538-8880
INTERNATIONAL OCEANOGRAPHIC TABLES.
(Prepared Under the Supervision of the Joint Panel
on Oceanographic Tables and Standards. Published
in Cooperation with the National Institute of
Oceanography, Great Britain) (Text in English,
French, Spanish and Russian) 1966. Unesco Press, 7
Place de Fontenoy, F-75700 Paris, France (Dist. in
U.S. by: Unipub, 345 Park Ave., S., New York, NY
10010)

551.4 IS ISSN 0304-7423
ISRAEL OCEANOGRAPHIC AND
LIMNOLOGICAL RESEARCH. ANNUAL
REPORT. (Text in English) 1972. a. Israel
Oceanographic and Limnological Research, Tel
Shikmona, Box 1793, Haifa, Israel.

551.46 JA
JAPAN OCEANOLOGY DIRECTORY/KAIYO
SANGYO JIMMEIROKU. 1971. irreg. 5000 Yen.
Research Institute for Ocean Economics - Kaiyo
Sangyo Kenkyu Kai, c/o Murufuji Bldg., 3-1-10
Shimbashi, Minato-ku, Tokyo 105, Japan.

551.46 US ISSN 0075-3858
JOHNS HOPKINS OCEANOGRAPHIC STUDIES.
1962. irreg. 1977, no. 6. price varies. Johns Hopkins
University Press, Baltimore, MD 21218.

551.4 623 333.7 GW ISSN 0452-7739
DIE KUESTE; Archiv fuer Forschung und Technik an
der Nord- und Ostsee. 1952. irreg. (1-2/yr.) price
varies. (Kuratorium fuer Forschung im
Kuesteningenieurwesen) Westholsteinische
Verlagsanstalt Boyens und Co., Am Wulf-Isebrand-
Platz, Postfach 1880, 2240 Heide, W. Germany
(B.R.D.) Ed. Harald Goehren. illus.

LABORATORIO DI TECNOLOGIA DELLA
PESCA. QUADERNI. see FISH AND FISHERIES

551.46 US
LECTURE NOTES ON COASTAL AND
ESTUARINE STUDIES. 1980. irreg. price varies.
Springer-Verlag, 175 Fifth Ave., New York, NY
10010 (Also Berlin, Heidelberg, Vienna) Ed.Bd.
(reprint service avail. from ISI)

551.46 CN
MCGILL UNIVERSITY, MONTREAL. MARINE
SCIENCES CENTRE. MANUSCRIPT REPORT.
1966. irreg. Can.$3 per no. ‡ McGill University,
P.O. Box 6070, Station a, Montreal H3C 3G1,
Canada. circ. controlled. Indexed: Ocean.Abstr.

551.4 IO ISSN 0079-0435
MARINE RESEARCH IN INDONESIA. (Text in
English; summaries in English and German) 1956.
irreg. $2. National Institute of Oceanography -
Lembaga Oseanologi Nasiona, Jalan Aktuarum, Box
580, Jakarta Barat, Indonesia. Ed. Gatot Rahadjo.

387 US ISSN 0198-9618
MARINER'S CATALOG. 1973. a. $7.95.
International Marine Publishing Co., 21 Elm St.,
Camden, ME 04843.

551.46 US ISSN 0085-0683
MEMOIRS OF THE HOURGLASS CRUISES. 1969.
irreg. free. Department of Natural Resources,
Marine Research Laboratory, 100-8th Ave. S.E., St.
Petersburg, FL 33701. charts. illus. circ. 1,000.
(tabloid format) Indexed: Aqua.Sci. & Fish Abstr.
Biol.Abstr. Deep Sea Res. & Oceanogr. Abstr.
Ocean Abstr. Zoo.Rec.

551.46 574.92 CN
MEMORIAL UNIVERSITY, ST. JOHN'S,
NEWFOUNDLAND. MARINE SCIENCES
RESEARCH LABORATORY. M.S.R.L.
BULLETIN. irreg. Memorial University, Marine
Sciences Research Laboratory., St. John's,
Newfoundland, Canada. stat.
Continues: Memorial University, St. John's
Newfoundland. Library Bulletin.

550 GW ISSN 0543-5900
"METEOR" FORSCHUNGSERGEBNISSE. REIHE
A. ALLGEMEINES, PHYSIK UND CHEMIE
DES MEERES. (Text in German; summaries in
English) 1966. irreg., no. 20, 1978. price varies.
(Deutsche Forschungsgemeinschaft) Gebrueder
Borntraeger Verlagsbuchhandlung, Johannesstr. 3A,
7000 Stuttgart 1, W. Germany (B.R.D.) Eds. W.
Hansen, G. Siedler, H. Walden. charts. illus.

"METEOR" FORSCHUNGSERGEBNISSE. REIHE
C. GEOLOGIE UND GEOPHYSIK. see EARTH
SCIENCES — Geophysics

"METEOR" FORSCHUNGSERGEBNISSE. REIHE
D. BIOLOGIE. see BIOLOGY

551.46 MX
MEXICO. DIRECCION GENERAL DE
OCEANOGRAFIA. CALENDARIO GRAFICO
DE MAREAS. 1971. a. $3. (Direccion General de
Oceanografia) Universidad Nacional Autonoma de
Mexico, Instituto de Geofisica, Circuito Exterior,
Ciudad Universitaria, Mexico 20, D.F., Mexico.

333.9 US ISSN 0095-6783
MISSISSIPPI MARINE RESOURCES COUNCIL.
ANNUAL REPORT. a. free. Mississippi Marine
Resources Council, Box 959, Long Beach, MS
39560. illus. Key Title: Annual Report - Mississippi
Marine Resources Council.

551.46 UN ISSN 0077-104X
MONOGRAPHS ON OCEANOGRAPHIC
METHODOLOGY. 1966. irreg., 1973, no. 3.
Unesco, 7-9 Place de Fontenoy, 75700 Paris, France
(Dist. in U.S. by: Unipub, 345 Park Ave. S., New
York, NY 10010)

551.46 UR ISSN 0076-4477
MORSKAYA GEOLOGIYA I GEOFIZIKA/
MARINE GEOLOGY AND GEOPHYSICS. (Text
in Russian; summaries in English) 1970. biennial.
$1. Vsesoyuznyi Issledovatel'skii Institut Morskoi
Geologii i Geofiziki, Ul. Lacpliesa, 13, Riga, U. S. S.
R. Ed. K. Springis.

MORSKI INSTYTUT RYBACKI, GDYNIA.
PRACE. SERIA A: OCEANOGRAFICZNO -
ICHTIOLOGICZNA. see FISH AND FISHERIES

551.46 NZ ISSN 0110-618X
N Z O I RECORDS. 1972. irreg. exchange basis. New
Zealand Oceanographic Institute, P.O. Box 12-346,
Wellington North, New Zealand. Ed. D.P. Gordon.

551.468 JA
NATIONAL INSTITUTE OF POLAR RESEARCH .
MEMOIRS. SERIES D: OCEANOGRAPHY.
(Text in English) 1964. irreg. exchange basis.
National Institute of Polar Research - Kokuritsu
Kyokuchi Kenkyujyo, 9-10 Kaga, 1-chome, Itabashi-
ku, Tokyo 173, Japan. Ed. Takesi Nagata. circ.
1,000. Indexed: Curr.Antarc.Lit.
Supersedes: Japanese Antarctic Research
Expedition, 1956-1962. Scientific Reports. Series D:
Oceanography (ISSN 0075-3386)

551.46 US ISSN 0361-2805
NATIONAL OCEAN SURVEY. COLLECTED
REPRINTS. irreg. U.S. National Ocean Survey,
Rockville, MD 20850. illus. Key Title: Collected
Reprints-National Ocean Survey.
Continues: Atlantic Oceanographic and
Meteorological Laboratories. Collected Reprints.

551.46 NZ ISSN 0083-789X
NEW ZEALAND OCEANOGRAPHIC INSTITUTE.
COLLECTED REPRINTS. 1952. a. exchange basis.
New Zealand Oceanographic Institute, P.O. Box 12-
346, Wellington North, New Zealand. Ed. D. P.
Gordon. index. Indexed: Ocean.Abstr. Pollut.Abstr.

551.46 NZ ISSN 0083-7903
NEW ZEALAND OCEANOGRAPHIC INSTITUTE.
MEMOIR. 1955. irreg. price varies. New Zealand
Oceanographic Institute, P.O. Box 12-346,
Wellington North, New Zealand. Ed. G.
Stephenson. index.

551.46 NL ISSN 0078-2130
O. R. S. T. O. M. RECUEIL DE TRAVAUX.
OCEANOGRAPHIE. (Text in French; summaries
in English) 1969. a. available on exchange. Office de
la Recherche Scientifique et Technique Outre-Mer,
Centre O.R.S.T.O.M., B.P. A5, Noumea, New
Caledonia. circ. 270.

623 US
OCEAN ENGINEERING: A WILEY SERIES. 1973.
irreg., latest, 1979. John Wiley & Sons, Inc., 605
Third Ave., New York, NY 10016. Ed. M.E.
McCormick.

623 US ISSN 0078-3137
OCEAN ENGINEERING INFORMATION
SERIES. 1969. irreg., vol. 7, 1975. price varies.
Ocean Engineering Information Service, P.O. Box
989, La Jolla, CA 92037. author index.

551.46 US
OCEAN SERIES. a. price varies. Gordon and Breach
Science Publishers, One Park Ave., New York, NY
10016. Ed. Donald A. Wilson.

551.46 US
OCEAN YEARBOOK. 1978. a. $35. (University of
Malta, International Ocean Institute, MM)
University of Chicago Press, 5801 S. Ellis Ave,
Chicago, IL 60637 (Orders to: 11030 Langley Ave.,
Chicago, IL 60628) Eds. Elisabeth Mann Borgese,
Norton M. Ginsburg. (reprint service avail. from
UMI,ISI)

551.46 SA ISSN 0078-320X
OCEANOGRAPHIC RESEARCH INSTITUTE,
DURBAN. INVESTIGATIONAL REPORT. 1961.
irreg., no. 46, 1976. price varies, free to qualified
personnel. ‡ Oceanographic Research Institute,
Durban, Centenary Aquarium Buildings, 2 West St.,
Durban 4000, South Africa. (Co-sponsor: South
African Association for Marine Biological Research)
circ. controlled. Indexed: Ocean.Abstr.
Aqua.Sci.&Fish.Abstr. Zoo.Rec.

EARTH SCIENCES — OCEANOGRAPHY

551.46 574.92 UK
OCEANOGRAPHY AND MARINE BIOLOGY: AN ANNUAL REVIEW. 1963. a. £35. Aberdeen University Press, Farmers Hall, Aberdeen AB9 2XT, Scotland. Ed. Margaret Barnes.
Formerly: Oceanography and Marine Biology (ISSN 0078-3218)

551.46 PL ISSN 0078-3234
OCEANOLOGIA. (Text in Polish and English; summaries in English) 1971. irreg., no. 11, 1979. 30 Zl. (Polska Akademia Nauk, Komitet Badan Morza) Ossolineum, Publishing House of the Polish Academy of Sciences, Rynek 9, 50-106 Wroclaw, Poland (Dist. by Ars Polona-Ruch, Krakowskie Przedmiescie 7, Warsaw, Poland) Ed. Stanislaw Szymborski.

551.46 UK
OCEANOLOGY INTERNATIONAL. CONFERENCE PAPERS. irreg. Society for Underwater Technology, 1 Birdcage Walk, London SW1H OJJ, England.

551.4 BU
OKEANOLOGIIA. 1975. irreg. 1 lv. per issue. (Bulgarska Akademiia na Naukite) Publishing House of the Bulgarian Academy of Sciences, Ul. Akad. G. Bonchev, 1113 Sofia, Bulgaria. circ. 500.

551.46 US ISSN 0078-7604
PACIFIC MARINE STATION, DILLON BEACH, CALIFORNIA. RESEARCH REPORT. 1961. irreg. University of the Pacific, Pacific Marine Station, Dillon Beach, CA 94929. circ. controlled. (processed)

551.46 US
PACIFIC RIM RESEARCH SERIES. vol. 2, 1977. irreg. price varies. D. C. Heath & Company, 125 Spring St., Lexington, MA 02173. index.

551.46 MM
PROCEEDINGS OF PACEM IN MARIBUS. 1971. a, 8th, 1977, Mexico. price varies. University of Malta, International Ocean Institute, Msida, Malta.

551.46 US ISSN 0079-6611
PROGRESS IN OCEANOGRAPHY. 1963. 4/yr. $70. Pergamon Press, Inc., Journals Division, Maxwell House, Fairview Park, Elmsford, NY 10523 (And Headington Hill Hall, Oxford OX3 OBW, England) Eds. Martin V. Angel, James O'Brien. index. (also avail. in microform from MIM,UMI) Indexed: Biol.Abstr. Chem.Abstr.

551.46 US
RADIONAVIGATION JOURNAL. 1975. a. $4. Wild Goose Association, 4 Townsend Road, Acton, MA 01720. circ. 1,200.

551.46 UN
REPORTS ON MARINE SCIENCE AFFAIRS. 1970. irreg. price varies. World Meteorological Organization, 41 Ave. Giuseppe Motta, 1211 Geneva 20, Switzerland (Dist. in U.S by: Unipub, 345 Park Ave. S., New York, NY 10010)
Formerly: Marine Science Affairs (ISSN 0076-4507)

551.46 US ISSN 0091-1518
S I O: A REPORT ON THE WORK AND PROGRAMS OF SCRIPPS INSTITUTION OF OCEANOGRAPHY. (Report year ends June 30) a. Scripps Institution of Oceanography, La Jolla, CA 92037. illus. Key Title: S.I.O.

551.46 US ISSN 0080-8318
SCRIPPS INSTITUTION OF OCEANOGRAPHY. BULLETIN. 1927. irreg. price varies. University of California Press, 2223 Fulton St., Berkeley, CA 94720.

551.46 US ISSN 0080-8326
SCRIPPS INSTITUTION OF OCEANOGRAPHY. CONTRIBUTIONS. 1893. a. available only on exchange with libraries and scientific institutions. Scripps Institution of Oceanography, La Jolla, CA 92037.

551.46 US ISSN 0080-8334
SCRIPPS INSTITUTION OF OCEANOGRAPHY. DEEP SEA DRILLING PROJECT. INITIAL REPORTS. irreg. Scripps Institution of Oceanography, La Jolla, CA 92037 (Dist. by: Supt. of Documents, Washington, DC 20402)

SEA TECHNOLOGY BUYERS GUIDE/ DIRECTORY. see *ENGINEERING*

551.4 US ISSN 0037-0118
SEAHORSE. 1964. irreg. free. Hydro Products, A Tetra Tech Co., 11777 Sorrento Valley Rd., San Diego, CA 92121. Ed. Irene Anderson. bk. rev. illus. tr.lit. circ. 25,000. Indexed: Ocean.Ind.

SEARS FOUNDATION FOR MARINE RESEARCH. MEMOIRS. see *BIOLOGY*

551.46 574.92 GW ISSN 0080-889X
SENCKENBERGIANA MARITIMA. ZEITSCHRIFT FUER MEERESGEOLOGIE UND MEERESBIOLOGIE. a. DM.72. (Senckenbergische Naturforschende Gesellschaft) Verlag Dr. Waldemar Kramer, Bornheimer Landwehr 57a, Postfach 600445, 6000 Frankfurt 60, W. Germany (B.R.D.) Eds. G. Hertweck, S. Little-Gadow. Indexed: Ocean.Abstr. Pollut.Abstr.

SNOWY MOUNTAINS ENGINEERING CORPORATION. ANNUAL REPORT. see *ENGINEERING*

551.46 US ISSN 0081-8720
STUDIES IN TROPICAL OCEANOGRAPHY. 1963. irreg., no. 12, 1974. price varies. Rosenstiel School of Marine and Atmospheric Science, University of Miami, 4600 Rickenbacker Causeway, Miami, FL 33149. Ed. William Richards. Indexed: Biol.Abstr. Zoo.Rec.

551.46 US ISSN 0082-2922
TEXAS A & M OCEANOGRAPHIC STUDIES. 1970. irreg., vol. 3, 1972. price varies. (Texas A & M University) Gulf Publishing Co., P.O. Box 2608, Houston, TX 77001.

551.46 US ISSN 0069-9640
TEXAS A & M UNIVERSITY. DEPARTMENT OF OCEANOGRAPHY. CONTRIBUTIONS IN OCEANOGRAPHY. 1950. irreg. $25 or exchange basis. Texas A & M University, Department of Oceanography, College Station, TX 77840. abstr. circ. controlled.

551.461 DK
TIDEVANDSTABELLER FOR GROENLAND. (Text in Danish and English) 1966. a. Kr.20. Farvandsdirektoratet, Nautisk Afdeling, Esplanaden 19, 1263 Copenhagen K, Denmark.

TOPICS IN OCEAN ENGINEERING. see *ENGINEERING*

551.46 639.3 TI ISSN 0579-7926
TUNISIA. INSTITUT NATIONAL SCIENTIFIQUE ET TECHNIQUE D'OCEANOGRAPHIE ET DE PECHE. BULLETIN. (Text in French; summaries in Arabic, English, and French) 1966(N.S.) irreg. Institut National Scientifique et Technique d'Oceanographie et de Peche, Salammbo, Tunisia. circ. 1,150. Indexed: Bull.Signal.

551.4 574.92 UN ISSN 0503-4299
UNESCO TECHNICAL PAPERS IN MARINE SCIENCE. 1965. irreg. Unesco, 7-9 Place de Fontenoy, F-75700 Paris, France.

551.46 US ISSN 0082-9625
U. S. COAST GUARD. OCEANOGRAPHIC REPORTS (CG-373 SERIES) 1962. irreg., no. 71, 1976. price varies. U.S. Coast Guard, Oceanographic Unit, 400 7th St., N.W., Washington, DC 20590 (Avail. from: NTIS, Springfield, VA 22151) circ. 500. (also avail. in microfiche) Indexed: Ocean.Abstr. Pollut.Abstr.

U. S. NATIONAL OCEANIC AND ATMOSPHERIC ADMINISTRATION. MANNED UNDERSEA SCIENCE AND TECHNOLOGY PROGRAM; REPORT. see *ENGINEERING*

U.S. NATIONAL OCEANIC AND ATMOSPHERIC ADMINISTRATION. NATIONAL CLIMATIC CENTER. MARINE CLIMATOLOGICAL SUMMARIES. see *METEOROLOGY*

551.46 US
U. S. NATIONAL OCEANIC AND ATMOSPHERIC ADMINISTRATION. TECHNICAL BULLETIN. 1964. irreg. free. ‡ U.S. National Oceanic and Atmospheric Administration, Engineering Support Office, Rockville, MD 20852. circ. 3,000.
Former titles: U.S. National Oceanic and Atmospheric Administration. Test and Evaluation Laboratory. Technical Bulletin; U. S. National Oceanographic Instrumentation Center. Technical Bulletin.

551.46 US
U. S. NATIONAL OCEANIC AND ATMOSPHERIC ADMINISTRATIONN. TECHNICAL MEMORANDUM. 1969. irreg. free. ‡ U. S. National Oceanic and Atmospheric Administration, Engineering Support Office, Rockville, MD 20852. circ. 3,000.
Former titles: U. S. National Oceanic and Atmospheric Adminnistration. Test and Evaluation Office. Technical Memorandum; U. S. National Oceanographic Instrumentation Center. Technical Memorandum.

551.46 US ISSN 0091-9500
U. S. NATIONAL OCEANOGRAPHIC DATA CENTER. KEY TO OCEANOGRAPHIC RECORDS DOCUMENTATION. 1973. irreg., no. 6, 1976. U. S. National Oceanographic Data Center, Washington, DC 20235.

U. S. NATIONAL WEATHER SERVICE. DATA ACQUISITION DIVISION. MARINE SURFACE OBSERVATIONS. see *METEOROLOGY*

551.46 574.92 CK
UNIVERSIDAD DE BOGOTA JORGE TADEO LOZANO. MUSEO DEL MAR. BOLETIN. (Text in Spanish; summaries in English) 1970. a. Col.$70($3) Universidad de Bogota Jorge Tadeo Lozano, Museo del Mar, Calle 23 No. 4-47, Bogota, Colombia. Ed. Jorge Barreto Soulier. bibl. illus. circ. 1,200(controlled) (cards)
Marine biology

551.46 VE ISSN 0590-3351
UNIVERSIDAD DE ORIENTE. INSTITUTO OCEANOGRAFICO. CUADERNOS OCEANOGRAFICOS. irreg. Bol.$12($3) Universidad de Oriente, Instituto Oceanografico, Biblioteca, Cumana, Venezuela.

551.46 VE
UNIVERSIDAD DE ORIENTE. INSTITUTO OCEANOGRAFICO. REGISTRO DE DATOS OCEANOGRAFICOS Y METEOROLOGICOS. 1971. irreg. $3 per no. Universidad de Oriente, Instituto Oceanografico, Apartado Postal 94, Cumana, Venezuela. Ed. J. M. Sellier Civrieux. circ. controlled.

551.46 BL ISSN 0373-5524
UNIVERSIDADE DE SAO PAULO. INSTITUTO OCEANOGRAFICO. BOLETIM. (Text in various languages; summaries in English) 1950. a. price varies; avail. on exchange. Universidade de Sao Paulo, Instituto Oceanografico, Cidade Universitaria, Butanta, 05508 Sao Paulo, SP, Brazil. circ. 650. Indexed: Biol.Abstr. Ocean.Abstr. Aqua.Sci. & Fish.Abstr. Deep Sea Res. & Oceanogr.Abstr. Zoo.Rec.

550 BL ISSN 0100-5146
UNIVERSIDADE DE SAO PAULO. INSTITUTO OCEANOGRAFICO. PUBLICACAO ESPECIAL. (Multilingual Text; summaries in English) 1972. irreg., no. 4, 1977. price varies; avail. on exchange. Universidade de Sao Paulo, Instituto Oceanografico, Cidade Universitaria, Butanta, 05508 Sao Paulo, SP, Brazil. circ. 800.

551 BL ISSN 0100-5197
UNIVERSIDADE DE SAO PAULO. INSTITUTO OCEANOGRAPHICO. RELATORIO DE CRUZEIROS. (Text in various languages; summaries in English) 1976. irreg.,no. 4, 1980. price varies; avail. on exchange. Universidade de Sao Paulo, Instituto Oceanografico, Cidade Universitaria, Butanta, 05508 Sao Paulo, S.P., Brazil. circ. 650.

551 BL ISSN 0100-5146
UNIVERSIDADE DE SAO PAULO. INSTITUTO
OCEANOGRAFICO. RELATORIO INTERNO.
(Text in various languages; summaries in English)
1974. irreg.; no. 9, 1980. price varies; avail. on
exchange. Universidade de Sao Paulo, Instituto
Oceanografico, Cidade Universitaria, Butanta, 05508
Sao Paulo, S.P., Brazil.

551.46 US
UNIVERSITY OF CALIFORNIA, SANTA CRUZ.
COASTAL MARINE LABORATORY. SPECIAL
PUBLICATION. vol. 3, 1975. irreg., no. 9, 1978.
University of California, Santa Cruz, Coastal Marine
Laboratory, Santa Cruz, CA 95064.

551.46 II
UNIVERSITY OF COCHIN. DEPARTMENT OF
MARINE SCIENCES. BULLETIN. (Text in
English) 1963. irreg. Rs.20 per no. University of
Cochin, Department of Marine Sciences, Foreshore
Rd., Ernakulam, Cochin 16, Kerala, India. Ed. C. V.
Kurian. (back issues avail)
 Formerly: University of Cochin. Department of
Marine Biology and Oceanography. Bulletin.

551.46 MM
UNIVERSITY OF MALTA. INTERNATIONAL
OCEAN INSTITUTE. OCCASIONAL PAPERS.
Short title: I O I Occasional Papers. 1973. irreg., no.
6, 1978. price varies. Malta University Press, Msida,
Malta. circ. 200. Indexed: Chem.Abstr.
Ocean.Abstr.

551.46 574.92 US
UNIVERSITY OF RHODE ISLAND. GRADUATE
SCHOOL OF OCEANOGRAPHY. COLLECTED
REPRINTS. 1958. irreg., vol. 10, 1973. exchange
only. ‡ University of Rhode Island, Graduate School
of Oceanography, Kingston, RI 02881. circ. 350.
 Vols. 1-6: University of Rhode Island.
Narragansett Marine Laboratory. Collected Reprints
(ISSN 0077-281X)

551.46 574.92 US
UNIVERSITY OF RHODE ISLAND. GRADUATE
SCHOOL OF OCEANOGRAPHY. MARINE
TECHNICAL REPORTS. 1950. irreg., latest issue,
no. 35. not available for distribution. University of
Rhode Island, Graduate School of Oceanography,
Kingston, RI 02881.
 Formerly: Narragansett Marine Laboratory.
Technical Reports (ISSN 0077-2836)

551.46 US ISSN 0077-2828
UNIVERSITY OF RHODE ISLAND.
NARRAGANSETT MARINE LABORATORY.
OCCASIONAL PUBLICATION. 1962. irreg.,
1973, no. 5. price varies. University of Rhode
Island, Graduate School of Oceanography, Kingston,
RI 02881.

551.46 US
UNIVERSITY OF SOUTH CAROLINA. BELLE W.
BARUCH LIBRARY IN MARINE SCIENCE
AND COASTAL RESEARCH. COLLECTED
PAPERS. 1973. irreg (approx. 2/yr) $27.50.
University of South Carolina Press, Columbia, SC
29208. charts. illus.

551.46 JA ISSN 0564-6898
UNIVERSITY OF TOKYO. OCEAN RESEARCH
INSTITUTE. BULLETIN/TOKYO DAIGAKU
KAIYO KENKYUSHO. (Text in English) 1967.
irreg. exchange basis. University of Tokyo, Ocean
Research Institute - Tokyo Daigaku Kaiyo
Kenkyusho, 1-15-1 Minamidai, Nakano-ku, Tokyo
164, Japan. stat.

551.46 US ISSN 0083-7520
UNIVERSITY OF WASHINGTON. DEPARTMENT
OF OCEANOGRAPHY. CONTRIBUTION. 1933.
a. University of Washington, Department of
Oceanography, Seattle, WA 98105.

551.46 US
VIRGINIA INSTITUTE OF MARINE SCIENCE,
GLOUCESTER POINT. SPECIAL REPORT IN
APPLIED MARINE SCIENCE AND OCEAN
ENGINEERING. 1955. irreg., no. 202, 1979. $1.
Virginia Institute of Marine Science, Gloucester
Point, VA 23062. (also avail. in microfiche)

551.46 UR
VSESOYUZNYI NAUCHNO-ISSLEDOVATEL'SKII
INSTITUT MORSKOGO RYBNOGO
KHOZYAISTVA I OKEANOGRAFII (VNIRO).
TRUDY. vol. 117, 1976. irreg. price varies.
Ul.Verkhnaya Krasnosel'skaya, 17, Moscow
107140, U.S.S.R. Ed. K. Yablonskaya. circ. 500.

551.46 UK
WHO'S WHO IN OCEAN AND FRESH WATER
SCIENCE. 1978. irreg. Longman Group Ltd.,
Longman House, Burnt Mill, Harlow, Essex CM20
2JE, England (Dist. in U.S. and Canada by: Gale
Research Co. Ltd., Book Tower, Detroit, MI 48226)

551.46 US
WILD GOOSE ASSOCIATION. ANNUAL
TECHNICAL SYMPOSIUM PROCEEDINGS.
1975. a. $10. Wild Goose Association, 4 Townsend
Road, Acton, MA 01720. circ. 1,200.

551.46 UN ISSN 0084-2001
WORLD METEOROLOGICAL ORGANIZATION.
REPORT ON MARINE SCIENCE AFFAIRS.
1970. irreg. price varies. World Meteorological
Organization, 41 Ave. Giuseppe Motta, 1211
Geneva 20, Switzerland (Dist. in U.S. by: Unipub,
345 Park Ave. S., New York, NY 10010)

ECONOMIC SITUATION AND CONDITIONS

see Business and Economics—Economic Situation and Conditions

ECONOMIC SYSTEMS AND THEORIES, ECONOMIC HISTORY

see Business and Economics—Economic Systems and Theories, Economic History

ECONOMICS

see Business and Economics

EDUCATION

see also Education—Adult Education;
Education—Guides to Schools and
Colleges; Education—Higher Education;
Education—International Education
Programs; Education—School
Organization and Administration;
Education—Special Education and
Rehabilitation; Education—Teaching
Methods and Curriculum

A F T ISSUES BULLETIN. (American Federation of
Teachers) see LABOR UNIONS

372 US ISSN 0517-3833
A M S. PROCEEDINGS OF THE NATIONAL
SEMINAR. irreg. price varies. American
Montessori Society, 150 Fifth Ave., New York, NY
10011.

370 US
A.O.E. DIRECTORY; membership list. 1955. a.
membership. Association of Overseas Educators,
Inc., c/o Dr. Norris C. Crook, Slippery Rock State
College, Slippery Rock, PA 16057. Ed. Dr.Norris C.
Crook. circ. 500. (looseleaf format)

A P U PRESS ALASKANA SERIES. (Alaska Pacific
University Press) see HISTORY

371 AT
A T F ANNUAL REPORT.* 1943. a. free. ‡
Australian Teachers' Federation, 300 Sussex St.,
Sydney, N. S. W. 2000, Australia. adv. circ.
controlled. (processed)
 Formerly: A T F Monthly Report (ISSN 0001-2726)

370 DK ISSN 0065-0145
AARBOG FOR DANSK SKOLEHISTORIE. 1967. a.
Kr.110. Selskabet for Dansk Skolehistorie, Lersoe
Parkalle 101, DK-2100 Copenhagen OE, Denmark.
Ed. Ingrid Markussen. bk. rev.

370 SW ISSN 0065-0196
AARSBOK FOER SKOLAN. 1964. a. price varies.
Sveriges Laerarfoerbund, Box 12239, S-102 26
Stockholm 12, Sweden. Ed. Nils Soederberg. circ.
12,000.
 Supersedes Title Issued 1920-63: Folkskolans
Aarsbok.

ABHANDLUNGEN ZUR PHILOSOPHIE,
PSYCHOLOGIE UND PAEDAGOGIK. see
PHILOSOPHY

370 US ISSN 0065-0625
ACADEMY FOR EDUCATIONAL
DEVELOPMENT. ACADEMY PAPERS. 1966.
irreg., 1973, no. 6. free. ‡ Academy for Educational
Development, 680 Fifth Ave., New York, NY
10019. Ed. Ronald Gross.

ACTA COLLOQUII DIDACTICII CLASSICI;
didactica classica gandensia. see LINGUISTICS

301 PL ISSN 0208-5267
ACTA UNIVERSITATIS NICOLAI COPERNICI.
SOCJOLOGIA WYCHOWANIA. (Text in Polish;
summaries in English) 1976. irreg. price varies.
Uniwersytet Mikolaja Kopernika, Fosa Staromiejska
3, Torun, Poland (Dist. by Osrodek
Rozpowszechniania Wydawnictw Naukowych PAN,
Palac Kultury i Nauki, 00-901 Warsaw, Poland)
 Formerly: Uniwersytet Mikolaja Kopernika,
Torun. Nauki Humanistyczno-Spoleczne. Socjologia.

ACTA UNIVERSITATIS SZEGEDIENSIS DE
ATTILA JOZSEF NOMINATAE. ACTA
BIBLIOTHECARIA. see LIBRARY AND
INFORMATION SCIENCES

370 PL ISSN 0137-1096
ACTA UNIVERSITATIS WRATISLAVIENSIS.
PRACE PEDAGOGICZNE. (Subseries of Acta
Universitatis Wratislaviensis) (Summaries in English,
French and Russian) 1973. irreg. price varies.
(Uniwersytet Wroclawski) Panstwowe Wydawnictwo
Naukowe, Oddzial we Wroclawiu, Ul. Pretficza 9/
11, 53-328 Wroclaw, Poland (Dist. by: Ars Polona,
Krakowskie Przedmiescie 7, 00-068 Warsaw,
Poland) circ. 600.
 Supersedes in part: Uniwersytet Wroclawski.
Prace Pedagogiczne i Psychologia.

370 ET ISSN 0072-9388
ADDIS ABABA UNIVERSITY. UNIVERSITY
TESTING CENTER. TECHNICAL REPORT.*
(Name of issuing body varies: Haile Sellassie I
University, University of Addis Ababa, National
University) (Text in English) 1967. irreg., 1971, no.
5. free. Addis Ababa University, University Testing
Center, Box 1176, Addis Ababa, Ethiopia.

372.21 US ISSN 0270-4021
ADVANCES IN EARLY EDUCATION AND DAY
CARE. 1980. a. J A I Press, Box 1285, 165 W.
Putnam Ave., Greenwich, CT 06830. Ed. Sally
Kilmer.

370 US
ADVANCES IN LIFELONG EDUCATION. 1976.
irreg., vol. 6, 1979. price varies. Pergamon Press,
Inc., Maxwell House, Fairview Park, Elmsford, NY
10523 (And Headington Hill Hall, Oxford OX3
0BW, England)

ADVENTURES IN WESTERN NEW YORK
HISTORY. see HISTORY — History Of North
And South America

AGRI EDUCATOR; the magazine for professionals
teaching vocational agriculture. see
AGRICULTURE

AGRICULTURE TEACHERS DIRECTORY AND
HANDBOOK. see AGRICULTURE

EDUCATION

370 NR ISSN 0065-4752
AHMADU BELLO UNIVERSITY. INSTITUTE OF EDUCATION. PAPER.* irreg. Ahmadu Bello University, Institute of Education, Zaria, Nigeria.

AISTHESIS; revista chilena de investigaciones esteticas. see *PHILOSOPHY*

ALBARREGAS. see *HUMANITIES: COMPREHENSIVE WORKS*

370 CN ISSN 0708-3106
ALBERTA. DEPARTMENT OF EDUCATION. EARLY CHILDHOOD SERVICES PROGRAM HIGHLIGHTS. 1975. irreg. Department of Education, Early Childhood Services Branch, Executive Bldg., Edmonton, Alta. T5J 2V2, Canada. illus.

371.1 CN ISSN 0706-9839
ALBERTA TEACHERS' ASSOCIATION. MEMBERS' HANDBOOK. a. Alberta Teachers' Association, Barnett House, 11010-142 St., Edmonton, Alta. T5N 2R1, Canada.

370 CN ISSN 0701-1237
ALBERTA TEACHERS' ASSOCIATION. RELIGIOUS STUDIES & MORAL EDUCATION COUNCIL. NEWSLETTER. 1974. 3-5/yr. Can.$15. Alberta Teachers' Association, Religious Studies & Moral Education Council, 11010 142nd St., Edmonton, Alta. T5N 2R1, Canada. circ. 220. (back issues avail.)

377.9 US ISSN 0002-6093
ALLIANCE REVIEW. vol.25,1973. irreg. membership. American Friends of the Alliance Israelite Universelle Inc., 161 Broadway, Suite 811, New York, NY 10006. Ed. Saadiah Cherniak. illus.
Religious

AMERICAN ARTIST DIRECTORY OF ART SCHOOLS & WORKSHOPS. see *ART*

370 410 US
AMERICAN ASSOCIATION OF TEACHERS OF ITALIAN. DIRECTORY. a. $3.75. American Association of Teachers of Italian, Department of French and Italian, SUNY at Stony Brook, Stony Brook, NY 11794.

370 US ISSN 0084-6333
AMERICAN COUNCIL ON INDUSTRIAL ARTS TEACHER EDUCATION. YEARBOOK. 1952. a. $11.20. ‡ American Council on Industrial Arts Teacher Education, c/o University of Northern Iowa, Department of Industrial Technology, Cedar Falls, IA 50613. Indexed: Educ.Ind.
Formerly: American Industrial Arts Association. Yearbook (ISSN 0065-8634)

AMERICAN COUNTRY LIFE ASSOCIATION. PROCEEDINGS OF THE ANNUAL CONFERENCE. see *SOCIOLOGY*

370 US ISSN 0084-6341
AMERICAN EDUCATIONAL RESEARCH ASSOCIATION. ANNUAL MEETING PAPER AND SYMPOSIA ABSTRACTS. 1969. a. $8. ‡ American Educational Research Association, 1230 17th St. N.W., Washington, DC 20036. circ. 3,500. (also avail. in microfiche from EDR)

AMERICAN FEDERATION OF TEACHERS. CONVENTION PROCEEDINGS (ABRIDGED) see *LABOR UNIONS*

370 FR
ANNUAIRE DE L'EDUCATION PERMANENTE. 1971. a. 88 F. Office National de Publications Culturelles, 3 bis Cite d'Hauteville, 75010 Paris, France. Ed. Jacques de Montjoye. circ. 8,000.
Formerly: Guide National de l'Education Permante.

ANNUAIRE DES COMMUNAUTES D'ENFANTS. see *CHILDREN AND YOUTH — About*

377 BE ISSN 0068-2942
ANNUAIRE ET STATISTIQUE DE L'ENSEIGNEMENT CATHOLIQUE. Dutch edition: Brussels. Nationaal Sekretariaat van Het Katholiek Onderwijs. Statisti Jaarboek van Het Katholiek Onderwijs. (Editions in Dutch and French) 1957. a. 500 Fr.($13) Nationaal Sekretariant van het Katholiek Onderwijs, Guimardstraat, Brussels, Belgium.

370 US ISSN 0095-5787
ANNUAL EDITIONS: READINGS IN EDUCATION. Short title: Readings in Education. a. $5.75. Dushkin Publishing Group, Sluice Dock, Box 426, Guilford, CT 06437. illus.

370 US ISSN 0085-4077
ANNUAL EDUCATIONAL SUMMARY, NEW YORK STATE. 1904. a. free. ‡ Education Department, Information Center on Education, Albany, NY 12234. stat. circ. controlled. (processed)

ANNUAL REPORT OF EDUCATIONAL PSYCHOLOGY IN JAPAN/KYOIKU SHINRIGAKU NEMPO. see *PSYCHOLOGY*

370 GW ISSN 0066-569X
ARBEITEN ZUR PAEDAGOGIK. 1963. irreg., vol. 19, 1975. price varies. Calwer Verlag, Schwarnhauser Str.44, 7000 Stuttgart 70, W. Germany (B.R.D.) Eds. Otto Duerr, Helmut Frik.

370 GW
ARBEITSGRUPPE FUER EMPIRISCHE BILDUNGSFORSCHUNG. UEBERSICHT UEBER DIE BISHERIGEN ARBEITEN. irreg. Arbeitsgruppe fuer Empirische Bildungsforschung, Zeppelinstr. 151, 6900 Heidelberg 1, W. Germany (B.R.D.)

370 060 PL ISSN 0066-6831
ARCHIWUM DZIEJOW OSWIATY. (Text in Polish) 1959. irreg., vol. 8, 1978. price varies. (Polska Akademia Nauk, Instytut Historii Nauki, Oswiaty i Techniki) Ossolineum, Publishing House of the Polish Academy of Sciences, Rynek 9, Wroclaw, Poland (Dist. by Ars Polona-Ruch, Krakowskie Przedmiescie 7, Warsaw, Poland) circ. 1,000.

370 AG ISSN 0066-7021
ARGENTINA. DEPARTAMENTO DE ESTADISTICA EDUCATIVA. BOLETIN INFORMATIVO. 1965. a. free. Ministerio de Cultura y Educacion, Departamento de Estadistica Educativa, Avda.Eduardo Madero 235, 1 Piso, Buenos Aires, Argentina.

379 US ISSN 0095-5310
ARIZONA. DEPARTMENT OF EDUCATION. ANNUAL REPORT OF THE SUPERINTENDENT OF PUBLIC INSTRUCTION. a. Department of Education, 1535 W. Jefferson, Phoenix, AZ 85007. illus. stat. Key Title: Annual Report of the Superintendent of Public Instruction.

371.9 US
ARIZONA STATE PLAN FOR THE EDUCATION OF MIGRATORY CHILDREN. Cover title: Education for Migrant Children; Arizona State Plan. 1967. irreg., latest issue, 1974. free. ‡ Department of Education, 1535 W. Jefferson, Phoenix, AZ 85007. illus. stat.

370 US ISSN 0066-7455
ARIZONA STATE UNIVERSITY. BUREAU OF EDUCATIONAL RESEARCH AND SERVICES. EDUCATIONAL SERVICES BULLETIN. 1962. irreg.; no. 54, 1977. $1-2. Arizona State University, College of Education, Tempe, AZ 85281. Ed. R. Merwin Deever.

370 US ISSN 0066-7463
ARIZONA STATE UNIVERSITY. BUREAU OF EDUCATIONAL RESEARCH AND SERVICES. RESEARCH AND SERVICES BULLETIN. (Some numbers issued by the Bureau under a variant name, Division of Educational Research and Field Services) 1959. irreg.; no. 36, 1976. $1-2.50. Arizona State University, College of Education, Tempe, AZ 85281. Ed. R. Merwin Deever.

370 UK ISSN 0066-8672
ASPECTS OF EDUCATION. 1964. irreg., no. 24, 1980. price varies. University of Hull, Institute of Education, 173, Cottingham Rd., Hull HU5 2EH, England. Indexed: SSCI. Br.Educ.Ind.

370 CN
ASSOCIATION DES COLLEGES DU QUEBEC ANNUAIRE. 1968. a. free. (Association des Colleges du Quebec) Centre d'Animation de Developpement et de Recherche en Education, 1940 est, Henri-Bourassa, Montreal, Que. H2B 1S2, Canada. adv. circ. 8,500.

373 CN ISSN 0066-8990
ASSOCIATION DES INSTITUTIONS D'ENSEIGNEMENT SECONDAIRE. ANNUAIRE. 1968. a. free. (Association des Institutions d'Enseignement Secondaire) Centre d'Animation de Developpement et de Recherche en Education, 1940 Est Blvd. Henri-Bourassa, Montreal, Que. H2B 1S2, Canada. adv. circ. 8,500.
Formerly: Annuaire des Institutions d'Enseignement Secondaire (ISSN 0084-6511)

370 301.16 US
ASSOCIATION FOR EDUCATIONAL COMMUNICATIONS AND TECHNOLOGY. MONOGRAPHS. no. 3 1967. irreg., no. 4, 1970. price varies. Association for Educational Communications and Technology, 1126 16th St. N.W., Washington, DC 20036.

370 AT
AUSTRALIA. ADVISORY COMMITTEE ON RESEARCH AND DEVELOPMENT IN EDUCATION. ANNUAL REPORT.* 1970/71. a. Aus.$0.44. Australian Government Publishing Service, Box 84, Canberra, A.C.T. 2600, Australia.

372 373 AT ISSN 0067-1150
AUSTRALIA. BUREAU OF STATISTICS. VICTORIAN OFFICE. PRIMARY AND SECONDARY EDUCATION. 1967. a. free. Australian Bureau of Statistics, Victorian Office, Box 2796Y, G.P.O. Melbourne, Victoria 3001, Australia. circ. 2,300.

370 AT
AUSTRALIAN COUNCIL FOR EDUCATIONAL RESEARCH. ANNUAL REPORT. a. membership. Australian Council for Educational Research, P.O. Box 210, Hawthorn, Vic. 3122, Australia.

370 AT ISSN 0067-1835
AUSTRALIAN COUNCIL FOR EDUCATIONAL RESEARCH. OCCASIONAL PAPERS. irreg. Australian Council for Educational Research, P.O. Box 210, Hawthorn, Victoria 3122, Australia. circ. 500.

370 AT
AUSTRALIAN COUNCIL FOR EDUCATIONAL RESEARCH. RESEARCH SERIES. irreg. Australian Council for Educational Research, Box 210, Hawthorn, Vic.3122, Australia.

370 AT
AUSTRALIAN EDUCATION REVIEW. irreg. standing orders. Australian Council for Educational Research, Box 210, Hawthorn, Victoria 3122, Australia. stat. Indexed: Aus.Educ.Ind.
Formerly: Quarterly Review of Australian Education. (ISSN 0033-5762)

370 AT
AUSTRALIAN RESEARCH GRANTS COMMITTEE. REPORT. a. price varies. Australian Government Publishing Service, P.O. Box 84, Canberra, A.C.T. 2600, Australia. stat. (back issues avail.)

AUSTRALIAN TEACHER OF THE DEAF. see *DEAF*

370 AU ISSN 0067-2289
AUSTRIA. BUNDESMINISTERIUM FUER UNTERRICHT UND KUNST. JAHRESBERICHT. 1957/58. a., not published 1968-1970. Bundesministerium fuer Unterricht und Kunst, Postfach 65, A-1014 Vienna, Austria.

370 AU
AUSTRIA. BUNDESMINISTERIUM FUER UNTERRICHT UND KUNST. SCHRIFTENREIHE. 1965. irreg. Bundesministerium fuer Unterricht und Kunst., Minoritenplatz 5, A-1010 Vienna, Austria.
Formerly: Austria. Bundesministerium fuer Unterricht und Kunst. Erziehung, Wissenschaft, Forschung (ISSN 0067-2270)

370 BF
BAHAMAS. MINISTRY OF EDUCATION AND CULTURE ANNUAL REPORT. a. Ministry of Education and Culture, N 7147, Nassau, Bahamas. illus.

370 US ISSN 0067-303X
BALDWIN LECTURES IN TEACHER EDUCATION. 1957. a. $1.50. Northeast Missouri State University, Kirksville, MO 63501.

370 150 US
BASIC CONCEPTS IN EDUCATIONAL
PSYCHOLOGY SERIES. irreg. price varies.
Brooks-Cole Publishing Co., 555 Abrego St.,
Monterey, CA 93940.

BASIC CONCEPTS IN PSYCHOLOGY SERIES. see
PSYCHOLOGY

379 GW ISSN 0005-7207
BAYERISCHES STAATSMINISTERIUM FUER
UNTERRICHT UND KULTUS. AMTSBLATT.
1865. irreg. DM.60 for Teil I, DM. 42 for Teil II.
(Staatsministerium fuer Unterricht und Kultus)
Kommunalschriften-Verlag J. Jehle, Isoldenstr. 38,
8000 Munich 40, W. Germany (B.R.D.) index. circ.
15,000. (tabloid format)

370 BE ISSN 0067-5598
BELGIUM. MINISTERE DE L'EDUCATION
NATIONALE ET DE LA CULTURE
FRANCAISE. RAPPORT ANNUEL.* a. Ministere
de l'Education Nationale et de la Culture Francaise,
Cite Administrative de l'Etat, Bd. Pacheco, 1010
Brussels, Belgium.

370 PL ISSN 0067-7671
BIBLIOTEKA KLASYKOW PEDAGOGIKI. 1955.
irreg., vol. 62, 1977. price varies. (Polska Akademia
Nauk, Komitet Nauk Pedagogicznych) Ossolineum,
Publishing House of the Polish Academy of
Sciences, Rynek 9, 50-106 Wroclaw, Poland (Dist.
by Ars Polona-Ruch, Krakowskie Przedmiescie 7,
Warsaw, Poland) Ed. Bogdan Suchodolski.

370 AU ISSN 0067-8589
BILDUNGSPLANUNG IN OESTERREICH/
EDUCATIONAL POLICY AND PLANNING.
AUSTRIA/POLITIQUE ET LA
PLANIFICATION DE L'ENSEIGNEMENT -
AUTRICHE. (Text in German; summaries in
English and French) 1967. irreg., no. 4, 1974. S.200.
Bundesministerium fuer Unterricht und Kunst,
Postfach 65, A-1014 Vienna, Austria.

370 CN
BISHOPS MITRE. 1893. irreg. Can.$1.25. Bishops
University, Cultural Affairs Committee, Lennoxville,
Que. J1M 1Z7, Canada. Ed. Damien Pettigrew.

379.156 US ISSN 0363-6518
BOOKS FOR KANSAS SCHOOLS. 1965. a. State
Department of Education, Topeka, KS 66612.

BOOKS FOR SECONDARY SCHOOL LIBRARIES.
see *LIBRARY AND INFORMATION SCIENCES*

371.4 CN ISSN 0705-8802
BRITISH COLUMBIA SCHOOL COUNSELLORS'
ASSOCIATION. NEWSLETTER. 1956. irreg.
membership. ‡ B.C. Teachers' Federation, No. 105,
2235 Burrard St., Vancouver, B. C. V6J 3H9,
Canada. circ. 450.
Formerly: British Columbia Counsellors'
Association. Newsletter (ISSN 0045-2947)

370 UK ISSN 0141-5972
BRITISH QUALIFICATIONS. 1970. a. £14.95.
Kogan Page Ltd., 120 Pentonville Rd., London N1
9JN, England.

C A I D NEWSLETTER. (Convention of American
Instructors of the Deaf) see *DEAF*

371.2 CN ISSN 0068-8657
C E A HANDBOOK/KI-ES-KI. (Text in French and
English) 1949. a. Can.$20. Canadian Education
Association, 252 Bloor St. W., Toronto, Ont. M5S
1V5, Canada. Ed. H. Goldsborough. circ. 2,500.
Formerly: Directory of Administrative Officials in
Public Education - Canada.

370
C E M A BULLETIN. (Organization formed by the
merger of C A V E A and Connecticut School
Library Association) 1976. a. $3. Connecticut
Educational Media Association, 25 Elmwood
Avenue, Trumbull, CT 06611. bibl. circ. 1,000.
Formerly (until no. 28, 1975): Connecticut
Audiovisual Education Association. Bulletin.

C G R B BULLETIN. (Citizens' Governmental
Research Bureau) see *PUBLIC
ADMINISTRATION — Municipal Government*

371.42 UY ISSN 0577-2931
C I N T E R F O R. ESTUDIOS Y
MONOGRAFIAS. 1967. irreg. price varies. Centro
Interamericano de Investigacion y Documentacion
Sobre Formacion Profesional, Rio Negro 1241,
Casilla de Correo 1761, Montevideo, Uruguay.
Indexed: CIRF Abstr.

370 CN ISSN 0315-727X
C S S E YEARBOOK. a. Canadian Society for the
Study of Education, c/o Faculty of Education,
University of British Columbia, Vancouver, B.C.
V6T 1Z5, Canada.

370 FR ISSN 0068-5119
CAHIERS DES UNIVERSITES FRANCAISES.
1971. irreg. price varies. Association d'Etude pour
l'Expansion de l'Enseignement Superieur, 173 Bd.
St. Germain, Paris 5e, France.

371.9 US ISSN 0363-7484
CALIFORNIA. DEPARTMENT OF HEALTH.
ANNUAL EVALUATION REPORT PROGRAM
INFORMATION. Cover title: Compensatory
Education Report. a. Health & Welfare Agency, 744
P St., Sacramento, CA 95814. illus. stat. Key Title:
Annual Evaluation Report Program Information.

370 UK ISSN 0068-6816
CAMBRIDGE TEXTS AND STUDIES IN THE
HISTORY OF EDUCATION. 1966. irreg., no. 15,
1974. price varies. Cambridge University Press, Box
110, Cambridge CB2 3RL, England (and 32 E. 57
St., New York, NY 10022) Ed. Bd.

704 CN ISSN 0068-9645
CANADIAN SOCIETY FOR EDUCATION
THROUGH ART. ANNUAL JOURNAL. a. $4. ‡
Canadian Society for Education Through Art, 112
Oakdale Ave., St. Catherines, Ont. L2P 3J9,
Canada. Ed. Arnel W. Pattemore. circ. 300.

371 US ISSN 0069-0651
CARNEGIE FOUNDATION FOR THE
ADVANCEMENT OF TEACHING. REPORT.
1906. a. free. ‡ Carnegie Foundation for the
Advancement of Teaching, 437 Madison Ave., New
York, NY 10022. circ. 2,800. (also avail. in
microform)

370 US
CASE STUDIES IN EDUCATION AND
CULTURE. irreg. price varies. Holt, Rinehart and
Winston, 383 Madison Ave., New York, NY 10017.

CATALOGO DE PUBLICACIONES
LATINOAMERICANAS SOBRE FORMACION
PROFESIONAL. see *OCCUPATIONS AND
CAREERS — Abstracting, Bibliographies, Statistics*

370 CJ
CAYMAN ISLANDS. EDUCATION
DEPARTMENT. REPORT OF THE CHIEF
EDUCATION OFFICER. a. Education
Department, Grand Cayman, Cayman Islands,
B.W.I. illus.

370 US
CENTER ON EVALUATION, DEVELOPMENT,
AND RESEARCH. OCCASIONAL PAPER
SERIES. 1968. irreg., no. 23, 1976. price varies.
(Center on Evaluation, Development, and Research)
Phi Delta Kappa, Inc., International Headquarters,
Eighth St. & Union Ave., Box 789, Bloomington, IN
47402. (back issues avail.)

370 US
CENTER ON HUMAN POLICY. NOTES FROM
THE CENTER. 1974. no. 4. irreg.; latest no. 7.
$0.50. Syracuse University, Center on Human
Policy, Box 127, University Sta., Syracuse, NY
13210. Ed. Douglas Biklen. bibl. charts. circ. 2,000.

370 SZ
CENTRE MEDICO-SOCIAL DE PRO FAMILIA;
educations sexuelle de la jeunesse. 1970. irreg. (1-2/
yr.); no. 16, 1979. 5 Fr. per no. Centre Medico-
Social de Pro Familia, Av. Georgette 1, 1003
Lausanne, Switzerland. Ed. Mary Anna Barbey. circ.
2,000.

370 FR ISSN 0069-2069
CENTRE REGIONAL DE DOCUMENTATION
PEDAGOGIQUE DE TOULOUSE. ANNALES;*
dossier d'information et de Perfectionnement
(Francais-Mathematiques) (Supplements its Bulletin
Regional d'Informations Universitaires) 1970. irreg.
price varies. Centre Regional de Documentation
Pedagogique de Toulouse, 3 rue Roquelaine, 31000
Toulouse, France.

371.42 016 UY
CENTRO INTERAMERICANO DE
INVESTIGACION Y DOCUMENTACION
SOBRE FORMACION PROFESIONAL. SERIE
BIBLIOGRAFICA. 1968. irreg. Centro
Interamericano de Investigacion y Documentacion
Sobre Formacion Profesional, Rio Negro 1241,
Casilla de Correo 1761, Montevideo, Uruguay. bk.
rev. abstr. bibl.

372 AT
CHANNELS. 1973. a. free. Department of Education,
Primary Curriculum Committee, P.O. Box 33,
North Quay, Qld. 4000, Australia. Eds. John E.
Fitzgerald and Jarvis Finger.

371.1 US ISSN 0069-2751
CHARLES W. HUNT LECTURE. 1960. irreg.
American Association of Colleges for Teacher
Education, 1 Dupont Circle, N.W., Washington, DC
20036. Ed. Esther Hemsing.

370 BL ISSN 0080-3103
COLEGIO MILITAR DO RIO DE JANEIRO.
REVISTA DIDACTICA.* 1902. a. free. Colegio
Militar do Rio de Janeiro, Rua Sao Francisco
Xavier 267 - ZC-11, Rio de Janeiro, Brazil.

373 IT ISSN 0069-5246
COLLANA "INSEGNARE". irreg. price varies. Casa
Editrice Felice le Monnier, Via Scipione Ammirato
100, C.P. 455, 50136 Florence, Italy.

COLLEGE THEOLOGY SOCIETY.
PROCEEDINGS. see *RELIGIONS AND
THEOLOGY — Roman Catholic*

370 CK
COLOMBIA. MINISTERIO DE EDUCACION
NACIONAL. EDUCACION PARA
DESARROLLO. irreg. Ministerio de Educacion
Nacional, Division de Educacion de Adultos,
Bogota, Colombia.

370 UK ISSN 0010-1842
COLSTONIAN. 1894. a. 50p. Colston's School,
Stapleton, Bristol, Eng. Ed. M. P. B. Tayler. adv.
illus. circ. 1,000.

370 SP
COMISION MIXTA DE COORDINACION
ESTADISTICA DE BARCELONA.
ESTADISTICAS DE ENSENANZA DE LA
PROVINCIA DE BARCELONA. (Subseries of:
Comision Mixta de Coordinacion Estadistica de
Barcelona. Serie Estadisticas) 1970/71. $3.
Comision Mixta de Coordinacion Estadistica, Urgel
187, Barcelona 11, Spain. circ. 1,000.

331.2 AT
COMMONWEALTH TEACHING SERVICE.
ANNUAL REPORT. (Subseries of: Australia.
Parliament. Parliamentary Papers) 1972. a. price
varies. Australian Government Publishing Service,
Box 84, Canberra, A.C.T. 2600, Australia. illus.

COMMUNITY-CLINICAL PSYCHOLOGY SERIES.
see *PSYCHOLOGY*

370 UK ISSN 0588-9049
COMPARATIVE EDUCATION SOCIETY IN
EUROPE. PROCEEDINGS OF THE GENERAL
MEETING. (Text in English and French) 1963.
biennial. £4($8) Comparative Education Society in
Europe, University of London Institute of
Education, c/o Dr. Brian Holmes, Malet St.,
London WC1E 7HS, England (Subscr. to: Prof.
Denis Kallen, University of Amsterdam,
Prinsengracht 225, Amsterdam) Eds. Brian Holmes
and Raymond Ryba. circ. controlled.

370 US
COMPREHENSIVE LISTING OF
RECOMMENDED PERIODICALS FOR
CATHOLIC SECONDARY SCHOOL
LIBRARIES. 1962. a. free. Seaboard Subscription
Agency, Box 1482, Allentown, PA 18105. L.
Heckenberger.

EDUCATION

370 US ISSN 0069-8547
CONFERENCE ON FRONTIERS IN EDUCATION. DIGEST. a. price varies. Institute of Electrical and Electronics Engineers, Inc., Education Group, 445 Hoes Lane, Piscataway, NJ 08854.

370 US ISSN 0084-9170
CONFERENCE ON THE ECONOMICS OF EDUCATION. PROCEEDINGS. 1967. irreg. free. ‡ Florida State University, Department of Education, 107 Gaines St., Tallahassee, FL 32306. Ed. Richard H.P. Kraft.

379 US ISSN 0363-650X
CONNECTICUT. ADVISORY COUNCIL ON VOCATIONAL AND CAREER EDUCATION. VOCATIONAL EDUCATION EVALUATION REPORT. 1969. a. Advisory Council on Vocational and Career Education., 56 Arbor St., Hartford, CT 06106. Ed. Richard G. Rausch. circ. 2,000. (also avail. in microfiche) Key Title: Vocational Education Evaluation Report.

379 US ISSN 0095-5329
CONSOLIDATED REPORT ON ELEMENTARY AND SECONDARY EDUCATION IN COLORADO. a. $4. Department of Education, State Office Bldg., 201 E. Colfax Ave., Denver, CO 80203. illus. stat.

370 US
CONTEMPORARY EDUCATIONAL ISSUES. irreg. price varies. McCutchan Publishing Corp., 2526 Grove St., Berkeley, CA 94704.

371.42 US ISSN 0069-9810
COOPERATIVE EDUCATION ASSOCIATION MEMBERSHIP DIRECTORY. 1965. a. free to members. Cooperative Education Association, c/o E. R. Pettebone, Exec. Sec., 247 Alumni Center, Indiana State University, Terre Haute, IN 47809. circ. 3,000. (reprint service avail. from UMI)

370 US ISSN 0010-843X
COOPERATIVE EDUCATION ASSOCIATION NEWSLETTER. 1969. 6/yr. $5 to non-members. Cooperative Education Association, c/o E. R. Pettebone, Exec. Sec., 247 Alumni Center, Indiana State University, Terre Haute, IN 47809. Ed. Edgar R. Pettebone. circ. 3,000. (tabloid format; reprint service avail. from UMI)

370 ZA
COPPERBELT EDUCATION. (Text in English) irreg.(1-2/yr.) P.O. Box 1552, Ndola, Zambia. illus.

370 US
CORRESPONDENCE EDUCATIONAL DIRECTORY. 1976. biennial. $10. Racz Publishing Co., Box 287, Oxnard, CA 93032. adv. bk. rev. circ. 10,000.

370 US ISSN 0070-069X
COUNCIL FOR BASIC EDUCATION. OCCASIONAL PAPERS. 1961. irreg., latest no. 31. $2 per no. Council for Basic Education, 725 15th St., N.W., Washington, DC 20005.

371.4 US
COUNSELOR EDUCATION DIRECTORY: PERSONNEL AND PROGRAMS. 1971. triennial, 3rd, 1977. $12.95. Accelerated Development Inc., Box 667, Muncie, IN 47305. Ed. Joseph W. Hollis.

CREATIVE DRAMA. see THEATER

370 US
CRITICAL ISSUES IN EDUCATION. irreg. price variess. Harper and Row Publishers, Inc., 10 East 53rd St, New York, NY 10022.

370 CL
CUADERNOS DE EDUCACION. 1973. irreg. Esc.250($16.80) Centro de Investigacion y Desarrollo de Educacion, Casilla 13608, Santiago 1, Chile. Ed. Francisco Alvarez Martin. adv. bk. rev. bibl. charts. illus. index. circ. 3,000.

370 VE ISSN 0070-1718
CUADERNOS DE PEDAGOGIA.* 1966. irreg. Bs.2($0.45) Universidad del Zulia, Facultad de Humanidades y Educacion, Apartado de Correos 415, Maracaibo, Venezuela.

379 US
CURRENT EDUCATION LAW. 1971. 9/yr. $29. Platte Publishing Co., Box 18195, Denver, CO 80218. Ed. Reese Miller. cum.index. circ. 800. (looseleaf format)

370 US ISSN 0094-1050
CURRICULUM IMPROVEMENT. 1950. a. $15. Professors of Curriculum, c/o Arizona State University, Education B Bldg., Rm. 412, Tempe, AZ 85281. Ed. James J. Jelinek. illus. circ. 2,000. (reprint service avail. from UMI) Indexed: ERIC.
Former titles: Philosophy of Education; Far Western Philosophy of Education Society. Proceedings (ISSN 0430-0661)

370 CN
CYCLOPEDIA. 1981. a. free contr. circ. Student Enterprises & Assistance League, Box 250, Station P., Toronto, Ont. M5S 2T9, Canada. illus. circ. 25,000.

370 DK
DANSKE SKOLEHAANDBOG. 1928. a. Kr.120.75. Finn Suenson Forlag, Rosenoerns Alle 18, 1970 Copenhagen V, Denmark. Ed. Claus Moldt. adv. circ. 4,500.

370 SP ISSN 0070-2897
DATOS Y CIFRAS DE LA ENSENANZA EN ESPANA. 1974. irreg. Ministerio de Educacion y Ciencia, Secretaria General Tecnica, Servicio de Publicaciones, Madrid 3, Spain.

370 US ISSN 0091-6188
DELAWARE. DEPARTMENT OF PUBLIC INSTRUCTION. EDUCATIONAL PERSONNEL DIRECTORY. 1921. a. contr. free circ. Department of Public Instruction, Division of Planning, Research & Evaluation, Townsend Building, Dover, DE 19901. Ed. Wilmer E. Wise. circ. 3,500.

370 US ISSN 0362-8787
DELAWARE. STATE BOARD OF EDUCATION. REPORT OF EDUCATIONAL STATISTICS. a. State Board of Education, Townsend Building, Dover, DE 19901. Key Title: Report of Educational Statistics.

370 PK ISSN 0080-1321
DEVELOPMENT OF EDUCATION IN PAKISTAN. (Text in English) 1965. a. Ministry of Education, Documentation Section, Curriculum Wing, Sector H-9, P.O. Shaigan, Industrial Area, Islamabad, Pakistan.
Title varies: Report on the Progress of Education in Pakistan.

371.42 US ISSN 0070-5357
DIRECTORY OF COOPERATIVE EDUCATION. 1968. a. Cooperative Education Association, c/o E. R. Pettebone, Exec. Sec., 247 Alumni Center, Indiana State University, Terre Haute, IN 47809. circ. 4,000. (reprint service avail. from UMI)

371.4 US ISSN 0094-7512
DIRECTORY OF COUNSELING SERVICES. 1969. a. $6. International Association of Counseling Services, Inc., Two Skyline Pl., Suite 400, 5203 Leesburg Pike, Falls Church, VA 22041. Ed. Jean P. Whittaker. circ. 5,000.
Formerly: Directory of Approved Counseling Agencies.

371 US ISSN 0362-5710
DIRECTORY OF DELAWARE SCHOOLS. a. $5. Department of Public Instruction, Townsend Building, Federal St. at Loockerman St., Dover, DE 19901 (Orders to: Public Information Office, Dept. of Public Instruction, Box 1402, Dover, DE 19901)

370.06 US ISSN 0160-0508
DIRECTORY OF EDUCATION ASSOCIATIONS. a. price varies; single copies free from USOE. U. S. Office of Education, Dept. of Health, Education, and Welfare, Washington, DC 20202 (Orders to: Supt. of Documents, Washington, DC 20402)
Formerly: Education Directory: Education Associations (ISSN 0083-2650)

370 CN ISSN 0070-5454
DIRECTORY OF EDUCATION STUDIES IN CANADA/ANNUAIRE D'ETUDES EN EDUCATION AU CANADA. (Text in English and French) 1968. a. Can.$25. Canadian Education Association, 252 Bloor St., West, Toronto, Ont. M5S 1V5, Canada. circ. 300. Indexed: Can.Educ.Ind.
Incorporating: Education Studies in Progress in Canadian Universities.

370 US
DIRECTORY OF EDUCATIONAL CONSULTANTS. a. price varies. School Management Study Group (Fremont), 4674 Richmond Ave, Fremont, CA 94536.

374 US ISSN 0084-991X
DIRECTORY OF EDUCATIONAL INSTITUTIONS IN NEW MEXICO. (Subseries of its Bulletin) 1966. a. free. Department of Education, Veterans Approval Division, Box 4277, Santa Fe, NM 87501. Dir. Rudy Silva.

370 US ISSN 0070-5616
DIRECTORY OF GRADUATE PROGRAMS IN THE SPEECH COMMUNICATION ARTS AND SCIENCES. 1967. biennial. $10. Speech Communication Association, 5105 Blacklick Rd., No. E, Annandale, VA 22003. Ed. Robert N. Hall. circ. 1,000. (reprint service avail. from UMI)

DIRECTORY OF MUSIC FACULTIES IN COLLEGES & UNIVERSITIES U.S. AND CANADA. see MUSIC

370 331 US
DIRECTORY OF WORKERS EDUCATION. a. $2. Workers Education Local 189, c/o Lee Balliet, Treas., Box 818, Morgantown, WV 26505. charts. illus. circ. 1,000.
Formerly: Directory of Labor Education.

371 US
DISCUSSIONS ON TEACHING. 1971. irreg. $1.50 per issue. ‡ American Historical Association, 400 A St. S.E., Washington, DC 20003. bibl. charts. illus.

370 US ISSN 0077-9210
DISTRIBUTION OF HIGH SCHOOL GRADUATES AND COLLEGE GOING RATE, NEW YORK STATE. 1967. a. free. ‡ Education Department, Information Center on Education, Albany, NY 12234. circ. controlled.

370 US
DOCUMENTS IN THE HISTORY OF EDUCATION. irreg. price varies. Harvard University Press, 79 Garden Street, Cambridge, MA 02138.

370 FR ISSN 0070-7139
DOSSIERS D'EDUCATION FAMILIALE. 1969. irreg. price varies. Editions de l' Ecole, 11 rue de Sevres, Paris 6e, France.

970.1 370 US ISSN 0070-7171
DOWNDRAFT. 1967. irreg. U. S. Bureau of Indian Affairs, 1951 Constitution Ave., N.W., Washington, DC 20245.
U.S. Indian Affairs Schools

370 GW ISSN 0070-7767
DURCH STIPENDIEN STUDIEREN. 1964. a. DM.10. Verein Freunde und Foerderer der Deutschen Studentenschaft e.V., Untere Hausbreite 11, 8000 Munich 45, W. Germany (B.R.D.) Ed. Gundolf Seidenspinner. adv.

370 US
E R I C CLEARINGHOUSE ON TEACHER EDUCATION. SPECIAL CURRENT ISSUES PUBLICATIONS. irreg. (4-5/yr.) E R I C Clearinghouse on Teacher Education, Suite 616, One Dupont Circle, Washington, DC 20036. (also avail. in microfiche)

370 US
E R I C CLEARINGHOUSE ON TESTS, MEASUREMENT, AND EVALUATION. T M REPORT SERIES. irreg., approx. 10/yr. E R I C, Clearinghouse on Tests, Measurement, & Evaluation - Educational Resources Information Center, Educational Testing Service, Princeton, NJ 08541. (also avail. in microfiche; back issues avail.) Indexed: Res.Educ.

370 BL
EDUCACAO E REALIDADE. 1976. a. Universidade Federal do Rio Grande do Sul, Faculdade de Educacao, Av Paulo Gama s/n, 90000 Porto Alegre, Brazil. illus.

370 GT
EDUCACION Y PLANEAMIENTO.* 1970. irreg. Oficina de Planeamiento Integral de la Educacion, 4A. Avenida 8-56, Zona 1, Guatemala, Guatemala.

370 SA
EDUCARE. (Text in Afrikaans and English) 1972. a. R.1.05. University of South Africa, Faculty of Education, P. O. Box 392, Pretoria 0001, South Africa. Ed. T.L. Verster. adv. bk. rev. circ. 5,500.

370.193 CN
EDUCATION ADVISORY. 1975. irreg. (approx. 2/yr) Can.$3 for 4 nos. 2267 Kings Ave., West Vancouver, B.C. V7V 2C1, Canada.

370 371.42 SA
EDUCATION & CAREERS IN SOUTH AFRICA. (Text in Afrikaans and English) a. R.10. Erudita Publications (Pty) Ltd., Box 2511, Marshalltown, Transvaal, South Africa. adv.

370.968 SA
EDUCATION & CULTURE/OPVOEDING EN KULTUUR. (Text in Afrikaans and English) 1976. irreg. free. Department of National Education, Private Bag X1 22, Pretoria 0001, South Africa. Ed. Mrs. S.M.M. Wurbrink. circ. 5,000.

370 UK ISSN 0070-9115
EDUCATION AND SCIENCE. a. £1.50. Department of Education and Science, Elizabeth House, York Rd., London SE1 7PH, England (Avail. from H.M.S.O., c/o Liaison Officer, Atlantic House, Holborn Viaduct, London EC1P 1BN, England)

370.58 UK ISSN 0070-9131
EDUCATION AUTHORITIES' DIRECTORY AND ANNUAL. 1902. a. £15.25. School Government Publishing Co. Ltd., Darby House, Bletchingley Rd., Merstham, Redhill RH1 3DN, England. Ed. J.R. Whittaker. circ. 9,000.

375 US ISSN 0424-5407
EDUCATION DEVELOPMENT CENTER. ANNUAL REPORT. 1967. a. Education Development Center, 55 Chapel Street, Newton, MA 02160. illus. circ. 6,500.

370 US
EDUCATION DIRECTORY. LOCAL EDUCATION AGENCIES. a. U.S. National Center for Education Statistics, U.S. Department of Education, 400 Maryland Ave., S.W., Washington, DC 20202 (Order to: Supt. of Documents, Washington, DC 20402)
Formerly: Education Directory. Public Schools (ISSN 0083-2677)

370 IE
EDUCATION ENVIRONMENT. 1973. irreg. £1.50. Regional & Technical Publications, 36 Morehampton Rd., Dublin 4, Ireland. Ed. Denis Bergin. adv. bk. rev. circ. 2,850.

370 UN
EDUCATION IN ASIA AND OCEANIA: REVIEWS, REPORTS AND NOTES. (Nos. 1-3 Issued as: Unesco Regional Office for Education in Asia. Bulletin. Supplement) (Text in English) 1972. approx. 2/yr. price varies. Unesco, Regional Office for Education in Asia and Oceania, Box 1425, Bangkok G.P.O., Thailand (Dist. in U.S. by: Unipub, Box 433, Murray Hill Station, New York, NY 10016) bk. rev. abstr. bibl. circ. 2,900 (combined)
Formerly: Education in Asia: Reviews, Reports and Notes.

370 FR ISSN 0070-9190
EDUCATION IN EUROPE. SECTION 2: GENERAL AND TECHNICAL EDUCATION. 1963. irreg. price varies; $1.50-$6. Council of Europe, Council for Cultural Co-Operation, Publications Section, Strasbourg, France (Dist. in U.S. by Manhattan Publishing Co., 225 Lafayette St., New York, N.Y. 10012)

370 FR ISSN 0070-9204
EDUCATION IN EUROPE. SECTION 3: OUT-OF-SCHOOL EDUCATION. 1963. irreg. price varies; $1.50-$4. Council of Europe, Council for Cultural Co-Operation, Publications in Section, Strasbourg, France (Dist. in U.S. by Manhattan Publishing Co., 225 Lafayette St., New York, N.Y. 10012)

370 FR ISSN 0070-9212
EDUCATION IN EUROPE. SECTION 4 (GENERAL) 1963. irreg. price varies; $1.50-$4.50. Council of Europe, Council for Cultural Co-Operation, Publications Section, Strasbourg, France (Dist. in U.S. by Manhattan Publishing Co., 225 Lafayette St., New York, N.Y. 10012)

370 II
EDUCATION IN INDIA. (Issued in 2 Vols.) (Text in English) 1950. irreg. price varies. Ministry of Education and Social Welfare, Department of Education, Shastri Bhavan, New Delhi 110001, India (Orders to: Controller of Publications, Government of India, Civil Lines, Delhi 100054, India)

370 JA ISSN 0070-9220
EDUCATION IN JAPAN; A GRAPHIC PRESENTATION. (Text in English) 1954. irreg., 1971, 8th ed. 1400 Yen. Ministry of Education, 3-2-2 Kasumigaseki, Chiyoda-ku, Tokyo 100, Japan (Subscr. to Government Publications Service Center, 1-2-1 Kasumigaseki, Chiyoda-ku, Tokyo 100, Japan)

370 UK ISSN 0424-5512
EDUCATION IN THE NORTH. a. 60p. Aberdeen College of Education, Hilton Place, Aberdeen AB9 1FA, Scotland. Eds. Alasdair Roberts, Neil Ferguson. adv. circ. 2,000. Indexed: Br.Educ.Ind.

370 340 US
EDUCATION LAW BULLETIN. 1975. irreg. $12 for 3 nos. Center for Law and Education, Inc., Gutman Library, 6 Appian Way, Cambridge, MA 02138.

EDUCATION NEWS FROM METROLOGIC. see INSTRUMENTS

EDUCATION SOCIAL WORKER. see SOCIAL SERVICES AND WELFARE

370 UK
EDUCATION STATISTICS FOR THE UNITED KINGDOM. a. £3.50. Department of Education and Science, Elizabeth House, 39 York Rd., London SE1 7PH, England (Avail. from H.M.S.O., c/o Liaison Offices, Atlantic House, Holborn Viaduct, London EC1P 1BN, England)

370 UK
EDUCATION YEAR BOOK. 1939. a. £18.95. (Society of Education Officers) Councils and Education Press Ltd. (Subsidiary of: Longman Group Ltd.) Fourth Ave., Harlow, Essex, England. Eds. Tudor David, Judith Hollingdale. adv.
Formerly: Education Committees Year Book (ISSN 0070-9158)

EDUCATIONAL AND PSYCHOLOGICAL INTERACTIONS. see PSYCHOLOGY

370 SW
EDUCATIONAL REPORTS UMEAA. (Text in English) 1973. irreg., no. 19, 1978. free. Umeaa Universitet, Pedagogiska Institutionen, S-901 87 Umeaa, Sweden.

370 IR
EDUCATIONAL RESEARCH AND STUDIES. irreg. Rs.150. Teacher Training College, Teheran, Educational Research Institute, 6 Sorayya Ave., Box 3071, Teheran, Iran.

370 JA
EDUCATIONAL STANDARDS IN JAPAN. (Text in English) 1959. irreg. Ministry of Education, 3-2-2 Kasumigaseki, Chiyoda-ku, Tokyo 100, Japan. illus. stat.

370 PK
EDUCATIONAL STATISTICS OF PUNJAB. (Text in English) a. unpriced. Bureau of Education, Lahore, Punjab, Pakistan. stat.

370 FR
EDUCATIONAL STATISTICS YEARBOOK. (Text in English) 1974. a. $3.75. Organization for Economic Cooperation and Development, Rue Andre-Pascal, 75775 Paris 16, France (U.S. orders to: O.E.C.D. Publications and Information Center, 1750 Pennsylvania Ave. N.W., Washington, D.C. 20006) (also avail. in microfiche)

370 UN ISSN 0070-9344
EDUCATIONAL STUDIES AND DOCUMENTS. (Text in English, French or Spanish) 1953. irreg; no. 15, 1974. price varies. Unesco, 7-9 Place de Fontenoy, 75700 Paris, France (Dist. in U.S. by: Unipub, 345 Park Ave. S., New York, NY 10010)

371.2 US ISSN 0091-8989
EDUCATIONAL TESTING SERVICE ANNUAL REPORT. 1949. a. free. ‡ Educational Testing Service, Princeton, NJ 08541. Ed. Peter B. Mann. illus. circ. 70,000. Key Title: Annual Report - Educational Testing Service.

372 373 US
EDUCATOR: OPEN COURT NEWSLETTER. 1967. 2-5/yr. free. ‡ Open Court Publishing Co., Box 599, La Salle, IL 61301. Ed. Robert J. Willmot. illus. circ. 30,000. (reprint service avail. from UMI)
Former titles: Bulletin: Open Court Newsletter; Open Court Newsletter (ISSN 0048-1912)

378.666 IV
ENSEIGNEMENT SUPERIEUR EN COTE-D'IVOIRE. a. Universite Nationale de Cote d'Ivoire, B.P. 8109, Abidjan, Ivory Coast.

370 SZ ISSN 0071-125X
ERZIEHUNG UND UNTERRICHT. 1967. irreg., no. 22, 1978. price varies. Paul Haupt AG, Falkenplatz 14, CH-3001 Berne, Switzerland. Ed.Bd.

370 GE ISSN 0075-2622
ERZIEHUNGS- UND SCHULGESCHICHTE JAHRBUCH. 1961. a. price varies. (Akademie der Paedagogischen Wissenschaften der DDR) Verlag Volk und Wissen, Berlin, E. Germany (D.D.R.)

370 PN ISSN 0378-4967
ESTADISTICA PANAMENA. SITUACION CULTURAL. SECCION 511. EDUCACION. 1967. a. Bl..30. Direccion de Estadistica y Censo, Contraloria General, Apartado 5213, Panama 5, Panama. circ. 1,100.

370 US ISSN 0071-3481
EXPLORATIONS IN EDUCATION. 1963. a. free. South Carolina State College, Orangeburg, SC 29115. Ed. Ernest W. Boston.

371 US ISSN 0092-461X
FACTS ABOUT MARYLAND PUBLIC EDUCATION. 1967. a. free. Department of Education, P.O. Box 8717, Baltimore-Washington International Airport, Baltimore, MD 21240. illus. circ. 10,000.
Formerly: Facts About Maryland Schools.

370 US ISSN 0015-0037
FERGUSON-FLORISSANT SCHOOLS. 1945. irreg. Ferguson-Florissant School District, Board of Education, 655 January Ave., Ferguson, MO 63135. Ed. Debra Rath. illus. circ. 23,000. (tabloid format)

370 FJ
FIJI. MINISTRY OF EDUCATION. REPORT. (Subseries of: Fiji. Parliament. Parliamentary Paper) a. Ministry of Education, Suva, Fiji.
Formerly (until 1977): Fiji. Ministry of Education, Youth and Sport. Report.

332 US ISSN 0430-4748
FINANCIAL AID NEWS. 1960. irreg. (approx 6/yr.) free. College Board, College Scholarship Service, 888 Seventh Ave., New York, NY 10019. Ed. Kathleen Brouder. bk. rev. circ. 20,000. (processed)

371 US
FLORIDA. DEPARTMENT OF EDUCATION. PROFESSIONAL PRACTICES COUNCIL. REPORT. 1969/70. a. free. Department of Education, Professional Practices Council, Tallahassee, FL 32304. Ed. Hugh Ingram. circ. 300.

370 335 GW ISSN 0067-589X
FREIE UNIVERSITAET BERLIN. OSTEUROPA-INSTITUT. ERZIEHUNGSWISSENSCHAFTLICHE VEROEFFENTLICHUNGEN. 1964. irreg., vol. 13, 1979. price varies. Verlag Otto Harrassowitz, Taunusstr. 6, Postfach 2929, 6200 Wiesbaden, W. Germany (B.R.D.) Eds. Oskar Anweiler, Siegfried Baske. circ. 1,000.

370 PO
FUNDACAO CALOUSTE GULBENKIAN. CENTRO DE INVESTIGACAO PEDAGOGICA. ESTUDOS.* 1972. a. Fundacao Calouste Gulbenkian, Centro de Investigacion Pedagogica, Avenida de Berna 56-3, Lisbon, Portugal.

374 II ISSN 0072-0720
GENERAL EDUCATION READING MATERIAL SERIES.* (Text in English and Hindi) 1959. irreg. price varies. Aligarh Muslim University, Aligarh, Uttar Pradesh, India.

370 GH
GHANA. MINISTRY OF EDUCATION. EDUCATIONAL STATISTICS. a. NC.2. Ministry of Education, Box M 45, Accra, Ghana. charts. stat.

371.9 US ISSN 0016-9870
GIFTED PUPIL; newsletter of programs for mentally gifted minors. 1965. irreg. free. Department of Education, Gifted and Talented Education Management Team, 721 Capitol Mall, Sacramento, CA 95814. Ed. Paul D. Plowman. bk. rev. bibl. illus. circ. 1,500.

370 SW ISSN 0436-1121
GOETEBORG STUDIES IN EDUCATIONAL SCIENCES. (Subseries of Acta Universitatis Gothoburgensis) (Text in English and Swedish) 1966. irreg., no. 35, 1980. price varies. Acta Universitatis Gothoburgensis, Box 5096, S-402 22 Goeteborg 5, Sweden (Dist. in U.S., Canada, and Mexico by: Humanities Press, Inc., 171 First Ave., Atlantic Highlands, NJ 07716) Eds. Kjell Haernqvist, Ference Marton, Karl Gustaf Stukat.

370 UK ISSN 0072-5897
GREAT BRITAIN. DEPARTMENT OF EDUCATION AND SCIENCE. EDUCATION SURVEYS. 1967. irreg. price varies. Department of Education and Science, Elizabeth House, York Rd., London SE1 7PH, England (Avail. from H.M.S.O., c/o Liaison Officer, Atlantic House, Holborn Viaduct, London EC1P 1BN, England).

370 UK ISSN 0072-5900
GREAT BRITAIN. DEPARTMENT OF EDUCATION AND SCIENCE. STATISTICS OF EDUCATION. 1961. a. in 6 pts. price varies. Department of Education and Science, Elizabeth House, York Rd., London SE1 7PH, England (Avail. from H.M.S.O., c/o Liaison Officer, Atlantic House, Holborn Viaduct, London EC1P 1BN, England)

373 UK ISSN 0072-7121
GREAT BRITAIN. SCHOOLS COUNCIL PUBLICATIONS. EXAMINATIONS BULLETINS. 1963. irreg. price varies. ‡ Methuen Educational, 11 New Fetter Lane, London EC4P 4EE. England.

370 UK ISSN 0072-713X
GREAT BRITAIN. SCHOOLS COUNCIL PUBLICATIONS. WORKING PAPERS. 1965. irreg. price varies. ‡ Methuen Educational, 11 New Fetter Lane, London EC4P 4EE, England.

GUIDE TO FREE-LOAN TRAINING FILMS (16 MM) see MOTION PICTURES

370 301 UK ISSN 0305-9839
HARD CHEESE; a journal of education. 1973. irreg. 20p.($1) ‡ c/o Ted Bowden, Ed., 95a Shooters Hill Rd., Blackheath, London SE3 8RL, England. adv. bk. rev. circ. 2,500.

370.25 US ISSN 0092-1777
HAWAII. DEPARTMENT OF EDUCATION. EDUCATIONAL DIRECTORY: STATE & DISTRICT OFFICE. a. $1.50. Department of Education, Liliuokalani Bldg., Honolulu, HI 96813. illus.

379.122 US ISSN 0090-9440
HAWAII. DEPARTMENT OF EDUCATION. OFFICE OF BUSINESS SERVICES. REPORT ON FEDERALLY CONNECTED PUPILS: HAWAII PUBLIC SCHOOLS. a. Department of Education, Office of Business Services, Honolulu, HI 96813. Key Title: Report on Federally Connected Pupils. Hawaii Public Schools.

371.2 US
HAWAII. DEPARTMENT OF EDUCATION. OFFICE OF BUSINESS SERVICES. STUDENT INFORMATION & RECORDS ADMINISTRATION BRANCH. PUBLIC AND PRIVATE SCHOOL ENROLLMENT. a. Department of Education, Office of Business Services, Honolulu, HI 96813.
Formerly: Hawaii. Department of Education. Office of Research and Planning. Information Systems Branch. Public and Private School Enrollment.

370 PK
HIGH SCHOOLS STATISTICS IN PUNJAB. 1973/74. irreg. Bureau of Education, Lahore, Punjab, Pakistan.

370 410 GW ISSN 0073-3792
HUEBER HOCHSCHULREIHE. 1971. irreg., vol. 35, 1975. price varies. Max Hueber Verlag, Max-Hueber-Str.4, 8045 Ismaning, W. Germany (B.R.D.)

373.1 SA
HUMAN SCIENCES RESEARCH COUNCIL. INSTITUTE FOR MANPOWER RESEARCH. PROJECT TALENT SURVEY: FINDINGS OF RESEARCH. (Subseries of Human Sciences Research Council. Institute of Manpower Research. Report MT) a. R.1. Human Sciences Research Council, Institute of Manpower Research, Private Bag X41, Pretoria 0001, South Africa. Ed. W. L. Roos. circ. 700 (English edt.); 900 (Afrikaans edt.)

370 150 US
HYMAN BLUMBERG SYMPOSIUM SERIES. 1973. irreg., no. 6, 1977. price varies. Johns Hopkins University Press, Baltimore, MD 21218.

I A S L CONFERENCE PROCEEDINGS. (International Association of School Librarianship) see LIBRARY AND INFORMATION SCIENCES

370 US ISSN 0073-8697
I/D/E/A MONOGRAPHS. 1967. irreg. $1-2 price varies. Institute for Development of Educational Activities, Inc., Informational Services, Box 446, Melbourne, FL 32901. (Affiliate: Charles F. Kettering Foundation)

370 US ISSN 0073-8700
I/D/E/A OCCASIONAL PAPERS. 1967. irreg. $1-2 price varies. Institute for Development of Educational Activities, Inc., Informational Services, Box 446, Melbourne, FL 32901. (Affiliate: Charles F. Kettering Foundation)

370 SP ISSN 0536-2512
IBERO-AMERICAN BUREAU OF EDUCATION. INFORMATION AND PUBLICATIONS DEPARTMENT SERIES V: TECHNICAL SEMINARS AND MEETINGS.* 1964. Ibero-American Bureau of Education, Avenida de los Reyes Catolicos, Ciudad Universitaria, Madrid 3, Spain.

371.9 US ISSN 0093-7223
IDAHO. STATE SUPERINTENDENT OF PUBLIC INSTRUCTION. ANNUAL REPORT. STATE OF IDAHO JOHNSON-O'MALLEY PROGRAM. Cover title: Indian Education Annual Report. irreg. State Superintendent of Public Instruction, Boise, ID 83720. Key Title: Annual Report: State of Idaho Johnson-O'Malley Program.

370 US ISSN 0073-4497
IDAHO EDUCATION ASSOCIATION. PROCEEDINGS. a. Idaho Education Association, 620 N. Sixth St., P.O.B. 2638, Boise, ID 83701.

379 US
ILLINOIS. STATE BOARD OF EDUCATION. ANNUAL REPORT. a. State Board of Education, 100 N. First St., Springfield, IL 62706. illus. stat.
Supersedes: Illinois. Department of Public Instruction. Annual State of Education Message (ISSN 0098-0269)

370 US
ILLINOIS EDUCATION REVIEW.* 1972. $3 per no. University of Illinois at Urbana-Champaign, College of Education, 140 Education Bldg., Urbana, IL 61801. Eds. Thomas L. McGreal, Dennis G. Wiseman. circ. 5,500. (tabloid format)

370 II
INDIA. MINISTRY OF EDUCATION AND SOCIAL WELFARE. DEPARTMENT OF EDUCATION. REPORT. 1948-49. a. free. Ministry of Education and Social Welfare, Department of Education, Shastri Bhavan, New Delhi 110001, India (Available from: Assistant Educational Adviser (Publications), Ministry of Education, Room No. 503, "C" Wing, Shastri Bhavan, New Delhi 110001, India) circ. 3,500.
Formerly: India. Ministry of Education and Social Welfare. Department of Education. Report (ISSN 0073-6201)

370 II ISSN 0579-6105
INDIA. MINISTRY OF EDUCATION AND SOCIAL WELFARE. PROVISIONAL STATISTICS OF EDUCATION IN THE STATES. (Text in English) 1954. a. controlled free circ. Ministry of Education and Social Welfare, Department of Education, Shastri Bhavan, New Delhi 110001, India (Available from: Assistant Educational Adviser (Publications), Ministry of Education, Room No. 503, "C" Wing, Shastri Bhavan, New Delhi 110001, India)

370 970.1 CN ISSN 0318-000X
INDIAN EDUCATION NEWSLETTER. vol. 5, 1975. irreg. contributions. (British Columbia Native Indian Teachers' Association) Indian Education Resources Centre, c/o Brock Hall 106, University of British Columbia, Vancouver, B.C. V6T 1W5, Canada. adv. bk. rev. film rev. bibl. illus. stat. circ. 5,000. (back issues avail.)

INDIANA DIRECTORY OF MUSIC TEACHERS. see MUSIC

370 US ISSN 0073-800X
INGLIS LECTURE. 1926. a. price varies. Harvard University Press, 79 Garden St., Cambridge, MA 02138.

370 US ISSN 0073-8123
INSIGHTS. 1964. irreg., vol. 16, 1979. membership. John Dewey Society, c/o Robert R. Sherman, Sec.-Treas., Norman Hall, University of Florida, Gainesville, FL 32611. Ed. B. Edward McClellan. circ. 350.

370 FR ISSN 0073-8174
INSTITUT COLLEGIAL EUROPEEN. BULLETIN. a. 30 Fr. Institut Collegial Europeen, Logis Royal de Loches, Loches, France.

INSTITUT FUER DEN WISSENSCHAFTLICHEN FILM. PUBLIKATIONEN ZU WISSENSCHAFTLICHEN FILMEN. SEKTION GESCHICHTE, PUBLIZISTIK. see MOTION PICTURES

INSTITUTUL PEDAGOGIC ORADEA. LUCRARI STIINTIFICE: SERIA PEDAGOGIE, PSIHOLOGIE, METODICA. see PSYCHOLOGY

370 500 US ISSN 0074-0829
INTER-AMERICAN COUNCIL FOR EDUCATION, SCIENCE, AND CULTURE. FINAL REPORT. (Text in Spanish, English, French, and Portuguese) a. $4. Organization of American States, Department of Publications, Washington, DC 20006. circ. 2,000.

373 CN ISSN 0020-563X
INTERMEDIATE TEACHER. 1962. a. membership. (Provincial Intermediate Teachers) B.C. Teachers' Federation, 105-2235 Burrard St., Vancouver, B.C. V6J 3H9, Canada. bk. rev. illus. circ. 1,000. Indexed: Can.Educ.Ind.

370 US
INTERNATIONAL AND INTERCULTURAL COMMUNICATION ANNUAL. 1975? a. $5. Speech Communication Association, 5105 Blacklick Rd., No. E, Annandale, VA 22003. (reprint service avail. from UMI)

370   SZ   ISSN 0074-1973
INTERNATIONAL BACCALAUREATE OFFICE. ANNUAL BULLETIN. (Editions in English, French) 1968. a. 8 Fr. International Baccalaureate Office - Office du Baccalaureat International, Palais Wilson, 1211 Geneva 14, Switzerland (Order in the U.S. from: International Baccalaureate North America, 888 Seventh Ave., New York, NY 10019) circ. 5,000 (approx.)
    Before 1972: International Baccalaureate Office. Semi-Annual Bulletin.

370   JA
INTERNATIONAL CHRISTIAN UNIVERSITY. INSTITUTE FOR EDUCATIONAL RESEARCH AND SERVICE. EDUCATIONAL STUDIES/ KOKUSAI KIRISUTOKYO DAIGAKU, KYOIKU KENKYU. (Text in Japanese and English) vol. 22, 1979. a. International Christian University, Institute for Educational Research and Service, 3-10-2 Osawa, Mitaka, Tokyo 181, Japan. Ed. Akira Miyake. circ. 500. (back issues avail.)

370   UN
INTERNATIONAL CONFERENCE ON EDUCATION. FINAL REPORT/CONFERENCE INTERNATIONAL DE L'EDUCATION. RAPPORT FINAL. (Editions in Arabic, English, French, Russian, and Spanish) 1934, 3rd (none 1940-45, 1969) a. until 33rd, 1971; thereafter biennial. free. Unesco, International Bureau of Education, Palais Wilson, CH-1211 Geneva 14, Switzerland. (also avail. in microfiche)
    Former titles: International Conference on Education. Proceedings (ISSN 0074-3275); Before no. 32, 1970: International Conference on Public Education. Proceedings.

371.9   US
INTERNATIONAL CONFERENCE ON PIAGETIAN THEORY AND THE HELPING PROFESSIONS. PROCEEDINGS. 8th, 1978. a. price varies. (Childrens Hospital of Los Angeles, University Affiliated Program) University of Southern California Press, c/o Bookstore, Mail Order Dept., University Park, Los Angeles, CA 90007.

428.4   US   ISSN 0538-933X
INTERNATIONAL READING ASSOCIATION. ANNUAL REPORT. a. International Reading Association, Inc., Box 8139, Newark, DE 19711. Key Title: Annual Report - International Reading Association.

370   US
INTERNATIONAL SCHOLARS DIRECTORY. 1972. irreg. $44.50. Marquis Academic Media, 200 E. Ohio St., Chicago, IL 60611 (And 4300 W. 62nd St., Indianapolis, Ind. 46268)

370   UN
INTERNATIONAL STUDIES IN EDUCATION. 1961. irreg., no. 36, 1979. price varies. Unesco Institute for Education - Unesco Institut fuer Paedagogik, Feldbrunnen Str. 58, 2000 Hamburg, 13, W. Germany (B.R.D.) (Dist. by: Swets & Zeitlinger B.V., Heerweg 347B, Lisse, Netherlands)

371.7   614.8   SZ   ISSN 0074-9524
INTERNATIONAL UNION OF SCHOOL AND UNIVERSITY HEALTH AND MEDICINE. CONGRESS REPORTS. quadrennial, 1975, 7th, Mexico City. International Union of School and University Health and Medicine, c/o Charles de Roche, Secr., 1M Sesselacker 73, CH-4059 Basel, Switzerland.

370   920   UK
INTERNATIONAL WHO'S WHO IN EDUCATION. 1980. irreg. price varies. Melrose Press Ltd., 17-21 Churchgate St., Soham, Ely, Cambridgeshire CB7 5DS, England (U.S. subscr. to: International Biographical Centre, 81 Adams Drive, Totowa, NJ 07512)

373   US
INVENTORY OF CONTINUING EDUCATION ACTIVITIES IN THE PUBLIC SCHOOL DISTRICTS OF PENNSYLVANIA. 1969. a. $3. (Department of Education) University of Pennsylvania, Department of Planning Studies in Continuing Education, University Park, PA 16802. Ed. B. M. Nead.
    Formerly: Inventory of Continuing Education Activities in Pennsylvania Secondary School Districts (ISSN 0085-2228)

379   US   ISSN 0091-8962
IOWA. DEPARTMENT OF PUBLIC INSTRUCTION. SUMMARY OF FEDERAL PROGRAMS. 1971. irreg. free. Department of Public Instruction, Grimes State Office Bldg, Des Moines, IA 50319. Ed. Earl Linden. circ. 600.

370   IE
IRISH COUNTRYWOMEN'S ASSOCIATION. AN GRIANAN PROGRAMME. 1954. a. 20p. per issue. Irish Countrywomen's Association, Ballsbridge, Dublin 4, Ireland. circ. 3,000.

370   IS   ISSN 0075-1081
ISRAEL. CENTRAL BUREAU OF STATISTICS. STUDENTS IN ACADEMIC INSTITUTIONS. (Subseries of its Special Series) 1964/65. a. I£90. Central Bureau of Statistics, Box 13015, Jerusalem, Israel.

J E B-POINTS. see *CHILDREN AND YOUTH — About*

370   MY
JOURNAL OF EDUCATIONAL RESEARCH/ JURNAL PENDIDIKAN. (Text mainly in English) 1970. a. National University of Malaysia, Box 1124, Jalan Pantai Baru, Kuala Lumpur 22-12, Malaysia.

JOURNALISM CAREER AND SCHOLARSHIP GUIDE; information on a journalism career and directory of college journalism programs. see *JOURNALISM*

370   LB
JULIUS C. STEVENS ANNUAL LECTURES IN EDUCATION. irreg. University of Liberia, William V. S. Tubman Teachers College, Monrovia, Liberia.

373   US   ISSN 0075-4560
JUNIOR HIGH SCHOOL ASSOCIATION OF ILLINOIS. STUDY. 1967. irreg., approx. a. price varies. ‡ Interstate Printers and Publishers, Inc., 19 N. Jackson St., Danville, IL 61832.

150   300   370   FI   ISSN 0075-4625
JYVASKYLA STUDIES IN EDUCATION, PSYCHOLOGY AND SOCIAL RESEARCH. (Text in Finnish or English; summaries in English) 1962. irreg. price varies. Jyvaskylan Yliopisto, Kirjasto - University of Jyvaskyla, Seminaarinkatu 15, 40100 Jyvaskyla 10, Finland. Ed. Lea Pulkkinen. circ. 400-500. Indexed: Psychol.Abstr.

370   JA
KANAZAWA UNIVERSITY. FACULTY OF EDUCATION. BULLETIN: HUMANITIES, SOCIAL AND EDUCATIONAL SCIENCES. (Text in Japanese; summaries and some articles in English) irreg. Kanazawa University, Faculty of Education - Kanazawa Daigaku Kyoikugabuku, 1-1 Marunouchi, Kanazawa 920, Japan.

370   US
KANSAS. STATE DEPARTMENT OF EDUCATION. BULLETIN. irreg. State Department of Education, Kansas State Education Bldg., 120 E. 10th St., Topeka, KS 66612.
    Continues: Kansas. State Department of Public Instruction. Bulletin (ISSN 0449-7953)

370   US   ISSN 0099-0728
KANSAS EDUCATIONAL DIRECTORY. (Subseries of its Bulletin) a. State Department of Education, Kansas State Education Bldg., 120 10th St., Topeka, KS 66612.

370   KE   ISSN 0075-5869
KENYA. MINISTRY OF EDUCATION. ANNUAL REPORT. a, latest 1975. Government Printing and Stationery Department, Box 30128, Nairobi, Kenya.

370   410   US
LANGUAGE IN EDUCATION. THEORY AND PRACTICE. 1978. irreg., approx. 10/yr. $40. Center for Applied Linguistics, 3520 Prospect St., N.W., Washington, DC 20007.

370   US   ISSN 0191-8850
LEARNING AND SOCIETY. 1981. a. $55. Pergamon Press, Inc., Journals Division, Maxwell House, Fairview Park, Elmsford, NY 10523 (And Headington Hill Hall, Oxford OX3 0BW, England) (also avail. in microform from MIM,UMI)

370   IT   ISSN 0075-8760
LEONARDO; almanacco di educazione popolare. 1952. a. L.1000. Ente Nazionale per le Biblioteche Popolari e Scholastiche, Via Michele Mercati, 4, 00197 Rome, Italy.

370   LO
LESOTHO. MINISTRY OF EDUCATION AND CULTURE. ANNUAL REPORT OF THE PERMANENT SECRETARY. 1966. a. Ministry of Education and Culture, Maseru, Lesotho.

370   SP   ISSN 0075-9201
LIBROS Y MATERIAL DE ENSENANZA. 1958. a. free. Instituto Nacional del Libro Espanol, Comision Asesora de Editores de Libros de Ensenanza, Santiago Rusinol, 8, Madrid-3, Spain. Ed. Ramon Grimaldo Huete. adv. bk. rev. circ. 10,000.

370   US
LOUISIANA PHILOSOPHY OF EDUCATION JOURNAL. vol. 5, 1979. a. $12. Louisiana Philosophy of Education Society, c/o Joe L. Green, Chairman, Department of Education, Louisiana State University in Shreveport, 8515 Youree Dr., Shreveport, LA 71115.

370   CN
M A C E NEWSLETTER. 1977. irreg. Manitoba Association of Confluent Educators, 13-2871 Ness Ave., Winnipeg, Man. R3J 1A9, Canada.
    Formerly: Confluent Education Newsletter (ISSN 0707-7920)

371   MM   ISSN 0076-3489
MALTA. CENTRAL OFFICE OF STATISTICS. EDUCATION STATISTICS. a. £0.17. Central Office of Statistics, Auberge de Castille, Valletta, Malta (Subscr. to: Department of Information, Auberge de Castille, Valletta, Malta)

370   CN
MANITOBA EDUCATIONAL RESEARCH COUNCIL. POLICY STUDY. 1977. a. Manitoba Educational Research Council, 693 Taylor Ave., Winnipeg, Man R3M 3T8, Canada.

370   NZ   ISSN 0076-4280
MAORI EDUCATION FOUNDATION. ANNUAL REPORT. 1962. a. free. Maori Education Foundation, P.O. Box 3745, Wellington, New Zealand.

MASSACHUSETTS ADVOCACY CENTER. ANNUAL REPORT. see *LAW*

370   016   US   ISSN 0076-5112
MASTER'S THESES IN EDUCATION. 1951. a. $20. Research Publications, Box 92, Cedar Falls, IA 50613. Ed. H. M. Silvey.

370   GW   ISSN 0076-5627
MAX-PLANCK-INSTITUT FUER BILDUNGSFORSCHUNG, BERLIN. STUDIEN UND BERICHTE. (Text usually in German; summaries in English) 1965. irreg., vol. 40, 1979. price varies. Max-Planck-Institut fuer Bildungsforschung, Lentzeallee 94, 1000 Berlin 33, W. Germany (B.R.D.)

370   AT   ISSN 0076-6275
MELBOURNE STUDIES IN EDUCATION. 1957. a. Aus.$15.60. (University of Melbourne, School of Education) Melbourne University Press, Box 278, Carlton South, Vic. 3053, Australia (Dist. by International Scholarly Book Services, Inc., Box 555, Forest Grove, Ore. 97116) Ed. Stephen Murray-Smith.

370   GO
MESSAGE; bulletin de liaison des enseignants gabonais. irreg. 600 Fr.CFA. Direction de l'Enseignement du Premier Degre, B.P. 221, Libreville, Gabon.
    Formerly: Tam-Tam.

370   MX
MEXICO. SECRETARIA DE EDUCACION PUBLICA. INFORME DE LABORES. irreg. Secretaria de Educacion Publica, Mexico D.F., Mexico.

370   US
MICHIGAN STATE UNIVERSITY. INSTITUTE FOR INTERNATIONAL STUDIES IN EDUCATION. PUBLICATIONS. 1962. irreg. Michigan State University, Institute for International Studies in Education, 513 Erickson Hall, E. Lansing, MI 48823.

370   PK
MIDDLE SCHOOLS STATISTICS IN PUNJAB. 1973/74. irreg. Bureau of Education, Lahore, Punjab, Pakistan.

370 US ISSN 0092-2986
MIDWEST HISTORY OF EDUCATION SOCIETY. JOURNAL. 1972. a. $3. University of Northern Iowa, College of Education, Education Center 513, Cedar Falls, IA 50613. Ed. Edward Rutkowski. circ. 100. Key Title: Journal of the Midwest History of Education Society.

373 US ISSN 0190-9185
MONITORING THE FUTURE; questionnaire responses from the nation's high school seniors. 1975. a. $15. University of Michigan, Institute for Social Research, Box 1248, Ann Arbor, MI 48106.
Secondary

370 UN ISSN 0077-1007
MONOGRAPHS ON EDUCATION. (Text in English, French and Spanish) 1962. irreg.; vol. 8, 1973. price varies. Unesco, 7-9 Place de Fontenoy, 75700 Paris, France (Dist. in U.S. by: Unipub, 345 Park Ave. S., New York, NY 10010)

370 GE ISSN 0077-1481
MONUMENTA PAEDAGOGICA. 1960. irreg., 1965, vol. 2. price varies. Akademie der Wissenschaften der DDR) Verlag Volk und Wissen, Berlin, E. Germany (D.D.R.)

370 CN ISSN 0027-7037
N T A JOURNAL. vol. 69, 1980. irreg. $5 (Includes NTA Bulletin) Newfoundland Teachers Association, 3 Kenmount Rd., St. John's, Nfld. A1B 1W1, Canada. Ed. Heber E. Walters. adv. bk. rev. charts. illus. circ. 8,500. Indexed: Can.Ind.

370 UK ISSN 0077-5932
N U S YEARBOOK. 1922. a. £5. National Union of Students, Communications Department, 3 Endsleigh Street, London WC1H 0DU, England. circ. 5,000.

370   II
NAGALAND EDUCATION BULLETIN. (Text in English) vol. 26, 1973. irreg. Directorate of Education, Kohima, Nagaland, India.

NATIONAL ADVISORY COUNCIL ON WOMEN'S EDUCATIONAL PROGRAMS. ANNUAL REPORT. see *WOMEN'S INTERESTS*

371 US ISSN 0550-7421
NATIONAL ASSOCIATION OF INDEPENDENT SCHOOLS. ANNUAL REPORT. 1963. a. National Association of Independent Schools, 18 Tremont St., Boston, MA 02108. stat. (reprint service avail. from UMI) Key Title: Annual Report - National Association of Independent Schools.

377.9 US
NATIONAL CATHOLIC EDUCATIONAL ASSOCIATION. OCCASIONAL PAPERS. 1975. irreg. price varies. National Catholic Educational Association, One Dupont Circle, Suite 350, Washington, DC 20036. (reprint service avail. from UMI)

NATIONAL COUNCIL OF TEACHERS OF MATHEMATICS. YEARBOOK. see *MATHEMATICS*

370.6 US ISSN 0092-5691
NATIONAL EDUCATION ASSOCIATION OF THE UNITED STATES. ANNUAL SUMMATIVE EVALUATION REPORT. 1973. a. National Education Association, 1201 16th St. N.W., Washington, DC 20036. Key Title: Annual Summative Evaluation Report - National Education Association.

370 US ISSN 0190-7662
NATIONAL EDUCATION ASSOCIATION OF THE UNITED STATES. PROCEEDINGS OF THE ANNUAL MEETING. 1860. a. $5. ‡ National Education Association, 1201 Sixteenth St., N.W., Washington, DC 20036 (Order from: N E A Order Dept., Academic Bldg., Saw Mill Rd., West Haven CT 06516) index. (also avail. in microfiche)
Formerly: National Education Association of the United States. Addresses and Proceedings (ISSN 0077-4243)

370 CE ISSN 0085-3747
NATIONAL EDUCATION SOCIETY OF SRI LANKA. JOURNAL.* (Text in English) a. Rs.31.($1) Metro Printers, 19 Austin Place, Borella, Colombo 8, Sri Lanka. Ed. Swarna Jayaweera.

370 JA ISSN 0085-378X
NATIONAL INSTITUTE FOR EDUCATIONAL RESEARCH. RESEARCH BULLETIN. (Text in English) 1959. irreg. free. National Institute for Educational Research, Planning Section, 6-5-22 Shimomeguro, Meguro-ku, Tokyo 153, Japan. Ed. Bd. charts. illus. stat. circ. controlled. (tabloid format) Indexed: Psychol.Abstr.

373.1 US ISSN 0360-0815
NATIONAL PANORAMA OF AMERICAN YOUTH. a. Josep Communications, Box 1286, Denver, CO 80201. illus. bibl.

370 500 CN ISSN 0316-4047
NATIONAL RESEARCH COUNCIL, CANADA. ANNUAL REPORT ON SCHOLARSHIPS AND GRANTS IN AID OF RESEARCH/CONSEIL NATIONAL DE RECHERCHES DU CANADA. COMPTE RENDU ANNUEL DES BOURSES ET SUBVENTIONS D'AIDE A LA RECHERCHE. (Text and summaries in English and French) 1958. a. Can.$2.50. National Research Council of Canada, Office of Grants & Scholarships, Ottawa, Ont. K1A 0R6, Canada. Ed. I. C. Macfarlane. stat.
Formerly: National Research Council, Canada. Annual Report on Support of University Research.

370 US ISSN 0077-5762
NATIONAL SOCIETY FOR THE STUDY OF EDUCATION. YEARBOOK. 1902. a. in 2 pts. price varies. University of Chicago Press, 5801 S. Ellis Ave., Chicago, IL 60637. Ed. Kenneth J. Rehage. (reprint service avail. from UMI,ISI)

370   CH
NATIONAL TAIWAN NORMAL UNIVERSITY. GRADUATE INSTITUTE OF EDUCATION. BULLETIN. (Text in English and Chinese) vol. 17, 1975. a. National Taiwan Normal University, Graduate Institute of Education, East Ho-Ping Road, Taipei, Taiwan, Republic of China.

372 NE ISSN 0077-6750
NEDERLANDSE JEUGD EN HAAR ONDERWIJS/NETHERLANDS YOUTH AND ITS EDUCATION. (Text in Dutch and English) 1947. a. fl.14.45. Centraal Bureau voor de Statistiek, Prinses Beatrixlaan 428, Voorburg, Netherlands (Orders to: Staatsuitgeverij, Christoffel Plantijnstraat, The Hague, Netherlands)

370 US ISSN 0548-1384
NEED A LIFT? 1951. a. $1 per no. ‡ American Legion, Education Program, Box 1055, Indianapolis, IN 46206. Ed. Mike Ayers. adv. circ. 150,000.

NEPAL. DEPARTMENT OF AGRICULTURAL EDUCATION AND RESEARCH. ANNUAL REPORT. see *AGRICULTURE*

370   NE
NETHERLANDS. CENTRAAL BUREAU VOOR DE STATISTIEK. STATISTIEK VAN HET BEROEPSONDERWIJS: BEROEPSBEGELEIDEND ONDERWIJS LEERLINGWEZEN. a. fl.6.30. Centraal Bureau voor de Statistiek, Prinses Beatrixlaan 428, Voorburg, Netherlands (Orders to: Staatsuitgeverij, Christoffel Plantijnstraat, The Hague, Netherlands) stat.

370   NE
NETHERLANDS. CENTRAAL BUREAU VOOR DE STATISTIEK. STATISTIEK VAN HET BEROEPSONDERWIJS: SOCIAAL-PEDAGOGISCH ONDERWIJS. (Text in Dutch and English) 1968/69. a. fl.10.25. Centraal Bureau voor de Statistiek, Prinses Beatrixlaan 428, Voorburg, Netherlands (Orders to: Staatsuitgeverij, Christoffel Plantijnstraat, The Hague, Netherlands)
Formerly: Netherlands. Centraal Bureau voor de Statistiek. Statistiek van het Sociaal-Pedagogisch Onderwijs. Statistics on Socio-Pedagogic Training (ISSN 0077-7374)

370   NE
NETHERLANDS. MINISTERIE VAN ONDERWIJS EN WETENSCHAPPEN. ONDERWIJSVERSLAG. 1973. a. fl.32. Staatsuitgeverij, Chr. Plantijnstraat, The Hague, Netherlands. (Prepared by: Ministerie van Onderwijs en Wetenschappen) circ. 1,000.

371.2 US ISSN 0362-5958
NEW JERSEY. DEPARTMENT OF EDUCATION. EDUCATIONAL ASSESSMENT PROGRAM STATE REPORT. a. Department of Education, Division of Operations Research and Evaluation, 225 W. State St., Trenton, NJ 08625. Key Title: Educational Assessment Program State Report.

370   US
NEW SCHOOLS EXCHANGE. DIRECTORY AND RESOURCE GUIDE. 1969. a. $5. New Schools Exchange, Pettigrew, AR 72752. Ed. Grace Dailey-Harwood. adv. bk. rev. film rev, bibl. cum. index. circ. 3,000. (back issues avail.)

370 PK ISSN 0077-8826
NEW TEACHER. (Text in English, Urdu and Pashto) 1952. a. Rs.8. University of Peshawar, College of Education, Peshawar, Pakistan. Ed. Bd.

370 379 NZ ISSN 0077-958X
NEW ZEALAND. CENTRAL ADVISORY COMMITTEE ON THE APPOINTMENTS AND PROMOTION OF PRIMARY TEACHERS. REPORT TO THE MINISTER OF EDUCATION. 1961. quinquennial. free. ‡ Central Advisory Committee, c/o Department of Education, Private Bag, Government Buildings, Wellington, New Zealand. circ. controlled.

NIHON KYOIKUHO GAKKAI NEMPO. see *LAW*

370 US ISSN 0077-9253
NONPUBLIC SCHOOL ENROLLMENT AND STAFF, NEW YORK STATE. 1966. a. free. ‡ Education Department, Information Center on Education, Albany, NY 12234. circ. controlled.
Formerly: Survey of Nonpublic Schools in New York State.

NORTHWEST ASSOCIATION OF SCHOOLS AND COLLEGES. PROCEEDINGS. see *EDUCATION — Higher Education*

370   CN
NOUVEAU POUVOIR. irreg., (approx. 10-12/yr.) Federation Nationale des Enseignants Quebecois, 1601 rue Delorimier, Montreal, Que. H2K 4M5, Canada. circ. controlled.

370   GW
NUMERUS CLAUSUS - FINESSEN. 1973. a. DM.10. Verein Freunde und Foerderer der Deutschen Studentenschaft e.V., Untere Hausbreite 11, 8000 Munich 45, W. Germany (B.R.D.) Ed. Gundolf Seidenspinner. adv.
Former titles: Numerus Clausus - Alternativen; Numerus Clausus - Ersatzstudiengaenge.

370 US ISSN 0095-6694
O.S.S.C. BULLETIN. irreg. Oregon School Study Council, 124 College of Education, University of Oregon, Eugene, OR 97403.
Formerly: Oregon School Study Council. Bulletin.

371 US ISSN 0078-4230
OHIO UNIVERSITY. CENTER FOR EDUCATIONAL RESEARCH AND SERVICE. PUPIL SERVICES SERIES.* irreg. price varies. Ohio University, Center for Educational Research & Service, Athens, OH 45701.

370.25 CN ISSN 0316-8549
ONTARIO DIRECTORY OF EDUCATION. a. Can.$8.03 per no. Ministry of Education, Toronto, Ont. M7A 1L2, Canada (Orders to: Publications Centre, Ministry of Government Services, 880 Bay St., Toronto, Ont. M7A 1N8, Canada)

370 NE ISSN 0077-6769
ONTWIKKELING VAN HET ONDERWIJS IN NEDERLAND/DEVELOPMENT OF EDUCATION IN THE NETHERLANDS. (Text in Dutch and English) 1966. irreg. fl.31. Centraal Bureau voor de Statistiek, Prinses Beatrixlaan 428, Voorburg, Netherlands (Orders to: Staatsuitgeverij, Christoffel Plantijnstraat, The Hague, Netherlands)

370 AT
OPEN BOOK. 1972. irreg. Aus.$5. 21 Smith St., Thornbury, Vic. 3071, Australia. Ed.Bd.

378.777 US ISSN 0093-3465
OPPORTUNITIES IN IOWA'S AREA SCHOOLS. a. Department of Public Instruction, Grimes State Office Building, Des Moines, IA 50319. illus. Indexed: ERIC.

374 US ISSN 0364-0027
OREGON. STATE ADVISORY COUNCIL FOR CAREER AND VOCATIONAL EDUCATION. ANNUAL EVALUATION REPORT. Variant title: Report on the Availability of Postsecondary and Adult Vocational Education to Oregon's Citizens. a. State Advisory Council for Career and Vocational Education, 304 Executive House, 325 Thirteenth St., N.E., Salem, OR 97310. Key Title: Annual Evaluation Report - State Advisory Council for Career and Vocational Education to Oregon's Citizens.

371 US ISSN 0078-5792
OREGON STATE MONOGRAPHS. STUDIES IN EDUCATION AND GUIDANCE. 1944. irreg. price varies. Oregon State University Press, 101 Waldo Hall, Corvallis, OR 97331.

372 AU
P A - KONTAKTE. (Text in German) 1972. irreg. International Institute for Children's Literature and Reading Research, Fuhrmannsgasse 18a, A-1080 Vienna, Austria. Ed. Richard Bamberger. bibl.

370 BE ISSN 0079-0370
PAEDAGOGICA BELGICA ACADEMICA; periodical survey of the Belgian University Studies in Education. (Text in Dutch, French, and English; summaries in Dutch or French) 1951. a. 350 Fr. Rijksuniversiteit te Gent, Seminaries voor Historische en voor Vergelijkende Pedagogiek, A. Baertsoenkaai 3, B-9000 Ghent, Belgium. Ed. H. Van daele. circ. 400.

370 US
PAIDEIA. 1972. a. $5. State University of New York at Buffalo, Department of Foundational Studies, 1300 Elmwood Ave., Buffalo, NY 14222. Ed. Albert Grande. adv. bk. rev. (back issues avail) Indexed: M.L.A.

370 PL ISSN 0137-3943
PAIDEIA; miedzynarodowy rocznik pedagogiczny. (Text in various languages) irreg., vol. 6, 1978. 60 Zl. (Polska Akademia Nauk, Komitet Nauk Pedagogicznych) Ossolineum, Publishing House of the Polish Academy of Sciences, Rynek 9, Wroclaw, Poland (Dist. by: Ars Polona-Ruch, Krakowskie Przedmiescie 7, Warsaw, Poland) Ed. B. Suchodolski.

370 PK ISSN 0078-7914
PAKISTAN. CENTRAL BUREAU OF EDUCATION. EDUCATIONAL STATISTICS BULLETIN SERIES. (Text in English) 1966. irreg. Central Bureau of Education, Sector H-9, Cultural Area, Islamabad, Pakistan.

370 PK ISSN 0078-8287
PAKISTAN. MINISTRY OF EDUCATION. YEARBOOK. (Text in English) a. unpriced. Ministry of Education, Documentation Section, Curriculum Wing, Sector H-9, P.O. Shaigan, Industrial Area, Islamabad, Pakistan.
Formerly: Pakistan. Central Bureau of Education. Yearbook (ISSN 0078-7922)

372.21 CN
PARENT COOPERATIVE PRESCHOOLS INTERNATIONAL. DIRECTORY. 1969. irreg. Can.$8 to individuals (3 nos.); Can.$7 for libraries. Parent Cooperative Preschools International, International Office, Whiteside Taylor Center for Cooperative Education, 20551 Lakeshore Road, Baie d'Urfe, Quebec H9X 1R3, Canada. Ed. Barbara Cantor. adv. bk. rev. circ. 6,000-7,000.

370 SW
PEDAGOGISK DEBATT UMEAA. 1972. irreg. free. Umeaa Universitet, Pedagogiska Institutionen, S-901 87 Umeaa, Sweden. circ. controlled.

370 SW
PEDAGOGISKA RAPPORTER UMEAA. 1969. irreg. free. Umeaa Universitet, Pedagogiska Institutionen, S-901 87 Umeaa, Sweden.

372 AT ISSN 0311-1490
PEN. 1973. irreg. Aus.$0.75 per issue. Primary English Teaching Association of New South Wales, Box 55, Gordon, N.S.W. 2072, Australia. Ed. R. D. Nalshe. circ. 5,000.

370 US ISSN 0079-0451
PENN STATE STUDIES. irreg. price varies. Pennsylvania State University Press, 215 Wagner Bldg., University Park, PA 16802. (reprint service avail. from UMI)

370 US ISSN 0085-4824
PENNSYLVANIA. OFFICE OF THE BUDGET. PROGRAM BUDGET. Cover title: Commonwealth of Pennsylvania. Executive Budget. (In 2 volumes) 1927. a. free. Office of the Budget, Main Capitol Bldg., Harrisburg, PA 17120.

370 US ISSN 0079-0508
PENNSYLVANIA SCHOOL STUDY COUNCIL. REPORTS. 1947. irreg. (20-25 per year) price varies (free to members) Pennsylvania School Study Council, 244 Chambers Bldg., Pennsylvania State University, University Park, PA 16802. Ed. Hugh W. Fraser. circ. 200.

370 US ISSN 0093-7568
PENNSYLVANIA STATE UNIVERSITY. RESEARCH PUBLICATIONS AND PROFESSIONAL ACTIVITIES. 1956. a. free. Pennsylvania State University, Vice President for Research & Graduate Studies, 207 Old Main Bldg., University Park, PA 16802. Ed. Harlan Berger. circ. 2,000.
Formerly: Pennsylvania State University. Council on Research. Research Publications and Other Contributions (ISSN 0079-0583)

370 PE
PERU. MINISTERIO DE EDUCACION PUBLICA. OFICINA SECTORIAL DE PLANIFICACION.PLAN BIENAL. irreg. Ministerio de Educacion Publica, Oficina Sectorial de Planificacion, Lima, Peru. illus.

PHILIPPINE NORMAL COLLEGE. LANGUAGE STUDY CENTER. OCCASIONAL PAPER. see *LINGUISTICS*

370 US ISSN 0079-1733
PHILOSOPHY OF EDUCATION SOCIETY. PROCEEDINGS OF THE ANNUAL MEETINGS. (Proceedings for 1st-13th meetings not published) 1958, 14th meeting proceedings. a. price varies. Philosophy of Education Society, c/o Prof. Thomas Nelson, Illinois State Univ., Normal, IL 61761. circ. 1,200.

370 PL ISSN 0079-340X
POLSKA AKADEMIA NAUK. ODDZIAL W KRAKOWIE. KOMISJA NAUK PEDAGOGICZNYCH. PRACE. (Text in Polish; summaries in English and Russian) 1958. irreg., no. 18, 1979. price varies. Ossolineum, Publishing House of the Polish Academy of Sciences, Rynek 9, 50-106 Wroclaw, Poland (Dist. by Ars Polona-Ruch, Krakowskie Przedmiescie 7, Warsaw, Poland)

370 PL ISSN 0079-3418
POLSKA AKADEMIA NAUK. ODDZIAL W KRAKOWIE. KOMISJA NAUK PEDAGOGICZNYCH. ROCZNIK. (Text in Polish; summaries in English, French, German, Russian) 1961. a. 50 Zl. Ossolineum, Publishing House of the Polish Academy of Sciences, Rynek 9, 50-106 Wroclaw, Poland (Dist. by Ars Polona-Ruch, Krakowskie Przedmiescie 7, Warsaw, Poland) Ed. Kamila Arozowska.

370 UN
POPULATION EDUCATION IN ASIA NEWSLETTER. 1974. 2/yr. free or on exchange basis. Unesco, Regional Office for Education in Asia and Oceania, Population Education Programme Service, Box 1425, Bangkok G.P.O., Thailand. circ. 2,000.
Supersedes: Unesco Regional Office for Education in Asia. Regional Conference Reports (ISSN 0503-4469)

370 PO ISSN 0079-4155
PORTUGAL. INSTITUTO NACIONAL DE ESTATISTICA. ESTATISTICAS DE EDUCACAO. 1940. a. $100. Instituto Nacional de Estatistica, Av. Antonio Jose de Almeida, Lisbon 1, Portugal (Orders to: Imprensa Nacional, Casa da Moeda, Direccao Comercial, rua D. Francisco Manuel de Melo 5, Lisbon 1, Portugal)

PRAJNAN. see *SCIENCES: COMPREHENSIVE WORKS*

370 RM
PROBLEME DE PEDAGOGIE CONTEMPORANA. 1970. 3-4/yr. free to Romanian schools; exchange basis to others. Biblioteca Centrala Pedagogica, Str. Zalomit Nr. 12, Bucharest, Romania. Ed. Alfred Lauterman. index. circ. 5,000.
Supersedes: Buletin de Informare Pedagogica (ISSN 0007-3792)

379.73 US
PROGRESS OF EDUCATION IN THE UNITED STATES OF AMERICA. (Editions in English, French, Russian, and Spanish) a. price varies. U. S. Office of Education, Dept. of Health, Education, and Welfare, Washington, DC 20202 (Orders to: Supt. of Documents, Washington, DC 20402)
Formerly: Progress of Public Education in the United States (ISSN 0079-6891)

PSYCHOLOGIA A SKOLA. see *PSYCHOLOGY*

370 US ISSN 0077-9229
PUBLIC SCHOOL PROFESSIONAL PERSONNEL REPORT, NEW YORK STATE. 1967-68. ‡ Education Department, Information Center on Education, Albany, NY 12234. circ. controlled.

372 AT ISSN 0310-4079
QUEENSLAND. DEPARTMENT OF EDUCATION. RESEARCH AND CURRICULUM BRANCH. CURRICULUM PAPER. 1973. irreg. free. Department of Education, Research and Curriculum Branch, P.O. Box 33, North Quay, Qld. 4001, Australia. Ed. J. Fitzgerald.

370 AT
QUEENSLAND. DEPARTMENT OF EDUCATION. RESEARCH BRANCH, RESEARCH SERIES. 1975. irreg. Department of Education, Research Branch, Box 33, North Quay, Qld. 4000, Australia.

370 AT ISSN 0313-8143
QUEENSLAND EDUCATION DIGEST. 1976. a. Department of Education, Information and Publications Branch, P.O. Box 33, North Quay, Qld. 4000, Australia. Ed. J. L. Finger.

507 MY
R E C S A M ANNUAL REPORT. (Text in English) a. Southeast Asian Ministers of Education Organisation, Regional Centre for Education in Science and Mathematics, Glugor, Penang, Malaysia. illus. circ. 200.

371 US ISSN 0085-4093
RACIAL/ETHNIC DISTRIBUTION OF PUBLIC SCHOOL STUDENTS AND STAFF, NEW YORK STATE. 1968-69. a. free. ‡ Education Department, Information Center on Education, Albany, NY 12234. circ. controlled.

370   SA
RANDSE AFRIKAANSE UNIVERSITEIT. JAARBOEK. 1968. a. free. Rand Afrikaans University, Box 524, Johannesburg 2000, South Africa. circ. controlled. (processed)

370   SA
RANDSE AFRIKAANSE UNIVERSITEIT. OP EN OM DIE KAMPUS. 1968. a. free. Rand Afrikaans University, Box 524, Johannesburg 2000, South Africa. adv. circ. controlled. (processed)

370   SA
RANDSE AFRIKAANSE UNIVERSITEIT. PROSPEKTUS. 1968. a. free. Rand Afrikaans University, Box 524, Johannesburg 2000, South Africa. circ. controlled. (processed)

371   US
READINGS FOR INTRODUCTION TO TEACHING. irreg. price varies. Harper and Row Publishers, Inc., 10 East 53rd St., New York, NY 10022.

370.15   US   ISSN 0363-5953
READINGS IN EDUCATIONAL PSYCHOLOGY: CONTEMPORARY PERSPECTIVES. (Subseries of: Contemporary Perspectives Reader Series) irreg. Harper & Row Publishers, Inc., 10 E. 53rd St., New York, NY 10022. illus.

370   UK
REPORTS ON EDUCATION. irreg (4-6/yr. free. Department of Education and Science, Information Division, Elizabeth House, 39 York Rd., London SE1 7PH 555 England (Avail. from H.M.S.O., c/o Liaison Officer, Atlantic House, Holborn Viaduct, London EC1P 1BN, England)

370.19   US   ISSN 0197-5080
RESEARCH IN SOCIOLOGY OF EDUCATION AND SOCIALIZATION; a research annual. 1980. a. J A I Press, Box 1285, 165 W. Putnam Ave., Greenwich, CT 06830.

REVIEW OF CHILD DEVELOPMENT RESEARCH. see CHILDREN AND YOUTH — About

370   II
REVIEW OF EDUCATION IN INDIA. 1950. a. Ministry of Education and Social Welfare, Department of Education, Shastri Bhavan, New Delhi 110001, India (Available from: Assistant Educational Adviser (Publications), Ministry of Education, Room No. 503, "C" Wing, Shastri Bhavan, New Delhi 110001, India)

371.8 332.7   CK
REVISTA A P I C E/A P I C E JOURNAL. (Text in Spanish; summaries in English) 1975. irreg. Bol.$340($8) Asociacion Panamericana de Instituciones de Credito Educativo, Calle 38 no. 8-56, Apdo. Aereo 17388, Bogota, Colombia. circ. 1,000. (back issues avail.)

REVISTA BRASILEIRA DE TELEDUCACAO. see COMMUNICATIONS — Radio And Television

377.8   BL
REVISTA DE EDUCACAO A E C. irreg. Associacao de Educacao Catolica do Brasil, Rua Martins Ferreira 23, Botafogo, 22271 Rio de Janeiro, Brazil.
Formerly: Associacao de Educacao Catolica do Brasil. Boletim.

370   BL   ISSN 0482-5527
REVISTA DE EDUCACAO E CULTURA. 1960. a. Secretaria de Estado de Educacao de Cultura, Rua Ulhoa Cintra s/n, Recife-Pernambuco, Brazil.

370   US   ISSN 0080-2751
RHODE ISLAND EDUCATION ASSOCIATION. JOURNAL. a. Rhode Island Education Association, 300 Hennessey Ave., North Providence, RI 02911.

370   IT
RICERCHE DI SOCIOLOGIA DELL'EDUCAZIONE E PEDAGOGIA COMPARATA. 1974. irreg. (Universita degli Studi di Messina, Istituto di Pedagogia) Peloritana Editrice, Messina, Italy. Dir. Giuseppe Catalfamo.
Educational sociology & comparative teaching

370   PL   ISSN 0137-9585
ROCZNIK PEDAGOGICZNY. irreg., vol. 6, 1980. 90 Zl. (Polska Akademia Nauk, Komitet Nauk Pedagogicznych) Ossolineum, Publishing House of the Polish Academy of Sciences, Rynek 9, Wroclaw, Poland (Dist. by: Ars Polona-Ruch, Krakowskie Przedmiescie 7, Warsaw, Poland) Ed. Wincenty Okon.

370   PL   ISSN 0080-4754
ROZPRAWY Z DZIEJOW OSWIATY. (Text in Polish; summaries in English or Russian) 1958. a. 60 Zl. (Polska Akademia Nauk, Instytut Historii Nauki, Oswiaty i Techniki, Pracownia Dziejow Oswiaty) Ossolineum, Publishing House of the Polish Academy of Sciences, Rynek 9, Wroclaw, Poland (Dist. by Ars Polona-Ruch, Krakowskie Przedmiescie 7, Warsaw, Poland) Ed. Jozef Miaso. bk. rev. circ. 600.
History

370   US
S C E A EMPHASIS. vol. 29, 1973. 14-18/yr. $3. South Carolina Education Association, 421 Zimalcrest Drive, Columbia, SC 29210. Ed. Patsy O. Towery. adv. bk. rev. circ. 26,000.
Formerly: South Carolina Education News Emphasis (ISSN 0038-3066)

370   NZ   ISSN 0110-6376
S E T: RESEARCH INFORMATION FOR TEACHERS. 1974. 2/yr. NZ.$10. New Zealand Council for Educational Research, Test and Book Sales Service, P. O. Box 3237, Wellington, New Zealand. (Co-sponsor: Australian Council for Educational Research) Ed. Llewelyn Richards. bibl. circ. 2,000. (looseleaf format)

370   US
S P E MONOGRAPHS. 1967? irreg., latest 1979. price varies. Society of Professors of Education, c/o George V. Guy, School of Education, Portland State University, Box 751, Portland, OR 97207. circ. controlled.
Supersedes (as of 1975): National Society of College Teachers of Education. Monographs.

370   US   ISSN 0081-3060
S R E B EDUCATIONAL BOARD. ANNUAL REPORT. a. free. Southern Regional Education Board, 130 6th St., N.W., Atlanta, GA 30313. Ed. Bruce Schultz. circ. 2,200.

370 301   US
SAGE ANNUAL REVIEW OF SOCIAL AND EDUCATIONAL CHANGE. 1977. a. $17.50 for hardcover; softcover $9.95. Sage Publications, Inc., 275 S. Beverly Dr., Beverly Hills, CA 90212 (And Sage Publications, Ltd., 28 Banner St., London EC1Y 8QE, England) Ed. Edmund King. (back issues avail.)

370   AG   ISSN 0080-6099
SANTA FE. CENTRO DE DOCUMENTACION E INFORMACION EDUCATIVA. BOLETIN DE INFORMACION EDUCATIVA. 1964. irreg; 1973, no. 15. free. ‡ Centro de Documentacion e Informacion Educativa, Centro Civico Gubernamental, San Martin 1153 - 2er.P., Santa Fe, Argentina. circ. 3,000.

379   BL
SAO PAULO, BRAZIL (STATE). SECRETARIA DA EDUCACAO. ATIVIDADES DESENVOLVIDAS. 1973. irreg. Secretaria da Educacao, Sao Paulo, Brazil.

370   UK   ISSN 0140-878X
SCHOLARSHIPS AT INDEPENDENT SCHOOLS. 1977. irreg. Truman and Knightley Educational Trust Ltd., 76-78 Notting Hill Gate, London, W11 3LJ, England. circ. 1,000.
Incorporating: Scholarships at Boys' Public Schools & Scholarships at Girls' Schools.

370   UK   ISSN 0306-1736
SCHOLARSHIPS GUIDE FOR COMMONWEALTH POSTGRADUATE STUDENTS. 1972. irreg. £4.95. Association of Commonwealth Universities, 36 Gordon Square, London WC1H OPF, England.

370 500   ZA
SCIENCE EDUCATION IN ZAMBIA. vol. 8, 1977. a. membership. ‡ Zambia Association of Science Education, Box R.W. 335, Lusaka, Zambia. (Co-sponsor: Zambia Agriculture Education Association) Ed. W. M. Gleeson. adv. bk. rev. illus. circ. 700.
Formerly: Z.A.S.E. Bulletin.

371.92   IT
SCIENZE PEDAGOGICHE. 1976. irreg. L.7500. (Universita Cattolica del Sacro Cuore) Vita e Pensiero, Largo A. Gemelli 1, Milan, Italy.

370   UK   ISSN 0080-8008
SCOTTISH COUNCIL FOR RESEARCH IN EDUCATION. PUBLICATIONS. 1930. irreg. price varies. University of London Press Ltd., Saint Paul's House, Warwick Lane, London EC4P 4AH, England (Dist. in U.S. by: Lawrence Verry Inc., River Rd., Mystic, CT 06355)

SELECTED LIST OF CATALOGUES FOR SHORT FILMS AND FILMSTRIPS. see MOTION PICTURES

370   II
SELECTIONS FROM EDUCATIONAL RECORDS OF THE GOVERNMENT OF INDIA. (Text in English) 1976. irreg. Jawaharlal Nehru University, Zakir Husain Centre for Educational Studies, New Delhi 110057, India. bibl.

032 370   AT   ISSN 0311-2373
SERIALS IN EDUCATION IN AUSTRALIAN LIBRARIES: A UNION LIST. 1972. irreg. Australian Council for Educational Research, Box 210, Hawthorn, Vic. 3122, Australia. Ed. Margaret A. Findlay.

370   AG
SERIE LEGISLACION EDUCATIVA ARGENTINA. no. 12, 1976. irreg. (Consejo Federal de Educacion) Argentina. Centro Nacional de Documentacion e Informacion Educativa, Avda. E. Madero 235, Buenos Aires, Argentina.

370   SL   ISSN 0080-9551
SIERRA LEONE. MINISTRY OF EDUCATION. REPORT. 1961-62. a. Ministry of Education, Freetown, Sierra Leone. circ. 1,200.

370   PK   ISSN 0560-0871
SIND UNIVERSITY JOURNAL OF EDUCATION. (Text in English) 1971, vol. 16. a. Rs.5($1.50) (University of Sind, Institute of Education & Research) Sind University Press, Jamshoro, Hyderabad 6, Pakistan. Ed. N. A. Baloch. bk. rev. bibl. circ. 1,000.

370   SI
SINGAPORE JOURNAL OF EDUCATION. (Text in English and Malay) 1978. irreg. (Institute of Education) Federal Publications (Pte) Ltd., No. 1 New Industrial Rd., Singapore 19, Singapore. illus.

370   NO   ISSN 0080-9950
SKOLENS AARBOK. 1965. a. Kr.105. Forlaget Tanum-Norli A-S, Kr. Augustsgt. 7 A, Oslo 1, Norway. Ed. Einar Ness. circ. 2,700.

370   CH
SOCIAL EDUCATION YEARLY.* (Text in Chinese) a. Social Education Society of China, c/o Social Education Dept, Ministry of Education, Chungshan S. Rd., Taipei, Taiwan, Republic of China. Ed.Shing Chou Wang. abstr. charts. stat. index. cum.ind. (processed)

370   UK   ISSN 0307-093X
SOCIAL SERVICES YEARBOOK. 1972. a. £18.50. (Association of County Councils) Councils & Education Press Ltd. (Subsidiary of: Longman Group Ltd.) Fourth Ave., Harlow, Essex, England. (Co-sponsor: Association of Metropolitan Authorities) Eds. Tudor David, Judith Hollingdale. adv.

370   US   ISSN 0081-0916
SOCIETE DES PROFESSEURS FRANCAIS EN AMERIQUE. BULLETIN ANNUEL. 1930. a. free. Societe des Professeurs Francais en Amerique, c/o Michel Coclet, 22 E. 60th St., New York, NY 10022.

370 GW
SONDERSCHULDIENST. 1964. 2/yr. free. Verlag Duerrsche Buchhandlung, Plittersdorfer Str. 91, 5300 Bonn 2, W. Germany (B.R.D.) adv. bk. rev. abstr. adv. bibl. illus. circ. 8,000. (looseleaf format)

370 US ISSN 0149-8924
SOURCEBOOK OF EQUAL EDUCATIONAL OPPORTUNITY. 1975/76. biennial. $39.50. Marquis Academic Media (Subsidiary of: Marquis Who's Who, Inc.) 200 E. Ohio St., Chicago, IL 60611.
Formerly: Yearbook of Equal Educational Opportunity.

370 SA ISSN 0081-2188
SOUTH AFRICA. DEPARTMENT OF BANTU EDUCATION. ANNUAL REPORT. 1963. irreg. price varies. Department of Bantu Education, Private Bag X212, Pretoria 0001, South Africa (Orders to: Government Printer, Bosman St., Private Bag X85, Pretoria 0001, South Africa)

370 SA
SOUTH AFRICA. DEPARTMENT OF NATIONAL EDUCATION. JAARVERSLAG/ANNUAL REPORT. (Text in Afrikaans and English) a. Government Printer, Bosman St., Private Bag X85, Pretoria 0001, South Africa. illus. stat.

SOUTHERN REGIONAL EDUCATION BOARD. STATE AND LOCAL REVENUE POTENTIAL. see BUSINESS AND ECONOMICS — Public Finance, Taxation

370 500 SP
SPAIN. MINISTERIO DE EDUCACION Y CIENCIA. GUIA. irreg. Ministerio de Educacion y Ciencia, Servicio de Publicaciones, Madrid, Spain.

370 SP ISSN 0561-4619
SPAIN. MINISTERIO DE EDUCACION Y CIENCIA. JUNTA NACIONAL CONTRA EL ANALFABETISMO. BOLETIN. 1951. a. Ministerio de Educacion y Ciencia, Junta Nacional Contra el Analfabetismo, Los Madrazo 17, Madrid, Spain. illus. stat.

370 BF
SPOTLIGHT. 1976. irreg. $1 per no. Ministry of Education and Culture, P.O. Box N 7147, Nassau, Bahamas.

370 US ISSN 0081-4237
STANDARD EDUCATION ALMANAC. 1968. a. $39.50. Marquis Academic Media (Subsidiary of: Marquis Who's Who, Inc.) 200 E. Ohio St., Chicago, IL 60611. charts, illus. index.

379.544 II
STATE INSTITUTE OF EDUCATION, RAJASTHAN. ANNUAL REPORT. (Text in English) a. State Institute of Education, Udaipur, Rajasthan, India.

370 US ISSN 0561-9440
STATISTICS & FACTS ABOUT NEBRASKA SCHOOLS. a. Department of Education, Division of Administrative Services, Statistical Services Section, Lincoln, NE 68508.

371 SO
STATISTICS OF EDUCATION IN SOMALIA.* irreg. Ministry of Education, Department of Planning, Mogadishu, Somalia. illus. stat.

370 US
STOPOUT: WORKING WAYS TO LEARN. 1978. triennial. $8.95. Garrett Park Press, Garrett Park, MD 20766. Ed. Joyce Slayton Mitchell.

370 PL ISSN 0081-6795
STUDIA PEDAGOGICZNE. 1954. irreg., vol. 41, 1979. price varies. (Polska Akademia Nauk, Komitet Nauk Pedagogicznych) Ossolineum, Publishing House of the Polish Academy of Sciences, Rynek 9, 50-106 Wroclaw, Poland (Dist. by Ars Polona-Ruch, Krakowskie Przedmiescie 7, Warsaw, Poland)

370 GW
STUDIEN UND DOKUMENTATIONEN ZUR DEUTSCHEN BILDUNGSGESCHICHTE. 1976. irreg. price varies. (Deutsches Institut fuer Internationale Paedagogische Forschung) Verlag Julius Beltz, Am Hauptbahnhof 10, Postfach 1120, 6940 Weinheim, W. Germany (B. R. D.) Eds. W. Mitter, C. Fuehr.

370 GW
DER STUDIENBEGINN. 1968. a. DM.10. Verein Freunde und Foerderer der Deutschen Studentenschaft e.V., Untere Hausbreite 11, 8000 Munich 45, W. Germany (B.R.D.) Ed. Gundolf Seidenspinner. adv.

STUDIENREIHE PAEDAGOGISCHE PSYCHOLOGIE. see PSYCHOLOGY

371.5 UN ISSN 0081-7783
STUDIES IN COMPULSORY EDUCATION. (Text in English or French) 1951. irreg. price varies. Unesco, 7-9 Place de Fontenoy, 75700 Paris, France (Dist. in U.S. by: Unipub, 345 Park Ave. S., New York NY 10010)

370 US
STUDIES IN EDUCATION. 1959. a. free to qualified personnel. West Texas State University, College of Education, Box 208, WT Station, Canyon, TX 79016. Ed. Robert W. Warren. circ. 300.

370 375 II
STUDIES IN EDUCATION AND TEACHING TECHNIQUES. 1979. irreg. Bahri Publications Pvt. Ltd., 57 Santnagar, New Delhi 110065, India. Ed. Ujjal Singh Bahri.

STUDIES IN LANGUAGE DISABILITY AND REMEDIATION. see LINGUISTICS

370 150 FR
STUDIES IN THE LEARNING SCIENCES. (Editions in English and French) 1973. irreg. price varies. Organization for Economic Cooperation and Development, Centre for Educational Research and Innovation, 2, rue Andre Pascal, 75775 Paris Cedex 16, France (U.S. orders to: O.E.C.D. Publications and Information Center, 1750 Pennsylvania Ave., N.W., Washington DC 20006)

379 US ISSN 0094-8268
SUMMARY OF EXPENDITURE DATA FOR MICHIGAN PUBLIC SCHOOLS. a. free. Department of Education, Lansing, MI 48933. charts. stat.

370 US ISSN 0362-6679
SUMMARY OF KENTUCKY EDUCATION STATISTICS. irreg. Department of Education, Bureau of Administration and Finance, Frankfort, KY 40601. stat. Key Title: Summary of Kentucky Education.

331.1 US ISSN 0094-2308
SUPPLY AND DEMAND: EDUCATIONAL PERSONNEL IN DELAWARE. Variant title: Educational Personnel in Delaware. a. Department of Public Instruction, Dover, DE 19901. illus.
Continues: Delaware. Department of Public Instruction. Teacher Supply and Demand.

370 SW
SWEDEN. STATISTISKA CENTRALBYRAAN. UTBILDNINGSSTATISTISK/SWEDISH EDUCATIONAL STATISTICS. irreg. Kr.29. Liber Foerlag, Fack, S-162 89 Vaellingby, Sweden.

370 US ISSN 0082-1217
SYSTEMS ENGINEERING OF EDUCATION SERIES. 1965. irreg., 1-2/yr. price varies. Education and Training Consultants Co. (ETC), Box 49899, Los Angeles, CA 90049. Ed. Leonard C. Silvern. circ. 1,000. (also avail. in microfiche from EDR) Indexed: ERIC.

370 HU ISSN 0082-1632
TANULMANYOK A NEVELESTUDOMANY KOREBOL. (Text in Hungarian; summaries in English and Russian) 1958. irreg. price varies. (Magyar Tudomanyos Akademia) Akademiai Kiado, Publishing House of the Hungarian Academy of Sciences, P.O. Box 24, H-1363 Budapest, Hungary.

371 AT
TEACHERS GUILD OF NEW SOUTH WALES. PROCEEDINGS. 1923. a. Aus.$2. Teachers' Guild of New South Wales, Assembly Hall, 44 Margaret St., Sydney, N.S.W. 2000, Australia. Ed. R. E. Kefford. adv. bk. rev. circ. 800. Indexed: Aus.Educ.Ind.
Formerly: Australian Teacher (ISSN 0045-091X)

370 UK ISSN 0085-7114
TEACHERS OF HISTORY IN THE UNIVERSITIES OF THE UNITED KINGDOM. a. £1. University of London, Institute of Historical Research, Senate House, London WC1E 7HU, England. circ. 300. (processed)

370 US
TEACHING OPPORTUNITIES OVERSEAS. 1959. biennial. $3. ‡ Hill International Publications, P.O. Box 79, East Islip, NY 11730.

379 US
TENNESSEE RESEARCH COORDINATING UNIT FOR VOCATIONAL EDUCATION. RESEARCH SERIES. irreg. Tennessee Research Coordinating Unit for Vocational Education, 909 Mountcastle St., Knoxville, TN 37916. illus.

372 US
TEXAS CHILD MIGRANT PROGRAM. ANNUAL REPORT. Variant title: Texas Migrant Program. Annual Report. 1966. a. free. Texas Education Agency, Division of Evaluation, 201 E. 11th St., Austin, TX 78701. charts. stat. circ. 2,000.

344 US ISSN 0362-6334
TEXAS PUBLIC SCHOOL LAW BULLETIN. irreg. Texas Education Agency, 201 E. 11th St., Austin, TX 78701.

370 940.1 US ISSN 0082-3732
TEXTS AND STUDIES IN THE HISTORY OF MEDIAEVAL EDUCATION. (Text in English and French; footnotes in Latin, German, French) 1953. irreg., no. 16, 1979. price varies. ‡ University of Notre Dame Press, Notre Dame, IN 46556. Ed. Astrik L. Gabriel.

378 US
TRANSFER CREDIT PRACTICES BY SELECTED EDUCATION INSTITUTIONS. a. $5. American Association of Collegiate Registrars and Admissions Officers, One Dupont Circle, N.W., Suite 330, Washington, DC 20036.
Formerly: Report on the Credit Given by Educational Institutions (ISSN 0569-2482)

370 TR ISSN 0082-6510
TRINIDAD AND TOBAGO. CENTRAL STATISTICAL OFFICE. DIGEST OF STATISTICS ON EDUCATION. 1958. a. T.T.$1.50. Central Statistical Office, Textel Building, Edward Street, Port of Spain, Trinidad (Orders to: Government Printing Office, 2 Victoria Ave., Port of Spain, Trinidad)

370 TU
TURKEY. DEVLET ISTATISTIK ENSTITUSU. MILLI EGITIM ISTATISTIKLERI: OGRETIM YILI BASI. (Subseries of its Yayin) 1970/71. a, latest 1972-74. free or on exchange basis. State Institute of Statistics, Necatibey Caddesi 114, Ankara, Turkey. stat.

370 UN
U I E MONOGRAPHS. 1973. irreg. price varies. Unesco Institute for Education, Feldbrunnen Str. 58, 2000 Hamburg 13, W. Germany (B.R.D.) (Dist. in U.S. by: Unipub, 345 Park Ave. S., New York, NY 10010)

370 UN
UNESCO. REGIONAL OFFICE FOR EDUCATION IN ASIA AND OCEANA. BULLETIN. (Text in English) 1966. a. price varies. Unesco, Regional Office for Education in Asia and Oceania, Box 1425, Bangkok G.P.O., Thailand (Dist. in U.S. by: Unipub, Box 433, Murray Hill Station New York, NY 10016) circ. 3,200 (combined)
Formerly: Unesco. Regional Office for Education in Asia.Bulletin. (ISSN 0503-4450)

370 AT ISSN 0311-4775
UNICORN. 1975. 4/yr. Aus.$15 to non-members. Australian College of Education, 914 Swanston St., Carlton, Victoria 3053, Australia. Ed. G.W. Bassett. bk. rev. circ. 5,600.
Incorporating: Australian College of Education. Proceedings of the Annual Conference and Annual Report (ISSN 0067-1770)

UNION NATIONALE DE L'ENSEIGNEMENT AGRICOLE PRIVE. ANNUAIRE. see AGRICULTURE

370.6   II
UNITED SCHOOLS ORGANISATION OF INDIA. ANNUAL REPORT.* (Text in English) 19th, 1969. a. United Schools Organisation of India, 1715 Arya Samaj Rd., New Delhi 5, India. illus.

370   US   ISSN 0093-7924
U.S. NATIONAL ADVISORY COUNCIL ON INDIAN EDUCATION. ANNUAL REPORT TO THE CONGRESS OF THE UNITED STATES. 1974. a. $1.40. U. S. National Advisory Council on Indian Education, Penn Building, Suite 326, 425 13th St. N.W., Washington, DC 20004 (Orders to: U. S. Superintendent of Documents, Washington, DC 20402) Key Title: Annual Report to the Congress of the United States from the National Council on Indian Education.

379   US
U.S. NATIONAL CENTER FOR EDUCATION STATISTICS. REVENUES AND EXPENDITURES FOR PUBLIC ELEMENTARY AND SECONDARY EDUCATION. (Report year ends June 30) U.S. National Center for Education Statistics, 400 Maryland Ave., S.W., Washington, DC 20201 (For Sale by the Supt. of Docs., G.P.O., Washington. D.C.)
    Formerly: U.S. National Center for Education Statistics. Expenditures and Revenues for Public Elementary and Secondary Education (ISSN 0090-7618)

372   373   US
U.S. NATIONAL CENTER FOR EDUCATION STATISTICS. STATISTICS OF PUBLIC ELEMENTARY AND SECONDARY DAY SCHOOLS. 1954. a. U.S. National Center for Education Statistics, U.S. Department of Education, 400 Maryland Ave., S.W., Washington, DC 20202 (Orders to: Supt. of Documents, Washington, DC 20402)

370   SP   ISSN 0078-8686
UNIVERSIDAD DE NAVARRA. INSTITUTO DE CIENCIAS DE LA EDUCACION. COLECCION I C E. 1969. irreg.; 1979, no. 24. price varies. Ediciones Universidad de Navarra, S.A., Plaza de los Sauces, 1 y 2 Baranain, Pamplona, Spain.

370   BL   ISSN 0085-0284
UNIVERSIDADE FEDERAL DO ESPIRITO SANTO. COMISSAO DE PLANEJAMENTO. DOCUMENTARIO ESTATISTICO SOBRE A SITUACAO EDUCACIONAL.* irreg. Universidade Federal do Espirito Santo, Sub-Reitoria de Planejamento e Desenvolvimento, Vitoria, Espirito Santo, Brazil.

370   BL   ISSN 0085-0292
UNIVERSIDADE FEDERAL DO ESPIRITO SANTO. COMISSAO DE PLANEJAMENTO. DOCUMENTARIO ESTATISTICO SOBRE A SITUACAO EDUCACIONAL. SUPPLEMENTO.* irreg. Universidade Federal do Espirito Santo, Sub Reitoria de Planejamento e Desenvolvimento, Vitoria, Espirito Santo, Brazil.

370   IT   ISSN 0082-6480
UNIVERSITA DEGLI STUDI DI TRIESTE. ISTITUTO DI PEDAGOGIA. QUADERNI. 1966. irreg. price varies. (Universita degli Studi di Trieste) Casa Editrice Felice le Monnier, Via Scipione Ammirato 100, C.P. 455, 50136 Florence, Italy.

370   BE   ISSN 0076-1281
UNIVERSITE CATHOLIQUE DE LOUVAIN. LABORATOIRE DE PEDAGOGIE EXPERIMENTALE. CAHIERS DE RECHERCHES. 1964. irreg., latest 1978. price varies. Universite Catholique de Louvain, Laboratoire de Pedagogie Experimentale, 20 Voie du Roman Pays, 1348 Louvain-la-Neuve, Belgium. Ed. Arthur Gille.

370   FR
UNIVERSITE DE BRETAGNE OCCIDENTALE. GUIDE DE L'ETUDIANT. 1971. a. free. Universite de Brest (Brestagne Occidentale), Rue de Archives, 29269 Brest, France. circ. controlled. (processed)

370   MY
UNIVERSITI KEBANGSAAN MALAYSIA. LAPURAU TAHUNAN/ANNUAL REPORT. (Text in English & Malay) 1971. a. free. National University of Malaysia - Universiti Kebangsaan Malaysia, Bangi, Kajang, Selangor, Malaysia. stat.

370   II   ISSN 0084-621X
UNIVERSITY OF ALLAHABAD. EDUCATION DEPARTMENT. RESEARCHES AND STUDIES. 1950. a. exchange basis. University of Allahabad, Education Department, Allahabad 211002, Uttar Pradesh, India. Ed. S.B. Adaval. circ. controlled.

370.71   US   ISSN 0066-751X
UNIVERSITY OF ARIZONA. COLLEGE OF EDUCATION. MONOGRAPH SERIES. 1971. irreg. $2. University of Arizona, College of Education, Bureau of Educational Services, Tucson, AZ 85721. Ed. Roy M. Claridge.

378   US   ISSN 0070-3044
UNIVERSITY OF DAYTON. SCHOOL OF EDUCATION. ABSTRACTS OF RESEARCH PROJECTS. 1968. a. free. University of Dayton, School of Education, Dayton, OH 45469. Ed. Louis J. Faerber. index.
    Projects completed by candidates for the M.S.

371.42   PH   ISSN 0070-8259
UNIVERSITY OF EASTERN PHILIPPINES. RESEARCH CENTER. REPORT. 1965. irreg. $2. University of Eastern Philippines, Research Center, University Town, Northern Samar, Philippines. Ed. Andres F. Celestino. circ. 3,000. (processed)

370   CN
UNIVERSITY OF GUELPH. CENTER FOR RESOURCES DEVELOPMENT. ANNUAL REPORT. 1969. a. Can.$1. University of Guelph, Center for Resources Development, Guelph, Ont. N1G 2W1, Canada.

378   150   US   ISSN 0073-1196
UNIVERSITY OF HAWAII. COUNSELING AND TESTING CENTER. REPORT. 1961. irreg., 1969, no. 12. free. University of Hawaii, Counseling and Testing Center, 2327 Dole St., Honolulu, HI 96822. Ed. George Y. Fujita.

370   FI   ISSN 0073-179X
UNIVERSITY OF HELSINKI. INSTITUTE OF EDUCATION. RESEARCH BULLETIN. (Text in English, French or German) 1957. irreg., no. 51, 1978. exchange basis only. Helsingin Yliopisto, Kasvatustieteen Laitos, Fabianinkatu 28, SF-00100 Helsinki 10, Finland. circ. 325.

370   UK   ISSN 0073-3806
UNIVERSITY OF HULL. INSTITUTE OF EDUCATION. AIDS TO RESEARCH. 1970. irreg., no. 2, 1975. price varies. University of Hull, Institute of Education, 173 Cottingham Rd., Hull HU5 2EH, England.

370   UK   ISSN 0073-3814
UNIVERSITY OF HULL. INSTITUTE OF EDUCATION. RESEARCH MONOGRAPHS. 1965. irreg., 1968, no. 2. price varies. University of Hull, Institute of Education, 173 Cottingham Rd., Hull HU5 2EH, England.

370   NR   ISSN 0073-4314
UNIVERSITY OF IBADAN. INSTITUTE OF EDUCATION. OCCASIONAL PUBLICATIONS. irreg. price varies. University of Ibadan, Institute of Education, Ibadan, Nigeria.

370   US   ISSN 0073-5388
UNIVERSITY OF ILLINOIS AT URBANA-CHAMPAIGN. OFFICE OF INSTRUCTIONAL RESOURCES. MEASUREMENT AND RESEARCH DIVISION. RESEARCH REPORT. irreg., latest issue no. 356. University of Illinois at Urbana-Champaign, Office of Instructional Resources, 307 Engineering Hall, Urbana, IL 61801.

370   UK   ISSN 0075-854X
UNIVERSITY OF LEEDS. INSTITUTE OF EDUCATION. PAPERS. 1955. irreg. price varies. ‡ University of Leeds, Institute of Education, Leeds, LS2 9JT, England.

370   UK   ISSN 0305-7984
UNIVERSITY OF MANCHESTER. SCHOOL OF EDUCATION. GAZETTE. a. free. University of Manchester, School of Education, Manchester MI3 9PL, England. Ed. Dr. James Rushton. circ. 1,500. (back issues avail.)

370   US
UNIVERSITY OF MICHIGAN. SCHOOL OF EDUCATION. BULLETIN. vol. 4, 1975. biennial. University of Michigan, School of Education, E. and S. University Aves., Ann Arbor, MI 48109. circ. 30,000.

370   US
UNIVERSITY OF MINNESOTA. CENTER FOR RESEARCH IN HUMAN LEARNING. REPORT AND FELLOWSHIP OFFERINGS. a. University of Minnesota, Center for Research in Human Learning, 205 Elliott Hall, Minneapolis, MN 55455.
    Formerly: University of Minnesota. Center for Research in Human Learning. Report (ISSN 0076-9282)

370   US
UNIVERSITY OF MONTANA. DIVISION OF EDUCATIONAL RESEARCH AND SERVICES. EDUCATION MONOGRAPH. irreg. $1.50 per no. University of Montana, School of Education, Missoula, MT 59812.

370   CS   ISSN 0083-4165
UNIVERZITA KOMENSKEHO. FILOZOFICKA FAKULTA. ZBORNIK: PAEDAGOGICA. (Text in Slovak; summaries in German and Russian) 1968. a. exchange basis. Univerzita Komenskeho, Filozoficka Fakulta, Gondova 2, 806 01 Bratislava, Czechoslovakia. Ed. Jozef Matej. circ. 700.

370   150   PL   ISSN 0072-047X
UNIWERSYTET GDANSKI. WYDZIAL HUMANISTYCZNY. ZESZYTY NAUKOWE. PEDAGOGIKA, PSYCHOLOGIA, HISTORIA WYCHOWANIA. 1966. irreg. 20 Zl. Uniwersytet Gdanski, Ul. Czerwonej Armii 110, 81-824 Sopot, Poland (Dist. by Ars Polona-Ruch, Krakowskie Przedmiescie 7, Warsaw, Poland)

UNIWERSYTET JAGIELLONSKI. ZESZYTY NAUKOWE. PRACE PSYCHOLOGICZNO-PEDAGOGICZNE. see *PSYCHOLOGY*

370   PL
UNIWERSYTET SLASKI W KATOWICACH. PRACE PEDAGOGICZNE. irreg., 1976, vol. 4. 25 Zl. Uniwersytet Slaski w Katowicach, Ul. Bankowa 14, 40-007 Katowice, Poland. Ed. Wlodzimierza Goriszowskiego. charts.

150   PL
UNIWERSYTET SLASKI W KATOWICACH. PRACE PSYCHOLOGICZNE. (Subseries of its: Prace Naukowe) (Text in Polish; summaries in English, German, Russian) 1971. irreg. available on exchange. Uniwersytet Slaski w Katowicach, Ul. Bankowa 14, 40-007 Katowice, Poland.

370   GW
DER UNTERMIETER. 1966. irreg. DM.5. Verein Freunde und Foerderer der Deutschen Studentenschaft e.V., Untere Hausbreite 11, 8000 Munich 45, W. Germany (B.R.D.) Ed. Peter Gantzer. adv.

370   GW
UNTERRICHTSWISSENSCHAFT. 4/yr. DM.60 to individuals; DM. 40 to students. Urban und Schwarzenberg, Pettenkoferstr. 18, Postfach 202440, D-8000 Munich, W. Germany (B.R.D.) (U.S. address: Urban and Schwarzenburg Inc., 7 East Redwood St., Baltimore MD 21202) Ed. H. J. Krumm.

370   SW   ISSN 0347-1314
UPPSALA STUDIES IN EDUCATION. (Subseries of Acta Universitatis Upsaliensis) (Text in English and Swedish; summaries in English) 1976. irreg. price varies. (Uppsala Universitet, Pedagogiska Institutionen - University of Uppsala, Department of Education) Almqvist & Wiksell International, Box 62, S-101 20 Stockholm, Sweden. Eds. Karl-Georg Ahlstroem, Urban Dahlloef, Erik Wallin. index. circ. 500-1,000.
    Supersedes: Studia Scientiae Paedagogicae Upsaliensis (ISSN 0081-6892)

370   VE
VENEZUELA. DEPARTAMENTO DE INVESTIGACIONES EDUCACIONALES. SECCION DE ESTADISTICA. ESTADISTICAS EDUCACIONALES.* 1971. a. Ministerio de Educacion, Departamento de Investigaciones Educacionales, Seccion de Estadistica, Caracas, Venezuela. illus. stat.

370 US
VERMONT EDUCATIONAL DIRECTORY. a. free. Department of Education, State Office Building, Montpelier, VT 05602. circ. 6,000.

370 NZ ISSN 0083-6036
VICTORIA UNIVERSITY OF WELLINGTON. AWARDS HANDBOOK. 1969. a. free. Victoria University of Wellington, c/o Administration Officer, Private Bag, Wellington, New Zealand.

370 US ISSN 0083-6354
VIRGINIA EDUCATIONAL DIRECTORY. a. $2. Department of Education, 9Th St. Office Building, Richmond, VA 23216.

371 SZ ISSN 0512-252X
W C O T P THEME STUDY. 1954. biennial. 10 Fr. per no. ‡ World Confederation of Organizations of the Teaching Profession, 5 Avenue du Moulin, 1110 Morges, Switzerland. Ed. John M. Thompson.

WARD'S BULLETIN. see *SCIENCES: COMPREHENSIVE WORKS*

370 US
WASHINGTON EDUCATION DIRECTORY. 1972/73. a. $10.50 prepaid; $11.50 invoiced. (Superintendent of Public Instruction) Barbara Krohn and Associates, 835 Securities Bldg., Seattle, WA 98101. circ. 7,000.

370 UK ISSN 0083-7946
WELSH STUDIES IN EDUCATION SERIES. 1968. irreg. price varies. (University College of Wales, Aberystwyth, Faculty of Education) University of Wales Press, 6 Gwennyth St., Cathays, Cardiff CF2 4YD, Wales. Ed. Prof. Jac L. Williams. (reprint service avail. from UMI)

370 US ISSN 0085-8099
WEST VIRGINIA EDUCATION DIRECTORY. 1934. a. free. ‡ Department of Education, Capitol Complex, Bldg. B-204, Charleston, WV 25305. Ed. Elnora Pepper. circ. 7,500.

370 UK ISSN 0140-6728
WESTMINSTER STUDIES IN EDUCATION. 1978. a. $45. Carfax Publishing Co., Haddon House, Dorchester-on-Thames, Oxford OX9 8JZ, England. Ed. Dr. Keith Dent. bk. rev. illus. stat. circ. 700. (reprint service avail. from ISI)

920 370 UK
WHO'S WHO IN EDUCATION. 1974. irreg. Melrose Press Ltd., 17-21 Churchgate St., Soham, Ely, Cambridgeshire CB7 5DS, England (U.S. subscr. to: International Biographical Centre, c/o Biblio Distribution Centre, 81 Adams Drive, Totowa, NJ 07512)

371.33 US ISSN 0361-2120
WISCONSIN. EDUCATIONAL COMMUNICATIONS BOARD. BIENNIAL REPORT. biennial. Educational Communications Board, 732 North Midvale Boulevard, Madison, WI 53705. Key Title: Biennial Report-Educational Communications Board.

WISCONSIN COUNCIL OF TEACHERS OF ENGLISH. SERVICE BULLETIN SERIES. see *LITERATURE*

370.7 US
WISCONSIN RESEARCH AND DEVELOPMENT CENTER FOR INDIVIDUALIZED SCHOOLING. PRACTICAL PAPERS. 1968. irreg., no.23, 1980. ‡ Wisconsin Research and Development Center for Individualized Schooling, 1025 West Johnson St., Madison, WI 53706 (Order from: ERIC Document Reproduction Service, Box 190, Arlington, VA 22210) (also avail. in microfiche; back issues avail.) Indexed: ERIC.
Formerly: Wisconsin Research and Development Center for Cognitive Learning. Practical Papers (ISSN 0084-0629)

370.7 US
WISCONSIN RESEARCH AND DEVELOPMENT CENTER FOR INDIVIDUALIZED SCHOOLING. TECHNICAL REPORTS. 1965. irreg., no. 570, 1980. ‡ Wisconsin Research and Development Center for Individualized Schooling, 1025 West Johnson St., Madison, WI 53706 (Order from: ERIC Document Reproduction Service, Box 190, Arlington, VA 22210) (also avail. in microfiche; back issues avail.) Indexed: ERIC.
Formerly: Wisconsin Research and Development Center for Cognitive Learning. Technical Reports (ISSN 0084-0645)

370.7 US
WISCONSIN RESEARCH AND DEVELOPMENT CENTER FOR INDIVIDUALIZED SCHOOLING. THEORETICAL PAPERS. (1966-67 issued as Occasional Papers) 1966. irreg., no. 90, 1980. ‡ Wisconsin Research and Development Center for Individualized Schooling, 1025 West Johnson St., Madison, WI 53706 (Order from: ERIC Document Reproduction Service, Box 190, Arlington, VA 22210) (also avail. in microfiche; back issues avail.) Indexed: ERIC.
Formerly: Wisconsin Research and Development Center for Cognitive Learning. Theoretical Papers (ISSN 0084-0637)

370 BE
WORLD ASSOCIATION FOR EDUCATIONAL RESEARCH. CONGRESS REPORTS. 1953. quadrennial, 7th, 1977, Ghent, published in 1979. 1200 Fr. World Association for Educational Research, Henri Dunantlaan 1, B-9000 Ghent, Belgium. Ed. M.-L. van Herreweghe.
Formerly: International Association for the Advancement of Educational Research. Congress Reports (ISSN 0074-154X)

370 US
WORLD EDUCATION SERIES (ARCHON) irreg. Archon Books, c/o Shoe String Press, 995 Sherman Ave., Hamden, CT 06514.

374 CN ISSN 0700-5350
WORLD LITERACY OF CANADA. NEWSLETTER. 1967. irreg. World Literacy of Canada, 692 Coxwell Ave., Toronto, Ont., Canada. illus.
Formerly: World Literacy of Canada, News and Views (ISSN 0705-8829)

370 SZ ISSN 0510-9175
WORLD O R T UNION. CONGRESS REPORT. (Organization for Rehabilitation Through Training) a. World O R T Union, 3 rue Varembe, Geneva, Switzerland (Dist. by: American O R T Federation, 817 Broadway, New York, NY 10003)

WORLD WHO'S WHO OF WOMEN IN EDUCATION. see *WOMEN'S INTERESTS*

371.4 US ISSN 0512-3879
WORLD-WIDE SUMMER PLACEMENT DIRECTORY. 1952. a. $10. Advancement & Placement Institute, 161 N. 9th St., Box 99, Greenpoint Sta., Brooklyn, NY 11222. Ed. A. L. Verssen. adv. illus.

370 UK ISSN 0084-2508
WORLD YEARBOOK OF EDUCATION. 1968. a. £12.50. Kogan Page Ltd., 120 Pentonville Rd., London N1 9JN, England.

370 US
WYOMING. DEPARTMENT OF EDUCATION. EDUCATION DIRECTORY. a. $2. Department of Education, Hathaway Bldg, Cheyenne, WY 82001.

370 US
YEARBOOK IN EDUCATION. 1973. a. $15. Arizona Association for Supervision and Curriculum Development, Dr. James John Jelinek, Ed., c/o College of Education, Arizona State University, Tempe, AZ 85281.

YEARBOOK OF HIGHER EDUCATION LAW. see *LAW*

YEARBOOK OF SCHOOL LAW. see *LAW*

370 JA ISSN 0513-5656
YOKOHAMA NATIONAL UNIVERSITY. EDUCATIONAL SCIENCES/YOKOHAMA KOKURITU DAIGAKU KYOIKU KIYO. (Text in English and Japanese) 1962. irreg. Yokohama National University, Faculty of Education - Yokohama Kokuritsu Daigaku Kyoikugakubu, 156 Tokiwadai, Hodogaya-ku, Yokohama 240, Japan. cum.index nos. 11-15, 1971-1975.

370 ZA ISSN 0084-487X
ZAMBIA. MINISTRY OF EDUCATION. ANNUAL REPORT. 1964. a. Ministry of Education, Box RW 93, Lusaka, Zambia (Orders to: Government Printer, Box 136, Lusaka, Zambia)

370 ZA ISSN 0084-5086
ZAMBIA. TEACHING SERVICE COMMISSION. ANNUAL REPORT. a. 5 n. Government Printer, P.O. Box 136, Lusaka, Zambia.

370 ZA
ZAMBIA EDUCATIONAL JOURNAL. 1971. a. free to Zambian educational institutions. Ministry of Education, Box RW 93, Lusaka, Zambia. Ed. P.D.M. Lombe. bk. rev. charts. illus.

370 RH ISSN 0080-2859
ZIMBABWE. MINISTRY OF EDUCATION. AFRICAN EDUCATION REPORT. a. Rhod.$1.05. Government Printer, P.O. Box 8062, Causeway, Zimbabwe.

370 PL ISSN 0084-5698
ZRODLA DO DZIEJOW MYSLI PEDAGOGICZNEJ. 1957. irreg., vol. 15, 1979. price varies. (Polska Akademia Nauk, Komitet Nauk Pedagogicznych) Ossolineum, Publishing House of the Polish Academy of Sciences, Rynek 9, Wroclaw, Poland (Dist. by Ars Polona-Ruch, Krakowskie Przedmiescie 7, Warsaw, Poland)

370 GW
ZULASSUNGSARBEIT. 1972. irreg. DM.10. Verein Freunde und Foerderer der Deutschen Studentenschaft e.V., Untere Hausbreite 11, 8000 Munich 45, W. Germany (B.R.D.) Ed. Gundolf Seidenspinner. adv.

370 GW
ZUSAMMENSTELLUNG STUDIENEINFUEHRENDER SCHRIFTEN. 1974. irreg. DM.1. Verein Freunde und Foerderer der Deutschen Studentenschaft e.V., Untere Hausbreite 11, 8000 Munich 45, W. Germany (B.R.D.) adv. bk. rev.

EDUCATION — Abstracting, Bibliographies, Statistics

A. A. T. E. GUIDE TO ENGLISH BOOKS. (Australian Association for the Teaching of English) see *LITERATURE — Abstracting, Bibliographies, Statistics*

016 371.2 US
AMERICAN ASSOCIATION OF SCHOOL ADMINISTRATORS. ANNOTATED BIBLIOGRAPHIES ON CRUCIAL ISSUES. irreg. price varies. American Association of School Administrators, 1801 N. Moore St., Arlington, VA 22209.

016 370 US
AMERICAN DISSERTATIONS ON FOREIGN EDUCATION; a bibliography with abstracts. irreg. price varies. Whitston Publishing Co. Inc., Box 958, Troy, NY 12181. Ed. Franklin Parker.

ANNUAL REPORT ON DENTAL AUXILIARY EDUCATION. see *MEDICAL SCIENCES — Abstracting, Bibliographies, Statistics*

ANNUAL REPORT ON DENTAL EDUCATION. see *MEDICAL SCIENCES — Abstracting, Bibliographies, Statistics*

378 319.4 AT
AUSTRALIA. BUREAU OF STATISTICS. COLLEGES OF ADVANCED EDUCATION. a. free. Australian Bureau of Statistics, Box 10, Belconnen, A.C.T. 2616, Australia. circ. 1,900.

379.121   AT
AUSTRALIA. BUREAU OF STATISTICS. EXPENDITURE ON EDUCATION. a. free. Australian Bureau of Statistics, P.O. Box 10, Belconnen, A.C.T. 2616, Australia. stat. circ. 2,000.

370 319.4   AT
AUSTRALIA. BUREAU OF STATISTICS. LEAVERS FROM SCHOOLS, UNIVERSITIES AND OTHER EDUCATIONAL INSTITUTIONS. 1973. irreg., latest Aug. 1978. free. Australian Bureau of Statistics, Box 10, Belconnen, A.C.T. 2616, Australia. circ. 3,000.
    Formerly: Australia. Bureau of Statistics. Survey of Leavers from Schools, Universities or Other Educational Institutions.

370 319.4   AT
AUSTRALIA. BUREAU OF STATISTICS. NEW SOUTH WALES OFFICE. EDUCATION. 1972. a. Australian Bureau of Statistics, N. S. W. Office, St. Andrews House, Sydney Square, George St., Sydney, N. S. W. 2000, Australia. charts, stat.

016   AT   ISSN 0311-323X
AUSTRALIAN AUDIO-VISUAL REFERENCE BOOK. 1974. a. Aus.$20. D. W. Thorpe Pty. Ltd., 384 Spencer St., Melbourne, Vic. 3003, Australia. Ed. Vivienne Brophy.

370 016   TH   ISSN 0067-3498
BANGKOK, THAILAND. COLLEGE OF EDUCATION. THESIS ABSTRACT SERIES.* (Editions in Thai and English) 1967/69. a. $1. Suan Sunsutha Teacher College, Samsen, Bangkok 4, Thailand.

370   BE
BELGIUM. MINISTERE DE L'EDUCATION NATIONALE ET DE LA CULTURE FRANCAISE. ANNUAIRE STATISTIQUE DE L'ENSEIGNEMENT. (Text in Dutch and French) 1957. a. 90 Fr. Ministere de l'Education Nationale et de la Culture Francaise, Cite Administrative de l'Etat, Bd. Pacheco, 1010 Brussels, Belgium.
    Formerly: Belgium. Institut National de Statistique. Annuaire Statistique de l'Enseignement (ISSN 0067-5423)

370 016   GE   ISSN 0067-6969
BIBLIOGRAPHIE DER PAEDAGOGISCHEN VEROEFFENTLICHUNGEN IN DER DEUTSCHEN DEMOKRATISCHEN REPUBLIK. a. price varies. Akademie der Paedagogischen Wissenschaften der DDR, Zentralstelle fuer Paedagogische Information und Dokumentation, Otto-Grotewohl-Str. 11, 108 Berlin, E. Germany (D.D.R.) Ed. Rosemarie Kohls.

370 016
BIBLIOGRAPHIES ON EDUCATIONAL TOPICS. irreg. (4-5/yr.) E R I C Clearinghouse on Teacher Education, One Dupont Circle, Suite 616, Washington, DC 20036. (also avail. in microfiche)

331.8 378 016   US
BIBLIOGRAPHY OF HIGHER EDUCATION COLLECTIVE BARGAINING INVOLVING OTHER THAN FACULTY PERSONNEL. s-a. (National Center for the Study of Collective Bargaining in Higher Education) City University of New York, Bernard M. Baruch College, 17 Lexington Ave., New York, NY 10010.

370 314   GW
BILDUNG IM ZAHLENSPIEGEL. 1974. a. DM.11.70. (Bundesministerium fuer Bildung und Wissenschaft) W. Kohlhammer-Verlag GmbH, Abt. Veroeffentlichungen des Statistischen Bundesamtes, Philipp-Reis-Str. 3, Postfach 421120, 6500 Mainz 42, W. Germany (B.R.D.) (Co-sponsor: Statistisches Bundesamt) stat.

370 318   BL
BRAZIL. MINISTERIO DA EDUCACAO E CULTURA. SERVICO DE ESTATISTICA DA EDUCACAO E CULTURA. 1971. irreg. Ministerio da Educacao e Cultura, Servico de Estatistica da Educacao e Cultura, Rua de Imprensa 16, 20030 Rio de Janeiro, Brazil. illus.

378   BL
BRAZIL. MINISTERIO DA EDUCACAO E CULTURA. SERVICO DE ESTATISTICA DA EDUCACAO E CULTURA. SINOPSE ESTATISTICA DO ENSINO SUPERIOR. 1972. irreg. Ministerio da Educacao e Cultura, Servico de Estatistica da Educacao e Cultura, Rua da Imprensa, 16 - 3o. Andar, 20030 Rio de Janeiro, Brazil.

372   BL
BRAZIL. SERVICO DE ESTATISTICA DA EDUCACAO E CULTURA. SINOPSE ESTATISTICA DO ENSINO PRIMARIO. irreg. Servico de Estatistica da Educacao e Cultura, Rio de Janeiro, Brazil.

375 650 016   US   ISSN 0068-4414
BUSINESS EDUCATION INDEX. 1941. a. $8. Delta Pi Epsilon Graduate Business Education Fraternity, National Office, Gustavus Adolphus College, St. Peter, MN 56082. Ed. Rose McCauley. circ. 11,000. (also avail. in microform from UMI; reprint service avail. from UMI)

371.2   CN   ISSN 0704-6596
CANADA. STATISTICS CANADA. ELEMENTARY-SECONDARY SCHOOL ENROLMENT/EFFECTIFS DES ECOLES PRIMAIRES ET SECONDAIRES. (Catalog 81-210) (Text in English and French) 1960/61. a. Can.$4.50($5.40) Statistics Canada, Publications Distribution, Ottawa, Ont. K1A 0V7, Canada. (also avail. in microform from MML)

378   CN   ISSN 0382-0920
CANADA. STATISTICS CANADA. ENROLLMENT IN COMMUNITY COLLEGES/ EFFECTIFS DES COLLEGES COMMUNAUTAIRES. (Catalogue 81-222) (Text in English and French) 1969. a. Can.$4.50($5.40) Statistics Canada, Publications Distribution, Ottawa, Ont. K1A 0V7, Canada. (also avail. in microform from MML)

310 370   CN   ISSN 0703-9328
CANADA. STATISTICS CANADA. FINANCIAL STATISTICS OF EDUCATION/STATISTIQUES FINANCIERES DE L'EDUCATION. (Catalog 81-208) (Text in English and French) 1954. a. Can.$6($7.20) Statistics Canada, Publications Distribution, Ottawa, Ont. K1A 0V7, Canada. (also avail. in microform from MML)

338.2   CN   ISSN 0318-3874
CANADA. STATISTICS CANADA. SALARIES AND QUALIFICATIONS OF TEACHERS IN PUBLIC, ELEMENTARY AND SECONDARY SCHOOLS/TRAITEMENTS ET QUALIFICATIONS DES ENSEIGNANTS DES ECOLES PUBLIQUES, PRIMAIRES ET SECONDAIRES. (Catalogue 81-202) (Text in English and French) 1936. a. Can.$6($7.20) Statistics Canada, Publications Distribution, Ottawa, Ont. K1A 0V7, Canada. (also avail. in microform from MML)

370 016   CN
CANADIAN TEACHERS' FEDERATION. BIBLIOGRAPHIES IN EDUCATION. irreg. price varies. Canadian Teachers' Federation, 110 Argyle Ave., Ottawa, Ont. K2P 1B4, Canada. circ. 750.

310 370   UK   ISSN 0307-0514
CHARTERED INSTITUTE OF PUBLIC FINANCE AND ACCOUNTANCY. EDUCATION ESTIMATES STATISTICS. 1974. a. £10. Chartered Institute of Public Finance and Accountancy, 1 Buckingham Place, London SW1E 6HS, England. (back issues avail.)

310 370   UK   ISSN 0309-5614
CHARTERED INSTITUTE OF PUBLIC FINANCE AND ACCOUNTANCY. EDUCATION STATISTICS. ACTUALS. 1948-49. a. £10. Chartered Institute of Public Finance and Accountancy, 1 Buckingham Place, London SW1E 6HS, England. stat. (back issues avail.)

370   UK
CHARTERED INSTITUTE OF PUBLIC FINANCE AND ACCOUNTANCY. EDUCATION STATISTICS. UNIT COSTS. 1980. a. £1.50. Chartered Institute of Public Finance and Accountancy, 1 Buckingham Place, London SW1E 6HS, England.

370 016   CL
CHILE. CENTRO DE DOCUMENTACION PEDAGOGICA. BIBLIOGRAFIA DE LA EDUCACION CHILENA. 1974. irreg. Centro de Documentacion Pedagogica, Morande 322, Santiago, Chile. Ed. Maria Cornejo Acosta. bibl.

378 011   US   ISSN 0578-4247
CLARK UNIVERSITY (WORCESTER, MASS.) DISSERTATIONS AND THESES. (Subseries of Clark University. Bulletin) 1929. N. S. 1953. a. Clark University, Graduate Board, 950 Main St., Worcester, MA 01610. Ed. Emil Brignola. circ. 400. (also avail. in microform) Indexed: D.A.

378.1   US   ISSN 0095-3377
COLLEGE BOARD. ADMISSIONS TESTING PROGRAM. NATIONAL REPORT ON COLLEGE-BOUND SENIORS. (Former name of issuing body: College Entrance Examination Board) irreg. College Board, Admissions Testing Program, 888 Seventh Ave., New York, NY 10019. illus. stat. Key Title: College Bound Seniors.

379   US
COMSEARCH: GEOGRAPHIC. (Avail. for 12 areas) 1980. a. price varies. Foundation Center, 888 Seventh Ave., New York, NY 10106.

379   US
COMSEARCH PRINTOUTS: SPECIAL TOPICS. 1976. a. Foundation Center, 888 Seventh Ave., New York, NY 10019. (also avail. in microfiche)

379 016   US
COMSEARCH PRINTOUTS: SUBJECTS. 1972. a. $12. Foundation Center, 888 Seventh Ave, New York, NY 10019. circ. 5,000. (also avail. in microfiche)
    Supersedes in part: Comsearch Printouts; Supersedes (since 1977): Foundation Grants Index; Subjects on Microfiche (ISSN 0090-1601)

370   US   ISSN 0098-4752
CONDITION OF EDUCATION; a statistical report on the condition of American education. 1975. a. U. S. National Center for Education Statistics, 400 Maryland Ave. S. W., Washington, DC 20202 (Orders to: Supt. of Documents, Washington, DC 20402) stat.

378.1   CN   ISSN 0382-912X
COUNCIL OF ONTARIO UNIVERSITIES. RESEARCH DIVISION. APPLICATION STATISTICS. 1973. a. Council of Ontario Universities, Research Division, 130 St. George St., Suite 8039, Toronto, Ont. M5S 2T4, Canada.

378   DK
DENMARK. UNDERVISNINGSMINISTERIET. OEKONOMISK-STATISTISKE KONSULENT. STATISTIK DE VIDEREGAENDE UDDANNELSER. irreg. price varies. Undervisningsministeriet, Oekonomisk-Statistiske Konsulent, Copenhagen, Denmark.

370 016   CH   ISSN 0419-3733
DIRECTORY OF THE CULTURAL ORGANIZATIONS OF THE REPUBLIC OF CHINA. (In four parts; Learned Societies, Universities and Colleges, Libraries, and Social Educational Centers) 5th ed. 1978. $8. National Central Library, Bureau of International Exchange of Publications, 43 Nan-Hai Rd., Taipei 107, Taiwan, Republic of China. circ. 1,000.

370   CN   ISSN 0706-3679
EDUCATION IN CANADA/EDUCATION AU CANADA. (Catalogue 81-229) (Text in English and French) 1973. a. Can.$7($8.40) Statistics Canada, Publications Distribution, Ottawa, Ont. K1A 0V7, Canada. (also avail. in microform from MML)

370
EDUCATION STATISTICS, NEW YORK STATE; prepared especially for members of the Legislature. 1968. a. free. ‡ Education Department, Information Center on Education, Albany, NY 12234. circ. controlled.

371.33 016   US
EDUCATIONAL FILMS. triennial (with yearly supplements) University of Michigan, Audio-Visual Education Center, 416 Fourth St., Ann Arbor, MI 48103.

016   US   ISSN 0070-9352
EDUCATIONAL TECHNOLOGY BIBLIOGRAPHY SERIES. 1971. irreg. Educational Technology Publications Inc., 140 Sylvan Ave., Englewood Cliffs, NJ 07632.

016   370   US   ISSN 0070-9565
EL HI TEXTBOOKS IN PRINT; including related teaching materials. 1969. a. $38. R.R. Bowker Company, 1180 Ave. of the Americas, New York, NY 10036 (Orders to P.O. Box 1807, Ann Arbor, Mich. 48106)
Formerly: Textbooks in Print.

370   318   MX
ESTADISTICA BASICA DEL SISTEMA EDUCATIVO NACIONAL. 1975. irreg. Secretaria de Educacion Publica, Mexico, D. F., Mexico.

370.982   318   AG
ESTADISTICAS DE LA EDUCACION. 1974. a. Ministerio de Cultura y Educacion, Departamento de Estadistica Educativa, Avenida E. Madero 235, Buenos Aires, Argentina. illus. stat.
Formerly: Estadistica Educativa.

314   370   CY   ISSN 0301-7559
FINANCIAL STATISTICS OF EDUCATION IN CYPRUS. (Text in English) 1970. a. Mils.250. Department of Statistics and Research, Ministry of Finance, Nicosia, Cyprus. circ. 200.

314   378   FI   ISSN 0355-2225
FINLAND. TILASTOKESKUS. KORKEAKOULUT/FINLAND. STATISTIKCENTRALEN. HOEGSKOLORA/FINLAND. CENTRAL STATISTICAL OFFICE. HIGHER EDUCATION. (Section XXXVII of Official Statistics of Finland) (Text in Finnish, Swedish and English) 1969. a. Fmk.20. Tilastokeskus, Annankatu 44, SF-00100 Helsinki 10, Finland (Subscr. to: Government Printing Centre, Box 516, SF-00100 Helsinki 10, Finland)

314   373   FI   ISSN 0355-2446
FINLAND. TILASTOKESKUS. YLEISSIVISTAVAT OPPILAITOKSET/FINLAND. STATISTIKCENTRALEN. ALLMAENBILDANDE LAEROANSTALTER/FINLAND. CENTRAL STATISTICAL OFFICE. GENERAL EDUCATION. (Section 10 of Official Statistics of Finland) (Text in Finnish, Swedish and English) 1973. a. Fmk.16. Tilastokeskus, Annankatu 44, SF-00100 Helsinki 10, Finland (Subscr. to: Government Printing Centre, Box 516, SF-00100 Helsinki 10, Finland)
Formed by the merger of: Finland. Tilastokeskus. Kansanopetus & Finland. Tilastokeskus. Oppikoulut.

379   US   ISSN 0094-1468
FLORIDA. DEPARTMENT OF EDUCATION. FLORIDA STATEWIDE ASSESSMENT PROGRAM: CAPSULE REPORT. 1972. irreg. Department of Education, Division of Elementary and Secondary Education, Student Evaluation Section, Tallahassee, FL 32304. stat. Key Title: Florida Statewide Assessment Program.

FOR YOUNGER READERS, BRAILLE AND TALKING BOOKS. see *BLIND — Abstracting, Bibliographies, Statistics*

370   FR
FRANCE. INSTITUT NATIONAL DE LA STATISTIQUE ET DES ETUDES ECONOMIQUES. L'ENSEIGNEMENT DANS LES DEPARTMENTS D'OUTRE-MER. irreg. Institut National de la Statistique et des Etudes Economiques, 97487 St. Denis, France.

370   GM
GAMBIA. CENTRAL STATISTICS DEPARTMENT. EDUCATION STATISTICS. a. d.8. Central Statistics Department, Wellington St., Banjul, Gambia. stat.
Former titles: Gambia. Education Department. Education Statistics; Gambia. Education Department. Annual Report and Statistics.

370   317   US   ISSN 0094-1557
GEORGIA. DEPARTMENT OF EDUCATION. STATISTICAL REPORT. a. Department of Education, State Office Bldg., Atlanta, GA 30334. stat. Key Title: Statistical Report - Georgia Department of Education.

370   314   GW   ISSN 0072-1778
GERMANY (FEDERAL REPUBLIC, 1949-) STATISTISCHES BUNDESAMT. FACHSERIE 11: BILDUNG UND KULTUR. (Consists of several subseries) 1960. a. price varies. W. Kohlhammer-Verlag GmbH, Abt. Veroeffentlichungen des Statistischen Bundesamtes, Philipp-Reis-Str. 3, Postfach 421120, 6500 Mainz 42, W. Germany (B.R.D.)

370   GR
GREECE. NATIONAL STATISTICAL SERVICE. EDUCATION STATISTICS. a., latest 1975/1976. $5. National Statistical Service, Publications and Information Division, 14-16 Lycourgou St., Athens 112, Greece.
Formerly: Greece. National Statistical Service. Annuaire Statistique de l'Enseignement (ISSN 0072-7407)

371.0025   016   US   ISSN 0072-8225
GUIDE TO AMERICAN EDUCATIONAL DIRECTORIES. 1964. triennial. $29.50. Todd Publications, Box 535, Rye, NY 10580. Ed. Barry Klein.

378   310   IS
ISRAEL. CENTRAL BUREAU OF STATISTICS. INPUTS IN RESEARCH AND DEVELOPMENT IN ACADEMIC INSTITUTIONS. (Text in English and Hebrew) 1970. irreg. I£110. Central Bureau of Statistics, P.O.B. 13015, Jerusalem, Israel. (Affiliate: Co-sponsor: National Council for Research and Development) charts. stat.

372   IS   ISSN 0075-1065
ISRAEL. CENTRAL BUREAU OF STATISTICS. SCHOOLS AND KINDERGARTENS. (Subseries of its Special Series) (Text in Hebrew and English) 1954/55. irreg., latest issue, no. 596, 1978. I£110. Central Bureau of Statistics, Box 13015, Jerusalem, Israel.

378   016   GE
JAHRESVERZEICHNIS DER HOCHSCHULSCHRIFTEN DER DDR, DER BRD UND WESTBERLINS. 1884. irreg. price varies. VEB Verlag fuer Buch- und Bibliothekswesen, Gerichtsweg 26, 701 Leipzig, E. Germany (D.D.R.)
Formerly: Jahresverzeichnis der Deutschen Hochschulschriften (ISSN 0075-2940)

378.1   US   ISSN 0098-9770
KENTUCKY. COUNCIL ON PUBLIC HIGHER EDUCATION. ORIGIN OF ENROLLMENTS, ACCREDITED COLLEGES AND UNIVERSITIES. a. free. Council on Public Higher Education, 1050 US 127 Bypass, Frankfort, KY 40601. charts, illus. stat. Key Title: Origin of Enrollments, Accredited Colleges and Universities.

370   315   KO
KOREA (REPUBLIC). MINISTRY OF EDUCATION. BASIC STATISTICS OF EDUCATION. a. Ministry of Education, Seoul, S. Korea. charts. stat.

370   315   KO
KOREA (REPUBLIC). MINISTRY OF EDUCATION. EDUCATIONAL DEVELOPMENT IN KOREA; a graphic presentation. irreg. Ministry of Education, Seoul, S. Korea. charts. illus.

370   016   KO
LIST OF THESES FOR THE DOCTOR'S AND MASTER'S DEGREE IN KOREA/HANKUK BAKSA MIT SEUKSA HAK WEE LONMUN CHONG MOKROK. (Text in Korean) 1969. a. free. National Assembly, Library, Processing & Reference Bureau, Yoido-Dong 1, Yeongdeungpo-gu, Seoul, S. Korea. circ. 700.

378   016   US   ISSN 0540-3847
MISSISSIPPI STATE UNIVERSITY ABSTRACTS OF THESES AND DISSERTATIONS. 1953. biennial. free. Mississippi State University, Graduate School, c/o Mitchell Memorial Library, P.O. Box 5408, Mississippi State, MS 39762. Ed. George R. Lewis. circ. controlled.
Formerly: Mississippi State University Abstracts of Theses (ISSN 0540-3847)

MUSIC THERAPY INDEX. see *MUSIC — Abstracting, Bibliographies, Statistics*

370   016   US
N I C E M INDEX TO EDUCATIONAL AUDIO TAPES. vol. 4, 1976. biennial. $54. National Information Center for Educational Media, University of Southern California, University Park, Los Angeles, CA 90007. (also avail. in microfiche)

370   016   US
N I C E M INDEX TO EDUCATIONAL OVERHEAD TRANSPARENCIES. vol. 5, 1976. biennial. $61. National Information Center for Educational Media, University of Southern California, University Park, Los Angeles, CA 90007. (also avail. in microfiche)

370   016   US
N I C E M INDEX TO EDUCATIONAL RECORDS. vol. 4, 1976. biennial. $47. National Information Center for Educational Media, University of Southern California, University Park, Los Angeles, CA 90007. (also avail. in microfiche)

370   016   US
N I C E M INDEX TO EDUCATIONAL SLIDES. vol. 3, 1976. biennial. $42.50. National Information Center for Educational Media, University of Southern California, University Park, Los Angeles, CA 90007. (also avail. in microfiche)

370   016   US
N I C E M INDEX TO EDUCATIONAL VIDEO TAPES. vol. 4, 1976. biennial. $29.50. National Information Center for Educational Media, University of Southern California, University Park, Los Angeles, CA 90007. (also avail. in microfiche)

370   016   US
N I C E M INDEX TO PRODUCERS AND DISTRIBUTORS. (National Information Center for Educational Media) see *MOTION PICTURES — Abstracting, Bibliographies, Statistics*

370   016   US
N I C E M INDEX TO 8MM MOTION CARTRIDGES. vol. 5, 1976. biennial. $47. National Information Center for Educational Media, University of Southern California, University Park, Los Angeles, CA 90007. (also avail. in microfiche)

370   016   US
N I C E M INDEX TO 16MM EDUCATIONAL FILMS. vol. 6, 1976. biennial. $109.50. National Information Center for Educational Media, University of Southern California, University Park, Los Angeles, CA 90007. (also avail. in microfiche)

370   016   US
N I C E M INDEX TO 35MM EDUCATIONAL FILMSTRIPS. vol. 6, 1976. biennial. $86.50. National Information Center for Educational Media, University of Southern California, University Park, Los Angeles, CA 90007. (also avail. in microfiche)

371   379   NE
NETHERLANDS. CENTRAAL BUREAU VOOR DE STATISTIEK. PER LEERLING BESCHIKBAAR GESTELDE BEDRAGEN VOOR HET LAGER ONDERWIJS. AMOUNTS PER PUPIL PROVIDED FOR PRIMARY EDUCATION. (Text in Dutch and English) 1949. a. fl.7.85. Centraal Bureau voor de Statistiek, Prinses Beatrixlaan 428, Voorburg, Netherlands (Orders to: Staatsuitgeverij, Christoffel Plantijnstraat, The Hague, Netherlands)
Formerly: Netherlands. Centraal Bureau voor de Statistiek. Statistiek van de Gemeentewege per Leerling Beschikbaar Gestelde Bedragenter Bestrijding van de Materiele Exploitatiekosten der Lagere Scholen. Statistics of the Amounts per Pupil Provided by the Municipality to Meet the Material Cost of Elementary Education (ISSN 0077-7226)

371.3   314   NE
NETHERLANDS. CENTRAAL BUREAU VOOR DE STATISTIEK. STATISTIEK VAN DE VOORLICHTING BIJ SCHOLEN EN BEROEPSKEUZE. STATISTICS OF VOCATIONAL GUIDANCE. 1946. a. fl.6.30. Centraal Bureau voor de Statistiek, Prinses Beatrixlaan 428, Voorburg, Netherlands (Orders to: Staatsuitgeverij, Christoffel Plantijnstraat, The Hague, Netherlands)
Formerly: Netherlands. Centraal Bureau voor de Statistiek. Statistiek van de Voorlichting Bij Beroepskeuze. Statistics of Vocational Guidance and Selection of Personnel (ISSN 0077-7218)

375 314　　　　　　　NE
NETHERLANDS. CENTRAAL BUREAU VOOR DE STATISTIEK. STATISTIEK VAN HET BEROEPSONDERWIJS: AGRARISCH ONDERWIJS. (Text in Dutch and English) 1940/41. a. fl.3.95. Centraal Bureau voor de Statistiek, Prinses Beatrixlaan 428, Voorburg, Netherlands (Orders to: Staatsuitgeverij, Christoffel Plantijnstraat, The Hague, Netherlands)
　　Former titles: Netherlands. Centraal Bureau voor de Statistiek. Statistiek van het Beroepsonderwijs: Landbouwonderwijs; Formerly: Netherlands. Centraal Bureau voor de Statistiek. Statistiek van het Land- en Tuinbouwonderwijs. Statistics Concerning Agricultural and Horticultural Education (ISSN 0077-7331)

378　　　　　　　　　NE
NETHERLANDS. CENTRAAL BUREAU VOOR DE STATISTIEK. STATISTIEK VAN HET BEROEPSONDERWIJS: OPLEIDINGSSCHOLEN KLEUTERLEIDSTERS EN PEDAGOGISCHE ACADEMIES. (Text in Dutch and English) 1943/44. a. fl.7.85. Centraal Bureau voor de Statistiek, Prinses Beatrixlaan 428, Voorburg, Netherlands (Orders to: Staatsuitgeverij, Christoffel Plantijnstraat, The Hague, Netherlands)
　　Formerly: Netherlands. Centraal Bureau voor de Statistiek. Statistiek. van het Kweekschoolonderwijs. Statistics on Teacher Training Colleges (ISSN 0077-7323)

375 314　　　　　　　NE
NETHERLANDS. CENTRAAL BUREAU VOOR DE STATISTIEK. STATISTIEK VAN HET BEROEPSONDERWIJS: TECHNISCH EN NAUTISCH ONDERWIJS. STATISTICS ON VOCATIONAL TRAINING. (Text in Dutch and English) 1968/69. a. price varies. Centraal Bureau voor de Statistiek, Prinses Beatrixlaan 428, Voorburg, Netherlands (Orders to: Staatsuitgeverij, Christoffel Plantijnstraat, The Hague, Netherlands)
　　Formerly: Netherlands. Centraal Bureau voor de Statistiek. Statistiek van het Beroepsonderwijs (ISSN 0077-7235)

373　　　　　　　　　NE
NETHERLANDS. CENTRAAL BUREAU VOOR DE STATISTIEK. VOORTGEZET ONDERWIJS REGIONAAL BEZIEN. 1949. a. fl.16. Centraal Bureau voor de Statistiek, Prinses Beatrixlaan 428, Voorburg, Netherlands (Orders to: Staatsuitgeverij, Christoffel Plantijnstraat, The Hague, Netherlands) circ. 500.

371.9　　　　US　　ISSN 0548-5150
NEW JERSEY. BUREAU OF STATISTICAL ANALYSIS AND SOCIAL RESEARCH. SCHOOLS FOR THE MENTALLY RETARDED. (Report year ends June 30) a. Bureau of Statistical Analysis and Social Research, Trenton, NJ 08625. Key Title: Schools for the Mentally Retarded (Trenton)

379　　　　　　　　　US
NORTH DAKOTA. DEPARTMENT OF PUBLIC INSTRUCTION. BIENNIAL REPORT OF THE SUPERINTENDENT OF PUBLIC INSTRUCTION. 1888. biennial. Department of Public Instruction, Bismarck, ND 58505.

371　　　　　　　　　NO
NORWAY. STATISTISK SENTRALBYRAA. UTDANNINGSSTATISTIKK: EDUCATIONAL STATISTICS. (Subseries of its Norges Offiseille Statistikk) (Text in Norwegian and English) 1952/53. a. price varies. Statistisk Sentralbyraa, Box 8131-Dep., Oslo 1, Norway. circ. 1,600.

370 314　　　　AU　　ISSN 0067-2343
OESTERREICHISCHE HOCHSCHULSTATISTIK. (Subseries of: Beitraege zur Oesterreichischen Statistik) 1965/66. a. S.140. ‡ (Oesterreichisches Statistisches Zentralamt) Oesterreichische Staatsdruckerei, Vienna, Austria. circ. 1,000.

370 318　　　　　　　PN
PANAMA. DIRECCION NACIONAL DE PLANEAMIENTO Y REFORMA EDUCATIVA. DEPARTAMENTO DE ESTADISTICA. SERIE: ANALISIS ESTADISTICO. irreg. Direccion Nacional de Planeamiento y Reforma Educativa, Departamento de Estadistica, Panama, Panama.

370 314　　　　PL　　ISSN 0079-2799
POLAND. GLOWNY URZAD STATYSTYCZNY. ROCZNIK STATYSTYCZNY SZKOLNICTWA. YEARBOOK OF EDUCATION STATISTICS. (Subseries of its: Statystyka Polski) 1967. a. Glowny Urzad Statystyczny, Al. Niepodleglosci 208, 00-925 Warsaw, Poland.

PRESS BRAILLE, ADULT. see *BLIND — Abstracting, Bibliographies, Statistics*

374 016　　　　US　　ISSN 0080-147X
REGISTER OF RESEARCH AND INVESTIGATION IN ADULT EDUCATION. 1968. irreg., latest 1971. $7. Adult Education Association of the United States of America, 810 18 St., N.W., Washington, DC 20006. (Co-Sponsor: ERIC Clearinghouse)

370 016　　　　UK　　ISSN 0080-1674
RESEARCH IN THE HISTORY OF EDUCATION: A LIST OF THESES FOR HIGHER DEGREES IN THE UNIVERSITIES OF ENGLAND AND WALES. (1969 Ed. includes Ireland) 1969. a. 30p. History of Education Society, c/o Mrs. B. Starkey, 4 Marydene Dr., Evington, Leicester LE5 6HD, England. Ed. D. A. Turner. circ. 250.

370.953　　　　　　　SU
SAUDI ARABIA. MINISTRY OF EDUCATION. EDUCATIONAL STATISTICS. (Text in Arabic and English) irreg. Ministry of Education, Statistics, Research and Education Documents Unit, Statistics Section, Box 2871, Riyadh, Saudi Arabia. illus.

370　　　　　　　　　SA
SOUTH AFRICA. DEPARTMENT OF STATISTICS. EDUCATION: COLOUREDS AND ASIANS. (Report No. 21-03) a., latest 1976. Department of Statistics, Private Bag X44, Pretoria 0001, South Africa (Orders to: Government Printer, Bosman St., Private Bag X85, Pretoria 0001, South Africa)

370　　　　　　　　　SA
SOUTH AFRICA. DEPARTMENT OF STATISTICS. EDUCATION: WHITES. (Report No. 21-02) a., latest 1976. R.3.50. Department of Statistics, Private Bag X44, Pretoria 0001, South Africa (Orders to: Government Printer, Bosman St., Private Bag X85, Pretoria 0001, South Africa)

613.7 015　　　　　　UK
SPORTS DOCUMENTATION CENTRE. ABSTRACT JOURNAL HOLDINGS. (Text in English and other languages) 1975. irreg. free. Sports Documentation Centre, Main Library, Box 363, University of Birmingham, Birmingham B15 2TT, England. Ed. Bd.
　　Formerly: National Documentation Centre for Sport, Physical Education and Recreation. Abstract Journal Holdings.
Physical education

370.19　　　　US　　ISSN 0091-8075
STATISTICAL PROFILE OF THE U.S. EXCHANGE PROGRAM. (Subseries of the bureau's annual report) 1962. irreg., latest issue, 1971. U.S. Department of State, Bureau of Education and Cultural Affairs, 2201 C St,NW, Washington, DC 20520. stat.

370 312　　　　　　　CY
STATISTICS OF EDUCATION IN CYPRUS. a. Mils.300. Department of Statistics and Research, Ministry of Finance, Nicosia, Cyprus.

370.967　　　　　　　GO
STATISTIQUES DE L'ENSEIGNEMENT AU GABON. a. Ministere de l'Education Nationale de la Jeunesse, des Sports et des Loisirs, Direction de l'Administration Generale et de la Planification, B.P. 334, Libreville, Gabon. illus.

370　　　　　　SW　　ISSN 0082-0342
SWEDEN. STATISTISKA CENTRALBYRAAN. STATISTISKA MEDDELANDEN. SUBGROUP U (EDUCATION AND CULTURE) (Text in Swedish; table heads and summaries in English) 1963 N.S. irreg. Kr.70. Liber Foerlag, Fack, S-162 89 Vaellingby, Sweden. circ. 2,000.

370　　　　　　　　　SZ
SWITZERLAND. STATISTISCHES AMT. SCHUELERSTATISTIK/STATISTIQUE DES ELEVES. (Subseries of Statistische Quellenwerke der Schweiz) (Text in French and German) 1976. a. Statistisches Amt., Hallwylstrasse 15, 3003 Berne, Switzerland.

TALKING BOOKS, ADULT. see *BLIND — Abstracting, Bibliographies, Statistics*

370　　　　　　　　　US
U.S. NATIONAL CENTER FOR EDUCATION STATISTICS. DEGEST OF EDUCATION STATISTICS. 1962. a. U.S. National Center for Education Statistics, U.S. Department of Education, 400 Maryland Ave., S.W., Washington, DC 20202 (Orders to: Supt. of Documents, Washington, DC 20402)
　　Formerly: U.S. National Center for Education Statistics. Digest of Educational Statistics (ISSN 0083-2634)

016.378768　　　　　　US
UNIVERSITY OF TENNESSEE. REPORT ON RESEARCH AND PUBLICATIONS. a. University of Tennessee, Knoxville, TN 37916. Key Title: Report on Research and Publications (Knoxville)

378 016　　　　　　　YU
UNIVERZITET U SARAJEVU. DOKTORSKE DISERTACIJE. REZIMEI. (Supplement to: Univerzitet u Sarajevu. Bilten) 1969. a. Univerzitet u Sarajevu, Vojvode Stepe obala 7/111, 71000 Sarajevo, Yugoslavia. illus.

378 016　　　　　　　US
VANDERBILT UNIVERSITY. ABSTRACTS OF THESES. irreg. Vanderbilt University, Publications Office, 117 Alumni Hall, Nashville, TN 37240.

378 016　　　　　　　CN
A VIEW OF UNIVERSITY FINANCING. (Text in English and French) 1978. a. Can.$2. Association of Universities and Colleges of Canada, 51 Slater St., Ottawa, Ont. K1P 5N1, Canada. circ. 350. (tabloid format)

013　　　　　　US　　ISSN 0083-6451
VIRGINIA MILITARY INSTITUTE, LEXINGTON. PUBLICATIONS, THESES, AND DISSERTATIONS OF THE STAFF AND FACULTY. 1963/64. irreg., 6th 1975. free. Virginia Military Institute, Preston Library, Lexington, VA 24450. Dir. Maj. Gen. Richard L. Irby. circ. 500.

082　　　　　　　　　KO
YONSEI UNIVERSITY. GRADUATE SCHOOL. ABSTRACTS OF FACULTY RESEARCH REPORTS. (Text in English) 1972. a. Yonsei University, Graduate School, Seoul, S. Korea.

370 314　　　　　　　YU
YUGOSLAVIA. SAVEZNI ZAVOD ZA STATISTIKU. OSNOVNA I SREDNJE. (Subseries of its Statisticki Bilten) 20 din.($1.11) Savezni Zavod za Statistiku, Uzun Mirkova 1, Belgrade, Yugoslavia. circ. 1,000.

370 314　　　　YU　　ISSN 0513-0832
YUGOSLAVIA. SAVEZNI ZAVOD ZA STATISTIKU. UCENICI U PRIVREDI. (Subseries of its Statisticki Bilten) 20 din.($1.11) Savezni Zavod za Statistiku, Uzun Mirkova 1, Belgrade, Yugoslavia. circ. 1,000.

EDUCATION — Adult Education

374.013　　　　　　　DK
AARBOG FOR ERHVERVSUDDANNELSERNE I DANMARK. 1975. a. Kr.84. Kroghs Skolehandbog, Gl. Landevej 13, 7100 Vejle, Denmark. illus.

374　　　　　　　　　US
ADULT & COMMUNITY EDUCATION ORGANIZATIONS & LEADERS DIRECTORY. 1977. a. $40. Today Publications and News Service, Inc., 621 National Press Building, Washington, DC 20045. Ed. Lester A. Barrer.

374 CN ISSN 0702-0066
ALBERTA. DEPARTMENT OF ADVANCED
EDUCATION AND MANPOWER. POST-
SECONDARY EDUCATION PROGRAMS. a.
Department of Advanced Education and Manpower,
Executive Bldg., Edmonton, Alta. T5J 2C8, Canada.

374 AT ISSN 0067-1630
AUSTRALIAN ASSOCIATION OF ADULT
EDUCATION. MONOGRAPH. 1969. irreg., no. 3,
1978. Aus.$6. Australian Association of Adult
Education, Box 1346, P.O. Canberra City, A.C.T.
2601, Australia. Ed. D. S. Robertson.

374 AT ISSN 0067-1649
AUSTRALIAN ASSOCIATION OF ADULT
EDUCATION. PROCEEDINGS OF THE
NATIONAL CONFERENCE. 1963, 3rd. a.
Aus.$6. Australian Association of Adult Education,
Box 1346, P.O. Canberra City, A.C.T. 2601,
Australia. Ed. D. S. Robertson.

374 BG ISSN 0070-8135
BANGLADESH. EDUCATION DIRECTORATE.
REPORT ON PILOT PROJECT ON ADULT
EDUCATION. Bengali; edition: Barshika Bibarani
Bayaska Siksha Parikshya Prakalpa Bangladesh.
(Text in English) 1964. a. Tk.2 per no. Education
Directorate, Adult Education Branch, B E E R I,
Dhanmond, Dacca 5, Bangladesh. circ. 500.
Supersedes: East Pakistan. Education Directorate.
Adult Education Branch. Report on Pilot Project on
Adult Education.

374 CN ISSN 0068-8274
C A A E ANNUAL REPORT. a. Can.$2 to non-
members. Canadian Association for Adult
Education, 29 Prince Arthur Ave., Toronto, Ont.
M5R 1B2, Canada. Ed. Ian Morrison. circ. 1,000.

374 II
C I I L ADULT LITERACY SERIES. (Text in
English) 1976. irreg., latest 1979. Central Institute
of Indian Languages, Manasagangotri, Mysore
570006, India. bibl.

374.4 CN ISSN 0068-855X
CANADIAN CORRESPONDENCE COURSES
FOR UNIVERSITY CREDIT.* 1957-58. a. free.
Canadian Association of Departments of Extension
and Summer School, Department of
Correspondence Courses, Saskatoon, Sask, Canada.

374 AT ISSN 0310-1649
CANBERRA PAPERS IN CONTINUING
EDUCATION. 1972. irreg. price varies. Australian
National University, Centre for Continuing
Education, Box 4, Canberra, A.C.T. 2600, Australia.
Ed. Dr. Nicolas Haines.

374.013 UY
CENTRO INTERAMERICANO DE
INVESTIGACION Y DOCUMENTACION
SOBRE FORMACION PROFESIONAL.
INFORMES. 1964. irreg. price varies. Centro
Interamericano de Investigacion y Documentacion
Sobre Formacion Profesional, Rio Negro 1241,
Casilla de Correo 1761, Montevideo, Uruguay.

370 US ISSN 0009-1464
CHANNEL (NEW PALTZ) 1950. a. $1. Mid-Hudson
School Study Council, Old Main Bldg., State
University College, New Paltz, NY 12561. Ed.
Marcia Norton. bk. rev. charts. illus. stat. tr.lit.
circ. 12,500.

374.013 UY
COLECCIONES BASICAS C I N T E R F O R.
(Text in Spanish and Portuguese) 1970. irreg. price
varies. Centro Interamericano de Investigacion y
Documentacion Sobre Formacion Profesional, Rio
Negro 1241, Casilla de Correo 1761, Montevideo,
Uruguay. Indexed: CIRF Abstr.

374 US ISSN 0084-9138
CONFERENCE FOR COLLEGE AND
UNIVERSITY LEADERS IN CONTINUING
EDUCATION. PROCEEDINGS. 1958. irreg.,
14th, 1972. price varies. Michigan State University,
Continuing Education Service, Kellogg Center for
Continuing Education, East Lansing, MI 48824.
Formerly: Seminar on Leadership in Continuing
Education.

374 301 BO
CUADERNOS C I P C A (SERIE POPULAR) 1974.
irreg. price varies. Centro de Investigacion y
Promocion del Campesinado, Sagarnaga 479, Casilla
5854, La Paz, Bolivia.
Study and teaching

374 PE
CUADERNOS DE CAPACITATION. 1979. irreg.
$40 includes subscr. to: Testimonios (en Historieta),
Cuadernos de Estudio and Cuadernos Populares.
Comision Evangelica Latinoamericana de Educacion
Cristiana, Av. General Garzon 2267, Lima 11, Peru.

374 PE
CUADERNOS POPULARES. 1977. irreg. $40
(includes subscr. to Testimonios (en Historieta),
Cuadernos de Capacitation, and Cuadernos de
Estudios) Comision Evangelica Latinoamericana de
Educacion Cristiana, Av. General Garzon 2267,
Lima 11, Peru.

374 GW
DEUTSCHER FACHHOCHSCHULFUEHRER.
1954. irreg., latest, 21st edition. DM.32. V D E-
Verlag GmbH, Bismarckstr. 33, 1000 Berlin 12, W.
Germany (B.R.D.) adv. bk. rev.

374 US ISSN 0094-095X
DIRECTORY OF CONTINUING EDUCATION
OPPORTUNITIES IN NEW YORK CITY. 1974.
irreg. $10. New York City Regional Center for Life-
Long Learning, Pace Plaza, New York, NY 10038.

374 US
EDUCATIONAL OPPORTUNITIES OF GREATER
BOSTON. 1923. a. $5.95 (summer supplement
$1.95) Educational Exchange of Greater Boston, 17
Dunster St., Cambridge, MA 02138.

374 UK
FLOODLIGHT; I L E A guide to evening classes.
1945. a. 30p. Inner London Education Authority, 1-
4 King St., London WC2E 8HN, England. Ed. Ted
Enever. adv. circ. 125,000.

374 UK ISSN 0260-3306
GREAT BRITAIN. ADVISORY COUNCIL FOR
ADULT AND CONTINUING EDUCATION.
ANNUAL REPORT. 1979. a. 2.50. H. M. S. O.,
P.O. Box 569, London SE1 9NH, England.

GUIDE TO COLLEGE COURSES IN FILM AND
TELEVISION. see MOTION PICTURES

374 UK
HANDBOOK OF ADULT EDUCATION IN
SCOTLAND. 1965. a. £1.50($3.50) Scottish
Institute of Adult Education, 4 Queensferry St.,
Edinburgh EH2 4PA, Scotland. Eds. J. C. Horobin,
Valerie Wilson. adv. bibl. stat.
Formerly: Yearbook of Adult Education in
Scotland.

374 US
HANDBOOK OF ADULT EDUCATION IN THE
UNITED STATES. irreg., latest ed. 1970. $15.
Adult Education Association of the United States of
America, 810 18th Street, N.W., Washington, DC
20006.

HANDBOOK OF TRADE AND TECHNICAL
CAREERS AND TRAINING. see
EDUCATION — Guides To Schools And Colleges

374.9 US ISSN 0362-2940
HAWAII. OFFICE OF INSTRUCTIONAL
SERVICES. SPECIAL PROGRAMS BRANCH.
ANNUAL PERFORMANCE REPORT ON
ADULT EDUCATION. a. Department of
Education, Office of Instructional Services, Special
Programs Branch, Honolulu, HI 96813. stat. Key
Title: Annual Performance Report on Adult
Education.

374 CN ISSN 0018-8891
I. C. E. A. CAHIERS. 1966. irreg. Institut Canadien
d'Education des Adultes, 506 Est rue Catherine,
Suite 800, Montreal, Que., Canada. illus.
Formerly: Education des Adultes (ISSN 0424-
5393)

379 US ISSN 0091-5882
IDAHO. STATE BOARD FOR VOCATIONAL
EDUCATION. ANNUAL DESCRIPTIVE
REPORT OF PROGRAM ACTIVITIES FOR
VOCATIONAL EDUCATION. 1963. a. State
Board for Vocational Education, 650 W. State St.,
Boise, ID 83720. Key Title: Annual Descriptive
Report of Program Activities for Vocational
Education.

374 US ISSN 0073-702X
INDIANA UNIVERSITY MONOGRAPH SERIES
IN ADULT EDUCATION. 1961. irreg. price
varies. ‡ Indiana University, Bureau of Studies in
Adult Education, Bloomington, IN 47401.

374.4 SW ISSN 0023-4125
KORRESPONDENS /UTBILDNINGSKONTAKT.
1901. irreg. Kr.25. Hermods Foundation, Fack, 205
10 Malmoe, Sweden. Eds. Borje Holmberg, Gunhild
Saellvin. adv. bk. rev. illus. circ. 12,000.

374 IR
LITERACY IN DEVELOPMENT; a series of training
monographs. irreg. $2. International Institute for
Adult Literacy Methods - Institut International pour
les Methodes d'Alphabetisation des Adultes, Box
1555, Teheran, Iran.

379 US ISSN 0094-1506
MICHIGAN STATE PLAN FOR VOCATIONAL
EDUCATION. a. Department of Education,
Division of Vocational Education, Box 30009,
Lansing, MI 48909. illus.

374 US
MICHIGAN STATE UNIVERSITY.
COOPERATIVE EXTENSION SERVICE.
ANNUAL REPORT. 1915. irreg., latest issue 1967.
free. Michigan State University, Cooperative
Extension Service, East Lansing, MI 48824.

374 US
MYRIN INSTITUTE FOR ADULT EDUCATION
PROCEEDINGS. 1954. irreg. $1.50 per no. Myrin
Institute for Adult Education, 521 Park Ave., New
York, NY 10021. Ed. Bd. bibl. circ. 2,000.

028 US
N C R A YEARBOOK. 1962. irreg., vol. 9, 1978.
North Central Reading Association, 190 Coffey
Hall, 1420 Eckles Ave., St. Paul, MN 55108. Ed.
David M. Wark. bk. rev. circ. 1,000.
Formerly: College and Adult Reading (ISSN
0069-553X)

379 US
NEVADA. STATE BOARD FOR VOCATIONAL
EDUCATION. ANNUAL PROGRAM PLAN
FOR VOCATIONAL EDUCATION. a. free. State
Board for Vocational Education, 400 W. King St.,
Carson City, NV 89710. illus. circ. 350.
Former titles: Nevada State Plan for Vocational
Education (ISSN 0094-1123) & Nevada State Plan
for Career Education.

379 US ISSN 0091-5114
PENNSYLVANIA STATE PLAN FOR THE
ADMINISTRATION OF VOCATIONAL-
TECHNICAL EDUCATION PROGRAMS. Cover
title: Vocational-Technical Education Programs.
(Vols. for 1973- issued in 2 parts: pt. 1,
Administrative Provisions; pt. 2, Annual and Long-
Range Program Provisions) a. free. Department of
Education, Bureau of Vocational, Technical and
Continuing Education, Box 911, Harrisburg, PA
17126. stat. circ. controlled; for official use only.

374 US ISSN 0079-7545
PUBLIC CONTINUING AND ADULT
EDUCATION ALMANAC. 1961. a. membership
(non-members $15) National Association for Public
Continuing and Adult Education, 1201 16 St. N.W.,
Washington, DC 20036. Ed. Leona L. Jones. adv.
circ. 2,500. (reprint service avail. from UMI)
From 1961-64 issued as: Focus.

374 US
RESOURCES FOR EDUCATORS OF ADULTS.
Variant title: International Handbook of Resources
for the Educators of Adults. no. 4, 1976. irreg. $20.
Syracuse University, Publications in Continuing
Education, 224 Huntington Hall, Syracuse, NY
13210. Ed. Alexander N. Charters. circ. 1,000.
(looseleaf format)

374   CE
SRI LANKA FOUNDATION INSTITUTE. NEWS. (Text in English, Sinhalese, or Tamil) irreg. Rs.3. Sri Lanka Foundation Institute, 100 Independence Square, Colombo 8, Sri Lanka.

374   TZ
STUDIES IN ADULT EDUCATION. 1971. irreg. price varies. Institute of Adult Education, Box 20679, Dar es Salaam, Tanzania. circ. 500.

374   US
SYRACUSE UNIVERSITY PUBLICATIONS IN CONTINUING EDUCATION. LANDMARK AND NEW HORIZONS SERIES. 1971. irreg. Syracuse University, Publications in Continuing Education, 224 Huntington Hall, 150 Marshall St., Syracuse, NY 13210.

374   US
SYRACUSE UNIVERSITY PUBLICATIONS IN CONTINUING EDUCATION. NOTES AND ESSAYS. no. 72, 1972. irreg. price varies. Syracuse University, Publications in Continuing Education, 224 Huntington Hall, 150 Marshall St., Syracuse, NY 13210. bibl. illus.

374   US   ISSN 0082-1179
SYRACUSE UNIVERSITY PUBLICATIONS IN CONTINUING EDUCATION. OCCASIONAL PAPERS. irreg., no. 46, 1976. Syracuse University, Publications in Continuing Education, 224 Huntington Hall, 150 Marshall St., Syracuse, NY 13210.

374   CN   ISSN 0707-9087
TEACHING OF ADULTS SERIES. 1977. irreg. University of Saskatchewan, Extension Division, Saskatoon, Sask., Canada.

378   630   UN
TRAINING FOR AGRICULTURE AND RURAL DEVELOPMENT. 1967. a. price varies. Food and Agriculture Organization of the United Nations, Agricultural Education and Training Service, Distribution and Sales Section, Via delle Terme di Caracalla, I-00100 Rome, Italy (Dist. in U.S. by: Unipub, 345 Park Ave. S., New York, NY 10010)
Formerly: Training for Agriculture; From 1971-72: Extension; Until 1971: Agricultural Education and Training.

374.9   US   ISSN 0360-8166
U.S. NATIONAL ADVISORY COUNCIL ON EXTENSION AND CONTINUING EDUCATION. ANNUAL REPORT. a. U.S. National Advisory Council on Extension and Continuing Education, 425 13th St. N.W., Suite 529, Washington, DC 20004 (For Sale by: Supt. of Documents, Washington, DC 20402) stat. Key Title: Annual Report-National Advisory Council on Extension and Continuing Education.

374   AG   ISSN 0075-742X
UNIVERSIDAD NACIONAL DE LA PLATA. INSTITUTO DE ESTUDIOS SOCIALES Y DEL PENSAMIENTO ARGENTINO. CUADERNOS DE EXTENSION UNIVERSITARIA.* 1957. irreg. price varies. Universidad Nacional de la Plata, Facultad de Humanidades y Ciencias de la Educacion, Calle 7 no. 776, La Plata, Argentina.

374.8   CN   ISSN 0068-1695
UNIVERSITY OF BRITISH COLUMBIA. CENTER FOR CONTINUING EDUCATION. OCCASIONAL PAPERS IN CONTINUING EDUCATION. 1968. irreg. price varies. ‡ University of British Columbia, Center for Continuing Education, Vancouver 8, B.C., Canada. circ. 300. Indexed: Can.Ind.

374.8   NR   ISSN 0075-7667
UNIVERSITY OF LAGOS. CONTINUING EDUCATION CENTRE. OCCASIONAL PAPERS.* 1970. irreg., no. 2, 1971. price varies. University of Lagos, Continuing Education Centre, Yaba, Lagos, Nigeria. Ed. E. A. Tugbiyele.

374.9   ZA
UNIVERSITY OF ZAMBIA. CENTRE FOR CONTINUING EDUCATION. REPORT OF THE ANNUAL RESIDENT TUTORS' CONFERENCE. a, 8th, 1976. University of Zambia, Centre for Continuing Education, Box 516, Lusaka, Zambia.
Formerly: University of Zambia. Centre for Continuing Education. Report of the Annual Staff Conference.

374   US
WADSWORTH CONTINUING EDUCATION SERIES. irreg. Wadsworth Publishing Co., 10 Davis Dr., Belmont, CA 94002.

374   US   ISSN 0084-2486
WORLD WIDE REGISTER OF ADULT EDUCATION; directory of home study schools. 1960. irreg., latest 1973 (with 1980 supp.) $8.95. ‡ Aurea Publications, Allenhurst, NJ 07711. Ed. Alex Sandri-White.

374   US
YEARBOOK OF ADULT AND CONTINUING EDUCATION. 1975/76. a. $39.50. Marquis Academic Media, 200 E. Ohio St., Chicago, IL 60611. charts, stat. index.

374   UK   ISSN 0084-3601
YEARBOOK OF ADULT EDUCATION. 1961. a. £2.75. National Institute of Adult Education, 19B de Montfort St., Leicester LE1 7GH, England. bk. rev. index. circ. 2,000.

EDUCATION — Guides To Schools And Colleges

378.0025   US
A C M ADMINISTRATIVE DIRECTORY OF COLLEGE AND UNIVERSITY COMPUTER SCIENCE/DATA PROCESSING PROGRAMS AND COMPUTER FACILITIES. a. $12. Association for Computing Machinery, Inc., 1133 Avenue of the Americas, New York, NY 10036 (Subscr. to: A C M Order Dept., Box 64145, Baltimore, MD 21264)
Formerly: Administrative Directory of College and University Computer Science Departments and Computer Centers.

378.025   US   ISSN 0361-9362
ACCREDITED INSTITUTIONS OF POSTSECONDARY EDUCATION. 1964. a. $12.50. American Council on Education, One Dupont Circle, N.W., Washington, DC 20036. circ. 8,000(approx.)
Former titles: Accredited Institutions of Postsecondary Education and Programs; Accredited Institutions of Post Secondary Education; Accredited Institutions of Higher Education (ISSN 0065-0862)

ACCREDITED JOURNALISM EDUCATION. see JOURNALISM

ADMISSION REQUIREMENTS OF U.S. AND CANADIAN DENTAL SCHOOLS. see MEDICAL SCIENCES — Dentistry

610   378.0025   US
ALLIED HEALTH EDUCATION DIRECTORY. 1968. biennial. $8. American Medical Association, 535 N. Dearborn St., Chicago, IL 60610. Ed. Patricia Dedman. circ. 10,000.
Formerly: Allied Medical Education Directory.

370   US   ISSN 0516-9313
AMERICAN ASSOCIATION OF COLLEGES FOR TEACHER EDUCATION. DIRECTORY. a. price varies. American Association of Colleges for Teacher Education, 1 du Pont Circle, N.W., Washington, DC 20036.

660   540   016   US
AMERICAN CHEMICAL SOCIETY. DIRECTORY OF GRADUATE RESEARCH. biennial. $30. American Chemical Society, Committee on Professional Training, 1155 16th St., N.W., Washington, DC 20036.

378   370.025   US   ISSN 0065-9029
AMERICAN JUNIOR COLLEGES. 1940. quadrennial. $20 8th ed. American Council on Education, One Dupont Circle, N.W., Washington, DC 20036. Ed. Edmond J. Gleazer, Jr. index.

370.025   378   US   ISSN 0066-0922
AMERICAN UNIVERSITIES AND COLLEGES. 1928. quadrennial. $42. American Council on Education, One Dupont Circle, N.W., Washington, DC 20036. Ed. W. Todd Furniss.

ASSOCIATION OF THEOLOGICAL SCHOOLS IN THE UNITED STATES AND CANADA. DIRECTORY. see RELIGIONS AND THEOLOGY

378.0025   US
BARRON'S GUIDE TO GRADUATE SCHOOLS; the social sciences and psychology. 1975. triennial. $5.95. Barron's Educational Series, Inc., 113 Crossways Park Drive, Woodbury, NY 11797.

378.0025   US
BARRON'S PROFILES OF AMERICAN COLLEGES. VOL. 1: DESCRIPTIONS OF THE COLLEGES. 11th edt., 1978. biennial. $23.95 hardbound; $9.95 paper. Barron's Educational Series, Inc., 113 Crossways Park Dr., Woodbury, NY 11797.

378.0025   US   ISSN 0533-1072
BARRON'S PROFILES OF AMERICAN COLLEGES. VOL. 2: INDEX TO MAJOR AREAS OF STUDY. 1973. biennial. $17.95 hardbound; $8.95 paperbound. Barron's Educational Series, Inc., 113 Crossways Park Drive, Woodbury, NY 11797.

BRICKER'S INTERNATIONAL DIRECTORY OF UNIVERSITY-SPONSORED EXECUTIVE DEVELOPMENT PROGRAMS. see BUSINESS AND ECONOMICS — Management

371.0025   US   ISSN 0162-9646
C I C'S SCHOOL DIRECTORIES. (Curriculum Information Center) (Published by state in 51 vols.) 1976. a. $650 per set; price varies per vol. Market Data Retrieval, Ketchum Pl., Westport, CT 06880. (back issues avail.)
Continues: School Universe Data Book (ISSN 0146-4329)

371.025   US   ISSN 0098-5147
CALIFORNIA PRIVATE SCHOOL DIRECTORY. 1969. a. $5. ‡ Department of Education, Bureau of Publications, State Education Bldg., 721 Capitol Mall, Sacramento, CA 95814. Ed. Theodore R. Smith. index. circ. 2,000. (back issues avail)
Formerly: Directory of Private Elementary Schools and High Schools in California.

370.025   US   ISSN 0068-5771
CALIFORNIA PUBLIC SCHOOL DIRECTORY. 1928. a. $11. Department of Education, Bureau of Publications, 721 Capitol Mall, Sacramento, CA 95814. Ed. Theodore R. Smith. index. circ. 9,000.
Before 1970: Directory of Administrative and Supervisory Personnel of California Public Schools.

CHRISTIAN SCHOOL DIRECTORY. see RELIGIONS AND THEOLOGY

378.0025   US
CHRONICLE FOUR-YEAR COLLEGE DATABOOK. 1974. a. $6.25. Chronicle Guidance Publications, Inc., Moravia, NY 13118.
Formerly: Guide to Four-Year College Databook (ISSN 0361-8927); Supersedes in part: Chronicle College Chart.

378.0025   US
CHRONICLE GUIDE FOR TRANSFERS. a. $8.50. Chronicle Guidance Publications, Inc., Aurora St., Moravia, NY 13118.
Formerly (until 1981): Chronicle College Counseling for Transfers (ISSN 0160-9300)

378.0025   US
CHRONICLE TWO-YEAR COLLEGE DATABOOK. 1974. a. $10. Chronicle Guidance Publications, Inc., Moravia, NY 13118.
Formerly(until 1978): Chronicle Guide to Two-Year College Majors and Careers; Guide to Two-Year College Majors and Careers (ISSN 0362-420X); Supersedes in part: Chronicle College Charts.

378.0025   US
CHRONICLE VOCATIONAL SCHOOL MANUAL. 1979. a. $10.50. Chronicle Guidance Publications, Inc., Moravia, NY 13118. Ed. Paul Downes. (also avail. in microfiche)
Formerly: Chronicle Annual Vocational School Manual (ISSN 0163-4100)

370.025   US   ISSN 0069-5572
COLLEGE BLUE BOOK. 1923. a. $85. Macmillan Publishing Co., Inc., 866 Third Ave., New York, NY 10022. Ed. William E. Burgess.

EDUCATION — GUIDES TO SCHOOLS AND COLLEGES

378.0025 US
COLLEGE TRANSFER GUIDE. a. $3. Catholic News Publishing Co., Inc., 80 W. Broad St., Mt. Vernon, NY 10552. Ed. V. L. Ridder, Jr. adv.

378.0025 US
COLLEGES AND UNIVERSITIES GRANTING DEGREES IN MICROBIOLOGY. 1973. irreg. (every 3-5 yrs.), latest issue 1980. $5. American Society for Microbiology, 1913 I St., N.W., Washington, DC 20006. circ. 2,000.

378.025 US ISSN 0075-4552
COMMUNITY, JUNIOR, AND TECHNICAL COLLEGE DIRECTORY. a. $10. American Association of Community and Junior Colleges, One Dupont Circle, N.W., Washington, DC 20036.
Former titles: Community and Junior College Directory (ISSN 0075-4552); Junior College Directory.

370 US
COMMUNITY, TECHNICAL, AND JUNIOR COLLEGE IN THE UNITED STATES: A GUIDE FOR FOREIGN STUDENTS. 1978. irreg. $3.50. Institute of International Education, 809 United Nations Plaza, New York, NY 10017.
Supersedes in part: Two-Year College in the United States; Community and Junior College in the U.S.

DANCE MAGAZINE DIRECTORY OF COLLEGE AND UNIVERSITY DANCE. see DANCE

370.025 GW
DEUTSCHER HOCHSCHULFUEHRER. 1925. a. DM.22. Verlag Dr. Josef Raabe GmbH und Co., Langer Graben Weg 1A, 5300 Bonn 1, W. Germany (B.R.D.). circ. 5,000.

378 US
DIRECTORY: A GUIDE TO COLLEGES, VOCATIONAL-TECHNICAL AND DIPLOMA SCHOOLS OF NURSING. 1966. biennial. free. Georgia Educational Improvement Council, Room 656, Seven M.L.K. Jr. Dr. S.W., Atlanta, GA 30334. circ. 5,000.
Formerly: Directory of Educational Opportunities in Georgia (ISSN 0419-2559)

378.1 US ISSN 0092-8526
DIRECTORY LISTING CURRICULUMS OFFERED IN THE COMMUNITY COLLEGES OF PENNSYLVANIA. 1967. irreg., 10th edt. 1977. free. ‡ Department of Education, Box 911, Harrisburg, PA 17126. Ed. Robert L. Sheppard. circ. 1,500.

370.025 US
DIRECTORY OF ACCREDITED HOME STUDY SCHOOLS. 1953. a. free. National Home Study Council, 1601 18 St. N.W., Washington, DC 20009. circ. 60,000.
Formerly: Directory of Accredited Private Home Study Schools (ISSN 0070-5055)

DIRECTORY OF ACCREDITED INSTITUTIONS. see BUSINESS AND ECONOMICS

DIRECTORY OF AEROSPACE EDUCATION. see AERONAUTICS AND SPACE FLIGHT

DIRECTORY OF BANKERS SCHOOLS. see BUSINESS AND ECONOMICS — Banking And Finance

370.025 UK ISSN 0070-5233
DIRECTORY OF CATHOLIC SCHOOLS AND COLLEGES. 1937. irreg. £1.25. Truman & Knightley Educational Trust Ltd., 76-78 Notting Hill Gate, London, W11 3LJ, England.

DIRECTORY OF EDUCATIONAL FACILITIES FOR THE LEARNING DISABLED. see EDUCATION — Special Education And Rehabilitation

370.025 US ISSN 0070-5675
DIRECTORY OF INSTITUTIONS OF HIGHER EDUCATION IN MISSOURI. 1968. a. Department of Higher Education, 600 Clark Ave., Jefferson City, MO 65101.

373.2 US ISSN 0098-096X
DIRECTORY OF OCCUPATIONAL EDUCATION PROGRAMS IN NEW YORK STATE. triennial. free. Education Department, Office of Occupational Education, 99 Washington Ave., Albany, NY 12224.

371.0025 US
DIRECTORY OF PUBLIC SCHOOLS IN THE U.S. a. $20 to non-members. Association for School, College and University Staffing, Box 4411, Madison, WI 53711. circ. 1,000.

371.0025 378.0025
371.42 US ISSN 0093-9501
DIRECTORY OF SPECIAL PROGRAMS FOR MINORITY GROUP MEMBERS; CAREER INFORMATION SERVICES, EMPLOYMENT SKILLS, BANKS, FINANCIAL AID SOURCES. 1974. a. $20. Garrett Park Press, Garrett Park, MD 20766. Ed. Willis L. Johnson. bibl.

370.025 US
EDUCATION DIRECTORY. (SCHOOL YEAR): COLLEGES AND UNIVERSITIES. 1967. a. U.S. National Center for Education Statistics, U.S. Department of Education, 400 Maryland Ave., Washington, DC 20202 (Orders to: Supt. of Documents, Washington, DC 20402)
Formerly: Directory of U.S. Institutions of Higher Education (ISSN 0070-654X)

370 US ISSN 0363-874X
EDUCATIONAL DIRECTORY OF MISSISSIPPI SCHOOLS. a. Department of Education, Jackson, MS 39205.
Formerly: Mississippi Educational Directory (ISSN 0092-7899)

378.025 US ISSN 0071-3643
FACTS ABOUT NEW ENGLAND COLLEGES, UNIVERSITIES AND INSTITUTES. 1957. a. $2. ‡ New England Board of Higher Education, 68 Walnut Rd., Wenham, MA 01984. circ. 15,000.

FLORIDA. STATE BOARD OF INDEPENDENT COLLEGES AND UNIVERSITIES. REPORT. see EDUCATION — Higher Education

370.025 US
FLORIDA EDUCATION DIRECTORY. a. Department of Education, Knott Building, Tallahassee, FL 32304.

FOREIGN MEDICAL SCHOOL CATALOGUE. see MEDICAL SCIENCES

370.025 FR ISSN 0071-8963
FRANCE. INSTITUT NATIONAL DE RECHERCHE ET DE DOCUMENTATION PEDAGOGIQUES. REPERTOIRE D'ETABLISSEMENTS PUBLICS D'ENSEIGNEMENT ET DE SERVICES. 1967. a. (Ministere de l'Education) France. Centre National de Documentation Pedagogique, 13 rue du Four, 75006 Paris, France.

377 SP
GUIA DE CENTROS EDUCATIVOS CATOLICOS. a. 1980 ptas.($33) Federacion Espanola de Religiosos de la Ensenanza, Servicio Estadistico, Conde de Penalver, 45, Madrid-6, Spain. stat.
Formerly: Guia de Centros Docentes de la Iglesia.

370 709 UY
GUIA DE LATINOAMERICA. (Text in English and Spanish) 1972. biennial. $50. Eduardo Darino, Ed. & Pub., Casilla de Correo 1677, Montevideo, Uruguay (U.S. Subscr. to: Darino, Box 1496-GC8s, New Yor, NY 10163) circ. 10,000.

GUIDE TO GRADUATE DEPARTMENTS OF GEOGRAPHY IN THE UNITED STATES AND CANADA. see GEOGRAPHY

378 650 US ISSN 0162-2463
GUIDE TO GRADUATE MANAGEMENT EDUCATION; a guide for prospective students. a. $4.95. ‡ (Graduate Management Admission Council) Educational Testing Service, P. O. Box 966, Princeton, NJ 08541.
Former titles: Graduate Study in Management; Programs of Graduate Study in Business.

378.025 US ISSN 0072-8500
GUIDE TO GRADUATE STUDY IN BOTANY FOR THE UNITED STATES AND CANADA. 1966. irreg.,latest 1977. $3. Botanical Society of America Inc., c/o School of Biological Sciences, University of Kentucky, Lexington, KY 40506.

370.025 374.4 US ISSN 0149-1083
GUIDE TO INDEPENDENT STUDY THROUGH CORRESPONDENCE INSTRUCTION. 1964. biennial. $4. (National University Extension Association) Peterson's Guides, Box 2123, Princeton, NJ 08540.
Formerly: Guide to Correspondence Studies in Colleges and Universities (ISSN 0072-8322)

370.025 US ISSN 0072-8705
GUIDE TO SUMMER CAMPS AND SUMMER SCHOOLS. 1936. biennial. $12 for cloth; paper $9. Porter Sargent Publishers, Inc., 11 Beacon St., Boston, MA 02108. index.

378.0025 US
HANDBOOK OF AMERICAN COLLEGE FINANCIAL AID. 1971. triennial. $7.95. Barron's Educational Services, Inc., 113 Crossways Park Dr., Woodbury, NY 11737. Ed. Carole Berglie. charts.

370.025 US ISSN 0072-9884
HANDBOOK OF PRIVATE SCHOOLS. 1915. a. $25. Porter Sargent Publishers, Inc., 11 Beacon St., Boston, MA 02108. Ed.Bd. index.

371.0025 US
HANDBOOK OF TRADE AND TECHNICAL CAREERS AND TRAINING. 1965. a. National Association of Trade and Technical Schools, 2021 K St., N.W., Washington, DC 20006. circ. 360,000.

373 370.025 US ISSN 0073-5779
INDEPENDENT SCHOOLS ASSOCIATION OF THE SOUTHWEST. MEMBERSHIP LIST. 1966. a. free. Independent Schools Association of the Southwest, Box 52297, Tulsa, OK 74152. Ed. Richard W. Ekdahl. circ. 500.
List of schools accredited by the Association

INTERNATIONAL DIRECTORY OF PROGRAMS IN BUSINESS AND COMMERCE. see BUSINESS AND ECONOMICS

370.025 IE ISSN 0075-0662
IRELAND (EIRE) DEPARTMENT OF EDUCATION. LIOSTA DE IAR-BHUNSCOILEANNA AITHEANTA. LIST OF RECOGNISED POST-PRIMARY SCHOOLS. 1968. a. price varies. Government Publications Sales Office, G.P.O. Arcade, Dublin 1, Ireland.

370 US ISSN 0091-0775
KENTUCKY SCHOOL DIRECTORY. a. $4.50. ‡ Department of Education, Capital Plaza Tower, Frankfort, KY 40601. stat. circ. controlled. (processed)

370.025 371.4 US ISSN 0076-1346
LOVEJOY'S CAREER AND VOCATIONAL SCHOOL GUIDE. 1955. irreg., latest issue 1975. $7.95 $3.95 pap. Simon and Schuster, Inc., 630 Fifth Ave., New York, NY 10020. Ed. Clarence E. Lovejoy.

370.025 US ISSN 0076-132X
LOVEJOY'S COLLEGE GUIDE. 1940. irreg., latest issue 1974. $8.95 cloth ($4.95-paper) Simon and Schuster, Inc., 630 Fifth Ave., New York, NY 10020. Ed. Clarence E. Lovejoy.

371 US ISSN 0459-925X
LOVEJOY'S PREP SCHOOL GUIDE. 3rd edt., 1968. irreg., 4th edt. 1974. $9.95 cloth; $5.95 paper. Simon & Schuster, Inc., 630 Fifth Ave., New York, NY 10020. Ed. Clarence E. Lovejoy.

378.774 US
MICHIGAN POSTSECONDARY ADMISSIONS & FINANCIAL ASSISTANCE HANDBOOK. a. Department of Education, Lansing, MI 48933. illus.
Formerly: Michigan. Department of Education. College Admissions & Financial Assistance Handbook (ISSN 0094-3754)

EDUCATION — GUIDES TO SCHOOLS AND COLLEGES

377.82   US   ISSN 0147-8044
N C E A GANLEY'S CATHOLIC SCHOOLS IN AMERICA. biennial. price varies. (National Catholic Educational Association) Curriculum Information Center, Brooks Towers, Suite 42C, 1020 15th St., Denver, CO 80202.
    Formerly: Catholic Schools in the United States (ISSN 0091-9527)

371.0025   700   US
NATIONAL ASSOCIATION OF SCHOOLS OF ART. DIRECTORY. 1977. a. free. National Association of Schools of Art, 11250 Roger Beacon Dr., No. 5, Reston, VA 22090.

378.1   US   ISSN 0098-1451
NATIONAL DIRECTORY OF SUMMER INTERNSHIPS FOR UNDERGRADUATE STUDENTS. a. $8.50. Bryn Mawr College and Haverford College, Career Planning Office, Haverford College, Haverford, PA 19041.

NATIONAL UNIVERSITY CONTINUING EDUCATION ASSOCIATION. HANDBOOK AND DIRECTORY. see *EDUCATION — Higher Education*

NETHERLANDS. CENTRAAL BUREAU VOOR DE STATISTIEK. STATISTIEK VAN HET BEROEPSONDERWIJS: KUNSTONDERWIJS. ART COLLEGES. see *EDUCATION — Higher Education*

373.2   US
OCCUPATIONAL EDUCATION: ENROLLMENTS AND PROGRAMS IN NONCOLLEGIATE POST SECONDARY SCHOOLS. 1971. irreg. U.S. National Center for Education Statistics, 400 Maryland Ave. S. W., Washington, DC 20202 (Orders to: Supt. of Documents, Washington, DC 20402)
    Formerly: Directory of Secondary Schools with Occupational Curriculums, Public and Nonpublic (ISSN 0091-3243)

370.025   US   ISSN 0078-5679
OREGON SCHOOL DIRECTORY. a. $5. Department of Education, 942 Lancaster Dr. N.E., Salem, OR 97310. circ. 8,000.
    Formerly (1972-73): Oregon School-Community College Directory.

370.025   US   ISSN 0079-0230
PATTERSON'S AMERICAN EDUCATION. 1904. a. $40. Educational Directories Inc., P.O. Box 199, Mount Prospect, IL 60056. Ed. Norman F. Elliott. index. circ. 4,000.
    Formerly: Patterson's American Educational Directory (ISSN 0163-2728)

371.0025   US   ISSN 0553-4054
PATTERSON'S SCHOOLS CLASSIFIED. (Also Incl. in Patterson's American Education) 1952. a. $6. Educational Directories Inc., P.O. Box 199, Mount Prospect, IL 60056. Ed. Norman F. Elliott. circ. 10,000. (processed)

370.025   378   US   ISSN 0147-8451
PETERSON'S ANNUAL GUIDE TO UNDERGRADUATE STUDY. 1970. a. $12. Peterson's Guides, Box 2123, Princeton, NJ 08540 (Orders to: Box 978, Edison, NJ 08817) Ed. Joan Hunter. circ. 15,000.
    Formerly: Annual Guide to Undergraduate Study (ISSN 0091-0465)

370.025   US
PETERSON'S GUIDES. ANNUAL GUIDES TO GRADUATE STUDY. BOOK 1: ACCREDITED INSTITUTIONS OFFERING GRADUATE WORK - AN OVERVIEW. 1980. a. $11. Peterson's Guides, Box 2123, Princeton, NJ 08540 (Orders to: Box 978, Edison, NJ 08817) Ed. Barbara A. Morrison. circ. 4,600.

370.025   650   US
PETERSON'S GUIDES. ANNUAL GUIDES TO GRADUATE STUDY. BOOK 2: HUMANITIES AND SOCIAL SCIENCES. 1974. a. $17. Peterson's Guides, Box 2123, Princeton, NJ 08540 (Orders to: Box 978, Edison, NJ 08817) Ed. Barbara A. Morrison. circ. 4,600.

370.025   570   US
PETERSON'S GUIDES. ANNUAL GUIDES TO GRADUATE STUDY. BOOK 3: BIOLOGICAL, AGRICULTURAL AND HEALTH SCIENCES. 1974. a. $17. Peterson's Guides, Box 2123, Princeton, NJ 08540 (Orders to: Box 978, Edison, NJ 08817) Ed. Sarah V. Weaver. circ. 3,900.

370.025   500   US
PETERSON'S GUIDES. ANNUAL GUIDES TO GRADUATE STUDY. BOOK 4: PHYSICAL SCIENCES. 1966. a. $14. Peterson's Guides, Box 2123, Princeton, NJ 08540 (Orders to: Box 978, Edison, NJ 08817) Ed. Margaret G. Butt. circ. 3,400.

370.025   620   US
PETERSON'S GUIDES. ANNUAL GUIDES TO GRADUATE STUDY. BOOK 5: ENGINEERING AND APPLIED SCIENCES. 1966. a. $15. Peterson's Guides, Box 2123, Princeton, NJ 08540 (Orders to: Box 978, Edison, NJ 08817) Ed. Margaret G. Butt. circ. 3,300.

370.025   US   ISSN 0079-5399
PRIVATE INDEPENDENT SCHOOLS; the Bunting and Lyon Blue Book. 1943. a. $40. Bunting and Lyon, 238 N. Main St., Wallingford, CT 06492.

371.0025   US   ISSN 0160-8126
PUBLIC EDUCATION DIRECTORY. a. Tomi Publications, 746 E. 79th St., Lock Box 95, Chicago, IL 60619.

378.0025   US
RANDAX EDUCATION GUIDE; a guide to colleges seeking students. 1971. a. $6.50. Education Guide, Inc., Box 421, Randolph, MA 02368. Ed. Stephen E. Marshall. adv. bk. rev. circ. 20,000.

378.0025   UK   ISSN 0306-1728
SCHEDULE OF POSTGRADUATE COURSES IN UNITED KINGDOM UNIVERSITIES. 1973. a. £3.15. Association of Commonwealth Universities, 36 Gordon Sq., London WC1H OPF, England. (Co-sponsor: Committee of Vice-Chancellors and Principals of the Universities of the United Kingdom)

370   US
SCHOOL GUIDE. 1935. a. $5. Catholic News Publishing Co., Inc., 80 W. Broad St., Mount Vernon, NY 10552. Ed. Victor L. Ridder, Jr. adv. stat. circ. 225.

370.025   UK   ISSN 0080-6897
SCHOOLS. 1924. a. £7. Truman and Knightley Educational Trust Ltd., 76-78 Notting Hill Gate, London, W11 3LJ, England. Ed. F.L. Hackston. circ. 3,000.
    Guide to independent schools in Great Britain

SCHOOLS IN THE UNITED STATES AND CANADA OFFERING GRADUATE EDUCATION IN PHARMACOLOGY. see *PHARMACY AND PHARMACOLOGY*

370.025   UK   ISSN 0080-6919
SCHOOLS OF ENGLAND, WALES, SCOTLAND AND IRELAND. (Includes: Continental Tutors and Special Training Sections) 1910. a. price varies. J. Burrow & Co. Ltd., Publicity House, Streatham Hill, London SW2 4TR, England.

378.0025   UK
SIGNPOST; I L E A guide to further and higher education. 1977/78. a. 35p. Inner London Education Authority, 1-4 King St., London WC2E 8HN, England. Ed. Ted Enever. adv. circ. 12,500.

370   SW
SKOLAN. a. Kr.94.50. (Laerarnas Riksfoerbund) LiberLaeromedel, Malmoe, 205 10 Malmoe, Sweden. Ed. Ingemar Ternbo. adv. charts. illus. stat. index. circ. 3,000.
    Formerly: Skolvaerldens Aarsbok.

370   US   ISSN 0363-9495
SOUTH CAROLINA SCHOOL DIRECTORY. irreg. $2. Department of Education, Planning and Dissemination Office, 1208 Rutledge Bldg., 1429 Senate St., Columbia, SC 29201.

STATE-APPROVED SCHOOLS OF NURSING - L. P. N./L. V. N. see *MEDICAL SCIENCES — Nurses And Nursing*

STATE-APPROVED SCHOOLS OF NURSING - R. N. see *MEDICAL SCIENCES — Nurses And Nursing*

371   US   ISSN 0363-4566
TEXAS SCHOOL DIRECTORY. irreg. $2. 201 E. 11 St., Austin, TX 78701.

371   US
UTAH PUBLIC SCHOOL DIRECTORY. a. $2. State Board of Education, 250 East 5th South, Salt Lake City, UT 84111. circ. 2,000.

378.0025   659.1   US
WHERE SHALL I GO TO COLLEGE TO STUDY ADVERTISING? a. $1. Advertising Education Publications, 3429 55th St., Lubbock, TX 79413. Eds. Billy I. Ross, Donald G. Hileman. circ. 5,000.

378   US
WHERE THE COLLEGES RANK. irreg., latest 1973. $2. College-Rater, Inc., 2121 South 12th St., Allentown, PA 18103.

370.025   UK   ISSN 0143-2214
WHERE TO LEARN ENGLISH IN GREAT BRITAIN. 1960. a. £2.50. Truman and Knightley Educational Trust Ltd., 76-78 Notting Hill Gate, London, W11 3LJ, England.
    Formerly: Schools of English in Great Britain (ISSN 0080-6927)
    Guide to schools specializing in the teaching of English as a foreign language

378.025   UK
WHICH DEGREE. 1963. a. £25. VNU Business Publications BV, 53-55 Frith St., London W1A 2HG, England (Dist. in U.S. by Barnes & Noble, Inc., 105 Fifth Ave., New York, NY 10003) Ed. Clive Carpenter.
    Formerly: Which University (ISSN 0083-923X)

371.0025   US   ISSN 0148-5059
WISCONSIN PUBLIC SCHOOL DIRECTORY. a. $2. ‡ Department of Public Instruction, 126 Langdon St., Madison, WI 53702. Ed. David R. Jamieson.

617.6   UN   ISSN 0512-2732
WORLD DIRECTORY OF DENTAL SCHOOLS. 1961. irreg. World Health Organization - Organization Mondiale de le Sante, Distribution and Sales Service, 20 Avenue Appia, CH-1211 Geneva 27, Switzerland.

610   378.0025   UN   ISSN 0512-2759
WORLD DIRECTORY OF MEDICAL SCHOOLS/ REPERTOIRE MONDIAL DES ECOLES DE MEDECINE. 1953. irreg., latest 1979. World Health Organization - Organisation Mondiale de la Sante, Distribution and Sales Service, 20 Avenue Appia, CH-1211 Geneva 27, Switzerland.

610.73   UN   ISSN 0512-2767
WORLD DIRECTORY OF POST-BASIC AND POST-GRADUATE SCHOOLS OF NURSING. 1965. irreg. World Health Organization - Organisation Mondiale de la Sante, Distribution and Sales Service, 20 Avenue Appia, CH-1211 Geneva 27, Switzerland.

615   375   UN   ISSN 0512-2775
WORLD DIRECTORY OF SCHOOLS OF PHARMACY. 1963. irreg. World Health Organization - Organisation Mondiale de la Sante, Distribution and Sales Service, 20 Avenue Appia, CH-1211 Geneva 27, Switzerland.

614   UN   ISSN 0512-2783
WORLD DIRECTORY OF SCHOOLS OF PUBLIC HEALTH. 1965. irreg. World Health Organization - Organisation Mondiale de la Sante, Distribution and Sales Service, 20 Avenue Appia, CH-1211 Geneva 27, Switzerland.

636   UN   ISSN 0512-2791
WORLD DIRECTORY OF VETERINARY SCHOOLS. 1963. irreg. World Health Organization - Organisation Mondiale de la Sante, Distribution and Sales Service, 20 Avenue Appia, CH-1211 Geneva 27, Switzerland.

370.025 378　　　UK　ISSN 0084-1889
WORLD LIST OF UNIVERSITIES, OTHER INSTITUTIONS OF HIGHER EDUCATION AND UNIVERSITY ORGANIZATIONS. 1952. biennial. £15. ‡ (International Association of Universities) Macmillan Press Ltd., 4 Little Essex St., London WC2R 3LF, England. Eds. H. M. R. Keyes, D. J. Aitken. index.

370.025　　　UK　ISSN 0084-2117
WORLD OF LEARNING. 1947. a. $105. Europa Publications, Ltd., 18 Bedford Squ., London WC1B 3JN, England.
　　Guide and directory of learned societies, research institutes, libraries, museums and universities

EDUCATION — Higher Education

see also College and Alumni

378　　　US　ISSN 0065-7123
A A C T E YEARBOOK. 1922. a. American Association of Colleges for Teacher Education, One Dupont Circle, Washington, DC 20036.

610 378　　　US　ISSN 0360-7437
A A M C DIRECTORY OF AMERICAN MEDICAL EDUCATION. a. $6. Association of American Medical Colleges, 1 du Pont Circle., N.W., Washington, DC 20036.

378　　　US　ISSN 0065-7344
A A S C U STUDIES. 1970. irreg. price varies. American Association of State Colleges and Universities, One Dupont Circle, N.W., Suite 700, Washington, DC 20036.

378　　　US　ISSN 0065-7832
A C T MONOGRAPH SERIES. 1967. irreg., no. 15, 1974. $3 per no. American College Testing Program, Box 168, Iowa City, IA 52243. (also avail. in microfiche from EDR) Indexed: Coll.Stud.Pers.Abstr. Eric.

378　　　US　ISSN 0569-3993
A C T RESEARCH REPORT. 1965. irreg., no. 81, 1981. price varies. American College Testing Program, P. O. Box 168, Iowa City, IA 52243. circ. 3,354. (also avail. in microfiche) Indexed: Col. Stud. Pers. Abstr. ERIC. Psychol. Abstr.
　　Formerly: A C T Research Service Report (ISSN 0065-7840)

A I CH E CONTINUING EDUCATION SERIES. (American Institute of Chemical Engineers) see ENGINEERING — Chemical Engineering

378 959　　　TH　ISSN 0066-9695
A S A I H L. SEMINAR REPORTS. 1963. irreg., latest issue, 1975. $3. Association of Southeast Asian Institutions of Higher Learning, Ratasastra Building, Chulalongkorn University, Henri Dunant Road, Bangkok, Thailand. circ. 600.

A S I L S INTERNATIONAL LAW JOURNAL. (Association of Student International Law Societies) see LAW

A T M OCCASIONAL PAPERS. (Association of Teachers of Management) see BUSINESS AND ECONOMICS — Management

378　　　FI　ISSN 0355-5798
AABO AKADEMI. AARSSKRIFT. 1917. a. Aabo Akademi, Domkyrkotorget 3, 20500 Aabo 50, Finland.

378　　　US
ABSTRACTS OF THESES ACCEPTED BY THE GRADUATE SCHOOL OF LOUISIANA TECH UNIVERSITY. 1968. a. $5. ‡ Louisiana Tech University, Prescott Library, Ruston, LA 71270. Ed. Sam A. Dyson. abstr. bibl. index; cum.index 1958-68; 1968-78. circ. 100.

378　　　SA　ISSN 0079-4317
ABSTRACTS OF THESES AND DISSERTATIONS ACCEPTED FOR HIGHER DEGREES IN THE POTCHEFSTROOM UNIVERSITY FOR CHRISTIAN HIGHER EDUCATION. (Cumulated edition covers 1956-1975) 1956. a. free. Potchefstroom University for Christian Higher Education, Potchefstroom, South Africa. index.

378　　　SZ
ACADEMICA HELVETICA. 1976. irreg. price varies. Paul Haupt AG, Falkenplatz 14, CH-3001 Berne, Switzerland.

060　　　IT
ACCADEMIA NAZIONALE DI SAN LUCA. ANNUARIO. a. Accademia Nazionale di San Luca, Piazza dell'Accademia di San Luca 77, Rome, Italy.

378.761　　　US　ISSN 0095-1285
ALABAMA. COMMISSION ON HIGHER EDUCATION. BIENNIAL REPORT TO THE GOVERNOR AND THE LEGISLATURE. 1973. biennial. Commission on Higher Education, Montgomery, AL 36104. illus. Key Title: Biennial Report to the Governor and the Legislature of the Alabama Commission on Higher Education.

378　　　US
AM I ELIGIBLE? THE EASY WAY TO CALCULATE THE B E O G INDEX. 1979. a. $1.25. Octameron Associates, Inc., Box 3437, Alexandria, VA 22302.

AMERICAN ASSEMBLY OF COLLEGIATE SCHOOLS OF BUSINESS. MEMBERSHIP DIRECTORY. see BUSINESS AND ECONOMICS

AMERICAN ASSOCIATION OF COLLEGES FOR TEACHER EDUCATION. DIRECTORY. see EDUCATION — Guides To Schools And Colleges

370.7　　　US　ISSN 0002-7413
AMERICAN ASSOCIATION OF COLLEGES FOR TEACHER EDUCATION. BULLETIN. 1947. irreg., latest Jan. 1979. American Association of Colleges for Teacher Education, One Dupont Circle, Suite 610, Washington, DC 20036. Ed. Ruth Barker. bk. rev. illus. circ. 8,000.
　　Teacher education

AMERICAN ASSOCIATION OF ENGINEERING SOCIETIES. ENGINEERING MANPOWER COMMISSION. SALARIES OF ENGINEERS IN EDUCATION. see ENGINEERING

378　　　US
AMERICAN ASSOCIATION OF STATE COLLEGES AND UNIVERSITIES. PROCEEDINGS. a. price varies. American Association of State Colleges and Universities, 1 du Pont Circle, N.W., Washington, DC 20036.

378　　　US　ISSN 0517-0680
AMERICAN COLLEGE TESTING PROGRAM. ANNUAL REPORT. 1959/60. a. free. American College Testing Program, 2201 N. Dodge St., Box 168, Iowa City, IA 52243.

378.1　　　US　ISSN 0065-7905
AMERICAN CONFERENCE OF ACADEMIC DEANS. PROCEEDINGS. 1946. a. $5. American Conference of Academic Deans, c/o Shelagh Casey, 1818 R St., N.W., Washington, DC 20009. circ. 750. (also avail. in microfilm from UMI)

378.242　　　US　ISSN 0065-809X
AMERICAN DOCTORAL DISSERTATIONS. 1934. a. $20. (Association of Research Libraries) University Microfilms International, 300 N. Zeeb Rd., Ann Arbor, MI 48106. Ed. Patricia M. Colling. author index. circ. 1,000. (microfiche)
　　Complete listing of all doctoral dissertations accepted by American and Canadian universities

378 327　　　US　ISSN 0066-1082
AMERICAN UNIVERSITIES FIELD STAFF. ANNUAL REPORT OF THE EXECUTIVE DIRECTOR. 1951-52. a. free. American Universities Field Staff, Inc., P.O. Box 150, Hanover, NH 03755. Ed. Manon L. Spitzer. circ. 2,000.

378.62　　　UA
AMERICAN UNIVERSITY IN CAIRO. PRESIDENT'S REVIEW. Variant title: American University in Cairo. Annual Report. (Text in English) a. American University in Cairo, 113 Sharia Kasr el-Aini, Cairo, Egypt.

378　　　FR　ISSN 0066-2771
ANNUAIRE DES CHERCHEURS FRANCAIS DU FONDS DE BOURSES DE RECHERCHE SCIENTIFIQUE ET TECHNIQUE DE L'ORGANISATION DU TRAITE DE L'ATLANTIQUE NORD. 1959. irreg. (North Atlantic Treaty Organization, Commission Francaise d'Attribution des Bourses de Recherche Scientifique) Conservatoire National des Arts et Metiers, 292 rue Saint-Martin, 75141 Paris Cedex 03, France. circ. 2,000.

378　　　FR　ISSN 0066-281X
ANNUAIRE DES DOCTEURS (LETTRES) DE L'UNIVERSITE DE PARIS ET AUTRES UNIVERSITES FRANCAISES;* bibliographie analytique des theses. 1967. a. Association Internationale des Docteurs (Lettres) de l'Universite de Paris, 29 rue d'Ulm, 75005 Paris, France.

378　　　US
A'S & B'S OF ACADEMIC SCHOLARSHIPS; a guide to current programs. 1978. a. $2.50. Octameron Associates, Inc., Box 3437, Alexandria, VA 22302.

378 630　　　BL
ASSOCIACAO BRASILEIRA DE EDUCAO AGRICOLA SUPERIOR. ANAIS DE REUNIAO ANUAL. no. 16, 1976. a. Associacao Brasileira de Educacao Agricola Superior, Praia do Flamengo 322, Caixa Postal 16074 ZC01, 2000 Rio de Janeiro, R.J., Brazil. (Instituto Interamericano de Ciencias Agricolas)
　　Agricultural education

378.1　　　US　ISSN 0066-8729
ASSOCIATED COLLEGES OF ILLINOIS. REPORT. a. Associated Colleges of Illinois, Suite A-2101, 175 W. Jackson Blvd., Chicago, IL 60604. charts. illus. stat.

378　　　US
ASSOCIATED WESTERN UNIVERSITIES. BIENNIAL REPORT. biennial. Associated Western Universities, Inc., 136 E. So. Temple, Suite 1005, Salt Lake City, UT 84111.
　　Formerly: Associated Western Universities. Annual Report (ISSN 0066-877X); Associated Western Universities. Report.

378.15　　　US
ASSOCIATION FOR CONTINUING HIGHER EDUCATION. PROCEEDINGS. 1939. a. $5. Association for Continuing Higher Education, c/o Dr. William D. Barton, Exec. V.P., 451 Communications Bldg., University of Tennessee, Knoxville, TN 37916. circ. 400.
　　Formerly: Association of University Evening Colleges. Proceedings (ISSN 0066-9741)

378　　　US　ISSN 0587-1948
ASSOCIATION FOR INSTITUTIONAL RESEARCH. ANNUAL FORUM ON INSTITUTIONAL RESEARCH. PROCEEDINGS. a. price varies. Association for Institutional Research, c/o Jean C. Chulak, Exec. Sec., 217 Education Bldg., Florida State University, Tallahassee, FL 32306.

ASSOCIATION FOR PROFESSIONAL EDUCATION FOR MINISTRY. REPORT OF THE BIENNIAL MEETING. see RELIGIONS AND THEOLOGY

370.71　　　NR　ISSN 0331-0388
ASSOCIATION FOR TEACHER EDUCATION IN AFRICA. WESTERN COUNCIL. REPORT OF THE ANNUAL CONFERENCE. a. Association for Teacher Education in Africa, Western Council, Lagos, Nigeria. illus.

378　　　GH
ASSOCIATION OF AFRICAN UNIVERSITIES. REPORT OF THE GENERAL CONFERENCE. 1967. irreg., 4th, 1976, Khartoum (in prep.) Association of African Universities, Box 5744, Accra, Ghana.

658.1　　　US
ASSOCIATION OF COLLEGE AND UNIVERSITY AUDITORS. PROCEEDINGS: ANNUAL CONFERENCE. a. $3. Association of College and University Auditors, Northwestern University, c/o Auditing Dept., 633 Clark St., Evanston, IL 60201. illus.

378 US
ASSOCIATION OF COLLEGE UNIONS-INTERNATIONAL. DIRECTORY. a. $15. Association of College Unions-International, P.O. Box 7286, Stanford, CA 94305.

378 US ISSN 0147-1120
ASSOCIATION OF COLLEGE UNIONS-INTERNATIONAL. PROCEEDINGS OF THE ANNUAL CONFERENCE. a. $20. Association of College Unions-International, P.O. Box 7286, Stanford, CA 94305.

378 UK ISSN 0066-9539
ASSOCIATION OF COLLEGES FOR FURTHER AND HIGHER EDUCATION. YEAR BOOK. 1894. a. membership. Association of Colleges for Further and Higher Education, 16 Balderton St., London W1Y 1TF, England.

378 UK ISSN 0307-2274
ASSOCIATION OF COMMONWEALTH UNIVERSITIES. ANNUAL REPORT OF THE COUNCIL TOGETHER WITH THE ACCOUNTS OF THE ASSOCIATION. 1931. a. free. Association of Commonwealth Universities, 36 Gordon Square, London WC1H 0PF, England.
  Formerly: Association of Commonwealth Universities. Report of the Council Together with the Accounts of the Association (ISSN 0571-6241)

378 TH ISSN 0066-9687
ASSOCIATION OF SOUTHEAST ASIAN INSTITUTIONS OF HIGHER LEARNING. HANDBOOK: SOUTHEAST ASIAN INSTITUTIONS OF HIGHER LEARNING. (Text in English) 1966. biennial. $10. Assn. of Southeast Asian Institutions of Higher Learning, Henri Dunant Rd., Bangkok, Thailand. circ. 600.

378 TH ISSN 0572-4325
ASSOCIATION OF SOUTHEAST ASIAN INSTITUTIONS OF HIGHER LEARNING. NEWSLETTER. 1969. irreg. $2. Association of Southeast Asian Institutions of Higher Learning, Ratasastra Building, Chulalongkorn University, Henri Dunant Road, Bangkok, Thailand. circ. 600.

378 CN ISSN 0066-9725
ASSOCIATION OF UNIVERSITIES AND COLLEGES OF CANADA. ANNUAL MEETING. PROCEEDINGS. 1965. a. Can.$3. ‡ Association of Universities and Colleges of Canada, 151 Slater St., Ottawa, Ont. K1P 5N1, Canada. Ed. Joan Rondeau. circ. 400. Indexed: Can.Educ.Ind.

378 US ISSN 0066-975X
ASSOCIATION OF UNIVERSITY SUMMER SESSIONS. SUMMARY REPORT. 1919. a. membership. ‡ Association of University Summer Sessions, Office of Summer Sessions, Indiana University, Bloomington, IN 47401.
  Formerly: Association of Summer Session Deans and Directors. Summary of Reports.

378 US
ASSOCIATION OF URBAN UNIVERSITIES. PROCEEDINGS. a. membership. Association of Urban Universities, Jacksonville University, Jacksonville, FL 32211. Ed. Lawrence H. Lium. circ. 600.

ATLANTIC PROVINCES INTER-UNIVERSITY COMMITTEE ON THE SCIENCES. NEWSLETTER. see *SCIENCES: COMPREHENSIVE WORKS*

378.94 AT
AUSTRALIA. BUREAU OF STATISTICS. UNIVERSITY STATISTICS. (In three parts) 1972. a. free. Australian Bureau of Statistics, P.O. Box 10, Belconnen, A.C.T. 2616, Australia.

378 AT ISSN 0311-3000
AUSTRALIAN COUNCIL ON AWARDS IN ADVANCED EDUCATION. BULLETIN. 1973. irreg. free. Australian Council on Awards in Advanced Education, P.O. Box 826, Woden, A.C.T. 2606, Australia.

378 AU
AUSTRIA. BUNDESMINISTERIUM FUER WISSENSCHAFT UND FORSCHUNG. HOCHSCHULBERICHT. irreg. free. Bundesministerium fuer Wissenschaft und Forschung, Minoritenplatz 5, A-1014 Vienna, Austria. stat.

378 UK ISSN 0144-4611
AWARDS FOR COMMONWEALTH UNIVERSITY ACADEMIC STAFF. 1971. irreg. £5.55. Association of Commonwealth Universities, 36 Gordon Sq., London WC1H OPF, England.
  Formerly: Awards for Commonwealth University Staff (ISSN 0305-8697)

378 US
B H M SUPPORT; directory of grants, awards, and loans. a. U.S. Bureau of Health Manpower, 5600 Fishers Lane, Rockville, MD 20852.

BACCALAUREATE EDUCATION IN NURSING: KEY TO A PROFESSIONAL CAREER IN NURSING. see *MEDICAL SCIENCES — Nurses And Nursing*

378 BE
BELGIUM. MINISTERE DES AFFAIRES ETRANGERES. REPERTOIRE DES THESES DE DOCTORAT/BELGIUM. MINISTERIE VAN BUITENLANDSE ZAKEN. REPERTORIUM VAN DE DOCTORALE PROEFSCHRIFTEN. (Text in Dutch,English,French,German,Italian and Spanish) 1972. a. free. Ministere des Affaires Etrangeres, 2 rue des Quatre Bras, 1000 Brussels, Belgium.

378 II
BHOPAL UNIVERSITY RESEARCH JOURNAL. (Text in English and Hindi) 1972. a. Rs.7. Bhopal University Research Council, Bhopal University, Bhopal, Madhya Pradesh, India. Ed. P. Shrotiya. circ. 200.

378 BL
BRAZIL. DEPARTAMENTO DE ASSUNTOS UNIVERSITARIOS. COORDENACAO DE AVALIACAO E CONTROLE. ATIVIDADES DAS INSTITUICOES FEDERAIS DE ENSINO SUPERIOR. a. Ministerio da Educacao e Cultura, Departamento de Assuntos Universitarios, Coordenacao de Avaliacao e Controle, Esplanada dos Ministerios, Bloco H, Brasilia, Brazil. charts. stat.

378 BL
BRAZIL. DEPARTAMENTO DE ASSUNTOS UNIVERSITARIOS. COORDENACAO DE AVAILIACAO E CONTROLE. CATALOGO GERAL DAS INSTITUICOES DE ENSINO SUPERIOR. 1973. irreg. Ministerio da Educacao e Cultura, Departamento de Assuntos Universitarios, Coordenacao de Avaliacao e Controle, Esplanada dos Ministerios, Bloco - H 7. andar, Brasilia, Brazil. stat.

052 PH ISSN 0115-1843
BUILDER OF PROGRESS. 1969. a. free. ‡ Saint Louis University, Box 71, Baguio City 0216, Philippines. Ed. Josefino Balatero. circ. 12,000. (processed)

C I E C PROCEEDINGS. (College Industry Education Conference) see *ENGINEERING*

378 US ISSN 0034-5393
CALIFORNIA UNIVERSITY CENTER FOR RESEARCH AND DEVELOPMENT IN HIGHER EDUCATION. RESEARCH REPORTER. 1966. irreg., latest vol. 10, no. 1, 1976. free. University of California, Berkeley, Center for Research and Development in Higher Education, 4603 Tolman Hall, Berkeley, CA 94720. Ed. Harriet Renaud. bibl. charts. illus. stat. circ. 14,000. (tabloid format)

CANADA. DEPARTMENT OF INDIAN AND NORTHERN AFFAIRS. INDIAN AND INUIT GRADUATE REGISTER. see *ETHNIC INTERESTS*

378 CN ISSN 0316-0149
CANADIAN THESES ON MICROFICHE (SUPPLEMENT)/THESES CANADIENNES SUR MICROFICHE (SUPPLEMENT) (Text in English and French) no. 18, 1977. irreg. free. National Library of Canada, Canadian Theses Division, 395 Wellington St., Ottawa Ont. K1A 0N4, Canada. Ed. Helena Vesely. circ. 250.

378 US
CARNEGIE COMMISSION ON HIGHER EDUCATION. COMMISSION REPORTS. irreg. price varies. Carnegie Commission on Higher Education, 2150 Shattuck Ave., Berkeley, CA 94704 (Dist. by: McGraw-Hill, Inc, 1221 Ave. of the Americas, New York, NY 10020)

378 US
CARNEGIE COMMISSION ON HIGHER EDUCATION. GENERAL REPORTS. irreg. price varies. Carnegie Commission on Higher Education, 2150 Shattuck Ave., Berkeley, CA 94704 (Dist. by: McGraw-Hill, Inc., 1221 Ave. of the Americas, New York, NY 10020)

378 US
CARNEGIE COMMISSION ON HIGHER EDUCATION. TECHNICAL REPORTS. irreg. price varies. Carnegie Commission on Higher Education, 2150 Shattuck Ave., Berkeley, CA 94704 (Dist. by: Carnegie Council on Policy Studies in Higher Education, 2150 Shattuck Ave., Berkeley, CA 94704)

378 US
CARNEGIE COUNCIL ON POLICY STUDIES IN HIGHER EDUCATION. CARNEGIE COUNCIL SERIES. irreg., latest 1981. Jossey-Bass, Inc. Publishers, 433 California St., San Francisco, CA 94104. (reprint service avail. from UMI)

378 US ISSN 0069-0783
CARSON AND NEWMAN COLLEGE, JEFFERSON CITY, TENNESSEE. FACULTY STUDIES. 1965. a. free; limited distribution. ‡ Carson-Newman College, Jefferson City, TN 37760. Ed. Charles C. Hobbs. circ. 600.

378 BL
CATALOGO DE PESQUISAS CONCLUIDAS E EM DESENVOLVIMENTO. 1975. irreg. (Universidade Federal de Pernambuco) Editora Universitaria, Recife, Brazil.

378 BL
CATALOGO DOS CURSOS DE POS-GRADUACAO NO BRASIL. 1975. irreg. Ministerio da Educacao e Cultura, Departamento de Assuntos Universitarios, Coordenacao do Aperfeicoamento de Pessoal de Nivel Superior, Brasilia, Brazil.

378 IE ISSN 0069-1399
CELTICA. 1946. irreg., vol. 10, 1974. price varies. Dublin Institute for Advanced Studies, 10 Burlington Rd., Dublin, 4, Ireland. Ed.Bd. bk. rev. circ. 212.

378 US ISSN 0025-911X
CENTER FOR RESEARCH ON LEARNING AND TEACHING. MEMO TO THE FACULTY. 1963. irreg. $4 for 6 nos. University of Michigan, Center for Research on Learning and Teaching, 109 E. Madison, Ann Arbor, MI 48109. Ed. Stanford C. Ericksen. bibl. circ. 15,000.

378 CF
CENTRE D'ENSEIGNEMENT SUPERIEUR DE BRAZZAVILLE. ANNALES. 1965. a. Centre d'Enseignement Superieur de Brazzaville, B.P. 69, Brazzaville, Congo.

CHEMICAL ENGINEERING FACULTIES OF CANADA AND THE UNITED STATES. see *ENGINEERING — Chemical Engineering*

378.3 US ISSN 0190-339X
CHRONICLE STUDENT AID ANNUAL. 1955. a. $12.50. Chronicle Guidance Publications, Inc., Moravia, NY 13118. circ. 10,000.
  Former titles: Student Aid Annual (ISSN 0585-4555); Student Aid Manual (ISSN 0145-8043)
  Alphabetical listing of scholarship titles

378 US ISSN 0077-894X
CITY COLLEGE PAPERS; contributions to knowledge in all fields originating in lectures, research and scholarship at the City College of New York. 1965. irreg, no. 12, 1974; later issues postponed. available on exchange. City College of New York, Library, Convent Ave. & 138th St., New York, NY 10031.

378 CN
CLAN MACDONALD ANNUAL. a. McGill University, MacDonald Campus, Students Council, Box 98, MacDonald College, Quebec, Que. H0A 1C0, Canada. Ed. Elizabeth Koessler. adv.

378.1 US
COLLEGE ADMISSIONS DATA SERVICE. Spine title: College Admissions Data. 1959. a. $80. Orchard House, Inc., Balls Hill Rd., Concord, MA 01742. Ed. Bruce Sylvester. circ. 2,500.

378 US ISSN 0147-5894
COLLEGE AND UNIVERSITY ADMISSIONS AND ENROLLMENT, NEW YORK STATE. 1948. a. free. ‡ Education Department, Information Center on Education, Albany, NY 12234. circ. controlled.
Formerly: College and University Enrollment in New York State (ISSN 0077-9180)

378 US ISSN 0077-9172
COLLEGE AND UNIVERSITY DEGREES CONFERRED, NEW YORK STATE. 1950. a. free. Education Department, Information Center on Education, Albany, NY 12234. circ. controlled.

378 US ISSN 0093-3414
COLLEGE AND UNIVERSITY EMPLOYEES, NEW YORK STATE. a. free. Education Department, Information Center on Education, Albany, NY 12234. charts. circ. controlled.
Formerly: Employees in Colleges and Universities, New York State.

378 FR ISSN 0069-5580
COLLEGE DE FRANCE. ANNUAIRE. 1901. a. College de France, 124 rue Henri Barbusse, 93308 Aubervilliers Cedex, France.

378 US ISSN 0069-5688
COLLEGE FACTS CHART. 1952. a. $2. ‡ National Beta Club, Box 730, Spartanburg, SC 29304. circ. 10,000.

360 US
COLLEGES AND UNIVERSITIES WITH ACCREDITED UNDERGRADUATE SOCIAL WORK PROGRAMS. a. free. Council on Social Work Education, 111 Eighth Ave., New York, NY 10011.

378 EI ISSN 0588-6953
COMMISSION OF THE EUROPEAN COMMUNITIES. EXPOSE ANNUEL SUR LES ACTIVITIES D'ORIENTATION PROFESSIONNELLE DANS LA COMMUNAUTE. (Editions also in German, Italian and Dutch) 1968. a. 5.60 F. Office for Official Publications of the European Communities, C.P. 1003, Luxembourg 1, Luxembourg (Dist. in U.S. by: European Community Information Service, 2100 M St., NW, Suite 707, Washington, DC 20037)

378 US ISSN 0069-6854
COMMITTEE ON INSTITUTIONAL COOPERATION. ANNUAL REPORT. 1961-62. a. free. ‡ Committee on Institutional Cooperation, 820 Davis St., Suite 130, Evanston, IL 60201. Ed. Robin S. Wilson. circ. controlled.

378 UK ISSN 0069-7745
COMMONWEALTH UNIVERSITIES YEARBOOK. 1914. a. £44. Association of Commonwealth Universities, 36 Gordon Sq., London WC1H 0PF, England (Dist. by International Publications Service, 114 East 32nd St. New York, N.Y. 10016) Eds. A. Christodoulou, T. Craig. index. circ. 5,500.

378 UK ISSN 0571-625X
COMPENDIUM OF UNIVERSITY ENTRANCE REQUIREMENTS FOR FIRST DEGREE COURSES IN THE UNITED KINGDOM. 1963. a. £4.70. Association of Commonwealth Universities, 36 Gordon Square, London WC1 H OPF, England (Avail. only from: Lund Humphries(A.C.U.), the Country Press, Drummond Rd., Bradford BD8 8DH, England) (Co-sponsor: Committee of Vice-Chancellors and Principals of the Universities of the United Kingdom) circ. 15,000.

378.54 II
CONFERENCE OF VICE-CHANCELLORS. REPORT. (Text in English) University Grants Commission, Publication Officer, 35 Ferozeshah Rd., New Delhi 110001, India.

378 150 910.03 US
CONFERENCE ON EMPIRICAL RESEARCH IN BLACK PSYCHOLOGY. 1974. a. U.S. National Institute of Education, Educational Equity Group, Washington, DC 20208.
Black interests

378 SZ
CONFERENCE UNIVERSITAIRE SUISSE. RAPPORT ANNUEL. German edition: Schweizerische Hochschulkonferenz. Jahresbericht. 1969. a. free. Conference Universitaire Suisse - Schweizerische Hochschulkonferenz, Wildhainweg 21, CH-3012 Berne, Switzerland. circ. 600 (German edt.); 300 (French edt.)

378 US ISSN 0069-9012
CONNECTICUT COLLEGE MONOGRAPH. irreg.; latest issue, no. 10. (Connecticut College) Shoe String Press, Inc., 995 Sherman Ave., Hamden, CT 06514.

378 VE
CONSEJO NACIONAL DE INVESTIGACIONES CIENTIFICAS Y TECNOLOGICAS. DEPARTAMENTO DE EDUCACION. DIRECTORIO NACIONAL DE CURSOS DE POSTGRADO. irreg. Consejo Nacional de Investigaciones Cientificas y Tecnologicas, Departamento de Educacion, Apartado 70617 Los Ruices, Caracas, Venezuela.

378 ES ISSN 0589-4301
CONSEJO SUPERIOR UNIVERSITARIO CENTROAMERICANO. ACTAS DE LA REUNION ORDINARIA.* irreg. Consejo Superior Universitaria Centroamericano, 5 Calle Oriente 220, San Salvador, El Salvador.

378 NQ ISSN 0589-4360
CONSEJO SUPERIOR UNIVERSITARIO CENTROAMERICANO. PUBLICACIONES.* irreg. Editorial Universitaria de la U N A N, Leon, Nicaragua.

378 IT
CONSORZIO UNIVERSITARIO. PUBBLICAZIONI. SEZIONE MISCELLANEA. 1975. irreg. exchange. Universita degli Studi di Udine, Biblioteca Centrale, Udine, Italy.

378.1 US
COUNCIL FOR ADVANCEMENT AND SUPPORT OF EDUCATION. MEMBERSHIP DIRECTORY. (Council formed by merger of American College Public Relations Association and American Alumni Council) a. $50. Council for Advancement and Support of Education, 11 Dupont Circle, Suite 400, Washington, DC 20036.
Formerly: Council for Advancement and Support of Education. Directory; Supersedes in part: American College Public Relations Association. Directory (ISSN 0065-7816)

378.15 US ISSN 0070-1076
COUNCIL OF GRADUATE SCHOOLS IN THE UNITED STATES. PROCEEDINGS OF THE ANNUAL MEETING. 1961. a. price varies. Council of Graduate Schools in the U.S., One Dupont Circle, Suite 310, Washington, DC 20036. Ed. John W. Ryan. Indexed: ERIC.

378 CN ISSN 0315-9590
COUNCIL OF ONTARIO UNIVERSITIES TRIENNIAL REVIEW. 1975. triennial. free. Council of Ontario Universities, Suite 8039, 130 St. George Street, Toronto, Ontario M5S 2T4, Canada. Ed. G. Grant Clarke. circ. 12,000.
Former titles: Council of Ontario Universities Biennial Review (ISSN 0084-8972); Council of Ontario Universities. Annual Review (ISSN 0315-9000)

378 060 VE ISSN 0070-170X
CUADERNOS DE ORIENTACION.* 1966. irreg. Universidad del Zulia, Facultad de Humanidades y Educacion, Apartado de Correos 415, Maracaibo, Venezuela.

378 US ISSN 0070-1971
CURRENT ISSUES IN HIGHER EDUCATION. (Based on presentations at annual National Conference on Higher Education) 1946. a. price varies. American Association for Higher Education, One Dupont Circle, Suite 780, Washington, DC 20036. index. circ. 9,000. (also avail. in microform from UMI)

CURRICULA IN THE ATMOSPHERIC AND OCEANOGRAPHIC SCIENCES. see METEOROLOGY

378 US
D.H.E. RESEARCH NOTE. 1975. irreg. Department of Higher Education, 225 West State St., Box 1293, Trenton, NJ 08625. charts. stat.
Formerly(until vol. 16, 1975): D.H.E. Data Briefs.

378 US
DANFORTH FOUNDATION. ANNUAL REPORT. a. Danforth Foundation, 222 S. Central Ave., St. Louis, MO 63105.

378 US ISSN 0098-5279
DATA BOOK ON ILLINOIS HIGHER EDUCATION. a. Board of Higher Education, 4 W. Old Capitol Sq., 500 Reisch Bldg., Springfield, IL 62701.

378 US ISSN 0092-3761
DATA ON IOWA'S AREA SCHOOLS. a. Department of Public Instruction, Grimes State Building, Des Moines, IA 50319. illus. stat. Indexed: ERIC. Key Title: Data on Iowa's Area Schools and Public Junior College.

378 US
DEGARMO LECTURES. 1975. a. price varies. Society of Professors of Education, c/o George V. Guy, School of Education, Portland State University, Box 751, Portland, OR 97207.

378.1 US
DEGREE PROGRAMS OFFERED BY WEST VIRGINIA INSTITUTIONS OF HIGHER EDUCATION. a. Board of Regents, 950 Kanawha Blvd. E., Charleston, WV 25301.

378.1 US ISSN 0092-606X
DEGREES CONFERRED BY WEST VIRGINIA INSTITUTIONS OF HIGHER EDUCATION. a. Board of Regents, 950 Kanawha Blvd. E., Charleston, WV 25301.

378 CN ISSN 0315-9248
DEVELOPMENT JOURNAL. 1970. irreg. Canadian Association of University Development Officers, University of Guelph, Guelph, Ont., Canada. illus.

378 CN ISSN 0706-2338
DIRECTORY OF CANADIAN UNIVERSITIES/ REPERTOIRE DES UNIVERSITES CANADIENNES. (Text in English and French) 1956. a. Can.$9($11) ‡ Association of Universities and Colleges of Canada, 151 Slater St., Ottawa, Ontario K1P 5N1, Canada. circ. 4,000.
Former titles: Directory of Canadian Universities and Colleges; Universities and Colleges of Canada (ISSN 0083-3932)

378 US ISSN 0084-988X
DIRECTORY OF COLLEGE STORES. 1956. biennial. $30. B. Klein Publications, Box 8503, Coral Springs, FL 33065.

378 US
DIRECTORY OF COOPERATIVE EDUCATION ACTIVITIES IN FLORIDA. 1972. biennial. free. ‡ Florida State University, Department of Education, 107 Gaines St., Tallahassee, FL 32304. Ed. Aaron D. Lucas.

DIRECTORY OF COUNSELING SERVICES. see EDUCATION

378 CN ISSN 0705-8160
DIRECTORY OF COURSES. TOURISM-HOSPITALITY-RECREATION. 1976. biennial. free. Department of Industry, Trade and Commerce, Office of Tourism, Ottawa, Ont. K1A OJ2, Canada. (Co-sponsors: Canadian Restaurant Association; Travel Industry Association of Canada)

DIRECTORY OF DENTAL EDUCATORS. see MEDICAL SCIENCES — Dentistry

378.3 II ISSN 0084-9936
DIRECTORY OF FULBRIGHT ALUMNI. (Text in English) 1969. triennial. free. United States Educational Foundation in India, Fulbright House, 12 Hailey Rd., New Delhi 110001, India. Ed. P. D. Sayal. cum.index 1950-70. circ. controlled.

EDUCATION — HIGHER EDUCATION

378   UK
DIRECTORY OF FURTHER EDUCATION. 1974. a. £30 hardback; £27.50 paperback. Hobsons Press, Bateman St., Cambridge CB2 1LZ, England.

378.774   US
DIRECTORY OF MICHIGAN INSTITUTIONS OF HIGHER EDUCATION. irreg. Department of Education, Lansing, MI 48933.

378 530   ISSN 0361-2228
DIRECTORY OF PHYSICS & ASTRONOMY STAFF MEMBERS. 1959/1960. a. $49. American Institute of Physics, 335 E. 45th St., New York, NY 10017. stat.
    Continues: Directory of Physics and Astronomy Faculties in North American Colleges & Universities (ISSN 0419-3253)

378   US
DIRECTORY OF PROFESSIONAL PERSONNEL: STATE HIGHER EDUCATION AGENCIES AND BOARDS. a. $5. Education Commission of the States, 300 Lincoln Tower, 1860 Lincoln St., Denver, CO 80203.

378   US   ISSN 0146-7336
DIRECTORY OF RESEARCH GRANTS. 1975. a. $37.50 Oryx Press, 2214 N. Central at Encanto, Suite 103, Phoenix, AZ 85004. Eds. Betty L. Wilson, William K. Wilson.

378   CN   ISSN 0708-2193
DIRECTORY OF UNIVERSITY CORRESPONDENCE COURSES. 1977. irreg. University of Saskatchewan, Department of Correspondence Courses, Saskatoon, Sask. S7N 0W0, Canada.

378   IT   ISSN 0391-5018
DOC; DOCUMENTAZIONE. 1972. biennial. L.60000. (Istituto Nazionale Informazione) Editoriale Italiana, Via Vigliena, 10, Rome, Italy. illus. circ. 5,000.

DOKUMENTE ZUM HOCHSCHULSPORT. see SPORTS AND GAMES

378   US
DON'T MISS OUT; the ambitious student's guide to scholarships and loans. 1976. a. $2.50. Octameron Associates, Inc., Box 3437, Alexandria, VA 22302. Ed. Robert Leider. bibl, illus, stat. circ. 200,000. (back issues avail.)

378   US
E M C DIRECTORY OF SUMMER SESSION COURSES ON EDUCATIONAL MEDIA. 1964. a (not published in 1974) free. Educational Media Council, 1346 Connecticut Ave. N.W., Washington, DC 20036. Ed. Harriet Lundgaard. circ. 7,500.

378   US   ISSN 0531-9315
E R I C CLEARINGHOUSE FOR JUNIOR COLLEGES. TOPICAL PAPER SERIES. 1968. irreg., 3-4/yr. free. E R I C Clearinghouse for Junior Colleges, 96 Powell Library Bldg., University of California, Los Angeles, CA 90024. Dir. Arthur M. Cohen. bibl. charts. stat. circ. 2,000. (also avail. in microfiche) Indexed: Res.Educ.

378   US   ISSN 0424-0227
E U M E N ACTION.* (Entr'aide Universitaire Mondiale) 1965. irreg. World University Service, 20 West 40th St., New York, NY 10018.

378 323   SA   ISSN 0070-8976
EDGAR BROOKES ACADEMIC AND HUMAN FREEDOM LECTURE.* 1965. a. University of Natal, Students Representative Council, Box 375, Pietermaritzburg, South Africa.

EDUCATION FOR NURSING: THE DIPLOMA WAY. see MEDICAL SCIENCES — Nurses And Nursing

378   FR   ISSN 0070-9182
EDUCATION IN EUROPE. SECTION 1: HIGHER EDUCATION AND RESEARCH. 1963. irreg. price varies; $1-$4.50. Council of Europe, Council for Cultural Co-Operation, Publications Section, Strasbourg, France (Dist. in U.S. by Manhattan Publishing Co., 225 Lafayette St., New York, N.Y. 10012)

378   AT
EDUCATION RESEARCH AND PERSPECTIVES. 1961. s-a. Aus.$3.50. (University of Western Australia, Department of Education) University of Western Australia Press, Nedlands, W.A. 6009, Australia (Dist. in U.S. by: International Scholarly Book Services, Box 555, Forest Grove, OR 97116) bk. rev.
    Formerly: Australian Journal of Highter Education.

ENGINEERING COLLEGE RESEARCH AND GRADUATE STUDY. see ENGINEERING

378   US
ENROLLMENT IN INSTITUTIONS OF HIGHER EDUCATION IN ILLINOIS. Variant title: Enrollment in Institutions of Higher Learning in Illinois. 1946. a. free. Board of Higher Education, 4 W. Old Capitol Sq., 500 Reisch Bldg., Springfield, IL 62701.

378   US   ISSN 0071-1187
ERNEST BLOCH LECTURES. 1969. irreg. price varies. University of California Press, 2223 Fulton St., Berkeley, CA 94720.

370.7   CL
ESTUDIOS PEDAGOGICOS. (Text in Spanish; summaries in English) 1976. irreg. exchange basis. Universidad Austral de Chile, Facultad de Letras y Educacion, Casilla 567, Valdivia, Chile. bibl, charts, stat.

378.761   US   ISSN 0095-0637
FACT BOOK. ALABAMA INSTITUTIONS OF HIGHER EDUCATION, UNIVERSITIES AND COLLEGES. Short title: Alabama Institutions of Higher Education, Universities and Colleges. 1972. irreg. Commission on Higher Education, Montgomery, AL 36104. illus.

378.754   US   ISSN 0093-8831
FACT BOOK AND REPORT OF THE WEST VIRGINIA STATE SYSTEM OF HIGHER EDUCATION. irreg. Board of Regents, 950 Kanawha Blvd. E., Charleston, WV 25301.

378   US
FACT BOOK FOR ACADEMIC ADMINISTRATORS. 1958. a. $25. American Council on Education, One Dupont Circle, Washington, DC 20036. Ed. Charles Anderson. stat. cum.index.
    Former titles: Fact Book for Academic Administration; Until 1980: Fact Book on Higher Education (ISSN 0363-6720); F B; A Fact Book on Higher Education (ISSN 0014-6501)

378   US   ISSN 0191-1643
FACT BOOK ON HIGHER EDUCATION IN THE SOUTH. 1965. biennial. $3. Southern Regional Education Board, 130 Sixth St., N.W., Atlanta, GA 30313. E. F. Schietinger.

378.1   US
FACULTY CHARACTERISTICS: PUBLIC COLLEGES AND UNIVERSITIES IN WEST VIRGINIA. a. Board of Regents, 950 Kanawha Blvd. E., Charleston, WV 25301.

378   US
FEDERAL GOVERNMENT & COOPERATIVE EDUCATION. 1979. a. $1.75. Octameron Associates, Inc., Box 3437, Alexandria, VA 22302.

378.3   US   ISSN 0085-0543
FINANCIAL AIDS TO ILLINOIS STUDENTS. 1968. biennial. Office of Education, 100 N. First St., Springfield, IL 62777. Ed. Thomas J. Denny.

020 378.3   US   ISSN 0569-6275
FINANCIAL ASSISTANCE FOR LIBRARY EDUCATION. a. $0.50. American Library Association, Standing Committee on Library Education, 50 E. Huron St., Chicago, IL 60611. circ. 8,000.

378   US
FINANCING HIGHER EDUCATION. 1959. irreg; no. 27, 1976. free. Southern Regional Education Board, 130 Sixth St., N.W., Atlanta, GA 30313. charts. stat.

378.759   US   ISSN 0093-1071
FLORIDA. STATE BOARD OF INDEPENDENT COLLEGES AND UNIVERSITIES. REPORT. 1972. a. free. Florida State Board of Independent Colleges and Universities, Tallahassee, FL 32304. circ. 500. Key Title: Report of the State Board of Indenpendent Colleges and Universities (Tallahassee)

371   US   ISSN 0071-5999
FLORIDA REQUIREMENTS FOR TEACHER CERTIFICATION. 1923. irreg. free. Department of Education, Knott Bldg., Tallahassee, FL 32304. Ed. Ralph D. Turlington.

016.05   US   ISSN 0428-6766
FLORIDA STATE UNIVERSITY. PUBLICATIONS OF THE FACULTY. Running title: F S U Faculty Publications. 1954. irreg. Florida State University, Office of the Dean, Graduate Studies & Research, Tallahassee, FL 32306. Ed. Clifton Paisley. circ. 2,500. Key Title: Publications of the Faculty - Research Council, Florida State University.
    Continues: Florida State University. Publications of the Faculty and Theses Directed.

378   AU   ISSN 0429-1573
FORSCHUNGEN ZUR INNSBRUCKER UNIVERSITAETSGESCHICHTE. (Subseries of: Universitaet Innsbruck. Veroeffentlichungen) 1962. irreg., vol, 10, 1971. price varies. (Universitaet Innsbruck) Oesterreichische Kommissionsbuchhandlung, Maximilianstrasse 17, A-6020 Innsbruck, Austria. Ed. Franz Huter.

FOUNDATION CENTER NATIONAL DATA BOOK. see SOCIAL SERVICES AND WELFARE

378   US
FOUNDATION GRANTS INDEX. 1970. a. $27. Foundation Center, 888 Seventh Ave., New York, NY 10106. Ed. Lee Noe. stat. index.

FOUNDATION GRANTS TO INDIVIDUALS. see SOCIAL SERVICES AND WELFARE

378   GE
GERMANY (DEMOCRATIC REPUBLIC, 1949-). MINISTERIUM FUER HOCH- UND FACHSCHULWESEN. VERFUEGUNGEN UND MITTEILUNGEN.* irreg. M.0.90. Ministerium fuer Hoch- und Fachschulwesen, Rechtsabteilung, Marx-Engels-Platz 2, Berlin 102, E. Germany (D.D.R.)

378   GH
GHANA. NATIONAL COUNCIL FOR HIGHER EDUCATION. ANNUAL REPORT. a. National Council for Higher Education, Accra, Ghana.

001.3 378   GW   ISSN 0085-1108
GOETTINGER UNIVERSITAETSREDEN. 1941. irreg. price varies. Vandenhoeck und Ruprecht, Theaterstr. 13, Postfach 77, 3400 Goettingen, W. Germany (B.R.D.)

378   US   ISSN 0072-4904
GOING-TO-COLLEGE HANDBOOK. 1946. a. $2. Outlook Publishers, Inc., 512 E. Main St., Richmond, VA 23219. Ed. Aubrey N. Brown, Jr. adv. bk. rev. circ. 40,000.

378 507   US   ISSN 0072-5250
GRADUATE FELLOWSHIP AWARDS ANNOUNCED BY NATIONAL SCIENCE FOUNDATION. a. free. U. S. National Science Foundation, 1800 G St., N.W., Washington, DC 20550 (Orders to: Supt. Doc., Washington, DC 20402)

GRADUATE PROGRAMS: PHYSICS, ASTRONOMY, AND RELATED FIELDS. see PHYSICS

378   UK   ISSN 0144-462X
GRANTS FOR STUDY VISITS BY UNIVERSITY ADMINISTRATORS AND LIBRARIANS. 1979. irreg. £1. Association of Commonwealth Universities, 36 Gordon Square, London WC1H 0PF, England.

378   UK
GRANTS REGISTER (UK) 1968. biennial. £9. St. James Press, 3 Percy St., London W.1., England (And St. Martins Press, 175 Fifth Ave., New York, NY 10010)

EDUCATION — HIGHER EDUCATION

GREAT BRITAIN. SOCIAL SCIENCE RESEARCH COUNCIL. BURSARY SCHEME. see *SOCIAL SCIENCES: COMPREHENSIVE WORKS*

GREAT BRITAIN. SOCIAL SCIENCE RESEARCH COUNCIL. STUDENTSHIP HANDBOOK. see *SOCIAL SCIENCES: COMPREHENSIVE WORKS*

378 UK ISSN 0072-7237
GREAT BRITAIN. UNIVERSITY GRANTS COMMITTEE. ANNUAL SURVEY. a. £1. University Grants Committee, 14 Park Crescent, London W1N 4DH, England (Avail. from H.M.S.O., c/o Liaison Officer, Atlantic House, Holborn Viaduct, London EC1P 1BN, England)

378 US ISSN 0046-6409
GREEN SHEET; University of Hawaii newsletter. 1968. irreg. free, attached to weekly University Bulletin. University of Hawaii, Office of University Relations and Development, 2500 Campus Rd., Hawaii 2, Honolulu, HI 96822. Ed. Gay Burk. charts. illus. circ. 3,700.

301.07 CN ISSN 0315-0895
GUIDE TO DEPARTMENTS OF SOCIOLOGY AND ANTHROPOLOGY IN CANADIAN UNIVERSITIES/ANNUAIRE DES DEPARTEMENTS DE SOCIOLOGIE ET D'ANTHROPOLOGIE AU CANADA. 1974. irreg. Canadian Sociology and Anthropology Association, Concordia University, 1455 Bd. de Maisonneuve W., Montreal, Que. H3G 1M8, Canada.

658 US ISSN 0098-9835
GUIDE TO PROFESSIONAL DEVELOPMENT OPPORTUNITIES FOR COLLEGE AND UNIVERSITY ADMINISTRATORS: SEMINARS, WORKSHOPS, CONFERENCES, AND INTERNSHIPS. irreg. $4. Academy for Educational Development, Management Division, 1414 22nd St., N.W., Washington, DC 20037 (Orders to: Ms. Sylvia Galloway, American Council on Education, One Dupont Circle, N.W., Washington, D.C. 20036) (Co-sponsor: American Council on Education. Office of Leadership Development in Higher Education)

378.3 US ISSN 0072-8721
GUIDE TO THE NATIONAL MERIT SCHOLARSHIP PROGRAM. 1961. a. free. National Merit Scholarship Corporation, 1 American Plaza, Evanston, IL 60201.

GUIDEBOOK OF U.S. & CANADIAN POSTDOCTORAL DENTAL PROGRAMS. see *MEDICAL SCIENCES — Dentistry*

378 GW
H I S BRIEF. 1969. irreg., no. 64, 1978. DM.20. (Hochschul-Informations-System GmbH) K.G. Saur Verlag KG, Poessenbacherstr. 12 B, Postfach 711009, 8000 Munich 71, W. Germany (B.R.D.) bibl.
Incorporating (since 1978): Hochschulplannung.

378 US ISSN 0146-5104
HANDBOOK FOR RECRUITING AT THE HISTORICALLY BLACK COLLEGES. irreg., approx. biennial. $9. College Placement Services, Inc., Box 2322, Bethlehem, PA 18001.

378 AU
HANDBUCH DER ALLGEMEINBILDENDEN HOEHEREN SCHULEN OESTERREICHS. 1954. biennial. S.150($10) Gewerkschaft der Oeffentlich Bediensteten, Bundessektion Hoehere Schule, Lackierergasse 7, A-1090 Vienna, Austria. adv.

378 US ISSN 0440-7881
HIGHER EDUCATION IN NEW ENGLAND. 1956. irreg.(formerly q.) free. New England Board of Higher Education, 68 Walnut Rd., Wenham, MA 01984.

378 942 UK ISSN 0144-5138
HISTORY OF UNIVERSITIES. (Text in English, French, German, Italian and Spanish) 1981. a. £16. Avebury Publishing Co. Ltd., Olympic House, 63 Woodside Rd., Amersham, Bucks HP6 6AA, England (Subscr. to: The Distribution Centre, Blackhorse Rd., Letchworth,Herts, SE6 1HN, England) Ed. Dr. Charles Schmitt. bk. rev. index. Indexed: Hist.Abstr.

HOME ECONOMICS IN INSTITUTIONS GRANTING BACHELORS OR HIGHER DEGREES. see *HOME ECONOMICS*

378 068 II
I I A S OCCASIONAL PAPERS. (Text in English) 1974. irreg. price varies. Indian Institute of Advanced Study, Rashtrapati Nivas, Summer Hill, Simla 171005, India.

378.773 US ISSN 0094-8322
ILLINOIS. BOARD OF HIGHER EDUCATION. DIRECTORY OF HIGHER EDUCATION. irreg. Board of Higher Education, 4 W. Old Capitol Sq., 500 Reisch Bldg., Springfield, IL 62701. Key Title: Directory of Higher Education.

378 US ISSN 0073-4756
ILLINOIS. BOARD OF HIGHER EDUCATION. REPORT. 1962. a. from 1970; previously irreg. free. Board of Higher Education, 4 W. Old Capitol Sq., 500 Reisch Bldg., Springfield, IL 62701.

378.1 US ISSN 0362-5524
ILLINOIS. BOARD OF HIGHER EDUCATION. STATEWIDE SPACE SURVEY. 1962. biennial. Board of Higher Education, 500 Reisch Bldg., 4 W. Old Capitol Sq., Springfield, IL 62701. Key Title: Statewide Space Survey.

378.1 US ISSN 0092-7783
ILLINOIS COMMUNITY COLLEGE BOARD. BIENNIAL REPORT. (Special issue of: Community College Bulletin) 1967? biennial. Community College Board, 3085 Stevenson Dr., Springfield, IL 62703. stat.
Supersedes: Illinois. Junior College Board. Annual Report (ISSN 0092-7783)

378 IO
INDONESIA. DIRECTORATE GENERAL OF HIGHER EDUCATION. ANNUAL REPORT/ INDONESIA. DIREKTORAT JENDERAL PENDIDIKAN TINGGI. LAPORAN TAHUNAN. (Text in Indonesian) a. Directorate General of Higher Education, Jakarta, Indonesia.

378 AU ISSN 0020-0077
INFORMATION FOR FOREIGN STUDENTS INTENDING TO STUDY AT AUSTRIAN UNIVERSITIES; fuer auslaendische Studienbewerber an oesterreichischen Hochschulen. 1961/1962. irreg. ‡ Oesterreichischer Auslandsstudentendienst, Dr. Karl Lueger-Ring 1, A-1010 Vienna, Austria. Ed. Robert Bauchinger. circ. 10,000-15,000.

378 PL
INFORMATOR DLA KANDYDATON NA STUDIA PODYPLOMOWE I DOKTORANCKIE. 1971/72. a. price varies. (Ministerstwo Nauki, Szkolnictwa Wyzszego i Techniki) Panstwowe Wydawnictwo Naukowe, Miodowa 10, Warsaw, Poland. Ed. Aleksander Malec. circ. 5,000.

378.1 US ISSN 0363-2601
INNOVATIVE GRADUATE PROGRAMS DIRECTORY. 1975. irreg. $4. Empire State College, Learning Resources Center, Saratoga Springs, NY 12866. circ. 1,000.

378 AU
INNSBRUCKER UNIVERSITAETSREDEN. (Subseries of: Universitaet Innsbruck. Veroeffentlichungen) 1969. irreg., vol. 8, 1974. price varies. (Universitaet Innsbruck) Oesterreichische Kommissionsbuchhandlung, Maximilianstrasse 17, A-6020 Innsbruck, Austria.

378 EI
INSTITUT DE LA COMMUNAUTE EUROPEENNE POUR LES ETUDES UNIVERSITAIRES. RECHERCHE. RESEARCH. no. 8, 1974. irreg. European Community Institute for University Studies - Institut de la Communaute Europeenne pour les Etudes Universitaires, 200 rue de la Loi, B-1040 Brussels, Belgium.

370.7 CK
INSTITUTO COLOMBIANO DE PEDAGOGIA. BOLETIN INFORMATIVO Y DE DOCUMENTACION. irreg. Instituto Colombiano de Pedagogia, Carrera 7a no. 27-52, Apartado Aereo 52976, Bogota, Colombia.

INSTITUTO COLOMBIANO PARA EL FOMENTO DE LA EDUCACION SUPERIOR. BOLETIN BIBLIOGRAFICO. see *BIBLIOGRAPHIES*

370.7 BL
INTER-ACAO. 1975. irreg. Universidade Federal de Goias, Faculdade de Educacao, Praca Universitaria s/n, 70000 Goiana, Brazil.
Teacher education

378 UK
INTERNATIONAL ASSOCIATION OF UNIVERSITIES. PAPERS & REPORTS. a. $9.50. Carfax Publishing Co., Haddon House, Dorchester-on-Thames, Oxford OX9 8JZ, England. (also avail. in microfiche; back issues avail., reprint service avail. from ISI)

378 UK ISSN 0018-8492
INTERNATIONAL ASSOCIATION OF UNIVERSITY PROFESSORS & LECTURERS. COMMUNICATION. (Text in English and French) 1944. irreg., no. 9, 1979. International Association of University Professors & Lecturers, Florence Boot Hall, University Park, Nottingham NG7 2QY, England. Ed. Jean P. Russell-Gebbett. adv. charts. cum.index. circ. 2,000.

378 FR ISSN 0579-3866
INTERNATIONAL FEDERATION OF CATHOLIC UNIVERSITIES. GENERAL ASSEMBLY. (REPORT) irreg., 1975, 11th Assembly, New Delhi. International Federation of Catholic Universities, Secretariat Permanent, 77 bis rue de Grenelle, 75007 Paris, France.

378 UK ISSN 0074-6215
INTERNATIONAL HANDBOOK OF UNIVERSITIES AND OTHER INSTITUTIONS OF HIGHER EDUCATION. Title varies: International Handbook of Universities. (Text in English) 1959. triennial, 8th ed., 1980. £45. ‡ (International Association of Universities) Macmillan Press Ltd., 4 Little Essex St., London WC2R 3LF, England. Eds. H. M. R. Keyes, D. J. Aitken. index.

INTERNATIONAL HIGHER EDUCATION. see *EDUCATION — International Education Programs*

371.8 CS ISSN 0074-9532
INTERNATIONAL UNION OF STUDENTS. CONGRESS RESOLUTIONS. (Editions in English, French and Spanish) a. price varies. International Union of Students, 17th November St., 110 01 Prague 1, Czechoslovakia.

378 CN ISSN 0318-8329
INVENTORY OF RESEARCH INTO HIGHER EDUCATION IN CANADA. (Text in English and French) 1974. a. Can.$5. Association of Universities and Colleges of Canada, 151 Slater St., Ottawa, Ont. K1P 5A3, Canada. Ed. J. F. Houwing. circ. 400.

378 US
ISSUES IN HIGHER EDUCATION. 1970. irreg; no. 9, 1975. free. Southern Regional Education Board, 130 Sixth St., N.W., Atlanta, GA 30313.

378 GW ISSN 0342-6300
JAHRBACH DEUTSCH ALS FREMDSPRACHE. 1975. a. DM.40. Julius Groos Verlag, Hertzstr. 6, Postfach 102423, D-6900 Heidelberg 1, W. Germany (B.R.D.) Ed. Alois Wierlacher. circ. 1,500. (back issues avail.)

378 FI ISSN 0355-6832
JOENSUUN KORKEAKOULU. JULKAISUJA. SARJA B2/UNIVERSITY OF JOENSUU. PUBLICATIONS. SERIES B2. 1975. irreg. price varies. Joensuun Korkeakoulu - University of Joensuu, Tulliportinkatu 1 A, PL 111, Joensuu 10, Finland. circ. 400.
Formerly: Joensuun Korkeakoulu. Julkaisuja. Sarja B (ISSN 0355-3957)

JOURNAL OF FINANCIAL EDUCATION. see *BUSINESS AND ECONOMICS — Banking And Finance*

378 NR
KENYATTA UNIVERSITY COLLEGE. DIRECTORY OF RESEARCH. 1975. a. supplements to base vol. free. Kenyatta University College, Box 43844, Nairobi, Kenya. Ed. J.M. Ng'Ang'A. circ. 200.

EDUCATION — HIGHER EDUCATION

378   SI   ISSN 0047-3383
KESATUAN BULLETIN. vol. 10, 1975. irreg. free. ‡ Kesatuan Akademis Universiti Singapura, Singapore, Singapore. Ed. Tham Seong Chee. adv. bk. rev. charts. circ. 1,000.

378   SA   ISSN 0024-4015
LINK-UP. (Text in English) 1966. irreg. (1-3/yr.) free. University of Pretoria, Director of Public Relations, Hillcrest, Pretoria, South Africa. adv. circ. 3,500.

378   US
LINZER UNIVERSITAETSSCHRIFTEN. 1969. irreg. price varies. Springer-Verlag, 175 Fifth Ave., New York, NY 10010 (also Berlin, Heidelberg, Vienna) (reprint service avail. from ISI)
    Formerly: Linzer Hochschulschriften (ISSN 0075-9724)

378   FR   ISSN 0457-9976
LISTE DES SOCIETES SAVANTES ET LITTERAIRES. 1975. irreg. Comite des Travaux Historiques et Scientifiques, 61 rue de Richelieu, 75002 Paris, France.

370.73   UG
MAKERERE UNIVERSITY. FACULTY OF EDUCATION. HANDBOOK. Added title: Teacher Education in Uganda. a. Makerere University, Faculty of Education, Box 7062, Kampala, Uganda. illus.

371.42   US
MAKING IT: A GUIDE TO STUDENT FINANCES. 1973. irreg. $4.95. E. P. Dutton & Co., Inc., 201 Park Ave. S., New York, NY 10003 (Subscr. to: Harvard Student Agencies, 4 Holyoke St., Cambridge MA 02138)

378   MY
MARA INSTITUTE OF TECHNOLOGY. ANNUAL REPORT/INSTITUT TEKNOLOGI MARA. LAPORAN TAHUNAN. (Text in Malay) a. Mara Institute of Technology, Shah Alam, Selangor, Malaysia.

378   US
MASTER PLAN FOR POSTSECONDARY EDUCATION IN ILLINOIS. 1964. irreg. free. Board of Higher Education, 119 S. 5th St., 500 Reisch Building, Springfield, IL 62701.
    Formerly: Master Plan for Higher Education in Illinois (ISSN 0076-5082)

MASTERS EDUCATION: ROUTE TO OPPORTUNITIES IN CONTEMPORARY NURSING. see *MEDICAL SCIENCES — Nurses And Nursing*

378   GW
MATERIALIEN ZUR HOCHSCHULPOLITIK. 1973. irreg. Universitaet Bremen, Bibliothekstr., 2800 Bremen 33, W. Germany (B.R.D.) Ed. Wolfgang Schmitz.

MELBOURNE UNIVERSITY MAGAZINE. see *LITERATURE*

371.42   US   ISSN 0076-7913
MICHIGAN. DIVISION OF VOCATIONAL EDUCATION. REPORT. 1918. a. free. Department of Education, Division of Vocational Education, Box 30009, Lansing, MI 48909. cum.index: 1917-18 thru 1968-69.
    Continues: Michigan. State Board of Control for Vocational Education. Annual Descriptive Report.

378   US
MIDWESTERN ASSOCIATION OF GRADUATE SCHOOLS. PROCEEDINGS OF THE ANNUAL MEETING. 1949. a. $5. Midwestern Association of Graduate Schools, Kansas State University, Graduate School, Manhattan, KS 66506. circ. 200.
    Supersedes: Midwest Conference on Graduate Study and Research. Proceedings.

378.1   US   ISSN 0076-9223
MINNESOTA PRIVATE COLLEGE FUND. REPORT.* a. Minnesota Private College Fund, 906 Northwestern Bank Bldg., Minneapolis, MN 55402.

MINORITY STUDENTS OPPORTUNITIES IN UNITED STATES MEDICAL SCHOOLS. see *MEDICAL SCIENCES*

370 338   US
N A B T E REVIEW. 1973. a. $3. ‡ (National Association for Business Teacher Education) National Business Education Association, 1906 Association Drive, Reston, VA 22091. Ed. Lawrence W. Erickson. bibl. circ. 12,000.

378.1   US   ISSN 0090-3965
NATIONAL ASSOCIATION OF COLLEGE ADMISSIONS COUNSELORS. MEMBERSHIP DIRECTORY. biennial. $20 to non-members. National Association of College Admissions Counselors, 9933 Lawler Ave., Suite 500, Skokie, IL 60076. Ed. Robert K. Long. Key Title: Membership Directory - National Association of College Admissions Counselors.
    Continues: Association of College Admissions Counselors. Membership Directory.

378.2   US   ISSN 0027-8416
NATIONAL ASSOCIATION OF COLLEGE ADMISSIONS COUNSELORS. NEWSLETTER. (Issued formerly under previous name of organization: Association of College Admissions Counselors) 1963. irreg. $4.50 to non-members. National Association of College Admissions Counselors, 9933 Lawler Ave., Skokie, IL 60076. Ed. Robert K. Long.

378.1   US   ISSN 0077-328X
NATIONAL ASSOCIATION OF COLLEGE DEANS AND REGISTRARS. PROCEEDINGS.* (Formerly: National Association of Collegiate Deans and Registrars in Negro Schools. Proceedings) a. free. Florida A & M University, Tallahassee, FL 32307. Ed. Edwin M. Thorpe.

378.1   US   ISSN 0077-3425
NATIONAL ASSOCIATION OF STATE UNIVERSITIES AND LAND-GRANT COLLEGES. APPROPRIATIONS OF STATE TAX FUNDS FOR HIGHER EDUCATION. a. $2.50 to nonmembers, 0.75 to members. National Association of State Universities and Land-Grant Colleges, One Dupont Circle, N.W., Suite 710, Washington, DC 20036.

378.15 379   US   ISSN 0077-3433
NATIONAL ASSOCIATION OF STATE UNIVERSITIES AND LAND-GRANT COLLEGES. PROCEEDINGS. 1887. a. free. National Association of State Universities and Land-Grant Colleges, One Dupont Circle, Suite 710, Washington, DC 20036. Ed. C. K. Arnold. circ. 1,000.

378 331   US   ISSN 0095-9294
NATIONAL CENTER FOR THE STUDY OF COLLECTIVE BARGAINING IN HIGHER EDUCATION. ANNUAL CONFERENCE PROCEEDINGS. 1973. s-a. $20. City University of New York, Bernard M. Baruch College, 17 Lexington Ave., New York, NY 10010. Ed. Joel M. Douglas. bibl. circ. 1,000.

507.2   LE
NATIONAL COUNCIL FOR SCIENTIFIC RESEARCH. ANNUAL REPORT. French edition: Conseil National de la Recherche Scientifique. Rapport Annuel. (Editions in Arabic, English and French) a, latest 1974. free to institutions. National Council for Scientific Research, Box 8281, Beirut, Lebanon.

378   US
NATIONAL DEAN'S LIST. 1978. a. $24.95. Educational Communications, Inc., 3105 MacArthur Blvd., Northbrook, IL 60062.

001.3   US   ISSN 0361-1221
NATIONAL ENDOWMENT FOR THE HUMANITIES. PROGRAM ANNOUNCEMENT. a. U.S. National Endowment for the Humanities, 806 15th St., N.W., Washington, DC 20006.

NATIONAL LEAGUE FOR NURSING. ASSOCIATE DEGREE EDUCATION FOR NURSING. see *MEDICAL SCIENCES — Nurses And Nursing*

378   US
NATIONAL UNIVERSITY CONTINUING EDUCATION ASSOCIATION. HANDBOOK AND DIRECTORY. 1974. a. $25. National University Continuing Education Association, 1 Dupont Circle, N.W., Ste. 360, Washington, DC 20036.
    Formerly: National University Extension Association. Handbook and Directory.

378   NE
NETHERLANDS. CENTRAAL BUREAU VOOR DE STATISTIEK. STATISTIEK VAN HET BEROEPSONDERWIJS: KUNSTONDERWIJS. ART COLLEGES. (Text in Dutch and English) 1966/67. a. fl.7.85. Centraal Bureau voor de Statistiek, Prinses Beatrixlaan 428, Voorburg, Netherlands (Orders to: Staatsuitgeverij, Christoffel Plantijnstraat, The Hague, Netherlands)
    Formerly: Netherlands. Centraal Bureau voor de Statistiek. Statistiek van het Kunstonderwijs. Statistics on Art Colleges (ISSN 0077-7307)

378   NE   ISSN 0077-7439
NETHERLANDS. CENTRAAL BUREAU VOOR DE STATISTIEK. STATISTIEK VAN HET WETENSCHAPPELIJK ONDERWIJS. STATISTICS OF UNIVERSITY EDUCATION. (Text in Dutch and English) 1937/38. a. fl.20.25. Centraal Bureau voor de Statistiek, Prinses Beatrixlaan 428, Voorburg, Netherlands (Orders to: Staatsuitgeverij, Christoffel Plantijnstraat, The Hague, Netherlands)

378 370.73   US   ISSN 0077-8168
NEW CAMPUS. 1922. a. $6. Association for Continuing Professional Education, c/o John J. Dlabal, Jr., Northern Illinois University, DeKalb, IL 60115. Eds. Earl Greene, George Hackler. cum.index vols. 1-33, 1948-1980. Indexed: ERIC.

378   US
NEW ENGLAND BOARD OF HIGHER EDUCATION. NEW ENGLAND REGIONAL STUDENT PROGRAM: ENROLLMENT REPORT. 1968. a. free. New England Board of Higher Education, 68 Walnut Rd., Wenham, MA 01984. Ed. Jeanne M. Burns.

378   US
NEW ENGLAND BOARD OF HIGHER EDUCATION. NEW ENGLAND REGIONAL STUDENT PROGRAM: GRADUATE LEVEL. 1955. a. ‡ New England Board of Higher Education, 68 Walnut Rd., Wenham, MA 01984. circ. 13,000.

378   US
NEW ENGLAND BOARD OF HIGHER EDUCATION. NEW ENGLAND REGIONAL STUDENT PROGRAM: UNDERGRADUATE LEVEL. 1955. a. ‡ New England Board of Higher Education, 68 Walnut Rd., Wenham, MA 01984. circ. 13,000.

378   US
NEW JERSEY. DEPARTMENT OF HIGHER EDUCATION. RESEARCH REPORT. 1976. irreg. Department of Higher Education, 225 West State St., Box 1293, Trenton, NJ 08625. charts. stat.

378   AT
NEW SOUTH WALES. HIGHER EDUCATION BOARD. ANNUAL REPORT. 1977. a. free. Higher Education Board, 13th Floor, 189 Kent St., Sydney, N. S. W. 2000, Australia. Ed. N. Booth.

378.669   NR
NIGERIA. NATIONAL UNIVERSITIES COMMISSION. ANNUAL REPORT. a. National Universities Commission, Private Mail Bag 12694, 18 Alhaji Ribadu Rd., Lagos, Nigeria.

378.1   US   ISSN 0078-1428
NORTH CAROLINA STATE UNIVERSITY. DEVELOPMENT COUNCIL. REPORT. 1958. a. free. North Carolina State University, Development Council, 12 Holiday Hall, Raleigh, NC 27607. Ed. Rudolph Pate. circ. 1,200.
    Formerly: North Carolina, University. State College of Agriculture and Engineering, Raleigh. Development Council. Report.

378.766   US
NORTHEASTERN OKLAHOMA STATE UNIVERSITY. FACULTY RESEARCH, PUBLICATIONS, IN-SERVICE ACTIVITIES. vol. 25, 1974. a. free. Northeastern Oklahoma State University, Tahlequa, OK 74464.

EDUCATION — HIGHER EDUCATION

378 US
NORTHWEST ASSOCIATION OF SCHOOLS AND COLLEGES. PROCEEDINGS. Variant name of organization: Northwest Association of Secondary and Higher Schools. 1926. a. $2.50. Northwest Association of Schools and Colleges, 3700-B University Way N.E., Seattle, WA 98105. Ed. James F. Bemis. circ. controlled.

374.013 NO
NORWAY. DIREKTORATET FOR ARBEIDSTILSYNET. FORSKRIFTER/ REGULATIONS. irreg. free. Direktoratet for Arbeidstilsynet, Fr. Nansens vei 14, Box 8103 Dep., Oslo 1, Norway. charts. illus.
Formerly: Norway. Statens Arbeidstilsyn Direktoratet. Verneregler.

378 US ISSN 0078-2904
OAK RIDGE ASSOCIATED UNIVERSITIES. REPORT. 1947. a. free. ‡ Oak Ridge Associated Universities, Inc., Information Services Department, P.O. Box 117, Oak Ridge, TN 37830. Ed. Robert A. Potter. circ. 3,000.

371.4 US ISSN 0360-5434
OCCUPATIONAL EDUCATION. (Included in College Blue Book series) 1972. biennial. $35. Macmillan Publishing Co., Inc., 866 Third Ave., New York, NY 10022. Ed. Max M. Russell.
Formerly: Blue Book of Occupational Education (ISSN 0067-9275)

OESTERREICHISCHER KRANKENPFLEGERVERBAND. FORTBILDUNGSPROGRAMM. see *MEDICAL SCIENCES* — Nurses And Nursing

379 US
OREGON. EDUCATIONAL COORDINATING COUNCIL. ANNUAL PROGRAM AMENDMENT FOR TITLE I, HIGHER EDUCATION ACT OF 1965; program impact. 1970. a. free. Educational Coordinating Commission, 495 State St., Salem, OR 97310. circ. 300.

OREGON STATE UNIVERSITY. SCHOOL OF ENGINEERING. GRADUATE RESEARCH AND EDUCATION. see *ENGINEERING*

378 US
OXFORD UNIVERSITY ALMANACK. a. price varies. Oxford University Press, 200 Madison Ave., New York, NY 10016 (And Ely House, 37 Dover St., London W1X 4AH, England)

378 US
OXFORD UNIVERSITY CALENDAR. a. price varies. Oxford University Press, 200 Madison Ave., New York, NY 10016 (And Ely House, 37 Dover St., London W1X 4AH, England)

378 US
OXFORD UNIVERSITY HANDBOOK. irreg. price varies. Oxford University Press, 200 Madison Ave., New York, NY 10016 (And Ely House, 37 Dover St., London W1X 4AH, England)

378 CN ISSN 0384-0972
P D B. (Professional Development Bulletin) irreg. Alberta Teachers' Association, Professional Development Department, Barnett House, 11010-142 St., Edmonton, Alta. T5N 2R1, Canada.

378 US ISSN 0078-7620
PACIFIC NORTHWEST CONFERENCE ON HIGHER EDUCATION. PROCEEDINGS. 1935; suspended 1943-1945; resumed 1946. a. $4. Oregon State University Press, 101 Waldo Hall, Corvallis, OR 97331. (back issues avail. since 1950)

378 US ISSN 0085-4816
PENNSYLVANIA. DEPARTMENT OF EDUCATION. OUR COLLEGES AND UNIVERSITIES TODAY. vol. 14, 1976. irreg., 7-8/yr. free. Department of Education, Bureau of Educational Statistics, Box 911, Harrisburg, PA 17126. Ed. Roger G. Hummell. charts. stat.

370.7 PH
PHILIPPINE NORMAL COLLEGE RESEARCH SERIES. 1976. irreg., no. 3, 1977. price varies. Philippine Normal School, Manila 2801, Philippines. charts. circ. 500.

378.1 US ISSN 0093-884X
PHYSICAL FACILITIES AT INSTITUTIONS OF HIGHER EDUCATION IN WEST VIRGINIA. irreg. Board of Regents, 950 Kanawha Blvd. E., Charleston, WV 25301.

378 530 US ISSN 0569-5716
PHYSICS MANPOWER - EDUCATION AND EMPLOYMENT STATISTICS. 1964. irreg. $10.00. American Institute of Physics, 335 E. 45th St., New York, NY 10017. Ed. Susanne D. Ellis. circ. 1,000.

378 PL ISSN 0458-1547
POLITECHNIKA LODZKA. ZESZYTY NAUKOWE. ZESZYT SPECJALNY. (Text in Polish; summaries in English and Russian) 1962. irreg. price varies. Politechnika Lodzka, Ul. Zwirki 36, 90-924 Lodz, Poland (Dist. by: Ars Polona-Ruch, Krakowskie Przedmiescie 7, Warsaw, Poland) Ed. Kazimierz Stepniewski. circ. 350.

378.748 US ISSN 0361-9419
POOR RICHARD'S RECORD. a. University of Pennsylvania, 3417 Spruce St., Philadelphia, PA 19174. illus.

378 US
POSTSECONDARY EDUCATION IN CALIFORNIA: INFORMATION DIGEST. a. Postsecondary Education Commission, 1020 12th St., Sacramento, CA 95814.

378 SA
POTCHEFSTROOM UNIVERSITY FOR CHRISTIAN HIGHER EDUCATION. WETENSKAPLIKE BYDRAES. REEKS H: INOUGURELE REDES. (Text in Afrikaans; sometimes in English) irreg. free. Potchefstroom University for Christian Higher Education, Potchefstroom, South Africa.

378 HO
PRESENCIA UNIVERSITARIA. irreg. Editorial Universitaria, Ciudad Universitaria, Tegucigalpa, Honduras. illus.

378.73 US ISSN 0364-3735
PRIVATE HIGHER EDUCATION; annual report on financial and educational trends in the private sector of American higher education. a. National Institute of Independent Colleges and Universities, 1717 Massachusetts Ave. N.W., Washington, DC 20036.

378 US
QUICK HELP FROM THE GOVERNOR: A DIRECTORY OF STATE FINANCIAL AID AGENCIES; names, addresses, phone numbers. 1979. a. $1.25. Octameron Associates, Inc., Box 3437, Alexandria, VA 22302.

370 SW ISSN 0347-4976
R & D IN HIGHER EDUCATION. (Text in English) 1971. irreg. free. National Board of Universities and Colleges, R & D Unit, Box 45501, S-104 30 Stockholm, Sweden. Ed. Kenneth Abrahamsson. circ. 600. Indexed: ERIC. Sociol.Educ.Abstr.
Former titles (1971-76): Sweden. Universitetskanslersaembetet. Educational Development (ISSN 0346-6175); Sweden. Universitetskanslersaembetet. Research and Development in Post- Secondary Education (ISSN 0082-0377)

378 GW ISSN 0067-5997
R I A S-FUNKUNIVERSITAET, BERLIN. FORSCHUNG UND INFORMATION. 1967. irreg. DM.19.80. Colloquium Verlag, Unter den Eichen 93, 1000 Berlin 45, W. Germany (B.R.D.) Ed. Ruprecht Kurzrock. circ. 3,000.

013 SA
RANDSE AFRIKAANSE UNIVERSITEIT. OPSOMMINGS VAN PROEFSKRIFTE EN VERHANDELINGE/ABSTRACTS OF DISSERTATIONS AND THESES. (Text in Afrikaans; summaries in Afrikaans, English, German) 1969/70. a. R.2. Rand Afrikaans University, Box 524, Johannesburg 2000, South Africa. circ. 400.

RED DEER COLLEGE. LEARNING RESOURCES CENTRE. WHAT'S THE USE...? see *EDUCATION* — Teaching Methods And Curriculum

378.3 US
REPORT: MASSACHUSETTS STATE SCHOLARSHIP PROGRAMS. Short title: Massachusetts State Scholarship Programs. irreg. Board of Higher Education, 182 Tremont St., Boston, MA 02111. stat.

378 AT ISSN 0085-5510
REPORT ON AUSTRALIAN UNIVERSITIES. 1958/63. irreg. price varies. Australian Government Publishing Service, Box 84, Canberra, A.C.T. 2600, Australia.

RESEARCH FIELDS IN PHYSICS AT UNITED KINGDOM UNIVERSITIES AND POLYTECHNICS. see *PHYSICS*

378 UK
RESEARCH STRENGTHS OF UNIVERSITIES IN THE DEVELOPING COUNTRIES OF THE COMMONWEALTH. 1976. irreg. £3.50. Association of Commonwealth Universities, 36 Gordon Square, London WC1H 0PF, England.

378 CN
RESOURCES FOR TOURISM/HOSPITALITY/ RECREATION. 1979. biennial. free. Department of Industry, Trade and Commerce, Office of Tourism, Ottawa, Ont. K1A 0J2, Canada.

378 BL
REVISTA UNIMAR. (Text in English, French, Portuguese) 1974. irreg. Universidade Estadual de Maringa, Maringa, Brazil. illus.

ROCHESTER CONFERENCE ON PROGRAMMED INSTRUCTION IN MEDICAL EDUCATION. PROCEEDINGS. see *MEDICAL SCIENCES*

378 AU ISSN 0080-5734
SALZBURGER UNIVERSITAETSREDEN. 1966. irreg., no. 68, 1980. price varies. (Universitaet Salzburg) Universitaetsverlag Anton Pustet, Bergstr. 12, Postschliessfach 144, A-5021 Salzburg, Austria.

378 GW ISSN 0344-0591
SAMMLUNG GROOS. 1977. irreg. price varies. Julius Groos Verlag, Hertzstr. 6, Postfach 102423, D-6900 Heidelberg, W. Germany (B.R.D.) circ. 500. (back issues avail.)

378.1 CN ISSN 0382-1838
SASKATCHEWAN UNIVERSITIES COMMISSION. ANNUAL REPORT. a. Saskatchewan Universities Commission, 2302 Arlington Ave., Saskatoon, Sask., Canada.

378.3 AU ISSN 0036-6374
SCHOLARSHIPS FOR FOREIGN STUDENTS AND UNIVERSITY GRADUATES AT AUSTRIAN INSTITUTIONS OF HIGHER LEARNING/STIPENDIEN FUER AUSLAENDISCHE STUDIERENDE UND AKADEMIKER AN OESTERREICHISCHEN HOCHSCHULEN. 1962. irreg. ‡ Oesterreichischer Auslandsstudentendienst, Dr. Karl Lueger-Ring 1, A-1010 Vienna, Austria. Ed. Robert Bauchinger. circ. 10,000.

360 US
SCHOOLS OF SOCIAL WORK WITH ACCREDITED MASTER'S DEGREE PROGRAMS. a. free. Council on Social Work Education, 111 Eighth Ave., New York, NY 10011. circ. 10,000.
Formerly: Graduate Professional Schools of Social Work in Canada and the U.S.A.

SCOTTISH GRADUATE. see *OCCUPATIONS AND CAREERS*

378.1 US ISSN 0091-5246
SELECT DATA ON STUDENTS, ALABAMA INSTITUTIONS OF HIGHER LEARNING. (Subseries of Alabama. State Commission for the Higher Education Facilities Act of 1963. Comprehensive Planning Study Publication) irreg. Division of Vocation Education and Community Colleges, c/o State Dept. of Education, Montgomery, AL 36104. stat.

SHAKESPEARE RESEARCH AND OPPORTUNITIES; REPORT OF THE MODERN LANGUAGE ASSOCIATION OF AMERICA CONFERENCE. see *LITERATURE*

EDUCATION — HIGHER EDUCATION

378   II   ISSN 0080-9322
SHRI CHHATRAPATI SHIVAJI UNIVERSITY. REPORT. (Text in English) 1963/64. a. Shri Chhatrapati Shivaji University, Kolhapur, India. circ. 218.

378   US
SOCIETY OF PROFESSORS OF EDUCATION. OCCASIONAL PAPERS. 1974. irreg., no. 11, 1979. price varies. Society of Professors of Education, c/o George V. Guy, School of Education, Portland State Univeristy, Box 751, Portland, OR 97207.

378   SA   ISSN 0081-220X
SOUTH AFRICA. DEPARTMENT OF HIGHER EDUCATION. ANNUAL REPORT.* (Text in Africaans and English) 1910. a. Government Printer, Bosman St., Private Bag X85, Pretoria 0001, South Africa.

378   379   US   ISSN 0081-3087
SOUTHERN REGIONAL EDUCATION BOARD. STATE LEGISLATION AFFECTING HIGHER EDUCATION IN THE SOUTH. 1961. irreg. price varies. Southern Regional Education Board, 130 Sixth St., N.W., Atlanta, GA 30313.

378   US   ISSN 0077-9350
STATE UNIVERSITY OF NEW YORK AT ALBANY. FACULTY SENATE. ANNUAL FACULTY ASSEMBLY PROCEEDINGS.* 1966. a. free. State University of New York at Albany, Faculty Senate, 8 Thurlow Terrace, Albany, NY 12201.

378   US   ISSN 0081-4644
STATISTICAL ABSTRACT OF HIGHER EDUCATION IN NORTH CAROLINA. 1968. a. free. ‡ University of North Carolina at Chapel Hill, Box 2688, Chapel Hill, NC 27514.

378   US
STUDENT ENROLLMENT IN NEW ENGLAND INSTITUTIONS OF HIGHER EDUCATION. 1971. irreg., latest 1978; a. supplements. free. New England Board of Higher Education, 68 Walnut Rd., Wenham, MA 01984.

378.1   US   ISSN 0091-8938
STUDENT ENROLLMENT REPORT; WEST VIRGINIA INSTITUTIONS OF HIGHER EDUCATION. 1970. a. ‡ Board of Regents, 950 Kanawha Blvd. E., Charleston, WV 25301.

370   150   GW   ISSN 0081-7392
STUDIENHEFTE PSYCHOLOGIE IN ERZIEHUNG UND UNTERRICHT. 1964. irreg. price varies. Ernst Reinhardt, GmbH und Co., Verlag. Kemnatenstr. 46, 8000 Munich 19, W. Germany (B.R.D) Eds. H. Nickel, A.-M. Tausch. (reprint service avail. from ISI and UMI)
    Formerly: Studienhefte der Paedagogischen Hochschule.

STUDIENSTIFTUNG. JAHRESBERICHT. see *SOCIAL SERVICES AND WELFARE*

378   SZ
STUDIERENDEN AN DEN SCHWEIZERISCHEN HOCHSCHULEN/LES ETUDIANTS DANS LES HAUTES ECOLES SUISSES. (Text in French and German) 1970. a. 5 Fr. Statistisches Amt., Hallwylstrasse 15, CH-3003 Berne, Switzerland.

378   CN   ISSN 0081-7988
STUDIES IN HIGHER EDUCATION IN CANADA. 1960. irreg. price varies. (National Conference of Canadian Universities and Colleges Committee) University of Toronto Press, Front Campus, Toronto, Ont. M5S 1A6, Canada. (also avail. in microfiche)

360   US
SUMMARY INFORMATION ON MASTER OF SOCIAL WORK PROGRAMS. a. $3. Council on Social Work Education, 345 E. 46th St., New York, NY 10017.

378   UK   ISSN 0302-3494
SUMMARY OF POSTGRADUATE DIPLOMAS AND COURSES IN MEDICINE. 1975. a. £3.50 per issue. Council for Postgraduate Medical Education in England & Wales, 7 Marylebone Rd., London NW1 5HH, England.

378   296   US
SURVEY OF CURRENT JEWISH RESEARCH. 1974. a. $1. World Jewish Congress, American Section, One Park Ave., Suite 418, New York, NY 10016. Ed. Mark Friedman. circ. 1,000.

378   SW
SWEDEN. UNIVERSITETSKANSLERSAEMBETET. HOEGRE UTBILDNING OCH FORSKNING. (Subseries of its Skriftserie) 1967/68. a. free. Universitetskanslersaembetet - Office of the Chancellor of the Swedish Universities, Box 45501, S-104 30 Stockholm, Sweden. illus. stat.

378   CN   ISSN 0082-2205
TEACHER EDUCATION. 1968. a. Can.$4. ‡ University of Toronto, Faculty of Education, 371 Bloor St. W., Toronto M5S 2R7, Ont., Canada. (Co-sponsor: Ontario Teachers' Federation) Ed. Dr. J. M. Paton. circ. 4,500. Indexed: Psychol.Abstr. Can.Educ.Ind.

371.42   US   ISSN 0082-2353
TECHNICIAN EDUCATION YEARBOOK. 1963. biennial. price varies. Prakken Publications, Inc., 416 Longshore Dr., Box 8623, Ann Arbor, MI 48107. Ed. Lawrence W. Prakken. adv. circ. 3,000. (reprint service avail. from UMI)

378   GW
TECHNISCHE UNIVERSITAET BRAUNSCHWEIG. BERICHTSBAND. FORSCHUNG. every 5 years. Technische Universitaet Braunschweig, Pockelsstr. 14, Postfach 3329, 3300 Braunschweig, W. Germany (B.R.D.) Ed. Ernst Henze.

378   IS
TEL-AVIV UNIVERSITY. PH.D. DEGREES AND ABSTRACTS. (Text in English and Hebrew) 1972. irreg. Tel-Aviv University, Tel-Aviv, Israel.

378   US
TENNESSEE. HIGHER EDUCATION COMMISSION. BIENNIAL REPORT. 1970. biennial. free. Higher Education Commission, Union Bldg., Suite 300, Nashville, TN 37219. Ed. Joel D.Fryer. circ. 1,000.

378   AG   ISSN 0325-0245
TESIS PRESENTADAS A LA UNIVERSIDAD DE BUENOS AIRES. 1961. biennial. Arg.$10000($4) Universidad de Buenos Aires, Instituto Bibliotecologico, Casilla de Correo 901, 1000 Buenos Aires, Argentina. Dir. Hans Gravenhorst. (also avail. in microfiche)

378   US   ISSN 0082-2981
TEXAS. COORDINATING BOARD. TEXAS COLLEGE AND UNIVERSITY SYSTEM. C B ANNUAL REPORT. 1965. a. free; selective distribution. Texas College and University System, Coordinating Board, Capitol Sta., Austin, TX 78711. Ed. Debby Bay. circ. 2,000 (controlled)

378   US   ISSN 0082-299X
TEXAS. COORDINATING BOARD. TEXAS COLLEGE AND UNIVERSITY SYSTEM. C B POLICY PAPER. 1968. irreg., 1973, no. 9. free; selective distribution. Texas College and University System, Coordinating Board, Capitol Sta., Box 12788, Austin, TX 78711. Ed. Debby Bay. circ. 2,000 (controlled)

378   US   ISSN 0082-3007
TEXAS. COORDINATING BOARD. TEXAS COLLEGE AND UNIVERSITY SYSTEM. C B STUDY PAPER. 1968. irreg., no. 29, 1980. free; selective distribution. Texas College and University System, Coordinating Board, Capitol Sta., Box 12788, Austin, TX 78711. Ed. Debby Bay. circ. 2,000 (controlled)

600   US   ISSN 0082-3198
TEXAS TECH UNIVERSITY. GRADUATE STUDIES. 1972. irreg. price varies. Texas Tech University, Lubbock, TX 79409 (Orders to:, Gift and Exchange Dept., Texas Tech University Library) Ed. Dilford C. Carter.

378   JA   ISSN 0082-4844
TOKYO UNIVERSITY OF FOREIGN STUDIES. SUMMARY.* 1954/55. a. exchange basis. Tokyo University of Foreign Studies - Tokyo Gaikogu Daigaku, 4-51-21 Nishigahara, Kitaku, Tokyo, Japan.

378   AT   ISSN 0156-1006
U N E CONVOCATION BULLETIN & ALUMNI NEWS. 1957. a. to graduates only. University of New England, Armidale, N.S.W. 2351, Australia. Ed. A. J. Barker. bk. rev. circ. 13,000.
    Former titles: U N E Bulletin; University of New England. Bulletin (ISSN 0084-6740)

378   IO
UDAYANA STATE UNIVERSITY BULLETIN. irreg. Udayana State University, Box 105, Jalan Jendral Sudirman, Denpasar, Indonesia.

UNICORN. see *EDUCATION*

378   GW
UNISPIEGEL. 1969. irreg. (approx. 8-10/yr.) free. Universitaet Heidelberg, Grabengasse 1, Postfach 105760, 6900 Heidelberg, W. Germany (B.R.D.) Ed. Roland J. Felleisen. adv. bk. rev. circ. 10,000.
    Formerly: Unispiegel Aktuell.

378   US   ISSN 0565-744X
U.S. NATIONAL CENTER FOR EDUCATION STATISTICS. EARNED DEGREES CONFERRED. 1948. a. U.S. National Center for Education Statistics, 400 Maryland Ave., S.W., Washington, DC 20202 (Subscr. to Supt. of Docs., Govt. Printing Off. Washington, DC 20402) Indexed: Educ.Ind. R.G.

378   US
U.S. NATIONAL CENTER FOR EDUCATION STATISTICS. FALL ENROLLMENT IN HIGHER EDUCATION. 1958. a. price varies. U.S. National Center for Education Statistics, U.S. Department of Education, 400 Maryland Ave., S.W., Washington, DC 20202 (Orders to: Supt. of Documents, Washington, DC 20402)
    Formerly: Opening Fall Enrollment in Higher Education (ISSN 0083-2758)

378   US
U.S. NATIONAL CENTER FOR EDUCATION STATISTICS. FINANCIAL STATISTICS OF INSTITUTIONS OF HIGHER EDUCATION. a. $1.55. U.S. National Center for Education Statistics, 400 Maryland Ave., S.W., Washington, DC 20202 (Orders to: Supt. of Documents, Washington DC 20402)

378   US
U.S. NATIONAL CENTER FOR EDUCATION STATISTICS. LIBRARY STATISTICS OF COLLEGES AND UNIVERSITIES. irreg. U.S. National Center for Education Statistics, U.S. Department of Education, 400 Maryland Ave., S.W., Washington, DC 20202 (Orders to: Supt. of Documents, Washington, DC 20402)

507   US   ISSN 0094-7881
U.S. NATIONAL SCIENCE FOUNDATION. GRADUATE SCIENCE EDUCATION STUDENT SUPPORT AND POSTDOCTORALS. (Subseries of NSF's Surveys of Science Resources Series) a. U. S. National Science Foundation, 1800 G St. N.W., Washington, DC 20550 (Orders to: Supt. of Documents, Washington, DC 20402) Key Title: Graduate Science Education Student Support and Postdoctorals.

378   DR
UNIVERSIDAD AUTONOME DE SANTO DOMINGO. COMISION PARA EL DESARROLLO Y REFORMA UNIVERSITARIOS.* irreg. Universidad Autonoma de Santo Domingo, Comision para el Desarrollo y Reforma Universitarios, Ciudad Universitaria, Apdo. 1355, Santo Domingo, Dominican Republic.

378   BO
UNIVERSIDAD BOLIVIANA GABRIEL RENE MORENO. REVISTA. vol. 18, 1974. irreg. Universidad Boliviana Gabriel Rene Moreno, Santa Cruz de la Sierra, Bolivia. illus.
    Formerly: Universidad Mayor Gabriel Rene Moreno. Revista.

378   BO
UNIVERSIDAD BOLIVIANA JUAN MISAEL SARACHO. INFORME DE LABORES. irreg. Universidad Boliviana Juan Misael Saracho, Av. Las Americas, Casilla 51, Tarija, Bolivia. charts. illus. stat.

EDUCATION — HIGHER EDUCATION

378   VE   ISSN 0083-5439
UNIVERSIDAD CENTRAL DE VENEZUELA. CONSEJO DE DESARROLLO CIENTIFICO Y HUMANISTICO. CATALOGO DE LA U. C. V.* (Title varies slightly: Catalogo de la Investigacion Universitaria) 1960-63. triennial. Universidad Central de Venezuela, Consejo de Desarrollo Cientifico y Humanistico, Ciudad Universitaria, Caracas, Venezuela.

378   CK
UNIVERSIDAD DE MEDELLIN. REVISTA. 1975. irreg. Universidad de Medellin, Apdo. Aereo 1983, Medellin, Colombia. illus.

378   PE
UNIVERSIDAD DEL PACIFICO. CENTRO DE INVESTIGACION. SERIE: MONOGRAFIAS. no. 2, 1975. irreg. Universidad del Pacifico, Centro de Investigacion, Lima, Peru.

378   PE
UNIVERSIDAD DEL PACIFICO. CENTRO DE INVESTIGACION. SERIE: TRABAJOS DE INVESTIGACION. no. 4, 1975. irreg. Universidad del Pacifico, Centro de Investigacion, Lima, Peru.

UNIVERSIDAD DEL ZULIA. REVISTA. see *LITERATURE*

378.46   SP   ISSN 0080-6145
UNIVERSIDAD INTERNACIONAL MENENDEZ PELAYO. PUBLICACIONES. 1947. biennial, no. 43, 1974. Universidad Internacional Menendez Pelayo, Palacio de la Magdalena, Santander, Spain. circ. 1,000.

505   PE
UNIVERSIDAD NACIONAL DEL CENTRO DEL PERU. ANALES CIENTIFICOS. 1971. a. price varies. Universidad Nacional del Centro del Peru, Departamento de Publicaciones e Impresiones, c/o Secretaria de Publicaciones, Calle Real 160, Huancayo, Peru. illus. circ. 1,000.

378 060   VE   ISSN 0076-4337
UNIVERSIDAD NACIONAL DEL ZULIA. FACULTAD DE HUMANIDADES Y EDUCACION. ARTES Y LETRAS.* 1966. irreg. price varies. Universidad del Zulia, Facultad de Humanidades y Educacion, Apartado de Correos 415, Maracaibo, Venezuela.

378 060   VE   ISSN 0076-4353
UNIVERSIDAD NACIONAL DEL ZULIA. FACULTAD DE HUMANIDADES Y EDUCACION. FUERA DE SERIE.* 1962. irreg. price varies. Universidad del Zulia, Facultad de Humanidades y Educacion, Apartado de Correos 415, Maracaibo, Venezuela.

378 060   VE   ISSN 0076-4361
UNIVERSIDAD NACIONAL DEL ZULIA. FACULTAD DE HUMANIDADES Y EDUCACION. MANUALES DE LA ESCUELA DE EDUCACION.* 1965. irreg. Bs.7.($1.60) Universidad del Zulia, Facultad de Humanidades y Educacion, Apartado de Correos 415, Maracaibo, Venezuela.

378 060   VE   ISSN 0076-437X
UNIVERSIDAD NACIONAL DEL ZULIA. FACULTAD DE HUMANIDADES Y EDUCACION. MONOGRAFIAS Y ENSAYOS.* 1963. irreg. price varies. Universidad del Zulia, Facultad de Humanidades y Educacion, Apartado de Correos 415, Maracaibo, Venezuela.

UNIVERSIDAD TECNOLOGICA DEL CHOCO. REVISTA. see *TECHNOLOGY: COMPREHENSIVE WORKS*

378   BL
UNIVERSIDADE ESTADUAL PAULISTA. DEPARTAMENTO DE EDUCACAO. BOLETIM. irreg. $20 per no. Universidade Estadual Paulista, Departamento de Educacao, Rua Roberto Simonsen 305, C.P. 957, Presidente Prudente, Brazil. illus.

378   BL
UNIVERSIDADE FEDERAL DE PERNAMBUCO. JORNAL. 1967. irreg. Universidade Federal de Pernambuco, Recife, Pernambaco, Brazil. (microfilm)

378   BL
UNIVERSIDADE FEDERAL DE PERNAMBUCO. RELATORIO DES ATTIVIDADES UNIVERSITARIAS. a. Universidade Federal de Pernambuco, Biblioteca Central, Cidade Universitaria, Recife, Pernambuco, Brazil. (also avail. in microfilm)

378   BL
UNIVERSIDADE FEDERAL DO PARA. RELATORIO ANUAL. a. Universidade Federal do Para, Belem, Para, Brazil.

378   IT
UNIVERSITA DEGLI STUDI DI MILANO. ANNUARIO. 1924. a. ‡ Universita degli Studi di Milano, Via Festa del Perdono 7, 20122 Milan, Italy. circ. 1,000.

378   IT   ISSN 0078-7752
UNIVERSITA DEGLI STUDI DI PADOVA. ISTITUTO PER LA STORIA. CONTRIBUTI. 1964. irreg:; no. 8, 1976. price varies. Editrice Antenore, Via G. Rusca 15, 35100 Padua, Italy.

378   IT   ISSN 0078-7760
UNIVERSITA DEGLI STUDI DI PADOVA. ISTITUTO PER LA STORIA. QUADERNI. 1968. irreg.; no. 8, 1975. price varies. Editrice Antenore, Via G. Rusca 15, 35100 Padua, Italy.

378   GW   ISSN 0070-7457
UNIVERSITAET DUESSELDORF. JAHRBUCH. 1969. a. DM.34. Triltsch Druck und Verlag GmbH und Co. KG, Herzstr. 53, 4000 Duesseldorf, W. Germany (B.R.D.) Ed. Hans Schadewaldt. adv.

378   GW   ISSN 0436-1202
UNIVERSITAET GOETTINGEN. JAHRESBERICHT. 1966/67. irreg. Universitaet Goettingen, Wilhelmsplatz 1, 3400 Goettingen, W. Germany (B.R.D.) stat.

378   GW   ISSN 0069-5890
UNIVERSITAET ZU KOELN. JAHRBUCH. 1966. a. DM.8. (Freunde und Foerderer der Universitaet zu Koeln) Drei Kronen Druck, Reifferscheidt GmbH und Co. KG, Rondorfer Str. 224, 5030 Huerth, W. Germany (B.R.D.) Ed. Wolfgang Mathias. adv. circ. 8,000.

054   CF   ISSN 0302-4814
UNIVERSITE DE BRAZZAVILLE. ANNALES. (Text in French; summaries in English) a. Universite de Brazzaville, B. P. 69, Brazzaville, Congo. illus.

378.494   SZ
UNIVERSITE DE NEUCHATEL. ANNALES. 1969/70. a. 15 Fr. Universite de Neuchatel, Av. du Premier Mars 26, 2000 Neuchatel, Switzerland. illus.

378.714   CN
UNIVERSITE DU QUEBEC (PROVINCE). RAPPORT ANNUEL. 1970. a. free. Universite du Quebec, 2875 Bd. Laurier, Ste. Foy, Que G1V 2M3, Canada. circ. 5,500.

378   US
UNIVERSITY IN CRISIS. irreg. University Centers for Rational Alternatives, 110 W. 40th St., New York, NY 10018.

378.794   US   ISSN 0092-0290
UNIVERSITY OF CALIFORNIA, BERKELEY. OFFICE OF INSTITUTIONAL RESEARCH. CAMPUS STATISTICS. 1966/67. irreg., latest 1976. free. University of California, Berkeley, Office of Institutional Research, Berkeley, CA 94720. circ. 200. Indexed: ERIC.

378   US   ISSN 0362-4706
UNIVERSITY OF CHICAGO RECORD. 1967. irreg., 6-9/yr. free. University of Chicago, Vice-President for Public Affairs, 5801 South Ellis Avenue, Chicago, IL 60637. Ed. Jack Wolowiec. charts. circ. 18,000.

378   US   ISSN 0071-6170
UNIVERSITY OF FLORIDA. UNIVERSITY COLLEGE SERIES.* 1967. irreg. University of Florida, University College, Gainesville, FL 32601.

378.669   NR
UNIVERSITY OF IBADAN. STUDENT AFFAIRS OFFICE. STUDENT HANDBOOK OF INFORMATION ON UNIVERSITY POLICIES AND PRACTICES. irreg. University of Ibadan, Student Affairs Office, Ibadan, Nigeria. illus.

378.549   II
UNIVERSITY OF KASHMIR. ANNUAL REPORT. (Text in English) a. University of Kashmir, Hazratbal, Srinagar 190006, India.

378.769   US   ISSN 0566-8719
UNIVERSITY OF KENTUCKY RESEARCH FOUNDATION. ANNUAL REPORT. Cover title: U K R F Annual Report. a. University of Kentucky, Research Foundation, Lexington, KY 40506. Ed. Susan H. Donohew. illus. stat. circ. 2,500. Key Title: Annual Report of the University of Kentucky Research Foundation.

378   KE
UNIVERSITY OF KENYA. BUREAU OF EDUCATIONAL RESEARCH. RESEARCH PROJECTS. 1973. a. University of Nairobi, Bureau of Educational Research, Box 30197, Nairobi, Kenya. stat.

378   II   ISSN 0076-2210
UNIVERSITY OF MADRAS. ENDOWMENT LECTURES.* a. University of Madras, Chepauk, Triplicane, Madras 600005, Tamil Nadu, India.

378.1   MW
UNIVERSITY OF MALAWI. CENTRE FOR EXTENSION STUDIES. ANNUAL REPORT. a. University of Malawi, Centre for Extension Studies, Box 86, Zomba, Malawi.

658.15   MM
UNIVERSITY OF MALTA. ANNUAL REPORT. a. University of Malta, Msida, Malta.

378   MF
UNIVERSITY OF MAURITIUS. ANNUAL REPORT. 1968/1969. a. University of Mauritius, Reduit, Mauritius. stat. circ. 450. (back issues avail.)

013.379   AT   ISSN 0548-6831
UNIVERSITY OF NEW SOUTH WALES, KENSINGTON. RESEARCH AND PUBLICATIONS. (Title Varies Slightly) a. University of New South Wales, Kensington, New South Wales, Australia.

378.669   NR
UNIVERSITY OF NIGERIA. ANNUAL REPORT. a. University of Nigeria, Nsukka, Nigeria.

378   IO
UNIVERSITY OF NORTH SUMATRA. BULLETIN/MAJALAH UNIVERSITAS SUMATERA UTARA. (Text in Indonesian) 1975. irreg.? University of North Sumatra, Jl. Universitas No. 9, Biro Rektor, Kampus, Medan, Indonesia.

378   AT
UNIVERSITY OF QUEENSLAND. COMBINED FACULTY DIRECTORY. irreg. University of Queensland, Brisbane, Qld., Australia.

378   AT
UNIVERSITY OF QUEENSLAND. HIGHER DEGREE HANDBOOK. irreg. Aus.$4.50. University of Queensland, Registrar, Brisbane, Qld., Australia (Subscr. address: University Bookstore, Circular Drive. University of Queensland, St. Lucia, Qld., 4067, Australia) circ. 1,400.
    Formerly: University of Queensland. Combined Higher Degree Handbook.

378   AT   ISSN 0079-9033
UNIVERSITY OF QUEENSLAND INAUGURAL LECTURES. 1965. irreg. price varies. ‡ University of Queensland Press, P.O. Box 42, St. Lucia, Queensland 4067, Australia.

378   UK
UNIVERSITY OF SUSSEX. CENTRE FOR CONTINUING EDUCATION. OCCASIONAL PAPER. irreg; no. 9, 1978. price varies. University of Sussex, Centre for Continuing Education, Falmer, Brighton, Sussex BN1 9RG, England.

016 378　　　　SA　ISSN 0067-9216
UNIVERSITY OF THE ORANGE FREE STATE. OPSOMMINGS VAN PROEFSKRIFTE EN VERHANDELINGE. ABSTRACTS OF DISSERTATIONS AND THESES. (Text in Afrikaans and English) a. University of the Orange Free State, P.O. Box 339, Bloemfontein, South Africa.

378　　　　US　ISSN 0083-4920
UNIVERSITY OF UTAH. OFFICE OF INSTITUTIONAL STUDIES. STATISTICAL SUMMARIES.* 1965. a. $2.50. University of Utah, Office of Institutional Studies, Salt Lake City, UT 84112. Ed. Harry P. Bluhm. cum.index.

378　　　　ZA
UNIVERSITY OF ZAMBIA. SCHOOL OF HUMANITIES AND SOCIAL SCIENCES. ANNUAL REPORT. a. School of Humanities and Social Sciences, School of Humanities and Social Science. Box 2379, Lusaka, Zambia.

378　　　　PL　ISSN 0083-7342
UNIWERSYTET WARSZAWSKI. ROCZNIKI/ANNALES UNIVERSITATIS VARSOVIENSIS. 1958. a. price varies. Uniwersytet Warszawski, Krakowskie Przedmiescie 26/28, Warsaw, Poland. Ed. Ludwik Bazylow. circ. 500.

378　　　　GW　ISSN 0083-565X
VEREINIGUNG FREUNDE DER UNIVERSITAET MAINZ. JAHRBUCH. 1952. biennial. price varies. Vereinigung Freunde der Universitaet Mainz, Ludwigstr. 8-10, 6500 Mainz, W. Germany (B.R.D.)

378　　　　NZ
VICTORIA UNIVERSITY OF WELLINGTON. VICE-CHANCELLOR'S REPORT. 1974. a. Victoria University of Wellington, Wellington, New Zealand.

378.776　　　　US　ISSN 0095-5744
VIKING. Cover title: Viking Retrospect. 1904. a. $5. St. Olaf College, Northfield, MN 55057. Ed. Kathleen L. Hahn. adv. illus. circ. 2,850. Key Title: Viking (Northfield)

371.42　　　　US　ISSN 0083-6575
VIRGINIA'S SUPPLY OF PUBLIC SCHOOL INSTRUCTIONAL PERSONNEL. 1968. a. free. Department of Education, Division of Teacher Education, 9Th St. Office Building, Richmond, VA 32316. circ. 5,000.

378.754　　　　US　ISSN 0091-6196
WEST VIRGINIA'S STATE SYSTEM OF HIGHER EDUCATION; ANNUAL REPORT, CURRENT OPERATING REVENUES AND EXPENDITURES. 1971. a. controlled free circ. Board of Regents, 950 Kanawha Blvd. E., Charleston, WV 25301.

378　　　　US　ISSN 0511-6848
WESTERN ASSOCIATION OF GRADUATE SCHOOLS. PROCEEDINGS OF THE ANNUAL MEETING. 19th, 1977, Albuquerque. a. $3. Western Association of Graduate Schools, c/o Lawrence H. Rice, Ed., Idaho State Univ., Pocatello, ID 83209. circ. 500.

607　　　　AT
WESTERN AUSTRALIA. TECHNICAL EDUCATION DIVISION. HANDBOOK. 1948. a. ‡ Education Department, Technical Education Division, 36 Parliament Place, West Perth W.A. 6005, Australia. circ. 1,500.

378　　　　US　ISSN 0083-9248
WHIDDEN LECTURES. 1956. a. (McMaster University, CN) Oxford University Press, 200 Madison Ave., New York, NY 10016 (And Ely House, 37 Dover St., London W1X 4AH England)

WHO'S WHO AMONG STUDENTS IN AMERICAN JUNIOR COLLEGES. see *BIOGRAPHY*

WHO'S WHO AMONG STUDENTS IN AMERICAN UNIVERSITIES AND COLLEGES. see *BIOGRAPHY*

378.3　　　　US　ISSN 0084-1137
WOODROW WILSON NATIONAL FELLOWSHIP FOUNDATION. NEWSLETTER. 1963. irreg.(approx. 3 times a year) free. Woodrow Wilson National Fellowship Foundation, 32 Nassau Street, Princeton, NJ 08540. Ed. Judith L. Pinch.

378.3　　　　US　ISSN 0084-1145
WOODROW WILSON NATIONAL FELLOWSHIP FOUNDATION. REPORT. 1958. irreg. free. Woodrow Wilson National Fellowship Foundation, 16 John St., Box 642, Princeton, NJ 08540.

378　　　　US　ISSN 0084-344X
YALE SCENE; UNIVERSITY SERIES. 1967. irreg., no. 3, 1974. price varies. Yale University Press, 92A Yale Sta., New Haven, CT 06520.

370　　　　US　ISSN 0084-3784
YEARBOOK OF HIGHER EDUCATION. 1969. a. $44.50. Marquis Academic Media, 200 E. Ohio St., Chicago, IL 60611. index.

EDUCATION — International Education Programs

370.19　　　　US　ISSN 0098-6356
ACADEMIC YEAR ABROAD IN EUROPE-AFRICA-AUSTRALIA. a. Center for Foreign Study, 216 S. State St., Ann Arbor, MI 48107. illus.

370.196　　　　US
AMERICAN FULBRIGHT SCHOLARS; university lecturing, advanced research abroad. a. free. Council for International Exchange of Scholars, 11 Dupont Circle, N.W., Washington, DC 20036. circ. 100,000.

370.196　　　　CY
CYPRIOT STUDENTS ABROAD. (Text in English and Greek) 1967. a. Mils.250. Department of Statistics and Research, Ministry of Finance, Nicosia, Cyprus.

378.35　　　　PK　ISSN 0070-606X
DIRECTORY OF PAKISTANI SCHOLARS ABROAD. (Text in English) 1965. a. Ministry of Education, Documentation Section, Curriculum Wing, Sector H-9, P.O. Shaigan, Industrial Area, Islamabad, Pakistan.

378.35　　　　US　ISSN 0098-1508
DIRECTORY OF VISITING FULBRIGHT SCHOLARS IN THE UNITED STATES. a. free. Council for International Exchange of Scholars, 11 Dupont Circle, Suite 300, Washington, DC 20036. (Affiliate: American Council on Education)
Former titles: Directory of Visiting Lecturers and Research Scholars in the United States Under the Mutual Educational Exchange Program (the Fulbright-Hays Act); Formerly: Directory of Visiting Scholars in the United States Awarded Grants Under the Mutual Educational and Cultural Exchange Act (the Fulbright-Hays Act) (ISSN 0070-6582)

370.196　　　　BE
E F I L DOCUMENTATION. irreg., no. 3, 1979. European Federation for Intercultural Learning, Bosmanslei 12, B-2000 Antwerp, Belgium.

370.196　　　　UK
EDUCATIONAL INTERNATIONAL. 1969. a. £2.50. ‡ Central Bureau for Educational Visits and Exchanges, 43 Dorset St., London W1H 3FN, England. Ed. James Platt. circ. 2,000.
Formed by the merger of: Education Exchange (ISSN 0046-1490) & Higher Education Exchange (ISSN 0305-3253)

371.39　　　　US
EXPERIMENT IN INTERNATIONAL LIVING. ANNUAL REPORT. 1960. a. free. ‡ Experiment in International Living, U S Office, Brattleboro, VT 05301. Ed. David J. Corey. circ. 2,000.
Formerly: Experiment in International Living. President's Report (ISSN 0071-3376)

370.196　　　　US
FULBRIGHT AWARDS ABROAD; lecturing and research. a. free. Council for International Exchange of Scholars, 11 Dupont Circle, N.W., Washington, DC 20036. circ. 100,000.

370　　　　UN　ISSN 0071-9862
FUNDAMENTALS OF EDUCATIONAL PLANNING. (English and French editions) 1966. irreg., no. 28, 1979. price varies. ‡ International Institute for Educational Planning, 7-9 rue Eugene Delacroix, 75016 Paris, France (Dist. in U.S. by: Unipub, 345 Park Ave. S., New York, NY 10010)

370　　　　UN　ISSN 0071-9870
FUNDAMENTALS OF EDUCATIONAL PLANNING. LECTURE-DISCUSSION SERIES. (Some titles in English; others in French) 1966. irreg., no. 63, 1979. price varies. ‡ International Institute for Educational Planning, 7-9 rue Eugene Delacroix, 75016 Paris, France.

378.3　　　　US　ISSN 0072-5471
GRANTS REGISTER. 1969. biennial. $32.50. St. Martins Press, 175 Fifth Avenue, New York, NY 10010 (And St. James Press, 3 Percy St., London W1P 9FA, England) Ed. Craig Alan Lerner.

378.3　　　　US　ISSN 0440-1948
HANDBOOK ON INTERNATIONAL STUDY FOR U.S. NATIONALS. VOL. 2: STUDY IN THE AMERICAN REPUBLICS AREA. 1977. irreg. $6.95 paper; $12 clothbound. Institute of International Education, 809 United Nations Plaza, New York, NY 10017.

940　　　　US　ISSN 0073-926X
INSTITUTE OF EUROPEAN STUDIES. ANNOUNCEMENTS. (Text in English; some parts in French, German and Spanish) 1962. a (biennial from 1965-69) free. Institute of European Studies, 710 N. Rush St., Chicago, IL 60611. Ed. Edward Hearne. index.

370.196　　　　US　ISSN 0073-9278
INSTITUTE OF EUROPEAN STUDIES. PAPERS AND ADDRESSES OF THE ANNUAL CONFERENCE AND ACADEMIC COUNCIL. 1966. irreg.(usually 1 per year) free. Institute of European Studies, 710 North Rush Street, Chicago, IL 60611. Ed. Thomas Roberts.

370.196　　　　AT　ISSN 0310-5571
INTERNATIONAL ASSOCIATION FOR THE EVALUATION OF EDUCATIONAL ACHIEVEMENT (AUSTRALIA). NEWSLETTER. 1971. irreg. free. Australian Council for Educational Research, P.O. Box 210, Hawthorn, Vic. 3122, Australia. Ed. Malcolm J. Rosier.

378.3　　　　GR　ISSN 0538-4427
INTERNATIONAL ASSOCIATION FOR THE EXCHANGE OF STUDENTS FOR TECHNICAL EXPERIENCE. ANNUAL REPORT. Short title: I A E S T E Annual Report. 1948. a. International Association for the Exchange of Students for Technical Experience, c/o National Technical University, 42 Patission Str., Athens, Greece. circ. 6,000.

370.196　　　　US
INTERNATIONAL FOUNDATION DIRECTORY. 1974. irreg., vol. 2, 1979. $65. Gale Research Company, Book Tower, Detroit, MI 48226. Ed. H. V. Hodson.

378　　　　UK
INTERNATIONAL HIGHER EDUCATION. (Text in English; summaries in French and German) 1978. a. £1($3) (Standing Conference on International Higher Education) North East London Polytechnic, Longbridge Rd., Dagenham, Essex, England. Ed. A. P. Hamilton. bk. rev. circ. 1,000. (back issues avail.)

370　　　　UN　ISSN 0074-6401
INTERNATIONAL INSTITUTE FOR EDUCATIONAL PLANNING. OCCASIONAL PAPERS. (Some titles in English; others in French) 1968. irreg., no. 39, 1979. price varies. ‡ International Institute for Educational Planning, 7-9 rue Eugene Delacroix, 75016 Paris, France.

371.39 378.35　　　　US
LEARNING TRAVELER. U.S. COLLEGE-SPONSORED PROGRAMS ABROAD: ACADEMIC YEAR. 1964. a. $8. ‡ Institute of International Education, 809 United Nations Plaza, New York, NY 10017. Ed. Gail A. Cohen. index.
Former titles: U S College-Sponsored Programs Abroad. Academic Year (ISSN 0082-8602); United States Academic Programs Abroad.

371.39　　　　US
LEARNING TRAVELER. VACATION STUDY ABROAD. 1947. a. $8. ‡ Institute of International Education, 809 United Nations Plaza, New York, NY 10017. Ed. Gail A. Cohen.
Formerly: Summer Study Abroad (ISSN 0081-9379)
University-level

371.3 US ISSN 0077-3190
N A F S A DIRECTORY. 1950. biennial. $10.
National Association for Foreign Student Affairs,
1860 19 St. N.W., Washington, DC 20009. Ed.
Georgia E. Stewart. index. circ. 4,500.

370.196 AU
OESTERREICHISCHER
AUSLANDSSTUDENTENDIENST.
RECHENSCHAFTSBERICHT. 1961. a. free. ‡
Oesterreichischer Auslandsstudentendienst, Dr.-Karl-Lueger-Ring 1, A-1010 Vienna, Austria. illus. stat. circ. 350.

378.3 US ISSN 0078-5172
OPEN DOORS; report on international exchange. 1955. a. $20. ‡ Institute of International Education, 809 United Nations Plaza, New York, NY 10017. Ed. Douglas Boyan.

371.39 US ISSN 0080-6900
SCHOOLS ABROAD. Variant title: Schools Abroad of Interest to Americans. 1959. irreg., 4th edt., 1979. $15. Porter Sargent Publishers, Inc., 11 Beacon St., Boston, MA 02108. index.

378.391 UN ISSN 0081-895X
STUDY ABROAD/ETUDES A L'ETRANGER/ ESTUDIOS EN EL EXTRANJERO; international scholarships and courses. (Text in English, French and Spanish) 1949. biennial; fol. 22, 1979. Unesco, 7-9 Place de Fontenoy, 75700 Paris, France (Dist. in U.S. by: Unipub, 345 Park Ave. S., New York NY 10010)

370.19 US
STUDY IN DENMARK. (Text in English) 1969. a. free. Danish Consulate General, Danish Information Office, 280 Park Ave., New York, NY 10017. circ. 6,000.
Formerly: Study in Denmark: Courses for Foreigners.

370.196 US
TEACHING ABROAD. 1973. irreg. $6. Institute of International Education, 809 United Nations Plaza, New York, NY 10017. Ed. Gail A. Cohen.

UNESCO. RECORDS OF THE GENERAL CONFERENCE. RESOLUTIONS. see POLITICAL SCIENCE — International Relations

UNESCO. REPORT OF THE DIRECTOR-GENERAL ON THE ACTIVITIES OF THE ORGANIZATION. see POLITICAL SCIENCE — International Relations

378.391 UN ISSN 0082-7487
UNESCO HANDBOOK OF INTERNATIONAL EXCHANGES. (Text in English, French, Russian and Spanish) 1965. biennial, 1967, 2nd ed. Unesco, 7-9 Place de Fontenoy, 75700 Paris, France (Dist. in U.S. by: Unipub, 345 Park Ave. S., New York NY 10010)
Supersedes: Directory of Cultural Relations Services and the Index of Cultural Agreements.

371.142 US
U.S. OFFICE OF EDUCATION. OPPORTUNITIES FOR TEACHERS ABROAD. a. price varies; .55 for 1977-78 edition. U. S. Office of Education, Dept. of Health, Education, and Welfare, Washington, DC 20202 (Orders to: Supt. of Documents, Washington, Dc 20402)
Formerly: Opportunities Abroad for Teachers (ISSN 0078-5458)

371.391 US ISSN 0070-1165
WHOLE WORLD HANDBOOK: A STUDENT GUIDE TO WORK, STUDY AND TRAVEL ABROAD. 1972. a. $3.95. ‡ (Council on International Educational Exchange) Frommer-Pasmantier Publishing Corp., 205 E. 42nd St., New York, NY 10017. Ed. Margaret E. Sherman. circ. 25,000.
Formerly: Council on International Educational Exchange. Summer Study, Travel and Work Programs.

060 US ISSN 0092-4261
WOODROW WILSON INTERNATIONAL CENTER FOR SCHOLARS. ANNUAL REPORT. 1970. a. free. ‡ Woodrow Wilson International Center for Scholars, Smithsonian Institution Building, Washington, DC 20560. Ed. William Dunn. illus. circ. 2,000. Key Title: Annual Report - Woodrow Wilson International Center for Scholars.

378.3 US ISSN 0084-2419
WORLD UNIVERSITY SERVICE. ANNUAL REPORT.* (Text in English) 1921. a. 1 Fr. World University Service, 20 West 40th St., New York, NY 10018. Ed. Roger Eggleston. index.

378.3 US ISSN 0084-2427
WORLD UNIVERSITY SERVICE. PROGRAMME OF ACTION.* (Text in English; occasionally issues in French and Spanish) 1950. biennial. 2 Fr. World University Service, 20 West 40th St., New York, NY 10018. Ed. Roger Eggleston.

370.196 UK
YOUTH INTERNATIONAL. 1976. a. £2.50. Central Bureau for Educational Visits and Exchanges, 43 Dorset St., London W1H 3FN, England. Ed. James Platt. circ. 2,000.
Formerly: Intercommunity - International Community Education (ISSN 0308-9231)

EDUCATION — School Organization And Administration

379.15 CN ISSN 0703-766X
A G M REPORTER. 1976. a. free. British Columbia School Trustees Association, 1155 West 8th Ave, Vancouver, B.C. V6H 1C5, Canada.
Formerly: B C S T A Convention Reporter (ISSN 0319-0684)

371 US ISSN 0066-9156
A S C U S ANNUAL-TEACHING OPPORTUNITIES FOR YOU. 1966. a. $6 to non-members. Association for School, College and University Staffing, Box 4411, Madison, WI 53711. circ. 100,000.

371 US ISSN 0066-9164
A S C U S DIRECTORY OF MEMBERSHIP AND SUBJECT FIELD INDEX. a. $10 to non-members. Association for School, College and University Staffing, Box 2151, Madison, WI 53701.

371.2 US
ACADEMIC COLLECTIVE BARGAINING INFORMATION SERVICE. MONOGRAPHS. irreg., latest no.7. Academic Collective Bargaining Information Service, Gateway 1 Bldg., Box 17230, Dulles International Airport, Washington, DC 20041.

371.2 US
ACADEMIC COLLECTIVE BARGAINING INFORMATION SERVICE. RESEARCH SUMMARY. 1975. irreg., latest no. 6. Academic Collective Bargaining Information Service, Gateway 1 Bldg., Box 17230, Dulles International Airport, Washington, DC 20041.

371.2 US
ACADEMIC COLLECTIVE BARGAINING INFORMATION SERVICE. SPECIAL REPORTS. irreg., latest no.35. Academic Collective Bargaining Information Service, Gateway 1 Bldg., Box 17230, Dulles International Airport, Washington, DC 20041.

378.3 US ISSN 0094-2227
AMERICAN COLLEGE TESTING PROGRAM. HANDBOOK FOR FINANCIAL AID ADMINISTRATORS. Spine title: A C T Handbook for Financial Aid Administrators. a. free. American College Testing Program, Box 168, Iowa City, IA 52243. stat.

371 379 US ISSN 0077-9342
ANALYSIS OF SCHOOL FINANCES, NEW YORK STATE SCHOOL DISTRICTS. a. free. Education Department, Bureau of Educational Finance Research, University of the State of New York, Albany, NY 12230. (Co-sponsor: University of the State of New York)

371 379 US ISSN 0066-4049
ANNUAL REGISTER OF GRANT SUPPORT. 1967. a. $57.50. Marquis Academic Media (Subsidiary of: Marquis Who's Who, Inc.) 200 E. Ohio St., Chicago, IL 60611. index.
Formerly: Grant Data Quarterly.

371 379 US ISSN 0066-8753
ASSOCIATED PUBLIC SCHOOLS SYSTEMS. YEARBOOK. 1951. a. $5. ‡ (Associated Public School Systems) Columbia University, Teachers College, 525 W. 120 St., New York, NY 10027. circ. 1,000.

ASSOCIATION FOR EDUCATIONAL DATA SYSTEMS. ANNUAL CONVENTION PROCEEDINGS. see COMPUTER TECHNOLOGY AND APPLICATIONS

ASSOCIATION FOR EDUCATIONAL DATA SYSTEMS. HANDBOOK AND DIRECTORY. see COMPUTER TECHNOLOGY AND APPLICATIONS

371.8 GW ISSN 0076-1745
ASTA-PRESS. 1971. irreg. Technische Universitaet Muenchen, Studentenvertretung, Arcisstr. 21, 8000 Munich 2, W. Germany (B.R.D.) adv. circ. 10,000.
Formerly: M S Z: Muenchener Studentenzeitung.

371 US
BEST OF E R I C (EDUCATIONAL MANAGEMENT) 1974. 6-9/yr. free. E R I C Clearinghouse on Educational Management, University of Oregon, Eugene, OR 97403. Ed. Stuart C. Smith. circ. 21,000. (tabloid format; also avail. in microfiche from EDR)

371 AG ISSN 0067-7922
BIBLIOTHECA DEL PLANEAMIENTO EDUCATIVO.* 1961. irreg. Ministerio de Cultura y Educacion, Departamento de Documentacion Informacion Educativa, Parera 55, Buenos Aires, Argentina.

370 GW ISSN 0006-9582
BREMER SCHULBLATT. 1954. irreg. price varies. Senator fuer Bildung, Rembertiring 8-12, 2800 Bremen, W. Germany (B.R.D.) abstr. cum-index. circ. 1,700. (looseleaf format)

371.2 CN ISSN 0381-5978
BRITISH COLUMBIA SCHOOL TRUSTEES ASSOCIATION. NEWSLETTER. 1967. irreg. British Columbia School Trustees Association, 1155 West 8th Ave., Vancouver 6,B.C., Canada.

353.9 US ISSN 0090-5593
CALIFORNIA. TEACHERS RETIREMENT BOARD. STATE TEACHER'S RETIREMENT SYSTEM; ANNUAL REPORT TO THE GOVERNOR AND THE LEGISLATURE. (Report Year Ends June 30.) 1963. a. $5. Teachers Retirement Board, Box 15275-C, Rm. 616, Sacramento, CA 95813. Ed. Michael N. Thome. circ. 1,500. Key Title: Annual Report to the Governor and Legislature - Teacher's Retirement Board.

CENTRO REGIONAL DE CONSTRUCCIONES ESCOLARES PARA AMERICA LATINA Y LA REGION DEL CARIBE. DOCUMENTOS TECNICOS. see EDUCATION — School Organization And Administration

371 MX
CENTRO REGIONAL DE CONSTRUCCIONES ESCOLARES PARA AMERICA LATINA Y LA REGION DEL CARIBE. DOCUMENTOS ASESORIA. irreg. price varies. Centro Regional de Construcciones Escolares para America Latina y la Region del Caribe, Apartado Postal 41-518, Mexico 10, D.F., Mexico.
Formerly: Centro Regional de Construcciones Escolares para America Latina. Documentos Asesoria.

690 371.6 MX
CENTRO REGIONAL DE CONSTRUCCIONES ESCOLARES PARA AMERICA LATINA Y LA REGION DEL CARIBE. DOCUMENTOS TECNICOS. 1967. irreg. price varies. Centro Regional de Construcciones Escolares para America Latina y la Region del Caribe, Apartado Postal 41-518, Mexico 10, D.F., Mexico. Ed. Alonso Barrientos Rodriguez. bk. rev.
Formerly: Centro Regional de Construcciones Escolares para America Latina. Documentos Tecnicos.

EDUCATION — SCHOOL ORGANIZATION AND ADMINISTRATION

378.3 US ISSN 0589-9087
COUNCIL FOR FINANCIAL AID TO EDUCATION. C.F.A.E. CORPORATION SUPPORT OF HIGHER EDUCATION. a. $3. Council for Financial Aid to Education, 680 Fifth Ave., New York, NY 10017. charts. stat.

371.6 US
DELAWARE STATE PLANNING OFFICE. SCHOOL FACILITIES PLANNING STUDY. 1969. a. free. Office of Management, Budget & Planning, Thomas Collins Bldg., Dover, DE 19901. Ed. Helen L. Gelog.

DEVELOPMENT JOURNAL. see EDUCATION — Higher Education

DIRECTORY OF NATIONAL ORGANIZATIONS CONCERNED WITH SCHOOL HEALTH. see PUBLIC HEALTH AND SAFETY

371.0025 US
DIRECTORY OF NONPUBLIC SCHOOLS AND ADMINISTRATORS, NEW YORK STATE. a. Education Department, Information Center on Education, Albany, NY 12234. circ. controlled.

371 US ISSN 0070-6035
DIRECTORY OF ORGANIZATIONS AND PERSONNEL IN EDUCATIONAL MANAGEMENT. 1968. irreg., approx. biennial, 6th edt., 1979. $5.95. ‡ E R I C Clearinghouse on Educational Management, University of Oregon, Eugene, OR 97403. Eds. Philip K. Piele, Stuart C. Smith. subject index. circ. 1,500. (also avail. in microfiche from EDR)
Formerly: Directory of Organizations and Personnel in Educational Administration.

378.1 US
DIRECTORY OF PUBLIC SCHOOLS AND ADMINISTRATORS, NEW YORK STATE. a. $1.50. Education Department, Information Center on Education, Albany, NY 12234.

378.3 US ISSN 0091-7168
EASTERN ASSOCIATION OF STUDENT FINANCIAL AID ADMINISTRATORS. DIRECTORY.* 1973. a. Eastern Association of Student Financial Aid Administrators, House of Printing, 8833 Brookville Road, Silver Spring, MD 20910. Key Title: Directory for the Eastern Association of Student Financial Aid Administrators.

371.2 UK
EDUCATIONAL ADMINISTRATION AND HISTORY MONOGRAPHS. 1973. irreg., no. 9, 1980. price varies. University of Leeds, School of Education, Rm. 4, Parkinson Court, Leeds LS2 9JT, England.

379 US
FEDERAL AID REFERENCE MANUAL. a. plus updates. Croft-N E I Publications, 24 Rope Ferry Rd., Waterford, CT 06386. (looseleaf format)

379 US ISSN 0095-3342
FEDERAL FUNDING GUIDE FOR ELEMENTARY AND SECONDARY EDUCATION. 1975. a. $27.95. Education Funding Research Council, 752 National Press Bldg. N.W., Washington, DC 20045. Ed. Jeanne M. Vonhof.

371.2 FR
FRANCE. INSTITUT NATIONAL DE RECHERCHE ET DE DOCUMENTATION PEDAGOGIQUES. CAHIERS DE DOCUMENTATION. 1960. irreg. price varies. Institut National de Recherche et de Documentation Pedagogiques, Centre National de Documentation Pedagogique, 29 rue d'Ulm, 75230 Paris Cedex 05, France (Orders to: Librairie du C.N.D.P., 13 rue du Four, 75006 Paris, France)

371 US
GEORGIA CONGRESS OF PARENTS AND TEACHERS. ANNUAL LEADERSHIP TRAINING CONFERENCE. WORKSHOP FOR P T A LEADERS. a., 52nd edt., 1974. $3. University of Georgia, Center for Continuing Education, Athens, GA 30602. circ. 700.
Formerly: Georgia Congress of Parents and Teachers. Annual Summer Institute. Handbook for P T A Leaders (ISSN 0072-1220)

371 UK ISSN 0072-4564
GIRLS SCHOOL YEAR BOOK; official book of reference of the Girls' Schools Association. 1906. a. £4.95. A. & C. Black(Publishers) Ltd., 35 Bedford Row, London WC1R 4JH, England. Ed. J. F. Burnet. adv. index.

371.6 UK ISSN 0260-0471
GREAT BRITAIN. DEPARTMENT OF EDUCATION AND SCIENCE. ARCHITECTS AND BUILDING BRANCH. BROADSHEET. 1980. irreg. free. Department of Education and Science, Architects and Building Branch, Elizabeth House, York Rd., London SE1 7PH, England.

371.6 UK ISSN 0072-5870
GREAT BRITAIN. DEPARTMENT OF EDUCATION AND SCIENCE. BUILDING BULLETINS. 1955-64, no.1-23. 1964 N.S. irreg. price varies. Department of Education and Science, Elizabeth House, York Rd., London SE1 7PH, England (Avail. from H.M.S.O., c/o Liaison Officer, Atlantic House, Holborn Viaduct, London EC1P 1BN, England)

371 US ISSN 0072-8101
GUIDE FOR PLANNING EDUCATIONAL FACILITIES. 1949. irreg; approx. quinquennial. $17.50. Council of Educational Facility Planners, 29 W. Woodruff Ave., Columbus, OH 43210. Ed. D. E. Gardner. index.
Formerly: Guide for Planning School Plants.

370 US
GUIDE TO THE EVALUATION OF EDUCATIONAL EXPERIENCES IN THE ARMED SERVICES. (3-vol. set) biennial. $18. American Council on Education, Office of Educational Credit, One Dupont Circle, Washington, DC 20036. Ed. Eugene J. Sullivan.

371 GW
HESSISCHER KULTUSMINISTER. BILDUNGSPOLITISCHE INFORMATIONEN. irreg. Kultusministerium, Luisenplatz 10, 6200 Wiesbaden, W. Germany (B.R.D.) Ed. Peter Ochs.

379 II
INDIA. DEPARTMENT OF CULTURE. DEMANDS FOR GRANTS/SAMSKRITI VIBHAGA KI ANUDANOM KI MANGEM. (Text in Hindi and English) 1971/72. a. Government of India Press, General Manager, Minto Rd., New Delhi, India.

378.3 US
IOWA. COLLEGE AID COMMISSION. BIENNIUM REPORT. 1967. biennial. College Aid Commission, 201 Jewett Building, Des Moines, IA 50309. stat. circ. 1,000.
Former titles (until 1978): Iowa. Higher Education Facilities Commission. Biennium Report; State of Iowa Scholarships, Tuition Grants. Biennium Report (ISSN 0091-3588)

379 US ISSN 0091-9802
KANSAS. STATE DEPARTMENT OF EDUCATION. ADMINISTRATION AND FINANCE DIVISION. ANNUAL STATISTICAL REPORT. a. State Department of Education, 120 E. 10th, Topeka, KS 66612.

371 US ISSN 0076-9460
MISSISSIPPI CONGRESS OF PARENTS AND TEACHERS. PROCEEDINGS. a. Mississippi Congress of Parents and Teachers, 401 First Federal Bldg., P.O. Box 1946, Jackson, MS 39201. circ. controlled.

371 US ISSN 0076-9479
MISSISSIPPI CONGRESS OF PARENTS AND TEACHERS. YEARBOOK. a. ‡ Mississippi Congress of Parents and Teachers, 401 First Federal Bldg., P.O. Box 1946, Jackson, MS 39201. circ. controlled.

371.16 US ISSN 0077-345X
NATIONAL ASSOCIATION OF TEACHERS' AGENCIES. LIST OF THE ACCREDITED MEMBERS. 1914. a. free. National Association of Teachers' Agencies, 1825 K St. N.W., Washington, DC 20006.
National listing of privately controlled teachers' agencies

371 US ISSN 0077-4472
NATIONAL FACULTY DIRECTORY. 1971. a. $135 for 2 vols. Gale Research Company, Book Tower, Detroit, MI 48226.

370 US
NATIONAL GUIDE TO EDUCATIONAL CREDIT FOR TRAINING PROGRAMS. 1976. a. $20. American Council on Education, Office on Educational Credit, One Dupont Circle, Washington, DC 20036. Ed. John J. Sullivan. (also avail. in microfiche)
Formerly: National Guide to Credit Recommendations for Noncollegiate Courses.

371 US ISSN 0077-569X
NATIONAL SCHOOL BOARDS ASSOCIATION. YEARBOOK. a. $7.50. National School Boards Association, 1055 Thomas Jefferson St. N.W., Washington, DC 20007.

371 379 NE ISSN 0077-7188
NETHERLANDS. CENTRAAL BUREAU VOOR DE STATISTIEK. STATISTIEK VAN DE UITGAVEN DER OVERHEID VOOR ONDERWIJS. STATISTICS OF THE EXPENDITURE OF THE STATE, THE PROVINCES AND THE MUNICIPALITIES ON EDUCATION. (Text in Dutch and English) 1964. a. fl.8.95. Centraal Bureau voor de Statistiek, Prinses Beatrixlaan 428, Voorburg, Netherlands (Orders to: Staatsuitgeverij, Christoffel Plantijnstraat, The Hague, Netherlands)

371 373 NE
NETHERLANDS. CENTRAAL BUREAU VOOR DE STATISTIEK. STATISTIEK VAN HET W V O, H A V O EN M A V O; INSTROOM, DOORSTROOM EN UITSTROOM VAN LEERLINGEN. (Text in Dutch and English) 1950-54. a. fl.12.10. Centraal Bureau voor de Statistiek, Prinses Beatrixlaan 428, Voorburg, Netherlands (Orders to: Staatsuitgeverij, Christoffel Plantijnstraat, The Hague, Netherlands)
Formerly: Netherlands. Centraal Bureau voor de Statistiek. Statistiek van het Voorbereidend Hoger en Middelbaar Onderwijs: Leraren. Statistics of Secondary Education: Teachers (ISSN 0077-7404)

371 372 NE ISSN 0077-6785
NETHERLANDS. CENTRAAL BUREAU VOOR DE STATISTIEK. VOORZIENING IN DE BEHOEFTE AAN ONDERWIJZERS BIJ HET LAGER ONDERWIJS. SUPPLYING THE NEED FOR TEACHERS IN ELEMENTARY EDUCATION. (Text in Dutch and English) 1950. a. fl.5. Centraal Bureau voor de Statistiek, Prinses Beatrixlaan 428, Voorburg, Netherlands (Orders to: Staatsuitgeverij, Christoffel Plantijnstraat, The Hague, Netherlands)

371.2 AT ISSN 0085-3976
NEW SOUTH WALES. DEPARTMENT OF EDUCATION. SCHOOL MANAGEMENT BULLETIN. 1958. irreg. contr. free circ. Department of Education, Box 33, Sydney, N.S.W. 2001, Australia. Ed. C. L. Macdonald. bk. rev. circ. 6,000.

371.2 FR
ORGANISATION DE L'ENSEIGNEMENT EN FRANCE. a. Institut National de Recherche et de Documentation Pedagogiques, 29 rue d'Ulm, 75230 Paris, France. illus.

379 US ISSN 0079-2071
PILOT STUDIES APPROVED FOR STATE AID IN PUBLIC SCHOOL SYSTEMS IN VIRGINIA. 1964. a. ‡ Department of Education, Division of Educational Research, Richmond, VA 23216. Ed. Dr. Mary F. Lovern.

PROGRESS IN LEARNING DISABILITIES. see EDUCATION — Special Education And Rehabilitation

371 UK ISSN 0079-7537
PUBLIC AND PREPARATORY SCHOOLS. YEARBOOK; official book of reference of the Headmasters Conference, the Incorporated Association of Preparatory Schools and the Society of Headmasters of Independent Schools. 1890. a. £6.95. A. & C. Black (Publishers) Ltd., 35 Bedford Row, London WC1R 4JH, England. Ed. J. F. Burnet. adv. index.

378.1 US
PUBLIC SCHOOL ENROLLMENT AND STAFF, NEW YORK STATE. 1961. a. free. ‡ Education Department, Information Center on Education, Albany, NY 12234. circ. controlled.
Formerly: New York (State) Education Department. Public School Professional Personnel Report (ISSN 0077-9245)

371.2 AT
QUEENSLAND. DEPARTMENT OF EDUCATION. INFORMATION AND PUBLICATIONS BRANCH. DOCUMENT. 1973. irreg. Department of Education, Information and Publications Branch, P.O. Box 33, North Quay, Qld. 4000, Australia. Ed. J. L. Finger.
Formerly: Queensland. Department of Education. Research and Curriculum Branch. Document (ISSN 0310-4087)

371 372 US ISSN 0080-1429
REQUIREMENTS FOR CERTIFICATION OF TEACHERS, COUNSELLORS, LIBRARIANS, ADMINISTRATORS FOR ELEMENTARY SCHOOLS, SECONDARY SCHOOLS, JUNIOR COLLEGES. 1935. a. price varies. University of Chicago Press, 5801 S. Ellis Ave., Chicago, IL 60637. Ed. E. H. Woellner. (reprint service avail. from UMI,ISI)

371.1 UN ISSN 0082-2213
TEACHERS' ASSOCIATIONS. ASSOCIATIONS D'ENSEIGNANTS. ASOCIACIONES DE PERSONAL DOCENTE. (Text in English, French and Spanish) 1961. irreg., 1971, 2nd ed. Unesco, 7-9 Place de Fontenoy, 75700 Paris, France (Dist. in U.S. by: Unipub, 345 Park Ave. S., New York NY 10010)

371 US ISSN 0083-3967
U C E A CASE SERIES IN EDUCATIONAL ADMINISTRATION. 1960. irreg., latest issue, 1975. price varies. University Council for Educational Administration, 29 W. Woodruff Ave., Columbus, OH 43210. (reprint service avail. from UMI, ISI)

378 US
U C E A CASE SERIES IN HIGHER EDUCATION. 1976. irreg. price varies. University Council for Educational Administration, 29 W. Woodruff Ave., Columbus, OH 43210. (reprint service avail. from UMI,ISI)

379 US ISSN 0362-3610
UNDERSTANDING FINANCIAL SUPPORT OF PUBLIC SCHOOLS. Cover title: Sharing of Total Public School Expenditures. 1967/68. irreg. free. Education Department, Bureau of Educational Finance Research, Albany, NY 12230. (Co-sponsor: University of the State of New York)

379 500 US
U.S. NATIONAL SCIENCE FOUNDATION. GUIDE TO PROGRAMS. 1966. a. $3.50. U.S. National Science Foundation, 1800 G. St. N.W., Washington, DC 20550 (Orders to: Supt. of Documents, Washington, DC 20402) circ. 25,000.

378 BL
UNIVERSIDADE FEDERAL DE PERNAMBUCO. ANUARIO ESTATISTICO. (Includes University Master Plan) 1972. a (with supplement) free. Universidade Federal de Pernambuco, Assessoria da Area de Informacao, Cidade Universitaria, Av. Prof. Morais Rego, Recife, Pernambuco, Brazil. stat.

371.2 US ISSN 0076-857X
UNIVERSITY OF CHICAGO. MIDWEST ADMINISTRATION CENTER. MONOGRAPH SERIES. 1954. irreg., latest issue. 1978. Univ. of Chicago, Midwest Administration Center, 5835 S. Kimbark Ave., Chicago, IL 60637. (back issues avail.; reprint service avail. from UMI)

371 US
UNIVERSITY OF OREGON. CENTER FOR EDUCATIONAL POLICY AND MANAGEMENT. MONOGRAPHS. irreg., latest 1977. University of Oregon, Center for the Advanced Study of Educational Administration, Center for Educational Policy and Management, Eugene, OR 97401.
Formerly: University of Oregon. Center for the Advanced Study of Educationl Administration. Monographs (ISSN 0078-6004)

379.792 US ISSN 0094-8314
UTAH. STATE BOARD OF EDUCATION. ANNUAL REPORT OF THE STATE SUPERINTENDENT OF PUBLIC INSTRUCTION. At head of title: Utah Public School System. a. State Board of Education, Publications Secretary, 250 East 5th South, Salt Lake City, UT 84111. illus. Key Title: Annual Report of the State Superintendent of Public Instruction Utah Public School System.

371.2 US ISSN 0093-0040
UTAH. STATE BOARD OF EDUCATION. OPINIONS OF THE UTAH STATE SUPERINTENDENT OF PUBLIC INSTRUCTION. 1963. irreg., latest issue 1972. State Board of Education, 250 East 5th South, Salt Lake City, UT 84111. Key Title: Opinions of the Utah State Superintendent of Public Instruction.

371 SZ ISSN 0084-1528
W C O T P ANNUAL REPORT. (Including the formal documents of the Assembly of Delegates) (Editions in English, French and Spanish) 1952. a. 6 Fr.($2) ‡ World Confederation of Organizations of the Teaching Profession, 5 Avenue du Moulin, 1110 Morges, Switzerland. Ed. John M. Thompson. circ. 1,400(combined)

371 AT
WESTERN AUSTRALIA. EDUCATION DEPARTMENT. SCHOOLS & STAFFING. a. Education Department, Perth, W.A., Australia.

EDUCATION — Special Education And Rehabilitation

see also Blind; Criminology and Law Enforcement; Deaf; Social Services and Welfare

A S H A DIRECTORY. (American Speech-Language-Hearing Association) see *MEDICAL SCIENCES — Otorhinolaryngology*

A S H A REPORTS. (American Speech-Language-Hearing Association) see *MEDICAL SCIENCES — Otorhinolaryngology*

371.9 US ISSN 0270-4013
ADVANCES IN SPECIAL EDUCATION. 1980. a. J A I Press, Box 1285, 165 W. Putnam Ave., Greenwich, CT 06830.

371.9 US
AMERICAN LECTURES IN SPECIAL EDUCATION. irreg. price varies. Charles C. Thomas, Publisher, 301-327 E. Lawrence Ave., Springfield, IL 62717.

371.9 US ISSN 0065-9800
AMERICAN PRINTING HOUSE FOR THE BLIND, LOUISVILLE, KENTUCKY. DEPARTMENT OF EDUCATIONAL RESEARCH. ANNUAL REPORT. 1958. a. free. ‡ American Printing House for the Blind, Department of Educational Research, P.O. Box 6085, Louisville, KY 40206. Ed. June E. Morris. circ. 800.

371.9 US ISSN 0198-7518
ANNUAL EDITIONS: EDUCATING EXCEPTIONAL CHILDREN. a. $6.95. Dushkin Publishing Group, Sluice Dock, Guilford, CT 06437. Key Title: Educating Exceptional Children.

371.911 US ISSN 0066-9105
ASSOCIATION FOR EDUCATION OF THE VISUALLY HANDICAPPED. SELECTED PAPERS FROM A E V H BIENNIAL CONFERENCES. 1874. biennial. $3. Association for Education of the Visually Handicapped, Inc., 919 Walnut St., 4th Fl., Philadelphia, PA 19109. Ed. Mary K. Bauman. cum.indexes: 1922-30, 1931, 1932-40, 1944-60. circ. 2,500.
Formerly: American Association of Instructors of the Blind. Biennial Conference Proceedings.

371 GW ISSN 0171-9718
BEHINDERTENHILFE DURCH ERZIEHUNG, UNTERRICHT UND THERAPIE. 1977. irreg., no. 11, 1980. price varies. Ernst Reinhardt, GmbH und Co., Verlag, Kemnatenstr. 46, 8000 Munich 19, W. Germany (B.R.D.) Ed. Otto Speck. (reprint service avail. from ISI and UMI)

371.9 CN ISSN 0068-9580
CANADIAN REHABILITATION COUNCIL FOR THE DISABLED. ANNUAL REPORT. 1963. a. free. Canadian Rehabilitation Council for the Disabled, Suite 2110, One Yonge St., Toronto, Ont. M5E 1E8, Canada. circ. 1,800.
Rehabilitation

370 US
CASE STUDIES IN BILINGUAL EDUCATION. Variant title: Studies in Bilingual Education. 1978. irreg. $15 for latest vol. Newbury House, Publishers, Inc., 68 Middle Road, Rowley, MA 01969. Eds. Bernard Spolsky and Robert L. Cooper.

CONVENTION OF AMERICAN INSTRUCTORS OF THE DEAF. PROCEEDINGS AND SELECTED PAPERS. see *DEAF*

371.9 136.7 US ISSN 0070-5012
DIRECTORY FOR EXCEPTIONAL CHILDREN; a listing of educational and training facilities. 1954. biennial. $25. Porter Sargent Publishers, Inc., 11 Beacon St., Boston, MA 02108. index.

371.9 US ISSN 0093-7703
DIRECTORY OF EDUCATIONAL FACILITIES FOR THE LEARNING DISABLED. 1968. biennial. free. Academic Therapy Publications, Inc., 20 Commercial Blvd., Novato, CA 94947. Ed. Betty Lou Kratoville. circ. 30,000.
Formerly: Directory of Facilities for the Learning Disabled (ISSN 0092-3257)

371.9 NZ
DIRECTORY OF SPECIAL EDUCATION AND GUIDANCE SERVICES IN NEW ZEALAND. a. free. Department of Education, Public Relations Section, Wellington, New Zealand.

371.9 US ISSN 0531-8327
EDUCATING THE DISADVANTAGED. 1970. irreg. price varies. A M S Press, Inc., 50 E. 13th St., New York, NY 10003. Ed. Erwin Flaxman. bibl. charts. stat.

371.9 US ISSN 0070-9379
EDUCATIONAL THERAPY; educational programs. 1966. irreg. $8.25 paper; hardcover prices vary. Special Child Publications, 4535 Union Bay Place N.E., Seattle, WA 98105. Ed. Marshall Rosenberg. index. (back issues available) Indexed: Except.Child Educ.Abstr. Ment.Retard.Abstr.

362.8 EI
EUROPEAN SOCIAL FUND. ANNUAL REPORT ON THE ACTIVITIES OF THE NEW EUROPEAN SOCIAL FUND. 1972. a. Office for Official Publications of the European Communities, Boite Postale 1003, Luxembourg, Luxembourg (Dist. in the U.S. by: European Community Information Service, 2100 M St., NW, Suite 707, Washington, DC 20037) stat.

379.155 US
INDIANA STATE PLAN FOR VOCATIONAL EDUCATION. ANNUAL PROGRAM PLAN. 1978. a. State Board of Vocational and Technical Education, 401 Illinois Bldg., 17 W. Market St., Indianapolis, IN 46204. stat. circ. 1,000.

371.9 FR ISSN 0074-1787
INTERNATIONAL ASSOCIATION OF WORKERS FOR MALADJUSTED CHILDREN. CONGRESS REPORTS. (Text in English, French, German) 1955. irreg., 1970, 7th, Versailles. $5. International Association of Workers for Maladjusted Children, 66 Chaussee d'Antin, Paris 9e, France.

INTERNATIONAL CONFERENCE ON PIAGETIAN THEORY AND THE HELPING PROFESSIONS. PROCEEDINGS. see *EDUCATION*

370 US
INTERNATIONAL INTERDISCIPLINARY SEMINAR ON PIAGETIAN THEORY AND ITS IMPLICATIONS FOR THE HELPING PROFESSIONS. PROCEEDINGS; emphasis: the handicapped child. 1970. a. $12. Children's Hospital of Los Angeles, University Affiliated Program, Piaget Conference Committee, Box 54700, Los Angeles, CA 90054. (Co-sponsor: University of Southern California, School of Education) Ed. James F. Magary. bibl. circ. 4,000. (back issues avail.) Indexed: P.A.I.S. Psychol.Abstr. SSCI. A.B.C.Pol.Sci. Can.Ind. Rehabil.Lit.

EDUCATION — SPECIAL EDUCATION AND REHABILITATION

INTERNATIONAL REVIEW OF RESEARCH IN MENTAL RETARDATION. see *MEDICAL SCIENCES — Psychiatry And Neurology*

371.9 US ISSN 0074-7939
INTERNATIONAL SEMINAR ON SPECIAL EDUCATION. PROCEEDINGS. third, 1966. irreg; 5th; 1972, Australia. Aus.$4.50. Rehabilitation International, 432 Park Avenue South, New York, NY 10016 (Dist. by: Rehabilitation International Information Service, Box 101 409, 6900 Heidelberg 1, B.R.D., W. Germany)

331.8 IS ISSN 0075-1383
ISRAEL SOCIETY FOR REHABILITATION OF THE DISABLED. ANNUAL. (Added title page in Hebrew: Shenaton) (Text in English and Hebrew) 1964. a. free. ‡ Israel Society for Rehabilitation of the Disabled, 10 Ibn Gvirol St., Tel Aviv, Israel. Ed. E. Chigier. adv. circ. 700-1,000.

371.9 US
IT'S HAPPENING. 1972. irreg. $10 to non-members. National Association for Creative Children and Adults, c/o Ann F. Issacs, 8080 Spring Valley Dr., Cincinnati, OH 45236. adv. circ. 2,000. (reprint service avail. from UMI)

371.9 FR ISSN 0075-4420
JOURNEE DE REEDUCATION. a. Expansion Scientifique, 15 rue St. Benoit, 75278 Paris Cedex 06, France. Eds. Prof. DeSeze, Prof. Debeyre, J. Levernieux.

371.9 KO
KOREA SOCIAL WORK COLLEGE. RESEARCH INSTITUTE FOR SPECIAL EDUCATION. JOURNAL/KWANG-EUNG YEO. (Text in Korean) vol. 6, 1978. a. Korea Social Work College, Research Institute for Special Education, 2288 Daemyung-dong Nam Gu, Daegu 634-00, S.Korea.

371.9 US ISSN 0075-8337
LEARNING DISORDERS. 1965. irreg. $8.25 paper; hardcover price varies. Special Child Publications, 4535 Union Bay Place N.E., Seattle, WA 98105. Ed. Barbara Bateman. index. (back issues avail.) Indexed: Except.Child.Educ.Abstr.

353.9 US ISSN 0095-8050
MASSACHUSETTS. REHABILITATION COMMISSION. EXPENDITURES REPORT. irreg. Rehabilitation Commission, 296 Boylston St., Boston, MA 02130. Key Title: Expenditures Report of the Massachusetts Rehabilitation Commission.

379 US ISSN 0093-9137
MICHIGAN. ADVISORY COUNCIL FOR VOCATIONAL EDUCATION. ANNUAL REPORT. a. Advisory Council for Vocational Education, Box 30008, Lansing, MI 48909. Key Title: Annual Report of the Michigan State Advisory Council for Vocational Education.

371.9 NE ISSN 0076-9916
MODERN APPROACHES TO THE DIAGNOSIS AND INSTRUCTION OF MULTI-HANDICAPPED CHILDREN. 1970. irreg., vol. 15, 1980. price varies. Swets Publishing Service (Subsidiary of: Swets en Zeitlinger B.V.) Heereweg 347B, 2161 CA Lisse, Netherlands (Dist. in the U.S. and Canada by: Swets North America, Inc., Box 517, Berwyn, PA 19312)

NATIONAL ASSOCIATION OF TRAINING SCHOOLS AND JUVENILE AGENCIES. PROCEEDINGS. see *CRIMINOLOGY AND LAW ENFORCEMENT*

370.11 US ISSN 0361-1507
NATIONAL INSTITUTE OF EDUCATION. CAREER EDUCATION PROGRAM: PROGRAM PLAN. irreg. U.S. National Institute of Education, 1200 19th St. N.W., Washington, DC 20208. Key Title: Career Education Program. Program Plan.

362.3 US ISSN 0096-3054
NEBRASKA. OFFICE OF MENTAL RETARDATION. DIRECTORY OF COMMUNITY-BASED MENTAL RETARDATION SERVICES. irreg. Office of Mental Retardation, State House Station, Box 94728, Lincoln, NE 68509. Key Title: Directory of Community-Based Mental Retardation Services.

371.9 372 NE
NETHERLANDS. CENTRAAL BUREAU VOOR DE STATISTIEK. STATISTIEK VAN HET BUITENGEWOON ONDERWIJS. STATISTICS OF SPECIAL EDUCATION. (Text in Dutch and English) 1939-47. a. price varies. Centraal Bureau voor de Statistiek, Prinses Beatrixlaan 428, Voorburg, Netherlands (Orders to: Staatsuitgeverij, Christoffel Plantijnstraat, The Hague, Netherlands)

373 US
NEVADA. ADVISORY COUNCIL FOR VOCATIONAL-TECHNICAL EDUCATION. ANNUAL EVALUATION REPORT. a. Advisory Council for Vocational-Technical Education, Nye Bldg., Capitol Complex, Carson City, NV 89701. illus.
Formerly: Nevada. Advisory Council for Manpower Training and Career Education. Annual Evaluation Report (ISSN 0093-9595)

370 US
NEW JERSEY STATE PLAN FOR VOCATIONAL EDUCATION. 1964. a. $2.50. Department of Education, Division of Vocational Education, Trenton, NJ 08608.

371.9 US
NEW YORK STATE ASSOCIATION FOR RETARDED CHILDREN. ANNUAL REPORT OF EXECUTIVE DIRECTOR. a. $0.50. New York State Association for Retarded Children, Inc., 175 Fifth Ave., New York, NY 10010.
Formerly: New York State Association for the Mentally Retarded. Annual Report of Executive Director.

362.8 US ISSN 0093-7843
NORTH DAKOTA STATE PLAN FOR REHABILITATION FACILITIES AND WORKSHOPS; annual modification. a. Division of Vocational Rehabilitation, Administrative Office, 1025 N. Third St., Bismarck, ND 58501. stat.

371.9 SZ
O R T YEARBOOK.* (Organization for Rehabilitation Through Training) 1971. a. World O R T Union, 1, rue de Varembe, 1211 Geneva 20, Switzerland. charts. illus. stat.

379 US ISSN 0098-5139
OHIO. ADVISORY COUNCIL FOR VOCATIONAL EDUCATION. ANNUAL REPORT. a. Advisory Council for Vocational Education, 5900 Sharon Woods Blvd., Columbus, OH 43229. illus. stat. Key Title: Annual Report, Ohio Advisory Council for Vocational Education.

371.9 US ISSN 0078-6624
ORTON SOCIETY. BULLETIN; an interdisciplinary journal of specific language disability. 1951. a. $6. Orton Society, Inc., 8415 Bellona Lane, Towson, MD 21204. Ed. Margaret Byrd Rawson. bk. rev. circ. 6,000. Indexed: Child Devel.Abstr. DSH Abstr. Lang. & Lang.Behav.Abstr. Psychol.Abstr.
Formerly: Orton Society. Monograph.

371.9 US ISSN 0099-0302
PENNSYLVANIA. DEPARTMENT OF EDUCATION. SPECIAL EDUCATION PROGRAMS-SERVICES. irreg. Department of Education, Box 911, Harrisburg, PA 17126. stat. Key Title: Special Education Programs-Services.

371.9 363.6 BL
PLANO NACIONAL DE EDUCACAO ESPECIAL. 1979. irreg. Ministerio da Educacao e Cultura, Centro Nacional de Educacao Especial, Brasilia, Brazil.

371.9 US ISSN 0079-6387
PROGRESS IN LEARNING DISABILITIES. 1967. irreg. Grune and Stratton, Inc. (Subsidiary of: Harcourt Brace Jovanovich, Inc.) 111 Fifth Avenue, New York, NY 10003. Ed. H. R. Myklebust.

REHA-RUNDBRIEF. see *BLIND*

371.9 GW ISSN 0080-0708
REHABILITATION DER ENTWICKLUNGSGEHEMMTEN. 1961. irreg., no. 9, 1978. price varies. Ernst Reinhardt, GmbH und Co., Verlag, Kemnatenstr. 46, 8000 Munich 19, W. Germany (B.R.D.) Ed. Gerhard Heese. (reprint service avail. from ISI and UMI)
Rehabilitation

371.9 US ISSN 0361-4166
REHABILITATION GAZETTE; international journal of independent living for the disabled. (Editions in English, French, German, Japanese, Portuguese, Spanish) 1958. a. $6 ($3.50 to disabled persons) Rehabilitation Gazette, Inc., 4502 Maryland Ave., St. Louis, MO 63108. Eds. Gini & Joe Laurie. bk. rev. film rev. abstr. illus. circ. 10,000. (also avail. in talking book; back issues avail.) Indexed: Excerp.Med.
Formerly: Toomey J Gazette (ISSN 0495-8667)

338 II ISSN 0080-0724
REHABILITATION INDUSTRIES CORPORATION. ANNUAL REPORT.* (Report year ends Mar. 31) (Text in English) 1959-60. a. Rehabilitation Industries Corporation Ltd., 25 Free School St., Calcutta 16, India.

371.9 US ISSN 0091-5580
REVIEW OF SPECIAL EDUCATION. 1973. a(approx.) price varies. ‡ Grune & Stratton, Inc. (Subsidiary of: Harcourt Brace Jovanovich, Inc.) 111 Fifth Ave., New York, NY 10003. Ed. Lester Mann.

SERIES IN CLINICAL AND COMMUNITY PSYCHOLOGY. see *PSYCHOLOGY*

371.9 US ISSN 0364-0035
SPECIAL EDUCATION DIRECTORY. irreg. Department of Education, Division of Special Education, Columbus, OH 43215.

808.5 US
SPEECH COMMUNICATION DIRECTORY. 1935. a. $10. Speech Communication Association, 5105 Blacklick Rd., No. E, Annandale, VA 22003. Ed. Robert N. Hall. circ. 1,500. (reprint service avail. from UMI)
Former titles: Speech Communication Directory of S C A and the Regional Speech Communicqtion Organizations; Speech Communication Association. Directory (ISSN 0081-3648); Speech Association of America. Directory.

371.9 US
SYRACUSE SPECIAL EDUCATION AND REHABILITATION MONOGRAPH SERIES. 1955. irreg; no. 12, 1977. price varies. Syracuse University Press, 1011 E. Water St., Syracuse, NY 13210. Ed. William M. Cruickshank. index.
Formerly: Special Education and Rehabilitation Monograph Series (ISSN 0081-3532)

379 US ISSN 0093-0903
TENNESSEE. STATE ADVISORY COUNCIL ON VOCATIONAL EDUCATION. ANNUAL EVALUATION REPORT. 1970. a. Advisory Council on Vocational Education, 909 Mountcastle St., Knoxville, TN 37916. Ed. Judy Statzer. illus. circ. 5,000. Key Title: Annual Evaluation Report of the Tennessee State Advisory Council on Vocational Education.

373.2 US ISSN 0093-9889
TENNESSEE. STATE BOARD FOR VOCATIONAL EDUCATION. INFORMATION SERIES. irreg. State Board for Vocational Education, Nashville, TN 37219. Key Title: Information Series - Tennessee State Board of Vocational Education.

618 IS
TIDINGS. (Text in German) 1951. a. free. Akim-Israel Association for Rehabilitation of the Mentally Handicapped, 116 Allenby St., Tel Aviv, Israel. Ed. Moshe Dayan. illus.

371.9 US ISSN 0099-1554
TRAINING DIRECTORY OF THE REHABILITATION RESEARCH AND TRAINING CENTERS. a. Rehabilitation Services Administration, Special Centers Office, Department of Health, Education and Welfare, 330 C. St. S.W., Washington, DC 20201. Ed. Joseph Fenton.

371.9 CN ISSN 0381-9612
TRUST. 1967. irreg. Saskatchewan Association for the Mentally Retarded, Regina Branch, 1602 12th Ave., Regina, Sask., Canada.

371.9 US ISSN 0070-6736
U S C ANNUAL DISTINGUISHED LECTURE SERIES MONOGRAPHS IN SPECIAL EDUCATION AND REHABILITATION. 1962. a. $4. (University of Southern California, School of Education) University of Southern California Press, c/o Bookstore, University Park, Los Angeles, CA 90007. Ed. James F. Magary. circ. 3,000. Indexed: ERIC. Except.Child Educ.Abstr. Rehabil.Lit.

371.9 US ISSN 0093-3430
U.S. DEPARTMENT OF HEALTH, EDUCATION AND WELFARE. ANNUAL REPORT TO THE CONGRESS OF THE UNITED STATES ON SERVICES PROVIDED TO HANDICAPPED CHILDREN IN PROJECT HEAD START. At head of title: Head Start Services to Handicapped Children. 1973. a. U.S. Administration for Children, Youth and Families, 330 Independence Ave., S.W., Washington, DC 20201. circ. 10,000. Key Title: Annual Report of the U.S. Department of Health, Education,and Welfare to the Congress of the United States on Services Provided to Handicapped Children in Project Head Start.

371.9 US
U.S. REHABILITATION SERVICES ADMINISTRATION. AUDIOVISUAL DIRECTORY OF THE RESEARCH AND TRAINING CENTERS. biennial. Rehabilitation Services Administration, Special Centers Office, Department of Health, Education and Welfare, 330 C St. S.W., Washington, DC 20201.

371.9 CS ISSN 0083-4211
UNIVERZITA KOMENSKEHO. ODDELENIE LIECEBNEJ A SPECIALNEJ PEDAGOGIKY. ZBORNIK: PAEDAGOGICA SPECIALIS. (Text in Slovak; summaries in English, German, Russian) 1970. irreg. exchange basis. Univerzita Komenskeho, Oddelenie Liecebnej a Specialnej Pedagogiky, Skolska ul., 800 00 Bratislava, Czechoslovakia. Ed. Juraj Brtka.

371.9 US
WADSWORTH SERIES IN SPECIAL EDUCATION. irreg. Wadsworth Publishing Co., 10 Davis Dr., Belmont, CA 94002.

362.8 US
WASHINGTON (STATE). VOCATIONAL REHABILITATION SERVICES DIVISION. STATE FACILITIES DEVELOPMENT PLAN. 1969. irreg. free. Vocational Rehabilitation Services Division, P.O. Box 1788, Olympia, WA 98504. circ. 1,000.
Formerly: Washington (State). Vocational Rehabilitation Services Division. State Facilities Plan (ISSN 0092-5543)

378.1 US ISSN 0148-6381
WHO'S WHO AMONG VOCATIONAL AND TECHNICAL STUDENTS IN AMERICA. 1975. a. $23.80. Randall Publishing Co., Box 2029, Tuscaloosa, AL 35401.
Formerly: Who's Who Among Students in American Vocational and Technical Schools (ISSN 0360-5248)

371.9 US
YEARBOOK OF SPECIAL EDUCATION. 1975/76. a. $39.50. Marquis Academic Media, 200 E. Ohio St., Chicago, IL 60611. bibl. index.

EDUCATION — Teaching Methods And Curriculum

see also specific subjects

A. A. M. C. CURRICULUM DIRECTORY. (Association of American Medical Colleges) see MEDICAL SCIENCES

375 US ISSN 0068-1180
A C T F L ANNUAL REVIEW OF FOREIGN LANGUAGE EDUCATION. 1969. a. $9 to non-members; members $6.75. (American Council on the Teaching of Foreign Languages) National Textbook Co., 8259 Niles Center Rd., Skokie, IL 60076 (And M L A Publications Center, 62 Fifth Ave., New York, NY 10011) Ed. Gilbert Jarvis.
Formerly: Britannica Review of Foreign Language Education.

A.V.C.D. - ANNUAIRE DE L'AUDIOVISUEL; guide de l'equipement et des fournisseurs. see COMMUNICATIONS

371.33 JA ISSN 0065-0102
A V E IN JAPAN. (Text in English) 1963. a. 1750 Yen. ‡ Japan Audio-Visual Education Association, 1-17-1 Toranomon, Minato-ku, Tokyo 105, Japan. Ed. Tatsuo Moriwaki. circ. 2,000.

ACADEMIC COURSES IN GREAT BRITAIN RELEVANT TO THE TEACHING OF ENGLISH TO SPEAKERS OF OTHER LANGUAGES. see LINGUISTICS

ALBERTA ENGLISH. see LINGUISTICS

ALBERTA HEALTH EDUCATION PROGRAMS. see PHYSICAL FITNESS AND HYGIENE

371.3 CN ISSN 0380-8491
ALBERTA TEACHERS' ASSOCIATION. LEARNING RESOURCES COUNCIL. NEWSLETTER. 1975. irreg. Alberta Teachers' Association, Learning Resources Council, Barnett House, 11010 142nd St., Edmonton, Alta. T5N 2R1, Canada.
Former titles: Alberta Teachers' Association. Audio-Visual Council. Newsletter (ISSN 0380-8513) & Alberta Teachers' Association. School Library Council. Newsletter (ISSN 0380-8505)

ALBERTA TEACHERS ASSOCIATION. MATHEMATICS MONOGRAPH. see MATHEMATICS

371.3 US
ALPHA NEWS. 1974. irreg. New Dimensions in Education, Inc., 83 Keeler Ave., Norwalk, CT 06854. Ed. Evelyn J. Bergstrom. charts. illus. circ. 20,000 (controlled)

371.42 US
AMERICAN VOCATIONAL ASSOCIATION. YEARBOOK. (Each vol. has distinctive title) 1971. a. $12. American Vocational Association, 2020 N. 14th St., Arlington, VA 22201. Ed. Gordon F. Law. bibl. charts. stat. circ. 5,000.

ANNUAL REPORT ON ADVANCED DENTAL EDUCATION. see MEDICAL SCIENCES — Dentistry

375 IT ISSN 0066-6106
ARCHIMEDE. QUADERNI. 1968. irreg. price varies. Casa Editrice Felice le Monnier, Via Scipione Ammirato 100, C.P. 202, 50136 Florence, Italy.

ARISTO - MITTEILUNGEN FUER INGENIEUR- UND HOCHSCHULEN. see MATHEMATICS

379 US ISSN 0091-8792
ARIZONA. STATE ADVISORY COUNCIL FOR VOCATIONAL EDUCATION. ANNUAL REPORT. 1970. a. free. Advisory Council for Vocational Education, P. O. Box 6694, 1810 W. Adams St., Phoenix, AZ 85005. circ. 2,500.

ARIZONA MODEL UNITED NATIONS. see LAW — International Law

371.3 UK ISSN 0141-5956
ASPECTS OF EDUCATIONAL TECHNOLOGY. 1975. a. £13.95. Kogan Page Ltd., 120 Pentonville Rd., London N1 9JN, England.

375 US
ASSOCIATION FOR EDUCATIONAL COMMUNICATIONS AND TECHNOLOGY. MEMBERSHIP DIRECTORY & DATA BOOK. a. $25 to non-members; members $12.50. Association for Educational Communications and Technology, 1126 16th St. N.W., Washington, DC 20036.

ASSOCIATION OF HISTORY TEACHERS IN NIGERIA. see HISTORY

371.3 IO
ATMA JAYA RESEARCH CENTRE. ANNUAL REPORT. (Text in English) a. Atma Jaya Research Centre - Pusat Penelitian Atma Jaya, Jalan Jenderal Sudirman 49a, Box 2639, Jakarta, Indonesia. illus.

371.33 AT
AUDIO-VISUAL BULLETIN. 1971. irreg. Catholic Secondary Schools' Association of N.S.W. and A.C.T., Educational Media Committee, Christian Brothers' High School, 68 the Boulevard, Lewisham, N.S.W. 2049, Australia.
Formerly: Catholic Secondary Schools' Association of N.S.W. and A.C.T. Educational Media Committee. Bulletin.

371.33 670 US ISSN 0571-8759
AUDIO-VISUAL EQUIPMENT DIRECTORY. 1953. a. $32.50 to commercial non-members; members and users, $21. National Audio-Visual Association, Inc., 3150 Spring Street, Fairfax, VA 22031. Ed. Sally Herickes. charts. illus. stat. index. circ. 14,000. (processed)

371.3 US ISSN 0067-0553
AUDIOVISUAL MARKET PLACE; A MULTIMEDIA GUIDE. 1969. a. since 1976; previously biennial. $32.50. R.R. Bowker Company, 1180 Ave. of the Americas, New York, NY 10036 (Orders to Box 1807, Ann Arbor, MI 48106) (reprint service avail. from UMI)

375.38 AT ISSN 0084-6961
AUSTRALASIAN COMMERCIAL TEACHERS' ASSOCIATION. JOURNAL.* 1968. a. $1. Australasian Commercial Teachers' Association, 20 Napoleon St., Roseberry, N.S.W. 2018, Australia.

507 375 AT ISSN 0157-244X
AUSTRALIAN SCIENCE EDUCATION RESEARCH ASSOCIATION. RESEARCH IN SCIENCE EDUCATION. 1971. a. Aus.$8. Australian Science Education Research Association, c/o Dr. J. Butler, Department of Education, University of Queensland, St. Lucia, Qld. 4067, Australia. Ed. C.N. Power. circ. 300.

371.33 AT
AUSTRALIAN SOCIETY FOR EDUCATION IN FILM AND TELEVISION. PRESIDENT'S NEWSLETTER. 1971. irreg. Australian Society for Education in Film and Television, G.P.O. Box 252c, Hobart, Tas. 7001, Australia.

AUSTRALIAN SOCIETY FOR MUSIC EDUCATION. REPORT OF PROCEEDINGS OF THE NATIONAL CONFERENCE. see MUSIC

371.3 AU
AUSTRIA. BUNDESMINISTERIUM FUER UNTERRICHT UND KUNST. SCHRIFTENREIHE. 1971. irreg. price varies. Manzsche Verlags- und Universitaetsbuchhandlung, Kohlmarkt 16, A-1014 Vienna, Austria.

BALAI PENDIDIKAN VDAN LATIHAN TENAGH SOCIAL. LAPORAN. see SOCIAL SERVICES AND WELFARE

370.1 707 CN ISSN 0316-1544
BRITISH COLUMBIA ART TEACHERS' ASSOCIATION. JOURNAL. 1960. irreg. membership. ‡ (B.C. Art Teachers' Association) B.C. Teachers' Federation, No. 105, 2235 Burrard St., Vancouver, B. C. V6J 3H9, Canada. adv. circ. 450. Indexed: Can.Educ.Ind.
Formerly: British Columbia Art Teachers' Association. Newsletter (ISSN 0045-2904)

371.3 US
C S E MONOGRAPH SERIES IN EVALUATION. 1973. irreg. $4.50 per no. University of California, Los Angeles, Center for the Study of Evaluation, 405 Hilgard Ave., 145 Moore Hall, Los Angeles, CA 90024. Indexed: ERIC.

371.3 US ISSN 0162-5977
C S P DIRECTORY OF SUPPLIERS OF EDUCATIONAL FOREIGN LANGUAGE MATERIALS. 1974. biennial. Cruzada Spanish Publications, Box 650909, Miami, FL 33165. Ed. Andres Rivero. circ. 5,000.
Formerly (until 1977): C S P Directory of Suppliers of Spanish Materials.

375 FR ISSN 0069-2050
CENTRE REGIONAL DE RECHERCHE ET DE DOCUMENTATION PEDAGOGIQUES DE LYON. ANNALES. 1970. irreg. price varies; depending on series. Centre Regional de Recherche et de Documentation Pedagogiques de Lyon, 47-49 rue Philippe-De-Lassalle, 69 Lyon (4e), France.

EDUCATION — TEACHING METHODS AND CURRICULUM

CENTRE UNIVERSITAIRE DE LA REUNION. CAHIER. see *LINGUISTICS*

CENTRO DE INVESTIGACIONES EN CIENCIAS DE LA EDUCACION. SECCION LENGUAS INDIGENAS. DOCUMENTO DE TRABAJO. see *LINGUISTICS*

370 510   FR   ISSN 0395-7837
CHANTIERS DE PEDAGOGIE MATHEMATIQUE. 1970. irreg. Association des Professeurs de Mathematiques de l'Enseignement Public, Regionale Parisienne, c/o Institut National de Recherche et de Documentation Pedagogiques, 29 rue d'Ulm, 75230 Paris Cedex 05, France.

420 371.3   US   ISSN 0550-5755
CLASSROOM PRACTICES IN TEACHING ENGLISH. 13th, 1975. a. National Council of Teachers of English, 1111 Kenyon Rd., Urbana, IL 61801.

COLLANA "INSEGNARE". see *EDUCATION*

COURSE GUIDE IN THE THEATRE ARTS AT THE SECONDARY SCHOOL LEVEL. see *THEATER*

CURRENT AUDIOVISUALS FOR MENTAL HEALTH EDUCATION. see *PSYCHOLOGY*

375 780   US   ISSN 0070-198X
CURRENT ISSUES IN MUSIC EDUCATION. 1963. irreg., 1970, no. 5. price varies. ‡ Ohio State University, School of Music, Div. of Music Education, Columbus, OH 43210.

371   US   ISSN 0095-2885
CURRENT TOPICS IN CLASSROOM INSTRUCTION SERIES. irreg., unnumbered, 9th vol., 1978. price varies. Macmillan Publishing Co., Inc., 866 Third Ave., New York, NY 10022.

016.375   US   ISSN 0095-4977
CURRICULUM MATERIALS CLEARINGHOUSE. INDEX AND CURRICULUM BRIEFS. 1974. irreg. University Microfilms International, 300 N. Zeeb Rd., Ann Arbor, MI 48106.

375 300   US
DATA BOOK OF SOCIAL STUDIES MATERIALS AND RESOURCES. 1971. a. $10. Social Science Education Consortium, 855 Broadway, Boulder, CO 80302. (Co-sponsor: ERIC Clearinghouse for Social Studies/Social Science Education) Ed. Judith E. Hedstrom. (also avail. in microform from EDR)
    Former titles: Social Studies Materials and Resources Data Book. Annual; (until vol. 4, 1979): Social Studies Curriculum Materials Data Book Supplement.

650   US   ISSN 0416-9336
DELTA PI EPSILON. RESEARCH BULLETIN. 1962. irreg. price varies. Delta Pi Epsilon Graduate Business Education Fraternity, National Office, Gustavus Adolphus College, St. Peter, MN 56082. circ. 10,000. (reprint service avail. from UMI) Indexed: Bus.Educ.Ind.

430.07 378   AU   ISSN 0012-1398
DEUTSCHKURSE/GERMAN LANGUAGE COURSES. 1961-1962. irreg. ‡ Oesterreichischer Auslandsstudentendienst, Dr. Karl Lueger-Ring 1, A-1010 Vienna, Austria. Ed. Robert Bauchinger. adv. circ. 10,000.

371.3   US   ISSN 0070-4881
DIMENSION: LANGUAGES; proceedings of the Southern Conference on Language Teaching. 1966. a. $4. Southern Conference on Language Teaching, c/o James G. Gates, Exec.Sec., Spelman College, Atlanta, GA 30314.

375   US
DIRECTORY OF PRIVATE POSTSECONDARY INSTITUTIONS IN CALIFORNIA. 1978. $1.50. Department of Education, Bureau of Publications, 721 Capitol Mall, Sacramento, CA 95814.
    Supersedes: Courses Offered by California Schools.

DIRECTORY OF SPORTS, RECREATION AND PHYSICAL EDUCATION. see *SPORTS AND GAMES*

353   US   ISSN 0098-1109
DIRECTORY OF U. S. GOVERNMENT AUDIOVISUAL PERSONNEL. 1969. a. $3. ‡ U.S. National Audiovisual Center, General Services Administration, Washington, DC 20409. circ. 3,000.

371.3   BB
EASTERN CARIBBEAN STANDING CONFERENCE ON TEACHER EDUCATION. REPORT. 1957. biennial. bds. 8. University of the West Indies, School of Education, Cave Hill, Barbados, W. Indies. Ed. R. M. Nicholson.
    Formerly: Conference on Teacher Education in the Eastern Caribbean. Report (ISSN 0069-8695)

371.3 330   US   ISSN 0070-8534
ECONOMIC EDUCATION EXPERIENCES OF ENTERPRISING TEACHERS; report developed from the entries in the International Paper Company Foundation awards program for the teaching of economics at K-12 level. 1963. a. $2. Joint Council on Economic Education, 1212 Ave. of the Americas, New York, NY 10036. Eds. Andrew T. Nappi, Anthony F. Suglia.

370   US
EDUCATION COMMISSION OF THE STATES. NATIONAL ASSESSMENT OF EDUCATIONAL PROGRESS. ASSESSMENT REPORTS. 1970. irreg. (approx. 10-25/yr.) price varies. Education Commission of the States, 700 Lincoln Tower, 1860 Lincoln St., Denver, CO 80203 (Subscr. to: Supt. of Documents, Govt. Printing Office, Washington, DC 20402) Eds. Rexford Brown, Theodore B. Pratt. bibl. charts. stat. circ. 10,000. (also avail. in microfiche from EDR) Indexed: ERIC.

EDUCATIONAL MATERIALS DIRECTORY. see *HOME ECONOMICS*

375   US
EDUCATIONAL MEDIA CATALOGS ON MICROFICHE. 1975. a. with s-a. updates. $87.50. Olympic Media Information, 70 Hudson St., Hoboken, NJ 07030. Ed. Walter J. Carroll. circ. 750.

371.33   US   ISSN 0000-037X
EDUCATIONAL MEDIA YEARBOOK. 1973. a. $20. Libraries Unlimited, Inc., Box 263, Littleton, CO 80160. Ed. James W. Brown.

371.3   US   ISSN 0070-9387
EDUCATORS GRADE GUIDE TO FREE TEACHING AIDS. 1955. a. $30.25. Educators Progress Service, Inc., Randolph, WI 53956. Ed. Michael Weller. index. (also avail. in looseleaf format)

371.3   US   ISSN 0160-1296
EDUCATORS GUIDE TO FREE AUDIO AND VIDEO MATERIALS. 1954. a. $12.25. Educators Progress Service, Inc., Randolph, WI 53956. Eds. James L. Berger, Walter A. Wittich.
    Formerly: Educators Guide to Free Tapes, Scripts, and Transcriptions (ISSN 0070-9441)

371.3   US   ISSN 0070-9395
EDUCATORS GUIDE TO FREE FILMS. 1941. a. $16.25. Educators Progress Service, Inc., Randolph, WI 53956. Eds. Mary Foley Horkheimer & John Diffor. index.

371.3   US   ISSN 0070-9409
EDUCATORS GUIDE TO FREE FILMSTRIPS. 1949. a. $11.75. Educators Progress Service, Inc., Randolph, WI 53956. Eds. Mary Foley Horkheimer & John Diffor. index.

371.42   US   ISSN 0070-9417
EDUCATORS GUIDE TO FREE GUIDANCE MATERIALS. 1962. a. $14.25. Educators Progress Service, Inc., Randolph, WI 53956. Ed. Bd.

371.3   US   ISSN 0424-6241
EDUCATORS GUIDE TO FREE HEALTH, PHYSICAL EDUCATION & RECREATION MATERIALS. 1968. a. $15. Educators Progress Service, Inc., Randolph, WI 53956. Eds. Foley A. Horkheimer, Louis E. Alley.

371.3   US   ISSN 0070-9425
EDUCATORS GUIDE TO FREE SCIENCE MATERIALS. 1960. a. $14. Educators Progress Service, Inc., Randolph, WI 53956. Eds. Mary Horkheimer Saterstrom & John W. Renner. index.

371.3   US   ISSN 0070-9433
EDUCATORS GUIDE TO FREE SOCIAL STUDIES MATERIALS. 1961. a. $15.25. Educators Progress Service, Inc., Randolph, WI 53956. Ed. Bd.

371.3   US
EDUCATORS INDEX OF FREE MATERIALS. 1937. a. $36. Educators Progress Service, Inc., Randolph, WI 53956. Eds. Charles R. Duvall, Wayne J. Krepel. (looseleaf format)

375   US   ISSN 0070-9980
ELEMENTARY TEACHERS GUIDE TO FREE CURRICULUM MATERIALS. 1944. a. $13.75. Educators Progress Service, Inc., Randolph, WI 53956. Ed. Patricia H. Suttles.

371.3 407   US   ISSN 0071-0601
ENGLISH LANGUAGE AND ORIENTATION PROGRAMS IN THE UNITED STATES; including a list of programs for training teachers of English as a second language. 1960. irreg., 7th edt. 1980. $4.50. ‡ Institute of International Education, 809 United Nations Plaza, New York, NY 10017.

373   IR
ENGLISH LANGUAGE TEACHERS ASSOCIATION. REVIEW/ANJOMAN-E DABIRAN-E ZABANHA-YE KHAREJI. NASHRIYEH. (Text in Persian & English) 1972. irreg. free. English Language Teachers Association, Box 33-59, Tajrish, Teheran, Iran. Ed. Gholam Hoseyn Kehtari.

ENGLISH STUDIES SERIES. see *LINGUISTICS*

ENGLISH-TEACHING INFORMATION CENTRE, LONDON. INFORMATION GUIDES. see *LINGUISTICS*

375   FR   ISSN 0071-2728
EUROPEAN CURRICULUM STUDIES. 1968. irreg. price varies; $2.-$4. Council of Europe, Council for Cultural Co-Operation, Publications Section, Strasbourg, France (Dist. in U.S. by Manhattan Publishing Co., 225 Lafayette St., New York, N.Y. 10012) charts, illus.

371.3   US
FEATURE FILMS ON 8MM, 16MM AND VIDEOTAPE. 1967. irreg., 6th edt., 1979. $26.25. R.R. Bowker Company, 1180 Ave. of the Americas, New York, NY 10036 (Orders to: P. O. Box 1807, Ann Arbor, MI 48106) (reprint service avail. from UMI)
    Formerly: Feature Films on 8mm and 16mm (ISSN 0071-4100)

375 770   US   ISSN 0071-4887
FILM-ENGLISH/HUMANITIES ASSOCIATION. JOURNAL.* a. incl. in membership fee, $1. Film-English-Humanities Association, 265 Ernst Bessey Hall, Michigan State University, East Lansing, MI 48823.

375   AT   ISSN 0310-6020
FILTER: A PAPER FOR SCIENCE TEACHERS. 1973. irreg. free. Education Department, Curriculum Branch, Claver House, 823 Wellington St., Perth, W.A. 6000, Australia. bk. rev. circ. 2,000.

371.3   US   ISSN 0071-9307
FREE AND INEXPENSIVE LEARNING MATERIALS. 1941. biennial. $3.50. George Peabody College for Teachers, Office of Educational Services, Nashville, TN 37203. Ed. Norman R. Moore. circ. 15,000.

613   JA
FUKUI UNIVERSITY. FACULTY OF EDUCATION. MEMOIRS. SERIES 6: PHYSICAL EDUCATION. (Text in Japanese) a. Fukui University, Faculty of Education, 9-1, 3-chome, Bunkyo, Fukui 910, Japan.

910   AT   ISSN 0085-0969
GEOGRAPHICAL EDUCATION. 1969. a. Aus.$3. Australian Geography Teachers' Association, c/o W.R. Wilson, Milpera College of Advanced Education, Box 108, Milperra, N.S.W. 2214, Australia. Indexed: Aus.Educ.Ind.

EDUCATION — TEACHING METHODS AND CURRICULUM

375   GW
GERMANY (FEDERAL REPUBLIC, 1949-) BUNDESANSTALT FUER ARBEIT. FOERDERUNG DER BERUFLICHEN BILDUNG; ERGEBNISSE DER TEILNEHMERSTATISTIK. (Supplement to the Amtliche Nachrichten of the Bundesanstalt fuer Arbeit) 1970. irreg. DM.9. ‡ Bundesanstalt fuer Arbeit, Regensburger Strasse 104, 8500 Nuernberg 1, W. Germany (B.R.D.)

370   SW   ISSN 0348-2219
GOETEBORGS UNIVERSITET. INSTITUTIONEN FOER PRAKTISK PEDAGOGIK. RAPPORT. 1966. irreg., no. 91, 1979. free. Goeteborgs Universitet, Institutionen foer Praktisk Pedagogisk, Box 1010, S-431 26 Moelndal, Sweden. Ed. K.G. Stukat.
Former titles: Laerarhoegskolan i Moelndal. Pedagogiska Institutionen. Rapport; Laerarhoegskolan i Goeteborg. Pedagogiska Institutionen. Rapport (ISSN 0534-042X)

375   UK   ISSN 0072-7113
GREAT BRITAIN. SCHOOLS COUNCIL PUBLICATIONS. CURRICULUM BULLETINS. 1965. irreg. price varies. ‡ Methuen Educational, 11 New Fetter Lane, London EC4P 4EE, England.

371   US
GREAT PLAINS NATIONAL INSTRUCTIONAL TELEVISION LIBRARY. RECORDED VISUAL INSTRUCTION. 1967. a. free. ‡ Great Plains National Instructional Television Library, P.O. Box 80669, Lincoln, NE 68501. (Affiliate: University of Nebraska) Ed. Richard L. Spence. circ. 7,000.
Formerly (until 1973): Catalog of Recorded Instruction for Television.

371.3   UK   ISSN 0072-8918
GUIDELINES FOR TEACHERS. 1967. irreg. price varies. National Council for Special Education, 1 Wood St., Stratford-Upon-Avon, Warwickshire CV37 6JE, England. Ed. R. Hermelin.

371.3   UK   ISSN 0073-1714
HELPS FOR STUDENTS OF HISTORY. 1950. irreg. £1.60. Historical Association, 59a Kennington Park Rd., London SE11 4JH, England. (reprint service avail. from UMI)

371.3   UK   ISSN 0073-2591
HISTORICAL ASSOCIATION, LONDON. AIDS FOR TEACHERS. 1957. irreg. 80p. Historical Association., 59a Kennington Park Rd., London SE11 4JH, England. (reprint service avail. from UMI)

907   AT   ISSN 0085-1558
HISTORY TEACHERS ASSOCIATION OF NEW SOUTH WALES. NEWSLETTER. 1965. irreg. History Teachers' Association of New South Wales, Box 87, Rozelle, N.S.W. 2039, Australia.

375   AT   ISSN 0310-558X
I. E. A. (AUSTRALIA) REPORT. 1973. irreg. price varies. Australian Council for Educational Research, P.O. Box 210, Hawthorn, Vic. 3122, Australia. Ed. Malcolm J. Rosier. Indexed: Aus.Educ.Ind.

379   US   ISSN 0091-8970
INDIANA. STATE ADVISORY COUNCIL FOR VOCATIONAL TECHNICAL EDUCATION. ANNUAL REPORT. a. State Advisory Council for Vocational Technical Education, 803 State Office Building, Indianapolis, IN 46206. illus.

371.26   US
INDIANA STUDIES IN HIGHER EDUCATION. 1961. irreg. $1. Indiana University, Bureau of Evaluative Studies and Testing, Bloomington, IN 47401. Ed. Clinton I. Chase. circ. 200.
Formerly: Indiana Studies in Prediction (ISSN 0073-6945)

378   US
INSIDE OUTSIDE BANKSTREET. irreg., 1-2/yr., not published 1977. free. Bank Street College of Education, 610 W. 112 St., New York, NY 10025. illus.

371.3   UK   ISSN 0307-9732
INTERNATIONAL YEARBOOK OF EDUCATIONAL & INSTRUCTIONAL TECHNOLOGY. 1976. biennial. £13.50. Kogan Page Ltd., 120 Pentonville Rd., London N1 9JN, England.

371.3 900   GW   ISSN 0074-9834
INTERNATIONALES JAHRBUCH FUER GESCHICHTS UND GEOGRAPHIEUNTERRICHT. (Text in German, English and French) 1951. a. $8. Institut fuer Internationale Schulbuchforschung, Rebenring 53, 3300 Braunschweig, W. Germany (B.R.D.) Ed. Georg Eckert. circ. 2,500.
Formerly: Internationales Jahrbuch fuer Geschichtsunterricht.

371   IS
ISRAEL. MINISTRY OF EDUCATION AND CULTURE. DEPARTMENT OF EDUCATIONAL TECHNOLOGY. BULLETIN/ALON LE-TECHNOLOGYAH BE-KHINUKH. (Text in Hebrew) irreg. Ministry of Education and Culture, Department of Educational Technology, Jerusalem, Israel.

371.3   US   ISSN 0098-7239
ISSUES IN MEDIA MANAGEMENT. a. free. Department of Education, Division of Library Development and Services, School Media Services Section, Baltimore, MD 21201. Ed. David R. Bender.

JOURNAL OF AGRONOMIC EDUCATION. see *AGRICULTURE — Crop Production And Soil*

KODALY INSTITUTE OF CANADA. MONOGRAPH; a selected bibliography of the Kodaly concept of music education. see *MUSIC — Abstracting, Bibliographies, Statistics*

371.3   JA
KYOKA KYOIKU KENKYU.* 1968. a. Kanazawa University, Faculty of Education - Kanazawa Daigaku Kyoikugakubu, 1-1 Marunouchi, Kanazawa 920, Japan. illus.

370   AT   ISSN 0023-9585
LEADER. vol.7, 1970. irreg. price varies. Department of Education, Bridge St., Sydney, N.S.W. Australia. Ed. H.T.B. Harris.

LIIKUNTAKASVATUS. see *PHYSICAL FITNESS AND HYGIENE*

MATHEMATICS IN SCHOOL. see *MATHEMATICS*

MENTAL MEASUREMENTS YEARBOOK. see *PSYCHOLOGY*

MISSOURI JOURNAL OF RESEARCH IN MUSIC EDUCATION. see *MUSIC*

MODERN ENGLISH JOURNAL/EIGO KYOIKU JAANARU. see *LINGUISTICS*

371.3   AT   ISSN 0085-3526
MODERN TEACHING. (Supplement) 1968. q. Aus.$10. Modern Teaching Methods Association, Box 243, 22 Boyana Cres., Croydon, Vic. 3136, Australia. adv. bk. rev. index. circ. 1,000. Indexed: Aus.Educ.Ind.

375   AT   ISSN 0310-5695
MONASH UNIVERSITY. HIGHER EDUCATION ADVISORY AND RESEARCH UNIT. NOTES ON HIGHER EDUCATION. 1970. irreg. free. Monash University, Higher Education Advisory and Research Unit, Clayton, Vic. 3168, Australia. Ed. Dr. Terry Hore. bk. rev. circ. 2,000.

371.3   GW
MONATSHEFTE FUER DIE UNTERRICHTSPRAXIS - DIE SCHOLLE. 1924. m. DM.25. R. Oldenbourg Verlag GmbH, Postfach 80 13 60, 8000 Munich, W. Germany (B.R.D.) (Subscr. to: Michael Proegel Verlag, Postfach 326, 8800 Ansbach, W. Germany (B.R.D.)) (Co-publisher: Michael Proegel Verlag) adv. bk. rev. illus. index. circ. 10,119. (back issues avail.)

371.3   PL   ISSN 0077-0558
MONOGRAFIE Z DZIEJOW OSWIATY. (Text in Polish; summaries in English, French or Russian) 1957. irreg., vol. 32, 1978. price varies. (Polska Akademia Nauk, Instytut Historii Nauki, Oswiaty i Techniki, Pracownia Dziejow Oswiaty) Ossolineum, Publishing House of the Polish Academy of Sciences, Rynek 9, 50-106 Wroclaw, Poland (Dist. by Ars Polona-Ruch, Krakowskie Przedmiescie 7, Warsaw, Poland) Ed. Jozef Miaso.

379.155   US   ISSN 0093-6472
MONTANA ADVISORY COUNCIL FOR VOCATIONAL EDUCATION. ANNUAL REPORT. 1970. a. free. Advisory Council for Vocational Education, Helena, MT 59601. Key Title: Annual Report - Montana Advisory Council for Vocational Education.

MUSIC IN HIGHER EDUCATION. see *MUSIC*

MUZYKAL'NOE VOSPITANIE V SHKOLE. see *MUSIC*

371.33   US
N A V A MEMBERSHIP DIRECTORY. 1947. a. $12. ‡ National Audio-Visual Association, Inc., 3150 Spring St., Fairfax, VA 22031. Ed. Susan Fischel. circ. 7,000.

613.7   US
N C P E A M PROCEEDINGS. 1897. a. $10. ‡ National College Physical Education Association for Men, 108 Cooke Hall, University of Minnesota, Minneapolis, MN 55455. Ed. C.E. Mueller. circ. 1,400(controlled)

N I C E M INDEX TO PSYCHOLOGY-MULTIMEDIA. (National Information Center for Educational Media) see *PSYCHOLOGY*

N I C E M INDEX TO VOCATIONAL AND TECHNICAL EDUCATION-MULTIMEDIA. (National Information Center for Educational Media) see *ABSTRACTING AND INDEXING SERVICES*

375 700   US   ISSN 0077-3174
NATIONAL ART EDUCATION ASSOCIATION. RESEARCH MONOGRAPH. 1965. irreg., 1972, no. 5. $1.50. National Art Education Association, 1916 Association Drive, Reston, VA 22091. Ed. John Mahlmann.

NATIONAL ASSOCIATION OF SCHOOLS OF MUSIC. DIRECTORY. see *MUSIC*

650 338   US   ISSN 0547-4728
NATIONAL BUSINESS EDUCATION YEARBOOK. no. 15, 1977. a. $10. ‡ National Business Education Association, 1906 Association Drive, Reston, VA 22091. Eds.W. Crews, Z.S. Dickerson, Jr. bibl. circ. 23,000. (also avail. in microform from UMI)

371.3   US   ISSN 0077-3719
NATIONAL CENTER FOR AUDIO TAPES. CATALOG. 1966. triennial. $4.50 for catalog; $1. for Guidelines for Audio Tape Libraries. National Center for Audio Tapes, University of Colorado, Stadium Bldg. 348, Boulder, CO 80302. Ed. Edward Tracy. subject index. circ. 10,000.
Continues: National Tape Recording Catalog.

910   US   ISSN 0469-9130
NATIONAL COUNCIL FOR GEOGRAPHIC EDUCATION. DO IT THIS WAY. irreg., no. 9, 1974. price varies. National Council for Geographic Education, c/o James W. Vining, Exec. Dir., Western Illinois University, Macomb, IL 61455.

910   US
NATIONAL COUNCIL FOR GEOGRAPHIC EDUCATION. INSTRUCTIONAL ACTIVITIES SERIES. irreg. National Council for Geographic Education, c/o James W. Vining, Exec. Dir., Western Illinois University, Macomb, IL 61455.

910   US   ISSN 0547-5643
NATIONAL COUNCIL FOR GEOGRAPHIC EDUCATION. SPECIAL PUBLICATIONS. irreg., no. 16, 1970. price varies. National Council for Geographic Education, c/o James W. Vining, Exec. Dir., Western Illinois University, Macomb, IL 61455.

910   US
NATIONAL COUNCIL FOR GEOGRAPHIC EDUCATION. TOPICS IN GEOGRAPHY. irreg., no. 5, 1970. price varies. National Council for Geographic Education, c/o James W. Vining, Exec. Dir., Western Illinois University, Macomb, IL 61455.

371.3   UK   ISSN 0077-5940
NATIONAL UNION OF TEACHERS. ANNUAL REPORT. 1870. a. L.1. National Union of Teachers, Hamilton House, Mabledon Place, London, WC1H 9BD, England.

EDUCATION — TEACHING METHODS AND CURRICULUM

371.3   PL   ISSN 0077-653X
NEODIDAGMATA. (Text in Polish, rarely in French, English or German; summaries in French, English, Russian) 1970. irreg., vol. 7, 1975. price varies. Uniwersytet im. Adama Mickiewicza w Poznaniu, Miedzywydzialowy Zaklad Nowych Technik Nauczania, Stalingradzka 1, 61-712 Poznan, Poland (Dist. by: Ars Polona, Krakowskie Przedmiescie 7, 00-068 Warsaw, Poland) Ed. Leon Leja. Indexed: Psychol.Abstr.

375   NE
NETHERLANDS. CENTRAAL BUREAU VOOR DE STATISTIEK. STATISTIEK VAN HET BEROEPSONDERWIJS: HUISHOUD- EN NIJVERHEIDSONDERWIJS. (Text in Dutch and English) 1946/47. a. fl.8.95. Centraal Bureau voor de Statistiek, Prinses Beatrixlaan 428, Voorburg, Netherlands (Orders to: Staatsuitgeverij, Christoffel Plantijnstraat, The Hague, Netherlands)
Formerly: Netherlands. Centraal Bureau voor de Statistiek. Statistiek van het Nijverheidsonderwijs (ISSN 0077-734X)

375   NE
NETHERLANDS. CENTRAAL BUREAU VOOR DE STATISTIEK. STATISTIEK VAN HET ERKENDE SCHRIFTELIJK ONDERWIJS. STATISTICS ON CORRESPONDENCE COURSES. (Text in Dutch and English) 1947. a. fl.7.50. Centraal Bureau voor de Statistiek, Prinses Beatrixlaan 428, Voorburg, Netherlands (Orders to: Staatsuitgeverij, Christoffel Plantijnstraat, The Hague, Netherlands)
Formerly: Netherlands. Centraal Bureau voor de Statistiek. Statistiek van het Schriftelijk Onderwijs. Statistics on Correspondence Courses (ISSN 0077-7366)

NEW TEACHER. see EDUCATION

371 500   UN
NEW TRENDS IN INTEGRATED SCIENCE TEACHING. (Text in English, Romance language) 1971. biennial. price varies. Unesco, 7-9 Place de Fontenoy, 75700 Paris, France (Dist. in U.S. by: Unipub, 345 Park Ave. S., New York, NY 10010) Ed. P. E. Richmond.

NEW YORK STATE ENGLISH COUNCIL. MONOGRAPH SERIES. see LITERATURE

379.155   US   ISSN 0094-8306
NORTH DAKOTA. STATE ADVISORY COUNCIL FOR VOCATIONAL EDUCATION. ANNUAL EVALUATION REPORT. a. State Advisory Council for Vocational Education, Box 5405, State University Station, Fargo, ND 58102. illus. Key Title: Annual Evaluation Report - North Dakota State Advisory Council for Vocational Education.

371.3   US   ISSN 0078-1665
NORTHEAST CONFERENCE ON THE TEACHING OF FOREIGN LANGUAGES. REPORTS OF THE WORKING COMMITTEES. 1954. a. $6. Northeast Conference on the Teaching of Foreign Languages, Box 623, Middlebury, VT 05753. adv. cum.index 1954-1975. circ. 5,000. Indexed: C.I.J.E.

O R T E S O L JOURNAL. (Oregon Teachers of English to Speakers of Other Languages) see LINGUISTICS

OKLAHOMA COUNCIL ON ECONOMIC EDUCATION NEWSLETTER. see BUSINESS AND ECONOMICS

375   CN   ISSN 0078-4680
ONTARIO ASSOCIATION FOR CURRICULUM DEVELOPMENT. ANNUAL CONFERENCE (REPORT) (Each volume has distinctive title) 1951. a. $2 per copy. Ontario Association for Curriculum Development, 1260 Bay St., 6th Floor, Toronto, Ont. M5R 2B1, Canada. Ed. S. Dubois.

371.33   CN   ISSN 0707-7777
P E. M. C. CATALOGUE: SUPPLEMENT. 1978. irreg. Provincial Educational Media Centre, Burnaby, B.C., Canada.
Formerly: British Columbia. Provincial Educational Media Centre. Videotape Supplement (ISSN 0707-7785)

371.3 410   US   ISSN 0078-7388
P I /L T; OCCASIONAL PAPERS ON PROGRAMMED INSTRUCTION AND LANGUAGE TEACHING. irreg. Behavioral Research Laboratories, Ladera Professional Center, Box 577, Palo Alto, CA 94302.

PAPERS IN JAPANESE LINGUISTICS. see LINGUISTICS

371.3   UK   ISSN 0141-5964
PERSPECTIVES ON ACADEMIC GAMING & SIMULATION. 1976. a. Kogan Page Ltd., 120 Pentonville Rd., London N1 9JN, England. index. circ. 1,500. (back issues avail.)

613   AT
PHYSICAL EDUCATION AND HEALTH. 1954. irreg. Department of Education, Corner Bridge and Loftus Streets, Sydney, N.S.W. 2000, Australia. Ed. Moira Whiteside. Indexed: Aus.Educ.Ind.
Formerly: Health and Physical Education Bulletin for Teachers in Secondary Schools (ISSN 0441-7933)

371.7   US   ISSN 0079-189X
PHYSICAL EDUCATION AROUND THE WORLD. MONOGRAPH. 1966. irreg., no. 7, 1976. $3. Phi Epsilon Kappa Fraternity, 9030 Log Run Drive N., Indianapolis, IN 46234. Ed. William Johnson. (reprint service avail. from UMI)

371.7   UK   ISSN 0079-1903
PHYSICAL EDUCATION ASSOCIATION OF GREAT BRITAIN AND NORTHERN IRELAND. REPORT. 1900. a. Physical Education Association of Great Britain and Northern Ireland, 10 Nottingham Place, London WIM 4AX, England. Ed. P. Sebastian. circ. controlled.

POLITISCHE BILDUNG. see POLITICAL SCIENCE

QUADERNI DI SESSUALITA. see BIOLOGY

375   AT
QUEENSLAND. DEPARTMENT OF EDUCATION. INFORMATION AND PUBLICATIONS BRANCH. INFORMATION STATEMENT. irreg. Department of Education, Information and Publications Branch, P.O. Box 33, North Quay, Qld. 4000, Australia. Ed. J. L. Finger.
Formerly: Queensland. Department of Education. Research and Curriculum Branch. Information Statement (ISSN 0310-5121)

375   AT
QUEENSLAND. DEPARTMENT OF EDUCATION. RESEARCH BRANCH. REPORTING RESEARCH. 1971. irreg. Department of Education, Research Branch, P.O. Box 33, North Quay, Qld. 4000, Australia. Ed. E. Cassin.
Formerly: Queensland. Department of Education. Research and Curriculum Branch. Reporting Research (ISSN 0310-4095)

910   AT   ISSN 0314-3457
QUEENSLAND GEOGRAPHER. 1966. s-a. Aus.$15. Geography Teachers Association of Queensland, Teachers' Bldg., 495-9 Boundary St., Spring Hill, Qld. 4000, Australia. Ed. Dr. Ian Macpherson. adv. bk. rev. circ. 400.
Formerly (until 1979): Geography Teachers Association of Queensland. Journal (ISSN 0085-0977)

R E C S A M ANNUAL REPORT. (Regional Centre for Education in Science and Mathematics) see EDUCATION

507   MY   ISSN 0126-7612
R E C S A M NEWS. 1967. q. free. Southeast Asian Ministers of Education Organisation, Regional Centre for Education in Science and Mathematics, Glugor, Penang, Malaysia. illus. circ. 1,800.
Formerly: R E C S A M Newsletter.

028   II
READING JOURNAL. (Text in English and Hindi) 1973. a. Rs.3($0.50) Indian Reading Association, J-15 Haus Khas Enclave, Mehrauli Road, New Delhi 16, India. Ed. K. Bose. bk. rev.

371.3 378   CN   ISSN 0380-5727
RED DEER COLLEGE. LEARNING RESOURCES CENTRE. WHAT'S THE USE...? 1973. a. free. Red Deer College, Learning Resources Centre, Red Deer, Alberta, Canada. Ed. Mary Lou Armstrong. illus. circ. 1,800.
Formerly: What's the Use of a Library.

REHOVOT. see SCIENCES: COMPREHENSIVE WORKS

375   CN   ISSN 0382-5914
REPERTOIRE DES COURS D'ETE; et cours permanents pour etrangers. (Text in French) 1969. a. Can.$3. Association des Universites Partiellement Ou Entierement de Langue Francaise, c/o Universite de Montreal, Box 6128, Montreal, Que. H3C 3J7, Canada. circ. 2,000.

370.78   US   ISSN 0091-732X
REVIEW OF RESEARCH IN EDUCATION. 1973. a. price varies. (American Educational Research Association) F. E. Peacock Publishers, 401 W. Irving Park Rd., Itasca, IL 60143. Ed. Lee S. Shulman. index.

RHOMBUS. see MATHEMATICS

371.3   US
S C I S NEWSLETTER. no. 30, 1977. irreg. Science Curriculum Improvement Study, Lawrence Hall of Science, University of California, Berkeley, CA 94720. illus.

371.3   US   ISSN 0068-5860
SAN FRANCISCO STATE UNIVERSITY. AUDIO-VISUAL CENTER. MEDIA CATALOG.* irreg. $3. San Francisco State University, Audio Visual Center, 1600 Holloway, San Francisco, CA 94132.

SCIENCE NOTES AND NEWS. see SCIENCES: COMPREHENSIVE WORKS

SELECTIVE GUIDE TO AUDIOVISUALS FOR MENTAL HEALTH AND FAMILY LIFE EDUCATION. see PSYCHOLOGY

SELECTIVE GUIDE TO PUBLICATIONS FOR MENTAL HEALTH AND FAMILY LIFE EDUCATION. see PSYCHOLOGY — Abstracting, Bibliographies, Statistics

370   MY   ISSN 0126-8155
SOUTHEAST ASIAN-MINISTERS OF EDUCATION ORGANISATION. REGIONAL CENTRE FOR EDUCATION IN SCIENCE AND MATHEMATICS. GOVERNING BOARD MEETING. FINAL REPORT. a. Southeast Asian Ministers of Education Organisation, Regional Centre for Education in Science and Mathematics, Glugor, Penang, Malaysia. circ. 200.

371.3   US
STANFORD CENTER FOR RESEARCH AND DEVELOPMENT IN TEACHING. OCCASIONAL PAPERS. 1975. irreg., no. 19, 1977. Stanford University, Stanford Center for Research and Development in Teaching, Stanford, CA 94305.

371.3   US
STANFORD CENTER FOR RESEARCH AND DEVELOPMENT IN TEACHING. RESEARCH AND DEVELOPMENT MEMORANDA. 1967. irreg., no. 151, 1977. Stanford University, Stanford Center for Research and Development in Teaching, Stanford, CA 94305.

371   US   ISSN 0081-6078
STUDENT JOURNALIST GUIDE SERIES. 1964. irreg. price varies. Richards Rosen Press, 29 E. 21st St., New York, NY 10010. Ed. Ruth C. Rosen.

375   TZ
STUDIES IN CURRICULUM DEVELOPMENT. irreg. price varies. ‡ University of Dar es Salaam, Institute of Education, Box 35094, Dar es Salaam, Tanzania. Ed. A. A. Lema. adv. bk. rev. bibl.

STUDIES IN EDUCATION AND TEACHING TECHNIQUES. see EDUCATION

370   US   ISSN 0090-4023
SUCCESSFUL VENTURES IN CONTEMPORARY EDUCATION IN OKLAHOMA. 1974. vol. 9. a. free. ‡ Department of Education, Curriculum Improvement Commission, Oliver Hodge Education Bldg., Suite 220, Oklahoma City, OK 73105.

371.33 UK ISSN 0306-7858
TAPE TEACHER; a magazine of audio visual teaching. 1971. a. avail. only in U.K. 3M United Kingdom Ltd., 3M House, Box 1, Bracknell, Berkshire RG12 1JU, England. Ed. Bryan Lewis. adv. illus. circ. 23,000.
Audio-visual

371.3 US ISSN 0082-223X
TEACHING. 1970. irreg.; no. 6, 1976. single copy free to educational organizations and professional personnel. ‡ Stanford University, Stanford Center for Research and Development in Teaching, School of Education, Stanford, CA 94305. Ed. Bruce Harlow. circ. 5,000.

371.3 UK ISSN 0073-2605
TEACHING OF HISTORY. 1961. irreg. Historical Association, 59a Kennington Park Rd., London SE11 4JH, England. (reprint service avail. from UMI)

370 UN ISSN 0502-9554
UNESCO SOURCE BOOKS ON CURRICULA AND METHODS. irreg. price varies. Unesco Press, 7 Place de Fontenoy, F-75700 Paris, France (Dist. in U.S. by: Unipub, 345 Park Ave. S., New York, NY 10010)

375 US
U.S. NATIONAL ENDOWMENT FOR THE HUMANITIES. EDUCATION PROGRAMS. 1974. a. U.S. National Endowment for the Humanities, 806 Fifteenth St. N.W., Washington, DC 20506. circ. 25,000.

371.3 FR ISSN 0077-2712
UNIVERSITE DE NANCY II. CENTRE DE RECHERCHES ET D'APPLICATIONS PEDAGOGIQUES EN LANGUES. MELANGES. Spine title: Melanges GRAPEL. (Text in French; occasionally in English) 1970. a. 105 F. individuals; institutions 180F (for 3 years) Universite de Nancy II, Centre de Recherches et d'Applications Pedagogiques en Langues, B.P. 33-97, 54015 Nancy, France. Ed. C. Heddesheimer. circ. 1,000. Indexed: Lang. & Lang.Behav.Abstr.

375 570 US ISSN 0072-1255
UNIVERSITY OF GEORGIA. ANTHROPOLOGY CURRICULUM PROJECT. OCCASIONAL PAPER SERIES. 1965. irreg. price varies. University of Georgia, Anthropology Curriculum Project, 107 Dudley Hall, Athens, GA 30602. Ed. Marion J. Rice.

910 375 US ISSN 0435-5113
UNIVERSITY OF GEORGIA. GEOGRAPHY CURRICULUM PROJECT PUBLICATIONS. 1968. irreg. price varies. University of Georgia, Geography Curriculum Project, 107 Dudley Hall, Athens, GA 30602. Ed. Marion J. Rice. (also avail. in microfiche) Indexed: ERIC.

371.33 US ISSN 0076-9274
UNIVERSITY OF MINNESOTA. AUDIO-VISUAL LIBRARY SERVICE. EDUCATIONAL RESOURCES BULLETIN. 1932. irreg. $6 per issue. University of Minnesota, Audio Visual Library Service, 3300 University Ave. S.E., Minneapolis, MN 55414. Ed. W. D. Philipson. circ. 25,000.

371.3 CN
UNIVERSITY OF WESTERN ONTARIO. INSTRUCTIONAL MEDIA CENTRE. NEWSLETTER. 1970. irreg. University of Western Ontario, Instructional Media Centre, London, Ont., Canada.

371.3 PL
UNIWERSYTET SLASKI W KATOWICACH. PRACE DYDAKTYCZNE. (Subseries of Its: Prace Naukowe) (Text in Polish; summaries in English, French, German, Russian) 1970. irreg. available on exchange. Uniwersytet Slaski w Katowicach, Ul. Bankowa 14, 40-007 Katowice, Poland. Ed. Zygmunt Surowiak. circ. 400.

375 AT ISSN 0085-7726
VICTORIA, AUSTRALIA. EDUCATION DEPARTMENT. CURRICULUM AND RESEARCH BRANCH. RESEARCH REPORTS. 1967. irreg. contr. free circ. Department of Education, Curriculum & Research Branch, 234 Queensberry St., Carlton, Vic. 3053, Australia. circ. 300. Indexed: Aus..Educ.Ind.

372 AT
VINCULUM. 1963. irreg. membership. Mathematical Association of Victoria, Clunies Ross House, 191 Royal Parade, Parkville, Vic. 3052, Australia. Ed. J. Foyster.

WADSWORTH GUIDES TO SCIENCE TEACHING. see SCIENCES: COMPREHENSIVE WORKS

375 US
WADSWORTH SERIES IN CURRICULUM AND INSTRUCTION. irreg. Wadsworth Publishing Co., 10 Davis Dr., Belmont, CA 94002.

371.3 US ISSN 0083-9116
WHAT RESEARCH SAYS TO THE TEACHER SERIES. 1953. irreg. price varies. ‡ National Education Association, 1201 Sixteenth St., N.W., Washington, DC 20036 (Order from: N E A Order Dept., Academic Bldg., Saw Mill Rd., West Haven, CT 06516) (also avail. in microfiche)

ELECTRICITY AND ELECTRICAL ENGINEERING

see also Communications — Radio and Television

621.3 FI ISSN 0001-6845
ACTA POLYTECHNICA SCANDINAVICA. ELECTRICAL ENGINEERING SERIES. (Text and summaries in English, German, and French) irreg (2-3/yr.) Fmk.60. Teknillisten Tieteiden Akatemia - Finnish Academy of Technical Sciences, Kansakoulukatu 10 A, SF-00100 Helsinki 10, Finland. Ed. Martti Tiuri. index; cum. index (1958-1979) circ. 250. (also avail. in microfilm from UMI; back issues avail.; reprint service avail. from UMI) Indexed: INSPEC.

537 US
ADVANCED TECHNIQUES IN FAILURE ANALYSIS SYMPOSIUM. PROCEEDINGS. irreg., latest 1976. $20. Institute of Electrical and Electronics Engineers Inc., 445 Hoes Lane, Piscataway, NJ 08854. charts. illus.

537.5 621.38 US ISSN 0065-2539
ADVANCES IN ELECTRONICS AND ELECTRON PHYSICS. 1948. irreg., vol. 55, 1981. price varies. Academic Press, Inc. (Subsidiary of: Harcourt Brace Jovanovich) 111 Fifth Ave., New York, NY 10003. Ed. L. Marton. index. cum.index: vol. 1-20(1948-1964) in vol. 20 (1964) (also avail. in microfiche)

537.5 621.38 US ISSN 0065-2547
ADVANCES IN ELECTRONICS AND ELECTRON PHYSICS. SUPPLEMENT. 1963. irreg., no. 12, 1979. price varies. Academic Press, Inc., 111 Fifth Ave., New York, NY 10003. Ed. L. Marton.

621.38 US ISSN 0094-7032
ADVANCES IN IMAGE PICKUP AND DISPLAY. 1974. irreg., vol. 3, 1977. Academic Press, Inc., 111 Fifth Ave., New York, NY 10003. Ed. B. Kazani. illus.

621.38 US ISSN 0094-7032
ADVANCES IN IMAGE PICKUP AND DISPLAY. SUPPLEMENTS. 1974. irreg., no. 1, 1974 latest. price varies. Academic Press, Inc., 111 Fifth Ave., New York, NY 10003.
Electronics

ADVANCES IN MAGNETIC RESONANCE. see PHYSICS

537.5 US ISSN 0065-2946
ADVANCES IN MICROWAVES. 1966. irreg., vol. 8, 1974. price varies. Academic Press, Inc., 111 Fifth Ave., New York, NY 10003. Ed. Leo Young. index.

537.5 621.38 US
ADVANCES IN MICROWAVES. SUPPLEMENTS. irreg. price varies. Academic Press, Inc., 111 Fifth Ave., New York, NY 10003.

537.5 US ISSN 0065-3284
ADVANCES IN QUANTUM ELECTRONICS. 1970. irreg., vol. 3, 1975. Academic Press Inc., 111 Fifth Ave., New York, NY 10003. Ed. D. W. Goodwin.

621.38 US
AMERICAN ELECTRONICS ASSOCIATION DIRECTORY. 1949. a. price varies. American Electronics Association, 2600 El Camino Real, Palo Alto, CA 94306. Ed. Barbara Tyler. adv. circ. 10,000.
Formerly (until 1977): W E M A Directory (ISSN 0509-5190)

621.32 FR ISSN 0066-264X
ANNUAIRE DE L'ECLAIRAGE. a. Association Francaise de l'Eclairage, 52 Bd. Malesherbes, 75008 Paris, France. adv. bk. rev. circ. 4,000.

621.3 US
ANNUAL ALLERTON CONFERENCE ON CIRCUIT AND SYSTEM THEORY. 1963. a. $15. ‡ University of Illinois at Urbana-Champaign, Department of Electrical Engineering, Urbana, IL 61801. circ. 2,000.

ANNUAL BOOK OF A S T M STANDARDS. PART 39. ELECTRICAL INSULATION--TEST METHODS: SOLIDS AND SOLIDIFYING FLUIDS. see ENGINEERING — Engineering Mechanics And Materials

ANNUAL BOOK OF A S T M STANDARDS. PART 40. ELECTRICAL INSULATION--SPECIFICATIONS: SOLIDS, LIQUIDS, AND GASES; TEST METHODS: LIQUIDS AND GASES. see ENGINEERING — Engineering Mechanics And Materials

ANNUAL BOOK OF A S T M STANDARDS. PART 43. ELECTRONICS. see ENGINEERING — Engineering Mechanics And Materials

621.3 US ISSN 0190-5600
ANNUAL ELECTRIC POWER SURVEY. 1949. a. $7. Edison Electric Institute, Electric Power Survey Committee, 1111 19th St. N.W., Washington, DC 20036. Ed. Carl Tobie. charts. illus. stat. circ. 4,000.
Former titles: Electric Power Survey (ISSN 0190-5619); Semi-Annual Electric Power Survey (ISSN 0190-5589)

338.4 UK
ANNUAL STATISTICAL SURVEY OF THE ELECTRONICS INDUSTRY. a. 65p. National Economic Development Office, Millbank Tower, Millbank St., London S.W.1, England (Avail. from H.M.S.O., c/o Liaison Officer, Atlantic House, Holborn Viaduct, London EC1P 1BN, England) illus. stat.

621.38 IT
ANNUARIO DI ELETTRONICA. 1978. a. L.20000. B P T Editori, Via Flavia 104, 00187 Rome, Italy. Ed. Pier Roberto Pais. adv. circ. 10,000.
Formerly: Elettronica.

683.83 US ISSN 0066-5401
APPLIANCE TECHNICAL CONFERENCE. PREPRINTS. a. Institute of Electrical and Electronics Engineers, Inc., 445 Hoes Lane, Piscataway, NJ 08854.
Appliances and equipment

621.38 US ISSN 0066-5533
APPLIED SOLID STATE SCIENCE; advances in materials and device research. 1969. irreg., vol. 6, 1976. price varies. Academic Press, Inc., 111 Fifth Ave., New York, NY 10003. Ed. R. Wolfe. (also avail. in microfiche)
Electronics

621.3 AG ISSN 0066-7277
ARGENTINA. OFICINA SECTORIAL DE DESARROLLO DE ENERGIA. ANUARIOS ESTADISTICOS: COMBUSTIBLE.* 1961. a. free. Oficina Sectorial de Desarrollo de Energia, Departamento de Informacion e Investigacion Aplicada, Av. Julio A. Roca 651, Sector 31, Buenos Aires, Argentina.

621.3 AG ISSN 0066-7285
ARGENTINA. OFICINA SECTORIAL DE DESARROLLO DE ENERGIA. ANUARIOS ESTADISTICOS. ENERGIA ELECTRICA.* 1961. a. free. Oficina Sectorial de Desarrollo de Energia, Departamento de Informacion e Investigacion Aplicada, Av. Julio A. Roca 651, Sector 31, Buenos Aires, Argentina.

ELECTRICITY AND ELECTRICAL ENGINEERING

621.3   AT
ASIA ELECTRONICS CONFERENCE.
PROCEEDINGS. no. 8, 1975. irreg. Aus.$1.50.
Asia Electronics Union, Melbourne, Vic., Australia.

621.3   US   ISSN 0571-3218
ASILOMAR CONFERENCE ON CIRCUITS AND
SYSTEMS. CONFERENCE RECORD. 1967. a.
$15.-$20 (University of Santa Clara) Western
Periodicals Co., 13000 Raymer St, North
Hollywood, CA 91605. (Co-sponsor: Naval Post-
Graduate School) Eds. Shu-Park Chan, S. R. Parker.

537   621.3   IT   ISSN 0066-9822
ASSOCIAZIONE ELETTROTECNICA ED
ELETTRONICA ITALIANA. RENDICONTI
DELLA RIUNIONE ANNUALE. 1926. a. price
varies. Associazione Elettrotecnica ed Elettronica
Italiana, Viale Monza, 259, 20126 Milan, Italy. circ.
1,200.

621.31   665.7   AT
AUSTRALIA. BUREAU OF STATISTICS.
ECONOMIC CENSUSES: ELECTRICITY AND
GAS ESTABLISHMENTS, DETAILS OF
OPERATIONS. 1968. irreg. free. Australian Bureau
of Statistics, Box 10, Belconnen, A.C.T. 2616,
Australia. stat. circ. 2,000.

AUTOMOBILE ELECTRONIC EQUIPMENT. see
TRANSPORTATION — Automobiles

621.3   US
AUTOTESTCON. 1965. a. price varies. Institute of
Electrical and Electronics Engineers, Inc.,
Aerospace and Electronic Systems Society, 445
Hoes Lane, Piscataway, NJ 08854.
Formerly: Automatic Support Systems
Symposium for Advanced Maintainability.
Proceedings (ISSN 0067-2491)

621.35   US
BATTERY REPLACEMENT DATA BOOK. 1972. a.
$2.80. ‡ Battery Council International, 111 E.
Wacker Dr., Chicago, IL 60601. illus. circ. 400,000.

621.3   001.6   US
BENCHMARK PAPERS IN ELECTRICAL
ENGINEERING & COMPUTER SCIENCE.
(Each vol. has distinctive title) 1973. irreg., vol.23,
1980. price varies. Dowden, Hutchinson & Ross,
Inc., 523 Sarah St., Stroudsburg, PA 18360 (Dist. by
Academic Press, Inc., 111 Fifth Ave., New York,
NY 10003) Ed. John B. Thomas.

621.3   YU
BEOGRADSKI UNIVERZITET.
ELEKTROTEHNICKI FAKULTET.
PUBLIKACIJE. SERIJA: ELEKTRONIKA,
TELEKOMUNIKACIJE, AUTOMATIKA. (Text in
English) 1971, no. 53/58. irreg. free or exchange
basis. Univerzitet u Beogradu, Elektrotehnicki
Fakultet, Studentski trg 1, Belgrade, Yugoslavia. Ed.
Milic Stojic. bk. rev. illus. circ. 1,000. Indexed:
Ref.Zh.
Continues: Belgrade. Univerzitet. Elektrotehnicki
Fakultet. Publikacije. Serija: Telekomunikacije i
Elektronika (ISSN 0409-0179)

BRENNSTOFFSTATISTIK DER
WAERMEKRAFTWERKE FUER DIE
OEFFENTLICHE
ELEKTRIZITAETSVERSORGUNG IN
OESTERREICH. see *PUBLIC
ADMINISTRATION*

621.38   US
BROWN BOVERI SYMPOSIA. PROCEEDINGS.
1969. irreg., latest, 1978. Plenum Press, 233 Spring
St., New York, NY 10013.

338.4   CN   ISSN 0527-5504
CANADA. STATISTICS CANADA.
MANUFACTURERS OF ELECTRIC WIRE AND
CABLE/FABRICANTS DE FILS ET DE
CABLES ELECTRIQUES. (Catalogue 43-209)
(Text in English and French) 1960. a.
Can.$4.50($5.40) Statistics Canada, Publications
Distribution, Ottawa, Ont. K1A 0V7, Canada. (also
avail. in microform from MML)

621.3   CN   ISSN 0576-5161
CANADIAN ELECTRICAL ASSOCIATION.
ENGINEERING AND OPERATING DIVISION.
TRANSACTIONS. 1962. a. Can.$50. Canadian
Electrical Association - Association Canadienne de
l'Electricite, 1 Westmount Sq, Suite 580, Montreal,
Que. H3Z 2P9, Canada.

621.38   CN
CANADIAN ELECTRONICS ENGINEERING
COMPONENTS AND EQUIPMENT
DIRECTORY. 1957. a. Can.$10. Maclean-Hunter
Ltd., 481 University Ave., Toronto, Ont. M5W
1A7, Ont., Canada. Ed. Ernie Welling.
Former titles: Canadian Electronics Engineering
Annual Buyers' Guide and Catalog Directory (ISSN
0075-5990); Key to Electronics Engineering
Purchasing in Canada.

CANADIAN HARDWARE, ELECTRICAL &
BUILDING SUPPLY DIRECTORY. see
BUILDING AND CONSTRUCTION

338.4   RH   ISSN 0069-147X
CENTRAL AFRICAN POWER CORPORATION.
ANNUAL REPORT AND ACCOUNTS. 1956. a.
‡ Central African Power Corporation, Box 630,
Club Chambers, Baker Ave., Salisbury, Zimbabwe.
index.

621.38   629.286   FR
CHAMBRE SYNDICALE NATIONALE DES
ELECTRICIENS ET SPECIALISTES DE
L'AUTOMOBILE. ANNUAIRE. 1948. a. 50 F.
Electricite Automobile, 59, rue du Faubourg
Poissonniere, 75009-Paris, France. Ed. Pierre
Carrette.

683.8   621.9   CH
CHINA (REPUBLIC). MACHINERY AND
ELECTRICAL APPARATUS INDUSTRY
YEARBOOK/CHUNG-HUA MIN KUO CHI CHI
YU TIEN KUNG CHI TSAI NIEN CHIEN. (Text
in Chinese and English) a. World Enterprise, 247
San Ming Road, Tai - Chung, Taiwan, Republic of
China.

621.38   CH
CHINA, REPUBLIC. TELECOMMUNICATION
LABORATORIES. TECHNICAL REPORTS.
(Text in Chinese and English) 1971. irreg. free.
Telecommunications Laboratories, Ministry of
Communications, Box 71, Chung-Li, Taiwan,
Republic of China. abstr. circ. 500.
Formerly: China, Republic. Telecommunication
Laboratories. Quarterly Report.

621.3   UY
COMISION DE INTEGRACION ELECTRICA
REGIONAL. DIRECTORIO DEL SECTOR
ELECTRICO. 1968. irreg.; 1978, no. 6. price varies.
Comision de Integracion Electrica Regional, Bulevar
Artigas 996, Montevideo, Uruguay.

621.39   BL
COMISSAO DE INTEGRACAO ELETRICA
REGIONAL. INFORME DO COORDENADOR
TECNICO; operacao e mantencao dos sistemas
eletricos nos paises membros da CIER. (Text in
Spanish, Portuguese) a. Comisso de Integracao
Eletrica Regional, Sub-Comite de Operacao e
Mantencao de Sistemas Eletricos - Comision de
Integracion Eletrica Regional, Sao Paulo, Brazil.
illus.

537   665.5   BE
COMITE DE CONTROLE DE L'ELECTRICITE ET
DU GAZ. RAPPORT ANNUEL. 1956. a. free.
Comite de Controle de l'Electricite et du Gaz -
Controle Comite voor de l'Electriceit en het Gas,
Boulevard du Regent 8, 1000 Brussels, Belgium.
charts. illus.

COMITE INTERNATIONAL DES POIDS ET
MESURES. COMITE CONSULTATIF
D'ELECTRICITE. (RAPPORT ET ANNEXES)
see *METROLOGY AND STANDARDIZATION*

621.3   US   ISSN 0381-095X
COMMUNICATOR; a TV technicians newsletter.
1958. irreg. ‡ Radio Corporation of America,
Technical Services Training, 600 North Sherman
Drive, Indianapolis, IN 46201. Ed. C. W. Mitchell.
illus. circ. 15,000. (looseleaf format)
Supersedes: R C A Plain Talk and Technical Tips
(ISSN 0048-6582)

621.3   BL
COMPANHIA DE ELECTRICIDADE DE
BRASILIA. RELATORIO DAS ATIVIDADES.
free. Companhia de Eletricidade de Brasilia, Quadra
04-Bloco A, Lotes 106 e 136, Brasilia-DF, Brazil.
charts. illus. circ. 3,000. (back issues avail)

537   BL
COMPANHIA PAULISTA DE FORCA E LUZ.
ASSESSORIA DE PLANEJAMENTO E GESTAO
EMPRESARIAL. RELATORIO ESTATISTICO
ANUAL; acompanhamento do mercado de energia
eletrica. a. Companhia Paulista de Forca e Luz,
Assessoria de Planejamento e Gestao Empresarial,
Avenida Angelica, 2565, Sao Paulo, Brazil. charts.
illus. stat.
Continues: Companhia Paulista de Forca e Luz.
Acompanhamento de Mercado.

621.31   BL
COMPANHIA PAULISTA DE FORCA E LUZ.
BOLETIM ESTATISTICO; acompanhamento do
mercado de energia eletrica. irreg. Companhia
Paulista de Forca e Luz, Assessoria de Planejamento
e Gestao Empresarial, Av. Angelica 2565, Sao
Paulo, Brazil. charts.

338.7   VE
COMPANIA ANONIMA DE ADMINISTRACION
Y FOMENTO ELECTRICO. INFORME ANUAL.
a. Compania Anonima de Administracion y
Fomento Electrico, Caracas, Venezuela. illus.

COMPUTER-AIDED DESIGN OF ELECTRONIC
CIRCUITS. see *COMPUTER TECHNOLOGY
AND APPLICATIONS*

621.319   621   US   ISSN 0084-9162
CONFERENCE ON ELECTRICAL INSULATION
AND DIELECTRIC PHENOMENA. ANNUAL
REPORT. 1952? a. $25. National Academy of
Sciences, Conference on Electrical Insulation and
Dielectric Phenomena, 2101 Constitution Ave.,
N.W., Washington, DC 20418.

621.31   US   ISSN 0069-875X
CONFERENCE ON UNDERGROUND
TRANSMISSION AND DISTRIBUTION.
RECORD. Variant title: Underground Transmission
and Distribution Conference. Record. a. $16.
Institute of Electrical and Electronics Engineers,
Inc., Power Engineering Society, 445 Hoes Lane,
Piscataway, NJ 08854.
Power transmission

621.32   BL
CONSUMO INDUSTRIAL DE ENERGIA
ELETRICA DO ESTADO DA BAHIA. 1975. a.
free. Secretaria das Minas e Energia, Coordenacao
de Energia, Av. Centro Administrativo da Bahia,
Av. Luiz Viana Filho, Salvador - Bahia, Brazil. stat.

621.3   US
CONVENTION OF ELECTRICAL AND
ELECTRONICS ENGINEERS IN ISRAEL.
PROCEEDINGS. 10th, 1977. a? Institute of
Electrical and Electronics Engineers, Inc., 445 Hoes
Lane, Piscataway, NJ 08854.

CONVERGENCE: INTERNATIONAL
COLLOQUIUM ON AUTOMOTIVE
ELECTRONIC TECHNOLOGY.
PROCEEDINGS. see *TRANSPORTATION —
Automobiles*

621.3   US   ISSN 0070-0002
CORNELL BIENNIAL ELECTRICAL
ENGINEERING CONFERENCE. 1967. biennial.
price varies (1979, $30) Cornell University, School
of Electrical Engineering, Phillips Hall, Ithaca, NY
14853.

621.38   US   ISSN 0148-7604
D A T A BOOK OF DISCONTINUED
SEMICONDUCTOR DIODES. Spine title:
Discontinued Semiconductor Diode D A T A Book.
1975. a. D.A.T.A., Inc., 45 U.S. Hwy. 46, Pine
Brook, NJ 07050.
Electronics

621.38   US   ISSN 0092-508X
D.A.T.A. BOOK OF DISCONTINUED
THYRISTORS. (Subseries of D.A.T.A. Book
Electronic Information Series) 1969. a. $15.50.
D.A.T.A., Inc. - Derivation and Tabulation
Associates, 45 U.S. Hwy 46, Box 602, Pine Brook,
NJ 07058.
Electronics

ELECTRICITY AND ELECTRICAL ENGINEERING

621.38   US   ISSN 0070-2498
D A T A BOOK OF DISCONTINUED TRANSISTORS. (Subseries of D.A.T.A.Book Electronic Information Series) 1965. a. $20.50. D A T A, Inc., U.S. Hwy 46, Box 602, Pine Brook, NJ 07058.
Type numbers and parameters of worldwide transistors discontinued since 1956

D I S A INFORMATION. MEASUREMENT AND ANALYSIS. see *METROLOGY AND STANDARDIZATION*

621.3   DK
DANSK ELFORSYNING. a. Danske Elvaerkers Forening - Danish Association of Electricity Supply Undertakings, Rosenoerns Allee 9, DK-1970 Copenhagen V, Denmark. illus.
Formerly: Dansk Elvaerksstatistik (ISSN 0070-2803)

623.043   US
DIRECTORY OF DEFENSE ELECTRONIC PRODUCTS AND SERVICES: UNITED STATES SUPPLIERS. 1975. a. $20. (Electronic Industries Association) Bermont Books, 815 15 St., N.W., Washington, DC 20005. illus.

621.31   665.5   US   ISSN 0092-4970
DIRECTORY OF ELECTRIC LIGHT AND POWER COMPANIES. 1972. a. $20. Midwest Oil Register, Inc., Drawer 7248, Tulsa, OK 74105. Ed. Ross G. Sloan.

621   US
DIRECTORY OF ELECTRONIC REPRESENTATIVES. 1936. a. $10. Electronic Representatives Association, 233 E. Erie St., Suite 1002, Chicago, IL 60611. Ed. Janet Hipp. adv. circ. 5,000(controlled)

537.5   NZ
DIRECTORY OF ELECTRONICS & INSTRUMENTATION. 1973. a. NZ.$10. Associated Group Media Ltd., Box 28349, Auckland 5, New Zealand.

621.3   JA
E B G. (Electronics Buyers Guide) 1968. a. $46. Dempa Publications Inc., 1-11-15 Higashi Gotanda, Shinagawa-ku, Tokyo 141, Japan (U. S. address: 380 Madison Ave., New York, NY 10017) adv.
Electronics

621.3   UK
E C A YEAR BOOK DESK DIARY. 1918. a. £4. Electrical Contractors' Association, 34 Palace Court, London W2 4HY, England. adv. circ. 4,000.
Formerly: Electrical Contractors' Year Book (ISSN 0070-9654)

338.4   US   ISSN 0093-3236
E C & M'S ELECTRICAL PRODUCTS YEARBOOK. (Electrical Construction and Maintenance) a. $2.50 (free to qualified personnel) McGraw Hill Publications Co., 1221 Avenue of the Americas, New York, NY 10020. Ed. William Novak. adv. illus. circ. 37,000. Key Title: Electrical Products Yearbook.

621.38   US   ISSN 0423-9938
E E M. (Electronic Engineers Master) 1957. a. $30. United Technical Publications, Inc., 645 Stewart Ave., Garden City, NY 11530. Ed. W. J. Evanzia. adv. circ. 85,993.

621.3   US
EASTERN PENNSYLVANIA, SOUTHERN DELAWARE AND EASTERN MARYLAND BLUE BOOK. 1977. a. $15. Gleason Publishing Co. Inc., Box 303, 162 Great Rd., Acton, MA 01720. index. circ. 15,000.

621.31   CN   ISSN 0070-8275
EATON ELECTRONICS RESEARCH LABORATORIES. TECHNICAL REPORT.* irreg. McGill University, Department of Physics, Eaton Lab., Rm 115, P.O. Box 6070, Station A, Montreal H3C 3G1, Que., Canada.
Electronics

621.31   338.4   US
EDISON ELECTRIC INSTITUTE. STATISTICAL YEARBOOK OF THE ELECTRIC UTILITY INDUSTRY. 1928. a. $15. Edison Electric Institute, Statistical Committee, 1111 19th St. N.W., Washington, DC 20036. Ed. J. David Bailey. charts. stat. circ. 3,200.

621.31   363.62   JA   ISSN 0420-9397
ELECTRIC POWER INDUSTRY IN JAPAN/ NIHON NO DENKI JIGYO. (Text in English) 1959. a. exchange basis. Overseas Electrical Industry Survey Institute - Kaigai Denryoku Chosakai, 1-1-13 Shinbashi, Minato-ku, Tokyo 105, Japan.

621.313   US
ELECTRIC UTILITY GENERATION PLANBOOK. Variant title: Power's Electric Utility Generation Planbook. 1972. a. $10. (McGraw-Hill Inc.) McGraw-Hill Publications Co., 1221 Avenue of Americas, New York, NY 10020. Ed. Bob Schwieger. adv. charts. illus. stat. circ. 17,000. (back issues avail)

621.3   UK   ISSN 0070-9638
ELECTRICAL AND ELECTRONIC TRADER YEAR BOOK. 1965. biennial. £5. I P C Electrical-Electronic Press Ltd., Dorset House, Stamford Street, London, SE1 9LU, England. Ed. Tony Hewitt-Hulin. adv. bk. rev.
Formerly: Wireless and Electrical Trader Year Book.

621.3   UK   ISSN 0070-9646
ELECTRICAL AND ELECTRONICS TRADES DIRECTORY. 1883. a. £25. Peter Peregrinus Ltd., Box 26, Hitchin, Herts. SG5 1SA, England (U.S. address: IEEE Service Center, 445 Hoes Lane, Piscataway, NJ 08854) adv.
Formerly: Electrical Trades Directory.

621.3   CN
ELECTRICAL BLUE BOOK. 1979. a. Can.$20. Kerrwil Publications Ltd., 20 Holly St., Suite 201, Toronto, Ont. M4S 2E6, Canada. circ. 7,000.

621.3   US
ELECTRICAL BLUE BOOK-DIRECTORY OF NEW YORK & NORTHERN NEW JERSEY'S ELECTRICAL MARKET. 1975. a. $15. Gleason Publishing Co. Inc., Box 303, 162 Great Road, Acton, MA 01720. index. circ. 15,000. (back issues avail.)

621.3   US
ELECTRICAL BUYER'S GUIDE. a. $20. A M C Publisher, 2506 Gross Point Rd., Evanston, IL 60201. Ed. D. Audrey Bond. adv. bk. rev. circ. 60,000. (also avail. in microfilm)

621.31   US
ELECTRICAL CONTACTS. Represents: Holm Seminar on Electrical Contacts. Proceedings. 1953. a. $35. Illinois Institute of Technology, Department of Electrical Engineering, 127 Siegel Hall, Chicago, IL 60616. illus.

621.31   US   ISSN 0070-9697
ELECTRICAL ELECTRONICS INSULATION CONFERENCE. RECORD. 1958. biennial. price varies. National Electrical Manufacturers Association, 2101 L St. N.W., Washington, DC 20037. (Co-Sponsor: Institute of Electrical and Electronic Engineers)
Formerly: Electrical Insulation Technical Conference. Record.

621.3   US
ELECTRICAL ENGINEERING AND ELECTRONICS; a series of reference books and textbooks. 1977. irreg., vol. 9, 1979. Marcel Dekker, Inc., 270 Madison Ave., New York, NY 10016. index.

621.3   US   ISSN 0070-9719
ELECTRICAL PROCESS HEATING IN INDUSTRY. TECHNICAL CONFERENCE. RECORD. Variant title: Conference on Electric Process Heating in Industry. Conference Record. biennial. $10. Institute of Electrical and Electronics Engineers, Inc., Industry Applications Society, 445 Hoes Lane, Piscataway, NJ 08854.

621.3   US
ELECTRICAL WORLD DIRECTORY OF ELECTRIC UTILITIES. 88th edt. 1979-80. a. $125. McGraw-Hill Publications Co., 1221 Ave. of the Americas, New York, NY 10020. Ed. Eileen Macdonald. stat.

338   537   FR   ISSN 0070-9735
ELECTRICITE DE FRANCE. RAPPORT D'ACTIVITE. a. Electricite de France, Service de l'Information et Relations Publiques, 2 rue Louis Murat, 75008 Paris, France.

338   537   FR   ISSN 0070-9751
ELECTRICITE DE FRANCE. STATISTIQUES DE LA PRODUCTION ET DE LA CONSOMMATION. a. Electricite de France, Direction de la Production et du Transport, Departement Statistiques, 6 rue de Messine, 75008 Paris, France.

537.5   UK   ISSN 0070-976X
ELECTRICITY SUPPLY HANDBOOK. 1948. a. £6. I P C Electrical Electronic Press Ltd., Dorset House, Stamford St., London SE1 9LU, England. Ed. Alan Jack. adv. circ. 9,500.

621.3   SI
ELECTRO. (Text Mainly in English; occasionally in Chinese) 1973. biennial. free contr. circ. Electrical & Electronic Engineering Society, Ngee Ann Technical College, 535, Clementi Road, Singapore 21, Singapore. illus.

621.3   FR
ELECTRO. ANNUAIRE; electricite, electronique, electromenager. a. 55 F. Societe Nouvelle d'Editions Publicitaires, 16, Av. de Verdun, 75010 Paris, France. adv. illus. index.

621.3   US
ELECTROMECHANICAL BENCH REFERENCE. 1974. a. included in subscr. to monthly Electrical Apparatus. Barks Publications, Inc., 400 N. Michigan Ave., Chicago, IL 60611. adv.

537.5   US
ELECTRON SPECTROSCOPY: THEORY, TECHNIQUES AND APPLICATIONS. 1977. irreg. price varies. Academic Press, Inc., 111 Fifth Ave., New York, NY 10003 (And Berkeley Square House, London W. 1, England) Eds. C. R. Brundle, A. D. Baker.

621.38   US   ISSN 0569-5503
ELECTRONIC COMPONENTS CONFERENCE. PROCEEDINGS. a. Institute of Electrical and Electronics Engineers, Inc., 445 Hoes Lane, Piscataway, NJ 08854.
Formerly: Electronics Components Conference. Record (ISSN 0070-9832)

621.38   US   ISSN 0145-0085
ELECTRONIC CONNECTOR STUDY GROUP. ANNUAL CONNECTOR SYMPOSIUM. PROCEEDINGS. 1968. a. $25. Electronic Connector Study Group, Inc., Box 167, Fort Washington, PA 19034. charts. illus. circ. 1,500. (also avail. in microfilm) Indexed: Ca.
Electronics

ELECTRONIC DESIGN'S GOLD BOOK. see *BUSINESS AND ECONOMICS — Trade And Industrial Directories*

621.38   US
ELECTRONIC EXPERIMENTER'S HANDBOOK. 1959. a. $2.50. Ziff-Davis Publishing Co., 1 Park Ave., New York, NY 10016. Ed. Arthur P. Salsberg. adv. illus. tr.lit.
Electronics

ELECTRONIC INDUSTRY TELEPHONE DIRECTORY. see *BUSINESS AND ECONOMICS — Trade And Industrial Directories*

621.38   338.4   US   ISSN 0070-9867
ELECTRONIC MARKET DATA BOOK. 1956. a. $50 to non-members; members $25. Electronic Industries Association, 2001 Eye St. N.W., Washington, DC 20006. cum.index.
Formerly: Electronic Industries Yearbook.

621.38   338   US   ISSN 0070-9875
ELECTRONIC NEWS FINANCIAL FACT BOOK AND DIRECTORY. 1962. a. $90. Fairchild Books (Subsidiary of: Fairchild Publications Inc.) 7 East 12th St., New York, NY 10003. Ed. Robin Feldman. circ. 2,000. (back issues avail.)

621.3   CN
ELECTRONIC PROCUREMENT INDEX FOR CANADA. a. Southam Communications Ltd., 1450 Don Mills Rd., Don Mills, Ont. M3B 2X7, Canada. Ed. Ron Glen. adv.

ELECTRONIC REPRESENTATIVES DIRECTORY. see *BUSINESS AND ECONOMICS — Trade And Industrial Directories*

ELECTRICITY AND ELECTRICAL ENGINEERING

620.7 621.38 629.1   US   ISSN 0531-6863
ELECTRONICS AND AEROSPACE SYSTEMS CONVENTION. E A S C O N RECORD. irreg., latest 1975. $32. Institute of Electrical and Electronics Engineers, Inc., 445 Hoes Lane, Piscataway, NJ 08854. illus. Key Title: E.A.S.C.O.N. Convention Record.

621.38 670   US   ISSN 0090-5291
ELECTRONICS BUYERS' GUIDE. 1945. a. $30. (McGraw-Hill Inc.) McGraw-Hill Publications Co., 1221 Ave. Americas, New York, NY 10020. Ed. Regina Hera. adv. stat. circ. 30,000 (controlled) (also avail. in microfilm)

621.38   US   ISSN 0424-8384
ELECTRONICS HOBBYIST. 1963. a. $1.95. Davis Publications, Inc., 380 Lexington Ave., New York, NY 10017. Ed. Julian S. Martin. adv. bk. rev. tr.lit.

537.5   JA   ISSN 0070-9913
ELECTRONICS IN JAPAN. (Text in English) 1959. a. $20. Electronics Association of Japan, 1 Toden Kyukan 1-chome, Shinbashi, Minato-ku, Tokyo 105, Japan. Ed. Mojiro Machida. adv. circ. 7,000.

ELECTRONICS NEW PRODUCT DIRECTORY. see BUSINESS AND ECONOMICS — Marketing And Purchasing

537.5   US
ELECTRONICS THEORY HANDBOOK. a. $1.95. Davis Publications Inc., 380 Lexington Ave., New York, NY 10017. Ed. Julian Martin. adv.

338.4   FR
ELECTRONIQUE FRANCAISE. 1971. a. free. Federation Nationale des Industries Electroniques, 11 rue Hamelin, 75783 Paris 16, France. stat. circ. 200.

621.3   GW
ELEKTRO-INDUSTRIE; Elektronik und Ihre Helfer. 1952. a. DM.38. Industrieschau-Verlagsgesellschaft, Berliner Allee 8, 6100 Darmstadt, W. Germany (B.R.D.) adv. charts. illus. circ. 7,000.

537.5   GW   ISSN 0070-9956
ELEKTRO-JAHR; eine Neuheiten-Dokumentation der Elektro-Industrie. 1957. a. DM.14. Vogel-Verlag KG, Max-Planck-Str. 7, Postfach 6740, 8700 Wuerzburg 1, W. Germany (B.R.D.) Ed. Ernst Pohl. adv. circ. 12,200.

621.3   DK
ELEKTRONIKINDUSTRIENS INDKOEBSBOG. 1974. a. Kr.150.30. Teknisk Forlag A-S, Skelbaeksgade 4, DK-1717 Copenhagen V, Denmark. adv. circ. 3,000.

621   UR
ELEKTROTECHNIKA IR MECHANIKA. (Text in Lithuanian or Russian; summaries in the other language) 1963. irreg. Aukstuju Mokyklu Mokslo Darbai, Vilnius, U. S. S. R. illus.
   Mechanika.

537   UR
ELEKTROVYMIRIUVALNA TEKHNIKA. (Subseries of: Kharkivskyi Politekhnichnyi Instytut. Vestnik) 1973. irreg. 0.53 Rub. Kharkivskyi Politekhnichnyi Instytut, Ul. Frunze, 21, Kharkov, U.S.S.R. illus.

621.3   HO
EMPRESA NACIONAL DE ENERGIA ELECTRICA. DATOS ESTADISTICOS. a. Empresa Nacional de Energia Electrica, Departamento de Planificacion Economica, Tegucigalpa, Honduras. stat.

621.32   IV
ENERGIE ELECTRIQUE DE LA COTE D'IVOIRE. RAPPORT ANNUEL. Variant title: Energie Electrique de la Cote d'Ivoire. Compte Rendu de Gestion. a. free. Energie Electrique de la Cote d'Ivoire, Boite Postale 1345, Abidjan, Ivory Coast.

ENERGY RESOURCES CONSERVATION BOARD. CUMULATIVE ANNUAL STATISTICS: ALBERTA ELECTRIC INDUSTRY. see ENERGY

621.3 388.3   BL
ESTADO DE SAO PAULO; AMALISE E ACOMPANHEMENTO DO MERCADO DE ENERGIA ELECTRICA DOS AUTOPRODUCTORES. irreg. Centrais Eletricas, Setor de Estudos de Mercado, Diretoria de Distribuicao, Sao Paulo, Brazil.

621.38 338.4   UK
EUROPEAN ELECTRONIC COMPONENT DISTRIBUTOR DIRECTORY. 1979. a. £30($75) Mackintosh Publications Ltd., Mackintosh House, Napier Rd., Luton, Beds. LU1 1RG, England. adv.
   Formerly: European Distributor Directory (ISSN 0143-2958)

EUROPEAN ORGANISATION FOR CIVIL AVIATION ELECTRONICS. GENERAL ASSEMBLY. ANNUAL REPORT. see AERONAUTICS AND SPACE FLIGHT

537.244   US
FERROELECTRICITY AND RELATED PHENOMENA. a. price varies. Gordon and Breach Science Publishers, One Park Ave., New York, NY 10016. Ed. I. Lefkowitz, G. W. Taylor.

621.3   FR
FRANCE. DIRECTION DES AFFAIRES EXTERIEURES ET DE LA COOPERATION. RAPPORT D'ACTIVITE-ELECTRICITE DE FRANCE. irreg. Direction des Affaires Exterieures et de la Cooperation, 68 rue du Faubourg St. Honore, 75008 Paris, France. illus.

537   JA
FUJIKURA TECHNICAL REVIEW. (Text in English) 1969. a. free. Fujikura Cable Works Co., Ltd. - Fujikura Densen K.K., 1-5-1 Kiba, Koto-ku, Tokyo 135, Japan. charts. illus.

GREAT BRITAIN. DEPARTMENT OF ENERGY. ELECTRICITY: ANNUAL REPORT. see ENERGY

621.3   UK
GREAT BRITAIN. DEPARTMENT OF ENERGY. ELECTRICITY: REPORT OF THE SECRETARY OF STATE FOR ENERGY. a. Department of Energy, Thames House, South Millbank, London SW1P 4Q (Avail. from H.M.S.O., c/o Liaison Officer, Atlantic House, London EC1P 1BW, England)

621.3   UK   ISSN 0307-1146
GREAT BRITAIN. ELECTRICITY COUNCIL. REPORT AND ACCOUNTS. 1958-59. a. free (Annual report); £1.80 (Accounts & Statistics) Electricity Council, 30 Millbank St., London SW1P 4RO, England (Avail. from H.M.S.O., c/o Liaison Officer, Atlantic House, Holborn Viaduct, London EC1P 1BN, England) illus. circ. 23,000.

621.38   II
GUIDE TO ELECTRONICS INDUSTRY IN INDIA. (Text in English) no. 2, 1974. irreg. Rs.50($10) per no. Statistics Investigations Bureau, 4-A Naaz Bldg., Lamington Rd., Bombay 400004, India. Ed. S. Swarn. illus.
   Continues: Guide to Radio Electronics & Components Trade and Industry in India (ISSN 0533-540X)

621.38 537.5   US   ISSN 0072-9795
HANDBOOK OF ELECTRONIC MATERIALS. 1971. irreg., 1972, vol. 9. price varies. Plenum Publishing Corp., I.F.I.--Plenum Data Co., 233 Spring St., New York, NY 10013.
   Electronics

621.3   JA   ISSN 0439-3465
HOKKAIDO UNIVERSITY. RESEARCH INSTITUTE OF APPLIED ELECTRICITY. MONOGRAPH SERIES. (Text in English) 1950. a. exchange basis. Hokkaido University, Research Institute of Applied Electricity - Hokkaido Daigaku Oyo Denki Kenkyusho, Nishi-6-chome, Kita-12-jo, Kita-ku, Sapporo 060, Japan.

621.38   UK   ISSN 0073-4136
HYBRID MICROELECTRONICS SYMPOSIUM. (PAPERS)* irreg. 1968, 3rd. price varies. International Society for Hybrid Microelectronics, c/o David Boswell, 20 Hale Lane, London NW 7, England.
   Title Varies: Symposium on Hybrid Microelectronics.
   Electronics

621.3   UK
I E E CONFERENCE PUBLICATION SERIES. 1962. irreg. (Institution of Electrical Engineers) Peter Peregrinus Ltd., Box 26, Hitchin, Herts. SG5 1SA, England (U.S. address: IEEE Service Center, 445 Hoes Lane, Piscataway, NJ 08854)

621.3   UK
I E E CONTROL ENGINEERING SERIES. 1976. irreg. (Institution of Electrical Engineers) Peter Peregrinus Ltd., Box 26, Hitchin, Herts. SG5 1SA, England (U.S. address: IEEE Service Center, 445 Hoes Lanes, Piscataway, NJ 08854)

621.3   US
I E E E INTERNATIONAL CONFERENCE ON ACOUSTICS, SPEECH AND SIGNAL PROCESSING. CONFERENCE RECORD. 4th, 1979. a. $30. Institute of Electrical and Electronics Engineers, Inc., 445 Hoes Lane, Piscataway, NJ 08854.

621.3   US   ISSN 0073-9138
I E E E INTERNATIONAL CONVENTION AND EXHIBITION. RECORD.* a. Institute of Electrical and Electronics Engineers, Inc., 445 Hoes Lane, Piscataway, NJ 08854.

621.38   US   ISSN 0090-7294
I E E E INTERNATIONAL CONVENTION DIGEST.* Cover title: I E E E Intercon Digest. (Synopses of papers presented at the international convention) a. $9. Institute of Electrical and Electronics Engineers, Inc, 445 Hoes Lane, Piscataway, NJ 08854. illus.

621.38   US
I E E E INTERNATIONAL SYMPOSIUM ON CIRCUITS AND SYSTEMS. PROCEEDINGS. a. $40. Institute of Electrical and Electronics Engineers, Inc, 445 Hoes Lane, Piscataway, NJ 08854.
   Supersedes: I E E International Symposium on Circuit Theory. Symposium Digest. Summaries of Papers (ISSN 0579-4234)
   Electronics

621.3   US
I E E E INTERNATIONAL SYMPOSIUM ON ELECTRICAL INSULATION. CONFERENCE RECORD. a. Institute of Electrical and Electronics Engineers, Inc., 445 Hoes Lane, Piscataway, NJ 08854. charts.

621.3   US   ISSN 0073-9146
I E E E MEMBERSHIP DIRECTORY.* 1966. a. $7. to members; $30. to non-members. Institute of Electrical and Electronics Engineers, Inc., 445 Hoes Lane, Piscataway, NJ 08854.

621.366   US   ISSN 0099-121X
I E E E/O S A CONFERENCE ON LASER ENGINEERING AND APPLICATIONS. DIGEST OF TECHNICAL PAPERS. biennial. price varies. Institute of Electrical and Electronics Engineers, Inc., Quantum Electronics Council, 445 Hoes Lane, Piscataway, NJ 08854. (Co-sponsor: Optical Society of America)
   Formerly: Conference on Laser Engineering and Applications (ISSN 0069-858X); Supersedes: Electron, Ion and Laser Beam Technology Conference. Record (ISSN 0070-9808)

621.3   US   ISSN 0073-9154
I E E E POWER ENGINEERING SOCIETY. WINTER MEETING. PREPRINTS. a. $3 each to non-members. Institute of Electrical and Electronics Engineers, Inc., 445 Hoes Lane, Piscataway, NJ 08854.

621.3   US   ISSN 0073-9170
I E E E REGION 3 CONFERENCE. RECORD. Variant title: Southeastcon. Record. a. Institute of Electrical and Electronics Engineers, Inc., 445 Hoes Lane, Piscataway, NJ 08854.

621.3   US   ISSN 0073-9197
I E E E REGION 5 CONFERENCE. RECORD. a. $20. Institute of Electrical and Electronics Engineers, Inc., 445 Hoes Lane, Piscataway, NJ 08854.
   Formerly: Institute of Electrical and Electronics Engineers. Southwestern I E E E Conference and Exhibition. Record.

ELECTRICITY AND ELECTRICAL ENGINEERING

621.3 US
I E E E REGION 6. CONFERENCE. PROCEEDINGS. a. Institute of Electrical and Electronics Engineers, Inc., 445 Hoes Lane, Piscataway, NJ 08854.
Supersedes: I E E E Region 6. Technical Conference. Record (ISSN 0073-9189)

621.31 US
I E E E RURAL ELECTRIC POWER CONFERENCE. PAPERS PRESENTED. 1956. a. Institute of Electrical and Electronics Engineers, Inc., Industry Applications Society, Rural Power Committee, 445 Hoes Lane, Piscataway, NJ 08854.

621.3 US ISSN 0073-9162
I E E E STANDARDS. irreg. Institute of Electrical and Electronics Engineers, Inc., 445 Hoes Lane, Piscataway, NJ 08854.

621.3 US ISSN 0362-4536
I E E E STUDENT PAPERS. 1975. a. $16. Institute of Electrical and Electronics Engineers, Inc., IEEE Service Center, 445 Hoes Lane, Piscataway, NJ 08865. illus.

621.3 US
I E E E VEHICULAR TECHNOLOGY GROUP. PROCEEDINGS OF THE ANNUAL CONFERENCE. vol. 26, 1976. a. $15. Institute of Electrical and Electronics Engineers, Inc., 445 Hoes Lane, Piscataway, NJ 08854. charts. illus.

620 UK
I E E ELECTROMAGNETIC WAVES SERIES. 1976. irreg. (Institution of Electrical Engineers) Peter Peregrinus Ltd., Box 26, Hitchin, Herts. SG5 1SA, England (U.S. address: IEEE Service Center, 445 Hoes Lane, Piscataway, NJ 08854)

621.3 UK ISSN 0073-9766
I E E MONOGRAPH SERIES. 1967. irreg., no. 18, 1976. (Institution of Electrical Engineers) Peter Peregrinus Ltd., Box 26, Hitchin, Herts. SG5 1SA, England (U.S. address: IEEE Service Center, 445 Hoes Lane, Piscataway, NJ 08854)

621.3 UK
I. E. E. REPRINT SERIES. 1975. irreg. (Institution of Electrical Engineers) Peter Peregrinus Ltd., Box 26, Hitchin, Herts. SG5 1SA, England (U.S. address: IEEE Service Center, 445 Hoes Lane, Piscataway, NJ 08854) Ed. P.J.B. Clarricoats.

621.32 US ISSN 0073-5469
I E S LIGHTING HANDBOOK. 1949. irreg. $40. Illuminating Engineering Society, 345 E. 47th St., New York, NY 10017. Eds. J. E. Kaufman, Jack F. Christensen. circ. 20,000.

621.3 US ISSN 0190-0943
I T E M. (Interference Technology Engineers Master) 1971. a. $15. (Robar Industries, Inc.) R. & B Enterprises, P.O. Box 328, Plymouth Meeting, PA 19462. Ed. R.D. Goldblum. adv. bibl. charts. illus. tr.lit. index. circ. 20,000(controlled) (record)

354 II
INDIA. RURAL ELECTRIFICATION CORPORATION. ANNUAL REPORT AND STATEMENT OF ACCOUNTS. (Text in English and Hindi) 1969/70. a. Rural Electrification Corporation, D-5 N.D.S.E. Part II, Ring Rd., New Delhi 110019, India. stat.

338.7 II ISSN 0377-7340
INDIAN ELECTRONICS DIRECTORY. (Text in English) 1974. biennial; 2nd ed. 1977. Rs.40($6) Electric Component Industries Association, C-40 South Extension 11, New Delhi 110049, India.

621.3 IO
INDONESIA. DEPARTMENT OF PUBLIC WORKS AND ELECTRIC POWER. ADMINISTRATION BUREAU. ANNUAL REPORT/INDONESIA. DEPARTEMEN PEKERJAAN UMUM DAN TENAGA LISTRIK. BIRO UMUM. LAPORAN TAHUNAN. (Text in Indonesian) a. Department of Public Works and Electric Power, Administration Bureau, Jl. K. H. Hasjim Asjhari 6-12, Jakarta, Indonesia.

621.3 US ISSN 0073-733X
INDUSTRIAL AND COMMERCIAL POWER SYSTEMS AND ELECTRICAL SPACE HEATING AND AIR CONDITIONING JOINT TECHNICAL CONFERENCE. RECORD.* 1964. a. Institute of Electrical and Electronics Engineers, Inc., 445 Hoes Lane, Piscataway, NJ 08854.

338.4 FR
INDUSTRIE ELECTRONIQUE FRANCAISE. irreg. Federation Nationale des Industries Electroniques, 11 rue Hamelin, 75783 Paris 16, France. stat.

621.3 FR
INDUSTRIES ELECTRIQUES ET ELECTRONIQUES. 1972. irreg. free. Federation des Industries Electriques et Electroniques, 75783 Paris Cedex 16, 75783 Paris, France. Ed. G. Tussau. adv. charts. illus. mkt. stat. circ. 5,200. Indexed: Eng.Ind.
Formerly: Construction Electrique (ISSN 0010-6747)

621.38 YU ISSN 0033-7536
INFORMACIJE RADE KONCAR. (Text in Croatian; summaries in English, French and Russian) 1954. irreg. free. Elektrotehnicki Institut Poduzeca "Rade Koncar", Fallerovo Set. 22, Zagreb, Yugoslavia. Ed. Nenad Marinovic. bibl. charts. illus. circ. 2,500(controlled)

537 380 CR ISSN 0074-0047
INFORME DE OPERACION DE LAS PRINCIPALES EMPRESAS PRODUCTORAS Y DISTRIBUIDORAS DE ENERGIA ELECTRICA DE COSTA RICA. 1958. a. free; limited distribution. Instituto Costarricense de Electricidad, Direccion de Planificacion Electrica, P.O. Box 10032, San Jose, Costa Rica. charts. stat. index. circ. controlled.

621.3 US
INFRARED INFORMATION EXCHANGE. PROCEEDINGS. vol. 2, 1975. biennial. A G A Corporation, 550 County Ave., Secaucus, NJ 07094. Ed. Cliff Warren. charts, illus, stat.

621.3 UK
INSPEC THESAURUS. irreg. Institution of Electrical Engineers, Information Services Division, Station House, Nightingale Rd., Hitchin, Herts. SG5 1RJ, England.

621.3 PL ISSN 0032-6216
INSTYTUT ELEKTROTECHNIKI. PRACE. (Text in Polish; summaries in English, French and Russian) 1951. irreg. per no. Instytut Elektrotechniki - Electrotechnical Research Institute, Ul. Pozaryskiego 28, 04-703 Warsaw, Poland (Dist. by: Ars Polona-Ruch, Krakowskie Przedmiescie 7, 00-068 Warsaw, Poland) Ed. Wieslaw Seruga. circ. 450. Indexed: Chem.Abstr.

621.38 691 US
INSULATION/CIRCUITS DESK MANUAL; for the electrical/electronic industries. 1961. a. $25. Lake Publishing Corporation, Box 159, 700 Peterson Rd., Libertyville, IL 60048. Ed. Lincoln R. Samelson. adv. circ. 33,000. Indexed: Chem.Abstr. Eng.Ind.
Former titles: Insulation Directory/Encyclopedia; Insulation/Circuits Directory/Encyclopedia (ISSN 0074-0659).
Electronics

621.3 US
INTERNATIONAL ANTENNA AND PROPAGATION SYMPOSIUM PROGRAM AND DIGEST. a. $48. Institute of Electrical and Electronics Engineers, Inc., 345 E. 47th St., New York, NY 10017 (Subscr. to: IEEE Service Center, 445 Hoes Lane, Piscataway, NJ 08854) charts. illus. stat. (also avail. in microfiche)

621.32 FR ISSN 0074-2724
INTERNATIONAL COMMISSION ON ILLUMINATION. PROCEEDINGS. 1900. quadrennial; 1975, 18th, London. International Commission on Illumination, 52 Bd. Malesherbes, 75008 Paris, France.

621.38 US
INTERNATIONAL CONFERENCE ON ION IMPLANTATION IN SEMICONDUCTORS. PROCEEDINGS. 1971. irreg, 1st, Thousand Oaks, CA, 1970. $48. Gordon and Breach Science Publishers, 1 Park Ave., New York, NY 10016. Eds. Fred H. Eisen, Lewis T. Chatterton. bibl. illus.
Electronics

621.31 FR ISSN 0074-3151
INTERNATIONAL CONFERENCE ON LARGE HIGH VOLTAGE ELECTRIC SYSTEMS. PROCEEDINGS. (Text in French and English) 1921. biennial, 1978, 27th. price varies. International Conference on Large High Voltage Electric Systems, 112 Bd. Haussmann, 75008 Paris, France.
Formerly: International Conference on Large High Tension Electric Systems. Proceedings.
Power transmission

537.622 FR ISSN 0074-3240
INTERNATIONAL CONFERENCE ON PHYSICS OF SEMICONDUCTORS. PROCEEDINGS. (Proceedings Published by Host Countries) irreg., 1974, 20th, Stuttgart. International Union of Pure and Applied Physics, c/o J. Bok, Groupe de Physique des Solides, Ecole Normale Superieure, 24 rue l'Homond, Paris 75, France (U.S. dist.: Four Continent Book Corp., 156 Fifth Ave., New York, NY 10010)

621.3 519.3 US
INTERNATIONAL CONFERENCE ON THE THEORY AND APPLICATIONS OF DIFFERENTIAL GAMES. PROCEEDINGS.* 1969. irreg., 1st, Amherst, 1969. $6. Institute of Electrical and Electronics Engineers, Inc, 445 Hoes Lane, Piscataway, NJ 08854.

621 US
INTERNATIONAL CONFERENCE ON THERMOELECTRIC ENERGY CONVERSION. PROCEEDINGS. 2nd, 1978. irreg. Institute of Electrical and Electronics Engineers, Inc., 445 Hoes Lane, Piscataway, NJ 08854.

621.38 US ISSN 0074-4670
INTERNATIONAL ELECTRON DEVICES MEETING. ABSTRACTS. a. Institute of Electrical and Electronics Engineers, Inc., 445 Hoes Lane, Piscataway, NJ 08854.
Electronics

621.3 SZ
INTERNATIONAL ELECTROTECHNICAL COMMISSION. ANNUAIRE/INTERNATIONAL ELECTROTECHNICAL COMMISSION. HANDBOOK. (Text in English and French) a. 15 Fr. International Electrotechnical Commission, 1, rue de Varembe, 1211 Geneva 20, Switzerland (Dist. in the U.S. by: American National Standards Institute, 1430 Broadway, New York, NY 10018)

621.3 SZ ISSN 0074-4697
INTERNATIONAL ELECTROTECHNICAL COMMISSION. REPORT ON ACTIVITIES. (Text in English and French) 1961. a. price varies. International Electrotechnical Commission, 1 rue de Varembe, 1211 Geneva 20, Switzerland (Dist. in the U.S. by: American National Standards Institute, 1430 Broadway, New York, NY 10018)
Formerly: International Electrotechnical Commission. Central Office Report (ISSN 0534-9907)

621.3 US
INTERNATIONAL GEOSCIENCE ELECTRONICS SYMPOSIUM DIGEST. a. $75. Institute of Electrical and Electronics Engineers, Inc., 345 E. 47th St., New York, NY 10017 (Subscr. to: IEEE Service Center, 445 Hoes Lane, Piscataway, Nj 08854) charts. illus. stat. (also avail. in microfiche)

621.38 US
INTERNATIONAL MICROWAVE POWER INSTITUTE. TRANSACTIONS. 1973. irreg. International Microwave Power Institute, 211 E. 43rd St., Ste. 2302, New York, NY 10017. Eds. W.A.G. Voss, W. R. Tinga.

621.38 US ISSN 0074-7009
INTERNATIONAL MICROWAVE SYMPOSIUM DIGEST. a. $25. Institute of Electrical and Electronics Engineers, Inc., 445 Hoes Lane, Piscataway, NJ 08854.

INTERNATIONAL OPTICAL COMPUTING CONFERENCE. DIGEST OF PAPERS. see *COMPUTER TECHNOLOGY AND APPLICATIONS*

621.3 US ISSN 0538-9275
INTERNATIONAL QUANTUM ELECTRONICS CONFERENCE. DIGEST OF TECHNICAL PAPERS. 1968? a? Institute of Electrical and Electronics Engineers, Inc., 445 Hoes Lane, Piscataway, NJ 08854. (Co-sponsor: Optical Society of America)

621.3 US ISSN 0074-803X
INTERNATIONAL SERIES OF MONOGRAPHS IN ELECTRICAL ENGINEERING.* irreg. price varies. Pergamon Press,Inc., Maxwell House, Fairview Park, Elmsford, NY 10523 (And Headington Hill Hall, Oxford OX3 0BW, England)

537.5 US ISSN 0538-9992
INTERNATIONAL SERIES ON ELECTROMAGNETIC WAVES. 1965. irreg., 1973, vol. 17. price varies. Pergamon Press, Inc., Maxwell House, Fairview Park, Elmsford, NY 10523. index.
Formerly: International Series of Monographs on Electro- Magnetic Waves.

INTERNATIONAL SERIES ON ELECTRONICS AND INSTRUMENTATION. see *PHYSICS*

537.622 US ISSN 0074-8315
INTERNATIONAL SERIES ON SEMICONDUCTORS. 1960. irreg., 1970, vol. 10. price varies. Pergamon Press, Inc., Maxwell House, Fairview Park, Elmsford, NY 10523. index.
Formerly: International Series of Monographs on Semiconductors.

621.38 US ISSN 0074-8587
INTERNATIONAL SOLID STATE CIRCUITS CONFERENCE. DIGEST. 1954. a. $30. Institute of Electrical and Electronics Engineers, Inc., 445 Hoes Lane, Piscataway, NJ 08854.
Electronics

621.38 US ISSN 0074-8811
INTERNATIONAL SYMPOSIUM ON ELECTROMAGNETIC COMPATIBILITY. RECORD. a. $25. Institute of Electrical and Electronics Engineers Inc., 445 Hoes Lane, Piscataway, NJ 08854.

621.38 UK
INTERNATIONAL SYMPOSIUM ON RESIDUAL GASES IN ELECTRON TUBES. PROCEEDINGS. irreg., 4th, Florence, 1971. $18. Academic Press Inc. (London) Ltd., 24-28 Oval Rd, Camden Town, London, NW 1 7DX, England. Eds. T.A. Giorgi, P. della Porta. bibl. illus.
Electronics

621.3 US
INTERNATIONAL SYMPOSIUM ON SUBSCRIBER LOOP AND SERVICES. PROCEEDINGS. irreg., 2nd, 1976. Institute of Electrical and Electronics Engineers, Inc., 445 Hoes Lane, Piscataway, NJ 08854.

INTERNATIONAL SYMPOSIUM ON WIND ENERGY SYSTEMS. PROCEEDINGS. see *ENERGY*

338.39 621.31 FR ISSN 0074-9486
INTERNATIONAL UNION OF PRODUCERS AND DISTRIBUTORS OF ELECTRICAL ENERGY. (CONGRESS PROCEEDINGS) triennial, 1979, Warsaw. International Union of Producers and Distributors of Electrical Energy, 39 Ave. de Friedland, 75008 Paris, France. 1976, Vienna.

338.4 US
JAPAN FACT BOOK. (Text in English) irreg. $10. Dempa Publications, Inc, 380 Madison Ave., New York, NY 10017.

621.3 US ISSN 0075-3939
JOINT AUTOMATIC CONTROL CONFERENCE. RECORD.* a. Institute of Electrical and Electronics Engineers Inc., 445 Hoes Lane, Piscataway, NJ 08854.

621.31 US
JOINT POWER GENERATION CONFERENCE. CONFERENCE RECORD. a. Institute of Electrical and Electronics Engineers, Inc., 445 Hoes Lane, Piscataway, NJ 08854. (Co-sponsor: American Society of Mechanical Engineers) Supersedes: Joint Power Generation Technical Conference. Preprint (ISSN 0075-398X)
Power transmission

621.3 UR
KHARKOVSKII GOSUDARSTVENNYI UNIVERSITET. RADIOFIZYKA I ELEKTRONIKA. (Subseries of its: Visnyk) 1972. irreg. 2.20 Rub. (Kharkovskii Gosudarstvennyi Universitet) Izdatel'stvo Vysshaya Shkola, Kharkov, U.S.S.R. Ed. L. Stepin. illus. circ. 1,000.

621.3 GW
KONTAKTE; Information fuer Fachhandel, Werkstaetten und Techniker. 1965. irreg., approx 4/yr. free to qualified personnel. ‡ Philips GmbH, Moenckebergstr. 7, Postfach 101420, 2000 Hamburg 1, W. Germany (B.R.D.) Ed. Heinz Bahr. circ. 12,500.

621.3 SZ ISSN 0023-7949
LANDIS UND GYR MITTEILUNGEN/REVUE LANDIS ET GYR/LANDIS & GYR REVIEW. (Text and summaries in English, French and German) 1953. irreg. free. ‡ L G Z Landis und Gyr Zug AG, CH-6301 Zug, Switzerland. Ed. U. Hofmann. charts. illus. circ. 4,500(English edt.); 4,500(French edt.); 7,300(German edt.)

621.366 US
LASER APPLICATIONS. 1971. irreg. Academic Press, Inc, 111 Fifth Ave., New York, NY 10003. Ed. Monte Ross. Indexed: Chem.Abstr.

621.35 AT
LEAD BATTERY POWER. 1965. irreg. free. Australian Lead Development Association, 95 Collins St., Melbourne, Vic. 3000, Australia. Ed. Colin J. Bain. circ. 7,500.

621.3 UR
MAGNITNOIMPULSNAYA OBRABOTKA METALLOV. (Subseries of: Kharkivskyi Politeknichnyi Instytut. Vestnik) 1971. irreg. 0.55 Rub. Kharkivskyi Politekhnichnyi Instytut, Ul. Frunze, 21, Kharkov, U.S.S.R. illus.

021.38 UR
MAGNITO-POLUPROVODNIKOVYE I ELEKTROMASHINNYE ELEMENTY AVTOMATIKI. 1974. irreg. 0.52 Rub. Ryazanskii Radiotekhnicheskii Institut, Ul. Gagarina 59/1, 390024 Ryazan, U.S.S.R.

MASCHINENWELT-ELEKTROTECHNIK. see *MACHINERY*

537.5 US
MASSACHUSETTS INSTITUTE OF TECHNOLOGY. RESEARCH LABORATORY OF ELECTRONICS. R L E PROGRESS REPORT. 1946. a. free. ‡ Massachusetts Institute of Technology, Research Laboratory of Electronics, Cambridge, MA 02139. circ. 1,000.
Formerly: Massachusetts Institute of Technology. Research Laboratory of Electronics. Quarterly Progress Report (ISSN 0025-4827)

354 MF
MAURITIUS. CENTRAL ELECTRICITY BOARD. ANNUAL REPORT. a. Central Electricity Board, Curepipe, Mauritius. illus.

MECHANICAL & ELECTRICAL COST DATA. see *BUILDING AND CONSTRUCTION*

621.3 690 SA
MERKEL'S ELECTRICIAN'S MANUAL. 1979. a. R.25. Thomson Publications S.A. (Pty) Ltd., Box 8308, Johannesburg 2000, South Africa. Ed. H. Merkel. adv.

METALMECANICA; metalurgia, electricidad y electronica. see *METALLURGY*

621.38 US
MICROWAVE POWER SYMPOSIUM. PROCEEDINGS. no. 8, 1973. a., 14th., 1979, Monaco. International Microwave Power Institute, 211 E. 43rd St., Ste. 2302, New York, NY 10017.
Electronics

621.38 US
MICROWAVES PRODUCT DATA DIRECTORY. 1973. a. $15. Hayden Publishing Co., Inc., 50 Essex St., Rochelle Park, NJ 07662. adv. illus. circ. 40,021.
Electronics

537 US
MIDWEST SYMPOSIUM ON CIRCUITS AND SYSTEMS. PROCEEDINGS. 1955. a. $79.50. Western Periodicals Co., 13000 Raymer St., North Hollywood, CA 91605. (back issues avail.)
Formerly (until 1975): Midwest Symposium on Circuit Theory. Proceedings.

621.3 621.38 US
MONOGRAPHS IN ELECTRICAL AND ELECTRONIC ENGINEERING. irreg. price varies. Oxford University Press, 200 Madison Ave., New York, NY 10016 (And Ely House, 37 Dover St., London W1X 4AH, England) Eds. P. Hammond, D. Walsh.

537.6 530.4 US ISSN 0544-8417
MONOGRAPHS IN SEMICONDUCTOR PHYSICS. (Translated from Russian) 1963. irreg. price varies. Plenum Press, 233 Spring St., New York, NY 10013.

621.4 US ISSN 0095-6481
NATIONAL CONFERENCE ON POWER TRANSMISSION. PROCEEDINGS. 1974. a. $30. Illinois Institute of Technology, National Conference on Power Transmission, 10 W. 32nd St., Chicago, IL 60616. illus. circ. 500. Key Title: Proceedings of the National Conference on Power Transmission.

621.38 US ISSN 0077-4421
NATIONAL ELECTRONICS CONFERENCE. RECORD. a. National Electronics Conference, Oakbrook Exec. Plaza, 1211 W. 22nd St., Oak Brook, IL 60521.
Electronics

537.5 621.38 US
NATIONAL ELECTRONICS CONFERENCE-NATIONAL COMMUNICATIONS FORUM. PROCEEDINGS. 1944. a. $25. (National Electronics Conference) National Engineering Consortium, Inc., 1211 W. 22nd St., Oak Brook, IL 60521. index. cum.index every 5 years.
Formerly (until vol. 33, 1979): National Electronics Conference. Proceedings (ISSN 0077-4413)
Electronics

621.38 UK ISSN 0305-2257
NATIONAL ELECTRONICS REVIEW; a survey of progress in electronics. vol. 6, 1970. a. National Electronics Council, Abell House, John Islip St., London SW1P 4LN, England. Ed.Bd. adv. bibl. charts. illus.
Formerly: National Electronics Council. Review (ISSN 0047-8857)
Electronics

621.3 II
NATIONAL HYDRO ELECTRIC POWER CORPORATION. ANNUAL REPORT. (Text in English) 1976. a. National Hydro Electric Power Corporation Ltd., Manjusha, 57 Nehru Place, New Delhi 110019, India.

621.38 US ISSN 0077-5401
NATIONAL RELAY CONFERENCE. PROCEEDINGS; Relay Conference Papers. 1952. a. $10. National Association of Relay Manufacturers, Box 1649, Scottsdale, AZ 85252. (also avail. in microfilm)
Electronics

621.3 US ISSN 0077-5657
NATIONAL RURAL ELECTRIC COOPERATIVE ASSOCIATION. GOVERNMENT RELATIONS DEPARTMENT. RESEARCH DIVISION. RESEARCH PAPERS AND CIRCULARS. 1964. irreg. free. ‡ National Rural Electric Cooperative Association, Massachusetts Ave., N.W., Washington, DC 20036. Ed. M. L. DuMars. circ. 200.
Formerly: National Rural Electric Cooperative Association. Legislative Research Staff. Research Paper; Formerly: National Rural Electric Cooperative Association. Legislation and Communications Department. Research Division. Research Papers and Circulars.

ELECTRICITY AND ELECTRICAL ENGINEERING

621.3   UK
NEW ELECTRONICS' DISTRIBUTOR PRODUCT FINDER AND GUIDE. 1977. a. £8.50. Juniper Journals Ltd., 49-50 Hatton Garden, London EC1N 8XS, England. Ed. Kim Bachmann.

621.3   US   ISSN 0548-4456
NEW ENGLAND ELECTRICAL BLUE BOOK. 1957. a. $20. Gleason Publishing Co., Inc., Box 303, 162 Great Road, Acton, MA 01720. Ed. Ann M. Courtright. adv. circ. 10,480.

621.3   JA   ISSN 0037-3745
NEW NIPPON ELECTRIC TECHNICAL REVIEW/ SHIN NIPPON DENKI GIHO. (Text in Japanese; summaries in English) 1972, vol. 7. a. New Nippon Electric Company Ltd. - Shin Nippon Denki K. K., 2-9-1 Seiran, Otsu 520, Shiga, Japan. Ed. Teruo Hayashi. illus. circ. 1,700.

621.38   NZ
NEW ZEALAND ELECTRONICS REVIEW. 1967. a. National Electronics Research Council (N.Z.), Wellington, New Zealand.

621.3   NR
NIGERIA. NATIONAL ELECTRIC POWER AUTHORITY. ANNUAL REPORT AND ACCOUNTS. a. National Electric Power Authority, Electricity Headquarters, 24/25 Marina, Lagos, Nigeria. charts. illus. stat.

621.38   US   ISSN 0078-1673
NORTHEAST ELECTRONICS RESEARCH AND ENGINEERING MEETING. RECORD.* a. Institute of Electrical and Electronics Engineers, Inc., 445 Hoes Lane, Piscataway, NJ 08854.
Electronics

621.312   CN   ISSN 0078-2459
NOVA SCOTIA POWER CORPORATION. ANNUAL REPORT. 1913. a. free. ‡ Nova Scotia Power Corporation, P.O. Box 910, Halifax, N.S., Canada. circ. 4,500.

621.3   UR
NOVYE ISSLEDOVANIYA V GORNOI ELEKTROMEKHANIKE. (Subseries of: Gornyi Institut, Leningrad. Nauchnye Trudy) irreg. 0.45 Rub. Leningradskii Gornyi Institut, Leningrad, U.S.S.R. illus.

621.3   US   ISSN 0095-7143
O.T.S.: OFF-THE-SHELF CATALOG OF ELECTRO PRODUCTS. irreg. United Technical Publications, Inc., 645 Stewart Ave., Garden City, NY 11530. Key Title: O.T.S.

621.3   US   ISSN 0078-3706
OFF-SHORE TECHNOLOGY CONFERENCE. RECORD. a. Institute of Electrical and Electronics Engineers, Inc., 445 Hoes Lane, Piscataway, NJ 08854.

621.3   US
ONE HUNDRED AND ONE ELECTRONICS PROJECTS; for under $15. a. $1.95. Davis Publications, Inc., 380 Lexington Ave., New York, NY 10017. Ed. Julian Martin.

363.6   CN   ISSN 0382-2834
ONTARIO HYDRO. STATISTICAL YEARBOOK. 1971. a. ‡ Ontario Hydro, 700 University Ave., Toronto, Ont. M5G 1X6, Canada. Ed. K. B. Wilson. stat. circ. 1,500.

338.39   FR   ISSN 0474-5477
ORGANIZATION FOR ECONOMIC COOPERATION AND DEVELOPMENT. ELECTRICITY SUPPLY INDUSTRY. L'INDUSTRIE DE L'ELECTRICITE. (Text in English and French) irreg. $9. Organization for Economic Cooperation and Development, 2 rue Andre Pascal, 75775 Paris 16, France (U. S. orders to: O.E.C.D. Publications and Information Center, 1750 Pennsylvania Ave., N. W., Washington, D. C. 20006) (also avail. in microfiche)

621.3   US
P C E A ANNUAL ENGINEERING & OPERATING CONFERENCE. (Each paper published separately) a. $5 per paper. Pacific Coast Electrical Association, Inc., 1545 Wilshire Blvd., Los Angeles, CA 90017. Ed. W. E. Vaughn, Jr. tr.lit.

621.3   AT
PHILIPS REPORTER. 1968. irreg. Philips Electrical Pty. Ltd., P.O. Box 34, Artarmon, NSW 2064, Australia.

536   US
PHYSICS OF QUANTUM ELECTRONICS; proceedings of summer schools. 1974. irreg., vol. 7, 1980. price varies. Addison-Wesley Publishing Co., Advanced Book Program, Reading, MA 01867. Ed. Bd. illus. bibl. Indexed: Chem.Abstr. Sci.Abstr. Nucl.Sci.Abstr.

629   PL   ISSN 0137-6977
POLITECHNIKA CZESTOCHOWSKA. ZESZYTY NAUKOWE. NAUKI TECHNICZNE. ELEKTROTECHNIKA. (Text in Polish; summaries in English and Russian) 1969. irreg. Politechnika Czestochowska, Ul. Deglera 31, 42-200 Czestochowa, Poland (Dist. by: Ars Polona-Ruch, Krakowskie Przedmiescie 7, Warsaw, Poland) Ed. Pawel Rolicz.

621.38   PL   ISSN 0418-3614
POLITECHNIKA GDANSKA. ZESZYTY NAUKOWE. ELEKTRONIKA. (Text in Polish; summaries in English and Russian) 1956. irreg. price varies. Politechnika Gdanska, Majakowskiego 11/12, 81-952 Gdansk 6, Poland (Dist. by: Osrodek Rozpowszechniania Wydawnctw Naukowych Pan, Palac Kultury i Nauki, 00-901 Warsaw, Poland)

621   PL
POLITECHNIKA GDANSKA. ZESZYTY NAUKOWE. ELEKTRYKA. (Text in Polish; summaries in English and Russian) 1955. irreg. price varies. Politechnika Gdanska, Majakowskiego 11/12, 81-952 Gdansk 6, Poland (Dist. by: Osrodek Rozpowszechniania Wydawnictw Naukowych Pan, Palac Kultury i Nauki, 00-901 Warsaw, Poland)

621.3   PL   ISSN 0459-682X
POLITECHNIKA LODZKA. ZESZYTY NAUKOWE. ELEKTRYKA. (Text in Polish; summaries in English and Russian) 1955. irreg. price varies. Politechnika Lodzka, Ul. Zwirki 36, 90-924 Lodz, Poland (Dist. by: Ars Polona-Ruch, Krakowskie Przedmiescie 7, Warsaw, Poland) Ed. Andrzej Czajkowski. circ. 383. Indexed: Chem.Abstr. Comput. & Contr. Abstr. Elec. & Electron. Abstr. Phys.Abstr. Sci. Abstr.

621.3   PL   ISSN 0079-4503
POLITECHNIKA POZNANSKA. ZESZYTY NAUKOWE. ELEKTRYKA. (Text in Polish; summaries in English and Russian) 1959. irreg. price varies. Politechnika Poznanska, Pl. Curie-Sklodowskiej 5, Poznan, Poland. Ed. Miroslaw Dabrowski. circ. 150.

537 621.3   PL   ISSN 0072-4688
POLITECHNIKA SLASKA. ZESZYTY NAUKOWE. ELEKTRYKA. (Text in Polish: summaries in English and Russian) 1954. irreg. price varies. Politechnika Slaska, W. Pstrowskiego 7, 44-100 Gliwice, Poland (Dist. by: Ars Polona, Krakowskie Przedmiescie 7, 00-068 Warsaw, Poland) Ed. Zofia Cichowska.

621.3   PL   ISSN 0324-9778
POLITECHNIKA WROCLAWSKA. INSTYTUT ENERGOELEKTRYKI. PRACE NAUKOWE. KONFERENCJE. (Text in Polish and English) 1973. irreg., 1978, no. 12. price varies. Politechnika Wroclawska, Wybrzeze Wyspianskiego 27, 50-370 Wroclaw, Poland (Dist. by: Ars Polona-Ruch, Krakowskie Przedmiescie 7, Warsaw, Poland) Ed. Marian Kloza. circ. 480.

621.3   PL   ISSN 0324-976X
POLITECHNIKA WROCLAWSKA. INSTYTUT ENERGOELEKTRYKI. PRACE NAUKOWE. MONOGRAFIE. (Text in Polish; summaries in English, French and Russian) 1972. irreg., no. 10, 1979. price varies. Politechnika Wroclawska, Wybrzeze Wyspianskiego 27, 50-370 Wroclaw, Poland (Dist. by: Ars Polona-Ruch, Krakowskie Przedmiescie 7, Warsaw, Poland) Ed. Marian Kloza.

621.3   PL   ISSN 0084-2826
POLITECHNIKA WROCLAWSKA. INSTYTUT ENERGOELEKTRYKI. PRACE NAUKOWE. STUDIA I MATERIALY. (Text in Polish; summaries in English, French, German, Russian) 1969. irreg., no. 30, 1979. Politechnika Wroclawska, Ul. Wybrzeze Wyspianskiego 27, 50-370 Wroclaw, Poland (Dist. by: Ars Polona-Ruch, Krakowskie Przedmiescie 7, Warsaw, Poland) Ed. Marian Kloza.

621.3 389   PL   ISSN 0324-9557
POLITECHNIKA WROCLAWSKA. INSTYTUT METROLOGII ELEKTRYCZNEJ. PRACE NAUKOWE. KONFERENCJE. (Text in Polish and English) 1973. irreg., no. 7, 1979. price varies. Politechnika Wroclawska, Wybrzeze Wyspianskiego 27, 50-370 Wroclaw, Poland (Dist. by : Ars Polona-Ruch, Krakowskie Przedmiescie 7, Warsaw, Poland) Ed. Marian Kloza. circ. 480.

621.3 389   PL   ISSN 0324-9549
POLITECHNIKA WROCLAWSKA. INSTYTUT METROLOGII ELEKTRYCZNEJ. PRACE NAUKOWE. MONOGRAFIE. (Text in Polish; summaries in English and Russian) 1974. irreg., no. 2, 1976. price varies. Politechnika Wroclawska, Wybrzeze Wyspianskiego 27, 50-370 Wroclaw, Poland (Dist. by: Ars Polona-Ruch, Krakowskie Przedmiescie 7, Warsaw, Poland) Ed. Marian Kloza. circ. 375.

621.3 389   PL   ISSN 0324-9530
POLITECHNIKA WROCLAWSKA. INSTYTUT METROLOGII ELEKTRYCZNEJ. PRACE NAUKOWE. PRZEMYSL. (Text in Polish; summaries in English and Russian) 1975. irreg., 1975, no. 1. price varies. Politechnika Wroclawska, Wybrzeze Wyspianskiego 27, 50-370 Wroclaw, Poland (Dist. by: Ars Polona-Ruch, Krakowskie Przedmiescie 7, Warsaw, Poland) Ed. Marian Kloza. circ. 375.

621.3 389   PL   ISSN 0084-2958
POLITECHNIKA WROCLAWSKA. INSTYTUT METROLOGII ELEKTRYCZNEJ. PRACE NAUKOWE. STUDIA I MATERIALY. (Text in Polish; summaries in English, Russian) 1970. irreg., no. 30, 1979. price varies. Politechnika Wroclawska, Wybrzeze Wyspianskiego 27, 50-370 Wroclaw, Poland (Dist. by: Ars Polona-Ruch, Krakowskie Przedmiescie 7, Warsaw, Poland) Ed. Marian Kloza.

621   PL   ISSN 0324-9441
POLITECHNIKA WROCLAWSKA. INSTYTUT PODSTAW ELEKTROTECHNIKI I ELEKTROTECHNOLOGII. PRACE NAUKOWE. KONFERENCJE. (Text in Polish; summaries in English and Russian) 1975. irreg., 1976, no. 3. price varies. Politechnika Wroclawska, Wybrzeze Wyspianskiego 27, 50-370 Wroclaw, Poland (Dist. by: Ars Polona-Ruch, Krakowskie Przedmiescie 7, Warsaw, Poland) Ed. Marian Kloza.

621   PL   ISSN 0324-945X
POLITECHNIKA WROCLAWSKA. INSTYTUT PODSTAW ELEKTROTECHNIKI I ELEKTROTECHNOLOGII. PRACE NAUKOWE. MONOGRAFIE. (Text in Polish; summaries in English and Russian) 1972. irreg., no. 6, 1978. price varies. Politechnika Wroclawska, Wybrzeze Wyspianskiego 27, 50-370 Wroclaw, Poland (Dist. by: Ars Polona-Ruch, Krakowskie Przedmiescie 7, Warsaw, Poland) Ed. Marian Kloza. circ. 250.

621.3   PL   ISSN 0370-0852
POLITECHNIKA WROCLAWSKA. INSTYTUT PODSTAW ELEKTROTECHNIKI I ELEKTROTECHNOLOGII. PRACE NAUKOWE. STUDIA I MATERIALY. (Text in Polish; summaries in English and Russian) 1970. irreg., no. 7, 1975. price varies. Politechnika Wroclawska, Wybrzeze Wyspianskiego 27, 50-370 Wroclaw, Poland (Dist. by: Ars Polona-Ruch, Krakowskie Przedmiescie 7, Warsaw, Poland) Ed. Marian Kloza. circ. 250.

621.3   PL
POLITECHNIKA WROCLAWSKA. INSTYTUT PODSTAW ELEKTROTECHNIKI I ELEKTROTECHNOLOGII. PRACE NAUKOWE. WSPOLPRACA. (Text in Polish; summaries in English and Russian) 1977. irreg. price varies. Politechnika Wroclawska, Wybrzeze Wyspianskiego 27, 50-370 Wroclaw, Poland. Ed. Marian Kloza. circ. 250.

621.38   PL   ISSN 0370-0887
POLITECHNIKA WROCLAWSKA. INSTYTUT TECHNOLOGII ELEKTRONOWEJ. PRACE NAUKOWE. KONFERENCJE. (Text in Polish; summaries in English, French and Russian) 1973. irreg., no. 3, 1979. price varies. Politechnika Wroclawska, Wybrzeze Wyspianskiego 27, 50-370 Wroclaw, Poland (Dist. by: Ars Polona-Ruch, Krakowskie Przedmiescie 7, Warsaw, Poland) Ed. Marian Kloza.

621.38   PL   ISSN 0084-280X
POLITECHNIKA WROCLAWSKA. INSTYTUT TECHNOLOGII ELEKTRONOWEJ. PRACE NAUKOWE. MONOGRAFIE. (Text in Polish; summaries in English, Russian) 1970. irreg., no. 7, 1979. price varies. Politechnika Wroclawska, Wybrzeze Wyspianskiego 27, 50-370 Wroclaw, Poland (Dist. by: Ars Polona-Ruch, Krakowskie Przedmiescie 7, Warsaw, Poland) Ed. Marian Kloza.

621.3   530   PL   ISSN 0084-2885
POLITECHNIKA WROCLAWSKA. INSTYTUT TECHNOLOGII ELEKTRONOWEJ. PRACE NAUKOWE. STUDIA I MATERIALY. (Text in Polish; summaries in English, Russian) 1970. irreg., no. 13, 1978. price varies. Politechnika Wroclawska, Wybrzeze Wyspianskiego 27, 50-370 Wroclaw, Poland (Dist. by: Ars Polona-Ruch, Krakowskie Przedmiescie 7, Warsaw, Poland) Ed. Marian Kloza.

621.38   534   PL   ISSN 0324-9344
POLITECHNIKA WROCLAWSKA. INSTYTUT TELEKOMUNIKACJI I AKUSTYKI. PRACE NAUKOWE. KONFERENCJE. (Text in Polish; summaries in English and Russian) 1973. irreg., no. 11, 1979. price varies. Politechnika Wroclawska, Wybrzeze Wyspianskiego 27, 50-370 Wroclaw, Poland (Dist. by: Ars Polona-Ruch, Krakowskie Przedmiescie 7, Warsaw, Poland) Ed. Marian Kloza.

621.38   534   PL   ISSN 0324-9328
POLITECHNIKA WROCLAWSKA. INSTYTUT TELEKOMUNIKACJI I AKUSTYKI. PRACE NAUKOWE. MONOGRAFIE. (Text in Polish; summaries in English and Russian) 1969. irreg., 1979, no. 19. price varies. Politechnika Wroclawska, Wybrzeze Wyspianskiego 27, 50-370 Wroclaw, Poland (Dist. by: Ars Polona-Ruch, Krakowskie Przedmiescie 7, Warsaw, Poland) Ed. Marian Kloza.

621.38   534   PL   ISSN 0324-9336
POLITECHNIKA WROCLAWSKA. INSTYTUT TELEKOMUNIKACJI I AKUSTYKI. PRACE NAUKOWE. STUDIA I MATERIALY. (Text in Polish; summaries in English and Russian) 1971. irreg., no. 11, 1977. price varies. Politechnika Wroclawska, Wybrzeze Wyspianskiego 27, 50-370 Wroclaw, Poland (Dist. by: Ars Polona-Ruch, Krakowskie Przedmiescie 7, Warsaw, Poland) Ed. Marian Kloza.

621.3   PL   ISSN 0324-931X
POLITECHNIKA WROCLAWSKA. INSTYTUT UKLADOW ELEKTROMASZYNOWICH. PRACE NAUKOWE. KONFERENCJE. (Text in Polish; summaries in English and Russian) 1973. irreg., 1977, no. 7. price varies. Politechnika Wroclawska, Wybrzeze Wyspianskiego 27, 50-370 Wroclaw, Poland (Dist. by: Ars Polona-Ruch, Krakowskie Przedmiescie 7, Warsaw, Poland) Ed. Marian Kloza.

621.3   PL   ISSN 0137-6284
POLITECHNIKA WROCLAWSKA. INSTYTUT UKLADOW ELEKTROMASZYNOWYCH. PRACE NAUKOWE. MONOGRAFIE. (Text in Polish; summaries in English and Russian) 1969. irreg., no. 4, 1979. price varies. Politechnika Wroclawska, Ul. Wybrzeze Wyspianskiego 27, 50-370 Wroclaw, Poland (Dist. by: Ars Polona-Ruch, Krakowskie Przedmiescie 7, Warsaw, Poland) Ed. Marian Kloza.

621.3   PL   ISSN 0137-6292
POLITECHNIKA WROCLAWSKA. INSTYTUT UKLADOW ELEKTROMASZYNOWYCH. PRACE NAUKOWE. PRZEMYSL. (Text in Polish; summaries in English and Russian) 1971. irreg., no. 5, 1973. price varies. Politechnika Wroclawska, Wybrzeze Wyspianskiego 27, 50-370 Wroclaw, Poland (Dist. by: Ars Polona-Ruch, Krakowskie Przedmiescie 7, Warsaw, Poland) Ed. Marian Kloza.

621.3   PL   ISSN 0084-294X
POLITECHNIKA WROCLAWSKA. INSTYTUT UKLADOW ELEKTROMASZYNOWYCH. PRACE NAUKOWE. STUDIA I MATERIALY. (Text in Polish; summaries in English and Russian) 1969. irreg., no. 15, 1979. price varies. Politechnika Wroclawska, Ul. Wybrzeze Wyspianskiego 27, 50-370 Wroclaw, Poland (Dist. by: Ars Polona-Ruch, Krakowskie Przedmiescie 7, Warsaw, Poland) Ed. Marian Kloza.

537.5   DK
POLYTEKNISKE LAEREANSTALT, DANMARKS TEKNISKE HOEJSKOLE. LABORATORIET FOR ELEKTRONIK. BERETNING. 1970. a. Polytekniske Laereanstalt, Danmarks Tekniske Hoejskole, Laboratoriet for Elektronik - Technical University of Denmark, Electronics Laboratory, Bygning 344, 2800 Lyngby, Denmark. Ed. Ole Trier Andersen.

537   PL   ISSN 0079-4260
POSTEPY NAPEDU ELEKTRYCZNEGO. 1960. irreg. price varies. (Polska Akademia Nauk) Panstwowe Wydawnictwo Naukowe, Miodowa 10, Warsaw, Poland (Dist. by Ars Polona-Ruch, Krakowskie Przedmiescie 7, Warsaw, Poland)

POWER INDUSTRY COMPUTER APPLICATIONS CONFERENCE. RECORD. see *COMPUTER TECHNOLOGY AND APPLICATIONS*

621.35   621.38   US   ISSN 0079-4457
POWER SOURCES SYMPOSIUM. PROCEEDINGS. 1956. biennial. $25. ‡ Electrochemical Society Inc., 10 S. Main St., Pennington, NJ 08534. circ. 1,000.

621.38   NP
POWER STATISTICS JOURNAL OF NEPAL.* (Text in English) 1970/71. irreg. Department of Electricity, Kathmandu, Nepal. illus. stat.

621.31   US
POWER TRANSMISSION DESIGN HANDBOOK. 1961/62. biennial. $27. Penton-IPC, 614 Superior Ave., W., Cleveland, OH 44113. Ed. Ro Lutz-Nagy. adv. circ. 20,335. (reprint service avail. from UMI)
Formerly: Power Transmission & Bearing Handbook (ISSN 0554-890X)
Power transmission

621.3   PL   ISSN 0079-4627
POZNANSKIE TOWARZYSTWO PRZYJACIOL NAUK. KOMISJA ELEKTROTECHNIKI. PRACE. 1968. irreg., 1972, vol. 1, no. 2. price varies. Panstwowe Wydawnictwo Naukowe, Miodowa 10, Warsaw, Poland (Dist. by Ars Polona, Ruch, Krakowskie Przedmiescie 7, Warsaw, Poland) bibl, charts.

621.38   GE   ISSN 0079-564X
PROBLEME DER FESTKOERPERELEKTRONIK. 1969. a. price varies. VEB Verlag Technik, Postfach 293, 102 Berlin, E. Germany (D.D.R.) (Dist. in U.S. by Atlas for Action Books, Inc., 162 Fifth Ave., New York, N.Y. 10010)

621.38   US
PROCESSES AND MATERIALS IN ELECTRONICS. a. price varies. Gordon and Breach Science Publishers, One Park Ave., New York, NY 10016. Ed. H. H. Manko.
Electronics

537.5   US   ISSN 0079-6727
PROGRESS IN QUANTUM ELECTRONICS. 1969. q. $66. Pergamon Press, Inc., Journals Division, Maxwell House, Fairview Park, Elmsford, NY 10523 (And Headington Hill Hall, Oxford OX3 0BW, England) Eds. S. Stenholm, T. S. Moss. (also avail. in microform from MIM,UMI) Indexed: Chem.Abstr.

621.3   US
PULSED POWER MODULATOR CONFERENCE (RECORD) biennial. $30. Institute of Electrical and Electronics Engineers, Inc., Electron Devices Society, 445 Hoes Lane, Piscataway, NJ 08854.
Formerly: Modulator Symposium (Record)

621.3   CN   ISSN 0075-6091
QUEEN'S UNIVERSITY AT KINGSTON. DEPARTMENT OF ELECTRICAL ENGINEERING. RESEARCH REPORT. 1962. irreg. free. ‡ Queen's University, Department of Electrical Engineering, Kingston, Ont. K7L 3N6, Canada. Ed. Dr. P.H. Wittke. (back issues avail.)

621.3   621   UK   ISSN 0432-2924
R E M E JOURNAL. 1952. a. 71p. Royal Electrical & Mechanical Engineers, Moat House, Arborfield, Reading, Berks RG2 9LN, England.

683.88   UK
REGULATIONS FOR THE ELECTRICAL EQUIPMENT OF BUILDINGS. 1966. irreg., 15th ed., 1981. £6.50. Institution of Electrical Engineers, Savoy Place, London WC2H 0BL, England.
Appliances and equipment

621.38   US
RELAY D.A.T.A.BOOK. every 18 months. $38.50. D. A. T. A. Inc., 45 U.S. Hwy 46, Box 602, Pine Brook, NJ 07058.
Formerly: Miniature and Subminiature Relay D.A.T.A. Book.
Electronics

621.3   US
RELIABILITY AND MAINTAINABILITY CONFERENCE. RECORD. 1964. a. price varies. Institute of Electrical and Electronics Engineers, Inc., 445 Hoes Lane, Piscataway, NJ 08854. (Co-Sponsor: American Society for Quality Control)

621.3   CN
REPERTOIRE DES PRODUITS ELECTRONIQUES. 1979. a. Can.$15. Kerrwil Publications Ltd., 20 Holly St., Suite 201, Toronto, Ont. M4S 2E8, Canada. circ. 5,000.

621.38   US
RINEHART PRESS SERIES IN ELECTRONIC TECHNOLOGY. irreg. price varies. Holt, Rinehart and Winston, 383 Madison Ave., New York, NY 10017.
Electronics

ROBOTRON TECHNISCHE MITTEILUNGEN. see *COMMUNICATIONS*

621.38   629   FR
S P E R ANNUAIRE.* 1962. irreg. Syndicat des Industries de Materiel Professionel Electronique et Radioelectrique, 11 rue Hamelin, 75783 Paris 16, France. (Co-sponsor: Federation des Industries Electriques et Electroniques)
Formerly: Syndicat des Industries de Material Professionnel Electronique et Radioelectrique. Annuaire (ISSN 0082-1020)

621.31   MY
SARAWAK ELECTRICITY SUPPLY CORPORATION. ANNUAL REPORT. (Text in English) 1957. a. M.6. Sarawak Electricity Supply Corporation - Perbadanan Pembekalan Letrik Sarawak, Box 149, Kuching, Sarawak, Malaysia. stat. circ. 750.

621.38   US   ISSN 0092-6302
SEMICONDUCTOR HEAT SINK, SOCKET & ASSOCIATED HARDWARE D.A.T.A. BOOK. (Subseries of: D.A.T.A. Reference Standards for Industry) a. $24. D.A.T.A., Inc., 32 Lincoln Ave., Orange, NJ 07050.
Electronics

621.381   US
SEMICONDUCTOR TEST SYMPOSIUM. DIGEST OF PAPERS. a. $20 to non-members; members $15. Institute of Electrical and Electronics Engineers, Inc., 445 Hoes Lane, Piscataway, NJ 08854.

621.38   US   ISSN 0080-8784
SEMICONDUCTORS AND SEMIMETALS. 1967. irreg., vol. 13, 1977. price varies. Academic Press Inc., 111 Fifth Ave., New York, NY 10003. Eds. R. K. Willardson, Albert C. Beer.
Electronics

621.3   UK   ISSN 0305-4543
SPON'S MECHANICAL & ELECTRICAL SERVICES PRICE BOOK. 1968. a. £15. E. & F. N. Spon Ltd., 11 New Fetter Lane, London EC4P 4EE, England. Ed. Bd. adv. circ. 5,000.

621.3   530   US
SPRINGER SERIES IN ELECTROPHYSICS. 1977. irreg., vol. 5, 1981. price varies. Springer-Verlag, 175 Fifth Ave., New York, NY 10010 (Also Berlin, Heidelberg, Vienna) Ed.Bd. (reprint service avail. from ISI)

621.3   US
STATE ELECTRICITY PROFILES. 2nd ed., 1979. a. $25. Electricity Consumers Resource Council, 1225 Connecticut Ave. N.W., Suite 314, Washington, DC 20036. stat.

621.35 US ISSN 0081-5802
STORAGE BATTERY MANUFACTURING INDUSTRY YEARBOOK. 1945. biennial. $3.75. ‡ Battery Council International, 111 E. Wacker Dr., Chicago, IL 60601.
Formerly: Association of American Battery Manufacturers. Yearbook.

621.3 NE
STUDIES IN ELECTRICAL AND ELECTRONIC ENGINEERING. 1978. irreg. price varies. Elsevier Scientific Publishing Co., Box 211, 1000 AE Amsterdam, Netherlands.

621.31 SW ISSN 0039-6931
SVENSKA KRAFTVERKSFOERENINGENS PUBLIKATIONER. (Text mainly in Swedish, occasionally in English and German) 1910. irreg. (8-12/yr.) Kr.35. Svenska Kraftverksfoereningen - Swedish Power Association, Box 1704, 111 87 Stockholm, Sweden. Ed. Hans Bostroem. charts. illus. index. circ. 1,200. Indexed: Sci.Abstr.
Formerly: Svenska Vattenkraftfoereningens Publikationer.

621.38 US ISSN 0082-0490
SWITCHING AND AUTOMATA THEORY CONFERENCE. RECORD.* a. Institute of Electrical and Electronics Engineers, Inc., 445 Hoes Lane, Piscataway, NJ 08854.
Electronics

621.3 US ISSN 0082-0814
SYMPOSIUM ON APPLICATIONS OF WALSH FUNCTIONS. RECORD.* a. Institute of Electrical and Electronics Engineers, Inc., 445 Hoes Lane, Piscataway, NJ 08854.

621.38 US ISSN 0082-092X
SYMPOSIUM ON RELIABILITY. PROCEEDINGS.* 1954. a. $18. Institute of Electrical and Electronics Engineers, Inc., 445 Hoes Lane, Piscataway, NJ 08854.

621.3 331.8 FR
SYNDICAT GENERAL DE LA CONSTRUCTION ELECTRIQUE. ANNUAIRE. a. (Federation des Industries Electriques et Electroniques, Syndicat General de la Construction Electrique) Union Francaise d'Annuaires Professionnels, 13 Ave. Vladimir Komarov, B.P. 36, 78190 Trappes, France.

621.3 US ISSN 0039-8314
T E C REPORT; for education in the efficient use of electrical energy, electrical products and electrical services. 1964. irreg. membership. The Electrification Council, 90 Park Ave, New York, NY 10016. Ed.Bd. charts. illus. circ. 3,000(controlled)
Formerly: Watts News.

537 GE
TECHNISCHE HOCHSCHULE KARL-MARX-STADT. WISSENSCHAFTLICHE SCHRIFTENREIHE. 1977. irreg. Technische Hochschule Karl-Marx-Stadt, Sektion Physik-Elektronische Bauelemente, P.F. 964, 90 Karl-Marx-Stadt, E. Germany (D.D.R.) Eds. H. G. Schneider, H. Wiegand, J. Fruehauf.

TEKNOLOGI. see *TECHNOLOGY: COMPREHENSIVE WORKS*

363.6 380 US
TENNESSEE VALLEY AUTHORITY. POWER PROGRAM SUMMARY. 1980. a. free. U.S. Tennessee Valley Authority, Power Reports and Information Office, 670 Chestnut St. Tower II, Chattanooga, TN 37041. circ. 10,000. Indexed: Amer.Stat.Ind.
Formed by the merger of, 1960-1980: Tennessee Valley Authority. Power Annual Report (ISSN 0082-2795); -1963-1980: Tennessee Valley Authority. Operations: Municipal and Cooperative Distributors of T.V.A. Power (ISSN 0362-3432)

621.3 US ISSN 0082-2809
TENNESSEE VALLEY AUTHORITY. TECHNICAL MONOGRAPHS. 1934. irreg. price varies. Tennessee Valley Authority, Engineering Reports and Information Office, Knoxville, TN 37902. circ. 600.

621.3 US ISSN 0082-2817
TENNESSEE VALLEY AUTHORITY. TECHNICAL REPORTS. 1940. irreg. price varies. Tennessee Valley Authority, Engineering Reports and Information Office, Knoxville, TN 37902. circ. 2,000.

621.3 FR ISSN 0154-0009
TEQUI ELECTRICITE ELECTRONIQUE; catalogue national du materiel electrique et electronique. 1928. a. 144 F. Editions du Cartel, 2 rue de Florence, 75008 Paris, France. Ed. A.L. Savu. circ. 12,000.

537.5 US
TEXAS ANNUAL OF ELECTRONICS RESEARCH. 1964/65. a. $6 per no. University of Texas at Austin, Electronics Research Center, Austin, TX 78712. Ed. Edward J. Powers. abstr. bibl. illus.
Formerly: Texas Biannual of Electronics Research (ISSN 0563-2625)

354 TU
TURKISH ELECTRICITY AUTHORITY. ANNUAL REPORT. (Text in English) a. Turkish Electricity Authority - Turkiye Elektrik Kurumu, Necatibey Caddesi No. 36, Ankara, Turkey. charts. illus. stat.

U.S. NATIONAL BUREAU OF STANDARDS. SEMICONDUCTOR MEASUREMENT TECHNOLOGY. see *METROLOGY AND STANDARDIZATION*

621.393 US ISSN 0083-3177
U. S. RURAL ELECTRIFICATION ADMINISTRATION. ANNUAL STATISTICAL REPORT. RURAL ELECTRIFICATION BORROWERS. a. free. U. S. Rural Electrification Administration, U.S. Dept. of Agriculture, Washington, DC 20250.

621.393 US ISSN 0083-3185
U. S. RURAL ELECTRIFICATION ADMINISTRATION. ANNUAL STATISTICAL REPORT. RURAL TELEPHONE PROGRAM. 1958. a. not for sale. ‡ U. S. Rural Electrification Administration, Dept. of Agriculture, Washington, DC 20250.

621.393 US ISSN 0083-3193
U. S. RURAL ELECTRIFICATION ADMINISTRATION. REPORT OF THE ADMINISTRATOR OF THE RURAL ELECTRIFICATION ADMINISTRATION. 1936. a. free. U. S. Rural Electrification Administration, Department of Agriculture, Washington, DC 20250.

621.3 AG ISSN 0082-6693
UNIVERSIDAD NACIONAL DE TUCUMAN. INSTITUTO DE INGENIERIA ELECTRICA. REVISTA. 1963. irreg. $1.50. Universidad Nacional de Tucuman, Instituto de Ingenieria Electrica, Avda. Independencia 1700, San Miguel de Tucuman, Argentina. bk. rev. index. circ. 1,500.

621.3 US ISSN 0568-0581
UNIVERSITY OF ILLINOIS AT URBANA-CHAMPAIGN. DEPARTMENT OF ELECTRICAL ENGINEERING. AERONOMY LABORATORY. AERONOMY REPORT. 1963. irreg. free. University of Illinois at Urbana-Champaign, Department of Electrical Engineering, Aeronomy Laboratory, Urbana, IL 61801. Ed. Belva Edwards. circ. controlled.

621.3 AT ISSN 0085-3259
UNIVERSITY OF MELBOURNE. DEPARTMENT OF ELECTRICAL ENGINEERING. RESEARCH REPORT. 1966. irreg. free. University of Melbourne, Department of Electrical Engineering, Parkville, Vic. 3052, Australia.

621.3 AT ISSN 0085-4158
UNIVERSITY OF NEWCASTLE. DEPARTMENT OF ELECTRICAL ENGINEERING. TECHNICAL REPORT EE. 1967. irreg. contr. free circ. ‡ University of Newcastle, Department of Electrical Engineering, Shortland, N.S.W. 2308, Australia. circ. 800.

621.3 CN ISSN 0082-514X
UNIVERSITY OF TORONTO. DEPARTMENT OF ELECTRICAL ENGINEERING. RESEARCH REPORT.* 1954. irreg. University of Toronto, Department of Electrical Engineering, Toronto, Ont., Canada.

621.3 GW
V D E W ARBEITSBERICHT. 1953. a. Vereinigung Deutscher Elektrizitaetswerke e.V., Stresemannallee 23, 6000 Frankfurt, W. Germany (B.R.D.) charts. stat. index. circ. controlled.

VALTION TEKNILLINEN TUTKIMUSKESKUS. SAHKO- JA ATOMITEKNIIKKA. JULKAISU. see *PHYSICS — Nuclear Energy*

621.3 FI ISSN 0355-3671
VALTION TEKNILLINEN TUTKIMUSKESKUS. SAHKOTEKNIIKAN LABORATORIO. TIEDONANTO/TECHNICAL RESEARCH CENTRE OF FINLAND. ELECTRICAL ENGINEERING LABORATORY. REPORT. (Text mainly in Finnish, some in English or Swedish) 1971. irreg. price varies. Valtion Teknillinen Tutkimuskeskus - Technical Research Centre of Finland, Vuorimiehentie 5, 02150 Espoo 15, Finland.

621.3 AT
VICTORIA, AUSTRALIA. STATE ELECTRICITY COMMISSION. SCIENCE REPORT. irreg. State Electricity Commission, Herman Central Scientific Laboratory, Howard St., Richmond, Victoria 3121, Australia. bibl. charts. illus.

537 UR
VOPROSY ELEKTRONIKI TVERDOGO TELA. vol. 7, 1978. irreg. 1.80 Rub. per no. Idatel'stvo Leningradskii Universitet, Universitetskaya Nab. 7/9, Leningrad B-164, U.S.S.R. abstr. bibl. circ. 1,500.

621.38 US
W E S C O N CONFERENCE RECORD. vol. 20, 1976. a. $95. (Western Electronic Show and Convention) Western Periodicals Co., 13000 Raymer St., North Hollywood, CA 91605.
Formerly (until 1977): W E S C O N Technical Papers (ISSN 0083-8837)
Electronics

363.6 US ISSN 0424-480X
YEAR-END SUMMARY OF THE ELECTRIC POWER SITUATION IN THE UNITED STATES. 1956. a. $7. Edison Electric Institute, Electric Power Survey Committee, 1111 19th St. N.W., Washington, DC 20036. Ed. Carl Tobie. illus. circ. 4,000.

354 ZA
ZAMBIA ELECTRICITY SUPPLY CORPORATION. ANNUAL REPORT. a, latest 1973-74. free. Zambia Electricity Supply Corporation, Box 3304, Lusaka, Zambia. stat.

ELECTRICITY AND ELECTRICAL ENGINEERING — Abstracting, Bibliographies, Statistics

621.3 314 UN ISSN 0066-3816
ANNUAL BULLETIN OF ELECTRIC ENERGY STATISTICS FOR EUROPE. (Supplemented by the Commision's Half-Yearly Bulletin of Electric Energy Statistics for Europe) (Text in English, French and Russian) 1956 (covering 1955. ;vol. 24, 1978. price varies. United Nations Economic Commission for Europe, Palais des Nations, 1200 Geneva 10, Switzerland (Or United Nations Publications, Room LX-2300, New York, NY 10017)

338.4 CN ISSN 0384-4161
CANADA. STATISTICS CANADA. ELECTRIC LAMP AND SHADE MANUFACTURERS/ INDUSTRIE DES LAMPES ELECTRIQUES ET DES ABAT-JOUR. (Catalogue 35-214) (Text in English and French) 1960. a. Can.$4.50($5.40) Statistics Canada, Publications Distribution, Ottawa, Ont. K1A 0V7, Canada. (also avail. in microform from MML)

338.4 621.31 CN ISSN 0380-951X
CANADA. STATISTICS CANADA. ELECTRIC POWER STATISTICS VOLUME 1: ANNUAL ELECTRIC POWER SURVEY OF CAPABILITY AND LOAD/STATISTIQUE DE L'ENERGIE ELECTRIQUE. VOLUME 1: ENQUETE ANNUELLE SUR LA PUISSANCE MAXIMALE ET SUR LA CHARGE DES RESEAUX. (Catalog 57-204) 1955. a. Can.$6($7.20) Statistics Canada, Publications Distribution, Ottawa, Ont. K1A 0V7, Canada. (also avail. in microform from MML)

621.3 690   CN   ISSN 0702-8083
CANADA. STATISTICS CANADA. ELECTRICAL CONTRACTING INDUSTRY/ ENTREPRENEURS D'INSTALLATIONS ELECTRIQUES. (Catalogue 64-205) (Text in English and French) 1969. a. Can.$6($7.20) Statistics Canada, Publications Distribution, Ottawa, Ont. K1A 0V7, Canada. (also avail. in microform from MML)

CANADA. STATISTICS CANADA. MANUFACTURERS OF ELECTRIC WIRE AND CABLE/FABRICANTS DE FILS ET DE CABLES ELECTRIQUES. see *ELECTRICITY AND ELECTRICAL ENGINEERING*

016   537.24   US   ISSN 0070-4865
DIGEST OF LITERATURE ON DIELECTRICS. 1936. a. $40. National Academy of Sciences, Conference on Electrical Insulation and Dielectric Phenomena, 2101 Constitution Ave. N.W., Washington, DC 20418. index.

621.3   016   CN   ISSN 0070-9662
ELECTRICAL ENGINEERING RESEARCH ABSTRACTS. CANADIAN UNIVERSITIES. (Summaries in English and French) 1962. a. free to Canadian companies. ‡ University of British Columbia, Electrical Engineering Department, Vancouver, B.C. V6T 1W5, Canada. Ed. J. Douglas. circ. 600.

621.3   016   SZ
I E C CATALOGUE OF PUBLICATIONS. (Text in English and French) 1960. a. with supplements twice per year. 9 Fr. International Electrotechnical Commission, 1, rue de Varembe, 1211 Geneva 20, Switzerland (Dist. in the U.S. by: American National Standards Institute, 1430 Broadway, New York, NY 10018) adv. index.

338.4   621.38   UK   ISSN 0306-5774
MACKINTOSH YEARBOOK OF WEST EUROPEAN ELECTRONICS DATA. 1973. a. £130($325) Mackintosh Publications Ltd., Mackintosh House, Napier Rd., Luton, Beds. LU1 1RG, England. adv. illus. stat.
Electronics

338.4   US
STATISTICS FOR ELECTRIC UTILITIES IN PENNSYLVANIA. a. free. Department of Commerce, Bureau of Statistics, Research and Planning, 630B Health & Welfare Bldg., Harrisburg, PA 17120. illus.

STATISTICS OF PRIVATELY OWNED ELECTRIC UTILITIES IN THE UNITED STATES. see *ENERGY — Abstracting, Bibliographies, Statistics*

621.381   US
U S S R REPORT: ELECTRONICS AND ELECTRICAL ENGINEERING. 1973. irreg. (approx. 8/yr.) $24. U.S. Joint Publications Research Service, 1000 N. Glebe Rd., Arlington, VA 22201 (Orders to: NTIS, Springfield, VA 22161)
Formerly: U S S R and Eastern Europe Scientific Abstracts: Electronics and Electrical Engineering; Which was formed by the merger of: U S S R Scientific Abstracts: Electronics and Electrical Engineering; East European Scientific Abstracts: Electronics and Electrical Engineering.

ELECTROCHEMISTRY

see *Chemistry — Electrochemistry*

ENCYCLOPEDIAS AND GENERAL ALMANACS

051   US
ALMANAC OF THE CITIES. 1977. a. $8.95. Serina Press, 70 Kennedy St., Alexandria, VA 22305.

035   IT
ALMANACCO REPUBBLICANO. a. L.3000. Edizioni della Voce s.r.l., Via Tomacelli 146, 00186 Rome, Italy. Ed. Giuseppe Ciranna. adv. illus. circ. 15,000.

031   920   CN   ISSN 0065-650X
ALMANACH DU PEUPLE. 1869. a. Can.$2.50. Librairie Beauchemin Limitee, 450 Avenue Beaumont, Montreal, Que. H3N 1T8, Canada. Ed. Raymond Bertram. adv. bk. rev. circ. 125,000.

808   CN   ISSN 0569-096X
ALMANACH MODERNE. Title varies: Almanach Moderne Eclair. 1956. a. Can.$2.50. ‡ Publications Eclair Ltee, 9393 Ave. Edison, Montreal, Quebec H1J 1T5, Canada. Ed. Paul Rochon. adv. circ. 145,000.

039   IO   ISSN 0301-7621
ALMANAK JAKARTA. irreg. Rps.2500. Badan Penerbit Almanak Jakarta, Jl. Gajahmada No. 25, Jakarta, Indonesia. illus.

ALMANAKH GOMONU UKRAINY. see *ETHNIC INTERESTS*

036   PR
ALMANAQUE PUERTORRIQUENO (YEAR) 1978. a. Editorial Edil, 1001 Ponce de Leon, P.O.B. 23088, Rio Piedras, PR 00931. Ed. Jose A. Toro Sugrones.

032   UK
ALTERNATIVE ENGLAND AND WALES. 1970. biennial (with quarterly supplements) £2.50. 65 Edith Grove, London SW10, England. Ed. Nicholas Saunders. bk. rev. charts. illus. index. circ. 30,000. (back issues avail.)
Formerly: Alternative London.

036.9   BL
ANNUARIO DELTA-LAROUSSE.* (Covers the events of the previous year) 1972. a. Editora Delta, Avda. Almirante Barroso 63, Rio de Janeiro, Brazil. illus.

007   US
AWARDS, HONORS AND PRIZES. (Vol. 1, U.S. and Canada; Vol. 2, International and Foreign) 1969. irreg., 4th edt., 1978. vol. 1, $50; vol. 2, $65. Gale Research Company, Book Tower, Detroit, MI 48226. Ed. Paul Wasserman. index.

031   US   ISSN 0068-1156
BRITANNICA BOOK OF THE YEAR. 1938. a. $15.95. Encyclopaedia Britannica, Inc., 425 N. Michigan Ave., Chicago, IL 60611. Ed. James Ertel.

CALIFORNIA HANDBOOK. see *SOCIAL SCIENCES: COMPREHENSIVE WORKS*

CARITAS-KALENDER. see *RELIGIONS AND THEOLOGY*

030   US   ISSN 0577-5728
CHASES' CALENDAR OF ANNUAL EVENTS; special days, weeks and months in the year. 1958. a. $9.95. Apple Tree Press, Box 1012, Flint, MI 48501. Ed. William D. Chase. index. circ. 20,000.

031   US   ISSN 0069-5793
COLLIER'S YEARBOOK. (Supplement To: Collier's Encyclopedia and Merit Students Encyclopedia) 1939. a. $8.95 to libraries. Macmillan, Inc., 866 Third Ave., New York, NY 10022. Ed. Maron L. Waxman. index.

031   US   ISSN 0069-8091
COMPTON YEARBOOK. 1958. a. $12.95. Encyclopaedia Britannica, Inc., 425 N. Michigan Ave., Chicago, IL 60611. Ed. James Ertel. index.

032   CN   ISSN 0315-7083
CORPUS ALMANAC OF CANADA. a. Can.$67 for 2 vols. Corpus Information Services Ltd., 1450 Don Mills Rd., Don Mills, Ont. M3B 2X7, Canada. Ed. Margot Fawcett. index. (back issues avail.)

030   UK   ISSN 0301-7761
DAILY MAIL YEAR BOOK. a. Associated Newspapers Group Ltd., Carmelite House, Carmelite St., London EC4Y 0JA, England. (back issues avail.)

DICTIONNAIRE DES COMMUNES (LAVAUZELLE ET CIE) see *PUBLIC ADMINISTRATION*

030   FR   ISSN 0073-4640
DICTIONNAIRES DU SAVOIR MODERNE; les idees, les oeuvres, les hommes. 1969. irreg. price varies. (Centre d'Etudes et de Promotion de la Lecture) Editions Denoel, 19 rue de l'Universite, Paris 7e, France.

032   CN   ISSN 0316-0734
DIRECTORY OF ASSOCIATIONS IN CANADA. 1974. a. Can.$37.50. University of Toronto Press, Toronto, Ont. M5S 1A6, Canada. Ed. Brian Land.

011   UK   ISSN 0070-5152
DIRECTORY OF BRITISH ASSOCIATIONS. 1965. irreg., 6th, 1980. £37.50($110) ‡ C.B.D. Research Ltd., 154 High St., Beckenham, Kent BR3 1EA, England (Dist. in U.S. by: Gale Research Co., Book Tower, Detroit, MI 48226) Eds. G. P. Henderson, S. P. A. Henderson. indexes. circ. 6,000.

035   IT
DIZIONARIO ENCICLOPEDICO D'INFORMAZIONI. 1977. a. L.7000. Rusconi Editori Associati S.p.A., Via Vitruvio 43, 20124 Milan, Italy.

ECONOMICS: ENCYCLOPEDIA. see *BUSINESS AND ECONOMICS*

028   US   ISSN 0361-1094
ENCYCLOPEDIA BUYING GUIDE. 1962. triennial. $22.50. R.R. Bowker Company, 1180 Ave. of the Americas, New York, NY 10036 (Orders to P.O. Box 1807, Ann Arbor, Mich. 48106) (reprint service avail. from UMI)
Supersedes: General Encyclopedias in Print (ISSN 0072-0739)

030   366   US   ISSN 0071-0202
ENCYCLOPEDIA OF ASSOCIATIONS. (In 3 vols: Vol 1, National Organizations of the U.S., Vol.2, Geographic-Executive Index; Vol 3, New Associations and Projects) 1956. a. vol. 1, $90; vol. 2, $75; vol. 3, $85. Gale Research Company, Book Tower, Detroit, MI 48226. Eds. Nancy Yakes, Denise Akey.
Formerly: Encyclopedia of American Associations (ISSN 0190-3071)

031   US
ENCYCLOPEDIA YEAR BOOK. 1947. a. $10.90. Grolier Incorporated, Sherman Turnpike, Danbury, CT 06816. Eds. Edward Humphrey, James E. Churchill, Jr. charts. illus. stat. index.

940   UK   ISSN 0071-2302
EUROPA YEAR BOOK; a world survey. 1926. a. $150 for 2 vols. Europa Publications Ltd., 18 Bedford Sq., London WC1B 3JN, England.

052   AT
FACTS ABOUT AUSTRALIA. 1952. irreg. Bank of New South Wales, 341 George St., Sydney, N.S.W. 2000, Australia.

030   US
FORD ALMANAC; for farm and home. 1954. a. $1.25. Almanac Co., 515 W. Jackson, Woodstock, IL 60098. Ed. Cliff Granschow. adv. illus. circ. 100,000.

FORD FOUNDATION ANNUAL REPORT. see *HUMANITIES: COMPREHENSIVE WORKS*

030   UK   ISSN 0071-8084
FOULSHAM'S ORIGINAL OLD MOORE'S ALMANACK. 1967. a. 12p. W. Foulsham & Co. Ltd., Yeovil Road, Slough, Bucks., England.

030   IE   ISSN 0072-0887
GENUINE IRISH OLD MOORE'S ALMANAC. 1764. a. 34p. John Arigho & Sons (1974) Ltd., 16 Firhouse Park, Templeogue, Dublin 14, Ireland. Ed. K. Ryan. adv. index. circ. 90,000.

036   320.531   MX
GUIA DEL TERCER MUNDO. 1979. a. Mex.$65($6) Periodistas del Tercer Mundo, Apdo. Postal 20-572, Mexico 20, D.F., Mexico.

032   MW
GUIDE TO PROFESSIONAL BODIES IN MALAWI. a. Centraf Associates Ltd., Box 3046, Chichiri, Blantyre 3, Malawi.

001.9 US
GUINNESS BOOK OF WORLD RECORDS.
(Editions in 16 other languages) 1955. a. $9.95. ‡
Sterling Publishing Co., Inc., Two Park Ave., New
York, NY 10016. bk. rev. illus. circ. 400,000.
Formerly: Guinness Book of Records (ISSN
0300-1679)

972.94 HT
HAITI-CULTURE. (Text in French) 1973. irreg.
Gde.4.00. Boite Postale T, Port-au-Prince, Haiti.
illus.

051 US
HAMMOND ALMANAC. 1964. a. $5.95 hard
bound; $2.75 soft cover. (Associated Press)
Hammond Almanac, Inc., Valley St., Maplewood,
NJ 07040 (Softcover edt. distr. by: Dell Publishing
Co., 1 Dag Hammarskjold Plaza, 245 E. 47 St.,
New York, NY 10017) Ed. Sylvia Westerman. adv.
bk. rev. illus. circ. 500,000.
Former titles, until 1979: C B S News Almanac
(ISSN 0361-5545); Until 1974: Official Associated
Press Almanac (ISSN 0090-208X)

350 AU ISSN 0440-2103
HANDBUCH DES OEFFENTLICHEN LEBENS IN
OESTERREICH. 1958. a. S.248. Verlag Dr. Adolf
Heinrich, Akademiestr. 3, A-1010 Vienna, Austria.
circ. 3,000.

032 II ISSN 0073-4284
I N F A PRESS AND ADVERTISERS YEAR
BOOK. (Text in English) 1962. a. $12. (India News
and Feature Alliance) I N F A Publications, Jeevan
Deep Bldg., New Delhi 110001, India. adv. circ.
2,000.

INEDITS RUSSES. see *LIBRARY AND
INFORMATION SCIENCES*

031 US ISSN 0073-7860
INFORMATION PLEASE ALMANAC. 1947. a.
$5.95 hardcover; $2.95 paper. (Dan Golenpaul
Associates) Simon and Schuster, Inc., 630 Fifth
Ave., New York, NY 10020 (Orders from: 1 W.
39th St., New York, N.Y. 10018)

050 PL
INFORMATOR ROBOTNICZY. 1973. a. 35 Zl.
Wydawnictwo "Ksiazka i Wiedza", Ul. Smolna 13,
Warsaw, Poland. illus.
Continues: Kalendarz Robotniczy.

035 IT
ISTITUTO DELLA ENCICLOPEDIA ITALIANA.
ANNUARIO. 1972. a. L.18000. Istituto della
Enciclopedia Italiana, Piazza Paganica 4, 00186
Rome, Italy.

035 IT
ISTITUTO DELLA ENCICLOPEDIA ITALIANA.
BIBLIOTHECA BIOGRAPHICA. irreg. price
varies. Istituto della Enciclopedia Italiana, Piazza
Paganica 4, 00186 Rome, Italy.

030 JA
JAPAN ALMANACH. (Text in English) 1972. a.
3200 Yen($17.50) (Mainichi Daily News) Mainichi
Newspapers, 1-1-1 Hitotsubashi, Chiyoda-ku, Tokyo
100, Japan. adv. charts. stat.

034 FR ISSN 0449-4733
JOURNAL DE L'ANNEE. 1966. a. Larousse, 17 rue
de Montparnasse, 75280 Paris Cedex 06, France.
Ed. Maurice Barrois. illus.

036 AG
LIBRO DEL ANO; almanaque de sucesos argentinos
y mundiales. 1974. a. $8.95. Editorial Huemul S.A.,
Chacabuco 860, Buenos Aires, Argentina. Ed. Eder
Julio Locco. charts. illus. stat.

089 HU
LUDAS MATYI EVKONYVE. 1970. a. $1.90.
Hirlapkiado Vallalat, Blaha Lujza ter 3, 1959
Budapest 8, Hungary (Subscr. to: Kultura, Box 149,
H-1389 Budapest, Hungary) Ed. Jozsef Arkus. adv.
illus. circ. 350,000.

017 US ISSN 0094-1484
MAGYAR NAPTAR (NEW YORK) (Text in
Hungarian) a. $3. Amerikai Magyar Szo, 130 E.
16th St., New York, NY 10003. illus.

039 YU ISSN 0541-9344
MAGYAR SZO NAPTARA. (Text in Hungarian)
1969. a. 58 din. Forum, Novi Sad, Vojvode Misica
1, Novi Sad, Yugoslavia. illus.

030 615 US
N A R D ALMANAC. 1915. a. National Association
of Retail Druggists, c/o Willard B. Simmons, 1E.
Wacker Dr., Chicago, IL 60601. Ed. Louis E.
Kazin. circ. 1,125,250 (controlled)

030 US ISSN 0196-0148
NEW BOOK OF KNOWLEDGE ANNUAL; the
young people's book of the year. 1940. a. $12.45.
Grolier Incorporated, Sherman Turnpike, Danbury,
CT 06816. Ed. William E. Shapiro. circ. 350,000.
(back issues avail.)

354 US
NEW MEXICO DIGEST. 1975. a. $3. J. R. Spencer,
2921 Axtell St., Clovis, NM 88101. illus. circ.
2,500.
Formerly: New Mexico Almanac (ISSN 0360-
1048)

031 631 US ISSN 0078-4516
OLD FARMER'S ALMANAC. 1792. a. $1. Yankee,
Inc., Dublin, NH 03444. Ed. Robert B. Thomas.
adv. circ. 3,000,000. (reprint service avail. from
UMI)

032 UK ISSN 0079-0362
PEARS CYCLOPAEDIA. 1897. a. £4.95. Pelham
Books Ltd., 44 Bedford Square, London W.C.1,
England. Ed. Dr. Chris Cook. circ. 100,000.

051 US ISSN 0362-8523
POOR JOE'S PENNSYLVANIA ALMANAC. a.
$0.75. Crabapple Press, 300 North St., Meadville,
PA 16335. illus.

948 038 NE ISSN 0079-8223
PYTTERSEN'S NEDERLANDSE ALMANAK;
jaarlijks verschijnend handboek van personen en
instellingen in Nederland en de Nederlandse
Antillen. (Text in Dutch; table of contents in
English) 1901. a. fl.99.50. Koninklijke Drukkerij van
de Garde B. V., Zaltbommel, Netherlands. Ed. M.
Paulissen. index. circ. 4,000.

031.02 US ISSN 0079-9831
READER'S DIGEST ALMANAC AND
YEARBOOK. 1966. a. $4.41. Readers Digest
Association, Inc., Pleasantville, NY 10570. Ed.
David C. Whitney. circ. 1,000,000.

REFERENCE ENCYCLOPEDIA OF THE
AMERICAN INDIAN. see *ETHNIC INTERESTS*

500 US ISSN 0080-7621
SCIENCE YEAR; World Book Science Annual. 1965.
a. $9.95-$10.95 price varies. World Book-Childcraft
International, Inc., 510 Merchandise Mart Plaza,
Chicago, IL 60654. Ed. Arthur G. Tressler.
cum.index for 3-yr period. circ. 750,000.

309.23 UV
SECRETARIAT PERMANENT DES
ORGANISATIONS NON
GOUVERNEMENTALES. RAPPORT
D'ACTIVITIES. 1976. a. Secretariat Permanent des
Organisations Non Gouvernementales, B.P. 131,
Ouagadougou, Upper Volta.

030 369 US ISSN 0080-8512
SEEKER'S GUIDE; a directory of unusual
organizations. 1961. irreg; latest edt., 1970. $5.60. ‡
Aurea Publications, Allenhurst, NJ 07711. Ed. Alex
Sandri White.

030 UK ISSN 0083-7067
WALKER'S OLD MOORE'S ALMANAC. 1844. a.
5p. W. Walker & Sons (Otley) Ltd., Victoria Works,
Otley, England.

032 UK ISSN 0083-9256
WHITAKER'S ALMANACK. 1869. a. £8.20. J.
Whitaker & Sons Ltd., 12 Dyott St., London WC1A
1DF, England (Dist. in U.S. by: Gale Research Co.,
Book Tower, Detroit, MI 48226) (reprint service
avail. from UMI)

031 US ISSN 0084-1382
WORLD ALMANAC AND BOOK OF FACTS.
1868. a. $3.95 paperback; $7.95 hardcover.
Newspaper Enterprise Association, Inc., World
Almanac Division, 200 Park Ave., New York, NY
10017. Ed. George E. Delury. index. circ.
1,000,000. (also avail. in microform from BLH)

031 US ISSN 0084-1439
WORLD BOOK YEAR BOOK. (Supplement To:
World Book Encyclopedia) 1922. a. $11.95-$13.95.
World Book-Childcraft International, Inc., 510
Merchandise Mart Plaza, Chicago, IL 60654. Ed.
Wayne Wille. cum.index for 3-yr. period. circ.
2,400,000.

ENCYCLOPEDIAS AND GENERAL ALMANACS — Abstracting, Bibliographies, Statistics

314 NE ISSN 0077-6858
STATISTICAL YEARBOOK OF THE
NETHERLANDS. 1942-46. a. fl.57.50. Centraal
Bureau voor de Statistiek, Prinses Beatrixlaan 428,
Voorburg, Netherlands (Orders to: Staatsuitgeverij,
Christoffel Plantijnstraat, The Hague, Netherlands)

030 FR ISSN 0083-5072
VADE-MECUM.* 1969. irreg. price varies. Editions
B. Arthaud, 6 rue de Mezieres, Grenoble, France.

ENDOCRINOLOGY

see *Medical Sciences—Endocrinology*

ENERGY

*Here are entered serials covering the
economic, social and technical aspects of
many types of energy sources.*

*see also Earth Sciences—Geology; Earth
Sciences—Geophysics; Electricity and
Electrical Engineering; Mines and
Mining Industry; Petroleum and Gas;
Physics—Nuclear Energy*

531.64 621.48 SW
A E. no. 511, 1975. irreg. A B Atomenergi, Fack, S-
611 01 Nykoeping 1, Sweden.

A E C L REPORT SERIES. (Atomic Energy of
Canada, Ltd.) see *PHYSICS — Nuclear Energy*

A I A ENERGY NOTEBOOK. (American Institute of
Architects) see *ARCHITECTURE*

330 531.64 US
ADVANCES IN THE ECONOMICS OF ENERGY
AND RESOURCES. 1979. a. $17.25 to individuals;
institutions $34.50. J A I Press, Box 1678, 165 W.
Putnam Ave., Greenwich, CT 06830. Ed. Robert S.
Pindyck. stat.

531.64 665.5 CN ISSN 0700-2645
ALBERTA. DEPARTMENT OF ENERGY AND
NATURAL RESOURCES, ANNUAL REPORT.
1976. a. free. Department of Energy and Natural
Resources, Petroleum Tower, South Tower, 9915
108th St., Edmonton, Alta. T5K 2C9, Canada.
Ed.Bd. charts. stat. circ. 2,500.

531.64 333.7 CN
ALBERTA. ENERGY RESOURCES
CONSERVATION BOARD. OPERATIONS
REPORT. 1978. a. Energy Resources Conservation
Board, 603 Sixth Ave. S.W., Calgary,Alta. T2P
CT4, Canada.

662 US ISSN 0071-027X
AMERICAN UNIVERSITY. ENERGY INSTITUTE.
PROCEEDINGS.* 1961. irreg. $7.50. American
University, School of Business Administration,
Washington, DC 20016.

ENERGY

531.6   US   ISSN 0362-1626
ANNUAL REVIEW OF ENERGY. 1976. a. $20. Annual Reviews Inc., 4139 El Camino Way, Palo Alto, CA 94306. Ed. Jack M. Hollander. bibl. index, cum.index. (back issues avail.; reprint service avail. from ISI) Indexed: CA.

621.47   US
ANNUAL SOLAR HEATING AND COOLING RESEARCH AND DEVELOPMENT BRANCH CONTRACTORS' MEETING. PROCEEDINGS. 3rd, 1979. a. U.S. Department of Energy, Washington, DC 20545.

ATOMIC ENERGY OF CANADA. ANNUAL REPORT. see *PHYSICS — Nuclear Energy*

AUSTRALIA. BUREAU OF STATISTICS. ECONOMIC CENSUSES: ELECTRICITY AND GAS ESTABLISHMENTS, DETAILS OF OPERATIONS. see *ELECTRICITY AND ELECTRICAL ENGINEERING*

531.64   BL
BALANCO ENERGETICO NACIONAL. irreg. Departamento Nacional de Aguase Energia, Brasilia, Brazil. stat.

500   US
BENCHMARK PAPERS ON ENERGY. 1973. irreg., vol. 7. 1979. price varies. Dowden, Hutchinson & Ross, Inc., 523 Sarah St., Stroudsburg, PA 18360 (Dist. by Academic Press, Inc., 111 Fifth Ave., New York, NY 10003) Eds. R. B. Lindsay, M. E. Hawley.

531.64   621.3   CN   ISSN 0703-086X
BRITISH COLUMBIA. ENERGY COMMISSION. ANNUAL REPORT. 1973. a. free. ‡ Energy Commission, 1177 West Hastings St, Vancouver, B. C. V 6E 2L7, Canada. stat. circ. 2,000.
    Supersedes: British Columbia Energy Board. Annual Report (ISSN 0524-5672)

531.54   US
CALIFORNIA. STATE ENERGY COMMISSION. BIENNIAL REPORT. 1977. biennial. Energy Commission, 1111 Howe Ave., Sacramento, CA 95825.

531.64   CN
CANADA. DEPARTMENT OF ENERGY, MINES AND RESOURCES. SOLAR HEATING CATALOGUE. no. 2, 1979. a. Can.$2($2.40) Department of Energy, Mines and Resources, Conservation and Renewable Energy Resources Branch, 580 Booth St., Ottawa, Ont. 51A 0E4, Canada. Ed. Michael Glover.

537   CN   ISSN 0068-7901
CANADA. NATIONAL ENERGY BOARD. ANNUAL REPORT. a. National Energy Board, Ottawa, Ont., Canada.

338.2   CN   ISSN 0315-8233
CANADIAN GAS ASSOCIATION. MEMBERSHIP DIRECTORY. a. membership only. Canadian Gas Association, 55 Scarsdale Rd., Don Mills, Ont., Canada. circ. controlled.

333.8   CN   ISSN 0316-3547
CANADIAN GAS FACTS. a. Canadian Gas Association, 55 Scarsdale Road, Don Mills, Ont. M3B 2R3, Canada.

665.5   CN   ISSN 0576-5269
CANADIAN GAS UTILITIES DIRECTORY. 1966. a. Canadian Gas Association, 55 Scarsdale Rd., Don Mills, Ont. M3B 2R3, Canada.
    Formerly: Directory of Gas Utilities (ISSN 0315-8349)

CENTRALE ELLETRONUCLEARE LATINA. RELAZIONE ANNUALE. see *PHYSICS — Nuclear Energy*

531.64   US
COAL/ENERGY NEWS. 1974. m. $7. Box 538, National Road West, St. Clairsville, OH 43950. Ed. Charles Callaway. adv. circ. 21,003.
    Formerly (until Sep. 1979): Coal Monthly and Energy News.

COLOMBIA. MINISTERIO DE MINAS Y ENERGIA. BOLETIN DE MINAS Y ENERGIA. see *MINES AND MINING INDUSTRY*

380   EI   ISSN 0531-304X
COMMISSION OF THE EUROPEAN COMMUNITIES. CONJONCTURE ENERGETIQUE DANS LA COMMUNAUTE. 1961. a. 5.50 F. (1970-1971 ed.) Office for Official Publications of the European Communities, C.P. 1003, Luxembourg 1, Luxembourg (Dist. in the U.S. by: European Community Information Service, 2100 M St., NW, Suite 707, Washington, DC 20037)
    Issued 1961-62 as: European Coal and Steel Community. High Authority. Rapport sur la Situation Energetique de la Communaute et Perspective d'Approvisionnement dans la Communaute en 1962.

330   EI   ISSN 0069-6714
COMMISSION OF THE EUROPEAN COMMUNITIES. ETUDES: SERIE ENERGIE.* 1968. irreg. Office for Official Publications of the European Communities, C.P. 1003, Luxembourg, Luxembourg (Dist. in U.S. by: European Community Information Service, 2100 M St., NW, Suite 707, Washington, DC 20037)

662   696   AT
COMMITTEE FOR ECONOMIC DEVELOPMENT OF AUSTRALIA. C E D A ENERGY PROJECT POSITION PAPERS. irreg. price varies. Committee for Economic Development of Australia, 186 Exhibition St., Melbourne, Vic 3000, N.S.W. 2000, Australia. Ed. Peter Gres. bibl. charts.

333.7   US   ISSN 0360-2257
CONNECTICUT. ENERGY ADVISORY BOARD. ANNUAL REPORT TO THE GOVERNOR AND GENERAL ASSEMBLY. EXECUTIVE SUMMARY. 1975. a. Energy Advisory Board, Hartford, CT 06115. illus. Key Title: Annual Report to the Governor and General Assembly. Executive Summary.

600   US
CONTROL OF POWER SYSTEMS CONFERENCE. CONFERENCE RECORD. 1977 called: Control of Power Systems Conference and Exposition. Conference Record. a. $12. Institute of Electrical and Electronics Engineers, Inc., 445 Hoes Lane, Piscataway, NJ 08854.

531.64   665.54   US
CRUDE-OIL AND PRODUCTS PIPELINES. triennial. free. U.S. Energy Information Administration, 1726 M St., N.W., Rm. 200, Washington, DC 20461.
    Formerly: Crude-Oil and Refined-Products Pipeline Mileage in the United States.

DENMARK. ATOMENERGIKOMMISSIONENS FORSOEGSANSLAEG, RISOE. RISOE REPORT. see *PHYSICS — Nuclear Energy*

333.8   UK   ISSN 0307-0603
DIGEST OF UNITED KINGDOM ENERGY STATISTICS. 1974. a. Department of Energy, Thames House, South Millbank, London SW1P 4QJ, England (Avail. from H.M.S.O., c/o Liaison Officer, Atlantic House, London EC1P 1BW, England) illus.
    Formerly: Great Britain. Department of Trade and Industry. Digest of Energy Statistics.

531.64   620   IT
E N I ANNUAL REPORT. a. Ente Nazionale Idrocarburi, Piazzale Enrico Mattei 1, 00144 Rome, Italy. illus.

531.6   US
EARTHMIND NEWSLETTER. 1975. a. $2. 4844 Hirsch Rd., Mariposa, CA 95338. Ed. Michael Hackleman. bk. rev. circ. 500.

531.64   NE
ENERGIEBESPARING; in bedrijf en instelling. 1980. m. fl.195. Ten Hagen B.V., Box 34, 2501 AG The Hague, Netherlands. Ed. F. Oremus. adv. bk. rev. illus. circ. 10,000.

531.64   020   CN   ISSN 0707-1000
ENERGY AND NATURAL RESOURCES LIBRARY JOURNALS. Variant title: E & N R Library Journals. 1978. irreg. Department of Energy and Natural Resources, Petroleum Plaza, South Tower, 9915 108th St., Edmonton, Alta. T5K 2C9, Canada. (also avail. in microfiche)

531.64   FR
ENERGY BALANCES OF O E C D COUNTRIES. (Text in English and French) 1976. a. $9. Organization for Economic Cooperation and Development, International Energy Agency, 2 rue Andre Pascal, 75775 Paris Cedex 16, France (U.S. subscr. to: O E C D Publications and Information Center, 1750 Pennsylvania Ave. N.W., Washington, DC 20006)

531.64   GW   ISSN 0342-5665
ENERGY DEVELOPMENTS; journal of energy engineering. (Text in English; summaries in Spanish) 1977. q. DM.48. Technischer Verlag Resch KG, Irminfriedstr. 20-22, 8032 Graefelfing, W. Germany (B.R.D.) (U.S. subscr. to: Lynn Western Inc., Box 2549, Rancho Palos Verdes, CA 90274) Ed.Helmut Sender. adv. charts. illus. patents.

621.4   US   ISSN 0163-5662
ENERGY GUIDEBOOK. a. $10. McGraw-Hill, Inc., 1221 Ave. of the Americas, New York, NY 10020. illus.

531.64   US
ENERGY INFORMATION LOCATOR; select guide to information centers, systems, data bases, abstracting services, directories, newsletters, binder services and journals. a. $35 (or with Energy Directory Update) Environment Information Center, Inc., 292 Madison Ave., New York, NY 10017.

531.64   US
ENERGY MAGAZINE'S ANNUAL INTERNATIONAL CONFERENCE ON ENERGY. PROCEEDINGS. 1978. a. $80 per vol. Business Communications Co., Inc. (Stamford), Box 2070C, Stamford, CT 06906. Ed. Roger Memmott.

531.64   US
ENERGY, POWER, AND ENVIRONMENT; a series of reference books and textbooks. 1977. irreg., vol. 4, 1979. Marcel Dekker, Inc., 270 Madison Ave., New York, NY 10016. Eds. Philip N. Powers, David T. Shaw.

333.1   US
ENERGY REPORT TO THE ILLINOIS GENERAL ASSEMBLY. 1975. irreg. Energy Resources Commission, Rm. 713, William G. Stratton Bldg., Springfield, IL 62706.
    Formerly: Illinois. Energy Resources Commission. Report to the General Assembly of the State of Illinois.

333.7   363.6   CN
ENERGY RESOURCES CONSERVATION BOARD. CUMULATIVE ANNUAL STATISTICS: ALBERTA ELECTRIC INDUSTRY. a. Can.$2. Energy Resources Conservation Board, 603 6th Ave., S.W., Calgary, Alta. T2P 0T4, Canada. illus.

531.64   US
ENERGY SOURCES. 1976. a. $10.95. Enercom, 1641 California, Ste. 300, Denver, CO 80202. Ed. Rita Blome. circ. 20,000.

531.64   US
ENERGY TECHNOLOGY REVIEW. 1974. irreg., no. 61, 1981. $32-64. Noyes Data Corporation, Noyes Bldg., Mill Rd. at Grand Ave., Park Ridge, NJ 07656.

531.64   PO
ESTATISTICAS DA ENERGIA: CONTINENTE E ILHAS ADJACENTES. (Text in French and Portuguese) irreg. $50 per no. Instituto Nacional de Estatistica, Servicos Centrais, Av. Antonio Jose de Almeida 1, Lisbon, Portugal (Orders to: Imprensa Nacional, Casa da Moeda, Direccao Comercial, rua D. Francisco Manuel de Melo 5, Lisbon 1, Portugal)

500   600   US
EXXON BACKGROUND SERIES. (Includes annual subseries: World Energy Outlook) irreg. Exxon Corporation, 1251 Ave. of the Americas, New York, NY 10020.

531.64   US   ISSN 0364-1678
FEDERAL GOVERNMENT. a. Environment Information Center, Inc., 292 Madison Ave., New York, NY 10017.

FINANCIAL POST SURVEY OF MINES AND ENERGY RESOURCES. see *MINES AND MINING INDUSTRY*

FRANCE. COMMISSARIAT A L'ENERGIE
ATOMIQUE. ANNUAL REPORT. see
PHYSICS — Nuclear Energy

662   531.6   US
FUEL AND ENERGY SCIENCE SERIES. irreg.
price varies. Elsevier North-Holland, Inc., New
York, 52 Vanderbilt Ave., New York, NY 10017.

531.64   665.538   US
FUEL OIL SALES. a. free. U.S. Energy Information
Administration, 1726 M St., N.W., Rm. 200,
Washington, DC 20461.
  Formerly: Sales of Fuel Oil and Kerosene.

333   AG
FUNDACION BARILOCHE. INSTITUTO DE
ECONOMIA DE LA ENERGIA.
PUBLICACIONES. irreg. price varies. Fundacion
Bariloche, Instituto de Economia de la Energia,
Casilla de Correo 138, 8400 San Carlos de
Bariloche - Rio Negro, Argentina. (Co-sponsor:
Grupo de Analisis de Sistemas. Ecologicos)
  Supersedes in part: Fundacion Bariloche.
Departamento de Recursos Naturales y Energia.
Publicaciones; Formerly: Fundacion Bariloche.
Programa de Recursos Naturales y Energia.
Publicaciones (ISSN 0071-9846)

531.64   US
FUSION-FISSION ENERGY SYSTEMS REVIEW
MEETING. PROCEEDINGS. 2nd, 1978. irreg.
$11.75. U.S. Department of Energy, Washington,
DC 20545 (Orders to: NTIS, Springfield, VA
22161) Ed. S. Locke Bogart. charts. illus. (also
avail. in microfiche)

GAS RESOURCE STUDIES. see *PETROLEUM
AND GAS*

621.312   UK
GREAT BRITAIN. DEPARTMENT OF ENERGY.
ELECTRICITY: ANNUAL REPORT. a. price
varies. Department of Energy, Thames House
South, Millbank, London SW1P 4QJ, England
(Avail. from H.M.S.O., c/o Liaison Officer, Atlantic
House, Holborn Viaduct, London EC1P 1BN,
England)
  Formerly: Great Britain. Ministry of Power.
Annual Report on Electricity (ISSN 0072-663X)

338.4   UK   ISSN 0307-6547
GREAT BRITAIN. DEPARTMENT OF ENERGY.
REPORT ON RESEARCH AND
DEVELOPMENT. 1972/73. a. price varies.
Department of Energy, Thames House South,
Millbank, London SW1P 4QJ, England (Avail. from
H.M.S.O., c/o Liaison Officer, Atlantic House,
Holborn Viaduct, London EC1P 1BN, England)
stat.
  Formerly: Great Britain. Department of Trade
and Industry. Report on Research and
Development.

363.6   II
INDIA. DEPARTMENT OF POWER. REPORT.
(Text in English) 1975. a. Department of Power,
Ministry of Energy, New Delhi, India.

INTER-AMERICAN NUCLEAR ENERGY
COMMISSION. FINAL REPORT. see
PHYSICS — Nuclear Energy

531.64   US   ISSN 0146-4566
INTERNATIONAL SOLAR ENERGY SOCIETY.
AMERICAN SECTION. ANNUAL MEETING.
PROCEEDINGS. a. International Solar Energy
Society, American Section, 205B McDowell Hall,
University of Delaware, Newark, DE 19711. Eds.
Gregory E. Franta, Barbara H. Glenn.

INTERNATIONAL SYMPOSIUM ON WAVE AND
TIDAL ENERGY. PROCEEDINGS. see *WATER
RESOURCES*

621.3   UK
INTERNATIONAL SYMPOSIUM ON WIND
ENERGY SYSTEMS. PROCEEDINGS. 1977.
irreg., 3rd, 1980. price varies. British
Hydromechanics Research Association, Cranfield,
Bedford MK43 0AJ, England (Dist. in U.S. by: Air
Science Co., Box 143, Corning, N.Y. 14830)

INTERSOCIETY ENERGY CONVERSION
CONFERENCE. PROCEEDINGS. see
PHYSICS — Nuclear Energy

338   IT   ISSN 0075-1650
ITALY. DIREZIONE GENERALE DELLE FONTI
DI ENERGIA E DELLE INDUSTRIE DI BASE.
BILANCI ENERGETICI. a. Direzione Generale
delle Fonti di Energia, Rome, Italy.

JAARBOEK VAN DE OPENBARE
GASVOORZIENING. see *PETROLEUM AND
GAS*

JAPAN PETROLEUM AND ENERGY
YEARBOOK. see *PETROLEUM AND GAS*

JOURNAL OF THE NEW ALCHEMISTS. see
TECHNOLOGY: COMPREHENSIVE WORKS

551   US
KANSAS GEOLOGICAL SURVEY. ENERGY
RESOURCES SERIES. 1973. irreg. $3 per no.
Geological Survey, 1930 Ave. "A", Campus West,
University of Kansas, Lawrence, KS 66044.

620   US   ISSN 0145-0093
KANSAS STATE UNIVERSITY. CENTER FOR
ENERGY STUDIES. REPORT. (Subseries of:
Institute for Systems Design and Optimization.
Report) irreg. Kansas State University, Center for
Energy Studies, Manhattan, KS 66502. illus. stat.

KERNENERGIECENTRALE VAN 50 MWE;
DOODEWARD. JAARVERSLAG. see
ENGINEERING

KERNKRAFT LINGEN. JAHRESBERICHT. see
PHYSICS — Nuclear Energy

KERNKRAFT ZENTRALE, GUNDREMMINGEN.
JAHRESBERICHTE. see *PHYSICS — Nuclear
Energy*

KERNKRAFTWERK OBRIGHEIM.
JAHRESBERICHT. see *PHYSICS — Nuclear
Energy*

531.64   665.538   US
LIQUIFIED PETROLEUM GAS SALES. a. free.
U.S. Energy Information Administration, 1726 M
St., N.W., Rm. 200, Washington, DC 20461.

531.64   333.9   TZ
MAJI REVIEW. (Text in English) 1974. irreg (approx.
a) Ministry of Water, Energy and Minerals,
Research and Training Division, Box 35066, Dar es
Salaam, Tanzania. illus.

621.3   GW   ISSN 0580-3403
MUSTERANLAGEN DER
ENERGIEWIRTSCHAFT. 1966. irreg. price varies.
Energiewirtschaft und Technik Verlagsgesellschaft
mbH, Wendelsteinstr. 8, Postfach 1229, 8032
Graefelfing, W. Germany (B.R.D.) Ed. Edmund
Graefen. bk. rev.

531.64   614.7   US
NATIONAL CONFERENCE ON ENERGY AND
THE ENVIRONMENT. PROCEEDINGS. 3rd,
1975. irreg. $22.50. (American Institute of Chemical
Engineers, Dayton & Ohio Valley Sections) Wright
State University, Eugene W. Kettering Center, 140
East Monument Ave., Dayton, OH 45402. charts.
illus.

621.3   622.338   US   ISSN 0470-3219
NATIONAL STRIPPER WELL SURVEY. a.
Interstate Oil Compact Commission, Box 53127,
Oklahoma City, OK 73152.

531.64   665.7   US
NATURAL GAS (ANNUAL) a. free. U.S. Energy
Information Administration, 1726 M St., N.W., Rm.
200, Washington, DC 20461.

333.7   NZ
NEW ZEALAND. MINISTRY OF ENERGY.
REPORT. 1973. irreg. NZ.$1.95. Government
Printing Office, Private Bag, Wellington, New
Zealand.
  Formerly: New Zealand. Ministry of Energy
Resources. Report.

NIHON UNIVERSITY. ATOMIC ENERGY
RESEARCH INSTITUTE. ANNUAL REPORT.
see *PHYSICS — Nuclear Energy*

ENERGY   363

531.64   CN   ISSN 0704-1551
NORTHERN CANADA POWER COMMISSION.
ANNUAL REVIEW/COMMISSION D'ENERGIE
DU NORD CANADIEN. REVUE ANNUELLE.
(Text in English and French) 1969. a. Northern
Canada Power Commission, Box 5700, rue L,
Edmonton, Alta. T6C 4J8, Canada. charts. illus.
  Formerly: Commission d'Energie du Nord
Canadien. Revue de l'Exploitation (ISSN 0704-
1543)

NUCLEAR FUEL CYCLE REQUIREMENTS. see
PHYSICS — Nuclear Energy

531.64   US
OCEAN THERMAL ENERGY CONVERSION
WORKSHOP. WORKSHOP PROCEEDINGS.
2nd, 1974. irreg. $30. University of Miami, Clean
Energy Research Institute, Coral Gables, FL 33124.
(also avail. in microfiche)

OIL AND ARAB COOPERATION. ANNUAL
REVIEW. see *PETROLEUM AND GAS*

621.3   CN
ONTARIO ENERGY BOARD. ANNUAL REPORT.
1962. a. Can.$2. Ontario Energy Board, 14 Carlton
St., Toronto, Ont. M5B 1J2, Canada. circ. 500.

ORGANIZATION FOR ECONOMIC
COOPERATION AND DEVELOPMENT.
NUCLEAR ENERGY AGENCY. ACTIVITY
REPORT. see *PHYSICS — Nuclear Energy*

531.64   FR
ORGANIZATION FOR ECONOMIC
COOPERATION AND DEVELOPMENT.
INTERNATIONAL ENERGY AGENCY.
ANNUAL REPORT ON ENERGY RESEARCH,
DEVELOPMENT AND DEMONSTRATION. a.
Organization for Economic Cooperation and
Development, International Energy Agency, 2 rue
Andre Pascal, 75775 Paris Cedex 16, France.

ORGANIZATION OF ARAB PETROLEUM
EXPORTING COUNTRIES. ANNUAL ENERGY
REPORT. see *PETROLEUM AND GAS*

531.64   US
PERSPECTIVES ON THE ENERGY CRISIS. 1977.
irreg. Ann Arbor Science Publishers, Inc., Box 1425,
Ann Arbor, MI 48106.

531.64   665.538   US
PETROLEUM STATEMENT (ANNUAL) a. free.
U.S. Energy Information Administration, 1726 M
St., N.W., Rm. 200, Washington, DC 20461.

621   PL   ISSN 0372-9796
POLITECHNIKA SLASKA. ZESZYTY NAUKOWE.
ENERGETYKA. (Text in Polish; summaries in
English and Russian) 1957. irreg. price varies.
Politechnika Slaska, W. Pstrowskiego 7, 44-100
Gliwice, Poland (Dist. by: Ars Polona, Krakowskie
Przedmiescie 7, 00-068 Warsaw, Poland) Ed.
Gerard Kosman.

658.8   US
POWER'S ENERGY MANAGEMENT
GUIDEBOOK. 1975. a. McGraw-Hill Publications
Co., 1221 Ave. of the Americas, New York, NY
10020. Ed. Bob Schwieger. circ. 17,000.

333.7   622   CN   ISSN 0380-4275
RESERVES OF COAL, PROVINCE OF ALBERTA.
1972. a. Can.$18. Energy Resources Conservation
Board, 603 Sixth Ave. S.W., Calgary, Alta. T2P
2M4, Canada. illus.

333.7   622.338   CN   ISSN 0380-4305
SCHEDULE OF WELLS DRILLED FOR OIL AND
GAS, PROVINCE OF ALBERTA. 1971. a. Energy
Resources Conservation Board, 603 Sixth Ave.
S.W., Calgary, Alta. T2P 2M4, Canada.

SCHEDULE OF WELLS DRILLED FOR OIL AND
NATURAL GAS IN BRITISH COLUMBIA. see
PETROLEUM AND GAS

333.8   GW
SCHRIFTENREIHE AKTUELLE FRAGEN DER
ENERGIEWIRTSCHAFT. irreg., no. 9, 1976. price
varies. R. Oldenbourg Verlag GmbH, Rosenheimer
Str. 145, 8000 Munich 80, W. Germany (B.R.D.)

531.64 GW
SCHRIFTENREIHE KERNENERGIE. 1979. irreg. price varies. (Landesamt fuer Umweltschutz) R. Oldenbourg Verlag GmbH, Rosenheimer Str. 145, 8000 Munich 80, W. Germany (B.R.D.)

621.47 US
SOLAR ENERGY RESEARCH AND DEVELOPMENT REPORTS. irreg. U.S. Department of Energy, Washington, DC 20545.

530 US
SURVEY OF THE EMERGING SOLAR ENERGY INDUSTRY. a. $60. Solar Energy Information Services, Box 204, San Mateo, CA 94401. Ed. Francis deWinter.

338.476 662.6 US
U S S R REPORT: RESOURCES. 1969. irreg. (approx. 84/yr.) $294. U.S. Joint Publications Research Service, 1000 N. Glebe Rd., Arlington, VA 22201 (Orders to: NTIS, Springfield, VA 22161)
Formerly: Translations on U S S R Resources.

531.6 US
U.S. DEPARTMENT OF ENERGY. DIRECTORY OF INFORMATION CENTERS. 1967. irreg. free. U.S. Department of Energy, Technical Information Center, Box 62, Oak Ridge, TN 37830.
Former titles: U.S. Energy Research and Development Administration. Directory of E R D A Information Centers; U.S. Atomic Energy Commission. Directory of U S A E C Information Analysis Centers; Atomic Energy Commission. Directory of U S A E C Specialized Information and Data Centers.

531.64 US ISSN 0190-1141
U.S. DEPARTMENT OF ENERGY. FOSSIL ENERGY RESEARCH AND DEVELOPMENT PROGRAM. a. U.S. Department of Energy, Office of Energy Technology, Washington, DC 20545. Key Title: Fossil Energy Research and Development Program of the U.S. Department of Energy.
Formerly: U.S. Energy Research Administration. Fossil Energy Research Program.

531.64 US ISSN 0161-1674
U.S. DEPARTMENT OF ENERGY. OFFICE OF STATE AND LOCAL PROGRAMS. ANNUAL REPORT TO THE PRESIDENT AND THE CONGRESS ON THE STATE ENERGY CONSERVATION PROGRAM. a. U.S. Department of Energy, Office of State and Local Programs, Washington, DC 20461. Key Title: Annual Report to the President and the Congress on the State Energy Conservation Program.

U.S. DEPARTMENT OF TRANSPORTATION. NATIONAL TRANSPORTATION STATISTICS. ANNUAL; a supplement to the summary of national transportation statistics. see STATISTICS

351.64 US
U. S. ENERGY INFORMATION ADMINISTRATION. ANNUAL REPORT TO CONGRESS. a. U.S. Energy Information Administration, Washington, DC 20461.

354.941 AT
WESTERN AUSTRALIA. STATE ENERGY COMMISSION. ANNUAL REPORT. 1976. a. State Energy Commission, Perth, W.A., Australia. illus.

530 US
WESTERN REGIONAL SOLAR ENERGY DIRECTORY. 1976. a. $2.35. California Solar Energy Association, 202 C St., 1A, San Diego, CA 92101. Eds. John Brand, Ildiko Demeter.

531.64 US
WILDERNESS ENERGY SURVEY. 1979. quadrennial. $3.50. (Rockefeller Foundation) World Priorities, Inc., Box 1003, Leesburg, VA 22075. Ed. Ruth Leger Sivard.

531.64 US
WIND ENERGY WORKSHOP. PROCEEDINGS. 3rd, 1978. biennial. U.S. Department of Energy, Division of Solar Technology, Washington, DC 20545 (Order from: Supt. of Documents, Washington DC 20402)

WOODSTOVE, COALSTOVE, FIREPLACE & EQUIPMENT DIRECTORY; the international sourcebook of wood and coal heating products. see HEATING, PLUMBING AND REFRIGERATION

531.64 UK
WORLD ENERGY CONFERENCE. DIRECTORY OF ENERGY INFORMATION CENTRES IN THE WORLD. (Text in English & French) 1976. triennial. £28. World Energy Conference, 34 St. James St., London SW1A 1HD, England.

363.6 UK ISSN 0084-1722
WORLD ENERGY CONFERENCE. PLENARY CONFERENCES. TRANSACTIONS. triennial, 11th, 1980, Munich. $125. World Energy Conference, 34 St. James St., London SW1A 1HD, England.

621.3 UK ISSN 0084-1730
WORLD ENERGY CONFERENCE. SURVEY OF ENERGY RESOURCES. (Text in English, French and German) 1962. every 6 years(updated statistical tables every 3 years) £25. World Energy Conference, 34 St. James St., London SW1A 1HD, England.

531.64 UK
WORLD ENERGY CONFERENCE. TECHNICAL DATA ON FUEL. every 6 yrs. £30. World Energy Conference, 34 St. James St., London SW1A 1HD, England. Eds. J.W. Rose, J.R. Cooper.

531.64 UK
WORLD ENERGY DIRECTORY. 1981. irreg. £70. Longman Group Ltd., Longman House, Burnt Mill, Harlow, Essex CM20 2JE, England (Dist. in U.S. and Canada by: Gale Research Co. Ltd., Book Tower, Detroit, MI 48226)

621.3 UN ISSN 0084-1749
WORLD ENERGY SUPPLIES. 1952. triennial; latest issue, 1969-72. price varies. United Nations, Department of Economic and Social Affairs, Secretariat, New York, NY 10017 (Dist. by: United Nations Publications, Room LX-2300, New York, NY 10017; or Distribution and Sales Section, Palais des Nations, CH-1211 Geneva 10, Switzerland)

ENERGY — Abstracting, Bibliographies, Statistics

ANNUAL BULLETIN OF ELECTRIC ENERGY STATISTICS FOR EUROPE. see ELECTRICITY AND ELECTRICAL ENGINEERING — Abstracting, Bibliographies, Statistics

338 314 UN
ANNUAL BULLETIN OF GENERAL ENERGY STATISTICS FOR EUROPE. (Text in English, French and Russian) 1970 (covering 1976 & 1968) a; vol. 11, 1978. price varies. United Nations Economic Commission for Europe, Palais des Nations, 1200 Geneva 10, Switzerland (Or United Nations Publications, Room LX-2300, New York, NY, 10017)

333.8 AG
ARGENTINA. DIRECCION GENERAL DE PLANIFICACION Y CONTROL ENERGETICO. ANUARIO ESTADISTICO. Cover title: Combustibles. a. Direccion General de Planificacion y Control Energetico, Avda. Julio A. Roca 651, 1322 Buenos Aires, Argentina. stat.
Formerly: Argentina. Direccion Nacional de Energia y Combustibles. Departamento de Estadistica. Anuario Estadistico Combustibles.

ATOMIC ENERGY OF CANADA. LIST OF PUBLICATIONS. see PHYSICS — Abstracting, Bibliographies, Statistics

531.64 AT
AUSTRALIA. BUREAU OF STATISTICS. VICTORIAN OFFICE. MANUFACTURING ESTABLISHMENTS: USAGE OF ELECTRICITY AND FUELS. 1969. a. free. Australian Bureau of Statistics, Victorian Office, Box 2796Y, G.P.O., Melbourne, Vic. 3001, Australia. Ed. H. L. Speagle. charts. stat. circ. 500.

531.64 AT
AUSTRALIAN ENERGY STATISTICS. 1981. a. Aus.$4.10. Australian Government Publishing Service, Box 84, Camberia, A.C.T. 2600, Australia.

531.64 639.9 016 AT ISSN 0155-9443
AUSTRALIAN RENEWABLE ENERGY RESOURCES INDEX. 1978. a. Aus.$5. C. S. I. R. O., Editorial and Publications Service, 314 Albert St., East Melbourne, Victoria 3002, Australia. Ed. Robert D. Clark. bibl. index. circ. 800. (microfiche; back issues avail.) Indexed: Aus.Sci.Ind.

CANADA. STATISTICS CANADA. ELECTRIC POWER STATISTICS VOLUME 1: ANNUAL ELECTRIC POWER SURVEY OF CAPABILITY AND LOAD/STATISTIQUE DE L'ENERGIE ELECTRIQUE. VOLUME 1: ENQUETE ANNUELLE SUR LA PUISSANCE MAXIMALE ET SUR LA CHARGE DES RESEAUX. see ELECTRICITY AND ELECTRICAL ENGINEERING — Abstracting, Bibliographies, Statistics

614.7 016 US ISSN 0094-6281
ENERGY INDEX. 1973. a. $125. Environment Information Center, Inc., 292 Madison Ave., New York, NY 10017. Ed. Monica Pronin. abstr, charts, stat. index. (also avail. in microfiche; magnetic tape; back issues avail.)

318.1 BL ISSN 0512-350X
ESTATISTICA BRASILEIRA DE ENERGIA/ BRAZILIAN ENERGY STATISTICS. (Text in Portuguese and English; summaries in English) 1965. a. free, controlled circulation. World Energy Conference, Comite Nacional Brasileiro, Av. Presidente Vargas, 642, Rio de Janeiro, Brazil. Eds. John R. Cotrim, Julius A. Wilberg. charts. stat. circ. 1,000. (back issues avail)

338 314 GW
GERMANY (FEDERAL REPUBLIC, 1949-) STATISTISCHES BUNDESAMT FACHSERIE 19, REIHE 2: WASSERVERSORGUNG UND ABWASSERBESEITIGUNG. (Consists of several subseries) irreg. price varies. W. Kohlhammer-Verlag GmbH, Abt. Veroeffentlichungen des Statistischen Bundesamtes, Philipp-Reis-Str. 3, Postfach 421120, 6500 Mainz 42, W. Germany (B.R.D.)

378 NO
NORWAY. STATISTISK SENTRALBYRAA. ELECTRISITESSTATISTIKK/ELECTRICITY STATISTICS. (Subseries of its Norges Offisielle Statistikk) 1937. a. Statistisk Sentralbyraa, Box 8131 Dep., Oslo 1, Norway.

621 FR
ORGANIZATION FOR ECONOMIC COOPERATION AND DEVELOPMENT. ENERGY STATISTICS. (Text in English and French) 1965. a. $12.50. Organization for Economic Cooperation and Development, 2 rue Andre - Pascal, 75775 Paris Cedex 16, France (U.S. orders to: O.E.C.D. Publications and Information Center, 1750 Pennsylvania Ave., N.W., Washington, D.C. 20006) (also avail. in microfiche)
Formerly: Organization for Economic Cooperation and Development. Statistics of Energy.

330 EI ISSN 0081-489X
STATISTICAL OFFICE OF THE EUROPEAN COMMUNITIES. ENERGY STATISTICS. YEARBOOK. (Text in German, French, Italian Dutch, English) a. B.P. 1907, Luxembourg, Luxembourg (Dist. in the U.S. by: European Community Information Service, 2100 M St., NW, Suite 707, Washington, DC 20037)

621.31 310 US ISSN 0161-9004
STATISTICS OF PRIVATELY OWNED ELECTRIC UTILITIES IN THE UNITED STATES. 1955. a. $12.50. U.S. Energy Information Administration, Washington, DC 20461 (Orders to: NTIS, Springfield, VA 22161) (also avail. in microfiche from NTI)
Formerly (until 1966): Statistics of Electric Utilities in the United States. Classes A and B Privately Owned Companies (ISSN 0083-0828)

318 531.64 VE
VENEZUELA. MINISTERIO DE ENERGIA Y MINAS. APENDICE ESTADISTICO. (Supplement to: Venezuela. Ministerio de Energia y Minas. Memoria) a. Ministerio de Energia y Minas, Oficina de Estudios Economicos Energeticos, Caracas, Venezuela. charts.

318 531.64 VE
VENEZUELA. MINISTERO DE ENERGIA Y MINAS. MEMORIA. a. Ministerio de Energia y Minas, Oficina de Estudios Economicos Energeticos, Caracas, Venezuela.

ENGINEERING

see also Engineering—Chemical Engineering; Engineering—Civil Engineering; Engineering—Engineering Mechanics and Materials; Engineering—Hydraulic Engineering; Engineering—Mechanical Engineering; Electricity and Electrical Engineering

A E. see ENERGY

620 690 US
A E M S SEMINAR (PAPERS) 1970. a. $12. American Engineering Model Society, Box 2066, Aiken, SC 29801. circ. 750.

A G E DIGEST. (Asian Information Center for Geotechnical Engineering) see EARTH SCIENCES

658.5 331 US
A I I E. INDUSTRIAL AND LABOR RELATIONS MONOGRAPH SERIES. irreg. price varies. American Institute of Industrial Engineers, Inc., Industrial and Labor Relations Division, 25 Technology Park, Norcross, GA 30071.

620 US
A S E E PROFILE. (Special issue of Engineering Education) a. $7.50. American Society for Engineering Education, Suite 400, One Dupont Circle, N. W., Washington, DC 20036. Ed. P. W. Samaras. adv. illus. circ. 12,000. (also avail. in microform) Indexed: Curr.Cont. Eng.Ind.
Formerly: American Society for Engineering Education. Review and Directory (ISSN 0092-4326)

671.7 US ISSN 0363-8065
ABRASIVE ENGINEERING SOCIETY. ABRASIVE USAGE CONFERENCE. PROCEEDINGS.* 1962. a. price varies. Abrasive Engineering Society, 1700 Painters Run Rd., Pittsburgh, PA 15243. index.
Formerly: American Society for Abrasive Methods. Technical Conference. Proceedings (ISSN 0066-006X)

660.63 US ISSN 0065-2210
ADVANCES IN BIOCHEMICAL ENGINEERING. 1971. irreg., no. 19, 1981. Springer-Verlag, 175 Fifth Ave., New York, NY 10010 (Also Berlin, Heidelberg, Vienna) Eds. T.K Ghose & A. Fiechter. (reprint service avail. from ISI)

ADVANCES IN BIOENGINEERING. see BIOLOGY

ADVANCES IN CRYOGENIC ENGINEERING. see PHYSICS — Heat

620 US ISSN 0272-4790
ADVANCES IN DRYING. 1980. irreg. $55. Hemisphere Publishing Corporation, 1025 Vermont Ave., N.W., Washington, DC 20005. Ed. A.S. Mujumdar. bibl. charts.

ADVANCES IN NUCLEAR SCIENCE AND TECHNOLOGY. see PHYSICS — Nuclear Energy

ALASKA. STATE BOARD OF REGISTRATION FOR ARCHITECTS, ENGINEERS AND LAND SURVEYORS. DIRECTORY OF ARCHITECTS, ENGINEERS AND LAND SURVEYORS. see ARCHITECTURE

ALLIANCE FOR ENGINEERING IN MEDICINE AND BIOLOGY. PROCEEDINGS OF THE ANNUAL CONFERENCE. see MEDICAL SCIENCES

AMERICAN ACADEMY OF ENVIRONMENTAL ENGINEERS. ROSTER. see ENVIRONMENTAL STUDIES

650 657 US ISSN 0065-7158
AMERICAN ASSOCIATION OF COST ENGINEERS. TRANSACTIONS OF THE ANNUAL MEETING. 1967. a. $35. American Association of Cost Engineers, 308 Monongahela Bldg, Morgantown, WV 26505. Ed. Kenneth K. Humphreys. circ. 1,250. (also avail. in microform from UMI)

620 US ISSN 0071-0393
AMERICAN ASSOCIATION OF ENGINEERING SOCIETIES. ENGINEERING MANPOWER COMMISSION. ENGINEERING AND TECHNOLOGY DEGREES. (Former name of organization: Engineers Joint Council) a. $100 (or Part 1, $25; Part 2, $75; Part 3, $25) American Association of Engineering Societies, Engineering Manpower Commission, 345 E. 47 St., New York, NY 10017.

331.7 620 US
AMERICAN ASSOCIATION OF ENGINEERING SOCIETIES. ENGINEERING MANPOWER COMMISSION. ENGINEERING ENROLLMENT DATA. (Former name of organization: Engineers Joint Council) a. $75 (or $45 each part) American Association of Engineering Societies, Engineering Manpower Commission, 345 E. 47 St., New York, NY 10017.
Formerly: Engineering and Technology Enrollments (ISSN 0071-0407)

331.7 620 US ISSN 0071-0415
AMERICAN ASSOCIATION OF ENGINEERING SOCIETIES. ENGINEERING MANPOWER COMMISSION. ENGINEERS' SALARIES: SPECIAL INDUSTRY REPORT. (Former Name of Organization: Engineers Joint Council) biennial. $60. American Association of Engineering Societies, Engineering Manpower Commission, 345 E. 47 St., New York, NY 10017.

331.7 620 US ISSN 0071-0423
AMERICAN ASSOCIATION OF ENGINEERING SOCIETIES. ENGINEERING MANPOWER COMMISSION. PROFESSIONAL INCOME OF ENGINEERS. (Former Name of Organization: Engineers Joint Council) 1953. biennial. $15. American Association of Engineering Societies, Engineering Manpower Commission, 345 E. 47 St., New York, NY 10017.

331.7 620 US
AMERICAN ASSOCIATION OF ENGINEERING SOCIETIES. ENGINEERING MANPOWER COMMISSION. PLACEMENT OF ENGINEERING AND TECHNOLOGY GRADUATES. a. $25. American Association of Engineering Societies, Engineering Manpower Commission, 345 E. 47 St., New York, NY 10017.
Formerly: Prospects of Engineering and Technology Graduates (ISSN 0071-0431)

331.7 620 US
AMERICAN ASSOCIATION OF ENGINEERING SOCIETIES. ENGINEERING MANPOWER COMMISSION. SALARIES OF ENGINEERING TECHNICIANS AND TECHNOLOGISTS. 1966. biennial. $75. American Association of Engineering Societies, Engineering Manpower Commission, 345 E. 47 St., New York, NY 10017.
Formerly: Salaries of Engineering Technicians (ISSN 0071-0474)

620 US
AMERICAN ASSOCIATION OF ENGINEERING SOCIETIES. ENGINEERING MANPOWER COMMISSION. SALARIES OF ENGINEERS IN EDUCATION. 1972. biennial. $10. ‡ American Association of Engineering Societies, Engineering Manpower Commission, 345 E. 47th St., New York, NY 10017. Ed. Patrick J. Sheridan.

658.5 US
AMERICAN INSTITUTE OF INDUSTRIAL ENGINEERS. ENGINEERING ECONOMY DIVISION. MONOGRAPH SERIES. irreg., latest no.5. price varies. American Institute of Industrial Engineers, Inc., 25 Technology Park/Atlanta, Norcross, GA 30092. (reprint service avail. from UMI)

621 US
AMERICAN INSTITUTE OF INDUSTRIAL ENGINEERS. FACILITIES PLANNING AND DESIGN DIVISION. MONOGRAPHS. irreg. price varies. American Institute of Industrial Engineers, Inc., 25 Technology Park/Atlanta, Norcross, GA 30092. (reprint service avail. from UMI)

621 US ISSN 0163-1810
AMERICAN INSTITUTE OF INDUSTRIAL ENGINEERS. FALL INDUSTRIAL ENGINEERING CONFERENCE. PROCEEDINGS. 1973? a. $40 to non-members; members $20. American Institute of Industrial Engineers, Inc., 25 Technology Park/Atlanta, Norcross, GA 30092. (reprint service avail. from UMI)
Supersedes: American Institute of Industrial Engineers. Systems Engineering Conference. Proceedings.

620 US
AMERICAN INSTITUTE OF INDUSTRIAL ENGINEERS. MANAGEMENT DIVISION. MONOGRAPHS. irreg. price varies. American Institute of Industrial Engineers, Inc., 25 Technology Park/Atlanta, Norcross, GA 30092. (reprint service avail. from UMI)

621 US
AMERICAN INSTITUTE OF INDUSTRIAL ENGINEERS. MANUFACTURING SYSTEMS DIVISION. MONOGRAPHS. irreg. price varies. American Institute of Industrial Engineers, Inc., 25 Technology Park/Atlanta, Norcross, GA 30092. (reprint service avail. from UMI)

658.5 US
AMERICAN INSTITUTE OF INDUSTRIAL ENGINEERS. MATERIAL HANDLING INSTITUTE. PROCEEDINGS. a. $30. American Institute of Industrial Engineers, Inc., 25 Technology Pk./Atlanta, Norcross, GA 30092. (reprint service avail. from UMI)
Formerly: Material Handling and Industrial Engineer (ISSN 0190-4302)

620 US
AMERICAN INSTITUTE OF INDUSTRIAL ENGINEERS. OPERATIONS RESEARCH DIVISION. MONOGRAPHS. irreg. price varies. American Institute of Industrial Engineers, Inc., 25 Technology Park/Atlanta, Norcross, GA 30092. (reprint service avail. from UMI)

658.5 US
AMERICAN INSTITUTE OF INDUSTRIAL ENGINEERS. PRODUCTION PLANNING AND CONTROL DIVISION. MONOGRAPHS. irreg., latest, no. 3. price varies. American Institute of Industrial Engineers, Inc., 25 Technology Park/Atlanta, Norcross, GA 30092. (reprint service avail. from UMI)

620 US
AMERICAN INSTITUTE OF INDUSTRIAL ENGINEERS. QUALITY CONTROL AND RELIABILITY ENGINEERING DIVISION. MONOGRAPHS. irreg. price varies. American Institute of Industrial Engineers, Inc., 25 Technology Park/Atlanta, Norcross, GA 30092. (reprint service avail. from UMI)

658.5 US
AMERICAN INSTITUTE OF INDUSTRIAL ENGINEERS. WORK MEASUREMENT AND METHODS ENGINEERING DIVISION. MONOGRAPHS. irreg., latest, no. 5. price varies. American Institute of Industrial Engineers,Inc., 25 Technology Park/Atlanta, Norcross, GA 30092. (reprint service avail. from UMI)

620 US ISSN 0190-1052
AMERICAN SOCIETY FOR ENGINEERING EDUCATION. ANNUAL CONFERENCE PROCEEDINGS. a. $30 to non-members; members $25. American Society for Engineering Education, One Dupont Circle, N.W., Suite 400, Washington, DC 20036.

620.86 US
AMERICAN SOCIETY OF SAFETY ENGINEERS. PROCEEDINGS. PROFESSIONAL CONFERENCE. a. $20. American Society of Safety Engineers, 850 Busse Highway, Park Ridge, IL 60068.

ENGINEERING

620   SP
ANALES DE LA UNIVERSIDAD HISPALENSE. SERIE: INGENIERIA. irreg. price varies. Universidad de Sevilla, San Fernando 4, Seville, Spain.

ANALYTICAL CALORIMETRY. see *PHYSICS — Heat*

ANNUAIRE DE L'ACTIVITE NUCLEAIRE FRANCAISE. see *PHYSICS — Nuclear Energy*

ANNUAL BOOK OF A S T M STANDARDS. PART 45. NUCLEAR STANDARDS. see *ENGINEERING — Engineering Mechanics And Materials*

ANNUAL REVIEW OF BIOPHYSICS AND BIOENGINEERING. see *BIOLOGY — Biophysics*

APPLIED PHYSICS AND ENGINEERING. see *PHYSICS*

658.5   US   ISSN 0570-9601
ARIZONA STATE UNIVERSITY. FACULTY OF INDUSTRIAL ENGINEERING. INDUSTRIAL ENGINEERING RESEARCH BULLETIN. 1965. a. ‡ Arizona State University, Faculty of Industrial Engineering, Tempe, AZ 85281. Ed. William C. Moor. abstr. charts. circ. 600 (controlled)

621.9   US   ISSN 0066-8702
ASSEMBLY ENGINEERING MASTER CATALOG. 1962. a. $25. Hitchcock Publishing Co., Hitchcock Bldg., Wheaton, IL 60187. Ed. Roland Laboissonniere. adv. circ. 42,000. (also avail. in microform from UMI; reprint service avail. from UMI)
Formerly: Assembly Directory and Handbook (ISSN 0066-8699)

620   IV
ASSOCIATION DES INGENIEURS ET TECHNICIENS AFRICAINS DE COTE D'IVOIRE. ANNUAIRE.* a. Association des Ingenieurs et Techniciens Africains de Cote d'Ivoire, Autoroute de Port-Bouet, Boite Postale 794, Abidjan, Ivory Coast.

620.2   II
ASSOCIATION OF INDIAN ENGINEERING INDUSTRY. HANDBOOK OF STATISTICS. (Text in English) 1963. a. price varies. Association of Indian Engineering Industry, Secretary, 172 Jorbaugh, New Delhi 110003, India.
Continues: Indian Engineering Association. Handbook of Statistics (ISSN 0073-6333)

620   AT   ISSN 0084-6996
AUSTRALASIAN SOCIETY OF ENGINEERS. ENGINEERS HANDBOOK.* 1954/55. a. contr. free circ. Australasian Society of Engineers, 422-424 Kent St., Sydney, N.S.W. 2000, Australia.

AUSTRALIA.ATOMIC ENERGY COMMISSION. RESEARCH ESTABLISHMENT. A A E C/E. see *PHYSICS — Nuclear Energy*

AUSTRALIA.ATOMIC ENERGY COMMISSION. RESEARCH ESTABLISHMENT. A A E C/M. see *PHYSICS — Nuclear Energy*

620   AT   ISSN 0084-7496
AUSTRALIAN NATIONAL UNIVERSITY, CANBERRA. DEPARTMENT OF ENGINEERING PHYSICS. PUBLICATION EP-RR. 1959. irreg. ‡ Australian National University, Research School of Physical Sciences, Dept. of Engineering Physics, Box 4, Canberra, A.C.T. 2600, Australia. Ed. Prof. S. Kaneff.

620   UK   ISSN 0067-5709
B E M A ENGINEERING DIRECTORY. 1937. a. £2.50 for non-members. Bristol and West of England Engineering Manufacturers Association Ltd., BEMA House, 4 Broad Plain, Bristol BS2 0NG, England. Ed. D.W.D. Steward.

658.5 600   UK   ISSN 0306-1450
B I A S JOURNAL. 1969. a. membership. Bristol Industrial Archaeological Society, c/o J. Powell, 22 Penrose, Whitchurch, Bristol BS14 0AQ, England. Ed. R. A. Buchanan. bk. rev. cum.index every 5 years. circ. 500.

620   BG   ISSN 0070-8186
BANGLADESH UNIVERSITY OF ENGINEERING AND TECHNOLOGY, DACCA. TECHNICAL JOURNAL.* (Supersedes the Technical Journal of the University of Dacca's Ahsanullah Engineering College) (Text in English) 1962. a. Bangladesh University of Engineering and Technology, Ramna, Dacca 2, Bangladesh.

BIOTECHNOLOGY & BIOENGINEERING SYMPOSIA. see *BIOLOGY*

620   TU
BOGAZICI UNIVERSITY JOURNAL: ENGINEERING. (Text in English or Turkish) 1973. a. $3. Bogazici Universitesi, Box 2, Istanbul, Turkey.

620   BL   ISSN 0067-9607
BOLETIM DE ENGENHARIA DE PRODUCAO.* 1962. irreg. Universidade de Sao Paulo, Departamento de Engenharia de Electricidade, Cidade Universitaria, "Armando de Salles Oliveira", C.P.8191, Sao Paulo, Brazil.

620   CL
BOLETIN INGENIERIA COMERCIAL. 1975. irreg. free. Universidad Catolica de Valparaiso, Escuela de Ingenieria Comercial, Pilcomayo 478, Cerro Concepcion, Valparaiso, Chile. adv. circ. 300.

620   US
BOLTON LANDING CONFERENCE. PROCEEDINGS. 3rd, 1970. irreg., 4th, 1975. $32. Claitor's Publishing Division, 3165 S. Arcadian, Box 3333, Baton Rogue, LA 80821. Eds. J. Walter, J. Westbrook, D. Woodford. illus.

620   US   ISSN 0068-1008
BRIGHAM YOUNG UNIVERSITY. COLLEGE OF ENGINEERING SCIENCES AND TECHNOLOGY. ANNUAL ENGINEERING SYMPOSIUM. ABSTRACTS. 1960. a. price varies. ‡ Brigham Young University Press, 205 University Press Bldg., Provo, UT 84602. circ. 500.

620 378   US
C I E C PROCEEDINGS. 1967. a. $12. ‡ American Society for Engineering Education, College Industry Education Conference, 1 Dupont Circle, Suite 400, Washington, DC 20036. circ. 1,000.
Supersedes (as of 1976): Industry-Engineering Education Series (ISSN 0073-7801) & Continuing Engineering Studies Series (ISSN 0069-956X)

620   US
CALIFORNIA INSTITUTE OF TECHNOLOGY. DIVISION OF ENGINEERING AND APPLIED SCIENCE. ANNUAL REPORT. 1953/54. a. free. California Institute of Technology, Division of Engineering and Applied Science, 1201 E. California Blvd., Pasadena, CA 91125. circ. 2,500.
Formerly: California Institute of Technology. Division of Engineering and Applied Science. Report of Research and Other Activities (ISSN 0068-5658)

620 621.9   CN   ISSN 0068-8665
CANADIAN ENGINEERING & INDUSTRIAL YEAR BOOK. 1945. a. Can.$28($40) Lloyd Publications of Canada, Box 262, West Hill, Ont. M1E 4R5, Canada. adv. index. circ. 9,500.
Formerly: Canadian Engineering & Machinery Year Book.

620   NZ   ISSN 0069-0201
CANTERBURY ENGINEERING JOURNAL. 1970. irreg., no. 5, 1975. price varies. University of Canterbury, School of Engineering, Private Bag, Christchurch, New Zealand. Ed. R.H.T. Bates. cum.index. circ. 400.

620 690   US
CATALOG OF MODEL SERVICES AND SUPPLIES. 1975. a. $5. American Engineering Model Society, Box 2066, Aiken, SC 29801. Ed. R. J. Hale. circ. 500.

CENTRAL NUCLEAIRE ARDENNES. see *PHYSICS — Nuclear Energy*

CENTRALE ELLETRONUCLEARE LATINA. RELAZIONE ANNUALE. see *PHYSICS — Nuclear Energy*

CENTRALE NUCLEARE GARIGLIANO. RELAZIONE ANNUALE. see *PHYSICS — Nuclear Energy*

620   FR   ISSN 0069-2611
CHAMBRE DES INGENIEURS-CONSEILS DE FRANCE. ANNUAIRE. 1955. a. 140 F. Chambre des Ingenieurs-Conseils de France, 3 rue Leon Bonnat, 75016 Paris, France.

681   US   ISSN 0163-0679
CHILTON'S CONTROL EQUIPMENT MASTER. Abbreviated title: C E M. 1976. a. $45. Chilton Co., Inc., Chilton Way, Radnor, PA 19089. Ed. Pat O'Donnell. adv. circ. 50,000.

COGWHEEL. see *COLLEGE AND ALUMNI*

620   SP
COLECCION TEMAS BASICOS DE INGENIERIA. irreg. Editorial Gustavo Gili, S.A., Rosellon 87-89, Barcelona 15, Spain.

620   II
COLLEGE OF ENGINEERING, TRIVANDRUM. MAGAZINE. (Text in English or Malayalam) 1942. a. Rs.10. College of Engineering, Trivandrum 16, Kerala, India. adv. illus.

658.5   US
COMPENSATION OF INDUSTRIAL ENGINEERS. 1972. a. $60 to non-members; members $35. American Institute of Industrial Engineers, Inc., 25 Technology Park/Atlanta, Norcross, GA 30092. (reprint service avail. from UMI)

CONFERENCE ON REMOTE SYSTEMS TECHNOLOGY. PROCEEDINGS. see *PHYSICS — Nuclear Energy*

620   UK   ISSN 0069-9225
CONSULTING ENGINEER WHO'S WHO AND YEAR BOOK. 1946. a. £13.50. Northwood Publications Ltd., Elm House, 10-16 Elm Street, London WC1X 0BP, England. Ed. J. H. Stephens. adv. circ. 2,000.

620   CN   ISSN 0317-6525
CONSULTING ENGINEERS-CANADA-INGENIEURS-CONSEILS. (Text in English and French and Spanish) 1958. irreg. $20. ‡ Association of Consulting Engineers of Canada, 130 Albert St., St. 616, Ottawa K1P 5G4, Canada. Ed. H. R. Pinault. circ. 2,500.
Formerly: Association of Consulting Engineers of Canada. Specialization Typical Projects (ISSN 0084-6899)

DENMARK. ATOMENERGIKOMMISSIONENS FORSOEGSANSLAEG, RISOE. RISOE REPORT. see *PHYSICS — Nuclear Energy*

621.8   US   ISSN 0190-2296
DESIGN NEWS. FASTENING. a. $6. Cahners Publishing Co. (Chicago), Division of Reed Holdings, Inc., 5 S. Wabash Ave., Chicago, IL 60603 (Subscr. address: 270 St. Paul St., Denver, CO 80206) adv.
Formerly: Design News Annual. Fastening Edition (ISSN 0190-2288)

620   US   ISSN 0070-5470
DIRECTORY OF ENGINEERING SOCIETIES AND RELATED ORGANIZATIONS. 1956. biennial. $23. Engineers Joint Council, 345 E. 47 St., New York, NY 10017. Ed. Jean Gregory. index.

DIRECTORY OF INDIAN ENGINEERING EXPORTERS. see *BUSINESS AND ECONOMICS — Trade And Industrial Directories*

DIRECTORY OF LAND DRILLING AND OILWELL SERVICING CONTRACTORS. see *PETROLEUM AND GAS*

DIRECTORY OF THE SCIENTISTS, TECHNOLOGISTS, AND ENGINEERS OF THE P C S I R. (Pakistan Council of Scientific and Industrial Research) see *SCIENCES: COMPREHENSIVE WORKS*

E N I ANNUAL REPORT. (Ente Nazionale Idrocarburi) see *ENERGY*

620   US   ISSN 0098-6305
E N R DIRECTORY OF DESIGN FIRMS. Cover title: Design Firms. 1974. a. (Engineering News-Record) McGraw-Hill Publications Co., 1221 Ave. of the Americas, New York, NY 10020. Ed. Jim Webber. illus. circ. 11,000.

621.8 US
ELECTRONIC PACKAGING AND PRODUCTION VENDOR SELECTION ISSUE. 1966. a. $10 (free to qualified personnel) Milton S. Kiver Publications, Inc., 222 W. Adams, Chicago, IL 60606. Ed. Donald J. Levinthal. adv. circ. controlled.
Formerly: Electronic Packaging and Production Buyers Guide; Electronic Production Aids Catalog (ISSN 0424-8287)

621.3 UR
ELEKTROENERGETIKA I AVTOMATIZATSIYA ENERGOUSTANOVOK. (Subseries of: Kharkivskyi Politekhnichnyi Instytut. Vestnik) 1971. irreg. 0.67 Rub. Kharkivskyi Politekhnichnyi Instytut, Ul. Frunze, 21, Kharkov, U.S.S.R. illus.

620 GW
ELSNERS HANDBUCH FUER STAEDTISCHES INGENIEURWESEN. 1973. a. DM.28.40. Otto Elsner Verlagsgesellschaft, Schoefferstr. 15, 6100 Darmstadt, W. Germany (B.R.D.) Ed. Otto Sill. circ. 3,500.
Formerly: Elsners Handbuch fuer Staedtischen Ingenieurbau.

620 UK ISSN 0071-0288
ENGINEER BUYERS GUIDE. 1897. a. £13.50. Morgan-Grampian Book Publishing Co., 30 Calderwood St., Calderwood Street, London SE18 6QH, England. Ed. Jane Doyle. adv. circ. 5,500.

620 301.24 US ISSN 0094-7288
ENGINEERING AND SOCIETY SERIES. 1973. irreg., no. 3, 1974. Washington State University, College of Engineering, Pullman, WA 99163. Ed. David C. Flaherty. illus.

620.7 370.58 US
ENGINEERING COLLEGE RESEARCH AND GRADUATE STUDY. (Supplement to Engineering Education) 1967. a. $10. American Society for Engineering Education, One Dupont Circle, Suite 400, Washington, DC 20036. Ed. Patricia W. Samaras. adv. index. circ. 13,000. (also avail. in microfiche; microfilm) Indexed: Curr.Cont. Eng.Ind.
Formerly: Directory of Engineering College Research and Graduate Study (ISSN 0070-5462)

ENGINEERING COMMITTEE ON OCEANIC RESOURCES. PROCEEDINGS OF THE GENERAL ASSEMBLY. see WATER RESOURCES

620 US
ENGINEERING DESIGN GUIDES. irreg. price varies. Oxford University Press, 200 Madison Ave., New York, NY 10016 (And Ely House, 37 Dover St., London W1X 4AH, England)

620 US
ENGINEERING FOUNDATION ANNUAL REPORT. 1915. a. free. Engineering Foundation, United Engineering Center, 345 East 47 Street, New York, NY 10017. circ. 3,000.

620 UK ISSN 0071-0342
ENGINEERING INDUSTRIES ASSOCIATION. CLASSIFIED DIRECTORY AND BUYERS GUIDE. 1949. biennial. £2. Northern Advertising Agency (Bradford) Ltd., 7 Tong Lane, Bradford, BD4 ORR, England.

620 SI
ENGINEERING JOURNAL OF SINGAPORE. 1973. a. S.$5($2.50) ‡ University of Singapore, Faculty of Engineering, Kent Ridge, Singapore 0511, Singapore. Ed. Bd. circ. 1,000. Indexed: Chem.Abstr. Eng.Ind.
Formerly: University of Singapore. Faculty of Engineering. Journal.

620 UN ISSN 0071-0350
ENGINEERING LABORATORIES SERIES. 1970. irreg. price varies. Unesco, 7-9 Place de Fontenoy, 75700 Paris, France (Dist. in U.S. by: Unipub, 345 Park Ave. S., New York, NY 10010)

620 US
ENGINEERING MANPOWER BULLETIN. no. 29, 1976. irreg., approx. 6/yr. $20. Engineers Joint Council, 345 E. 47th St., New York, NY 10017.

620 CN
ENGINEERING MANPOWER NEWS/MAIN D'OEUVRE EN GENIE BULLETIN. (Text in English and French) 1974. irreg. Can.$10. Canadian Council of Professional Engineers, 116 Albert St., Suite 401, Ottawa, Ont. K1P 5G3, Canada. Ed. John Butcher. circ. 600.

620 US ISSN 0149-0605
ENGINEERING RESEARCH HIGHLIGHTS. 1966. a. free. Iowa State University, Engineering Research Institute, Ames, IA 50011. Ed. R. E. Welch.
Formerly: Iowa State Engineering Research (ISSN 0075-0409)

620 II
ENGINEERING TIMES ANNUAL DIRECTORY. (Text in English) 14th ed., 1974/75. a. Engineering Times Publications Pvt. Ltd., Wachel Molla Mansion, 8 Lenin Sarani, Calcutta 700013, India.
Continues: Indian Engineering & Industries Register.

620 CN ISSN 0430-8247
FOCUS (WATERLOO) 1965. irreg. University of Waterloo, Undergraduate Engineering Society "B", Waterloo, Ont., Canada. illus.

FRANCE. COMMISSARIAT A L'ENERGIE ATOMIQUE. ANNUAL REPORT. see PHYSICS — Nuclear Energy

620 SA ISSN 0071-979X
FULCRUM. a. free. University of the Witwatersrand, Johannesburg, Student Engineers Council, South West Engineering Block, Room B1, 1 Jan Smuts Ave., Johannesburg 2001, South Africa. Ed. P. Harrod.

620 NE
FUNDAMENTAL STUDIES IN ENGINEERING. 1978. irreg. price varies. Elsevier Scientific Publishing Co., Box 211, 1000 AE Amsterdam, Netherlands.

620.005 GY
G.A.P.E. irreg. Guyana Association of Professional Engineers, Georgetown, Guyana. illus.

620 FR ISSN 0072-0844
GENIE INDUSTRIEL; CATALOGUE DE L'INGENIERIE. (Text mainly in French; one section in English, Arabic, French and Spanish) 1960. a. 380 F. Documentations Industrielles et Techniques, 11 rue de Madrid, 75 Paris 8, France. Ed. Gaston Berard. circ. controlled.

620 BL
GRANDES VULTOS DA ENGENHARIA BRASILEIRA. 1975. a. $12. Clube de Engenharia, Av. Rio Branco 124, Rio de Janeiro, Gb, Brazil.

HACETTEPE FEN VE MUHENDISLIK BILIMLERI DERGISI. see SCIENCES: COMPREHENSIVE WORKS

620 JA ISSN 0073-2311
HIROSHIMA UNIVERSITY. FACULTY OF ENGINEERING. MEMOIRS. (Text in English, French and German) 1957. a. not for sale. Hiroshima University, Faculty of Engineering - Hiroshima Daigaku Kogakubu, Senda-machi 3, Hiroshima 730, Japan. Ed. Kaizo Kuwabara. circ. 650. Indexed: Chem.Abstr.

620 JA
HOKKAIDO UNIVERSITY. FACULTY OF ENGINEERING. MEMOIRS. (Text in European languages) 1927. a. exchange basis. Hokkaido University, Faculty of Engineering, Nishi-8-chome, Kita-13-jo, Kita-ku, Sapporo 060, Japan.

I A T U L PROCEEDINGS. (International Association of Technological Universities Libraries) see LIBRARY AND INFORMATION SCIENCES

620 FR ISSN 0066-8982
I C A M ANNUAIRE.* 1970. a. price varies. Institut Catholique d'Arts et Metiers de Lille, 6 rue Auber, Lille, France.

620 US
I E E E INTERNATIONAL PULSED POWER CONFERENCE. DIGEST OF TECHNICAL PAPERS. 1976. biennial. Institute of Electrical and Electronics Engineers, Inc., 345 E. 47th St., New York, NY 10017 (Subscr. to: 445 Hoes Lane, Piscataway, NJ 08854) Ed. A.H. Guenther. (reprint service avail. from ISI)
Formerly (until 1979): I E E E International Pulsed Power Conference. Proceedings.

620 II ISSN 0073-6554
INDIAN JOURNAL OF ENGINEERS. ANNUAL FOUNDRY NUMBER. (Text in English) 1960. a. Rs.25 in India; Rs.40 elsewhere. Technical and General Press, Engineers' Bureau, c/o Jyotsnmay Guha Thakurta, 21B Lansdowne Terrace, Calcutta 26, India. Ed. A.K. Bose.

658.5 US ISSN 0073-7445
INDUSTRIAL ENGINEERING CONFERENCE. PROCEEDINGS.* (Issued as a subseries of West Virginia University. Engineering Experiment Station. Bulletin) 1950. a. West Virginia University, Engineering Experiment Station, College of Engineering, Morgantown, WV 26506.

620 CK ISSN 0073-7992
INGENIERIA. BOLETIN INFORMATIVO.* 1962. irreg. free. Universidad Nacional de Colombia, Facultad de Ingenieria, Secretario, Apartado Nal. 1537, Bogota, Colombia.
Issued formerly as: Colombia. Universidad, Bogota. Facultad de Ingenieria Boletin Informative.

620 US
INGENIEURWISSENSCHAFTLICHE BIBLIOTHEK/ENGINEERING SCIENCE LIBRARY. 1964. irreg.; vol. 13, 1971. price varies. Springer-Verlag, 175 Fifth Ave., New York, NY 10010 (Also Berlin, Heidelberg, Vienna) (reprint service avail. from ISI)

621.48 GW
INSTITUT FUER REAKTORSICHERHEIT DER TECHNISCHEN UEBERWACHUNGS-VEREINE. TAETIGKEITSBERICHT. a. Institut fuer Reaktorsicherheit der Technischen Ueberwachungs-Vereine, Glockengasse 2, 5000 Cologne 1, W. Germany (B.R.D.) illus.

INSTITUTE OF ENVIRONMENTAL SCIENCES. ANNUAL MEETING. PROCEEDINGS. see ENVIRONMENTAL STUDIES

INSTITUTE OF ENVIRONMENTAL SCIENCES. TUTORIAL SERIES. see ENVIRONMENTAL STUDIES

INSTITUTE OF NUCLEAR MATERIALS MANAGEMENT. PROCEEDINGS OF ANNUAL MEETING. see PHYSICS — Nuclear Energy

620 II ISSN 0073-9782
INSTITUTION OF ENGINEERS (INDIA). DIRECTORY. (Text in English) 1967-68. quadrennial. Rs.20. Institution of Engineers (India), 8 Gokhale Rd., Calcutta 700020, India. Ed. B. T. Nagrani. circ. 25,000.
Formerly: Institution of Engineers (India). Yearbook.

620 BG ISSN 0073-9219
INSTITUTION OF ENGINEERS. YEAR BOOK.* (Text in English) a. Institution of Engineers, Ramna, Dacca 2, Bangladesh.

620 AT
INSTITUTION OF ENGINEERS, AUSTRALIA. GENERAL ENGINEERING TRANSACTIONS. 1977. irreg. Aus.$4 to non-members. Institution of Engineers, Australia, 11 National Circuit, Barton, A.C.T. 2600, Australia. Eds. G. D. Butler, J. Rory Gibson.

620 AT
INSTITUTION OF ENGINEERS, AUSTRALIA. NATIONAL CONFERENCE PUBLICATIONS. irreg. Institution of Engineers, Australia, 157 Gloucester St., Sydney, N.S.W. 2000, Australia. charts. stat.

620 IE
INSTITUTION OF ENGINEERS OF IRELAND.
REGISTER OF CHARTERED ENGINEERS
AND MEMBERS. 1960. a. £6. Irish Engineering
Publications Ltd., 22 Clyde Road, Ballsbridge,
Dublin, 4, Ireland. adv. circ. 2,500.
Formerly: Directory of Engineers (ISSN 0070-5489)

620 IE ISSN 0073-9790
INSTITUTION OF ENGINEERS OF IRELAND.
TRANSACTIONS. 1835. a. £3. Irish Engineering
Publications Ltd., 22 Clyde Road, Ballsbridge,
Dublin, 4, Ireland. circ. 3,500.

620 SI
INSTITUTION OF ENGINEERS, SINGAPORE.
JOURNAL. (Text in English) irreg. S.$3.60.
Graphic Publications, Singapore Professional Centre,
Block 23, 2nd Floor, Outram Park 3, Singapore 3,
Singapore.

620 CE
INSTITUTION OF ENGINEERS, SRI LANKA.
YEAR BOOK. 1973. a. Institution of Engineers, Sri
Lanka, 120-15 Wijerama Mawatha, Colombo 1, Sri
Lanka.

629.8 PL ISSN 0084-2788
INSTYTUT AUTOMATYKI SYSTEMOW
ENERGETYCZNYCH. PRACE. 1964. irreg.,
1972, no. 24. Instytut Automatyki Systemow
Energetycznych, Wystawowa 1, 51-618 Wroclaw,
Poland.

INTER-AMERICAN NUCLEAR ENERGY
COMMISSION. FINAL REPORT. see
PHYSICS — Nuclear Energy

INTERNATIONAL ATOMIC ENERGY AGENCY.
ANNUAL REPORT. see PHYSICS — Nuclear
Energy

INTERNATIONAL ATOMIC ENERGY AGENCY.
PANEL PROCEEDINGS SERIES. see
PHYSICS — Nuclear Energy

INTERNATIONAL ATOMIC ENERGY AGENCY.
POWER REACTORS IN MEMBER STATES. see
PHYSICS — Nuclear Energy

INTERNATIONAL ATOMIC ENERGY AGENCY.
PROCEEDINGS SERIES. see PHYSICS —
Nuclear Energy

INTERNATIONAL ATOMIC ENERGY AGENCY.
TECHNICAL DIRECTORIES. see PHYSICS —
Nuclear Energy

INTERNATIONAL ATOMIC ENERGY AGENCY.
TECHNICAL REPORT SERIES. see PHYSICS —
Nuclear Energy

620 US ISSN 0272-880X
INTERNATIONAL CENTRE FOR HEAT AND
MASS TRANSFER. PROCEEDINGS. 1972. irreg.,
no. 14, 1981. price varies. (International Centre for
Heat and Mass Transfer) Hemisphere Publishing
Corporation, 1025 Vermont Ave., N.W.,
Washington, DC 20005 (Subscr. to Hemisphere, 19
W.44 St., New York, NY 10036) Eds. Z.P. Zaric,
C.L. Tien. bibl. illus. (back issues avail.) Indexed:
Chem.Abstr.

620.41 US ISSN 0074-3062
INTERNATIONAL CONFERENCE ON
ENGINEERING IN THE OCEAN
ENVIRONMENT. DIGEST. Abbreviated title:
Ocean. a. Institute of Electrical and Electronics
Engineers, Inc., 445 Hoes Lane, Piscataway, NJ
08854.

INTERNATIONAL CONFERENCE ON
SHIELDING AROUND HIGH ENERGY
ACCELERATORS. PAPERS. see PHYSICS —
Nuclear Energy

620 US ISSN 0074-5774
INTERNATIONAL ENGINEERING DIRECTORY.
(Text in English, French and Spanish) 1965.
biennial. $10. American Consulting Engineers
Council, 1155 15th St., N.W., Washington, DC
20005. Ed. Bruce Roberts. circ. 5,000.

621 PL
INTERNATIONAL SYMPOSIUM ON
SWITCHING ARC PHENOMENA.
PROCEEDINGS. (Text in English, German,
Russian; summaries in English) irreg., 1973, 2nd.
price varies. Politechnika Lodzka, Ul. Zwirki 36, 90-924 Lodz, Poland. (Co-sponsor: Stowarzyszenie
Elektrykow Polskich) illus.

620 CN
INTERNATIONAL TOWING TANK
CONFERENCE. PROCEEDINGS. vol. 14, 1975.
a. Can.$180. National Research Council of Canada,
Ottawa, Ont. K1A 0R6, Canada. illus.

620 US ISSN 0075-0433
IOWA STATE UNIVERSITY. ENGINEERING
RESEARCH INSTITUTE. ENGINEERING
RESEARCH REPORT. 1949/50. irreg. price varies.
Iowa State University, Engineering Research
Institute, Ames, IA 50011.

620 UR
ISSLEDOVANIE, KONSTRUIROVANIE I
RASCHET REZBOVYKH SOEDINENII. 1973.
irreg. 0.50 Rub. per no. (Ulyanovskii
Politekhnicheskii Institut) Privolzhskoe Knizhnoe
Izdatel'stvo, Ul. Goncharova, 52, Ulyanovsk,
U.S.S.R.

620 JA ISSN 0085-2325
IWATE UNIVERSITY. FACULTY OF
ENGINEERING. TECHNOLOGY REPORTS/
IWATE DAIGAKU KOGAKUBU KENKYU
HOKOKU. (Text in English) 1965. irreg. Iwate
University, Faculty of Engineering - Iwate Daigaku
Kogakubu, 4-3-5 Ueda, Morioka 020, Iwate, Japan.
Ed. Tatuo Chubachi. Indexed: Appl.Mech.Rev.

JAPAN ATOMIC ENERGY COMMISSION.
ANNUAL REPORT/GENSHIRYOKU NENPO.
see PHYSICS — Nuclear Energy

620 658.3 US
JOINT ENGINEERING MANAGEMENT
CONFERENCE. CONFERENCE RECORD.
1952. a. $16. Institute of Electrical and Electronics
Engineers, Inc., 445 Hoes Lane, Piscataway, NJ
08854.
Formerly: Joint Engineering Societies
Management Conference. Proceedings (ISSN 0075-3955)

621 UR
KAZANSKII UNIVERSITET. SBORNIK
ASPIRANTSKIKH RABOT: TEORIYA PLASTIN
I OBOLOCHEK. 1971. irreg. 0.67 Rub. Kazanskii
Universitet, Ul. Lenina, 4/5, Kazan, U.S.S.R. illus.

620 JA
KEIO ENGINEERING REPORTS. (Text in English,
French and German) 1948. irreg. exchange only.
Keio University, Faculty of Engineering - Keio
Gijuku Daigaku Kogakubu, Matsushita Memorial
Library, 832 Hiyoshi-cho, Kohoku-ku, Yokohama
223, Japan. Ed. Prof. Tameyoshi Mori. charts. illus.
stat. circ. 1,000. Indexed: Chem.Abstr. Math.R.
Formerly: Keio University. Fujihara Memorial
Faculty of Engineering. Proceedings. (ISSN 0016-2507)

620 UK ISSN 0075-5400
KEMPE'S ENGINEERS YEAR BOOK. (In two
volumes) 1894. a. £29.50. Morgan-Grampian Book
Publishing Co., 30 Calderwood St., London SE18
6QH, England. Ed. John P. Quayle. adv. bibl, illus.
index. circ. 7,300.

621.48 EI
KERNENERGIECENTRALE VAN 50 MWE;
DOODEWARD. JAARVERSLAG. (Text in Dutch
only) 1964. a. (European Atomic Energy
Community) Office for Official Publications of the
European Communities, C.P. 1003, Luxembourg 1,
Luxembourg (Dist. in U.S. by European Community
Information Service, 2100 M St., N.W., Suite 707,
Washington, D.C. 20037)

KERNFORSCHUNGSZENTRUM KARLSRUHE.
ERGEBNISBERICHT UEBER FORSCHUNG
UND ENTWICKLUNG. see PHYSICS — Nuclear
Energy

KERNKRAFT LINGEN. JAHRESBERICHT. see
PHYSICS — Nuclear Energy

KERNKRAFT ZENTRALE, GUNDREMMINGEN.
JAHRESBERICHTE. see PHYSICS — Nuclear
Energy

KERNKRAFTWERK OBRIGHEIM.
JAHRESBERICHT. see PHYSICS — Nuclear
Energy

KJELLER REPORT. see PHYSICS — Nuclear
Energy

KOBE UNIVERSITY OF MERCANTILE MARINE.
REVIEW. PART 2. NAVIGATION, MARINE
ENGINEERING, NUCLEAR ENGINEERING
AND SCIENTIFIC SECTION. see SCIENCES:
COMPREHENSIVE WORKS

DIE KUESTE; Archiv fuer Forschung und Technik an
der Nord- und Ostsee. see EARTH SCIENCES —
Oceanography

620 JA ISSN 0023-5334
KUMAMOTO UNIVERSITY. FACULTY OF
ENGINEERING. MEMOIRS/KUMAMOTO
DAIGAKU KOGAKUBU KIYO. (Text in English)
1954. 1-3/yr. free. Kumamoto University, Faculty of
Engineering, 2-39-1 Kurokami, Kumamoto 860,
Japan. bibl. charts. illus.

620 JA ISSN 0369-0512
KYUSHU INSTITUTE OF TECHNOLOGY.
MEMOIRS: ENGINEERING. (Text in English)
1971. a. exchange basis. Kyushu Institute of
Technology - Kyushu Kogyo Daigaku, 1-1 Sensui-cho, Tobata, Kitakyushu 804, Japan.

620 500 US
LOS ANGELES COUNCIL OF ENGINEERS &
SCIENTISTS. PROCEEDINGS SERIES. 1975.
irreg. $25. Los Angeles Council of Engineers &
Scientists, 1052 W. 6th St., Suite 334, Los Angeles,
CA 90017.

620 US ISSN 0076-1060
LOUISIANA STATE UNIVERSITY. DIVISION OF
ENGINEERING RESEARCH. ENGINEERING
RESEARCH BULLETIN.* irreg., 1967, no. 92.
Louisiana State University, College of Engineering,
Baton Rouge, LA 70803.

620 GW
M.A.N. FORSCHEN, PLANEN, BAUEN. English
edition: M.A.N. Research, Engineering,
Manufacturing. (Editions Also in French & Spanish)
1970. a. free. Maschinenfabrik Augsburg-Nuernberg
AG, 8900 Augsburg, W. Germany (B.R.D.) Ed.
Udo Gorontzy. illus. circ. 40,000(comb.)

620 UK ISSN 0076-3705
MANCHESTER ASSOCIATION OF ENGINEERS.
TRANSACTIONS. 1861. a. £5. Manchester
Association of Engineers, M.T.A. Office, U.M.I.S.T.,
Box 88, Sackville St., Manchester M60 1QD,
England. Ed. J. F. C. Morden. circ. 300.

MANITOBA CONSTRUCTION INDUSTRY
DIRECTORY. PURCHASING GUIDE. see
BUILDING AND CONSTRUCTION

658.5 670 US ISSN 0363-700X
MANUFACTURING ENGINEERING
TRANSACTIONS. Title varies: Society of
Manufacturing Engineers. S M E Transactions.
(Includes: North American Metalworking Research
Conference Proceedings) 1972. a. $65. Society of
Manufacturing Engineers, 20501 Ford Rd.,
Dearborn, MI 48128. Ed. Daniel B. Dallas. (reprint
service avail. from UMI)

620 US
MARINE SCIENCES INSTRUMENTATION. irreg.,
vol. 5, 1973. $9. Instrument Society of America,
400 Stanwix St., Pittsburgh, PA 15222.

MATERIALS RESEARCH AND ENGINEERING/
WERKSTOFF- FORSCHUNG UND -TECHNIK.
see METALLURGY

620.11 NE
MATERIALS SCIENCE MONOGRAPHS. 1978.
irreg., vol. 6, 1980. price varies. Elsevier Scientific
Publishing Co., Box 211, 1000 AE Amsterdam,
Netherlands.

MATHEMATICS IN SCIENCE AND
ENGINEERING; series of monographs and
textbooks. see MATHEMATICS

621　　　　　SW　ISSN 0025-6609
MECMAN-TECHNIQUE. (Editions in Danish, English, Finnish, French, Italian, German, Hungarian, Japanese, Norwegian, and Swedish) 1965. irreg. free. A B Mecman, Box 32 035, S-126 11 Stockholm 32, Sweden. Ed. Carl Eric Beckman. charts. illus. circ. 100,000.
Formerly: Mecman-Teknik.

380.1　　　　AT　ISSN 0314-1586
METAL & ENGINEERING INDUSTRY YEAR BOOK. a. Aus.$40. (Metal & Engineering Industry Association) Peter Isaacson Publications, 46-49 Porter St., Prahran, Vic. 3181, Australia. adv.

620　　　　　JA　ISSN 0540-4924
MIYAZAKI UNIVERSITY. FACULTY OF ENGINEERING. MEMOIRS/MIYAZAKI DAIGAKU KOGAKUBU KIYO. (Text in English) 1956. irreg. exchange basis. Miyazaki University, Faculty of Engineering - Miyazaki Daigaku Kogakubu, 1-1-1 Kirishima, Miyazaki 880, Japan.

MONOGRAPH SERIES ON METALLURGY IN NUCLEAR TECHNOLOGY. see ENGINEERING — Engineering Mechanics And Materials

620　530　　　UK
MONOGRAPHS IN PHYSICAL MEASUREMENT. 1978. irreg. £12.50. Academic Press Inc.(London) Ltd., 24-28 Oval Rd., London NW1 7DX, England. Ed. A. H. Cook.

620　　　　　US　ISSN 0276-1459
MULTIPHASE SCIENCE AND TECHNOLOGY. 1981. irreg. price varies. Hemisphere Publishing Corporation, 1025 Vermont Ave., N.W., Washington, DC 20005 (Orders to: 19 W. 44th St., New York, Ny 10036) Ed.Bd. bibl. charts.

620　　　　　US　ISSN 0077-4081
NATIONAL COUNCIL OF ENGINEERING EXAMINERS. PROCEEDINGS. a. National Council of Engineering Examiners, Box 1099, Seneca, SC 29678.

620　　　　　CN　ISSN 0077-5428
NATIONAL RESEARCH COUNCIL, CANADA. ASSOCIATE COMMITTEE ON GEOTECHNICAL RESEARCH. TECHNICAL MEMORANDUM. 1945. irreg. price varies. National Research Council of Canada, Associate Committee on Geotechnical Research, Ottawa, Ontario K1A OR6, Canada. (back issues avail.) Indexed: Eng.Ind. Arct.Bibl.

620　　　　　CH
NATIONAL TAIWAN UNIVERSITY. COLLEGE OF ENGINEERING. BULLETIN. (Text in Chinese and English) no. 18, 1975. a. National Taiwan University, College of Engineering, Taipei, Taiwan, Republic of China. Ed. Chao Yung-Cheng.

NATIONAL WASTE PROCESSING CONFERENCE. PROCEEDINGS; with discussions. see PUBLIC HEALTH AND SAFETY

620　600　　　UK　ISSN 0372-0187
NEWCOMEN SOCIETY FOR THE STUDY OF THE HISTORY OF ENGINEERING AND TECHNOLOGY. TRANSACTIONS. 1922. a. £10. Newcomen Society for the Study of the History of Engineering and Technology, Science Museum, South Kensington, London SW7 2DD, England. bibl. charts. illus. (also avail. in microfilm)

620　　　　　CN　ISSN 0384-1898
NEWFOUNDLAND AND LABRADOR ENGINEER. 1966. irreg. Association of Professional Engineers of Newfoundland, Box 8414, Sta. A, St. John's, Nfld. A1B 3N7, Canada. illus.

NIHON UNIVERSITY. ATOMIC ENERGY RESEARCH INSTITUTE. ANNUAL REPORT. see PHYSICS — Nuclear Energy

NORTHWESTERN ONTARIO CONSTRUCTION INDUSTRY DIRECTORY. PURCHASING GUIDE. see BUILDING AND CONSTRUCTION

NUCLEAR ENGINEERING. see PHYSICS — Nuclear Energy

NUCLEAR SCIENCE TECHNOLOGY MONOGRAPH SERIES. (American Nuclear Society) see PHYSICS — Nuclear Energy

O E C D HALDEN REACTOR PROJECT. (Organization for Economic Cooperation and Development) see PHYSICS — Nuclear Energy

OCEAN ENGINEERING: A WILEY SERIES. see EARTH SCIENCES — Oceanography

OCEAN ENGINEERING INFORMATION SERIES. see EARTH SCIENCES — Oceanography

620　　　　　CN
ONTARIO DIGEST. irreg. membership. Association of Professional Engineers of Ontario, 1027 Yonge St., Toronto, Ont. M4W 3E5, Canada.

ONTARIO GOLDEN HORSESHOE CONSTRUCTION INDUSTRY DIRECTORY. PURCHASING GUIDE. see BUILDING AND CONSTRUCTION

OPTICAL PHYSICS AND ENGINEERING. see PHYSICS — Optics

620　378　　　US　ISSN 0078-5938
OREGON STATE UNIVERSITY. SCHOOL OF ENGINEERING. GRADUATE RESEARCH AND EDUCATION. 1957. irreg., 1970, Jan., no. 39. $0.50. Oregon State University, School of Engineering, Corvallis, OR 97331. Ed. James G. Knudsen.

620　　　　　US　ISSN 0078-5946
OREGON STATE UNIVERSITY. SCHOOL OF ENGINEERING. RESEARCH ACTIVITIES.* 1960. biennial. $0.35. Oregon State University, School of Engineering, Corvallis, OR 97331. Ed. James G. Knudsen.

ORGANIZATION FOR ECONOMIC COOPERATION AND DEVELOPMENT. NUCLEAR ENERGY AGENCY. ACTIVITY REPORT. see PHYSICS — Nuclear Energy

620　　　　　JA　ISSN 0078-6659
OSAKA CITY UNIVERSITY. FACULTY OF ENGINEERING. MEMOIRS/OSAKA-SHIRITSU DAIGAKU KOGAKUBU OBUN KIYO. (Text and summaries in English) 1959. a. free. Osaka City University, Faculty of Engineering - Osaka-shiritsu Daigaku Kogakubu, 459 Sugimoto-cho, Sumiyoshi-ku, Osaka 558, Japan. circ. 1,000.

620　　　　　US
OXFORD ENGINEERING SCIENCE SERIES. irreg. price varies. Oxford University Press, 200 Madison Ave., New York, NY 10016 (And Ely House, 37 Dover St., London W1X 4AH, England) Ed.Bd.

620　551　　　CN　ISSN 0030-7912
PEGG/PROFESSIONAL ENGINEER, GEOLOGIST, GEOPHYSICIST. a. Can.$10 to non-members. ‡ Association of Professional Engineers, Geologists & Geophysicists of Alberta, 1010 One Thornton Court, Edmonton, Alta. T5J 2E7, Canada. Ed. A. M. Ibrahim. adv. charts. stat. circ. 20,000.
Formerly: Alberta Professional Engineer.

620　　　　　US　ISSN 0079-0869
PERGAMON UNIFIED ENGINEERING SERIES.* irreg. price varies. Pergamon Press, Inc., Maxwell House, Fairview Park, Elmsford, NY 10523 (And Headington Hill Hall, Oxford OX3 0BW, England) Eds. J. P. Hartnett, T. F. Irvine, Jr.

PETERSON'S GUIDES. ANNUAL GUIDES TO GRADUATE STUDY. BOOK 5: ENGINEERING AND APPLIED SCIENCES. see EDUCATION — Guides To Schools And Colleges

PION APPLIED PHYSICS SERIES. see PHYSICS

658.5　　　　US　ISSN 0554-2693
PLANT ENGINEERING DIRECTORY & SPECIFICATIONS CATALOG. 1965. a. $30. Technical Publishing Co., 1301 So. Grove Ave., Barrington, IL 60010. Ed. Leo F Spector. adv. charts. illus. circ. controlled.

620　　　　　PL　ISSN 0079-323X
POLISH ACADEMY OF SCIENCES. INSTITUTE OF FUNDAMENTAL TECHNOLOGICAL RESEARCH. SCIENTIFIC ACTIVITIES. (Text in English) 1962. a. (Polska Akademia Nauk, Instytut Podstawowych Problemow Techniki) Panstwowe Wydawnictwo Naukowe, Middowa 10, Warsaw, Poland. Ed. Marek Sokolowski. bibl. illus.

620　　　　　PL　ISSN 0574-9069
POLITECHNIKA CZESTOCHOWSKA. ZESZYTY NAUKOWE. NAUKI PODSTAWOWE. (Text in Polish; summaries in English and Russian) 1960. irreg. Politechnika Czestochowska, Ul. Deglera 31, 42-200 Czestochowa, Poland (Dist. by: Ars Polona-Ruch, Krakowskie Przedmiescie 7, Warsaw, Poland) Ed. Boleslaw Wyslocki.

628　　　　　PL　ISSN 0324-9719
POLITECHNIKA WROCLAWSKA. INSTYTUT INZYNIERII OCHRONY SRODOWISKA. PRACE NAUKOWE. KONFERENCJE. 1972. irreg., no. 10, 1977. price varies. Politechnika Wroclawska, Wybrzeze Wyspianskiego 27, 50-370 Wroclaw, Poland (Dist. by: Ars Polona-Ruch, Krakowskie Przedmiescie 7, Warsaw, Poland) Ed. Marian Kloza.

628　　　　　PL　ISSN 0084-2877
POLITECHNIKA WROCLAWSKA. INSTYTUT INZYNIERII OCHRONY SRODOWISKA. PRACE NAUKOWE. STUDIA I MATERIALY. (Text in Polish; summaries in English, French, German and Russian) 1969. irreg., 1978, no. 20. price varies. Politechnika Wroclawska, Wybrzeze Wyspianskiego 27, 50-370 Wroclaw, Poland (Dist. by: Ars Polona-Ruch, Krakowskie Przedmiescie 7, Warsaw, Poland) Ed. Marian Kloza.

620　　　　　EC　ISSN 0032-3055
POLITECNICA; revista de informacion tecnico - cientifica. (Text in Spanish; summaries in English) 1967. a. $2. Escuela Politecnica Nacional, Isabel la Catolica y Veintimilla, Apdo. 2759, Quito, Ecuador. Ed.Bd. bibl. charts. illus. Indexed: Biol.Abstr. Chem.Abstr.

POLSKA ADAKEMIA NAUK. CENTRUM BADAN NAUKOWYCH W WOJEWODZTWIE KATOWICKIM. PRACE I STUDIA. see HUMANITIES: COMPREHENSIVE WORKS

POLSKA AKADEMIA NAUK. INSTYTUT PODSTAW INZYNIERII SRODOWISKA. PRACE I STUDIA. see ENVIRONMENTAL STUDIES

671.73　　　　US　ISSN 0092-0479
POWDER COATING CONFERENCE. (Some vols. issued in parts) 1965. irreg.; latest issue 1976. $45. Society of Manufacturing Engineers, 20501 Ford Road, Dearborn, MI 48128. illus. circ. 36,000. (also avail. in microfiche; reprint service avail. from UMI)

620　　　　　SW
POWER SYSTEMS COMPUTATION CONFERENCE. P S C C PROCEEDINGS. 1968. triennial, 5th, 1975, Cambridge; next conference, 6th, 1978, Darmstadt. $35. Kungliga Tekniska Hoegskolan, Power Systems Research Group - Royal Institute of Technology, 100 44 Stockholm 70, Sweden. Ed. J.A. Bubenko.

620　658.8　　US
PREVIEW/ENGINEERING; technical information, new products, ideas, literature. 1978. irreg. free. Ampersand, Box 388, Rockville Centre, NY 11570. illus.

620　　　　　SA　ISSN 0555-6945
PULSE. vol. 22, 1975. a. membership. University of Natal, Students Engineering Society, King George IV Ave., Durban 4001, South Africa. Ed. V. N. Hatley.

PURE AND APPLIED PHYSICS; a series of monographs and textbooks. see PHYSICS

RADIONAVIGATION JOURNAL. see EARTH SCIENCES — Oceanography

ENGINEERING

620   JA
RESOURCES EXPLOITATION INSTITUTE. BULLETIN/SHIGEN SOGO KAIHATSU KENKYUSHO OBUN HOKOKU. (Text in English) irreg. exchange basis. Resources Exploitation Institute - Shigen Sogo Kaihatsu Kenkyusho, Shibuya Paru Homu, 29-25 Sakuragaoka-cho, Shibuya-ku, Tokyo 150, Japan.

RIKKYO UNIVERSITY. INSTITUTE FOR ATOMIC ENERGY. REPORT. see *PHYSICS — Nuclear Energy*

ROZPRAWY HYDROTECHNICZNE. see *WATER RESOURCES*

620   US   ISSN 0080-4975
RUTGERS UNIVERSITY.BUREAU OF ENGINEERING RESEARCH. ANNUAL REPORT. 1927. a. free. ‡ Rutgers University, College of Engineering, Bureau of Engineering Research, New Brunswick, NJ 08903. Ed. R. C. Ahlert. index. circ. 500.

S F S CATALOGUE; catalogue of Finnish national standards. (Suomen Standardisoimisliitto) see *METROLOGY AND STANDARDIZATION*

S H E. (Subject Headings for Engineering) see *LIBRARY AND INFORMATION SCIENCES*

621.38   US   ISSN 0097-966X
S I D INTERNATIONAL SYMPOSIUM. DIGEST OF TECHNICAL PAPERS. 1970. a. $30 (members $20) Society for Information Display, 654 North Sepulveda Blvd., Los Angeles, CA 90049. circ. 2,000. Key Title: Digest of Technical Papers.
Formerly: Symposium on Information Display. Digest of Technical Papers (ISSN 0082-0830)

SASKATCHEWAN CONSTRUCTION INDUSTRY DIRECTORY. PURCHASING GUIDE. see *BUILDING AND CONSTRUCTION*

623   US
SEA TECHNOLOGY BUYERS GUIDE/DIRECTORY. 1967. a. $18. Compass Publications, Inc. (Arlington), 1117 N. 19th St., Suite 1000, Arlington, VA 22209. adv. circ. 10,000. (reprint service avail. from UMI)
Formerly: Sea Technology Handbook and Directory.

620   US
SERIES ON BULK MATERIALS HANDLING. 1975. irreg. (3-5/yr.) price varies. Trans Tech Publications, 16 Bearskin Neck, Rockport, MA 01966. Ed. R. H. Wohlbier. adv. circ. 3,000-10,000.
Formerly: Series on Bulk Materials Engineering.

620   JA
SHINSHU UNIVERSITY. FACULTY OF TEXTILE SCIENCE AND TECHNOLOGY. JOURNAL. SERIES B: ENGINEERING. (Text in European languages) 1952. irreg. exchange basis. Shinshu University, Faculty of Textile Science and Technology - Shinshu Daigaku Sen'i Gakubu, 3-15-1 Tokida, Ueda, Nagano 386, Japan.

620   SI
SINGAPORE POLYTECHNIC ENGINEERING SOCIETY. JOURNAL. 1963. a. free. ‡ Singapore Polytechnic Engineering Society, c/o Singapore Polytechnic Students Union, 9 Prince Edward Rd., Singapore, Singapore. adv. illus. circ. 3,000.

328.94   338.7   AT
SNOWY MOUNTAINS ENGINEERING CORPORATION. ANNUAL REPORT. a. price varies. Australian Government Publishing Service, Box 84, Canberra, A.C.T. 2600, Australia. illus.

620   PE
SOCIEDAD DE INGENIEROS. INFORMACIONES Y MEMORIAS. 1975. irreg. Sociedad de Ingenieros, Avda. Nicolas de Pierola 788, Lima, Peru.

620   SA
SOUTH AFRICAN ASSOCIATION OF CONSULTING ENGINEERS. DIRECTORY OF REGISTERED FIRMS/SUID-AFRICAANSE VERENIGING VAN RAADGEWENDE INGENIEURS. GIDS VAN GEREGISTREEDE FIRMAS. (Text in Afrikaans and English) 1967. irreg. R.5. ‡ South African Association of Consulting Engineers, 9 Keyes Ave., Rosebank, Johannesburg 2196, South Africa. circ. 3,000.
Formerly: South African Association of Consulting Engineers. Directory of Members' Firms/Gids van Lede Se Firmas.

SOUTH AFRICAN MINING AND ENGINEERING YEARBOOK. see *MINES AND MINING INDUSTRY*

SOUTH CENTRAL ONTARIO CONSTRUCTION INDUSTRY DIRECTORY. PURCHASING GUIDE. see *BUILDING AND CONSTRUCTION*

620   UK   ISSN 0038-3570
SOUTH WALES INSTITUTE OF ENGINEERS. PROCEEDINGS. 1857. a. £1. South Wales Institute of Engineers, Park Place, Cardiff, Wales. adv. charts. illus. index. Indexed: Chem.Abstr. Eng.Ind. Met.Abstr.

620   US   ISSN 0038-4364
SOUTHERN METHODIST UNIVERSITY. INDUSTRIAL INFORMATION SERVICES. NEWSLETTER. 1966. irreg. ‡ Southern Methodist University, Industrial Information Services, Science Information Center, Dallas, TX 75275. Ed. Devertt D. Bickston. bk. rev. abstr. bibl. pat. circ. 1,100(controlled) (processed)

SOUTHWESTERN ONTARIO CONSTRUCTION INDUSTRY DIRECTORY. PURCHASING GUIDE. see *BUILDING AND CONSTRUCTION*

STUDIECENTRUM VOOR KERNENERGIE. ANNUAL SCIENTIFIC REPORT. see *PHYSICS — Nuclear Energy*

620   US
SWEET'S SYSTEM FOR THE ENGINEERING MARKET. 1976. a. McGraw-Hill Information Systems Co., Sweet's Division, 1221 Ave. of the Americas, New York, NY 10020. adv. circ. 11,000.

338.4   US   ISSN 0092-8763
SWEET'S SYSTEM FOR THE INDUSTRIAL CONSTRUCTION & RENOVATION MARKET. 1974. a. McGraw-Hill Information Systems Co., Sweet's Division, 1221 Avenue of the Americas, New York, NY 10020. illus.
Continues: Sweet's Plant Engineering Extension Industrial Construction and Renovation File (ISSN 0092-8763); Sweet's Industrial Construction Catalog File (ISSN 0090-7626)

620.1   SW
T L I-INGENJOEREN. 1949. 4-6/yr. Kr.25($3) Ingenjoersfoerbundet T L I, Fack, S-103 10 Stockholm, Sweden. Ed. Hans Roedin. adv. pat. tr.lit. circ. 4,000. (tabloid format)
Formerly: Gymnasieingenjoeren (ISSN 0017-5919)

620   GW   ISSN 0082-1926
TASCHENBUCH FUER INGENIEURE UND TECHNIKER IM OEFFENTLICHEN DIENST. 1968. a. DM.26.95. (Deutsche Angestellten-Gewerkschaft) Walhalla- und Praetoria-Verlag Georg Zwichenpflug, Dolomitenstr. 1, Postfach 301, 8400 Regensburg 1, W. Germany (B.R.D.) Ed. F. W. Schmidt. adv.

620   GW   ISSN 0082-1918
TASCHENBUCH FUER INGENIEURE UND TECHNIKER IN INDUSTRIE UND WIRTSCHAFT. 1968. a. DM.27.95. Walhalla- und Praetoria-Verlag Georg Zwichenpflug, Dolomitenstr. 1, Postfach 301, 8400 Regensburg 1, W. Germany (B.R.D.) Ed. Werner Frischholz.

620   GE   ISSN 0040-1528
TECHNISCHE HOCHSCHULE KARL-MARX-STADT. WISSENSCHAFTLICHE ZEITSCHRIFT. 1958-59. a. M.58. Technische Hochschule Karl-Marx-Stadt, Bibliothek, Postfach 964, 901 Karl-Marx-Stadt, E. Germany (D.D.R.) Ed. Christine Haeckel. charts. index. circ. 1,100.
Formerly: Hochschule fuer Maschinenbau Karl-Marx-Stadt. Wissenschaftliche Zeitschrift.

620   NE
TECHNISCHE HOGESCHOOL TE DELFT. BIBLIOTHEEK. LIJST VAN LOPENDE TIJDSCHRIFTABONNEMENTEN. 1967. a. fl.4. ‡ Technische Hogeschool te Delft, Bibliotheek, P.O.B. 98, Delft, Netherlands. index. circ. 1,000.

620   JA   ISSN 0040-8883
TOKUSHIMA UNIVERSITY. FACULTY OF ENGINEERING. BULLETIN. (Text in English) 1964. a. Tokushima University, Faculty of Engineering - Tokushima Daigaku Kogakubu, 2-1 Nanjo Mishima-machi, Tokushima 770, Japan. charts. circ. 600.

TOPICS IN APPLIED PHYSICS. see *PHYSICS*

623   551.46   US   ISSN 0085-7297
TOPICS IN OCEAN ENGINEERING. 1969. irreg., vol. 3, 1976. price varies. (University of Hawaii) Gulf Publishing Co., Box 2608, Houston, TX 77001. Ed. Charles Bretschneider. illus. index.

TORONTO & AREA CONSTRUCTION INDUSTRY DIRECTORY. PURCHASING GUIDE. see *BUILDING AND CONSTRUCTION*

620   US
U.E.E.S. REPORT. 1978. irreg. University of Utah, Utah Engineering Experiment Station, Salt Lake City, UT 84112.

ULTRASONICS SYMPOSIUM. PROCEEDINGS. see *PHYSICS — Sound*

UNITED KINGDOM ATOMIC ENERGY AUTHORITY. ANNUAL REPORT. see *PHYSICS — Nuclear Energy*

620   US   ISSN 0083-0313
U.S. ARMY. CORPS OF ENGINEERS. TECHNICAL REPORTS, T R (SERIES)* irreg. U.S. Army, Corps of Engineers, Washington, DC 20310 (Order from: National Technical Information Service, 5285 Port Royal Rd., Springfield, VA 22151)

U.S. ATOMIC ENERGY COMMISSION. MONOGRAPHS. see *PHYSICS — Nuclear Energy*

623   US   ISSN 0092-8917
U. S. NATIONAL OCEANIC AND ATMOSPHERIC ADMINISTRATION. MANNED UNDERSEA SCIENCE AND TECHNOLOGY PROGRAM; REPORT. 1971/72. a. $1. U.S. National Oceanic and Atmospheric Administration, 6010 Executive Blvd., Rockville, MD 20852 (Order to: NTIS, 5285 Port Royal Rd., Springfield, VA 22161) Ed. Kurt Stehling. illus. circ. 1,000. (also avail. in microfiche) Key Title: Manned Undersea Science and Technology Program.

620   610   001.3   CK   ISSN 0120-0852
UNIVERSIDAD INDUSTRIAL DE SANTANDER. REVISTA - INVESTIGACIONES. (Summaries in English, French, German and Spanish) 1959. irreg. P.100($2.) per no. or exchange basis. Universidad Industrial de Santander, Centro de Documentacion y Bibliografia, Apartado Aereo 678, Nal. 162, Bucaramanga, Colombia. adv. bk. rev. bibl. charts. illus. stat. cum.ind. every 5 yrs. circ. 1,200. Indexed: Met.Abstr.
Supersedes in part (since 1969): Universidad Industrial de Santander. Revista (ISSN 0041-8587)

620   US   ISSN 0068-631X
UNIVERSITY OF CALIFORNIA ENGINEERING AND PHYSICAL SCIENCES EXTENSION SERIES. 1959. irreg. latest vol. 1972. price varies. John Wiley & Sons, Inc., 605 Third Ave., New York, NY 10016.

620   US   ISSN 0073-5272
UNIVERSITY OF ILLINOIS AT URBANA - CHAMPAIGN. ENGINEERING EXPERIMENT STATION. BULLETIN. 1904. irreg., 1970, no. 505. price varies. University of Illinois at Urbana - Champaign, Engineering Publications Office, 112 Engineering Hall, Urbana, IL 61801.

620   US   ISSN 0073-5280
UNIVERSITY OF ILLINOIS AT URBANA-CHAMPAIGN. ENGINEERING EXPERIMENT STATION. SUMMARY OF ENGINEERING RESEARCH. 1958. a. free. University of Illinois at Urbana-Champaign, Engineering Publications Office, 112 Engineering Hall, Urbana, IL 61801. Ed. Ann Sapoznik.

620   MY
UNIVERSITY OF MALAYA. FACULTY OF ENGINEERING. JOURNAL/UNIVERSITI MALAYA. FAKULTI KEJURUTERAAN. JERNAL. 1958. a. University of Malaya, Faculty of Engineering, Lembah Pantai, Kuala Lumpur 22-11, Malaysia. adv. illus.
Formerly: University of Malaya. Department of Engineering. Journal.

620   US   ISSN 0542-9307
UNIVERSITY OF MASSACHUSETTS. SCHOOL OF ENGINEERING. ANNUAL REPORT. 1950. a. University of Massachusetts, School of Engineering, Amherst, MA 01002.

VACUUM METALLURGY CONFERENCE. PROCEEDINGS. see METALLURGY

691   FI   ISSN 0357-7031
VALTION TEKNILLINEN TUTKIMUSKESKUS. RAKENNETEKNIIKAN LABORATORIO. TIEDONANTO/TECHNICAL RESEARCH CENTRE OF FINLAND. LABORATORY OF STRUCTURAL ENGINEERING. REPORT. (Text mainly in Finnish, some in English or Swedish) 1979. irreg. price varies. Valtion Teknillinen Tutkimuskeskus - Technical Research Centre of Finland, Vuorimiehentie 5, 02150 Espoo 15, Finland.

624   552   UR
VOPROSY TEORII RAZRABOTKI MESTOROZHDENII POLEZNYKH ISKOPAEMYKH. a. 0.85 Rub. Akademiya Nauk S. S. S. R., Institut Fiziki Zemli, B. Gruzinskaya ul. 10, Moscow, U.S.S.R.

621   CS
VYSOKA SKOLA BANSKA. SBORNIK VEDECKYCH PRACI: RADA STROJNI. (Text in Czech; summaries also in English, German and Russian) 1967. irreg., vol. 20, 1974. 25 Kcs.($1) per issue. Statni Pedagogicke Nakladatelstvi, Ostrovni 30, 113 01 Prague 1, Czechoslovakia. Ed. L. Kuchar. charts. illus. index. circ. 600.

620   US
W B K. (Text in German) 1980. irreg. (Univeritaet Karlsruhe, Institut fuer Werkzeugmaschinen und Betriebstechnik, GW) Springer-Verlag, 175 Fifth Ave., New York, NY 10010 (Also Berlin, Heidelberg, Vienna) Ed. H. Victor. (reprint service avail. from ISI)

WASEDA UNIVERSITY. SCHOOL OF SCIENCE AND ENGINEERING. MEMOIRS/WASEDA DAIGAKU RIKOGAKUBU KIYO. see SCIENCES: COMPREHENSIVE WORKS

WASEDA UNIVERSITY. SCIENCE AND ENGINEERING RESEARCH LABORATORY. REPORT. see SCIENCES: COMPREHENSIVE WORKS

WEST COAST BRITISH COLUMBIA CONSTRUCTION INDUSTRY DIRECTORY. PURCHASING GUIDE. see BUILDING AND CONSTRUCTION

620   US   ISSN 0083-8640
WEST VIRGINIA UNIVERSITY. ENGINEERING EXPERIMENT STATION. BULLETIN.* 1918. irreg. West Virginia University, Engineering Experiment Station, College of Engineering, Morgantown, WV 26506.
Formed by the Merger in 1968 of Its Research Bulletin and Its Technical Bulletin Series.

620   US   ISSN 0083-8659
WEST VIRGINIA UNIVERSITY. ENGINEERING EXPERIMENT STATION. REPORT.* 1968. irreg., 1970, no.11. West Virginia University, Engineering Experiment Station, College of Engineering, Morgantown, WV 26506.

620   US   ISSN 0149-7537
WHO'S WHO IN ENGINEERING. 1970. triennial. $50. Engineers Joint Council, 345 E. 47 St., New York, NY 10017. Ed. Jean Gregory.
Formerly: Engineers of Distinction (ISSN 0149-7545)

WILD GOOSE ASSOCIATION. ANNUAL TECHNICAL SYMPOSIUM PROCEEDINGS. see EARTH SCIENCES — Oceanography

WILEY SERIES IN HUMAN FACTORS. see PSYCHOLOGY

620.7   US   ISSN 0084-019X
WILEY SERIES ON SYSTEMS ENGINEERING AND ANALYSIS. 1965. irreg., unnumbered, latest 1980. price varies. John Wiley & Sons, Inc., 605 Third Ave., New York, NY 10016. Ed. H. Chestnut.

621.45   US
WIND ENGINEERING RESEARCH DIGEST. 1974. a. University of Hawaii, Department of Engineering, 2540 Dole St., Honolulu, HI 96822 (Orders to: National Technical Information Service, Springfield, VA 22161) (Co-Sponsor: National Science Foundation) Ed. Arthur N. L. Chiu. circ. controlled. (also avail. in microfiche)

620   338   US   ISSN 0512-5405
WIRE JOURNAL DIRECTORY/CATALOG. 1969. a. $10 to non-members. (Wire Association International) Wire Journal, Inc., 1570 Boston Post Rd., Guilford, CT 06437. Ed. Anita M. Oliva. adv. abstr. tr.lit. index. circ. 10,000.

620   GW   ISSN 0340-2703
WISSENSCHAFTLICHE FORSCHUNGSBERICHTE. REIHE 2. ANWENDUNGSTECHNIK UND ANGEWANDTE WISSENSCHAFT/CURRENT TOPICS IN SCIENCE. REIHE 2. ENGINEERING. 1972. irreg. price varies. Dr. Dietrich Steinkopff Verlag, Saalbaustr. 12, Postfach 11 1008, 6100 Darmstadt 11, W. Germany(B.R.D.) Ed. W. Bruegel. circ. 2,000.

WORLDWIDE DIRECTORY OF PIPELINES AND CONTRACTORS. see PETROLEUM AND GAS

620   JA   ISSN 0513-2592
YOKOHAMA NATIONAL UNIVERSITY. FACULTY OF ENGINEERING. BULLETIN/YOKOHAMA KOKURITSU DAIGAKU KOGAKUBU KIYO. (Text in English and European languages) 1951. a. exchange basis. Yokohama National University, Faculty of Engineering - Yokohama Kokuritsu Daigaku Kogakubu, 156 Tokiwadai Hodogaya-ku, Yokohama 240, Japan.

YORK-SIMCOE ONTARIO CONSTRUCTION INDUSTRY DIRECTORY. PURCHASING GUIDE. see BUILDING AND CONSTRUCTION

ENGINEERING — Abstracting, Bibliographies, Statistics

624.173   016   US   ISSN 0363-5732
ABSTRACT JOURNAL IN EARTHQUAKE ENGINEERING. 1972. a. $30. University of California, Berkeley, Earthquake Engineering Research Center, 1301 South 46th Street, Richmond, CA 94804. Ed. Ruth C. Denton. index. circ. 835. (back issues avail.) Indexed: Bibl.Seismol.

669.141   US
AMERICAN IRON AND STEEL INSTITUTE. ANNUAL STATISTICAL REPORT. a. price varies. American Iron and Steel Institute, 1000 16 St., N.W., Washington, DC 20036.

676   016   GW
AUSZUEGE AUS DER LITERATUR DER ZELLSTOFF- UND PAPIER-ERZEUGUNG UND CELLULOSEVERARBEITUNG. 1934. a. membership. (Verein der Zellstoff- und Papier-Chemiker und Ingenieure) Eduard Roether Verlag, Berliner Allee 56, 6100 Darmstadt, W. Germany (B.R.D.) abstr. pat. index.

620   016   BL   ISSN 0100-0705
BIBLIOGRAFIA BRASILEIRA DE ENGENHARIA. 1970. a. Cr.$100($15) Instituto Brasileiro de Informacao em Ciencia e Tecnologia, Av. General Justo 171,4 Andar, 20000 Rio de Janeiro RJ, Brazil. circ. 500.

624   016   PO   ISSN 0067-6756
BIBLIOGRAFIA PORTUGUESA DE CONSTRUCAO CIVIL. (Text in Portuguese and English) 1963. a. not for sale. Laboratorio Nacional de Engenharia Civil, Avenida do Brasil, Lisbon 5, Portugal. bk. rev. circ. 750.

624   US
BIBLIOGRAPHY ON COLD REGIONS SCIENCE AND TECHNOLOGY. 1951. a. ‡ U.S. Army Cold Regions Research and Engineering Laboratory, P.O. Box 282, Hanover, NH 03755 (Orders to: National Technical Information Service, Springfield, VA 22151) Ed. Geza T. Thuronyi. index. cum.index:1951-1963;1969-1973. circ. controlled. (also avail. in microfiche)

624   625   CN   ISSN 0706-2451
CANADA. STATISTICS CANADA. HIGHWAY, ROAD, STREET AND BRIDGE CONTRACTING INDUSTRY/ENTREPRENEURS DE GRANDE ROUTE, CHEMIN, RUE ET PONT. (Catalogue 64-206) (Text in English and French) 1970. a. Can.$6($7.20) Statistics Canada, Publications Distribution, Ottawa, Ont. K1A 0V7, Canada. (also avail. in microform from MML)

338.4   CN   ISSN 0527-5539
CANADA. STATISTICS CANADA. MANUFACTURERS OF INDUSTRIAL CHEMICALS/FABRICANTS DE PRODUITS CHIMIQUES INDUSTRIELS. (Catalog 46-219) (Text in English and French) 1960. a. Can.$4.50($5.40) Statistics Canada, Publications Distribution, Ottawa, Ont. K1A 0V7, Canada. (also avail. in microform from MML)

690   CN   ISSN 0576-0097
CANADA. STATISTICS CANADA. MECHANICAL CONTRACTING INDUSTRY/LES ENTREPRENEURS D'INSTALLATIONS MECANIQUES. (Catalogue 64-204) (Text in English and French) 1967. a. Can.$6($7.20) Statistics Canada, Publications Distribution, Ottawa, Ont. K1A 0V7, Canada. (also avail. in microform from MML)

620.1   GW   ISSN 0340-3475
DOKUMENTATION TRIBOLOGIE/DOCUMENTATION TRIBOLOGY; verschleiss, reibung und schmierung. (Text in German and English) 1967. a. $108. Bundesanstalt fuer Materialpruefung, Unter den Eichen 87, 1000 Berlin 45, W. Germany (B.R.D.) Ed. Harald Tischer. index. circ. 500. (back issues from no. 5/1968 available)
Formerly: Dokumentation Verschleiss, Reibung und Schmierung (ISSN 0070-7023)

620   016   US   ISSN 0145-207X
ENGINEERING INDEX. NOTES & COMMENT. 1974. irreg. included with subscr. to Engineering Index. Engineering Index, Inc., Engineering Center, 345 E. 47th St., New York, NY 10017. Ed. Nancy F. Hardy. bibl. circ. 5,000.

620   US   ISSN 0360-8557
ENGINEERING INDEX ANNUAL. 1884. a. $530. Engineering Index, Inc., 345 E. 47 St., New York, NY 10017. (also avail. in microfilm; magnetic tape; back issues avail.)

620   016   UK
ENGINEERING SCIENCES DATA UNIT INDEX. 1966. a. £5. Engineering Sciences Data Unit Ltd., 251-259 Regent St., London W1R 7AD, England. (Co-sponsors: Royal Aeronautical Society; Institutions of Chemical, Mechanical and Structural Engineers) Ed. J.A. Shaw. cum.index.:1943-1979. circ. 6,000. Indexed: Chem.Abstr.
Formerly: Engineering Sciences Data Index (ISSN 0071-0377)

627.4   016   US   ISSN 0071-5735
FLOOD DAMAGE PREVENTION; AN INDEXED BIBLIOGRAPHY. 1963. irreg., 8th edt. 1976. free. Tennessee Valley Authority, Technical Library, Knoxville, TN 37902. circ. 2,000.

INDIAN LITERATURE IN ENVIRONMENTAL
ENGINEERING; annual bibliography. see
*ENVIRONMENTAL STUDIES — Abstracting,
Bibliographies, Statistics*

016 620 US ISSN 0085-4581
P I E. (Publications Indexed for Engineering) a. $10.
Engineering Index, Inc., 345 E. 47 St., New York,
NY 10017. Ed. John. E. Creps, Jr.

620 US
U S S R REPORT: ENGINEERING AND
EQUIPMENT. 1973. irreg. (approx. 11/yr.) $44.
U.S. Joint Publications Research Service, 1000 N.
Glebe Rd., Arlington, VA 22201 (Orders to: NTIS,
Springfield, VA 22161)
   Formerly: U S S R and Eastern Europe Scientific
Abstracts: Engineering and Equipment; Which was
formed by the merger of: U S S R Scientific
Abstracts: Engineering and Equipment; East
European Scientific Abstracts: Engineering and
Equipment.

620.11 669 US
U S S R REPORT: MATERIALS SCIENCE AND
METALLURGY. 1973. irreg. (approx. 7/yr.) $28.
U.S. Joint Publications Research Service, 1000 N.
Glebe Rd., Arlington, VA 22201 (Orders to: NTIS,
Springfield, VA 22161)
   Formerly: U S S R and Eastern Europe Scientific
Abstracts: Materials Science and Metallurgy; Which
was formed by the merger of: U S S R Scientific
Abstracts: Materials Science and Metallurgy; East
European Scientific Abstracts: Materials Science
and Metallurgy.

ENGINEERING — Chemical Engineering

see also Plastics

660 378 US ISSN 0065-8790
A I CH E CONTINUING EDUCATION SERIES.
1967. irreg., no. 5, 1971. price varies. American
Institute of Chemical Engineers, 345 E. 47 St., New
York, NY 10017. Ed. H. I. Abramson. circ. 500-
2,000.

660.2 542 US ISSN 0569-5473
A I CH E EQUIPMENT TESTING PROCEDURES.
1952. irreg. price varies. American Institute of
Chemical Engineers, Equipment Testing Procedures
Committee, 345 E. 47 St., New York, NY 10017.

660 US ISSN 0065-8812
A I CH E SYMPOSIUM SERIES. 1951. irreg.
American Institute of Chemical Engineers, 345 E.
47 St., New York, NY 10017. Ed. Sylvia
Fourdrinier.
   Supersedes: Chemical Engineering Progress
Symposium Series (ISSN 0069-2948)

660.2 US ISSN 0065-2377
ADVANCES IN CHEMICAL ENGINEERING.
1956. irreg., vol. 10, 1978. price varies. Academic
Press, Inc., 111 Fifth Ave., New York, NY 10003.
Eds. Thomas B. Drew, John W. Hoopes, Jr. index.

ADVANCES IN ELECTROCHEMISTRY AND
ELECTROCHEMICAL ENGINEERING. see
CHEMISTRY — Electrochemistry

ADVANCES IN POLYMER SCIENCE/
FORTSCHRITTE DER HOCHPOLYMEREN-
FORSCHUNG. see *CHEMISTRY — Organic
Chemistry*

AKTUELLE PROBLEME DER POLYMER-
PHYSIK. see *CHEMISTRY — Organic Chemistry*

661 US ISSN 0360-7011
AMMONIA PLANT SAFETY AND RELATED
FACILITIES. 1959. a. price varies. American
Institute of Chemical Engineers, 345 E. 47 St., New
York, NY 10017. Ed. Larry Resen. circ. 2,000.
   Formerly: Chemical Engineering Progress. Safety
in Air and Ammonia Plants (ISSN 0069-293X)

ANNUAL BOOK OF A S T M STANDARDS.
PART 29. PAINT - FATTY OILS AND ACIDS,
SOLVENTS, MISCELLANEOUS; AROMATIC
HYDROCARBONS; NAVAL STORES. see
*ENGINEERING — Engineering Mechanics And
Materials*

ANNUAL BOOK OF A S T M STANDARDS.
PART 30. SOAP; ENGINE COOLANTS;
POLISHES; HALOGENATED ORGANIC
SOLVENTS; ACTIVATED CARBON;
INDUSTRIAL CHEMICALS. see
*ENGINEERING — Engineering Mechanics And
Materials*

660 UK ISSN 0066-541X
APPLIED CHEMISTRY SERIES. 1970. irreg.
Business Books Ltd., 24 Highbury Crescent, London
N5 1RX, England (Dist. by: Cahners Books, 89
Franklin St., Boston, MA 02110)

668.4 US ISSN 0066-5517
APPLIED POLYMER SYMPOSIUM. PAPERS.
1965. irreg., no. 35, 1979. price varies. (Brooklyn
Polytechnic Institute) John Wiley & Sons, Inc., 605
Third Ave., New York, NY 10016. (also avail. in
microfilm)

660 665.5 AT
AUSTRALIAN CONFERENCE ON CHEMICAL
ENGINEERING. PROCEEDINGS. 1973. a. price
varies. Institution of Chemical Engineers in
Australia, Box 9, Killara, N.S.W. 2071, Australia.
circ. 2,500. (back issues avail.)

660 AT ISSN 0310-1444
BELL BRYANT NEWS. 1972. irreg. Bell Bryant Pty.
Ltd., 37 Herbert St., St. Leonards, NSW 2065,
Australia.

662 UK
BRITISH CARBONIZATION RESEARCH
ASSOCIATION. ANNUAL REPORT. a. British
Carbonization Research Association, Chesterfield,
Derbyshire, England.

CANADIAN CHEMICAL REGISTER. see
CHEMISTRY

660.2 US
CANADIAN SOCIETY FOR CHEMICAL
ENGINEERING SYMPOSIUM SERIES. a. price
varies. Plenum Publishing Corp., 233 Spring
St., New York, NY 10013.

662 UK ISSN 0305-9545
CARBONIZATION RESEARCH REPORT. 1959.
irreg. £10 per no. British Carbonization Research
Association, Chesterfield, Derbyshire, England. circ.
500. Indexed: Chem.Abstr.
   Formerly: Coke Research Report (ISSN 0010-
0528)

661 US
CHEMICAL ENGINEERING CATALOG. 1916. a.
$27. Penton-IPC, 614 Superior Ave., W., Cleveland,
OH 44113. adv. circ. 35,180. (also avail. in
microfilm; reprint service avail. from UMI)

660.2 378 US
CHEMICAL ENGINEERING FACULTIES OF
CANADA AND THE UNITED STATES. a. price
varies. American Institute of Chemical Engineers,
Chemical Engineering Education Projects
Committee, 345 E. 47 St., New York, NY 10017.

660 US ISSN 0069-2921
CHEMICAL ENGINEERING PROGRESS.
REPRINT MANUALS. 1965. irreg. price varies.
American Institute of Chemical Engineers, 345 E.
47 St., New York, NY 10017. Ed. Larry Resen.
circ. 2,000(approx.)

660 US ISSN 0069-2956
CHEMICAL ENGINEERING PROGRESS.
TECHNICAL MANUALS. 1960. irreg. price
varies. American Institute of Chemical Engineers,
345 E. 47 St., New York, NY 10017. Ed. Larry
Resen. circ. 2,000.

338.4 II
CHEMICAL INDIA ANNUAL. (Text in English) a.
Rs.5. c/o S. K. Bhanot, 640 Double Storey, New
Rajinder Nagar, New Delhi, India. illus.

660 UK ISSN 0069-2980
CHEMICAL INDUSTRY DIRECTORY. 1923. a.
£20. Benn Publications Ltd., 25 New Street Square,
London EC4A 3JA, England (Orders to: Directories
Dept., Sovereign Way, Tonbridge, Kent TN9 1RW,
England) Ed. A. J. Mulvaney. adv. index. circ.
2,200.

540 US
CHEMICAL TECHNOLOGY REVIEW. 1973. irreg.,
no. 179, 1981. $32-72. Noyes Data Corporation,
Noyes Bldg., Mill Rd. at Grand Ave., Park Ridge,
NJ 07656.
   Formerly: Chemical Processing Review.

660 AT ISSN 0312-9225
COMMONWEALTH SCIENTIFIC AND
INDUSTRIAL RESEARCH ORGANIZATION.
DIVISION OF CHEMICAL TECHNOLOGY.
RESEARCH REVIEW. 1974. irreg. C. S. I. R. O.,
Division of Chemical Technology, 69 Yarra Bank
R., South Melbourne, Vic. 3205, Australia. illus.

660 FR ISSN 0430-2222
CONGRESS F A T I P E C. Variant title: Federation
d'Associations de Techniciens des Industries des
Peintures, Vernis, Emaux et Encres d'Imprimerie de
l'Europe Continentale. Congress Proceedings. 1951.
biennial; 15th, Amsterdam, 1980. Federation
d'Associations de Techniciens des Industries des
Peintures, Vernis, Emaux et Encres d'Imprimerie de
l'Europe Continentale, Maison de la Chimie, 28 rue
Saint Dominique, 75007 Paris, France.

660.28 CN ISSN 0070-525X
DIRECTORY OF CHEMICAL ENGINEERING
RESEARCH IN CANADIAN UNIVERSITIES.
(Text in English and French) 1961. a. Can.$7 to
non-members. Canadian Society for Chemical
Engineering, 151 Slater St., Ottawa, Ont., K1P 5H3,
Canada. Ed. D. E. Seborg. circ. 400.

660 CK
ENLACE. 1976. irreg. Universidad Pontificia
Bolivariana, Facultad de Ingenieria Quimica,
Medellin, Colombia. Ed.Bd.

660 GW
EUROPEAN FEDERATION OF CHEMICAL
ENGINEERING. ANNUAL REPORT. (Editions
in English, French, German) biennial. price varies.
European Federation of Chemical Engineering, c/o
DECHEMA, Postfach 970146, 6000 Frankfurt 97,
W. Germany (B.R.D.)

660.2 GW ISSN 0071-3112
EUROPEAN SYMPOSIUM ON CHEMICAL
REACTION ENGINEERING. PROCEEDINGS.
(First and Second published by Pergamon Press in
Chemical Engineering Science; Third and Fourth-in
supplement to Chemical Engineering Science; Fifth-
by Elsevier; Sixth-by the Federation itself) irreg.
6th, 1976, Heidelberg. European Federation of
Chemical Engineering, Theodor Heuss-Allee 25,
6000 Frankfurt, W. Germany (B.R.D.)

660 BE ISSN 0425-9076
FEDERATION DES INDUSTRIES CHIMIQUES
DE BELGIQUE. ANNUAIRE. (Text in French,
Flemish, German and English) irreg., latest edition
1978-79. 1200 Fr. Federation des Industries
Chimiques de Belgique, Square Marie Louise 49, B-
1040 Brussels, Belgium. adv. circ. 4,500.

660.28 BE ISSN 0085-0489
FEDERATION DES INDUSTRIES CHIMIQUES
DE BELGIQUE. RAPPORT. (Text in French)
1928. a. free. Federation des Industries Chimiques
de Belgique, 49 Square Marie-Louise, B-1040
Brussels, Belgium. Ed. Paul-F. Smets.

660.284 US
FILTRATION ENGINEERING CATALOG. 1971. a.
$10. 25 W. 45th St., New York, NY 10036. Ed.
Michael Sparks. adv. circ. controlled.

662 SW ISSN 0348-6613
FOEREDRAG VID PYROTEKNIKDAGEN. (Text
in English and Swedish) biennial. Svenska
Nationalkommitten foer Mekanik, Sektionen foer
Detonik och Foerbraenning, Box 608, S-551 02
Joenkoeping, Sweden. illus. Indexed: Chem.Abstr.
Explosives

FUEL AND ENERGY SCIENCE SERIES. see
ENERGY

GLASNIK HEMICARA I TEHNOLOGA BOSNE I
HERCEGOVINE. see *CHEMISTRY*

ENGINEERING — CHEMICAL ENGINEERING

660   II
GUIDE TO INDIAN CHEMICAL PLANTS AND EQUIPMENT. Bound with: Indian Chemical Directory (ISSN 0073-6295) (Text in English) 1966. irreg. Rs.100 for Indian Chemical Directory. Technical Press Publications, 5 Convent St., Colaba, Bombay 1, India. Ed. J. P. de Sousa. adv. circ. 10,000.
    Formerly: Catalogue of Indian Chemical Plants (ISSN 0069-1151)

HIGH POLYMERS; a series of monographs on the chemistry, physics and technology of high polymeric substances. see *CHEMISTRY — Organic Chemistry*

660   FR
I M P H O S CONGRESS PROCEEDINGS/ WORLD PHOSPHATE ROCK INSTITUTE. PROCEEDINGS. (Institut Mondial du Phosphate) (Text in English, French) 1978. irreg; 2nd, 1980, Boston, Mass. 250 F. World Phosphate Rock Institute, 8 rue de Penthievre, 75008 Paris, France. (back issues avail)

660 540   II   ISSN 0073-6295
INDIAN CHEMICAL DIRECTORY. (Text in English) 1955. 11th edt., 1975. Rs.100. Technical Press Publications, 5 Convent St., Colaba, Bombay 1, India. Ed. J. P. de Sousa. adv. circ. 10,000.

500 662   UK
INSTITUTE OF ENERGY. SYMPOSIUM SERIES. 1975. irreg. £7. Institute of Energy, 18 Devonshire St., London W1N 2AU, England.
    Formerly: Institute of Fuel. Symposium Series.

INSTRUMENTATION IN THE CHEMICAL AND PETROLEUM INDUSTRY. see *INSTRUMENTS*

INTERNATIONAL CONGRESS OF PURE AND APPLIED CHEMISTRY. (LECTURES) see *CHEMISTRY*

665   US
INTERNATIONAL OZONE INSTITUTE. WORKSHOP SERIES. vol. 2, 1976. irreg. International Ozone Institute, Inc., Merrill Lane, Skytop Complex, Syracuse, NY 13210.

660   US   ISSN 0074-8021
INTERNATIONAL SERIES ON CHEMICAL ENGINEERING. 1960. irreg., vol. 13, 1973. price varies. Pergamon Press, Inc., Maxwell House, Fairview Park, Elmsford, NY 10523. index.
    Formerly: International Series of Monographs in Chemical Engineering.

660   GE   ISSN 0075-0336
IONENAUSTAUSCHER IN EINZELDARSTELLUNGEN. 1962. irreg., vol. 8, 1970. price varies. Akademie-Verlag, Leipziger Str. 3-4, 108 Berlin, E. Germany (D.D.R.) Ed. Hans Reuter.

660   IT
ITALY. ENTE NAZIONALE IDROCARBURI. CHIMICA. SOMMARIO STATISTICO. (Text in Italian; summaries in English) irreg. (Ente Nazionale Idrocarburi) Staderini S.p.A., Pomezia, Italy. charts.

660   JA   ISSN 0075-319X
JAPAN CHEMICAL ANNUAL. (Text in English) a. 3000 Yen($16) Chemical Daily Co., Ltd. - Kagaku Kogyo Nipposha, 3-19-16 Shibaura, Minato-ku, Tokyo 108, Japan. Ed. Hayao Kitani.

660   JA   ISSN 0075-3203
JAPAN CHEMICAL DIRECTORY. (Text in English) 1963. a. 18000 Yen($70) Chemical Daily Co., Ltd. - Kagaku Kogyo Nipposha, 3-19-16 Shibaura, Minato-ku, Tokyo 108, Japan.

660   JA   ISSN 0448-858X
JAPAN CHEMICAL REVIEW. (Text in English) a. Chemical Daily Co., Ltd. - Kagaku Kogyo Nipposha, 3-19-16 Shibaura, Minato-ku, Tokyo 108, Japan.

668.4   US   ISSN 0570-4898
JOURNAL OF APPLIED POLYMER SCIENCE. SYMPOSIA. Short title: Applied Polymer Symposia. 1965. irreg., no. 35, 1979. price varies. John Wiley & Sons, Inc., 605 Third Ave., New York, NY 10016.

660   US
KLINE GUIDE TO THE CHEMICAL INDUSTRY. 1971. triennial. $147. Charles H. Kline & Co., Inc., 330 Passaic Ave., Fairfield, NJ 07006. Ed. Susan Rich.
    Formerly: Marketing Guide to the Chemical Industry (ISSN 0076-4582)

665   US   ISSN 0077-4022
NATIONAL COTTONSEED PRODUCTS ASSOCIATION. TRADING RULES. 1897. a. $10 to non-members. National Cottonseed Products Association, P.O. Box 12023, Memphis, TN 38112. Ed. John Devine. circ. 1,000.

NEW SOUTH WALES. DEPARTMENT OF MINES. CHEMICAL LABORATORY. REPORT. see *MINES AND MINING INDUSTRY*

662   NO
NORWAY. STATENS SPRENGSTOFFINSPEKSJON. AARSBERETNING. a. Statens Sprengstoffinspeksjon, Postboks 355, 3101 Toensberg, Norway. illus.
    Formerly: Norway. Sprengstoffinspeksjonen. Aarsberetning.

NOVYE ISSLEDOVANIYA V KHIMII, METALLURGII I OBOGASHCHENII. see *METALLURGY*

660   US
PACIFIC CHEMICAL ENGINEERING CONGRESS. PROCEEDINGS. irreg., 2nd, 1977. American Institute of Chemical Engineers, 345 E. 47th St., New York, NY 10017.

660 655   US   ISSN 0079-1288
PETROLEUM AND CHEMICAL INDUSTRY TECHNICAL CONFERENCE. RECORD. a. Institute of Electrical and Electronics Engineers, Inc., 445 Hoes Lane, Piscataway, NJ 08854.

668.4   SI
PLASTICHEM. 1969. a. free to qualified personnel. Singapore Polytechnic Polymer Society, Dover Rd., Singapore 5, Singapore. Ed. Tang Sook Mui. adv. circ. 1,000 (controlled)
    Formerly: Polymer Journal.

660.2   PL
POLITECHNIKA LODZKA. ZESZYTY NAUKOWE. INZYNIERIA CHEMICZNA. (Text in Polish; summaries in English and Russian) 1973. irreg. price varies. Politechnika Lodzka, Ul. Zwirki 36, 90-924 Lodz, Poland (Dist. by: Ars Polona-Ruch, Krakowskie Przedmiescie 7, Warsaw, Poland) Ed. Czeslaw Strumillo. circ. 350.

665   PL   ISSN 0324-9867
POLITECHNIKA WROCLAWSKA. INSTYTUT CHEMII I TECHNOLOGII NAFTY I WEGLA. PRACE NAUKOWE. KONFERENCJE. (Text in Polish and English) 1975. irreg., 1978, no. 4. price varies. Politechnika Wroclawska, Wybrzeze Wyspianskiego 27, 50-370 Wroclaw, Poland (Dist. by: Ars Polona-Ruch, Krakowskie Przedmiescie 7, Warsaw, Poland) Ed. Marian Kloza. circ. 375.

665   PL   ISSN 0324-9859
POLITECHNIKA WROCLAWSKA. INSTYTUT CHEMII I TECHNOLOGII NAFTY I WEGLA. PRACE NAUKOWE. MONOGRAFIE. (Text in Polish; summaries in English, French and Russian) 1972. irreg., 1978, no. 12. price varies. Politechnika Wroclawska, Wybrzeze Wyspianskiego 27, 50-370 Wroclaw, Poland (Dist. by: Ars Polona-Ruch, Krakowskie Przedmiescie 7, Warsaw, Poland) Ed. Marian Kloza.

665   PL   ISSN 0084-2818
POLITECHNIKA WROCLAWSKA. INSTYTUT CHEMII I TECHNOLOGII NAFTY I WEGLA. PRACE NAUKOWE. STUDIA I MATERIALY. (Text in Polish; summaries in English, Russian) 1969. irreg., 1976, no. 19. price varies. Politechnika Wroclawska, Wybrzeze Wyspianskiego 27, 50-370 Wroclaw, Poland (Dist. by: Ars Polona-Ruch, Krakowskie Przedmiescie 7, Warsaw, Poland) Ed. Marian Kloza.

660 697   PL
POLITECHNIKA WROCLAWSKA. INSTYTUT INZYNIERII CHEMICZNEJ I URZADZEN CIEPLNYCH. PRACE NAUKOWE. KONFERENCJE. (Text in Polish; summaries in English, French and Russian) 1972. irreg., 1977, no. 4. price varies. Politechnika Wroclawska, Wybrzeze Wyspianskiego 27, 50-370 Wroclaw, Poland (Dist. by: Ars Polona-Ruch, Krakowskie Przedmiescie 7, Warsaw, Poland) Ed. Marian Kloza.

660 697   PL   ISSN 0084-2850
POLITECHNIKA WROCLAWSKA. INSTYTUT INZYNIERII CHEMICZNEJ I URZADZEN CIEPLNYCH. PRACE NAUKOWE. MONOGRAFIE. (Text in Polish; summaries in English, French and Russian) 1970. irreg., 1977, no. 18. price varies. Politechnika Wroclawska, Wybrzeze Wyspianskiego 27, 50-370 Wroclaw, Poland (Dist. by: Ars Polona-Ruch, Krakowskie Przedmiescie 7, Warsaw, Poland) Ed.Marian Kloza.

660 697   PL   ISSN 0324-9751
POLITECHNIKA WROCLAWSKA. INSTYTUT INZYNIERII CHEMICZNEJ I URZADZEN CIEPLNYCH. PRACE NAUKOWE. STUDIA I MATERIALY. (Text in Polish: Summaries in English and Russian) 1970. irreg., 1976, no. 13. price varies. Politechnika Wroclawska, Wybrzeze Wyspianskiego 27, 50-370 Wroclaw, Poland (Dist. by: Ars Polona-Ruch, Krakowskie Przedmiescie 7, Warsaw Poland) Ed. Marian Kloza.

660   PL   ISSN 0084-2893
POLITECHNIKA WROCLAWSKA. INSTYTUT TECHNOLOGII NIEORGANICZNEJ I NAWOZOW MINERALNYCH. PRACE NAUKOWE. KONFERENCJE. 1972. irreg., no. 7, 1979. price varies. Politechnika Wroclawska, Wybrzeze Wyspianskiego 27, 50-370 Wroclaw, Poland (Dist. by: Ars Polona-Ruch, Krakowskie Przedmiescie 7, Warsaw, Poland) Ed. Marian Kloza.

660   PL   ISSN 0084-2907
POLITECHNIKA WROCLAWSKA. INSTYTUT TECHNOLOGII NIEORGANICZNEJ I NAWOZOW MINERALNYCH. PRACE NAUKOWE. MONOGRAFIE. (Text in Polish; summaries in English, Russian) 1971. irreg., no. 4, 1977. price varies. Politechnika Wroclawska, Wydawnictwo, Wybrzeze Wyspianskiego 27, 50-370 Wroclaw, Poland.

660   PL   ISSN 0084-2915
POLITECHNIKA WROCLAWSKA. INSTYTUT TECHNOLOGII NIEORGANICZNEJ I NAWOZOW MINERALNYCH. PRACE NAUKOWE. STUDIA I MATERIALY. (Text in Polish; summaries in English, Russian) 1970. irreg., 1976, no. 4. price varies. Politechnika Wroclawska, Wybrzeze Wyspianskiego 27, 50-370 Wroclaw, Poland (Dist. by: Ars Polona-Ruch, Krakowskie Przedmiescie 7, Warsaw, Poland) Ed. Marian Kloza.

668.4   PL   ISSN 0137-1398
POLITECHNIKA WROCLAWSKA. INSTYTUT TECHNOLOGII ORGANICZNEJ I TWORZYW SZTUCZNYCH. PRACE NAUKOWE. KONFERENCJE. (Text in Polish; summaries in English and Russian) 1972. irreg., no. 10, 1979. price varies. Politechnika Wroclawska, Wybrzeze Wyspianskiego 27, 50-370 Wroclaw, Poland (Dist. by: Ars Polona-Ruch, Krakowskie Przedmiescie 7, Warsaw, Poland) Ed. Marian Kloza.

668.4   PL   ISSN 0370-0879
POLITECHNIKA WROCLAWSKA. INSTYTUT TECHNOLOGII ORGANICZNEJ I TWORZYW SZTUCZNYCH. PRACE NAUKOWE. MONOGRAFIE. (Text in Polish; summaries in English and Russian) 1971. irreg., no. 7, 1979. price varies. Politechnika Wroclawska, Wybrzeze Wyspianskiego 27, 50-370 Wroclaw, Poland (Dist. by: Ars Polona-Ruch, Krakowskie Przedmiescie 7, Warsaw, Poland) Ed. Marian Kloza.

660.2   US   ISSN 0079-3728
POLYMER ENGINEERING AND TECHNOLOGY SERIES. 1964. irreg., unnumbered, latest 1971. price varies. John Wiley & Sons, Inc., 605 Third Ave., New York, NY 10016. Ed. D.V. Rosato.

660   US   ISSN 0079-5054
PRESSURE GAUGE. 1962. irreg; latest issue, 1975. Aerosol Techniques, Inc., Old Gate Lane, Milford, CT 06460. Ed. Hugh W. Johnson. circ. 3,500.

662   380.1   UK
PROCESS ENGINEERING DIRECTORY. 1977. a. £15. Morgan- Grampian Book Publishing Co., 30 Calderwood St, Woolwich, London SE18 6QH, England. Ed. Jane Doyle. adv. circ. 1,500.

660   MX
PRODUCCION QUIMICA MEXICANA. 1963. a. 300($15) Editorial Innovacion, Espana 396, Mexico 13, D.F., Mexico. Ed. Cesar Macazaga. adv. index; cum. index. circ. 5,000.

660   MX
PRODUCTOS QUIMICOS. 1958. a. 150($180) Editorial Cosmos, Espana 396, Mexico 13, D.F., Mexico. Ed. Cesar Macazaga. adv.

PROGRESS IN POLYMER SCIENCE. see CHEMISTRY — Organic Chemistry

660   UK   ISSN 0456-4804
RAMSAY SOCIETY OF CHEMICAL ENGINEERS. JOURNAL. 1949. a. £1.50. ‡ Ramsay Society of Chemical Engineers, Dept. of Chemical Engineering, University College London, Torrington Place, London WC1E 7JE, England. Ed. D. J. C. Flower. adv. illus. circ. 600. (tabloid format)

660   IT
REPERTORIO CHIMICO ITALIANO; industriale e commerciale. biennial. Edizioni Ariminum, Via Negroli 51, 20133 Milan, Italy.

660   677   JA   ISSN 0559-8621
SHINSHU UNIVERSITY. FACULTY OF TEXTILE SCIENCE AND TECHNOLOGY. JOURNAL. SERIES C: CHEMISTRY. (Text in English) 1951. irreg. exchange basis. Shinshu University, Faculty of Textile Science and Technology - Shinshu Daigaku Sen'i Gakubu, 3-15-1 Tokida, Ueda, Nagano 386, Japan.

333.7   665   UK
SYMPOSIUM ON FLAMES AND INDUSTRY. PROCEEDINGS. no. 4, 1972. irreg. £15($37.50) Institute of Fuel, British Flame Research Committee, 18 Devonshire St., London W1N 2AU, England.

660   US   ISSN 0082-1144
SYNTHETIC ORGANIC CHEMICALS, UNITED STATES PRODUCTION AND SALES. 1918. a. price varies. U.S. International Trade Commission, 701 E St. N.W., Washingto, DC 20436 (Orders to: Supt. Doc., Washington, DC 20402)

660   CK   ISSN 0120-100X
UNIVERSIDAD INDUSTRIAL DE SANTANDER. REVISTA - ION. 1953. a. Col.$120($3) per no. or exchange basis. Universidad Industrial de Santander, Centro de Estudios de Ingenieria Quimica, Apdo. Aereo 678, Bucaramanga, Colombia. adv. bk. rev. bibl. charts. illus. circ. 600.

660   FI   ISSN 0355-3574
VALTION TEKNILLINEN TUTKIMUSKESKUS. KEMIAN LABORATORIO. TIEDONANTO/ TECHNICAL RESEARCH CENTRE OF FINLAND. CHEMICAL LABORATORY. REPORT. (Text mainly in Finnish, some in English or Swedish) 1971. irreg. price varies. Valtion Teknillinen Tutkimuskeskus - Technical Research Centre of Finland, Vuorimiehentie 5, 02150 Espoo 15, Finland.

669   HU   ISSN 0083-5277
VASKOHASZATI ENCIKLOPEDIA. 1954. irreg. price varies. (Magyar Tudomanyos Akademia) Akademiai Kiado, Publishing House of the Hungarian Academy of Sciences, P.O. Box 24, H-1363 Budapest, Hungary.

WISSENSCHAFTLICHE FORSCHUNGSBERICHTE. REIHE 2. ANWENDUNGSTECHNIK UND ANGEWANDTE WISSENSCHAFT/CURRENT TOPICS IN SCIENCE. REIHE 2. ENGINEERING. see ENGINEERING

ENGINEERING — Civil Engineering

see also Building and Construction; Transportation—Roads and Traffic

A R T B A OFFICIALS AND ENGINEERS DIRECTORY, TRANSPORTATION AGENCY PERSONNEL. (American Road and Transportation Builders Association) see TRANSPORTATION — Roads And Traffic

690   FI   ISSN 0355-2705
ACTA POLYTECHNICA SCANDINAVICA. CIVIL ENGINEERING AND BUILDING CONSTRUCTION SERIES. (Text in English, French, German) 1958. irreg. (2-3/yr.) Fmk.60. Teknillisten Tieteiden Akatemia - Finnish Academy of Technical Sciences, Kansakoulukatu 10 A, SF-00100 Helsinki 10, Finland. Ed. Leo Keinonen. index; cum index (1958-1979) price. 250. (also avail. in microfilm from UMI; back issues avail.; reprint service avail. from UMI)

ALBERTA RESEARCH COUNCIL. HIGHWAY RESEARCH. see TRANSPORTATION — Roads And Traffic

627.1   551.44   CN
ALBERTA RESEARCH COUNCIL. RIVER ENGINEERING AND SURFACE HYDROLOGY REPORTS. irreg. $2. Alberta Research Council, Publications Department, 11315-87 Avenue, Edmonton, Alberta T6G 2C2, Canada. Formerly: Alberta Research. Highways and River Engineering Reports (ISSN 0080-1550)

624   US   ISSN 0065-9932
AMERICAN PUBLIC WORKS ASSOCIATION. RESEARCH FOUNDATION. SPECIAL REPORTS. irreg.; latest issue. 1977. price varies. ‡ American Public Works Association, 1313 E. 60 St., Chicago, IL 60637.

624   US   ISSN 0569-7948
AMERICAN SOCIETY OF CIVIL ENGINEERS. CONSTRUCTION DIVISION. JOURNAL. Short title: Construction. 1956. q. $25.50 to non-members. American Society of Civil Engineers, 345 E. 47th St., New York, NY 10017. (reprint service avail. from UMI)

624   US
AMERICAN SOCIETY OF CIVIL ENGINEERS. ENERGY DIVISION. JOURNAL. Short title: Energy. 1956. irreg. (2-3/yr) $19.50 to non-members. American Society of Civil Engineers, 345 E. 47th St., New York, NY 10017. (reprint service avail. from UMI)
Formerly (until 1978): American Society of Civil Engineers. Power Division. Journal (ISSN 0569-8030)

624   US   ISSN 0003-1119
AMERICAN SOCIETY OF CIVIL ENGINEERS. PROCEEDINGS. (Consists of the Journals of the various Divisions of the Society) 1873. m. $195. American Society of Civil Engineers, 345 E. 47th St., New York, NY 10017. abstr. bibl. charts. illus. stat. index. cum.index every 5 yrs. circ. 105,000(total 15 journals) (also avail. in microfilm from UMI) Indexed: A.S. & T.Ind. Appl.Mech.Rev. Chem.Abstr. Eng.Ind.

625.72   US   ISSN 0569-8073
AMERICAN SOCIETY OF CIVIL ENGINEERS. SURVEYING AND MAPPING DIVISION. JOURNAL. Short title: Surveying and Mapping. 1956. irreg. (2-3/yr.) $15 to non-members. American Society of Civil Engineers, 345 E. 47th St., New York, NY 10017. (reprint service avail. from UMI)
Surveying

624   US
AMERICAN SOCIETY OF CIVIL ENGINEERS. TECHNICAL COUNCILS. JOURNAL. 1978. irreg.(2-3/yr.) $19.50 to non-members. American Society of Civil Engineers, 345 E. 47th St., New York, NY 10017. (reprint service avail. from UMI)

624   US   ISSN 0066-0604
AMERICAN SOCIETY OF CIVIL ENGINEERS. TRANSACTIONS. a. $45. American Society of Civil Engineers, 345 E. 47th St., New York, NY 10017. (reprint service avail. from UMI) Indexed: Appl.Mech.Rev.

ANNUAIRE BATIMENT ET TRAVAUX PUBLICS. see BUILDING AND CONSTRUCTION

ARIZONA LAND SURVEYORS CONFERENCE. PROCEEDINGS. see GEOGRAPHY

625.8   US   ISSN 0066-9466
ASSOCIATION OF ASPHALT PAVING TECHNOLOGISTS. PROCEEDINGS. Vol. 43 (1974): Asphalt Paving Technology. 1928. a. $30. Association of Asphalt Paving Technologists, 155 Experimental Engineering Bldg, University of Minnesota, Minneapolis, MN 55455. Ed. E. L. Skok, Jr. cum.index through vol. 43. (back issues avail.)
Roads and streets

624.151   US
ASSOCIATION OF ENGINEERING GEOLOGISTS. SPECIAL PUBLICATIONS. irreg. price varies. Association of Engineering Geologists, c/o Floyd T. Johnston, Exec. Dir., 8310 San Fernando Way, Dallas, TX 75218.

625.72   CN   ISSN 0700-5989
ASSOCIATION OF ONTARIO LAND SURVEYORS. ANNUAL REPORT. a. Can.$10. Association of Ontario Land Surveyors, 6070 Yonge St., Willowdale, Ont. M2M 3Z3, Canada.
Surveying

AUSTRALIAN ROAD RESEARCH BOARD. PROCEEDINGS. see TRANSPORTATION — Roads And Traffic

625.7   AT   ISSN 0705-9213
AUSTRALIAN ROAD RESEARCH IN PROGRESS. 1980. a. 10. Australian Road Research Board, Box 156 (Bag 4), Nunawading, Vic. 3131, Australia.
Roads and streets

624   BF
BAHAMAS. MINISTRY OF WORKS. ANNUAL REPORT. a. $2. Ministry of Works, P.O. Box N8156, Nassau, Bahamas (Orders to: Government Publications Office, Bank Lane, Nassau, Bahamas) charts. illus. stat. circ. 100(approx.)

624.183   GW   ISSN 0067-6365
BETON- UND FERTIGTEIL-JAHRBUCH. 1951. a. DM.19.50. Bauverlag GmbH, Wittelsbacherstr. 10, 6200 Wiesbaden, W. Germany (B.R.D.)
Formerly: Betonstein-Jahrbuch.

627.8   UK   ISSN 0525-4205
BRITISH NATIONAL COMMITTEE ON LARGE DAMS. NEWS AND VIEWS. a. £2($4) (Institution of Civil Engineers) Thomas Telford Ltd., Publications Division, 26-34 Old St., London EC1V 9AD, England. Ed. H. W. Baker. adv. bk. rev. charts. illus. index.

624   UK   ISSN 0069-9209
C I R I A ANNUAL REPORT. 1964. a. free. Construction Industry Research and Information Association, 6 Storey's Gate, London SW1P 3AU, England.
Formerly: C I R I A. Bulletin.

CALIFORNIA TRANSPORTATION AND PUBLIC WORKS CONFERENCE. PROCEEDINGS. see TRANSPORTATION — Roads And Traffic

624   CN   ISSN 0318-0522
CANADIAN STRUCTURAL ENGINEERING CONFERENCE. PROCEEDINGS. 1968. biennial. Canadian Steel Industries Construction Council, 1815 Yonge St., Toronto, Ont. M4T 2A3, Canada.

627   JA   ISSN 0578-5634
COASTAL ENGINEERING IN JAPAN. (Text in English) 1958. a. 1,600 Yen. Japan Society of Civil Engineers - Doboku Gakkai, 1-chome, Yotsuya, Shinjuku-ku, Tokyo 160, Japan.

COMMONWEALTH SCIENTIFIC AND INDUSTRIAL RESEARCH ORGANIZATION. DIVISION OF APPLIED GEOMECHANICS. TECHNICAL PAPER. see MINES AND MINING INDUSTRY

COMMONWEALTH SCIENTIFIC AND INDUSTRIAL RESEARCH ORGANIZATION. DIVISION OF APPLIED GEOMECHANICS. TECHNICAL REPORT. see MINES AND MINING INDUSTRY

ENGINEERING — CIVIL ENGINEERING

624.176 AT
COMMONWEALTH SCIENTIFIC AND INDUSTRIAL RESEARCH ORGANIZATION. INSTITUTE OF EARTH RESOURCES. ANNUAL REPORT. 1980. a. free. C. S. I. R. O., Institute of Earth Resources, Box 225, Dickson, A.C.T. 2602, Australia. Ed. J. North. circ. 2,000(controlled)

624.151 NE
DEVELOPMENTS IN GEOTECHNICAL ENGINEERING. 1972. irreg., vol. 27, 1979. price varies. Elsevier Scientific Publishing Co., Box 211, 1000 AE Amsterdam, Netherlands.

624 US
E E R C REPORTS. irreg. $240 per annual series. University of California, Berkeley, Earthquake Engineering Research Center, 47th St. & Hoffman Blvd., Richmond, CA 94804 (Single copies from: NTIS, Springfield, VA 22161)

ECONOMIE FRANCAISE EN PERSPECTIVES SECTORIELLES: FILIERE BATIMENT, GENIE CIVIL, MATERIAUX DE CONSTRUCTION. see *BUILDING AND CONSTRUCTION*

625.7 GW
ELSNERS HANDBUCH FUER STRASSENWESEN. 1937. a. DM.28.40. Otto Elsner Verlagsgesellschaft, Schoefferstr. 15, 6100 Darmstadt, W. Germany (B.R.D.) Ed. E. W. Goerner. adv. circ. 12,500.
Formerly: Elsner; Handbuch fuer Strassenbau und Strassenverkehrstechnik (ISSN 0071-0067)
Roads and streets

624 BL
ENGENHARIA CIVIL. 1974. m. Cr.$10000($12) Engetec Ltda., Rua Nestor Pestana 125, Sao Paulo, Brazil. illus.
Supersedes in part: Engenharia (ISSN 0013-7707)

624.151 US ISSN 0071-0318
ENGINEERING GEOLOGY AND SOILS ENGINEERING SYMPOSIUM. PROCEEDINGS. 1963. a. $8. Transportation Department, Division of Highways, P.O.B. 7129, Boise, ID 83707. Ed. Robert G. Charboneau. circ. 500.
Formerly: Engineering Geology Symposium. Proceedings.

624.151 US ISSN 0071-0326
ENGINEERING GEOLOGY CASE HISTORIES. (Each vol. has distinctive title) 1957. irreg., no. 10, 1974. price varies. Geological Society of America, 3300 Penrose Place, Boulder, CO 80301.

625.7 FR
EUROPEAN SYMPOSIUM ON CONCRETE PAVEMENTS. REPORTS. 1969. irreg.; 3rd, Besancon(France), 1977. 360 F.($30.00) Cembureau, 2, rue Saint Charles, 75740 Paris, France. circ. 1,140.
Roads and streets

624.176 CN
FIRST CANADIAN CONFERENCE ON EARTHQUAKE ENGINEERING. PROCEEDINGS. 1971. quadrennial. Can.$15. University of British Columbia, Department of Civil Engineering, Vancouver 8, B.C., Canada. Ed. S. Cherry. charts, illus. circ. 1,000.

625.7 016 GW ISSN 0340-3998
FORSCHUNG IM STRASSENWESEN. 1972. irreg. DM.50. ‡ Forschungsgesellschaft fuer das Strassenwesen e.V., Maastrichter Str. 45, 5000 Cologne 1, W. Germany (B.R.D.) Ed. Herbert Kuehn. bibl. circ. 3,000.
Roads and streets

FORSCHUNG UND KONSTRUKTION IM STAHLBAU/RESEARCH AND CONSTRUCTION ON STEEL-ENGINEERING/ ETUDE DES OUVRAGES EN ACIER ET CONSTRUCTION METALLIQUE. see *ENGINEERING — Engineering Mechanics And Materials*

625.8 GW ISSN 0426-9918
FORSCHUNGSGESELLSCHAFT FUER DAS STRASSENWESEN. ARBEITSGRUPPE ASPHALT- UND TEERSTRASSEN. SCHRIFTENREIHE. 1948. irreg. price varies. (Forschungsgesellschaft fuer das Strassenwesen e.V.) Kirschbaum Verlag, Siegfriedstr. 28, Postfach 210209, 5300 Bonn 2, W. Germany (B.R.D.)
Roads and streets

625.8 GW ISSN 0429-1816
FORSCHUNGSGESELLSCHAFT FUER DAS STRASSENWESEN. ARBEITSGRUPPE BETONSTRASSEN. SCHRIFTENREIHE. 1950. irreg. price varies. (Forschungsgesellschaft fuer das Strassenwesen e.V.) Kirschbaum Verlag, Siegfriedstr. 28, Postfach 210209, 5300 Bonn 2, W. Germany (B.R.D.)
Roads and streets

624 FR ISSN 0085-2643
FRANCE. LABORATOIRES DES PONTS ET CHAUSEES. RAPPORT DE RECHERCHE. (Text in French; summaries in French, English, German, Russian and Spanish) 1969. irreg., 1979, no. 86. free. Laboratoire Central des Ponts et Chaussees, 58 Blvd. Lefebre, 75732 Paris Cedex 15, France.

625.7 GW
GERMANY (FEDERAL REPUBLIC, 1949-) BUNDESANSTALT FUER STRASSENWESEN, ERFAHRUNGSAUSTAUCH UEBER ERDARBEITEN IM STRASSENBAU. a. free. Bundesanstalt fuer Strassenwesen, Bruehler Str. 1, 5000 Cologne 51, W. Germany (B.R.D.)
Roads and streets

624 UK ISSN 0072-6850
GREAT BRITAIN. DEPARTMENT OF THE ENVIRONMENT. ENGINEERING SPECIFICATIONS. irreg. price varies. Department of the Environment, 2 Marsham St., London SW1P 3EB, England (Avail. from H.M.S.O. c/o Liaison Officer, Atlantic House, Holborn Viaduct, London EC1P 1BN, England)

624 US ISSN 0072-9264
HAFENBAUTECHNISCHE GESELLSCHAFT. JAHRBUCH. vol. 19, 1951. irreg., vol. 36, 1979. price varies. (GW) Springer-Verlag, 175 Fifth Ave., New York, NY 10010 (Also Berlin, Heidelberg, Vienna) (reprint service avail. from ISI)

625.7 US ISSN 0073-2176
HIGHWAY PLANNING NOTES. 1962. irreg. U. S. Federal Highway Administration, Management Systems Branch, 400 Seventh St. S.W., Washington, DC 20591. (newsletter format)
Roads and streets

625.7 II
HIGHWAY RESEARCH RECORD; general report on road research work done in India during (year). (Text in English) 1975. a. Indian Roads Congress, Highway Research Board, Jamnagar House, Shahjahan Rd., New Delhi 110011, India. Ed. P.C. Bhasin.

624 UK ISSN 0308-4159
I C E YEARBOOK. a. £12.50($34) (Institution of Civil Engineers) Thomas Telford, Ltd., 26-34 Old St., London, EC1V 9AD, England (U.S. subscr. to: International Scholarly Book Services, Box 555, Forest Grove, OR 97116) adv.

625.7 US ISSN 0095-6686
ILLINOIS. DEPARTMENT OF TRANSPORTATION. PHYSICAL RESEARCH REPORT. irreg. Department of Transportation, Springfield, IL 62706. Key Title: Physical Research Report.
Roads and streets

624 US
INGENIEURBAUTEN. 1971. irreg.; vol. 8, 1976. price varies. Springer-Verlag, 175 Fifth Ave., New York, NY 10010 (Also Berlin, Heidelberg, Vienna) Eds. K. Sattler, P. Stein. (reprint service avail. from ISI)

624 UK ISSN 0073-9847
INSTITUTION OF STRUCTURAL ENGINEERS. YEARBOOK. a. Institution of Structural Engineers, 11 Upper Belgrave St., London SW1X 8BH, England.

624 SZ ISSN 0074-1418
INTERNATIONAL ASSOCIATION FOR BRIDGE AND STRUCTURAL ENGINEERING. FINAL REPORT (OF CONGRESS) (Text in English, French or German; summaries in English, French and German) 1932. quadrennial, 11th, 1980, Vienna. International Association for Bridge and Structural Engineering, ETH-Hoenggerberg, CH-8093 Zurich, Switzerland.

624 SZ ISSN 0074-1434
INTERNATIONAL ASSOCIATION FOR BRIDGE AND STRUCTURAL ENGINEERING. PRELIMINARY REPORT (OF CONGRESS) (Text in English, French or German; summaries in English, French and German) 1932. quadrennial. International Association for Bridge and Structural Engineering, ETH-Hoenggerberg, CH-8093 Zurich, Switzerland.

624 SZ ISSN 0074-1442
INTERNATIONAL ASSOCIATION FOR BRIDGE AND STRUCTURAL ENGINEERING. REPORTS OF THE WORKING COMMISSIONS. (Text in English, French and German) 1964. irreg., no. 32, 1979. price varies. International Association for Bridge and Structural Engineering, ETH-Hoenggerberg, CH-8093 Zurich, Switzerland.

624 SP ISSN 0538-4400
INTERNATIONAL ASSOCIATION FOR SHELL AND SPATIAL STRUCTURES. BULLETIN. (Text in English or French) 1960. irreg. membership. International Association for Shell and Spatial Structures., Alfonson XII 3, Madrid 7, Spain.

627.8 US ISSN 0074-4115
INTERNATIONAL COMMISSION ON LARGE DAMS. TRANSACTIONS. triennial since 1961; 1979, 13th, India. United States Committee on Large Dams, c/o American Association of Engineering Societies, 345 E. 47 St., New York, NY 10017.

627.8 FR ISSN 0534-8293
INTERNATIONAL COMMISSION ON LARGE DAMS. BULLETIN. irreg. International Commission on Large Dams, 22 et 30 Ave. de Wagram, F-75008 Paris, France.

624 MX ISSN 0074-3313
INTERNATIONAL CONFERENCE ON SOIL MECHANICS AND FOUNDATION ENGINEERING. PROCEEDINGS. (Text in English and French) 1936. biennial; 7th, 1974. price varies. (International Conference on Soil Mechanics and Foundation Engineering) Sociedad Mexicana de Mecanica de Suelos, Londres 44, Coyoacan, Mexico 21, D.F., Mexico.
Proceedings available only from the Mexican Society for Soil Mechanics

INTERNATIONAL INSTITUTE OF SEISMOLOGY AND EARTHQUAKE ENGINEERING. BULLETIN. see *EARTH SCIENCES — Geophysics*

INTERNATIONAL INSTITUTE OF SEISMOLOGY AND EARTHQUAKE ENGINEERING. EARTHQUAKE REPORT. see *EARTH SCIENCES — Geophysics*

INTERNATIONAL INSTITUTE OF SEISMOLOGY AND EARTHQUAKE ENGINEERING. LECTURE NOTE. see *EARTH SCIENCES — Geophysics*

INTERNATIONAL INSTITUTE OF SEISMOLOGY AND EARTHQUAKE ENGINEERING. PROGRESS REPORT. see *EARTH SCIENCES — Geophysics*

INTERNATIONAL INSTITUTE OF SEISMOLOGY AND EARTHQUAKE ENGINEERING. REPORT OF INDIVIDUAL STUDY BY PARTICIPANTS OF I I S E E. see *EARTH SCIENCES — Geophysics*

INTERNATIONAL INSTITUTE OF SEISMOLOGY AND EARTHQUAKE ENGINEERING. YEAR BOOK. see *EARTH SCIENCES — Geophysics*

INTERNATIONAL ROAD CONGRESSES. PROCEEDINGS. see *TRANSPORTATION — Roads And Traffic*

624 UK
INTERNATIONAL SAFETY CONFERENCE. PROCEEDINGS. no. 3, 1975. irreg. Institution of Civil Engineers, Publications Division, 26-34 Old St., London EC1V 9AD, England.
Safety in the construction industry

ENGINEERING — CIVIL ENGINEERING

624   US   ISSN 0538-9887
INTERNATIONAL SERIES ON CIVIL ENGINEERING. 1966. irreg., 1972, vol. 5. price varies. Pergamon Press, Inc., Maxwell House, Fairview Park, Elmsford, NY 10523. index. Formerly: International Series of Monographs on Civil Engineering.

624.151   PO   ISSN 0074-848X
INTERNATIONAL SOCIETY FOR ROCK MECHANICS. CONGRESS. PROCEEDINGS. (Proceedings avail. from countries in Which Congresses Were held) (Text in English, French and German) 1966. irreg; 6th Lisbon, 1974. price varies. International Society for Rock Mechanics, Laboratorio Nacional de Engenharia Civil, Avenida do Brasil. Lisbon 5, Portugal.

625.732   US   ISSN 0074-8498
INTERNATIONAL SOCIETY FOR TERRAIN-VEHICLE SYSTEMS. PROCEEDINGS OF INTERNATIONAL CONFERENCE. 1961. irreg.; 5th, Detroit, Mich., 1975. $55. International Society for Terrain-Vehicle Systems, 711 Hudson St., Hoboken, NJ 07030. Ed. N. W. Radforth.
Roads and streets

624 380 5   UK
INTERNATIONAL SYMPOSIUM ON THE AERODYNAMICS AND VENTILATION OF VEHICLE TUNNELS. PROCEEDINGS. irreg., 3rd, 1979. price varies. British Hydromechanics Research Association, Cranfield, Bedford MK43 0AJ, England (Dist. in U.S. by: Air Science Co., Box 143, Corning, N.Y. 14830)

624   JA
JAPAN. PUBLIC WORKS RESEARCH INSTITUTE. JOURNAL OF RESEARCH/DOBOKU KENKYUSHO HOKOKU. (Text in English) 1954. irreg. available to public organizations on exchange basis. Public Works Research Institute - Kensetsusho Doboku Kenkyusho, Ministry of Construction, 2-28-32 Honkomagome, Bunkyo-ku, Tokyo 113, Japan.

624   JA   ISSN 0047-1798
JAPAN SOCIETY OF CIVIL ENGINEERS. TRANSACTIONS. (Text in English and Occidental languages) 1969. a. $10. Japan Society of Civil Engineers - Dobuku Gakkai, 1-chome, Yotsuya, Shinjuku-ku, Tokyo 160, Japan. Ed. Bd.

K B S-RAPPORTER. see *HOUSING AND URBAN PLANNING*

624   JA   ISSN 0075-7365
KYOTO UNIVERSITY. RESEARCH ACTIVITIES IN CIVIL ENGINEERING AND RELATED FIELDS. (Text in English) 1963. triennial. free. Kyoto University, Department of Civil Engineering, Sakyo-ku, Kyoto 606, Japan.

354   LB   ISSN 0304-7296
LIBERIA. MINISTRY OF LANDS AND MINES. ANNUAL REPORT. Ministry of Lands and Mines, Monrovia, Liberia.

624   BE   ISSN 0025-9195
MEMOIRES C.E.R.E.S. N.S. 1961. irreg. price varies. Université de Liege, Centre d'Etudes de Recherches, d'Essais Scientifiques de Genie Civil, 6 Quai Banning, 4000 Liege, Belgium. adv. bk. rev. abstr. bibl. stat. index. circ. 500-600. (also avail. in microform) Indexed: Appl. Mech. Rev.

557   US   ISSN 0076-9606
MISSOURI DIVISION OF GEOLOGICAL SURVEY AND WATER RESOURCES. ENGINEERING GEOLOGY SERIES. 1969. irreg., 1973, no. 5. price varies. Department of Natural Resources, Division of Geology and Land Survey, Box 250, Rolla, MO 65401.

526.9 625.72   SA
NATIONAL CONFERENCE OF SOUTH AFRICAN SURVEYORS. PROCEEDINGS/NASIONALE KONFERENSIE VAN SUID-AFRIKAANSE OPMETERS. VERRIGTINGE. irreg. R.10.50. National Conference of South African Surveyors, Institute of Land Surveyors of the Cape Province, Box 462, Cape Town, South Africa.
Surveying

NATIONAL COOPERATIVE HIGHWAY RESEARCH PROGRAM REPORTS. see *TRANSPORTATION — Roads And Traffic*

NATIONAL COOPERATIVE HIGHWAY RESEARCH PROGRAM SYNTHESIS OF HIGHWAY PRACTICE. see *TRANSPORTATION — Roads And Traffic*

625   SA   ISSN 0379-6124
NATIONAL INSTITUTE FOR TRANSPORT AND ROAD RESEARCH. ANNUAL REPORT/NASIONALE INSTITUUT VIR VERVOER- EN PADNAVORSING. JAARVERSLAG. (Text in English and Afrikaans) 1961. a. free. National Institute for Transport and Road Research, P.O. Box 395, Pretoria 0001, South Africa. Ed. B. M. Davies. bibl. charts. illus. circ. 1,500.
Formerly: National Institute for Road Research. Annual Report.

NATIONAL INSTITUTE FOR TRANSPORT AND ROAD RESEARCH. USER MANUALS FOR COMPUTER PROGRAMS/NASIONALE INSTITUUT VIR VERVOER- EN PADNAVORSING. GEBRUIKERSHANDBOEKE VIR REKENAARPROGRAMME. see *TRANSPORTATION — Roads And Traffic*

388   US
NEBRASKA. DEPARTMENT OF ROADS. CHALLENGE OF THE 80'S; one and six-year program. 1970. a. Department of Roads, So. Jct. N-2 & U.S. 77, Box 94759, Lincoln, NE 68509. Ed. Robert Munger. charts. illus. stat. circ. controlled. (processed)
Formerly: Focus on Nebraska Highways.

625.8   US   ISSN 0079-0273
PAVING CONFERENCE. PROCEEDINGS. 1962. a. $8. University of New Mexico, Department of Civil Engineering, Albuquerque, NM 87131. Ed. J. E. Martinez. circ. 200. (back issues avail.)
Roads and streets

624 690   PL
POLITECHNIKA GDANSKA. ZESZYTY NAUKOWE. BUDOWNICTWO LADOWE. (Text in Polish; summaries in English and Russian) 1956. irreg. price varies. Politechnika Gdanska, Majakowskiego 11/12, 81-952 Gdansk 6, Poland (Dist. by: Osrodek Rozpowszechniania Wydawnictw Naukowych Pan, Palac Kulturi Nauki, 00-901 Warsaw, Poland)

624   PL   ISSN 0076-0323
POLITECHNIKA LODZKA. ZESZYTY NAUKOWE. BUDOWNICTWO. (Text in Polish; summaries in English and Russian) 1967. irreg. price varies. Politechnika Lodzka, Ul. Zwirki 36, 90-924 Lodz, Poland (Dist by Ars Polona-Ruch, Krakowskie Przedmiescie 7, Warsaw, Poland) Ed. Stefan Przewlocki. circ. 383. (also avail. in microfilm)

624   PL
POLITECHNIKA POZNANSKA. ZESZYTY NAUKOWE. BUDOWNICTWO. (Text in Polish; summaries in English and Russian) 1956. irreg. price varies. Politechnika Poznanska, Pl. Curie Sklodowskiej 5, Poznan, Poland. Ed. Romuald Switka. circ. 150.
Formerly: Politechnika Poznanska. Zeszyty Naukowe. Budownictwo Ladowe (ISSN 0079-449X)

624   PL   ISSN 0434-0779
POLITECHNIKA SLASKA. ZESZYTY NAUKOWE. BUDOWNICTWO. (Text in Polish; summaries in English and Russian) 1956. irreg. price varies. Politechnika Slaska, W. Pstrowskiego 7, 44-100 Gliwice, Poland (Dist. by: Ars Polona, Krakowskie Przedmiescie 7, 00-068 Warsaw, Poland) Ed. Zdzislaw Trojan. circ. 265.

624   PL   ISSN 0324-9743
POLITECHNIKA WROCLAWSKA. INSTYTUT INZYNIERII LADOWEJ. PRACE NAUKOWE. KONFERENCJE. (Text in Polish; summaries in English) 1973. irreg., no. 8, 1978. price varies. Politechnika Wroclawska, Wybrzeze Wyspianskiego 27, 50-370 Wroclaw, Poland (Dist. by: Ars Polona-Ruch, Krakowskie Przedmiescie 7, Warsaw, Poland) Ed. Marian Kloza. illus.

624   PL   ISSN 0324-9727
POLITECHNIKA WROCLAWSKA. INSTYTUT INZYNIERII LADOWEJ. PRACE NAUKOWE. MONOGRAFIE. (Text in Polish; summaries in English and Russian) 1972. irreg., no. 7, 1978. price varies. Politechnika Wroclawska, Wybrzeze Wyspianskiego 27, 50-370 Wroclaw, Poland (Dist. by: Ars Polona-Ruch, Krakowskie Przedmiescie 7, Warsaw, Poland) Ed. Marian Kloza.

624   PL   ISSN 0370-0844
POLITECHNIKA WROCLAWSKA. INSTYTUT INZYNIERII LADOWEJ. PRACE NAUKOWE. STUDIA I MATERIALY. (Text in Polish; summaries in English and Russian) 1970. irreg., 1973, no. 10. price varies. Politechnika Wroclawska, Wybrzeze Wyspianskiego 27, 50-370 Wroclaw, Poland (Dist. by: Ars Polona-Ruch, Krakowskie Przedmiescie 7, Warsaw, Poland) Ed. Marian Kloza.

PORT AND HARBOUR TECHNICAL RESEARCH INSTITUTE. GUIDE/KOWAN GIJUTSU KENKYUSHO. GUIDE. see *TRANSPORTATION — Ships And Shipping*

625.735   US   ISSN 0091-0813
POTENTIALLY REACTIVE CARBONATE ROCKS; PROGRESS REPORT. 1962. irreg. U.S. Federal Highway Administration, 400 Seventh St., S. W., Washington, DC 20590. (also avail. in microfiche from NTI) Key Title: Potentially Reactive Carbonate Rocks.

624   US   ISSN 0079-8096
PURDUE UNIVERSITY. CIVIL ENGINEERING REPRINTS. 1940. irreg., no. 306, 1978. single copies free. Purdue University, School of Civil Engineering, West Lafayette, IN 47907.

625.7   US   ISSN 0079-810X
PURDUE UNIVERSITY. ENGINEERING EXPERIMENT STATION. JOINT HIGHWAY RESEARCH PROJECT. RESEARCH REPORTS. (Issues not numbered consecutively) 1937. irreg., no. 24, 1978. $5. Purdue University, School of Civil Engineering, Joint Highway Research Project, West Lafayette, IN 47907. (Co-Sponsor: Indiana State Highway Commission) circ. 100.
Roads and streets

624   AT   ISSN 0311-9491
QUEENSLAND. DEPARTMENT OF LOCAL GOVERNMENT. CONFERENCE OF LOCAL AUTHORITY ENGINEERS. PROCEEDINGS. a. Department of Local Government, Brisbane, Qld., Australia. illus.

624   SP
RELACION DE INGENIEROS DE CAMINOS, CANALES Y PUERTOS. (Vols. for 1970- issued in pts.) irreg. 3000 ptas. Colegio de Ingenieros de Caminos, Canales y Puertos, Almagro, 42, Madrid 4, Spain. illus.

624.151   US   ISSN 0080-2018
REVIEWS IN ENGINEERING GEOLOGY. 1961. irreg., vol. 3, 1977. price varies. Geological Society of America, 3300 Penrose Place, Boulder, CO 80301. index.

624   SP
REVISTA A T E M C O P. ESPECIAL ALQUILADORES. 1976. a. $10. Asociacion Espanola de Tecnicos de Maquinaria para la Construccion y Obra Publicas, Cruz del Sur 3, Madrid 30, Spain. Ed. Ignacio Vega Alonso. illus.

625.7   US   ISSN 0080-3278
ROAD BUILDER'S CLINIC. PROCEEDINGS. 1950. a. $7.50. ‡ Washington State University, Engineering Extension Service, College of Engineering, Pullman, WA 99164. (Co-sponsor: University of Idaho, College of Engineering)
Roads and streets

ROAD NOTES. see *TRANSPORTATION — Roads And Traffic*

SAO PAULO, BRAZIL (STATE). DEPARTAMENTO DE EDIFICIOS E OBRAS PUBLICAS. RELATORIO DE ATIVIDADES. see *PUBLIC ADMINISTRATION*

SCOTTISH BUILDING & CIVIL ENGINEERING YEAR BOOK. see *BUILDING AND CONSTRUCTION*

SERIES ON ROCK AND SOIL MECHANICS. see
EARTH SCIENCES

624 FR ISSN 0081-0886
SOCIETE DES INGENIEURS CIVILS DE
FRANCE. ANNUAIRE. 1883. irreg. price varies.
Societe des Ingenieurs Civils de France, 19 rue
Blanche, 75009 Paris, France.

711.7 624 US
STANDARD SPECIFICATIONS FOR HIGHWAY
BRIDGES. a. price varies. American Association of
State Highway and Transportation Officials, 444 N.
Capitol St. N.W., Suite 225, Washington, DC
20001.

620 PL
STUDIA Z ZAKRESU INZYNIERII. 1958. irreg.
price varies. (Polska Akademia Nauk, Komitet
Inzynierii Ladowej i Wodnej) Panstwowe
Wydawnictwo Naukowe, Miodowa 10, Warsaw,
Poland (Dist. by Ars Polona-Ruch, Krakowskie
Przedmiescie 7, Warsaw, Poland)
Formerly: Studia z Zakresu Budownictwa (ISSN
0081-7139)

SWEDEN. STATENS RAAD FOER
BYGGNADSFORSKNING. DOCUMENT. see
BUILDING AND CONSTRUCTION

SWEDEN. STATENS RAAD FOER
BYGGNADSFORSKNING.
INFORMATIONSBLAD. see *BUILDING AND
CONSTRUCTION*

SWEDEN. STATENS RAAD FOER
BYGGNADSFORSKNING. RAPPORT. see
BUILDING AND CONSTRUCTION

SWEDEN. STATENS RAAD FOER
BYGGNADSFORSKNING.
VERKSAMHETSPLAN. see *BUILDING AND
CONSTRUCTION*

THOM'S DUBLIN & COUNTY STREET
DIRECTORY. see *GEOGRAPHY*

TRANSPORT AND ROAD RESEARCH. see
TRANSPORTATION — Roads And Traffic

TRANSPORTATION RESEARCH BOARD
SPECIAL REPORT. see *TRANSPORTATION —
Roads And Traffic*

TRANSPORTATION RESEARCH RECORD. see
TRANSPORTATION — Roads And Traffic

625.7 US ISSN 0073-2184
U.S. FEDERAL HIGHWAY ADMINISTRATION.
HIGHWAY PLANNING TECHNICAL
REPORTS. 1963. irreg. free. ‡ U.S. Federal
Highway Administration, Dept. of Transportation,
800 Independence Ave. S.W., Washington, DC
20590 (Subscr. to Supt. of Documents, Government
Printing Office, Washington, DC 20402)
Roads and streets

625.7 US ISSN 0092-3389
U.S. FEDERAL HIGHWAY ADMINISTRATION.
HIGHWAY TRANSPORTATION RESEARCH
AND DEVELOPMENT STUDIES. irreg. $4.20. U.
S. Federal Highway Administration, 400 Seventh St.
S. W., Washington, DC 20590 (Orders to: Supt. of
Documents, Washington, DC 20402) Key Title:
Highway Transportation Research and Development
Studies.
Roads and streets

625.7 US ISSN 0098-0234
U.S. FEDERAL HIGHWAY ADMINISTRATION
RESEARCH AND DEVELOPMENT PROGRAM.
a. U.S. Federal Highway Administration, Dept. of
Transportation, Washington, DC 20591. illus. Key
Title: Research and Developement Program.
Roads and streets

624 US
U.S. WATER AND POWER RESOURCES
SERVICE. ENGINEERING AND RESEARCH
CENTER. TECHNICAL RECORDS OF DESIGN
AND CONSTRUCTION. irreg. price varies. U.S.
Water and Power Resources Service, Engineering
and Research Center, Box 25007, Denver Federal
Center, Denver, CO 80225. (back issues avail.)
Formerly: U.S. Bureau of Reclamation.
Engineering and Research Center. Technical
Records of Design and Construction.

624.176 CN ISSN 0068-1709
UNIVERSITY OF BRITISH COLUMBIA.
DEPARTMENT OF CIVIL ENGINEERING.
REPORT. SOIL MECHANICS SERIES. 1966.
irreg. free to universities & government research
labs. ‡ University of British Columbia, Department
of Civil Engineering, Vancouver 8, B.C., Canada.

624 CN
UNIVERSITY OF BRITISH COLUMBIA.
DEPARTMENT OF CIVIL ENGINEERING.
STRUCTURAL RESEARCH SERIES. 1970. irreg.
free to university and government research labs.
University of British Columbia, Department of Civil
Engineering, Vancouver 8, B.C., Canada.

624 CN
UNIVERSITY OF BRITISH COLUMBIA.
DEPARTMENT OF CIVIL ENGINEERING.
TRANSPORTATION RESEARCH SERIES. 1972.
irreg. free to qualified personnel. University of
British Columbia, Department of Civil Engineering,
Vancouver 8, B.C., Canada.

624 CN
UNIVERSITY OF CALGARY. DEPARTMENT OF
CIVIL ENGINEERING RESEARCH REPORT.
1971. irreg (25/yr) free. University of Calgary,
Department of Civil Engineering, Calgary T2N
1N4, Alta, Canada.

624 US
UNIVERSITY OF ILLINOIS AT URBANA-
CHAMPAIGN. CIVIL ENGINEERING
STUDIES. HYDRAULIC ENGINEERING
RESEARCH SERIES. 1951. irreg., no. 33, 1978.
price varies. University of Illinois at Urbana-
Champaign, Department of Civil Engineering,
Engineering Documents Center, B106 C. E. Bldg.,
Urbana, IL 61801. (also avail. in microform from
NTI)

624 US
UNIVERSITY OF ILLINOIS AT URBANA-
CHAMPAIGN. CIVIL ENGINEERING
STUDIES. PHOTOGRAMMETRY SERIES. 1963.
irreg., no. 43, 1976. price varies. University of
Illinois at Urbana-Champaign, Department of Civil
Engineering, Engineering Documents Center, B106
C. E. Bldg., Urbana, IL 61801. (also avail. in
microform from NTI)

624.1 US ISSN 0069-4274
UNIVERSITY OF ILLINOIS AT URBANA-
CHAMPAIGN. CIVIL ENGINEERING
STUDIES. STRUCTURAL RESEARCH SERIES.
1950. irreg., no. 452, 1978. University of Illinois at
Urbana-Champaign, Department of Civil
Engineering, Engineering Documents Center, B106
C. E. Bldg., Urbana, IL 61801. (also avail. in
microform from NTI)

624 US
UNIVERSITY OF ILLINOIS AT URBANA-
CHAMPAIGN. CIVIL ENGINEERING
STUDIES. TRANSPORTATION ENGINEERING
SERIES. 1972. irreg., no. 23, 1978. price varies.
University of Illinois at Urbana-Champaign,
Department of Civil Engineering, Engineering
Documents Center, B106 C. E. Bldg., Urbana, IL
61801. (also avail. in microform from NTI)

624 AT ISSN 0085-3240
UNIVERSITY OF MELBOURNE. DEPARTMENT
OF CIVIL ENGINEERING. DEPARTMENTAL
REPORT. 1962. irreg. price varies. ‡ University of
Melbourne, Department of Civil Engineering,
Parkville, Vic. 3052, Australia.

624 AT ISSN 0077-8796
UNIVERSITY OF NEW SOUTH WALES. SCHOOL
OF CIVIL ENGINEERING. U N I C I V
REPORTS. SERIES I. 1963. irreg. Aus.$5
combined subscription for series I. & R. University
of New South Wales, Box 1, P.O., Kensington,
N.S.W. 2033, Australia. circ. 220.

624 AT ISSN 0077-880X
UNIVERSITY OF NEW SOUTH WALES. SCHOOL
OF CIVIL ENGINEERING. U N I C I V
REPORTS. SERIES R. 1963. irreg. Aus.$25
combined subscription for Series I. & R.; free to
qualified libraries. University of New South Wales,
School of Civil Engineering, P.O. Box 1,
Kensington, N.S.W. 2033, Australia. circ. 220.

624 GE
VERMESSUNGS-INFORMATIONEN/
SURVEYING NEWS/INFORMATIONS
TOPOGRAFIQUES. (Editions in German, English,
French) 1955. irreg. free. Jenoptik Jena GmbH,
Carl-Zeiss-Str. 1, 69 Jena, E. Germany (D.D.R.) Ed.
H. Strosche. abstr. illus. (also avail. in microfiche)

VIRGINIA HIGHWAY AND TRANSPORTATION
CONFERENCE. PROCEEDINGS. see
TRANSPORTATION — Roads And Traffic

ENGINEERING — Engineering Mechanics And Materials

620.1 US ISSN 0066-0515
A S T M PROCEEDINGS. 1898. a. $19. American
Society for Testing and Materials, 1916 Race St.,
Philadelphia, PA 19103. Ed. R. Lukens. circ. 2,000.
(also avail. in microform from UMI) Indexed:
Appl.Mech.Rev.

ADVANCES IN APPLIED MECHANICS. see
PHYSICS — Mechanics

620.112 US ISSN 0065-2474
ADVANCES IN CORROSION SCIENCE AND
TECHNOLOGY. 1970. irreg. price varies. Plenum
Press, 233 Spring St., New York, NY 10013. Eds.
M. G. Fontana, R. W. Staehle.

ADVANCES IN X-RAY ANALYSIS. see
METALLURGY

620.1 690 US ISSN 0066-0523
AMERICAN SOCIETY FOR TESTING AND
MATERIALS. COMPILATION OF A S T M
STANDARDS IN BUILDING CODES. 1952.
irreg., 16th edt. 1978. $100. American Society for
Testing and Materials, 1916 Race St., Philadelphia,
PA 19103. Ed. R. Lukens. circ. 2,000.

620.1 US ISSN 0066-0531
AMERICAN SOCIETY FOR TESTING AND
MATERIALS. DATA SERIES PUBLICATIONS.
1964. irreg., no. 58, 1975. American Society for
Testing and Materials, 1916 Race St., Philadelphia,
PA 19103.

620.1 US ISSN 0066-054X
AMERICAN SOCIETY FOR TESTING AND
MATERIALS. FIVE-YEAR INDEX TO A S T M
TECHNICAL PAPERS AND REPORTS.
(Supplements the A.S.T.M. 50-Year Index) 1950.
quinquennial. American Society for Testing and
Materials, 1916 Race St., Philadelphia, PA 19103.
circ. 2,000.

620.1 US ISSN 0066-0558
AMERICAN SOCIETY FOR TESTING AND
MATERIALS. SPECIAL TECHNICAL
PUBLICATIONS. 1911. irreg., no. 686, 1979.
American Society for Testing and Materials, 1916
Race St., Philadelphia, PA 19103.

620.1 US ISSN 0066-0183
ANNUAL BOOK OF A S T M STANDARDS.
PART 1. STEEL PIPING, TUBING, AND
FITTINGS. 1898. a. $34. American Society for
Testing and Materials, 1916 Race St., Philadelphia,
PA 19103. Ed. R. Lukens.

620.1 669 US ISSN 0066-0191
ANNUAL BOOK OF A S T M STANDARDS.
PART 2. FERROUS CASTINGS, FERRO-
ALLOYS. a. $24. American Society for Testing and
Materials, 1916 Race St., Philadelphia, PA 19103.

620.1 US
ANNUAL BOOK OF A S T M STANDARDS.
PART 3. STEEL PLATE, SHEET, STRIP AND
WIRE, METALLIC COATED PRODUCTS. a.
$34. American Society for Testing and Materials,
1916 Race St., Philadelphia, PA 19103.
Formerly: Annual Book of A S T M Standards.
Part 3. Steel Strip, Bar, Rod, Wire, Chain, and
Spring: Wrought Iron; Metallic Coated Products;
Ferrous Surgical Implants (ISSN 0066-0205)

620.1 US
ANNUAL BOOK OF A S T M STANDARDS.
PART 4. STRUCTURAL STEEL; CONCRETE REINFORCING STEEL; PRESSURE VESSEL PLATE AND FORGINGS; STEEL RAILS, WHEELS, AND TIRES; STEEL FASTENERS. a. $33. American Society for Testing and Materials, 1916 Race St., Philadelphia, PA 19103.
Formerly: Annual Book of A S T M Standards. Part 4. Structural Steel; Concrete Reinforcing Steel; Pressure Vessel Plate; Steel Rails; Wheels, and Tires; Bearing Steel; Steel Forgings. (ISSN 0066-0213)

620.1 US
ANNUAL BOOK OF A S T M STANDARDS.
PART 5. STEEL BARS, CHAIN, AND SPRINGS; BEARING STEEL; STEEL FORGINGS. a. $33. American Society for Testing and Materials, 1916 Race St., Philadelphia, PA 19103.

620.1 US ISSN 0066-0221
ANNUAL BOOK OF A S T M STANDARDS.
PART 6. COPPER AND COPPER ALLOYS (INCLUDING ELECTRICAL CONDUCTORS) a. $38. American Society for Testing and Materials, 1916 Race St., Philadelphia, PA 19103.

620.1 US ISSN 0066-023X
ANNUAL BOOK OF A S T M STANDARDS.
PART 7. DIE-CAST METALS; LIGHT METALS AND ALLOYS (INCLUDING ELECTRICAL CONDUCTORS) a. $38. American Society for Testing and Materials, 1916 Race St., Philadelphia, PA 19103.

620.1 US
ANNUAL BOOK OF A S T M STANDARDS.
PART 8. NONFERROUS METALS--NICKEL, LEAD, AND TIN ALLOYS, PRECIOUS METALS, PRIMARY METALS; REACTIVE METALS. a. $32. American Society for Testing and Materials, 1916 Race St., Philadelphia, PA 19103.
Formerly: Annual Book of A S T M Standrads. Part 7. Nonferrous Metals and Alloys (Including Corrosion Tests); Electrodeposited Metallic Coatings; Metal Powders; Surgical Implants. (ISSN 0066-0248)

620.1 US
ANNUAL BOOK OF A S T M STANDARDS.
PART 9. ELECTRODEPOSITED METALLIC COATINGS; METAL POWDERS, SINTERED P/M STRUCTURAL PARTS. a. $22. American Society for Testing and Materials, 1916 Race St., Philadelphia, PA 19103.

620.1 669 US
ANNUAL BOOK OF A S T M STANDARDS.
PART 10. METALS - MECHANICAL, FRACTURE, AND CORROSION TESTING; FATIGUE; EROSION; EFFECT OF TEMPERATURE. a. $34. American Society for Testing and Materials, 1916 Race St., Philadelphia, PA 19103.
Formerly: Annual Book of A S T M Standards. Part 31. Metals - Physical, Mechanical, Nondestructive, and Corrosion Tests, Metallography, Fatigue, Effect of Temperature. (ISSN 0066-0477)

620.1 US
ANNUAL BOOK OF A S T M STANDARDS.
PART 11. METALLOGRAPHY; NONDESTRUCTIVE TESTING. a. $28. American Society for Testing and Materials, 1916 Race St., Philadelphia, PA 19103.

620.1 542 US ISSN 0066-0485
ANNUAL BOOK OF A S T M STANDARDS.
PART 12. CHEMICAL ANALYSIS OF METALS; SAMPLING AND ANALYSIS OF METAL BEARING ORES. a. $32. American Society for Testing and Materials, 1916 Race St., Philadelphia, PA 19103.

620.1 690 US
ANNUAL BOOK OF A S T M STANDARDS.
PART 13. CEMENT; LIME; CEILINGS AND WALLS (INCLUDING MANUAL OF CEMENT TESTING) a. $23. American Society for Testing and Materials, 1916 Race St., Philadelphia, PA 19103.
Formerly: Annual Book of A S T M Standards. Part 9. Cement; Lime; Gypsum (ISSN 0066-0256)

620.1 690 US ISSN 0066-0264
ANNUAL BOOK OF A S T M STANDARDS.
PART 14. CONCRETE AND MINERAL AGGREGATES (INCLUDING MANUAL OF CONCRETE TESTING) a. $27. American Society for Testing and Materials, 1916 Race St., Philadelphia, PA 19103.

620.1 US
ANNUAL BOOK OF A S T M STANDARDS.
PART 15. ROAD AND PAVING MATERIALS; BITUMINOUS MATERIALS FOR HIGHWAY CONSTRUCTION, WATERPROOFING AND ROOFING, AND PIPE; SKID RESISTANCE. a. $38. American Society for Testing and Materials, 1916 Race St., Philadelphia, PA 19103.
Formerly: Annual Book of A S T M Standards. Part 11. Bituminous Materials for Highway Construction, Waterproofing and Roofing: Soil and Rock; Skid Resistance (ISSN 0066-0272)

620.1 691 US
ANNUAL BOOK OF A S T M STANDARDS.
PART 16. CHEMICAL-RESISTANT NONMETALLIC MATERIALS. VITRIFIED CLAY AND CONCRETE PIPE AND TILE; MASONRY MORTARS AND UNITS; ASBESTOS-CEMENT PRODUCTS. a. $21. American Society for Testing and Materials, 1916 Race St., Philadelphia, PA 19103.
Formerly: Annual Book of A S T M Standards. Part 12. Chemical-Resistant Nonmetallic Materials; Clay and Concrete Pipe and Tile; Masonry Mortars and Units; Asbestos-Cement Products; Natural Building Stones (ISSN 0066-0280)

620.1 US ISSN 0066-0299
ANNUAL BOOK OF A S T M STANDARDS.
PART 17. REFRACTORIES, GLASS AND OTHER CERAMIC MATERIALS; MANUFACTURED CARBON AND GRAPHITE PRODUCTS. a. $34. American Society for Testing and Materials, 1916 Race St., Philadelphia, PA 19103.

620.1 US ISSN 0066-0302
ANNUAL BOOK OF A S T M STANDARDS.
PART 18. THERMAL AND CRYOGENIC INSULATING MATERIALS; BUILDING SEALS AND SEALANTS; FIRE TESTS; BUILDING CONSTRUCTIONS; ENVIRONMENTAL ACOUSTICS. a. $41. American Society for Testing and Materials, 1916 Race St., Philadelphia, PA 19103.

620.1 US
ANNUAL BOOK OF A S T M STANDARDS.
PART 19. NATURAL BUILDING STONES; SOIL AND ROCK; PEATS, MOSSES, AND HUMUS. a. $21. American Society for Testing and Materials, 1916 Race St., Philadelphia, PA 19103.

620.1 US
ANNUAL BOOK OF A S T M STANDARDS.
PART 20. PAPER; PACKAGING; BUSINESS COPY PRODUCTS. a. $29. American Society for Testing and Materials, 1916 Race St., Philadelphia, PA 19103.
Formerly: Annual Book of A S T M Standards. Part 15. Paper; Packaging; Cellulose; Casein; Flexible Barrier Materials; Carbon Paper; Leather (ISSN 0066-0310)

620.1 US
ANNUAL BOOK OF A S T M STANDARDS.
PART 21. CELLULOSE; LEATHER; FLEXIBLE BARRIER MATERIALS. a. $19. American Society for Testing and Materials, 1916 Race St., Philadelphia, PA 19103.

620.1 US ISSN 0066-0329
ANNUAL BOOK OF A S T M STANDARDS.
PART 22. WOOD; ADHESIVES. a. $37. American Society for Testing and Materials, 1916 Race St., Philadelphia, PA 19103.
Formerly: Annual Book of A S T M Standards. Part 16. Structural Sandwich Constructions; Wood; Adhesives.

620.1 665.5 US
ANNUAL BOOK OF A S T M STANDARDS.
PART 23. PETROLEUM PRODUCTS AND LUBRICANTS (1) a. $37. American Society for Testing and Materials, 1916 Race St., Philadelphia, PA 19103.
Formerly: Annual Book of A S T M Standards. Part 17. Petroleum Products - Fuels; Solvents; Burner Fuel Oils; Lubricating Greases; Hydraulic Fluids (ISSN 0066-0337)

620.1 665.5 US
ANNUAL BOOK OF A S T M STANDARDS.
PART 24. PETROLEUM PRODUCTS AND LUBRICANTS (2) a. $37. American Society for Testing and Materials, 1916 Race St., Philadelphia, PA 19103.
Formerly: Annual Book of A S T M Standards. Part 18. Petroleum Products - Measurement and Sampling; Liquefied Petroleum Gases; Light Hydrocarbons; Plant Spray Oils; Aerospace Materials; Sulfonates; Crude Petroleum; Petroleum; Wax; Graphite (ISSN 0066-0345)

620.1 665.5 629.3 US
ANNUAL BOOK OF A S T M STANDARDS.
PART 25. PETROLEUM PRODUCTS AND LUBRICANTS (3); AEROSPACE MATERIALS. a. $38. American Society for Testing and Materials, 1916 Race St., Philadelphia, PA 19103.

620.1 US
ANNUAL BOOK OF A S T M STANDARDS.
PART 26. GASEOUS FUELS; COAL AND COKE; ATMOSPHERIC ANALYSIS. a. $34. American Society for Testing and Materials, 1916 Race St., Philadelphia, PA 19103.
Formerly: Annual Book of A S T M Standards. Part 26. Gaseous Fuels; Coal and Coke (ISSN 0066-0353)

620.1 667.4 US ISSN 0066-037X
ANNUAL BOOK OF A S T M STANDARDS.
PART 27. PAINT - TESTS FOR FORMULATED PRODUCTS AND APPLIED COATINGS. a. $33. American Society for Testing and Materials, 1916 Race St., Philadelphia, PA 19103.

620.1 667.4 US
ANNUAL BOOK OF A S T M STANDARDS.
PART 28. PAINT - PIGMENTS, RESINS AND POLYMERS. a. $22. American Society for Testing and Materials, 1916 Race St., Philadelphia, PA 19103.

620.1 US
ANNUAL BOOK OF A S T M STANDARDS.
PART 29. PAINT - FATTY OILS AND ACIDS, SOLVENTS, MISCELLANEOUS; AROMATIC HYDROCARBONS; NAVAL STORES. a. $32. American Society for Testing and Materials, 1916 Race St., Philadelphia, PA 19103.
Formerly: Annual Book of A S T M Standards. Part 20. Paint, Varnish, Lacquer, and Related Products - Materials Specifications and Tests; Naval Stores; Industrial Aromatic Hydrocarbons and Related Chemicals (ISSN 0066-0361)

620.1 US ISSN 0066-0388
ANNUAL BOOK OF A S T M STANDARDS.
PART 30. SOAP; ENGINE COOLANTS; POLISHES; HALOGENATED ORGANIC SOLVENTS; ACTIVATED CARBON; INDUSTRIAL CHEMICALS. a. $38. American Society for Testing and Materials, 1916 Race St., Philadelphia, PA 19103.

620.1 US
ANNUAL BOOK OF A S T M STANDARDS.
PART 31. WATER. a. $38. American Society for Testing and Materials, 1916 Race St., Philadelphia, PA 19103.
Formerly: Annual Book of A S T M Standards. Part 23. Water; Atomspheric Analysis (ISSN 0066-0396)

620.1 677 US ISSN 0066-040X
ANNUAL BOOK OF A S T M STANDARDS.
PART 32. TEXTILES--YARN, FABRICS, AND GENERAL TEST METHODS. a. $29. American Society for Testing and Materials, 1916 Race St., Philadelphia, PA 19103.

620.1 677 US ISSN 0066-0418
ANNUAL BOOK OF A S T M STANDARDS.
PART 33. TEXTILES--FIBERS, ZIPPERS; HIGH MODULUS FIBERS. a. $28. American Society for Testing and Materials, 1916 Race St., Philadelphia, PA 19103.

ENGINEERING — ENGINEERING MECHANICS AND MATERIALS

620.1 668.4 690 US
ANNUAL BOOK OF A S T M STANDARDS. PART 34. PLASTIC PIPE. a. $28. American Society for Testing and Materials, 1916 Race St., Philadelphia, PA 19103.

620.1 668.4 US ISSN 0066-0434
ANNUAL BOOK OF A S T M STANDARDS. PART 35. PLASTICS - GENERAL TEST METHODS; NOMENCLATURE. a. $36. American Society for Testing and Materials, 1916 Race St., Philadelphia, PA 19103.

620.1 668.4 US
ANNUAL BOOK OF A S T M STANDARDS. PART 36. PLASTICS--MATERIALS, FILM, REINFORCED AND CELLULAR PLASTICS; HIGH MODULUS FIBERS AND THEIR COMPOSITES. a. $36. American Society for Testing and Materials, 1916 Race St., Philadelphia, PA 19103.
Formerly: Annual Book of A S T M Standards. Part 26. Plastics - Specifications; Methods of Testing Pipe, Film, Reinforced and Cellular Plastics (ISSN 0066-0426)

620.1 678.2 US
ANNUAL BOOK OF A S T M STANDARDS. PART 37. RUBBER, NATURAL AND SYNTHETIC--GENERAL TEST METHODS; CARBON BLACK. $31. American Society for Testing and Materials, 1916 Race St., Philadelphia, PA 19103.

620.1 678.2 US
ANNUAL BOOK OF A S T M STANDARDS. PART 38. RUBBER PRODUCTS, INDUSTRIAL-- SPECIFICATIONS AND RELATED TEST METHODS; GASKETS; TIRES. a. $29. American Society for Testing and Materials, 1916 Race St., Philadelphia, PA 19103.
Formerly: Annual Book of A S T M Standards. Part 28. Rubber; Carbon Black; Gaskets (ISSN 0066-0442)

620.1 US
ANNUAL BOOK OF A S T M STANDARDS. PART 39. ELECTRICAL INSULATION--TEST METHODS: SOLIDS AND SOLIDIFYING FLUIDS. a. $33. American Society for Testing and Materials, 1916 Race St., Philadelphia, PA 19103.
Formerly: Annual Book of A S T M Standards. Part 39. Electrical Insulating Materials--Test Methods (ISSN 0066-0450)

620.1 US
ANNUAL BOOK OF A S T M STANDARDS. PART 40. ELECTRICAL INSULATION-- SPECIFICATIONS: SOLIDS, LIQUIDS, AND GASES; TEST METHODS: LIQUIDS AND GASES. $38. American Society for Testing and Materials, 1916 Race St., Philadelphia, PA 19103.

620.1 US
ANNUAL BOOK OF A S T M STANDARDS. PART 41. GENERAL TEST METHODS, NONMETAL; STATISTICAL METHODS; SPACE SIMULATION; PARTICLE SIZE MEASUREMENT; GENERAL LABORATORY APPARATUS; DURABILITY OF NONMETALLIC MATERIALS; METRIC PRACTICE. a. $38. American Society for Testing and Materials, 1916 Race St., Philadelphia, PA 19103.
Formerly: Annual Book of A S T M Standards. Part 41. General Test Methods (Nonmetal); Statistical Methods; Space Simulation; Particle Size Measurement; Deterioration of Nonmetallic Materials (ISSN 0066-0469)

620.1 542 US
ANNUAL BOOK OF A S T M STANDARDS. PART 42. EMISSION, MOLECULAR, AND MASS SPECTROSCOPY; CHROMATOGRAPHY; RESINOGRAPHY; MICROSCOPY. $21. American Society for Testing and Materials, 1916 Race St., Philadelphia, PA 19103.

620.1 621.38 US
ANNUAL BOOK OF A S T M STANDARDS. PART 43. ELECTRONICS. $36. American Society for Testing and Materials, 1916 Race St., Philadelphia, PA 19103.

620.1 US
ANNUAL BOOK OF A S T M STANDARDS. PART 44. MAGNETIC PROPERTIES AND MAGNETIC MATERIALS; METALLIC MATERIALS FOR THERMOSTATS AND FOR ELECTRICAL RESISTANCE, HEATING, AND CONTACTS; TEMPERATURE MEASUREMENT; ILLUMINATING STANDARDS. a. $43. American Society for Testing and Materials, 1916 Race St., Philadelphia, PA 19103.
Formerly: Annual Book of A S T M Standards. Part 8. Magnetic Properties; Metallic Materials for Thermostats and Contacts Materials for Electron Devices and Microelectronics (ISSN 0066-0507)

620.1 621.48 US
ANNUAL BOOK OF A S T M STANDARDS. PART 45. NUCLEAR STANDARDS. $48. American Society for Testing and Materials, 1916 Race St., PA 19103.

620.1 US
ANNUAL BOOK OF A S T M STANDARDS. PART 46. END USE AND CONSUMER PRODUCTS. $51. American Society for Testing and Materials, 1916 Race St., Philadelphia, PA 19103.

620.1 US
ANNUAL BOOK OF A S T M STANDARDS. PART 47. TEST METHODS FOR RATING MOTOR, DIESEL, AND AVIATION FUELS. $24. American Society for Testing and Materials, 1916 Race St., Philadelphia, PA 19103.

620.1 US ISSN 0066-0493
ANNUAL BOOK OF A S T M STANDARDS. PART 48. INDEX. a. $6. American Society for Testing and Materials, 1916 Race St., Philadelphia, PA 19103.

620.1 US ISSN 0066-538X
APPALACHIAN UNDERGROUND CORROSION SHORT COURSE, WEST VIRGINIA UNIVERSITY. PROCEEDINGS. (Issued as subseries in its Bulletin series) 1956. irreg. a. $6. West Virginia University, Engineering Experiment Station, College of Engineering, Morgantown, WV 26506. Ed. Donald M. Bondurant. circ. 1,200.

620.1 BE ISSN 0066-8818
ASSOCIATION BELGE POUR L'ETUDE, L'ESSAI ET L'EMPLOI DES MATERIAUX. PROCES VERBAL DE L'ASSEMBLEE GENERALE ORDINAIRE. (Subseries of its publication A.B.E.M.) (Text in French, Dutch) 1931. a. price varies. Association Belge pour l'Etude, l'Essai et l'Emploi des Materiaux, 53 rue d'Arlon, 1040 Brussels, Belgium.

620.1 BE ISSN 0066-8796
ASSOCIATION BELGE POUR L'ETUDE, L'ESSAI ET L'EMPLOI DES MATERIAUX. PUBLICATION A.B.E.M. (Text in Dutch, English, French; summaries in French and Dutch) 1927. irreg. price varies. Association Belge pour l'Etude, l'Essai et l'Emploi des Materiaux, 53 rue d'Arlon, 1040 Brussels, Belgium.

620.1 FR ISSN 0066-9792
ASSOCIATION SCIENTIFIQUE DE LA PRECONTRAINTE. SESSIONS D'ETUDES. 1956. irreg. Association Scientifique de la Precontrainte, 1, Place Genevieres, 59000 Lille, France.

620.106 US
BATTELLE INSTITUTE MATERIALS SCIENCE COLLOQUIA. 1972. irreg. price varies. Plenum Press, 233 Spring St., New York, NY 10013.

620.1 PL ISSN 0067-7701
BIBLIOTEKA MECHANIKI STOSOWANEJ. (Text in Polish and English) 1956. irreg. price varies. (Polska Akademia Nauk, Instytut Podstawowych Problemow Techniki) Panstwowe Wydawnictwo Naukowe, Miodowa 10, Warsaw, Poland (Dist. by Ars Polona-Ruch, Krakowskie Przedmiescie 7, Warsaw, Poland) Ed. Witold Nowacki.

621.8 US ISSN 0360-2877
CONCRETE PIPE INDUSTRY STATISTICS. 1974. a. $350. American Concrete Pipe Association, 8320 Old Courthouse Rd., Vienna, VA 22180. illus.

620.11 SZ
EIDGENOESSISCHE TECHNISCHE HOCHSCHULE ZUERICH. INSTITUT FUER BAUSTATIK UND KONSTRUKTION. ALLGEMEINE BERICHTE. (Text in English and German; summaries in English, French, and German) irreg., no. 88, 1978. price varies. (Swiss Federal Institute of Technology, Institute of Structural Engineering) Birkhaeuser Verlag, Elisabethenstr. 19, CH-4010 Basel, Switzerland. bibl.

620.111 SZ
EIDGENOESSISCHE TECHNISCHE HOCHSCHULE ZUERICH. INSTITUT FUER BAUSTATIK UND KONSTRUKTION. VERSUCHSBERICHTE. (Text in English and German; summaries in English, French and German) irreg. price varies. (Swiss Federal Institute of Technology, Institute of Structural Engineering) Birkhaeuser Verlag, Elisabethenstr. 19, CH-4010 Basel, Switzerland.

ELECTRICITY SUPPLY HANDBOOK. see *ELECTRICITY AND ELECTRICAL ENGINEERING*

531 620.1 US ISSN 0071-3422
EXPERIMENTAL MECHANICS; PROCEEDINGS. 1961. irreg., 3rd, Los Angeles, 1973. Society for Experimental Stress Analysis, 14 Fairfield Dr., Brookfield Center, CT 06805.
Represents: International Congress on Experimental Mechanics. Proceedings.

620.1 US ISSN 0071-4046
FASTENER STANDARDS. 1941. irreg., 5th ed., 1970. $30. Industrial Fasteners Institute, 1505 E. Ohio Bldg., 1717 E. Ninth St., Cleveland, OH 44114. Ed. Richard B. Belford. index. circ. 20,000.

620.1 US ISSN 0428-7738
FLUID POWER HANDBOOK & DIRECTORY. 1956. biennial. $27. Penton-IPC, 614 Superior Ave., W., Cleveland, OH 44113. Ed. Tobi Goldoftas. adv. charts. illus. stat. tr.lit. circ. 34,000. (also avail. in microform; reprint service avail. from UMI)

620.1 SZ ISSN 0071-7649
FORSCHUNG UND KONSTRUKTION IM STAHLBAU/RESEARCH AND CONSTRUCTION ON STEEL-ENGINEERING/ ETUDE DES OUVRAGES EN ACIER ET CONSTRUCTION METALLIQUE. (Text in German, French or English) no. 37, 1967. irreg. Buchdruckerei und Verlag Leemann AG, Arbenzstr. 20, 8034 Zurich, Switzerland. Indexed: Appl.Mech.Rev.

620.1 GW ISSN 0341-0528
GERMANY (FEDERAL REPUBLIC, 1949-) BUNDESANSTALT FUER MATERIALPRUEFUNG. JAHRESBERICHT. 1957. a. DM.5. ‡ Bundesanstalt fuer Materialpruefung, Unter den Eichen 87, 1000 Berlin 45, W. Germany (B.R.D.) illus. index. circ. 1,500.

HANDBOOK OF ELECTRONIC MATERIALS. see *ELECTRICITY AND ELECTRICAL ENGINEERING*

INTERNATIONAL CONFERENCE ON PRESSURE VESSEL TECHNOLOGY. PAPERS. see *TECHNOLOGY: COMPREHENSIVE WORKS*

620 US ISSN 0074-3437
INTERNATIONAL CONGRESS FOR STEREOLOGY. PROCEEDINGS. 1963. irreg., 1971, 3rd, Switzerland. price varies. International Society for Stereology, c/o Dr. Anna-Mary Carpenter, Treas., Department of Anatomy, 4-125 Jackson Hall, University of Minnesota, Minneapolis, MN 55455. circ. 400.

620.1 UK ISSN 0074-6045
INTERNATIONAL FEDERATION OF PRESTRESSING. CONGRESS PROCEEDINGS. 1974. quadrennial, 8th, 1978, London. price varies. International Federation of Prestressing - Federation Internationale de la Precontrainte, Wexham Springs, Slough SL3 6PL, England. Ed. P. Maxwell-Cook.

620.1 JA ISSN 0514-5171
JAPAN CONGRESS ON MATERIALS
RESEARCH. PROCEEDINGS/ZAIRYO
KENKYU RENGO KOENKAI RONBUNSHU.
(Text in English) 1957. a. price varies. Japan
Society of Materials Science - Nihon Zairyo Gakkai,
1-101 Yoshida Izumidono-cho, Sakyo-ku, Kyoto
606, Japan.

551 JA
KYUSHU UNIVERSITY. RESEARCH INSTITUTE
FOR APPLIED MECHANICS. ABSTRACTS OF
PAPERS. (Text in English and Japanese) 1974. a.
on exchange basis. Kyushu University, Research
Institute for Applied Mechanics - Kyushu Daigaku
Oyorikigaku Kenkyusho, 87, Hakozaki, Higashi-ku,
Fukuoka 812, Japan. Ed.Bd. circ. 600.

620.1 US
LAWRENCE BERKELEY LABORATORY.
MATERIALS AND MOLECULAR RESEARCH
DIVISION. ANNUAL REPORT. a. University of
California, Berkeley, Lawrence Berkeley Laboratory,
Berkeley, CA 94720 (Order from: National
Technical Information Service, 5285 Port Royal
Rd., Springfield, VA 22151) illus.
 Formerly: Lawrence Berkeley Laboratory.
Inorganic Materials Research Division. Annual
Report (ISSN 0092-6248)

620.1 CN ISSN 0076-2059
MCMASTER UNIVERSITY, HAMILTON,
ONTARIO. INSTITUTE FOR MATERIALS
RESEARCH. ANNUAL REPORT. 1967. a. free. ‡
McMaster University, Institute for Materials
Research, 1280 Main St. W., Hamilton Ont. L8S
4M1, Canada.

620 BU
MATERIALOZNANIE I TEKHNOLOGIIA. 1975.
irreg. 1 lv. per issue. (Bulgarska Akademiia na
Naukite) Publishing House of the Bulgarian
Academy of Sciences, Ul. Akad. G. Bonchev, 1113
Sofia, Bulgaria. circ. 600.

620 CN
MATERIALS RESEARCH IN A E C L. 1969. a.
Atomic Energy of Canada Ltd., Technical
Information Branch, S.D.D.O., Station 14, Chalk
River, Ont. K0J 1J0, Canada. charts. illus. circ.
controlled. (also avail. in microfiche; back issues
avail.) Indexed: INIS Atomind. Nucl.Sci.Abstr.

620.1 US ISSN 0079-8126
MATERIALS RESEARCH IN SCIENCE AND
ENGINEERING AT PURDUE UNIVERSITY.
PROGRESS REPORT. 1962. a. free. Purdue
University, Materials Research Business Office,
Physics Bldg., West Lafayette, IN 47907. Ed. J. M.
Honig. circ. 200.
 Continues: Materials Research in Science and
Engineering at Purdue University. Annual Report.

620.1 US ISSN 0076-5201
MATERIALS SCIENCE RESEARCH. 1963. irreg.
price varies. Plenum Press, 233 Spring St., New
York, NY 10013. Ed. Bd.

620.11 US ISSN 0465-2886
MATERIALS SELECTOR. (Reference issue of
Materials in Design Engineering) 1957. a. $10.
Reinhold Publishing Co., Inc., 600 Summer St.,
Stamford, CT 06904. Ed. J. E. Hauck. adv. circ.
60,547.

620.1 US
METRIC FASTENER STANDARDS. 1976. irreg.,
2nd edt. 1980. $35. Industrial Fasteners Institute,
1505 E. Ohio Bldg., 1717 E. Ninth St., Cleveland,
OH 44114.

620.1 US ISSN 0077-0000
MODERN MATERIALS. ADVANCES IN
DEVELOPMENT AND APPLICATIONS. 1958.
irreg., 1970, vol. 7. price varies. Academic Press,
Inc, 111 Fifth Ave., New York, NY 10003. Ed. B.
W. Gonser. index.

669 621.48 US
MONOGRAPH SERIES ON METALLURGY IN
NUCLEAR TECHNOLOGY. irreg. price varies.
Gordon and Breach Science Publishers, 1 Park
Avenue, New York, NY 10016.

620.1 US ISSN 0077-0744
MONOGRAPHS AND TEXTBOOKS IN
MATERIAL SCIENCE. 1971. irreg., vol. 8, 1977.
price varies. Marcel Dekker, Inc., 270 Madison
Ave., New York, NY 10016. Eds. A. Sosin and
R.R.Bunshah.

620.1 AT
N. A. T. A. DIRECTORY. 1968. a. Aus.$20. National
Association of Testing Authorities, 688 Pacific
Highway, Chatswood, N.S.W. 2067, Australia.
 Continues: N. A. T. A. Index.

620.1 US ISSN 0081-1556
NATIONAL S A M P E TECHNICAL
CONFERENCE SERIES. N S T C PREPRINT
SERIES. (Fall conferences) 1969. a. price varies.
Society for the Advancement of Material and
Process Engineering, P. O. Box 613, Azusa, CA
91702. Ed. Marge Smith.
 Formerly: Society of Aerospace Material and
Process Engineers. National S A M P E Technical
Conference. N S T C Preprint Series.

NORSKE VERITAS CLASSIFICATION AND
REGISTRY OF SHIPPING. PUBLICATION. see
TRANSPORTATION — Ships And Shipping

620 US
NORTHWESTERN UNIVERSITY. MATERIALS
RESEARCH CENTER. ANNUAL TECHNICAL
REPORT. 1961. a. free. ‡ National Science
Foundation, Northwestern University, Materials
Research Center, 2145 Sheridan Rd., Evanston, IL
60201. circ. controlled. (processed)

620.1 DK ISSN 0105-922X
POLYTEKNISKE LAEREANSTALT, DANMARKS
TEKNISKE HOEJSKOLE. AFDELINGEN FOR
BAERENDE KONSTRUKTIONER. RAPPORT R.
(Text in Danish and English) 1967. irreg. (5-8/yr.);
no. 109, 1979. Kr.60. Polytekniske Laereanstalt,
Danmarks Tekniske Hoejskole, Afdelingen for
Baerende Konstruktioner - Technical University of
Denmark, Structural Research Laboratory,
Lundtoftevej 100, Bygning 118, DK-2800 Lyngby,
Denmark. circ. 300. Indexed: Appl.Mech.Rev.
Eng.Ind. Ref.Zh.

620.1 US ISSN 0079-6425
PROGRESS IN MATERIALS SCIENCE. 1949. 4/yr.
$80. Pergamon Press, Inc., Journals Division,
Maxwell House, Fairview Park, Elmsford, NY
10523 (And Headington Hill Hall, Oxford OX3
0BW, England) Ed. Bruce Chalmers. index. (also
avail. in microform from MIM,UMI) Indexed:
Chem.Abstr. Eng.Ind.

620.1 US ISSN 0080-7559
SCIENCE OF ADVANCED MATERIAL AND
PROCESS ENGINEERING SERIES. (Spring
Symposia) 1959. a. price varies. Society for the
Advancement of Material and Process Engineering,
P.O. Box 613, Azusa, CA 91702. Ed. Marge Smith.
Indexed: Chem.Abstr.

621.9 US ISSN 0081-1645
SOCIETY OF MANUFACTURING ENGINEERS.
COLLECTED PAPERS AND TECHNICAL
PAPERS PRESENTED AT WESTERN METAL
AND TOOL EXPOSITION AND
CONFERENCE. 1965. irreg., latest issue 1975.
$57.75. Society of Manufacturing Engineers, 20501
Ford Rd., Dearborn, MI 48128. circ. 36,000.
(reprint service avail. from UMI)

620.1 US ISSN 0081-430X
STANDARDS ENGINEERS SOCIETY.
PROCEEDINGS OF ANNUAL MEETING. 1951.
a. $20 to non-members; members $15. Standards
Engineers Society, 6700 Penn Ave. S., Minneapolis,
MN 55423. Ed. Raymond E. Monahan. index. circ.
1,000.

530 620.1 US
SYMPOSIUM ON NONDESTRUCTIVE
EVALUATION. PROCEEDINGS. 1962. s-a. price
varies. Southwest Research Institute, Nondestructive
Testing Data Support Center, 8500 Culebra, San
Antonio, TX 78284. circ. 500.
 Formerly: Symposium on Physics and
Nondestructive Testing, San Antonio. Proceedings
(ISSN 0082-0903)

620.1 530 US ISSN 0073-5264
T & A M REPORT. 1946. irreg., no. 437, 1979.
controlled circ. University of Illinois at Urbana-
Champaign, Department of Theoretical and Applied
Mechanics, 216 Talbot Laboratory, Urbana, IL
61801. circ. 120.

620.1 US
TREATISE ON MATERIALS SCIENCE &
TECHNOLOGY. 1971. irreg (approx 1/yr.)
Academic Press, Inc., 111 Fifth Ave, New York,
NY 10003. Ed. H. Herman.

624.17 GW
UNIVERSITAET HANNOVER. INSTITUT FUER
STATISTIK. MITTEILUNGEN. 1959. irreg., no.
23, 1977. price varies. Universitaet Hannover,
Institut fuer Statik, Callinstrasse 32,II, 3000
Hannover 1, W. Germany (B.R.D.) Ed. A. Pflueger.
 Formerly: Technische Universitaet Hannover.
Institut fuer Statistik. Mitteilungen (ISSN 0073-
0300)

669 GW
UNIVERSITAET HANNOVER. LEHRSTUHL
FUER STAHLBAU. SCHRIFTENREIHE. 1960.
irreg. price varies. Universitaet Hannover, Lehrstuhl
fuer Stahlbau, Callinstr. 32, 3000 Hannover 1, W.
Germany (B.R.D.)
 Formerly: Technische Universitaet Hannover.
Lehrstuhl fuer Stahlbau. Schriftenreihe (ISSN 0073-
0289)

620.1 CN
UNIVERSITY OF WATERLOO. SOLID
MECHANICS DIVISION. STUDIES SERIES. no.
13, 1978. irreg. price varies. University of Waterloo,
Solid Mechanics Division, Waterloo, Ont. N2L
3G1, Canada. Ed. M. Z. Cohn.

620.1 CN
UNIVERSITY OF WATERLOO. SOLID
MECHANICS DIVISION. TECHNICAL NOTES.
1951, no. 2. irreg. free. University of Waterloo,
Solid Mechanics Division, Waterloo, Ont. N2L
3G1, Canada.

620.1 US ISSN 0084-0203
WILEY SERIES ON THE SCIENCE AND
TECHNOLOGY OF MATERIALS. 1958. irreg.,
latest 1978. price varies. John Wiley & Sons, Inc.,
605 Third Ave., New York, NY 10016. Ed.Bd.

ENGINEERING — Hydraulic Engineering

627 NZ ISSN 0571-9291
AUSTRALASIAN CONFERENCE ON
HYDRAULICS AND FLUID MECHANICS.
PROCEEDINGS. 1962. triennial; 6th Adelaide,
Australia, 1977. University of Canterbury,
Christchurch, New Zealand (Proceedings published
by host)
 1st Perth, Univ. of Western Australia, 1962; 2nd
Auckland, Univ. of Auckland, 1965; 3rd Sydney,
Institution of Engineers, 1968; 4th Melbourne,
Monash Univ., 1971; 5th Christchurch, N.Z., 1974.

627 UK
B. H. R. A. FLUID ENGINEERING SERIES. irreg.
price varies. British Hydromechanics Research
Association, Cranfield, Bedford MK43 0AJ,
England (Dist. in U.S. by: Air Science Co., Box
143, Corning,N.Y. 14830)

627 UK
BRITISH HYDROMECHANICS RESEARCH
ASSOCIATION. PROCEEDINGS OF
HYDROTRANSPORT. irreg., 7th, 1980. price
varies. British Hydromechanics Research
Association, Cranfield, Bedford MK43 0AJ,
England (Dist. in U.S. by: Air Science Co., Box
143, Corning, NY 14830)

627 UK
BRITISH HYDROMECHANICS RESEARCH
ASSOCIATION. PROCEEDINGS OF
PNEUMOTRANSPORT. 1972. irreg., 5th. 1977.
price varies. British Hydromechanics Research
Association, Cranfield, Bedford MK43 0AJ,
England (Dist. in U.S. by: Air Science Co., Box
143, Corning, N.Y. 14830)

620.106 UK
BRITISH PUMP MANUFACTURERS ASSOCIATION. TECHNICAL CONFERENCE PROCEEDINGS. irreg., 6th, 1979. price varies. British Hydromechanics Research Association, Cranfield, Bedford MK43 0AJ, England (Dist. in U.S. by: Air Science Co., Box 143, Corning, N.Y. 14830)

D N O C S-FINS E ATIVIDADES. (Departamento Nacional de Obras Contra as Secas) see *AGRICULTURE — Crop Production And Soil*

EIDGENOESSISCHE TECHNISCHE HOCHSCHULE ZUERICH. VERSUCHSANSTALT FUER WASSERBAU, HYDROLOGIE UND GLAZIOLOGIE. JAHRESBERICHT. see *EARTH SCIENCES — Hydrology*

EIDGENOESSISCHE TECHNISCHE HOCHSCHULE ZUERICH. VERSUCHSANSTALT FUER WASSERBAU, HYDROLOGIE UND GLAZIOLOGIE. MITTEILUNGEN. see *EARTH SCIENCES — Hydrology*

627 UK ISSN 0071-6278
FLUID POWER SYMPOSIUM. PROCEEDINGS. 1969. irreg., 6th, 1981. price varies. British Hydromechanics Research Association, Fluid Engineering, Cranfield, Bedfordshire, England (Dist. in U.S. by: Air Science Co., Box 143, Corning, N.Y. 14830) Ed. H. S. Stephens.

627 628 UK ISSN 0073-4187
GREAT BRITAIN. HYDRAULICS RESEARCH STATION. REPORTS. 1956. a. price varies. Hydraulics Research Station, Wallingford, Berkshire, England (Avail. from H.M.S.O., Atlantic House, Holborn Viaduct, London EC1P 1BN, England)

627.027 US ISSN 0094-1832
HYDRAULIC RESEARCH IN THE UNITED STATES AND CANADA. 1951. a. price varies. U. S. National Bureau of Standards, Washington, DC 20234 (Orders to: Supt. Doc., Washington, DC 20402)
Formerly: Hydraulic Research in the United States (ISSN 0073-4160)

627 GW ISSN 0073-7755
INDUSTRIEABWAESSER. 1958. a. DM.7. Deutscher Kommunal-Verlag GmbH, Roseggerstr. 5a, 4000 Duesseldorf 30, W. Germany (B.R.D.)

627 UR
INSTITUT VODNOGO TRANSPORTA, LENINGRAD. GIDROTEKHNICHESKAYA LABORATORIYA. MATERIALY. (Subseries of: Institut Vodnogo Transporta, Leningrad. Trudy) irreg. 0.85 Rub. Izdatel'stvo Transport, Leningradskoe Otdelenie, Ul. Dekabristov, 33, 190121 Leningrad, U. S. S. R. illus.

627 NE ISSN 0074-1477
INTERNATIONAL ASSOCIATION FOR HYDRAULIC RESEARCH. CONGRESS PROCEEDINGS. 1937. biennial, 19th, 1981, New Delhi. $150 for 6 issues. International Association for Hydraulic Research, Rotterdamseweg 185, P.O. Box 177, 2600 MH Delft, Netherlands.
Proceedings published in host country

627.52 II ISSN 0074-2732
INTERNATIONAL COMMISSION ON IRRIGATION AND DRAINAGE. CONGRESS REPORTS. 1951. triennial since 1969; 1978, 10th Athens. price varies. International Commission on Irrigation and Drainage - Commission Internationale des Irrigations et du Drainage, 48 Nyaya Marg, Chanakyapuri, New Delhi 1100021, India. (back issues avail.)

627 UK
INTERNATIONAL SYMPOSIUM ON DREDGING TECHNOLOGY. PROCEEDINGS. 1976. irreg., 3rd, 1980. price varies. British Hydromechanics Research Association, Cranfield, Bedford MK43 0AJ, England (Dist. in U.S. by: Air Science Co., Box 143, Corning, N.Y. 14830)

INTERNATIONAL SYMPOSIUM ON URBAN HYDROLOGY, HYDRAULICS AND SEDIMENT CONTROL. PROCEEDINGS. see *EARTH SCIENCES — Hydrology*

628.1 US ISSN 0074-9575
INTERNATIONAL WATER CONFERENCE. PROCEEDINGS. 1941. a. $20. Engineers' Society of Western Pennsylvania, Wm. Penn Hotel, 530 William Penn Pl., Pittsburgh, PA 15219. Ed. Richard Lampl. adv. 35-yr. cum.index. circ. 1,500.

NATIONAL CONFERENCE ON FLUID POWER. PROCEEDINGS. see *MEETINGS AND CONGRESSES*

627.8 US ISSN 0078-4508
OKLAHOMA'S GRAND RIVER DAM AUTHORITY. ANNUAL REPORT. 1967. a. free. Grand River Dam Authority, Drawer G, Vinita, OK 74301.

621.3 PK ISSN 0083-8349
PAKISTAN. WATER AND POWER DEVELOPMENT AUTHORITY. REPORT. (Text in English) 1958-59. a. Water and Power Development Authority, WAPDA House, Shara-e-Quaid-e-Azam, Lahore, Pakistan. circ. 1,000.

627 UR
POLIMERY V MELIORATSII I VODNOM KHOZYAISTVE. 1974. irreg. 0.44 Rub. Latviiskii Nauchno-issledovatel'skii Institut Gidrotekniki i Melioratsii - Latvijas Hidrotehnikas Un Melioracijas Zinatnisti Petnieciskais Instituts, Ul. Revoliutsiias, 43, Elgava, Latvia, U.S.S.R. illus.

627 PL ISSN 0416-7295
POLITECHNIKA GDANSKA. ZESZYTY NAUKOWE. BUDOWNICTWO WODNE. (Text in Polish; summaries in English and Russian) 1956. irreg. price varies. Politechnika Gdanska, Majakowskiego 11/12, 81-952 Gdansk 6, Poland (Dist. by: Osrodek Rozpowszechniania Wydawnictw Naukowych Pan, Palac Kultury i Nauki, 00-901 Warsaw, Poland)

PROJECT SKYWATER. ANNUAL REPORT. see *WATER RESOURCES*

627 US ISSN 0146-0854
SERIES IN THERMAL AND FLUIDS ENGINEERING. 1976. irreg., unnumbered, latest 1980. Hemisphere Publishing Corporation, 1025 Vermont Ave., Washington, DC 20005. (Co-publisher: McGraw-Hill) (reprint service avail. from UMI) Indexed: Chem.Abstr. Eng.Ind.

621.2 UK
SYMPOSIUM ON JET PUMPS & EJECTORS AND GAS LIFT TECHNIQUES. PROCEEDINGS. irreg., 2nd 1975 Cambridge. £19. British Hydromechanics Research Association, Cranfield, Bedford MK43 0AJ, England (Dist. in U.S. by: Air Science Co., Box 143, Corning, N.Y. 14830)

627 II ISSN 0080-4045
U. P. IRRIGATION RESEARCH INSTITUTE. GENERAL ANNUAL REPORT.* (Issued in its Technical Memorandum Series) a. U. P. Irrigation Research Institute, Roorkee, Uttar Pradesh, India.

627 II ISSN 0080-4053
U.P. IRRIGATION RESEARCH INSTITUTE. TECHNICAL MEMORANDUM.* (Text in English) irreg. U. P. Irrigation Research Institute, Roorkee, Uttar Pradesh, India.

627 US
U.S. WATER AND POWER RESOURCES SERVICE. ENGINEERING MONOGRAPH. no. 6, 1950. irreg. U.S. Water and Power Resources, Engineering and Research Center, Box 25007, Denver Federal Center, Denver, CO 80225.
Formerly: U.S. Bureau of Reclamation. Engineering Monograph.
Land reclamation

627 NO ISSN 0082-6618
UNIVERSITETET I TRONDHEIM. NORGES TEKNISKE HOEGSKOLE. VASSDRAGS- OG HAVNELABORATORIET. MEDDELELSE. English edition: University of Trondheim. Norwegian Institute of Technology. River and Harbour Laboratory. Bulletin. (Editions in Norwegian and English) 1959. a. free. Universitetet i Trondheim, Norges Tekniske Hoegskole. Vassdrags- og Havnelaboratoriet, Klaebuveien 153, 7034 Trondheim, Norway. Ed. F. Johansen. circ. 700.

VODNI PROBLEMI. see *WATER RESOURCES*

627 BE
VON KARMAN INSTITUTE FOR FLUID DYNAMICS. LECTURE SERIES. irreg. 4500 Fr. Von Karman Institute for Fluid Dynamics - Institut von Karman de Dynamique des Fluides, Chaussee de Waterloo 72, B-1640 Rhode Saint Genese, Belgium.

627 UK ISSN 0307-1782
WATER SERVICES HANDBOOK. 1929. a. £13.50. Fuel and Metallurgical Journals Ltd., Queensway House, 2 Queensway, Redhill, Surrey RH 1 1QS, England. Ed. Derrek Eddowes. adv.
Formerly: Water Engineer's Handbook (ISSN 0083-7644)

627 RH ISSN 0080-2832
ZIMBABWE. MINISTRY OF WATER DEVELOPMENT. HYDROLOGICAL SUMMARIES. 1965. quinquennial; latest 1969-70. $2 ($3) Ministry of Water Development, c/o Chief Hydrological Engineer, P.O. Box 8132, Causeway, Salisbury, Zimbabwe.

551 RH ISSN 0080-2840
ZIMBABWE. MINISTRY OF WATER DEVELOPMENT. HYDROLOGICAL YEAR BOOK. 1956-57. a. $3. Ministry of Water Development, c/o Chief Hydrological Engineer, P.O. Box 8132, Causeway, Salisbury, Zimbabwe.

ENGINEERING — Mechanical Engineering

see also Machinery

621 FI ISSN 0001-687X
ACTA POLYTECHNICA SCANDINAVICA. MECHANICAL ENGINEERING SERIES. (Text and summaries in English, German and French) irreg. (2-3/yr.) Fmk.60. Teknillisten Tieteiden Akatemia - Finnish Academy of Technical Sciences, Kansakoulukatu 10 A, SF-00100 Helsinki 10, Finland. Ed. Henrik Ryti. index; cum index (1958-1979) circ. 250. (also avail. in microfilm from UMI; back issues avail.; reprint service avail. from UMI)

621 US ISSN 0517-5356
AMERICAN SOCIETY OF MECHANICAL ENGINEERS. MACHINE DESIGN DIVISION. PAPERS. 1956. irreg. price varies. American Society of Mechanical Engineers, Machine Design Division, 345 E. 47 St., New York, NY 10017.

AUSTRALIAN GAS INDUSTRY DIRECTORY. see *PETROLEUM AND GAS*

621.8 GW ISSN 0522-0629
BALL AND ROLLER BEARING ENGINEERING. German edition: Waelzerlagertechnik (ISSN 0511-0653); French edition: Technique du Roulement (ISSN 0170-303X); Spanish edition: Technica de los Rodamientos (ISSN 0170-3056); Italian edition: Cuscinetti Volventi (ISSN 0170-3048) (Text in English) 1962. 1-3/yr. Fag Kugelfischer Georg Schaefer und Co., Postfach 1260, 8720 Schweinfurt 1, W. Germany (B.R.D.) Indexed: Eng.Ind.

621 AT ISSN 0069-7486
COMMONWEALTH SCIENTIFIC AND INDUSTRIAL RESEARCH ORGANIZATION. DIVISION OF MECHANICAL ENGINEERING. CIRCULAR. 1959. irreg. free. ‡ C.S.I.R.O., Division of Mechanical Engineering, P.O. Box 26, Highett, Victoria 3190, Australia.

621 AT ISSN 0069-7508
COMMONWEALTH SCIENTIFIC AND INDUSTRIAL RESEARCH ORGANIZATION. DIVISION OF MECHANICAL ENGINEERING. REPORT. 1959-60. a. free. ‡ C. S. I. R. O., Division of Mechanical Engineering, P.O. Box 26, Highett, Vic. 3190, Australia.

621 AT
COMMONWEALTH SCIENTIFIC AND INDUSTRIAL RESEARCH ORGANIZATION. DIVISION OF MECHANICAL ENGINEERING. TECHNICAL REPORTS. 1954. irreg. free. ‡ C. S. I. R. O., Division of Mechanical Engineering, P.O. Box 26, Highett, Vic. 3190, Australia.
Formerly: Commonwealth Scientific and Industrial Research Organization. Division of Mechanical Engineering. Engineering Development Reports (ISSN 0069-7494)

ENGINEERING — MECHANICAL ENGINEERING

621   US   ISSN 0070-4822
DIESEL AND GAS TURBINE WORLD WIDE CATALOG. 1935. a. $45. Diesel Engines, Inc., Box 26308, Milwaukee, WI 54902.

621.9   US   ISSN 0070-5772
DIRECTORY OF MACHINE TOOLS AND RELATED PRODUCTS; built by members of the National Machine Tool Builders' Assn. a. National Machine Tool Builders' Association, 7901 Westpark Drive, McLean, VA 22102. circ. 30,000.

ELEKTROTECHNIKA IR MECHANIKA. see *ELECTRICITY AND ELECTRICAL ENGINEERING*

621   UK
EUROPEAN CONFERENCE ON MIXING AND CENTRIFUGAL SEPARATION. PROCEEDINGS. 1975. irreg., 3rd, 1980. price varies. British Hydromechanics Research Association, Cranfield, Bedford MK43 0AJ, England (Dist. in U.S. by: Air Science Co., Box 143, Corning, N.Y. 14830)

621.8   US
FLUID METERS: THEIR THEORY AND APPLICATION. irreg., 6th, 1971. price varies. American Society of Mechanical Engineers, Research Committee on Fluid Meters, 345 E. 47 St., New York, NY 10017.

629.8   NE
I F A C SYMPOSIUM ON MULTIVARIABLE TECHNICAL CONTROL SYSTEMS. PROCEEDINGS.* 1968. irreg. (International Federation of Automatic Control) North Holland Publishing Co., P.O.B. 211, 1000 AE Amsterdam, Netherlands (Inquire: Kenneth Derbyshire, Dunraven St., Park Lane, London W1, England) Ed. H. Schwarz. bibl.

621   UK   ISSN 0020-3483
INSTITUTION OF MECHANICAL ENGINEERS. PROCEEDINGS. 1847. q. £59($230) Mechanical Engineering Publications Ltd., Box 24, Northgate Ave., Bury St. Edmunds, Suffolk 1P32 6BW, England. Ed. F. Whiteley. bibl. illus. index;cum.index irreg. (also avail. in microform from UMI) Indexed: A.S. & T.Ind. Appl.Mech.Rev. Br.Tech.Ind. Chem.Abstr. Eng.Ind. Math.R. Met.Abstr. Sci.Abstr.

621   US
INTERNATIONAL CENTRE FOR MECHANICAL SCIENCES (CISM). COURSES AND LECTURES. (Text mainly in English) 1969. irreg., no. 265, 1981. price varies. (IT) Springer-Verlag, 175 Fifth Ave., New York, NY 10010 (Also Berlin, Heidelberg, Vienna) (reprint service avail. from ISI)

621 532   UK   ISSN 0074-3089
INTERNATIONAL CONFERENCE ON FLUID SEALING. PROCEEDINGS. 1961. irreg., 9th. 1981. price varies. British Hydromechanics Research Association, Fluid Engineering, Cranfield, Bedford MK 43 0AJ, England (Dist. in U.S. by: Air Science Co., Box 143, Corning, N.Y. 14830)

621   UK
INTERNATIONAL CONFERENCE ON PRESSURE SURGES. PROCEEDINGS. 1973. irreg., 3rd, 1980. $45.50 latest vol. British Hydromechanics Research Association, Cranfield, Bedford MK43 0AJ, England (Dist. in U.S. by: Air Science Co., Box 143, Corning, N. Y. 14830)

621.4   FR   ISSN 0074-4077
INTERNATIONAL CONGRESS ON COMBUSTION ENGINES. PROCEEDINGS. 1951. irreg., 12th, 1977, Tokyo. price varies. International Council on Combustion Engines - Conseil International des Machines a Combustion, 10 Avenue Hoche, 75008 Paris, France (Proceedings of 12th Congress avail. from: N. Kajitani, Japan Internal Combustion Engine Federation, 11-5, 1-Chome, Shinbashi, Minato-Ku, Tokyo 105, Japan)
Proceedings published by organizing committee

INTERNATIONAL GAS BEARING SYMPOSIUM. PROCEEDINGS. see *PETROLEUM AND GAS*

621   UK
INTERNATIONAL SYMPOSIUM ON JET CUTTING TECHNOLOGY. PROCEEDINGS. 1972. irreg., 5th, 1980. price varies. British Hydromechanics Research Association, Cranfield, Bedford MK43 0AJ, England (Dist. in U. S. by: Air Science Co., Box 143, Corning, N.Y. 14830)

621   GW
JAHRBUCH SCHLEIFFEN, HONEN, LAEPPEN UND POLIEREN, VERFAHREN UND MASCHINEN. 1932. a. DM.56. Vulkan- Verlag Dr. W. Classen, Hollestr. 1G, Postfach 103962, 4300 Essen, W. Germany (B.R.D.) Ed. E. Salje. adv. circ. 2,500.
Former titles: Jahrbuch der Schleiff-, Hon-, Laepp- und Poliertechnik (ISSN 0075-2398); Jahrbuch der Schleif- und Poliertechnik und der Oberflaechenbehandlung.

621   CN   ISSN 0076-1966
MCGILL UNIVERSITY, MONTREAL. MECHANICAL ENGINEERING RESEARCH LABORATORIES. REPORT. 1962. irreg. free when avail. McGill University, Mechanical Engineering Department, 817 Sherbrooke St. W., Montreal, Que. H3A 2K6, Canada. Indexed: Sci. & Tech.Aerosp.Rep.

621   CN   ISSN 0076-1974
MCGILL UNIVERSITY, MONTREAL. MECHANICAL ENGINEERING RESEARCH LABORATORIES. TECHNICAL NOTE. 1962. irreg. free when avail. McGill University, Mechanical Engineering Department, 817 Sherbrooke St. W., Montreal, Que. H3A 2K6, Canada. Indexed: Sci. & Tech.Aerosp.Rep.

621   US
MACHINE DESIGN REFERENCE ISSUES. (Set includes 5 separate issues: Materials, Electric Motors and Controls, Mechanical Drives, Fluid Power, Fastening and Joining) a. $6. Penton-IPC, Penton Plaza, 1111 Chester Ave., Cleveland, OH 44114. (reprint service avail. from UMI)

621   UK   ISSN 0305-3121
MACHINERY'S BUYERS' GUIDE. 1926. a. £3.75. Machinery Publishing Co. Ltd., New England House, New England St., Brighton BN1 4HN, England. Ed. F.A.J. Browne. adv. circ. 8,000.
Formerly: Machinery's Annual Buyer's Guide (ISSN 0076-2040)

620.1 690   PL   ISSN 0324-9182
MECHANIKA I BUDOWNICTWO LADOWE/ MECHANICS AND BUILDING ENGINEERING. (Subseries of its: Zeszyty Naukowe) (Text in Polish; summaries in English and Russian) 1974. irreg. price varies. Akademia Rolniczo-Techniczna, Blok 21, 10-957 Olsztyn-Kortowo, Poland. illus.

621   UR
MEKHANICHESKAYA TEKHNOLOGIYA/ MECHANINE TECHNOLOGIJA. (Text in Lithuanian or Russian) irreg. Aukstuju Mokyklu Mokslo Darbai, Vilnius, U.S.S.R. illus.

338.45 621.9   US
MODERN MACHINE SHOP NC/CAM GUIDEBOOK. 1970. a. $5. Gardner Publications Inc., 600 Main St., Cincinnati, OH 45202. Ed. Ken M. Gettelman. (also avail. in microform from UMI; reprint service avail. from UMI)
Formerly: Modern Machine Shop N C Guidebook and Directory (ISSN 0076-9991)

621   CN   ISSN 0077-555X
NATIONAL RESEARCH COUNCIL, CANADA. NATIONAL AERONAUTICAL ESTABLISHMENT. MECHANICAL ENGINEERING REPORTS. 1947. irreg. free. National Research Council of Canada, Ottawa, Ont. K1A OR6, Canada. circ. 300-1,200. Indexed: Sci.&Tech.Aerosp.Rep.

338.47 621.3   FR   ISSN 0474-5353
ORGANIZATION FOR ECONOMIC COOPERATION AND DEVELOPMENT. SURVEY OF ELECTRIC POWER EQUIPMENT. ENQUETE SUR L'EQUIPMENT ELECTRIQUE. (Text in French and English) 1950. irreg. Organization for Economic Cooperation and Development, 2 rue Andre Pascal, 75775 Paris 16, France (U. S. orders to: O.E.C.D. Publications and Information Center, 1750 Pennsylvania Ave., N. W., Washington, D. C. 20006) (also avail. in microfiche)

629   PL   ISSN 0137-6969
POLITECHNIKA CZESTOCHOWSKA. ZESZYTY NAUKOWE. NAUKI TECHNICZNE. MECHANIKA. (Text in Polish; summaries in English and Russian) 1969. irreg. Politechnika Czestochowska, Ul. Deglera 31, 42-200 Czestochowa, Poland (Dist. by: Ars Polona-Ruch, Krakowskie Przedmiescie 7, Warsaw, Poland) Ed. Ryszard Parkitny.

621   PL   ISSN 0072-0380
POLITECHNIKA GDANSKA. ZESZYTY NAUKOWE. MECHANIKA. (Text in Polish; summaries in English and Russian) 1955. irreg. price varies. Politechnika Gdanska, Majakowskiego 11/12, 81-952 Gdansk 6, Poland (Dist. by: Osrodek Rozpowszechniania Wydawnictw Naukowych Pan, Palac Kultury i Nauki, 00-901 Warsaw, Poland)

621.8   PL
POLITECHNIKA LODZKA. ZESZYTY NAUKOWE. CIEPLNE MASZYNY PRZEPLYWOWE. (Text in Polish; summaries in English and Russian) irreg. price varies. Politechnika Lodzka, Ul. Zwirki 36, 90-924 Lodz, Poland (Dist. by: Ars Polona-Ruch, Krakowskie Przedmiescie 7, Warsaw, Poland) Ed. Ryszard Przybylski. circ. 350.

621   PL   ISSN 0458-1563
POLITECHNIKA LODZKA. ZESZYTY NAUKOWE. MECHANIKA. (Text in Polish; summaries in English and Russian) 1954. irreg. price varies. Politechnika Lodzka, Ul. Zwirki 36, 90-924 Lodz, Poland (Dist. by: Ars Polona-Ruch, Krakowskie Przedmiescie 7, Warsaw, Poland) Ed. Zdzislaw Orzechowski. circ. 350. Indexed: Chem.Abstr.

620   PL   ISSN 0434-0817
POLITECHNIKA SLASKA. ZESZYTY NAUKOWE. MECHANIKA. (Text in Polish; summaries in English and Russian) 1955. irreg. price varies. Politechnika Slaska, W. Pstrowskiego 7, 44-100 Gliwice, Poland (Dist. by: Ars Polona, Krakowskie Przedmiescie 7, 00-068 Warsaw, Poland) Ed. Jan Darlewski.

621   PL   ISSN 0324-9573
POLITECHNIKA WROCLAWSKA. INSTYTUT MATERIALOZNAWSTWA I MECHANIKI TECHNICZNEJ. PRACE NAUKOWE. KONFERENCJE. (Text in Polish; summaries in English and Russian) 1974. irreg., no. 2, 1973. Politechnika Wroclawska, Wybrzeze Wyspianskiego 27, 50-370 Wroclaw, Poland (Dist. by: Ars Polona-Ruch, Krakowskie Przedmiescie 7, Warsaw, Poland) Ed. Marian Kloza. illus.

621   PL   ISSN 0324-9379
POLITECHNIKA WROCLAWSKA. INSTYTUT TECHNOLOGII BUDOWY MASZYN. PRACE NAUKOWE. KONFERENCJE. (Text in Polish; summaries in English and Russian) 1975. irreg., no. 4, 1979. price varies. Politechnika Wroclawska, Wybrzeze Wyspianskiego 27, 50-370 Wroclaw, Poland (Dist. by: Ars Polona-Ruch, Krakowskie Przedmiescie 7, Warsaw, Poland)

621   PL
POLITECHNIKA WROCLAWSKA. INSTYTUT TECHNOLOGII BUDOWY MASZYN. PRACE NAUKOWE. MONOGRAFIE. (Text in Polish; summaries in English and Russian) 1972. irreg., no. 3, 1978. price varies. Politechnika Wroclawska, Wybrzeze Wyspianskiego 27, 50-370 Wroclaw, Poland (Dist. by: Ars Polona-Ruch, Krakowskie Przedmiescie 7, Warsaw, Poland) Ed. Marian Kloza.

621   PL   ISSN 0324-9360
POLITECHNIKA WROCLAWSKA. INSTYTUT
TECHNOLOGII BUDOWY MASZYN. PRACE
NAUKOWE. STUDIA I MATERIALY. (Text in
Polish; summaries in English and Russian) 1970.
irreg., no. 3, 1978. price varies. Politechnika
Wroclawska, Wybrzeze Wyspianskiego 27, 50-370
Wroclaw, Poland (Dist. by: Ars Polona-Ruch,
Krakowskie Przedmiescie 7, Warsaw, Poland) Ed.
Marian Kloza.

621   PL   ISSN 0079-3205
POLSKA AKADEMIA NAUK. INSTYTUT
MASZYN PRZEPLYWOWYCH. PRACE. (Text in
Polish; summaries in English and Russian) 1960.
irreg. price varies. Panstwowe Wydawnictwo
Naukowe, Ul. Miodowa 10, Warsaw, Poland. Ed.
Kazimierz Steller. bibl, charts, illus.

R E M E JOURNAL. (Royal Electrical & Mechanical
Engineers) see *ELECTRICITY AND
ELECTRICAL ENGINEERING*

621   US   ISSN 0272-4804
SERIES IN COMPUTATIONAL METHODS IN
MECHANICS AND THERMAL SCIENCES.
1980. irreg. $22.50. Hemisphere Publishing
Corporation, 1025 Vermont Ave., N.W.,
Washington, DC 20005. Eds. W.J. Minkowycz,
E.M. Sparrow. bibl. charts.

621   US   ISSN 0146-2059
STRUCTURAL MECHANICS SOFTWARE SERIES.
1977. irreg. $25. (University of Virginia,
Department of Engineering Science and Systems)
University Press of Virginia, Box 3608 University
Sta., Charlottesville, VA 22903. Eds. Nicholas
Perrone, Walter Pilkey. index. circ. 1,500.

623.82   YU   ISSN 0350-3097
SVEUCILISTE U ZAGREBU. FAKULTET
STROJARSTVA I BRODOGRADNJE. ZBORNIK
RADOVA. (Summaries in English or German)
1970. a. free. Sveuciliste u Zagrebu, Fakultet
Strojarstva i Brodogradnje, Djure Salaja 5, Zagreb,
Yugoslavia. illus.

621   GW   ISSN 0082-1810
TASCHENBUCH DER WERKZEUGMASCHINEN
UND WERKZEUGE. 1953. a. DM.32. Fachverlag
Schiele und Schoen GmbH, Markgrafenstr. 11, 1000
Berlin 61, W. Germany (B.R.D.) Ed. J. Paschke.
adv. circ. 3,000.

621   GW   ISSN 0170-303X
LA TECHNIQUE DU ROULEMENT. English
edition: Ball and Roller Bearing Engineering (ISSN
0522-0629); German edition: Waelzlagertechnik
(ISSN 0511-0653); Italian edition: Cuscinetti
Volventi (ISSN 0170-3048); Spanish edition:
Tecnica de los Rodamientos (ISSN 0170-3056)
(Text in French) 1962. 1-3/yr. Fag Kugelfischer
Georg Schaefer und Co., Postfach 1260, 8720
Schweinfurt 1, W. Germany (B.R.D.)

621   GW   ISSN 0170-3056
LA TECNICA DE LOS RODAMIENTOS. English
edition: Ball and Roller Bearing Engineering (ISSN
0522-0629); French edition: La Technique du
Roulement (ISSN 0170-303X); German edition:
Waelzlagertechnik (ISSN 0511-0653); Italian
edition: Cuscinetti Volventi (ISSN 0170-3048) (Text
in Spanish) 1962. 1-3/yr. Fag Kugelfischer Georg
Schaefer und Co., Postfach 1260, 8720 Schweinfurt
1, W. Germany (B.R.D.)

621.8   UK   ISSN 0082-6405
TRIBOLOGY CONVENTION. PROCEEDINGS.
1962. a. £12($29.80) Institution of Mechanical
Engineers, Tribology Group, 1 Birdcage Walk,
London SW1H 9JJ, England. Ed. J. C. Mundy.
Issued previously as: Lubrication and Wear
Convention. Proceedings.

621.4   US
TURBOMACHINERY CATALOG AND
WORKBOOK. 1963. a. $35. Turbomachinery
Publications,Inc., 22 S. Smith St., Norwalk, CT
06855. Ed. Kurt Hallberg.
Former titles: Sawyer's Gas Turbine Catalog &
Gas Turbine Catalog (ISSN 0072-0267)

UNIVERSITAET STUTTGART. INSTITUT FUER
STEUERUNGSTECHNIK DER
WERKZEUGMASCHINEN UND
FERTIGUNGSEINRICHTUNGEN. I S W
BERICHTE. see *MACHINERY*

621.8   RM
UNIVERSITATEA DIN BRASOV. BULETINUL.
SERIA A. MECANICA APLICATA-
CONSTRUCTII DE MASINI. (Text in Romanian;
summaries in English, French, German) v. 18, 1976.
a. price varies. Universitatea din Brasov, Bd. Gh.
Gheorghiu-Dej, Nr. 29, Brasov, Romania. bibl.
illus.

621.8   RM
UNIVERSITATEA DIN BRASOV. BULETINUL.
SERIA A/3. MECANICA APLICATA -
CONSTRUCTII DE MASINI. CONSTRUCTIA
DE MASINI SI TEHNOLOGIA PRELUCRARII
METALELOR. (Text in Romanian; summaries in
English, French, German) vol.18, 1976. a. price
varies. Universitatea din Brasov, Bd. Gh.
Gheorghiu-Dej, Nr. 29, Brasov, Romania. bibl.
illus.

621   CN   ISSN 0082-5182
UNIVERSITY OF TORONTO. DEPARTMENT OF
MECHANICAL ENGINEERING. TECHNICAL
PUBLICATION SERIES. 1962. irreg. University of
Toronto, Department of Mechanical Engineering,
Toronto, Ont., Canada.

621   SA
UNIVERSITY OF WITWATERSRAND,
JOHANNESBURG. SCHOOL OF
MECHANICAL ENGINEERING. REPORTS.
1957. irreg. free. University of the Witwatersrand,
Johannesburg, School of Mechanical Engineering,
Jan Smuts Ave., Johannesburg, South Africa. Ed. E.
Bunt. circ. 200.

629.2   UK
VEHICLE BUILDERS & REPAIRERS
ASSOCIATION. DIRECTORY OF MEMBERS &
BUYERS GUIDE. a. $9. Vehicle Builders &
Repairers Association, Belmont House, 102 Finkle
Lane, Gildersome, Leeds LS27 7TW, England. Ed.
Robert Hadfield. adv. circ. 5,500.
Former titles: Vehicle Builders and Repairers
Association. Yearbook (ISSN 0083-5331); Vehicle
Builders and Repairers Association. Directory.

620.1   UR
VOPROSY INZHENERNOI GEOLOGII I
GRUNTOVEDENIYA; proceedings of the seminar
of the chair of the theory elasticity under the
guidance A.A. Ilushin. 1963. biennial. 4.20 Rub.
Moskovskii Universitet, Kafedra Gruntovedeniya i
Inzhenernoi Geologii, Leninskie Gory, Moscow V-
234, U.S.S.R. Ed. P. U. Ogibalov.

621   GW   ISSN 0511-0653
WAELZLAGERTECHNIK. English edition: Ball and
Roller Bearing Engineering (ISSN 0522-0629);
French edition: La Technique du Roulement (ISSN
0170-303X) Italian edition: Cuscinetti Volventi
(ISSN 0170-3048); Spanish edition: La Tecnica de
los Rodamientos (ISSN 0170-3056) (Text in
German; French Edition: Technique of Roulement;
Spanish Edition: Tecnica de los Rodamientos;
Italian Edition: Cuscinetti Volventi; English Edition:
Ball and Roller Bearing Engineering; Issn 0522-
0629) 1962. 1-3/yr. Fag Kugelfischer Georg
Schaefer und Co., Postfach 1260, 8720 Schweinfurt
1, W. Germany (B.R.D.)

621   GW   ISSN 0083-9299
WER BAUT MASCHINEN/WHO MAKES
MACHINERY. (Editions in English, French,
German, Spanish) 1928. a. DM.20. (Verein
Deutscher Maschinenbau-Anstalten e.V.) Verlag
Hoppenstedt und Co., Havelstr. 9, Postfach 4006,
6100 Darmstadt, W. Germany (B.R.D.) Ed. K.
Schidlo. adv.

ENTOMOLOGY

see *Biology—Entomology*

ENVIRONMENTAL STUDIES

see also *Biology; Conservation; Public
Health and Safety; Water Resources*

614.7   US
A.P.C.A. PROCEEDINGS DIGEST. 1970. a. $5. Air
Pollution Control Association, 4400 Fifth Ave.,
Pittsburgh, PA 15213.

574.5   UK   ISSN 0065-2504
ADVANCES IN ECOLOGICAL RESEARCH. 1962.
irreg. price varies. Academic Press Inc. (London)
Ltd., 24-28 Oval Rd., London N.W. 1, England
(and 111 Fifth Ave., New York, N.Y. 10003) Ed. J.
B. Cragg.

600   US
ADVANCES IN ENVIRONMENTAL SCIENCE
AND ENGINEERING. irreg., vol. 3 in prep. $50
per vol. Gordon and Breach Science Publishers, One
Park Ave., New York, NY 10016. Eds. J.R. Pfafflin,
E.N. Ziegler.

614.7   US   ISSN 0065-2563
ADVANCES IN ENVIRONMENTAL SCIENCE
AND TECHNOLOGY. 1969. irreg., vol. 10, 1980.
price varies. John Wiley & Sons, Inc., 605 Third
Ave., New York, NY 10016. Ed. J. N. Pitts, R. L.
Metcalf.
Advances in Environmental Sciences (ISSN
0095-4535)

614.77   US   ISSN 0065-3535
ADVANCES IN WATER POLLUTION
RESEARCH. 1964. irreg., 6th, 1973. price varies.
(International Association on Water Pollution
Research) Pergamon Press Inc., Maxwell House,
Fairview Park, Elmsford, NY 10523.
Represents: International Conference on Water
Pollution Research. International Congress
Proceedings.

301.31   SG
AFRICAN ENVIRONMENT. OCCASIONAL
PAPERS/ETUDES ET RECHERCHES. (Text in
English and French) irreg. 1700 Fr.CFA($20) for 10
nos. African Institute for Economic Development
and Planning, Environment Training Programme,
Box 3370, Dakar, Senegal. (Co-sponsor:
International African Institute)

614.7   UK   ISSN 0309-345X
AFRICAN ENVIRONMENT SPECIAL REPORTS.
1974. irreg. International African Institute, 210
High Holborn, London WC1V 7BW, England. bk.
rev. bibl.

614.7   US
AIR QUALITY DATA FOR ARIZONA. 1972. a. ‡
Department of Health Services, Bureau of Air
Quality Control, 1740 W. Adams St., Phoenix, AZ
85007. Ed. James L. Guyton. illus. circ. controlled.
Formerly: Air Pollution Effects Surveillance
Network Data Report (ISSN 0092-1009); Air
Quality Monitoring Network Data.

363.6   US   ISSN 0361-5650
AIR QUALITY IN MINNESOTA. 1973. a. Pollution
Control Agency, 1935 West County Rd., Roseville,
MN 55113. illus.

614.71 628.53   US
AIR QUALITY INSTRUMENTATION. 1972. irreg.
price varies. Instrument Society of America, 400
Stanwix St., Pittsburgh, PA 15222. Ed. J. W. Scales.

614.71   US   ISSN 0568-3653
AIR QUALITY MONOGRAPH SERIES. 1969. irreg.
price varies. American Petroleum Institute,
Commttee on Medicine and Biological Sciences,
2101 L St., N.W., Washington, DC 20037.

333.7   US
ALASKA'S LAND. a. Joint Federal-State Land Use
Planning Commission for Alaska, 733 West Fourth
Ave., Anchorage, AK 99501.
Formerly (1972-1973): Joint Federal-State Land
Use Planning Commission for Alaska. Annual
Report (ISSN 0094-9515)

354   CN   ISSN 0383-3739
ALBERTA. DEPARTMENT OF THE
ENVIRONMENT. ANNUAL REPORT. a.
Department of the Environment, 9820 106th St.,
Edmonton, Alta. T5K 2J6, Canada.

ENVIRONMENTAL STUDIES

614.7 333.7   CN   ISSN 0705-5811
ALBERTA. ENVIRONMENT COUNCIL OF ALBERTA. ANNUAL REPORT. 1977. a. Environment Council of Alberta, 2100 College Plaza Tower 3, 8215 112th St., Edmonton, Alta. T6G 2M4, Canada. circ. 1,500. (also avail. in microform from MML)

333.7   CN   ISSN 0707-2783
ALBERTA. FISH AND WILDLIFE DIVISION. FISHERIES POLLUTION REPORT. 1978. irreg. Fish and Wildlife Division, Lethbridge, Alta., Canada. bibl. charts. illus.
Formerly: Alberta. Fish and Wildlife Division. Pollution Report (ISSN 0707-2791)

614.7   NO
AMBIO. SPECIAL REPORTS. (Text in English) 1972. irreg. price varies. Kungliga Svenska Vetenskapsakademien, SW - Royal Swedish Academy of Sciences, Box 50005, S-104 05 Stockholm, Sweden. Ed. Ulla Magnusson. charts, illus. stat.

614.7 620   US   ISSN 0065-6860
AMERICAN ACADEMY OF ENVIRONMENTAL ENGINEERS. ROSTER. 1956. a. membership. American Academy of Environmental Engineers, P.O. Box 1278, Rockville, MD 20850. bk. rev.

614.7   US
AMERICAN LECTURES IN ENVIRONMENTAL STUDIES. irreg. price varies. Charles C. Thomas, Publisher, 301-327 E. Lawrence Ave., Springfield, IL 62717.

614.7   CN   ISSN 0707-5723
ANALYSIS. 1977. irreg. Ministry of the Environment, Laboratory Services Branch, Box 213, Rexdale, Ont. M9W 5L1, Canada. illus.

ANNUAL BOOK OF A S T M STANDARDS. PART 31. WATER. see *ENGINEERING — Engineering Mechanics And Materials*

614.7   US   ISSN 0196-4542
ANNUAL EDITIONS: READINGS IN ENVIRONMENT. 1980. a. $6.95. Dushkin Publishing Group, Sluice Dock, Guilford, CT 06437.
Key Title: Readings in Environment.

574.5   US   ISSN 0066-4162
ANNUAL REVIEW OF ECOLOGY AND SYSTEMATICS. 1970. a. $20. Annual Reviews Inc., 4139 El Camino Way, Palo Alto, CA 94306. Ed. Richard F. Johnston. bibl. index; cum.index. (back issues avail.; reprint service avail. from ISI)
Indexed: Biol.Abstr. Chem.Abstr. Field Crop.Abstr. Herb.Abstr. M.M.R.I.

614.7   PL   ISSN 0324-8461
ARCHIWUM OCHRONY SRODOWISKA. (Text in Polish; summaries in English and Russian) irreg., no. 3/4 1977. 180 Zl. (Polska Akademia Nauk, Instytut Podstaw Inzynierii Srodowiska) Ossolineum, Publishing House of the Polish Academy of Sciences, Rynek 9, Wroclaw, Poland (Dist. by: Ars Polona-Ruch, Krakowskie Przedmiescie 7, Warsaw, Poland) Ed. Stanislaw Jarzebski.

363.6   US
ARIZONA. GOVERNOR'S COMMISSION ON ARIZONA ENVIRONMENT. ANNUAL REPORT. a. Governor's Commission on Arizona Environment, 206 S. 17th Ave., Rm. 105-A, Phoenix, AZ 85007. illus.
Formerly: Arizona. Advisory Commission on Arizona Environment. Annual Report (ISSN 0097-9953)

614.7   US   ISSN 0360-8778
ATMOSPHERIC QUALITY IMPROVEMENT TECHNICAL BULLETIN. irreg. National Council of the Paper Industry for Air and Stream Improvement, Inc., 260 Madison Ave., New York, NY 10016.
Continues: Atmospheric Pollution Technical Bulletin.

614.7 333.7   AT
AUSTRALIA. DEPARTMENT OF THE ENVIRONMENT AND CONSERVATION. REPORT. 1974. irreg. Aus.$2.25. Department of the Environment and Conservation, Canberra, A.C.T. 2600, Australia.

614.7   UK   ISSN 0459-7400
BARTLETT SOCIETY. TRANSACTIONS.* 1962-63. a (approx.) £1. University of London, School of Environmental Studies, Gower St., London WC1E 6BT, England.

BEITRAEGE ZUR GEOGRAPHIE. see *GEOGRAPHY*

614.7   GW   ISSN 0340-9716
BEITRAEGE ZUR UMWELTGESTALTUNG. REIHE A. irreg. price varies. Erich Schmidt Verlag (Berlin), Genthiner Str. 30G, 1000 Berlin 30, W. Germany (B.R.D.)

614.7   GW   ISSN 0340-949X
BEITRAEGE ZUR UMWELTGESTALTUNG. REIHE B. irreg. price varies. Erich Schmidt Verlag(Berlin), Genthiner Str. 30G, 1000 Berlin 30, W. Germany(B.R.D.)

614.7 910   NE
BIOGEOGRAPHICA. 1973. irreg., vol. 18, 1980. price varies. Dr. W. Junk Publishers, Box 13713, 2501 ES The Hague, Netherlands. Ed. J. Schmithuesen. circ. 1,000.

614.7   AT
BOTANY BAY PROJECT. WORKING PAPER. no. 3, 1977. irreg. Australian National University Press, Box 4, Canberry City, A.C.T., Australia. Ed. N. G. Butlin.

BRADWELL ABBEY FIELD CENTRE FOR THE STUDY OF ARCHAEOLOGY, NATURAL HISTORY & ENVIRONMENTAL STUDIES. OCCASIONAL PAPERS. see *SCIENCES: COMPREHENSIVE WORKS*

BRITISH COLUMBIA. MINISTRY OF THE ENVIRONMENT. NORTHEAST COAL STUDY PRELIMINARY ENVIRONMENTAL REPORT. see *MINES AND MINING INDUSTRY*

614.7   CN
BRITISH COLUMBIA. MINISTRY OF THE ENVIRONMENT. ANNUAL REPORT. a. Ministry of the Environment, Provincial Parliament Bldgs., Victoria, B.C. V8V 1X5, Canada. charts. illus.

614.7   US
C. C. FURNAS MEMORIAL CONFERENCE PROCEEDINGS. 1972. irreg., vol. 5, 1977. Marcel Dekker, Inc., 270 Madison Ave., New York, NY 10016. Ed. J. Szekely.

628.53   US   ISSN 0068-5496
CALIFORNIA. AIR RESOURCES BOARD. ANNUAL REPORT. a. free. ‡ Air Resources Board, Box 2815, Sacramento, CA 95812.

614.7   US
CALIFORNIA. AIR RESOURCES BOARD. FACT SHEETS. 1972. irreg. free. Air Resources Board, Information Office, Box 2815, Sacramento, CA 95812.

614.7   US
CALIFORNIA AIR BASINS. 1969. irreg. free. ‡ Air Resources Board, Box 2815, Sacramento, CA 95812. charts. illus. stat. (processed)

614.71   US   ISSN 0008-0861
CALIFORNIA AIR ENVIRONMENT. 1969. irreg. free. Statewide Air Pollution Research Center, University of California, Riverside, CA 92521. Ed. Marian C. Carpelan. bibl. charts. circ. 3,500.

301.31   US   ISSN 0148-0324
CALIFORNIA ENVIRONMENTAL DIRECTORY; a guide to organization and resources. 1973. irreg., 3rd edt. 1980. $18.50. California Institute of Public Affairs, Box 10, Claremont, CA 91711. (Affiliate: Claremont Colleges) illus. index. circ. 1,000(approx.)
Formerly: California Enviromental Yearbook & Directory (ISSN 0092-1343)

363.6   CN   ISSN 0381-2995
CANADA. AIR POLLUTION CONTROL DIRECTORATE. ANNUAL SUMMARY: NATIONAL AIR POLLUTION SURVEILLANCE. (Subseries of: Canada. Environmental Protection Service. Surveillance Report - Environmental Protection Service) (Text in English and French) 1970. a. Air Pollution Control Directorate, Ottawa, Ont. K1A 1C8, Canada. illus. circ. 600. (also avail. in microfiche)

354.7 614.7   CN
CANADA. ANTI-DUMPING TRIBUNAL. ANNUAL REPORT. (Text in English and French) a. Ottawa, Ont. K1A 0S9, Canada.

333.7   CN   ISSN 0381-2146
CANADA. ENVIRONMENTAL PROTECTION SERVICE. CANADA-ONTARIO AGREEMENT RESEARCH REPORT. (Text in English and French) 1972. irreg. Environmental Protection Service, 135 St. Clair Ave. West, Ottawa, Ont. M4V 1P5, Canada. abstr. bibl. illus.

363.6   CN
CANADA. FISHERIES AND ENVIRONMENT CANADA. OCCASIONAL PAPER. (Text in English and French) 1975. irreg. Fisheries and Environment Canada, Ottawa, Canada.

550   CN
CANADIAN ENVIRONMENTAL ADVISORY COUNCIL. ANNUAL REVIEW. a. Canadian Environmental Advisory Council, Ottawa, Ont. K1A OH3, Canada.

550   CN
CANADIAN ENVIRONMENTAL ADVISORY COUNCIL. REPORTS. irreg. Canadian Environmental Advisory Council, Ottawa K1A 0H3, Canada.

614.772 628   CN   ISSN 0576-6176
CANADIAN SYMPOSIUM ON WATER POLLUTION RESEARCH. WATER POLLUTION RESEARCH IN CANADA. PROCEEDINGS. 1968. a. price varies. University of Toronto, Institute for Environmental Studies, Publications and Information, Toronto, Ont. M5S 1A4, Canada.

CAPE OF GOOD HOPE. DEPARTMENT OF NATURE CONSERVATION AND MUSEUM SERVICES. ANNUAL REPORT. see *CONSERVATION*

CENTRE ECONOMIE, ESPACE, ENVIRONNEMENT. CAHIERS. see *BUSINESS AND ECONOMICS*

711   UK   ISSN 0069-1917
CENTRE FOR ENVIRONMENTAL STUDIES, LONDON. CONFERENCE PAPER. irreg. Centre for Environmental Studies, 62 Chandos Place, London WC2N 4HH, England.

711   UK
CENTRE FOR ENVIRONMENTAL STUDIES, LONDON. OCCASIONAL PAPER. irreg. price varies. Centre for Environmental Studies, 62 Chandos Place, London WC2N 4HH, England.

CHALMERS TEKNISKA HOGSKOLA. INSTITUTIONEN FOER VATTENFOERSOERJNINGS OCH AVLOPPSTEKNIK. PUBLIKATIONSSERIE B; Current reports on research in water supply and sewage disposal. see *WATER RESOURCES*

614.7   US
CHESAPEAKE BAY JOURNAL. a. Chesapeake Bay Foundation, 162 Prince George St., Annapolis, MD 21401.

CHILDHOOD CITY NEWSLETTER. see *PSYCHOLOGY*

614.71   UK   ISSN 0301-9039
CLEAN AIR CONFERENCE (GT. BRIT.) a. £6. National Society for Clean Air, 136 North St., Brighton, Sussex BN1 1RG, England.

614.7   US
COASTAL NOTES. 1976. irreg. price varies. Rutgers University, Center for Coastal & Environmental Studies, Doolittle Hall, Box 1179, Piscataway, NJ 08854. (Co-sponsor: New Jersey Department of Environmental Protection. Division of Coastal Resources) circ. 300.

COMPANHIA ESTADUAL DE TECNOLOGIA DE SANEAMENTO BASICO E DE DEFESA DO MEIO AMBIENTE. DIRECTORIA RELATORIA ANUAL. see *PUBLIC HEALTH AND SAFETY*

614.7 US
CONFERENCE ON PREVENTION AND
CONTROL OF OIL SPILLS. PROCEEDINGS.
Variant title: A P I Joint Conference on Prevention
and Control of Oil Spills. Proceedings. Oil Spill
Conference(Prevention, Behavior, Control, Cleanup)
1969. biennial. $10-25. ‡ American Petroleum
Institute, 2101 L St. N.W., Washington, DC 20037.
(Co-sponsors: Environmental Protection Agency;
U.S. Coast Guard) Ed. Bd. bibl. charts. illus.

614 US ISSN 0069-8741
CONFERENCE ON TRACE SUBSTANCES IN
ENVIRONMENTAL HEALTH. PROCEEDINGS.
1967. a. $20 price varies. ‡ University of Missouri-
Columbia, Environmental Health Center and
Extension Division, 206 Whitten Hall, Columbia,
MO 65201. Ed. Delbert D. Hemphill. index. circ.
2,000.

363.6 US ISSN 0095-4624
CONNECTICUT. COUNCIL ON
ENVIRONMENTAL QUALITY. ANNUAL
REPORT. a.; none published 1977. Council on
Environmental Quality, State Office Bldg., Hartford,
CT 06115. Key Title: Annual Report - State of
Connecticut, Council on Environmental Quality.

628 614.7 US ISSN 0065-4604
CORNELL AGRICULTURAL WASTE
MANAGEMENT CONFERENCE.
PROCEEDINGS. price varies. New York State
College of Agriculture and Life Sciences, Cornell
University, Ithaca, NY 14853. (Co-sponsors: U.S.
Environmental Protection Agency, National Waste
Treatment Research Program; National Canners
Association)
Formerly: Cornell University Conference on
Agricultural Waste Management.

614.7 US
CORVALLIS ENVIRONMENTAL RESEARCH
LABORATORY. RESEARCH HIGHLIGHTS.
1973. irreg. Corvallis Environmental Research
Laboratory, 200 S.W. 35 St., Corvallis, OR 97330.
bibl. circ. 2,000. (processed)
Formerly: Coastal Pollution Research Highlights.

CURRENT TOPICS IN ENVIRONMENTAL AND
TOXICOLOGICAL CHEMISTRY. see
CHEMISTRY

747 UK ISSN 0306-6185
D I A YEARBOOK - DESIGN ACTION. 1916. a.
£1. Design and Industries Association, Nash House,
12 Carlton House Terrace, London, SW1, England.
Ed. Raymond Plummer. circ. 2,000.
Formerly: Design and Industries Association.
Year Book and Membership List (ISSN 0070-3834)

614.7 GW
DATEN UND DOKUMENTE ZUM
UMWELTSCHUTZ/DATA AND DOCUMENTS
ABOUT ENVIRONMENT PROTECTION. 1972.
irreg. price varies. Universitaet Hohenheim,
Dokumentationsstelle, Paracelsusstr. 2, Postfach
106, 7000 Stuttgart 70, W. Germany (B.R.D.) Ed.
H.-J. Friede. abstr. bibl. circ. 130-650. Indexed:
Nutr.Abstr.

333.7 US ISSN 0084-9642
DELAWARE. DEPARTMENT OF NATURAL
RESOURCES AND ENVIRONMENTAL
CONTROL. ANNUAL REPORT. 1970. a. free.
Department of Natural Resources and
Environmental Control, Dover, DE 19901. Ed.
Michael Bickler. circ. 100.

363.6 US
DIRECTORY OF GOVERNMENTAL AIR
POLLUTION AGENCIES. a. $2.50. Air Pollution
Control Association, 4400 5th Ave., Pittsburgh, PA
15213.
Formerly: A.P.C.A. Directory and Resource Book
(ISSN 0094-9191); Continues: A P C A Directory.

628 333.7 US ISSN 0084-9987
DIRECTORY OF NATIONAL ORGANIZATIONS
CONCERNED WITH LAND POLLUTION
CONTROL. 1970. a. $18. Freed Publishing Co.,
Box 1144, FDR Station, New York, NY 10022. Ed.
Laura E. Freed.

DIRECTORY OF OFFICIAL ARCHITECTURE
AND PLANNING. see ARCHITECTURE

614.7 US
DIRECTORY OF STATE AGENCIES
CONCERNED WITH LAND POLLUTION
CONTROL. 1971. biennial. $12. Freed Publishing
Co., Box 1144 FDR Station, New York, NY 10022.
Ed. Laura E. Freed.

333.9 FR ISSN 0419-3865
DIRECTORY OF WATER POLLUTION
RESEARCH LABORATORIES. irreg. Organization
for Economic Cooperation and Development,
Central Service for International Cooperation in
Scientific Research, 2, rue Andre- Pascal, 75775
Paris 16, France (U. S. orders to: O.E.C.D.
Publications and Information Center, 1750
Pennsylvania Ave., N.W., Washington, D. C.
20006) (also avail. in microfiche)

614.7 US
DISCUSSIONS IN ENVIRONMENTAL HEALTH
PLANNING. 1977? irreg., latest 1980. Cornell
University, Program in Urban and Regional Studies,
209 W. Sibley Hall, Ithaca, NY 14853. (Co-sponsor:
Cornell University Department of City and Regional
Planning, Environmental Health Training Program)

620.8 US
DISTRICT OF COLUMBIA. AIR MONITORING
DIVISION. ANNUAL REPORT ON THE
QUALITY OF THE AIR IN WASHINGTON, D.
C. a. free. Department of Environmental Services,
Air Monitoring Division, 5010 Overlook Ave., S.W.,
Washington, DC 20032.

614 CL
DOCUMENTOS TALLER MULTIDISCIPLINARIO
DEL MEDIO AMBIENTE. 1978. a. free.
Universidad Catolica de Valparaiso, Vicerrectoria
Academica Direccion General de Investigacion,
Casilla 4059, Valparaiso, Chile. Ed.Bd. abstr. circ.
1,000.

614.7 US ISSN 0161-8490
E P A ACTIVITIES UNDER THE RESOURCE
CONSERVATION AND RECOVERY ACT OF
1976; annual report to the President and Congress.
1977. a. U.S. Environmental Protection Agency,
1401 M St., N.W., Washington, DC 20460.

614.7 US
E P A RESEARCH REVIEW. 1977. a. free. U.S.
Environmental Protection Agency, Gulf Breeze
Environmental Research Laboratory, Sabine Island,
Gulf Breeze, FL 32561. Ed. Betty P. Jackson. circ.
1,000.

EARTH AND YOU; vehicle of current ideas for
modern men. see LITERARY AND POLITICAL
REVIEWS

ENERGY, POWER, AND ENVIRONMENT; a
series of reference books and textbooks. see
ENERGY

614.7 US
ENFO. 1971. irreg., 6 or more per yr. $12 to
individuals; institutions $25. (Florida Conservation
Foundation) Environmental Information Center of
Florida, 935 Orange Ave., Winter Park, FL 32789.
Ed. William R. Barada. circ. 1,200.

ENVIROFACTS. see PACKAGING

614.7 TR
ENVIRON; patterns of progress in the Caribbean.
1977. a. $6.50. Key Caribbean, 1 El Socorro
Extension Rd., Kirpalani's Complex, San Juan,
Trinidad (Subscr. to: P.O. Box 21, Port of Spain,
Trinidad) Ed. Roy Boyke. circ. 5,000. (back issues
avail)

614.7 US ISSN 0090-0486
ENVIRONMENT FILM REVIEW; a critical guide to
ecology films. 1972. irreg. $20. Environment
Information Center Inc., 292 Madison Ave., New
York, NY 10017. film rev. index.

614.7 CN ISSN 0381-646X
ENVIRONMENT PROBE. 1975. q. Can.$5
membership. Saskatoon Environmental Society, Box
1372, Saskatoon, Sask. S7K 3N9, Canada. Ed.
Warren Steck. adv. bk. rev. illus. circ. 1,000.
Formerly: Probe (ISSN 0316-0033)

614.7 917.9 US
ENVIRONMENTAL ASSESSMENT OF THE
ALASKAN CONTINENTAL SHELF. ANNUAL
REPORTS SUMMARY. a. U.S. National Oceanic
and Atmospheric Administration, Environmental
Research Laboratories, 6010 Executive Blvd.,
Rockville, MD 20852. (Co-sponsor: U.S. Bureau of
Land Management)

ENVIRONMENTAL CHEMISTRY; specialist
periodical reports. see CHEMISTRY

301.31 US ISSN 0091-9837
ENVIRONMENTAL DEFENSE FUND. ANNUAL
REPORT. a. membership. Environmental Defense
Fund, 475 Park Ave. S., New York, NY 10016.
illus.

ENVIRONMENTAL DESIGN PERSPECTIVES;
viewpoints on the profession, education and
research. see ARCHITECTURE

614.7 US ISSN 0071-089X
ENVIRONMENTAL HEALTH SERIES: AIR
POLLUTION.* irreg. U.S. Public Health Service,
5600 Fishers Lane, Rockville, MD 10852.

614.7 333.7 US
ENVIRONMENTAL HOTLINE. m. (sometimes
more) $10. Ohio Environmental Council, Inc., 850
Michigan Ave., Columbus, OH 43215. Ed. Steve
Sedam. circ. 400. (tabloid format; back issues avail.)

026.3636 614.7 US ISSN 0094-3231
ENVIRONMENTAL INFORMATION SYSTEMS
DIRECTORY. a. $0.95 per no. U.S. Environmental
Protection Agency, Room 3101, 401 M St., S.W.,
Washington, DC 20460.

614.7 AT
ENVIRONMENTAL LAW REFORM GROUP.
PUBLICATION. no. 2, 1972. irreg. Environmental
Law Reform Group, c/o Dr. R.J. K. Chapman,
Dept. of Political Science, University of Tasmania,
Box 252c, Hobart, Tas. 7001, Australia. circ. 500.

614.7 333.7 US
ENVIRONMENTAL LEGISLATIVE BULLETIN.
irreg. $5. Ohio Environmental Council, Inc., 850
Michigan Ave., Columbus, OH 43215. Ed. Steve
Sedam. (looseleaf format; back issues avail.)

574.5 CN ISSN 0316-0661
ENVIRONMENTAL MANAGEMENT FOR THE
PUBLIC HEALTH INSPECTOR. 1961. a. Can.$5.
Dalhousie University, Institute of Public Affairs,
Halifax, N.S. B3H 3J5, Canada. (Co-sponsors:
Departments of Health-Nova Scotia-New
Brunswick-Prince Edward Island-Newfoundland)
circ. 300.
Formerly: Environmental Hygiene for the Public
Health Inspector (ISSN 0071-092X)

333.7 SZ
ENVIRONMENTAL POLICY AND LAW PAPERS.
1972. irreg.(2-3/yr.); no. 12, 1976. price varies.
International Union for Conservation of Nature and
Natural Resources, 1110 Morges, Switzerland (Dist.
in U.S. by: Unipub, Inc., 345 Park Ave. S., New
York, NY 10010) Ed. Sir Hugh Elliott. circ. 1,000.
Formerly: Environmental Law Papers.

614.7 US
ENVIRONMENTAL PROTECTION DIRECTORY.
1973. irreg., 2nd 1975. $46.50. Marquis Academic
Media (Subsidiary of: Marquis Who's Who, Inc.)
200 E. Ohio St., Chicago, IL 60611.
Supersedes in part: Directory of Consumer
Protection and Environmental Agencies.

614.7 UK
ENVIRONMENTAL PROTECTION SURVEY. irreg.
£2. Process Engineering, 30 Calderwood St.,
London SE18 6QH, England. illus.

363.6 US ISSN 0509-769X
ENVIRONMENTAL RADIATION
SURVEILLANCE IN WASHINGTON STATE;
ANNUAL REPORT. a. Department of Social and
Health Services, Health Services Division, Box 1788
Olympia Airport, Olympia, WA 98504. illus.

614.7 SW
ENVIRONMENTAL RESEARCH. (Biennial English edt. ceased in 1975) 1972. a. price varies. Statens Naturvaardsverk - National Environment Protection Board, Fack, S-171 20 Solna 1, Sweden (Dist. by: Liber Foerlag, Fack, S-162 89 Vaellingby, Sweden) Ed. Eva Ahnland.

614.7 628.5 US
ENVIRONMENTAL SCIENCE AND TECHNOLOGY: A WILEY-INTERSCIENCE SERIES OF TEXTS AND MONOGRAPHS. 1969. irreg., unnumbered, latest vol., 1976. price varies. John Wiley & Sons, Inc., 605 Third Ave., New York, NY 10016. Ed. Bd.

614.7 US
ENVIRONMENTAL SCIENCE SERIES. 1972. irreg. Elsevier North-Holland, Inc., New York, 52 Vanderbilt Ave., New York, NY 10017. Ed. A. K. Biswas.

614.7 US
ENVIRONMENTAL SCIENCES AND APPLICATIONS. 1977. irreg., vol. 9, 1980. price varies. Pergamon Press, Inc., Maxwell House, Fairview Park, Elmsford, NY 10523 (And Headington Hill Hall, Oxford OX3 0BW, England)

614.7 CN
ENVIRONNEMENT. 1973. irreg. Can.$5. Societe pour Vainore la Pollution, B.P. 65, Place d'Armes, Montreal, Que., Canada. circ. 5,000.
Formerly: Bulletin - S V P (ISSN 0382-5302); Supersedes: Societe pour Vaincre la Pollution. Bulletin de Liaison (ISSN 0382-5310)

614.71 FR ISSN 0071-1942
ETUDES DE POLLUTION ATMOSPHERIQUE A PARIS ET DANS LES DEPARTMENTS PERIPHERIQUES. 1964. a. free. Prefecture de Police, Laboratoire Central, 39 bis rue de Dantzig, Paris 15e, France.

614.7 US ISSN 0272-4626
EUROPEAN APPLIED RESEARCH REPORTS; a journal of European science and technology. irreg. $89.50 per volume. Harwood Academic Publishers GmbH, Box 786 Cooper Station, New York, Ny 10276. (Co-sponsor: Commission of the European Communities)

614.7 UK ISSN 0428-304X
FIELD STUDIES. 1959. a. £8 to non-members. Field Studies Council, 62 Wilson St., London EC2A 4HT, England. Ed. J. H. Crothers. bibl. cum.index every 5th year. circ. 2,000(approx.)

363.6 FR
FRANCE. MINISTERE DE LA CULTURE ET DE L'ENVIRONNEMENT. BILAN D'ACTIVITE DES AGENCES FINANCIERES DE BASSIN. irreg. Ministere de la Culture et de l'Environnement, Service de l'Information des Relations et de l'Action Educative, 3 rue de Valois, 75042 Paris, France. illus.

614.7 AG
FUNDACION BARILOCHE. GRUPO DE ANALISIS DE SISTEMAS ECOLOGICOS. PUBLICACIONES. irreg. price varies. Fundacion Bariloche, Grupo de Analisis de Sistemas Ecologicos, Casilla de Correo 138, 8400 San Carlos de Bariloche - Rio Negro, Argentina.
Supersedes in part: Fundacion Bariloche. Departamento de Recursos Naturales y Energia. Publicaciones.

GEOECOLOGICAL RESEARCH. see EARTH SCIENCES

614.7 UK
GOLDEN LIST OF BEACHES; believed to be free from sewage pollution. 1960. quinquennial. £2. Coastal Anti-Pollution League, Alverstoke, Greenway Lane, Bath, Somerset, England. Ed. J. Wakefield. circ. 2,000.

614.77 UK ISSN 0072-5803
GREAT BRITAIN. DEPARTMENT OF THE ENVIRONMENT. COMMITTEE ON SYNTHETIC DETERGENTS. PROGRESS REPORT. 1956. a. price varies. Department of the Environment, Committee on Synthetic Detergents, 2 Marsham St., London SW1P 3EB, England (Avail. from H.M.S.O., c/o Liaison Officer, Atlantic House, Holborn Viaduct, London EC1P 1BN, England)

301.31 UK
GREAT BRITAIN. DEPARTMENT OF THE ENVIRONMENT. REPORT ON RESEARCH AND DEVELOPMENT. 1973. a. price varies. ‡ Department of the Environment, 2 Marsham St., London SW1P 3EB, England (Avail. from H.M.S.O., c/o Liaison Officer, Atlantic House, Holborn Viaduuct, London EC1P 1BN, England)

628.5 UK ISSN 0141-3279
GREAT BRITAIN. WARREN SPRING LABORATORY. ANNUAL REVIEW. a. free. Warren Spring Laboratory, P.O. Box 20, Gunnels Wood Rd., Stevenage, Herts SG1 2BX, England.

628.5 UK ISSN 0585-2730
GREAT BRITAIN. WARREN SPRING LABORATORY. INVESTIGATION OF AIR POLLUTION: NATIONAL SURVEY, SMOKE AND SULPHUR DIOXIDE. Short title: National Survey, Smoke and Sulphur Dioxide. a. price varies. Warren Spring Laboratory, P.O. Box 20, Gunnels Wood Rd., Stevenage, Herts. SG1 2BX, England.

GREEN PAGES: DIRECTORY OF NON-GOVERNMENT ENVIRONMENTAL GROUPS IN AUSTRALIA. see CONSERVATION

GREENLAND BIOSCIENCES. see BIOLOGY

614.7 JA
HOKKAIDO RESEARCH INSTITUTE FOR ENVIRONMENTAL POLLUTION. REPORT/ HOKKAIDO KOGAI BOSHI KENKYUJO HO. (Text in Japanese; summaries in English or Japanese.) 1975. irreg. Hokkaido Research Institute for Environmental Pollution - Hokkaido Kogai Boshi Kenkyujo., Nishi 12-chome, Kita 19-Jo, Kita-ku, Sapporo 060, Japan. illus.

574.5 NE
I T C-U N E S C O INTERNATIONAL SEMINAR. PROCEEDINGS. 1966. a.; latest 1974. price varies. International Institute for Aerial Survey and Earth Sciences, P.O. Box 6, Enschede, Netherlands.
Former titles: International Seminar on Integrated Surveys. Proceedings & Seminar on Integrated Surveys of Environment. Proceedings (ISSN 0080-8830)

614.7 US
IDAHO ENVIRONMENTAL OVERVIEW. irreg. Department of Water Resources, 1365 N. Orchard St., Boise, ID 83720. bibl. charts. illus.

614.7 US
ILLINOIS. DIVISION OF AIR POLLUTION CONTROL. ANNUAL AIR QUALITY REPORT. 1968. a. free. Environmental Protection Agency, Division of Air Pollution Control, Ambient Air Monitoring Section, 2200 Churchill Rd., Springfield, IL 62706. circ. 1,500.
Former titles, until 1975: Illinois Air Quality Report (ISSN 0360-9162); Incorporating: Illinois. Division of Air Pollution Control. Semi-Annual Report; Until 1974: Illinois Air Sampling Network Report (ISSN 0092-3281)

363.6 US ISSN 0362-8795
ILLINOIS. ENVIRONMENTAL PROTECTION AGENCY. OPERATOR CERTIFICATION SECTION. DIGESTER; to promote optimum operation and maintenance of every waste water treatment facility in Illinois. vol. 28, 1974. irreg. Environmental Protection Agency, Operator Certification Section, 2200 Churchill Rd., Springfield, IL 62706. illus.
Continues: Illinois. Department of Public Health. Digester.

363.6 US ISSN 0091-4541
ILLINOIS. ENVIRONMENTAL PROTECTION AGENCY. WATER POLLUTION CONTROL PLAN. irreg. free. Environmental Protection Agency, Division of Water Pollution Control, 2200 Churchill Rd., Springfield, IL 62706. Key Title: Water Pollution Control Plan (Springfield)

333.7 US ISSN 0090-8967
ILLINOIS INSTITUTE FOR ENVIRONMENTAL QUALITY. ANNUAL REPORT. 1972. a. free. Illinois Institute for Environmental Quality, 309 West Washington, Chicago, IL 60606. illus. Key Title: Annual Report - Illinois Institute for Environmental Quality.

628.168 US ISSN 0073-5450
ILLINOIS WATER QUALITY NETWORK. SUMMARY OF DATA. 1965. a. free. Environmental Protection Agency, Division of Water Pollution Control, 2200 Churchill Rd., Springfield, IL 62706. Ed. Ronald Barganz. circ. 350. (also avail. in microfiche)

614.7 NE
IMG-TNO RESEARCH INSTITUTE FOR ENVIRONMENTAL HYGIENE. ANNUAL REPORT. (Text in English) 1942. biennial. IMG-TNO Research Institute for Environmental Hygiene, Box 214, Schoemakerstraat 97, Delft, Netherlands. bibl. charts. illus. circ. 1,200.
Formerly: IG-TNO Research Institute for Environmental Hygiene. Annual Report.

614.7 UK
INDEX OF CURRENT GOVERNMENT AND GOVERNMENTAL-SUPPORTED RESEARCH IN ENVIRONMENTAL POLLUTION IN GREAT BRITAIN. irreg. Department of the Environment, Headquarters Library, Research Section, 2 Marsham St., London SW1P 3EB, England (Avail. from H.M.S.O., c/o Liaison Officer, Atlantic House, Holborn Viaduct, London EC1P 1BN, England)

333.7 US ISSN 0094-5749
INDIANA. ENVIRONMENTAL MANAGEMENT BOARD. ANNUAL REPORT. 1973. free. Environmental Management Board, 1330 W. Michigan St., Indianapolis, IN 46206.

333 350 US
INDIANA UNIVERSITY. SCHOOL OF PUBLIC AND ENVIRONMENTAL AFFAIRS. OCCASIONAL PAPERS. 1972. irreg., no. 5, 1976. $3. Indiana University, School of Public and Environmental Affairs, 400 E. Seventh, Bloomington, IN 47401. Ed. Richard S. Howe. circ. controlled. (back issues avail.)

614.76 628.168 US ISSN 0073-7682
INDUSTRIAL WASTE CONFERENCE, PURDUE UNIVERSITY, LAFAYETTE, INDIANA. PROCEEDINGS. 1944. a. $39.95. Purdue University, School of Civil Engineering, West Lafayette, IN 47907 (Distr. by: Ann Arbor Science Publishers, Inc., Ann Arbor, MI 48106) Ed. John M. Bell.

574.5 US ISSN 0073-9227
INSTITUTE OF ENVIRONMENTAL SCIENCES. ANNUAL MEETING. PROCEEDINGS. 1960. a. $25. Institute of Environmental Sciences, 940 E. Northwest Hwy., Mt. Prospect, IL 60056. Ed. B.L. Peterson.
Ecology

574.5 US ISSN 0073-9251
INSTITUTE OF ENVIRONMENTAL SCIENCES. TUTORIAL SERIES. irreg. price varies. Institute of Environmental Sciences, 940 E. Northwest Hwy., Mt. Prospect, IL 60056.
Ecology

614 US
INTERNATIONAL BANFF CONFERENCE ON MAN AND HIS ENVIRONMENT. PROCEEDINGS. Short title: Man and His Environment. 2nd, 1974. irreg. Pergamon Press, Inc., Maxwell House, Fairview Park, Elmsford, NY 10523 (And Headington Hill Hall, Oxford OX3 0BW, England) Ed. M. F. Mohtadi.

614.71 US ISSN 0085-2090
INTERNATIONAL CLEAN AIR CONGRESS. PROCEEDINGS. 1966, 1st, London. irreg., 1970, 2nd, Washington, D.C. (International Union of Air Pollution Prevention Associations) Academic Press, Inc., 111 Fifth Ave., New York, NY 10013 (Inquire: the Union, c/o Air Pollution Control Association, 4400 Fifth Ave., Pittsburgh, Pa. 15213) Ed. Harold M. Englund.
Proceedings published in host country

614.7 US
INTERNATIONAL CONFERENCE ON THE ENVIRONMENTAL IMPACT OF AEROSPACE OPERATIONS IN THE HIGH ATMOSPHERE. (PROCEEDINGS) 1973. irreg., 2nd, 1974, San Diego. $20. American Meteorological Society, 45 Beacon St., Boston, MA 02108. (Co-sponsor: American Institute of Aeronautics and Astronautics)

ENVIRONMENTAL STUDIES

614.7 US
INTERNATIONAL CONFERENCE ON WATER POLLUTION RESEARCH. PROCEEDINGS. vol. 6, 1973. irreg. Pergamon Press, Inc., Maxwell House, Fairview Park, Elmsford, NY 10523.

INTERSTATE COMMISSION ON THE POTOMAC RIVER BASIN. PROCEEDINGS. see *WATER RESOURCES*

628.168 US
INTERSTATE COMMISSION ON THE POTOMAC RIVER BASIN. TECHNICAL REPORTS. 1977. irreg. Interstate Commission on the Potomac River Basin, 1055 First St., Rockville, MD 20850.
Supersedes: Interstate Commission on the Potomac River Basin. Technical Bulletin (ISSN 0074-9966)

628 IS ISSN 0334-3162
ISRAEL. ENVIRONMENTAL PROTECTION AGENCY. EKHUT HA-SEVIVAH BE-YISRAEL. DUAKH SHNATI. (Text in Hebrew) 1973. a. Environmental Protection Agency, Ministry of the Interior, Box 6158, Jerusalem, Israel. Ed. Shalom K. Eilati. circ. 3,500.

JOURNAL OF FRESHWATER. see *WATER RESOURCES*

551.48 614.7 US ISSN 0380-1330
JOURNAL OF GREAT LAKES RESEARCH. 1975. a. $15. International Association for Great Lakes Research, 1300 Elmwood Ave., Buffalo, NY 14222 (Subscr. to: T. M. Dick, NWRI/CCIW, Box 5050, Burlington, Ont. L7R 4A6, Canada) Ed. Dr. James R. Kramer. circ. 1,000. (also avail. in microfilm from UMI) Indexed: Pollut.Abstr. Meteor. & Geoastrophys.Abstr.
Supersedes: Conference on Great Lakes Research. Proceedings (ISSN 0045-8058)

333.77 CN ISSN 0381-0984
JOURNAL OF NATURAL RESOURCE MANAGEMENT AND INTERDISCIPLINARY STUDIES. vol. 2, 1977. a. Can.$6. Natural Resource Institute, University of Manitoba, 177 Dysant Rd., Winnipeg, Man. R3T 2N2, Canada. Ed. Paul E. Nickel.

JOURNAL OF THE NEW ALCHEMISTS. see *TECHNOLOGY: COMPREHENSIVE WORKS*

614.7 US
KANSAS. ADVISORY COUNCIL ON ECOLOGY. ANNUAL REPORT. 1970. a. free. ‡ Advisory Council on Ecology, Room 459 W, State Office Bldg., Topeka, KS 66612. Ed. Dr. Richard D. Davis. circ. 1,500. (processed)

614.7 II
KERALA (INDIA). BOARD FOR PREVENTION AND CONTROL OF WATER POLLUTION. ANNUAL REPORT. (Text in English) a. Board for Prevention and Control of Water Pollution, Trivandrum 685001, India. stat.

DIE KUESTE; Archiv fuer Forschung und Technik an der Nord- und Ostsee. see *EARTH SCIENCES — Oceanography*

614.7 US ISSN 0094-6311
LAKE MICHIGAN SHORE AND OPEN WATER REPORT. irreg. Environmental Protection Agency, Springfield, IL 62706. illus.

551.4 614.7 US ISSN 0361-8188
LAKE MICHIGAN WATER QUALITY REPORT. a. Environmental Protection Agency, 2200 Churchill Road, Springfield, MI 62706. Indexed: Chem. Abstr.

340 574.5 US
LAND USE AND ENVIRONMENT LAW REVIEW. 1970. a. $45. Clark Boardman Co., Ltd, 435 Hudson St., New York, NY 10014. Ed. Frederic Strom. index. circ. 1,400.
Formerly: Environment Law Review (ISSN 0071-0830)

614.7 GW ISSN 0340-4900
LITERATURBERICHTE UEBER WASSER, ABWASSER, LUFT UND FESTE ABFALLSTOFFE. irreg. DM.175 per vol. (4 issues) Gustav Fischer Verlag, Wollgrasweg 49, Postfach 720143, 7000 Stuttgart 70, W. Germany (B.R.D.)

333.9 AU
LUDWIG BOLTZMANN-INSTITUT FUER UMWELTWISSENSCHAFTEN UND NATURSCHUTZ. MITTEILUNGEN. 1975. irreg. Ludwig Boltzmann-Institut fuer Umweltwissenschaften und Naturschutz, Peinrichstr. 5, A-8010 Graz, Austria.

614.7 GW ISSN 0460-2374
LUFTVERUNREINIGUNG. 1973. a. DM.7. Deutscher Kommunal-Verlag GmbH, Roseggerstr. 5a, 4000 Duesseldorf 30, W. Germany (B. R. D.) Ed. H-J. Schumacher. adv. bk. rev. charts. illus.

614.7 333.77 US
MAN-ENVIRONMENT SYSTEMS/FOCUS SERIES. price varies. Association for the Study of Man-Environment Relations, P.O. Box 57, Orangeburg, NY 10962.

354 CN ISSN 0380-9803
MANITOBA. ENVIRONMENTAL COUNCIL. ANNUAL REPORT. 1973. a. free. Environmental Council, Box 139, 139 Tuxedo Avenue, Winnipig, Man. R3N 0H6, Canada. Ed. J. J. Keleher. illus. circ. 900. (also avail. in microfiche from MML)

354 CN ISSN 0380-979X
MANITOBA. ENVIRONMENTAL COUNCIL. STUDIES. 1973. irreg. free. Environmental Council, Box 139, 139 Tuxedo Ave., Winnipeg, Man. R3N 0H6, Canada. illus. circ. 1,000. (also avail. in microform from MML)

363.6 US
MARYLAND AIR QUALITY PROGRAMS. DATA REPORT. Cover title: Maryland Air Quality Data Report. 1971. a. free. Air Quality Programs, 201 W. Preston St., Baltimore, MD 21201. Ed. Douglas Proctor. illus.
Former titles: Maryland. Bureau of Air Quality and Noise Control. Data Report; Until 1977: Maryland. Bureau of Air Quality Control. State-Local Cooperative Air Sampling Program Yearly Data Report (ISSN 0094-4629)

301.3 CL
MEDIO AMBIENTE. (Text in Spanish; summaries in English) 1975. irreg. Universidad Austral de Chile, Instituto de Ecologia y Evolucion, Casilla 567, Valdivia, Chile.

614.7 SP
MEDIO AMBIENTE EN ESPANA. vol. 2, 1978. irreg. Ministerio de Obras Publicas y Urbanismo, Servicio de Publicaciones, Avda. del Generalisimo 3, Madrid 3, Spain.

614.7 NE
MENS EN MILIEU. irreg., no. 2, 1977. price varies. Van Gorcum, Box 43, Assen, Netherlands. Ed. Bd.

628 US ISSN 0544-0327
MID-ATLANTIC INDUSTRIAL WASTE CONFERENCE PROCEEDINGS. 1968. irreg., 8th, 1976. $10. University of Delaware, Department of Civil Engineering, John M. Clayton Hall, Newark, DE 19711. Ed. Richard I. Dick.

614 JA
MIE PREFECTURE. ENVIRONMENTAL SCIENCE INSTITUTE. ANNUAL REPORT/ MIE-KEN KOGAI SENTA NEMPO. (Text in Japanese) 1973. a. Environmental Science Institute, 8-ban 12-jo Shinjo 4-chome, Yokkaichi, Japan.

614.7 DK ISSN 0105-3094
MILJOE-PROJEKTER. 1975. irreg., no. 19, 1979. price varies. Miljoestyrelsen, Strandgade 29, 1401 Copenhagen K, Denmark (Orders to: Danske Boghendleres Kommissionsanstalt, Siljangade 6, 2300 Copenhagen S, Denmark)

301.31 US ISSN 0094-1697
MINNESOTA. GOVERNOR. ANNUAL REPORT ON THE QUALITY OF THE ENVIRONMENT. 1974. a. State Planning Agency, Environmental Planning Section, Capitol Square Building, 550 Cedar St., St. Paul, MN 55155. bibl. Key Title: Annual Report on the Quality of the Environment (St. Paul)

614.7 US ISSN 0091-0457
MONTANA. ENVIRONMENTAL QUALITY COUNCIL. ANNUAL REPORT. Cover title: Montana Environmental Indicators. vol. 4, 1975. a. Environmental Quality Council, Helena, MT 59601. charts. illus. stat.

628.1 US ISSN 0077-2178
MUNICIPAL WASTE FACILITIES IN THE U. S. irreg. $1. limited copies free. U.S. Environmental Protection Agency, 401 M St. N.W., Washington, DC 20460 (Orders to: Supt. Doc., Washington, DC 20402)

MUSIC OF THE ENVIRONMENT SERIES. see *PHYSICS — Sound*

614.7 US
N E I W P C C ANNUAL REPORT. a. New England Interstate Water Pollution Control Commission, 607 Boylston St., Boston, MA 02116. illus.

614.7 UK ISSN 0305-8336
N E R C NEWS JOURNAL. 1970. irreg. free. ‡ National Environmental Research Council, Alhambra House, 27-33 Charing Cross Rd., London WC2H 0AX, Eng. Ed. Bd. bk. rev. charts. illus.

614.71 628.53 UK ISSN 0140-6795
N. S. C. A. REFERENCE BOOK; comprehensive guide to all aspects of air pollution control. 1978. next edition Feb. 1982. National Society for Clean Air, 136 North Brighton, Sussex BN1 1RG, England. Ed. J. Dunmore. adv. index.
Former titles: N. S. C. A. Yearbook; Clean Air Year Book (ISSN 0069-4606)

614 JA
NAGOYA. ENVIRONMENTAL POLLUTION RESEARCH INSTITUTE. ANNUAL REPORT. (Text in Japanese; summaries in English) 1972. a. Environmental Pollution Research Institute, Nagoya, Japan.

NAGOYA UNIVERSITY. RESEARCH INSTITUTE OF ENVIRONMENTAL MEDICINE. ANNUAL REPORT/NAGOYA DAIGAKU KANKYO IGAKU KENKYUSHO NENPO. see *MEDICAL SCIENCES*

614.7 US
NATIONAL AIR QUALITY EMISSIONS TRENDS. REPORT. 1973. a. U.S. Environmental Protection Agency, Office of Air Quality Planning and Standards, Air Pollution Technical Information Center, Research Triangle Park, NC 27709 (Orders to: NTIS, Springfield, VA 22161) (also avail. in microfiche from NTI) Indexed: Air Pollut.Abstr.
Until 1977: National Air Monitoring Program Air Quality and Emissions Trends. Report (ISSN 0092-9670)

NATIONAL CONFERENCE ON ENERGY AND THE ENVIRONMENT. PROCEEDINGS. see *ENERGY*

628.44 US ISSN 0160-6662
NATIONAL CONFERENCE ON INDIVIDUAL ONSITE WASTEWATER SYSTEMS. PROCEEDINGS. 1974. a. (National Sanitation Foundation) Ann Arbor Science Publishers, Inc., Box 1425, Ann Arbor, MI 48106. (Co-sponsor: U.S. Environmental Protection Agency, Technology Transfer Program) Indexed: Chem.Abstr. Key Title: Individual Onsite Wastewater Systems.

301.31 CN ISSN 0316-0114
NATIONAL RESEARCH COUNCIL, CANADA. ASSOCIATE COMMITTEE ON SCIENTIFIC CRITERIA FOR ENVIRONMENTAL QUALITY. STATUS REPORT/CONSEIL NATIONAL DE RECHERCHES, CANADA, COMITE ASSOCIE SUR LES CRITERES SCIENTIFIQUES. RAPPORT D'ACTIVITE. (Text in English and French) 1972. irreg. National Research Council of Canada, Associate Committee on Scientific Criteria for Environmental Quality, Ottawa, Ont., Canada. illus.

622 JA
NATIONAL RESEARCH INSTITUTE FOR POLLUTION AND RESOURCES. ANNUAL REPORT/KOGAI SHIGEN KENKYUSHO NENPO. (Text in Japanese) 1952. a. National Research Institute for Pollution and Resources - Tsusho Sangyo-sho Kogyo Gijutsu-in Kogai Shigen Kenkyusho, 3-1-1 Kawaguchi, Kawaguchi-shi, Saitama 332, Japan. illus. circ. 1,800.
Continues: Shigen Gijutsu Shikenjo Nempo.

622 JA
NATIONAL RESEARCH INSTITUTE FOR POLLUTION AND RESOURCES. SCIENCE REPORT/KOGAI SHIGEN KENKYUSHO HOKOKU. (Text in Japanese; summaries in English) 1970. irreg. National Research Institute for Pollution and Resources - Tsusho Sangy-cho Kogyo Gijutsu-in Kogai Shigen Kenktusho, 3-1-1 Kawaguchi, Kawaguchi-shi, Saitama 332, Japan.

614.7 SP
NATURALIA HISPANICA. (Text in Spanish; summaries in English, French, German) 1974. irreg. price varies. Instituto Nacional para la Conservacion de la Naturaleza, Gran via San Francisco 35, Madrid 5, Spain. Ed. P. Ceballos. charts. illus. circ. 100. (back issues avail.) Indexed: Biol.Abstr. Chem.Abstr. Curr.Cont. Aqua.Sci. & Fish.Abstr. Wild Life Rev. Zoo.Rec.

NATURE CONSERVATION COUNCIL OF N. S. W. BULLETIN. (Nature Conservation Council of New South Wales) see CONSERVATION

353.9 US ISSN 0092-3311
NEW JERSEY. DEPARTMENT OF ENVIRONMENTAL PROTECTION. ANNUAL REPORT. 1971/72. a. free. Department of Environmental Protection, John Fitch Plaza, Trenton, NJ 08625. illus. circ. 5,000. Key Title: Annual Report - Department of Environmental Protection (Trenton)

614.71 US ISSN 0077-8451
NEW JERSEY CLEAN AIR COUNCIL. REPORT. a. Department of Environmental Protection, New Jersey Clean Air Council, John Fitch Plaza, Trenton, NJ 08625.

628 US ISSN 0362-6210
NEW YORK (STATE). ENVIRONMENTAL QUALITY RESEARCH AND DEVELOPMENT UNIT. TECHNICAL PAPER. irreg. Department of Environmental Conservation, Environmental Quality Research and Development Unit, Albany, NY 12205. illus. Key Title: Technical Paper-New York State, Department of Environmental Conservation, Environmental Quality Research and Development Unit.

NEW ZEALAND WHOLE EARTH CATALOGUE. see BUSINESS AND ECONOMICS — Trade And Industrial Directories

614.7 IT ISSN 0546-2347
NOISE AND SMOG NEWS. (Text in English, Italian) 1952. a. N.A.N.S., Belvedere Golfo Paradiso 21, 16036 Recco, Genoa, Italy. adv. circ. 18,595.
Formerly: Audiotecnica News.

NOISE REGULATION REPORTER. (Bureau of National Affairs, Inc.) see LAW

628.5 BE ISSN 0377-7669
NORTH ATLANTIC TREATY ORGANIZATION. EXPERT PANEL ON AIR POLLUTION MODELING. PROCEEDINGS. (Subseries of: Air Pollution) a. North Atlantic Treaty Organization, Committee on the Challenges of Modern Society, 1110 Brussels, Belgium.

614.7 US ISSN 0048-0746
NORTHEASTERN REGIONAL ANTIPOLLUTION CONFERENCE. PROCEEDINGS. 1970, 3rd. a. price varies. (University of Rhode Island) Technomic Publishing Co., Inc., 265 Post Rd. W., Westport, CT 06880. charts. illus. stat. Indexed: Chem.Abstr. Eng.Ind. Pollut.Abstr.

354 CN ISSN 0317-3526
NOVA SCOTIA. ENVIRONMENTAL CONTROL COUNCIL. ANNUAL REPORT. 1973. a. Environmental Control Council, Box 2107, Halifax, N.S. B3K 3B7, Canada.

614.7 CN ISSN 0704-2701
OCEAN DUMPING REPORT. (Text in English; summaries in English and French) 1978. irreg. free. Fisheries and Oceans, 240 Sparks St., 7th Floor West, Ottawa, Ont. K1A 0E6, Canada. Ed. Dr. J. Watson. bibl. illus. circ. 300. (back issues avail.)

354 CN
ONTARIO. MINISTRY OF THE ENVIRONMENT. ANNUAL REPORT. 1973. a. Can.$1. Ministry of the Environment, 135 St. Clair Ave. W., Toronto, Ont., Canada. charts. illus.

628.44 CN ISSN 0078-4893
ONTARIO. MINISTRY OF THE ENVIRONMENT. INDUSTRIAL WASTE CONFERENCE. PROCEEDINGS. 1954. a. controlled circulation, free. ‡ Ministry of the Environment, Water Resources Branch, 135 St. Clair Ave., Toronto, Ont. M4V 1P5, Canada. Ed. M. F. Cheetham.

614.7 CN ISSN 0078-5148
ONTARIO. MINISTRY OF THE ENVIRONMENT. POLLUTION CONTROL BRANCH. RESEARCH PUBLICATION. 1959. irreg. free. Ministry of the Environment, Pollution Control Branch, 135 St. Clair Ave., Toronto, Ont. M4V 1P5, Canada. circ. 300.

333.9 US
OREGON. DEPARTMENT OF FISH AND WILDLIFE. ENVIRONMENTAL MANAGEMENT SECTION. SPECIAL REPORT. Cover title: Environmental Investigations Special Report. 1969. irreg., no. 4, 1972. $2. ‡ Department of Fish and Wild Life, 506 S.W. Mill St., Box 3503, Portland, OR 97208. illus.

301.31 US ISSN 0092-7937
PENNSYLVANIA. CITIZENS ADVISORY COUNCIL TO THE DEPARTMENT OF ENVIRONMENTAL RESOURCES. ANNUAL REPORT. 1971/72. a. free. Citizens Advisory Council to the Pennsylvania Department of Environmental Resources, Box 2357, 816 Executive House, Harrisburg, PA 17120. Ed. Mark M. McClellan. stat. circ. 2,500. Key Title: Annual Report - Citizens Advisory Council (Harrisburg)

PHILIPPINES. DEPARTMENT OF NATURAL RESOURCES. PLANS AND PROGRAMS. see CONSERVATION

614.7 333.7 PH
PHILIPPINES. DEPARTMENT OF NATURAL RESOURCES. ANNUAL REPORT. a. Department of Natural Resources, Diliman, Quezon City, Philippines.

614.7 US
POLLUTION CONTROL CONFERENCE. PROCEEDINGS. vol. 3, 1975. irreg. Ann Arbor Science Publishers, Inc., Box 1425, Ann Arbor, Mi 48106.

614.7 500 UK
POLLUTION RESEARCH INDEX. 1974. irreg., 2nd edt. 1979. Longman Group Ltd., Longman House, Burnt Mill, Harlow, Essex, England (Dist. in U.S. and Canada by: Gale Research Co. Ltd., Book Tower, Detroit, MI 48226)

614.7 620 PL
POLSKA AKADEMIA NAUK. INSTYTUT PODSTAW INZYNIERII SRODOWISKA. PRACE I STUDIA. irreg., no. 19, 1978. 18 Zl. Ossolineum, Publishing House of the Polish Academy of Sciences, Rynek 9, Wroclaw, Poland (Dist. by: Ars Polona-Ruch, Krakowskie Przedmiescie 7, Warsaw, Poland) Ed. Stefan Jarzebski.

614.7 PO
PORTUGAL. MINISTERIO DA HABITACAO E OBRAS PUBLICAS. COMISSAO NACIONAL DO AMBIENTE. RELATORIO DE ACTIVIDADES. 1973. a. free. Ministerio do Equipamento Social e do Ambiente, Comissao Nacional do Ambiente, Praca Duque de Saldanha 31, 1096 Lisboa Codex, Portugal. circ. 200.
Formerly: Portugal. Ministerio do Equipamento Social e do Ambiente. Comissao Nacional do Ambiente. Relatorio de Actividades.

POTOMAC RIVER BASIN WATER QUALITY REPORTS. see WATER RESOURCES

628 CN ISSN 0085-5138
PRINCE EDWARD ISLAND. DEPARTMENT OF THE ENVIRONMENT. ANNUAL REPORT. 1970. a. Department of the Environment, Box 2000, Charlottetown, Prince Edward Island, Canada. circ. 150.
Formerly: Prince Edward Island Water Authority. Annual Report.

624 US
PUBLIC WATER SUPPLY ENGINEERS CONFERENCE (PROCEEDINGS) 1959. a. price varies. University of Illinois at Urbana-Champaign, Engineering Publications Office, 112 Engineering Hall, Urbana, IL 61801. circ. 1,000.
Formerly (from 12th to 17th): Water Quality Conference.Proceedings (ISSN 0080-6013); (until 12th, 1970): Sanitary Engineering Conference.

628.71 US
PURDUE AIR QUALITY CONFERENCE. PROCEEDINGS. 1961. a. Purdue University, School of Civil Engineering, W. Lafayette, IN 47907. (Co-sponsor: Indiana State Board of Health) Ed. Dr. Robert B. Jacko.

QUEBEC (PROVINCE) MINISTERE DES RICHESSES NATURELLES. RAPPORT. see CONSERVATION

354 AT
QUEENSLAND. AIR POLLUTION COUNCIL. ANNUAL REPORT. a. Queensland. Government Printer, Brisbane, Australia. illus.

628.44 IT
REPERTORIO TECNICHE AMBIENTALI. a. L.25000. Etas Kompass Periodici Tecnici S.p.A., Via Mantegna 6, 20154 Milan, Italy.
Former titles: Tecniche Ambientali; Annuario Dell Tecniche Ambientali.

614.7 574 UK
RESOURCE AND ENVIRONMENTAL SCIENCE SERIES. 1977. irreg. price varies. Edward Arnold (Publishers) Ltd., 41 Bedford Square, London WC1B 3DQ, England.

614.7 MX
REUNION NACIONAL SOBRE PROBLEMAS DE CONTAMINACION AMBIENTAL. MEMORIA. 1973. irreg. Secretaria de Salubridad y Asistencia, Direccion General de Planeacion, Mexico City, Mexico. illus.

ROCENKA ZNECISTENI OVZDUSI NA UZEMI C S R. see METEOROLOGY

550 BL
SAO PAULO, BRAZIL (STATE). SUPERINTENDENCIA DE SANEAMENTO AMBIENTAL. RELATORIO ANUAL DE ATIVIDADES. a. Superintendencia de Saneamento Ambiental, Secretaria de Estado da Saude, Sao Paulo, Brazil.

354 CN ISSN 0317-4611
SASKATCHEWAN. DEPARTMENT OF THE ENVIRONMENT. ANNUAL REPORT. 1973. a. free. Department of the Environment, Regina, Sask., Canada. illus. stat. circ. 400.

SCHRIFTENREIHE AUS DEN NATURSCHUTZGEBIETEN BAYERNS. see CONSERVATION

614.7 GW
SCHRIFTENREIHE CHEMISCHE ANALYTIK UND UMWELTTECHNOLOGIE. irreg. price varies. (Landesamt fuer Umweltschutz) R. Oldenbourg Verlag GmbH, Rosenheimer Str. 145, 8000 Munich 80, W. Germany (B.R.D.)

614.7 GW
SCHRIFTENREIHE LUFTREINHALTUNG. irreg., vol. 3, 1979. price varies. (Landesamt fuer Umweltschutz) R. Oldenbourg Verlag GmbH, Rosenheimer Str. 145, 8000 Munich 80, W. Germany (B.R.D.)

SCHRIFTENREIHE NATURSCHUTZ UND LANDSCHAFTSPFLEGE. see CONSERVATION

628.168 US ISSN 0083-050X
SEWAGE FACILITIES CONSTRUCTION. a. $1. limited copies free. U.S. Environmental Protection Agency, Office of Water Program Operations, M St. N.W., Washington, DC 20460 (Orders to: Supt. Doc., Washington, DC 20402)

614 US
SHORELINE/COASTAL ZONE MANAGEMENT. 1976. m. Department of Ecology, Olympia, WA 98504.

SKENECTADA. see BIOLOGY

ENVIRONMENTAL STUDIES

614.7   SP
SPAIN. INSTITUTO NACIONAL PARA LA CONSERVACION DE LA NATURALEZA. MONOGRAFIAS. 1978. irreg. price varies. Instituto Nacional para la Conservacion de la Naturaleza, Gran via San Francisco 35, Madrid 5, Spain. bibl. charts. illus. circ. 1,000. (back issues avail.) Indexed: Biol.Abstr. Chem.Abstr. Curr.Cont. Aqua.Sci. & Fish.Abstr. Wild Life Rev. Zoo.Rec.

614.7   US
SPRINGER SERIES ON ENVIRONMENTAL MANAGEMENT. 1979. irreg. price varies. Springer-Verlag, 175 Fifth Ave., New York, NY 10010 (Also Berlin, Heidelberg, Vienna) Ed. Dr. Robert DeSanto. (reprint service avail. from ISI)

614.7   US
STATE OF VIRGINIA'S ENVIRONMENT: ANNUAL REPORT. a. Council on the Environment, Box 790, Richmond, VA 23206.

614.2   US   ISSN 0360-8751
STREAM IMPROVEMENT TECHNICAL BULLETIN. 1971. irreg. $150. National Council of the Paper Industry for Air and Stream Improvement, Inc., 260 Madison Ave., New York, NY 10016.
Continues: National Council of the Paper Industry for Air and Stream Improvement. Technical Bulletin.

614.7   NE
STUDIES IN ENVIRONMENTAL SCIENCE. 1978. irreg. price varies. Elsevier Scientific Publishing Co., Box 211, 1000 AE Amsterdam, Netherlands.

614.7 301.31   CN   ISSN 0225-4123
STUDIES IN LAND USE HISTORY AND LANDSCAPE CHANGE. 1973. irreg. University of Waterloo, Faculty of Environmental Studies, Waterloo Ont. N2L 3G1, Canada.

614.7   SW   ISSN 0587-1433
SWEDISH NATURAL SCIENCE RESEARCH COUNCIL. ECOLOGICAL BULLETINS. (Text in English) 1968. irreg. (2-3/yr.) Naturvetenskapliga Forskningsraadet, Ecological Research Committee, Editorial Service, Box 23136, S-104 35 Stockholm, Sweden. Ed. Thomas Rosswall. Indexed: Biol.Abstr.

614.7 616   US   ISSN 0164-0968
TASK FORCE ON ENVIRONMENTAL CANCER AND HEART AND LUNG DISEASE. ANNUAL REPORT TO CONGRESS. 1978. a. U.S. Environmental Protection Agency, Technical Information Office, Washington, DC 20460. Key Title: Annual Report to Congress by the Task Force on Environmental Cancer and Heart and Lung Disease.

628.168   AT   ISSN 0082-2094
TASMANIA. METROPOLITAN WATER BOARD. REPORT. 1963. a. free. ‡ Metropolitan Water Board, G.P.O. Box 179, Hobart, Tasmania, Australia.

TOPICS IN ENVIRONMENTAL HEALTH. see *BIOLOGY*

614.   GW   ISSN 0341-1206
UMWELTMAGAZIN. 1971. 8/yr. DM.76. Vogel-Verlag KG, Max-Planck-Str. 7, 8700 Wuerzburg 1, W. Germany (B.R.D.) Ed. J. Jobst. adv. circ. 11,200(controlled)
Formerly: U - das Technische Umweltmagazin.

614.7   US   ISSN 0092-0320
U.S. COAST GUARD. POLLUTING INCIDENTS IN AND AROUND U.S. WATERS. a. free contr. circ. U. S. Coast Guard, 1300 E St. N.W., Washington, DC 20591.

353.008   US   ISSN 0360-4543
U.S. DEPARTMENT OF THE INTERIOR. OIL SHALE ENVIRONMENTAL ADVISORY PANEL. ANNUAL REPORT. 1975. a. U. S. Department of the Interior, Oil Shale Environmental Advisory Panel, Box 25007, Room 690, Bldg. 67, Denver Federal Center, Denver, CO 80225. Key Title: Annual Report-Oil Shale Environmental Adivsory Panel.

U.S. ENVIRONMENTAL PROTECTION AGENCY. WATER PLANNING DIVISION. WATER QUALITY STRATEGY PAPER. see *WATER RESOURCES*

628.168   US   ISSN 0071-5506
U. S. ENVIRONMENTAL PROTECTION AGENCY. FISH KILLS CAUSED BY POLLUTION. a. $1. U. S. Environmental Protection Agency, Office of Water Programs, 401 M St. N.W., Washington, DC 20460 (Orders to: Supt. Doc., Washington, DC 20402)

614.7   US
U.S. ENVIRONMENTAL PROTECTION AGENCY. OFFICE OF RESEARCH AND DEVELOPMENT. PROGRAM GUIDE. 1977? a. Environmental Protection Agency, Office of Research and Development, Washington, DC 20460.

614.7   US   ISSN 0161-7796
U.S. ENVIRONMENTAL PROTECTION AGENCY. RADIATION PROTECTION ACTIVITIES. a. U.S. Environmental Protection Agency, Office of Radiation Programs, Washington, DC 20460. Key Title: Radiation Protection Activities.
Formerly: U.S. Environmental Protection Agency. Radiation Protection.

614.7   US   ISSN 0363-9819
U.S. ENVIRONMENTAL PROTECTION AGENCY. RADIOLOGICAL QUALITY OF THE ENVIRONMENT IN THE UNITED STATES. a. U.S. Environmental Protection Agency, Office of Radiation Programs, Washington, DC 20460. Key Title: Radiological Quality of the Environment.

671.7   US   ISSN 0092-9689
U. S. ENVIRONMENTAL PROTECTION AGENCY. UPGRADING METAL-FINISHING FACILITIES TO REDUCE POLLUTION. 1973. irreg. U. S. Environmental Protection Agency, Washington, DC 20460. illus. Key Title: Upgrading Metal Finishing Facilities to Reduce Pollution.

333.9   US   ISSN 0098-4922
U.S. NATIONAL OCEANIC AND ATMOSPHERIC ADMINISTRATION. REPORT TO THE CONGRESS ON OCEAN POLLUTION, OVERFISHING, AND OFFSHORE DEVELOPMENT. 1973. a. $1.45. 6010 Executive Blvd., Rockville, MD 20852 (Orders to: NTIS, 5285 Port Royal Rd., Springfield, VA 22161) Key Title: Report to the Congress on Ocean Pollution, Overfishing, and Offshore Development.
Formerly: U.S. National Oceanic and Atmospheric Administration. Report to the Congress on Ocean Dumping and Other Man-Induced Changes to Ocean Ecosystems (ISSN 0094-5196)

385.1 614.7   UK
UNIVERSITY OF BIRMINGHAM. DEPARTMENT OF TRANSPORTATION AND ENVIRONMENTAL PLANNING. RESEARCH JOURNAL. 1969-71. biennial. 90p. University of Birmingham, Department of Transportation & Environmental Plannning, P.O. Box 363, Birmingham B15 2TT, England.

560   CN   ISSN 0068-5437
UNIVERSITY OF CALGARY. ARCHAEOLOGICAL ASSOCIATION. PALEO-ENVIRONMENTAL WORKSHOP. PROCEEDINGS. 1969. a. price varies. ‡ University of Calgary, Archaeological Association, Department of Archaeology, 2920-24th Ave. N.W., Calgary, Alta. T2N 1N4, Canada.

614 301.32   TZ   ISSN 0084-960X
UNIVERSITY OF DAR ES SALAAM. BUREAU OF RESOURCE ASSESSMENT AND LAND USE PLANNING. ANNUAL REPORT. 1968. a. free. University of Dar es Salaam, Bureau of Resource Assessment and Land Use Planning, Box 35097, Dar es Salaam, Tanzania. Ed. Adolfo Mascarenhas. circ. 250.

614 301.32   TZ   ISSN 0084-9626
UNIVERSITY OF DAR ES SALAAM. BUREAU OF RESOURCE ASSESSMENT AND LAND USE PLANNING. RESEARCH PAPER. 1968. irreg., no. 60, 1979. $50. University of Dar es Salaam, Bureau of Resource Assessment and Land Use Planning, Box 35097, Dar es Salaam, Tanzania. Ed. Adolfo Mascarenhas. circ. 200.

614 301.32   TZ   ISSN 0084-9634
UNIVERSITY OF DAR ES SALAAM. BUREAU OF RESOURCE ASSESSMENT AND LAND USE PLANNING. RESEARCH REPORT. 1969. irreg., no. 39, 1979 (N.S.) price varies. University of Dar es Salaam, Bureau of Resource Assessment and Land Use Planning, Box 35097, Dar es Salaam, Tanzania. Ed. Adolfo Mascarenhas. circ. 200. Indexed: Geo.Abstr.

574.5   US   ISSN 0094-9205
UNIVERSITY OF GEORGIA. INSTITUTE OF ECOLOGY. ANNUAL REPORT. Cover title: Ecology. a. free. University of Georgia, Institute of Ecology, Athens, GA 30602. Ed. Lorraine Edwards. bibl. Key Title: Annual Report - University of Georgia, Institute of Ecology.

614.7   US
UNIVERSITY OF LOUISVILLE. SPEED SCIENTIFIC SCHOOL. ENVIRONMENTAL ENGINEERING AND SCIENCE CONFERENCE. PROCEEDINGS. 1971. a. $20. University of Louisville, Speed Scientific School, Director of Professional Development, Louisville, KY 40208.

614.7   US
UNIVERSITY OF NORTH DAKOTA. INSTITUTE OF ECOLOGICAL STUDIES. RESEARCH REPORT. 1971. irreg., no. 29, 1979. price varies. University of North Dakota, Institute for Ecological Studies, Grand Forks, ND 58202. Ed. Dr. P. B. Kannowski. circ. 200.

614.7   US   ISSN 0079-0699
UNIVERSITY OF PENNSYLVANIA. INSTITUTE FOR ENVIRONMENTAL STUDIES. REPORT.*
1965. irreg. price varies. University of Pennsylvania, Institute for Environmental Studies, 3400 Walnut St., Philadelphia, PA 19104.

614.7   US   ISSN 0079-8207
UNIVERSITY OF PITTSBURGH. PYMATUNING LABORATORY OF ECOLOGY. SPECIAL PUBLICATION. 1956. irreg., no.5, 1978. $2-$4.50. University of Pittsburgh, Pymatuning Laboratory of Ecology, Linesville, PA 16424. Ed. R. T. Hartman. index. circ. 1,000.

333.77   CN
UNIVERSITY OF WATERLOO. FACULTY OF ENVIRONMENTAL STUDIES. WORKING PAPER SERIES. 1977. irreg. Faculty of Environmental Studies, Waterloo, Ont. N2L 3G1, Canada.

614.7   US
UNIVERSITY OF WISCONSIN, MADISON. INSTITUTE OF ENVIRONMENTAL STUDIES. I E S REPORTS. 1972. irreg., no. 106, 1979. University of Wisconsin-Madison, Institute for Environmental Studies, 610 Walnut St., Madison, WI 53706. (Co-sponsors: College of Engineering, School of Business) circ. 300. (also avail. in microform from NTI)

614.7 627   US   ISSN 0093-6332
VANDERBILT UNIVERSITY. DEPARTMENT OF ENVIRONMENTAL AND WATER RESOURCES ENGINEERING. TECHNICAL REPORTS. 1962. irreg., 1977, no. 40. price varies. Vanderbilt University, Department of Environmental and Water Resources Engineering, Box 6304, Station B, Nashville, TN 37235.

VEREIN FUER WASSER-, BODEN- UND LUFTHYGIENE. SCHRIFTENREIHE. see *CONSERVATION*

350   US
VERMONT RESOURCES RESEARCH CENTER SERIES. irreg., latest, no. 20. University of Vermont, Cooperative Extension Service, Morrill Hall, Burlington, VT 05401.

VIRGINIA. STATE WATER CONTROL BOARD. ANNUAL REPORT. see *WATER RESOURCES*

614   US   ISSN 0362-6369
WASHINGTON (STATE). DEPARTMENT OF ECOLOGY. WATER QUALITY ASSESSMENT REPORT. 1975. a. Department of Ecology, Olympia, WA 98504. Key Title: Water Quality Assessment Report.

614.7   US
WATCH IT. 1969. irreg. free to members. Wilderness Watch, Box 3184, Green Bay, WI 54303. Ed. Nancy Delavantes.

614.7   US
WATER POLLUTION: A SERIES OF MONOGRAPHS. irreg. Academic Press, Inc., 111 Fifth Ave., New York, NY 10003. Eds. K. S. Speigler, J. Bregman.

614.77 628.168   UK   ISSN 0083-7660
WATER POLLUTION RESEARCH. a. price varies. Water Pollution Research Laboratory, Stevenage, Hertfordshire, England (Avail. from H.M.S.O., c/o Liaison Officer, Atlantic House, Holborn Viaduct, London EC1P 1BN, England) cum. index 1952-64 in 1964 report.

628.168 614.77   UK   ISSN 0083-7679
WATER POLLUTION RESEARCH LABORATORY, STEVENAGE, ENGLAND. TECHNICAL PAPERS. irreg. price varies. Water Pollution Research Laboratory, Stevenage, Hertfordshire, England (Avail. from H.M.S.O., Atlantic House, Holborn Viaduct, London EC1P 1BN, England)

WATER QUALITY DATA FOR ONTARIO STREAMS & LAKES. see *WATER RESOURCES*

363.6   US   ISSN 0097-7519
WATER QUALITY MONITORING DATA FOR GEORGIA STREAMS. a. Department of Natural Resources, Environmental Protection Division, Water Quality Control Section, 270 Washington St. S.W., Atlanta, GA 30334.

628.168   UK   ISSN 0143-2443
WATER RESEARCH CENTRE. ANNUAL REPORT. 1974. a. Water Research Centre, Stevenage Laboratory, Elder Way, Stevenage, Herts SG1 1TH, England.
    Formed by the merger: Water Research Association. Report & Water Pollution Research.

614.7 551   US
WEST VIRGINIA ENVIRONMENTAL GEOLOGY BULLETINS. 1973. irreg. Geological and Economic Survey, Box 879, Morgantown, WV 26505.
    Formerly: West Virginia Geological Survey. Environmental Geology Bulletin.

WESTERN AUSTRALIA. CONSERVATION AND ENVIRONMENT COUNCIL. ANNUAL REPORT. see *CONSERVATION*

WESTERN GEOGRAPHICAL SERIES. see *GEOGRAPHY*

614.7   US   ISSN 0362-5354
WISCONSIN. DEPARTMENT OF NATURAL RESOURCES. ANNUAL WATER QUALITY REPORT TO CONGRESS. a. Department of Natural Resources, Box 7721, Madison, WI 53701. illus. Key Title: Annual Water Quality Report to Congress.

333.7   US   ISSN 0092-0908
WORLD DIRECTORY OF ENVIRONMENTAL ORGANIZATIONS. 1973. irreg., 2nd. edt. 1975. $25. (Sierra Club International Program) California Institute of Public Affairs, Box 10, Claremont, CA 91711. (Co-sponsor: International Union for Conservation of Nature and Natural Resources) Eds. Thaddeus C. Trzyna, Eugene V. Coan.

614.7   US   ISSN 0094-4742
WORLD ENVIRONMENTAL DIRECTORY. 1974. biennial. $67.50. Business Publishers, Inc., P.O. Box 1067, Silver Spring, MD 20910. Ed. Beverly E. Gough. adv. circ. 5,000.

WORLD GUIDE TO POLLUTION CONTROL IN THE FERTILIZER INDUSTRY. see
    AGRICULTURE — Crop Production And Soil

551.5 614.7   UN
WORLD METEOROLOGICAL ORGANIZATION. SPECIAL ENVIRONMENTAL REPORTS. (Subseries of: World Meteorological Organization. W M O (Publications)) irreg. World Meteorological Organization, 41 Ave. Giuseppe Motta, CH-1211 Geneva 20, Switzerland. illus.

300   US
WORLDWATCH PAPERS. 1975. irreg., no. 24, 1978. $25. Worldwatch Institute, 1776 Massachusetts Ave., N.W., Washington, DC 20036. Ed. Linda Starke. circ. 5,000. (back issues avail.)

614.7   US
WORLDWIDE REPORT: ENVIRONMENTAL QUALITY. 1973. irreg. (approx. 36/yr.) $126. U.S. Joint Publications Research Service, 1000 N. Glebe Rd., Arlington, VA 22201 (Orders to: NTIS, Springfield, VA 22161)
    Formerly: Translations on Environmental Quality. Focus primarily on USSR, Eastern Europe and Japan

353.9   US   ISSN 0099-1279
WYOMING. DEPARTMENT OF ENVIRONMENTAL QUALITY. ANNUAL REPORT. 1974. a. Department of Environmental Quality, Cheyenne, WY 82002. Key Title: Annual Report of the Department of Environmental Quality.

333.9   US   ISSN 0098-0846
WYOMING. WATER QUALITY DIVISION. WYOMING STATE PLAN. a. Department of Environmental Quality, Water Quality Division, Cheyenne, WY 82002. Key Title: Wyoming State Plan.

628   GW   ISSN 0539-1539
ZAHLESTAFELN DER PHYSIKALISCH-CHEMISCHEN UNTERSUCHUNGEN DES RHEINS SOWIE DER MOSEL/TABLEAUX NUMERIQUES DES ANALYSES PHYSICO-CHIMIQUES DES EAUX DU RHIN AINSI QUE DE LA MOSELLE. (Text in German and French) 1963. a. free. International Commission for the Protection of the Rhine Against Pollution - Internationale Kommission zum Schutzes des Rheins gegen Verunreinigung, Kaiserin-Augusta-Anlagen 15, Postfach 309, 5400 Koblenz, W. Germany (B.R.D.)

37 DESIGN & ENVIRONMENT PROJECTS. see *ARCHITECTURE*

ENVIRONMENTAL STUDIES —
Abstracting, Bibliographies, Statistics

614.7 016   US   ISSN 0092-5756
BIBLIOGRAPHY OF NOISE. (Supplement to Bibliography of Noise 1965-1970) 1971. a. price varies. Whitston Publishing Co. Inc., Box 958, Troy, NY 12181. Ed. Dorothy Barnes.

614.7   US
E I S CUMULATIVE. (Environmental Impact Statement) 1977. a. varies. Information Resources Press (Subsidiary of: Herner & Co.) 1700 N. Moore St., Suite 700, Arlington, VA 22209.

ENERGY INDEX. see *ENERGY — Abstracting, Bibliographies, Statistics*

614.7 016   US
ENVIRONMENT INDEX; a guide to the key environmental literature of the year. 1971. a. $125. Environment Information Center, Inc., 292 Madison Ave., New York, NY 10017.

614.7 016   FR
FRANCE. MINISTERE DE LA QUALITE DE LA VIE. BULLETIN DE DOCUMENTATION. irreg. (Ministere de la Qualite de la Vie) Documentation Francaise, 29-31 Quai Voltaire, 75340 Paris Cedex 7, France.

301.31 016   UK   ISSN 0141-2604
GREAT BRITAIN. DEPARTMENTS OF THE ENVIRONMENT AND TRANSPORT. LIBRARY SERVICES. ANNUAL LIST OF PUBLICATIONS. 1971. a. price varies. Departments of the Environment and Transport, 2 Marsham Street, Room P3/178, London SW1P 3EB, England. bibl. circ. 6,900.
    Formerly: Great Britain. Department of the Environment. Library Services. D. O. E. Annual List of Publications.

340 333.7 016   GW
I C E L REFERENCES; to publications concerning legal, administrative and policy aspects of environmental conservation. (Text in various languages) 1970. 17-20/yr. membership. International Council on Environmental Law, 214 Adenauerallee, 5300 Bonn, W. Germany (B. R. D.) circ. 300(controlled) (cards)

614.7 016   II
INDIAN LITERATURE IN ENVIRONMENTAL ENGINEERING; annual bibliography. (Text in English) 1971. a. Rs.10($5) National Environmental Engineering Research Institute, Documentation and Library Services, Nehru Marg, Nagpur 440020, India. (Affiliate: Council of Scientific and Industrial Research) Eds. S. K. Kesarwani, S. G. Bhat. author and geographical indexes. (processed)

614.7 016   US
N I C E M INDEX TO ENVIRONMENTAL STUDIES-MULTIMEDIA. biennial. $40. National Information Center for Educational Media, University of Southern California, University Park, Los Angeles, CA 90007. cum.index. (also avail. in microfiche)
    Formerly: Index to Ecology.

333.7   CN
ONTARIO. MINISTRY OF NATURAL RESOURCES. STATISTICS. irreg. Ministry of Natural Resources, Parliament Bldgs., Toronto, Ont., Canada.

016 614.7   US
U. S. ENVIRONMENTAL PROTECTION AGENCY. OFFICE OF RESEARCH AND DEVELOPMENT. INDEXED BIBLIOGRAPHY. (Subseries of Water Pollution Control Research series) irreg. free. U. S. Environmental Protection Agency, Publications Staff, Washington, DC 20460. (also avail. in microfiche from NTI)
    Formerly: U. S. Environmental Protection Agency. Office of Research and Development. Bibliography of Water Quality Research Reports (ISSN 0090-2055)

016.6 614.7   US   ISSN 0090-6808
U.S. ENVIRONMENTAL PROTECTION AGENCY. OFFICE OF RESEARCH AND DEVELOPMENT. SELECTED IRRIGATION RETURN FLOW QUALITY ABSTRACTS. (Environmental Protection Technology series) 1968/69. a. price varies. U.S. Environmental Protection Agency, Washington (For sale by the Supt. of Docs., G.P.O., Washington, D.C. 20240) (also avail. in microfiche from NTI) Key Title: Selected Irrigation Return Flow Quality Abstacts.

016 614.7   US
WATER POLLUTION CONTROL FEDERATION CONFERENCE. ABSTRACTS OF TECHNICAL PAPERS. 46th, 1973. a. Water Pollution Control Federation, 2626 Pennsylvania Ave. N.W., Washington, DC 20037.

ETHNIC INTERESTS

296   US   ISSN 0364-0094
A J S REVIEW. Short title: A J S Review. 1975. a. $20. (Association for Jewish Studies) Ktav Publishing House, 75 Varick St., New York, NY 10013. Ed. Charles Berlin. bk. rev. bibl. circ. 1,500.
    Jewish interests

960   US
A S A PAPERS. 1960? a. African Studies Association, Brandeis University, Epstein Service Bldg., Waltham, MA 02154.

960   US
A S A REVIEW OF BOOKS. 1975. a. $15. African Studies Association, Brandeis University, Epstein Service Bldg., Waltham, MA 02154. Eds. Barbara Lewis, Allen Howard.

960   UK   ISSN 0141-3341
AFRICA YEAR BOOK AND WHO'S WHO. 1977. a. £16. Africa Journal Ltd., Kirkman House, 54A Tottenham Court Rd., London W1P OBT, England. illus.

AFRICAN-AMERICAN HERITAGE SERIES. see
HISTORY — History Of North And South
America

309 301.45   US
AFRICAN-AMERICAN LIBRARY SERIES. irreg.
price varies. Collier Books, 866 Third Ave., New
York, NY 10022.

960   US   ISSN 0002-0206
AFRICAN STUDIES REVIEW. 1958. a. membership.
African Studies Association, c/o Alan Smith, Ed.,
Brandeis University, Epstein Service Bldg.,
Waltham, MA 02154. adv. bk. rev. circ. 2,500.
Incorporating: African Studies Bulletin.
African studies

973   US   ISSN 0360-5388
AIS-EIRI; the magazine of Irish-America. 1975. irreg.
$7.50 for 4 nos. to individuals; institutions $10. An
Claidheamh Soluis, Inc., 553 W. 51 St., New York,
NY 10019. Ed. Robert G. Lowery. adv. bk. rev.
illus. circ. 2,500.
Formerly: Sword of Light.
Irish interests

947   US   ISSN 0516-3145
AKADEMISKA DZIVE/ACADEMIC LIFE. (Text in
Latvian; summaries in English) 1958. a. $5.
Association of Latvian Academic Societies, One
Vincent Ave. S., Minneapolis, MN 55405. Ed.Bd.
bk. rev. illus. circ. 1,100. Indexed: Hist.Abstr.
Amer.Hist.&Life.

057.91   CN   ISSN 0441-1196
ALMANAKH GOMONU UKRAINY. 1956
(Suspended during 1974) irreg. Homin Ukrainy
Publishing Co., 140 Bathurst St., Toronto, Ont.
M5V 2R3, Canada. illus.

917.306   US
AMERICAN CROAT/AMERICKI HRVAT. vol. 11,
1975. q. $6. ‡ (Croatian Information Service) Peter
Radielovic, Ed. & Pub., Box 3025, Arcadia, CA
91006. Ed. Petar Radielovic. bk. rev. illus. circ.
3,000. (back issues avail.)
Croation interests

AMERICAN INDIAN LAW REVIEW. see *LAW*

970.1   US   ISSN 0193-8207
AMERICAN INDIAN LIBRARIES NEWSLETTER.
1976. irreg. American Library Association, Office
for Library Service to the Disadvantaged, 50 E.
Huron St., Chicago, IL 60611. Ed. Dr. Cheryl
Metoyer-Duran. circ. 1,700.
American Indian interests

917.306   US
AMERICAN ITALIAN HISTORICAL
ASSOCIATION. PROCEEDINGS. (Each vol. has
distinctive title.) 1968. a. $5 or membership.
American Italian Historical Association, 209 Flagg
Pl., Staten Island, NY 10304. circ. 300-400.
Italian interests

296   AG
ANALES DE LA COMUNIDAD ISRAELITA DE
BUENOS AIRES. Cover title: Pinkes Fun der
Kehile in Buenos Ayres. (Text in English and
Spanish) a. Asociacion Mutual Israelita Argentina,
Kultur Departament bay der Kehile in Buenos
Ayres, Pasteur 633, Buenos Aires, Argentina.
Jewish interests

915.306   CN   ISSN 0706-7917
ARAB DIRECTORY/DALIL EL ARAB. (Text and
summaries in Arabic and English) 1979. a.
Can.$4.95($5.95) Allam Arabic Publishing &
Advertising Co., 834 Yonge St., Suite 204, Toronto,
Ont. M4W 2H1, Canada. Ed. Salah Allam. adv.
illus. circ. 4,000. (back issues avail.)

919.4 052   AT
AUSTRALIA. DEPARTMENT OF ABORIGINAL
AFFAIRS. REPORT. 1974. a. Aus.$2.65.
Australian Government Publishing Service, P.O.
Box 84, Canberra, A.C.T. 2600, Australia. illus.
Native Australian interests

914.406   AT
AUSZTRALIAI MAGYAR UJSAF. HUNGARIAN
WEEKLY. 1950. irreg. Aus.$0.20. c/o F. Antal,
Ed., P.O. Box 66, Fitzroy, Vic. 3065, Australia.
Hungarian interests

910.03   SA
B L A C. (Text in English and Afrikaans) irreg. Black
Literature and Arts Congress, 1 Long St., Mowbray,
South Africa.

910.03   US
B R I C S BRACS; a quarterly reviewing journal of
Afro-American resources. 1977. q. $15. Black
Resources Information Coordinating Services, Inc.,
614 Howard Ave., Box 6353, Tallahassee, FL
32304. Ed. Emily A. Copeland. adv. bk. rev. film
rev, play rev, abstr, bibl, illus. index, cum. index.
Black interests

BAYAVAYA USKALOS; Byelorussian literary
magazine. see *LITERATURE*

BEBOP DRAWING CLUB BOOK. see *ART*

BELARUSKI INSTYTUT NAVUKI MACTATSTVA.
ZAPISY/BYELORUSSIAN INSTITUTE OF ARTS
AND SCIENCES. ANNALS. see HISTORY —
History Of Europe

BIOGRAPHICAL DIRECTORY OF AMERICANS
AND CANADIANS OF CROATIAN DESCENT.
see *BIOGRAPHY*

910.03 330   US
BLACK ECONOMIC RESEARCH CENTER.
OCCASIONAL PAPER. irreg. Black Economic
Research Center, 112 W. 120th St., New York, NY
10027. charts, stat.

BLACK FORUM. see *LITERARY AND
POLITICAL REVIEWS*

BLACK JACK. see *LITERATURE*

910.03   US
BLACK PAGES PAMPHLET SERIES. 1973. irreg.
$1.50 per copy. Institute of Positive Education,
7524 So. Cottage Grove Ave., Chicago, IL 60619.
Ed. Haki Madhubuti. bibl. illus. circ. 5,000.

960   SA
BLACK REVIEW. irreg. Black Community
Programmes, 86 Beatrice St., Durban, South Africa.
Black interests

301.45   US
BLACK STUDIES SERIES. 1972. irreg. $13.50.
Edward L. Jones & Associates, 5517 17th Ave.
N.E., Seattle, WA 98105. Ed. E. L. Jones.
Black studies

BLACKS IN AMERICAN JOURNALISM SERIES.
see *JOURNALISM*

910.03   US
BLACKS IN THE NEW WORLD. irreg. University
of Illinois Press, 54 E. Gregory, Box 5081, Station
A, Champaign, IL 61820. (reprint service avail.
from UMI)
Black interests

914.406 320   FR
BUDESHTE/AVENIR. 1973. m. $60. Parizh, 18 bis
rue Brunel, 75017 Paris, France. Ed. Tsenko Barev.
bk. rev. circ. 3,000.
Bulgarian interests

970.1 378   CN
CANADA. DEPARTMENT OF INDIAN AND
NORTHERN AFFAIRS. INDIAN AND INUIT
GRADUATE REGISTER. a. Department of Indian
and Northern Affairs, 400 Laurier Ave. W., Ottawa,
Ont. K1A OH4, Canada.
Canadian Indian interests

296   CN   ISSN 0576-5528
CANADIAN JEWISH ARCHIVES (NEW SERIES)
1955. N.S. 1974. irreg. Can.$5 per no. Canadian
Jewish Congress, 1590 McGregor, Montreal, Que.
H3G 1C5, Canada. Ed. David Rome. circ. 500.

CANADIAN MUSLIM. see *RELIGIONS AND
THEOLOGY — Islamic*

918 784.6 700   US   ISSN 0098-8340
CANTO LIBRE; a bilingual trimester of Latin
American people's art. (Text in English and
Spanish) 1974. irreg. membership. Center for Cuban
Studies, 220 East 23rd St., New York, NY 10010.
Ed. Susan Ortega. adv. bk. rev. illus. circ. 1,500.
(back issues avail.) Indexed: Alt.Press Ind.

ETHNIC INTERESTS   391

CENTER FOR HOLOCAUST STUDIES
NEWSLETTER. see HISTORY — History Of
Europe

917.306   US
CHINESE CULTURE ASSOCIATION,
MAGAZINE. (Text in Chinese) 1966. a. $5.
Chinese Culture Association, Box 1272, Palo Alto,
CA 94302. Ed. P. F. Tao. adv. circ. 2,500.

917.306   US
CHINESE HISTORICAL SOCIETY OF AMERICA.
ANNIVERSARY BULLETIN. a. $1. Chinese
Historical Society of America, 17 Adler Place, off
1140 Grant Ave., San Francisco, CA 94133. Ed.
Thomas W. Chinn.

914.606   SP
COLECCION ILLARGI AMANDREA. 1977. irreg.
price varies. Editorial Txertoa, Plaza de las
Armerias 4, San Sebastian, Spain. illus.
Basque interests

296   US   ISSN 0160-7057
CONFERENCE OF PRESIDENTS OF MAJOR
AMERICAN JEWISH ORGANIZATIONS.
REPORT. 1965. a. free. Conference of Presidents of
Major American Jewish Organizations, 515 Park
Ave., New York, NY 10022. Ed. Richard Cohen.
illus.
Formerly: Conference of Presidents of Major
American Jewish Organizations. Annual Report
(ISSN 0160-7049)

CONFERENCE ON EMPIRICAL RESEARCH IN
BLACK PSYCHOLOGY. see *EDUCATION —
Higher Education*

CORNISH BIOLOGICAL RECORDS. see
BIOLOGY

970.1   US   ISSN 0084-9421
COYOTE. 1970. irreg. $0.25. ‡ Native American
Student Alliance, Rt 1, Box 2170, Davis, CA 95616.
Eds. Andrea J. Kelsey, Frank Lee. adv. bk. rev. circ.
2,000. (also avail. in microform from UMI)
American Indian interests

296   AG
CUADERNOS DE ESTUDIOS JUDIOS. 1973. irreg.
Arg.$1.50. Comite Judio Americano, Oficina
Sudamericana, Bartolome Mitre 1943, 1-B, Buenos
Aires, Argentina. Eds. Natalio Mazar, Santiago E.
Kovadloft.
Jewish interests

960.07   US   ISSN 0147-9466
DIRECTORY OF AFRICAN AND AFRO-
AMERICAN STUDIES IN THE UNITED
STATES. 1971. irreg., approx biennial, 5th edt.,
1976. $25. African Studies Association, Research
Liaison Committee, 218 Shiffman Center, Epstein
Service Bldg., Waltham, MA 02154.
Formerly (until 1976): Directory of African
Studies in the United States.
African studies

DIRECTORY OF SPECIAL PROGRAMS FOR
MINORITY GROUP MEMBERS; CAREER
INFORMATION SERVICES, EMPLOYMENT
SKILLS, BANKS, FINANCIAL AID SOURCES.
see *EDUCATION — Guides To Schools And
Colleges*

960   US
ETHIOPIAN MONOGRAPH SERIES. irreg., no. 9,
1980. price varies. Michigan State University,
African Studies Center, Committee on Northeast
African Studies, Rm. 100, Center for International
Programs, East Lansing, MI 48824.

971.004   CN
ETHNIC DIRECTORY OF CANADA. 1976. irreg.
Western Publishers, Box 30193 Sta. B, Calgary,
Alta., Canada.

917.306   US
ETHNIC REVIEW. irreg. Hungarian Freedom
Fighters (Guardian) World Federation, Inc., Box
441, Gracie Sta., New York, NY 10028.

FOLK LITERATURE OF THE SEPHARDIC JEWS.
see *LITERATURE*

DE FRANSE NEDERLANDEN/PAYS-BAS
FRANCAIS. see *SCIENCES: COMPREHENSIVE
WORKS*

917.309 US
FURDEK. 1971, vol. 10. a. First Catholic Slovak Union, 3289 East 55th St., Cleveland, OH 44127. Ed. Joseph C. Krajsa. bibl. index.
Slovak-American interests

296 IS
GAL-ED; on the history of the Jews in poland. (Text in Hebrew; summaries in English) 1973. irreg., vol. 5, 1978. $12. Tel Aviv University, Diaspora Research Institute, c/o Publication Department, Tel-Aviv, Israel. Ed. Moshe Mishkinsky.
Jewish interests

917.1 CN ISSN 0316-8603
GERMAN-CANADIAN YEARBOOK/ DEUTSCHKANADISCHES JAHRBUCH. (Text in English and German) 1973. a. Can.$16. Historical Society of Mecklenburg Upper Canada, Box 193, Station K, Toronto, Ont. M6M 2X9, Canada. Ed. Dr. Hartmut Froeschle. illus. circ. 2,000.
German-Canadian interests

GLENBOW-ALBERTA INSTITUTE. OCCASIONAL PAPER. see *HISTORY — History Of North And South America*

028.5 920 US ISSN 0046-6077
GOLDEN LEGACY; illustrated history magazine series. 1966. irreg. $4 for each set of 16 titles. Fitzgerald Publishing Co., Inc., 527 Madison Ave., New York, NY 10022. Ed. Bertram A. Fitzgerald.
Black interests

296 US ISSN 0149-8487
GRATZ COLLEGE ANNUAL OF JEWISH STUDIES. 1972. a. $5. Gratz College, 10th St. & Tabor Road, Philadelphia, PA 19141. Eds. Isidore D. Passow, Samuel T. Lachs.
Formerly: Annual of Jewish Studies.
Jewish interests

910.03 US
GUIDE TO AFRO-AMERICAN RESOURCES. 1973. biennial. $50. Black Resources Information Coordinating Services, Inc., 614 Howard Ave., Box 6353, Tallahassee, FL 32304. Ed. Emily A. Copeland.
Formerly: Guide to Minority Resources.
Black interests

914 BE
GUIDE TOURISTIQUE EUROPEEN POUR ISRAELITES/EUROPEAN TRAVEL GUIDE FOR JEWS. (Text in English and French) a. 120 Fr. Belgisch Israelitisch Weekblad, Pelikaanstraat 104-108, Antwerp, Belgium. (Co-sponsor: Belgian National Tourist Office) illus.

296 US ISSN 0533-5620
GUIDES TO JEWISH SUBJECTS IN SOCIAL AND HUMANISTIC RESEARCH; doctoral dissertations and master's theses accepted by American institutions of higher learning. 1966. a. $5. YIVO Institute for Jewish Research, 1048 Fifth Ave., New York, NY 10028. Ed. Phyllis Disenhouse. circ. 1,500. (processed)

HAMBONE. see *THEATER*

296 US
HARVARD JUDAIC MONOGRAPHS. 1975. irreg. price varies. Harvard University Press, 79 Garden St., Cambridge, MA 02138.

917.306 US
HARVARD UKRAINIAN RESEARCH INSTITUTE. MINUTES OF THE SEMINAR IN UKRAINIAN STUDIES. a. Harvard Ukrainian Research Institute, 1581-1583 Massachusetts Ave., Cambridge, MA 02138. Ed. Uliana Pasicznyk.

296 956.94 US ISSN 0360-9049
HEBREW UNION COLLEGE ANNUAL. (Text in English, Hebrew, French, German) 1924. a. $15. Hebrew Union College-Jewish Institute of Religion, 3101 Clifton Ave., Cincinnati, OH 45220. Eds. Sheldon H. Blank, Matitiahu Tsevat. cum.index (1924-1974) in 1975 vol. circ. 2,250. (also avail. in microfilm; back issues avail.) Indexed: Old Test.Abstr.

296 US
HEBREW UNION COLLEGE ANNUAL SUPPLEMENTS. 1976. irreg. Hebrew Union College-Jewish Institute of Religion, 3101 Clifton Ave., Cincinnati, OH 45220 (Dist. by: Ktav Publishing House, Inc., 75 Varick St., New York, NY 10013) Eds. Sheldon H. Blank, Matitiahu Tsevat.

HOLY BEGGARS' GAZETTE; journal of Chassidic Judaism. see *RELIGIONS AND THEOLOGY — Judaic*

I W G I A DOCUMENTS; documentation of oppression of ethnic groups in various countries. (International Work Group for Indigenous Affairs) see *ANTHROPOLOGY*

I W G I A NEWSLETTER. (International Work Group for Indigenous Affairs) see *ANTHROPOLOGY*

IDAHO. STATE SUPERINTENDENT OF PUBLIC INSTRUCTION. ANNUAL REPORT. STATE OF IDAHO JOHNSON-O'MALLEY PROGRAM. see *EDUCATION*

INDIAN BOOK REVIEW DIGEST. see *PUBLISHING AND BOOK TRADE*

INDIAN EDUCATION NEWSLETTER. see *EDUCATION*

970.1 US
INDIGENA; news from Indian America. 1973. irreg. $8 to institutions for 4 issues. P.O. Box 4073, Berkeley, CA 94704. Ed. William Meyer. bk. rev. film rev. charts. illus. circ. 6,000. (tabloid format; also avail. in microform from UMI; back issues avail.) Indexed: Alt.Press. Ind.
American Indian interests

914.106 UK
INSTITUTE OF CORNISH STUDIES. SPECIAL BIBLIOGRAPHY. no. 2, 1973. irreg. 30p. Institute of Cornish Studies, Trevenson House, Pool, Redruth, Cornwall TR15 3RE, England.

910.03 US
INSTITUTE OF THE BLACK WORLD. BLACK PAPER. vol. 2, 1970. irreg. $3. Institute of the Black World, Distribution Department, 87 Chestnut St. S.W., Atlanta, GA 30314.
Black interests

910.03 US
INSTITUTE OF THE BLACK WORLD. OCCASIONAL PAPER SERIES. irreg. Institute of the Black World, 87 Chestnut St. S.W., Atlanta, GA 30314.

301.1 US
INSTITUTE ON PLURALISM AND GROUP IDENTITY. WORKING PAPER SERIES. no. 17, 1976. irreg. $1.25 per no. Institute on Pluralism and Group Identity, 165 E. 56th St., New York, NY 10022. (Affiliate: American Jewish Committee)

914.467 SP
INSTITUTO DE ESTUDIOS GERUNDENSES. ANALES. (Text in Spanish and Catalan) 1946. a. 300 ptas.($10) Instituto de Estudios Gerundenses, Plaza Aceite 7, Gerona, Spain. bk. rev. (back issues avail)

914.467 SP
INSTITUTO DE ESTUDIOS GERUNDENSES. SERIE MONOGRAFICA. 1947. irreg. price varies. Instituto de Estudios Gerundenses, Plaza Aceite 7, Gerona, Spain.

323.1 947 IS
ITALIA; literature and culture of Italian Jews. (Text in English, French, Hebrew, and Italian) 1976. s-a. I£50($8) Hebrew University of Jerusalem, Institute of Languages and Literatures) Magnes Press, Hebrew University, Jerusalem, Israel. Eds. R. Bonfil and M.M. Mayer. abstr.

JAPAN-AMERICA SOCIETY OF WASHINGTON. BULLETIN. see *POLITICAL SCIENCE — International Relations*

917.309 US ISSN 0085-2368
JEWISH BOSTON; guide to Jewish life in the greater Boston Jewish community with a Massachusetts supplement. 1969. biennial? $2.50. Jewish Boston, Inc., 233 Bay State Road, Boston, MA 02215. Eds. Morey Schapira, Chaim Casper. adv. bk. rev. illus. circ. 10,000.
Formerly: Jewish Boston and New England Jewry.

296 US
JEWISH HISTORICAL SOCIETY OF NEW YORK. PUBLICATIONS. 1976. irreg., no. 3, 1979. Jewish Historical Society of New York, 8 W. 70th St., New York, NY 10023.

917.1 296 CN ISSN 0317-1655
JEWISH HISTORICAL SOCIETY OF WESTERN CANADA. ANNUAL PUBLICATION. (Text in English; summaries in Yiddish) 1970. a. Jewish Historical Society of Western Canada, 365 Hargrave St., Rm. 406, Winnipeg, Man. R3B 2K3, Canada.

296 US
JEWISH PICKLE. 1976. irreg. American University, Jewish Studies Program, Washington, DC 20016. Ed. Ron Brown. (tabloid format)

917.306 US ISSN 0093-8920
LATVIJA SODIEN. 1972. a. $3 per no. World Federation of Free Latvians, 400 Hurley Ave., Box 16, Rockville, MD 20850. Ed. Dr. I. Spilners. bk. rev. illus. circ. 2,000.

960 UK
LIBRARY OF PEASANT STUDIES. 1975. irreg. £6.95($20.09) Frank Cass & Co. Ltd., Gainsborough House, 11 Gainsborough Rd., London E11 1RS, England (Dist. by: International Scholarly Book Services, 10300 S.W. Allen Blvd., Beaverton, OR 97005) bibl. index.

971.004 CN ISSN 0317-6983
MALTESE DIRECTORY: CANADA, UNITED STATES. 1954. irreg. Malta Service Bureau, Box 826 Station B, Ottawa, Ont. K1P 5P9, Canada. Ed. George Bonavia. circ. 1,000.

914.206 UK ISSN 0306-8536
MANXMAN. no. 8, 1977. irreg. Shearwater Press Ltd., Welch House, Church Rd., Onchan, Isle of Man, England. Eds. Ian Faulds, Mona Douglas.

377 IS ISSN 0543-1786
MA'AYANOT. 1952. irreg; latest issue, no. 4. price varies. World Zionist Organization, P.O. Box 92, Jerusalem, Israel.

970.1 US
MEETING GROUND. 1973. a. Newberry Library, Center for the History of the American Indian, 60 W. Walton, Chicago, IL 60610. Ed. William Swagerty. circ. 2,500.

917.206 US
MEXICAN AMERICAN MONOGRAPH SERIES. 1975. irreg. price varies. University of Texas at Austin, Center for Mexican American Studies, Austin, TX 78712. Ed.Bd. circ. 1,000.

296 IS
MICHAEL; on the history of the Jews in the Diaspora. (Text in Italian, French, German, Hebrew, English) 1972. irreg., vol. 5, 1978. $25 per volume. Tel-Aviv University, Diaspora Research Institute, Sales Division, Tel Aviv, Israel. Ed. Bd.

917.306 US
MINORITY ORGANIZATIONS: A NATIONAL DIRECTORY. 1978. biennial. $15. Garrett Park Press, Garrett Park, MD 20766. Ed. Katherine W. Cole.

026 960 US ISSN 0047-8350
MUNGER AFRICANA LIBRARY NOTES. 1970. irreg., 5-6/yr. $12 per vol. California Institute of Technology, Munger Africana Library, Pasadena, CA 91109. Ed. Edwin S. Munger. charts. illus. cum.index (every 5 yrs.) circ. controlled. Indexed: Hist.Abstr.

NADA. see *HISTORY — History Of Africa*

NATIONAL ROSTER OF BLACK ELECTED OFFICIALS. see *POLITICAL SCIENCE*

NAVAJO HISTORICAL PUBLICATIONS. BIOGRAPHICAL SERIES. see *BIOGRAPHY*

ETHNIC INTERESTS

970.3 US
NAVAJO HISTORICAL PUBLICATIONS. CULTURAL SERIES. 1972. irreg. $1. Navajo Tribal Museum, Box 308, Window Rock, AZ 86515.

970.3 US
NAVAJO HISTORICAL PUBLICATIONS. DOCUMENTARY SERIES. 1971. irreg. $1. Navajo Tribal Museum, Box 308, Window Rock, AZ 86515.

970.3 US
NAVAJO HISTORICAL PUBLICATIONS. HISTORICAL SERIES. 1971. irreg. $1. Navajo Tribal Museum, Box 308, Window Rock, AZ 86515.

353.9 US ISSN 0360-683X
NEBRASKA. INDIAN COMMISSION. REPORT. 1972. irreg. Indian Commission, Lincoln, NE 68509. illus. circ. 100. (also avail. in microform) Key Title: Report of the Nebraska Indian Commission.

910.03 CK
NEGRITUD. 1977. irreg. Centro para la Investigacion de la Cultura Negra, Calle 22 no. 1-90E, Apdo. Aereo 2363, Bogota, Colombia. Ed. Amir Smith Cordoba.
Black interests

296 US
NIVIM; University of Minnesota journal of unlimited Jewish expression. vol. 2, 1975. irreg. B'nai B'rith Hillel Foundation, 1521 University Ave. S.E., Minneapolis, MN 55414. bk. rev. (tabloid format)

NORTH-SOUTH; Canadian journal of Latin American studies. see *POLITICAL SCIENCE — International Relations*

390 YU
NOVA DUMKA. 1971. irreg. Sojuz Rusinoh i Ukraincoh Gorvatskej, Pionirske Naselene 10, Vukovar, Yugoslavia. Ed. Vladd Kostelnik.

OKYEAME; Ghana's literary magazine. see *LITERATURE*

371.9 US ISSN 0090-1059
OREGON. DEPARTMENT OF EDUCATION. RACIAL AND ETHNIC SURVEY. 1971. a. $1. Department of Education, 942 Lancaster Drive NE, Salem, OR 97310. illus. circ. 1,500. Key Title: Racial and Ethnic Survey.

971.3 CN ISSN 0315-0771
OTTAWA ETHNIC GROUPS DIRECTORY. 1971. a. free to qualified personnel. Ottawa-Carleton Immigrant Services Organization, 425 Gloucester St., Ottawa, Ont. K1R 5E9, Canada. Ed. G. Bonavia. circ. 1,000.

OXBRIDGE DIRECTORY OF ETHNIC PERIODICALS. see *BIBLIOGRAPHIES*

PANGNIRTUNG. see *ART*

PROSPECTS; annual journal of American cultural studies. see *HISTORY — History Of North And South America*

PROUD BLACK IMAGES. see *LITERATURE*

LA RAZA LAW REVIEW. see *LAW*

RAZON MESTIZA. see *WOMEN'S INTERESTS*

970.1 US
REFERENCE ENCYCLOPEDIA OF THE AMERICAN INDIAN. triennial. $47.50 per set. Todd Publications, Box 535, Rye, NY 10580. Ed. Barry Klein.

960 US ISSN 0360-7410
RENAISSANCE TWO; JOURNAL OF AFRO-AMERICAN STUDIES. 1972. a. $3.50. Yale University, Afro- American Cultural Center, 211 Park St., New Haven, CT 06520. adv. bk. rev. illus. circ. 10,000. Key Title: Renaissance 2.
African studies

970.1 US
RENEGADE.* 1968. irreg. $5. Survival of American Indians Association, Box 719, Tacoma, WA 98401. Ed. H.L. Adams. illus. stat. circ. 8,000. (looseleaf format)

296 UK ISSN 0306-9567
REPORT ON CZECHOSLOVAK JEWRY. 1970. irreg. $20 (includes ICJC Newsletter) International Council of Jews from Czechoslovakia, 12-13 Henrietta St., London WC2E 8LH, England. adv. bk. rev. circ. 5,000.

296 US ISSN 0556-8609
RHODE ISLAND JEWISH HISTORICAL NOTES. 1954. a. $7. ‡ Rhode Island Jewish Historical Association, 130 Sessions St., Providence, RI 02906. Ed. Seebert J. Goldowsky, M.D. bk. rev. bibl. charts. illus. stat. cum.index (every 4 issues) circ. 550. (processed) Indexed: Hist.Abstr. Amer.Hist. & Life.

RHODES DIRECTORY OF BLACK DENTISTS REGISTERED IN THE UNITED STATES. see *MEDICAL SCIENCES — Dentistry*

353.9 US ISSN 0093-9951
ROSTER OF BLACK ELECTED OFFICIALS IN THE SOUTH. irreg. Voter Education Project Inc., 52 Fairlie St. N.W., Atlanta, GA 30303.

ROYAL ONTARIO MUSEUM. ETHNOGRAPHY MONOGRAPH. see *ANTHROPOLOGY*

917.306 US
SCOTIA; American-Canadian journal of Scottish studies. 1977. a. $5. Old Dominion University, Institute on Scottish Studies, Arts and Letters Building, Norfolk, VA 23508. Ed. Charles H. Haws. Supersedes (1973-1976): Conference on Scottish Studies. Proceedings.

SEMANA INTERNACIONAL DE ANTROPOLOGIA VASCA. ACTAS. see *ANTHROPOLOGY*

892.49 956.94 US
SEPHARDIC SCHOLAR. 1973. a. $5. (American Society of Sephardic Studies) Yeshiva University, Sephardic Studies Program, 500 West 185 St., New York, NY 10033. Ed. Rachel Dalven. bk. rev. circ. 5,000.
Formerly: American Society of Sephardic Studies Series.

918.8 GE
SERBSKA PRATYJA. (Text in Serbian) 1971. a. VEB Domowina Verlag, Tuchmacherstr. 27, 86 Bautzen, E. Germany(D.D.R.) illus.

296 IS
SHVUT; Jewish problems in the USSR and Eastern Europe. (Text in Hebrew; summaries in English) 1973. a. $6. ‡ Tel-Aviv University, Diaspora Research Institute, Sales Division, Tel Aviv, Israel. Ed. Y. A. Gilboa. bk. rev. circ. 1,500.

917.309 US ISSN 0037-6914
SLOVAK PRESS DIGEST. 1968. irreg. free. ‡ Slovak-American Cultural Center, Box 291, New York, NY 10008. Ed. Jozef Ihnat. bk. rev. abstr. bibl. stat. tr.lit. circ. 500. (looseleaf format)
Slovak-American interests

943.7 US ISSN 0583-5623
SLOVAKIA. 1951. a. $5 softbound; $7 hardbound. Slovak League of America, Rifle Camp Rd., West Paterson, NJ 07424. Ed. Michael Novak. bk. rev. bibl. circ. 3,000. (also avail. in microform from UMI)

SLOVANSKE STUDIE. see *HISTORY — History Of Europe*

296 920 SA
SOUTH AFRICAN JEWRY AND WHO'S WHO. a. R.20($20) Alex White and Co. (Pty) Ltd., Box 4886, Johannesburg 2000, South Africa. Ed. Leon Feldberg.

SOUTH DAKOTA INDIAN RECIPIENTS OF SOCIAL WELFARE. see *SOCIAL SERVICES AND WELFARE*

296 807 US
STUDIES IN AMERICAN JEWISH LITERATURE. 1975. a. $10 to individuals; institutions $25. State University of New York Press, State University Plaza, Albany, NY 12246. Ed. Daniel Walden. circ. 400.
Jewish interests

301.45 US
STUDIES IN AMERICAN NEGRO LIFE. irreg., latest no. 35, 1975. price varies. Atheneum Publishers, 122 E. 42nd St., New York, NY 10017. Ed. August Meier.

970.1 US
SUN TRACKS. 1971. a. $5. University of Arizona, Department of English, Tucson, AZ 85720. Ed. Larry Evers. bk. rev. circ. 1,000.
American Indian interests

SURVEY OF CURRENT JEWISH RESEARCH. see *EDUCATION — Higher Education*

087 366 CN ISSN 0317-4018
SVETOVY KONGRES SLOVAKOV. BULLETIN. (Text mainly in Slovak; Some English) 1971. irreg. Svetovy Kongres Slovakov, 4 King St., Toronto, Ont., Canada. illus.

TALLADEGAN. see *COLLEGE AND ALUMNI*

917.306 US
TEREM; problemy ukrainskoi kultury. (Text in Ukrainian, summaries in English) 1963. irreg. price varies. Institute of Ukrainian Culture, 13588 Sunset St., Detroit, MI 48212. Ed. Yurij Tys - Krochmaluk. illus. circ. 1,500.

THEATA. see *ANTHROPOLOGY*

950 US ISSN 0363-311X
TIBET SOCIETY NEWSLETTER. 1967. irreg. membership. Tibet Society, Goodbody Hall, Indiana University, Bloomington, IN 47405.

TODAA. see *WOMEN'S INTERESTS*

970.1 US
TOSAN; American Indian people's inter-tribal news. (Text in English; Occasionally in Cree Syllabic & Shawnee) 1971. irreg. (5-7/yr) free to Indians. Shawnee Nation, c/o Tukemas, Ed., P.O. Box 609, Xenia, OH 45385. adv. bk. rev. charts. illus. circ. 309. (processed; also avail. in microfilm from MCA)

TRY US; national minority business directory. see *BUSINESS AND ECONOMICS*

296 US
TZADDIKIM REVIEW. no. 9, 1978. a. $2. Judaic Book Service, 3726 Virden Ave., Oakland, CA 94619. Ed. Steven L. Maimes.

908 US
UKRAINIAN ARCHIVES. (Text in Ukrainian; summaries in English) no. 27, 1974. irreg. membership. Shevchenko Scientific Society, 302 W. 13 St., New York, NY 10014.

UKRAINIAN ART DIGEST/NOTATKI Z MISTETSTBA. see *ART*

U.S. NATIONAL ADVISORY COUNCIL ON INDIAN EDUCATION. ANNUAL REPORT TO THE CONGRESS OF THE UNITED STATES. see *EDUCATION*

338.04 US ISSN 0091-4630
U.S. OFFICE OF MINORITY BUSINESS ENTERPRISE. MINORITY ENTERPRISE PROGRESS REPORT. a. U. S. Office of Minority Business Enterprise, U.S. Dept. of Commerce, Washington, DC 20230. Key Title: Progress Report. The Minority Business Enterprise Program.

UNIVERSITE DE BORDEAUX II. CENTRE D'ETUDES ET DE RECHERCHES ETHNOLOGIQUES. CAHIERS. see *SOCIOLOGY*

296 956.94 UK
UNIVERSITY COLLEGE LONDON. INSTITUTE OF JEWISH STUDIES. BULLETIN. 1973. 1-2/yr. $4.50. University College London, Institute of Jewish Studies, Gower St., London WC1E 6BT, England. Eds. R. Loewe, C. Abramsky. bk. rev. circ. 400.

UNIVERSITY OF ABERDEEN. AFRICAN STUDIES GROUP. OCCASIONAL PUBLICATIONS. see *HISTORY — History Of Africa*

917.109 CN ISSN 0705-1867
VANI. (Text in Telugu) 1970. a. Can.$2.50 per no. Andhra Cultural Association, Box 3282, Station D, Edmonton, Alta. T5L 4J7, Canada. illus.
East Indian interests

943 GW
VEREIN FUER NIEDERSAECHSISCHES VOLKSTUM. MITTEILUNGEN. 1925. irreg. membership. Verein fuer Niedersaechsisches Volkstum, Am Wall 187, 2800 Bremen 1, W. Germany (B.R.D.) Ed. Karl Dillschneider. circ. 1,000.

296 US
VIEWPOINTS. 1977. irreg. American Jewish Congress, 15 E. 84th St., New York, NY 10028.

057.9 CN
VILNE SLOVO ANNUAL. (Text in Ukrainian) 1961. biennial. $3.50. Toronto Free Press Publications Ltd., 156 Bathurst St., Toronto, Ont. M5T 2R8, Canada Ed. Dr. Stephen Rosocha. adv. abstr. bibl. charts. illus. stat. circ. 5,000(controlled)

910.03 US
WADSWORTH SERIES: EXPLORATIONS IN THE BLACK EXPERIENCE. irreg. Wadsworth Publishing Co., 10 Davis Dr., Belmont, CA 94002.

353.9 US ISSN 0360-4837
WASHINGTON (STATE). INDIAN ASSISTANCE DIVISION.INDIAN ECONOMIC EMPLOYMENT ASSISTANCE PROGRAM. ANNUAL REPORT. a. Indian Assistance Division, Office of Community Development, 1677 2nd Ave., Tumwater, WA 98504. illus. Key Title: Annual Report, the Indian Economic Employment Assistance Program.

WASHINGTON LETTER. see *POLITICAL SCIENCE*

WHO'S WHO IN AMERICAN JEWRY. see *BIOGRAPHY*

296 AT
WIZO REVIEW. 1955. irreg. Australian Federation of Wizo, 584 St. Kilda Road, Melbourne, Vic. 3004, Australia. Ed. Sylvia White.

296 US
WORKING PAPERS IN YIDDISH AND EAST EUROPEAN JEWISH STUDIES/IN GANG FUN ARBET: YIDISH UN MIZRAKH EYROPEISHE YIDISHE SHTUDIES. (Text in various languages) 1974. irreg. $12 to institutions. YIVO Institute for Jewish Research, Max Weinreich Center for Advanced Jewish Studies, 1048 Fifth Ave., New York, NY 10028. Ed. Joan Bratkowsky. circ. 125.

296 US
ZEIREI FORUM. vol. 6, 1976. irreg. $5. Zeirei Agudath Israel of America, 5 Beekman St., New York, NY 10038. Ed. David Zwiebel. adv. illus.

296 IS
ZION. (Text in Russian) irreg. Israel Public Council for Soviet Jewry, 4A Chissin St., Tel-Aviv, Israel. Ed. Rafael Nudelman.
Jewish interests

ETHNIC INTERESTS — Abstracting, Bibliographies, Statistics

910.03 016 US ISSN 0360-2710
BIBLIOGRAPHIC GUIDE TO BLACK STUDIES. 1975. a. G.K. Hall & Co., 70 Lincoln Ave., Boston, MA 02111.

910.03 016 US
BLACK LIST; the concise and comprehensive reference guide to black journalism, radio and television. educational and cultural organizations in the USA, Africa and the Caribbean. 1970. a. $20. Box 3552, New York City, NY 10017. Ed. S. O. Battle. bk. rev. bibl. charts.

016 910.03 US
BLACK PRESS PERIODICAL DIRECTORY. Variant title: Black Communicators. 1973. a. $25. Systems Catalog, Inc., 566 Springfield Ave., Newark, NJ 07103. Ed. Lawrence T. Jackson. adv. stat. circ. 3,000. (looseleaf format)

016 US
BURT FRANKLIN ETHNIC BIBLIOGRAPHICAL GUIDES. vol. 2, 1977. irreg. price varies. Burt Franklin & Co., Inc., 235 E. 44th St., New York, NY 10017. Eds. Francesco Cordasco, William W. Brickman.

917.306 US
DIRECTORY OF ETHNIC PUBLISHERS AND RESOURCE ORGANIZATIONS. 1976. irreg., 2nd edt. 1979. American Library Association, Office for Library Service to the Disadvantaged, 50 E. Huron St., Chicago, IL 60611. Ed. Marjorie K. Joramo.

970.1 016 US ISSN 0091-7346
INDEX TO LITERATURE ON THE AMERICAN INDIAN. 1970. irreg. $8 (hardbound $10) (American Indian Historical Society, Inc.) Indian Historian Press, 1451 Masonic Ave., San Francisco, CA 94117. Ed. Jeannette Henry. circ. 3,000.

029 US ISSN 0161-8245
INDEX TO PERIODICAL ARTICLES BY AND ABOUT BLACKS. 1960. a. price varies. (Central State University, Hallie Q. Brown Memorial Library) G. K. Hall & Co., 70 Lincoln St., Boston, MA 02111. (Co-sponsor: Schomburg Collection of Negro Literature and History)
 Former titles: Index to Periodical Articles by and About Negroes (ISSN 0073-5973) & Index to Selected Periodicals.

659.1 US
MINORITY/ETHNIC MEDIA GUIDE; ethnic and minority media and markets in the U. S. 1977. a. $65. Directories International, 1718 Sherman Ave., Evanston, IL 60201. Ed. Marilyn Justman.
 Formerly: Minority Group Media Guide (ISSN 0149-9572)

016 910.03 US
MINORITY INFORMATION TRADE ANNUAL; publishers and producers lists of Afro-American material. 1977. m. $35. Black Resources Information Coordinating Services, Inc., 614 Howard Ave., Box 6353, Tallahassee, FL 32304. Ed. Emily A. Copeland.

016.342 US
NATIONAL INDIAN LAW LIBRARY. CATALOGUE; an index to Indian legal materials and resources. 1973/74. a. $30. ‡ Native American Rights Fund, 1506 Broadway, Boulder, CO 80302. bibl. circ. 850.
 Formerly: Native American Rights Fund. Catalogue (ISSN 0092-3419)

STUDIES IN BIBLIOGRAPHY AND BOOKLORE. see *RELIGIONS AND THEOLOGY — Abstracting, Bibliographies, Statistics*

TZADDIKIM; a catalogue of Chassidic, Kabbalistic and selected Judaic books. see *RELIGIONS AND THEOLOGY — Abstracting, Bibliographies, Statistics*

EXPERIMENTAL MEDICINE, LABORATORY TECHNIQUE

see *Medical Sciences — Experimental Medicine, Laboratory Technique*

FASHIONS

see *Clothing Trade — Fashions*

FEED, FLOUR AND GRAIN

see *Agriculture — Feed, Flour and Grain*

FIRE PREVENTION

614.84 AT
AUSTRALIAN NATIONAL CONFERENCE ON FIRE. CONFERENCE PAPERS. vol. 6, 1977. a. Australian Fire Protection Association, 49 Chetwynd St., West Melbourne, Vic. 3003, Australia.

614.84 US
DIRECTORY OF FIRE RESEARCH. 7th edt., 1975. biennial. National Academy of Sciences, Committee on Fire Research, 2101 Constitution Ave., Washington, DC 20418.
 Formerly: Directory of Fire Research in the United States (ISSN 0419-2648)

628.92 164.84 GW ISSN 0071-4674
FEUERWEHR-JAHRBUCH; ein Jahresbericht ueber das Feuerwehrwesen in der Bundesrepublik Deutschland. 1964. a. DM.7. Deutscher Feuerwehrverband, Hochkreuzallee 89, 5300 Bonn-Bad Godesberg, W. Germany (B.R.D.) Ed. Benno Ladwig. adv.
 Formerly: Freiwilliger Feuerwehren.

634.9 CN ISSN 0428-4666
FIRE CONTROL NOTES. 1956. biennial. Can.$7. Canadian Forestry Association of British Columbia, Suite 410, 1200 W. Pender St., Vancouver, B.C. V6E 2S9, Canada.

628.9 US ISSN 0090-5313
FIRE MARSHALS ASSOCIATION OF NORTH AMERICA. YEAR BOOK. a. membership. Fire Marshals Association of North America, 470 Atlantic Ave., Boston, MA 02210. Ed. Ronald K. Melott. circ. 1,000(controlled)

614.84 CN ISSN 0071-5395
FIRE PREVENTION NEWS. a. Joint Fire Prevention Publicity Committee Inc., 196 Bronson Ave., Suite 111, Ottawa, Ont. K1R 6H4, Canada. (Co-sponsors: Canadian Association of Fire Chiefs; Association of Fire Commissioners and Fire Marshalls)

614.84 UK ISSN 0071-5409
FIRE PROTECTION DIRECTORY. 1940. a. £15. Benn Publications Ltd., 25 New Street Square, London EC4A 3JA, England. Ed. J. L. Eades. adv. index.

614.84 US ISSN 0071-5417
FIRE PROTECTION HANDBOOK. 1896. quintennial. $43.50. National Fire Protection Association, 470 Atlantic Ave, Boston, MA 02210. Ed. Gordon P. McKinnon. index. (reprint service avail. from UMI)

614.84 US ISSN 0071-5425
FIRE PROTECTION HANDBOOK STUDY GUIDE. 1962. irreg., latest 1976. $15. Davis Publishing Co., 250 Potrero St., Santa Cruz, CA 95060. Ed. S. Davis.

614.84 US ISSN 0361-8382
FIRE PROTECTION REFERENCE DIRECTORY. 1975. a. National Fire Protection Association, 470 Atlantic Ave., Boston, MA 02210. adv. index. circ. 75,000. (reprint service avail. from UMI)

693.82 US
FIRE SAFETY ASPECTS OF POLYMERIC MATERIALS. 1977. irreg. price varies. (National Academy of Sciences, National Materials Advisory Board) Technomic Publishing Co., Inc., 265 Post Rd. W., Westport, CT 06880.

352.3 US ISSN 0071-5468
FIRE YEARBOOK. 1961. a. $7. Davis Publishing Co., 250 Potrero St., Santa Cruz, CA 95060. Eds. Robert Ford, Robert A. Davis, Sr.
 Civil Service questions

614.84 UK ISSN 0307-2118
FITECH; the international equipment guide for the emergency services. (Text in English, French, German, Spanish, Arabic & other languages) 1971. a. $17.50. Unisaf Publications Ltd., Queensway House, 2 Queensway, Redhill, Surrey RH1 1QS, England. Ed. H. Klopper. circ. controlled.

614.84 690 UK
GREAT BRITAIN. BUILDING RESEARCH ESTABLISHMENT. REPORTS. 1961. irreg. price varies. Building Research Establishment, Garston, Watford WD2 7JR, England.
Replaces: Great Britain. Department of the Environment. Fire Research Station. Fire Notes (ISSN 0071-5379) & Great Britain. Department of the Environment. Fire Research Station. Technical Papers (ISSN 0071-545X)

614.84 FR ISSN 0337-5781
GUIDE DU FEU. 1962. a. 95 F. France-Selection, 9-13 rue du Departement, 75921 Paris Cedex 19, France. adv.
Formerly: Guide du Feu et de la Protection Civile (ISSN 0072-8047)

353.9 US ISSN 0095-8247
ILLINOIS. FIRE PROTECTION PERSONNEL STANDARDS AND EDUCATION COMMISSION. ANNUAL REPORT. a. Fire Protection Personnel Standards and Education Commission, 628 E. Adams St., Springfield, IL 62701. Key Title: Annual Report - Illinois Fire Protection Personnel Standards and Education Commission.

INSULATION HANDBOOK. see *BUILDING AND CONSTRUCTION*

614.84 US ISSN 0077-4553
N F P A TECHNICAL COMMITTEE. REPORT. 1917. s-a. first copy free. National Fire Protection Association, 470 Atlantic Ave., Boston, MA 02210. Ed. Richard E. Stevens. index. (reprint service avail. from UMI)

614.84 UK ISSN 0077-4537
NATIONAL FIRE PREVENTION GAZETTE. 1962. a. Unisaf Publications Ltd., UNISAF House, Dudley Road, Tunbridge Wells, Kent, England.

614.84 US ISSN 0077-4545
NATIONAL FIRE PROTECTION ASSOCIATION. NATIONAL FIRE CODES. (Issued in 16 Vols.) 1951. a. $10 per vol., $95 per set. National Fire Protection Association, 470 Atlantic Ave., Boston, MA 02210. index. (also avail. in microfiche; reprint service avail. from UMI) Key Title: National Fire Codes.
All codes, standards, recommended practices, and manuals by technical committees of the N F P A

614.84 NE ISSN 0077-6955
NETHERLANDS. CENTRAAL BUREAU VOOR DE STATISTIEK. STATISTIEK DER BRANDEN. FIRE STATISTICS. (Text in Dutch and English) 1950. a. fl.16.25. Centraal Bureau voor de Statistiek, Prinses Beatrixlaan 428, Voorburg, Netherlands (Orders to: Staatsuitgeverij, Christoffel Plantijnstraat, The Hague, Netherlands)

614.84 CN ISSN 0085-4395
NOVA SCOTIA. FIRE MARSHAL. ANNUAL REPORT. a. Department of Labour, Box 697, Halifax, Nova Scotia, Canada.

614.84 US ISSN 0048-5497
PROGRESS IN FIRE RETARDANCY. 1972. irreg. price varies. Technomic Publishing Co., Inc., 265 Post Rd. W., Westport, CT 06880. charts. illus. stat. index. Indexed: Chem.Abstr. Eng.Ind.

614.85 364.4 SA
SECURITY AND PROTECTION MANUAL. 1978. a. R.40. Thomson Publications S.A. (Pty) Ltd., Box 8308, Johannesburg 2000, South Africa. Ed. Carola Tonetti. adv.

U.S. FOREST SERVICE. COOPERATIVE FIRE PROTECTION. WILDFIRE STATISTICS. see *FORESTS AND FORESTRY*

628.92 FI ISSN 0355-3485
VALTION TEKNILLINEN TUTKIMUSKESKUS. PALOTEKNIIKAN LABORATORIO. TIEDONANTO/TECHNICAL RESEARCH CENTRE OF FINLAND. FIRE TECHNOLOGY LABORATORY. REPORT. (Text mainly in Finnish, some in English or Swedish) 1970. irreg. price varies. Valtion Teknillinen Tutkimuskeskus - Technical Research Centre of Finland, Vuorimiehentie 5, 02150 Espoo 15, Finland.

FIRE PREVENTION — Abstracting, Bibliographies, Statistics

363.3 UK ISSN 0309-622X
CHARTERED INSTITUTE OF PUBLIC FINANCE AND ACCOUNTANCY. FIRE SERVICE STATISTICS. ACTUALS. 1948. a. £5. Chartered Institute of Public Finance and Accountancy, 1 Buckingham Place, London SW1E 6HS, England. stat. (back issues avail.)

310 UK ISSN 0307-0573
CHARTERED INSTITUTE OF PUBLIC FINANCE AND ACCOUNTANCY. FIRE SERVICE STATISTICS. ESTIMATES. 1974. a. £5. Chartered Institute of Public Finance and Accountancy, 1 Buckingham Place, London SW1E 6HS, England. (back issues avail.)

016.6289 614.84 UK ISSN 0306-5766
REFERENCES TO SCIENTIFIC LITERATURE ON FIRE. 1947. s-a. £3 per no. Fire Research Station, Boreham Wood, Herts WD6 2BL, England. Ed. P. K. Mealing. circ. 500-600. (also avail. in microfiche)

FISH AND FISHERIES

see also Biology—Zoology

799.1 UK ISSN 0044-8257
A.C.A. REVIEW. 1948. a. membership. ‡ Anglers Cooperative Association, Midland Bank Chambers, Westgate, Grantham, Lincs NG31 6LE, England. Ed. Ken Sutton. adv. bk. rev. circ. 10,000.

639.9 US ISSN 0095-4632
A. D. F. &. G. TECHNICAL DATA REPORT. irreg. Department of Fish and Game, Subport Bldg., Juneau, AK 99801. illus.

639 NO
AARSBERETNING VEDKOMMENDE NORGES FISKERIER. 1894. a. price varies. Fiskeridirektoratet - Directorate of Fisheries, Box 185, 5001bergen, Norway.

ACTA ADRIATICA. see *EARTH SCIENCES — Oceanography*

338.4 US
ALASKA. DEPARTMENT OF FISH AND GAME. COMMERCIAL OPERATORS. Title varies: Alaska Fisheries Commercial Operators. 1967. a. Department of Fish and Game, Juneau, AK 99801. illus.

ALBERTA. FISH AND WILDLIFE DIVISION. FISHERIES POLLUTION REPORT. see *ENVIRONMENTAL STUDIES*

639.2 US
AMERICAN FISHERIES DIRECTORY AND REFERENCE BOOK. 1978. biennial. $42. Journal Publications (Camden), 21 Elm St., Camden, ME 04843. Ed. James Martin. (reprint service avail. from UMI)

639.2 US ISSN 0097-0638
AMERICAN FISHERIES SOCIETY. SPECIAL PUBLICATIONS. irreg. price varies. American Fisheries Society, 5410 Grosvenor Lane, Bethesda, MD 20014.

639 FR ISSN 0066-2623
ANNUAIRE DE L'ARMEMENT A LA PECHE; guide de la peche francaise. 1956. a. 230 F. Editions Maritimes, 190 Boulevard Haussmann, 75008 Paris, France. Ed. Christian Moreux. index.

639 FR ISSN 0066-2542
ANNUAIRE DE LA MAREE. 1930. a. 270 F. Editions Maritimes, 190, Boulevard Haussmann, Paris 75008, France. Ed. Christian Moreux. index.

338.3 CN ISSN 0382-2249
ANNUAL STATISTICAL REVIEW OF CANADIAN FISHERIES/REVUE STATISTIQUE ANNUELLE DES PECHES CANADIENNES. (Text in English and French) a. Fisheries and Marin Service, 116 Lisgar St., Ottawa, Ont. K1A 0H3, Canada.

639.3 CN
AQUACULTURE REVIEW. a. Department of Tourism and Renewable Resources, Fisheries and Wildlife Branch, 1825 Lorne St., Regina, Sask. S4P 3V7, Canada. illus.
Formerly: Fish Farming Review.

639.3 CH
AQUICULTURE. (Text in Chinese or English) 1970. irreg. Taiwan Fisheries Research Institute, Tungkang Marine Laboratory, Tungkang, Pingtung, Taiwan, Republic of China. Ed. I-Chiu Liao.

639.2 GW ISSN 0003-9063
ARCHIV FUER FISCHEREIWISSENSCHAFT. 1949. irreg., vol. 26, 1975. price varies. (Bundesforschungsanstalt fuer Fischerei) H. Heenemann GmbH, Bessemerstr. 83, 1000 Berlin 42, W. Germany (B.R.D.) Eds. Klaus Tiews, Dietrich Sahrhage. adv. bk. rev. charts. illus. maps. Indexed: Biol.Abstr. Chem.Abstr.

639.3 AG
ARGENTINA. SERVICIO NACIONAL DE PESCA. MONOGRAFIAS DE RECURSOS PESQUEROS.* 1973, no.2. irreg. Servicio Nacional de Pesca, Ministerio de Agricultura y Ganaderia, Buenos Aires, Argentina. Ed. Bd. bibl. charts. stat.

639.97 CN ISSN 0707-5162
ATLANTIC SALMON DIRECTORY. 1978. a. $3. International Atlantic Salmon Foundation, Box 429, St. Andrews, N.B. E0G 2X0, Canada.

639.2 US
ATLANTIC STATES MARINE FISHERIES COMMISSION. SPECIAL REPORT. 1976. irreg., no. 2, 1977. Atlantic States Marine Fisheries Commission, 1717 Massachusetts Ave. N.W., Washington, DC 20036.

639.2 AT
AUSTRALIA. BUREAU OF STATISTICS. WESTERN AUSTRALIAN OFFICE. FISHERIES. 1968-69. a. free. Australian Bureau of Statistics, Western Australian Office, 1-3 St. George's Tce., Perth 6000, W.A., Australia. Ed. E. Binns. circ. 300. (processed)

328.94 639 AT
AUSTRALIA. FISHING INDUSTRY RESEARCH COMMITTEE. ANNUAL REPORT. a. price varies. Australian Government Publishing Service, Box 84, Canberra, A.C.T. 2600, Australia. illus.

639.2 AT ISSN 0084-7356
AUSTRALIAN FISHERIES PAPER. 1966. irreg. price varies; free to qualified personnel. Department of Primary Industry, Fisheries Division, Broughton St., Barton, Canberra, A.C.T. 2600, Australia. Indexed: Aus.Sci.Ind.

639.3 BE ISSN 0303-9072
BELGIUM. RIJKSSTATION VOOR ZEEVISSERIJ. MEDEDELINGEN. 1969. irreg. free. Rijksstation voor Zeevisserij, Ankerstraat 1, B-8400 Oostende, Belgium. circ. 500. (back issues avail) Indexed: Biol. & Agr.Ind.

639 591 CL ISSN 0067-8767
BIOLOGIA PESQUERA. 1961. irreg. exchange basis. Servicio Nacional de Pesca, Casilla 4088, Santiago, Chile. circ. controlled. (also avail. in microform)

639 IE ISSN 0068-0265
BORD IASCAIGH MHARA. TUARASCAIL AGUS CUNTAISI/IRISH SEA FISHERIES BOARD. ANNUAL REPORT. (Text in English and Gaelic) 1953. a. contr. free circ. to libraries & institutions. Irish Sea Fisheries Board, Box 275 Hume House, Ballsbridge, Dublin 4, Ireland.

639 BL ISSN 0068-0850
BRAZIL. SERVICO DE PISCICULTURA. PUBLICACAO.* (Text in Portuguese; occasionally in English) 1910. irreg. available on exchange. Departamento Nacional de Obras Contras as Secas, Servico de Piscicultura, Rio de Janeiro, Brazil.

CAL-NEVA WILDLIFE; TRANSACTIONS. see *CONSERVATION*

639 CN ISSN 0068-7375
CANADA. FISHERIES AND ENVIRONMENT CANADA. ANNUAL REPORT. 1931. a. Fisheries and Environment Canada, Vancouver, B.C., Canada.

FISH AND FISHERIES

639 574.92   CN   ISSN 0068-7510
CANADA. FISHERIES AND MARINE SERVICE. BIOLOGICAL STATION, ST. ANDREWS, NEW BRUNSWICK. GENERAL SERIES CIRCULAR. (Text in English; some French editions) 1947. irreg. free. Fisheries and Marine Service, 116 Lisgar St., Ottawa, Ont. K1A 0E6, Canada. circ. 300. Indexed: Biol.Abstr. Schem.Abstr.

639 574.92   CN   ISSN 0068-7537
CANADA. FISHERIES AND MARINE SERVICE BULLETIN SERIES. (Text in English; occasionally in French; summaries in English and French) 1918. irreg., no. 197, 1976. price varies. Fisheries and Marine Service, 116 Lisgar St., Ottawa, Ont. K1A 0E6, Canada. Ed. J. C. Stevenson. circ. 2,500-15,000. Indexed: Biol.Abstr. Chem.Abstr. Arct.Bibl.

388.3   CN
CANADA. FISHERIES AND MARINE SERVICE. PACIFIC REGION. ANNUAL SUMMARY OF BRITISH COLUMBIA CATCH STATISTICS. a. Fisheries and Marine Service, 116 Lisgar St., Ottawa, Ont. K1A 0E6, Canada.

639   CN
CANADA. FISHERIES AND MARINE SERVICE. RESOURCE MANAGEMENT BRANCH-CENTRAL REGION. ANNUAL REPORT. 1972. a. Fisheries and Marine Service, 116 Lisgar St, Ottawa, Ont. K1A 0E6, Canada. illus.

639 574.92   CN   ISSN 0068-7553
CANADA. FISHERIES AND MARINE SERVICE. TECHNICAL REPORT SERIES. (Text in English, occasionally in French; summaries in English and French) 1967. irreg., no. 651, 1976. free. Fisheries and Marine Service, 116 Lisgar St, Ottawa, Ont. K1A 0E6, Canada. circ. 500. Indexed: Biol.Abstr. Chem.Abstr.

639   CN
CANADA. FISHERIES RESEARCH BOARD ANNUAL. (Text in English and French) 1925. a. free. Fisheries and Marine Service, 116 Lisgar St., Ottawa, Ont. K1A 0E6, Canada. Ed. J. C. Stevenson. circ. 4,000.
   Formerly: Canada. Fisheries & Marine Service Annual. (ISSN 0068-7499)

639.2   CN
CANADA. FISHERIES RESEARCH BOARD. MISCELLANEOUS SPECIAL PUBLICATION SERIES. 1929. irreg., no. 33, 1976. price varies. Fisheries and Marine Service, 116 Lisgar St., Ottawa, Ont. K1A 0E6, Canada. Ed. J. C. Stevenson. circ. 2,000-15,000. Indexed: Biol.Abstr. Chem.Abstr.

639.2   US
CANNED FISHERY PRODUCTS. 1921. a. free. U. S. National Marine Fisheries Service, Statistics and Market News Division, National Oceanic and Atmospheric Administration, Washington, DC 20235. circ. 1,000. (also avail. in microfiche) Indexed: Amer.Stat.Ind. C.I.S.Ind.

639.2   II   ISSN 0008-9427
CENTRAL INLAND FISHERIES RESEARCH INSTITUTE. BULLETIN. 1963. irreg. exchange basis. Central Inland Fisheries Research Institute, Barrackpore 743101, West Bengal, India. abstr. bibl. circ. 132. (processed) Indexed: Biol.Abstr. Sci.Cit.Ind.

597 551.46   II   ISSN 0577-084X
CENTRAL MARINE FISHERIES RESEARCH INSTITUTE. BULLETIN. 1968. irreg., no. 25, 1973. price varies. Central Marine Fisheries Research Institute, Marine Fisheries P.O., Mandapam Camp, Tamil Nadu, India. circ. 500 (controlled) (looseleaf format) Indexed: Biol.Abstr.

639 591   CL
CHILE. SERVICIO NACIONAL DE PESCA. ANUARIO ESTADISTICO DE PESCA. 1944. a. exchange basis. Servicio Nacional de Pesca, Casilla 4088, Santiago, Chile. circ. controlled. (also avail. in microform)
   Former titles: Chile. Servicio Agricola y Ganadero. Division Proteccion Pesquera. Anuario Estadistico (ISSN 0069-3537) & Chile. Direccion de Agricultura y Pesquera. Departamento Estadistica. Anuario Estadistico de Pesca.

COMMONWEALTH SCIENTIFIC AND INDUSTRIAL RESEARCH ORGANIZATION. DIVISION OF FISHERIES AND OCEANOGRAPHY. CIRCULAR. see EARTH SCIENCES — Oceanography

COMMONWEALTH SCIENTIFIC AND INDUSTRIAL RESEARCH ORGANIZATION. DIVISION OF FISHERIES AND OCEANOGRAPHY. FISHERIES SYNOPSIS. see BIOLOGY — Zoology

639 551.46   AT   ISSN 0069-7397
COMMONWEALTH SCIENTIFIC AND INDUSTRIAL RESEARCH ORGANIZATION. DIVISION OF FISHERIES AND OCEANOGRAPHY. ANNUAL REPORT. 1960/61. a. free. C. S. I. R. O., Division of Fisheries and Oceanography, P.O. Box 21, Cronulla 2230, N.S.W., Australia. circ. 1,000.

639 551.46   AT   ISSN 0069-7370
COMMONWEALTH SCIENTIFIC AND INDUSTRIAL RESEARCH ORGANIZATION. DIVISION OF FISHERIES AND OCEANOGRAPHY. REPORT. 1956. irreg. free. C. S. I. R. O., Division of Fisheries and Oceanography, P.O.B. 21, Cronulla 2230, N.S.W., Australia. circ. 1,000. Indexed: Ocean.Abstr.

639   FR   ISSN 0069-889X
CONGRES NATIONAL DES PECHES ET INDUSTRIES MARITIMES. COMPTE RENDU.* 1952, vol. 14. irreg. Confederation des Industries du Traitement des Produits des Peches Maritimes, 3 rue de Logelbach, Paris 17e, France.

354.564   CY
CYPRUS. DEPARTMENT OF FISHERIES. ANNUAL REPORT ON THE DEPARTMENT OF FISHERIES AND THE CYPRUS FISHERIES. (Text in English) a. Department of Fisheries, Nicosia, Cyprus.
   Supersedes: Cyprus. Department of Fisheries. Annual Report of the Cyprus Fisheries.

639   DK   ISSN 0106-553X
DENMARK. DANMARKS FISKERI- OG HAVUNDERSOEGELSER. DANA. (Text in English) 1952. irreg. price varies. Danmarks Fiskeri-og Havundersoegelser - Danish Institute for Fisheries and Marine Research, Charlottenlund Castle, 2920 Charlottenlund, Denmark. Ed. E. Hoffmann. index, cum.index 1904-1979.
   Formerly: Denmark. Danmarks Fiskeri- og Havundersoegelser. Meddeleser (ISSN 0070-3435)

639 574.92   DK   ISSN 0070-3605
DENMARK. FISKERIMINISTERIET. FORSOEGSLABORATORIUM. AARSBERETING/ANNUAL REPORT. (Text in Danish and English) 1952. a. free. Fiskeriministeriet, Forsoegslaboratorium - Ministry of Fisheries, Technological Laboratory, Polytekniske Laereanstalt, Danmarks Tekniske Hoejskole, Building 221, 2800 Lyngby, Denmark. circ. 2,000. Indexed: Chem.Abstr. Aqua.Sci. & Fish.Abstr. Food Sci. & Tech.Abstr.

639.21   UG   ISSN 0070-7953
EAST AFRICAN FRESHWATER FISHERIES RESEARCH ORGANIZATION. ANNUAL REPORT. 1948. a. $1.50. East African Freshwater Fisheries Research Organization, P.O. Box 343 (Nile Crescent), Jinja, Uganda.

639.2   UN   ISSN 0429-9329
F A O FISHERIES CIRCULARS. irreg.; 1973, no. 314. price varies. Food and Agriculture Organization of the United Nations, Distribution and Sales Section, Via delle Terme di Caracalla, I-00100 Rome, Italy (Dist. in U.S. by: Unipub, 345 Park Ave. S., New York, NY 10010)

639.2   UN   ISSN 0429-9337
F A O FISHERIES REPORTS. irreg.; 1973, no. 132. price varies. Food and Agriculture Organization of the United Nations, Distribution and Sales Section, Via delle Terme di Caracalla, I-00100 Rome, Italy (Dist. in U.S. by: Unipub, 345 Park Ave. S., New York, NY 10010)

639   UN   ISSN 0071-7037
F A O FISHERIES STUDIES. (Text in English, French and Spanish) irreg., 1966, no. 12. price varies. Food and Agriculture Organization of the United Nations, Distribution and Sales Section, Via delle Terme di Caracalla, 00100 Rome, Italy (Dist. in U.S. by: Unipub, 345 Park Ave. S., New York, NY 10010) Ed. Chris A. Theodore.

639   UN   ISSN 0429-9345
F A O FISHERIES TECHNICAL PAPER. 1960. Food and Agriculture Organization of the United Nations, Distribution and Sales Section, Via delle Terme di Caracalla, I-00100 Rome, Italy (Dist. in U.S. by: Unipub, 345 Park Ave. S., New York, NY 10010)

639   UN   ISSN 0071-7061
F A O MANUALS IN FISHERIES SCIENCE. (Text in English, French and Spanish) 1965. irreg., 1972, no. 5. price varies. Food and Agriculture Organization of the United Nations, Distribution and Sales Section, Via delle Terme di Caracalla, 00100 Rome, Italy (Dist. in U.S. by: Unipub, 345 Park Ave. S., New York, NY 10010)

639.2   UK
F. O. S. YEAR BOOK & ANNUAL REPORT. 1972. a. £2.50 to non-members. Fisheries Organization Society Ltd., 558 London Rd., North Cheam, Sutton, Surrey SM3 9AA, England. Ed. E. B. Hamley. adv. bk. rev. charts. illus. stat. tr.lit. index. circ. 1,500(controlled) (back issues avail.)

639   FI   ISSN 0301-908X
FINNISH FISHERIES RESEARCH. (Text and Summaries in English) 1972. irreg. exchange basis. Finnish Game and Fisheries Research Institute, Fisheries Division, Box 193, SF-00131 Helsinki 13, Finland. Ed. Pekka Tuunainen. circ. 1,500. Indexed: Biol.Abstr. Aqua.Sci. & Fish.Abstr. Commer.Fish.Abstr. Sport Fish.Abstr.

639.2   AT
FISH AND WILDLIFE GAZETTE. 1962. irreg. New South Wales Institute of Freshwater Fishermen, P.O. Box 195, Lindfield, NSW 2070, Australia. Ed. R. B. Hungerford. circ. controlled.

639   US   ISSN 0071-5492
FISH DISEASE LEAFLETS. 1966. irreg., no. 44, 1975. $1. U.S. Fish and Wildlife Service, Dept. of the Interior, Washington, DC 20240. (looseleaf format)

639.3   NZ
FISHDEX. 1980. irreg. free. Ministry of Agriculture and Fisheries, Media Services, Box 2298, Wellington, New Zealand. Ed. C. Rumble. illus.

639 333.7   AT   ISSN 0071-5522
FISHERIES AND WILDLIFE PAPER. VICTORIA. 1971. irreg. free. Ministry for Conservation, Fisheries and Wildlife Division, Box 41, East Melbourne, Vic. 3002, Australia (Subscr. to: Scientific Editor, Fisheries and Wildlife Division, P.O. Box 137, Heidelberg, Vic. 3084 Australia) circ. 250.

639   CN   ISSN 0317-1817
FISHERIES FACT SHEET. irreg. Fisheries and Marine Service, Ottawa, Ont., Canada. illus.

639   UK   ISSN 0080-1283
FISHERIES OF SCOTLAND REPORT. 1882. a. price varies. Department of Agriculture and Fisheries, Marine Laboratory, P.O. Box 101, Victoria Rd., Aberdeen AB9 8DB, Scotland (Avail. from: H.M.S.O., Avail. from H.M.S.O., 13a Castle St., Edinburgh EH2 3AR, Scotland)

338.3   US
FISHERIES OF THE UNITED STATES. 1942. a. U. S. National Marine Fisheries Service, National Oceanic and Atmospheric Administration, Washington, DC 20235 (Orders to: Supt. of Documents, Government Printing Office, Washington, DC 20402) stat. circ. 1,700. (also avail. in microfiche) Indexed: Amer.Stat.Ind. C.I.S.Ind.
   Formerly: Fishery Statistics of the United States (ISSN 0071-5603); Which superseded: U. S. Bureau of Commercial Fisheries. United States Fisheries.

639   ZA   ISSN 0084-4713
FISHERIES RESEARCH BULLETIN OF ZAMBIA. (Text in English) 1962/63. irreg. Central Fisheries Research Institute, Box 100, Chilanga, Zambia.

639 338.1 JA ISSN 0071-5581
FISHERIES STATISTICS OF JAPAN. (Text in English) 1963. a. Ministry of Agriculture and Forestry, Statistics Bureau - Norin-sho Norin Keizai-Kyoku Tokei Joho-bu, 11-14 2-Chome, Meguro-Ku, Tokyo 153, Japan (Orders to: Government Publications Service Center, 1-2-1 Kasumigaseki, Chiyoda-Ku, Tokyo 100, Japan) cum.index: 1963-67.

639.2 IO
FISHERMAN UNION OF INDONESIA. CENTRAL GOVERNING BOARD. ANNUAL REPORT/HIMPUNAN NELAYAN SELURAH INDONESIA. DEWAN PIMPANAN PUSAT. LAPORAN KEGIATAN. (Text in Indonesian) a. Fisherman Union of Indonesia, Central Governing Board, Jl. Imam Bonjol, Jakarta, Indonesia.

639.22 UK ISSN 0308-0935
FISHING PROSPECTS. 1969. a. free. Ministry of Agriculture, Fisheries and Food, Fisheries Laboratory, Lowestoft, Suffolk NR33 0HT, England. illus. Indexed: Aqua.Sci. Fish Abstr.

639 574.92 DK ISSN 0105-9211
FISK OG HAV. 1972. a. $4. Danmarks Fiskeri- og Havundersoegelser - Danish Institute for Fisheries and Marine Research, Charlottenlund Castle, DK-2920 Charlottenlund, Denmark. Ed. Erik Hoffmann. cum.index: 1904-52.
Formerly: Denmark. Danmarks Fiskeri og Havundersoegelser. Skrifter.

FISKE. see *SPORTS AND GAMES*

639 NO ISSN 0071-5638
FISKEN OG HAVET. (Reports previously published in Fiskets Gang) (Text in Norwegian; summaries in English) 1959. irreg. Fiskeridirektoratet, Havforskningsinstituttet - Directorate of Fisheries, Box 1870-72, N-5011 Bergen-Nordnes, Norway. Ed. Erling Bratberg.

639.2 UN
FOOD AND AGRICULTURE ORGANIZATION OF THE UNITED NATIONS. COMMITTEE FOR INLAND FISHERIES OF AFRICA. CIFA REPORTS. (Represents Its Report of the Session) 1973. irreg. unpriced. Food and Agriculture Organization of the United Nations, Distribution and Sales Section, Via delle Terme di Caracalla, I-00100 Rome, Italy (Dist. in U.S. by: Unipub, 345 Park Ave., S., New York, NY 10010)

639.2 UN
FOOD AND AGRICULTURE ORGANIZATION OF THE UNITED NATIONS. COMMITTEE FOR INLAND FISHERIES OF AFRICA. CIFA TECHNICAL PAPERS. 1972. irreg.; 1973, no. 2. unpriced. Food and Agriculture Organization of the United Nations, Distribution and Sales Section, Via delle Terme di Caracalla, I-00100 Rome, Italy.

639 UN ISSN 0532-9396
FOOD AND AGRICULTURE ORGANIZATION OF THE UNITED NATIONS. EUROPEAN INLAND AND FISHERIES ADVISORY COMMISSION. E I F A C NEWSLETTER. 1963. Food and Agriculture Organization of the United Nations, Distribution and Sales Section, Via delle Terme di Caracalla, I-00100 Rome, Italy.

639.2 US ISSN 0091-8105
FOOD FISH MARKET REVIEW AND OUTLOOK. 1964. irreg. (2-3/yr.) free. U.S. National Marine Fisheries Service, National Oceanographic and Atmospheric Administration, Washington, DC 20235. charts. mkt. stat. circ. 6,500. (processed; also avail. in microform from MIM) Indexed: Ind.U.S.Gov.Per.
Formerly: Food Fish Situation and Outlook (ISSN 0015-640X)

639 UN ISSN 0072-0747
GENERAL FISHERIES COUNCIL FOR THE MEDITERRANEAN. PROCEEDINGS AND TECHNICAL PAPERS. DEBATS ET DOCUMENTS TECHNIQUES. (Text in English and French) 1952. irreg., 1969, no. 10. Food and Agriculture Organization of the United Nations, Distribution and Sales Section, Via delle Terme di Caracalla, 00100 Rome, Italy (Dist. in U.S. by: Unipub, 345 Park Ave. S., New York, NY 10010)

639 UN ISSN 0072-0755
GENERAL FISHERIES COUNCIL FOR THE MEDITERRANEAN. REPORTS OF THE SESSIONS. 1968. irreg., no. 12, 1974. price varies. Food and Agriculture Organization of the United Nations, Distribution and Sales Section, Via delle Terme di Caracalla, 00100 Rome, Italy (Dist. in U.S. by: Unipub, 345 Park Ave. S., New York, NY 10010) Indexed: Aqua.Sci. & Fish.Abstr.

639 UN ISSN 0433-3519
GENERAL FISHERIES COUNCIL FOR THE MEDITERRANEAN. STUDIES AND REVIEWS. 1957. irreg., no. 56, 1977. price varies. Food and Agriculture Organization of the United Nations, Distribution & Sales Section, Via delle Terme di Caracalla, I-00100 Rome, Italy (Dist. in U.S. by: Unipub, 345 Park Ave. S., New York, NY 10010)

639.22 UK ISSN 0308-5589
GREAT BRITAIN. MINISTRY OF AGRICULTURE, FISHERIES AND FOOD. FISHERIES RESEARCH TECHNICAL REPORT. 1971. irreg. free. Ministry of Agriculture, Fisheries and Food, Fisheries Laboratory, Lowestoft, NR33 0HT, England. Indexed: Chem.Abstr. Aqua. Sci. & Fish Abstr.

639.22 UK ISSN 0072-6699
GREAT BRITAIN. MINISTRY OF AGRICULTURE, FISHERIES AND FOOD. LABORATORY LEAFLET. irreg., no.49,1979. free. Ministry of Agriculture, Fisheries and Food, Fisheries Laboratory, Lowestoft, Suffolk NR33 0HT, England.

639.22 UK
GREAT BRITAIN. MINISTRY OF AGRICULTURE, FISHERIES AND FOOD. REPORT OF THE DIRECTOR OF FISHERIES RESEARCH. irreg. free. Ministry of Agriculture, Fisheries and Food, Fisheries Laboratory, Lowestoft, Suffolk NR33 0HT, England.

639 UK ISSN 0072-7261
GREAT BRITAIN. WHITE FISH AUTHORITY. ANNUAL REPORT AND ACCOUNTS. 1951/52. a. price varies. White Fish Authority, Sea Fisheries House, 10 Young St., Edinburgh EH2 4JQ, Scotland (Avail. from H.M.S.O., c/o Liaison Officer, Atlantic House, Holborn Viaduct, London EC1P 1BN, England) Ed. Richard Murray. circ. 2,500.

639 US ISSN 0072-7296
GREAT LAKES FISHERY COMMISSION (UNITED STATES AND CANADA) ANNUAL REPORT. 1956. a. free. Great Lakes Fishery Commission, 1451 Green Rd., Ann Arbor, MI 48105. circ. 500.

639 US ISSN 0072-730X
GREAT LAKES FISHERY COMMISSION (UNITED STATES AND CANADA) TECHNICAL REPORT. 1961. irreg., no. 28, 1975. free. Great Lakes Fishery Commission, 1451 Green Rd., Ann Arbor, MI 48105. circ. 500.

639 US ISSN 0072-9019
GULF AND CARIBBEAN FISHERIES INSTITUTE. ANNUAL PROCEEDINGS. 1948. a. $20. University of Miami, Gulf and Caribbean Fisheries Institute, 4600 Rickenbacker Causeway, Miami, FL 33149. Ed. B. Higman. cum.index: 1948-64. circ. 1,000.

HOKKAIDO UNIVERSITY. FACULTY OF FISHERIES. DATA RECORD OF OCEANOGRAPHIC OBSERVATIONS AND EXPLORATORY FISHING/KAIYO CHOSA GYOGYO SHIKEN YOHO. see *EARTH SCIENCES — Oceanography*

639 HK ISSN 0065-0269
HONG KONG. FISHERIES RESEARCH STATION. BULLETIN. (Text in English) 1970. irreg., no. 4, 1974. price varies. ‡ Fisheries Research Station, 100A Shek Pai Wan Rd., Aberdeen, Hong Kong.

IDAHO. DEPARTMENT OF FISH AND GAME. FEDERAL AID INVESTIGATION PROJECTS. PROGRESS REPORTS AND PUBLICATIONS. see *CONSERVATION*

597 II ISSN 0537-2003
INDIAN JOURNAL OF FISHERIES. (Text in English) 1954. a. $7. Central Marine Fisheries Research Institute, Marine Fisheries P. O., Mandapam Camp, Tamil Nadu, India. circ. 300. (looseleaf format) Indexed: Biol.Abstr. Chem.Abstr. Ocean.Abstr. Pollut.Abstr.

639.2 UN
INDIAN OCEAN FISHERY COMMISSION. REPORT OF THE SESSION. irreg., 1972, 3rd, Colombo. unpriced. Food and Agriculture Organization of the United Nations, Distribution and Sales Section, Via delle Terme di Caracalla, I-00100 Rome, Italy.
Scheduled 4th, 1975, Colombo

639 UN ISSN 0537-3654
INDO-PACIFIC FISHERIES COUNCIL. REGIONAL STUDIES. 1965. irreg. Food and Agriculture Organization of the United Nations, Regional Office for Asia and the Far East, Maliwan Mansion, Phra Atit Road, Bangkok 2, Thailand.

639.2 US ISSN 0093-8726
INDUSTRIAL FISHERY PRODUCTS. 1921. a. free. U. S. National Marine Fisheries Service, Statistics and Market News Division, National Oceanic and Atmospheric Administration, Washington, DC 20235. circ. 1,000. (also avail. in microfiche) Indexed: Amer.Stat.Ind. C.I.S.Ind.

639 MR ISSN 0069-0821
INSTITUT DES PECHES MARITIMES. BULLETIN. (Text in French) 1953. irreg., July 1969, no. 17. Institut des Peches Maritimes, Rue de Tiznit, Casablanca, Morocco. (Affiliate: Office National des Peches)

639 CL
INSTITUTO DE FOMENTO PESQUERO. INFORMES PESQUERO. 1965. irreg.; no. 66, 1978. $5. ‡ Instituto de Fomento Pesquero, Jose Domingo Canas 2277, Casilla 1287, Santiago, Chile. abst. bibl. charts. illus. stat. circ. 700.
Formerly: Santiago de Chile. Instituto de Fomento Pesquero Publicacion (ISSN 0080-6153)

639 BL ISSN 0046-9939
INSTITUTO DE PESCA, SAO PAULO. BOLETIM. (Text in Portuguese; summaries in English) 1971. irreg. free. Instituto de Pesca, Secao de Biblioteca, Av. Francisco Matarazzo, 455, 05001 Sao Paulo, S.P., Brazil. Ed. Dr. Newton Castagnolli. adv. 639. circ. 1,000.

630 BL
INSTITUTO DE PESCA, SAO PAULO. BOLETIM. SERIE DE DIVULGACAO. 1972. irreg. free. Instituto de Pesca, Secao de Biblioteca, Av. Francisco Matarazzo, 455, 05001 Sao Paulo, S. P., Brazil. Ed. Dr. Albino Joaquim Rorigues. circ. 1,000.

639.1 639.2 PE ISSN 0458-7766
INSTITUTO DEL MAR DEL PERU. BOLETIN. (Text in Spanish; summaries in English) 1960. irreg (4-5 per year) $8. Instituto del Mar del Peru, Biblioteca, Apartado 3734, Lima, Peru.

639.2 639.3 PE ISSN 0458-7774
INSTITUTO DEL MAR DEL PERU. INFORME. (Text in Spanish; summaries in English) 1965. irreg (4-5 per year) $10. Instituto del Mar del Peru, Biblioteca, Apartado 37-34, Lima, Peru. bibl. charts. illus. stat.

639.2 AG ISSN 0325-6987
INSTITUTO NACIONAL DE INVESTIGACION Y DESARROLLO PESQUERO. MEMORIA. a. Instituto Nacional de Investigacion y Desarrollo Pesquero, Casilla de Correo 175, 7600 Mar del Plata, Argentina.

639 US ISSN 0538-3609
INTER-AMERICAN TROPICAL TUNA COMMISSION. DATA REPORT. (Text in English and Spanish) 1966. irreg., no. 6, 1980. price varies. Inter-American Tropical Tuna Commission, Scripps Institution of Oceanography, La Jolla, CA 92093. Ed. Clifford L. Peterson. circ. 500 (approx.)

FISH AND FISHERIES

639   US   ISSN 0074-1000
INTER-AMERICAN TROPICAL TUNA COMMISSION. INFORME ANUAL. ANNUAL REPORT. (Text in English and Spanish) 1951. a. $2. Inter-American Tropical Tuna Commission, c/o Scripps Institution of Oceanography, La Jolla, CA 92093. Ed. Clifford L. Peterson. circ. 1,200.

639   US   ISSN 0074-0993
INTER-AMERICAN TROPICAL TUNA COMMISSION. BULLETIN/COMISION INTERAMERICANA DEL ATUN TROPICAL. BOLETIN. (Text in English and Spanish) 1954. irreg., no. 7, 1980. price varies. Inter-American Tropical Tuna Commission, c/o Scripps Institution of Oceanography, La Jolla, CA 92093. Ed. Clifford L. Peterson. circ. 1,000. Indexed: Biol.Abstr.

639.2   333.7   CN
INTERNATIONAL ATLANTIC SALMON FOUNDATION. SPECIAL PUBLICATION SERIES. 1971. irreg. price varies. International Atlantic Salmon Foundation, P.O. Box 429, St. Andrews, N. B. E0G 2X0, Canada. (back issues avail.) Indexed: Ocean.Abstr.

639   CN   ISSN 0074-7165
INTERNATIONAL NORTH PACIFIC FISHERIES COMMISSION. ANNUAL REPORT. (Editions in English and Japanese) 1954. a. available on exchange. ‡ International North Pacific Fisheries Commission, 6640 N.W. Marine Dr., Vancouver, B.C. V6T 1X2, Canada. circ. 1,000. Indexed: Biol.Abstr.   Aqua.Sci. & Fish.Abstr.

639   CN   ISSN 0074-7157
INTERNATIONAL NORTH PACIFIC FISHERIES COMMISSION. BULLETIN. (Edts. in English and Japanese) 1955. irreg. available on exchange. ‡ International North Pacific Fisheries Commission, 6640 N.W. Marine Dr., Vancouver, B.C. V6T 1X2, Canada. circ. 1,000. Indexed: Biol.Abstr.   Aqua.Sci. & Fish.Abstr.

639   CN   ISSN 0535-1588
INTERNATIONAL NORTH PACIFIC FISHERIES COMMISSION. STATISTICAL YEARBOOK. 1970. a. exchange basis. International North Pacific Fisheries Commission, 6640 N.W. Marine Drive, Vancouver, B.C. V6T 1X2, Canada. circ. 500.

639   US   ISSN 0074-7238
INTERNATIONAL PACIFIC HALIBUT COMMISSION (U.S. AND CANADA). ANNUAL REPORT. 1969. a. free. International Pacific Halibut Commission, P.O. Box 5009, University Station, Seattle, WA 98105. circ. 2,000. (back issues avail.)

639   US   ISSN 0074-7246
INTERNATIONAL PACIFIC HALIBUT COMMISSION (U.S. AND CANADA). SCIENTIFIC REPORTS. no. 62, 1976. irreg. free. International Pacific Halibut Commission, P.O. Box 5009, University Station, Seattle, WA 98105. circ. 1,500.

639   US   ISSN 0579-3920
INTERNATIONAL PACIFIC HALIBUT COMMISSION (U.S. AND CANADA). TECHNICAL REPORTS. 1969. irreg., no. 13, 1975. free. International Pacific Halibut Commission, P.O. Box 5009, University Station, Seattle, WA 98105. circ. 1,500.
    Formerly: International Pacific Halibut Commission. Report (ISSN 0096-1221)

639   CN   ISSN 0074-7254
INTERNATIONAL PACIFIC SALMON FISHERIES COMMISSION. ANNUAL REPORT. 1937. a. International Pacific Salmon Fisheries Commission, Box 30, New Westminster, B.C. V3L 4X9, Canada.

639   CN   ISSN 0074-7262
INTERNATIONAL PACIFIC SALMON FISHERIES COMMISSION. BULLETIN. 1945. irreg. International Pacific Salmon Fisheries Commission, Box 30, New Westminster, B.C. V3L 4X9, Canada.

639   CN   ISSN 0074-7270
INTERNATIONAL PACIFIC SALMON FISHERIES COMMISSION. PROGRESS REPORT. 1956. irreg. International Pacific Salmon Fisheries Commission, Box 30, New Westminster, B.C. V3L 4X9, Canada.

639.28   UK   ISSN 0074-9591
INTERNATIONAL WHALING COMMISSION. REPORT. 1950. a. free. International Whaling Commission, The Red House, Station Rd., Histon, Cambridge CB4 4NP, England. Ed. R. Stacey.

639   630   IE   ISSN 0075-0654
IRELAND (EIRE) DEPARTMENT OF AGRICULTURE AND FISHERIES. JOURNAL. 1900. a. price varies. Government Publications Sales Office, G.P.O. Arcade, Dublin 1, Ireland.

639   IS   ISSN 0075-1189
ISRAEL. MINISTRY OF AGRICULTURE. DEPARTMENT OF FISHERIES. ISRAEL FISHERIES IN FIGURES/HA-DAYIG BE-YISRAEL BE-MISPARIM. (Text in Hebrew and English) 1964. a. Ministry of Agriculture, Dept. of Fisheries, P.O.B. 21170, Tel Aviv 62263, Israel.

639   GW   ISSN 0075-2851
JAHRESBERICHT UEBER DIE DEUTSCHE FISCHWIRTSCHAFT. 1949. a. DM.38. Bundesministerium fuer Ernaehrung, Landwirtschaft und Forsten, 5300 Bonn, W. Germany (B.R.D.)

639   TH   ISSN 0075-5206
KASETSART UNIVERSITY, BANGKOK, THAILAND. FACULTY OF FISHERIES. NOTES. (Text in English) 1965. irreg. free on exchange. Kasetsart University, Museum of Fisheries, Faculty of Fisheries, Bangkok 9, Thailand.

639   KE
KENYA FISHERIES REPORTS. irreg. Ministry of Tourism and Wildlife, Box 30027, Nairobi, Kenya.

639.2   591   JA   ISSN 0453-0314
KYUSHU UNIVERSITY. CONTRIBUTIONS FROM THE DEPARTMENT OF FISHERIES AND THE FISHERY RESEARCH LABORATORY/KYUSHU DAIGAKU NOGAKUBU SUISANGAKKA GYOSEKISHU. (Text in Japanese and English) 1959. a. exchange basis. Kyushu University, Department of Fisheries - Kyushu Daigaku Nogakubu Suisan Gakka, 3575-1 Hakozaki, Higashi-ku, Fukuoka 812, Japan.

639.3   551.46   IT
LABORATORIO DI TECNOLOGIA DELLA PESCA. QUADERNI. (Summaries in English, French, Italian) 1970. irreg. avail only on exchange basis. Laboratorio di Tecnologia della Pesca, Molo Mandracchio, 60100 Ancona, Italy. circ. 500.

639   US
MAINE. DEPARTMENT OF MARINE RESOURCES. FISHERIES CIRCULARS. 1947. irreg., no. 30, 1977. Department of Marine Resources, State House Annex, Augusta, ME 04330.
    Incorporating: Maine. Department of Sea and Shore Fisheries. General Bulletin (ISSN 0076-2636)

639.2   US
MAINE. DEPARTMENT OF MARINE RESOURCES. FISHERY BULLETIN. vol. 74, 1976. irreg. free. Department of Marine Resources, State House Annex, Augusta, ME 04330.

639.2   US
MAINE. DEPARTMENT OF MARINE RESOURCES. RESEARCH BULLETIN. 1949. irreg. free. Department of Marine Resources, State House Annex, Augusta, ME 04330.

639.2   MW
MALAWI. FISHERIES DEPARTMENT. FISHERIES BULLETIN. 1971. irreg. Fisheries Department, Ministry of Agriculture and Natural Resources, Capital City, Box 30134, Lilongwe 3, Malawi. illus.

639.2   MY
MALAYSIA. MINISTRY OF AGRICULTURE. FISHERIES DIVISION. ANNUAL FISHERIES STATISTICS/MALAYSIA. KEMENTERIAN PERTANIAN. BAHAGIAN PERIKANAN. PERANGKAAN TAHUNAN PERIKANAN. (Text in English and Malay) a. M.$2. Ministry of Agriculture, Fisheries Division, Swettenham Rd., Kuala Lumpur 10-02, Malaysia. illus.

MALAYSIA. MINISTRY OF AGRICULTURE. TECHNICAL AND GENERAL BULLETINS. see AGRICULTURE

639.2   US   ISSN 0161-522X
MARINE RECREATIONAL FISHERIES. 1976. a. $15. Sport Fishing Institute, 608 13th St., N.W., Washington, DC 20005. Ed. Henry Clepper. circ. 1,500. (back issues avail.)

639.2   US   ISSN 0542-7029
MARINE RESOURCES OF THE ATLANTIC COAST. 1965. irreg., latest no. 20. price varies. Atlantic States Marine Fisheries Commission, 1717 Massachusetts Ave., N.W., Washington, DC 20036. Ed. Albert C. Jensen. charts. illus. circ. controlled.

639   US   ISSN 0076-7905
MICHIGAN. DEPARTMENT OF NATURAL RESOURCES. INSTITUTE FOR FISHERIES RESEARCH. MISCELLANEOUS PUBLICATION. 1944. irreg. Department of Natural Resources, Institute for Fisheries Research, Univ. Museums Annex, Ann Arbor, MI 48109.

639   JA   ISSN 0539-998X
MIE PREFECTURAL UNIVERSITY. FACULTY OF FISHERIES. BULLETIN/MIE-KENRITSU DAIGAKU SUISAN GAKUBU KIYO. (Text in Japanese and English; summaries in English) 1950. a. exchange. Mie Prefectural University, Faculty of Fisheries - Mie-kenritsu Suisan Gakubu, 2-158 Edobashi, Tsu-shi 514, Japan. circ. controlled.

639   US   ISSN 0076-9150
MINNESOTA FISHERIES INVESTIGATIONS. 1958. irreg. free to qualified personnel. ‡ Department of Natural Resources, Division of Fish and Wildlife, Section of Fisheries, St. Paul, MN 55155. Ed. C. R. Burrows.
    Formerly: Minnesota Fish and Game Investigations. Fish Series.

353.9   US   ISSN 0098-7840
MISSISSIPPI. STATE GAME AND FISH COMMISSION. ANNUAL REPORT TO THE REGULAR SESSION OF THE MISSISSIPPI LEGISLATURE. a. Game and Fish Commission, Box 451, Jackson, MS 39205. Key Title: Annual Report of the Mississippi Game and Fish Commission to the Regular Session of the Mississippi Legislature.

639   551.4   PL   ISSN 0072-0496
MORSKI INSTYTUT RYBACKI, GDYNIA. PRACE. SERIA A: OCEANOGRAFICZNO - ICHTIOLOGICZNA. (Supersedes in part its Prace, published 1937-57, and continues its numbering) (Text in Polish; summaries in English, Russian) 1937. a. Morski Instytut Rybacki - Maritime Fishing Institute, Al. Zjednoczenia 1, Gdynia, Poland (Dist. by Ars Polona-Ruch, Krakowskie Przedmiescie 7, Warsaw, Poland) circ. 400. Indexed: Aqua.Sci.&Fish.Abstr.

639   PL   ISSN 0072-050X
MORSKI INSTYTUT RYBACKI, GDYNIA. PRACE. SERIA B: TECHNIKA RYBACKA I TECHNOLOGIA RYB. (Supersedes in part its Prace, published 1937-57, and continues its numbering) (Text in Polish; summaries in English, Russian) 1953. a. Morski Instytut Rybacki - Maritime Fishing Institute, Al. Zjednoczenia 1, Gdynia, Poland (Dist. by Ars Polona-Ruch, Krakowskie Przedmiescie 7, Warsaw, Poland) circ. 400. Indexed: Aqua.Sci.&Fish.Abstr.

639   338.2   PL   ISSN 0072-0518
MORSKI INSTYTUT RYBACKI, GDYNIA. PRACE. SERIA C: EKONOMIKA RYBACKA. 1956. a. Morski Instytut Rybacki - Maritime Fishing Institute, Al. Zjednoczenia 1, Gdynia, Poland (Dist. by Ars Polona-Ruch, Krakowskie Przedmiescie 7, Warsaw, Poland) circ. 400. Indexed: Aqua.Sci.&Fish.Abstr.

639   CN   ISSN 0704-4798
N A F O ANNUAL REPORT. 1951. a. price varies. International Commission for the Northwest Atlantic Fisheries, P.O. Box 638, Dartmouth, N.S. B2Y 3Y9, Canada. Ed. W. H. Champion.
    Former titles (until vol. 29, 1980): International Commission for the Northwest Atlantic Fisheries. Annual Report (ISSN 0303-4151); International Commission for the Northwest Atlantic Fisheries. Annual Proceedings (ISSN 0074-2627)

639 CN ISSN 0250-7811
N A F O LIST OF FISHING VESSELS. 1953. triennial. price varies. Northwest Atlantic Fisheries Organization, P.O. Box 638, Dartmouth, N.S. B2Y 3Y9, Canada.
 Formerly (until 1980): International Commission for the Northwest Atlantic Fisheries. List of Fishing Vessels (ISSN 0074-2635)

639 CN ISSN 0704-4771
N A F O MEETING PROCEEDINGS. 1963. a. price varies. Northwest Atlantic Fisheries Organization, P.O. Box 638, Dartmouth, N.S. B2Y 3Y9, Canada.
 Formerly(until 1979): International Commission for the Northwest Atlantic Fisheries. Meetings Proceedings.

639 CN ISSN 0250-6424
N A F O SAMPLING YEARBOOK. 1958. a. price varies. Northwest Atlantic Fisheries Organization, P.O. Box 638, Dartmouth, N.S. B2Y 3Y9, Canada.
 Formerly (until 1980): International Commission for the Northwest Atlantic Fisheries. Sampling Yearbook.

639 CN ISSN 0250-6416
N A F O SCIENTIFIC COUNCIL MEETING REPORTS. 1958. a. limited distribution. Northwest Atlantic Fisheries Organization, P.O. Box 638, Dartmouth, N. S. B2Y 3Y9, Canada. Ed. V. M. Hodder.
 Formerly (until Dec. 1980): International Commission for the Northwest Atlantic Fisheries. Redbook (ISSN 0074-2643)

639 CN ISSN 0250-6432
N A F O SCIENTIFIC COUNCIL STUDIES. 1976. a. price varies. Northwest Atlantic Fisheries Organization, P.O. Box 638, Dartmouth, N.S. B2Y 3Y9, Canada. Ed. V. M. Hodder.
 Formerly (until 1980): International Commission for the Northwest Atlantic Fisheries. Selected Papers (ISSN 0380-4933)

639 CN ISSN 0250-6394
N A F O STATISTICAL BULLETIN. 1952. a. price varies. International Commission for the Northwest Atlantic Fisheries, P.O. Box 638, Dartmouth, Nova Scotia, B2Y 3Y9, Canada. Ed. V. M. Hodder.
 Formerly (until vol. 28, 1980): International Commission for the Northwest Atlantic Fisheries. Statistical Bulletin (ISSN 0074-266X)

639 US ISSN 0077-457X
NATIONAL FISHERMAN. YEARBOOK ISSUE. 1968. a. $3. Journal Publications (Camden), 21 Elm St., Camden, ME 04843. Ed. David R. Getchell. adv. circ. 68,000. (reprint service avail. from UMI)

639.3 CH
NATIONAL TAIWAN UNIVERSITY. INSTITUTE OF FISHERY BIOLOGY. REPORT. (Text and summaries in Chinese or English) 1956. irreg (approx. biennial) free on exchange basis. National Taiwan University, Institute of Fishery Biology, Taipei, Taiwan 107, Republic of China. (back issues avail)

353.9 US ISSN 0092-1696
NEBRASKA. FISHERIES PRODUCTION DIVISION. ANNUAL REPORT. 1971. a. Game and Parks Commission, Fisheries Division, Box 30370, Lincoln, NE 68503. illus.

639 NE ISSN 0077-7242
NETHERLANDS. CENTRAAL BUREAU VOOR DE STATISTIEK. STATISTIEK VAN DE VISSERIJ. STATISTICS OF FISHERIES. (Text in Dutch and English) 1950. a. fl.7.85. Centraal Bureau voor de Statistiek, Prinses Beatrixlaan 428, Voorburg, Netherlands (Orders to: Staatsuitgeverij, Christoffel Plantijnstraat, The Hague, Netherlands)

639 CN ISSN 0077-8036
NEW BRUNSWICK DEPARTMENT OF FISHERIES. ANNUAL REPORT. (Text in English and French) 1964. a. free. Department of Fisheries, Box 600, Fredericton, N.B. E3B 5H1, Canada.

NEW HAMPSHIRE. FISH AND GAME DEPARTMENT. MANAGEMENT AND RESEARCH. BIOLOGICAL SURVEY BULLETIN. see *BIOLOGY*

NEW HAMPSHIRE. FISH AND GAME DEPARTMENT. MANAGEMENT AND RESEARCH. TECHNICAL CIRCULAR SERIES. see *BIOLOGY*

639.3 NZ ISSN 0110-1749
NEW ZEALAND. MINISTRY OF AGRICULTURE AND FISHERIES. FISHERIES RESEARCH DIVISION. BULLETIN. irreg. Ministry of Agriculture and Fisheries, P.O. Box 19062, Wellington, New Zealand. illus.

639.3 NZ ISSN 0110-4519
NEW ZEALAND. MINISTRY OF AGRICULTURE AND FISHERIES. FISHERIES RESEARCH DIVISION: INFORMATION LEAFLET. irreg. free. Ministry of Agriculture and Fisheries, Box 19062, Wellington, New Zealand.

639.2 NZ
NEW ZEALAND. MINISTRY OF AGRICULTURE AND FISHERIES. FISHERIES TECHNICAL REPORT. 1974, no. 117. irreg. free. ‡ Ministry of Agriculture and Fisheries, Wellington, New Zealand. bibl. illus. circ. 600.

354 CN
NEWFOUNDLAND. DEPARTMENT OF FISHERIES. ANNUAL REPORT. a. Department of Fisheries, St. John's, Newfoundland, Canada. illus.

639.2 NR
NIGERIA. FEDERAL DEPARTMENT OF FISHERIES. FEDERAL FISHERIES OCCASIONAL PAPER. (Continues occasional paper issued by the Dept. of Fisheries Research of Nigeria) 1969. irreg.; latest issue, 1974. price varies. Federal Department of Fisheries, P.M.B. 12529, Lagos, Nigeria.

639.2 799.1 NO
NORSK FISKARALMANAKK. 1903. a. Kr.68. (Selskabet for de Norske Fiskeriers Fremme) A-S Nordanger-Bergen & Park Forlag, Postboks 731, 5001 Bergen, Norway. adv. circ. 7,000.

639 US ISSN 0094-128X
NORTHEAST PACIFIC PINK AND CHUM SALMON WORKSHOP. PROCEEDINGS. (Subseries of: Alaska. Department of Fish and Game. Information Leaflet) biennial. Department of Fish and Game, Subport Bldg., Juneau, AK 99801. illus. Key Title: Proceedings of the Northeast Pacific Pink Salmon Workshop.

639 NO
NORWAY. FISKERIDIREKTORATET. FISKEFLAATEN. (Subseries of Aarsberetning Vedkommende Norges Fiskerier) 1952. a. price varies. Fiskeridirektoratet - Directorate of Fisheries, Box 185, 5001 Bergen, Norway.

639 574.92 NO ISSN 0015-3117
NORWAY. FISKERIDIREKTORATET. SKRIFTER. SERIE HAVUNDERSOEKELSER. (Text in English and Norwegian; summaries in English) 1900. irreg., vol. 17, no. 3, 1981. price varies. Fiskeridirektoratet, Havforskningsinstituttet - Directorate of Fisheries, Box 1870-72, N-5011 Bergen-Nordnes, Norway. Ed. Erling Bratberg. Indexed: Biol.Abstr. Chem.Abstr.
 Report on Norwegian fishery & marine investigations

639.2 CN ISSN 0708-3629
NOVA SCOTIA FISHERMAN. 1977. irreg. free contr. circ. Department of Fisheries, Box 2223, Halifax, N.S. B3J 3C4, Canada.

639 US ISSN 0078-4370
OKLAHOMA. FISHERY RESEARCH LABORATORY, NORMAN. BULLETIN. 1964. irreg., 1968, no.8. free. (Department of Wildlife Conservation) Oklahoma Fishery Research Laboratory, 1416 Planck St., Norman, OK 73069. (Co-Sponsor: University of Oklahoma Biological Survey)

639 US ISSN 0078-7574
PACIFIC MARINE FISHERIES COMMISSION. ANNUAL REPORT. 1949. a. free. Pacific Marine Fisheries Commission, 528 S.W. Mill St., Portland, OR 97201. Ed. Clarence G. Pautzke. circ. 1,050.

639 US ISSN 0078-7582
PACIFIC MARINE FISHERIES COMMISSION. BULLETIN. 1948. irreg., no. 8, 1972. free. Pacific Marine Fisheries Commission, 528 S.W. Mill St., Portland, OR 97201. Ed. Leon A. Verhoeven.

639 US ISSN 0078-7590
PACIFIC MARINE FISHERIES COMMISSION. NEWSLETTER. 1962. irreg., no. 31, 1978. free. Pacific Marine Fisheries Commission, 528 S.W. Mill St., Portland, OR 97201. Ed. Clarence G. Pautzke.

639 PO
PORTUGAL. INSTITUTO NACIONAL DE ESTATISTICA. ESTATISTICAS DA PESCA/ STATISTIQUES DE LA PECHE; continente e ilhas adjacentes. (Text and summaries in French and Portuguese) 1969. a. Esc.40($2) per issue. Instituto Nacional de Estatistica, Av. Antonio Jose de Almeida, Lisbon, Portugal (Orders to: Imprensa Nacional, Casa da Moeda, Direccao Comercial, rua D. Francisco Manuel de Melo 5, Lisbon 1, Portugal) stat. (processed)

639 CN ISSN 0079-5143
PRINCE EDWARD ISLAND. DEPARTMENT OF FISHERIES. ANNUAL REPORT. 1959/60. a. Department of Fisheries, Charlottetown, P.E.I. C1A 7N8, Canada.

639.2 US
PROPAGATION & DISTRIBUTION OF FISHES FROM NATIONAL FISH HATCHERIES. (Subseries of Fish Distribution Report) 1872. a. free. U. S. Fish & Wildlife Service, Division of Fish Hatcheries, Dept. of the Interior, Washington, DC 20240. stat. circ. 1,275.

639.2 GW ISSN 0438-4555
PROTOKOLLE ZUR FISCHEREITECHNIK. (Text & summaries in German & English) 1962. 1-3/yr. DM.2.50. Bundesforschungsanstalt fuer Fischerei, Institut fuer Fangtechnik, Palmaille 9, 2000 Hamburg 50, W. Germany (B.R.D.) Ed. Dr. Steinberg. stat. circ. 400(controlled) Indexed: Biol.Abstr. Aqua.Sci.&Fish Abstr.

574 PR
PUERTO RICO. DEPARTMENT OF AGRICULTURE. AGRICULTURAL AND FISHERIES CONTRIBUTIONS/PUERTO RICO. DEPARTAMENTO DE AGRICULTURA. CONTRIBUCIONES AGROPECUARIAS Y PESQUERAS. (Text and summaries in Spanish and English) 1969. irreg. free. Commercial Fisheries Laboratory, Box 3665, Mayaguez, PR 00708. abstr. bibl. charts. illus. stat. index.

639 US ISSN 0083-7555
RESEARCH IN FISHERIES. (Represents the College's Annual Report) 1958. a. free. ‡ University of Washington, College of Fisheries and Fisheries Institute, Seattle, WA 98105. index. circ. 2,000.

338.3 FR ISSN 0078-6241
REVIEW OF FISHERIES IN OECD MEMBER COUNTRIES. 1967. a. price varies. Organization for Economic Cooperation and Development, 2 rue Andre-Pascal, 75775 Paris 16, France (U. S. orders to: O.E.C.D. Publications and Information Center, 1750 Pennsylvania Ave., N. W., Washington, D. C. 20006) (also avail. in microfiche)

639.2 FI ISSN 0355-0648
RIISTA- JA KALATALOUDEN TUTKIMUSLAITOS. KALANTUTKIMUSOSASTO. TIEDONANTOJA. (Text in Finnish; tables in English) 1971. irreg. exchange basis. Finnish Game and Fisheries Research Institute, Fisheries Division, Box 193, SF-00131 Helsinki 13, Finland. Ed. Viljo Nylund. stat. circ. 2,500 (controlled) (back issues avail.)

639 PL ISSN 0080-3723
ROCZNIKI NAUK ROLNICZYCH. SERIA H. RYBACTWO. (Test in Polish; summaries in English and Russian) 1903. irreg., 1975, vol. 97, no. 1. price varies. (Polska Akademia Nauk, Komitet Nauk Zootechnicznych) Panstwowe Wydawnictwo Naukowe, Ul. Miodowa 10, Warsaw, Poland (Dist. by Ars Polona-Ruch, Krakowskie Przedmiescie 7, Warsaw, Poland) Ed. Boleslaw Dabrowski. bibl. index.

RURAL INDUSTRY DIRECTORY. see *AGRICULTURE*

639 UK ISSN 0140-5004
SCOTLAND. DEPARTMENT OF AGRICULTURE AND FISHERIES. FRESHWATER FISHERIES TRIENNIAL. triennial. Department of Agriculture and Fisheries, Marine Laboratory, P.O. Box 101, Victoria Rd., Aberdeen AB9 8DB, Scotland.

FISH AND FISHERIES

639   UK   ISSN 0140-5012
SCOTLAND. DEPARTMENT OF AGRICULTURE AND FISHERIES. TRIENNIAL REVIEW OF RESEARCH. 1968. triennial. Department of Agriculture and Fisheries, Marine Laboratory, P.O. Box 101, Victoria Rd., Aberdeen AB9 8DB, Scotland.
Formerly (until 1972): Scotland. Directorate of Fisheries Research. Annual Report (ISSN 0072-6141)

639   UK   ISSN 0559-1791
SCOTTISH FISHERIES BULLETIN. 1952. 1-2/yr. free. Department of Agriculture and Fisheries, Marine Laboratory, P.O. Box 101, Victoria Rd., Aberdeen AB9 8DB, Scotland. charts. illus.

639   UK   ISSN 0309-9105
SCOTTISH FISHERIES INFORMATION PAMPHLETS. 1977 N.S. irreg., no. 2, 1978. Department of Agriculture and Fisheries, Marine Laboratory, P.O. Box 101, Victoria Rd., Aberdeen AB9 8DB, Scotland.

639   UK
SCOTTISH FISHERIES RESEARCH REPORTS. 1975. irreg. Department of Agriculture and Fisheries, Marine Laboratory, P.O. Box 101, Victoria Rd., Aberdeen AB9 8DB, Scotland. charts.

639   UK   ISSN 0080-8202
SCOTTISH SEA FISHERIES STATISTICAL TABLES. 1939. a. price varies. Department of Agriculture and Fisheries, Marine Laboratory, P.O. Box 101, Victoria Rd., Aberdeen AB9 8DB, Scotland (Avail. from: H.M.S.O., 13a Castle St., Edinburgh EH2 3AR, Scotland)

SEA GRANT PUBLICATIONS INDEX. see *EARTH SCIENCES — Abstracting, Bibliographies, Statistics*

639.2   CL
SERIE INVESTIGACION PESQUERA. (Text in Spanish; Summaries in English) 1965. irreg.; no. 27, 1977. $5. ‡ Instituto de Fomento Pesquero, Seccion Edicion y Publicaciones, Jose Domingo Canas 2277, Casilla 1287, Santiago, Chile. abstr. bibl. charts. stat. circ. 600. (processed) Indexed: Biol.Abstr.
Formerly: Instituto de Fomento Pesquero. Boletin Cientifico (ISSN 0020-3882)

639.54   IO
SHRIMP CULTURE RESEARCH CENTRE. BULLETIN. (Text in English; summaries in Indonesian) 1975. irreg. Shrimp Culture Research Centre - Pusat Penelitian Udang, Box 1, Jepara, Indonesia.

639   SA
SOUTH AFRICA. SEA FISHERIES BRANCH. ANNUAL REPORT. (Text in Afrikaans and English) 1921. a, latest 1971. exchange basis. ‡ Sea Fisheries Branch, Beach Rd., Sea Point 8001, Cape Town, South Africa. circ. 2,400 (combined) Indexed: Biol.Abstr.
Formerly; South Africa. Division of Sea Fisheries. Annual Report (ISSN 0081-2218)

639   SA
SOUTH AFRICA. SEA FISHERIES BRANCH. FISHERIES BULLETIN. (Text in Afrikaans and English) 1935. irreg., no. 12, 1979. exchange basis. Sea Fisheries Branch, Beach Rd., Sea Point 8001, Cape Town, South Africa. Eds. H. Boonstra, A. Payne. circ. 1,500.
Formerly: South Africa. Division of Sea Fisheries. Fisheries Bulletin.

639   SA
SOUTH AFRICA. SEA FISHERIES INSTITUTE. INVESTIGATIONAL REPORT. (Text in English and Afrikaans) 1934. irreg., no. 120, 1979. exchange basis. Sea Fisheries Institute, Private Bag X2, Rogge Bay 8012, Cape Town, South Africa. Ed. H. Boonstra. circ. 1,500. Indexed: Biol.Abstr. Ocean.Atstr.
Former titles: South Africa. Sea Fisheries Branch. Investigational Report; South Africa. Division of Sea Fisheries. Investigational Report (ISSN 0081-2234)

639.2   SA   ISSN 0080-5076
SOUTH AFRICAN FISHING INDUSTRY HANDBOOK AND BUYER'S GUIDE. Variant title: S.A. Fishing Industry Handbook and Buyer's Guide. 1951. biennial. R.30. Thomson Publications S.A. (Pty) Ltd., P.O. Box 8308, Johannesburg 2000, South Africa. Ed. Heinz Engelhardt. adv.

639   PH
SOUTHEAST ASIAN FISHERIES DEVELOPMENT CENTER. REPORT OF THE MEETING. no. 4, 1971. a. Southeast Asian Fisheries Development Center, Manila, Philippines. charts. stat.

639   SI
SOUTHEAST ASIAN FISHERIES DEVELOPMENT CENTER MARINE FISHERIES RESEARCH DEPARTMENT. ANNUAL REPORT. (Text in English) 1969. a. free on exchange. ‡ Southeast Asian Fisheries Development Center, Marine Fisheries Research Department, Changi Point, Singapore 17, Singapore. circ. 200.

639.2   SP
SPAIN. DIRECCION GENERAL DE PESCA MARITIMA. PUBLICACIONES TECNICAS. irreg. Direccion General de Pesca Martima, Madrid, Spain. illus.

639   SP   ISSN 0081-3362
SPAIN. INSTITUTO NACIONAL DE ESTADISTICA. INDUSTRIAS DERIVADAS DE LA PESCA. a. Instituto Nacional de Estadistica, Avda. Generalisimo 91, Madrid 16, Spain.

639   FI   ISSN 0085-6940
SUOMEN KALATALOUS. (Text in Finnish; summaries in Swedish and English) 1912. irreg., vol. 47, 1974. exchange basis only. Finnish Game and Fisheries Research Institute, Fisheries Division, Box 193, SF-00131 Helsinki 13, Finland. Ed. Kai Westman. circ. 2,000. Indexed: Biol.Abstr. Commer.Fish.Abstr.

639   CH   ISSN 0082-1489
TAIWAN. FISHERIES RESEARCH INSTITUTE, KEELUNG. BULLETIN. (Text mainly in Chinese; occasionally in English) 1953. irreg., no. 28, 1977. not for sale. Taiwan Fisheries Research Institute, 199 Hou-Ih Rd., Keelung, Taiwan, Republic of China.

639 574   CH   ISSN 0082-1497
TAIWAN. FISHERIES RESEARCH INSTITUTE, KEELUNG. LABORATORY OF FISHERY BIOLOGY. REPORT. (Text in English) 1951. irreg., no. 28, 1976. not for sale. Taiwan Fisheries Research Institute, 199 Hon-Ih Rd., Keelung, Taiwan, Republic of China.

338   JA   ISSN 0563-8372
TOKYO UNIVERSITY OF FISHERIES. REPORT/ TOKYO SUISAN DAIGAKU RONSHU. (Text mainly in Japanese; summaries in English) 1966. a. Tokyo University of Fisheries - Tokyo Suisan Daigaku, 4-5-7 Konan, Minato-ku, Tokyo 108, Japan. Ed. Kozo Iwamoto. illus.

639 919.9 551.4   JA
TOKYO UNIVERSITY OF FISHERIES. TRANSACTIONS. (Text in English or Japanese; summaries in English) 1958. irreg. Tokyo University of Fisheries - Tokyo Suisan Daigaku, 4-5-7 Konan, Minato-ku, Tokyo 108, Japan. Ed. Kozo Iwamoto.
Supersedes (1974): Tokyo University of Fisheries. Journal. Special Edition (ISSN 0082-4836)

639 607   UK   ISSN 0082-5352
TORRY RESEARCH STATION, ABERDEEN, SCOTLAND. ANNUAL REPORT. 1958. a. free. Torry Research Station, P.O. Box 31, 135 Abbey Rd., Aberdeen, Scotland. circ. 3,000.

639   CN   ISSN 0082-609X
TRAVAUX SUR LES PECHERIES DU QUEBEC. (Text in French and English) 1964. irreg., no. 45, 1976. available on exchange. ‡ Ministere de l'Industrie et du Commerce, 2700 Einstein, 555 Boul. Henri IV, Quebec G1P 3W8, Canada. Ed. J. Bergeron. circ. 1,100. Indexed: Biol.Abstr. Ocean.Ind.

TUNISIA. INSTITUT NATIONAL SCIENTIFIQUE ET TECHNIQUE D'OCEANOGRAPHIE ET DE PECHE. BULLETIN. see *EARTH SCIENCES — Oceanography*

639   BE
UITKOMSTEN VAN DE BELGISCHE ZEEVISSERIJ. 1957. a. free. Dienst voor de Zeevisserij, Koninginnelaan 59, 8400 Oostende, Belgium. stat.

U. S. FISH AND WILDLIFE SERVICE. SPORT FISHERY AND WILDLIFE RESEARCH. see *SPORTS AND GAMES — Outdoor Life*

639   US   ISSN 0565-0704
U. S. FISH AND WILDLIFE SERVICE. INVESTIGATIONS IN FISH CONTROL. no. 25, 1969. irreg., no. 82, 1977. U. S. Fish and Wildlife Service, U. S. Dept. of the Interior, Washington, DC 20242. Key Title: Investigations in Fish Control.

639   US   ISSN 0083-0941
U. S. FISH AND WILDLIFE SERVICE. RESEARCH REPORTS. 1941. irreg., no. 79, 1976. U.S. Fish and Wildlife Service., Department of the Interior, Washington, DC 20240 (Orders to: Supt. Doc., Washington, DC 20402)

639   US   ISSN 0094-7008
U.S. NATIONAL MARINE FISHERIES SERVICE. GRANT-IN-AID FOR FISHERIES: PROGRAM ACTIVITIES. a. free. U.S. National Marine Fisheries Service, 3300 Whitehaven St. N.W., Washington, DC 20235.

639.2   US
U. S. NATIONAL MARINE FISHERIES SERVICE. IMPORTS AND EXPORTS OF FISHERY PRODUCTS. a. U. S. National Marine Fisheries Service, Statistics and Market News Division, National Oceanic and Atmospheric Administration, Washington, DC 20235. circ. 200-2,000.

639.2   US   ISSN 0093-9412
U.S. NATIONAL MARINE FISHERIES SERVICE. REPORT. U.S. National Marine Fisheries Service, National Oceanographic and Atmospheric Administration, Washington, DC 20235 (Orders to: Supt. of Documents, Washington, DC 20402) bibl.

639.2   US   ISSN 0085-7939
UNIVERSITY OF WASHINGTON PUBLICATIONS IN FISHERIES. 1962, N.S. irreg., vol. 6, 1975. price varies. (University of Washington, College of Fisheries) University of Washington Press, Seattle, WA 98105.

UPPER VOLTA. DIRECTION DES EAUX ET FORETS ET DE LA CONSERVATION DES SOLS. RAPPORT ANNUEL. see *FORESTS AND FORESTRY*

639   US   ISSN 0083-7474
WASHINGTON (STATE) DEPARTMENT OF FISHERIES. TECHNICAL REPORT. 1970. irreg., no. 24, 1977. free. Department of Fisheries, Olympia, WA 98504.

639   AT
WESTERN AUSTRALIA. DEPARTMENT OF FISHERIES AND WILDLIFE. FISHERIES RESEARCH BULLETIN. 1941. irreg. not for sale; free to government agencies. Department of Fisheries and Wildlife, 108 Adelaide Terrace, Perth, W.A. 6000, Australia. circ. 600.
Formerly part of: Western Australia. Fisheries and Fauna Department. Bulletin (ISSN 0083-8683)

639.2 639.9   AT
WESTERN AUSTRALIA. DEPARTMENT OF FISHERIES & WILDLIFE. REPORT. 1964. irreg. free to government and conservation agencies. Department of Fisheries & Wildlife, 108 Adelaide Terrace, Perth, W.A. 6000, Australia. circ. 1,000.

597   US
WORLD RECORD GAME FISHES. 1946. a. $5.95. ‡ International Game Fish Association, 3000 E. Las Olas Blvd., Fort Lauderdale, FL 33316. Ed. M. B. McCracken. adv. illus. stat. circ. 25,000.
Formerly: World Record Marine Fishes (ISSN 0084-2214)

639.2   UN   ISSN 0084-375X
YEARBOOK OF FISHERY STATISTICS. (Text in English, French, and Spanish) 1947. a. price varies. Food and Agriculture Organization of the United Nations, Distribution and Sales Section, Via delle Terme di Caracalla, Rome, Italy (Dist. in U.S. by: Unipub, 345 Park Ave. S., New York, NY 10010)

639   ZA   ISSN 0514-8731
ZAMBIA. CENTRAL STATISTICAL OFFICE. FISHERIES STATISTICS (NATURAL WATERS). 1965. a, latest 1971 (vol. 1) K.1. Central Statistical Office, P.O. Box 1908, Lusaka, Zambia.

FISH AND FISHERIES — Abstracting, Bibliographies, Statistics

318 639.2   CL
AGRICULTURA E INDUSTRIAS AGROPECUARIAS Y PESCA. 1911-12. a; latest edition, 1974-75. $5. Instituto Nacional de Estadisticas, Casilla 7597-Correo 3, Santiago, Chile. stat. (processed)

354.71 310   CN
CANADA. FISHERIES AND MARINE SERVICE. RECREATIONAL FISHERIES BRANCH. STATISTICS ON SALES OF SPORT FISHING LICENCES IN CANADA. (Text in English and French) 1971. a. Fisheries and Marine Service, 116 Lisgar St., Ottawa, Ont. K1A 0E6, Canada.

639.2 664.94   CN   ISSN 0527-5172
CANADA. STATISTICS CANADA. FISH PRODUCTS INDUSTRY/INDUSTRIE DE LA TRANSFORMATION DU POISSON. (Catalogue 32-216) (Text in English & French) 1949. a. Can.$4.50($5.40) Statistics Canada, Publications Distribution, Ottawa, Ont. K1A 0V7, Canada. (also avail. in microform from MML)

639.2 310   US   ISSN 0162-6108
FROZEN FISHERY PRODUCTS. ANNUAL SUMMARY. a. U.S. National Marine Fisheries Service, National Oceanic and Atmospheric Administration, Washington, DC 20235.

639 338.2   GW   ISSN 0072-3673
GERMANY (FEDERAL REPUBLIC, 1949-) STATISTISCHES BUNDESAMT. FACHSERIE 3, REIHE 4.5: FISCHEREI. (Includes subseries: Hochsee- und Kuestenfischerei; Bodenseefischerei) m, a. price varies. W. Kohlhammer-Verlag GmbH, Abt. Veroeffentlichungen des Statistischen Bundesamtes, Philipp-Reis-Str. 3, Postfach 421120, 6500 Mainz 42, W. Germany (B.R.D.)

639.2   GR
GREECE. NATIONAL STATISTICAL SERVICE. RESULTS OF SEA FISHERY SURVEY BY MOTOR VESSELS. (Text in English and Greek) 1964. a., latest 1974/1975. $1. National Statistical Service, Publications and Information Division, 14-16 Lycourgou St., Athens 112, Greece.

338.476   CK
INSTITUTO DE DESARROLLO DE LOS RECURSOS NATURALES RENOVABLES. OFICINA DE PLANEACION. ESTADISTICAS PESQUERAS. a. Instituto de Desarrollo de los Recursos Naturales Renovables, Oficina de Planeacion, Bogota, Colombia.

390 016   GW   ISSN 0074-9737
INTERNATIONALE VOLKSKUNDLICHE BIBLIOGRAPHIE/INTERNATIONAL FOLKLORE BIBLIOGRAPHY/BIBLIOGRAPHIE INTERNATIONALE DES ARTS ET TRADITIONS POPULAIRES. (Entries in various languages) 1954. irreg., 1981, covering 1977/78. price varies. Rudolf Habelt Verlag, Am Buchenhang 1, 5300 Bonn 1, W. Germany (B.R.D.) Ed. Robert Wildhaber.

338.3   CN
PECHE HAUTURIERE AU QUEBEC. irreg. Bureau of Statistics, Division des Peches, Quebec, P.Q., Canada. illus.

639 338   SP
SPAIN. DIRECCION GENERAL DE PESCA MARITIMA. ANUARIO DE PESCA MARITIMA. 1973. a. Direccion General de Pesca Maritima, Madrid, Spain.
    Formed by the merger of: Spain. Direccion General de Pesca Maritima. Estadistica de Pesca & Spain. Direccion General de Pesca Maritima. Flota Pesquera Espanola.

FLORIST TRADE

see Gardening and Horticulture—Florist Trade

FOLKLORE

398   SW   ISSN 0065-0897
ACTA ACADEMIAE REGIAE GUSTAVI ADOLPHI. (Text in English, German and Swedish; summaries in English) 1933. irreg., no. 55, 1977. price varies. Kungliga Gustav Adolfs Akademien, Klostergatan 2, S-753 21 Uppsala, Sweden. Ed. Folke Hedblom.

301.2 398 943   CS
ACTA ETHNOLOGICA SLOVACA. 1974. irreg. price varies. (Slovenska Akademia Vied, Narodopisny Ustav) Veda, Publishing House of the Slovak Academy of Sciences, Klemensova 19, 895 30 Bratislava, Czechoslovakia (Dist. by Oddleenia Wymeny Publikaci, Ustredna Kniznica Sav, Dlemensova 27, 895 19 Bratislava)

398   UR
AKADEMIYA NAUK BELARUSSKOI SSR. BELARUSSKII ETNOGRAFICHESKII SBORNIK. SERIYA FOL'KLORA I ETNOGRAFII. (Text in Belarussian) 1958. a. (Akademiya Nauk Belarusskoi SSR, Institut Mastatstvaznaustva) Izdatel'stvo Akademii Nauk BSSR, Minsk, U.S.S.R.

398   SP   ISSN 0065-6127
ALCOY; FIESTA DE MOROS Y CRISTIANOS.* 1940. a. 75 ptas. (Asociacion de San Jorge de Alcoy) Casa de Escritores, Pablo Aranda 3, Madrid 6, Spain.

398   GW
ALTES HANDWERK. 1972. irreg., no. 50, 1980. price varies. (Gesellschaft fuer Volkskunde, Basel, Abteilung Film, SZ) Rudolf Habelt Verlag, Am Buchenhang 1, 5300 Bonn 1, W. Germany (B.R.D.) Ed. Paul Hugger.

ANUARIO DE EUSKO-FOLKLORE; etnografia y paletnografia. see ANTHROPOLOGY

ARCHIV FUER VOELKERKUNDE. see ANTHROPOLOGY

398   VE   ISSN 0570-7196
ARCHIVOS VENEZOLANOS DE FOLKLORE. 1951. a. (Universidad Central de Venezuela, Instituto de Antropologia e Historia) Edicion Edime, Comision Editora, Caracas, Venezuela. (Co-sponsor: Instituto de Filologia Andres Bello) bibl.

398   SW   ISSN 0066-8176
ARV/JOURNAL OF SCANDINAVIAN FOLKLORE; journal of Scandinavian folklore/ tidskrift foer nordisk folkminnesforskning. (Text in English and German; summaries in English) 1945. a. Ref.55. (Kungliga Gustav Adolfs Akademien - Royal Gustavus Adolphus Academy) Almqvist & Wiksell International, Box 62, S-101 20 Stockholm, Sweden. Ed. Dag Stromback. bk. rev. circ. 500.

ASTRADO; revue bilingue de Provence. see LITERATURE

ATLAS POLSKICH STROJOW LUDOWYCH. see ANTHROPOLOGY

B R A D S. (Bollettino del Repertorio e dell'Atlante Demologico Sardo) see HISTORY — History Of Europe

398 745   GW   ISSN 0067-4591
BAUERNHAEUSER DER SCHWEIZ. 1965. irreg., no. 7, 1979. price varies. Rudolf Habelt Verlag, Am Buchenhang 1, 5300 Bonn 1, W. Germany (B.R.D.)

398   GW   ISSN 0067-4729
BAYERISCHES JAHRBUCH FUER VOLKSKUNDE. 1950. a. price varies. (Bayerische Akademie der Wissenschaften, Institut fuer Volkskunde) Karl Hart, 8712 Volkach, W. Germany (B.R.D) Ed. T. Gerhard. bk. rev. circ. 800.

398 301.2   BL
BIBLIOGRAFICA FOLCLORICA. 1977. irreg. Instituto Nacional do Folclore, Rua do Catete 179 ZC-01, 20-000 Rio de Janeiro RJ, Brazil. Ed.Bd. bk. rev.

BIBLIOTECA DE CULTURA VASCA. see HISTORY — History Of North And South America

398   BL
BOLETIM ALAGOANO DE FOLCLORE. 1977. irreg. Comissao Alagoana de Folclore, Av. Tomas Espindola 489, Farol, Maceio, Brazil. illus.

398   BU
BULGARSKI FOLKLOR. (Text in various languages) 1975. irreg. 1.50 lv. per issue. (Bulgarska Akademiia na Naukite) Publishing House of the Bulgarian Academy of Sciences, Ul. Akad. G. Bonchev, 1113 Sofia, Bulgaria. Ed. P. Dinekov. circ. 1,000.

398   II
C I I L FOLKLORE SERIES. (Text in English) 1975. irreg., latest 1977. Central Institute of Indian Languages, Manasagangotri, Mysore 570006, India. bibl.

CAHIERS BRETONS/AR GWYR. see SOCIAL SCIENCES: COMPREHENSIVE WORKS

CANU GWERIN/FOLK SONG. see MUSIC

200 900   US   ISSN 0528-1458
CARL NEWELL JACKSON LECTURES. a. price varies. Harvard University Press, 79 Garden St., Cambridge, MA 02138.

COMUNIDADES Y CULTURAS PERUANAS. see ANTHROPOLOGY

COSTUME SOCIETY OF ONTARIO. NEWSLETTER. see CLOTHING TRADE — Fashions

COUNTRY DANCE AND SONG. see MUSIC

398   PE
CUADERNOS DEL TALLER DE FOLKLORE. 1977. irreg. Universidad Nacional Federico Villareal, Direccion Universitaria de Proyeccion Social, Lima, Peru.

398   CN   ISSN 0701-0184
CULTURE & TRADITION. (Text in English and French) 1976. a. Can.$3. Memorial University of Newfoundland, St. John's, Nfld. A1C 5S7, Canada. illus.

398   DK   ISSN 0070-2765
DANMARKS FOLKEMINDER. 1908. irreg. price varies. Akademisk Forlag, 8 St. Kannikestraede, DK 1169 Copenhagen, Denmark. circ. 1,000.

DATOS ETNO-LINGUISTICOS. see LINGUISTICS

398   GW
DEUTSCHE GESELLSCHAFT FUER VOLKSKUNDE. D G V INFORMATIONEN. 1970. irreg. membership. Deutsche Gesellschaft fuer Volkskunde e.V., Schloss, L. Uhland-Institut, D-7400 Tuebingen, W. Germany(B.R.D.) Ed. Hermann Bausinger. bk. rev. circ. 900.
    Continues Its Mitteilungen.

398   US
EROTIC FOLKLORE NEWSLETTER. 1975. irreg. free. c/o Frank A. Hoffmann, Ed., Dept. of English, State University College at Buffalo, 1300 Elmwood Ave., Buffalo, NY 14222. bk. rev. circ. 150.

398   MX   ISSN 0071-1683
ESTUDIOS DE FOLKLORE. 1961. irreg; latest issue, 1971. price varies. ‡ Universidad Nacional Autonoma de Mexico, Instituto de Investigaciones Esteticas, Ciudad Universitaria, Mexico 20, D.F., Mexico.

398   PY
ESTUDIOS FOLKLORICOS PARAGUAYOS. 1978. irreg. Casilla Postal 611, Asuncion, Paraguay.

ETHNOLOGIA. see ANTHROPOLOGY

398   PL
ETNOGRAFIA. (Text in Polish; summaries in various languages) 1961. irreg. price varies. Uniwersytet im. Adama Mickiewicza w Poznaniu, Stalingradzka 1, 61-712 Poznan, Poland (Dist. by: Ars Polona, Krakowskie Przedmiescie 7, 00-068 Warsaw, Poland)
    Formerly: Uniwersytet im. Adama Mickiewicza w Poznaniu. Wydzial Filozoficzno-Historyczny. Seria Etnografia.

EUROPAEISCHE VOLKSMUSIKINSTRUMENTE. HANDBUCH. see MUSIC

FOLKLORE

398   FI   ISSN 0014-5815
F F COMMUNICATIONS. (Folklore Fellows) (Text mainly in English; occasionally in French and German) 1910. 2-5/yr. price varies. Suomalainen Tiedeakatemia - Academia Scientiarum Fennica, Snellmaninkatu 9-11, 00170 Helsinki 17, Finland. Ed. Lauri Honko. cum.index. circ. 500-600. (back issues avail.; reprint service avail. from UMI) Indexed: Bull.Signal. M.L.A. Ref.Zh. Abstr.Fclk.Stud.

398   DK   ISSN 0105-1024
FOLK OG KULTUR. 1972. a. Kr.60. (Danmarks Fulkeminder) Akademisk Forlag, 8 St. Kannikestraede, DK-1169 Copenhagen, Denmark. Eds. L. Bodker, Chr. Lisse. bk. rev. bibl. circ. 600.

398   SW   ISSN 0071-6766
FOLKLIVSSKILDRINGAR OCH BYGDESSTUDIER. 1934. irreg., no. 10, 1978. price varies. Kungliga Gustav Adolfs Akademien, Klostergatan 2, S-753 21 Uppsala, Sweden. Ed. Folke Hedblom.

398   UR
FOL'KLOR URALA. vol. 2, 1976. irreg. 0.65 Rub. per issue. Ural'skii Gosudarstvennyi Universitet, Pr. Lenina 51, Sverdlovsk, U.S.S.R. circ. 600.

398   US   ISSN 0162-6280
FOLKLORE AND MYTHOLOGY STUDIES. 1977. a. $2.50. University of California, Los Angeles, Folklore Graduate Students' Association, Los Angeles, CA 90024.

398   US   ISSN 0071-6782
FOLKLORE ANNUAL. 1969. a. free on exchange. (University Folklore Association) University of Texas at Austin, Center for Intercultural Studies in Folklore and Oral History, S.W.B. 306, Austin, TX 78712. bk. rev. circ. 500.

398   BE
FOLKLORE DU MONDE. 1969. irreg., no. 2, 1975. Librairie-Editions Thanh-Long, 34 rue Dekens, 1040 Brussels, Belgium.

398   US   ISSN 0071-6804
FOLKTALES OF THE WORLD. 1963. irreg., 1970, no. 12. price varies. University of Chicago Press, 5801 S. Ellis Ave., Chicago, IL 60637. Ed. Richard M. Dorson. (reprint service avail. from UMI,ISI)

FORSCHUNGEN ZUR RECHTSARCHAEOLOGIE UND RECHTLICHEN VOLKSKUNDE. see *LAW*

394.2   US
GOOD OLD DAYS CHRISTMAS ANNUAL. Short title: Christmas Annual. 1966. a. $1. Tower Press, Inc., Box 428, Seabrook, NH 03874. illus.

398   IS   ISSN 0075-3661
HEBREW UNIVERSITY OF JERUSALEM. FOLKLORE RESEARCH CENTER. STUDIES. (Text in Hebrew and English) 1970. irreg., vol. 5, 1975. Magnes Press, Hebrew University of Jerusalem, Jerusalem, Israel. Eds. Dov Noy & I. Ben-Ami.

390   GW   ISSN 0075-0468
I P E K/ANNUAL REVIEW OF PREHISTORIC AND ETHNOGRAPHICAL ART. (Jahrbuch fuer Praehistorische und Ethnographische Kunst) irreg., vol. 25, 1980. $77.60 price varies. (Deutsche Forschungsgemeinschaft) Walter de Gruyter und Co., Genthiner Str. 13, 1000 Berlin 30, W. Germany (B.R.D.) Ed. Herbert Kuehn. adv. bk. rev.

398   US   ISSN 0073-6996
INDIANA UNIVERSITY. FOLKLORE INSTITUTE. MONOGRAPH SERIES. 1933. irreg., 1970, vol. 23. price varies. ‡ Indiana University, Folklore Institute, 504 N. Fess, Bloomington, IN 47405. Ed. Richard M. Dorson.

398   AU
INSTITUT FUER GEGENWARTSVOLKSKUNDE. MITTEILUNGEN. (Issues also published in other series of the Akademie) 1974. irreg., no. 6, 1979. price varies. Verlag der Oesterreichischen Akademie der Wissenschaften, Dr. Ignaz Seipel-Platz 2, A-1010 Vienna, Austria. (Affiliate: Oesterreichische Akademie der Wissenschaften)

398   AG
INSTITUTO NACIONAL DE INVESTIGACIONES FOLKLORICAS. CUADERNOS. 1960. a. Instituto Nacional de Investigaciones Folkloricas, Sanchez de Bustamente 2663, Buenos Aires, Argentina. bibl.

INTERNATIONAL FOLK MUSIC COUNCIL. YEARBOOK. see *MUSIC*

JAHRBUCH FUER MUSIKALISCHE VOLKS- UND VOELKERKUNDE. see *MUSIC*

398   301.2   GW   ISSN 0075-2738
JAHRBUCH FUER OSTDEUTSCHE VOLKSKUNDE. 1962. a. price varies. (Deutsche Gesellschaft fuer Volkskunde e.V., Kommission fuer Ostdeutsche Volkskunde) N.G. Elwert Verlag, Reitgasse 7/9, Postfach 1128, 3550 Marburg, W. Germany (B.R.D.) Ed. Erhard Riemann. circ. 1,000.

398   AU   ISSN 0022-7560
KAERNTNER HEIMATLEBEN. 1959. irreg. price varies. Landesmuseum fuer Kaernten, Museumgasse 2, A-9010 Klagenfurt, Austria. circ. 600.

398   US   ISSN 0075-5508
KENTUCKY FOLKLORE SERIES. 1965. irreg., no. 6, 1975. price varies. Kentucky Folklore Society, Box U-169, Western Kentucky University, Bowling Green, KY 42101. Ed. Camilla A. Collins. circ. 250-300.

KINAADMAN/WISDOM; a journal of the Southern Philippines. see *HISTORY — History Of Asia*

398   FR   ISSN 0075-7160
KRYPTADIA: JOURNAL OF EROTIC FOLKLORE. (Text in English) 1883. approx. a. $15. ‡ La Cle des Champs, Valbonne (Alpes-Maritimes), France. Ed. G. Legman.

390   GW   ISSN 0075-7942
LANDSCHAFTSVERBAND WESTFALEN-LIPPE. VOLKSKUNDLICHE KOMMISSION. SCHRIFTEN. 1937. irreg. price varies. Aschendorffsche Verlagsbuchhandlung, Soester Str. 13, 4400 Muenster, W. Germany (B.R.D.)

390   IT   ISSN 0075-8019
LARES. BIBLIOTECA. 1955. irreg., no. 43, 1974. price varies. Casa Editrice Leo S. Olschki, Casella Postale 66, 50100 Florence, Italy. Ed. G. B. Bronzini. adv. bk. rev. circ. 1,000.

390   572   PL   ISSN 0076-0382
LODZKIE STUDIA ETNOGRAFICZNE. (Text in Polish; summaries in French) 1959. irreg.; 1972, vol. 14. price varies. (Polskie Towarzystwo Ludoznawcze, Oddzial w Lodzki) Panstwowe Wydawnictwo Naukowe, Ul. Miodowa 10, Warsaw, Poland. Ed. Kazimiera Zawistowicz-Adamska. bibl. illus.

390   US   ISSN 0459-8962
LOUISIANA FOLKLORE MISCELLANY. 1958. irreg. $5. Louisiana Folklore Society, c/o Department of English, University of New Orleans, New Orleans, LA 70122.

MAERCHEN DER EUROPAEISCHEN VOELKER. see *LITERATURE*

MAKEDONIKA. see *CLASSICAL STUDIES*

069   398   GW
MUSEUM FUER VOELKERKUNDE IN HAMBURG. MITTEILUNGEN. (Not published 1940-1949) 1905. a. price varies. Museum fuer Voelkerkunde und Vorgeschichte, Binderstr. 14, 2000 Hamburg, W. Germany (B.R.D.)

MUZYKAL'NAYA FOLKLORISTIKA. see *MUSIC*

NAPRSTKOVO MUZEUM ASIJSKYCH, AFRICKYCH A AMERICKYCH KULTUR. ANNALS. see *ANTHROPOLOGY*

NAPRSTKOVO MUZEUM ASIJSKYCH, AFRICKYCH A AMERICKYCH KULTUR. ANTHROPOLOGICAL PAPERS. see *ANTHROPOLOGY*

398   HU
NEPMUVESZET EVSZAZADAI/JAHRHUNDERTE DER VOLKSKUNST. (Text in German and Hungarian) irreg. Istvan Kiraly Muzeum, Szekesfehervar, Hungary. illus.

NEPRAJZI KOZLEMENYEK. see *ANTHROPOLOGY*

390   DK   ISSN 0008-1345
NORD NYTT; Nordic periodical for folklife studies. (Text in Danish; summaries in English) 1963. irreg. (8-10/yr.) price varies. N E F A-Norden, Institut for Europaeisk Folkelivsforskning, Brede Alle 69, DK-2800 Lyngby, Denmark (Subscr. to: Museumstjenesten, Lysgaard, DK-8800 Viborg, Denmark) Ed. Soergen Burchardt. adv. bk. rev. bibl. illus. index. circ. 1,500.
Ethnology

398   US   ISSN 0078-1681
NORTHEAST FOLKLORE. (Text in English; occasionally in French) 1962. a. $5. Northeast Folklore Society, South Stevens Hall, University of Maine, Orono, ME 04469. Ed. Edward D. Ives. cum.index being planned. circ. 400. Indexed: Abstr.Folk.Stud.

398   AU
OESTERREICHISCHE VOLKSKUNDLICHE BIBLIOGRAPHIE. 1966. irreg., no. 7/8, 1976. price varies. Verband der Wissenschaftlichen Gesellschaften Oesterreichs, Verein fuer Volkskunde, Lindengasse 37, A-1070 Vienna, Austria. Ed. Klaus Beitl.

398   AU
OESTERREICHISCHES MUSEUM FUER VOLKSKUNDE: VEROEFFENTLICHUNGEN. 1952. irreg. price varies. Verlag Ferdinand Berger und Soehne OHG, Wiener Str. 21-23, A-3580 Horn, Austria. circ. 1,000.

QUELLENWERKE ZUR ALTEN GESCHICHTE AMERIKAS. see *HISTORY — History Of North And South America*

398   AU
RAABSER MAERCHEN-REIHE. 1974. irreg., vol. 3, 1977. Oesterreichisches Museum fuer Volkskunde, Laudongasse 15-19, A-1080 Vienna, Austria. Eds. Leopold Schmidt, Klaus Beitl. circ. 800.

398   EC   ISSN 0556-6436
REVISTA DEL FOLKLORE ECUATORIANO. (Text and summaries in Castellano) 1965. irreg. $1.50. Instituto Ecuatoriano de Folklore, Apartado 2140, Quito, Ecuador. bk. rev. bibl. illus. (processed)

REVISTA INSTITUTO INTERAMERICANO DE ETNOMUSICOLOGIA Y FOLKLORE. see *MUSIC*

398   GW   ISSN 0080-2697
RHEINISCHES JAHRBUCH FUER VOLKSKUNDE. 1950. a. price varies. (Rheinische Vereinigung fuer Volkskunde) Ferdinand Duemmlers Verlag, Kaiserstr. 31-37, Postfach 1480, 5300 Bonn 1, W. Germany (B.R.D.) Ed. H. L. Cox. bk. rev.

398   PL   ISSN 0080-3561
ROCZNIK SADECKI. (Text in Polish; summaries in English, French, Russian) 1938. a. 100 Zl. Polskie Towarzystwo Historyczne, Oddzial w Nowy Sacz, Rynek Ratusz, Nowy Sacz, Poland. bk. rev. circ. 1,500.

398   SW
SAGA OCH SED. 1932. a. Jungliga Gustav Adolfs Akademien, Klostergatan 2, S-753 21 Uppsala, Sweden. Ed. Folke Hedblom.

SAGA OF THE SANPITCH. see *HISTORY — History Of North And South America*

398   GW   ISSN 0080-732X
SCHWEIZERISCHE GESELLSCHAFT FUER VOLKSKUNDE. SCHRIFTEN. 1902. irreg., no. 65, 1980. price varies. (SZ) Rudolf Habelt Verlag, Am Buchenhang 1, 5300 Bonn 1, W. Germany (B.R.D.)

SCOTTISH STUDIES. see *HISTORY — History Of Europe*

398   BL
SERIE THESAURUS-FOLCLORE. 1976. irreg. Thesaurus Editora e Sistemas Audio Visuais Ltda., SCLRN 703, Bloque F, C.P. 04.326, 70000 Brasilia, Brazil.

309 950 US ISSN 0582-8155
SERIES ON CONTEMPORARY JAVANESE LIFE.
1960. irreg. price varies. Macmillan Publishing Co.,
Inc., 866 Third Ave., New York, NY 10022.

398 MX
SOCIEDAD FOLKLORICA DE MEXICO.
ANUARIO. 1945. a. Sociedad Folklorica de
Mexico, Avenida Amsterdam 130, Mexico 11, D.
F., Mexico.

SPROG OG KULTUR. see *LINGUISTICS*

398 GW ISSN 0081-5608
STIMMEN INDIANISCHER VOELKER. 1968.
irreg., vol. 2, 1976. price varies. (Ibero-
Amerikanisches Institut Preussischer Kulturbesitz
Berlin) Gebr. Mann Verlag, Lindenstr. 76, Postfach
110303, 1000 Berlin 61, W. Germany (B.R.D.) Ed.
Gerdt Kutscher.

390 IT ISSN 0081-5837
STORIA, COSTUMI E TRADIZIONI. 1962. irreg.,
vol. 4, 1980. price varies. ALFA Edizioni, Via Santo
Stefano 13, I-40125 Bologna, Italy. Ed. Andrea
Emiliani. circ. 4,000.

301.2 NO
STUDIA NORVEGICA ETHNOLOGICA ET
FOLKLORISTICA. (Text in English and
Norwegian) irreg. Universitetsforlaget, Kolstadgt. 1,
Box 2959-Toeyen, Oslo 6, Norway (U.S. address:
Box 258, Irvington-on-Hudson, NY 10533)
Continues: Studia Norvegica.

SUEDOSTDEUTSCHES ARCHIV. see *HISTORY —
History Of Europe*

SULU STUDIES. see *ANTHROPOLOGY*

398 US ISSN 0082-3023
TEXAS FOLKLORE SOCIETY. PUBLICATIONS.
1916. a. price varies. Texas Folklore Society, Box
13007 SFA Sta., Nacogdoches, TX 75962. Ed.
Francis E. Abernethy. index.

THEATA. see *ANTHROPOLOGY*

390 YU
TRADITIONES. (Text in Slovenian; summaries in
English, French, German, Italian) 1972. irreg. price
varies. Slovenska Akademija Znanosti in Umetnosti,
Razred za Filoloske in Literarne Vede, Novi Trg 5/
1, Ljubljana, Yugoslavia (Dist. by: Trubarjev
Antikvariat, Mestni Trg 25, 61000 Ljubljana) illus.
bibl. circ. 1,000.

398 GW ISSN 0068-0893
UEBERSEE-MUSEUM, BREMEN.
VEROEFFENTLICHUNGEN. REIHE B:
VOELKERKUNDE. 1950. irreg., vol. 3. 1973. price
varies. Uebersee-Museum, Bremen, Bahnhofsplatz
13, 2800 Bremen, W. Germany (B.R.D.)

UJ MAGYAR NEPKOLTESI GYUJTEMENY. see
LITERATURE — Poetry

398 UK ISSN 0082-7347
ULSTER FOLKLIFE. 1955. a. £3. Ulster Folk and
Transport Museum, Cultra Manor, Holywood,
County Down BT18 0EU, N. Ireland. Ed. Dr. Alan
Gailey. bk. rev. circ. 750.

398 780 CK ISSN 0067-9534
UNIVERSIDAD NACIONAL DE COLOMBIA.
CENTRO DE ESTUDIOS FOLKLORICOS.
MONOGRAFIAS. irreg.; latest issue, 1973. $40
free. Universidad Nacional de Colombia, Facultad
de Artes, Conservatorio de Musica, Bogota,
Colombia. Ed. Guillermo Abadia Morales. circ.
2,000.

398 IT ISSN 0069-1186
UNIVERSITA DEGLI STUDI DI CANTANIA.
ISTITUTO DI STORIA DELLE TRADIZIONI
POPOLARI. STUDI E TESTI. 1964. irreg., 1964,
no. 2. price varies. Casa Editrice Leo S. Olschki,
Casella Postale 66, 50100 Florence, Italy - Ed.
Sebastiano Lo Nigro. circ. 1,000.

398 CN ISSN 0085-5243
UNIVERSITE LAVAL. ARCHIVES DE
FOLKLORE. (Text and summaries in French)
1946. irreg., 1972, no. 14. price varies. Presses de
l'Universte Laval, C.P. 2447, Quebec 2, Canada.
Ed. Luc Lacourciere. bibl. circ. processed.

398 US ISSN 0068-6247
UNIVERSITY OF CALIFORNIA, LOS ANGELES.
CENTER FOR THE STUDY OF
COMPARATIVE FOLKLORE AND
MYTHOLOGY. PUBLICATIONS. irreg.
University of California Press, Berkeley, CA 94720.

398 US
UNIVERSITY OF CALIFORNIA PUBLICATIONS.
FOLKLORE & MYTHOLOGY STUDIES. 1953.
irreg. price varies. University of California Press,
2223 Fulton St., Berkeley, CA 94720.
Formerly: University of California Publications.
Folklore Studies (ISSN 0068-6360)

UNIVERZITA KOMENSKEHO. FILOZOFICKA
FAKULTA. ZBORNIK: ETHNOLOGIA
SLAVICA; an international review of Slavic
ethnology. see *ANTHROPOLOGY*

398 AU
VEREIN FUER VOLKSKUNDE IN WIEN.
SONDERSCHRIFTEN. 1955. irreg., vol. 3, 1978.
Verein fuer Volkskunde, Laudongasse 19, A-1080
Vienna, Austria. Eds. Leopold Schmidt, Klaus Beitl.
circ. 600.

398 909 GE
VEROEFFENTLICHUNGEN ZUR VOLKSKUNDE
UND KULTURGESCHICHTE. 1950. irreg., no.
64, 1977. price varies. Akademie-Verlag, Leipziger
Str. 3-4, 108 Berlin, E. Germany (D.D.R.) Eds. R.
Peesch, H. Strohbach, B. Weissel.
Continues: Akademie der Wissenschaften, Berlin.
Volkskundliche Veroeffentlichungen (ISSN 0065-
5228)

VOLHYNIAN BIBLIOGRAPHIC CENTER.
PUBLICATIONS. see *HISTORY — History Of
Europe*

390 AU
VOLKSKUNDLICHE STUDIEN. (Subseries of:
Universitaet Innsbruck. Veroeffentlichungen) 1970.
irreg. price varies. (Universitaet Innsbruck)
Oesterreichische Kommissionsbuchhandlung,
Maximilianstrasse 17, A-6020 Innsbruck, Austria.
Ed. Karl Ilg.

398 GW ISSN 0083-6877
VOLKSTUM DER SCHWEIZ. 1941. irreg., no. 12,
1979. price varies. Rudolf Habelt Verlag, Am
Buchenhang 1, 5300 Bonn 1, W. Germany (B.R.D.)

WESTFAELISCHE FORSCHUNGEN. see
HISTORY — History Of Europe

WHITLOCK'S WESSEX. see *HISTORY — History
Of Europe*

390 AU ISSN 0084-0068
WIENER VOELKERKUNDLICHE
MITTEILUNGEN. 1953. a. S.72($4)
(Oesterreichische Ethnologische Gesellschaft)
Museum fuer Voelkerkunde, Neue Hofburg, A-1014
Vienna, Austria. adv. circ. 500.

398 301.32 YU ISSN 0581-751X
ZEMALJSKI MUZEJ BOSNE I HERCEGOVINE.
GLASNIK. ETNOLOGIJA. (Vols. for 1965-66,
1969-70 issued in combined form) (Summaries in
French or German, 1965-68) 1974. a. Zemaljski
Muzej Bosne i Hercegovine, Vojvode Putnika 7,
Sarajevo, Yugoslavia. Ed. Vlajko Palavestra. illus.
Continues the publication with the same title
issued by the museum under its earlier name:
Zemaljski Muzej u Sarajevu.

FOLKLORE — Abstracting, Bibliographies, Statistics

BIBLIOGRAPHIE ZUR SYMBOLIK,
IKONOGRAPHIE UND MYTHOLOGIE. see
*ANTHROPOLOGY — Abstracting, Bibliographies,
Statistics*

398 016 US ISSN 0272-8494
FOLKLORE BIBLIOGRAPHY FOR (YEAR)
(Subseries of: Indiana University. Folklore Institute.
Monograph Series) 1976. irreg., vol. 32, 1981.
$17.50. (Indiana University, Folklore Institute)
Institute for the Study of Human Issues, Inc., 3401
Science Center, Philadelphia, PA 19104. Ed. R.
Dorson. circ. 500-700.

INTERNATIONAL ARTHURIAN SOCIETY.
BIBLIOGRAPHICAL BULLETIN. see
*LITERATURE — Abstracting, Bibliographies,
Statistics*

M L A DIRECTORY OF PERIODICALS; a guide to
journals and series in languages and literatures.
(Modern Language Association of America) see
*LITERATURE — Abstracting, Bibliographies,
Statistics*

FOOD AND FOOD INDUSTRIES

see also *Food and Food Industries—Bakers
and Confectioners; Food and Food
Industries—Grocery Trade; Agriculture;
Fish and Fisheries; Home Economics;
Hotels and Restaurants; Nutrition and
Dietetics*

664 VE ISSN 0084-683X
A T A V E BOLETIN INFORMATIVO.* irreg. free.
Asociacion de Tecnicos Azucareros de Venezuela,
Estacion Experimental de Occidente, Yaritaguce,
Yaracuy, Venezuela.

664 US ISSN 0065-2628
ADVANCES IN FOOD RESEARCH. 1948. irreg.,
vol. 25, 1979. price varies. Academic Press, Inc.,
111 Fifth Ave., New York, NY 10003. Eds. E. M.
Mrak, George F. Stewart. index. (also avail. in
microfiche)

664 US ISSN 0065-2636
ADVANCES IN FOOD RESEARCH.
SUPPLEMENT. 1969. irreg., 1972, no. 3. price
varies. Academic Press, Inc., 111 Fifth Ave., New
York, NY 10003.

664 PL
AKADEMIA ROLNICZA, POZNAN. ROCZNIK.
TECHNOLOGIA ROLNO-SPOZYWCZA.
(Summaries in English and Russian) 1960. irreg.
price varies. Akademia Rolnicza, Poznan, Ul.
Wojska Polskiego 28, 60-637 Poznan, Poland.
Indexed: Bibl.Agri.

664 MX
ALIMENTARIA. 1963. a. 125($90) Editorial
Innovacion, Espana 396, Mexico 13, D.F., Mexico.
Ed. Cesar Macazaga. adv.

664.7 US ISSN 0065-7107
AMERICAN ASSOCIATION OF CEREAL
CHEMISTS. MONOGRAPH SERIES. irreg., latest
no. 6. American Association of Cereal Chemists,
Inc., 3340 Pilot Knob Road, St. Paul, MN 55121.

664 US ISSN 0084-635X
AMERICAN FROZEN FOOD INSTITUTE.
MEMBERSHIP DIRECTORY. 1943. a. $65. ‡
American Frozen Food Institute, 919 - 18th Street
N.W., Washington, D.C. Ed. Barbara B. Noveau.
adv. circ. 3,000 (controlled)

636 US
AMERICAN MEAT SCIENCE ASSOCIATION.
RECIPROCAL MEAT CONFERENCE.
PROCEEDINGS. 1948. a. $8. ‡ National Live
Stock and Meat Board, 444 N. Michigan Ave.,
Chicago, IL 60611. Ed. H. Kenneth Johnson. circ.
650.

664.028 FR
ANNUAIRE INTERPROFESSIONNEL DE LA
SURGELATION ET DE LA CONGELATION. a.
Federation des Industries et Commerces Utilisateurs
des Basses Temperatures, 3 rue de Logelbach, 75847
Paris Cedex 17, France.

664 FR ISSN 0084-652X
ANNUAIRE NATIONAL DES INDUSTRIES DE
LA CONSERVE. 1952. a. 198 F. Editions
Comindus, 1 rue Descombes, Paris 17, France.

338.1 US
ANNUAL REPORT OF THE CONVENIENCE
STORE INDUSTRY. 1971. a. $10. Progressive
Grocer Publishing Co., 708 Third Ave., New York,
NY 10017. Ed. Robert Rossner. adv. charts. stat.
(back issues avail.)
Formerly: Convenience Store Study.

ASSOCIATION EURATOM-ITAL. ANNUAL REPORT. see *AGRICULTURE*

664 US ISSN 0094-8764
ASSOCIATION OF AMERICAN PLANT FOOD CONTROL OFFICIALS. OFFICIAL PUBLICATION. 1947. a. $6. Association of American Plant Food Control Officials, Department of Biochemistry, Purdue University, Lafayette, IN 47907. circ. 400.

641.38 AT ISSN 0067-1894
AUSTRALIAN HONEY BOARD. ANNUAL REPORT. 1963/64. a. free. Australian Honey Board, 647 George St., Sydney, N.S.W., Australia.
Honey

AUSTRALIAN MEAT RESEARCH COMMITTEE. ANNUAL REPORT. see *AGRICULTURE — Poultry And Livestock*

664.1 AT
AUSTRALIAN SOCIETY OF SUGAR CANE TECHNOLOGISTS. PROCEEDINGS. 1930. a. Aus.$15. Australian Society of Sugar Cane Technologists, G.P.O. Box 608, Brisbane, Qld. 4001, Australia. Ed. O.W. Sturgess. cum. index every 5 years. circ. 1,000.
Formerly (until April 1978): Queensland Society of Sugar Cane Technologists. Proceedings (ISSN 0079-8851)

664.1 AT ISSN 0067-2173
AUSTRALIAN SUGAR YEAR BOOK. 1941. a. Aus.$19.10. Strand Publishing Pty. Ltd., 432 Queen St., Brisbane, Qld. 4000, Australia.
Sugar

664.1 BG
BANGLADESH SUGAR MILLS CORPORATION. ANNUAL REPORT. (Text in English) a. Tk.20. Bangladesh Sugar Mills Corporation, Shilpa Bhaban, Motijheel Commercial Area, Dacca 2, Bangladesh. stat.

664 607 UK ISSN 0067-8651
BINSTED'S DIRECTORY OF FOOD TRADE MARKS AND BRAND NAMES. 1959. a. £14.50. Food Trade Press Ltd., 29 High St., Green Street Green, Orpington, Kent BR6 6LS, England. Ed. Adrian Binsted. adv. circ. 2,500.

664.028 UK
BRITISH FROZEN FOOD FEDERATION. YEAR BOOK. 1968. a. $25. ‡ British Frozen Food Federation, Honeypot Lane, Colsterworth, Grantham, Lincolnshire NG33 5LY, England. Ed. Patrick G. Howell. adv. circ. 1,000.

664 CN ISSN 0068-7308
CANADA. AGRICULTURE CANADA. FOOD RESEARCH INSTITUTE, OTTAWA. RESEARCH REPORT. 1962-64. irreg. free. Agriculture Canada, Food Research Institute, Ottawa, Canada. circ. 200.

664 CN ISSN 0068-8150
CANADA'S MEAT INDUSTRY. triennial. free. Meat Packers Council of Canada, 5233 Dundas St. W., Islington, Ont. M9B 1A6, Canada.

664 CN ISSN 0068-8754
CANADIAN FOOD AND PACKAGING DIRECTORY. 1924. a. Can.$20($30) Lloyd Publications of Canada, Box 262, West Hill, Ont. M1E 4R5, Canada. Ed. J. Lloyd. adv. index. index. circ. 8,500.

664.1 338.1 CN ISSN 0068-8770
CANADIAN FRUIT WHOLESALERS' ASSOCIATION. YEARBOOK. 1925. a. Can.$30. Canadian Fruit Wholesalers Association, 1568 Carling Ave., Ottawa, Ont. K1Z 7M5, Canada. Ed. H. R. Taylor. adv. circ. 1,200.

CANNED FISHERY PRODUCTS. see *FISH AND FISHERIES*

635 UK ISSN 0069-0988
CASTLE'S GUIDE TO THE FRUIT, FLOWER, VEGETABLE AND ALLIED TRADES. 1912. biennial. £8. Castle Publishing Co., 314 Gray's Inn Rd., London W.C. 1, England.

663.92 GH ISSN 0300-1385
COCOA RESEARCH INSTITUTE. ANNUAL REPORT. 1962. a. Cocoa Research Institute, Box 8, Tafo, Ghana.

664 SP
COLECCION SIURELL. SERIE DE COCINA. no. 5, 1974. irreg. price varies. Luis Ripoll Ed. & Pub., Calatrava 34, Palma de Mallorca, Spain.

664 AT ISSN 0069-7419
COMMONWEALTH SCIENTIFIC AND INDUSTRIAL RESEARCH ORGANIZATION. DIVISION OF FOOD RESEARCH. REPORT OF RESEARCH. (Before 1969 entitled Annual Report) 1959-60. a. Aus.$2. ‡ C. S. I. R. O., Division of Food Research, Box 89, East Melbourne, Vic. 3002, Australia.

664 AT ISSN 0069-7427
COMMONWEALTH SCIENTIFIC AND INDUSTRIAL RESEARCH ORGANIZATION. DIVISION OF FOOD RESEARCH. TECHNICAL PAPER. 1956. irreg. Aus.$1.50. ‡ C. S. I. R. O., Division of Food Research, Box 89, East Melbourne, Vic. 3002, Australia. Indexed: Chem.Abstr.

637 US ISSN 0070-2587
DAIRY INDUSTRIES CATALOG. 1927. a. $20. Magazines for Industry, Inc., 747 Third Ave., New York, NY 10017. Ed. Margaret Futch. adv. circ. 10,000.

338.1 US
DIRECTORY OF CONVENIENCE STORE COMPANIES. 1978. a. $65. Progressive Grocer Publishing Co., 708 Third Ave., New York, NY 10017. Ed. Lillyan Forman.

664 658.8 US ISSN 0070-6213
DIRECTORY OF RESEARCH REPORTS RELATING TO PRODUCE PACKAGING AND MARKETING. 1960. irreg. $10. Produce Marketing Association, 700 Barksdale Plaza, Newark, DE 19711. Ed. Jesse S. Raybourn.

DIRECTORY OF THE CANNING, FREEZING, PRESERVING INDUSTIRES. see *BUSINESS AND ECONOMICS — Trade And Industrial Directories*

664 UN ISSN 0071-7010
F A O FOOD ADDITIVE CONTROL SERIES. (Text in English, French and Spanish) 1969. irreg., 1969, no. 8. price varies. Food and Agriculture Organization of the United Nations, Distribution and Sales Section, Via delle Terme di Caracalla, 00100 Rome, Italy (Dist. in U.S. by: Unipub, 345 Park Ave. S., New York, NY 10010)

F D A CLINICAL EXPERIENCE ABSTRACTS. (U. S. Food and Drug Administration) see *PHARMACY AND PHARMACOLOGY*

664 615 US
F D A COMPLIANCE POLICY GUIDE. base vol. plus 12 updates. $100. (U.S. Food and Drug Administration) U.S. National Technical Information Service, 5285 Port Royal Rd., Springfield, VA 22161.

664.028 FR
FEDERATION INTERPROFESSIONNELLE DE LA CONGELATION ULTRA-RAPIDE. RAPPORT STATISTIQUE ANNUEL. a. Federation des Industries et Commerces Utilisateurs des Basses Temperatures, 3 rue de Logelbach, 75847 Paris Cedex 17, France.

664 658.8 GW ISSN 0014-9691
FEINKOST-REVUE; Deutsche Milchhandels- und Feinkost-Zeitung. 1967. a. DM.48. Verlagshaus Sponholz, Grosser Hasenpfad 42-48, Postfach 701040, 6000 Frankfurt 70, W. Germany (B.R.D.) adv. bk. rev. bibl. charts. illus. circ. 7,200.

633.6 FJ
FIJI SUGAR YEAR BOOK. (Text in English, Fijian and Hindi) 1979. a. Fiji Sugar Industry, Box 644, Suva, Fiji. Ed. D. V. Tarte. charts. illus. stat. tr.lit. circ. 5,000.

664.7 UK ISSN 0071-6243
FLOUR MILLING AND BAKING RESEARCH ASSOCIATION. ANNUAL REPORT AND ACCOUNTS. 1968. a. membership. Flour Milling and Baking Research Association, Chorleywood, Herts WD3 5SH, England. circ. 2,000.
Issued formerly under previous name of organization: British Baking Industries Research Association. Annual Report.

664 FR ISSN 0474-537X
FOOD CONSUMPTION IN THE O. E. C. D. COUNTRIES/CONSOMMATION DE DENREES ALIMENTAIRES DANS LES PAYS DE L'OCDE. (Text in English and French) irreg. $19. Organization for Economic Cooperation and Development, 2 rue Andre Pascal, 75775 Paris 16, France (U.S. orders to: O.E.C.D. Publications and Information Center, 1750 Pennsylvania Ave. N.W., Washington, D.C. 20006) (also avail. in microfiche)

664 SA
FOOD INDUSTRIES YEARBOOK AND BUYERS' GUIDE. 1952. biennial. R.25($36) Thomson Publications S. A. (Pty) Ltd., P.O. Box 8308, Johannesburg 2000, South Africa. Ed. H. Engelhardt. adv.
Former titles: Food Industries Yearbook and Buyers' Directory; Food Industries of S.A. Buyers' Guide (ISSN 0071-7185); Food Industries of South Africa Manual and Buyer's Guide.

664 UN ISSN 0071-7193
FOOD INDUSTRY STUDIES. 1969. irreg. price varies. United Nations Industrial Development Organization, Lerchenfelderstrasse 1, Box 707, A-1011 Vienna, Austria (Orders from Europe, Africa and Middle East to: Distribution and Sales Section, Palais des Nations, 1211 Geneva 10 Switzerland. Orders from Asia, the Pacific and North and South America to: United Nations Publications, Room LX-2300, New York, NY 10017)

664 UK
FOOD PROCESSING INDUSTRY DIRECTORY. 1954. a. £10. Consumer Industries Press Ltd., 40 Bowling Green Lane, London EC1R 0NE, England. Ed. Hazel Blake. adv. index.
Formerly: Food Processing and Packaging Directory (ISSN 0071-7207)

664 US ISSN 0071-7223
FOOD SCIENCE SERIES. 1971. irreg., vol. 6, 1979. price varies. Marcel Dekker, Inc., 270 Madison Ave., New York, NY 10016. Ed. O. Fennema.

664 US
FOOD SERVICE RESEARCH ABSTRACTS. 1971. a. $7.50. Society for the Advancement of Food Service Research, 2710 N. Salisbury St., West Lafayette, IN 47906. Ed. Robert D. Buchanan. circ. 250. (back issues avail.)

664 US ISSN 0093-0075
FOOD TECHNOLOGY REVIEW. 1973. irreg., no. 54, 1981. $32-48. Noyes Data Corporation, Noyes Bldg., Mill Rd. at Grand Ave., Park Ridge, NJ 07656.
Formerly: Food Processing Review (ISSN 0071-7215)

664 UK ISSN 0071-7231
FOOD TRADES DIRECTORY, FOOD BUYER'S YEARBOOK. 1958. biennial. £21. Newman Publishing Ltd., 48 Poland St., London W1V 4PP, England.

338.1 UN ISSN 0071-934X
FREEDOM FROM HUNGER CAMPAIGN. BASIC STUDIES. (Text in English, French and Spanish) 1963. irreg., 1970, no. 24. price varies. Food and Agriculture Organization of the United Nations, Distribution and Sales Section, Via delle Terme di Caracalla, Rome, Italy (Dist. in U.S. by: Unipub, 345 Park Ave. S., New York, NY 10010)

664.02 338.47 US ISSN 0071-9684
FROZEN FOOD FACTBOOK AND DIRECTORY. 1948. a. $50. National Frozen Food Association, Inc., One Chocolate Ave., Hershey, PA 17033. Ed. Dorothy Williamson. adv. index. circ. 3,500.

664.028 DK
FROZEN FOODS IN DENMARK. 1963. a. free. Dybfrostinstituttet - Frozen Food Institute, Kastelvej 11, 2100 Copenhagen OE, Denmark. stat.

664.028 641 UK ISSN 0071-9692
FROZEN FOODS YEAR BOOK. 1957. a. £12. Retail Journals Ltd., Queensway House, 2 Queensway, Redhill, Surrey RH1 1QS, England. circ. 2,500.

FOOD AND FOOD INDUSTRIES

664   GW   ISSN 0341-0498
GRUNDLAGEN UND FORTSCHRITTE DER LEBENSMITTELUNTERSUCHUNG UND LEBENSMITTELTECHNOLOGIE. 1953. irreg. price varies. Verlag Paul Parey (Berlin), Lindenstr. 44-47, 1000 Berlin 61, W. Germany (B.R.D.) Ed. Friedrich Kiermeier. bibl. illus. index. Indexed: Biol.Abstr.
Formerly: Grundlagen und Fortschritte der Lebensmitteluntersuchung (ISSN 0432-7454)

641.5   US
HANDBOOK OF FOOD PREPARATION. irreg., 8th, 1980. $6. American Home Economics Association, 2010 Massachusetts Ave., N.W., Washington, DC 20036.

664   UK   ISSN 0142-1824
HOTEL, RESTAURANT AND CATERING SUPPLIES. 1964. a. £10. Sell's Publications Ltd., Sell's House, 39 East Street, Epsom KT17 1BQ, Surrey, England. adv. bk. rev. circ. 3,500.
Former titles: Sell's Hotel, Restaurant and Canteen Supplies (ISSN 0073-3504); Hotel, Restaurant and Canteen Supplies.

664   US   ISSN 0073-9286
I F T WORLD DIRECTORY AND GUIDE. 1967. a. membership. Institute of Food Technologists, 221 N. La Salle St., Chicago, IL 60601. Ed. John B. Klis. adv. circ. 20,000.

642.5   US
INSITE (YEAR) 1980. a. $35 to non-members. National Association of Concessionaires, 35 E. Wacker Dr., Chicago, IL 60601. Ed. Lisa Eisenberg. adv. charts. stat. circ. 3,500.

664 641   BL   ISSN 0100-350X
INSTITUTO DE TECNOLOGIA DE ALIMENTOS. COLETANEA. 1965. a. Cr$60. Instituto de Tecnologia de Alimentos, Caixa Postal 139, Campinas S.P., Brazil. circ. 500.

664   AU   ISSN 0074-1450
INTERNATIONAL ASSOCIATION FOR CEREAL CHEMISTRY. WORKING AND DISCUSSION MEETINGS REPORTS. 1958. biennial; 8th, Vienna, 1974. free. International Association for Cereal Chemistry, Schmidgasse 3-7, A-2320 Schwechat, Austria.

664.1   UK
INTERNATIONAL COMMISSION FOR UNIFORM METHODS OF SUGAR ANALYSIS. REPORT OF THE PROCEEDINGS OF THE SESSION. irreg., 17th, 1978, Montreal (published in 1979) £6. International Commission for Uniform Methods of Sugar Analysis, Box 35, Wharf Rd., Peterborough PE2 9PU, England. Ed. D. Hibbert.
Sugar

664.1   BE   ISSN 0074-2708
INTERNATIONAL COMMISSION OF SUGAR TECHNOLOGY. PROCEEDINGS OF THE GENERAL ASSEMBLY. (Text in English, French, German) 1953. irreg., 15th, 1979, Amsterdam. 1800 Fr. International Commission of Sugar Technology - Commission Internationale Technique de Sucrerie, c/o R. Pieck, General Secretary-Treasurer, 1 Aandorenstraat, B-3300 Tienen, Belgium.
Sugar

641 664   US   ISSN 0074-3666
INTERNATIONAL CONGRESS OF FOOD SCIENCE AND TECHNOLOGY. PROCEEDINGS. 1962. quadriennial; 1978, 5th, Kyoto, Japan. price varies. ‡ International Union of Food Science and Technology, c/o C. L. Wiley, Institute of Food Technologists, 221 N. La Salle St., Chicago, IL 60601 (For 5th Congress inquire: Prof. Hisateru Mitsuda, 64 Takanawate-Cho, Kamigamo, Kita-Ku, Kyoto, 603, Japan) circ. 3,000.

664   US   ISSN 0074-3968
INTERNATIONAL CONGRESS OF SUGARCANE TECHNOLOGISTS. PROCEEDINGS.* 1965. triennial, 1974, 15th, Durban. International Society of Sugarcane Technologists, Box 1057, Alea, HI 96701.

641 664   FR   ISSN 0074-4034
INTERNATIONAL CONGRESS ON CANNED FOODS. REPORT. irreg., 6th, 1972, Paris. Permanent International Committee on Canned Foods, 3 rue de Logelbach, 75017 Paris, France.

664   FR   ISSN 0534-9257
INTERNATIONAL CONGRESS ON CANNED FOODS. TEXTS OF PAPERS PRESENTED AND RESOLUTIONS/CONGRES INTERNATIONAL DE LA CONSERVE. TEXTES DES COMMUNICATIONS. (Text in English and French; Summaries in English and German) irreg.; 6th, Paris, 1972. International Permanent Committee on Canned Foods, French Delegation - Comite International Permanent de la Conserve, 3, rue de Logelbach, 75 Paris 17, France.

663   FR   ISSN 0535-0182
INTERNATIONAL FEDERATION OF FRUIT JUICE PRODUCERS. PROCEEDINGS. BERICHTE. RAPPORTS.* (Text in English, French, or German with Summaries in the other languages) 1958. irreg. International Federation of Fruit Juice Producers, 10 rue de Liege, 75009 Paris, 75009 Paris.

INTERNATIONAL SUGAR ORGANIZATION. ANNUAL REPORT. see *AGRICULTURE — Crop Production And Soil*

664   NE
INTERNATIONAL SYMPOSIUM ON NITRITE IN MEAT PRODUCTS. PROCEEDINGS. irreg., 2nd, 1973, Zeist, Netherlands. fl.65. Centre for Agricultural Publishing and Documentation, Box 4, 6700 AA Wageningen, Netherlands.

INTERNATIONAL UNION OF FOOD AND ALLIED WORKERS' ASSOCIATIONS. MEETING OF THE EXECUTIVE COMMITTEE. I. DOCUMENTS OF THE SECRETARIAT. II. SUMMARY REPORT. see *LABOR UNIONS*

338.4   JA
JAPAN SUGAR YEARBOOK. (Text in English) 1958. a. free. Mitsui & Co., Ltd., C.P.O. Box 822, Tokyo 100-91, Japan. adv. charts, illus, stat. circ. 600.

JOINT F A O/W H O CODEX ALIMENTARIUS COMMISSION. REPORT OF THE SESSION. see *PUBLIC HEALTH AND SAFETY*

641 664   UN   ISSN 0075-3963
JOINT F A O/W H O EXPERT COMMITTEE ON FOOD ADDITIVES REPORT. (Issued in F A O Nutrition Meetings Report Series) 1957. a. Food and Agriculture Organization of the United Nations, Distribution and Sales Section, Via delle Terme di Caracalla, 00100 Rome, Italy (Dist. in U.S. by: Unipub, 345 Park Ave. S., New York, NY 10010)

KOMPASS ALIMENTATION. see *BUSINESS AND ECONOMICS — Trade And Industrial Directories*

664   JA   ISSN 0452-9995
KYOTO UNIVERSITY. RESEARCH INSTITUTE FOR FOOD SCIENCE. MEMOIRS/SHOKURYO KAGAKU KENKYUSHO KIYO. (Text in European languages) 1951. irreg. exchange basis. Kyoto University, Research Institute for Food Science - Kyoto Daigaku Shokuryo Kogaku Kenkyusho, Gokasho, Uji 611, Japan.

664   US
LATIN AMERICAN FOOD PRODUCTION CONFERENCE SUMMARY REPORT. 9th, 1973. a? International Minerals and Chemicals Corporation, IMC Plaza, Libertyville, IL 60048.

664 658.8   US   ISSN 0146-9223
MARKET SCOPE. Variant title: Progressive Grocer's Market Scope. 1975. a. $139. Progressive Grocer Publishing Co., 708 Third Ave., New York, NY 10017. Ed. Norman Bussel. index. (back issues avail.)

664.9   UK
MEAT RESEARCH INSTITUTE. BIENNIAL REPORT. 1977. biennial. Meat Research Institute, Langford, Bristol BS18 7DY, England. illus.
Meat

664   US   ISSN 0090-5631
MEAT SCIENCE INSTITUTE. PROCEEDINGS. 1972. a. $10 price varies. (National Independent Meat Packers Association) University of Georgia, Center for Continuing Education, Dept. of Food Sciences, Athens, GA 30602. Ed. John A. Carpenter.

636   UK   ISSN 0082-7967
MEAT TRADE YEARBOOK. 1959. a. £3.15. (National Federation of Meat Traders) Wheatland Journals Ltd., 177 Hagden Lane, Watford, WD1 8LW, England. Ed. Victor Lilley. adv. circ. 4,500.
Formerly: United Kingdom Meat Trade Annual.

664.9 331.88   AT   ISSN 0310-6721
MEATWORKER. 1971. irreg. Australasian Meat Industry Employees Union, Queensland Branch, Trades Hall, Brisbane, Qld. 4000, Australia. Ed. C. A. Maxwell. (newspaper)

MOVEMENT OF CALIFORNIA FRUITS AND VEGETABLES BY RAIL, TRUCK, AND AIR. see *TRANSPORTATION*

664   NE
NETHERLANDS. MINISTERIE VAN VOLKSGEZONDHEID EN MILIEUHYGIENE. VERSLAG LEVENSMIDDELEN EN KEURING VAN WAREN. (Subseries of: Netherlands. Ministerie van Volksgezondheid en Milieuhygiene. Verslagen, Adviezen, Rapporten) irreg. Ministerie van Volksgezondheid en Milieuhygiene - Ministry of Public Health and Environmental Hygiene, The Hague, Netherlands.

613 641   ZA   ISSN 0078-284X
NUTRITION NEWS IN ZAMBIA. (Text in English) 1969. irreg.(approx. 2-4 issues per year) free. National Food and Nutrition Commission, Box 2669, Lusaka, Zambia. bk. rev. circ. 1,500.

664   PL   ISSN 0528-9254
POLITECHNIKA LODZKA. ZESZYTY NAUKOWE. CHEMIA SPOZYWCZA. (Text in Polish; summaries in English and Russian) 1955. irreg. price varies. Politechnika Lodzka, Ul. Zwirki 36, 90-924 Lodz, Poland (Dist. by: Ars Polona-Ruch, Krakowskie Przedmiescie 7, Warsaw, Poland) Ed. Mieczyslaw Boruch. circ. 283. Indexed: Chem.Abstr.

664 668.8   US
PRODUCE MARKETING ALMANAC. 1976. a. $15. Produce Marketing Association, 700 Barksdale Plaza, Newark, DE 19711. Ed. Jesse Raybourn. adv. circ. 4,000.
Formerly: Produce Marketing Association Almanac; Supersedes(1968-1976): Produce Marketing Association. Yearbook (ISSN 0079-5860); Which was formerly titled: Produce Packaging and Marketing Association. Yearbook.

338.1   US   ISSN 0079-6921
PROGRESSIVE GROCER'S MARKETING GUIDEBOOK. 1967. a. $159. Progressive Grocer Publishing Co., 708 Third Ave., New York, NY 10017. Ed. Lucy Tarzian. adv. index. (back issues avail.)

664.028   US   ISSN 0079-9289
QUICK FROZEN FOODS DIRECTORY OF FROZEN FOOD PROCESSORS. 1945-46. a. $20. Harcourt Brace Jovanovich, Inc., 757 3rd Ave., New York, NY 10017. Ed. Sam Martin.

664.028 380.1   US
QUICK FROZEN FOODS DIRECTORY OF WHOLESALE DISTRIBUTORS. 1949. biennial. $40 per copy. Harcourt Brace Jovanovich, Inc., 757 Third Ave., New York, NY 10017. Ed. Sam Martin. adv. index. circ. 1,000. (looseleaf format)

664   FR
REPERTOIRE DES CENTRES DE RECHERCHE ALIMENTAIRE. a. 315 F. Societe d'Edition et de Promotion Agricoles, Industrielles et Commerciales, 42 rue du Louvre, 75001 Paris, France.

664   US
S I C 20 BUYER'S GUIDE. 1975. a. $15. S I C Publishing Co., Box 6042, Lawrenceville, NJ 08648. Ed. P. C. Hereld. adv. circ. 17,500.

664.028   SW
S I K INFORMATION. (Text in English) 1972. irreg. free. Svenska Livsmedelsinstitutet - Swedish Food Institute, Box 27022, S-400 23 Goeteborg, Sweden. circ. 700.

SAMMLUNG LEBENSMITTELRECHTLICHER ENTSCHEIDUNGEN. see *LAW*

664 SZ
SCHWEIZERISCHER ERNAEHRUNGSBERICHT. 1975. irreg. Verlag Hans Huber, Laenggassstr. 76 und Marktgasse 9, 3000 Berne 9, Switzerland. charts, stat.

642 US ISSN 0081-1483
SOCIETY FOR THE ADVANCEMENT OF FOOD SERVICE RESEARCH. PROCEEDINGS. 1959. a. $10 price may vary. Society for the Advancement of Food Service Research, 2710 N. Salisbury St., West Lafayette, IN 47906. Ed. Charles E. Eshbach.

664.1 SA
SOUTH AFRICAN SUGAR YEAR BOOK. a. R.6. South African Sugar Association, Box 1209, Durban 4000, South Africa. Ed. M.S. Morgan. adv.
Sugar

664 US
SPECTRUM. 1974. a. $25. National Renderers Association, 3150 Des Plaines Ave., Des Plaines, IL 60018. Ed. Robert J. Werner. adv. circ. 5,000.
  Supersedes: Renderers' Yearbook (ISSN 0080-0910)

634 NE
SPRENGER INSTITUUT. COMMUNICATIONS. (Text in Dutch; Summaries in English, French and German) vol. 35, 1976. irreg. price varies. Sprenger Instituut, Postbus 17, 6700 AA Wageningen, Netherlands. (back issues avail.)

634 664 NE ISSN 0081-3850
SPRENGER INSTITUUT. JAARVERSLAG/ANNUAL REPORT. (Text in Dutch and English) 1956. a. price varies. ‡ Sprenger Instituut, Postbus 17, 6700 AA Wageningen, Netherlands. Indexed: Food Sci.&Tech.Abstr. Hort.Abstr.

634 NE
SPRENGER INSTITUUT. RAPPORTEN. irreg. price varies. Sprenger Instituut, Postbus 17, 6700 AA Wageningen, Netherlands. (back issues avail.)

664 GW ISSN 0081-9174
SUESSWAREN JAHRBUCH; Wer und Was in der deutschen Suesswarenindustrie. 1949. a. DM.78. B. Behr's Verlag GmbH, Averhoffstr. 10, 2000 Hamburg 76, W. Germany (B.R.D.)

664 TR ISSN 0302-4555
SUGAR TECHNOLOGISTS' ASSOCIATION OF TRINIDAD AND TOBAGO. PROCEEDINGS. 1967. a. free. ‡ Sugar Technologists' Association of Trindad & Tobago, 80 Abercromby St., P.O. Box 230, Port of Spain, Trinidad. Ed. M.Y. Khan. circ. controlled. (processed)

664.1 US ISSN 0081-9212
SUGAR Y AZUCAR YEARBOOK. (Text in English, Spanish) a. $30. Palmer Publications, 25 W. 45 St., New York, NY 10036.
Sugar

664 SW
SWEDISH FOOD INSTITUTE. ANNUAL REPORT. Short title: S I K Annual Report. (Text in English and Swedish) 1951. a. Svenska Livsmedelsinstitutet - Swedish Food Institute, Box 27022, S-400 23 Goeteborg, Sweden. circ. 2,500.

338.1 CH ISSN 0492-1712
TAIWAN SUGAR. irreg. $5. Good Earth Press, P.O. Box 697, Taipei, Taiwan, Republic of China. illus.

TASMANIAN MEAT INDUSTRY JOURNAL. see *AGRICULTURE — Poultry And Livestock*

641 IS ISSN 0068-0761
TECHNION-ISRAEL INSTITUTE OF TECHNOLOGY. BRAVERMAN MEMORIAL LECTURE.* 1963. irreg. Technion-Israel Institute of Technology, Department of Food Engineering and Biotechnology, Haifa, Israel.

664.9 UY
URUGUAY. INSTITUTO NACIONAL DE CARNES. DEPARTAMENTO DE EXPORTACIONES. ANUARIO. 1975. a. Instituto Nacional de Carnes, Departamento de Exportaciones, Rincon 549, Montevideo, Uruguay.

664 FI ISSN 0355-3558
VALTION TEKNILLINEN TUTKIMUSKESKUS. ELINTARVIKELABORATORIO. TIEDONANTO/TECHNICAL RESEARCH CENTRE OF FINLAND. FOOD RESEARCH LABORATORY. REPORT. (Text mainly in Finnish, some in English or Swedish) 1972. irreg. price varies. Valtion Teknillinen Tutkimuskeskus - Technical Research Centre of Finland, Vuorimiehentie 5, 02150 Espoo 15, Finland.

338.1 US
WORLD FOOD CRISIS: AN INTERNATIONAL DIRECTORY OF ORGANIZATIONS AND INFORMATION RESOURCES. 1977. irreg. $20. California Institute of Public Affairs, Box 10, Claremont, CA 91711. Eds. Thaddeus C. Trzyna, Joan Dickson Smith, Judith Ruggles.

338.1 UN ISSN 0084-179X
WORLD FOOD PROBLEMS. (Text in English, French, and Spanish) 1956. irreg., 1971, no. 14. price varies. Food and Agriculture Organization of the United Nations, Distribution and Sales Section, Via delle Terme di Caracalla, Rome, Italy (Dist. in U.S. by: Unipub, 345 Park Ave. S., New York, NY 10010)

641 ZA ISSN 0084-4969
ZAMBIA. NATIONAL FOOD AND NUTRITION COMMISSION. ANNUAL REPORT. (Text in English) 1968. a. free. ‡ National Food and Nutrition Commission, Box 2669, Lusaka, Zambia. circ. 2,000.

664 GW ISSN 0084-5736
ZUCKERWIRTSCHAFTLICHES TASCHENBUCH/SUGAR ECONOMY/ECONOMIE SUCRIERE. 1954. a. DM.29. Verlag Dr. Albert Bartens, Lueckhoffstr. 16, 1000 Berlin 38, W. Germany (B.R.D.) adv. circ. 2,200.

FOOD AND FOOD INDUSTRIES —
Abstracting, Bibliographies, Statistics

338.1 339 AT
AUSTRALIA. BUREAU OF STATISTICS. APPARENT CONSUMPTION OF FOODSTUFFS AND NUTRIENTS. 1948. a. free. Australian Bureau of Statistics, P.O. Box 10, Belconnen, A.C.T. 2616, Australia. circ. 2,200. (processed)

339.4 AT
AUSTRALIA. BUREAU OF STATISTICS. APPARENT CONSUMPTION OF TEA AND COFFEE. 1972-73. a. free. Australian Bureau of Statistics, P.O. Box 10, Belconnen, A.C.T. 2616, Australia. circ. 1,400. (processed)

664.9 319.4 AT
AUSTRALIA. BUREAU OF STATISTICS. TASMANIAN OFFICE. MEAT PRODUCTION. a. Australian Bureau of Statistics, Tasmanian Office, Box 66A, Hobart, Tasmania 7001, Australia. circ. 590.
  Formerly: Australia. Bureau of Statistics. Tasmanian Office. Production of Meat in Tasmania.

664 658.8 CN ISSN 0316-9537
BLUE BOOK OF FOOD STORE OPERATORS & WHOLESALERS. a. Can.$12. Sanford Evans Publishing Ltd., 1077 St. James St., Box 6900, Winnipeg, Man, R3C 3B1, Canada. Ed. C. B. Wagner. circ. 1,000.

338.4 CN ISSN 0527-4869
CANADA. STATISTICS CANADA. BREWERIES/BRASSERIES. (Catalog 32-205) (Text in English and French) 1919. a. Can.$4.50($5.40) Statistics Canada, Publications Distribution, Ottawa, Ont. K1A 0V7, Canada. stat. (also avail. in microform from MML)

338.4 CN ISSN 0384-2843
CANADA. STATISTICS CANADA. CANE AND BEET SUGAR PROCESSORS/TRAITEMENT DU SUCRE DE CANNE ET DE BETTERAVES. (Catalogue 32-222) (Text in English & French) 1918. a. Can.$4.50($5.40) Statistics Canada, Publications Distribution, Ottawa, Ont. K1A 0V7, Canada. (also avail. in microform from MML)

CANADA. STATISTICS CANADA. FISH PRODUCTS INDUSTRY/INDUSTRIE DE LA TRANSFORMATION DU POISSON. see *FISH AND FISHERIES — Abstracting, Bibliographies, Statistics*

338.4 CN ISSN 0700-0324
CANADA. STATISTICS CANADA. FLOUR AND BREAKFAST CEREAL PRODUCTS INDUSTRY/MEUNERIE ET FABRICATION DE CEREALES DE TABLE. (Catalog 32-228) (Text in English and French) 1970. a. Can.$4.50($5.40) Statistics Canada, Publications Distribution, Ottawa, Ont. K1A 0V7, Canada. (also avail. in microform from MML)

664 CN ISSN 0384-4420
CANADA. STATISTICS CANADA. FRUIT AND VEGETABLE PROCESSING INDUSTRIES/PREPARATION DE FRUITS ET DE LEGUMES. (Catalogue 32-218) (Text in English and French) 1918. a. Can.$4.50($5.40) Statistics Canada, Publications Distribution, Ottawa, Ont. K1A 0V7, Canada. (also avail. in microform from MML)

664 CN ISSN 0384-3696
CANADA. STATISTICS CANADA. MISCELLANEOUS FOOD PROCESSORS/TRAITMENT DES PRODUITS ALIMENTAIRES DIVERS. (Catalogue 32-224) (Text in English and French) 1918. a. Can.$4.50($5.40) Statistics Canada, Publications Distribution, Ottawa, Ont. K1A 0V7, Canada. (also avail. in microform from MML)

338.4 CN ISSN 0384-4951
CANADA. STATISTICS CANADA. SLAUGHTERING AND MEAT PROCESSORS/ABATTAGE ET CONDITIONNEMENT DE LA VIANDE. (Catalogue 32-221) (Text in English and French) 1917. a. Can.$4.50($5.40) Statistics Canada, Publications Distribution, Ottawa, Ont. K1A 0V7, Canada. (also avail. in microform from MML)

338.4 CN ISSN 0527-6403
CANADA. STATISTICS CANADA. VEGETABLE OIL MILLS/MOULINS A HUILE VEGETALE. (Catalogue 32-223) (Text in English and French) 1918. a. Can.$4.50($5.40) Statistics Canada, Publications Distribution, Ottawa, Ont. K1A 0V7, Canada. (also avail. in microform from MML)

664.8 US ISSN 0069-018X
CANNED FOOD PACK STATISTICS. 1960. a. $13. ‡ (National Food Processors Association) Technical Services Corporation, 1133 20th St. N.W., Washington, DC 20036. Ed. Yuli Wexler. circ. 1,000.

664 016 US ISSN 0146-3780
FOOD PUBLICATIONS ROUND-UP. 1977. irreg. $30. Special Libraries Association, Food & Nutrition Division, Food & Nutrition Division (St. Louis), Jefferson Memorial Sta., 14 S. 4th St., St. Louis, MO 63102. Ed. Larry R. Walton. circ. 100.

664 NE
NETHERLANDS. CENTRAAL BUREAU VOOR DE STATISTIEK. PRODUKTIESTATISTIEKEN: SUIKERFABRIEKEN. a. fl.7.10. Centraal Bureau voor de Statistiek, Prinses Beatrixlaan 428, Voorburg, Netherlands (Orders to: Staatsuitgeverij, Christoffel Plantijnstraat, The Hague, Netherlands)

FOOD AND FOOD INDUSTRIES —
Bakers And Confectioners

664.752 US ISSN 0066-0582
AMERICAN SOCIETY OF BAKERY ENGINEERS. PROCEEDINGS OF THE ANNUAL MEETING. 1925. a. free to members. ‡ American Society of Bakery Engineers, Rm. 1921, 2 N. Riverside Plaza, Chicago, IL 60606. Ed. Robert A. Fischer. index,cum.index every 10 yrs. circ. 3,000.

664.15 FR
ANNUAIRE SUCRIER. a. 275 F. Societe d'Edition et de Promotion Agricoles, Industrielles et Commerciales, 42 rue du Louvre, 75001 Paris, France.

664 US
CANDY & SNACK INDUSTRY BUYING GUIDE. 1944. a. $15. Magazines for Industry, Inc., 747 Third Ave., New York, NY 10017. Ed. Myron Lench. adv. bk. rev. abstr. circ. 3,500.

664.15 380.1 US
CANDY BUYERS DIRECTORY. 1932. a. $25.
Manufacturing Confectioner Publishing Co.,
Directory Division, 175 Rock Rd., Glen Rock, NJ
07452. Ed. Allen R. Allured. adv. circ. 10,000.
(tabloid format)
Including: Directory of Candy Brokers.

663 BE ISSN 0535-1626
REPORT OF THE GENERAL ASSEMBLY OF
THE MEMBERS OF THE INTERNATIONAL
OFFICE OF COCOA AND CHOCOLATE AND
THE INTERNATIONAL SUGAR
CONFECTIONARY MANUFACTURERS'
ASSOCIATION. irreg., latest 1976, Munich. 250
Fr. International Office of Cocoa and Chocolate,
Avenue de Cortenbergh 172, 1040 Brussels,
Belgium. (Co-sponsor: International Sugar
Confectionary Manufacturers' Association)

664 UK ISSN 0080-7974
SCOTTISH BAKERS' YEAR BOOK. 1894. a. ‡
Scottish Association of Master Bakers, 19 Atholl
Crescent, Edinburgh, EH3 8HJ, Scotland.

664.752 AT
SOUTH AUSTRALIAN BAKER AND
PASTRYCOOK. 1969. biennial. (Baking Trade
Federation of Australia, South Australian Branch)
Percival Publishing Co. Pty. Ltd., 17 Currie St.,
Adelaide, S.A. 5000, Australia. Ed. James Fryer.

FOOD AND FOOD INDUSTRIES — Grocery Trade

AGENDA VINICOLA & DELLE INDUSTRIE
ALIMENTARI. see *BEVERAGES*

658.86 US ISSN 0091-9152
CHAIN STORE GUIDE DIRECTORY: FOOD
SERVICE DISTRIBUTORS.* 1973. irreg. $49.
Business Guides, Inc., 425 Park Ave., New York,
NY 10022.

658.8 US ISSN 0084-9294
CONVENIENCE STORE INDUSTRY REPORT.
1970. a. $10. ‡ B M T Publications, Inc., 254 W.
31st St., New York, NY 10001. Ed. Barbara J.
Bagley. adv.

658.8 US
CO-OP DIRECTORY. 1979. irreg. $7. Co-Operative
Directory Association, Box 4218, Albuquerque, NM
87196. adv. circ. 8,000.
Supersedes (1973-1978): Food Co-Op Directory.

664 658.8 US ISSN 0081-9522
FACTS ABOUT NEW SUPER MARKETS. 1953. a.
$15. Food Marketing Institute, 1750 K St. N.W.,
Washington, DC 20006. Ed. Patricia Shinko.

664 658.8 US ISSN 0190-3349
FOOD MARKETING INDUSTRY SPEAKS. 1949. a.
$7.50. Food Marketing Institute, 1750 K St. N.W.,
Washington, DC 20006. Ed. Patricia Shinko.
Formerly: Supermarket Industry Speaks (ISSN
0081-9530)

658.8 US
FOOD SERVICE DIRECTORY AND BUYERS
GUIDE FOR FRESH PRODUCE. 1974. irreg. $3.
Produce Marketing Association, 700 Barksdale
Plaza, Newark, DE 19711. Ed. Steve Ahlberg.

658.8 UK
GROCER MARKETING DIRECTORY. 1954. a. £5.
William Reed Ltd., 5 Southwark St., London SE1
1RQ, England. Ed. Margaret Beddall. circ. 5,000.
Former titles: Grocer Directory; Grocer
Directory of Multiples and Co-Operatives (ISSN
0072-7695)

658.8 380 FR
GUIDOR. (Guide Annuaire Officiel du Complexe de
Rungis) a. Compagnie de Documentation, 17 rue de
Paradis, 75010 Paris, France. charts.

658.86 GW
HESSE. MINISTERIUM FUER
LANDWIRTSCHAFT UND UMWELT.
ERNTEN, MAERKTE, PREISE.
JAHRESBERICHT. 1954. a. free. Ministerium fuer
Landwirtschaft und Umwelt, 6200 Wiesbaden, W.
Germany (B.R.D.) circ. 5,000.

658.8 US
MAINE STATE GROCERS BULLETIN. 1938. a.
Maine State Grocers Association, c/o Arthur H.
Charles, Ed., 320 Baxter Blvd., Portland, ME
04101. adv. circ. 1,200.

658.8 US
PROGRESSIVE GROCER'S ANNUAL REPORT
OF THE GROCERY INDUSTRY. 1922. a. $15.
Progressive Grocer Publishing Co., 708 Third Ave.,
New York, NY 10017. Ed. Edgar B. Walzer. adv.
charts. stat. circ. 83,000. (back issues avail.)
Formerly: Progressive Grocer's Annual Report of
the Grocery Trade.

658.8 GW ISSN 0343-3226
SELBSTBEDIENUNG--DYNAMIK IM HANDEL.
1957. m. DM.78.50. (Institut fuer Selbstbedienung
und Warenwirtschaft e.V.) Gesellschaft fuer
Selbstbedienung, Burgmauer 53, 5000 Cologne 1, W.
Germany (B.R.D.) Ed.H.K. Henksmeier. adv. bk.
rev. charts. illus. stat. index. circ. 5,844. (back
issues avail.)
Formerly: Selbstbedienung und Supermarkt (ISSN
0582-4761)

658.8 US ISSN 0163-4488
SUPERMARKET TRENDS. irreg. $25. Food
Marketing Institute, Research Division, 1750 K St.
N.W., Washington, DC 20006.

338.4 US ISSN 0082-4151
THOMAS GROCERY REGISTER. (3-vol. set) 1898.
a. $69. Thomas Publishing Co., One Penn Plaza,
New York, NY 10001. Ed. John Kovac. adv. bk.
rev. circ. 5,000.

FORENSIC SCIENCES

see *Medical Sciences — Forensic Sciences*

FORESTS AND FORESTRY

see also *Forests and Forestry — Lumber and Wood; Conservation*

634.9 IT ISSN 0515-2178
ACCADEMIA ITALIANA DI SCIENZE
FORESTALI. ANNALI. 1953. a. Accademia
Italiana di Scienza Forestali, Piazza Edison II,
50133 Florence, Italy. Dir. Generoso Patrone.

634.9 PL ISSN 0065-0927
ACTA AGRARIA ET SILVESTRIA. SERIES
SILVESTRIS. (Text in Polish; summaries in English
and Russian) 1961. irreg., 1975, vol. 15. price
varies. (Polska Akademia Nauk, Oddzial w
Krakowie, Komisja Nauk Rolniczych i Lesnych)
Panstwowe Wydawnictwo Naukowe, Miodowa 10,
Warsaw, Poland (Dist. by Ars Polona-Ruch,
Krakowskie Przedmiescie 7, Warsaw, Poland) Ed.
Jerzy Fabijanowski. bibl, charts, illus.

634.9 CS
ACTA FACULTATIS FORESTALIS, ZVOLEN/
VYSOKA SKOLA LESNICKA A DREVARSKA
VO ZVOLENE. LESNICKA FAKULTA.
ZBORNIK VEDECKYCH PRAC. (Text and
summaries in English, German, Russian, Slovak)
1957. irreg. exchange basis. Vysoka Skola Lesnicka
a Drevarska vo Zvolene, Lesnicka Fakulta, Sturova
2, Zvolen, Czechoslovakia. Ed. Stefan Smelko.
charts. illus. circ. 300.

634.9 FI ISSN 0001-5636
ACTA FORESTALIA FENNICA. (Text in English,
Finnish and German) 1913. irreg. (5-8/yr.) Fmk.15
per no. Suomen Metsatieteellinen Seura - Society of
Forestry in Finland, Unioninkatu 40 B, SF-00170
Helsinki 17, Finland. illus. cum. index (1913-1972)
circ. 1,050. Indexed: Biol.Abstr. Chem.Abstr.
Forest.Abstr.

634.9 674 PL
AKADEMIA ROLNICZA, POZNAN. ROCZNIK.
LESNICTWO. (Summaries in English and Russian)
1957. irreg. price varies. Akademia Rolnicza,
Poznan, Ul. Wojska Polskiego 28, 60-637 Poznan,
Poland. Indexed: Bibl.Agri. Forest.Abstr.

634.9 YU
ANNALES FORESTALES/ANALI ZA
SUMARSTVO. vol. 6, 1974. a. price varies.
Jugoslavenska Akademija Znanosti i Umjetnosti,
Razred za Prirodne Znanosti, Zrinski trg 11, Zagreb,
Yugoslavia. Ed. Mirko Vidakovic. circ. 800.
Indexed: Forest.Abstr.

634.9 AG
ARGENTINA. DIRECCION DE
INVESTIGACIONES FORESTALES. FOLLETO
TECNICO FORESTAL. 1959. irreg., no. 52, 1977.
exchange basis. Instituto Forestal Nacional,
Pueyrredon 2446, Buenos Aires, Argentina. circ.
controlled.
Formerly: Argentina. Direccion de
Investigaciones Forestales. Notas Tecnologicas
Forestales (ISSN 0066-7110)

634.9 AG ISSN 0066-7102
ARGENTINA. DIRECCION DE
INVESTIGACIONES FORESTALES. NOTAS
SILVICOLAS. 1959. irreg; no. 23, 1967. available
on exchange. Instituto Forestal Nacional, Direccion
de Investigaciones Forestales, Pueyrredon 2446,
Buenos Aires, Argentina. circ. controlled.

634.9 AG ISSN 0066-7099
ARGENTINA. DIRECCION DE
INVESTIGACIONES FORRESTALES.
MISCELENEAS FORESTALES. 1960. irreg; latest
issue, no. 15, 1975. exchange basis. Instituto
Forestal Nacional, Pueyrredon 2446, Buenos Aires,
Argentina. circ. controlled.

634.9 AG ISSN 0518-4142
ARGENTINA. INSTITUTO FORESTAL
NACIONAL. ANUARIO DE ESTADISTICA
FORESTAL. irreg.latest,1976. exchange. Instituto
Forestal Nacional, Pueyrredon 2446, Buenos Aires,
Argentina. Ed.Bd. charts. stat.

634.9 US ISSN 0066-7404
ARIZONA FORESTRY NOTES. 1966. irreg., no. 12,
1974. ‡ Northern Arizona University, School of
Forestry, Box 4098, Flagstaff, AZ 86001. charts.
stat. circ. 800.

ARIZONA LANDMARKS. see *AGRICULTURE*

634.9 CN ISSN 0066-9644
ASSOCIATION OF REGISTERED
PROFESSIONAL FORESTERS OF NEW
BRUNSWICK. PAPERS AND REPORTS. 1937. a.
free. Association of Registered Professional
Foresters of New Brunswick, P.O. Box 23,
Fredericton, N.B., Canada. circ. 200.

634.9 AT
AUSTRALIAN FOREST RESOURCES. 1977. a. free.
Department of Primary Industry, Forest and Timber
Bureau, Banks St., Yarralumla, A. C. T. 2600,
Australia (Subscr. to: Australian Government
Publishing Service, Sales & Dist. Sect., P. O. Box
84, Canberra, A.C.T. 2600, Australia) bk. rev. circ.
700(controlled) Indexed: Forest.Abstr.
Former titles: Forest Resources; Commonwealth
Scientific and Industrial Research Organization.
Division of Forest Research. Forest Resources
Newsletter; Australia. Forestry and Timber Bureau.
Forest Resources Newsletter (ISSN 0067-1460)

634.9 GW ISSN 0067-4710
BAYERISCHES FORSTDIENST-TASCHENBUCH.
1966. a. DM.51.95. (Bund Deutscher Forstmaenner,
Landesverband Bayern e.V.) Walhalla- und
Praetoria-Verlag Georg Zwichenpflug, Dolomitenstr.
1, Postfach 301, 8400 Regensburg 1, W. Germany
(B.R.D.)

BIOLOGISCHE BUNDESANSTALT FUER LAND-
UND FORSTWIRTSCHAFT, BERLIN-DAHLEM.
MITTEILUNGEN. (Biologische Bundesanstalt fuer
Land- und Forstwirtschaft in Berlin-Dahlem) see
AGRICULTURE

634.9 BS ISSN 0068-0486
BOTSWANA. FOREST DEPARTMENT. REPORT.
a. R.1($0.10) Forest Department, Gaborone,
Botswana.

634.9 674 BL
BRASIL MADEIRA. irreg. Cr.$900. Caixa Postal
1425, 80000 Curitiba, Brazil. illus.

FORESTS AND FORESTRY

634.9   CN
BRITISH COLUMBIA. MINISTRY OF FORESTS. ANNUAL REPORT. 1912. a. Ministry of Forests, Information B, Parliament Building, Victoria, B.C. V8W 3E7, Canada. index.
Formerly: British Columbia. Forest Service. Annual Report (ISSN 0068-1490)

634.9   CN
BRITISH COLUMBIA. MINISTRY OF FORESTS. RESEARCH NOTES. 1938, N.S. irreg., 1970, no. 54. free. Ministry of Forests, Information Branch, Victoria, B.C. V8W 3E7, Canada.
Formerly: British Columbia. Forest Service. Research Notes (ISSN 0068-1520)

634.9   CN
BRITISH COLUMBIA. MINISTRY OF FORESTS. RESEARCH REVIEW. 1957. a. Forest Service, Information Branch, Parliament Buildings, Victoria, B.C. V8W 3E7, Canada. index.
Formerly: British Columbia. Forest Service. Research Review (ISSN 0068-1539)

634.9   US   ISSN 0068-5569
CALIFORNIA. DEPARTMENT OF FORESTRY. RANGE IMPROVEMENT STUDIES. 1954. irreg., 1970, no. 20. free. ‡ Department of Forestry, 1416 Ninth St., Sacramento, CA 95814. index: 1954-70. circ. 200-500.

634.9   US   ISSN 0068-5577
CALIFORNIA. DEPARTMENT OF FORESTRY. STATE FOREST NOTES. 1960. irreg.; no. 64, Nov. 1976. free. Department of Forestry, 1416 Ninth St., Sacramento, CA 95814. index: 1960-71. circ. 1,500-3,500.

634.961   US
CALIFORNIA FIRE PREVENTION NOTES. 1968. irreg. free. Department of Forestry, 1416 Ninth St., Sacramento, CA 95814. bibl.

634.9   CN   ISSN 0071-7495
CANADA. DEPARTMENT OF THE ENVIRONMENT. FOREST MANAGEMENT INSTITUTE. PROGRAM REVIEW. 1965. biennial. free. Forest Management Institute, Ottawa, Ont. K1A OH3, Canada. Ed. B. E. Silverside. circ. 900.

634.96   CN   ISSN 0226-9759
CANADA. DEPARTMENT OF THE ENVIRONMENT. INSECT AND DISEASE CONDITIONS IN CANADA. French edition (ISSN 0226-9767) (Editions in English and French) 1980. a. free. ‡ Canadian Forestry Service, Ottawa, Ont. K1A 1G5, Canada.
Supersedes: Canada. Department of the Environment. Forest Insect and Disease Survey. Annual Report (ISSN 0068-7588)

634.961   CN   ISSN 0068-757X
CANADA. FOREST FIRE RESEARCH INSTITUTE. INFORMATION REPORT (FF-X) 1966. irreg. free. Forest Fire Research Institute, 240 Bank St., Ottawa, Ont. K2P 1X4, Canada. Indexed: Fire Res.Abstr. & Rev. Forest.Abstr. Forest Fire Control.Abstr.

634.9 595   CN   ISSN 0704-769X
CANADA. MARITIMES FOREST RESEARCH CENTRE, FREDERICTON, NEW BRUNSWICK. INFORMATION REPORT M-X. French Edition (ISSN 0706-4195) (Editions in English and French) 1966. irreg (10-12/yr.) free. Maritimes Forest Research Centre, P.O. Box 4000, Fredericton, N.B., Canada. Ed. M. D. Cameron. circ. 500-100. (also avail. in microform from MML) Indexed: Forest.Abstr.

634.9   CN   ISSN 0704-7673
CANADA. NORTHERN FOREST RESEARCH CENTRE. INFORMATION REPORT. 1971. irreg. (approx. 100/yr.) free. Northern Forest Research Centre, 5320-122 St., Edmonton, Alta. T6H 3S5, Canada. Ed. P. Logan. circ. controlled. Indexed: Biol. Abstr. Forest.Abstr.
Formerly: Canadian Forestry Service Dept. of Fisheries & Forestry Prairies Region. Information Report.

634.9   CN
CANADA. NORTHERN FOREST RESEARCH CENTRE. FORESTRY REPORT. 1971. irreg. (approx 5-6/yr.) free. Northern Forest Research Centre, 5320-122 St., Edmonton, Alta. T6H 3S5, Canada. Ed. R. Waldron. circ. 3,000.
Formerly: Canadian Forestry Service. Prairies Region. Forestry Report.

634.9   CN
CANADA. PACIFIC FOREST RESEARCH CENTRE. INFORMATION REPORT. (Text in English and French) 1971. irreg. free. Pacific Forest Research Centre, 506 West Burnside Rd., Victoria, B.C. V8Z 1M5, Canada. abstr. bibl. charts. illus.

634.9   CN
CANADIAN FOREST FIRE WEATHER INDEX. irreg. free. Pacific Forest Research Centre, 506 West Burnside Rd., Victoria, B.C. V8Z 1M5, Canada. (back issues avail.)

634.9   CN   ISSN 0068-8991
CANADIAN INSTITUTE OF FORESTRY. ANNUAL REPORT. Included in: Forestry Chronicle (ISSN 0015-7546) irreg. Canadian Institute of Forestry, Box 5000, Macdonald College, Quebec H0A 1C0, Canada. Ed. J. D. Macarthur. adv. bk. rev. circ. 2,700.

634.9 574.5   BE
CENTRE D'ECOLOGIE FORESTIERE ET RURALE. COMMUNICATIONS. (Text in French; summaries in German, English) 1943. irreg., N.S. no. 24, 1979. price varies. Centre d'Ecologie Forestiere et Rurale, 59 Ave. de la Faculte d'Agronomie, 5800 Gembloux, Belgium. circ. 200. Indexed: Forest.Abstr. Herb.Abstr.
Formerly: Centre de Cartographie Phytosociologique. Communications (ISSN 0069-1747)

634.9   BE
CENTRE D'ECOLOGIE FORESTIERE ET RURALE. NOTES TECHNIQUES. A: FORESTIERES. 1968. irreg., no. 32, 1978. price varies. Centre d'Ecologie Forestiere et Rurale, 59 Ave. de la Faculte d'Agronomie, 5800 Gembloux, Belgium.
Supersedes in part: Centre d'Ecologie Forestiere. Notes Techniques (ISSN 0069-1801)

634.9   BE
CENTRE D'ECOLOGIE FORESTIERE ET RURALE. NOTES TECHNIQUES. B: HERBAGERES. 1968. irreg., no. 10, 1978. price varies. Centre d'Ecologie Forestiere et Rurale, 59 Ave. de la Faculte d'Agronomie, 5800 Gembloux, Belgium. Indexed: Forest.Abstr. Herb.Abstr.
Supersedes in part: Centre d'Ecologie Forestiere. Notes Techniques (ISSN 0069-1801)

634.9   CM
CENTRE TECHNIQUE FORESTIERE TROPICAL DU CAMEROUN. RAPPORT ANNUEL. a. free. Centre Technique Forestier Tropical du Cameroun, B.P. 832, Douala, Cameroon.

634.9   US
CLEMSON UNIVERSITY. DEPARTMENT OF FORESTRY. FOREST RESEARCH SERIES. irreg., no. 34, 1980. Clemson University, Department of Forestry, Clemson, SC 29631.

634.9   US   ISSN 0093-0083
CLEMSON UNIVERSITY. DEPARTMENT OF FORESTRY. FORESTRY BULLETIN. 1967. irreg., no. 23, 1981. free. Clemson University, Department of Forestry, Clemson, SC 29631. Ed. Robert M. Allen. charts. illus. stat. circ. 500(controlled) (back issues avail.)

634.9   US
CLEMSON UNIVERSITY. DEPARTMENT OF FORESTRY. TECHNICAL PAPER. irreg., no. 12, 1980. Clemson University, Department of Forestry, Clemson, SC 29631.

634.9 333.7   CN   ISSN 0381-3932
CLOVER LEAFLET. 1972. N.S. 1976. irreg. Department of Recreation, Parks and Wildlife, 4-H and Junior Forest Ranger Branch, Edmonton, Alberta, Canada. illus.
Formerly: Alberta 4-H Club News.

338.4   US   ISSN 0362-191X
COMMODITY DRAIN REPORT OF FLORIDA'S PRIMARY FOREST INDUSTRIES. 1960. biennial. free. Department of Agriculture and Consumer Services, Division of Forestry, Collins Bldg., Tallahassee, FL 32301. Ed. H.S. Friensehner. stat. circ. 1,200.

634.9   UK   ISSN 0069-7060
COMMONWEALTH FORESTRY BUREAU. TECHNICAL COMMUNICATION. 1942. irreg. price varies. (Commonwealth Forestry Bureau) Commonwealth Agricultural Bureaux, Farnham House, Farnham Royal, Slough SL2 3BN, England.

CONSERVATION TOPICS. see *CONSERVATION*

634.96   GW
DEUTSCHER FORSTVEREIN. JAHRESBERICHT. 1950. biennial. Deutscher Forstverein, Josefstr. 10, 7710 Donaueschingen, W. Germany (B.R.D.) illus.

630 634.9   NE
DEVELOPMENTS IN AGRICULTURAL AND MANAGED FOREST ECOLOGY. 1975. irreg. price varies. Elsevier Scientific Publishing Co., Box 211, 1000 AE Amsterdam, Netherlands.

634.9 676   UN   ISSN 0532-0283
F A O FORESTRY AND FOREST PRODUCTS STUDIES. 1950. Food and Agriculture Organization of the United Nations, Distribution and Sales Section, Via delle Terme di Caracalla, 00100 Rome, Italy (Dist. in U.S. by: Unipub, 345 Park Ave. S., New York, NY 10010)

634.9   UN   ISSN 0071-7029
F A O FORESTRY DEVELOPMENT PAPERS. (Text in English, French and Spanish) 1954. irreg., 1971, no. 17. price varies. Food and Agriculture Organization of the United Nations, Distribution and Sales Section, Via delle Terme di Caracalla, 00100 Rome, Italy (Dist. in U.S. by: Unipub, 345 Park Ave. S., New York, NY 10010)

582.16 634.9 635.977   CS
FOLIA DENDROLOGICA. irreg, vol. 3, 1977. price varies. (Slovenska Akademia Vied, Ustav Dendrobiologie) Veda, Publishing House of the Slovak Academy of Sciences, Klemensova 19, 895 30 Bratislava, Czechoslovakia. (Co-sponsor: Arboretum Mlynany) Ed. Frantisek Bencat.

634.9   PL   ISSN 0071-6677
FOLIA FORESTALIA POLONICA. SERIES A. LESNICTWO. (Text in Polish; summaries in English, German or Russian) 1958. a. price varies. (Polska Akademia Nauk) Panstwowe Wydawnictwo Naukowe, Miodowa 10, Warsaw, Poland (Dist. by Ars Polona-Ruch, Krakowskie Przedmiescie 7, Warsaw, Poland) Ed. Wieslaw Grochowski.

634.9   UN   ISSN 0532-0666
FOOD AND AGRICULTURE ORGANIZATION OF THE UNITED NATIONS. FOREST TREE SEED DIRECTORY. 1954. irreg., latest 1975. Food and Agriculture Organization of the United Nations, Distribution and Sales Section, Via delle Terme di Caracalla, I-00100 Rome, Italy (Dist. in U.S. by: Unipub, 345 Park Ave. S., New York, NY 10010)

634.9   US   ISSN 0071-7444
FOREST ENGINEERING SYMPOSIUM. PROCEEDINGS.* (Issued as a subseries of West Virginia University. Engineering Experiment Station. Bulletin) 1966. a. West Virginia University, Engineering Experiment Station, College of Engineering, Morgantown, WV 26506.

634.9   US   ISSN 0071-7452
FOREST FARMER. MANUAL EDITION. 1950. biennial. $12.50. Forest Farmers Association, Box 95385, 4 Executive Park East, N.E., Atlanta, GA 30347. Ed. J. Walter Myers Jr. adv. index. circ. 4,000.

634.96   US
FOREST INSECT AND DISEASE LEAFLETS. 1955. irreg. free. U.S. Forest Service, Department of Agriculture, Washington, DC 20250.
Formerly: Forest Pest Leaflets (ISSN 0071-7509)

634.96   US   ISSN 0071-7487
FOREST INSECT CONDITIONS IN THE UNITED STATES. 1954. U.S. Forest Service, Department of Agriculture, Washington, DC 20250.
Formerly: Forest Insect and Disease Conditions in the United States.

634.9   II   ISSN 0071-7533
FOREST RESEARCH IN INDIA. (Pt. 1: Forest Research Institute; Pt. 2: Reports from Indian States) (Text in English) 1919-20. a. price varies. ‡ Forest Research Institute & Colleges, P.O. New Forest, Dehra Dun, India. circ. 500. Indexed: Biol.Abstr. Forest.Abstr. Indian Sci.Abstr.

634.9   US   ISSN 0071-7568
FOREST SCIENCE MONOGRAPHS. 1959. irreg., 1969, no. 16. included in subscription to Forest Science. ‡ Society of American Foresters, 5400 Grosvenor Lane, Bethesda, MD 20014. Ed. William E. Miller. bk. rev. circ. 1,567. Indexed: Biol.Abstr. Biol. & Agri.Ind. Chem.Abstr.

634.9   US   ISSN 0071-7576
FOREST TREE NURSERIES IN THE UNITED STATES. triennial. U. S. Forest Service, c/o Dept. of Agriculture, Washington, DC 20250.

634.9   AT
FORESTRY LOG. 1968. a. Aus.$4. Australian National University, Forestry Department, Forestry Students Society, Canberra, A.C.T. 2600, Australia. Ed. John Kelley. adv. circ. 600.

634.9   UN   ISSN 0532-0747
FORESTRY NEWSLETTER OF THE ASIA-PACIFIC REGION. Food and Agriculture Organization of the United Nations, Regional Office for Asia and the Far East, Maliwan Mansion, Phra Atit Road, Bangkok 2, Thailand.

FORSCHUNGSSTELLE FUER JAGDKUNDE UND WILDSCHADENVERHUETUNG. SCHRIFTENREIHE. see *SPORTS AND GAMES — Outdoor Life*

634.9   DK   ISSN 0085-0837
FORSTLIGE FORSOEGSVAESEN I DANMARK. (Text in Danish; summaries in English) 1905. irreg. Kr.20 per vol. (4-5 parts) Statens Forstlige Forsoegsvaesen - Danish Forest Experiment Station, Springforbivej 4, 2930 Klampenborg, Denmark. Ed. Erik Holmsgaard. charts. illus. circ. 800. Indexed: Forest.Abstr.

634.9   GW   ISSN 0071-772X
FORSTWISSENSCHAFTLICHE FORSCHUNGEN; Beihefte zum Forstwissenschaftlichen Centralblatt. 1952. irreg., no. 36, 1976. price varies. (Forstliche Forschungsanstalt Muenchen) Verlag Paul Parey (Hamburg), Spitalerstr. 12, 2000 Hamburg 1, W. Germany (B.R.D.) Ed. U. Ammer. (reprint service avail. from ISI) Indexed: Biol.Abstr.

338.4 634.9   FR
FRANCE. DIRECTION DES FORETS. PRODUCTION DE LA BRANCHE EXPLOITATION FORESTIERE ET PRODUCTION DES BRANCHES SCIENCE ET CARBONISATION EN FORET. a. free. Direction des Forets, 1 Ave. de Lowendal, 75007 Paris, France.

333.7 634.9   FR
FRANCE. DIRECTION DES FORETS. RAPPORT SUR LE FONDS FORESTIER NATIONAL; rapport au Comite de Controle pour l'annee. 1948. a. free. Direction des Forets, 1 Ter. Ave. de Lowendal, 75007 Paris, France. stat.

634.9   US   ISSN 0072-4556
GIRIOS AIDAS/ECHO OF THE FOREST. (Text in Lithuanian; summaries in English) 1950. biennial. $1.-$1.50. Association of Lithuanian Foresters in Exile, 2740 W. 43 St., Chicago, IL 60632. Ed. J. Kuprionis. bk. rev.

634.9   CN   ISSN 0072-9140
H. R. MACMILLAN LECTURESHIP IN FORESTRY. 1950. a. free. University of British Columbia, Faculty of Forestry, 2075 Wesbrook Mall, Vancouver, B.C V6T 1W5, Canada. Indexed: Forest.Abstr.

HORACE M. ALBRIGHT CONSERVATION LECTURESHIP. see *CONSERVATION*

353.9   US
ILLINOIS. DIVISION OF FIRE PREVENTION. ANNUAL REPORT. 1918. a. Division of Fire Prevention, 601 Armory Bldg., Springfield, IL 62706.
Supersedes: Illinois. State Fire Marshal. Annual Report.

634.9   II   ISSN 0073-635X
INDIAN FOREST BULLETIN (NEW SERIES) (Text in English) 1911. irreg., no. 276, 1979. price varies. ‡ Forest Research Institute & Colleges, P.O. New Forest, Dehra Dun, India. circ. 500. Indexed: Biol.Abstr. Forest.Abstr. Indian Sci.Abstr.

634.9   II   ISSN 0073-6368
INDIAN FOREST LEAFLETS (NEW SERIES) (Text in English) 1941. irreg., no. 196, 1977. price varies. ‡ Forest Research Institute & Colleges, P.O. New Forest, Dehra Dun, India. circ. 500. Indexed: Biol.Abstr. Forest.Abstr. Indian Sci.Abstr.

634.9   II   ISSN 0073-6406
INDIAN FOREST RECORDS (NEW SERIES) FOREST PATHOLOGY. (Text in English) 1950. irreg., vol. 2, no. 11, 1973. price varies. Forest Research Institute & Colleges, P.O. New Forest, Dehra Dun, India. circ. 500. Indexed: Biol.Abstr. Forest.Abstr. Indian Sci.Abstr.
Formerly: Indian Forest Records (New Series) Mycology.

634.9   II   ISSN 0073-6422
INDIAN FOREST RECORDS (NEW SERIES) SILVICULTURE. (Text in English) 1936. irreg., vol. 13, no. 1, 1974. price varies. ‡ Forest Research Institute & Colleges, P.O. New Forest, Dehra Dun, India. circ. 500. Indexed: Biol.Abstr. Forest.Abstr. Indian Sci.Abstr.

634.9   II   ISSN 0073-6430
INDIAN FOREST RECORDS (NEW SERIES) STATISTICAL. (Text in English) 1960. irreg., 1970, vol. 1, no. 3. price varies. ‡ Forest Research Institute & Colleges, P.O. New Forest, Dehra Dun, India. circ. 500. Indexed: Biol.Abstr. Forest.Abstr. Indian Sci.Abstr.

634.9   IO
INDONESIAN STATISTICS ON TRADE OF FOREST PRODUCTS. 1971. a. Rps.1500($4) Directorate General of Forestry, Forest Product Marketing Development Project, Jl. Salemba Raya 16, Jakarta, Indonesia.
Formerly (1971-1975): Forest Products Trade Statistics of Indonesia (ISSN 0302-203X)

634.9   KO   ISSN 0073-9294
INSTITUTE OF FOREST GENETICS, SUWON, KOREA. RESEARCH REPORT. (Text in Korean and English) 1959. a. free. Institute of Forest Genetics, Breeding Section, Director, Suwon, S. Korea.

634.9   BL   ISSN 0100-3151
INSTITUTO FLORESTAL. BOLETIM TECNICO. 1972. irreg. Instituto Florestal, C.P. 1322, Sao Paulo 01000, Brazil. stat. circ. 600(approx.)

634.9   UN   ISSN 0074-7475
INTERNATIONAL POPLAR COMMISSION. SESSION REPORTS. (Text in English) irreg.; 11th, 1976. Food and Agriculture Organization of the United Nations, Viale delle Terme di Caracalla, Rome, Italy.

634.9   GW   ISSN 0074-9400
INTERNATIONAL UNION OF FOREST RESEARCH ORGANIZATIONS. CONGRESS PROCEEDINGS/RAPPORTS DU CONGRES/ KONGRESSBERICHTE. quinquenniql, 17th, 1981, Japan. International Union of Forest Research Organizations, c/o Walter Liese, Pres., Bundesforschungsanstalt fuer Forst- und Holzwirtschaft, Leuschnerstrasse 91 D, D-2057 Hamburg 80, W. Germany (B.R.D.)

634.9   IT   ISSN 0075-1707
ITALY. ISTITUTO CENTRALE DI STATISTICA. ANNUARIO DI STATISTICA FORESTALE. a. L.6500. Istituto Centrale di Statistica, Via Cesare Balbo 16, 00100 Rome, Italy. circ. 850.

634.9   JA
JAPAN. FORESTRY AND FOREST PRODUCTS RESEARCH INSTITUTE. ANNUAL REPORT/ NORINSHO RINGYO SHIKENJO NENPO. (Text in Japanese) 1963. a. Forestry and Forest Products Research Institute, P.O. Box 2, Ushiku, Ibaraki 300-12, Japan.
Formerly: Japan. Government Forest Experiment Station, Tokyo. Annual Report (ISSN 0557-0352)

634.9   JA
JAPAN. FORESTRY AND FOREST PRODUCTS RESEARCH INSTITUTE. BULLETIN. irreg; 8-10/yr. Forestry and Forest Products Research Institute, P.O. Box 2, Ushiku, Ibaraki 300-12, Japan.

634.9   JA   ISSN 0557-0395
JAPAN. GOVERNMENT FOREST EXPERIMENT STATION. KYUSHU BRANCH. ANNUAL REPORT/RINGYO SHIKENJO KYUSHU SHIJO NENPO. (Text in Japanese) 1960. a. Government Forest Experiment Station, Kyushu Branch - Rin'yacho Ringyo Shikenjo Kyushu Shijo, 4-11-16 Kurokami, Kumamoto 860, Japan.

JAPAN. MINISTRY OF AGRICULTURE AND FORESTRY. ANNUAL REPORT/NORIN-SHO NENPO. see *AGRICULTURE*

630 634.9   NO   ISSN 0075-7853
LANDBRUKETS AARBOK. JORDBRUK, HAGEBRUK, SKOGBRUK. 1962. a. Kr.105. Forlaget Tanum-Norli A-S, Kr. Augustsgt. 7A, Oslo 1, Norway. Ed. A. Bruaset. circ. 3,800.
Incorporating: Landbrukets Aarbok. Skogbruk (ISSN 0075-7861)

634.9   US   ISSN 0076-1095
LOUISIANA STATE UNIVERSITY. SCHOOL OF FORESTRY AND WILDLIFE MANAGEMENT. ANNUAL FORESTRY SYMPOSIUM. PROCEEDINGS. 1952. a. price varies. Louisiana State University, Division of Continuing Education, Baton Rouge, LA 70803. circ. 750.

634.9   MW   ISSN 0076-3071
MALAWI. DEPARTMENT OF FORESTRY AND GAME. REPORT.* irreg.(approx.) a) $0.84. Government Printer, P.O. Box 37, Zomba, Malawi. cum.index: 1960-65.

634.9   FI   ISSN 0356-343X
METSATILASTOLLINEN VUOSIKIRJA/ YEARBOOK OF FOREST STATISTICS. (Subseries of Folia Forestalia. Section XVII A of Official Statistics of Finland) (Text in English and Finnish) Metsantutkimuslaitos - Finnish Forest Research Institute, Unioninkatu 40 A, SF-00170 Helsinki 17, Finland. Ed. Matti Uusitalo. charts. stat.

634.9   US   ISSN 0077-2046
MULTILINGUAL FORESTRY TERMINOLOGY SERIES. 1971. irreg. $15. ‡ Society of American Foresters, 5400 Grosvenor Lane, Bethesda, MD 20014.

634.9   AT   ISSN 0085-3984
NEW SOUTH WALES. FORESTRY COMMISSION. RESEARCH NOTES. 1958. irreg. Forestry Commission, 95-99 York St., Sydney, N.S.W. 2000, Australia. Indexed: Aus.Sci.Ind.

634.9   NZ   ISSN 0077-9997
NEW ZEALAND. FOREST RESEARCH INSTITUTE. REPORT. 1952. a. free. Forest Research Institute, Private Bag, Rotorua, New Zealand. charts. illus. circ. 3,000. (back issues avail.) Indexed: Forest.Abstr.

634.9   NZ   ISSN 0078-0006
NEW ZEALAND. FOREST RESEARCH INSTITUTE. TECHNICAL PAPER. 1954. irreg., no. 69, 1979. free. Forest Research Institute, Private Bag, Rotorua, New Zealand. charts. illus. circ. 700. (back issues avail.) Indexed: Biol.Abstr. Forest.Abstr.

634.9   NZ   ISSN 0078-0014
NEW ZEALAND. FOREST SERVICE. REPORT OF THE DIRECTOR GENERAL OF FORESTS. 1919. a. price varies. Government Printing Office, Private Bag, Wellington, New Zealand.

634.9　　　　　　　NR　ISSN 0300-2403
NIGERIA. FEDERAL DEPARTMENT OF FOREST RESEARCH. RESEARCH PAPER. (Includes 3 series: Forest Series, Savanna Series, Forest Products Series) (Text and summaries in English) 1965. irreg. exchange basis. Federal Department of Forest Research, Private Mail Bag No. 5054, Ibadan, Nigeria. Ed.Bd. circ. 700.

634.9　　　　　　　US　ISSN 0090-0664
NORTH CAROLINA STATE UNIVERSITY. SCHOOL OF FOREST RESOURCES. TECHNICAL REPORT. 1950. 3-4/yr. free. North Carolina State University, School of Forest Resources, Raleigh, NC 27607. circ. 300(controlled) Indexed: Forest.Abstr.

634.9　　　　　　　CN
ORDRE DES INGENIEURS FORESTIERS DU QUEBEC. CONGRES ANNUEL. TEXTE DES CONFERENCES. 1928. a. free. Ordre Professionnelle des Ingenieurs Forestiers du Quebec, C.P. 57, Sillery, Que. G1T 2P7, Canada. circ. 1,200.
　　Formerly: Corporation des Ingenieurs Forestiers du Quebec. Congres Annuel. Texte des Conferences (ISSN 0070-0304)

634.9　　　　　　　US　ISSN 0078-5865
OREGON STATE UNIVERSITY. FOREST RESEARCH LABORATORY. ANNUAL REPORT. 1958. a. free. Oregon State University, Forest Research Laboratory, Corvallis, OR 97331. Ed. Ralph E. McNees. index. (reprint service avail. from UMI)

634.9　　　　　　　US　ISSN 0078-5903
OREGON STATE UNIVERSITY. FOREST RESEARCH LABORATORY. RESEARCH BULLETIN. 1949. irreg., no. 34, 1979. free. Oregon State University, Forest Research Laboratory, Corvallis, OR 97331. Ed. Ralph E. McNees. circ. 2,000. (reprint service avail. from UMI) Indexed: Forest.Abstr.

634.9　　　　　　　US　ISSN 0078-5911
OREGON STATE UNIVERSITY. FOREST RESEARCH LABORATORY. RESEARCH NOTE. 1949. irreg., no. 66, 1978. free. Oregon State University, Forest Research Laboratory, Corvallis, OR 97331. Ed. Ralph E. McNees. (reprint service avail. from UMI) Indexed: Forest.Abstr.

634.9　　　　　　　US　ISSN 0078-592X
OREGON STATE UNIVERSITY. FOREST RESEARCH LABORATORY. RESEARCH PAPER. 1965. irreg., no. 42, 1979. free. Oregon State University, Forest Research Laboratory, Corvallis, OR 97331. Ed. Ralph E. McNees. circ. 2,000. (also avail. in microform from UMI; reprint service avail. from UMI) Indexed: Chem.Abstr. Forest.Abstr.

634.9　　　　　　　US
OXFORD FORESTRY MEMOIRS. irreg. price varies. Oxford University Press, 200 Madison Ave., New York, NY 10016 (And Ely House, 37 Dover St., London W1X 4AH, England)

634.96　　　　　　　CN
PACIFIC FOREST RESEARCH CENTRE. PEST LEAFLET. no. 68, 1981. irreg. free. Pacific Forest Reseach Centre, 506 West Burnside Rd., Victoria, B.C. V8Z 1M5, Canada. Ed. Alister McEwan. (back issues avail.)

634.9　　　　　　　CN
PACIFIC FOREST RESEARCH CENTRE. PEST REPORT. irreg. free. Pacific Forest Research Centre, 506 West Burnside Rd., Victoria, B.C. V8Z 1M5, Canada.

634.92　　　　　　　PK　ISSN 0078-8147
PAKISTAN FOREST INSTITUTE, PESHAWAR. ANNUAL PROGRESS REPORT. (Text in English) 1950. a. Pakistan Forest Institute, Peshawar, Pakistan. circ. 500. Indexed: Biol.Abstr. Chem.Abstr. Forest. Abstr.

POZNANSKIE TOWARZYSTWO PRZYJACIOL NAUK. KOMISJA NAUK ROLNICZYCH I KOMISJA NAUK LESNYCH. PRACE. see
AGRICULTURE

634.9　338.7　　　　YU
PRIRODNJACKI MUZEJ U BEOGRADU. GLASNIK. SERIJA C: SUMARSTVO I LOV. vol. 30, 1975. irreg. Prirodnjacki Muzej u Beogradu, Njegoseva 51, Belgrade, Yugoslavia. Ed. Zivomir Vasic.

634.9　　　　　　　CN
QUEBEC (PROVINCE) MINISTERE DE L'ENERGIE ET DES RESSOURCES. SERVICE DE LA RECHERCHE FORESTIERE. GUIDE. (Text in French; summaries in English and French) 1970. irreg. free. Ministere de l'Energie et des Ressources, Service de la Recherche Forestiere, 2700 rue Einstein, Sainte-Foy, Que. G1P 3W8, Canada.

634.9　　　　　　　CN
QUEBEC(PROVINCE) MINISTERE DE L'ENERGIE ET DES RESSOURCES. SERVICE DE LA RECHERCHE FORESTIERE. NOTE. (Text in French; summaries in English and French) 1972. irreg. free. Ministere de l'Energie et des Ressources, Service de la Recherche Forestiere, 2700 rue Einstein, Sainte-Foy, Que. G1P 3W8, Canada. charts. illus. circ. 900.

634.9　　　　　　　CN
QUEBEC (PROVINCE) MINISTERE DE L'ENERGIE ET DES RESSOURCES. SERVICE DE LA RECHERCHE. MEMOIRE/QUEBEC (PROVINCE) DEPARTMENT OF LANDS AND FORESTS. RESEARCH SERVICE. MEMOIRE. (Text in French; summaries in English and French) 1970. irreg. free. Ministere de l'Energie et des Ressources, Service de la Recherche Forestiere, 2700 rue Einstein, Sainte-Foy, Que. G1P 3W8, Canada. circ. 900. (back issues avail)

634.9　333.7　　　CN　ISSN 0700-3749
QUEBEC (PROVINCE) MINISTERE DES TERRES ET FORETS. CONSEIL CONSULTATIF DES RESERVES ECOLOGIQUES. RAPPORT ANNUEL. 1975/76. a. Ministere des Terres et Forets, Conseil Consultatif des Reserves Ecologiques, 200 B, chemin Ste-Foy, Quebec, P.Q. G1R 4X7, Canada.

634.9　　　　　　　AT　ISSN 0157-809X
QUEENSLAND. DEPARTMENT OF FORESTRY. RESEARCH PAPER. 1971. irreg. Department of Forestry, Box 5, Brisbane, Qld. 4000, Australia. Indexed: Aus.Sci.Ind. Forest Abstr.

333.7　　　　　　　II
RAJASTHAN FOREST STATISTICS. (Text in English) irreg. Forest Department, Jaipur, Rajasthan, India.

634.9　　　　　　　US
REPORT OF FOREST PLANTING, SEEDING AND SILVICAL TREATMENTS IN THE UNITED STATES. a. U.S. Forest Service, U. S. Department of Agriculture, Washington, DC 20250.
　　Formerly: Report of Forest and Windbarrier Planting in the United States (ISSN 0080-1259)

RURAL INDUSTRY DIRECTORY. see
AGRICULTURE

634.9　　　　　　　US　ISSN 0080-5092
S. J. HALL LECTURESHIP IN INDUSTRIAL FORESTRY. 1969. a. free. University of California, Berkeley, Department of Forestry and Conservation, 145 Mulford Hall, Berkeley, CA 94720.

634.9　　　　　　　MY　ISSN 0080-5211
SABAH. FOREST DEPARTMENT. ANNUAL REPORT. (Text in English) 1963. a. M.$3. Forest Department, Sandakan, Sabah, Malaysia. circ. controlled.

634.9　　　　　　　CN
SASKATCHEWAN. DEPARTMENT OF TOURISM AND RENEWABLE RESOURCES. TECHNICAL BULLETINS. 1953. irreg. Department of Tourism and Renewable Resources, 1825 Lorne St., Regina, Sask. S4P 3V7, Canada.
　　Formerly: Saskatchewan. Department of Natural Resources. Forestry Branch. Technical Bulletins (ISSN 0080-6528)

634.9　　　　　　　NR
SAVANNA FORESTRY RESEARCH STATION, NIGERIA. ANNUAL REPORT. a, latest 1973/74. Savanna Forestry Research Station, P.M.B. 1039, Samaru, Zaria, Nigeria (Orders to: Forestry Research Institute of Nigeria, P.M.B. 5054, Ibadan, Nigeria) (Co-sponsors: Food and Agriculture Organization of the United Nations; United Nations Development Programme) illus.

634.9　　　　　　　SZ
SCHWEIZERISCHER FORSTVEREIN. ZEITSCHRIFT. BEIHEFTE. irreg. price varies. Schweizerischer Forstverein, Binzstr. 39, 8045 Zurich, Switzerland.

634.9　　　　　　　BL　ISSN 0583-3132
SILVICULTURA EM SAO PAULO. 1962. irreg. Instituto Florestal, Sao Paulo, S.P., Brazil. circ. 1,500(approx.)

634.9　　　　　　　AT
SOUTH AUSTRALIA. DEPARTMENT OF WOODS AND FORESTS. BULLETIN. 1928. irreg. price varies. Department of Woods and Forests, 135 Waymouth St., Adelaide, South Australia, Australia. Indexed: Aus.Sci.Ind.

634.9　　　　　　　US　ISSN 0490-8287
STATE AGENCIES COOPERATING WITH THE U.S. DEPARTMENT OF AGRICULTURE FOREST SERVICE IN ADMINISTRATION OF VARIOUS FORESTRY PROGRAMS. 1972. a. U.S. Forest Service, U. S. Department of Agriculture, Washington, DC 20250.

634.9　　　　　　　US　ISSN 0082-318X
STEPHEN F. AUSTIN STATE UNIVERSITY. SCHOOL OF FORESTRY. BULLETIN. 1957. irreg., 1972, no. 25. price varies. Stephen F. Austin State University, School of Forestry, Nacogdoches, TX 75961.

634.9　　　　　　　SW　ISSN 0039-3150
STUDIA FORESTALIA SUECICA. (Text & summaries in English, German & Swedish) 1963. irreg., no. 117, 1974. price varies. (Sveriges Lantbruksuniversitet, Institutionen foer Virkeslaera - Swedish University of Agricultural Sciences, Department of Forest Products) Liber Foerlag, Fack, S-162 10 Vaellingby 1, Sweden. charts. circ. 1,400. Indexed: Biol.Abstr. Chem.Abstr.

634.9　　　　　　　SW　ISSN 0085-6983
SVENSKA TRAEFORSKNINGSINSTITUTET. MEDDELANDE. SERIES A. (Text and summaries in Swedish, German and English) 1969. irreg. exchange basis. Svenska Traeforskningsinstitutet - Swedish Forest Products Research Laboratory, Box 5604, S-114 86 Stockholm, Sweden. illus. cum.index: 1969-1978. circ. 500.

634.9　674　　　　　SW
SVERIGES LANTBRUKSUNIVERSITET. INSTITUTION FOER VIRKESLAERA. UPPSATSER. (Text in English and Swedish) 1954. irreg. price varies. Sveriges Lantbruksuniversitet, Institutionen foer Virkeslaera - Swedish University of Agricultural Sciences. Department of Forestry Products, Box 7008, S-750-07 Uppsala, Sweden.
　　Formerly (until 1977): Kungliga Skogshoegskolan. Institutionen foer Virkeslaera. Uppsatser (ISSN 0082-0059)

634.9　674　　　　SW　ISSN 0348-4599
SVERIGES LANTBRUKSUNIVERSITET. INSTITUTIONEN FOER VIRKESLAERA. RAPPORTER. (Text in Swedish; some nos. have English summaries) 1955. irreg., no. 115, 1980. Sveriges Lantbruksuniversitet, Institutionen foer Virkeslaera - Swedish University of Agricultural Sciences, Department of Forest Products, Box 7008, S-750 07 Uppsala, Sweden.
　　Formerly (until 1977): Kungliga Skogshoegskolan. Institutionen foer Virkeslaera. Rapporter (ISSN 0082-0040)

634.9　　　　　　　SZ
SWITZERLAND. EIDGENOESSISCHE ANSTALT FUER DAS FORSTLICHE VERSUCHSWESEN. BERICHTE. irreg. (approx. 15/yr.) price varies. Eidgenoessische Anstalt fuer das Forstliche Versuchswesen - Swiss Federal Institute of Forest Research, CH-8903 Birmensdorf, Switzerland.

634.9　　　　　　　SZ
SWITZERLAND. EIDGENOESSISCHE ANSTALT
FUER DAS FORSTLICHE VERSUCHSWESEN.
MITTEILUNGEN. 1891. irreg. (approx. 4/yr.)
price varies. ‡ Eidgenoessische Anstalt fuer das
Forstliche Versuchswesen - Swiss Federal Institute
of Forest Research, CH-8903 Birmensdorf,
Switzerland. Ed. Walter Bosshard. index, cum.
index. circ. 1,400.
　　Formerly: Switzerland. Schweizerische Anstalt
fuer das Forstliche Versuchswesen. Mitteilungen
(ISSN 0080-7257)

634.94　　　　US　ISSN 0082-1527
TALL TIMBERS FIRE ECOLOGY CONFERENCE.
PROCEEDINGS. 1969. a. price varies. Tallahassee
Tall Timbers Research Station, Route 1, Box 160,
Tallahassee, FL 32303. Ed. Roy Komarek.

634.928　　　　US　ISSN 0082-3031
TEXAS. FOREST SERVICE. COOPERATIVE
FOREST TREE IMPROVEMENT PROGRAM.
PROGRESS REPORT. 1953. a. (Texas Forest
Service) Texas A & M University, College Station,
TX 77843. Ed. J. P. van Buijtenen.
　　Forest genetics research project

634.9　　　　US　ISSN 0082-304X
TEXAS FORESTRY PAPERS. 1970. irreg., no. 16,
1972. Stephen F. Austin State University, School of
Forestry, Nacogdoches, TX 75961.

634　336.2　　US　ISSN 0563-5446
TIMBER TAX JOURNAL. 1967. a. $25. Forest
Industries Committee on Timber Valuation and
Taxation, 1250 Connecticut Ave., Washington, DC
20036 (Distr. by: International Scholarly Book
Services, Inc., 2130 Pacific Ave., Forest Grove, OR
97116) charts. stat. cum,index.

634.9　　　　JA　ISSN 0082-4720
TOKYO METROPOLITAN AGRICULTURAL
EXPERIMENT STATION, ITSUKAICHI
OFFICE. FORESTRY EXPERIMENTAL
BULLETIN/RINGYO SHIKEN KENKYU
HOKOKU. (Text and summaries in English,
French, German and Japanese) 1904. irreg. (8-10
vols. per year) available on exchange. Tokyo
Metropolitan Agricultural Experiment Station,
Itsukaichi Office - Tokyo-to Nogyo Shikenjo
Itsukaichi Bunjo, 853 Tokura, Itsukaichi-machi,
Nishitama-gun, Tokyo 190-01, Japan.

634.9　　　　JA　ISSN 0082-5379
TOTTORI UNIVERSITY FORESTS. BULLETIN/
TOTTORI DAIGAKU NOGAKUBU FUZOKU
ENSHURIN HOKOKU. (Text in Japanese;
summaries in English) 1958. biennial. Tottori
University Forests - Tottori Daigaku Nogakubu
Fuzoku Enshurin, 1-1 Koyama-cho, Tottori 680,
Japan.

634.9　　　　UG　ISSN 0082-7177
UGANDA. FORESTRY DEPARTMENT. ANNUAL
REPORT. 1904. a, latest 1973/74. EAs.20. Forestry
Department, P.O. Box 31, Entebbe, Uganda.
cum.index. Indexed: Forest.Abstr.

634.9　　　　UG　ISSN 0082-7193
UGANDA. FORESTRY DEPARTMENT.
TECHNICAL NOTES. 1953. irreg., latest no. 219,
1977. free. Forestry Department, P.O. Box 31,
Entebbe, Uganda. cum.index: 1953-71. Indexed:
Forest.Abstr.

634.9　　　　US　ISSN 0083-1026
U.S. FOREST SERVICE. ANNUAL FIRE REPORT
FOR NATIONAL FORESTS. 1941. a. free. U. S.
Forest Service, U. S. Department of Agriculture,
Washington, DC 20250.

634.9　　　　US　ISSN 0360-8034
U.S. FOREST SERVICE. COOPERATIVE FIRE
PROTECTION. WILDFIRE STATISTICS. 1941. a.
free. U. S. Forest Service, U.S. Department of
Agriculture, Washington, DC 20013.
　　Supersedes: U.S. Forest Service. Division of
Cooperative Fire Protection. Forest Fire Statistics
(ISSN 0083-1034)

634.9　　　　US　ISSN 0090-239X
U.S. FOREST SERVICE. FOREST SERVICE
RESEARCH ACCOMPLISHMENTS. 1968. a.
free. U. S. Forest Service, U.S. Dept. of Agriculture,
Washington, DC 20250. circ. 3,000.
　　Supersedes: Forest Resources Reports (ISSN
0071-755X)

634.9　　　　US　ISSN 0092-9654
U.S. FOREST SERVICE. GENERAL TECHNICAL
REPORT INT. irreg. U. S. Forest Service,
Intermountain Forest and Range Experiment
Station, 507 25th St, Ogden, UT 84401. bibl.

634.92　　　　US
U. S. FOREST SERVICE. NATIONAL FOREST
SYSTEM AREAS. 1905. a. U.S. Forest Service.,
Department of Agriculture, Washington, DC 20250.
　　Formerly: U. S. Forest Service. National Forest
Areas (ISSN 0083-1042)

634.9　　　　US　ISSN 0502-5001
U.S. FOREST SERVICE. RESEARCH PAPER RM.
1963. irreg., no. 198, 1977. free. U. S. Forest
Service, Rocky Mountain Forest and Range
Experiment Station, 240 W. Prospect, Fort Collins,
CO 80521.

634.9　　　　US　ISSN 0502-4994
U.S. FOREST SERVICE. RESEARCH NOTE RM.
1963. irreg., no. 351, 1977. free. U. S. Forest
Service, Rocky Mountain Forest and Range
Experiment Station, 240 W. Prospect, Fort Collins,
CO 80521.

634.9　　　　US
U.S. FOREST SERVICE. RESOURCE BULLETIN
PNW. 1963. irreg. free. ‡ U.S. Forest Service,
Pacific Northwest Forest and Range Experiment
Station, 1809 N E. Sixth Ave., Portland, OR 97232.
Ed. George M. Hansen. stat. circ. 2,000.

634.9　　　　US
U.S. FOREST SERVICE. SOUTHERN FOREST
EXPERIMENT STATION. RESEARCH
ACCOMPLISHED. 1976. irreg. free. U.S. Forest
Service, Southern Forest Experiment Station, 701
Loyola Ave., New Orleans, LA 70113. Ed. Howard
Mobley. bk. rev. circ. 16,000.
　　Formed by the merger of: Forest Research News
for the South (ISSN 0071-7541) & U.S. Forest
Service. Southern Forest Experiment Station.
Recent Publications.

634.9　　　　US　ISSN 0083-1077
U. S. FOREST SERVICE. TECHNICAL
EQUIPMENT REPORTS. 1958. irreg. U.S. Forest
Service., U.S. Dept. of Agriculture, Washington, DC
20250.

634.9　　　　PR
U.S. INSTITUTE OF TROPICAL FORESTRY.
ANNUAL LETTER. (Text in English and Spanish)
a. U.S. Institute of Tropical Forestry, P. P. Box AQ,
Rio Piedras, PR 00928. Dir. Frank H. Wadsworth.

634.9　　　　CN　ISSN 0079-838X
UNIVERSITE LAVAL. FONDS DE RECHERCHES
FORESTIERES. CONTRIBUTION. (Text in
English and French) 1956. irreg. exchange basis. ‡
Universite Laval, Fonds de Recherches Forestieres,
3083 Quatre-Bourgeois, Ste-Foy, Que. G1W 2K6,
Canada. Ed. Louis Laneville. index. circ. 2,000.

634.9　　　　UK　ISSN 0065-0277
UNIVERSITY OF ABERDEEN. DEPARTMENT
OF FORESTRY. ECONOMIC SURVEY OF
PRIVATE FORESTRY. 1952(1st series); 1963(2nd
series); 1978(combined series) a. University of
Aberdeen, Department of Forestry, St. Machar Dr.,
Old Aberdeen AB9 2UU, Scotland. circ. 250.
Indexed: Forest.Abstr.

634.9　　　　CN　ISSN 0318-9171
UNIVERSITY OF BRITISH COLUMBIA.
FACULTY OF FORESTRY. BULLETIN. 1951.
irreg. University of British Columbia, Faculty of
Forestry, 2075 Wesbrook Mall, Vancouver, B.C.
V6T 1W5, Canada. Indexed: Forest.Abstr.
　　Formerly: University of British Columbia. Faculty
of Foresty. Bulletin (ISSN 0068-1776)

634.9　　　　CN　ISSN 0068-1784
UNIVERSITY OF BRITISH COLUMBIA.
FACULTY OF FORESTRY. RESEARCH NOTES.
1950. irreg. free. University of British Columbia,
Faculty of Forestry, 2075 Wesbrook Mall,
Vancouver, B.C. V6T 1W5, Canada. Indexed:
Forest.Abstr.

634.9　　　　CN　ISSN 0068-1792
UNIVERSITY OF BRITISH COLUMBIA.
FACULTY OF FORESTRY. RESEARCH
PAPERS. 1952. irreg. free. University of British
Columbia, Faculty of Forestry, 2075 Wesbrook
Mall, Vancouver, B.C. V6T 1W5, Canada. Indexed:
Forest.Abstr.

634.9　　　　CN　ISSN 0068-1806
UNIVERSITY OF BRITISH COLUMBIA.
FACULTY OF FORESTRY. TRANSLATIONS.
1953. irreg. free. University of British Columbia,
Faculty of Forestry, 2075 Wesbrook Mall,
Vancouver, B.C. V6T 1W5, Canada. Indexed:
Forest.Abstr.

634.9　　　　CN　ISSN 0407-2294
UNIVERSITY OF BRITISH COLUMBIA. FOREST
CLUB. RESEARCH NOTE. 1950. irreg. University
of British Columbia, Forest Club, Vancouver, B.C.,
Canada.

634.9　　　　CN　ISSN 0084-8069
UNIVERSITY OF BRITISH COLUMBIA.
RESEARCH FOREST ANNUAL REPORT. 1962.
a. free. University of British Columbia, Faculty of
Forestry, 2075 Wesbrook Mall, Vancouver, B.C.
V6T 1W5, Canada. Indexed: Forest.Abstr.

634.9　575.1　　US
UNIVERSITY OF FLORIDA. SCHOOL OF
FOREST RESOURCES & CONSERVATION.
COOPERATIVE FOREST GENETICS
RESEARCH PROGRAM. PROGRESS REPORT.
(Subseries of its Research Report) 1957. irreg.,
22nd, 1980. free. University of Florida, School of
Forest Resources & Conservation, Gainesville, FL
32601. Ed. R. E. Goddard. circ. 300.
　　Formerly: University of Florida. School of
Forestry. Cooperative Forest Genetics Research
Program. Progress Report (ISSN 0071-6146)

634.9　　　　US　ISSN 0077-1155
UNIVERSITY OF MONTANA. FOREST AND
CONSERVATION EXPERIMENT STATION,
MISSOULA. BULLETIN. 1949. irreg., no. 43,
1979. price varies. University of Montana, School of
Forestry, Montana Forest and Conservation
Experiment Station, Missoula, MT 59801. Ed. Linda
Harbine.

634.9　　　　US　ISSN 0077-1163
UNIVERSITY OF MONTANA. FOREST AND
CONSERVATION EXPERIMENT STATION,
MISSOULA. RESEARCH NOTES. 1964. irreg.,
no. 13, 1980. free. University of Montana, School of
Forestry, Montana Forest and Conservation
Experiment Station, Missoula, MT 59801. Ed. Linda
Harbine.

634.9　　　　CN　ISSN 0082-5190
UNIVERSITY OF TORONTO. FACULTY OF
FORESTRY. TECHNICAL REPORTS. 1959. irreg.
free. ‡ University of Toronto, Faculty of Forestry,
Toronto, Ont., Canada. circ. 500. Indexed:
Forest.Abstr.

354　　　　　UV
UPPER VOLTA. DIRECTION DES EAUX ET
FORETS ET DE LA CONSERVATION DES
SOLS. RAPPORT ANNUEL. a. Direction des
Eaux et Forets et de la Conservation des Sols,
Ouagadougou, Upper Volta. stat.

VEGETATION UNGARISCHER
LANDSCHAFTEN. see *BIOLOGY — Botany*

634.9　　　　AT　ISSN 0085-7742
VICTORIA, AUSTRALIA. FORESTS
COMMISSION. BULLETIN. 1922. irreg. free.
Forests Commission, 601 Bourke St., Melbourne,
Vic. 3001, Australia. Ed. M. L. Huebner. Indexed:
Aus.Sci.Ind.

634.9　　　　AT　ISSN 0083-5978
VICTORIA, AUSTRALIA. FORESTS
COMMISSION. FORESTRY TECHNICAL
PAPERS. 1963. irreg. free. Forests Commission,
601 Bourke St., Melbourne, Vic. 3001, Australia.
Ed. M. L. Huebner. Indexed: Forest.Abstr.

WASHINGTON (STATE). DEPARTMENT OF
REVENUE. FOREST TAX REPORT. see
*BUSINESS AND ECONOMICS — Public
Finance, Taxation*

WEST VIRGINIA. AGRICULTURAL AND
FORESTRY EXPERIMENT STATION.
BULLETIN. see *AGRICULTURE*

WEST VIRGINIA. AGRICULTURAL AND
FORESTRY EXPERIMENT STATION.
RESOURCE MANAGEMENT SERIES. see
AGRICULTURE

634.9   AT   ISSN 0085-8129
WESTERN AUSTRALIA. FORESTS
DEPARTMENT. BULLETIN. 1919. irreg. free. ‡
Forests Department, Conservator of
Forests, 4th Floor, R. & I. Bank Bldg., Barrack St., Perth, W.A.
6000, Australia. Ed. M.R.L. Lewis. circ. 1,000.
(back issues avail.) Indexed: Aus.Sci.Ind.

634.9   AT
WESTERN AUSTRALIA. FORESTS
DEPARTMENT RESEARCH PAPER. 1971. irreg.
free. Forests Department, 54 Barrack St., Perth,
W.A. 6014, Australia. Ed. M. R. L. Lewis. circ.
1,000(controlled) (back issues avail.)

634.9   US
WESTERN FORESTRY CENTER. ANNUAL
REPORT. a. free. Western Forestry Center, 4033 S.
W. Canyon Rd., Portland, OR 97221.

634.9   US
WESTERN FORESTRY CONFERENCE.
EXECUTIVE SUMMARIES OF PROCEEDINGS.
1930. a. $2 (individual papers avail. and priced
separately) Western Forestry and Conservation
Association, 1326 American Bank Bldg., Portland,
OR 97205. Ed. Steele Barnett. circ. 600.
Supersedes (as of 1977): Western Forestry
Conference. Proceedings; Includes: Western Forest
Fire Committee. Proceedings (ISSN 0511-750X) &
Western Forest Pest Committee. Proceedings (ISSN
0511-7518) & Western Reforestation Coordinating
Committee. Proceedings (ISSN 0511-7526) &
Western Stand Management Committee.
Proceedings.

634.9   US   ISSN 0511-9723
WILLIAM L. HUTCHESON MEMORIAL FOREST.
BULLETIN. irreg. price varies. Rutgers University,
Department of Botany, New Brunswick, NJ 08903.

639.9   UG
WOODSMAN. 1964. a, latest no. 31, 1977. free.
Forestry Department, Box 31, Entebbe, Uganda.

634.9   US   ISSN 0361-4425
YALE UNIVERSITY. SCHOOL OF FORESTRY.
BULLETIN. 1912. irreg. Yale University, School of
Forestry, New Haven, CT 06511.

634.9   ZA   ISSN 0084-4616
ZAMBIA. DEPARTMENT OF FORESTRY.
REPORT. 1964. a. 25 n. Government Printer, Box
136, Lusaka, Zambia.

FORESTS AND FORESTRY —
Abstracting, Bibliographies, Statistics

634.9 016   JA
ABSTRACTS OF JAPANESE LITERATURE IN
FOREST GENETICS AND RELATED FIELDS.
PART A. (Text in Japanese and English) 1970.
irreg. 5,000 Yen. (Government Forest Experiment
Station, Tokyo - Ringyo Shikenjo) Noorin Syuppan
Co. Ltd., 5-33-2 Sinbasi, Minato-ku, Tokyo 105,
Japan. abstr.

634.9 016   JA
ABSTRACTS OF JAPANESE LITERATURE IN
FOREST GENETICS AND RELATED FIELDS.
PART B. (Text in Japanese and English) 1972.
irreg. 7,000 Yen. (Government Forest Experiment
Station, Tokyo - Ringyo Shikenjo) Noorin Syuppan
Co. Ltd., 5-33-2 Sinbasi, Minato-ku, Tokyo 105,
Japan. abstr.

634.9 016   CN   ISSN 0068-7561
CANADA. FOREST FIRE RESEARCH
INSTITUTE. BIBLIOGRAPHY. SUPPLEMENT.
a. Forest Fire Research Institute, 240 Bank St.,
Ottawa, Ont. K2P 1X4, Canada. Eds. G. S.
Ramsey, N. G. Bruce.

634.9   CN   ISSN 0384-4633
CANADA. STATISTICS CANADA. PULP AND
PAPER MILLS/USINES DE PATES ET
PAPIERS. (Catalog 36-204) (Text in English and
French) 1917. a. Can.$4.50($5.40) Statistics Canada,
Publications Distribution, Ottawa, Ont. K1A 0V7,
Canada. (also avail. in microform from MML)

338.4   CN   ISSN 0318-7128
CANADA. STATISTICS CANADA. SAWMILLS
AND PLANING MILLS AND SHINGLE
MILLS/SCIERIES ET ATELIERS DE
RABOTAGE ET USINES DE BARDEAUX.
(Catalog 35-204) (Text in English and French)
1917. a. Can.$6($7.20) Statistics Canada,
Publications Distribution, Ottawa, Ont. K1A 0V7,
Canada. stat. (also avail. in microform from MML)

634.9 016   UK   ISSN 0069-7052
COMMONWEALTH FORESTRY BUREAU
ANNOTATED BIBLIOGRAPHIES. 1966. irreg.
price varies. (Commonwealth Forestry Bureau)
Commonwealth Agricultural Bureaux, Farnham
House, Farnham Royal, Slough SL2 3BN, England.
Ed. W. Finlayson. Indexed: Forest.Abstr.

634.9 016   UK   ISSN 0071-7584
FORESTRY ABSTRACTS. LEADING ARTICLE
REPRINT SERIES. 1942. irreg. price varies.
(Commonwealth Forestry Bureau) Commonwealth
Agricultural Bureaux, Farnham House, Farnham
Royal, Slough SL2 3BN, England.

634.9 314   GW   ISSN 0084-7690
FORSTATISTISCHES JAHRBUCH. 1953. a. DM.35.
Ministerium fuer Ernaehrung, Landwirtschaft und
Umwelt, Marienstr. 41, 7000 Stuttgart 1, W.
Germany (B.R.D.)

634.9   CL
INSTITUTO FORESTAL. BOLETIN
ESTADISTICO. 1973. a. $6. Instituto Forestal,
Division Estudios Economicos, Huerfanos 554,
Casilla 3085, Santiago, Chile. stat. circ. 1,000.

634.9   NO
NORWAY. STATISTISK SENTRALBYRAA.
SKUGSTATSTIKK/FORESTRY STATISTICS.
(Subseries of its Norges Offisielle Statistikk) 1952.
a. Statistisk Sentralbyraa, Box 8131 Dep., Oslo 1,
Norway.

634.9 314   PL   ISSN 0079-2721
POLAND. GLOWNY URZAD STATYSTYCZNY.
ROCZNIK STATYSTYCZNY LESNICTWA.
YEARBOOK OF FORESTRY STATISTICS.*
(Issued in its Seria Roczniki Branzowe. Branch
Yearbooks) irreg. Glowny Urzad Statystyczny, Al.
Niepodleglosci 208, 00-925 Warsaw, Poland.

674 310   SQ
SWAZILAND. CENTRAL STATISTICAL OFFICE.
COMMERCIAL TIMBER PLANTATION AND
WOOD PRODUCTS STATISTICS. 1970. a, latest
1977. Central Statistical Office, Box 456, Mbabane,
Swaziland. charts. stat.

634.9 016   US
U.S. FOREST SERVICE. NORTH CENTRAL
FOREST EXPERIMENT STATION. LIST OF
PUBLICATIONS. 1966. a. free. ‡ U.S. Forest
Service, North Central Forest Experiment Station,
1992 Folwell Ave., St.Paul, MN 55108. Ed. Robert
D. Wray. circ. 2,500.
Formerly: U. S. Forest Service. North Central
Forest Experiment Station, St. Paul, Minnesota.
Annual Report (ISSN 0083-2472)

634.961 310   US
WASHINGTON (STATE). DEPARTMENT OF
NATURAL RESOURCES. ANNUAL FIRE
STATISTICS. a. Department of Natural Resources,
Olympia, WA 98504.

674 310   US   ISSN 0195-931X
WESTERN WOOD PRODUCTS ASSOCIATION.
STATISTICAL YEARBOOK. a. $7.50. Western
Wood Products Association, 1500 Yeon Building,
Portland, OR 97204.

FORESTS AND FORESTRY — Lumber
And Wood

see also Paper and Pulp

674   CN   ISSN 0065-0013
A B C BRITISH COLUMBIA LUMBER TRADE
DIRECTORY AND YEAR BOOK. 1916. biennial.
Can.$33. Progress Publishing Co. Ltd., 355 Burrard
St., Vancouver, B.C. V6C 2G6, Canada.

674   US
ALASKA FOREST PRODUCTS NEWSLETTER.
vol. 6, 1975. irreg. free. University of Alaska,
Cooperative Extension Service, Fairbanks, AK
99701. Eds. Kenneth Kilborn, James A. Smith. bk.
rev. bibl. circ. 1,900. (looseleaf format)

ANNUAL BOOK OF A S T M STANDARDS.
PART 22. WOOD; ADHESIVES. see
*ENGINEERING — Engineering Mechanics And
Materials*

674   BG
BANGLADESH FOREST INDUSTRIES
DEVELOPMENT CORPORATION. ANNUAL
REPORT. (Text in English) a. Bangladesh Forest
Industries Development Corporation, 186 Circular
Rd, Motijheel, Dacca 2, Bangladesh.

BRASIL MADEIRA. see *FORESTS AND
FORESTRY*

674   CN   ISSN 0068-1601
BRITISH COLUMBIA LUMBERMAN'S
GREENBOOK. 1970. a. Can.$35. Journal of
Commerce Ltd., 2000 West 12th Ave., Vancouver
9, B.C., Canada. Ed. Jean Sorenson. adv. circ.
8,024.

674   US   ISSN 0008-1094
CALIFORNIA FORESTRY AND FOREST
PRODUCTS; technical notes. 1957. irreg., latest,
no. 48, 1973. free or on exchange basis. University
of California, Berkeley, Forest Products Library,
47th St. & Hoffman Blvd., Richmond, CA 94804.
Ed.Bd. Indexed: Chem.Abstr.

674   AT
COMMONWEALTH SCIENTIFIC AND
INDUSTRIAL RESEARCH ORGANIZATION.
FOREST PRODUCTS LABORATORY. FOREST
PRODUCTS NEWSLETTER. 1941. irreg. C. S. I.
R. O., Forest Products Laboratory, Box 310, South
Melbourne, Vic. 3205, Australia. Indexed:
Aus.Sci.Ind.

674   GH   ISSN 0586-8440
COUNCIL FOR SCIENTIFIC AND INDUSTRIAL
RESEARCH, GHANA. FOREST PRODUCTS
RESEARCH INSTITUTE. ANNUAL REPORT. a.
Council for Scientific and Industrial Research,
Forest Products Research Institute, University P. O.
Box 63, Kumasi, Ghana. bibl.

F A O FORESTRY AND FOREST PRODUCTS
STUDIES. see *FORESTS AND FORESTRY*

674   FJ
FIJI TIMBERS AND THEIR USES. irreg. free.
Department of Forestry, Suva, Fiji. index.

674.8   PL   ISSN 0071-6685
FOLIA FORESTALIA POLONICA. SERIES B.
DRZEWNICTWO. (Text in Polish; summaries in
English and Russian) 1959. irreg.; 1975, no. 12.
price varies. (Polska Akademia Nauk, Oddzial w
Krakowie, Komisja Drzewnictwa) Panstwowe
Wydawnictwo Naukowe, Miodowa 10, Warsaw,
Poland (Dist. by Ars. Polona-Ruch, Krakowskie
Przedmiescie 7, Warsaw, Poland) Ed. Wieslaw
Grochowski.

674   CN   ISSN 0226-0786
FORINTEK CANADA CORPORATION,
WESTERN LABORATORY. REVIEW REPORTS.
1979. irreg. free. Forintek Canada Corporation,
Western Laboratory, 6620 Northwest Marine Drive,
Vancouver, B.C. V6T 1X2, Canada. Ed. Robert H.
Forbes.

674   CN   ISSN 0226-1170
FORINTEK CANADA CORPORATION,
WESTERN LABORATORY. SPECIAL
PUBLICATIONS. 1979. irreg. free. Forintek
Canada Corporation, Western Laboratory, 6620
Northwest Marine Drive, Vancouver, B.C. V6T
1X2, Canada. Ed. Robert H. Forbes. circ. 200-
2,000.

FORESTS AND FORESTRY — LUMBER AND WOOD

674   CN   ISSN 0708-6172
FORINTEK CANADA CORPORATION, WESTERN LABORATORY. TECHNICAL REPORTS. 1965. irreg. free. ‡ Forintek Canada Corporation, Western Laboratory, 6620 Northwest Marine Drive, Vancouver, B.C. V6T 1X2, Canada. Ed. Robert H. Forbes. circ. 200-2,000. Indexed: Bibl.Agri. Forest.Abstr.
     Former titles(until Apr. 1979): Canada. Western Forest Products Laboratory. Information Reports (ISSN 0045-429X); Canada. Forest Products Laboratory. Information Reports.

GREAT BRITAIN. BUILDING RESEARCH ESTABLISHMENT. REPORTS. see *FIRE PREVENTION*

674   SW   ISSN 0072-9922
HANDBOOK OF THE NORTHERN WOOD INDUSTRIES. (Text in English) 1887. biennial. Kr.140. AB Svensk Traevarutidning, Observatoriegatan 17, 113 29 Stockholm, Sweden. Ed. Rune Lindqvist. index.

674   GW   ISSN 0518-0147
HANDBUCH HOLZ. 1950. a. DM.15. Wirtschafts- und Forstverlag Euting KG, Tannenstr. 1, 5451 Strassenhaus, W. Germany (B.R.D.)

674   380.1   US
HARDWOOD PURCHASING HANDBOOK. 1971. a. $26.40. International Wood Trade Publications, Inc., 1235 Shady Grove, Box 34908, Memphis, TN 38134. Ed. Bd. bk. rev.
     Formerly: Hardwood Purchasing Directory.

674   382   US
IMPORT/EXPORT WOOD PURCHASING GUIDE. 3rd edt., 1976. $25. International Wood Trade Publications, Inc., 1235 Shady Grove, Box 34908, Memphis, TN 38134.

674   II   ISSN 0073-6384
INDIAN FOREST RECORDS (NEW SERIES) COMPOSITE WOOD. (Text in English) 1952. irreg., 1964, vol. 1, no. 2. price varies. ‡ Forest Research Institute & Colleges, P. O. New Forest, Dehra Dun, India. circ. 500. Indexed: Biol.Abstr. Forest.Abstr. Indian Sci.Abstr.

674   II   ISSN 0073-6414
INDIAN FOREST RECORDS (NEW SERIES) LOGGING. (Text in English) 1966. irreg., 1972, vol. 1, no. 3. price varies. ‡ Forest Research Institute & Colleges, P.O. New Forest, Dehra Dun, India. circ. 500. Indexed: Biol.Abstr. Forest.Abstr. Indian Sci.Abstr.

674   II   ISSN 0073-6449
INDIAN FOREST RECORDS (NEW SERIES) TIMBER MECHANICS. (Text in English) 1952. irreg., 1972, vol. 2, no. 2. price varies. ‡ Forest Research Institute & Colleges, P.O. New Forest, Dehra Dun, India. circ. 500. Indexed: Biol.Abstr. Forest.Abstr. Indian Sci.Abstr.

674   US   ISSN 0076-1109
L S U WOOD UTILIZATION NOTES. 1960. irreg.; no. 30, 1976. free. ‡ Louisiana State University, School of Forestry and Wildlife Management, Baton Rouge, LA 70803. Ed. Peter J. Fogg. circ. 250.

674   US   ISSN 0076-9509
MISSISSIPPI STATE UNIVERSITY. FOREST PRODUCTS UTILIZATION LABORATORY. INFORMATION SERIES. 1965. irreg. Mississippi State University, Forest Products Utilization Laboratory, Drawer F P, Mississippi State, MS 39762.

674   US   ISSN 0026-640X
MISSISSIPPI STATE UNIVERSITY. FOREST PRODUCTS UTILIZATION LABORATORY. RESEARCH REPORT. 1966. irreg. free. Mississippi State University, Forest Products Utilization Laboratory, Drawer F P, Mississippi State, MS 39762.

674.2   US   ISSN 0094-9329
MODERN SAWMILL TECHNIQUES; proceedings. 1973. a. price varies. (Sawmill Clinic) Miller Freeman Publications, Inc., 500 Howard St., San Francisco, CA 94105. illus.

674   CN   ISSN 0704-0970
NEW BRUNSWICK. FOREST PRODUCTS COMMISSION. PROGRESS REPORT. 1972. irreg. Forest Products Commission, Box 6700, Fredericton, N.B., Canada.

338.1   US   ISSN 0094-2782
NEW MEXICO FOREST PRODUCTS DIRECTORY. irreg. Department of State Forestry, Box 2167, Santa Fe, NM 87501.

674   US   ISSN 0078-1797
NORTHWEST WOOD PRODUCTS CLINIC. PROCEEDINGS. 1945. a. $7.50. ‡ Washington State University, Engineering Extension Service, College of Engineering, Pullman, WA 99164. (Co-sponsors: University of Idaho; University of Montana)

674   PL   ISSN 0079-4724
POZNANSKIE TOWARZYSTWO PRZYJACIOL NAUK. KOMISJA TECHNOLOGII DREWNA. PRACE. (Text in Polish; summaries in English) a. price varies. Poznanskie Towarzystwo Przyjaciol Nauk, Mielzynskiego 27/29, 61-725 Poznan, Poland (Dist. by Ars Polona-Ruch, Krakowskie Przedmiescie 7, Warsaw, Poland) Indexed: Biol.Abstr.

674   US   ISSN 0485-9960
RANDOM LENGTHS YEARBOOK. 1965. a. $16.50. Random Lengths Publications, Inc., Box 867, Eugene, OR 97440. Ed. David S. Evans. charts. stat.

674   387   UK   ISSN 0080-9284
SHIPPING MARKS ON TIMBER. 1894. triennial (approx.) £18. Benn Publications Ltd., 25 New Street Square, London EC4A 3JA, England. Ed. John Topham. adv. index. circ. 2,500.
     Lists timber shippers their shipping marks and agents throughout the world

674   NO
SKOGBRUKETS OG SKOGINDUSTRIENES FORSKNINGSRAAD. AARBOK. no. 28, 1975. a. Skogbrukets og Skogindustrienes Forskningsraad, Box 250, Vinderen, Oslo 3, Norway.
     Continues: Skogbrukets og Skogindustrienes Forsknings-Forening. Arbok.

674   SW   ISSN 0346-7090
SVENSKA TRAESKYDDSINSTITUTET. MEDDELANDEN/SWEDISH WOOD PRESERVATION INSTITUTE. REPORTS. (Text in English and Swedish) 1952. irreg., no. 134, 1979. $60. Svenska Traeskyddsinstitutet - Swedish Wood Preservation Institute, Drottning Kristinas Vaeg 47c, S-114 28 Stockholm, Sweden. Ed. Joeran Jermer. circ. 400-1,500.

674   US   ISSN 0082-089X
SYMPOSIUM ON PARTICLEBOARD. PROCEEDINGS. 1967. a. $35. Washington State University, Engineering Extension Service, Pullman, WA 99164. Ed. Tom Maloney.

674   US
SYRACUSE WOOD SCIENCE SERIES. irreg. Syracuse University Press, 1011 E. Water St., Syracuse, NY 13210. Ed. Wilfred A. Cote.

674.2   674.8   UK   ISSN 0082-433X
TIMBER AND PLYWOOD. BOARD NEWS ANNUAL. (Annual number of Timber and Plywood Weekly) 1885. a. 65p. Middlesex Publishing Co., Ltd., 21 New Street, London EC2 M 4NT, England. Ed. W. G. Potter. index.

TIMBER TRADES DIRECTORY. see *BUSINESS AND ECONOMICS — Trade And Industrial Directories*

674   UK   ISSN 0082-4364
TIMBER TRADES JOURNAL. ANNUAL SPECIAL ISSUE. 1879. a. £5.50. Benn Publications Ltd., 25 New Street Square, London EC4A 3JA, England. adv. circ. 7,000.

674   691.1   CN
TREATED WOOD PERSPECTIVES/ PERSPECTIVES DES BOIS TRAITES. 1973. irreg. free; selected distribution. ‡ Canadian Institute of Timber Construction, Suite 702, the Juliana, 100 Bronson Ave., Ottawa, Ont. K1R 6G8, Canada. Ed. D. R. Douglas. circ. 4,200.
     Supersedes: Modern Wood (ISSN 0077-0175)

674   US   ISSN 0083-1018
U.S. FOREST SERVICE. FOREST PRODUCTS LABORATORY, MADISON, WISCONSIN. REPORT OF RESEARCH AT THE FOREST PRODUCTS LABORATORY. 1962. irreg. free; limited distribution. U.S. Forest Service, Forest Products Laboratory, Box 5130, Madison, WI 53705. circ. 20,000.
     Formerly: U.S. Forest Service. Forest Products Laboratory, Madison, Wisconsin. Annual Report of Research at the Forest Products Laboratory.

674   CN   ISSN 0079-8355
UNIVERSITE LAVAL. DEPARTEMENT D'EXPLOITATION ET UTILISATION DES BOIS. NOTE DE RECHERCHES. 1967. irreg. free. Universite Laval, Faculte de Foresterie, Quebec, Que, Canada. Ed. Dr. Marcel Goulet. circ. 500-1,500.

674   CN   ISSN 0079-8363
UNIVERSITE LAVAL. DEPARTEMENT D'EXPLOITATION ET UTILISATION DES BOIS. NOTE TECHNIQUE. (Text in French and English) 1967. irreg. free. ‡ Universite Laval, Faculte de Foresterie, Quebec, Que, Canada. Ed. Dr. Marcel Goulet. circ. 500-1,500.

674.1   690   US   ISSN 0083-6508
VIRGINIA POLYTECHNIC INSTITUTE AND STATE UNIVERSITY. WOOD RESEARCH AND WOOD CONSTRUCTION LABORATORY. SPECIAL REPORT. 1949. irreg. price varies. Virginia Polytechnic Institute and State University, Wood Research and Wood Construction Laboratory, Blacksburg, VA 24061. Ed. E. G. Stern.

674   US
WESTERN DRY KILN CLUBS. PROCEEDINGS. 1948. a. membership. West Coast Dry Kiln Association, Oregon State University, School of Forestry, Corvallis, OR 97331. Ed. Charles J. Kozlik. circ. 700.

WESTERN WOOD PRODUCTS ASSOCIATION. STATISTICAL YEARBOOK. see *FORESTS AND FORESTRY — Abstracting, Bibliographies, Statistics*

WHERE TO BUY HARDWOOD PLYWOOD AND VENEER. see *BUILDING AND CONSTRUCTION — Carpentry And Woodwork*

674   634.98   JA   ISSN 0083-9272
WHITE PAPER ON JAPAN'S FOREST INDUSTRIES. Title varies: Directory of Asian Forest Products. (English edition) 1965. decennial. $36. Japan Lumber Journal, Inc., C.P.O. Box 1945, Tokyo 100-91, Japan. Ed. Satoshi Ogawa.

674   US
WOOD & WOOD PRODUCTS REFERENCE BUYING GUIDE. 1963. a. $2.50. Vance Publishing Corporation (Chicago), 300 W. Adams St., Chicago, IL 60606. Ed. Monte Mace. circ. 30,000. (also avail. in microform from UMI)
     Formerly: Wood & Wood Products Reference Data/Buying Guide (ISSN 0084-1080)

674   JA   ISSN 0049-7916
WOOD RESEARCH/MOKUZAI KENKYU. (Text in English) 1949. irreg. (1-2/yr.) exchange basis. Wood Research Institute, Kyoto University, Gokansho, Uji, Kyoto 611, Japan. Ed.Bd. charts. stat. Indexed: Biol.Abstr. Chem.Abstr. Forest.Abstr.

338.4   UK
WOODWORKING INDUSTRY /BUYERS' GUIDE. 1945. a. £5 or free with subscr. to Woodworking Industry Journal. Benn Publications Ltd., 25 New Street Square, London EC4A 3JA, England. Ed. John Topnam. adv. circ. 5,000.
     Formerly: Woodworking Industry /Directory (ISSN 0084-120X)

674   US
WORLD WOOD. LATIN AMERICAN EDITION. 1975. a. $3. Miller Freeman Publications, Inc., 500 Howard St., San Francisco, CA 94105. Ed. Hugh R. Fraser. adv. circ. 4,542.

674   UN   ISSN 0084-3768
YEARBOOK OF FOREST PRODUCTS. (Text in English, French and Spanish) 1947. a. price varies. Food and Agriculture Organization of the United Nations, Distribution and Sales Section, Via delle Terme di Caracalla, Rome, Italy (Dist. in U.S. by: Unipub, 345 Park Ave. S., New York, NY 10010)

FUNERALS

614.6   US   ISSN 0065-7565
AMERICAN BLUE BOOK OF FUNERAL DIRECTORS. 1966. biennial. $50. Kates-Boylston Publications, Inc., 1501 Broadway, New York, NY 10036.

614.6   UK   ISSN 0305-9537
CREMATION SOCIETY HANDBOOK AND DIRECTORY OF CREMATORIA. 1969. a. £4. Cremation Society of Great Britain, Woodcut House, Ashford Rd., Hollingbourne, Maidstone, Kent ME17 IXH, England. Ed. K.G.C. Prevette. adv. circ. 1,000.
     Formerly: Directory of Crematoria in the British Isles & Overseas Cremation Societies.
     Cremation

614.6   UK   ISSN 0070-1475
CREMATION SOCIETY OF GREAT BRITAIN. CONFERENCE REPORT. 1922. a. £4. Cremation Society of Great Britain, Woodcut House, Ashford Rd., Hollingbourne, Maidstone, Kent ME17 1XH, England. Ed. Kenneth G. C. Prevette. adv. circ. 500.
     Cremation

614.6   US   ISSN 0074-2155
INTERNATIONAL CEMETERY DIRECTORY. 1961. triennial. $12. ‡ American Cemetery Association, 250 Broad St., Columbus, OH 43215. Ed. John P. Danglade. adv.
     Lists 10,000 cemeteries in U.S., Canada and other nations

393   US
MANUAL OF DEATH EDUCATION AND SIMPLE BURIAL. 1962. biennial. $2. (Continental Association of Funeral and Memorial Societies) Celo Press, Rt. 5, Burnsville, NC 28714. Ed. Ernest Morgan. adv. bk. rev. bibl. stat. circ. 50,000.
     Formerly: Manual of Simple Burial.

381   US   ISSN 0098-3322
YELLOW BOOK OF FUNERAL DIRECTORS & SERVICES. Cover title: National Yellow Book of Funeral Directors & Suppliers. a. $15 to advertisers; $25 to non-advertisers. Nomis Publications Inc., Box 5122, Youngstown, OH 44514. illus.

FUNERALS — Abstracting, Bibliographies, Statistics

338.4   CN   ISSN 0527-4915
CANADA. STATISTICS CANADA. COFFIN AND CASKET INDUSTRY/INDUSTRIE DES CERCUEILS. (Catalog 35-210) (Text in English & French) 1960. a. Can.$4.50($5.40) Statistics Canada, Publications Distribution, Ottawa, Ont. K1A 0V7, Canada. (also avail. in microform from MML)

393   US   ISSN 0270-7543
DIRECTORS ENCYCLOPEDIA OF NEWSPAPERS; the funeral directors reference guide of United States newspapers. a. Poston & Poston, 13940 N. Dale Mabry, Tampa, FL 33618.

FURNITURE AND HOUSE FURNISHINGS

see Interior Design and Decoration— Furniture and House Furnishings

GARDENING AND HORTICULTURE

see also Gardening and Horticulture— Florist Trade; Agriculture—Crop Production and Soil; Biology—Botany

635   UK
A. G. S. GUIDES. irreg. price varies. Alpine Garden Society, c/o D. K. Haselgrove, 278-280 Hoe St., Walthamstow, London E17 9PL, England. illus. cum. index. (back issues avail.)

634   SA
A P G A ANNUAL/A P K V JAARBLAD. (Text in Afrikaans and English) a. Apricot, Peach and Pear Growers' Association, 258 Main St., Box 414, Paarl 7620, South Africa. Ed. P. F. Greeff. adv.

635   580.7   RM   ISSN 0068-3329
ACTA BOTANICA HORTI BUCURESTIENSIS. (Text and summaries in Romanian, English, German, French) 1958. a. available on exchange. Gradina Botanica a Universitatii Bucuresti, Soseaua Cotroceni Nr. 32, Bucharest, Romania. circ. 500.

635   NE   ISSN 0567-7572
ACTA HORTICULTURAE. 1963. irreg., latest no. 104. price varies. International Society for Horticultural Science, Bezuidenhoutseweg 73, Box 20401, 2500 EK The Hague, Netherlands.

635   PL
AKADEMIA ROLNICZA, POZNAN. ROCZNIK. OGRODNICTWO. (Summaries in English and Russian) 1959. irreg. price varies. Akademia Rolnicza, Poznan, Ul. Wojska Polskiego 28, 60-637 Poznan, Poland. Indexed: Bibl.Agri.

635   PL   ISSN 0083-7288
AKADEMIA ROLNICZA, WARSAW. ZESZYTY NAUKOWE. OGRODNICTWO. (Text in Polish; summaries in English and Russian) 1957. irreg. Akademia Rolnicza, Warsaw, Ul. Rakowiecka 26/30, Warsaw, Poland. Ed. J.R. Starck. Indexed: Hort.Abstr.

635   CN   ISSN 0706-3369
ALBERTA. HORTICULTURAL RESEARCH CENTER. ANNUAL REPORT. (Previously included in: Alberta. Department of Agriculture. Annual Report) 1970. a. free. ‡ Department of Agriculture, Horticultural Research Center, Communications Branch, 9718-107th St., Edmonton, Alta. T5K 2C8, Canada. stat. circ. controlled.

ALLERTONIA; a series of occasional papers. *see BIOLOGY — Botany*

338.1   US   ISSN 0098-793X
ALLIED LANDSCAPE INDUSTRY MEMBER DIRECTORY. a. $8 to non-members. American Association of Nurserymen, 230 Southern Bldg., 15th & H St. N.W., Washington, DC 20005.

635.9   US   ISSN 0065-762X
AMERICAN CAMELLIA YEARBOOK. 1946. a. $7.50. American Camellia Society, Box 1217, Fort Valley, GA 31030. Ed. Milton H. Brown. index. cum.index from 1946. circ. 5,200.
     Camellias

635.9   US   ISSN 0066-0000
AMERICAN ROSE ANNUAL. 1916. a. $8.50. American Rose Society, Inc., P.O. Box 30,000, Shreveport, LA 71130. Ed. Harold S. Goldstein. index. cum.index 1916-41.
     Roses

635   MX   ISSN 0066-0116
AMERICAN SOCIETY FOR HORTICULTURAL SCIENCE. TROPICAL REGION. PROCEEDINGS OF THE ANNUAL MEETING. (Text and summaries in English and Spanish) 1957. a. $5. American Society for Horticultural Science, Londres 40, Mexico 6, D.F., Mexico. Ed. Dr. C. E. Fernandez. index. cum.index: vols. 1-12(1957-68) cum.index. circ. 700. Indexed: Hort.Abstr. Trop.Abstr.
     Formerly: American Society for Horticultural Science. Caribbean Region. Proceedings of the Annual Meeting.

635   621.9   FR   ISSN 0224-2478
ANNUAIRE REPERTOIRE DE LA MOTOCULTURE DE PLAISANCE JARDINAGE. 1979. a. 80 F. Societe d'Edition pour Engins a Moteur, Jalna, Parc d'Ausnieres, 74500 Evian-les-Bains, France. Ed. A. de Crecy. adv. circ. 4,000.

635.9   AT
AUSTRALIAN ROSE ANNUAL. 1928. a. (National Rose Society of Australia) Ramsay Ware Stockland Pty. Ltd., 552 Victoria St., North Melbourne, Vic. 3051, Australia.
     Roses

BAILEYA; a journal of horticultural taxonomy. *see BIOLOGY — Botany*

635   BE   ISSN 0303-903X
BELGIUM. RIJKSSTATION VOOR SIERPLANTENTEELT. MEDEDELINGEN. (Text in Dutch; summaries in English, French, and German) 1961. irreg. (1-3/yr.) 250 Fr. Rijksstation voor Sierplantenteelt, Caritasstraat 21, B-9230 Melle, Belgium. circ. 400. Indexed: Biol.&Agr.Ind. Hort.Abstr.

635   GW   ISSN 0303-1241
BETRIEBS- UND MARKTWIRTSCHAFT IM GARTENBAU. 1974. irreg. price varies. Verlag Paul Parey (Berlin), Lindenstr. 44-47, 1000 Berlin 61, W. Germany (B.R.D.). bibl. illus. index.

635   640   US
BETTER HOMES AND GARDENS GARDEN IDEAS AND OUTDOOR LIVING. 1940. a. $1.95 per no. (not sold through subscr.) Meredith Corporation, 1716 Locust St., Des Moines, IA 50036. adv. illus.

BETTER HOMES AND GARDENS HUNDREDS OF IDEAS. *see INTERIOR DESIGN AND DECORATION — Furniture And House Furnishings*

635   PL
BIULETYN WARZYWNICZY. (Text in Polish; summaries in English and Russian) 1953. irreg. 40 Zl. Instytut Warzywnictwa - Research Institute of Vegetable Crops, Ul. 22 Lipca 1/3, 96-100 Skierniewice, Poland. Ed. E. Chroboczek. charts. illus. cum.index. (tabloid format; also avail. in cards) Indexed: Ref.Zh. Hort.Abstr.

634   CN   ISSN 0701-757X
BRITISH COLUMBIA FRUIT GROWERS ASSOCIATION. HORTICULTURAL FORUM PROCEEDINGS. 1969. a. British Columbia Fruit Growers Association, 1473 Water Street, Kelowna, B.C. V1Y 7N6, Canada.
     Formerly: British Columbia Fruit Growers Association. Horticultural Conference Proceedings (ISSN 0068-1555)

634   CN   ISSN 0068-1563
BRITISH COLUMBIA FRUIT GROWERS ASSOCIATION. MINUTES OF THE PROCEEDINGS OF THE ANNUAL CONVENTION. 1890. a. British Columbia Fruit Growers Association, 1473 Water Street, Kelowna, B. C. W1Y 7N6, Canada.

635   US
BROWN THUMBER'S HANDBOOK OF HOUSE PLANTS. 1977. a. $1.50. Snibbe Publications, Inc., 523 Lakeview Rd., Clearwater, FL 33516. Ed. Gil Whitton. circ. 200,000.

635   630   SI
BULLETIN OF AGRI-HORTICULTURE. (Text in English and Chinese) irreg. Tri-Products Private Ltd., 33-A Phillip St., Singapore 1, Singapore. adv. circ. 5,000.

635.9   CN   ISSN 0319-1915
CANADIAN GLADIOLUS SOCIETY. ANNUAL. 1921. a. Can.$3.50($3.50) Canadian Gladiolus Society, 1274 129 A St., Ocean Park, B.C., Canada. Ed. Grant Wilson.
     Gladiolas

635   CN   ISSN 0068-8908
CANADIAN HORTICULTURAL COUNCIL. ANNUAL MEETING REPORTS. 1922. a. Can.$20. Canadian Horticultural Council, 1568 Carling Ave., Ottawa, Ont. K1Z 7M5, Canada.

635   CN   ISSN 0068-8916
CANADIAN HORTICULTURAL COUNCIL. COMMITTEE ON HORTICULTURAL RESEARCH. ANNUAL REPORTS. 1963. a. Can.$20. Canadian Horticultural Council, 1568 Carling Ave., Ottawa, Ont. K1Z 7M5, Canada. Ed. C. J. Bishop, W. Daman.

635   CN   ISSN 0315-6877
CANADIAN SOCIETY FOR HORTICULTURAL SCIENCE. JOURNAL. a. membership. Canadian Society for Horticultural Science, c/o E. W. Toop, Dept. of Plant Science, Univ. of Alberta, Edmonton, Alta. T6G 2H4, Canada.

GARDENING AND HORTICULTURE

635   JA   ISSN 0069-3227
CHIBA UNIVERSITY. FACULTY OF HORTICULTURE. TECHNICAL BULLETIN/ CHIBA DAIGAKU ENGEIGAKUBU GAKUJUTSU HOKOKU. (Text in Japanese; summaries and tables of contents in English) 1953. a. Chiba University, Faculty of Horticulture - Chiba Daigaku Engeigakubu, 648 Matsudo, Matsudo-shi, Chiba 271, Japan. circ. 750.

635   UK   ISSN 0069-6986
COMMONWEALTH BUREAU OF HORTICULTURE AND PLANTATION CROPS. HORTICULTURAL REVIEW. 1969. irreg. price varies. (Commonwealth Bureau of Horticulture and Plantation Crops) Commonwealth Agricultural Bureaux, Farnham House, Farnham Royal, Slough SL2 3BN, England.

635   UK   ISSN 0069-6994
COMMONWEALTH BUREAU OF HORTICULTURE AND PLANTATION CROPS. RESEARCH REVIEW. 1966. irreg. price varies. (Commonwealth Bureau of Horticulture and Plantation Crops) Commonwealth Agricultural Bureaux, Farnham House, Farnham Royal, Slough SL2 3BN, England.

633 635   UK   ISSN 0069-7001
COMMONWEALTH BUREAU OF HORTICULTURE AND PLANTATION CROPS. TECHNICAL COMMUNICATIONS. 1930. irreg. price varies. (Commonwealth Bureau of Horticulture and Plantation Crops) Commonwealth Agricultural Bureaux, Farnham House, Farnham Royal, Slough SL2 3BN, England.

635   AT   ISSN 0069-7435
COMMONWEALTH SCIENTIFIC AND INDUSTRIAL RESEARCH ORGANIZATION. DIVISION OF HORTICULTURAL RESEARCH. REPORT. 1962/63. biennial. free. ‡ C. S. I. R. O., Division of Horticultural Research, Box 350, G.P.O., Adelaide 5001, S. Australia. circ. 3,000. Indexed: Hort.Abstr.

634   US
CORNELL RECOMMENDATIONS FOR COMMERCIAL TREE-FRUIT PRODUCTION. 1950. a. $1.75. ‡ New York State College of Agriculture and Life Sciences, Cornell University, Ithaca, NY 14853. Ed. Ms. Merle Gold. circ. 4,000.
Formerly: Tree Fruit Production Recommendations (ISSN 0070-0118)

635   UK
DAFFODIL SOCIETY. JOURNAL. 1960. a. £1. ‡ Daffodil Society, c/o D. J. Pearce, 1, Noak's Cross, Cottages, Great Braxted, Witham, Essex, England. adv. stat. circ. controlled.
Daffodils

635.9   UK   ISSN 0070-2544
DAFFODILS. 1913. a. £1.50. Royal Horticultural Society, Vincent Sq., London SW1P 2PE, England. (Co-sponsor: Daffodil Society) Ed. Elspeth Napier. circ. 1,000.
Formerly: Daffodil and Tulip Year Book.
Daffodils

DAILY PLANET ALMANAC. see *ASTROLOGY*

635   UK
DELPHINIUM SOCIETY YEARBOOK. 1929. a. £1($2) ‡ Delphinium Society, 11 Long Grove, Seer Green, Beaconsfield, Bucks HP9 2YN, England. Ed. C. R. Edwards. adv. bk. rev. circ. 2,500.

635   GW   ISSN 0341-2091
DEUTSCHER GARTENBAU; ueberregionale Fachzeitschrift fuer alle Sparten des Gartenbaus. 1947. w. DM.164.40. Verlag Eugen Ulmer, Wollgrasweg 41, Postfach 700561, 7000 Stuttgart 70, W. Germany (B.R.D.) Ed.Gerd Heinrichs. adv.
Formerly: Erwerbsgaertner.

635 016   US   ISSN 0417-5522
DIRECTORY OF AMERICAN HORTICULTURE. irreg. $7.50. American Horticultural Society, Mount Vernon, VA 22121.

635   UK   ISSN 0070-6787
DO-IT-YOURSELF GARDENING ANNUAL. 1960. a. 75p. Link House Publications Ltd., Link House, Dingwall Ave., Croydon CR9 2TA, England. Ed. Tony Wilkins. adv.

635.9   US   ISSN 0418-2057
DWARF IRIS SOCIETY PORTFOLIO. 1952. a. $2. ‡ Dwarf Iris Society, c/o Elsie A. Zuercher, Ed., 121 E. Union St, Portland, IN 47371. illus. circ. 300. (processed)

FOLIA DENDROLOGICA. see *FORESTS AND FORESTRY*

634   AT   ISSN 0085-090X
FRUIT WORLD ANNUAL AND ORCHARDISTS GUIDE. 1920. a. Aus.$0.75. Fruit World Pty. Ltd., Box 1944, Melbourne, Vic. 3001, Australia. Ed. L. Thornton. adv. bk. rev. circ. 9,000.

635   UK   ISSN 0071-9730
FUCHSIA ANNUAL. 1938. a. £1.00. British Fuchsia Society, The Bungalow, Brookwood Military Cemetery, Brookwood, Surrey, England. Ed. E. J. Goulding. adv. bk. rev. circ. 5,000.

635   GW   ISSN 0301-2719
GAERTNERISCHE BERUFSPRAXIS. (Series A: Produktionsgartenbau: Series B: Landschafts- und Sportplatzbau) 1937. irreg. price varies. Verlag Paul Parey (Berlin), Lindenstr. 44-47, 1000 Berlin 61, W. Germany (B.R.D.) bibl. illus. index.

635   CN
GARDEN FAX. 1976. irreg. Department of Agriculture, Printmedia Branch, 9718 107th St., Edmonton, Alta. T5K 2C8, Canada. illus.

635   US
GARDEN SUPPLY RETAILER GREEN BOOK. 1950. a. $10. ‡ Miller Publishing Co., 2501 Wayzata Blvd., Box 67, Minneapolis, MN 55440. adv. bk. rev. index. circ. 40,000(controlled) (also avail. in microfilm from UMI; reprint service avail. from UMI)
Formerly: Home & Garden Supply Merchandiser Green Book.

635   US   ISSN 0016-4631
GARDEN WRITERS BULLETIN. vol.17,1970. 1-6/yr. membership. Garden Writers Association of America, 101 Park Ave., New York, NY 10017. Ed. Derek Fell. circ. 400.
Organization news

790   UK   ISSN 0141-2361
GARDENS OPEN TO THE PUBLIC IN ENGLAND AND WALES. 1930. a. price varies. National Gardens Scheme Charitable Trust, 57 Lower Belgrave St., London SW1W 0LR, England. Ed. Organising Secretary. adv. index. circ. 75,000.
Formerly(until 1979): Gardens of England and Wales Open to the Public (ISSN 0072-0186)

635   UK
GARDENS TO VISIT. 1956. a. 30p.($2) ‡ Gardeners' Sunday Organisation, White Witches, Claygate Road, Dorking, Surrey, England. (Co-sponsors: Gardeners' Royal Benevolent Society; Gardeners' Orphan Fund) Ed. K. Collett. adv. circ. 50,000.

635   GW   ISSN 0072-7717
DER GROSSE GARTENKATALOG. 1970. a. DM.19.80. Fachschriften-Verlag GmbH, Hoehenstr. 17, Postfach 1329, 7012 Fellbach, W. Germany (B.R.D.)

635   UK   ISSN 0440-5757
HEATHER SOCIETY. YEARBOOK. 1963. a. membership. Heather Society, Harvest House, 62 London Rd., Reading, Berks RG1 5AS, England. Ed. A. J. Stow. adv. bibl. illus. index. 1963-1972. cum.index: 1963-1972. circ. 1,000.

635   US
HERB COLLECTOR'S MANUAL & MARKETING GUIDE; gingseng growers and collectors' handbook. 1946. irreg., 5th edt., 1977. $3.95. J. Kelly, Box 7, Looneyville, WV 25259.

635   US
HERBARIST. 1935. a. $2.75. Herb Society of America, 300 Massachusetts Ave., Boston, MA 02115. adv. bk. rev. illus. circ. 2,000. (back issues avail)

635   NE   ISSN 0441-7461
HORTICULTURAL RESEARCH INTERNATIONAL; directory of horticultural research institutes and their activities in 54 countries. irreg., latest 1972. fl.60. Centre for Agricultural Publishing and Documentation, P.O. Box 4, 6700 AA Wageningen, Netherlands.

635   US   ISSN 0163-7851
HORTICULTURAL REVIEWS. 1979. a. $33. AVI Publishing Company, 250 Post Rd. East, Box 831, Westport, CT 06881. Ed. Jules Janick. circ. 4,000.

635   US   ISSN 0147-8591
HOUSE & GARDEN GARDENING GUIDE. a. $2. Conde Nast Publications Inc., 350 Madison Ave., New York, NY 10017. Ed. Louis O. Gropp. adv. index.

635   US   ISSN 0073-3563
HOUSE BEAUTIFUL'S GARDENING AND OUTDOOR LIVING. 1940. a. $1.50. Hearst Magazines, House Beautiful, 250 W. 55th St., New York, NY 10019. Ed. Richard Beatty. circ. 175,000.

635   NE   ISSN 0074-6231
INTERNATIONAL HORTICULTURAL CONGRESS. PROCEEDINGS. 1899. quadrennial; 20th, 1978, Sydney, Australia. fl.23. International Society for Horticultural Science, C/O Dr. G. de Bakker, Bezuidenhoutseweg 73, Box 20401, 2500 EK The Hague, Netherlands.
Proceedings published by organizing committee

634.3   US   ISSN 0074-7203
INTERNATIONAL ORGANIZATION OF CITRUS VIROLOGISTS. PROCEEDINGS OF THE CONFERENCE. 1957. irreg. price varies. University Presses of Florida, 15 N.W. 15th St., Gainesville, FL 32603. Ed. W. C. Price.

635   US   ISSN 0075-0700
IRIS YEAR BOOK. 1924. a. price varies. British Iris Society, 67 Bushwood Rd., Kew, Richmond, Surrey TW9 3BG, England. Ed. C. E. E. Bartlett. adv. bk. rev. circ. 1,000.
Irises

635.9   UK
JANUARY BULLETIN. a. £3.64($5) National Dahlia Society (Great Britain), 26 Burns Rd., Lillington, Leamington Spa, Warks, England.

635.9   CN   ISSN 0319-3098
JARDIN BOTANIQUE DE MONTREAL. ANNUELLES ET LEGUMES: RESULTATS DES CULTURES D'ESSAI. (Text in French) 1969. a. free to botanical and horticultural institutions. Jardin Botanique de Montreal, 4101 est, rue Sherbrooke, Montreal, Que. H1X 2B2. illus.
Formerly: Jardin Botanique de Montreal. Annuelle (ISSN 0319-3101)

JARDIN BOTANIQUE DE MONTREAL. MEMOIRE. see *BIOLOGY — Botany*

635.93   UK   ISSN 0075-949X
LILIES AND OTHER LILIACEAE. 1932. a. £1.50. Royal Horticultural Society, Vincent Sq., London SW1P 2PE, England. Ed. Elspeth Napier. index. circ. 1,000.
Formerly: Lily Year Book.
Lilies

635   NZ   ISSN 0069-3820
LINCOLN COLLEGE. DEPARTMENT OF HORTICULTURE. BULLETIN. 1967. irreg. price varies. Lincoln College, Department of Horticulture, Canterbury, New Zealand. circ. 500-5,000. Indexed: Bibl.Agri. Hort.Abstr.

LLEWELLYN'S MOON SIGN BOOK. see *ASTROLOGY*

LONGWOOD PROGRAM SEMINARS. see *BIOLOGY — Botany*

MORTON ARBORETUM QUARTERLY. see *BIOLOGY — Botany*

635   UK
N. C. S. YEARBOOK. a. membership. National Chrysanthemum Society, 65 St. Margaret's Ave., Whetstone, London N20 9HT, England.
Chrysanthemums

635   UK   ISSN 0077-4189
NATIONAL DAHLIA SOCIETY ANNUAL. a. £3.64($5) ‡ National Dahlia Society (Great Britain), 26 Burns Road, Lillington, Leamington Spa, England. Ed. Philip Damp. adv. bk. rev. circ. 5,000-6,000.
Dahlias

635 US ISSN 0077-5088
NATIONAL JUNIOR HORTICULTURAL
ASSOCIATION. NEWSLETTER. 1940. irreg. free.
(American Horticultural Society) National Junior
Horticultural Association, Mount Vernon, VA
22121. Ed. Murray Keene. circ. 5,000-7,000.

635 US
NEW YORK STATE HORTICULTURAL SOCIETY.
PROCEEDINGS. vol. 122, 1977. a. $4.50. New
York State Horticultural Society, 900 Jefferson Rd.,
Rochester, NY 14623.

PLANT PROTECTION CENTER. ANNUAL
REPORT. see AGRICULTURE — Crop
Production And Soil

635 US
PRIMER FOR HERB GROWING. 1952. irreg. $0.50.
Herb Society of America, 300 Massachusetts Ave.,
Boston, MA 02115. bibl.

635 NE
PRODUKTSCHAP VOOR SIERGEWASSEN.
JAARVERSLAG/STATISTIEK. 1947. a. ‡
Produktschap voor Siergewassen, Bezuidenhoutse
Weg 153, Postbus 361, The Hague, Netherlands.
Formed by the merger of: Produktschap voor
Siergewassen. Jaarverslag (ISSN 0077-7609) &
Produktschap voor Siergewassen. Statistiek (ISSN
0556-543X)

635 UK ISSN 0080-441X
R. H. S. GARDENER'S DIARY. 1912. a. 99p. Royal
Horticultural Society, Vincent Square, London
SW1P 2PE, England. circ. 66,000.

635.9 UK ISSN 0080-2891
RHODODENDRONS, WITH MAGNOLIAS AND
CAMELLIAS. 1946. a. £1.50. Royal Horticultural
Society, Vincent Sq., London SW1P 2PE, England.
Eds. Elspeth Napier, James Platt. index. circ. 1,250.
Formerly: Rhododendron and Camellia Yearbook.

635 US ISSN 0485-2044
RIO GRANDE VALLEY HORTICULTURAL
SOCIETY. JOURNAL. 1946. a. $10. Rio Grande
Valley Horticultural Society, Box 107, Weslaco, TX
78596. Ed. Robert Leyden. charts. illus. stat.
index; cum.index: v. 25, 1946-1971. circ. 400. (back
issues avail.) Indexed: Biol.Abstr. Chem.Abstr.

635 UK ISSN 0483-3686
ROSE ANNUAL. 1910. a. membership; libraries £1.
Royal National Rose Society, Chiswell Green Lane,
St. Albans, Hertfordshire AL2 3NR, England. Ed.
Ken Lemmon. adv. bk. rev. circ. 65,000.

580.744 CN ISSN 0072-9647
ROYAL BOTANICAL GARDENS, HAMILTON,
ONT. SPECIAL BULLETIN. 1947. a. free. Royal
Botanical Gardens, P.O. Box 399, Hamilton, Ont.
L8N 3H8, Canada. Ed. Dr. Leslie Laking. circ.
3,000. (back issues avail)

ROYAL BOTANICAL GARDENS, HAMILTON,
ONT. TECHNICAL BULLETIN. see
BIOLOGY — Botany

635 NZ ISSN 0110-5760
ROYAL NEW ZEALAND INSTITUTE OF
HORTICULTURE. ANNUAL JOURNAL. 1973. a.
NZ.$6. Royal New Zealand Institute of
Horticulture, P.O. Box 12, Lincoln College,
Canterbury, New Zealand. bk. rev. illus. circ. 500.
Supersedes: Royal New Zealand Institute of
Horticulture. Journal (ISSN 0557-6601)

635 UK ISSN 0080-7737
SCIENTIFIC HORTICULTURE. 1932. a. £1.
(Horticultural Education Association) Elvy & Gibbs,
11 Best Lane, Canterbury, Kent, England.

SEED SAVERS EXCHANGE. see HOBBIES

635 US
SOCIETY FOR LOUISIANA IRISES. SPECIAL
PUBLICATIONS. 1952. irreg. $3. Society for
Louisiana Irises, Box 4-0175, U.S.L., Lafayette, LA
70504. Ed. Barbara F. Nelson. illus. circ. 250.
Irises

635 US
SUNSET GARDEN IDEAS AND ANSWERS. 1976.
a. $1.75. Lane Publishing Co., 85 Willow Rd.,
Menlo Park, CA 94025. adv.
Formerly: Sunset Joy of Gardening.

635 AT ISSN 0082-2124
TATURA, AUSTRALIA. HORTICULTURAL
RESEARCH STATION. ANNUAL RESEARCH
REPORT. 1962/63. a. Horticultural Research
Station, Tatura, Australia.

635 GW
TECHNISCHE UNIVERSITAET MUENCHEN.
INSTITUT FUER WIRTSCHAFTSLEHRE DES
GARTENBAUES. FORSCHUNGSBERICHTE
ZUR OEKONOMIE IN GARTENBAU. 1968.
irreg. Technische Universitaet Muenchen, Institut
fuer Wirtschaftslehre des Gartenbaues,
Weihenstephan, 8000 Munich, W. Germany
(B.R.D.)

635 US ISSN 0073-3075
U.S. DEPARTMENT OF AGRICULTURE. HOME
AND GARDEN BULLETIN. 1950. irreg. price
varies. U.S. Department of Agriculture, Washington,
DC 20250.

635 CN ISSN 0042-3092
VEGETABLES NEWSLETTER. 1967. irreg.
Department of Agriculture & Rural Development,
Horticulture Division, Plant Industry Branch,
Fredericton, N.B., Canada. Ed. C. F. Harding.

635 US
WASHINGTON STATE HORTICULTURAL
ASSOCIATION. PROCEEDINGS. 68th, 1972. a.
Washington State Horticultural Association, Box
136, Wenatchee, WA 98801.

WEED CONTROL MANUAL AND HERBICIDE
GUIDE. see AGRICULTURE — Crop Production
And Soil

635 631 AT
WESTERN AUSTRALIA VEGETABLES. a.
Australian Bureau of Statistics, Western Australian
Office, 1-3 St. George's Terrace, Perth, W.A. 6000,
Australia.

635 CN ISSN 0083-8810
WESTERN CANADIAN SOCIETY FOR
HORTICULTURE. REPORT OF PROCEEDINGS
OF ANNUAL MEETING. 1943. a. $10. ‡ Western
Canadian Society for Horticulture, Plant Science
Dept., University of Manitoba, Winnipeg, Man. R3T
2N2, Canada.

635 US ISSN 0090-9319
WOMAN'S DAY 101 GARDENING & OUTDOOR
IDEAS. 1972. a. $1.25. Fawcett Publications, Inc.,
1515 Broadway, New York, NY 10036. Frank
Bowers. adv. illus. Key Title: 101 Gardening and
Outdoor Ideas.

635 AT ISSN 0085-8382
YOUR AUSTRALIAN GARDEN. 1965. irreg. price
varies. ‡ David G. Stead Memorial Wildlife
Research Foundation of Australia, Box 4840,
Sydney, N.S.W. 2001, Australia. Ed. Thistle Y.
Stead. bk. rev. circ. 3,000.

GARDENING AND HORTICULTURE — Abstracting, Bibliographies, Statistics

338.1 635 CN ISSN 0318-5184
CANADA. STATISTICS CANADA. SURVEY OF
CANADIAN NURSERY TRADES INDUSTRY/
ENQUETE SUR L'INDUSTRIE DES
PEPINIERES CANADIENNES. (Catalogue 22-
203) (Text in English and French) 1919. a.
Can.$4.50($5.40) Statistics Canada, Publications
Distribution, Ottawa, Ont. K1A 0V7, Canada. (also
avail. in microform from MML)

635 US
FARM AND GARDEN PERIODICALS ON
MICROFILM. 1978. a. Minnesota Scholarly Press,
Box 224, Mankato, MN 56001.

GERMANY (FEDERAL REPUBLIC, 1949-)
STATISTISCHES BUNDESAMT. FACHSERIE 3,
REIHE 3: PFLANZLICHE ERZEUGUNG. see
AGRICULTURE — Abstracting, Bibliographies,
Statistics

635 310 NE
LANDBOUW-ECONOMISCH INSTITUUT.
TUINBOUWCIJFERS. a. price varies. Landbouw-
Economisch Instituut, Conradkade 175, 2517 CL
The Hague, Netherlands.

GARDENING AND HORTICULTURE — Florist Trade

636.9 CN
CANADIAN FLORIST, KEITH'S DIRECTORY &
HORTICULTURAL GUIDE. 1932. a.
Can.$10($20) to florist trade. Horticulture
Publications Ltd., Box 697, Streetsville, Ont. L5M
2C2, Canada. Ed. W. E. Bowman. adv. circ. 2,250.

EDGAR BROOKES ACADEMIC AND HUMAN
FREEDOM LECTURE. see EDUCATION —
Higher Education

635 SI
NANYANG ORCHID. (Text in Chinese) 1966. a.
membership. Nanyang Orchid Association, 33
Phillip St., Singapore 0104, Singapore. Ed. Low
Siew Liap. adv. circ. 5,000. (back issues avail)

745.92 JA
TOKYO NO IKEBANA. (Text in Japanese) a. Tokyo-
to Kado Kyokai, c/o Shinkosha Bldg., 2-1-8 Koraku,
Bunkyo-ku, Tokyo, Japan. illus.
Flower arrangement

WHO'S WHO IN FLORICULTURE. see
BIOGRAPHY

GASTROENTEROLOGY

see Medical Sciences — Gastroenterology

GENEALOGY AND HERALDRY

929 CN
ALBERTA GENEALOGICAL SOCIETY.
ANCESTOR INDEX. 1975. a. Alberta
Genealogical Society, Box 12015, Edmonton, Alta.
T5J 3L2, Canada.
Formerly: Alberta Genealogical Society.
Surnames Register (ISSN 0704-9145)

929.6 US
AMERICAN HERALDIC CHALLENGER-
INFORMER. 1976. irreg. $7.50. Rte.1, Box 124A,
Crockett, TX 75835. illus.

929 CN
AMIS DE L'HISTOIRE DE LA PERADE.
COLLECTION "NOS VIELLES FAMILLES".
(Text in French) no. 2, 1973. irreg. Can.$3.90. Amis
de l'Histoire de la Perade, Case Postale 157, Sainte-
Anne de la Perade, Que. G0X 2J0, Canada. illus.
circ. 1,000.

929 FR ISSN 0066-2569
ANNUAIRE DE LA NOBLESSE DE FRANCE ET
D'EUROPE. 1843. Nobiliaire, 120 Av. du Roule,
92200 Neuilly sur Seine, France. Eds. M. Martin, J.
Koenig.

ASSOCIATION FOR GRAVESTONE STUDIES.
NEWSLETTER. see ART

929 US
BE-NE-LUX GENEALOGIST. 1977. irreg. $3.
Augustan Society, Inc., 1510 Cravens Ave.,
Torrance, CA 90501. bibl.

929 GW ISSN 0067-5261
BEITRAEGE ZUR WESTFAELISCHEN
FAMILIENFORSCHUNG. irreg. price varies.
(Westfaelische Gesellschaft fuer Genealogie und
Familienforschung) Aschendorffsche
Verlagsbuchhandlung, Soester Str. 13, 4400
Muenster, W. Germany (B.R.D.) Ed. August
Schroeder. bk. rev.

GENEALOGY AND HERALDRY

929   US
BIBB EAGLE. 3rd ed., 1977. irreg. membership. Bibb County Heritage Association, Box270, Brent, AL 35034. Ed. Frances Lynn Hamric. illus.

BIBLIOTHECA EMBLEMATICA. see *ART*

929   US
BOURLAND BULLETIN. vol. 2, 1978. irreg. Bourland Society, Box 2072, Warner Robins, GA 31093. illus.

928   UK
BURKE'S FAMILY INDEX. 1976. irreg. £8.50. Burke's Peerage Ltd., 56 Walton St., London SW3 1RB, England (Dist. in U.S. by: British Book Centre, Fairview Park, Elmsford, NY 10523) Ed. Hugh Montgomery-Massingberd.

929   UK
BURKE'S IRISH FAMILY RECORDS. 1976. irreg. £38($110) Burke's Peerage Ltd., 56 Walton St., London SW3 1RB, England (Dist. in U.S. by: British Book Centre, Fairview Park, Elmsford, N.Y. 10523) illus.

929   US
BUTSON FAMILY NEWSLETTER. 1979. irreg. $8 to institutions; individuals by donation. c/o W. Wesley Johnston, Ed., 1524 S. Holmes Ave., Springfield, IL 62704. charts.

929   AT   ISSN 0314-7894
CANDY FAMILY HISTORY NEWSLETTER. 1977. irreg. membership. c/o Philip C. Candy, 147 Seventh Ave., Royston Park, S.A. 5070, Australia.

929   UK   ISSN 0260-8391
CARAHER FAMILY HISTORY SOCIETY. JOURNAL. 1980. a. £2.50. Caraher Family History Society, Gowanlea, Willoughby St., Muthill, Perthshire PH5 2AB, Scotland.

929   FR
CENTRE GENEALOGIQUE DE MIDI-PROVENCE. CAHIER GENEALOGIQUE. 1973. irreg. price varies. Centre Genealogique de Midi-Provence, 13110 Port-de-Bouc, France. Ed. Yvan Malarte. circ. 300(controlled)

929   FR
CENTRE GENEALOGIQUE DU MIDI-PROVENCE. FICHES TECHNIQUES. 1978. irreg. price varies. Centre Genealogique du Midi-Provence, Centre Culturel Elsa Triolet, 13110 Port de Bouc, France. Ed. Yvan Malarte.

929   US
CRANE-CRANE BULLETIN. irreg. Elizabeth Prather Ellsberry, Box 206, Chillicothe, MO 64601. (processed)

929   US
CROVER FAMILY HISTORY AND GENEALOGY. 1975. a. $3. c/o Willard R. Berry, Ed., 609 Spruce Ave., Tillamook, OR 97141. adv. bk. rev.

929   DK   ISSN 0084-9561
DANMARKS ADELS AARBOG. 1886. biennial. Kr.160. J. H. Schultz Forlag, Vognmagergade 2, 1120 Copenhagen K, Denmark. Eds. Sven Houmoeller, Albert Fabritius. circ. 1,000.

929   US
DIRECTORY OF GENEALOGICAL SOCIETIES IN THE USA & CANADA. 1976. biennial. $8.50. 297 Cove Road, Pasadena, MD 21122. Ed. Mary K. Meyer. adv. circ. 1,500.

929   US
DIRECTORY OF PROFESSIONAL GENEALOGISTS AND RELATED SERVICES. 1979. irreg. $7.75 to non-members. Association of Professional Genealogists, Box 11601, Salt Lake City, UT 84147. (Co-sponsor: Utah Genealogical Association, Professional Genealogists Chapter)

929   US
EAST ASIAN GENEALOGIST. irreg. Augustan Society, Inc., 1510 Cravens Ave., Torrance, CA 90501.

929   US
EASTERN EUROPEAN GENEALOGIST. 1977. a. $7. Augustan Society, Inc., 1510 Cravens Ave., Torrance, CA 90501. Ed. Rodney Hartwell.

929   US
ELDER BREWSTER PRESS. 1979. a. membership. Brewster Society, c/o Chester Arthur Johnson, Ed., 5 Chestnut St., Binghamton, NY 13905 (Also c/o Robert Stevens, 20 Free St., Portland, ME 04101)

929   UK   ISSN 0140-7503
ESSEX FAMILY HISTORIAN. 1974. irreg. $4. Essex Society for Family History, 57 Coopers Hill, Ongar, Essex, England. Ed. Margaret Baker. bk. rev.

929   FR
ETAT DE LA NOBLESSE FRANCAISE SUBSISTANTE. 1972. a. 125 F. J. Dell'Acquo-Bascourt, Les Frenes 52, 55 Bd. de Charonne, 75011 Paris, France. circ. 300.

929   GW   ISSN 0014-7176
FAMILIENVERBAND AVENARIUS. FAMILIENZEITSCHRIFT. 1961. irreg. DM.20. Familienverband Avenarius e.V., Kampstrasse 6, 4520 Melle, W. Germany (B.R.D.) Ed. Gert Avenarius. charts. illus. stat. circ. 200. (tabloid format)

929   US
FAMILY NOTES: A JOURNAL OF THE HUECK FAMILIES. 1968. a. $10 to libraries. ‡ Hueck Family Association, 413 One Office Park Bldg, Mobile, AL 36609. Ed. George T. de Hueck. circ. 200.

929   US
FEDERATION OF GENEALOGICAL SOCIETIES. MONOGRAPH. 1976. irreg. Federation of Genealogical Societies, Chicago Regional Office, Box 743, Midlothian, IL 60445.

929   US   ISSN 0190-8189
FOLK AND KINFOLK OF HARRIS COUNTY. 1975. a. Harris County High School, Box 448, Hamilton, GA 38188. illus.

929   US   ISSN 0071-7738
FORT BELKNAP GENEALOGICAL ASSOCIATION. BULLETIN. 1962. a. $2. ‡ Fort Belknap Genealogical Association, Murray Rte., Graham, TX 76046. Ed. Barbara Ledbetter. circ. 100.

929   US
FRENCH GENEALOGIST. 1977. irreg. $6. Augustan Society, Inc., 1510 Cravens Ave., Torrance, CA 90501.

929   NE
FRYSKE NAMEN. 1978. irreg. Fryske Akademy, Doelestrjitte 8, 8911 DX Ljouwert/Leeuwarden, Netherlands. Ed.Bd.

929   US
GEESAMAN COUSINS. vol. 3, 1977. irreg. Geesaman Family Association, Box 175, Quincy, PA 17247. Eds. Richard F. Kirkpatrick, Bernadine N. Geesaman.

929   US
GENEALOGICAL SOCIETY OF GREATER MIAMI. NEWSLETTER. vol. 2, 1976. irreg. Genealogical Society of Greater Miami, 1100 S.W. 2nd Ave., Miami, FL 33130. Ed. Blanche E. Reinhardt. (processed)

929   GW   ISSN 0085-0934
GENEALOGISCHES HANDBUCH DES BAYERISCHEN ADELS. 1950. biennial. DM.80. (Vereinigung des Adels in Bayern) Verlag Degener und Co., Nuernberger Str. 27, Postfach 1340, 8530 Neustadt /Aisch, W. Germany (B.R.D.)

929   AU   ISSN 0073-1897
HERALDISCH-GENEALOGISCHE GESELLSCHAFT ADLER. JAHRBUCH. 1946. irreg., 3rd series, vol. 9, 1974/78. S.300. Heraldisch-Genealogische Gesellschaft Adler, Haarhof 4a, A-1010 Vienna, Austria.

HISTORISCHER VEREIN DES KANTONS BERN. ARCHIV. see *HISTORY — History Of Europe*

929.2   US   ISSN 0363-8847
HUDSON FAMILY ASSOCIATION, SOUTH. BULLETIN. irreg. Hudson Family Association (South), Route Seven, Del Monte Place, Longview, TX 75601. illus. Key Title: Bulletin - Hudson Family Association, South.

HUGUENOT HISTORIAN; a journal of Huguenot history and genealogy. see *HISTORY — History Of North And South America*

HUGUENOT SOCIETY OF LONDON. PROCEEDINGS. see *HISTORY*

HUGUENOT SOCIETY OF LONDON, QUARTO SERIES. see *HISTORY*

929   UK
I'ANSON TIMES. 1976. irreg. membership. c/o Thomas Henry Wolstencroft, 29 Meadowfield, Whaley Bridge, Stockport, Cheshire (England)

929   US   ISSN 0090-905X
IOWA GENEALOGICAL SOCIETY. SURNAME INDEX. 1973. irreg. $10. Iowa Genealogical Society, P.O. Box 3815, Des Moines, IA 50322 (Orders to: Mrs. Bertlyn C. Johnston, 1215 McKinley Dr., Ames, IA 50010) illus. circ. 1,200.

929   US
ITALIAN GENEALOGIST. 1977. irreg. $6. Augustan Society, Inc., 1510 Cravens Ave., Torrance, CA 90501.

929   UK   ISSN 0308-9037
KENT FAMILY HISTORY SOCIETY. RECORD PUBLICATION. 1976. irreg. Kent Family History Society, c/o Colin J. Perry, 53 St. Lawrence Forstal, Canterbury, Kent, England.

929   UK   ISSN 0140-9301
LEICESTERSHIRE FAMILY HISTORY CIRCLE. NEWSLETTER. no. 10, 1977. irreg. membership. Leicestershire Family History Circle, 11 Coniston Rd., Barrow-upon-Soar, Loughborough, Leics. LE12 8PS, England. Ed. Mrs. P. C. Baker. circ. 260.

929.6
LYLES OFFICIAL ARMS & ARMOUR REVIEW. a. $18.95. Apollo Book, 391 South Rd., Poughkeepsie, NY 12601.

929   CN
M G S NEWS. 1976. irreg. membership. Manitoba Genealogical Society, Box 2066, Winnipeg, Man. R3C 3R4, Canada.

929   US
MASH FAMILY BULLETIN. 1967. irreg. 3755 Robinhood Rd., Houston, TX 77005. Ed. Robert M. Hess. (processed)

929   NE
NIET ZO BENAUWD. (Summaries in English) 1959. a. fl.5($2) ‡ Stichting Familieclub Johannes van der Linden - Foundation Family Club Johannes van der Linden, c/o Guus van der Linden, Wagendwarsstraat 74, Utrecht, Netherlands. Ed. M. E. Leegwater-van der Linden. adv. illus. circ. 150 (controlled) (processed)

929   NR
NIGERIAN NAMES. 1972. irreg. Daystar Press, Box 1261, Ibadan, Nigeria.

929 913 940   UK   ISSN 0141-6340
NOMINA; a newsletter of name studies relating to Great Britain and Ireland. 1977. a. £1($3) English Name Studies, English Department, University of Hull, Hull, England. Ed. Peter McClure. bk. rev. bibl. circ. 165. (looseleaf format; back issues avail.)

929   DK
NORDISK FLAGGSKRIFT. no. 2, 1976. irreg. C. F. Pederson, Listedvej 84, Kastrup, Denmark.

929   US
NYE FAMILY NEWSLETTER. 1966. a. $3. Nye Family of America Association, East Sandwich, MA 02537. Ed. L. Bert Nye, Jr. illus. circ. 3,000.

PANORAMA. see *HISTORY — History Of Europe*

929   BE
PARCHEMIN. RECUEIL GENEALOGIQUE ET HERALDIQUE. 1952. a. price varies. Office Genealogique et Heraldique de Belgique, c/o Musees Royaux d'Art et d'Histoire, Parc du Cinquantenaire 10, B-1040 Brussels, Belgium. Ed. Chevalier Xavier de Ghellinck Vaernewyck. charts. illus. cum.index (1952-1960; 1961-1973)

929   US
ROBINSON NEWSLETTER. 1976. irreg. Genealogical Reference Builders, Box 249, Post Falls, ID 83854. Ed. Elaine Walker. (processed)

929.6   US
ROLL OF ARMS. no. 8, 1976. irreg. $12.50. New England Genealogical Society, Committee on Heraldry, 101 Newbury St., Boston, MA 02116. illus.

976   US
SEAHORN LORE. irreg. c/o Denton M. Starr, Route 1, Stilwell, OK 74960. illus.

929   US
SEELEY GENEALOGICAL SOCIETY (NEWSLETTER) vol. 23, 1976. irreg. Seely Genealogical Society, c/o Esther H. Houtz, Box 131, Allenspark, CO 80510. stat.

929 970
SONS AND DAUGHTERS OF THE SODDIES. REPORTS;* sod houses and dugouts in North America. 1955. irreg. (1-2/yr.) $2 (2 yrs) Sod House Society of America, Sod House Survey, Colby, KS 67701. Ed. R.E. Thiel. illus. stat. tr.lit. circ. 10,000. (processed)

929 977   US
SOUTHSUBKIN. vol. 5, 1977. irreg. South Suburban Genealogical and Historical Society, Box 96, South Holland, IL 60473. Ed. Willard Siville.

929   UK
TABARD. 1977. irreg. Bath Heraldic Society, 5 Bloomfield Ave., Bath BA2 3AB, England.

929
TOWNSEND SOCIETY OF AMERICA. NEWSLETTER. vol. 2, 1977. irreg. membership. Townsend Society of America, c/o Ethel Townsend, 14 Glen St., Glen Cove, NY 11542. (back issues avail.)

929   US   ISSN 0091-6455
TRAILS AND TALES. 1973. irreg. $2 per no. Upton Country Genealogical Society, P.O. Box 6, Rankin, TX 79778. Ed. Kaye Skiles. circ. 45.

929   US
ULSTER GENIE. 1976. irreg. Ulster County Genealogical Society, Box 84, Stone Ridge, NY 12484. (processed)

929   US   ISSN 0091-6706
WOOD - WOODS FAMILY MAGAZINE. 1973. a. $8. c/o Virginia W. Alexander, Ed., 903 Myers Ave., Columbia, TN 38401. bk. rev. circ. 300.

929   UK
YORKSHIRE ARCHAEOLOGICAL SOCIETY PARISH REGISTER SERIES. 1899. a. £10. Yorkshire Archaeological Society, Claremont, Clarendon Road, Leeds LS2 9NZ, England. Ed. D.J.H. Michelmore. index. circ. 300.

929   US   ISSN 0085-8390
YOUR TEXAS ANCESTORS. (Annual cumulation of weekly column in Fort Worth Star Telegram) 1968. a. $6. Fort Worth Star Telegram, P.O. Box 1870, Fort Worth, TX 76101. Ed. Damon Veach. adv. index. (processed)

GENEALOGY AND HERALDRY — Abstracting, Bibliographies, Statistics

929 016 026   US
FINDING AIDS TO THE MICROFILMED MANUSCRIPT COLLECTION OF THE GENEALOGICAL SOCIETY OF UTAH. 1978. irreg. price varies. University of Utah Press, Salt Lake City, UT 84112.

GENERAL INTEREST PERIODICALS — Africa

see also General Interest Periodicals — Libya; General Interest Periodicals — Malagasy Republic

GENERAL INTEREST PERIODICALS — Australasia

see also General Interest Periodicals — Oceania

GENERAL INTEREST PERIODICALS — Bangladesh

051   BG
DHAKA BISVABIDYALAYA PATRIKA. Added title: Dacca Visva Vidyalaya Patrika. (Text in Bengali) 1973. a. University of Dacca, Ramna, Dacca 2, Bangladesh.

GENERAL INTEREST PERIODICALS — Canada

054   CN   ISSN 0707-8021
POINT DE MIRE. (Text mainly in French) 1978. irreg. (3-4/yr) Can.$5. Federation Quebecoise de Tir, 1415 rue Jarry, E., Montreal, Que. H2E 2Z7, Canada. Ed. Danielle Evans. bk. rev. circ. 500. Formerly: Pistolier.

GENERAL INTEREST PERIODICALS — Central America

056.1   HO
HONDURAS AL DIA. (Text in English and Spanish) 1978. irreg. free. Junta Militar de Gobierno, Secretaria de Prensa, Apdo. Postal 403, Tegucigalpa, D.C., Honduras. Eds. Alma Luz Rodezno, Wilfredo Mayorga, Carlos Rivas.

056.1   CR
PENSAMIENTO COSTARRICENSE. 1977. irreg. Ministerio de Cultura, Juventud y Deportes, Dept. de Publicaciones, Apdo. 10227, San Jose, Costa Rica.

GENERAL INTEREST PERIODICALS — Colombia

056   CK
REVISTA UNIVERSIDAD LA GRAN COLOMBIA. N.S.1975. irreg. Universidad La Gran Colombia, Apartado Aereo No. 7909, Bogota, Colombia. Ed. Consuelo Zapata. illus.

GENERAL INTEREST PERIODICALS — Great Britain

942   UK
CAMBRIDGE TOWN, GOWN & COUNTY SERIES. 1976. irreg. price varies. Oleander Press, 17 Stansgate Ave., Cambridge CB2 2QZ, England (U.S. address: 210 Fifth Ave., New York, N.Y. 10010) Eds. Audrey Ward and Philip Ward. circ. 2,500.

GENERAL INTEREST PERIODICALS — India

059   II
ALOKA BHARATI. (Text in Hindi) 1971. a. Rs.22. K-15 Green Park, New Delhi 16, India. Ed. Bd. adv. charts. illus.

059   II
MADHYA PRADESH YEARBOOK. (Text in Hindi) 1973/74. a. Rs.32.50. c/o Kamla Kundra, E-32, 45 Bungalows, Bhopal 462003, India. Ed. Prakash Kundra. circ. 1,500.
Formerly: Madhya Pradesh Varshiki.

052   II
RABINDRA BHARATI JOURNAL. (Text in English) 1968. irreg., latest issue, 1973. Rs.2. Rabindra Bharati University, 6/4 Dwarkanath Tagore Lane, Calcutta 700007, India. Ed. Ramendranath Mullick. circ. 500.
Essays and poems

GENERAL INTEREST PERIODICALS — Indonesia

059   IO
SELECTION SKETSMASA. 1974. irreg. Rps.85. Jl. Kawung 2, Surabaya, Indonesia. adv. illus.
Supersedes: Selection; Sketsmasa.

GENERAL INTEREST PERIODICALS — Italy

055.1   IT
LECCIO - PRESS AGENCY. 1953. irreg. Mario Cesare Guidi, Ed. & Pub., Via di Cammori 54, 50145 Florence, Italy. adv. circ. 1,500. (reprint service avail. from UMI,ISI)

GENERAL INTEREST PERIODICALS — Libya

320.9   ZR
CAHIERS ZAIROIS DE LA RECHERCHE ET DU DEVELOPPEMENT. 1967. irreg. $8.00. Office National de la Recherche et du Developpement, B.P. 16706, Kinshasa, Zaire. bk. rev. illus. circ. 2,000.
Continues: Cahiers Congolais de la Recherche et du Developpement.

GENERAL INTEREST PERIODICALS — Malagasy Republic

916.9   MG
KIANJA.* (Text in French or Malagasy) 1972. irreg. FMG.200. B.P. 3153, Antananarivo, Malagasy Republic. stat.

GENERAL INTEREST PERIODICALS — Oceania

NEW GUINEA PERIODICAL INDEX; guide to current periodical literature about New Guinea. see *ABSTRACTING AND INDEXING SERVICES*

GENERAL INTEREST PERIODICALS — Pakistan

059   PK
SARANG MAGAZINE. (Text in English, Sindhi or Urdu) vol. 8, 1974. a. Sind Agriculture College, Tandojam, Pakistan.

GENERAL INTEREST PERIODICALS — Peru

056.1   PE   ISSN 0567-753X
ACTA HEREDIANA. 1968. a. Universidad Peruana Cayetano Heredia, Direccion de Biblioteca Publicaciones y Museos, Avda. Honorio Delgado 932, Apdo. 2563, Lima 100, Peru.

ORGANIZATION FOR ECONOMIC COOPERATION AND DEVELOPMENT. CATALOGUE OF PUBLICATIONS. see *BIBLIOGRAPHIES*

GENERAL INTEREST PERIODICALS — Puerto Rico

972.95   PR   ISSN 0033-4049
PUERTO RICO LIVING. 1963. a. $3.50. Box 6756, Loiza Sta., Santurce, PR 00914. Ed. Alex Glass. adv. illus. stat. circ. 10,000(6mos) (also avail. in microfilm from UMI)

GENERAL INTEREST PERIODICALS — Singapore

052   SI   ISSN 0585-3923
STRAITS TIMES ANNUAL. (Text in English) 1905. a. S.$6. Times Periodicals Private Ltd., 422 Thomson Rd., Singapore 1129, Singapore. bk. rev. circ. 47,000.

GENERAL INTEREST PERIODICALS — South America

see also *General Interest Periodicals— Colombia; General Interest Periodicals— Peru; General Interest Periodicals— Venezuela*

GENERAL INTEREST PERIODICALS — United States

979   US   ISSN 0191-328X
ALASKA TODAY. 1973. a. $20. University of Alaska, Department of Journalism and Broadcasting, Fairbanks, AK 99701. circ. 6,000.

051   US
BAY AREA MEN'S RESOURCE CATALOG. every 18 mos. $1.25. Bay Area Men's Resource Catalog Collective, Box 6072, San Francisco, CA 94101. adv. bibl. illus. tr.lit. circ. 6,000.

051   US
CONVERSATIONS WITH. 1977. irreg. $22 per no. Gale Research Company, Book Tower, Detroit, MI 48226. Eds. Matthew J. Bruccoli, C. E. Frazer Clark, Jr. illus.

973   US   ISSN 0017-3673
GREAT PLAINS JOURNAL. 1961. a. $7.50 includes s-a. newsletter. Museum of the Great Plains, Box 68, Lawton, OK 73502. Ed. Steve Wilson. adv. bk. rev. bibl. circ. 1,000. (tabloid format; also avail. in microform from UMI) Indexed: Hist.Abstr.

051   US
RESOURCES(CAMBRIDGE) 1974. irreg. $5 for 12 issues. Box 134, Harvard Square, Cambridge, MA 02138. Ed. Richard Gardner. bk. rev.

051   US
SPECTATOR. 1970. irreg. (2-5/yr) $5. Tasmania Press, Inc., 4375 Beverly Blvd., Los Angeles, CA 90004. Ed. Donald Mishell. circ. 100.

GENERAL INTEREST PERIODICALS — Venezuela

056.1   VE
ESTO ES VENEZUELA. a. Ediciones Castellon S.A., Edificio Malak, Calle Real de Sabana Grande, Caracas, Venezuela. Eds. Juan V. Guerra, Jose R.Aldaris.

GENERAL INTEREST PERIODICALS — West Indies

052   BB
CHALLENGES IN THE NEW CARIBBEAN. Also called: Issues in the New Caribbean. irreg. Cedar Press, Box 616, Bridgetown, Barbados, W.I. (Affiliate: Caribbean Conference of Churches)

GENETICS

see *Biology—Genetics*

GEOGRAPHY

see also *History; Travel and Tourism*

551   HU   ISSN 0567-7475
ACTA GEOGRAPHICA DEDRECINA. (Text in English, French, German, Hungarian, Russian) 1962. irreg., vol. 15, 1979. Kossuth Lajos Tudomanyegyetem, P.O. Box 9, H-4010 Debrecen, Hungary. Ed. L. Kadar.

910   PL   ISSN 0065-1249
ACTA GEOGRAPHICA LODZIENSIA. (Text in Polish; summaries in English and French) 1947. irreg., no. 41, 1979. price varies. Ossolineum, Publishing House of the Polish Academy of Sciences, Rynek 9, Wroclaw, Poland (Dist. by: Ars Polona - Ruch, Krakowskie Przedmiescie 7, Warsaw, Poland) Ed. Halina Klatkowa.

949.3   BE   ISSN 0065-1257
ACTA GEOGRAPHICA LOVANIENSIA. 1961. irreg., latest no. 16. price varies. Universite Catholique de Louvain, Institut de Geographie, Batiment Mercator, 3 Place Louis Pasteur, 1348 Louvain-la-Neuve, Belgium. Eds. Th. Brulard, M. Goosens. circ. 250. Indexed: Geo.Abstr.

ACTA HUMBOLDTIANA. SERIES GEOGRAPHICA ET ETHNOGRAPHICA. see *ANTHROPOLOGY*

ACTA PHYTOGEOGRAPHICA SUECICA. see *BIOLOGY — Botany*

910   HU   ISSN 0567-7467
ACTA UNIVERSITATIS SZEGEDIENSIS DE ATTILA JOZSEF NOMINATAE. ACTA GEOGRAPHICA. (Text in English, French and German) 1955. a. 100 Ft. exchange price. Jozsef Attila Tudomanyegyetem, Foldrajzi Tanszek, Egyetem U. 2, Szeged, Hungary (Subscr. to: Kultura, Box 149, H-1389 Budapest, Hungary) Ed. Gyula Krajko. bibl. charts. illus. circ. 500.

AFRICA SOUTH OF THE SAHARA. see *HISTORY — History Of Africa*

910   NR   ISSN 0065-4698
AHMADU BELLO UNIVERSITY. DEPARTMENT OF GEOGRAPHY. OCCASIONAL PAPER.* 1965. irreg. Ahmadu Bello University, Department of Geography, Zaria, Nigeria.

526.1   GE
AKADEMIE DER WISSENSCHAFTEN DER DDR. ZENTRALINSTITUT FUER PHYSIK DER ERDE. VEROEFFENTLICHUNGEN. 1949. irreg. exchange basis. Akademie der Wissenschaften der DDR, Zentralinstitut fuer Physik der Erde, Telegrafenberg A17, 45 Potsdam, E. Germany (D.D.R.) Ed. H. Kautzleben.
Formerly (1949-1969): Akademie der Wissenschaften der DDR. Geodaetisches Institut. Veroeffentlichungen (ISSN 0065-5015)

910   CN   ISSN 0065-6097
ALBERTAN GEOGRAPHER. 1965. a. Can.$1.25. ‡ University of Alberta, Department of Geography, Edmonton, Alta. T6G 2H4, Canada. circ. 300.

915   HK   ISSN 0072-4939
ALL-ASIA GUIDE. 1961. irreg. HK.$40($7.95) Far Eastern Economic Review Ltd., Box 160, Hong Kong, Hong Kong.
Formerly: Golden Guide to South and East Asia.

914   UK   ISSN 0065-6569
ALPINE JOURNAL. 1863. a. £8 hardcover; £6.50 paperback. ‡ Alpine Club, 74 S. Audley St., London W1Y 5FF, England. Ed. Edward Pyatt. adv. bk. rev. index. circ. 2,500. Indexed: Br.Hum.Ind.

526   US   ISSN 0161-0945
AMERICAN CONGRESS ON SURVEYING AND MAPPING. PROCEEDINGS. 1968. 2/yr. $50 includes journal Surveying and Mapping. ‡ American Congress on Surveying and Mapping, 210 Little Falls St., Falls Church, VA 22046. index. circ. 3,500.
Incorporating: American Congress on Surveying and Mapping. Papers from the Annual Meetings (ISSN 0065-7913)

910   US   ISSN 0065-8413
AMERICAN GEOGRAPHICAL SOCIETY OF NEW YORK. OCCASIONAL PUBLICATION. 1962. irreg., 1969, no. 4. price varies. ‡ American Geographical Society, Broadway at 156 St., New York, NY 10032.

910   US   ISSN 0065-8421
AMERICAN GEOGRAPHICAL SOCIETY OF NEW YORK. RESEARCH SERIES. 1921. irreg. price varies. ‡ American Geographical Society, Broadway at 156 St., New York, NY 10032.

910   US   ISSN 0065-843X
AMERICAN GEOGRAPHICAL SOCIETY OF NEW YORK. SPECIAL PUBLICATION. 1915. irreg. price varies. ‡ American Geographical Society, Broadway at 156 St., New York, NY 10032.

796.552   US
AMERICAN INSTITUTE FOR EXPLORATION. EXPEDITION FIELD REPORTS. 1955. a. $7 (including World Exploration) ‡ Quest Productions, 1809 Nichols Rd., Kalamazoo, MI 49007. (Co-Sponsors: American Heritage Research (California), Exploration Club of Hokkaido University (Japan)) Eds. Ted P. Bank, II, Jay Ellis Ransom. bk. rev. film rev. bibl. charts. illus. circ. 250 (controlled) Indexed: Biol.Abstr.

910   US
AMERICAN INSTITUTE FOR EXPLORATION. OCCASIONAL CONTRIBUTIONS. 1954. irreg. (approx. 1-2/yr.) $2-4 to non-members. Quest Productions, 1809 Nichols Rd., Kalamazoo, MI 49007. Eds. Ted Bank, Dr. Peter Hamill. bibl. charts. illus. circ. 1,000 (controlled) Indexed: Biol.Abstr.
Formerly: American Institute for Exploration. Occasional Papers.

910   US
AMERICAN INSTITUTE FOR EXPLORATION. REPRINT SERIES. 1960. irreg. (approx. 1-2/yr.) $2-4 to non-members. Quest Productions, 1809 Nichols Rd., Kalamazoo, MI 49007. Eds. Ted Bank, Dr. Peter Hamill. bibl. charts. illus. circ. 1,000 (controlled) Indexed: Biol.Abstr.

526.982   US   ISSN 0066-0663
AMERICAN SOCIETY OF PHOTOGRAMMETRY. TECHNICAL PAPERS FROM THE ANNUAL MEETING. a. $10 to non-members; members $5. American Society of Photogrammetry, 105 N. Virginia Ave., Falls Church, VA 22046. index. *Photogrammetry*

GEOGRAPHY

AMERICAN TRAIL SERIES. see *TRAVEL AND TOURISM*

910   MX
ANALES DE GEOGRAFIA. 1975. a. Universidad Nacional Autonoma de Mexico, Instituto de Geografia, Villa Obregon, Ciudad Universitaria, Mexico 20, D.F., Mexico. illus.

911   US
ANDREW H. CLARK SERIES IN THE HISTORICAL GEOGRAPHY OF NORTH AMERICA. irreg. price varies. Oxford University Press, 200 Madison Ave., New York, NY 10016 (And Ely House, 37 Dover St., London, W1X 4AH, England) Ed. Andrew H. Clark.

910 551   PL   ISSN 0137-1983
ANNALES UNIVERSITATIS MARIAE CURIE-SKLODOWSKA. SECTIO B. GEOGRAPHIA, GEOLOGIA, MINERALOGIA ET PETROGRAPHIA. (Text in Polish or English; summaries in English, French, German, Russian) 1946. a. Uniwersytet Marii Curie-Sklodowskiej, Plac Marii Curie-Sklodowskiej 5, 20-031 Lublin, Poland. Ed. A. Malicki. Indexed: Doc.Geogr. Geo.Abstr.

914.4   FR
ANNUAIRE DES NOTABLES REGIONAUX. 1975. Editions Dany Thibaud, 52 rue Labrouste, 75015 Paris, France.

919   US   ISSN 0066-4626
ANTARCTIC BIBLIOGRAPHY. 1965. every 18 mos. price varies. U. S. National Science Foundation, Office of Polar Programs, 10 First St., Washington, DC 20550. Ed. Geza T. Thuronyi. circ. 1,500.

919.9   US   ISSN 0066-4634
ANTARCTIC RESEARCH SERIES. 1964. irreg., no. 29,1978. price varies. American Geophysical Union, 2000 Florida Ave. N.W., Washington, DC 20009. Ed.Bd. (reprint service avail. from ISI)

919.8   AG   ISSN 0302-5691
ANTARTIDA. 1971. a. Instituto Antartico Argentino, Cerrito 1248, Buenos Aires, Argentina. Ed. Juan Alberto Nadaud. charts. illus.

910.02   US   ISSN 0066-4812
ANTIPODE: A RADICAL JOURNAL OF GEOGRAPHY. 1969. irreg. (approx. 3/yr.) $7-15 for 3 nos. Box 339, West Side Station, Worcester, MA 01602. Eds. Phillip O'Keefe, Richard Peet. bk. rev. circ. 2,000. (back issues avail.) Indexed: Alt.Press Ind.

917.203   MX
ANUARIO BAJA CALIFORNIA Y SUS HOMBRES. 1975. a. Mex.$500. Calle 1 no. 134, Apdo. Postal 3-500, Mexicali, B.C., Mexico. circ. 3,000.

ANUARIO GEOGRAFICO DEL PERU. see *HISTORY — History Of North And South America*

914.3   GW   ISSN 0373-7187
ARBEITEN ZUR RHEINISCHEN LANDESKUNDE. 1950. irreg. price varies. (Universitaet Bonn, Geographisches Institut) Ferd. Duemmlers Verlag, Postfach 1480-Kaiserstr. 31-37, D-5300 Bonn 1, W. Germany (B.R.D.)

919.8 500   CN   ISSN 0066-6971
ARCTIC INSTITUTE OF NORTH AMERICA. RESEARCH PAPER. 1959. irreg, latest no. 63, 1973. $2 per no., o.p. issues avail. on inter-library loan basis from Arctic Institute Library, Calgary. Arctic Institute of North America, University Library Tower, 2920 24th Ave. N.W., Calgary, Alta. T2N 1N4, Canada (And 3426 N. Washington Blvd., Arlington, VA 22201) (reprint service avail. from UMI)

526.9 625.72   US   ISSN 0066-7439
ARIZONA LAND SURVEYORS CONFERENCE. PROCEEDINGS.* 1954. biennial. $2. (American Congress on Surveying and Mapping, Arizona Section) University of Arizona, Civil Engineering Department, Engineering Experiment Station, Tuscon, AZ 85721.

910   US   ISSN 0571-5962
ASSOCIATION OF AMERICAN GEOGRAPHERS. HANDBOOK - DIRECTORY. 1956. irreg., latest 1978. price varies. Association of American Geographers, 1710 16th St., N.W., Washington, DC 20009. (reprint service avail. from UMI)

910   US   ISSN 0066-9393
ASSOCIATION OF AMERICAN GEOGRAPHERS. MONOGRAPH SERIES. 1959. irreg., no. 8, 1976. price varies. Association of American Geographers, 1710 16th St., N.W., Washington, DC 20009. (reprint service avail. from UMI)

912   CN   ISSN 0318-2851
ASSOCIATION OF CANADIAN MAP LIBRARIES. BULLETIN. (Text in English and French) 1969. q. membership. Association of Canadian Map Libraries, c/o National Map Collection, Public Archives of Canada, 395 Wellington St., Ottawa, Ont. K1A 0N3, Canada. circ. 350.
    Incorporating: Association of Canadian Map Libraries. Annual Conference Proceedings (ISSN 0066-9474); Formerly: Association of Canadian Map Libraries. Newsletter (ISSN 0066-9482)

910   JA   ISSN 0066-958X
ASSOCIATION OF JAPANESE GEOGRAPHERS. SPECIAL PUBLICATION. (Text in English) 1966. irreg., 1971, no. 2. price varies. Association of Japanese Geographers - Nippon Chiri Gakkai, c/o Japan Academic Societies Centre, 2-4-16 Yayoi, Bunkyo-ku, Tokyo 113, Japan. index.

910   US   ISSN 0066-9628
ASSOCIATION OF PACIFIC COAST GEOGRAPHERS. YEARBOOK. 1935. a. $7. Oregon State University Press, 101 Waldo Hall, Corvallis, OR 97331. Ed. James Scott. abstr, bibl, charts, illus. cum. index: vols. 27, 35 and 40. circ. 800. (also avail. in microform from UMI; back issues avail.)

917   US
ATLAS OF THE PACIFIC NORTHWEST. 1953. every 4-5 yrs., 6th, 1979. $20 clothbound; $8 paperback. Oregon State University Press, 101 Waldo Hall, Corvallis, OR 97331. Ed. Richard Highsmith Jr. chart. illus. stat.

AUSTRALIA. BUREAU OF MINERAL RESOURCES, GEOLOGY, AND GEOPHYSICS. PUBLICATIONS. see *BIBLIOGRAPHIES*

910   PL   ISSN 0067-2807
BADANIA FIZJOGRAFICZNE NAD POLSKA ZACHODNIA. SERIA A. GEOGRAFIA FIZYCZNA. (Text in Polish; summaries in English, French or German) 1948. irreg., vol. 26, 1973. price varies. (Poznanskie Towarzystwo Przyjaciol Nauk) Panstwowe Wydawnictwo Naukowe, Ul. Miodowa 10, Warsaw, Poland (Dist. by Ars Polona-Ruch, Krakowskie Przedmiescie 7, Warsaw, Poland) Ed. Bogumil Krygowski.

910   SZ   ISSN 0067-4486
BASLER BEITRAEGE ZUR GEOGRAPHIE. (Text in German; summaries in French or English) 1968. irreg. Verlag Wepf und Co., Eisengasse 5, CH-4001 Basel, Switzerland.

910   GE
BEITRAEGE ZUR GEOGRAPHIE. 1951. a. M.35. (Akademie der Wissenschaften der DDR, Institut fuer Geographie und Geooekologie) Akademie-Verlag, Leipziger Str. 3-4, 108 Berlin, E. Germany (D.D.R.)
    Formerly (until 1979): Akademie der Wissenschaften der DDR. Institut fuer Geographie und Geooekologie. Wissenschaftliche Veroeffentlichungen.

915   BG
BHUGOLA SAMAYIKI. (Text in Bengali) 1974. a. Tk.10. Bangladesh National Geographical Association, c/o Dept. of Geography, Dacca College, Dhanmondi, Dacca 2, Bangladesh.

BIOGEOGRAPHICA. see *ENVIRONMENTAL STUDIES*

910   UK   ISSN 0067-9232
BLOOMSBURY GEOGRAPHER. 1968. every 18 mos. 50p. University College London, Department of Geography, c/o Gareth M. Hadley, 25 Gordon St., London, WC1H OAH, England. circ. 450. (back issues avail.)

910   BL   ISSN 0006-6079
BOLETIM PAULISTA DE GEOGRAFIA. 1941. irreg; 2-3/yr. $2 (for 4 nos.) Associacao dos Geografos Brasileiros, Secao Regional de Sao Paulo, C.P. 8. 105, 01000 Sao Paulo, Brazil. Dir. Myrna T. Rego Viana. bibl. charts. illus. circ. 2,000. Indexed: Hist.Abstr.

910   GW   ISSN 0373-0468
BONNER GEOGRAPHISCHE ABHANDLUNGEN. 1948. irreg. price varies. Duemmlers Verlag, Postfach 1480-Kaiserstr. 31-37, D-5300 Bonn 1, W. Germany (B.R.D.)

BOOKS FOR YOUNG EXPLORERS SERIES. see *CHILDREN AND YOUTH — For*

910   GW   ISSN 0524-2444
BRAUNSCHWEIGER GEOGRAPHISCHE STUDIEN. 1964. irreg. price varies. Verlag Erich Goltze GmbH und Co. KG, Stresemannstr. 28, 3400 Goettingen, W. Germany (B.R.D.) Ed. Arno Beuermann.

912   US   ISSN 0068-1148
BRITANNICA ATLAS. (Text in English,French,German,Portuguese and Spanish) 1969. biennial. $59.50. Encyclopaedia Britannica, Inc., 425 N. Michigan Ave., Chicago, IL 60611. Ed. William A. Cleveland.

910   CN   ISSN 0068-1571
BRITISH COLUMBIA GEOGRAPHICAL SERIES: OCCASIONAL PAPERS IN GEOGRAPHY. 1960. irreg. price varies. ‡ (Canadian Association of Geographers, Western Division) Tantalus Research Ltd., P.O. Box 34248, Vancouver, B.C. V6J 4N8, Canada. Ed. W. G. Hardwick. circ. 300-500.

508.3   UK   ISSN 0521-1573
BRITISH SCHOOLS EXPLORING SOCIETY. REPORT. a. British Schools Exploring Society, 175 Temple Chamber, Temple Ave., London E.C. 44, England. illus.

BROADS BOOK. see *TRAVEL AND TOURISM*

910   BU   ISSN 0068-3744
BULGARSKA AKADEMIIA NA NAUKITE. GEOGRAFSKI INSTITUT. IZVESTIIA. (Summaries in various languages) 1951. irreg. 2.13 lv. per issue. Publishing House of the Bulgarian Academy of Sciences, Ul. Akad. G. Bonchev, 1113 Sofia, Bulgaria (Dist. by: Hemus, 6, Rouski Blvd., 1000 Sofia, Bulgaria) circ. 500.

910 301.3   UK   ISSN 0306-6142
C A T M O G. (Concepts and Techniques in Modern Geography) 1975. irreg. (5/yr approx.) price varies. Geo Books, c/o Geo Abstracts Ltd., University of East Anglia, Norwich NR4 7TJ, England. (back issues avail.)

526   US
C H C PUBLICATION. (Collection for the History of Cartography) vol. 5, 1976. irreg. California State University, Fullerton, Library, Special Collections Division, Fullerton, CA 92634.

910   FR   ISSN 0526-8133
CAHIERS DES EXPLORATEURS. 1957. a. membership only. Societe des Explorateurs et des Voyageurs Francais, 184 Bd. St. Germain, 75006 Paris, France.

910   UK   ISSN 0068-6654
CAMBRIDGE GEOGRAPHICAL STUDIES. 1969. irreg., no. 14, 1981. $39.50 for latest vol. Cambridge University Press, Box 110, Cambridge CB2 3RL, England (and 32 E. 57 St., New York, N.Y. 10022) Ed.Bd. index.

916.7   CM   ISSN 0301-7753
CAMEROON YEAR BOOK. (Text in English) 1973. a. 300 Fr.CFA. United Publishers, P.O. Box 200, Victoria, Cameroon. Ed. Jennie Gwellem. adv. illus. stat. circ. 10,000.

910   CN
CANADIAN ASSOCIATION OF GEOGRAPHERS. DIRECTORY. (Text in English and French) 1964. a. Can.$5. Canadian Association of Geographers, McGill University, 805 Sherbrooke St. W., Montreal, Que. H3A 2K6, Canada. Ed. B. M. Barr. circ. 1,400.
    Formerly: Canadian Association of Geographers. Newsletter (ISSN 0068-8312)

910   CN
CANADIAN CULTURE SERIES. 1974. irreg. price varies. Tantalus Research Ltd., P.O. Box 34248, 2405 Pine St., Vancouver, B.C. 46J 4N8, Canada. Ed. Francis C. Hardwick.

CARIBBEAN CONFERENCE SERIES. see HISTORY — *History Of North And South America*

910   US
CAROLINA GEOGRAPHICAL SYMPOSIUM. PAPERS. (Subseries of Studies in Geography) 1974. irreg., 4th, 1978. price varies. University of North Carolina at Chapel Hill, Department of Geography, 203 Saunders Hall, Chapel Hill, NC 27514.

CENTRE EUROPEEN D'ETUDES BURGONDO-MEDIANES. PUBLICATION. see HISTORY — *History Of Europe*

910   CN
COLLECTION "ATLAS". 1976. irreg. Can.$9. Editions Naaman, C.P. 697, Sherbrooke, Que. J1H 5K5, Canada.

916   FR   ISSN 0069-5378
COLLECTION ETUDES ET TRAVAUX DE LA REVUE "MEDITERRANEE". 1964. irreg. Universite d'Aix-Marseille I (Universite de Provence), Institut de Geographie, Service des Publications, 13621 Aix en Provence, France.

910   GW   ISSN 0588-3253
COLLOQUIUM GEOGRAPHICUM. 1952. irreg. price varies. (Geographisches Institut) Ferd. Duemmlers Verlag, Kaiserstr. 31, D-5300, Bonn 1, W. Germany (B.R.D.).

910   FR   ISSN 0071-8424
COMITE DES TRAVAUX HISTORIQUES ET SCIENTIFIQUES. SECTION DE GEOGRAPHIE. ACTES DU CONGRES NATIONAL DES SOCIETES SAVANTES. 1961 (Congress of 1960) a. price varies. Bibliotheque Nationale, 58 rue Richelieu, 75084 Paris Cedex 02, France. circ. 600.

COMITE NATIONAL FRANCAIS DE GEODESIE ET GEOPHYSIQUE. COMPTES-RENDUS. see EARTH SCIENCES — *Geophysics*

COMITE NATIONAL FRANCAIS DE GEODESIE ET GEOPHYSIQUE. RAPPORT NATIONAL FRANCAIS A L'U G G I. see EARTH SCIENCES — *Geophysics*

910   UK   ISSN 0069-7109
COMMONWEALTH INSTITUTE, LONDON. ANNUAL REPORT. 1926. a. free. ‡ Commonwealth Institute, Kensington High St., London W.8, England. Ed. F. Lightfoot. index. circ. controlled.

338   FR   ISSN 0396-2024
CONNAISSANCE DE L'OUEST. 1971. irreg. Association pour le Developpment Industriel de l'Ouest Atlantique, Immeuble Neptune, 44000 Nantes, France.

910   US
CONTEMPORARY PROBLEMS IN GEOGRAPHY. irreg. price varies. Oxford University Press, 200 Madison Ave., New York, NY 10016 (And Ely House, 37 Dover St., London W1X 4AH, England) Ed.Bd.

COSTA RICA. ARCHIVO NACIONAL. REVISTA. see HISTORY

910   SP   ISSN 0210-5462
CUADERNOS GEOGRAFICOS. (Includes: monographic supplements) (Text in Spanish; summaries in English, French) 1971. a. 650 ptas. Universidad de Granada, Secretariado de Publicaciones, Hospital Real, Granada, Spain. Ed. Francisco Villegas Molina.

918.3   CL
CUADERNOS GEOGRAFICOS DEL SUR. 1971. irreg. $2. Universidad de Concepcion, Departamento de Geografia, Casilla 1257, Concepcion, Chile.

526   GW   ISSN 0065-5309
DEUTSCHE GEODAETISCHE KOMMISSION. VEROEFFENTLICHUNGEN: REIHE A. THEORETISCHE GEODAESIE. 1952. irreg. price varies. Deutsche Geodaetische Kommission, Marstallplatz 8, 8000 Munich 22, W. Germany (B.R.D.)

526   GW   ISSN 0065-5317
DEUTSCHE GEODAETISCHE KOMMISSION. VEROEFFENTLICHUNGEN: REIHE B. ANGEWANDTE GEODAESIE. 1952. irreg. price varies. Deutsche Geodaetische Kommission, Marstallplatz 8, 8000 Munich 22, W. Germany (B.R.D.)

526   GW   ISSN 0065-5325
DEUTSCHE GEODAETISCHE KOMMISSION. VEROEFFENTLICHUNGEN: REIHE C. DISSERTATIONEN. 1952. irreg. price varies. Deutsche Geodaetische Kommission, Marstallplatz 8, 8000 Munich 22, W. Germany (B.R.D.)

526   GW   ISSN 0065-5333
DEUTSCHE GEODAETISCHE KOMMISSION. VEROEFFENTLICHUNGEN: REIHE D. TAFELWERKE. 1956. irreg. price varies. Deutsche Geodaetische Kommission, Marstallplatz 8, 8000 Munich 22, W. Germany (B.R.D.)

526   GW   ISSN 0065-5341
DEUTSCHE GEODAETISCHE KOMMISSION. VEROEFFENTLICHUNGEN: REIHE E. GESCHICHTE UND ENTWICKLUNG DER GEODAESIE. 1961. irreg. price varies. Deutsche Geodaetische Kommission, Marstallplatz 8, 8000 Munich 22, W. Germany (B.R.D.)

910   GW
DEUTSCHE GEOGRAPHISCHE BLAETTER. N.S. 1977. irreg. price varies. Uebersee-Museum, Bremen, Bahnhofsplatz 13, 2800 Bremen, W. Germany (B.R.D.)
Formerly: Uebersee-Museum, Bremen. Veroeffentlichungen. Reihe C: Geographie (ISSN 0341-9258)

910   US   ISSN 0012-3234
DIRECTIONS. 1953/54. a. $2. (New Jersey Council for Geographic Education) Glassboro State College, Department of Geography, Glassboro, NJ 08028. Ed. Charles Stansfield. adv. bk. rev. charts. illus. stat. circ. 700.

912   CN   ISSN 0070-5217
DIRECTORY OF CANADIAN MAP COLLECTIONS. (Text in English and French) 1969. irreg. Association of Canadian Map Libraries, c/o National Map Collection, Public Archives of Canada, 395 Wellington St., Ottawa, Ont. K1A 0N3, Canada. Ed. Lorraine Dubreuil.

DOCUMENTS DE CARTOGRAPHIE ECOLOGIQUE. see BIOLOGY

910   UK
DRUMLIN. 1955. a. 50p. c/o Department of Geography, University of Glasgow, Glasgow G12 8QQ, Scotland. Ed. G. Kennedy. circ. 300.

916.76   UG   ISSN 0070-7961
EAST AFRICAN GEOGRAPHICAL REVIEW. 1963. a. $8. Uganda Geographical Association, P.O. Box 7062, Kampala, Uganda. Ed. J. B. Kabera. adv. bk. rev. circ. 1,000.

917   US   ISSN 0070-8127
EAST LAKES GEOGRAPHER. 1964. a. $3. Bowling Green State University, Department of Geography, Bowling Green, OH 43403. (Co-sponsor: Association of American Geographers, East Lakes Division) Ed. John Hiltner. circ. 500.

910   US   ISSN 0531-786X
ECUMENE; a geographical publication of East Texas State University. 1968. a. $5 for 2 nos. East Texas State University, Box 3036, E.T. Sta., Commerce, TX 75428. Ed. John A. Johnson. charts. illus. circ. 300.

910   US
ENCYCLOPEDIA OF GEOGRAPHIC INFORMATION SOURCES. (Companion to Encyclopedia of Business Information Sources) irreg., 3rd edt., 1978. Gale Research Company, Book Tower, Detroit, MI 48226. Ed. Paul Wasserman.

ENVIRONMENTAL ASSESSMENT OF THE ALASKAN CONTINENTAL SHELF. ANNUAL REPORTS SUMMARY. see ENVIRONMENTAL STUDIES

910   GW   ISSN 0425-1741
ERDKUNDLICHES WISSEN; Schriftenfolge fuer Forschung und Praxis. (Supplement to Geographische Zeitschrift) 1952. irreg., vol. 54, 1981. price varies. Franz Steiner Verlag GmbH, Friedrichstr. 24, Postfach 5529, 6200 Wiesbaden, W. Germany (B.R.D.) Eds. Emil Meynen, Ernst Plewe.

ERETZ-ISRAEL. ARCHAEOLOGICAL, HISTORICAL AND GEOGRAPHICAL STUDIES. see ARCHAEOLOGY

FAR EAST AND AUSTRALASIA. see HISTORY — *History Of Australasia And Other Areas*

910   HU   ISSN 0071-6642
FOLDRAJZI MONOGRAFIAK. (Text in Hungarian; occasional summaries in French, German or Russian) 1955. irreg. price varies. (Magyar Tudomanyos Akademia) Akademiai Kiado, Publishing House of the Hungarian Academy of Sciences, P.O. Box 24, H-1363 Budapest, Hungary.

910   HU   ISSN 0071-6650
FOLDRAJZI TANULMANYOK. 1964. irreg. price varies. (Magyar Tudomanyos Akademia) Akademiai Kiado, Publishing House of the Hungarian Academy of Sciences, P.O. Box 24, H-1363 Budapest, Hungary.

910   PL   ISSN 0071-6707
FOLIA GEOGRAPHICA. GEOGRAPHICA-OECONOMICA. (Text in Polish; summaries in English) 1968. a. 40 Zl. (Polska Akademia Nauk, Oddzial w Krakowie, Komisja Nauk Geograficznych) Ossolineum, Publishing House of the Polish Academy of Sciences, Rynek 9, Wroclaw, Poland. Ed. Antoni Wrzosek.

910   PL   ISSN 0071-6715
FOLIA GEOGRAPHICA. GEOGRAPHICA-PHYSICA. (Text in Polish; summaries in English) 1967. a. 30 Zl. (Polska Akademia Nauk, Oddzial w Krakowie, Komisja Nauk Geograficznych) Ossolineum, Publishing House of the Polish Academy of Sciences, Rynek 9, Wroclaw, Poland. Ed. Mieczyslaw Klimaszewski. circ. 600.

914   DK   ISSN 0071-6693
FOLIA GEOGRAPHICA DANICA. (Text in Danish and English; summaries in English and Danish) 1940. irreg., (approx. 1 per year) price varies. Kongelige Danske Geografiske Selskab - Royal Danish Geographical Society, Haraldsgade 68, DK-2100 Copenhagen OE, Denmark (Subscr. to: C. A. Reitzels Forlag, Noerre Soegade 35, DK-1370 Copenhagen K, Denmark) Ed. Dr. N. Kingo Jacobsen. abstr. bibl. charts. illus. (reprint service avail. from UMI) Indexed: Geo.Abstr.

526.982   SW   ISSN 0071-8068
FOTOGRAMMETRISKA MEDDELANDEN/ PHOTOGRAMMETRIC INFORMATION. (Text in English, German, Swedish; summaries in English) 1944. irreg. Kr.40. Kungliga Tekniska Hoegskolan, Institutionen foer Fotogrammetri - Royal Institute of Technology, Department of Photogrammetry, S-100 44 Stockholm 70, Sweden. Ed. Kennert Torlegaard. cum.index: 1944-69. circ. 200.
Photogrammetry

FOTOINTERPRETACJA W GEOGRAFII. see PHOTOGRAPHY

914   GW   ISSN 0071-8173
FRAENKISCHE GEOGRAPHISCHE GESELLSCHAFT. MITTEILUNGEN. 1954. a, or biennial. price varies. Fraenkische Geographische Gesellschaft, Kochstr. 4, D-8520 Erlangen, W. Germany (B.R.D.) Ed. F. Linnenberg. adv. bk. rev. circ. 1,000.

910   FR   ISSN 0071-8432
FRANCE. COMITE DES TRAVAUX HISTORIQUES ET SCIENTIFIQUES. SECTION DE GEOGRAPHIE. BULLETIN. 1913. irreg., vol. 83, 1978. price varies. Bibliotheque Nationale, 58, rue de Richelieu, 75084 Paris Cedex 02, 58 rue Richelieu. cum.index: 1886-1916. circ. 650. (back issues available)

526.8 910   FR   ISSN 0071-8262
FRANCE. SERVICE DE DOCUMENTATION ET DE CARTOGRAPHIE GEOGRAPHIQUES. MEMOIRES ET DOCUMENTS. 1966 N.S. irreg. price varies. Centre National de la Recherche Scientifique, 15 Quai Anatole-France, 75700 Paris, France.

910   GW   ISSN 0071-9234
FRANKFURTER GEOGRAPHISCHE HEFTE. irreg. price varies. (Frankfurter Geographische Gesellschaft) Verlag Dr. Waldemar Kramer, Bornheimer Landwehr 57a, 6000 Frankfurt 60, W. Germany (B.R.D.)

910   GW   ISSN 0071-9447
FREIBURGER GEOGRAPHISCHE HEFTE. 1963. irreg., vol. 17, 1980. price varies. Universitaet Freiburg, Geographisches Institut, Werderring 4, 7800 Freiburg, W. Germany (B.R.D.) Ed. W. Weischet.

910   SP
FUENTES CARTOGRAFICAS ESPANOLAS. irreg. 200 ptas.($3-4) per copy. Instituto de Geografia Aplicada, Serrano 115, Madrid-6, Spain. circ. 1,500. (tabloid format)

GALLIA PREHISTOIRE. SUPPLEMENT. see ARCHAEOLOGY

917.1   CN   ISSN 0576-1999
GAZETTEER OF CANADA. (Text in English; some issues have text in English and French) 1952. irreg. price varies. Permanent Committee on Geographical Names, Surveys and Mapping Branch, c/o Dept. of Energy, Mines and Resources, Ottawa, Ont., Canada (Orders to: Canadian Government Publishing Centre, Department of Supply and Services, Hull, Que. K1A 0S9, Canada) maps.

910   UK
GEO ABSTRACTS. ANNUAL INDEX. 1972. a. price varies. Geo Abstracts Ltd., University of East Anglia, Norwich NR4 7TJ, England.
Continues: Geographical Abstracts: Annual Index.

910   PL
GEOGRAFIA. (Text in Polish; summaries in English and German) 1957. irreg. Uniwersytet im. Adama Mickiewicza w Poznaniu, Stalingradzka 1, 61-712 Poznan, Poland. (also avail. in microfilm)
Formerly: Uniwersytet im. Adama Mickiewicza w Poznaniu. Wydzial Biologii i Nauk o Ziemi. Zeszyty Naukowe. Geografia (ISSN 0554-8063)

526   BL   ISSN 0100-7912
GEOGRAFIA. (Text in Portuguese: summaries in English and French) 1976. s-a. $10 or exchange. Associacao de Geografia Teoretica, Caixa Postal 178, 13500 Rio Claro, Brazil. Eds. A. Christofoletti, L.H.O. Gerardi, M.C. Sanchez. Indexed: Ref.Zh. Geo.Abstr.

900   AG
GEOGRAFICA. 1972. a.; no. 3, 1974. $4. ‡
Universidad Nacional del Nordeste, Instituto de Geografia, Las Heras, 727, Resistencia, Argentina. Ed.Bd. illus. circ. 1,000.

910 550   UR   ISSN 0072-0976
GEOGRAFIJA IR GEOLOGIJA. (Proceedings of the Lithuanian High Schools: Lietuvos TSR Aukstuju Mokyklu Mokslo Darbai) (Text in Lithuanian; summaries in German and Russian) 1961. irreg. $2. Vilnius Universitet, Ciurlionio g-ve 21/27, Vilnius 31, U.S.S.R. Ed. A. Basalykas. Indexed: Ref.Zh.

910   UR   ISSN 0072-0917
GEOGRAFINIS METRASTIS/GEOGRAPHICAL ANNUAL. (Text in Lithuanian; summaries in English, German and Russian) 1958. irreg. price varies. Akademiya Nauk Litovskoi S. S. R., Lenino Prospektas 3, Vilnius, U.S.S.R. Ed. K. Bieliukas.

910   UK   ISSN 0308-6992
GEOGRAPHERS; biobibliographical studies. 1977. a. price varies. (International Geographical Union, Commission on the History of Geographical Thought) Mansell Publishing, 3 Bloomsbury Place, London WC1A 2QA, England (Dist. in U.S. by: Mansell, Merrimack Book Service, 99 Main St., Salem, NH 03079) Eds. T.W. Freeman, Philippe Pinchemel.

910 610   HU   ISSN 0435-3730
GEOGRAPHIA MEDICA. Title varies: Geographia Medica Hungarica. 1970. a. (approx.) $6. Magyar Foldrajzi Tarsasag, Nepkoztarsasag utja 62, Budapest, Hungary (Subscr. to: Kultura, Box 149, H-1389 Budapest, Hungary) Ed. Illes Desi.

910   MY
GEOGRAPHICA. (Text in English) 1965. a. M.$3.50($4) University of Malaya, Geographical Society, Kuala Lumpur 22-11, Malaya. adv. bibl. charts. illus. circ. 500.

GEOGRAPHICAL EDUCATION. see EDUCATION — Teaching Methods And Curriculum

914.2   UK   ISSN 0078-2084
GEOGRAPHICAL FIELD GROUP (NOTTINGHAM). REGIONAL STUDIES. 1957. irreg., no. 19, 1975. price varies. Geographical Field Group, University of Nottingham, Dept. of Geography, Nottingham NG7 2RD, England. Ed. P. T. Wheeler. circ. 500.

910   NP
GEOGRAPHICAL JOURNAL OF NEPAL. 1978. a. Rs.15($2.50) Tribhuvan University, Geography Instruction Committee, Kirtipur, Nepal.

910   II   ISSN 0072-0925
GEOGRAPHICAL OBSERVER. (Text in English and Hindi) 1965. a. Rs.15($5) plus postage. Meerut College Geographical Society, c/o Department of Geography, Meerut College, Meerut, Uttar Pradesh, India. Ed. V. S. Chauhan. Indexed: Doc.Geogr. Geo.Abstr.

910   GW   ISSN 0072-0941
GEOGRAPHISCHE GESELLSCHAFT, MUNICH. MITTEILUNGEN. 1900. a. DM.50. Geographische Gesellschaft e.V., Muenchen, Heinrich Voglstr. 7, 8000 Munich 71, W. Germany (B.R.D.) Ed. Hans Fehn. bk. rev. circ. 600.

910   GE   ISSN 0072-095X
GEOGRAPHISCHES JAHRBUCH. a. VEB Hermann Haack, Geographisch-Kartographische Anstalt Gotha-Leipzig, Justus-Pertes-Str. 3-9, 58 Gotha, E. Germany (D.D.R.)

910   GW   ISSN 0072-0968
GEOGRAPHISCHES TASCHENBUCH. 1949. irreg., 1981/82. price varies. Franz Steiner Verlag GmbH, Postfach 5529, Friedrichstr. 24, 6200 Wiesbaden, W. Germany (B.R.D.) Eds. Emil Meynen, Eckhart Ehlers.

914   UK
GEOGRAPHY OF THE BRITISH ISLES SERIES. irreg. price varies. Cambridge University Press, Box 110, Cambridge CB2 3RL, England (And 32 E. 57th St., New York NY 10022) Ed. A. V. Hardy.

910   HU
GEOGRAPHY OF WORLD AGRICULTURE. (Text in English) 1972. irreg., vol. 7, 1977. price varies. (Magyar Tudomanyos Akademia) Akademiai Kiado, Publishing House of the Hungarian Academy of Sciences, P.O. Box 24, H-1363 Budapest, Hungary.

910   US   ISSN 0418-3975
GEOGRAPHY PUBLICATIONS AT DARTMOUTH. 1964. irreg., latest, no. 10. price varies. Dartmouth College, Department of Geography, Hanover, NH 03755. Eds. Robert E. Huke, John W. Sommer. circ. 750.

916   GH   ISSN 0016-9536
GHANA GEOGRAPHICAL ASSOCIATION. BULLETIN. 1957. a. membership. Ghana Geographical Association, University of Ghana, Department of Geography, Legon, Accra, Ghana. Ed. E. Ardayfio-Schandorf. adv. bk. rev. circ. 500.

526   AU   ISSN 0436-0664
GLOBUSFREUND. (Text in English, French, German; summaries in Russian) 1952. irreg., 1-3/yr. membership. Internationale Coronelli-Gesellschaft fuer Globen- und Instrumentenkunde, Schwindgasse 6, A-1040 Vienna, Austria. bk. rev. charts. illus. stat. index.

910   US   ISSN 0072-8497
GUIDE TO GRADUATE DEPARTMENTS OF GEOGRAPHY IN THE UNITED STATES AND CANADA. a. $6. Association of American Geographers, 1710 16th St., N.W., Washington, DC 20009. Ed. Teresa Mulloy. (reprint service avail. from UMI)

526   US   ISSN 0073-0610
HARVARD PAPERS IN THEORETICAL GEOGRAPHY. 1967. irreg., no. 57, 1972. price varies. Harvard University, Laboratory for Computer Graphics and Spatial Analysis, Graduate School of Design, 520 Gund Hall, 48 Quincy St., Cambridge, MA 02138. circ. 500.

910   NP
HIMALAYAN REVIEW. (Text in English) 1968. a. Rs.10($1.00) Nepal Geographical Society, Tribhuvan University, Dept. of Geography, Tripureswar, Kathmandu, Nepal. Ed. Mangal S. Mananchar. adv. bk. rev. bibl. circ. 1,000.

911   UK   ISSN 0143-683X
HISTORICAL GEOGRAPHY RESEARCH SERIES. 1979. irreg (3-4/yr) Geo Books, c/o Geo Abstracts Ltd., University of East Anglia, Norwich NR4 7TJ, England.

900   FR   ISSN 0073-3202
HOMMES ET LA TERRE. 1956. irreg. price varies. Editions de l' Ecole des Hautes Etudes en Sciences Sociales, 131 Bd. Saint Michel, F-75005 Paris, France, France.

910   HK
HONG KONG GEOGRAPHICAL ASSOCIATION. BULLETIN. 1971. a. membership. Hong Kong Geographical Association, Dept of Geography and Geology, Hong Kong University, Hong Kong, Hong Kong. Ed. Lam Kia Che. adv. bk. rev. charts. illus. circ. 400(controlled)

914.3   GW   ISSN 0441-5302
HYDRONYMIA GERMANIAE. irreg., vol. 12, 1978. price varies. (Akademie der Wissenschaften und Literatur, Mainz) Franz Steiner Verlag GmbH, Friedrichstr. 24, Postfach 5529, 6200 Wiesbaden, W. Germany (B.R.D.) Ed.Wolfgang P. Schmid.

526.9   NE   ISSN 0536-2113
I T C INFORMATION BOOKLETS. 1961. irreg. free. International Institute for Aerial Survey and Earth Sciences, Box 6, 7500 AA Enschede, Netherlands.

526.9   NE   ISSN 0074-915X
I T C - PUBLICATIONS. SERIES A (PHOTOGRAMMETRY) (International Training Centre for Aerial Survey) (Some numbers are issued combined with ITC - Publications, Series B (Photo-Interpretation), and are called ITC-Publications, Series A/B) 1960. irreg.; latest issue, 1974. price varies. International Institute for Aerial Survey and Earth Sciences, Box 6, 7500 AA Enschede, Netherlands. (back issues avail.)

526.9   NE   ISSN 0539-0893
I T C PUBLICATIONS. SERIES B. PHOTO-INTERPRETATION. 1960. irreg. price varies. International Institute for Aerial Survey and Earth Sciences, Box 6, Enschede, Netherlands.

910   MY
ILMU ALAM. (Text and summaries in Malay and English) 1972. a. M.$9($4) National University of Malaysia, Department of Geography, Bangi, Selangor, Malaysia. (Co-sponsor: Geographical Society of the National University of Malaysia) Ed. Abd. Hamid Abdullah. bk. rev. circ. 400. Indexed: Geo.Abstr.

910   UK   ISSN 0308-5694
IMAGO MVNDI; a review of early cartography. (Text and summaries in English) 1935. a. fl.10($25) (Calouste Gulbenkian Foundation, PO) Imago Mundi Ltd., c/o Hary Margary, Lympne Castle, Kent, England. Ed. C. Koeman. adv. bk. rev. charts. illus. circ. 400.

917.3 557   US   ISSN 0073-6937
INDIANA STATE UNIVERSITY. DEPARTMENT OF GEOGRAPHY AND GEOLOGY. PROFESSIONAL PAPERS. 1968. a. price varies. Indiana State University, Department of Geography and Geology, Terre Haute, IN 47809. Ed. B.K. Barton. circ. 1,000.

GEOGRAPHY

910 US ISSN 0073-6953
INDIANA UNIVERSITY. DEPARTMENT OF GEOGRAPHY. GEOGRAPHIC MONOGRAPH SERIES. 1966. irreg. Indiana University, Department of Geography, Kirkwood Hall 208, Bloomington, IN 47401.

526 GW ISSN 0071-9196
INSTITUT FUER ANGEWANDTE GEODAESIE. MITTEILUNGEN. 1952. irreg. price varies. Institut fuer Angewandte Geodaesie, Richard-Strauss-Allee 11, 6000 Frankfurt 70, W. Germany (B.R.D.) circ. 700.

916.75 526.8 ZR ISSN 0443-3173
INSTITUT GEOGRAPHIQUE DU ZAIRE. RAPPORT ANNUEL. 1953. a. Institut Geographique du Zaire, B.P. 3086, Kinshasa, Zaire. illus.
   Continues: Institut Geographique du Congo. Rapport.

910 UK ISSN 0073-9006
INSTITUTE OF BRITISH GEOGRAPHERS. SPECIAL PUBLICATION. (Text in English; summaries in English, French and German) 1968. a. price varies. Institute of British Geographers, 1, Kensington Gore, London SW7 2AR, England. Indexed: Geo.Abstr.

918.602 CK
INSTITUTO GEOGRAFICO AGUSTIN CODAZZI. INFORME DE LABORES. a. Instituto Geografico Agustin Codazzi, Carrera 30 No. 48-51, Apdo. Aero 6721, Bogota, Colombia. illus.

914 RM
INSTITUTUL PEDAGOGIC ORADEA. LUCRARI STIINTIFICE: SERIA GEOGRAFIE. (Continues in part its Lucrari Stiintifice: Seria A and Seria B (1969-70), and its Lucrari Stiintifice (1967-68)) (Text in Rumanian, occasionally in English or French; summaries in Rumanian, French, English or German) 1967. a. Institutul Pedagogic Oradea, Calea Armatei Rosii Nr. 5, Oradea, Romania.

526 GR ISSN 0081-0312
INTERNATIONAL ASSOCIATION OF GEODESY. CENTRAL BUREAU FOR SATELLITE GEODESY. INFORMATION BULLETIN. 1966. irreg. International Association of Geodesy, Central Bureau for Satellite Geodesy, National Technical University, K. Zographou 9, Athens 624, Greece.

526 BE ISSN 0542-6766
INTERNATIONAL ASSOCIATION OF GEODESY. COMMISSION PERMANENTE DES MAREES TERRESTRES. MAREES TERRESTRES BULLETIN D'INFORMATION. 1957. irreg. 500 Fr. International Association of Geodesy, Commission Permanente des Marees Terrestres, c/o Observatoire Royal de Belgique, 3 Avenue Circulaire, 1180 Brussels, Belgium. Ed. P. Melchior.

910 UR ISSN 0074-6134
INTERNATIONAL GEOGRAPHICAL UNION. REPORT OF CONGRESS. 1968. quadrennial; 23rd, Moscow 1976. ‡ International Geographical Union, Inquire: Dr. Yuri/Medvedkov.,Sec. Gen., Soviet Organizing Committee, Staromonetnyi Per. 29, Moscow 109017, U.S.S.R. circ. 2,000.

910 AU ISSN 0074-8471
INTERNATIONAL SOCIETY FOR RESEARCH ON THE MOORS. REPORT OF CONGRESS.* irreg., 1970, 10th Rome. International Society for Research on the Moors, Graben 2, Postf. 67, A-4810 Gmunden, Austria.

INTERNATIONAL STRAITS OF THE WORLD. see *POLITICAL SCIENCE — International Relations*

526 551 CN ISSN 0539-1016
INTERNATIONAL UNION OF GEODESY AND GEOPHYSICS. MONOGRAPH.* (Text in English and French) irreg. International Union of Geodesy and Geophysics, University of Toronto, Geophysics Laboratory, Toronto 5, Canada.

526 551 FR ISSN 0074-9419
INTERNATIONAL UNION OF GEODESY AND GEOPHYSICS. PROCEEDINGS OF THE GENERAL ASSEMBLY. (Text in English and French) 1921. quadrennial. $16. International Union of Geodesy and Geophysics, Publications Office, 39 ter rue Gay Lussac, 75005 Paris, France. circ. 3,000.

526.8 GW ISSN 0341-0986
INTERNATIONALES JAHRBUCH FUER KARTOGRAPHIE. (Text in English, French, German) 1961. a. DM.60 price varies. (International Cartographic Association) Kirschbaum Verlag, Siegfriedstr. 28, Postfach 210209, 5300 Bonn 2, W. Germany (B.R.D.) Ed. K.-H. Meine. circ. 2,000.

919.8 NE ISSN 0074-1035
INTER-NORD; REVUE INTERNATIONALE D'ETUDES ARCTIQUES ET NORDIQUES. (Text in English and French) 1960. a(in 2 pts) (Fondation Francaise d'Etudes Nordiques, FR) Mouton Publishers, Noordeinde 41, 2514 GC The Hague, Netherlands (U.S. addr.: Mouton Publishers, c/o Walter de Gruyter, Inc., 200 Saw Mill River Road, Hawthorne, NY 10532) Ed. Jean Malaurie. adv. bk. rev. circ. 400.

914 IE ISSN 0075-0778
IRISH GEOGRAPHY; bulletin of the Geographical Society of Ireland. 1944. a. £6($11) Geographical Society of Ireland, Department of Geography, Trinity College, Dublin 2, Ireland. Ed. John H. Andrews. bk. rev. circ. 750. Indexed: Geo.Abstr.

910.5 SA
ISIZWE. 1974. a. University of Natal, Students Geographical Society, Durban, South Africa. illus.

526.8 IS
ISRAEL. DEPARTMENT OF SURVEYS. CARTOGRAPHIC PAPERS. (Text in Hebrew; with English abstracts) 1965. irreg. $1 per no. Department of Surveys, P.O.B. 14171, Tel-Aviv 61140, Israel. Ed. N. Kadmon.

526.8 IS ISSN 0075-1138
ISRAEL. DEPARTMENT OF SURVEYS. GEODETIC PAPERS. (Text in Hebrew; summaries in English) 1965. irreg. $1 per no. Department of Surveys, P. O. B. 14171, Tel Aviv 61140, Israel. Ed. N. Kadmon.

526.8 IS
ISRAEL. DEPARTMENT OF SURVEYS. PHOTOGRAMMETRIC PAPERS. (Text in Hebrew; with English Abstract) 1976. irreg. $1 per no. Department of Surveys, P.O.B. 14171, Tel-Aviv 61140, Israel.

913 SZ ISSN 0075-2002
ITINERA ROMANA; Beitraege zur Strassengeschichte des roemischen Reiches. 1967. irreg. price varies. Kuemmerly und Frey AG, Hallerstrasse 6-10, CH-3001 Berne, Switzerland. Ed. Gerold Walser.

910 NZ ISSN 0075-210X
J. T. STEWART LECTURE IN PLANNING. 1967. a. price varies. ‡ New Zealand Geographical Society (Inc.), Manawatu Branch, c/o Dept. of Geography, Massey University, Palmerston North, New Zealand.

910 AT
JAMES COOK UNIVERSITY OF NORTH QUEENSLAND. DEPARTMENT OF GEOGRAPHY. MONOGRAPH SERIES. 1970. irreg (approx. 2/yr) price varies. James Cook University of North Queensland, Department of Geography, Box 999, Douglas 4811, Australia. Ed. Dr. David Hopley. circ. 300. Indexed: Geo.Abstr.

914.3 GW ISSN 0075-4528
JUGENDHERBERGS-VERZEICHNIS. 1920. a. DM.4. Deutsches Jugendherbergswerk, Buelowstr. 26, 4930 Detmold 1, W. Germany (B.R.D.) Ed. Bert Pichel.

JUNIOR EAGLE. see *SOCIAL SCIENCES: COMPREHENSIVE WORKS*

917 US
KANSAS GEOGRAPHER. 1958. a. free. Kansas Council for Geographic Education, c/o Dept. of Geography, Kansas State University, Manhattan, KS 66506. Ed. Stephen L. Stover. circ. 600.

900 910 GW
LAENDERMONOGRAPHIEN. 1969. irreg. price varies. (Institut fuer Auslandsbeziehungen, Stuttgart) Horst Erdmann Verlag, Hartmeyerstr. 117, Postfach 1380, 7400 Tuebingen, W. Germany (B.R.D.) circ. 4,000.

912 GW ISSN 0457-0715
LANDESKUNDLICHE LUFTBILDAUSWERTUNG IM MITTELEUROPAEISCHEN RAUM. 1952. irreg., vol. 13, 1977. price varies. Bundesforschungsanstalt fuer Landeskunde und Raumordnung, Am Michaelshof 8, Postfach 200130, 5300 Bonn 2, W. Germany(B.R.D.) circ. 800.

914.503 IT
LIGURIA TERRITORIO E CIVILTA. no. 4, 1977. irreg. Sagep Editrice S.p.A., Piazza della Vittoria 14, 16121 Genoa, Italy. Ed. Gaspare De Fiore.

914 UK ISSN 0076-0498
LONDON RED GUIDE. 1903. irreg. £1.95. Ward Lock, Ltd., Warwick House, 116 Baker St., London W.1, England (Dist. in U.S. by: International Publications Service, 114 E. 32nd St., New York, NY 10016) Ed. Reginald J. W. Hammond. index.

910 UK ISSN 0076-0641
LONDON SCHOOL OF ECONOMICS AND POLITICAL SCIENCE. DEPARTMENT OF GEOGRAPHY. GEOGRAPHICAL PAPERS. 1964. irreg., latest 1976. price varies. London School of Economics & Political Science, Dept. of Geography, Houghton St., Aldwych, London WC2A 2AE, England.

917.94 US ISSN 0076-096X
LOS ANGELES GEOGRAPHICAL SOCIETY. PUBLICATION. 1964. irreg. $6.95. Pacific Books, Publishers, P.O. Box 558, Palo Alto, CA 94302. Ed. J.E. Spencer.

910.02 910 SW ISSN 0076-146X
LUND STUDIES IN GEOGRAPHY. SERIES A. PHYSICAL GEOGRAPHY. (Text in English and German) 1950. irreg., no. 56, 1977. price varies. (Lunds Universitet, Department of Geography) C.W.K. Gleerup (Subsidiary of: LiberLaeromedel) Box 1205, 221 05 Lund, Sweden. index. cum.index: 1950-54, 1956-58, 1960-66.

LUND STUDIES IN GEOGRAPHY. SERIES B. HUMAN GEOGRAPHY. see *BIOLOGY*

910 526 SW ISSN 0076-1486
LUND STUDIES IN GEOGRAPHY. SERIES C. GENERAL AND MATHEMATICAL GEOGRAPHY. (Text in English) 1962. irreg., no. 12, 1971. price varies. (Lunds Universitet, Department of Geography) C.W.K. Gleerup (Subsidiary of: LiberLaeromedel) Box 1205, 221 05 Lund, Sweden. index. cum.index: 1962-65.

917.1 CN ISSN 0076-1982
MCGILL SUB-ARCTIC RESEARCH PAPERS. 1956. irreg. Can.$3 per no. McGill University, P. O. Box 6070, Montreal, Que. 101, Canada (Dist. by McGill Sub-Arctic Research Laboratory, P.O. Box 790, Schefferville, Que. Canada) circ. 500.

914 HU ISSN 0076-2512
MAGYARORSZAG TAJFOLDRAJZA. 1967. irreg. price varies. (Magyar Tudomanyos Akademia) Akademiai Kiado, Publishing House of the Hungarian Academy of Sciences, P.O. Box 24, H-1363 Budapest, Hungary.

910 UG ISSN 0075-4722
MAKERERE UNIVERSITY. DEPARTMENT OF GEOGRAPHY. OCCASIONAL PAPER. 1967. irreg., no. 71, 1977. price varies. Makerere University, Department of Geography, P.O. Box 7062, Kampala, Uganda. adv. bk. rev.

910 UK ISSN 0140-7961
MATTER OF DEGREE; a guide to geography courses in the United Kingdom. 1971. a. £1.50. Geo Books, c/o Geo Abstracts Ltd., University of East Anglia, Norwich NR4 7TJ, England. circ. 2,000.

910.9 CN
MAWDSLEY MEMOIRS. 1973. irreg. price varies. Institute for Northern Studies, University of Saskatchewan, Saskatoon, Sask. S7N 0W0, Canada. bibl.

915 IS
MERHAVIM; collection of geographical research about Israel and the Middle East. (Text in Hebrew; summaries in English) 1974. irreg. Tel Aviv University, Department of Geography, Tel Aviv, Israel. illus.

526.8 SZ
METHODES DE LA CARTOGRAPHIE THEMATIQUE. 1976. irreg. Editions Universitaires de Fribourg, 36 Bd. de Perolles, 1700 Fribourg, Switzerland.

910 US ISSN 0076-7948
MICHIGAN GEOGRAPHICAL PUBLICATIONS. 1970. irreg., approx. s-a., no. 24, 1977. $4-5. University of Michigan, Department of Geography, Ann Arbor, MI 48109. Eds. John Kolars, Tom Detwyler.

MIDDLE EAST AND NORTH AFRICA; survey and Directory of Lands of Middle East and North Africa. see HISTORY — History Of The Near East

917 US
MISSISSIPPI GEOGRAPHER. 1973. a. $2. (Mississippi Council for Geographic Education) University of Southern Mississippi, Geography Department, Box 8464, Hattiesburg, MS 39401. Ed. Jesse O. McKee. adv. bk. rev. bibl. charts. illus. stat. circ. 700. Indexed: Sociol.Abstr. Geo.Abstr.

910 AT
MONASH UNIVERSITY. PUBLICATIONS IN GEOGRAPHY. 1972. 3-6/yr. Aus.$1.50. Monash University, Department of Geography, Clayton, Australia. bibl. illus. index. circ. 100.

910 GW
MUENCHENER GEOGRAPHISCHE ABHANDLUNGEN. 1970. 3-4 copies per year. price varies. (Universitaet Muenchen, Institut fuer Geographie) Geo-Buch Verlag, Rosental 6, 8000 Munich 2, W. Germany (B.R.D.) circ. 600.

910.1 GW ISSN 0077-1902
MUENCHNER STUDIEN ZUR SOZIAL- UND WIRTSCHAFTSGEOGRAPHIE. (Text in German; summaries in English, French and Russian) 1966. irreg. price varies. (Universitaet Muenchen, Wirtschaftsgeographisches Institut) Verlag Michael Lassleben, Lange Gasse 19, Postfach 20, 8411 Kallmuenz, W. Germany (B.R.D.)

MUSEUM NATIONAL D'HISTOIRE NATURELLE, PARIS. NOTES ET MEMOIRES SUR LE MOYEN-ORIENT. see EARTH SCIENCES — Geology

MUSEUM OF ANTIQUITIES OF TEL-AVIV-YAFO. PUBLICATIONS. see ARCHAEOLOGY

526 GW ISSN 0469-4236
NACHRICHTEN AUS DEM KARTEN- UND VERMESSUNGSWESEN. REIHE 1: ORIGINALBEITRAEGE. 1956. irreg. price varies. Institut fuer Angewandte Geodaesie, Richard-Strauss-Allee 11, 6000 Frankfurt 70, W. Germany (B.R.D.) bk. rev. circ. 500.
Supersedes in part: Nachrichten aus dem Karten- und Vermessungswesen (ISSN 0071-920X)

914 SW ISSN 0077-2704
NAMN OCH BYGD; journal for Nordic place-name research. (Text in English, German and Swedish; summaries in English) 1913. a. Kr.45($11) Kungliga Gustav Adolfs Akademien - Royal Gustavus Adolphus Academy, Tiundagatan 39, S-752 30 Uppsala, Sweden. Ed. Harry Staahl. bk. rev. circ. 500.

NATIONAL CONFERENCE OF SOUTH AFRICAN SURVEYORS. PROCEEDINGS/ NASIONALE KONFERENSIE VAN SUID-AFRIKAANSE OPMETERS. VERRIGTINGE. see ENGINEERING — Civil Engineering

NATIONAL COUNCIL FOR GEOGRAPHIC EDUCATION DO IT THIS WAY. see EDUCATION — Teaching Methods And Curriculum

NATIONAL COUNCIL FOR GEOGRAPHIC EDUCATION. INSTRUCTIONAL ACTIVITIES SERIES. see EDUCATION — Teaching Methods And Curriculum

910 US
NATIONAL COUNCIL FOR GEOGRAPHIC EDUCATION. PACESETTER SERIES. 1970. a. price varies. National Council for Geographic Education, c/o James W. Vining, Exec. Dir., Western Illinois University, Macomb, IL 61455. Ed. Clyde F. Kohn. Indexed: Educ.Ind.
Formerly: National Council for Geographic Education. Yearbook (ISSN 0077-4030)

NATIONAL COUNCIL FOR GEOGRAPHIC EDUCATION. SPECIAL PUBLICATIONS. see EDUCATION — Teaching Methods And Curriculum

NATIONAL COUNCIL FOR GEOGRAPHIC EDUCATION. TOPICS IN GEOGRAPHY. see EDUCATION — Teaching Methods And Curriculum

910 II ISSN 0470-0929
NATIONAL GEOGRAPHER. (Text in English) 1958. a. $12. Allahabad Geographical Society, University of Allahabad, Department of Geography, Allahabad 211002, Uttar Pradesh, India. Ed. R. N. Singh. bk. rev. illus. circ. 450.

910 US ISSN 0077-4618
NATIONAL GEOGRAPHIC BOOKS (SERIES) Also known as: National Geographic Society. Special Publications Series. 1966. 4/yr. National Geographic Society, 17 & M Sts. N.W., Washington, DC 20036.

NATIONAL GEOGRAPHIC SOCIETY RESEARCH REPORTS. see SCIENCES: COMPREHENSIVE WORKS

508.98 US ISSN 0361-2279
NATIONAL RESEARCH COUNCIL. COMMITTEE ON POLAR RESEARCH. REPORT ON UNITED STATES ANTARCTIC RESEARCH ACTIVITIES. Added title: Polar Research. a. free. National Research Council, Polar Research Board, National Academy of Sciences, 2101 Constitution Ave., Washington, DC 20418. illus. Key Title: Report on United States Antarctic Research Activities.

910 CH
NATIONAL TAIWAN UNIVERSITY. DEPARTMENT OF GEOGRAPHY. SCIENCE REPORTS.* (Text and summaries in English or Chinese) 1962. irreg. $2.50 free. National Taiwan University, Department of Geography, Taipei Taiwan, Republic of China.

910 US ISSN 0082-5166
NATURAL HAZARD RESEARCH WORKING PAPERS. 1968. irreg., no. 36, 1979. $2 per no. (Natural Hazards Research and Applications Information Center) University of Colorado, Institute of Behavioral Science, Boulder, CO 80309. Ed. Gilbert F. White. circ. 130. Indexed: Geo.Abstr.

910 CS
NAUKA O ZEMI. SERIA GEOGRAPHICA. (Text in Slovak; summaries in English and Russian) 1966. irreg. (Slovenska Akademia Vied) Veda, Publishing House of the Slovak Academy of Sciences, Klemensova 19, 895 30 Bratislava, Czechoslovakia.

526 NE ISSN 0077-7625
NETHERLANDS. RIJKSCOMMISSIE VOOR GEODESIE. PUBLICATIONS ON GEODESY. NEW SERIES. (Text usually in English) 1961. irreg. price varies. ‡ Rijkscommissie voor Geodesie - Netherlands Geodetic Commission, Thijsseweg 11, Delft, Netherlands.

919.31 NZ ISSN 0078-0022
NEW ZEALAND GEOGRAPHICAL SOCIETY. MISCELLANEOUS SERIES. 1950. irreg., 1970, no. 11. price varies. New Zealand Geographical Society Inc., Dept. of Geography, University of Canterbury, Private Bag, Christchurch, New Zealand.

919.31 NZ ISSN 0078-0030
NEW ZEALAND GEOGRAPHY CONFERENCE PROCEEDINGS SERIES. 1955. biennial; up to 1971 triennial; 1971, no. 6. price varies. ‡ New Zealand Geographical Society Inc., Dept. of Geography, University of Canterbury, Private Bag, Christchurch, New Zealand. circ. 950.

NORSK POLARINSTITUTT. AARBOK. see EARTH SCIENCES — Geology

NORSK POLARINSTITUTT. MEDDELELSER. see EARTH SCIENCES — Geology

NORSK POLARINSTITUTT. POLARHAANDBOK. see EARTH SCIENCES — Geology

NORSK POLARINSTITUTT. SKRIFTER. see EARTH SCIENCES — Geology

913 UK ISSN 0078-1649
NORTH STAFFORDSHIRE JOURNAL OF FIELD STUDIES. irreg. £3.50. University of Keele, Keele, Staffordshire ST5 5BG, England. Ed. A.D.M. Phillips.

910 II
NORTH EASTERN GEOGRAPHER. (Text in English) vol. 10, 1978. s-a. Rs.10($2) North East India Geographical Society, c/o Department of Geography, Gauhati University, Gauhati 781014, Assam, India. Ed. N. N. Bhattacharyya. bk. rev. bibl. charts. illus. circ. 250.
Formerly: North East India Geographical Society. Journal.

917 US
NORTHERN ARIZONA SCENE; a pictorial and prose profile of Arizona's northlands. 1976. a. $2. Halamar Publications, 9800 Flint Rock Road, Manassas, VA 22110. Ed. Hal Sundstrom. illus. circ. 50,000.

910 GW
NUERNBERGER WIRTSCHAFTS-UND SOZIALGEOGRAPHISCHE ARBEITEN. (Text in German; summaries in English) 1957. irreg., vol. 31, 1979. price varies. Friedrich-Alexander-Universitaet, Nuernberg, Wirtschafts- und Sozialgeographisches Institut, Lange Gasse 20, 8500 Nuernberg, West Germany (B.R.D.) Eds. Ernst Weigt, Wigand Ritter. circ. 700.

910 UK ISSN 0078-3056
OCCASIONAL PAPERS IN GEOGRAPHY. 1965. irreg. individually priced. University of Hull Publications Committee, Hull HU6 7RX, England. Ed. H. R. Wilkinson. Indexed: SSCI.

910 US ISSN 0094-9043
OHIO GEOGRAPHERS: RECENT RESEARCH THEMES. 1973. a. $2. (Ohio Academy of Science, Ohio Geography Section) University of Akron, Department of Geography, 302 E. Buchtel Ave., Akron, OH 44325. Ed. Vern Harnapp. circ. 100(controlled) Indexed: ERIC.

919 US ISSN 0472-6979
OHIO STATE UNIVERSITY. INSTITUTE OF POLAR STUDIES. CONTRIBUTION SERIES. 1961. irreg., no. 402, 1981. free. Ohio State University, Institute of Polar Studies, 125 S. Oval Mall, Columbus, OH 43210.

919 US
OHIO STATE UNIVERSITY. INSTITUTE OF POLAR STUDIES. MISCELLANEOUS SERIES. 1958. irreg., no. 150, 1981. free. Ohio State University, Institute of Polar Studies, 125 S. Oval Mall, Columbus, OH 43210.

919 US ISSN 0078-415X
OHIO STATE UNIVERSITY. INSTITUTE OF POLAR STUDIES. REPORT SERIES. 1962. irreg., no. 80, 1981. price varies. ‡ Ohio State University, Institute of Polar Studies, 103 Mendenhall, 125 S. Oval Mall, Columbus, OH 43210. circ. 500.

917.6 US
OKLAHOMA LAKE LIVING. 1979. a. $2 per no. Oklahoma Lake Living Magazine, Box 1781, Muskogee, OK 74401. adv. circ. 50,000.

917 CN ISSN 0078-4850
ONTARIO GEOGRAPHY. 1967. irreg. Can.$2. University of Western Ontario, Department of Geography, London, Ont. N6A 5C2, Canada. Ed. Nigel Waters. bk. rev. circ. 800. Indexed: Geo.Abstr.

910 AT ISSN 0085-4506
OONDOONA.* 1959. irreg. $0.50. University of Sydney Geographical Society, Sydney, N.S.W. 2006, Australia.

910　　　　　　　　　GW　ISSN 0030-4395
ORBIS GEOGRAPHICUS; world directory of geography. (Text in German, English, French) 1952. irreg. price varies. (International Geographical Union) Franz Steiner Verlag GmbH, Friedrichstr. 24, Postfach 5529, 6200 Wiesbaden, W. Germany (B.R.D.) Ed. E. Meynen.

526.9　　　　　　　　US
ORTHOPHOTO WORKSHOP. PAPERS. 1971. irreg., 3rd, 1975. $10 to non-members; members $5. American Society of Photogrammetry, Cartography Division, 105 North Virginia Ave., Falls Chruch, VA 22046. (Affiliate: American Congress on Surveying and Mapping) illus.
 Vol. for 1971, sponsored by Potomac Region, American Society of Photogrammetry and the Cartography Division, American Congress on Surveying and Mapping; 1973- sponsored by the Northern California Region of the Society and the Northern California Section of the Congress.

910　　　　　　　NZ　ISSN 0078-690X
OTAGO GEOGRAPHER. 1968. irreg. NZ.$1. University of Otago, Geography Students Assn., c/o Geography Dept., Box 56, Dunedin, New Zealand. Ed. G. O. Crombie. circ. 200.

910　　　　　　　　　US
OXFORD RESEARCH STUDIES IN GEOGRAPHY. irreg. price varies. Oxford University Press, 200 Madison Ave., New York, NY 10016 (And Ely House, 37 Dover St., London W1X 4AH, England) Ed.Bd.

910　　　　　　　NZ　ISSN 0553-738X
PERSPECTIVE. no. 11, 1976. irreg. NZ.$0.30 per no. New Zealand Geographical Society (Inc.), Manawatu Branch, c/o Department of Geography, Massey University, Palmerston North, New Zealand. Ed. M. J. Sheperd. (back issues avail.)

910　　　　　　　　　US
PERSPECTIVES IN GEOGRAPHY. 1971. irreg. price varies. Northern Illinois University Press, 515 Garden Road, Dekalb, IL 60115.

POLITICAL HANDBOOK OF THE WORLD. see POLITICAL SCIENCE

910　　　　　　　PL　ISSN 0373-6547
POLSKA AKADEMIA NAUK. INSTYTUT GEOGRAFII I PRZESTRZENNEGO ZAGOSPODAROWANIA. PRACE GEOGRAFICZNE. (Text in Polish; summaries in English and Russian) 1954. irreg., no. 131, 1979. price varies. Ossolineum, Publishing House of the Polish Academy of Sciences, Rynek 9, Wroclaw, Poland. Ed. M. Kielczewska-Zaleska.
 Formerly: Polska Akademia Nauk. Instytut Geografii. Prace Geograficzne (ISSN 0554-5749)

526　　　　　　　PL　ISSN 0079-3299
POLSKA AKADEMIA NAUK. ODDZIAL W KRAKOWIE. KOMISJA GORNICZO-GEODEZYJNA. PRACE: GEODEZJA. (Text in Polish; summaries in English and Russian) 1964. irreg., no. 27, 1978. price varies. Ossolineum, Publishing House of the Polish Academy of Sciences, Rynek 9, Wroclaw, Poland (Dist. by Ars Polona-Ruch, Krakowskie Przedmiescie 7, Warsaw, Poland) Ed. Jozef Jachimski.

910.02　　　　　　PL　ISSN 0137-2939
POLSKA AKADEMIA NAUK. ODDZIAL W KRAKOWIE. OSRODEK DOKUMENTACJI FIZJOGRAFICZNEJ. STUDIA. 1972. a. 90 Zl. Ossolineum, Publishing House of the Polish Academy of Sciences, Rynek 9, Wroclaw, Poland. Dist. by: Ars Polona-Ruch, Krakowskie Przedmiescie 7, Warsaw, Poland. Ed. Antoni Kleczkowski.

914.7　　　　　　　　PL
POMORSKIE MONOGRAFIE TOPONOMASTYCZNE. (Text in Polish; summaries in English and Russian) irreg., vol. 3, 1977. price varies. (Gdanskie Towarzystwo Naukowe) Ossolineum, Publishing House of the Polish Academy of Sciences, Rynek 9, Wroclaw, Poland (Dist. by: Ars Polona-Ruch, Krakowskie Przedmiescie 7, Warsaw, Poland) Ed. H. Gornowicz. circ. 950.

POZNANSKIE TOWARZYSTWO PRZYJACIOL NAUK. KOMISJA GEOGRAFICZNO-GEOLOGICZNA. PRACE. see EARTH SCIENCES — Geology

915.7 919.8　　　CN　ISSN 0079-5771
PROBLEMS OF THE NORTH. 1960. irreg. price varies. ‡ National Research Council of Canada, Ottawa, K1A OS2, Canada. Ed. G. Belkov. circ. 300.

910　　　　　　　CN　ISSN 0079-7758
PUBLICATIONS IN TROPICAL GEOGRAPHY SAVANNA RESEARCH SERIES. 1964. irreg. Can.$100. McGill University, Department of Geography, 805 Sherbrooke St. West, Montreal, Que. H3A 2K6, Canada. Ed. Dr. Theo L. Hills.

910　　　　　　　　　PL
QUAESTIONES GEOGRAPHICAE. (Text in English) 1974. a. price varies. Uniwersytet im. Adama Mickiewicza w Poznaniu, Stalingradzka 1, 61-712 Poznan, Poland. Ed. Stefan Kozarski. circ. 1,000. (also avail. in microfilm) Indexed: Geo.Abstr.

910　　　　　　　UK　ISSN 0306-2740
QUEEN MARY COLLEGE. DEPARTMENT OF GEOGRAPHY. OCCASIONAL PAPERS. 1974. irreg. price varies. Queen Mary College, Department of Geography, Mile End Rd., London E1 4NS, England. Ed. Philip E. Ogden. circ. 600.

QUEENSLAND GEOGRAPHER. see EDUCATION — Teaching Methods And Curriculum

910　　　　　　　　　AT
QUEENSLAND GEOGRAPHICAL JOURNAL. 1885. irreg. Aus.$0.75 non-members $1. Royal Geographical Society of Australia, Queensland Branch, 117 Ann St., Brisbane, Qld 4000, Australia. Ed. R. S. Dick.

RAND MCNALLY COMMERCIAL ATLAS AND MARKETING GUIDE. see BUSINESS AND ECONOMICS — Marketing And Purchasing

910　　　　　　　UK　ISSN 0309-3263
READING GEOGRAPHER. 1970. a. University of Reading, Department of Geography, White Knights, Reading RG6 2AB, England. Indexed: Geo.Abstr.

526　　　　　　　FR　ISSN 0180-9970
RECUEIL DES CORRECTIONS DE CARTES (YEAR) 1978. a. price varies. Service Hydrographique et Oceanographique de la Marine, 3 Ave. Octave Gerard, 75200 Paris Naval, France (Subscr. address: E.P.S.H.O.M., B.P. 426, 29275 Brest Cedex, France)
 Cartography

910　　　　　　　　　CN
REGINA GEOGRAPHICAL STUDIES. 1977. irreg. price varies. University of Regina, Department of Geography, Regina, Sask, Canada. Indexed: Chem.Abstr.

910　　　　　　　　　FR
REPERTOIRE DES GEOGRAPHES DE FRANCE. 1969. irreg (every 2-3 years) Centre National de la Recherche Scientifique, Laboratoire "Intergeo", 191 rue Saint-Jacques, 75005 Paris, France.
 Formerly (until 1978): Annuaire des Geographes de la France et de l'Afrique Francophone (ISSN 0066-2844)

910　　　　　　　　　US
RESEARCH IN CONTEMPORARY AND APPLIED GEOGRAPHY; a discussion series. 1977. irreg. State University of New York at Binghamton, Department of Geography, Binghamton, NY 13901. Ed. John Frazier.

910　　　　　　　　　AT
RESEARCH PAPERS IN GEOGRAPHY. no. 24, 1979. irreg. University of Newcastle, Department of Geography, Newcastle, N.S.W. 2308, Australia.

526.982　　　　　　CK　ISSN 0120-2499
REVISTA CENTRO INTERAMERICANO DE FOTOINTERPRETACION. Short title: Revista C I A F. 1972. a. $12. Centro Interamericano de Fotoinerpretacion, Carrera 30 No. 47a-57, Apdo. Aereo 53754, Bogota, Colombia. adv. illus. circ. 1,000.

910　　　　　　　CL　ISSN 0034-9577
REVISTA GEOGRAFICA DE VALPARAISO. 1967. a. (Universidad Catolica de Valparaiso, Instituto de Geografia) Ediciones Universitarias de Valparaiso, Monttsaavedra 44, Casilla 1415, Valparaiso, Chile. Ed. Vladimir Flores B. charts. illus. circ. 1,000.

910　　　　　　　BE　ISSN 0035-0796
REVUE BELGE DE GEOGRAPHIE. 1876. irreg. (3-7/yr.) 600 Fr. for non-members. Societe Royale Belge de Geographie, 87 Av. Adolphe Buyl, 1050 Brussels, Belgium. Ed. Christian van der Motten. bk. rev. charts. illus. circ. 800. Indexed: Geo.Abstr.
 Formerly: Bulletin de Societe Royale Belge de Geographie.

910　　　　　　　GW　ISSN 0080-2662
RHEIN-MAINISCHE FORSCHUNGEN. irreg. price varies. (Universitaet Frankfurt, Geographisches Institut) Verlag Dr. Waldemar Kramer, Bornheimer Landwehr 57a, Postfach 600445, 6000 Frankfurt 60, W. Germany (B.R.D.) Eds. A. Krenzlin, A. Semmel, K. Wolf.

910　　　　　　　AT　ISSN 0085-5790
ROYAL GEOGRAPHICAL SOCIETY OF AUSTRALASIA. SOUTH AUSTRALIAN BRANCH. PROCEEDINGS. 1886. a. membership. Royal Geographical Society of Australasia, South Australian Branch, State Library Bldg., North Terrace, Adelaide, S.A. 5000, Australia. Ed. Roger Brown. bk. rev. cum. index: vols. 1-40. circ. 400. Indexed: Aus.Sci.Ind.

910　　　　　　　　　US
SCIENCE IN GEOGRAPHY. irreg. price varies. Oxford University Press, 200 Madison Ave., New York, NY 10016 (And Ely House, 37 Dover St., London W1X 4AH, England) Ed. Brian P. FitzGerald.

910　　　　　　　　　UK
SCIENTIFIC EXPLORATION SOCIETY. NEWSLETTER. 1969. irreg. (approx. 10/yr.) £3. ‡ Daily Telegraph Ltd., 135 Fleet St, London EC4P 4BS, England. Ed. Richard Snailham. circ. 250. (looseleaf format)

914.502　　　　　　　IT
SCIENZE GEOGRAFICHE. 1975. irreg. (Universita Cattolica del Sacro Cuore) Vita e Pensiero, Largo Gemelli 1, 20123 Milan, Italy.

SEE AUSTRALIA. see TRAVEL AND TOURISM

916.64　　　　　　SL　ISSN 0583-239X
SIERRA LEONE GEOGRAPHICAL JOURNAL. Title varies, no. 1-10: Sierra Leone Geographical Association. Bulletin. 1967. a. Le.2.50($3) Sierra Leone Geographical Association, c/o Fourah Bay College Bookshop, Freetown, Sierra Leone. Ed.Bd. adv. bk. rev. charts.

SOCIAAL-GEOGRAFISCHE STUDIEN. see ANTHROPOLOGY

910　　　　　　　　　AG
SOCIEDAD ARGENTINA DE ESTUDIOS GEOGRAFICOS BOLETIN. 1931. irreg. free. Sociedad Argentina de Estudios Geograficos, Av. Santa Fe 1145, Buenos Aires, Argentina (Distr. by: LIBRART, Casilla Corre Central 5047, Buenos Aires 1000, Argentina) bk. rev. circ. controlled. (looseleaf format)

914　　　　　　　FR　ISSN 0081-0789
SOCIETE DE GEOGRAPHIE DE MARSEILLE. BULLETIN. 1877. biennial. 35 F. Societe de Geographie de Marseille, 2 rue Beauvan, 13001 Marseille, France. circ. 350.

910　　　　　　　FR　ISSN 0081-086X
SOCIETE DES EXPLORATEURS ET DES VOYAGEURS FRANCAIS. ANNUAIRE GENERAL. 1962. irreg. membership. Societe des Explorateurs et des Voyageurs Francais, 184 Bd. St. Germain, 75006 Paris, France. bk. rev. circ. 3,000.

910　　　　　　　BE　ISSN 0583-8622
SOCIETE GEOGRAPHIQUE DE LIEGE. BULLETIN. (Text in French, summaries in French and English) 1965. a. 500 Fr. Societe Geographique de Liege, 7, Place du Vingt-Aout, B-4000 Liege, Belgium. Ed. F. Dussart. bk. rev. circ. 1,000.
 Supersedes: Universite de Liege. Seminaire de Geographie. Travaux; Travaux Geographigues de Liege.

910　　　　　　　　　BU
SOFIISKI UNIVERSITET. GEOLOGO-GEOGRAFSKI FAKULTET. GEOGRAFIIA. GODISHNIK. (Text in Bulgarian and Russian; summaries in English, French, German) 1905. irreg. 3.22 lv. per issue. Izdatelstvo Nauka i Izkustvo, 6, Rouski Blvd., Sofia, Bulgaria. circ. 542.

526.982   SA   ISSN 0085-6398
SOUTH AFRICAN JOURNAL OF PHOTOGRAMMETRY. (Text in Afrikaans and English) 1959. a. R.8 to non-members. Photogrammetric Society of South Africa, Box 2830, Johannesburg, South Africa. Ed. T.R. van Rooyen. adv. bk. rev. circ. 500(approx.)
Photogrammetry

910   US   ISSN 0073-4950
SOUTHERN ILLINOIS UNIVERSITY, CARBONDALE. DEPARTMENT OF GEOGRAPHY. DISCUSSION PAPER. 1969. irreg., no. 6, 1979. ‡ Southern Illinois University, Carbondale, Department of Geography, Carbondale, IL 62901.

910   US   ISSN 0073-4969
SOUTHERN ILLINOIS UNIVERSITY, CARBONDALE. OCCASIONAL PAPER SERIES IN GEOGRAPHY. 1963. irreg. price varies. ‡ Southern Illinois University, Carbondale, Department of Geography, Carbondale, IL 62901.

914.7   US   ISSN 0094-2863
SOVIET UNION/UNION SOVIETIQUE. (Text in English, French, German and Russian) 1974. irreg.(2-4/yr.) $2 to institutions. Russian and East European Publications, c/o Charles Schlacks, Jr., Ed., Arizona State Univ., 120B McAllister Ave., Tempe, AZ 85281. adv. bk. rev. bibl. index. circ. 500. (also avail. in microform from UMI) Key Title: Soviet Union (Pittsburgh)

914.38   PL   ISSN 0081-640X
STUDIA GEOGRAFICZNE. (Issued as a subseries of its Acta Universitatis Wratislaviensis) (Text in Polish; summaries in English, French) 1963. irreg., 1976, vol. 22. price varies. (Uniwersytet Wroclawski) Panstwowe Wydawnictwo Naukowe, Miodowa 10, Warsaw, Poland (Dist. by Ars Polona-Ruch, Krakowskie Przedmiescie 7, Warsaw, Poland) Ed. H. Migaczowa. charts. illus. circ. 480.

STUDIA GEOGRAFICZNO-FIZYCZNE Z OBSZARU OPOLSZCZYZNY. see *EARTH SCIENCES — Geology*

910   550   PL   ISSN 0082-5549
STUDIA SOCIETATIS SCIENTIARUM TORUNENSIS. SECTIO C (GEOGRAFIA ET GEOLOGIA) (Text in Polish; summaries in English) 1953. irreg., 1977, vol. 9, no. 1. price varies. (Towarzystwo Naukowe w Toruniu) Panstwowe Wydawnictwo Naukowe, Ul. Miodowa 10, Warsaw, Poland. Ed. Rajmund Galon. charts. illus. circ. 680.

STUDIA UNIVERSITATIS "BABES-BOLYAI". GEOLOGIA. GEOGRAPHIA. see *EARTH SCIENCES — Geology*

910   US
STUDIES IN GEOGRAPHY. 1970. irreg., no. 14, 1980. price varies. University of North Carolina at Chapel Hill, Department of Geography, 203 Saunders Hall, Chapel Hill, NC 27514.

910   HU   ISSN 0081-7961
STUDIES IN GEOGRAPHY IN HUNGARY. (Text in English) 1964. irreg., vol. 14, 1978. price varies. (Magyar Tudomanyos Akademia) Akademiai Kiado, Publishing House of the Hungarian Academy of Sciences, P.O. Box 24, H-1363 Budapest, Hungary.

915.69   IS   ISSN 0081-8585
STUDIES IN THE GEOGRAPHY OF ISRAEL/MEHKARIM BE-GE'OGRAFYAH SHEL ERETS-YISRAEL. (Text in Hebrew; table of contents and summaries in English) 1960, vol. 11, 1977. irreg. $8. Israel Exploration Society, Box 7041, Jerusalem, Israel. (Co-publisher: Hebrew Unuiversity of Jerusalem, Department of Geography) circ. 1,500.

STUDIES IN URBAN GEOGRAPHY. see *HOUSING AND URBAN PLANNING*

910   GW
STUTTGARTER GEOGRAPHISCHE STUDIEN. 1924. 2-3/yr. price varies (DM. 6-DM.36) Universitaet Stuttgart, Geographisches Institut, Silcherstr. 9, 7000 Stuttgart 1, W. Germany (B.R.D.) Eds. W. Meckelein & Ch. Borcherdt. charts. illus. stat. circ. 500-1,000.

526.982   SR
SURINAM. CENTRAAL BUREAU LUCHTKARTERING. JAARVERSLAG. (Text in Dutch) irreg. Centraal Bureau Luchtkartering, Paramaribo, Surinam.

910   UK   ISSN 0081-9980
SWANSEA GEOGRAPHER. 1959. a. price varies. University College of Swansea, Department of Geography, Singleton Park, Swansea, Glam. SA2 8PP, Wales. Eds. Shirley E. Tomlinson, John. W. Raine.

910   US   ISSN 0082-1160
SYRACUSE GEOGRAPHICAL SERIES. 1965. irreg; no. 4, 1975. price varies. (Syracuse University, Department of Geography) Syracuse University Press, 1011 E. Water St., Syracuse, NY 13210.

THAMES BOOK. see *TRAVEL AND TOURISM*

914.1   625.7   IE
THOM'S DUBLIN & COUNTY STREET DIRECTORY. 1851. a. $40. Thom's Directories Ltd., 38 Merrion Sq., Dublin 2, Ireland. Ed. J. L. Wootton.

910   JA   ISSN 0386-8710
TOKYO METROPOLITAN UNIVERSITY. DEPARTMENT OF GEOGRAPHY. GEOGRAPHICAL REPORTS/TOKYO-TORITSU DAIGAKU CHIRIGAKU HOKOKU. (Text in European languages) 1966. a. price varies. Tokyo Metropolitan University, Department of Geography - Tokyo-toritsu Daigaku Rigakubu Chirigaku Kyoshitsu, 2-1-1 Fukazawa, Setagaya-ku, Tokyo 158, Japan. Eds. I. Maejima, T. Tamura & S. Iwata. bibl. charts. illus. circ. 1,000. Indexed: Geo.Abstr.

TOKYO UNIVERSITY OF EDUCATION. FACULTY OF SCIENCE. SCIENCE REPORTS. SECTION C: GEOGRAPHY, GEOLOGY AND MINERALOGY. see *EARTH SCIENCES — Geology*

916   FR   ISSN 0336-5522
TRAVAUX ET DOCUMENTS DE GEOGRAPHIE TROPICALE. 1971. irreg. price varies. Centre d'Etudes de Geographie Tropicale, Domaine Universitaire, Esplanade des Antilles, 33405 Talence Cedex, France. (also avail. in microfiche)

526.3   UR
TSENTRAL'NYI NAUCHNO-ISSLEDOVATEL'SKII INSTITUT GEODEZII, AEROS"EMKI I KARTOGRAFII. TRUDY. vol. 218, 1977. irreg. Ul.Onezhskaya 26, Moscow 125413, U.S.S.R. circ. 500.

910   GW   ISSN 0564-4232
TUEBINGER GEOGRAPHISCHE STUDIEN. 1958. irreg. (approx. 5/yr) price varies. Universitaet Tuebingen, Geographisches Institut, Hoelderlinstr. 12, 7400 Tuebingen, W. Germany (B.R.D.) Ed. Bd. bibl. charts. illus. stat.

TURUN YLIOPISTO. JULKAISUJA. SARJA A. II. BIOLOGICA- GEOGRAPHICA- GEOLOGICA. see *BIOLOGY*

526   UK
UNITED KINGDOM GEODESY REPORT. 1963. quadrennial. free. (British National Committee for Geodesy and Geophysics. Geodesy Subcommittee.) Royal Society, 6 Carlton House Terrace, London SW1Y 5AG, England. Ed. Lt. Col. J. W. Williams. circ. 600.

526.8   UN   ISSN 0082-836X
UNITED NATIONS REGIONAL CARTOGRAPHIC CONFERENCE FOR ASIA AND THE FAR EAST. PROCEEDINGS OF THE CONFERENCE AND TECHNICAL PAPERS. 1955. irreg.; 6th, vol. 2, 1972. price varies. United Nations Publications, LX 2300, New York, NY 10017 (Or Distribution and Sales Section, CH-1211 Geneva 10, Switzerland)

526   US   ISSN 0364-7064
U.S. NATIONAL CARTOGRAPHIC INFORMATION CENTER. NEWSLETTER. 1975. irreg. free. U.S. National Cartographic Information Center, U.S. Geological Survey, 507 National Center, Reston, VA 22092. Ed. N. B. Faries. bk. rev. bibl. circ. 7,000.

918.7   VE   ISSN 0076-6569
UNIVERSIDAD DE LOS ANDES. INSTITUTO DE GEOGRAFIA Y CONSERVACION DE RECURSOS NATURALES. CUADERNOS GEOGRAFICOS. (Text in Spanish; summaries in English) 1961. irreg. price varies. Universidad de Los Andes, Instituto de Geografia y Conservacion de Recursos Naturales, Merida, Venezuela. circ. 2,000.

910   MX
UNIVERSIDAD NACIONAL AUTONOMA DE MEXICO. INSTITUTO DE GEOGRAFIA. ANUARIO DE GEOGRAFIA. Mex.$25($2.50) Universidad Nacional Autonoma de Mexico, Colegio de Geografia, Ciudad Universitaria, Mexico 20, D.F., Mexico. circ. 1,500.

917.2   MX   ISSN 0076-7190
UNIVERSIDAD NACIONAL AUTONOMA DE MEXICO. INSTITUTO DE GEOGRAFIA. BOLETIN. 1969. a. $4. Universidad Nacional Autonoma de Mexico, Instituto de Geografia, Ciudad Universitaria, Mexico, 20, D.F., Mexico.

910   AG   ISSN 0041-8684
UNIVERSIDAD NACIONAL DE ROSARIO. FACULTAD DE CIENCIAS, INGENIERIA Y ARQUITECTURA. INSTITUTO DE FISIOGRAFIA Y GEOLOGIA. PUBLICACIONES. (Text in Spanish; summaries in English, French) 1937. a. exchange basis. Universidad Nacional de Rosario, Avenida Pellegrini 250, Rosario, Argentina. Dir. Pierina Pasotti. charts. illus. bibl.

910   BL
UNIVERSIDADE DE SAO PAULO. MUSEU PAULISTA COLECAO. SERIE DE GEOGRAFIA. irreg. Universidade de Sao Paulo, Museu Paulista, Caixa Postal 42503, Parque da Independencia, 04263 Sao Paulo SP, Brazil.
     Supersedes in part (since 1975): Museu Paulista. Colecao (ISSN 0080-6382)

910   BL
UNIVERSIDADE ESTADUAL PAULISTA. DEPARTAMENTO DE GEOGRAFIA.BOLETIM. no. 6, 1974. a. Universidade Estadual Paulista, Departamento de Geografia, Rua Roberto Simonsen 305, C.P. 957, Presidente Prudente, Brazil.

910   GW
UNIVERSITACT KIEL. GEOGRAPHISCHES INSTITUT. SCHRIFTEN. 1932. irreg. price varies. Universitaet Kiel, Geographisches Institut, Neue Universitaet, Olshausenstr. 40-60, 2300 Kiel, W. Germany (B.R.D.) Ed. Bd. bk. rev.

910   GW   ISSN 0563-1491
UNIVERSITAET DES SAARLANDES. GEOGRAPHISCHES INSTITUT. ARBEITEN. (Text in German; summaries in English, French and Spanish) 1956. irreg., vol. 26, 1978. price varies. Universitaet des Saarlandes, Geographisches Institut, 6600 Saarbruecken 11, W. Germany (B.R.D.) Ed. Bd. bibl. charts. illus. circ. 1,000.

910.1   GW   ISSN 0077-2127
UNIVERSITAET MUENCHEN. WIRTSCHAFTSGEOGRAPHISCHES INSTITUT. "W G I"-BERICHTE ZUR REGIONALFORSCHUNG. (Text in German; summaries in English) 1970. irreg., no. 14, 1974. price varies. Geo-Buch Verlag, Rosental 6, 8000 Munich 2, W. Germany (B.R.D.)

914   RM
UNIVERSITATEA "AL. I. CUZA" DIN IASI. ANALELE STIINTIFICE. SECTIUNEA 2C: GEOGRAFIE. (Text in Romanian; summaries in foreign languages) 1955. a. $10. Universitatea "Al. I. Cuza" din Iasi, Calea 23 August Nr.11, Jassy, Romania (Subscr. to: ILEXIM, Str. 13 Decembrie Nr. 3, P.O. Box 136-137, Bucharest, Romania) bk. rev. abstr. charts. illus.

910   CN
UNIVERSITE LAVAL. DEPARTEMENT DE GEOGRAPHIE. TRAVAUX. 1970. irreg (approx. biennial) Presses de l'Universite Laval, B.P. 2447, Quebec 2, P.Q., Canada. bibl. charts. illus. stat. circ. 1,500.

900   IV
UNIVERSITE NATIONALE DE COTE D'IVOIRE. ANNALES. SERIE G: GEOGRAPHIE. 1969. irreg, vol. 6, 1974. price varies. Universite Nationale de Cote d'Ivoire, Tropical Geography Institute, c/o Bibliotheque Universitaire, B.P. 8859, Abidjan, Ivory Coast. Ed. Bd. bibl. charts. illus.
Formerly: Universite d'Abidjan. Annales. Serie G: Geographie.

910   NE   ISSN 0066-1317
UNIVERSITEIT VAN AMSTERDAM. FYSISCH GEOGRAFISCH EN BODEMKUNDIG LABORATORIUM. PUBLIKATIES. (Text in English and German; summaries in English, Dutch, French and German) no. 27, 1978. irreg. $5-$10. Universiteit van Amsterdam, Fysisch Geografish en Bodemkundig Laboratorium, Dapperstraat 115, Amsterdam, Netherlands.

910   NR   ISSN 0083-3975
UNIVERSITY GEOGRAPHER. 1956. a. Ibadan University Geographical Society, Ibadan, Nigeria.

910   CN
UNIVERSITY OF ALBERTA. STUDIES IN GEOGRAPHY. MONOGRAPHS. irreg. price varies. University of Alberta, Department of Geography, Edmonton, Alta. T6G 2H4, Canada.

910   NZ
UNIVERSITY OF AUCKLAND. DEPARTMENT OF GEOGRAPHY. OCCASIONAL PAPERS. 1961. irreg., no. 10, 1977. price varies. University of Auckland, Department of Geography, Private Bag, Auckland, New Zealand. Ed. Dr. Warwick Neville. circ. 200.

910   US   ISSN 0068-6441
UNIVERSITY OF CALIFORNIA PUBLICATIONS IN GEOGRAPHY. 1913. irreg. price varies. University of California Press, 2223 Fulton St., Berkeley, CA 94720.

910   US   ISSN 0069-3340
UNIVERSITY OF CHICAGO. DEPARTMENT OF GEOGRAPHY. RESEARCH PAPERS. 1947. irreg.,, no. 190, 1979. $8 per no. University of Chicago, Department of Geography, 5828 S. University Ave., Chicago, IL 60637. Ed. Bob Smith. (also avail. in microform from UMI)

UNIVERSITY OF COLORADO. INSTITUTE OF ARCTIC AND ALPINE RESEARCH. OCCASIONAL PAPERS. see EARTH SCIENCES

UNIVERSITY OF GEORGIA. GEOGRAPHY CURRICULUM PROJECT PUBLICATIONS. see EDUCATION — Teaching Methods And Curriculum

916   CN
UNIVERSITY OF GUELPH. DEPARTMENT OF GEOGRAPHY. GEOGRAPHICAL PUBLICATION. (Text in English and French) 1971. irreg. University of Guelph, Department of Geography, Guelph, Ont., Canada (Sole Distributor: Geo Abstracts Ltd., University of East Anglia, Norwich NOR 88C, England) circ. 500.

312   UK   ISSN 0441-4004
UNIVERSITY OF HULL. DEPARTMENT OF GEOGRAPHY. MISCELLANEOUS SERIES IN GEOGRAPHY. 1965. irreg. (approx. 2/yr.) price varies. University of Hull, Department of Geography, Hull, Yorkshire HU6 7RX, England. Ed. H.R. Wilkinson. bibl. charts. illus. circ. 400.

910   UK   ISSN 0076-0056
UNIVERSITY OF LIVERPOOL. DEPARTMENT OF GEOGRAPHY. RESEARCH PAPER. 1966. irreg., 1972, no. 9. price varies. University of Liverpool, Department of Geography, Roxby Bldg., Liverpool, England. Ed. R. M. Prothero. circ. 300.

910   AT   ISSN 0066-7706
UNIVERSITY OF NEW ENGLAND. DEPARTMENT OF GEOGRAPHY. MONOGRAPH SERIES IN GEOGRAPHY. 1963. irreg., 1966, no. 2. Aus.$3($4.25) University of New England, Department of Geography, Armidale, N.S.W. 2351, Australia. Ed. M.J. Cooper.

910   AT
UNIVERSITY OF NEW ENGLAND. DEPARTMENT OF GEOGRAPHY. STUDIES IN APPLIED GEOGRAPHICAL RESEARCH. 1977. irreg. price varies. University of New England, Department of Geography, Armidale, N.S.W. 2351, Australia. Ed. M.J. Cooper.

910 325   UK   ISSN 0078-026X
UNIVERSITY OF NEWCASTLE-UPON-TYNE. DEPARTMENT OF GEOGRAPHY. RESEARCH SERIES. 1954. irreg. price varies. University of Newcastle-Upon-Tyne, Department of Geography, Newcastle-Upon-Tyne NE1 7RU, England. Ed. J. A. Hellen. circ. 500-1,000. Indexed: Geo.Abstr.

914.2   UK
UNIVERSITY OF NEWCASTLE-UPON-TYNE. EXPLORATION SOCIETY JOURNAL. 1964. a. University of Newcastle-Upon-Tyne, Exploration Society, Daysh Building, Newcastle-Upon-Tyne NE1 7RO, England. bibl. charts.

910   CN
UNIVERSITY OF OTTAWA. DEPARTMENT OF GEOGRAPHY AND REGIONAL PLANNING. NOTES DE RECHERCHES/RESEARCH NOTES. (Text in English or French) 1971. irreg. price varies. University of Ottawa, Department of Geography and Regional Planning, Ottawa, Ont. K1N 6N5, Canada.

910   CN
UNIVERSITY OF OTTAWA. DEPARTMENT OF GEOGRAPHY. OCCASIONAL PAPERS. (Text in French and English) 1971. irreg. price varies. University of Ottawa Press, 65 Hastey Ave., Ottawa, Ont. K1N 6N5, Canada. charts. illus. (tabloid format)

910   UK   ISSN 0305-8190
UNIVERSITY OF OXFORD. SCHOOL OF GEOGRAPHY. RESEARCH PAPERS. 1972. irreg. £1.25 per no. University of Oxford, School of Geography, Mansfield Road, Oxford OX1 3TB, England. Ed. Bd. charts. circ. 500.

910   PP
UNIVERSITY OF PAPUA NEW GUINEA. DEPARTMENT OF GEOGRAPHY. OCCASIONAL PAPERS IN GEOGRAPHY. 1970. irreg. (2-3/yr) price varies. ‡ University of Papua New Guinea, Department of Geography, Box 4820, University P.O., Papua New Guinea. Ed. Bd. bibl. charts. illus.

910   JA   ISSN 0082-478X
UNIVERSITY OF TOKYO. DEPARTMENT OF GEOGRAPHY. BULLETIN/TOKYO DAIGAKU CHIRIGAKU KYOSHITSU KAIHO. (Text in English) 1969. a. available on exchange. University of Tokyo, Department of Geography - Tokyo Daigaku Chirigaku Kyoshitsu, 7-3-1 Hongo, Bunkyo-ku, Tokyo 113, Japan. bibl. charts. circ. 800. Indexed: Geo.Abstr.

910   CN   ISSN 0317-9893
UNIVERSITY OF TORONTO. DEPARTMENT OF GEOGRAPHY. DISCUSSION PAPER SERIES. 1970. irreg., no. 25, 1979. University of Toronto, Department of Geography, Toronto, Ont. M5S 1A1, Canada. Ed. Prof. J. Britton.

910   CN   ISSN 0082-5174
UNIVERSITY OF TORONTO. DEPARTMENT OF GEOGRAPHY. RESEARCH PUBLICATIONS. 1968. irreg., 1970, no. 5. $5. price varies. University of Toronto Press, Front Campus, Toronto, Ont. M5S 1A6, Canada (and 33 E. Tupper St., Buffalo, N.Y. 14203) Ed. Ian Burton. (also avail. in microfiche)

526 917   US
UNIVERSITY OF WISCONSIN, MADISON. CARTOGRAPHIC LABORATORY. PAPER. 1975. irreg. $3.50 per no. University of Wisconsin, Madison, Cartographic Laboratory, Science Hall, Madison, WI 53706. charts.

914.38   PL
UNIWERSYTET GDANSKI. WYDZIAL BIOLOGII I NAUK O ZIEMI. ZESZYTY NAUKOWE. GEOGRAFIA. 1970. irreg. 20 Zl. Uniwersytet Gdanski, Ul. Czerwonej Armii 110, 81-824 Sopot, Poland (Dist. by Ars Polona-Ruch, Krakowskie Przedmiescie 7, Warsaw, Poland) Ed. Jerzy Szukalski. bk. rev. circ. 300.

910   PL   ISSN 0083-4343
UNIWERSYTET JAGIELLONSKI. ZESZYTY NAUKOWE. PRACE GEOGRAFICZNE. 1960. irreg., 1972, vol. 28. price varies. ‡ (Instytut Geografii) Panstwowe Wydawnictwo Naukowe, Miodowa 10, Warsaw, Poland (Dist. by Ars Polona-Ruch, Krakowskie Przedmiescie 7, Warsaw, Poland) circ. 700. (also avail. in microfilm) Indexed: Ref.Zh.

910   PL   ISSN 0083-7326
UNIWERSYTET WARSZAWSKI. INSTYTUT GEOGRAFICZNY. PRACE I STUDIA. 1959. irreg. price varies. Uniwersytet Warszawski, Krakowskie Przedmiescie 26/28, Warsaw, Poland (Subscription to: Ars Polona-Ruch, Krakowskie Przedmiescie 7, Warsaw, Poland) Eds. J. Kondracki, R. Czarnecki. circ. 350.

910.02   PL
UNIWERSYTET WROCLAWSKI. INSTYTUT GEOGRAFICZNE. PRACE. SERIA A: GEOGRAFIA FIZYCZNA. (Subseries of its: Acta Universitatis Wratislaviensis) irreg., 1974, no. 236. price varies. Uniwersytet Wroclawski, Plac Uniwersytecki 1, Wroclaw, Poland.

910   PL
UNIWERSYTET WROCLAWSKI. INSTYTUT GEOGRAFICZNE. PRACE. SERIA B: GEOGRAFIA SPOLECZNA I EKONOMICZNA. (Subseries of its: Acta Universitatis Wratislaviensis) 1975. irreg. price varies. Uniwersytet Wroclawski, Plac Uniwersytecki 1, Wroclaw, Poland.

910   BG
UPOKUL. (Text in Bengali and English) 1972. irreg. Dacca University Geography Association, Ramna, Dacca 2, Bangladesh. adv. illus.

910   NE   ISSN 0376-4001
UTRECHTSE GEOGRAFISCHE STUDIES. (Text in Dutch or English; summaries in English) 1976. irreg. Rijksuniversiteit Te Utrecht, Geografisch Instituut, Box 80115, 3508 TC Utrecht, Netherlands. Ed. J. G. Borchert. Indexed: Geo.Abstr.
Formerly: Rijksuniversiteit te Utrecht. Geografisch Instituut. Bulletin. Serie 1: Sociale Geografie.

910   GW   ISSN 0083-5684
VERHANDLUNGEN DES DEUTSCHEN GEOGRAPHENTAGES. 1881. biennial. price varies. (Zentralverband der Deutschen Geographen) Franz Steiner Verlag GmbH, Friedrichstr. 24, Postfach 5529, 6200 Wiesbaden, W. Germany (B.R.D.)

915   UR
VOPROSY GEOGRAFII. vol. 103, 1977. irreg. 1.25 Rub. per no. Izdatel'stvo Mysl', Leninskii Prospekt 15, 117071 Moscow B-71, U.S.S.R. Ed. S. Kovalev. bibl. charts. circ. 9,800.

WERTE UNSERER HEIMAT; Ergebnisse der heimatkundlichen Bestandsaufnahme in der DDR. see HISTORY — History Of Europe

914.2   UK   ISSN 0083-8136
WESSEX GEOGRAPHICAL YEAR.* 1959. a. Hurad Ltd., Christchurch, England.

910   AT   ISSN 0313-8860
WESTERN GEOGRAPHER. 2/yr. Geographical Association of Western Australia, Box 152, Nedlands, W.A. 6009, Australia.

910   CN   ISSN 0315-2022
WESTERN GEOGRAPHICAL SERIES. 1970. irreg. (approx. 2-4/yr.) Can.$4 per vol. University of Victoria, Department of Geography, Victoria, B.C. V8W 2Y2, Canada. Ed. Dr. Harold D. Foster. circ. 1,000. (tabloid format)

910   AU   ISSN 0083-9957
WIENER GEOGRAPHISCHE SCHRIFTEN. (Summaries in English) 1957. irreg., no. 48, 1976. price varies. (Geographisches Institut der Hochschule fuer Welthandel) Verlag Ferdinand Hirt GmbH, Widerhofergasse 8, Postfach 39, A-1094 Vienna, Austria. Ed. Leopold Scheidl.

581   GW   ISSN 0084-0912
WISSENSCHAFTLICHE ALPENVEREINSHEFTE. 1897. irreg. Deutscher Alpenverein, Praterinsel 5, 8000 Munich 22, W. Germany (B.R.D.)

526   UN   ISSN 0084-1471
WORLD CARTOGRAPHY. 1951. irreg.; vol 12, 1972. price varies. United Nations Publications, LX 2300, New York, NY 10017 (Or Distribution and Sales Section, CH-1211 Geneva 10, Switzerland)

796.552   US
WORLD EXPLORATIONS. 1955. irreg.; (approx. 1/yr.) $5 (including Expedition Field Reports) (American Institute for Exploration) Quest Productions, 1809 Nichols Rd., Kalamazoo, MI 49007. (Co Sponsor: World Explorations Program of Richard Williams) Eds. Ted P. Bank, II, Jay Ellis Ransom. bk. rev. film rev. bibl. charts. illus. circ. 250(controlled) Indexed: Biol.Abstr.

910   GW   ISSN 0510-9833
WUERZBURGER GEOGRAPHISCHE ARBEITEN. 1953. irreg., (approx. 3-4/yr.) price varies. Universitaet Wuerzburg, Geographisches Institut, Am Hubland, 8700 Wuerzburg, W. Germany (B.R.D.) (Co-sponsor: Geographische Gesellschaft, Wuerzburg) Ed. Bd. illus. (tabloid format) Indexed: Geo. Abstr.
    Supersedes: Fraenkische Studien.

910   SW   ISSN 0044-0477
YMER. 1881. a. Kr.70. (Svenska Saellskapet foer Antropologi och Geografi) Generalstabens Lithografiske Anstalt, Box 22069, 104 22 Stocklhom, Sweden. Ed. Dagny Torbrand. bk. rev. bibl. charts. illus. index. circ. 1,200.

910   ZA
Z G A OCCASIONAL STUDIES. Variant title: Z G A Occasional Studies and Special Publications. 1968. irreg., no. 9, 1978. price varies. Zambia Geographical Association, Box RW 287, Lusaka, Zambia. Ed. G. J. Williams. bk. rev. charts. circ. 500. (back issues avail.) Indexed: Geo.Abstr.

526.9   ZA   ISSN 0084-5078
ZAMBIA. SURVEY DEPARTMENT. REPORT. a. 20 n. Government Printer, P.O. Box 136, Lusaka, Zambia.

968.94   ZA
ZAMBIA GEOGRAPHICAL ASSOCIATION. REGIONAL HANDBOOK. Cover title: Z G A Regional Handbook. irreg. Zambia Geographical Association, Box RW 287, Lusaka, Zambia. illus. (back issues avail.)
    Formerly: Zambia Geographical Association. Conference Handbook.

910   ZA
ZAMBIAN GEOGRAPHICAL JOURNAL. (Text and summaries in English) 1967. a. K.8($15) Zambia Geographical Association, Box RW 287, Lusaka, Zambia. Ed. G. J. Williams. bk. rev. bibl, charts. circ. 500. (tabloid format; back issues avail.) Indexed: Geo.Abstr.
    Formerly: Z G A Magazine.

GEOGRAPHY — Abstracting, Bibliographies, Statistics

526 016   GW   ISSN 0340-0409
BIBLIOGRAPHIA CARTOGRAPHICA; international documentation of cartographical literature. 1957. a. DM.36. (Staatsbibliothek Preussischer Kulturbesitz) K.G. Saur Verlag KG, Poessenbacherstr. 12 B, Postfach 711009, 8000 Munich 71, W. Germany (B.R.D.) (Co-sponsor: Deutsche Gesellschaft fuer Kartographie e.V.) Ed. Lothar Zoegner.
    Formerly: Bibliotheca Cartographica.

526 016   GR
INTERNATIONAL ASSOCIATION OF GEODESY. CENTRAL BUREAU FOR SATELLITE GEODESY. BIBLIOGRAPHY. 1965. irreg. free. International Association of Geodesy, Central Bureau for Satellite Geodesy, National Technical University, K. Zographou 9, Athens 624, Greece.
    Formerly: Bibliography on Satellite Geodesy and Related Subjects (ISSN 0067-7353)

317   NQ
NICARAGUA. OFICINA EJECUTIVA DE ENCUESTOS Y CENSOS. COMPENDIO ESTADISTICO. a. C.$100($20) Oficina Ejecutiva de Encuestos y Censos, Apdo. 4031, Managua, Nicaragua.

317 917.3   US
U S STATISTICAL ATLAS. 1969. biennial. $15. Williams Market Analysis, P.O. Box 170, Elmwood, NE 68349. Ed. Joe B. Williams. stat. circ. 2,500.

011 910   ZA
Z G A BIBLIOGRAPHIC SERIES. 1974. irreg., no. 3, 1978. price varies. Zambia Geographical Association, P.O. Box R.W. 287, Lusaka, Zambia. Ed. G. J. Williams. (back issues avail.) Indexed: Geo.Abstr.

GEOLOGY

see Earth Sciences — Geology

GEOPHYSICS

see Earth Sciences — Geophysics

GERONTOLOGY AND GERIATRICS

301.435 618.97   US   ISSN 0065-2709
ADVANCES IN GERONTOLOGICAL RESEARCH. 1964. irreg., 1972, vol. 4. price varies. Academic Press, Inc., 111 Fifth Ave., New York, NY 10003. Ed. B. Strehler. index.

612.67   US   ISSN 0361-0179
AGING (NEW YORK) 1975. irreg; vol. 10 1979. price varies. Raven Press, 1140 Ave. of the Americas, New York, NY 10036. Indexed: Curr.Cont. Sci.Cit.Ind.

618.97   GW   ISSN 0084-6252
ALTERN UND ENTWICKLUNG/AGING AND DEVELOPMENT. 1971. irreg; vol. 4, 1972. price varies. Akademie der Wissenschaften und der Literatur, Mainz, Geschwister-Scholl-Str. 2, 6500 Mainz, W. Germany(B.R.D.) Eds. H. Bredt, J. W. Rohen.

618.97   US
AMERICAN LECTURES IN GERIATRICS. irreg. price varies. Charles C. Thomas, Publisher, 301-327 E. Lawrence Ave., Springfield, IL 62717.

353.9   US   ISSN 0090-6077
CONNECTICUT. DEPARTMENT ON AGING. REPORT TO THE GOVERNOR AND GENERAL ASSEMBLY. (Report Year Ends June 30) 1969. a. Department on Aging, 80 Washington St., Hartford, CT 06115. Ed. Nelson N. Dion. circ. 500.

612.67   US   ISSN 0419-8093
DUKE UNIVERSITY. COUNCIL ON AGING AND HUMAN DEVELOPMENT. PROCEEDINGS OF SEMINARS. 1955. quinquennial. $7.50. Duke University, Center for the Study of Aging and Human Development, P.O. Box 3003, Durham, NC 27710. Ed. Frances C. Jeffers.

FLORIDA'S LOCAL RETIREMENT SYSTEMS: A SURVEY. see PUBLIC ADMINISTRATION

612.67   FI   ISSN 0072-4157
GERON. (Text in English, German or French) 1949. irreg. Fmk.20. Societas Gerontologica Fennica, Siltavuurendenger 20-A, Helsinki 17, Finland. Ed. Dr. Eva Hirsjarvi. circ. 300. Indexed: Ind.Med.

301.435 323.4   US
GRAY PANTHER NEWS. 1975. irreg. $2. Gray Panthers, 3700 Chestnut St., Philadelphia, PA 19104. illus. (tabloid format)

HAWAII. COMMISSION ON AGING. REPORT OF ACHIEVEMENTS OF PROGRAMS FOR THE AGING. see SOCIAL SERVICES AND WELFARE

610   SZ   ISSN 0074-1132
INTERDISCIPLINARY TOPICS IN GERONTOLOGY. (Text in English) 1968. irreg. (approx. 2/yr.) 90 Fr.($54) per vol. (1981 price) S. Karger AG, Allschwilerstrasse 10, P.O. Box, CH-4009 Basel, Switzerland. Ed. H. P. von Hahn. (reprint service avail. from ISI) Indexed: Biol.Abstr. Chem.Abstr. Curr.Cont. Ind.Med.

612.67   SZ   ISSN 0379-1068
KARGER HIGHLIGHTS: GERONTOLOGY; reprinted selected top articles. 1979. a. 15 Fr.($9) (1981 price) S. Karger AG, Allschwilerstrasse 10, P.O. Box, CH-4009 Basel, Switzerland. Ed. H. P. von Hahn. bibl. charts. illus. (reprint service avail. from ISI)

353.9   US   ISSN 0363-9207
OHIO. COMMISSION ON AGING. ANNUAL REPORT. a. Commission on Aging, 34 N. High St., Columbus, OH 43215. Key Title: Annual Report - Ohio Commission on Aging.

362.6   UK
OLD AGE: A REGISTER OF SOCIAL RESEARCH. 1955. a. Centre for Policy on Ageing, Nuffield Lodge, Regent's Park, London NW1 4RS, England. Ed. Hilary Todd.

PENNSYLVANIA. ADMINISTRATION ON AGING. STATE PLAN ON AGING. see SOCIAL SERVICES AND WELFARE

301.435   CN
TIDBITS. 1974. irreg., 8th ed. 1976. Good Neighbours Retired Citizens Association, 25 Palmer St., Truro, N.S. B2N 4E8, Canada. Ed. Patricia Irving.
    To promote interest in arts, crafts, recreation, health

353.008   US   ISSN 0098-8405
U.S. ADMINISTRATION ON AGING. ANNUAL REPORT. a. U.S. Administration on Aging, Dept. of Health, Education, and Welfare, Office of Human Development, Washington, DC 20201. Key Title: Annual Report - Administration on Aging.

618.97 301.435   US   ISSN 0071-6103
UNIVERSITY OF FLORIDA. CENTER FOR GERONTOLOGY. STUDIES AND PROGRAMS. 1951. irreg. price varies. University Presses of Florida, 15 N.W. 15th St., Gainesville, FL 32603. Ed. Carter C. Osterbind.

301.4 612   US
UNIVERSITY OF MICHIGAN. INSTITUTE OF GERONTOLOGY. OCCASIONAL PAPERS IN GERONTOLOGY. 1968. irreg., no. 10, 1975. $1.50. University of Michigan, Institute of Gerontology, 520 E. Liberty St., Ann Arbor, MI 48109. Ed. Eloise Snyder. circ. controlled.

612.67 618.97   JA
YOKUFUKAI GERIATRIC JOURNAL/ YOKUFUKAI CHOSA KENKYU KIYO. (Text in Japanese; summaries in English) 1930. a. free. Yokufukai Geriatric Hospital - Yokufukai Byoin, 1-12-1 Nishi Takaido, Suginami-ku, Tokyo 168, Japan. Indexed: Biol.Abstr. Chem.Abstr.
    Formerly: Acta Gerontologica Japonica (ISSN 0001-5768)

618.97 362.6   GE   ISSN 0084-5272
ZEITSCHRIFT FUER ALTERNSFORSCHUNG. SUPPLEMENTBAENDE. 1970. irreg. price varies. VEB Verlag Volk und Gesundheit, Neue Gruenstr. 18, 8053 Dresden, E. Germany (D.D.R.)

GERONTOLOGY AND GERIATRICS — Abstracting, Bibliographies, Statistics

362.6 310   US
U.S. ADMINISTRATION ON AGING. STATISTICAL REPORTS ON OLDER AMERICANS. no. 4, 1978. irreg. U.S. Administration on Aging, U. S. Dept. of Health, Education and Welfare, Office of Human Development Services, Washington, DC 20201.
    Formed by the merger of: U. S. Administration on Aging. Facts and Figures on Older Americans & U.S. Administration on Aging. Statistical Memos.

GIFTWARE AND TOYS

688   UK   ISSN 0068-2624
B T M A DIRECTORY. 1969. a. £1. British Toy & Hobby Manufacturers Association, 80 Camberwell Rd., London SE5 OEG, England. Ed. J. K. Horbury. adv.

688   CN   ISSN 0068-9955
CANADIAN VARIETY & MERCHANDISE DIRECTORY. 1924. a. Can.$20($30) Lloyd Publications of Canada, Box 262, West Hill, Ont. M1E 4R5, Canada. Ed. J. Lloyd. adv. index. circ. 6,000.
    Formerly: Canadian Toy, Notion and Stationery Directory.

688   US   ISSN 0072-4505
GIFT AND DECORATIVE ACCESSORIES BUYERS DIRECTORY. 1877. a. incl. in subscr. to Gifts and Decorative Accessories. Geyer-McAllister Publications, 51 Madison Ave., New York, NY 10010. Ed. Phyllis Sweed. adv. circ. 32,000.

658.72   US   ISSN 0148-9437
GIFT AND TABLEWARE REPORTER. GIFT GUIDE; a buyers' guide. a. $10. Gralla Publications, 1515 Broadway, New York, NY 10036. Ed. Jack McDermott.

688   UK
GIFTS INTERNATIONAL BUYERS' GUIDE. 1972. a. £7.50. Benn Publications Ltd., c/o T. E. Coffey, 25 New Street Square, London EC4A 3JA, England. Ed. John Hedges. adv. circ. 5,200.
    Formerly: Gifts Annual Buyers' Guide.

658.8   HK
HONG KONG TOYS. (Text in English) 1970. a. free to qualified personnel. Hong Kong Trade Development Council, Connaught Centre, Connaught Place, Hong Kong, Hong Kong. Ed.Bd. adv. illus. stat. circ. 20,000 (controlled)

688   FR   ISSN 0075-4056
JOUETS ET JEUX. (Text in French; summaries in German, Italian, English, Spanish) 1950. a. 96 F. Creations, Editions et Productions Publicitaires, 1, Place d'Estienne d'Orves, 75009 Paris, France. Ed. Georges Prieux. adv. circ. 8,500.

658.72 643   US
NATIONWIDE DIRECTORY OF GIFT AND HOUSEWARES BUYERS. a. with 3 supplements. $90. Salesman's Guide, Inc., 1140 Broadway, New York, NY 10001.

688.72   US   ISSN 0079-2349
PLAYTHINGS DIRECTORY. 1903. a. $12. Geyer-McAllister Publications, 51 Madison Ave., New York, NY 10010. Ed. Frank Reysen, Jr. adv. circ. 11,900.

688   SP
RUTAS DE CATALUNA; boletin catalogo comercial. 1954. a. free. Calle de Guardia 6, Barcelona 1, Spain. Ed. Roberto Ciurana. adv. circ. 2,000.

688   CN   ISSN 0317-9443
TOY AND DECORATION FAIR. (Text in English and French) a. free. Canadian Toy Manufacturers Association, Box 294, Kleinburg, Ont. L0J 1C0, Canada. circ. 2,000.
    Formerly: Canadian Toy Fair. Trade Show Directory (ISSN 0068-9890)

688   UK   ISSN 0082-5611
TOY TRADER YEAR BOOK. 1953. a. £6.20 (includes subscription to Toy Trader) Trade Papers Ltd., 157, Hagden Land, Watford WD1 8LW, England. Ed. Malcolm Naish. adv. circ. 5,000.
    Incorporating: Pram and Nursery Trader Year Book (ISSN 0306-6541)

688   US
TOYS, HOBBIES & CRAFTS DIRECTORY ISSUE. 1917. a. $5. Harcourt Brace Jovanovich, Inc., 757 Third Ave., New York, NY 10017. Ed. Richard Rothstein. adv. stat.
    Supersedes (as of 1978): Toys Directory.

745.5   US
WOMAN'S DAY BEST IDEAS FOR CHRISTMAS. a. $1.25. Fawcett Publications, Inc., 1515 Broadway, New York, NY 10036. Ed. Dan Blue. adv. illus.
    Formerly: Woman's Day Gifts You Can Make for Christmas (ISSN 0092-3850)

GROCERY TRADE

see Food and Food Industries—Grocery Trade

GUIDES TO SCHOOLS AND COLLEGES

see Education—Guides to Schools and Colleges

HARDWARE

see Building and Construction—Hardware

HEAT

see Physics—Heat

HEATING, PLUMBING AND REFRIGERATION

697   US   ISSN 0066-0620
A S H R A E HANDBOOK & PRODUCT DIRECTORY. (In 4 vols.: Fundamentals, Systems, Equipment, Applications) 1922. quadrennial. $50. American Society of Heating, Refrigerating and Air-Conditioning Engineers Inc., 345 E. 47 St., New York, NY 10017. Ed. Thomas Elliott. adv. index. circ. 35,000.
    Formerly: A S H R A E Handbook of Fundamentals; Supersedes in part: A S H R A E Guide and Data Book. Fundamentals and Equipment.

620   BL
ANUARIO BRASILEIRO DO FRIO. 1973. irreg. Editora Publicacoes Technicas Ltda., Av. Sao Joao 1113, Sao Paulo, Brazil. illus.

697   UK
B S R I A APPLICATION GUIDES. TECHNICAL NOTES. 1959. irreg. price varies; free to members. Building Services Research and Information Association, Old Bracknell Lane, Bracknell, Berks RG12 4AH, England. Ed. A. R. Eaves. bk. rev. circ. 1,300. Indexed: Int.Build.Serv.Abstr.
    Formerly: Heating and Ventilating Research Association. Laboratory Reports (ISSN 0438-8887)

697   UK   ISSN 0309-0248
B S R I A TECHNICAL NOTES. 1959; 1971 N.S. irreg., 1973, no. 38. price varies. Building Services Research and Information Association, Old Bracknell Lane, Bracknell, Berks. RG12 4AH, England. circ. 1,300.
    Formerly: Heating and Ventilating Research Association. Technical Notes (ISSN 0437-133X)

697   FR   ISSN 0153-999X
CATALOGUE NATIONAL DU GENIE CLIMATIQUE-CHAUFFAGE ET CONDITIONNEMENT D'AIR/NATIONAL CATALOGUE OF HEATING AND AIR CONDITIONING/NAZIONALER KATALOG DER HEIZUNG UND KLIMATISIERUNG. 1952. a. 36 F. Editions du Cartel, 2 rue de Florence, 75008 Paris, France. Ed. A. L. Savu. adv. circ. 12,000.
    From 1966-1973: Catalogue Nationale du Chauffage et du Conditionnement d'Air; From 1952-1966: Annuaire-Guide du Chauffage et du Conditionnement d'Air.

697   UK   ISSN 0307-4625
CENTERPIECE; what's new in home heating. no. 19, 1976. irreg. Solid Fuel Advisory Service, Hobart House, Grosvenor Place, London SW1X 7AE, England.

621.56   US   ISSN 0070-6167
DIRECTORY OF PUBLIC REFRIGERATED WAREHOUSES. 1930. a. $35 free to warehouse customers. Inter-National Association of Refrigerated Warehouses, 7315 Wisconsin Avenue, Suite 700-W, Washington, DC 20014. Dir. Richard Powell. adv. circ. 6,000.

697   SW   ISSN 0015-3400
FLAKTEN. English edition: Flakt Review. 1936. a. free. A B Svenska Flaktfabriken, Box 20-040, S-104 60 Stockholm 20, Sweden. Ed. Olle Edner.

H M T: THE SCIENCE AND APPLICATION OF HEAT MASS TRANSFER; reports,reviews & computer programs. see PHYSICS — Heat

697 696   US
H P A C INFO-DEX. (Heating/Piping/Air Conditioning Mechanical Systems Information Index) 1972. a. $9 includes 12 monthly issues of Heating/Piping/Air Conditioning Magazine. Reinhold Publishing Co., Inc., 600 Summer St., Stamford, CT 06904. Ed.Robert T. Korte. adv. bk. rev. circ. 23,000. (also avail. in microfilm) Indexed: Eng.Ind.

697   UK
H V A C RED BOOK OF HEATING, VENTILATING AND AIR CONDITIONING EQUIPMENT. 1971. biennial. £20. Heating and Ventilating Publications Ltd., Faversham House, 111 St. James Rd., Croydon, Surrey CR9 2TH, England. Ed. J. V. T. Gould. adv. circ. 1,500.
    Formerly(until 1979): Air Conditioning, Ventilating and Heating Equipment (ISSN 0065-4809)

696   CN   ISSN 0382-6996
HEATING, PLUMBING, AIR CONDITIONING BUYERS' GUIDE. a. Can.$21($30) Southam Communications Ltd., 1450 Don Mills Rd., Don Mills, Ont. M3B 2X7, Canada. adv. circ. 12,000.

697   UK   ISSN 0306-3585
HEATING, VENTILATING AND AIR CONDITIONING YEAR BOOK. 1968. a. £2.50. ‡ Heating and Ventilating Contractors' Association, Coastal Chambers, 172 Buckingham Palace Road, London SW1W 9TD, England. (Co-sponsors: H E V A C Association; Institution of Heating and Ventilating Engineers; Heating and Ventilating Research Association) Ed. J. M. Paynton. circ. 5,000.
    Formerly: Heating and Ventilating Year Book (ISSN 0073-1552)

696   US
I C B O PLUMBING CODE. triennial. price varies. International Conference of Building Officials, 5360 S. Workman Mill Rd., Whittier, CA 90601.

697 331.8   US   ISSN 0569-4043
INDUSTRIAL VENTILATION; A MANUAL OF RECOMMENDED PRACTICE. 1951. irreg. price varies. American Conference of Governmental Industrial Hygienists, Committee on Industrial Ventilation, Box 16153, Lansing, MI 48901.

621.56   UK   ISSN 0073-9677
INSTITUTE OF REFRIGERATION, LONDON. PROCEEDINGS. 1900. a. £3. Institute of Refrigeration, 272 London Road, Wallington, Surrey, England. index. circ. 2,000.

636 637 US
INTERNATIONAL BUYER'S GUIDE OF MOBILE
AIR CONDITIONING. 1971. a. $10. ‡
International Mobile Air Conditioning Association,
Box 567, Lansdale, PA 19446. Ed. Stanley A.
Rodman. adv. bk. rev. charts. illus. pat. stat.
tr.lit. circ. 10,000.
  Supersedes (as of 1977): Mobile Air
Conditioning.

697 US ISSN 0074-4638
INTERNATIONAL DISTRICT HEATING
ASSOCIATION. PROCEEDINGS. 1909. a. $50
free to members. ‡ International District Heating
Association, 1735 Eye St. N.W., Washington, DC
20006. circ. 500. Indexed: Therm.Abstr.

621.56 FR ISSN 0074-6541
INTERNATIONAL INSTITUTE OF
REFRIGERATION. PROCEEDINGS OF
COMMISSION MEETINGS. irreg. price varies.
International Institute of Refrigeration - Institut
International du Froid, 177 Boulevard Malesherbes,
75017 Paris, France.

697 621.56 US ISSN 0538-9895
INTERNATIONAL SERIES ON HEATING,
VENTILATION AND REFRIGERATION. 1966.
irreg., vol. 13, 1978. price varies. Pergamon Press,
Inc., Maxwell House, Fairview Park, Elmsford, NY
10523. index.
  Formerly: International Series of Monographs on
Heating, Ventilation and Refrigeration.

696 SA
MERKEL'S S.A. PLUMBER'S COSTING
MANUAL. 1977. a. R.20. Thomson Publications
S.A. (Pty) Ltd., Box 8308, Johannesburg 2000,
South Africa. adv.

697 621.56 UK ISSN 0305-0777
REFRIGERATION AND AIR CONDITIONING
YEAR BOOK. a. price varies. Refrigeration Press,
Ltd., Davis House, 69-77 High St., Croydon CR9
1QH, Surrey, England. Ed. T. A. O'Gorman. adv.
index. circ. 5,200. (also avail. in microfilm)
  Formerly: Refrigeration and Air Conditioning
Directory (ISSN 0080-0503)

621.56 AT ISSN 0080-0511
REFRIGERATION ANNUAL. 1964. a. (Australian
Institution of Refrigeration, Air Conditioning and
Heating) Page Publications Pty. Ltd., Box 606
G.P.O., Sydney, N.S.W. 2001, Australia.

697 US
TENNESSEE PLUMBING, HEATING, COOLING
CONTRACTOR; convention program. a. free.
Tennessee Association of Plumbing-Heating-Cooling
Contractors, Inc., c/o Gladys E. Kiss, Ed., 1410
Walton Road, Memphis, TN 38117. adv. circ.
2,000.
  Formerly: Tennessee Plumbing, Heating &
Mechnical Contractor.

600 US
WHOLESALER PRODUCT DIRECTORY; the who-
what-where of the plumbing, heating, piping, air-
conditioning & refrigeration industry. 1972. a. $25.
Scott Periodicals Corp., 135 Addison Ave.,
Elmhurst, IL 60126. Ed. Edwin A. Scott, Jr. adv.
circ. 8,300 (controlled)

697 US ISSN 0271-5090
WOODSTOVE, COALSTOVE, FIREPLACE &
EQUIPMENT DIRECTORY; the international
sourcebook of wood and coal heating products.
Spine title: Woodstove Directory. 1978. a. $2.95.
Energy Communications Press, Inc., Box 4474,
Manchester, NH 03108. Ed. C. R. Martel, Jr. adv.
charts. illus. stat. tr.lit. index. circ. 220,000. (back
issues avail.)

HEMATOLOGY

see Medical Sciences—Hematology

HIGHER EDUCATION

see Education—Higher Education

HISTORY

see also History—History of Africa;
History—History of Asia; History—
History of Australasia and Other Areas;
History—History of Europe; History—
History of North and South America;
History—History of the Near East;
Anthropology; Archaeology; Folklore;

also specific subjects

979.8 US
A P U PRESS ALASKANA SERIES. 1963. irreg., no.
36, 1979. price varies. Alaska Pacific University
Press, Anchorage, AK 99504. Ed. O. W. Frost.
index. circ. 3,000. (also avail. in microform from
UMI)
  Former titles: A M U Press Alaskana Series
(Alaska Methodist University) (ISSN 0002-4554);
Alaska Review.

900 CH
ACADEMIA SINICA. INSTITUTE OF MODERN
HISTORY. BULLETIN/CHUNG YANG YEN
CHIU YUAN. CHIU TAI SHIH YEN CHIU SO
CHI K'AN. (Text in Chinese) 1969. irreg. NT.$15.
Academia Sinica, Institute of Modern History,
Nankang, Taipei, Taiwan, Republic of China.

ACADEMIE DES INSCRIPTIONS ET BELLES-
LETTRES. ETUDES ET COMMENTAIRES. see
LINGUISTICS

ACADEMIE INTERNATIONALE D'HISTOIRE
DES SCIENCES. COLLECTION DES
TRAVAUX. see SCIENCES: COMPREHENSIVE
WORKS

900 GW ISSN 0567-7599
ACTA HUMBOLDTIANA. SERIES HISTORICA.
1966. irreg. price varies. (Deutsche Ibero-Amerika-
Stiftung) Franz Steiner Verlag GmbH, Friedrichstr.
24, Postfach 5529, 6200 Wiesbaden, W. Germany
(B.R.D.) Ed.Wolfgang Haberland.

960 950 BL ISSN 0002-0591
AFRO-ASIA. (Text in Portuguese; summaries in
English and French) 1965. irreg. exchange.
Universidade Federal da Bahia, Centro de Estudos
Afro-Orientais, C. P. 1163, 4000 Salvador, Bahia,
Brazil. Ed. Leovigildo Filgueiras. bk. rev. bibl.
charts. illus. circ. 1,000.

AKADEMIE DER WISSENSCHAFTEN,
GOETTINGEN. NACHRICHTEN 1.
PHILOLOGISCH-HISTORISCHE KLASSE. see
LINGUISTICS

900 US ISSN 0065-8669
AMERICAN INSTITUTE FOR MARXIST
STUDIES. HISTORICAL SERIES. no. 9, 1974.
irreg., no. 10, 1978. (American Institute for Marxist
Studies) Humanities Press, Inc., 171 First Avenue,
Atlantic Highlands, NJ 07716.

938 US ISSN 0362-8914
AMERICAN JOURNAL OF ANCIENT HISTORY.
(Text in English, Greek or Latin) 1976. irreg.,
approx. s-a. $14.50. Robinson Hall, Harvard
University, Cambridge, MA 02138. Ed. E. Badian.
adv.

973 US
AMERICAN PROBLEMS STUDIES. irreg. price
varies. Holt, Rinehart and Winston, 383 Madison
Ave., New York, NY 10017.

900 BL
ANAIS DE HISTORIA. (Text in English, French,
Portuguese, Spanish) 1968-69. a. Cr.$85.
Universidade Estadual Paulista "Julio de Mesquita
Filho", Instituto de Letras, Historia e Psicologia de
Assis, Assis, Sao Paulo, Brazil. bk. rev. circ. 1,000.

ANCIENT CULTURE AND SOCIETIES. see
ANTHROPOLOGY

ANCIENT GREEK CITIES REPORT. see
HOUSING AND URBAN PLANNING

930 BE ISSN 0066-1619
ANCIENT SOCIETY. (Text in English, French,
Dutch, German, Italian) 1970. a. 600 Fr. Katholieke
Universiteit te Leuven, c/o H. Verdin, Ed.,
Eikenboslaan 19, B-3200 Kessel-Lo, Belgium. circ.
500. (back issues avail.)

ANGLO-AMERICAN FORUM. see LITERATURE

900 016 UK ISSN 0066-3832
ANNUAL BULLETIN OF HISTORICAL
LITERATURE. 1911. a. £9.60. Historical
Association, 59a Kennington Park Rd., London
SE11 4JH, England. Ed. Mrs. I. Collins. index.
(reprint service avail. from UMI)

913 IT ISSN 0066-4766
ANTICHITA CLASSICA E CRISTIANA. 1965.
irreg., latest issue no. 16. price varies. Paideia
Editrice, Via Corsica 58/M, Brescia, Italy.

930 GW ISSN 0066-4839
ANTIQUITAS. REIHE 1. ABHANDLUNGEN ZUR
ALTEN GESCHICHTE. (Text in English, French,
German and Italian) 1955. irreg., no. 32, 1980. price
varies. Rudolf Habelt Verlag, Am Buchenhang 1,
5300 Bonn 1, W. Germany (B.R.D.) Eds. V. Burr, J.
Straub, A. Alfoeldi.

930 GW ISSN 0066-4847
ANTIQUITAS. REIHE 2. ABHANDLUNGEN AUS
DEM GEBIETE DER VOR- UND
FRUEHGESCHICHTE. 1955. irreg., no. 12, 1981.
price varies. Rudolf Habelt Verlag, Am Buchenhang
1, 5300 Bonn 1, W. Germany (B.R.D.) Eds. A.
Alfoeldi, K. Tackenberg.

930 913 GW ISSN 0066-4855
ANTIQUITAS. REIHE 3. ABHANDLUNGEN ZUR
VOR- UND FRUEHGESCHICHTE, ZUR
KLASSISCHEN UND PROVINZIAL-
ROEMISCHEN ARCHAEOLOGIE UND ZUR
GESCHICHTE DES ALTERTUMS. (Text in
German and French) 1960. irreg., no. 25, 1979.
price varies. Rudolf Habelt Verlag, Am Buchenhang
1, 5300 Bonn 1, W. Germany (B. R. D.) Ed.Bd.

930 GW ISSN 0066-4863
ANTIQUITAS. REIHE 4. BEITRAEGE ZUR
HISTORIA-AUGUSTA-FORSCHUNG. (Text in
German, English, French, Italian) 1963. irreg., vol.
14, 1980. price varies. Rudolf Habelt Verlag, Am
Buchenhang 1, 5300 Bonn 1, W. Germany (B. R.
D.) Eds. J. Straub, A. Alfoeldi.

909 SP ISSN 0210-9603
ANUARIO DE HISTORIA MODERNA Y
CONTEMPORANEA. 1974. a. 300 ptas.
Universidad de Granada, Secretariado de
Publicaciones, Hospital Real, Granada, Spain. Ed.
Pedro Herrera Puga.

913 931 GE ISSN 0066-6459
ARCHIV FUER PAPYRUSFORSCHUNG UND
VERWANDTE GEBIETE. 1907. irreg. price varies.
(Staatliche Museen zu Berlin) Teubner
Verlagsgesellschaft, Sternwartenstr. 8, 701 Leipzig,
E. Germany (D.D.R.) bk. rev.

900 US
ARCHIVE FOR REFORMATION HISTORY/
ARCHIV FUER
REFORMATIONSGESCHICHTE. 1909. a. $23
($35 in combination with Literature Review)
American Society for Reformation Research, 6477
San Bonita, St. Louis, MO 63105. Ed. Hans J.
Hillerbrand. bk. rev. bibl. circ. 500.

900 FR
ARCHIVUM; revue internationale des archives. 1951.
a. 60 rue des Francs Bourgeois, 75141 Paris Cedex
3, France. Eds. Michel Duchein, Ariane Ducrot.
Archives

950 US ISSN 0587-3606
ASIA FOUNDATION. PRESIDENT'S REVIEW.
1968. a. free. Asia Foundation, Box 3223, San
Francisco, CA 94119. Ed. Gray Gibson. illus. circ.
5,000.

930 309 US
ASPECTS OF GREEK AND ROMAN LIFE. irreg.
price varies. Cornell University Press, 124 Roberts
Place, Ithaca, NY 14850.

900 UK
ASSOCIATION OF CONTEMPORARY
HISTORIANS. BULLETIN. 1969. irreg. £1.50($5)
Association of Contemporary Historians, c/o
Secretary, Prof. D.C. Watt, London School of
Economics, Aldwych, London WC2A 2AE,
England. Ed. Dr. Neville Waites. circ. 100-150
(controlled)

HISTORY

900   NR
ASSOCIATION OF HISTORY TEACHERS IN NIGERIA. 1971. a. S.10. Educational Research Institute, Box 277, Ibadan, Nigeria. Ed. Od Olusola Akintagy.

901   US   ISSN 0067-0588
AUGUSTANA HISTORICAL SOCIETY, ROCK ISLAND, ILLINOIS. PUBLICATIONS. 1930. irreg., no. 27, 1979. price varies. Augustana Historical Society, c/o Augustana College, Rock Island, IL 61201. Ed. Ernest M. Espelie. bk. rev. circ. 1,000.

BALLENA PRESS PUBLICATIONS IN ARCHAEOLOGY, ETHNOLOGY AND HISTORY. see *ARCHAEOLOGY*

900   SZ
BASLER BEITRAEGE ZUR GESCHICHTSWISSENSCHAFT. 1938. irreg. price varies. Helbing und Lichtenhahn Verlag AG, Steinentorstr. 13, CH-4010 Basel, Switzerland.

940   GW
BEITRAEGE ZUR SOZIAL- UND WIRTSCHAFTSGESCHICHTE. 1970. a. price varies. Verlag Walter G. Muehlau, Holtenauer Str. 116, 2300 Kiel, W. Germany (B. R. D.) Ed. Wilhelm Koppe.

970   US
BERKSHIRE STUDIES IN AMERICAN HISTORY. (Subseries of Berkshire Studies in History) irreg. price varies. Holt, Rinehart and Winston, 383 Madison Ave., New York, NY 10017.

942 016   UK   ISSN 0067-7191
BIBLIOGRAPHY OF HISTORICAL WORKS ISSUED IN THE UNITED KINGDOM. 1957. quinquennial. £6. University of London, Institute of Historical Research, Senate House, London WC1E 7HU, England. (Co-sponsor: Anglo-American Conference of Historians) circ. 900.

930   GW   ISSN 0067-8201
BIBLIOTHEK DER KLASSISCHEN ALTERTUMSWISSENSCHAFTEN. NEUE FOLGE. 1963. irreg. price varies. Carl Winter Universitaetsverlag, Lutherstr. 59, 6900 Heidelberg, W. Germany (B.R.D.)

909 016   GW   ISSN 0081-900X
BIBLIOTHEK FUER ZEITGESCHICHTE, STUTTGART. SCHRIFTEN. 1962. irreg. price varies. Bernard und Graefe Verlag, Hubertusstr. 5, 8000 Munich 19, W. Germany (B.R.D.)

900   FR
BIBLIOTHEQUE HISTORIQUE. 1976. irreg. $20.20. Editions Payot, 106 Bd. Saint-Germain, Paris 6e, France.

930   NE
BULLETIN ANTIEKE BESCHAVING. Short title: Babesch. 1926. a. fl.150. Stichting Bulletin Antieke Beschaving, Rapenburg 26, 2311 EW Leiden, Netherlands. adv. bk. rev.
Supersedes: Vereniging tot Bevordering der Kennis van de Antieke Beschaving. Bulletin.

BULLETIN OF MEDIEVAL CANON LAW. NEW SERIES. see *LAW*

BURT FRANKLIN ART HISTORY AND ART REFERENCE SERIES. see *ART*

900 300 330   US   ISSN 0068-4317
BURT FRANKLIN ESSAYS IN HISTORY, ECONOMICS, AND SOCIAL SCIENCES. (Text in various languages) 1962; 1972 n.S. irreg. price varies. Lenox Hill Publishing and Distributing Corporation, 235 E. 44th St., New York, NY 10017. (back issues avail.)

900   US   ISSN 0068-4341
BURT FRANKLIN RESEARCH AND SOURCE WORKS SERIES. (Text in various languages) 1960; 1972 N.S. irreg. price varies. Lenox Hill Publishing and Distributing Corporation, 235 E. 44th St., New York, NY 10017.

CAHIERS CULTURELS. see *LINGUISTICS*

900 001.3 300   UK
CAMBRIDGE COMMONWEALTH SERIES. irreg. price varies. Cambridge University Press, Box 110, Cambridge CB2 3RL, England (And 32 E. 57th St., New York NY 10022) Ed. E. T. Stokes.

909   UK   ISSN 0084-8336
CAMBRIDGE STUDIES IN EARLY MODERN HISTORY. 1970. irreg. price varies. Cambridge University Press, Box 110, Cambridge CB2 3RL, England (and 32 E. 57th St., New York, N.Y. 10022) Eds. J. H. Elliot, H. G. Koenigsberger.

CAMBRIDGE UNIVERSITY LIBRARY. HISTORICAL BIBLIOGRAPHY SERIES. see *BIBLIOGRAPHIES*

900   CN   ISSN 0316-1900
CANADA. NATIONAL MUSEUM OF MAN. MERCURY SERIES. HISTORY DIVISION. PAPERS/CANADA. MUSEE NATIONAL DE L'HOMME. COLLECTION MERCURE. DIVISION DE L'HISTOIRE. DOSSIERS. (Text in English or French) 1972. irreg. free. (National Museum of Man, History Division) National Museums of Canada, Ottawa, Ontario K1A 0M8, Canada.

013 900   CN   ISSN 0068-8088
CANADA. PUBLIC ARCHIVES. REGISTER OF POST GRADUATE DISSERTATIONS IN PROGRESS IN HISTORY AND RELATED SUBJECTS. 1966. a. Can.$2. (Public Archives) Canadian Historical Association, c/o Public Archives of Canada, 395 Wellington St., Ottawa, Ontario K1A 0N3, Canada. Ed. P. Yurkiw. circ. 800.

CANADIAN CHURCH HISTORICAL SOCIETY JOURNAL. see *RELIGIONS AND THEOLOGY*

971   CN   ISSN 0068-8878
CANADIAN HISTORICAL ASSOCIATION. HISTORICAL PAPERS; a selection from the papers presented at the annual meeting. (Text in English and French) 1923. a. $6. ‡ Canadian Historical Association, c/o Public Archives of Canada, 395 Wellington St., Ottawa, Ont. K1A 0N3, Canada. Eds. T. Cook, C. Lacelle. cum.index: 1922-1959. circ. 3,000. Indexed: Can.Ind.

900   CN
CANADIAN WAR MUSEUM. HISTORICAL PUBLICATIONS. (Text in English and French) 1968. irreg. price varies. (National Museum of Man) National Museums of Canada, Ottawa, Ont. K1A 0M8, Canada.

900   ISSN 0069-1461
CENTERS OF CIVILIZATION SERIES. 1958. irreg. price varies. University of Oklahoma Press, 1005 Asp Ave., Norman, OK 73019. Indexed: M.L.A.

900   IT   ISSN 0069-0026
CENTRO DI DOCUMENTAZIONE SUL MOVIMENTO DEI DISCIPLINATI. QUADERNI. 1965. irreg.; no. 20, 1978. Centro di Documentazione Sul Movimento dei Disciplinati, Casella Postale 73, Perugia 06100, Italy. Ed. Prof. Giovanni Cecchini. adv. bk. rev. bibl. illus.

900   UK   ISSN 0069-2263
CEREDIGION. 1950. a. £2.50. Ceredigion Antiquarian Society, 24 Alban Square, Aberaeron, Dyfed, SA46 0AJ, Wales. Ed. David Jenkins. bk. rev. circ. 800.

900   CN   ISSN 0069-2646
CHAMPLAIN SOCIETY, TORONTO. REPORT. 1906. a. membership. Champlain Society, Royal York Hotel, 100 Front St. W., Toronto, Ont., M5J 1E3, Canada.

978   US   ISSN 0162-217X
CHARLES REDD MONOGRAPHS IN WESTERN HISTORY. 1972. irreg (1-2/yr.) price varies. (Charles Redd Center for Western Studies) Brigham Young University Press, 205 University Press Bldg., Provo, UT 84602. Eds. Thomas Alexander, Leonard J. Arrington.

500 610   US   ISSN 0073-2745
CHICAGO HISTORY OF SCIENCE AND MEDICINE. 1971. irreg., vol. 3, 1978. price varies. University of Chicago Press, 5801 S. Ellis Ave., Chicago, IL 60637. Ed. Allen G. Debus. (reprint service avail. from UMI,ISI)
History

900 309   US
CIVILIZATION AND SOCIETY: STUDIES IN SOCIAL, ECONOMIC AND CULTURAL HISTORY. irreg. D.C. Heath & Company, 125 Spring St., Lexington, MA 02173.

940   FR   ISSN 0069-5343
COLLECTION D'HISTOIRE CONTEMPORAINE. 1969. irreg. price varies. ‡ Librarie A. Hatier, 8 rue d'Assas, 75278 Paris, France. bk. rev.

930   FR   ISSN 0069-5491
COLLECTION U. SERIE HISTOIRE ANCIENNE. 1969. irreg. price varies. Librairie Armand Colin, 103 Bld. Saint-Michel, Paris 5e, France.

907   US
COLUMBIA UNIVERSITY ORAL HISTORY COLLECTION INDEX PART 1. 1979. irreg. $95. Microfilming Corporation of America, 1620 Hawkins Ave., Box 10, Sanford, NC 27330.

COMITATUS; A JOURNAL OF MEDIEVAL AND RENAISSANCE STUDIES. see *LITERATURE*

COMPARATIVE STUDIES IN SOCIETY AND HISTORY. see *SOCIAL SCIENCES: COMPREHENSIVE WORKS*

900   FR
CONFLUENTS. no. 2, 1976. irreg. Societe d'Edition les Belles Lettres, 95 Bd. Raspail, Paris 6e, France. illus.

949.3   BE   ISSN 0010-602X
CONNAITRE LA WALLONIE/TO KNOW WALLONY. Alternate title: Institut Jules Destree. Collection: Connaitre la Wallonie. 1960. irreg., price varies. Institut Jules Destree, Rue du Chateau 3, 6100 Mont-sur-Marchienne Charleroi, Belgium.

900   US
CONSPECTUS OF HISTORY. 1974. a. $4.95. Ball State University, Department of History, Muncie, IN 47306. Eds. Dwight W. Hoover, John Koumoulides.

909   UK   ISSN 0069-942X
CONTEMPORARY ISSUES SERIES.* 1969. a. Peter Owen Ltd., 20, Holland Park Ave, London W.11 3Q V, England (Dist in U. S. by: Humanities Press Inc., 450 Park Ave. So., New York, NY 10010)

972.86   CR   ISSN 0034-9003
COSTA RICA. ARCHIVO NACIONAL. REVISTA. 1936. a. free. Archivo Nacional, Calle 7, Ave. 4, Apdo. 5028, San Jose, Costa Rica. charts. illus. index. circ. 2,100.

900   US
CRITICAL PERIODS OF HISTORY SERIES. irreg. price varies. J. B. Lippincott Co., East Washington Square, Philadelphia, PA 19105.

900   SP
CUADERNOS DE ESTUDIOS MEDIEVALES. (Text in Spanish, French; summaries in English, French) 1973. a. Universidad de Granada, Departamento de Historia Medieval, Secretariado de Publicaciones, Hospital Real, Granada, Spain. Ed. Cristobal Torres. circ. 750-1,000.

900   UK
CYFRES LLYGAD Y FFYNNON. (Text in Welsh) 1972. irreg. price varies. (Welsh Joint Education Committee) University of Wales Press, 6 Gwennyth St., Cathays, Cardiff CF2 4YD, Wales. Ed. Hugh Thomas. (reprint service avail. from UMI)

900   NE
DAT WAS DE TOESTAND IN DE WERELD. 1973. a. B.V. Uitgeversmaatschappij Annoventura, Box 152, Amsterdam, Netherlands. illus.
Supersedes: Toestand in de Wereld.

930   FR
DIALOGUES D'HISTOIRE ANCIENNE. (Subseries of Besancon, France. Universite. Annales Litteraires) 1969. a. price varies. (Universite de Besancon, Centre de Recherches d'Histoire Ancienne) Societe d'Edition les Belles Lettres, 95 Boulevard Raspail, 75006 Paris, France.

909   PK   ISSN 0070-4873
DIGEST OF WORLD EVENTS. (Text in English) 1957. a. Rs.3.25. Modern Book Depot, Sialkot Cantt, Pakistan.

900   IT
DOCUMENTI E TESTIMONIANZE DI STORIA CONTEMPORANEA. 1976. irreg. Editrice la Scuola S.p.A., Via Cadorna 11, 25100 Brescia, Italy.

900   US
DOCUMENTS OF MODERN HISTORY. irreg. price varies. Saint Martins Press, 175 Fifth Ave., New York, NY 10010.

DOCUMENTS OF REVOLUTION. see *POLITICAL SCIENCE*

900   US   ISSN 0070-7562
DUMBARTON OAKS TEXTS. (English translation of original Greek) 1968. irreg. price varies. (Dumbarton Oaks Center for Byzantine Studies) J. J. Augustin, Inc., Locust Valley, NY 11560.

900   SZ   ISSN 0078-964X
ECOLE PRATIQUE DES HAUTES ETUDES. QUATRIEME SECTION. HISTORIQUES ET PHILOLOGIQUES. ANNUAIRE. 1880. a. price varies. (FR) Librarie Droz, 11, rue Massot, 1211 Geneva 12, Switzerland.

930   AT   ISSN 0085-0187
EDUBBA; studies ancient history. 1967. a. price varies. University of Sydney, Department of History, Sydney, N.S.W. 2006, Australia. circ. 500.

EDUCATIONAL ADMINISTRATION AND HISTORY MONOGRAPHS. see *EDUCATION — School Organization And Administration*

960   GH   ISSN 0013-712X
ENCYCLOPAEDIA AFRICANA. INFORMATION REPORT. 1962. irreg., no. 18, 1979. free. Encyclopaedia Africana Project, Box 2797, Accra, Ghana.

900   GW   ISSN 0071-0989
EPIGRAPHISCHE STUDIEN. 1967. irreg., vol. 12, 1979. Rheinland-Verlag, Kennedy-Ufer 2, 5000 Cologne 21, W. Germany (B.R.D.) (Distr. by: Rudolf Habelt Verlag, Am Buchenhang 1, 5300 Bonn, W. Germany (B.R.D.))

900   HU   ISSN 0071-1233
ERTEKEZESEK A TORTENETI TUDOMANYOK KOREBOL. UJ SOROZAT. 1957. irreg. price varies. (Magyar Tudomanyos Akademia) Akademiai Kiado, Publishing House of the Hungarian Academy of Sciences, P.O. Box 24, H-1363 Budapest, Hungary.

975.9   US   ISSN 0014-0376
ESCRIBANO. 1955. a. membership; institutions & libraries $3. ‡ St. Augustine Historical Society, 271 Charlotte St., St. Augustine, FL 32084. Ed. Mark E. Fretwell. illus. circ. 450(approx.)

900   US   ISSN 0071-1411
ESSAYS IN HISTORY. 1954. a. $43.50. University of Virginia, Corcoran Department of History, Randall Hall, Charlottesville, VA 22903. Ed. Donald McCracken. cum.index: vols. 1-20. circ. 250. (also avail. in microform from UMI; back issues avail)

ESSAYS IN PUBLIC WORKS HISTORY. see *PUBLIC ADMINISTRATION*

ESTUDOS ITALIANOS EM PORTUGAL. see *ART*

900   HU   ISSN 0071-2108
ETUDES HISTORIQUES. (Text in English, German, Russian, French) 1960. quinquennial. (Magyar Tudomanyos Akademia) Akademiai Kiado, Publishing House of the Hungarian Academy of Sciences, P.O. Box 24, H-1363 Budapest, Hungary. Represents: International Congress of Historical Sciences. Proceedings.

ETUDES MILITAIRES. see *MILITARY*

025 946.9   PO   ISSN 0430-4497
FILMOTECA ULTRAMARINA PORTUGUESA. BOLETIM * irreg., 1971, no. 44. Junta de Investigacaoes do Ultramar, Centro de Estudos Historicos Ultramarinos, Av. de Ilha de Madeira, Lisbon, Portugal. Ed. A. da Silva Rego. bibl.

320   SA
FOCUS ON POLITICS. irreg., no. 2, 1976. University of the Orange Free State, Institute for Contemporary History - Universiteit van die Oranje-Vrystaat, Instituut vir Eietydse Geskiedenis, Box 2320, Bloemfontein 9300, South Africa. Ed. Bd.

943.6   AU
FORSCHUNGEN UND BEITRAEGE ZUR WIENER STADTGESCHICHTE; Sonderreihe der Wiener Geschichtsblaetter. 1978. 2-3/yr. price varies. Verein fuer Geschichte der Stadt Wien, Rathaus, A-1082 Vienna, Austria. Ed. Felix Czeike. circ. 2,100.

930   GW   ISSN 0071-7665
FORSCHUNGEN ZUR ANTIKEN SKLAVEREI. 1967. irreg., vol. 13, 1981. price varies. (Akademie der Wissenschaften und der Literatur, Mainz, Kommission fuer Geschichte des Altertums) Franz Steiner Verlag GmbH, Friedrichstr. 24, Postfach 5529, 6200 Wiesbaden, W. Germany (B.R.D.) Eds. Joseph Vogt, Heinz Bellen.

901   FR
FRANCE. COMITE DES TRAVAUX HISTORIQUES ET SCIENTIFIQUES. SECTION D'HISTOIRE MODERNE ET CONTEMPORAINE. NOTICES, INVENTAIRES ET DOCUMENTS. irreg. (Comite des Travaux Historiques et Scientifiques, Section d'Histoire Moderne et Contemporaine) Bibliotheque Nationale, 58 rue Richelieu, 75084 Paris Cedex 2, France.

900   UK   ISSN 0533-9685
GREAT BRITAIN. ROYAL COMMISSION ON HISTORICAL MANUSCRIPTS.SECRETARY'S REPORT TO THE COMMISSIONERS. 1968-69. a. price varies. Royal Commission on Historical Manuscripts, Quality House, Chancery Lane, London WC2A 1HP, England (Avail. from: H. M. S. O., c/o Liaison Officer, Atlantic House, London EC1P 1BN, England)

909 031   US   ISSN 0072-7288
GREAT IDEAS TODAY. 1961. a. $11.95. Encyclopaedia Britannica, Inc., 425 N. Michigan Ave, Chicago, IL 60611. Ed. John Van Doren.

930   GW   ISSN 0072-9175
HABELTS DISSERTATIONSDRUCKE. REIHE ALTE GESCHICHTE. 1963. irreg., no. 13, 1978. price varies. Rudolf Habelt Verlag, Am Buchenhang 1, 5300 Bonn 1, W. Germany (B.R.D.) Eds. H. Schmitt & J. Straub.

930   GW   ISSN 0072-9213
HABELTS DISSERTATIONSDRUCKE. REIHE MITTELALTERLICHE GESCHICHTE. 1965. irreg., no. 2, 1979. price varies. Rudolf Habelt Verlag, Am Buchenhang 1, 5300 Bonn 1, W. Germany (B.R.D.)

900   GW   ISSN 0072-9558
HAMBURGER HISTORISCHE STUDIEN. 1969. irreg., no. 8, 1979. price varies. Verlag Helmut Buske, Schlueterstr. 14, 2000 Hamburg 13, W. Germany (B.R.D.)

943   GW   ISSN 0073-0149
HANDBUCH DER SUDETENDEUTSCHEN KULTURGESCHICHTE. 1961. irreg., vol. 6, 1973. price varies. (Collegium Carolinum) Verlag Robert Lerche, Waltherstr. 27, 8000 Munich 15, W. Germany (B.R.D.)

900   US   ISSN 0073-0521
HARVARD HISTORICAL MONOGRAPHS. 1932. irreg., 1973, no. 68. price varies. (Harvard University, Department of History) Harvard University Press, 79 Garden St., Cambridge, MA 02138.

900   US   ISSN 0073-053X
HARVARD HISTORICAL STUDIES. 1886. irreg., 1972, no. 88. price varies. (Harvard University, Department of History) Harvard University Press, 79 Garden St., Cambridge, MA 02138.

737   SZ   ISSN 0073-0963
HAUTES ETUDES NUMISMATIQUES. 1966. irreg., 1967, no. 2. (Ecole Pratique des Hautes Etudes, Centre de Recherches d'Histoire et de Philologie, FR) Librarie Droz, 11, rue Massot, 1211 Geneva 12, Switzerland. circ. 1,000.

090   SZ   ISSN 0073-2419
HISTOIRE ET CIVILISATION DU LIVRE. 1966. irreg., no. 9, 1976. price varies. (Ecole Pratique des Hautes Etudes, Centre de Recherches d'Histoire et de Philologie, FR) Librarie Droz, 11, rue Massot, 1211 Geneva 12, Switzerland. circ. 1,000.

900   GW   ISSN 0341-0056
HISTORIA. EINZELSCHRIFTEN. (Supplement to Historia) (Text in English, French, German) irreg., vol. 38, 1981. price varies. Franz Steiner Verlag GmbH, Friedrichstr. 24, Postfach 5529, 6200 Wiesbaden, W. Germany (B.R.D.)

909   SP
HISTORIA UNIVERSAL. 1979. irreg. price varies. Ediciones Universidad de Navarra, S.A., Plaza de los Sauces 1 y 2, Baranain, Pamplona, Spain.

900   FI   ISSN 0439-2183
HISTORIAN AITTA. 1929. irreg., latest no. 19. Historian Ystavain Liitto - Society of the Friends of History, Museokatu 46 B 42, 00100 Helsinki 10, Finland. Indexed: Hist.Abstr.

900   PH   ISSN 0073-2613
HISTORICAL CONSERVATION SOCIETY. PUBLICATIONS. 1961. irreg., latest issue, 1975. price varies. Historical Conservation Society, Manila, Philippines (Dist. by: Cellar Book Shop, 18090 Wyoming, Detroit, MI 48221)

900   SI
HISTORICAL MISCELLANY. (Text in Chinese and English) 1967. a. S.$2($1) (Historical Society of Nanyang University) Nanyang University, Jurong Road, Singapore 22, Singapore.

900   US   ISSN 0046-7553
HISTORICAL MUSINGS. 1971. irreg. Indiana University of Pennsylvania, Department of History, Indiana, PA 15701.

901   UK   ISSN 0073-2621
HISTORICAL PROBLEMS: STUDIES AND DOCUMENTS. 1968. irreg. price varies. George Allen & Unwin (Publishers) Ltd., 40 Museum St., London W. C. 1, England (U.S. Address: Allen & Unwin Inc., 198 Ash St., Reading, MA 01867)

900   UK   ISSN 0308-7417
HISTORICAL RESEARCH FOR UNIVERSITY DEGREES IN THE UNITED KINGDOM. PART 1: THESES COMPLETED. 1967. a. £1. University of London, Institute of Historical Research, Senate House, London WC1E 7HU, England. Ed. Joyce M. Horn. circ. 750.

900   UK   ISSN 0308-7425
HISTORICAL RESEARCH FOR UNIVERSITY DEGREES IN THE UNITED KINGDOM. PART 2: THESES IN PROGRESS. 1967. a. £2. University of London, Institute of Historical Research, Senate House, London WC1E 7HU, England. Ed.Joyce M. Horn. circ. 750.

900   GW   ISSN 0440-9558
HISTORISCHE FORSCHUNGEN. (Text in English, French, and German) irreg., vol. 6, 1978. price varies. (Akademie der Wissenschaften und der Literatur, Mainz, Historische Kommission) Franz Steiner Verlag GmbH, Friedrichstr. 24, Postfach 5529, 6200 Wiesbaden, W. Germany (B.R.D.) Ed. Bd.

900   GW   ISSN 0067-5857
HISTORISCHE KOMMISSION ZU BERLIN. EINZELVERDEFFENTLICHUNGEN. 1968. irreg. price varies. Colloquium Verlag, Unter den Eichen 93, 1000 Berlin 45, W. Germany (B.R.D.) circ. 1,000.

909.82   US   ISSN 0098-163X
HISTORY IN NEWSPAPER FRONT PAGES. 1974. a. $2.95. Drake Publishers, Inc., 801 Second Ave., New York, NY 10017. illus.

900   UK
HISTORY OF CIVILIZATION. irreg. price varies. Routledge & Kegan Paul Ltd., Broadway House, Newtown Rd., Henley-on-Thames, Oxon. RG9 1EN, England (U.S. address: Routledge Journals, 9 Park St., Boston, MA 02108)

HISTORY TEACHERS ASSOCIATION OF NEW SOUTH WALES. NEWSLETTER. see *EDUCATION — Teaching Methods And Curriculum*

HOLIDAY BOOK. see *RELIGIONS AND THEOLOGY*

HOMMES ET LA TERRE. see *GEOGRAPHY*

900 UK ISSN 0309-8346
HUGUENOT SOCIETY OF LONDON.
PROCEEDINGS. 1885. a. membership. Huguenot Society of London, c/o Barclay's Bank Ltd., 1 Pall Mall East, London SW1Y 5AX, England. Ed. Irene Scouloudi. bk. rev. illus. cum.index.

900 UK ISSN 0309-8354
HUGUENOT SOCIETY OF LONDON, QUARTO SERIES. 1885. every 2-4/yrs. Huguenot Society of London, c/o Barclays Bank Ltd., 1 Pall Mall East, London SW1Y 5AX, England. Ed. Irene Scouloudi.

940 US
HUMANA CIVILITAS; sources and studies relating to the Middle Ages and the Renaissance. 1976. irreg. price varies. (University of California, Los Angeles, Center for Medieval and Renaissance Studies) Undena Publications, Box 97, Malibu, CA 90265. Eds. Michael J.B.Allan, Robert L. Benson, Fredi Chiapelli.

I P E K/ANNUAL REVIEW OF PREHISTORIC AND ETHNOGRAPHICAL ART. (Jahrbuch fuer Praehistorische und Ethnographische Kunst) see *FOLKLORE*

900 UK ISSN 0306-977X
ILKESTON AND DISTRICT LOCAL HISTORY SOCIETY. OCCASIONAL PAPER. no. 5, 1975. irreg. £1.40. Ilkeston and District Local History Society, Ilkeston, Derbyshire DE7 5RE, England.

950 II
INDIAN ASSOCIATION OF AMERICAN STUDIES. PAPERS. 1973, no. 7. a. Indian Association of American Studies, c/o Dwijendra Tripathi, Indian Institute of Management, Vastrapur, Ahmedabad 380015, India. bibl.
Formerly: Indian Congress of American History. Papers.

INSTITUT FUER DEN WISSENSCHAFTLICHEN FILM. PUBLIKATIONEN ZU WISSENSCHAFTLICHEN FILMEN. SEKTION GESCHICHTE, PUBLIZISTIK. see *MOTION PICTURES*

900 GW ISSN 0170-365X
INSTITUT FUER EUROPAEISCHE GESCHICHTE, MAINZ. VEROEFFENTLICHUNGEN. ABTEILUNG UNIVERSALGESCHICHTE. BEIHEFTE. (Text in English, French, and German) irreg., vol. 12, 1981. price varies. Franz Steiner Verlag GmbH, Friedrichstr. 24, Postfach 5529, 6200 Wiesbaden, W. Germany (B.R.D.) Ed. K.O. von Aretin.

900 200 GW
INSTITUT FUER EUROPAEISCHE GESCHICHTE, MAINZ. VEROEFFENTLICHUNGEN. ABTEILUNG UNIVERSALGESCHICHTE UND ABTEILUNG RELIGIONSGESCHICHTE. (Text in English, French, and German) irreg., vol. 104, 1981. price varies. Franz Steiner Verlag GmbH, Friedrichstr. 24, Postfach 5529, 6200 Wiesbaden, W. Germany (B.R.D.) Eds. K. O. von Aretin, P. Meinhold.
Formerly: Institut fuer Europaeische Geschichte, Mainz. Veroeffentlichungen. Abteilung Universitaetsgeschichte und Abteilung fuer Abendlaendische Religionsphilosophie (ISSN 0537-7919)

900 200 GW
INSTITUT FUER EUROPAEISCHE GESCHICHTE, MAINZ. VORTRAEGE. ABTEILUNG UNIVERSALGESSCHICHTE UND ABTEILUNG RELIGIONSGESCHICHTE. (Text in English, French, and German) irreg., vol. 74, 1981. price varies. Franz Steiner Verlag GmbH, Friedrichstr. 24, Postfach 5529, 6200 Wiesbaden, W. Germany (B.R.D.) Eds. K. O. von Aretin, P. Meinhold.
Formerly: Institut fuer Europaeische Geschichte, Mainz. Vortraege. Abteilung Universalgeschichte und Abteilung fuer Abendlaendische Religionsphilosophie (ISSN 0537-7927)

940.27 FR ISSN 0020-2371
INSTITUT NAPOLEON. REVUE. 1933. a. 55 F.($11) Societe d'Etudes Napoleoniennes, Ecole Pratique des Hautes Etudes, Section IV, 45 rue des Ecoles, Paris (5e), France. Ed. Jean Tulard. bk. rev. illus. index. circ. 100,000. (also avail. in microfilm)

954 II
INSTITUTE FOR REWRITING INDIAN HISTORY. ANNUAL REPORT AND GENERAL MEETING INVITATION. (Text in English) 1965. a. $2. Institute for Rewriting Indian History, N-128 Greater Kailash I, New Delhi 110048, India. Ed. P. N. Oak. adv. bk. rev. circ. 1,100.

900 MX ISSN 0076-762X
INSTITUTO NACIONAL DE ANTROPOLOGIA E HISTORIA. SERIE CULTURAS DEL MUNDO. 1966. irreg. price varies. Instituto Nacional de Antropologia e Historia, Cordoba 45, Mexico 7,D.F., Mexico.

940 RM
INSTITUTUL PEDAGOGIC ORADEA. LUCRARI STIINTIFICE: SERIA ISTORIE. (Continues in part its Lucrari Stiintifice: Seria Istorie, Stiinte Sociale, Pedagogie (1971-72), its Lucrari Stiintifice: Seria A and Seria B (1969-70), and its Lucrari Stiintifice (1967-68)) (Text in Rumanian, occasionally in English or French; summaries in Rumanian, French, English or German) a. Institutul Pedagogic Oradea, Calea Armatei Rosii Nr. 5, Oradea, Romania.

900 FR ISSN 0074-2783
INTERNATIONAL COMMITTEE FOR HISTORICAL SCIENCE. BULLETIN D'INFORMATION. 1953. irreg.; no. 11, May 1980. International Committee for Historical Science, c/o Michel Francois, Sec. Gen, 270 Bd. Raspail, 75014 Paris, France (Subscr. to: Jean-Charles Biaudet, la Folie, CH 1605 Chexbres, Switzerland)

949.5 GR ISSN 0074-3542
INTERNATIONAL CONGRESS FOR BYZANTINE STUDIES. ACTS/CONGRES INTERNATIONAL DES ETUDES BYZANTINES. ACTES.*
(Published in host country) irreg., 1971, 14th, Bucharest. International Association for Byzantine Studies, Rue Sissimi 31, Athens 612, Greece.

942 500.9 UI
ISLE OF MAN NATURAL HISTORY AND ANTIQUARIAN SOCIETY. PROCEEDINGS. 1888. biennial. £2. ‡ Isle of Man Natural History and Antiquarian Society, c/o Manx Museum, Douglas, Isle of Man. Ed. R. A. Curphey. index; cum.index. circ. 300.

930 IT ISSN 0075-1502
ISTITUTO ELLENICO DI STUDI BIZANTINI E POSTBIZANTINI, VENICE. BIBLIOTECA. 1962. irreg., no. 10, 1979. prices varies. Istituto Ellenico di Studi Bizantini e Post-Bizantini, Castello 3412, 3412 Venezia, Italy. circ. 1,500.

930 IT
ISTITUTO ITALIANO DI PREISTORIA E PROTOSTORIA. ATTI DELLA RIUNIONE SCIENTIFICA. no. 15, 1973. a. L.10000. Istituto Italiano di Preistoria e Protostoria, Florence, Italy.

900 UR
ISTORICHESKIE ZAPISKI. vol. 97, 1976. irreg. 1.62 Rub. (Akademiya Nauk S.S.S.R., Institut Istorii S.S.S.R.) Izdatel'stvo Nauka, Podsosenskii Per., 21, Moscow K-62, U.S.S.R. Ed. A. Samsonov. circ. 2,050.

900 RM ISSN 0075-1626
ISTORIE SI CIVILIZATIE. 1970. irreg. (Academia Republicii Socialiste Romania) Editura Academiei Republicii Socialiste Romania, Calea Victoriei 125, Bucharest, Romania (Subscr. to: ILEXIM, Str. 13 Decembrie Nr. 3, P.O. Box 136-137, Bucharest, Romania)

902 GW ISSN 0075-2835
JAHRESBERICHT DER BAYERISCHEN BODENDENKMALPFLEGE. 1960. a. price varies. (Landesamt fuer Denkmalpflege) Rudolf Habelt Verlag, Am Buchenhang 1, 5300 Bonn 1, W. Germany (B.R.D.)

900 US ISSN 0075-3610
JEROME LECTURES. 1933. irreg. not avail. by subscription. University of Michigan Press, Box 1104, 839 Greene St., Ann Arbor, MI 48106.

900 US ISSN 0075-3874
JOHNS HOPKINS SYMPOSIA IN COMPARATIVE HISTORY. 1970. irreg. price varies. Johns Hopkins University Press, Baltimore, MD 21218.

900 320 US ISSN 0075-3904
JOHNS HOPKINS UNIVERSITY STUDIES IN HISTORICAL AND POLITICAL SCIENCE. 1882. irreg. price varies. Johns Hopkins University Press, Baltimore, MD 21218. (also avail. in microform from UMI)

900 491 PL
KATOLICKI UNIWERSYTET LUBELSKI WYDZIAL HISTORYCZNO-FILOLOGICZNY. ROZPRAWY. (Text in Polish; summaries in German) 1947. irreg. price varies. Katolicki Uniwersytet Lubelski, Towarzystwo Naukowe, Chopina 29, 20-023 Lublin, Poland. index. circ. 450.

900 SA ISSN 0023-2084
KLEIO. (Text in Afrikaans, Dutch and English) 1969. a. R.0.70. University of South Africa, Department of History, Box 392, Pretoria 0001, South Africa. Ed. K. W. Smith. adv. bk. rev. bibl. illus. cum.index (vol. 1-4 in vol. 6, no. 2, 1974) circ. 2,000. Indexed: Hist.Abstr. Amer.Hist.& Life. Ind.S.A.Per.

930 GE ISSN 0075-6334
KLIO; Beitraege zur alten Geschichte. bi-a. M.103. (Akademie der Wissenschaften der DDR, Zentralinstitut fuer Alte Geschichte und Archaeologie) Akademie-Verlag, Leipziger Str. 3-4, 108 Berlin, E. Germany (D.D.R.)

900 II
KOODAL HISTORICAL SERIES. (Text in English) irreg. Koodal Publishers, 217-A South Masi St., Madurai 625001, Tamilnadu, India. Ed. N. Subrahmanian. bibl.

900 GW
KRITISCHE STUDIEN ZUR GESCHICHTSWISSENSCHAFT. irreg. price varies. Vandenhoeck und Ruprecht, Theaterstr. 13, Postfach 77, 3400 Goettingen, W. Germany (B.R.D.)

300 900 GW
KULTUR UND GESELLSCHAFT; Neue historische Forschungen. 1976. irreg. price varies. Friedrich Frommann Verlag Guenther Holzboog GmbH and Co., Postfach 500460, Koenig-Karl-Str. 27, 7000 Stuttgart 50, W. Germany (B.R.D.) Ed. R. van Duelmen. bibl.

KUNSTHISTORISCHES INSTITUT IN FLORENZ. MITTEILUNGEN. see *ART*

LAENDERMONOGRAPHIEN. see *GEOGRAPHY*

900 US ISSN 0075-7772
LAMAR LECTURE SERIES. 1958. a. price varies. (Eugenia Dorothy Blount Lamar Lectures at Mercer University, Macon, Georgia) University of Georgia Press, Athens, GA 30602. (reprint service avail. from UMI)

LECCIONES DE HISTORIA JURIDICA. see *LAW*

942 UK ISSN 0024-0664
LEICESTERSHIRE HISTORIAN. 1967. a. £0.70. Leicestershire Local History Council, c/o Mrs. J. M. Mason, Ramses, Walton, Lutterworth, Leics. LE17 5RP, England. Ed. J. Goodacre. bk. rev. bibl. circ. 500.
Local

900 NE ISSN 0458-998X
LEIDSE HISTORISCHE REEKS. 1953. irreg., vol. 21, 1977. price varies. Leiden University Press, c/o Martinus Nijhoff, Box 566, 2501 CN The Hague, Netherlands.

LINGUARUM MINORUM DOCUMENTA HISTORIOGRAPHICA. see *LINGUISTICS*

900 UK ISSN 0076-0544
LONDON HISTORY STUDIES. 1968. irreg. price varies. University of London Press Ltd., Saint Paul's House, Warwick Lane, London EC4P 4AH, England. Ed. R. Ben Jones.

LONGITUDE; a magazine of the Seven Seas. see *TRANSPORTATION — Ships And Shipping*

900 SW ISSN 0076-1494
LUND STUDIES IN INTERNATIONAL HISTORY. (Text in English and German) 1970. irreg. price varies. Esselte Studium AB, Scheelegatan 24, S-112 85 Stockholm, Sweden. Eds. Goeran Rystad, Sven Taegil. index.

| 900 | | II | ISSN 0464-5030 |

MAHARAJA SAYAJIRAO UNIVERSITY OF BARODA. DEPARTMENT OF HISTORY SERIES. 1958. irreg. price varies. Maharaja Sayajirao University of Baroda, Department of History, Baroda 390002, Gujarat, India. Ed. Satish C. Misra. circ. 500.

| 900 | | US | |

MAKING OF THE TWENTIETH CENTURY. irreg. St. Martin's Press, 175 Fifth Ave., New York, NY 10010.

| 900 | | US | ISSN 0076-4981 |

MASSACHUSETTS HISTORICAL SOCIETY. PROCEEDINGS. 1859. a. $15 paper, $20 cloth. Massachusetts Historical Society, 1154 Boylston St., Boston, MA 02215. Ed. Malcolm Freiberg. circ. 750. Indexed: Amer.Hist. & Life. Hist.Abstr.

| 900 | | IT | |

MATERIALI DI STORIA URBANA. 1978. irreg. Officina Edizioni, Passeggiata di Ripetta 25, 00186 Rome, Italy.

| 900 | | PL | |

MATERIALY HISTORYCZNO-METODYCZNE. 1966. irreg. price varies. Politechnika Poznanska, Pl. Curie Sklodowskiej 5, Poznan, Poland.
    Formerly: Politechnika Poznanska. Materialy Historyczno-Metodyczne. Studia Filozoficzne (ISSN 0079-4481)

| 942.5 410 | | IE | |

MEDIAEVAL AND MODERN BRETON SERIES. no. 3, 1975. irreg. £6. Dublin Institute for Advanced Studies, Dublin, Ireland.

| 900 | | US | ISSN 0361-946X |

MEDIAEVALIA. 1975. a. $15. State University of New York at Binghamton, Center for Medieval and Early Renaissance Studies, Binghamton, NY 13901. Ed. Bernard S. Levy. circ. 400. (reprint service avail. from ISI) Indexed: M.L.A.

| 909 | | IT | |

MEDIOEVO: SAGGI E RASSEGNE. 1975. a. price varies. (Universita degli Studi di Cagliari, Istituto di Storia Medioevale) Editrice Sarda Fossataro, Viale Elmas 154, 09100 Cagliari, Italy.

| 940 | | GW | ISSN 0340-8140 |

MENDELSSOHN STUDIEN; Beitraege zur neueren deutschen Kultur- und Wirtschaftsgeschichte. (Text in English and German) 1972. irreg., vol. 2, 1975. price varies. (Mendelssohn-Gesellschaft e. V.) Duncker und Humblot, Dietrich-Schaefer-Weg 9, Postfach 410329, 1000 Berlin 41, W. Germany (B.R.D.) Ed. Cecile Lowenthal-Hensel.

| 900 | | BU | |

METODOLOGICHESKI I ISTORIOGRAFSKI PROBLEMI NA ISTORICHESKATA NAUKA. (Summaries in Russian, English, French and German) 1973. biennial. 2.84 lv.($2) (Bulgarska Akademiia na Naukite, Institut za Istoriia) Publishing House of the Bulgarian Academy of Sciences, Ul. Akad. G. Bonchev, 1113 Sofia, Bulgaria (Dist. by: Hemus, 6, Rouski Blvd., 1000 Sofia, Bulgaria) circ. 1,000.

| 900 | | US | |

MILESTONES OF HISTORY. 1974. irreg. $7.95 per issue. ‡ Newsweek Books, 444 Madison Ave., New York, NY 10022. adv. bk. rev. bibl. charts. illus.

MISCELLANEA MEDIAEVALIA. see PHILOSOPHY

| 330.1 | | FR | ISSN 0077-0434 |

MONNAIES, PRIX, CONJONCTURE. 1952. irreg., 1968, no. 7. price varies. Editions de l' Ecole des Hautes Etudes en Sciences Sociales, 131 Bd. Saint-Michel, 75005 Paris, France.

| 900 | | US | |

MONOGRAPHS ON THE ANCIENT NEAR EAST. 1974. irreg. $17. Undena Publications, P.O. Box 97, Malibu, CA 90265. Ed. Bd.

| 930 | | GW | ISSN 0077-2003 |

MUENSTERSCHE BEITRAEGE ZUR VOR- UND FRUEHGESCHICHTE. 1964. irreg. price varies. (Universitaet Muenster) Verlag August Lax, Postfach 8847, 3200 Hildesheim, W. Germany (B. R. D.) Eds. K Tackenberg, K. J. Narr.
    Formerly: Muenstersche Beitraege zur Vorgeschichtsforschung.

| 900 | | SP | ISSN 0077-2054 |

MUNDO ANTIGUO. 1962. irreg.; 1979, no. 4. price varies. (Universidad de Navarra, Departamento de Historia Antigua) Ediciones Universidad de Navarra, S.A., Plaza de los Sauces, 1 y 2, Baranain, Pamplona, Spain.

| 901 | | BE | |

MUSEE ROYAL DE L'AFRIQUE CENTRALE. ANNALES. SERIE IN 8. SCIENCES HISTORIQUES/KONINKLIJK MUSEUM VOOR MIDDEN-AFRIKA. ANNALEN. REEKS IN 8. HISTORISCHE WETENSCHAPPEN. 1964. irreg., latest no. 4, 1971. Musee Royal de l'Afrique Centrale, 13 Steenweg op Leuven, B-1980 Tervuren., Belgium. charts. illus.

| 900 | | IT | ISSN 0082-6863 |

MUSEO EGIZIO, TURIN. CATALOGO. SERIE PRIMA: MONUMENTI E TESTI. 1967. irreg. price varies. Casa Editrice Felice le Monnier, Via Scipione Ammirato 100, C.P.455, 50136 Florence, Italy.

| 913 069 | | GE | ISSN 0079-4376 |

MUSEUM FUER UR- UND FRUEHGESCHICHTE DES BEZIRKES POTSDAM, FRANKFURT/ ODER UND COTTBUS. VEROEFFENTLICHUNGEN. 1962. a. price varies. (Museum fuer Ur- und Fruehgeschichte, Potsdam) VEB Deutscher Verlag der Wissenschaften, Postfach 1216, 108 Berlin, E. Germany (D.D.R.) Ed. Bernhard Gramsch.

NARODNI TECHNICKE MUZEUM. ROZPRAVY. see TECHNOLOGY: COMPREHENSIVE WORKS

| 943 | | GW | |

NEUZEIT IM AUFBAU; Darstellung und Dokumentation. 1977. irreg. price varies. Friedrich Frommann Verlag Guenther Holzboog GmbH und Co., Postfach 500460, Koenig-Karl-Str. 27, 7000 Stuttgart 50, W. Germany (B.R.D.) Ed.Bd.

| 900 | | US | |

NEW PERSPECTIVES IN HISTORY. irreg. price varies. Houghton Mifflin Co., One Beacon St., Boston, MA 02107.

| 071 | | US | |

NEW YORK TIMES SCHOOL MICROFILM COLLECTION INDEX. irreg. Microfilming Corporation of America, 1620 Hawkins Ave., Box 10, Sanford, NC 27330. Ed. Jack Heher. illus.
    Formerly: New York Times School Microfilm Collection Index by Reels (ISSN 0095-5663)

NORDISK ARKIVKUNSKAB. see LIBRARY AND INFORMATION SCIENCES

| 900 | | NO | ISSN 0029-2311 |

NORSKE VIDENSKAPS-AKADEMI. HISTORISK-FILOSOFISK KLASSE. AVHANDLINGER TWO. (Text in several languages) 1925. irreg. price varies. (Norwegian Academy of Sciences and Letters) Universitetsforlaget, Kolstadgt. 1, Box 2959-Toeyen, Oslo 6, Norway (Dist. in the U.S. by: Columbia University Press, 136 South Broadway, Irvington, NY 10533) bibl. circ. 775.

| 900 | | GW | ISSN 0078-2238 |

NOVA HEDWIGA, BEIHEFTE. (Text in English, French, German) 1962. irreg. price varies. J. Cramer, In den Springaeckern 2, 3300 Braunschweig, W. Germany (B.R.D.) Ed. Johannes Gerloff. circ. 400.

| 900 | | GW | ISSN 0078-2742 |

NUNTIATURBERICHTE AUS DEUTSCHLAND NEBST ERGAENZENDEN AKTENSTUECKEN. (Text in German and Latin) 1959. irreg. price varies. (Deutsches Historisches Institut in Rom, IT) Max Niemeyer Verlag, Pfrondorfer Str.4, 7400 Tuebingen, W. Germany (B.R.D.)

NUOVA UNIVERSALE STUDIUM. see LITERATURE

| 900 | | US | ISSN 0094-0798 |

ORAL HISTORY REVIEW. (Contains selections from its Proceedings) 1973. a. $5. Oral History Association, Box 13734, North Texas State University, Denton, TX 76203. circ. 1,700.
    Formerly (1966-72): National Colloquium on Oral History. Proceedings (ISSN 0077-3832)

| 900 | | US | ISSN 0078-5822 |

OREGON STATE MONOGRAPHS. STUDIES IN HISTORY. 1938. irreg., no. 8, 1981. price varies. Oregon State University Press, 101 Waldo Hall, Corvallis, OR 97331.

ORESTES BROWNSON SERIES ON CONTEMPORARY THOUGHT AND AFFAIRS. see PHILOSOPHY

| 900 | | US | ISSN 0078-7205 |

OXFORD HISTORICAL SERIES. irreg. Oxford University Press, 200 Madison Ave., New York, NY 10016 (and Ely House, 37 Dover St., London W1X 4AH, England) Ed.Bd.

| 930 | | IT | |

PAPYROLOGICA FLORENTINA. 1976. irreg. Edizioni Gonnelli, Florence, Italy. illus.

| 900 | | GW | |

PAPYROLOGISCHE TEXTE UND ABHANDLUNGEN. 1968. irreg., no. 27, 1980. price varies. Rudolf Habelt Verlag, Am Buchenhang 1, 5300 Bonn 1, W. Germany (B.R.D.) Ed. Bd.

| 900 | | BL | ISSN 0553-8491 |

PESQUISAS: PUBLICACOES DE HISTORIA. (Numbering is in continuation of articles published in Pesquisas) no. 12, 1960. irreg. price varies (or exchange) (Universidade do Vale do Rio dos Sinos, Instituto Anchietano de Pesquisas) Unisinos, Praca Tiradentes, 35, Sao Leopoldo RS, Brazil.
    Supersedes in part: Pesquisas.

| 909 | | US | ISSN 0094-4998 |

POINT OF REFERENCE. 1974. a. $2. Alexandrian Society, c/o History Department, Virginia Commonwealth University, 926 Park Ave., Richmond, VA 23284.

| 800 900 | | PL | ISSN 0079-3302 |

POLSKA AKADEMIA NAUK. ODDZIAL W KRAKOWIE. KOMISJA HISTORYCZNOLITERACKA. ROCZNIK. (Text in Polish; summaries in English, French, German, Russian) 1963. a. 42 Zl. Ossolineum, Publishing House of the Polish Academy of Sciences, Rynek 9, 50-106 Wroclaw, Poland (Dist. by Ars Polona-Ruch, Krakowskie Przedmiescie 7, Warsaw, Poland) Ed. Marian Stepien. circ. 580.

| 900 | | PL | ISSN 0079-337X |

POLSKA AKADEMIA NAUK. ODDZIAL W KRAKOWIE. KOMISJA NAUK HISTORYCZNYCH. MATERIALY. (Text in Polish and Russian) 1958. irreg., no. 27, 1979. price varies. Ossolineum, Publishing House of the Polish Academy of Sciences, Rynek 9, 50-106 Wroclaw, Poland (Dist. by Ars Polona-Ruch, Krakowskie Przedmiescie 7, Warsaw, Poland)

| 930 | | | |

PROBLEMS IN ANCIENT HISTORY. irreg. price varies. Macmillan Publishing Co., Inc., 866 Third Ave., New York, NY 10022.

PROBLEMS OF THE CONTEMPORARY WORLD/PROBLEMES DU MONDE CONTEMPORAIN/PROBLEMAS DEL MUNDO CONTEMPORANEO. see SOCIAL SCIENCES: COMPREHENSIVE WORKS

PROBLEMY POLONII ZAGRANICZNEJ. see POLITICAL SCIENCE

| 900 | | UY | ISSN 0079-8061 |

PUPILA: LIBROS DE NUESTRO TIEMPO.* irreg. Editorial Arca, Colonia 1263, Montevideo, Uruguay.

| 900 | | FR | ISSN 0249-5619 |

RECHERCHES D'HISTOIRE ET DE SCIENCES SOCIALES/STUDIES IN HISTORY AND SOCIAL SCIENCES. 1980. irreg. Editions de l' Ecole des Hautes Etudes en Sciences Sociales, Departement Diffusion, 131 Bd. Saint-Michel, F-75005 Paris, France.

| 909 342 | | GW | ISSN 0486-1493 |

RECHT UND GESCHICHTE. (Contains vol. 7, 1978. price varies. (Universitaet Mainz, Institut fuer Rechts- und Verfassungsgeschichte) Franz Steiner Verlag GmbH, Friedrichstr. 24, Postfach 5529, 6200 Wiesbaden, W. Germany (B.R.D.) Ed. Johannes Baermann.

900 US ISSN 0080-0287
RECORDS OF CIVILIZATION. SOURCES AND STUDIES. 1915. irreg., latest no. 96. price varies. Columbia University Press, 136 South Broadway, Irvington-On-Hudson, NY 10533.

900 UK ISSN 0080-0554
REGESTA REGUM SCOTTORUM. (Text in Latin; commentary and introduction in English) 1960. irreg. price varies. Edinburgh University Press, George Sq., Edinburgh EH8 9LF, Scotland. Ed. G. H. Barrow.

900 CK
REVISTA DE HISTORIA. 1977. irreg. Libreria y Editorial America Latina, Avda Caracas 55-16, Apdo Aereo 53613, Bogota 2, Colombia.

REVUE D'EGYPTOLOGIE. see ARCHAEOLOGY

RHODE ISLAND JEWISH HISTORICAL NOTES. see ETHNIC INTERESTS

900 069 GW ISSN 0076-275X
ROEMISCH-GERMANISCHES ZENTRALMUSEUM, MAINZ. KATALOGE VOR- UND FRUEHGESCHICHTLICHER ALTERTUEMER. 1909. irreg., no. 19, 1979. price varies. Rudolf Habelt Verlag, Am Buchenhang 1, 5300 Bonn 1, W. Germany (B.R.D.).

ROSENBERG LIBRARY BULLETIN. see LIBRARY AND INFORMATION SCIENCES

900 AT ISSN 0085-5804
ROYAL HISTORICAL SOCIETY OF QUEENSLAND. JOURNAL. 1914. a. Aus.$7. Royal Historical Society of Queensland, Box 1811, Brisbane, Qld. 4001, Australia. Ed. H.J. Summers. circ. 600.

900 700 CN ISSN 0316-1269
ROYAL ONTARIO MUSEUM. HISTORY, TECHNOLOGY AND ART MONOGRAPHS. 1973. irreg. price varies. Royal Ontario Museum, 100 Queen's Park, Toronto, Ont. M5S 2C6, Canada.

ROYAL SOCIETY OF TASMANIA, HOBART. PAPERS AND PROCEEDINGS. see SCIENCES: COMPREHENSIVE WORKS

930 GW ISSN 0080-5181
SAARBRUECKER BEITRAEGE ZUR ALTERTUMSKUNDE. 1964. irreg., no. 25, 1980. price varies. Rudolf Habelt Verlag, Am Buchenhang 1, 5300 Bonn 1, W. Germany (B.R.D.) Eds. R. Hachmann, W. Schmitthenner.

SAECHSISCHE AKADEMIE DER WISSENSCHAFTEN, LEIPZIG. PHILOLOGISCH-HISTORISCHE KLASSE. ABHANDLUNGEN. see LINGUISTICS

SAECHSISCHE AKADEMIE DER WISSENSCHAFTEN, LEIPZIG. PHILOLOGISCH-HISTORISCHE KLASSE. SITZUNGSBERICHTE. see LINGUISTICS

930 001.3 GW ISSN 0343-2009
SAECULA SPIRITALIA. (Text in English, French, German, Italian, Latin) 1979. irreg., vol. 4, 1981. price varies. Verlag Valentin Koerner, H-Sielcken-Str. 36, Postfach 304, D-7570 Baden-Baden 1, W. Germany(B.R.D.) Ed. Dieter Wuttke.

900 GW ISSN 0080-5319
SAECULUM; Jahrbuch fuer Universalgeschichte. 1950. a. DM.68. Karl Alber GmbH, Hermann-Herder-Str. 4, 7800 Freiburg, W. Germany (B.R.D.) Ed. Oskar Koehler.

SALZBURGER BEITRAEGE ZUR PARACELSUSFORSCHUNG. see PHILOSOPHY

900 320 US
SCHOULER LECTURES IN HISTORY AND POLITICAL SCIENCE. irreg. price varies. Johns Hopkins University Press, Baltimore, MD 21218.

SCHRIFTEN UND QUELLEN DER ALTEN WELT. see ARCHAEOLOGY

900 930 GE
SCHRIFTEN ZUR UR- UND FRUEHGESCHICHTE. 1953. irreg., vol. 29, 1976. price varies. (Akademie der Wissenschaften der DDR, Zentralinstitut fuer Alte Geschichte und Archaeologie) Akademie-Verlag, Leipziger Str. 3-4, 108 Berlin, E. Germany (D.D.R.)
Continues: Akademie der Wissenschaften, Berlin. Sektion fuer Vor- und Fruehgeschichte. Schriften (ISSN 0065-5198)

900 320 GW ISSN 0080-7168
SCHRIFTENREIHE ZUR GESCHICHTE UND POLITISCHEN BILDUNG. 1965. irreg., 1971, vol. 7. price varies. Aloys Henn Verlag KG, Bahnhofstr. 17, Postfach 1180, 5448 Kastellaun, W. Germany (B.R.D.)

SCRIPTORES BYZANTINI. see LITERATURE

942 UK
SEAX SERIES OF TEACHING PORTFOLIOS. 1969. a. price varies. ‡ Essex County Council, Essex Record Office, County Hall, Essex, Chelmsford CM1 1LX, England. Ed. V. W. Gray. circ. 1,200.

SELDEN SOCIETY, LONDON. HANDBOOK: PUBLICATIONS, LIST OF MEMBERS AND RULES. see LAW

SELDEN SOCIETY, LONDON. LECTURES. see LAW

SELDEN SOCIETY, LONDON. MAIN (ANNUAL) SERIES. see LAW

SELDEN SOCIETY, LONDON. SUPPLEMENTARY SERIES. see LAW

900 US ISSN 0080-939X
SHORT OXFORD HISTORY OF THE MODERN WORLD. 1970. irreg., latest vol., 1978. Oxford University Press, 200 Madison Ave., New York, NY 10016 (and Ely House, 37 Dover St., London W1X 4AH, England) Ed. J. M. Roberts.

900 US ISSN 0081-0193
SMITH COLLEGE STUDIES IN HISTORY. 1915. irreg., vol. 47, 1975. price varies. Smith College Library, Office of Technical Services, Northhampton, MA 01063. (reprint service avail. from UMI)

900 600 US ISSN 0081-0258
SMITHSONIAN STUDIES IN HISTORY AND TECHNOLOGY. 1969. irreg. Smithsonian Institution Press, Washington, DC 20560. Ed. Albert L. Ruffin Jr. circ. 1,600. (reprint service avail. from UMI)

900 IT ISSN 0085-6231
SOCIETA STORICA VALTELLINESE. BOLLETTINO. 1921. a. L.6000($8) Societa Storica Valtellinese, c/o Renzo Sertoli Salis, Via Gorizia 29, Sondrio, Italy. bk. rev.

900 FR ISSN 0081-0975
SOCIETE D'HISTOIRE MODERNE. ANNUAIRE. 1957. irreg. $10. Societe d'Histoire Moderne, 5 Villa Poirier, 75015 Paris, France.

526.8 SZ ISSN 0078-9518
SOCIETE DE L'ECOLE DES CHARTES. MEMOIRES ET DOCUMENTS. 1896. irreg. price varies. Librarie Droz, 11, rue Massot, 1211 Geneva 12, Switzerland. circ. 1,000.

900 CN ISSN 0081-1130
SOCIETE HISTORIQUE DE QUEBEC. TEXTES. 1968. irreg. Can.$1. Societe Historique de Quebec, C.P. 460, Quebec, P.Q. G1R 4R7, Canada. circ. 500. Indexed: RADAR.

930 FR
SOCIETE SPELEOLOGIQUE ET PREHISTORIQUE DE BORDEAUX. MEMOIRE. 1975. irreg. Societe Speleologique et Prehistorique de Bordeaux, Hotel des Societes Savantes, 71 rue du Loup, Bordeaux, France. illus.

930 AT ISSN 0081-2110
SOURCES IN ANCIENT HISTORY. 1967. irreg. price varies. ‡ Sydney University Press, Press Bldg., University of Sydney, New South Wales, Australia (Dist. by: International Scholarly Book Services, Inc., Box 555, Forest Grove, OR 97116) Ed. E. A. Judge.

SOUTH STAFFORDSHIRE ARCHAEOLOGICAL AND HISTORICAL SOCIETY. TRANSACTIONS. see ARCHAEOLOGY

900 CN
STATE AND ECONOMIC LIFE SERIES. 1979. irreg. price varies. University of Toronto Press, Front Campus, Toronto, Ont. M5S 1A6, Canada. Eds. Mel Watkins, Leo Panitch.

930 950 IT ISSN 0081-6124
STUDI CLASSICI E ORIENTALI. 1951. irreg. L.36000($65) (Universita degli Studi di Pisa, Instituto per le Scienze dell'Antichita) Giardini Editori e Stampatori, Istituti per le Scienze dell'Antichita, 56100 Pisa, Italy. Ed. Graziano Arrighetti.

STUDI GENUENSI. see ARCHAEOLOGY

900 VC
STUDIA ET DOCUMENTA HISTORIAE ET IURIS. 1935. a. L.40000. Pontificia Universita Lateranense, Pontificio Istituto Utriusque Iuris, Piazza S. Giovanni in Laterano 4, 00184 Rome, Italy. Ed. Gabrio Lombardi. bk. rev. bibl. index. (tabloid format)

900 HU ISSN 0076-2458
STUDIA HISTORICA ACADEMIAE SCIENTIARUM HUNGARICAE. (Text in English, French, German, Russian) 1951. irreg., vol.130,1979. price varies. (Magyar Tudomanyos Akademia) Akademiai Kiado, Publishing House of the Hungarian Academy of Sciences, P.O. Box 24, H-1363 Budapest, Hungary.

900 RM ISSN 0039-3428
STUDIA UNIVERSITATIS "BABES-BOLYAI". HISTORIA. (Text in Romanian; summaries in English, French, German, Italian or Russian) 1956. s-a. exchange basis. Universitatea Babes-Bolyai, Biblioteca Centrala Universitara, Str. Clinicilor Nr. 2, Cluj-Napoca, Romania. bk. rev. charts. illus. index.

950 325 GE
STUDIEN UEBER ASIEN, AFRIKA UND LATEINAMERIKA. 1972. irreg., vol. 22, 1976. price varies. (Zentraler Rat fuer Asien-, Afrika- und Lateinamerikawissenschaften in der DDR) Akademie-Verlag, Leipziger Str. 3-4, 108 Berlin, E. Germany (D.D.R.) Ed. Lothar Rathmann.
Formerly: Studien zur Geschichte Asiens, Afrikas und Lateinamerikas. (ISSN 0081-7287)

900 GW ISSN 0081-7309
STUDIEN ZUR GESCHICHTE DES NEUNZEHNTEN JAHRHUNDERTS. irreg. price varies. R. Oldenbourg Verlag GmbH, Rosenheimer Str. 145, 8000 Munich 80, W. Germany (B.R.D.)

900 GW
STUDIEN ZUR MODERNEN GESCHICHTE. irreg., vol. 24, 1980. price varies. R. Oldenbourg Verlag GmbH, Rosenheimer Str. 145, 8000 Munich 80, W. Germany (B.R.D.)

930 NE ISSN 0081-7546
STUDIES IN ANCIENT HISTORY. irreg. price varies. Mouton Publishers, Noordeinde 41, 2514 GC The Hague, Netherlands (U.S. addr: Mouton Publishers, c/o Walter de Gruyter, Inc., 200 Saw Mill River Road, Hawthorne, NY 10532)

930 US
STUDIES IN CHRISTIAN ANTIQUITY. irreg., vol. 20, 1980. price varies. (Catholic University of America) Catholic University of America Press, 620 Michigan Ave. N.E., Washington, DC 20064.

STUDIES IN EIGHTEENTH CENTURY CULTURE; American Society for Eighteenth Century Studies. Proceedings of the Annual Meeting. see HUMANITIES: COMPREHENSIVE WORKS

900 100 US ISSN 0148-6543
STUDIES IN HISTORY AND PHILOSOPHY. PAMPHLET SERIES. 1965. irreg. $1 per no. Institute for Humane Studies, 177 University Dr., Menlo Park, CA 94025. bibl. circ. 5,000. (back issues avail.)

900 800 US ISSN 0085-6878
STUDIES IN MEDIEVAL CULTURE. 1964. irreg. price varies. ‡ Western Michigan University, Medieval Institute, Kalamazoo, MI 49008. charts. illus. stat. circ. 1,000. (tabloid format)

900 CN ISSN 0081-850X
STUDIES IN SOCIAL HISTORY. 1961. irreg. price varies. University of Toronto Press, Front Campus, Toronto, Ontario M5S 1A6, Canada (and 33 East Tupper St., Buffalo, N.Y. 14203) Ed. Harold Perkin. (also avail. in microfiche)

900 US
STUDIES IN THE REFORMATION. 1977. irreg. Ohio University Press, Athens, OH 45701. (Cosponsor: Wayne State University Press) Ed. Robert C. Walton.

SURMACH. see *MILITARY*

SVENSKA ARKIVSAMFUNDET. SKRIFTSERIE. see *LIBRARY AND INFORMATION SCIENCES*

839.7 920 FI ISSN 0039-6842
SVENSKA LITTERATURSAELLSKAPET I FINLAND. SKRIFTER. (Text mainly in Swedish; occasionally in other languages) 1886. irreg. (4-8/ yr.) price varies. Svenska Litteratursaellskapet i Finland, Snellmansg. 9-11, 00170 Helsinki 17, Finland.

900 GE ISSN 0082-1950
TASCHENBUCHREIHE GESCHICHTE. 1969. irreg. price varies. VEB Deutscher Verlag der Wissenschaften, Postfach 1216, 108 Berlin, E. Germany (D.D.R.)

TEACHING OF HISTORY. see *EDUCATION — Teaching Methods And Curriculum*

900 US ISSN 0082-2884
TERRAE INCOGNITAE. (Text in English) 1969. a. $13. (Society for the History of Discoveries) Wayne State University Press, 5959 Woodward Ave., Detroit, MI 48202. Ed. Douglas W. Marshall. adv. bk. rev. bibl. charts. illus. cum.index. circ. 500. (back issues avail.)

900 US ISSN 0082-2973
TEXAS CHRISTIAN UNIVERSITY MONOGRAPHS IN HISTORY AND CULTURE. 1966. irreg., no. 14, 1978. ‡ Texas Christian University Press, Box 30783 T C U Sta., Fort Worth, TX 76129. Ed. Donald E. Worcester. circ. 1,000.

930 US ISSN 0082-3759
TEXTS FROM CUNEIFORM SOURCES. 1966. irreg. price varies. J. J. Augustin, Inc., Locust Valley, NY 11560. Ed. A. Leo Oppenheimer. index.
 Up-to-date editions of Akkadian, Sumerian, Hittite and other sources written in Cuneiform

930 IT ISSN 0082-4097
THESAURISMATA. (Text in Greek and other languages; summaries in Italian) 1962. a. L.16000($20) Istituto Ellenico di Studi Bizantini e Post-Bizantini, Castello 3412, 3412 Venezia, Italy. circ. 1,000.

900 UK ISSN 0082-4232
THORESBY SOCIETY, LEEDS, ENGLAND. PUBLICATIONS. 1891. a. price varies. ‡ Thoresby Society, Claremont, 23 Clarendon Rd., Leeds LS2 9NZ, England. Eds. Mrs. R. S. Mortimer, Mrs. W. B. Stephens. circ. 530. (back issues avail.) Indexed: Br.Hum.Ind.

TOOLS AND TILLAGE; a journal on the history of the implements of cultivation and other agricultural processes. see *AGRICULTURE*

TOWARZYSTWO NAUKOWE W TORUNIU. FONTES. see *HISTORY — History Of Europe*

900 SZ ISSN 0082-6073
TRAVAUX D'HISTOIRE ETHICO-POLITIQUE. 1963. irreg., no. 30, 1976. price varies. Librarie Droz, 11, rue Massot, 1211 Geneva 12, Switzerland. Ed. Alain Dufour. circ. 1,000.

930 GW ISSN 0170-348X
UEBERSETZUNGEN AUSLAENDISCHER ARBEITEN ZUR ANTIKEN SKLAVEREI. irreg., vol. 3, 1978. price varies. (Akademie der Wissenschaften und der Literatur, Mainz, Kommission fuer Geschichte des Altertums) Franz Steiner Verlag GmbH, Friedrichstr. 24, Postfach 5529, 6200 Wiesbaden, W. Germany (B.R.D.) Eds. Herbert Braeuer, Joseph Vogt.

900 US ISSN 0083-1611
U. S. LIBRARY OF CONGRESS. MANUSCRIPT DIVISION. REGISTER OF PAPERS. 1958. irreg. free to libraries. ‡ U. S. Library of Congress, Washington, DC 20540. circ. 400.

UNIVERS HISTORIQUE. see *SCIENCES: COMPREHENSIVE WORKS*

900 BL ISSN 0070-1815
UNIVERSIDADE DO PARANA. DEPARTAMENTO DE HISTORIA. BOLETIM.*
Title varies: Historia Moderna e Contemporanea. (Text in Portuguese; summaries in English) 1962. irreg., 1969, no. 8. available on exchange. Universidade Federal do Parana, Departamento de Historia, Curitiba, Parana, Brazil.

909 IT ISSN 0068-4805
UNIVERSITA DEGLI STUDI DI CAGLIARI. ISTITUTO DI STORIA MEDIOEVALE. PUBLICAZIONI. 1961. irreg., no. 25, 1977. price varies. (Universita degli Studi di Cagliari, Istituto di Storia Medioevale) Casa Editrice Dott. Antonio Milani, Via Jappelli 5, 35100 Padua, Italy. circ. 600-1,000.

930 IT
UNIVERSITA DEGLI STUDI DI GENOVA. FONDAZIONE NOBILE AGOSTINO POGGI (PUBBLICAZIONE) 1940. irreg., no. 14, 1979. Casa Editrice Dott. A. Giuffre, Via Statuto 2, 20121 Milan, Italy.
 Roman empire

900 IT ISSN 0078-7744
UNIVERSITA DEGLI STUDI DI PADOVA ISTITUTO DI STORIA ANTICA. PUBBLICAZIONI. 1953. irreg., no. 13, 1979. price varies. Erma di "Bretschneider", Via Cassiodoro, 19, 00193 Rome, Italy.

090 GW ISSN 0072-4491
UNIVERSITAET GIESSEN. BIBLIOTHEK. KURZBERICHTE AUS DEN PAPYRUS-SAMMLUNGEN. (Text in various languages) 1956. irreg., no. 35, 1975. price varies. Universitaet Giessen, Bibliothek, Bismarckstr. 37, Giessen, W. Germany (B.R.D.) Ed. H. Schueling.

900 CN ISSN 0079-8398
UNIVERSITE LAVAL. INSTITUT D'HISTOIRE. CAHIERS. 1959. irreg. Presses de l'Universite Laval, Quebec, Que., Canada.

900 CN
UNIVERSITY OF CALGARY STUDIES IN HISTORY. irreg. University of Calgary, Department of History, 2920 24th Ave., Calgary, Alta. T2N 1N4, Canada.

900 US ISSN 0068-6239
UNIVERSITY OF CALIFORNIA, LOS ANGELES. CENTER FOR MEDIEVAL AND RENAISSANCE STUDIES. CONTRIBUTIONS. irreg. price varies. University of California Press, 2223 Fulton St., Berkeley, CA 94720.

900 US ISSN 0068-6220
UNIVERSITY OF CALIFORNIA, LOS ANGELES. CENTER FOR MEDIEVAL AND RENAISSANCE STUDIES. PUBLICATIONS. irreg. price varies. University of California Press, 2223 Fulton St., Berkeley, CA 94720.

900 UK ISSN 0076-0692
UNIVERSITY OF LONDON HISTORICAL STUDIES. 1954. irreg., no. 38, 1975. price varies. Athlone Press, 90-91 Great Russell St., London WC1B 3PY, England (Dist. in U.S. by: Humanities Press, Inc., 171 First Ave., Atlantic Highlands, NJ 07716)

900 AT ISSN 0085-7629
UNIVERSITY OF NEWCASTLE HISTORICAL JOURNAL. 1974. irreg. (vol. 3, no. 2) a. Aus.$2. University of Newcastle, Department of History, Newcastle, N.S.W. 2308, Australia. bk. rev.

900 CS ISSN 0083-4122
UNIVERZITA KOMENSKEHO. FILOZOFICKA FAKULTA. ZBORNIK: HISTORICA. (Text in Slovak; summaries in German and Russian) 1958. irreg. exchange basis. Univerzita Komenskeho, Filozoficka Fakulta, Gondova 2, 806 01 Bratislava, Czechoslovakia. Ed. Branislav Varsik. bk. rev. circ. 700.

UNIWERSYTET GDANSKI. WYDZIAL HUMANISTYCZNY. ZESZYTY NAUKOWE. PRACE HISTORYCZNO-LITERACKIE. see *LITERATURE*

900 PL
UNIWERSYTET SLASKI W KATOWICACH. PRACE HISTORYCZNE. irreg., 1975, no. 4. 10 Zl. Uniwersytet Slaski w Katowicach, Ul. Bankowa 14, 40-007 Katowice, Poland. Ed. Jana Pachonskiego. charts. illus.

VERDI. see *MUSIC*

900 US ISSN 0083-5897
VIATOR; Medieval and Renaissance Studies. (Contributions in English and other major modern languages) 1970. a. (University of California, Los Angeles, Center for Medieval and Renaissance Studies) University of California Press, 2223 Fulton St, Berkeley, CA 94720. Ed.Bd.

900 UK ISSN 0083-6087
VICTORIAN SOCIETY. CONFERENCE REPORTS. 1964. irreg. price varies. ‡ Victorian Society, 1 Priory Gardens, Bedford Park, London W4 1TT, England.

VIERTELJAHRSCHRIFT FUER SOZIAL-UND WIRTSCHAFTSGESCHICHTE. BEIHEFTE. see *SOCIAL SCIENCES: COMPREHENSIVE WORKS*

040 US
WALKER-AMES LECTURES. 1958. irreg., latest 1978. price varies. University of Washington Press, Seattle, WA 98105.

900 US ISSN 0083-713X
WALTER PRESCOTT WEBB MEMORIAL LECTURES. 1968; vol. 11, 1977. a. price varies. (University of Texas at Arlington) University of Texas Press, Box 7819, University Sta., Austin, TX 78712. (reprint service avail. from UMI)

031 US ISSN 0512-5804
WHAT THEY SAID. 1969. a. $19.50. Monitor Book Co. Inc., 195 So. Beverly Dr., Beverly Hills, CA 90212. Eds. Alan F. Pater, Jason R. Pater.

900 913 700 US
WILBOUR MONOGRAPHS. 1968. irreg., no. 7, 1974. Brooklyn Museum, Department of Egyptian and Classical Art, The Book Shop, 188 Eastern Pkwy., Brooklyn, NY 11238. circ. 1,000.

900 320 US
WORLD CHRONOLOGIES SERIES. 1973. irreg. $7.50 per vol. Oceana Publications, Inc., Dobbs Ferry, NY 10522. charts. stat.

900 US ISSN 0084-3350
YALE HISTORICAL PUBLICATIONS (MISCELLANY) 1914. irreg., no.125,1980. price varies. Yale University Press, 92A Yale Sta., New Haven, CT 06520.

909.82 US ISSN 0094-9027
YOUNG STUDENTS ENCYCLOPEDIA YEARBOOK. 1974. a. $4.59. Funk & Wagnalls (Subsidiary of: Dun & Bradstreet Corporation) 666 Fifth Ave., New York, NY 10019. Ed. Harold Blum. illus. circ. 30,000.

900 UN ISSN 0084-4322
YOUR UNITED NATIONS. 1952. irreg. $2.50. United Nations Publications, LX 2300, New York, NY 10017 (Or Distribution and Sales Section, CH-1211 Geneva 10, Switzerland)

HISTORY — Abstracting, Bibliographies, Statistics

960 016   US
AFRICA SOUTH OF THE SAHARA: INDEX TO PERIODICAL LITERATURE. SUPPLEMENTS. 1973. irreg., latest, 1973. $65. G. K. Hall and Co., 70 Lincoln Street, Boston, MA 02111.

960 015   US   ISSN 0065-3926
AFRICAN BIBLIOGRAPHIC CENTER, WASHINGTON, D.C. CURRENT READING LIST SERIES. 1963. irreg., latest, vol. 12, 1976-78. price varies. African Bibliographic Center, P.O. Box 13096, Washington, DC 20009. Ed. Daniel G. Matthews.

960 015   US   ISSN 0065-3934
AFRICAN BIBLIOGRAPHIC CENTER, WASHINGTON, D.C. SPECIAL BIBLIOGRAPHIC SERIES. 1963; N.S. 1975. irreg. Greenwood Press, 88 Post Rd. W., Westport, CT 06881. Ed. Daniel G. Matthews.

016 960   US
AFRICAN BIBLIOGRAPHY SERIES. 1971. irreg. Africana Publishing Co. (Subsidiary of: Holmes & Meier Publishers, Inc.) 30 Irving Pl., New York, NY 10003. (back issues avail.)

970 016   US   ISSN 0363-1249
AMERICA: HISTORY AND LIFE. PART C: AMERICAN HISTORY BIBLIOGRAPHY. a. price based on annual book fund of library. American Bibliographical Center-Clio Press, 2040 Alameda Padre Serra, Box 4397, Santa Barbara, CA 93103. index.

016 940   US   ISSN 0569-3497
AMERICAN BIBLIOGRAPHY OF SLAVIC AND EAST EUROPEAN STUDIES. Title varies: American Bibliography of Russian and East European Studies. 1956. a. price varies. American Association for the Advancement of Slavic Studies, Rm. 731 SEO Bldg., University of Illinois at Chicago Circle, Chicago, IL 60680. Ed. David Kraus. bibl.

973 015   US
AMERICAN HERITAGE INDEX. a. $5. American Heritage Publishing Co., Inc., 10 Rockefeller Plaza, New York, NY 10020.

319 994   AT   ISSN 0067-1118
AUSTRALIA. BUREAU OF STATISTICS. VICTORIAN OFFICE. GENERAL STATISTICS OF LOCAL GOVERNMENT AREAS. 1964. irreg. free. Australian Bureau of Statistics, Victorian Office, Box 2796Y, G.P.O. Melbourne, Victoria 3001, Australia. circ. 1,500.

319   AT   ISSN 0067-1215
AUSTRALIA. BUREAU OF STATISTICS. VICTORIAN OFFICE. VICTORIAN STATISTICAL PUBLICATIONS. 1970. irreg. free. Australian Bureau of Statistics, Victorian Office, Box 2796Y, G.P.O. Melbourne, Victoria 3001, Australia. adv. circ. 3,000.

994 319   AT
AUSTRALIA. BUREAU OF STATISTICS. WESTERN AUSTRALIAN OFFICE. STATISTICS OF WESTERN AUSTRALIA-LOCAL GOVERNMENT. 1960. a. Aus.$0.75. Australian Bureau of Statistics, Western Australian Office, 1-3 St. George's Terrace, Perth, W.A. 6000, Australia. Ed. E. Binns. index. circ. 800.
Formerly: Australia. Bureau of Statistics. Western Australian Office. Abstract of Statistics of Local Government Areas. (ISSN 0067-124X)

016 943.8   PL   ISSN 0067-6721
BIBLIOGRAFIA HISTORII POLSKIEJ. 1962. irreg., bibliography for 1975 and 1976 published in 1978. (Polska Akademia Nauk, Instytut Historii) Ossolineum, Publishing House of the Polish Academy of Sciences, Rynek 9, Wroclaw, Poland (Dist. by Ars Polona-Ruch, Krakowskie Przedmiescie 7, Warsaw, Poland) Ed.Bd. circ. 1,500.

016 943.8   PL   ISSN 0409-3453
BIBLIOGRAFIA POMORZA ZACHODNIEGO. (Text in Polish; summaries in English and Russian) irreg., vol. 9, 1977. 50 Zl. Wojewodzka i Miejska Biblioteka Publiczna-Biblioteka Glowna im. S. Staszica, Podgorna 15, 70-952 Szczecin, Poland. Ed. Stanislaw Krzywicki.

970 016   US   ISSN 0147-6491
BIBLIOGRAPHIC GUIDE TO NORTH AMERICAN HISTORY. a. G.K. Hall & Co., 70 Lincoln St., Boston, MA 02111.

960 016   FR
BIBLIOGRAPHIE ANALYTIQUE DE L'AFRIQUE ANTIQUE. 1969. irreg. Diffusion de Boccard, 11 rue de Medicis, Paris 6e, France (U.S. Subscr. to: Institute for the Arts, Rice University, Box 1892, Houston, Tx 77001) Eds. Jehan Desanges, Serge Lancel.

944   FR   ISSN 0067-6918
BIBLIOGRAPHIE ANNUELLE DE L'HISTOIRE DE FRANCE. 1955. a. 200 F. price varies. Centre National de la Recherche Scientifique, 15 Quai Anatole-France, 75700 Paris, France.

949.4   SZ
BIBLIOGRAPHIE DER BERNER GESCHICHTE/ BIBLIOGRAPHIE DE L'HISTOIRE BERNOISE. (Text in French & German) 1975. a. 6 Fr. Burgerbibliothek Bern - Bibliotheque de la Bourgeoisie de Berne, Muenstergasse 63, CH 3000 Berne 7, Switzerland. circ. 1,200.

949.35 016   LU   ISSN 0067-7043
BIBLIOGRAPHIE ZUR GESCHICHTE LUXEMBURGS/BIBLIOGRAPHIE D'HISTOIRE LUXEMBOURGEOISE. (Text and summaries in French and German) 1964. a. 100 Fr. Bibliotheque Nationale, 37, Boulevard F.-D. Roosevelt, Luxembourg, Luxembourg. circ. 500.

960 016   BE
BIBLIOGRAPHIES ANALYTIQUES SUR L'AFRIQUE CENTRALE. 1977. irreg. 1000 Fr. Centre d'Etudes et de Documentation Africaines, 7 Place Royale, 1000 Brussels, Belgium. abstr. index.

950 016   US   ISSN 0067-7159
BIBLIOGRAPHY OF ASIAN STUDIES. 1954. a. $35. Association for Asian Studies, Inc., 1 Lane Hall, University of Michigan, Ann Arbor, MI 48109. Ed. Louis Jacob. circ. 6,000. (also avail. in microform from UMI)

948 448   DK   ISSN 0067-7213
BIBLIOGRAPHY OF OLD NORSE-ICELANDIC STUDIES. (Text in several languages) 1964. a. price varies. Kongelige Bibliotek, 8 Christians Brygge, DK-1219 Copenhagen K, Denmark. Ed. Hans Bekker-Nielsen. circ. 600.

BIBLIOGRAPHY OF PERIODICAL ARTICLES ON MARITIME AND NAVAL HISTORY. see *TRANSPORTATION — Abstracting, Bibliographies, Statistics*

900 016   GW   ISSN 0081-8992
BIBLIOTHEK FUER ZEITGESCHICHTE, STUTTGART. JAHRESBIBLIOGRAPHIE; Neue Folge der Buecherschau de Weltkriegsbuecherei. 1961. irreg. price varies. (Bibliothek fuer Zeitgeschichte, Stuttgart) Bernard und Graefe Verlag, Hubertusstr. 5, 8000 Munich 19, W. Germany (B.R.D.)

960 016   BE   ISSN 0067-5601
BIBLIOTHEQUE AFRICAINE. CATALOGUE DES ACQUISITIONS. CATOLOGUS VAN DE AANWINSTEN. 1949. a. Bibliotheque Africaine, Place Royale, 7, B-1000 Brussels, Belgium. circ. 400.

959 016   SI   ISSN 0068-0176
BOOKS ABOUT SINGAPORE. 1963. biennial. free. National Library, Stamford Road, Singapore 0617, Singapore. circ. 3,000.
Formerly: Books About Malaysia.

972.9 016   PR   ISSN 0069-0465
CARIBBEAN BIBLIOGRAPHY. 1970. irreg. price varies. Universidad de Puerto Rico, Institute of Caribbean Studies, Rio Piedras, PR 00931.

016.5 950   US
COLUMBIA UNIVERSITY. SOUTHERN ASIAN INSTITUTE. OCCASIONAL BIBLIOGRAPHIC PAPERS. irreg. price varies. Columbia University, Southern Asian Institute, 535 West 114th St., New York, NY 10027.

015.729 016   PR   ISSN 0070-1866
CURRENT CARIBBEAN BIBLIOGRAPHY/ BIBLIOGRAFIA ACTUAL DEL CARIBE/ BIBLIOGRAPHIE COURANTE DE LA CARAIBE. (Text in English, French, Spanish) 1951. a. $8. Department of State, Caribbean Regional Library, Av. Ponce de Leon 452, Apdo. 1050, Hato Rey, PR 00919. Ed. Maria Elena A. Cardona. index. circ. 500.

948.9   DK
DANSK HISTORISK AARSBIBLIOGRAFI. 1967. irreg. Kr.38.60. Dansk Historisk Faellesforening, H.C. Andersens Boulevard 38, DK-1553 Copenhagen V, Denmark.

016 940   US   ISSN 0070-8097
EAST EUROPE IN GERMAN BOOKS; a bulletin listing new books on East Europe published in the German language. 1971. irreg., vol. 5, 1977. Park College, Governmental Research Bureau, Kansas City, MO 64152. Ed. Jerzy Hauptmann.

900   US
FACTS ON FILE. YEARBOOK. 1941. a. $65. Facts on File, Inc., 119 W. 57 St., New York, NY 10019. 5-year cum. index. (back issues avail.)

940 016   GW   ISSN 0067-5881
FREIE UNIVERSITAET BERLIN. OSTEUROPA-INSTITUT. BIBLIOGRAPHISCHE MITTEILUNGEN. 1959. irreg., no. 11, 1975. price varies. Freie Universitaet Berlin, Osteuropa Institut, Garystr. 55, 1000 Berlin 33 (Dahlem), W. Germany (B. R. D.) circ. 500.

016   US
FRENCH 17; an annual descriptive bibliography of French 17th Century studies. 1953. a. $3. (Modern Language Association of America, Seventeenth Century French Division) Colorado State University, Department of Foreign Languages, Fort Collins, CO 80523. circ. 400.
Formerly: French III.

090 942   UK
GREAT BRITAIN. ROYAL COMMISSION ON HISTORICAL MANUSCRIPTS. ACCESSIONS TO REPOSITORIES AND REPORTS ADDED TO THE NATIONAL REGISTER OF ARCHIVES. a. price varies. Royal Commission on Historical Manuscripts, Quality House, Quality Court, Chancery Lane, London WC2A 1HP, England (Avail. from: H.M.S.O., c/o Liason Officer, Atlantic House, Holborn Viaduct, London EC1P 1BN, England)

942 090 015   UK   ISSN 0072-7083
GREAT BRITAIN. ROYAL COMMISSION ON HISTORICAL MANUSCRIPTS. COMMISSIONERS' REPORTS TO THE CROWN. 1870. irreg. price varies. Royal Commission on Historical Manuscripts, Quality House, Quality Court, Chancery Lane, London WC2A 1HP, England (Avail. from H.M.S.O., c/o Liaison Officer, Atlantic House, Holborn Viaduct, London EC1P 1BN, England)

090 942 015   UK   ISSN 0072-7091
GREAT BRITAIN. ROYAL COMMISSION ON HISTORICAL MANUSCRIPTS. JOINT PUBLICATION. 1962. irreg. price varies. Royal Commission on Historical Manuscripts, Quality House, Quality Court, Chancery Lane, London WC2A 1HP, England (Avail. from H.M.S.O., c/o Liaison Officer, Atlantic House, Holborn Viaduct, London EC1P 1BN, England)

090 994 016   AT
GUIDE TO COLLECTIONS OF MANUSCRIPTS RELATING TO AUSTRALIA. 1964. irreg. Aus.$7 per part; binders Aus. $5. National Library of Australia, Sales and Subscription Unit, Canberra, A.C.T. 2600, Australia. (looseleaf format)
Formerly: Guide to Manuscripts Relating to Australia.

016 960 SZ
GUIDE TO THE SOURCES OF THE HISTORY OF THE NATIONS. B: AFRICA. (Text in English, French and German) irreg. price varies. Inter-Documentation Company, Poststrasse 14, Zug, Switzerland.

980 US ISSN 0361-5502
HISPANIC AMERICAN PERIODICAL INDEX. 1978. a. $100. University of California, Los Angeles, Latin American Center, 405 Hilgard Ave., Los Angeles, CA 90024. Ed. Barbara G. Valk.

960 016 ZA
HISTORY IN ZAMBIA. irreg.(appox. a.), no. 8, 1978. free. Historical Association of Zambia, c/o University of Zambia, Box 2379, Lusaka, Zambia. Ed. R. B. Boeder. bibl.

016.909 US ISSN 0362-8671
INDEX TO BOOK REVIEWS IN HISTORICAL PERIODICALS. irreg., 1977 edt., 1979. Scarecrow Press, Inc., 52 Liberty St., Box 656, Metuchen, NJ 08840. Eds. John W. Brewster, Deborah Gentry.

954 016 II
INDIA AND WORLD AFFAIRS: AN ANNUAL BIBLIOGRAPHY. (Part 1: India's Foreign Policy and Relations with Other Countries of the World; Part 2: Indian Opinions on World Events) (Text in English) 1958. a. not for sale. Jawaharlal Nehru University, School of International Studies, New Mehrauli Rd., New Delhi 110057, India.

900 FR ISSN 0074-2015
INTERNATIONAL BIBLIOGRAPHY OF HISTORICAL SCIENCES. (Text in French and English) 1947. irreg. price varies. Librairie Armand Colin, 103, Bd.St.-Michel, Paris 5e, France.

315 KO ISSN 0075-6873
KOREA STATISTICAL YEARBOOK/HANGUK TONGGYE YONGAM. (Text in Korean and English) 1952. a. 4050 Won. Bureau of Statistics, Economic Planning Board, Gyeongun-Dong, Jongro-Gu, Seoul, S. Korea. Ed. Heung-Koo Kang. circ. 2,000.

016 980 UK ISSN 0085-2694
LATIN AMERICAN STUDIES IN THE UNIVERSITIES OF THE UNITED KINGDOM. 1966/7. a. free. University of London, Institute of Latin American Studies, 31 Tavistock Sq., London WC1H 9HA, England. Ed. Miss D. F. Rodger.

016 980 300 UK ISSN 0085-2708
LATIN AMERICAN STUDIES IN THE UNIVERSITIES OF THE UNITED KINGDOM. STAFF RESEARCH IN PROGRESS OR RECENTLY COMPLETED IN THE HUMANITIES AND THE SOCIAL SCIENCES. 1968/9. a. free. ‡ University of London, Institute of Latin American Studies, 31 Tavistock Sq., London WC1H 9HA, England. Ed. Miss D. F. Rodger.

015 MY ISSN 0126-5210
MALAYSIAN NATIONAL BIBLIOGRAPHY/BIBLIOGRAFI NEGARA MALAYSIA. (Text in English and Malay) 1967. q. (plus annual cumulation) M.$55 for full service; M. $35 for annual comulation only. National Library, National Bibliography Division, Jalan Perdana, Kuala Lumpur 10-06, Malaysia (Orders to: Parry's Book Centre, Box 960, Hotel Hilton, Kuala Lumpur, Malaysia) Ed. Shellatay Devadason. circ. 500.

951 US ISSN 0076-7808
MICHIGAN ABSTRACTS OF CHINESE AND JAPANESE WORKS ON CHINESE HISTORY. (Summary-Translations of Chinese and Japanese Historical Monographs) 1970. irreg; no. 5, 1976. $4. University of Michigan, Center for Chinese Studies, Lane Hall, Ann Arbor, MI 48109. Ed. Mark Elvin.

940 016 UK ISSN 0077-0280
MONARCHIST BOOK REVIEW; an annotated list of new and reprinted books dealing with various aspects of monarchy. 1968. a. 30p.($0.75) Monarchist Press Association, 7 Sutherland Rd., West Ealing London W13 0DX, England. Ed. James Page. circ. 600.

016 US
NEW MEXICO. STATE RECORDS CENTER & ARCHIVES. PUBLICATIONS AND RULES FILED. 1969. irreg. $12. ‡ State Records Center and Archives, Publications Management Division, 404 Montezuma, Santa Fe, NM 87503.
 Formerly: New Mexico State Records Center and Archives. Publications Filed (ISSN 0090-0931)

NEWS DICTIONARY. see *POLITICAL SCIENCE*

990 US ISSN 0085-459X
PACIFIC ISLANDS STUDIES AND NOTES. 1971. irreg. free to selected libraries. ‡ N.L.H. Krauss, Ed. & Pub., 2437 Parker Place, Honolulu, HI 96822. circ. 500.

319 993.1 NZ ISSN 0079-2411
POCKET DIGEST OF NEW ZEALAND STATISTICS. 1914. a. NZ.$1.20. Department of Statistics, Private Bag, Wellington, New Zealand (Subscr. to: Government Printing Office, Publications, Private Bag, Wellington, New Zealand) circ. 5,000.

950 011 UK ISSN 0308-7395
QUARTERLY INDEX ISLAMICUS; current books, articles, and papers on Islamic Studies. (Text in all languages) 1977. q. £15.50($32.50) (University of London, School of Oriental and African Studies) Mansell Publishing, 3 Bloomsbury Place, London WC1A 2QA, England. Ed. J. D. Pearson. index.

015 948 SW ISSN 0347-4585
R A-NYTT. (Two series: Enskilda Arkiv and Riksarkivets Myndighetsservice) 1969. irreg. (3-4/yr.) free. Riksarkivet - National Swedish Record Office, Box 34104, 100 26 Stockholm, Sweden. cum. index.

974.7 016 US ISSN 0080-1488
RESEARCH AND PUBLICATIONS IN NEW YORK STATE HISTORY. 1969. a. free. Education Department, Division of Historical Services, New York State Museum, Ed. Stefan Bielinski, Albany, NY 12230. Ed. Thomas E. Felt.

951 016 NE ISSN 0080-2484
REVUE BIBLIOGRAPHIQUE DE SINOLOGIE. (Text in Chinese and French) 1955. a. price varies. (Ecole des Hautes Etudes en Sciences Sociales, Centre d'Etudes Chinoise, FR) Mouton Publishers, Noordeinde 41, 2514 GC The Hague, Netherlands (U.S. addr.: Mouton Publishers, c/o Walter de Gruyter, Inc., 200 Saw Mill River Road, Hawthorne, NY 10532) Ed. D. Holzmann. adv. bk. rev. circ. 400.

942 015 UK ISSN 0308-4558
ROYAL HISTORICAL SOCIETY. ANNUAL BIBLIOGRAPHY OF BRITISH AND IRISH HISTORY. 1976. a. $18.85. Harvester Press Ltd., 16 Ship St., Brighton, Sussex BN1 1AD, England. Ed. G. Elton.

200 016 US
SIXTEENTH CENTURY BIBLIOGRAPHY. 1975. irreg. $7.50. Center for Reformation Research, 6477 San Bonita Ave., St. Louis, MO 63105. Ed. William Maltby. circ. 150.
 Formerly: Foundation for Reformation Research. Bulletin of the Library (ISSN 0015-8941)

011 960 SA
SOUTH AFRICA. OFFICE OF THE DIRECTOR OF ARCHIVES. ANNUAL REPORT OF THE DIRECTOR OF ARCHIVES/SOUTH AFRICA. KANTOOR VAN DIE DIREKTEUR VAN ARGIEWE. JAARVERSLAG VAN DIE DIREKEUR VAN ARGIEWE. a. Office of the Director of Archives, Private Bag X236, Union Buildings, Pretoria 0001, South Africa. bibl.

968 312 SA ISSN 0302-0681
SOUTH AFRICA. OFFICIAL YEARBOOK OF THE REPUBLIC OF SOUTH AFRICA. a. Department of Foreign Affairs and Information, Private Bag X152, Pretoria 0001, South Africa. Ed. Bettie van Wyk.

318 US ISSN 0081-4687
STATISTICAL ABSTRACT OF LATIN AMERICA. 1956. a (plus supplements) price varies. University of California, Los Angeles, Latin American Center, Los Angeles, CA 90024. Ed. James W. Wilkie.

947.1 FI ISSN 0081-9417
SUOMEN HISTORIALLINEN SEURA. KASIKIRJOJA. (Text in Finnish) 1925. irreg., no. 8, 1975. price varies. Suomen Historiallinen Seura - Finnish Historical Society, Snellmaninkatu 9-11, 00170 Helsinki 17, Finland. circ. 350.

SWEDEN. STATISTISKA CENTRALBYRAAN. STATISTISKA MEDDELANDEN. SUBGROUP BE (POPULATION) see *POPULATION STUDIES — Abstracting, Bibliographies, Statistcs*

016 973 JA
TOKYO LINCOLN CENTER. REPORT. (Text in English & Japanese) 1962. a. Tokyo Lincoln Book Center, Japan Publications Trading Co. Bldg., 1-2-1 Sarugaku-cho, Chiyoda-ku, Tokyo 101, Japan. Ed. Masaharu Mochizuki. circ. 150.
 Formerly: Tokyo Lincoln Book Center. Report.

940 016 CN ISSN 0082-5042
TORONTO MEDIEVAL BIBLIOGRAPHIES. 1967. irreg. price varies. (University of Toronto, Centre for Medieval Studies) University of Toronto Press, Front Campus, Toronto, Ont. M5S 1A6, Canada. Ed. J. Leyerle. (also avail. in microfiche)

016 950 PH
UNIVERSITY OF THE PHILIPPINES. ASIAN CENTER. BIBLIOGRAPHY. 1970. irreg. price varies. ‡ University of the Philippines, Asian Center, Diliman, Quezon City 3004, Philippines. circ. 1,000.

973 016 US
WRITINGS ON AMERICAN HISTORY; a subject bibliography of articles. 1962. a. $31. (American Historical Association) Kraus International Publications, Rt. 100, Millwood, NY 10546. Ed. Cecelia J. Dadian. (back issues avail.)

942 UK ISSN 0084-2753
WRITINGS ON BRITISH HISTORY. (Text in various languages; notes in English) 1937. irreg. price varies. University of London, Institute of Historical Research, Senate House, London WC1E 7HU, England.

HISTORY — History Of Africa

960 SA
A.S.I. COMMUNICATIONS. irreg., no. 5, 1977. University of the Witwatersrand, Johannesburg, African Studies Institute, Jan Smuts Ave., Johannesburg 2001, South Africa.

968.94 ZA ISSN 0065-0374
ABOUT ZAMBIA. 1964. irreg. free. Information Services, Box RW 20, Lusaka, Zambia (Orders to: Government Printer, Box 136, Lusaka, Zambia)

960 SA ISSN 0065-3829
AFRICA AT A GLANCE: A QUICK REFERENCE OF FACTS AND FIGURES ON AFRICA. 1973. irreg. R.3. Africa Institute of South Africa, P. O. Box 630, Pretoria 0001, South Africa. circ. 5,000.

330 960 US ISSN 0065-3845
AFRICA CONTEMPORARY RECORD, ANNUAL SURVEY AND DOCUMENTS. 1968/69. a. $95. Africana Publishing Co. (Subsidiary of: Holmes & Meier Publishers, Inc.) 30 Irving Pl., New York, NY 10003 (U.K. address: 131 Trafalgar Rd., Greenwich, London SE10 9TX, England) Ed. Colin Legum. adv. circ. 3,000.

960 309 US
AFRICA IN THE MODERN WORLD. irreg. price varies. Cornell University Press, 124 Roberts Place, Ithaca, NY 14850.

960 SA
AFRICA INSTITUTE. CHAIRMAN'S REPORT. Variant title: Africa Institute of South Africa. Chairman's Report. a. Africa Institute of South Africa, P. O. Box 630, Pretoria 0001, South Africa.
 Formerly: Africa Institute. Annual Report (ISSN 0065-3853)

960 SA ISSN 0065-3861
AFRICA INSTITUTE. COMMUNICATIONS. Variant title: Africa Institute of South Africa. Communications. 1964. irreg., no. 32, 1978. price varies. Africa Institute of South Africa, P.O. Box 630, Pretoria 0001, South Africa.

HISTORY — HISTORY OF AFRICA

960   SA
AFRICA INSTITUTE. OCCASIONAL
PUBLICATIONS. Variant title: Africa Institute of
South Africa. Occasional Papers. 1968. irreg., no.
44, 1979. price varies. Africa Institute of South
Africa, Box 630, Pretoria 0001, South Africa.
Supersedes: Africa Institute. Special Publications
(ISSN 0065-3888)

960   KE
AFRICA INTERNATIONAL. 1974. irreg. Kenya
Literature Bureau, Box 30022, Nairobi, Kenya.

960   UK   ISSN 0065-3896
AFRICA SOUTH OF THE SAHARA. 1971. a. $75.
Europa Publications Ltd., 18 Bedford Sq., London
WC1B 3JN, England.

AFRICAN BIOGRAPHIES. see *BIOGRAPHY*

960   US
AFRICAN DOCUMENTS SERIES. 1969. irreg., no.
4, 1976. Boston University, African Studies Center,
10 Lenox St., Brookline, MA 02146.

AFRICAN FREEDOM. ANNUAL. see *POLITICAL SCIENCE*

960   NR   ISSN 0568-1332
AFRICAN HISTORIAN. 1963. a. (University of Ife,
Historical Society) African Education Press, Box
4061, Ibadan, Nigeria.

960   US
AFRICAN HISTORICAL DICTIONARIES. 1974.
irreg., no. 17, 1978. price varies. Scarecrow Press,
Inc., 52 Liberty Street, P.O. Box 656, Metuchen, NJ
08840.

AFRICAN LANGUAGE STUDIES. see *LINGUISTICS*

960   US
AFRICAN RESEARCH STUDIES. 1958. irreg., no.
14, 1980. Boston University, African Studies Center,
10 Lenox St., Brookline, MA 02146.

960   CH
AFRICAN STUDIES. (Text in Chinese & English) no.
2, 1973. a. free on exchange. National Chengchi
University, Program of African Studies, Social
Sciences Materials Center, Taipei, Taiwan 116,
Republic of China. Ed.Bd.

960   UK   ISSN 0065-406X
AFRICAN STUDIES SERIES. 1971. irreg., no. 28,
1980. $45 for latest vol. Cambridge University
Press, Box 110, Cambridge CB2 3RL, England
(And 32 E. 57th St., New York, NY 10022) Ed.Bd.

960   SA   ISSN 0065-4116
AFRICANA COLLECTANEA SERIES.
irreg.(approx. 4 vols. per year) price varies. ‡ C.
Struik Africana Publishers, P.O. Box 1144, Cape
Town, South Africa. index. circ. 1,000.
Collection of long out-of-print Africana items

968.005   SA
AFRICANA SOCIETY OF PRETORIA.
YEARBOOK/AFRICANA VERENIGING VAN
PRETORIA. JAARBOEK. (Text in Afrikaans and
English) 1975. a. R.20 to institutions. Africana
Society of Pretoria, Box 3239, Pretoria 0001, South
Africa. Ed. W. Punt. adv. bk. rev. circ. 250.

AFRIKANO-AZIATSKI PROBLEMI. see
HISTORY — History Of Asia

950   UA   ISSN 0065-4191
AFRO-ASIAN PEOPLES' CONFERENCE.
PROCEEDINGS. (Text in English, French, Arabic)
1957. irreg., 1965, 4th, Winneba, Ghana. Afro-Asian
Peoples' Solidarity Organization, 89 Abdel Aziz al-
Saoud St., Manial, Cairo, Egypt.

950 960   UA   ISSN 0078-6233
AFRO-ASIAN PEOPLES' SOLIDARITY
ORGANIZATION. COUNCIL. DOCUMENTS
OF THE SESSION. (Subseries of Afro-Asian
Publications) irreg, 12th, 1975, Moscow. Afro-
Asian Peoples' Solidarity Organization, 89, Abdel
Aziz al Saoud St., Manial, Cairo, Egypt.

961   UA   ISSN 0515-6327
AFRO-ASIAN PUBLICATIONS.* irreg. Afro-Asian
Peoples' Solidarity Organization, 89 Abdel Aziz al
Saoud, 89 Abdel Aziz al-Saoud St., Cairo, Egypt.

966.9   NR
AHMADU BELLO UNIVERSITY. NORTHERN
HISTORY RESEARCH SCHEME. INTERIM
REPORT. 1966. irreg., 4th, 1978. £N3 approx.
Ahmadu Bello University, Northern History
Research Scheme, Zaria, Nigeria. circ. 2,000.
Formerly: Ahmadu Bello University. Northern
History Research Scheme. Papers (ISSN 0065-4760)

960   FR   ISSN 0569-0870
ALMANACH AFRICAIN. (Text in French) 1974.
biennial. 95 F. Agence de Cooperation Culturelle et
Technique, 19 Av. de Messine, 75008 Paris, France.
circ. 60,000.

960 913   FR   ISSN 0066-4871
ANTIQUITES AFRICAINES. 1967. a. price varies.
Centre National de la Recherche Scientifique, 15
Quai Anatole-France, 75700 Paris, France.

960   MZ
ANUARIO DO ESTADO DE MOCAMBIQUE;
informacoes oficias, comerciais, geograficas e
historicas. A.W. Bayly & Ca., Lda., Av. 25 de
Setembro 195-197, C.P. 185, Maputo, Mozambique.
Formerly: Anuario da Provincia de Mocambique
(ISSN 0570-4022)

960   GW
ARBEITSKREIS DER DEUTSCHEN AFRIKA-
FORSCHUNGS- UND
DOKUMENTATIONSSTELLEN. RUNDBRIEF.
1967. irreg. free. I F O Institut fuer
Wirtschaftsforschung, Poschingerstr. 5, 8000
Munich 80, W. Germany (B.R.D.)

ASIAN AND AFRICAN STUDIES. see *ORIENTAL STUDIES*

ASIEN - AFRIKA - LATEINAMERIKA.
JAHRBUCH. see *HISTORY — History Of Asia*

967 913   KE   ISSN 0067-270X
AZANIA. 1966. a. $19. ‡ British Institute in Eastern
Africa, P.O. Box 30710, Nairobi, Kenya. Ed. H. N.
Chittick. index, cum.index: 1966-68. (back issues
avail.)

960   SZ   ISSN 0170-5091
BASLER AFRIKA BIBLIOGRAPHIEN.
MITTEILUNGEN/BASEL AFRICA
BIBLIOGRAPHY. COMMUNICATIONS. 1972.
0irreg. (1-3/yr.), vol. 22, 1979. price varies. Basler
Afrika Bibliographien, Postfach 2037, CH-4001
Basel, Switzerland. Ed. Bd. adv. bk. rev. bibl.

960   SZ   ISSN 0171-1660
BEITRAEGE ZUR AFRIKAKUNDE. 1978. irreg.
price varies. Basler Afrika Bibliographien, Postfach
2037, CH-4001 Basel, Switzerland. circ. 300.

960   SZ   ISSN 0067-7825
BIBLIOTHECA AFRICANA DROZ. 1969. irreg.
price varies. Librarie Droz, 11, rue Massot, 1211
Geneva 12, Switzerland.

960   US
BOSTON UNIVERSITY PAPERS ON AFRICA.
1964. irreg., no. 6, 1975. Boston University, African
Studies Center, 10 Lenox St., Brookline, MA 02146.

968.1   BS   ISSN 0525-5090
BOTSWANA NOTES AND RECORDS. 1968. a.
R.3.50($7) Botswana Society, Box 71, Gaborone,
Botswana. Ed. Doreen Nteta. adv. bk. rev. circ.
1,000. Indexed: Key Word Ind.Wildl.Res.

967.6   KE   ISSN 0068-2152
BRITISH INSTITUTE IN EASTERN AFRICA.
ANNUAL REPORT. 1959. a. British Institute in
Eastern Africa, Box 30710, Nairobi, Kenya.
Formerly: British Institute of History and
Archaeology in East Africa. Report.

960   KE
BRITISH INSTITUTE IN EASTERN AFRICA.
MEMOIRS. irreg., no. 7, 1978. price varies. British
Institute in Eastern Africa, Box 30710, Nairobi,
Kenya.

916.8   SA
CABO. (Text in Afrikaans or English) 1972. a. R.1.80.
Historical Society of Cape Town, P.O. Box 2615,
Cape Town, South Africa.

960   UK   ISSN 0069-0899
CASS LIBRARY OF AFRICAN STUDIES.
GENERAL STUDIES. 1962. irreg, no. 137, 1973.
price varies. Frank Cass & Co. Ltd., Gainsborough
House, 11 Gainsborough Rd., London E11 1RS,
England (Dist. in U.S. by: Biblio Distribution
Center, 81 Adams Drive, Totowa, N.J. 07512)

960   UK   ISSN 0069-0902
CASS LIBRARY OF AFRICAN STUDIES.
RESEARCHES AND TRAVELS. 1968. irreg., no.
25, 1973. price varies. Frank Cass & Co. Ltd.,
Gainsborough House, 11 Gainsborough Rd., London
E11 1RS, England (Dist. in U.S. by: Biblio
Distribution Center, 81 Adams Drive, Totowa, N.J.
07512)

960 916   UK   ISSN 0069-0910
CASS LIBRARY OF AFRICAN STUDIES. SOUTH
AFRICAN STUDIES. 1968. irreg., no. 6, 1970.
price varies. Frank Cass & Co. Ltd., Gainsborough
House, 11 Gainsborough Rd., London E11 1RS,
England (Dist. in U.S. by: Biblio Distribution
Center, 81 Adams Drive, Totowa, N.J. 07512)

960 916   UK   ISSN 0069-0929
CASS LIBRARY OF AFRICAN STUDIES.
TRAVELS AND NARRATIVES. 1964. irreg., no.
73, 1968. price varies. Frank Cass & Co. Ltd.,
Gainsborough House, 11 Gainsborough Rd., London
E11 1RS, England (Dist. in U.S. by: Biblio
Distribution Center, 81 Adams Drive, Totowa, N.J.
07512)

960   BE   ISSN 0069-1763
CENTRE INTERNATIONAL DE
DOCUMENTATION ECONOMIQUE ET
SOCIALE AFRICAINE. MONOGRAPHIES
DOCUMENTAIRES. 1967. irreg. International
Centre for African Social and Economic
Documentation, Place Royale 7, 1000 Brussels,
Belgium.

960   BE   ISSN 0069-1755
CENTRE INTERNATIONAL DE
DOCUMENTATION ET SOCIALE AFRICAINE.
ENQUETES BIBLIOGRAPHIQUES. 1959. irreg.,
1970, vol.17. price varies. International Centre for
African Social and Economic Documentation, Place
Royale 7, 1000 Brussels, Belgium. bk. rev. circ.
2,000. (also avail. in micropaque)

960   NE
CHANGE AND CONTINUITY IN AFRICA. irreg.
price varies. (Afrika-Studiecentrum) Mouton
Publishers, Noordeinde 41, 2514 GC The Hague,
Netherlands (U.S. addr: Mouton Publishers, c/o
Walter de Gruyter, Inc., 200 Saw Mill River Road,
Hawthorne, NY 10532)

960   AO
COLECCAO N'GOLA. a. price varies. Livrangol
Editores, Ave. dos Restauradores 21-1, Luanda,
Angola. illus.

960   KE   ISSN 0069-9330
CONTEMPORARY AFRICAN MONOGRAPHS.
1965. irreg. (East African Institute of Social and
Cultural Affairs) East African Publishing House,
Box 30571, Lusaka Close, off Lusaka Rd., Nairobi,
Kenya. circ. 3,000.

CONTRIBUTIONS A LA CONNAISSANCE DES
ELITES AFRICAINES. see *BIOGRAPHY*

960 361   US   ISSN 0069-9624
CONTRIBUTIONS IN AFRO-AMERICAN AND
AFRICAN STUDIES. 1970. irreg. 51 Riverside
Ave., Westport, CT 06880. Ed. Hollis Lynch.

960   SG
COTE D'IVOIRE EN CHIFFRES. a. 10000 Fr.CFA.
Societe Africaine d'Edition, 16 bis, rue de Thiong,
Dakar, Senegal (And 32 rue de l'Echiquier, Paris,
France)

960   CM
CULTURE CAMEROUNAISE/CAMEROONIAN
CULTURE. 1969. irreg, vol. 2, 1971. Direction des
Affaires Culturelle, Ministere de l'Education, de la
Culture et de la Formation Professionelle, Yaounde,
Cameroon. illus. (processed)

ECOLE DES HAUTES ETUDES EN SCIENCES
SOCIALES. DOSSIERS AFRICAINS. see
ANTHROPOLOGY

HISTORY — HISTORY OF AFRICA

967.5   BE
ENQUETES ET DOCUMENTS D'HISTOIRE AFRICAINE. irreg. Universite Catholique de Louvain, Centre d'Histoire de l'Afrique, Maria-Theresiastraat 21, B-3000 Louvain, Belgium.

ETHIOPIAN MONOGRAPH SERIES. see *ETHNIC INTERESTS*

960   BE   ISSN 0071-187X
ETUDES AFRICAINES. 1953. irreg. price varies. (Universite Libre de Bruxelles, Institut de Sociologie) Editions de l'Universite de Bruxelles, Parc Leopold, 1040 Brussels, Belgium.

960   ZR   ISSN 0071-1993
ETUDES D'HISTOIRE AFRICAINE/STUDIES IN AFRICAN HISTORY. 1970. a. price varies. Universite Nationale du Zaire, Lubumbashi, Department d'Histoire, B.P. 1825, Lubumbashi, Zaire. (Co-sponsor: Musee Royale de l'Afrique Centrale, Belgium) Ed. Dr. J. L. Vellut. adv. bk. rev. circ. 1,000.

ETUDES MAURITANIENNES. see *ANTHROPOLOGY*

ETUDES SENEGALAISES. see *SOCIOLOGY*

962 961   FR   ISSN 0153-5021
ETUDES SUR L'EGYPTE ET LE SOUDAN ANCIENS. 1973. a. (Universite de Lille III, Institut de Papyrologie et d'Egyptologie) Presses Universitaires de Lille, 9 rue Auguste Angellier, 59000 Lille, France. illus.

969   RE
FONDATION POUR LA RECHERCHE ET LE DEVELOPPEMENT DANS L'OCEAN INDIEN. DOCUMENTS ET RECHERCHES. 1975. irreg. 118 Fr.CFA. Fondation pour la Recherche et le Developpement dans l'Ocean Indien, Bibliotheque Departementale, Rue Roland Garros, St. Denis, Reunion.

960   GH   ISSN 0433-969X
GHANA YEAR BOOK. 1953. a. NC.1. Graphic Corporation, Box 742, Accra, Ghana. Ed. Alhaji Sule Raji. adv. bibl. stat. index.

960   GW
HAMBURGER BEITRAEGE ZUR AFRIKA-KUNDE. 1965. irreg. (Institut fuer Afrika-Kunde) Afrika Verlag, Tuerltorstr. 14, Postfach 86, 8068 Pfaffenhofen, W. Germany (B.R.D.)

HISTOIRE ET CIVILISATION ARABE. see *HISTORY — History Of Asia*

960   KE
HISTORICAL ASSOCIATION OF KENYA. PAMPHLET. 1977. irreg. Kenya Literature Bureau, Box 30022, Nairobi, Kenya.

960   KE   ISSN 0440-9264
HISTORICAL ASSOCIATION OF TANZANIA. PAPERS. irreg. (TZ) East African Publishing House, Box 30571, Lusaka Close, off Lusaka Rd., Nairobi, Kenya. bibl.

960   RH
HISTORICAL ASSOCIATION OF ZIMBABWE. LOCAL SERIES PAMPHLETS. 1959. a. Historical Association of Zimbabwe, University of Zimbabwe, Private Bag MP 167, Salisbury, Zimbabwe.
Formerly: Central Africa Historical Association. Local Series Pamphlets (ISSN 0577-036X)

960   US   ISSN 0361-5413
HISTORY IN AFRICA. 1974. a. $15. African Studies Association, Brandeis University, Epstein Service Bldg., Waltham, MA 02154. Ed. David P. Henige. bk. rev. bibl. charts.

960   US
HISTORY IN AFRICA; an annual journal of method. 1974. a. $15. c/o Memorial Library, University of Wisconsin, Madison, WI 53706 (Subscr. to African Studies Association, Epstein Bldg., Brandeis University, Waltham, MA 02154) Ed. David Henige. bk. rev. bibl. circ. 400. Indexed: Curr.Cont. Hist.Abstr.

960   NR   ISSN 0073-3385
HORIZON.* 1961. a. Ibadan Renaissance Society, University College, Ibadan, Nigeria.

960   US
HOWARD UNIVERSITY. AFRICAN STUDIES DEPARTMENT. SEMINAR PAPERS ON AFRICAN STUDIES. 1974. a. $8. Howard University, African Studies Department, Washington, DC 20059. circ. 500.

960   US
INDIANA UNIVERSITY PUBLICATIONS. AFRICAN SERIES. vol. 6, 1976. irreg., vol. 8, 1977. $18. (Indiana University) Humanities Press, Inc., 171 First Ave., Atlantic Highlands, NJ 07716.

960   SG   ISSN 0070-2617
INSTITUT FONDAMENTAL D'AFRIQUE NOIRE. CATALOGUES ET DOCUMENTS. 1947. irreg., no. 22, 1972. price varies. Institut Fondamental d'Afrique Noire, Boite Postale 206, Dakar, Senegal.

960   SG   ISSN 0070-2625
INSTITUT FONDAMENTAL D'AFRIQUE NOIRE. INITIATIONS ET ETUDES AFRICAINES. Short title: Initiations et Etudes Africaines. 1955. irreg., no. 31, 1974. price varies. Institut Fondamental d'Afrique Noire, Boite Postale 206, Dakar, Senegal.

960   SG   ISSN 0070-2633
INSTITUT FONDAMENTAL D'AFRIQUE NOIRE. MEMOIRES. 1939. irreg., no. 89, 1975. price varies. Institut Fondamental d'Afrique Noire, Boite Postale 206, Dakar, Senegal.

960   US   ISSN 0534-655X
INTERNATIONAL AFRICAN SEMINAR. STUDIES PRESENTED AND DISCUSSED. 1959. a, 13th, 1975. price varies. Oxford University Press, 200 Madison Ave., New York, NY 10016 (And Ely House, 37 Dover St., London W1X 4AH, England)

955   IR   ISSN 0075-0476
IRAN ALMANAC AND BOOK OF FACTS. (Text in English) 1961. a. $25. Echo of Iran, 4 Kuche Khalkhali, Hafez Ave., P.O. Box 2008, Teheran, Iran. Ed. Jehangir Behrooz. adv.
Formerly: Echo of Iran.

960   IV
IVORY COAST. ANNUAIRE INTERNATIONAL/INTERNATIONAL DIRECTORY. biennial. Chastrusse et Co., Rue Andre-Devaud, Brive, Ivory Coast. adv. illus.

960   JA   ISSN 0065-4140
JOURNAL OF AFRICAN STUDIES/AFURIKA KENKYU. 1964. irreg. 600 Yen. Japan Association of Africanists - Nihon Afrika Gakkai, c/o University of Tokyo, Dept. of Geography, Hongo, Bunkyo-ku, Tokyo 113, Japan. Ed. Shoji Hasegawa.

960   KE
KENYA. MINISTRY OF INFORMATION AND BROADCASTING. ANNUAL REPORT. 1963. a. Ministry of Information and Broadcasting, Box 30025, Nairobi, Kenya (Orders to: Government Printing and Stationery Department, Box 30128, Nairobi, Kenya)
Former titles: Kenya. Ministry of Information, Broadcasting and Tourism. Annual Report; Kenya. Ministry of Information. Annual Report (ISSN 0075-5885)

967.6   KE
KENYA NATIONAL ACADEMY FOR ADVANCEMENT OF ARTS AND SCIENCES. RESEARCH INFORMATION CIRCULARS. 1968. a., no. 9, 1978. EAs.40($5) Kenya National Academy for Advancement of Arts and Sciences, Box 47288, Nairobi, Kenya.
Formerly: East African Research Information Centre. E A R I C Information Circular (ISSN 0070-8011)

967.62 500.9   KE
KENYA PAST AND PRESENT. 1971. a, no. 11, 1979. EAs.20 per no. Kenya Museum Society, c/o Kenya National Museums, P.O. Box 40658, Nairobi, Kenya. Eds. Chryssee MacCasler, Perry Martin. adv. illus. circ. 2,000.

960   KE
KENYA REGIONAL STUDIES. irreg., no. 2, 1975. Kenya Literature Bureau, Box 30022, Nairobi, Kenya.

960   KE   ISSN 0378-2158
KENYA UHURU YEARBOOK. (Supplements avail.) 1973. a. EAs.40($20) Newspread International, Box 46854, Nairobi, Kenya. Ed. Kul Bhushan. adv. bk. rev. circ. 5,000.

960   NR   ISSN 0075-7640
LAGOS NOTES AND RECORDS;* a journal of African studies. 1967. irreg., vol. 5, 1974. University of Lagos, School of African Studies, Faculty of Arts, Lagos, Nigeria.

MCGILL UNIVERSITY, MONTREAL. CENTRE FOR DEVELOPING-AREA STUDIES. BIBLIOGRAPHY SERIES. see *BIBLIOGRAPHIES*

968.97   MW
MALAWI. DEPARTMENT OF INFORMATION. YEAR IN REVIEW. Short title: Year in Review. 1969. a. Department of Information, P.O. Box 494, Blantyre, Malawi. illus. circ. 10,000.
Formerly (until 1975): Malawi Year Book (ISSN 0076-3012)

MUNGER AFRICANA LIBRARY NOTES. see *ETHNIC INTERESTS*

MUSEUM FUER VOELKERKUNDE, BERLIN. VEROEFFENTLICHUNGEN. NEUE FOLGE. ABTEILUNG: AFRIKA. see *ANTHROPOLOGY*

960   RH   ISSN 0085-3658
NADA. 1923. a. Rhod.$2. Ministry of Home Affairs, Management Committee, Private Bag 7702, Causeway, Salisbury, Zimbabwe. Ed. E. E. Burke. adv. bk. rev. circ. 1,000.

960   SA   ISSN 0085-3674
NATALIA. 1971. a. R.3. Natal Society, Box 415, Pietermaritzburg, Natal, South Africa. Ed. John M. Sellers. adv. bk. rev. bibl. illus. circ. 500. (tabloid format)

NATIONAL ARCHIVES OF ZAMBIA. ANNUAL REPORT. see *LIBRARY AND INFORMATION SCIENCES*

960   ZA
NATIONAL ARCHIVES OF ZAMBIA. NATIONAL ARCHIVES OCCASIONAL PAPER. 1973, no. 2. irreg. 45 n. ‡ National Archives, Box RW 10, Ridgeway, Lusaka, Zambia. Ed. Robin Palmer. bibl. circ. 500(approx.)

968   NE   ISSN 0077-6416
NEDERLANDS-ZUIDAFRIKAANSE VERENIGING. JAARVERSLAG. 1882. a. fl.25. Nederlands-Zuidafrikaanse Vereniging, Keizersgracht 141, Amsterdam C, Netherlands.

960 383   GH   ISSN 0072-9825
OFFICIAL HANDBOOK OF GHANA.* a. Information Services Department, P.O. Box 745, Accra, Ghana.

960   UK
OPUS. 1970. irreg. Star Research (Publications) Society, 34 Oxford Garden, Chiswick, London W.4, England.

960   US
OXFORD STUDIES IN AFRICAN AFFAIRS. irreg. price varies. Oxford University Press, 200 Madison Ave., New York, NY 10016 (And Ely House, 37 Dover St., London W1X 4AH, England) Eds. John D. Hargreaves, George Shepperson.

960 301.2   KE
PEOPLES OF EAST AFRICA. irreg. East African Publishing House, Box 30571, Lusaka Close, off Lusaka Rd., Nairobi, Kenya. bibl. illus.

PERSPECTIVES ON SOUTHERN AFRICA. see *POLITICAL SCIENCE*

962   GW   ISSN 0481-0023
QUELLEN ZUR GESCHICHTE DES ISLAMISCHEN AEGYPTENS. 1978. irreg., vol. 2, 1981. price varies. (Deutsches Archaeologisches Institut, Cairo, UA) Franz Steiner Verlag GmbH, Friedrichstr. 24, Postfach 5529, 6200 Wiesbaden, W. Germany (B.R.D.)

RECHERCHES VOLTAIQUES; collection de travaux de sciences humaines sur la Haute-Volta. see *ANTHROPOLOGY*

967   CM
REPUBLIQUE UNIE DU CAMEROUN: ANNUAIRE INTERNATIONAL/UNITED REPUBLIC OF CAMEROON INTERNATIONAL YEAR BOOK. Cover title: Cameroun Annuaire International. (Subseries of Collection Inf-Afrique) (Text in English or French) a. Les 4 Points Cardinaux, B.P. 513, Douala, Cameroon. illus.

960   AE   ISSN 0556-7343
REVUE D'HISTOIRE ET DE CIVILISATION DU MAGHREB. (Text in French and Arabic) irreg. (3-4/yr.) Societe Historique Algerienne, 3 Bd. Zirout Youcef, Algiers, Algeria. Ed. M. Kaddache.

SAGE SERIES ON AFRICAN MODERNIZATION AND DEVELOPMENT. see *BUSINESS AND ECONOMICS — International Development And Assistance*

960   SW   ISSN 0080-6706
SCANDINAVIAN INSTITUTE OF AFRICAN STUDIES. ANNUAL SEMINAR PROCEEDINGS. 1964. a. price varies. Nordiska Afrikainstitutet - Scandinavian Institute of African Studies, Box 2126, S-750 02 Uppsala, Sweden (Dist. by: Almqvist & Wiksell International, 26 Gamla Brogatan, Box 62, 101 20 Stockholm, Sweden) circ. 1,500.

960   SW   ISSN 0080-6714
SCANDINAVIAN INSTITUTE OF AFRICAN STUDIES. RESEARCH REPORT. (Text in English) 1967. irreg., no. 38, 1977. Kr.5. Nordiska Afrikainstitutet - Scandinavian Institute of African Studies, Box 2126, S-750 02 Uppsala, Sweden. circ. 1,000.

960   SG
SENEGAL EN CHIFFRES. a. 12500 Fr.CFA. Societe Africaine d'Edition, 15 bis rue de Thiong, Dakar, Senegal (And 32 rue de l'Echiquier, Paris, France)

SHILOACH CENTER FOR MIDDLE EASTERN & AFRICAN STUDIES. MONOGRAPH SERIES. see *HISTORY — History Of The Near East*

SOCIAAL-HISTORISCHE STUDIEN. see *SOCIAL SCIENCES: COMPREHENSIVE WORKS*

SOUTH AFRICAN BIOGRAPHICAL AND HISTORICAL STUDIES. see *BIOGRAPHY*

960   SA
SOUTH AFRICAN HISTORICAL JOURNAL. (Text in Afrikaans and English; summaries in English) 1969. a. R.1.50. South African Historical Society, University of the Orange Free State, Department of History, Bloemfontein 9301, South Africa. Ed. M. C. E. van Schoor. bk. rev. bibl. index. circ. 500.

960 309   US
STUDIES IN EAST AFRICAN SOCIETY AND HISTORY. irreg. price varies. N O K Publishers, Ltd., 150 Fifth Ave., New York, NY 10011.

960   KE
STUDIES IN THE DEVELOPMENT OF AFRICAN RESOURCES. irreg. $5.25. Oxford University Press (East African Branch), Box 72532, Nairobi, Kenya.

STUDIES IN ZAMBIAN SOCIETY. see *SOCIOLOGY*

968.3   SQ
SWAZILAND NATIONAL MUSEUM. YEARBOOK. a, latest 1976. Swaziland National Centre, Box 100, Lobamba, Swaziland. illus.
Formerly (until Aug. 1976): Swaziland National Centre. Yearbook.

SYRACUSE UNIVERSITY. MAXWELL SCHOOL OF CITIZENSHIP AND PUBLIC AFFAIRS. FOREIGN AND COMPARATIVE STUDIES: AFRICAN SERIES. see *SOCIAL SCIENCES: COMPREHENSIVE WORKS*

969.1   MG
TANTARA. 1973. FMG.400. Societe d'Histoire de Madagascar, B.P. 3384, Antananarivo, Malagasy Republic.

960   TZ
TANZANIAN STUDIES. irreg. Tanzania Publishing House, Box 2138, Dar es Salaam, Tanzania.

968   SA
TOPOSCOPE. (Text in English) 1970. a. $0.90. ‡ Lower Albany Historical Society, 24 Colgate St., Port Alfred 6170, South Africa. Ed. A.S. Basson. bk. rev. circ. 250.

960   LB
TORCH. no. 9, 1976. irreg. Torch Services, Box 1394, Monrovia, Liberia. Ed. Bill Frank Enoanyi. adv. illus.

960   KE
TRANSAFRICA HISTORICAL PAPERS. 960. irreg. Transafrica Publishers Ltd., Box 42990, Nairobi, Kenya.

960   GW   ISSN 0344-4317
UEBERSEE-MUSEUM, BREMEN. VEROEFFENTLICHUNGEN. REIHE F: BREMER AFRIKA-ARCHIV. Short title: B A A. 1977. irreg., vol. 7, 1979. price varies. Uebersee-Museum, Bremen, Bahnhofsplatz 13, 2800 Bremen, W. Germany(B.R.D.)

967.61   UG   ISSN 0041-574X
UGANDA JOURNAL. 1934. irreg. S.50 membership. Uganda Society, Box 4980, Kampala, Uganda. Ed.Bd. adv. bk. rev. bibl. index. circ. 400-500.

960   US   ISSN 0083-0003
U. S. DEPARTMENT OF STATE. AFRICAN SERIES. (Subseries of its Departmental Series) 1960. irreg. price varies. U.S. Department of State, Bureau of Public Affairs, Washington, DC 20250 (Orders to Supt. of Documents, Washington, DC 20402)

960   UK
UNIVERSITY OF ABERDEEN. AFRICAN STUDIES GROUP. OCCASIONAL PUBLICATIONS. irreg. price varies. University of Aberdeen, African Studies Group, Kings College, Aberdeen AB9 2UB, Scotland.

960   US   ISSN 0068-6190
UNIVERSITY OF CALIFORNIA, LOS ANGELES. AFRICAN STUDIES CENTER. OCCASIONAL PAPER. 1965. irreg. price varies. ‡ University of California, Los Angeles, African Studies Center, 405 Hilgard Ave, Los Angeles, CA 90024.

960   SA
UNIVERSITY OF CAPE TOWN. CENTRE FOR AFRICAN STUDIES. COMMUNICATIONS. 1979. irreg., no. 2, 1979. R.2.75 per no. University of Cape Town, Centre for African Studies, Rondebosch 7700, South Africa.

960 330.9   KE   ISSN 0547-1788
UNIVERSITY OF NAIROBI. INSTITUTE FOR DEVELOPMENT STUDIES. DISCUSSION PAPERS. 1965. irreg., no. 266, 1978. price varies. University of Nairobi, Institute for Development Studies, Box 30197, Nairobi, Kenya.

960 330.9   KE
UNIVERSITY OF NAIROBI. INSTITUTE FOR DEVELOPMENT STUDIES. WORKING PAPERS. irreg., no. 353, 1979. University of Nairobi, Institute for Development Studies, Box 30197, Nairobi, Kenya.

968   SA
UNIVERSITY OF THE ORANGE FREE STATE. INSTITUTE FOR CONTEMPORARY HISTORY. ANNUAL REPORT. a. University of the Orange Free State, Institute for Contemporary History - Univesiteit van die Oranje-Vrystaat, Instituut vir Eietydse Geskiedenis, Box 2320, Bloemfontein 9300, South Africa.

968   UK
UNIVERSITY OF YORK. CENTRE FOR SOUTHERN AFRICAN STUDIES. COLLECTED PAPERS. 1974. irreg. £1 per vol. University of York, Centre for Southern African Studies, Heslington, York YO1 5DD, England. Eds. Anne V. Akeroyd, Christopher R. Hill.

320   GW   ISSN 0341-275X
VEREINIGUNG VON AFRIKANISTEN IN DEUTSCHLAND. SCHRIFTEN. 1969. irreg., vol. 8, 1976. price varies. Verlag Helmut Buske, Schlueterstr. 14, 2000 Hamburg 13, W. Germany (B.R.D.)

916.605   NR   ISSN 0083-8144
WEST AFRICA ANNUAL. (Text in English) 1963. a. $10.50. John West Publications Ltd., 212 Yakubu Gowon Street, Lagos, Nigeria (Dist. in U.S. by: International Publications Service, 114 E. 32nd St., New York, NY 10016) Ed. L. K. Jakende. adv. circ. 5,000.

960   US
WORKING PAPERS IN AFRICAN STUDIES. 1976. irreg., no. 42, 1981. Boston University, African Studies Center, 10 Lenox St., Brookline, MA 02146.

960   US   ISSN 0084-2281
WORLD TODAY SERIES: AFRICA. 1966. a. $2.95. Stryker-Post Publications Inc., 888 Seventeenth St., N.W., Washington, DC 20006. Ed. Pierre Etienne Dostert. circ. 10-15,000.

960   ZA   ISSN 0084-4810
ZAMBIA. INFORMATION SERVICES. ANNUAL REPORT.* 1964. a. Information Services, Box RW 20, Lusaka, Zambia (Orders to: Government Printer, Box 136, Lusaka, Zambia)

960 572   ZA
ZAMBIA. NATIONAL MUSEUMS BOARD. OCCASIONAL PAPER SERIES. irreg. price varies. National Museums Board, Livingstone Museum, Box 498, Livingstone, Zambia.

960 916   ZA
ZAMBIA MUSEUMS PAPERS SERIES. irreg. price varies. National Museums Board, Livingstone Museum, Box 498, Livingstone, Zambia.

968.94   ZA   ISSN 0084-5124
ZAMBIAN PAPERS. 1967. irreg. price varies. (University of Zambia, Institute for African Studies) Manchester University Press, Box 30900, Lusaka, Zambia. Eds. M. E. Kashoki, Q. N. Parsons.
Supersedes: Rhodes-Livingstone Papers.

968.9 069   RH
ZIMBABWE. NATIONAL ARCHIVES. ANNUAL REPORT. 1971. a. free. ‡ National Archives, Private Bag 7729, Causeway, Salisbury, Zimbabwe. circ. 350.

968.9 069   RH   ISSN 0035-4716
ZIMBABWE. NATIONAL ARCHIVES. OCCASIONAL PAPERS. 1963. irreg. Rhod.$0.75. ‡ National Archives, Private Bag 7729, Causeway, Salisbury, Zimbabwe. circ. 750.
Formerly: Southern Rhodesia. National Archives. Occasional Papers.

HISTORY — History Of Asia

see also Oriental Studies

954   US   ISSN 0360-3687
A I I S ANNUAL REPORT. a. American Institute of Indian Studies, 1130 E. 59th St., Chicago, IL 60637. Key Title: Annual Report - American Institute of Indian Studies.

950   US
A M S ASIAN STUDIES. 1976. irreg. price varies. A M S Press, Inc., 56 E. 13th St., New York, NY 10003.

A S A I H L. SEMINAR REPORTS. (Association of Southeast Asian Institutions of Higher Learning) see *EDUCATION — Higher Education*

950   KO   ISSN 0066-8311
A S P A C SEMINAR ON AUDIO-VISUAL EDUCATION. PROCEEDINGS. 1969. irreg., 1970, 3rd. free. Asian and Pacific Council, Cultural and Social Centre, I.P.O. Box 3129, Seoul, S. Korea. circ. 1,200.

953.3   YS   ISSN 0065-1923
ADEN MAGAZINE/MAGALLAT ADEN. (Editions in Arabic and English) 1959. a. free; selected distribution. British Petroleum Refinery (Aden) Ltd., P.O.Box 3003, Aden, Southern Yemen. bk. rev. circ. 3,000 (Arabic edt.); 100 (English edt.)

958.1   GW
AFGHANISCHE STUDIEN. 1969. irreg, no 19, 1980. price varies. Verlag Anton Hain GmbH, Adelheidstr. 2, Postfach 1220, 6240 Koenigstein, W. Germany (B.R.D.) Ed. Bd.

HISTORY — HISTORY OF ASIA

958.1 AF ISSN 0304-6133
AFGHANISTAN REPUBLIC ANNUAL. (Text in English) a. Ministry of Information and Culture, Kabul, Afghanistan. illus.

950 960 BU
AFRIKANO-AZIATSKI PROBLEMI. 1970. irreg. 1.44 lv. per issue. (Bulgarska Akademiia na Naukite, Nauchnoizsledovatelski Tsentur za Africa i Aziia) Publishing House of the Bulgarian Academy of Sciences, Ul. Akad. G. Bonchev, 1113 Sofia, Bulgaria. Ed. Evgeni G.. Kamenov. circ. 600.

AFRO-ASIAN PEOPLES' CONFERENCE. PROCEEDINGS. see *HISTORY — History Of Africa*

AFRO-ASIAN PEOPLES' SOLIDARITY ORGANIZATION. COUNCIL. DOCUMENTS OF THE SESSION. see *HISTORY — History Of Africa*

959 US ISSN 0065-6259
ALIGARH MUSLIM UNIVERSITY, ALIGARH, INDIA. DEPARTMENT OF HISTORY. PUBLICATION. (Text in English) 1963. irreg. price varies. (II) Asia Publishing House, Inc., 141 E. 44th St., New York, NY 10017.

954 GW ISSN 0170-3242
ALT- UND NEU-INDISCHE STUDIEN. irreg., vol. 23, 1981. price varies. (Universitaet Hamburg, Seminar fuer Kultur und Geschichte Indiens) Franz Steiner Verlag GmbH, Friedrichstr. 24, Postfach 5529, 6200 Wiesbaden, W. Germany (B.R.D.) Ed.Bd.

950 US ISSN 0065-9541
AMERICAN ORIENTAL SERIES. 1925. irreg. price varies. American Oriental Society, 329 Sterling Memorial Library, Yale Station, New Haven, CT 06520. bk. rev.

996.1 913 NE ISSN 0066-1554
ANATOLICA. 1967. a. price varies. Nederlands Instituut voor het Nabije Oosten, Noordeindsplein 4a, Leiden, Netherlands. Ed. Bd. bk. rev. circ. 500.

954 II
ANDHRA HISTORICAL RESEARCH SOCIETY. JOURNAL. (Text in English) 1926. a. Department of Archaeology and Museums, Hyderabad 500001, Andhra Pradesh, India (Or: Publications Bureau, Directorate of Government Printing, Chanchalguda, Hyderabad, India)

ANDHRA PRADESH, INDIA. DEPARTMENT OF ARCHAEOLOGY AND MUSEUMS. EPIGRAPHY SERIES. see *ARCHAEOLOGY*

ANDHRA PRADESH, INDIA. DEPARTMENT OF ARCHAEOLOGY AND MUSEUMS. MUSEUM OBJECTS AND NUMISMATICS SERIES. see *HOBBIES — Numismatics*

950 US
ARIZONA STATE UNIVERSITY. CENTER FOR ASIAN STUDIES. OCCASIONAL PAPERS. 1967. irreg.; no. 10, 1977. price varies. Arizona State University, Center for Asian Studies, Tempe, AZ 85281. Dir. Yung-Hwan Jo.

950.06 US ISSN 0098-1214
ASIA SOCIETY. ANNUAL REPORT. a. Asia Society, 112 E. 64th St., New York, NY 10021. illus. Key Title: Annual Report - Asia Society.

ASIAN AND AFRICAN STUDIES. see *ORIENTAL STUDIES*

950 KO ISSN 0066-8303
ASIAN AND PACIFIC COUNCIL. CULTURAL AND SOCIAL CENTRE. ANNUAL REPORT. 1969. irreg.; latest issue, 1973. free. Asian and Pacific Council, Cultural and Social Centre, I.P.O. Box 3129, Seoul, S. Korea. Ed. Mario T. Gatbonton. circ. 2,000.

950 JA ISSN 0454-2150
ASIAN CULTURAL STUDIES. (Text in English or Japanese) 1960. irreg. Kokusai Christian University - Kokusai Kirisutokyo Daigaku, Mitaka, Japan. illus.

951 CH ISSN 0571-2939
ASIAN PEOPLES' ANTI-COMMUNIST LEAGUE. CHARTS ABOUT CHINESE COMMUNISTS ON THE MAINLAND. 1955. irreg. $3. World Anti-Communist League, Asian People's Anti-Communist League - China Chapter, 1 Tsingtao East Rd., Taipei, Taiwan, Republic of China.

950 US ISSN 0066-8486
ASIAN STUDIES AT HAWAII MONOGRAPH SERIES. 1965. irreg., no. 23, 1979. price varies. (University of Hawaii, Asian Studies Program) University Press of Hawaii, 2840 Kolowalu St., Honolulu, HI 96822. Ed. Philip Jenner. (reprint service avail. from UMI,ISI)

950 CN
ASIAN STUDIES MONOGRAPHS SERIES. 1981. irreg. price varies. University of British Columbia Press, 303-6344 Memorial Rd., Vancouver, B.C. V6T 1W5, Canada.

959 SZ
ASIAN STUDIES SERIES. (Text in English and French) 1979. irreg. price varies. Universite de Geneve, Institut Universitaire de Hautes Etudes Internationales, Centre Asiatique - University of Geneva, Graduate Institute of International Studies, Asian Centre, Case Postale 53, 1211 Geneva 21, Switzerland. Ed.Bd. circ. 400.
Supersedes (1973-1977, vol.2, no.6-7-8): Centre de Documentation et de Recherche sur l'Asie. Etudes et Documents.

950 GW ISSN 0571-320X
ASIATISCHE FORSCHUNGEN. 1959. irreg., vol. 69, 1980. price varies. Verlag Otto Harrassowitz, Taunusstr. 6, Postfach 2929, 6200 Wiesbaden, W. Germany (B.R.D.) Ed. Walther Heissig.

950 960 980 GE
ASIEN - AFRIKA - LATEINAMERIKA. JAHRBUCH. 1969. a. price varies. (Zentraler Rat fuer Asien-, Afrika- und Lateinamerikawissenschaften in der DDR) VEB Deutscher Verlag der Wissenschaften, Johannes-Dieckmann-Str. 10, Postfach 1216, 108 Berlin, E. Germany (D.D.R.) Ed. L. Rathmann. bk. rev.
Formerly: Asien - Afrika - Lateinamerika (ISSN 0066-8508)

950 US
ASSOCIATION FOR ASIAN STUDIES. ENDURING SCHOLARSHIP. REFERENCE SERIES. 1972. irreg. price varies. Association for Asian Studies, Inc., University of Michigan, 1 Lane Hall, Ann Arbor, MI 48109.

320 US ISSN 0066-9059
ASSOCIATION FOR ASIAN STUDIES. MONOGRAPHS. 1951. irreg., no. 36, 1979. price varies. University of Arizona Press, Box 3398, Tucson, AZ 85722. adv. bk. rev.

950 AT ISSN 0067-2041
AUSTRALIAN NATIONAL UNIVERSITY, CANBERRA. FACULTY OF ASIAN STUDIES. OCCASIONAL PAPERS. 1963. irreg. Aus.$3.50. Australian National University, Faculty of Asian Studies, Box 4, Canberra City, A.C.T. 2600, Australia. circ. 300.
Formerly: Australian National University, Canberra. Centre of Oriental Studies. Occasional Papers.

954 II
B. R. P. T. BULLETIN. (Text in Bengali or English) 1974. a. Rs.2.50. Bureau of Research and Publications on Tripura, No. 2 Ramnagar Rd., Agartala 799002, India.

954.9 BG
BANGLADESH ITIHAS SAMITI. JOURNAL/ITIHASA SAMITI PATRIKA. (Text in Bengali or English) no. 2, 1973. a. Tk.15. Bangladesh Itihas Samiti, c/o Dept. of History, University of Dacca, Dacca 2, Bangladesh.

BEITRAEGE ZUR JAPANOLOGIE. see *ORIENTAL STUDIES*

950 GW ISSN 0170-3137
BEITRAEGE ZUR SUEDASIEN FORSCHUNG. 1974. irreg., vol. 61, 1981. price varies. (Universitaet Heidelberg, Suedasien-Institut) Franz Steiner Verlag GmbH, Friedrichstr. 24, Postfach 5529, 6200 Wiesbaden, W. Germany (B.R.D.)

954 UK ISSN 0575-6863
CAMBRIDGE SOUTH ASIAN STUDIES. 1966. irreg., no. 24, 1981. $39.50 for latest vol. Cambridge University Press, Box 110, Cambridge CB2 3RL, England (and 32 E. 57 St., New York NY 10022) index.

951 UK
CAMBRIDGE STUDIES IN CHINESE HISTORY, LITERATURE AND INSTITUTIONS. 1970. irreg. price varies. Cambridge University Press, Box 110, Cambridge CB2 3RL, England (And 32 E. 57th St., New York, NY 10022) Eds. P. Hanan. D. Twitchett.

950 930 UK ISSN 0068-6891
CAMBRIDGE UNIVERSITY. ORIENTAL PUBLICATIONS. 1956. irreg., no. 30, 1981. $39 for latest vol. (Cambridge University,Faculty of Oriental Languages) Cambridge University Press, Box 110, Cambridge CB2 3RL, England (and 32 E. 57 St., New York, NY 10022) index.

956 BE ISSN 0077-0353
CENTRE POUR L'ETUDE DES PROBLEMES DE MONDE MUSULMAN CONTEMPORAIN. INITIATIONS. 1962. irreg. price varies. ‡ Centre pour l'Etude des Problemes du Monde Musulman Contemporain, Ave. Jeanne, 44, 1050 Brussels, Belgium. circ. 1,500.

950 MX ISSN 0066-8249
CENTRO DE ESTUDIOS ORIENTALES. ANUARIO. 1968. a. price varies. Universidad Nacional Autonoma de Mexico, Facultad de Filosofia y Letras, Ciudad Universitaria, Mexico 20, D.F., Mexico. Ed. Lothar Knauth.

958 CE ISSN 0577-4691
CEYLON HISTORICAL JOURNAL. (Text in English) 1951. irreg. Tisara Prakaskayo Ltd, 137 Dutugemunu St., Dehiwala, Sri Lanka.

CHINA FACTS AND FIGURES ANNUAL. see *POLITICAL SCIENCE*

951 US ISSN 0069-3693
CHINA RESEARCH MONOGRAPHS. 1967. irreg., no. 15, 1979. University of California, Berkeley, Center for Chinese Studies, Institute of East Asian Studies, Berkeley, CA 94720. (reprint service avail. from UMI)

CHINESE HISTORICAL SOCIETY OF AMERICA. ANNIVERSARY BULLETIN. see *ETHNIC INTERESTS*

CHINESE SCIENCE; an informal and irregular journal dedicated to the study of traditional Chinese science, technology, and medicine. see *SCIENCES: COMPREHENSIVE WORKS*

952 IT ISSN 0529-7451
CINA. (Includes: Supplements) 1956. irreg., vol. 17, 1980. L.800. (Istituto Italiano per Il Medio ed Estremo Oriente) Herder Editrice e Libreria S.r.L., Piazza Montecitorio 120, 00186 Rome, Italy. Ed. Lionello Lanciotti.

951 IT ISSN 0069-4312
CIVILTA ASIATICHE. 1960. irreg., 1963, no.5. price varies. (Fondazione Giorgio Cini, Centro di Cultura e Civilta) Casa Editrice Leo S. Olschki, 50100 Florence, Italy. circ. 500.

959.7 BE
COLLECTION VIETNAMIENNE. 1973. irreg., no. 5, 1980. 110 Fr. per no. Librairie-Editions Thanh-Long, 34 rue Dekens, 1040 Brussels, Belgium.

COLUMBIA UNIVERSITY. EAST ASIAN INSTITUTE. STUDIES. see *ORIENTAL STUDIES*

951 HK ISSN 0069-7788
COMMUNIST CHINA PROBLEM RESEARCH SERIES. (Editions in English and Chinese) 1953. irreg. price varies. Union Cultural Organization Ltd., No. 9 College Road, Kowloon, Hong Kong. Ed. William Hsu. circ. 600.

951 HK ISSN 0069-7796
COMMUNIST CHINA YEARBOOK SERIES. (Included in: Communist China Problems Research Series) (English Edition) 1955. irreg. $12. Union Cultural Organization Ltd., No. 9 College Road, Kowloon, Hong Kong. Ed. William Hsu. circ. 600.

HISTORY — HISTORY OF ASIA

951   HK   ISSN 0069-9535
CONTINENTAL RESEARCH SERIES. (Text in English) 1970. irreg. Continental Research Institute, 199/203 Hennessy Rd., Hong Kong, Hong Kong.

950   US   ISSN 0070-0215
CORNELL UNIVERSITY. SOUTHEAST ASIA PROGRAM. DATA PAPERS. 1951. irreg., no. 114, 1980. price varies. Cornell University, Southeast Asia Program, 120 Uris Hall, Ithaca, NY 14853. (also avail. in microform from UMI)

959.3   US   ISSN 0070-0223
CORNELL UNIVERSITY. THAILAND PROJECT. INTERIM REPORTS SERIES. (Subseries of: Cornell University. Southeast Asia Program. Data Papers) 1953. irreg., 1971, no. 14. price varies; 1971, no. 14, $3.50. Cornell University, Southeast Asia Program, 120 Uris Hall, Ithaca, NY 14853. (also avail. in microform from UMI)

950   US
CORNELL UNIVERSITY EAST ASIA PAPERS. 1973. irreg., no. 24, 1981. price varies. Cornell University, China-Japan Program, 140 Uris Hall, Ithaca, NY 14853.

956   BE   ISSN 0070-0517
CORRESPONDANCE D'ORIENT. 1960. irreg. price varies. ‡ Centre pour l'Etude des Problemes du Monde Musulman Contemporain, Ave. Jeanne, 44, 1050 Brussels, Belgium. bk. rev. circ. 500.
Formerly: Centre pour l'Etude des Problemes du Monde Musulman Contemporain. Revue Annuelle.

DECCAN COLLEGE. POSTGRADUATE & RESEARCH INSTITUTE. BULLETIN. see *SOCIAL SCIENCES: COMPREHENSIVE WORKS*

DHANIRAM BHALLA GRANTHAMALA. see *ORIENTAL STUDIES*

DIRECTORY OF EAST ASIAN COLLECTIONS IN NORTH AMERICAN LIBRARIES. see *LIBRARY AND INFORMATION SCIENCES*

951   US   ISSN 0362-5028
EARLY CHINA. 1975. a. $7. Society for the Study of Early China, c/o University of California, Department of History, Berkeley, CA 94720. Ed. David N. Keightley. adv. bk. rev. abstr. bibl. charts. illus. circ. 350(controlled)
Supersedes: Society for the Study of Pre-Han China. Newsletter (ISSN 0361-9613)

ERETZ-ISRAEL. ARCHAEOLOGICAL, HISTORICAL AND GEOGRAPHICAL STUDIES. see *ARCHAEOLOGY*

490 950   GW   ISSN 0340-6261
FREIBURGER BEITRAEGE ZUR INDOLOGIE. 1968. irreg., vol. 14, 1980. price varies. Verlag Otto Harrassowitz, Taunusstr. 6, Postfach 2929, 6200 Wiesbaden, W. Germany (B.R.D.) Ed. Ulrich Schneider.

954   342   KE   ISSN 0072-0143
GANDHI MEMORIAL LECTURES. irreg., 1969, series 1. Oxford University Press (East African Branch), Box 72532, Nairobi, Kenya.

950   II   ISSN 0072-0348
GAZETEER OF INDIA. (3 volume series,; Vol. 1: Land and People; Vol. 2: History and Culture; Vol. 3: Economic Structure and Activities) (Text in English) 1965. irreg. price varies per vol. India Ministry of Education and Social Welfare., Ministry of Information and Broadcasting, Publications Division, Patiala House, Tilak Marg, New Delhi 110001, India (U.S. subscr.: M/S Inter Culture Association, Thompson, CT 06377) Ed. P. N. Chopra. circ. 5,000 (per vol.)

952   IT
GIAPPONE. 1963. a. L.3000. (Japanese Institute of Culture) Herder Editrice e Libreria s.r.l., Piazza di Montecitorio 120, 00186 Rome, Italy. Ed. Adolfo Tamburello.

GOETTINGER ORIENTFORSCHUNGEN. REIHE I: SYRIACA. see *ORIENTAL STUDIES*

GOETTINGER ORIENTFORSCHUNGEN. REIHE III: IRANICA. see *ORIENTAL STUDIES*

GOETTINGER ORIENTFORSCHUNGEN. REIHE IV: AEGYPTEN. see *ORIENTAL STUDIES*

950   US   ISSN 0073-0483
HARVARD EAST ASIAN MONOGRAPHS. irreg., 1973, no. 48. price varies. (Harvard University, East Asian Research Center) Harvard University Press, 79 Garden St., Cambridge, MA 02138. Ed. John K. Fairbank.

950   US   ISSN 0073-0491
HARVARD EAST ASIAN SERIES. (Title varies no. 1-10(1959-61) Harvard East Asian Studies) 1959. irreg., 1972, nos. 65-70. price varies. (Harvard University, East Asian Research Center) Harvard University Press, 79 Garden St., Cambridge, MA 02138. Ed. John K. Fairbank.

956   US   ISSN 0073-0572
HARVARD MIDDLE EASTERN MONOGRAPHS. 1959. irreg., 1973, no. 22. price varies. (Harvard University, Center for Middle Eastern Studies) Harvard University Press, 79 Garden St., Cambridge, MA 02138.

950   US   ISSN 0073-0599
HARVARD ORIENTAL SERIES. (Text in English, German or Sanskrit) 1883. irreg., 1968, no. 47. price varies. Harvard University Press, 79 Garden St., Cambridge, MA 02138. Ed. Daniel H. H. Ingalls.

959   US
HARVARD STUDIES IN AMERICAN-EAST ASIAN RELATIONS. 1972. irreg., no. 6, 1974. $15. Harvard University Press, 79 Garden St., Cambridge., MA 02138.

951   US   ISSN 0073-084X
HARVARD-YENCHING INSTITUTE. MONOGRAPH SERIES. irreg., vol. 22, 1975. Harvard University Press, 79 Garden St., Cambridge, MA 02138.

951   US   ISSN 0073-0858
HARVARD-YENCHING INSTITUTE. STUDIES. 1950. irreg., 1972, nos. 27, 28. price varies. Harvard University Press, 79 Garden St., Cambridge, MA 02138.

950 960   FR   ISSN 0073-2400
HISTOIRE ET CIVILISATION ARABE. 1969. irreg. price varies. Editions Cujas, 4,6,8 rue de la Maison-Blanche, 75013 Paris, France.

354.9   PK
HISTORICAL STUDIES (PAKISTAN) SERIES. 1976. irreg. price varies. National Commission on Historical and Cultural Research, Islamabad, Pakistan.

954   SZ
HULL MONOGRAPHS ON SOUTH-EAST ASIA. irreg., no. 4, 1971. price varies. Interdocumentation Company, Poststrasse 14, Zug, Switzerland.

954   US
INDIA FORUM. 1975. irreg. $5 for 5 nos. Box 8221, Emeryville Station, Oakland, CA 94662 (Subscr addr.: Box 4141, Berkeley, CA 94704) Ed. Bd. adv. circ. 1,200. (back issues avail.)

INDIAN YEARBOOK OF INTERNATIONAL AFFAIRS. see *POLITICAL SCIENCE — International Relations*

915.95   MY
INFORMATION MALAYSIA. 1963. a. M.$8. New Straits Times Press (Malaysia) Berhad, No. 31, Jalan Riong, Kuala Lumpur 22-03, Malaysia (Dist. in U.S. by International Publications Service, 303 Park Ave. South, New York, N.Y. 10010)
Incorporating: Malaysia Year Book (ISSN 0076-339X)

950   KO
INQUIRY INTO THE FUTURE. (Text in English or Korean) 1970. a. $5. (Korean Society for Future Studies) Seoul National University Press, Graduate School of Environmental Studies, Rm. 13-211, Seoul National University, Seoul 151, S. Korea. Ed. An-Jae Kim. bk. rev. circ. 200.

954 891.2   II   ISSN 0073-8352
INSTITUT FRANCAIS D'INDOLOGIE. PUBLICATIONS. 1956. irreg., no. 57, 1977. price varies. Institut Francais d'Indologie, B.P. No. 33, Pondicherry 605001, India.

950   GW   ISSN 0073-8387
INSTITUT FUER ASIENKUNDE. SCHRIFTEN. (Text in German; summaries in English) 1957. irreg., no. 44, 1978. price varies. Verlag Otto Harrassowitz, Taunusstr. 6, Postfach 2929, 6200 Wiesbaden, W. Germany(B.R.D.)

935 913   NE   ISSN 0073-8549
INSTITUT HISTORIQUE ET ARCHEOLOGIQUE NEERLANDAIS DE STAMBOULL. PUBLICATIONS. (Text in English, French and German) 1956. irreg., 1974, vol. 36. price varies. (TU - Netherlands Institute for the Near East) Nederlands Instituut voor Het Nabije Oosten, Noordeindsplein 42, Leiden, Netherlands. Ed. Bd.

950   FR
INSTITUT NATIONAL DES LANGUES ET CIVILISATIONS ORIENTALES. LIVRET DE L'ETUDIANT. 1970. a. $2. Institut National des Langues et Civilisations Orientales, 4 rue de Lille, 75007 Paris, France. Ed. A. Schneider. adv. circ. 4,000.

956.94   US
INSTITUTE FOR PALESTINE STUDIES. ARABIC ANNUAL DOCUMENTARY SERIES. Variant title: Palestine Documents. (Text in Arabic) 1966. a. $25. Institute for Palestine Studies, Box 19449, Washington, DC 20036 (Or Box 11-7164, Beirut, Lebanon) index. (back issues avail)

956   US   ISSN 0073-8794
INSTITUTE FOR PALESTINE STUDIES. BASIC DOCUMENTS SERIES. Variant title: U N Resolutions on Palestine. (Text in Arabic, English and French) 1967. a. $5. Institute for Palestine Studies, Box 19449, Washington, DC 20036 (Or Box 11-7164, Beirut, Lebanon)

956.94   US   ISSN 0073-8808
INSTITUTE FOR PALESTINE STUDIES. INTERNATIONAL ANNUAL DOCUMENTARY SERIES. Variant title: International Documents on Palestine. (Text in English) 1967. a. $35. Institute for Palestine Studies, Box 19449, Washington, DC 20036 (Or Box 11-7164, Beirut, Lebanon)
Formerly: United Nations Annual Documentary Series.

956   US   ISSN 0073-8816
INSTITUTE FOR PALESTINE STUDIES. MONOGRAPH SERIES. (Text mainly in English; occasionally in Arabic or French) 1969. irreg., no. 48, 1978. price varies. Institute for Palestine Studies, Box 19449, Washington, DC 20036 (Or Box 11-7164, Beirut, Lebanon)

956.94   US
INSTITUTE FOR PALESTINE STUDIES. YEARBOOK SERIES. Title varies: Palestine Yearbook. (Text in Arabic) 1965. a. $30. Institute for Palestine Studies, Box 19449, Washington, DC 20036. Ed. Burhan Dajani. index. (back issues avail)

959   SI
INSTITUTE OF SOUTHEAST ASIAN STUDIES. ANNUAL REPORT. (Text in English) 1969. a. free. Institute of Southeast Asian Studies, Heng Mui Keng Terrace, Pasir Panjang, Singapore 0511, Singapore.

959   SI
INSTITUTE OF SOUTHEAST ASIAN STUDIES. ANNUAL REVIEW. (Text in English) 1974. a., no. 7, 1980. price varies. Institute of Southeast Asian Studies, Heng Mui Keng Terrace, Pasir Panjang, Singapore 0511, Singapore.

959   SI
INSTITUTE OF SOUTHEAST ASIAN STUDIES. CURRENT ISSUES SEMINAR SERIES. (Text in English) 1973. irreg., no. 7, 1978. price varies. Institute of Southeast Asian Studies, Heng Mui Keng Terrace, Pasir Panjang, Singapore 0511, Singapore.

959   SI
INSTITUTE OF SOUTHEAST ASIAN STUDIES. FIELD REPORTS SERIES. (Text in English) 1973. irreg., no. 14, 1978. price varies. Institute of Southeast Asian Studies, Heng Mui Keng Terrace, Pasir Panjang, Singapore 0511, Singapore.

959 SI
INSTITUTE OF SOUTHEAST ASIAN STUDIES. MONOGRAPHS SERIES. (Text in English) 1973. irreg., no. 19, 1979. price varies. Institute of Southeast Asian Studies, Heng Mui Keng Terrace, Pasir Panjang, Singapore 0511, Singapore.

959 SI ISSN 0073-9731
INSTITUTE OF SOUTHEAST ASIAN STUDIES. OCCASIONAL PAPER. (Text in English) 1970. irreg., no. 62, 1980. price varies. Institute of Southeast Asian Studies, Heng Mui Keng Terrace, Pasir Panjang, Singapore 0511, Singapore. Indexed: Bibl.Asian Stud.

959 SI
INSTITUTE OF SOUTHEAST ASIAN STUDIES. ORAL HISTORY PROGRAMMES. (Text in English) 1973. irreg. price varies. Institute of Southeast Asian Studies, Heng Mui Keng Terrace, Pasir Panjang, Singapore 0511, Singapore.

959 SI
INSTITUTE OF SOUTHEAST ASIAN STUDIES. PROCEEDINGS AND INTERNATIONAL CONFERENCES. (Text in English) 1973. irreg., no. 4, 1978. price varies. Institute of Southeast Asian Studies, Heng Mui Keng Terrace, Pasir Panjang, Singapore 0511, Singapore.

959 SI
INSTITUTE OF SOUTHEAST ASIAN STUDIES. RESEARCH NOTES AND DISCUSSION SERIES. (Text in English) 1976. irreg., no. 13, 1979. price varies. Institute of Southeast Asian Studies, Heng Mui Keng Terrace, Pasir Panjang, Singapore 0511, Singapore.

954 II ISSN 0074-123X
INTERNATIONAL ACADEMY OF INDIAN CULTURE. REPORT. (Text in English) 1951. a. free. International Academy of Indian Culture, J-22 Hauz Khas Enclave, New Delhi 16, India. circ. 100.

956 UK ISSN 0075-093X
ISLAMIC SURVEYS. 1962. irreg., no. 1976. price varies. Edinburgh University Press, 22 George Square, Edinburgh EH8 9LF, Scotland. Ed. A. M. Watt. circ. 4,000.

915.69 IS ISSN 0075-1413
ISRAEL YEARBOOK. 1950/51. a. $25. Israel Yearbook Publications, Box 1199, Tel Aviv, Israel (Dist. in U.S. by International Publications Service, 303 Park Ave. So., New York, N.Y. 10010) Eds. L. Berger, R. Levin, S. Yedidyah. adv.

952 IT ISSN 0080-391X
ISTITUTO GIAPPONESE DI CULTURA, ROME. ANNUARIO. (Text in Western languages) 1963. a. free. (Kokusai Koryu Kikin) Istituto Giapponese di Cultura in Roma, Via Antonio Gramsci 74, 00197 Roma, Italy.

952 IT ISSN 0080-3928
ISTITUTO GIAPPONESE DI CULTURA, ROME. NOTIZIARIO. 1965. a. free. (Kokusai Koryu Kikin) Istituto Giapponese di Cultura in Roma, Via Antonio Gramsci 74, 00197 Roma, Italy.

956.1 NE ISSN 0075-2118
JAARBERICHT "EX ORIENTE LUX; annuaire de la Societe Orientale Neerlandaise "Ex Oriente Lux". 1933. a. fl.80($30) (Vooraziatisch-Egyptisch Genootschap "Ex Oriente Lux") Nederlands Instituut voor Het Nabije Oosten, Noordeindsplein 42, Leiden, Netherlands. Ed. K. R. Veenhof. circ. 800.

959 MY
JEBAT. 1971/72. a. National University of Malaysia, Historical Society - Universiti Kebangsaan Malaysia, Persatuan Sejarah, c/o Jabatan Sejarah, Bangi, Kajang, Selangor, Malaysia. Ed. Bd. bibl. illus.

959 MY
JERNAL SEJARAH. (Text in English and Malay) 1960. a. $2.50. University of Malaya, Historical Society - Universiti Malaya, Persatuan Sejarah, Lembah Pantai, Kuala Lumpur 22-11, Malaysia. bibl.

950 IS
JERUSALEM STUDIES ON ASIA. irreg. $5. (Hebrew University of Jerusalem, Harry S. Truman Research Institute, Asia Research Unit) Jerusalem Academic Press, Box 3640, Jerusalem, Israel. Ed. Martin Rudner.

954 II ISSN 0075-4110
JOURNAL OF ANCIENT INDIAN HISTORY. 1967-68. a. Rs.30($6) University of Calcutta, Centre of Advanced Study in Ancient Indian History and Culture, 51-2 Hazra Rd., Calcutta 19, India. Ed. D. C. Sircar.

954.9 320 PK
JOURNAL OF HISTORY AND POLITICAL SCIENCE. (Text in English) 1971. a. Government College, Department of History and Political Science, Lahore, Pakistan. Ed. S. Razi Wasti. bk. rev. circ. 500.

952 JA
KAGOSHIMA UNIVERSITY. HISTORICAL SCIENCE REPORTS. (Text in Japanese) a. Kagoshima University, Uerata-cho, Korimoto 1-chome, Kagoshima 890, Japan.

950 913 GE ISSN 0075-532X
KEILSCHRIFTURKUNDEN AUS BOGHAZKOEI. 1953. irreg., vol. 13, 1977. price varies. (Akademie der Wissenschaften der DDR, Zentralinstitut fuer Geschichte) Akademie-Verlag, Leipziger Str. 3-4, 108 Berlin, E. Germany (D.D.R.)

959 398 PH
KINAADMAN/WISDOM; a journal of the Southern Philippines. 1979. a. P.35($9.50) Xavier University, Cagayan de Oro City, Philippines (Dist. in the U.S. by: Cellar Book Shop, 18090 Wyoming, Detroit, MI 48221) Ed. Miguel A. Bernad. bk. rev. bibl. circ. 800.

951.9 US
KOREA RESEARCH MONOGRAPHS. 1980. irreg. University of California, Berkeley, Center for Chinese Studies, Institute of East Asian Studies, Berkeley, CA 94720. (reprint service avail. from UMI)

951.9 US ISSN 0145-840X
KOREAN STUDIES. 1977. a. (University of Hawaii, Center for Korean Studies) University Press of Hawaii, 2840 Kolowalu St., Honolulu, HI 96822. bk. rev. (reprint service avail. from UMI,ISI) Indexed: Amer.Hist.& Life. Hist.Abstr.

950 490 HU ISSN 0075-6911
KOROSI CSOMA KISKONYVTAR. 1966. irreg. price varies. (Magyar Tudomanyos Akademia) Akademiai Kiado, Publishing House of the Hungarian Academy of Sciences, P.O. Box 24, H-1363 Budapest, Hungary.

930 520 FR
KTEMA; civilisations de l 'Orient, de la Grece et de Rome Antiques. 1976. a. 50 F. (Universite de Strasbourg II, Groupe de Recherche d'Histoire Romaine) A. E. C. R., Box 350R9, 67009 Strasbourg Cedex, France. Ed. Edmond Frezouls, Edmond Levy.

950 PH ISSN 0459-4835
LIPUNAN JOURNAL. (Text in English and Filipino) 1965. irreg. University of the Philippines, Asian Center, Diliman, Quezon City 3004, Philippines. bibl.

954 II ISSN 0076-2547
MAHARASHTRA ARCHIVES BULLETIN. (Text in English and Marathi) 1962. irreg. price varies. Department of Archives, Governmental Printing and Stationery, Charni Road Gardens, Bombay 400004, Maharashtra, India. Ed. Shri V. G. Khobrekar.

954 II ISSN 0076-2571
MAHRATTA. (Text in English) 1881. a. Kesari-Mahratta Trust Publication, The Kesari and the Mahratta Office, 568 Narayan, Poona 2, India. Ed. J. S. Tilak.

915.95 MY ISSN 0301-7095
MALAYSIA IN BRIEF. (Text in English) irreg. Ministry of Foreign Affairs - Kementerian Luar Negeri, Jalan Wisma Putra, Kuala Lumpur, Malaysia. illus. circ. 60,000.

959.5 MY ISSN 0076-3373
MALAYSIA OFFICIAL YEAR BOOK. (Text in English and Malay) a. $11.50. Government Printer, Jalan Chan Sow Ling, Kuala Lumpur, Malaysia. (Prepared by: Federal Department of Information)

329.9 MY ISSN 0542-397X
MALAYSIAN CHINESE ASSOCIATION. ANNUAL REPORT. (Text in English) 1963. a. Malaysian Chinese Association, 67, Jln. Ampang, 5th Fl., Kuala Lumpur, Malaysia.

950 US ISSN 0146-6798
MATERIALS AND STUDIES FOR KASSITE HISTORY. 1976. irreg. price varies. University of Chicago, Oriental Institute, 1155 E. 58th St., Chicago, IL 60637.

959 US ISSN 0076-6119
MEDIEVAL INDIA; A MISCELLANY. (Text in English) 1970. irreg., 1975, vol. 3. price varies. (Aligarh Muslim University, Center for Advanced Study, II) Asia Publishing House, Inc., 141 E. 44th St., New York, NY 10017. Ed. K. A. Nizami. bk. rev.

959.7 BE
MESSAGE D'EXTREME-ORIENT. 1976. irreg., no. 2, 1977. Librairie-Editions Thanh-Long, 34 rue Dekens, 1040 Brussels, Belgium.

951 US ISSN 0076-8065
MICHIGAN PAPERS IN CHINESE STUDIES. 1968. irreg; no. 29, 1976. $4-$5. University of Michigan, Center for Chinese Studies, Lane Hall, Ann Arbor, MI 48109. (back issues avail.)
Continues: University of Michigan. Center for Chinese Studies. Occasional Papers.

959 US
MICHIGAN PAPERS ON SOUTH AND SOUTHEAST ASIA. 1970. irreg., no. 14, 1978. price varies per vol. University of Michigan, Center for South and Southeast Asian Studies, 130 Lane Hall, Ann Arbor, MI 48104. adv. bk. rev.

950 US ISSN 0076-812X
MICHIGAN STATE UNIVERSITY. ASIAN STUDIES CENTER. OCCASIONAL PAPERS: EAST ASIAN SERIES. 1969. irreg., no. 6, 1979. Michigan State University, Asian Studies Center, 101 International Center, East Lansing, MI 48824.

950 US ISSN 0076-8138
MICHIGAN STATE UNIVERSITY. ASIAN STUDIES CENTER. OCCASIONAL PAPERS: SOUTH ASIAN SERIES. 1965. irreg., no. 29, 1980. Michigan State University, Asian Studies Center, 101 International Center, E. Lansing, MI 48824.

956 US ISSN 0076-8537
MIDDLE EASTERN MONOGRAPHS. 1957. irreg., no. 11, 1973. (Royal Institute of International Affairs, UK) Oxford University Press, 200 Madison Ave., New York, NY 10016 (and Ely House, 37 Dover St., London W1X 4AH, England) Indexed: SSCI.

956 US ISSN 0077-0027
MODERN MIDDLE EAST SERIES. 1970. irreg., no. 4, 1979. Columbia University Press, 136 South Broadway, Irvington-On-Hudson, NY 10533.

959 320 AT
MONASH PAPERS ON SOUTHEAST ASIA. 1972. irreg. price varies. Monash University, Centre of Southeast Asian Studies, Clayton, Victoria 3168, Australia.

951 US ISSN 0077-0396
MONGOLIA SOCIETY. OCCASIONAL PAPERS. 1964. irreg. $2-15 to non-members. Mongolia Society, Inc., Drawer 606, Bloomington, IN 47402. Ed. John R. Krueger. circ. 300-500.

954 GW ISSN 0077-1880
MUENCHENER INDOLOGISCHE STUDIEN. 1955. irreg., vol. 6, 1969. price varies. Verlag Otto Harrassowitz, Taunusstr. 6, Postfach 2929, 6200 Wiesbaden, W. Germany (B.R.D.) Ed. H. Hoffmann.

025.17 MY ISSN 0076-3381
NATIONAL ARCHIVES OF MALAYSIA. ANNUAL REPORT/ARKIB NEGARA MALAYSIA. PENYATA TAHUNAN. (Text in Malay and English) 1963. a. M.$3. National Archives, Federal Government Building, Jalan Sultan, Petaling Jaya, Malaysia.
Supersedes: Malaya (Federation) Public Records Office and National Archives. Report.

NEUINDISCHE STUDIEN. see *LINGUISTICS*

950 II ISSN 0078-0855
NITYANAND UNIVERSAL SERIES. (Text in Hindi and Sanskrit) 1960. irreg., vol. 11, 1976. price varies. Vishveshvaranand Vedic Research Institute, P. O. Sadhu Ashram, Hoshiarpur 146021, Punjab, India. Ed. Vishva Bandhu.

959 US
NORTHERN ILLINOIS UNIVERSITY. CENTER FOR SOUTHEAST ASIAN STUDIES. OCCASIONAL PAPERS SERIES. 1974. irreg., no. 7, 1979. price varies. Northern Illinois University, Center for Southeast Asian Studies, DeKalb, IL 60115 (Dist. by Cellar Bookshop, 18090 Wyoming, Detroit MI 48221) Ed. Donn V. Hart. circ. 400-500.

959 US ISSN 0073-4934
NORTHERN ILLINOIS UNIVERSITY. CENTER FOR SOUTHEAST ASIAN STUDIES. SPECIAL REPORT SERIES. 1969. irreg., no. 18, 1979. price varies. Northern Illinois University, Center for Southeast Asian Studies, De Kalb, IL 60115 (Dist. by Cellar Bookshop, 18090 Wyoming, Detroit, MI 48221) Ed. Donn V. Hart. adv. circ. 400-500.

950 US ISSN 0146-678X
ORIENTAL INSTITUTE COMMUNICATIONS. 1922. irreg., vol. 23, 1978. price varies. University of Chicago, Oriental Institute, 1155 E. 58th St., Chicago, IL 60637 (Vols. published before 1977 avail. from: University of Chicago Press, 5801 Ellis Ave., Chicago IL 60637)

950 JA ISSN 0082-562X
ORIENTAL LIBRARY. RESEARCH DEPARTMENT. MEMOIRS/ZAIDAN HOJIN TOYO BUNKO. (Text in English) 1926. a. 4500 Yen($18) Oriental Library - Toyo Bunko, 2-28-21 Honkomagome, Bunkyo-ku, Tokyo 113, Japan. Ed. Kazuo Enoki. circ. 500.

950 935 IS ISSN 0078-6543
ORIENTAL NOTES AND STUDIES. 1951. irreg. price varies. Israel Oriental Society, Hebrew University, Jerusalem, Israel.

950 309 US
OXFORD IN ASIA; CURRENT AFFAIRS. irreg. price varies. Oxford University Press, 200 Madison Ave., New York, NY 10016 (And Ely House, 37 Dover St., London W1X 4AH, England)

950
OXFORD IN ASIA; HISTORICAL REPRINTS. irreg. price varies. Oxford University Press, 200 Madison Ave., New York, NY 10016 (And Ely House, 37 Dover St., London W1X 4AH, England) Eds. John Bastin, D. C. Twitchett.

950 PK ISSN 0078-8481
PAKISTAN. SURVEY OF PAKISTAN. GENERAL REPORT.* (Text in English) a. $3. Survey of Pakistan, Rawalpindi, Pakistan.

954.7 PK ISSN 0078-8171
PAKISTAN HISTORICAL SOCIETY. MEMOIR. (Text in English) 1953. a. Rs.100. Pakistan Historical Society, 30 New Karachi Co-operative Housing Society, Karachi 5, Pakistan. adv. circ. 1,000. (back issues avail.)

954.7 PK ISSN 0078-818X
PAKISTAN HISTORICAL SOCIETY. PROCEEDINGS OF THE PAKISTAN HISTORY CONFERENCE.* (Text in English) 1953. a. Rs.100. Pakistan Historical Society, 30 New Karachi Co-operative Housing Society, Karachi 5, Pakistan. adv. bk. rev. circ. 1,000. (back issues avail.)

PANJAB UNIVERSITY INDOLOGICAL SERIES. see ORIENTAL STUDIES

930 NE ISSN 0079-0893
PERSICA. (Text in English, French and German) 1963. a. fl.125. Genootschap Nederland-Iran - Netherlands-Iranian Society, c/o K. B. Kremer, Ed., Rozemarijntuin 47, Leiderdorp, Netherlands. adv. bk. rev. circ. 1,000. (back issues avail.)

PHILIPPINES CHINESE HISTORICAL ASSOCIATION. ANNALS. see POLITICAL SCIENCE — International Relations

PUBLICATIONS IN NEAR AND MIDDLE EAST STUDIES. SERIES B. see LINGUISTICS

956 490 NE ISSN 0079-7707
PUBLICATIONS IN NEAR AND MIDDLE EAST STUDIES. SERIES A. irreg. price varies. (Columbia University, Department of Middle East Languages and Cultures, US) Mouton Publishers, Noordeinde 41, 2514 GC The Hague, Netherlands (U.S. addr.: Mouton Publishers, c/o Walter de Gruyter, Inc., 200 Saw Mill River Road, Hawthorne, NY 10532) (Co-sponsor: Middle East Institute)

950 US ISSN 0079-7782
PUBLICATIONS ON ASIA. Title varies: Studies on Asia. 1952. irreg., no. 33, 1978. price varies. (University of Washington, School for International Studies) University of Washington Press, Seattle, WA 98105.

954 II ISSN 0079-9572
RAJASTHAN YEAR BOOK AND WHO'S WHO.* (Text in English) 1962. a. Rs.60. Samriddhi Publications, C-5 Bapunagar, Jaipur 4, India. Ed. Milap Chand Dandia. adv. circ. 2,000.

950 GW ISSN 0340-6687
RUHR-UNIVERSITAET BOCHUM. OSTASIEN INSTITUT. VEROEFFENTLICHUNGEN. irreg., vol. 26, 1980. price varies. Verlag Otto Harrassowitz, Taunusstr. 6, Postfach 2929, 6200 Wiesbaden, W. Germany (B.R.D.)

958 NE ISSN 0080-4916
RUSSIAN SERIES ON SOCIAL HISTORY. 1970. irreg. price varies. (International Institute for Social History) D. Reidel Publishing Co., P.O. Box 17, 3300 AA Dordrecht, Netherlands (And Lincoln Building, 160 Old Derby St., Hingham, MA 02043) Ed. Boris Sapir.

958 II ISSN 0080-6137
SANTAKUTI VEDIC RESEARCH SERIES. (Text in English and Sanskrit) 1935. irreg., no. 24, 1972. price varies. Vishveshvaranand Vedic Research Institute, P. O. Sadhu Ashram, Hoshiarpur 146021, Punjab, India. Ed. Vishva Bandhu.

950 US
SAROJINI NAIDU MEMORIAL LECTURE SERIES. irreg., latest vol. 1977. price varies. Asia Publishing House, Inc., 141 E. 44th St., New York, NY 10017.

950 II ISSN 0080-6471
SARVADANAND UNIVERSAL SERIES. (Text in English, Hindi and Sanskrit) 1950. irreg., vol. 67, 1975. price varies. Vishveshvaranand Vedic Research Institute, P. O. Sadhu Ashram, Hoshiarpur 146021, Punjab, India. Ed. Vishva Bandhu.

950 GE ISSN 0080-6994
SCHRIFTEN ZUR GESCHICHTE UND KULTUR DES ALTEN ORIENT. 1971. irreg., vol. 12, 1977. price varies. (Akademie der Wissenschaften der DDR, Zentralinstitut fuer Alte Geschichte und Archaeologie) Akademie-Verlag, Leipziger Str. 3-4, 108 Berlin, E. Germany (D.D.R.)

SCRIPTA MONGOLICA. see LITERATURE

954 890 II
SERIES IN SIKH HISTORY AND CULTURE. 1979. irreg. price varies. Bahri Publications Pvt.Ltd., 57 Santnagar, New Delhi 110065, India. Ed. Ujjal Singh Bahri.

959.5 SI ISSN 0080-9691
SINGAPORE FACTS AND PICTURES. 1963. a. S.$1.50. Ministry of Culture, 3Rd Floor, Govt. Offices, St. Andrew's Road, Singapore, 6, Singapore (Orders to: Singapore National Printers, Box 485, Singapore, Singapore) circ. 28,000.

SINOLOGICA COLONIENSIA; Ostasiatische Beitraege der Universitaet zu Koeln. see ORIENTAL STUDIES

SLAVISTIC PRINTING AND REPRINTINGS. see LITERATURE

954 AT ISSN 0085-6401
SOUTH ASIA; JOURNAL OF SOUTH ASIAN STUDIES. 1971. a. Aus.$11. (South Asian Studies Association of Australia & New Zealand, Center for South and South-East Asian Studies) University of Western Australia, Nedlands, W.A. 6009, Australia. (Co-sponsor: University of Heidelberg, South Asia Institute) Ed. Hugh Owen. adv. bk. rev. circ. 900.

SOUTH ASIAN STUDIES. see ORIENTAL STUDIES

991 SI ISSN 0081-2889
SOUTH SEAS SOCIETY. JOURNAL. (Text in Chinese and English) 1940. s-a. $5. ‡ South Seas Society, P. O. Box 709, Singapore, Singapore. Ed. Gwee Yee Hean. bk. rev. circ. 1,000.

991 SI ISSN 0081-2897
SOUTH SEAS SOCIETY. MONOGRAPH. (Text in Chinese and English) 1959. irreg., no. 22, 1980. price varies. ‡ South Seas Society, P. O. Box 709, Singapore, Singapore. Ed. Gwee Yee Hean. circ. 1,000.

959 SI
SOUTHEAST ASIAN AFFAIRS. (Text in English) 1974. a. price varies. Institute of Southeast Asian Studies, Heng Mui Keng Terrace, Pasir Panjang, Singapore 0511, Singapore. Ed. Christine Tan. circ. 2,000.

950 MY ISSN 0085-6509
SOUTHEAST ASIAN ARCHIVES. (Text in English) 1968. a. $6. International Council on Archives, Southeast Asian Regional Branch, c/o National Archives of Malaysia, Federal Government Building, Jalan Sultan, Petaling Jaya, Malaysia. Ed. Habibah Zon. adv. bk. rev.

959 SI
SOUTHEAST ASIAN PERSPECTIVE SERIES. (Text in English) 1973. irreg., no. 4, 1978. price varies. Institute of Southeast Asian Studies, Heng Mui Keng Terrace, Pasir Panjang, Singapore 0511, Singapore.

950 490 II ISSN 0081-3907
SRI VENKATESWARA UNIVERSITY. ORIENTAL JOURNAL. (Text in English, Hindi, Sanskrit, Tamil and Telugu) 1958. a.(issued in 2 pts.) Rs.15($4) Sri Venkateswara University, Oriental Research Institute, Tirupati 517502, District Chittoor, India. Ed. J. Chenna Reddy. cum.index: vols. 1-10(1958-67)

STUDI CLASSICI E ORIENTALI. see HISTORY

956 410 GW ISSN 0341-4191
STUDIEN ZUR INDOLOGIE UND IRANISTIK. (Text in English, French and German) 1975. a. DM.27.50. Dr. Inge Wezler Verlag fuer Orientalistische Fachpublikationen, Bernhard-Ihnen-Str. 18, D-2057 Reinbek, W. Germany (B.R.D.) Ed.Bd. circ. 200-250.

952 GW ISSN 0585-6094
STUDIEN ZUR JAPANOLOGIE. 1959. irreg., vol. 14, 1978. price varies. Verlag Otto Harrassowitz, Taunusstr. 6, Postfach 2929, 6200 Wiesbaden, W. Germany (B.R.D.) Ed. Horst Hammitzsch.

931 US ISSN 0081-7554
STUDIES IN ANCIENT ORIENTAL CIVILIZATION. 1931. irreg., no. 40, 1977. price varies. University of Chicago, Oriental Institute, 1155 E. 58th St., Chicago, IL 60637 (Vols. published before 1977 avail. from: University of Chicago Press, 5801 Ellis Ave., Chicago, IL 60637)

952 US ISSN 0081-8127
STUDIES IN JAPANESE CULTURE. (Subseries of Center's Occasional Papers) (Text in English and Japanese) 1965. irreg. price varies. (University of Michigan, Center for Japanese Studies) University of Michigan Press, Box 1104, 839 Greene St., Ann Arbor, MI 48104.

930 390 US ISSN 0081-8321
STUDIES IN ORIENTAL CULTURE. 1967. irreg., no. 14, latest. Columbia University Press, 136 South Broadway, Irvington-On-Hudson, NY 10533.

954 II
STUDIES IN RAJPUT HISTORY AND CULTURE SERIES. 1976. irreg. Rs.50. Bharatiya Publishing House, 42-43 V. B. Jawabarnagar, Delhi 110007, India. bibl.

SUI YUAN WEN HSIEN. see ORIENTAL STUDIES

900 II
SWARBICA JOURNAL. (Text in English) 1978. a. Rs.15. International Council of Archives, South and West Asian Regional Branch, c/o National Archives of India, Janpath, New Delhi 110001, India.

HISTORY — HISTORY OF ASIA

TAMKANG COLLEGE. INSTITUTE OF AREA STUDIES. AREA STUDIES. see *ORIENTAL STUDIES*

959 TH ISSN 0563-3737
THAILAND YEAR BOOK. (Text in English) 1964. a. $15. Temple Publicity Services, 4Th Floor, British Airways Building, 133/19 Gaysorn Road, P.O. Box 316, Bangkok, Thailand. Ed. Ivan Mudannayake. circ. 5,000.

950 700 II ISSN 0082-4437
TIMES OF INDIA ANNUAL. (Text in English) Rs.12($1.50) Bennett, Coleman & Co., Times of India, 7 Bahadur Shah Zaffar Marg, New Delhi 110002, India (U.S. subscr. address: India Publications, Ltd., 307 Fifth Ave., New York, NY 10016) Ed. Sham Lal.
Art journal covering India's cultural history

954 II ISSN 0082-4445
TIMES OF INDIA DIRECTORY AND YEARBOOK INCLUDING WHO'S WHO. (Text in English) a. $19. Bennett, Coleman & Co., Times of India, 7 Bahadur Shah Zaffar Marg, New Delhi 110002, India (U.S. subscr.: India Publications, Ltd., 307 Fifth Ave., New York, NY 10016) Ed Mr. Shamlal. index.

950 CN ISSN 0082-5123
TORONTO SEMITIC TEXTS AND STUDIES. 1971. irreg. price varies. University of Toronto Press, Front Campus, Toronto, Ont. M5S 1A6, Canada. (also avail. in microfiche)

959 SI ISSN 0082-6316
TRENDS IN SOUTHEAST ASIA. (Text in English) 1971. irreg., no. 9, 1978. price varies. Institute of Southeast Asian Studies, Heng Mui Keng Terrace, Pasir Panjang, Singapore 0511, Singapore. Indexed: Bibl.Asian Stud.

950 956 US
U.S. DEPARTMENT OF STATE. NEAR EAST AND SOUTH ASIAN SERIES. 1948. irreg. price varies. U.S. Department of State, Bureau of Public Affairs, Washington, DC 20250 (Orders to Supt. of Documents, Washington, DC 20402)
Supersedes: U.S. Department of State. Near and Middle Eastern Series (ISSN 0083-0151)

950 GW ISSN 0440-601X
UNIVERSITAET HEIDELBERG. SUEDASIEN-INSTITUT. SCHRIFTENREIHE. (Text in English and German) irreg., vol. 29, 1981. price varies. Franz Steiner Verlag GmbH, Friedrichstr. 24, Postfach 5529, 6200 Wiesbaden, W. Germany (B.R.D.)

UNIVERSITAET ZU KOELN. KUNSTHISTORISCHES INSTITUT. ABTEILUNG ASIEN. PUBLIKATIONEN. see *ART*

950 BE ISSN 0076-1265
UNIVERSITE CATHOLIQUE DE LOUVAIN. INSTITUT ORIENTALISTE. PUBLICATIONS. Short title: P.I.O.L. Variant title: Institute Orientaliste de Louvain. Publications. 1970. irreg., no. 20, 1979. price varies. Universite Catholique de Louvain, Institut Orientaliste, College Erasme, Place Blaise Pascal 1, B-1348 Louvain-la-Neuve, Belgium. adv.
Supersedes (1932-1968): Bibliotheque du Museon.

950 CN ISSN 0068-1687
UNIVERSITY OF BRITISH COLUMBIA LIBRARY. ASIAN STUDIES DIVISION. LIST OF CATALOGUED BOOKS. SUPPLEMENT. (Text in Chinese, Japanese and Korean) 1966. irreg., 1972, no. 4. free. University of British Columbia Library, Asian Studies Division, Vancouver, B.C. V6T 1W5, Canada. Ed. Tung-King Ng. circ. 150.

954 II ISSN 0068-5380
UNIVERSITY OF CALCUTTA. CENTRE OF ADVANCED STUDY IN ANCIENT INDIAN HISTORY AND CULTURE. LECTURES. 1965. irreg., 1969, no. 3. price varies. University of Calcutta, Centre of Advanced Study in Ancient Indian History and Culture, 51-2 Hazra Rd., Calcutta 19, West Bengal, India.

954 II ISSN 0068-5399
UNIVERSITY OF CALCUTTA. CENTRE OF ADVANCED STUDY IN ANCIENT INDIAN HISTORY AND CULTURE. PROCEEDINGS OF SEMINARS. 1966, vol. 2. irreg., 1973, vol. 11. price varies. University of Calcutta, Centre of Advanced Study in Ancient Indian History and Culture, 51-2 Hazra Rd., Calcutta 19, West Bengal, India.

950 US ISSN 0068-600X
UNIVERSITY OF CALIFORNIA. CENTER FOR SOUTH AND SOUTHEAST ASIA STUDIES. OCCASIONAL PAPERS. 1969. irreg., no. 11, 1973. University of California, Berkeley, Center for South and Southeast Asia Studies, Berkeley, CA 94720 (Dist. by: the Cellar Bookshop, 18090 Wyoming, Detroit, MI 48221)

950 US ISSN 0068-6018
UNIVERSITY OF CALIFORNIA. CENTER FOR SOUTH AND SOUTHEAST ASIA STUDIES. RESEARCH MONOGRAPH SERIES. 1970. irreg., no. 18, 1979. University of California, Berkeley, Center for South and Southeast Asia Studies, 2420 Bowditch St., Berkeley, CA 94720 (Dist. by: the Cellar Bookshop, 18090 Wyoming, Detroit, MI 48221)

956 US ISSN 0068-6514
UNIVERSITY OF CALIFORNIA PUBLICATIONS. NEAR EASTERN STUDIES. irreg. price varies. University of California Press, 2223 Fulton St., Berkeley, CA 94720.

950 US ISSN 0069-3367
UNIVERSITY OF CHICAGO ORIENTAL INSTITUTE. PUBLICATIONS. 1924. irreg., vol. 100, 1979. price varies. University of Chicago, Oriental Institute, 1155 E. 58th St., Chicago, IL 60637 (Vols. published before 1977 avail. from: University of Chicago Press, 5801 Ellis Ave., Chicago, IL 60637) (also avail. in microfiche)

950 US ISSN 0070-8070
UNIVERSITY OF KANSAS. CENTER FOR EAST ASIAN STUDIES. INTERNATIONAL STUDIES: EAST ASIAN SERIES. REFERENCE SERIES. 1967. irreg., no. 2, 1975. price varies. University of Kansas, Center for East Asian Studies, 106 Strong Hall, Lawrence, KS 66045 (Dist. by: Paragon Book Gallery, Ltd., 14 E. 38th St., New York, NY 10016)

950 US ISSN 0070-8062
UNIVERSITY OF KANSAS. CENTER FOR EAST ASIAN STUDIES. INTERNATIONAL STUDIES: EAST ASIAN SERIES. RESEARCH SERIES. 1967. irreg., no. 9, 1978. price varies. University of Kansas, Center for East Asian Studies, Lawrence, KS 66044 (Dist. by: Paragon Book Gallery, Ltd., 14 E. 38th St., New York, NY 10016)

950 II ISSN 0076-2229
UNIVERSITY OF MADRAS. HISTORICAL SERIES.* 1919. irreg. University of Madras, Chepauk, Triplicane, Madras 600005, Tamil Nadu, India.

952 US ISSN 0076-8340
UNIVERSITY OF MICHIGAN. CENTER FOR JAPANESE STUDIES. BIBLIOGRAPHICAL SERIES. (Text in English and Japanese) 1950. irreg. price varies. University of Michigan Press, Box 1104, 839 Greene St., Ann Arbor, MI 48106. circ. 47.

952 US ISSN 0076-8359
UNIVERSITY OF MICHIGAN. CENTER FOR JAPANESE STUDIES. OCCASIONAL PAPERS. 1951. irreg. price varies. University of Michigan Press, Box 1104, 839 Greene St., Ann Arbor, MI 48106. Ed. Richard K. Beardsley. circ. 111.

959 MY
UNIVERSITY OF SCIENCE OF MALAYSIA HISTORY FORUM/UNIVERSITI SAINS MALAYSIA FORAM SEJARAH. (Text in English or Malay) 1971. irreg. University of Science of Malaysia, School of Humanities - Universiti Sains Malaysia, Pusat Pengajian Ilmu Kemanusiaan, Minden, Malaysia.

951 SI ISSN 0080-9667
UNIVERSITY OF SINGAPORE. CHINESE SOCIETY. JOURNAL.* (Text in Chinese and English) 1961. a. M.$2. University of Singapore, Chinese Society, c/o Dept. of Chinese Studies, Cluny Rd., Singapore 10, Singapore.

950 SI ISSN 0085-610X
UNIVERSITY OF SINGAPORE. HISTORY SOCIETY. JOURNAL. 1963. a. S.$1.50. University of Singapore History Society, History Dept., University, Bukit Timah Road, Singapore, 10, Singapore. Ed. Lulie Tan. adv. cum index. circ. controlled. Indexed: Hist.Abstr.

950 PH ISSN 0079-9238
UNIVERSITY OF THE PHILIPPINES. ASIAN CENTER. MONOGRAPH SERIES. (Text in English) 1965. irreg. price varies. ‡ University of the Philippines, Asian Center, Diliman, Quezon City 3004, Philippines. circ. 1,000.

950 PK ISSN 0079-8029
UNIVERSITY OF THE PUNJAB. ARABIC AND PERSIAN SOCIETY. JOURNAL.* (Text in English, Arabic or Persian) a. University of the Punjab, Arabic and Persian Society, Lahore, Pakistan.

959.7 VN ISSN 0085-7823
VIETNAMESE STUDIES.* vol. 8, 1972. irreg. Vietnamese Studies, Xunhasaba 32, Hai Ba Trung, Socialist Republic of Vietnam, Vietnam. Ed. Nguyen Khac Vien. illus.

VISHVA VICHARAMALA. see *ORIENTAL STUDIES*

954 II ISSN 0083-6613
VISHVESHVARANAND INDOLOGICAL PAPER SERIES. (Text in English, Hindi and Sanskrit) 1950. irreg., no. 325, 1977. price varies. Vishveshvaranand Vedic Research Institute, P. O. Sadhu Ashram, Hoshiarpur 146021, Punjab, India. Ed. Vishva Bandhu.

VISHVESHVARANAND INDOLOGICAL SERIES. see *LINGUISTICS*

VISHVESHVARANAND VEDIC RESEARCH INSTITUTE. RESEARCH AND GENERAL PUBLICATIONS. see *ORIENTAL STUDIES*

954 NP
VOICE OF HISTORY. (Text in English or Nepali) 1975. a. Rs.10.50. (Tribhuvan University History Association) Tribhuvan University, Kirtipur, Nepal. bibl.

935 NE
VOORAZIATISCH-EGYPTISCH GENOOTSCHAP "EX ORIENTE LUX". MEDEDELINGEN EN VERHANDELINGEN. (Text in English, French, German, Dutch) 1943, no. 5. irreg., 1968, no. 17. price varies. (Netherlands Institute for the Near East) Nederlands Instituut voor Het Nabije Oosten, Noordeindsplein 42, Leiden, Netherlands. Eds. A.A. Kampman, K.R. Veenhof.
Formerly: Mededelingen "Ex Oriente Lux" (ISSN 0081-1211)

951 920 HK ISSN 0083-9477
WHO'S WHO IN COMMUNIST CHINA. 1966. irreg., 1969, 2nd ed. vols. 1 & 2. $18. Union Cultural Organization Ltd., No. 9 College Road, Kowloon, Hong Kong. Ed. William Hsu. index. circ. 2,000.

WIENER ZEITSCHRIFT FUER DIE KUNDE SUEDASIENS UND ARCHIV FUER INDISCHE PHILOSPHIE. see *PHILOSOPHY*

951 US ISSN 0084-053X
WISCONSIN CHINA SERIES. (Text in English and Chinese) 1966. irreg., latest, no. 3. $3. University of Wisconsin-Madison, Department of East Asian Languages and Literature, 1212 Van Hise Hall, Madison, WI 53706. Ed. Tse-tsung Chow.

950 980 US ISSN 0084-229X
WORLD TODAY SERIES: FAR EAST AND SOUTHWEST PACIFIC. 1968. a. $2.95. Stryker-Post Publications Inc., 888 Seventeenth St., N.W., Washington, DC 20006. Ed. Harold C. Hinton. circ. 10-15,000.

950 US ISSN 0084-2311
WORLD TODAY SERIES: MIDDLE EAST AND
SOUTH ASIA. a. $2.95. Stryker-Post Publications
Inc., 888 Seventeenth St., N.W., Washington, DC
20006. Ed. Ray L. Cleveland. circ. 10-15,000.

959 US ISSN 0084-3466
YALE SOUTHEAST ASIA STUDIES. 1965. irreg.,
no. 8, 1978. price varies. Yale University Press, 92A
Yale Sta., New Haven, CT 06520.

950 GW ISSN 0514-857X
ZENTRALASIATISCHE STUDIEN. 1967. a. price
varies. (Seminar fuer Sprach- und
Kulturwissenschaft Zentralasiens) Verlag Otto
Harrassowitz, Taunusstr. 6, Postfach 2929, 6200
Wiesbaden, W. Germany (B.R.D.)

HISTORY — History Of Australasia And Other Areas

994 AT ISSN 0001-2068
A N U HISTORICAL JOURNAL. 1964. a. Aus.$3.
Australian National University, Historical Society,
Box 1112, Canberra, A.C.T. 2601, Australia. Ed. P.
D. Hurst. adv. bk. rev. index. circ. 500. (back issues
avail.) Indexed: Aus.P.A.I.S.

969.005 FR
ANNUAIRE DES PAYS DE L'OCEAN INDIEN.
(Text in French; summaries in English) 1974. a.
(Universite d'Aix-Marseille III (Universite de Droit
d'Economie et des Sciences), Centre d'Etudes et de
Recherches sur les Societes de l'Ocean Indien)
Presses Universitaires d'Aix Marseille, 3 Av. Robert
Schuman, 13621 Aix en Provence, France. bk. rev.
illus.

994 AT ISSN 0084-6732
ARMIDALE AND DISTRICT HISTORICAL
SOCIETY. JOURNAL AND PROCEEDINGS.
1961. a. membership. Armidale and District
Historical Society, c/o B. Mitchel, Department of
History, Univ. of New England, Armidale, N.S.W.
2351, Australia. Ed.Bd. bk. rev. circ. 400. Indexed:
Hist.Abstr. Amer.Hist. & Life.

990 AT
AUSTRALASIAN AND PACIFIC SOCIETY FOR
EIGHTEENTH-CENTURY STUDIES.
NEWSLETTER. 1971. irreg. Aus.$7.50
(membership); students Aus. $7.50; institutions Aus.
$10. Australasian and Pacific Society for
Eighteenth-Century Studies, Humanities Research
Centre, Australian National University, P.O. Box 4,
Canberra City, A.C.T. 2601, Australia. Ed. J. C.
Eade. bk. rev. circ. 100.

994 AT ISSN 0082-2116
AUSTRALIA. BUREAU OF STATISTICS.
TASMANIAN OFFICE. TASMANIAN YEAR
BOOK. 1967. a. Aus.$8. ‡ Australian Bureau of
Statistics, Tasmanian Office, Box 66A, G.P.O.,
Hobart, Tasmania 7001, Australia. Ed. D. Maclaine.
index. circ. 2,700.

AUSTRALIA. BUREAU OF STATISTICS.
VICTORIAN OFFICE. CAUSES OF DEATH. see
POPULATION STUDIES

AUSTRALIA. BUREAU OF STATISTICS.
VICTORIAN OFFICE. PRIMARY AND
SECONDARY EDUCATION. see *EDUCATION*

AUSTRALIA. BUREAU OF STATISTICS.
VICTORIAN OFFICE. ROAD TRAFFIC
ACCIDENTS INVOLVING CASUALTIES. see
TRANSPORTATION — Roads And Traffic

309.1 AT ISSN 0572-0494
AUSTRALIA. DEPARTMENT OF TERRITORIES.
TERRITORY OF NORFOLK ISLAND;
REPORT.* (Subseries of: Australia. Parliament.
Parliamentary Papers) irreg. price varies. Australian
Government Publishing Service, P.O. Box 84,
Canberra, 2600 A.C.T., Australia. illus. stat.

994 AT ISSN 0067-1495
AUSTRALIA HANDBOOK. 1970. a. price varies.
Australian Government Publishing Service, Sales
and Distribution Branch, Box 84, Canberra, A.C.T.
2600, Australia.

994 AT ISSN 0084-7259
AUSTRALIAN CATHOLIC HISTORICAL
SOCIETY. JOURNAL. 1954. a. Aus.$3. ‡
Australian Catholic Historical Society, 154
Elizabeth St., Sydney, N.S.W. 2000, Australia. Ed.
A. Cahill. adv. bk. rev. circ. 300.

994 AT ISSN 0067-2246
AUSTRALIANA FACSIMILE EDITIONS. 1962.
irreg. price varies. Libraries Board of South
Australia, Box 419 G.P.O., Adelaide, S. A. 5001,
Australia.

994 NE ISSN 0067-7876
BIBLIOTHECA AUSTRALIANA. 1967. irreg., vol.
76, 1976. price varies. N. Israel, Keizersgracht 526,
1017 EK Amsterdam, Netherlands. circ. 500.

990 AT ISSN 0310-1584
CABBAGES AND KINGS. 1973. a. Aus.$5. Murray
Park College of Advanced Education, Department
of History and Australian Studies, 15 Lorne Ave.,
Magill, SA 5072, Australia.

950 999 UK ISSN 0071-3791
FAR EAST AND AUSTRALASIA. 1969. a. $84.
Europa Publications Ltd., 18 Bedford Sq., London
WC1B 3JN, England.

990 320 AT
FLINDERS JOURNAL OF HISTORY AND
POLITICS. 1969. a. Aus.$1.20 80 cents for
students. Flinders University of South Australia,
History and Politics Society, School of Social
Sciences, Bedford Park, S. A. 5042, Australia. Ed.
Michael Clark.

990 US
HAWAIIAN HISTORICAL SOCIETY. ANNUAL
REPORT. 1893. a. price varies: $1.50-$5. Hawaiian
Historical Society, 560 Kawaiahao St., Honolulu, HI
96813. (back issues avail.)

990 US ISSN 0440-5145
HAWAIIAN JOURNAL OF HISTORY; devoted to
the history of Hawaii, Polynesia and the Pacific
area. 1967. a. $5. Hawaiian Historical Society, 560
Kawaiahao St., Honolulu, HI 96813. illus. circ.
800(controlled)

990 AT ISSN 0311-8924
HISTORICAL JOURNAL. 1975. irreg. Wollongong
University, Historical Society, Box 1144,
Wollongong, N.S.W. 2500, Australia. Ed. C. J.
Krawczyk. circ. 1,000.

HOCKEN LECTURE. see *ANTHROPOLOGY*

999 CL ISSN 0073-9863
INSTITUTO ANTARTICO CHILENO. BOLETIN.
1965. irreg; no. 10. 1977. available on exchange.
Instituto Antartico Chileno, Luis Thayer Ojeda 814,
Casilla 16521, Correo 9, Santiago, Chile.

999 CL ISSN 0073-9871
INSTITUTO ANTARTICO CHILENO.
CONTRIBUTION. SERIE CIENTIFICA. (Text in
Spanish; summaries in English) 1964; n.s. 1969.
irreg; vol. 5, no. 2, 1977. available on exchange.
Instituto Antartico Chileno, Luis Thayer Ojeda 814,
Casilla 16521, Correo 9, Santiago, Chile.
Supercedes: Instituto Antartico Chileno.
Publicacion.

990 AT
LA TROBE HISTORICAL STUDIES. 1971. irreg.
Aus.$1. La Trobe University, Historical Association,
La Trobe University, Bundoora, Vic. 3083,
Australia. Ed. Ron Adams. Indexed: Aus.P.A.I.S.

994 AT ISSN 0076-6232
MELBOURNE HISTORICAL JOURNAL. 1961. a.
$2. University of Melbourne, Historical Society,
Parkville, Victoria 3052, Australia. bk. rev. circ.
500-600.

MUSEUM FUER VOELKERKUNDE, BERLIN.
VEROEFFENTLICHUNGEN. NEUE FOLGE.
ABTEILUNG: SUEDSEE. see *ANTHROPOLOGY*

994 AT
NATIONAL TRUST OF AUSTRALIA (WESTERN
AUSTRALIA) ANNUAL REPORT. a. National
Trust of Australia (Western Australia), Perth W.A.,
Australia.

919.31 NZ ISSN 0078-0170
NEW ZEALAND OFFICIAL YEAR-BOOK. 1892. a.
NZ.$7.50. Department of Statistics, Private Bag,
Wellington, New Zealand (Subscr. to: Government
Printing Office, Publications, Private Bag,
Wellington, New Zealand) circ. 16,000.

994.42 AT ISSN 0078-0243
NEWCASTLE HISTORY MONOGRAPHS. 1966.
irreg., 1973, no. 7. price varies. Newcastle Region
Public Library, P.O. Box 489g, Newcastle N. S. W.
2300, Australia. Ed.Bd. circ. 500. (back issues avail.)

990 AT ISSN 0078-7523
PACIFIC ISLANDS YEAR BOOK. 1930. irreg., 14th
ed., 1981. Aus.$29.95. Pacific Publications
(Australia) Pty. Ltd., G.P.O. Box 3408, Sydney,
N.S.W. 2001, Australia. Ed. Stuart Inder. adv.
Formerly: Pacific Islands Year Book and Who's
Who.

994 AT ISSN 0085-4670
PAPERS ON THE HISTORY OF BOURKE. 1966.
irreg. Aus.$4 per no. Bourke & District Historical
Society, Bourke, N.S.W. 2840, Australia. Ed. W.J.
Cameron. circ. 200.

994 AT ISSN 0085-5375
QUIRINDI AND DISTRICT HISTORICAL NOTES.
1965. a. price varies. Quirindi & District Historical
Society, P.O. Box 57, Quirindi, N.S.W. 2343,
Australia. Ed. Dorothy Durrant. index. circ. 500.

990 355 AT ISSN 0310-4141
R. M. C. HISTORICAL JOURNAL. 1972. a. Royal
Military College of Australia, Department of
History, Duntroon, A.C.T. 2600, Australia. Ed. R.
C. Thompson.

994 AT ISSN 0080-4738
ROYAL WESTERN AUSTRALIAN HISTORICAL
SOCIETY. JOURNAL AND PROCEEDINGS.
1926. a. Aus.$6. ‡ Royal Western Australian
Historical Society, 49 Broadway, Nedlands, 6009
WA, Australia. Ed. Ronald P. Wright. circ. 1,500.
Indexed: Aus. P.A.I.S.

993.5 BP
SOLOMON ISLANDS RESEARCH REGISTER.
1972. a. University of the South Pacific, Solomon
Islands Centre, Box 460, Honiara, British Solomon
Islands. circ. 2,000.

994 052 AT ISSN 0083-7016
TASMANIAN ALMANAC. 1863. a. Aus.$12.
Mercury-Walch Pty. Ltd., 5-7 Bowen Road,
Moonah, Tasmania 7009, Australia. Ed. T.A.
Collins. circ. 1,500.
Formerly: Walch's Tasmanian Almanac.

990 AT
TIDE OF TIME. 1968. a. Aus.$2. Inverell and
District Historical Society, P.O. Box 396, Inverell,
NSW 2360, Australia. Ed. P. N. Whish.

990 GW ISSN 0342-6610
UEBERSEE-MUSEUM BREMEN.
VEROEFFENTLICHUNGEN. REIHE G:
BREMER SUEDPAZIFIK-ARCHIV. 1977. irreg.,
vol. 2, 1978. price varies. Uebersee-Museum,
Bremen, Bahnhofsplatz 13, 2800 Bremen, W.
Germany(B.R.D.)

994 NZ ISSN 0067-0480
UNIVERSITY OF AUCKLAND HISTORICAL
SOCIETY. ANNUAL. 1967. a. NZ.$0.85.
University of Auckland, Department of History,
Private Bag, Auckland, New Zealand.
Student contributions

994 AT ISSN 0085-7858
WAGGA WAGGA AND DISTRICT HISTORICAL
SOCIETY. JOURNAL. 1968. a. $1 per no. Wagga
Wagga & District Historical Society, Box 90, Wagga
Wagga, N.S.W. 2650, Australia.

994 PP ISSN 0085-7866
WAIGANI SEMINAR. PAPERS. 1969. irreg. price
varies. University of Papua New Guinea, Box 4820,
University, Papua New Guinea. charts. illus. index.
circ. 1,000.

994 330 AT ISSN 0083-8756
WESTERN AUSTRALIAN POCKET YEARBOOK.
1919. a. Aus.$0.75. Australian Bureau of Statistics,
Western Australian Office, 1-3 St. George's Terrace,
Perth, W.A. 6000, Australia. Ed. E. Binns. circ.
3,000.

994 330 AT ISSN 0083-8772
WESTERN AUSTRALIAN YEARBOOK. NEW
SERIES. Title varies: Official Year Book of Western
Australia. 1957. a. Aus.$7.50. Australian Bureau of
Statistics, Western Australian Office, 1-3 St.
George's Terrace, Perth, W.A. 6000, Australia. Ed.
E. Binns. circ. 2,650.

993 NZ
WHAKATANE & DISTRICT HISTORICAL
SOCIETY. MONOGRAPHS. no 4, 977. irreg.
Whakatane & District Historical Society, Box 203,
Whakatane, New Zealand.

HISTORY — History Of Europe

see also Classical Studies

943 GW ISSN 0065-0137
AACHENER GESCHICHTSVEREIN.
ZEITSCHRIFT. 1879. a. membership. Aachener
Geschichtsverein, Fischmarkt 3, 5100 Aachen, W.
Germany (B.R.D.) Ed. Bernhard Poll. bk. rev.
index. circ. 1,500.

948.1 NO ISSN 0587-4076
AARBOK FOR TELEMARK. a. Kr.32. Telemark
Maalkontor, Dag Bondeheim, Skien, Norway.

942 UK
ABERTAY HISTORICAL SOCIETY. SERIES OF
MONOGRAPHS. 1954. a. price varies. ‡ Abertay
Historical Society, c/o Dept. of History, The
University, Dundee DD1 4HN, Scotland. Ed. Dr.
Anette Smith. bk. rev. circ. 3,000-5,000.

330 940 GE ISSN 0065-0358
ABHANDLUNGEN ZUR HANDELS- UND
SOZIALGESCHICHTE. 1958. irreg., vol. 19, 1980.
price varies. (Historiker-Gesellschaft der DDR,
Hansische Arbeitsgemeinschaft) Hermann Boehlaus
Nachfolger, Meyerstr. 50a, 53 Weimar, E. Germany
(D.D.R.)

949.8 913 RM ISSN 0065-048X
ACADEMIA DE STIINTE SOCIALE SI POLITICE.
INSTITUTUL DE ISTORIE SI ARHEOLOGIE
CLUJ-NAPOCA. ANUARUL. 1958. a. $10.
Editura Academiei Republicii Socialiste Romania,
Calea Victoriei 125, Bucharest, Romania (Subscr. to:
ILEXIM, Str. 13 Decembrie Nr. 3, P.O. Box 136-
137, Bucharest, Romania) Ed. Stefan Pascu. circ.
600.

940 PO
ACADEMIA PORTUGUESA DA HISTORIA.
ANAIS. 1940. a; vol. 24, 1977. price varies.
Academia Portuguesa da Historia, Palacio da Rosa,
Largo da Rosa 5, Lisbon 1100, Portugal. circ. 550.

940 IT
ACADEMIE DE FRANCE A ROME.
CORRESPONDANCE DES DIRECTEURS.
NOUVELLE SERIE. (Text in French) 1979. a.
price varies. Edizioni dell' Elefante, Piazza de
Caprettari 70, 00186 Rome, Italy. Ed. Georges
Brunel.

937.5 IT ISSN 0065-0730
ACCADEMIA ETRUSCA DI CORTONA.
ANNUARIO. 1935. a. price varies. Casa Editrice
Leo S. Olschki, Viuzzo del Pozzetto (Viale Europa),
50126 Florence, Italy (And Casella Postale 66,
50100 Florence, Italy) Ed. Celestino Bruschetti.
circ. 500.

940 GW ISSN 0567-7289
ACTA BALTICA. 1961. a. price varies. Institutum
Balticum, Haus der Begegnung, Bischof-Kaller-Str.
3, 6240 Koenigstein, W. Germany (B.R.D.) bk. rev.
index.

947 301 PL ISSN 0065-1044
ACTA BALTICO-SLAVICA. irreg., vol. 12, 1979. 90
Zl. (Polska Akademia Nauk, Instytut
Slowianoznawstwa) Ossolineum, Publishing House
of the Polish Academy of Sciences, Rynek 9,
Wroclaw, Poland (Dist. by: Ars Polona-Ruch,
Krakowskie Przedmiescie 7, Warsaw, Poland) Ed.
Jan Safarewicz.

940 NE ISSN 0065-129X
ACTA HISTORIAE NEERLANDICAE. (Text in
English) 1966. a. price varies. (Dutch Historical
Association) Martinus Nijhoff, Box 566, 2501 CN
The Hague, Netherlands.

949.8 IT ISSN 0065-1303
ACTA HISTORICA. (Contributions in Italian,
English, French and German) 1959. irreg. price
varies. Societa Accademica Romena, Foro Traiano
1a, 00187 Rome, Italy.

940 PL
ACTA MEDIAEVALIA. (Text in Latin or Polish;
summaries in French) 1973. irreg. price varies.
Katolicki Uniwersytet Lubelski, Towarzystwo
Naukowe, Chopina 29, 20-023 Lublin, Poland.

940 GW ISSN 0065-146X
ACTA PACIS WESTPHALICAE. 1962. irreg. price
varies. (Rheinisch-Westfaelische Akademie der
Wissenschaften) Aschendorffsche
Verlagsbuchhandlung, Soester Str. 13, 4400
Muenster, W. Germany (B.R.D.) (Co-sponsor:
Vereinigung zur Erforschung der Neueren
Geschichte e.V.) Ed. Konrad Repgen.

943.8 PL ISSN 0137-5830
ACTA UNIVERSITATIS NICOLAI COPERNICI.
HISTORIA. 1965. irreg. price varies. Uniwersytet
Mikolaja Kopernika, Fosa Staromiejska 3, Torun,
Poland (Dist. by Osrodek Rozpowszechniania
Wydanictw Naukowych PAN, Palac Kultury i
Nauki, 00-901 Warsaw, Poland)
Formerly: Uniwersytet Mikolaja Kopernika,
Torun. Nauki Humanistyczno-Spoleczne. Historia
(ISSN 0083-4491)

948.5 SW
ACTA VISBYENSIA; Visby-symposiet foer historiska
vetenskaper. (Text in German) 1963. irreg.
Kr.65.50($6) Foereningen Gotlands Fornvaenner,
Box 83, S-62101 Visby, Sweden. circ. 1,500.

948.9 DK ISSN 0065-3667
AELDRE DANSKE TINGBOEGER. 1954. irreg.
price varies. Landbohistorisk Selskab, H. C.
Andersens Boulevard 38, DK-1553 Copenhagen K,
Denmark.

380 332 FR ISSN 0065-3799
AFFAIRES ET GENS D'AFFAIRES. 1952. irreg.
price varies. Editions de l' Ecole des Hautes Etudes
en Sciences Sociales, 131 Bd. Saint Michel, F-75005
Paris, France, France.

940 GE ISSN 0065-5236
AKADEMIE DER WISSENSCHAFTEN DER DDR.
ZENTRALINSTITUT FUER GESCHICHTE.
SCHRIFTEN. (Vol. 1-37, 1957-1972: under
Subtitle: Reihe 1: Allgemeine und Deutsche
Geschichte) 1957. irreg., vol. 52, 1977. price varies.
Akademie-Verlag, Leipziger Str. 3-4, 108 Berlin, E.
Germany (D.D.R.)

949 YU
AKADEMIJA NAUKA I UMJETNOSTI BOSNE I
HERCEGOVINE. CENTAR ZA
BALKANOLOSKA ISPITIVANJA. GODISNJAK.
vol. 12, 1975. a. 168 din. Akademija Nauka i
Umjetnosti Bosne i Hercegovine, Centar za
Balkanoloska Ispitivanja, Sarajevo, Yugoslavia. Ed.
Alojz Benac.

949 891 491 YU
AKADEMIJA NAUKA I UMJETNOSTI BOSNE I
HERCEGOVINE. ODJELJENJE ISTORIJSKO
FILOLOSKIH NAUK. DJELA. irreg.
Akademija Nauka i Umjetnosti Bosne i
Hercegovine, Odjeljenje Istorijsko Filoloskih Nauk,
Obala Vojvode Stepe 42, Sarajevo, Yugoslavia.

AKADEMISKA DZIVE/ACADEMIC LIFE. see
ETHNIC INTERESTS

949 NE
ALKMAARSE HISTORISCHE REEKS. 1977. a.
price varies. Walburg Pers, Zaadmarkt 842,
Zutphen, Netherlands. Ed. Bd.

940 GW
ALLENSBACHER ALMANACH. 1950. free.
Arbeitsgemeinschaft Allensbach e.V., Kappeler-Berg-
Str. 54, 7753 Allensbach, W. Germany (B.R.D.) Ed.
Julius Boltze. bk. rev. illus.

340 GW
ALLGAEUER GESCHICHTSFREUND. 1888. a.
DM.8. (Heimatbund Allgaeu) Verlag fuer
Heimatpflege, Koenigstr. 25, 8960 Kempten, W.
Germany (B.R.D.) Ed. Wolfgang Haberl. illus.
index. circ. 1,200.

940 GE ISSN 0065-6585
ALT-THUERINGEN. 1953-1954. irreg. (every 1-2
yrs.), vol. 17, 1980. price varies. (Museum fuer Ur-
und Fruehgeschichte Thueringens) Hermann
Boehlaus Nachfolger, Meyerstr. 50a, 53 Weimar, E.
Germany (D.D.R.) Ed. Guenter Behm-Blancke.
Formerly: Museum fuer Ur- und Fruehgeschichte
Thueringens. Jahreschrift.

940 US ISSN 0516-9240
AMERICAN ASSOCIATION FOR THE
ADVANCEMENT OF SLAVIC STUDIES.
DIRECTORY OF MEMBERS. irreg. membership.
American Association for the Advancement of
Slavic Studies, Rm. 731 SEO Bldg., University of
Illinois at Chicago Circle, Chicago, IL 60680.

949 NE
AMSTERDAM. GEMEENTELIJKE
ARCHIEFDIENST. JAARVERSLAG. a.
Gemeentelijke Archiefdienst, Amsterdam,
Netherlands.

AMSTERDAMER BEITRAEGE ZUR NEUEREN
GERMANISTIK. see *LITERATURE*

ANALECTA CARTUSIANA; review for Carthusian
history and spirituality. see *RELIGIONS AND
THEOLOGY*

930 DK ISSN 0066-1392
ANALECTA ROMANA INSTITUTI DANICI. (Text
in English, French, Italian) 1960. irreg., no. 8, 1978.
price varies. Odense University Press, 36,
Pjentedamsgade, DK-5000 Odense, Denmark. index.

930 DK ISSN 0066-1406
ANALECTA ROMANA INSTITUTI DANICI.
SUPPLEMENTUM. (Text in English, French,
Italian) 1960. irreg., no. 8, 1978. price varies.
Odense University Press, 36, Pjentedamsgade, DK-
5000 Odense, Denmark.

942 UK ISSN 0072-5625
ANCIENT MONUMENTS BOARD FOR
ENGLAND. ANNUAL REPORT. 1954. a. price
varies. Ancient Monuments Board, Fortress House,
23 Savile Row, London W1X 2HE, England (Avail.
from H.M.S.O., c/o Liaison Officer, Atlantic House,
Holborn Viaduct, London EC1P 1BN, England)
illus.

940 913 690 UK
ANCIENT MONUMENTS SOCIETY
TRANSACTIONS. 1924. a. £5. Ancient
Monuments Society, St. Andrew-by-the-Wardrobe,
Queen Victoria St., London EC4V 5DE, England.
Ed. Michael McGarvie. bk. rev. bibl. circ. 2,000.

943.8 PL ISSN 0066-2224
ANNALES SILESIAE. (Text in English and Polish)
1960. irreg., vol. 8, 1978. 24 Zl. (Wroclawskie
Towarzystwo Naukowe) Ossolineum, Publishing
House of the Polish Academy of Sciences, Rynek 9,
50-106 Wroclaw, Poland (Dist. by Ars Polona-Ruch,
Krakowskie Przedmiescie 7, Warsaw, Poland) Ed. J.
Trzynadlowski.

940 US
ANNALS OF THE FRENCH REVOLUTION. 1978.
a. $10 to individuals; institutions $15. University of
Southwestern Louisiana, Institute of French Studies,
Box 4-0831, Lafayette, LA 70504. Ed. John B.
Cameron, Jr. bk. rev.

943 IT ISSN 0066-4642
ANTEMURALE; annual periodical devoted to the
history of Central and Eastern Europe. 1954. a.
price varies. Institutum Historicum Polonicum
Romae - Polish Historical Institute, Via Virginio
Orsini 19, 00192 Rome, Italy. cum. index.

946 SP ISSN 0066-5061
ANUARIO DE ESTUDIOS MEDIEVALES. (Text in
Romance Languages; summaries in English and
French) 1964. a. 2000 ptas.($41) Universidad de
Barcelona, Instituto de Historia Medievales,
Barcelona, Spain. Ed. Emilio Saez. adv. bk. rev.
indexes. circ. 1,000.

HISTORY — HISTORY OF EUROPE

940 341   SP
ANUARIO DE HISTORIA DEL DERECHO ESPANOL. 1924. a. 1000 ptas. Instituto Nacional de Estudios Juridicos, Duque de Medinaceli, 6, Madrid, Spain. bk. rev. bibl. index.

949   RM
APULUM. At head of title: Acta Musei Apulensis. (Text in English, French, German, Italian, Romanian; summaries in English, French, German, Italian) 1939/42. a. Muzeul de Istorie si Arheologie Alba Julia, Str. Mihai Vieazul nr. 12-14, Alba Julia, Romania. illus.

940   PL   ISSN 0066-6041
ARCHEION; czasopismo naukowe poswiecone sprawom archiwalnym. (Text in Polish; summaries in English and Russian) 1927. irreg., vol. 62, 1975. price varies. (Naczelna Dyrekcja Archiwow Panstwowych) Panstwowe Wydawnictwo Naukowe, Ul. Miodowa 10, Warsaw, Poland (Dist. by Ars Polona-Ruch, Krakowskie Przedmiescie 7, Warsaw, Poland) Ed. Piotr Bankowski. cum. index: vols. 1-50 (issued in 1969) circ. 820. Indexed: Hist.Abstr.

ARCHITECTURAL AND ARCHAEOLOGICAL SOCIETY OF DURHAM AND NORTHUMBERLAND. TRANSACTIONS. NEW SERIES. see *ARCHAEOLOGY*

940   GW   ISSN 0066-6297
ARCHIV FUER DIPLOMATIK, SCHRIFTGESCHICHTE, SIEGEL- UND WAPPENKUNDE. 1955. a. price varies. Boehlau Verlag GmbH, Niehler Str. 272-274, 5000 Cologne 60, W. Germany (B.R.D.) Eds. W. Heinemeyer, K. Jordan.

943   GW   ISSN 0066-6335
ARCHIV FUER GESCHICHTE VON OBERFRANKEN. 1827. a. price varies. Historischer Verein fuer Oberfranken, Ludwigstr. 21, Neues Schloss, 8580 Bayreuth, W. Germany (B.R.D.) Ed. Erwin Herrmann. bk. rev.

943   GW   ISSN 0066-636X
ARCHIV FUER HESSISCHE GESCHICHTE UND ALTERTUMSKUNDE. 1835. a. DM.32 for members. Historischer Verein fuer Hessen, Staatsarchiv, Schloss, 6100 Darmstadt, W. Germany (B.R.D.) (Co-sponsor: Technische Hochschule Darmstadt) bk. rev. circ. 900.

940   GW   ISSN 0066-6505
ARCHIV FUER SOZIALGESCHICHTE. 1960. a. DM.108. (Friedrich-Ebert Stiftung) Verlag Neue Gesellschaft GmbH, Godesberger Allee 143, 5300 Bonn 2, W. Germany (B.R.D.) (Co-sponsor: Institut fuer Sozialgeschichte) bk. rev. circ. 1,500.

900   AU   ISSN 0003-9462
ARCHIV FUER VATERLAENDISCHE GESCHICHTE UND TOPOGRAPHIE. 1849. irreg. price varies. Geschichtsverein fuer Kaernten, Museumgasse 2, A-9020 Klagenfurt, Austria. Ed. Wilhelm Neumann. bk. rev.

940   NE   ISSN 0066-6548
ARCHIVES BAKOUNINE/BAKUNIN-ARCHIV. 1961. irreg., vol. 7, 1981. price varies. (International Institute for Social History) E. J. Brill, Oude Rijn 33a-35, Leiden, Netherlands. Ed. Arthur Lehning.

945   IT   ISSN 0066-6718
ARCHIVIO STORICO ITALIANO. BIBLIOTECA. 1949. irreg., vol. 21, 1979. price varies. Casa Editrice Leo S. Olschki, Casella Postale 66, 50100 Florence, Italy. circ. 1,000.

945   IT   ISSN 0004-0347
ARCHIVIO STORICO LODIGIANO. 1881. a. L.5000. Comune di Lodi, Biblioteca Comunale Laudense, Corso Umberto 63, 20075 Lodi, Milan, Italy. bk. rev. index. circ. 300.
Local

945   IT   ISSN 0066-6807
ARCHIVUM ROMANICUM. BIBLIOTECA. SERIE 1: STORIA LETTERATURA-PALEOGRAFIA. (Text in French, German, or Italian) 1921. irreg., vol. 153, 1979. price varies. Casa Editrice Leo S. Olschki, Casella Postale 66, 50100 Florence, 50100 Florence. circ. 1,000.

949.8 571   RM   ISSN 0066-7358
ARHEOLOGIA MOLDOVEI/ARCHEOLOGIE DE LA MOLDAVIE. (Text in Rumanian; summaries in French) 1961. irreg. (Academia de Stiinte Sociale si Politice) Editura Academiei Republicii Socialiste Romania, Calea Victoriei 125, Bucharest, Romania (Subscr. to: ILEXIM, Str. 13 Decembrie Nr. 3, P.O. Box 136-137, Bucharest, Romania) (Co-sponsor: Institutul de Istorie si Arheologie A.D. Xenopol)

949   YU
ARHIVSKI VJESNIK. (Text in Croatian; summaries in French, German, English, Italian) 1899. a. 200 din. Arhiv Hrvatske, Marulicev trg 21, 41000 Zagreb, Yugoslavia. Ed. Bernard Stulli. bk. rev. illus. circ. 700.

ARS SUECICA. see *ART*

940   US   ISSN 0572-4287
ASSOCIATION FOR THE ADVANCEMENT OF BALTIC STUDIES. PUBLICATIONS. 1969. irreg. price varies. Association for the Advancement of Baltic Studies, 366 86th St., Brooklyn, NY 11220.

943   US
ASSOCIATION FOR THE ADVANCEMENT OF POLISH STUDIES. BULLETIN. vol. 3,1978. irreg. Association for the Advancement of Polish Studies, Alliance College, Cambridge Springs, PA 16403.

940   SZ   ISSN 0571-6322
ASSOCIATION OF INSTITUTES FOR EUROPEAN STUDIES. ANNUAIRE.* 1957. a. Association of Institutes for European Studies, European Cultural Centre, 122 rue de Lausanne, Geneva, Switzerland.

378 940   SZ   ISSN 0571-6330
ASSOCIATION OF INSTITUTES FOR EUROPEAN STUDIES. YEAR-BOOK.* a. Association of Institutes for European Studies, European Cultural Centre, 122 rue de Lausanne, Geneva, Switzerland.

947   US   ISSN 0066-9717
ASSOCIATION OF THE RUSSIAN-AMERICAN SCHOLARS IN U.S.A. ZAPISKI RUSSKOI AKADEMICHESKOI GRUPPY V S. SH. A. TRANSACTIONS.* (Text and summaries in English and Russian) 1967. a. $7.50. Association of Russian-American Scholars in U.S.A., 85-20 114 St., Richmond Hill, NY 11418.

945   IT
ASSOCIAZIONE NAZIONALE PER LA TUTELA DEL PATRIMONIO STORICO ARTISTICO E NATURALE DELLA NAZIONE. ATTI DI CONVEGNI. irreg; no. 13, 1975. price varies. Associazione Nazionale per la Tutela del Patrimonio Storico Artistico e Naturale della Nazione, Corso Vittorio Emanuele 287, 00186 Rome, Italy.

945   IT
ASSOCIAZIONE NAZIONALE PER LA TUTELA DEL PATRIMONIO STORICO ARTISTICO E NATURALE DELLA NAZIONE. DOCUMENTI. irreg. L.2000. Associazione Nazionale per la Tutela del Patrimonio Storico Artistico e Naturale della Nazione, Corso Vittorio Emanuele 287, 00186 Rome, Italy.

945   IT
ASSOCIAZIONE NAZIONALE PER LA TUTELA DEL PATRIMONIO STORICO ARTISTICO E NATURALE DELLA NAZIONE. QUADERNI. irreg. L.2000. Associazione Nazionale per la Tutela del Patrimonio Storico Artistico e Naturale della Nazione, Corso Vittorio Emanuele 287, 00186 Rome, Italy.

945   IT
ASSOCIAZIONE NAZIONALE PER LA TUTELA DEL PATRIMONIO STORICO ARTISTICO E NATURALE DELLA NAZIONE. STUDI. 1962. irreg; no. 143, 1976. L.1000. Associazione Nazionale per la Tutela del Patrimonio Storico Artistico e Naturale della Nazione, Corso Vittorio Emanuele 287, 00186 Rome, Italy.

943.6 015   US   ISSN 0067-236X
AUSTRIAN HISTORICAL BIBLIOGRAPHY/ OESTERREICHISCHE HISTORISCHE BIBLIOGRAPHIE. 1965. a. $37.75. American Bibliographical Center- Clio Press, 2040 Alameda Padre Serra, Box 4397, Santa Barbara, CA 93103. Ed. Eric H. Boehm. cum. index every 5 yrs.

943.6   US   ISSN 0067-2378
AUSTRIAN HISTORY YEARBOOK. 1965. a. price varies. Rice University, Houston, TX 77001. (Co-Sponsor: Conference Group for Central European History) Ed. R. John Rath. bk. rev. circ. 900-1,000. Indexed: Hist.Abstr.
Supersedes: Austrian History Newsletter.

945 398   IT   ISSN 0067-9860
B R A D S. (Bollettino del Repertorio e dell'Atlante Demologico Sardo) 1966. irreg.; no. 8, 1978. L.4000 or exchange. Universita degli Studi di Cagliari, Cattedra di Storia delle Tradizioni Popolari, Cagliari, Italy (Dist. by: Agenzia Libraria Cosentino, via Gallura 15, I-09100 Cagliari, Italy) Ed. Enrica Delitala. bk. rev. circ. 500.

940   PL   ISSN 0067-2793
BADANIA Z DZIEJOW SPOLECZNYCH I GOSPODARCZYCH. (Text in Polish; summaries in English, French or German) irreg. price varies. (Poznanskie Towarzystwo Przyjaciol Nauk) Panstwowe Wydawnictwo Naukowe, Miodowa 10, Warsaw, Poland (Dist. by Ars Polona-Ruch, Krakowskie Przedmiescie 7, Warsaw, Poland)

949   YU
BALCANICA. vol. 5, 1974. a. Srpska Akademija Nauka i Umetnosti, Koordinacioni Medjuakademski Odbor za Balkanologiju, Belgrade, Yugoslavia. (Co-sponsor: Srpska Akademija Nauka i Umetnosti. Balkanoloski Institut) Ed. Mehmed Begovic.

943   US   ISSN 0360-2206
BALKANISTICA; occasional papers in Southeast European studies. 1975. irreg. $8.95. (American Association for Southeast European Studies) Slavica Publishers, Inc., Box 14388, Columbus, OH 43214. Ed. Kenneth E. Naylor. charts. illus. circ. 525.

949.6   UR
BALKANSKIE ISSLEDOVANIYA. 1974. irreg. 1.61 Rub. per issue. (Akademiya Nauk S.S.S.R., Institut Slavyanovedeniya i Balkanistiki) Izdatel'stvo Nauka, Podsosenskii Per., 21, Moscow K-62, U.S.S.R. Ed. V. Vinogradov. circ. 1,700.

940   GW   ISSN 0067-3099
BALTISCHE STUDIEN. 1835. a. DM.21. (Gesellschaft fuer Pommersche Geschichte, Altertumskunde und Kunst) Christoph von der Ropp, Wulfsdorfer Weg 17, 2000 Hamburg 67, W. Germany (B.R.D.) Eds. D. Kausche, E.v. Puttkamer, A. Holtz. bk. rev. circ. 1,000.

940   GW   ISSN 0341-3918
BAYERISCHE VORGESCHICHTSBLAETTER. (Text in German, English, French) 1921. a. price varies. (Bayerische Akademie der Wissenschaften, Kommission fuer Bayerische Landesgeschichte) C. H. Beckshe Verlagsbuchhandlung, Wilhelmstr. 9, 8000 Munich 40, W. Germany (B.R.D.) Ed. H.-J. Kellner. bk. rev. bibl. illus. circ. 600.

942   UK   ISSN 0067-4826
BEDFORDSHIRE HISTORICAL RECORD SOCIETY. PUBLICATIONS. 1913. a. L.3. Bedfordshire Historical Record Society, White Crescent Press, Luton, Beds., England. Ed. Patricia Bell. circ. 750.

947   BE   ISSN 0373-1537
BEDI KARTLISA; revue de kartvelologie; etudes georgiennes et caucasiennes. a. 450 Fr.($15) Editions Peeters s.p.r.l., B.P. 41, B-3000 Louvain, Belgium.

274.3   GW   ISSN 0408-8344
BEITRAEGE ZUR GESCHICHTE DER REICHSKIRCHE IN DER NEUZEIT. irreg., vol. 10, 1981. price varies. Franz Steiner Verlag GmbH, Friedrichstr. 24, Postfach 5529, 6200 Wiesbaden, W. Germany (B.R.D.) Ed. Rudolf Reinhardt.

940   GE   ISSN 0522-6562
BEITRAEGE ZUR GESCHICHTE DER UNIVERSITAET ERFURT (1392-1816) 1956. irreg., vol. 18, 1978. price varies. (Medizinische Akademie Erfurt) Johann Ambrosius Barth Verlag, Salomonstr. 186, 701 Leipzig, E. Germany (D.D.R.)

943.08   GW   ISSN 0408-8379
BEITRAEGE ZUR GESCHICHTE DER UNIVERSITAET MAINZ. irreg., vol. 13, 1981. price varies. (Universitaet Mainz) Franz Steiner Verlag GmbH, Friedrichstr. 24, Postfach 5529, 6200 Wiesbaden, W. Germany (B.R.D.) Ed.Bd.

HISTORY — HISTORY OF EUROPE

943   GW   ISSN 0078-2785
BEITRAEGE ZUR GESCHICHTE UND KULTUR DER STADT NUERNBERG. 1959. irreg. price varies. Stadtbibliothek, Egidien-Platz 23, 8500 Nuernberg 2, W. Germany (B.R.D.) Eds. R. Fritzsch, G. Thomann.

940   GW
BEITRAEGE ZUR HEIMATKUNDE DER STADT SCHWELM UND IHRER UMGEBUNG. 1951. a. price varies. Verein fuer Heimatkunde Schwelm, Haynauer Str. 3, 5830 Schwelm, W. Germany (B.R.D.) Ed. Kurt Wollmerstaedt.

943   GW   ISSN 0067-5164
BEITRAEGE ZUR OBERPFALZFORSCHUNG. 1965. irreg. price varies. Verlag Michael Lassleben, Lange Gasse 19, Postfach 20, 8411 Kallmuenz, W. Germany (B.R.D.) Ed. Heinz K. Rademacher.

947   917.306   US   ISSN 0510-3746
BELARUSKI INSTYTUT NAVUKI MACTATSTVA. ZAPISY/BYELORUSSIAN INSTITUTE OF ARTS AND SCIENCES. ANNALS. (Text in Byelorussian; summaries in English) 1952. a. $10 per no. Byelorussian Institute of Arts and Sciences, Inc., 3441 Tibbett Ave., Bronx, NY 10463. Ed. Vitaut Tumash. adv. bk. rev. bibl. illus. stat. circ. 1,000. (back issues avail)

943   GW   ISSN 0067-5792
BERGISCHER GESCHICHTSVEREIN. ZEITSCHRIFT. 1863. irreg. DM.15. Bergischer Geschichtsverein e. V., Kolpingstrasse 8, 5600 Wuppertal-Elberfeld, W. Germany (B.R.D.) Ed. Wolfgang Koelmann. bk. rev. circ. 2,700.

940   US
BERKSHIRE STUDIES IN EUROPEAN HISTORY. (Subseries of Berkshire Studies in History) irreg. price varies. Holt, Rinehart and Winston, 383 Madison Ave., New York, NY 10017.

949.50   930   GE   ISSN 0067-6055
BERLINER BYZANTINISTISCHE ARBEITEN. (Text in German; occasionally in Greek) 1956. irreg., no. 47, 1976. price varies. (Akademie der Wissenschaften der DDR, Zentralinstitut fuer Alte Geschichte und Archaeologie) Akademie-Verlag, Leipziger Strasse 3-4, 108 Berlin, E. Germany (D.D.R.) (Co-sponsor: Martin-Luther-Universitaet, Halle/Wittenberg)

943   GW   ISSN 0067-6071
BERLINER HISTORISCHE KOMMISSION. VEROEFFENTLICHUNGEN. 1960. irreg., vol. 50, 1981. price varies. Walter de Gruyter und Co., Genthiner Str. 13, 1000 Berlin 30, W. Germany (B.R.D.) adv.

943.8   PL   ISSN 0067-6470
BIALOSTOCKIE TOWARZYSTWO NAUKOWE. PRACE.* 1963. irreg. Bialostockie Towarzystwo Naukowe, Dom Technika, Sklodowskiej - Curie 2, 15-097 Bialystok, Poland (Dist by Ars Polona-Ruch, Krakowskie Przedmiescie 7, Warsaw, Poland)

949.4   016   SZ   ISSN 0067-6772
BIBLIOGRAFIA TICINESE.* 1960. a. price varies. Biblioteca Cantonale Lugano, Viale Carlo Cattaneo, CH-6900 Lugano, Switzerland. index.

940   US
BIBLIOGRAPHIC GUIDE TO SOVIET AND EUROPEAN STUDIES. (Text in Czech,Slovak,Ukranian,Latvian,Bulgarian, Russian,Polish,English) 1978. a. $250. G. K. Hall & Co., 70 Lincoln St., Boston, MA 02111.

BIBLIOGRAPHIE LUXEMBOURGEOISE. see *BIBLIOGRAPHIES*

945   IT   ISSN 0067-7442
BIBLIOTECA DI STORIA TOSCANA MODERNA E CONTEMPORANEA STUDI E DOCUMENTI. 1965. irreg., vol. 21, 1979. price varies. (Unione Regionale delle Provincie Toscane, Florence) Casa Editrice Leo S. Olschki, Casella Postale 66, 50100 Florence, Italy. circ. 1,000.

949.8   RM   ISSN 0067-7493
BIBLIOTECA ISTORICA. 1957. irreg. (Academia de Stiinte Sociale si Politice, Institutul de Istorie "N. Iorga") Editura Academiei Republicii Socialiste Romania, Calea Victoriei 125, Bucharest, Romania (Subscr. to: ILEXIM, Str. 13 Decembrie Nr. 3, P.O. Box 136-137, Bucharest, Romania)

945   940.27   IT
BIBLIOTECA NAPOLETANA DI STORIA E ARTE. 1976. irreg. price varies. Congedo Editore, Galatina, Italy. Dir. Franco Strazzullo.

946   SP   ISSN 0405-9212
BIBLIOTECA PROMOCION DEL PUEBLO. 1965. irreg. no. 100, 1977. Zero S.A., Artasamina 12, Bilbao, Spain (Dist. by: ZYX S.A., Lerida 80, Madrid 20, Spain)

945   IT
BIBLIOTECA STATALE E LIBRERIA CIVICA DI CREMONA. AANNALI. 1948. a. price varies. Biblioteca Statale e Libreria Civica di Cremona, Via Ugolani Dati 4, Cremona, Italy. Ed. Rita Barbisotti. circ. 1,780.

945   IT
BIBLIOTECA STATALE E LIBRERIA CIVICA DI CREMONA. MOSTRE. 1978. irreg., no. 6, 1979. exchange basis. Biblioteca Statale e Libreria Civica di Cremona, Via Ugolani Dati 4, Cremona, Italy. Ed. Rita Barbisotti. circ. 1,780.

945   IT
BIBLIOTECA STORICA ELBANA. 1976. irreg. Casa Editrice Leo S. Olschki, Casella Postale 66, 0100 Florence, Italy.

945   IT
BIBLIOTECA STORICA TOSCANA. SERIE I. 1923. irreg., no. 19, 1978. price varies. (Deputazione Toscane di Storia Patria) Casa Editrice Leo S. Olschki, Casella Postale 66, 50100 Florence, Italy. circ. 1,000.
Formerly (until 1977): Biblioteca Storica Toscana (ISSN 0067-7523)

945   IT
BIBLIOTECA STORICA TOSCANA. SERIE II. 1977. irreg. (Societa Toscana per la Storia del Risorgimento) Casa Editrice Leo S. Olschki, Casella Postale 66, 0100 Florence, Italy.

BIBLIOTEKA KRAKOWSKA. see *ART*

949.8   RM   ISSN 0067-799X
BIBLIOTHECA HISTORICA ROMANIAE. MONOGRAPHIES. (Text in English, French, German, Russian) 1963. irreg. (Academia Republicii Socialiste Romania) Editura Academiei Republicii Socialiste Romania, Calea Victoriei 125, Bucharest, Romania (Subscr. to: ILEXIM, Str. 13 Decembrie Nr. 3, P.O. Box 136-137, Bucharest, Romania) (Co-sponsor: Academia de Stiinte Sociale si Politice) Eds. St. Pascu, St. Stefanescu.

949.8   RM   ISSN 0067-7981
BIBLIOTHECA HISTORICA ROMANIAE. STUDIES. (Text in English, French, German, Russian) 1963. irreg. (Academia Republicii Socialiste Romania) Editura Academiei Republicii Socialiste Romania, Calea Victoriei 125, Bucharest, Romania (Subscr. to: ILEXIM, Str. 13 Decembrie Nr. 3, P.O. Box 136-137, Bucharest, Romania) (Co-sponsor: Academia de Stiinte Sociale si Politice) Eds. St. Pascu, St. Stefanescu.

940   PL   ISSN 0067-8031
BIBLIOTHECA LATINA MEDII ET RECENTIORI AEVI. (Text in Latin) 1960. irreg. price varies. (Polska Akademia Nauk, Komitet Nauk o Kulturze Antycznej) Ossolineum, Publishing House of the Polish Academy of Sciences, Rynek 9, 50-106 Wroclaw, Poland (Dist. by Ars Polona-Ruch, Krakowskie Przedmiescie 7, Warsaw, Poland) Ed. C.F. Kumaniecki.

940   GW
BIBLIOTHECA RERUM HISTORICARUM. 1970. irreg. price varies. Scientia Verlag, Postfach 1660, 7080 Aalen, W. Germany (B.R.D.) Ed.Karl August Eckhardt.

940   SZ   ISSN 0067-8406
BIBLIOTHEQUE HISTORIQUE VAUDOISE. 1940. irreg., no. 58, 1977. price varies. Petit-Chene 18, 1002 Lausanne, Switzerland. cum.index (1940-present) in each vol.

948   NE   ISSN 0165-0505
BIJDRAGEN EN MEDEDELINGEN BETREFFENDE DE GESCHIEDENIS DER NEDERLANDEN. vol. 95, 1980. 3/yr. fl.50.50. (Nederlands Historisch Genootschap) Martinus Nijhoff, Box 566, 2501 CN The Hague, Netherlands. Ed.Bd. bk. rev.

949.2   NE   ISSN 0067-8554
BIJDRAGEN TOT DE GESCHIEDENIS VAN ARNHEM. 1966. irreg., 1972. no. 4. price varies. Gemeentearchief - Arnhem Municipal Archives, Koningstraat 23 II, Arnhem, Netherlands. circ. 1,000.

940   069   GE
BILDUNG IM GESCHICHTSMUSEUM. no. 10, 1974. a. Museum fuer Geschichte der Stadt Dresden, Ernst--Thaelmann--Str. 2, 801 Dresden, E. Germany (D.D.R.) bibl. illus.

942   UK
BIRTH OF MODERN BRITAIN SERIES. irreg. price varies. Routledge & Kegan Paul Ltd., Broadway House, Newtown Rd., Henley-om-Thames, Oxon. RG9 1EN, England (U.S. address: Routledge Journals, 9 Park St., Boston, MA 02108)

BLAETTER FUER WUERTTEMBERGISCHE KIRCHENGESCHICHTE. see *RELIGIONS AND THEOLOGY*

948.9   630   DK   ISSN 0067-9550
BOL OG BY. 1956; 1977 (N.S.) irreg. price varies. Landbohistorisk Selskab, H. C. Andersens Boulevard 38, DK-1553 Copenhagen K, Denmark. Ed. Erik Helmer Pedersen.

943   GW   ISSN 0068-0052
BONNER GESCHICHTSBLAETTER. 1937. a. DM.18. Bonner Heimat- und Geschichtsverein, Berliner Platz 2, 5300 Bonn 1, W. Germany (B.R.D.) (Co-sponsor: Stadtarchiv Bonn) Ed. Dietrich Hoeroldt.

948   DK   ISSN 0084-7976
BORNHOLMSKE SAMLINGER. irreg. Kr.25. William Dams Bookshop, 3700 Roenne, Bornholm, Denmark. Ed. C.H. Kibsgaard. bk. rev. circ. 600.

942   UK   ISSN 0084-7984
BOROUGH OF TWICKENHAM LOCAL HISTORY SOCIETY. PAPERS. 1965. irreg. price varies. Twickenham Local History Society, 59 Park House Gardens, Twickenham Middlesex, England. Ed. A.C.B. Urwin. circ. 200-1,000.

914.221   UK   ISSN 0520-6790
BOURNE SOCIETY LOCAL HISTORY RECORDS. 1962. a. £1. Bourne Society, c/o 17 Manor Ave., Caterham, Surrey CR3 6AP, England. Ed. M. Alderton. adv. bibl. charts. illus. index. circ. 4,000.

946.9   PO   ISSN 0006-8640
BRACARA AUGUSTA; revista cultural de Regionalismo e historia. 1949. irreg. price varies. (Camara Municipal de Braga) Livraria Cruz, Rua D. Diogo de Sousa 129-133, Braga, Portugal. Ed.Bd. bibl. illus. index.
Local

943   GW   ISSN 0068-0745
BRAUNSCHWEIGISCHES JAHRBUCH. 1902. a. DM.32. Braunschweiger Geschichtsverein, Schriftleitung, Forstweg 2, 3340 Wolfenbuettel, W. Germany (B.R.D.) Ed. J. Koenig. circ. 1,300.

941   IE   ISSN 0068-0877
BREIFNE; journal of Cumann Seanchais Bhreifne. (Texts in English and Gaelic) 1958. a. £2($5) Breifne Historical Society, St. Patrick's College, Cavan, Co.Cavan, Ireland. Ed. Rev. Sean Brady. bk. rev. circ. 800.

940   GW   ISSN 0341-9622
BREMISCHES JAHRBUCH. 1863. a. price varies. Staatsarchiv Bremen, Praesident-Kennedy-Platz 2, 2800 Bremen 1, W. Germany (B.R.D.) (Co-sponsor: Historische Gesellschaft Bremen) Ed. Wilhelm Luehrs. bk. rev. illus. circ. 1,500.

BRISTOL AND GLOUCESTERSHIRE ARCHAEOLOGICAL SOCIETY, BRISTOL, ENGLAND. TRANSACTIONS. see *ARCHAEOLOGY*

942   UK   ISSN 0068-1075
BRITAIN: AN OFFICIAL HANDBOOK. a. £5. Central Office of Information, Hercules Rd., London SE1 7DU, England (Avail. from H.M.S.O., c/o Liaison Officer, Atlantic House, Holborn Viaduct, London EC1P 1BN, England) illus.

942 US ISSN 0068-1105
BRITAIN IN THE WORLD TODAY. 1962. irreg. price varies. Johns Hopkins University Press, Baltimore, MD 21218 (Exclusive Commonwealth edition from Chatto and Windus, 40-42 William IV St., London W. C. 2, England) index.

940 UK ISSN 0068-113X
BRITANNIA. (Includes annual survey of Romano-British excavations) 1970. a. membership. Society for the Promotion of Roman Studies, 31-34 Gordon Sq., London WC1H 0PP, England. Ed. J. J. Wilkes. adv. bk. rev. circ. 1,800.
Devoted to Romano-British and connected studies

943 HU ISSN 0068-3337
BUDAPEST VAROSTORTENETI MONOGRAFIAI. 1956. irreg. price varies. (Magyar Tudomanyos Akademia) Akademiai Kiado, Publishing House of the Hungarian Academy of Sciences, P.O. Box 24, H-1363 Budapest, Hungary.

949.75 BL ISSN 0007-3946
BULGARIAN REVIEW. (Text in English) 1961. a. $20. Foyer Bulgare, Caixa Postal 14590-ZC-95, Rio de Janeiro, Brazil (Subscr. Also Through: Bulgarian Historical Institute, Chase Manhattan Bank, National Div., Madison Ave. at 64 St., N.Y. 10021) bk. rev. circ. 1,000.

949 BU ISSN 0068-3779
BULGARSKA AKADEMIIA NA NAUKITE. INSTITUT ZA ISTORIIA. IZVESTIIA. (Summaries in various languages) 1951. irreg. 2.90 lv. Publishing House of the Bulgarian Academy of Sciences, Ul. Akad. G. Bonchev, 1113 Sofia, Bulgaria (Dist. by: Hemus, 6, Rouski Blvd., 1000 Sofia, Bulgaria) Ed. D. Kosev. circ. 800.

947 BU ISSN 0081-1122
BULGARSKO ISTORICHESKO DRUZHESTVO. IZVESTIIA. (Summaries in French) 1905. irreg. 5.08 lv. per no. Publishing House of the Bulgarian Academy of Sciences, Ul. Akad. G. Bonchev, 1113 Sofia, Bulgaria (Dist. by: Hemus, 6, Rouski Blvd., 1000 Sofia, Bulgaria) (Co-sponsor: Bulgarska Akademiia na Naukite) Ed. D. Kosev. circ. 2,131.

944 FR ISSN 0068-4058
BULLETIN D'HISTOIRE ECONOMIQUE ET SOCIALE DE LA REVOLUTION FRANCAISE. 1961. a. price varies. (Commission d'Histoire Economique et Sociale de la Revolution Francaise) Bibliotheque Nationale, 58 rue Richelieu, 75084 Paris Cedex 02, France. cum.index: 1907-21. circ. 650.

948 NO ISSN 0084-8212
BY OG BYGD; Norsk Folkemuseums aarbok. (Text in Norwegian; summaries in English and German) 1943. a. price varies. Norsk Folkemuseum, Bygdoey, Oslo 2, Norway.

943.8 PL ISSN 0068-4589
BYDGOSKIE TOWARZYSTWO NAUKOWE. WYDZIAL NAUK HUMANISTYCZNYCH. PRACE. SERIA C (HISTORIA I ARCHEOLOGIA) 1963. irreg. price varies. Bydgoskie Towarzystwo Naukowe, Jezuicka 4, Bydgoszcz, Poland (Dist. by Ars Polona-Ruch, Krakowskie Przedmiescie 7, Warsaw, Poland)

949 NE ISSN 0525-4507
BYZANTINA NEERLANDICA. 1969. irreg. price varies. E. J. Brill, Oude Rijn 33a-35, Leiden, Netherlands. Eds. G. H. Blanken, H. J. Scheltema, H. Hennephof.

940 FR ISSN 0068-5011
CAHIERS DE CIVILISATION MEDIEVALE. SUPPLEMENT. 1958. irreg. 150 F. Universite de Poitiers, Centre d'Etudes Superieures de Civilisation Medievale, 24, rue de la Chaine, 86022 Poitiers, France. adv. bk. rev. cum.index.

940 FR
CAHIERS FRANCO-ECOSSAIS DE NORMANDIE.* (Text in French & occasionally in English) 1972. 10 F. c/o Rene Soyer, Ed., Residence Jeanne-d'Arc, 43 Route d'Ifs, Caen-14, France.

942 UK ISSN 0068-6786
CAMBRIDGE STUDIES IN MEDIEVAL LIFE AND THOUGHT. THIRD SERIES. 1969. irreg., no. 14, 1980. $42.50 for latest vol. Cambridge University Press, Box 110, Cambridge CB2 3RL, England (and 32 E. 57 St., New York, NY 10022) Ed. Walter Ullmann. index.

942 UK ISSN 0068-6905
CAMDEN FOURTH SERIES. 1838, Fourth Series 1964. a. membership. Royal Historical Society, University College London, Gower St., London WC1E 6BT, England.

940 UK ISSN 0305-4756
CAMDEN HISTORY REVIEW. 1973. a. £1 per no. Camden History Society, Swiss Cottage Library, Avenue Rd., London N.W. 3, England. Ed. Christopher Wade. bk. rev. bibl. circ. 3,000.
Regional English history

940.53 US
CENTER FOR HOLOCAUST STUDIES NEWSLETTER. 1976. irreg., 1-2/64. per no. Center for Holocaust Studies, 1609 Ave. J, Brooklyn, NY 11230. bk. rev. film rev. play rev. bibl.

940 BE ISSN 0076-1192
CENTRE BELGE HISTOIRE RURALE. PUBLICATIONS/BELGISCH CENTRUM VOOR LANDELIJKE GESCHIEDENIS. PUBLIKATIES. (Text in French, Dutch, English) 1963. irreg., no. 53, 1977. Centre Belge Histoire Rurale, Blijde-Indomststraat, 29, 3000 Louvain, Belgium.

920 BE
CENTRE D'HISTOIRE ET D'ART DE LA THUDINIE. PUBLICATIONS. 1977. irreg. (1-2/ yr.) 150 Fr. Centre d'Histoire et d'Art de la Thudinie, 7 rue Louis Cambier, Bte. 14, 6530 Thuin, Belgium. illus.

940 SZ ISSN 0069-1895
CENTRE EUROPEEN D'ETUDES BURGONDO-MEDIANES. PUBLICATION. (Text in French and German) 1953. a. 20 Fr. Centre Europeen d'Etudes Burgondo-Medianes, Birfelderstr. 4, CH-4132 Muttenz, Switzerland. cum.index: 1959-1969.

CENTRE INTERNATIONAL DE DOCUMENTATION OCCITANE. SERIE BIBLIOGRAPHIQUE. see *BIBLIOGRAPHIES*

944 FR ISSN 0398-3765
CENTRE INTERNATIONAL DE DOCUMENTATION OCCITANE. SERIE ETUDES. 1978. irreg. Centre International de Documentation Occitane, Beziers, France. Ed. C. Bonnet, S. Drouin, F. Pic.

949.3 BE
CERCLE D'HISTOIRE ET D'ARCHEOLOGIE DE SAINT-GHISLAIN ET DE LA REGION. ANALES. a. Cercle d'Histoire et d'Archeologie de Saint-Ghislain et de la Region, Saint-Ghislain, Belgium. adv.
Supersedes: Cercle d'Histoire et d'Archeologie de Saint-Ghislain et de la Region. Miettes d'Histoire.

949.5 US ISSN 0577-5574
CHARIOTEER; an annual review of modern Greek culture. 1960. a. $4. Parnassos, Greek Cultural Society of New York, 2928 Grand Central Station, New York, NY 10017. Eds. Andonis Decavalles & Bebe Spanos. adv. bk. rev. illus. circ. 1,500.

940 AU
CHORHERRENSTIFT KLOSTERNEUBURG. JAHRBUCH. 1961. a. DM.66. Hermann Boehlaus Nachf., Schmalzhofgasse 4, Postfach 167, A-1061 Vienna, Austria. circ. 200.

946 SP
CHRONICA NOVA. 1968. irreg. price varies. Universidad de Granada, Secretariado de Publicaciones, Hospital Real, Granada, Spain. Ed. Pedro Gan Jiminez.

CIVILTA VENEZIANA. FONTI E TESTI. SERIE PRIMA: FONTI E TESTI PER LA STORIA DELL'ARTE VENETA. see *ART*

945 IT ISSN 0069-4347
CIVILTA VENEZIANA. FONTI E TESTI. SERIE TERZA. 1959. irreg., no. 3, 1973. price varies. (Fondazione Giorgio Cini) Casa Editrice Leo S. Olschki, Casella Postale 66, 50100 Florence, Italy. circ. 500.

945 IT ISSN 0069-4371
CIVILTA VENEZIANA. SAGGI. 1955. irreg., vol. 25, 1979. price varies. (Fondazione Giorgio Cini) Casa Editrice Leo S. Olschki, Casella Postale 66, 50100 Florence, Italy. circ. 1,000.

945 IT ISSN 0069-438X
CIVILTA VENEZIANA. STUDI. 1953. irreg., vol. 34, 1978. price varies. (Fondazione Giorgio Cini) Casa Editrice Leo S. Olschki, Casella Postale 66, 50100 Florence, Italy. circ. 1,000.

CLASSICS OF BRITISH HISTORICAL LITERATURE. see *LITERATURE*

940 GW ISSN 0084-8808
COBURGER LANDESSTIFTUNG. JAHRBUCH. 1956. a. DM.20. Coburger Landesstiftung, Schloss Ehrenburg, 8630 Coburg, W. Germany (B.R.D.) Ed. Georg Aumann. bk. rev. bibl. illus. circ. controlled.

946 SP
COLECCION ARAGON. no. 10, 1977. irreg. Libreria General, Independencia 22, Zaragoza 1, Spain.

946 SP ISSN 0069-5106
COLECCION HISTORICA. 1958. irreg.; 1979, no. 4. price varies. (Universidad de Navarra, Facultad de Filosofia y Letras) Ediciones Universidad de Navarra, S.A., Plaza de los Sauces, 1 y 2 Baranain, Pamplona, Spain.

946 SP
COLECCION TEXTOS RECUPERADOS. 1976. irreg. Editorial Hispanamerica, Calle Libertad 27, Madrid 4, Spain.

940 IT ISSN 0391-3279
COLLANA DI STORIA MODERNA E CONTEMPORANEA. 1978. irreg., no. 4, 1979. price varies. Liguori Editore s.r.l., Via Mezzocannone 19, 80134 Naples, Italy. Ed. Aurelio Lepre.

940 GW
COLLEGIUM CAROLINUM. BOHEMIA-JAHRBUCH. vol. 17, 1976. a. DM.65. R. Oldenbourg Verlag GmbH, Rosenheimer Str. 145, 8000 Munich 80, W. Germany (B.R.D.) Ed. G. Hanke.

940 GW
COLLEGIUM CAROLINUM. VEROEFFENTLICHUNGEN. vol. 30, 1977. irreg. price varies. R. Oldenbourg Verlag GmbH, Rosenheimer Str. 145, 8000 Munich 80, W. Germany (B.R.D.)

943 947 US
COLUMBIA UNIVERSITY. INSTITUTE ON EAST CENTRAL EUROPE. EAST CENTRAL EUROPEAN STUDIES. irreg., latest 1968. price varies. Columbia University Press, 136 South Broadway, Irvington-on-Hudson, NY 10533.

947 US ISSN 0588-5477
COLUMBIA UNIVERSITY. RUSSIAN INSTITUTE. STUDIES. 1953. irreg. price varies. Columbia University, Russian Institute, 420 W. 118th St., New York, NY 10027.

940 BE ISSN 0572-9327
COMITE INTERNATIONAL DE DACHAU. BULLETIN. 1960. irreg. International Dachau Committee, 65 rue de Haerne, 1040 Brussels, Belgium.

COMMISSION DEPARTEMENTALE DES MONUMENTS HISTORIQUES DU PAS-DE-CALAIS. BULLETIN. see *ARCHITECTURE*

940 NE
COMPARATIVE STUDIES IN OVERSEAS HISTORY. (Text in English) 1978. irreg. price varies. (Leiden Centre for the History of European Expansion) Leiden University Press, c/o Martinus Nijhoff, Box 566, 2501 CN The Hague, Netherlands. Ed. H.L. Wesseling.

HISTORY — HISTORY OF EUROPE

941.5 UK ISSN 0069-908X
CONNOLLY'S SUPPRESSED WRITINGS.* 1967. irreg. price varies. (Irish Communist Organization) Connolly Books Ltd., 28 Mercer Rd., London N.19, England. Ed. James Connolly.

COSTUME. see CLOTHING TRADE — Fashions

270 940 UK ISSN 0070-1394
COURTENAY LIBRARY OF REFORMATION CLASSICS. 1964. irreg., no. 9, 1980. price varies. Sutton Courtenay Press, Appleford, Abingdon, Oxford OX14 4PB, England. Ed. G. E. Duffield.

230 940 UK
COURTENAY REFORMATION FACSIMILES. 1973. irreg. price varies. Sutton Courtenay Press, Appleford, Abingdon, Oxford OX14 4PB, England. Formerly: Courtenay Facsimiles.

230 940 UK ISSN 0070-1408
COURTENAY STUDIES IN REFORMATION THEOLOGY. 1966. irreg., no. 3, 1981. price varies. Sutton Courtenay Press, Appleford, Abingdon, Oxford OX 14 4PB, England. Ed. G. E. Duffield.

942 UK
COVENTRY EVENING TELEGRAPH YEAR BOOK & WHO'S WHO. 1966. a. £2. Coventry Newspapers Ltd., Corporation St., Coventry CV1 1BR, Warwickshire, England. Ed. E. B. Newbold. adv. stat. index. circ. 1,150.

940 BE
CREDIT COMMUNAL DE BELGIQUE. ACTES DES COLLOQUES INTERNATIONAUX. COLLECTION HISTOIRE. SERIES IN 8. 1964. biennial. Credit Communal de Belgique, 44 Bd Pacheco, Brussels, Belgium.

940 UK ISSN 0307-5583
CROMWELLIANA. 1968-69. a. membership. Cromwell Association, Combe Lodge, Ringley Park Ave., Reigate, Surrey, England. bk. rev.

940 SP
CUADERNOS DE TRABAJO DE HISTORIA. 1973. irreg.; 1979, no. 8. price varies. (Universidad de Navarra, Departamento de Historia Medieval) Ediciones Universidad de Navarra, S.A., Plaza de los Sauces 1 y 2, Baranain, Pamplona, Spain.

945 IT
CULTURA SARDA. 1975. irreg. Libreria Dessi Editrice, Sassari, Italy.

948.5 SW
CURRENT SWEDEN. 1970. irreg. (35-40/yr.) free. Svenska Institutet - Swedish Institute, Box 7434, 103 91 Stockholm, Sweden (U.S. dist: Swedish Information Service, 825 Third Ave., New York, NY 10022) circ. 400 (English edt.); 1,000 (French edt.); 1,000 (German edt.); 800 ((Spanish edt.) (processed)
Incorporates: Environment Planning and Conservation in Sweden.

940 PL ISSN 0070-2471
CZASOPISMO PRAWNO-HISTORYCZNE. (Text in Polish; summaries in French) 1948. irreg., 1972, vol. 24. price var.es. (Polska Akademia Nauk, Instytut Historii, Komisja Historii Panstwa i Prawa) Panstwowe Wydawnictwo Naukowe, Ul. Miodowa 10, Warsaw, Poland (Dist. by Ars Polona-Ruch, Krakowskie Przedmiescie 7, Warsaw, Poland) Ed. Michal Sczaniecki. bk. rev. bibl. charts.

948.9 DK ISSN 0070-2846
DANSKE MAGAZIN. (In 8 series; series 1-6 out of print) 1745. a. Kr.40. Kongelige Danske Selskab for Faedrelandets Historie, H.C. Andersens Boulevard 38, 1552 Copenhagen V, Denmark. Ed. Viggo Sjoegvist. index. circ. 300.

943 GW
DARMSTAEDTER ARCHIVSCHRIFTEN. 1975. irreg., no. 5, 1980. price varies. Historischer Verein fuer Hessen, Staatsarchiv, Schloss, 6100 Darmstadt, W. Germany (B.R.D.) (Co-sponsors: Hessisches Staatsarchiv; Stadtarchiv Darmstadt)

940 NE
DAVIS MEDIEVAL TEXTS AND STUDIES. 1978. irreg., vol. 3, 1980. price varies. E.J. Brill, Oude Rijn 332-35, Leiden, Netherlands. Ed.Bd.

945 IT ISSN 0300-4422
DEPUTAZIONE DI STORIA PATRIA PER L'UMBRIA. BOLLETTINO. 1895. a. L.8000. Deputazione di Storia Patria per l'Umbria, Palazzo dei Priori, C.P. 130, 06100 Perugia, Italy. Ed. Pier Lorenzo Meloni. bk. rev. bibl. circ. 500.

943 430 GE ISSN 0070-3893
DEUTSCH-SLAWISCHE FORSCHUNGEN ZUR NAMENKUNDE UND SIEDLUNGSGESCHICHTE. irreg., vol. 31, 1972. price varies. (Saechsische Akademie der Wissenschaften, Leipzig, Historische Kommission) Akademie-Verlag, Leipziger Str. 3-4, 108 Berlin, E. Germany (D.D.R.)

943 GW
DEUTSCHE ANNALEN. 1972. a. DM.14.40. Druffel-Verlag, Assenbucher Str. 19, 8131 Berg-Leoni, W. Germany (B.R.D.) Ed. Gert Sudholt. illus. circ. 11,500.

940 GE ISSN 0075-286X
DEUTSCHE GESCHICHTE. JAHRESBERICHTE. 1952. a. price varies. (Akademie der Wissenschaften der DDR, Zentralinstitut fuer Geschichte, Abteilung Information und Dokumentation) Akademie-Verlag, Leipziger Str. 3-4, 108 Berlin, E. Germany (D.D.R.)

943 GW ISSN 0170-3080
DEUTSCHE HANDELSAKTEN DES MITTELALTERS UND DER NEUZEIT. irreg., vol. 15, 1978. price varies. (Bayerische Akademie der Wissenschaften, Historische Kommission) Franz Steiner Verlag GmbH, Friedrichstr. 24, Postfach 5529, 6200 Wiesbaden, W. Germany (B.R.D.) Ed.Bd.

940 270 GW ISSN 0344-2934
DEUTSCHER HUGENOTTEN-VEREIN E.V. GESCHICHTSBLAETTER. 1890. irreg. price varies. Deutscher Hugenotten-Verein E.V., Schoeneberger Str. 15, 3400 Goettingen, W. Germany (B.R.D.) Ed. Helmut Kimmel.

940 GW ISSN 0340-8396
DEUTSCHES MITTELALTER, KRITISCHE STUDIENTEXTE DER MONUMENTA GERMANIAE HISTORICA. (Text in German and Latin) 1937. irreg. price varies. Anton Hiersemann Verlag, Rosenbergstr. 113, Postfach 723, 7000 Stuttgart 1, W. Germany (B.R.D.)

DIPLOMACIAI IRATOK MAGYARORSZAG KULPOLITIKAJAHOZ. see POLITICAL SCIENCE — International Relations

948.9 DK ISSN 0070-4938
DIPLOMATARIUM DANICUM. Danish translation: Danmarks Riges Breve (ISSN 0070-2773) (Text generally in Latin) 1938. irreg. Danske Sprog- og Litteraturselskab - Danish Society of Language and Literature, Frederiksholms Kanal 18 A, 1220 Copenhagen K, Denmark (Subscr. to: C. A. Reitzel, Booksellers, 20 Noerregade, DK-1165 Copenhagen K, Denmark) circ. 600.

949.8 RM ISSN 0070-6825
DOCUMENTA ROMANIAE HISTORICA. SERIE A: LA MOLDAVIE. 1969. irreg. (Academia de Stiinte Sociale si Politice) Editura Academiei Republicii Socialiste Romania, Calea Victoriei 125, Bucharest, Romania (Subscr. to: ILEXIM, Str. 13 Decembrie Nr. 3, P.O. Box 136-137, Bucharest, Romania)

949.8 RM ISSN 0070-6833
DOCUMENTA ROMANIAE HISTORICA. SERIE B: LA VALACHIE. 1966. irreg. (Academia de Stiinte Sociale si Politice) Editura Academiei Republicii Socialiste Romania, Calea Victoriei 125, Bucharest, Romania (Subscr. to: ILEXIM, Str. 13 Decembrie Nr. 3, P.O. Box 136-137, Bucharest, Romania)

949.8 RM ISSN 0070-6884
DOCUMENTE ISTORICE. irreg. (Academia de Stiinte Sociale si Politice) Editura Academiei Republicii Socialiste Romania, Calea Victoriei 125, Bucharest, Romania (Subscr. to: ILEXIM, Str. 13 Decembrie Nr. 3, P.O. Box 136-137, Bucharest, Romania)

DOKUMENTE ZUR DEUTSCHLANDPOLITIK. see POLITICAL SCIENCE

DOKUMENTE ZUR DEUTSCHLANDPOLITIK. BEIHEFTE. see POLITICAL SCIENCE

943 GW ISSN 0070-7074
DONAUSCHWAEBISCHES SCHRIFTTUM. 1953. irreg., no. 17, 1972. price varies. Landsmannschaft der Donauschwaben, Goldmuehlestr. 30, 7032 Sindelfingen, W. Germany (B.R.D.) adv. bk. rev. circ. 1,000.

942 UK ISSN 0070-7430
DUDLEY, ENGLAND (WEST MIDLANDS) PUBLIC LIBRARIES. ARCHIVES DEPARTMENT. TRANSCRIPTS. 1960. irreg., no. 17, 1973. price varies. Dudley Public Libraries, St. James's Rd., Dudley, West Midlands DY1 1HR, England.

914.92 NE
DUTCH STUDIES; annual review of the language, literature and life in the low countries. 1974. irreg. (International Association for Dutch Studies) Martinus Nijhoff, Box 566, 2501 CN The Hague, Netherlands.

943.8 PL ISSN 0419-8816
DZIEJE LUBLINA. 1965. irreg. price varies. Wydawnictwo Lubelskie, Okopowa 7, Lublin, Poland.

943.8 PL ISSN 0070-7791
DZIEJE POLSKIEJ GRANICY ZACHODNIEJ. 1961. irreg. Instytut Zachodni, Stary Rynek 78/79, 61-772 Poznan, Poland (Dist. by Ars Polona-Ruch, Krakowskie Przedmiescie 7, Warsaw, Poland) circ. 1,500.

EALING OCCASIONAL PAPERS IN THE HISTORY OF LIBRARIES. see LIBRARY AND INFORMATION SCIENCES

940 US ISSN 0094-3037
EAST CENTRAL EUROPE/EUROPE DU CENTRE EST. (Text in English, French, German, and Russian) 1974. 2-4/yr. $20 to institutions. Russian and East European Publications, c/o Charles Schlacks, Jr., Ed., Arizona State Univ., 120B McAllister Ave., Tempe, AZ 85281. adv. bk. rev. index. circ. 450. (also avail. in microform from UMI; back issues avail.) Indexed: Hist.Abstr.

942 UK ISSN 0070-8208
EAST YORKSHIRE LOCAL HISTORY SERIES. 1952. irreg. £2 price varies. East Yorkshire Local History Society, Purey Cust Chambers, York YO1 2EJ, England. Ed. K. J. Allison.

EASTERN EUROPEAN GENEALOGIST. see GENEALOGY AND HERALDRY

ECONOMISCH- EN SOCIAAL-HISTORISCH JAARBOEK. see BUSINESS AND ECONOMICS — Economic Systems And Theories, Economic History

943.8 IT ISSN 0070-9972
ELEMENTA AD FONTIUM EDITIONES; unpublished sources to mediaeval and modern European history, 14th-17th centuries. (Text in Latin, English, Italian, Spanish, Swedish) 1960. irreg., vol. 46, 1979. price varies. Institutum Historicum Polonicum Romae - Polish Historical Institute, Via Virginio Orsini 19, 00192 Rome, Italy. cum. index.

942 US ISSN 0085-0225
ELIZABETHAN CLUB SERIES. 1960. irreg., 1972, no. 5. price varies. Yale University Press, 92A Yale Sta., New Haven, CT 06520.

940 FR ISSN 0071-0156
EN DIRECT AVEC L'HISTOIRE.* 1969. irreg. price varies. Editions B. Arthaud, 6 rue de Mezieres, Grenoble, France.

942 US ISSN 0071-058X
ENGLISH HISTORICAL DOCUMENTS. irreg. price varies. Oxford University Press, 200 Madison Ave., New York, NY 10016 (and Ely House, 37 Dover St., London W1X 4AH, England) Ed. David C. Douglas.

942 US ISSN 0071-0628
ENGLISH MONARCH SERIES. 1964. irreg. price varies. University of California Press, 2223 Fulton St., Berkeley, CA 94720.

946   SP
ESPANA - SUS MONUMENTOS Y ARTES; SU NATURALEZA E HISTORIA. 1977. a. $500. Ediciones el Albir, Calle de los Angeles 8, Barcelona 1, Spain.
Local

946   SP
ESTUDIOS HISTORICOS Y DOCUMENTOS DE LOS ARCHIVOS DE PROTOCOLOS. (Text and summaries in Spanish and Catalan) 1948. a. 1000 ptas.($20) (Colegio Notarial de Barcelona) Ediciones el Albir, Calle de los Angeles 8, Barcelona 1, Spain.

ETUDES DE PHILOLOGIE ET D'HISTOIRE. see *LITERATURE*

940   FR   ISSN 0071-206X
ETUDES FOREZIENNES. 1968. irreg (every year) price varies. Universite de Saint Etienne, Centre d'Etudes Foreziennes, 1 rue de la Convention, 42100 Saint-Etienne, France.

941.5   FR
ETUDES IRLANDAISES; revue bilingue d'histoire, civilisation et litterature irlandaises. (Text and summaries in English and French) 1972. a. 30 F. Universite de Lille III, Boite Postale 149, 59653 Villeneuve d'Ascq Cedex, France. Eds. Patrick Rafroidi, Pierre Joannon. adv. bk. rev. bibl. circ. 800. (back issues avail.)

944   FR   ISSN 0071-2140
ETUDES PICARDES. 1957. irreg. (Societe d'Emulation Historique et Litteraire d'Abbeville) Editions A. et J. Picard, 82 Rue Bonaparte, 75006 Paris, France.

944   FR
ETUDES SAVOISIENNES. no.2, 1975. irreg. 100 F. Institut d'Etudes Savoisiennes, Centre Universitaire de Savoie, B.P. 143, 73000 Chambery, France. (Co-Sponsor: Societe Savoisienne d'Histoire et d'Archeologie) Dir. Jacques Lovie. bibl. illus.

940   NE
EUROPE IN THE MIDDLE AGES; selected studies. (Text in English) 1977. irreg. price varies. North-Holland Publishing Co., Box 211, Amsterdam, Netherlands. Ed. Richard Vaughan.

940   FR   ISSN 0071-3155
EUROPINION;* revue annuelle. 1965. a. 2 rue Michel Ange, Paris 16e, France.

948   DK   ISSN 0085-0365
EXCERPTA HISTORICA NORDICA. 1955. irreg, no. 8, 1975. Kr.50. Gyldendalske Boghandel - Nordisk Forlag A-S, Klareboderne 3, DK-1001 Copenhagen K, Denmark.

940   PL   ISSN 0071-4038
FASCICULI HISTORICI. (Text in English, French, German and Russian) 1968. irreg., vol. 7, 1974. price varies. Uniwersytet Warszawski, Instytut Historyczny, Krakowskie Przedmiescie 26/28, Warsaw, Poland (Dist. by: Ars Polona-Ruch, Krakowskie Przedmiescie 7, Warsaw, Poland) Ed. Aleksander Gieysztor. circ. 500.

FIGURA. NOVA SERIES; Uppsala studies in the history of art. see *ART*

949   BE   ISSN 0069-5386
FIGURES DE WALLONIE. Alternate title: Institute Jules Destree. Collection: Figures de Wallonie. irreg., latest F 15. price varies. Institut Jules Destree, Rue du Chateau 3, 6100 Mont-sur Marchienne Charleroi, Belgium.

947.1   FI   ISSN 0356-827X
FINLAND; books and publications in politics, political history and international relations. (Text in English) 1965. a. Turun Yliopisto, Poliittisen Historian Laitos, SF-20500 Turku 50, Finland. bk. rev. circ. 3,000.

322 323   GE
FIRST HAND INFORMATION. (Text in English) irreg. Panorama DDR - Auslandspresseagentur GmbH, Wilhelm Pieck Str. 49, 1054 Berlin, E. Germany (D.D.R.) illus.

942   UK   ISSN 0140-8429
FLINTSHIRE HISTORICAL SOCIETY. PUBLICATIONS, JOURNAL AND RECORD SERIES. 1909. biennial. membership. ‡ Flintshire Historical Society, 50, Hafod Park, Mold, Clwyd CH7 1QW, Wales. Ed. Prof. J. Gwynn Williams. bk. rev. circ. 750.

947   300   US
FLORIDA STATE UNIVERSITY. CENTER FOR YUGOSLAV-AMERICAN STUDIES, RESEARCH, AND EXCHANGES. PROCEEDINGS AND REPORTS OF SEMINARS AND RESEARCH. 1967. a. $4. Florida State University, Center for Yugoslav-American Studies, Research, and Exchanges, 930 W. Park Ave., Tallahassee, FL 32306. Ed. George Macesich.
Formerly: Florida State University. Slavic Papers (ISSN 0430-7291)

940   HU   ISSN 0133-6622
FOLIA HISTORICA. 1972. a. exchange basis. Magyar Nemzeti Muzeum, Muzeum-krt. 14-16, 1370 Budapest 8, Hungary. Ed. Ferenc Fulep. illus. circ. 700.

FONTES ARCHAEOLOGICI POSNANIENSES/ ANNALES MUSEI ARCHAEOLOGICI POSNANIENSIS. see *ARCHAEOLOGY*

943   AU   ISSN 0071-6871
FONTES RERUM AUSTRIACARUM. REIHE 1. SCRIPTORES. (Text in German and Latin) 1855. irreg. price varies. (Oesterreichische Akademie der Wissenschaften, Historische Kommission) Verlag der Oesterreichischen Akademie der Wissenschaften, Dr. Ignaz Seipel-Platz 2, A-1010 Vienna, Austria.

943   AU   ISSN 0071-688X
FONTES RERUM AUSTRIACARUM. REIHE 2. DIPLOMATARIA ET ACTA. (Text in German and Latin) 1849. irreg. price varies. (Oesterreichische Akademie der Wissenschaften, Historische Kommission) Verlag der Oesterreichischen Akademie der Wissenschaften, Dr. Ignaz Seipel-Platz 2, A-1010 Vienna, Austria.

943   340   AU   ISSN 0071-6898
FONTES RERUM AUSTRIACARUM. REIHE 3. FONTES JURIS. (Text in German and Latin) 1953. irreg. price varies. (Oesterreichische Akademie der Wissenschaften, Historische Kommission) Verlag der Oesterreichischen Akademie der Wissenschaften, Ignaz Seipelplatz 2, A-1010 Vienna, Austria.

FONTI E STUDI PER LA STORIA DI BOLOGNA E DELLE PROVINCE EMILIANE E ROMAGNOLE. see *ART*

945   IT   ISSN 0071-6901
FONTI SUI COMUNI RURALI TOSCANI. 1962. irreg., 1970, no. 7. price varies. (Deputazione di Storia Patria, Florence) Casa Editrice Leo S. Olschki, Casella Postale 66, 50100 Florence, Italy. Ed. Niccolo Rodolico. circ. 500.

948.1   NO   ISSN 0071-7436
FORENINGEN TIL NORSKE FORTIDSMINNESMERKERS BEVARING. AARBOK. (Text in English and Norwegian) 1845. a. Kr.90. Foreningen til Norske Fortidsminnesmerkers Bevaring, Dronningsgt. 11, Oslo 1, Norway.

940   GE   ISSN 0071-7673
FORSCHUNGEN ZUR MITTELALTERLICHEN GESCHICHTE. 1956. irreg., vol. 23, 1975. price varies. Akademie-Verlag, Leipziger Strasse 3-4, 108 Berlin, E. Germany (D.D.R.)

940   956   UK
FOUNDATIONS OF MEDIEVAL HISTORY. 1979. irreg. price varies. Edward Arnold(Publishers) Ltd., 41 Bedford Square, London WC1B 3DQ, England. Ed. M.T. Clanchy.

948   DK   ISSN 0085-0845
FRA ALS OG SUNDEVED. 1928. irreg., no. 56, 1978. price varies. Historisk Samfund for Als og Sundeved, Soenderborg Slot, DK-6400 Soenderborg, Denmark. Ed. Y. Slettebo. illus. circ. 1,500-2,000.
Local

948   DK
FRA HOLBACK AMT: HISTORISKE AARBOEGER. 1907. a. Kr.40($6) Historisk Samfund for Holbaek Amt, Museet for Holbaek og Omegn, Klosterstraede 14-16, 4300 Holbaek, Denmark. Ed.Ove Bruun Joergensen. adv. bk. rev. charts. illus. circ. 500.
Local

948   DK   ISSN 0085-0853
FRA VIBORG AMT. AARBOG. 1929. a. Kr.45. Historisk Samfund for Viborg Amt, Landsarkivet, 8800 Viborg, Denmark. Ed. Paul G. Oerberg. adv. bk. rev.
Local

944   FR   ISSN 0071-819X
FRANCE. ARCHIVES NATIONALES. CENTRE D'INFORMATION DE LA RECHERCHE HISTORIQUE EN FRANCE. BULLETIN. 1953. a. Archives Nationales, Services de Renseignements, 60 rue des Francs-Bourgeois, Paris 3e, France. index.

944   440   FR   ISSN 0071-8408
FRANCE. COMITE DES TRAVAUX HISTORIQUES ET SCIENTIFIQUES. BULLETIN PHILOLOGIQUE ET HISTORIQUE (JUSQU'A 1610) 1960. irreg., latest 1977. price varies. Bibliotheque Nationale, 58 rue Richelieu, 75084 Paris Cedex 02, France. cum.index: 1882-1915. circ. 650.
Formerly: France. Comite des Travaux Historiques et Scientifiques. Bulletin Philologique (Jusqu'a 1715) (ISSN 0399-5569)

940   FR   ISSN 0071-8440
FRANCE. COMITE DES TRAVAUX HISTORIQUES ET SCIENTIFIQUES. SECTION D'HISTOIRE MODERNE ET CONTEMPORAINE. ACTES DU CONGRES NATIONAL DES SOCIETES SAVANTES. 1951. a. price varies. Bibliotheque Nationale, 58 rue Richelieu, 75084 Paris Cedex 02, France. cum.index: 1950-60. circ. 650.

944   FR   ISSN 0071-8459
FRANCE. COMITE DES TRAVAUX HISTORIQUES ET SCIENTIFIQUES. SECTION D'HISTOIRE MODERNE ET CONTEMPORAINE. BULLETIN. 1965. irreg., 1978 no. 11. price varies. Bibliotheque Nationale, 58 rue Richelieu, 75084 Paris Cedex 02, France. cum.index: 1956-60. circ. 650. (back issues available)
Formerly: France. Comite des Travaux Historiques et Scientifiques. Section d'Histoire Moderne et Contemporaine (Depuis 1610). Bulletin (ISSN 0399-9726)

944   FR
FRANCE. COMMISSION DEPARTEMENTALE DES MONUMENTS HISTORIQUES DU PAS DE CALAIS. BULLETIN. 1849; N.S. 1889. a. Commission Departementale des Monuments Historiques du Pas de Calais, Archives Departementales, Prefecture du Pas de Calais, 62020 Arras Cedex, France.
Local

944   FR
FRANCE. COMMISSION DEPARTEMENTALE DES MONUMENTS HISTORIQUES DU PAS DE CALAIS. MEMOIRES. irreg., no. 20, 1979-1980. price varies. Commission Departementale des Monuments Historiques du Pas de Calais, Archives Departementales, Prefecture du Pas de Calais, 62020 Arras Cedex, France.
Local

940   FR   ISSN 0082-5417
FRANCE-IBERIE RECHERCHE. THESES ET DOCUMENTS. 1970. irreg. price varies. Universite de Toulouse II (le Mirail), Institut d'Etudes Hispaniques, Hispanoamericaines, 109 bis, rue Vauquelin, 31081 Toulouse Cedex, France.

940   GW
FRANKFURTER ALTHISTORISCHE STUDIEN. 1968. irreg. price varies. (Universitaet Frankfurt, Seminar fuer Alte Geschichte) Verlag Michael Lassleben, Lange Gasse 19, Postfach 8, 8411 Kallmuenz, W. Germany (B. R. D.) Eds. Jochen Bleicken, Helga Gesche.

942 UK
FREEMEN. 1908. a. membership. ‡ Guild of Freemen of the City of London, 40a Ludgate Hill, London EC4M 7DE, England. Ed. C. R. Coward. circ. 3,000.

FREIE UNIVERSITAET BERLIN. OSTEUROPA-INSTITUT. BERICHTE. see *HUMANITIES: COMPREHENSIVE WORKS*

947 GW ISSN 0067-5903
FREIE UNIVERSITAET BERLIN. OSTEUROPA-INSTITUT. HISTORISCHE VEROEFFENTLICHUNGEN; Forschungen zur Osteuropaeischen Geschichte. 1954. irreg., vol. 13, 1980. price varies. Verlag Otto Harrassowitz, Taunusstr. 6, Postfach 2929, 6200 Wiesbaden 1, W. Germany (B.R.D.) Ed. H.-I.Torke.

944 US
FRENCH COLONIAL HISTORICAL SOCIETY. PROCEEDINGS OF THE MEETING. (Text in English and French) 1976. a. University Press of America, 4710 Auth Pl., S.E., Washington, DC 20023. Ed. James J. Cooke. circ. 300.

940 GW ISSN 0071-9706
FRUEHMITTELALTERLICHE STUDIEN; Jahrbuch. 1967. a. price varies. (Universitaet Muenster, Institut fuer Fruehmittelalterforschung) Walter de Gruyter und Co., Genthiner Str. 13, 1000 Berlin 30, W. Germany (B.R.D.) Ed. Karl Hauck. adv. bk. rev.

948 DK ISSN 0085-0918
FYNSKE AARBOEGER. 1939. a. Kr.35. Historisk Samfund for Fyns Stift, c/o H. H. Jacobsen, Ed., Nyvej 71, Ulboelle, DK-5762 V. Skerninge, Denmark. bk. rev.
Local

948.1 NO
GAULDALSMINNE; arbok for bygdehistorie og folkeminne. irreg. Kr.30. Gauldal Historielag, c/o Jens Haukdal, 7450 Soknedal, Norway.

943.8 913 PL ISSN 0072-0410
GDANSKIE TOWARZYSTWO NAUKOWE. WYDZIAL I. NAUK SPOLECZNYCH I HUMANISTYCZNYCH. KOMISJA ARCHEOLOGICZNA. PRACE. (Text in Polish; summaries in English and German) 1959. irreg., no. 9, 1977. price varies. (Gdanskie Towarzystwo Naukowe) Ossolineum, Publishing House of the Polish Academy of Sciences, Rynek 9, Wroclaw, Poland (Dist. by Ars Polona-Ruch, Krakowskie Przedmiescie 7, Warsaw, Poland) Ed. Bd. charts. illus. circ. 500.

943.8 PL ISSN 0433-230X
GDANSKIE TOWARZYSTWO NAUKOWE. WYDZIAL I. NAUK SPOLECZNYCH I HUMANISTYCZNYCH. SERIA MONOGRAFII. 1959. irreg., no. 70, 1979. price varies. (Gdanskie Towarzystwo Naukowe) Ossolineum, Publishing House of the Polish Academy of Sciences, Rynek 9, Wroclaw, Poland (Dist. by: Ars Polona-Ruch, Krakowskie Przedmiescie 7, Warsaw, Poland) Ed. Bd. bibl. illus. circ. 1,500.

943.8 PL ISSN 0072-0429
GDANSKIE TOWARZYSTWO NAUKOWE. WYDZIAL I. NAUK SPOLECZNYCH I HUMANISTYCZNYCH. SERIA POPULARNONAUKOWA "POMORZE GDANSKIE". 1965. irreg., no. 12, 1979. price varies. (Gdanskie Towarzystwo Naukowe) Ossolineum, Publishing House of the Polish Academy of Sciences, Rynek 9, Wroclaw, Poland (Dist. by Ars Polona-Ruch, Krakowskie Przedmiescie 7, Warsaw, Poland) Ed. Z. Ciesielski. circ. 740.

943.8 PL ISSN 0072-0437
GDANSKIE TOWARZYSTWO NAUKOWE. WYDZIAL I. NAUK SPOLECZNYCH I HUMANISTYCZNYCH. SERIA ZRODEL. irreg., 1976, no. 10. (Gdanskie Towarzystwo Naukowe) Ossolineum, Publishing House of the Polish Academy of Sciences, Rynek 9, Wroclaw, Poland (Dist. by Ars Polona-Ruch, Krakowskie Przedmiescie 7, Warsaw, Poland) Ed. Z. Binerowski. circ. 600.

940 NE
GENOOTSCHAP AMSTELODAMUM. JAARBOEK. 1902. a. fl.35 includes the Jaarboek and six bimonthly issues. De Bussy, Eilerman Harms N. V., Warmoesstraat 151, Amsterdam, Netherlands. Ed. J.H.A. Ringeling. bibl. illus.

943 GW ISSN 0072-4203
GESCHICHTLICHE LANDESKUNDE. 1964. irreg., vol. 21, 1981. price varies. (Universitaet Mainz, Institut fuer Geschichtliche Landeskunde) Franz Steiner Verlag GmbH, Friedrichstr. 24, Postfach 5529, 6200 Wiesbaden, W. Germany (B.R.D.) Ed. Bd. (back issues avail.)

941 UK
GLAMORGAN COUNTY HISTORY SERIES. 1971. irreg. price varies. Glamorgan County History Trust Ltd., Dept. of History, University College of Swansea, Singleton Park, Swansea SA2 8PP, Wales. Ed. Glanmor Williams.

949 YU
GLASNIK ARHIVA I DRUSTAVA ARHIVSKIH RADNIKA BOSNE I HERCEGOVINE. 1961. a. price varies. Arhiv, Save Kovacevica 6, 71000 Sarajevo, Yugoslavia. Ed. Bozo Madzar. bk. rev. circ. 350.

943 GW ISSN 0072-4882
GOETTINGER JAHRBUCH. 1952. a. price varies. (Geschichtsverein fuer Goettingen und Umgebung) Reise Verlag, Hanssenstr. 24, Postfach 359, 3400 Goettingen, W. Germany (B.R.D.) Ed. W. Roehrbein.

940 FR ISSN 0072-5404
GRANDES FIGURES DE LA CHARITE.* 1970. irreg. price varies. Editions S.O.S., 106 rue du Bac, 75007 Paris, France.

942 UK ISSN 0072-5722
GREAT BRITAIN. CENTRAL OFFICE OF INFORMATION. REFERENCE DIVISION. REFERENCE PAMPHLETS. 1955. irreg. price varies. Central Office of Information, Reference Division, Hercules Rd., London SE1 7DU, England (Avail. from H.M.S.O., c/o Liaison Officer, Atlantic House, Holborn Viaduct, London EC1P 1BN, England)

GREAT BRITAIN. DEPARTMENT OF THE ENVIRONMENT. ARCHAEOLOGICAL REPORTS. see *ARCHAEOLOGY*

942 020 UK ISSN 0072-6516
GREAT BRITAIN. KEEPER OF PUBLIC RECORDS. ANNUAL REPORT OF THE KEEPER OF PUBLIC RECORDS ON THE WORK OF THE PUBLIC RECORD OFFICE AND THE REPORT OF THE ADVISORY COUNCIL ON PUBLIC RECORDS. 1959. a. price varies. H.M.S.O., Atlantic House, Holborn Viaduct, London EC1P 1BN, England.

942 571 UK ISSN 0072-7067
GREAT BRITAIN. ROYAL COMMISSION ON THE ANCIENT AND HISTORICAL MONUMENTS AND CONSTRUCTIONS OF ENGLAND. INTERIM REPORT. irreg., 34th, 1977. price varies. Royal Commission on the Ancient and Historical Monuments and Constructions of England, Fortress House, 23 Saville Row, London W.1, England (Avail. from H.M.S.O., c/o Liaison Officer, Atlantic House, Holborn Viaduct, London EC1P 1BN, England)

942 571 UK ISSN 0072-7075
GREAT BRITAIN. ROYAL COMMISSION ON THE ANCIENT AND HISTORICAL MONUMENTS AND CONSTRUCTIONS OF WALES AND MONMOUTHSHIRE. INTERIM REPORT. irreg. price varies. Royal Commission on the Ancient and Historical Monuments and Constructions of Wales and Monmouthshire, Edleston House, Queens Rd., Aberystwyth, Wales (Avail. from H.M.S.O., c/o Liaison Officer, Atlantic House, Holborn Viaduct, London EC1P 1BN, England)

940 GE
GREIFSWALD-STRALSUNDER JAHRBUCH. 1955. irreg., vol. 12, 1979. price varies. (Kulturhistorisches Museum Stralsund) Herman Boehlaus Nachfolger, Meyerstr. 50a, 53 Weimar, E. Germany (D.D.R.)

949.4 SZ ISSN 0072-7725
GROSSE HEIMATBUECHER. (Text in German, English, French) 1965. irreg. 58 Fr. Paul Haupt AG, Falkenplatz 14, CH-3001 Berne, Switzerland.

944 914 FR
GWECHALL. a. 50 F. (to non-members) Societe Finisterienne d'Histoire et d'Archeologie, 4 rue du Palais, Quimper, France.

942 UK ISSN 0306-3151
GWYNEDD ARCHIVES SERVICE. BULLETIN. (Text in English and Welsh) no. 4, 1980. irreg. £1. Gwynedd Archives Service, Gwynedd County Council, Caernarfon, Gwynedd LL55 1SH, Wales.

HAMPSHIRE FIELD CLUB AND ARCHAEOLOGICAL SOCIETY PROCEEDINGS. see *ARCHAEOLOGY*

940 GW ISSN 0073-0327
HANSISCHE GESCHICHTSBLAETTER. 1882. a. price varies. (Hansischer Geschichtsverein) Boehlau Verlag GmbH, Niehler Str. 272-274, 5000 Cologne 60, W. Germany (B.R.D.) Ed. P. Johansen.

948 DK ISSN 0046-6840
HARDSYSSELS AARBOG. 1907; N.S. 1967. a. Kr.45 for members; Kr. 60 for non-members. Historisk Samfund for Ringkoebing Amt, c/o Kr. Bjerregaard, Holstebro Bibliotek, 7500 Holstebro, Denmark. Ed. Knut Erik Nielsen. bk. rev. bibl. illus. index, cum. index 1907-1966. circ. 2,000.
Local

940 US ISSN 0073-0459
HARVARD ARMENIAN TEXTS AND STUDIES. 1965. irreg., 1970, no. 3. price varies. Harvard University Press, 79 Garden St., Cambridge, MA 02138. Ed. Avedis K. Sanjian.

947 491.8 891.8 US
HARVARD SLAVIC MONOGRAPHS. 1975. irreg. price varies. Harvard University Press, 79 Garden St., Cambridge, MA 02138.

947 US ISSN 0073-0831
HARVARD UNIVERSITY. RUSSIAN RESEARCH CENTER. RUSSIAN RESEARCH CENTER STUDIES. (Text in English; one vol. in Russian) 1950. irreg., no. 74, 1974. price varies. Harvard University Press, 79 Garden St., Cambridge, MA 02138.

943 GW ISSN 0073-0882
HARZ-ZEITSCHRIFT. 1868. N.S. 1948. a. DM.24. Harzverein fuer Geschichte und Altertumskunde, Zehnstr. 24, 3380 Goslar /Hartz, W. Germany (B.R.D.) (Affiliate: Braunschweigisches Landesmuseum fuer Geschichte und Volkstum) Ed. K. W. Sanders.

940 SZ ISSN 0073-0955
HAUTES ETUDES MEDIEVALES ET MODERNES. 1964. irreg. price varies. (Ecole Pratique des Hautes Etudes, Centre de Recherches d'Histoire et de Philologie, FR) Libraire Droz, 11, rue Massot, 1211 Geneva 12, Switzerland. circ. 1,000.

947.5 GW ISSN 0440-6230
HEIMATGRUSS. 1956. a. DM.4.50. Landsmannschaft der Deutschen aus Litauen, c/o Alfred Franzkeit and Edith Kunfert, Eds. & Pubs., 2839 Freistatt, W. Germany (B.R.D.) circ. 2,000.

943 GW
HEIMATKUNDLICHES JAHRBUCH FUER DEN KREIS SEGEBERG. 1955. a. DM.19.80. (Heimatverein des Kreises Segeberg) Verlag C. H. Waeser, Lindenstr. 24b, 2360 Bad Segeberg, W. Germany (B.R.D.) Ed. Horst Tschentscher. bk. rev. bibl. illus. circ. 1,200.

943 GW ISSN 0073-196X
HERFORDER JAHRBUCH; BEITRAEGE ZUR GESCHICHTE DER STADT UND DES STIFTES HERFORD. 1960. a. DM.124. (Herforder Verein fuer Heimatkunde) Maximilian Verlag, Steintorwall 17, Postfach 371, 4900 Herford, W. Germany (B.R.D.)

943 331.88 GW
HESSISCHE BEITRAEGE ZUR GESCHICHTE DER ARBEITERBEWEGUNG. irreg. price varies. Historischer Verein fuer Hessen, Staatsarchiv, Schloss, 6100 Darmstadt, W. Germany (B.R.D.)

943 GW ISSN 0073-2001
HESSISCHES JAHRBUCH FUER
LANDESGESCHICHTE. 1951. a. price varies.
Hessisches Landesamt fuer Geschichtliche
Landeskunde, Krummbogen 28c, 3550 Marburg, W.
Germany (B.R.D.) bk. rev.

944 FR
HISTOIRE ET THEORIE. irreg. price varies. Editions
Syros, 1 rue de Varenne, 75006 Paris, France.

HISTORIA ARCHAEOLOGICA. see
ARCHAEOLOGY

946 SP
HISTORIA GRAFICA DE CATALUNYA DIA A
DIA. 1978. a. Edicions 62, Provença 278,
Barcelona-8, Spain.

947.1 FI ISSN 0073-2540
HISTORIALLINEN ARKISTO. (Text in Finnish or
Swedish; summaries in English or German) 1866.
irreg., no. 74, 1978. price varies. Suomen
Historiallinen Seura - Finnish Historical Society,
Snellmaninkatu 9-11, 00170 Helsinki 17, Finland.
cum.index: nos. 1-50(1886-1944) circ. 350.

947.1 FI ISSN 0073-2559
HISTORIALLISIA TUTKIMUKSIA. (Text in Finnish:
summaries in English or German) 1918/1920. irreg.,
no. 108, 1978. price varies. Suomen Historiallinen
Seura - Finnish Historical Society, Snellmaninkatu
9-11, 00170 Helsinki 17, Finland. circ. 300.

940 US
HISTORIANS OF EARLY MODERN EUROPE.
NEWSLETTER. a. Historians of Early Modern
Europe, c/o Robert V. Schnucker, Ed., 115
Laughlin Bldg., Northeast Missouri State University,
MO 03501. (Co-sponsor: American Society for
Reformation Research) circ. 500.
    Incorporating: American Society for Reformation
Research. Newsletter.

942 UK
HISTORIC HOUSES, CASTLES AND GARDENS
IN GREAT BRITAIN AND IRELAND. 1952. a.
£1.40. A B C Historic Publications, Oldhill, London
Rd., Dunstable, Bedfordshire LU6 3EB, England.
adv. circ. 112,000.
    Formerly: Historic Houses, Castles and Gardens
(ISSN 0073-2567)

942 UK ISSN 0140-332X
HISTORIC SOCIETY OF LANCASHIRE AND
CHESHIRE. TRANSACTIONS. 1848. a.
membership. ‡ Historic Society of Lancashire and
Cheshire, School of History, University of
Liverpool, P.O. Box 147, Liverpool L69 3BX,
England (Subscr. to: Hon. Sec. P. Andrews, 15
Woodley Fold, Penketh, Warrington WA5 2JB,
England) Eds. Dr. C. B. Phillips, Mrs. J. I. Kernode.
bk. rev. charts. illus. index; cum.index. circ. 600.

HISTORICA CARPATICA. see POLITICAL
SCIENCE

HISTORICAL ASSOCIATION, LONDON. AIDS
FOR TEACHERS. see EDUCATION — Teaching
Methods And Curriculum

HISTORICAL SOCIETY OF THE CHURCH IN
WALES. JOURNAL. see RELIGIONS AND
THEOLOGY — Protestant

HISTORICAL SOCIETY OF THE PRESBYTERIAN
CHURCH OF WALES. JOURNAL. see
RELIGIONS AND THEOLOGY — Protestant

943.7 CS ISSN 0440-9515
HISTORICKE STUDIE. (Text in Slovak; summaries
in German and Russian) irreg., vol. 22, 1977. fl.35
per no. (Slovenska Akademia Vied, Historicky
Ustav) Veda, Publishing House of the Slovak
Academy of Sciences, Klemensova 19, 895 30
Bratislava, Czechoslovakia (Distributor in Western
Countries: John Benjamins B.V., Amsteldijk 44,
Amsterdam (Z.), Netherlands) Ed. Vladimir Matula.

949 NE
HISTORISCH JAARBOEK VLAARDINGEN. 1977.
a. $17. (Historische Vereniging Vlaardingen)
Uitgeverij De Draak, Vlaardingen, Netherlands. circ.
1,200.
    Supersedes: Historische Verenigning Vlaardingen.
Tijdschrift.

943 GW
HISTORISCHE STUDIEN. irreg., vol. 432, 1978.
price varies. Matthiessen Verlag GmbH,
Nordbahnhofstr. 2, 2250 Husum, W. Germany
(B.R.D.) Ed. Wilhelm Berges.

943 GW ISSN 0073-2680
HISTORISCHER VEREIN DER PFALZ.
MITTEILUNGEN. 1870. a. price varies.
Historischer Verein der Pfalz, Gr. Pfaffengasse 7,
6720 Speyer, W. Germany (B.R.D.) Ed. Otto
Roller.

949.4 SZ
HISTORISCHER VEREIN DES KANTONS BERN.
ARCHIV. 1848. a. Historischer Verein des Kantons
Bern, Stadt- und Universitaetsbibliothek,
Muenstergasse 61, CH-3000 Berne 7, Switzerland.
charts. illus. cum. index (vol. 1-38; vol. 39-55) circ.
1,700.

949 SZ
HISTORISCHER VEREIN DES KANTONS ST.
GALLEN. NEUJAHRSBLAETT. 1861. a. price
varies. ‡ Verlag Fehr'sche Buchhandlung,
Schmiedgasse 16, 9001 St. Gallen, Switzerland. Ed.
Bd. bibl. illus. circ. 300.

943 GW ISSN 0073-2699
HISTORISCHER VEREIN DILLINGEN AN DER
DONAU. JAHRBUCH. 1888. a. price varies.
Historischer Verein Dillingen an der Donau,
Oertelstr. 10, 8880 Dillingen, W. Germany (B.R.D)
Ed. Adolf Layer. bk. rev. circ. 1,000.

943.6 AU ISSN 0440-9736
HISTORISCHES JAHRBUCH DER STADT LINZ.
1935. a. S.300. Archiv der Stadt Linz, Hauptplatz 1,
Rathaus, A-4010 Linz, Austria. Eds. Fritz
Mayrhofer, Willibald Katzinger. bk. rev. cum.index.

948 DK ISSN 0046-7588
HISTORISK AARBOG FOR SKIVE OG OMEGN.
1909. a. Kr.15. Historisk Samfund for Skive og
Omegn, Folkebiblioteket, Skive, Denmark. Eds.
Otto L. Sorensen, Johs. Bang, Sv. Mortensen.
Local

940 DK
HISTORISKE MEDDELELSER OM
KOEBENHAVN. 1907. a. Kr.40. Stadsarkiv,
Raadhuset, DK-1599 Copenhagen V, Denmark
(Subscr. to: G.E.C. Gad, Vimmelskaftet 32, DK-
1161 Copenhagen K, Denmark) Ed. Helle Linde.
bk. rev. bibl. illus. cum. index (every 4 yrs.) circ.
1,450. (back issues avail.)
Local

948.1 NO ISSN 0105-7154
HISTORISKE STUDIER FRA FYN. 1977. irreg. (1-
2/yr.) price varies. (Historisk Samfund for Fyns
Stift) Landsarkivet for Fyn, Jernbanegade 36, DK-
5000 Odense C, Denmark. Ed. Anne Riising. circ.
200. (back issues avail.)
Local

HISTORY OF UNIVERSITIES. see
EDUCATION — Higher Education

940 PL ISSN 0073-277X
HISTORYKA; STUDIA METODOLOGICZNE.
(Text in Polish; summaries in English, French and
Russian) 1967. a. 30 Zl. per volume. (Polska
Akademia Nauk, Oddzial w Krakowie, Komisja
Nauk Historycznych) Ossolineum, Publishing House
of the Polish Academy of Sciences, Rynek 9,
Wroclaw, Poland (Dist. by: Ars Polona-Ruch,
Krakowskie Przedmiescie 7, Warsaw, Poland) Ed.
Celina Bobinska. bk. rev.

942 UK
HORNSEY HISTORICAL SOCIETY.
OCCASIONAL PAPERS. 1976. N.S. 1978. irreg.
Hornsey Historical Society, 16 Barnard Hill,
London N.10, England.

IBSEN AARBOKEN/IBSEN YEARBOOK. see
LITERATURE

946 SP
INSTITUCION PRINCIPE DE VIANA.
COLECCION HISTORIA. no. 3, 1974. irreg. 350
ptas. Diputacion Foral de Navarra, Institucion
Principe de Viana, Avda. Carlos III, 2, Pamplona,
Spain.

943 FR ISSN 0079-0001
INSTITUT D'ETUDES SLAVES, PARIS.
COLLECTION HISTORIQUE. 1920. irreg., vol.
27, 1980. price varies. Institut d'Etudes Slaves, 9
rue Michelet, F-75006 Paris, France.

INSTITUT D'ETUDES SLAVES, PARIS.
TRAVAUX. see LITERATURE

949 BE ISSN 0073-8522
INSTITUT HISTORIQUE BELGE DE ROME.
BIBLIOTHEQUE. 1949. irreg. price varies. Institut
Historique Belge de Rome, c/oArchives Generales
du Royaume, 2-6 rue de Ruysbroeck, B-1000
Brussels, Belgium.

949 BE ISSN 0073-8530
INSTITUT HISTORIQUE BELGE DE ROME.
BULLETIN. (Text in French or Italian) 1919. a.
price varies. Institut Historique Belge de Rome, c/o
Archives Generales du Royaume, 2-6 rue de
Ruysbroeck, B-1000 Brussels, Belgium. circ.
controlled.

949 BE ISSN 0073-8557
INSTITUT JULES DESTREE. ETUDES ET
DOCUMENTS. Alternate title: Institut Jules
Destree. Collection: Etudes et Documents. irreg.,
latest E 15. price varies. Institut Jules Destree, Rue
du Chateau 3, 6100 Mont-sur-Marchienne
Charleroi, Belgium.

945 GR ISSN 0073-862X
INSTITUTE FOR BALKAN STUDIES.
PUBLICATIONS/IDRYMA MELETON
CHERSONESOU AIMOU. EKTHOSEIS. (Text in
English, French, German and Greek) 1953. irreg.,
no. 171, 1977. price varies. Institute for Balkan
Studies, 45 Tsimiski St., Thessaloniki, Greece. Ed.
Prof. K. Mitsakis.

946.73 SP ISSN 0534-3364
INSTITUTO DE ESTUDIOS TARRACONENSES
RAMON BERENGUER IV. PUBLICACION.
1952. irreg. Instituto de Estudios Tarraconenses
Ramon Berenguer IV, Diputacion Provincial de
Tarragona, Calle Santa Ana 8, Tarragona, Spain.
bibl. illus.

946 SP
INSTITUTO PROVINCIAL DE
INVESTIGACIONES Y ESTUDIOS
TOLEDANOS. PUBLICACIONES. no. 4, 1976.
irreg. Instituto Provincial de Investigaciones y
Estudios Toledanos, Servicios Culturales, Diputacion
Provincial de Toledo, Plaza de la Merced 4, Toledo,
Spain.

INSTITUTUL DE ISTORIE SI ARHEOLOGIE "A.
D. XENOPOL". ANUARUL. see
ARCHAEOLOGY

943 PL ISSN 0074-0616
INSTYTUT SLASKI. KOMMUNIKATY. SERIA
NIEMCOZNAWCZA. (Text in Polish, occasionally
in English) 1961. irreg. price varies. Instytut Slaski,
Instytut Naukowo-Badawczy, Ul. Luboszycka 3, 45-
036 Opole, Poland (Dist. by Ars Polona,
Krakowskie Przedmiescie 7, Warsaw, Poland) index.

943.8 PL ISSN 0074-0632
INSTYTUT SLASKI. WYDAWNICTWA. 1958. irreg.
price varies. Instytut Slaski, Instytut Naukowo-
Badawczy, Ul. Luboszycka 3, 45-036 Opole, Poland
(Distributed by: Ars Polona-Ruch, Krakowskie
Przedmiescie 7, Warsaw, Poland)

949.5 GR ISSN 0571-5857
INTERNATIONAL ASSOCIATION FOR
BYZANTINE STUDIES. BULLETIN
D'INFORMATION ET DE COORDINATION.
1964. irreg. International Association for Byzantine
Studies, c/o D. A. Zakythinos, Pres., Rue Sissini 31,
Athens 612, Greece. Ed. Helene Ahrweiler. circ.
1,000.

940 CN
INTERUNIVERSITY CENTRE FOR EUROPEAN
STUDIES. INTERNATIONAL COLLOQUIUM
PROCEEDINGS. 1974. irreg. Can.$8.50.
Interuniversity Centre for European Studies, Box
8892, Montreal, Quebec H3C 3P8, Canada. Ed.
Frederick Krantz.

949.3 BE
INVENTAIRE DES ARCHIVES HISTORIQUES/ INVENTARIS VAN HET HISTORISCH ARCHIEF. 1961. irreg., no. 7, 1977. price varies. Musee Royal de l'Afrique Centrale, 13 Steenweg op Leuven, B-1980 Tervuren, Belgium. illus.

949.2 BE ISSN 0075-0166
INVENTARIS VAN HET KUNSTPATRIMONIUM VAN OOST-VLAANDEREN. 1951. irreg., no. 10, 1979. price varies. Kunstpatrimonium, Bisdomplein 3, 9000 Ghent, Belgium. index.

946 SP
INVESTIGACIONES HISTORICAS. 1975. irreg. Universidad de Valladolid, Valladolid, Spain. circ. 500.
Formerly (until 1979): Cuadernas Simancas de Investigaciones Historicas. Monografias.

941 300 UK
IRISH ECONOMIC AND SOCIAL HISTORY. 1974. a. $20. Economic and Social History Society of Ireland, c/o Hon. Treasurer, 66 Balmoral Ave., Belfast BT9 6NY, N. Ireland. Eds. D. Dickson, P. Roebuck. adv. bk. rev. abstr. bibl. stat. circ. 550. (back issues avail.)

949.5 IT ISSN 0075-1545
ISTITUTO SICILIANO DI STUDI BIZANTINI E NEOELLENICI. QUADERNI. 1965. irreg., no. 10, 1978. price varies. Istituto Siciliano di Studi Bizantini e Neoellenici, Via Noto, 34, 90141 Palermo, Italy.

949.5 880 IT ISSN 0075-1553
ISTITUTO SICILIANO DI STUDI BIZANTINI E NEOELLENICI. TESTI E MONUMENTI. TESTI. 1954. irreg., 1976, no. 12. price varies. Istituto Siciliano di Studi Bizantini e Neoellenici, Via Noto, 34, 90141 Palermo, Italy.

940 IT ISSN 0085-2287
ISTITUTO STORICO ARTISTICO ORVIETANO. BOLLETTINO. 1945. a. L.5000 (free to institutions) Istituto Storico Artistico Orvietano, Piazza Febei N.1, Orvieto 05018, Italy. Dir. Franco Crisanti. adv. circ. controlled.

945 323 IT ISSN 0075-1561
ISTITUTO STORICO DELLA RESISTENZA IN MODENA E PROVINCIA. QUADERNI. 1960. irreg. price varies. Istituto Storico della Resistenza, Via. C. Battisti, 12, 41100 Modena, Italy. Ed. Ennio Pacchioni.

907 947 UR
ISTOCHNIKOVEDENIE OTECHESTVENNOI ISTORII. 1973. irreg. 1.92 Rub. (Akademiya Nauk S.S.S.R., Sektor Istochnikovedeniya i Vspomogatel'nykh Istoricheskikh Distsiplin) Izdatel'stvo Nauka, Podsosenskii per., 21, Moscow K-62, U. S. S. R. bibl.

ITALIAN GENEALOGIST. see GENEALOGY AND HERALDRY

940 BU
IZSLEDOVANIIA PO BULGARSKA ISTORIIA. 1976. irreg. 3 lv. per issue. (Bulgarska Akademiia na Naukite, Institut za Istoriia) Publishing House of the Bulgarian Academy of Sciences, Ul. Akad. G. Bonchev, 1113 Sofia, Bulgaria. circ. 2,000.

943 GW ISSN 0075-2436
JAHRBUCH DES BALTISCHEN DEUTSCHTUMS. 1952. a. Nordland-Druck, Am Sande 18, Postfach 2343, 3140 Lueneburg, W. Germany (B.R.D.)

943 GW ISSN 0448-150X
JAHRBUCH FUER DEN KREIS PINNEBERG. 1967. a. DM.19.50. (Heimatverband fuer den Kreis Pinneberg) A. Beig Verlag, Damm 11, Postfach 1220, 2080 Pinneberg, W. Germany (B.R.D.) Ed. Mannfred Peters. bk. rev. bibl. illus. circ. 1,000.

940 GE
JAHRBUCH FUER GESCHICHTE DES FEUDALISMUS. vol. 2, 1978. a. 48. (Akademie der Wissenschaften der DDR, Zentralinstitut fuer Geschichte) Akademie-Verlag, Leipziger Strasse 3-4, 108 Berlin, E. Germany (D.D.R.)

940 GE ISSN 0085-2341
JAHRBUCH FUER REGIONALGESCHICHTE. 1965. irreg., vol. 8, 1981. price varies. (Saechsische Akademie der Wissenschaften, Leipzig, Historische Kommission) Hermann Boehlaus Nachfolger, Meyerstr. 50A, 53 Weimar, E. Germany (D.D.R.) bk. rev.

943 GW ISSN 0075-2754
JAHRBUCH FUER SALESIANISCHE STUDIEN. 1963. a. (Arbeitsgemeinschaft fuer Salesianische Studien) Franz-Sales-Verlag, Rosental 1, Abholfach, D-8078 Eichstaett/Bay., W. Germany (B.R.D.) bk. rev.

940 GW ISSN 0170-2025
JAHRBUCH FUER WESTDEUTSCHE LANDESGESCHICHTE. 1975. a. price varies. Landesarchivverwaltung, Karmeliterstr. 1/3, 5400 Koblenz, W. Germany (B.R.D.)

940 GE
JAHRBUCH ZUR GESCHICHTE DRESDENS. (Subseries of the Institute's Informationsdienst) a. M.4. Institut und Museum fuer Geschichte der Stadt Dresden, Ernst-Thaelmann-Str. 2, 801 Dresden A 1, E. Germany (D.D.R.) bk. rev. bibl. illus.

947 UK ISSN 0075-4161
JOURNAL OF BYELORUSSIAN STUDIES. (Text in English, Byelorussian) 1965. a. (£2.50) Anglo-Byelorussian Society, 39 Holden Rd., London N12 8HS, England. Ed. J. Dingley. adv. bk. rev. cum.index: 1965-68, 1969-72. circ. 800.

949.7 US ISSN 0075-4218
JOURNAL OF CROATIAN STUDIES; annual review of the Croatian Academy of America. 1960. a. $12. Croatian Academy of America, Inc., Box 1767 Grand Central Station, New York, NY 10017. Eds. Jerome Jareb And Karlo Mirth. bk. rev. circ. 1,000.

940 MM ISSN 0075-4285
JOURNAL OF MALTESE STUDIES. (Text in Italian, French and English) 1961. irreg. price varies. University of Malta, Department of Maltese and Oriental Languages, Msida, Malta. Ed. J. Aquilina. bk. rev. circ. 400.

947 YU ISSN 0449-3648
JUGOSLAVENSKA AKADEMIJA ZNANOSTI I UMJETNOSTI. HISTORIJSKI INSTITUT, DUBROVNIK. ANALI. (Text in Croatian; summaries in French, English or Other Languages) 1952. a. Jugoslavenska Akademija Znanosti i Umjetnosti, Historijski Institut, Dubrovnik., Yugoslavia. Ed.Bd. illus.

941 UK ISSN 0260-583X
KINGSTON HISTORY SOCIETY. PAPERS. Variant title: Kingston History Society. Annual Papers. 1977. a. membership. Kingston History Society, c/o R. J. Jenkins, 5 Wishlades Row, Kingston, Herefordshire, England.

948.9 DK ISSN 0525-6844
KOEBENHAVNS UNIVERSITET. HISTORISKE INSTITUT. SKRIFTER. 1957. irreg., no. 5, 1975. Koebenhavns Universitet, Historiske Institut, Bispetorvet 3, DK-1167 Copenhagen K, Denmark.

KOELNER ROEMER-ILLUSTRIERTE. see MUSEUMS AND ART GALLERIES

940 309 330 GW
KOELNER VORTRAEGE ZUR SOZIAL- UND WIRTSCHAFTSGESCHICHTE. 1969. irreg., no. 28, 1977. price varies. Universitaet zu Koeln, Forschungsinstitut fuer Sozial- und Wirtschaftsgeschichte, Unter Sachsenhausen 10-26, 5000 Cologne 1, W. Germany (B.R.D.)

943 GW ISSN 0067-2831
KOMMISSION FUER GESCHICHTLICHE LANDESKUNDE IN BADEN-WUERTTEMBERG. VEROEFFENTLICHUNGEN. REIHE A. QUELLEN. 1958. irreg. price varies. Kommission fuer Geschichtliche Landeskunde in Baden-Wuerttemberg, Konrad-Adenauer-Str. 4, 7000 Stuttgart 1, W. Germany (B.R.D.) circ. 500-1,000.

943 GW ISSN 0521-9884
KOMMISSION FUER GESCHICHTLICHE LANDESKUNDE IN BADEN-WUERTTEMBERG. VEROEFFENTLICHUNGEN. REIHE B: FORSCHUNGEN. 1958. irreg. price varies. Kommission fuer Geschichtliche Landeskunde in Baden-Wuerttemberg, Konrad-Adenauer-Str. 4, 7000 Stuttgart 1, W. Germany (B.R.D.) circ. 500-1,000.

943.6 AU
KOMMISSION FUER NEUERE GESCHICHTE OESTERREICHS. VEROEFFENTLICHUNGEN. 1924. irreg., vol. 68, 1979. price varies. Hermann Boehlaus Nachf, Schmalzhofgasse 4, Postfach 167, A-1061 Vienna, Austria. Ed. Erich Zoellner. circ. 700. (back issues avail.)

943.8 PL ISSN 0075-7020
KRAKOW DAWNIEJ I DZIS. 1952. irreg., vol. 20, 1978. price varies. Towarzystwo Milosnikow Historii i Zabytkow Krakowa, Ul. Sw. Jana 12, 31-018 Krakow, Poland (Dist. by Ars Polona-Ruch, Krakowskie Przedmiescie 7, Warsaw, Poland) Ed. Jan M. Malecki.

948.5 SW ISSN 0083-6796
KUNGLIGA VITTERHETS-, HISTORIE- OCH ANTIKVITETS AKADEMIEN. AARSBOK. 1926. a. Kr.50. Kungliga Vitterhets-, Historie- och Antikvitets Akademien - Royal Academy of Letters, History and Antiquities, Villagatan 3, 114 32 Stockholm, Sweden.

948.5 SW ISSN 0083-6737
KUNGLIGA VITTERHETS-, HISTORIE- OCH ANTIKVITETS AKADEMIEN. ANTIKVARISKT ARKIV. (Text in English, German and Swedish) 1954. irreg., no. 70, 1980. price varies. Kungliga Vitterhets-, Historie- och Antikvitets Akademien - Royal Academy of Letters, History and Antiquities, Villagatan 3, 114 32 Stockholm, Sweden. index.

948.5 SW ISSN 0083-6761
KUNGLIGA VITTERHETS-, HISTORIE- OCH ANTIKVITETS AKADEMIEN. HANDLINGAR. ANTIKVARISKA SERIEN/ROYAL ACADEMY OF LETTERS, HISTORY AND ANTIQUITIES. PROCEEDINGS. ANTIQUARIAN SERIES. (Text in English, French, German, Swedish) 1954. irreg., no. 30, 1977. price varies. Kungliga Vitterhets-, Historie- och Antikvits Akademien, Villagatan 3, 114 32 Stockholm, Sweden.

940 SW ISSN 0083-6788
KUNGLIGA VITTERHETS-, HISTORIE- OCH ANTIKVITETS AKADEMIEN. HANDLINGAR. HISTORISKA SERIEN/ROYAL ACADEMY OF LETTERS, HISTORY AND ANTIQUITIES. PROCEEDINGS. HISTORICAL SERIES. (Text in German and Swedish; summaries in English and French) 1957. irreg., no. 21, 1979. price varies. Kungliga Vitterhets-, Historie- och Antikvits Akademien, Villagatan 3, 114 32 Stockholm, Sweden. index.

940 SW ISSN 0083-6753
KUNGLIGA VITTERHETS-, HISTORIE- OCH ANTIKVITETS AKADEMIEN. HISTORISKT ARKIV. (Text in English, French, German or Swedish) 1954. irreg., no. 16, 1975. price varies. Kungliga Vitterhets-, Historie- och Antikvits Akademien - Royal Academy of Letters, History and Antiquities, Villagatan 3, 114 32 Stockholm, Sweden. index.

LANDESMUSEUM FUER VORGESCHICHTE, DRESDEN. VEROEFFENTLICHUNGEN. see MUSEUMS AND ART GALLERIES

LANDESMUSEUM FUER VORGESCHICHTE, HALLE. VEROEFFENTLICHUNGEN. see MUSEUMS AND ART GALLERIES

940 720 UK ISSN 0143-3768
LANDSCAPE HISTORY. 1979. a. £7 membership. Society for Landscape Studies, 3 Benjamin St., Wakefield WF2 9AN, England. Ed. Dr. Margaret L. Faull. charts. illus. circ. 300. Indexed: Br. Archaeol.Abstr. Geo.Abstr.

LEEDS MEDIEVAL STUDIES. see LITERATURE

LEICESTERSHIRE ARCHAEOLOGICAL AND HISTORICAL SOCIETY. TRANSACTIONS. see ARCHAEOLOGY

HISTORY — HISTORY OF EUROPE

LEO BAECK INSTITUTE. YEAR BOOK. see
RELIGIONS AND THEOLOGY — Judaic

947 US ISSN 0091-4347
LIETUVIU TAUTOS PRAEITIS/LITHUANIAN HISTORICAL REVIEW. (Text in Lithuanian, English, German, French) 1959. a. price varies. Lithuanian Historical Society, Inc., 10425 S. Kenton, Oak Lawn, IL 60453. Eds. Juozas Jakstas, John A. Rackauskas. bk. rev. circ. 1,000. Indexed: Hist.Abstr.

940 FR ISSN 0075-9376
LIEUX ET LES DIEUX.* 1970. irreg. price varies. Editions Julliard, 8 rue Garanciere, Paris 6e, France.

LINCOLNSHIRE HISTORY AND ARCHAEOLOGY. see *ARCHAEOLOGY*

949 NE
LINSCHOTEN-VEREENIGING. WERKEN. vol. 80, 1977. irreg. price varies. Martinus Nijhoff, Box 566, 2501 CN The Hague, Netherlands. (back issues avail.)

943.7 CS ISSN 0075-9988
LITOMERICKO; vlastivedny sbornik. 1964. a. 15 Kcs. Okresni Vlastivedne Muzeum, Mirove nam. 171, 412 01 Litomerice, Czechoslovakia. Ed. Eva Stibrova.

949.6 UR
LITUANISTIKA V. S.S.S.R. ISTORIYA. 1977. irreg. 1.7 Rub. per issue. Akademiya Nauk Litovskoi S.S.R., Institut Filosofii, Sotsiologii i Prava, Lenino Prospektas, 3, Vilnius., U.S.S.R. Ed. A. Bal'Sis. circ. 500.

942 UK ISSN 0085-283X
LONDON RECORD SOCIETY. OCCASIONAL PUBLICATIONS. 1970. irreg. £1($5) to non-members. London Record Society, c/o Institute of Historical Research, Senate House, London WC1E 7HU, England. circ. 350.

942 UK ISSN 0085-2848
LONDON RECORD SOCIETY. PUBLICATIONS. 1965. a. price varies. London Record Society, c/o Institute of Historical Research, Senate House, London WC1E 7HU, England. Ed. William Kellaway. circ. 350. (back issues avail.)

940 PL ISSN 0076-1516
LUSTRACJE DOBR KROLEWSKICH XVI-XVIII WIEKU. 1959. irreg. price varies. (Polska Akademia Nauk, Instytut Historii) Panstwowe Wydawnictwo Naukowe, Miodowa 10, Warsaw, Poland (Dist. by Ars Polona-Ruch, Krakowskie Przedmiescie 7, Warsaw, Poland) Ed. Leonid Zytkowicz.

948 DK
M I V: MUSEERNE I VIBORG AMT. 1971. a. Viborg Stiftsmuseum, DK-8800 Viborg, Denmark (Subscr. to: Moseumstjenesten, Sjorupvej, Lysgaard, DK-8800 Viborg, Denmark) Ed. Marianne Bro-Joergensen. illus. circ. 1,000.

943 HU ISSN 0076-2407
MAGYAR KOZLONY; official gazette. irreg. $54.50. (Minisztertanacs) Kultura (Distributor), P.O. Box 149, H-1389 Budapest, Hungary.

MAGYARORSZAG MUEMLEKI TOPOGRAFIAJA. see *ART*

943 709 GW ISSN 0076-2725
MAINFRAENKISCHES JAHRBUCH FUER GESCHICHTE UND KUNST. 1949. a. DM.40. Freunde Mainfraenkischer Kunst und Geschichte, Friedensstr. 47, 8700 Wuerzburg, W. Germany (B.R.D.) Ed. Ernst. G. Krenig. bk. rev. circ. 900.

MAINZER ZEITSCHRIFT; Mittelrheinisches jahrbuch fuer Archaeologie, Geschichte und Kunst. see *ART*

MAKEDONIKA. see *CLASSICAL STUDIES*

942 UK ISSN 0076-4264
MANX MUSEUM, DOUGLAS, ISLE OF MAN. JOURNAL. 1924. irreg. Manx Museum and National Trust, Douglas, Isle of Man, U.K. Eds. A. M. Cubbon And Ann M. Harrison. index. circ. 750.

944 US ISSN 0076-4671
MARQUETTE SLAVIC STUDIES. 1955. irreg. price varies. (Marquette University, Slavic Institute) Marquette University Press, 1324 W. Wisconsin Ave., Milwaukee, WI 53233.

MATERIALE SI CERCETARI ARHEOLOGICE. see *ARCHAEOLOGY*

940 AU
MATERIALIEN ZUR WIRTSCHAFTS- UND SOZIALGESCHICHTE. 1978. irreg. Verlag fuer Geschichte und Politik, Neulinggasse 26, A-1030 Vienna, Austria. Eds. Alfred Hoffmann, Herbert Matis, Michael Mitterauer.

940 PL ISSN 0076-5236
MATERIALY ZACHODNIO-POMORSKIE. (Text in Polish; summaries in German, English, French) 1957. a. price varies. Muzeum Narodowe, Szczecin, Staromlynska 27, 70-561 Szczecin, Poland (Dist. by: Ars Polona- Ruch, Krakowskie Przedmiescie 7, Warsaw, Poland) Ed. Wladyslaw Filipowiak. bk. rev. circ. 700.

948 DK ISSN 0076-5864
MEDIAEVAL SCANDINAVIA. (Text in English) 1968. a. price varies. Odense University Press, 36, Pjentedamsgade, DK-5000 Odense, Denmark. Ed. Hans Bekker-Nielsen.

MEDIAEVAL SOURCES IN TRANSLATION. see *LITERATURE*

940 CN ISSN 0076-5872
MEDIAEVAL STUDIES. (Text in English; occasionally in French, German, Latin and other languages) 1939. a. $20. Pontifical Institute of Mediaeval Studies, 59 Queen's Park Crescent E., Toronto, Ont.M5S 2C4, Canada. Ed. Virginia Brown. cum.index: vols. 1-25; supplement index: vols. 26-30. circ. 1,100. Indexed: M.L.A.

940 BE
MEDIAEVALIA LOVANIENSIA. SERIES I. (Text in English, French, German, and Dutch) 1972. a. price varies. (Katholieke Universiteit te Leuven, Instituut voor Middeleeuwse Studies) Leuven University Press, Krakenstraat 3, 3000 Louvain, Belgium.

940 US
MEDIEVAL ACADEMY BOOKS. 1928. irreg., no. 90, 1980. Medieval Academy of America, 1430 Massachusetts Ave., Cambridge, MA 02138.
Formerly: Medieval Academy of America. Publications (ISSN 0076-583X)

940 US
MEDIEVAL ACADEMY REPRINTS FOR TEACHING. 1978. irreg., no. 10, 1980. price varies. (Medieval Academy of America) University of Toronto Press, Front Campus, Toronto, Ont. M5s 1A6, Canada.

MEDIEVAL ARCHAEOLOGY. see *ARCHAEOLOGY*

946 NE ISSN 0076-6100
MEDIEVAL IBERIAN PENNINSULA. 1961. irreg., 1971, no. 4. price varies. E. J. Brill, Oude Rijn 33a-35, Leiden, Netherlands.

970 US ISSN 0543-5056
MERCHANT EXPLORER. 1961. a. membership. James Ford Bell Library, 472 Wilson Library, University of Minnesota, Minneapolis, MN 55455. Ed. John Parker. bk. rev. bibl. circ. 500.

940 US
MIDDLE AGES. 1897. irreg., latest 1977. University of Pennsylvania, Department of History, Philadelphia, PA 19104. Ed. Edward M. Peters.
Supersedes: Translations and Reprints from the Original Sources of European History (ISSN 0082-593X)

942 UK ISSN 0047-729X
MIDLAND HISTORY. 1971. a. £6. University of Birmingham, School of History, Box 363, Birmingham B15 2TT, England. Ed. C. Dyer. adv. bk. rev. circ. 500.

948.5 355 SW
MILITAERHISTORISK TIDSKRIFT. (Text in Swedish; summaries in English; sometimes French or German) 1963. a. Kungliga Militaerhoegskolan, Militaerhistoriska Avdelningen - Royal Armed Forces Staff College, 100 45 Stockholm 90, Sweden. Formerly (until 1979): Aktuellt och Historiskt (ISSN 0065-5619)

946 SP
MISCELANEA DE TEXTOS MEDIEVALES. 1972. irreg. $8 price varies. Universidad de Barcelona, Instituto de Historia Medievales, Departamento de Estudios Medievales, Egipciacas 15, Barcelona, Spain. adv. bk. rev. bibl. circ. 1,000.

949.5 809 GW ISSN 0076-9347
MISCELLANEA BYZANTINA MONACENSIA. 1965. irreg., no. 23, 1978. price varies. Universitaet Muenchen, Institut fuer Byzantinistik und Neugriechische Philologie, Geschwister Scholl Platz 1, 8000 Munich 22, W. Germany (B.R.D.) Eds. Hans-Georg Beck, Armin Hohlweg. index.

940 GE ISSN 0075-2932
MITTELDEUTSCHE VORGESCHICHTE. JAHRESSCHRIFT. 1964. a. price varies. VEB Deutscher Verlag der Wissenschaften, Postfach 1216, 108 Berlin, E. Germany (D.D.R.) Ed. H. Behrens.

940 NE ISSN 0076-9754
MITTELLATEINISCHE STUDIEN UND TEXTE. 1965. irreg., vol. 11, 1980. price varies. E. J. Brill, Oude Rijn 33a-35, Leiden, Netherlands. Ed. K. Langosch.

940 US
MODERN SCHOLARSHIP ON EUROPEAN HISTORY. irreg. price varies. New Viewpoints, c/o Franklin Watts, Inc., 730 Fifth Ave, 8th Floor, New York, NY 10019.

942 UK ISSN 0077-0299
MONARCHIST PRESS ASSOCIATION. HISTORICAL SERIES. 1964. irreg. 40 n.p($1. Monarchist Press Association, 7 Sutherland Rd., West Ealing, London, W13 0DX, England. circ. 3,000.

943.8 PL ISSN 0077-0523
MONOGRAFIE SLASKIE OSSOLINEUM. 1960. irreg., vol. 32, 1979. price varies. Ossolineum, Publishing House of the Polish Academy of Sciences, Rynek 9, 50-106 Wroclaw, Poland (Dist By. Ars Polona-Ruch, Krakowskie Przedmiescie 7, Warsaw, Poland) Ed. Jan Gierowski.

MONOGRAFIE SLAWISTYCZNE. see *LITERATURE*

940 GW ISSN 0080-6951
MONUMENTA GERMANIAE HISTORICA. SCHRIFTEN. 1938. irreg., vol. 28, 1980. price varies. Anton Hiersemann Verlag, Rosenbergstr. 113, Postfach 723, 7000 Stuttgart 1, W. Germany (B.R.D.) circ. 1,200.

940 GW ISSN 0340-8035
MONUMENTA GERMANIAE HISTORICA. STAATSSCHRIFTEN DES SPAETEREN MITTELALTERS. (Text in German and Latin) 1941. irreg. price varies. Anton Hiersemann Verlag, Rosenbergstr. 113, Postfach 723, 7000 Stuttgart 1, W. Germany (B.R.D.)

943 HU ISSN 0077-1430
MONUMENTA HISTORICA BUDAPESTINENSIA. (Text in Hungarian, French and German) 1959. irreg. price varies. (Magyar Tudomanyos Akademia) Akademiai Kiado, Publishing House of the Hungarian Academy of Sciences, P.O. Box 24, H-1363 Budapest, Hungary.

940 UK ISSN 0545-0373
MORGANNWG. 1957. a. £2. Glamorgan History Society, c/o Miss Hilary Thomas, County Record Office, Mid-Glamorgan County Hall, Cathays Park, Cardiff, S. Glamorgan, Wales. Eds. B. L. James, G. E. Jones. bk. rev. illus. circ. 300.

943 GW ISSN 0170-8929
MUENCHNER ZEITSCHRIFT FUER BALKANOLOGIE. 1978. a. DM.76. Dr. Rudolf Trofenik Verlag, Elsabethstr. 18, 8000 Munich 40, W. Germany (B.R.D.) Ed.Peter Bartl. bk. rev.

946 SP
MUSEO CANARIO. 1879. a. $4. Sociedad de Ciencias, Letras y Artes, Dr. Chil 25, Las Palmas, Canary Islands, Spain. Ed. Agustin Millares Carlo. bk. rev. bibl. circ. 1,000.

943.8 PL ISSN 0077-2577
MUZEA WALKI. 1968. a. 25 Zl. Muzeum Historii Polskiego Ruchu Rewolucyjnego, Plac Dzierzynskiego 1, 00-139 Warsaw, Poland (Dist. by: Ars Polona-Ruch, Krakowskie Przedmiescie 7, Warsaw, Poland) Ed.Bd. circ. 800.

943.8 PL ISSN 0068-4651
MUZEUM GORNOSLASKIE W BYTOMIU. ROCZNIK. SERIA HISTORIA. 1963. irreg. price varies. Muzeum Gornoslaskie, Pl. Thaelmanna 2, 41-902 Bytom, Poland (Dist. by Ars Polona-Ruch, Krakowskie Przedmiescie 7, Warsaw, Poland)

947 UR
MYNULE I SUCHASNE PIVNICHNOI BUKOVYNY/PROSHLOE I NASTOYASCHCHEE SEVERNOI BUKOVINY. 1972. irreg. 0.95 Rub. (Akademiya Nauk Ukrainskoi S.S.R., Institut Istorii) Izdatel'stvo Naukova Dumka, Ul. Repina, 3, Kiev, U.S.S.R.

943 GW ISSN 0077-2887
NASSAUISCHE ANNALEN. 1827. a. DM.72. Verein fuer Nassauische Altertumskunde und Geschichtsforschung, Mainzer Str. 80, 6200 Wiesbaden, W. Germany (B.R.D.) Ed. Hans-Joachim Haebel. adv. bk. rev. circ. 1,800.

948.1 NO
NES OG HELG YA. 1977. a. Kr.25. Nes Historielag, Ekebergvn. 292-21 A, Oslo 11, Norway.

949 NE
NETHERLANDS. RIJKSINSTITUUT VOOR OORLOGSDOCUMENTATIE. PROGRESS REPORT. no. 8, 1979. irreg. Rijksinstituut voor Oorlogsdocumentatie - Netherlands State Institute for War Documentation, Herengracht 474, 1000 GT Amsterdam, Netherlands.

940 GW ISSN 0077-7706
NEUE MUENSTERSCHE BEITRAEGE ZUR GESCHICHTSFORSCHUNG. 1957. irreg. price varies. Aschendorffsche Verlagsbuchhandlung, Soester Str. 13, 4400 Muenster, W. Germany (B.R.D.) Ed. Heinz Gollwitzer.

943 GW
NEUES TRIERISCHES JAHRBUCH FUER HEIMATPFLEGE UND HEIMATGESCHICHTE. 1961. a. DM.9.50. Verein Trierisch e.V., Loewenbrueckener Str. 23, 5500 Trier, W. Germany (B.R.D.) Ed. Claus Zander.
Neues Trierisches Jahrbuch (ISSN 0077-7765)

943 GW ISSN 0077-7862
NEUSSER JAHRBUCH FUER KUNST, KULTURGESCHICHTE UND HEIMATKUNDE. 1956. a. DM.9. Clemens-Sels-Museum, Im Obertor, 4040 Neuss, W. Germany (B.R.D.)

947 CN ISSN 0381-9140
NEW REVIEW OF EAST-EUROPEAN HISTORY. 1974. irreg. A. Pidhainy, Box 31, Postal Sta. E, Toronto, Ont. M6H 4E1, Canada. bibl.
Formerly: New Review (ISSN 0028-6605)

940 GW ISSN 0078-0561
NIEDERSAECHSISCHES JAHRBUCH FUER LANDESGESCHICHTE. 1925. a. (Historische Kommission fuer Niedersachsen und Bremen) Verlag August Lax, Postfach 8847, 3200 Hildesheim, W. Germany (B.R.D.)

NOMINA; a newsletter of name studies relating to Great Britain and Ireland. see *GENEALOGY AND HERALDRY*

943 GW ISSN 0078-1037
NORDELBINGEN; Beitraege zur Kunst- und Kulturgeschichte. a. price varies. (Gesellschaft fuer Schleswig-Holsteinische Geschichte) Westholsteinische Verlagsanstalt Boyens und Co., Am Wulf-Isebrand-Platz, Postfach 1880, 2240 Heide, W. Germany (B.R.D.) Eds. O. Klose, E. Redlefsen, R. Zoellner.

949.2 GW ISSN 0078-1045
NORDFRIESISCHES JAHRBUCH. 1965. a. price varies. Nordfriisk Instituut, Osterstr. 63, 2257 Bredstedt, W. Germany (B.R.D.) Eds. Tams Joergensen and Ingwer E. Momsen. bk. rev. circ. 950.

942 UK ISSN 0078-1169
NORFOLK RECORD SOCIETY. PUBLICATIONS. 1931. a. membership. Norfolk Record Society, 425 Unthank Rd., Norwich NR4 7QB, England. Eds. A. Hassell Smith And R. Virgoe. circ. 300.

359 NO
NORSK SJOEFARTSMUSEUM. AARSBERETNING. (Text in Norwegian; summaries in English) 1965. a. Kr.50. Norsk Sjoefartsmuseum, Bygdoeynesveien 37, Oslo 2, Norway. Ed. Baard Kolltveit. adv. illus. cum.index. circ. 2,000.

NORTH STAFFORDSHIRE JOURNAL OF FIELD STUDIES. see *GEOGRAPHY*

914.2 UK ISSN 0140-9131
NORTHAMPTONSHIRE PAST AND PRESENT. 1948. a. membership. Northamptonshire Record Society, Delapre Abbey, Northampton, England. Ed. Bd. adv. bk. rev. illus. cum.index every 5 or 6 years. circ. 3,000.
Local

942 UK ISSN 0078-172X
NORTHERN HISTORY; a review of the history of the North of England. 1966. a. £6.50($20) University of Leeds, School of History, Leeds, England. Ed. G. C. F. Forster. bk. rev. circ. 800.

940 UK ISSN 0078-2122
NOTTINGHAM MEDIEVAL STUDIES. 1957. a. £3.50($7) University of Nottingham, Nottingham, England. Ed. Antonia Gransden. circ. 500.

943 GW ISSN 0078-2653
NUERNBERGER FORSCHUNGEN. irreg. price varies. Verein fuer Geschichte der Stadt Nuernberg, Egidienplatz 23, 8500 Nuernberg, W. Germany (B.R.D.) Ed. Gerhard Hirschmann. circ. 700.

940 IT ISSN 0391-6049
NUOVO MEDIOEVO. 1976. irreg., no. 9, 1979. price varies. Liguori Editore s.r.l., Via Mezzocannone 19, 80134 Naples, Italy. Ed. Massimo Oldoni.

949 NE
O S G N WETENSCHAPPELIJKE PUBLIKATIE. irreg., no. 4, 1977. price varies. Organisatie van Studenten in de Geschiedenis van Nederland, Groningen, Netherlands. (Co-sponsor: Stichting Ter Bevordering van de Studie in de Geschiedenis van Nederland)

949.4 SZ
OBWALDNER GESCHICHTSBLAETTER. irreg. Historisch-Antiquarischer Verein Obwalden, CH-6060 Sarnen, Switzerland. illus.

942 UK ISSN 0078-303X
OCCASIONAL PAPERS IN ENGLISH LOCAL HISTORY. 1969. irreg., 3rd series, no. 5, 1980. price varies. ‡ Leicester University Press, Fielding Johnson Bldg., Univ. of Leicester, University Rd., Leicester, England. Ed. Alan Everitt.

OCCASIONAL PAPERS IN GERMAN STUDIES. see *LITERATURE*

OCCASIONAL PAPERS IN MODERN DUTCH STUDIES. see *POLITICAL SCIENCE*

900 300 DK ISSN 0078-3307
ODENSE UNIVERSITY STUDIES IN HISTORY AND SOCIAL SCIENCES. (Text in Danish and English; summaries in English) 1970. irreg., no. 68, 1980. price varies. Odense University Press, 36, Pjentedamsgade, DK-5000 Odense, Denmark.

947 PL ISSN 0029-8514
ODRODZENIE I REFORMACJA W POLSCE. 1956. irreg., vol. 24, 1979. 60 Zl. (Polska Akademia Nauk, Instytut Historii) Ossolineum, Publishing House of the Polish Academy of Sciences, Rynek 9, Wroclaw, Poland (Dist. by: Ars Polona-Ruch, Krakowskie Przedmiescie 7, Warsaw, Poland) Ed. J. Tazbir.

943.6 AU
OESTERREICH ARCHIV. 1959. irreg. price varies. (Institut fuer Oesterreichkunde) Verlag fuer Geschichte und Politik, Neulinggasse 26, A-1030 Vienna, Austria. Ed. Erich Zoellner.

943.6 AU ISSN 0003-9322
OESTERREICHISCHE AKADEMIE DER WISSENSCHAFTEN. ARCHIV FUER OESTERREICHISCHE GESCHICHTE. 1848. irreg. price varies. (Oesterreichische Akademie der Wissenschaften, Historische Kommission) Verlag der Oesterreichischen Akademie der Wissenschaften, Ignaz Seipelplatz 2, A-1010 Vienna, Austria.

940 930 AU
OESTERREICHISCHE AKADEMIE DER WISSENSCHAFTEN. KOMMISSION FUER DIE TABULA IMPERII BYZANTINI. VEROEFFENTLICHUNGEN. (Subseries of: Oesterreichische Akademie der Wissenschaften. Philosophisch-Historische Klasse. Denkschriften) 1973. irreg. price varies. Verlag der Oesterreichischen Akademie der Wissenschaften, Ignaz Seipel-Platz 2, A-1010 Vienna, Austria. bibl. illus.

940 100 AU ISSN 0065-5368
OESTERREICHISCHE AKADEMIE DER WISSENSCHAFTEN. PHILOSOPHISCH-HISTORISCHE KLASSE. ANZEIGER. 1848. a. price varies. Verlag der Oesterreichischen Akademie der Wissenschaften, Dr. Ignaz Seipel-Platz 2, A-1010 Vienna, Austria. circ. 800.

940 AU ISSN 0065-5376
OESTERREICHISCHE AKADEMIE DER WISSENSCHAFTEN. PRAEHISTORISCHE KOMMISSION. MITTEILUNGEN. 1887. irreg., vol. 15/16, 1974. price varies. Verlag der Oesterreichischen Akademie der Wissenschaften, Dr. Ignaz Seipel-Platz 2, A-1010 Vienna, Austria. circ. 600-800.

949.5 AU ISSN 0075-2355
OESTERREICHISCHE BYZANTINISTIK. JAHRBUCH. (Text in German, English, French, ancient and modern Greek, Latin) 1951. a. price varies. (Oesterreichische Akademie der Wissenschaften, Kommission fuer Byzantinistik) Verlag der Oesterreichischen Akademie der Wissenschaften, Dr. Ignaz Seipel-Platz 2, A-1010 Vienna, Austria. Ed. Herbert Hunger. bk. rev.
Formerly: Oesterreichische Byzantinische Gesellschaft Jahrbuch.

940 AU ISSN 0078-3641
OESTERREICHISCHES KULTURINSTITUT, ROM. ABTEILUNG FUER HISTORISCHE STUDIEN. PUBLIKATIONEN I. ABTEILUNG: ABHANDLUNGEN. (Text in English, French and German) 1954. irreg. price varies. (IT) Verlag der Oesterreichischen Akademie der Wissenschaften, Dr. Ignaz Seipel-Platz 2, A-1010 Vienna, Austria. Eds. Leo Santifaller, H. Schmidinger.

940 AU ISSN 0078-365X
OESTERREICHISCHES KULTURINSTITUT, ROM. ABTEILUNG FUER HISTORISCHE STUDIEN. PUBLIKATIONEN II. ABTEILUNG: QUELLEN. 1968. irreg. price varies. (IT) Verlag der Oesterreichischen Akademie der Wissenschaften, Dr. Ignaz Seipel-Platz 2, A-1010 Vienna, Austria. circ. 500.

940 AU ISSN 0078-3439
OESTERREICHISCHES OST- UND SUEDOSTEUROPA INSTITUT. SCHRIFTENREIHE. 1967. irreg., vol. 5, 1975. price varies. ‡ Verlag fuer Geschichte und Politik, Neulinggasse 26, A-1030 Vienna, Austria. Eds. R. G. Plaschka, K. Mack.

940 020 AU ISSN 0067-2297
OESTERREICHISCHES STAATSARCHIV. MITTEILUNGEN. (Supplements avail.) (Text in German, English, French, Italian) 1948. a. price varies. Verlag Ferdinand Berger und Soehne OHG, Wienerstr. 21-23, A-3580 Horn, Austria. Eds. Gerhard Rill, Christiane Thomas. bk. rev. bibl. illus. cum.index 25 yrs. circ. 500(controlled)

940 GW ISSN 0078-3714
OFFA-JAHRBUCH; VOR- UND FRUEHGESCHICHTE. a. Karl Wachholtz Verlag, Gaensemarkt 1, Postfach 255, 2350 Neumuenster, W. Germany (B.R.D.) circ. 500.

HISTORY — HISTORY OF EUROPE

941   IE   ISSN 0475-1388
OLD ATHLONE SOCIETY JOURNAL. 1969. biennial (approx) membership; non-members £2. ‡ Old Athlone Society, c/o Miss N. C. Egan, Lara, Court Devenish, Athlone, Ireland. Ed. G. O'Brien. adv. charts. illus. circ. 500.

940   FR   ISSN 0078-4591
OMBRES DE L'HISTOIRE.* 1969. irreg. price varies. R. Laffont, 6 Place Saint-Sulpice, Paris 6e, France.

944   FR
OR DU RHINE. 1977. irreg. Editions Copernic, B.P. 129, 75326 Paris Cedex 07, France. Ed. Alain de Benoist.

943   GW   ISSN 0078-6845
OSTBAIRISCHE GRENZMARKEN. 1957. a. DM.25. Universitaet Passau, Institut fuer Ostbairische Heimatforschung, Michaelisgasse 13, 8390 Passau, W. Germany (B.R.D.) Ed. August Leidl. bk. rev. circ. 600.

940   GW   ISSN 0078-687X
OSTEUROPA INSTITUT, MUNICH. VEROEFFENTLICHUNGEN. REIHE GESCHICHTE. 1953. irreg., vol. 48, 1979. Verlag Otto Harrassowitz, Taunusstr. 6, Postfach 2929, 6200 Wiesbaden, W. Germany (B.R.D.) Ed. G. Stadtmueller. (back issues avail.)

910   AU   ISSN 0078-6896
OSTPANORAMA. 1965. a. S.290. Gesellschaft fuer Ost- und Suedostkunde, Bismarckstr. 5, A-4020 Linz, Austria. Ed. Georg Dox. circ. 5,000.

943.6   AU
OTTOKARFORSCHUNGEN. a., n.s. vol. 44/45, 1978/79. S.360. Verein fuer Landeskunde von Niederoesterreich und Wien, Herrengasse 11, A-1010 Vienna, Austria.

OXFORD ENGLISH MEMOIRS AND TRAVELS. see *BIOGRAPHY*

940   US
OXFORD HISTORICAL MONOGRAPHS. irreg. price varies. Oxford University Press, 200 Madison Ave., New York, NY 10016 (And Ely House, 37 Dover St., London W1X 4AH, England) Ed.Bd.

942   US
OXFORD HISTORY OF ENGLAND. irreg. price varies. Oxford University Press, 200 Madison Ave., New York, NY 10016 (And Ely House, 37 Dover St., London W1X 4AH, England) Ed. Sir George Clark.

940   US
OXFORD HISTORY OF MODERN EUROPE. irreg. price varies. Oxford University Press, 200 Madison Ave., New York, NY 10016 (And Ely House, 37 Dover St., London W1X 4AH, England) Eds. Alan Bullock, F.W.D. Deakin.

OXONIENSIA. see *ARCHAEOLOGY*

940 929   UK
PANORAMA. 1956. a. 40p.($2) Thurrock Local History Society, Thurrock Museums Dept., Orsett Rd., Grays, Essex RM17 5DX, England. Ed. Randal Bingley. circ. 400.
Local

943   GW   ISSN 0078-9410
PAPYROLOGICA COLONIENSIA. 1964. (Rheinisch-Westfaelische Akademie der Wissenschaften) Westdeutscher Verlag GmbH, Faulbrunnenstr. 13, 6200 Wiesbaden, W. Germany (B.R.D.)

940   UK   ISSN 0479-8244
PEMBROKESHIRE HISTORIAN. 1959. irreg. membership. (Pembrokeshire Local History Society) Dyfed Rural Council, 4 Victoria Place, Haverfordwest, Dyfed, Wales. Ed. Dillwyn Miles. bk. rev. circ. 1,000.

940   PL   ISSN 0079-3388
POLSKA AKADEMIA NAUK. ODDZIAL W KRAKOWIE. KOMISJA NAUK HISTORYCZNYCH. PRACE. (Text in Polish; summaries in English, French or Russian) 1958. irreg., no. 42, 1978. price varies. Ossolineum, Publishing House of the Polish Academy of Sciences, Rynek 9, Wroclaw, Poland (Dist. by Ars Polona-Ruch, Krakowskie Przedmiescie 7, Warsaw, Poland)

947   PL
POLSKA KLASA ROBOTNICZA. STUDIA HISTORYCZNA. irreg., 1976, vol. 7. $10. (Polska Akademia Nauk, Instytut Historii) Panstwowe Wydawnictwo Naukowe, Miodowa 10, Warsaw, Poland (Dist. by: Ars Polona-Ruch, Krakowskie Przedmiescie 7, Warsaw, Poland) Ed. S. Kalabinski. charts.

POLSKA 2000. see *SOCIOLOGY*

947   PL   ISSN 0556-0691
POMARANIA ANTIQUA. irreg., vol. 9, 1979. 60 Zl. (Muzeum Archeologiczne, Gdansk) Ossolineum, Publishing House of the Polish Academy of Sciences, Rynek 9, Wroclaw, Poland (Dist. by: Ars Polona-Ruch, Krakowskie Przedmiescie 7, Warsaw, Poland) Ed. L. Luka.

940   CN   ISSN 0082-5328
PONTIFICAL INSTITUTE OF MEDIAEVAL STUDIES. STUDIES AND TEXTS. 1955. irreg. price varies. Pontifical Institute of Mediaeval Studies, 59 Queen's Park Crescent E., Toronto Ontario M5S 2C4, Canada. circ. 500.

940   UK   ISSN 0554-7598
PORTSMOUTH PAPERS. 1970. 7/reg., no. 26, 1977. price varies. Portsmouth City Council, Civic Offices, Portsmouth, England. Ed. Dr. E. Course. bibl. illus.

940   GW   ISSN 0079-421X
PORTUGIESISCHE FORSCHUNGEN DER GOERRESGESELLSCHAFT. REIHE 1: AUFSAETZE ZUR PORTUGIESISCHEN KULTURGESCHICHTE. 1960. irreg. price varies. (Goerres-Gesellschaft) Aschendorffsche Verlagsbuchhandlung, Soester Str. 13, 4400 Muenster, W. Germany (B.R.D.) Ed. Hans Flasche.

940   GW   ISSN 0079-4228
PORTUGIESISCHE FORSCHUNGEN DER GOERRESGESELLSCHAFT. REIHE 2: MONOGRAPHIEN. 1961. irreg. price varies. (Goerres-Gesellschaft) Aschendorffsche Verlagsbuchhandlung, Soester Str. 13, 4400 Muenster, W. Germany (B.R.D.) Ed. Hans Flasche.

940   PL   ISSN 0079-4465
POWSTANIE STYCZNIOWE. MATERIALY I DOKUMENTY. irreg., vol. 24, 1978. price varies. (Polska Akademia Nauk, Instytut Historii i Akademia Nauk ZSRR) Ossolineum, Publishing House of the Polish Academy of Sciences, Rynek 9, 50-106 Wroclaw, Poland (Dist. by Ars Polona-Ruch, Krakowskie Przedmiescie 7, Warsaw, Poland)

940   PL   ISSN 0079-4651
POZNANSKIE TOWARZYSTWO PRZYJACIOL NAUK. KOMISJA HISTORYCZNA. PRACE. (Text in Polish; summaries in German) irreg., 1976, vol. 29. price varies. Panstwowe Wydawnictwo Naukowe, Miodowa 10, Warsaw, Poland (Dist. by Ars Polona-Ruch, Krakowskie Przedmiescie 7, Warsaw, Poland) Ed.Bd. bibl. charts. illus. circ. 840.

943.64   LH   ISSN 0048-5306
PRINCIPALITY OF LIECHTENSTEIN: A DOCUMENTARY HANDBOOK. (Text in German, English, French) 1966. triennial. 10 Fr. Press and Information Office, Fl-9490 Vaduz, Principality of Liechtenstein. circ. 9,000.

937   IT   ISSN 0079-5682
PROBLEMI E RICERCHE DE STORIA ANTICA. 1951. irreg., no. 8, 1981. price varies. Erma di "Bretschneider", Via Cassiodoro 19, 00193 Rome, Italy.

PROBLEMS IN EUROPEAN CIVILIZATION. see *HUMANITIES: COMPREHENSIVE WORKS*

940   US
PROBLEMS IN EUROPEAN HISTORY. irreg. price varies. Oxford University Press, 200 Madison Ave., New York, NY 10016 (And Ely House, 37 Dover St., London Ww1X 4AH, England) Eds. John F. Naylor, Richard Bienvenu.

940   GW   ISSN 0079-709X
PROVINZIALINSTITUT FUER WESTFAELISCHE LANDES- UND VOLKSFORSCHUNG. VEROEFFENTLICHUNGEN. 1937. irreg. price varies. Aschendorffsche Verlagsbuchhandlung, Soester Str. 13, 4400 Muenster, W. Germany (B.R.D.) Eds. Alfred Hartlieb von Wallthor, Karl-Heinz Kirchhoff.

PUBBLICAZIONI DI VERIFICHE. see *PHILOSOPHY*

930   IT
PUTEOLI; studi di storia antica. (Text in English, French and Italian) 1977. a. price varies. Azienda Autonoma di Cura, Soggiorno e Turismo, Via Campi Flegrei (S.S. Domiziana), 3, 80078 Pozzuoli (NA), Italy. Ed. Vitantonio Sirago. circ. 1,000. (back issues avail.)

945   IT
QUADERNI DI CULTURA MATERIALE. 1977. irreg., vol. 2, 1981. Erma di Bretschneider, Via Cassiodora 19, 00193 Rome, Italy. Ed. Andrea Carandini.

940   IT
QUADERNI DI STUDI STORICI TOSCANI. irreg.; 3-4/yr. price varies. (Centro di Studi Storici Toscani) Libreria L. del Re, Via dei Pucci 45 R., Florence, Italy. Ed. M. Leopps Pegna. bibl. charts. illus. circ. 500.

945 300   IT   ISSN 0066-2283
QUADERNI INTERNAZIONALI DI STORIA ECONOMICA E SOCIALE/INTERNATIONAL JOURNAL OF ECONOMIC AND SOCIAL HISTORY/CAHIERS INTERNATIONAUX D'HISTOIRE ECONOMIQUE ET SOCIALE. (Text in Italian, English, French, German, Spanish) 1960. a. £10000($15) Istituto Italiano per la Storia dei Movimenti Sociali e delle Structure Sociali, Via G.B. Ruoppolo 69, Naples, Italy (and Librairie Droz, rue Massot 11, Geneva, Switzerland) adv. bk. rev.
Formerly: Annali di Storia Economica e Sociale.

949.4   SZ   ISSN 0079-9076
QUELLEN UND FORSCHUNGEN ZUR BASLER GESCHICHTE. 1966. irreg., no. 9, 1977. price varies. (Staatsarchiv) Friedrich Reinhardt Verlag, Missionsstr. 36, 4012 Basel, Switzerland. Ed. Andreas Staehelin. circ. 500.

940   GW   ISSN 0170-3595
QUELLEN UND STUDIEN ZUR GESCHICHTE DES OESTLICHEN EUROPA. irreg., vol. 16, 1981. price varies. Franz Steiner Verlag GmbH, Friedrichstr. 24, Postfach 5529, 6200 Wiesbaden, W. Germany (B.R.D.) Eds.M. Hellman, E. Oberlaender.

940   GE   ISSN 0079-9114
QUELLEN UND STUDIEN ZUR GESCHICHTE OSTEUROPAS. 1958. irreg., vol. 18, 1977. price varies. Akademie-Verlag, Leipziger Str. 3-4, 108 Berlin, E. Germany (D.D.R.) Eds. Edward Winter, Heinz Lemke.

942   UK   ISSN 0306-848X
RADNORSHIRE SOCIETY. TRANSACTIONS. 1931. a. £1.75. Radnorshire Society, c/o Radnor College of Further Education, Llandrindod Wells, Radnorshire, England. Ed. C.W. Newman. bk. rev. circ. 500. (also avail. in microform from UMI) Indexed: Br.Hum.Ind.

940   UK   ISSN 0079-9866
READING UNIVERSITY STUDIES ON CONTEMPORARY EUROPE.* 1968. irreg., 1970, vol. 4. 63 s.-70s($7.95 hardback; $2.45 pap) (Reading University, Graduate School of Contemporary European Studies) Weidenfeld and Nicolson Ltd., 5 Winsley St., Oxford Circus, London W.1, England (Dist. in U.S. by: Humanities Press, Inc., 303 Park Ave. S., New York, NY 10010)

943   GW
RECHTSRHEINISCHES KOELN; Jahrbuch fuer Geschichte und Volkskunde. 1975. a. price varies. Heimatverein Porz e.V., Aachener Str. 27, 5000 Cologne 90, W. Germany (B.R.D.) Eds. Gebhard Aders, Wilhelm Becker. adv. bk. rev. circ. 2,000.

940   UK
REIGN OF CHARLEMAGNE-DOCUMENTS OF MEDIEVAL HISTORY. no. 2, 1975. irreg. £9.50. Edward Arnold (Publishers) Ltd., 441 Bedford Sq., London WC1B 3DQ, England. Eds. G.W.S. Barrow, Edward Miller.
Formerly: Documents of Medieval History.

942 UK ISSN 0080-0880
REMAINS, HISTORICAL AND LITERARY,
CONNECTED WITH THE PALATINE
COUNTIES OF LANCASTER AND CHESTER.
1843. irreg. £4 membership. ‡ (Chetham Society)
Manchester University Press, Oxford Rd.,
Manchester M13 9PL, England.

940 FR ISSN 0080-1151
REPERTOIRE INTERNATIONAL DES
MEDIEVISTES. 1965. irreg. 120 F.($28.80) Centre
d'Etudes Superieures de Civilisation Medievale,
Hotel Berthelot, 24, rue de la Chaine, 86000
Poitiers, France. adv. cum.index. in vol. published in
1971.

940 FR ISSN 0080-133X
REPORTAGES FANTASTIQUES. 1969. irreg. price
varies. Editions B. Arthaud, 23 Grande rue, 38
Grenoble, France.

944 FR ISSN 0556-7335
REVUE ANNUELLE D'HISTOIRE DU
QUATORZIEME ARRONDISSEMENT DE
PARIS. 1955. a. 35 F. Societe Historique du
Quatorzieme Arrondissement de Paris, 2 Pl.
Ferdinand Brunot, 75675 Paris Cedex 14, France.
Ed. G. N. Perroy. adv. illus.

REVUE BELGE DE NUMISMATIQUE ET DE
SIGILLOGRAPHIE. see HOBBIES —
Numismatics

944 FR
REVUE DE LA SAINTONGE ET DE L'AUNIS.
1975. a. Sciete d'Archeologie et d'Histoire de la
Charente Maritime, Musee Archeologique,
Esplanade A. Malraux, 17100 Saintes, France.

949.4 SZ
REVUE DU VIEUX GENEVE. a. c/o Paul Loosli,
Rue Philippe - Plantamour, 1-3, Geneva,
Switzerland. Ed. E. Dumont. adv. bibl. charts.
illus.
Formerly: Almanach du Vieux Geneve.

944 FR
REVUE HISTORIQUE DE BORDEAUX ET DU
DEPARTEMENT DE LA GIRONDE. 1952, N.S.
a. 60 F. Archives Municipales, 71, rue du Loup,
33000 Bordeaux, France. bk. rev. circ. 450. (back
issues avail. (1908-1945))

REVUE HISTORIQUE ET ARCHEOLOGIQUE DU
MAINE. see ARCHAEOLOGY

REVUE HISTORIQUE VAUDOISE. see
ARCHAEOLOGY

943 GW ISSN 0067-9976
RHEINISCHES LANDESMUSEUM IN BONN.
BONNER JAHRBUECHER. 1846. irreg., 1979
covering 1975-1976. price varies. Rheinland-Verlag,
Kennedy-Ufer 2, 5000 Cologne 21, W. Germany
(B.R.D.) (Dist. by: Rudolf Habelt Verlag, Am
Buchenhang 1, 5300 Bonn 1, W. Germany (B.R.D.))
cum.index.

945 IT
RICHERCHE DI STORIA MODERNA. 1976. irreg.
(Universita degli Studi di Pisa, Istituto di Storia
Medioevale e Moderna) Pacini Editore, Via della
Faggiola 17, Pisa, Italy.

949 NE
RIJKS GESCHIEDKUNDIGE PUBLICATIEN.
GROTE SERIE. vol. 163, 1978. irreg. price varies.
Martinus Nijhoff, Box 566, 2501 CN The Hague,
Netherlands.

949 NE
RIJKS GESCHIEDKUNDIGE PUBLICATIEN.
KLEINE SERIE. vol. 44, 1976. irreg. price varies.
Martinus Nijhoff, Box 566, 2501 CN The Hague,
Netherlands.

940 NE ISSN 0066-1287
RIJKSINSTITUUT VOOR
OORLOGSDOCUMENTATIE. DOCUMENTEN.
1967. irreg. Martinus Nijhoff, Box 566, 2501 CN
The Hague, Netherlands.

940 NE ISSN 0066-1295
RIJKSINSTITUUT VOOR
OORLOGSDOCUMENTATIE.
MONOGRAFIEEN. price varies. Martinus
Nijhoff, Box 566, 2501 CN The Hague,
Netherlands.

RINASCIMENTO. see HUMANITIES:
COMPREHENSIVE WORKS

943.8 PL ISSN 0080-3421
ROCZNIK BIALOSTOCKI. (Text in Polish;
summaries in English and Russian) 1961. a. price
varies. (Muzeum w Bialymstoku) Panstwowe
Wydawnictwo Naukowe, Miodowa 10, Warsaw,
Poland (Dist. by: Ars Polona-Ruch, Krakowskie
Przedmiescie 7, Warsaw, Poland)

940 PL ISSN 0080-3456
ROCZNIK GDANSKI. (Text in Polish; summaries in
English, French, Russian) 1927. irreg., vol. 39, 1979.
price varies. (Gdanskie Towarzystwo Naukowe)
Ossolineum, Publishing House of the Polish
Academy of Sciences, Rynek 9, Wroclaw, Poland
(Dist. by Ars Polona-Ruch, Krakowskie
Przedmiescie 7, Warsaw, Poland) Ed. Andrzej
Bukowski. illus. circ. 750.

943.8 PL ISSN 0080-3464
ROCZNIK GRUDZIADZKI.* 1960. a. price varies.
Polskie Towarzystwo Historyczne, Oddzial w
Grudziadzu, Murowa 29, Grudziadz, Poland (Dist.
by Ars Polona-Ruch, Krakowskie Przedmiescie 7,
Warsaw, Poland) Eds. Marian Biskup, Adam
Wolnikowski.

943.8 PL ISSN 0080-3480
ROCZNIK JELENIOGORSKI. 1963. a. 30 Zl.
(Towarzystwo Przyjaciol Ziemi Jeleniogorskiej)
Ossolineum, Publishing House of the Polish
Academy of Sciences, Rynek 9, 50-106 Wroclaw,
Poland (Dist. by Ars Polona-Ruch, Krakowskie
Przedmiescie 7, Warsaw, Poland) Ed. Stanislaw
Lejde.

940 PL ISSN 0137-3501
ROCZNIK KALISKI. (Summaries in French and
Russian) 1968. irreg. price varies. (Polskie
Towarzystwo Historyczne, Oddzial w Kalisz)
Wydawnictwo Poznanskie, Ul. Fredry 8, Poznan,
Poland. bk. rev. illus. circ. 1,000.

940 PL ISSN 0080-3499
ROCZNIK KRAKOWSKI. 1898. irreg., vol. 49, 1978.
price varies. (Towarzystwo Milosnikow Historii i
Zabytkow Krakowa) Ossolineum, Publishing House
of the Polish Academy of Sciences, Rynek 9,
Wroclaw, Poland (Dist. by Ars Polona-Ruch,
Krakowskie Przedmiescie 7, Warsaw, Poland) Ed.
Karol Estreicher. circ. 600.

943.8 PL
ROCZNIK KULTURALNY ZIEMI GDANSKIEJ.
1965. irreg., 1973, vol. 6. 15 Zl. per volume.
(Gdanskie Towarzystwo Przyjaciol Sztuki)
Wydawnictwo Morskie, Szeroka 38-40, 80-835
Gdansk, Poland.
Formerly: Gdanski Rocznik Kulturalny (ISSN
0435-1568)

943 PL ISSN 0080-3502
ROCZNIK LODZKI. 1958. a. price varies. (Polskie
Towarzystwo Historyczne, Oddzial w Lodzki)
Panstwowe Wydawnictwo Naukowe, Miodowa 10,
Warsaw, Poland. Ed. Ryszard Rosin. bk. rev. charts.

943.8 PL ISSN 0080-3510
ROCZNIK LUBELSKI. (Text in Polish; summaries in
French, Russian) 1959. a. price varies. (Polskie
Towarzystwo Historyczne, Oddzial w Lublinie -
Polish Historical Society) Wydawnictwo Lubelskie,
Okopowa 7, Lublin, Poland (Dist. by Ars Polona-
Ruch, Krakowskie Przedmiescie 7, Warsaw, Poland)
Ed. Kazimierz Myslinski. circ. 500.

943.8 PL ISSN 0080-3537
ROCZNIK OLSZTYNSKI. (Text in Polish; summaries
in English and Russian) 1958. a. 120 Zl. Muzeum
Warmii i Mazur, Ul. Zamkowa 2, 10-074 Olsztyn,
Poland (Dist. by Ars Polona-Ruch, Krakowskie
Przedmiescie 7, Warsaw, Poland) Ed. Wladyslaw
Ogrodzinski. bk. rev.

ROCZNIK SADECKI. see FOLKLORE

943.8 PL ISSN 0080-3618
ROCZNIK WROCLAWSKI. 1957. a. (Towarzystwo
Milosnikow Wroclawia) Ossolineum, Publishing
House of the Polish Academy of Sciences, Rynek 9,
50-106 Wroclaw, Poland.

947 PL
ROCZNIK ZIEMI KLODZKIEJ. a. 45 Zl.
(Towarzystwo Milosnikow Ziemi Klodzkiej)
Ossolineum, Publishing House of the Polish
Academy of Sciences, Rynek 9, Wroclaw, Poland
(Dist. by: Ars Polona-Ruch, Krakowskie
Przedmiescie 7, Warsaw, Poland)

940 PL ISSN 0080-3634
ROCZNIKI DZIEJOW SPOLECZNYCH I
GOSPODARCZYCH. (Text in Polish; summaries in
French) 1931. irreg, 1972, vol. 33. price varies.
(Poznanskie Towarzystwo Przyjaciol Nauk)
Panstwowe Wydawnictwo Naukowe, Ul. Miodowa
10, Warsaw, Poland (Dist. by Ars Polona-Ruch,
Krakowskie Przedmiescie 7, Warsaw, Poland) Ed.
Wladyslaw Rusinski. bk. rev. bibl. charts.

900 069 GW ISSN 0076-2741
ROEMISCH-GERMANISCHES
ZENTRALMUSEUM, MAINZ. JAHRBUCH.
1954. a. DM.35. Rudolf Habelt Verlag, Am
Buchenhang 1, 5300 Bonn 1, W. Germany (B.R.D.)
bk. rev.

940 AU ISSN 0080-3790
ROEMISCHE HISTORISCHE MITTEILUNGEN.
1958. a. price varies. (Oesterreichisches
Kulturinstitut, Rom, IT) Verlag der
Oesterreichischen Akademie der Wissenschaften,
Dr. Ignaz Seipel-Platz 2, A-1010 Vienna, Austria.
circ. 500.

ROMANTIZM V RUSSKOI I SOVETSKOI
LITERATURE. see LITERATURE

940 UK ISSN 0306-1140
ROMFORD RECORD. 1971. no. 4. a. 25p. Romford
and District Historical Society, c/o Central Library,
Romford, Essex, England. Ed. Brian D. Evans.
charts. illus.

942 UK ISSN 0080-4398
ROYAL HISTORICAL SOCIETY. GUIDES AND
HANDBOOKS. (Supplementary Series) 1938. N.S.
1974. irreg. membership. Royal Historical Society,
University College London, Gower St., London
WC1E 6BT, England.

942 UK ISSN 0080-4401
ROYAL HISTORICAL SOCIETY.
TRANSACTIONS. FIFTH SERIES. 1872. a.
membership. Royal Historical Society, University
College London, Gower St., London WC1E 6BT,
England.

ROYAL IRISH ACADEMY. PROCEEDINGS.
SECTION C: ARCHAEOLOGY, CELTIC
STUDIES, HISTORY, LINGUISTICS AND
LITERATURE. see ARCHAEOLOGY

947 NE
RUMANIAN STUDIES; an international annual of
the humanities and social sciences. 1970. irreg. price
varies. E.J. Brill, Oude Rijn 33a-35, Leiden,
Netherlands. illus.

942 US ISSN 0080-4886
RUSSIAN AND EAST EUROPEAN STUDIES.
1958. irreg. price varies. University of California
Press, 2223 Fulton St., Berkeley, CA 94720.

949.5 US
RUTGERS BYZANTINE SERIES. 1957. irreg., 1970,
no. 7. price varies. Rutgers University Press, 30
College Ave., New Brunswick, NJ 08903.

947 SZ
SAMISDAT; stimmen aus den "anderen Russland".
1972. irreg. price varies. Kuratorium Geistige
Freiheit, Postfach 227, 3601 Thun, Switzerland. Ed.
Udo Robe. circ. 1,500.
Supersedes: Russischer Samisdat.

SCHATZKAMMER; der deutschen Sprachlehre,
Dichtung und Geschichte. see HISTORY —
History Of North And South America

940 GW ISSN 0340-6490
SCHRIFTEN ZUR GEISTESGESCHICHTE DES
OESTLICHEN EUROPA. 1967. irreg., vol. 13,
1979. price varies. Verlag Otto Harrassowitz,
Taunusstr. 6, Postfach 2929, 6200 Wiesbaden, W.
Germany (B.R.D.) Ed.Bd.

943 SZ ISSN 0080-7273
SCHWEIZERISCHE BEITRAEGE ZUR
ALTERTUMSWISSENSCHAFT. (Text in German
and French) 1942. irreg., no. 15, 1979. price varies.
Friedrich Reinhardt Verlag, Missionsstr. 36, CH-
4012 Basel, Switzerland (Dist. by: Albert J. Phiebig
Books, Box 352, White Plains, NY 10602) Ed.
Bernhard Wyss. circ. 1,000.

930 SZ ISSN 0080-7311
SCHWEIZERISCHE GESELLSCHAFT FUER UR-
UND FRUEHGESCHICHTE. INSTITUT FUER
UR- UND FRUEHGESCHICHTE DER
SCHWEIZ. JAHRBUCH. (Text in German, French,
Italian) 1908. a. 90 Fr.($25) ‡ Huber und Co. AG,
Promenadenstr. 16, 8500 Frauenfeld, Switzerland.
bk. rev. index.

940 SZ ISSN 0080-7397
SCHWEIZERISCHE ZEITSCHRIFT FUER
GESCHICHTE. BEIHEFTE/REVUE SUISSE
D'HISTOIRE. SUPPLEMENT. 1943. irreg., no. 16,
1976. price varies. Buchdruckerei und Verlag
Leemann AG, Arbenzstr. 20, 8034 Zurich,
Switzerland.

941 301 UK ISSN 0036-9411
SCOTTISH STUDIES. (Text in English; occasionally
in Scots and Gaelic) 1957. a. £5($13) ‡ University
of Edinburgh, School of Scottish Studies, 27 George
Square, Edinburgh EH8 9LD, Scotland. Ed. John
MacQueen. bk. rev. illus. circ. 800.

941 CN
SCOTTISH TRADITION. 1968. a. Can.$10. Canadian
Association for Scottish Studies, Interdepartmental
Committee on Scottish Studies, Department of
History, University of Guelph, Guelph, Ont.,
Canada. Eds. Dr. W.W. Straka, Edward Cowan. bk.
rev. circ. 250.
Incorporating: Colloquium on Scottish Studies.
Proceedings (ISSN 0069-5823)

947 CN
SHORTER STUDIES IN EAST-EUROPEAN
HISTORY. 1967. irreg. Can.$10($10) New Review
Books, Box 31, Sta. E, Toronto, Ont. M6H 4E1,
Canada. Ed. Dr. Oleh S. Pidhainy. (back issues
avail.)

940 NE
SIR THOMAS BROWNE INSTITUUT.
PUBLICATIONS. GENERAL SERIES AND
SPECIAL SERIES. 1962. irreg. Leiden University
Press, c/o Martinus Nijhoff, Box 566, 2501 CN The
Hague, Netherlands.
Formerly: Sir Thomas Browne Instituut.
Publications. General Series (ISSN 0080-9799)

940 NO ISSN 0080-9888
SJOEFARTSHISTORISK AARBOK/NORWEGIAN
YEARBOOK OF MARITIME HISTORY. (Text in
English and Norwegian; summaries in English)
1965. a. Kr.35. Bergens Sjoefart Museum - Bergen
Maritime Museum, Box 2736, 5010 Bergen,
Norway. Eds. Lauritz Pettersen, Atle Thowsen. circ.
1,100. Indexed: Hist.Abstr.

947 PL
SLASKIE STUDIA HISTORYCZNE. 1975. irreg.,
1975, vol. 1. 53 Zl. Uniwersytet Slaski w
Katowicach, Slaski Instytut Naukowy, Ul. Bankowa
14, 40-007 Katowice, Poland. Ed. Jozefa
Chlebowczyka. charts. illus.

572 943.7 CS ISSN 0081-0061
SLOVACI V ZAHRANICI. (Text in Slovak;
summaries in English and Russian) 1971. a. price
varies. Matica Slovenska, Mudronova 35, 036 52
Martin, Czechoslovakia. bk. rev.

947 CS ISSN 0081-007X
SLOVANSKE HISTORICKE STUDIE. (Text in
Czech; summaries in English, French, German,
Russian) 1955. irreg., vol. 10, 1974. price varies.
(Ceskoslovenska Akademie Ved) Academia,
Publishing House of the Czechoslovak Academy of
Sciences, Vodickova 40, 112 29 Prague 1,
Czechoslovakia.

947 CS ISSN 0583-564X
SLOVANSKE STUDIE. vol. 17, 1976. irreg. fl.45.
(Slovenska Akademia Vied, Udesk Sav) Veda,
Publishing House of the Slovak Academy of
Sciences, Klemensova 19, 895 30 Bratislava,
Czechoslovakia (Distributor in Western countries:
John Benjamins B.V., Amsteldijk 44, Amsterdam
(Z.), Netherlands) Ed. J. Hroziencik.

945 IT ISSN 0081-0681
SOCIETA DI STUDI ROMAGNOLI. GUIDE. 1967.
irreg., 1975, no. 4. L.2500. Biblioteca Malatestiana,
47023 Cesena, Italy. circ. controlled.

SOCIETE ARCHEOLOGIQUE DE TOURAINE.
MEMOIRES. see ARCHAEOLOGY

SOCIETE D'ARCHEOLOGIE, D'HISTOIRE ET DE
FOLKLORE DE NIVELLES ET DU BRABANT
WALLON. ANNALES. see ARCHAEOLOGY

944 FR
SOCIETE D'EMULATION DE MONTBELIARD.
MEMOIRES. 1852. a. 120 F. Societe d'Emulation
de Montbeliard, Musee Beurnier, 8, Place Saint-
Martin, 25200 Montbeliard, France. circ. 700.
Local

944 FR ISSN 0081-0819
SOCIETE D'EMULATION HISTORIQUE ET
LITTERAIRE D'ABBEVILLE. BULLETIN. 1888.
a. 50 F.($10) Societe d'Emulation Historique et
Litteraire d'Abbeville, Hotel de Ville, 80101
Abbeville, France. cum.index (at approx 4-5 yr.
intervals)

944 FR ISSN 0081-0940
SOCIETE D'HISTOIRE DE FRANCE. ANNUAIRE.
1834. a. price varies. Editions Klincksieck, 11 rue
de Lille, Paris 7e, France. Ed. Michel Francois.

SOCIETE D'HISTOIRE ET D'ARCHEOLOGIE DE
LA GOELE. BULLETIN D'INFORMATION. see
ARCHAEOLOGY

914.4 FR
SOCIETE D'HISTOIRE ET D'ARCHEOLOGIE DE
LA LORRAINE. ANNUAIRE. vol. 73, 1973. a. 50
F. subscription includes quarterly publication
Cahiers Lorvains. ‡ Archives Prefecture, F. 57034
Metz, France. (Affiliate: Academie Nationale de
Metz) bibl. illus.

944 FR
SOCIETE DES ANTIQUAIRES DE L'OUEST.
MEMOIRES. 1834. irreg. price varies. Societe des
Antiquaires de l'Ouest, Rue Paul Guillon, B.P. 179,
86004 Poitiers Cedex, France.
Local

944 FR
SOCIETE DES ANTIQUAIRES DE PICARDIE.
MEMOIRES. 1855. irreg. price varies. Societe des
Antiquaires de Picardie, Musee de Picardie, 48 rue
de la Republique, Amiens, France.

942 UI
SOCIETE GUERNESIAISE. REPORT AND
TRANSACTIONS. (Text in English) 1882. a. £7.
Societe Guernesiaise, Priaulx Library, Guernsey, C.
I., Channel Islands. bibl. illus. index. circ. 800.

944 FR
SOCIETE HISTORIQUE DE VILLIERS SUR
MARNE ET DE LA BRIE FRANCAISE.
REVUE.* 1968. a. 10 F. Centre Culturel du
Belvedere, 94350 Villiers S/Marne, France.

949.2 NE ISSN 0085-6266
SOCIETE HISTORIQUE ET ARCHEOLOGIQUE
DANS LE LIMBOURG. PUBLICATIONS. (Text
in Dutch) 1864. a. fl.60. Limburgs Geschied- en
Oudheidkundig Genootschap, Bogaardenstraat 43,
Postbus 83, 6200 AB Maastricht, Netherlands. bk.
rev. circ. 2,000.

944 FR
SOCIETE HISTORIQUE ET ARCHEOLOGIQUE
DE PONTOISE, DU VAL D'OISE ET DU
VEXIN. MEMOIRES. irreg. Societe Historique et
Archeologique de Pontoise, du Val d'Oise et du
Vexin, 43 rue de la Roche, Pontoise, France. illus.

944 FR
SOCIETE PHILOMATIQUE VOSGIENNE.
BULLETIN. 1875. a. 45 F. Societe Philomatique
Vosgienne, Bibliotheque Municipale, Rue St.-
Charles, 88100 Saint-die, France.

945 US ISSN 0081-1424
SOCIETY FOR ITALIAN HISTORICAL STUDIES.
NEWSLETTER. 1963. a. free to members. ‡
Society for Italian Historical Studies, c/o Alan
Reinerman, Ed., Dept. of History, Boston College,
Chestnut Hill, MA 02167. circ. 200.

SOCIETY FOR LINCOLNSHIRE HISTORY AND
ARCHAEOLOGY. ANNUAL REPORT AND
STATEMENT OF ACCOUNTS. see
ARCHAEOLOGY

947 407 US
SOCIETY FOR SLOVENE STUDIES.
DOCUMENTATION SERIES. 1975. irreg. Society
for Slovene Studies, 420 W. 118 St., New York, NY
10027. Ed. Rado L. Lencek. index.

942 UK ISSN 0081-1564
SOCIETY OF ANTIQUARIES OF SCOTLAND.
PROCEEDINGS. 1851. a. £10 to non-members.
Society of Antiquaries of Scotland, National
Museum of Antiquities of Scotland, Queen Street,
Edinburgh EH2 1JD, Scotland. Ed. Dr. David
Clarke. index. circ. 2,000. Indexed:
Br.Archaeol.Abstr.

480 938 CY ISSN 0081-1580
SOCIETY OF CYPRIOT STUDIES. BULLETIN/
KYPRIAKAI SPOUDAI. (Text in Greek and other
languages) 1937. a. Mils.5000($14) Society of
Cypriot Studies, P.O. Box 1436, Nicosia, Cyprus.
Ed. Theodore Papadopoullos. bk. rev. circ. 500.

948 DK ISSN 0085-6339
SOELLEROEDBOGEN. 1942. a. Kr.50. Historisk-
Topografisk Selskab for Soelleroed Kommune,
Soelleroed Kommunebibloteker, Biblioteksalleen 1-
5, 2850 Naerum, Denmark.

948.5 SW
SOERMLANDSBYGDEN. a. Soedermanlands
Hembygdsfoerbund, Nykoeping, Sweden. Ed. Hans
Nilsson.

940 GW
SOESTER BEITRAEGE. 1949. irreg. price varies.
Verein fuer Geschichte und Heimatpflege Soest,
Stadtarchiv, 4770 Soest, W. Germany (B.R.D.) bibl.

940 GW
SOESTER ZEITSCHRIFT. 1886. a. DM.15. Verein
fuer Geschichte und Heimatpflege Soest,
Stadtarchiv, 4770 Soest, W. Germany (B.R.D.)

940 BU ISSN 0081-184X
SOFIISKI UNIVERSITET. FILOSOFSKI
FAKULTET. GODISHNIK/L'UNIVERSITE DE
SOFIA. FACULTE DE PHILOSOPHIE.
ANNUAIRE. (Summaries in various languages) vol.
67, 1974. 3.95 lv. Publishing House of the Bulgarian
Academy of Sciences, Ul. Akad. G. Bonchev, 1113
Sofia, Bulgaria. circ. 594.
Continues in part: Sofiiski Universitet. Filosofski-
Istoricheski Fakultet. Godishnik.

940 UK ISSN 0142-4688
SOUTHERN HISTORY. 1979. a. Alan Sutton
Publishing Ltd., 17a Brunswick Rd., Gloucester
GL1 1HG, England.

947 US ISSN 0085-6533
SOVIET AFFAIRS SYMPOSIUM. 1967. a. free. ‡
U.S. Army Russian Institute, APO, NY 09053. circ.
controlled. (processed)

940 NE
SOVIETICA. PUBLICATIONS AND
MONOGRAPHS. (Text in German and English)
1959. irreg. price varies. (Universite de Fribourg,
Institute of East-European Studies, SZ) D. Reidel
Publishing Co., P.O. Box 17, 3300 AA Dordrecht,
Netherlands (And Lincoln Building, 160 Old Derby
St., Hingham, MA 02043) Eds. T. J. Blakeley, G.
Kueng, N. Lobkowicz.
Formed by the merger of: Sovietica. Publication
(ISSN 0081-3206) & Sovietica. Monographs (ISSN
0081-3192)

946 GW ISSN 0081-3486
SPANISCHE FORSCHUNGEN DER
GOERRESGESELLSCHAFT. REIHE 1:
GESAMMELTE AUFSAETZE ZUR
KULTURGESCHICHTE SPANIENS. 1928. irreg.
price varies. (Goerres-Gesellschaft) Aschendorffsche
Verlagsbuchhandlung, Soester Str. 13, 4400
Muenster, W. Germany (B.R.D.) Ed. Odilo Engels.

946 GW ISSN 0081-3494
SPANISCHE FORSCHUNGEN DER
GOERRESGESELLSCHAFT. REIHE 2:
MONOGRAPHIEN. 1931. a. price varies.
(Goerres-Gesellschaft) Aschendorffsche
Verlagsbuchhandlung, Soester Str. 13, 4400
Muenster, W. Germany (B.R.D.) Ed. Odilo Engels.

909.07 US
SPECULUM ANNIVERSARY MONOGRAPHS. 1977. irreg., no. 7, 1981. price varies. Medieval Academy of America, 1430 Massachusetts Ave., Cambridge, MA 02138.

SRPSKI ETNOGRAFSKI ZBORNIK. NASELJA I POREKLO STANOVNISTVA. see *ANTHROPOLOGY*

SRPSKI ETNOGRAFSKI ZBORNIK. RASPRAVE I GRADJA. see *ANTHROPOLOGY*

SRPSKI ETNOGRAFSKI ZBORNIK. SRPSKE NARODNE UMOTVORINE. see *ANTHROPOLOGY*

SRPSKI ETNOGRAFSKI ZBORNIK. ZIVOT I OBICAJI NARODNI. see *ANTHROPOLOGY*

060 GW ISSN 0081-5578
STIFTUNG PREUSSISCHE KULTURBESITZ. JAHRBUCH. 1962. a. G. Grote'sche Verlagsbuchhandlung KG (Stuttgart), Urbanstr. 12-16, Postfach 747, 7000 Stuttgart 1, W. Germany (B.R.D.)

STILLE SCHAR. see *RELIGIONS AND THEOLOGY — Roman Catholic*

945 IT
STORIA E SOCIETA. 1976. irreg. (Istituto di Storia Contemporanea del Movimento Operaio e Contadino di Ferrera) Ricardo F. Levi Editore S.p.A., 1085-2 via Vaciglio, 41010 Modena, Italy.

945 IT
STORIA, LETTERATURA E ARTE NEL MEZZOGIORNO. irreg., no. 4, 1976. L.2000. Edizioni Dehoniane, Via Marechiaro 46, Naples, Italy. Ed. Fiorenzo F. Mastroianni.

945 IT
STUDI E DOCUMENTI. 1974. irreg. (Universita degli Studi della Calabria, Dipartimento di Storia) Editori Meridionali Riuniti, Reggio Calabria, Italy.

940 IT
STUDI ETRUSCHI. 1927. a. price varies. Casa Editrice Leo S. Olschki, Casella Postale 66, 50100 Florence, Italy. Eds. M. Pallottino, A. Neppi Modona.

945 IT ISSN 0081-6205
STUDI ROMAGNOLI. 1950. a. L.20000. (Societa di Studi Romagnoli) Biblioteca Malatestiana, 47023 Cesena, Italy.

945 IT ISSN 0081-6213
STUDI ROMAGNOLI. ESTRATTI DI SEZIONE. 1951. irreg. price varies. (Societa di Studi Romagnoli) Biblioteca Malatestiana, 47023 Cesena, Italy.

945 IT ISSN 0081-6221
STUDI ROMAGNOLI. QUADERNI. 1962. irreg.; 1977, no. 10. price varies. (Societa di Studi Romagnoli) Biblioteca Malatestiana, 47023 Cesena, Italy.

945 IT ISSN 0081-6248
STUDI SECENTESCHI. 1960. a. price varies. Casa Editrice Leo S. Olschki, Casella Postale 66, 50100 Florence, Italy. Eds. Uberto Limentani, Carmine Jannaco. bk. rev. index. circ. 1,000.

945 IT ISSN 0081-6264
STUDI VENEZIANI. 1959. a. price varies. (Fondazione Giorgio Cini) Giardini Editori e Stampatori, Via Santa Bibbiana 28, 56100 Pisa, Italy. Ed. A. Pertusi. bk. rev. circ. 1,000.
Continues: Societa e Dello Stato Veneziano. Istituto di Storia. Bollettino.

947 BU ISSN 0081-6329
STUDIA BALCANICA. (Text in English, French, German and Russian) irreg., 1970, no. 3. 2.50 lv. price varies. Publishing House of the Bulgarian Academy of Sciences, Ul. Akad. G. Bonchev, 1113 Sofia, Bulgaria.

STUDIA CAUCASICA. see *LINGUISTICS*

STUDIA ET DOCUMENTA HISTORIAE ET IURIS. see *LAW*

STUDIA HIBERNICA. see *LITERATURE*

947.1 FI ISSN 0081-6493
STUDIA HISTORICA. (Text in English, German or French) 1959. irreg., no. 8, 1978. price varies. Suomen Historiallinen Seura - Finnish Historical Society, Snellmaninkatu 9-11, 00170 Helsinki 17, Finland. circ. 350.

945 IT ISSN 0081-6507
STUDIA HISTORICA. 1964. irreg., no. 124, 1979. price varies. Erma di "Bretschneider", Via Cassiodoro, 19, 00193 Rome, Italy.

948.5 SW ISSN 0081-6515
STUDIA HISTORICA GOTHOBURGENSIA. (Text in Swedish; usually summaries in English or French) 1963. irreg., no. 14, 1972. price varies. Goeteborgs Universitet, Historiska Institutionen, Bengt Lidnersgatan 7, S-412 56 Goeteborg, Sweden. Ed. Erik Loennroth.

947.1 FI ISSN 0081-6523
STUDIA HISTORICA JYVASKYLAENSIA. (Text in English, Finnish, French, German and Swedish; summaries in English and German) 1962. irreg. price varies. Jyvaskylan Yliopisto, Kirjasto - University of Jyvaskyla, Seminaarinkatu 15, 40100 Jyvaskyla 10, Finland. Ed. Mauno Jokipii. circ. 400-500.

918 930 PL
STUDIA HISTORICA SLAVO-GERMANICA. (Text in Polish and German; summaries in German) 1973. irreg., vol. 5, 1976. price varies. Uniwersytet im. Adama Mickiewicza w Poznaniu, Stalingradzka 1, 61-712 Poznan, Poland (Dist. by: Ars Polona, Krakowskie Przedmiescie 7, 00-068 Warsaw, Poland) Ed. Antoni Czubinski. bk. rev. bibl.

940 SW ISSN 0081-6531
STUDIA HISTORICA UPSALIENSIS. (Subseries of Acta Universitatis Upsala) (Text in French, English, German, Norwegian, Swedish; summaries in English, French and German) 1960. irreg., vol. 103, 1978. price varies. (Uppsala Universitet, Historiska Institutionen) Almqvist & Wiksell International, Box 62, S-101 20 Stockholm, Sweden. Eds. Sven A. Nilson, Sten Carlsson, Carl Goeran Andrae. index.

943.8 PL ISSN 0081-654X
STUDIA I MATERIALY DO DZIEJOW WIELKOPOLSKI I POMORZA. (Text in Polish; summaries in German) 1955. irreg. price varies. (Polskie Towarzystwo Historyczne, Oddzial w Poznaniu) Panstwowe Wydawnictwo Naukowe, Ul. Miodowa 10, Warsaw, Poland. Ed. Zdzislaw Kaczmarczyk. bk. rev.

STUDIA I MATERIALY Z DZIEJOW NAUKI POLSKIEJ. SERIA A. HISTORIA NAUK SPOLECZNYCH. see *SOCIAL SCIENCES: COMPREHENSIVE WORKS*

943.8 PL ISSN 0081-6620
STUDIA I MATERIALY Z DZIEJOW POLSKI W OKRESIE OSWIECENIA. (Text in Polish; summaries in French) 1957. irreg. price varies. (Polska Akademia Nauk, Instytut Historii) Panstwowe Wydawnictwo Naukowe, Miodowa 10, Warsaw, Poland (Dist. by Ars Polona-Ruch, Krakowskie Przedmiescie 7, Warsaw, Poland) Ed. B. Lesnodorski.

947 US
STUDIA LITUANICA. (Text in English, German or Lithuanian) vol. 3, 1976. irreg. $15. Lithuanian Research Institute, Inc., 29 W. 57th St., New York, NY 10019. Ed. Martin Brakas. circ. 100.

914.38 PL ISSN 0081-6752
STUDIA NAD ZAGADNIENIAMI GOSPODARCZYMI I SPOLECZNYMI ZIEM ZACHODNICH. 1960. irreg. price varies. Instytut Zachodni, Stary Rynek 78/79, 61-772 Poznan, Poland (Dist. by Ars Polona-Ruch, Krakowskie Przedmiescie 7, Warsaw, Poland)

949.7 US ISSN 0585-5543
STUDIA SLOVENICA. 1958. irreg., no. 13, 1980. Studia Slovenica, Box 232, New York, NY 10032 (And Box 4531, Washington, DC 20017) Ed. John A. Arnez.

949.7 US ISSN 0081-6922
STUDIA SLOVENICA. SPECIAL SERIES. 1966. irreg., no. 3, 1971. $5-9. Studia Slovenica, P. O. Box 232, New York, NY 10032 (and P. O. Box 4531, Washington, D. C. 20017) Ed. John A. Arnez.

940 PL ISSN 0081-7023
STUDIA WARSZAWSKIE. 1968. irreg., 1971, vol. 9, no. 2. price varies. (Polska Akademia Nauk, Instytut Historii) Panstwowe Wydawnictwo Naukowe, Miodowa 10, Warsaw, Poland (Dist. by Ars Polona-Ruch, Krakowskie Przedmiescie 7, Warsaw, Poland)

943.8 PL ISSN 0081-7058
STUDIA Z DZIEJOW OSADNICTWA. (Subseries of Polska Akademia Nauk. Instytut Historii Kultury Materialnej. Studia i Materialy) 1963. irreg. price varies. (Polska Akademia Nauk, Instytut Historii Kultury Materialnej) Ossolineum, Publishing House of the Polish Academy of Sciences, Rynek 9, 50-106 Wroclaw, Poland (Dist. by Ars Polona-Ruch, Krakowskie Przedmiescie 7, Warsaw, Poland)

947 PL ISSN 0081-7082
STUDIA Z DZIEJOW ZSRR I EUROPY SRODKOWEJ. (Text in Polish; summaries in English and Russian) 1966. irreg., vol. 15, 1979. 60 Zl. (Polska Akademia Nauk, Instytut Historii) Ossolineum, Publishing House of the Polish Academy of Sciences, Rynek 9, Wroclaw, Poland (Dist. by Ars Polona-Ruch, Krakowskie Przedmiescie 7, Warsaw, Poland) Ed. J. Zarnowski. bk. rev. circ. 700.

943.8 PL ISSN 0081-7147
STUDIA ZRODLOZNAWCZE. (Text in Polish; summaries in Russian and one western language) 1957. irreg. price varies. (Polska Akademia Nauk, Instytut Historii) Panstwowe Wydawnictwo Naukowe, Ul. Miodowa 10, Warsaw, Poland. bk. rev.

940 AU
STUDIEN UND QUELLEN ZUR OESTERREICHISCHEN ZEITGESCHICHTE. 1978. irreg. (Wissenschaftliche Kommission des Theodor-Koerner-Stiftungsfonds und des Leopold-Kunschak-Preises zur Erforschung der Oesterreichischen Geschichte der Jahre 1918 bis 1938) Verlag fuer Geschichte und Politik, Neulinggasse 26, A-1030 Vienna, Austria.

940 NE ISSN 0585-5837
STUDIEN UND TEXTE ZUR GEISTESGESCHICHTE DES MITTELALTERS. (Text in German and English) 1950. irreg., vol. 13, 1980. price varies. E. J. Brill, Oude Rijn 33a-35, Leiden, Netherlands.

940 GW ISSN 0081-7252
STUDIEN ZUR EUROPAEISCHEN GESCHICHTE. 1955. irreg. price varies. Colloquium Verlag, Unter den Eichen 93, 1000 Berlin 45, W. Germany (B.R.D.) circ. 1,000.

940 NE ISSN 0081-7317
STUDIEN ZUR GESCHICHTE OSTEUROPAS/ STUDIES IN EAST EUROPEAN HISTORY. 1954. irreg., vol. 21, 1977. price varies. E. J. Brill, Oude Rijn 33a-35, Leiden, Netherlands (Dist. in U.S. by: Humanities Press, Inc., 171 First Ave., Atlantic Highlands, NJ 07716)

942 UK ISSN 0585-6515
STUDIES IN ANGLESEY HISTORY. 1966. irreg. (approx. biennial) price varies. Anglesey Antiquarian Society and Field Club, c/o Hon. Secretary, 22 Lon Ganol, Menai Bridge, Anglesey, Wales. Ed. Helen Ramage. bk. rev.

942 US ISSN 0081-7619
STUDIES IN BRITISH HISTORY AND CULTURE. 1968. irreg., 1970, no. 3. (Conference on British Studies) Archon Books (Subsidiary of: Shoe String Press, Inc.) 995 Sherman Ave., Hamden, CT 06514. (Co-sponsor: Wittenberg University)

947 NE
STUDIES IN EAST EUROPEAN SOCIAL HISTORY. (Text in English, German and French) 1977. biennial. price varies. E.J. Brill, Oude Rijn 33a-35, Leiden, Netherlands. Ed. Keith Hitchins.

940 NE ISSN 0081-7910
STUDIES IN EUROPEAN HISTORY. 1964. irreg. price varies. Mouton Publishers, Noordeinde 41, 2514 GC The Hague, Netherlands (U.S. addr: Mouton Publishers, c/o Walter de Gruyter, Inc., 200 Saw Mill River Road, Hawthorne, NY 10532)

941 CN ISSN 0081-8097
STUDIES IN IRISH HISTORY. 1960. irreg. price varies. University of Toronto Press, Front Campus, Toronto, Ont. M5S 1A6. Eds. T. W. Moody, J. C. Beckett, T. D. Williams. (also avail. in microfiche)

940.1 CN ISSN 0081-8224
STUDIES IN MEDIEVAL AND RENAISSANCE HISTORY. 1964. a. Can.$18 per vol. University of British Columbia, Committee for Medieval Studies, Vancouver, B.C. V6T 1W5, Canada.

940 US ISSN 0098-275X
STUDIES IN MODERN EUROPEAN HISTORY AND CULTURE. 1975. a. $9. Institute for the Study of Nineteenth Century Europe, 188 Lawton Rd., Riverside, IL 60546. bk. rev. circ. 500. (also avail. in microform from UMI) Indexed: Hist.Abstr.

940 UK
STUDIES IN RUSSIAN AND EAST EUROPEAN HISTORY. irreg. price varies. (University of London, School of Slavonic and East European Studies) Macmillan Press Ltd., 4 Little Essex St., London WC2R 3LF, England.

940 UK ISSN 0141-030X
STUDIES IN WELSH HISTORY. 1977. irreg. price varies. (Board of Celtic Studies) University of Wales Press, 6 Gwennyth St., Cathays, Cardiff CF2 4YD, Wales. Ed.Bd. (reprint service avail. from UMI)

943 RM
STUDII ISTORICE SUD-EST EUROPENE. (Text in Romanian; summaries in French) 1974. irreg. (Institutul de Studii Sud-Est Europene) Editura Academiei Republicii Socialiste Romania, Calea Victoriei 125, Bucharest, Romania (Subscr. to: ILEXIM, Str. 13 Decembrie Nr. 3, P.O. Box 136-137, Bucharest, Romania)

949 RM
STUDII SI ARTICOLE DE ISTORIE. irreg. Societatea de Stiinte Istorice din Republica Socialista Romania, Bd. Republicii Nr. 55, Bucharest, Romania. illus.
Formerly: Societatea de Stiinte Istorice si Filologice Din R.P.R. Studii si Articole de Istorie.

940 RM
STUDII SI MATERIALE DE ISTORIE MEDIE. (Text in Romanian; summaries in English, French, German, Russian) 1956. irreg. (Academia de Stiinte Sociale si Politice) Editura Academiei Republicii Socialiste Romania, Calea Victoriei 125, Bucharest, Romania (Subscr. to: ILEXIM, Str. 13 Decembrie Nr. 3, P.O. Box 136-137, Bucharest, Romania) adv. bk. rev. circ. 800.

940 RM
STUDII SI MATERIALE DE ISTORIE MODERNA. (Text in Romanian; summaries in French) 1970. irreg. (Academia de Stiinte Sociale si Politice, Institutul de Istorie "N. Iorga") Editura Academiei Republicii Socialiste Romania, Calea Victoriei 125, Bucharest, Romania (Subscr. to: ILEXIM, Str. 13 Decembrie Nr. 3, P.O. Box 136-137, Bucharest, Romania) Ed. N. Adadiloaie, D. Berindei. adv. bk. rev.

940 PL ISSN 0081-8941
STUDIUM NIEMCOZNAWCZE. (Text in Polish; summaries in English or Russian) 1946. irreg., vol. 26, 1975. price varies. Instytut Zachodni, Stary Rynek 78/79, 61-772 Poznan, Poland (Dist. by Ars Polona-Ruch, Krakowskie Przedmiescie 7, Warsaw, Poland) Ed. Maria Morkowska. circ. 1,500-2,000.

947 UK
STUDY GROUP ON EIGHTEENTH-CENTURY RUSSIA. NEWSLETTER. 1973. a. £2($5) to individuals; £3($7.50) to institutions. Study Group on Eighteenth-Century Russia, c/o Dr. A. G. Cross, School of Modern Languages and European History, University of East Anglia, Norwich NR4 7TJ, England. bk. rev. bibl. circ. 200.

940 CN ISSN 0316-0769
SUBSIDIA MEDIAEVALIA. 1972. irreg. price varies. Pontifical Institute of Mediaeval Studies, 59 Queen's Park Crescent E., Toronto, Ont. M5S 2C4, Canada. circ. 600.

943.7 GW ISSN 0081-9077
SUEDOST-FORSCHUNGEN; Internationale Zeitschrift fuer Geschichte, Kultur und Landeskunde Suedosteuropas. (Text in English, French and German) 1936. a. DM.85. Suedost-Institut, Guellstr. 7, 8000 Munich 2, W. Germany (B.R.D.) Ed. Mathias Bernath. bk. rev.

940 GW
SUEDOSTDEUTSCHE HISTORISCHE KOMMISSION. BUCHREIHE. 1958. irreg. price varies. R. Oldenbourg Verlag GmbH, Rosenheimer Str. 145, 8000 Munich 80, W. Germany (B.R.D.) Ed. Adam Wandruzska.

940 398 GW ISSN 0081-9085
SUEDOSTDEUTSCHES ARCHIV. 1958. a. DM.40. (Suedostdeutsche Historische Kommission) R. Oldenbourg Verlag GmbH, Rosenheimer Str. 145, 8000 Munich 80, W. Germany (B.R.D.) Ed. Adam Wandruszka, Felix v. Schroeder.

943 GW ISSN 0081-9093
SUEDOSTDEUTSCHES KULTURWERK, MUNICH. KLEINE SUEDOSTREIHE. 1957. irreg. price varies. Suedostdeutsches Kulturwerk, Guellstr. 7, 8000 Munich 2, W. Germany (B.R.D.)

943 831 GW ISSN 0081-9107
SUEDOSTDEUTSCHES KULTURWERK, MUNICH. SCHRIFTENREIHEN. REIHE A. KULTUR UND DICHTUNG. 1953. irreg. price varies. Suedostdeutsches Kulturwerk, Guellstr. 7, 8000 Munich 2, W. Germany (B.R.D.)

943 830 GW ISSN 0081-9115
SUEDOSTDEUTSCHES KULTURWERK, MUNICH. SCHRIFTENREIHEN. REIHE B. WISSENSCHAFTLICHE ARBEITEN. 1954. irreg. price varies. Suedostdeutsches Kulturwerk, Guellstr. 7, 8000 Munich 2, W. Germany (B.R.D.)

940 GW ISSN 0081-9123
SUEDOSTDEUTSCHES KULTURWERK, MUNICH. SCHRIFTENREIHEN. REIHE C. ERINNERUNGEN UND QUELLEN. 1958. irreg. price varies. Suedostdeutsches Kulturwerk, Guellstr. 7, 8000 Munich 2, W. Germany (B.R.D.)

940 GW ISSN 0081-914X
SUEDOSTEUROPA-JAHRBUCH. 1957. irreg., 1973, vol. 10. price varies. Suedosteuropa-Gesellschaft e.V., Widenmayerstr. 49, 8000 Munich 22, W. Germany (B.R.D.)

940 GW ISSN 0081-9158
SUEDOSTEUROPA-SCHRIFTEN. 1959. irreg., 1968, vol. 9. price varies. Suedosteuropa-Gesellschaft e. V., Widenmayerstr. 49, 8000 Munich 22, W. Germany (B.R.D.)

940 GW ISSN 0081-9166
SUEDOSTEUROPA-STUDIEN. 1962. irreg., no. 24, 1976. price varies. Suedosteuropa-Gesellschaft e.V., Widenmayerstr. 49, 8000 Munich 22, W. Germany (B.R.D.)

940 GW
SUEDOSTEUROPAEISCHE ARBEITEN. no. 13, 1937. irreg., vol. 76, 1978. price varies. (Suedost-Institut) R. Oldenbourg Verlag GmbH, Rosenheimer Str. 145, 8000 Munich 80, W. Germany (B.R.D.) Ed. M. Bernath.

947.1 FI ISSN 0081-9425
SUOMEN HISTORIAN LAEHTEITAE/SOURCE MATERIAL OF FINNISH HISTORY. (Text in Finnish or Swedish) 1936. irreg., 1973, no. 8. price varies. Suomen Historiallinen Seura - Finnish Historical Society, Snellmaninkatu 9-11, 00170 Helsinki 17, Finland. circ. 342.

948.5 SW
SVENSKA HISTORISKA FOERENINGEN. SKRIFTER. irreg., no. 8, 1978. price varies. Almqvist & Wiksell International, Box 62, S-101 20 Stockholm, Sweden.

SWEDEN. RIKSARKIVET. MEDDELANDEN. see LIBRARY AND INFORMATION SCIENCES

944 FR ISSN 0082-1403
TABLE RONDE FRANCAISE. ANNUAIRE. 1964/65. a. (Table Ronde Francaise) S.E.P.A.L., 23 rue du Renard, 75004 Paris, France.

914.3 GW ISSN 0082-1829
TASCHENBUCH DES OEFFENTLICHEN LEBENS. 1950. a. price varies. Festland-Verlag, Postfach 200841, 5300 Bonn 2, W. Germany (B.R.D.) Ed. Albert Oeckl. adv. circ. 14,000.

943.8 UK ISSN 0085-4956
TEKI HISTORYCZNE. (Text in Polish; summaries in English) 1947. a. Polish Historical Society in Great Britain, 20 Princes Gate, London SW7 1QA, England.

943 IS
TEL AVIV UNIVERSITY. INSTITUT FUER DEUTSCHE GESCHICHTE. JAHRBUCH. (Text in German; summaries in Hebrew) 1972. a. I£112($17) Tel-Aviv University, Institute for German History, Tel-Aviv, Ramat-Aviv, Israel. Ed. Walter Grab. bk. rev. circ. 1,200.

946 SP
TEMAS DE HISTORIA Y POLITICA CONTEMPORANEAS. no. 4, 1978. irreg. Ediciones Peninsula, Provenza 278, Barcelona 8, Spain.

940.5472 CS
TEREZINSKE LISTY.* (Text in Czech; summaries in English, German and Russian) 1970. a. 10 Kcs. (Pamatnik Terezin) Severoceske Nakladatelstvi, Alcova 1, Liberec, Czechoslovakia. illus.

945 IT
TESTI MEDIEVALI DI INTERESSE DANTESCO. 1977. irreg., vol. 2, 1978. (Istituto Dantesco Europeo) Casa Editrice Leo S. Olschki, Casella Postale 66, 50100 Florence, Italy. Ed. Bd.

TEXTS AND STUDIES IN THE HISTORY OF MEDIAEVAL EDUCATION. see EDUCATION

940 NE
THORBECKE-COLLEGES. 1975. irreg., vol. 3, 1977. price varies. Leiden University Press, c/o Martinus Nijhoff, Box 566, 2501 CN The Hague, Netherlands.

THOROTON SOCIETY OF NOTTINGHAMSHIRE. TRANSACTIONS. see ARCHAEOLOGY

947 RM
TIBISCUS. SERIA ISTORIE. (Text in Romanian: summaries in German) a. Muzeul Banatului, Piata Huniade Nr. 1, Timisoara, Romania.

943.6 AU
TIROLER ORTSCHRONIKEN. 1973. irreg., 2-3/yr. price varies. Tiroler Landesarchiv, Herrengasse 1, A-6010 Innsbruck, Austria. Ed. Fridolin Doerrer.

943.6 AU
TIROLOER GESCHICHTSQUELLEN. 1976. irreg., 2-3/yr. price varies. Tiroler Landesarchiv, Herrengasse, A-6010 Innsbruck, Austria. Ed. Fridolin Doerrer.

TORONTO MEDIAEVAL LATIN TEXTS. see LITERATURE

940 PL ISSN 0082-5506
TOWARZYSTWO NAUKOWE W TORUNIU. FONTES. 1897. irreg., 1968, vol. 60. price varies. Panstwowe Wydawnictwo Naukowe, Ul. Miodowa 10, Warsaw, Poland (Dist. by Ars Polona-Ruch, Krakowskie Przedmiescie 7, Warsaw, Poland) Ed. Artur Hutnikiewicz.

940 US ISSN 0362-1529
TRADITIO; studies in ancient and medieval history, thought, and religion. 1943. a. $30. Fordham University Press, University Box L, Bronx, NY 10458. circ. 1,000. (back issues available)

940 800 900 SZ ISSN 0082-6081
TRAVAUX D'HUMANISME ET RENAISSANCE. irreg., no. 154, 1977. price varies. Librarie Droz, 11, rue Massot, 1211 Geneva 12, Switzerland. circ. 1,000.

948 FI ISSN 0085-7440
TURUN HISTORIALLINEN ARKISTO. Variant title: Turun Historiallisen Yhdistyksen Julkaisuja. 1924. a. $10-20. Turun Historiallinen Yhdistys, Turun Yliopisto, SF-20500 Turku 50, Finland. circ. 600. Indexed: Hist.Abstr.

HISTORY — HISTORY OF EUROPE

947 US
U C I S SERIES IN RUSSIAN & EAST EUROPEAN STUDIES. 1977. irreg. University of Pittsburgh, University Center for International Studies, G-6 Mervis Hall, Pittsburgh, PA 15260.

941.6 UK ISSN 0082-7363
ULSTER-SCOT HISTORICAL SERIES. 1966. irreg., 1969, no. 2. ‡ Routledge & Kegan Paul Ltd., Broadway House, Newtown Rd., Henley-on-Thames, Oxon. RG9 1EN, England (U.S. orders to: Routledge Journals, 9 Park St., Boston, MA 02108) Ed. J. C. Beckett, Kenneth Darwin.

940 UK ISSN 0082-7371
ULSTER YEAR BOOK. a. price varies. H.M.S.O. (N. Ireland), 80 Chichester Street, Belfast BT1 4JY, Northern Ireland.

943.91 GW ISSN 0082-755X
UNGARN-JAHRBUCH; Zeitschrift fuer die Kunde Ungarns und Verwandte Gebiete. 1969. a. DM.35. (Ungarisches Institut) V. Hase und Koehler Verlag, Clemensstr. 2, 8000 Munich 40, W. Germany (B.R.D.) bk. rev.

943.1 US
UNICORN GERMAN SERIES. (Text in English and German) 1968. irreg. $5 paper; $15 cloth. Unicorn Press, Inc., Box 3307, Greensboro, NC 27402. Ed. Teo Savory. (back issues avail.)

940 US ISSN 0083-0070
U. S. DEPARTMENT OF STATE. EUROPEAN AND BRITISH COMMONWEALTH SERIES. 1948. irreg. price varies. U.S. Department of State, Bureau of Public Affairs, Washington, DC 20250 (Orders to Supt. of Documents, Washington, DC 20402)

944 FR
UNIVERS DE LA FRANCE ET DES PAYS FRANCOPHONES. vol. 44, 1979. irreg. Editions Edouard Privat, 14 rue des Arts, 31000 Toulouse, France. Dir. Philippe Wolff.

946 SP
UNIVERSIDAD DE LA LAGUNA. COLECCION ESTUDIOS DE HISTORIA. no. 2, 1976. irreg. Universidad de la Laguna, Secretariado de Publicaciones, Laguna, Canary Islands, Spain.

940 SP
UNIVERSIDAD DE OVIEDO. CENTRO DE ESTUDIOS DEL SIGLO XVIII. BOLETIN. 1973. irreg. $5. Universidad de Oviedo, Centro de Estudios del Siglo XVIII, Calle San Francisco, Oviedo, Spain.

945 IT
UNIVERSITA CATTOLICA DEL SACRO CUORE. ISTITUTO DI STORIA ANTICA. CONTRIBUTI. 1972. irreg. L.9500. (Universita Cattolica del Sacro Cuore, Istituto di Storia Antica) Vita e Pensiero, Largo Gemelli 1, 20123 Milan, Italy. illus.

900 IT ISSN 0072-0860
UNIVERSITA DEGLI STUDI DI GENOVA. ISTITUTO DI PALEOGRAFIA E STORIA MEDIEVALE. COLLANA. STORICA DI FONTI E STUDI. 1958. irreg. price varies. Universita degli Studi di Genova, Istituto di Paleografia e Storia Medievale, Via Cairoli, 18, 16124 Genoa, Italy (Dist. by: Libreria Bozzi, via Cairoli 2, Genoa, Italy) circ. 300-500.

930 940 IT ISSN 0076-6631
UNIVERSITA DEGLI STUDI DI MESSINA. ISTITUTO DI STORIA MEDIEVALE E MODERNA. PUBBLICAZIONI. 1959. irreg. price varies. Casa Editrice Felice le Monnier, Via Scipione Ammirato 100, C.P.455, 50136 Florence, Italy.

945 IT ISSN 0078-771X
UNIVERSITA DEGLI STUDI DI PADOVA. CENTRO PER LA STORIA DELLA TRADIZIONE ARISTOTELICA NEL VENETO. SAGGI E TESTI. 1961. irreg.; no. 14, 1977. price varies. Editrice Antenore, Via G. Rusca 15, 35100 Padua, Italy.

UNIVERSITATEA BUCURESTI. ANALELE. FILOZOFIE. ISTORIE. DREPT. see *PHILOSOPHY*

940 FR ISSN 0065-5007
UNIVERSITE D'AIX-MARSEILLE III. INSTITUT D'HISTOIRE DES PAYS D'OUTRE-MER. ETUDES ET DOCUMENTS. 1970. irreg. price varies. Universite d'Aix-Marseille III (Universite de Droit, d'Economie et des Sciences), Institut d'Histoire des Pays d'Outre-Mer, 3 Avenue Robert Schuman, 13621 Aix- en- Provence, France. (also avail. in microform)

949.4 SZ
UNIVERSITE DE FRIBOURG. HISTORISCHE SCHRIFTEN. 1976. irreg. Editions Universitaires de Fribourg, 36 Bd. de Perolles, 1700 Fribourg, Switzerland.

940 SZ ISSN 0072-0836
UNIVERSITE DE GENEVE. SECTION D'HISTOIRE. DOCUMENTS. 1966. irreg., no. 10, 1976. price varies. Librarie Droz, 11, rue Massot, 1211 Geneva 12, Switzerland. circ. 1,600.

UNIVERSITE DE HAUTE BRETAGNE. CENTRE D'ETUDES HISPANIQUES, HISPANO-AMERICAINES ET LUSO-BRESILIENNES. TRAVAUX. see *LITERATURE*

944 FR
UNIVERSITE DE NANTES. CENTRE DE RECHERCHES SUR L'HISTOIRE DE LA FRANCE ATLANTIQUE. ENQUETES ET DOCUMENTS. 1971. a. 59 F. Universite de Nantes, Centre de Recherches sur l'Histoire de la France Atlantique, Chemin de la Sensive du Tertre, Boite Postal 1025, 44036 Nantes Cedex, France. bk. rev. illus. stat.

940 FR ISSN 0079-256X
UNIVERSITE DE POITIERS. CENTRE D'ETUDES SUPERIEURES DE CIVILISATION MEDIEVALE. PUBLICATIONS. 1960. irreg. price varies. Universite de Poitiers, Centre d'Etudes Superieures de Civilisation Medievale, 24 rue de la Chaine, 86022 Poitiers, France.

944 FR
UNIVERSITE DE RENNES. INSTITUT ARMORICAIN DE RECHERCHES ECONOMIQUES ET HUMAINES. (PUBLICATION) 1966. irreg. price varies. Editions Klincksieck, 11, rue de Lille, Paris 7e, France. Ed. Prof. Delumeau.
Formerly: Institut Armoricain de Recherches Historiques, Rennes. (Publication) (ISSN 0073-8220)

949.3 BE
UNIVERSITE LIBRE DE BRUXELLES. GROUPE D'ETUDE DU DIX-HUITIEME SIECLE. ETUDES SUR LE DIX-HUITIEME SIECLE. 1974. irreg. (Groupe d'Etude de Dix-Huiteme Siecle) Editions de l'Universite de Bruxelles, Parc Leopold, 1040 Brussels, Belgium.

949.3 BE
UNIVERSITE LIBRE DE BRUXELLES. INSTITUT POUR L'ETUDE DE LA RENAISSANCE ET DE L'HUMANISME. COLLOQUES. 1963. irreg., 5th, 1976. Editions de l'Universite de Bruxelles, Parc Leopold, 1040 Brussels, Belgium.

940 UK ISSN 0076-082X
UNIVERSITY OF LONDON. INSTITUTE OF HISTORICAL RESEARCH BULLETIN. SPECIAL SUPPLEMENT. 1936, no. 3. irreg., no. 11, 1976. free with I.H.R. Bulletin. University of London, Institute of Historical Research, London WC1E 7HU, England. circ. 1,500.

940 UK ISSN 0141-0008
UNIVERSITY OF NOTTINGHAM. DEPARTMENT OF ADULT EDUCATION. BULLETIN OF LOCAL HISTORY, EAST MIDLANDS REGION. 1966. a. price varies. University of Nottingham, Department of Adult Education, Publications Unit, 14-22 Shakespeare St., Nottingham NG1 4FJ, England. Ed. John H. Davies. bibl. cum.index. circ. 300.

940 UK ISSN 0079-9858
UNIVERSITY OF READING. GRADUATE SCHOOL OF CONTEMPORARY EUROPEAN STUDIES. OCCASIONAL PUBLICATION. 1968. irreg. University of Reading, Graduate School of Contemporary European Studies, Faculty of Letters and Social Sciences, White Knights, Reading, Berks RG6 2AB, England.

940 340 UK
UNIVERSITY OF WALES. BOARD OF CELTIC STUDIES. HISTORY AND LAW SERIES. 1929. irreg. University of Wales Press, 6 Gwennyth St., Cathays, Cardiff CF2 4YD, Wales. Ed. Glanmor Williams. (reprint service avail. from UMI)

943.8 PL ISSN 0072-0461
UNIWERSYTET GDANSKI. WYDZIAL HUMANISTYCZNY. ZESZYTY NAUKOWE. HISTORIA. 1965. irreg. Uniwersytet Gdanski, Ul. Czerwonej Armii 110, 81-824 Sopot, Poland (Dist. by Ars Polona-Ruch, Krakowskie Przedmiescie 7, Warsaw, Poland)

943.8 PL ISSN 0083-4351
UNIWERSYTET JAGIELLONSKI. ZESZYTY NAUKOWE. PRACE HISTORYCZNE. (Text in Polish; summaries in English, French, German, Russian) 1955. irreg., 1972, vol. 39. price varies. Panstwowe Wydawnictwo Naukowe, Miodowa 10, Warsaw, Poland (Dist by Ars Polona-Ruch, Krakowskie Przedmiescie 7, Warsaw, Poland) Ed. Jerzy Wyrozumski. circ. 600.

940 300 UK ISSN 0306-0845
URBAN HISTORY YEARBOOK. 1974. a. price varies. Leicester University Press, Fielding Johnson Bldg., Univ. of Leicester, University Rd., Leicester, England.

948.5 SW
VAESTERBOTTENS NORRA FORNMINNESFOERENING. SKELLEFTEA MUSEUM. MEDDELANDE. no. 37, 1975. irreg. Kr.18.50. Vaesterbottens Norra Fornminnesfoerening, Skelleftea Museum, Skelleftea, Sweden. Ed. Peter Gustafsson, Stig-Henrik Viklund. illus.

940 NO
VALDRES HISTORIELAG. AARBOK. 1916. a. price varies. Valdres Historielag, 2967 Lomen, Norway. Ed. Bd. bk. rev. bibl. illus. circ. 2,500.

948 DK ISSN 0085-7645
VENDSYSSEL AARBOG. 1915. a. Kr.25($5) ‡ Historisk Samfund for Vendsyssel, Sct.Annavej 3, DK-9800 Hjoerring, Denmark. Ed. Joergen Joergensen. circ. 3,200.
Formerly: Vendsysselske Aarboeger.
Local

943 GW ISSN 0083-5579
VEREIN FUER GESCHICHTE DER STADT NUERNBERG. MITTEILUNGEN. 1879. a. price varies. Verein fuer Geschichte der Stadt Nuernberg, Egidienplatz 23, 8500 Nuernberg, W. Germany (B. R. D.) Ed. G. Hirschmann. bk. rev. circ. 1,100.

943.6 AU
VEREIN FUER GESCHICHTE DER STADT WIEN. JAHRBUCH. 1939. a. Verein fuer Geschichte der Stadt Wien, Rathaus, A-1082 Vienna, Austria. Ed. Peter Czendes. circ. 1,700.

943 GW ISSN 0083-5587
VEREIN FUER HAMBURGISCHE GESCHICHTE. ZEITSCHRIFT. 1841. a. DM.30. Verein fuer Hamburgische Geschichte, ABC-Str. 19, 2000 Hamburg 36, W. Germany (B. R. D.) adv. bk. rev. cum.index. circ. 1,500.

943 GW ISSN 0083-5609
VEREIN FUER LUEBECKISCHE GESCHICHTE UND ALTERTUMSKUNDE. ZEITSCHRIFT. a. DM.30. ‡ Max Schmidt-Roemhild Verlag, Mengstr. 16, 2400 Luebeck 1, W. Germany (B.R.D.) Ed. A. Grassmann. bk. rev.

949 SZ ISSN 0083-5641
VEREINIGUNG PRO SIHLTAL. BLAETTER. 1951. a. 12 Fr. Vereinigung Pro Sihltal, Postfach, 8039 Zurich Selnau, Switzerland. cum. index (1951-1979)

940 342 SZ
VERFASSUNGSGESCHICHTE. 1975. irreg. Verlag Peter Lang AG, Muenzgraben 2, Postfach, CH-3000 Berne 7, Switzerland. Ed. Bd.

VIENNA CIRCLE COLLECTION. see *BIOGRAPHY*

948 UK ISSN 0305-9219
VIKING SOCIETY FOR NORTHERN RESEARCH. SAGA BOOK. a. £6.50. Viking Society for Northern Research, c/o Dept. of Scandinavian Studies, University College, London WC1E 6BT, England.

VLASTIVEDNY ZBORNIK. see *HUMANITIES: COMPREHENSIVE WORKS*

947 398 US
VOLHYNIAN BIBLIOGRAPHIC CENTER. PUBLICATIONS. (Text in Ukrainian; summaries in English) 1968. a. price varies ($5-$10 per no.) Volhynian Bibliographic Center, 307 N. Overhill Drive, Bloomington, IN 47401. Ed. Dr. Max Boyko. circ. 100. (processed)
Formerly (until 1970): Volhynian Bibliographic Center, Proceedings.

947 UR
VOPROSY ISTORII DAL'NEGO VOSTOKA, KHABAROVSK, GOS. PED. INSTITUT. 1972. irreg. Khabarovskii Gosudarstvennyi Pedagogicheskii Institut, Khabarovsk, U.S.S.R.

940 UK ISSN 0307-5281
WATFORD AND DISTRICT INDUSTRIAL HISTORY SOCIETY. JOURNAL. 1971. a. price varies. ‡ Watford and District Industrial History Society, c/o Mr. R.C. Kennell, 37 Kindersley Way, Abbots Langley, Hertsfordshire WD5 0DG, England. Ed. D.G.N. English. charts. illus. circ. 100.
Formerly: Watford and District Industrial History Society Bulletin.
Local

940 910 GE ISSN 0083-8063
WERTE UNSERER HEIMAT; Ergebnisse der heimatkundlichen Bestandsaufnahme in der DDR. 1957. irreg., no. 30, 1977. DM.12,50. (Akademie der Wissenschaften der DDR, Geographisches Institut) Akademie-Verlag, Leipziger Str. 3-4, 108 Berlin, E. Germany (D.D.R.)

942 UK ISSN 0143-8158
WEST MIDLANDS ARCHIVES NEWSLETTER. 1979. irreg. Walsall Library & Museums Service, Central Library, Lichfield St., Walsall WS1 1TR, England. illus.
Local

944 US ISSN 0099-0329
WESTERN SOCIETY FOR FRENCH HISTORY. PROCEEDINGS OF THE ANNUAL MEETING. 1974. a. $25. (Western Society for French History) New Mexico State University Press, c/o J.D. Falk, 2726 Cuesta Rd., Santa Barbara, CA 93105. circ. 250. Indexed: Hist.Abstr. Key Title: Proceedings of the Annual Meeting of the Western Society for French History.

943 GW ISSN 0083-9027
WESTFAELISCHE FORSCHUNGEN. a. price varies. (Provinzialinstitut fuer Westfaelische Landes- und Volksforschung) Aschendorffsche Verlagsbuchhandlung, Soester Str. 13, Postfach 1124, 4400 Muenster, W. Germany (B. R. D.) Ed. K. H. Kirchhoff. bk. rev.

943 GW ISSN 0083-9043
WESTFAELISCHE ZEITSCHRIFT. 1948. irreg. DM.36. (Verein fuer Geschichte und Altertumskunde Westfalens) Verlag Regensberg, Daimlerweg 58, Postfach 6748/6749, 4400 Muenster, W. Germany (B.R.D.) Eds. Klemens Honselmann, Alfred Hartlieb von Wallthor. circ. ,3,000.

WESTFALIA SACRA; Quellen und Forschungen zur Kirchengeschichte Westfalens. see *RELIGIONS AND THEOLOGY*

943 GW ISSN 0511-8484
WESTPREUSSEN-JAHRBUCH. 1950. a. DM.22. (Landsmannschaft Westpreussen e.V.) Verlagsgesellschaft C. J. Fahle, Neubrueckenstr. 8-11, 4400 Muenster, W. Germany (B.R.D.) bibl. illus. stat. circ. 2,000.

942.2 UK
WHITLOCK'S WESSEX. 1975. a. $2.95. Moonraker Press, 26 St. Margarets St., Bradford-on-Avon, Wiltshire, England. illus.
Local

WIENER RINGSTRASSE-BILD EINER EPOCHE; Die Erweiterung der Inneren Stadt Wien unter Kaiser Franz Joseph. see *ART*

940 UK
WINCHESTER STUDIES. 1976. irreg. Oxford University Press, Press Rd., Neasden, London NW10 0DD, England. Ed. Martin Biddle.

940 AU
WISSENSCHAFTLICHE KOMMISSION DES THEODOR-KOERNER-STIFTUNGSFONDS UND DES LEOPOLD-KUNSCHAK-PREISES ZUR ENFORSCHUNG DER OESTERREICHISCHEN GESCHICHTE DER JAHRE 1918 BIS 1938. VEROEFFENTLICHUNGEN. 1973. irreg. price varies. Verlag fuer Geschichte und Politik, Neulinggasse 26, A-1030 Vienna, Austria. Eds. R. Neck, A. Wandrustka.

940 US ISSN 0084-232X
WORLD TODAY SERIES: SOVIET UNION AND EASTERN EUROPE. a. $2.95. Stryker-Post Publications Inc., 888 Seventeenth St., N.W., Washington, DC 20006. Ed. Samuel L. Sharp.

940 US ISSN 0084-2338
WORLD TODAY SERIES: WESTERN EUROPE. a. $2.95. Stryker-Post Publications Inc., 888 Seventeenth St., N.W., Washington, DC 20006. Ed. Claire Z. Carey.

943 GW ISSN 0084-2613
DER WORMSGAU; Zeitschrift der Kulturinstitute der Stadt Worms und des Altertumsvereins Worms. 1926. a. DM.15. Stadtbibliothek, Marktplatz 10, 6520 Worms, W. Germany (B.R.D.) Dir. Fritz Reuter. bk. rev.

943 GW ISSN 0084-3067
WUERTTEMBERGISCH FRANKEN. 1847. a. DM.25. Historischer Verein fuer Wuerttembergisch Franken, Dr. G. Wunder, Postfach 664, 7170 Schwaebisch Hall, W. Germany (B.R.D.) bk. rev.

943 GW
WUERZBURGER DIOEZESANGESCHICHTSBLAETTER. 1933. a. DM.20. Wuerzburger Dioezesangeschichtsverein, Domerschulstrasse, 8700 Wuerzburg 1, W. Germany (B.R.D.) bk. rev. charts. illus. circ. 800. (tabloid format)

945 IT
YEARBOOK OF ITALIAN STUDIES. 1971. irreg. price varies. (Italian Cultural Institute, CN) Casalini Libri, 50014 Fiesole, Italy. Eds. Antonio d'Andrea, Dante della Terza. circ. 1,500.

YEARBOOK OF ROMANIAN STUDIES. see *LITERATURE*

942 UK ISSN 0084-4047
YEARBOOK OF THE COMMONWEALTH. 1969 under new title. a. H.M.S.O., P.O. Box 569, London SE1 9NH, England.
Supersedes: Great Britain. Commonwealth Office. Yearbook.

940 UK
YORKSHIRE ARCHAEOLOGICAL SOCIETY RECORD SERIES. 1885. a. £10. Yorkshire Archaeological Society, Claremont, Clarendon Road, Leeds LS2 9NZ, England. Ed. J. Taylor. index. circ. 350.

949.7 YU ISSN 0084-5191
ZBORNIK ZA ISTORIJU, JEZIK I KNJIZEVNOST SRPSKOG NARODA. FONTES RERUM SLAVORUM MERIDIONALIUM. (Text in Serbo-Croatian; summaries in French, German or Russian) 1932. irreg. price varies. Srpska Akademija Nauka i Umetnosti, Knez Mihailova 35, 11001 Belgrade, Yugoslavia (Dist. by: Prosveta, Terazije 16, Belgrade, Yugoslavia) circ. 800.

949.7 YU ISSN 0084-5213
ZBORNIK ZA ISTORIJU, JEZIK I KNJIZEVNOST SRPSKOG NARODA. SPOMENICI NA TUDJIM JEZICIMA. (Text in Serbo-Croatian; summaries in French, English, German or Russian) 1904. irreg. price varies. Srpska Akademija Nauka i Umetnosti, Knez Mihailova 35, 11001 Belgrade, Yugoslavia (Dist. by: Prosveta, Terazije 16, Belgrade, Yugoslavia) circ. 600.

943 GW
ZEITSCHRIFT FUER DIE GESCHICHTE DES OBERRHEINS. 1850. a. DM.58. Kommission fuer Geschichtliche Landeskunde in Baden-Wuerttemberg, Konrad-Adenauer-Str. 4, 7000 Stuttgart 1, W. Germany(B.R.D.) bk. rev. circ. 500.

943 YU
ZENTAI FUZETEK. 1960. irreg. 25 din.($3) Udruzenje Prijatelja Muzeja i Arhiva "Dudas Gyula", 24400 Senta, Yugoslavia (Dist. by: Forum NIP, Vojvode Misica 1, 21000 Novi Sad, Yugoslavia) Ed. Janos Szloboda. circ. 250-1,000.
Local

943 PL ISSN 0084-5493
ZIEMA KOZIELSKA. STUDIA I MATERIALY. 1971. irreg. 60 Zl. Instytut Slaski, Instytut Naukowo-Badawczy, Lubozycka 3, Opole, Poland.

943.8 PL ISSN 0084-5507
ZIEMIE ZACHODNIE. STUDIA I MATERIALY. (Text in Polish; summaries in English, Russian) 1957. irreg. price varies. Instytut Zachodni, Stary Rynek 78/79, 61-772 Poznan, Poland (Dist. by Ars Polona-Ruch, Krakowskie Przedmiescie 7, Warsaw, Poland) circ. 2,000.

943.8 PL ISSN 0084-568X
ZRODLA DO DZIEJOW BYDGOSZCZY. 1963. irreg. price varies. Bydgoskie Towarzystwo Naukowe, Jezuicka 4, Bydgoszcz, Poland (Dist. by Ars Polona-Ruch, Krakowskie Przedmiescie 7, Warsaw, Poland)

949.4 SZ ISSN 0084-5809
ZUR LAGE DER SCHWEIZ; beitrage zueinem Rueckblick. 1962. a. 7 Fr. Schweizerischer Aufklaerungs-Dienst, Feldeggstrasse 65, 8034 Zurich, Switzerland.

940 NE
ZWISCHEN HAUSMANNSTURM UND WALBECKER WARTE. (Text in German) vol. 17, 1976. irreg. price varies. Europese Bibliotheek, Gasthuisstr. 12, Box 49, Zaltbommel, Netherlands. Ed. R. Schaper.

942 UK
1745 ASSOCIATION AND NATIONAL MILITARY HISTORY SOCIETY. QUARTERLY NOTES. 1967. 3-4/yr. £2. 1745 Association and National Military History Society, c/o Ed. Barbara Fairweather, Inevloe House, Glencoe, Argyll, Scotland (Subscr. to: Mrs Hart, 45 Ann St.,Edinburgh, Scotland) bk. rev. circ. 300-350.

HISTORY — History Of North And South America

973 AT
A J A S: AUSTRALIAN JOURNAL OF AMERICAN STUDIES. 1979. irreg. Aus.$10. Australian and New Zealand American Studies Association, c/o Dept. of History, University of Sydney, Sydney, N.S.W., Australia. Eds. N. Meangy, R. Waterhouse. bk. rev. circ. 400.
Former titles: A. N. Z. A. S. A. Bulletin; A. N. Z. A. S. A. Newsletter.

972.9 DR ISSN 0567-5871
ACADEMIA DOMINICANA DE LA HISTORIA. PUBLICACIONES. 1955. irreg; vol. 49, 1978. price varies. Academia Dominicana de la Historia, Calle de la Mercedes 50, Santo Domingo, Dominican Republic.

972 MX
ACADEMIA MEXICANA DE LA HISTORIA. MEMORIAS. vol. 30, 1978. irreg. Academia Mexicana de la Historia, Plaza de Carlos Pacheco 21, Mexico 1, D.F., Mexico. Ed. Edmundo O'Gorman.

987 VE
ACADEMIA NACIONAL DE LA HISTORIA. BIBLIOTECA. SERIE: ESTUDIOS MONOGRAFIAS Y ENSAYOS. 1976. irreg. Academia Nacional de la Historia, Biblioteca, Antigua Palacio de las Academias, Caracas, Venezuela. Dir. Hector para Marquez.

HISTORY — HISTORY OF NORTH AND SOUTH AMERICA

982　　　　　　　　AG　ISSN 0567-6029
ACADEMIA PROVINCIAL DE LA HISTORIA.
BOLETIN.* 1971, no. 6. a. Academia Provincial de la Historia, Avda. Jose I de la Roza, San Juan, Argentina. Ed. Bd. bk. rev. bibl.

986　　　　　　　　EC
ACTAS DEL CABILDO COLONIAL DE GUAYAQUIL. 1972. irreg. Archivo Historico del Guayas, Casilla 1333, Guayaquil, Ecuador.

974.7　C28.5　　US　ISSN 0001-883X
ADVENTURES IN WESTERN NEW YORK HISTORY. 1960. irreg. $1.25 per no. Buffalo and Erie County Historical Society, 25 Nottingham Court, Buffalo, NY 14216. bibl. illus.
  Junior high school level

960　301.45　　US
AFRICAN-AMERICAN HERITAGE SERIES. irreg. price varies. Alkebu-Lan Books, 209 W. 125th St., Room 218, New York, NY 10027.

976.1　　　　　　US　ISSN 0002-4236
ALABAMA HISTORICAL QUARTERLY. 1930. irreg., approx. quarterly. free contr.circ. ‡ Department of Archives and History, 624 Washington Ave., Montgomery, AL 36130. Ed. Milo B. Howard, Jr. bk. rev. illus. index. circ. 1,000. (also avail. in microfiche) Indexed: Hist.Abstr.

979.8　　　　　　US　ISSN 0084-6139
ALASKA. STATE LIBRARY, JUNEAU. HISTORICAL MONOGRAPHS. 1970. irreg. Department of Education, Division of State Libraries and Museums, Pouch G, Juneau, AK 99811. Ed. Phyllis Demuth. circ. controlled. (tabloid format)

971　　　　　　　CN　ISSN 0707-705X
ALBERTA HISTORICAL RESOURCES FOUNDATION. NEWS & VIEWS. 1977. irreg. Alberta Historical Resources Foundation, 121 8th Ave. S.W., Calgary, Alta., Canada.

996.9　　　　　　　US　ISSN 0065-6453
ALMANAC OF HAWAIIANA.* 1969. a. since 1970-72. $2.50. Hawaiiana Almanac Publishing Co., 1021 University Ave., Honolulu, HI 96814. Ed. Mitsuo Uyehara. index.

972.95　　　　　　PR
ALMANAQUE BORICUA; libro de informacion general sobre Puerto Rico. 1972. irreg. $2.95. ‡ Editorial Cordillera, Inc., Ave. F.D. Roosevelt, 237, Hato Rey, Puerto Rico. Ed. Hector E. Serrano. circ. 5,000.

918.5　　　　　　　PE
ALMANAQUE DEL PERU.* 1973. a. Selecciones Tauro S.A., Jr. Huancavelica 421, Of. 402, Lima, Peru. illus. stat.

973　340　　　　　US
AMERICAN CONSTITUTIONAL AND LEGAL HISTORY. irreg. price varies. Da Capo Press, Inc., 227 W. 17 St., New York, NY 10011.

973　　　　　　　US　ISSN 0065-8014
AMERICAN CULTURE. 1969. irreg., 1970, no. 6. $7.50. George Braziller, Inc., One Park Ave., New York, NY 10016. Ed. Ed Seaver. adv. bk. rev.

973　　　　　　　US
AMERICAN DIPLOMATIC HISTORY SERIES. irreg. price varies. Macmillan Publishing Co., Inc., 866 Third Ave., New York, NY 10022.

910　917　　　　US　ISSN 0065-8219
AMERICAN EXPLORATION AND TRAVEL. 1937. irreg. price varies. University of Oklahoma Press, 1005 Asp Ave., Norman, OK 73019. Indexed: M.L.A.

973　　　　　　　US
AMERICAN FOREIGN POLICY LIBRARY. irreg. price varies. Harvard University Press, 79 Garden St., Cambridge, MA 02163.

970　　　　　　　US　ISSN 0065-8561
AMERICAN HISTORICAL ASSOCIATION. ANNUAL REPORT. a. American Historical Association, 400 A St. S. E., Washington, DC 20003. (also avail. in microform from UMI)

973　　　　　　　US
AMERICAN HISTORY RESEARCH SERIES. irreg. price varies. Wadsworth Publishing Co., 10 Davis Dr., Belmont, CA 94002.

970　　　　　　　US　ISSN 0065-8936
AMERICAN JEWISH COMMUNAL HISTORY. 1954. irreg., 1969, no. 5. price varies. ‡ American Jewish Historical Society, 2 Thornton Rd., Waltham, MA 02154. index. circ. 1,000.

970　　　　　　　US　ISSN 0193-6859
AMERICAN POPULAR CULTURE. irreg. price varies. Greenwood Press, 8 Post Rd. W., Westport, CT 06881. Ed. M. Thomas Inge.

973　　　　　　　II　ISSN 0066-0795
AMERICAN STUDIES RESEARCH CENTRE. NEWSLETTER. (Text in English) 1964. irreg. membership. American Studies Research Centre, Osmania University Campus, Hyderabad 500007, India. circ. 3,000.

970.1　　　　　　US　ISSN 0066-121X
AMERICANS BEFORE COLUMBUS. 1969. irreg.(approx. m.) membership. National Indian Youth Council, 201 Hermosa N.E., Albuquerque, NM 87108. Ed. Joy Harjo. bk. rev. circ. 5,000.

980　　　　　　　MQ　ISSN 0517-855X
ANNALES DES ANTILLES. 1950. irreg. Societe d'Histoire de la Martinique, Boite Postale 52, Fort-de-France, Martinique.

917.3　　　　　　US　ISSN 0090-4511
ANNUAL EDITIONS: READINGS IN AMERICAN HISTORY. 1972/73. a. $5.75 per vol. (2 vols.) Dushkin Publishing Group, Sluice Dock, Guilford, CT 06437. illus.

973　　　　　　　US　ISSN 0066-4618
ANSON G. PHELPS LECTURESHIP ON EARLY AMERICAN HISTORY. 1932. irreg., latest 1980. price varies. New York University Press, Washington Square, New York, NY 10003.

979.4　　　　　　US　ISSN 0044-8362
ANTEPASADOS. (Text in English and Spanish) 1970. s-a. $10. Los Californianos, Inc., Box 5155, San Francisco, CA 94101. Ed. Rudecinda Lo Buglio. illus. circ. 250. (processed; back issues avail.)

970　918.5　　　PE　ISSN 0066-5223
ANUARIO GEOGRAFICO DEL PERU. 1962. a. price varies. Sociedad Geografica de Lima, Jiron Puno 456, Apartado 1176, Lima, Peru.

977　　　　　　　US
ARCHAEOLOGICAL COMPLETION REPORT SERIES. 1977. irreg.,approx.a. $15. Mackinac Island State Park Commission, Box 30028, Lansing, MI 48909. Ed. David A. Armour. bibl. illus. circ. 300.

986.6　　　　　　EC
ARCHIVO HISTORICO DEL GUAYAS. COLECCION MONOGRAFICA. 1972. irreg. Archivo Historico del Guayas, Casilla 1333, Guayaquil, Ecuador.

ARGENTINA. DEPARTAMENTO DE ESTUDIOS HISTORICOS NAVALES. SERIE E: DOCUMENTOS. see *MILITARY*

ARGENTINA. INSTITUTO ETNICO NACIONAL. ANALES. see *ANTHROPOLOGY*

355　982　　　　AG　ISSN 0066-7293
ARGENTINA. SECRETARIA DE GUERRA. DIRECCION DE ESTUDIOS HISTORICOS. BOLETIN BIBLIOGRAFICO.* 1967. irreg. $350. Secretaria de Guerra, Comando en Jefe del Ejercito, Azopardo 250 Planta Baja, Buenos Aires, Argentina.

979.1　　　　　　US
ARIZONA HISTORICAL SOCIETY. HISTORICAL MONOGRAPHS. 1973. irreg., no. 6, 1977. price varies. Arizona Historical Society, 949 E. Second St., Tucson, AZ 85719.

970　　　　　　　US
ARIZONA HISTORICAL SOCIETY. MUSEUM MONOGRAPH SERIES. 1964. irreg., no. 7, 1976. price varies. Arizona Historical Society, 949 East Second St., Tucson, AZ 85719. Ed. Bd. bibl. charts. illus.

975.5　　　　　　US　ISSN 0066-7684
ARLINGTON HISTORICAL MAGAZINE. 1957. a. $4. Arlington Historical Society, Inc., P.O. Box 402, Arlington, VA 22210. index. cum.index: 1957 to present.

ARQUEOLOGICAS. see *ANTHROPOLOGY*

ASIEN - AFRIKA - LATEINAMERIKA. JAHRBUCH. see *HISTORY — History Of Asia*

970　　　　　　　CN　ISSN 0066-992X
ASTICOU. 1968. 2-3/yr. Can.$5. ‡ Societe Historique de l'Ouest du Quebec, C.P. 7, Hull, Que., Canada. Ed. Gauvin. circ. 1,000-1,500.

BAJA CALIFORNIA TRAVEL SERIES. see *TRAVEL AND TOURISM*

BAMPTON LECTURES IN AMERICA. see *RELIGIONS AND THEOLOGY*

972.9　　　　　　BB　ISSN 0005-5891
BARBADOS MUSEUM AND HISTORICAL SOCIETY. JOURNAL. 1933. a. $10. ‡ Barbados Museum and Historical Society, St. Ann's Garrison, Barbados, W. Indies. Ed. P. F. Campbell. bk. rev. circ. 500.

971　　　　　　　CN　ISSN 0702-634X
BASILIAN HISTORICAL BULLETINS. irreg., no. 10, 1977. Can.$1. Basilian Press, 95 St. Joseph St., Toronto, Ont. M5S 2R9, Canada.

979.2　　　　　　US
BEEHIVE HISTORY. 1975. a. $1.50. Utah State Historical Society, 307 W. Second South, Salt Lake City, UT 84101. Ed. Miriam B. Murphy. circ. 3,000.

917.49　　　　　　US　ISSN 0094-7989
BERGEN COUNTY HISTORY. 1970. a. $4.75 to non-members. Bergen County (New Jersey) Historical Society, Box 55, River Edge, NJ 07661. Ed. Mrs. Claire K. Tholl. illus. circ. 600.

980　　　　　　　BM　ISSN 0409-2163
BERMUDA HISTORICAL SOCIETY. OCCASIONAL PUBLICATIONS. irreg., 1972, no. 8. price varies. Bermuda Historical Society, Museum Par La Ville, Hamilton, Bermuda. Ed. Bd.

979.4　　　　　　US　ISSN 0045-1851
BIBLIO-CAL NOTES. 1967. a. institutions $7.50; individuals $3. Southern California Local History Council, Box 909, Anaheim, CA 92805. Ed. Richard B. Dimmitt. bk. rev. circ. 175.

982　　　　　　　AG　ISSN 0067-7396
BIBLIOTECA DE CULTURA VASCA. 1942. irreg. (approx. s-a.) price varies. Editorial Vasca Ekin s.r.l., Belgrano 1144, Buenos Aires 1092, Argentina.

972.9　　　　　　GP
BIBLIOTHEQUE D'HISTOIRE ANTILLAISE. no. 3, 1978. irreg. Societe d'Histoire de la Guadeloupe, Basse-Terre, Guadeloupe.

977　　　　　　　US
BLOOMING GROVE COURIER. 1972. irreg. membership. Historic Blooming Grove Historical Society, Inc., 1000 Nichols Rd., Monona, WI 53716. Ed. Jeannette L. Mundstock. circ. 125.

982　020.6　　　AG
BOLETIN INTERAMERICANO DE ARCHIVOS. 1974. irreg. Universidad Nacional de Cordoba, Facultad de Filosofia y Humanidades, Estafeta 32, Cordoba, Argentina. Ed. Aurelio Tanodi. bk. rev. bibl.

984　　　　　　　UK　ISSN 0067-981X
BOLIVIA INFORMATION HANDBOOK. 1971. a. free. (Embassy of Bolivia, London) Diplomatist Associates Ltd., Shooter's Lodge, Windsor Forest, Berks, England. Ed. B. Fernandez-Armesto. adv. bk. rev. circ. 26,000.

BOLSILIBROS. see *LITERATURE*

917.3　　　　　　US　ISSN 0092-4571
BORDER STATES. 1973. a. $4. American Studies Association, Kentucky-Tennessee Chapter, c/o William Berge, Oral History Center, Easter Kentucky University, Richmond, KY 40475.

HISTORY — HISTORY OF NORTH AND SOUTH AMERICA

971   CN   ISSN 0068-0303
BOREAL INSTITUTE, EDMONTON.
OCCASIONAL PUBLICATIONS. 1964. irreg.
price varies. ‡ Boreal Institute for Northern Studies, University of Alberta, Edmonton, Alberta T6G 2E9, Canada.

971   CN   ISSN 0316-7828
BOREAL INSTITUTE, EDMONTON. REPORT OF ACTIVITIES. 1963-64. a. free. ‡ Boreal Institute for Northern Studies, University of Alberta, Edmonton, Alberta T6G 2E9, Canada.
Formerly: Boreal Institute, Edmonton. Annual Report (ISSN 0068-0281)

980   US   ISSN 0520-6294
BORZOI BOOKS ON LATIN AMERICA. irreg. price varies. Alfred A. Knopf (Subsidiary of: Random House, Inc.) 201 E. 50 St., New York, NY 10022.

973   US
BORZOI SERIES IN UNITED STATES CONSTITUTIONAL HISTORY. irreg. price varies. Alfred A. Knopf (Subsidiary of: Random House, Inc.) 201 E. 50 St., New York, NY 10022.

974   US
BOSTONIAN SOCIETY. PROCEEDINGS. 1881. irreg., latest 1976. $3. ‡ Bostonian Society, Old State House, 206 Washington Street, Boston, MA 02109. circ. 1,200 (controlled)

970   CN   ISSN 0068-0524
BOUNDARY HISTORICAL SOCIETY. REPORT. 1958. every four or five years. Can.$3.50. Boundary Historical Society, 12 Street, S.E., Grand Forks, B.C., Canada.

973   BL
BRAZIL. ARQUIVO NACIONAL. SERIE DE PUBLICACOES. irreg. Arquivo Nacional, Praca da Republica 26, Rio de Janeiro, R.J., Brazil. illus.

980   BL   ISSN 0068-0788
BRAZIL. DIRETORIA DO PATRIMONIO HISTORICO E ARTISTICO NACIONAL. REVISTA.* irreg. Ministerio da Educacao e Cultura, Directoria do Patromonio Historico e Artistico Nacional, Esplanada dos Ministerios, Bloco L, Brasilia, D.F., Brazil.

971   CN
BRITISH COLUMBIA HISTORICAL DOCUMENTS SERIES. 1975. irreg. price varies. University of British Columbia Press, 303-6344 Memorial Rd., Vancouver, B.C. V6T 1W5, Canada. Ed. Bd.

971   CN   ISSN 0381-6206
BROME COUNTY HISTORICAL SOCIETY. PUBLICATION. 1937. irreg. Brome County Historical Society, Knowlton, Que., Canada. illus. Key Title: Publication - Brome County Historical Society.

974   US
BROOKSIDE COLUMNS. irreg. Saratoga County Historical Society, Ballston Spa, NY 12020.

971   CN   ISSN 0084-8115
BRUCE COUNTY HISTORICAL SOCIETY. YEAR BOOK. 1967. a. Can.$2.50. Bruce County Historical Society, c/o Mrs Mary Anne Ellenton, Box 182, Tiverton, Ont. N0G 2T0, Canada. Ed. Mrs. Clarence McGillivray. adv. illus.

982   AG   ISSN 0524-9864
BUENOS AIRES (PROVINCE). ARCHIVO HISTORICO. PUBLICACIONES. SEXTA SERIE. 1951. irreg. Ministerio de Educacion, Archivo Historico, La Plata, Argentina.

970   US   ISSN 0068-4287
BURT FRANKLIN AMERICAN CLASSICS IN HISTORY AND SOCIAL SCIENCES. 1966. irreg., 1973, no. 246. price varies. Lenox Hill Publishing and Distributing Corporation, 235 E. 44th St., New York, NY 10017. (back issues avail.)

981   BL
CADERNOS DE DEBATE. 1976. irreg. Editora Brasiliense, Rua Barao de Itapetininga 93, 01042 Sao Paulo, Brazil. Ed. Flavio Aguiar.

971   CN   ISSN 0009-7489
CAHIERS DE CITE LIBRE. vol. 18, 1967. irreg. Editions du Jour, 6765 rue de Marseille, Montreal, Que. H1N 1M4, Canada.
Supersedes: Cite Libre (ISSN 0383-0470)

987   VE   ISSN 0068-5259
CAIN.* 1969. a. Bs.3($0.70) Universidad del Zulia, Facultad de Humanidades y Educacion, Maracaibo, Venezuela.

980   UK   ISSN 0068-6689
CAMBRIDGE LATIN AMERICAN STUDIES. 1967. irreg., no. 38, 1980. $41.50 for latest vol. Cambridge University Press, Box 110, Cambridge CB2 3RL, England (and 32 E. 57th St., New York, NY 10022) Ed. Malcolm Deas.

971.9   CN   ISSN 0319-583X
CANADA NORTH ALMANAC. 1975. irreg. Research Institute of Northern Canada, Box 188, Yellowknife, N.W.T. X0E 1HO, Canada.

971   CN   ISSN 0068-8193
CANADIAN ALMANAC AND DIRECTORY. 1847. a. Can.$34.95. Copp Clark Publishing Co., 517 Wellington St. W., Toronto, Ont. M5V 1G1, Canada. Ed. Susan Walters. index. circ. 8,000.

971   CN   ISSN 0315-1433
CANADIAN ANNUAL REVIEW OF POLITICS AND PUBLIC AFFAIRS. 1961. a. price varies. University of Toronto Press, Front Campus, Toronto, Ont. M5S 1A6, Canada (and 33 East Tupper St., Buffalo, N. Y. 14023) Ed. John Saywell. index. (also avail. in microfiche)
Formerly: Canadian Annual Review (ISSN 0068-8215)

971   CN   ISSN 0315-0062
CANADIAN FRONTIER; Canada's national history magazine. 1972. a. Can.$3.95. Antonson Publishing Co., Ltd., P.O. Box 157, New Westminster, B.C. V3L 4Y4, Canada. Ed. Brian Antonson. bk. rev. cum.index. circ. 3,000. (back issues available)

CANADIAN HISTORIC SITES; OCCASIONAL PAPERS IN ARCHAEOLOGY AND HISTORY. see *ARCHAEOLOGY*

971   CN   ISSN 0068-886X
CANADIAN HISTORICAL ASSOCIATION. HISTORICAL BOOKLETS. BROCHURES HISTORIQUES. (Text in English and French) 1953. irreg. $0.50 ea. or $0.35 ea. for bulk orders of 10 copies or more. ‡ Canadian Historical Association, C/O Public Archives of Canada, 395 Wellington St., Ottawa, Ont. K1A 0N3, Canada. Eds. P. Gillis, A. Vachon. circ. 4,000.

970 016   CN   ISSN 0068-9165
CANADIAN LOCAL HISTORIES TO 1950. A BIBLIOGRAPHY. HISTOIRES LOCALES ET REGIONALES CANADIENNES DES ORIGINES A 1950. 1967. irreg. price varies. (Centennial Commission) University of Toronto Press, Front Campus, Toronto, Ont. M5S 1A6, Canada (and 33 East Tupper St., Buffalo, N. Y. 14203) Ed. W.F.E. Morley. (also avail. in microfiche)

971.006   CN   ISSN 0383-6894
CANADIAN ORAL HISTORY ASSOCIATION. JOURNAL. (Text in English and French) 1976. irreg. Can.$5 to non-members. Canadian Oral History Association, P.O. Box 31, Sta. A, Ottawa, Ont. K1N 8V3, Canada. Ed. Richard Lockhead. bk. rev. circ. 300.

971   CN   ISSN 0068-9793
CANADIAN STUDIES IN HISTORY AND GOVERNMENT. 1961. irreg. price varies. (Social Science Research Council of Canada) University of Toronto Press, Front Campus, Toronto, Ont. M5S 1A6, Canada (and 33 East Tupper St., Buffalo, N. Y. 14023) Ed. G. S. French. (also avail. in microfiche)

CANADIAN WAR MUSEUM. HISTORICAL PUBLICATIONS. see *MILITARY*

972   US   ISSN 0069-0457
CARIBBEAN CONFERENCE SERIES. Issued also as (1-17, 1950-1966): Conference on the Caribbean, University of Florida. Papers. 1951-1967, vols.1-17 a. price varies. University Presses of Florida, 15 N. W. 15th St., Gainesville, FL 32603. Ed. A. Curtis Wilgus. index.

972.9   PR   ISSN 0069-0473
CARIBBEAN DOCUMENTS. 1970. irreg. price varies. Universidad de Puerto Rico, Institute of Caribbean Studies, Rio Piedras, PR 00931. (Co-sponsor: Institute of International Relations, University of the West Indies)

972.9   PR   ISSN 0069-0511
CARIBBEAN MONOGRAPH SERIES. 1964. irreg; no. 9, 1978. price varies. Universidad de Puerto Rico, Institute of Caribbean Studies, Rio Piedras, PR 00931.

972.9 574   VI
CARIBBEAN RESEARCH INSTITUTE. REPORT. 1965. irreg; latest, tenth anniv. issue, 1975. free. College of the Virgin Islands, Caribbean Islands Research Institute, St. Thomas, Virgin Islands, VI 00801.
Formerly: Caribbean Islands Research Institute. Annual Report (ISSN 0069-0503)

972.9   PR   ISSN 0069-052X
CARIBBEAN SCHOLARS' CONFERENCE. PROCEEDINGS. 1962. biennial. price varies; no.3, $4.00. Universidad de Puerto Rico, Institute of Caribbean Studies, Rio Piedras, PR 00931.

972.8   US   ISSN 0069-0538
CARIBBEAN SERIES. 1959. irreg., no. 15, 1975. price varies. Yale University Press, 92A Yale Sta., New Haven, CT 06520.

CARIBBEAN YEAR BOOK. see *TRAVEL AND TOURISM*

972.91   CU
CENTRO DE ESTUDIOS MARTIANOS. ANUARIO. 1969. a. Centro de Estudios Martianos, Apartado Postal 6640, Havana 6, Cuba. bk. rev. bibl.
Supersedes (last issued 1977, no.7): Anuario Martiano (ISSN 0066-524X)

989.5   VE   ISSN 0411-5023
CENTRO DE HISTORIA DEL TACHIRA. BOLETIN. 1943. irreg. exchange basis. Centro de Historia del Tachira, Avda. 19 Abril No. 9-111, San Cristobal, Tachira, Venezuela. Ed. Xuan T. Garcia-Tamayo. circ. 1,000.

971   CN   ISSN 0316-6724
CHARLOTTES. irreg. price varies. Queen Charlotte Islands Musuem Society, Box 130, Masset, B.C. V0T 1M0, Canada. Ed. L. L. Simpson. circ. 2,500.

970   US   ISSN 0069-3278
CHICAGO HISTORY OF AMERICAN CIVILIZATION. 1956. irreg., latest 1977. price varies. University of Chicago Press, 5801 S. Ellis Ave., Chicago, IL 60637. Ed. Daniel J. Boorstin. adv. bk. rev. (reprint service avail. from UMI,ISI)

970.1   US   ISSN 0069-4304
CIVILIZATION OF THE AMERICAN INDIAN. 1932. irreg. price varies. University of Oklahoma Press, 1005 Asp Ave., Norman, OK 73019.

917.97   US   ISSN 0090-449X
CLARK COUNTY HISTORY. 1960. a. $3. ‡ Fort Vancouver Historical Society, P.O. Box 1834, Vancouver, WA 98663. Eds. Paul Aldinger, Richard Hawkins. bibl. circ. 1,000.

974   US
CLINTON HISTORICAL SOCIETY. NEWSLETTER. irreg. Clinton Historical Society, Box 282, Clinton, NY 13323.

981   BL
COLECAO BERNARDO PEREIRA DE VASCONCELLOS. SERIE ESTUDOS HISTORICOS. irreg. Senado Federal, Praca dos Tres Poderes, 7000 Brasilia D.F., Brazil.

981   BL
COLECAO DE ESTUDOS HISTORICOS. 1978. irreg. Fundacao Casa de Rui Barbosa, Rua Sao Clemente 134, Botafogo 22260, Rio de Janeiro RJ, Brazil. Dir. Washington Luis Neto.

981   BL
COLECAO TEMAS BRASILEIROS. no. 13, 1972. irreg. Conquista, Av. 28 de Setembro 174, Rio de Janeiro GB, Brazil. Dir. Arthur C. Ferreira Reis. illus.

982   AG
COLECCION CONOCIMIENTO DE LA ARGENTINA. 1974. irreg. Editorial Biblioteca, Alem 3078, Rosario, Argentina.

987   VE   ISSN 0069-5084
COLECCION "FOROS Y SEMINARIOS." SERIE FOROS. 1965. irreg., 1968, no. 5. ‡ Universidad Central de Venezuela, Direccion de Cultura, Departamento de Distribucion de Publicaciones, Edificio de la Biblioteca Central, Apdo. 59004, Los Chaguaramos, Caracas, Venezuela.

987   VE   ISSN 0069-5092
COLECCION "FOROS Y SEMINARIOS." SERIE SEMINARIOS. 1964. irreg., no. 2, 1966. Universidad Central de Venezuela, Direccion de Cultura, Departamento de Distribucion de Publicaciones, Edificio de la Biblioteca Central, Apdo. 59004, Los Chaguaramos, Caracas, Venezuela.

971   CN   ISSN 0069-5513
COLLECTIONS: LES IDEES DU JOUR. 1961. irreg. Editions du Jour, 6765 rue de Marseille, Montreal, Que. H1N 1M4, Canada.

086.1   CK
COLOMBIA. INSTITUTO COLOMBIANO DE CULTURA. ARCHIVO NACIONAL. REVISTA. 1977 n.s. a. Instituto Colombiano de Cultura, Archivo Nacional, Calle 24 no. 5-60, Bogota, Colombia. Ed. Alberto Lee Lopez.
Archives

974   US
COLONIAL SOCIETY OF MASSACHUSETTS. PUBLICATIONS. (Transactions and Collections) 1895. irreg., vol. 51, 1979. $20. Colonial Society of Massachusetts, 87 Mount Vernon St., Boston, MA 02108. Ed. Frederick S. Allis, Jr.

COLONIAL WILLIAMSBURG ARCHAEOLOGICAL SERIES. see *ARCHAEOLOGY*

978.8   US
COLORADO HERITAGE. 1923. biennial. membership. ‡ Colorado Historical Society, Colorado Heritage Center, 1300 Broadway, Denver, CO 80203. Ed. Cathryne Johnson. bk. rev. bibl.illus.index. circ. 4,500. Indexed: Amer.Hist. & Life.
Formerly(until 1981): Colorado Magazine (ISSN 0010-1648)

976   US
COLORADO STATE UNIVERSITY. DEPARTMENT OF HISTORY. GERMANS FROM RUSSIA IN COLORADO STUDY PROJECT. MONOGRAPHS, PAPERS AND REPORTS SERIES. irreg., no. 3, 1977. Colorado State University, Department of History, Germans from Russia in Colorado Study Project, Fort Collins, CO 80523.

979.5   US   ISSN 0069-6293
COLUMBIA COUNTY HISTORY (OREGON) 1962. a. $2.40. Columbia County Historical Society, Old Courthouse Museum, 45 S. 21st St., St. Helens, OR 97051. index. (back issues avail.)

970   US   ISSN 0069-9357
CONTEMPORARY AMERICAN HISTORY SERIES. 1969. irreg., 1977, no. 10. Columbia University Press, 136 South Broadway, Irvington-On-Hudson, NY 10533. Ed. William E. Leuchtenburg.

973   US   ISSN 0084-9219
CONTRIBUTIONS IN AMERICAN HISTORY. 1970. irreg. price varies. Greenwood Press, 88 Post Rd. W., Westport, CT 06881. Ed. Jon L. Wakelyn.

973   US   ISSN 0084-9227
CONTRIBUTIONS IN AMERICAN STUDIES. 1969. irreg. price varies. Greenwood Press, 88 Post Rd. W., Westport, CT 06881. Ed. Robert H. Walker.

970   US   ISSN 0163-3813
CONTRIBUTIONS IN COMPARATIVE COLONIAL STUDIES. irreg. price varies. Greenwood Press, 8 Post Rd. W., Westport, CT 06881. Ed. Robin Winks.

CORPUS ANTIQUATATUM AMERICANENSIUM. see *ARCHAEOLOGY*

979.4   US   ISSN 0574-3680
COVERED WAGON. a. $2. Shasta Historical Society, P.O. Box 277, Redding, CA 96001. illus.

972   MX   ISSN 0070-1750
CUADERNOS DEL MEXICO PREHISPANICO. 1968. irreg. price varies. Instituto Nacional de Antropologia e Historia, Cordoba 45, Mexico 7,D.F., Mexico.

917.56   US   ISSN 0091-9640
CURRITUCK COUNTY HISTORICAL SOCIETY. JOURNAL. 1973. a. $4. ‡ Currituck County Historical Society, Jarisburg, NC 27947. Ed. Roy E. Sawyer, Jr. illus. circ. 1,000.

970   GW
DEUTSCHE GESELLSCHAFT FUER AMERIKASTUDIEN. MITTEILUNGSBLATT. (Text in German and English) 1954. a. Deutsche Gesellschaft fuer Amerikastudien - German Association for American Studies, Marburg, W. Germany (B.R.D.) Ed. H. Thies. bk. rev.

972   MX
DEVENIR. CUADERNOS DEL SEMINARIO DE HISTORIA. 1955. irreg., 1966, no. 14. price varies. Universidad Nacional Autonoma de Mexico, Instituto de Investigaciones Historicas, Villa Obregon, Ciudad Universitaria, Mexico 20, D.F., Mexico.
Formerly: Universidad Nacional Autonoma de Mexico. Instituto de Investigaciones Historicas. Cuadernos Serie Historica.

918   US   ISSN 0091-3235
DIRECTORY OF A S U LATIN AMERICANISTS. 1972/73. a. free. Arizona State University, Center for Latin American Studies, Tempe, AZ 85281. Ed. J. R. Ladman.
Formerly: Directory of Latin Americanists (ISSN 0091-3235)

973   US   ISSN 0070-5659
DIRECTORY OF HISTORICAL SOCIETIES AND AGENCIES IN THE UNITED STATES AND CANADA. triennial. $28. American Association for State and Local History, 1400 Eighth Ave. S., Nashville, TN 37203. Ed. Tracey Linton Craig.

DOWNDRAFT. see *EDUCATION*

975   US
DROVER'S POST. irreg. membership. Spartanburg County Historical Association, c/o Mrs. John Edmunds, Jr., 407 Forest Ave., Spartanburg, SC 29302.

970   US   ISSN 0070-8089
EAST CAROLINA UNIVERSITY PUBLICATIONS IN HISTORY. 1964. irreg., vol. 4, 1976. $3.45 for vol. 4. ‡ East Carolina University, Department of History, Greenville, NC 27834. Ed. Roy N. Lokken. circ. 500.
Formerly: East Carolina College Publications in History.

970   US   ISSN 0361-6193
EAST TENNESSEE HISTORICAL SOCIETY'S PUBLICATIONS. 1929. a. $7 membership. East Tennessee Historical Society, Lawson McGhee Library, Knoxville, TN 37902. Ed. William J. MacArthur, Jr. bk. rev. circ. 1,032.

974.7   US   ISSN 0071-0091
EMPIRE STATE HISTORICAL PUBLICATIONS. irreg.; no. 9208, 1978. Ira J. Friedman (Subsidiary of: Kennikat Press Corp.) 90 S. Bayles Ave., Port Washington, NY 11050.

970.1   MX   ISSN 0071-1667
ESTUDIOS DE CULTURA MAYA. (Text in Spanish and English) 1960. a. Mex.$70($6.) Universidad Nacional Autonoma de Mexico, Centro de Estudios Mayas, Torre de Humanidades II, Ciudad Universitaria, Mexico 20, D.F., Mexico. bk. rev. circ. 1,500.

972   MX   ISSN 0014-147X
ESTUDIOS DE HISTORIA MODERNA Y CONTEMPORANEA DE MEXICO. 1965. irreg; vol. 5, 1976. price varies. Universidad Nacional Autonoma de Mexico, Instituto de Investigaciones Historicas, Villa Obregon, Ciudad Universitaria, Mexico 20, D.F., Mexico. Ed.Bd. bk. rev. bibl. illus. index. circ. 1,500.

972   MX
ESTUDIOS DE HISTORIA NOVOHISPANA. 1947. irreg; no. 26, 1976. price varies. Universidad Nacional Autonoma de Mexico, Instituto de Investigaciones Historicas, Villa Obregon, Ciudad Universitaria, Mexico 20, D.F., Mexico.
Formerly: Universidad Nacional Autonoma de Mexico. Instituto de Investigaciones Historicas. Serie de Historia Novohispana (ISSN 0076-7379)

986.6 572   EC
ESTUDIOS ETNOHISTORICOS DEL ECUADOR. 1976. irreg. Casa de la Cultura Ecuatoriana, Nucleo de Guayas, Quito, Ecuador.

980   PL   ISSN 0137-3080
ESTUDIOS LATINOAMERICANOS. (Text in Spanish, Portugese, English) irreg., vol. 5, 1979. 60 Zl. (Polska Akademia Nauk, Instytut Historii) Ossolineum, Publishing House of the Polish Academy of Sciences, Rynek 9, Wroclaw, Poland (Dist. by: Ars Polona-Ruch, Krakowskie Przedmiescie 7, Warsaw, Poland) Ed. Tadeusz Lepkowski.

980   BL
ESTUDOS HISTORICOS. no. 14, 1975. irreg. exchange. Universidade Estadual Paulista "Julio de Mesquito Filho", Faculdade de Filosofia, Ciencias e Letras de Marilia, Departamento de Historia, Avda. Vicente Ferreira 1278, Caixa Postal 420, 17500 Marilia, S.P., Brazil. Ed. Bd. bk. rev. bibl. charts.

973.04   US   ISSN 0071-1780
ETHNIC CHRONOLOGY SERIES. 1971. irreg. $7.50. Oceana Publications Inc., Dobbs Ferry, New York, NY 10522.

975.9   US   ISSN 0085-0659
FLORIDA. BUREAU OF HISTORIC SITES AND PROPERTIES. BULLETIN. 1970. a. free. Department of State, Bureau of Historic Sites and Properties, The Capitol, Tallahassee, FL 32301. Ed. Tom Llewellyn. bibl. charts. illus. circ. 3,000.

971   CN   ISSN 0383-2708
FOCUS ON VANCOUVER. 1970. irreg. Vancouver Historical Society, Vancouver, B.C., Canada.

982   AG   ISSN 0325-8238
FOLIA HISTORICA DEL NORDESTE. 1974. irreg. Universidad Nacional del Nordeste, Instituto de Historia, Casilla de Correo 128, 3400 Corrientes, Argentina. (Co-sponsor: Instituto de Investigaciones Geohistoricas) Eds. E. J. Maeder, A.S. Bolsi, R. Gutierrez. bk. rev. circ. 500.

978.9   US   ISSN 0071-7754
FORT BURGWIN RESEARCH CENTER. PUBLICATIONS. 1961. irreg. price varies. Fort Burgwin Research Center, Inc., Southern Methodist University, Dallas, TX 75275. bk. rev. circ. 1,000.

976.4   US   ISSN 0046-4651
FORT CONCHO REPORT; news from the frontier fort on the Conchos. 1969. 3-4/yr. free. ‡ Fort Concho National Historic Landmark, 213 E. Avenue D, San Angelo, TX 76901. Eds. Tilly Chandler, Wayne Daniel. bk. rev. circ. 1,200. (processed)
Local

970   GW
FREIE UNIVERSITAET BERLIN. JOHN F. KENNEDY-INSTITUT FUER NORDAMERIKA STUDIEN. MATERIALIEN. (Text in English) 1972. irreg., no. 2, 1973. price varies. Freie Universitaet Berlin, John F. Kennedy-Institut fuer Nordamerika-Studien, Lansstr. 7-9, 1000 Berlin 33, W. Germany (B.R.D.) bibl. circ. 300-500.

970   CN   ISSN 0069-1771
FRENCH-CANADIAN CIVILIZATION RESEARCH CENTER. CAHIERS/CENTRE DE RECHERCHE EN CIVILISATION CANADIENNE-FRANCAISE. CAHIERS. 1968. irreg. price varies. University of Ottawa Press, 65 Hastey Ave., Ottawa, Ont. K1N 6N5, Canada. Eds. J. Menard, J. Hare.
Formerly: Centre de Recherche en Litterature Canadienne-Francaise. Cahiers.

FRONTIER MILITARY SERIES. see *MILITARY*

970.1 MX ISSN 0071-9773
FUENTES INDIGENAS DE LA CULTURA
NAHUATL. (Title varies: Fuentes Indigenas de la
Cultura Nahuatl. Textos de los Informantes de
Sahagun) 1958. irreg; 1969, no. 7. price varies.
Universidad Nacional Autonoma de Mexico,
Instituto de Investigaciones Historicas, Villa
Obregon, Ciudad Universitaria, Mexico 20, D.F.,
Mexico. Ed.Bd. circ. 3,000.
Translations from Classic Nahuatl language texts

981.6 BL
FUNDACAO CULTURAL DE CURITIBA.
RELATORIO. 1974. irreg. Fundacao Cultural de
Curitiba, Curitiba, Brazil. illus.

GERMAN-CANADIAN YEARBOOK/
DEUTSCHKANADISCHES JAHRBUCH. see
ETHNIC INTERESTS

970.1 CN ISSN 0072-467X
GLENBOW-ALBERTA INSTITUTE.
OCCASIONAL PAPER. 1966. irreg. Glenbow-
Alberta Institute, First St. S.E. & 9th Ave., Calgary,
Alta. T2G OP3, Canada. illus.
Formerly: Glenbow Foundation. Occasional
Paper (ISSN 0700-6365)

970.1 CN
GLENBOW MUSEUM. ARCHIVES SERIES. 1974,
no. 6. irreg. free. Glenbow-Alberta Institute, 9Th
Ave. & First St. S.E., Calgary, Alta. T2G 0P3,
Canada. Ed. William McKee. illus. circ. 500.
Formerly: Glenbow Foundation. Archives Series
(ISSN 0436-0605)

971 CN ISSN 0316-2702
GRAND MANAN HISTORIAN. 1934. a. Can.$3. ‡
Grand Manan Historical Society, c/o Secretary,
Grand Manan, New Brunswick EOG ILO, Canada.
Ed. L. Keith Ingersoll. circ. 300.

970 US ISSN 0148-771X
GRASS ROOTS PERSPECTIVES ON AMERICAN
HISTORY. irreg. price varies. Greenwood Press, 8
Post Rd. W., Westport, CT 06881. Ed. David
Thelen.

978 970.1 US ISSN 0072-7342
GREAT WEST AND INDIAN SERIES. 1945. irreg.
price varies. ‡ Westernlore Press, 5117 Eagle Rock
Blvd., Los Angeles, CA 90041. Ed. Paul D. Bailey.

977.5 US
GUIDES TO HISTORICAL RESOURCES. irreg.
State Historical Society of Wisconsin, 816 State St.,
Madison, WI 53706.

946.9 PO
GUIMARAES. ARQUIVO MUNICIPAL
"ALFREDO PIMENTO." BOLETIM DE
TRABALHOS HISTORICOS; elementos para a
historia Vimaranese. a. Esc.400. Arquivo Municipal
"Alfredo Pimenta", Largo Conego Jose Maria
Gomes, 4800 Guimaraes, Portugal. Ed. Manuel
Alves de Oliveira.

973 US
GULF COAST CONFERENCE PROCEEDINGS.
1969. irreg. $$10.95 for cloth; paper $6.95. (Gulf
Coast History and Humanities Conference)
University of West Florida, John C. Pace Library,
Pensacola, FL 32504. (back issues avail.)

972 US ISSN 0072-9833
HANDBOOK OF LATIN AMERICAN STUDIES: A
SELECTED AND ANNOTATED GUIDE TO
RECENT PUBLICATIONS. 1935. a. beginning
with no. 36, even numbered volumes cover
humanities; odd numbered volumes cover social
sciences. price varies. (Hispanic Foundation)
University of Florida, Center for Latin American
Studies, 15 N.W. 15 St., Gainesville, FL 32603.
Eds. Martin Moyano, Dolores Moyano. bk. rev.
circ. 1,350.

996.9 US ISSN 0073-1145
HAWAII SERIES. 1968. irreg., no. 6, 1978. price
varies. (University of Hawaii, Social Science
Research Institute) University Press of Hawaii, 2840
Kolowalu St., Honolulu, HI 96822. (reprint service
avail. from UMI,ISI)

976 US
HEMPSTEAD COUNTY HISTORICAL SOCIETY.
(PUBLICATION) vol. 1, 1977. irreg. Hempstead
County Historical Society, Box 95, Washington, AR
71862.

983 CL ISSN 0073-2435
HISTORIA. 1961. a. $20. Universidad Catolica de
Chile, Instituto de Historia, Casilla 114-D, Santiago,
Chile. Ed.Bd. adv. bk. rev. circ. 1,000.

981 BL
HISTORIA, CADERNOS DE PESQUISA. 1977.
irreg. (Associacao dos Universitarios para a Pesquisa
em Historia do Brasil) Editora Brasiliense, Rua
Barao de Itapetining 93, 01042 Sao Paulo, Brazil.
Ed. Jose Antonio Segatto.

989.5 UY
HISTORIA URUGUAYA. SEGUNDA SERIE: LOS
HOMBRES. 1976. irreg. Ediciones de la Banda
Oriental, Yi 1364, Montevideo, Uruguay.

985 PE ISSN 0073-2486
HISTORIA Y CULTURA. 1965. irreg. $10. Museo
Nacional de Historia, Plaza Bolivar, Pueblo Libre,
Apdo. 1992, Lima, Peru. Ed. Maria Rostworowski
de Diez Canseco. Indexed: Hist.Abstr.

974 US
HISTORIC BETHLEHEM. NEWSLETTER. no. 13,
1977. irreg. Historic Bethlehem, Inc., 516 Main St.,
Bethlehem, PA 18018. Ed. Joan L. Ward. illus.

970 980 US
HISTORIC DOCUMENTS. 1972. a. $39.
Congressional Quarterly Inc., 1414 22nd St. N.W.,
Washington, DC 20037. Ed. Bob Diamond. bibl.

977.5 US ISSN 0361-574X
HISTORIC MADISON. JOURNAL. 1975. a. $1.50.
Historic Madison, Inc., Box 2031, Madison, WI
53701. Ed. Gordon Orr, Jr. illus. Key Title: Journal
of Historic Madison, Inc. of Wisconsin.

970 US
HISTORICAL SOCIETY OF PRINCETON, NEW
JERSEY. NEWS & NOTES. vol.4, 1980. irreg.
membership. Historical Society of Princeton, New
Jersey, Bainbridge House, 158 Nassau St.,
Princeton, NJ 08540. Ed. Florence L. Peters.

929 US ISSN 0199-9583
HUGUENOT HISTORIAN; a journal of Huguenot
history and genealogy. 1982. biennial. Huguenot
Society of New Jersey, c/o Mrs. Lyman P. Hill,
Ed., English Village, Cranford, NJ 07016.

980 US ISSN 0073-4349
IBERO-AMERICANA. 1932. irreg. price varies.
University of California Press, 2223 Fulton St.,
Berkeley, CA 94720. circ. 260.

980 860 460 CS
IBEROAMERICANA PRAGENSIA. 1966. approx.
every 18 mo. price varies. Universita Karlova,
Centro de Estudios Iberoamericanos, Nam.
Krasnoarmejcu 2, 116 38 Prague 1, Czechoslovakia.

973 II ISSN 0301-9101
IDEAS; Indian doctoral engagements in American
studies. (Text in English) 1971. irreg. membership.
American Studies Research Centre, Osmania
University Campus, Hyderabad 500007, India. abstr.
circ. 3,000.

ILLINOIS. STATE MUSEUM. SCIENTIFIC
PAPERS SERIES. see EARTH SCIENCES —
Geology

INDIANA; contributions to ethnology and linguistics,
archaeology and physical anthropology of Indian
America. see ANTHROPOLOGY

973 US ISSN 0073-6880
INDIANA HISTORICAL COLLECTIONS. 1916.
irreg. price varies. Indiana Historical Bureau, 408
State Library and Historical Bldg., 140 N. Senate
Ave., Indianapolis, IN 46204. bk. rev. index. circ.
600.

973 US ISSN 0073-6902
INDIANA HISTORICAL SOCIETY.
PUBLICATIONS. 1897. irreg., vol. 26, no. 1, 1980.
price varies. Indiana Historical Society, 315 W.
Ohio St., Indianapolis, IN 46202. Ed. Gayle
Thornbrough. circ. 5,000.

977 US
INDIANA HISTORY RESOURCE SERIES. 1980.
irreg. price varies. Indiana Historical Bureau, 408
State Library and Historical Bldg., 140 N. Senate
Ave., Indianapolis, IN 46204. index. circ. 600.

973 US ISSN 0085-1833
INDUSTRIAL CITIES NEWS SERVICE; an
independent, socialist news service. 1967. irreg.
price varies. Industrial Cities News Service, Box
592, Chicago, IL 60690. Ed. Charles G. Doehrer.
bk. rev. film rev. circ. 125. (processed)

980 PE
INEDITA. 1973. irreg. Universidad Nacional de San
Agustin, Direccion Universitaria de Investigacion,
Apdo. 23, Arequipa, Peru. Ed. Alejandro Malaga
Medina.

977 US
INSCRIPTIONS. 1972. irreg. Wisconsin State Old
Cemetery Society, c/o F. Winston Luck, Ed., 4319
N. 70th St., Milwaukee, WI 53216.

980 300 FR ISSN 0073-828X
INSTITUT DES HAUTES ETUDES DE
L'AMERIQUE LATINE. CENTRE D'ETUDES
POLITIQUES, ECONOMIQUES ET SOCIALES.
PUBLICATIONS MULTIGRAPHIEES. 1962. no.
7. irreg., 1973, no. 14. price varies. Institut des
Hautes Etudes de l'Amerique Latine, 28 rue Saint
Guillaume, 75007 Paris, France.

980 972 FR ISSN 0073-8298
INSTITUT DES HAUTES ETUDES DE
L'AMERIQUE LATINE. TRAVAUX ET
MEMOIRES. 1957. irreg., 1978, no. 31. price
varies. Institut des Hautes Etudes de l'Amerique
Latine, 28 rue Saint-Guillaume, 75007 Paris, France.

970 UK ISSN 0306-5499
INSTITUTE OF UNITED STATES STUDIES
MONOGRAPHS. 1974. irreg., no. 2, 1975. price
varies. Athlone Press, 90-91 Great Russell St.,
London WC1B 3PY, England.

972.86 CR ISSN 0074-0039
INSTITUTO COSTARRICENSE DE CULTURA
HISPANICA. PUBLICACION.* irreg. Instituto
Costarricense de Cultura Hispanica, Apartado 4860,
San Jose, Costa Rica.

INSTITUTO DE ANTROPOLOGIA E HISTORIA.
ANUARIO. see ANTHROPOLOGY

980 PE
INSTITUTO DE ESTUDIOS PERUANOS.
HISTORIA ANDINA. 1973. irreg. $5. I E P
Ediciones, Horacio Urteaga 694 (Campo de Marte),
Lima 11, Peru.

983 574 CL ISSN 0085-1922
INSTITUTO DE LA PATAGONIA. ANALES. (Text
in Spanish; summaries in English) 1970. a. $20.
Instituto de la Patagonia, Casilla de Correo 102-D,
Punta Arenas, Magallanes, Chile. adv. bk. rev. bibl.
charts. illus. circ. 1,000 (controlled) Indexed:
Biol.Abstr. Chem.Abstr. Aqua.Sci.&Fish. Abstr.

INSTITUTO FEMENINO DE INVESTIGACIONES
HISTORICAS. ANUARIO. see WOMEN'S
INTERESTS

INSTITUTO NACIONAL DE ANTROPOLOGIA E
HISTORIA. ANALES. see ANTHROPOLOGY

INSTITUTO NACIONAL DE ANTROPOLOGIA E
HISTORIA. OBRAS VARIAS. see
ANTHROPOLOGY

972 MX ISSN 0077-1228
INSTITUTO TECNOLOGICO Y DE ESTUDIOS
SUPERIORES. PUBLICACIONES. SERIE
HISTORIA. (Text in Spanish. one number in
German) 1963. 1970, no. 12. Instituto Tecnologico
y de Estudios Superiores de Monterrey, Sucursal de
Correos "J", Monterrey, N.L., Mexico.

980 300 US ISSN 0074-0918
INTER-AMERICAN ECONOMIC AND SOCIAL
COUNCIL. FINAL REPORT OF THE ANNUAL
MEETING AT THE MINISTERIAL LEVEL.
(Text in Spanish, English, French and Portuguese)
1962. a. $2. Organization of American States,
Department of Publications, Washington, DC
20006. circ. 2,000.

980 GW ISSN 0075-2673
JAHRBUCH FUER GESCHICHTE VON STAAT,
WIRTSCHAFT UND GESELLSCHAFT
LATEINAMERIKAS. 1964. a. price varies.
Boehlau Verlag GmbH, Niehler Str. 272-274, 5000
Cologne 60, W. Germany (B.R.D.) Ed. R.
Konetzke.

HISTORY — HISTORY OF NORTH AND SOUTH AMERICA

989   JM
JAMAICAN HISTORICAL REVIEW. 1946. a; 1973, vol. 10. Jam.$2.50($4) Jamaican Historical Society, c/o Institute of Jamaica, 12-16 East St., Kingston, Jamica. Ed. D.J. Buisseret. adv. bk. rev. illus. circ. 600.

973   US   ISSN 0075-3599
JEFFERSON MEMORIAL LECTURE SERIES. 1962. irreg. price varies. University of California Press, 2223 Fulton St., Berkeley, CA 94720.

980   US
JOHNS HOPKINS STUDIES IN ATLANTIC HISTORY AND CULTURE. 1977. irreg. price varies. Johns Hopkins University Press, Baltimore, MD 21218. Eds. Richard Price, Franklin W. Knight.

JOURNAL OF LIBRARY HISTORY. STATE LIBRARY HISTORY BIBLIOGRAPHY SERIES. see *LIBRARY AND INFORMATION SCIENCES*

979.4   US   ISSN 0047-2581
JOURNAL OF MEXICAN AMERICAN HISTORY. 1970. a. $15. Joseph Peter Navarro, Ed. & Pub., Box 13861 (UCSB), Santa Barbara, CA 93107. Ed. Kathleen O'Connor. adv. bk. rev. bibl. circ. 1,000. (also avail. in microform from UMI) Indexed: Hum.Ind. Amer.Hist.& Life.

975   US   ISSN 0094-8039
JOURNAL OF MUSCLE SHOALS HISTORY. 1973. a. price varies. Tennessee Valley Historical Society, University of North Alabama, Florence, AL 35630. Ed. Kenneth R. Johnson. circ. 800.

980   AG   ISSN 0076-6380
JUNTA DE ESTUDIOS HISTORICOS DE MENDOZA. REVISTA. 1934. biennial. price varies. Junta de Estudios Historicos de Mendoza, Calle Montevideo 544, 5500 Mendoza, Argentina. Ed. Dr. Edmundo Correas. bk. rev. illus.

KENTUCKY. ADJUTANT-GENERAL'S OFFICE. REPORT. see *MILITARY*

978   US
LAKE CHELAN HISTORY NOTES. vol. 5, 1977. irreg. Lake Chelan Historical Society, Box 697, Chelan, WA 98816. Ed. James E. Lindston.

980   US
LATIN AMERICAN HISTORICAL DICTIONARIES SERIES. 1967. irreg., no.20, 1979. price varies. Scarecrow Press, Inc., 52 Liberty St., Box 656, Metuchen, NJ 08840. Ed. A. Curtis Wilgus.

980   US
LATIN AMERICAN HISTORIES. irreg. price varies. Oxford University Press, 200 Madison Ave., New York, NY 10016 (And Ely House, 37 Dover St., London W1X 4AH, England) Ed. James R. Scobie.

LATIN AMERICAN INTERNATIONAL AFFAIRS. see *POLITICAL SCIENCE — International Relations*

970   US   ISSN 0075-8108
LATIN AMERICAN MONOGRAPHS. 1965. irreg; no. 24, 1976. price varies. (University of Florida, Center for Latin American Studies) University Presses of Florida, 15 N. W. 15 St., Gainesville, FL 32603. Ed.Bd. Indexed: SSCI.

972 016   US
LATIN AMERICAN STUDIES WORKING PAPERS. (Text in English & Spanish) 1972. irreg. price varies. Indiana University, Latin American Studies Program, Lindley Hall 311, Bloomington, IN 47401. Ed. Richard C. Burke. (back issues avail.)

LATINOAMERICANA. see *BIBLIOGRAPHIES*

977   US
LEE COUNTY HISTORICAL SOCIETY. HISTORICAL YEARBOOK. 1972? a. price varies. Lee County Historical Society, Box 58, Dixon, IL 61021. Ed. Marion Snively. illus.

971   CN   ISSN 0383-9133
LILLOOET DISTRICT HISTORICAL SOCIETY. BULLETIN. 1974. irreg. membership. Lillooet District Historical Society, Box 441, Lillooet, B.C. V0K 1V0, Canada. Ed. Renee Haweis Chipman. circ. 100-150.

974.4   US   ISSN 0024-8185
M.H.S. MISCELLANY. 1955. irreg. free. Massachusetts Historical Society, 1154 Boylston St., Boston, MA 02215. Ed. Malcolm Freiberg. circ. 1,500.

976 016   US   ISSN 0076-9525
M V C BULLETIN. (Mississippi Valley Collection) 1968. irreg., approx. a. $7.50. ‡ (Memphis State University, John Willard Brister Library) Memphis State University Press, Memphis, TN 38152. Ed. Eleanor McKay. circ. 300. (back issues avail.)

978   US   ISSN 0541-6507
MACKINAC HISTORY; an informal series of illustrated vignettes. 1963. irreg. (2-3/yr.), latest, vol. 2, no. 5. $0.50 per no. ‡ Mackinac Island State Park Commission, Box 30028, Lansing, MI 48909. bibl. illus. (looseleaf format)

975   US   ISSN 0076-2342
MAGAZINE OF ALBEMARLE COUNTY HISTORY. 1940. a. $5. ‡ Albemarle County Historical Society, 220 Court Sq., Charlottesville, VA 22901. Ed. Frederick Schmidt. bk. rev. cum.index: v. 1-20 (1940-1962) circ. 1,000. (back issues avail.)

974.1   US   ISSN 0076-2652
MAINE HERITAGE SERIES. 1970. irreg. (Maine State Museum) Bond Wheelwright Co., Box 296, Freeport, ME 04032.

974.1   US
MAINE HISTORICAL SOCIETY. RESEARCH SERIES. 1977. irreg. price varies. Maine Historical Society, 485 Congress St., Portland, ME 04111.

MALTESE DIRECTORY: CANADA, UNITED STATES. see *ETHNIC INTERESTS*

971   CN   ISSN 0076-3896
MANITOBA RECORD SOCIETY. PUBLICATIONS. (Text in English: occasionally French) 1965. a. Can.$16. Manitoba Record Society, 500 Dysart Rd., Winnipeg, Man. R3T 2M8, Canada. Ed. A. B. McKillop. circ. 1,000.

MAWDSLEY MEMOIRS. see *GEOGRAPHY*

MEETING GROUND. see *ETHNIC INTERESTS*

980   US   ISSN 0076-8189
MICHIGAN STATE UNIVERSITY. LATIN AMERICAN STUDIES CENTER. MONOGRAPH SERIES. irreg. price varies. ‡ Michigan State University, Latin American Studies Center, 200 International Center, East Lansing, MI 48824. (reprint service avail. from UMI)

980   US   ISSN 0076-8200
MICHIGAN STATE UNIVERSITY. LATIN AMERICAN STUDIES CENTER. RESEARCH REPORTS. 1968. irreg. price varies. ‡ Michigan State University, Latin American Studies Center, 200 International Center, East Lansing, MI 48824. (reprint service avail. from UMI)

977   US
MIDDLETOWN HISTORICAL SOCIETY. NEWSLETTER. no. 17, 1977. irreg. Middletown Historical Society, 7426 Hubbard Ave., Middletown, WI 53562.

970   US   ISSN 0076-9630
MISSOURI HANDBOOK SERIES. 1961. irreg., 1964, no. 5. price varies. University of Missouri Press, 107 Swallow Hall, Columbia, MO 65201.

973   US   ISSN 0076-9894
MODERN AMERICA. 1964. irreg., no. 4, 1975. price varies. Ohio State University Press, 2070 Neil Ave., Columbus, OH 43210. Eds. John Braeman, Robert H. Bremmer, David Brody.

MONUMENTA AMERICANA. see *ARCHAEOLOGY*

572 069   BL
MUSEU DO INDIO. DOCUMENTACAO. 1976. irreg. Museu do Indio, Biblioteca Marechal Rondon, Rua Mata Machado, 127, Maracana, Rio de Janeiro, Brazil.

980 860   UY   ISSN 0077-2844
NARRATIVA LATINOAMERICANA.* irreg. Editorial Arca, Colonia 1263, Montevideo, Uruguay.

973 320   US   ISSN 0077-7935
NEVADA STUDIES IN HISTORY AND POLITICAL SCIENCE. 1960. irreg. no. 14 in prep. price varies. ‡ (University of Nevada, Departments of History and Political Science) University of Nevada Press, Reno, NV 89557. Ed. Wilbur S. Shepperson.

978.9   US   ISSN 0196-3929
NEW MEXICO BLUE BOOK. 1882. biennial. free. ‡ Secretary of State, Legislative-Executive Building, Santa Fe, NM 87503. bibl. charts. illus. stat. circ. 4,000.
Formerly: Historical Blue Book of New Mexico.

971   CN   ISSN 0078-1053
NORDICANA. (Text and summaries in English and French) 1964. irreg. (approx. 3-5 nos. per year) price varies. Universite Laval, Centre d'Etudes Nordiques, Quebec C1K 7P4, Canada. Ed. C. Morissoneau.
Until No. 30(1971) Issued As: Quebec (City) Universite Laval. Centre d'Etudes Nordiques. Travaux Divers.

982   AG
NORTE. 1975 (third series) irreg. Consejo Provincial de Difusion Cultural, Departamento de Literatura, San Miguel de Tucuman, Argentina.

NORTH AMERICAN SOCIETY FOR SPORT HISTORY. PROCEEDINGS. see *SPORTS AND GAMES*

973   US   ISSN 0078-1789
NORTHWEST HISTORICAL SERIES. 1923. irreg. price varies. Arthur H. Clark Co., 1264 S. Central Ave., Glendal, CA 91204. index.

900 325   US   ISSN 0078-1967
NORWEGIAN-AMERICAN HISTORICAL ASSOCIATION. NEWSLETTER. 1934. irreg. free. ‡ Norwegian-American Historical Association, St. Olaf College, Northfield, MN 55057. Ed. Lloyd Hustvedt. circ. 1,100.

948 973   US   ISSN 0085-4352
NORWEGIAN-AMERICAN HISTORICAL ASSOCIATION. TOPICAL STUDIES. 1971. irreg. ‡ Norwegian-American Historical Association, St. Olaf College, Northfield, MN 55057. Ed. Kenneth O. Bjork. circ. 1,500. (also avail. in microform from UMI)

900   US   ISSN 0078-1975
NORWEGIAN AMERICAN HISTORICAL ASSOCIATION. TRAVEL AND DESCRIPTION SERIES. 1926. irreg., vol. 8, 1973. price varies. ‡ Norwegian-American Historical Association, St. Olaf College, Northfield, MN 55057. Ed. Kenneth O. Bjork. circ. 1,500.

900   US   ISSN 0078-1983
NORWEGIAN-AMERICAN STUDIES. 1926. irreg.; vol. 27, 1976. price varies. ‡ Norwegian-American Historical Association, St. Olaf College, Northfield, MN 55057. Ed. Kenneth O. Bjork. circ. 1,500. (also avail. in microform from UMI)
Formerly: Norwegian-American Studies and Records.

980   US   ISSN 0078-6403
O A S. GENERAL SECRETARIAT. ANNUAL REPORT. 1960. a. $20. Organization of American States, General Secretariat, Department of Publications, 17th and Constitution Ave. N.W., Washington, DC 20006.

976   US
OKLAHOMA SERIES. vol. 4, 1976. irreg. price varies. Oklahoma Historical Society, Historical Building, 2100 North Lincoln, Oklahoma City, OK 73105. illus.

970   US
OLD GLORY; the story of our flag. 1972. a. $1.50. Snibbe Publications, Inc., 523 Lakeview Rd., Clearwater, FL 33516. Ed. M.R. Bennett.

975.6   US   ISSN 0078-4540
OLD SALEM GLEANER. 1957. irreg. not available to general public. Old Salem, Inc., Drawer F, Salem Station, Winston-Salem, NC 27108. Ed. Frances Griffin. circ. 2,000.
Title varies; 1957-1962: Old Salem Newsletter.

HISTORY — HISTORY OF NORTH AND SOUTH AMERICA

974 US ISSN 0078-4559
OLD STURBRIDGE VILLAGE BOOKLET SERIES. 1955. irreg., no. 29, 1972. Old Sturbridge Village, Sturbridge, MA 01566. Ed. Catherine Fennelly. circ. 12,000. Indexed: Hist.Abstr.

971 CN ISSN 0078-5091
ONTARIO SERIES. 1957. irreg. membership. (Champlain Society) University of Toronto Press, Front Campus, Toronto, Ont. M5S 1A6, Canada. (also avail. in microfiche)

980 016 US ISSN 0078-642X
ORGANIZATION OF AMERICAN STATES. OFFICIAL RECORDS. INDICE Y LISTA GENERAL. Spanish edition: Documentos Oficiales de la Organizacion de los Estados Americanos: Lista General Indice Analitico (ISSN 0078-6365) (Editions Also in French, Portuguese) 1960. a. price varies. Organization of American States, General Secretariat, Department of Publications, 17th and Constitution Ave. N.W., Washington, DC 20006. circ. 2,000.

980 341.8 US ISSN 0078-6438
ORGANIZATION OF AMERICAN STATES. PERMANENT COUNCIL. DECISIONS TAKEN AT MEETINGS (CUMULATED EDITION) (Text in Spanish and English) 1951. a. price varies. Organization of American States, Department of Publications, Washington, DC 20006. circ. 1,000.

917.47 US ISSN 0092-9549
OSWEGO COUNTY HISTORICAL SOCIETY. JOURNAL. 1939. a. $7.50. Oswego County Historical Society, Richardson-Bates House, 135 E. 3rd St., Oswego, NY 13126. Dir. Philip C. Kwiatkowski. illus. circ. 500. Key Title: Journal - Oswego County Historical Society.

972 800 382 US ISSN 0190-2229
PACIFIC COAST COUNCIL ON LATIN AMERICAN STUDIES. PROCEEDINGS. (Text in English, Spanish, Portuguese) 1972. a. $10. Campanile Press, San Diego State University, San Diego, CA 92182. Ed. Roger L. Cunniff. adv. film rev. bibl. circ. 600(controlled) (back issues avail.)

971 CN
PACIFIC MARITIME STUDIES SERIES. 1980. irreg. price varies. University of British Columbia Press, 303-6344 Memorial Rd., Vancouver, B.C. V6T 1W5, Canada.

980 MX ISSN 0078-8813
PAN AMERICAN INSTITUTE OF GEOGRAPHY AND HISTORY. COMMISSION ON HISTORY. BIBLIOGRAFIAS. (Text in English, Spanish, Portugese or French) 1953. irreg., 1970, vol. 4. price varies. Instituto Panamericano de Geografia e Historia, Ex-Arzobispedo 29, Mexico 18, D.F., Mexico.

980 MX ISSN 0078-8821
PAN AMERICAN INSTITUTE OF GEOGRAPHY AND HISTORY. COMMISSION ON HISTORY. GUIAS. (Text in Spanish, English, Portugese or French) 1949. irreg., 1967, vol. 4. price varies. Instituto Panamericano de Geografia e Historia, Commission on History, Ex-Arzobispedo 29, Mexico 18, D.F., Mexico.

980.2 MX ISSN 0078-883X
PAN AMERICAN INSTITUTE OF GEOGRAPHY AND HISTORY. COMMISSION ON HISTORY. HISTORIOGRAFIAS AMERICANAS. 1953. irreg.; 1977, vol. 9. Instituto Panamericano de Geografia e Historia, Ex-Arzobispedo 29, Mexico 18, D.F., Mexico.

980 MX ISSN 0078-8848
PAN AMERICAN INSTITUTE OF GEOGRAPHY AND HISTORY. COMMISSION ON HISTORY. HISTORIADORES DE AMERICA. (Text in Spanish, English, Portugese or French) 1949. irreg., 1967, vol. 12. price varies. Instituto Panamericano de Geografia e Historia, Commission on History, Ex-Arzobispedo 29, Mexico 18, D.F., Mexico.

980.2 MX ISSN 0078-8856
PAN AMERICAN INSTITUTE OF GEOGRAPHY AND HISTORY. COMMISSION ON HISTORY. MONUMENTOS HISTORICOS Y ARQUEOLOGICOS. 1950. irreg.; 1974 vol. 17. price varies. Instituto Panamericano de Geografia e Historia, Commission on History, Ex-Arzobispedo 29, Mexico 18, D.F., Mexico.

PENNSYLVANIA. HISTORICAL AND MUSEUM COMMISSION. ANTHROPOLOGICAL SERIES. see *ANTHROPOLOGY*

973 US ISSN 0079-0990
PERSPECTIVES IN AMERICAN HISTORY. 1967. a. $10. Harvard University, Charles Warren Center for Studies in American History, Robinson Hall, Cambridge, MA 02138. Ed. Donald Fleming. circ. 2,000.

974 US
PETTAQUAMSCUTT REPORTER. vol. 13, 1977. irreg. membership. Pettaquamscutt Historical Society, c/o William D. Metz, Ed., Box 59, Kingston, RI 02881. circ. 300.

917.4 US
PINERY. 1956, N.S. 1977. irreg., aprox. 3-4/yr. membership. ‡ Portage County Historical Society, University of Wisconsin, Stevens Point, WI 54481. Ed. William G. Paul. bk. rev. bibl. circ. 200.
Local

970 CN
PIONEER DAYS. 1903. irreg., 3rd ed. 1975. $2.75. Bruce County Historical Society, c/o Mrs Mary Anne Ellenton, Box 182, Tiverton, Ont. N0G 2T0, Canada. Ed. David Kennedy.

970 US ISSN 0193-6891
POPULAR CULTURE BIO-BIBLIOGRAPHIES. irreg. price varies. Greenwood Press, 8 Post Rd. W., Westport, CT 06881. Ed. M. Thomas Inge.

917.8 US ISSN 0092-8313
PRAIRIE SCOUT. 1973. a. $12.95. Westerners, Kansas Corral, P.O. Box 531, Abilene, KS 67410. illus. circ. 500 (controlled)

PROBLEMS IN AMERICAN CIVILIZATION. see *HUMANITIES: COMPREHENSIVE WORKS*

390 973 US ISSN 0361-2333
PROSPECTS; annual journal of American cultural studies. 1975. a. $24.95. Burt Franklin & Co., Inc., 235 E. 44th St., New York, NY 10017.

973 US ISSN 0079-7014
PROSPECTS FOR AMERICA. 1961. irreg. William-Frederick Press, 308 E. 79th St., New York, NY 10021.

973 US ISSN 0085-5227
PUBLICATIONS IN THE AMERICAN WEST. 1969. irreg., latest issue, 1978. price varies. (American West Center) University of Utah Press, Salt Lake City, UT 84112. Ed. Brigham D. Madsen.

970 980 GW ISSN 0079-9157
QUELLENWERKE ZUR ALTEN GESCHICHTE AMERIKAS. irreg., vol. 12, 1977. price varies. (Ibero-Amerikanisches Institut Preussischer Kulturbesitz Berlin) Gebr. Mann Verlag, Lindenstr. 76, Postfach 110303, 1000 Berlin 61, W. Germany (B.R.D.) Ed. Gerdt Kutscher.

980 EC
QUITUMBE. 1971. a; no. 2, 1972. S/40($2) Pontificia Universidad Catolica del Ecuador, Departamento de Historia y Geografia, Avda. 12 de Octubre 1076 y Carrion, Apdo. 2184, Quito, Ecuador. adv. circ. 1,000.

971 CN ISSN 0315-2804
RAINCOAST CHRONICLES. 1972. irreg. Can.$8. Raincoast Historical Society, Box 119, Madeira Park, B.C. VON 2HO, Canada. Ed. Howard White. bk. rev. illus. circ. 5,000.

973 US
RAYFORD W. LOGAN LECTURE SERIES. vol. 6, 1975. a. $2. Howard University, Department of History, Washington, DC 20059.

981 BL
RECIFE, BRAZIL. SECRETARIA DE EDUCACAO E CULTURO. ARQUIVOS. irreg. Secretaria de Educacao e Cultura, Recife, Pernambuco, Brazil.
Archives

977 917 US
REPORTS IN MACKINAC HISTORY AND ARCHAEOLOGY. 1972. irreg., approx. a. $2-3. ‡ Mackinac Island State Park Commission, Box 30028, Lansing, MI 48909. Ed. David A. Armour. bibl. illus.

980 CL ISSN 0080-2093
REVISTA CHILENA DE HISTORIA Y GEOGRAFIA. 1911. a. $15. Sociedad Chilena de Historia y Geografia, Casilla 1386, Santiago, Chile. Ed. Ricardo Donoso. cum.index.

990 CR
REVISTA DE HISTORIA. 1975. irreg. Col.35($6.50) Universidad Nacional, Escuela de Historia, Apartado 86, Heredia, Costa Rica. bibl charts, stat. circ. 800. (back issues avail.)

986.6 EC ISSN 0556-5987
REVISTA DE HISTORIA DE LAS IDEAS. 1959. irreg. Instituto Panamericano de Geografia e Historia, Casa de la Cultura Ecuatoriana, Quito, Ecuador.

982 AG ISSN 0556-5995
REVISTA DE HISTORIA DE ROSARIO. 1963. a. $5. Sociedad de Historia de Rosario, 1 de Mayo 1082, 2000 Rosario, Argentina. Ed. Wladimir C. Mikielievich. adv. bk. rev. circ. 1,100.

989 UY
REVISTA HISTORICA. vol. 67, 1973. a. Museo Historico Nacional, Casa Rivera, Rincon 437, Montevideo, Uruguay. Ed.Bd.

975.5 US
REVOLUTIONARY VIRGINIA: THE ROAD TO INDEPENDENCE. 1973. irreg., vol. 4, 1978. (Virginia Independence Bicentennial Commission) University Press of Virginia, Box 3608 University Sta., Charlottesville, VA 22903.
Formerly: Virginia Independence Bicentennial Publications.

RIPLEY P. BULLEN MONOGRAPHS IN ANTHROPOLOGY AND HISTORY. see *ANTHROPOLOGY*

975.5 US
ROANOKE VALLEY HISTORICAL SOCIETY JOURNAL. 1964. a. $3.50 to non-members; members $2.50. ‡ Roanoke Valley Historical Society, Box 1904, Roanoke, VA 24008. Ed. George Kegley. illus. circ. 500(approx.) (back issues avail.)
Formerly: Roanoke Historical Society. Journal (ISSN 0035-7359)

970 US ISSN 0080-3383
ROCKBRIDGE HISTORICAL SOCIETY, LEXINGTON, VIRGINIA. PROCEEDINGS. 1939. irreg., vol.8, 1979. $16. Rockbridge Historical Society, 101 E. Washington St., Lexington, VA 24450. Ed. Larry I. Bland. cum.index: vols. 1-6 in vol. 6. circ. 750.

980 US ISSN 0081-2951
S E C O L A S ANNALS. 1970. a. membership. Southeastern Conference on Latin American Studies, c/o Ed. Eugene R. Huck, Kennesaw College, Box 444, Marietta, GA 30061. circ. 500. (also avail. in microfilm from UMI) Indexed: Hist.Abstr. Amer.Hist.&Life.

979.2 US
SAGA OF THE SANPITCH. 1969. a. $1.50. ‡ Church of Jesus Christ of Latter-day Saints, Manti Region, 94 W. 400 South, Manti, UT 84642. Eds. Ruth B. Scow, Eleanor P. Madsen. illus. index. circ. 1,500.

977.3 US ISSN 0095-3911
ST. CLAIR COUNTY HISTORICAL SOCIETY. JOURNAL. a. $1.75. St. Clair County Historical Society, c/o Rose Mansfield Ed., 20 Sherwood Forest, Belleville, IL 62223. illus. (back issues avail.) Key Title: Journal of the St. Clair County Historical Society.

978 US
SANTA ANA MOUNTAIN SERIES. 1977. irreg. price varies. California Classics, Box 291, Trabuco Canyon, CA 92678.

970 940 430 375.4 US
SCHATZKAMMER; der deutschen Sprachlehre, Dichtung und Geschichte. 1975. a. $3.50. c/o Werner Kitzler, Mg. Ed., Department of Modern Languages, University of South Dakota, Vermillion, SD 57069. Ed. Duane V. Keilstrup. adv. bk. rev. circ. 1,000.
German-American history

973   US
SCHUYLERITE. vol.4,1975. a. $5. Schuyler County Historical Museum, Corner Congress and Madison St., Rushville, IL 62681. Ed. Edward Y. Crandall.

SEMINAR ON THE ACQUISITION OF LATIN AMERICAN LIBRARY MATERIALS. FINAL REPORT AND WORKING PAPERS. see *LIBRARY AND INFORMATION SCIENCES*

981   BL
SERIE CADERNOS DE HISTORIA. no. 2, 1977. irreg. Thesaurus Editora e Sistemas Audio Visuais Ltda., SCLRN 703, Bloque F, C.P. 04.326, 70000 Brasilia, Brazil.

979.4   US   ISSN 0583-4449
SISKIYOU PIONEER AND YEARBOOK. 1946. a. $7 (including monthly newsletter, Nuggets) Siskiyou County Historical Society, 910 S. Main St., Yreka, CA 96097. adv. charts. illus. circ. 1,500. (also avail. in microform from UMI)

971   CN   ISSN 0085-6207
SOCIAL HISTORY OF CANADA. 1971. irreg. price varies. University of Toronto Press, Front Campus, Toronto, Ont. M5S 1A6, Canada (and 33 East Tupper St., Buffalo, N.Y. 14203) Ed. Prof. H.V. Nelles. (also avail. in microfiche)

SOCIEDAD GEOLOGICA DEL PERU. BOLETIN. see *EARTH SCIENCES — Geology*

572   SZ   ISSN 0582-1592
SOCIETE SUISSE DES AMERICANISTES.BULLETIN/ SCHWEIZERISCHE AMERIKANISTEN-GESELLSCHAFT. BULLETIN. (Text and summaries in French and German) 1950; N.S. 1980. a. 25 Fr. Societe Suisse des Americanistes - Schweizerische Amerikanisten-Gesellschaft, 65-67, Boulevard Carl-Vogt, 1205 Geneva, Switzerland. Ed. Rene Fuerst. bibl. charts. illus. circ. 750.

980   UK   ISSN 0308-1540
SOCIETY FOR LATIN AMERICA STUDIES. BULLETIN. irreg. £3.60. Portsmouth Polytechnic, Department of Geography, Ravelin House, Museum Rd., Portsmouth, Hants PO1 2QQ, England.

970 355   US
SOCIETY OF COLONIAL WARS. BULLETIN. 1934. q. membership. Society of Colonial Wars, 122 East 58th St., New York, NY 10022. Ed. Robert G. Collier. bibl.

SONS AND DAUGHTERS OF THE SODDIES. REPORTS; sod houses and dugouts in North America. see *GENEALOGY AND HERALDRY*

975   US
SOUTH CAROLINA. DEPARTMENT OF ARCHIVES AND HISTORY. ANNUAL REPORT. a. Department of Archives and History, Box 11669, Columbia, SC 29211.

975   US   ISSN 0361-6207
SOUTH CAROLINA HISTORICAL ASSOCIATION. PROCEEDINGS. 1932. a. $6.50. South Carolina Historical Association, Box 28662, Furman University, Greenville, SC 29613. circ. 500. (also avail. in microfilm; back issues avail.) Key Title: Proceedings of the South Carolina Historical Association.

977   US   ISSN 0081-2773
SOUTH DAKOTA STATE HISTORICAL SOCIETY. COLLECTIONS. 1902. biennial. price varies. South Dakota State Historical Society, Memorial Bldg., Pierre, SD 57501. Ed. Nancy Koupal. circ. 1,000. (reprint service avail. from UMI)
Former titles: South Dakota. Department of History. Historical Collections; (until 1974): South Dakota. Department of History. Report and Historical Collections (ISSN 0092-198X)

977   US
SOUTH WOOD COUNTY HISTORICAL CORPORATION. NEWSLETTER. irreg. free. South Wood County Historical Corporation, 540 Third St. So., Wisconsin Rapids, WI 54494.

976.3   US   ISSN 0098-9193
SOUTHEAST LOUISIANA HISTORICAL ASSOCIATION. PAPERS. 1974. irreg. Southeast Louisiana Historical Association, Box 1937, Hammond, LA 70401. Key Title: Papers - Southeast Louisiana Historical Association.

SOUTHSUBKIN. see *GENEALOGY AND HERALDRY*

SPECTRUM (ST. PAUL) see *POPULATION STUDIES*

971   CN   ISSN 0081-4369
STANSTEAD COUNTY HISTORICAL SOCIETY. JOURNAL. 1965. biennial. Can.$3.50. Stanstead County Historical Society, Box 210, Stanstead, Que. J0B 3E0, Canada. circ. 600.

STIMMEN INDIANISCHER VOELKER. see *FOLKLORE*

STORIES FROM THE HILLS. see *LITERATURE*

973   IT   ISSN 0085-6819
STUDI AMERICANI. (Text and summaries in English and Italian) 1955. a. price varies. Edizioni di Storia e Letteratura, Via Lancellotti 18, Rome 00186, Italy. Ed. Agostino Lombardo.

970   NE   ISSN 0081-7503
STUDIES IN AMERICAN HISTORY. 1963. irreg. price varies. Mouton Publishers, Noordeinde 41, 2514 GC The Hague, Netherlands (U.S. addr: Mouton Publishers, c/o Walter de Gruyter, Inc., 200 Saw Mill River Road, Hawthorne, NY 10532)

SURVEY OF SOURCES NEWSLETTER. see *BIOLOGY*

975.9   US
TEQUESTA. 1941. a. $20 includes Update. ‡ Historical Association of Southern Florida, 3280 S. Miami Ave., Bldg. B, Miami, FL 33129. Eds. Arva Moore Parks, Thelma Peters. bibl. circ. 1,800.

985   PE
TESTIMONIOS (EN HISTORIETA) 1979. irreg. $40 includes subscr. to: Cuadernos de Estudio, Cuadernos de Capacitation and Cuadernos Populares. Comision Evangelica Latinoamericana de Educacion Cristiana, Av. General Garzon 2267, Lima 11, Peru.

976.4   US
TEXAS ALMANAC AND STATE INDUSTRIAL GUIDE. 1857. biennial. $6.75 hardbound, $4.75 paperbound. A.H. Belo Corp., Communications Center, Dallas, TX 75265. Ed. Fred Pass. adv. illus. stat. circ. 100,000. (also avail. in microform)

THESES IN LATIN AMERICAN STUDIES AT BRITISH UNIVERSITIES IN PROGRESS AND COMPLETED. see *BIBLIOGRAPHIES*

970   CN   ISSN 0082-4283
THUNDER BAY HISTORICAL MUSEUM SOCIETY. PAPERS AND RECORDS. 1908. irreg. Can.$2. Thunder Bay Museum, 219 S. May St., Thunder Bay, Ont. P7E 1B5, Canada.

971   CN   ISSN 0226-7209
TORONTO HISTORICAL BOARD. YEAR BOOK. 1975. a. Toronto Historical Board, General Office, Stanley Barracks, Toronto, Ont. M6K 3C3, Canada. illus.

973   SP
TRABAJOS MONOGRAFICOS SOBRE LA INDEPENDENCIA DE NORTEAMERICA. 1977. irreg. Ministerio de Asuntos Exteriores, Direccion General de Relaciones Culturales, Madrid, Spain.

970   US
TRAIL GUIDE. 1955. irreg., (approx. q.) $6 to non-members. (Westerners, Kansas City Posse) Lowell Press, 115 E. 31st St., Kansas City, MO 64141. Ed. Payson W. Lowell. bibl. cum.index in prep. circ. 250-300.

980   VE
UNIVERSIDAD CENTRAL DE VENEZUELA. INSTITUTO DE ESTUDIOS HISPANOAMERICANOS. ANUARIO. 1974. a. Universidad Central de Venezuela, Instituto de Investigaciones Historicas, Av. Libertador, Qta. Cantabria, los Caobos, Caracas 105, Venezuela. Ed. Eduardo Arcila Farias.

989.5   UY
UNIVERSIDAD DE LA REPUBLICA. FACULTAD DE HUMANIDADES Y CIENCIAS. REVISTA. SERIE HISTORIA. N.S. 1979. irreg. Universidad de la Republica, Facultad de Humanidades y Ciencias, Seccion Revista, Tristan Narvaja 1674, Montevideo, Uruguay. Dir. Beatriz Martinez Osorio. Supersedes in part: Universidad de la Republica. Facultad de Humanidades y Ciencias. Revista.

972.9   PR   ISSN 0079-788X
UNIVERSIDAD DE PUERTO RICO. INSTITUTE OF CARIBBEAN STUDIES. SPECIAL STUDIES. 1965. irreg. price varies; no. 8, $4.00. Universidad de Puerto Rico, Institute of Caribbean Studies, Rio Piedras, PR 00931.

970.1   MX   ISSN 0076-7166
UNIVERSIDAD NACIONAL AUTONOMA DE MEXICO. CENTRO DE ESTUDIOS MAYAS. CUADERNOS. (Text in Spanish and English) 1969. irreg. Mex.$20($1.93) Universidad Nacional Autonoma de Mexico, Centro de Estudios Mayas, Torre de Humanidades II, Ciudad Universitaria, Mexico 20, D.F., Mexico. Ed. Alberto Ruz Lhuillier. bk. rev. circ. 2,000.

972   MX   ISSN 0076-7271
UNIVERSIDAD NACIONAL AUTONOMA DE MEXICO. INSTITUTO DE INVESTIGACIONES HISTORICAS. CUADERNOS SERIE DOCUMENTAL. 1963. irreg., 1968, no. 6. price varies. Universidad Nacional Autonoma de Mexico, Instituto de Investigaciones Historicas, Departamento de Distribucion de Libros Universitarias, Insurgentes sur 299, Mexico 11, D.F., Mexico.

972   MX   ISSN 0076-7301
UNIVERSIDAD NACIONAL AUTONOMA DE MEXICO. INSTITUTO DE INVESTIGACIONES HISTORICAS. SERIE BIBLIOGRAFICA. 1948. irreg., 1969, no. 5. price varies. Universidad Nacional Autonoma de Mexico, Instituto de Investigaciones Historicas, Departamento de Distribucion de Libros Universitarias, Insurgentes sur, 299, Mexico 11, D.F., Mexico.

972   MX   ISSN 0076-731X
UNIVERSIDAD NACIONAL AUTONOMA DE MEXICO. INSTITUTO DE INVESTIGACIONES HISTORICAS. SERIE DOCUMENTAL. 1947. irreg; no. 11, 1974. price varies. Universidad Nacional Autonoma de Mexico, Instituto de Investigaciones Historicas, Departamento de Distribucion de Libros Universitarias, Insurgentes sur, 299, Mexico 11, D.F., Mexico.

972   MX   ISSN 0076-7328
UNIVERSIDAD NACIONAL AUTONOMA DE MEXICO. INSTITUTO DE INVESTIGACIONES HISTORICAS. SERIE DE CULTURES MESOAMERICANAS. 1967. irreg; no. 2, 1968. price varies. Universidad Nacional Autonoma de Mexico, Instituto de Investigaciones Historicas, Departamento de Distribucion de Libros Universitarias, Insurgentes sur 299, Mexico 11, D.F., Mexico.

972   MX   ISSN 0071-1675
UNIVERSIDAD NACIONAL AUTONOMA DE MEXICO. INSTITUTO DE INVESTIGACIONES HISTORICAS. SERIE DE CULTURA NAHUATL. ESTUDIOS DE CULTURA NAHUATL. 1959. irreg; 1976, vol. 12. price varies. Universidad Nacional Autonoma de Mexico, Instituto de Investigaciones Historicas, Villa Obregon, Ciudad Universitaria, Mexico 20, D.F., Mexico.

972   MX   ISSN 0076-7212
UNIVERSIDAD NACIONAL AUTONOMA DE MEXICO. INSTITUTO DE INVESTIGACIONES HISTORICAS. SERIE DE CULTURA NAHUATL. FUENTES. 1958. irreg., 1969, no. 7. price varies. Universidad Nacional Autonoma de Mexico, Instituto de Investigaciones Historicas, Departamento de Distribucion de Libros Universitarias, Insurgentes sur 299, Mexico 11, D.F., Mexico.

HISTORY — HISTORY OF NORTH AND SOUTH AMERICA

972   MX   ISSN 0076-7344
UNIVERSIDAD NACIONAL AUTONOMA DE MEXICO. INSTITUTO DE INVESTIGACIONES HISTORICAS. SERIE DE CULTURA NAHUATL. MONOGRAFIAS. 1959. irreg; no. 19, 1975. price varies. Universidad Nacional Autonoma de Mexico, Instituto de Investigaciones Historicas, Departamento de Distribucion de Libros Universitarias, Insurgentes sur 299, Mexico 11, D.F., Mexico.

972   MX   ISSN 0076-7352
UNIVERSIDAD NACIONAL AUTONOMA DE MEXICO. INSTITUTO DE INVESTIGACIONES HISTORICAS. SERIE DE HISTORIA GENERAL. 1949. irreg; no. 8, 1972. Universidad Nacional Autonoma de Mexico, Instituto de Investigaciones Historicas, Departamento de Distribucion de Libros Universitarias, Insurgentes sur 299, Mexico 11, D.F., Mexico.

972   MX   ISSN 0076-7387
UNIVERSIDAD NACIONAL AUTONOMA DE MEXICO. INSTITUTO DE INVESTIGACIONES HISTORICAS. SERIE DE HISTORIADORES Y CRONISTAS. 1967. irreg; no. 6, 1977. price varies. Universidad Nacional Autonoma de Mexico, Instituto de Investigaciones Historicas, Departamento de Distribucion de Libros Universitarias, Insurgentes sur 299, Mexico 11, D.F., Mexico.

985   PE
UNIVERSIDAD NACIONAL FEDERICO VILLAREAL. DEPARTAMENTO DE CIENCIAS HISTORICO SOCIALES. PUBLICACIONES. 1976. irreg. Universidad Nacional Federico Villareal, Departamento de Ciencias Historico Sociales, Colmena 412, Lima, Peru.

981   BL
UNIVERSIDADE DE SAO PAULO. DEPARTAMENTO DE HISTORIA. BOLETIM. no. 11 (no. 18 n.s.) 1977. Universidade de Sao Paulo, Departamento de Historia, Caixa Postal 8.105, Sao Paulo, Brazil. Dir. Myriam Ellis. bibl.

981   BL   ISSN 0020-3874
UNIVERSIDADE DE SAO PAULO. INSTITUTO DE ESTUDOS BRASILEIROS. REVISTA. 1966. a. $2. ‡ Universidade de Sao Paulo, Instituto de Estudos Brasileiros, Caixa Postal 11 154, 01000 Sao Paulo, Brazil. Ed Jose Aderaldo Castello. bk. rev. bibl. charts. illus. Indexed: Hist.Abstr.

980.2   BL   ISSN 0080-6374
UNIVERSIDADE DE SAO PAULO. MUSEU PAULISTA. ANAIS. (Text in Portuguese; summaries in English) 1922. a. Universidade de Sao Paulo, Museu Paulista, C.P. 42.503, 04263 Sao Paulo, Brazil.

708   BL
UNIVERSIDADE DE SAO PAULO. MUSEU PAULISTA. COLECAO. SERIE DE HISTORIA. 1963. irreg. Universidade de Sao Paulo, Museu Paulista, C.P. 42503, Parque da Independencia, 04263 Sao Paulo, Brazil. Ed. Setembrino Petri.
Supersedes in part (since 1975): Museu Paulista. Colecao (ISSN 0080-6382)

981   BL
UNIVERSIDADE FEDERAL DO RIO GRANDE DO SUL. GABINETE DE PESQUISA DE HISTORIA. BOLETIM. 1973. irreg. Universidade Federal do Rio Grande do sul, Gabinete de Pesquisa de Historia, 90000 Porto Alegre, Rio Grande do Sul, Brazil.

UNIVERSITE CATHOLIQUE DE LOUVAIN. CENTRE D'ETUDES POLITIQUES. WORKING GROUP "AMERICAN FOREIGN POLICY." CAHIER. see *POLITICAL SCIENCE — International Relations*

UNIVERSITE DE BORDEAUX III. CENTRE DE RECHERCHES SUR L'AMERIQUE ANGLOPHONE. ANNALES. see *POLITICAL SCIENCE*

800   980   FR
UNIVERSITE DE STRASBOURG. INSTITUT D'ETUDES LATINO-AMERICAINES. TRAVAUX. 1960. a. Universite de Strasbourg, Institut d'Etudes Latino-Americaines, 25 rue du Soleil, 67 Strasbourg, France.

971   CN   ISSN 0079-8347
UNIVERSITE LAVAL. CENTRE D'ETUDES NORDIQUES. TRAVAUX ET DOCUMENTS. (Text in English, Eskimo and French; summaries in English and French) 1963. irreg., 1970, no. 5. price varies: $6.-$15. Presses de l'Universite Laval, C.P. 2447 Quebec 2, Canada.

972   US   ISSN 0045-3994
UNIVERSITY OF CALIFORNIA, LOS ANGELES. CHICANO STUDIES CENTER. MONOGRAPHS. 1970. irreg. price varies. University of California, Los Angeles, Chicano Studies Center, 405 Hilgard Ave., Los Angeles, CA 90024. Ed. Carlos Velez, Ray Rocco. (reprint service avail. from UMI)

980   US   ISSN 0075-8132
UNIVERSITY OF CALIFORNIA, LOS ANGELES. LATIN AMERICAN CENTER. LATIN AMERICAN STUDIES SERIES. 1965. irreg., no. 46, 1979. price varies. University of California, Los Angeles, Latin American Center, 405 Hilgard Ave., Los Angeles, CA 90024. Ed. Johannes Wilbert.

980   US   ISSN 0068-6263
UNIVERSITY OF CALIFORNIA, LOS ANGELES. LATIN AMERICAN CENTER. REFERENCE SERIES. 1962. irreg; vol. 8, 1976. price varies. University of California, Los Angeles, Latin American Center, 405 Hilgard Ave., Los Angeles, CA 90024. Ed. Ludwig Lauerhass, Jr.

970   US
UNIVERSITY OF CHICAGO PRESS DOCUMENTS IN AMERICAN HISTORY. 1973. irreg. price varies. University of Chicago Press, 5801 S. Ellis Ave., Chicago, IL 60637. Ed. Arthur Mann. adv. bk. rev. (reprint service avail. from UMI,ISI)

972.6   980   016   US   ISSN 0071-6138
UNIVERSITY OF FLORIDA. LIBRARIES. TECHNICAL PROCESSES DEPARTMENT. CARIBBEAN ACQUISITIONS. 1957/58. irreg. $3. ‡ University of Florida, Library, Gainesville, FL 32611. Ed. Berta L. Clarke. circ. 170.

980   US   ISSN 0075-4986
UNIVERSITY OF KANSAS. CENTER FOR LATIN AMERICAN STUDIES. GRADUATE STUDIES ON LATIN AMERICA. 1963. irreg. $2 per issue. ‡ University of Kansas, Center for Latin American Studies, 106 Strong Hall, Lawrence, KS 66044. Ed. Charles L. Stansifer.

980   UK   ISSN 0076-0846
UNIVERSITY OF LONDON. INSTITUTE OF LATIN AMERICAN STUDIES. MONOGRAPHS. 1969. irreg., no. 9, 1978. Athlone Press, 90-91 Great Russell St., London WC1B 3PY, England (Dist. in U.S. by: Humanities Press, Inc., 171 First Ave., Atlantic Highlands, NJ 07716)

UNIVERSITY OF MISSOURI MONOGRAPHS IN ANTHROPOLOGY. see *ANTHROPOLOGY*

970   980   US
UNIVERSITY OF NEBRASKA. INSTITUTE FOR INTERNATIONAL STUDIES. OCCASIONAL PUBLICATIONS. (Text in English, French and Spanish) 1976. irreg. University of Nebraska-Lincoln, Institute for International Studies, 1034 Oldfather Hall, Lincoln, NE 68588. circ. 500.

980   US   ISSN 0075-8140
UNIVERSITY OF PITTSBURGH. CENTER FOR INTERNATIONAL STUDIES: LATIN AMERICAN STUDIES. OCCASIONAL PAPERS. (Text in English or Spanish) 1970. irreg., no. 10, 1974. free. ‡ University of Pittsburgh, University Center for International Studies, 261 Mervis Hall, Pittsburgh, PA 15260. Ed. Harold D. Sims. circ. 500.

980   US
UNIVERSITY OF WISCONSIN-MILWAUKEE. CENTER FOR LATIN AMERICA. BUSINESS SERIES. 1976. irreg. price varies. University of Wisconsin-Milwaukee, Center for Latin America, Milwaukee, WI 53201.
Formerly: University of Wisconsin-Milwaukee. Center for Latin America. Conference Series.

980   US   ISSN 0146-258X
UNIVERSITY OF WISCONSIN, MILWAUKEE. CENTER FOR LATIN AMERICA. DISCUSSION PAPERS. 1968. irreg., no. 66, 1979. $1. ‡ University of Wisconsin-Milwaukee, Center for Latin America, Milwaukee, WI 53201.
Formerly: University of Wisconsin, Milwaukee. Language and Area Center for Latin America. Discussion Papers. (ISSN 0084-0831)

980   US   ISSN 0084-084X
UNIVERSITY OF WISCONSIN, MILWAUKEE. CENTER FOR LATIN AMERICA. ESSAY SERIES. 1968. irreg; no. 7, 1976. $2. University of Wisconsin, Milwaukee, Center for Latin America, Milwaukee, WI 53201. Key Title: Center Essay Series.

980   US   ISSN 0146-2598
UNIVERSITY OF WISCONSIN-MILWAUKEE. CENTER FOR LATIN AMERICA. SPECIAL PAPERS SERIES. 1974. irreg., no. 4, 1976. $1 per no. University of Wisconsin-Milwaukee, Center for Latin America, Milwaukee, WI 53201. (back issue avail.)

980   US
UNIVERSITY OF WISCONSIN, MILWAUKEE. CENTER FOR LATIN AMERICA. SPECIAL STUDIES SERIES. 1970. irreg., no. 3, 1977. price varies. ‡ University of Wisconsin-Milwaukee, Center for Latin America, Milwaukee, WI 53201.
Formerly: University of Wisconsin, Milwaukee. Language and Area Center for Latin America. Special Studies Series (ISSN 0084-0858)

979.2   US
UTAH STATE HISTORICAL SOCIETY. ANTIQUITIES SECTION. SELECTED PAPERS. 1975. irreg. $5.50. Utah State Historical Society, 307 W. Second South, Salt Lake City, UT 84101. Ed. David B. Madsen.

971   CN
VANCOUVER HISTORICAL SOCIETY. OCCASIONAL PAPERS. irreg. Vancouver Historical Society, Vancouver, B.C., Canada.

980   US   ISSN 0083-5234
VANDERBILT UNIVERSITY. CENTER FOR LATIN AMERICAN STUDIES. OCCASIONAL PAPERS. (No. 1 issued by the Center under its earlier name: Graduate Center for South American Studies) 1964. irreg. ‡ Vanderbilt University, Center for Latin American Studies, Box 1806, Nashville, TN 37235.

973   US   ISSN 0083-5781
VERMONT YEAR BOOK. 1818. a. $14.95. ‡ National Survey, Chester, VT 05143. Ed. John Henneberger. adv.
Formerly: Walton's Register.

972.9   VI
VIRGIN ISLANDS (U.S.) BUREAU OF LIBRARIES, MUSEUMS AND ARCHAEOLOGICAL SERVICES. OCCASIONAL PAPER SERIES. no. 3, 1978. irreg. Bureau of Libraries, Museums and Archaeological Services, Department of Conservation and Cultural Affairs, P.O. Box 390, St. Thomas, VI 00801.

975.5   US   ISSN 0083-6524
VIRGINIA. STATE LIBRARY. PUBLICATIONS. 1956. irreg. State Library, 12th & Capital Streets, Richmond, VA 23219.

975.5   US   ISSN 0083-6389
VIRGINIA HISTORICAL SOCIETY. DOCUMENTS. 1961. irreg., vol. 13, 1977. price varies. University Press of Virginia, Box 3608, University Sta., Charlottesville, VA 22903. circ. 1,500.

973   US   ISSN 0083-7121
WALTER LYNWOOD FLEMING LECTURES IN SOUTHERN HISTORY. 1937. irreg. price varies. Louisiana State University Press, University Station, Baton Rouge, LA 70803.

975.3   US   ISSN 0083-7393
WASHINGTON; a comprehensive directory of the Nation's Capital, its people and institutions. 1966. biennial. $27.50. Potomac Books, Inc., Publishers, Box 40604, Palisades Sta., Washington, DC 20016. Eds. Cary T. Grayson, Jr., Susan Lukowski. index.

975.3 US
WASHINGTON INFORMATION DIRECTORY.
1976. a. $19.50. Congressional Quarterly Inc., 1414
22nd St. N.W., DC 20037.

971 CN ISSN 0083-7733
WATERLOO HISTORICAL SOCIETY. REPORT.
1913. a. membership. Waterloo Historical Society,
c/o Mrs. Robert Woolner, 49 Stirling Ave. N.,
Kitchener, Ont. N2H 3G4, Canada. Ed.Bd. circ.
600.
Local history-Regional Muncipality of Waterloo

976 US
WEST TENNESSEE HISTORICAL SOCIETY.
PAPERS. 1947. a. $5. ‡ West Tennessee Historical
Society, c/o James Alex Baggett, Union University,
Jackson, TN 38301. (Affiliate: Tennessee Historical
Commission) adv. bk. rev. bibl. illus. circ. 500.

978 US ISSN 0083-887X
WESTERN FRONTIER LIBRARY. 1953. irreg. price
varies. University of Oklahoma Press, 1005 Asp
Ave., Norman, OK 73019. Indexed: M.L.A.

973 US ISSN 0083-8888
WESTERN FRONTIERSMEN SERIES. 1937. irreg.
price varies. Arthur H. Clark Co., 1264 Central
Ave, Glendale, CA 91204. index.

978 971 US ISSN 0513-1545
WESTERN HISTORICAL SERIES. vol. 5, 1972.
irreg. Yale University Library, New Haven, CT
06520.

973 US ISSN 0083-8985
WESTERN RESERVE HISTORICAL SOCIETY,
CLEVELAND. PUBLICATIONS. irreg., 1968, no.
120. Western Reserve Historical Society, Quail
Bldg., Cleveland, OH 44106.

979 US ISSN 0083-9019
WESTERNLORE GHOST TOWN SERIES. 1963.
irreg. price varies. Westernlore Press, 5117 Eagle
Rock Blvd., P.O. Box 41073, Los Angeles, CA
90041. Ed. Paul Bailey.

971 CN ISSN 0382-0831
WESTMORLAND HISTORICAL SOCIETY.
NEWSLETTER. 1965. irreg. Westmorland
Historical Society, c/o F. McManus, 291 Highfield
St., Moncton, N.B., Canada.

973 US ISSN 0084-0181
WILEY AMERICAN REPUBLIC SERIES. 1969.
irreg., latest, 1979. price varies. John Wiley & Sons,
Inc., 605 Third Ave., New York, NY 10016. Ed.
D.E. Fehrenbacher.

975.5 US ISSN 0084-0297
WILLIAMSBURG IN AMERICA SERIES. 1950.
irreg; vol. 10, 1975. University Press of Virginia,
Box 3608, University Station, Charlottesville, VA
22903.

975 US ISSN 0084-0300
WILLIAMSBURG RESEARCH STUDIES. 1965.
irreg., unnumbered. price varies. ‡ Colonial
Williamsburg Foundation, Williamsburg, VA 23185.
Ed. Cary Carson. index.

973 US ISSN 0084-067X
WISCONSIN STATE HISTORICAL SOCIETY.
URBAN HISTORY GROUP. NEWSLETTER.
1954. irreg. Wisconsin State Historical Society, c/o
History Department, University of Wisconsin,
Milwaukee, WI 53201.

980 US ISSN 0084-2303
WORLD TODAY SERIES: LATIN AMERICA. a.
$2.95. Stryker-Post Publications Inc., 888
Seventeenth St., N.W., Washington, DC 20006. Ed.
Jon D. Cozean. circ. 10-15,000.

975.8 920 US ISSN 0084-2621
WORMSLOE FOUNDATION. PUBLICATIONS.
1955. irreg, no. 11 (vol. 3), 1972. price varies.
University of Georgia Press, Athens, GA 30602.
(reprint service avail. from UMI)

973 US ISSN 0084-3393
YALE PUBLICATIONS IN AMERICAN STUDIES.
1957. irreg., no. 20, 1970. price varies. Yale
University Press, 92A Yale Sta., New Haven, CT
06520.

978 US ISSN 0084-3563
YALE WESTERN AMERICANA SERIES. 1962.
irreg., no. 30, 1977. price varies. Yale University
Press, 92A Yale Sta., New Haven, CT 06520.

970 US
YORKER (1976) q. $2. New York State Historical
Association, Cooperstown, NY 13326. Ed. Margaret
P. Misencik.
Formerly (1974-1975): Yorker Annual; Yorker
News; Which superseded in part: Yorker (ISSN
0044-0574)

HISTORY — History Of The Near East

932 GW ISSN 0568-0476
AEGYPTOLOGISCHE ABHANDLUNGEN. 1960.
irreg., vol. 36, 1980. price varies. Verlag Otto
Harrassowitz, Taunusstr. 6, Postfach 2929, 6200
Wiesbaden, W. Germany (B.R.D.) Ed. Wolfgang
Helck.

930 913 722 US
AEGYPTOLOGISCHE FORSCHUNGEN. irreg. vol.
1-25, 1973. price varies. J.J. Augustin, Inc., Locust
Valley, NY 11560.

956 US
AIDS AND RESEARCH TOOLS IN ANCIENT
NEAR EASTERN STUDIES. Short title:
ARTANES. irreg. Undena Publications, Box 97,
Malibu, CA 90265. Ed. Giorgio Buccellati.

930 GE
ALTORIENTALISCHE FORSCHUNGEN.
(Subseries of: Schriften zur Geschichte und Kultur
des Alten Orients) (Text in English, German, Italian
and Russian) 1974. irreg. price varies. (Akademie
der Wissenschaften der DDR, Zentralinstitut fuer
Alte Geschichte und Archaeologie.) Akademie-
Verlag, Leipziger Strasse 3-4, Berlin 108, E.
Germany (D.D.R.) bibl. illus.

950 US ISSN 0066-0035
AMERICAN SCHOOLS OF ORIENTAL
RESEARCH. ANNUAL. irreg., latest issue 1977.
American Schools of Oriental Research, 126 Inman
St., Cambridge, MA 02139. (also avail. in
microform from UMI)

956 UK
ARABIA PAST & PRESENT SERIES. 1972. irreg.
(approx. 2/yr) price varies. Oleander Press, 17
Stansgate Ave., Cambridge CB2 2QZ, England (U.S.
address: 210 Fifth Ave., New York, N.Y. 10010)
Ed. Philip Ward. circ. 1,500.

953 320 UK ISSN 0305-036X
ARABIAN STUDIES. 1974. a. price varies.
(Cambridge University, Middle East Centre) C.
Hurst & Co.(Publishers) Ltd., 1-2 Henrietta St.,
London WC2E 8PS, England. Eds. R. B. Serjeant
and R. L. Bidwell. bk. rev. bibl. charts. circ. 1,000.

956 AU ISSN 0066-6440
ARCHIV FUER ORIENTFORSCHUNG;
Internationale Zeitschrift fuer die Wissenschaft vom
Vorderen Orient. irreg., vol. 26, 1978/79. price
varies. Verlag Ferdinand Berger and Soehne OHG,
Postfach 11, A-3580 Horn, A 3580 Horn, Austria.

956 297 US
ARCHIVUM OTTOMANICUM. a. Cyrco Press, Inc.,
342 Madison Ave., New York, NY 10017. Eds.
Tibor Halasi-Kun, Halil Inalcik.

956 US
ASSUR. (Subseries of: Monographic Journals of the
Near East) irreg. $17. Undena Publications, Box 97,
Malibu, CA 90265. Eds. K. Deller, P.Garelli, C.
Saporetti.

BEER-SHEVA. see RELIGIONS AND
THEOLOGY — Judaic

950 GW ISSN 0067-4931
BEIRUTER TEXTE UND STUDIEN. (Text in
Arabic and German) 1964. irreg., vol. 25, 1981.
price varies. (Deutsche Morgenlaendische
Gesellschaft Beirut, Orient-Institut, LE) Franz
Steiner Verlag GmbH, Friedrichstr. 24, Postfach
5529, 6200 Wiesbaden, W. Germany (B.R.D.)

956 US
BIBLIOTHECA MESOPOTAMICA. irreg. Undena
Publications, Box 97, Malibu, CA 90265. Ed.
Giorgio Buccellati.

956 II
BIHAR RESEARCH SOCIETY. JOURNAL.* (Text
in English) 1971, vol. 57. a. Rs.30. Bihar Research
Society, Patna, India. Ed. S.V. Sohoni. bk. rev.

956 US
BYZANTINA KAI METABYZANTINA. irreg.
Undena Publications, Box 97, CA 90265. Ed.
Speros Vyronis, Jr.

026 296 IS
CENTRAL ARCHIVES FOR THE HISTORY OF
THE JEWISH PEOPLE NEWSLETTER/HA-
ARKHIYON HA-MERKAZI LE-TOLDOT HA-
AM HA-YEHUDI. YEDIOT. a. $3. Central
Archives for the History of the Jewish People,
Hebrew University Campus, Sprinzak Bldg., P.O.
Box 1149, Jerusalem, Israel. illus.

956 US
COMPUTER AIDED RESEARCH IN ANCIENT
NEAR EASTERN STUDIES. Short title:
CARANES. (Subseries of: Monographic Journals of
the Near East) irreg. $17. Undena Publications, Box
97, Malibu, CA 90265. Ed. J.-G. Heintz.

956.94 BE
CONNAISSANCE D'ISRAEL. 1977. irreg. $25.
Centre Interuniversitaire de Recherches sur Israel,
16 rue de la Bienfaisance, Charleroi, Belgium.

950 US ISSN 0360-649X
COPTS. (Text in Arabic or English) 1974. irreg.
American Coptic Association, Box 9119, G. L. S.,
Jersey City, NJ 07304.

915.69 IS ISSN 0071-3635
FACTS ABOUT ISRAEL. (Text in English) 1952.
irreg., latest edt. 1979. free. Ministry for Foreign
Affairs, Jerusalem, Israel (Dist. in U. S. by Israel
Office of Information, 11 East 70 Street, New York,
N.Y. 10021) Ed. Gad Mazor. circ. 50,000.
Title Varies: Facts and Figures in Israel.

FOUNDATIONS OF MEDIEVAL HISTORY. see
HISTORY — History Of Europe

FRANKFURTER TURKOLOGISCHE
ARBEITSMITTEL. see ORIENTAL STUDIES

350 GW ISSN 0340-6369
GIORGIO LEVI DELLA VIDA CONFERENCES.
1970. irreg. price varies. (University of California,
Los Angeles, Near Eastern Center, US) Verlag
Otto Harrassowitz, Taunusstr. 6, Postfach 2929,
6200 Wiesbaden, W. Germany (B.R.D.)

956 US
GULF HANDBOOK; a guide to the eight Persian
Gulf countries. 1977. a. $15.95. Garrett Park Press,
Garrett Park, MD 20766. Eds. Peter Kilner,
Jonathan Wallace. illus.

932 GW
HABELTS DISSERTATIONSDRUCKE. REIHE
AEGYPTOLOGIE. 1976. irreg. price varies. Rudolf
Habelt Verlag, Am Buchenhang 1, 5300 Bonn 1, W.
Germany (B.R.D.)

955 US
HARVARD IRANIAN SERIES. 1973. irreg. price
varies. Harvard University Press, 79 Garden St.,
Cambridge, MA 02138.

956 US ISSN 0073-0580
HARVARD MIDDLE EASTERN STUDIES. 1958.
irreg., 1972, no. 16. price varies. (Harvard
University, Center for Middle Eastern Studies)
Harvard University Press, 79 Garden St.,
Cambridge, MA 02138.

930 US ISSN 0073-0645
HARVARD SEMITIC SERIES. 1912. irreg., 1970,
no. 21. price varies. Harvard University Press, 79
Garden St., Cambridge, MA 02138.

950 SZ ISSN 0073-0947
HAUTES ETUDES ISLAMIQUES ET
 ORIENTALES D'HISTOIRE COMPAREE. 1970.
 irreg. price varies. (Ecole Pratique des Hautes
 Etudes, Centre de Recherches d'Histoire et de
 Philologie, FR) Librarie Droz, 11 rue Massot, 1211
 Geneva 12, Switzerland. Ed. Jean Aubin. circ.
 1,000.

HOLY PLACES OF PALESTINE. see *RELIGIONS AND THEOLOGY*

950 IS
INSTITUTE FOR ARAB STUDIES.
 PUBLICATIONS AND STUDIES. (Text mainly in
 Hebrew) 1966. irreg., no. 29, 1979. Institute for
 Arab Studies, Giv'at Haviva, Israel. Dir. Moshe
 Gabbay.
  Formerly: Arab and Afro-Asian Monograph
 Series (ISSN 0066-5622)

INTERNATIONAL ASSOCIATION FOR
 BYZANTINE STUDIES. BULLETIN
 D'INFORMATION ET DE COORDINATION.
 see *HISTORY — History Of Europe*

956 US
INVITED LECTURES ON THE MIDDLE EAST
 AT THE UNIVERSITY OF TEXAS AT AUSTIN.
 irreg. Undena Publications, Box 97, Malibu, CA
 90265.

956 319 IR
IRAN YEARBOOK; a complete directory and
 encyclopedia of facts, data and statistics on Iran. a.
 Kayhan Group of Newspapers, Kayhan Research
 Associates, Ferdowsi Ave., Teheran, Iran.

JAMES TERRY DUCE MEMORIAL SERIES. see
 POLITICAL SCIENCE

KENTRON EPISTEMONIKON EREUNION.
 EPETERIS/CYPRUS RESEARCH CENTER.
 ANNUAL. see *LINGUISTICS*

943 GW ISSN 0344-449X
MATERIALIA TURCICA. 1975. irreg. price varies.
 (Ruhr-Universitaet, Bochum,
 Sprachwissenschaftliches Institut, Lektorat fuer
 Tuerksprachen) Studienverlag Dr. N. Brockmeyer,
 Querenburger Hoehe 281, 4630 Bochum, W.
 Germany (B. R. D.) Ed. Hermann Vary. bk. rev.

932 950 GW ISSN 0543-1719
MAX FREIHERR VON OPPENHEIM-STIFTUNG.
 SCHRIFTEN. 1955. irreg., vol. 10, 1978. price
 varies. Verlag Otto Harrassowitz, Taunusstr. 6,
 Postfach 2929, 6200 Wiesbaden, W. Germany
 (B.R.D.)

916 UK ISSN 0076-8502
MIDDLE EAST AND NORTH AFRICA; survey and
 Directory of Lands of Middle East and North
 Africa. 1948. a. £70. Europa Publications Ltd., 18
 Bedford Sq., London WC1B 3JN, England.

956 US ISSN 0163-5476
MIDDLE EAST CONTEMPORARY SURVEY.
 1976/77. a. $85. Holmes & Meier Publishers, Inc.,
 30 Irving Place, New York, NY 10003 (U.K.
 address: 131 Trafalgar Rd., Greenwich, London
 SE10 9TX, England) Eds. Colin Legum, Haim
 Shaked. adv. charts. illus. stat. circ. 2,000.

956 IS ISSN 0076-8529
MIDDLE EAST RECORD. 1960. irreg., vol. 5, 1977.
 (Tel-Aviv University, Shiloah Center for Middle
 Eastern and African Studies) Keter Publishing
 House Ltd., Box 7145, Jerusalem, Israel (U.S.
 Orders to: Transaction Books, Edison, NJ)

956 US
MIDDLE EAST SERIES. 1971. irreg., vol. 5, 1975.
 price varies. Elsevier North-Holland, Inc., New
 York, 52 Vanderbilt Ave., New York, NY 10017.

MUENCHNER ZEITSCHRIFT FUER
 BALKANOLOGIE. see *HISTORY — History Of Europe*

956 NE
NEAR AND MIDDLE EAST MONOGRAPHS.
 1973. irreg. price varies. Mouton Publishers,
 Noordeinde 41, 2514 GC The Hague, Netherlands
 (U.S. addr.: Mouton Publishers, c/o Walter de
 Gruyter, Inc., 200 Saw Mill River Road,
 Hawthorne, NY 10532)

NETHERLANDS INSTITUTE OF
 ARCHAEOLOGY AND ARABIC STUDIES IN
 CAIRO. PUBLICATIONS. see *ARCHAEOLOGY*

PALESTINE! see *POLITICAL SCIENCE*

PALESTINE-JORDANIAN BIBLIOGRAPHY. see
 BIBLIOGRAPHIES

956 US ISSN 0085-4662
PAPERS ON ISLAMIC HISTORY. 1970. irreg.,
 1972, no. 3. (University of Pennsylvania, Near East
 Center) International Scholarly Book Services Inc.,
 Box 555, Forest Grove, OR 97116. (Co-sponsor:
 Near Eastern History Group, Oxford)

935.63 319 QA
QATAR YEARBOOK. (Text in English) a. Ministry
 of Information, Box 1836, Doha, Qatar.

QUADERNI DE "LA TERRA SANTA". see
 RELIGIONS AND THEOLOGY

932 950 GW ISSN 0340-8450
RECORDS OF THE ANCIENT NEAR EAST. (Text
 in English) 1972. irreg., vol. 2, 1976. price varies.
 Verlag Otto Harrassowitz, Taunusstr. 6, Postfach
 2929, 6200 Wiesbaden, W. Germany (B.R.D.)

956 TU ISSN 0578-9761
SARKIYAT MECMUASI. 1956. irreg. TL.34. Istanbul
 University, Sarkiyat Enstitusu, Istanbul, Turkey. bk.
 rev. circ. 1,000.

915.3 UK
SEMINAR FOR ARABIAN STUDIES.
 PROCEEDINGS. 1971. a. £6. Seminar for Arabian
 Studies, 31-34 Gordon Square, London WC1H 0PY,
 England. circ. 200.

956 960 US
SHILOACH CENTER FOR MIDDLE EASTERN &
 AFRICAN STUDIES. MONOGRAPH SERIES.
 irreg., unnumbered, latest vol. 1973. Halsted Press
 (Subsidiary of: John Wiley & Sons, Inc.) 605 Third
 Ave., New York, NY 10016.

956 NE ISSN 0085-6193
SOCIAL, ECONOMIC AND POLITICAL STUDIES
 OF THE MIDDLE EAST. 1971. irreg., vol. 28,
 1979. price varies. E. J. Brill, Oude Rijn 33a-35,
 Leiden, Netherlands (Dist. in U.S. by: Humanities
 Press, Inc., 171 First Ave., Atlantic Highlands, NJ
 07716)

956 US
SOURCES FROM THE ANCIENT NEAR EAST.
 1974. irreg. $17. Undena Publications, Box 97,
 Malibu, CA 90265. Ed.Bd.

950 960 US
STUDIES IN MIDDLE EASTERN HISTORY. 1974.
 irreg., no. 4, 1979. price varies. Bibliotheca Islamica,
 Inc., Box 1536, Chicago, Minneapolis, IL 60690.

956 SJ
SUDAN NOTES AND RECORDS. (Text in English)
 1918. a, latest 1973. $12. Box 555, Khartoum,
 Sudan. Ed. Yusuf Fadl Hasan. bk. rev. (back issues
 avail.)

956 US
SYRO-MESOPOTAMIAN STUDIES. (Subseries of:
 Monographic Journals of the Near East) irreg. $17.
 Undena Publications, Box 97, Malibu, CA 90265.
 Ed. M. Kelly-Buccelatti.

930 GW
TUEBINGER AEGYPTOLOGISCHE BEITRAEGE.
 1973. irreg., no. 2, 1976. price varies. Rudolf Habelt
 Verlag, Am Buchenhang 1, 5300 Bonn 1, W.
 Germany (B.R.D.) Eds. Hellmut Brunner, Ingrid
 Gamer-Wallert.

956 TU ISSN 0085-7432
TURKIYAT MECMUASI. 1925. irreg. price varies.
 Istanbul University, Institute of Turcology - Istanbul
 Universitesi, Turkiyat Enstitusu, Ayniyat, Istanbul,
 Turkey. Ed. M. Kaplan. circ. 1,000.

913.39 AG ISSN 0325-1209
UNIVERSIDAD DE BUENOS AIRES. INSTITUTO
 DE HISTORIA ANTIGUA ORIENTAL.
 REVISTA. 1972. a. Universidad de Buenos Aires,
 Instituto de Historia Antigua Oriental, 25 de Mayo
 217, Buenos Aires, Argentina. bk. rev. bibl. illus.
 circ. 800.

UNIVERSITE SAINT-JOSEPH. MELANGES. see
 ARCHAEOLOGY

955 IR
UNIVERSITY OF TEHERAN. FACULTY OF
 LETTERS AND HUMANITIES. BULLETIN OF
 IRANIAN STUDIES/DANESHGAH-E TEHRAN.
 DANESHKADE-YE ADABIYAT VA 'OLUM-E
 ENSANI. MAJALLE-YE IRANSHENASI. Short
 title: Bulletin of Iranian Studies. (Text in Persian)
 1963. irreg. price varies. University of Teheran,
 Faculty of Letters and Humanities, Shahreza Ave.,
 Teheran, Iran. Ed. Fereydun Badre'I.

930 GW
VETUS TESTAMENTUM COPTICE. 1973. irreg.
 price varies. Rudolf Habelt Verlag, Am Buchenhang
 1, 5300 Bonn 1, W. Germany (B.R.D.)

VICINO ORIENTE. see *ORIENTAL STUDIES*

956 IR
WISDOM OF PERSIA. irreg., no. 9, 1977. McGill
 University, Teheran Branch, Institute of Islamic
 Studies, Box 14/1133, Teheran, Iran.

956 US ISSN 0084-3385
YALE NEAR EASTERN RESEARCHES. 1967.
 irreg; no. 7, 1977. price varies. Yale University
 Press, 92A Yale Sta., New Haven, CT 06520. Ed.
 William W. Hallo.

935 US
YALE ORIENTAL SERIES. BABYLONIAN
 TEXTS. 1915. irreg., vol. 14, 1978. Yale University
 Press, 92A Yale Sta., New Haven, CT 06520.

HOBBIES

see also *Hobbies—Antiques; Hobbies—
 Needlework; Hobbies—Numismatics;
 Hobbies—Philately; Sports and Games*

629.133 UK ISSN 0065-3691
AEROMODELLER ANNUAL. 1948. a. £3.25. Argus
 Books Ltd., Argus House, St. James Rd., Watford,
 Hertfordshire, England. Ed. R. G. Moulton.

793.8 II
ALL INDIA MAGIC CIRCLE BULLETIN. 1961. m.
 Rs.12($2) (Society of Indian Magicians) All India
 Magic Circle, 276-1 Rash Behary Ave., Ballyganj,
 Calcutta 700019, India. Ed. Madhab Choudhuri.
 adv. bk. rev. illus. circ. 5,000.
 Magic

683 US ISSN 0362-9457
AMERICAN SOCIETY OF ARMS COLLECTORS.
 BULLETIN. irreg. American Society of Arms
 Collectors, 4823 Ellenberg Dr., Dallas, TX 75234.
 illus. Key Title: Bulletin - American Society of
 Arms Collectors.

790.132 760 US
AMERICAN SOCIETY OF BOOKPLATE
 COLLECTORS AND DESIGNERS. YEAR
 BOOK. 1922. irreg. price varies. American Society
 of Bookplate Collectors and Designers, 605 N.
 Stoneman Ave., No. F, Alhambra, CA 91801. Ed.
 Audrey Spencer Arellanes. bk. rev. bibl. illus.
 cum.index 1922-1950;1951-1972. circ. 200. (also
 avail. in microfilm; some back issues available)

AMERICAN WINE SOCIETY. BULLETIN. see
 BEVERAGES

790.13 FR
ANNUAIRE INTERNATIONAL DES
 COLLECTIONNEURS. 1973. a. Editions Dany
 Thibaud, 52 rue Labrouste, 75015 Paris, France.

629.221 US ISSN 0092-6256
AURORA AFX ROAD RACING HANDBOOK.
 1973. a. $2.50. Auto World, Inc., 701 N. Keyser
 Ave., Scranton, PA 18508. Ed. Oscar Koveleski.
 circ. 40,000.

B T M A DIRECTORY. (British Toy & Hobby
 Manufacturers Association) see *GIFTWARE AND
 TOYS*

BETTER HOMES AND GARDENS CHRISTMAS
 IDEAS. see *HOME ECONOMICS*

745.5   US
BETTER HOMES AND GARDENS HOLIDAY
CRAFTS. 1974. a. $1.75. Meredith Corporation,
1716 Locust St., Des Moines, IA 50336. adv.

790.13   US
COMIC BOOK PRICE GUIDE. 1970. a. $9.95. c/o
Bob Overstreet, Ed., 780 Hunt Cliff Dr., N.W.,
Cleveland, TN 37311 (Dist. by: Crown Publishers,
One Park Ave., New York, NY 10016) adv. illus.
stat. tr.lit. circ. 50,000.

623.4   US   ISSN 0590-6776
CORD SPORTFACTS GUNS GUIDE. Short title:
Guns Guide. irreg. Cord Communications Corp., 25
W. 43rd St., New York, NY 10022. illus.

790.13   UK   ISSN 0142-0097
CRAFT AND HOBBY TRADE DIRECTORY. 1978.
a. £0.75 (free to subscribers of Craft and Hobby
Dealer) Elliot Publications Ltd., 9 Queen Victoria
St., Reading RG1 1SY, England.

790.2   US
CRAFT, MODEL & HOBBY INDUSTRY ANNUAL
TRADE DIRECTORY. a. $10. Hobby Publications,
Inc., 225 W. 34th St., New York, NY 10001.
    Formerly: Annual Basic Hobby Industry Trade
Directory (ISSN 0066-3778)

740   US
CRAFTS ANNUAL. 1972. a. $1.50 per no. New
York State Craftsmen, Inc., 27 W. 53 St., New
York, NY 10019.

ELECTRONICS HOBBYIST. see *ELECTRICITY
AND ELECTRICAL ENGINEERING*

745.5   US
GOODFELLOW CATALOG OF WONDERFUL
THINGS. 1974. triennial. $17.50. ‡ Goodfellow,
Box 4520, Berkeley, CA 94704. adv. illus. circ.
100,000.

HOB-NOB ANNUAL. see *LITERATURE*

745.5   US   ISSN 0095-5337
ILLINOIS HANDCRAFTS DIRECTORY. 1973. a.
$1.50. Box 157, Bondville, IL 61815. illus.

790.13   US
INTERNATIONAL DIRECTORY OF
CONCHOLOGISTS. biennial. Shell Cabinet, Box
29, Falls Church, VA 22046. Eds. Isabelle E.
Welch, M.E. Young.

748.8   US
KOVEL'S OFFICIAL BOTTLE PRICE LIST. a.
$7.95. Crown Publishers, Inc., One Park Ave., New
York, NY 10016. Eds. Ralph Kovel, Terry Kovel.

629.22   US
MINI-AUTO INTERNATIONAL; the magazine for
the adult collector of fine miniature vehicles. 1974;
temporarily suspended 1975-76. irreg., no. 4, 1977?
$10. David Sinclair Publications, 3831 West 12th
Street, Erie, PA 16505. adv. bk. rev. illus. (back
issues avail.)
    Formerly: Exact Scale Quarterly.

790   US
MINIATURES CATALOG. 1978. a. $13.95. Boynton
& Associates, Clifton House, Clifton, VA 22024. Ed.
Joan Craun.

625.19 385   UK
MODEL RAILWAY CONSTRUCTOR ANNUAL.
1978. a. price varies. Ian Allan Ltd., Terminal
House, Shepperton, Middlesex TW17 8AS, England.
Ed. S.W. Stevens Stratten. circ. 12,500.

NATIONAL OUTDOOR LIVING DIRECTORY. see
CONSERVATION

NEW COLLECTOR'S DIRECTORY. see *CLUBS*

790.132   US
NEWES. 1950. irreg. $2 for 4 issues. International
Newspaper Collectors' Club, Box 7271, Phoenix,
AZ 85011. Ed. Charles J. Smith. adv. bk. rev. illus.
circ. 150. (processed)

790.13   US
SCANDAL SHEET. 1971. irreg. $2. Scandalous
Bohemians of New Jersey, c/o Norman Nolan, 68
Crest Rd., Middletown, NJ 07748. Ed. Robert A.
W. Lowndes. (back issues avail.)
    Sherlockiana

790.132 635   US
SEED SAVERS EXCHANGE. 1976. a. $2. c/o Kent
Whealy, Ed., RFD 2, Princeton, MO 64673. circ.
3,000.
    Formerly: True Seed Exchange.

355   US
SOLDIER SHOP ANNUAL. 1972. a. $5. ‡ Soldier
Shop, 1013 Madison Ave., New York, NY 10021.
Ed. Peter J. Blum. bk. rev. charts. illus. circ.
15,000.
    Formerly: Soldier Shop Quarterly.

SPORTS COLLECTORS DIRECTORY. see *SPORTS
AND GAMES*

790.13   US   ISSN 0090-2578
SUNSET CHRISTMAS IDEAS AND ANSWERS.
1971. a. $1.50 per no. Lane Publishing Co., 85
Willow Rd., Menlo Park, CA 94025. Ed. Elton
Welke. adv. illus. circ. 450,000.

VINTAGE AIRCRAFT DIRECTORY. see
AERONAUTICS AND SPACE FLIGHT

VINTAGE AUTO ALMANAC. see
TRANSPORTATION — Automobiles

790.13   US
WHERE-TO-SELL-IT DIRECTORY. 1979. irreg.
$3.50. Pilot Books, 347 Fifth Ave., New York, NY
10016.

790.132 917   US
WHO'S WHO IN INDIAN RELICS. 1960. every 4
or 5 years. $20. Ben W. Thompson, Ed. & Pub.,
1757 W. Adams, St. Louis, MO 63122. illus. circ.
3,000.

643   US
WOODWORKER PROJECTS & TECHNIQUES.
1960. a. $1.35 plus postage $.25. Davis Publications,
Inc., 380 Lexington Ave., New York, NY 10017.
Ed. Joe Daffron. circ. 60,000.
    Formerly: Woodworker (ISSN 0084-1188)

HOBBIES — Abstracting, Bibliographies, Statistics

029   US   ISSN 0073-5930
INDEX TO HOW TO DO IT INFORMATION; a
periodical index. 1963. a. with q. supplements. $12.
‡ Norman Lathrop Enterprises, 2342 Star Dr., Box
198, Wooster, OH 44691. Eds. Mary Lou &
Norman Lathrop. cum. index every 5 yrs.
    Formerly: Aids Index to How to do It
Information.

745   US
INDEX TO MODEL MAKING & MINIATURES.
1980. a. $15. Norman Lathrop Enterprises, 2342
Star Dr., Box 198, Wooster, OH 44691. Eds. Mary
Lou & Norman Lathrop.

HOBBIES — Antiques

see also Art

745.1   NE
ANTIEKWERELD; maandelijks informatiemagazine
voor de antiek- en kunstliefhebber. 1976. m. fl.65.
Uitgeversmaatschappij de Tijdstroom, Box 14,
Lochem, Netherlands. Ed. Bd. adv. bk. rev. illus.
index. circ. 15,000.

ARMS STUDY SERIES. see *MILITARY*

745.1   US   ISSN 0084-6783
ART AT AUCTION; THE YEAR AT SOTHEBY'S
AND PARKE-BERNET. 1967. a. $25. Sotheby
Parke Bernet Publications, c/o Biblio Distribution
Centre, 81 Adams Dr., Totowa, NJ 07512. Eds.
Philip Wilson, Russell Chambers. illus. index.

745.1   UK
BRITISH ART & ANTIQUES YEARBOOK. 1949. a.
£8.50($22) Art & Antiques Yearbooks, 72
Broadwick St., London W1V 2BP, England. Ed.
Marcelle d'Argy Smith. adv. illus. index. circ. 10,000.

745 355   US   ISSN 0094-1182
CIVIL WAR COLLECTORS' DEALER
DIRECTORY. 1974. irreg., 3rd edt. 1980/81.
$7.95. Essential Press, 10453 Medina Road,
Richmond, VA 23235. Ed. C. L. Batson. adv. circ.
1,000.

745.1   US
FLEA MARKET ALMANAC; official U.S. flea
market directory. 1973. a. $6. Maverick
Publications, Box 243, Bend, OR 97701. Ed.
Kenneth Asher. adv. bk. rev. illus. circ. 15,000.
    Formerly: Flea Market Quarterly.

381   US   ISSN 0364-023X
FLEA MARKET TRADER. 1977. irreg. $5.95.
Collector Books, Box 3009, Paducah, KY 42001.
illus.

739.7 355   SP   ISSN 0436-029X
GLADIUS; etudes sur les armes anciennes,
l'armement, l'art militaire et la vie culturelle en
Orient et Occident. (Text in English, French,
German, Spanish) 1961. a. price varies. (Consejo
Superior de Investigaciones Cientificas) Instituto de
Estudios sobre Armas Antiguas, P.O. Box 4,
Jarandilla (Caceres), Spain. Ed. Ada Bruhn de
Hoffmeyer. bk. rev. bibl. illus. index. cum.index.
circ. 500-750.

745.1   UK
GUIDE TO THE ANTIQUE SHOPS OF BRITAIN.
a. £6.95. Antique Collectors' Club, 5 Church St.,
Woodbridge, Suffolk, England. illus.

HISTORICAL ARMS SERIES. see *MILITARY*

745.1   UK
HOLBROOKS GUIDE TO THE ANTIQUE TRADE
IN SCOTLAND. 1977. a. £2.50. Aberdeen
Advertiser, 6 1/2 St. Mary's Place, Aberdeen AB1
2HN, Scotland. Ed. Bernard Holbrook. adv. bk. rev.

INTERNATIONAL WHO'S WHO IN ART AND
ANTIQUES. see *ART*

745.1   US
KOVEL'S COMPLETE ANTIQUES PRICE LIST. a.
$7.95. Crown Publishers, Inc., One Park Ave., New
York, NY 10016. Eds. Ralph Kovel, Terry Kovel.

KUNSTPREIS-JAHRBUCH. see *ART*

745.1   US
LYLE OFFICIAL ANTIQUES REVIEW. 1971/72. a.
$15. Apollo Book, 391 South Rd., Poughkeepsie,
NY 12601. Ed. Tony Curtis. adv. illus. index. circ.
30,000.

737   PO   ISSN 0085-364X
N U M U S NUMISMATICA, MEDALHISTICA,
ARGUEOLOGIA. (Text in Portuguese, English,
French; summaries in French & English) 1952. a.
Esc.250. Sociedade Portuguesa de Numismatica,
Rua de Costa Cabral, 664, 4200 Porto, Portugal.
Eds. R.M.S. Centeno, M. C. Hipolito, M. J. P.
Ferro. bk. rev. bibl. charts. illus. cum.index 1968-
72. circ. 2,000.

NATIONAL CAROUSEL ASSOCIATION
CAROUSEL CENSUS. see *ART*

739.7   DK
VAABENHISTORISKE AARBOEGER. (Text in
English; summaries in English and German) 1934.
a. Kr.125. Vaabenhistorisk Selskab, Danish Arms
and Armour Society, "Brobyvang", Freerslev, DK-
3400 Hilleroed, Denmark. Ed. Finn Askgaard. bk.
rev. cum. index (vols. 1-10 in vol. 10; vols. 11-20 in
vol. 20)

HOBBIES — Needlework

746   US
SPINNING AROUND THE WORLD; international
handspinning directory and handbook. 1971. irreg.,
latest 1975. $6.50. Doloria M. Chapin, Ed. & Pub.,
2178 Pompey-Fabius Rd., R.D.1, Fabius, NY 13063.
adv. illus, stat.
    Formerly: Let's Go Spinning.

746.43　　　　FR　ISSN 0183-3928
TOUT LE TRICOT - TRICOT D'ART. 1977.
biennial. 13 F. per no. Editions E.G.E., 23 rue
Chalopin, 69007 Lyon, France. Ed. J. Deschavanne.
circ. 70,000.

793　　　　US
WOMAN'S DAY GRANNY SQUARES. 1973. a.
$1.29 per no. Fawcett Publications, Inc., 1515
Broadway, New York, NY 10036. Ed. Ellene
Saunders. adv.

746.4　　　　US
WOMAN'S DAY 101 SWEATERS YOU CAN KNIT
& CROCHET. no.14, 1981. a. Fawcett Publications,
Inc. (Subsidiary of: C B S Publications) 1515
Broadway, 14th Fl., New York, NY 10036. Ed.
Susan Weinkrantz. circ. 763,000.

HOBBIES — Numismatics

730　　　　US
ALMANZAR'S COINS OF THE WORLD. vol. 16,
1975. a. Bank of San Antonio, Suite 208, One
Romana Plaza, San Antonio, TX 78205.

737　　　　US　ISSN 0569-6720
AMERICAN NUMISMATIC SOCIETY. ANNUAL
REPORT. a. free. American Numismatic Society,
Broadway at 155th St., New York, NY 10032. illus.
(reprint service avail. from UMI)

737.4　　　　US
ANCIENT COINS IN NORTH AMERICAN
COLLECTIONS. 1969. irreg. price varies.
American Numismatic Society, Broadway at 155th
St., New York, NY 10032. Ed. Leslie A. Elam.
(reprint service avail. from UMI)
  Formerly: Greek Coins in North American
Collections (ISSN 0072-744X)

737　954　　　II
ANDHRA PRADESH, INDIA. DEPARTMENT OF
ARCHAEOLOGY AND MUSEUMS. MUSEUM
OBJECTS AND NUMISMATICS SERIES. (Text
in English) 1961. irreg., no. 18, 1975-76. price
varies. Department of Archaeology and Museums,
Hyderabad 500001, Andhra Pradesh, India (Or:
Publications Bureau, Directorate of Government
Printing, Chanchalguda, Hyderabad, Andhra
Pradesh, India)
  Formerly: Andhra Pradesh, India. Department of
Archaeology. Museum Series (ISSN 0066-166X)

737　　　　AT　ISSN 0313-9611
AUSTRALIAN BANKNOTE CATALOGUE. 1977.
irreg., vol. 2, 1979. Aus.$8.95. Hawthorn Press Pty.
Ltd., 601 Little Bourke St., Melbourne, Vic. 3000,
Australia. Ed. Alan Nicholson.

737　　　　AT　ISSN 0084-7267
AUSTRALIAN COIN CATALOGUE. 1964. irreg.
per no. Hawthorn Press Pty. Ltd., 601 Little Bourke
St., Melbourne, Vic. 3000, Australia. Ed. John
Gartner. circ. 5,000.

737　　　　AT　ISSN 0004-9875
AUSTRALIAN NUMISMATIC JOURNAL; devoted
to the study of coins, tokens, paper money and
medals, particularly the issues of Australia. 1949. a.
membership. South Australian Numismatic Society,
Box 80 G.P.O., Adelaide, South Australia, Australia.
Ed. G. W. Tomlinson. bk. rev. index. cum.index.
circ. 200.

737.4　　　　GW
BERLINER NUMISMATISCHE ZEITSCHRIFT.
1949. irreg., vol. 4, no 41, 1979. price varies.
Numismatische Gesellschaft zu Berlin,
Warnemunder Str. 2, 1000 Berlin 33, W. Germany
(B.R.D.) Ed.Bd. adv. bk. rev. illus. circ. 500.

737　　　　UK
BRITISH NUMISMATIC JOURNAL. (Includes the
Society's Annual Proceedings) 1905. a. £12($25)
membership. British Numismatic Society, c/o W.
Slayter, Hon. Sec., 63 West Way, Edgeware, Middx.
HA8 9LA, England. Eds. M. Delme-Radcliffe, N.J.
Mayhew. adv. bk. rev. bibl. charts. illus. index;
cum.index every 10 vols. circ. 650. Indexed:
Br.Hum.Ind.

737　　　　US　ISSN 0068-4562
BUYING AND SELLING UNITED STATES
COINS. 1970. a. $1.50. Western Publishing Co.,
Inc., 1220 Mound Ave., Racine, WI 53404. Eds.
Ken Bressett & R. S. Yeoman. index.

737　　　　US　ISSN 0069-102X
CATALOG OF MODERN WORLD COINS. 1957.
irreg. (every 18 mos.-2 years) $7. Western
Publishing Co., Inc., 1220 Mound Ave., Racine, WI
53404. Ed. R. S. Yeoman. index.

737　　　　BE　ISSN 0069-2247
CERCLE D'ETUDES NUMISMATIQUES.
TRAVAUX. 1964. irreg. price varies. Cercle
d'Etudes Numismatiques, 4 Boulevard de
l'Empereur, B-1000 Brussels, Belgium.

737.4　　　　US　ISSN 0361-0845
COIN WORLD ALMANAC. 1976. irreg. $10. Amos
Press, Inc., Box 150, Sidney, OH 45367. illus.

737.4　　　　UK　ISSN 0307-6571
COIN YEARBOOK. 1968. a. £7.95. Numismatic
Publishing Co., Sovereign House, Brentwood, Essex
CM14 4SE, England. Ed. David Couldridge. illus.
circ. 27,500.

737.4　　　　UK　ISSN 0069-4983
COINS MARKET VALUES. a. £1. Link House
Publications Ltd., Link House, Dingwall Ave,
Croydon, CR9 2TA, England. Ed. Heather Salter.
adv. circ. 24,000.
  Formerly: Coins Annual.

737　　　　US　ISSN 0070-1882
CURRENT COINS OF THE WORLD. 1966. irreg.
$5.50. Western Publishing Co., Inc., 1220 Mound
Ave., Racine, WI 53404. Ed. R. S. Yeoman. index.

737　　　　US
FRANKLIN MINT. LIMITED EDITIONS. 1965/69.
a. $6. ‡ Franklin Mint, Franklin Center, PA 19091.
Ed. Herman Baron. illus. stat. index. cum.index:
1965-1973.
  Until 1974: Franklin Mint. Numismatic Issues
(ISSN 0090-4058)

737　　　　UK
GOLD CIRCLE NUMISMATICS.* 1973. irreg.
Academy for Arts, Ashurstwood Abbey, East
Grinstead, Sussex RH19 3SD, England. Ed. Jean
Straker. circ. controlled.

737.4　　　　US　ISSN 0072-8802
GUIDEBOOK OF ENGLISH COINS,
NINETEENTH AND TWENTIETH
CENTURIES. 1962. irreg; 8th ed., 1975. $3.50.
Western Publishing Co., Inc., 1220 Mound Ave.,
Racine, WI 53404. Ed. Kenneth E. Bressett. index.

737.4　　　　US　ISSN 0072-8810
GUIDEBOOK OF MODERN UNITED STATES
CURRENCY. 1965. irreg; 7th ed., 1975. $3.
Western Publishing Co., Inc., 1220 Mound Ave.,
Racine, WI 53404. Ed. Neil Shafer. index.

737.4　　　　US　ISSN 0072-8829
GUIDEBOOK OF UNITED STATES COINS. 1946.
a. $3.95. Western Publishing Co., Inc., 1220 Mound
Ave., Racine, WI 53404. Ed. R. S. Yeoman. index.

737　　　　GW　ISSN 0072-9523
HAMBURGER BEITRAEGE ZUR NUMISMATIK.
1947. a. price varies. Hamburger Museumsverein,
Holstenwall 24, 2000 Hamburg 36, W. Germany
(B.R.D.) Eds. Walter Haevernick, Gert Hatz.

737.4　　　　US　ISSN 0072-9949
HANDBOOK OF UNITED STATES COINS. 1941.
a. $2.95. Western Publishing Co., Inc., 1220 Mound
Ave., Racine, WI 53404. Ed. R. S. Yeoman. index.

737　　　　GW　ISSN 0075-2711
JAHRBUCH FUER NUMISMATIK UND
GELDGESCHICHTE. (Text in German;
occasionally in English, French) 1949. a. price
varies. (Bayerische Numismatische Gesellschaft)
Verlag Michael Lassleben, Lange Gasse 19, Postfach
20, 8411 Kallmuenz, W. Germany (B.R.D.) Ed. J.
Kellner.

737　　　　US　ISSN 0022-2976
JOURNAL OF NECROMANTIC NUMISMATICS.
1966. a. free (sent to contributors only) ‡ F. William
Kuethe, Jr., Ed. & Pub., 700 Glenview Ave., S.W.,
Glen Burnie, MD 21061. bk. rev. illus. 5 yr
cum.index. circ. 16. (processed)

737　　　　US
LINN'S WORLD STAMP ALMANAC. 1977.
biennial. $15. Amos Press Inc., Box 29, OH 45367.
Ed. Edwin O. Neuce.

737　　　　IQ　ISSN 0002-4058
AL-MASKUKAT. 1969. a. ID. 3000($12) State
Antiquities Organization, Jamal Abdul Nasr St.,
Baghdad, Iraq.

737　　　　SP
MONOGRAFIAS SOBRE NUMISMATICA
ANTIGUA. 1962. irreg.; no. 5, 1974. price varies.
Asociacion Numismatica Espanola, Avda. Jose
Antonio 627, Barcelona 10, Spain.

737　　　　CS　ISSN 0077-152X
MORAVSKE NUMISMATICKE ZPRAVY. (Text in
Czech; summaries in English, French, German)
1956/57. irreg., no. 15, 1980. price varies. Moravske
Muzeum, Numismaticke Oddeleni, Nam.25, Unora
6, 65937 Brno, Czechoslovakia. (Co-sponsor: Ceska
Numismaticka Spolecnost Pobocka Brno) circ.
1,200.

737.4　　　　US　ISSN 0145-1413
MUSEUM NOTES (NEW YORK) a. membership.
American Numismatic Society, Broadway at 155th
St., New York, NY 10032. (reprint service avail.
from UMI)

737　　　　NZ　ISSN 0028-8527
NEW ZEALAND NUMISMATIC JOURNAL. 1947.
irreg. membership. Royal Numismatic Society of
New Zealand, Inc., G.P.O. Box 23, Wellington,
New Zealand. Ed. C. R. H. Taylor. adv. bk. rev.
illus. cum.index: 1947-1966. circ. 500.

737　　　　GR
NOMISMATIKA CHRONICA. (Summaries in
English) 1972. irreg. $6. Hellenic Numismatic
Society, Box 736, Athens, Greece. circ. 1,000.

737　　　　NO　ISSN 0078-107X
NORDISK NUMISMATISK AARSSKRIFT/
SCANDINAVIAN NUMISMATIC JOURNAL.
(Text in English and Scandinavian languages;
summaries in English) 1936. biennial. price varies.
(Kungliga Vitterhets-, Historie- och Antikvitets
Akademien, SW - Royal Academy of Letters,
History and Antiquities) Universitetsforlaget,
Kolstadgt. 1, Box 2959-Toeyen, Oslo 6, Norway
(U.S. address: Box 258, Irvington-on-Hudson, NY
10533) (Co-sponsor: Nordisk Numismatisk Union)
Eds. Brita Malmer, Ulla Westermark. cum.index:
1936-1970 in vol. 1971.

737　　　　CK
NUMIS-NOTAS. no. 4, Sep., 1976. irreg. Circulo
Numismatico Antioqueno, Edificio La Bastilla,
Medellin, Colombia. Eds. Ricardo Jaramillo,
German Rodriguez.

737　　　　US
NUMISMATIC BOOKS IN PRINT. a. $5 hardbound;
$3 paper. Sanford J. Durst Numismatic Publications,
133 E. 58th St., New York, NY 10022. Ed. Sanford
J. Durst.

737　　　　UK　ISSN 0078-2696
NUMISMATIC CHRONICLE AND JOURNAL.
1839. a. £8 to non-members. Royal Numismatic
Society, British Museum, London, WC1B 3DG,
England. Ed. Dr. D. M. Metcalf. adv. bk. rev. circ.
1,400. (also avail. in microfilm)

737　　　　US　ISSN 0078-2718
NUMISMATIC NOTES AND MONOGRAPHS.
1920. irreg., no. 161, 1979. price varies. American
Numismatic Society, Broadway at 155th St., New
York, NY 10032. (reprint service avail. from UMI)

737　　　　US　ISSN 0517-404X
NUMISMATIC STUDIES. irreg. price varies.
American Numismatic Society, Broadway at 155th
St., New York, NY 10032. (reprint service avail.
from UMI)

737　　　　CS　ISSN 0078-2726
NUMISMATICA MORAVICA. (Text in Czech;
summaries also in English, French, German,
Russian) 1965. irreg., no. 5, 1976. price varies.
Moravske Muzeum, Numismaticke Oddeleni,
Nam.25, Unora 6, 65937 Brno, Czechoslovakia.
(Co-Sponsor: Ceska Numismaticka Spolecnost,
Pobocka Brno) illus. index. circ. 1,200.

478 HOBBIES — PHILATELY

737   SW   ISSN 0078-2734
NUMISMATISKA MEDDELANDEN/
NUMISMATIC COMMUNICATIONS. (Text in Swedish; summaries in English, French and occasionally German) 1874. irreg. price varies. Svenska Numismatiska Foereningen, Oestermalmsgatan 81, 114 50 Stockholm, Sweden. index. circ. 1,000.

737   AU
OESTERREICHISCHE AKADEMIE DER WISSENSCHAFTEN. NUMISMATISCHE KOMMISSION. VEROEFFENTLICHUNGEN. (Subseries of: Oesterreichische Akademie der Wissenschaften. Philosophisch-Historische Klasse. Denkschriften) 1973. irreg. Verlag der Oesterreichischen Akademie der Wissenschaften, Dr. Ignaz-Seipel Platz 2, A-1010 Vienna, Austria. illus.

737   BE
REVUE BELGE DE NUMISMATIQUE ET DE SIGILLOGRAPHIE. 1842. a. 1200 Fr. Societe Royale de Numismatique de Belgique, 28A Ave. Leopold, 1330 Rixensart, Belgium. Ed.Bd. adv. bk. rev. cum.index (nos. 1-110) circ. 500.

737   FR   ISSN 0484-8942
REVUE NUMISMATIQUE. 1836. a. 170 F. (Societe Francaise de Numismatique) Societe d'Edition les Belles Lettres, 95 Boulevard Raspail, 75006 Paris, France. bk. rev.

737   SZ   ISSN 0035-4163
REVUE SUISSE DE NUMISMATIQUE/ SCHWEIZERISCHE NUMISMATISCHE RUNDSCHAU. (Text in English, French and German) 1890. a. 50 Fr. Societe Suisse de Numismatique - Schweizerische Numismatische Gesellschaft, c/o Colin Martin, Petit-Chene 18, 1002 Lausanne, Switzerland. adv. illus. circ. 1,000.

737.4   UK
SEABY'S STANDARD CATALOGUE OF BRITISH COINS. 1978? irreg. £6. B.A. Seaby Ltd., Audley House, 11 Margaret St., London W1N 8AT, England. illus.

737   CS   ISSN 0081-0088
SLOVENSKA NUMIZMATIKA. (Text in Slovak; summaries in German) 1970. approx. biennial. 35 Kcs. (Slovenska Akademia Vied) Veda, Publishing House of the Slovak Academy of Sciences, Klemensova 19, 895 30 Bratislava, Czechoslovakia. Ed. Josef Hlinka.

737   US   ISSN 0037-9948
SOCIETY OF MEDALISTS. NEWS BULLETIN. 1930. a. free. Society of Medalists, West Branch Rd., Weston, CT 06880. Ed. Mary Louise Cram. circ. 2,500(approx.)

737   AT   ISSN 0085-6606
STANDARD AUSTRALIAN COIN CATALOGUE. 1965. irreg., vol. 8, 1979. Aus.$1 per no. Hawthorn Press Pty. Ltd., 601 Little Bourke St., Melbourne, Vic. 3000, Australia. Ed. John Gartner. circ. 25,000.

737   CS   ISSN 0081-6779
STUDIA NUMISMATICA ET MEDAILISTICA. (Text in Czech; summaries in English, French, German and Russian) 1970. irreg., no. 3, 1979. price varies. Moravske Muzeum, Numismaticke Oddeleni, Nam.25, Unora 6, 65937 Brno, Czechoslovakia. (Co-sponsor: Ceska Numismaticka Spolecnost, Pobocka Brno) illus. index. circ. 1,200.

737   RM   ISSN 0081-8887
STUDII SI CERCETARI DE NUMISMATICA. 1957. irreg., 1975, vol. 6. (Academia Republicii Socialiste Romania) Editura Academiei Republicii Socialiste Romania, Calea Victoriei 125, Bucharest, Romania (Subscr. to: ILEXIM, Str. 13 Decembrie Nr. 3, P.O. Box 136-137, Bucharest, Romania)

737   US   ISSN 0271-3993
SYLLOGE NUMMORUM GRAECORUM. Short title: S N G A N S. 1972. irreg., vol. 6, 1981. price varies. American Numismatic Society, Broadway at 155th St., New York, NY 10032.

SYLLOGE NUMMORUM GRAECORUM DEUTSCHLAND. see ARCHAEOLOGY

737   US   ISSN 0082-0628
SYLLOGE OF COINS OF THE BRITISH ISLES. 1958. irreg. Oxford University Press, 200 Madison Ave., New York, NY 10016 (and Ely House, 37 Dover St., London W1X 4AH, England)

069.9 737   BL
UNIVERSIDADE DE SAO PAULO. MUSEU PAULISTA. COLECAO. SERIE DE NUMISMATICA. 1975. irreg. Universidade de Sao Paulo, Museu Paulista, Caixa Postal 42503, Parque da Independencia, 04263 Sao Paulo SP, Brazil. Ed. Antonio Rocha Penteado.
   Supersedes in part (since 1975): Museu Paulista. Colecao (ISSN 0080-6382)

HOBBIES — Philately

769.56   DK
A F A OESTEUROPA FRIMAERKEKATALOG. Title varies: Oesteuropa Frimaerkekatalog. irreg. Aarhus Frimaerkehandel, Bruunsgade 42, 8000 Aarhus C, Denmark. illus.
   Supersedes in part: A F A Europe Frimaerkekatolog.

769.56   DK
A F A VESTEUROPA FRIMAERKEKATALOG. Title varies: Vesteuropa Frimaerkekatalog. 1974. irreg. Aarhus Frimaerkehandel, Bruunsgade 42, 8000 Aarhus C, Denmark. illus.
   Supersedes in part: A F A Europa Frimaerkekatalog.

769.54   FR   ISSN 0074-1698
A. I. J. P. YEARBOOK. a. price varies. International Association of Philatelic Journalists, c/o Secretary General Henri Trachtenberg, 115 rue Hoche, 94200 Ivry, Seine, France.

769.56   US
AERO PHILATELIST ANNALS. vol. 19, 1975. a. included in subscr. to Airpost Journal. American Air Mail Society, c/o George D. Kingdom, P. O. Box 499, Conneaut, OH 44030. Ed. Philip Silver. bk. rev. illus.

769.56   US
AMERICAN PHILATELIC CONGRESS. CONGRESS BOOK. 1935. a. $10 to non-members. ‡ American Philatelic Congress, Box 3646, Wilmington, NC 28401. Ed. James P. Harris. bk. rev. charts, illus. cum.index every 5 yrs. circ. 1,000.

769.56   US
AMERICAN STAMP CATALOG. a. price varies. Minkus Publications Inc., 116 W. 32 St., New York, NY 10001.

760   AT   ISSN 0313-9603
AUSTRALIAN COMMONWEALTH SPECIALISTS' CATALOGUE. 1926. a. Aus.$7.95. Hawthorn Press Pty Ltd, 601 Little Bourke Street, Melbourne, Vic. 3000, Australia. Ed. J. P. Meara.

760   AT
AUSTRALIAN STAMP BULLETIN. 1979. irreg. free. Post-Master General's Department., Philatelic Service Section, Australian Post Office Headquarters, Box 302, Carlton South, Vic. 3053, Australia (Subscriptions to: Philatelic Mailing List, Post Office Box 259, S. Melbourne, Vic. 3205) Ed. J. K. McKay. circ. 340,000.
   Formerly: Stamp Preview.

769.56   UK   ISSN 0305-4039
BALE CATALOGUE OF PALESTINE AND ISRAEL POSTAGE STAMPS. 1969. a. price varies. Michael H. Bale, Ed. & Pub., 41 High St., Ilfracombe, England (Dist. in U.S. by: Barry D. Hoffman, 739 Boylston St., Boston, MA 02116) circ. 3,500.
   Formerly: Bale Catalogue of Israel Stamps (ISSN 0067-3048)

769.56   GW   ISSN 0005-4364
BALLON KURIER. 1952. a. free. ‡ Pestalozzi Kinder- und Jugenddorf Wahlwies, 7768 Stockach 14, W. Germany (B.R.D.) Ed. H. J. Scheer. adv. bk. rev. illus. circ. 3,000. (looseleaf format)

769.56   US
BOOKLET. 1944. 3-4/yr. $2. Booklet Pane Society, P.O. Box 222, Forest Hills, NY 11375. Ed. Harry H. Moskovitz. adv. bk. rev. illus. circ. 125. (processed)

737   UK   ISSN 0068-1903
BRITISH COMMONWEALTH STAMP CATALOGUE. 1865. a. £12.50. ‡ Stanley Gibbons Publications Ltd., 391 Strand, London WC2R OLX, England. Ed. James Negus.

769.56   UK
BRITISH JOURNAL OF RUSSIAN PHILATELY. (Text in English; summaries occasionally in transliterated Russian) 1937. a. £5($10) membership. British Society of Russian Philately, c/o John Lloyd, The Retreat, West Bergholt, Colchester, Essex C06 3HE, England. Ed. I. L. G. Baillie. bk. rev. index. circ. 250(controlled)

769.56   CS
CESKOSLOVENSKO.* Spine title: Katalog Ceskoslovenskych Znamek. irreg. 40 Kcs. (Postovni Filatelisticka Sluzba) Nakladatelstvi Dopravy a Spoju, Hybernska 5, 115 78 Prague 1, Czechoslovakia. illus.

769.56   UK   ISSN 0142-5625
CHANNEL ISLANDS SPECIALISED CATALOGUE. 1979. irreg. £6. Stanley Gibbons Publications Ltd., 391 Strand, London WC2R OLX, England. Ed. James Negus.

769.56   UK   ISSN 0306-5103
COLLECT CHANNEL ISLANDS STAMPS. 1972. a. £1.25. Stanley Gibbons Publications Ltd., 391 Strand, London WC2R OLX, England. Ed. James Negus.

769.56   UK   ISSN 0307-7098
COLLECT ISLE OF MAN STAMPS. 1976. a. £1.25. Stanley Gibbons Publications Ltd., 391 Strand, London WC2R OLX, England. Ed. James Negus.

769.56   US   ISSN 0069-5521
COLLECTORS CLUB HANDBOOKS. irreg., 1973, no. 24. Collectors Club, Inc., 22 E. 35th St., New York, NY 10016.

769.56   UK   ISSN 0142-7830
COMMONWEALTH CATALOGUE OF QUEEN ELIZABETH STAMPS. 1952. a. price varies. Urch, Harris & Co. Ltd., 7 Richmond Hill Ave., Clifton, Bristol BS8 1BQ, England. adv. illus. circ. 10,000.

769.56   UK   ISSN 0071-0024
ELIZABETHAN STAMP CATALOGUE. 1965. a. £9.50. ‡ Stanley Gibbons Publications, Ltd., 391 Strand, London WC2R OLX, England. Ed. James Negus.

760   AT
GREAT WALL. 1956. irreg. China Stamp Collector's Club of Australasia, c/o Norman S. Hale, P.O. Box H137, Australia Square, Sydney, N.S.W. 2000, Australia. Ed. S. R. Tyler.

769.56   GT   ISSN 0046-6549
GUATEMALA FILATELICA. 1932. a. Q.12($3) ‡ Asociacion Filatelica de Guatemala, Apartado Postal 39, Guatemala, Guatemala. Ed. Eduardo Escobar. adv. bk. rev. charts. illus. stat. circ. 500.

383.2   US   ISSN 0072-9981
HANDBOOK ON U. S. LUMINESCENT STAMPS. 1970. irreg. (every 2-3 yrs.) latest, 1975. $4. ‡ Alfred G. Boerger, Ed. & Pub., P.O. Box 23822, Ft. Lauderdale, FL 33307. adv. bk. rev. circ. 3,000.

769   US
HEBERT'S CATALOGUE OF PLATE NUMBER SINGLES. 8th edt., 1975. irreg., approx. triennial. $6. Trans Pacific Stamp Co., Box 48215, Los Angeles, CA 90048. Ed. George G. Shapiro. illus.
   Former titles: Hebert's Catalogue of Used Plate Number Singles (ISSN 0098-2326); Catalogue of Used Plate Number Singles.

769.56   FR   ISSN 0074-1701
INTERNATIONAL ASSOCIATION OF PHILATELIC JOURNALISTS. BULLETIN. (Text in English, French, German) 1962. approx. a. free to members. International Association of Philatelic Journalists, c/o Secretary General Henri Trachtenberg, 115 rue Hoche, 94200 Ivry, Seine, France.

769.56 FR ISSN 0074-171X
INTERNATIONAL ASSOCIATION OF
PHILATELIC JOURNALISTS. MINUTES OF
ANNUAL CONGRESSES. (Text in English,
French, German) 1962. a. International Association
of Philatelic Journalists, c/o Secretary General
Henri Trachtenberg, 115 rue Hoche, 94200 Ivry,
Seine, France.

769.56 LU ISSN 0074-7343
INTERNATIONAL PHILATELIC FEDERATION.
GENERAL ASSEMBLY. PROCES-VERBAL.
1973. 5-6 per year. free to members. International
Philatelic Federation - Federation Internationale de
Philatelie, 38 rue du Cure, Luxembourg,
Luxembourg. adv. bk. rev.

769.56 UK
JOHN LISTER QUEEN ELIZABETH II STAMP
CATALOGUE. 1964. a. £4.25($6) Compton Press
Ltd., The Old Brewery, Tisbury, Nr. Salisbury,
Wilts. SP3 6NH, England.

769.56 GW ISSN 0076-7727
MICHEL-BRIEFMARKEN-KATALOGE. 1910. a
and irreg. price varies. Schwaneberger Verlag
GmbH, Muthmannstr. 4, 8000 Munich 45, W.
Germany (B.R.D.)

769.56 US ISSN 0076-9061
MINKUS NEW AMERICAN STAMP CATALOG.
1953. a. $7.50. Minkus Publications, Inc., 116 W.
32 St., New York, NY 10001. Ed. Ben Blumenthal.

769.56 US ISSN 0076-907X
MINKUS NEW WORLD WIDE STAMP
CATALOG. 1955. a. $16.50 per vol. Minkus
Publications, Inc., 116 W 32 St., New York, NY
10001. Ed. George Tlamsa.

769.56 US ISSN 0078-091X
NOBLE OFFICIAL CATALOG OF CANADA
PRECANCELS. 1923. irreg., 12th ed., 1978. $2.
Gilbert W. Noble, Ed. & Pub., Box 931, Winter
Park, FL 32789. circ. 1,000.

769.56 US ISSN 0078-0928
NOBLE OFFICIAL CATALOG OF UNITED
STATES BUREAU PRECANCELS. 1926. a. $5.
Gilbert W. Noble, Ed. & Pub., Box 931, Winter
Park, FL 32789. circ. 1,000.

769.56 PK ISSN 0078-8422
PAKISTAN POSTAGE STAMPS. (Text in English)
1960. irreg., latest issue, 1966. Rs.1.50. Post Office
Department, Karachi, Pakistan. adv. circ. 6,000.

769.56 PK
PAKSTAMPAGE CATALOGUE. Other title:
Pakistan Postage Stamp Catalogue. (Text in English)
1977. a. Rs.15. Pakstampage Publishers, Lyallpur,
Pakistan.

769.56 US
PHILATELIC DIRECTORY; a handbook for the
philatelic writer. 1976. biennial. $12. (Society of
Philaticians) Gustav Detjen Jr., Ed. & Pub., 154
Laguna Court, St. Augustine Shores, FL 32084. adv.
circ. 1,000. (reprint service avail. from UMI)

383.2 US ISSN 0079-4244
POSTAGE STAMPS OF THE UNITED STATES.
1927. biennial. $16. U. S. Postal Service, 475
l'Enfant Plaza West S.W., Washington, DC 20260
(Orders to: Supt. Doc., Washington, DC 20402)

769.56 UK ISSN 0140-8003
PRIVATE POST. 1977. a. £3. Cinderella Stamp Club,
30 Dunstan Rd., London NW11 8AB, England. Ed.
L. N. Williams. bibl. illus. circ. 600. (back issues
avail.)

769 SA
R. S. A. POSTAGE STAMP CATALOGUE. 1969.
irreg. R.3.25. Arcade Stamp Shop, Investment Bldg.,
97 Commissioner St., Johannesburg, South Africa.
Eds. N. Dorn, C. Slagt. illus. circ. 3,000.

769.56 RH
RHODESIA STAMP CATALOGUE. 1971. a.
Rhod.$5.75($8.40) Rhodesian Philatelic Agencies
(Pvt) Ltd., Box 3415, Salisbury, Zimbabwe. Ed.
D.G. Pollard. illus. index. circ. 7,000.

769.56 CN ISSN 0319-5465
SANAVIK COOPERATIVE. BAKER LAKE
PRINTS. 1974. a. Sanavik Cooperative, c/o
Canadian Arctic Producers Ltd., Box 4130, Station
E, Ottawa, Ont. K1S 5B2, Canada. illus.

769.56 UK ISSN 0080-8164
SCOTTISH POSTMARK GROUP. HANDBOOK.*
1962. irreg. price varies. Scottish Postmark Group,
David C. Jefferies, 11 Craigcrook Ave., Edinburgh
EH4 3QE, Scotland.

769.56 UK ISSN 0081-4210
STAMPS OF THE WORLD. 1934. a. £12.50. ‡
Stanley Gibbons Publications Ltd., 391 Strand,
London WC2R 0LX, England. Ed. James Negus.

769.56 US ISSN 0090-7286
TOPICAL NEW ISSUES. (Subseries of: American
Topical Association. Topical Handbook) a.
American Topical Association, Inc., 3306 N. 50th
St., Milwaukee, WI 53216. illus.

769.56 US ISSN 0049-4135
TOPICAL STAMP HANDBOOKS. 1951. irreg., no.
102, 1981. price varies. American Topical
Association, Inc., 3306 N. 50th St., Milwaukee, WI
53216. Ed. Jerome Husak. index, cum. index. every
5 yrs.

HOME ECONOMICS

see also *Interior Design and Decoration;
Nutrition and Dietetics*

747 200 US ISSN 0405-6590
BETTER HOMES AND GARDENS CHRISTMAS
IDEAS. 1952. a. $1.75 per no. Meredith
Corporation, 1716 Locust St., Des Moines, IA
50336. adv.

BETTER HOMES AND GARDENS GARDEN
IDEAS AND OUTDOOR LIVING. see
GARDENING AND HORTICULTURE

641.8 US ISSN 0361-0896
CELEBRATE; the annual for cake decorators. Variant
title: Wilton Cake Decorating Yearbook. 1975. a.
Wilton Enterprises, 833 W. 115th St., Chicago, IL
60643. illus.

CONSUMER-FARMER COOPERATOR. see
AGRICULTURE

641 FR ISSN 0339-7963
CUISINE CHEZ SOL. 1975. irreg. 7 F. per no.
Editions Beaulieu, 1 Place Alphonse Deville, 75006
Paris, France. Ed. Andre Guerber.

643 UK ISSN 0070-6779
DO-IT-YOURSELF. ANNUAL; do-it-yourself and
home improvement. 1959. a. 65p. per no. Link
House Publications Ltd., Link House, Dingwall
Ave., Croydon CR9 2TA, England. Ed. Tony
Wilkins. adv. circ. 80,000.

640 370 US
EDUCATIONAL MATERIALS DIRECTORY.
Variant title: Clothing and Textiles Educational
Materials Directory. 1975. a. $1. (American Home
Sewing Association) Homesewing Trade News, 330
Sunrise Highway, Rockville Centre, NY 11570. Ed.
Senta Mead. adv. circ. 15,000.

640 JA
FUKUI UNIVERSITY. FACULTY OF
EDUCATION. MEMOIRS. SERIES 5: APPLIED
SCIENCE AND HOME ECONOMICS. (Text in
Japanese; summaries in English & Japanese) 1964. a.
Fukui University, Faculty of Education, 9-1, 3-
chome, Bunkyo, Fukui 910, Japan.

HANDBOOK OF FOOD PREPARATION. see
FOOD AND FOOD INDUSTRIES

640 US
HOME APPLIANCE TRADE-IN BLUE BOOK.
1948. a. $12. Dealerscope, 23868 Hawthorne Blvd.,
Suite 100, Torrance, CA 90505. adv. (also avail. in
microform from UMI)
Formerly: Home Appliance Blue Book (ISSN
0085-1574)

640 US ISSN 0073-3105
HOME ECONOMICS IN INSTITUTIONS
GRANTING BACHELORS OR HIGHER
DEGREES. 1965. biennial. $6. ‡ American Home
Economics Association, 2010 Massachusetts Ave.,
N.W., Washington, DC 20036. Ed. Laura Jane
Harper.

640 AT
HOME SCIENCE FOR TEACHERS IN
SECONDARY SCHOOLS. 1957. irreg. Department
of Education, Bridge and Loftus Sts., Sydney, NSW
2000, Australia. Eds. H. J. Smith and J. M. Clare.
Indexed: Aus.Educ.Ind.
Formerly: New South Wales. Department of
Education. Home Economics Bulletin for Teachers
in Secondary Schools.

640 US
HOMEMAKER'S HANDBOOK. 1970. a. $1.50.
Snibbe Publications, Inc., 523 Lakeview Rd.,
Clearwater, FL 33516. Eds. John M. Benson Jr. and
Bern Fleming. circ. 700,000.
Former titles: Four Things Every Woman Should
Know (ISSN 0073-3156) & Homemaker's Guide.

640 FR ISSN 0074-3712
INTERNATIONAL CONGRESS OF HOME
ECONOMICS. REPORT. (Text in English, French
and German) quadrennial; 1980, 14th, Manila. 30 F.
International Federation for Home Economics, 5
Av. de la Porte Brancion, 75015 Paris, France.

640 NE ISSN 0074-4360
INTERNATIONAL COUNCIL OF HOMEHELP
SERVICES. REPORTS OF CONGRESS.* 1959.
every 3-4 yrs., 1975, 6th, Stockholm. International
Council of Home Help Services, c/o Dr. J. M. B.
Scholten, Cornelis Houtmanstr. 21, Utrecht,
Netherlands.

IOWA STATE UNIVERSITY. IOWA
AGRICULTURE AND HOME ECONOMICS
EXPERIMENT STATION. RESEARCH
BULLETIN SERIES. see *AGRICULTURE*

640 FR
JAMS GUIDE DE LA DEMEURE ET DES
JEUNES MARIES. a. Editions JAMS, 30 Cours
Lafayette, 69001 Lyon, France.

641.5 US ISSN 0094-0305
MCCALL'S COOKING SCHOOL. 1973. a. $1.50 per
no. McCall Publishing Co., 230 Park Ave., New
York, NY 10017. illus.

640 US
MCCALL'S HOLIDAY BAKE-IT BOOK. 1979. a.
$1.75. McCall Publishing Co., 230 Park Ave., New
York, NY 10017.

MAGAZIN POLOVNIKA. see *SPORTS AND
GAMES — Outdoor Life*

NATIONWIDE DIRECTORY OF GIFT AND
HOUSEWARES BUYERS. see *GIFTWARE AND
TOYS*

640 CN ISSN 0548-4081
NEW BRUNSWICK HOME ECONOMICS
ASSOCIATION. NEWSLETTER. 1966. irreg. New
Brunswick Home Economics Association, Bathurst,
N.B., Canada. illus. Key Title: Newsletter - New
Brunswick Home Economics Association.

013 640 US ISSN 0082-4534
TITLES OF DISSERTATIONS AND THESES
COMPLETED IN HOME ECONOMICS.
(Formerly an annual compilation published in the
Journal of Home Economics) 1962-63. a. $7.50. ‡
American Home Economics Association, 2010
Massachusetts Ave., N.W., Washington, DC 20036
(Order from University Microfilms International, Box
1764, Ann Arbor, MI 48106)

640 JA
TOKYO COLLEGE OF DOMESTIC SCIENCE.
BULLETIN/TOKYO KASEI DAIGAKU
KENKYU KIYO. (Text in Japanese or English)
1960. a. Tokyo College of Domestic Science -
Tokyo Kasei Daigaku, 1-18-1 Kaga, Itabashi-ku,
Tokyo 173, Japan.

640 US ISSN 0073-3113
U.S. DEPARTMENT OF AGRICULTURE. HOME
ECONOMICS RESEARCH REPORT. 1957. irreg.
U.S. Department of Agriculture, Washington, DC
20250.

HOME ECONOMICS — Abstracting, Bibliographies, Statistics

641.5   IT
VIAGGI INTORNO ALLA TAVOLA. 1975. irreg. Edizioni Il Formichiere s.r.l., Via del Lauro 3, 20121 Milan, Italy.

HOME ECONOMICS — Abstracting, Bibliographies, Statistics

301.5   645   CN   ISSN 0318-5273
CANADA. STATISTICS CANADA. HOUSEHOLD FACILITIES AND EQUIPMENT/ L'EQUIPMENT MENAGER. (Catalogue 64-202) (Text in English and French) 1947. a. Can.$4.50($5.40) Statistics Canada, Publications Distribution, Ottawa, Ont. K1A 0V7, Canada. (also avail. in microform from MML)

640   016   US   ISSN 0018-4020
HOME ECONOMICS RESEARCH ABSTRACTS. 1966. a. $37.50. ‡ American Home Economics Association, 2010 Massachusetts Ave., N.W., Washington, DC 20036 (Order from: University Microfilms International, 300 N. Zeeb Rd., Ann Arbor, MI 48106) (processed)

315   640   SI
SINGAPORE. DEPARTMENT OF STATISTICS. REPORT ON THE HOUSEHOLD EXPENDITURE SURVEY. 1972. quinquennial. S.$6. Department of Statistics, Government Publications Bureau, Fullerton Bldg., Singapore, Singapore. charts. stat.

HOMOSEXUALITY

301.41   US
B S J. (Broad St. Journal) 1971. irreg. $8. Broad Street Publishing, 1009 Broad St., Milliken, CO 80543 (Subscr. address: Box 310, Evans, CO 80620) adv. bk. rev. illus. stat. (looseleaf format)

301   US
DIRECTORY OF HOMOSEXUAL ORGANIZATIONS AND PUBLICATIONS. a. $3. Homosexual Information Center, 6715 Hollywood Blvd., No. 210, Hollywood, CA 90028. Ed. Ursula Enters Copely. (back issues avail.)

323.4   301   US
HOMOSEXUAL INFORMATION CENTER. NEWSLETTER. irreg. free. Homosexual Information Center, 6715 Hollywood Blvd., No. 210, Hollywood, CA 90028. bk. rev. (back issues avail.)

323.4
N G T F ACTION REPORT. irreg. membership. National Gay Task Force, 80 Fifth Ave., New York, NY 10011. Ed. Dave Perry.

301.41   323.4   CN
SEQUEL. vol. 2, 1974. s-m. Can.$12. c/o K. Vaughn, Box 1267 Station A, Toronto, Ont. M5W 1G7, Canada. Ed. Karl H. von Harten. adv. bk. rev. circ. 400.
    Former titles: South of Tuk (ISSN 0382-8522); Christian Nationalist Party News.

HOMOSEXUALITY — Abstracting, Bibliographies, Statistics

011   301   US
SELECTED BIBLIOGRAPHY OF HOMOSEXUALITY. biennial. $0.35. Homosexual Information Center, 6715 Hollywood Blvd., No. 210, Hollywood, CA 90028. Ed. Leslie Colfar. (back issues avail.)

HORSES AND HORSEMANSHIP

see Sports and Games — Horses and Horsemanship

HOSPITALS

see also Medical Sciences; Nutrition and Dietetics

362.1   AT
A H A HEALTH SERVICES MONOGRAPHS. irreg. Australian Hospital Association, The Science Centre, 35 Clarence St., Sydney, N.S.W. 2000, Australia.

ALASKA NATIVE MEDICAL CENTER. ANNUAL REPORT. see SOCIAL SERVICES AND WELFARE

AMERICAN ANIMAL HOSPITAL ASSOCIATION. ANNUAL MEETING SCIENTIFIC PROCEEDINGS. see VETERINARY SCIENCE

362   US   ISSN 0065-7794
AMERICAN COLLEGE OF HOSPITAL ADMINISTRATORS. DIRECTORY. 1960. biennial. $25 to non-members. American College of Hospital Administrators, 840 N. Lake Shore Dr., Chicago, IL 60611. Ed. Mary Lou Rollins. circ. 4,000.

362   US   ISSN 0098-2377
AMERICAN GROUP PRACTICE ASSOCIATION DIRECTORY. 1952. biennial. $25. American Group Practice Association, 20 S. Quaker Lane, Alexandria, VA 22314.
    Formerly: American Association of Medical Clinics. Directory (ISSN 0569-2679)

ANNUAIRE MEDICAL DE L'HOSPITALISATION FRANCAISE. see MEDICAL SCIENCES

362   AT   ISSN 0312-7907
AUSTRALIA. BUREAU OF STATISTICS. WESTERN AUSTRALIAN OFFICE. HOSPITAL IN-PATIENT STATISTICS. 1971. a. free. Australian Bureau of Statistics, Western Australian Office, 1-3 St. George's Tce., Perth, W.A. 6000, Australia. Ed. E. Binns. circ. 300.

362.1   AT
AUSTRALIAN HOSPITAL ASSOCIATION. PROCEEDINGS-NATIONAL CONGRESS. 1977. a. Aus.$3.75. Australian Hospital Association, The Science Centre, 35 Clarence St., Sydney, N.S.W. 2000, Australia. circ. 1,000.

362.1   AT   ISSN 0312-5599
AUSTRALIAN HOSPITALS AND HEALTH SERVICES YEARBOOK. 1967. a. Aus.$30 per no. (University of New South Wales, School of Health Administration) Peter Isaacson Publications, 46-49 Porter St., Prahran, Vic. 3181, Australia. Ed. C. Grant. adv. circ. 2,500.
    Formerly: Australian and New Zealand Hospitals and Health Services Yearbook (ISSN 0084-7208)

362.11   CN
B. C. HEALTH ASSOCIATION. PROCEEDINGS OF THE ANNUAL CONFERENCE. 1919. a. ‡ British Columbia Health Association, 440 Cambie, Vancouver, B.C., Canada. Ed. Marilyn Dimeo. circ. 300.
    Formerly: B. C. Association of Hospitals and Health Organizations. Proceedings of the Annual Conference & British Columbia Hospitals' Association. Proceedings of the Annual Conference (ISSN 0068-158X)

658   BL
BRAZIL. COORDENACAO DE ASSISTENCIA MEDICA E HOSPITALAR. CADASTRO HOSPITALAR BRASILEIRO. irreg. Ministerio da Saude, Coordenacao de Assistencia Medica e Hospitalar, Brasilia, Brazil. stat.

362   368.4   UK   ISSN 0068-2098
BRITISH HOSPITALS CONTRIBUTORY SCHEMES ASSOCIATION. DIRECTORY OF HOSPITALS CONTRIBUTORY SCHEME BENEFITS. 1954. biennial. £1. ‡ British Hospitals Contributory Schemes Association, 30 Lancaster Gate, London W2 3LT, England. Ed. A.A. Case. circ. 500.

362   UK   ISSN 0068-2101
BRITISH HOSPITALS CONTRIBUTORY SCHEMES ASSOCIATION. REPORT.* 1949. a. 5p. British Hospitals Contributory Schemes Association, 30 Lancaster Gate, London W2 3LT, England. Ed. A.A. Case.

362.1   US
CALIFORNIA STATE HEALTH PLAN. a. Office of Statewide Health Planning Development, 714 P St., Rm. 1000, Sacramento, CA 95814. stat.
    Former titles: California State Plan for Hospitals and Related Health Facilities (ISSN 0526-9288); California State Plan for Hospitals (ISSN 0575-2221)

362   CN   ISSN 0068-8932
CANADIAN HOSPITAL DIRECTORY/ ANNUAIRE DES HOPITAUX DU CANADA. (Text in English and French) 1953. a. Can.$35. ‡ Canadian Hospital Association, 410 Laurier Ave. W., Suite 800, Ottawa, Ont. K1R 7T6, Canada. Ed. E. Sawyer. adv. circ. 4,200.

610   GW
DEUTSCHE KRANKENHAUSGESELLSCHAFT. JAHRESBERICHT. biennial. free. Deutsche Krankenhausgesellschaft, Tersteegenstr. 9, 4000 Duesseldorf 30, W. Germany (B.R.D.)

362.1   US   ISSN 0095-5191
DIRECTORY OF INVESTOR-OWNED HOSPITALS AND HOSPITAL MANAGEMENT COMPANIES. a. Federation of American Hospitals, 1405 N. Pierce St., Ste. 311, Little Rock, AR 72207. (reprint service avail. from UMI)

362.11   US   ISSN 0093-8041
GEORGIA STATE UNIVERSITY. INSTITUTE OF HEALTH ADMINISTRATION. OCCASIONAL PUBLICATION. 1965. irreg. price varies. Georgia State University, Hospital Administration Program, Atlanta, GA 30303. Ed. George R. Wren.
    Formerly: Georgia State University. Hospital Administration Program. Occasional Publication (ISSN 0072-1247)

362   UK   ISSN 0072-5978
GREAT BRITAIN. DEPARTMENT OF HEALTH AND SOCIAL SECURITY. CAPRICODE CAPITAL PROJECTS CODE. HOSPITAL BUILDING PROCEDURE NOTES. (Joint publication with the Welsh Office) 1970. irreg. price varies. H.M.S.O., P.O. Box 569, London SE1 9NH, England.

362.11   UK
GREAT BRITAIN. DEPARTMENT OF HEALTH AND SOCIAL SECURITY. HEALTH BUILDING NOTES. 1961. irreg. price varies. H.M.S.O., P.O. Box 569, London SE1 9NH, England.
    Formerly: Great Britain. Department of Health and Social Security. Hospital Building Notes (ISSN 0072-601X)

362.11   UK   ISSN 0141-1403
GREAT BRITAIN. DEPARTMENT OF HEALTH AND SOCIAL SECURITY. HEALTH EQUIPMENT NOTES. 1975. irreg. price varies. H.M.S.O., P.O. Box 569, London SE1 9NH, England.
    Formerly: Great Britain. Department of Health and Social Security. Hospital Equipment Notes (ISSN 0072-6028)

362   UK
GREAT BRITAIN. DEPARTMENT OF HEALTH AND SOCIAL SECURITY. NOTES ON GOOD PRACTICES. 1975. irreg. price varies. H.M.S.O., P.O. Box 569, London SE1 9NH, England. abstr. charts, illus. stat. (looseleaf format) Indexed: Hosp.Abstr.
    Former titles (until 1977): Abstracts of Efficiency Studies in the National Health Service; Abstracts of Efficiency Studies in the Hospital Service (ISSN 0001-3552)

362.1 614 UK
GREAT BRITAIN. DEPARTMENT OF HEALTH AND SOCIAL SECURITY. STATISTICAL AND RESEARCH REPORT SERIES. 1965. irreg. price varies. H.M.S.O., P.O. Box 569, London SE1 9NH, England.
Formerly (until 1972): Great Britain. Department of Health and Social Security. Statistical Report Series (ISSN 0072-6125)

362 UK
GREAT BRITAIN. NATIONAL HEALTH SERVICE. HEALTH SERVICE COSTING RETURNS. a. £3.50. National Health Service, Alexander Fleming House, Elephant and Castle, London SE1 6BY, England (Avail. from H.M.S.O., c/o Liaison Officer, Atlantic House, Holborn Viaduct, London EC1P 1BN, England)
Formerly: Great Britain. National Health Service. Hospital Costing Returns (ISSN 0072-6966)

610 FR ISSN 0072-8144
GUIDE MEDICAL ET HOSPITALIER. 1959. a. 300 F. Editions Boileau, 9 rue Clauzel, Paris (9e), France. adv.

362 US ISSN 0094-8969
GUIDE TO THE HEALTH CARE FIELD. 1945. a. $50 to non-members; members $40. American Hospital Association, 840 N. Lake Shore Dr., Chicago, IL 60611. Ed. Frank Sabatino. adv. stat. tr. lit. circ. 32,000.

362 US ISSN 0090-2535
GUIDEBOOK OF CATHOLIC HOSPITALS. a. $10. Catholic Health Association, 4455 Woodson Rd., St. Louis, MO 63134. circ. 2,500. (reprint service avail. from UMI)

362 US
HAWAII. DEPARTMENT OF HEALTH. WAIMANO TRAINING SCHOOL AND HOSPITAL DIVISION (REPORT) 1962. a. free. Department of Health, Waimano Training School and Hospital Division, Box 3378, Honolulu, HI 96801.
Former titles: Hawaii. Department of Health. Division of Mental Health. Children's Health Services (ISSN 0362-6296); Hawaii, Department of Health Research and Planning Statistical Office. (Report on) Waimano Training School and Hospital (ISSN 0073-1056)

362 658.8 US ISSN 0073-1412
HAYES DIRECTORY OF PHYSICIAN AND HOSPITAL SUPPLY HOUSES. 1935. a. $55. Edward N. Hayes, Ed. & Pub., 4229 Birch St., Newport Beach, CA 92660.

362.1 UK ISSN 0140-5748
HEALTH SERVICE BUYERS GUIDE. 1966. a. £12. Sell's Publications Ltd., Sell's House, 39 East Street, Epsom, Surrey, England. adv. bk. rev. circ. 4,000.
Former titles: Sell's Health Service Buyers Guide (ISSN 0308-7107); Sell's Hospital and Surgical Supplies (ISSN 0073-3458)

362 610.73 SA ISSN 0441-2613
HOSPITAL AND NURSING YEARBOOK OF SOUTHERN AFRICA. Title varies: Hospital and Nursing Year Book of South Africa. 1960. a. R.40($36) Thomson Publications S. A. (Pty) Ltd., Box 8308, Johannesburg 2000, South Africa. Ed. Heinz Engelhardt. adv.

658 BL
HOSPITAL-ESCOLA SAO CAMILO E SAO LUIS. BOLETIM. a. Hospital-Escola Sao Camilo e Sao Luis, Macapa, Brazil.

362 UK ISSN 0073-3474
HOSPITALS & HEALTH SERVICES YEAR BOOK AND DIRECTORY OF HOSPITAL SUPPLIERS. 1973. a. £29.40($72) Institute of Health Service Administrators, 75 Portland Place, London W1N 4AN, England. Ed. N. W. Chaplin. adv.
Continues: Hospitals Year Book and Directory of Hospital Suppliers.

331 US
IN CARE; for the people who care for patients in mental hospitals. 1971. irreg. membership only. California State Employees Association, Psychiatric Technician Occupational Council, 1108 O St., Sacramento, CA 95814. circ. 15,000(controlled) (tabloid format; back issues avail.)
Formerly: Outlook.

362 SZ ISSN 0074-977X
INTERNATIONALER SPITALBEDARF. 1958. a. 18 Fr. Vogt-Schild AG, Dornacherstr. 39, 4501 Solothurn 1, Switzerland. adv. circ. 3,800.

ISRAEL. CENTRAL BUREAU OF STATISTICS. DIAGNOSTIC STATISTICS OF HOSPITALIZED PATIENTS. see *SOCIAL SERVICES AND WELFARE*

362 AU ISSN 0075-7063
JAHRBUCH KRANKENHAUS. 1964. a. S.240. Dieter Goeschl Buch- und Zeitschriftenverlag, Klopstockgasse 34, A-1170 Vienna, Austria. Ed. R. M. Tornar. adv. index. circ. 2,400.
Formerly: Unser Krankenhaus.

362 JA ISSN 0408-0904
JAPANESE HOSPITAL DIRECTORY/BYOIN YORAN. (Text in Japanese) 1958/59-1964; 1976. 8500 Yen. (Ministry of Health and Welfare - Koseisho Imukyoku Somuka) Igaku Shoin Ltd., 5-24-3 Hongo, Bunkyo-ku, Tokyo 113-91, Japan.

KING'S GAZETTE; the journal of King's College Hospital. see *MEDICAL SCIENCES*

362 HU
MAGYAR KORHAZAK ES KLINIKAK EVKONYVE. 1970. every 5 yrs. 250. Magyar Korhazszovetseg, Budapest, Hungary. Ed. G. Aczel. illus. circ. 1,000.

MODERN NURSING HOME DIRECTORY OF NURSING HOMES IN THE UNITED STATES, U.S. POSSESSIONS AND CANADA. see *SOCIAL SERVICES AND WELFARE*

362 SA ISSN 0078-5547
ORANGE FREE STATE. DIRECTOR OF HOSPITAL SERVICES. REPORT/ORANGE FREE STATE. DIREKTEUR VAN HOSPITALDIENSTE. VERSLAG. 1965. a. R.9.50 approx. ‡ Director of Hospital Services, Box 517, Bloemfontein 9300, South Africa. circ. controlled.

658 AT
PERMAIL HOSPITAL BOOK. 1965. biennial. Aus.$50. Permail Pty. Ltd., Box 56, Artarmon, NSW 2064, Australia.

362 PR
PUERTO RICO. DIVISION OF HEALTH FACILITIES. PLAN FOR HOSPITAL AND MEDICAL FACILITIES. (Text in English; summaries in English) 1949. a. Department of Health, Division of Health Facilites, Stop 19, Santurce, PR 00907. circ. 250. (processed)

362.11 CN
QUEEN ALEXANDRA HOSPITAL FOR CHILDREN. ANNUAL REPORT. 1927. a. free. Queen Alexandra Solarium for Crippled Children Society, 2400 Arbutus Road, Victoria, B.C. V8W 2P3, Canada. Ed. George O. Thomas. circ. 100. (processed)
Formerly: Queen Alexandra Solarium for Crippled Children Annual Report (ISSN 0085-526X)

RHODE ISLAND. DEPARTMENT OF MENTAL HEALTH, RETARDATION AND HOSPITALS. MENTAL HEALTH, RETARDATION AND HOSPITALS. see *PUBLIC HEALTH AND SAFETY*

610 UK ISSN 0036-2840
SAINT GEORGE'S HOSPITAL GAZETTE. 1893. a. £1.05. St. George's Hospital Medical School, Cranmer Terrace, Tooting, London S.W. 17, England. Ed.Bd. adv. bk. rev. charts. illus. cum.index. circ. 1,000.

362.1 US ISSN 0081-2692
SOUTH CAROLINA STATE PLAN FOR FRANCHISING, CONSTRUCTION AND MODERNIZATION OF HOSPITAL AND RELATED MEDICAL FACILITIES. 1947. a. free. Department of Health and Environmental Control, Bureau of Health Facilities and Services, J. Marion Sims Bldg., 2600 Bull St., Columbia, SC 29201. circ. 900.
Formerly (until 1974): South Carolina State Plan for Construction and Modernization of Hospital and Medical Facilities.

362 618.92 US
STANDARDS AND RECOMMENDATIONS FOR HOSPITAL CARE OF NEWBORN INFANTS. 5th edt., 1971. irreg. (every 2-3 yrs.) $6. American Academy of Pediatrics, Committee on Fetus and Newborn, Box 1034, Evanston, IL 60204.

U.S. NATIONAL CENTER FOR HEALTH STATISTICS. VITAL AND HEALTH STATISTICS. SERIES 13. DATA ON HEALTH RESOURCES UTILIZATION. see *PUBLIC HEALTH AND SAFETY*

658 614 US ISSN 0073-1439
UNIVERSITY OF IOWA. GRADUATE PROGRAM IN HOSPITAL AND HEALTH ADMINISTRATION. HEALTH CARE RESEARCH SERIES. 1966. irreg., 1975, no. 21. ‡ University of Iowa, Graduate Program in Hospital and Health Administration, S-517 Westlawn, Iowa City, IA 52241.

360 CN
VISTAS FOR VOLUNTEERS. no. 17, 1977. a. Can.$5. International Alliance of Hospital Volunteers, Suite 323, 1117 St. Catherine St. W., Montreal, P.Q. H3B 1H9, Canada. Ed. Catherine B. Draper. illus.

362 UN ISSN 0510-8845
WORLD HEALTH ORGANIZATION. REGIONAL OFFICE FOR THE WESTERN PACIFIC. REPORT ON THE REGIONAL SEMINAR ON THE ROLE OF THE HOSPITAL IN THE PUBLIC HEALTH PROGRAMME.* 1963. irreg. World Health Organization, Regional Office for the Western Pacific, P.O. Box 2932, Manila, Philippines.

HOSPITALS — Abstracting, Bibliographies, Statistics

362 016 US ISSN 0194-4908
ABSTRACTS OF HEALTH CARE MANAGEMENT STUDIES. 1963-64. q. $47.50. Health Administration Press, School of Public Health, University of Michigan, Ann Arbor, MI 48109. Ed. Gene Regenstreif. abstr. index. circ. 2,000. (also avail. in microfilm from UMI; reprint service avail. from UMI)
Formerly: Abstracts of Hospital Management Studies (ISSN 0001-3595)

362.1 319 AT
AUSTRALIA. BUREAU OF STATISTICS. QUEENSLAND OFFICE. HOSPITAL MORBIDITY. a. Australian Bureau of Statistics, Queensland Office, 345 Ann St., Brisbane, Qld. 4000, Australia.
Formerly: Australia. Bureau of Statistics. Queensland Office. Patients Treated in Hospitals.

658 CN ISSN 0381-8802
CANADA. STATISTICS CANADA. HOSPITAL STATISTICS: PRELIMINARY ANNUAL REPORT/STATISTIQUE HOSPITALIERE: RAPPORT ANNUEL PRELIMINAIRE. (Catalogue 83-217) (Text in English and French) 1961. a. Can.$3($3.60) Statistics Canada, Publications Distribution, Ottawa, Ont. K1A 0V7, Canada. (also avail. in microform from MML)

362.1 CN ISSN 0225-5642
CANADA. STATISTICS CANADA. LIST OF CANADIAN HOSPITALS AND SPECIAL CARE FACILITIES/LISTE DES HOPITAUX CANADIENS ET DES ETABLISSEMENTS DE SOINS SPECIAUX. (Catalogue 83-201) (Text in English and French) 1942. a. Can.$10($12) Statistics Canada, Publications Distribution, Ottawa, Ont. K1A 0V7, Canada. (also avail. in microform from MML)
Formerly: Canada. Statistics Canada. Hospitals Section. List of Canadian Hospitals and Related Institutions and Facilities/Liste des Hopitaux Canadiens et des Etablissements et Installations Connexes (ISSN 0319-8014)

362.2 US ISSN 0094-2294
FLORIDA. MENTAL HEALTH PROGRAM OFFICE. STATISTICAL REPORT OF HOSPITALS. (Former name of issuing body: Division of Mental Health) a. Mental Health Program Office, 1323 Winewood Blvd., Tallahassee, FL 32301. Key Title: Statistical Report of Hospitals (Tallahassee)

362 NZ ISSN 0548-9938
HOSPITAL AND SELECTED MORBIDITY DATA. a. price varies. National Health Statistics Centre, Box 6314, Te Aro, Wellington 1, New Zealand.

362 NZ ISSN 0110-1900
NEW ZEALAND. DEPARTMENT OF HEALTH. HOSPITAL MANAGEMENT DATA. 1926. a. price varies. National Health Statistics Centre, P. O. Box 6314, Wellington, New Zealand. circ. controlled.
 Formerly: Hospital Statistics of New Zealand (ISSN 0073-3466)

362 UY ISSN 0041-8455
UNIVERSIDAD DE LA REPUBLICA. HOSPITAL DE CLINICAS. INFORME ESTATISTICO. (Text in Spanish) 1962. a. $1. Hospital de Clinicas "Dr. Manuel Quintela", Universidad de la Republica, Avda. Italia S/N, Montevideo, Uruguay. Ed. Bd. circ. 400.

HOTELS AND RESTAURANTS

see also *Nutrition and Dietetics; Travel and Tourism*

647 910 UK
AGENT'S HOTEL GAZETTEER: AMERICA. a. £12.50. C.H.G. Travel Publications, 30 Grove Rd., Beaconsfield, Bucks, England.

647 910 UK
AGENT'S HOTEL GAZETTEER: RESORTS. (In two parts) a. £17.50. C. H. G. Travel Publications, 30 Grove Rd., Beaconsfield, Bucks., England. illus.

647 UK ISSN 0308-9584
AGENT'S HOTEL GAZETTEER: TOURIST CITIES. (In Two Parts) a. £17.50. C. H. G. Travel Publications, 30 Grove Rd., Beaconsfield, Bucks., England. illus.

647.9 US
AMERICAN HOTEL AND MOTEL ASSOCIATION. BUYERS GUIDE FOR HOTELS & MOTELS. 1975. a. American Hotel and Motel Association, 888 Seventh Ave., New York, NY 10019. Ed. Robert Cummings. adv. illus. circ. 11,000.
 Supersedes: American Hotel and Motel Association. Product News. (ISSN 0032-9789)

919.4 AT
AUSTRALIAN ACCOMMODATION GUIDE. 1963/64. a. $1.50 ea. ‡ Royal Automobile Association of South Australia Inc., 41 Hindmarsh Sqe., Adelaide, S.A. 5000, Australia. (Co-sponsor: Royal Automobile Club of Victoria) adv. circ. 135,000.
 Formerly: Royal Automobile Association of South Australia. Accommodation Guide (ISSN 0085-5782)

642.47 AT
AUSTRALIAN HOTEL, MOTEL, CLUB CATERING RESTAURANT HANDBOOK AND BUYERS GUIDE. 1962. a. Aus.$10. David Boyce Publishing & Associates, 44 Regent St., Redfern, N.S.W. 2016, Australia. Ed. D. W. Boyce. adv. circ. 4,000.

B A H R E P INTERNATIONAL HOTEL DIRECTORY. (British Association of Hotel Representatives) see *TRAVEL AND TOURISM*

647 916.8 SA
C V R TRAVEL AND HOTEL GUIDE TO SOUTHERN AFRICA. (Text in Afrikaans and English) 1966. a. R.7.50. Chris van Rensburg Publications (Pty) Ltd., P.O. Box 25272, Ferreirasdorp 2048, South Africa.
 Formerly: Guide to Hotels in South Africa (ISSN 0533-5450)

642.56 CN ISSN 0706-5310
CALGARY GASTRONOMIC. 1977. a. $3.50. Between the Lines Publishing Co., 3320 34th Ave S.W., Calgary, Alta T3E OZ4, Canada. adv.

647.9 CN ISSN 0381-5765
CANADIAN HOTEL, RESTAURANT, INSTITUTION & STORE EQUIPMENT DIRECTORY. 1925. a. Can.$20($30) Lloyd Publications of Canada, Box 262, West Hill, Ont. M1E 4R5, Canada. Ed. J. Lloyd. adv. index. circ. 8,300.

647.95 642.47 UK ISSN 0069-1194
CATERING & HOTEL MANAGEMENT YEAR BOOK & DIARY. 1960. a. £3. Blandford Business Press, Pembroke House, Wellesley Rd., Croydon CR9 2BX, England.
 Formerly: Hotel and Catering Executives Year Book and Diary.

DAWSONS GUIDE TO AUSTRALIAN & WORLDWIDE HOTELS. see *TRAVEL AND TOURISM*

647 US
DIRECTORY OF HOTEL AND MOTEL SYSTEMS. a. $15. American Hotel and Motel Association, 888 7th Ave., New York, NY 10019.

647.954 UK
EGON RONAY'S LUCAS GUIDE TO HOTELS, RESTAURANTS AND INNS IN GREAT BRITAIN AND IRELAND. 1957. a. £4.75($9.95) Egon Ronay Organisation Ltd., Greencoat House, Francis St., London SW1P 1DH, England. adv. circ. 100,000.
 Former titles: Egon Ronay's Dunlop Guide to Hotels and Restaurants in the British Isles (ISSN 0070-9468); Egon Ronay's Guide to Hotels, Restaurants, Pubs and Inns.

647.94 UK
FARM HOLIDAY GUIDE. (In three editions: England; Scotland; Wales & Ireland) 1948. a. Farm Holiday Guides Ltd., 18 High Street, Paisley PA1 2BX, Scotland.

647.9 UK ISSN 0308-8464
FINANCIAL TIMES WORLD HOTEL DIRECTORY. 1975/76. a. £15.95. Longman Group Ltd., Longman House, Burnt Mill, Harlow, Essex CM20 2JE, England.

647.94 UK
GOFF'S GUIDE TO MOTELS AND MOTORWAYS IN GREAT BRITAIN AND IRELAND. 1963. a. 60p. London and Continental Publishing Co., 15 Albert Mews, London W8 5RY, England. Ed. R. Redman. adv. circ. 30,000.
 Formerly: Goff's Guide to Motels in Great Britain and Europe (ISSN 0072-4890)

647.95 UK ISSN 0072-5005
GOOD FOOD GUIDE. 1951. a. £5.95. Consumers' Association, 14 Buckingham St., London W.C.2, England (Subscr. to: Caxton Hill, Hertford SG13 7LZ, England) Ed. Christopher Driver. circ. 60,000. (also avail. in microfiche)
 Over 1000 recommended eating places in Great Britain, Ireland, and Channel Isles

647.95 UK
GOOD HOTEL GUIDE. a. Consumers Association, 14 Buckingham St., London WC2N 6DS, England (Subscr. to: Caxton Hill, Hertford SG13 7LZ, England)

GUIDE DES RELAIS ROUTIERS. see *TRAVEL AND TOURISM*

GUIDE KLEBER FRANCE. see *TRAVEL AND TOURISM*

647 US ISSN 0093-4585
GUIDE TO THE RECOMMENDED COUNTRY INNS OF NEW ENGLAND. 1974. a. $5.95. Globe Pequot Press, Old Chester Rd., Chester, CT 06412. Ed. Linda Kennedy. illus.

647.94 US
H.S.M.A. HOTEL FACILITIES DIGEST. a. $5. ‡ Hotel Sales Management Association, 362 Fifth Ave., New York, NY 10001. Ed. Frank W. Berkman. adv. circ. 25,000.
 Formerly: H.S.M.A. Hotel-Motel Directory and Facilities Guide (ISSN 0072-9167)

647.94 II ISSN 0073-0386
HARDY'S ENCYCLOPAEDIA HOTELS OF INDIA AND NEPAL.* (Text in English) 1964. a. price varies. Hardy & Ally, 8-44 Regal Bldg., Box 184, New Delhi 1, India. Ed. K. N. Malhotra.

919.4 AT ISSN 0085-1485
HERALD MOTEL GUIDE. 1965. a. Aus.$1 ea. Herald Travel Bureau, Newspaper House, 247 Collins St., Melbourne, Vic. 3000, Australia. Ed. D.H. Day.

647.94 UK ISSN 0073-2982
HOLIDAY CHALETS AND CARAVANS DIRECTORY MAGAZINE. 1957. a. 50p. Stone and Cox (Publications) Ltd., 44 Fleet Street, London EC4Y 1BS, England.

647.94 CN ISSN 0704-6359
HOSPITALITE. (Text in French) 1977. a. Can.$17. Maclean-Hunter Ltd., 481 University Ave., Toronto, Ont. M5W 1A7, Canada. Ed. Peter Bouwer. adv. circ. 5,017.

650 640 AT
HOSPITALITY BUYERS GUIDE. a. Aus.$25. Peter Isaacson Publications, 46-49 Porter St., Prahran, Vic. 3181, Australia. Ed. Les Griffiths.
 Former titles: Hospitality Buyers Guide & Diary; Hospitality Yearbook (ISSN 0311-2969)

647.94 US ISSN 0073-3490
HOTEL AND MOTEL RED BOOK; hotels and motels which are members of the American Hotel and Motel Association; also many foreign hotels. 1886. a. $25. (American Hotel and Motel Association) American Hotel Association Directory Corp., 888 Seventh Ave, New York, NY 10019. Ed. G.M. Barbara Rugowski. adv. index. circ. 30,000.

919.4 AT
HOTEL, MOTEL AND TRAVEL DIRECTORY. 1965. a. Aus.$15. Peter Isaacson Publications, 46-49 Porter St., Prahran, Vic. 3181, Australia.
 Formerly: Hotel and Motel Directory (ISSN 0085-1612)

914 GW
HOTELFUEHRER DEUTSCHLAND. irreg. Allgemeiner Deutscher Automobil-Club e.V., Baumgartnerstr. 53, 8000 Munich 70, W. Germany (B.R.D.) (Co-sponsor: Oesterreichischer Automobil-, Motorrad- und Touring-Club)

647.94 647.95 UK
HOTELS AND RESTAURANTS IN BRITAIN. a. £4.25 to non-members. Automobile Association, Fanum House, Basingstoke, Hants RG21 2EA, England. adv.
 Former titles: Hotel and Restaurant Guide; Guide to Hotels and Restaurants in Great Britain (ISSN 0072-8527)

647.94 647.95 UK ISSN 0073-3512
HOTELS AND RESTAURANTS IN BRITAIN. (Explanatory Notes in French, German, Spanish, Italian, English) a. £1.90. British Tourist Authority, 64-65 St. James's St., London SW1A 1NF, England. Ed. R. T. FitzGerald. cum.index.

647.94 FR
HOTELS DE LA FRANCE. 1962. a. 80 F. Hotels de la France, 83 rue Amelot, 75011 Paris, France.
 Formerly: Hotels de la France et d'Outre-Mer (ISSN 0073-3539)

I A T A TRAVEL AGENTS DIRECTORY OF EUROPE. see *TRAVEL AND TOURISM*

647.9 642 UK ISSN 0073-7364
INDUSTRIAL CATERING. 1955. a. £2. Blandford Business Press, Pembroke House, Wellesley Rd., Croydon CR9 2BX, England.

647.94 FR ISSN 0074-624X
INTERNATIONAL HOTEL GUIDE. 1948. a. 90 F. International Hotel Association, 89, Faubourg-Saint-Honore, 75008 Paris, France. circ. 14,000.

647 JA ISSN 0446-6217
JAPAN HOTEL GUIDE. (Text in English) irreg. Japan Tourist Association, 1 Marunouchi, Chuo-ku, Tokyo, Japan. illus.

647.954 UK
JUST A BITE; Egon Ronay's Lucas guide for gourmets on a family budget. 1979. a. £1.95($4.50) Egon Ronay Organisation Ltd., Greencoat House, Francis St., London SW1P 1DH, England.

647.94 UK ISSN 0075-8876
LET'S HALT AWHILE IN GREAT BRITAIN. 1933. a. £2.60 plus 40p postage. Michael Joseph, 52 Bedford Sq., London W.C. 1, England. Ed. Ashley Courtenay. index.

MICHELIN RED GUIDE SERIES: GREATER LONDON. see *TRAVEL AND TOURISM*

647 US ISSN 0095-0386
MORT'S GUIDE TO LOW-COST VACATIONS & LODGINGS ON COLLEGE CAMPUSES. 1974. irreg. $5. C M G Publications, Box 630, Princeton, NJ 08540. illus.

647.94 GW
MOTELFUEHRER INTERNATIONAL; ADAC-Reisefuehrer. (Text in English, Dutch, French, and German) 1975. irreg. DM.16.80. ADAC Verlag GmbH, Baumgartnerstr. 53, 8000 Munich 70, W. Germany (B.R.D.)

647 US ISSN 0099-0205
N A A WHERE TO STAY BOOK. irreg. National Automobile Association, Box 29037, Atlanta, GA 30329. illus.

647.94 US
NATIONAL DIRECTORY OF BUDGET MOTELS; a nation-wide guide to low-cost chain motel accommodations. 1975. a. $3.50. Pilot Books, 347 Fifth Ave., New York, NY 10016. Ed. Raymond Carlson.

NIGERIA TOURIST GUIDE/GUIDE DU TOURISME NIGERIEN. see *TRAVEL AND TOURISM*

674.94 UK ISSN 0307-062X
OFFICIAL GUIDE TO HOTELS & RESTAURANTS IN GREAT BRITAIN, IRELAND AND OVERSEAS. a. £1. British Hotels, Restaurants and Caterers Association, 13 Cork St., London W1X 2BH, England.
Formerly: B H R C A Guide to Hotels and Restaurants (ISSN 0068-2128)

647.9 642.5 PK
PAKISTAN HOTEL AND RESTAURANT GUIDE. (Text in English) 1980. a. Rs.15($3) Maulai Enterprise, 5-6/2, al-Naseer, Sharifabad, Federal B Area, Blk. No. 1, Karachi 19, Pakistan. Ed. Syed Wali Ahmad Maulai. adv. stat. circ. 5,000.

658.91 US
RESORTS & PARKS PURCHASING GUIDE. 1965. a. Klevens Publications, Inc., 7600 Ave. V, Littlerock, CA 93543. adv.
Formerly: Resorts & R V Parks Purchasing Guide.

647 US ISSN 0098-4507
SAV-ON-HOTELS. Cover title: Sav-on-Hotels Across Europe. a. $3. Traveltips, Box 11061, Oakland, CA 94611.

919.6 FJ
STATISTICS ON TOURISM AND HOTEL INDUSTRY IN FIJI. (Text in English) 1969. a. $1.25. Bureau of Statistics, Box 2221, Suva, Fiji. stat. circ. 500.
Incorporating: Statistics on Visitor and Other Arrivals & Statistics on the Hotel Industry in Fiji.

642.5 US
TABLE SERVICE RESTAURANT OPERATIONS; annual study of the financial performance of restaurants. 1976. a. free. (National Restaurant Association) Laventhol & Horwath, 1845 Walnut St., Philadelphia, PA 19103. charts. circ. 10,000.
Formerly: Restaurant Operations.

642.5 US
TABLESERVICE RESTAURANT OPERATIONS REPORT. a. National Restaurant Association, 1 IBM Plaza, Suite 2600, Chicago, IL 60611.

TRAVELER'S DIRECTORY OF FAST-FOOD RESTAURANTS. see *TRAVEL AND TOURISM*

647 TU
TURKEY: HOTELS-CAMPING. (Text in English, French, German, Italian and Turkish) 1964. a. free. Ministry of Tourism and Information - Turizm ve Tanitma Bakanligi, Gazi Mustafa Kemal Bulvari 33, Ankara, Turkey. adv. circ. 20,000.
Formerly: Hotel Guide to Turkey.

658.91 US ISSN 0361-2198
U. S. LODGING INDUSTRY; annual report on hotel and motor hotel operations. 1932. a. free. Laventhol & Horwath, 1845 Walnut St., Philadelphia, PA 19103. charts. circ. 20,000.
Formerly: Lodging Industry.

642.56 CN ISSN 0706-5302
VANCOUVER GASTRONOMIC. 1977. a. $5 per no. Apogee Enterprises Ltd, Box 48525, Sta. Bentall, Vancouver, B.C. V7X 1A2, Canada.

647.94 UK ISSN 0083-6273
VILLA GUIDE. 1970. a. 25p. Villa Guide Ltd., 51 Brompton Road, London, SW3, England.
Formerly: Euro Property.

642.5 915 SI
WHERE TO EAT & ENTERTAIN-SINGAPORE. 1980. a. S.$4. Times Directories Private Ltd., 530 Cuppage Centre, 55 Cuppage Rd., Singapore 0922, Singapore. circ. 12,000.

642 917.1 CN ISSN 0315-3088
WHERE TO EAT IN CANADA. 1971. a. $8.95. Oberon Press, 401a Inn of the Provinces, Ottawa, Ont. K1R 7S8, Canada. Ed. Anne Hardy.

647.95 UK ISSN 0083-9205
WHERE TO EAT IN LONDON. 1939. a. 60p. Regency Press, 43 New Oxford St., London WC1A 1BH, England.

338.4 US ISSN 0361-218X
WORLDWIDE LODGING INDUSTRY; annual report on international hotel operations. 1971. a. free. Laventhol & Horwath, 1845 Walnut St., Philadelphia, PA 19103. charts. circ. 12,000.

647.94 CN
WRIGLEY'S HOTEL-MOTEL DIRECTORY. 1910. a. Can.$8.50. Wrigley Directories Ltd., 7385 Laburnum St., Vancouver, B.C. V6P 5N2, Canada. adv.

647 YU
YUGOSLAVIA; HOTEL AND TOURIST DIRECTORY. Spine title: Hotelsko-Turisticki Adresar. (Text in English, French, German, Serbocroatian) irreg. Privredni Pregled, Marsala Birjuzova 3, Belgrade, Yugoslavia. illus.

HOTELS AND RESTAURANTS — Abstracting, Bibliographies, Statistics

647.94 310 JO
JORDAN. DEPARTMENT OF STATISTICS. HOTEL STATISTICS. (Text in Arabic and English) 1975. a. $5. Department of Statistics, Amman, Jordan.

HOUSING AND URBAN PLANNING

see also *Building and Construction; Real Estate*

352.7 US
ALABAMA PLANNING RESOURCE CHECKLIST; county/counties and substate planning and development districts in Alabama. 1976. a. $25. Development Office, State Capitol, Montgomery, AL 36130. (Co-sponsor: U.S. Department of Housing and Urban Development) Ed. Mark Worsham. bibl. cum.index. circ. 275. (back issues avail.)

711 AT ISSN 0310-7299
ALBURY/WODONGA. 1973-1974 (no. 11) irreg. free. Victoria Town and Country Planning Board, 235 Queen St., Melbourne, Vic. 3000, Australia.

624 US ISSN 0569-8081
AMERICAN SOCIETY OF CIVIL ENGINEERS. URBAN PLANNING AND DEVELOPMENT DIVISION. JOURNAL. Short title: Urban Planning and Development. 1956. irreg.(2-3/yr.) $15 to non-members. American Society of Civil Engineers, 345 E. 47th St., New York, NY 10017. circ. 4,400. (reprint service avail. from UMI)

352.7 301.15 949.5 GR
ANCIENT GREEK CITIES REPORT. 1971. irreg., no. 24, 1978. price varies. Athens Center of Ekistics, 24, Strat. Syndesmou St., Box 471, Athens 136, Greece.

352.7 360 FR
ANNUAIRE H L M. (Habitations a Loyer Modere) Short title: Guide Annuaire des H.L.M. 1968. a. 180 F. Union Nationale des Federations d'Organismes d'Habitations a Loyer Modere, 14 rue Lord Byron, 75008 Paris, France. adv. index. circ. 5,600.

350.865 AG
ARGENTINA. CAJA FEDERAL DE AHORRO Y PRESTAMO PARA LA VIVIENDA. MEMORIA Y BALANCE. a. free. Caja Federal de Ahorro y Prestamo para la Vivienda, Alsina 301 E.P., Buenos Aires, Argentina. Dir. Salomon Herman. charts. stat.

388.3 US
ARIZONA MOBILE HOME & RECREATIONAL VEHICLE PARK GUIDE. 1956. a. $4.50. ‡ Arizona Trailer Publications, 4110 E. Van Buren, Phoenix, AZ 85008. Ed. Ruth C. Kaseman. adv. circ. 10,000.
Formerly: Arizona Trailer Guide.

711 GR ISSN 0067-0073
ATHENS CENTER OF EKISTICS. RESEARCH REPORT. 1967. irreg., latest no. 13, 1973. price varies. Athens Center of Ekistics, 24, Strat. Syndesmou Street, P.O. Box 471, Athens 136, Greece. circ. 250-300.

711 AT ISSN 0067-1517
AUSTRALIA. NATIONAL CAPITAL DEVELOPMENT COMMISSION. ANNUAL REPORT. 1958. a. price varies. ‡ National Capital Development Commission, Box 373, Canberra City, A.C.T. 2601, Australia. circ. 2,500.

352.7 CN
B. C. PLANNING PAPERS. 1981. irreg. University of British Columbia, School of Community and Regional Planning, Vancouver, B.C. V6T 1W5, Canada.
Supersedes: University of British Columbia. School of Community and Regional Planning. Planning Papers; Formerly: University of British Columbia. School of Community and Regional Planning. Occasional Papers.

352.7 BL
BANCO NACIONAL DA HABITACAO. RELATORIO DE ATIVIDADES. irreg. Banco Nacional da Habitacao, Secretaria de Divulgacao, Av. Republica do Chile 230, Rio de Janeiro, Brazil. charts. stat.

352.7 SZ
BERICHTE ZUR ORTS- , REGIONAL- UND LANDESPLANUNG. 1968. irreg. price varies. Eidgenoessische Technische Hochschule Zuerich, Institut fuer Orts-, Regional- und Landesplanung - Swiss Federal Institute of Technology, Institute for Local, Regional and National Planning, Hoenggerberg HIL, 8093 Zurich, Switzerland.

352.7 IT
BIBLIOTECA MARSILIO: ARCHITETTURA E URBANISTICA. no. 26, 1974. irreg. $8300. Biblioteca Marsilio, Marsilio, Padua, Italy. bibl. charts. stat.

309.26 BL
BRAZIL. SUPERINTENDENCIA DO DESENVOLVIMENTO DO NORDESTE. SUDENE PLANO DE ACAO. Cover title: SUDENE Plano de Acao. irreg. Superintendencia do Desenvolvimento do Nordeste, Av. Prof. Moraes Rego, Cidade Universitaria, Recife-PE, Brazil. illus.
Regional planning

352.7 BG
C U S BULLETIN. (Text in English) biennial. Centre for Urban Studies, c/o Dept. of Geography, University of Dacca, Ramna, Dacca 2, Bangladesh.

HOUSING AND URBAN PLANNING

352　　　　　CN　ISSN 0226-0336
CANADA MORTGAGE AND HOUSING
CORPORATION. ANNUAL REPORT. a. Canada
Mortgage and Housing Corporation, Montreal Rd.,
Ottawa, Ont. K1A 0P7, Canada.
　　Formerly: Central Mortgage and Housing
Corporation. Annual Report.

711　　　　　AT
CARLTON NEWSLETTER. 1967. irreg. Aus.$2.
Carlton Association, P.O. Box 52, North Carlton,
Vic. 3054, Australia. Ed. Richard Malone.

352.7　　　　　US
CENTRAL MISSISSIPPI PLANNING AND
DEVELOPMENT DISTRICT. ANNUAL
REPORT. a. free. Central Mississippi Planning and
Development District, 2675 River Ridge Rd., Box
2470, Jackson, MS 39205. Ed. Kathy Pearson.

711　　　　　UK　ISSN 0069-1925
CENTRE FOR ENVIRONMENTAL STUDIES,
LONDON. INFORMATION PAPER. 1968. irreg.
Centre for Environmental Studies, 62 Chandos
Place, London WC2N 4HH, England. circ. 500.
City planning

CENTRE FOR ENVIRONMENTAL STUDIES,
LONDON. OCCASIONAL PAPER. see
ENVIRONMENTAL STUDIES

352.946　　　　　VE
CENTRO DE ESTUDIOS URBANOS.
CUADERNOS. irreg. Centro de Estudios Urbanos,
Apdo. 14559, Caracas, Venezuela.

338.4　　　　　FR
CHAMBRE DE COMMERCE ET D'INDUSTRIE
DE PARIS. CONTRIBUTION DES
EMPLOYEURS A L'EFFORT DE
CONSTRUCTION. irreg. free. Chambre de
Commerce et d'Industrie de Paris, 27 Av. de
Driedland, 75008 Paris, France.

352.7　　　　　UK　ISSN 0260-4086
CHARTERED INSTITUTE OF PUBLIC FINANCE
AND ACCOUNTANCY. HOUSING ESTIMATE
STATISTICS. 1975. a. £5. Chartered Institute of
Public Finance and Accountancy, 1 Buckingham
Place, London SW1E 6HS, England. (back issues
avail.)

352.7　　　　　UK　ISSN 0307-0468
CHARTERED INSTITUTE OF PUBLIC FINANCE
AND ACCOUNTANCY. HOUSING
MAINTENANCE & MANAGEMENT.
ACTUALS STATISTICS. 1967. a. £10. Chartered
Institute of Public Finance and Accountancy, 1
Buckingham Place, London SW1E 6HS, England.
(back issues avail.)

711.59　　　　　SP　ISSN 0069-5068
COLECCION CIENCIA URBANISTICA. irreg.
(Laboratorio de Urbanismo de la Escuela Tecnica
Superior de Arquitectura de Barcelona) Editorial
Gustavo Gili, S.A., Rosellon 87-89, Apdo. de
Correos 35.149, Barcelona 29, Spain.

711　　　　　MX
COLECCION PROYECTO Y PLANIFICACION.
irreg. Ediciones G. Gili, S.A., Amores 2027-Colonia
del Valle, Apartado Postal 73-339, Mexico 12, D.F.,
Mexico.

350.086　　　　　IT
COLLANA DI STUDI SU PROBLEMI
URBANISTICI FIORENTINO. no. 2, 1974. irreg.
L.5500. Ufficio della Provincia, Florence, Italy. bibl.
illus.

COLUMBIA UNIVERSITY. CENTER FOR
ADVANCED RESEARCH IN URBAN AND
ENVIRONMENTAL AFFAIRS. WORKING
PAPERS. see *SOCIOLOGY*

352.7　　　　　US
CONDOMINIUM DEVELOPMENT GUIDE
(SUPPLEMENT) supplements issued periodically to
update base volume. $27.50 for base volume.
Warren, Gorham and Lamont, Inc., 210 South St.,
Boston, MA 02111.

CONSTRUCTION INDUSTRY EUROPE. see
BUILDING AND CONSTRUCTION

352　　　　　BL
CONTRIBUICOES EM DESENVOLVIMENTO
URBANO. irreg. Editora Campus Ltda (Subsidiary
of: Elsevier North-Holland Inc.) Rua Japeri 35,
20000 Rio de Janeiro R.J., Brazil.

333.77　　　　　US
CORNELL UNIVERSITY. PROGRAM IN URBAN
AND REGIONAL STUDIES. OCCASIONAL
PAPERS. 1974. irreg., no. 10, 1980. Cornell
University, Program in Urban and Regional Studies,
209 W. Sibley Hall, Ithaca, NY 14853.
　　Supersedes (as of 1976): Cornell University.
Center for Urban Development Research.
Occasional Papers.

352.7　333.77　　　　　US
CORNELL UNIVERSITY. PROGRAM IN URBAN
AND REGIONAL STUDIES. RESEARCH
REPORTS. 1955. irreg., latest 1981. Cornell
University, Program in Urban and Regional Studies,
209 W. Sibley Hall, Ithaca, NY 14853.
　　Supersedes (as of 1970): Cornell University.
Center for Housing and Environmental Studies.
Research Reports (ISSN 0070-0061)

333.77　　　　　UK　ISSN 0143-8190
COUNTRYSIDE PLANNING YEARBOOK. 1980. a.
£9.50($21.85) paperback;£12.50($28.75) hardcover.
Geo Books, c/o Geo Abstracts Ltd., University of
East Anglia, Norwich NR4 7TJ, England. Ed. A.
W. Gilg.

350.086　　　　　US
CURRENT CONSTRUCTION REPORTS:
HOUSING UNITS AUTHORIZED FOR
DEMOLITION IN PERMIT-ISSUING PLACES.
(Series C-45) 1968. a. price varies. U.S. Bureau of
the Census, Publications Dist. Section, Washington,
DC 20233. stat. circ. 500. (also avail. in microfiche)

301.5　　　　　US
CURRENT HOUSING REPORTS. $3.60. U.S.
Bureau of the Census, Washington, DC 20233
(Combined subscription for H-111 and H-121
available from: Supt. of Documents, Washington,
DC 20402, Other reports in the series available
from Bureau's Subscriber Services Section)

352　301.5　　　　　US　ISSN 0498-8450
CURRENT HOUSING REPORTS: HOUSING
CHARACTERISTICS. (Series H-121) irreg. $3.60
(with H-111: Housing Vacancies) U.S. Bureau of the
Census, U.S. Dept. of Commerce, Washington, DC
20233 (Subsciptions to: Supt. of Documents,
Washington, DC 20402)

301.5　　　　　US　ISSN 0498-8469
CURRENT HOUSING REPORTS: HOUSING
VACANCIES. Quarterly reports are titled: Housing
Units in the United States. Annual reports are titled:
Vacancy Rates and Characteristics of Housing in
the United States. (Series H-111) quarterly and
annual. $3.60 with H-121. U.S. Bureau of the
Census, Washington, DC 20233 (Subsciptions to:
Supt. of Documents, Washington, DC 20402)

D M G OCCASIONAL PAPERS. see
ARCHITECTURE

352.7　　　　　US
D P E D NEWSLETTER. irreg. free. Department of
Planning and Economic Development, Box 2359,
Honolulu, HI 96804.

DESIGN RESEARCH INTERACTIONS. see
ARCHITECTURE

712　711　　　　　NE
DEVELOPMENTS IN LANDSCAPE
MANAGEMENT AND URBAN PLANNING.
1975. irreg., vol. 3, 1976. price varies. Elsevier
Scientific Publishing Co., Box 211, 1000 AE
Amsterdam, Netherlands.

301.35　　　　　US　ISSN 0362-4366
DIRECTORY: COMMUNITY DEVELOPMENT
EDUCATION AND TRAINING PROGRAMS
THROUGHOUT THE WORLD. irreg. $2.
Community Development Society, 720 Clark Hall,
University of Missouri, Columbia, MO 65201.

352.7　　　　　US
DIRECTORY OF HOUSING COOPERATIVES IN
THE UNITED STATES. irreg. $5 to individuals;
institutions $50. National Association of Housing
Cooperatives, 1012 14th St. N.W., Washington, DC
20005.

301.5　　　　　AT
DIRECTORY: RESEARCH IN HOUSING -
AUSTRALIA AND NEW ZEALAND. (Subseries
of: Ian Buchan Fell Research Project on Housing.
Report) irreg. Aus.$2. Ian Buchan Fell Research
Project on Housing, Sydney, Australia.

DISCUSSIONS IN ENVIRONMENTAL HEALTH
PLANNING. see *ENVIRONMENTAL STUDIES*

301.54　　　　　FR　ISSN 0081-1262
FEDERATION NATIONALE DES SOCIETES
D'ECONOMIE MIXTE DE CONSTRUCTION,
D'AMENAGEMENT ET DE RENOVATION.
ANNUAIRE. (Special number of Collectivites et
Habitations) 1965. triennial. Federation Nationale
des Societes d'Economie Mixte de Construction,
d'Amenagement et de Renovation, 66 Bld.
Malesherbes, 75008 Paris, France. adv.

331.83　　　　　FJ
FIJI. HOUSING AUTHORITY. REPORT. (Subseries
of: Fiji Parliament. Parliamentary Paper) 1959. a.
$1.50. Housing Authority, Box 1263, Suva, Fiji.
circ. 550.

301.5　　　　　US
FLORIDA. DIVISION OF LOCAL RESOURCE
MANAGEMENT. COMMUNITY PROGRAM
DEVELOPMENT AND MANAGEMENT
SERIES. 1973. irreg., no. 22, 1978. Department of
Veteran and Community Affairs, Division of Local
Resource Management, 2571 Executive Center
Circle East, Tallahassee, FL 32301.

301.5　　　　　US
FLORIDA. DIVISION OF LOCAL RESOURCE
MANAGEMENT. TECHNICAL PAPER SERIES.
1978? irreg., no.9, 1979. free. Department of
Veteran and Community Affairs, Division of Local
Resource Management, 2571 Executive Center
Circle, East, Tallahassee, FL 32301.

309.2　　　　　US
FLORIDA. DIVISION OF STATE PLANNING.
ANNUAL REPORT ON STATE AND
REGIONAL PLANNING. 1973. a. free.
Department of Administration, Division of State
Planning, 660 Apalachee Pkwy., Tallahassee, FL
32301.

301.5　　　　　US　ISSN 0091-9942
FLORIDA. GOVERNOR. ANNUAL REPORT ON
STATE HOUSING GOALS. Title varies: Housing
in Florida. 1973. a. free. Department of Veteran and
Community Affairs, Division of Local Resource
Management, 2571 Executive Center Circle, East,
Tallahassee, FL 32301. (back issues avail.)

352.7　　　　　US
FLORIDA HOUSING AND COMMUNITY
DEVELOPMENT SERIES. 1977. irreg., latest no.
8. Department of Veteran and Community Affairs,
Division of Local Resource Management, 2571
Executive Center Circle, East, Tallahassee, FL
32301.
　　Formed by the merger of: Florida Housing
Assistance Series & Florida Housing Rehabilitation
Series.

350　　　　　GW　ISSN 0341-244X
FORSCHUNGEN ZUR RAUMENTWICKLUNG.
1975. irreg. vol. 7, 1978. price varies.
Bundesforschungsanstalt fuer Landeskunde und
Raumordnung, Am Michaelshof 8, Postfach 200130,
5300 Bonn 2, W. Germany(B.R.D.)
　　Formerly(1953-1974): Institut fuer Raumordnung.
Mitteilungen.

GA HOUSES. see *ARCHITECTURE*

350　　　　　GW
GESELLSCHAFT FUER
REGIONALFORSCHUNG.
SEMINARBERICHTE. irreg., no.10,1974.
Gesellschaft fuer Regionalforschung, Spanische
Allee 95E, 1000 Berlin 38, W. Germany (B.R.D.)
Ed. Herwig Birg.

GOLD BOOK OF MULTI HOUSING. see
BUILDING AND CONSTRUCTION

HOUSING AND URBAN PLANNING

690 UK
GREAT BRITAIN. DEPARTMENT OF THE ENVIRONMENT. HOUSING AND CONSTRUCTION. DESIGN BULLETIN. 1962. irreg. price varies. Department of the Environment, Housing and Construction, 2 Marsham St., London SW1P 3EB, England (Avail. from H.M.S.O., c/o Liaison Officer, Atlantic House, Holborn Viaduct, London EC1P 1BN, England)
Formerly: Great Britain. Ministry of Housing and Local Government. Design Bulletin (ISSN 0085-1191)

711 UK
GREAT BRITAIN. DEPARTMENT OF THE ENVIRONMENT. HOUSING AND CONSTRUCTION. PLANNING BULLETIN. 1962. irreg. price varies. Department of the Environment, Housing and Construction., 2 Marsham St., London SW1P 3EB, England (Avail. from H.M.S.O., c/o Liaison Officer, Atlantic House, Holborn Viaduct, London EC1P 1BN, England)
Formerly: Great Britain. Ministry of Housing and Local Government. Planning Bulletin (ISSN 0072-6796)

711 352 UK ISSN 0072-6818
GREAT BRITAIN. DEPARTMENT OF THE ENVIRONMENT. STATISTICS FOR TOWN AND COUNTRY PLANNING. SERIES 1. (Joint publication with the Welsh Office) 1969. irreg. price varies. Department of the Environment, 2 Marsham St., London SW1P 3EB, England (Avail. from H.M.S.O., c/o Liaison Officer, Atlantic House, Holborn Viaduct, London EC1P 1BN, England)

711 352 UK ISSN 0072-6826
GREAT BRITAIN. DEPARTMENT OF THE ENVIRONMENT. STATISTICS FOR TOWN AND COUNTRY PLANNING. SERIES 2. (Joint publication with the Welsh Office) 1968. irreg. price varies. Department of the Environment, 2 Marsham St., London SW1P 3EB, England (Avail. from H.M.S.O., c/o Liaison Officer, Atlantic House, Holborn Viaduct, London EC1P 1BN, England)

301.54 FR
GUIDE DE L'HABITAT ET DE L'AMENAGEMENT RURAL. 1967. a. Federation Nationale de l'Habitat Rural et de l'Amenagement du Territoire Rural, 27 rue La Rochefoucauld, 75009 Paris, France.
Former titles: Guide de l'Habitat Rural; Annuaire des Organismes d'Habitat Rural (ISSN 0066-2917)

301.363 US
HARVARD STUDIES IN URBAN HISTORY. irreg. price varies. Harvard University Press, 79 Garden St., Cambridge, MA 02138.

333.7 KE
HIGHLANDS FIELD STATION REPORT. 1978. irreg., latest no. 2. University of Nairobi, Department of Urban and Regional Planning, Box 30197, Nairobi, Kenya.

352.7 US
HOUSING. 1972. irreg. price varies. A M S Press, Inc., 56 E. 13th St., New York, NY 10003. Eds. George Sternlieb, Lynne B. Sagalyn. bibl. charts. stat. cum. index 1970-0974.

711 331.83 US ISSN 0073-3652
HOUSING AND URBAN DEVELOPMENT LEGISLATION IN NEW YORK STATE. 1950. a. free. Community Service Society of New York, Committee on Housing and Urban Development, 105 East 22nd St., New York, NY 10010. circ. 2,000.
Supersedes: Housing Legislation in New York State.

352.7 332 KE
HOUSING FINANCE COMPANY OF KENYA. ANNUAL REPORT AND ACCOUNTS. 1970. a. Housing Finance Company of Kenya, Rehani House, Kenyatta Ave., Box 30088, Nairobi, Kenya.

I U L A (PUBLICATION) (International Union of Local Authorities) see PUBLIC ADMINISTRATION

352.7 US ISSN 0090-3248
ILLINOIS. HOUSING DEVELOPMENT AUTHORITY. ANNUAL REPORT. 1970. a. free. Housing Development Authority, 130 E. Randolph, Suite 510, Chicago, IL 60601. Ed. Don Rose. charts. illus. stat. circ. 5,000.

711 352 IT ISSN 0019-3399
INCHIESTE DI URBANISTICA E ARCHITETTURA; rivista di studi e informazioni. 1957. irreg. L.3000. Istituto Editoriale Pubblicazioni Internazionali, Piazza Ruggero di Sicilia 1, 00162 Rome, Italy. Ed. Salvo Tomaselli. adv. bk. rev. bibl. charts. illus.

331.83 IO
INDONESIA. DIREKTORAT PERUMAHAN RAKJAT. LAPORAN KERDJA. 1970. a. free. Direktorat Perumahan Rakjat, Jalan Wijaya I/68, Kebayoran Baru, Jakarta, Indonesia. circ. controlled.

INSTITUT ZA ARHITEKTURU I URBANIZAM SRBIJE. ZBORNIK RADOVA. see ARCHITECTURE

711 AG ISSN 0074-0330
INSTITUTO TORCUATO DI TELLA. CENTRO DE ESTUDIOS URBANOS REGIONALES. DOCUMENTOS DE TRABAJO. 1969. irreg. price varies. Instituto Torcuato di Tella, Conde 1717, Buenos Aires, Argentina. circ. 200.

301.5 NE
INTERNATIONAL FEDERATION FOR HOUSING AND PLANNING. DIRECTORY. (Text in English, French or German) 1972. irreg. membership. ‡ International Federation for Housing and Planning, Wassenaarseweg 43, 2596 CG The Hague, Netherlands. circ. 2,000(controlled)
Former titles: International Federation for Housing and Planning. Yearbook; International Federation for Housing and Planning. List of Members.

333.77 US
INTERNATIONAL STUDIES IN PLANNING. 1978. irreg. Cornell University, Program in Urban and Regional Studies, 209 W. Sibley Hall, Ithaca, NY 14853. (Co-sponsor: Cornell University Department of City and Regional Planning, Program on International Studies in Planning)

711 JA ISSN 0074-8897
INTERNATIONAL SYMPOSIUM ON REGIONAL DEVELOPMENT. PAPERS AND PROCEEDINGS. (Text in English) 1967. irreg., 1974, 4th. 3700 Yen. Japan Center for Area Development Research - Nihon Chiiki Kaihatsu Senta, Iino Bldg., 2-1-1 Uchisaiwaicho, Chiyoda-ku, Tokyo 100, Japan. circ. 500.

301.54 IS ISSN 0075-109X
ISRAEL. CENTRAL BUREAU OF STATISTICS. SURVEY OF HOUSING CONDITIONS. (Subseries of its Special Series) (Text in Hebrew and English) 1963. irreg., latest issue, no. 533, 1974. I£160. Central Bureau of Statistics, Box 13015, Jerusalem, Israel.

JERUSALEM URBAN STUDIES. see SOCIOLOGY

309.26 US ISSN 0075-3947
JOINT CENTER FOR URBAN STUDIES. PUBLICATIONS. irreg. Harvard University Press, 79 Garden St., Cambridge, MA 02138. (Co-publisher: M I T Press)

301.36 US ISSN 0098-5244
JOINT CENTER FOR URBAN STUDIES. RESEARCH REPORT FROM M I T-HARVARD. 1972. irreg. Joint Center for Urban Studies, 53 Church St., Cambridge, MA 02138. Ed. Charlotte Moore. circ. 1,200. Key Title: Research Report from M I T-Harvard Joint Center for Urban Studies.

352.7 JA
JUTAKU SANGYO HANDOBUKKU; handbook for Japanese housing industry. (Text in Japanese) 1976. a. 2800 Yen($12.50) Jutaku Sangyo Johoh Services, 23 Mori Bldg., 1-23-7, Toranomon, Minato-ku, Tokyo 105, Japan. Ed. Tsuneshi Miwa. adv. (back issues avail)

354.4 SW ISSN 0022-7293
K B S-RAPPORTER. 1961. irreg. (5-15/yr.) price varies. Byggnadsstyrelsen - National Board of Public Building, S-106 43 Stockholm, Sweden.

352.7 KE
KENYA. MINISTRY OF HOUSING. ANNUAL REPORT. 1967. a. Government Printing and Stationery Department, P.O. Box 30128, Nairobi, Kenya.
Supersedes in part: Kenya. Ministry of Health and Housing. Annual Report (ISSN 0075-5877)

350.865 KE
KENYA. NATIONAL HOUSING CORPORATION. ANNUAL REPORT. a. EAs.4. National Housing Corporation, Box 30257, Nairobi, Kenya. charts. illus. stat.

LEGAL SERVICES OCCASIONAL. see LAW

309.26 UK ISSN 0076-0633
LONDON PAPERS IN REGIONAL SCIENCE. 1969. irreg. price varies. Pion Ltd., 207 Brondesbury Park, London NW2 5JN, England (Dist. by: Methuen Ltd., 11 New Fetter Lane, London EC4P 4EE, England and Methuen Inc., 733 Third Ave., New York, NY 10017)

352 UK ISSN 0024-6158
LONDON SOCIETY. JOURNAL. 1913. a. £2. London Society, City University, Room G307, St. John St., London EC1V 4PB, England. bk. rev. illus. index. Indexed: Br.Hum.Ind.

352.7 US
M S H D A REVIEW. 1978. irreg. free. State Housing Development Authority, Office of Communications, Box 30044, Lansing, MI 48909. Ed. Larrestine M. Trimm. illus.

331.83 MW ISSN 0581-0892
MALAWI HOUSING CORPORATION. ANNUAL REPORT AND ACCOUNTS. 1964. a. Malawi Housing Corporation, Box 414, Blantyre, Malawi.

MAN-ENVIRONMENT SYSTEMS/FOCUS SERIES. see ENVIRONMENTAL STUDIES

331.83 US ISSN 0076-499X
MASSACHUSETTS HOUSING FINANCE AGENCY. ANNUAL REPORT. 1969. a. free. Massachusetts Housing Finance Agency, Old City Hall, 45 School St., Boston, MA 02108. Ed. Joy Conway. circ. 7,000.

352.7 SP
MATERIALES DE LA CIUDAD. irreg. Editorial Gustavo Gili, S.A., Rosellon 87-89, Barcelona 15, Spain.

333 711 MF ISSN 0076-552X
MAURITIUS. MINISTRY OF HOUSING, LANDS AND TOWN AND COUNTRY PLANNING. ANNUAL REPORTS. a. price varies. Government Printing Office, Elizabeth II Ave., Port Louis, Mauritius.

361 US
MICHIGAN HOUSING MARKET INFORMATION SYSTEM MONOGRAPH SERIES. (Subseries of: Michigan. Department of Social Services. D S S Publication) 1975. irreg. State Housing Development Authority, Plaza One, Fourth Fl., 401 S. Washington Square, Box 30044, Lansing, MI 48909. stat.

353.9 US
MICHIGAN STATE HOUSING DEVELOPMENT AUTHORITY. ANNUAL REPORT. 1970. a. State Housing Development Authority, Plaza One, Fourth Floor, 401 South Washington Square, Box 30044, Lansing, MI 48909. illus. stat.

352.7 US
MODERN CONSTRUCTION FORMS (SUPPLEMENT) supplements issued periodically to update base volume. $37.50 for base volume. Warren, Gorham and Lamont, Inc., 210 South St., Boston, MA 02111.

352.7 BO
MONOGRAFIAS URBANAS. 1975. irreg. $12. Centro de Investigaciones Sociales, Casilla 6931 - Correo Central, La Paz, Bolivia.

309.2 NO ISSN 0085-4263
N I B R RAPPORT. (Text in Norwegian; summaries in English) 1965. irreg. price varies. Norsk Institutt for By- og Regionforskning - Norwegian Institute of Urban and Regional Research, Nycoveien 1, Box 15 Grefsen, Oslo 4, Norway.

301.36 US
NATIONAL URBAN LEAGUE ANNUAL REPORT. a. $1. National Urban League, 500 E. 62nd St., New York, NY 10021. illus.
Formerly: National Urban League Progress Report (ISSN 0098-7735)

HOUSING AND URBAN PLANNING

301.5   NE
NETHERLANDS. MINISTERIE VAN VOLKSHUISVESTING EN RUIMTELIJKE ORDENING. AFDELING VOORLICHTING. CURRENT TRENDS AND POLICIES IN HOUSING AND BUILDING. Variant title: Netherlands - Current Trends and Policies in Housing and Building. (Text in English) irreg (latest 1975) Ministerie van Volkshuisvesting en Ruimtelijke Ordening, Afdeling Voorlichting - Ministry of Housing and Physical Planning, Information Department, The Hague, Netherlands.

352.7   AT
NEW SOUTH WALES. COMMONWEALTH HOUSING COMMISSION. ANNUAL REPORT. a. Commonwealth Housing Commission, Sydney, N.S.W., Australia. illus.

NEW YORK STATE BUSINESS FACT BOOK. PART 2: POPULATION AND HOUSING. see *BUSINESS AND ECONOMICS — Economic Situation And Conditions*

346   US   ISSN 0550-7006
NORTH CAROLINA. LAWS, STATUTES, ETC. PLANNING LEGISLATION IN NORTH CAROLINA. 1957. biennial. $2. ‡ University of North Carolina at Chapel Hill, Institute of Government, Box 990, Chapel Hill, NC 27514. Ed. Philip P. Green, Jr. Indexed: P.A.I.S.

352.7   US
NORTH CENTRAL REGIONAL CENTER FOR RURAL DEVELOPMENT. RESEARCH REPORT. no. 4, 1976. irreg. North Central Regional Center for Rural Development, 108 Curtiss Hall, Iowa State University, Ames, IA 50011.

711   CK
NOTICIERO I.D.U.N. 1976. irreg. Instituto de Desarrollo Urbano, Division de Documentacion, Comunicacion y Archivo, Apartado Aereo 034176, Bogota, Colombia.

350.086   BL
NUCLEO DE ESTUDOS SOCIAIS PARA HABITACAO E URBANISMO. Variant title: N E U R B. irreg. Pontificia Universidade Catolica do Rio de Janeiro, Nucleo de Estudos Sociais para Habitacao e Urbanismo, Rua Marques de Sao Vicente 209, 20000 Rio de Janeiro, Brazil. Dir. Alexandre Luiz Mandina.

333.77   US
O D C PLANNING REPORTS. no. 86, 1976. irreg. membership. Oahu Development Conference, 119 Merchant St., Honolulu, HI 96813.

333.77   US
OAHU DEVELOPMENT CONFERENCE. ANNUAL REPORT. a. membership. Oahu Development Conference, 119 Merchant St., Honolulu, HI 96813. illus.

711   AU   ISSN 0078-3617
OESTERREICHISCHES INSTITUT FUER RAUMPLANUNG. TAETIGKEITSBERICHT. 1957. a. free. Oesterreichisches Institut fuer Raumplanung, Franz Josefs Kai 27, A-1011 Vienna, Austria. Ed. Michael Sauberer. circ. 1,300.

309.26   301   AU   ISSN 0078-3625
OESTERREICHISCHES INSTITUT FUER RAUMPLANUNG. VEROEFFENTLICHUNGEN. 1957. irreg. price varies. Oesterreichisches Institut fuer Raumplanung, Franz Josefs Kai 27, A-1011 Vienna, Austria. Ed. Michael Sauberer.

301.54   CN   ISSN 0078-4885
ONTARIO. MINISTRY OF HOUSING. ANNUAL REPORT. 1966. a. Can.$1 per no. Ministry of Housing, 56 Wellesley St. W., Toronto, Ont. M7A 2K4, Canada. circ. 2,000.

352.7   PK
PAKISTAN. BUILDING RESEARCH STATION. BIENNIAL REPORT. (Text in English) 1972/1973. biennial. Building Research Station, Ministry of Science and Technology, Council for Works and Housing Research, Karachi, Pakistan.

352.7   PN
PANAMA. MINISTERIO DE VIVIENDA. MEMORIA. a. Instituto de Vivienda y Urbanismo, Panama City, Panama. illus. stat.
     Supersedes (since 1973): Instituto de Vivienda y Urbanismo. Memoria Presentada por el Director General.

301.54   SP   ISSN 0067-4168
PATRONATO MUNICIPAL DE LA VIVIENDA DE BARCELONA. MEMORIA. 1947. a. free. Patronato Municipal de la Vivienda, Plaza F. de Lesseps, 12, Barcelona 6, Spain. Ed. Fernando Aramburo Campoy. bk. rev. index. circ. 1,500.

330.9   US
PENNSYLVANIA JOURNAL OF URBAN ECONOMIC DEVELOPMENT. 1977. irreg. free. Department of Commerce, 415 South Office Bldg., Harrisburg, PA 17120. (Co-sponsor: Pennsylvania Council for Urban Economic Development) Ed. John B. Koller. circ. 200.

352   711   CN
PLAN CANADA. (Text in English and French) 1959. 3-4/yr. Can.$15 to individuals; Can. $25 to institutions. Canadian Institute of Planners, 46 Elgin St., Ste. 30, Ottawa, Ont. K1P 5K6, Canada. Ed. H. Hightower. bk. rev. illus. cum.ind. circ. 3,000.
     Formerly: Plan (ISSN 0032-0544)

309.2   NO
PLAN DATA. 1968. irreg. Kr.175. Norsk Institutt for By- og Regionforskning - Norwegian Institute of Urban and Regional Research, Nycoveien 1, Box 15 Grefsen, Oslo 4, Norway. (looseleaf format)

352.7   CK
PLANEACION REGIONAL. 1974. irreg. exchange. Departamento Administrativo de Planeacion, Oficina 107, Medellin, Colombia. Ed.Bd. charts. stat. circ. 800.

309.2   SI
PLANEWS. 1972. irreg., latest issue, 1975. S.$2 per no. ‡ Singapore Institute of Planners, Box 3600, Singapore, Singapore. Eds. Lee Lai Choo, Ole Johan Dale. illus. circ. 300.
     Formerly: Singapore Institute of Planners. Newsletter.

352.7   MX
PLANIFICACION. irreg. $10. Sociedad Mexicana de Planificacion, Insurgentes sur 1991, Mexico 20, D.F., Mexico. illus.

309.1   NZ
PLANNING RESEARCH INDEX. 1969. a. free. ‡ Town and Country Planning Division, P.O. Box 12041, Wellington North, New Zealand. Ed. M.S. McDonald. abstr. circ. 600.

711.4   PL   ISSN 0079-3493
POLSKA AKADEMIA NAUK. KOMITET PRZESTRZENNEGO ZAGOSPODAROWANIA KRAJU. BIULETYN. 1960. irreg., 1971, no. 65. price varies. Panstwowe Wydawnictwo Naukowe, Ul. Miodowa 10, Warsaw, Poland (Dist. by Ars Polona-Ruch, Krakowskie Przedmiescie 7, Warsaw, Poland) Ed. Michal Kaczorowski. index.

711   PL   ISSN 0079-3507
POLSKA AKADEMIA NAUK. KOMITET PRZESTRZENNEGO ZAGOSPODAROWANIA KRAJU. STUDIA. (Text in Polish, English, French or Russian: summaries in English and Russian) 1961. irreg., 1973, vol. 43. price varies. Panstwowe Wydawnictwo Naukowe, Ul. Miodowa 10, Warsaw, Poland (Dist by Ars Polona-Ruch, Krakowskie Przedmiescie 7, Warsaw, Poland) Ed. Michal Kaczorowski.

POLSKA AKADEMIA NAUK. ODDZIAL W KRAKOWIE. KOMISJA URBANISTYKI I ARCHITEKTURY. TEKA. see *ARCHITECTURE*

312   US   ISSN 0362-5079
POPULATION AND OCCUPIED DWELLING UNITS IN SOUTHEAST MICHIGAN. 1972. a. Southeast Michigan Council of Governments, 800 Book Bldg., Detroit, MI 48226.
     Supersedes: Southeast Michigan Council of Governments. Planning Division. Planning Data. Series C: Population and Occupied Dwelling Units in the Detroit Region. Report.

301.5   PO
PORTUGAL. INSTITUTO NACIONAL DE ESTATISTICA. SERVICOS CENTRAIS. RECENSEAMENTO DA HABITACAO: CONTINENTE E ILHAS ADJACENTES. 1970. irreg. $50. Instituto Nacional de Estatistica, Servicos Centrais, Av. Antonio Jose de Almeida, Lisbon 1, Portugal (Orders to: Imprensa Nacional, Casa da Moeda, Direccao Comercial, rua D. Francisco Manuel de Melo 5, Lisbon 1, Portugal)

350.086   US   ISSN 0163-8602
PRESIDENT'S NATIONAL URBAN POLICY REPORT. 1978. biennial. U.S. Department of Housing and Urban Development, Washington, DC 20410.

240   AU
PROBLEME GRENZNAHER RAEUME. 1973. Universitaet Innsbruck, Institut fuer Staedtebau und Raumordnung, A-6020 Innsbruck, Austria. Ed. Franz Heigl.

711   309.62   US   ISSN 0305-9006
PROGRESS IN PLANNING. 1973. 3/yr. $45. Pergamon Press, Inc., Journals Division, Maxwell House, Fairview Park, Elmsford, NY 10523 (And Headington Hill Hall, Oxford OX3 0BW, England) Eds. D. Diamond, T.B. McLoughlin. (also avail. in microform from MIM,UMI)

352.7   SI
PUBLIC HOUSING IN SINGAPORE: A MULTI-DISCIPLINARY STUDY. irreg. S.$39. Housing and Development Board, National Development Bldg., Maxwell Rd., Singapore 1, Singapore. Ed. Stephen H. K. Yeh. charts. stat.

350.086   PR
PUERTO RICO. DEPARTAMENTO DE LA VIVIENDA. SECRETARIA AUXILIAR DE PLANIFICATION Y PROGRAMACION. INFORME ANUAL. a. Departamento de la Vivienda, Urban Renewal and Housing Corporation, San Juan, Puerto Rico.

711.59   IT
QUADERNI DI RINNOVAMENTO VENETO. 1976. irreg. Marsilio Editori S.p.A., Fondamenta Santa Chiara, Santa Croce 518-A, 30125 Venice, Italy.

352   US
R P A NEWS. 1929. irreg. $4 per no. to non-members. Regional Plan Association, Inc., 235 E. 45th St, New York, NY 10017. Ed. Wm. B. Shore. bk. rev. charts. illus. circ. 3,500. Indexed: P.A.I.S.
     Former titles: R P A Bulletin (ISSN 0483-7738); Regional Plan News (ISSN 0034-3374); Regional Plan Association. News Letter.

352.7   614   SZ
RAUMPLANUNG UND UMWELTSCHUTZ IM KANTON ZURICH. (Text in German) 1964. irreg. free. Amt fuer Raumplanung, Stampfenbach Str. 14, 8090 Zurich, Switzerland. (Co-sponsor: Amt fuer Regionalplanung) bibl. charts. illus.
     Formerly (no. 1-7): Regionalplanung in Kanton Zurich.

309.26   NE
RECHERCHE URBAINE. 1973. irreg. price varies. (Ecole des Hautes Etudes en Sciences Sociales, FR) Mouton Publishers, Noordeinde 41, 2514 GC The Hague, Netherlands (U.S. addr.: Mouton Publishers, c/o Walter de Gruyter, Inc., 200 Saw Mill River Road, Hawthorne, NY 10532)

333.77   US
REGIONAL SCIENCE DISSERTATION AND MONOGRAPH SERIES. 1972. irreg., latest 1981. Cornell University, Program in Urban and Regional Studies, 209 W. Sibley Hall, Ithaca, NY 14853. (Co-sponsor: Cornell University Field of Regional Science)

352   US   ISSN 0034-3420
REGION'S AGENDA. irreg. $0.75 per no. to non-members. Regional Plan Association, Inc., 235 E. 45th St, New York, NY 10017.

HOUSING AND URBAN PLANNING

352.7 JA
REPORT ON URBAN RESEARCH/TOSHI KENKYU HOKOKU. (Text in Japanese) 1969. irreg. free. Tokyo Metropolitan University - Tokyotoritsu Daigaku, 1-1-1 Yakumo, Meguro-ku, Tokyo 152, Japan. illus.

350.865 VE
REVISTA INTERNACIONAL DE VIVIENDA RURAL/INTERNATIONAL RURAL HOUSING JOURNAL. (Text in English and Spanish) 1970. a (with bi-m. supplements) $10. ‡ International Rural Housing Association, Apto. 16224, Caracas, Venezuela. Ed. Arturo R. Ortiz. adv. bk. rev. charts. illus. circ. 6,000.

354 AT ISSN 0310-4923
RURAL RECONSTRUCTION AUTHORITY OF WESTERN AUSTRALIA. ANNUAL REPORT. 1971/72. a. free. Rural Reconstruction Authority of Western Australia, Central Government Building, Barrack Street, Perth, W.A. 6000, Australia. stat.

352 US ISSN 0094-050X
S C A G ANNUAL REPORT. 1967. a. free. ‡ Southern California Association of Governments, 600 S. Commonwealth Ave., Suite 1000, Los Angeles, CA 90005. illus. stat.
Formerly: S C A G: a Record of Accomplishment.

711 AT
S. P. A. N. (State Planning Authority News) 1966. irreg. free. State Planning Authority of New South Wales, G.P.O. Box 3927, Sydney, N.S.W. 2001, Australia.

338.7 CN
SASKATCHEWAN HOUSING CORPORATION. ANNUAL REPORT. 1973. a. free. Saskatchewan Housing Corporation, 2024 Albert St., Regina, Sask. S4P 3P4, Canada. illus. stat.

711.4 338.9 AU ISSN 0558-9746
SCHRIFTENREIHE FUER RAUMFORSCHUNG UND RAUMPLANUNG. 1957. irreg., vol. 17, 1979. Amt der Kaerntner Landesregierung, Abteilung Landesplanung, A-9010 Klagenfurt, Austria. Ed. Oskar Glanzer. circ. 300.
Regional planning

352.7 SZ
SCHRIFTENREIHE ZUR ORTS-, REGIONAL- UND LANDESPLANUNG. 1970. irreg. price varies. Eidgenoessische Technische Hochschule Zuerich Institut fuer Orts- , Regional- und Landesplanung - Swiss Federal Institute of Technology, Institute for Local, Regional and National Planning, Hoenggerberg HIL, 8093 Zurich, Switzerland.

352.7 GW
SIN-STAEDTEBAUINSTITUT. INFORMATION. Short title: S I N Information. irreg. DM.10 per no. SIN-Staedtebauinstitut Forschungsgesellschaft mbH, Neutorgraben 1A, 8500 Nuernberg 111, W. Germany (B.R.D.) (looseleaf format)

352.7 GW
SIN-STAEDTEBAUINSTITUT. JAHRESBERICHTE. Short title: S I N Jahresberichte. a. free. SIN-Staedtebauinstitut Forschungsgesellschaft mbH, Neutorgraben 1A, 8500 Nuernberg 111, W. Germany (B.R.D.)

711 690 GW ISSN 0078-2807
SIN-STAEDTEBAUINSTITUT. SCHRIFTENREIHE. 1965. irreg. price varies. SIN-Staedtebauinstitut Forschungsgesellschaft mbH, Neutorgraben 1A, 8500 Nuernberg 111, W. Germany (B.R.D.) Ed. Gerhard G. Dittrich.

711 690 GW ISSN 0078-2815
SIN-STAEDTEBAUINSTITUT. STUDIENHEFTE. 1965. irreg. price varies. SIN-Staedtebauinstitut Forschungsgesellschaft mbH, Neutorgraben 1A, 8500 Nuernberg 111, W. Germany (B.R.D.) Ed. Gerhard G. Dittrich.

711 690 GW ISSN 0078-2823
SIN-STAEDTEBAUINSTITUT. WERKBERICHTE. 1968. irreg. free. SIN-Staedtebauinstitut Forschungsgesellschaft mbH, Neutorgraben 1A, 8500 Nuernberg 111, W. Germany (B.R.D.) Ed. Gerhard G. Dittrich.

350.086 SI
SINGAPORE. HOUSING AND DEVELOPMENT BOARD. ANNUAL REPORT. (Text in English) 1960. a. S.$12. Housing and Development Board, National Development Building, Maxwell Road, Singapore 1, Singapore. charts. illus. stat. circ. controlled. (back issues avail.)

352.7 SI
SINGAPORE. MINISTRY OF NATIONAL DEVELOPMENT. ANNUAL REPORT. 1975. a. Ministry of National Development, National Development Bldg., Maxwell Rd., Singapore 0106, Singapore. circ. 1,500.

352.7 AG
SOCIEDAD INTERAMERICANA DE PLANIFICACION. EDICIONES SIAP. 1974. irreg. (Sociedad Interamericana de Planificacion) Ediciones S.I.A.P., Chenaut 1968, 1426 Buenos Aires, Argentina (Distrib. by: Ediciones Nueva Vision, Viamonte 494, Buenos Aires, Argentina) Dir. Martha S. de Kaplan. circ. 3,000.

352.7 VE ISSN 0583-7774
SOCIEDAD VENEZOLANA DE PLANIFICACION. CUADERNOS. 1962. irreg. Sociedad Venezolana de Planificacion, Apdo. 10861, Caracas, Venezuela.

352 BE ISSN 0067-5652
SOCIETE NATIONAL DU LOGEMENT. RAPPORT ANNUEL. Dutch edition: Nationale Maatschappij voor de Huisvesting. Jaarverslag (ISSN 0522-7739) 1920 (French edt.; 1934 (Dutch edt.) a. free. Institut National du Logement, Rue Breydel 12, 1040 Brussels, Belgium.

352.7 US
SOUTH ATLANTIC URBAN STUDIES. 1977. a. College of Charleston, Urban Studies Center, Charleston, SC 29401. Eds. Jack R. Censer, N. Steven Steinert.

711 US ISSN 0073-4993
SOUTHERN ILLINOIS UNIVERSITY, EDWARDSVILLE. CENTER FOR URBAN AND ENVIRONMENTAL RESEARCH AND SERVICES. C U E R S. REPORT. 1969. irreg., no. 10, 1979. Southern Illinois University, Edwardsville, Center for Urban and Environmental Research and Services, Edwardsville, IL 62026.

352 711 GW
DIE STADT. 1972. irreg. price varies. SIN-Staedtebauinstitut Forschungsgesellschaft mbH, Neutorgraben 1A, 8500 Nuernberg 111, W. Germany (B.R.D.) Ed. Gerhard G. Dittrich. adv.

352 333 US
STATE OF FLORIDA LAND DEVELOPMENT GUIDE. a. free. Department of Administration, Division of State Planning, Bureau of Comprehensive Planning, 660 Apalachee Pkwy, Tallahassee, FL 32304. charts. illus.

STUDIA I MATERIALY DO TEORII I HISTORII ARCHITEKTURY I URBANISTYKI. see ARCHITECTURE

352.7 SZ
STUDIENUNTERLAGEN ZUR ORTS- , REGIONAL- UND LANDESPLANUNG. 1971. irreg. price varies. Eidgenoessische Technische Hochschule Zuerich, Institut fuer Orts- , Regional- und Landesplanung - Swiss Federal Institute of Technology, Institute for Local, Regional and National Planning, Hoenggerberg HIL, 8093 Zurich, Switzerland.

910 US ISSN 0586-5107
STUDIES IN URBAN GEOGRAPHY. 1969. irreg. price varies. American Geographical Society, 3755 Broadway, New York, NY 10032.

301.364 US ISSN 0081-8801
STUDIES OF URBAN SOCIETY. 1968. irreg., latest 1978. price varies. University of Chicago Press, 5801 S. Ellis Ave., Chicago, IL 60637. Ed. David P. Street. (reprint service avail. from UMI,ISI)

SWEDEN. STATENS RAAD FOER BYGGNADSFORSKNING. DOCUMENT. see BUILDING AND CONSTRUCTION

SWEDEN. STATENS RAAD FOER BYGGNADSFORSKNING. INFORMATIONSBLAD. see BUILDING AND CONSTRUCTION

SWEDEN. STATENS RAAD FOER BYGGNADSFORSKNING. RAPPORT. see BUILDING AND CONSTRUCTION

SWEDEN. STATENS RAAD FOER BYGGNADSFORSKNING. VERKSAMHETSPLAN. see BUILDING AND CONSTRUCTION

352.7 UK
SYMPOSIUM ON URBAN RENEWAL. PAPERS. 1965. irreg. University of Salford, Department of Engineering, Salford, Lancs. M5 4WT, England. Ed. Stanley Millward.

350.086 TZ
TANZANIA. CAPITAL DEVELOPMENT AUTHORITY. REPORT AND ACCOUNTS. 1974. a. EAs.10. Capital Development Authority, Box 913, Dodoma, Tanzania. illus.

354 TZ
TANZANIA. MINISTRY OF LANDS, HOUSING AND URBAN DEVELOPMENT. URBAN PLANNING DIVISION. ANNUAL REPORT. 1974. a. Ministry of Lands, Housing and Urban Development, Urban Planning Division, Box 20671, Dar es Salaam, Tanzania. Ed. I. J. Mitiro.

TECHNICAL UNIVERSITY OF DENMARK. INSTITUTE OF ROADS, TRANSPORT AND TOWN PLANNING. REPORT. see TRANSPORTATION — Roads And Traffic

711 HU ISSN 0040-2680
TELEPULESTUDOMANYI KOZLEMENYEK. (Text in Hungarian; summaries in English, German & Russian) 1952. a. free. (Budapesti Muszaki Egyetem, Varosepitesi Tanszek) Muszaki Konyvkiado, Bajcsy-Zsilinszky Ut 22, 1051 Budapest, Hungary. (Co-sponsors: Magyar Urbanisztikai Tarsasag, Varosepitesi Tudomanyos es Tervezo Intezet) Ed. Dr. Kalman Farago. bk. rev. bibl. charts. illus. circ. 1,030.

309.2 UK ISSN 0308-082X
TOWN AND COUNTRY PLANNING ASSOCIATION. ANNUAL REPORT. a. 75p.($1.80) Town and Country Planning Association, 17 Carlton House Terrace, London SW1Y 5AS, England. (reprint service avail. from UMI)

711 UK ISSN 0078-2114
TOWN AND COUNTRY PLANNING SUMMER SCHOOL; REPORT OF PROCEEDINGS. 1936. a. £3. Royal Town Planning Institute, 26 Portland Place, London W1N 4BE, England. Ed. Margaret Cox. circ. 12,000.

309.2 US
TRI-STATE REGIONAL PLANNING COMMISSION. ANNUAL REGIONAL REPORT. 1971/72. a. ‡ Tri-State Regional Planning Commission, One World Trade Center, New York, NY 10048. circ. 5,000.
Formerly: Tri-State Regional Planning Commission. Annual Regional Report (ISSN 0092-2358)

309.2 US
TRI-STATE REGIONAL PLANNING COMMISSION. REGIONAL PROFILE. 1966. irreg., unnumbered after vol. 3, 1975; latest 1977. Tri-State Regional Planning Commission, One World Trade Center, New York, NY 10048.

352.7 TT
TRUST TERRITORY OF THE PACIFIC ISLANDS. TERRITORIAL HOUSING COMMISSION. ANNUAL REPORT. (Text in English) a. Territorial Housing Commission, Capitol Hill, Saipan 96950, Mariana Islands.

350.865 US ISSN 0565-2820
U. S. DEPARTMENT OF HOUSING AND URBAN DEVELOPMENT. ANNUAL REPORT. 1965. a. U.S. Department of Housing and Urban Development., Washington, DC 20410 (Orders to: Supt. Doc., Washington, DC 20402)

352.7 US
U.S. DEPARTMENT OF HOUSING AND URBAN DEVELOPMENT. OCCASIONAL PAPERS IN HOUSING AND COMMUNITY AFFAIRS. vol. 2, 1978. irreg. U.S. Department of Housing and Urban Development, Washington, DC 20410 (Orders to: NTIS, Springfield, VA 22161)

352.7 US
U.S. DEPARTMENT OF HOUSING AND URBAN DEVELOPMENT. OFFICE OF INTERNATIONAL AFFAIRS. INTERNATIONAL BULLETIN. 1978. irreg. U.S. Department of Housing and Urban Development, 451 Seventh St., S.W., Washington, DC 20410.

352.7 US
U.S. DEPARTMENT OF HOUSING AND URBAN DEVELOPMENT. OFFICE OF INTERNATIONAL AFFAIRS. INTERNATIONAL REVIEW. 1978. irreg. U.S. Department of Housing and Urban Development, 451 Seventh St., S.W., Washington, DC 20410.

301.54 US ISSN 0091-4932
U.S. FEDERAL HOUSING ADMINISTRATION. F H A HOMES; data for states on characteristics of FHA operations under Section 203. 1956. irreg. U. S. Federal Housing Administration, 451 Seventh St., S.W., Washington, DC 20410. stat. circ. 1,500. Key Title: F.H.A. Homes.

350.086 CL
UNIVERSIDAD CATOLICA DE CHILE. INSTITUTO DE PLANIFICACION DEL DESARROLLO URBANO. DOCUMENTOS DE TRABAJO. irreg. price varies. Universidad Catolica de Chile, Instituto de Planificacion del Desarrollo Urbano, Los Navegantes 1919, Casilla 16002-Correo 9, Santiago, Chile.

350.086 PR
UNIVERSIDAD DE PUERTO RICO. GRADUATE SCHOOL OF PLANNING. PLANNING SERIES E. no. 2, 1977. irreg. Editorial Universitaria, Apdo. Postal X, Rio Piedras, San Juan, PR 00931. Dir. Gerardo Navas.

309 711.4 UK ISSN 0067-8953
UNIVERSITY OF BIRMINGHAM. CENTRE FOR URBAN AND REGIONAL STUDIES. OCCASIONAL PAPERS. 1968 N.S. 1981. irreg., no. 3, 1981. University of Birmingham, Centre for Urban and Regional Studies, J. G. Smith Bldg., Box 363, Birmingham B15 2TT, England.

309 711.4 UK ISSN 0067-8961
UNIVERSITY OF BIRMINGHAM. CENTRE FOR URBAN AND REGIONAL STUDIES. URBAN AND REGIONAL STUDIES. 1971. irreg., no. 7, 1976. George Allen & Unwin (Publishers) Ltd., 40 Museum St., London W.C. 1, England.

309 711.4 UK
UNIVERSITY OF BIRMINGHAM. CENTRE FOR URBAN AND REGIONAL STUDIES. WORKING PAPER. irreg., no. 79, 1981. price varies. University of Birmingham, Centre for Urban and Regional Studies, J.G. Smith Bldg., Box 363, Birmingham B15 2TT, England.

309.2 US ISSN 0094-0801
UNIVERSITY OF FLORIDA. GROWTH CONFERENCE. PREPARED PAPERS. 1973. irreg., no. 8, 1977. University of Florida, College of Architecture, Gainesville, FL 32611. stat. Key Title: Prepared Papers - University of Florida Growth Conference.

711 US
UNIVERSITY OF ILLINOIS AT CHICAGO CIRCLE. COLLEGE OF URBAN SCIENCES. OCCASIONAL PAPER SERIES. 1968. irreg. price varies. ‡ University of Illinois at Chicago Circle, College of Urban Sciences, P.O. Box 4348, Chicago, IL 60680. Dir. Ashish K. Sen.
Formerly: University of Illinois at Chicago Circle. Center for Urban Studies. Occasional Paper Series (ISSN 0083-4017)

UNIVERSITY OF OTTAWA. DEPARTMENT OF GEOGRAPHY. OCCASIONAL PAPERS. see *GEOGRAPHY*

309.26 US ISSN 0079-0680
UNIVERSITY OF PENNSYLVANIA. INSTITUTE FOR ENVIRONMENTAL STUDIES. CITY PLANNING SERIES.* University of Pennsylvania, Institute for Environmental Studies, 3400 Walnut St., Philadelphia, PA 19104.

350 711 CN
UNIVERSITY OF TORONTO. DEPARTMENT OF URBAN & REGIONAL PLANNING. PAPERS ON PLANNING & DESIGN. 1971. irreg. University of Toronto, Department of Urban & Regional Planning, Toronto, Ont. M5S 1A1, Canada. Ed. Allen J. Scott.

UNIVERSITY OF WATERLOO. FACULTY OF ENVIRONMENTAL STUDIES. WORKING PAPER SERIES. see *ENVIRONMENTAL STUDIES*

UPPER MIDWEST ECONOMIC STUDY. URBAN REPORT. see *BUSINESS AND ECONOMICS — Economic Situation And Conditions*

711.4 301.3 US ISSN 0083-4688
URBAN AFFAIRS ANNUAL REVIEWS. 1967. biennial. $18.50 for hardcover; softcover $8.95. Sage Publications Inc., 275 S. Beverly Dr., Beverly Hills, CA 90212 (And Sage Publications, Ltd., 28 Banner St., London EC1Y 8QE, England) (back issues avail.)

352.7 US
URBAN AFFAIRS PAPERS. 1976. irreg., no. 3, 1977. $1.50 per no. National Association of Schools of Public Affairs and Administration, 1225 Connecticut Ave., N.W., Suite 306, Washington, DC 20036.

711.4 US
URBAN AND REGIONAL PLANNING SERIES. 1970. irreg., vol. 22, 1980. price varies. Pergamon Press, Inc., Maxwell House, Fairview Park, Elmsford, NY 10523 (And Headington Hill Hall, Oxford OX3 0BW, England)
Regional planning

338.7 JM
URBAN DEVELOPMENT CORPORATION. ANNUAL REPORT. a. free. Urban Development Corporation, 12 Ocean Blvd., Kingston, Jamaica. illus.

352.7 US
URBAN INSIGHTS MONOGRAPH SERIES. 1979. irreg., 5th 1980. Loyola University of Chicago, Center for Urban Policy, 820 N. Michigan Ave., Chicago, IL 60611.

309.2 US ISSN 0092-7481
URBAN INSTITUTE. ANNUAL REPORT. 1969-1970. a. Urban Institute, 2100 M. Street, N. W., Washington, DC 20037. Ed. Chisholm Gentry. circ. 3,000. Key Title: Urban Institute Report.

711 AT
URBAN ISSUES. 1970. irreg. Aus.$5 to libraries. Australian Institute of Urban Studies, Queensland Division, c/o Department of Geography, University of Queensland, St. Lucia, Qld. 4067, Australia (Subscr. address: Hon. Secretary, AIUS (Qld. Division), G.P.O. Box 1989, Brisbane, Qld. 4001, Australia) Ed. J. H. A. Dick. Indexed: Aus.P.A.I.S.

350.086 CN
URBAN ISSUES (WINNIPEG) 1971. irreg. University of Winnipeg, Institute of Urban Studies, 515 Portage Ave., Winnipeg, Man. R3B 2E9, Canada. illus.

352.7 US
URBAN PROBLEMS AND URBAN TECHNOLOGY SERIES. 1973. irreg., vol. 2, 1975. Marcel Dekker, Inc., 270 Madison Ave., New York, NY 10016. Ed. Herbert Fox.

711 AT ISSN 0310-5601
URBANOLOGY. 1971. irreg. University of New South Wales, School of Town Planning, P.O. Box 1, Kensington, NSW 2033, Australia. Ed. J. H. Shaw.

352.7 SZ
VADEMECUM. 1970. biennial. 2 Fr. Eidgenoessische Technische Hochschule Zuerich, Institut fuer Orts-Regional- und Landesplanung - Swiss Federal Institute of Technology, Hoenggerberg HIL, CH-8093 Zurich, Switzerland.

711 FI ISSN 0355-3477
VALTION TEKNILLINEN TUTKIMUSKESKUS. MAANKAYTON LABORATORIO. TIEDONANTO/TECHNICAL RESEARCH CENTRE OF FINLAND. LABORATORY OF LAND USE. REPORT. (Text mainly in Finnish, some in English or Swedish) 1970. irreg. price varies. Valtion Teknillinen Tutkimuskeskus - Technical Research Centre of Finland, Vuorimiehentie 5, 02150 Espoo 15, Finland.

333.9 US ISSN 0085-798X
WASHINGTON UNIVERSITY. INSTITUTE FOR URBAN AND REGIONAL STUDIES. WORKING PAPER. 1967. irreg., 1970, no. 8. price varies. Washington University, Institute for Urban & Regional Studies, St. Louis, MO 63130. circ. 500.

630 US
WORKING PAPERS IN PLANNING. 1979. irreg., latest 1981. Cornell University, Program in Urban and Regional Studies, 209 W. Sibley Hall, Ithaca, NY 14853. (Co-sponsor: Cornell University Department of City and Regional Planning)

309.26 301.364 US ISSN 0084-3520
YALE STUDIES OF THE CITY. 1969. irreg. Yale University Press, 92A Yale Sta., New Haven, CT 06520.

HOUSING AND URBAN PLANNING — Abstracting, Bibliographies, Statistics

352.7 016 BL
BANCO NACIONAL DA HABITACAO. ASSESSORIA TECNICA DE DOCUMENTACAO. BOLETIM BIBLIOGRAFICO. 1976. irreg. Banco Nacional da Habitacao, Assessoria Tecnica de Documentacao, Biblioteca, Av. Chile 230, Rio de Janeiro, Brazil. bibl.
City planning

352.7 016 AT
BIBLIOGRAPHY OF URBAN STUDIES IN AUSTRALIA. 1971. a. Aus.$7.50. Australian Institute of Urban Studies, P.O. Box 809, Canberra City, A.C.T. 2601, Australia. Ed. Sue Sutherland. index. circ. controlled. (back issues avail.)

301.54 CN ISSN 0068-8940
CANADIAN HOUSING STATISTICS. 1955. a with monthly supplements. free. Canada Mortgage and Housing Corporation, Montreal Road, Ottawa, Ont. K1A OP7, Canada.

352.7 UK
CHARTERED INSTITUTE OF PUBLIC FINANCE AND ACCOUNTANCY. HOMELESSNESS STATISTICS. 1980. a. £5. Chartered Institute of Public Finance and Accountancy, 1 Buckingham Place, London SW1E 6HS, England.

352.7 UK ISSN 0260-4078
CHARTERED INSTITUTE OF PUBLIC FINANCE AND ACCOUNTANCY. HOUSING REVENUE ACCOUNTS. ACTUALS STATISTICS. 1951. a. £10. Chartered Institute of Public Finance and Accountancy., 1 Buckingham Place, London SW1E 6HS, England. (back issues avail.)
Formerly: Chartered Institute of Public Finance and Accountancy. Housing Part 2: Revenue Accounts. Actuals Statistics (ISSN 0307-1316)

352.7 UK ISSN 0260-406X
CHARTERED INSTITUTE OF PUBLIC FINANCE AND ACCOUNTANCY. HOUSING RENTS. STATISTICS. 1969. a. £10. Chartered Institute of Public Finance and Accountancy, 1 Buckingham Place, London SW1E 6HS, England. (back issues avail.)
Formerly: Chartered Institute of Public Finance and Accountancy. Housing Part 1: Rents. Actuals Statistics (ISSN 0307-1308)

314   352.7   FI   ISSN 0355-2152
FINLAND. TILASTOKESKUS.
ASUNTOTUOTANTO/FINLAND.
STATISTIKCENTRALEN.
BOSTADSPRODUKTIONEN/FINLAND.
CENTRAL STATISTICAL OFFICE.
PRODUCTION OF DWELLINGS. (Section XVIII
D of Official Statistics of Finland) (Text in Finnish,
Swedish and English) 1968. a. Fmk.14.
Tilastokeskus, Annakatu 44, SF-00100 Helsinki 10,
Finland (Subscr. to: Government Printing Centre,
Box 516, SF-00100 Helsinki 10, Finland)

350.865 312   PH
PHILIPPINES. NATIONAL CENSUS AND
STATISTICS OFFICE. LISTING OF CITIES,
MUNICIPALITIES AND MUNICIPAL
DISTRICTS BY PROVINCE. irreg. P.12($4)
National Census and Statistics Office, Ramon
Magsaysay Blvd., Box 779, Manila, Philippines.

301.54   PL   ISSN 0079-2659
POLAND. GLOWNY URZAD STATYSTYCZNY.
ROCZNIK STATYSTYCZNY GOSPODARSKI
MIESZKANIOWEJ I KOMUNALNEJ. (Subseries
of its: Statystyka Polski) 1967. irreg. 39 Zl. Glowny
Urzad Statystyczny, Al. Niepodleglosci 208, 00-925
Warsaw, Poland.

352.7   US
SAN DIEGO COUNTY PLANNING AND LAND
USE DEPARTMENT. COUNTY DATA BASE.
1965. irreg. free. County Planning and Land Use
Department, 1600 Pacific Highway, San Diego, CA
92101. charts. stat. circ. controlled. (looseleaf
format)
　Formerly: San Diego County Planning
Department. Planning Data.

301.54   SA
SOUTH AFRICA. DEPARTMENT OF
STATISTICS. STATISTICS OF HOUSES AND
DOMESTIC SERVANTS AND OF FLATS.
(Report No. 11-03) (Text in Afrikaans and English)
a., latest 1978. R.2.40. Department of Statistics,
Private Bag X44, Pretoria 0001, South Africa
(Orders to: Government Printer, Bosman St.,
Private Bag X85, Pretoria 0001, South Africa)

352.7   310   SW
SWEDEN. STATISTISKA CENTRALBYRAAN.
ALLMAAN FASTIGHETSTAXERING. 1975. a.
Liber Foerlag, Fack, S-162 89 Vaellingby, Sweden.

301.54   US   ISSN 0082-9366
U. S. BUREAU OF THE CENSUS. CENSUS OF
HOUSING. (Issued in several series such as:
Housing Characteristics, Residential Finance,
Subject Reports) 1940. decennial. price varies. U.S.
Bureau of the Census, Dept. of Commerce,
Washington, DC 20233 (Orders to: Supt. of
Documents, Washington, DC 20402)

352.7 310   US   ISSN 0147-7870
U.S. DEPARTMENT OF HOUSING AND URBAN
DEVELOPMENT. STATISTICAL YEARBOOK.
a. $4.10. U.S. Department of Housing and Urban
Development, Washington, DC 20410 (Orders to:
Supt. Doc., Washington, DC 20402) Key Title:
Statistical Yearbook of the U.S. Department of
Housing and Urban Development.
　Formerly: H U D Statistical Yearbook (ISSN
0190-275X)

HUMANITIES: COMPREHENSIVE WORKS

001.3   GW
DAS ABENDLAND; Forschung zur Geschichte
europaeischen Geisteslebens. Neue Folge. 1972.
irreg., vol. 12, 1981. price varies. Vittorio
Klostermann, Frauenlobstr. 22, Postfach 900601,
6000 Frankfurt 90, W. Germany (B.R.D.) Eds. E.
Heftrich, W. Hempel.

001.3   500   BE
ACADEMIE ROYALE DES SCIENCES, DES
LETTRES ET DES BEAUX-ARTS DE
BELGIQUE. ANNUAIRE. 1835. a. 200 Fr.
Academie Royale des Sciences, des Lettres et des
Beaux-Arts de Belgique, 43 Av. des Arts, B-1040
Brussels, Belgium (Subscr. to: Office International
de Librairie, 30 Av. Marnix, 1050 Brussels,
Belgium)

001.3   BE
ACADEMIE ROYALE DES SCIENCES, DES
LETTRES ET DES BEAUX-ARTS DE
BELGIQUE. CLASSE DES BEAUX-ARTS.
MEMOIRES. irreg. price varies. (Academie Royale
des Sciences, des Lettres et des Beaux-Arts de
Belgique., Classe des Beaux-Arts) Editions et
Imprimerie J. Duculot S.A., 43 Av-des Arts, B-1040
Brussels, Belgium (Subscr. to: Office International
de Librairie, 30 Av. Marnix, 1050 Brussels,
Belgium)

001.3   BE
ACADEMIE ROYALE DES SCIENCES, DES
LETTRES ET DES BEAUX-ARTS DE
BELGIQUE. CLASSE DES LETTRES ET DES
SCIENCE MORALES ET POLITIQUES.
MEMOIRES. irreg. price varies. Academie Royale
des Sciences, des Lettres et des Beaux-Arts de
Belgique., Classe des Lettres et des Science Morales
et Politiques, 43 Av. des Arts, B-1040 Brussels,
Belgium (Subscr. to: Office International de
Librairie, 30 Av. Marnix, 1050 Brussels, Belgium)

055.1   IT
ACCADEMIA DEI CINQUECENTO PER LE
ARTI, LETTERE, SCIENZE E CULTURA.
ANALI. irreg. Accademia dei Cinquecento per le
Arti, Lettere, Scienze e Cultura, Via Trebio Littore,
11, 00152 Rome, Italy.

ACCADEMIA LIGURE DI SCIENZE E LETTERE.
ATTI. see SCIENCES: COMPREHENSIVE
WORKS

001.3   FI   ISSN 0355-578X
ACTA ACADEMIAE ABOENSIS. SERIES A:
HUMANIORA. 1920. irreg. Aabo Akademi,
Domkyrkotorget 3, 20500 Aabo 50, Finland.

001.3   SW   ISSN 0072-4823
ACTA REGIAE SOCIETATIS SCIENTIARUM ET
LITTERARUM GOTHOBURGENSIS.
HUMANIORA. (Contributions in various
languages) 1967. irreg., no. 16, 1980. price varies;
also exchange basis. Goeteborgs Kungliga
Vetenskaps- och Vitterhets-Samhaelle, c/o
Goeteborgs Universitetsbibliotek, P.O. Box 5096, S-
402 22 Goeteborg 5, Sweden (Dist. in U.S., Canada
and Mexico by: Humanities Press, Inc., 171 First
Ave., Atlantic Highlands, NJ 07716)
　Supersedes in part: Goeteborgs Kungliga
Vetenskaps- och Vitterhets- Samhaelle. Handlingar.

001.3   500   SW   ISSN 0347-4925
ACTA REGIAE SOCIETATIS SCIENTIARUM ET
LITTERARUM GOTHOBURGENSIS.
INTERDISCIPLINARIA. 1977. irreg., no. 2, 1979.
Goeteborgs Kungliga Vetenskaps- och Vitterhets-
Samhaelle, c/o Goeteborgs Universitetsbibliotek,
Box 5096, S-402 22 Goeteborg 5, Sweden (Dist. in
U.S., Canada and Mexico by: Humanities Press,
Inc., 171 First Ave., Atlantic Highlands, NJ 07716)

001.3   SJ   ISSN 0302-8844
ADDAB JOURNAL. (Text in English & French)
1972. a. (University of Khartoum, Faculty of Arts)
Khartoum University Press, Box 321, Khartoum,
Sudan. Ed. Ali Abdalla Abbas. bk. rev.

AKADEMIE DER WISSENSCHAFTEN UND DER
LITERATUR, MAINZ. JAHRBUCH. see
SCIENCES: COMPREHENSIVE WORKS

300 001.3   GW   ISSN 0002-2977
AKADEMIE DER WISSENSCHAFTEN UND DER
LITERATUR. GEISTES- UND
SOZIALWISSENSCHAFTLICHE KLASSE.
ABHANDLUNGEN. 1950. irreg. price varies.
Franz Steiner Verlag GmbH, Friedrichstr. 24,
Postfach 5529, 6200 Wiesbaden, W. Germany
(B.R.D.) bibl. charts. illus. index.

001.3   370   VE
ALBARREGAS. 1976. irreg. Universidad de los
Andes, Facultad de Humanidades y Educacion,
Avda. Universidad, Merida, Venezuela (Orders to:
Oficina Distribucion de Publicaciones, Av. Andres
Bello-Via la Parroquia, Merida, Venezuela) Ed.
Ramon Palomares. circ. 2,500.

001.3   378   GW   ISSN 0342-6785
ALEXANDER VON HUMBOLT-STIFTUNG.
JAHRESBERICHT. 1954. a. free. Alexander von
Humboldt-Stiftung, Jean-Paul-Str. 12, 5300 Bonn 2,
W. Germany (B.R.D.) Ed. Heinrich Pfeiffer. index;
cum.index: 1953-1978.

001.3   US   ISSN 0065-6216
ALFRED P. SLOAN FOUNDATION. REPORT. a.
free. ‡ Alfred P. Sloan Foundation, 630 Fifth Ave.,
New York, NY 10020. circ. 9,000.

001.3   061   US   ISSN 0145-8493
AMERICAN ACADEMY AND INSTITUTE OF
ARTS AND LETTERS. PROCEEDINGS. 1951
N.S. a. $10. American Academy and Institute of
Arts and Letters, 633 W. 155 St., New York, NY
10032. Ed. Sarah Faunce. circ. 600.
　Formerly: American Academy of Arts and
Letters. Proceedings (ISSN 0065-6836)

ANALES DE LA UNIVERSIDAD HISPALENSE.
SERIE: FILOSOFIA Y LETRAS. see SCIENCES:
COMPREHENSIVE WORKS

060   US   ISSN 0066-1694
ANDREW W. MELLON FOUNDATION. REPORT.
(Supersedes Report of the Avalon Foundation and
Report of the Old Dominion Foundation) 1969. a.
free. Andrew W. Mellon Foundation, 140 E. 62nd
St., New York, NY 10021.
　Supersedes: Avalon Foundation. Report & Old
Dominion Foundation. Report.

942   UK
ANGLO-SAXON ENGLAND. 1972. a. $56 for latest
vol. Cambridge University Press, Box 110,
Cambridge CB2 3RL, England (And 32 E. 57th St.,
New York, NY 10022) Ed. P. Clemoes.

001.3   FI   ISSN 0355-113X
ANNALES ACADEMIAE SCIENTIARUM
FENNICAE. DISSERTATIONES HUMANARUM
LITTERARUM. (Text in English, French and
German) 1973. irreg. Suomalainen Tiedeakatemia -
Academia Scientiarum Fennicae, Snellmanikatu 9-
11, 00170 Helsinki 17, Finland. Ed. Yrjo Blomstedt.
circ. 500. (reprint service avail. from UMI)

001.3   PL   ISSN 0137-2033
ANNALES UNIVERSITATIS MARIAE CURIE-
SKLODOWSKA. SECTIO F. HUMANIORA.
(Text in English or Polish; summaries in English,
French, German, Russian) 1946. a. Uniwersytet
Marii Curie-Sklodowskiej, Plac Marii-Curie-
Sklodowskiej 5, 20-031 Lublin, Poland. Ed. J.
Willaume. Indexed: Hist.Abstr.

900   FR   ISSN 0066-3247
ANNUAIRE INTERNATIONAL DES DIX-
HUITIEMISTES. 1969. a. 80 F. International
Society for 18th Century Studies, 23 Quai de
Grenelle, 75015 Paris, France. Ed. Roland Desne.
adv. circ. 2,500.

353.9   US   ISSN 0098-7387
ARIZONA COMMISSION ON THE ARTS &
HUMANITIES. REPORT TO THE GOVERNOR.
a. free. Commission on the Arts and Humanities,
6330 N. 7th St., Phoenix, AZ 85014. illus. Key
Title: Report to the Governor - Arizona
Commission on the Arts & Humanities.

020   US   ISSN 0067-057X
AUGUSTANA LIBRARY PUBLICATIONS. Variant
title: Augustana College Library Publications. 1898.
irreg. price varies. Augustana College, Library, Rock
Island, IL 61201. Ed. John Caldwell. circ. 1,000.

001.3   AT   ISSN 0067-1592
AUSTRALIAN ACADEMY OF THE
HUMANITIES. PROCEEDINGS. 1970. a. price
varies. ‡ Sydney University Press, Press Bldg.,
University of Sydney, N.S.W. 2006, Australia. Ed.
G. A. Wilkes.

370   US   ISSN 0073-6821
BALL STATE MONOGRAPHS. 1963. irreg., no. 30,
1980. free. ‡ Ball State University, Publications
Office, Muncie, IN 47306. Ed. Gertrude Kane. circ.
900. (reprint service avail. from UMI) Indexed:
Abstr.Engl.Stud.
　Earlier issues under former name of organization:
Indiana Ball State Teachers College.

BAYERISCHE AKADEMIE DER
WISSENSCHAFTEN. PHILOSOPHISCH-
HISTORISCHE KLASSE. SITZUNGSBERICHTE.
see SCIENCES: COMPREHENSIVE WORKS

080   IT   ISSN 0067-7434
BIBLIOTECA DI LABEO. 1964. irreg. price varies.
Casa Editrice Dott. Eugenio Jovene, Via
Mezzocannone, 109, Naples 80134, Italy. Ed. Bd.
bk. rev.

HUMANITIES: COMPREHENSIVE WORKS

080 PO ISSN 0067-7469
BIBLIOTECA DO EDUCADOR PROFISSIONAL. 1968. irreg. price varies. Livros Horizonte, Rua das Chagas, 17, Lisbon 2, Portugal. Ed. Rogenio Mendes de Moura.

001.3 SP
BIBLIOTECA N T; coleccion cultural de bolsillo. 1975. irreg.; 1979, no. 73. 1995 ptas. (for 10 nos.) Ediciones Universidad de Navarra S.A., Plaza de los Sauces 1 y 2, Baranain, Pamplona, Spain.
Formerly: Temas N T.

001.3 CN
BIBLIOTHEQUE DES LETTRES QUEBECOISES. irreg. price varies. Presses de l'Universite de Montreal, C.P. 6128, Succ. A, Montreal, Que. H3C 3J7, Canada. (reprint service avail. from UMI)

BIDRAG TILL KAENNEDOM AV FINLANDS NATUR OCH FOLK. see *SOCIAL SCIENCES: COMPREHENSIVE WORKS*

742 CN ISSN 0068-029X
BOREAL INSTITUTE, EDMONTON. MISCELLANEOUS PUBLICATIONS. 1969. irreg. price varies. Boreal Institute for Northern Studies, University of Alberta, Edmonton, Alberta T6G 2E9, Canada.

981 BL
CADERNOS DE ESTUDOS BRASILEIROS. 1972. irreg. Cr.$3. Universidade Federal do Rio de Janeiro, Forum de Ciencia e Cultura., Av. Pasteur 250, Praia Vermelha, Rio de Janeiro, Brazil. illus. stat. circ. 5,000.

CAMBRIDGE COMMONWEALTH SERIES. see *HISTORY*

001.3 CN
CANADIAN FEDERATION FOR THE HUMANITIES. ANNUAL REPORT. 1945. a. free. ‡ Canadian Federation for the Humanities, 151 Slater St., Ottawa K1P 5H3, Canada. circ. 800.
Formerly: Humanities Research Council of Canada. Report (ISSN 0073-3946)

001.3 US ISSN 0069-0635
CARNEGIE CORPORATION OF NEW YORK. ANNUAL REPORT. 1921. a. free. Carnegie Corporation of New York, 437 Madison Ave., New York, NY 10022. Ed. Avery Russell. circ. 18,000.

060 UK ISSN 0069-0686
CARNEGIE UNITED KINGDOM TRUST. ANNUAL REPORT. 1913. a. free. Carnegie United Kingdom Trust, Comely Park House, Dunfermline, Fife KY12 7EJ, Scotland. index.

001.3 US ISSN 0098-0900
CENTER FOR HERMENEUTICAL STUDIES IN HELLENISTIC AND MODERN CULTURE. PROTOCOL SERIES OF THE COLLOQUIES. 1970. irreg., 3-7/yr. $4 per no. Center for Hermeneutical Studies, 2465 Le Conte Ave., Berkeley, CA 94709. (Co-Sponsors: Graduate Theological Union; University of California, Berkeley) Ed. Edward Hobbs. circ. 200. (back issues avail.) Indexed: New Test.Abstr.

001.3 FR ISSN 0069-1976
CENTRE NATIONAL DE LA RECHERCHE SCIENTIFIQUE. COLLOQUES INTERNATIONAUX. SCIENCES HUMAINES. irreg; several a year. price varies. Centre National de la Recherche Scientifique, 15 Quai Anatole-France, 75700 Paris, France.

001.3 300 US ISSN 0069-2727
CHARLES E. MERRILL MONOGRAPH SERIES IN THE HUMANITIES AND SOCIAL SCIENCES. 1967. irreg., vol. 3, no. 1, 1973. price varies. Brigham Young University Press, 205 University Press Bldg., Provo, UT 84602.

001.3 US
CHARLES ELIOT NORTON LECTURES. 1938/39. a. Harvard University Press, 79 Garden St., Cambridge, MA 02138.

051 US ISSN 0069-2786
CHARTER; Gonzaga University's journal of Liberal Arts. 1961. a. $0.50. ‡ Gonzaga University, Spokane, WA 99258. circ. 500.

700 US ISSN 0009-7349
CIRCULO; revista de cultura. (Text in English and Spanish) 1970. a. $8. Circulo de Cultura Panamericano, 16 Malvern Pl., Verona, NJ 07044. Ed. Elio Alba-Buffill. adv. bk. rev. abstr. bibl. cum.index. circ. 750. Indexed: M.L.A.

001.3 VE ISSN 0069-5114
COLECCION "HUMANISM Y CIENCIA". (Some vols. issued in more than one part) irreg.,1977, no.12. Universidad Central de Venezuela, Direccion de Cultura, Departamento de Distribucion de Publicaciones, Edificio de la Biblioteca Central, Apdo. 59004, Los Chaguaramos, Caracas, Venezuela.

001.3 SP
COLECCION KARPOS. no. 5, 1977. irreg. (Instituto de Ciencias del Hombre) Editorial Karpos, Ayala 132, Madrid 6, Spain. Ed. Rafael Lapesa.

001.3 100 CN
COLLECTED WORKS OF ERASMUS. 1974. irreg. (approx. 2/yr.) price varies. University of Toronto Press, Toronto, Ont. M5S 1A6, Canada. (also avail. in microfiche)

001.3 FI ISSN 0069-6587
COMMENTATIONES HUMANARUM LITTERARUM. 1923. irreg. price varies. Societas Scientiarum Fennica, Snellmansgatan 9-11, SF-00170 Helsinki 17, Finland. Ed. Henrik Zilliacus. circ. 1,000 (approx.) Indexed: Abstr.Engl.Stud. Bull.Signal. Lang. & Lang.Behav.Abstr.

001.3 PL ISSN 0079-3167
CONFERENZE. (Text in Italian) irreg., vol. 77, 1979. price varies. (Polska Akademia Nauk, Stacja Naukowa w Rzymie, IT) Ossolineum, Publishing House of the Polish Academy of Sciences, Rynek 9, 50-106 Wroclaw, Poland (Dist. by Ars Polona-Ruch, Krakowskie Przedmiescie 7, Warsaw, Poland)

CONNECTICUT ACADEMY OF ARTS AND SCIENCES. MEMOIRS. see *SCIENCES: COMPREHENSIVE WORKS*

700 060 500 US ISSN 0069-8989
CONNECTICUT ACADEMY OF ARTS AND SCIENCES. TRANSACTIONS. 1866. irreg., 1976, vol. 46. price varies. Archon Books, 995 Sherman Ave, Hamden, CT 06514. Ed. Dorothea Rudnick. cum.index in vol. 38(1949)

CONTEMPORY ESSAY SERIES. see *LITERATURE*

CONTRIBUTIONS TO ASIAN STUDIES. see *SOCIAL SCIENCES: COMPREHENSIVE WORKS*

001.3 IT
COSCIENZA DEL TEMPO. irreg. price varies. Edizioni Studium-Vita Nova, Via Crescenzio 63, 00193 Rome, Italy.

800 IS ISSN 0084-9456
CRITICISM AND INTERPRETATION; journal for literature, linguistics. history and aesthetics. (Text in Hebrew; summaries in English) 1970. 2/yr. Bar-Ilan University, Ramat-Gan, Israel. Ed. A. Shanan.

001.3 IT
CULTURA. no. 20, 1979. irreg. price varies. Edizioni Studium-Vita Nova, Via Crescenzio 63, 00193 Rome, Italy.

001.3 VE
CULTURA UNIVERSITARIA. 1968 no. 98-99. 3/yr. Universidad Central de Venezuela, Direccion de Cultura, Departamento de Distribucion de Publicaciones, Edificio de la Biblioteca Central, Apdo. 59004, Los Chaguaramos, Caracas, Venezuela.

001.3 300 US ISSN 0590-417X
CURRENT RESEARCH IN BRITISH STUDIES BY AMERICAN AND CANADIAN SCHOLARS. 1953. irreg. price varies. Robin Higham, Ed. & Pub., Eisenhower Hall, Kansas State University, Manhattan, KS 66506. (Co-sponsors: Conference on British Studies, and the journals Military Affairs, Aerospace Historian) (reprint service avail. from UMI,ISI)

001.3 NE
CURRENT RESEARCH IN THE NETHERLANDS: HUMANITIES. 1973. irreg. Nederlandse Organisatie voor Zuiver-Wetenschappelijk Onderzoek - Netherlands Organisation for the Advancement of Pure Research (Z.W.O.), Juliana van Stolberglaan 148, The Hague, Netherlands. Ed. S. T. Groenman.

001.3 US ISSN 0070-2536
DAEDALUS LIBRARY. 1964. irreg., 1968, vol. 12. American Academy of Arts and Sciences, 165 Allandale St., Jamaica Plain Sta., Boston, MA 02130.

001.3 GW
DEUTSCHE UNESCO-KOMMISSION. SEMINARBERICHT. (Text in German and English) irreg., no. 30, 1978. price varies. K.G. Saur Verlag KG, Poessenbacherstr. 12 B, Postfach 711009, 8000 Munich 71, W. Germany (B.R.D.)

940 FR ISSN 0070-6760
DIX-HUITIEME SIECLE. 1969. a. 95 F. per no. (Societe Francaise d'Etude du Dix Huitieme Siecle) Editions Garnier Freres, 19 rue des Plantes, 75014-Paris, France. Ed. Roland Desne. adv. bk. rev. circ. 2,500. Indexed: M.L.A.

001.4 US ISSN 0419-8050
DUKE ENDOWMENT. ANNUAL REPORT. 1963. a. free. ‡ Duke Endowment, 30 Rockefeller Plaza, New York, NY 10020. illus.

100 CN ISSN 0071-1063
ERASMUS IN ENGLISH. 1970. a. free. University of Toronto Press, Front Campus, Toronto, Ont. M5S 1A6, Canada. Eds. R. M. Schoeffel, P. Tracy. bk. rev.

001.3 BL
ESTUDOS UNIVERSITARIOS. 1970. irreg; latest 1973. (Faculdades Unidas Catolicas de Mato Grosso, Faculdade Dom Aquino de Filosofia, Ciencias e Letras) Edicoes F U C M T, Av. Mato Grosso 491, Caixa Postal 801, Campo Grande, Mato Grosso, Brazil, Brazil. Dir. A. Maria da Gloria Sa Rosa. illus.

060 370 US ISSN 0071-7274
FORD FOUNDATION ANNUAL REPORT. a. free. Ford Foundation, 320 E. 43rd St., New York, NY 10017.

940 335 GW ISSN 0067-5873
FREIE UNIVERSITAET BERLIN. OSTEUROPA-INSTITUT. BERICHTE. 1952. irreg. price varies. Freie Universitaet Berlin, Osteuropa-Institut, Garystr. 55, 1000 Berlin 33 (Dahlem), W. Germany (B.R.D.) circ. 300.

001.3 DK
GEORG BRANDES AARBOG. 1975. a. Georg Brandes Biblioteket, Smallegade 43, 2000 Copenhagen F, Denmark.

551 SW ISSN 0436-113X
GOETEBORGS KUNGLIGA VETENSKAPS- OCH VITTERHETS-SAMHAELLET. 1967. a. exchange basis. Goeteborgs Kungliga Vetenskaps- och Vitterhets-Samhaelle, Box 5096, S-402 22 Goeteborg 5, Sweden (Dist. in U.S., Canada, and Mexico by: Humanities Press, 171 First Ave., Atlantic Highlands, NJ 07716)
Formerly: Goeteborgs Kungliga Vetenskaps- och Vitterhets- Samhaelles Handligar. Bihang.

001.3 JA ISSN 0386-4294
GUMMA UNIVERSITY. FACULTY OF EDUCATION. ANNUAL REPORT: CULTURAL SCIENCE SERIES. 1950. a. exchange basis. Gumma University, Faculty of Education, Gunma University Library, 1375 Aramaki, Maebashi, Gumma 371, Japan.

001.3 JA ISSN 0367-4061
GUNMA JOURNAL OF LIBERAL ARTS AND SCIENCES. 1967. a. exchange basis. Gumma University, Faculty of General Studies, Gunma University Library, 1375 Aramaki, Maebashi, Gumma 371, Japan.

001.3 980 US
HANDBOOK OF LATIN AMERICAN STUDIES. HUMANITIES. biennial. price varies. University Presses of Florida, 15 N.W. 15th St., Gainesville, FL 32603.

040 001.3 US ISSN 0073-022X
HANEY FOUNDATION SERIES. 1964. irreg., latest issues (2) published in 1977. University of Pennsylvania Press, 3933 Walnut St., Philadelphia, PA 19104.

001.3 081 300 US ISSN 0073-0602
HARVARD PAPERBACKS. irreg., no. 86, 1972. price varies. Harvard University Press, 79 Garden St., Cambridge, MA 02138.

001.3 US
HEBREW ANNUAL REVIEW; a journal of studies of Hebrew language and literature. 1977. a. $15. Ohio State University, Department of Judaic and Near Eastern Languages and Literatures, 1841 Millikin Road, Columbus, OH 43210 (Orders to: Ohio State Univ. Press, 2070 Neil Ave., Columbus, OH 43210) Ed. Dr. Yehiel Hayon. adv. circ. 750.

HELLENIKA; Zeitschrift fuer deutsch-griechische kulturelle und wirtschaftliche Zusammenarbeit. see LITERATURE

060 UK
HERIOT-WATT UNIVERSITY LECTURES.* 1968. a. £1. Heriot-Watt University, Publications Office, Edinburgh EH1 1HX, Scotland. Ed. D. C. MacDonald. circ. 500. (back issues avail)

300 JA
HIROSHIMA UNIVERSITY. FACULTY OF GENERAL EDUCATION. MEMOIRS: STUDIES IN HUMANITIES AND SOCIAL SCIENCES. (Text in Japanese; summaries in English) a. Hiroshima University, Faculty of General Education, 1-89 1-chome Higashisenda, Hiroshima 730, Japan.

001.3 FI ISSN 0073-2702
HISTORISKA OCH LITTERATURHISTORISKA STUDIER. (Subseries of: Svenska Litteratursaellskapet i Finland. Skrifter) (Text in Swedish) 1925. a. Fmk.30. Svenska Litteratursaellskapet i Finland, Snellmansgatan 9-11, 00170 Helsinki 17, Finland. Ed. Torsten Steinby.

HITOTSUBASHI JOURNAL OF ARTS AND SCIENCES. see SCIENCES: COMPREHENSIVE WORKS

001.3 HK ISSN 0073-375X
HSIN-YA HSUEH PAO/NEW ASIA JOURNAL. (Text in Chinese; summaries in English) 1955. a. HK.$30($6.) New Asia Institute of Advanced Chinese Studies and Research, Chinese University of Hong Kong, 6 Farm Rd., Kowloon, Hong Kong.

HUMAN SCIENCES RESEARCH COUNCIL. ANNUAL REPORT. see SOCIAL SCIENCES: COMPREHENSIVE WORKS

HUMAN SCIENCES RESEARCH COUNCIL. GENERAL INFORMATION. see SOCIAL SCIENCES: COMPREHENSIVE WORKS

001.3 MX
HUMANIDADES. 1973. s-a. Mex.$70($5) Universidad Iberoamericana, Division de Humanidades, Av. Cerro de las Torres 395, Mexico 21, D.F., Mexico.

001.3 DK ISSN 0105-5216
HUMANIORA. 1975. biennial. Kr.60.10. Statens Humanistiske Forskningsraad, Holmens Kanal 7, 1060 Copenhagen K, Denmark. Eds. Sven Tito Achen, Gunver Kyhn. illus. circ. 1,800.

HUMANISTIC STUDIES IN THE COMMUNICATIONS ARTS. see COMMUNICATIONS

I I A S OCCASIONAL PAPERS. (Indian Institute of Advanced Study) see EDUCATION — Higher Education

054 001.3 FR ISSN 0339-4212
I N E S INFORMATIONS. no. 43, 1976. irreg. free to members and to universities. Institut d'Etudes Slaves, 9, rue Michelet, F-75006 Paris, France. bibl.

001.3 060 II ISSN 0073-6465
INDIAN INSTITUTE OF ADVANCED STUDY. TRANSACTIONS AND MONOGRAPHS. 1965. irreg. price varies. Indian Institute of Advanced Study, Rashtrapati Nivas, Summer Hill, Simla 171005, India.

001.3 II
INDIAN INSTITUTE OF WORLD CULTURE. ANNUAL REPORT. no. 18, 1977. a. Indian Institute of World Culture, 6 Shri B.P. Wadia Rd., Box 402, Basavangudi, Bangalore 560004, India.

INSTITUT DE FRANCE. ANNUAIRE. see SCIENCES: COMPREHENSIVE WORKS

054.1 SZ
INSTITUT NATIONAL GENEVOIS. ACTS. irreg. free. Institut National Genevois, 1, Promenade du Pin, Geneva, Switzerland.

001.3 CK
INSTITUTO CARO Y CUERVO. PUBLICACIONES. 1944. irreg., no. 56, 1980. price varies. Instituto Caro y Cuervo, Apdo. Aero 20002, Bogota, Colombia.

001.3 SP ISSN 0584-6374
INSTITUTO DE ESTUDIOS MADRILENOS. ANALES. 1966. irreg. price varies. (Consejo Superior de Investigaciones Cientificas, Instituto de Estudios Madrilenos) Espasa-Calpe, S.A., Carretera de Irun, Km. 12,200, Variente de Fuencarral, Apartado 547, Madrid 34, Spain.

001.3 BL
INSTITUTO DO PATRIMONIO HISTORICO E ARTISTICO NACIONAL. PUBLICACOES. 1937. irreg. Instituto do Patrimonio Historico e Artistico Nacional, Palacio da Cultura, Rua da Imprensa 16, Rio de Janeiro, Brazil. Dir.Renato Soeiro. bibl. charts. illus.

001.3 II
INTERCULTURAL RESEARCH INSTITUTE TRANSLATION SERIES. 1976. irreg. Simant Publications, 3958 Roshan Pura, Nai Sarak, Delhi 110006, India (Dist. by: National Publishing House, 23 Daryaganj, Delhi 110006, India)

001.3 FR ISSN 0074-6819
INTERNATIONAL LITERARY AND ARTISTIC ASSOCIATION. PROCEEDINGS AND REPORTS OF CONGRESS. (Text in English and French) irreg., 1972, 54th, Paris. International Literary and Artistic Association, c/o A. Francon, 55 rue des Mathurins, 75008 Paris, France.

800 AU ISSN 0574-6817
INTERNATIONALES INSTITUT FUER DEN FRIEDEN. CULTURAL ANNIVERSARIES SERIES.* 1958. irreg. Internationales Institut fuer den Frieden, Moellwaldplatz 5, A-1040 Vienna, Austria.

001.3 JA
JAPAN FOUNDATION ANNUAL REPORT. (Text in English) a. free. Japan Foundation, Park Bldg., 3-6, Kioi-cho, Chiyoda-ku, Tokyo 102, Japan.

001.3 060 JA ISSN 0084-5515
JIMBUN. (Text in English or French) 1957. a. Kyoto University, Research Institute for Humanistic Studies - Kyoto Daigaku Jimbun Kagaku Kenkyujo, 50 Kitashirakawa Oiwake-cho, Sakyo-ku, Kyoto 606, Japan. circ. controlled.

060 JA ISSN 0521-7903
JOURNAL OF CULTURAL SCIENCES/BUNKA KAGAKU KIYO. (Text in Japanese) 1959. a. Chiba University, Faculty of Humanities and Social Sciences, 1-33 Yayoicho, Chiba 280, Japan.

700 UK ISSN 0075-4390
JOURNAL OF THE WARBURG AND COURTAULD INSTITUTES. 1937. a. £15. Warburg Institute, University of London, Woburn Square, London, WC1H 0AB, England. Ed. Bd. index; cum.index: vols. 1-37. circ. 1,300.

089 JA
KANAGAWA UNIVERSITY. INSTITUTE OF HUMANITIES. BULLETIN. (Text in Japanese; summaries in English) 1965. a. Kanagawa University, Institute of Humanities, 3-chome Rokkaku-bashi, Kanagawa-ku, Yokahama, Japan.

001.3 II ISSN 0075-515X
KARNATAK UNIVERSITY, DHARWAD, INDIA. JOURNAL. HUMANITIES. (Text mainly in English; occasionally in French, German and Sanskrit) 1957. a. Rs.8($4) Karnatak University, C. S. Kanavi, Director, Prasaranga, Dharwad 580003, Karnataka, India. Ed. K. Krishnamoorthy. circ. 500.

001.3 080 US ISSN 0075-5265
KATHERINE ASHER ENGEL LECTURES. 1958 in Hudson Review, v.12, spring, 1959; since by Smith College. irreg. price varies. Smith College Library, Office of Technical Services, Northhampton, MA 01063. (reprint service avail. from UMI)

001.3 US ISSN 0078-4222
KENT STATE UNIVERSITY. LIBRARIES. OCCASIONAL PAPER. 1968. irreg., no. 9, 1972. $1.25-$3. (Kent State University Libraries) Kent State University Press, Kent, OH 44242. Ed. Alex Gildzen. (reprint service avail. from UMI)

001.3 KE
KENYA NATIONAL ACADEMY FOR ADVANCEMENT OF ARTS AND SCIENCES. FOUNDATION LECTURES. 1965. irreg. no. 6, 1974. Kenya National Academy for Advancement of Arts and Sciences, Box 47288, Nairobi, Kenya.
Formerly: East African Academy. Foundation Lectures.

001.3 060 KE
KENYA NATIONAL ACADEMY FOR ADVANCEMENT OF ARTS AND SCIENCES. PROCEEDINGS. 1964. a. EAs.70($9) Kenya National Academy for Advancement of Arts and Sciences, Box 47288, Nairobi, Kenya.
Formerly: East African Academy. Proceedings (ISSN 0070-7945)

001.3 300 JA
KOBE UNIVERSITY OF MERCANTILE MARINE. REVIEW. PART 1. STUDIES IN HUMANITIES AND SOCIAL SCIENCE. (Text in Japanese, Abstracts in English) 1952. a. Kobe University of Mercantile Marine, 5-1-1 Fukae-Minami-machi, Higashinada-ku, Kobe 658, Japan.

001.3 SZ ISSN 0075-6520
KOELNER ROMANISTISCHE ARBEITEN. 1958, no. 9. irreg., no. 49, 1976. price varies. (Universitaet zu Koeln, Romanisches Seminar, GW) Librarie Droz, 11, rue Massot, 1211 Geneva 12, Switzerland. circ. 500.

001.3 100 DK ISSN 0106-0481
KONGELIGE DANSKE VIDENSKABERNES SELSKAB. HISTORISK-FILOSOFISKE MEDDELELSER. (Text in English, French, German and Danish) 1917. irreg., vol. 49, no. 4, 1979. price varies. Kongelige Danske Videnskabernes Selskab - Royal Danish Academy of Sciences and Letters, Dantes Plads 5, DK-1556 Copenhagen V, Denmark (Orders to: Munksgaard Boghandel, Noerregade 6, DK-1165 Copenhagen K, Denmark) Ed.Bd. bibl.

001.3 DK ISSN 0023-3307
KONGELIGE DANSKE VIDENSKABERNES SELSKAB. HISTORISK-FILOSOFISKE SKRIFTER. (Text in English, French, German and Danish) 1943. irreg., vol. 10, no. 2, 1979. price varies. Kongelige Danske Videnskabernes Selskab - Royal Danish Academy of Sciences and Letters, Dantes Plads 5, DK-1556 Copenhagen V, Denmark (Orders to: Munksgaards Boghandel, Noerregade 6, DK-1165 Copenhagen K, Denmark) bibl. illus. index.

001.3 DK ISSN 0023-3315
KONGELIGE DANSKE VIDENSKABERNES SELSKAB. OVERSIGT OVER SELSKABETS VIRKSOMHED. (Text in Danish; summaries in English) 1814. a. Kongelige Danske Videnskabernes Selskab - Royal Danish Academy of Sciences and Letters, Dantes Plads 5, DK-1556 Copenhagen V, Denmark (Orders to: Munksgaards Boghandel, Noerregade 6, DK-1165 Copenhagen K, Denmark) illus. Indexed: Biol.Abstr. Chem.Abstr.

KONGELIGE NORSKE VIDENSKABERS SELSKAB. FORHANDLINGER. see SCIENCES: COMPREHENSIVE WORKS

KONGELIGE NORSKE VIDENSKABERS SELSKAB. SKRIFTER/ROYAL NORWEGIAN SOCIETY OF SCIENCES. PUBLICATIONS. see SCIENCES: COMPREHENSIVE WORKS

001.3 NE ISSN 0065-5511
KONINKLIJKE NEDERLANDSE AKADEMIE VAN WETENSCHAPPEN. AFDELING LETTERKUNDE. VERHANDELINGEN. NIEUWE REEKS. (Text in English, French, German and Dutch) 1896. irreg., vol. 102, 1980. price varies. ‡ North-Holland Publishing Co., P.O. Box 211, 1000 AE Amsterdam, Netherlands. Ed. A. M. Verheggen. adv. bk. rev. circ. 1,000.

001.3 PL ISSN 0075-7179
KSIAZKA W DAWNEJ KULTURZE POLSKIEJ. 1951. irreg., vol. 28, 1978. price varies. (Polska Akademia Nauk, Instytut Badan Literackich) Ossolineum, Publishing House of the Polish Academy of Sciences, Rynek 9, 50-106 Wroclaw, Poland (Dist. by Ars Polona-Ruch, Krakowskie Przedmiescie 7, Warsaw, Poland) Ed.Bd.

001.3 JA ISSN 0075-7381
KYOTO PREFECTURAL UNIVERSITY. SCIENTIFIC REPORTS: HUMANITIES/KYOTO-FURITSU DAIGAKU GAKUJUTSU HOKOKU JIMBUN. (Text in Japanese; summaries in English) 1952. irreg., no. 28, 1976. available on exchange. Kyoto Prefectural University - Kyoto-furitsu Daigaku, Shimogamo Hangi-cho, Sakyo-ku, Kyoto 606, Japan. Ed. Z. Hayashino.

300 JA ISSN 0453-0349
KYUSHU INSTITUTE OF TECHNOLOGY. BULLETIN: HUMANITIES, SOCIAL SCIENCES/KYUSHU KOGYO DAIGAKU KENKYU HOKOKU, JINBUN-SHAKAI-KAGAKU. (Text in Japanese, English or German) 1953. a. exchange basis. Kyushu Institute of Technology - Kyushu Kogyo Daigaku, 1-1 Sensui-cho, Tobata, Kitakyushu 804, Japan.

001.3 US
LAST MONTH'S NEWSLETTER. 1968. irreg. free to members. ‡ Procrastinators' Club of America, 1111 Broad-Locust Bldg., Philadelphia, PA 19102. Ed. Bd. circ. 3,500.

001.3 NE
LEIDSE VOORDRACHTEN. irreg., vol. 56, 1977. price varies. Leiden University Press, c/o Martinus Nijhoff, Box 566, 2501 CN The Hague, Netherlands.

001.3 PL
LUBELSKIE TOWARZYSTWO NAUKOWE. WYDZIAL HUMANISTYCZNY. PRACE. MONOGRAFIE. irreg., t. 6, 1977. (Lubelskie Towarzystwo Naukowe) Panstwowe Wydawnictwo Naukowe, Miodowa 10, 00-251 Warsaw, Poland. bibl.

001.3 700 GW
MASSSTAEBE. 1964. irreg. DM.21.50. Verlag der Massstaebe, Hafenstr. 6, Postfach 143, 2890 Nordenham, W. Germany (B.R.D.) Ed. Norbert Weiss. bk. rev.

001.3 GW
MINERVA; INTERNATIONALES VERZEICHNIS WISSENSCHAFTLICHER INSTITUTIONEN. 1891. irreg. price varies. Walter de Gruyter und Co., Genthiner Str. 13, 1000 Berlin 30, W. Germany (B.R.D.) adv.
Formerly: Minerva; Jahrbuch der Gelehrten Welt (ISSN 0076-8960)

001.3 US ISSN 0076-9215
MINNESOTA MONOGRAPHS IN THE HUMANITIES. 1966. irreg., no. 11, 1980. price varies. University of Minnesota Press, Minneapolis, MN 55455. Ed. Leonard Unger.

001.3 UK
MODERN HUMANITIES RESEARCH ASSOCIATION. PUBLICATIONS. 1969. a. price varies. Modern Humanities Research Association, King's College, Strand, London WC2R 2LS, England.
Formerly: Modern Humanities Research Association. Monograph (ISSN 0076-9983)

060 VE
MONTALBAN. 1972. a. Bs.120($40) ‡ Universidad Catolica Andres Bello, Facultad de Letras, Departamento de Humanidades, Apartado 29068, Caracas, Venezuela. Ed. Jose del Ray Fayardo. circ. 1,200.

001.3 300 BE
MUSEE ROYAL DE L'AFRIQUE CENTRALE. ANNALES. SERIE IN 8. SCIENCES HUMAINES/KONINKLIJK MUSEUM VOOR MIDDEN-AFRIKA. ANNALEN. REEKS IN 8. MENSELIJKE WETENSCHAPPEN. irreg., no. 104, 1980. price varies. Musee Royal de l'Afrique Centrale, 13 Steenweg op Leuven, B-1980 Tervuren, Belgium.

001.3 US ISSN 0083-2111
NATIONAL ENDOWMENT FOR THE HUMANITIES. ANNUAL REPORT. 1966. a. U.S. National Endowment for the Humanities, 806 15th St., N.W., Washington, DC 20506. circ. 5,000.

001.3 PY
NEMITY; revista bilingue de cultura. 1977. irreg. $1. Distribuidora Comuneros, Pte. Franco 480, Casella 930, Asuncion, Paraguay.

NORTHERN ILLINOIS UNIVERSITY. CENTER FOR SOUTHEAST ASIAN STUDIES. OCCASIONAL PAPERS SERIES. see HISTORY — History Of Asia

NORTHERN ILLINOIS UNIVERSITY. CENTER FOR SOUTHEAST ASIAN STUDIES. SPECIAL REPORT SERIES. see HISTORY — History Of Asia

NORWEGIAN RESEARCH COUNCIL FOR SCIENCE AND THE HUMANITIES. ANNUAL REPORT. see SCIENCES: COMPREHENSIVE WORKS

001.3 IT ISSN 0078-2769
NUOVI SAGGI. 1953. irreg., no. 78, 1981. price varies. Edizioni dell' Ateneo S.p.A., P.O. Box 7216, 00100 Rome, Italy. circ. 2,000.

OESTERREICHISCHE AKADEMIE DER WISSENSCHAFTEN. ALMANACH. see SCIENCES: COMPREHENSIVE WORKS

083 AU
OESTERREICHISCHE AKADEMIE DER WISSENSCHAFTEN. IRANISCHE KOMMISSION. VEROEFFENTLICHUNGEN. (Subseries of: Oesterreichische Akademie der Wissenschaften. Philosophisch-Historische Klasse. Sitzungsberichte) 1973. irreg. Verlag der Oesterreichischen Akademie der Wissenschaften, Ignaz Seipelplatz 2, A-1010 Vienna, Austria.

100 001.3 830 GW ISSN 0078-5539
OPUSCULA - AUS WISSENSCHAFT UND DICHTUNG. 1962. irreg. DM.7.80. Verlag Guenther Heske, Kloster, 7417 Pfullingen, W. Germany (B.R.D.)

OXFORD ENGLISH MONOGRAPHS. see LITERATURE

001.3 US ISSN 0078-723X
OXFORD PAPERBACKS UNIVERSITY SERIES. irreg., no. 69, 1974. Oxford University Press, 200 Madison Ave., New York, NY 10016 (and Ely House, 37 Dover St., London W1X 4AH, England) Eds. D.R. Newth, Anthony Quinton.

001.3 PL ISSN 0079-3582
POLSKA ADAKEMIA NAUK. CENTRUM BADAN NAUKOWYCH W WOJEWODZTWIE KATOWICKIM. PRACE I STUDIA. 1969. irreg., 1971, vol. 10. price varies. Ossolineum, Publishing House of the Polish Academy of Sciences, Rynek 9, 50-106 Wroclaw, Poland (Dist. by Ars Polona-Ruch, Krakowskie Przedmiescie 7, Warsaw, Poland) Ed. Jan Paluch.
Formerly: Polska Akademia Nauk. Zaklad Badan Naukowych Gornoslaskiego Okregu Przemyslowego. Prace i Studia.

001.3 PL ISSN 0079-3531
POLSKA AKADEMIA NAUK. ODDZIAL W KRAKOWIE. ROCZNIK. 1959. a. price varies. Ossolineum, Publishing House of the Polish Academy of Sciences, Rynek 9, 50-106 Wroclaw, Poland (Dist. by Ars Polona-Ruch, Krakowskie Przedmiescie 7, Warsaw, Poland)

POLSKIE TOWARZYSTWO NAUKOWE NA OBCZYZNIE. ROCZNIK. see SCIENCES: COMPREHENSIVE WORKS

001.3 SA ISSN 0079-4333
POTCHEFSTROOM UNIVERSITY FOR CHRISTIAN HIGHER EDUCATION. WETENSKAPLIKE BYDRAES. REEKS A: GEESTESWETENSKAPPE. (Text in Afrikaans and English) 1971. irreg. free. Potchefstroom University for Christian Higher Education, Potchefstroom, South Africa. circ. 350.

001.3 701.18 US
PRINCETON ESSAYS ON THE ARTS. 1975. irreg. price varies. Princeton University Press, Princeton, NJ 08540. (reprint service avail. from UMI)

001.3 NE
PRIX NOBEL. NOBEL PRIZES. (Text in English and French) 1967. a. price varies. (Nobel Foundation, SW) Elsevier Scientific Publishing Co., Box 211, 1000 AE Amsterdam, Netherlands.

PROBLEMATA. see PHILOSOPHY

909 001.3 970 US
PROBLEMS IN AMERICAN CIVILIZATION. irreg. $2.95 per no. D.C. Heath & Company, 25 Spring St., Lexington, MA 02173.

909 001.3 US
PROBLEMS IN EUROPEAN CIVILIZATION. irreg. $2.95 per no. D.C. Heath & Company, 125 Spring St., Lexington, MA 02173.

PSYCHIATRY AND THE HUMANITIES. see MEDICAL SCIENCES — Psychiatry And Neurology

001.3 AT
QUADERNI. (Text in Italian and English) 1965. irreg., no. 5, 1975. ‡ Istituto Italiano di Cultura - Italian Cultural Institute, 233 Domain Rd., South Yarra, Vic. 3141, Australia. circ. 1,000.

001.3 UK ISSN 0079-919X
QUESTION. 1968. a. £1($2.50) Rationalist Press Association, 88 Islington High St., London N1 8EW, England. Ed. G. A. Wells. circ. 3,000. (also avail. in microfilm from UMI)
Supersedes: Rationalist Annual.

060 BG ISSN 0483-9218
RAJSHAHI UNIVERSITY STUDIES.* 1972, vol. 4. a. University of Rajshahi, c/o M. Rahman, Rajshahi, Bangladesh. Ed. A.F.S. Ahmed. adv.

001.3 UK ISSN 0486-3720
RENAISSANCE AND MODERN STUDIES. 1957. a. £6.75. (University of Nottingham) Sisson and Parker Ltd., 25 Wheeler Gate, Nottingham NG1 2NF, England. Eds. G.A.G. Parffitt, P. J. Coveney. adv. bibl. circ. 500. (also avail. in microfilm from UMI)

REPERTOIRE INTERNATIONAL DES MEDIEVISTES. see HISTORY — History Of Europe

378.54 II
RESEARCH JOURNAL: HUMANITIES AND SOCIAL SCIENCES. (Text in English and Hindi) 1972. irreg. Rs.5. University of Indore, University House, Indore 452001, Madhya Pradesh, India. bibl. illus.

001.3 JA
REVIEW ON LIBERAL ARTS/KYOYO RONSHU. (Text in English or Japanese) 1975. irreg. Kokushikan University, Society of Liberal Arts - Kokushikan Daigaku Kyoyo Gakkai, 4-28-1 Setagaya, Setagaya-ku, Tokyo 154, Japan.

001.3 056.1 PR ISSN 0378-7974
REVISTA DE ESTUDIOS HISPANICOS. 1971. a. $3.50 (students $1) Universidad de Puerto Rico, Departamento de Estudios Hispanicos, Departamento de Estudios Hispanicos, Box 21787, University Station, Rio Pedras, PR 00931. Ed. Daisy Caraballo. bk. rev. bibl. circ. 1,000.

001.3 AG ISSN 0080-2387
REVISTA HUMANIDADES. 1923. irreg. price varies. Universidad Nacional de la Plata, Facultad de Humanidades y Ciencias de la Educacion, La Plata, Argentina. index.

001.3 VE
REVISTA NACIONAL DE CULTURA. irreg. Instituto Nacional de Cultura y Bellas Artes, Apartado 50995, Caracas, Venezuela.

001.3 FR
REVUE DE PAU ET DU BEARN. 1973. a. 40 F. Societe de Sciences, Lettres et Arts de Pau, 13 Avenue Trespoey, 64000 Pau, France. Ed. Bd. bibl. illus.

001.3 IT ISSN 0080-3073
RINASCIMENTO. (Text in English, French, German and Italian) 1938. a. L.17000. (Istituto Nazionale di Studi sul Rinascimento) Casa Editrice G. C. Sansoni Editore Nuova S.p.A., Via Benedetto Varchi 47, 50132 Florence, Italy. Ed. Eugenio Garin.
Formerly (until 1950): Rinascita.

001.3 PL
ROCZNIK DOLNOSLASKI. 1972. irreg. 40 Zl. (Dolnoslaskie Towarzystwo Oswiatowe) Ossolineum, Publishing House of the Polish Academy of Sciences, Rynek 9, Wroclaw, Poland. bk. rev. illus. circ. 1,800.

SAECULA SPIRITALIA. see *HISTORY*

060 II ISSN 0080-5416
SAHITYA AKADEMI, NEW DELHI. REPORT. (Text in English) 1954/55. a. free. National Academy of Letters - Sahitya Akademi, Rabindra Bhavan, New Delhi 110001, India.

001.3 II
SAMBALPUR UNIVERSITY JOURNAL: HUMANITIES. (Text in English or Oriya) vol. 5, 1972. a. Rs.5. Sambalpur University, Budharaja Hills, Sambalpur 768001, Orissa, India.

300 SZ ISSN 0080-5807
SAMMLUNG DALP. 1946. irreg., vol. 105, 1976. price varies. ‡ Francke Verlag, Postfach, CH-3000 Berne 26, Switzerland.

100 060 SZ ISSN 0080-729X
SCHWEIZERISCHE GEISTESWISSENSCHAFTLICHE GESELLSCHAFT. SCHRIFTEN. (Text in French or German) 1957. irreg. price varies. ‡ Francke Verlag, Postfach, CH-3000 Berne 26, Switzerland.

040 IS ISSN 0080-8369
SCRIPTA HIEROSOLYMITANA. (Text in English) 1954. irreg. price varies. (Hebrew University of Jerusalem) Magnes Press, Jerusalem, Israel.

001.3 FR ISSN 0085-6037
SEMITICA. 1948. a. price varies. (Universite de Paris III (Sorbonne-Nouvelle), Institut d'Etudes Semitiques) Adrien Maisonneuve, 11 rue St Sulpice, 75006 Paris, France. (Co-sponsor: Centre National de la Recherche Scientifique) Ed.Bd.

001.3 500 PK ISSN 0080-9314
SHIVAJI UNIVERSITY, KOLHAPUR, INDIA. JOURNAL. HUMANITIES AND SCIENCES. (Text in English) 1968. a.(in 2 parts) Rs.10. Shivaji University, Registrar, Kolhapur 4, Pakistan. Eds. R. N. Patil & S. K. Desai. circ. 377. Indexed: Chem.Abstr.

001.3 BE ISSN 0085-6169
SNOECK'S ALMANACH. 1782. a. 60 Fr. Snoeck-Ducaju en Zoon N.V., Begijnhoflaan 440, B-9000 Ghent, Belgium. Ed. Serge Snoeck. adv. circ. 100,000.

001.3 BE ISSN 0085-6177
SNOECK'S; LITERATUUR KUNST FILM TONEEL MODE REIZEN. 1923. a. 29 Fr. Snoeck-Ducaju en Zoon N.V., Begijnhoflaan 440, B-9000 Ghent, Belgium. Ed. Serge Snoeck. adv. bk. rev. circ. 126,000.

001.3 CH
SOOCHOW JOURNAL OF HUMANITIES. 1976. irreg. $7 per no. Soochow University, Wai Shuang Shi, Shih Lin, Taipei, Taiwan, Republic of China.

068 AT ISSN 0311-290X
SOUTHEAST ASIAN RESEARCH MATERIALS GROUP. NEWSLETTER. 1972. irreg. free. Southeast Asian Research Materials Group, National Library of Australia, Canberra, A.C.T. 2601, Australia. Ed. P. Crawcour. circ. 350.

001.3 500 YU ISSN 0081-4032
SRPSKA AKADEMIJA NAUKA I UMETNOSTI SPOMENICA. (Text in Serbo-Croatian; summaries in French, English, German or Russian) 1888. irreg. price varies. Srpska Akademija Nauka i Umetnosti, Knez Mihailova 35, 11001 Belgrade, Yugoslavia (Dist. by: Prosveta., Terazije 16, Belgrade, Yugoslavia) circ. 700.

301.2 UN ISSN 0586-6898
STUDIES AND DOCUMENTS ON CULTURAL POLICIES. (Subseries of Unesco. Documents) irreg. Unesco Press, 7 Place de Fontenoy, 75700 Paris, France (Dist. in U.S. by: Unipub, 345 Park Ave. S., New York, NY 10010)

001.3 900 US
STUDIES IN EIGHTEENTH CENTURY CULTURE; American Society for Eighteenth Century Studies. Proceedings of the Annual Meeting. (Vols 1-3 published by Case Western Reserve) irreg., vol. 7, 1978. price varies. University of Wisconsin Press, 114 N. Murray St., Madison, WI 53715.

909 US
STUDIES IN WORLD CIVILIZATION. irreg. price varies. Alfred A. Knopf, c/o Random House, 201 E. 50th St., New York, NY 10022.

001.3 500 300 SJ ISSN 0453-8129
SUDAN RESEARCH INFORMATION BULLETIN. (Issued in two sections) 1965. irreg. University of Khartoum, Sudan Unit, Box 321, Khartoum, Sudan.

SURREALIST TRANSFORMACTION. see *ART*

060 US
SURVEY OF GRANT-MAKING FOUNDATIONS. 3rd edt., 1977. a. $10. Public Service Materials Center, 415 Lexington Ave., New York, NY 10017.

001.3 US ISSN 0564-7169
T A I U S. (Texas A & I University Studies) 1968. a. ‡ Texas A & I University, Jernigan Library, Kingsville, TX 78363. circ. 3,000. (tabloid format)

080 SA ISSN 0082-1330
T. B. DAVIE MEMORIAL LECTURE. 1959. a. R.0.50. University of Cape Town, Private Bag, Rondebosch 7700, South Africa.

001.3 US ISSN 0082-2779
TENNESSEE TECH JOURNAL. 1966. a. free. ‡ Tennessee Technological University, Box 5146, Cookeville, TN 38501. Ed. Nolan Fowler. abstr. circ. 950. (back issues avail)

300 700 800 US ISSN 0049-4127
TOPIC; a journal of the liberal arts. 1961. a. $1. Washington & Jefferson College, Washington, PA 15301. Ed. Walter S. Sanderlin. circ. 1,000.

TRADITIO; studies in ancient and medieval history, thought, and religion. see *HISTORY — History Of Europe*

TURKIYAT MECMUASI. see *HISTORY — History Of The Near East*

001.3 FI ISSN 0082-6987
TURUN YLIOPISTO. JULKAISUJA. SARJA B. HUMANIORA. (Latin title: Annales Universitatis Turkuensis) (Text in English, German, French, Finnish) 1923. irreg. price varies. Turun Yliopisto - University of Turku, SF-20500 Turku 50, Finland.

001.3 500 FI ISSN 0082-6995
TURUN YLIOPISTO. JULKAISUJA. SARJA C. SCRIPTA LINGUA FENNICA EDITA. (Latin title: Annales Universitatis Turkuensis) (Text in Finnish; summaries in English, German, French) 1965. irreg. price varies. Turun Yliopisto, SF-20500 Turku 50, Turku 50, Finland.

001.3 SW
UMEAA STUDIES IN THE HUMANITIES. (Subseries of Acta Universitatis Umensis) 1975. irreg., no. 8, 1975. Kr.37.25. Umeaa Universitet, Bibliotek, Box 718, S-901 10 Umeaa, Sweden.

060 BE ISSN 0074-9346
UNION ACADEMIQUE INTERNATIONALE. COMPTE RENDU DE LA SESSION ANNUELLE DU COMITE. 1920. a, 53rd, 1979, Berne. International Union of Academies, Palais des Academies, 1 rue Ducale, 1000 Brussels, Belgium.

001.3 CK
UNIVERSIDAD DE ANTIOQUIA. DEPARTAMENTO DE HUMANIDADES. COLECCION PAPELES DE TRABAJO. 1977. irreg. Universidad de Antioquia, Departmento de Humanidades, Medellin, Colombia.

001.3 SP ISSN 0072-5382
UNIVERSIDAD DE GRANADA. COLLECCION MONOGRAFICA. 1970. irreg. price varies. Universidad de Granada, Departamento de Historia del Arte, Secretariado de Publicaciones, Granada, Spain.

700 800 500 UY ISSN 0041-8447
UNIVERSIDAD DE LA REPUBLICA. FACULTAD DE HUMANIDADES Y CIENCIAS. PUBLICACIONES. (Text in English, French and Spanish) 1956. exchange basis. Universidad de la Republica, Facultad de Humanidades y Ciencias, Departamento de Documentacion y Biblioteca, Seccion Revista, Tristan Narvaja 1674, Montevideo, Uruguay. bibl. charts.

001.3 GT
UNIVERSIDAD DE SAN CARLOS ANUAL. 1945. a. Universidad de San Carlos de Guatemala, Ciudad Universitaria, Guatemala 12, Guatemala. Ed. Bd. bk. rev. bibl.

001.3 080 AG ISSN 0068-3485
UNIVERSIDAD DEL SALVADOR. ANALES. 1963. a. $3. Universidad del Salvador, Alberti 158, Buenos Aires, Argentina.

001.3 VE
UNIVERSIDAD DEL ZULIA. REVISTA. 1947; N. S. 1958. irreg. Universidad del Zulia, Direccion de Cultura, Apartado 526, Maracaibo, Venezuela.

UNIVERSIDAD INDUSTRIAL DE SANTANDER. REVISTA - INVESTIGACIONES. see *ENGINEERING*

001.3 CK ISSN 0120-095X
UNIVERSIDAD INDUSTRIAL DE SANTANDER. REVISTA - HUMANIDADES. (Text in Spanish; Summaries in English, French, German and Spanish) 1969. irreg. $2 per no. or exchange basis. Universidad Industrial de Santander, Apartado Aereo 678, Bucaramanga, Colombia. adv. bk. rev. bibl. charts. illus. cum. index every 5 yrs.
Supersedes in part: Universidad Industrial de Santander. Revista.

001.3 MX
UNIVERSIDAD NACIONAL AUTONOMA DE MEXICO. INSTITUTO DE INVESTIGACIONES ESTETICAS. MONOGRAFIAS. SERIE MAYOR. 1977. irreg; latest issue, 1977. Universidad Nacional Autonoma de Mexico, Instituto de Investigaciones Esteticas, Torre I de Humanidades, Ciudad Universitaria, Mexico 20, D.F., Mexico.

060 AG ISSN 0564-4070
UNIVERSIDAD NACIONAL DE TUCUMAN. FACULTAD DE FILOSOFIA Y LETRAS. CUADERNOS DE HUMANITAS.* 1959. irreg., 1972, no. 40. Universidad Nacional de Tucuman, Facultad de Filosofia y Letras, Ayacucho 482, San Miguel de Tucuman, Argentina. Ed. Bd. bibl.

001.3 VE ISSN 0076-4345
UNIVERSIDAD NACIONAL DEL ZULIA. FACULTAD DE HUMANIDADES Y EDUCACION. CONFERENCIAS Y COLOQUIOS.* irreg. Bs.7($1.60) Universidad del Zulia, Facultad de Humanidades y Educacion, Apartado 526, Maracaibo, Venezuela.

060 IT
UNIVERSITA DEGLI STUDI CAGLIARI. FACOLTA DI LETTERE-FILOSOFIA. ANNALI. 1976. irreg. L.10000. Universita degli Studi di Cagliari, Facolta di Lettere-Filosofia, Cagliari, Italy (Orders to: Libreria Cocco, Bargo Carlo Felice 76, I-09100 Cagliari, Italy) abstr. illus. circ. 425.
Supersedes in part(1936-1975): Universita di Cagliari. Facolta di Lettere-Filosofia e Magistero. Annali.

060　　　　　　　IT
UNIVERSITA DEGLI STUDI DI CAGLIARI. FACOLTA DI MAGISTERO. ANNALI. 1976. irreg.; no. 2, 1977. Universita degli Studi di Cagliari, Facolta di Magistero, 09100 Cagliari, Italy. abstr. illus. circ. 425.
　　Supersedes in part (1936-1975): Universita di Cagliari. Facolta di Lettere-Filosofia e Magistero. Annali.

001.3　　　　　IT　ISSN 0076-1818
UNIVERSITA DEGLI STUDI DI MACERATA. FACOLTA DI LETTERE E FILOSOFIA. ANNALI. 1968. a. L.15000($9.) Universita degli Studi di Macerata, Facolta di Lettere e Filosofia, Macerata, Italy. Ed. Lidio Gasperini. bk. rev. circ. 500.

001.3　　　　　IT
UNIVERSITA DEGLI STUDI DI PADOVA. FACOLTA DI LETTERE E FILOSOFIA. ANNALI. 1976. irreg., vol. 2, 1978. Casa Editrice Leo S. Olschki, Casella Postale 66, 50100 Florence, Italy.

085　　　　　　　RM
UNIVERSITATEA DIN CRAIOVA. ANALELE: SERIA ISTORIE, GEOGRAFIE, FILOLOGIE. (Text in Rumanian; summaries in French and/Or English, German, Italian, Russian) 1972. irreg. $10. Universitatea din Craiova, Str. Al.I. Cuza Nr. 13, Craiova, Romania (Subscr. to: ILIXIM, Str. 13 Decembrie Nr. 3, P.O. Box 136-137, Bucharest, Romania) illus.

001.3 060　　　　FR　ISSN 0065-4973
UNIVERSITE D'AIX-MARSEILLE I. FACULTE DES LETTRES ET SCIENCES HUMAINES. ANNALES. 1907. 1953 N. S. a. price varies. Universite d'Aix-Marseille I (Universite de Provence), Faculte des Lettres et Sciences Humaines, Service des Publications, 13621 Aix en Provence, France.

001.3　　　　　IT　ISSN 0072-7652
UNIVERSITE DE GRENOBLE. INSTITUT FRANCAIS DE FLORENCE. PUBLICATION. SERIE 1: COLLECTION D'ETUDES D'HISTOIRE.* 1910. irreg., 1968, no. 31. price varies. (FR) Casa Editrice G. C. Sansoni Editore Nuova S.p.A., Via Benedetto Varchi 47, 50132 Florence, Italy.

001.3　　　　　BE
UNIVERSITE DE LIEGE. FACULTE DE PHILOSOPHIE ET LETTRES. PUBLICATIONS. irreg. Universite de Liege, Faculte de Philosophie et Lettres, Place du 20-Aout, Liege, Belgium.

UNIVERSITE DE PARIS. FACULTE DES LETTRES ET SCIENCES HUMAINES. PUBLICATIONS. SERIE ACTA. see SCIENCES: COMPREHENSIVE WORKS

001.3　　　　　FR
UNIVERSITE DE SAINT ETIENNE. CENTRE JEAN PALERNE. MEMOIRES. 1978. irreg. Universite de Saint Etienne, Centre Jean Palerne, 2 rue Trefilerie, 42100 Saint Etienne, France.

UNIVERSITE DE STRASBOURG II. INSTITUT DE PHONETIQUE. TRAVAUX. see LINGUISTICS

001.3　　　　　BE
UNIVERSITE LIBRE DE BRUXELLES. FACULTE DE PHILOSOPHIE ET LETTRES. SOURCES ET INSTRUMENTS. 1978. irreg., no. 2, 1978. price varies. Editions de l'Universite de Bruxelles, Parc Leopold, B-1040 Brussels, Belgium.

001.3　　　　　BE
UNIVERSITE LIBRE DE BRUXELLES. FACULTE DE PHILOSOPHIE ET LETTRES. TRAVAUX. 1930. irreg., vol. 67, 1977. Editions de l'Universite de Bruxelles, Parc Leopold, 1040 Brussels, Belgium.

060　　　　　　　US　ISSN 0068-6522
UNIVERSITY OF CALIFORNIA PUBLICATIONS. OCCASIONAL PAPERS. 1964. irreg. University of California Press, 2223 Fulton Street, Berkeley, CA 94720.

001.3　　　　　SA　ISSN 0070-7740
UNIVERSITY OF DURBAN-WESTVILLE. JOURNAL/UNIVERSITEIT VAN DURBAN-WESTVILLE. TYDSKRIF. (Text in English and Afrikaans) 1965. a. exchange basis. University of Durban-Westville, Private Bag X54001, Durban 4000, South Africa. Ed. A. L. Behr. circ. 1,000. Indexed: Ind.S.A.Per.

001.3　　　　　US　ISSN 0071-6189
UNIVERSITY OF FLORIDA MONOGRAPHS. HUMANITIES. 1959. irreg. price varies. University Presses of Florida, 15 N.W. 15 St., Gainesville, FL 32603.

001.3　　　　　NR
UNIVERSITY OF IFE. FACULTY OF ARTS. LECTURE SERIES. 1974. irreg. University of Ife, Faculty of Arts, Ile-Ife, Nigeria.

001.3　　　　　US　ISSN 0085-2473
UNIVERSITY OF KANSAS HUMANISTIC STUDIES. 1912. irreg., (approx. a.) price varies. ‡ University of Kansas, Library Exchange and Gift Section, Lawrence, KS 66045.

001.3　　　　　NR　ISSN 0075-7675
UNIVERSITY OF LAGOS. HUMANITIES SERIES. 1971. irreg. price varies. University of Lagos, Yaba, Lagos, Nigeria.

001.3　　　　　NR　ISSN 0075-7659
UNIVERSITY OF LAGOS. INAUGURAL LECTURE SERIES. 1968. irreg. price varies. University of Lagos, Yaba, Lagos, Nigeria.

001.3　　　　　MM　ISSN 0035-9297
UNIVERSITY OF MALTA. FACULTY OF ARTS. JOURNAL. 1957. irreg., latest 1976. University of Malta, Faculty of Arts, Msida, Malta.

001.3　　　　　US　ISSN 0076-9703
UNIVERSITY OF MISSOURI STUDIES. 1926. irreg., no. 68, 1978. price varies. University of Missouri Press, 107 Swallow Hall, Columbia, MO 65201.

001.3　　　　　US　ISSN 0077-6386
UNIVERSITY OF NEBRASKA STUDIES. NEW SERIES. 1946. irreg., no. 62, 1979. available on exchange basis only. University of Nebraska-Lincoln, Libraries, Serials Department, Lincoln, NE 68508. circ. 600. (also avail. in microform from UMI)

060　　　　　　　SA
UNIVERSITY OF PORT ELIZABETH. PUBLICATIONS. BIBLIOGRAPHIES. (Text in English or Afrikaans) 1977. irreg., E 1, 1977. University of Port Elizabeth, Library, Private Bag X6058, Port Elizabeth 6000, South Africa. Ed.Bd.

001.3 060　　　　SA　ISSN 0079-3957
UNIVERSITY OF PORT ELIZABETH. PUBLICATIONS. GENERAL SERIES. (Text in English and Afrikaans) 1965. irreg., no. A 14, 1978. price varies. University of Port Elizabeth, Library, Private Bag X6058, Port Elizabeth 6000, South Africa. Ed. Bd.

001.3　　　　　SA　ISSN 0085-5022
UNIVERSITY OF PORT ELIZABETH. PUBLICATIONS. INAUGURAL AND EMERITUS ADDRESSES. (Text in Afrikaans and English) 1971. irreg., no. D 12, 1976. price varies. University of Port Elizabeth, Library, Private Bag X6058, Port Elizabeth 6000, South Africa. Ed. Bd.

001.3 060　　　　SA　ISSN 0079-3965
UNIVERSITY OF PORT ELIZABETH. PUBLICATIONS. RESEARCH PAPERS. (Text in English and Afrikaans) 1970. irreg., no. C 17,1980. price varies University of Port Elizabeth, Library, Private Bay X6058, Port Elizabeth 6000, South Africa. Ed. Bd.

001.3 060　　　　SA
UNIVERSITY OF PORT ELIZABETH. PUBLICATIONS. SYMPOSIA, SEMINARS, AND LECTURES. (Text in English and Afrikaans) 1969. irreg., no. B 7, 1980. price varies. University of Port Elizabeth, Library, Private Bag X6058, Port Elizabeth 6000, South Africa. Ed. Bd.
　　Formerly: University of Port Elizabeth. Publications. Symposia and Seminars (ISSN 0079-3973)

001.3　　　　　PH　ISSN 0069-1321
UNIVERSITY OF SAN CARLOS. SERIES A: HUMANITIES. (Text in English) 1964. irreg., no. 10, 1975. price varies. (University of San Carlos) San Carlos Publications, Cebu City 6401, Philippines (Dist. by: Cellar Book Shop, 18090 Wyoming, Detroit, MI 48221) Ed. Rudolf Rahmann. circ. 547.

001.3　　　　　PH　ISSN 0069-1356
UNIVERSITY OF SAN CARLOS. SERIES D: OCCASIONAL MONOGRAPHS. (Text in English) 1966. irreg., no. 3, 1976. price varies. (University of San Carlos) San Carlos Publications, Cebu City 6401, Philippines (Dist. by: Cellar Book Shop, 18090 Wyoming, Detroit, MI 48221) Ed. Rudolf Rahmann. circ. 160.

UNIVERSITY OF SIND. RESEARCH JOURNAL. ARTS SERIES: HUMANITIES AND SOCIAL SCIENCES. see ART

UNIVERSITY OF WISCONSIN, MILWAUKEE. CENTER FOR LATIN AMERICA. SPECIAL STUDIES SERIES. see HISTORY — History Of North And South America

UNIVERSITY OF WYOMING PUBLICATIONS. see SCIENCES: COMPREHENSIVE WORKS

001.3　　　　　PL　ISSN 0076-034X
UNIWERSYTET LODZKI. PRACE. irreg. price varies. Uniwersytet Lodzki, Narutowicza 65, Lodz, Poland (Dist. by Ars Polona-Ruch, Krakowskie Przedmiescie 7, Warsaw, Poland)

001.4　　　　　US　ISSN 0083-5242
VARIA.* 1963. a. free. North Carolina Central University, Faculty Research Committee, Durham, NC 27707. Eds. Ruth N. Horry, Ross E. Townes. circ. 600.

001.3　　　　　IT
VERIFICHE E PROPOSTE. 1975. irreg. Tringale Editore, Via Vecchia Ognina 90, 95129 Catania, Italy. Ed. Ermanno Scuderi.

001.3　　　　　US
VICTORIANS INSTITUTE.JOURNAL. 1972. a. $2. Victorians Institute Journal, Old Dominion University, Norfolk, VA 23508. Ed. Conrad Festa. circ. 600.

943.7　　　　　CS
VLASTIVEDNY ZBORNIK. (Text in Slovak: summaries in German and Russian) 1973. irreg. 25.50. Matica Slovenska, Mudronova 35, 036 52 Martin, Czechoslovakia. illus.

700　　　　　　　UK　ISSN 0083-7199
WARBURG INSTITUTE. STUDIES. 1939. irreg. price varies. Warburg Institute, University of London, Woburn Square, London WC1H 0AB, England.

060　　　　　　　US　ISSN 0083-9167
WHERE AMERICA'S LARGE FOUNDATIONS MAKE THEIR GRANTS; who gets them and how much each receives. 1971-2. irreg., latest 1980-81. $34.50. Public Service Materials Center, 415 Lexington Ave., New York, NY 10017. Ed. Joseph Dermer.

WHIDDEN LECTURES. see EDUCATION — Higher Education

001.3　　　　　AU　ISSN 0083-9965
WIENER HUMANISTISCHE BLAETTER. (Text in German, Latin and Ancient Greek) 1956. a. DM.6. (Wiener Humanistische Gesellschaft) Hermann Boehlaus Nachf., Schmalzhofgasse 4, Postfach 167, A-1061 Vienna, Austria. Ed. Walther Kraus. bk. rev. illus. circ. 800.

920　　　　　　　UK　ISSN 0084-0270
WILLIAM MORRIS SOCIETY. REPORT. 1956. a. membership. William Morris Society, Kelmscott House, 26 Upper Mall, Hammersmith, London W6, England.

082　　　　　　　US　ISSN 0084-2168
WORLD PERSPECTIVES.* 1954. irreg., vol. 48, 1974. price varies. Harper & Row Publishers, Inc., 49 E. 33rd St., New York, NY 10016. Ed. Ruth Nanda Anshen.

001.3 PL ISSN 0084-3016
WROCLAWSKIE TOWARZYSTWO NAUKOWE. PRACE. SERIA A. HUMANISTYKA. (Text in Polish, English, French and German; summaries in English, French and German) 1947. irreg., no. 200, 1979. price varies. Ossolineum, Publishing House of the Polish Academy of Sciences, Rynek 9, Wroclaw, Poland (Dist. by Ars Polona-Ruch, Krakowskie Przedmiescie 7, Warsaw, Poland)

001.3 PH ISSN 0084-3229
XAVIER UNIVERSITY. MUSEUM AND ARCHIVES PUBLICATIONS. 1970. irreg., no. 18, latest issue. price varies. Xavier University, Cagayan de Oro City, Philippines. Ed. Francisco Demetrio y Radaza. (processed)

001.3 080 US ISSN 0084-3318
YALE COLLEGE SERIES. 1964. irreg; no. 14, 1976. price varies. Yale University Press, 92A Yale Station, New Haven, CT 06520.

001.3 JA ISSN 0085-834X
YAMAGATA UNIVERSITY. BULLETIN. (Bulletin issued in 6 parts) (Text in Japanese, English, German; summaries in English and German) 1950. a. Yamagata University, Main Library, 1-4-12 Koshirakawa-machi, Yamagata City, Japan.

001.3 800 UK ISSN 0306-2473
YEARBOOK OF ENGLISH STUDIES. 1971. a. $45 for vols. 1-11. Modern Humanities Research Association, King's College, Strand, London WC2R 2CS, England. Eds. G. K. Hunter, C. J. Rawson. bk. rev. bibl.

YEARBOOK ON HUMAN RIGHTS. see POLITICAL SCIENCE — Civil Rights

001.3 PL ISSN 0084-5221
ZE SKARBCA KULTURY. 1951. s-a. price varies. (Polska Akademia Nauk, Biblioteka, Zaklad Narodowy Im. Ossolinskich) Ossolineum, Publishing House of the Polish Academy of Sciences, Rynek 9, 50-106 Wroclaw, Poland (Dist. by Ars Polona-Ruch, Krakowskie Przedmiescie 7, Warsaw, Poland) Ed. J. Albin.

001.3 CK
ZUMBAMBICO; gaceta cultural. 1976. irreg. c/o Alberto Restrepo, Apdo. Aereo 3301, Medellin, Colombia.

HUMANITIES: COMPREHENSIVE WORKS — Abstracting, Bibliographies, Statistics

001.3 016 US ISSN 0069-2824
CHECKLISTS IN THE HUMANITIES AND EDUCATION. 1971. irreg. Trinity University Press, Trinity University, 715 Stadium Dr., San Antonio, TX 78284. Ed. Harry B. Caldwell. index.

001.3 016 II
INDEX ASIA SERIES IN HUMANITIES. 1965. irreg. price varies. Centre for Asian Dokumentation, Box 11215, Calcutta 700014, India. Ed. S. Chaudhuri. bk. rev. index.
Bibliographies and indexes

001.3 028 US ISSN 0073-5892
INDEX TO BOOK REVIEWS IN THE HUMANITIES. 1960. a. $20. Phillip Thomson, Ed. & Pub., 836 Georgia St., Williamston, MI 48895. circ. 1,300. (back issues avail)

001.3 314 PL
POLAND. GLOWNY URZAD STATYSTYCZNY. ROCZNIK STATYSTYCZNY KULTURY. STATISTICAL YEARBOOK OF CULTURE. (Subseries of its: Statystyka Polski) 1969. irreg. Glowny Urzad Statystyczny, Al. Niepodleglosci 208, 00-925 Warsaw, Poland.
Formerly: Poland. Glowny Urzad Statystyczny. Kultura (ISSN 0079-2713)

HYDRAULIC ENGINEERING

see Engineering — Hydraulic Engineering

HYDROLOGY

see Earth Sciences — Hydrology

INDUSTRIAL HEALTH AND SAFETY

see also Business and Economics — Labor and Industrial Relations

614.7 US
AMERICAN CONFERENCE OF GOVERNMENTAL INDUSTRIAL HYGIENISTS. TRANSACTIONS OF THE ANNUAL MEETING. 1976, vol. 39. a. $5. American Conference of Governmental Industrial Hygienists, P.O. Box 1937, Cincinnati, OH 45201. circ. 1,800. (back issues avail)

ARBEITSMEDIZIN; Abhandlungen ueber Berufskrankheiten und deren Verhuetung. see MEDICAL SCIENCES

610 II ISSN 0518-8857
ASIAN CONFERENCE ON OCCUPATIONAL HEALTH. PROCEEDINGS. 1950. irreg.; latest issue, 1974. $3. Society for the Study of Industrial Medicine, 8 Tala Park Ave., Calcutta 700002, India. Ed. Dr. P. K. Ghosh. adv. bk. rev. circ. 1,000.

613.62 FR ISSN 0066-927X
ASSOCIATION FRANCAISE DES TECHNICIENS ET INGENIEURS DE SECURITE ET DES MEDECINS DU TRAVAIL. ANNUAIRE. (Suspended publication 1974-1978) 1964/65. a. 60 F. Imprimerie Rouille, 3 Ter, rue de la Gare, 28240-la Loupe, France. adv.

614.85 US ISSN 0090-7480
BEST'S SAFETY DIRECTORY; safety-industrial hygiene-security. 1946. a. $35. A. M. Best Co., Ambest Rd., Oldwick, NJ 08858. Ed. John Burridge. adv. circ. 19,500.

BRITISH COLUMBIA. DEPARTMENT OF LABOUR. NEGOTIATED WORKING CONDITIONS. see BUSINESS AND ECONOMICS — Labor And Industrial Relations

CALIFORNIA. DEPARTMENT OF INDUSTRIAL RELATIONS. ANNUAL REPORT. see BUSINESS AND ECONOMICS — Labor And Industrial Relations

613.62 EI ISSN 0530-749X
COMMISSION OF THE EUROPEAN COMMUNITIES. COLLECTION D'HYGIENE ET DE MEDECINE DU TRAVAIL. Italian ed: Collezione di Igiene e di Medicina del Lavro (ISSN 0591-1559); Dutch ed: Reeks Arbeidshygiene en Arbeidsgeneeskunds (ISSN 0486-2082) (Editions in French, German, Italian and Dutch) 1961. irreg., 1917, no. 14. price varies. Office for Official Publications of the European Communities, C.P. 1003, Luxembourg 1, Luxembourg (Dist. in the U.S. by: European Community Information Service, 2100 M St., NW, Suite 707, Washington, DC 20037)

613.62 669 EI
GENERAL COMMISSION ON SAFETY AND HEALTH IN THE IRON AND STEEL INDUSTRY. REPORT. (First edition in French only; later editions in German, French, Italian and Dutch) 1966. a. General Commission on Safety and Health in the Iron and Steel Industry, Rue de la Loi 200, 1040 Brussels, Belgium. circ. controlled.

614.85 CN ISSN 0073-7305
INDUSTRIAL ACCIDENT PREVENTION ASSOCIATION. ANNUAL REPORT. 1918. a. Industrial Accident Prevention Association, 2 Bloor St. E., Toronto, Ont. M4W 3C2, Canada. circ. 6,000.

613.62 US ISSN 0073-7488
INDUSTRIAL HEALTH FOUNDATION. CHEMICAL-TOXICOLOGICAL SERIES. BULLETIN. 1947. irreg., 1969, no. 8. price varies. ‡ Industrial Health Foundation, Inc., 5231 Centre Ave., Pittsburgh, PA 15232.
Formerly: Industrial Hygiene Foundation. Chemical-Toxicological Series. Bulletin (ISSN 0537-5215)

613.2 US ISSN 0073-7496
INDUSTRIAL HEALTH FOUNDATION. ENGINEERING SERIES. BULLETIN. 1936. irreg., no. 8, 1971. price varies. ‡ Industrial Health Foundation, Inc., 5231 Centre Ave., Pittsburgh, PA 15232.

331.8 613.62 US ISSN 0073-750X
INDUSTRIAL HEALTH FOUNDATION. LEGAL SERIES BULLETIN. 1936. irreg., 1972, no. 9. price varies. ‡ Industrial Health Foundation, Inc., 5231 Centre Ave., Pittsburgh, PA 15232.
Formerly: Industrial Hygiene Foundation of America. Legal Series Bulletin.

613.62 US ISSN 0073-7518
INDUSTRIAL HEALTH FOUNDATION. MEDICAL SERIES. BULLETIN. 1937. irreg., no. 20, 1979. price varies. ‡ Industrial Health Foundation, Inc., 5231 Centre Ave., Pittsburgh, PA 15232.

613.62 US
INDUSTRIAL HEALTH FOUNDATION. NURSING SERIES. BULLETINS. 1965. irreg., 1971, no. 3. price varies. Industrial Health Foundation, Inc., 5231 Centre Ave., Pittsburgh, PA 15232.
Formerly: Industrial Hygiene Foundation. Nursing Series. Bulletins (ISSN 0073-7526)

331 614 US
INDUSTRIAL HEALTH FOUNDATION. TECHNICAL BULLETIN. MANAGEMENT SERIES. 1971. irreg., no. 2, 1978. price varies. Industrial Health Foundation, Inc., 5231 Centre Ave., Pittsburgh, PA 15232. (back issues avail.)

INDUSTRIAL VENTILATION; A MANUAL OF RECOMMENDED PRACTICE. see HEATING, PLUMBING AND REFRIGERATION

614 JA ISSN 0074-4131
INTERNATIONAL CONGRESS ON OCCUPATIONAL HEALTH. PROCEEDINGS. (Text in English or French) triennial, 1969, 16th, Tokyo. $30. (Permanent Commission and International Association on Occupational Health - Congres International de Medecine du Travail) Japan Industrial Safety Association, 35-4 Shiba, 5-chome, Minato-ku, Tokyo 108, Japan.
Proceedings published in host country

331.8 614.8 UN ISSN 0579-8140
INTERNATIONAL DIRECTORY OF OCCUPATIONAL SAFETY AND HEALTH SERVICES AND INSTITUTIONS. (Subseries of the office's Occupational Safety and Health Series) a. International Labour Office, Publications Sales Service, CH-1211 Geneva 22, Switzerland (U.S. Distributor: I L O Branch Office, 1750 New York Ave. N.W., Washington, DC 20006)

613.62 331 US ISSN 0092-6299
IOWA. BUREAU OF LABOR. OCCUPATIONAL INJURIES AND ILLNESSES SURVEY. 1973. a. free. Bureau of Labor, Research and Statistics Division, East 7th and Court, Des Moines, IA 50319. stat. circ. 300. (processed)

MINES SAFETY AND HEALTH COMMISSION. REPORT/ORGANE PERMANENT POUR LA SECURITE DANS LES MINES E HOUILLE. RAPPORT. see MINES AND MINING INDUSTRY

613.62 US
MONOGRAPHS ON INDUSTRIAL HYGIENE. irreg. price varies. Academic Press, Inc., 111 Fifth Avenue, New York, NY 10003.

613.62 UK ISSN 0141-7568
OCCUPATIONAL HYGIENE MONOGRAPHS.
1978. irreg. Science Reviews Ltd., 40 The Fairway, Northwood, Middx. HAG 3DY, England. Ed. Dr. Donald Hughes. (back issues avail.)

344 US ISSN 0092-3435
OCCUPATIONAL SAFETY AND HEALTH DECISIONS. 1973. irreg. $27.50. Commerce Clearing House, Inc., 4025 W. Peterson Ave., Chicago, IL 60646.

613.62 UN ISSN 0078-3129
OCCUPATIONAL SAFETY AND HEALTH SERIES. (Editions in English, French and Spanish) 1963. irreg. free. International Labour Office, Publications Sales Service, CH-1211 Geneva 22, Switzerland (U.S. Distributor: I L O Branch Office, 1750 New York Ave. N.W., Washington, DC 20006)

614.85 UK
PROTECTION DIRECTORY OF INDUSTRIAL & ENVIRONMENTAL PERSONNEL. vol. 3, 1978/79. a. £5($10.50) (Institution of Industrial Safety Offices) Alan Osborne & Associates, 6 Tranquil Passage, Blackheath, London S.E. 3, England. (reprint service avail. from UMI)

615 US
REGISTRY OF TOXIC EFFECTS OF CHEMICAL SUBSTANCES. 1971. a. U.S. National Institute for Occupational Safety and Health, 5600 Fishers Lane, Rockville, MD 20857. Ed. Richard J. Lewis. abstr. bibl. index. circ. 10,000. (processed; also avail. in microform)

614.8 CN
SECURITE INDUSTRIELLE. 1975. a. Cash Crop Farming Publications Ltd., 222 Argyle Ave., Delhi, Ont. N4B 2Y2, Canada. Ed. D.G. Glendinning. adv.

SECURITY AND PROTECTION MANUAL. see FIRE PREVENTION

331.1 JA ISSN 0081-928X
SUMITOMO BULLETIN OF INDUSTRIAL HEALTH/SUMITOMO SANGYO EISEI. (Text in Japanese; summaries in English or French) 1965. a. $15 approx. Institute of Industrial Health, Sumitomo Hospital, 5-2-2 Nakanoshima, Kita-ku, Osaka 530, Japan. Ed. Dr. J. Kotani. bk. rev. Indexed: Ind.Med.

614.8 SZ ISSN 0084-165X
WORLD CONGRESS ON THE PREVENTION OF OCCUPATIONAL ACCIDENTS AND DISEASES. PROCEEDINGS. (Proceedings published by national organizing committee) 1955. triennial, 1971, 6th, Vienna. International Social Security Association, Box 1, 1211 Geneva 22, Switzerland.

331.8 US ISSN 0093-1241
WYOMING. DEPARTMENT OF LABOR AND STATISTICS. SURVEY OF OCCUPATIONAL INJURIES AND ILLNESSES. 1968. a. free. Department of Labor and Statistics, Barrett Bldg., Cheyenne, WY 82002. charts. stat. circ. 200. (processed)
Formerly: Wyoming Work Injury Report (ISSN 0085-8331)

INDUSTRIAL HEALTH AND SAFETY — Abstracting, Bibliographies, Statistics

658.2 614.85 AT ISSN 0314-1721
AUSTRALIA. BUREAU OF STATISTICS. TASMANIAN OFFICE. INDUSTRIAL ACCIDENT STATISTICS. a. Australian Bureau of Statistics, Tasmanian Office, Box 66A, Hobart, Tasmania 7001, Australia. circ. 500.

AUSTRALIA. BUREAU OF STATISTICS. WESTERN AUSTRALIAN OFFICE. INDUSTRIAL ACCIDENTS. SERIES A: ABSENCE FROM WORK FOR ONE DAY OR MORE. see BUSINESS AND ECONOMICS — Abstracting, Bibliographies, Statistics

AUSTRALIA. BUREAU OF STATISTICS. WESTERN AUSTRALIAN OFFICE. INDUSTRIAL ACCIDENTS. SERIES B: ABSENCE FROM WORK FOR ONE WEEK OR MORE. see BUSINESS AND ECONOMICS — Abstracting, Bibliographies, Statistics

331.8 016 613 UN ISSN 0074-2147
INTERNATIONAL CATALOGUE OF OCCUPATIONAL SAFETY AND HEALTH FILMS. (Subseries of Occupational Safety and Health Series) (Text in English, French and Spanish) 1969. irreg. International Labour Office, Publications Sales Service, CH-1211 Geneva 22, Switzerland (U.S. Distributor: I L O Branch Office, 1750 New York Ave. N.W., Washington, DC 20006)

312.39 614 US ISSN 0095-8174
VIRGINIA. DEPARTMENT OF LABOR AND INDUSTRY. DIVISION OF RESEARCH AND STATISTICS. OCCUPATIONAL INJURIES AND ILLNESSES BY INDUSTRY. a. free. Department of Labor and Industry, Division of Research and Statistics, Box 1814, Richmond, VA 23214. stat. Key Title: Occupational Injuries and Illnesses by Industry.

INORGANIC CHEMISTRY

see Chemistry — Inorganic Chemistry

INSTRUMENTS

see also Jewelry, Clocks and Watches; Metrology and Standardization

681.2 US ISSN 0065-2814
ADVANCES IN INSTRUMENTATION. (Consists of: Instrument Society of America. International Conference Proceedings) a. price varies. Instrument Society of America, 400 Stanwix St., Pittsburgh, PA 15222.

ADVANCES IN TEST MEASUREMENT; with Instrumentation in the Aerospace Industry. see METROLOGY AND STANDARDIZATION

AIR QUALITY INSTRUMENTATION. see ENVIRONMENTAL STUDIES

681 IT ISSN 0004-7309
ATTUALITA DI LABORATORIO. 1955. irreg. free. Dott. G. Terzano & Co. S.p.A., Via Darwin 19-21, Milan, Italy. charts. illus. Indexed: Chem.Abstr.

BIOMEDICAL SCIENCES INSTRUMENTATION. see MEDICAL SCIENCES

681 CN
CANADIAN CONTROLS & INSTRUMENTS CONTROL/INSTRUMENTS BUYERS' GUIDE. 1962. a. Can.$18. Maclean-Hunter Ltd., 481 University Ave., Toronto, Ont. M5W 1A7, Canada. Ed. Tom Kelly.
Formerly: Canadian Controls & Instrumentation Control/Instrumentation Buyers' Guide (ISSN 0068-8525)

CHILTON'S CONTROL EQUIPMENT MASTER. see ENGINEERING

CLINICAL LABORATORY REFERENCE. see MEDICAL SCIENCES — Experimental Medicine, Laboratory Technique

681.2 607 US ISSN 0046-144X
EDUCATION NEWS FROM METROLOGIC. 1971. a. free. ‡ Metrologic Instruments Inc., 143 Harding Ave., Bellmawr, NJ 08030. Ed. Herbert H. Gottlieb. adv. bk. rev. charts. illus. circ. 5,000.

681 US ISSN 0074-0500
I S A TRANSDUCER COMPENDIUM. 1963. irreg., 1968-1972, 2nd ed. $72. Instrument Society of America, 400 Stanwix St., Pittsburgh, PA 15222. Ed. Glenn F. Harvey. index.

681 US
INDUSTRIAL AND CONTROL APPLICATIONS OF MICROPROCESSORS. PROCEEDINGS. At head of title: I C E I(Year) a. Institute of Electrical and Electronics Engineers, Inc., Industrial Electronics and Control Instrumentation Group, 5855 Naples Plaza, No. 301, Long Beach, CA 90803.
Formerly: Industrial Applications of Microprocessors.

681 US ISSN 0074-0497
INSTRUMENT AND CONTROL SYSTEMS BUYERS GUIDE. 1939. a. $5 avail. to subscribers of Instruments and Control Systems. $4. Chilton Co., Inc., Chilton Way, Radnor, PA 19089. circ. 70,000.

681 US
INSTRUMENT MAINTENANCE MANAGEMENT. a. $8. Instrument Society of America, 400 Stanwix St., Pittsburgh, PA 15222.

681 US ISSN 0091-7699
INSTRUMENT SOCIETY OF AMERICA. I S A FINAL CONTROL ELEMENTS SYMPOSIUM. FINAL CONTROL ELEMENTS; PROCEEDINGS. 1970. irreg., latest 1977. price varies. Instrument Society of America, 400 Stanwix St., Pittsburgh, PA 15222. illus.

681.2 US ISSN 0074-0527
INSTRUMENT SOCIETY OF AMERICA. STANDARDS AND PRACTICES FOR INSTRUMENTATION. 1963. irreg., 1977, 5th ed. $100. Instrument Society of America, 400 Stanwix St., Pittsburgh, PA 15222. Ed. Mark T.Yothers. index.

681 660 US ISSN 0074-0551
INSTRUMENTATION IN THE CHEMICAL AND PETROLEUM INDUSTRY. (Includes: International Instrument Society of America Chemical and Petroleum Instrumentation Syposium Prodeedings) 1965. a. price varies. Instrument Society of America, 400 Stanwix St., Pittsburgh, PA 15222.

681 US
INSTRUMENTATION IN THE CRYOGENIC INDUSTRY; proceedings of the biennial Symposium on Cryogenic Instrumentation. 1976. biennial. $10. Instrument Society of America, 400 Stanwix St., Pittsburgh, PA 15222.

681.7 US ISSN 0074-056X
INSTRUMENTATION IN THE POWER INDUSTRY. (Includes: International Instrument Society of America Power Symposium Proceedings) 1967. a. price varies. Instrument Society of America, 400 Stanwix St., Pittsburgh, PA 15222.

681 US ISSN 0020-4412
INSTRUMENTS AND EXPERIMENTAL TECHNIQUES. English translation of: Pribory i Tekhnika Eksperimenta. 1958. m. $365. (Akademiya Nauk S.S.S.R., UR) Consultants Bureau (Subsidiary of: Plenum Publishing Corp.) 233 Spring St., New York, NY 10013. Ed. A.I. Shalnikov. Indexed: Appl. Mech. Rev. Chem. Abstr. Eng. Ind. Sci. Abstr.

338.4 UK
LABORATORY EQUIPMENT DIRECTORY. 1972. a. £15. Morgan-Grampian Book Publishing Co., 30 Calderwood St., Woolwich, London SE18 6QH, England. Ed. Jane Doyle. circ. 2,500.
Formerly: Laboratory Equipment Directory & Buyers Guide.

OXFORD MEDICAL ENGINEERING SERIES. see MEDICAL SCIENCES

681 FR
REVUE FRANCAISE DES LABORATOIRES. 1972. a. 242 F. Labo-France, 7 rue Godot de Mauroy, 75009 Paris, France. adv. circ. 14,000.
Formerly: Revue Francaise des Fournisseurs de Laboratoires.

681.2 542 US
SCIENCE GUIDE TO SCIENTIFIC
INSTRUMENTS. 1964. a. $6. American
Association for the Advancement of Science, 1515
Massachusetts Ave N.W., Washington, DC 20005.
Ed. Richard Sommer. adv. circ. 160,000. (also avail.
in microfiche from BLH; microfiche from UMI;
microfilm from UMI; back issues avail)
   Formerly: Guide to Scientific Instruments (ISSN
0533-5426)

681 681 UK
SIRA INSTITUTE. ANNUAL REPORT. 1969-70. a.
Sira Institute, Ltd., South Hill, Chislehurst, Kent
BR7 5EH, England. circ. 1,500.
   Supersedes: British Scientific Instrument Research
Association. Annual Report.

SOCIETY OF PHOTO-OPTICAL
INSTRUMENTATION ENGINEERS.
PROCEEDINGS. see PHYSICS — Optics

681 FI ISSN 0355-3434
VALTION TEKNILLINEN TUTKIMUSKESKUS.
KOJETEKNIIKAN LABORATORIO.
TIEDONANTO/TECHNICAL RESEARCH
CENTRE OF FINLAND. INSTRUMENT
LABORATORY. REPORT. (Text mainly in
Finnish, some in English or Swedish) 1974. irreg.
price varies. Valtion Teknillinen Tutkimuskeskus -
Technical Research Centre of Finland,
Vuorimiehentie 5, 02150 Espoo 15, Finland.

WATER QUALITY INSTRUMENTATION. see
WATER RESOURCES

INSTRUMENTS — Abstracting, Bibliographies, Statistics

338.4 CN ISSN 0384-4242
CANADA. STATISTICS CANADA. SCIENTIFIC
AND PROFESSIONAL EQUIPMENT
INDUSTRIES/FABRICATION DE MATERIEL
SCIENTIFIQUE ET PROFESSIONNEL.
(Catalogue 47-206) (Text in English and French)
1960. a. Can.$6($7.20) Statistics Canada,
Publications Distribution, Ottawa, Ont. K1A 0V7,
Canada. (also avail. in microform from MML)

INSURANCE

368 AT ISSN 0084-697X
A. I. J. MANUAL OF AUSTRALASIAN LIFE
ASSURANCE. (Australasian Insurance Journal)
1930/31. a. $1.60. Bushell Publishing Co. Pty. Ltd.,
Box 14, Haberfield, N.S.W. 2045, Australia.

368.4 SZ ISSN 0379-7074
AFRICAN NEWS SHEET. French edition: Cahiers
Africains. 1967. irreg. International Social Security
Association, Box 1, 1211 Geneva 22, Switzerland.
   Formerly: African Social Security Series (ISSN
0065-4043)

368.012 US ISSN 0065-4272
AGENT'S AND BUYER'S GUIDE. 1947. a. $11.50.
National Underwriter Co., 420 E. Fourth St.,
Cincinnati, OH 45202. adv.

368.4 US ISSN 0095-4667
ALASKA MEDICAID STATUS REPORT. 1973. a.
free. Department of Health and Social Services,
Division of Public Assistance, Pouch H-01, Juneau,
AK 99811. illus.
   Formerly: Alaska. Division of Medical
Assistance. Medicaid Annual Status Report (ISSN
0095-4675)

368.382 CN
ALBERTA. HEALTH CARE INSURANCE PLAN.
ANNUAL REPORT. 1970. a. Health Care
Insurance Commission, 118th Ave & Groat Rd.,
Edmonton, Alta. T5J 2M3, Canada. illus.
   Formerly (until 1978): Alberta. Health Care
Insurance Commission. Annual Report (ISSN 0383-
3615)
   Health

368 333.33 CN ISSN 0705-596X
ALBERTA. OFFICE OF THE SUPERINTENDENT
OF INSURANCE AND REAL ESTATE.
ANNUAL REPORT. 1976. irreg. Office of the
Superintendent of Insurance and Real Estate, 10065
Jasper Ave., Edmonton, Alta. T5J 3B1, Canada.
stat.

ALBERTA HAIL AND CROP INSURANCE
CORPORATION. ANNUAL REPORT. see
AGRICULTURE — Crop Production And Soil

368.4 NE ISSN 0401-331X
ALGEMEEN WERKLOOSHEIDSFONDS.
JAARVERSLAG. a. Algemeen Werkloosheidsfonds,
President Kennedylaan 21, 2517 JK The Hague,
Netherlands.

AMERICAN COUNCIL OF LIFE INSURANCE.
ECONOMIC AND INVESTMENT REPORT. see
BUSINESS AND ECONOMICS — Investments

368 US
AMERICAN INSURANCE ASSOCIATION.
ENGINEERING AND SAFETY SERVICE.
SPECIAL INTEREST BULLETIN. 1933. irreg., no.
294, 1976. $6 per set. American Insurance
Association, 85 John St., New York, NY 10038.
(looseleaf format)

331.2 US ISSN 0094-422X
AMERICAN SOCIETY OF PENSION
ACTUARIES. TRANSCRIBINGS. ANNUAL
CONFERENCE. a. $10. American Society of
Pension Actuaries, 1700 K St. N.W., Suite 404,
Washington, DC 20006. stat. Key Title:
Transcribings. Annual Conference - American
Society of Pension Actuaries.

368 EC
ANALISIS TECNICO DEL SEGURO PRIVADO
EN EL ECUADOR. irreg. Superintendencia de
Bancos, Avda. 10 de Agosto 251, Casilla 424,
Quito, Ecuador. charts.

ANALYSIS OF WORKERS' COMPENSATION
LAWS. see SOCIAL SERVICES AND WELFARE

368 FR
ANNUAIRE DES ASSURANCES ET
L'ASSUREUR-CONSEIL. a. 2 rue de Chateaudun,
75009 Paris, France.

368 CH
ANNUAL REPORT OF LIFE INSURANCE,
REPUBLIC OF CHINA. (Text in Chinese and
English) 1972. a. free. Taipei Life Insurance
Association, 5Th Floor, Suite 152, Sung Chiang Rd.,
Taipei, Taiwan, Republic of China.

368 IT ISSN 0084-6635
ANNUARIO ITALIANO DELLE IMPRESE
ASSICURATRICI. 1949. a. L.13000. Associazione
Nazionale fra le Imprese Assicuratrici, Via della
Frezza, 70, 00186 Rome, Italy. Ed. Francesco
Ciraci. circ. 4,000.

368 SP
ANUARIO ESPANOL DE SEGUROS. 1910. a. 3500
ptas. Club del Ejecutivo de Seguros, Santa Engracia,
151, Madrid 3, Spain.

368 SP
ANUARIO IBEROAMERICANO DE SEGUROS.
1980. a. 2500 ptas. Club del Ejecutivo de Seguros,
Santa Engracia, 151, Madrid 3, Spain.

368.4 NE
ARBEIDSONGESCHIKTHEIDSFONDS.
JAARVERSLAG. a. Arbeidsongeschiktheidsfonds,
President Kennedylaan 21, 2517 JK The Hague,
Netherlands.

368.1 US ISSN 0360-8921
ARGUS F. C. & S. CHART. (Fire Casualty & Surety)
a. $8.80. National Underwriter Co., Statistical
Department, 420 E. 4th St., Cinncinnati, OH 45202.
   Formerly: Argus Insurance Chart.

368.3 US ISSN 0066-9598
ASSOCIATION OF LIFE INSURANCE MEDICAL
DIRECTORS OF AMERICA. TRANSACTIONS.
1889. a. $15. Association of Life Insurance Medical
Directors, 200 Berkley St., Boston, MA 02117. Ed.
Paul S Entmacher, M.D. cum. index: quinquennial.
circ. 1,000(controlled) (also avail. in microform from
UMI) Indexed: Ind.Med.

368 NE ISSN 0515-0361
ASTIN BULLETIN; international journal for actuarial
studies in non-life insurance and risk theory. (Text
in English or French) 3/yr. fl.75. (International
Actuarial Association, Astin Section) E. J. Brill,
Oude Rijn 33a-35, Leiden, Netherlands. Ed. P ter
Berg.

368.4 AT
AUSTRALIA. DEPARTMENT OF SOCIAL
SECURITY. ANNUAL REPORT OF THE
DIRECTOR-GENERAL. 1972/73. a. Australian
Government Publishing Service, Publishing Branch,
P.O. Box 84, Canberra 2600, A.C.T., Australia.
illus. stat.

328.94 368.9 AT
AUSTRALIA. INSURANCE COMMISSIONER.
ANNUAL REPORT. a. price varies. Australian
Government Publishing Service, Box 84, Canberra,
A.C.T. 2600, Australia. illus. stat.

368 AT ISSN 0084-7453
AUSTRALIAN INSURANCE INSTITUTE.
JOURNAL. 1919. a. Aus.$5. ‡ Australian Insurance
Institute, 257 Collins St., Melbourne, Vic. 3000,
Australia. Ed. P. Kell. bk. rev.

AUSTRALIAN SUPERANNUATION AND
EMPLOYEE BENEFITS GUIDE. see SOCIAL
SERVICES AND WELFARE

368 UY
BANCOSEGUROS. 1975. irreg. Banco de Seguros,
Agremiacion de Funcionarios, Calle Sarandi 356,
Montevideo, Uruguay. illus.
   Organization news

368.4 BE
BELGIUM. INSTITUT NATIONAL
D'ASSURANCES SOCIALES POUR
TRAVAILLEURS INDEPENDANTS. RAPPORT
ANNUEL. Flemish edition: Belgium. Rijkinstituut
voor de Sociale Verzekeringen der Zelfstandigen.
Jaarverslag. 1970. a. free. Institut National
d'Assurances Sociales pour Travailleurs
Independants, Bibliotheque - Bureau 7-6 (Wat.),
Place Jean Jacobs, 6, 1000 Brussels, Belgium.

368 BE
BELGIUM. INSTITUT NATIONAL
D'ASSURANCES SOCIALES POUR
TRAVAILLEURS INDEPENDANTS.
STATISTIQUES DES BENEFICIAIRES DE
PRESTATIONS DE RETRAITE ET DE SURVIE/
BELGIUM. RIJKINSTITUUT VOOR DE SOCIAL
VERZEKERINGEN DER ZELFSTANDIGEN.
STATISTIEK VAN DE PERSONEN DIE EEN
RUST- EN OVERLEVINGSPRESTATIE
GENIETEN. (Text in Flemish and French) 1970. a.
free. Institut National d'Assurances Sociales pour
Travailleurs Independants, Bibliotheque - Bureau 7-6
(Wat.), Place Jean Jacobs, 6, 1000 Brussels,
Belgium. stat.

368.4 BE
BELGIUM. INSTITUT NATIONAL
D'ASSURANCES SOCIALES POUR
TRAVAILLEURS INDEPENDANTS.
STATISTIQUES DES PERSONNES
ASSUJETTIES AU STATUT SOCIAL DES
TRAVAILLEURS INDEPENDANTS/BELGIUM.
RIJKSINSTITUUT VOOR DE SOCIALE
VERZEKERINGEN DER ZELFSTANDIGEN.
STATISTIEK VAN DE PERSONEN DIE
ONDER DE TOEPASSING VALLEN VAN HET
SOCIAAL STATUUT VAN DE
ZELFSTANDIGEN. (Text in Flemish and French)
1970. a. free. Institut National d'Assurances Sociales
pour Travailleurs Independants, Bibliotheque -
Bureau 7-6 (Wat.), Place Jean Jacobs, 6, 1000
Brussels, Belgium.

368.4 BE ISSN 0067-558X
BELGIUM. MINISTERE DE LA PREVOYANCE
SOCIALE. RAPPORT GENERAL SUR LA
SECURITE SOCIALE/ALGEMEEN VERSLAG
OVER DE SOCIALE ZEKERHEID. (Text in
French and Flemish) 1962. a. 200 Fr. Ministere de
la Prevoyance Sociale, Rue de la Vierge Noire 3 C,
B-1000 Brussels, Belgium.

368 US ISSN 0094-9973
BEST'S AGENTS GUIDE TO LIFE INSURANCE
COMPANIES. 1974. a. $12. A. M. Best Co.,
Oldwick, NJ 08858. Ed. C. Burton Kellogg. stat.

INSURANCE

368 US
BEST'S INSURANCE REPORT: LIFE-HEALTH. 1906. $225. A. M. Best Co., Oldwick, NJ 08858. Ed. C. Burton Kellogg. stat.

368 US ISSN 0148-3218
BEST'S INSURANCE REPORT: PROPERTY-CASUALTY. 1900. a. $375. A. M. Best Co., Oldwick, NJ 08858. Ed. Robert J. Schraeder. stat.
Formerly: Best's Insurance Report: Property-Liability.

368 US ISSN 0091-830X
BEST'S RECOMMENDED INDEPENDENT INSURANCE ADJUSTERS. 1930. a. $15. ‡ A. M. Best Co., Oldwick, NJ 08858. Ed. John J. Liwok. circ. 12,000.
Continues: Best's Recommended Insurance Adjusters.

368 US
BEST'S RECOMMENDED INSURANCE ATTORNEYS. 1928. a. $25. A.M. Best Co., Oldwick, NJ 08858. Ed. John J. Liwok.

368 BO
BOLIVIA. SUPERINTENDENCIA NACIONAL DE SEGUROS Y REASEGUROS. COLECCION ESTUDIOS. 1976. irreg. Superintendencia Nacional de Seguros y Reaseguras, La Paz, Bolivia.

368.4 BL
BRAZIL. INSTITUTO NACIONAL DE PREVIDENCIA SOCIAL. BALANCO GERAL. a. Instituto Nacional de Assistencia Medica da Previdencia Social, Secretaria de Contabilidade e Autonoma, Rua Mexico 128, Caixa Postal 1290, Rio de Janeiro, Brazil. charts, stat.
Social security

368.4 CN
BRITISH COLUMBIA. WORKERS' COMPENSATION BOARD. WORKERS' COMPENSATION REPORTER. 1973. irreg. Can.$35. Workers' Compensation Board, Information Services, 5255 Heather St., Vancouver, B.C. 45Z 3L8, Canada. circ. 750.

368 CN ISSN 0068-1598
BRITISH COLUMBIA INSURANCE DIRECTORY. INSURANCE COMPANIES, AGENTS AND ADJUSTERS. 1964. a. Can.$17. ‡ Arbutus Publications Ltd., P.O. Box 35070, Sta. E, Vancouver, B.C. V6M 4G1, Canada. Ed. W. D. S. Earle. adv. bk. rev. circ. 1,400.

368 AG
BRUJULA. Variant title: Compania Argentina de Seguros. Memoria y Balance General. no. 14,1975. irreg. Compania Argentina de Seguros, San Martin 439, Buenos Aires, Argentina.

368 US
BUYER STUDY; a market study of new insured and ordinary life insurance purchased. (In 2 edts., U.S. and Canada) a. $25. Life Insurance Marketing and Research Association (LIMRA), 170 Sigourney St., Hartford, CT 06105.

368.012 US ISSN 0066-0590
C L U FORUM REPORT. 1967. a. $7. American Society of Chartered Life Underwriters, 270 Bryn Mawr Ave., Box 59, Bryn Mawr, PA 19010. Ed. Edward H. Armsby. circ. 2,500.

CALIFORNIA. EMPLOYMENT DATA AND RESEARCH DIVISION. TAXABLE AND TOTAL WAGES, REGULAR BENEFITS PAID, EMPLOYER CONTRIBUTIONS EARNED, AND AVERAGE COVERED EMPLOYMENT, BY INDUSTRY. see *BUSINESS AND ECONOMICS — Labor And Industrial Relations*

332 358 CN ISSN 0068-7383
CANADA. DEPARTMENT OF INSURANCE. REPORT. CO-OPERATIVE CREDIT ASSOCIATIONS. 1956. a. price varies. Supply and Services Canada, Publishing Centre, Hull, Que. K1A 0S5, Canada.

368 CN ISSN 0068-7405
CANADA. DEPARTMENT OF INSURANCE. REPORT OF THE SUPERINTENDENT OF INSURANCE. (Issued in 3 vols) a. price varies. Supply and Services Canada, Publishing Centre, Hull, Que. K1A 0S5, Canada.

332 CN ISSN 0068-7413
CANADA. DEPARTMENT OF INSURANCE. REPORT. SMALL LOANS COMPANIES AND MONEY-LENDERS. a. price varies. Supply and Services Canada, Publishing Centre, Hull, Que. K1A 0S5, Canada.

332.1 368 CN ISSN 0068-7391
CANADA. DEPARTMENT OF INSURANCE. REPORT. TRUST AND LOAN COMPANIES. a. price varies. Supply and Services Canada, Publishing Centre, Hull, Que. K1A 0S5, Canada.

368 CN ISSN 0068-8975
CANADIAN INSTITUTE OF ACTUARIES. YEARBOOK. a. membership. Canadian Institute of Actuaries, Suite 506, 116 Albert St., Ottawa, Ont. K1P 5G3, Canada.

368 CN ISSN 0068-9025
CANADIAN INSURANCE. ANNUAL STATISTICAL ISSUE. 1924. a. Can.$6. Stone and Cox Ltd., 100 Simcoe St., Toronto, Ont. M5H 3G2, Canada. Ed. M. Steeler. adv. circ. 11,700.

368.91 CN ISSN 0068-9033
CANADIAN INSURANCE LAW BULLETIN SERVICE. 1929. irreg. Can.$75. Stone & Cox Ltd., 100 Simcoe St., Toronto, Ont. M5H 3G2, Canada. Ed. B. C. F. Fraser. circ. 800.

368 CN ISSN 0707-6150
CANADIAN LIFE INSURANCE ASSOCIATION. DIRECTORY/ASSOCIATION CANADIENNE DES COMPAGNIES D'ASSURANCE. ANNUAIRE. (Text in English and French) a. free. Canadian Life Insurance Association, Box 2110, Toronto, Ont. M5W 1H1, Canada.

368 CN ISSN 0068-9157
CANADIAN LIFE INSURANCE FACTS; an authoritative source of factual information about life insurance in Canada. (Text in English and French) 1955. a. free. ‡ Canadian Life Insurance Association, Box 2110, Toronto, Ont. M5W 1H1, Canada. Ed. Hugh A. MacLean. circ. 9,000.

368.4 CL
CHILE. SUPERINTENDENCIA DE SEGURIDAD SOCIAL. SEGURIDAD SOCIAL: ESTADISTICAS. 1969. irreg. exchange basis. Superintendenica de Seguridad Social, Santiago, Chile.
Continues: Chile. Superintendencia de Seguridad Social. Boletin de Estadisticas de Seguridad.

368.01 US ISSN 0069-5718
COLLEGE OF INSURANCE. GENERAL BULLETIN. 1962-63. biennial. free. ‡ College of Insurance, 123 William St., New York, NY 10038. circ. 20,000.

COLOMBIA. MINISTERIO DE TRABAJO Y SEGURIDAD SOCIAL. MEMORIA. see *BUSINESS AND ECONOMICS — Labor And Industrial Relations*

COLOMBIA. SUPERINTENDENCIA BANCARIA. SEGUROS Y CAPITALIZACION. see *BUSINESS AND ECONOMICS*

368 CN ISSN 0315-8098
CORPORATE INSURANCE IN CANADA. vol. 2, 1974. a. Can.$2. Stone & Cox Ltd., 100 Simcoe St., Toronto, Ont. M5H 3G2, Canada. Ed. M.S. Steeler. adv. illus. circ. 6,300.

368.4 331 US ISSN 0070-0290
CORPORATE PENSION FUND SEMINAR. PROCEEDINGS. 1964. a. Donaldson, Lufkin and Jenrette, Inc, 140 Broadway, New York, NY 10005. (Co-sponsor: Alliance Capital Management Corp.) circ. 2,000.

CYPRUS. MINISTRY OF LABOUR AND SOCIAL INSURANCE. ANNUAL REPORT. see *BUSINESS AND ECONOMICS — Labor And Industrial Relations*

368 DK
DANSK FORSIKRINGS AARBOG. a. Kr.100. Tidsskriftet Forsikring, Amaliegade 10, DK-1256 Copenhagen K, Denmark. Eds. Arne Midtgaard, Erik Heimann Olsen.

368.8 II ISSN 0304-6966
DEPOSIT INSURANCE CORPORATION. ANNUAL REPORT: DIRECTORS' REPORT, BALANCE SHEET AND ACCOUNTS. (Text in English) a. Deposit Insurance Corporation, Vidyut Bhavan, P.B. No. 2810, Pathakwadi, Bombay 2, India.

368 GW ISSN 0070-4237
DIE DEUTSCHE LEBENSVERSICHERUNG. a. free. (Verband der Lebensversicherungsunternehmen e.V.) Verlag Versicherungswirtschaft e.V., Klosestr. 22, 7500 Karlsruhe, W. Germany (B.R.D.) circ. 22,000.

368 GW ISSN 0417-3228
DEUTSCHER SOZIALVERSICHERUNGS-KALENDER. (Title Varies--1963: Deutscher Krankenkassen-Kalender) a. DM.49.95. Walhalla- und Praetoria-Verlag Georg Zwichenpflug, Dolomitenstr. 1, Postfach 301, 8400 Regensburg 1, W. Germany (B.R.D.)

368 US ISSN 0070-5691
DIRECTORY OF INSURANCE COMPANIES LICENSED IN NEW YORK STATE. a. $1 per no. (single copies free to NY residents) Insurance Department, Empire State Plaza, Agency Bldg. No. 1, Albany, NY 12257.

368 ES
EL SALVADOR. SUPERINTENDENCIA DE BANCOS Y OTRAS INSTITUCIONES FINANCIERAS. ESTADISTICAS: SEGUROS, FIANZAS, BANCOS. Variant title: Estadisticas, Seguros, Fianzas, Bancos. 1963. irreg. free. Superintendencia de Bancos y Otras Instituciones Financieras, Asesoria Actuarial y Estadistica, Junta Monetaria, Edificio B C R, San Salvador, El Salvador. charts. circ. 750.
Formerly (until 1976, no. 14): El Salvador. Superintendencia de Bancos y Otras Instituciones Financieras. Estadisticas: Seguros, Finanzas, Capitalizacion (ISSN 0067-3234)

368 UK
EXECUTIVE PENSIONS AND BENEFITS. 1976. irreg. £7.75. Fundex Ltd., Minster Hous, Arthur St, London, England. Ed. Nia Sweeney. circ. 4,500. (tabloid format)

368.08 UK ISSN 0071-3686
FACULTY OF ACTUARIES IN SCOTLAND. TRANSACTIONS. 1901. irreg (approx 4/yr) £2 per issue. Faculty of Actuaries in Scotland, 23 St. Andrew Sq., Edinburgh EH2 1AQ, Scotland. Ed. A. M. Robertson. bk. rev. index. circ. 1,100.

368.8 332.2 US ISSN 0428-1365
FEDERAL SAVINGS AND LOAN INSURANCE CORPORATION. LIST OF MEMBER INSTITUTIONS. 1962. a. U. S. Federal Home Loan Bank Board, 1700 G St., N.W., Washington, DC 20552. Ed. Elizabeth M. Miller. circ. 500. Key Title: List of Member Institutions - Federal Saving and Loan Insurance Corporation.

368.4 NE ISSN 0071-4151
FEDERATIE VAN BEDRIJFSVERENIGINGEN. JAARVERSLAG. 1930. a. free. Federatie van Bedrijfsvereningingen, Postbus 8300, Amsterdam, Netherlands. circ. 400.

368 657 US ISSN 0148-8880
FINANCIAL REPORTING TRENDS: LIFE INSURANCE. 1974. a. free. Ernst & Whinney, 2000 National City Center, Cleveland, OH 44114. charts. stat.

657 369 US
FINANCIAL REPORTING TRENDS: PROPERTY/CASUALTY INSURANCE. a. free. Ernst & Whinney, 2000 National City Center, Cleveland, OH 44114. stat.
Formerly (until 1979): Financial Reporting Trends: Fire and Casualty Insurance (ISSN 0093-5751)

368 UK ISSN 0309-751X
FINANCIAL TIMES WORLD INSURANCE YEAR BOOK. a. £35. Longman Group Ltd., Longman House, Burnt Mill, Harlow, Essex CM20 2JE, England.

FINLAND. KANSANELAKELAITOS. JULKAISUJA. SARJA E. see *MEDICAL SCIENCES*

INSURANCE

FINLAND. KANSANELAKELAITOS. JULKAISUJA. SARJA M. see *MEDICAL SCIENCES*

368.4   FI   ISSN 0430-5205
FINLAND. KANSANELAKELAITOS. JULKAISUJA. SARJA A. (Text in Finnish and English; summaries in English) 1967. irreg., no. A14, 1978. Kansanelakelaitos - Social Insurance Institution of Finland, Research Institute of Social Security, Olavinkato 1 A, SF 00100 Helsinki 10, Finland. bibl.

368.1   FI   ISSN 0355-5003
FINLAND KANSANELAKELAITOS. TOIMINTA KERTOMUS. English edition: Finland. Social Insurance Institution. Annual Report. Swedish edition: Finland. Folkpensionsanstalt. Beraettelse. 1938. a. Kansanelakelaitos, Research Institute of Social Security, Olavinkato 1 A, SF-00100 Helsinki 10, Finland. circ. 17,000.

368.01   US   ISSN 0071-9293
FRATERNAL ACTUARIAL ASSOCIATION. PROCEEDINGS. 1918. a. Fraternal Actuarial Association, 222 W. College Ave., Appleton, WI 54911. Ed. Bartley L. Munson.

368   AG
GALICIA Y RIO DE LA PLATA. COMPANIA DE SEGUROS. MEMORIA Y BALANCE GENERAL. 1974. a. Compania de Seguros, Rivadavia 717, Buenos Aires, Argentina. stat.

368   GW   ISSN 0525-1737
GERMANY (FEDERAL REPUBLIC, 1949-) BUNDESAUFSICHTSAMT FUER DAS VERSICHERUNGSWESEN. GESCHAEFTSBERICHT. (Text in German; summaries in French) 1953. a. price varies. Bundesaufsichtsamt fuer das Versicherungswesen, Ludwigkirchplatz 3-4, Postfach 180, 1000 Berlin 15, W. Germany (B.R.D.) bk. rev. stat. index. circ. 1,300.

368   UK   ISSN 0308-499X
GREAT BRITAIN. DEPARTMENT OF TRADE. INSURANCE BUSINESS: ANNUAL REPORT. a. H.M.S.O., P.O.Box 569, London SE1 9NH, England. stat.
    Continues: Great Britain. Board of Trade. Insurance Business: Annual Report (ISSN 0072-5684)

368.3   CN   ISSN 0317-2678
GUIDE DE REUSSITE DANS LE CARRIERE D'ASSUREUR-VIE. English edition: Guide to a Successful Life Insurance Career (ISSN 0381-6532) (Text in French) 1971. a. Life Underwriters Association of Canada - Association des Assureurs-Vie du Canada, 41 Lesmill Rd., Don Mills, Ont. M3B 2T3, Canada.
    Formerly: Guide d'Une Carriere a Succes (ISSN 0317-2686)

368.32   CN   ISSN 0381-6532
GUIDE TO A SUCCESSFUL LIFE INSURANCE CAREER. French edition: Guide de Reussite dans la Carriere d'Assureur-Vie (ISSN 0317-2678) 1971. a. Life Underwriters Association of Canada, 41 Lesmill Rd., Don Mills, Ont. M3B 2T3, Canada.

368   GY
GUYANA. NATIONAL INSURANCE BOARD. ANNUAL REPORT. a. National Insurance Board, Georgetown, Guyana.

368   US   ISSN 0073-1110
HAWAII. INSURANCE DIVISION. REPORT OF THE INSURANCE COMMISSIONER OF HAWAII. 1903. a. free. Department of Regulatory Agencies, Insurance Division, Box 3614, Honolulu, HI 96811. circ. 1,000.

368.3   US   ISSN 0017-9027
HEALTH INSURANCE VIEWPOINTS. 1961. irreg. free. Health Insurance Association of America, Consumer and Professional Relations Div., 919 Third Ave., New York, NY 10022. Ed. Louis A. Orsini. charts. circ. 30,000.

HINE'S INSURANCE COUNSEL. see *LAW*

368   GW   ISSN 0073-3350
HOPPENSTEDT VERSICHERUNGS-JAHRBUCH. 1957. a. DM.285. Verlag Hoppenstedt und Co., Havelstr. 9, Postfach 4006, 6100 Darmstadt, W. Germany (B.R.D.) adv.

368   US
HUEBNER FOUNDATION MONOGRAPH. 1972. irreg. University of Pennsylvania, Wharton School of Finance and Commerce. S.S. Huebner Foundation for Insurance Education, 3641 Locust Walk-CE, Philadelphia, PA 19174 (Dist. by: Richard D. Irwin, Inc., Homewood, IL 60430) Ed. David Cummins.

368   US   ISSN 0073-7127
INDIANA UNIVERSITY. SESQUICENTENNIAL SERIES ON INSURANCE. 1971. irreg., no. 4, 1971. price varies. Indiana University, School of Business, Division of Research, Bloomington, IN 47401.

368.01   UK   ISSN 0073-8980
INSTITUTE OF ACTUARIES. YEAR BOOK. 1929. a. £1.50($5) Institute of Actuaries, Staple Inn Hall, High Holborn, London, WC1V 7QJ, England. Ed. M. C. Allanach. bk. rev. circ. 7,500.

368.01   AT
INSTITUTE OF ACTUARIES OF AUSTRALIA. TRANSACTIONS. 1963. a. Aus.$22.50. ‡ Institute of Actuaries of Australia, 5 Moorina Rd., St. Ives, N.S.W. 2075, Australia. Ed. B. K. Timbrell. circ. 800.
    Formerly: Institute of Actuaries of Australia and New Zealand. Transactions (ISSN 0073-8972)

368   UK   ISSN 0020-269X
INSTITUTE OF ACTUARIES STUDENTS' SOCIETY. JOURNAL. 1916. a. £4($10) Alden Press Ltd., Osney Mead, Oxford OX2 OEF, England. Ed. S.F. Wood. bk. rev. charts. stat. index. cum.index. circ. 2,500.

368.4   HO   ISSN 0074-0233
INSTITUTO HONDURENO DE SEGURIDAD SOCIAL. DEPARTAMENTO DE ESTADISTICA Y PROCESAMIENTO DE DATOS. ANUARIO ESTADISTICO. a (with supplements) exchange. Instituto Hondureno de Seguridad Social, Departamento de Estadistica y Actuarial, Apartado 555, Tegucigalpa, D.C., Honduras.

368.4   CR
INSTITUTO NACIONAL DE SEGUROS MEMORIA ANUAL. 1934. a. free. Instituto Nacional de Seguros, Apdo. 10061, San Jose, Costa Rica. charts. illus. stat. circ. 2,000.
    Former titles: Instituto Nacional de Seguros. Memoria Anual I.N.S & Instituto Nacional de Seguros. Informe Anual (ISSN 0074-0268)

368   US   ISSN 0074-0675
INSURANCE ALMANAC; WHO, WHAT, WHEN AND WHERE IN INSURANCE. 1912. a. $35. Underwriter Printing and Publishing Co., 50 E. Palisade Ave., Englewood, NJ 07631. Ed. Donald E. Wolff. adv. circ. 10,000.

368   US   ISSN 0074-0683
INSURANCE CASEBOOK. 1956. a. $35. Underwriter Printing and Publishing Co., 50 E. Palisade Ave., Englewood, NJ 07631. circ. 7,500.

368   UK   ISSN 0074-0691
INSURANCE DIRECTORY AND YEAR BOOK. 1841. a. £12.50. Buckley Press Ltd., The Butts, Half Acre, Brentford, Middlesex TW8 8BN, England.
    Formerly: Post Magazine Almanack. Insurance Directory.

368   NZ
INSURANCE DIRECTORY OF NEW ZEALAND. a. NZ.$2. Mercantile Gazette of New Zealand Ltd., Box 20-034, Christchurch 5, New Zealand. Ed. E. R. Edmonds.

368.01   US   ISSN 0074-0713
INSURANCE FACTS. 1961. a. free. Insurance Information Institute, 110 William St., New York, NY 10038.
    Compilation of statistics about property-liability insurance and related fields

368   AT
INSURANCE IN AUSTRALIA AND NEW ZEALAND. 1966. a. Aus.$13. McCarron Bird Pty. Ltd, 594 Lonsdale St., Melbourne, Vic. 3000, Australia. Ed.Bd.

368   CN   ISSN 0074-0721
INSURANCE INSTITUTE OF CANADA. REPORT. a. Insurance Institute of Canada, 55 University Ave., Toronto, Ont. M5J 2H7, Canada.

368   JA   ISSN 0085-1930
INSURANCE LIFE/NON-LIFE ANNUAL STATISTICS. 1947. a. $7.50. Insurance Research Institute Ltd. - Hoken Kenkyujo Ltd., 17-3 1-chome Honmachi, Shibuya-ku, Tokyo, Japan. circ. 25,000.

368   US   ISSN 0538-2629
INSURANCE MARKET PLACE; the agents and brokers guide to non-standard & specialty lines, aviation, marine & international insurance. 12th ed., 1974. a. free. Rough Notes Co., Inc., 1200 No. Meridian St., Indianapolis, IN 46206. Ed. Wallace L. Clapp, Jr. circ. 110,000.

368   CN   ISSN 0317-1272
INSURANCE MARKETER. a. Wadham Publications Ltd., 109 Vanderhoof Ave., Suite 101, Toronto, Ont. M4G 2J2, Canada. Ed. K. E. MacLeod. adv. circ. 10,444.

368.3   US   ISSN 0095-5221
INTEREST-ADJUSTED INDEX; life insurance payment and cost comparisons. 1969. a. $18.25. National Underwriter Co., 420 E. 4th St., Cincinnati, OH 45202.

368   SZ   ISSN 0074-1264
INTERNATIONAL ACTUARIAL CONGRESS. TRANSACTIONS. (Published by host country) quadrennial, 21st, 1980, Zurich. International Actuarial Association, c/o J. Kupper, Sec.-Gen., Box 653, CH-8022 Zurich, Switzerland.

368   US
INTERNATIONAL CLAIM ASSOCIATION PROCEEDINGS. a. $5. International Claim Association, c/o Penn Life Insurance Co., Independence Square, Philadelphia, PA 19172. Ed. Dudley W. Moseley.

368.3 610   SZ   ISSN 0074-3747
INTERNATIONAL CONGRESS OF LIFE ASSURANCE MEDICINE. PROCEEDINGS. triennial, 12th, 1976, Munich. Permanent International Committee for the Study of Life Assurance Medicine, c/o Dr. E. Tanner, Secretary-General, Swiss Reinsurance Company, 60 Mythenquai, Box 172, 8022 Zurich, Switzerland. Eds. M. Leffkowitz, H. Steinitz.

368.4   SZ
INTERNATIONAL SOCIAL SECURITY ASSOCIATION. ETUDES ET RECHERCHES/ STUDIES AND RESEARCH. (Editions in English and French) 1970. irreg. (1-2/yr.) 20 Fr. per no. International Social Security Association, Box 1, CH-1211 Geneva 22, Switzerland.

368.4   SZ   ISSN 0074-8439
INTERNATIONAL SOCIAL SECURITY ASSOCIATION. TECHNICAL REPORTS OF ASSEMBLIES. triennial, 19th, 1977, Madrid. price varies. International Social Security Association, Box 1, 1211 Geneva 22, Switzerland.

368   IS   ISSN 0077-5037
ISRAELI LIFE TABLE. (Text in English) 1969. irreg. National Insurance Institute, Weizmann Ave., Jerusalem, Israel.

368   NE
JAARBOEK/VADEMECUM VOOR HET VERZEKERINGSWEZEN. (Issued in 2 Parts) vol. 71, 1979/80. a. fl.195. Drukkerij Korthuis, Marnixstraat 16, The Hague, Netherlands. adv.
    Formed by merger of: Vademecum voor Het Nederlandsche Verzekeringswezen; Jaarboek voor Het Assurantie- en Hypotheekwezen.

368   JM
JAMAICA. MINISTRY OF SOCIAL SECURITY. REPORT. irreg. free. Ministry of Social Security, 14 National Heroes Circle, Box 10, Kingston 5, Jamaica.
    Formerly: Jamaica. Ministry of Pensions and Social Security. Report; Incorporating: Jamaica. National Insurance Scheme. Annual Reports (ISSN 0077-5053)

368   CN   ISSN 0318-8116
L U A C MONITOR. French Edition (ISSN 0318-8213) (Editions in English and French) 1957. irreg. membership. ‡ Life Underwriters Association of Canada, 41 Lesmill Rd., Don Mills, Ont. M3B 2T3, Canada. circ. 14,000 (English edt.); 4,400 (French edt.)

INSURANCE

368   US   ISSN 0072-0607
LIFE AGENCY MANAGEMENT PROGRAM BROCHURE. 1962. a. $2.50. National Association of Life Underwriters, General Agents and Managers Conference, 1922 F St., N.W., Washington, DC 20006. Ed. R. Humphreys. circ. 8,000 (controlled) (back issues avail.)

368.3   US   ISSN 0075-9406
LIFE INSURANCE FACT BOOK. 1946. a. single copy free; additional copies $1 ea. American Council of Life Insurance, 1850 K St. N.W., Washington, DC 20006. circ. 120,000.

368   CN
LIFE INSURANCE INSTITUTE OF CANADA. ANNUAL REPORT. a. membership. Life Insurance Institute of Canada, 15th Floor, 44 King St. W., Toronto, Ont. M5H 1E2, Canada.

368.3   US
LIFE INSURANCE MARKETING AND RESEARCH ASSOCIATION. PROCEEDINGS OF THE ANNUAL MEETING. 1946. a. free. ‡ Life Insurance Marketing and Research Association (LIMRA), 170 Sigourney St., Hartford, CT 06015. Ed. M. B. Petersen. circ. 1,000.
    Formerly: Life Insurance Agency Management Association. Proceedings of the Annual Meeting (ISSN 0075-9392)

368.3   US   ISSN 0075-9414
LIFE INSURERS CONFERENCE. ANNUAL PROCEEDINGS. 1910. a. free. Life Insurers Conference, 1004 N. Thompson St., Box 6856, Richmond, VA 23230. Ed. G. Mason Connell, Jr.

368.32   US
LIFE OFFICE MANAGEMENT ASSOCIATION. ANNUAL CONFERENCE. PROCEEDINGS OF CONCURRENT SESSIONS. 1924. a. Life Office Management Association, 100 Colony Sq, Atlanta, GA 30361. Ed. Nancy L. McCloskey. circ. 1,000.
    Formerly: Life Office Management Association. Annual Conference. Highlights.

368   US
LIFE RATES & DATA. 1971. a. $12.25. National Underwriter Co., 420 E. Fourth St., Cincinnati, OH 45202.

368   LU
LUXEMBOURG. INSPECTION GENERALE DE LA SECURITE SOCIALE. RAPPORT GENERAL SUR LA SECURITE SOCIALE AU GRAND-DUCHE DE LUXEMBOURG. 1974. a. Inspection Generale de la Securite Sociale, Ministere du Travail et de la Securite Sociale, Luxembourg, Luxembourg. circ. 750.

368   MW   ISSN 0076-3349
MALAWI. REGISTRAR OF INSURANCE. REPORT. a, latest 1972. K.0.50. Government Printer, P.O. Box 37, Zomba, Malawi.

368   CN   ISSN 0381-3215
MANITOBA. PENSION COMMISSION. ANNUAL REPORT. 1975. a. Pension Commission, Winnipeg, Man., Canada. circ. 200.

368 631   CN   ISSN 0542-5395
MANITOBA CROP INSURANCE CORPORATION. ANNUAL REPORT. 1962. a. free. Manitoba Crop Insurance Corporation, 886 St. James St., Winnipeg, Man. R3G 3J7, Canada. charts.

368   MF
MAURITIUS. REGISTRAR OF INSURANCE. ANNUAL REPORT. a. Rs.10. Registrar of Insurance, Treasury Building, Port Louis, Mauritius (Orders to: Government Printing Office, Elizabeth II Ave., Port Louis, Mauritius) stat.

368   MX
MEXICO. COMISION NACIONAL BANCARIA Y DE SEGUROS. ANUARIO ESTADISTICO DE SEGUROS. 1945. a. free. Comision Nacional Bancaria y de Seguros, Republica de el Salvador No. 47, Mexico 1 D.F., Mexico. stat. index.

368   US
MISSOURI. DIVISION OF INSURANCE. ANNUAL REPORT AND STATISTICAL DATA. 1870. a. free. Division of Insurance, Box 690, Jefferson City, MO 65101. circ. 1,800.

368.01   IS   ISSN 0075-1324
NATIONAL INSURANCE INSTITUTE, JERUSALEM. FULL ACTUARIAL REPORT. (Text in English and Hebrew) triennial. price varies. National Insurance Institute, Jerusalem, Israel.

368   UK
NATIONAL UNION OF INSURANCE WORKERS. PRUDENTIAL SECTION. GAZETTE. irreg. National Union of Insurance Workers, Prudential Section, 91-93 Gray's Inn Rd., London WC1X 8TX, England.
    Continues: Prudential Staff Gazette.

368   NE   ISSN 0077-5975
NATIONALE-NEDERLANDEN. ANNUAL REPORT. (Text in Dutch and English) 1963. a. free. Nationale-Nederlanden N.V., Prinses Beatrixlaan 15, Box 90504, 2509 LM the Hague, Netherlands.

368   NE   ISSN 0077-6874
NEDERLANDSE SCHADEVERZEKERINGSMAATSCHAPPIJEN/ NETHERLANDS NON-LIFE INSURANCE COMPANIES. (Text in Dutch and English) 1967. irreg. fl.11.25. Centraal Bureau voor de Statistiek, Prinses Beatrixlaan 428, Voorburg, Netherlands (Orders to: Staatsuitgeverij, Christoffel Plantijnstraat, The Hague, Netherlands)

368.4 314   NE   ISSN 0077-6742
NETHERLANDS. CENTRAAL BUREAU VOOR DE STATISTIEK. DIAGNOSESTATISTIEK BEDRIJFSVERENIGINGEN (OMSLAGLEDEN). SOCIAL INSURANCE SICKNESS STATISTICS. (Text in Dutch and English) 1958. a. fl.14.45. Centraal Bureau voor de Statistiek, Prinses Beatrixlaan 428, Voorburg, Netherlands (Orders to: Staatsuitgeverij, Christoffel Plantijnstraat, The Hague, Netherlands)

368.382   NE   ISSN 0489-2992
NETHERLANDS. SOCIALE VERZEKERINGSRAAD. VERSLAG VAN DE STAND DER ZIEKENGELDVERZEKERING. irreg. free. Sociale Verzekeringsraad, President Kennedylaan 21, 2517 JK The Hague, Netherlands.

368   GW   ISSN 0077-7773
NEUMANNS JAHRBUCH DER DEUTSCHEN VERSICHERUNGSWIRTSCHAFT. TEIL 1: PERSONENVERSICHERUNG (LEBENS- UND KRANKENVERSICHERUNG. 1879. a. DM.75. Verlag Versicherungswirtschaft e.V., Klosestr. 22, 7500 Karlsruhe, W. Germany (B. R. D.) adv. circ. 500.

368   GW   ISSN 0077-7781
NEUMANNS JAHRBUCH DER DEUTSCHEN VERSICHERUNGSWIRTSCHAFT. TEIL 2: SCHADEN- UND RUECKVERSICHERUNG. 1879. a. DM.120. Verlag Versicherungswirtschaft e.V., Klosestr. 22, 7500 Karlsruhe, W. Germany (B. R. D.) adv. circ. 500.

368   GW   ISSN 0077-779X
NEUMANNS JAHRBUCH DER DEUTSCHEN VERSICHERUNGSWIRTSCHAFT. TEIL 3: INSTITUTIONEN, UEBERSICHTEN UND ANSCHRIFTEN. 1879. a. DM.79. Verlag Versicherungswirtschaft e.V., Klosestr. 22, 7500 Karlsruhe, W. Germany (B. R. D.) adv. circ. 500.

368.4   US
NEW JERSEY. STATE AGENCY FOR SOCIAL SECURITY. ANNUAL REPORT. a. State Agency for Social Security, 20 W. Front St., Trenton, NJ 08625.

368   US
NEW YORK (STATE) INSURANCE DEPARTMENT. ANNUAL REPORT OF THE SUPERINTENDENT OF INSURANCE TO THE NEW YORK LEGISLATURE. a. free. Insurance Department, Empire State Plaza, Agency Bldg. No. 1, Albany, NY 12257. circ. 2,500.

368   US
NEW YORK (STATE) INSURANCE DEPARTMENT. FEES AND TAXES CHARGED INSURANCE COMPANIES UNDER THE LAWS OF NEW YORK TOGETHER WITH ABSTRACTS OF FEES, TAXES AND OTHER REQUIREMENTS OF OTHER STATES. 1906. a. $2.50. Insurance Department, Empire State Plaza, Agency Bldg. No. 1, Albany, NY 12257. circ. 2,000.

368   US
NEW YORK (STATE) INSURANCE DEPARTMENT. LOSS AND EXPENSE RATIOS. 1951. a. $2.50. Insurance Department, Empire State Plaza, Agency Bldg. No. 1, Albany, NY 12257. Ed. Jess Strash. circ. 3,000. (back issues avail)

368.4   US
NEW YORK (STATE) WORKMEN'S COMPENSATION BOARD. SUMMARY OF ACTIVITIES. a. free. Workmen's Compensation Board, Two World Trade Center, New York, NY 10047.

368   US
NEW YORK INSURANCE BROKERS DIRECTORY. 1971. a. $12.50. American Underwriter, 12 S. 12th St., Philadelphia, PA 19107.
    Formerly: New York (State) Insurance Department. Directory of Insurance Brokers Licensed in New York State.

336.2   US
OREGON UNEMPLOYMENT INSURANCE TAX RATES; tax rate comparisons for rate years. 1966. irreg. (every 2-3 yrs.) free. Department of Human Resources, Employment Division, Research & Statistics Section, 875 Union St., N.E., Salem, OR 97310. Ed. Charles Crane. circ. 230.

368   MX
P Y S; Prevision y Seguridad. 1970. a. Carpartado 484, Monterrey, Mexico. Ed. Manuel L. Barr.

368   PK   ISSN 0078-8236
PAKISTAN INSURANCE YEAR BOOK. (Text in English) a. Rs.3. Department of Insurance, Karachi, Pakistan (Order from: Manager of Publications, Government of Pakistan, 2nd Floor, Ahmad Chamber, Tariq Rd., P.E.C.H.S., Karachi 29, Pakistan)

368   PH
PHILIPPINES. INSURANCE COMMISSION. ANNUAL REPORT. a. Insurance Commission, P P L Building, United Nations Ave., Box 3589, Manila, Philippines.

368   CN
PROVINCIAL RESULTS IN CANADA OF GENERAL INSURANCE COMPANIES. (Text in English and French) 1935. a. Can.$40. Stone & Cox Ltd., 100 Simcoe St., Toronto, Ont. M5H 3G2, Canada. Ed. John S. Wyndham. circ. 400.
    Formerly: Provincial Results in Canada of Fire & Casualty Companies.

368   US
RALPH H. BLANCHARD MEMORIAL ENDOWMENT SERIES. 1977. irreg. $10 for vol. 1. (University of Pennsylvania, Wharton School of Finance and Commerce. Pension Research Council) Richard D. Irwin, Inc., Homewood, IL 60430.

368.4   MX   ISSN 0482-6876
REVISTA MEXICANA DE SEGURIDAD SOCIAL. 1971. irreg. Mex.$15. Instituto Mexicano del Seguro Social, San Jeronimo Lidice, Mexico 20, D.F., Mexico. stat. circ. 1,500.

368   US   ISSN 0036-3464
SALES/SLANTS. no.41-6,june 1967. irreg. price not given. Rough Notes Co., Inc., 1200 N. Meridian St., Indianapolis, IN 46206. adv. charts. illus.

368.3   CN   ISSN 0080-6544
SASKATCHEWAN. MEDICAL CARE INSURANCE COMMISSION. ANNUAL REPORT. 1962. a. free. Medical Care Insurance Commission, T.C. Douglas Bldg., 3475 Albert St., Regina, Sask. S4S 6X6, Canada.

SASKATCHEWAN. PRESCRIPTION DRUG PLAN. ANNUAL REPORT. see *PHARMACY AND PHARMACOLOGY*

368   UK
SELF-EMPLOYED PENSIONS. 1975. irreg. £8.50. Fundex Ltd., Minister House, Arthur St, London EC4R 9AX, England. Ed. Niall Sweeney. circ. 3,500. (tabloid format)
    Formerly: Handbook of Self-Employed Pensions.

SINGAPORE BANKING, FINANCE & INSURANCE. see *BUSINESS AND ECONOMICS — Banking And Finance*

368 SZ ISSN 0379-704X
SOCIAL SECURITY DOCUMENTATION:
AFRICAN SERIES. 1977. irreg. free. International
Social Security Association, Box 1, CH-1211
Geneva 22, Switzerland.

368 SZ
SOCIAL SECURITY DOCUMENTATION: ASIAN
SERIES. 1979. irreg. free. International Social
Security Association, Box 1, Ch-1211 Geneva 22,
Switzerland (Dist. by: Regional Office for Asia and
Oceania, R-39 Greater Kailash-I, New Delhi
110048, India)

368 SZ
SOCIAL SECURITY DOCUMENTATION:
EUROPEAN SERIES. (Editions in English, French,
German and Spanish) 1979. irreg. 20 Fr. per no.
International Social Security Association, Box 1,
CH-1211 Geneva 22, Switzerland.

368.4 US ISSN 0081-0495
SOCIAL SECURITY HANDBOOK. 1944. a. $1.25. ‡
Research and Review Service of America, Inc, Box
1727, Indianapolis, IN 46206. Ed. John D. Wells.
Social security

368 US ISSN 0037-9794
SOCIETY OF ACTUARIES. TRANSACTIONS.
1949. a. $7.50. Society of Actuaries, 208 S. La Salle
St., Chicago, IL 60604. Ed. K. Arne Eide. bk. rev.
abstr, bibl, charts. index, cum. index every 10 yrs.
circ. 3,000.

368.4 331.2 SA
SOUTH AFRICA. UNEMPLOYMENT
INSURANCE FUND. REPORT/SOUTH
AFRICA.
WERKLOOSHEIDVERSEKERINGSFONDS.
VERSLAG. (Text in Afrikaans and English) a.
R.0.60. Unemployment Insurance Fund, Box 1851,
Pretoria 0001, South Africa.

368.4 US ISSN 0099-2100
STATE HEALTH BENEFITS PROGRAM OF NEW
JERSEY. ANNUAL REPORT. a. State Health
Benefits Commission, 20 W. Front St., Trenton, NJ
08625.

368 CN
STONE AND COX GENERAL INSURANCE
REGISTER. 1920. a. Can.$15. Stone and Cox Ltd.,
100 Simcoe St., Toronto, Ont. M5H 3G2, Canada.
Ed. J. S. Wyndham. adv. circ. 3,000.
Formerly: Stone and Cox General Insurance Year
Book (ISSN 0081-5772)

368.3 CN ISSN 0081-5780
STONE AND COX LIFE INSURANCE TABLES.
(Text in English and French) 1912. a. Can.$14.50.
Stone and Cox Ltd., 100 Simcoe St., Toronto, Ont.
M5H 3G2, Canada. Ed. J. S. Wyndham. adv. circ.
5,000.

368 PL
STUDIA UBEZPIECZENIOWE. 1973. irreg., 1976,
vol. 3. price varies. Panstwowe Wydawnictwo
Naukowe, Miodowa 10, Warsaw, Poland.

368 FI ISSN 0356-7826
SUOMEN VAKUUTUSVUOSIKIRJA/FINNISH
INSURANCE YEARBOOK. Swedish edition:
Foersaekringsaarsbok foer Finland (ISSN 0356-
7834) (Text in Finnish and Swedish with English
glossary) 1912. a. Fmk.70. Suomen
Vakuutusyhdistys, Bulevardi 28, 00120 Helsinki 12,
Finland. Ed. Veikko Olli. stat. circ. 1,200 (Finnish
edt.); 600 (Swedish edt.)

SURVEY OF RETIREMENT, THRIFT AND
PROFIT SHARING PLANS COVERING
SALARIED EMPLOYEES OF THE 50 LARGEST
U. S. INDUSTRIAL COMPANIES. see *BUSINESS
AND ECONOMICS — Labor And Industrial
Relations*

368 SW ISSN 0081-9794
SVENSK FOERSAEKRINGS-AARSBOK/SWEDISH
INSURANCE YEAR-BOOK. 1916. a. Kr.70.
Svenska Foersaekringsfoereningen - Swedish
Insurance Societies, Birger Jarlsgatan 5, S-111 45
Stockholm, Sweden. Ed. Tage Larsson. adv. circ.
1,600.

368.4 SW ISSN 0082-0075
SWEDEN. RIKSFOERSAEKRINGSVERKET.
ALLMAEN FOERSAEKRING. (Text in Swedish;
summaries in English) 1963. a. Kr.65($39)
Riksfoersaekringsverket - National Social Insurance
Board, S-103 5 Stockholm, Sweden (Orders to:
Liber Foerlag, Fack, S-162 89 Vaellingby, Sweden)

368.4 SW ISSN 0562-861X
SWEDEN. RIKSFOERSAEKRINGSVERKET.
YRKESSKADOR. (Text in Swedish., summaries in
English) 1955. a. Kr.28. Riksfoersaekringsverket -
National Social Insurance Board, Fack, S-103 60
Stockholm 3, Sweden (Orders to: Liber Foerlag,
Fack, S-162 89 Vaellingby, Sweden)

368 SW
SWEDEN. STATENS ARBETSGIVARVERK.
FOERESKRIFTER OM STATLIGT
TJAENSTEPENSIONERING; F S P. 1970. a.
Statens Arbetsgivarverk - National Swedish Agency
for Government Employers, Box 2243, S-103 16
Stockholm, Sweden (Dist. by: Liber Foerlag, Fack,
S-162 89 Vaellingby, Sweden)
Former titles (until 1979): Sweden. Statens
Avtalsverk. Foereskrifter om Statlight
Tjaenstepensionering; F S P; Sweden. Statens
Avtalsverk Foerfattningar om Statligt
Tjaenstepensionering; F S P.

368.4 SW ISSN 0082-0083
SWEDISH SOCIAL SECURITY SCHEME. (Text in
English) 1969. a. Riksfoersaekringsverket - National
Social Insurance Board, 5-103 51 Stockholm,
Sweden.

368 US
TELEPHONE TICKLER FOR INSURANCE MEN
AND WOMEN. a. $5. Underwriter Printing and
Publishing Co., 50 E. Palisade Ave., Englewood, NJ
07631. Ed. Donald E. Wolff. adv. circ. 27,500.
Formerly: Telephone Tickler for Insurance Men
(ISSN 0082-2663)

368.32 US
TEXAS BLUE BOOK OF LIFE INSURANCE
STATISTICS. 1944. a. $12. Record Publishing Co.
(Dallas), Box 5770, Dallas, TX 75222.

368 AG
TUTORA. MEMORIA Y BALANCE GENERAL.
no. 13, 1975. a. Compania Sudamericana de
Seguros, Rivadavia 717, Buenos Aires, Argentina.

368.012 CN ISSN 0082-7452
UNDERWRITING RESULTS IN CANADA.
(Composed of two parts: Blue Chart federal; Brown
Chart provincial) 1930. a. Can.$40. Stone and Cox
Ltd., 100 Simcoe St., Toronto, Ont. M5H 3G2,
Canada. Ed. J. S. Wyndham. circ. 400.

368 CN ISSN 0576-4157
UNEMPLOYMENT INSURANCE CANADA.
ANNUAL REPORT/ASSURANCE-CHOMAGE
CANADA. RAPPORT ANNUEL. (Text in English
and French) 1973, no. 32. a. free. Unemployment
Insurance Commission, c/o Public Relations, 222
Nepean, Ottawa K1A 0J5, Canada. charts. stat.
circ. 10,000.

368 UK
UNIT-LINKED SAVINGS PLANS. 1973/74. a.
£8.45. Fundex Ltd., Minister House, Arthur St,
London EC4R 9AX, England. Ed. Niall Sweeney.
adv. circ. 3,000. (tabloid format)
Former titles: Regular Savings Plans (ISSN 0305-
8220); Equity Linked Life Insurance; Equity Linked
Assurance.

UNITED CHURCH OF CHRIST. PENSION
BOARDS (ANNUAL REPORT) see *RELIGIONS
AND THEOLOGY — Other Denominations And
Sects*

332.17 368.85 US ISSN 0083-0658
U. S. FEDERAL DEPOSIT INSURANCE
CORPORATION. ANNUAL REPORT. 1934. a.
single copy free. U.S. Federal Deposit Insurance
Corporation, 550 17th St., N.W., Washington, DC
20429.

368 US ISSN 0043-4612
WHAT'S NEWS IN REINSURANCE. irreg.(approx.
3/yr.) free. Republic National Life Insurance Co.,
Box 6210, Dallas, TX 75222. adv. charts. illus.
stat.

368 US
WHO WRITES WHAT. a. $10.50. National
Underwriter Co., 420 E. Fourth St., Cincinnati, OH
45202. adv.

368 US
WHO'S WHO AMONG PROFESSIONAL
INSURANCE AGENTS. 1977. a. $30. Underwriter
Printing and Publishing Co., 50 E. Palisade Ave.,
Englewood, NJ 07631. Ed. Donald E. Wolff. circ.
1,000.

368 US ISSN 0083-9574
WHO'S WHO IN INSURANCE. a. $35. Underwriter
Printing and Publishing Co., 50 E. Palisade Ave.,
Englewood, NJ 07631. Ed. Donald E. Wolff. circ.
10,000.

368 US
WHO'S WHO IN RISK MANAGEMENT. 1971. a.
$30. Underwriter Printing and Publishing Co., 50 E.
Palisade Ave., Englewood, NJ 07631. Ed. Donald
E. Wolff. circ. 10,000.

368 ZA
ZAMBIA STATE INSURANCE CORPORATION.
REPORT AND ACCOUNTS. 1971. a. Zambia
State Insurance Corporation, Box 894, Lusaka,
Zambia. circ. 3,000.

368 RH ISSN 0556-8692
ZIMBABWE. REGISTRAR OF INSURANCE.
REPORT. (Text in English) a, latest 1975.
Rhod.$1.50. Registrar of Insurance, Private Bag
7705, Causeway, Salisbury, Zimbabwe. stat.
Formerly: Rhodesia. Central Statistical Office.
Insurance Statistics.

INSURANCE — Abstracting, Bibliographies, Statistics

368 319 332 HO
BANCO CENTRAL DE HONDURAS. SECCION
DE SEGUROS. BOLETIN DE ESTADISTICAS
DE SEGUROS. 1974. irreg. (Banco Central de
Honduras) Honduras. Superintendencia de Bancos,
Seccion de Seguros, Tegucigalpa, Honduras.

314 368.4 BE
BELGIUM. INSTITUT NATIONAL
D'ASSURANCES SOCIALES POUR
TRAVAILLEURS INDEPENDANTS.
STATISTIQUE DES ENFANTS BENEFICIAIRES
D'ALLOCATIONS FAMILIALES/BELGIUM.
RIJKSINSTITUUT VOOR DE SOCIALE
VERZEKERINGEN DER ZELFSTANDIGEN.
STATISTIEK VAN DE KINDEREN DIE RECHT
GEVEN OP KINDERBIJSLAG. (Text in Dutch
and French) 1970. a. Institut National d'Assurances
Sociales pour Travailleurs Independants, Place Jean
Jacobs 6, 1000 Brussels, Belgium.

368.4 314 FI ISSN 0071-5247
FINLAND. KANSANELAKELAITOS.
TILASTOLLINEN VUOSIKIRJA/FINLAND.
FOLKPENSIONSANSTALT. STATISTIK
AARSBOK/FINLAN. SOCIAL INSURANCE
INSTITUTION. STATISTICAL YEARBOOK.
(Subseries of its Julkaisuja. Series T: 1) (Text in
Finnish and Swedish; summaries in English) 1965.
a. Fmk.23.80. Kansanelakelaitos - Social Insurance
Institution of Finland, Research Institute of Social
Security, Olavinkato 1 A, SF-00100 Helsinki 10,
Finland (Or Salomonkatu 17 B, 00100 Helsinki 10,
Finland) Ed. F. Gustafsson. charts. stat. circ. 4,000.

368.4 314 FR
FRANCE. CAISSE NATIONALE DE
L'ASSURANCE MALADIE DES
TRAVAILLEURS SALARIES. STATISTIQUES
DE L'ANNEE. a. Caisse Nationale de l'Assurance
Maladie des Travailleurs Salaries, 44-46, Boulevard
de Grenelle, 75015 Paris, France. illus.

368 314 GW ISSN 0435-7442
GESAMTSTATISTIK DER
KRAFTFAHRTVERSICHERUNG. 1958. a. free.
Verband der Haftpflicht-, Unfall- und
Kraftverkehrsversicherer e.V., Glockengiesserwall 1,
2000 Hamburg 1, W. Germany (B.R.D.) stat. circ.
600.

368 314 AU
HANDBUCH DER OESTERREICHISCHEN SOZIALVERSICHERUNG. 1971. irreg. Hauptverband der Oesterreichischen Sozialversicherungstraeger, Traungasse 14-16, A-1037 Vienna, Austria.
Formerly: Statistiches Handbuch der Oesterreichischen Sozialversicherung; Which superseded in part: Jahrbuch der Oesterreichischen Sozialversicherung.

368 016 US ISSN 0074-073X
INSURANCE PERIODICALS INDEX. (Cumulation of the index published monthly in Best's Review) 1964. a. $25. Special Libraries Association, Insurance Division (New York), c/o Robert Enequist, College of Insurance, 123 William St., New York, NY 10003. circ. 300.

368 319 FJ
INSURANCE STATISTICS OF FIJI. 1969. a. free. Bureau of Statistics, Box 2221, Suva, Fiji. stat. circ. 200.

368 KO
INSURANCE STATISTICS YEARBOOK. (Text in English and Korean) 1972. a. free. Korea Non-Life Insurance Association, 1-614 Yeoyido-dong, Yeongdeungpo-Ku, Seoul, S. Korea. Ed. Sang-Yong Lee. circ. 500.

368 315 IS ISSN 0074-0705
ISRAEL. CENTRAL BUREAU OF STATISTICS. INSURANCE IN ISRAEL/ISKE HA-BITUAH BE-YISRAEL. (Subseries of the Bureau's Special Series) (Text in Hebrew and English) 1950-52. a. I£90. Central Bureau of Statistics, Box 13015, Jerusalem, Israel.

368 315 IS
ISRAEL. CENTRAL BUREAU OF STATISTICS. KUPOT GEMEL BE-YISRAEL. Added title: Social Insurance Funds in Israel. (Text in English and Hebrew.) 1969. irreg., no. 436, 1971-72. I£90. Central Bureau of Statistics, Jerusalem, Israel.

368 314 IT ISSN 0075-1790
ITALY. ISTITUTO CENTRALE DI STATISTICA. ANNUARIO STATISTICO DELL'ASSISTENZA E DELLA PREVIDENZA SOCIALE. irreg., 1974-75 in prep. L.9000. Istituto Centrale di Statistica, Via C. Balbo, 16, 00100 Rome, Italy. circ. 850.

368 317 US
NEW YORK (STATE) INSURANCE DEPARTMENT. STATISTICAL TABLES FROM ANNUAL STATEMENTS. 1944. a. $6.50. Insurance Department, Empire State Plaza, Agency Bldg. No. 1, Albany, NY 12257. Ed. Jess Strash. circ. 2,000. (back issues avail)

368 NZ
NEW ZEALAND. DEPARTMENT OF STATISTICS. LIFE ANNUITY TABLES. quinquennial. NZ.$0.60. Department of Statistics, Private Bag, Wellington, New Zealand (Subscr. to: Government Printing Office, Publications, Private Bag, Wellington, New Zealand)

368 319 NZ ISSN 0110-3474
NEW ZEALAND, DEPARTMENT OF STATISTICS. INSURANCE STATISTICS. a. NZ.$1.20. Department of Statistics, Private Bag, Wellington, New Zealand (Subscr. to: Government Printing Office, Publications, Private Bag, Wellington, New Zealand)

368.4 319 PP
PAPUA NEW GUINEA. BUREAU OF STATISTICS. WORKERS' COMPENSATION CLAIMS. (Text in English) 1966. a. free. Bureau of Statistics, P.O. Wards Strip, Papua New Guinea. Ed. J. J. Shadlow. circ. 367.
Former titles: Papua New Guinea. Bureau of Statistics. Industrial Accidents; Papua New Guinea. Bureau of Statistics. Workers' Compensation Statistics (ISSN 0078-9265)

368 CN ISSN 0701-5488
PENSION PLANS IN CANADA/REGIMES DE PENSIONS AU CANADA. (Catalogue 74-401) (Text in English and French) 1970. biennial. Can.$7($8.40) Statistics Canada, Publications Distribution, Ottawa, Ont. K1A 0V7, Canada. circ. 10,000. (also avail. in microform from MML)

368 314 PL ISSN 0079-2853
POLAND. GLOWNY URZAD STATYSTYCZNY. UBEZPIECZENIA MAJATKOWE I OSOBOWE. PROPERTY AND PERSONAL INSURANCE. 1969. a. Glowny Urzad Statystyczny, Al. Niepodleglosci 208, 00-925 Warsaw, Poland.

368.4 317 CN
QUEBEC (PROVINCE) HEALTH INSURANCE BOARD. ANNUAL STATISTICS/REGIE DE L'ASSURANCE MALADE. STATISTIQUES ANNUELLES. (Text in French and English) 1971. a. free. ‡ Health Insurance Board, Case Postale 6600, Quebec, Que. G1A 7T3, Canada. circ. 10,000.

INTERIOR DESIGN AND DECORATION

see also *Interior Design and Decoration — Furniture and House Furnishings*

AUSTRIA. BUNDESMINISTERIUM FUER BAUTEN UND TECHNIK. WOHNBAUFORSCHUNG. see *ARCHITECTURE*

747 UK
BATHROOMS AND KITCHENS. (Architects & Specifiers Guide Series) 1975. a. £3.50. Builder Group, 23 Pemberton Row, London W.C.3, England.

747 US ISSN 0164-0186
BETTER HOMES AND GARDENS BEDROOM AND BATH DECORATING IDEAS. 1977. a. $1.75. Meredith Corporation, 1716 Locust St., Des Moines, IA 50336. adv. illus.

747 US ISSN 0092-7961
BETTER HOMES AND GARDENS FURNISHINGS AND DECORATING IDEAS. s-a. $1.95 per no. (not sold through subscr.) Meredith Corporation, 1716 Locust St., Des Moines, IA 50336. illus. Key Title: Furnishings and Decorating Ideas.

643.3 US
BETTER HOMES AND GARDENS KITCHEN & BATH IDEAS. irreg. $1.50. Meredith Corporation, 1716 Locust St., Des Moines, IA 50336. illus.

747 UK
CEILINGS & PARTITIONS. (Architects & Specifiers Guide Series) 1971. a. £3.50. Builder Group, 23 Pemberton Row, London W.C.3, England. Ed. Christopher Sykes. adv. circ. 5,000.

747 SP
COLOR Y DECORACION EN EL HOGAR. irreg. Editorial Gustavo Gili S.A., Rosellon 87-89, Barcelona 15, Spain.

747 UK ISSN 0069-9578
CONTRACT CARPETING. (Architects & Specifiers Guide Series) 1970. a. £7.50. Benn Publications Ltd., Press House, 25 High St., Edenbridge, Kent, England. Ed. Carolyn Vignoles.

747 UK ISSN 0070-3192
DECORATING CONTRACTOR ANNUAL DIRECTORY. 1903. a. £5.50. Ridgway Press, Elmbank, Walton Lane, Lower Halliford, Shepperton, Middlesex TW17 8LQ, England. Ed. Freda Troughton.

747 US
DECORATING MADE EASY. a. $1.75 per no. (no subscr. avail.) Family Circle, Inc., (Subsidiary of: New York Times Company, Inc.) 488 Madison Ave., New York, NY 10022.
Formerly: Family Circle's Home Decorating Guide (ISSN 0090-8630)

747 UK ISSN 0070-3206
DECORATIVE ART AND MODERN INTERIORS. (Text in English; Introduction in English, Spanish, French, German, Japanese) 1906. a. £19.95. Studio Vista (Subsidiary of: Cassell Ltd.) 35 Red Lion Square, London WC1R 4SG, England (Dist. in U.S. by: William Morrow & Co. Inc., 105 Madison Ave., New York, N.Y. 10016) Ed. Maria Schofield. circ. 20,000.

DESIGN DIRECTORY; a listing of firm and consultants in industrial, graphic, interior and environmental design. see *BUSINESS AND ECONOMICS — Trade And Industrial Directories*

DESIGN FROM SCANDINAVIA; a Scandinavian production in furniture, textiles, illumination, arts and crafts and industrial design. see *INTERIOR DESIGN AND DECORATION — Furniture And House Furnishings*

747 FI ISSN 0418-7717
DESIGNED IN FINLAND. 1960. a. Fmk.27($10) Finnish Foreign Trade Association, Arkadiankatu 4-6B, 00100 Helsinki 10, Finland. illus. circ. 40,000.

747 CN
DESIGNER. 1969. a. Southam Communications Ltd., 1450 Don Mills Rd., Don Mills, Ont. M3B 2X7, Canada. adv.

747 US ISSN 0420-011X
DESIGNERS WEST RESOURCE DIRECTORY. 1970. a. $5. Designers West, 9200 Sunset Blvd., Los Angeles, CA 90069. Ed. Mary N. Brown. adv. illus. circ. 8,000.

DOORS & WINDOWS. see *BUILDING AND CONSTRUCTION*

747 US
HOMEBOOK. 1979. a. McGraw-Hill Information Systems Co., 1221 Ave. of the Americas, New York, NY 10020. adv. circ. 300,000.

747 US ISSN 0147-832X
HOUSE & GARDEN KITCHEN & BATH GUIDE. a. Conde Nast Publications Inc., 350 Madison Ave., New York, NY 10017. Ed. Louis O. Gropp. adv. index.

747 UK
INTERIOR DESIGN CATALOGUES; catalogue of 2000 items of contract furniture and furnishings. a. £15. Standard Catalogue Information Services Ltd., Medway Wharf Rd., Tonbridge, Kent TN9 1QR, England.

747 IT
LIBRO DI CASA. 1935. a. L.3000($8) Editoriale Domus, Via Grandi 5/7, 20089 Rozzano (MI), Italy. Ed. Gianni Mazzocchi. adv.

747 UK
SCOTTISH DECORATORS' YEAR BOOK AND REVIEW. a. Scottish Decorators' Federation, 249 W. George St., Glasgow G2 4RB, Scotland.
Formerly: Scottish Decorators' Review.

747 US
TRADITIONAL HOME IDEAS. 1978. a. $1.95. Meredith Corporation, 1716 Locust St., Des Moines, IA 50336. adv. circ. 600,000.

747 US ISSN 0363-5406
WINDOW & WALL DECORATING IDEAS. irreg. $1.75. Meredith Corporation, 1716 Locust St., Des Moines, IA 50336. illus.
Formerly: Better Homes and Gardens Window Wall Ideas.

747 645 GE
WOHNEN. 1978. a. M.7. Verlag Fuer die Frau, Friedrich-Ebert-Str. 76-78, 701 Leipzig, E. Germany (D.D.R.)

747.05 US ISSN 0361-638X
WOMAN'S DAY HOME DECORATING IDEAS. Short title: Home Decorating Ideas. a. $1.39. Fawcett Publications, Inc., 1515 Broadway, New York, NY 10036. adv. illus.

INTERIOR DESIGN AND DECORATION — Abstracting, Bibliographies, Statistics

684.1 338.4 CN ISSN 0300-1199
CANADA. STATISTICS CANADA. HOUSEHOLD FURNITURE MANUFACTURERS/INDUSTRIE DES MEUBLES DE MAISON. (Catalog 35-211) (Text in English & French) 1960. a. Can.$4.50($5.40) Statistics Canada, Publications Distribution, Ottawa, Ont. K1A 0V7, Canada. (also avail. in microform from MML)

338.4   CN   ISSN 0384-4080
CANADA. STATISTICS CANADA. OFFICE FURNITURE MANUFACTURERS/INDUSTRIE DES MEUBLES DE BUREAU. (Catalog 35-212) (Text in English and French) 1960. a. Can.$4.50($5.40) Statistics Canada, Publications Distribution, Ottawa, Ont. K1A 0V7, Canada. (also avail. in microform from MML)

INTERIOR DESIGN AND DECORATION — Furniture And House Furnishings

see also Hobbies—Antiques

684   FR
ANNUAIRE DE L'AMEUBLEMENT ET DES INDUSTRIES S'Y RATTACHANT. 1908. a. 135 F. Editions Louis Johanet, 68 rue Boursault, Paris 17e, France.
    Formerly: Annuaire de l'Ameublement (ISSN 0066-2615)

747   US   ISSN 0090-6433
BETTER HOMES AND GARDENS HUNDREDS OF IDEAS. s-a. $1.50. Meredith Corporation, 1716 Locust St., Des Moines, IA 50303. illus. Key Title: Hundreds of Ideas.

381   AG
CAMARA DE COMERCIANTES EN ARTEFACTOS PARA EL HOGAR. REVISTA. irreg. Camara de Comerciantes en Artefactos para el Hogar, Bartolome Mitre 2162, Buenos Aires, Argentina. illus.

338.4   US
CARPET AND RUG INSTITUTE. INDUSTRY REVIEW. a. $3. Carpet and Rug Institute, Box 2048, Dalton, GA 30720.
    Formerly: Carpet and Rug Institute. Review--State of the Industry (ISSN 0092-0495)

338.4   IT   ISSN 0069-9764
CONVEGNO NAZIONALE DEI COMMERCIANTI DE MOBILI. ATTI E RELAZIONI.* 1960, 5th. a. Camera di Commercio, Industria, Artigianato e Agricoltura di Pesaro, Corso XI Settembre 116, 61100 Pesaro, Italy.

747   DK   ISSN 0011-9369
DESIGN FROM SCANDINAVIA; a Scandinavian production in furniture, textiles, illumination, arts and crafts and industrial design. (Text in English, French & German) 1966. a. $10. World Pictures A-S, Martinsvej 8, 1926 Copenhagen V, Denmark. Ed. Kirsten Bjerregaard. illus. circ. 50,000.
    Formerly: Design from Denmark.

643.6   UK   ISSN 0070-5179
DIRECTORY OF BRUSH AND ALLIED TRADES. a. $40 includes subscription to Brushes International. Wheatland Journals Ltd., Penn House, Penn Place, Arickmansworth, Herts WD3 1SN, England. Ed. Joan Barraclough. adv. circ. 3,000.

684.1   UK   ISSN 0070-6604
DIRECTORY TO THE FURNISHING TRADE; cabinet maker directory. 1957. a. £23. Benn Publications Ltd., 25 New Street Square, London EC4A 3JA, England (Orders to: Directories Dept., Sovereign Way, Tonbridge, Kent TN9 1RW, England) Ed. D. Syms. adv. index. circ. 3,515.

747   UK
FABRICS, WALLCOVERINGS & FURNITURE. (Architects & Specifiers Guide Series) a. £3.50. Builder Group, 23 Pemberton Row, London W.C.3, England.

INTERIOR DESIGN CATALOGUES; catalogue of 2000 items of contract furniture and furnishings. see INTERIOR DESIGN AND DECORATION

JAMS GUIDE DE LA DEMEURE ET DES JEUNES MARIES. see HOME ECONOMICS

645   US
KITCHEN & BATH IMPROVEMENTS. a. $1.35. Davis Publications, Inc., 380 Lexington Ave., New York, NY 10017. Ed. Marcia Spires.

677   US
LINENS, DOMESTICS & BATH PRODUCTS ANNUAL DIRECTORY. 1927. a. $5. Columbia Communications, Inc., 370 Lexington Ave., New York, NY 10017. adv. circ. 10,011.

684   GW   ISSN 0077-0205
MOEBEL-INDUSTRIE UND IHRE HELFER. 1957. a. DM.38. Industrieschau-Verlagsgesellschaft, Berliner Allee 8, 6100 Darmstadt, W. Germany (B.R.D.)

747 720   US
OLD HOUSE CATALOG; 2500 products, services, and suppliers for restoring, decorating and furnishing the period house. 1976. biennial. $7.95. Universe Books, 381 Park Ave. South, New York, NY 10016. Ed. Lawrence Grow. illus. circ. 75,000.

TABLEWARE REFERENCE BOOK. see CERAMICS, GLASS AND POTTERY

UNIVERSIDADE DE SAO PAULO. MUSEU PAULISTA. COLECAO. SERIE DE MOBILIARIO. see MUSEUMS AND ART GALLERIES

WOMAN'S DAY HOME DECORATING IDEAS. see INTERIOR DESIGN AND DECORATION

684   UK   ISSN 0084-1196
WOODWORKER ANNUAL. a. £5.95. Argus Books Ltd., Argus House, St. James Rd., Watford, Hertfordshire, England. Ed. Geoffrey Pratt.

INTERNATIONAL COMMERCE

see Business and Economics—International Commerce

INTERNATIONAL DEVELOPMENT AND ASSISTANCE

see Business and Economics—International Development and Assistance

INTERNATIONAL EDUCATION PROGRAMS

see Education—International Education Programs

INTERNATIONAL LAW

see Law—International Law

INTERNATIONAL RELATIONS

see Political Science—International Relations

INVESTMENTS

see Business and Economics—Investments

ISLAM

see Religions and Theology—Islamic

JEWELRY, CLOCKS AND WATCHES

553.82 739   US
AMERICAN DIAMOND AND JEWELRY TRADE DIRECTORY. 1945. a. price varies. Mesquita and Silver, Inc., 49 W. 47th St., New York, NY 10036. adv. circ. 10,000.

736.2   US   ISSN 0065-8405
AMERICAN GEM SOCIETY. MEMBER SUPPLIERS.* a. American Gem Society, 2960 Wilshire Blvd., Los Angeles, CA 90010.

736   FR   ISSN 0066-3581
ANNUAIRE PARIS: BIJOUX. 1913. a. 62 rue Beaubourg, Paris 3e, France.

681.11   SP   ISSN 0066-510X
ANUARIO DE RELOJERIA Y ARTE EN METAL PARA ESPANA E HISPANOAMERICA. 1959. a. 4000 ptas. Ediciones CEDEL, Calle Mallorca 257, Barcelona 8, Spain.
    Formerly: Anuario de la Relojeria en Espana.

681.1   GW   ISSN 0070-4040
DEUTSCHE GESELLSCHAFT FUER CHRONOMETRIE. JAHRBUCH. 1950. a. DM.35. Deutsche Gesellschaft fuer Chronometrie e.V., Christophstr. 5, Postfach 590, 7000 Stuttgart 1, W. Germany (B.R.D.)

739 681   GW   ISSN 0070-4814
DIEBENERS GOLDSCHMIEDE- UND UHRMACHER-JAHRBUCH. 1903. a. DM.18. Ruehle-Diebener Verlag GmbH und Co. KG, Wolfschlugener Str. 5a, Postfach 700450, 7000 Stuttgart 70, W. Germany (B.R.D.) adv. circ. 3,500.

739.27   SA
DIRECTORY OF JEWELLERY AND PRECIOUS METALS. 1979. a. R.27. Thomson Publications S.A. (Pty) Ltd., Box 8308, Johannesburg 2000, South Africa. Ed. Marianne Kruit. adv.

681.11   SZ   ISSN 0071-4259
FEDERATION HORLOGERE SUISSE. ANNUAL REPORT. 1925. a. free. ‡ Federation Horlogere Suisse - Federation of Swiss Watch Manufacturers, 6 rue d'Argent, 2501 Bienne, Switzerland (Dist. in the U.S. by Watchmakers of Switzerland Information Center, Inc., Cellule d'Information Fh, 608 Fifth Ave., 8th Fl., NY 10020) circ. 3,300.

736 553.8   II
GEM & JEWELLERY YEARBOOK. 1974. a. Rs.80($20) Gem and Jewellery Information Centre of India, A-95 Janta Colony, Jaipur 302004, India. Eds. Vidya Vinod Kala and Alok Kala. adv. bk. rev. charts. illus. stat. tr.lit.

681.11   SZ
GUIDE DES ACHETEURS: HORLOGERIE, BIJOUTERIE ET BRANCHES ANNEXES/ BUYERS' GUIDE: WATCH INDUSTRY, JEWELLERY AND ALLIED TRADES. (Text in English, French, German, and Spanish) a. $20. Hugo Buchser S.A., Tour-de-l'Ile 4, 1211 Geneva 11, Switzerland.
    Continues: Guide des Acheteurs pour l'Horlogerie et les Branches Annexes.

553.87 739.27   US
INTERNATIONAL TURQUOISE ANNUAL. Variant title: Turquoise Annual. a. $2.95. (International Turquoise Association) Impart Publishers, 175 West Moana Lane, Box 5212, Reno, NV 89502. illus.

739.27   US
JEWELRY FASHION GUIDE. 1976. a. Gralla Publications, 1515 Broadway, New York, NY 10036. Ed. Gerry Gewirtz. adv. illus. circ. 26,188 (controlled)

681.114   SZ   ISSN 0077-1309
MONTRE SUISSE. ANNUAIRE/WATCH REVIEW. CURRICULUM. (Text in French and German)

646 US
NATIONAL JEWELER ANNUAL FASHION GUIDE. 1976. a. Gralla Publications, 1515 Broadway, New York, NY 10036. adv. circ. 28,000.

736 FR ISSN 0078-9496
PARIS-BIJOUX EXPORTATION. 1913, 9th ed. a. free. 62 rue Beaubourg, 75003 Paris, France. Ed. M. Cangardel. adv.

681.114 US
POCKET WATCH PRICE INDICATOR. 1976. a. price varies. Heart of America Press, Box 9808, 10101 Blue Ridge Blvd., Kansas City, MO 64134. Ed. R. Ehrhardt. adv. illus. circ. 10,000.

681.11 GW ISSN 0082-7290
UHRMACHER-JAHRBUCH FUER HANDWERK UND HANDEL. 1950. a. DM.5. Bielefelder Verlagsanstalt KG, Niederwall 53, Postfach 1140, 4800 Bielefeld, W. Germany (B.R.D.) adv. circ. 4,000.

681.1 739.27 UK ISSN 0083-7628
WATCHMAKER, JEWELLER AND SILVERSMITH DIRECTORY OF TRADE NAMES AND PUNCH MARKS. 1931. a. £2. I P C Consumer Industries Press Ltd., 40 Bowling Green Lane, London EC1, England. Ed. Ken Blakemore. adv.

JOURNALISM

071 US
A P S DIRECTORY. 1980. biennial. $6. Alternative Press Syndicate, Inc., Box 775, Madison Sq. Sta., New York, NY 10159.

070 GW ISSN 0065-0323
ABHANDLUNGEN UND MATERIALEN ZUR PUBLIZISTIK. 1962. irreg. price varies. (Freie Universitaet Berlin, Institut fuer Publizistik) Colloquium Verlag, Unter den Eichen 93, 1000 Berlin 45, W. Germany (B.R.D.) Ed. Fritz Eberhard. circ. 1,000.

070 US
ACCREDITED JOURNALISM EDUCATION. 1910. a. free. American Council on Education for Journalism, c/o Sec.-Treas. Milton Gross, University of Missouri, School of Journalism, Columbia, MO 65201.
Former titles: Education for a Journalism Career; Accredited Programs in Journalism (ISSN 0079-6018)
Includes list of schools and departments, careers bibliography; History, membership and criteria of American Council on Education for Journalism

AGRUPACION DE PERIODISTAS DE INFORMACION ECONOMICA. INFORME. see *BUSINESS AND ECONOMICS*

070 US
AMERICAN NEWSPAPER MARKETS CIRCULATION. Cover title: Circulation. 1962. a. $25. American Newspaper Markets, Inc., Box 182, Northfield, IL 60093. Ed. Mrs. Thomas A. Sinding. circ. controlled.

070 FR ISSN 0066-2585
ANNUAIRE DE LA PRESSE ET DE LA PUBLICITE. 1879. a. 24 Place du General Catroux, 75017 Paris, France. adv.
Before 1969: Annuaire de la Presse Francaise et Etrangere.

070.172 CL
ANUARIO DE LA PRENSA CHILENA. 1974. a. Esc.400($12) Direccion de Bibliotecas Archivos y Museos, Biblioteca Nacional, Alameda 651, Santiago, Chile. bibl. circ. 1,000.

079 KO
ASIAN PRESS.* a. $3. Institute for Communication Research, Readership Research Center, Seoul National University, Dong Song-Dong, Seoul, S. Korea. illus.

ASSEMBLING; a collection of otherwise unpublishable creative work. see *PUBLISHING AND BOOK TRADE*

ASSOCIATION DES JOURNALISTES AGRICOLES. ANNUAIRE. see *AGRICULTURE*

BEITRAEGE ZUR KOMMUNIKATIONSWISSENSCHAFT UND MEDIENFORSCHUNG. see *COMMUNICATIONS*

070 659.1 UK ISSN 0141-1772
BENN'S PRESS DIRECTORY. (In two volumes: Vol. 1 U.K. Media; Vol. 2 Overseas Press) 1846. a. £30 for both vols. Benn Publications Ltd., 25 New Street Square, London EC4A 3JA, England. Ed. David Linton. adv. index. index. circ. 4,200.
Formerly: Newspaper Press Directory (ISSN 0078-043X)

070 CS
BIBLIOTHEK DER JOURNALISTEN. (Text in German) vol. 3, 1971. irreg. price varies. International Organization of Journalists, Parizska 9, 110 01 Prague 1, Czechoslovakia (Subscr. to: Artia, Ve Smeckach 30, 111 27 Prague 1) Eds. F. M. Fischer, Jaroslav Chladek. illus.

071 US ISSN 0147-2828
BLACK PRESS INFORMATION HANDBOOK. biennial. $5. National Newspaper Publishers Association, 770 National Press Building, Washington, DC 20045.

070 910.03 US
BLACKS IN AMERICAN JOURNALISM SERIES. vol. 2, 1975. irreg. $1.25 per no. Indiana University, Afro-American Arts Institute, 109 N. Jordan Ave., Bloomington, IN 47401. adv. bibl. illus.

070 UK ISSN 0007-0238
BRITISH AMATEUR JOURNALIST. 1890. irreg. membership. ‡ British Amateur Press Association, BM/BAPA, London W. C. I, England. bk. rev. circ. 200.

070 US ISSN 0362-3238
C B S NEWS INDEX. 1975. a. $60. (Dataflow Systems, Inc.) Microfilming Corporation of America, 1620 Hawkins Ave., Box 10, Sanford, NC 27330.

070 US
CALIFORNIA NEWSPAPER PUBLISHERS' ASSOCIATION. DIRECTORY AND RATE BOOK. 1923. a. $20. California Newspaper Publishers Association, Inc., 1127 11th St., Ste. 1040, Sacramento, CA 95814. Ed. Jacki Nava. adv. circ. 2,800.
Formerly: California Newspaper Publishers' Association. Newspaper Directory; Which supersedes: California Newspaper Directory (ISSN 0068-5763)

810 071.1 CN
CANADIAN WRITERS AND CRITICS. irreg. price varies. Forum House Publishing Co., 90 Ronson Dr., Rexdale, Ont., M9W 1C1, Canada.

070 FR
CEUX QUI FONT LA PRESSE. 1979. biennial. 447 F. Societe d'Etudes et de Publications Industrielles, 15 Square de Vergennes, 75015 Paris, France. (Affiliate: France Expansion)

070 US
CHICAGO MEDIA DIRECTORY. a. free. Chicago Convention and Tourism Bureau, Inc., McCormick Place on the Lake, Chicago, IL 60616. Ed. John Clegg. circ. 1,000.

070 BL
COLECAO JORNALISMO CATARINENSE. 1978. irreg. (Sindicato dos Jornalistos) Editora Lunardelli, Rua Victor Meirelles 28, 880000 Florianopolis SC, Brazil.

072 UK
COMMONWEALTH PRESS UNION. RECORD OF QUADRENNIAL CONFERENCE. 1925. quadrennial; 1974, Hong Kong. price varies. Commonwealth Press Union, Studio House, 184 Fleet St., London EC4A 2DU, England.

CONGRES INTERNATIONAL D'HISTOIRE DES SCIENCES. ACTES. see *SCIENCES: COMPREHENSIVE WORKS*

070 II
COOPERATIVE PRESS IN SOUTH-EAST ASIA. 1965. irreg. Rs.7.50($1) International Co-Operative Alliance, Regional Office and Education Centre for South-East Asia, Box 3312, 43 Friends Colony, New Delhi 110014, India.

073 GW ISSN 0417-9994
DORTMUNDER BEITRAEGE ZUR ZEITUNGSFORSCHUNG. 1958. irreg., no. 29, 1979. price varies. K.G. Saur Verlag KG, Poessenbacherstr. 12 B, Postfach 711009, 8000 Munich 71, W. Germany (B.R.D.) Ed. Kurt Koszyk.

070 FR ISSN 0070-8321
ECOLE FRANCAISE DES ATTACHES DE PRESSE. ASSOCIATION DES ANCIENS ELEVES. ANNUAIRE.* 1962, 2nd ed. a. price varies. Association des Anciens Eleves de l'Ecole Francaise des Attaches de Presse, 61 rue Pierre-Charron, Paris 8e, France.

EDITOR & PUBLISHER INTERNATIONAL YEAR BOOK; encyclopedia of the newspaper industry. see *COMMUNICATIONS*

EDITORIAL EYE; focusing on publications standards and practices. see *PUBLISHING AND BOOK TRADE*

070 FR ISSN 0071-2299
EUROPA. REVUE DE PRESSE EUROPEENNE.* 1969. irreg. 0.50 f. each. Cercle Europe de la Faculte de Droit et des Sciences Economiques de Paris, 92 rue d'Assas, Paris 6e, France.

070 US ISSN 0160-063X
FACE THE NATION (ANNUAL) vol. 18, 1975. a. (C B S Inc.) Scarecrow Press, Inc., 52 Liberty St., Box 656, Metuchen, NJ 08840.

070 US
FEATURE EDITOR'S DIRECTORY. 1977. a. (with m. updates) $30. Andrew R. Alaways, Ed. & Pub., 164-30 Hillside Ave., Suite 16-J, Jamaica, NY 11432. circ. 2,000. (looseleaf format; also avail. in magnetic tape)

070 FR ISSN 0071-4305
FEDERATION NATIONALE DES AGENCES DE PRESSE. ANNUAIRE. 1967. a. Federation Francaise des Agences de Presse, 4 Bis, Rue de Clery, 75002 Paris, France.

070.5 FJ
FIJI. PRINTING DEPARTMENT REPORT. (Text in English) a. price varies. Government Printing Department, Box 98, Suva, Fiji.

070 FI ISSN 0071-5301
FINLAND. POSTI-JA LENNATINLAITOS. ULKOMAISTEN SANOMALEHTIEN HINNASTO. UTLANDSK TIDNINGSTAXA. (Text in Finnish and Swedish) 1853. a. Fmk.7. Posti- ja Lennatinlaitos - General Direction of Posts and Telegraphs, Mannerheimintie 11, SF-00100 Helsinki 10, Finland. index.

070 US
FOLIO: ANNUAL. a. $20. Folio Magazine Publishing Corp., 125 Elm St., Box 697, New Canaan, CT 06840.

GADNEY'S GUIDE TO 1800 INTERNATIONAL CONTESTS, FESTIVALS & GRANTS IN FILM & VIDEO, PHOTOGRAPHY, TV-RADIO BROADCASTING, WRITING, POETRY, PLAYWRITING & JOURNALISM. see *MOTION PICTURES*

GENERAL DIRECTORY OF THE PRESS AND PERIODICALS IN JORDAN AND KUWAIT. see *PUBLISHING AND BOOK TRADE*

GENERAL DIRECTORY OF THE PRESS AND PERIODICALS IN SYRIA. see *PUBLISHING AND BOOK TRADE*

070 384 US
GREATER BOSTON MEDIA DIRECTORY. 1981. a. $17.50. New England Newsclip Agency, Inc., 5 Auburn St., Framingham, MA 01701. Ed. Thomas M. Georgon. adv.

070 UK ISSN 0072-8748
GUIDE TO THE PRESS OF THE WORLD. 1887. a. free. Wm. Dawson and Sons Ltd., Cannon House, Folkestone, Kent CT19 5EE, England.

070 US ISSN 0441-389X
HUDSON'S WASHINGTON NEWS MEDIA
CONTACTS DIRECTORY. 1968. a. $48. ‡
Newsletter Clearinghouse (Washington), 2626
Pennsylvania Ave. N.W., Washington, DC 20037.
Eds. Howard Penn Hudson, Mary Elizabeth
Hudson. adv.

070 HK ISSN 0082-7789
INDEX TO TITLES OF ENGLISH NEWS
RELEASES OF HSINHUA NEWS AGENCY.
(Text in English) 1967. irreg. HK.$90. Union
Cultural Organization Ltd., No. 9 College Rd.,
Kowloon, Hong Kong. Ed. William Hsu. circ. 200.

079 II
INDIAN & EASTERN NEWSPAPER SOCIETY
PRESS HANDBOOK. Spine title: I. E. N. S. Press
Handbook. (Text in English) irreg. Rs.25. Indian
and Eastern Newspaper Society, I. E. N. S. Bldgs.,
Rafi Marg, New Delhi 110001, India.

INTER-AMERICAN PRESS ASSOCIATION.
COMMITTEE ON FREEDOM OF THE PRESS.
REPORT. see *POLITICAL SCIENCE*

070 US
INTER-AMERICAN PRESS ASSOCIATION.
MINUTES OF THE ANNUAL MEETING. a.
$10. Inter-American Press Association, 2911 N.W.
39th St., Miami, FL 33142.

INTERNATIONAL FEDERATION OF
JOURNALISTS AND TRAVEL WRITERS.
OFFICIAL LIST/REPERTOIRE OFFICIEL. see
TRAVEL AND TOURISM

070 US
INTERNATIONAL LABOR PRESS
ASSOCIATION. DIRECTORY OF MEMBER
PUBLICATIONS. 1955. a. $10. International Labor
Press Association, 815 16th St. N.W., Washington,
DC 20006. circ. 700. (looseleaf format)

070 UK ISSN 0085-2198
INTERNATIONAL PRESS INSTITUTE. SURVEY.
1952. irreg., no. 8, 1976. price varies. International
Press Institute, City University, 280 St. John St.,
London EC1V 4PB, England.

INTERNATIONAL SPORTING PRESS
ASSOCIATION. BULLETIN. N.S. see *SPORTS
AND GAMES*

JEWISH PRESS IN AMERICA. see *ADVERTISING
AND PUBLIC RELATIONS*

070 016 US ISSN 0075-4412
JOURNALISM ABSTRACTS; M.A., M.S., and Ph.D.
theses in journalism and mass communications.
1963. a. $7 to non-members. Association for
Education in Journalism, c/o Susanne Shaw, Bus.
Mgr., Pubs., School of Journalism, University of
Kansas, Lawernce, KS 66045. circ. 500. (also avail.
in microform from UMI)

070 US
JOURNALISM CAREER AND SCHOLARSHIP
GUIDE; information on a journalism career and
directory of college journalism programs. 1973,
13th. a. single copies free. ‡ Newspaper Fund, Inc.,
P.O. Box 300, Princeton, NJ 08540. bibl. stat.
index.
 Formerly: Journalism Scholarship Guide (ISSN
0449-3362)

070 NE ISSN 0022-555X
JOURNALIST. 1946. a. fl.72. Nederlandse Vereniging
van Journalisten - Netherlands Association of
Journalists, Johannes Vermeerstraat 55, Amsterdam,
Netherlands. adv. bk. rev. circ. 6,000.

073 GW
JOURNALISTEN-HANDBUCH. At head of title:
Wer Schreibt und Spricht worueber? irreg. Verlag
Chmielorz GmbH und Co, Wilhelmstr. 42, 6200
Wiesbaden, W. Germany.
 Formerly: Wer Schreibt worueber? Journalisten-
Handbuch.

070 US ISSN 0075-5060
KAPPA TAU ALPHA YEARBOOK. 1945. a. free. ‡
Kappa Tau Alpha, National Headquarters,
University of Missouri, School of Journalism, Box
838, Columbia, MO 65201. Ed. William H. Taft.
circ. 1,600.
 National society honoring scholarship in
journalism

073 GW
KOMMUNIKATION UND POLITIK. irreg., no. 10,
1978. K.G. Saur Verlag KG, Poessenbacherstr. 12 B,
Postfach 711009, 8000 Munich 71, W. Germany
(B.R.D.) (And 175 Fifth Ave., New York, NY
10010) Ed.Bd.

052 MY
LEADER. 1972. irreg. $4 single issue. Malaysian Press
Institute, Kuala Lumpur, Malaysia. adv. bk. rev.
illus. circ. 2,000.

659.1 US
MEDIA ENCYCLOPEDIA; working press of the
nation. (Published in 5 vols.) a. $205. Automated
Marketing Systems, Inc., 310 S. Michigan Ave.,
Chicago, IL 60604. Ed. Beverly J. Fike. (also avail.
in microfiche)

070 US
MEDIA PERSONNEL DIRECTORY. 1979. irreg.
Gale Research Company, Book Tower, Detroit, MI
48226. Ed. Alan E. Abrams.

070 US ISSN 0077-1147
MONTANA JOURNALISM REVIEW. (Title varies:
no. 1-5, Journalism Review) 1958. a. free. ‡
University of Montana, School of Journalism,
Missoula, MT 59812. Ed. Warren J. Brier. circ.
4,000.

070.172 US
N N A NATIONAL DIRECTORY OF WEEKLY
NEWSPAPERS. 1921. a. $30. National Newspaper
Association, 1627 K St., N.W., Suite 400,
Washington, DC 20006. adv. charts. stat.

070 US
NACHRICHTENTECHNIK. 1977. irreg., vol. 7,
1980. price varies. Springer-Verlag, 175 Fifth Ave.,
New York, NY 10010 (Also Berlin, Heidelberg,
Vienna) Ed. H. Marko. (reprint service avail. from
ISI)

NEWES. see *HOBBIES*

070 US
NEWSLETTER YEARBOOK DIRECTORY. 1977. a.
$35. Newsletter Clearinghouse (Rhinebeck), 144 W.
Market St., Rhinebeck, NY 12572. Ed. Howard
Penn Hudson. adv.

070.4 US ISSN 0090-2209
NEWSPAPER GUILD. ANNUAL T.N.G.
CONVENTION OFFICERS' REPORT. a.
Newspaper Guild, 1125 15th St., N.W., Washington,
DC 20005. Key Title: Annual T N G Convention
Officers' Report.

070.4 US
NEWSPAPER GUILD. PROCEEDINGS OF THE
ANNUAL CONVENTION. 1940. a. Newspaper
Guild, A F L - C I O, 1125 15th St. N.W.,
Washington, DC 20036.

070 US ISSN 0083-1646
NEWSPAPERS CURRENTLY RECEIVED AND
PERMANENTLY RETAINED IN THE
LIBRARY OF CONGRESS. 1968. irreg., 4th ed.
1974. $0.95. U.S. Library of Congress, Serial Record
Division, 10 First St. S.E., Washington, DC 20540
(Orders to: Supt. of Documents, Washington, DC
20402)

OESTERREICHS PRESSE, WERBUNG, GRAPHIK.
see *PUBLISHING AND BOOK TRADE*

OVERSEAS MEDIA GUIDE. see *ADVERTISING
AND PUBLIC RELATIONS*

070 CH
P C O T BULLETIN. 1967. irreg. not for sale. ‡
National Press Council of the Republic of China, 4,
Lane 9, 3rd Floor, Nanch'ang Rd., Section 1,
Taipei, Taiwan 107, Republic of China. Ed. Bd. circ.
3,000(controlled)

079 AT ISSN 0079-5046
PRESS RADIO AND T.V. GUIDE. 1914. biennial.
Aus.$19.50 per no. Country Press Ltd., 44 Pitt St.,
Sydney, N.S.W. 2000, Australia. Ed. Ian Cook.
 Formerly: Press Directory of Australia and New
Zealand.

070 US
PROBLEMS OF JOURNALISM. (Proceedings of the
Society's annual convention) a. $6.25. American
Society of Newspaper Editors, Box 551, 1350
Sullivan Trail, Easton, PA 18042.

070 800 US
PROFESSIONAL FREELANCE WRITERS
DIRECTORY. 1979. a. $6. National Writers Club,
1450 S. Havana, Aurora, CO 80012. Ed. Donald E.
Bower. bk. rev. circ. 1,000. (processed)
 Supersedes: National Writers Club. Bulletin for
Professional Members (ISSN 0028-0429)

073 GW
PUBLIZISTIK-HISTORISCHE BEITRAEGE. irreg.,
no. 4, 1975. DM.58. K.G. Saur Verlag KG,
Poessenbacherstr. 12 B, Postfach 711009, 8000
Munich 71, W. Germany (B.R.D.) Ed.Heinz-
Dietrich Fischer.

070 SZ
REPERTOIRE DE LA PRESSE SUISSE/
LEITFADEN DER SCHWEIZER PRESSE. (Text
in French, German or Italian) 1970. a. Data
Information Services S. A., 81, Route de l'Aire, CH-
1211 Geneva 26, Switzerland.

070 384 US
RHODE ISLAND MEDIA DIRECTORY. 1980. a.
$15. New England Newsclip Agency, Inc., 5
Auburn St., Framingham, MA 01701 (Subscr. to:
AD/COM, Box 9488, Providence, RI 02940) Ed.
Thomas M. Georgon. adv.

SCRIBE. see *LABOR UNIONS*

073 GW ISSN 0585-6175
STUDIEN ZUR PUBLIZISTIK. BREMER REIHE.
1958. irreg., vol. 24, 1978. price varies. (Deutsche
Presseforschung) K. G. Saur Verlag KG,
Peossenbacherstr. 2, 8000 Munich 71, W. Germany
(B.R.D.) Ed. Elger Bluehm.

STUDIES IN MEDIA MANAGEMENT. see
BUSINESS AND ECONOMICS — Management

070 US
SYNDICATED COLUMNISTS. 1975. biennial. $3
includes semi-annual revisions. Richard Weiner,
Inc., 888 Seventh Ave., New York, NY 10019. Ed.
Richard Weiner. bibl. circ. 1,000.

TASCHENBUCH FUER AGRARJOURNALISTEN.
see *AGRICULTURE*

070 SP ISSN 0078-8724
UNIVERSIDAD DE NAVARRA. FACULTAD DE
CIENCIAS DE LA INFORMACION.
CUADERNOS DE TRABAJO. 1964. irreg.; 1979,
no. 33. price varies. Ediciones Universidad de
Navarra, S.A., Plaza de los Sauces, 1 y 2 Baranain,
Pamplona, Spain.
 Formerly: Universidad de Navarra. Instituto de
Periodismo. Cuadernos de Trabajo.

070 SP ISSN 0078-8783
UNIVERSIDAD DE NAVARRA. FACULTAD DE
CIENCIAS DE LA INFORMACION.
MANUALES: PERIODISMO. 1967. irreg.; 1979,
no. 8. price varies. Ediciones Universidad de
Navarra, S.A., Plaza de los Sauces, 1 y 2 Baranain,
Pamplona, Spain.

070 US ISSN 0077-6378
UNIVERSITY OF NEBRASKA. SCHOOL OF
JOURNALISM. DEPTH REPORT. 1961. a. free.
University of Nebraska-Lincoln, School of
Journalism, Lincoln, NE 68508.

070 CS ISSN 0083-422X
UNIVERZITA KOMENSKEHO. FILOZOFICKA
FAKULTA. ZBORNIK: ZURNALISTIKA. (Text in
Slovak; summaries in German and Russian) 1968.
irreg. exchange basis. Univerzita Komenskeho,
Filozoficka Fakulta, Gondova 2, 806 01 Bratislava,
Czechoslovakia. Ed. Frano Ruttkay. circ. 674.

070 384 US
VERMONT MEDIA DIRECTORY. 1979. a. $15.
New England Newsclip Agency, Inc., 5 Auburn St.,
Framingham, MA 01701. Ed. Thomas M. Georgon.
adv.

JOURNALISM — ABSTRACTING, BIBLIOGRAPHIES, STATISTICS

070 US ISSN 0084-1323
WORKING PRESS OF THE NATION. (Issued in 5 vols.: Vol. I The Newspaper Directory, Vol. II The Magazine Directory, Vol. III The Radio and Television Directory, Vol. IV The Feature Writers and Syndicate Directory, Vol. V Internal Publications Directory) 1949. a. $71 per vol., $198 per set. National Research Bureau, Inc., 424 N. Third St., Burlington, IA 52601. Ed. Milton A. Paule. circ. 2,500.

070 GR
YEARBOOK OF GREEK PRESS. 1965. a. free. ‡ Secretariat General of Press and Information, Zalokosta 1, Athens, Greece. annual index. circ. 5,000. (tabloid format; also avail. in microfilm)

070 IS
ZSHURNALIST. (Text in Yiddish) 1974. irreg. World Federation of Jewish Journalists, Jerusalem, Israel. (Co-sponsor: World Zionist Organization. Information Department)

JOURNALISM — Abstracting, Bibliographies, Statistics

070 SA
ADVERTISING AND PRESS ANNUAL OF SOUTHERN AFRICA; the blue-book of advertising. (Text in English) 1948. a. R.40($48) incl. Business Systems & Equipment. Communications Group, Business Press Division, White-Ray House, 51 Wale St., Box 335, Cape Town 8000, South Africa. Ed. F. M. Botha. adv.
Formerly: Advertising and Press Annual of Africa (ISSN 0065-3594)

070.172 US ISSN 0093-1179
ATLANTA CONSTITUTION: A GEORGIA INDEX. 1971. a. price varies. (Georgia State University, Library) Microfilming Corporation of America. 1620 Hawkins Ave., Box 10, Sanford, NC 27330. (back issues avail.)

070 011 EC
CATALOGO COLECTIVO DE PUBLICACIONES PERIODICAS. irreg. Superintendencia de Bancos, Biblioteca, 10 de Agosto 251, Casilla 424, Quito, Ecuador. Dir. Ruth Mazon de Pazmino.

015 070 GW
DEUTSCHE BIBLIOGRAPHIE. ZEITSCHRIFTEN-VERZEICHNIS; in Deutschland erscheinende periodische Veroeffentlichungen sowie deutschsprachige Periodika Oesterreichs, der Schweiz und anderer Laender. 1945/1952 (1958) irreg. price varies. (Deutsche Bibliothek) Buchhaendler-Vereinigung GmbH, Gr. Hirschgraben 17-21, 6000 Frankfurt 1, W. Germany (B.R.D.) bibl. index. circ. 1,600.

070 016 TH
INDEX TO THAI NEWSPAPERS. (Text in Thai) 1964. irreg. price varies. National Institute of Development Administration, Library and Information Center, Klongjan, Bangkapi, Bangkok 24, Thailand. index. circ. 500.

070 016 US
LIBRARIANS' GUIDE TO BACK ISSUES OF INTERNATIONAL PERIODICALS; originals & reprints, featuring science, technology, medicine, the humanities. 1974. irreg. free to libraries. Microforms International Marketing Corporation (Subsidiary of: Pergamon Press, Inc.) Fairview Park, Elmsford, NY 10523. Ed. Edward Gray. adv. bibl. circ. 15,000.
Formerly: Reference Guide & Comprehensive Catalog of International Serials (ISSN 0094-0151)

070 016 GW ISSN 0552-6981
PUBLIZISTIK WISSENSCHAFTLICHER REFERATEDIENST. Short title: P R D. 1966. a. DM.40. (Freie Universitaet Berlin, Institut fuer Publizistik und Dokumentationswissenschaft) K.G. Saur Verlag KG, Poessenbacherstr. 12 B, Postfach 711009, 3000 Munich 71, W. Germany (B.R.D.) circ. 1,000.

JUDAISM

see Religions and Theology — Judaic

LABOR AND INDUSTRIAL RELATIONS

see Business and Economics — Labor and Industrial Relations

LABOR UNIONS

see also Business and Economics — Labor and Industrial Relations

331.88 370 US
A F T ISSUES BULLETIN. irreg. American Federation of Teachers, 11 Dupont Circle N.W., Washington, DC 20036. (reprint service avail. from UMI)

791 US
A G V A NEWSLETTER. 1958. irreg. membership. American Guild of Variety Artists, 1540 Broadway, New York, NY 10036. adv. bk. rev. illus. circ. 16,000-17,000.
Formerly: A G V A News (ISSN 0001-1371)

A T F ANNUAL REPORT. (Australian Teachers' Federation) see EDUCATION

331.88 370 US
AMERICAN FEDERATION OF TEACHERS. CONVENTION PROCEEDINGS (ABRIDGED) a. price varies. American Federation of Teachers, 11 Dupont Circle, N.W., Washington, DC 20036. (reprint service avail. from UMI)

792.028 331.88 AG
ASOCIACION ARGENTINA DE ACTORES. MEMORIA Y BALANCE. no. 58, 1977. a. free. Asociacion Argentina de Actores, Viamonte 1443, 1055 Buenos Aires, Argentina. circ. 3,000.

331 AT
AUSTRALIAN CONGRESS OF TRADE UNIONS. DECISIONS. biennial. free to qualified personnel. Australian Council of Trade Unions, 254 la Trobe St., Melbourne, Vic. 3000, Australia.

331 AT ISSN 0310-5296
AUSTRALIAN LABOR PARTY (NSW BRANCH). LABOR YEAR BOOK. 1973. a. (Labor Council of New South Wales) Mass Communications Pty. Ltd., Labor Council Building, 377 Sussex St., Sydney, NSW 2000, Australia.

331.88 AT
AUSTRALIAN WORKERS' UNION. OFFICIAL REPORT OF THE ANNUAL CONVENTION. 1886. a. Aus.$5. Australian Workers' Union, Box a-252, Sydney S., N. S. W. 2000, Australia. Ed. F.V. Mitchell.

DER BANKANGESTELLTE. see BUSINESS AND ECONOMICS — Banking And Finance

331.88 622 GW ISSN 0343-0510
BERGBAU-BERUFSGENOSSENSCHAFT. GESCHAEFTSBERICHT. 1887. a. free. Bergbau-Berufsgenossenschaft, Hunscheidtstr. 18, 4630 Bochum, W. Germany (B.R.D.) stat.

331.88 US ISSN 0069-1615
CENTRAL CONFERENCE OF TEAMSTERS. OFFICERS' REPORT.* 1954. irreg. Central Conference of Teamsters, 8550 W. Bryn Mawr Ave., Suite 707, Chicago, IL 60631.
Formerly: Central Conference of Teamsters. Chairman's Report.

331.88 SP
COLECCION PRIMERO DE MAYO. no. 6, 1977. irreg. price varies. Editorial Laia S.A., Constitucion 18-20, Barcelona 14, Spain.

301.16 331.88 BL
CONFEDERACAO NACIONAL DOS TRABALHADORES EM COMUNICACOES E PUBLICIDADE. RELATORIO ANUAL. 1967. a. Confederacao Nacional dos Trabalhadores Em Comunicacoes e Publicidade, Edificio Serra Dourada, Conj. 705, Brasilia, Brazil. illus. circ. 1,500.
Trade unions telecommunication

331.88 CN ISSN 0316-0688
DALHOUSIE LABOUR INSTITUTE FOR THE ATLANTIC PROVINCES. PROCEEDINGS. 1959. irreg. Dalhousie University, Institute of Public Affairs, Halifax, N.S. B3H 3J5, Canada. circ. 170. (back issues avail.)

331.88 CN ISSN 0075-7578
DIRECTORY OF LABOUR ORGANIZATIONS IN CANADA/REPERTOIRE DES ORGANISATIONS DE TRAVAILLEURS AU CANADA. (Text in French and English) 1911. a. Can.$4($4.80) Labour Canada, Ottawa, Ont. K1A 0J2, Canada. circ. 10,500.

331.8 US
DIRECTORY OF MAINE LABOR ORGANIZATIONS. (Subseries of: Maine. Bureau of Labor. B L Bulletin) 1969. a. Department of Manpower Affairs, State Office Bldg., Augusta, ME 04333. circ. 600.

DIRECTORY OF WORKERS EDUCATION. see EDUCATION

331.88 BL
FEDERACAO DOS TRABALHADORES NA AGRICULTURA DO ESTADO DO PARANA. RELATORIO. irreg. Federacao dos Trabalhadores na Agricultura do Estado do Parana, Curitiba, Brazil.

HESSISCHE BEITRAEGE ZUR GESCHICHTE DER ARBEITERBEWEGUNG. see HISTORY — History Of Europe

331.88 II ISSN 0073-2273
HIND MAZDOOR SABHA. REPORT OF THE ANNUAL CONVENTION. 1952. a. price varies($3. approx.) Hind Mazdoor Sabha, Nagindas Chambers, 167 P. d'Mello Rd., Bombay 400001, India.

I M F STUDIES. (International Metalworkers Federation) see METALLURGY

331.88 UK
I T F PANORAMA. (Editions in English, French, German and Swedish) 1978. irreg. £5. International Transport Worker's Federation, 133-135 Great Suffolk St., London SE1 1PD, England. Ed. K.A. Golding. index. circ. 2,500(Eng.edt.); 500(Fr.edt.); 500(Ger.edt.); 500(Swedish edt)

331.88 EI ISSN 0073-7909
INFORMATION SERVICE OF THE EUROPEAN COMMUNITIES. TRADE UNION NEWS.* 1965. irreg.; (approx. 4/yr) limited distribution. Commission of the European Communities, Direction Generale de la Presse et Information, Rue de la Loi 200, B-1049 Brussels, Belgium.

331.8 GW ISSN 0084-9782
INSTITUT DER DEUTSCHEN WIRTSCHAFT. GEWERKSCHAFTSREPORT. 8/yr. DM.70. Deutscher Instituts-Verlag GmbH, Gustav-Heinemann-Ufer 84-88, Postfach 510670, 5000 Cologne 51, W. Germany (B.R.D.)
Formerly: Deutsches Industrieinstitut. Berichte zu Gewerkschaftsfragen.

331.88 BE ISSN 0538-5946
INTERNATIONAL CONFEDERATION OF FREE TRADE UNIONS. FEATURES. 1963. irreg. free. International Confederation of Free Trade Unions, 37-47 rue Montagne aux Herbes Potageres, B-1000 Brussels, Belgium.

331.88 BE ISSN 0074-2872
INTERNATIONAL CONFEDERATION OF FREE TRADE UNIONS. WORLD CONGRESS REPORTS. 1949. irreg., 11th, 1975, Mexico City. $15. International Confederation of Free Trade Unions, 37-47 rue Montagne aux Herbes Potageres, 1000 Brussels, Belgium. Ed. Otto Kersten, General Secretary.

INTERNATIONAL FEDERATION OF PLANTATION, AGRICULTURAL AND ALLIED WORKERS. REPORT OF THE SECRETARIAT TO THE I F P A A W WORLD CONGRESS. see AGRICULTURE — Agricultural Economics

331.88　　　　　SZ　ISSN 0074-6177
INTERNATIONAL GRAPHICAL FEDERATION. REPORT OF ACTIVITIES. (Text in English, French, German, Swedish) 1950. triennial. ‡ International Graphical Federation, Monbijoustrasse 73, CH-3007 Berne, Switzerland. Ed. Heinz Goeke.

INTERNATIONAL LABOR PRESS ASSOCIATION. DIRECTORY OF MEMBER PUBLICATIONS. see JOURNALISM

331.88　　　　　BE　ISSN 0538-9755
INTERNATIONAL SECRETARIAT OF ENTERTAINMENT TRADE UNIONS. NEWSLETTER.* irreg. International Secretariat of Entertainment Trade Unions, c/o Allan J. Forrest, Secretary, C I S L, 37-41 rue Montagne-aux-Herbes-Potageres, 1000 Brussels, Belgium.

INTERNATIONAL TRADE UNION COMMITTEE OF SOLIDARITY WITH THE WORKERS AND PEOPLE OF CHILE. BULLETIN. see POLITICAL SCIENCE — International Relations

INTERNATIONAL TRADE UNION CONFERENCE FOR ACTION AGAINST APARTHEID. RESOLUTION. see POLITICAL SCIENCE — Civil Rights

331.88　　　　　UK　ISSN 0539-0915
INTERNATIONAL TRANSPORT WORKERS' FEDERATION REPORT ON ACTIVITIES. (Editions in English, French, German, Swedish, Spanish) 1897. irreg. £6. ‡ International Transport Workers' Federation, 133-135 Great Suffolk St., London SE1 1PD, England. circ. 500 (approx.) (controlled)

331.88　664　　SZ　ISSN 0579-8299
INTERNATIONAL UNION OF FOOD AND ALLIED WORKERS' ASSOCIATIONS. MEETING OF THE EXECUTIVE COMMITTEE. I. DOCUMENTS OF THE SECRETARIAT. II. SUMMARY REPORT. a. International Union of Food and Allied Workers' Associations - Union Internationale des Travailleurs de l'Alimentation et des Branches Connexes, Secretariat, Rampe du Pont-Rouge 8, CH-1213 Petit-Lancy/Geneva, Switzerland.

INTERNATIONAL YEARBOOK OF ORGANIZATIONAL DEMOCRACY. see POLITICAL SCIENCE

331.88　　　　　CS
KALENDAR ODBORARA. a. 8 Kcs. (Slovenska Odborova Rada) Praca, Publishing House of the Slovak Trade Unions Council, Moskevska 17, 897 17 Bratislava, Czechoslovakia.

331.88　　　　　CN　ISSN 0383-3437
LABOUR ORGANIZATIONS IN NOVA SCOTIA. 1970. a. free. Department of Labour, Economics and Research Division, P.O. Box 697, Halifax, Nova Scotia, Canada. (processed)
　　Formerly: Directory of Labour Unions in Nova Scotia.

331.8　　　　　SW
LANDSORGANISATIONEN I SVERIGE. YTTRANDEN TILL OFFENTLIG MYNDIGHET. irreg. Landsorganisationen i Sverige, Barnhusgatan 18, 105 53 Stockholm, Sweden.

MAGYAR MUNKASMOZGALMI MUZEUM. EVKONYV. see POLITICAL SCIENCE

MAIN DECK. see TRANSPORTATION — Ships And Shipping

MEATWORKER. see FOOD AND FOOD INDUSTRIES

NATIONAL CENTER FOR THE STUDY OF COLLECTIVE BARGAINING IN HIGHER EDUCATION. ANNUAL CONFERENCE PROCEEDINGS. see EDUCATION — Higher Education

331.8　　　　　US　ISSN 0545-6061
NEW YORK CITY TRADE UNION HANDBOOK. 1950. irreg., 1981 latest edt. free. New York City Central Labor Council AFL-CIO, 386 Park Ave. S., New York, NY 10016. Ed. Sally Genn.

331.88　　　　　NZ
NEW ZEALAND FEDERATION OF LABOUR. OFFICIAL TRADE UNION DIRECTORY. 1971. a. New Zealand Federation of Labour, Box 6161, Lukes Lane, Wellington, New Zealand. Ed. Bd.

331.88　　　　　NZ
NEW ZEALAND TRADE UNION DIRECTORY. a. P.O. Box 27-113, Wellington, New Zealand.

331.88　　　　　DK
NORDISKA SAMARBETSORGAN. 1975. irreg. Nordisk Raad, Christiansborg Ridebane 10, DK-1218 Copenhagen, Denmark.

331.88　　　　　CN　ISSN 0316-0386
NOTES ON UNIONS. French edition: Cahiers Syndicaux (ISSN 0316-0394) (Editions in English and French) 1974. irreg. Canadian Labour Congress, 2841 Riverside Drive, Ottawa, Ont. K1V 8X7, Canada.

331.88　　　　　CN　ISSN 0078-4826
ONTARIO FEDERATION OF LABOUR. REPORT OF PROCEEDINGS. 1957. a. free. ‡ Ontario Federation of Labour, 15 Gervais Dr., Don Mills, Ont. M3C 1Y8, Canada. circ. 1,500.

331.8　　　　　FR
PAGES JURIDIQUES DE LA VIE OUVRIERE. a. Vie Ouvriere, 33 rue Bouret, 75940 Paris Cedex, France.

331.88　　　　　PE
PONTIFICIA UNIVERSIDAD CATOLICA. TALLER DE ESTUDIOS URBANO INDUSTRIALES. SERIE: ESTUDIOS SINDICALES. no. 3, 1976. irreg. Pontificia Universidad Catolica, Taller de Estudios Urbanos Industriales, Fundo Pando s/n, Lima, Peru.

331.88　　　　　PR
PUERTO RICO. DEPARTMENT OF LABOR. DIRECTORIO DE ORGANIZACIONES DEL TRABAJO. 1965. a. free. Department of Labor, Bureau of Labor Statistics, Office of Public Relations, 414 Barbosa Ave., Hato Rey, PR 00917. Ed. Federico Irizarry. circ. 800-1,000. (also avail. in microform)

331.88　　　　　CS　ISSN 0557-1693
ROCENKA ODBORARA. a. 15 Kcs. (Slovenska Odborova Rada) Praca, Publishing House of the Slovak Trade Unions Council, Moskevska 17, 897 17 Bratislava, Czechoslovakia.

331　079　　　AT
SCRIBE. 1963. irreg. Aus.$0.20. Australian Journalists' Association, Western Australia District, 104 St. George's Terrace, Perth, W.A. 6000, Australia. Ed. Malcolm Hollingsworth.

331.88　　　　　US
SERVICE EMPLOYEES INTERNATIONAL UNION. INTERNATIONAL CONVENTION. OFFICIAL PROCEEDINGS. 16th, 1976. quadrennial. Service Employees International Union, 2020 K St., N.W., Washington, DC 20006.

STEUER-GEWERKSCHAFTS-HANDBUCH. see BUSINESS AND ECONOMICS — Public Finance, Taxation

331.8　　　　　SW
STUDIER I ARBETARROERELSENS HISTORIA. irreg. Saellskapet foer Studier i Arbetarroerelsens Historia, Box 16 393, Stockholm, Sweden.

331.8　　　　　SW
SWEDEN. STATENS ARBETSGIVARVERK. FOERFATTNINGAR OM STATLIGT REGLERADETJAENSTER; F S T. 1969. a. Statens Arbetsgivarverk - National Swedish Agency for Government Employers, Box 2243, S-103 16 Stockholm, Sweden (Dist. by: Liber Foerlag, Fack, S-162089 Vaellingby, Sweden)
　　Formerly (until 1979): Sweden. Statens Avtalsverk. Foerfattningar om Statlight Regleradetjaenster; F S T.

SYNDICAT GENERAL DE LA CONSTRUCTION ELECTRIQUE. ANNUAIRE. see ELECTRICITY AND ELECTRICAL ENGINEERING

331.88　　　　　UK　ISSN 0307-7543
TRADE UNION REGISTER. 1970. irreg. Spokesman Books, Bertrand Russell House, Gamble St., Nottingham, England. stat.

331.88　　　　　II　ISSN 0445-6289
TRADE UNIONS IN INDIA. (Text in English) biennial. Rs.34($12.24) Labour Bureau, Simla 171004, India (Order from: Controller of Publications, Government of India, Civil Lines, Delhi 110054, India)
　　Supersedes: Review on the Working of the Trade Unions Act, 1926.

331.88　　　　　HU　ISSN 0084-1544
TRADE UNIONS INTERNATIONAL OF CHEMICAL, OIL AND ALLIED WORKERS. INTERNATIONAL TRADE CONFERENCE. DOCUMENTS. irreg., 7th, Tarnow, Poland. free. ‡ Trade Unions International of Chemical, Oil and Allied Workers, Benczur u. 45, Budapest 6, Hungary.

331.8　　　　　AT
TRADES UNION DIRECTORY. 1970. a. Trades and Labor Council of Queensland, Room 1, Trades Hall, Edward Street, Brisbane, Qld. 4000, Australia.

331.1　　　　　US
UNION DEMOCRACY REVIEW. 1972. irreg., approx. a. $5. Association for Union Democracy, 215 Park Ave. So., New York, NY 10003. Ed. H. W. Benson. bk. rev. circ. 3,000.
　　Supersedes: Union Democracy in Action (ISSN 0041-6835)

331.8　　　　　SZ　ISSN 0503-2334
UNION MONDIALE DES ORGANISATIONS SYNDICALES SUR BASES ECONOMIQUE ET SOCIALE LIBERALES. CONFERENCES: RAPPORT. 1960. a, latest 23rd, 1975, Locarno. World Union of Liberal Trade Union Organisations, 41 Badenerstrasse, 8004 Zurich, Switzerland.

331　　　　　AT
UNITY. 1952? irreg. Australian Boot Trade Employees Federation, 485-489 Queensberry St., North Melbourne, Vic. 3051, Australia.

331.88　　　　　MY
WHO'S WHO IN THE LABOUR MOVEMENT. (Text in English) 1975. irreg. $3. A. Ragunathan, 5-15e Jalan Chantek, Petaling Java, Kuala Lumpur, Malaysia. illus.

LABOR UNIONS — Abstracting, Bibliographies, Statistics

BIBLIOGRAPHY OF HIGHER EDUCATION COLLECTIVE BARGAINING INVOLVING OTHER THAN FACULTY PERSONNEL. see EDUCATION — Abstracting, Bibliographies, Statistics

331.881　314　　NE　ISSN 0077-6904
OMVANG DER VAKBEWEGING IN NEDERLAND/STATISTICS OF THE TRADE UNIONS IN THE NETHERLANDS. (Text in Dutch and English) 1946. a. fl.7.85. Centraal Bureau voor de Statistiek, Prinses Beatrixlaan 428, Voorburg, Netherlands (Orders to: Staatsuitgeverij, Christoffel Plantijnstraat, The Hague, Netherlands)

LABORATORY TECHNIQUE

see Medical Sciences—Experimental Medicine, Laboratory Technique

LAW

see also Law—International Law; Criminology and Law Enforcement; Patents, Trademarks and Copyrights;

also specific subjects

A A L S LIBRARY STATISTICS. (Association of American Law Schools) see LIBRARY AND INFORMATION SCIENCES

346 US ISSN 0361-3763
A B A LAWYERS' TITLE GUARANTY FUNDS NEWSLETTER. irreg. $1 per no. American Bar Association, Standing Committee on Lawyers' Title Guaranty Funds, 1155 East 60th St., Chicago, IL 60637.

340 AT
A L R C REPORT SERIES. (Australia Law Reform Commission) 1975. irreg. price varies. Australian Government Publishing Service, Box 84, Canberra, A.C.T. 2600, Australia. Indexed: Aus.Leg.Mon.Dig.

340 US ISSN 0161-1402
A S I L S INTERNATIONAL LAW JOURNAL. 1977. a. $7. Association of Student International Law Societies, Tillar House, 2223 Massachusetts, Ave.. N.W., Washington, DC 20008. circ. 500.

340 GW ISSN 0065-0307
ABHANDLUNGEN AUS DEM GESAMTEN BUERGERLICHEN RECHT, HANDELSRECHT UND WIRTSCHAFTSRECHT. 1954. irreg., no. 49, 1979. price varies. Verlagsgesellschaft Recht und Wirtschaft mbH, Haeusserstr. 14, Postfach 105960, 6900 Heidelberg 1, W. Germany (B.R.D.) Eds. E. Steindorf, P. Ulmer.

340 BL
ACADEMIA PAULISTA DE DIREITO. REVISTA. 1972. irreg. Universidade de Sao Paulo, Faculdade de Direito, Largo de Sao Francisco, 95, Sao Paulo, Brazil.

340 320 HU
ACTA FACULTATIS POLITICO-JURIDICAE UNIVERSITATIS SCIENTIARUM BUDAPESTIENSIS DE ROLANDO EOTVOS NOMINATAE. (Text in Hungarian; summaries in French, German, Russian) 1959. irreg. Eotvos Lorand Tudomanyegyetem, Allam- es Jogtudomanyi Kar, Egyetem ter 1-3, Budapest 5, Hungary.

340 SA ISSN 0065-1346
ACTA JURIDICA. 1958. irreg., latest issue 1980. R.20. (University of Cape Town, Faculty of Law) Juta & Co. Ltd., Box 30, Cape Town, South Africa. Ed. W. de Vos. circ. 500. Indexed: Leg.Per.

340 PL ISSN 0208-5283
ACTA UNIVERSITATIS NICOLAI COPERNICI. PRAWO. 1961. irreg. price varies. Uniwersytet Mikolaja Kopernika, Fosa Staromiejska 3, Torun, Poland (Dist. by Osrodek Rozpowszechniania Wydawnictw Naukowych PAN, Palac Kultury i Nauki, 00-901 Warsaw, Poland)
Formerly: Uniwersytet Mikolaja Kopernika, Torun. Nauki Humanistyczno-Spoleczne. Prawo (ISSN 0083-4513)

346 066 US
ADVERTISING LAW ANTHOLOGY. vol. 5, 1978. a. $59.95. International Library, 2425 Wilson Blvd., Arlington, VA 22201.

340 US ISSN 0462-3134
ADVOCACY INSTITUTE. PROCEEDINGS. 23rd, 1972. a. price varies. University of Michigan Law School, Institute of Continuing Legal Education, 625 South State, Ann Arbor, MI 48104.

340 CN ISSN 0382-456X
ADVOCATE. 1964. irreg. University of Toronto, Faculty of Law, Toronto, Ont. M5S 1A1, Canada.

342 AF
AFGHANISTAN. MINISTRY OF JUSTICE. OFFICIAL GAZETTE/RASMI JARIDAH. (Text in Persian) irreg. $15. Ministry of Justice, Darrul Aman, Kabul, Afghanistan.

340 BL
AJURIS. 1974. irreg. (Associacao dos Juizes do Rio Grande do Sul) Livraria Sulina, Av. Borges de Medeiros 1030-1036, Porto Alegre, Brazil.

ALBANY BULLETIN ON HEALTH AND WELFARE LEGISLATION. see *SOCIAL SERVICES AND WELFARE*

340 CN ISSN 0319-7980
ALBERTA DECISIONS, CIVIL AND CRIMINAL CASES. 1974. a(updated monthly) Can.$110 to individuals; Can. $190 to libraries. Western Legal Publications Ltd., 301-1 Alexander St., Vancouver, B.C. V6A 1B2, Canada.

340 BE
ALGEMENE PRACTISCHE RECHTVERZAMELING. Short title: A.P.R. 1972. irreg. price varies. E. Story-Scientia, Prudens van Duyseplein 8, B-9000 Ghent, Belgium.

AMERICAN AUTOMOBILE ASSOCIATION. DIGEST OF MOTOR LAWS. see *TRANSPORTATION — Automobiles*

342 US ISSN 0090-3647
AMERICAN BAR ASSOCIATION. SECTION OF ADMINISTRATIVE LAW. ANNUAL REPORTS OF COMMITTEES. 1964. a. American Bar Association, Section of Administrative Law, 1155 East 60th St., Chicago, IL 60637. Ed. Herbert Forrest. circ. 700. Key Title: Annual Reports of Committees.
Formerly: American Bar Association. Section of Administrative Law. Annual Reports of Divisions and Committees (ISSN 0569-3098)

AMERICAN BAR ASSOCIATION. SECTION OF LABOR RELATIONS LAW. COMMITTEE REPORTS. see *BUSINESS AND ECONOMICS — Labor And Industrial Relations*

347.9 331.1 US
AMERICAN BAR ASSOCIATION. SECTION OF LABOR RELATIONS LAW. PROCEEDINGS. a. $6. American Bar Association, Section of Labor Relations Law, 1155 E. 60th St., Chicago, IL 60637. circ. 8,300.

342.73 US ISSN 0587-2936
AMERICAN BAR ASSOCIATION. SECTION OF LOCAL GOVERNMENT LAW. COMMITTEE REPORTS. a. American Bar Association, Section of Local Government Law, 1155 E. 60th, Chicago, IL 60637. Key Title: Committee Reports - Local Government Law Section of the American Bar Assocation.

340 016 US ISSN 0065-7549
AMERICAN BAR FOUNDATION. RESEARCH CONTRIBUTIONS. 1967. irreg.,1-10/yr. $2-5 per no. American Bar Foundation, 1155 E. 60 St., Chicago, IL 60637. Ed. Spencer L. Kimball. (reprint service avail. from UMI)

340 US ISSN 0160-2578
AMERICAN BENCH-JUDGES OF THE NATION. 1977. a. $80. Reginald Bishop Forster Company, 121 W. Franklin, Minneapolis, MN 55404. Eds. Mary E. Reincke, Jeaneen Wilhelmi.

AMERICAN CONSTITUTIONAL AND LEGAL HISTORY. see *HISTORY — History Of North And South America*

340 970.1 US ISSN 0094-002X
AMERICAN INDIAN LAW REVIEW. 1973. s-a. $6.50. University of Oklahoma, College of Law, 300 Timberdell Rd., Norman, OK 73019. Ed. Sharon Claassen. adv. bk. rev. circ. 1,000.

340 US ISSN 0065-8995
AMERICAN JOURNAL OF JURISPRUDENCE. 1956. a. $7.50. University of Notre Dame, Notre Dame, IN 46556. Eds. Charles E. Rice, Robert E. Rodes. adv. bk. rev. circ. 1,000. (also avail. in microform from UMI)
Formerly: Natural Law Forum.

340 US ISSN 0065-9045
AMERICAN LAW INSTITUTE. ANNUAL MEETING. PROCEEDINGS. 1923. a. $25. American Law Institute, 4025 Chestnut St., Philadelphia, PA 19104. index from 1967.

AMERICAN LECTURES IN BEHAVIORAL SCIENCE AND LAW. see *PSYCHOLOGY*

020 340 US
AMERICAN LIBRARY LAWS. irreg., 4th, 1973. price varies. American Library Association, 50 E. Huron St., Chicago, IL 60611. Ed. Alex Ladenson.

340 SP
ANALES DE LA UNIVERSIDAD HISPALENSE. SERIE: DERECHO. irreg. price varies. Universidad de Sevilla, San Fernando 4, Seville, Spain.

340 BL
ANALISE JURISPRUDENCIAL. 1976. irreg. Instituto dos Advogados de Sao Paulo, Editora / Resenha Tributaria, Rue Xavier de Toledo 210, Sao Paulo, Brazil.

ANALYSIS OF WORKERS' COMPENSATION LAWS. see *SOCIAL SERVICES AND WELFARE*

340 PL ISSN 0458-4317
ANNALES UNIVERSITATIS MARIAE CURIE-SKLODOWSKA. SECTIO G. IUS. (Text in Polish, English, French, German; summaries in French, German, Polish, Russian) 1946. a. price varies. Uniwersytet Marii Curie-Sklodowskiej, Plac Marii Curie-Sklodowskiej 5, 20-031 Lublin, Poland. Ed. W. Skrzydlo.

340 GW
ANNALES UNIVERSITATIS SARAVIENSIS. RECHTSWISSENSCHAFTLICHE ABTEILUNG. SCHRIFTENREIHE. 1963. irreg., vol. 87, 1976. price varies. (Universitaet des Saarlandes, Rechtswissenschaftliche Fakultaet) Carl Heymanns Verlag KG, Gereonstr. 18-32, 5000 Cologne 1, W. Germany (B.R.D.)

ANNALS OF AIR AND SPACE LAW/ANNUAIRE DE DROIT AERIEN ET SPATIAL. see *AERONAUTICS AND SPACE FLIGHT*

340 FR ISSN 0066-2658
ANNUAIRE DE LEGISLATION FRANCAISE ET ETRANGERE. a. Centre National de la Recherche Scientifique, Service de Recherches Juridiques Comparatives, 15 Quai Anatole-France, 75700 Paris, France.

340 FR ISSN 0396-2318
ANNUAIRE DES AVOCATS. 1975. a. Edition Publi-Team-Elysees, 34 Av. des Champs-Elysees, 75008 Paris, France.

347.75 BE
ANNUAIRE MARITIME. a. Lloyd Anversois S.A., Eiermarkt 23, B-2000 Antwerp, Belgium. illus.

340 UK ISSN 0066-4405
ANNUAL SURVEY OF AFRICAN LAW. 1970. a. price varies. Rex Collings, 6 Paddington St., London W.1., England. Eds. N.N. Rubin, E. Cotran. index.

345 US ISSN 0066-4413
ANNUAL SURVEY OF AMERICAN LAW. 1942. 4/yr. $10. New York University, Law Publications, 137 Macdougal St., New York, NY 10012. circ. 3,200.

340 US
ANNUAL SURVEY OF ILLINOIS LAW. a. $5. De Paul University, 25 E. Jackson Blvd., Chicago, IL 60604.

340 II ISSN 0570-2666
ANNUAL SURVEY OF INDIAN LAW. (Text in English) 1965. a. Rs.30. Indian Law Institute, Bhagwandas Rd., New Delhi 110001, India. bibl.

340 US ISSN 0570-2674
ANNUAL SURVEY OF MASSACHUSETTS LAW. 1954. a. $24.50. Boston College, School of Law, 885 Centre St., Newton Centre, MA 02159.

340.5 IT ISSN 0003-5149
ANNUARIO DI DIRITTO COMPARATO E DI STUDI LEGISLATIVI. (Text in English, French and Italian) 1927. a. L.16000. Istituto Italiano di Studi Legislativi, Via Bertolini, 8, 00197 Rome, Italy. Dir. Riccardo Monaco. index. circ. 500.

340 UK
ANTHONY AND BERRYMAN'S MAGISTRATES' COURT GUIDE. a. Butterworth & Co. (Publishers) Ltd., 88 Kingsway, London WC2B 6AB, England. Ed. C. J. Acred.

340 SP
ANUARIO DE FILOSOFIA DEL DERECHO. 1953. a. Instituto Nacional de Estudios Juridicos, Seccion de Publicaciones, Duque de Medinaceli, 6, Madrid 14, Spain. Ed. L. Legaz Lacambra.

340 301 SP
ANUARIO DE SOCIOLOGIA Y PSICOLOGIA JURIDICAS. 1975. a. (Colegio de Abogados de Barcelona) Instituto de Psicologia y Sociologia Juricas, Calle Mallorca 283, Barcelona, Spain. bk. rev. bibl. circ. 1,000.

340 GW ISSN 0402-6802
ANWALTSVERZEICHNIS. 1952. biennial.
DM.65.80. (Deutscher Anwaltverein e.V.)
Juristischer Verlag W. Ellinghaus und Co. GmbH,
Bocholder Str. 259, 4300 Essen 11, W. Germany
(B.R.D.) circ. 20,000.

340 CE
AQUINAS LAW JOURNAL.* (Text in English)
1972. irreg. Rs.15. Aquinas College of Higher
Studies, Colombo 8, Sri Lanka.

340 GW ISSN 0066-5703
ARBEITEN ZUR RECHTSVERGLEICHUNG. 1958.
irreg., vol. 92, 1977. price varies. (Gesellschaft fuer
Rechtsvergleichung) Alfred Metzner Verlag GmbH,
Zeppelinallee 43, Postfach 970148, 6000 Frankfurt
97, W. Germany (B.R.D.) Eds. Ernst von
Caemmerer, Hans-Heinrich Jeschek.

ARBEITSRECHT DER GEGENWART. see
BUSINESS AND ECONOMICS — Labor And
Industrial Relations

ARCHIV FUER RECHTS- UND
SOZIALPHILOSOPHIE. BEIHEFTE. NEUE
FOLGE. see PHILOSOPHY

340 FR ISSN 0066-6564
ARCHIVES DE PHILOSOPHIE DU DROIT. 1952.
a. Editions Sirey, 22 rue Soufflot, 75005 Paris,
France. Ed. Michel Villey.

340 PL ISSN 0066-6882
ARCHIVUM IURIDICUM CRACOVIENSE. (Text
in English, French, German, Polish and Russian;
summaries in English, French, German and Russian)
1968. a. 60 Zl. (Polska Akademia Nauk, Oddzial w
Krakowie, Komisja Nauk Prawnych) Ossolineum,
Publishing House of the Polish Academy of
Sciences, Rynek 9, Wroclaw, Poland (Dist. by Ars
Polona-Ruch, Krakowskie Przedmiescie 7, Warsaw,
Poland) Ed. Franciszek Studnicki. circ. 600.

ARGENTINA. INSTITUTO NACIONAL DE
DERECHO AERONAUTICO Y ESPACIAL. see
TRANSPORTATION — Air Transport

348 US ISSN 0094-4246
ARIZONA LEGISLATIVE SERVICE. Cover title: A
R S Legislative Service. irreg. West Publishing Co.,
Box 3526, St. Paul, MN 55165.

348
ARIZONA REPORTS. 1913. irreg. (Supreme Court)
West Publishing Co., Box 3526, St. Paul, MN
55165.
Formerly: Report of Cases Argued and
Determined in the Supreme Court of the State of
Arizona.

340 NO ISSN 0004-2102
ARKIV FOR SJOERETT/SCANDINAVIAN
JOURNAL OF MARITIME LAW. (Text in
English and Scandinavian languages) 1951. irreg. (4-
5/vol.) Kr.120($24) per vol. (Norske Sjoeretts-
Forening) Universitetsforlaget, Kolstadgt. 1, Box
2959-Toeyen, Oslo 6, Norway (U.S. address: Box
258, Irvington-on-Hudson, NY 10533) Ed. Thor
Falkanger. adv. bk. rev. circ. 1,500.

340 US
ASIAN LAW SERIES. 1969. irreg., no. 6, 1978. price
varies. University of Washington Press, Seattle, WA
98105.

346 US ISSN 0066-9407
ASSOCIATION OF AMERICAN LAW SCHOOLS.
PROCEEDINGS. 1901. a. $2-3 per vol. ‡
Association of American Law Schools, Suite 370, 1
Dupont Circle, N.W., Washington, DC 20036. 50-
yr. cum.index. (processed)

340 US
ASSOCIATION OF TRIAL LAWYERS OF
AMERICA. LAW JOURNAL. 1946. biennial. $35.
‡ Association of Trial Lawyers of America, 1050
31st St. N.W., Washington, DC 20007. Ed. Thomas
F. Lambert, Jr. bk. rev. circ. 35,000.

346 NZ ISSN 0067-0510
AUCKLAND UNIVERSITY LAW REVIEW. 1967.
a. NZ.$5. ‡ Auckland University Law Students
Society, Inc., Private Bag, Auckland, New Zealand.
Ed. R. L. Towner. adv. bk. rev. circ. 1,100. Indexed:
Leg.Per.

338.7 340 GW ISSN 0067-0669
AUSLAENDISCHE AKTIENGESETZE. 1955. irreg.
price varies. (Gesellschaft fuer Rechtsvergleichung)
Alfred Metzner Verlag GmbH, Zeppelinallee 43,
Postfach 970148, 6000 Frankfurt 97, W. Germany
(B.R.D.)

340 AT ISSN 0312-1356
AUSTRALIA. BUREAU OF STATISTICS.
TASMANIAN OFFICE. PUBLIC JUSTICE. a.
free. Australian Bureau of Statistics, Tasmanian
Office, Box 66A, G.P.O., Hobart, Tasmania 7001,
Australia. circ. 380.

AUSTRALIA. FISHING INDUSTRY RESEARCH
COMMITTEE. ANNUAL REPORT. see FISH
AND FISHERIES

340 AT
AUSTRALIA. LAW REFORM COMMISSION.
ANNUAL REPORT. 1975. a. price varies.
Australian Government Publishing Service, Box 84,
Canberra, A.C.T. 2600, Australia. (back issues
avail.) Indexed: Aus.Leg.Mon.Dig.

346 AT ISSN 0067-1843
AUSTRALIAN DIGEST; a digest of all the Australian
law reports. 1961. irreg., vol. 33, 1980. Aus.$65.
Law Book Co. Ltd., 31 Market St., Sydney, N.S.W.
2000, Australia. Ed. J.M. Jelbart.

347 AT
AUSTRALIAN FAMILY LAW CASES. 1977. a.
Aus.$52. C C H Australia Ltd., P.O. Box 230,
North Ryde, N.S.W. 2113, Australia. charts.

345.01 AT
AUSTRALIAN LEGAL AID REVIEW
COMMITTEE. REPORT. 1974. a. Australian Legal
Aid Review Committee, 187 Macquarie St., Sydney,
N.S.W. 2000, Australia.

328.94 328.9 AT
AUSTRALIAN PARLIAMENTARY SEMINAR.
SUMMARY REPORT OF PROCEEDINGS. 1972.
biennial. free. Commonwealth Parliamentary
Association, Canberra, Australia.

AUSTRALIAN TAX CASES. see BUSINESS AND
ECONOMICS — Public Finance, Taxation

340 AU ISSN 0567-1477
AUSTRIA. OBERLANDESGERICHT WIEN IM
LEISTUNGSSTREITVERFAHREN ZWEITER
INSTANZ DER SOZIALVERSICHERUNG (SSV).
ENTSCHEIDUNGEN. 1961. a. price varies.
Manzsche Verlags- und Universitaetsbuchhandlung,
Kohlmarkt 16, A-1014 Vienna, Austria. circ.
2,000(approx.)

347 US ISSN 0099-1244
B A R-B R I BAR REVIEW. CIVIL PROCEDURE.
a. B A R-B R I Bar Review, 11801 W. Olympic
Blvd., Los Angeles, CA 90064. Key Title: Civil
Procedure.

346 US
B A R-B R I BAR REVIEW. COMMUNITY
PROPERTY. a. B A R-B R I Bar Review, 11801
W. Olympic Blvd., Los Angeles, CA 90064.

342.73 US ISSN 0098-7638
B A R-B R I BAR REVIEW. CONSTITUTIONAL
LAW. a. B A R-B R I Bar Review, 11801 W.
Olympic Blvd., Los Angeles, CA 90064. Key Title:
Constitutional Law.

346.73 US ISSN 0098-762X
B A R-B R I BAR REVIEW. CONTRACTS. a. B A
R-B R I Bar Review, 11801 W. Olympic Blvd., Los
Angeles, CA 90064. Key Title: Contracts.

346 US ISSN 0099-1236
B A R-B R I BAR REVIEW. CORPORATIONS. a. B
A R-B R I Bar Review, 11801 W. Olympic Blvd.,
Los Angeles, CA 90064. Key Title: Corporations.

347.73 US
B A R-B R I BAR REVIEW. EVIDENCE. a. B A R-
B R I Bar Review, 11801 W. Olympic Blvd., Los
Angeles, CA 90064.

174 US
B A R-B R I BAR REVIEW. PROFESSIONAL
RESPONSIBILITY. a. B A R-B R I Bar Review,
11801 W. Olympic Blvd., Los Angeles, CA 90064.
Formerly: Bay Area Review Course. Legal Ethics
(ISSN 0098-7980)

346.73 US
B A R-B R I BAR REVIEW. REAL PROPERTY. a.
B A R-B R I Bar Review, 11801 W. Olympic Blvd.,
Los Angeles, CA 90064.

347 US ISSN 0098-7999
B A R-B R I BAR REVIEW. REMEDIES. irreg. B A
R-B R I Bar Review, 11801 W. Olympic Blvd., Los
Angeles, CA 90064. Key Title: Remedies.

346 US
B A R-B R I BAR REVIEW. WILLS. a. B A R-B R I
Bar Review, 11801 W. Olympic Blvd., Los Angeles,
CA 90064.

340 US
B N A'S LAW REPRINTS: CRIMINAL LAW
SERIES. 1969. irreg. $250. Bureau of National
Affairs, Inc., 1231 25th St. N.W., Washington, DC
20037. Ed. Mildred Mason.
Formerly: Law Reprints: Criminal Law Series.

340 US
B N A'S LAW REPRINTS: LABOR SERIES. 1967.
irreg. $215. Bureau of National Affairs, Inc., 1231
25th St. N.W., Washington, DC 20037. Ed. Mildred
Mason.
Formerly: Law Reprints: Labor Series.

340 US
B N A'S LAW REPRINTS: PATENT,
TRADEMARK & COPYRIGHT SERIES. 1977.
irreg. $215. Bureau of National Affairs, Inc., 1231
25th St. N.W., Washington, DC 20037. Ed. Mildred
Mason.
Formerly: Law Reprints, Patent, Trademark and
Copyright Series.

340 US
B N A'S LAW REPRINTS: SECURITIES
REGULATION SERIES. 1976. irreg. $215. Bureau
of National Affairs, Inc., 1231 25th St. N.W.,
Washington, DC 20037. Ed. Mildred Mason.
Formerly: Law Reprints. Securities Regulation
Series.

340 US
B N A'S LAW REPRINTS: TAX SERIES. 1968.
irreg. $215. Bureau of National Affairs, Inc., 1231
25th St. N.W., Washington, DC 20037. Ed. Mildred
Mason.
Formerly: Law Reprints. Tax Series.

342 BG
BANGLADESH JATIYA AINJIBI SAMITY
SOUVENIR. Variant title: Bangladesh Jatiya Ainjibi
Samity. Annual Law Journal. (Text in English or
Bengali) 1977. a. Tk.25. Bangladesh Jatiya Ainjibi
Samity - National Bar Associaton of Bangladesh,
Bangladesh Supreme Court, Room no. 42, Dacca 2,
Bangladesh.

340 UK ISSN 0308-8219
BAR LIST OF THE UNITED KINGDOM. a. £10.75.
Sweet & Maxwell Stevens Journals, 11 New Fetter
Lane, London EC4P 4EE, England (Dist. in U.S. &
Canada by: Carswell Co. Ltd., 233 Midland Ave.,
Agincourt, Ont., Canada) adv. circ. 6,000.
Continues: Law List.

340.1 NR
BARRISTER.* (Suspended 1968-70) 1967. irreg.
University of Nigeria, Law Student's Association,
Nsukka, Nigeria.

340 SZ
BASLER STUDIEN ZUR
RECHTSWISSENSCHAFT. 1932. irreg. price
varies. Helbing und Lichtenhahn Verlag AG,
Steinentorstr. 13, CH-4010 Basel, Switzerland.

BEITRAEGE ZUM RUNDFUNKRECHT. see
COMMUNICATIONS — Radio And Television

340 SP
BOLETIN DE PEQUENA JURISPRUDENCIA.
1965. irreg. (approx. m.) free. Ilustre Colegio
Provincial de Abogados de San Sebastian,
Fuenterrabia A-2, Guipuzcoa, Spain. bibl. circ. 800.

BRAZIL. INSTITUTO DO ACUCAR E DO
ALCOOL. CONSELHO DELIBERATIVO.
COLETANEA DE RESOLUCOES (E)
PRESIDENCIA. COLETANEA DE ATOS. see
AGRICULTURE — Crop Production And Soil

340 BL
BRAZIL. SUPREMO TRIBUNAL FEDERAL.
JURISCIVEL DO S.T.F. 1972. irreg. Cultural
Distribuidora de Livros, Rua Sergipe, No. 1.466,
Sao Joaquim da Barra, Brazil.

340 BL
BRAZIL. SUPREMO TRIBUNAL FEDERAL.
RELATORIO DOS TRABALHOS REALIZADOS.
a. Supremo Tribunal Federal, Brasilia, Brazil.

340 BL
BRAZIL. SUPREMO TRIBUNAL FEDERAL.
INDICES DA LEGISLACAO FEDERAL.
(Subseries of: D.I.N.-Divulgacao) a. price varies.
Supremo Tribunal Federal, Departamento de
Imprensa Nacional, Brasilia, Brazil.

340 CN ISSN 0317-297X
BRITISH COLUMBIA PROVINCIAL JUDGES'
ASSOCIATION. ANNUAL CONFERENCE.
1972. a. British Columbia Provincial Judges'
Association, Vancouver, B.C., Canada. Key Title:
Annual Conference of the British Columbia
Provincial Judges' Association.

164 UK ISSN 0068-2160
BRITISH INSTITUTE OF INTERNATIONAL AND
COMPARATIVE LAW. COMPARATIVE LAW
SERIES.* 1961. irreg. price varies. British Institute
of International and Comparative Law, 32 Furnival
St., London EC4A 1JN, England.
Formerly: Common Market European and
Comparative Law Series.

340 BU ISSN 0068-3884
BULGARSKA AKADEMIIA NA NAUKITE.
INSTITUT ZA PRAVNI NAUKI. IZVESTIIA.
(Summaries in various languages) 1950. irreg. 2.61
lv. per issue. Publishing House of the Bulgarian
Academy of Sciences, Ul. Akad. G. Bonchev, 1113
Sofia, Bulgaria (Dist. by: Hemus, 6, Rouski Blvd.,
1000 Sofia, Bulgaria) Ed. K. Liutov. circ. 650.

348 US
BULLETIN OF MEDIEVAL CANON LAW. NEW
SERIES. (Text in English, French, German, Italian,
Latin and Spanish) 1971. a. $9. Institute of
Medieval Canon Law, University of California,
Berkeley, Boalt Hall, Berkeley, CA 94720. Ed.
Stephan Kuttner. bibl. circ. 500. Indexed: Canon
Law Abstr.

340.093 NZ ISSN 0110-070X
BUTTERWORTHS CURRENT LAW. (Supplement
to: New Zealand Law Journal) fortn. Butterworths
of New Zealand Ltd., 77/85 Customhouse Quay,
Wellington, New Zealand. Ed. Tony Black.

CAISSES CENTRALES DE MUTUALITE
SOCIALE AGRICOLE. STATISTIQUES. see
SOCIOLOGY

347.9 US ISSN 0068-5488
CALIFORNIA. ADMINISTRATIVE OFFICE OF
THE CALIFORNIA COURTS. ANNUAL
REPORT. (Incorporates report of Judicial Council)
1962. a. free. Administrative Office of the California
Courts, 601 McAllister St., San Francisco, CA
94102. (Co-sponsor: Judicial Council of California)
circ. 4,000.

340 US
CALIFORNIA. LAW REVISION COMMISSION.
REPORTS, RECOMMENDATIONS AND
STUDIES. 1955. irreg., vol. 14, 1978. pamphlets
free; bound vols. $11.98. Law Revision Commission,
Stanford Law School, Stanford University, Stanford,
CA 94305 (Bound vols. and priced pamphlets avail.
from Department of General Services, Documents
Section, Box 1015, North Highlands, CA 95660)
index. circ. 1,500.
Includes its Annual Reports, Recommendations
and Studies issued as pamphlets; bound every 2 yrs.

CALIFORNIA. STATE BOARD OF
COSMETOLOGY. RULES AND
REGULATIONS. see BEAUTY CULTURE

340 352 US ISSN 0068-5879
CALIFORNIA COUNTY LAW LIBRARY BASIC
LIST. 1961. irreg. free. ‡ State Library, Box 2037,
Sacramento, CA 95809. circ. 600.

340 UK ISSN 0084-8328
CAMBRIAN LAW REVIEW. 1970. a. £3. University
College of Wales, Department of Law, Aberystwyth,
Wales. Ed. J. E. Trice. adv. bk. rev. illus. circ. 700.

410 UK
CAMBRIDGE STUDIES IN ENGLISH LEGAL
HISTORY. irreg. price varies. Cambridge University
Press, Box 110, Cambridge CB2 3RL, England
(And 32 E. 57th St., New York NY 10022) Ed. D.
C. Yale.

340 341 UK ISSN 0068-6751
CAMBRIDGE STUDIES IN INTERNATIONAL
AND COMPARATIVE LAW. 1967. irreg., no. 9,
1972. $37.50 for latest vol. Cambridge University
Press, Box 110, Cambridge CB2 3RL, England (and
32 E. 57 St., New York, NY 10022) Ed. R. Y.
Jennings. index.

340 CN
CANADA. LAW REFORM COMMISSION.
ADMINISTRATIVE LAW SERIES. STUDY
PAPERS. (Text in English and French) 1976. irreg.
free. Law Reform Commission, 130 Albert St.,
Ottawa, Ont. K1A 0L6, Canada. (back issues avail.)

340 CN ISSN 0382-1463
CANADA. LAW REFORM COMMISSION.
ANNUAL REPORT. (Text in English and French)
1971/72. a. free. Law Reform Commission, 130
Albert St., Ottawa, Ont. K1A 0L6, Canada.

343 CN
CANADA. LAW REFORM COMMISSION.
CRIMINAL LAW SERIES. STUDY PAPERS.
(Text in English and French) irreg. free. Law
Reform Commission, 130 Albert St., Ottawa, Ont.
K1A 0L6, Canada.

340 CN
CANADA. LAW REFORM COMMISSION.
MODERNIZATION OF STATUTES. STUDY
PAPERS. (Text in English and French) 1981. irreg.
free. Law Reform Commission, 130 Albert St.,
Ottawa, Ont. K1A 0L6, Canada.

340 CN
CANADA. LAW REFORM COMMISSION.
PROTECTION OF LIFE SERIES. STUDY
PAPERS. (Text in English and French) 1979. irreg.
free. Law Reform Commission, 130 Albert St.,
Ottawa, Ont. K1A 0L6, Canada. (back issues avail.)

340 CN
CANADA. LAW REFORM COMMISSION.
REPORT TO PARLIAMENT. (Text in English and
French) 1975. irreg. free. Law Reform Commission,
130 Albert St., Ottawa, Ont. K1A 0L6, Canada.
(back issues avail.)

340 CN
CANADA. LAW REFORM COMMISSION.
WORKING PAPER. (Text in English and French)
irreg. free. Law Reform Commission, 130 Albert St.,
Ottawa, Ont. K1A 0L6, Canada. circ.
10,000(controlled) (back issues avail.)

346.71 CN ISSN 0317-6649
CANADA BUSINESS CORPORATIONS ACT
WITH REGULATIONS. vol. 4, 1979. irreg.
Can.$5.50. C C H Canadian Ltd., 6 Garamond Ct.,
Don Mills, Ont. M3C 1Z5, Canada. index.

340 CN ISSN 0045-4230
CANADA SUPREME COURT REPORTS/
RECUEIL DES ARRETS DE LA COUR
SUPREME DU CANADA. (Text in English and
French) 1877. 2 vols. per yr. Can.$42. Supreme
Court of Canada, Ottawa, Ont. K1A 0J1, Canada.
Ed. Mills Shipley.

340 CN
CANADIAN BAR ASSOCIATION. ANNUAL
REPORT OF PROCEEDINGS. a. Can.$20.
Canadian Bar Foundation, Suite 1700, 130 Albert
St., Ottawa, Ont. K1P 0L6, Canada.

340 CN ISSN 0384-5753
CANADIAN BAR ASSOCIATION. BRITISH
COLUMBIA BRANCH. PROGRAM REPORT.
1971. irreg. Canadian Bar Association, British
Columbia Branch, 1010-777 Hornby St., Vancouver,
B.C. V6Z 1S4, Canada.

340 CN ISSN 0704-0857
CANADIAN COMMUNITY LAW JOURNAL/
REVUE CANADIENNE DE DROIT
COMMUNAUTAIRE. (Text in English and
French) 1977. a. University of Windsor, Faculty of
Law, Windsor, Ont. N9B 3P4, Canada.

340 CN ISSN 0084-8573
CANADIAN LAW LIST. a. Can.$35. ‡ Canada Law
Book Ltd., 80 Cowdray Court, Agincourt, Ont.
M1S 1S5, Canada. Ed. Mrs. P. Egan.

340 CN
CANADIAN LEGAL MANUAL SERIES. irreg.
price varies. Butterworth & Co. (Canada) Ltd., 2265
Midland Ave., Scarborough, Toronto, Ont., Canada.

340 CN ISSN 0576-5625
CANADIAN LEGAL STUDIES SERIES. 1964. irreg.
price varies. Butterworth & Co. (Canada) Ltd., 2265
Midland Ave., Scarborough, Toronto, Ont., Canada.

CAPITULO CRIMINOLOGICO. see
CRIMINOLOGY AND LAW ENFORCEMENT

340 US
CASES AND MATERIALS ON
CONSTITUTIONAL LAW. irreg. price varies.
Foundation Press, Inc., 170 Old Country Rd.,
Mineola, NY 11501.

340 US
CASES AND MATERIALS ON TRADE
REGULATION. irreg. price varies. Foundation
Press, Inc., 170 Old Country Rd., Mineola, NY
11501.

345 347.9 US ISSN 0069-0872
CASES DECIDED IN THE COURT OF CLAIMS
OF THE UNITED STATES. 1863. irreg. $5.
United States Court of Claims, 717 Madison Place
N.W., Washington, DC 20005. starting with vol.
110, cumulative indexes are contained in every
tenth volume.

344 RM
CENTRUL DE STIINTE SOCIALE DIN CLUJ.
SERIA DREPT. (Subseries of: Studia Napocensia)
1974. irreg. Editura Academiei Republicii Socialiste
Romania, Calea Victoriei 125, Bucharest, Romania
(Subscr. to: Ilexim, Str. 13 Decembrie Nr. 3, P.O.
Box 136-137, Bucharest, Romania)

CHRONICLE OF PARLIAMENTARY ELECTIONS
AND DEVELOPMENTS. see POLITICAL
SCIENCE

340 US
CLARENDON LAW SERIES. irreg. price varies.
Oxford University Press, 200 Madison Ave., New
York, NY 10016 (And Ely House, 37 Dover St.,
London W1X 4AH, England) Ed. Herbert L. A.
Hart.

349 BE ISSN 0010-0188
CODES LARCIER. (Includes Mise a Jour) a. 15950
Fr. Maison Ferdinand Larcier, S.A., Rue des
Minimes 39, 1000 Brussels, Belgium. charts. index.

340 BL ISSN 0530-0657
COLECAO DE ESTUDOS JURIDICOS. 1956. irreg.
Fundacao Casa de Rui Barbosa, Rua Sao Clemente
134, Botafogo 22260, Rio de Janeiro RJ, Brazil. Dir.
Washington Luis Neto.

340 SP ISSN 0069-5122
COLECCION JURIDICA. 1954. irreg.; 1979, no. 75.
price varies. (Universidad de Navarra, Facultad de
Derecho.) Ediciones Universidad de Navarra, S.A.,
Plaza de los Sauces, 1 y 2 Baranain, Pamplona,
Spain. index: vols. 1-6.

340 CK
COLEGAS. irreg. Colegio Antioqueno de Abogados,
Edificio Bolsa de Medellin, Carrera 50 no. 50-48,
Medellin, Colombia.

340 FR ISSN 0069-5467
COLLECTION U. SERIE DROIT DES AFFAIRES
ET DE L'ECONOMIE. 1970. irreg. price varies.
Librairie Armand Colin, 103 Bld. Saint-Michel,
Paris 5e, France.

340 CE ISSN 0069-5939
COLOMBO LAW REVIEW.* 1969. a. Rs.15($3) (Sri
Lanka University Law Review Association) Hansa
Publishers Ltd., Clifford Ave., Colombo 3, Sri
Lanka. Ed. M. Sonnarajah.

COMMISSION OF THE EUROPEAN
COMMUNITIES. COLLECTION DU DROIT DU
TRAVAIL. see *BUSINESS AND
ECONOMICS — Labor And Industrial Relations*

346　　　　AT　　ISSN 0069-7133
COMMONWEALTH LAW REPORTS. 1903.
irreg.(approx. 10 issues per year) Aus.$58.50. Law
Book Co. Ltd., 31 Market St., Sydney, N.S.W.
2000, Australia. index; cum. index:vol.1-127.
Indexed: Curr.Aus.N.Z.Leg.Lit.Ind.

347.01　　　　UK　　ISSN 0307-6539
COMMONWEALTH MAGISTRATES'
CONFERENCE. REPORT. irreg., 4th, 1975, Kuala
Lumpur. Commonwealth Magistrates' Association,
28 Fitzroy Square, London W1P 6DD, England.

340　　　　US　　ISSN 0069-7893
COMPARATIVE JURIDICAL REVIEW. (Text in
English and Spanish) 1964. a. free. (Rainforth
Foundation) Pan American Institute of Comparative
Law, 3001 Ponce de Leon Blvd., Coral Gable, FL
33134. Ed. Mario Diaz Cruz. bk. rev. cum. index in
vol. 11, 1973. circ. 1,000.

340　　　　US
COMPILATION OF STATE AND FEDERAL
PRIVACY LAWS. 1975. a. $14.50. Robert Ellis
Smith, Box 8844, Washington, DC 20003. circ.
2,000. (reprint service avail. from UMI)

COMPLIANCE AND LEGAL SEMINAR.
PROCEEDINGS. see *BUSINESS AND
ECONOMICS — Investments*

COMPUTER LAW MONOGRAPH SERIES. see
*COMPUTER TECHNOLOGY AND
APPLICATIONS*

COMPUTER UND RECHT. see *COMPUTER
TECHNOLOGY AND APPLICATIONS*

340　350　　　TT
CONGRESS OF MICRONESIA. SENATE.
JOURNAL. (Text in English) irreg. Senate, Capitol
Hill, Saipan 96950, Mariana Islands.

353.9　　　　US　　ISSN 0098-8138
CONNECTICUT. JUDICIAL DEPARTMENT.
REPORT. irreg., approx. biennial. Judicial
Department, Box 1350, Hartford, CT 06101. illus.
Key Title: Report of the Judicial Department, State
of Connecticut.

342　　　　US
CONSORTIUM FOR COMPARATIVE
LEGISLATIVE STUDIES. PUBLICATIONS. 1975.
irreg. price varies. Duke University Press, Box 6697,
College Sta., Durham, NC 27708. Ed. Lloyd D.
Musolf.

340　　　　US　　ISSN 0147-1074
CONTRIBUTIONS IN LEGAL STUDIES. 1978.
irreg. Greenwood Press, 88 Post Rd. W., Westport,
CT 06881. Ed. Paul L. Murphy.

340　　　　SP　　ISSN 0589-8056
CORPUS HISPANORUM DE PACE. 1963. irreg.
Consejo Superior de Investigaciones Cientificas,
Instituto Francisco de Vitoria, Medinaceli 4,
Madrid, Spain (Orders to: Consejo Superior de
Investigaciones Cientificas. Distribution de
Publicaciones, Viturbio 8, Madrid 6, Spain)

340　011　　UK　　ISSN 0305-411X
COUNCIL OF LEGAL EDUCATION.
CALENDAR. 1901-2. a. price varies. Council of
Legal Education, 4, Gray's Inn Place, London
WC1R 5DX, England. circ. 5,000.

340　　　　UK
COUNTY COURT PRACTICE. a. Butterworth &
Co. (Publishers) Ltd., 88 Kingsway, London WC2B
6AB, England. Ed. Bd.

343　　　　US　　ISSN 0145-7322
CRIMINAL LAW OUTLINE. 1966. a. $4. National
Judicial College, Judicial College Bldg., University
of Nevada, Reno, NV 89557. Ed. William A.
Grimes.

340　　　　UK
CROWN COURT; an index of common penalties and
formalities. 1951. a. since 1974. £4.75($16.40) ‡
Barry Rose (Publishers) Ltd., Little London,
Chichester, Sussex PO19 1PG, England. Eds. Peter
Morrish, Ian McLean. circ. 2,000.

342　　　　AG
CUADERNOS DE LOS INSTITUTOS. 1957. irreg.
Universidad Nacional de Cordoba, Instituto de
Derecho Constitucional, Calle Obispo Trejo y
Sanabria 242, Cordoba, Argentina.

CURRENT EDUCATION LAW. see *EDUCATION*

340　　　　UK　　ISSN 0070-1998
CURRENT LEGAL PROBLEMS. 1948. a. price
varies. (University College, London) Sweet &
Maxwell Stevens Journals, 11 New Fetter Lane,
London, EC4, England (Dist. in U.S. & Canada by:
Carswell Co Ltd., 233 Midland Ave., Agincourt,
Ont., Canada) Eds. Lord Lloyd of Hampstead,
Roger Rideout.

CURRENT MUNICIPAL PROBLEMS. see *PUBLIC
ADMINISTRATION — Municipal Government*

340　　　　TZ　　ISSN 0418-3770
DAR ES SALAAM UNIVERSITY LAW JOURNAL.
1963. irreg. EAs.27. University of Dar es Salaam,
Faculty of Law, Box 35034, Dar es Salaam,
Tanzania. Ed. Ernest L. Kembela Mwipopo.
Formerly (until 1971): Denning Law Society.
Journal.

348　　　　US　　ISSN 0091-5564
DELAWARE REPORTER. (Vol. numbering adopted
from That of the Atlantic Reporter) irreg. West
Publishing Co., Box 3526, St. Paul, MN 55165.
Supersedes: Delaware. Court of Chancery.
Delaware Chancery Reports & Delaware. Courts.
Delaware Reports.

346.861　　　CK
DERECHO FINANCIERO. 1975. irreg. Asociacion
Nacional de Instituciones Financieras, Calle 35, No.
4-89, Apdo. Aereo 29677, Bogota, Colombia. Ed.
Belisario Betancur. illus.

340　　　　PE
DERECHOS SOCIALES. 1973. irreg. Asociacion
Peruana de Derechos Sociales, Jiron de la Union
No. 1011, Lima, Peru.

340　　　　GW
DEUTSCHER JUSTIZ-KALENDER. 1954. a.
DM.52.50. Walhalla- und Praetoria-Verlag Georg
Zwichenpflug, Dolomitenstr. 1, Postfach 301, 8400
Regensburg 1, W. Germany (B.R.D.)

340　382　　US　　ISSN 0419-1285
DIGEST OF COMMERCIAL LAWS OF THE
WORLD. 1966. irreg. $142.50. (National
Association of Credit Management) Oceana
Publications, Inc., Dobbs Ferry, NY 10522. Ed.
George Kohlik. bibl. (looseleaf format)

347　　　　IT　　ISSN 0070-4857
DIGEST OF LEGAL ACTIVITIES OF
INTERNATIONAL ORGANIZATIONS AND
OTHER INSTITUTIONS. 1969. a. $75. Unidroit
(International Institute for the Unification of Private
Law), Via Panisperna 28, 00184 Rome, Italy (Dist.
by: Oceana Publications, Inc., Dobbs Ferry, NY
10522)

340　　　　IS　　ISSN 0070-4903
DINE ISRAEL; an annual of Jewish and Israeli family
law. (Absorbed Current Bibliography of Hebrew
Law with No. 8, 1969) (Text in Hebrew and
English) 1969. a. $14. Tel Aviv University, Faculty
of Law, Tel Aviv, Israel. Eds. Ze'Ev W. Falk &
Aaron Kirschenbaum. bk. rev. circ. 500.

020　　　　US
DIRECTORY OF LAW LIBRARIES. 1946. biennial.
$5 to members; $10 to non-members. American
Association of Law Libraries, 53 W. Jackson Blvd.,
Room 1201, Chicago, IL 60604. Ed.Bd. circ. 3,000.

340　378　　US　　ISSN 0070-573X
DIRECTORY OF LAW TEACHERS. 1922. a. $15. ‡
(Association of American Law Schools) West
Publishing Co., Box 3526, St. Paul, MN 55165
(Order from: Association of American Law Schools,
One Dupont Circle, Suite 370, Washington, DC
20036)

340　　　　CN　　ISSN 0383-8358
DIRECTORY OF LAW TEACHERS/ANNUAIRE
DES PROFESSEURS DE DROIT. (Text in English
and French) 1972. a. Association of Canadian Law
Teachers, c/o Faculty of Law, Queen's University,
Kingston, Ont., Canada.

340　　　　US
DIRECTORY OF NORTH DAKOTA LAWYERS. a.
free. State Bar Board, State Capitol, Bismarck, ND
58501.

340　　　　US　　ISSN 0092-9174
DIRECTORY OF SAN FRANCISCO ATTORNEYS.
a. $20 to non-members; $5 to members. Bar
Association of San Francisco, 220 Bush St., San
Francisco, CA 94104. adv. circ. 5,000.

340　　　　IT　　ISSN 0390-8542
DIRITTO E SOCIETA (NAPLES) (Numbers not
published consecutively) 1977. irreg., no. 6, 1980.
price varies. Liguori Editore s.r.l., Via
Mezzocannone 19, 80134 Naples, Italy. Ed.
Gustavo Minervini.

340　　　　FR
DOCUMENTS D'ETUDES. (Includes 3 Series: Droit
Constitutionnel et Institutions Politiques; Droit
Administratif. Droit International Public) 1970. irreg
(10-14/yr) Documentation Francaise, 29-31 Quai
Voltaire, 75340 Paris Cedex 07, France. Ed. J-L.
Cremieux-Brilaac. bibl.

340　　　　US　　ISSN 0012-5938
DRAKE LAW REVIEW. Fourth issue titled:
Insurance Law Symposium. 1951. q. $15. Drake
University, Law School, Cartwright Hall, Des
Moines, IA 50311. Ed.Bd. adv. bk. rev. circ. 3,000.
(also avail. in microform from MIM) Indexed:
Leg.Per. C.C.L.P.

EDUCATION LAW BULLETIN. see *EDUCATION*

340　　　　AU　　ISSN 0531-674X
EHE- UND FAMILIENRECHTLICHE
ENTSCHEIDUNGEN. 1966. a. price varies.
Manzsche Verlags- und Universitaetsbuchhandlung,
Kohlmarkt 16, A-1014 Vienna, Austria. Eds.
Friedrich Hluze, Paul Litzlfellner. circ.
2,500(approx.)

342　　　　US　　ISSN 0091-9101
ELECTION LAWS OF HAWAII. a. free. Office of
the Lieutenant Governor, State Capitol, Honolulu,
HI 96813.

340　　　　SZ
ENGLISH LEGAL MANUSCRIPTS. 1975. irreg.
Inter-Documentation Company, Poststrasse 14, Zug,
Switzerland.

ENTSCHEIDUNGEN DES
BUNDESOBERSEEAMTES UND DER
SEEAMTER DER BUNDESREPUBLIK
DEUTSCHLAND. see *TRANSPORTATION —
Ships And Shipping*

340　　　　UK　　ISSN 0071-1586
ESTATES GAZETTE DIGEST OF LAND AND
PROPERTY CASES. a. £25. Estates Gazette Ltd.,
151 Wardour Street, London, W1V 4BN, England.

340　　　　NR
ETHIOPE LAW SERIES. no. 4, 1976. irreg. Ethiope
Publishing Corporation, 34 Murtala Mohammed St.,
P. M. B. 1192, Benin City, Nigeria. Ed. T. O. Elias.

340　　　　BE
ETUDES DE LOGIQUE JURIDIQUE. irreg., latest
no. 7. price varies. Etablissements Emile Bruylant,
67 rue de la Regence, 1000 Brussels, Belgium.

349　940　　FR　　ISSN 0531-2671
EUROPEAN ASPECTS, LAW SERIES; a collection
of studies relating to European integration. 1962.
irreg. Council of Europe, Publications Section,
67000 Strasbourg, France (Dist. in U. S. by
Manhattan Publishing Co., 225 Lafayette St., New
York, N. Y. 10012)

342.4　　　　FR
EUROPEAN COMMISSION OF HUMAN RIGHTS.
ANNUAL REVIEW/COMPTE RENDU
ANNUAL. (Text in English and French) 1972. a.
$2. European Commission of Human Rights, 67006
Strasbourg, France (Dist. in U. S. by Manhattan
Publishing Co., 225 Lafayette St., New York, N. Y.
10012)

340　　　　NE
EUROPEAN STUDIES IN LAW. 1977. irreg., vol. 8,
1978. price varies. North-Holland Publishing Co.,
Box 211, 1000 AE Amsterdam, Netherlands. Ed. A.
G. Chloros.

340 NE
EUROPEAN UNIVERSITY INSTITUTE SERIES. 1978. irreg. price varies. Sijthoff & Noordhoff International Publishers b.v., Box 4, 2400 MA Alphen aan den Rijn, Netherlands (Subscr. to: Box 66, 9700 AB Groningen, Netherlands; U.S. address: 20010 Century Blvd., Germantown, MD 20767)

340 301 NE
EUROPEAN YEARBOOK IN LAW AND SOCIOLOGY. 1977. a. price varies. Martinus Nijhoff, Box 566, 2501 CN The Hague, Netherlands. Eds. B. M. Blegvad, C. M. Campbell, C. J. Schuyt.

340 UK
EVERYMANS OWN LAWYER. 1856. triennial. £15. Macmillan Press Ltd., 4 Little Essex St., London WC2R 3LF, England.

348 CN ISSN 0380-2639
F M COMPILATION OF THE STATUTES OF CANADA. (Text in English and French) 1972. a. Municipal Forms Ltd., Farnham, Que. J2N 2R6, Canada. Ed. Pierrette Gregoire. adv. bk. rev. (looseleaf format)

340 BE
FACULTE DE DROIT DE NAMUR. TRAVAUX. no. 12, 1975. irreg. price varies. (Societe d'Etudes Morales, Sociales et Juridiques) Maison Ferdinand Larcier S.A., Rue des Minimes 39, 1000 Brussels, Belgium.

342 AT ISSN 0085-0462
FEDERAL LAW REPORTS. 1956. irreg. Aus.$58.50. Law Book Co. Ltd., 31 Market St., Sydney, N.S.W. 2000, Australia. Indexed: Curr.Aus.N.Z.Leg.Lit.Ind.

FEDERAL MARITIME COMMISSION SERVICE. see TRANSPORTATION — Ships And Shipping

328.96 FJ
FIJI. OFFICE OF THE OMBUDSMAN. ANNUAL REPORT OF THE OMBUDSMAN. (Text in English) 1973. a. Office of the Ombudsman, Suva, Fiji.

328 US ISSN 0090-1520
FLORIDA. LEGISLATURE. JOINT LEGISLATIVE MANAGEMENT COMMITTEE. SUMMARY OF GENERAL LEGISLATION. 1955. a. free. ‡ Legislature, Joint Legislative Management Committee, 701, The Capitol, Tallahassee, FL 32304. circ. 500. (processed)

328.759 US ISSN 0093-4089
FLORIDA SENATE. biennial. free. Legislature, Senate, Tallahassee, FL 32304. illus. stat.

340 SW
FOERTECKNING OEVER ADVOKATER OCH ADVOKATBYRAAER. a. free. ‡ Sveriges Advokatsamfund - Swedish Bar Association, Box 1339, 111 83 Stockholm, Sweden.

FONTES RERUM AUSTRIACARUM. REIHE 3. FONTES JURIS. see HISTORY — History Of Europe

340 HO
FORO HONDURENO. 1930. 12/yr (some issues quadruple) Sociedad de Abogados, Tegucigulpa, D.C., Honduras. Dir. A. Alvarado Ordanez.

340 US ISSN 0071-7657
FORSCHUNGEN AUS STAAT UND RECHT. irreg., vol. 48, 1979. price varies. Springer-Verlag, 175 Fifth Ave., New York, NY 10010 (also Berlin, Heidelberg, Vienna) (reprint service avail. from ISI)

340 AU
FORSCHUNGEN ZUR EUROPAEISCHEN UND VERGLEICHENDEN RECHTSGESCHICHTE. 1977. irreg., vol. 2, 1979. price varies. Hermann Boehlaus Nachf., Schmalzhofgasse 4, Postfach 167, A-1061 Vienna, Austria. Ed. Berthold Sutter. circ. 600. (back issues avail.)

340 SZ
FORSCHUNGEN ZUR RECHTSARCHAEOLOGIE UND RECHTLICHEN VOLKSKUNDE. 1978. irreg. price varies. Schulthess Polygraphischer Verlag AG, Zwingliplatz 2, 8001 Zurich, Switzerland.

340.05 US ISSN 0360-2044
FORUM LAW JOURNAL. University of Baltimore, School of Law, 1420 N. Charles St., Baltimore, MD 21202.
Formerly: Forum (Baltimore) (ISSN 0094-1948)

FRANCE. CENTRE NATIONAL POUR L'EXPLOITATION DES OCEANS. PUBLICATIONS. SERIE: RAPPORTS ECONOMIQUES ET JURIDIQUES. see EARTH SCIENCES — Oceanography

340 GW
FREIE UNIVERSITAET BERLIN. OSTEUROPA-INSTITUT. RECHTSWISSENSCHAFTLICHE VEROEFFENTLICHUNGEN. 1974. irreg. price varies. Freie Universitaet Berlin, Osteuropa-Institut, Garystr. 55, 1000 Berlin 33 (Dahlem), W. Germany (B.R.D.) Eds. Klaus Westen, Herwig Roggemann. circ. 500.

340 US ISSN 0164-1255
FUNDAMENTAL CONCEPTS OF ESTATE ADMINISTRATION. a. Practising Law Institute, 810 Seventh Ave., New York, NY 10019.

FUNDHEFT FUER ARBEITSRECHT. see BUSINESS AND ECONOMICS — Labor And Industrial Relations

340 GW ISSN 0071-9919
FUNDHEFT FUER OEFFENTLICHES RECHT. 1948. a. price varies. C. H. Beck'sche Verlagsbuchhandlung, Wilhelmstr. 9, 8000 Munich 40, W. Germany (B.R.D.) Ed. Otto Stroessenreuther. circ. 3,000.

340 GW ISSN 0071-9927
FUNDHEFT FUER ZIVILRECHT. 1948. a. price varies. C. H. Beck'sche Verlagsbuchhandlung, Wilhelmstr. 9, 8000 Munich 40, W. Germany (B.R.D.) Ed. Heinz Thomas. circ. 2,900.

GANDHI MEMORIAL LECTURES. see HISTORY — History Of Asia

344 US ISSN 0362-5931
GEORGIA LEGISLATIVE REVIEW. 1974. irreg. Southern Center for Studies in Public Policy, Clark College, Atlanta, GA 30314.

340 AU
GESAMTREGISTER MIT DEN RECHTSSAETZEN UND FUNDSTELLEN DER ENTSCHEIDUNGEN DER ZEITSCHRIFT FUER VERKEHRSRECHT. 1968. irreg. price varies. Manzsche Verlags- und Universitaetsbuchhandlung, Kohlmarkt 16, Postfach 163, A-1014 Vienna, Austria. circ. 2,400.

340 938 AU
GESELLSCHAFT FUER GRIECHISCHE UND HELLENISTISCHE RECHTSGESCHICHTE. AKTEN. irreg. Hermann Boehlaus Nachf., Schmalzhofgasse 4, Postfach 167, A-1061 Vienna, Austria.

340 US ISSN 0193-922X
GILBERT LAW SUMMARIES. CRIMINAL PROCEDURE. 1968. irreg. $10.50. Gilbert Law Summaries Law Distributors, 14415 S. Main St., Gardena, CA 90248. Key Title: Criminal Procedure.

343 IT
GIURISPRUDENZA ANNOTATA DI DIRITTO INDUSTRIALE. (Issued in pts) 1972. a. price varies. Casa Editrice Dott. A. Giuffre, Via Statuto 2, 20121 Milan, Italy.

340 IT
GIUSTIZIA CIVILE. REPERTORIO GENERALE ANNUALE. 1955. a. price varies. Casa Editrice Dott. A. Giuffre, Via Statuto 2, 20121 Milan, Italy. Ed. Angelo Jannuzzi.

340 GW
GOETTINGER STUDIEN ZUR RECHTSGESCHICHTE. 1969. irreg. price varies. Muster-Schmidt-Verlag, Brauweg 36a, Postfach 421, 3400 Goettingen, W. Germany (B.R.D.) Ed. Dr. Kroeschell.

340 UK
GREAT BRITAIN. OFFICE OF FAIR TRADING. REPORT. 1975. a. H.M.S.O., P.O. Box 569, London SE1 9NH, England.

349 UK ISSN 0080-7915
GREAT BRITAIN. SCOTTISH LAW COMMISSION. ANNUAL REPORT. 1965/66. a. price varies. Scottish Law Commission, 140 Causewayside, Edinburgh EH9 1PR, Scotland (Avail. from H.M.S.O., c/o Liaison Officer, Atlantic House, Holborn Viaduct, London EC1P 1BN, England) circ. 1,000.

340 US ISSN 0072-842X
GUIDE TO FOREIGN LEGAL MATERIALS SERIES. 1959. irreg., 1968, no. 3. price varies. (Columbia University, Parker School of Foreign and Comparative Law) Oceana Publications Inc., Dobbs Ferry, NY 10522.

GUIDEBOOK TO LABOR RELATIONS. see BUSINESS AND ECONOMICS — Labor And Industrial Relations

340 GY
GUYANA. OMBUDSMAN. REPORT. 1970. a. Office of the Ombudsman, 18/20 Croal St. Stabroek, Georgetown, Guyana.

340 UK ISSN 0308-4388
HALSBURY'S LAWS OF ENGLAND ANNUAL ABRIDGMENT. Short title: Laws of England Annual Abridgment. 1974. a. Butterworth & Co. (Publishers) Ltd., 88 Kingsway, London WC2B 6AB, England.

340 GW ISSN 0072-9507
HAMBURGER ABHANDLUNGEN. irreg., no. 63, 1974. price varies. (Universitaet Hamburg, Seminar fuer Oeffentliches Recht und Staatslehre) Gerold und Appel Verlagsgesellschaft, Neumann-Reichardt-Str. 29-33, 2000 Hamburg 70, W. Germany (B.R.D.) Eds. Rudolf Laun, Hans Peter Ipsen.

340 GW ISSN 0341-3179
HAMBURGER JURISTISCHE STUDIEN. 1970. irreg., no. 4, 1980. price varies. Verlag Helmut Buske, Schlueterstr. 14, 2000 Hamburg 13, W. Germany (B.R.D.)

340 341 GW ISSN 0072-9574
HAMBURGER OEFFENTLICH-RECHTLICHE NEBENSTUNDEN. 1960. irreg., vol.31, 1975. price varies. (Universitaet Hamburg, Institut fuer Internationale Angelegenheiten) Alfred Metzner Verlag GmbH, Zeppelinallee 43, Postfach 970148, 6000 Frankfurt 97, W. Germany (B.R.D.) Ed. Herbert Krueger.

340 350 GW ISSN 0438-5004
HANDAKTEN FUER DIE STANDESAMTLICHE ARBEIT. 1962. irreg. price varies. Verlag fuer Standesamtswesen GmbH und Co. KG, Hanauer Landstr. 197, 6000 Frankfurt 1, W. Germany (B.R.D.) Eds. August Simader, Rudolf Suppa.

340 GW ISSN 0073-0092
HANDBUCH DER JUSTIZ. 1953. a. DM.48. (Deutscher Richterbund) R. v. Decker's Verlag, G. Schenck GmbH, Im Weiher 10, 6900 Heidelberg, W. Germany (B.R.D.) Ed. R. Ziegler. adv.

340 AU ISSN 0567-1469
HANDELSRECHTLICHE ENTSCHEIDUNGEN. 1961. a. price varies. Manzsche Verlags- und Universitaetsbuchhandlung, Kohlmarkt 16, A-1014 Vienna, Austria. Ed. Gerhard Friedl. circ. 2,000(approx.)

340 AU
HANS KELSEN-INSTITUT. SCHRIFTENREIHE. 1974. irreg., vol. 3, 1978. price varies. Manzsche Verlags- und Universitaetsbuchhandlung, Kohlmarkt 16, A-1014 Vienna, Austria.

340 US
HARVARD ENVIRONMENTAL LAW REVIEW. 1976. a. $15. Harvard University Law School, Austin Hall, Cambridge, MA 02138. Ed. W. Ralph Canada, Jr.

016 016 US ISSN 0073-0793
HARVARD UNIVERSITY. LAW SCHOOL. LIBRARY. ANNUAL LEGAL BIBLIOGRAPHY. 1961. a. $75. Harvard University, Law School Library, Langdell Hall L-331, Cambridge, MA 02138. Ed. Margaret M. Moody. circ. 700.

347.9 US
HAWAII. JUDICIARY DEPARTMENT. ANNUAL REPORT. a. Judiciary Department, Box 2560, Honolulu, HI 96811. illus. stat.

348　　　　　　US　ISSN 0095-6619
HAWAII. LEGISLATIVE REFERENCE BUREAU.
DIGEST AND INDEX OF LAWS ENACTED. a.
price varies. Legislative Reference Bureau, State
Capitol, Honolulu, HI 96813.

HAWAII. STATE COMMISSION ON THE STATUS
OF WOMEN. ANNUAL REPORT. see
WOMEN'S INTERESTS

HEALTH LAW BULLETIN. see *PUBLIC HEALTH
AND SAFETY*

347　　　　　IS　ISSN 0075-9740
HEBREW UNIVERSITY OF JERUSALEM.
LIONEL COHEN LECTURES. (Text in English)
1953. irreg. price varies. Magnes Press, Hebrew
University of Jerusalem, Jerusalem, Israel.

340　　　　　　GW
HEIDELBERGER RECHTSVERGLEICHENDE
UND WIRTSCHAFTSRECHLICHE STUDIEN.
1967. a. price varies. Carl Winter
Universitaetsverlag, Lutherstr. 59, 6900 Heidelberg,
W. Germany (B.R.D.)

340　　　　　GW　ISSN 0073-165X
HEIDELBERGER
RECHTSWISSENSCHAFTLICHE
ABHANDLUNGEN. NEUE FOLGE. 1957. irreg.
price varies. (Universitaet Heidelberg, Juristische
Fakultaet) Carl Winter Universitaetsverlag,
Lutherstr. 59, 6900 Heidelberg, W. Germany
(B.R.D.)

340　　　　　　US
HINE'S INSURANCE COUNSEL. 1908. a. $15.
Hine's Legal Directory, Inc., 443 Duane St., P.O.
Box 71, Glen Ellyn, IL 60137. Ed. James R.
Collins. adv. circ. 8,000.

320　340　　　JA　ISSN 0073-2796
HITOTSUBASHI JOURNAL OF LAW AND
POLITICS. 1960. irreg. 1500 Yen. Hitotsubashi
University, Hitotsubashi Academy, 2-1 Naka,
Kunitachi, Tokyo 186, Japan. Ed. C. Hosoya. circ.
940.

340　　　　　　US
HOW TO BECOME A CITIZEN OF THE UNITED
STATES. 1922. biennial. American Council for
Nationalities Service, 20 W. 40th St., New York,
NY 10018. circ. 10,000.

347　　　　　US　ISSN 0536-3713
ILLINOIS. ADMINISTRATIVE OFFICE OF
ILLINOIS COURTS. ANNUAL REPORT TO
THE SUPREME COURT OF ILLINOIS. a.
Administrative Office of Illinois Courts, Supreme
Court Bldg., Springfield, IL 62706. stat. Key Title:
Annual Report to the Supreme Court of Illinois.

340　　　　　US　ISSN 0094-9795
ILLINOIS. LEGISLATIVE INVESTIGATING
COMMISSION. ANNUAL REPORT. 1967. a.
free. Legislative Investigating Commission, 300 W.
Washington St., Chicago, IL 60606. circ. 2,000.

347.7　　　　US　ISSN 0073-5000
ILLINOIS STATE BAR ASSOCIATION.
ANTITRUST LAW NEWSLETTER. 1959. irreg.,
1970, vol. 12, no. 1. membership. ‡ Illinois State
Bar Association, Illinois Bar Center, Springfield, IL
62701. Eds. Mark Crane And Nathan P. Owen.
circ. 1,000(controlled) (back issues avail.)

352　　　　　US　ISSN 0073-5035
ILLINOIS STATE BAR ASSOCIATION. LOCAL
GOVERNMENT LAW NEWSLETTER. 1962.
irreg., 1970, vol. 8, no. 1. membership. ‡ Illinois
State Bar Association, Illinois Bar Center,
Springfield, IL 62701. circ. 800. (back issues avail.)

340　　　　　CE　ISSN 0073-5728
INCORPORATED LAW SOCIETY OF SRI
LANKA. ANNUAL REPORT.* 1960/61. a.
Incorporated Law Society of Sri Lanka, 129/5
Hultsdorf St., Colombo 12, Sri Lanka.

340　　　　　CE　ISSN 0073-5736
INCORPORATED LAW SOCIETY OF SRI
LANKA. JOURNAL.* irreg. Incorporated Law
Society of Sri Lanka, 129/5 Hultsdorf St., Colombo
12, Sri Lanka.

340　　　　　　AU
INDEX DER
RECHTSMITTELENTSCHEIDUNGEN UND
DES SCHRIFTTUMS. 1947. a. price varies.
Manzsche Verlags- und Universitaetsbuchhandlung,
Kohlmarkt 16, Postfach 163, A-1014 Vienna,
Austria. circ. 2,400.

347　　　　　AT　ISSN 0312-4029
INDUSTRIAL ARBITRATION SERVICE. 1948.
irreg. price varies. Law Book Co. Ltd., 31 Market
St., Sydney, N.S.W. 2000, Australia.

INDUSTRIAL HEALTH FOUNDATION. LEGAL
SERIES BULLETIN. see *INDUSTRIAL HEALTH
AND SAFETY*

346.066　　　　UK
INDUSTRIAL PROPERTY LAW. ANNUAL. 1975.
irreg. price varies. European Law Centre Ltd., 4
Bloomsbury Square, London WC1A 2RL, England.

340　　　　　　GW
INDUSTRIEGESELLSCHAFT UND RECHT. 1974.
irreg., vol. 5, 1975. price varies. Gieseking-Verlag,
Deckerstr. 2, Postfach 42, 4813 Bielefeld-Bethel, W.
Germany (B.R.D.) Eds. Manfred Rehbinder, Bernd
Rebe.

340　　　　　　CU
INFORMACION JURIDICA. 1975. irreg. Fiscalia
General de la Republica, San Rafael 3, Havana,
Cuba. illus.

INSTITUT FUER KONFLIKTFORSCHUNG.
SCHRIFTENREIHE. see *SOCIOLOGY*

340　　　　　GW　ISSN 0073-8492
INSTITUT FUER OSTRECHT. STUDIEN. 1958.
irreg. price varies. Horst Erdmann Verlag,
Hartmeyerstr. 117, Postfach 1380, 7400 Tuebingen,
W. Germany (B.R.D.) circ. 1,000.

INSTITUTE OF PATENT ATTORNEYS OF
AUSTRALIA. ANNUAL PROCEEDINGS. see
PATENTS, TRADEMARKS AND COPYRIGHTS

340　　　　　　SP
INSTITUTO DE ESTUDIOS TARRACONENSES
RAMON BERENGUER IV. SECCION DE
ESTUDIOS JURIDICOS. PUBLICACION. (Text
in Catalan and/or Castilian) 1972. irreg. Instituto de
Estudios Tarraconenses Ramon Berenguer IV, Calle
Santa Ana 8, Tarragona, Spain.

INSTITUTO PERUANO DE DERECHO
AGRARIO. CUADERNOS AGRARIOS. see
AGRICULTURE

340　　　　　　US
INTER-AMERICAN BAR ASSOCIATION.
CONFERENCE PROCEEDINGS. 1941. irreg.,
20th, 1977, Atlanta. $6. Inter-American Bar
Association, Suite 315, 1730 K St. N.W.,
Washington, DC 20006.

340　　　　　　US
INTER-AMERICAN BAR ASSOCIATION.
LETTER TO MEMBERS. (Text in English and
Spanish) 1967. irreg. (3-4/yr.) $5. Inter-American
Bar Association, Suite 315, 1730 K St., N.W.,
Washington, DC 20006. Ed. John O. Dahlgren. circ.
3,000. (processed)

340　　　　　BE　ISSN 0074-1604
INTERNATIONAL ASSOCIATION OF
DEMOCRATIC LAWYERS. CONGRESS
REPORT. quadrennial, 10th 1975, Algiers.
International Association of Democratic Lawyers,
49 Av. Jupiter, 1190 Brussels, Belgium.

340　539　　　UN　ISSN 0074-1868
INTERNATIONAL ATOMIC ENERGY AGENCY.
LEGAL SERIES. (Text in English) 1959. irreg.
price varies. International Atomic Energy Agency -
Agence Internationale de l'Energie Atomique,
Wagramer Str. 5, Box 100, A-1400 Vienna, Austria
(Dist. in U.S. by: Unipub, 345 Park Ave. S., New
York, NY 10010)

340　　　　　　US
INTERNATIONAL COMMERCIAL LAW OF
NATIONS. irreg. price varies. Simon and Schuster,
Inc., 630 5th Ave., New York, NY 10020.

347.9　　　　　NE
INTERNATIONAL LABOUR LAW REPORTS.
1978. a. $87.50 per vol. Sijthoff & Noordhoff
International Publishers b.v., Box 4, 2400 MA
Alphen Aan den Rijn, Netherlands (Subscr. to: Box
66, 9700 AB Groningen, Netherlands; U.S. Address:
20010 Century Blvd., Germantown, MD 20767)
Ed.Bd.

340　　　　　CN　ISSN 0074-8722
INTERNATIONAL SYMPOSIA ON
COMPARATIVE LAW. PROCEEDINGS/
COLLOQUES INTERNATIONAUX DE DROIT
COMPARE. TRAVAUX. 1963. irreg. University of
Ottawa Press, 65 Hastey Ave., Ottawa, Ont. K1N
6N5, Canada. Ed. Clarence Smith.

340　　　　　　AU
INTERNATIONALE GESELLSCHAFT FUER
URHEBERRECHT. SCHRIFTENREIHE. 1955.
irreg., vol. 57, 1979. price varies. (GW -
International Copyright Society) Manzsche Verlags-
und Universitaetsbuchhandlung, Kohlmarkt 16, A-
1014 Vienna, Austria.

340　　　　　US　ISSN 0578-6533
IOWA ADVOCATE. irreg. University of Iowa,
College of Law, Iowa City, IA 52240. (Co-Sponsor:
Iowa Law School Foundation) illus.

347.9　　　　IS　ISSN 0075-1030
ISRAEL. CENTRAL BUREAU OF STATISTICS.
JUDICIAL STATISTICS. (Subseries of its Special
Series) (Text in Hebrew and English) 1951. irreg.,
latest issue, no. 617, 1978. I£90. Central Bureau of
Statistics, Box 13015, Jerusalem, Israel.

ISRAEL YEARBOOK ON HUMAN RIGHTS. see
POLITICAL SCIENCE — Civil Rights

340　　　　　　IT
ISTITUTO DI DIRITTO ROMANO. BULLETTINO.
(Text in various European Languages) 1888. a.
L.30000. Casa Editrice Dott. A. Giuffre, Via Statuto
2, Milan 20121, Italy. Ed. Prof. Edoardo Volterra.
adv. bk. rev. index. circ. 500.

340　　　　　IT　ISSN 0075-1715
ITALY. ISTITUTO CENTRALE DI STATISTICA.
ANNUARI DI STATISTICHE GIUDIZIARIE.
1962. a. L.8500. Istituto Centrale di Statistica, Via
Cesare Balbo 16, 00100 Rome, Italy. circ. 850.

340　　　　　IT　ISSN 0021-3241
IURA; rivista internazionale di diritto romano e antico.
(Text in various languages) 1950. irreg. price varies.
Casa Editrice Dott. Eugenio Jovene, 109 via
Mezzocannone, Naples, Italy. Ed. Prof. Cesare
Sanfilippo. bk. rev.

340　　　　　GW　ISSN 0579-2428
IUS COMMUNE. irreg., vol. 9, 1981. price varies.
Vittorio Klostermann, Frauenlobstr. 22, Postfach
900601, D-6000 Frankfurt 90, W. Germany
(B.R.D.)

340　　　　　　GW
IUS COMMUNE. SONDERHEFTE. irreg. price
varies. Vittorio Klostermann, Frauenlobstr. 22,
Postfach 900601, D-6000 Frankfurt 90, W.
Germany (B.R.D.)

340　　　　　IT　ISSN 0075-2037
IUS ROMANUM MEDII AEVI. (Text in English,
French, German, Italian and Spanish) 1961. irreg.
price varies. Casa Editrice Dott. A. Giuffre, Via
Statuto, 2, 20121 Milan, Italy.

340　　　　　　YU
IZVORI SRPSKOG PRAVA/SOURCES DE DROIT
SERBE/SERBISCHE RECHTSQUELLEN.
(Subseries of: Srpska Akademija Nauka i Umetnosti.
Odeljenje Drustvenih Nauka. Posebna Izdanja)
(Text in Serbian; summaries in French and German)
1967. irreg. Srpska Akademija Nauka i Umetnosti,
Odeljenje Drustvenih Nauka, Knez Mihailova 35,
11001 Belgrade, Yugoslavia. illus.

344　　　　　US　ISSN 0021-3519
J A G JOURNAL. 1947. irreg. U.S. Department of
the Navy, Office of the Judge Advocate General,
Washington, DC 20370 (Orders to: Supt. of
Documents, Washington DC 20402) Ed. W. D.
Cohen, LCDR. illus. index. cum.ind. every 4
years. circ. 11,000. (also avail. in microform from
UMI) Indexed: Leg.Per. Ind.U.S.Gov.Per.
Martial law

340 GW ISSN 0075-2517
JAHRBUCH DES OEFFENTLICHEN RECHTS DER GEGENWART. N.S. 1951. a. price varies. Verlag J.C.B. Mohr (Paul Siebeck), Wilhelmstr. 18, Postfach 2040, 7400 Tuebingen, W. Germany (B.R.D.) Ed. Gerhard Leibholz.

340 GW ISSN 0075-2746
JAHRBUCH FUER OSTRECHT. 1960. annual in 2 pts. DM.48. (Institut fuer Ostrecht, Munich) Horst Erdmann Verlag, Hartmeyerstr. 117, Postfach 1380, 7400 Tuebingen, W. Germany (B.R.D.) Ed. Erhardt Gralla. circ. 750.

JAHRESFACHKATALOG RECHT-WIRTSCHAFT-STEUERN. see *BUSINESS AND ECONOMICS*

340 JM
JAMAICAN BAR ASSOCIATION. ANNUAL REPORT. a. Jamaican Bar Association, 11 Duke Street, Kingston, Jamaica.

340 320 JA ISSN 0075-3157
JAPAN ANNUAL OF LAW AND POLITICS. (Text in English) 1952. a. exchange basis. Science Council of Japan - Nihon Gakujutsu Kaigi, 7-22-34 Roppongi, Minato-ku, Tokyo 106, Japan.

JEWISH LAW ANNUAL. see *RELIGIONS AND THEOLOGY — Judaic*

JORNADAS NACIONALES DE DERECHO AERONAUTICO Y ESPACIAL. TRABAJOS. see *TRANSPORTATION — Air Transport*

347.9 JA ISSN 0075-4188
JOURNAL OF CIVIL PROCEDURE/MINJI SOSHO ZASSHI. (Text in Japanese; summaries in English or German) 1954. a. 1500 Yen. (Japan Association of Civil Procedure - Minji Soshoho Gakkai) Horitsu Bunka Sha, 71 Kamigamo-Iwagz-Kakiuchi-Cho, Kita-ku, Kyoto, Japan. adv. bk. rev. circ. 1,500.

340 PL ISSN 0075-4277
JOURNAL OF JURISTIC PAPYROLOGY. (Text in English, German, Italian and Russian) 1949. irreg., vol. 18, 1974. $15 per volume) (Uniwersytet Warszawski, Instytut Papirologii i Prawa Antycznego - Warsaw University, Institute of Papyrology and Ancient Laws) Panstwowe Wydawnictwo Naukowe, Ul. Miodowa 10, Warsaw, Poland (Dist. by Ars Polona-Ruch, Krakowskie Przedmiescie 7, Warsaw, Poland) Ed. H. Kupiszewski. bk. rev.

340 US ISSN 0160-2098
JOURNAL OF JUVENILE LAW. 1977. a. $3.75. University of La Verne, College of Law, 1950 3rd St., La Verne, CA 91750. Ed. Mary Smith. adv. bk. rev. circ. 2,000. (back issues avail.)

340 JA
JOURNAL OF LAW AND POLITICS/DAITO HOGAKU. (Text in Japanese) 1974. a. Daito Bunka University, Law Society - Daito Bunka Daigaku Hogakkai, 1-9-1 Takashimadaira, Itabashi-ku, Tokyo, Japan.

347.016 US
JOURNAL OF NOTARIAL ACTS AND RECORDKEEPING PRACTICES. 1974. a. $6.85. National Notary Association, 23012 Ventura Blvd., Woodland Hills, CA 91364. Ed. Bd.
Supersedes in part: Customs and Practices of Notaries Public and Digest of Notary Laws in the U.S.

340 US
JOURNAL OF THE LEGAL PROFESSION. 1976. a. $6. University of Alabama, School of Law, Box 1976, University, AL 35486.

347.91 US ISSN 0148-4982
JUDICIAL FUNCTION OUTLINE. 1977. a. $4. National Judicial College, Judicial College Bldg., University of Nevada, Reno, NV 89557. Ed.Bd.

347.9 US
JUDICIAL FUNCTION OUTLINE FOR ADMINISTRATIVE LAW JUDGES. a. a. $4. National Judicial College, Judicial College Building, University of Nevada, Reno, NV 89557.

340 MX
JURIDICA. 1969. a. Mex.$300. Universidad Iberoamericana, Departamento de Derecho, Av. Cerro de las Torres No. 395, Mexico 21, D.F., Mexico.

348.46 SP
JURISPRUDENCIA ARAGONESA. 1972. a. Colegio de Abogados de Zaragoza., Zaragoza, Spain.

340 AG
JURISPRUDENCIA ARGENTINA. (In 5 vols. including an index) a. $100 per volume. Jurisprudencia Argentina S.A., Talcahuano 650, 1013 Buenos Aires, Argentina.
Formerly: Anuario de Jurisprudencia Argentina.

340 SP
JURISPRUDENCIA Y TEXTOS LEGALES. 1973. irreg.; 1979, no. 4. price varies. Ediciones Universidad de Navarra S.A., Plaza de los Sauces 1 y 2, Baranain, Pamplona, Spain.

340 GW ISSN 0449-4342
JURISTISCHE ABHANDLUNGEN. 1964. irreg., vol. 16, 1980. price varies. Vittorio Klostermann, Frauenlobstr. 22, Postfach 900601, 6000 Frankfurt 90, W. Germany (B.R.D.).

JUSTICE DEPARTMENT WATCH. see *POLITICAL SCIENCE — Civil Rights*

340 US
JUSTICE IN AMERICA SERIES. 1969. irreg. $9.20 (6 vols.) (Law in American Society Foundation) Houghton Mifflin Co., One Beacon Street, c/o Guest Perry, Boston, MA 02107. Ed. Robert H. Ratcliffe. bibl. illus.
Formerly: Justice in Urban America Series.

347.9 364 US
JUVENILE LAW LITIGATION DIRECTORY. 1972. a. free. Institute of Judicial Administration, Juvenile Justice Standards Project, 80 Fifth Avenue, Room 1501, New York, NY 10011. (Co-Sponsor: American Bar Association) Ed. Patricia Pickrel.

KANAZAWA UNIVERSITY. FACULTY OF LAW AND LITERATURE. STUDIES AND ESSAYS. see *LITERATURE*

KANO STATE OF NIGERIA GAZETTE. see *PUBLIC ADMINISTRATION*

340 PK ISSN 0075-5095
KARACHI LAW JOURNAL. (Text in English or Urdu) 1964. irreg. price varies. Pakistan Law House, Pakistan Chowk, Box 90, Karachi 1, Pakistan. (back issues avail.)

340 UK ISSN 0308-8987
KITCHIN'S ROAD TRANSPORT LAW. 1959. a. Butterworth & Co.(Publishers) Ltd., 88 Kingsway, London WC2B 6AB, England. Ed. James Duckworth.

340 JA ISSN 0075-6423
KOBE UNIVERSITY LAW REVIEW. INTERNATIONAL EDITION. (Text in English, French, German and other languages) 1961. irreg., vol. 11, 1977. available on exchange. Kobe University Law Review Association, Faculty of Law, Kobe University, Rokkodai-cho, Nadu-ku, Kobe, Japan. Ed. T. Hayakawa. circ. 500.

340 PL ISSN 0023-4478
KRAKOWSKIE STUDIA PRAWNICZE. (Text in Polish; summaries in English, German or French) 1968. a. 40 Zl. (Polska Akademia Nauk, Oddzial w Krakowie, Komisja Nauk Prawnych) Ossolineum, Publishing House of the Polish Academy of Sciences, Rynek 9, Wroclaw, Poland (Dist. by: Ars Polona-Ruch, Krakowskie Przedmiescie 7, Warsaw, Poland) Ed. Josez Filipek.

340 II
KURUKSHETRA LAW JOURNAL. (Text in English) 1971. a. Rs.5($1.50) Kurukshetra University, Faculty of Law, Kurukshetra 132118, Haryana, Punjab, India.

340 029 GW ISSN 0340-5982
KYBERNETIK - DATENVERARBEITUNG - RECHT. 1971. irreg., vol.7, 1977. price varies. (Forschungstelle fuer Juristische Dokumentation, Frankfurt) Alfred Metzner Verlag GmbH, Zeppelinallee 43, Postfach 970148, 6000 Frankfurt 97, W. Germany (B.R.D.) Ed. Spiros Simitis.

LABOUR LAW CASES. see *BUSINESS AND ECONOMICS — Labor And Industrial Relations*

LAND LAWS SERVICE. see *REAL ESTATE*

LANSKY: BIBLIOTHEKSRECHTLICHE VORSCHRIFTEN. see *LIBRARY AND INFORMATION SCIENCES*

340 NZ
LAW. irreg. New Zealand Law Society, Box 5041, 26 Waring Taylor St., Wellington, New Zealand. illus.

340 US
LAW AND ETHICS SERIES. 1977. irreg. Academy for Contemporary Problems, 1501 Neil Ave., Columbus, OH 43201.

340 320 KO
LAW AND POLITICAL REVIEW. (Text in Korean; table of contents in English) 1958. a. Ewha Women's University, College of Law and Political Science, 11-1 Dai-Hyun Dong, Seodaimoon Ku, Seoul, S. Korea. bibl.

340 300 616.8 US ISSN 0098-5961
LAW AND PSYCHOLOGY REVIEW. 1975. a. $5.50. University of Alabama, School of Law and Department of Psychology, Box 1435, University, AL 35486. Ed. Bd. adv. bk. rev. circ. 1,200. Indexed: Psychol.Abstr.

323.42 US
LAW & WOMEN SERIES. 1972. irreg. $2 per no. Today Publications & News Service, Inc., 621 National Press Building, Washington, DC 20045. Ed. Myra E. Barrer.

340 016 US ISSN 0075-8221
LAW BOOKS IN PRINT. (Supplemented 3-4 times a year by Law Books Published) 1957. irreg., revised every two-three years. $306 for 4-vol. set. Glanville Publishers, Inc., 75 Main St., Dobbs Ferry, NY 10522. Eds. J. Myron Jacobstein, Meira G. Pimsleur. index.

340 NR ISSN 0458-8592
LAW IN SOCIETY. 1964. irreg (1-2/yr.) Ahmadu Bello University, Law Society, Zaria, Nigeria.

340 CN ISSN 0316-5310
LAW SOCIETY OF UPPER CANADA. SPECIAL LECTURES. 1950. a. Law Society of Upper Canada, c/o R. de Boo, Osgoode Hall, 130 Queen St. W., Toronto, Ont. M5H 2N6, Canada.

340 US ISSN 0091-0430
LAWYER-TO-LAWYER CONSULTATION PANEL. 1973. a. $10. Lawyer to Lawyer Consultation Panel, 5325 Naiman Pkwy, Solon, OH 44139. Ed. C. A. Hermann. circ. 25,000.

340 US
LAWYERS IN THE UNITED STATES. DISTRIBUTION AND INCOME. (Supplement: Lawyer Statistical Report) irreg. price varies. American Bar Foundation, Publications Dept., 1155 E. 60th St., Chicago, IL 60637.

340 UK
LAWYER'S REMEMBRANCE. a. Butterworth & Co. (Publishers) Ltd., 88 Kingsway, London WC2B 6AB, England. Ed. G.R.N. Cusworth.

340 900 AG
LECCIONES DE HISTORIA JURIDICA. irreg. (Universidad de Buenos Aires, Instituto de Historia del Derecho Ricardo Levene) Editorial Perrot, Azcuenaga 1846, Buenos Aires, Argentina.

342 341 AG
LECCIONES Y ENSAYOS. 1956. irreg. Universidad de Buenos Aires, Facultad de Derecho y Ciencias Sociales, Av. Figueroa Alcorta 2263, Buenos Aires, Argentina. illus.

345.01 CN ISSN 0381-2049
LEGAL AID NEW BRUNSWICK ANNUAL REPORT/ASSISTANCE JUDICIAIRE NOUVEAU-BRUNSWICK RAPPORT ANNUEL. (Text in English and French) 1972. a. Barristers' Society of New Brunswick, Fredericton, N.B., Canada. circ. 1,500.

340 US ISSN 0075-8582
LEGAL ALMANAC SERIES. 1952. irreg. $5.95. Oceana Publications Inc., Dobbs Ferry, NY 10522.

340 US ISSN 0270-3424
LEGAL CONNECTION: CORPORATIONS AND LAW FIRMS; a directory of publicly-held corporations and their law firms. 1979. a. Box 801, Menlo Park, CA 94025. Ed. S.P. Harris.

340 352.7 US
LEGAL SERVICES OCCASIONAL. 1969. irreg., approx. 3/yr. $5. Massachusetts Law Reform Institute, 2 Park Square, Boston, MA 02116.
Formerly: Legal Services Monthly.

340 NE ISSN 0458-9998
LEIDSE JURIDISCHE REEKS. 1954. irreg., vol. 14, 1975. price varies. Leiden University Press, c/o Martinus Nijhoff, Box 566, 2501 CN The Hague, Netherlands.

340 LB
LIBERIA. MINISTRY OF JUSTICE. ANNUAL REPORT TO THE LEGISLATURE. 1973. a. Ministry of Justice, Monrovia, Liberia.

340 301 US ISSN 0075-9120
LIBRARY OF LAW AND CONTEMPORARY PROBLEMS. 1961. irreg., no. 19, 1974. price varies. (Duke University, School of Law) Oceana Publications Inc., Dobbs Ferry, NY 10522.

LOCAL GOVERNMENT LAW BULLETIN. see PUBLIC ADMINISTRATION — Municipal Government

345 622 US ISSN 0076-1087
LOUISIANA STATE UNIVERSITY. LAW SCHOOL. INSTITUTE ON MINERAL LAW. PROCEEDINGS. 1954. a. $15. Louisiana State University, Law School, Institute of Continuing Legal Education, Law Building, Baton Rouge, LA 70803. Ed. Thomas A. Harrell. index.

340 BL
M P. vol. 8, 1979. a. Ministerio Publico, Curitaba, Parana, Brazil. Eds. L. Branco Lacerda, J. Porto, Lona Cleto, R. A. Botelho. bibl.

340 UG ISSN 0075-4781
MAKERERE UNIVERSITY. FACULTY OF LAW. HANDBOOK. 1970/71. a. Makerere University, Faculty of Law, Box 17062, Kampala, Uganda.

347.9 MW ISSN 0076-3160
MALAWI. MINISTRY OF JUSTICE. ANNUAL REPORT. a, latest 1969. K.0.60. Government Printer, P.O. Box 37, Zomba, Malawi.

340 CN ISSN 0380-0008
MANITOBA DECISIONS, CIVIL AND CRIMINAL CASES. 1975. a (updated monthly) Can.$95 to individuals; Can.$155 to libraries. Western Legal Publications Ltd., 301-1 Alexander St., Vancouver, B.C. V6A 1B2, Canada.

340 CK
MANUAL DE IMPUESTOS. 1974. a. Col.$900($30) Avda. Jimenez 4-49, Apdo. Aereo 1465, Bogota, Colombia. Ed. Alejandro Restrepo Correa. adv. circ. 15,000.

340 US
MARTINDALE-HUBBELL LAW DIRECTORY. (In 7 vols.) 1868. a. $120. ‡ Martindale-Hubbell, Inc., 1 Prospect St., Summit, NJ 07901.

348.752 US ISSN 0093-0520
MARYLAND. STATE DEPARTMENT OF LEGISLATIVE REFERENCE. SYNOPSIS OF LAWS ENACTED BY THE STATE OF MARYLAND. 1916. a. $5.25. Department of Legislative Reference, 90 State Circle, Annapolis, MD 21401. Key Title: Synopsis of Laws Enacted by the State of Maryland.

340 US ISSN 0542-836X
MARYLAND LAWYER'S MANUAL. 1968. a. $15 to non-members. ‡ Maryland State Bar Association, 905 Keyser Building, Calvert & Redwood St., Baltimore, MD 21202. Ed. Claire Blackburn. adv. circ. 10,000.

353.9 US ISSN 0362-1383
MASSACHUSETTS ADVOCACY CENTER. ANNUAL REPORT. 1974. a. Massachusetts Advocacy Center, 2 Park Square, Boston, MA 02116. Key Title: Annual Report - Massachusetts Advocacy Center.

340 GW
MAX-PLANCK-INSTITUT FUER AUSLAENDISCHES OEFFENTLICHES RECHT UND VOELKERRECHT. FONTES IURIS GENTIUM. (Deutsche Rechtssprechung Zum Voelkerrecht 1879-1960) 1931. irreg. price varies. Max-Planck-Institut fuer Auslaendisches Oeffentliches Recht und Voelkerrecht, Berliner Str. 48, 6900 Heidelberg, W. Germany (B.R.D.) Eds. Hermann Mosler, Rudolf Bernhardt.
Formerly: Max-Planck-Institut fuer Auslaendisches Oeffentliches Recht und Voelkerrecht. Fontes (ISSN 0076-5651)

344.041 AT ISSN 0047-6587
MEDICO-LEGAL SOCIETY OF NEW SOUTH WALES. PROCEEDINGS. 1960/62. triennial. Aus.$50($61) per vol. Medico-Legal Society of New South Wales, 10th Floor, 180 Phillip St., Sydney, N.S.W. 2000, Australia.

340 FR
MEMENTO PRATIQUE DES SOCIETES COMMERCIALES. a. Editions Francis Lefebvre, 15 rue Viete, 75849 Paris Cedex 17, France.

340 296 US ISSN 0094-9701
HA-MESIVTA. (Text in Hebrew) 1940. a. $4. Yeshivath Torah Vodaath, Inc., 452 E. 9th St., Brooklyn, NY 11218. Ed. Elie Goldberg. circ. 1,000.

346 AU
MIETERECHTLICHE ENTSCHEIDUNGEN. Abbreviated title: MietSlg. 1951. irreg., vol. 30, 1979. price varies. Manzsche Verlags- und Universitaetsbuchhandlung, Kohlmarkt 16, Postfach 163, A-1014 Vienna, Austria. Ed. Viktor Heller. (back issues avail.)

348 US ISSN 0191-1562
MINNESOTA STATUTES. 1941. biennial. $250. Office of Revisor of Statutes, 3 State Capitol, St. Paul, MN 55155. circ. 3,200.

348 US ISSN 0094-1727
MINNESOTA STATUTES. SUPPLEMENT. 1973. biennial. $35. Office of Revisor of Statutes, 3 State Capitol, St. Paul, MN 55155.

340 SP ISSN 0077-0442
MONOGRAFIAS DE FILOSOFIA JURIDICA Y SOCIAL/MONOGRAPHS OF SOCIAL AND LEGAL PHILOSOPHY.* 1967. a. 70 ptas.($1.) Universidad de Granada, Facultad de Derecho, Granada, Spain.

340 CN ISSN 0077-0728
MONOGRAPHIES JURIDIQUES. 1967. irreg. price varies. (University of Ottawa, Faculty of Law) University of Ottawa Press, 65 Hastey Ave., Ottawa, Ont. K1N 6N5, Canada. Ed. Alain Bisson.

340 NE
MONOGRAPHS IN ASIAN LAW. 1978. irreg. price varies. Sijthoff & Noordhoff International Publishers b.v., Box 4, 2400 MA Alphen Aan den Plijn, Netherlands (Subscr. to Box 66, 9700 AB Groningen, Netherlands; U.S. address: 20010 Century Blvd., Germantown, MD 20767)

MONOGRAPHS ON INDUSTRIAL PROPERTY AND COPYRIGHT LAW. see PATENTS, TRADEMARKS AND COPYRIGHTS

MUNICIPAL RESEARCH AND SERVICES CENTER OF WASHINGTON. INFORMATION BULLETINS. see PUBLIC ADMINISTRATION — Municipal Government

340 US ISSN 0098-2857
NATIONAL BAR EXAMINATION DIGEST. 1975. a. $1. Harcourt Brace Jovanovich Legal and Professional Publications, Inc., 1909 K St. N.W., Washington, DC 20006.

340 US
NATIONAL CENTER FOR STATE COURTS. PUBLICATIONS. irreg. National Center for State Courts, 300 Newport Ave., Williamsburg, VA 23185.

347 US ISSN 0095-2028
NATIONAL COLLEGE OF THE STATE JUDICIARY. a. University of Nevada, Judicial College Bldg., Reno, NV 89507. illus.

340 US
NATIONAL CONFERENCE OF COMMISSIONERS ON UNIFORM STATE LAWS. HANDBOOK AND PROCEEDINGS. 1892. a. price varies. National Conference of Commissioners on Uniform State Laws, 645 N. Michigan Ave., Suite 510, Chicago, IL 60611. Ed. Leslie B. Turner. circ. 800.

340 CN
NATIONAL REPORTER. (Text in English; occasionally in French) irreg. (6 vols. per year) Can.$40 per vol. Maritime Law Book Co., Box 302, Fredericton, N.B. E3B 4Y9, Canada. Ed. Eric B. Appleby.

340 US
NEBRASKA TRANSCRIPT. irreg. University of Nebraska-Lincoln, College of Law, Lincoln, NE 68508. illus.

340 NP
NEPAL MISCELLANEOUS SERIES. (Text in English) 1964. irreg. Rs.600($50) per year. Regmi Research(Pvt.) Ltd., Lazimpat, Kathmandu, Nepal. Ed. Mahesh C. Regmi. (also avail. in microfilm from LCP)
Formerly: Nepal Law Translation Series (ISSN 0077-6572)

418.02 NP
NEPAL RECORDER. (Text in English) 1957. irreg. (2-3/mo.) Rs.600($50) Nepal Press Digest (Pvt) Ltd., Lazimpat, Kathmandu, Nepal. Ed. Mahesh C. Regmi. index. (also avail. in microfilm from LCP)
Formerly: Nepal Gazette Translation Service (ISSN 0028-2707)

340 MY
NERACA. (Text in English and Malaysian) 1973. a. University of Malaya, Law Society - Universiti Malaya, Persatuan Undang-Undang, Lembah Pantai, Kuala Lumpur 22-11, Malaysia. bk. rev.

347.9 NE ISSN 0077-684X
NETHERLANDS. CENTRAAL BUREAU VOOR DE STATISTIEK. JUSTITIELE STATISTIEK. JUDICIAL STATISTICS. (Text in Dutch and English) 1951. a. fl.14.45. Centraal Bureau voor de Statistiek, Prinses Beatrixlaan 428, Voorburg, Netherlands (Orders to: Staatsuitgeverij, Christoffel Plantijnstraat, The Hague, Netherlands)

340 US
NEW JERSEY. ADMINISTRATIVE OFFICE OF THE COURTS. ANNUAL REPORT OF THE ADMINISTRATIVE DIRECTOR OF THE COURTS. a. Administrative Office of the Courts, State House Annex, Trenton, NJ 08625. illus.

353.9 US ISSN 0093-9986
NEW JERSEY. LEGISLATURE. OFFICE OF FISCAL AFFAIRS. ANNUAL REPORT. 1973. a. free. State Legislature, Office of Fiscal Affairs, Trenton, NJ 08625. Key Title: Annual Report - New Jersey State Legislature. Office of Fiscal Affairs.

348.94 AT
NEW LEGISLATION OF THE AUSTRALIAN PARLIAMENT. 1973. irreg. Aus.$12. Reporter Newspapers Co., Box 2557 G.P.O., Sydney, Australia. illus.

340.3 AT ISSN 0085-400X
NEW SOUTH WALES. LAW REFORM COMMISSION. REPORT. 1966. irreg., 1972, no. 15. price varies. Law Reform Commission, Goodsell Bldg., 8-12 Chifley Square, Sydney 2000, Australia.

340 AT
NEW SOUTH WALES BAR ASSOCIATION. ANNUAL REPORT. a. membership. New South Wales Bar Association, Selbourne Chambers, 174 Phillip St., Syndey, N.S.W. 2000, Australia.

348 AT ISSN 0548-6793
NEW SOUTH WALES DISTRICT COURT REPORTS. 1965. irreg. price on application. ‡ (Council of Law Reporting for New South Wales) Butterworths Pty. Ltd., 586 Pacific Highway, Chatswood, Sydney 2067, Australia. Ed. O. M. L. Davies. index.

340　　　　　　US
NEW YORK (STATE) OPINIONS OF THE
ATTORNEY GENERAL. 1890. a. $10.
Department of Law, Office of the Attorney General,
Justice Bldg, Empire State Plaza, Albany, NY
12224.

340　　　　　　NZ　ISSN 0110-3482
NEW ZEALAND. DEPARTMENT OF
STATISTICS. JUSTICE STATISTICS. a. NZ.$3.15.
Department of Statistics, Private Bag, Wellington,
New Zealand (Subscr. to: Government Printing
Office, Publications, Wellington, New Zealand)

349　　　　　　NZ
NEW ZEALAND. LAW REVISION COMMISSION.
REPORT. 1970/71. a. price varies. Government
Printing Office, Private Bag, Wellington, New
Zealand.

346　　　　　　NZ　ISSN 0078-0081
NEW ZEALAND LAW REGISTER. 1950. a.
NZ.$18. Sweet and Maxwell (N.Z.) Ltd., Private
Bag, Auckland, New Zealand. circ. 2,500.

347.7　　　　　　NQ
NICARAGUA. CORTE SUPREMA DE JUSTICIA.
BOLETIN JUDICIAL. irreg. Corte Suprema de
Justicia, Managua, Nicaragua.

340　　　　　　UK　ISSN 0078-0774
NIGERIAN LAW JOURNAL. 1964. a. price varies.
Sweet & Maxwell Stevens Journals, 11 New Fetter
Lane, London EC4, England. Ed. A. B. Kasunmu.
adv. bk. rev.

370.26　　　　　　JA
NIHON KYOIKUHO GAKKAI NEMPO. Added
title: Educational Law Review. 1972. a. 1000 Yen.
(Nihon Kyoikuho Gakkai) Yuhikaku Publishing Co.
Ltd., 2-17 Kanda Jimbocho, Chiyoda-ku, Tokyo
101, Japan. circ. 2,000.

340　　　　　　CE
NITI VIMAMSA. (Text in Sinhalese) a. Rs.12. Sri
Lanka Nitivedi Shishya Sanvidhanaya, Sevana,
Seeduwa North, Sri Lanka.

344.73　　　　　　US　ISSN 0148-7957
NOISE REGULATION REPORTER. 1974. fortn.
$244. Bureau of National Affairs, Inc., 1231 25th
St., N.W., Washington, DC 20037. Ed. Michael H.
Blake. (looseleaf format)
　　Formerly: B N A Noise Regulation Reporter.

340　　　　　　SW　ISSN 0300-3094
NORDISK STATUTSAMLING. (Subseries of
Nordisk Utredningsserie) (Text in Danish, Finnish,
Icelandic, Norwegian, or Swedish) 1970. a.
Nordiska Raadet, Box 19506, S-104 32 Stockholm,
Sweden.

340　　　　　　NO　ISSN 0085-4220
NORDISKE DOMME I
SJOFARTSANLIGGENDER. 1900. irreg., latest
1977 (pub. 1978) Kr.150. Nordisk
Skibsrederforening, Kristinelundvei 22, Oslo 2,
Norway. Ed. Per Gram. adv. index, cum. index
every 10 yrs. circ. 900. (tabloid format)

347　　　　　　US
NORTH DAKOTA. JUDICIAL COUNCIL.
ANNUAL REPORT. a. Judicial Council, State
Capitol, Bismarck, ND 58505. stat.
　　Formerly: North Dakota. Judicial Council.
Statistical Compilation and Report (ISSN 0095-
6120)

347.016　　　　　　US
NOTARY PUBLIC PRACTICES & GLOSSARY.
1978. biennial. $13.95. National Notary Association,
23012 Venture Blvd., Woodland Hills, CA 91364.
Ed. Raymond C. Rothman.
　　Supersedes in part: Customs and Practices of
Notaries Public and Digest of Notary Laws in the
U.S.

NOTICIAS DEL TRABAJO. see BUSINESS AND
ECONOMICS — Labor And Industrial Relations

340　　　　　　US　ISSN 0078-3552
OESTERREICHISCHE ZEITSCHRIFT FUER
OEFFENTLICHES RECHT. SUPPLEMENT.
1971. irreg., no. 4, 1976. Springer-Verlag, 175 Fifth
Ave., New York, NY 10010 (also Berlin,
Heidelberg, Vienna) (reprint service avail. from ISI)

353.9　　　　　　US　ISSN 0098-8820
OHIO. ATTORNEY GENERAL'S OFFICE.
REPORT. irreg. Attorney General's Office, State
House Annex, Columbus, OH 43215. illus.

340　　　　　　US　ISSN 0078-4095
OHIO STATE UNIVERSITY. COLLEGE OF LAW.
LAW FORUM SERIES. 1961. irreg., no. 10, 1977.
price varies. Ohio State University Press, 2070 Neil
Ave., Columbus, OH 43210.

340　　　　　　US　ISSN 0475-0926
OKLAHOMA. ATTORNEY GENERAL'S OFFICE.
OPINIONS OF THE ATTORNEY GENERAL.
1968. a. price varies. Attorney General's Office,
Rm. 112, State Capitol, Oklahoma City, OK 73105.
circ. 750-850. (back issues avail.)

340　　　　　　US
OMBUDSMAN AND OTHER COMPLAINT-
HANDLING SYSTEMS SURVEY. Short title:
Ombudsman Survey. 1972. a. free. International Bar
Association, Ombudsman Committee, c/o Bernard
Frank, Ed., 931 Hamilton Mall, Box 419,
Allentown, PA 18105 (Or Peter L. Freeman, Co-
Ed., Law Center, University of Alberta, Edmonton,
Alberta T6G 2H5, Canada) (Co-sponsor:
International Ombudsman Institute) circ. 2,000.

340　　　　　　CN
ONTARIO ANNUAL PRACTICE. a. Can.$18.50. ‡
Canada Law Book Ltd., 80 Cowdray Court,
Agincourt, Ontario M1S 1S5, Canada.
　　Formerly: Chitty's Ontario Annual Practice
(ISSN 0084-8751)

340　　　　　　NZ　ISSN 0078-6918
OTAGO LAW REVIEW. 1965. a. NZ.$5. Otago Law
Review Trust Board, c/o Faculty of Law, University
of Otago, Dunedin, New Zealand (Dist. in U.S. by:
Wm. M. Gaunt & Sons, Inc., Gaunt Bldg., 3011
Gulf Drive, Holmes Beach, FL 33510) Ed. J.F.
Corkery. adv. bk. rev. circ. 1,200. Indexed: Leg.Per.

340　　　　　　CN　ISSN 0475-1671
OYEZ. 1970. irreg. University of Windsor, Faculty of
Law, Student Law Society, Windsor, Ont., Canada.
illus.

PAKISTAN. NATIONAL ASSEMBLY. DEBATES.
OFFICIAL REPORT. see PUBLIC
ADMINISTRATION

340　　　　　　PK　ISSN 0078-785X
PAKISTAN ANNUAL LAW DIGEST. (Text in
English) 1947. a. Rs.60. P.L.D. Publishers, Church
Rd., Lahore 1, Pakistan.

340　　　　　　IO
PANTA-RHEI. 1975. irreg. University of North
Sumatra, Faculty of Law - Universitas Sumatera
Utara, Fakultas Hukum, Jalan Universitas 4, Medan,
Indonesia.

340　　　　　　AT　ISSN 0085-4689
PAPUA AND NEW GUINEA LAW REPORTS.
1963. irreg. Aus.$60. Law Book Co. Ltd., 31
Market St., Sydney, N.S.W. 2000, Australia.

345　　　　　　US
PARKER DIRECTORY OF CALIFORNIA
ATTORNEYS. 1925. a. price varies. Parker and
Son Publications, Inc., Box 60001, Los Angeles, CA
90060. Ed. Linda Mancini Jones. adv. circ. 35,000.
　　Formerly: Parker Directory of Attorneys (ISSN
0079-0044)

346　　　　　　UK　ISSN 0079-0095
PARLIAMENT HOUSE BOOK. (In 2 vols) 1824. a.
£50. W. Green and Son Ltd., St. Giles St.,
Edinburgh EH1 1PU, Scotland. Ed. D. Purdom.
individual index to each section.

340　　　　　　UK
PATERSON'S LICENSING ACTS. a. price varies.
Butterworth & Co. (Publishers) Ltd., 88 Kingsway,
London WC2B 6AB, England. Ed. J. N. Martin.

340　　　　　　SP
PERSONA Y DERECHO. 1975. a. 1500 ptas.($30)
Ediciones Universidad de Navarra, S.A., Plaza de
los Sauces, 1 y 2, Baranain, Pamplona, Spain. Dir.
Javier Hervada.

340　150　　　　　　US
PERSPECTIVES IN LAW AND PSYCHOLOGY.
1977. irreg. price varies. Plenum Press, 233 Spring
St., New York, NY 10013. Ed. Bruce Dennis Sales.
bibl.

340　　　　　　PE
PERU. CONSEJO NACIONAL DE JUSTICIA.
MEMORIA. irreg. Consejo Nacional de Justicia,
Lima, Peru.

PLANO DA SAFRA ACUCAR E ALCOOL. see
AGRICULTURE — Crop Production And Soil

340　　　　　　PO
PORTUGAL. MINISTERIO DA JUSTICIA.
BOLETIN. no. 241, 1974. a. Esc.1500. Ministerio
da Justicia, Praca do Comercio, Lisbon, Portugal.
bk. rev. bibl.

340　　　　　　AT　ISSN 0048-508X
PRACTICAL FORMS AND PRECEDENTS (NEW
SOUTH WALES) 1957. irreg., 1972, vol. 7. price
varies. Law Book Co. Ltd., 31 Market St., Sydney,
N.S.W. 2000, Australia.

340　　　　　　CS　ISSN 0079-4929
PRAVNEHISTORICKE STUDIE. (Text in Czech;
summaries in French, German, Russian) 1955.
irreg., vol. 18, 1974. price varies. (Ceskoslovenska
Akademie Ved) Academia, Publishing House of the
Czechoslovak Academy of Sciences, Vodickova 40,
112 29 Prague 1, Czechoslovakia.

340　　　　　　PL
PRAWO. (Text in Polish; summaries in Russian and
English or French) 1961. irreg., no 74, 1977. price
varies. Uniwersytet im. Adama Mickiewicza w
Poznaniu, Stalingradzka 1, 61-712 Poznan, Poland
(Dist. by: Ars Polona, Krakowskie Przedmiescie 7,
00-068 Warsaw, Poland)
　　Formerly: Uniwersytet im. Adama Mickiewicza w
Poznaniu. Wydzial Prawa. Prace (ISSN 0083-4262)

340　　　　　　US　ISSN 0075-8264
PRE-LAW HANDBOOK. OFFICIAL LAW
SCHOOL GUIDE. 1967. a. $3. ‡ Association of
American Law Schools, Law School Admission
Council, Suite 370, 1 Dupont Circle, N.W.,
Washington, DC 20036 (Dist. by: Educational
Testing Service, Box 944, Princeton, NJ 08540)
(processed)
　　Formerly: Law Study and Practice in the United
States: Pre-Law Handbook.

340　　　　　　YU
PREGLED SUDSKE PRAKSE. (Issued as
Supplement to Nasa Zakonitost, by Ustavni Sud
Hrvatske and Other Legislative Bodies) 1972. irreg.
(Vrhovni Sud) Narodne Novine, Zagreb, Ratkajev
Prolaz 4, Zagreb, Yugoslavia. (Co-sponsors: Croatia.
Ustavni Sud; Visi Privredni Sud u Zagrebu)

340　　　　　　US　ISSN 0555-0963
PREVENTIVE LAW NEWSLETTER. 1965. a.
University of Southern California Law Center,
University Park, Los Angeles, CA 90007. Ed. Louis
M. Brown. circ. 700. (back issues avail)

340　　　　　　IT
PROCESSO LEGISLATIVO NEL PARLAMENTO
ITALIANO. no. 3, 1974. irreg. (Universita degli
Studi di Firenze, Facolta di Scienze Politiche) Casa
Editrice Dott. A. Giuffre, Via Statuto 2, 20121
Milan, Italy. Ed. Alberto Predieri.

343　　　　　　US　ISSN 0340-7349
PUBLIC INTERNATIONAL LAW. (Text in English)
1975. 1 vol. per yr., 2 nos. per vol. $38. Springer-
Verlag, 175 Fifth Ave., New York, NY 10010 (Also
Berlin, Heidelberg, Vienna) bibl. (reprint service
avail. from ISI)

340　　　　　　US
PUBLIC UTILITIES LAW ANTHOLOGY. vol. 4,
1978. a. $59.95. International Library, 2425 Wilson
Blvd., Arlington, VA 22201.

340　　　　　　PR
PUERTO RICO. COMISION DE DERECHOS
CIVILES. ESTUDIOS Y MONOGRAFIAS. 1967.
irreg. free. Comision de Derechos Civiles - Civil
Rights Commission, Aptdo 1016, Estacion de Hato
Rey, Hato Rey, San Juan, PR 00919. Ed. Bd.
charts. circ. 3,000.

340   PR
PUERTO RICO. COMISION DE DERECHOS CIVILES. INFORME ANUAL. 1965. a. Comision de Derechos Civiles, Aptdo 1016, Estacion de Hato Rey, Hato Rey, San Juan, PR 00919.

340   IT
QUADERNI CAMERTI DI STUDI ROMANISTICI. INDEX/INTERNATIONAL SURVEY OF ROMAN LAW. INDEX. (Vols. for 1970-72 issued by the Facolte Giuridica (under a variant name: Facolta di Giurisprudenza), Universita di Camerino) (Text in Italian, English, French, German and Spanish) 1970. a. L.12000. Edizioni Scientifiche Italiane S.p.A., Via Chiatamone, Naples, Italy.

354   CN
QUEBEC (PROVINCE) COMMISSION DES SERVICES JURIDIQUES. RAPPORT ANNUEL. a. Commission des Services Juridiques, C.P. 123, Succursale Desjardins, Montreal, Que. H5B 1B3, Canada.

340   AT
QUEENSLAND LEGAL DIRECTORY. 1895. a. Aus.$8. Incorporated Council of Law Reporting for the State of Queensland, Box 19, Brisbane, North Quay. 4000, Queensland, Australia. circ. 400.
  Formerly (1895-1974): Queensland Law Almanac (ISSN 0079-8827)

343.04   GW
R W P STEUERRECHT. AUSGABE A. (Rechts- und Wirtschafts-Praxis.) a. with supplements. price varies. Forkel-Verlag GmbH, Postfach 104, Postfach 700231, W. Germany (B.R.D.) Ed.Friedrich Vohl. abstr. stat.
  Tax case histories

343.04   GW
R W P STEUERRECHT. AUSGABE B. (Rechts- und Wirtschafts-Praxis) m. DM.42.50. Forkel-Verlag GmbH, Postfach 104, 7000 Stuttgart 70, W. Germany (B.R.D.) Ed. W. Westenberger.
  Tax rulings

340 332.1   US
RAND MCNALLY LIST OF BANK-RECOMMENDED ATTORNEYS. 1872. a. $10. Rand McNally & Co., Bank Publications Division, 8255 N. Central Park Ave., Skokie, IL 60076 (Orders to: Box 7600, Chicago, IL 60680) circ. 15,000.

340   US
LA RAZA LAW REVIEW. 1972. a. $5.50. (Chicano Law Student Association) University of California, Los Angeles, School of Law, Los Angeles, CA 90024. Ed. Bernice Hernandez. adv. circ. 600.
  Formerly: Chicano Law Review.

340 333.33   US
REAL ESTATE LAW DIGEST (SUPPLEMENT) supplements issued periodically to update base volume. $34.50 for base volume. Warren, Gorham and Lamont, Inc., 210 South St., Boston, MA 02111.

340 320   US   ISSN 0080-0163
RECHTS- UND STAATSWISSENSCHAFTEN. 1947. irreg., vol. 24, 1975. price varies. Springer-Verlag, 175 Fifth Ave., New York, NY 10010 (also Berlin, Heidelberg, Vienna) (reprint service avail. from ISI)

340   NE
RECHTSHISTORISCHE STUDIES. 1976. irreg., vol. 4, 1978. price varies. Leiden University Press, c/o Martinus Nijhoff, Box 566, 2501 CN The Hague, Netherlands.

340   GW   ISSN 0080-018X
RECHTSPFLEGE JAHRBUCH. 1954. a. Gieseking-Verlag, Deckerstr. 2-10, Postfach 42, 4813 Bielefeld-Bethel, W. Germany (B.R.D.)

RECHTSSTAAT IN DER BEWAEHRUNG. see
LAW — International Law

340 320   AU   ISSN 0486-1558
RECHTSWISSENSCHAFT UND SOZIALPOLITIK. 1966. irreg., vol. 13, 1978. price varies. Manzsche Verlags- und Universitaetsbuchhandlung, Kohlmarkt 16, A-1014 Vienna, Austria. Eds. H. Floretta, R. Strasser.

370   BL
RECIFE, BRAZIL. SECRETARIA DE ASSUNTOS JURIDICOS. REVISTA. irreg. Secretaria de Assuntos Juridicos, Recife, Brazil. illus.

340   SP
RECOPILACION DE DOCTRINA LEGAL. a. price varies. (Consejo de Estado) Spain. Boletin Oficial del Estado, Eloy Gonzalo, 19, Madrid 10, Spain.

342   BE
RECUEIL ANNUEL DE JURISPRUDENCE BELGE. 1950. a. price varies. Maison Ferdinand Larcier S.A., Rue des Minimes 39, 1000 Brussels, Belgium.

340   FR
RECUEIL PERIODIQUE DES JURIS-CLASSEURS: DROIT CIVIL. irreg. $268. Editions Techniques, 123, rue d'Alesia, 75014 Paris, France.
  Continues: Juris-Classeurs. Droit Civil.

346   UK
REFORM IN NORTHERN IRELAND. irreg. (approx. 1/yr.) H.M.S.O. (N. Ireland), Chichester House, Chichester St., Belfast BT1 4JY, N. Ireland.

340   CK
REGIMEN LEGAL TRIBUTARIO. irreg. Col.320($10) (for 6 nos.) Editores y Distribuidores Asociados Ltda., Avda. Jimenez No. 4-49, Apdo. 14965, Bogota, Colombia.

REGISTER OVER GAELLANDE SFS-FOERFATTNINGAR. see LIBRARY AND INFORMATION SCIENCES

343   SZ
REIHE STRAFRECHT. 1976. irreg. Verlag Rueegger, 8253 Diessenhofen, Switzerland.

340   IT
REPERTORIO DEL FORO ITALIANO. 1876. a. price varies. Zanichelli Editore, Via Irnerio 34, Bologna 40126, Italy. abstr. bibl.

342   IT
REPERTORIO DELLE DECISIONI DELLA CORTE COSTITUZIONALE. 1956. biennial. price varies. Casa Editrice Dott. A. Giuffre, Via Statuto 2, 20121 Milan, Italy. Ed. Nicola Lipari.

347.9   IT
REPERTORIO DI GIURISPRUDENZA DEL LAVORO. 1968. biennial. price varies. Casa Editrice Dott. A. Giuffre, Via Statuto 2, 20121 Milan, Italy. Eds. Mario Pacifico, Enrico Pacifico.

348   US   ISSN 0094-7148
REPORT OF CASES DETERMINED IN THE SUPREME COURT AND COURT OF APPEALS OF THE STATE OF NEW MEXICO. Spine title: New Mexico Reports. 1968. irreg. (Supreme Court) West Publishing Co., Box 3526, St. Paul, MN 55165.

RESEARCH IN LAW AND ECONOMICS. see
BUSINESS AND ECONOMICS

340.1 301   US
RESEARCH IN LAW, DEVIANCE AND SOCIAL CONTROL. 1978. a. $17.25 to individuals; institutions $34.50. J A I Press, Box 1678, 165 W. Putnam Ave., Greenwich, CT 06830. Ed. Rita J. Simon.
  Formerly (until 1981): Research in Law and Sociology (ISSN 0163-6588)

340   SA   ISSN 0486-5588
RESPONSA MERIDIANA; an annual law review. (Text in English and Afrikaans) 1964. a. University of Cape Town, Student Law Society, Cape Town 7700, South Africa. (Co-sponsor: University of Stellenbosch, Student Law Society)

340   US
RESTATEMENT IN THE COURTS. POCKET PARTS. a. price varies. American Law Institute, 4025 Chestnut St., Philadelphia, PA 19104.
  Formerly (until 1976): Restatement in the Courts. Supplements.

340   AG   ISSN 0325-0601
REVISTA DE CIENCIAS JURIDICAS SOCIALES. 1922. irreg. exchange or free. Universidad Nacional del Litoral, Facultad de Ciencias Juridicas y Sociales, Candido Pujato 2751, 3000 Santa Fe, Argentina. bk. rev. circ. 500.

LAW   517

340   HO
REVISTA DE DERECHO. 1969. a. Universidad Nacional Autonoma de Honduras, Facultad de Ciencias Juridicas y Sociales, Bloque de Aulas, 2, Ciudad Universitaria, Tegucigalpa, D.C., Honduras.

340   AG
REVISTA DE DERECHO PUBLICO. 1950. irreg. Universidad Nacional de Tucuman, Instituto de Derecho Publico, Tucuman, Buenos Aires.

340   EC   ISSN 0484-6923
REVISTA DE DERECHO SOCIAL ECUATORIANO. (Suspended publication 1956, resumed publ. 1958) 1952. irreg. Universidad Central del Ecuador, Box 2349, Quito, Ecuador. Ed. H. Valencia.

340 630   VE
REVISTA DE DERECHO Y REFORMA AGRARIA. 1969. a. $7. Universidad de los Andes, Instituto Iberoamericano de Derecho Agrario y Reforma Agraria, Merida, Venezuela. bk. rev. bibl. circ. 1,200.

340   BL
REVISTA DE DIREITO DO TRABALHO.* 1973. irreg. Industrias Graficas Centrograf Ltd, Rua Alencar Lima, 35- Grupo 903/7, Petropolis, Brazil. "doctrina, jurisprudencia, legislacao"

340   AG
REVISTA DE HISTORIA DE DERECHO. 1973. a. (Instituto de Investigaciones de Historia del Derecho) Librart s.r.l., Departamento de Publicaciones Cientificas Argentinas, Avda. Corrientes 127, Casilla Correo Central 5047, Buenos Aires, Argentina. Dir. Ricardo Zorraquin Becu.

340   SP
REVISTA DE HISTORIA DEL DERECHO. a. Universidad de Granada, Secretariado de Publicaciones, Hospital Real, Granada, Spain. Ed. Jose M. Perez Prendes.

340   AG   ISSN 0034-8481
REVISTA DE LEGISLACION ARGENTINA. Variant title: Anuario de Legislacion Argentina. (In 2 volumes) 1966. a. $100 per volume. Jurisprudencia Argentina S.A., Buenos Aires 1013, Buenos Aires, Argentina. Ed.Bd. adv. charts. illus. stat.

340   CL
REVISTA DE STUDIOS HISTORICO JURIDICO. 1976. a. $7. (Universidad Catolica de Valparaiso, Escuel a de Derecho) Ediciones Universitarias de Valparaiso, Casilla 1415, Valparaiso, Chile. Ed. Alejandro Guzman B. bk. rev. circ. 500.

340   PN   ISSN 0302-6655
REVISTA JURIDICA PANAMENA. 1-2/yr. $3 per issue. Universidad de Panama, Centro de Investigacion Juridica, Estafeta Universitaria, Panama, Panama.

340   CN   ISSN 0080-2514
REVUE DE DROIT COMPARE.* 1964. a. Association Quebecoise pour l'Etude Comparative du Droit, 5451 Durocher, Montreal, Quebec, Canada.

340   AT   ISSN 0310-6861
ST. THOMAS MORE SOCIETY. JOURNAL. 1971. irreg. St. Thomas More Society, Box 282 G.P.O., Sydney, N.S.W. 2001, Australia. Ed. John D. Traill.

340 320   GW   ISSN 0080-5823
SAMMLUNG GELTENDER STAATSANGEHOERIGKEITSGESETZE. 1949. irreg., vol. 36, 1975. price varies. (Universitaet Hamburg, Institut fuer Internationale Angelegenheiten) Alfred Metzner Verlag GmbH, Zeppelinallee 43, Postfach 970148, 6000 Frankfurt 97, W. Germany (B.R.D.)

340 664   GW   ISSN 0080-5831
SAMMLUNG LEBENSMITTELRECHTLICHER ENTSCHEIDUNGEN. 1959. irreg., vol. 10, 1978. DM.500. Carl Heymanns Verlag KG, Gereonstr 18-32, 5000 Cologne 1, W. Germany (B.R.D.) Eds. Holthoefer and K.H. Nuese.

340 SZ
ST. GALLER STUDIEN ZUM WETTBEWERBS UND IMMATERIALGUETERRECHT. 1971. irreg. price varies. Verlag Ostschweiz, Oberer Graben 8, Postfach 716, CH-9001 St. Gallen, Switzerland. Ed. Mario M. Pedrazzini.

SAO PAULO, BRAZIL (STATE). SECRETARIA DA EDUCACAO. ATIVIDADES DESENVOLVIDAS. see *EDUCATION*

340 CN ISSN 0319-7999
SASKATCHEWAN DECISIONS, CIVIL AND CRIMINAL CASES. 1975. a(updated monthly) Can.$105 to individuals; Can.$145 to libraries. Western Legal Publications Ltd., 301-1 Alexander St., Vancouver, B.C. V6A 1B2, Canada.

340 GE ISSN 0084-5264
SAVIGNY-STIFTUNG FUER RECHTSGESCHICHTE. ZEITSCHRIFT. GERMANISTISCHE, ROMANISTISCHE UND KANONISTISCHE ABTEILUNG. 1861. a, vol. 96, 1979. M.210. ‡ Hermann Boehlaus Nachfolger, Meyerstr. 50a, 53 Weimar, E. Germany (D.D.R.) Eds. T. Mayer-Maly, D. Noerr, W. Ogris. bk. rev.

340 SW ISSN 0085-5944
SCANDINAVIAN STUDIES IN LAW. (Text in English) 1957. a. Kr.120. (Stockholms Universitet) Almqvist & Wiksell International, Box 62, S-101 20 Stockholm, Sweden. Ed. F. Schmidt. bibl.

340 320 GW ISSN 0080-7060
SCHRIFTEN ZUR RECHTSLEHRE UND POLITIK. 1948. irreg., vol. 66, 1974. DM.28. Bouvier Verlag Herbert Grundmann, Am Hof 32, Postfach 1268, 5300 Bonn 1, W. Germany (B.R.D.) Ed. Ernst Von Hippel.

SCHRIFTENREIHE FINANZWIRTSCHAFT UND FINANZRECHT. see *BUSINESS AND ECONOMICS — Banking And Finance*

SCHRIFTENREIHE FUER AGRARWIRTSCHAFT. see *AGRICULTURE*

340 AU
SCHRIFTENREIHE: GESELLSCHAFT UND BETRIEB. 1974. irreg., vol. 3, 1979. price varies. (Institut fuer Partnerschaftliche Betriebsverfassung) Manzsche Verlags- und Universitaetsbuchhandlung, Kohlmarkt 16, A-1014 Vienna, Austria. circ. 1,800(approx.)

346 UK ISSN 0080-8083
SCOTTISH LAW DIRECTORY. 1892. a. £13. William Hodge & Co. Ltd., 34/6 No. Frederick St., Glasgow G1 2BT, Scotland.

SECURITIES LAW REVIEW. see *BUSINESS AND ECONOMICS — Banking And Finance*

942 UK
SELDEN SOCIETY, LONDON. HANDBOOK: PUBLICATIONS, LIST OF MEMBERS AND RULES. 1952. every 4-5 years. £2 to non-members. Selden Society, Queen Mary College, Faculty of Laws, Mile End Rd., London E1 4NS, England.

942 UK
SELDEN SOCIETY, LONDON. LECTURES. 1953. every 2-3 years. price varies. Selden Society, Queen Mary College, Faculty of Laws, Mile End Rd., London E1 4NS, England.

942 UK
SELDEN SOCIETY, LONDON. MAIN (ANNUAL) SERIES. (Text in English, Latin, French; summaries in English) 1887. a. £5($35) to individuals; £6 ($40) to libraries. Selden Society, Queen Mary College, Faculty of Laws, Mile End Road, London E1 4NS, England. bibl. charts. illus. cum.index: vols. 1-79. circ. 1,500.

942 UK ISSN 0582-4788
SELDEN SOCIETY, LONDON. SUPPLEMENTARY SERIES. 1965. irreg. price varies. Selden Society, Queen Mary College, Faculty of Laws, Mile End Rd., London E1 4NS, England.

SERIE LEGISLACION EDUCATIVA ARGENTINA. see *EDUCATION*

340 UK ISSN 0085-6061
SHAW'S DIRECTORY OF COURTS IN ENGLAND AND WALES. 1970. a. £3.50. Shaw & Sons Ltd., Shaway House, Bell Green Lane, London SE26 5AE, England. bk. rev.
Formerly: Shaw's Directory of Magistrates' Courts & Crown Courts & Directory of Magistrates Courts.

345 US ISSN 0080-9233
SHEPARD'S ACTS AND CASES BY POPULAR NAMES, FEDERAL AND STATE. 1968. irreg., with annual supplement. $55. Shepard's, Inc. of Colorado Springs (Subsidiary of: McGraw-Hill, Inc.) Box 1235, Colorado Springs, CO 80901.

340 US
SIGNIFICANT STATE APPELLATE DECISIONS OUTLINE. 1976. a. $4. National Judicial College, Judicial College Bldg., University of Nevada, Reno, NV 89557. Ed.Bd.

349 SI ISSN 0080-9705
SINGAPORE LAW REVIEW.* (Text in English) 1969. a. $5. University of Singapore, Law Society, c/o Law Faculty, Singapore 10, Singapore. Ed. Philip Nalliah Pillai.
Supersedes title issued 1958-69: Me Judice.

SOCIEDADES POR ACOES. see *BUSINESS AND ECONOMICS*

340 IT ISSN 0391-3260
SOCIETA E DIRITTO DI ROMA. 1975. irreg., no. 5, 1979. price varies. Liguori Editore s.r.l., Via Mezzocannone 19, 80134 Naples, Italy. Ed. Antonio Guarino.

340 FR ISSN 0081-0843
SOCIETE DES AUTEURS, COMPOSITEURS, EDITEURS POUR LA GERANCE DES DROITS DE REPRODUCTION MECANIQUE. (BULLETIN) (Title varies: A.C.E. Bulletin) irreg. price varies. Societe des Auteurs, Compositeurs, Editeurs pour la Gerance des Droits de Reproduction Mecanique, 62 rue Blanche, Paris 9e, France.

340 UK ISSN 0038-0016
SOCIETY OF PUBLIC TEACHERS OF LAW. JOURNAL. N.S. 1947. a. price varies. Butterworth & Co. (Publishers) Ltd., 88 Kingsway, London WC2B 6AB, England. Ed. J. A. Jolowicz. bk. rev. circ. 1,900. Indexed: Leg.Per.

340 BU ISSN 0081-1866
SOFIISKI UNIVERSITET. IURIDICHESKI FAKULTET. GODISHNIK. (Summaries in English, French, and German) irreg., vol. 61, 1970. 1.40 lv. price varies. Publishing House of the Bulgarian Academy of Sciences, Ul. Akad. G. Bonchev, 1113 Sofia, Bulgaria. Ed. B. Cholakova. circ. 600.

340 CH
SOOCHOW LAW REVIEW. (Text in Chinese or English) 1976. irreg. $7 per no. Soochow University, Wai Shuang Hsi, Shih Lin, Taipei, Taiwan, Republic of China.

340.3 SA
SOUTH AFRICA. LAW COMMISSION. JAARVERSLAG VAN DIE SUID-AFRIKAANSE REGSKOMMISSIE/ANNUAL REPORT OF THE SOUTH AFRICAN LAW COMMISSION. (Text in Afrikaans and English) 1974. a. Government Printer, Bosman St., Private Bag X85, Pretoria 0001, South Africa.

340 AU
SOZIALVERSICHERUNGSRECHTLICHE ENTSCHEIDUNGEN. 1953. a. price varies. Manzsche Verlags- und Universitaetsbuchhandlung, Kohlmarkt 16, A-1014 Vienna, Austria. Eds. Albert Nowak, Hellmut Teschner. circ. 2,000(approx.)

340 SA ISSN 0584-8652
SPECULUM JURIS. (Text in Afrikaans and English) a. R.2. (University of Fort Hare, Faculty of Law) Fort Hare University Press, Private Bag 1322, Alice, Cape Province 5700, South Africa. Ed. J. Labuscmagne. bibl.

340.115 CS
STAT A PRAVO. 1956. irreg. price vaies. (Ceskoslovenska Akademie Ved, Ustav Statu a Prava) Academia, Publishing House of the Czechoslovak Academy of Sciences, Vodickova 40, 112 29 Prague 1, Czechoslovakia.

340.06 US ISSN 0099-1058
STATE BAR OF ARIZONA. NEWSLETTER. 1972. irreg. State Bar of Arizona, 234 N. Central Ave., Phoenix, AZ 85004. Key Title: Newsletter-State Bar of Arizona.

344.73 US ISSN 0163-2914
STATE LAWS AND REGULATIONS. a. Environment Information Center, Inc., 292 Madison Ave., New York, NY 10017. illus.

340 UK
STONE'S JUSTICES' MANUAL. a. Butterworth & Co. (Publishers) Ltd., 88 Kingsway, London WC2B 6AB, England. Eds. S. J. Richman, A. T. Draycott.

340 945 IT
STUDIA ET DOCUMENTA HISTORIAE ET IURIS. (Suspended from 1905 to 1935) 1880. a. L.20000. Istituto Utriusque Iuris, Facolta di Diritto Civile, Piazza Montecitorio 120, 00186 Rome, Italy. Ed. Gabrio Lombardi.

340 PL ISSN 0081-6671
STUDIA IURIDICA. (Text in Polish; summaries in English, French and German) 1962. irreg. price varies. Towarzystwo Naukowe w Toruniu, Ul. Slowackiego 8, 87-100 Torun, Poland (Dist. by: Ars Polona-Ruch, Krakowskie Przedmiescie 7, Warsaw, Poland) circ. 500.

340 HU
STUDIA IURIDICA AUCTORIATATE UNIVERSITATIS PECS PUBLICATA. (Text in Hungarian; summaries in French, German, Russian) 1958. irreg., no. 87, 1977. exchange basis. Pecsi Tudomanyegyetem, Allam- es Jogtudomanyi Kar, 48-as ter 1, Pecs, Hungary. Ed. Antal Adam.

347.9 IT ISSN 0081-6698
STUDIA IURIDICA. 1964. irreg., no. 83, 1979. price varies. Erma di "Bretschneider", Via Cassiodoro, 19, 00193 Rome, Italy.

340 PL ISSN 0081-6841
STUDIA PRAWNO - EKONOMICZNE. (Text in Polish; summaries in English) 1968. irreg., vol. 21, 1979. price varies. (Lodzkie Towarzystwo Naukowe) Ossolineum, Publishing House of the Polish Academy of Sciences, Rynek 9, Wroclaw, Poland (Dist. by Ars Polona-Ruch, Krakowskie Przedmiescie 7, Warsaw, Poland) (Co-sponsor: Polska Akademia Nauk) Eds. Jerzy Wroblewski and Wladyslaw Welfe. bk. rev. circ. 500.

340 RM ISSN 0578-5464
STUDIA UNIVERSITATIS "BABES-BOLYAI" IURISPRUDENTIA. (Text in Romanian; summaries in English, French and Russian) 1958. s-a. exchange basis. Universitatea "Babes-Bolyai", Biblioteca Centrala Universitara, Str. Clinicilor nr. 2, Cluj-Napoca, Romania. bk. rev. cum.index:(1956-1963) (1964-1970)

900 340 330 AU
STUDIEN ZUR RECHTS-, WIRTSCHAFTS- UND KULTURGESCHICHTE. (Subseries of: Universitaet Innsbruck. Veroeffentlichungen) 1969. irreg., vol. 10, 1974. price varies. (Universitaet Innsbruck) Oesterreichische Kommissionsbuchhandlung, Maximilianstr. 17, A-6020 Innsbruck, Austria. Ed. Nikolaus Grass.

340.2 296 US ISSN 0085-686X
STUDIES IN JEWISH JURISPRUDENCE. (Text in English and German) 1971. irreg. price varies. Sepher-Hermon Press, Inc., 53 Park Place, New York, NY 10007. Eds. Edward M. Gershfield, William Fuss. adv. bk. rev. circ. 500. (also avail. in microfilm from UMI; reprint service avail. from UMI)

340 US ISSN 0148-6551
STUDIES IN LAW. 1967. irreg. $1 per no. Institute for Humane Studies, 1177 University Drive, Menlo Park, CA 94025. bibl. circ. 5,000. (back issues avail.)

340 US
STUDIES IN LEGAL HISTORY. 1973. irreg. price varies. (American Society for Legal History) Harvard University Press, 79 Garden St., Cambridge, MA 02138. Ed. Stanley N. Katz.

LAW

340 US
STUDIES IN TRANSNATIONAL LEGAL POLICY.
Variant title: American Society of International Law. Occasional Papers. irreg., latest no. 17. price varies. American Society of International Law, 2223 Massachusetts Ave, N.W., Washington, DC 20008.

340 SW ISSN 0348-1964
STUDIES OF LAW IN SOCIAL CHANGE AND DEVELOPMENT. 1977. irreg. price varies. Nordiska Afrikainstitutet - Scandinavian Institute of African Studies, Box 2126, S-750 02 Uppsala, Sweden. (Co-sponsor: International Legal Centre, New York)

343 US ISSN 0362-2983
STUDY OF FEDERAL TAX LAW. INCOME TAX VOLUME: BUSINESS ENTERPRISES. 1975. irreg. $18.50. Commerce Clearing House, Inc., 4025 W. Peterson Ave., Chicago, IL 60646.
Continues in part: Study of Federal Tax Law. Income Tax Volume.

343 US ISSN 0362-5230
STUDY OF FEDERAL TAX LAW. INCOME TAX VOLUME: INDIVIDUALS. 1975. irreg. $18.50. Commerce Clearing House, Inc., 4025 W. Peterson Ave., Chicago, IL 60646.
Supersedes in part: Study of Federal Tax Law. Income Tax Volume.

340 SJ ISSN 0585-8631
SUDAN LAW JOURNAL AND REPORTS. 1956. a. Judiciary, Khartoum, Sudan.

344 II
SUMMARIES IN IMPORTANT LABOUR JUDGEMENTS. (Text in English) 1970. biennial. Punjab, Haryana & Delhi Chamber of Commerce and Industry, Phelps Bldg., 9-A Connaught Pl., New Delhi 110001, India. Ed. Shri B. P. Gupta.

340 AT
SUPREME COURT GAZETTE. 1973. irreg., vol. 4, 1975. free. Supreme Court, Sydney, Australia.

347 US ISSN 0362-5249
SUPREME COURT HISTORICAL SOCIETY. YEARBOOK. 1976. a. Supreme Court Historical Society, 1629 K St., Washington, DC 20006. illus. Key Title: Yearbook - Supreme Court Historical Society.

340 CN ISSN 0228-0108
SUPREME COURT LAW REVIEW. (Text in English and French) 1980. a. Butterworth & Co. (Canada) Ltd., 2265 Midland Ave., Scarborough, Ont. M1P 4S1, Canada. Eds. E. P. Belobaba, E. Gertner.

340 UK ISSN 0039-5978
SUPREME COURT PRACTICE. 1967. triennial. price varies. Sweet & Maxwell Stevens Journals, 11 New Fetter Lane, London E.C.4, England. Ed.Bd.
Formerly: Annual Practice.

345 347.9 US ISSN 0081-9557
SUPREME COURT REVIEW. 1960. a. $30. University of Chicago Press, 5801 Ellis Ave., Chicago, IL 60637. Eds. Philip B. Kurland, Gerhard Casper. (reprint service avail. from UMI,ISI)

347 AT ISSN 0082-0512
SYDNEY LAW REVIEW. 1953. a. Aus.$10. University of Sydney, Faculty of Law, 173 Phillip St., Sydney, 2000, Australia (Subscr. to: Law Book Co. Ltd., St. Martins Tower, 31 Market St., Sydney, N.S.W. 2000, Australia) Ed. Bd. adv. bk. rev. index. circ. 1,250. (also avail. in microform from UMI)
Indexed: Leg.Per. SSCI. Aus.P.A.I.S.

340 AT ISSN 0085-7106
TASMANIAN STATE REPORTS. 1905. a. Aus.$41.50. Law Book Co. Ltd., 31 Market St., Sydney, N.S.W. 2000, Australia.

340 FR
TEXTES D'INTERET GENERAL. irreg. Direction des Journaux Officiels, 26 rue Desaix, 75732 Paris Cedex 15, France.

346.73 US ISSN 0092-6175
TRANSPORTATION AND PRODUCTS LEGAL DIRECTORY.* 1973. a. Spangler, Jennings, Spangler & Dougherty, 250 North Main Street, Crown Point, IN 46307.

TRANSPORTATION LAW SEMINAR. PAPERS AND PROCEEDINGS. see *TRANSPORTATION*

349 FR ISSN 0071-9129
TRIBUNAL DE COMMERCE, PARIS. ANNUAIRE.* 1969. a. price varies. Tribunal de Commerce de Paris, 1 Bld. du Palais, Paris, France.

340 GW ISSN 0082-6731
TUEBINGER RECHTSWISSENSCHAFTLICHE ABHANDLUNGEN. 1961. irreg. price varies. (Universitaet Tuebingen, Rechts- und Wirtschaftswissenschaftliche Fakultaet) Verlag J.C.B. Mohr (Paul Siebeck), Wilhelmstr. 18, Postfach 2040, 7400 Tuebingen, W. Germany (B.R.D.)

340 BE
TWEETALIGE LOSBLADIGE WETBOEKEN. 1965. irreg. price varies. E. Story-Scientia, Prudens van Duyseplein 8, B-9000 Ghent, Belgium.

340 330 US ISSN 0082-7088
TWENTIETH CENTURY LEGAL PHILOSOPHY SERIES. irreg., 1970, no. 8. Harvard University Press, 79 Garden St., Cambridge, MA 02138.

340 BB
U W I STUDENTS' LAW REVIEW. 1976. a. $5 bds. $4. University of the West Indies, Faculty of Law, Student's Law Review Committee, Cave Hill Campus, P.O. Box 64, Bridgetown, Barbados. Ed. Rudolph Muir. adv. bk. rev.

347 US ISSN 0097-7977
U.S. ADMINISTRATIVE OFFICE OF THE UNITED STATES COURTS. REPORT ON APPLICATIONS FOR ORDERS AUTHORIZING OR APPROVING THE INTERCEPTION OF WIRE OR ORAL COMMUNICATIONS. 1972. irreg. U.S. Administrative Office of the United States Courts, U.S. Supreme Court Bldg., Washington, DC 20544. Key Title: Report on Applications for Orders Authorizing or Approving the Interception of Wire or Oral Communications.

341.1 US ISSN 0082-8769
U. S. ARMS CONTROL AND DISARMAMENT AGENCY. ANNUAL REPORT TO CONGRESS. 1961. a. U.S. Arms Control and Disarmament Agency, Dept. of State Bldg., Washington, DC 20451 (Also available from: Supt. of Documents, Washington DC 20402)

340 658.8 663.1 US
U. S. BUREAU OF ALCOHOL, TOBACCO AND FIREARMS. ANNUAL REPORT. a. U.S. Department of the Treasury, Bureau of Alcohol, Tobacco and Firearms, Washington, DC 20226.

345 US ISSN 0082-9943
U. S. DEPARTMENT OF JUSTICE. ANNUAL REPORT OF THE ATTORNEY GENERAL OF THE UNITED STATES. 1870. a. price varies. U.S. Department of Justice., Constitution & 10th St. N.W., Washington, DC 20530 (Orders to: Supt of Documents, Washington, DC 20402)

345 US ISSN 0082-9951
U. S. DEPARTMENT OF JUSTICE. OPINIONS OF ATTORNEY GENERAL. 1789. irreg. price varies. U.S. Department of Justice., Constitution & 10th St. N.W., Washington, DC 20530 (Orders to: Supt. of Documents, Washington, DC 20402) cum. indexes issued separately.

344.73 US ISSN 0361-6673
U.S. ENVIRONMENTAL PROTECTION AGENCY. OFFICE OF GENERAL COUNSEL. A COLLECTION OF LEGAL OPINIONS. 1973. a. U.S. Environmental Protection Agency, 401 M St., S.W., Washington, DC 20460.

U. S. FEDERAL TRADE COMMISSION. COURT DECISIONS PERTAINING TO THE FEDERAL TRADE COMMISSION. see *BUSINESS AND ECONOMICS — Domestic Commerce*

U. S. FEDERAL TRADE COMMISSION. FEDERAL TRADE COMMISSION DECISIONS, FINDINGS, ORDERS AND STIPULATIONS. see *BUSINESS AND ECONOMICS — Domestic Commerce*

346 US ISSN 0093-4631
U.S. FISH AND WILDLIFE SERVICE. SELECTED LIST OF FEDERAL LAWS AND TREATIES RELATING TO SPORT FISH AND WILDLIFE. irreg. $0.30. U.S. Fish & Wildlife Service, Washington, DC 20240 (Orders to: Supt. of Documents, Washington, DC 20402) (looseleaf format) Key Title: Selected List of Federal Laws and Treaties Relating to Sport Fish and Wildlife.

342 US
U.S. JUDICIAL CONFERENCE OF THE UNITED STATES. REPORT OF THE PROCEEDINGS. 1927. a. Administrative Office of the United States Courts, United States Supreme Court Bldg., 1 First Avenue N.E., Washington, DC 20544 (Orders to: Supt. Documents, Washington DC 20402)

353 US ISSN 0083-2960
U. S. OFFICE OF THE FEDERAL REGISTER. CODE OF FEDERAL REGULATIONS. 1938. revised at least once each calender year and issued quarterly. $525. U. S. Office of the Federal Register, National Archives and Records Service, Washington, DC 20408 (Orders to: Supt. of Documents, Washington, DC 20402) index.

353 US
U.S. OFFICE OF THE FEDERAL REGISTER. FEDERAL REGISTER: WHAT IT IS AND HOW TO USE IT. 1978. biennial. $3.50. U.S. Office of the Federal Register, National Archives & Records Service, Washington, DC 20408 (Orders to: Supt. of Documents, Washington, DC 20402) circ. 10,000.

345 US ISSN 0083-2979
U. S. OFFICE OF THE FEDERAL REGISTER. GUIDE TO RECORD RETENTION REQUIREMENTS. 1955. a. $4.75. U. S. Office of the Federal Register, National Archives and Records Service, Washington, DC 20408 (Orders to: Supt. of Documents, Washington, DC 20402)

345 US ISSN 0083-3401
UNITED STATES STATUTES AT LARGE. 1873. a. U.S. Office of the Federal Register, National Archives and Records Service, Washington, DC 20408 (Orders to: Supt. of Documents, Washington, DC 20402) (also avail. in microform from UMI)
Cumulation of daily slip law prints, annotated pamphlets of public laws enacted by congress

340 CL
UNIVERSIDAD CATOLICA DE VALPARAISO. REVISTA DE DERECHO. 1977. a. $7. (Universidad Catolica de Valparaiso, Escuela de Derecho) Ediciones Universitarias de Valparaiso, Casilla 1415, Valparaiso, Chile. Ed. Mauricio Bezanilla. circ. 500.

UNIVERSIDAD DE ANTIOQUIA. ESCUELA INTERAMERICANA DE BIBLIOTECOLOGIA. PUBLICACIONES. SERIE: LEGISLACION BIBLIOTECARIA. see *LIBRARY AND INFORMATION SCIENCES*

340 SP ISSN 0075-773X
UNIVERSIDAD DE LA LAGUNA. FACULTAD DE DERECHO. ANALES. 1963. a. 150 ptas. Universidad de la Laguna, Secretariado de Publicaciones, Laguna, Canary Islands, Spain.

340 VE ISSN 0076-6550
UNIVERSIDAD DE LOS ANDES. FACULTAD DE DERECHO. ANUARIO. 1970. irreg. Universidad de Los Andes, Facultad de Derecho, Centro de Investigaciones Juridicas, Merida, Venezuela. Ed.Bd. bibl.
Supersedes: Merida, Venezuela (City) Universidad de Los Andes. Facultad de Derecho. Revista.

340 SP
UNIVERSIDAD DE MURCIA. DEPARTAMENTO DE DERECHO POLITICO. PUBLICACIONES. SERIE MONOGRAFIAS. 1977. irreg. Universidad de Murcia, Departamento de Derecho Politico, Murcia, Spain.

349 SP
UNIVERSIDAD DE NAVARRA. MANUALES DE DERECHO. irreg; 1976, no. 10. price varies. Ediciones Universidad de Navarra, S.A., Plaza de los Sauces 1 y 2, Baranain, Pamplona, Spain.
Formerly: Universidad de Navarra. Manuales: Derecho Notarial Espanol (ISSN 0078-8767)

340 PN
UNIVERSIDAD DE PANAMA. CENTRO DE INVESTIGACION JURIDICA. ANUARIO. a. price varies. Universidad de Panama, Centro de Investigacion Juridica, Estafeta Universitaria, Panama, Panama.

340 PN
UNIVERSIDAD DE PANAMA. CENTRO DE INVESTIGACION JURIDICA. LEGISLACION PANAMENA. INDICES CRONOLOGICOS Y ANALITICO DE LEYES(O DECRETOS EJECUTIVOS) 1958. quinquennial. price varies. Universidad de Panama, Centro de Investigacion Juridica, Estafeta Universitaria, Panama, Panama. Dir. Aura G. de Villalaz.

340 327 PN
UNIVERSIDAD DE PANAMA. FACULTAD DE DERECHO Y CIENCIAS POLITICAS. CUADERNOS. 1960. irreg. Universidad de Panama. Facultad de Derecho y Ciencias Politicas, Oficina de Informacion y Publicaciones, Panama City, Panama.

340 658 SP ISSN 0582-8929
UNIVERSIDAD DE SEVILLA. INSTITUTO GARCIA OVIEDO. PUBLICACIONES. irreg. price varies. Universidad de Sevilla, Instituto Garcia Oviedo, San Fernando 4, Seville, Spain.

340 VE
UNIVERSIDAD DEL ZULIA. FACULTAD DE DERECHO. REVISTA. (Not Published 1976, 1977) 1961. irreg; no. 49, 1977. Bs.15($3.50) Universidad del Zulia, Facultad de Derecho, Apdo. 526, Maracaibo, Venezuela. Dir. Alice Adrianza Alvarez. circ. 2,500. Indexed: P.A.I.S.

340 PO
UNIVERSIDADE DE LISBOA. FACULDADE DE DIREITO. REVISTA. 1944. a. Universidade de Lisboa, Faculdade de Direito, Lisbon, Portugal. bk. rev.

340 BL ISSN 0080-6250
UNIVERSIDADE DE SAO PAULO. FACULDADE DE DIREITO. REVISTA. 1893. a. Cr.$30. Universidade de Sao Paulo, Faculdade de Direito, 95 Largo de Sao Francisco, 3 andar, Sao Paulo, Brazil. bk. rev. circ. 1,500.

340 RM
UNIVERSITATEA "AL. I. CUZA" DIN IASI. ANALELE STIINTIFICE. SECTIUNEA 3D: STIINTE JURIDICE. (Text in Romanian; summaries in foreign languages) 1955. a. $10. Universitatea "Al. I. Cuza" din Iasi, Calea 23 August Nr. 11, Jassy, Romania (Subscr. to: ILEXIM, Str. 13 Decembrie Nr. 3, P.O. Box 136-137, Bucharest, Romania) bk. rev. abstr. charts. illus.

UNIVERSITATEA BUCURESTI. ANALELE. FILOZOFIE. ISTORIE. DREPT. see PHILOSOPHY

347 FR
UNIVERSITE DE NANCY II. FACULTE DE DROIT ET DES SCIENCES ECONOMIQUES. ETUDES ET TRAVAUX. SERIE DROIT PRIVE. 1973. irreg. 35 F. Universite de Nancy II, Faculte de Droit et des Sciences Economiques, Service des Publications, B.P. 454, 54001 Nancy, France. adv. circ. 500.

340 CN
UNIVERSITE DE SHERBROOKE. REVUE DE DROIT. (Text in English & French) 1970. a. $7 price varies. Universite de Sherbrooke, Faculte de Droit, Sherbrooke, Que J1K 2R1, Canada. adv. bk. rev. circ. 1,250. (also avail. in microform from UMI) Indexed: Leg.Per.

340 FR
UNIVERSITE JEAN MOULIN. ANNALES. 1968. irreg. price varies. Editions Hermes, 31 Pasteur, 69007 Lyon, France. bk. rev. circ. 500.
Former titles (until 1975): Universite de Lyon III. Faculte de Droit. Annales (ISSN 0336-1357) & Universite de Lyon. Faculte de Droit et des Sciences Economiques. Annales (ISSN 0076-1664)

340 BE ISSN 0068-3019
UNIVERSITE LIBRE DE BRUXELLES. INSTITUT D'ETUDES EUROPEENNES. THESES ET TRAVAUX JURIDIQUES. (Text in French or English) 1968. irreg. price varies. Editions de l'Universite de Bruxelles, Parc Leopold, 1040 Brussels, Belgium.

340 ZR
UNIVERSITE NATIONALE DU ZAIRE, KINSHASA. FACULTE DE DROIT. ANNALES. 1972. a. Universite Nationale du Zaire, Kinshasa, Faculte de Droit, B.P. 125, Kinshasa XI, Zaire.

347.9 US ISSN 0069-3332
UNIVERSITY OF CHICAGO. CENTER FOR STUDIES IN CRIMINAL JUSTICE. ANNUAL REPORT.* 1965-66. a. University of Chicago, Center for Studies in Criminal Justice, Chicago, IL 60637.

340 US ISSN 0083-4025
UNIVERSITY OF KANSAS LAW REVIEW. 1952. a.(issued in 4 parts) $14 ea. ‡ (University of Kansas) Kansas Law Review, Inc., Green Hall, Lawrence, KS 66045. Ed. John P. Bowman. adv. bk. rev. cum. index for 5 yr. period. circ. 1,000. Indexed: Leg.Per.

346 UK ISSN 0076-0714
UNIVERSITY OF LONDON LEGAL SERIES. 1953. irreg., no. 12, 1978. price varies. Athlone Press, 90-91 Great Russell St., London WC1B 3PY, England (Dist. in U.S. by: Humanities Press Inc., 171 First Ave., Atlantic Highlands, NJ 07716)

346 US ISSN 0537-9768
UNIVERSITY OF MIAMI, CORAL GABLES. LAW CENTER. ANNUAL INSTITUTE ON ESTATE PLANNING. 1967. a. $42.50. Matthew Bender & Co., Inc., 235 E. 45 St., New York, NY 10017. Ed. Philip Heckerling. (back issues avail.)

346 CN ISSN 0077-8141
UNIVERSITY OF NEW BRUNSWICK. LAW JOURNAL. 1947. a. Can.$8. University of New Brunswick, Faculty of Law, Box 4400, Fredericton. N.B. E3B 5A3, Canada (Subscr. to: Carswell Co. Ltd., 2330 Midland Ave., Agincourt Ont., Canada) Ed. Dr. John W. Reynolds. bk. rev. adv. circ. 1,650. (also avail. in microform from UMI)

UNIVERSITY OF OSAKA PREFECTURE. BULLETIN. SERIES D: SCIENCES OF ECONOMY, COMMERCE AND LAW. see BUSINESS AND ECONOMICS

340 AT ISSN 0083-4041
UNIVERSITY OF QUEENSLAND LAW JOURNAL. 1948. a. Aus.$10($12) University of Queensland Press, P.O. Box 42, St. Lucia, Queensland 4067, Australia. Eds. M. Cope, W. Herd. adv. bk. rev. circ. 750. (also avail. in microfilm from UMI) Indexed: Leg.Per.

340 AT ISSN 0082-2108
UNIVERSITY OF TASMANIA LAW REVIEW. Title varies: Tasmanian University Law Review. 1958. a. Aus.$4. University of Tasmania, Law Review, Box 252 C, Hobart, Tas. 7001, Australia. Ed. F. A. Bates. adv. bk. rev. index. circ. 450. Indexed: Leg.Per. Aus. P.A.I.S. C.C.L.P. Curr.Aus.N.Z.Leg.Lit.Ind.

UNIVERSITY OF WALES. BOARD OF CELTIC STUDIES. HISTORY AND LAW SERIES. see HISTORY — History Of Europe

340 US ISSN 0083-4068
UNIVERSITY OF WEST LOS ANGELES LAW REVIEW. 1967? a. $4. University of West Los Angeles, Law Review, 10811 Washington Blvd., Culver City, CA 90230.

340 PL
UNIWERSYTET GDANSKI. WYDZIAL PRAWA I ADMINISTRACJI. ZESZYTY NAUKOWE. PRAWO. (Text in Polish; summaries in English and Russian) 1972. 10.00 Zl. Uniwersytet Gdanski, Ul. Czerwonej Armii 110, 81-824 Sopot, Poland.

349 PL ISSN 0083-4394
UNIWERSYTET JAGIELLONSKI. ZESZYTY NAUKOWE. PRACE PRAWNICZE. (Text in Polish; summaries in English, Russian) 1955. irreg., no. 65, 1975. price varies. Panstwowe Wydawnictwo Naukowe, Miodowa 10, Warsaw, Poland (Dist. by Ars Polona-Ruch, Krakowskie Przedmiescie 7, Warsaw, Poland) Ed. Tadeusz Hanousek. circ. 600-800.

340 PL
UNIWERSYTET SLASKI W KATOWICACH. PRACE PRAWNICZE. irreg., 1975, no. 6. 13 Zl. Uniwersytet Slaski w Katowicach, Ul. Bankowa 14, 40-007 Katowice, Poland. Ed. Mieczyslawa Sosniaka.

340 GW ISSN 0083-4572
UNTERSUCHUNGEN ZUR DEUTSCHEN STAATS- UND RECHTSGESCHICHTE. NEUE FOLGE. 1962. irreg., vol. 22, 1978. price varies. Scientia Verlag, Postfach 1660, 7080 Aalen, W. Germany (B.R.D.)

340 BG
UP-TO-DATE CIVIL REFERENCE. (Text in English) irreg. Tk.30. Dacca Law Reports Office, Malibagh, Dacca, Bangladesh.
Bangladesh legal system

340.05 US ISSN 0091-9691
UTAH BAR JOURNAL. 1973. irreg. State Bar of Utah, 564 Kennecott Building, Salt Lake City, UT 84111. Ed. D. Ray Owen, Jr. adv. bk. rev. illus. circ. 3,000.

VERFASSUNG UND VERFASSUNGSWIRKLICHKEIT. see POLITICAL SCIENCE

VERFASSUNGSGESCHICHTE. see HISTORY — History Of Europe

340 AT
VICTORIAN BAR COUNCIL. ANNUAL REPORT. a. membership. Victorian Bar Council, Owen Dixon Chambers, 205 William St., Melbourne, Vic. 3000, Australia.

342 US ISSN 0360-7453
VIOLATIONS OF HUMAN RIGHTS IN SOVIET OCCUPIED LITHUANIA; a report. 1971. a. $5. Lithuanian American Community of USA, Inc., 708 Custis Rd., Glenside, PA 19038. Eds. Thomas Remeikis, Bronius Nainys. circ. 4,000.

353.9 US
VIRGINIA. CRIMINAL JUSTICE SERVICES COMMISSION. ANNUAL REPORT. a. free. Criminal Justice Services Commission, 9 N. Twelfth St., Richmond, VA 23219.
Former titles (1974-1976): Virginia. Criminal Justice Officers Training and Standards Commission. Biennial Report; Until 1974: Virginia. Law Enforcement Officers Training Standards Commission. Biennial Report (ISSN 0095-1846)

340 US
VIRGINIA LEGAL STUDIES. irreg. University Press of Virginia, Box 3608 University Sta., Charlottesville, VA 22903.

WASHINGTON (STATE) LEGISLATURE. TRANSPORTATION COMMITTEE. REPORT. see TRANSPORTATION

WASHINGTON WANT ADS; a guide to legal careers in the federal government. see OCCUPATIONS AND CAREERS

WASSERRECHT UND WASSERWIRTSCHAFT. see WATER RESOURCES

340 AT
WESTERN AUSTRALIA. LAW REFORM COMMISSION. ANNUAL REPORT. 1973. a. free. Law Reform Commission, City Centre Tower, 16th Fl., 44 St. Georges Terrace, Perth, W.A. 6000, Australia. stat.

340 AT ISSN 0085-8161
WESTERN AUSTRALIA LAW ALMANAC. 1913. a. Aus.$2. Crown Law Department, 109 William St., Perth, W.A. 6000, Australia. circ. 800.

346 AT ISSN 0083-8764
WESTERN AUSTRALIAN REPORTS. 1899. irreg., with annual cumulation. price on application. Butterworths Pty. Ltd., 586 Pacific Hwy, Chatswood 2067, Australia.

340 AT ISSN 0085-820X
WHITEACRE.* 1967. irreg. free. University of Sydney, Law Graduates Association, 173-175 Phillip St., Sydney, N.S.W. 2000, Australia.

340 US
WHO'S WHO IN AMERICAN LAW. 1977. biennial. $57.50. Marquis Who's Who Inc., 200 E. Ohio St., Chicago, IL 60611 (And 4300 W. 62nd St., Indianapolis, IN 46268)

340 AU ISSN 0084-0025
WIENER RECHTSWISSENSCHAFTLICHE STUDIEN. 1964. irreg., no. 17, 1979. price varies. (Universitaet Wien, Institut fuer Rechtsvergleichung) Manzsche Verlags- und Universitaetsbuchhandlung, Kohlmarkt 16, A-1014 Vienna, Austria. (Co-sponsor: Oesterreichische Gesellschaft fuer Rechtsvergleichung) Ed. Fritz Schwind.

WIRTSCHAFTSWISSENSCHAFTLICHE UND WIRTSCHAFTSRECHTLICHE UNTERSUCHUNGEN. see BUSINESS AND ECONOMICS

340 GW
WISSENSCHAFT UND GEGENWART. JURISTISCHE REIHE. 1970. irreg., no. 6, 1973. price varies. Vittorio Klostermann, Frauenlobstr. 22, Postfach 900601, 6000 Frankfurt 90, W. Germany (B.R.D.)

301 340 GW ISSN 0084-0939
WISSENSCHAFTLICHE GESELLSCHAFT FUER PERSONENSTANDSWESEN UND VERWANDTE GEBIETE. SCHRIFTENREIHE. NEUE FOLGE. 1960. irreg. price varies. Verlag fuer Standesamtswesen GmbH und Co. KG, Hanauer Landstr. 197, 6000 Frankfurt 1, W. Germany (B. R. D.) Eds. Hans Doelle, Hans G. Ficker, Friedrich A. Knost.

347 US ISSN 0074-0837
WORK ACCOMPLISHED BY THE INTER-AMERICAN JURIDICICAL COMMITTEE DURING ITS MEETING. (Editions in Spanish, English, French and Portuguese) a. price varies. Organization of American States, Department of Publications, Washington, DC 20006. circ. 2,000.

355 GW ISSN 0084-3083
WUERZBURGER WEHRWISSENSCHAFTLICHE ABHANDLUNGEN. 1967. irreg., vol. 5, 1975. price varies. (Universitaet Wuerzburg, Institut fuer Wehrrecht) Holzner-Verlag, Neubaustr. 12, Postfach 130, 8700 Wuerzburg 1, W. Germany (B.R.D.)

YALE LAW SCHOOL STUDIES. see POLITICAL SCIENCE

340 US
YEARBOOK OF HIGHER EDUCATION LAW. 1977. a. $1.95. National Organization on Legal Problems of Education, 5401 S.W. 7th Ave., Topeka, KS 66606. Ed. D. Parker Young. circ. 2,000.

340 US
YEARBOOK OF SCHOOL LAW. 1933. a. $11.95. National Organization on Legal Problems of Education, 5401 S.W. 7th Ave., Topeka, KS 66606. Ed. Philip Piele. circ. 3,000.

342 II
YEARLY SUPREME COURT DIGEST. (Supplement to Shree Krishan Agarwal's "Twenty-One Years Supreme Court Digest, 1950-1970") (Text in English) 1966. a. Rs.45. Law Book Co., Sardar Patel Marg, Box 4, Allahabad 1, India. Ed. S. K. Agarwal. circ. 2,600.

328.675 ZR
ZAIRE. CONSEIL LEGISLATIF NATIONAL. COMPTE RENDU ANALYTIQUE. 1972. irreg. Conseil Legislatif National, Kinshasa, Zaire. Continues: Zaire. Assemblee Nationale. Compte Rendu Analytique.

348 ZA
ZAMBIA LAW REPORTS. a. Council on Law Reporting, Box RW 67, Lusaka, Zambia.

340 SZ ISSN 0084-540X
ZEITSCHRIFT FUER SCHWEIZERISCHES RECHT/REVUE DE DROIT SUISSE. (Text in German and French) 1860. irreg. (8-10/yr.) 80 Fr. Helbing und Lichtenhahn Verlag AG, Steinentorstr. 13, CH-4010 Basel, Switzerland. Ed.Bd. bk. rev. index. cum.index every 10 years.

LAW — Abstracting, Bibliographies, Statistics

347.788 US ISSN 0094-7504
ANNUAL STATISTICAL REPORT OF THE COLORADO JUDICIARY. a. Office of the Court Administrator, 323 State Capitol, Denver, CO 80203.

340 AU
AUSTRIA. STATISTISCHES ZENTRALAMT. STATISTIK DER RECHTSPFLEGE. a. S.310. Carl Ueberreuter, Alserstr. 24, Postfach 60, A-1095 Vienna, Austria.

340 BE
BELGIUM. INSTITUT NATIONAL DE STATISTIQUE. STATISTIQUES JUDICIAIRES. irreg. 200 Fr. Institut National de Statistique, 44 rue de Louvain, 1000 Brussels, Belgium.

340 016 BL ISSN 0067-6616
BIBLIOGRAFIA BRASILEIRA DE DIREITO. (Formerly issued in Bibliografia Brasileira de Ciencias Sociais) 1970. irreg. Cr.$100($5) Instituto Brasileiro de Informacao em Ciencia e Tecnologia, Rio de Janeiro, Brazil. bk. rev. circ. 300.

340 016 US ISSN 0360-2745
BIBLIOGRAPHIC GUIDE TO LAW. 1975. a. G.K. Hall & Co., 70 Lincoln St., Boston, MA 02111.

341 016 EI ISSN 0590-7233
BIBLIOGRAPHIE DE JURISPRUDENCE EUROPEENNE CONCERNANT LES DECISIONS JUDICIARES RELATIVES AUX TRAITES INSTITUTANT LES COMMUNAUTES EUROPEENNES. 1967. a. 100 Fr. (Court of Justice of the European Communities) Office for Official Publications of the European Communities, C.P. 1003, Luxembourg 1, Luxembourg (Dist. in the U.S. by: European Community Information Service, 2100 M St., NW, Suite 707, Washington, DC 20037)
Annual supplement to a 1965 publication of the same title

349 016 SZ
BIBLIOGRAPHIE DES SCHWEIZERISCHEN RECHT. (Text in German, French, Italian) a. price varies. Helbing und Lichtenhahn Verlag AG, Steinentorstr. 13, CH-4010 Basel, Switzerland. Ed. Alfred Muller. bibl. index. cum.index every 5 years.

340 016 FR ISSN 0067-6985
BIBLIOGRAPHIE EN LA LANGUE FRANCAISE D'HISTOIRE DU DROIT DE 987 A 1875. vol. 18, 1979. since 1962) price varies. c/o Mme. Boulet-Sautel, Universite de Paris II(Universite de Droit d'Economie et des Science's Social), 12 Place du Pantheon, 75005 Paris, France. Eds. M. Sautel, G. Sautel and A. Vandenbossche.

016 US ISSN 0067-7329
BIBLIOGRAPHY ON FOREIGN AND COMPARATIVE LAW : BOOKS AND ARTICLES IN ENGLISH. 1955. quinquennial with annual supplements. (Columbia University, Parker School of Foreign and Comparative Law) Oceana Publications, Inc., Dobbs Ferry, NY 10522. Ed. Charles Szladits.

COMPUTER LAW BIBLIOGRAPHY. see COMPUTER TECHNOLOGY AND APPLICATIONS — Abstracting, Bibliographies, Statistics

347.9 IT ISSN 0419-4632
DIZIONARIO BIBLIOGRAFICO DELLE RIVISTE GIURIDICHE ITALIANE. 1956. a. price varies. Casa Editrice Dott. A. Giuffre, Via Statuto 2, 20121 Milan, Italy. Ed. Vincenzo Napoletano.

340 016 FR
EXCHANGE OF INFORMATION ON RESEARCH IN EUROPEAN LAW/ECHANGE D'INFORMATIONS SUR LES RECHERCHES EN DROIT EUROPEEN. (Text in English & French) 1971. a. Council of Europe, Directorate of Legal Affairs - Conseil de l'Europe, Publications Section, 67006 Strasbourg, France (Dist. in U. S. by Manhattan Publishing Co., 225 Lafayette St., New York, N. Y. 10012)

340 314 GW ISSN 0072-1859
GERMANY (FEDERAL REPUBLIC, 1949-) STATISTISCHES BUNDESAMT. FACHSERIE 10. RECHTSPFLEGE. (Consists of several subseries) 1959. a. price varies. W. Kohlhammer-Verlag GmbH, Abt. Veroeffentlichungen des Statistischen Bundesamtes, Philipp-Reis-Str. 3, Postfach 421120, 6500 Mainz 42, W. Germany (B.R.D.)

I C E L REFERENCES; to publications concerning legal, administrative and policy aspects of environmental conservation. (International Council on Environmental Law) see ENVIRONMENTAL STUDIES — Abstracting, Bibliographies, Statistics

340 016 CH
INDEX TO CHINESE LEGAL PERIODICALS. 1970. a. $12. Soochow University, Wai Shuang Hsi, Taipei, Taiwan, Republic of China.

340 010 SP
INSTITUTO INTERNACIONAL DE HISTORIA DEL DERECHO INDIANO. ACTAS Y ESTUDIOS. triennial. Instituto Nacional de Estudios Juridicos, Duque de Medinacelli St. No. 6, Madrid, Spain.
History

347 US ISSN 0098-7875
MICHIGAN. OFFICE OF THE COURT ADMINISTRATOR. JUDICIAL STATISTICS. 1961. a. Office of the Court Administrator, Box 30048, Lansing, MI 48909. Key Title: Judicial Statistics.

341 016 EI
PUBLICATIONS JURIDIQUES CONCERNANT L'INTEGRATION EUROPEENNE; BIBLIOGRAPHIE JURIDIQUE. SUPPLEMENT. (Annual supplement to a 1966 publication of the same title) 1967. a. 150 Fr. (Court of Justice of the European Communities) Office for Official Publications of the European Communities, C.P. 1003, Luxembourg 1, Luxembourg (Dist. in the U.S. by: European Community Information Service, 2100 M St., NW, Suite 707, Washington, DC 20037).

016 340 SZ
RECHTSBIBLIOGRAPHIE/BIBLIOGRAPHIE JURIDIQUE/LAW BIBLIOGRAPHY. (In 2 vols.: Vol.1 Switzerland; Vol.2 Austria, Liechstenstein) 1978. a. 31 Fr. per vol. Studio Verlag, CH-8023 Zurich, Switzerland. (also avail. in microfiche)

340 016 GE ISSN 0081-3680
SPEZIALBIBLIOGRAPHIEN ZU FRAGEN DES STAATES UND DES RECHTS. 1963. irreg. price varies. Akademie fuer Staats- und Rechtswissenschaft der DDR, Informationszentrum Staat und Recht, August-Bebel-Str. 89, 1502 Potsdam-Babelsberg, E. Germany (D.D.R.)

340 SW ISSN 0082-0318
SWEDEN. STATISTISKA CENTRALBYRAAN. STATISTISKA MEDDELANDEN. SUBGROUP R (JUDICIAL STATISTICS. LAW AND SOCIAL WELFARE) (Text in Swedish; table heads and summaries in English) 1963 N.S. irreg. Kr.70. Liber Foerlag, Fack, S-162 89 Vaellingby, Sweden. circ. 1,400.

016 340 US ISSN 0085-7092
UNIVERSITY OF TEXAS, AUSTIN. TARLTON LAW LIBRARY. LEGAL BIBLIOGRAPHY SERIES. 1970. irreg., no. 20, 1980. price varies. University of Texas at Austin, Tarlton Law Library, 2500 Red River St., Austin, TX 78705. Ed. Judith Helburn. bibl. (processed)

LAW — International Law

341 US ISSN 0066-0647
AMERICAN SOCIETY OF INTERNATIONAL LAW. PROCEEDINGS. 1907. a. $9. American Society of International Law, 2223 Massachusetts Ave. N.W., Washington, DC 20008. index. cum.index: 1907-1920, 1921-1940, 1941-1960. (also avail. in microform from UMI) Indexed: Leg.Per.

341 FR ISSN 0066-3085
ANNUAIRE FRANCAIS DE DROIT INTERNATIONAL. 1955. a. price varies. (Academie de Droit International de la Haye, Groupe Francais des Anciens Auditeurs, NE) Centre National de la Recherche Scientifique, 15 Quai Anatole-France, 75700 Paris, France.

341 SP
ANUARIO DE DERECHO INTERNACIONAL. 1975. a. 1700 ptas.($30) (Universidad de Navarra, Departamento de Derecho Internacional) Ediciones Universidad de Navarra, S.A., Plaza de los Sauces, 1 y 2, Baranain, Pamplona, Spain. Dir. Enrique Pecourt.

ANUARIO DE HISTORIA DEL DERECHO ESPANOL. see *HISTORY — History Of Europe*

341 EC ISSN 0570-4251
ANUARIO ECUATORIANO DE DERECHO INTERNACIONAL. 1964. a. Universidad Central del Ecuador, Instituto Ecuatoriano de Derecho Internacional, Apdo. 1025, Quito, Ecuador. Ed. Mario A. Gomez de la Torre. circ. 2,000.

341 US
ANUARIO INTERAMERICANO DE DERECHOS HUMANOS/INTER-AMERICAN YEARBOOK ON HUMAN RIGHTS. (Text in Spanish and English) 1960-67. biennial. $15. (Inter-American Commission on Human Rights) Organization of American States, Department of Publications, Washington, DC 20006.

341.13 375 US ISSN 0066-7447
ARIZONA MODEL UNITED NATIONS. 1964. a. free. University of Arizona, Department of Political Science, Tucson, AZ 85721. circ. 1,000.

347.7 UK ISSN 0571-5873
ASSOCIATION INTERNATIONALE DU DROIT COMMERCIAL ET DU DROIT AFFAIRES. GROUPE FRANCAIS. TRAVAUX.* irreg. International Law Association, 3 Paper Buildings, Temple, London EC4Y 7EU, England.

341 NE ISSN 0066-8923
ASSOCIATION OF ATTENDERS AND ALUMNI OF THE HAGUE ACADEMY OF INTERNATIONAL LAW. YEARBOOK. 1925. a. price varies. (Association of Attenders and Alumni of the Hague Academy of International Law) Martinus Nijhoff, Box 566, 2501 CN The Hague, Netherlands.

341.18 FR ISSN 0519-3125
ATLANTIC MAIL.* irreg. Atlantic Treaty Association, c/o Jean de Madre, 185 rue de la Pompe, 75116 Paris, France.

341 SZ
AUGSBURGER SCHRIFTEN ZUM STAATS- UND VOELKERRECHT. 1975. irreg. Verlag Peter Lang AG, Muenzgraben 2, Postfach, CH-3000 Berne 7, Switzerland. Ed. Dieter Blumenwitz.

341.2 AT
AUSTRALIAN TREATY SERIES. irreg. price varies. Australian Government Publishing Service, Box 84, Canberra, A.C.T. 2600, Australia.
Formerly: Australian Treaty List.

341 AT ISSN 0084-7658
AUSTRALIAN YEARBOOK OF INTERNATIONAL LAW. 1965. irreg. price on application. Butterworths Pty. Ltd., 586 Pacific Hwy., Chatswood 2067, Australia (Dist. in U.S. by: Oceana Publications, Inc., Dobbs Ferry, NY 10522)

B N A'S LAW REPRINTS: TRADE REGULATION. see *BUSINESS AND ECONOMICS — International Commerce*

341 US
BEITRAEGE ZUM AUSLAENDISCHEN OEFFENTLICHEN RECHT UND VOELKERRECHT. (Text Mainly in German) vol. 60, 1974. irreg., vol. 77, 1981. price varies. Springer-Verlag, 175 Fifth Ave., New York, NY 10010 (Also Berlin, Heidelberg, Vienna) (reprint service avail. from ISI)

341 US ISSN 0067-8562
BILATERAL STUDIES IN PRIVATE INTERNATIONAL LAW. 1956. irreg., no. 17, 1968. $7.50. (Columbia University, Parker School of Foreign and Comparative Law) Oceana Publications Inc., Dobbs Ferry, NY 10522.

341 US ISSN 0161-2832
BOSTON COLLEGE INTERNATIONAL AND COMPARATIVE LAW JOURNAL. 1977. a. $5. Boston College, School of Law, 885 Centre St., Newton Centre, MA 02159. Ed. Steven P. Ross.

BRITISH INSTITUTE OF INTERNATIONAL AND COMPARATIVE LAW. COMPARATIVE LAW SERIES. see *LAW*

341 UK ISSN 0068-2179
BRITISH INSTITUTE OF INTERNATIONAL AND COMPARATIVE LAW. INTERNATIONAL LAW SERIES.* irreg. price varies. British Institute of International and Comparative Law, 32 Furnival St., London EC4A 1JN, England.

341 US ISSN 0068-2195
BRITISH INTERNATIONAL LAW CASES. 1964. irreg., 1973, no. 9. price varies. (International Law Fund) Oceana Publications Inc., Dobbs Ferry, NY 10522. (Co-sponsor: British Institute of Foreign and Comparative Law) Ed. C. Parry.

341 UK ISSN 0007-1676
BRITISH PRACTICE IN INTERNATIONAL LAW.* 1962. irreg. price varies. British Institute of International and Comparative Law, 32 Furnival St., London EC4H, England. Ed. E. Lauterpacht. Indexed: Leg.Per.
Formerly: Contemporary Practice of the United Kingdom in the Field of International Law.

341.058 US ISSN 0068-2691
BRITISH YEAR BOOK OF INTERNATIONAL LAW. 1920? a. or biennial. price varies. (Royal Institute of International Affairs, UK) Oxford University Press, 200 Madison Ave., New York, NY 10016 (and Ely House, 37 Dover St., London W1X 4AH, England) Eds. H. Waldock, R.Y. Jennings.

341 US
CANADA-UNITED STATES LAW JOURNAL. 1978. a. $4. Case Western Reserve University, School of Law, Cleveland, OH 44106. Ed. David C. Indiano. circ. 650. Indexed: Leg.Per. C.C.L.P. Foreign Leg.Per.

341 CN ISSN 0317-9087
CANADIAN COUNCIL ON INTERNATIONAL LAW. PROCEEDINGS OF THE ANNUAL CONFERENCE. (Text in English and French) 1972. a. Canadian Council on International Law, c/o University of Ottawa, Faculty of Law, Ottawa, Ont., Canada.

341 CN ISSN 0069-0058
CANADIAN YEARBOOK OF INTERNATIONAL LAW/ANNUAIRE CANADIEN DE DROIT INTERNATIONAL. (Editions in English and French) 1963. a. Can.$28. University of British Columbia Press, 303-6344 Memorial Rd., Vancouver, B.C. V6T 1W5, Canada. Ed. C.B. Bourne. bk. rev. Indexed: Can.Ind. Foreign Leg.Per.

341.11 BE ISSN 0503-2407
COLLECTION OF DOCUMENTS FOR THE STUDY OF INTERNATIONAL NON-GOVERNMENTAL RELATIONS. Alternate title: Union of International Associations. Documents. (Text in English or French) 1956. irreg. Union of International Associations, 1 rue aux Laines, 1000 Brussels, Belgium.

COLLOQUIUM ON THE LAW OF OUTER SPACE. PROCEEDINGS. see *AERONAUTICS AND SPACE FLIGHT*

341.11 EI ISSN 0591-1745
COMMISSION OF THE EUROPEAN COMMUNITIES. DIRECTORY. 1968. a. 50 Fr. Office for Official Publications of the European Communities, Boite Postale 1003, Luxembourg, Luxembourg (Dist. in the U.S. by: European Community Information Service, 2100 M St., NW, Suite 707, Washington, DC 20037)

341.18 EI ISSN 0590-6563
COMMISSION OF THE EUROPEAN COMMUNITIES. COMMUNITY LAW. (Editions also in German, French, Italian and Dutch) 1968. a. free. Commission of the European Communities, Service de Renseignement et de Diffusion des Documents, Rue de la Loi 200, 1049 Brussels, Belgium.
Extracts from its General Report on the Activities of the Communities

341.8 FR ISSN 0589-9508
COUNCIL OF EUROPE. CONCISE HANDBOOK.* 1951. irreg. Council of Europe, Publications Section, 67000 Strasbourg, France (Dist. in U. S. by Manhattan Publishing Co., 225 Lafayette St., New York, N. Y. 10012)

341.18 FR ISSN 0070-105X
COUNCIL OF EUROPE. EUROPEAN TREATY SERIES. (Text in English and French) 1949. irreg; no. 101, 1978. $2. Council of Europe, Publications Section, Strasbourg, France (Dist. in U.S. by Manhattan Publishing Co., 225 Lafayette St., New York, N.Y. 10012)

341.8 FR ISSN 0589-9362
COUNCIL OF EUROPE. EXCHANGE OF INFORMATION BETWEEN THE MEMBER STATES ON THEIR LEGISLATIVE ACTIVITY AND REGULATIONS (NEW SERIES) 1967. irreg; no. 10, 1978. Council of Europe, Publications Section, 67000 Strasbourg, France (Dist. in U. S. by Manhattan Publishing Co., 225 Lafayette St., New York, N. Y. 10012) (processed)

341.18 FR
COUNCIL OF EUROPE. PARLIAMENTARY ASSEMBLY. DOCUMENTS; WORKING PAPERS/DOCUMENTS DE SEANCE. (Text in English and French) 1949. a. $12. Council of Europe, Parliamentary Assembly, Publications Section, Strasbourg, France (Dist. in U.S. by Manhattan Publishing Co., 225 Lafayette St., New York, N.Y. 10012)
Continues (since v. 26, pt. 3, 1974): Council of Europe. Consultative Assembly. Documents; Working Papers/Documents de Seance (ISSN 0070-1009)

341.18 FR
COUNCIL OF EUROPE. PARLIAMENTARY ASSEMBLY. ORDERS OF THE DAY, MINUTES OF PROCEEDINGS/ORDRES DU JOUR, PROCES VERBAUX. (Text in English and French) 1949. a. $5. Council of Europe, Publications Section, Strasbourg, France (Dist. in U.S. by Manhattan Publishing Co., 225 Lafayette St., New York, N.Y. 10012)
Continues (since 1974): Council of Europe. Consultative Assembly. Orders of the Day, Minutes of Proceedings/Ordres du Jour, Proces Verbaux (ISSN 0070-1017)

341.18 FR
COUNCIL OF EUROPE. PARLIAMENTARY ASSEMBLY. TEXTS ADOPTED BY THE ASSEMBLY/TEXTES ADOPTES PAR L'ASSEMBLEE. (Text in English and French) 1949. a. $5. Council of Europe, Parliamentary Assembly, Publications Section, Strasbourg, France (Dist. in U.S. by Manhattan Publishing Co., 225 Lafayette St., New York, N.Y. 10012)
Continues (since 1974): Council of Europe. Consultative Assembly. Texts Adopted by the Assembly/Textes Adoptes Par l'Assemblee (ISSN 0070-1033)

341 EI ISSN 0070-1386
COURT OF JUSTICE OF THE EUROPEAN COMMUNITIES. RECUEIL DE LA JURISPRUDENCE. (Text in French, German, Italian, Dutch) 1954. a. Office for Official Publications of the European Communities, Boite Postal 1003, Luxembourg, Luxembourg (Dist. in the U.S. by: European Community Information Service, 2100 M St., NW, Suite 707, Washington, DC 20037)

LAW — INTERNATIONAL LAW

341　　　　　　　　　　　　UY
CUADERNOS DE DERECHO INTERNACIONAL PRIVADO. 1975. irreg. Fundacion de Cultura Universitaria, 25 de Mayo no. 537, Montevideo, Uruguay.

341.18　330　　　EI　　ISSN 0071-3015
DEBATES OF THE EUROPEAN PARLIAMENT. 1958. irreg. 750 Fr.($18.10) (European Parliament) Office for Official Publications of the European Communities, Boite Postale 1003, Luxembourg, Luxembourg (Dist. in the U.S. by: European Community Information Service, 2100 M St., NW, Suite 707, Washington, DC 20037)

341　　　　　　　　　　　　NE
DIGEST OF THE DECISIONS OF THE INTERNATIONAL COURT. (Text in Dutch, English and French) 1974. irreg. price varies. Martinus Nijhoff, Box 566, 2501 CN The Hague, Netherlands. Ed. Krystyna Marek.

341　　　　　US　　ISSN 0095-3369
DIGEST OF THE UNITED STATES PRACTICE IN INTERNATIONAL LAW. 1973. a. $11. U. S. Department of State, 2201 C St. N.W., Washington, DC 20250 (Orders to: Supt. of Documents, Washington, DC 20402)

341.4　　　　　UA　　ISSN 0080-259X
EGYPTIAN REVIEW OF INTERNATIONAL LAW/REVUE EGYPTIENNE DE DROIT INTERNATIONAL. (Text in Arabic, French, English) 1945. a. $30. Egyptian Society of International Law, 16 Ramses St., Cairo, Egypt (Dist. by Oceana Publications, Inc., Dobbs Ferry, NY 10522) bk. rev. cum.index: 1945-49.

341.1　　　　　FR　　ISSN 0589-9575
EUROPEAN CO-OPERATION. irreg. Council of Europe, Publications Section, 67000 Strasbourg, France (Dist. in U. S. by Manhattan Publishing Co., 225 Lafayette St., New York, N. Y. 10012)

341.18　　　　　EI　　ISSN 0071-3023
EUROPEAN PARLIAMENT. DOCUMENTS DE SEANCE. 1958. irreg. Office for Official Publications of the European Communities, Boite Postale 1003, Luxembourg, Luxembourg (Dist. in the U.S. by: European Community Information Service, 2100 M St., NW, Suite 707, Washington, DC 20037)

341.18　　　　　EI　　ISSN 0531-4321
EUROPEAN PARLIAMENT. INFORMATIONS. (Editions also in German, Italian, Dutch occasionally in English) 1967. irreg.; issued in relation to its sessions. free. European Parliament, Secretariat, Centre Europeen, Case Postale 1601, Luxembourg, Luxembourg.

341　　　　　US　　ISSN 0428-903X
FONTES IURIS GENTIUM. (Text in English, French and German) irreg. price varies. Springer-Verlag, 175 Fifth Ave., New York, NY 10010 (Also Berlin, Heidelberg, Vienna) Eds. H. Mosler, R. Bernhardt. (reprint service avail. from ISI)

341　　　　　FR　　ISSN 0071-8971
FRANCE. MINISTERE DES AFFAIRES ETRANGERES. RECUEIL DES TRAITES ET ACCORDS DE LA FRANCE. 1961. a. price varies. Ministere des Affaires Etrangeres, 37, Quai d'Orsay, 75700 Paris, France.

341　　　　　　　　　　　　GW
DAS GELTENDE SEEVOELKERRECHT IN EINZELDARSTELLUNGEN. 1970. irreg., vol. 9, 1974. price varies. (Universitaet Hamburg, Institut fuer Internationale Angelegenheiten) Alfred Metzner Verlag GmbH, Zeppelinallee 43, Postfach 970148, 6000 Frankfurt 97, W. Germany (B.R.D.)
Formerly: Geltende Seekriegsrecht in Einzeldarstellungen (ISSN 0435-1924)

341　　　　　　　　　　　　GW
GERMAN YEARBOOK OF INTERNATIONAL LAW. 1948. a. price varies. (Universitaet Kiel, Institut fuer Internationales Recht) Duncker und Humblot, Dietrich-Schaefer-Weg 9, Postfach 410329, 1000 Berlin 41, W. Germany (B.R.D.)
Formerly: Jahrbuch fuer Internationales Recht (ISSN 0021-3993)

341　　　　　　　　　　　　UN
GILBERTO AMADO MEMORIAL LECTURE. 1972. a. unpriced. (United Nations International Law Commission) United Nations International Law Seminar, Secretary, Palais des Nations, CH-1211 Geneva 10, Switzerland. circ. 500.

341　　　　　NE　　ISSN 0072-9272
HAGUE CONFERENCE ON PRIVATE INTERNATIONAL LAW. ACTES ET DOCUMENTS. (In Three Vols.) (Text in English and French) 1893. quadrennial since 1951; 1972, 12th. $80. Hague Conference on Private International Law, Permanent Bureau, Javastraat 2C, The Hague, Netherlands.

HAMBURGER OEFFENTLICH-RECHTLICHE NEBENSTUNDEN. see LAW

341　　　　　II　　ISSN 0073-6678
INDIAN SOCIETY OF INTERNATIONAL LAW. PUBLICATIONS. 1960. irreg. $20. Indian Society of International Law, 7-8 Scindia House, Kasturba Gandhi Marg, New Delhi 110001, India. Ed. M. K. Nawaz. adv. bk. rev. circ. 1,500.

341　　　　　SZ　　ISSN 0073-8182
INSTITUT DE DROIT INTERNATIONAL. ANNUAIRE. (Text in English and French) 1876. a. 190 Fr.($114) per vol. (1981 price) (BE) S. Karger AG, Allschwilerstrasse 10, P.O. Box, CH-4009 Basel, Switzerland. index. circ. 900. (reprint service avail. from ISI)

341　　　　　　　　　　　　SZ
INSTITUT FUER INTERNATIONALES RECHT UND INTERNATIONALE BEZIEHUNGEN. SCHRIFTENREIHE. (Text mainly in German; occasionally in English or French) 1939. irreg. price varies. Helbing und Lichtenhahn Verlag AG, Steinentorstr. 13, CH-4010 Basel, Switzerland.

INTERNATIONAL CENTRE FOR SETTLEMENT OF INVESTMENT DISPUTES. ANNUAL REPORT. see BUSINESS AND ECONOMICS — Investments

341　　　　　UN　　ISSN 0074-445X
INTERNATIONAL COURT OF JUSTICE. YEARBOOK. (Editions in English and French) 1946/47. a. price varies. International Court of Justice, Peace Palace, 2517 KJ The Hague, Netherlands (Or United Nations Publications, New York, NY 10017; or Distribution and Sales Section, Palais des Nations, CH-12 Geneva, Switzerland) Ed.Bd. circ. 2,000.

341.7　　　　　　　　　　　　NE
INTERNATIONAL FISCAL ASSOCIATION. YEARBOOK. a. membership. International Fiscal Association, c/o General Secretariat, P.O. Box 1738, Burg. Oudlaan 50, 3000 DR Rotterdam, Netherlands.

341　　　　　　　　　　　　US
INTERNATIONAL LAW ASSOCIATION. AMERICAN BRANCH. PROCEEDINGS. biennial. $25. International Law Association, American Branch, 14 Wall St., New York, NY 10005. Ed. James P. Beggans, Jr. bibl. circ. 650.

341　　　　　UK　　ISSN 0074-6738
INTERNATIONAL LAW ASSOCIATION. REPORTS OF CONFERENCES. (Text in English; some papers in French) 1875. biennial; 59th. 1978, Manila. price varies. International Law Association, 3 Paper Bldgs., The Temple, London EC4 7EU, England. cum.index (1873-1972) circ. 4,000.

341　　　　　GW　　ISSN 0020-9503
INTERNATIONALES RECHT UND DIPLOMATIE. (Text mainly in German with quotations from other languages) 1956. irreg. DM.35($14) Verlag Wissenschaft und Politik Berend von Nottbeck, Salierring 14, 5000 Cologne 1, W. Germany (B.R.D) Ed. Boris Meissner. adv. bk. rev. index. cum.index. circ. 1,000.

341　　　　　　　　　　　　IT
ISTITUTO DI DIRITTO INTERNAZIONALE-D. ANZILOTTI. PUBBLICAZIONI. no. 5, 1975. irreg. Casa Editrice Dott. A. Giuffre, Via Statuto 2, 20121 Milan, Italy.

341　　　　　　　　　　　　IT
ISTITUTO DI STUDI E DOCUMENTAZIONI SULL'EST EUROPEO. SERIE GIURIDICA. 1969. irreg; latest issue, no. 5. price varies. Istituto di Studi e Documentazione sull'Est Europeo, Corso Italia 27, 34122 Trieste, Italy. circ. 400-1,000.

341　　　　　UK　　ISSN 0075-6040
KIME'S INTERNATIONAL LAW DIRECTORY. 1892. a. £10($20) Kime's International Law Directory, Ltd, 170 Sloane St., London SW1X 9QG, England. Ed. James M. Matthews. index.

341　　　　　FR　　ISSN 0085-2686
LANGUE INTERNATIONALE. 1950. a. F.20. ‡ Societe Idiste Francaise, c/o Georges Moureaux, Ed., 11 rue J. Donier, 01100 Oyonnax, France. bk. rev. (processed)

340　　　　　NE　　ISSN 0075-823X
LAW IN EASTERN EUROPE. (Text in English) 1958. irreg., no. 19, 1975. price varies. (Rijksuniversiteit te Leiden, Documentation Office for East European Law) Sijthoff & Noordhoff International Publishers b.v., Box 4, 2400 MA Alphen aan den Rijn, Netherlands (U.S. address: 20010 Century Blvd., Germantown, MD 20767) Ed. F.J. Feldbrugge. index. circ. 900.

LECCIONES Y ENSAYOS. see LAW

341.2　　　　　MW　　ISSN 0076-3357
MALAWI TREATY SERIES. (Text in English) a, latest 1970/71. K.0.60. Government Printer, Box 37, Zomba, Malawi. Ed. James S. Friedlander. cum.index (1964-69)

341　　　　　UK　　ISSN 0076-6313
MELLAND SCHILL LECTURES ON INTERNATIONAL LAW. 1961. irreg. price varies. ‡ Manchester University Press, Oxford Rd., Manchester M13 9PL, England.

341　　　　　NE　　ISSN 0077-6440
NEDERLANDSE VERENIGING VOOR INTERNATIONAAL RECHT. MEDEDELINGEN. 1911. biennial. price varies. Kluwer B.V., Box 23, Deventer, Netherlands. Ed. M. Bos.

341　　　　　　　　　　　　NE
NETHERLANDS YEARBOOK OF INTERNATIONAL LAW. (Text in English) 1970. a. price varies. (T.M.C. Asser Institute) Sijthoff & Noordhoff International Publishers b.v., Box 4, 2400 MA Alphen aan den Rijn, Netherlands (U.S. address: 20010 Century Blvd., Germantown MD 20767) Ed. Ko Swan Sik. bk. rev. bibl. circ. 750. Indexed: Foreign Leg.Per.

ORGANIZATION OF AMERICAN STATES. PERMANENT COUNCIL. DECISIONS TAKEN AT MEETINGS (CUMULATED EDITION) see HISTORY — History Of North And South America

341.18　　　　　US　　ISSN 0553-0326
PAN AMERICAN ASSOCIATIONS IN THE UNITED STATES; A DIRECTORY WITH SUPPLEMENTARY LISTS OF OTHER ASSOCIATIONS. INTER-AMERICAN AND GENERAL. 1955. irreg. $1. Organization of American States, Department of Publications, Washington, DC 20006. circ. 2,000.

341　　　　　　　　　　　　PH
PHILIPPINE YEARBOOK OF INTERNATIONAL LAW. vol. 3, 1974. a. P.18($7) Philippine Society of International Law, University of the Philippines, College of Law, Diliman, Quezon City, Philippines. Ed. Esteban B. Bautista. bibl. stat.

341　　　　　PL　　ISSN 0554-498X
POLISH YEARBOOK OF INTERNATIONAL LAW/ANNUAIRE POLONAIS DE DROIT INTERNATIONAL. (Text in English and French) 1966/67. a. 120 Zl. (Polska Akademia Nauk, Instytut Nauk Prawnych) Ossolineum, Publishing House of the Polish Academy of Sciences, Rynek 9, Wroclaw, Poland (Dist. by: Ars Polona-Ruch, Krakowskie Przedmiescie 7, Warsaw, Poland) Ed. Janusz Symonides.

PRINCETON UNIVERSITY. CENTER OF INTERNATIONAL STUDIES. RESEARCH MONOGRAPH SERIES. see POLITICAL SCIENCE — International Relations

341 327   US   ISSN 0079-5267
PRINCETON UNIVERSITY. CENTER OF
INTERNATIONAL STUDIES POLICY
MEMORANDUM. 1952. irreg., no. 39, 1974. ‡
Princeton University, Center of International
Studies, Princeton, NJ 08544.

PRIVATE INVESTORS ABROAD; problems and
solutions in international business. see *BUSINESS
AND ECONOMICS — Investments*

341   NE
PROBLEMS IN PRIVATE INTERNATIONAL
LAW. 1977. irreg., vol. 2, 1978. price varies. North-
Holland Publishing Co., Box 211, 1000 AE
Amsterdam, Netherlands.

PUBLIC INTERNATIONAL LAW. see *LAW*

340 341   GW
RECHTSSTAAT IN DER BEWAEHRUNG. 1975.
irreg. price varies. C. F. Mueller Juristischer Verlag
GmbH, Im Weiher 10, Postfach 102640, 6900
Heidelberg 1, W. Germany (B.R.D.)

341   GW
SCHMERZENSGELD-BETRAEGE. biennial. DM.28.
ADAC Verlag GmbH, 8 Munich 70,
Baumgartnerstr. 53, Postfach 700086, W. Germany
(B.R.D.)

341   SA
SOUTH AFRICAN YEARBOOK OF
INTERNATIONAL LAW/SUID-AFRIKAANSE
JAARBOEK VIR VOLKEREG. 1975. a. R.13.50.
VerLoren van Themaat Centre for Public
International Law, University of South Africa,
Institute of Foreign and Comparative Law, Box 392,
Pretoria 0001, South Africa. Ed. H. Booysen. bk.
rev.

341   US   ISSN 0081-4326
STANFORD JOURNAL OF INTERNATIONAL
STUDIES. 1966. a. $5. Stanford University,
Stanford Law School, Stanford, CA 94305. bk. rev.
circ. 500. Indexed: Leg.Per. P.A.I.S. SSCI.
A.B.C.Pol.Sci. Ind.Per.Art.Relat.Law.

341   US   ISSN 0585-6795
STUDIES IN INTER-AMERICAN LAWS. 1968.
irreg. price varies. (Institute for Inter-American
Legal Studies) University of Miami, School of Law,
Coral Gables, FL 33124.

STUDIES IN INTERNATIONAL AFFAIRS. see
POLITICAL SCIENCE — International Relations

341   UN
U N I T A R CONFERENCE REPORTS. 1973.
irreg. price varies. United Nations Institute for
Training and Research, Publications Office, 801
United Nations Plaza, New York, NY 10017 (Order
from: United Nations Publications, Room LX-2300,
New York, NY 10017; or Distribution and Sales
Section, Palais des Nations, CH 1211 Geneva 10,
Switzerland) bk. rev.

341.7   UN
UNITED NATIONS. COMMISSION ON
INTERNATIONAL TRADE LAW. REPORT ON
THE WORK OF ITS SESSION. (Subseries of
United Nations. General Assembly. Official
Records. Supplement) 1968. a; latest issue, 1974. $2.
United Nations, Commission on International Trade
Law, United Nations Publications, Room LX-2300,
New York, NY 10017 (Or Distribution and Sales
Section, Palais des Nations, CH-1211 Geneva 10,
Switzerland)

341 382   UN
UNITED NATIONS. COMMISSION ON
INTERNATIONAL TRADE LAW. YEARBOOK.
a.; vol. 4, 1974. price varies. United Nations,
Commission on International Trade Law, United
Nations Publications, Room LX-2300, New York,
NY 10017 (Or Distribution and Sales Section,
Palais des Nations, CH-1211 Geneva 10,
Switzerland) bibl.

341   UN   ISSN 0082-8289
UNITED NATIONS. INTERNATIONAL LAW
COMMISSION. YEARBOOK. (Issued in 2
Volumes) (Text in English, French and Spanish)
1949. a. price varies. United Nations Publications,
LX 2300, New York, NY 10017 (Or Distribution
and Sales Section, Palais des Nations, CH-1211
Geneva 10, Switzerland)

341.2   UN   ISSN 0082-8319
UNITED NATIONS. MULTILATERAL TREATIES
IN RESPECT OF WHICH THE SECRETARY-
GENERAL PERFORMS DEPOSITARY
FUNCTIONS. (Text in English and French) 1959.
irreg.; annex., suppl. no. 6-31 Dec., 1974. price
varies. United Nations Publications, LX 2300, New
York, NY 10017 (Or Distribution and Sales Section,
Palais des Nations, CH-1211 Geneva 10,
Switzerland)

341   UN   ISSN 0082-8297
UNITED NATIONS JURIDICAL YEARBOOK.
(Text in English, French and Spanish) 1965. a. price
varies. United Nations Publications, LX 2300, New
York, NY 10017 (Or Distribution and Sales Section,
CH-1211 Geneva 10, Switzerland)

341   UN   ISSN 0082-8300
UNITED NATIONS LEGISLATIVE SERIES. 1948.
irreg.; vol. 16, 1974. price varies. United Nations
Publications, LX 2300, New York, NY 10017 (Or
Distribution and Sales Section, CH-1211 Geneva
10, Switzerland)

327 341.2   US   ISSN 0083-0186
U. S. DEPARTMENT OF STATE. TREATIES AND
OTHER INTERNATIONAL ACTS SERIES. 1946.
irreg., vol. 26, pt. 3, 1975. price varies. U.S.
Department of State, Bureau of Public Affairs,
Washington, DC 20250 (Orders to Supt. of
Documents, Washington, DC 20402)

341.2   US   ISSN 0083-0194
U. S. DEPARTMENT OF STATE. TREATIES IN
FORCE. 1956. a. price varies. U.S. Department of
State, Bureau of Public Affairs, Washington, DC
20250 (Orders to Supt. of Documents, Washington,
DC 20402)

327 341.2   US   ISSN 0083-3487
UNITED STATES TREATIES AND OTHER
INTERNATIONAL AGREEMENTS. 1950. a.
price varies. U.S. Department of State, Bureau of
Public Affairs, 2201 C St. N.W., Washington, DC
20250 (Orders to Supt. of Documents, Washington,
DC 20402)

341 327   GW   ISSN 0341-3241
UNIVERSITAET HAMBURG. INSTITUT FUER
INTERNATIONALE ANGELEGENHEITEN.
WERKHEFTE. 1965. irreg., vol. 33, 1976. price
varies. Alfred Metzner Verlag GmbH, Zeppelinallee
43, Postfach 970148, 6000 Frankfurt 97, W.
Germany (B.R.D.) (Co-Sponsor: Deutscher Verein
fuer Internationales Seerecht)
 Formerly: Forschungstelle fuer Voelkerrecht und
Auslaendisches Oeffentliches Recht. Werkhefte
(ISSN 0072-9493)

341   FR
UNIVERSITE DE NANCY II. FACULTE DE
DROIT ET DES SCIENCES ECONOMIQUES.
ETUDES ET TRAVAUX. SERIE DROIT
INTERNATIONAL PUBLIC. 1973. irreg. 35 F.
Universite de Nancy II, Faculte de Droit et des
Sciences Economiques, Service des Publications,
B.P. 454, 54001 Nancy, France. circ. 200.

WIENER RECHTSWISSENSCHAFTLICHE
STUDIEN. see *LAW*

341.448   US
WORLDWIDE REPORT: LAW OF THE SEA. irreg.
(approx. 23/yr.) $115. U.S. Joint Publications
Research Service, 1000 N. Glebe Rd., Arlington,
VA 22201 (Orders to: NTIS, Springfield, VA
22161)
 Formerly: Translations on Law of the Sea.

LEATHER AND FUR INDUSTRIES

see also *Clothing Trade; Shoes and Boots*

675.2   NE   ISSN 0067-4834
BEDRIJFSCHAP VOOR DE
LEDERWARENINDUSTRIE. JAARVERSLAG.
1957. a. fl.10. ‡ Bedrijfschap voor de
Lederwarenindustrie, Reitseplein 1, Tilburg,
Netherlands. Ed. L. Ploeger. circ. 400.

636.088   US
BLUE BOOK OF FUR FARMING. 1943. a. $12.
Communications Marketing, Inc., 5100 Edina
Industrial Blvd., Edina, MN 55435. adv. circ. 3,100.

685.2   CN
CANADIAN FUR TRADE DIRECTORY. 1978. a.
Can.$20. Publicon Publishing Ltd., 4626 St.
Catherine W., Montreal, Que. H3Z 1S3, Canada.
Ed. Elizabeth Ruggier. adv. circ. 6,000. (back issues
avail.)

685   US
CLASSIFIED FUR SOURCE DIRECTORY. 1939. a.
Fur Age Weekly, 127 W. 30th St., New York, NY
10001.

385   NE
ECONOMISCH INSTITUUT VOOR HET
MIDDEN- EN KLEINBEDRIJF.
BEDRIJFSGEGEVENS VOOR DE
DETAILHANDEL IN KOFFERS EN
LEDERWAREN. (Subseries of:
Bedrijfseconomische Publicaties) irreg. Economisch
Instituut voor het Midden- en Kleinbedrijf,
Neuhuyskade 94, Postbus 96818, 2509 JE The
Hague, Netherlands.

685   GW   ISSN 0070-9530
EINKAUFSFUEHRER DURCH DIE PELZ- UND
LEDERMODE. 1968. a. DM.31. Otto Teubel
Verlag, Heinrich-Stamme-Str. 6, 3000 Hannover, W.
Germany (B.R.D.)

675   BL
INSTITUTO BRASILEIRO DO COURO,
CALCADOS E AFINS. SISTEMA DE
INFORMACAO ESTATISTICA PARA E
INDUSTRIA NACIONAL DE COUROS:
BOLETIM DE INFORMACOES. irreg. Instituto
Brasileiro do Couro, Calcados e Afins, Caixa Posta,
48, Estancia Velha 93600, Brazil. stat.

675   SA   ISSN 0085-2724
L I R I RESEARCH BULLETIN. 1942. irreg.
(approx. 20/yr.) price varies. Rhodes University,
Leather Industries Research Institute, Box 185,
Grahamstown 6140, South Africa. charts. illus.

675   SA
L I R I TECHNICAL BULLETIN. 1975. irreg.(10/
yr.) Rhodes University, Leather Industries Research
Institute, Box 185, Grahamstown 6140, South Africa.

685 685.31   JA
LEATHER & FOOTWEARS/KAWA TO
HAKIMONO. (Text in Japanese) irreg. Tokyo-to
Sangyo Rodo Kaikan, 1-1-6 Hashiba, Taito-ku,
Tokyo, Japan. illus.

675.2   US   ISSN 0075-8345
LEATHER BUYERS GUIDE AND LEATHER
TRADE MARKS. 1963. a. $8 (free with subscr. to
Leather and Shoes) Rumpf Publishing Division
(Subsidiary of: Nickerson & Collins Co.) 1800
Oakton St., Des Plaines, IL 60018. Ed. Elmer J.
Rumpf. index.

675.2   UK
LEATHER GUIDE. 1970. a. £18. Benn Publications
Ltd., 25 New Street Square, London EC4A 3JA,
England. Ed. A. Mulvany. adv. index. circ. 1,104.
 Formerly: European Leather Guide (ISSN 0071-
2906)

685   II
LEXPORT. vol. 11, 1974/75. a. Export Promotion
Council for Finished Leather & Leather
Manufacturers, 15-46 Civil Lines, Box 198, Kanpur
208001, India.

675   UK
MASTER SADDLERS YEARBOOK. 1968. a.
membership. Society of Master Saddlers, 9 St
Thomas Street, London S.E.1, England. Ed. Roy
Britter. adv.

338.7   II   ISSN 0302-4881
RAJASTHAN STATE TANNERIES LIMITED.
ANNUAL REPORT. (Text in English) 1973. a.
Rajasthan State Tanneries Limited, P-6 Tilak Marg,
C Scheme, Jaipur, India. Key Title: Annual Report-
Rajasthan State Tanneries Limited.

675.3   CN   ISSN 0581-8389
SASKATCHEWAN FUR MARKETING SERVICE.
ANNUAL REPORT. 1958. a. Saskatchewan Fur
Marketing Service, Regina, Sask., Canada.

LEATHER AND FUR INDUSTRIES — Abstracting, Bibliographies, Statistics

338.4   CN   ISSN 0384-4811
CANADA. STATISTICS CANADA. MISCELLANEOUS LEATHER PRODUCTS MANUFACTURERS/FABRICANTS D'ARTICLES DIVERS EN CUIR. (Catalogue 33-205) (Text in English & French) 1920. a. Can.$4.50($5.40) Statistics Canada, Publications Distribution, Ottawa, Ont. K1A 0V7, Canada. (also avail. in microform from MML)

636.088   CN   ISSN 0318-7888
CANADA. STATISTICS CANADA. REPORT ON FUR FARMS/RAPPORT SUR LES FERMES A FOURRURE. (Catalog 23-208) (Text in English and French) 1919. a. Can.$4.50($5.40) Statistics Canada, Publications Distribition, Ottawa, Ont. K1A 0V7, Canada. (also avail. in microform from MML)

LIBRARY AND INFORMATION SCIENCES

see also Bibliographies

026   US
A A L S LIBRARY STATISTICS. a. Association of American Law Schools, Committee on Libraries, One Dupont Circle, Suite 370, Washington, DC 20036. illus.

020   GW   ISSN 0340-3440
A B T INFORMATIONEN. (Arbeitsberichte zur Bibliothekstechnik) 1969. irreg., no. 23, 1977. free. Deutsches Bibliotheksinstitut, Bereich Anwendung der Datenverarbeitung, Potsdamer Str. 33, 1000 Berlin 30, W. Germany (B.R.D.) Ed. Christoph Mueller. circ. 950(controlled)

020   FR   ISSN 0066-9210
A D B S ANNUAIRE. 1966. a. 50 F. Association Francaise des Documentalistes et des Bibliothecaires Specialises, 63 bis, rue du Cardinal-Lemoine, 75005 Paris, France. circ. 1,500.

020   EI   ISSN 0571-6357
A I L/DOC. irreg. Association of International Libraries, c/o Commission of the European Communities, Library Luxembourg, Batiment Jean Monnet, Boite Postale 1907, Luxembourg.

020   US   ISSN 0065-907X
A L A STUDIES IN LIBRARIANSHIP. 1971. irreg., 1971, no. 2. price varies. American Library Association, 50 E. Huron St., Chicago, IL 60611.

020   US   ISSN 0001-1746
A L A WASHINGTON NEWSLETTER. 1949. irreg., minimum 12/yr. $10. American Library Association, Washington Office, Box 54, 110 Maryland Ave., N.E., Washington, DC 20002. Ed. Eileen D. Cooke, Carol C. Henderson. circ. 1,900. (processed)

020.6   US   ISSN 0364-1597
A L A YEARBOOK; a review of library events of previous year. 1976. a. price varies. American Library Association, 50 E. Huron St., Chicago, IL 60611. illus. index.

020.6   US   ISSN 0361-5669
A R L ANNUAL SALARY SURVEY. 1968. a. $5. Association of Research Libraries, 1527 New Hampshire Ave., N.W., Washington, DC 20036. Ed. Carol A. Mandel.

020   CN   ISSN 0316-0963
A. S. T. E. D. NOUVELLES. (Text in English and French) 1973. irreg. membership. A. S. T. E. D. Inc., 360 rue le Moyne, Montreal, Que. H2Y 1Y3, Canada. circ. 1,000. (looseleaf format; back issues avail.)

029   IS
ABSTRACTING AND INDEXING SERVICES IN SPECIAL LIBRARIES IN ISRAEL. irreg. I£100($25) (National Council for Research and Development) National Center of Scientific and Technological Information, P.O. Box 20125, Tel-Aviv, Israel. Ed. L. Vilentchuk.

020   SW   ISSN 0065-1060
ACTA BIBLIOTHECAE REGIAE STOCKHOLMIENSIS. 1961. irreg. price varies. Kungliga Biblioteket, Box 5039, 102 41 Stockholm, Sweden.

020   SW   ISSN 0065-1079
ACTA BIBLIOTHECAE UNIVERSITATIS GOTHOBURGENSIS. 1941. irreg., no. 19, 1977. price varies; also exchange basis. Goeteborgs Universitet, Universitetsbibliotek, Centralbiblioteket, Box 5096, S-402 22 Goeteborg 5, Sweden (Dist. in U.S., Canada and Mexico by: Humanities Press, Inc., 171 First Ave., Atlantic Highlands, NJ 07716) Formerly: Acta Bibliothecae Gothoburgensis.

010 020   HU   ISSN 0001-7175
ACTA UNIVERSITATIS SZEGEDIENSIS DE ATTILA JOZSEF NOMINATAE. ACTA BIBLIOTHECARIA. (Text in Hungarian, German or English; summaries in English, French, German, Italian or Russian) 1955. irreg., vol. 8, 1979. 50 Ft.($4.) exchange price. Jozsef Attila Tudomanyegyetem, Kozponti Konyvtar, Dugonics ter 13, Szeged, Hungary (Subscr. to: Kultura, Box 149, H-1389 Budapest, Hungary) Ed. Bela Karacsonyi. circ. 500.

029.7 651.8   US   ISSN 0065-2784
ADVANCES IN INFORMATION SYSTEMS SCIENCE. 1969. irreg. price varies. Plenum Press, 233 Spring St., New York, NY 10013. Ed. J. T. Tou.

020   US   ISSN 0065-2830
ADVANCES IN LIBRARIANSHIP. 1970. irreg., vol. 8, 1978. price varies. Academic Press, Inc., 111 Fifth Ave., New York, NY 10003. Ed. Melvin J. Voigt. (also avail. in microfiche)

020   IS
AL SAFARIM VE-KORIM/ON BOOKS AND READERS; mivhar avodot talmidin/students' theses and papers. 1970. irreg. price varies. Hebrew University of Jerusalem, Graduate School of Library & Archive Studies, Box 503, Jerusalem, Israel. Ed. Bd. adv. circ. 500.

027.4   US
ALABAMA. PUBLIC LIBRARY SERVICE. ANNUAL REPORT. 1956. a. Public Library Service, 6030 Monticello Dr., Montgomery, AL 36130. (also avail. in microform from EDR) Supersedes: Alabama. Public Library Service. Basic State Plan and Annual Program (ISSN 0095-361X)

020   US
ALABAMA DEPARTMENT OF EDUCATION. LIBRARY MEDIA OUTPUT. vol.2,1975. irreg. free. Department of Education, Montgomery, AL 36104.

021   US
ALASKA LIBRARIES AND LIBRARY PERSONNEL DIRECTORY. 1973. a. Alaska Library Association, c/o Audrey Kolb, Ed., 1215 Cowles St., Fairbanks, AK 99701 (Subscr. to: University Library, University of Alaska, Fairbanks, Ak 99701) circ. controlled.

027.5   CN   ISSN 0704-8734
ALBERTA. GOVERNMENT LIBRARIES COUNCIL. ANNUAL REVIEWS. 1975. a. Government Libraries Council, 406 Natural Resources Bldg., 109th St. & 99th Ave., Edmonton, Alta. T5K 2E1, Canada.

027   CN   ISSN 0383-3712
ALBERTA. LEGISLATURE LIBRARY. ANNUAL REPORT. 1975. a. free. Legislative Assembly, Library, 216 Legislature Bldg., Edmonton, Alta. T5K 2B6, Canada. circ. 250.

AMERICAN INDIAN LIBRARIES NEWSLETTER. see *ETHNIC INTERESTS*

020   US
AMERICAN LIBRARY ASSOCIATION. ANNUAL CONFERENCE PROGRAM. a. American Library Association, Conference Arrangements Office, 50 E. Huron St., Chicago, IL 60611. Ed. Mary Cilluffo. adv. circ. 8,000-14,000.

020   US   ISSN 0065-910X
AMERICAN LIBRARY DIRECTORY. 1908. a. $59.95. (Jaques Cattell Press) R. R. Bowker Company, 1180 Ave. of the Americas, New York, NY 10036 (Orders to: Box 1807, Ann Arbor, MI 48106) (reprint service avail. from UMI)

AMERICAN LIBRARY LAWS. see *LAW*

AMERICAN PETROLEUM INSTITUTE. CENTRAL ABSTRACTING AND INDEXING SERVICE. THESAURUS. see *PETROLEUM AND GAS*

020   CN   ISSN 0318-9937
AMERICAN SOCIETY FOR INFORMATION SCIENCE, WESTERN CANADA CHAPTER. ANNUAL MEETING PROCEEDINGS. 1969. a. price varies. American Society for Information Science, Western Canada Chapter, c/o G. A. Cooke, 8734 119th St., Edmonton, Alta. T6G 1W8, Canada. circ. 150. (back issues avail.)

025   US   ISSN 0066-0868
AMERICAN THEOLOGICAL LIBRARY ASSOCIATION. CONFERENCE. SUMMARY OF PROCEEDINGS. 1947. a. $10. American Theological Library Association, Lutheran Theological Seminary, 7301 Germantown Ave., Philadelphia, PA 19119. Ed. Rev. David J. Wartluft. 25 yr. cum. index 1973. circ. 675(a p) (also avail. in microfilm) Indexed: Rel.Ind.One.

001.5   US   ISSN 0066-4200
ANNUAL REVIEW OF INFORMATION SCIENCE AND TECHNOLOGY. 1966. a. $42.50 to nonmembers. (American Society for Information Science) Knowledge Industry Publications Inc., 701 Westchester Ave., White Plains, NY 10604. Ed. Martha E. Williams. bibl. index; cum.index vols.1-10. Indexed: SSCI.

027.4 026   SP
ANUARIO DE LA BIBLIOTECA DE LA CATALUNA Y DE LAS POPULARES Y ESPECIALES DE BARCELONA. 1939. a. 350 ptas. Diputacion Provincial de Barcelona, Servicios de Bibliotecas, Biblioteca de Catalunya, Carmen, No. 47, Barcelona 1, Spain. stat.

020   US
APPLICATIONS OF LIBRARY SCIENCE. 1970. irreg., vol. 5, 1975. price varies. Armadillo Press, P.O. Box 8131, University of Texas Station, Austin, TX 78712.

020   GW   ISSN 0518-2220
ARBEITSGEMEINSCHAFT DER PARLAMENTS- UND BEHOERDENBIBLIOTHEKEN. ARBEITSHEFTE. 1958. a. Arbeitsgemeinschaft der Parlaments- und Behoerdenbibliotheken, Bibliothek des Deutschen Bundestages, Bundeshaus, 5300 Bonn, W. Germany (B.R.D.)

027.7   GW
ARBEITSGEMEINSCHAFT KATHOLISCH-THEOLOGISCHER BIBLIOTHEKEN. MITTEILUNGSBLATT. 1952. 2/yr. DM.12. Arbeitsgemeinschaft Katholisch-Theologischer Bibliotheken, Erzbischoefliche Dioezesanbibliothek, Gereonstr. 2-4, 5000 Cologne 1, W. Germany (B.R.D.) Ed.Wilhelm Schoenartz. bk. rev. cum.index. circ. 250.

025.17   UK   ISSN 0066-653X
ARCHIVES AND THE USER. 1970. irreg. price varies. British Records Association, The Charterhouse, Charterhouse Sq., London EC1M 6AU, England. Ed. Andrew S. Cook.

029   PH
ARCHIVINIANA. (Text in English) 1968. a. National Archives, Bureau of Records Management, c/o National Library Building, Box 779, Manila, Philippines. Ed. Dr. Domingo Abella. circ. 500.

930.25   AG   ISSN 0325-2868
ARCHIVO GENERAL DE LA NACION. REVISTA. (Suspended during 1975) 1971. a. Arg.$3000. Archivo General de la Nacion, Leandro N. Alem 246, 1003 Buenos Aires, Argentina. Ed. Cesar A. Garcia. bk. rev. bibl. circ. 1,000.
Archives

LIBRARY AND INFORMATION SCIENCES

020   GW   ISSN 0066-6793
ARCHIVUM; REVUE INTERNATIONALE DES ARCHIVES. (Text in English, French, German, Spanish, Italian) 1951. a. $26.80. (International Council on Archives, FR.) Verlag Dokumentation, Poessenbacherstr. 2, Postfach 711009, 8000 Munich 71, W. Germany (B.R.D.) Ed. Michel Duchein. Indexed: Hist.Abstr. A.B.C.Pol.Sci. Amer.Hist. & Life.

020   UK   ISSN 0066-8524
ASLIB MEMBERSHIP LIST. irreg. Aslib, 3 Belgrave Sq., London SW1X 8PL, England.

020   UK   ISSN 0066-8532
ASLIB OCCASIONAL PUBLICATIONS. 1968. irreg.; no. 23, 1980. Aslib, 3 Belgrave Square, London SW1X 8PL, England.

020   CR   ISSN 0004-4784
ASOCIACION COSTARRICENSE DE BIBLIOTECARIOS. BOLETIN. 1955. irreg. free. ‡ Asociacion Costarricense de Bibliotecarios, Apdo. 3308, San Jose, Costa Rica. circ. 500. Indexed: Lib.Sci.Abstr.

020.6   MX
ASOCIACION DE BIBLIOTECARIOS DE INSTITUCIONES DE ENSENANZA SUPERIOR E INVESTIGACION. ARCHIVOS. 1976. irreg. Asociacion de Bibliotecarios de Instituciones de Ensenanza Superior e Investigaciones, Apartado Postal 5-611, Mexico 5, D.F., Mexico.

020.6   MX
ASOCIACION DE BIBLIOTECARIOS DE INSTITUCIONES DE ENSENANZA SUPERIOR E INVESTIGACIONES. CUADERNOS. 1976. irreg. Asociacion de Bibliotecarios de Instituciones de Ensenanza Superior e Investigaciones, Apartado Postal 5-611, Mexico 5,D.F., Mexico.

026   NQ
ASOCIACION DE BIBLIOTECAS UNIVERSITARIAS Y ESPECIALIZADAS DE NICARAGUA. BOLETIN. 1971. a. free. ‡ Asociacion de Bibliotecas Universitarias y Especializadas de Nicaragua, Apartado 68, Leon, Nicaragua. Ed. Walterio Lopez Adaros. illus. circ. 400.

ASOCIACION INTERAMERICANA DE BIBLIOTECARIOS Y DOCUMENTALISTAS AGRICOLAS. BOLETIN ESPECIAL. see *AGRICULTURE*

020   VE   ISSN 0066-8591
ASOCIACION VENEZOLANA DE ARCHIVEROS. COLECCION DOCTRINA.* 1970. irreg. Asociacion Venezolana de Archiveros, Archivo General de la Nacion, Santa Capilla a Carmelitas 15, Av. Urdaneta, Caracas 100, Venezuela.

020   FR   ISSN 0066-8877
ASSOCIATION DE L'ECOLE NATIONALE SUPERIEURE DES BIBLIOTHECAIRES. ANNUAIRE. 1969. biennial. 40 F. ‡ Association de l'Ecole Nationale Superieure des Bibliothecaires, 17-21 Bd. du 11 Novembre, 69100 Villeurbanne, France. adv. circ. 1,200.

020.6   FR   ISSN 0066-8931
ASSOCIATION DES BIBLIOTHECAIRES FRANCAIS. ANNUAIRE. 1906. triennial. Editions Person, 34 rue de Penthievre, 75008 Paris, France. circ. 3,000.

020   US
ASSOCIATION OF AMERICAN LIBRARY SCHOOLS. DIRECTORY. (Special annual edition of Journal of Education for Librarianship) a. $5. Association of American Library Schools, 471 Park Lane, State College, PA 16801. Ed. Janet Phillips. circ. 2,000.

020   US
ASSOCIATION OF JEWISH LIBRARIES. PROCEEDINGS OF THE ANNUAL CONVENTION. a. price varies. Association of Jewish Libraries, c/o National Foundation for Jewish Culture, 122 E. 42nd St., Rm. 1512, New York, NY 10017.

020   658   US
ASSOCIATION OF RESEARCH LIBRARIES. UNIVERSITY LIBRARY MANAGEMENT STUDIES OFFICE. MANAGEMENT SUPPLEMENT. 1972. irreg. $5 per no. Association of Research Libraries, Office of University Library Management Studies, 1527 New Hampshire N.W., Washington, DC 20036. Ed. Maxine K. Sitts. circ. 500. (back issues avail.)

025   US   ISSN 0091-4479
ASSOCIATION OF RESEARCH LIBRARIES. UNIVERSITY LIBRARY MANAGEMENT STUDIES OFFICE. OCCASIONAL PAPER. 1971. irreg. $5 per issue. Association of Research Libraries, Office of University Library Management Studies, 1527 New Hampshire Ave. N.W., Washington, DC 20036. Ed. Maxine K. Sitts. Key Title: Occasional Papers - Office of University Library Management Studies.

020   CN   ISSN 0316-0955
ASSOCIATION POUR L'AVANCEMENT DES SCIENCES ET DES TECHNIQUES DE LA DOCUMENTATION. RAPPORT. 1945. a. Association pour l'Avancement des Sciences et des Techniques de la Documentation, 360, Rue le Moyne, Montreal H2Y 1Y3, Quebec, Canada. circ. 1,200.
Formerly: Association Canadienne des Bibliothecaires de Langue Francaise. Rapport (ISSN 0066-8826)

020   IT   ISSN 0519-2048
ASSOCIAZIONE ITALIANA BIBLIOTECHE. QUADERNI DEL BOLLETTINO D'INFORMAZIONI. (Supplement to: Associazione Italiana Biblioteche. Bollettino d'Informazioni) 1965. irreg., no. 6, 1978. price varies. Associazione Italiana Biblioteche, c/o Istituto di Patologia del Libro, Via Milano 76, 00184 Rome, Italy. Ed. Olga Marinelli. circ. 1,000. (back issues avail)

026   CN   ISSN 0708-0263
AT A GLANCE. 1978. irreg. free contr. circ. Canadian Association of Special Libraries and Information Services, Edmonton Chapter, 82 Fairway Drive, Edmonton, Alta. T6J 2C5, Canada.

027.5   AT   ISSN 0312-259X
AUSTRALIA. NATIONAL LIBRARY. ACQUISITIONS NEWSLETTER. 1970. irreg. National Library of Australia, Sales and Subscriptions Unit, Canberra, A.C.T. 2600, Australia.

020   AT   ISSN 0069-0082
AUSTRALIA. NATIONAL LIBRARY. ANNUAL REPORT OF THE COUNCIL. 1961. a. Aus.$2.50. National Library of Australia, Sales and Subscription Unit, Canberra, A.C.T. 2600, Australia.

021   AT   ISSN 0310-8856
AUSTRALIAN ADVISORY COUNCIL ON BIBLIOGRAPHICAL SERVICES. LIBRARY SERVICES FOR AUSTRALIA. 1971. a. Aus.$5.95. Australian Advisory Council on Bibliographical Services, c/o National Library of Australia, Canberra, A.C.T. 2600, Australia. circ. 500.

027   US   ISSN 0067-3412
BANCROFTIANA. 1950. 3-4/yr. membership. (Friends of the Bancroft Library) University of California, Berkeley, Bancroft Library, Berkeley, CA 94720. cum.index: 1950-1966.

020   FR   ISSN 0067-3951
BANQUE DES MOTS. irreg. 105 F. (Conseil International de la Langue Francaise) Presses Universitaires de France, 108 Bd. Saint Germain, 75279 Paris Cedex 6, France (Service des Periodiques, 12 rue Jean de Beauvais, 75005 Paris)

020   GW   ISSN 0342-0221
BAYERISCHE STAATSBIBLIOTHEK, MUNICH. JAHRESBERICHT. 1972. a. Bayerische Staatsbibliothek, Ludwigstr. 16, 8000 Munich 34, W. Germany (B.R.D.)

020   GW   ISSN 0408-8107
BEITRAEGE ZUM BUCH- UND BIBLIOTHEKSWESEN. 1965. irreg., vol. 17, 1979. price varies. Verlag Otto Harrassowitz, Taunusstr. 6, Postfach 2929, 6200 Wiesbaden, W. Germany (B.R.D.) Ed. Carl Wehmer.

020   GW
BEITRAEGE ZUR INFORMATIONS- UND DOKUMENTATIONSWISSENSCHAFT. irreg., vol. 12, 1978. price varies. (Freie Universitaet Berlin, Institut fuer Publizistik) K.G. Saur Verlag KG, Poessenbacherstr. 12 B, Postfach 711009, 8000 Munich 71, W. Germany (B.R.D.) (And 175 Fifth Ave., New York, NY 10010) Ed. Gernot Wersig.

BEITRAEGE ZUR INKUNABELKUNDE. DRITTE FOLGE. see *PUBLISHING AND BOOK TRADE*

026   US   ISSN 0362-6881
BENTLEY LIBRARY ANNUAL. a. University of Michigan, Bentley Historical Library, Ann Arbor, MI 48104. illus.

020   016   GE
BERGAKADEMIE FREIBERG. WISSENSCHAFTLICHES INFORMATIONSZENTRUM. VEROEFFENTLICHUNGEN. 1964. irreg., no. 68, 1975. Bergakademie Freiberg, Wissenschaftliches Informationszentrum, Akademiestr. 6, 92 Freiberg, E. Germany (D.D.R.) Ed. Dieter Schmidmaier.

020   US   ISSN 0067-6357
BETA PHI MU CHAPBOOK. 1953. irreg., no. 10, 1974. price varies. Beta Phi Mu, International Honor Society, c/o University of Pittsburgh, Graduate School of Library and Information Sciences, Pittsburgh, PA 15260. Ed. Wayne A. Wiegand. Indexed: LISA. Lib.Lit.

020   GW
BETRIEBSSTATISTIK WISSENSCHAFTLICHER BIBLIOTHEKEN. 1974. a. DM.10. Deutsches Bibliotheksinstitut, Bundesallee 185, 1000 Berlin 31, W. Germany (B.R.D.) (Co-sponsor: Verein Deutscher Bibliothekare e.V.) Ed. R.H. Meyer.

015   029.7   BL   ISSN 0067-6624
BIBLIOGRAFIA BRASILEIRA DE DOCUMENTACAO. 1811; N.S. 1960. irreg. Cr.$250($12) Instituto Brasileiro de Informacao em Ciencia e Tecnologia, Rio de Janeiro, Brazil. bk. rev. circ. 300.

020   CN   ISSN 0067-687X
BIBLIOGRAPHICAL SOCIETY OF CANADA. FACSIMILE SERIES. 1951. irreg. Can.$10 for latest no. Bibliographical Society of Canada, Box 1878, Guelph, Ont. N1H 7A1, Canada. circ. 360.

020   CN   ISSN 0067-6888
BIBLIOGRAPHICAL SOCIETY OF CANADA. MONOGRAPHS. 1957. irreg. price varies. Bibliographical Society of Canada, Box 1878, Guelph, Ont. N1H 7A1, Canada. circ. 360.

020   SP
BIBLIOTECA ESTUDIOS ESCELICER. 1973. irreg. 457 ptas. Escelicer S.A., Comandante Azcarraga s/n, Madrid 16, Spain.

020   AO
BIBLIOTECA NACIONAL DE ANGOLA. NOVAS.* irreg. Biblioteca Nacional, Caixa Postal 2915, Luanda, Angola. illus.

020   PO
BIBLIOTECAS E ARQUIVOS DE PORTUGAL. 1969. irreg. free. Direccao Geral do Patrimonio Cultural, Rua Occidental Ao Campo Grande 83, 1799 Lisbon Codex, Portugal.

020   MX
BIBLIOTECAS Y ARCHIVOS. a. $4. Escuela Nacional de Biblioteconomia y Archivonomia, Viaducto M. Aleman 155, Col. Alamos, Mexico 13, D.F., Mexico. Ed. Guillermo Oropeza Quiroz. bibl. charts. circ. 1,200. (back issues avail.) Indexed: Ref.Zh. I.R.E.B.I. Lib.Sci.Abstr.

020.7   SP   ISSN 0006-1778
BIBLIOTECONOMIA. 1944. irreg. 1975, no. 79. price varies. Escuela de Bibliotecarias, Diputacion Provincial de Barcelona, 56 Calle Hospital, Barcelona 1, Spain. bk. rev. bibl. illus. index. Indexed: Lib.Lit.

LIBRARY AND INFORMATION SCIENCES

020 PL ISSN 0067-768X
BIBLIOTEKA KORNICKA. PAMIETNIK. (Text in Polish; summaries in English) 1929. irreg., vol. 15, 1979. price varies. (Polska Akademia Nauk) Ossolineum, Publishing House of the Polish Academy of Sciences, Rynek 9, Wroclaw, Poland (Dist. by Ars Polona-Ruch, Krakowskie Przedmiescie 7, Warsaw, Poland) (Co-Sponsor: Biblioteka Kornicka) Eds. Stefan Weyman and Marceli Kosman. circ. 700. (also avail. in microfilm)

020 PL ISSN 0083-7261
BIBLIOTEKA NARODOWA. ROCZNIK. (List of contents in English, French, German, Russian; summaries in English) 1964. a. 90 Zl. Biblioteka Narodowa, Ul. Hankiewicza 1, 00-973 Warsaw, Poland. Ed. Witold Stankiewicz. bk. rev. circ. 860.

020 PL
BIBLIOTEKA SLASKA. BIULETYN INFORMACYJNY. 1956. a. free of charge. Biblioteka Slaska, Ul. Francuska 12, 40-015 Katowice, Poland. bk. rev. bibl. cum. index (5 yrs.)

020 UR
BIBLIOTEKOVEDENIE, BIBLIOGRAFIYA I INFORMATIKA. 1974. irreg. 0.60 Rub. Moskovskii Gosudarstvennyi Institut Kul'tury, Moscow, U.S.S.R.

020 016 BU
BIBLIOTEKOZNANIE, BIBLIOGRAFIIA, KNIGOZNANIE, NAUCHNA INFORMATSIIA. 1968. a. $2 per volume. Narodna Biblioteka "Kiril i Metodii", 11, Tolbukhin Blvd., 1504 Sofia, Bulgaria. Ed. Snezina Kotova. circ. 500.

027 DK ISSN 0084-957X
BIBLIOTEKSAARBOG. 1939. a. Kr.113($20) Danmarks Biblioteksforening - Danish Library Association, Trekronergade 15, DK-2500 Copenhagen V, Denmark. Ed. Christian Goetzsche. circ. 1,700.

070 GW ISSN 0340-8051
BIBLIOTHEK DES BUCHWESENS (B B) 1972. irreg., vol. 7, 1981. price varies. Anton Hiersemann Verlag, Rosenbergstr. 113, Postfach 723, 7000 Stuttgart 1, W. Germany (B.R.D.) Ed. R. W. Fuchs.

020 GW ISSN 0067-8236
BIBLIOTHEK UND WISSENSCHAFT. (Text in English, French, German and Italian) 1964. a. DM.98 (approx.) (Deutsche Forschungsgemeinschaft) Verlag Otto Harrassowitz, Taunusstr. 6, Postfach 2929, 6200 Wiesbaden, W. Germany (B.R.D.) Eds. Udo Hoegy, Hellmut Vogeler. adv. circ. 600.

020 GW ISSN 0069-5858
BIBLIOTHEKAR-LEHRINSTITUT DES LANDES NORDRHEIN-WESTFALEN. ARBEITEN AUS DEM B L I. 1953. irreg. price varies. Greven Verlag Koeln, Neue Weyerstr. 1-3, 5000 Cologne 1, W. Germany (B.R.D.)

020 GW ISSN 0300-287X
BIBLIOTHEKSPRAXIS. irreg., vol. 22, 1978. price varies. K.G. Saur Verlag KG, Poessenbacherstr. 12 B, Postfach 711009, 8000 Munich 71, W. Germany (B.R.D.) (And 175 Fifth Ave., New York, NY 10010) Ed.Bd.

020 GW
BIBLIOTHEKSSTUDIEN. irreg, no. 2, 1974. price varies. K.G. Saur Verlag KG, Poessenbacherstr. 12 B, Postfach 711009, 8000 Munich 71, W. Germany (B.R.D.) (And 175 Fifth Ave., New York, NY 10010) Ed. Harro Heim.

027.4 SZ
BIBLIOTHEQUE PUBLIQUE ET UNIVERSITAIRE DE GENEVE.COMPTE RENDU. 1878. a. free. Bibliotheque Publique et Universitaire de Geneve, Promenade des Bastions, CH-1211 Geneva 4, Switzerland. (Co-sponsor: Institut et Musee Voltaire) stat.

025 BE ISSN 0524-7624
BIBLIOTHEQUE ROYALE ALBERT 1ER. ACQUISITIONS MAJEURES. Dutch edition: Koninklijke Bibliotheek Albert I. Voorname Aanwinsten. (Former name of issuing body: Bibliotheque Royale de Belgique) (Text in French or Dutch) 1964. a. free to institutions. ‡ Bibliotheque Royale Albert 1er, Boulevard de l'Empereur, 4, B-1000 Brussels, Belgium. illus.

020 BE
BIBLIOTHEQUE ROYALE ALBERT 1ER. RAPPORT ANNUEL. Dutch edition: Koninklijke Bibliotheek Albert I. Jaarverslag. a. free to institutions. Bibliotheque Royale Albert 1er, 4 blvd. de l'Empereur, 1000 Brussels, Belgium. stat.
Formerly: Bibliotheque Royale de Belgique. Rapport Annuel.

020 BE ISSN 0067-8538
BIJDRAGEN TOT DE BIBLIOTHECKWETENSCHAP/ CONTRIBUTIONS TO LIBRARY SCIENCE. 1961. irreg., no. 3, 1967. price varies. Rijksuniversiteit te Gent, Centrale Bibliotheek, B-9000 Ghent, Belgium.

029 UK ISSN 0520-2795
BLISS CLASSIFICATION BULLETIN. 1954. a. £4($10) to schools; individuals £2 ($5) Bliss Classification Association, c/o Library, Commonwealth Institute, Kensington High St., London W8 6NQ, England. Ed. J. Mills. circ. 200.

020 UK ISSN 0067-9488
BODLEIAN LIBRARY RECORD. 1938. irreg. price varies. Bodleian Library, Oxford OX1 3BG, England. Ed. Miss G. M. Briggs. index. circ. 2,000. (also avail. in microfilm from UMI) Indexed: Br.Hum.Ind. M.L.A.

BOLETIN INTERAMERICANO DE ARCHIVOS. see HISTORY — History Of North And South America

020 GW ISSN 0068-0028
BONNER BEITRAEGE ZUR BIBLIOTHEKS- UND BUECHERKUNDE. 1954. irreg., vol. 27, 1978. price varies. Bouvier Verlag Herbert Grundmann, Am Hof 32, Postfach 1268, 5300 Bonn 1, W. Germany (B.R.D.) Ed. Richard Mummendey.

021.7 US ISSN 0006-7393
BOOKMARK. 1944. irreg., no. 46, 1976. free. (Friends of the University of North Carolina Library) University of North Carolina, Library, Wilson Library 024-A, Chapel Hill, NC 27515. Ed. Dr. Harry Bergholz.

020 US ISSN 0006-7407
BOOKMARK; news about library services. 1949. irreg., approx. q. $1.50. State Library, Albany, NY 12224. Ed. R. Edwin Berry. bibl. circ. 5,000. (also avail. in microform from UMI) Indexed: Lib.Lit. P.A.I.S.

020 686 AT ISSN 0310-0391
BOOKMARK. 1974. a. price varies. Australian Library Promotions Council, State Library of Victoria, 328 Swanston St., Melbourne, Vic. 3000, Australia. Eds. J. S. Hamilton and M. Dugan. adv. bk. rev. circ. 1,650.

027.7 US ISSN 0006-7458
BOOKS AND LIBRARIES AT THE UNIVERSITY OF KANSAS. 1952. irreg., approx. 3/yr. free. University of Kansas Libraries, Dean of Libraries, Lawrence, KS 66045. Ed. Georgann Eglinski. bibl. illus. circ. controlled.

027.8 070.5 US ISSN 0068-0184
BOOKS FOR SECONDARY SCHOOL LIBRARIES. 1961. irreg., 6th edt., 1981. $29.95. R. R. Bowker Company, 1180 Ave. of the Americas, New York, NY 10036 (Orders to P. O. Box 1807, Ann Arbor, Mich. 48106) (reprint service avail. from UMI)
Formerly: Three Thousand Books for Secondary School Libraries.

028.5 US ISSN 0068-0192
BOOKS FOR THE TEEN AGE. 1929. a. $3. New York Public Library, Office of Young Adult Services, 8 East 40th St., New York, NY 10016. Ed. Lillian Morrison. index. circ. 15,000.

020 US
BOOKS IN LIBRARY AND INFORMATION SCIENCE. 1972. irreg., vol. 29, 1979. price varies. Marcel Dekker, Inc., 270 Madison Ave., New York, NY 10016. Ed. A. Kent.

026 BS
BOTSWANA. NATIONAL ARCHIVES. REPORT ON THE NATIONAL ARCHIVES. a. National Archives, Box 239, Gaborone, Botswana.

021 BS
BOTSWANA. NATIONAL LIBRARY SERVICE. REPORT. (Text in English) National Library Service, Private Bag 0036, Gaborone, Botswana. illus.

020 070.5 US ISSN 0068-0540
BOWKER ANNUAL; of library and book trade information. 1955. a. $32.50. R. R. Bowker Company, 1180 Ave. of the Americas, New York, NY 10036 (Orders to P. O. Box 1807, Ann Arbor, Mich. 48106) cum. index 1972-1976 in 1976 edt. (reprint service avail. from UMI)

020 BL ISSN 0100-1922
BRAZIL. BIBLIOTECA NACIONAL. ANAIS. 1876. a. Biblioteca Nacional, Av. Rio Branco 219, 20042 Rio de Janeiro, Brazil. circ. 1,000.

020 BL
BRAZIL. INSTITUTO NACIONAL DO LIVRO. RELATORIO DE ATIVIDADES. 1974. a. Instituto Nacional do Livro, Brasilia, D.F., Brazil.

021 BL
BRAZIL. MINISTERIO DAS RELACOES EXTERIORES. BIBLIOTECA. AQUISICOES BIBLIOGRAFICAS. 1958. irreg. free. Ministerio das Relacoes Exteriores, Biblioteca, 70000 Brasilia, D.F., Brazil.
Formerly: Brazil. Ministerio das Relacoes Exteriores. Biblioteca. Bibliografia Anual (ISSN 0068-0834)

020 UK ISSN 0071-5662
BRITISH LIBRARIANSHIP & INFORMATION SCIENCE. 1972. quinquennial. price varies. Library Association Publishing Ltd., 7 Ridgmount St., London WC1E 7AE, England. Ed. H. A. Whatley. index.
Formerly: Five Years Work in Librarianship.

027 UK ISSN 0305-7887
BRITISH LIBRARY. BOARD. ANNUAL REPORT. 1974. a. free. Store St., London WC1E 7DG, England. circ. 6,000.

020 BU ISSN 0068-3671
BULGARSKA AKADEMIIA NA NAUKITE. TSENTRALNA BIBLIOTEKA. IZVESTIIA. (Summaries in various languages) vol. 6, 1970. 1.66 lv. per issue. Publishing House of the Bulgarian Academy of Sciences, Ul. Akad. G. Bonchev, 1113 Sofia, Bulgaria (Dist. by: Hemus, 6, Rouski Blvd., 1000 Sofia, Bulgaria) circ. 800.

BUY BOOKS WHERE, SELL BOOKS WHERE; a directory of out of print booksellers and their specialties. see PUBLISHING AND BOOK TRADE

C A M L NEWSLETTER/A C B M NOUVELLES. (Canadian Association of Music Libraries) see MUSIC

020 US ISSN 0068-4708
C. C. WILLIAMSON MEMORIAL LECTURE. 1966. irreg., no. 9, 1974. $2. George Peabody College for Teachers, School of Library Science, Nashville, TN 37203.

026 UK ISSN 0069-9829
C I C R I S DIRECTORY AND GUIDE TO RESOURCES. 1968. biennial, 4th 1977. £1.25. Cooperative Industrial and Commercial Reference and Information Service, Acton District Library, High St., London W3 6NA, England. Ed. Peter E. Jones. circ. 200.

020 CN
C L A DIRECTORY. 1950. irreg. price varies. Canadian Library Association, 151 Sparks St., Ottawa, Ont K1P 5E3, Canada.
Former titles: C L A Organization Handbook and Membership List (ISSN 0068-9130); Canadian Library Directory.

020 US ISSN 0034-1169
C L R RECENT DEVELOPMENTS. 1957; N.S. 1972. irreg. free to qualified personnel. ‡ Council on Library Resources, Inc., One Dupont Circle, Suite 620, Washington, DC 20036. Ed. Nancy E. Gwinn. circ. 4,000.

LIBRARY AND INFORMATION SCIENCES

020 US
CALIFORNIA LIBRARY STATISTICS AND DIRECTORY. 1976. a. $8. State Library, Box 2037, Sacramento, CA 95809 (Subscr. address: California State Department of Education, Publications Sales, Box 271, Sacramento, CA 95802) Ed. Collin Clark. stat. circ. 2,000 (controlled) (also avail. in microfilm from UMI; back issues avail.) Indexed: Lib.Lit. Lib.Sci.Abstr.

029 BL
CAMARA BRASILEIRA DO LIVRO. CENTRO DE CATALOGACO NA FONTE. OFICINA DE LIVROS: NOVIDADES CATALOGADAS NA FONTE. 1974. irreg. Camara Brasileira do Livro, Centro de Catalogacao na Fonte, Av. Ipiranga, 1267, 10 andar, Sao Paulo 01039, Brazil. bk. rev. bibl. circ. 1,000.

020 UK
CAMBRIDGE UNIVERSITY LIBRARY LIBRARIANSHIP SERIES. irreg. £1 per no. Cambridge University Library, West Rd., Cambridge CB3 9DR, England.

CANADA. EARTH PHYSICS BRANCH. LIBRARY. LIBRARY NEWS. see *EARTH SCIENCES*

020 CN ISSN 0708-9325
CANADA. PRAIRIE FARM REHABILITATION ADMINISTRATION. LIBRARY. NEWSLETTER/NOUVELLES DE LA BIBLIOTHEQUE. (Text in English and French) 1970. irreg. Prairie Farm Rehabilitation Administration, Library, Regina, Sask., Canada. Key Title: P F R A Library Newsletter.

020 CN ISSN 0703-3249
CANADIAN CONFERENCE ON INFORMATION SCIENCE. PROCEEDINGS. 1973. a. Can.$16.50. Canadian Association for Information Science, Box 776, Station G, Calgary, Alta. T3A 2G6, Canada.

020 CN ISSN 0380-9218
CANADIAN JOURNAL OF INFORMATION SCIENCE/REVUE CANADIENNE DES SCIENCES DE INFORMATION. (Text in English and French) 1976. a. Can.$12. Canadian Association for Information Science, Box 776, Station G, Calgary, Alta. T3A 2G6, Canada. Ed. Bd. illus.

020 CN ISSN 0068-9092
CANADIAN LIBRARY ASSOCIATION. OCCASIONAL PAPERS. 1953. irreg. price varies. Canadian Library Association, 151 Sparks St., Ottawa, Ont. K1P 5E3, Canada.

020 CN ISSN 0315-2693
CANADIAN LIBRARY PROGRESS: A SELECTION OF THE BEST WRITINGS FROM CANADIAN LIBRARY PUBLICATIONS/PROGRES DES BIBLIOTHEQUES CANADIENNES: UNE SELECTION DES MEILLEURES OEUVRES DE PUBLICATIONS CANADIENNES DE BIBLIOTHECONOMIE. (Text in English, French) 1973. a. institutions Can. $10; individuals Can. $7.50. Versatile Publishing Co. Ltd., 151 W. Hastings, Vancouver, B.C. V6B 1H4, Canada. Ed. P.H. Connolly. bk. rev. circ. 500.

021.7 US ISSN 0008-6894
CARRELL. 1960. a. since 1974. $2 per no. (Friends of the University of Miami Library) University of Miami Library, Box 248214, Coral Gables, FL 33124. Ed. George W. Rosner. bibl. illus. cum. index vol. 1-13, 1972. circ. 600. Indexed: Bibl.Engl.Lang. & Lit.

CASSETTE BOOKS. see *BLIND*

020 US
CENTER FOR RESEARCH LIBRARIES. HANDBOOK. irreg. Center for Research Libraries, 5721 Cottage Grove Ave., Chicago, IL 60637. index.

020 MX
CENTRO DE BIBLIOTECOLOGIA, ARCHIVOLOGIA E INFORMACION. ANUARIO. 1961. a. Universidad Nacional Autonoma de Mexico, Centro de Bibliotecologia, Archivologia e Informacion, Villa Obregon, Ciudad Universitaria, Mexico 20, D.F., Mexico. Ed. Alicia Perales de Mercado. bk. rev. cum. index. circ. 1,000. (back issues avail)
Formerly: Anuario de Bibliotecologia, Archivologia e Informatica.

CERCLE BELGE DE LA LIBRAIRIE. ANNUAIRE. see *PUBLISHING AND BOOK TRADE*

010 020 CS ISSN 0577-3490
CESKA BIBLIOGRAFIE; sbornik stati a materialu. (Text in Czech; summaries in English, French, German, Russian) 1959. a. price varies. Statni Knihovna CSR, Klementinum 190, 113 07 Prague 1, Czechoslovakia. Ed. Josef Bleha.

020 US
CHANGING CONCEPT SERIES. irreg., no. 2, 1973. price varies. Indiana State University, Department of Library Science, Terre Haute, IN 47809.

027 US ISSN 0069-4215
CIRCUM-SPICE. 1965. irreg. (3 issues per year) free. City College of New York, Convent Ave. & West 135 St., New York, NY 10031. Eds. M. Cope, A. Meister. circ. 1,400.

025 UK ISSN 0578-4565
CLASSIFICATION SOCIETY BULLETIN. 1965. a. membership. University of Leicester, Department of Microbiology, University Rd., Leicester LE1 7RH, England. Ed. Prof. P.H.A. Sneath. adv. bk. rev. bibl. circ. 500.

020 US ISSN 0009-885X
CLEVELAND PUBLIC LIBRARY STAFF ASSOCIATION. NEWS AND VIEWS. 1937. irreg. membership. Cleveland Public Library Staff Association, 325 Superior Ave., Cleveland, OH 44114. bk. rev. circ. 350. (processed)

020 US ISSN 0084-8905
COLORADO STATE UNIVERSITY LIBRARIES. PUBLICATION. 1966. irreg., no. 22, 1979. free. ‡ Colorado State University, University Library, Fort Collins, CO 80523. circ. 300.

347 SI
CONFERENCE OF SOUTHEAST ASIAN LIBRARIANS. PROCEEDINGS. 1972. irreg., 1970, 1st, Singapore. price varies. Chopmen Enterprises, 428-429 Katong Shopping Centre (4th Fl.), Mountbatten Road, Singapore 1543, Singapore.

020.6 SP
CONGRESO NACIONAL DE BIBLIOTECAS. PONENCIAS, COMUNICACIONES Y CRONICA. 1966. irreg. 250 ptas. Asociacion Nacional de Bibliotecarios, Archiveros y Arqueologos, Avda. de Calvo Sotelo, 22, Madrid 1, Spain.

029.7 BL
CONGRESO REGIONAL SOBRE DOCUMENTACAO. ANAIS. a., 3rd, Lima, 1971. Instituto Brasileiro de Informacao em Ciencia e Tecnologia, Avenida General Justo 171, 4 Andar, Rio de Janeiro, Brazil.

027.4 US
CONNECTICUT LIBRARY ASSOCIATION. MEMO. vol. 3,1978. 10/yr. Connecticut Library Association, Inc., Connecticut State Library, Rm. L-216, 231 Capitol Ave., Hartford, CT 06115. Ed. Joyce Reid. (reprint service avail. from UMI)

020 CN ISSN 0084-9197
CONSEIL SUPERIEUR DU LIVRE. ANNUAIRE. 1965. a. free. Edi-Quebec Inc., 1151 Alexandre DeSeve, Montreal, Que. H2L 2T7, Canada. Ed. Jean-Pierre Bedard. circ. 4,000.

025 US ISSN 0069-9136
CONSERVATION OF LIBRARY MATERIALS. (Subseries of: American Library Association. Library Technology Program. L T P Publications) 1967. irreg. American Library Association, Library Technology Program, 50 E. Huron St., Chicago, IL 60611.

029.7 US ISSN 0084-9243
CONTRIBUTIONS IN LIBRARIANSHIP AND INFORMATION SCIENCE. 1972. irreg. price varies. Greenwood Press, 88 Post Rd. W., Westport, CT 06881. Ed. Paul Wasserman.

020 IS
CONTRIBUTIONS TO INFORMATION SCIENCE. (Text in English and Hebrew) 1967. irreg. $5 per no. Israel Society of Special Libraries and Information Centers, Box 20125, Tel-Aviv, Israel. Indexed: LISA.

020 US ISSN 0069-9683
CONTRIBUTIONS TO LIBRARY LITERATURE. 1955. irreg., latest issue. 1977. price varies. ‡ Shoe String Press Inc., 995 Sherman Ave., Hamden, CT 06514. Ed. John David Marshall.

025 US
COUNCIL ON LIBRARY RESOURCES ANNUAL REPORT. 1957. a. free. ‡ Council on Library Resources, Inc., One Dupont Circle, Suite 620, Washington, DC 20036. Ed. Nancy E. Gwinn. circ. 4,600. (also avail. in microform from EDR) Indexed: ERIC.
Formerly: Council on Library Resources Report (ISSN 0070-1181)

COUNTWAY LIBRARY ASSOCIATES HISTORICAL PUBLICATIONS. see *MEDICAL SCIENCES*

027.8 IE ISSN 0007-8565
CUMANN LEABHARLANNAITHE SCOILE. C L S BULLETIN. (Text in English and Irish) 1962. a. membership; non-members $2. Cumann Leabharlannaithe Scoile, 75 Mobhi Rd., Glasnevin, Dublin 9, Dublin, Ireland. Ed. Mary Carroll. adv. bk. rev. bibl. index. circ. 300.

029 GW
D G D SCHRIFTENREIHE. irreg., no. 8, 1978. price varies. (Deutsche Gesellschaft fuer Dokumentation e.V.) K.G. Saur Verlag KG, Poessenbacherstr. 12 B, Postfach 711009, 8000 Munich 71, W. Germany (B.R.D.)

020 US
D.H. HILL LIBRARY FOCUS. 1964. irreg. free. North Carolina State University, D.H. Hill Library, P.O. Box 5007, Raleigh, NC 27650. Ed. Ebba F. Kraar. circ. 650. (processed)

020 001.6 CN ISSN 0318-7403
DALHOUSIE UNIVERSITY. SCHOOL OF LIBRARY SERVICE. OCCASIONAL PAPERS. irreg., nos. 21-25, 1979. price varies. Dalhousie University, School of Library Service, Halifax, N.S. B3H 4H8, Canada. Ed. Norman Horrocks.

020 CN ISSN 0701-8894
DALHOUSIE UNIVERSITY. SCHOOL OF LIBRARY SERVICE. Y-A HOTLINE. 1977. irreg. Can.$3.50 for 6 nos. Dalhousie University, School of Library Service, Halifax, N.S. B3H 4H8, Canada. Ed. L.J. Amey. circ. 250.

027 DK
DANMARKS BIBLIOTEKSFORENING. BIBLIOTEKSVEJVISER/GUIDE TO DANISH LIBRARIES. (Subtitles and index in English) 1970. a. Kr.100($18) Danmarks Biblioteksforening - Danish Library Association, Trekronergade 15, DK-2500 Copenhagen V, Denmark (Subscr. to: Bibliotekscentralen, Telegrafvej 5, DK-2750 Ballerup, Denmark) Ed. Christian Goetzsche. illus. circ. 2,000.

020 DK ISSN 0069-9861
DANMARKS BIBLIOTEKSSKOLE. SKRIFTER. 1965. a. price varies. Danmarks Biblioteksskole, 6 Birketinget, 2300 Copenhagen S, Denmark. bk. rev.

020 DK
DANMARKS BILIOTEKSSKOLE. STUDIER. 1974. irreg. (8-10/yr.) price varies. Danmarks Biblioteksskole, 6 Birketinget, 2300 Copenhagen S, Denmark.

027 DK ISSN 0069-9896
DENMARK. KONGELIGE BIBLIOTEK. FUND OG FORSKNING. (Text in Danish; summaries in English) 1954. a. price varies. Kongelige Bibliotek, Christians Brygge 8, DK-1219 Copenhagen K, Denmark. cum. index; 1954-73.
Findings and research in the collections of the Royal Library

029 070.5 GE ISSN 0323-374X
DEUTSCHES BUECHERVERZEICHNIS. 1911/14. every five years. (Deutsche Buecherei) VEB Verlag fuer Buch- und Bibliothekswesen, Gerichtsweg 26, 701 Leipzig, E. Germany (D.D.R.)

LIBRARY AND INFORMATION SCIENCES

025.4 US ISSN 0083-1573
DEWEY DECIMAL CLASSIFICATION ADDITIONS, NOTES AND DECISIONS. 1959. irreg. ‡ U. S. Library of Congress, Decimal Classification Division, Washington, DC 20541 (Free to subscr. of LC Card Service, purchasers of 18th edition of Dewey Decimal Classification, and teachers of library science, upon request to: Forest Press, 85 Watervliet Ave., Albany, NY 12206)

026 CK
DIRECTORIO COLOMBIANO DE UNIDADES DE INFORMACION. 1976. irreg. (Fondo Colombiano de Investigaciones Cientificas y Proyectos Especiales) Impresa Nacional, Carrera 13 no. 60-34, Apdo. Aereo 051580, Bogota, Colombia.

020 US ISSN 0162-0290
DIRECTORY AND STATISTICS OF OREGON LIBRARIES. 1913. a. $3. State Library, Salem, OR 97310. Ed. Alice M. Nielsen. circ. 800.
Formerly: Directory of Oregon Libraries.

DIRECTORY OF CANADIAN MAP COLLECTIONS. see GEOGRAPHY

023 US
DIRECTORY OF CHINESE AMERICAN LIBRARIANS. (Text in English and Chinese) 1977. irreg. $5. (Chinese-American Librarians Association) Chinese Culture Service, Inc., Box 444, Oak Park, IL 60303. Ed. Tze-chung Li. circ. 500.

027 US ISSN 0070-5276
DIRECTORY OF COLLEGE AND UNIVERSITY LIBRARIES IN NEW YORK STATE. 1965. a. free to libraries in New York State; on exchange basis with other libraries. State Library, Division of Library Development, Albany, NY 12224. Ed. E. J. Josey.

020 US ISSN 0094-8403
DIRECTORY OF COLORADO LIBRARIES. a. $5. State Library, 1362 Lincoln St., Denver, CO 80203. Ed. Phyllis Baker.

026 959 US ISSN 0148-0065
DIRECTORY OF EAST ASIAN COLLECTIONS IN NORTH AMERICAN LIBRARIES. a. $3. Association for Asian Studies, Inc., Committee on East Asian Libraries, Ann Arbor, MI 48104.

020 US ISSN 0147-1678
DIRECTORY OF FEE-BASED INFORMATION SERVICES. a. $6.95. Information Alternative, Box 657, Woodstock, NY 12498. Ed. Kelly Warnken.

DIRECTORY OF GEOSCIENCE LIBRARIES, U.S. AND CANADA. see EARTH SCIENCES

026 610 US
DIRECTORY OF HEALTH SCIENCES LIBRARIES. 1969. irreg., latest 1973. $15. American Medical Association, 535 N. Dearborn St., Chicago, IL 60610. (Co-sponsors: Medical Library Association; American Hospital Association) Ed. Susan Crawford.

020 US
DIRECTORY OF INSTITUTIONS OFFERING OR PLANNING PROGRAMS FOR THE TRAINING OF LIBRARY TECHNICAL ASSISTANTS. 1968. triennial; latest, 1976. $7. Council on Library-Media Technical Assistants, c/o School Management Institute, 750 Brooksedge Blvd., Westerville, OH 43081. Ed. Mrs. Noel R. Grego. stat. (also avail. in microfiche)
Formerly (until 1971): Council on Library Technology. Directory of Institutions in the United States and Canada Offering or Developing Courses in Library Technology.

DIRECTORY OF LAW LIBRARIES. see LAW

027 US
DIRECTORY OF LIBRARIES AND LIBRARY RESOURCES IN THE SOUTH CENTRAL RESEARCH LIBRARY COUNCIL REGION. 1969. a. $3. South Central Research Library Council, DeWitt Bldg., 215 N. Cayuga St., Ithaca, NY 14850. Ed. Janet E. Steiner. circ. 700.
Formerly: South Central Research Library Council. Library Directory (ISSN 0081-2722)

021 CN ISSN 0317-8536
DIRECTORY OF LIBRARIES IN MANITOBA. 1973. biennial. Public Library Services, 139 Hamelin St., Winnipeg, Man.R3T 4H4, Canada.

778.1 US ISSN 0160-6077
DIRECTORY OF LIBRARY REPROGRAPHIC SERVICES. 1959. biennial. $12.95. Microform Review, Inc., Box 405, Saugatuck Sta., Westport, CT 06880.

026 US
DIRECTORY OF LIBRARY SCIENCE COLLECTIONS. 1975. irreg., 2nd edt. 1977. $2.50. (Association of College and Research Libraries) American Library Association, 50 E. Huron St., Chicago, IL 60611. Ed. Carol S. Nielsen. charts, stat.
Formerly: Directory of Library Science Libraries.

027 US ISSN 0070-5810
DIRECTORY OF MEDICAL LIBRARIES IN NEW YORK STATE. 1967. irreg. free to libraries in New York State; on exchange basis with other libraries. State Library, Division of Library Development, Albany, NY 12224. Ed. E. J. Josey.

027 US ISSN 0092-4067
DIRECTORY OF MISSOURI LIBRARIES; public, college, university & special libraries. 1965. a. free. State Library, 308 E. High St., Jefferson City, MO 65101. stat. (reprint service avail. from UMI)

027.7 US
DIRECTORY OF NEW ENGLAND COLLEGE, UNIVERSITY AND INSTITUTE LIBRARIES. 1969. a. $1. New England Board of Higher Education, 68 Walnut Rd., Wenham, MA 01984.

027 US ISSN 0070-5950
DIRECTORY OF NEW YORK STATE PUBLIC LIBRARY SYSTEMS. 1960. a. free to libraries in New York State; on exchange basis with other libraries. New York State Education Department, State Library, Division of Library Development, Albany, NY 12224. Ed. E. J. Josey.

027 US ISSN 0070-6183
DIRECTORY OF REFERENCE AND RESEARCH LIBRARY RESOURCES SYSTEMS IN NEW YORK STATE. 1967. a. free to libraries in New York State; on exchange basis to other libraries. ‡ State Library, Division of Library Development, Albany, NY 12224. Ed. E. J. Josey. circ. 1,500.

026 GH
DIRECTORY OF RESEARCH AND SPECIAL LIBRARIES IN GHANA. 1974. biennial (approx.) Council for Scientific and Industrial Research, Box M-32, Accra, Ghana. Ed. L. Agyei-Gyane. circ. 500.
Formerly: Directory of Special Libraries in Ghana.

026 US ISSN 0070-6361
DIRECTORY OF SPECIAL LIBRARIES AND INFORMATION CENTERS IN THE U.S. & CANADA. (In 3 vols.) 1963. biennial. vol. 1, $95; vol. 2, $80; vol. 3, $90. Gale Research Company, Book Tower, Detroit, MI 48226. Eds. Margaret L. Young, Harold C. Young.

026 IO ISSN 0376-8600
DIRECTORY OF SPECIAL LIBRARIES IN INDONESIA. (Text in Indonesian & English) irreg., latest issue 1978. $10 per no. National Scientific Documentation Centre - Pusat Dokumentasi Ilmiah Nasional, Jalan Jenderal Gatot Subroto, Box 3065/Jkt., Jakarta, Indonesia.

026 IS ISSN 0070-637X
DIRECTORY OF SPECIAL LIBRARIES IN ISRAEL. (Text in English and Hebrew) 1961. irreg., 4th edt., 1976. $15. (National Council for Research and Development) National Center of Scientific and Technological Information, Box 20125, Tel-Aviv, Israel. 2 indexes.

020 CN ISSN 0070-6396
DIRECTORY OF SPECIAL LIBRARIES IN MONTREAL. (Text in English and French) biennial. Can.$5. Special Libraries Association, Montreal Chapter, Box 10, Jardins Sta., Montreal, Que. H5B 1C8, Canada.

020 US ISSN 0070-6663
DISCOURSE UNITS IN HUMAN COMMUNICATION FOR LIBRARIANS. 1969. irreg., no. 16, 1980. price varies. University of Pittsburgh, Communications Media Research Center, c/o Patrick R. Penland, Graduate School of Library and Information Science, 135 No. Bellefield, Pittsburgh, PA 15260. Ed. Patrick R. Penland. (back issues avail.) Indexed: Lib.Lit. ERIC.

020 AG ISSN 0070-6841
DOCUMENTACION BIBLIOTECOLOGICA. 1970. irreg; latest issue, 1974. $2. available on exchange. Universidad Nacional del sur, Centro de Documentacion Bibliotecologica, Av. Alem 1253, Bahia Blanca, Argentina. Ed. Atilio Peralta. circ. 300.

020 UN
DOCUMENTATION, LIBRARIES AND ARCHIVES: STUDIES AND RESEARCH. (Editions in English, French and Spanish) 1972. irreg. price varies. Unesco Press, 7 Place de Fontenoy, F-75700 Paris, France (Dist. in U.S. by: Unipub, 345 Park Ave., S., New York, NY 10010)
Formerly (1951-1971): Unesco Manuals for Libraries (ISSN 0082-7495)

020 FR ISSN 0066-894X
DOCUMENTS A B F. 1969. irreg. Association des Bibliothecaires Francais, 65 rue de Richelieu, 75002 Paris, France.

027 IE ISSN 0332-0006
DUBLIN. NATIONAL LIBRARY OF IRELAND. COUNCIL OF TRUSTEES REPORT. a. price varies. National Library of Ireland, Kildare St., Dublin, Ireland (Avail. from H.M.S.O., c/o Liaison Officer, Atlantic House, Holborn Viaduct, London EC1P 1BN, England) illus.

027.7 US ISSN 0012-7108
DUKE UNIVERSITY LIBRARY NEWSLETTER. 1953. irreg. free. Duke University, Library, Perkins Library, Durham, NC 27706.

027.4 SA
DURBAN MUNICIPAL LIBRARY. ANNUAL REPORT. 1854. a. free. Durban Municipal Library, Box 917, Durban 4000, South Africa.

020 UK
EALING OCCASIONAL PAPERS IN THE HISTORY OF LIBRARIES. 1972. irreg. £1 per no. Ealing School of Library and Information Studies, Woodlands Ave., London W.5, England. Eds. J. B. Tooley, S. Sayed. circ. 200. Indexed: LISA.

020 SZ ISSN 0514-0668
EIDGENOESSISCHE TECHNISCHE HOCHSCHULE ZUERICH. BIBLIOTHEK. SCHRIFTENREIHE. 1948. irreg. Eidgenoessische Technische Hochschule Zuerich, Bibliothek, Raemistr. 101, 8092 Zurich, Switzerland. Ed. B. Glans. circ. 100.

029 020 GE ISSN 0070-9522
EINFUEHRUNG IN DIE INFORMATION UND DOKUMENTATION. irreg., no. 13, 1976. price varies. VEB Bibliographisches Institut, Gerichtsweg 26, 701 Leipzig, E. Germany (D.D.R.)

ENERGY AND NATURAL RESOURCES LIBRARY JOURNALS. see ENERGY

ENVIRONMENTAL INFORMATION SYSTEMS DIRECTORY. see ENVIRONMENTAL STUDIES

020 CK ISSN 0071-1314
ESCUELA INTERAMERICANA DE BIBLIOTECOLOGIA. ESTADISTICAS. a. free. Universidad de Antioquia, Apartado Aereo 1226, Medellin, Colombia.

020.6 US
EXHIBIT NEWSLETTER. 1955? irreg., vol. 25, 1981. membership only. American Library Association, Exhibits Round Table, 50 E. Huron St., Chicago, IL 60611. Ed. Tom Sutherland. circ. 425. (also avail. in microfilm)

029 NE ISSN 0014-5424
EXTENSIONS AND CORRECTIONS TO THE U D C. (Text in English, French, German) 1950. a. fl.195. International Federation for Documentation, Box 30115, 2500 GC The Hague, Netherlands. circ. 800.

020 010   NE   ISSN 0074-5804
F.I.D./C.R. REPORT SERIES. 1964. irreg., no. 18, 1978. price varies. International Federation for Documentation, Committee on Classification Research, Box 30115, 2500 GC The Hague, Netherlands (Orders to: FID/CR Secretariat, c/o Dr. I. Dahlberg, Woogstrasse 36a, D-6000 Frankfurt 50, W. Germany)

029.7   NE   ISSN 0379-3680
F I D DIRECTORY. 1958. biennial. fl.25. International Federation for Documentation, Box 30115, 2500 GC The Hague, Netherlands. circ. 1,000.
    Formerly: F I D Yearbook (ISSN 0074-5839)

029   UR
F I D/R I MEETINGS REPORTS. 1970. irreg., no. 2, 1974. fl.35. International Federation for Documentation, Committee on Research on the Theoretical Basis of Information, Hofweg 7, 2511 AA The Hague, Netherlands (And Vsesoyuznyi Institut Nauchno-Tekhnicheskoi Informatsii, Ul. Baltiiskaya 14, Moscow, U.S.S.R.)

029   NE
F I D/R I SERIES ON PROBLEMS OF INFORMATION SCIENCE. 1969. irreg., no. 5, 1979. fl.30. International Federation for Documentation, Committee on Research on the Theoretical Basis of Information, Box 30115, 2500 GC The Hague, Netherlands (And Vsesoyuznyi Institut Nauchno-Tekhnicheskoi Informatsii, Ul. Baltiiskaya 14, Moscow, U.S.S.R.) Ed. A. I. Mikhailov. circ. 300.
    Formerly: F I D /R I Series of Collected Articles.

020   US   ISSN 0014-5939
F L C NEWSLETTER. 1965. irreg. free. ‡ U. S. Library of Congress, Federal Library Committee, Washington, DC 20540. Ed. James Riley. bk. rev. stat. circ. controlled. (processed) Indexed: Lib.Lit.

070.5   GW   ISSN 0071-3627
FACHLITERATUR ZUM BUCH- UND BIBLIOTHEKSWESEN/INTERNATIONAL BIBLIOGRAPHY OF THE BOOK TRADE AND LIBRARIANSHIP. 1961. irreg., 11th edition, 1976. DM.148. K.G. Saur Verlag KG, Poessenbacherstr. 12 B, Postfach 711009, 8000 Munich 71, W. Germany (B.R.D.) Eds. Helga Lengenfelder, Gitta Hausen. adv.
    Formerly: Literature About the Book and Librarianship.

028   PE   ISSN 0015-0002
FENIX; revista. 1944. a; no. 27, 1979. $6. Biblioteca Nacional, Apartado 2335, Lima, Peru. Ed. Lucila Valderrama. bk. rev. music rev. bibl. cum.index. circ. 1,000.

020   FJ
FIJI LIBRARY DIRECTORY. a. free. Fiji Library Association, Box 1168, Suva, Fiji. (Co-sponsor: Library Service of Fiji) Ed. Pierina Parise. circ. 55. (looseleaf format)

FINANCIAL ASSISTANCE FOR LIBRARY EDUCATION. see EDUCATION — Higher Education

026 820   US   ISSN 0428-8211
FOLGER SHAKESPEARE LIBRARY ANNUAL REPORT. 1969. n.s. a. Folger Shakespeare Library, 201 E. Capitol St., S.E., Washington, DC 20003. stat. annual index. circ. 800.

020 070   UK
FRIENDS OF THE NATIONAL LIBRARIES. ANNUAL REPORT. 1932. a. £6($12) Friends of the National Libraries, c/o British Library, Great Russell St., London WC1B 3DG, England. circ. 700.

020   PE   ISSN 0433-0730
GACETA BIBLIOTECARIA DEL PERU. 1963. irreg; no. 25, 1975. Instituto Nacional de Cultura, Biblioteca Nacional, Oficina Nacional de Bibliotecas Publicas, Apartado 2335, Lima, Peru. Ed. Carmen Checa de Silva. illus. circ. 1,000.

020   US   ISSN 0072-0801
GENESEO STUDIES IN LIBRARY AND INFORMATION SCIENCE. 1969. irreg. $5 per volume. State University of New York, College at Geneseo, School of Library and Information Science, Geneseo, NY 14454 (Order from: College Bookstore, SUNY at Geneseo, NY, 14454)

027.4   CN   ISSN 0380-8068
GEORGIAN BAY REGIONAL LIBRARY SYSTEM. DIRECTORY-MEMBER LIBRARIES. 1968. irreg. Georgian Bay Regional Library System, 30 Morrow Rd., Barrie, Ont. L4N 3V8, Canada.

020   SW   ISSN 0347-884X
GOETEBORGS UNIVERSITET. UNIVERSITETSBIBLIOTEK. AARSBERAETTELSE. 1907-27; N.S. 1930. a. Goeteborgs Universitet, Universitetsbibliotek, Centralbiblioteket, Box 5096, S-402 22 Goeteborg 5, Sweden.

026 950   II
GOVERNMENT ORIENTAL MANUSCRIPTS LIBRARY. BULLETIN. (Text in English and various Indic languages) 1948. a. Rs.14. Government Oriental Manuscripts Library, Curator, University Library Buildings, Chepauk, Madras 600005, India. Ed. R. N. Sampata. bk. rev.

GREAT BRITAIN. KEEPER OF PUBLIC RECORDS. ANNUAL REPORT OF THE KEEPER OF PUBLIC RECORDS ON THE WORK OF THE PUBLIC RECORD OFFICE AND THE REPORT OF THE ADVISORY COUNCIL ON PUBLIC RECORDS. see HISTORY — History Of Europe

025.17   UK   ISSN 0072-7016
GREAT BRITAIN. PUBLIC RECORD OFFICE. HANDBOOKS. 1954. irreg. price varies. H.M.S.O., Atlantic House, Holborn Viaduct, London EC1P 1BN, England.

027.4   US   ISSN 0017-4610
GROSSE POINTE PUBLIC LIBRARY. NEWSLETTER. 1955. irreg (2-4/yr.) $3. (Friends of the Grosse Pointe Public Library) Grosse Point Public Library, 10 Kercheval Ave., Grosse Pointe, MI 48236. Ed. Edward T. Gushee, Jr. bk. rev. illus. circ. 2,000.

027.5   UN   ISSN 0072-8608
GUIDE TO NATIONAL BIBLIOGRAPHICAL INFORMATION CENTRES. (Text in English and French) 1962. irreg., 1970, 3rd ed. 23 F. Unesco, 7-9 Place de Fontenoy, 75700 Paris, France (Dist. in U.S. by: Unipub, 345 Park Ave. S., New York, NY 10010)

029   GW   ISSN 0340-1332
HANDBUCH DER INTERNATIONALEN DOKUMENTATION UND INFORMATION. irreg., no. 15, 1978. price varies. K.G. Saur Verlag KG, Poessenbacherstr. 12 B, Postfach 711009, 8000 Munich 71, W. Germany (B.R.D.)
    Formerly: Handbuch der Technischen Dokumentation und Bibliographie.

029   GW   ISSN 0073-0106
HANDBUCH DER KLASSIFIKATION. irreg. price varies. (Deutsches Institut fuer Normung e.V.) Beuth Verlag GmbH, Burggrafenstr 4-7, 1000 Berlin 30, W. Germany (B.R.D.)

020   GW   ISSN 0301-9225
HANDBUCH DER OEFFENTLICHEN BIBLIOTHEKEN. 1952. biennial. DM.41.50. Deutsches Bibliotheksinstitut, Bundesallee 185, 1000 Berlin 31, W. Germany (B.R.D.) Eds. Werner Beck, Helmut Roesner. stat. circ. 1,200. (back issues avail.)

510.78 410   US   ISSN 0073-0769
HARVARD UNIVERSITY. COMPUTATION LABORATORY. MATHEMATICAL LINGUISTICS AND AUTOMATIC TRANSLATION; REPORT TO NATIONAL SCIENCE FOUNDATION. 1959. irreg., 1970, no. 27. free. Harvard University, Aiken Computation Laboratory, Cambridge, MA 02138 (Orders to: National Technical Information Service, Operations Division, Springfield, VA 22151) Ed. Susumu Kuno.

020   US   ISSN 0073-103X
HAWAII. DEPARTMENT OF EDUCATION. OFFICE OF LIBRARY SERVICES. REPORT. 1962-63. a. free. Department of Education, Office of Library Services, P.O. Box 2360, Honolulu, HI 96804.

020   US   ISSN 0017-8586
HAWAII LIBRARY ASSOCIATION JOURNAL. 1944. a. $4 to non-members. Hawaii Library Association, Box 4441, Honolulu, HI 96813. charts. illus. circ. 600. (also avail. in microfilm from UMI) Indexed: LISA. Lib.Lit.

027   FI   ISSN 0355-1350
HELSINGIN YLIOPISTO. KIRJASTO. JULKAISUJA/HELSINGFORS UNIVERSITET. BIBLIOTEK. SKRIFTER/UNIVERSITY OF HELSINKI. LIBRARY. PUBLICATION. 1918. irreg., no. 43, 1980. Helsingin Yliopisto, Kirjasto, Box 312, 00171 Helsinki 17, Finland.

020   JA   ISSN 0018-3431
HOKKAIDO LIBRARIANS STUDY CIRCLE. BULLETIN/HOKKAIDO TOSHOKAN KENKYUKAI. KAIHO. (Text in Japanese) 1954. a. 1000 Yen. Hokkaido Librarians Study Circle - Hokkaido Toshokan Kenkyukai, c/o Sapporo Ika Daigaku Fuzoku Toshokan, Nishi-17-chome, Minami 1-jo, Sapporo, Japan. adv. circ. 300.

020   HK   ISSN 0073-3237
HONG KONG LIBRARY ASSOCIATION. JOURNAL. (Text in English and Chinese) 1969. irreg. price varies. Hong Kong Library Association, c/o Univ. of Hong Kong Library, Pokfulum Rd., Hong Kong, Hong Kong. Ed. M. Quinn. circ. 300.

027   US   ISSN 0082-6790
HOWARD-TILTON MEMORIAL LIBRARY. REPORT. 1960-61. a. free. ‡ Tulane University, Library, New Orleans, LA 70118. Ed. John H. Gribbin. circ. 250.

020   GE
HUMBOLDT-UNIVERSITAET ZU BERLIN. UNIVERSITAETSBIBLIOTHEK. SCHRIFTENREIHE. 1967. irreg., no. 30, 1979. price varies. Humboldt-Universitaet zu Berlin, Universitaets-Bibliothek, Clara-Zetkin-Str. 27, 108 Berlin, E. Germany (D.R.R.)

020   US
I A S L CONFERENCE PROCEEDINGS. 1972. a. $3.75. International Association of School Librarianship, c/o Secretariate, School of Librarianship, Western Michigan University, Kalamazoo, MI 49008. Ed. J. Lowrie. circ. 250. (looseleaf format; back issues avail.)

026   II   ISSN 0073-6279
I A S L I C SPECIAL PUBLICATION; working papers of seminars and conferences. (Working papers of Conferences/Seminars) (Text in English) 1960. a. price varies. Indian Association of Special Libraries and Information Centres, P-291 C.I.T. Scheme No. 6M, Kankurgachi, Calcutta 700054, India.

026   II   ISSN 0073-6260
I A S L I C TECHNICAL PAMPHLETS. 1964. a. price varies. Indian Association of Special Libraries and Information Centres, P-291 C.I.T. Scheme No. 6M, Kankurgachi, Calcutta 700054, India.

020   SW   ISSN 0018-8476
I A T U L PROCEEDINGS. 1963. irreg. Kr.40. International Association of Technological Universities Libraries, Chalmers University of Technology, S-412 96 Goeteborg, Fack, S-402 20 Goeteborg 5, Sweden. Ed. Nancy Fjaellbrant. adv. bk. rev. bibl. illus. circ. 300. Indexed: LISA. Lib.Lit. Inform.Sci.Abstr.
    Formerly: I A T U L Newsletter.

020   SZ
I F I P INFORMATION BULLETIN. irreg (approx. 2/yr.) International Federation for Information Processing, Secretariat, 3 rue du Marche, CH-1204 Geneva, Switzerland. bibl.

020   SZ
I F I P SUMMARY. 1971. every 18 mos. International Federation for Information Processing, Secretariat, 3 rue du Marche, CH-1204 Geneva, Switzerland.

LIBRARY AND INFORMATION SCIENCES

020 GW ISSN 0074-5987
I F L A ANNUAL; proceedings of the General Council Meetings. (Text in English) 1927. a. DM.58. (International Federation of Library Associations and Institutions) K.G. Saur Verlag KG, Poessenbacherstr. 12 B, Postfach 711009, 8000 Munich 71, W. Germany (B.R.D.) Eds. W.R.H. Koops, P. Havard-Williams, W.E.S. Coops. cum.index: vol. XXX, 1928-64.

020 NE ISSN 0074-6002
I F L A DIRECTORY. 1969. a. fl.30. International Federation of Library Associations and Institutions, Box 82128, 2508 EC The Hague, Netherlands. circ. 2,000 (approx.)

025 GW
I F L A PUBLICATIONS. (Text in English and French) 1974. irreg. vol. 17, 1979. (International Federation of Library Associations and Institutions) K.G. Saur Verlag KG, Poessenbacherstr. 12 B, Postfach 711009, 8000 Munich 71, W. Germany (B.R.D.) W.R. Koops, P. Havard-Williams.

539 UN
I N I S REFERENCE SERIES. 1969. irreg; no. 15, 1975. price varies. International Atomic Energy Agency, International Nuclear Information System, Kaerntner Ring 11, Box 590, A-1011 Vienna, Austria (Dist. in U.S. by: Unipub, 345 Park Ave. S., New York, NY 10010) (some issues also avail. in microfiche)

I S B N REVIEW. (International Standard Book Number) see *PUBLISHING AND BOOK TRADE*

027 IC
ICELAND. LANDSBOKASAFN ISLANDS. ARBOK. NYR FLOKKUR. N.S. 1976. a. Kr.40($6) Landsbokasafn Islands - National Library of Iceland, Safnahusinu, Hverfisgotu 15, 101 Reykjavik, Iceland. Ed. Finnbogi Gudmundsson.
Supersedes in part: Iceland. Landsbokasafn Islands. Arbok.

020 AT ISSN 0158-0876
INCITE. 1980. irreg. membership (Aus.$1 to non-members) Library Association of Australia, 35 Clarence St., Sydney, N.S.W. 2000, Australia. adv.

020 UN ISSN 0073-6074
INDEX TRANSLATIONUM. (Text in English and French) 1950. a; vol. 28, 1978. price varies. Unesco, 7-9 Place de Fontenoy, 75700 Paris, France (Dist. in U.S. by: Unipub, 345 Park Ave. S., New York, NY 10010)

020 II ISSN 0067-3439
INDIAN STATISTICAL INSTITUTE. DOCUMENTATION RESEARCH AND TRAINING CENTRE. ANNUAL SEMINAR. 1963. a. price varies. Indian Statistical Institute, Documentation Research and Training Centre, 31 Church St, Malleswaram, Bangalore 560001, India. circ. 500. (also avail. in microfilm; microfiche) Indexed: LISA. Inform.Sci.Abstr.

020 US
INDIANA LIBRARY ASSOCIATION MEMBERSHIP DIRECTORY. a. Indiana Library Association, 1100 W. 42 St., Indianapolis, IN 46208. Ed. Elbert L. Watson. circ. 900.

026 UK
INDUSTRIAL GROUP NEWSLETTER. irreg. membership. Library Association, Industrial Group, c/o Mrs. D. Palmer, Technical Librarian, Smith Kline & French Laboratories Ltd., Welwyn Garden City, Herts., England.

020 FR ISSN 0073-7828
INEDITS RUSSES. 1970. irreg. price varies. Librairie des Cinq Continents, 18 rue de Lille, Paris 7e, France.

651.8 IS ISSN 0073-7879
INFORMATION PROCESSING ASSOCIATION OF ISRAEL. NATIONAL CONFERENCE ON DATA PROCESSING. PROCEEDINGS. (Text in Hebrew and English) 1964. a. £15. Information Processing Association of Israel, Box 13009, Jerusalem, Israel.

020 US
INFORMATION SCIENCES SERIES. 1963. irreg., latest, 1979. price varies. John Wiley & Sons, Inc., 605 Third Ave., New York, NY 10016. Eds. R.M. Hayes, J. Becker.
Formerly: Hayes & Becker Information Sciences Series.

020 GE
INFORMATIONSDIENST UEBERSETZUNGEN. irreg. Zentralinstitut fuer Information und Dokumentation, Koepeniker Str. 325, 117 Berlin, E. Germany (D.D.R.) (microfiche)

029.7 FR
INFORMATIQUE DANS LES ENTREPRISES PUBLIQUES. a. (Direction General de l'Industrie, Mission a l'Informatique) Documentation Francaise, 29-31 Quai Voltaire, 75340 Paris, France. (Co-sponsor: Mission Interministrielle pour la Promotion de l'Informatique)

020 651.8 001.6 UK ISSN 0308-8111
INSPEC REPORTS. irreg. price varies. Institution of Electrical Engineers, Information Services Division, Station House, Nightingale Rd., Hitchin, Herts. SG5 1RJ, England.

020 SI ISSN 0073-9723
INSTITUTE OF SOUTHEAST ASIAN STUDIES. LIBRARY BULLETIN. (Text in English) 1971. irreg., no. 11, 1976. price varies. Institute of Southeast Asian Studies, Heng Mui Keng Terrace, Pasir Panjang, Singapore 0511, Singapore. Indexed: Bibl.Asian Stud.

020 US
INTERCOM; THE NEWSLETTER FOR CALIFORNIA COMMUNITY COLLEGE LIBRARIANS. 1965. irreg. (5-10/yr.) $1. c/o Solano Community College, Box 246, Suisun City, CA 94585. circ. 525(controlled)

026 US
INTERNATIONAL ASSOCIATION OF LAW LIBRARIES. DIRECTORY. irreg., latest edt. 1977. $12.50. International Association of Law Libraries, c/o Vanderbilt University, School of Law Library, Nashville, TN 37203.

020 US
INTERNATIONAL BIBLIOGRAPHICAL AND LIBRARY SERIES. irreg., vol. 3, 1973. price varies. Academic Press, Inc., 111 5th Ave., New York, NY 10003. Ed. G. Chandler.

025 FR ISSN 0074-3518
INTERNATIONAL CONGRESS OF ARCHIVES. PROCEEDINGS. (Published in the Council's periodical Archivum) quadrennial; 8th Congress, Washington, 1976. International Council on Archives - Conseil Internationale des Archives, 60 rue des Francs Bourgeois, 75003 Paris, France (Order from: Verlag Dokumentation Saur KG, P.O.B. 711009, D-8000 Munich 71, W. Germany(B.R.D.)

026 NE
INTERNATIONAL CONGRESS ON MEDICAL LIBRARIANSHIP. PROCEEDINGS.* (Published in Excerpta Medica International Congress Series) 1953. irreg. $39.50. Excerpta Medica, P.O.B. 211, Amsterdam, Netherlands (Dist. in the U.S. and Canada by: Elsevier North-Holland, Inc., New York, 52 Vanderbilt Ave., New York, NY 10017) Eds. K.E. Davis, W.D. Sweeney.

026 KE
INTERNATIONAL COUNCIL ON ARCHIVES. EAST AND CENTRAL AFRICA REGIONAL BRANCH. GENERAL CONFERENCE PROCEEDINGS. no. 3, 1974, Lusaka, Zambia. irreg. International Council on Archives, East and Central African Regional Branch, c/o Kenya National Archives, Jogou House "A", Box 30520, Nairobi, Kenya.

025.17 SP
INTERNATIONAL COUNCIL ON ARCHIVES. MICROFILM COMMITTEE. BULLETIN. (Text in English, French or Spanish with summaries in one of the other languages or German) 1972. a. free. (International Council on Archives, FR) Centro Nacional de Microfilm, c/o Sra. Carmen Crespo Nogueira, Ed., Serrano 115, Madrid 6, Spain. illus. circ. 2,100-2,600.

029 NE ISSN 0378-7656
INTERNATIONAL FEDERATION FOR DOCUMENTATION. P-NOTES. 1931. 30-40/yr. fl.40. International Federation for Documentation, Box 30115, 2500 GC The Hague, Netherlands.

029.7 NE ISSN 0074-5812
INTERNATIONAL FEDERATION FOR DOCUMENTATION. PROCEEDINGS OF CONGRESS. 1895. irreg., latest issue 1978. price varies. International Federation for Documentation, Box 30115, 2500 GC The Hague, Netherlands.

029.7 006 US ISSN 0074-820X
INTERNATIONAL SERIES IN LIBRARY AND INFORMATION SCIENCES. 1964. irreg., vol. 16, 1976. price varies. Pergamon Press, Inc., Maxwell House, Fairview Park, Elmsford, NY 10523.
Formerly: International Series of Monographs on Library and Information Sciences.

INTERNATIONAL SOCIETY FOR PERFORMING ARTS. LIBRARIES AND MUSEUMS. CONGRESS PROCEEDINGS. see *ART*

020 GW ISSN 0000-0221
INTERNATIONALES BIBLIOTHEKS-HANDBUCH/WORLD GUIDE TO LIBRARIES. (Text in English and German) 1966. irreg., 5th ed., 1980. DM.360($68) K.G. Saur Verlag KG, Poessenbacherstr. 12 B, Postfach 711009, 8000 Munich 71, W. Germany (B.R.D.) adv.

027 US ISSN 0075-0425
IOWA STATE UNIVERSITY. LIBRARY. ANNUAL REPORT. 1968. a. ‡ Iowa State University Library, Ames, IA 50010. Ed. Warren B. Kuhn.

026 025 IE
IRISH ARCHIVES BULLETIN. (Text in English & Gaelic) 1971. a. £2. Irish Society for Archives, 82 St. Stephen's Green, Dublin 2, Ireland. Ed. S. C. McMenamin. bk. rev. circ. 200. (back issues avail.)

050 070 IS ISSN 0078-0448
ISRAEL. GOVERMENT PRESS OFFICE. NEWSPAPERS AND PERIODICALS APPEARING IN ISRAEL. (Text in English) 1965. a. Government Press Office, Agron House, 37 Hillel St., Jerusalem, Israel.

020 US
ISSUES IN THE LIBRARY AND INFORMATION SCIENCES. 1972. irreg., no. 2, 1975. Rutgers University, Graduate School of Library and Information Studies, 4 Huntington St., New Brunswick, NJ 08903. Ed. Henry Voos.

016 IT
ITALY. ISTITUTO DI STUDI SULLA RICERCA E DOCUMENTAZIONE SCIENTIFICA. NOTE BIBLIOGRAFIA E DOCUMENTAZIONE SCIENTIFICA. 1955. irreg., vol. 36, 1979. price varies. Istituto di Studi sulla Ricerca e Documentazione Scientifica, Via Cesare do Lollis 12, 00185 Rome, Italy. Ed. Maria Pia Carosella. Indexed: Bull.Signal.
Formerly: Italy. Laboratorio di Studi sulla Ricerca e sulla Documentazione. Note di Bibliografia e Documentazione Scientifiche (ISSN 0085-2309)

JAHRBUCH DER AUKTIONSPREISE; fuer Buecher, Handschriften und Autographen. see *MUSEUMS AND ART GALLERIES*

020 GE ISSN 0075-2215
JAHRBUCH DER BIBLIOTHEKEN, ARCHIVE UND INFORMATIONSTELLEN DER DEUTSCHEN DEMOKRATISCHEN REPUBLIK. Title varies: Jahrbuch der Bibliotheken, Informationsstellen und Archive der D D R. 1959. biennial. M.33. Bibliographisches Institut, Hermann-Matern-Str. 57, 104 Berlin, E. Germany (D.D.R.) (Co-Sponsor: Bibliotheksverband der DDR) Eds. Heinz Gittig, Wolfgang Horscht. adv. bk. rev. circ. 3,500.

020 GW ISSN 0075-2223
JAHRBUCH DER DEUTSCHEN BIBLIOTHEKEN. 1902. biennial. DM.68 (approx.) (Verein Deutscher Bibliothekare) Verlag Otto Harrassowitz, Taunusstr. 6, Postfach 2929, 6200 Wiesbaden, W. Germany (B.R.D.) adv. circ. 2,400.

020.6 JM
JAMAICA LIBRARY ASSOCIATION. BULLETIN. 1950. a. Jamaica Library Association, P.O. Box 58, Kingston 5, Jamaica.
Formerly: Jamaica Library Association. Annual Bulletin (ISSN 0448-2174)

027 JA ISSN 0385-325X
JAPAN. NATIONAL DIET LIBRARY. ANNUAL REPORT/KOKURITSU KOKKAI TOSHOKAN NENPO. 1948. a. National Diet Library - Kokuritsu Kokkai Toshokan, 1-10-1 Nagata-cho, Chiyoda-ku, Tokyo 100, Japan. circ. 2,300.

027.4 SA
JOHANNESBURG PUBLIC LIBRARY. ANNUAL REPORT. (Text in English) 1891. a. free. Johannesburg Public Library, Market Square, Johannesburg 2001, South Africa. (back issues avail.)

050 US ISSN 0362-4544
JOURNAL HOLDINGS IN THE WASHINGTON-BALTIMORE AREA. 1969. biennial. $135. Interlibrary Users Association, c/o Metropolitan Washington Council of Governments, Information Center, 1225 Connecticut Ave., N.W., Washington, DC 20036. charts. circ. 160 (controlled) (processed; also avail. in microfiche)

020 970 US
JOURNAL OF LIBRARY HISTORY. STATE LIBRARY HISTORY BIBLIOGRAPHY SERIES. irreg. Florida State University, School of Library Science, Tallahassee, FL 32306.

020 US
JUNIOR HIGH SCHOOL LIBRARY CATALOG. 3rd edt., 1975. quinquennial, plus a. supplements. $42. H. W. Wilson Co., 950 University Ave., Bronx, NY 10452. Eds. Richard H. Isaacson, Gary L. Bogart.

020 US
JUST B'TWX US: AN INTERLIBRARY LOAN NEWSLETTER. 1970. irreg., vol. 5, no. 1, 1979. $5 for 2 yrs. University of Colorado Libraries, Interlibrary Loan Service, Boulder, CO 80309. Ed. Virginia Boucher. circ. 350. (processed)
Formerly: Just B'twx Us: An Interlibrary Loan Service Newsletter (ISSN 0075-4587)

020 US ISSN 0075-5311
KEEPSAKE. (Each issue has also a distinctive title) 1966. irreg., no. 9, 1979. $30. ‡ (Library Associates of the University Library, Davis) University of California, Davis, University Library, Davis, CA 95616.

020 KE ISSN 0075-5923
KENYA. NATIONAL LIBRARY SERVICE BOARD. ANNUAL AND AUDIT REPORT.* 1967/68. a. available on exchange. National Library Service Board, P.O. Box 30573, Nairobi, Kenya.

020 KE
KENYA LIBRARY ASSOCIATION CHAIRMAN'S ANNUAL REPORT. a. Kenya Library Association, Box 46031, Nairobi, Kenya.

020 CS
KNIHA. 1976. a. 25 Kcs. Matica Slovenska, Mudronova 35, 036 52 Martin, Czechoslovakia.
Formerly: Knizna Kultura.

020 CS ISSN 0075-6369
KNIZNICNY ZBORNIK/LIBRARY STUDIES. (Text in Slovak; summaries in German and Russian) 1957. irreg. price varies. Matica Slovenska, Mudronova 35, 036 52 Martin, Czechoslovakia. bk. rev.

020 HU ISSN 0075-6784
KONYVTARTUDOMANYI TANULMANYOK. (Text in Hungarian; summaries in English and Russian) 1958. irreg. price varies. (Orszagos Konyvtarugyi es Dokumentacios Tanacs) Nepmuvelesi Propaganda Iroda, Gorkij fasor 45, Budapest VII, Hungary. Eds. Mate Kovacs and Ararka Racz.

020 US ISSN 0094-615X
L A C U N Y OCCASIONAL PAPERS. 1972. irreg. incl. with subscr. to Urban Academic Librarian. Library Association of the City University of New York, c/o Kathleen Meier, Hunter College Library, 695 Park Ave., New York, NY 10021. Ed. Marguerite Iskenderian. circ. 600. Indexed: Lib.Lit.

020 US ISSN 0362-448X
L J SPECIAL REPORTS. 1976. irreg., no. 18, 1981. price varies. R. R. Bowker Company, 1180 Ave. of the Americas, New York, NY 10036 (Orders to: Box 1807, Ann Arbor, MI 48106) (reprint service avail. from UMI)

020 US ISSN 0095-4721
L.S.C.A. ANNUAL PROGRAM, HAWAII STATE LIBRARY SYSTEM. (Library Services and Construction Act) a. free to libraries. State Library, Office of Public Library Services, Research & Evaluation Servicess552478 S. King St., Honolulu, HI 96813.

023 NR ISSN 0047-3901
LAGOS LIBRARIAN. 1966. irreg., latest vol.7, 1978 (pub.1979) ‡ Nigerian Library Association, Lagos Division, c/o University Library, University of Lagos, Yaba, Lagos, Nigeria. adv. bk. rev. circ. 400.

020 340 GW
LANSKY: BIBLIOTHEKSRECHTLICHE VORSCHRIFTEN. irreg., 3rd, 1980. price varies. Vittorio Klostermann, Frauenlobstr. 22, Postfach 900601, D-6000 Frankfurt 90, W. Germany(B.R.D.)

020 US
LECTURE NOTES IN CONTROL AND INFORMATION SCIENCES. 1978. irreg., vol. 31, 1981. price varies. Springer-Verlag, 175 Fifth Ave., New York, NY 10010 (Also Berlin, Heidelberg, Vienna) Eds. A. V. Balakrishnan, M. Thoma. (report service avail. from ISI)

020 UK
LIBRARIES IN THE UNITED KINGDOM & THE REPUBLIC OF IRELAND. irreg. price varies. Library Association Publishing Ltd., 7 Ridgmount St., London WC1E 7AE, England.

LIBRARIES, MUSEUMS AND ART GALLERIES YEAR BOOK. see MUSEUMS AND ART GALLERIES

021 US ISSN 0092-833X
LIBRARIES OF MAINE; DIRECTORY AND STATISTICS. 1966. a. free. ‡ State Library, Department of Educational and Cultural Services, State House Sta. No. 64, Augusta, ME 04333. illus. stat.

020 JA
LIBRARY AND INFORMATION SCIENCE. (Text in English and Japanese) 1963. a. $15. Mita Society for Library and Information Science - Mita Toshokan Joho Gakkai, c/o Keio University, 2-15-15 Mita, Minato-ku, Tokyo 108, Japan. Ed. Yutaka Kobayashi. bk. rev. bibl. cum.index: nos. 1-10. circ. 1,150. Indexed: Curr.Cont. Lib.Lit. Lib.Sci.Abstr.

020.622 UK
LIBRARY ASSOCIATION. PROCEEDINGS, PAPERS AND SUMMARIES OF DISCUSSIONS AT THE ... CONFERENCE. a. Library Association Publishing Ltd., 7 Ridgmount St., London WC1E 7AE, England.

020 MM
LIBRARY ASSOCIATION (VALLETTA). GHAQDA BIBLJOTEKARJI/LIBRARY ASSOCIATION YEARBOOK. (Text in English) 1971. biennial. £1.70($4.50) Library Association (Valletta), c/o John XXIII Library, 226 St. Paul Street, Valletta, Malta. adv. circ. 500. Indexed: LISA.
Formerly: Malta Library Association Yearbook.

020.6 MM
LIBRARY ASSOCIATION (VALLETTA). GHAQDA BIBLJOTEKARJI/LIBRARY ASSOCIATION NEWSLETTER. (Text in English) 1969. irreg. membership. Library Association (Valletta), c/o John XXIII Library, 226 St. Paul Street, Valletta, Malta. Ed. Anthony F. Sapienza. bk. rev.
Formerly (until no. 30, 1978): Malta Library Association Newsletter.

020 UK ISSN 0075-9066
LIBRARY ASSOCIATION. YEAR BOOK. 1892. a. price varies. Library Association Publishing Ltd., 7 Ridgmount St., London WC1E 7AE, England.

020 UK
LIBRARY ASSOCIATION: A LIBRARIAN'S HANDBOOK. irreg., vol.2, 1980. price varies. Library Association Publishing Ltd., 7 Ridgmount St., London WC1E 7AE, England.

020 CN ISSN 0075-904X
LIBRARY ASSOCIATION OF ALBERTA. OCCASIONAL PAPERS. 1969. irreg. Can.$10. Library Association of Alberta, 1122 Crescent Rd N.W., Calgary 41, Alberta, Canada. bk. rev. circ. 700.

020 AT
LIBRARY ASSOCIATION OF AUSTRALIA. HANDBOOK. a. Aus.$7.50. Library Association of Australia, Science Centre, 35 Clarence St., Sydney, N.S.W. 2000, Australia.

020.6 BB
LIBRARY ASSOCIATION OF BARBADOS. BULLETIN. 1968. a. bds. $1. Library Association of Barbados, P.O. Box 827E, Bridgetown, Barbados, W. Indies.

020.6 BB
LIBRARY ASSOCIATION OF BARBADOS. OCCASIONAL NEWSLETTER. 1974. irreg. membership. Library Association of Barbados, Box 827E, Bridgetown, Barbados, W. Indies.

020 CH
LIBRARY ASSOCIATION OF CHINA. BULLETIN. no. 31, 1979. a. $5. Library Association of China, c/o National Central Library, 43 Nan Hai Rd., Taipei 107, Taiwan, Republic of China. adv. bk. rev. circ. 2,000.

020 TR ISSN 0521-9590
LIBRARY ASSOCIATION OF TRINIDAD AND TOBAGO. BULLETIN. 1964. a. T.T.$1. Library Association of Trinidad and Tobago, P.O. Box 1177, Port of Spain, Trinidad. Eds. Daphne Ottley & Yvonne Bobb.

029 US
LIBRARY BIBLIOGRAPHIES AND INDEXES. 1975. irreg. $58. Gale Research Company, Book Tower, Detroit, MI 48226. Eds. Paul Wasserman, Esther Herman.

020 US ISSN 0094-8829
LIBRARY DEVELOPMENT IN ALASKA: LONG RANGE PROGRAM. a. $5. Department of Education, Division of State Libraries and Museums, Pouch G.-State Office Building, Juneau, AK 99811.

020 MY
LIBRARY INDUSTRY. 1971. irreg. $2 per no. Melville Jayathissa, Ed. & Pub., No. 19, Road SS 1/7, Sungei Way - Subang, Selangor, Malaysia. adv. circ. controlled.

020 070.5 CN
LIBRARY INNOVATOR. 1972. irreg. Can.$20. Bibliotheca Polyglotta, P.O. Box 202, Postal Station A, Montreal, P.Q. H3C 2S1, Canada.

028 US ISSN 0075-9082
LIBRARY JOURNAL BOOK REVIEW. 1968. a. $35. R.R. Bowker Company, 1180 Ave. of the Americas, New York, NY 10036 (Orders to P. O. Box 1807, Ann Arbor, Mich. 48106) (reprint service avail. from UMI)

020 II
LIBRARY LITERATURE IN INDIA SERIES. no. 2, 1975. irreg. price varies. Library Literature House, Chandigarh, India. illus.

020 US
LIBRARY LOG. 1963. a. free. Friends of the Oak Park Public Library, 834 Lake St., Oak Park, IL 60301. circ. 20,000.

025 US
LIBRARY NETWORKS. 1974. biennial. $29.50. Knowledge Industry Publications, Inc., 701 Westchester Ave., White Plains, NY 10604. Ed. Susan K. Martin. bibl.

027.7 US ISSN 0024-2438
LIBRARY NOTES. 1936. irreg., no. 46, 1976. membership. (Friends of Duke University Library) Duke University, Library, Durham, NC 27706. Ed. John L. Sharpe. bibl. circ. 1,500. (also avail. in microfilm)

020　　　　　　　US　ISSN 0162-6426
LIBRARY OF CONGRESS; a brief summary of major activities. 1976. a. free. U.S. Library of Congress, Washington, DC 20540.

027　　　　　　　US　ISSN 0364-1236
LIBRARY RESOURCES FOR THE BLIND AND PHYSICALLY HANDICAPPED. 1968. a. free. U.S. Library of Congress, National Library Service for the Blind and Physically Handicapped, 1291 Taylor St., N.W., Washington, DC 20542. Indexed: ERIC.
Formerly: Directory of Library Resources for the Blind and Physically Handicapped.

021　　　　　　　UK
LIBRARY RESOURCES IN SCOTLAND. 1968. irreg. £5. Scottish Library Association, The Mitchell Library, North St., Glasgow G3 7DN, Scotland.

025　　　　　　　US　ISSN 0095-4098
LIBRARY RESOURCES NOTES. 1974. irreg. U.S. Library of Congress, Reference Department, Washington, DC 20540.

020　　　　　　　US　ISSN 0453-2406
LIBRARY SCHOOL REVIEW. 1954. irreg. $2 per no.; free to qualified personnel. Emporia State University, School of Library Science, Emporia, KS 66801. Ed. Marylouise D. Meder. circ. 500.

LIBRARY TELECOMMUNICATIONS DIRECTORY: CANADA - UNITED STATES. see *COMMUNICATIONS*

020　　　　　　　US
LIBRARY TRUSTEE; a practical guidebook. 2nd edt., 1969. irreg., latest edt. 1978. $15.95. R. R. Bowker Company, 1180 Ave. of the Americas, New York, NY 10036 (Orders to: Box 1807, Ann Arbor MI 48106) Ed. Virginia G. Young. (reprint service avail. from UMI)

027　　　　　　　US　ISSN 0085-2759
LOUISIANA STATE UNIVERSITY. LIBRARY. LIBRARY LECTURES. 1965. irreg., no. 6, 1979. free. Louisiana State University Library, Baton Rouge, LA 70803. Ed. Caroline Wire. circ. controlled. (also avail. in microform from EDR) Indexed: LISA. Lib.Lit. Inform.Sci.Abstr.

027.7　　　　　　US
LOUISIANA STATE UNIVERSITY. LIBRARY. REPORT OF THE DIRECTOR. 1943. a. free. Louisiana State University Library, Baton Rouge, LA 70803. circ. 300(controlled)

027.4　　　　　　ZA
LUSAKA CITY LIBRARY. ANNUAL REPORT. 1977. a. free. Lusaka City Library, Box 1304, Katondo Rd., Lusaka, Zambia. circ. 150. (processed)

027.7　　　　　　CN　ISSN 0024-9270
MCMASTER UNIVERSITY LIBRARY RESEARCH NEWS. 1969. irreg. Can.$6 for 3 nos. ‡ McMaster University Library Press, Mills Memorial Library, Hamilton, Ont. L8S 4L6, Canada. Ed. Wm. Ready. illus.

026.025　　　　　US　ISSN 0091-0759
MAINE. STATE LIBRARY. SPECIAL SUBJECT RESOURCES IN MAINE. irreg., latest issue 1972. State Library, State House Sta. No. 64, Augusta, ME 04333. Key Title: Special Subject Resources in Maine.

020　　　　　　　MY　ISSN 0126-7809
MAJALLAH PERPUSTAKAAN MALAYSIA. (Text in English and Malay) 1972. a. M.8. Persatuan Perpustakaan Malaysia, Box 2545, Kuala Lumpur, Malaysia. Ed. Lim Hucktee. bk. rev. circ. 500. Indexed: LISA.

026　610　　　　　UG
MAKERERE UNIVERSITY. ALBERT COOK LIBRARY. LIBRARY BULLETIN AND ACCESSION LIST. irreg., no. 2, 1977. free. Makerere University, Albert Cook Library, Makerere Medical School, Box 7072, Kampala, Uganda. Ed. Goretty Byaruhanga. circ. controlled. (processed; back issues avail.)

020　　　　　　　UG　ISSN 0075-4854
MAKERERE UNIVERSITY. LIBRARY. MAKERERE LIBRARY PUBLICATIONS. Short title: Makerere Library Publications. 1961. irreg. free. Makerere University, Library, Box 16002, Kampala, Uganda.

027.5689　　　　　MW
MALAWI. NATIONAL LIBRARY SERVICE. ANNUAL REPORT. 1969. a. contr.free circ. National Library Service, Box 30314, Capital City, Lilongwe 3, Malawi. circ. controlled.
Formerly: Malawi. National Library. Annual Report (ISSN 0581-0906)

021　　　　　　　CN　ISSN 0706-7798
MANITOBA. PUBLIC LIBRARY SERVICES. NEWSLETTER. 1978. irreg. Public Library Services, 139 Hamelin St., Winnipeg, Man. R3T 4H4, Canada.

021.7　　　　　　US
MARGINAL NOTES; an interim newsletter. no. 17, Nov. 1977. irreg. Friends of the Duke University Library, Durham, NC 27706.

MARIAN LIBRARY STUDIES. NEW SERIES. see *RELIGIONS AND THEOLOGY*

020　　　　　　　MF　ISSN 0076-5481
MAURITIUS. ARCHIVES DEPARTMENT. ANNUAL REPORT. (Includes yearly supplement Bibliography of Mauritius) (Text in English; bibliographical supplement in English and French) 1950 (covers 1949) a. Rs.10. Archives Department, Sunray Hotel, Coromandel, Beau-Bassin, Mauritius (Orders to: Government Printing Office, Elizabeth II Ave., Port Louis, Mauritius)

020　500　600　330　CS　ISSN 0322-7243
METODICKY ZPRAVODAJ CS. SOUSTAVY VEDECKYCH, TECHNICKYCH A EKONOMICKYCH INFORMACI. 1973. irreg. free. Ustredni Vedeckych Technickych a Ekonomickych Informaci, Konviktska 5, 113 57 Prague 1, Czechoslovakia. Ed. Bohumila Grogerova. circ. 1,000.

020　　　　　　　US　ISSN 0363-1257
METRO C.A.P. CATALOG; a dictionary catalog of materials purchased through the Cooperative Acquisitions Program. 1976. a. price varies. New York Metropolitan Reference and Research Library Agency, 33 W. 42nd St., New York, NY 10036.

026　　　　　　　US　ISSN 0076-7018
METRO; NEW YORK METROPOLITAN REFERENCE AND RESEARCH LIBRARY AGENCY. METRO MISCELLANEOUS PUBLICATIONS SERIES. 1968. irreg., latest no. 28. ‡ New York Metropolitan Reference & Research Library Agency, 33 W. 42nd St., New York, NY 10036.

020　　　　　　　US　ISSN 0076-7050
METROPOLITAN LIBRARY SERVICE AGENCY. ANNUAL REPORT. 1970. a. Metropolitan Library Service Agency, Griggs-Midway Bldg., Room S-275, 1821 University Ave., St. Paul, MN 55104.

020　　　　　　　MX
MEXICO. ARCHIVO GENERAL DE LA NACION. ARCHIVO HISTORICO DE HACIENDA. COLECCION DOCUMENTAL. 1975. irreg. Archivo General de la Nacion, Mexico, D.F., Mexico.

021　　　　　　　US　ISSN 0076-8081
MICHIGAN LIBRARY DIRECTORY & STATISTICS. 1967. a. free. Department of Education, State Library Services, Box 30007, Lansing, MI 48909. Ed. Donald C. Leaf. circ. 1,000.
Formerly the library's: Michigan Library News.

020　　　　　　　US　ISSN 0076-8324
MICHIGAN TECHNOLOGICAL UNIVERSITY. LIBRARY. LIBRARY PUBLICATION. 1965. irreg., 1973, no. 7. free. ‡ Michigan Technological University, Library, Houghton, MI 49931.

778.1　　　　　　US　ISSN 0362-0999
MICROFORM MARKET PLACE. Short title: M M P. 1974. biennial. $20.95. Microform Review, Inc., Box 405, Saugatuck Sta., Westport, CT 06880. Ed. Ardis V. Carleton. adv.

778.315　　　　　US　ISSN 0002-6530
MICROFORM REVIEW. Cumulated Every 5 Yrs (ISSN 0162-0940) 1972. q. $40 (with microfiche edition $75) Microform Review, Inc., Box 405, Saugatuck Station, Westport, CT 06880. Ed. Allen B. Veaner. adv. bk. rev. index. circ. 1,800. (also avail. in microform from MIM) Indexed: Inform.Sci.Abstr. LISA. Lib.Lit.
Reprography

020　　　　　　　US　ISSN 0362-1006
MICROGRAPHICS EQUIPMENT REVIEW. 1976. a. $175 (institutional price varies) Microform Review, Inc., Box 405, Saugatuck Station, Westport, CT 06880. Ed. William Saffady. index.

MODSZERTANI KIADVANYOK/METHODS OF INFORMATION AND DOCUMENTATION. see *TECHNOLOGY: COMPREHENSIVE WORKS*

021　　　　　　　US　ISSN 0094-873X
MONTANA LIBRARY DIRECTORY, WITH STATISTICS OF MONTANA PUBLIC LIBRARIES. a. State Library, 930 E. Lyndale Ave., Helena, MT 59601. Ed. Jo Ann Fallang. stat.

020　　　　　　　US
MONTANA NEWSLETTER. 1965. irreg. free. State Library, 930 East Lyndale Ave., Helena, MT 59601. Ed. Jo Ann Fallang. bibl. circ. (controlled)

020　060　　　　　AU　ISSN 0077-2208
MUSEION. 1957. irreg. price varies. (Oesterreichische Nationalbibliothek) Brueder Hollinek, Gallgasse 40A, A-1130 Vienna, Austria.

026　　　　　　　US　ISSN 0094-5099
MUSIC LIBRARY ASSOCIATION. TECHNICAL REPORTS; information for music media specialists. 1973. irreg. price varies. Music Library Association, 2017 Walnut St., Philadelphia, PA 19103. Ed. Lenore Coral. circ. 150. Indexed: RILM.

020　　　　　　　US　ISSN 0161-1704
MUSIC O C L C USERS GROUP. NEWSLETTER. 1977. irreg. $3 to individuals; institutions $5. Music O C L C Users Group, c/o Pamela Berlin, Mills Music Library, University of Wisconsin, 728 State St., Madison, WI 53706.

020　　　　　　　UN
N A T I S-NEWS. French edition: N A T I S-Nouvelles. Spanish edt.: N A T I S Noticias. (Newsletter containing information on the implementation in Unesco member states of national information systems) (Text in English, French, Spanish) 1975. irreg. free. Unesco, 7-9 Place de Fontenoy, 75700 Paris, France.

020　　　　　　　YU　ISSN 0350-3569
NARODNA IN UNIVERZITETNA KNJIZNICA, LJUBLJANA. ZBORNIK. (Text in Slovenian; summaries in French and German) 1974. irreg. Narodna in Univerzitetna Knjiznica, Turjaska 1, 61001 Ljubljana, Yugoslavia. Ed. Tomo Martelanc. illus.

025.17　　　　　　ZA　ISSN 0084-4942
NATIONAL ARCHIVES OF ZAMBIA. ANNUAL REPORT. 1964. a; latest 1974. National Archives, Box RW 10, Ridgeway, Lusaka, Zambia.

020　　　　　　　RH
NATIONAL FREE LIBRARY SERVICE. ANNUAL REPORT. 1961/62. a. free on exchange. ‡ National Free Library Service, P.O. Box 1773, Bulawayo, Zimbabwe. circ. 450.
Formerly: National Free Library of Rhodesia. Annual Report (ISSN 0068-3612)

027.571　　　　　CN　ISSN 0078-7000
NATIONAL LIBRARY OF CANADA. ANNUAL REPORT. (Text in English and French) 1963. a. free. ‡ National Library of Canada, Public Relations Office, 395 Wellington St., Ottawa, Ont. K1A 0N4, Canada. circ. 6,000.

020　　　　　　　US　ISSN 0093-0393
NATIONAL LIBRARY OF MEDICINE. PROGRAMS AND SERVICES. a. free. ‡ U.S. National Library of Medicine, National Institutes of Health, 8600 Rockville Pike, Bethesda, MD 20209. (reprint service avail. from UMI)
Formerly (until 1972): U.S. National Library of Medicine. Annual Report (ISSN 0083-2243)

025　　　　　　　US　ISSN 0547-8448
NATIONAL REGISTER OF MICROFORM MASTERS. 1965. a. $100 for 1979 edition; 1965-75 cummulation; $190 (no separate 1975 cumulation) ‡ U.S. Library of Congress, Catalog Publication Division, 10 First St. S.E., Washington, DC 20540 (Orders to: LC Cataloging Distribution Service, Building, No. 159, Navy Yard Annex, Washington DC 20541) Ed. Imre T. Jarmy. circ. 3,500.

021 US ISSN 0099-0299
NEBRASKA LIBRARY COMMISSION. ANNUAL REPORT. a. Library Commission, 1420 P St, Lincoln, NE 68508. Key Title: Annual Report - Nebraska Library Commission.

027.4 NE
NETHERLANDS. CENTRAAL BUREAU VOOR DE STATISTIEK. STATISTIEK VAN DE OPENBARE BIBLIOTHEKEN. a. fl.21. Centraal Bureau voor de Statistiek, Prinses Beatrixlaan 428, Voorburg, Netherlands (Orders to: Staatsuitgeverij, Christoffel Plantijnstraat, The Hague, Netherlands) stat.

029 US ISSN 0160-9742
NETWORK PLANNING PAPER. 1978. irreg., no. 5, 1979. U.S. Library of Congress, Network Development Office, Cataloging Distribution Service, Customer Services Section, Navy Yard Annex, Bldg. 159, Washington, DC 20541. Ed. David C. Hartman. bibl. charts.

020 US
NEVADA LIBRARY DIRECTORY AND STATISTICS. 1975. a. free. State Library, Capitol Complex, Carson City, NV 89710.

025 US ISSN 0147-1090
NEW DIRECTIONS IN LIBRARIANSHIP. 1978. irreg. $75. Greenwood Press, 88 Post Rd. W., Westport, CT 06881. Ed. Daniel Gore.

021 US ISSN 0362-2967
NEW JERSEY AREA LIBRARY DIRECTORY. irreg. State Library, 185 W. State St., Trenton, NJ 08625. Ed. Vianne Connor. illus.

022 UK ISSN 0307-9767
NEW LIBRARY BUILDINGS. 1963. irreg. price varies. Library Association Publishing Ltd., 7 Ridgmount St., London WC1E 7AE, England. Ed. Herbert Ward.
Formerly: Library Buildings (ISSN 0075-9074)

027 US ISSN 0077-930X
NEW YORK. STATE LIBRARY, ALBANY. DIVISION OF LIBRARY DEVELOPMENT. EXCERPTS FROM THE NEW YORK STATE EDUCATION LAW, RULES OF THE BOARD OF REGENTS, AND REGULATIONS OF THE COMMISSIONER OF EDUCATION PERTAINING TO PUBLIC AND FREE ASSOCIATION LIBRARIES, LIBRARY SYSTEMS, TRUSTEES AND LIBRARIANS. 1959. a. free to libraries in New York State; on exchange basis with other libraries. State Library, Division of Library Development, Albany, NY 12224. Ed. E. J. Josey.

027 US ISSN 0077-9318
NEW YORK. STATE LIBRARY, ALBANY. DIVISION OF LIBRARY DEVELOPMENT. INSTITUTION LIBRARIES STATISTICS. 1954. irreg. free to libraries in New York State; on exchange basis with other libraries. ‡ State Library, Division of Library Development, Albany, NY 12224. Ed. E. J. Josey. circ. 1,000.

027 US ISSN 0077-9326
NEW YORK. STATE LIBRARY, ALBANY. DIVISION OF LIBRARY DEVELOPMENT. PUBLIC AND ASSOCIATION LIBRARIES STATISTICS. (Title varies: 1950-1955, Its Statistics of Public and Association Libraries) 1950. a. free to libraries in New York State; on exchange basis with other libraries. State Library, Division of Library Development, Albany, NY 12224. Ed. E. J. Josey.

020 US ISSN 0362-8744
NEW YORK METROPOLITAN REFERENCE & RESEARCH LIBRARY AGENCY. DIRECTORY OF MEMBERS. 1970. every 2-3 yrs. price varies. ‡ New York Metropolitan Reference & Research Library Agency, 33 W. 42nd St., New York, NY 10036. Ed. L. Dawn Pohlman. circ. 1,000.

020 US ISSN 0077-9016
NEW YORK PUBLIC LIBRARY. FILMS; a catalogue of the film collection. 1953. irreg., latest supplement 1978. $4. New York Public Library, Office of Branch Libraries, 8 E. 40th St., New York, NY 10018. Ed. William Sloan. index.

026 US
NEW YORK STATE LIBRARY, ALBANY. MISCELLANEOUS PUBLICATION. no. 2, 1977. irreg. State Library, Albany, NY 12224.

026 US ISSN 0077-9490
NEW YORK UNIVERSITY. LIBRARIES. BULLETIN OF THE TAMIMENT LIBRARY. 1957. irreg., no. 49, 1974. free. ‡ New York University, Tamiment Library, 70 Washington Sq. So., New York, NY 10012. Ed. Dorothy Swanson. circ. 500. (also avail. in microfilm) Indexed: P.A.I.S.

020 US
NEWBERRY LIBRARY BULLETIN. 1944. irreg. free. Newberry Library, 60 W. Walton St., Chicago, IL 60610. Ed. James M. Wells. cum index. circ. 2,500.

025 GW ISSN 0072-4866
NIEDERSAECHSISCHE STAATS- UND UNIVERSITAETSBIBLIOTHEK, GOETTINGEN. ARBEITEN. 1954. irreg., no. 17, 1980. DM.38. (Niedersaechsische Staats- und Universitaetsbibliothek) Vandenhoeck und Ruprecht, Theaterstr. 13, 3400 Goettingen, W. Germany (B.R.D.)

027 US ISSN 0094-8977
NON SOLUS. 1974. a. $5 to non-members. University of Illinois at Urbana-Champaign, Library Friends, Library Publications Office, 249 Armory, Champaign, IL 61820. Ed. Scott Bennett. illus.

020 DK
NORDISK ARKIVKUNSKAB. (Text in Scandinavian languages) 1972. irreg (approx. a) price varies. Landsarkivet for Sjaelland, Jagtvej 10, 2200 Copenhagen N, Denmark. Ed. Harald Joergensen. circ. 800.

020 US ISSN 0029-2699
NORTH COUNTRY REFERENCE & RESEARCH RESOURCES COUNCIL. NEWSLETTER. 1968. irreg. membership. ‡ North Country Reference & Research Resources Council, Box 568, Canton, NY 13617. Ed. Richard H. Kimball. stat. circ. 200. (processed)

020 US ISSN 0048-0789
NORTHERN LIBRARIES BULLETIN. 1972. irreg. (approx. 3/yr.) free. ‡ Department of Education, Division of State Libraries and Museums, Pouch G, Juneau, AK 99811. Ed. Phyllis Demuth. bk. rev. bibl. circ. 150.

020 NO
NORWAY. RIKSBIBLIOTEKTJENESTEN. AARSMELDING. a. free. Riksbibliotektjenesten, Box 2439, Solli, Oslo 2, Norway.

020 US ISSN 0078-2025
NOTES FOR MEDICAL CATALOGERS. 1965. irreg. $5. ‡ U.S. National Library of Medicine, National Institutes of Health, 8600 Rockville Pike, Bethesda, MD 20209 (Distributed by: Medical Library Association, 919 N. Michigan Ave., Suite 3208, Chicago, IL 60611) circ. 1,000.

021.6 US ISSN 0090-8673
O C L C. ANNUAL REPORT. a. free. O C L C, 6565 Frantz Rd., Dublin, OH 43017. Ed. Philip Schieber. Key Title: Annual Report - Ohio College Library Center.

023 AT ISSN 0078-3080
OCCASIONAL PAPERS IN LIBRARIANSHIP. 1965. irreg. price varies. Libraries Board of South Australia, Box 419 G.P.O., Adelaide, S. Australia 5001, Australia.

026 016 AU
OESTERREICHISCHES STAATSARCHIV. PUBLIKATIONEN; Inventare oesterreichischer staatlicher Archive. 1909. irreg. price varies. Verlag Ferdinand Berger und Soehne OHG, Wiener Str. 21-23, A-3580 Horn, Austria.

020 US
OHIO. STATE LIBRARY. STATE LIBRARY REVIEW. 1972. a. free. State Library, 65 S. Front St., Columbus, OH 43215. Ed. Claudine M. Smith. charts. illus. stat.

020 US ISSN 0066-4065
OKLAHOMA. DEPARTMENT OF LIBRARIES. ANNUAL REPORT AND DIRECTORY OF LIBRARIES IN OKLAHOMA. 1955. a. free. ‡ Department of Libraries, 200 N. E. 18th St., Oklahoma City, OK 73105. Ed. Jan Blakely.

020 US ISSN 0078-6373
ORGANIZATION OF AMERICAN STATES. DEPARTMENT OF CULTURAL AFFAIRS. ESTUDIOS BIBLIOTECARIOS. 1958. irreg. $3. Organization of American States, Department of Publications, Washington, DC 20006.

020 US ISSN 0078-6381
ORGANIZATION OF AMERICAN STATES. DEPARTMENT OF CULTURAL AFFAIRS. MANUALES DEL BIBLIOTECARIO. 1961. irreg., latest no. 9. $15. Organization of American States, Department of Publications, Washington, DC 20006. circ. 2,000.

020 HU ISSN 0524-8868
ORSZAGOS SZECHENYI KONYVTAR. EVKONYV. (Text in Hungarian; summaries in English, French, German, Russian) 1958. a. 120 Ft. Orszagos Szechenyi Konyvtar, Muzeum korut 14-16, 1088 Budapest, Hungary. Ed. Bd.

020 US ISSN 0146-2237
P L A REPORT. 1973. a. free. Post Library Association, Long Island Univ., C.W. Post Center, Greenvale, NY 11548. Ed. Joan H. Huntoon. bk. rev. bibl. illus. circ. 2,000.

020 US ISSN 0079-0656
PENNSYLVANIA STATE UNIVERSITY. LIBRARIES. BIBLIOGRAPHIC SERIES. 1969. irreg., latest no. 7. price varies. ‡ Pennsylvania State University, University Libraries, University Park, PA 16802. Ed. Charles H. Ness. circ. 500.

050 016 US
PERIODICAL PERIODICAL. 1972. irreg. $2. ‡ Los Angeles Valley College Library, Periodicals Department, 5800 Fulton, Van Nuys, CA 91401. Ed. Barbara Toohey. circ. 570. (processed)
Formerly(until Oct. 1979): Periodicals Periodical.

PERU. BIBLIOTECA NACIONAL. BOLETIN. see BIBLIOGRAPHIES

027.4 PE ISSN 0031-6067
PERU. BIBLIOTECA NACIONAL. BOLETIN. 1943. a. $3. Instituto Nacional de Cultura, Biblioteca Nacional, Av. Abancay, 4a. Cuadra, Apdo. 2335, Lima, Peru. Ed. Lucila Valderrama. bibl. stat. circ. 1,000.

020 PH
PHILIPPINE LIBRARY ASSOCIATION. BULLETIN. (Text in English) vol. 8, 1973. a. P.10($6) Philippine Library Association, c/o National Library, T.M. Kalaw St., Manila, Philippines. Ed. Rev. Paul M. de Vera, OSB. circ. 1,000. (back issues avail.)

PHILIPPINES. GOVERNMENT PRINTING OFFICE. ITEMIZATION OF PERSONAL SERVICES AND ORGANIZATIONAL CHARTS. see PUBLIC ADMINISTRATION

027 US
PITTSBURGH REGIONAL LIBRARY CENTER. NEWSLETTER. no. 43, 1978. irreg. Pittsburgh Regional Library Center, Chatham College, Beatty Hall, Pittsburgh, PA 15232. circ. 350.

020 US
POINTS NORTHWEST. 1972. 4-6/yr. $5 to non-members. American Society for Information Science, Pacific Northwest Chapter, c/o Agnes M. Grady, Ed., Library, Oregon State University, Corvallis, OR 97331. circ. 120.

026 060 PL ISSN 0079-3140
POLSKA AKADEMIA NAUK. BIBLIOTEKA, KRAKOW. ROCZNIK. (Text in Polish; summaries in English and Russian) 1955. a. 75 Zl.($8) Ossolineum, Publishing House of the Polish Academy of Sciences, Rynek 9, 50-106 Wroclaw, Poland (Dist. by Ars Polona-Ruch, Krakowskie Przedmiescie 7, Warsaw, Poland) Ed. Zbigniew Jablonski. index.

020 UR
PROGNOZIROVANIE RAZVITYA BIBLIOTECHNOGO DELA V S.S.S.R. 1972. irreg. 0.53 Rub. Moskovskaya Publichnaya Biblioteka, Moscow, U.S.S.R.

PROGRESS IN COMMUNICATION SCIENCES. see COMMUNICATIONS

020   US   ISSN 0555-6031
PUBLIC LIBRARY REPORTER. Title varies; 1954-58: P L D Reporter. 1954. irreg. price varies. (Public Library Association) American Library Association, 50 East Huron Street, Chicago, IL 60611.

020   CN   ISSN 0380-7150
Q L A BULLETIN. (Text in English and French) 1971. irreg. Quebec Library Association, c/o Dawson College Library, 1001 Sherbrooke St. E., Montreal, Que. H2L 1L3, Canada.

020   CN   ISSN 0079-8428
QUEBEC LIBRARY ASSOCIATION. NEWSLETTER.* (Formerly: Q L A Bulletin) (Text in English and French) 1954. irreg. free. Agence de Publicite Media Ltee., 1460 Ave. Union, Montreal, Que., Canada.

020   US   ISSN 0146-8677
QUEENS COLLEGE STUDIES IN LIBRARIANSHIP. 1977. irreg. (approx. 1/yr.) price varies. Queens College Press, Flushing, NY 11367. Ed. Robert A. Colby. (back issues avail.)

027.7   CN
QUEEN'S UNIVERSITY AT KINGSTON. ANNUAL REPORT ON THE LIBRARIES. a. Queen's University, Kingston, Ont., Canada.

020 940   GW   ISSN 0079-9068
QUELLEN UND FORSCHUNGEN AUS ITALIENISCHEN ARCHIVEN UND BIBLIOTHEKEN. (Text in German, Greek, Italian, Latin) a. price varies. (Deutsches Historisches Institut in Rom, IT) Max Niemeyer Verlag, Pfrondorfer Str. 4, 7400 Tuebingen, W. Germany (B.R.D.)

027   UR
RAIONNYE BIBLIOTEKI BELORUSSII; analiz sostoyaniya raboty i metodicheskie rekomendatsii. 1957. a. free. Gosudarstvennaya Biblioteka Belorusskoi S. S. R. im V. I. Lenina, Krasnozmanennaya ul., 9, Minsk, U.S.S.R. Ed. E. N. Tsygankov. circ. 370. (also avail. in microfilm)

028   US   ISSN 0080-0430
REFERENCE AND SUBSCRIPTION BOOKS REVIEWS. 1960. a. $10. American Library Association, Reference and Subscription Books Review Committee, 50 E. Huron St., Chicago, IL 60611. Ed. Helen K. Wright. circ. 4,000.
    Supersedes: Subscription Books Bulletin Reviews.

016.34   SW
REGISTER OVER GAELLANDE SFS-FOERFATTNINGAR. irreg. Liber Foerlag, Fack, 162 89 Stockholm, Sweden.

020   US   ISSN 0080-1739
RESEARCH STUDIES IN LIBRARY SCIENCE. 1970. irreg., latest 1978. Libraries Unlimited, Inc., P.O. Box 263, Littleton, CO 80160. Ed. Bohdan S. Wynar.

027   US   ISSN 0080-3227
RIVER BEND LIBRARY SYSTEM. REPORT OF THE DIRECTOR. 1966. a. free. ‡ River Bend Library System, Box 125, Coal Valley, IL 61240. Ed. G.A. Curtis. circ. 20. (back issues avail.)

020   US   ISSN 0035-8312
ROSENBERG LIBRARY BULLETIN. 1969. irreg. $10. ‡ Friends of the Rosenberg Library, 2310 Sealy Ave., Galveston, TX 77550. Ed. Ken Bonham. bk. rev. bibl. illus. circ. 600.

027.7   GW
RUNDSCHREIBEN. q. Verein der Diplom-Bibliothekare an Wissenschaftlichen Bibliotheken, e.V., c/o Universitaetsbibliothek, Postfach 102148, 4630 Bochum 1, W. Germany (B.R.D.)

020.6   US
S H A R E. (Sisters Have Resources Everywhere); a directory of feminist library workers. 1975. biennial. $5. Women Library Workers, Box 9052, Berkeley, CA 94709. Ed. Carole Leita. index. circ. 1,000.

620 025.33   US
S H E. (Subject Headings for Engineering) 1972. irreg. plus supplements. $20. Engineering Index, Inc., 345 East 47th Street, New York, NY 10017.

020   US
S L A STATE-OF-THE-ART REVIEW SERIES. 1973. irreg., no.6, 1977. price varies. Special Libraries Association, 235 Park Ave. S., New York, NY 10003. (reprint service avail. from UMI)

020   US
S U N Y L A NEWSLETTER. 1968. irreg. (approx. 4/yr.) free. State University of New York Librarians Association, Drake Memorial Library, State University College at Brockport, Brockport, NY 14420. Ed. Virginia Cameron. bibl. circ. 315.

010   NE   ISSN 0581-2674
SAFAHO-MONOGRAPHS. 1962. irreg. price varies. (Safaho-Stiftung zur Foerderung Bibliographischer Forschung) Erasmus Antiquariaat & Boekhandel, Spui 2, Amsterdam, Netherlands. Ed. A. Horodisch.
    Formerly (1962-1969): Safaho-Monographien.

025.2 500   US   ISSN 0080-746X
SCIENCE AND TECHNOLOGY; a purchase guide for branch and public libraries. 1963. a. $4. Carnegie Library of Pittsburgh, Director's Office, 4400 Forbes Ave., Pittsburgh, PA 15213. Ed. Robert K. Matlack. circ. 540. (also avail. in microform from EDR) Indexed: Lib.Lit.
    Continues: Basic Collection of Science and Technology Books.
    Annotated bibliography

027   UK   ISSN 0080-8091
SCOTTISH LIBRARIES. 1966. triennial. £1.25. Scottish Library Association, The Mitchell Library, North St., Glasgow G3 7DN, Scotland. Eds. Christian E. G. Wright, Ian R. M. Mowatt. adv. circ. 600.

027.4   MY
SELANGOR PUBLIC LIBRARY. ANNUAL REPORT/PERBADANAN PERPUSTAKAAN AWAM SELANGOR. LAPURAN TAHUNAN. 1972. a. Selangor Public Library, 21 Jalan Raja, Kuala Lumpur 01-02, Malaysia. stat. circ. 500.

025   US   ISSN 0080-8849
SEMINAR ON THE ACQUISITION OF LATIN AMERICAN LIBRARY MATERIALS. FINAL REPORT AND WORKING PAPERS. Variant title: Reuniones Bibliotecologicas. 1956. a. $30 to non-members. ‡ Seminar on the Acquisition of Latin American Library Materials, SALALM Secretariat, c/o Benson Latin American Collection, University of Texas at Austin, Austin, TX 78712. cum.index(nos. 1-15) Indexed: Lib.Lit.

070 980   US   ISSN 0080-8857
SEMINAR ON THE ACQUISITION OF LATIN AMERICAN LIBRARY MATERIALS. MICROFILMING PROJECTS NEWSLETTER. 1964. a. $3. Seminar on the Acquisition of Latin American Library Materials, c/o Benson Latin American Collection, University of Texas at Austin, Austin, TX 78712. Ed. Suzanne Hodgman. cum.index (nos. 1-10; 11-15) circ. 300-350. (processed) Indexed: Lib.Lit.

026   SG
SENEGAL. ARCHIVES. RAPPORT ANNUEL. a. Archives du Senegal, Immeuble Administratif, Av. Roume, Dakar, Senegal.

020   US
SENIOR HIGH SCHOOL LIBRARY CATALOG. quinquennial, with a. supplements. $50. ‡ H. W. Wilson Co., 950 University Ave., Bronx, New York, NY 10452. Ed. Estelle A. Fidell. bk. rev.

SERIALS IN EDUCATION IN AUSTRALIAN LIBRARIES: A UNION LIST. see EDUCATION

016.05   US   ISSN 0148-4451
SERIALS IN TRANSITION. 1977. a. $8. F.W. Faxon Co., Inc., Publishing Division, 15 Southwest Park, Westwood, MA 02090.

SERIALS UPDATING SERVICE ANNUAL. see BIBLIOGRAPHIES

020   SL   ISSN 0583-2268
SIERRA LEONE. LIBRARY BOARD. REPORT. 1961. a, latest 1973/74. $0.40. Library Board, Box 326, Freetown, Sierra Leone. (back issues avail.)

020   SI   ISSN 0080-9721
SINGAPORE. NATIONAL LIBRARY. ANNUAL REPORT. 1875. a. exchange basis. National Library, Stamford Road, Singapore 0617, Singapore. circ. 1,000.

027   SI   ISSN 0085-6118
SINGAPORE LIBRARIES. (Text in English, Chinese Malay and Tamil) 1971. a. S.$16($10) Library Association of Singapore, c/o National Library, Stamford Road, Singapore 0617, Singapore. Ed. Michael Cheng. adv. bk. rev. circ. 500. Indexed: Lib.Lit.

020.6   US
SOLINET. ANNUAL REPORT. a. free. Southeastern Library Network, 615 Peachtree St. N.E., Atlanta, GA 30308. charts. stat.
    Formerly: Southeastern Library Network. Annual Report (ISSN 0099-085X)

020   US   ISSN 0038-1853
SOUNDINGS (SANTA BARBARA); collections of the University Library. 1969. a. $2 to non-members. ‡ University of California, Santa Barbara, Library, Santa Barbara, CA 93106. Ed. Donald E. Fitch. bibl. illus. circ. 600. Indexed: M.L.A.

027   US   ISSN 0085-6347
SOURCE (ANN ARBOR) 1972. irreg. ‡ University Microfilms International, 300 North Zeeb Rd., Ann Arbor, MI 48106. Ed. Stevens Rice. circ. 15,000. (also avail. in microform from UMI)

027.568   SA
SOUTH AFRICA. STATE LIBRARY COUNCIL. REPORT/VERSLAG. (Text in English and Afrikaans) irreg. free. State Library, P.O. Box 397, Pretoria, South Africa. illus.

020.6   SA
SOUTH AFRICAN LIBRARY ASSOCIATION. ANNUAL REPORT/SUID-AFRIKAANSE BIBLIOTEEKVERENIGING. JAARVERSLAG. (Text in English and Afrikaans) a. South African Library Association, c/o Ferdinand Postma Library, Potchefstroom University for Christian Higher Education, Potchefstroom 2520, South Africa. bibl. charts.

025   AT   ISSN 0081-2633
SOUTH AUSTRALIA. LIBRARIES BOARD. ANNUAL REPORT. 1884/5. a. free. Libraries Board of South Australia, Box 419 G.P.O., Adelaide, S. Australia 5001, Australia. circ. 450-500. Indexed: Aus.P.A.I.S.

027   US
SOUTH CAROLINA STATE LIBRARY. ANNUAL REPORT. 1943. a. free. State Library, 1500 Senate St., P.O. Box 11469, Columbia, SC 29211. Ed. Estellene P. Walker. circ. 500(controlled)

020 950   UK   ISSN 0308-4035
SOUTH EAST ASIA LIBRARY GROUP NEWSLETTER. 1968. irreg. (approx. 2/yr.) free. ‡ South East Asia Library Group, c/o British Library Reference Division, Department of Oriental Manuscripts and Printed Books, London WC1B 3DG, England. bk. rev. bibl. circ. 200.

020   CN   ISSN 0707-6894
SOUTHEAST REGIONAL LIBRARY (SASK.) LIBRARY DIRECTORY. Variant title: Directory of Libraries in Southeast Saskatchewan. 1975. a. free contr. circ. Southeast Regional Library (Sask.), Box 550, Weyburn, Sask. S4H 2K7, Canada. illus.

026   US   ISSN 0093-9587
SPECIAL LIBRARIES DIRECTORY OF GREATER NEW YORK. 13th edition, 1974. biennial. $15. Special Libraries Association, New York Chapter, c/o Dorothy Kasman, Coopers & Lybrand Library, 1251 Ave. of Americas, New York, NY 10020.

020   US
SPRINGER SERIES IN INFORMATION SCIENCES. 1980. irreg. Springer-Verlag, 175 Fifth Ave., New York, NY 10010 (Also Berlin, Heidelberg, Vienna) Ed. K. S. Fu, T. S. Huang. (reprint service avail. from ISI)

LIBRARY AND INFORMATION SCIENCES

026   GW   ISSN 0340-0700
STAATSBIBLIOTHEK PREUSSISCHER KULTURBESITZ. AUSSTELLUNGSKATALOGE. 1970. irreg. price varies. Staatsbibliothek Preussischer Kulturbesitz, Potsdamer Str. 33, Postfach 1407, 1000 Berlin 30, W. Germany (B.R.D.) (Order from: Dr. Ludwig Reichert Verlag, Reissrt. 10,6200 Wiesbaden, W. Germany(B.R.D.))

027   US
STANFORD UNIVERSITY. LIBRARIES. ANNUAL REPORT. a. Stanford University, Library, Stanford, CA 94305.

020   US
STATE UNIVERSITY OF NEW YORK AT ALBANY. SCHOOL OF LIBRARY AND INFORMATION SCIENCE. BULLETIN. 1967-68. biennial. State University of New York at Albany, School of Library and Information Science, 1400 Washington Ave., Albany, NY 12222. illus. circ. 3,000.

027   BU
STATISTICESKI DANNI ZA BIBLIOTEKITE V BULGARIA/STATISTICAL DATA ON LIBRARIES IN BULGARIA. 1965. a. $3 per volume. Narodna Biblioteka "Kiril i Metodii", 11, Tolbukhin Blvd., 1504 Sofia, Bulgaria. Ed. Zdravko Mitov. charts. stat. circ. 350. (processed)

027   US   ISSN 0081-5152
STATISTICS OF INDIANA LIBRARIES. 1954. a. free. ‡ State Library, 140 N. Senate Ave., Indianapolis, IN 46204. Ed. Anne Ross. circ. 550.

027.4   US
STATISTICS OF VIRGINIA PUBLIC LIBRARIES AND INSTITUTIONAL LIBRARIES. a. free. State Library, Library Development Branch, Richmond, VA 23219.
    Formerly: Statistics of Virginia Public Libraries (ISSN 0095-3490)

020   AU
STUDIEN ZUR BIBLIOTHEKSGESCHICHTE. 1973. irreg. price varies. Akademische Druck- und Verlagsanstalt, Auersperggasse 12, 8011 Graz, Austria.

020   US . ISSN 0081-8151
STUDIES IN LIBRARIANSHIP. 1961. irreg., no. 9, 1973. price varies. University of Denver, Graduate School of Librarianship, Publications Dept., Denver, CO 80210.

020   US
STUDIES IN LIBRARY MANAGEMENT. 1972. irreg., vol. 4, 1977. price varies. Shoe String Press, Inc., 995 Sherman Ave., Hamden, CT 06514.

025   UK   ISSN 0307-0808
STUDIES IN LIBRARY MANAGEMENT. 1972. irreg. price varies. Clive Bingley Ltd., 1-19 New Oxford St., London WC1A 1NE, England.

020   VI
STUDIES IN VIRGIN ISLANDS LIBRARIANSHIP. 1971. irreg.; 1978, no. 14. price varies. ‡ St. Croix Library Association, Box 6760, Sunny Isles, St. Croix, VI 00820. Ed. Bd. bk. rev. circ. controlled. (processed)

026   US
SUBJECT DIRECTORY OF SPECIAL LIBRARIES AND INFORMATION CENTERS. 1975. biennial. $200 for 5-vol. set; $48 per vol. Gale Research Company, Book Tower, Detroit, MI 48226. Eds. Margaret L. Young, Harold C. Young.

020   SA
SUID-AFRIKAANSE ARGIEFBLAD/SOUTH AFRICAN ARCHIVES JOURNAL. (Text in Afrikaans and English) 1959. a. R.2. South African Society of Archivists, c/o Treasurer, Government Archives, Union Buildings, Private Bag X236, Pretoria 0001, South Africa. Eds. P. J. du Plessls, P. A. Myburgh. adv. bk. rev. bibl. circ. 300.

500   FR
SURVEY OF THE ACTIVITIES OF SCIENTIFIC UNIONS; SPECIAL AND SCIENTIFIC COMMITTEES OF I C S U IN THE FIELD OF INFORMATION. 1966. biennial. $18. International Council of Scientific Unions, Abstracting Board, 17 rue Mirabeau, 75016 Paris, France.

020   SW   ISSN 0562-7451
SVENSKA ARKIVSAMFUNDET. SKRIFTSERIE. 1953. a., no. 17, 1975. Kr.30. Svenska Arkivsamfundet - Swedish Archives Association, Riksarkivet, Fack, 100 26 Stockholm 34, Sweden. Ed. Jan Lindroth. bk. rev. circ. 500.

SVENSKA BARNBOKSINSTITUTET. SKRIFTER/ SWEDISH INSTITUTE FOR CHILDREN'S BOOKS. STUDIES. see *CHILDREN AND YOUTH* — For

SWARBICA JOURNAL. see *HISTORY* — History Of Asia

020 651 940   SW   ISSN 0039-6893
SWEDEN. RIKSARKIVET. MEDDELANDEN. 1877. irreg. Kr.15. Riksarkivet - National Swedish Record Office, Box 34104, 100 26 Stockholm 34, Sweden.

020   CN   ISSN 0380-2973
TALKING BOOKS IN THE PUBLIC LIBRARY SYSTEMS OF METROPOLITAN TORONTO. 1974. irreg. Can.$20. Metropolitan Toronto Library Board, 789 Yonge St., Toronto, Ont. M4W 2G8, Canada. bibl.

TANZANIA NATIONAL BIBLIOGRAPHY. see *BIBLIOGRAPHIES*

026   US   ISSN 1661-2434
TEAMWORK. 1970. irreg., latest 1979. $4. ‡ (Southeastern Pennsylvania Theological Library Association) Krauth Memorial Library, Lutheran Theological Seminary, 7301 Germantown Ave., Philadelphia, PA 19119. Ed. Rev. David J. Wartluft. bibl. circ. 100. (processed)

027.4   US   ISSN 0363-7158
TENNESSEE PUBLIC LIBRARY STATISTICS. a. free. State Library and Archives, Public Libraries Section, Nashville, TN 37219.

029   US
TEXAS LIST OF SCIENTIFIC AND TECHNICAL SERIAL PUBLICATIONS. 1965. a. $250. Wilson Data Service, 1939 West Gray, Houston, TX 77019. Ed. Lois Bebout. circ. 200. (also avail. in microfiche; back issue avail.)

027   US   ISSN 0082-3120
TEXAS PUBLIC LIBRARY STATISTICS. 1965. a. free. ‡ State Library, Library Development Division, Box 12927, Capitol Station, Austin, TX 78711. circ. 1,650.

026   US   ISSN 0082-3163
TEXAS SPECIAL LIBRARIES DIRECTORY. 1969. biennial. free. State Library, Texas Archives and Library Bldg., Box 12927, Capitol Sta., Austin, TX 78711. (Co-sponsor: Special Library Association, Texas Chapter) Ed. Jay Bowen. circ. 800.

020   II   ISSN 0563-5489
TIMELESS FELLOWSHIP; annual journal of comparative librarianship. (Text in English) 1964. a. Rs.40($9) Karnatak University Library Association, Karnatak University, Dharwar 580003, Karnataka, India. Eds. K. S. Deshpande, M. R. Kumbhar. adv. bk. rev. circ. 500. Indexed: LISA.

020   UK
TOP 1,000 DIRECTORIES USED IN BRITISH LIBRARIES. 1980. a (monthly updates) £12.50. Alan Armstrong & Associates Ltd., 8 Queen Victoria St., Reading, Berkshire RG1 1TG, England.

020   KO
TOSOGUIAN HAK. (Text in Korean) a. 400 Won($1) Korean Library Science Society, c/o Ewha Women University Library, Seoul 120, S. Korea.

029   HU   ISSN 0373-5354
TUDOMANYOS TAJEKOZTATAS ELMELETE ES GYAKORLATA/THEORY AND PRACTICE OF SCIENTIFIC INFORMATION. (Text in Hungarian; summaries in English, German, Russian) 1966. irreg., no. 21, 1976. price varies. Orszagos Muszaki Konyvtar es Dokumentacios Kozpont - Hungarian Central Technical Library and Documentation Centre, Reviczky u. 6, Box 12, 1428 Budapest, Hungary.

020 060   FI   ISSN 0082-7010
TURUN YLIOPISTO. KIRJASTO. JULKAISUJA. (Text in Finnish, English, French; summaries in English, French, German) 1948. irreg; no. 11, 1975. price varies. Turun Yliopisto, Kirjasto - University of Turku, SF-20500 Turku 50, Finland. circ. 300.

020   MX
U N A M DIRECTORIO DE BIBLIOTECAS. 1976. biennial. $8 (or exchange) Universidad National Autonoma de Mexico, Direccion General de Bibliotecas, Ciudad Universitaria, Mexico 20, D.F., Mexico.

355   US
U S M A LIBRARY BULLETIN. 1945. irreg., no. 14A, 1978. controlled circ. ‡ U.S. Military Academy Library, West Point, NY 10996. Ed. Egon A. Weiss. bibl. illus. circ. 750.

027   DK   ISSN 0106-3014
U VEJVISER. 1979. a. Kr.7($1.50) Danmarks Biblioteksforening - Danish Library Association, Trekronergade 15, DK-2500 Copenhagen V, Denmark. Eds. Helle Leth-Moeller, Bente Melbye.

027.4   UG
UGANDA. PUBLIC LIBRARIES BOARD. PROCEEDINGS. irreg. Public Libraries Board, Box 4262, Kampala, Uganda.

020 025   US   ISSN 0083-1565
U. S. LIBRARY OF CONGRESS. ANNUAL REPORT OF THE LIBRARIAN OF CONGRESS. 1866. a. price varies. U.S. Library of Congress, Washington, DC 20540 (Free to libraries Upon request to LC Central Services Division; foreign libraries apply to LC Exchange and Gift Division, Also available from Supt. of Documents, Washington DC 20402)

027.5   US   ISSN 0092-8429
U.S. LIBRARY OF CONGRESS. PROCESSING DEPARTMENT. NEWSLETTER. U.S. Library of Congress, 10 First St. S.E., Washington, DC 20540. stat. Key Title: Newsletter - Processing Department (Washington)

020   CK
UNIVERSIDAD DE ANTIOQUIA. ESCUELA INTERAMERICANA DE BIBLIOTECOLOGIA. PUBLICACIONES. SERIE: LEGISLACION BIBLIOTECARIA. 1972. irreg. $3. Universidad de Antioquia, Escuela Interamericana de Bibliotecologia, Medellin, Colombia.

020   SP
UNIVERSIDAD DE BARCELONA. BIBLIOTECA. MEMORIA ANUAL. 1969/70. a. free. Universidad de Barcelona, Biblioteca, Av. Jose Antonio 585, Barcelona, Spain. illus. circ. controlled.

020   AG   ISSN 0068-3493
UNIVERSIDAD DE BUENOS AIRES INSTITUTO BIBLIOTECOLOGICO. PUBLICACION. irreg; no. 54, 1978. Universidad de Buenos Aires, Instituto Bibliotecologico, Casilla de Correo 901, 1000 Buenos Aires, Argentina. Ed. Hans Gravenhorst.

020   SP   ISSN 0078-8740
UNIVERSIDAD DE NAVARRA. ESCUELA DE BIBLIOTECARIAS. MANUALES: BIBLIOTECARIAS. 1969. irreg.; 1979, no. 4. price varies. Ediciones Universidad de Navarra, S.A., Plaza de los Sauces 1 y 2, Baranain, Pamplona, Spain.

020   MX
UNIVERSIDAD NACIONAL AUTONOMA DE MEXICO. INSTITUTO DE INVESTIGACIONES BIBLIOGRAFICA. INSTRUMENTA BIBLIOGRAPHICA. 1973. irreg. price varies. Universidad Nacional Autonoma de Mexico, Instituto de Investigaciones Bibliograficas, Apdo. Postal 29-124, Mexico 1, D. F., Mexico. (Co-sponsor: Biblioteca Nacional) (back issues avail)

020 010   AG   ISSN 0076-6402
UNIVERSIDAD NACIONAL DE CUYO. BIBLIOTECA CENTRAL. CUADERNOS DE LA BIBLIOTECA. 1961. irreg; no. 6, 1978. available on exchange. ‡ Universidad Nacional de Cuyo, Biblioteca Central, Centro Universitario-C.C. 420, Mendoza, Argentina.

020 PO
UNIVERSIDADE DE COIMBRA. ARQUIVO. BOLETIM. 1973. irreg. Universidade de Coimbra, Arquivo, Paco das Escolas, Coimbra, Portugal. Ed. Antonio de Oliveira.

027 GW ISSN 0072-4483
UNIVERSITAET GIESSEN. BIBLIOTHEK. BERICHTE UND ARBEITEN. (Text in various languages) 1962-63. irreg. price varies. Universitaet Giessen, Bibliothek, Bismarckstr. 37, 6300 Giessen, W. Germany (B. R. D.) Ed. H. Schueling.

020 GE
UNIVERSITAETS- UND LANDESBIBLIOTHEK SACHSEN-ANHALT. ARBEITEN. 1952. irreg., vol. 24, 1980. price varies. Universitaets- und Landesbibliothek Sachsen-Anhalt, August-Bebelstr. 13/50, Halle, E. Germany (D.D.R.)

020 CN ISSN 0077-1341
UNIVERSITE DE MONTREAL. ECOLE DE BIBLIOTHECONOMIE. PUBLICATIONS. (Text in French) 1965. irreg. price varies. Universite de Montreal, Ecole de Biblotheconomie, C.P. 6128, Succ. A, Montreal, P.Q. H3C 3J7, Canada.

020 FR ISSN 0081-5926
UNIVERSITE DE STRASBOURG. CENTRE DE RECHERCHE ET DE DOCUMENTATION DES INSTITUTIONS CHRETIENNES. BULLETIN DU CERDIC. 1970. a. price varies. Universite de Strasbourg II, Centre de Recherche et de Documentation des Institutions Chretiennes, 9, Place de l'Universite, 67084 Strasbourg Cedex, France. Eds. Jean Schlick & Marie Zimmermann. bk. rev. circ. 500.

027.7 NO
UNIVERSITETET I TRONDHEIM. BIBLIOTEKET. AVDELING B. RAPPORT. 1971. irreg. Universitetet i Trondheim, Biblioteket. Avdeling B, Trondheim, Norway. Indexed: LISA.

020 US
UNIVERSITY OF ARIZONA LIBRARY. OCCASIONAL PAPERS. 1974. irreg. $1 per no. University of Arizona Library, Tucson, AZ 85721. circ. 200.

027 NR
UNIVERSITY OF BENIN. LIBRARY. ANNUAL REPORT. (Title varies slightly) 1970/71. a. University of Benin, Library, P.M.B. 1154, Eken Wan Rd., Benin City, Nigeria. stat.

027 CN ISSN 0068-1857
UNIVERSITY OF BRITISH COLUMBIA LIBRARY. REFERENCE PUBLICATION. 1956. irreg. controlled circulation, available on exchange. University of British Columbia, Library, 2075 Westbrook Mall, Vancouver, B.C. V6T 1W5, Canada.

020 US ISSN 0068-6476
UNIVERSITY OF CALIFORNIA PUBLICATIONS IN LIBRARIANSHIP. 1951. irreg. price varies. University of California Press, 2223 Fulton St., Berkeley, CA 94720.

027.7 SA ISSN 0576-6885
UNIVERSITY OF CAPE TOWN. LIBRARIES. STATISTICAL REPORT. a. free. University of Cape Town, Libraries, Rondebosch 7700, South Africa.

020 SA
UNIVERSITY OF CAPE TOWN. LIBRARIES. VARIA SERIES. (Text in English) 1959. irreg. University of Cape Town, Libraries, Rondebosch 7700, South Africa.

020 US ISSN 0069-3375
UNIVERSITY OF CHICAGO STUDIES IN LIBRARY SCIENCE. 1939. irreg., latest 1980. price varies. University of Chicago Press, 5801 S. Ellis Ave., Chicago, IL 60637. Ed. Don R. Swanson. (back issues avail.; reprint service avail. from UMI,ISI)

027 US ISSN 0069-6161
UNIVERSITY OF COLORADO LIBRARIES. REPORT. 1966/67. a. free. ‡ University of Colorado Libraries, Boulder, CO 80309.

UNIVERSITY OF FLORIDA. LIBRARIES. TECHNICAL PROCESSES DEPARTMENT. CARIBBEAN ACQUISITIONS. see *HISTORY — History Of North And South America*

020 GH
UNIVERSITY OF GHANA. DEPARTMENT OF LIBRARY AND ARCHIVAL STUDIES. OCCASIONAL PAPERS. irreg., no. 15, 1976. University of Ghana, Department of Library and Archival Studies, Box 60, Legon, Ghana.

027 NR ISSN 0073-4322
UNIVERSITY OF IBADAN. LIBRARY. ANNUAL REPORT. 1948. a. free. University of Ibadan, Library, Ibadan, Nigeria. bk. rev. circ. 750.

025 US ISSN 0069-4789
UNIVERSITY OF ILLINOIS AT URBANA-CHAMPAIGN. CLINIC ON LIBRARY APPLICATIONS OF DATA PROCESSING. PROCEEDINGS. 1963. a. $9 (prices vary) University of Illinois at Urbana-Champaign, Graduate School of Library Science, 249 Armory Bldg., Champaign, IL 61820. index. (back issues avail.)

020 US ISSN 0536-4604
UNIVERSITY OF ILLINOIS AT URBANA-CHAMPAIGN. GRADUATE SCHOOL OF LIBRARY SCIENCE. ALLERTON PARK INSTITUTE. PAPERS. 1954. a. $9. University of Illinois at Urbana-Champaign, Graduate School of Library Science, 249 Armory Bldg., Champaign, IL 61820. index. (back issues avail)

020 US
UNIVERSITY OF ILLINOIS AT URBANA-CHAMPAIGN. GRADUATE SCHOOL OF LIBRARY SCIENCE. DOWNS FUND PUBLICATIONS SERIES. 1972. irreg. price varies. University of Illinois at Urbana-Champaign, Graduate School of Library Science, 249 Armory Bldg., Champaign, IL 61820. Ed. Scott Bennett. Indexed: Lib.Lit. M.L.A.

020 US ISSN 0073-5361
UNIVERSITY OF ILLINOIS AT URBANA-CHAMPAIGN. GRADUATE SCHOOL OF LIBRARY SCIENCE. LIBRARY RESEARCH CENTER. ANNUAL REPORT. 1961-62. a. free. University of Illinois at Urbana-Champaign, Graduate School of Library Science, 249 Armory Bldg., Champaign, IL 61820.

020 US ISSN 0073-5302
UNIVERSITY OF ILLINOIS AT URBANA-CHAMPAIGN. GRADUATE SCHOOL OF LIBRARY SCIENCE. MONOGRAPH SERIES. 1963. irreg. price varies. University of Illinois at Urbana-Champaign, Graduate School of Library Science, 249 Armory Bldg., Champaign, IL 61820.

020 US ISSN 0073-5310
UNIVERSITY OF ILLINOIS AT URBANA-CHAMPAIGN. GRADUATE SCHOOL OF LIBRARY SCIENCE. OCCASIONAL PAPERS. 1949. irreg.(5-6/yr.) $7. ‡ University of Illinois at Urbana-Champaign, Graduate School of Library Science, Publications Office, 249 Armory Bldg., Champaign, IL 61820. Ed. Rolland E. Stevens. circ. 600. (back issues avail.)

020 US ISSN 0041-9648
UNIVERSITY OF IOWA. SCHOOL OF LIBRARY SCIENCE. NEWSLETTER. 1966. a. free. University of Iowa, School of Library Science, Iowa City, IA 52242. Ed. Ethel Bloesch. bibl. circ. 4,000.

020 US ISSN 0075-5001
UNIVERSITY OF KANSAS LIBRARIES. LIBRARY SERIES. 1958. irreg. price varies. University of Kansas Libraries, Lawrence, KS 66045. Ed. James Helyar.

020 AT
UNIVERSITY OF KENSINGTON. SCHOOL OF LIBRARIANSHIP. OCCASIONAL PAPER. 1975. irreg. Aus.$2 per no. University of Kensington, School of Librarianship, P. O. Box 1, Kensington, New South Wales, Australia.

020 NR ISSN 0075-7705
UNIVERSITY OF LAGOS. LIBRARY. ANNUAL REPORT. 1962/63. a. free. University of Lagos, Library, Yaba, Lagos, Nigeria. Ed. E. B. Bankole. circ. 1,000.

026 UK ISSN 0076-079X
UNIVERSITY OF LONDON. INSTITUTE OF EDUCATION. LIBRARY. EDUCATION LIBRARIES BULLETIN SUPPLEMENTS. 1958. irreg., no. 22, 1981. price varies. University of London, Institute of Education Library, 11-13 Ridgmount St., London WC1E 7AH, England. Ed. Norman W. Beswick. circ. 500-1,000.

027 MW ISSN 0085-3038
UNIVERSITY OF MALAWI.LIBRARY. REPORT TO THE SENATE ON THE UNIVERSITY LIBRARIES. 1968. a. free. University of Malawi, Library, Box 280, Zomba, Malawi. circ. 200. (processed)

020 US ISSN 0076-4833
UNIVERSITY OF MARYLAND. COLLEGE OF LIBRARY AND INFORMATION SERVICES. CONFERENCE PROCEEDINGS. 1968. irreg. price varies. University of Maryland, College of Library and Information Services, College Park, MD 20742. Indexed: Lib.Lit.

020 US ISSN 0076-4841
UNIVERSITY OF MARYLAND. COLLEGE OF LIBRARY AND INFORMATION SERVICES. STUDENT CONTRIBUTION SERIES. 1967. irreg., no. 10, 1977. price varies. University of Maryland, College of Library and Information Services, College Park, MD 20742. Indexed: Lib.Lit.

027.7 US
UNIVERSITY OF MISSOURI, COLUMBIA. LIBRARY SERIES. 1908. irreg., no. 27, 1978. exchange basis. University of Missouri-Columbia, Ellis Library, Columbia, MO 65201. circ. 500.

020 610 AT ISSN 0155-0187
UNIVERSITY OF NEW SOUTH WALES. BIOMEDICAL LIBRARY. NEWSLETTER. 1968. a. free. University of New South Wales, Biomedical Library, Box 1, Kensington, N.S.W. 2033, Australia.

020 AT ISSN 0313-427X
UNIVERSITY OF NEW SOUTH WALES. LIBRARY. ANNUAL REPORT. 1978 (1975 report) a. free. University of New South Wales, Library, Box 1, Kensington, N.S.W. 2033, Australia. circ. 300.

027.7 AT
UNIVERSITY OF NEW SOUTH WALES. LIBRARY. INFORMATION BULLETIN. 1965. irreg. free. University of New South Wales, Library, P.O. Box 1, Kensington, NSW 2033, Australia. Eds. Robin Sheely-Jones and Bill McBain.

020 CN ISSN 0078-7027
UNIVERSITY OF OTTAWA. LIBRARY. ANNUAL REPORT. a. free. University of Ottawa, General Library, 65 Hastey, Ottawa, Ont. K1N 9A5, Canada.

020 US
UNIVERSITY OF RHODE ISLAND. LIBRARY. LIBRARY LETTER. 1967. a. free to qualified personnel. University of Rhode Island, Association of Friends of the Library, Kingston, RI 02881. Ed. Frederick Jackson. circ. controlled.

027.7 US ISSN 0041-9974
UNIVERSITY OF ROCHESTER LIBRARY BULLETIN. 1945. irreg. membership. University of Rochester, Rush Rhees Library, Rochester, NY 14627. Ed. Bd. illus. circ. 1,500. Indexed: Lib.Lit.

027 US ISSN 0081-2706
UNIVERSITY OF SOUTH CAROLINA. LIBRARIES. REPORT OF THE DIRECTOR OF LIBRARIES. 1960. a. free; limited distribution. ‡ University of South Carolina Libraries, Director of Libraries, Columbia, SC 29208. Ed. Kenneth Toombs. circ. 350.

025 UK ISSN 0081-2935
UNIVERSITY OF SOUTHAMPTON. LIBRARY. AUTOMATION PROJECT REPORT. 1970. irreg. price varies. University of Southampton, Library, Highfield, Southampton, Hants S09 5NH, England. circ. 400. Indexed: LISA.

020   IR   ISSN 0497-1000
UNIVERSITY OF TEHERAN. CENTRAL LIBRARY. LIBRARY BULLETIN/ DANESHGAH-E TEHRAN. KETABKHANE-YE MARKAZI. NASHRIYE-YE KETABKHANEH. (Text in Persian) 1966. irreg. price varies. University of Teheran, Central Library, Shahreza Ave., Teheran, Iran. Ed. Iraj Afshar.

013   US   ISSN 0270-059X
UNIVERSITY OF TENNESSEE. LIBRARY LECTURES. 1952. triennial. $2 per copy. University of Tennessee, Publications Service Bureau, 293 Communications Building, Knoxville, TN 37916. circ. 1,500. Key Title: Library Lectures(Knoxville)

027   SA   ISSN 0075-3807
UNIVERSITY OF THE WITWATERSRAND, JOHANNESBURG. LIBRARY. ANNUAL REPORT OF THE UNIVERSITY LIBRARIAN. 1932. a. free. ‡ University of the Witwatersrand, Johannesburg, Library, Private Bag 31550, Braamfontein 2017, South Africa.

027.7   SA
UNIVERSITY OF THE WITWATERSRAND, JOHANNESBURG. LIBRARY. HISTORICAL AND LITERARY PAPERS: INVENTORIES OF COLLECTIONS. irreg., no. 9, 1981. University of the Witwatersrand, Johannesburg, Library, Private Bag 31550, Braamfontein 2017, South Africa.

027.7   SA
UNIVERSITY OF THE WITWATERSRAND, JOHANNESBURG. LIBRARY. OCCASIONAL PUBLICATIONS. 1976. irreg., no. 7, 1980. University of the Witwatersrand, Johannesburg, Library, Private Bag 31550, Braamfontein 2017, South Africa.

020   CN   ISSN 0082-531X
UNIVERSITY OF TORONTO. LIBRARY. ANNUAL REPORT. 1954-55. a. free. University of Toronto, Library, Toronto, Ont., Canada. circ. 1,200.

020   UK
UNIVERSITY OF WARWICK LIBRARY. OCCASIONAL PUBLICATIONS. 1971. irreg. price varies. ‡ University of Warwick Library, Coventry, Warwickshire, CV4 7AL, England. circ. controlled. (processed)

027   AT   ISSN 0083-8713
UNIVERSITY OF WESTERN AUSTRALIA. LIBRARY. REPORT ON THE LIBRARY. 1960. a. free to libraries. University of Western Australia, Perth. W. A, Australia.

020   CN   ISSN 0076-0595
UNIVERSITY OF WESTERN ONTARIO. D. B. WELDON LIBRARY. LIBRARY BULLETIN. 1941. irreg., no. 9, 1976. free. University of Western Ontario, D. B. Weldon Library, London, Ont., Canada. Ed. Edward Phelps. circ. 500.

020   JA   ISSN 0566-2680
UNTEI. (Text in Japanese) 1958. a. 800 Yen($3) Tenri University, 1050 Somanouchi-cho, Tenri, Nara 632, Japan. Ed. Shigeomi Takahashi. bk. rev. circ. 1,000. (back issues avail.)

500   BE
VADE-MECUM FOR INFORMATION SCIENTISTS. (Subseries of A.S.T.R.I.D. General Reference and Practical Information Science Series) 1979. a. Herman-Karel de Jarger Publications, K. Astriclaan 89, B-9000 Ghent, Belgium. Ed. Herman-Karel de Jaeger.
Formed by the 1979 merger of: Practical Information Science & Science Information Sources & Recent Key Publications for Retrieving Essential Sources of Information Covering All Fields of Human Endeavour.

026 600   FI   ISSN 0355-3701
VALTION TEKNILLINEN TUTKIMUSKESKUS. TEKNILLINEN INFORMAATIOPALVELULAITOS. TIEDONANTO/TECHNICAL RESEARCH CENTRE OF FINLAND. TECHNICAL INFORMATION SERVICE. REPORT. (Text mainly in Finnish, some in English or Swedish) 1975. irreg. price varies. Valtion Teknillinen Tutkimuskeskus - Technical Research Centre of Finland, Vuorimiehentie 5, 02150 Espoo 15, Finland.

027.4   CN   ISSN 0707-2031
VIDEORECORDINGS AVAILABLE IN THE PUBLIC LIBRARIES OF METROPOLITAN TORONTO. 1979. irreg. Can.$13. Metropolitan Toronto Library Board, 789 Yonge St., Toronto, Ont. M4W 2G8, Canada.

027.4 029   VN
VIETNAM. DIRECTORATE OF ARCHIVES AND LIBRARIES. CATALOGUE OF BOOKS. (Text in Vietnamese) a. Directorate of Archives and Libraries, P.O. Box 2094, Saigon, Socialist Republic of Vietnam. Ed. Father A. Celinas.

020   US
VIRGINIA STATE LIBRARY NEWS. 1971. irreg. State Library, 12th & Capitol St., Richmond, VA 23219. Ed. Mary Alice Seemeyer. circ. 1,200(controlled) (looseleaf format; reprint service avail. from)

001.4   UR
VOPROSY INFORMATSIONNOI TEORII I PRAKTIKI. irreg. 0.65 Rub. Vsesoyuznyi Institut Nauchno-Tekhnicheskoi Informatsii (Viniti), Ul. Baltiiskaya, 14, Moscow, U. S. S. R. illus.

015   UK   ISSN 0065-0293
WALES. NATIONAL LIBRARY. HANDLIST ON MANUSCRIPTS IN THE NATIONAL LIBRARY OF WALES. (Supplement Series 2 of the National Library of Wales Journal) 1940. a. (occasionally irreg.) price varies. National Library of Wales, Aberystwyth, Dyfed SY23 3BU, Wales. index. circ. 550.

026 610   US
WAYNE STATE UNIVERSITY, DETROIT. MEDICAL SCHOOL LIBRARY. REPORT. 1964. irreg., no. 62, 1974. price varies; some copies free. Wayne State University Medical School Library, 4325 Brush St., Detroit, MI 48201. Ed. James F. Williams, II. (also avail. in microfiche from EDR)
Formerly: Wayne State University. Medical Library. Report (ISSN 0083-775X)

020   US
WESTERN ASSOCIATION OF MAP LIBRARIES. OCCASIONAL PAPERS. 1973. irreg., no. 5, 1978. price varies. Western Association of Map Libraries, c/o Stanley D. Stevens, University Library, University of California, Santa Cruz, CA 95064.

020   US
WESTERN MICHIGAN UNIVERSITY. SCHOOL OF LIBRARIANSHIP. BULLETIN. 1948. a. Western Michigan University, School of Librarianship, Kalamazoo, MI 49008. Ed. Mrs. Ardith B. Embs.

020   US   ISSN 0083-9892
WIDENER LIBRARY SHELFLIST. (Listings in various languages) 1965. irreg., 1973, nos. 42-46. price varies. (Harvard University, Widener Library) Harvard University Press, 79 Garden St., Cambridge, MA 02138.

025.5   US   ISSN 0361-2848
WISCONSIN LIBRARY SERVICE RECORD. (Subseries of: Wisconsin. Department of Public Instruction. Bulletin) 1973. a. $1. Department of Public Instruction, Division for Library Services, Dept. of Public Instruction, 125 S. Webster St., 4th Fl., Madison, WI 53702. (reprint service avail. from UMI)

020   GW   ISSN 0300-2012
WOLFENBUETTLER BEITRAEGE. 1972. irreg., vol. 3, 1978. price varies. (Herzog-August-Bibliothek, Wolfenbuettel) Vittorio Klostermann, Frauenlobstr. 22, 6000 Frankfurt 90, W. Germany (B.R.D.) Ed. Paul Raabe. circ. 1,500.

020   UK   ISSN 0084-1285
WORK OF ASLIB: ANNUAL REPORT. a. free. Aslib, 3 Belgrave Sq., London SW1X 8PL, England.

025.3   US
WORK RELATED ABSTRACTS SUBJECT HEADING LIST. 1972. a. $15. Information Coordinators, Inc., 1435-37 Randolph St., Detroit, MI 48226. circ. 500.
Until 1973: Employment Relations Abstracts: Subject Heading List (ISSN 0092-1432)

029   US
WORLD GUIDE TO ABBREVIATIONS OF ORGANIZATIONS. 1974, 5th ed. irreg. $28. Gale Research Company, Book Tower, Detroit, MI 48226. Ed. F.A. Buttress.

026   US
WORLDWIDE DIRECTORY OF FEDERAL LIBRARIES. 1973. irreg. $29.50. Marquis Academic Media, 200 E. Ohio St., Chicago, IL 60611.

020   GW   ISSN 0514-6364
ZEITSCHRIFT FUER BIBLIOTHEKSWESEN UND BIBLIOGRAPHIE. SONDERHEFTE. 1963. irreg. price varies. Vittorio Klostermann, Frauenlobstr. 22, Postfach 900601, D-6000 Frankfurt 90, W. Germany(B.R.D.)

LIBRARY AND INFORMATION SCIENCES — Abstracting, Bibliographies, Statistics

027   US   ISSN 0147-2135
A R L STATISTICS. 1964. a. $5. Association of Research Libraries, 1527 New Hampshire Ave., N.W., Washington, DC 20036. Ed. Carol A. Mandel. circ. 600. (back issues avail.)
Formerly: Academic Library Statistics (ISSN 0571-6519)

020   CN   ISSN 0080-1569
ALBERTA RESEARCH COUNCIL. LIST OF PUBLICATIONS. 1968. a. free. Alberta Research Council, Library Publications Dept., 11315-87 Ave., Edmonton, Alberta T6G 2C2, Canada.

016   US   ISSN 0065-9959
AMERICAN REFERENCE BOOKS ANNUAL. 1970. a. $31.50. Libraries Unlimited, Inc., Box 263, Littleton, CO 80160. Ed. Bodhan S. Wynar. cum.index every 5 yrs.

020 016   AG   ISSN 0067-656X
BIBLIOGRAFIA BIBLIOTECOLOGICA ARGENTINA. 1963. irreg. price varies. Universidad Nacional del sur, Centro de Documentacion Bibliotecologica, Av. Alem 1253, Bahia Blanca, Argentina. bk. rev. author index in each issue. circ. 300.
Argentine bibliography on library science

027.7 015   US
BIBLIOGRAPHICAL SERIES FROM THE YALE UNIVERSITY LIBRARY COLLECTIONS. vol. 3, 1973. irreg. Yale University Library, New Haven, CT 06520.

029.7 010   AT   ISSN 0084-7852
BIBLIOGRAPHICAL SOCIETY OF AUSTRALIA AND NEW ZEALAND. BULLETIN. 1970. s-a. membership. Bibliographical Society of Australia & New Zealand, c/o Trevor Mills, Secy., 117 St. Georges Rd., North Fitzroy, Vic 3068, Australia. Ed. B.J. McMullin. adv. bk. rev. circ. 180.

BIBLIOGRAPHY NEWSLETTER. see *PUBLISHING AND BOOK TRADE — Abstracting, Bibliographies, Statistics*

027   CN
BRITISH COLUMBIA PUBLIC LIBRARIES, STATISTICS. 1965. a. free. Library Services Branch, Parliament Buildings, Victoria, B.C. V8V 1X4, Canada. stat. circ. 750.
Formerly: British Columbia. Library Development Commission. Public Libraries, Statistics (ISSN 0084-8034)

016.051 020   CN   ISSN 0000-0345
CANADIAN SERIALS DIRECTORY/REPERTORIE DES PUBLICATIONS SERIEES CANADIENNES. (Text in English and French) a. University of Toronto Press, Toronto, Ont., Canada. bibl.

011   US   ISSN 0163-2280
CENSORED. 1973. irreg., 9th edt., 1979. $7 per no. Box 1526, Bonita Springs, FL 33923. Ed. Bayliss Corbett. circ. 500.
Formerly: Some Hard-to-Locate Sources of Information on Current Affairs.

020　　　　　　　　US　　ISSN 0084-6902
CENTER FOR CHINESE RESEARCH
MATERIALS. BIBLIOGRAPHICAL SERIES.
irreg. price varies. Association of Research Libraries,
Center for Chinese Research Materials, 1527 New
Hampshire Ave., N.W., Washington, DC 20036. Ed.
P. K. Yu.

310　　　　　　　UK　　ISSN 0309-6629
CHARTERED INSTITUTE OF PUBLIC FINANCE
AND ACCOUNTANCY. PUBLIC LIBRARY
STATISTICS. ACTUALS. 1957-58. a. £10.
Chartered Institute of Public Finance and
Accountancy, 1 Buckingham Place, London SW1E
6HS, England. stat. (back issues avail.)

310　　　　　　　UK　　ISSN 0307-0522
CHARTERED INSTITUTE OF PUBLIC FINANCE
AND ACCOUNTANCY. PUBLIC LIBRARY
STATISTICS. ESTIMATES. 1974. a. £5. Chartered
Institute of Public Finance and Accountancy, 1
Buckingham Place, London SW1E 6HS, England.
(back issues avail.)

015　　　　　　　UK　　ISSN 0084-8085
CHECKLIST OF BRITISH OFFICIAL SERIAL
PUBLICATIONS. 1967. irreg (approx. annual)
£3.50. ‡ British Library, Reference Division, Great
Russell St., London WC1B 3DG, England. circ.
4,000(controlled)

011 020　　　　US
COLLEGE READING ASSOCIATION.
MONOGRAPHS. irreg. College Reading
Association, c/o Dr. George McNinch, Pub. Bus.
Mgr., University of Southern Mississippi, Southern
Sta., Box 26, Hattiesburg, MS 39401. (reprint
service avail. from UMI)

020 011　　　　US
DIRECTORY OF DIRECTORIES. 1980. biennial.
Information Enterprises, Drawer 829, Detroit, MI
48231 (Dist. by Gale Research Co., Book Tower,
Detroit, MI 48226) Ed. James M. Ethridge.

010 020　　　　UN
DOCUMENTATION, LIBRARIES AND
ARCHIVES: BIBLIOGRAPHIES AND
REFERENCE WORKS. 1972. irreg. price varies.
Unesco Press, Place de Fontenoy, F-75700 Paris,
France (Dist. in U.S. by: Unipub, 345 Park Ave. S.,
New York, NY 10010)
　　Formerly: Unesco Bibliographical Handbooks
(ISSN 0082-7460)

FINDING AIDS TO THE MICROFILMED
MANUSCRIPT COLLECTION OF THE
GENEALOGICAL SOCIETY OF UTAH. see
GENEALOGY AND HERALDRY — Abstracting,
Bibliographies, Statistics

029 011　　　　SA
GREY BIBLIOGRAPHIES. irreg., no. 10, 1977.
South African Library, Queen Victoria St., Cape
Town 8001, South Africa.

020 011　　　CR　　ISSN 0487-1596
I C A P LISTA DE NUEVAS ADQUISICIONES.
1958. irreg. Instituto Centroamericano de
Administracion Publica, Departamento de
Biblioteca, Apartado 10025, San Jose, Costa Rica.

026 610 016　　US　　ISSN 0148-0650
ILLINOIS HEALTH SCIENCES LIBRARIES
SERIALS HOLDINGS LIST. a. $25. University of
Illinois at the Medical Center, Library of the Health
Sciences, Box 7509, Chicago, IL 60680.

029　　　　　　　KO
INDEX TO THE NATIONAL ASSEMBLY
RECORDS/KUK HOE HOE EU ROK SAEGIN.
(Text in Korean) 1963. irreg. free. National
Assembly, Library, Processing & Reference Bureau,
Yoido-Dong 1, Yoengdeungpo-gu, Seoul, S. Korea.
circ. 700.

020 016　　　　SZ　　ISSN 0074-1019
INTER-DOCUMENTATION COMPANY.
NEWSLETTER. (Separate newsletters for various
areas e.g. Slavic Newsletter, Asia Newsletter,
Indonesia Newsletter, Chinese Studies Newsletter,
etc.) (Text in English) 1969. irreg. free. Inter-
Documentation Company, Poststrasse 14, Zug,
Switzerland. Ed. J. Juttermans. circ. 10,000.
　　News about microform projects

020　　　　　　　US
INTERNATIONAL MICROGRAPHICS SOURCE
BOOK. 1972. a. $49.50. Microfilm Publishing, Inc.,
Box 313, Wykagyl Station, New Rochelle, NY
10804. adv. bk. rev. illus. stat.
　　Former titles: International Microfilm Source
Book (ISSN 0362-4498); Microfilm Source Book
(ISSN 0090-2861)

020 016　　　　IT　　ISSN 0075-0026
INVENTARI DEI MANOSCRITTI DELLE
BIBLIOTECHE D'ITALIA. 1890. irreg., vol. 94,
1979. price varies. Casa Editrice Leo S. Olschki,
Casella Postale 66, 50100 Florence, Italy. Eds. A.
Sorbelli, L. Ferrari. cum.index in prep. circ. 1,000.

016 500 600　　US
IOWA STATE UNIVERSITY. LIBRARY. SERIES
IN BIBLIOGRAPHY. 1971. irreg. price varies. ‡
Iowa State University Library, Ames., IA 50010.

020 011　　　　IC
ISLENZK BOKASKRA/ICELANDIC NATIONAL
BIBLIOGRAPHY. 1975. a. Kr.40($6)
Landsbokasafn Islands - National Library of Iceland,
Safnahusinu, Hverfisgotu 15, 101 Reykjavik,
Iceland.
　　Supersedes in part: Iceland. Landsbokasafn
Islands. Arbok.

025 323　　　　US　　ISSN 0075-8973
LIBRARIANS, CENSORSHIP AND
INTELLECTUAL FREEDOM; an annual
annotated bibliography. 1969. irreg. $2. American
Library Association, 50 E. Huron, Chicago, IL
60611. Eds. James A. Harvey, Patricia R. Harris.
Indexed: Lib.Lit.

029 011　　　　NE
LIBRARY, DOCUMENTATION AND ARCHIVES
SERIALS. irreg., 4th ed., 1975. International
Federation for Documentation, Box 30115, 2500
GC The Hague, Netherlands.

020　　　　　　　US　　ISSN 0085-2767
LIBRARY LIT. 1971. a. $12. Scarecrow Press, Inc.,
Box 656, 52 Liberty Street, Metuchen, NJ 08840.
Ed. William A. Katz. circ. 1,500.

020　　　　　　　US
LIBRARY OF CONGRESS CLASSIFICATION
SCHEDULES: A CUMULATION OF
ADDITIONS AND CHANGES. 1971. irreg. price
varies. Gale Research Company, Book Tower,
Detroit, MI 48226. Ed. Helen Savage.

LITERARY AND LIBRARY PRIZES. see
LITERATURE — Abstracting, Bibliographies,
Statistics

020 310　　　　US　　ISSN 0093-1098
NEW JERSEY PUBLIC LIBRARIES. STATISTICS.
1958. a. free. State Library, 185 W. State St.,
Trenton, NJ 08625. Ed. Hugo Knezevich. circ.
2,000.

027　　　　　　　NZ
NEW ZEALAND. DEPARTMENT OF
STATISTICS. CENSUS OF LIBRARIES.
quinquennial. NZ.$2. Department of Statistics,
Private Bag, Wellington, New Zealand (Subscr. to:
Government Printing Office, Publications, Private
Bag, Wellington, New Zealand)

021 027.7　　　US
NORTH DAKOTA LIBRARY STATISTICS. a. free.
State Library, Bismarck, ND 58505.
　　Formerly: North Dakota Academic Library
Statistics. (ISSN 0094-5455)

011 020　　　　UK
P S A LIBRARY BIBLIOGRAPHIES. (Includes
various titles: Current Information on Energy
Conservation(in 4 parts); Current Information on
Maintenance(in 6 parts.)) irreg. price varies.
Property Services Agency, c/o PSA Library Sales
Office, Room C109, Block C, Whitgift Centre,
Croydon CR9 3LY, England.

020　　　　　　　US
PUBLIC LIBRARY CATALOG. quinquennial, with a.
supplements. $110. ‡ H. W. Wilson Co., 950
University Ave., Bronx, New York, NY 10452. Ed.
Gary L. Bogart. bk. rev.
　　Formerly: Standard Catalog for Public Libraries.

020　　　　　　　CN　　ISSN 0075-6113
QUEEN'S UNIVERSITY AT KINGSTON.
DOUGLAS LIBRARY. OCCASIONAL PAPERS.
1969. irreg. Can.$3. Queen's University, Douglas
Library, Kingston, Ontario, Canada. circ. 300. (also
avail. in microfilm)

350 016　　　　US
RHODE ISLAND. STATE LIBRARY. CHECK-LIST
OF PUBLICATIONS OF STATE AGENCIES.
1972. biennial. free. State Library, State House,
Documents Division, Providence, RI 02903. bibl.
cum. index. (processed)

011 029　　　　SL
SIERRA LEONE PUBLICATIONS. 1964. a. $0.10.
Library Board, Box 326, Freetown, Sierra Leone.
(back issues avail.)

010　　　　　　　US　　ISSN 0081-7600
STUDIES IN BIBLIOGRAPHY. 1948. a. $20.
(Bibliographical Society of the University of
Virginia) University Press of Virginia, Box 3608
University Station, Charlottesville, VA 22903. Eds.
Fredson Bowers, A. Beaurline. circ. 2,000.

026　　　　　　　US　　ISSN 0000-0140
SUBJECT COLLECTIONS; a guide to special book
collections and subject emphasis in libraries. 1958.
irreg., 5th edt., 1978. $72.50. R.R. Bowker
Company, 1180 Ave. of the Americas, New York,
NY 10036 (Orders to P. O. Box 1807, Ann Arbor,
Mich. 48106) Ed. Lee Ash. subject index. (reprint
service avail. from UMI)

020 016　　　　US　　ISSN 0083-1603
U. S. LIBRARY OF CONGRESS. LIBRARY OF
CONGRESS PUBLICATIONS IN PRINT. 1935. a.
free. ‡ U. S. Library of Congress, Publications
Office, Washington, DC 20540. circ. 10,000.

LINGUISTICS

see also Classical Studies; Oriental Studies

410　　　　　　　US　　ISSN 0567-4263
A T A PROFESSIONAL SERVICES DIRECTORY.
1965. irreg., 3rd edt., 1976. $16 to non-members;
members $3. American Translators Association, Box
129, Croton-on-Hudson, NY 10520.

400 060　　　　HO　　ISSN 0065-0471
ACADEMIA HONDURENA DE LA LENGUA.
BOLETIN. 1955. a. L.10. ‡ Academia Hondurena
de la Lengua, Apartado Postal 38, Tegucigalpa,
Honduras. Ed. Ramon E. Cruz. bk. rev. circ. 1,000.

ACADEMIA PAULISTA DE LETRAS. REVISTA.
see LITERATURE

428　　　　　　　UK
ACADEMIC COURSES IN GREAT BRITAIN
RELEVANT TO THE TEACHING OF ENGLISH
TO SPEAKERS OF OTHER LANGUAGES. 1968.
a. 50p. ‡ British Council, English-Teaching
Information Centre, 10 Spring Gardens, London
SW1A 2BN, England.

840 913　　　　FR　　ISSN 0065-0544
ACADEMIE DES INSCRIPTIONS ET BELLES-
LETTRES. ETUDES ET COMMENTAIRES.
1946. irreg. price varies. Editions Klincksieck, 11
rue de Lille, Paris 7e, France. (also avail. in
microfiche)

840　　　　　　　BE　　ISSN 0567-6584
ACADEMIE ROYALE DE LANGUE ET DE
LITTERATURE FRANCAISES. ANNUAIRES. a.
price changes. Academie Royale de Langue et de
Litterature Francaises, Palais des Academies, 1 rue
Ducale, Brussels, Belgium. Ed. Bd. bibl.

492.4　　　　　　IS　　ISSN 0065-0692
ACADEMY OF THE HEBREW LANGUAGE.
SPECIALIZED DICTIONARIES. irreg. Academy
of the Hebrew Language, P.O.B.3449, Jerusalem,
Israel.

492.4　　　　　　IS
ACADEMY OF THE HEBREW LANGUAGE.
TEXTS & STUDIES. irreg. Academy of the Hebrew
Language, P.O.B. 3449, Jerusalem, Israel.
　　Formerly: Academy of the Hebrew Language.
Linguistic Studies (ISSN 0075-9643)

LINGUISTICS

410 860   CK
ACOPEL; temas de linguistica y literatura. irreg. Asociacion Colombiana de Profesores de Espanol y Literatura a Nivel Superior, Calle 31 no. 83B-150, Medellin, Colombia.

423.1   US
ACRONYMS, INITIALISMS AND ABBREVIATIONS DICTIONARY; a guide to alphabetic designations, contractions, acronyms, initialisms, and similar condensed appellations. biennial. $54. Gale Research Company, Book Tower, Detroit, MI 48226. Ed. Ellen T. Crowley.
     Formerly (until 1976): Acronyms and Initialisms Dictionary (ISSN 0065-0889)

410   SA   ISSN 0065-1141
ACTA CLASSICA. (Text mainly in English; occasionally in Afrikaans, French or German) 1958. a. fl.35($17.50) per vol. (Classical Association of South Africa) A. A. Balkema Ltd., P.O. Box 3117, Cape Town 8000, South Africa (And Box 1675, Rotterdam, Netherlands; in the U.S. and Canada, 99 Main St., Salem, NH 03079) Ed. H.L. Gonin.

480 470   BE
ACTA COLLOQUII DIDACTICII CLASSICI; didactica classica gandensia. (Text in Dutch, English, French, German and Latin) 1963. a. 150-250 Fr. International Bureau for the Study of the Problems in the Teaching of Greek and Latin, Blandijnberg, B-9000 Ghent, Belgium. Ed. J. Veremans.

410   SA   ISSN 0065-1273
ACTA GERMANICA; jahrbuch des Sudafrikansichen Germanistenverbandes. (Text in German) 1966. a. fl.35($17.50) per vol. (S.A. Germanistenverband) A. A. Balkema Ltd., P.O. Box 3117, Cape Town 8000, South Africa (And Box 1675, Rotterdam, Netherlands; in the U.S. and Canada, 99 Main St., Salem, NH 03079) Ed. Walter Boeddinghaus.

459   IT   ISSN 0065-1516
ACTA PHILOLOGICA. (Contributions in Italian, Rumanian, English, French, German and Spanish) 1958. irreg. price varies. Societa Accademica Romena, Foro Traiano 1a, 00187 Rome, Italy.

410   PL   ISSN 0065-1524
ACTA PHILOLOGICA. (Text in Polish, German; summaries in German) 1968. irreg., 1970. vol. 2. price varies. Uniwersytet Warszawski, Wydzial Filologii Obcych, Krakowskie Przedmiescie 26/28, Warsaw, Poland (Dist. by: Ars Polona-Ruch, Krakowskie Przedmiescie 7, Warsaw, Poland) Ed. J. Reychman. circ. 300.

489   AU   ISSN 0065-1532
ACTA PHILOLOGICA AENIPONTANA. 1962. irreg., vol. 4, 1979. price varies. ‡ (Gesellschaft fuer Klassische Philologie in Innsbruck) Universitaetsverlag Wagner, Andreas-Hofer-Str. 13, Postfach 219, A-6010 Innsbruck, Austria. (Co-sponsor: Oesterreichische Humanistische Gesellschaft) Ed. Robert Muth. circ. 600.

439   DK   ISSN 0001-6691
ACTA PHILOLOGICA SCANDINAVICA; tidsskrift for nordisk sprogforskning. (Text in several languages; summaries in English) 1926. irreg. 120 price varies. Munksgaard, Noerre sogade 35, DK-1370 Copenhagen K, Denmark. Ed.Bd. bk. rev. bibl. illus. index. circ. 300. (reprint service avail. from ISI) Indexed: Curr.Cont.

410   BL
ACTA SEMIOTICA ET LINGUISTICA. 1977. irreg. exchange basis. (Sociedade Brasileira de Professores de Linguistica) Editora de Humanismo, Ciencia e Tecnologia, Alameda Jau 404, Sao Paulo 01420, Brazil. Ed. Cidmar T. Pais. bk. rev. abstr.

491.85   PL   ISSN 0208-5321
ACTA UNIVERSITATIS NICOLAI COPERNICI. FILOLOGIA POLSKA. 1959. irreg. price varies. Uniwersytet Mikolaja Kopernika, Fosa Staromiejska 3, Torun, Poland (Dist. by Osrodek Rozpowszechniania Wydawnictw Naukowych PAN, Palac Kultury i Nauki, 00-901 Warsaw, Poland)
     Formerly: Uniwersytet Mikolaja Kopernika, Torun. Nauki Humanistyczno-Spoleczna. Filologia Polska (ISSN 0083-4483)

410   DK
ACTUALITATES. (Text in Danish and Interlingua) 1960. irreg.(1-4/yr.) Kr.5. Dansk Interlingua Union, Ellegaardspark 79, DK-3520 Farum, Denmark (Subscr. to: Information Interlingua, Juvelvej 25, DK-5210 Odense NV, Denmark) Ed. J. Kofod-Jensen. bk. rev.

496   UK   ISSN 0065-3985
AFRICAN LANGUAGE STUDIES. 1960. irreg. price varies. University of London, School of Oriental and African Studies, Malet St., London WC1E 7HP, England. Ed. G. Innes.

AFRO-ASIA. see *HISTORY*

492   US
AFROASIATIC DIALECTS. no. 2, 1975. irreg. Undena Publications, Box 97, Malibu, CA 90265. Ed. Thomas Penchoen.

492   US
AFROASIATIC LINGUISTICS. (Subseries of: Monographic Journals of the Near East) (Text in Syriac, Arabic, Hebrew, Aramaic and related languages) 1974. irreg., 7-10/yr. $17. Undena Publications, Box 97, Malibu, CA 90265. Eds. Robert Hetzron, R. Schuh.

400 900   GW   ISSN 0065-5287
AKADEMIE DER WISSENSCHAFTEN, GOETTINGEN. NACHRICHTEN 1. PHILOLOGISCH-HISTORISCHE KLASSE. (Text in English, German, occasionally French) 1893. irreg. price varies. Vandenhoeck und Ruprecht, Theaterstr. 13, Postfach 77, 3400 Goettingen, W. Germany (B.R.D.). index.

AKADEMIJA NAUKA I UMJETNOSTI BOSNE I HERCEGOVINE. ODJELJENJE ISTORIJSKO FILOLOSKIH NAUK. DJELA. see *HISTORY — History Of Europe*

491   UR
AKTUAL'NYE PROBLEMY LEKSIKOLOGII I SLOVOOBRAZOVANIYA. 1972. irreg. 0.70 Rub. Novosibirskii Gosudarstvennyi Universitet, Novosibirsk, 99 Akademgorodok, U.S.S.R. bibl. illus.

420   CN   ISSN 0382-5191
ALBERTA ENGLISH. 1960. irreg. (approx. 3-4/yr.) Can.$3. Alberta Teachers' Association, English Council, 11010 - 142 St., Edmonton, Alta. T5N 2R1, Canada. Ed. Tom Gee. bk. rev. illus. play rev. circ. 500-600. (tabloid format; also avail. in cards) Indexed: Can.Educ.Ind.
     Formerly: English Teacher.

400 800   BL   ISSN 0002-5216
ALFA. (Text in English, French, German and Portuguese) 1962. a. $8 per no. or exchange basis. Faculdade de Filosofia, Ciencias e Letras de Marilia, Caixa Postal 420, Marilia, SP, Brazil. bk. rev. bibl. index. circ. 2,000. (looseleaf format; also avail. in microform)

400   II
ALL-INDIA CONFERENCE OF LINGUISTS. PROCEEDINGS. (Text in English) 1970. a. price varies. Linguistic Society of India, c/o Deccan College Postgraduate and Research Institute, Poona 411006, India.

400   II
ALL-INDIA CONFERENCE OF LINGUISTS. SOUVENIR. 1970. irreg. $2. Linguistic Society of India, c/o Deccan College Postgraduate and Research Institute, Poona 411006, India. adv.

AMERICAN ASSOCIATION OF TEACHERS OF ITALIAN. DIRECTORY. see *EDUCATION*

420 375.4   US
AMERICAN DIALECT SOCIETY. PUBLICATION. Abbreviated title: P A D S. 1889. irreg. American Dialect Society, c/o James Hartman, Ed., Department of English, University of Kansas, Lawrence, KS 66044. circ. 800.

400   US   ISSN 0044-779X
AMERICAN PHILOLOGICAL ASSOCIATION. DIRECTORY OF MEMBERS. 1970. irreg. (approx. biennial) price varies. (American Philological Association) Scholars Press, Box 5207, Missoula, MT 59806. circ. 3,000.

480 478   US   ISSN 0065-9703
AMERICAN PHILOLOGICAL ASSOCIATION. SPECIAL PUBLICATIONS. 1946. irreg. price varies. Scholars Press, Box 5207, Missoula, MT 59806.

406   US   ISSN 0360-5949
AMERICAN PHILOLOGICAL ASSOCIATION. TRANSACTIONS. 1870. a. $30. (American Philological Association) Scholars Press, Box 5207, Missoula, MT 59806. Ed. Douglas E. Gerber. cum. index: 1869-1969. circ. 3,000.
     Formerly: American Philological Association. Transactions and Proceedings (ISSN 0065-9711)

AMERINDIA; revue d'ethnolinguistique amerindien. see *ANTHROPOLOGY*

410   NE   ISSN 0304-0712
AMSTERDAM STUDIES IN THE THEORY AND HISTORY OF LINGUISTIC SCIENCE. SERIES 1: AMSTERDAM CLASSICS IN LINGUISTICS, 1800-1925. Short title: A C I L. (Text in English and German) 1974. irreg., vol. 14, 1978. price varies. John Benjamins B. V., Box 52519, 1007 HA Amsterdam, Netherlands. Ed. E.F.K. Koerner.

410   NE   ISSN 0304-0720
AMSTERDAM STUDIES IN THE THEORY AND HISTORY OF LINGUISTIC SCIENCE. SERIES 3: STUDIES IN THE HISTORY OF LINGUISTICS. Short title: S I H O L. 1974. irreg., vol. 22, 1981. price varies. John Benjamins B. V., Box 52519, 1007 HA Amsterdam, Netherlands. Ed. E.F.K. Koerner.

410   NE   ISSN 0304-0763
AMSTERDAM STUDIES IN THE THEORY AND HISTORY OF LINGUISTIC SCIENCE. SERIES 4: CURRENT ISSUES IN LINGUISTIC THEORY. Short title: C I L T. (Text in English) 1975. irreg., vol. 19, 1981. price varies. John Benjamins B. V., Box 52519, 1007 HA Amsterdam, Netherlands. Ed. E. F. K. Koerner.

AMSTERDAMER PUBLIKATIONEN ZUR SPRACHE UND LITERATUR. see *LITERATURE*

440 840   GW   ISSN 0569-986X
ANALECTA ROMANICA. (Beihefte zu den Romanischen Forschungen) 1955. irreg., vol. 47, 1981. price varies. Vittorio Klostermann, Frauenlobstr. 22, Postfach 900601, 6000 Frankfurt 90, W. Germany (B.R.D.) Ed. Fritz Schalk.

430 792   UK
ANGLICA GERMANICA: SERIES 2. irreg. price varies. Cambridge University Press, Box 110, Cambridge CB2 3RL, England (And 32 E. 57th St., New York NY 10022) Ed.Bd.

ANGLO-AMERICAN FORUM. see *LITERATURE*

420 820   HU   ISSN 0570-0973
ANGOL FILOLOGIAI TANULMANYOK/ HUNGARIAN STUDIES IN ENGLISH. (Text in English) 1967. irreg., vol. 10, 1976. Kossuth Lajos Tudomanyegyetem, Angol Tanszek, Nagyerdei korut, Debrecen 10, Hungary. bibl. illus.

470   FR   ISSN 0066-2348
ANNEE EPIGRAPHIQUE; REVUE DES PUBLICATIONS EPIGRAPHIQUES RELATIVES A L'ANTIQUITE ROMAINE. 1962. a. 160 F. (Academie des Inscriptions et Belles-Lettres) Presses Universitaires de France, 108 Bd. Saint Germaine, 75279 Paris Cedex6, France (Service des Periodiques, 12 rue Jean Beauvais, 75005 Paris)

ANTICHITA CLASSICA E CRISTIANA. see *HISTORY*

400   VE   ISSN 0066-507X
ANUARIO DE FILOLOGIA.* 1962. a; biennial. Bs.10($2.25) Universidad del Zulia, Facultad de Humanidades y Educacion, Apdo. 526, Maracaibo, Venezuela.

400   SP   ISSN 0210-1343
ANUARIO DE FILOLOGIA. (Text in various European languages) 1975. a. 1200 ptas.($20) Universidad de Barcelona, Facultad de Filologia, Barcelona, Spain. Ed. Fernando Diaz Esteban. cum.index. circ. 300. (back issues avail.)
     Formerly: Universidad de Barcelona. Facultad de Filologia. Anuario.

491.8 AU ISSN 0066-5282
ANZEIGER FUER SLAVISCHE PHILOLOGIE.
1966. irreg., 1972 vol. 6. Akademische Druck- und Verlagsanstalt, Auersperggasse 12, 8010 Graz, Austria.

410 NE ISSN 0066-5576
APPROACHES TO SEMIOTICS. 1969. irreg. price varies. Mouton Publishers, Noordeinde 41, 2514 GC The Hague, Netherlands (U.S. addr: Mouton Publishers, c/o Walter de Gruyter, Inc., 200 Saw Mill River Road, Hawthorne, NY 10532)

492.7 370 US
AL-ARABIYYA. (Text in Arabic and English) 1967. a. $7.50 to individuals; institutions $15. American Association of Teachers of Arabic, c/o C. G. Killean, Exec. Sec., Near Eastern Languages, Oriental Institute, 1155 E. 58th St., Chicago, IL 60637. bk. rev. bibl. circ. 150. (processed)
Formerly (until vol. 8): Al-Nashra (ISSN 0003-2387)

450 IT ISSN 0066-6696
ARCHIVIO LINGUISTICO VENETO. QUADERNI. 1962. irreg., 1969, no. 5. price varies. (Fondazione Giorgio Cini) Casa Editrice Leo S. Olschki, Casella Postale 66, 50100 Florence, Italy. circ. 1,000.

450 IT ISSN 0066-6815
ARCHIVUM ROMANICUM. BIBLIOTECA. SERIE 2: LINGUISTICA. (Text in French, German or Italian) 1921. irreg., no. 36, 1977. price varies. Casa Editrice Leo S. Olschki, Casella Postale 66, 50100 Florence, Italy. circ. 1,000.

ARCHIWUM FILOLOGICZNE. see CLASSICAL STUDIES

491.85 891.85 PL
ARCHIWUM TLUMACZEN Z TEORII LITERATURY I METODOLOGII BADAN LITERACKICH. 1966. irreg. price varies. Katolicki Uniwersytet Lubelski, Chopina 29, 20-023 Lublin, Poland. index. circ. 125.

ARCTOS; ACTA PHILOLOGICA FENNICA. see CLASSICAL STUDIES

439 SW ISSN 0066-7668
ARKIV FOR NORDISK FILOLOGI/ARCHIVES FOR SCANDINAVIAN PHILOLOGY. (Text in Danish, English, French, German, Norwegian and Swedish) 1882. a. Kr.95. C.W.K. Gleerup (Subsidiary of: LiberLaeromedel) Box 1205, S-221 05 Lund, Sweden. Ed. Bengt Pamp. bk. rev. circ. 470.

ARNAMAGNAEAN INSTITUTE AND DICTIONARY. BULLETIN. see LITERATURE

408 UK ISSN 0587-3584
ART-LANGUAGE. irreg. £6. Art & Language Press, 13 Milverton Crescent, Leamington Spa, Warwickshire, England.

410 CK
ARTICULOS EN LINGUISTICA Y CAMPOS AFINES. 1974. irreg. Instituto Linguistico de Verano, Division Operativa de Asuntos Indigenas, Lomalinda, Meta, Colombia.

410 SP
ASOCIACION DE ACADEMIAS DE LA LENGUA ESPANOLA. COMISION PERMANENTE. BOLETIN. no. 22, 1975. irreg. 300 ptas. Comision Permanente, Calle de Felipe IV 4, Madrid 14, Spain. Ed. Bd. bibl.

400 CN ISSN 0066-9016
ASSOCIATION DES TRADUCTEURS ET INTERPRETES DE L'ONTARIO. ANNUAIRE. 1970. a. Can.$4. Association des Traducteurs et Interpretes de l'Ontario, 1 Nicholas, Suite 1406, Ottawa, Ont. K1N 7B7, Canada. adv. circ. 1,500.

400 CN ISSN 0381-5781
ASSOCIATION DES TRADUCTEURS ET INTERPRETES DE L'ONTARIO. INFORMATIO. (Text in English and French) 1971. irreg. Association des Traducteurs et Interpretes de l'Ontario, 1 Nicholas, Suite 1406, Ottawa, Ont. K1N 7B7, Canada. circ. 600.

410 US ISSN 0066-9903
ASSYRIOLOGICAL STUDIES. 1931. irreg., vol. 21, 1980. price varies. University of Chicago, Oriental Institute, 1155 E. 58th St., Chicago, IL 60637 (Vols. published before 1977 avail. from: University of Chicago Press, 5801 Ellis Ave., Chicago, IL 60637)

430 GE
BAUSTEINE ZUR SPRACHGESCHICHTE DES NEUHOCHDEUTSCHEN. 1970. irreg. price varies. (Akademie der Wissenschaften der DDR, Zentralinstitut fuer Sprachwissenschaft) Akademie-Verlag, Leipziger Strasse 3-4, 108 Berlin, E. Germany (D.D.R.)
Formerly: Bausteine zur Geschichte des Neuhochdeutschen (ISSN 0067-463X)

480 GW
BEITRAEGE ZUR KLASSISCHEN PHILOLOGIE. 1960. irreg., no. 119, 1980. price varies. Verlag Anton Hain GmbH, Adelheid Str. 2, Postfach 1220, 6240 Koenigstein, W. Germany (B.R.D.) Ed. Bd.

409 LU
BEITRAEGE ZUR LUXEMBURGISCHEN SPRACH- UND VOLKSKUNDE. (Text in French, German) 1925. irreg. price varies. Institut Grand-Ducal de Luxembourg, Section de Linguistique, de Folklore et de Toponymie, 5 rue Large, Luxembourg, Luxembourg. circ. 500-1,000. (back issues avail.)

479 GW ISSN 0067-5202
BEITRAEGE ZUR ROMANISCHEN PHILOLOGIE DES MITTELALTERS. 1968. irreg. price varies. Wilhelm Fink Verlag, Nikolaistr. 2, 8000 Munich 40, W. Germany (B.R.D.) Eds. Hans-Wilhelm Klein, Ernstpeter Ruhe.

BIBLIOGRAPHIE PAPYROLOGIQUE SUR FICHES. see ARCHAEOLOGY

400 SP
BIBLIOTECA DE FILOLOGIA HISPANICA ONOMASTICA Y TOPONIMIA. 1975. irreg. Ediciones el Albir, Calle de los Angeles 8, Barcelona 1, Spain. circ. 500.

499.9 IT ISSN 0067-7450
BIBLIOTECA DI STUDI ETRUSCHI. 1963. irreg., vol. 11, 1979. price varies. (Istituto di Studi Etruschi, Florence) Casa Editrice Leo S. Olschki, Casella Postale 66, 50100 Florence, Italy. circ. 500.

410 SP
BIBLIOTECA FILOLOGICA. ENSAYOS. irreg. Editorial Bello, Barcas 5, Valencia, Spain.

410 SP
BIBLIOTECA FILOLOGICA. MANUALES. no. 4, 1977. irreg. Editorial Bello, Barcas 5, Valencia, Spain.

450 IT ISSN 0067-7868
BIBLIOTHECA ATHENA. 1965. irreg., no. 24, 1979. price varies. (Universita degli Studi di Roma, Scuola di Filologia Classica) Edizioni dell' Anteneo S.P.A., P.O. Box 7216, 00100 Rome, Italy. circ. 2,500.

430 324 SZ ISSN 0067-7477
BIBLIOTHECA GERMANICA. HANDBUECHER, TEXTE UND MONOGRAPHIEN AUS DEM GEBIETE DER GERMANISCHEN PHILOLOGIE. 1951. irreg., no. 21, 1978. price varies. ‡ Francke Verlag, Postfach, CH-3000 Berne 26, Switzerland. Eds. Friedrich Maurer, Heinz Rupp, Max Wehrli.

400 SZ ISSN 0067-8120
BIBLIOTHECA PHONETICA. (Text in English, French and German) 1964. irreg. (approx. 1/yr) 100 Fr.($60) per vol. (1981 price) S. Karger AG, Allschwilerstrasse 10, P.O. Box, CH-4009 Basel, Switzerland. Ed.Bd. (reprint service avail. from ISI) Indexed: Biol.Abstr. Chem.Abstr. Curr.Cont. Ind.Med.

430 440 SZ ISSN 0067-7515
BIBLIOTHECA ROMANICA. (Text in French, Italian or German) 1945. irreg., vol. 13, 1977. price varies. ‡ Francke Verlag, Postfach, CH-3000 Berne 26, Switzerland. Ed. C. Th. Gossen.

800 GW ISSN 0341-3217
BIBLIOTHECA RUSSICA. 1979. irreg., no. 2, 1979. price varies. Verlag Helmut Buske, Schlueterstr. 14, 2000 Hamburg 13, W. Germany (B.R.D.) Ed. Irene Nowikowa.

491 943 FR ISSN 0067-8325
BIBLIOTHEQUE D'ETUDES BALKANIQUES. 1925. irreg., 1965, vol. 8. price varies. Institut d'Etudes Slaves, 9 rue Michelet, F 75006 Paris, France.

496 FR ISSN 0081-1238
BIBLIOTHEQUE DE LA S E L A F. 1967. 6/yr. price varies. Societe d'Etudes Linguistiques et Anthropologiques de France, 5, rue de Marseille, 75010 Paris, France.
Before 1969: Societe pour l'Etude des Langues Africaines. Bulletin.

800 479 FR ISSN 0067-8384
BIBLIOTHEQUE FRANCAISE ET ROMANE. SERIE E: LANGUE ET LITTERATURE FRANCAISES AU CANADA. 1966. irreg, 1973, no. 8. price varies. (Universite de Strasbourg II, Centre de Philologie et de Litteratures Romanes) Editions Klincksieck, 11 rue de Lille, Paris 7e, France. Ed. Georges Straka.

440 FR ISSN 0067-8341
BIBLIOTHEQUE FRANCAISE ET ROMANE. SERIE A: MANUELS ET ETUDES LINGUISTIQUES. 1960. irreg. price varies. (Universite de Strasbourg II, Centre de Philologie et de Litteratures Romanes) Editions Klincksieck, 11 rue de Lille, Paris 7, France. Ed. Georges Straka.

491.85 PL ISSN 0067-8996
BIULETYN FONOGRAFICZNY/BULLETIN PHONOGRAPHIQUE. (Supplement to Lingua Posnaniensis) (Text in English, French, German, Polish and Russian) 1953/60. irreg; 1972, no. 13. price varies. (Poznanskie Towarzystwo Przyjaciol Nauk) Panstwowe Wydawnictwo Naukowe, Ul. Miodowa 10, Warsaw, Poland. Ed. Ludwik Zabrocki.

400 BL
BOLETIM DE LINQUISTICA. 1974. irreg. Circulo de Estudos Linguisticos, Universidade Estadual de Londrina, Centro de Ciencias Humanas, Caixa Postal 2003, Londrina, Brazil.

400 CL ISSN 0067-9674
BOLETIN DE FILOLOGIA. (Text in Spanish, French, English, German) 1934. a. $12. Universidad de Chile, Departamento de Linguistica y Filologia, Departamento de Linguistica y Filologia, Casilla 10136, Correo Central, Santiago, Chile. Ed. Dr. Mario Ferreccio Podesta. adv. bk. rev. cum.ind. circ. 1,000. Indexed: M.L.A.

420 820 CS
BRNO STUDIES IN ENGLISH. 1957. irreg. price varies. Universita J. E. Purkyne, Filosoficka Fakulta, A. Novaka 1, 602 00 Brno, Czechoslovakia. bk. rev. circ. 600. Indexed: Bull.Signal.

491.81 BU ISSN 0068-3787
BULGARSKA AKADEMIIA NA NAUKITE. INSTITUT ZA BULGARSKI EZIK. IZVESTIIA. (Summaries in various languages) no. 19, 1970. a. 9.08 lv. Publishing House of the Bulgarian Academy of Sciences, Ul. Akad. G. Bonchev, 1113 Sofia, Bulgaria (Dist. by: Hemus, 6, Rouski Blvd., 1000 Sofia, Bulgaria) circ. 800.

412 BU
BULGARSKI ETIMOLOGICHEN RECHNIK. 1962. irreg. price varies. (Bulgarska Akademiia na Naukite, Institut za Bulgarski Ezik) Publishing House of the Bulgarian Academy of Sciences, Ul. Akad. G. Bonchev, 1113 Sofia, Bulgaria (Dist. by: Hemus, 6, Rouski Blvd., 1000 Sofia, Bulgaria)

800 479 FR ISSN 0068-4031
BULLETIN DES JEUNES ROMANISTES. 1960. irreg. price varies. (Association des Jeunes Romanistes) Editions Klincksieck, 11 rue de Lille, Paris 7, France. (Co-sponsor: Universite de Strasbourg II. Centre de Philologie et des Litteratures Romanes)

410 572 LU ISSN 0068-4066
BULLETIN LINGUISTIQUE ET ETHNOLOGIQUE. (Text in French, German, Luxembourgeois) 1953. irreg. price varies. Institut Grand-Ducal de Luxembourg, Section de Linguistique, de Folklore et de Toponymie, 5 rue Large, Luxembourg, Luxembourg. circ. 500. (back issues avail.)

400 800   PL   ISSN 0068-4570
BYDGOSKIE TOWARZYSTWO NAUKOWE.
WYDZIAL NAUK HUMANISTYCZNYCH.
PRACE. SERIA B (JEZYK I LITERATURA)
1965. irreg. price varies. Bydgoskie Towarzystwo
Naukowe, Jezuicka 4, Bydgoszcz, Poland (Dist. by
Ars Polona-Ruch, Krakowskie Przedmiescie 7,
Warsaw, Poland)

410 800   UK   ISSN 0307-0131
BYZANTINE AND MODERN GREEK STUDIES.
(Text in English; quotations in Greek) 1975. a.
£8($17) Basil Blackwell, Publisher, Ltd., 108
Cowley Rd., Oxford OX4 1JF, England. Ed.
Donald M. Nicol.

407   II
C I I L BILINGUAL HINDI SERIES. (Text in
English) 1976. irreg. Central Institute of Indian
Languages, Manasagangotri, Mysore 570006, India.
bibl.

491   II
C I I L GRAMMAR SERIES. 1975. irreg., latest
1980. Rs.10. Central Institute of Indian Languages,
Mysore 6, India. bibl.
Study and teaching

491   II
C I I L OCCASIONAL MONOGRAPH SERIES. no.
8, 1974. irreg., latest 1980. Central Institute of
Indian Languages, Mysore 6, India.

410   BL
CADERNOS DE ESTUDOS LINGUISTICOS. 1978.
irreg. Universidade Estadual de Campinas, Instituto
de Estudos da Linguagem, Departamento de
Linguistica, Caixa Postal 1170, 13100 Campinas SP,
Brazil. bibl. charts.

491   CN
CAHIERS CULTURELS. (Text in English and
French) 1956. a. Can.$6. Institut des Civilisations
Comparees de Montreal, 5214 Av. du Parc,
Montreal, Que. H2V 4G7, Canada. Ed. Prof.
Theodore F. Domaradzki. adv. bk. rev. bibl. charts.
index. circ. 1,000. (also avail. in microform)
Indexed: P.A.I.S. SSCI.
   Formerly (until 1978): Etudes Slaves et Est-
Europeennes (ISSN 0014-2190)

CAHIERS D'ETUDES MONGOLES ET
SIBERIENNES. see *ANTHROPOLOGY*

410   FR
CAHIERS DE LINGUISTIQUE HISPANIQUE
MEDIEVALE. 1976. irreg., no. 3, 1978. (Universite
de Paris XIII) Editions Klincksieck, 11 rue de Lille,
Paris 7, France.

400   FR   ISSN 0153-5048
CAHIERS DE PHILOLOGIE. (Includes supplements)
1976. irreg. (Universite de Lille III, Centre de
Recherche Philologique) Presses Universitaires de
Lille, 9 rue Auguste Angellier, 59000 Lille, France.
Dir. Jean Bollack.

400   CN   ISSN 0068-5070
CAHIERS DE PSYCHOMECANIQUE DE
LANGAGE. irreg. price varies. (Universite Laval,
Department de Linguistique) Presses de l'Universite
Laval, C. P. 2447, Quebec 2, Que., Canada.
   Formerly: Cahiers de Linguistique Structurale.

410   SZ   ISSN 0068-516X
CAHIERS FERDINAND DE SAUSSURE; review de
linguistique general. 1941. irreg., no. 30, 1976. price
varies. (Cercle Ferdinand de Saussure) Librarie
Droz, 11, rue Massot, 1211 Geneva 12, Switzerland.
bk. rev. circ. 1,000.

470 870   UK
CAMBRIDGE LATIN TEXTS. irreg. price varies.
Cambridge University Press, Box 110, Cambridge
CB2 3RL, England (And 32 E. 57th St., New York
NY 10022)

CAMBRIDGE PHILOLOGICAL SOCIETY.
PROCEEDINGS. see *CLASSICAL STUDIES*

CAMBRIDGE PHILOLOGICAL SOCIETY.
PROCEEDINGS. SUPPLEMENT. see
CLASSICAL STUDIES

400   UK   ISSN 0068-676X
CAMBRIDGE STUDIES IN LINGUISTICS. 1969.
irreg., no. 32, 1981. $75 for latest vol. Cambridge
University Press, Box 110, Cambridge CB2 3RL,
England (and 32 E. 57 St., New York, NY 10022)
Ed. Bd. index.

410   ZR
CENTRE D'ETUDES ETHNOLOGIQUES.
PUBLICATIONS. SERIE 3: TRAVAUX
LINGUISTIQUES. 1972. irreg., no. 5, 1975. C E E
B A Publications, Bandundu, Zaire. circ. 700.

410   FR
CENTRE INTERNATIONAL DE
DOCUMENTATION OCCITANE.
BIBLIOTHEQUE. CATALOGUE. (Text in French
and Occitan) 1976. irreg. Centre International de
Documentation Occitane, Bibliotheque, Boite
Postale 4202, 34325 Beziers Cedex, France.

440   RE   ISSN 0337-6176
CENTRE UNIVERSITAIRE DE LA REUNION.
CAHIER. 1971. irreg., no. 10, 1979. price varies.
Centre Universitaire de la Reunion, 12 rue de la
Victoire, 97489 Saint-Denis, Reunion. bk. rev.

407   AG
CENTRO DE INVESTIGACIONES EN CIENCIAS
DE LA EDUCACION. SECCION LENGUAS
INDIGENAS. DOCUMENTO DE TRABAJO.
no.9, 1975. irreg. Centro de Investigaciones en
Ciencias de la Educacion, Seccion Lenguas
Indigenas, Superi 1761, 1426 Buenos Aires,
Argentina. (Affiliate: Instituto Torcuato di Tella)

410   US   ISSN 0577-7240
CHICAGO LINGUISTIC SOCIETY. PAPERS
FROM THE REGIONAL MEETINGS. 1965. a.
price varies. Chicago Linguistic Society, 1050 E.
59th St., Chicago, IL 60637. (back issues avail.)

410   US   ISSN 0163-2809
CHILDREN'S LANGUAGE. 1978. a. $24.95.
Gardner Press, Inc., 19 Union Sq. W., New York,
NY 10003. Ed. Keith Nelson. circ. 2,000.

450   IT   ISSN 0069-4339
CIVILTA VENEZIANA. DIZIONARI DIALETTALI
E STUDI LINGUISTICI. 1960. irreg., 1969, no. 4.
price varies. (Fondazione Giorgio Cini) Casa
Editrice Leo S. Olschki, Casella Postale 66, 50100
Florence, Italy. circ. 1,000.

410 150   US
COGNITION AND LANGUAGE; a series in
psycholinguistics. 1979. irreg. price varies. Plenum
Publishing Corp., 233 Spring St., New York, NY
10013. Ed. R. W. Rieber.

400   BL   ISSN 0587-6435
COLECAO DE ESTUDOS FILOLOGICOS. 1956.
irreg. Fundacao Casa de Rui Barbosa, Rua Sao
Clemente 134, Botafogo 22260, Rio de Janeiro RJ,
Brazil. Dir. Washington Luis Neto.

410   FR
COLLECTION ORALITES-DOCUMENTS. 1978.
irreg. Societe d'Etudes Linguistiques et
Anthropologiques de France, 5 rue de Marseille,
75010 Paris, France.

460   US
COLLOQUIUM ON HISPANIC LINGUISTICS.
PROCEEDINGS. irreg., 2nd, 1976, Tampa.
(Linguistic Society of America) Georgetown
University Press, Washington, DC 20057.

400   JA   ISSN 0069-598X
COLOQUIO DE ESTUDOS LUSO BRASILEIROS.
ANAIS. (Text in Portuguese) 1967. a. $8.
Associacao Japonesa de Estudos Luso-Brasileiros,
Brazilian Center, Sophia University, 7-1 Kioicho,
Chiyoda-Ku, Tokyo 102, Japan. Ed. Vendelino
Lorscheiter. bk. rev. bibl. index(1976) circ. 220.
(back issues avail.)

420 375.4   US
COLUMBIA UNIVERSITY. AMERICAN
LANGUAGE PROGRAM. BULLETIN; instruction
in English as a foreign language. 1953. biennial.
free. Columbia University, School of General
Studies, American Language Program, 505
Lewisohn Hall, New York, NY 10027. Ed. Louis
Levi. circ. 6,000.

418   EI
COMMISSION OF THE EUROPEAN
COMMUNITIES. TERMINOLOGY OFFICE.
TERMINOLOGY BULLETIN/BULLETIN DE
TERMINOLOGIE. (Text in English, French,
German, Italian and Dutch) 1964. irreg.; latest
issue, no. 24, 1975. free. Commission of the
European Communities, Terminology Office,
Monterey Palace, Av. Monterey, Luxembourg,
Luxembourg. bk. rev.

410 001.6   NE
COMPUTATIONAL LINGUISTICS AND
COMPUTER LANGUAGES. Short title: C L C L.
no. 12, 1978. irreg. fl.42 per no. (Akademiai Kiado,
Publishing House of the Hungarian Academy of
Sciences, Computer and Automation Institute, HU)
John Benjamins B.V., Box 52519, 1007 HA
Amsterdam, Netherlands. Eds. T. Frey, T. Vamos.

CONTRIBUTIONS TO THE SOCIOLOGY OF
LANGUAGE. see *SOCIOLOGY*

420 810   SZ   ISSN 0069-9780
COOPER MONOGRAPHS ON ENGLISH AND
AMERICAN LANGUAGE AND LITERATURE.
(Text in English or German) 1956. irreg., vol. 28,
1978. price varies. ‡ Francke Verlag, Postfach, CH-
3000 Berne 26, Switzerland. Ed. R. Stamm.

410   NE
CORNELL LINGUISTIC CONTRIBUTIONS. (Text
in English) 1977. irreg., vol. 3, 1980. price varies.
(Cornell University, US) E. J. Brill, Oude Rijn 33a-
35, Leiden, Netherlands. Eds. Frans van Coetsem,
Linda R. Waugh.

492   US   ISSN 0070-1203
COUNCIL ON THE TEACHING OF HEBREW.
BULLETIN. (Text in Hebrew; title page in English)
1968-69. irreg.; latest issue, nos. 4-6, 1972. $1. Council
on the Teaching of Hebrew, Department of
Education and Culture, 515 Park Ave., New York,
NY 10022. Ed. Ben-Zion Fischler.

400   IT   ISSN 0391-1535
CRONACHE ERCOLANESI. (Text in English,
French, German, Italian) 1971. a. L.18000. Gaetano
Macchiaroli Editore, Via Carducci 59, Naples
80121, Italy.
   Study of papyri

410   MX
CUADERNOS DE LINGUISTICA. 1975. irreg. price
varies. Universidad Nacional Autonoma de Mexico,
Instituto de Investigaciones Filologicas, Centro de
Linguistica Hispanica, Torre de Humanidades II,
Ciudad Universitaria, Mexico 20, D.F., Mexico
(Order from: Departamento de Distribucion,
Libreria Universitaria, Insurgentes sur 299, Mexico
11, D.F., Mexico) (Co-sponsor: Asociacion de
Linguistica y Filologia de la America Latina) Ed.
Juan M. Lope Blanch.

410   UY
CUADERNOS DE SEMIOTICA. 1978. irreg.
Editorial Anfora Solar, Garibaldi 2844, Montevideo,
Uruguay. Eds. Pilar Barreiro Muracchle, Luis
Ernesto Behares.

410   CN
CURRENT INQUIRY INTO LANGUAGE AND
LINGUISTICS. irreg., no. 25, 1979. price varies.
Linguistic Research Inc., Box, 5677, Sta. L.,
Edmonton, Alta. T6C 4G1, Canada. Ed. Anthony
L. Vanek. bibl. charts. (also avail. in microform
from UMI)

840 440   GW
DACOROMANIA; Jahrbuch fuer oestliche Latinitaet.
1973. a. Karl Alber GmbH, Hermann-Herder-Str. 4,
7800 Freiburg, W. Germany (B. R. D.) Ed. Paul
Miron.

410   PE
DATOS ETNO-LINGUISTICOS. irreg., no.67, 1979.
price varies. Instituto Linguistico de Verano,
Departamento de Estudios Etno-Linguisticos, Casilla
2492, Lima 100, Peru. (microfilm)

DECCAN COLLEGE. POSTGRADUATE &
RESEARCH INSTITUTE. BULLETIN. see
*SOCIAL SCIENCES: COMPREHENSIVE
WORKS*

400 FR ISSN 0070-3338
DELPHICA.* 1971. irreg. price varies. Editions la
Tete de Feuille, 68 rue de Babylone, 75007 Paris,
France.

491.7 NE ISSN 0070-3826
DESCRIPTION AND ANALYSIS OF
CONTEMPORARY STANDARD RUSSIAN.
irreg. price varies. Mouton Publishers, Noordeinde
41, 2514 GC The Hague, Netherlands (U.S. addr:
Mouton Publishers, c/o Walter de Gruyter, Inc.,
200 Saw Mill River Road, Hawthorne, NY 10532)

DEUTSCH-SLAWISCHE FORSCHUNGEN ZUR
NAMENKUNDE UND
SIEDLUNGSGESCHICHTE. see *HISTORY —
History Of Europe*

491 GW ISSN 0070-3923
DEUTSCHE AKADEMIE FUER SPRACHE UND
DICHTUNG. JAHRBUCH. 1953. a. price varies.
Verlag Lambert Schneider, Hausackerweg 16, 6900
Heidelberg 1, W. Germany (B. R. D.) Ed. Ernst
Johann.

430 375.4 GW ISSN 0170-3153
DEUTSCHE SPRACHE IN EUROPA UND
UEBERSEE. irreg., vol. 8, 1981. price varies.
(Institut fuer Deutsche Sprache, Mannheim) Franz
Steiner Verlag GmbH, Friedrichstr. 24, Postfach
5529, 6200 Wiesbaden, W. Germany (B.R.D.) Eds.
L. Auburger, H. Kloss, H. Rupp.

447.9 BE
DIALECTES DE WALLONIE. Spine title: D W.
(Text in French) 1972. a. 300 Fr. Societe de Langue
et de Litterature Wallonnes, Place du Vingt-Aout 7,
B-4000 Liege, Belgium. Ed. Jean Lechanteur. bibl.
illus. circ. 600.

410 US ISSN 0270-3750
DICTIONARY, ENCYCLOPEDIA & HANDBOOK
REVIEW. 1981. a. $5 to individuals; institutions
$10. Translation Research Institute, 5914 Pulaski
Ave., Philadelphia, PA 19144. Ed. Charles Parsons.
bk. rev.

DICTIONARY OF CONTEMPORARY
QUOTATIONS. see *LITERATURE*

DIMENSION: LANGUAGES; proceedings of the
Southern Conference on Language Teaching. see
*EDUCATION — Teaching Methods And
Curriculum*

DIRECTORY OF PERIODICALS PUBLISHING
ARTICLES ON ENGLISH AND AMERICAN
LITERATURE AND LANGUAGE. see
LITERATURE

428 UK ISSN 0307-1006
DISCOURSE ANALYSIS MONOGRAPHS. 1976.
irreg. £1.50. University of Birmingham, English
Language Research, Birmingham, Birmingham B15
2TT. Ed. R. M. Coulthard. circ. 400.

400 FR ISSN 0085-4786
DOCUMENTS DE LINGUISTIQUE
QUANTITATIVE. 1969. irreg. price varies.
(Association Jean-Favard pour le Developpement de
la Linguistique Quantitative) Editions Jean Favard,
37 rue du Four a Chaux, 91910 St. Sulpice de
Favieres, France. Ed. Daniel J. Herault. circ. 850.
Indexed: Bull.Signal.

400 800 US
DUQUESNE STUDIES. LANGUAGE AND
LITERATURE. 1960. irreg. price varies. Duquesne
University Press, 600 Forbes Ave., Pittsburgh, PA
15219 (Dist. by Humanities Press, Inc., Atlantic
Highlands, NJ 07716) Ed. Foster Provost.
Formerly (until vol. 17): Duquesne Studies.
Philological Series (ISSN 0070-7694)

EDITIONES ARNAMAGNAEANAE. SERIES A.
see *LITERATURE*

EDITIONES ARNAMAGNAEANAE. SERIES B.
see *LITERATURE*

410 US ISSN 0163-3848
EDWARD SAPIR MONOGRAPH SERIES IN
LANGUAGE, CULTURE, AND COGNITION.
(Supplement to: Forum Linguiticum) 1977. irreg.
price varies. (Linguistic Association of Canada and
the United States) Jupiter Press, Box 101, Lake
Bluff, IL 60044. Ed. Adam Makkai. circ. 1,000.
(back issues avail.)

493 GW ISSN 0340-627X
ENCHORIA; Zeitschrift fuer Demotistik und
Koptologie. 1971. a. DM.58 (approx.) Verlag Otto
Harrassowitz, Taunusstr. 6, Postfach 2929, 6200
Wiesbaden, W. Germany (B.R.D.) Ed. E.
Lueddeckens, H.-J. Thissen, K.-Th. Zauzich. circ.
400. (back issues avail.)

400 GW ISSN 0071-0490
ENGLISH AND AMERICAN STUDIES IN
GERMAN; summaries of theses and monographs.
(Supplement To: Anglia - Zeitschrift fuer Englische
Philologie) 1969. a. price varies.
(German Congress of Scholars of English) Max
Niemeyer Verlag, Pfrondorfer Str. 4, 7400
Tuebingen, W. Germany (B.R.D.) Ed. Werner
Habicht.

410 UK ISSN 0308-0129
ENGLISH PHILOLOGICAL STUDIES. irreg. price
varies. (University of Birmingham) Heffers Printers
Ltd., Kings Hedges Rd., Cambridge CB4 2PQ,
England. Ed. Allan S.C. Ross. bibl.
Formerly: English and Germanic Studies.

420 422 UK ISSN 0071-0636
ENGLISH PLACE-NAME SOCIETY. 1922. irreg.
membership. ‡ English Place-Name Society, c/o
Mrs. M. D. Pattison, School of English Studies,
University of Nottingham, Nottingham NG7 2RD,
England. Ed. Kenneth Cameron. index. circ. 740.

420 375.4 US ISSN 0071-0644
ENGLISH STUDIES SERIES. irreg., no. 9, 1971.
Oxford University Press, 200 Madison Ave., New
York, NY 10016 (and Ely House, 37 Dover St.,
London W1X 4AH, England) Ed. Ronald Mackin.
English language study and teaching

428 UK
ENGLISH-TEACHING INFORMATION CENTRE,
LONDON. INFORMATION GUIDES. 1971.
irreg. price varies. ‡ British Council, English-
Teaching Information Centre, 10 Spring Gardens,
London SW1A 2BN, England. bk. rev.

410 BL
ENSAIOS LINGUISTICOS. 1978. irreg. price varies.
Summer Institute of Linguistics, Departamento de
Estudos Tecnicos, C. P. 14-2221, Brasilia 7000,
Brazil.

EPIGRAPHIC SOCIETY. OCCASIONAL
PUBLICATIONS. see *ARCHAEOLOGY*

407 FR
ESPERANTO-ACTUALITES. a. Union Francaise
pour l'Esperanto, 4 bis, rue de la Cerisaie, 75004
Paris, France.

499.992 NE ISSN 0165-2575
ESPERANTO DOCUMENTS. NEW SERIES.
Esperanto edition: Esperanto-Dokumentoj. Nova
Serio (ISSN 0165-2524); French edition: Documents
sur l'Esperanto. Nouvelle Serie (ISSN 0165-2621)
(Text in English) 1976. irreg. fl.31.25($17)
Universala Esperanto Asocio - Universal Esperanto
Association, Nieuwe Binnenweg 176, 3015 BJ
Rotterdam, Netherlands. circ. 500.

410 NE
ESSAIS DE DIALECTOLOGIE INTERLINGUALE.
1978. irreg. price varies. Van Gorcum, Box 43,
Assen, Netherlands.

408 JA
ESSAYS IN FOREIGN LANGUAGES AND
LITERATURES/GAIKOKUGO GAIKOKU
BUNGAKU KENKYU. (Text in Japanese, English,
French, or German) irreg. Hokkaido University,
Faculty of Literature, Library, Kita-10, Nishi-7,
Kita-ku, Sapporo 060, Japan.

460 375.4 MX
ESTUDIOS DE LINGUISTICA Y LITERATURA.
irreg., no. 7, 1978. Colegio de Mexico, Camino al
Ajusco 20, Mexico 20, D.F., Mexico. (reprint
service avail. from UMI)

400 CL ISSN 0071-1713
ESTUDIOS FILOLOGICOS. 1965. a. Esc.160($6)
Universidad Austral de Chile, Facultad de Letras y
Educacion, Casilla 567, Valdivia, Chile. Dir.
Claudio Wagner.

400 CL ISSN 0071-1721
ESTUDIOS FILOLOGICOS. ANEJO. 1968. irreg.,
1972, no. 4. price varies. Universidad Austral de
Chile, Faculdad de Filosofia y Letras, Valdivia,
Chile.

410 860 SP
ESTUDIOS ROMANICAS. 1978. irreg. 350 ptas.($7)
(Universidad de Murcia, Departamento de Filologia
Romanica) Ediciones el Albir, Calle de los Angeles
8, Barcelona 1, Spain.

400 FR
ETUDES CELTIQUES. (Text in English and French)
a. 100 F. Centre National de la Recherche
Scientifique, 15 Quai Anatole France, 75007 Paris,
France. Ed. Edward Bachellery. bk. rev. bibl. illus.
cum.index.

ETUDES FINNO-OUGRIENNES. see
LITERATURE

400 FR ISSN 0071-2124
ETUDES LINGUISTIQUES. 1962. irreg. price varies.
Editions Klincksieck, 11 rue de Lille, Paris 7,
France.

ETUDES VOLTAIQUES. see *ANTHROPOLOGY*

410 IT
EUROASIATICA; journal of neohistorical linguistics.
(Text in various European languages) 1970. irreg.;
vol. 4, 1978. price varies. Giardini Editori e
Stampatori, Via Santa Bibbiana 28, 56100 Pisa,
Italy. Ed.Nullo Minissi.

410 UK
EXPLORATIONS IN LANGUAGE STUDY. 1973.
irreg. price varies. Edward Arnold (Publishers) Ltd.,
41 Bedford Square, London WC1B 3DQ, England.

370.19 CN ISSN 0705-1026
FEDERATION DES ASSOCIATIONS DE
PARENTS ET INSTITUTEURS LANGUES
FRANCAISE DE L'ONTARIO. LIAISON. (Text
in French) 1973. irreg. free. Federation des
Associations de Parents et Instituteur de Langue
Francaise de l'Ontario, Bureau 296, Rue Dalhousie,
Ottawa, Ont. K1N 7E4, Canada.

490 GW ISSN 0341-311X
FENNO-UGRICA. 1973. irreg. price varies. Verlag
Helmut Buske, Schlueterstr. 14, 2000 Hamburg 13,
W. Germany (B.R.D.) Eds. Harald Haarmann,
Anna-Liisa Varri Haarmann.

400 AG ISSN 0071-495X
FILOLOGIA. 1949. a. exchange basis. Instituto de
Filologia y Literaturas Hispanicas "Dr. Amado
Alonso", 25 de Mayo 217, Buenos Aires, Argentina.
Ed. Frida Weber De Kurlat. bk. rev.

420 PL
FILOLOGIA ANGIELSKA. (Text in English, Polish;
summaries in English) 1972. irreg. price varies.
Uniwersytet im. Adama Mickiewicza w Poznaniu,
Stalingradzka 1, 61-712 Poznan, Poland (Dist. by:
Ars Polona, Krakowskie Przedmiescie 7, 00-068
Warsaw, Poland) Ed. Jacek Fisiak. bk. rev. circ.
500-2,000.
Formerly: Uniwersytet im. Adama Mickiewicza w
Poznaniu. Wydzial Filologiczny. Seria Filologia
Angielska.

491.9 891.9 PL
FILOLOGIA BALTYCKA/BALTIC PHILOLOGY.
(Text in Polish, Baltic languages) 1977. irreg., no. 2,
1977. price varies. Uniwersytet im. Adama
Mickiewicza w Poznaniu, Stalingradzka 1, 61-712
Poznan, Poland (Dist. by: Ars Polona, Krakowskie
Przedmiescie 7, 00-068 Warsaw, Poland)

450 IT ISSN 0071-4968
FILOLOGIA E CRITICA. 1965. irreg., no. 39, 1981.
price varies. Edizioni dell' Ateneo S.p.A., P.O. Box
7216, 00100 Rome, Italy. Ed. Bruno Gentili. circ.
3,000.

480 880 PL
FILOLOGIA KLASYCZNA. (Text in Polish;
summaries in various languages) 1966. irreg. price
varies. Uniwersytet im. Adama Mickiewicza w
Poznaniu, Stalingradzka 1, 61-712 Poznan, Poland
(Dist. by: Ars Polona, Krakowskie Przedmiescie 7,
00-068 Warsaw, Poland)
Formerly: Uniwersytet im. Adama Mickiewicza w
Poznaniu. Wydzial Filologiczny. Seria Filologia
Klasyczna.

400 CK ISSN 0071-4976
FILOLOGOS COLOMBIANOS. 1954. irreg., no. 9, 1979. Instituto Caro y Cuervo, Apartado Aereo 20002, Bogota, Colombia.

400 GW ISSN 0430-862X
FOLIA LINGUISTICA. 1967. a. DM.72. European Society of Linguistics, c/o Peter Hartmann, Universitaet Konstanz, W. Germany (B.R.D.) circ. 1,000(approx.)

410 US ISSN 0160-9394
FOLIA SLAVICA. 1977. irreg. (approx. 3/yr.) $20 to individuals; institutions $30. Slavica Publishers, Inc., Box 14388, Columbus, OH 43214. Ed. Charles E. Gribble. bk. rev. circ. 200. (back issues avail.)

459 RM ISSN 0071-6855
FONETICA SI DIALECTOLOGIE. 1958. irreg. (Acaçemia Republicii Socialiste Romania, Centrul de Cercetari Fonetice si Dialectale) Editura Academiei Republicii Socialiste Romania, Calea Victoriei 125, Bucharest, Romania (Subscr. to: ILEXIM, Str. 13 Decembrie Nr. 3, P.O. Box 136-137, Bucharest, Romania) Ed. B. Cazacu. bk. rev. circ. 1,100.

410 NE ISSN 0071-7592
FORMAL LINGUISTICS SERIES. 1970. irreg. price varies. D. Reidel Publishing Co., P.O. Box 17, 3300 AA Dordrecht, Netherlands (And Lincoln Building, 160 Old Derby St., Hingham, MA 02043) Eds. Henry Hiz, Henry M. Hoenigswald, and Zellig S. Harris.

400 GW ISSN 0071-7681
FORSCHUNGEN ZUR ROMANISCHEN PHILOLOGIE. 1957. irreg. price varies. Aschendorffsche Verlagsbuchhandlung, Soester Str. 13, 4400 Muenster, W. Germany (B.R.D.) Ed. Heinrich Lausberg.

410 SZ
FORUM LINGUISTICUM. (Text in English and German; summaries in English) 1974. irreg., no. 19, 1977. price varies. Verlag Peter Lang AG, Muenzgraben 2, Postfach, CH-3000 Berne 7, Switzerland. Ed. Christoph Gutknecht. bk. rev. abstr. bibl. circ. 400 (controlled) (back issues avail.)

410 GW ISSN 0341-3144
FORUM PHONETICUM. 1973. irreg., no. 24, 1981. price varies. Verlag Helmut Buske, Schlueterstr. 14, 2000 Hamburg 13, W. Germany (B.R.D.) Eds. H.W. Wodarz, G. Heike, M. Mangold.

FRANCE. COMITE DES TRAVAUX HISTORIQUES ET SCIENTIFIQUES. BULLETIN PHILOLOGIQUE ET HISTORIQUE (JUSQU'A 1610) see *HISTORY — History Of Europe*

FRANCE. DELEGATION GENERALE A LA RECHERCHE SCIENTIFIQUE ET TECHNIQUE. REPERTOIRE NATIONAL DES CHERCHEURS: SCIENCES SOCIALES ET HUMAINES. TOME 1: ETHNOLOGIE, LINGUISTIQUE, PSYCHOLOGIE, PSYCHOLOGIE SOCIALE, SOCIOLOGIE. see *SOCIOLOGY*

491.7 GW ISSN 0473-5277
FRANKFURTER ABHANDLUNGEN ZUR SLAVISTIK. irreg., vol. 24, 1978. price varies. Franz Steiner Verlag GmbH, Friedrichstr. 24, Postfach 5529, 6200 Wiesbaden, W. Germany (B.R.D.) Ed.Alfred Rammelmeyer.

FRANKFURTER BEITRAEGE ZUR GERMANISTIK. see *LITERATURE*

FREIBURGER BEITRAEGE ZUR INDOLOGIE. see *HISTORY — History Of Asia*

FREIE UNIVERSITAET BERLIN. OSTEUROPA-INSTITUT. SLAVISTISCHE VEROEFFENTLICHUNGEN. see *LITERATURE*

400 FR ISSN 0072-0356
GAZETO. 1957. irreg. price varies. Centre National Esperanto, 46 bis, Bld. Alexandre-Martin, 45000 Orleans, France.

423.1 UK ISSN 0072-0542
GEIRIADUR PRIFYSGOL CYMRU. (Text in Welsh and English) 1953. a. £2 per part. (Board of Celtic Studies) University of Wales Press, 6 Gwennyth St., Cathays, Cardiff CF2 4YD, Wales. Ed. G. A. Bevan. circ. 1,500. (reprint service avail. from UMI) Dictionary of the Welsh language

412 US ISSN 0072-0771
GENERAL SEMANTICS BULLETIN. 1950. a. $20 contribution(libraries $15) Institute of General Semantics, R.R. 1, Box 215, Lakeville, CT 06039. Ed. Robert Pula. bk. rev. cum.index (1-37) circ. 600. Indexed: Sociol.Abstr.
For information and inter-communication among workers in the non-aristotelian discipline formulated by Alfred Korzybski

400 US ISSN 0196-7207
GEORGETOWN UNIVERSITY ROUND TABLE ON LANGUAGES AND LINGUISTICS. 1951. a. price varies. (Georgetown University, School of Languages and Linguistics) Georgetown University Press, Washington, DC 20057. circ. 2,000.
Former titles: Georgetown University. Institute of Languages and Linguistics. Report of the Annual Round Table Meeting on Linguistics and Language Studies (ISSN 0072-1212); Monograph Series on Languages and Linguistics (ISSN 0077-0612)

430 GW ISSN 0072-1492
GERMANISTISCHE LINGUISTIK. 1969-70. irreg., no. 3/4, 1976. price varies. (Forschunginstitut fuer Deutsche Sprache, Marburg) Georg Olms Verlag GmbH, Hagentorwall 7, 3200 Hildesheim, W. Germany (B.R.D.) (Dist. by: Adler's Foreign Books, Inc., 462 Fifth Ave., New York, NY 10010) Eds. Ludwig E. Schmitt et al. adv. annual index. circ. 1,000.

400 PL ISSN 0072-4769
GLOTTODIDACTICA; AN INTERNATIONAL JOURNAL OF APPLIED LINGUISTICS. (Text in German, French, Russian and English) 1966. irreg., 1975, vol. 8. price varies. Uniwersytet im. Adama Mickiewicza w Poznaniu, Ul. Stalingradzka 1, 61-712 Poznan, Poland (Dist. by: Ars Polona, Krakowskie Przedmiescie 7, 00-068 Warsaw, Poland) Ed. Ludwik Zabrocki. bk. rev. circ. 1,500.

430 830 SW ISSN 0072-4793
GOETEBORGER GERMANISTISCHE FORSCHUNGEN. (Subseries of Acta Universitatis Gothoburgensis) (Text in German) 1955. irreg., no. 18, 1978. price varies; also exchange basis. (Goeteborg Universitaet, Germanisches Seminar) Acta Universitatis Gothoburgensis, Box 5096, S-402 22 Goeteborg 5, Sweden (Dist. in U. S., Canada, and Mexico by: Humanities Press, Inc., 171 First Ave., Atlantic Highlands, NJ 07716) Ed. Maerta Aasdahl Holmberg.

430 GW ISSN 0072-4858
GOETHE-INSTITUT ZUR PFLEGE DEUTSCHER SPRACHE UND KULTUR IM AUSLAND. JAHRBUCH. 1965. a. DM.11. Goethe-Institut zur Pflege Deutscher Sprache und Kultur im Ausland, Lenbachplatz 3, 8000 Munich 2, W. Germany (B.R.D.) circ. 4,000.

GOROG ES LATIN IROK TARA/SCRIPTORES GRAECI ET LATINI. see *CLASSICAL STUDIES*

410 SW
GOTHENBURG MONOGRAPHS IN LINGUISTICS. 1975. irreg. Goeteborgs Universitet, Department of Linguistics, Erik Dahlbergsgatan 11 B, 411 26 Goeteborg, Sweden.

400 830 SW ISSN 0072-503X
GOTHENBURG STUDIES IN ENGLISH. (Subseries of Acta Universitatis Gothoburgensis) 1952. irreg., no. 45, 1978. price varies; also exchange basis. Acta Universitatis Gothoburgensis, Box 5096, S-402 22 Goeteborg 5, Sweden (Dist. in U. S., Canada, and Mexico by: Humanities Press, Inc., 171 First Ave., Atlantic Highlands, NJ 07716) Eds. Alvar Ellegaard, Erik Frykman.

440 FR
GRAMMATICA. (Subseries of Universite de Toulouse-Le Mirail. Annales) 1972. irreg. 22 F. (single issue) Universite de Toulouse II (le Mirail), 109 bis, rue Vauquelin, 31081 Toulouse Cedex, France.

410 FR
GROUPE LINGUISTIQUE D'ETUDES CHAMITO-SEMITIQUES. COMPTES RENDUS. (Suspended publication 1940-1945) 1934. irreg. (Groupe Linguistique d'Etudes Chamito-Semitiques) Librarie Orientaliste Paul Geuthner, 12 rue Vavin, 75006 Paris, France.

410 US
GUIDE TO PROGRAMS IN LINGUISTICS. 1962. a. $7. Linguistic Society of America, 3520 Prospect St., N.W., Washington, DC 20007.
Former titles: University Resources in the United States and Canada for the Study of Linguistics & University Resources in the United States for Linguistics and the Teaching of English as a Foreign Language (ISSN 0511-3040)

480 GW ISSN 0072-9191
HABELTS DISSERTATIONSDRUCKE. REIHE KLASSISCHE PHILOLOGIE. 1953. irreg., no. 31, 1980. price varies. Rudolf Habelt Verlag, Am Buchenhang 1, 5300 Bonn 1, W. Germany (B.R.D.) Eds. W. Schetter, W. Schmid.

491.7 GW ISSN 0072-9515
HAMBURGER BEITRAEGE FUER RUSSISCHLEHRER. 1964. irreg., no. 20, 1981. price varies. Verlag Hemlmut Buske, Schlueterstr. 14, 2000 Hamburg 13, W. Germany (B.R.D.) Ed. Irene Nowikowa.

430 GW ISSN 0072-9582
HAMBURGER PHILOLOGISCHE STUDIEN. 1966. irreg., no. 51, 1980. price varies. Verlag Helmut Buske, Schlueterstr. 14, 2000 Hamburg 13, W. Germany (B.R.D.)

410 GW ISSN 0341-3187
HAMBURGER PHONETISCHE BEITRAEGE; Untersuchungen zur Phonetik und Linguistik. (Text in German, English, French) 1972. irreg., no. 36, 1981. price varies. Verlag Helmut Buske, Schlueterstr. 14, 2000 Hamburg 13, W. Germany (B.R.D.)

496 NR
HARSUNAN NIJERIYA. (Text in English and Hausa) 1971. a. $2. Ahmadu Bello University, Centre for the Study of Nigerian Languages, Private Bag 3011, Zaria, Nigeria. Ed. Roxana Ma Newman. circ. 500. (processed)

400 US ISSN 0073-0432
HARTFORD STUDIES IN LINGUISTICS. 1961. irreg., latest issue no. 24. price varies. Hartford Seminary Foundation, 111 Sherman St., Hartford, CT 06015.

HARVARD ENGLISH STUDIES. see *LITERATURE*

492 220 US ISSN 0073-0637
HARVARD SEMITIC MONOGRAPHS. 1968. irreg., 1972, no. 3. price varies. Harvard University Press, 79 Garden St., Cambridge, MA 02138.

HARVARD SLAVIC MONOGRAPHS. see *HISTORY — History Of Europe*

489 US ISSN 0073-0688
HARVARD STUDIES IN CLASSICAL PHILOLOGY. 1890. a. price varies. Harvard University Press, 79 Garden St., Cambridge, MA 02138.

479.1 US ISSN 0073-0718
HARVARD STUDIES IN ROMANCE LANGUAGES. irreg., 1972, no. 32. price varies. (Harvard University, Department of Romance Languages and Literature) Harvard University Press, 79 Garden St., Cambridge, MA 02138.

HARVARD-YENCHING INSTITUTE. MONOGRAPH SERIES. see *HISTORY — History Of Asia*

HAUTES ETUDES DU MONDE GRECO-ROMAIN. see *CLASSICAL STUDIES*

492.4 IS
HEBREW COMPUTATIONAL LINGUISTICS. (Text in English & Hebrew) 1969. 1-2/yr. I£6($3.50) Bar Ilan University, Department of Hebrew and Semitic Languages, Ramat Gan, Israel. Ed. Ora Schwarzwald. bibl. circ. 400. Indexed: MLA.

480 GW ISSN 0341-0064
HERMES-EINZELSCHRIFTEN. (Supplement to: Hermes) (Text in English and German) irreg., vol. 44, 1981. price varies. Franz Steiner Verlag GmbH, Friedrichstr. 24, Postfach 5529, 6200 Wiesbaden, W. Germany (B.R.D.)

HERON; essays on language & literature. see *LITERATURE*

430   GW   ISSN 0073-201X
HEUTIGES DEUTSCH. REIHE I: LINGUISTISCHE GRUNDLAGEN. 1971. irreg., vol. 6, 1975. price varies. (Institut fuer Deutsche Sprache) Max Hueber Verlag, Max-Hueber-Str.4, 8045 Ismaning, W. Germany (B.R.D.) (Co-sponsor: Goethe-Institut, Munich) Eds. Ulrich Engel, Hugo Moser, Hugo Steger.

410   914   SP   ISSN 0437-5602
HISPANIA ANTIQUA EPIGRAPHICA. 1950. irreg. (or exchange) Consejo Superior de Investigaciones Cientificas, Instituto Espanol de Arqueologia, Medinaceli 4, Madrid 14, Spain. Ed. A. Beltran. bibl.

HISPANO-ITALIC STUDIES. see *LITERATURE*

400   410   US   ISSN 0073-2710
HISTORY AND STRUCTURE OF LANGUAGES. 1967. irreg., no. 4, 1978. price varies. University of Chicago Press, 5801 S. Ellis Ave., Chicago, IL 60637. Ed. Eric P. Hamp. (reprint service avail. from UMI,ISI)

HUEBER HOCHSCHULREIHE. see *EDUCATION*

400   US   ISSN 0361-3399
I J A L NATIVE AMERICAN TEXTS SERIES. (International Journal of American Linguistics) 1976. irreg.; 3-4/vol. University of Chicago Press, 11030 Langley Ave., Chicago, IL 60628 (Orders to: University Microfilms International, 300 N. Zeeb Rd., Ann Arbor, MI 48106) Ed. Eric P. Hamp. (reprint service avail. from UMI,ISI) Indexed: Lang. & Lang.Behav.Abstr. Key Title: Native American Texts Series.
American Indian language and literature

ILLINOIS STUDIES IN LANGUAGE AND LITERATURE. see *LITERATURE*

410   IT
INCONTRI LINGUISTICI. 1974. a. L.12000($14) (Universita degli Studi di Udine e Trieste) Licosa S.p.A., Via A. Lamarmora 45, 50121 Florence, Italy. Ed. Bd. adv. bk. rev. circ. 3,000.

491   II   ISSN 0073-6589
INDIAN LINGUISTICS MONOGRAPH SERIES. (Text in English) 1958. irreg. price varies. Linguistic Society of India, c/o Deccan College Postgraduate and Research Institute, Poona 411006, India.

096   US   ISSN 0073-7062
INDIANA UNIVERSITY. RESEARCH CENTER FOR LANGUAGE AND SEMIOTIC STUDIES. AFRICAN SERIES. Short title: African Series. (Text in African languages and English) 1970. irreg. price varies. Indiana University, Research Center for Language and Semiotic Studies, 516 E. 6th St., Bloomington, IN 47405. Ed. Carleton T. Hodge.
Formerly: Indiana University. Research Center for the Language Sciences. African Studies (ISSN 0065-4051)

400   US   ISSN 0073-7097
INDIANA UNIVERSITY. RESEARCH CENTER FOR LANGUAGE AND SEMIOTIC STUDIES. URALIC AND ALTAIC SERIES. Short title: Uralic and Altaic Series. (Text in Uralic and Altaic Languages and English) 1960. irreg., 1970, vol. 109. price varies. ‡ Indiana University, Research Center for Language and Semiotic Studies, 516 E. 6th St., Bloomington, IN 47405. Ed. John R. Krueger.

494   950   HU   ISSN 0073-7194
INDICES VERBORUM LINGUAE MONGOLIAE MONUMENTIS TRADITORUM. (Text in Mongolian with transcriptions in Roman letters and introduction in French) 1970. irreg. price varies. (Magyar Tudomanyos Akademia) Akademiai Kiado, Publishing House of the Hungarian Academy of Sciences, P.O. Box 24, H-1363 Budapest, Hungary. Ed. L. Ligeti.

430   GW   ISSN 0019-7262
INDOGERMANISCHE FORSCHUNGEN; Zeitschrift fuer Indogermanistik und allgemeine Sprachwissenschaft. (Text in English, French, German and Italian) 1891. irreg., vol. 83, 1979. DM.92($46) Walter de Gruyter und Co., Genthiner Str. 13, 1000 Berlin 30, W. Germany (B.R.D.) Ed. Wolfgang P. Schmid. adv. bk. rev. charts. illus. index.

439.3   NE
INFORMATIE NEDERLANDSE LEXIKOLOGIE. 1970. irreg. free. Instituut voor Nederlandse Lexicologie, Afdeling Thesaurus, Plantsoen 41-43-45, Box 132, Leiden, Netherlands. Ed. P. van Sterkenburg. bibl. charts.

418   GW
INFOTERM SERIES. irreg., no. 4, 1978. price varies. (International Information Centre for Terminology, Vienna, AU) K.G. Saur Verlag KG, Poessenbacherstr. 12 B, Postfach 711009, 8000 Munich 71, W. Germany (B.R.D.)

400   FR   ISSN 0073-8018
INITIATION A LA LINGUISTIQUE. SERIE A. LECTURES. 1970. irreg. price varies. Editions Klincksieck, 11 rue de Lille, Paris 7e, France. Ed. Pierre Guiraud, Alain Rey.

400   FR   ISSN 0073-8026
INITIATION A LA LINGUISTIQUE. SERIE B. PROBLEMES ET METHODES. 1970. irreg. price varies. Editions Klincksieck, 11 rue de Lille, Paris 7e, France. Eds. Pierre Guiraud, Alain Rey.

410   FR   ISSN 0154-0157
INSTITUT D'ETUDES SLAVES. LEXIQUES. 1978. irreg.,vol.4, 1980. price varies. Institut d'Etudes Slaves, 9 rue Michelet, F-75006 Paris, France.

491   FR   ISSN 0078-9984
INSTITUT D'ETUDES SLAVES, PARIS. COLLECTION DE GRAMMAIRES. 1921. irreg., vol. 7, 1980. price varies. Institut d'Etudes Slaves, 9 rue Michelet, F - 75006 Paris, France.

491   943   FR   ISSN 0078-9992
INSTITUT D'ETUDES SLAVES, PARIS. COLLECTION DE MANUELS. 1923. irreg., vol. 7, 1976. price varies. Institut d'Etudes Slaves, 9 rue Michelet, F -75006 Paris, France.

375.4   FR   ISSN 0300-2594
INSTITUT D'ETUDES SLAVES, PARIS. DOCUMENTS PEDAGOGIQUES. 1970. irreg., vol. 23, 1980. price varies. Institut d'Etudes Slaves, 9 rue Michelet, F-75006 Paris, France.

INSTITUT D'ETUDES SLAVES, PARIS. TRAVAUX. see *LITERATURE*

400   BE
INSTITUT DE LINGUISTIQUE DE LOUVAIN. BIBLIOTHEQUE DE LA C I L L. 1976. irreg., no. 11, 1977. Editions Peeters s.p.r.l., B.P. 41, B-3000 Brussels, Belgium.

400   BE
INSTITUT DE LINGUISTIQUE DE LOUVAIN. CAHIERS. COURS ET DOCUMENTS. no. 7, 1974. irreg., no. 13, 1975. Editions Peeters s.p.r.l., B.P. 41, B-3000 Brussels, Belgium.

410   CK
INSTITUTO CARO Y CUERVO. SEMINARIO ANDRES BELLO. CUADERNOS. 1978. irreg. Instituto Caro y Cuervo, Apdo. Aereo 51502, Bogota, Colombia.

INSTITUTO CARO Y CUERVO. SERIES MINOR. see *LITERATURE*

460   PE
INSTITUTO LINGUISTICO DE VERANO. DOCUMENTOS DE TRABAJO. 1978. irreg., no. 16, 1979. price varies. Instituto Linguistico de Verano, Departamento de Estudios Etno-Linguisticos, Casilla 2492, Lima 100, Peru. Ed. Mary Ruth Wise. (back issues avail)

407   CK
INSTITUTO LINGUISTICO DE VERANO. SERIE SINTACTICA. 1975. irreg. Instituto Linguistico de Verano, Lomalinda, Meta, Colombia.
South American Indian languages

410   RM
INSTITUTUL PEDAGOGIC ORADEA. LUCRARI STIINTIFICE: SERIA LINGVISTICA. (Continues in part its Lucrari Stiintifice: Seria Filologie (1971-72), its Lucrari Stiintifice: Seria A and Seria B (1969-1970), and its Lucrari Stiintifice (1967-68).) (Text in Rumanian, occasionally in English or French; summaries in Rumanian, French, English or German) a. Institutul Pedagogic Oradea, Calea Armatei Rosii Nr. 5, Oradea, Romania.

410   BE   ISSN 0074-2791
INTERNATIONAL COMMITTEE OF ONOMASTIC SCIENCES. CONGRESS PROCEEDINGS. (Proceedings published in host country) 1938. triennial, 13th, 1978, Krakow. price varies. International Centre of Onomastics, Blijde-Inkomststr. 5, 3000 Louvain, Belgium.

410   NE   ISSN 0074-3755
INTERNATIONAL CONGRESS OF LINGUISTS. PROCEEDINGS. (Published in host country) 1928. quinquennial, 11th, 1974, Bologna. price varies. Permanent International Committee of Linguists, c/o E. M. Uhlenbeck, Stationsplein 10, Leiden, Netherlands.

400   800   FR   ISSN 0074-5855
INTERNATIONAL FEDERATION FOR MODERN LANGUAGES AND LITERATURE. CONGRESS REPORTS. 1932. triennial; 13th, Sydney, Australia, 1975. price varies. ‡ International Federation for Modern Languages and Literature - Federation Internationale des Langues et Litteratures Modernes, c/o Prof. A. M. Rousseau, 9 rue du Quatre Septembre, 13100 Aix-en-Provence, France. circ. 600-2,000 (approx.)
Reports published in host country

491   891   NE   ISSN 0020-7632
INTERNATIONAL JOURNAL OF SLAVIC LINGUISTICS AND POETICS. (Text in English, French, German and all Slavic languages) 1959. irreg. $10 per no. (University of California, Los Angeles, Department of Slavic Languages, US) Peter de Ridder Press, Box 168, 2160-AD-Lisse, Netherlands (Dist. in the U.S. by: Humanities Press, 171 Fifth Ave., Atlantic Highlands, NJ 07716) Ed. Prof. Dean S. Worth. adv. bk. rev. charts. illus. circ. 550.

400   US   ISSN 0074-6797
INTERNATIONAL LINGUISTIC ASSOCIATION. MONOGRAPH.* (Supplement to: Word) 1951. irreg. International Linguistic Association, Dept. of English, Clark University, Worcester, MA 01610.

400   US   ISSN 0074-6800
INTERNATIONAL LINGUISTIC ASSOCIATION. SPECIAL PUBLICATIONS.* 1964. irreg. International Linguistic Association, Dept. of English, Clark University, Worcester, MA 01610.

418.02   IT
INTERPRETE. (Text in English or Italian) irreg. Angelo Longo Editore, Via Rocca Ai Fossi 6, Casella Postale 431, 48100 Ravenna, Italy. Ed. Aldo Scaglione.

491   IT   ISSN 0077-2771
ISTITUTO UNIVERSITARIO ORIENTALE DI NAPOLI. ANNALI. SEZIONE SLAVA. 1958. a. Giardini Editori e Stampatori, Via Santa Bibbiana 28, 56100 Pisa, Italy. Ed. Nullo Minissi.

459   RM   ISSN 0075-160X
ISTORIA LIMBII ROMANE. 1965. irreg. (Academia Republicii Socialiste Romania) Editura Academiei Republicii Socialiste Romania, Calea Victoriei 125, Bucharest, Romania (Subscr. to: ILExIM, Str. 13 Decembrie Nr. 3, P.O. Box 136-137, Bucharest, Romania)

457   IT   ISSN 0085-2295
ITALIA DIALETTALE; rivista di Dialettologia Italiana. 1925. a. L.10000. (Universita degli Studi di Pisa, Istituto di Glottologia) Giardini Editori e Stampatori, Via S. Maria 36, Pisa, Italy. Ed. Tristano Bolelli. bk. rev.

JAHRBACH DEUTSCH ALS FREMDSPRACHE. see *EDUCATION — Higher Education*

410   NE
JANUA LINGUARUM. SERIES ANASTATICA. irreg. price varies. Mouton Publishers, Noordeinde 41, 2514 GC The Hague, Netherlands (U.S. addr.: Mouton Publishers, c/o Walter de Gruyter, Inc., 200 Saw Mill River Road, Hawthorne, NY 10532)

400   NE   ISSN 0075-3092
JANUA LINGUARUM. SERIES CRITICA. 1971. irreg. price varies. Mouton Publishers, Noordeinde 41, 2514 GC The Hague, Netherlands (U.S. addr.: Mouton Publishers, c/o Walter de Gruyter, Inc., 200 Saw Mill River Road, Hawthorne, NY 10532)

400 410   NE ISSN 0075-3106
JANUA LINGUARUM. SERIES DIDACTICA.
1973. irreg. price varies. Mouton Publishers,
Noordeinde 41, 2514 GC The Hague, Netherlands
(U.S. addr.: Mouton Publishers, c/o Walter de
Gruyter, Inc., 200 Saw Mill River Road,
Hawthorne, NY 10532)

400   NE ISSN 0075-3114
JANUA LINGUARUM. SERIES MAJOR. 1959.
irreg. price varies. Mouton Publishers, Noordeinde
41, 2514 GC The Hague, Netherlands (U.S. addr.:
Mouton Publishers, c/o Walter de Gruyter, Inc.,
200 Saw Mill River Road, Hawthorne, NY 10532)

400 410   NE ISSN 0075-3122
JANUA LINGUARUM. SERIES MINOR. irreg.
price varies. Mouton Publishers, Noordeinde 41,
2514 GC The Hague, Netherlands (U.S. addr.:
Mouton Publishers, c/o Walter de Gruyter, Inc.,
200 Saw Mill River Road, Hawthorne, NY 10532)

410   NE ISSN 0075-3130
JANUA LINGUARUM. SERIES PRACTICA. 1963.
irreg. price varies. Mouton Publishers, Noordeinde
41, 2514 GC The Hague, Netherlands (U.S. addr.:
Mouton Publishers, c/o Walter de Gruyter, Inc.,
200 Saw Mill River Road, Hawthorne, NY 10532)

410   NE ISSN 0075-3491
JARLIBRO. (Text in Esperanto) 1908. a. fl.25($13.60)
Universala Esperanto Asocio, Nieuwe Binnenweg
176, 3015 BJ Rotterdam, Netherlands. adv. index.
circ. 7,000. (back issues avail)

400 491.87   CS ISSN 0448-9241
JAZYKOVEDNE STUDIE. (Text in Slovak;
summaries in German and Russian) irreg., vol. 13,
1976. fl.25 per no. (Slovenska Akademia Vied,
Jazykovedny Ustav L. Stura) Veda, Publishing
House of the Slovak Academy of Sciences,
Klemensova 19, 895 30 Bratislava, Czechoslovakia
(Distributor in Western countries: John Benjamins
B.V., Amsteldijk 44, Amsterdam (Z.), Netherlands)

410   PL
JEZYKOZNAWSTWO STOSOWANE/APPLIED
LINGUISTICS. 1975. irreg., vol. 2, 1976. price
varies. Uniwersytet im. Adama Mickiewicza w
Poznaniu, Stalingradzka 1, 61-712 Poznan, Poland
(Dist. by: Ars Polona, Krakowskie Przedmiescie 7,
00-068 Warsaw, Poland)

420   US ISSN 0075-4242
JOURNAL OF ENGLISH LINGUISTICS. 1967. a.
$3. Western Washington University, Bellingham,
WA 98225. Ed. Robert A. Peters. adv. bk. rev. circ.
600. Indexed: M.L.A. Lang.& Lang.Behav.Abstr.

JOURNAL OF HELLENIC STUDIES. see
CLASSICAL STUDIES

KATOLICKI UNIWERSYTET LUBELSKI
WYDZIAL HISTORYCZNO-FILOLOGICZNY.
ROZPRAWY. see HISTORY

KEILSCHRIFTTEXTE AUS BOGHAZKOI. see
ARCHAEOLOGY

400 956.4   CY ISSN 0071-0954
KENTRON EPISTEMONIKON EREUNION.
EPETERIS/CYPRUS RESEARCH CENTER.
ANNUAL. (Text in Greek, English, French,
German) 1967/1968. a. Mils.10000. Cyprus
Research Centre, Box 1436, Nicosia, Cyprus. Ed.
Theodore Papadopoullos. bk. rev. bibl. charts. illus.
circ. 500. (back issues avail)

491   UR
KHARKOVSKII GOSUDARSTVENNYI
UNIVERSITET. FILOLOHIYA. (Subseries of its
Visnyk) irreg. Kharkovskii Gosudarstvennyi
Universitet, Kharkov, U.S.S.R.

410 800   GW
KLAUS-GROTH-GESELLSCHAFT.
JAHRESGABEN. 1964. a. price varies.
Westholsteinische Verlagsanstalt Boyens und Co.,
Am Wulf-Isebrand-Platz, Postfach 1880, 2240
Heide, W. Germany (B.R.D.) Ed.Bd. illus.

410 510   DK
KOEBENHAVNS UNIVERSITET. INSTITUT FOR
ANVENDT OG MATEMATISK LINGVISTIK.
SKRIFTER. 1974. irreg. Koebenhavns Universitet,
Institut for Anvendt og Matematisk Lingvistik, 1168
Copenhagen, Denmark.

400   NE ISSN 0083-3851
KONGRESA LIBRO. (Text in Esperanto) 1905. a.
fl.12($5) Universala Esperanto-Asocio, Nieuwe
Binnenweg 176, 3015 BJ Rotterdam, Netherlands.
adv. circ. 1,000-4,000.

410 800   BE
KONINKLIJKE ACADEMIE VOOR
NEDERLANDSE TAAL- EN LETTERKUNDE.
JAARBOEK. 1887. a. price varies. Koninklijke
Academie voor Nederlandse Taal- en Letterkunde,
Koningstraat 18, B-9000 Ghent, Belgium.

410   DK ISSN 0105-0257
KOPENHAGENER BEITRAEGE ZUR
GERMANISTISCHEN LINGUISTIK. 1970. irreg.
price varies. (Koebenhavns Universitet) Akademisk
Forlag, St. Kannikestraede 8, DK-1169 Copenhagen
K, Denmark. Ed. Karl Hyldgaard Jensen. bibl. circ.
600.

KOROSI CSOMA KISKONYVTAR. see
HISTORY — History Of Asia

400   SW ISSN 0083-6745
KUNGLIGA VITTERHETS- , HISTORIE- OCH
ANTIKVITETS AKADEMIEN. FILOLOGISKT
ARKIV. (Text in English, French, German, Spanish
or Swedish) 1955. irreg., no. 22, 1979. price varies.
Kungliga Vitterhets-, Historie- och Antikvitets
Akademien - Royal Academy of Letters, History
and Antiquities, Villagatan 3, 114 32 Stockholm,
Sweden. index.

400 100   SW ISSN 0083-677X
KUNGLIGA VITTERHETS- , HISTORIE- OCH
ANTIKVITETS AKADEMIEN. HANDLINGAR.
FILOLOGISK-FILOSOFISKA SERIEN/ROYAL
ACADEMY OF LETTERS, HISTORY AND
ANTIQUITIES. PROCEEDINGS.
PHILOLOGICAL-PHILOSOPHICAL SERIES.
(Text in English, German and Swedish) 1954. irreg.,
no. 18, 1979. price varies. Kungliga Vitterhets-,
Historie, och Antikvitets Akademien, Villagatan 3,
114 32 Stockholm, Sweden. index.

410   US
L A C U S FORUM. 1974. a. $10.95. (Linguistic
Association of Canada and the United States)
Hornbeam Press, Inc., 6520 Courtwood Dr.,
Columbia, SC 29206.

410   UK ISSN 0307-9341
LAKELAND DIALECT SOCIETY. BULLETIN. no.
39, 1977. a. 60p.($1.20) Lakeland Dialect Society,
c/o Miss N. Dawson, 8 Barras Close, Morton Park,
Carlisle CA2 6PR, England. Ed. Ted Relph. bk. rev.
circ. 600.

427   UK ISSN 0075-7799
LANCASHIRE DIALECT SOCIETY. JOURNAL.
1951. a. £1.50. ‡ Lancashire Dialect Society, c/o
Bob Dobson, 3 Staining Rise, Staining, Blackpool,
England. Ed. Peter Wright. bk. rev. cum.index: from
nos. 1-14 (1951-65) in no. 15. circ. 300.

400   SI
LANGUAGE. (Text in Chinese or English) 1972?
irreg. price varies. (Singapore Linguistic Society)
Educational Publications Bureau, 175a-179a Outram
Park, Singapore 0316, Singapore.

410   UK
LANGUAGE AND THOUGHT SERIES. 1976. a.
$16.90. Harvester Press Ltd., 16 Ship St., Brighton,
Sussex BN1 1AD, England.

410   II
LANGUAGE FORUM MONOGRAPH SERIES.
1978. irreg. price varies. Bahri Publications Pvt.
Ltd., 57 Santnagar, New Delhi 110065, India. Ed.
Ujjal Singh Bahri.

LANGUAGE IN EDUCATION. THEORY AND
PRACTICE. see EDUCATION

400   NE ISSN 0075-7969
LANGUAGE SCIENCE MONOGRAPHS. 1968.
irreg., 1970, Sep., vol. 6. price varies. ‡ (Indiana
University, Research Center for the Language
Sciences, US) Mouton Publishers, Noordeinde 41,
2514 GC The Hague, Netherlands (U.S. addr.:
Mouton Publishers, c/o Walter de Gruyter, Inc.,
200 Saw Mill River Road, Hawthorne, NY 10532)
Ed. Carl F. Voegelin.

410 301.2   FR
LANGUE ET CIVILISATION A TRADITION
ORALE. 1972. irreg. Societe d'Etudes Linguistiques
et Anthropologiques de France, 5 rue de Marseille,
75010 Paris, France.

410   SZ ISSN 0085-2678
LANGUE ET CULTURES; etudes et documents.
(Text and summaries in French or English) 1971.
irreg., no. 8, 1977. price varies. Librarie Droz, 11
rue Massot, 1211 Geneva 12, Switzerland. circ.
1,000.

410   CM
LANGUES DU CAMEROUN. irreg., no. 5, 1976.
B.P. 5351, Douala, Cameroun.

LANGUES ET STYLES. see LITERATURE

420   UK ISSN 0075-8574
LEEDS TEXTS AND MONOGRAPHS. 1967. a.
price varies. University of Leeds, School of English,
Leeds LS2 9JT, England. Ed. P. Meredith.

479 879   NE ISSN 0075-8647
LEIDSE ROMANISTISCHE REEKS. (Text in
French, Spanish and Italian) 1954. irreg., vol. 22,
1975. price varies. Leiden University Press, c/o
Martinus Nijhoff, Box 566, 2501 CN The Hague,
Netherlands.

450   IT ISSN 0075-8825
LESSICO INTELLETTUALE EUROPEO. 1969.
irreg., no. 24, 1981. price varies. Edizioni dell'
Ateneo S.p.A., P.O. Box 7216, 00100 Rome, Italy.
circ. 1,500.

400 800   GW
LILI. BEIHEFTE. (Zeitschrift fuer
Literaturwissenschaft und Linguistik) 1975. irreg.,
no. 11, 1980. price varies. Vandenhoeck und
Ruprecht, Theaterstr. 13, Postfach 77, 3400
Goettingen, W. Germany (B.R.D.)

400   RM ISSN 0583-8045
LIMBA SI LITERATURA. irreg. 18 lei. Societatea de
Stiinte Filologice din Republica Socialista Romania,
Bd. Republicii Nr. 55, Bucharest, Romania. bk. rev.
bibl.
Continues: Societatea de Stiinte Istorice si
Filologice Din R. P. R. Limba si Literatura.

496   SA ISSN 0024-3558
LIMI. (Text and summaries in Afrikaans and English)
1966. a. R.1.55. University of South Africa,
Department of African Languages, Box 392,
Pretoria 0001, South Africa. adv. bk. rev. bibl.
index. circ. 848. Indexed: M.L.A.

400 800   BL ISSN 0047-4711
LINGUA E LITERATURA. (Text in various
languages) 1972. a. Universidade de Sao Paulo,
Faculdade de Filosofia, Letras e Ciencias Humanas,
Ciudade Universitaria, C.P. 01000, Sao Paulo,
Brazil. Eds.Aida Costa, Carlos Drumond, Paulo
Vizioli. bk. rev. charts. illus. bibl. circ. 1,000.

491.85   PL ISSN 0079-4740
LINGUA POSNANIENSIS. (Text in various
languages) 1949. a. price varies. Poznanskie
Towarzystwo Przyjaciol Nauk, Mielzynskiego 27/
29, 61-725 Poznan, Poland. Indexed: Lang. &
Lang.Behav.Abstr.

410 900   GW ISSN 0341-3225
LINGUARUM MINORUM DOCUMENTA
HISTORIOGRAPHICA. irreg., no. 4, 1981.
price varies. Verlag Helmut Buske, Schlueterstr. 14,
2000 Hamburg 13, W. Germany (B.R.D.) Ed. H.
Haarmann.

400   IT
LINGUE E ISCRIZIONI DELL'ITALIA ANTICA.
1977. irreg. Casa Editrice Leo S. Olschki, Viuzzo
del Pozzetto, Casella Postale 66, 50100 Florence,
Italy. Dir. Aldo Prosdocimi.

410 800   NE ISSN 0165-7712
LINGUISTIC & LITERARY STUDIES IN
EASTERN EUROPE. Short title: L L S E E. 1979.
irreg., vol. 8, 1981. price varies. John Benjamins
B.V., Box 52519, 1007 HA Amsterdam,
Netherlands. Ed. John Odmark.

410 CN ISSN 0075-9597
LINGUISTIC CIRCLE OF MANITOBA AND
NORTH DAKOTA. PROCEEDINGS. 1959.
approx. a. membership. ‡ University of Manitoba,
Department of Classics, 500 Dysart Rd., Winnipeg,
Man. R3T 2N2, Canada. (Co-sponsors: University
of North Dakota; University of Winnipeg) Ed. Ben
L. Collins. circ. 500.

491 II ISSN 0075-9627
LINGUISTIC SOCIETY OF INDIA. BULLETIN.
(Supplement to Indian Linguistics) 1958. irreg.,
1970, no. 3. included with subscription to Indian
Linguistics. Linguistic Society of India, c/o Deccan
College Postgraduate and Research Institute, Poona
411006, India.

400 YU ISSN 0024-3922
LINGUISTICA. (Text in various languages) 1955.
irreg., vol. 18, 1978. $7. Univerza Edvarda Kardelja
v Ljubljani, Filozofska Fakulteta, Askerceva 12,
Ljubljana, Yugoslavia. Ed. Mitja Skubic. circ. 600.

410 PL
LINGUISTICA SILESIANA. (Text in English, French
or Russian) 1975. irreg., 1975, vol. 1. 16 Zl. per
volume. Uniwersytet Slaski w Katowicach, Ul.
Bankowa 14, 40-007 Katowice, Poland.

410 NE ISSN 0166-0829
LINGUISTIK AKTUELL; Amsterdamer Arbeiten zur
theoretischen und angewandten Linguistik. 1980.
irreg., vol. 2 1981. price varies. John Benjamins
B.V., Box 52519, 1007 HA Amsterdam,
Netherlands. Ed. Werner Abraham.

410 GW ISSN 0075-9686
LINGUISTISCHE REIHE. 1970. irreg., vol. 22, 1975.
price varies. Max Hueber Verlag, Max-Hueber-Str.4,
8045 Ismaning, W. Germany (B.R.D.) Eds. Klaus
Baumgaertner, Hugo Steger.

410 440 NE
LINGUISTICAE INVESTIGACIONES:
SUPPLEMENTA; studies in French and general
linguistics/etudes en linguistique francaise et
generale. (Companion series to Lingvisticae
Investigationes) 1979. irreg. price varies. (Universite
de Paris VIII (Paris-Vincennes), Departement de
Linguistique, FR) John Benjamins B.V., Box 52519,
1007 HA Amsterdam, Netherlands. (Co-sponsor:
Laboratoire d'Automatique Documentaire et
Linguistique (C.N.R.S.)) Eds.Jean-Claude Chevalier,
Maurice Gross, Christian Leclere.

410 440 NE ISSN 0378-4169
LINGVISTICAE INVESTIGATIONES; revue
internationale de linguistique francaise et de
linguistique generale. (Text in French and English)
1977. s-a. fl.80 to individuals; institutions fl. 130.
(Universite de Paris VIII (Paris-Vincennes),
Departement de Linguistique, FR) John Benjamins
B.V., Amsteldijk 44, Box 52519, 1007 HA
Amsterdam, Netherlands. (Co-sponsor: Laboratoire
d'Automatique Documentaire et Linguistique
(C.N.R.S.)) Eds. J. C. Chevalier, M. Gross, Chr.
Leclere. adv. bk. rev. bibl. index. (back issues avail.)

410 UR ISSN 0301-6900
LINGVISTICHESKIE ISSLEDOVANIYA. irreg. 0.96
Rub. Akademiya Nauk S. S. S. R., Institut
Yazykoznaniya, Ul. Marksa i Engel'sa 1/14,
Moscow, U.S.S.R.

410 CS
LINGVISTICKE CITANKY/READINGS IN
LINGUISTICS. 1970. irreg. 10 Kcs. Universita
Karlova, Filosoficka Fakulta, Nam. Krasnoarmejcu
1, 116 38 Prague 1, Czechoslovakia. Ed. Bohumil
Palek. circ. 500.

499.992 AT ISSN 0024-3965
LINGVOLOGIA REVUO. (Text in Esperanto) 1966.
irreg. free. ‡ Emil Hanhinemi, Ed. & Pub., c/o Emil
Hanhiniemi, Box 764, Ingham, Qld, 4850, Australia.
Ed. Emil Hanhiniemi. bk. rev. abstr. circ. 465.
(looseleaf format)

400 PL ISSN 0076-0390
LODZKIE TOWARZYSTWO NAUKOWE.
KOMISJI JEZYKOWEJ. ROZPRAWY. 1954.
irreg., vol. 23, 1977. price varies. Ossolineum,
Publishing House of the Polish Academy of
Sciences, Rynek 9, 50-106 Wroclaw, Poland (Dist.
by Ars Polona-Ruch, Krakowskie Przedmiescie 7,
00-068 Warsaw, Poland) (Co-sponsor: Polska
Akademia Nauk) Ed. Karol Dejna. circ. 500.

420 SW ISSN 0076-1451
LUND STUDIES IN ENGLISH. 1933. irreg., no. 51,
1977. price varies. C.W.K. Gleerup (Subsidiary of:
LiberLaeromedel) Box 1205, S-222 38 Lund, S-221
05 Lund. Eds. Claes Schaar, Jan Svartvik.

439.5 SW
LUNDASTUDIER I NORDISK
SPRAAKVETENSKAP. SERIE D:
MEDDELANDEN. 1972. irreg. price varies. Lunds
Universitet, Institutionen foer Nordiska Spraak,
Helgonabacken 14, S-223 62 Lund, Sweden. Eds.
Often Bertil Ejder, Goesta Holm. bk. rev. bibl. circ.
300.

M L A INTERNATIONAL BIBLIOGRAPHY OF
BOOKS AND ARTICLES ON THE MODERN
LANGUAGES AND LITERATURES. (Modern
Language Association of America) see
BIBLIOGRAPHIES

407 AT ISSN 0310-9674
M. L. T. A. NEWS. 1973. irreg. Modern Language
Teachers' Association of New South Wales, c/o
School of Modern Languages, Macquarie University,
North Ryde, NSW 2113, Australia. Ed. K. A. B.
Strong. circ. 650(controlled)

M S H A. (Michigan Speech and Hearing Association)
see *DEAF*

400 GW ISSN 0542-1551
MAINZER ROMANISTISCHE ARBEITEN. (Text in
English, French, and German) irreg., vol. 11, 1978.
price varies. Franz Steiner Verlag GmbH,
Friedrichstr. 24, Postfach 5529, 6200 Wiesbaden,
W. Germany (B.R.D.) Eds. W. T. Elwert, H. Kroell.

400 GW ISSN 0170-3560
MAINZER STUDIEN ZUR SPRACH- UND
VOLKSFORSCHUNG. irreg., vol. 4, 1981. price
varies. (Universitaet Mainz, Institut fuer
Geschichtliche Landeskunde) Franz Steiner Verlag
GmbH, Friedrichstr. 24, Postfach 5529, 6200
Wiesbaden, W. Germany (B.R.D.) Eds. G. Bellman,
W. Kleiber, H. Schwedt.

418.02 US ISSN 0363-9037
MALEDICTA PRESS PUBLICATIONS. 1976. irreg.,
vol. 5, 1979. price varies. Maledicta Press, 331 S.
Greenfield Ave., Waukesha, WI 53186. Ed.
Reinhold Aman. circ. 2,000.

410 FR
MATERIAUX POUR L'ETUDE DE L'ASIE
ORIENTALE MODERNE ET
CONTEMPORAINE. ETUDES
LINGUISTIQUES. 1966. irreg.,latest 1980. price
varies. Editions de l' Ecole des Hautes Etudes en
Sciences Sociales, Departement Diffusion, 131 Bd.
Saint-Michel, F-75005 Paris, France.

MEDIAEVAL AND MODERN BRETON SERIES.
see *HISTORY*

491.7 891.7 AT ISSN 0076-6267
MELBOURNE SLAVONIC STUDIES. (Text in
English and Russian) 1967. a. Aus.$5. University of
Melbourne, Department of Russian Language and
Literature, Parkville, Victoria 3052, Australia. Ed.
Nina Christesen. circ. 100. (also avail. in microfilm
from UMI) Indexed: M.L.A.

410 US
MICHIGAN LINGUISTIC SOCIETY. PAPERS.
1971. a. $5. ‡ Central Michigan University,
Department of English, Mount Pleasant, MI 48859.
Ed. David Lawton. bibl. charts. circ. 200.
(processed)
Formerly: Michigan Linguistic Society. Annual
Report.

950 800 410 US
MICHIGAN SERIES IN SOUTH AND
SOUTHEAST ASIAN LANGUAGES AND
LINGUISTICS. 1974. irreg. price varies. University
of Michigan, Center for South and Southeast Asian
Studies, 130 Lane Hall, Ann Arbor, MI 48104. adv.
bk. rev.

MICHIGAN SLAVIC MATERIALS. see
LITERATURE

410 US
MID-AMERICA LINGUISTICS CONFERENCE.
PAPERS. (Publisher varies) 1971. a. $7. Mid-
America Linguistics Conference, c/o Curt
Brandhorst, Rm. 156 Nebraska Center for
Continuing Education, Univ. of Nebraska, Lincoln,
NE 68581. circ. 500.
Formerly (until 1973): Kansas Linguistics
Conference. Papers (ISSN 0075-4919)

470 GW ISSN 0076-9762
MITTELLATEINISCHES JAHRBUCH. 1964. a.
Anton Hiersemann Verlag, Rosenbergstr. 113,
Postfach 723, 7000 Stuttgart 1, W. Germany
(B.R.D.) Ed. Karl Langosch. circ. 500.

420 375.4 JA
MODERN ENGLISH JOURNAL/EIGO KYOIKU
JAANARU. 1974. vol. 5. a. 900 Yen($3.50) Seido
Language Institute, 12-6 Funado-cho, Ashiya,
Hyogo 659, Japan. Ed. David Sell. adv. bk. rev.
circ. 3,000. (also avail. in microform from UMI)
Indexed: Lang.&Lang.Behav.Abstr.
English language study and teaching

410 HU ISSN 0076-9967
MODERN FILOLOGIAI FUZETEK. 1966. irreg.
price varies. (Magyar Tudomanyos Akademia)
Akademiai Kiado, Publishing House of the
Hungarian Academy of Sciences, P.O. Box 24, H-
1363 Budapest, Hungary.

410 US ISSN 0147-5207
MON-KHMER STUDIES. (Text in English, French
and German) vol. 6, 1977. a. price varies. University
Press of Hawaii, 2840 Kolowalu St., Honolulu, HI
96822. Ed. Philip N. Jenner.

400 NE ISSN 0077-1031
MONOGRAPHS ON LINGUISTIC ANALYSIS.
1965. irreg. price varies. (Ohio State University,
Project on Linguistic Analysis, US) Mouton
Publishers, Noordeinde 41, 2514 GC The Hague,
Netherlands (U.S. addr.: Mouton Publishers, c/o
Walter de Gruyter, Inc., 200 Saw Mill River Road,
Hawthorne, NY 10532)

410 NE
MONUMENTA LEXICOGRAPHICA
NEERLANDIA. REEK 3: STUDIES. 1975. irreg.
price varies. Martinus Nijhoff, Box 566, 2501 CN
The Hague, Netherlands.

400 GW ISSN 0077-1910
MUENCHENER STUDIEN ZUR
SPRACHWISSENSCHAFT. (Text in German,
English and French) 1954. irreg. (one or two issues/
yr) price varies. R. Kitzinger, Schellingstr. 25, 8000
Munich 13, W. Germany (B.R.D.) Ed. K.
Hoffmann.

MUENCHNER GERMANISTISCHE BEITRAEGE.
see *LITERATURE*

400 NE
MUSEUM PHILOLOGUM LONDINIENSE. 1975.
irreg., no. 2, 1977. price varies. J. C. Gieben,
Uithoorn, Netherlands. Ed. Giuseppe Giangrande.

430 GW ISSN 0027-514X
MUTTERSPRACHE; Zeitschrift zur Pflege und
Erforschung der deutschen Sprache. 1886. irreg.
DM.80. Gesellschaft fuer Deutsche Sprache,
Postfach 2669, 6200 Wiesbaden 1, W. Germany
(B.R.D.) Ed. Gerhard Mueller. adv. bk. rev. bibl.
index. circ. 1,600.

400 917.57 US ISSN 0077-2690
NAMES IN SOUTH CAROLINA. 1954. a. $3.50 in
South Carolina; outside state $4. University of
South Carolina, Department of English, Columbia,
SC 29208. Ed. Claude Henry Neuffer. circ. 1,100.
Indexed: M.L.A.

400 JA
NATIONAL LANGUAGE RESEARCH
INSTITUTE. ANNUAL REPORT/KOKURITSU
KOKUGO KENKYUSHO NENPO. 1951. a.
National Language Research Institute - Kokuritsu
Kokugo Kenkyusho, 3-9-14 Nisigaoka, Kita-ku,
Tokyo 115, Japan.

410 YU
NAUCNI SASTANAK SLAVISTA U VUKOVE
DANE. REFERATI I SAOPSTENJA. 1971. a.
Medjunarodni Slavisticki Centar SR Srbije,
Studetski trg 3/1, Belgrade, Yugoslvaia. ill.

440   CN   ISSN 0380-9366
NEOLOGIE EN MARCHE. SERIE A. LANGUE GENERALE. 1973. irreg., no. 8, 1978. Office de la Langue Francaise, 700bd. Saint-Cyrille Est, 2e, Quebec, P.Q. G1R 5A9, Canada. illus.

440   CN   ISSN 0701-7995
NEOLOGIE EN MARCHE. SERIE B. LANGUES DE SPECIALITIES. 1976. irreg., no. 10, 1978. Office de la Langue Francaise, 700 Bd. Saint-Cyrille Est, 2e, Quebec, P.Q. G1R 5A9, Canada.

420   GW   ISSN 0077-7684
NEUE BEITRAEGE ZUR ENGLISCHEN PHILOLOGIE. 1963. irreg. price varies. Aschendorffsche Verlagsbuchhandlung, Soester Str. 13, 4400 Muenster, W. Germany (B.R.D.) Ed. Edgar Mertner.

490 350   GW   ISSN 0340-6385
NEUINDISCHE STUDIEN. 1970. irreg., vol. 6, 1979. price varies. Verlag Otto Harrassowitz, Taunusstr. 6, Postfach 2929, 6200 Wiesbaden, W. Germany (B.R.D.) Ed. Bd.

NEUROLINGUISTICS; international series devoted to speech physiology and speech pathology. see MEDICAL SCIENCES — Psychiatry And Neurology

423.1   US
NEW ACRONYMS, INITIALISMS AND ABBREVIATIONS. (Supplement to Acronyms, Initialisms and Abbreviations Dictionary) a. $45 for 2 yrs. Gale Research Company, Book Tower, Detroit, MI 48226. Ed. Ellen T. Crowley.
    Formerly (until 1976): New Acronyms and Initialisms (ISSN 0077-7986)

NEW CEYLON WRITING; creative and critical writing of Sri Lanka. see LITERATURE

439   GW   ISSN 0078-0545
NIEDERDEUTSCHES WORT; Beitraege zur niederdeutschen Philologie. 1960. irreg. price varies. Aschendorffsche Verlagsbuchhandlung, Soester Str. 13, 4400 Muenster, W. Germany (B.R.D.) Ed. Jan Goossens.

439   SW   ISSN 0078-1134
NORDISTICA GOTHOBURGENSIA. (Subseries of Acta Universitatis Gothoburgensis) (Text in Swedish; summaries in English and German) 1965. irreg., no. 11, 1979. price varies; also exchange basis. Acta Universitatis Gothoburgensis, Box 5096, S-402 22 Goeteborg 5, Sweden (Dist. in U. S., Canada, and Mexico by: Humanities Press, Inc., 171 First Ave., Atlantic Highlands, NJ 07716) Ed. Sven Benson.

410   SW   ISSN 0346-6728
NORNA - RAPPORTER. 1973. irreg. free. Nordiska Samarbetskommitten foer Namnforskning, Johannesgatan 11, S-752 21 Uppsala, Sweden. bk. rev. charts.

400   NE   ISSN 0078-1592
NORTH-HOLLAND LINGUISTIC SERIES. 1970. irreg., vol. 4, 1979. price varies. North-Holland Publishing Co., P.O. Box 211, 1000 AE Amsterdam, Netherlands.

NORTHEAST CONFERENCE ON THE TEACHING OF FOREIGN LANGUAGES. REPORTS OF THE WORKING COMMITTEES. see EDUCATION — Teaching Methods And Curriculum

NORWEGIAN STUDIES IN ENGLISH. see LITERATURE

400   IT
NOVANTIQUA; biblioteca di filologia, curiosita e dialettologia. 1977. irreg., no. 5, 1978. price varies. Societa Editrice Napoletana s.r.l., Corso Umberto I 34, Naples, Italy. Ed. Antonio Altamura.

410   IO   ISSN 0126-2874
NUSA; linguistic studies in Indonesian and languages in Indonesia. (Text in English) 1975. irreg., vol. 6, 1978 (no.7 in prep.) price varies. J. W. M. Verhaar, Ed. & Pub., Box 2811/Jkt, Jakarta-Pusat, Indonesia. adv. circ. 450. (back issues avail.)

410   HU   ISSN 0078-2858
NYELVESZETI TANULMANYOK. 1951. irreg. price varies. (Magyar Tudomanyos Akademia) Akademiai Kiado, Publishing House of the Hungarian Academy of Sciences, P.O. Box 24, H-1363 Budapest, Hungary.

410   HU   ISSN 0078-2866
NYELVTUDOMANYI ERTEKEZESEK. 1953. irreg. price varies. (Magyar Tudomanyos Akademia, Nyelvtudomanyi Intezet) Akademiai Kiado, Publishing House of the Hungarian Academy of Sciences, P.O. Box 24, H-1363 Budapest, Hungary.

420 375.4   US   ISSN 0192-401X
O R T E S O L JOURNAL. 1979. a. $9.95. (Oregon Teachers of English to Speakers of Other Languages) ORTESOL, c/o Joe E. Pierce, Ed., The HaPi Press, 512 S.W. Maplecrest Drive, Portland, OR 97219. bk. rev. circ. 300. (back issues avail.)

OCCASIONAL PAPERS IN GERMAN STUDIES. see LITERATURE

410   US
OCCASIONAL PAPERS IN LINGUISTICS. 1972. irreg., no. 3, 1978. price varies. University of California, Los Angeles, Department of Linguistics, 405 Hilgard Ave., Los Angeles, CA 90024.

410   UK   ISSN 0308-2075
OCCASIONAL PAPERS IN LINGUISTICS AND LANGUAGE LEARNING. 1976. irreg. price varies. New University of Ulster, Board of Studies in Linguistics, Coleraine, N. Ireland. bibl. circ. 150-200.

499   US   ISSN 0078-3188
OCEANIC LINGUISTICS. SPECIAL PUBLICATIONS. 1966. irreg., no. 16, 1978. price varies. (University of Hawaii, Social Science Research Institute) University Press of Hawaii, 2840 Kolowalu St., Honolulu, HI 96822. Ed. Prof. Donald M. Topping. (reprint service avail. from UMI, ISI)

410   DK   ISSN 0078-3277
ODENSE UNIVERSITY SLAVIC STUDIES. 1970. irreg. price varies. Odense University Press, 36, Pjentedamsgade, DK-5000 Odense, Denmark.

420   DK   ISSN 0078-3293
ODENSE UNIVERSITY STUDIES IN ENGLISH. (Text in English) 1969. irreg., no. 4, 1979. price varies. Odense University Press, 36, Pjentedamsgade, DK-5000 Odense, Denmark.

400   DK   ISSN 0078-3315
ODENSE UNIVERSITY STUDIES IN LINGUISTICS. 1968. irreg., no. 4, 1979. price varies. Odense University Press, 36, Pjentedamsgade, DK-5000 Odense, Denmark.

439.5 839.5   DK   ISSN 0078-3331
ODENSE UNIVERSITY STUDIES IN SCANDINAVIAN LANGUAGES AND LITERATURES. (Text in Danish) 1968. irreg., no. 9, 1977. price varies. Odense University Press, 36, Pjentedamsgade, DK-5000 Odense, Denmark.

410 401   AU
OESTERREICHISCHE AKADEMIE DER WISSENSCHAFTEN. KOMMISSION FUER LINGUISTIK UND KOMMUNIKATIONSFORSCHUNG. VEROEFFENTLICHUNGEN. (Subseries of: Oesterreichische Akademie der Wissenschaften. Philosophisch-Historische Klasse. Sitzungsberichte) 1973. irreg. Verlag der Oesterreichischen Akademie der Wissenschaften, Dr.-Ignaz-Seipel-Platz 2, A-1010 Vienna, Austria.

420   US   ISSN 0078-4052
OHIO SPEECH JOURNAL. 1962. a. $2.50. Speech Communication Association of Ohio, c/o Dr. James R. Phipps, Speech Department, Cedarville College, Cedarville, OH 45314. Ed. Donald B. Morlan. adv. circ. 400.

491.79   PL   ISSN 0078-4648
ONOMASTICA; pismo poswiecone nazewnictwu geograficznemu i osobowemu. (Text in English, German, Polish and Russian; summaries in French) 1955. a. 50 Zl.($11) (Polska Akademia Nauk, Komitet Jezykoznawstwa) Ossolineum, Publishing House of the Polish Academy of Sciences, Rynek 9, 50-106 Wroclaw, Poland (Dist. by Ars Polona-Ruch, Krakowskie Przedmiescie 7, Warsaw, Poland) Ed. Kazimierz Rymut.

OREGON STATE MONOGRAPHS. STUDIES IN LITERATURE AND LANGUAGE. see LITERATURE

410   IT
ORIENTAMENTI LINGUISTICI. 1977. irreg. price varies. (Universita degli Studi di Pisa, Istituto di Glottologia) Giardini Editori e Stampatori, Via Santa Bibbiana 28, 56100 Pisa, Italy. Ed. Tristano Bolelli.

460 375.4   CN
OTTAWA HISPANICA. 1979. a. University of Ottawa, Department of Slavic Studies and Modern Languages, Ottawa, Ont. K1N 6N5, Canada. Ed. Rodolfo A. Borello.

OXFORD GERMAN STUDIES. see LITERATURE

417.7   US
OXFORD PALEOGRAPHICAL HANDBOOKS. irreg. price varies. Oxford University Press, 200 Madison Ave., New York, NY 10016 (And Ely House, 37 Dover St., London W1X 4AH, England) Ed.Bd.

P I /L T; OCCASIONAL PAPERS ON PROGRAMMED INSTRUCTION AND LANGUAGE TEACHING. see EDUCATION — Teaching Methods And Curriculum

400   US   ISSN 0078-7469
PACIFIC COAST PHILOLOGY. (Text mainly in English; occasionally in French and German) 1966. a. $4. Philological Association of the Pacific Coast, c/o Arlene N. Okerlund, Sec.-Treas., School of Humanities and the Arts, San Jose State University, San Jose, CA 95192. circ. 1,200.

499   AT   ISSN 0078-7531
PACIFIC LINGUISTICS. SERIES A: OCCASIONAL PAPERS. 1963. irreg., no. 61, 1980. price varies. (Linguistic Circle of Canberra) Australian National University, Research School of Pacific Studies, Dept. of Linguistics, Box 4, Canberra, A.C.T. 2600, Australia. Ed. S. A. Wurm. cum.index: 1963-70 in Series D, no. 9.

499   AT   ISSN 0078-754X
PACIFIC LINGUISTICS. SERIES B: MONOGRAPHS. 1963. irreg., no. 74, 1980. price varies. (Linguistic Circle of Canberra) Australian National University, Research School of Pacific Studies, Dept. of Linguistics, Box 4, Canberra, A.C.T. 2600, Australia. Ed. S. A. Wurm. cum.index: 1963-1970 in Series D, no. 9.

499   AT   ISSN 0078-7558
PACIFIC LINGUISTICS. SERIES C: BOOKS. 1965. irreg., no. 65, 1980. price varies. (Linguistic Circle of Canberra) Australian National University, Research School of Pacific Studies, Dept. of Linguistics, Box 4, Canberra, A.C.T. 2600, Australia. Ed. S. A. Wurm. cum.index: 1963-1970 in Series D, no. 9.

499   AT   ISSN 0078-7566
PACIFIC LINGUISTICS. SERIES D: SPECIAL PUBLICATIONS. 1964. irreg., no. 29, 1980. price varies. (Linguistic Circle of Canberra) Australian National University, Research School of Pacific Studies, Dept. of Linguistics, Box 4, Canberra, A.C.T. 2600, Australia. Ed. S. A. Wurm. cum.index: 1963-70 in Series D, no. 9.

400   US   ISSN 0363-8391
PACIFIC NORTHWEST COUNCIL ON FOREIGN LANGUAGES. PROCEEDINGS. (Issued in 2 Vols.) 1950. a. $8 per vol. Pacific Northwest Conference on Foreign Languages, c/o Franz Langhammer, Bus.Mgr., Dept. of Foreign Languages & Literatures, Portland State University, Portland, OR 97207. circ. 300. Indexed: M.L.A.
    Formerly: Pacific Northwest Conference on Foreign Languages. Proceedings (ISSN 0078-7612)

499 GE
PACO; bulteno de la Mondpaka Esperantista Movado, sekcio de G D R. (Text in Esperanto) a. Kulturbund der DDR, Zentraler Arbeitskreis Esperanto, Charlottenstr. 60, 108 Berlin, E. Germany (D.D.R.) (U.S. Subscr. to: J. M. Deer, 12946 N.E. Nancock, Portland, OR 97230) Ed. Detlev Blanke. illus.

410 II
PAKHA SANJAM. (Text in English or Panjabi) 1968. s-a. Punjabi University, Department of Linguistics, Patiala 4, Punjab, India. Ed. Harjeet Singh Gill. adv. bk. rev. circ. 500.

491.8 PL ISSN 0078-866X
PAMIETNIK SLOWIANSKI. (Text in Polish or Czech; summaries in French and Russian) 1950. a. 45 Zl.($7) (Polska Akademia Nauk, Komitet Slowianoznawstwa) Ossolineum, Publishing House of the Polish Academy of Sciences, Rynek 9, 50-106 Wroclaw, Poland (Dist. by Ars Polona-Ruch, Krakowskie Przedmiescie 7, Warsaw, Poland) Ed. Ludwik Bazylow.

PANAMIN FOUNDATION RESEARCH SERIES. see *ANTHROPOLOGY*

410 811 US
PAPER AIR. 1976. a. $8 for 3 nos. to individuals; institutions $10. Singing Horse Press, 825 Morris Rd., Blue Bell, PA 19422. Ed. Gil Ott. adv. bk. rev. bibl. illus. circ. 500. (back issues avail.)

410 US
PAPERS AND REPORTS ON CHILD LANGUAGE DEVELOPMENT. no. 8, 1974. irreg. Stanford University, Committee on Linguistics, Stanford, CA 94305 (Available from: E R I C, National Institute of Education, U.S. Dept. of H.E.W., Washington DC 20208)

410 PL
PAPERS AND STUDIES IN CONTRASTIVE LINGUISTICS. (Text in English) 1973. irreg., vol. 6, 1977. price varies. Uniwersytet im. Adama Mickiewicza w Poznaniu, Stalingradzka 1, 61-712 Poznan, Poland (Dist. by: Ars Polona, Krakowskie Przedmiescie 7, 00-068 Warsaw, Poland) (Co-sponsor: Center for Applied Linguistics, Arlington, VA, USA) Ed. Jacek Fisiak.

499 AT ISSN 0078-9062
PAPERS IN AUSTRALIAN LINGUISTICS. (Subseries of Pacific Linguistics. Series A: Occasional Papers) 1967. irreg., no. 13, 1980. price varies. (Linguistic Circle of Canberra) Australian National University, Research School of Pacific Studies, Dept. of Linguistics, Box 4, Canberra, A.C.T. 2600, Australia. Ed. S. A. Wurm. cum.index: 1963-1970 in Pacific Linguistics, Series D, no. 9.

499 AT ISSN 0078-9070
PAPERS IN BORNEO LINGUISTICS. (Subseries of Pacific Linguistics. Series A: Occasional Papers) 1969. irreg., no. 2, 1977. price varies. (Linguistic Circle of Canberra) Australian National University, Research School of Pacific Studies, Dept. of Linguustics, Box 4, Canberra, A.C.T. 2600, Australia. Ed. S. A. Wurm. cum.index: 1963-1970 in Pacific Linguistics, Series d, no. 9.

410 375.4 US
PAPERS IN JAPANESE LINGUISTICS. (Text in English) 1972. a. $10. University of Southern California, Department of Linguistics, Japanese Linguistics Workshop, Los Angeles, CA 90007. Ed. Masayoshi Shibatani. bk. rev. circ. 300.

499.5 AT ISSN 0078-9127
PAPERS IN LINGUISTICS OF MELANESIA. (Subseries of Pacific Linguistics. Series A: Occasional Papers) 1968. irreg. price varies. (Linguistic Circle of Canberra) Australian National University, Research School of Pacific Studies, Dept. of Linguistics, Box 4, Canberra, A.C.T. 2600, Australia. Ed. S. A. Wurm. cum.index: 1963-70 in Pacific Linguistics, Series D, no. 9.

499 AT ISSN 0078-9135
PAPERS IN NEW GUINEA LINGUISTICS. (Subseries of Pacific Linguistics. Series A: Occasional Papers) 1964. irreg., no. 20, 1980. price varies. (Linguistic Circle of Canberra) Australian National University, Research School of Pacific Studies, Dept. of Linguistics, Box 4, Canberra, A.C.T. 2600, Australia. Ed. S. A. Wurm. cum.index: 1963-1970 in Pacific Linguistics, Series D, no. 9.

499 AT ISSN 0078-9143
PAPERS IN PHILIPPINE LINGUISTICS. (Subseries of Pacific Linguistics. Series A: Occasional Papers) 1966. irreg., no. 10, 1979. price varies. (Linguistic Circle of Canberra) Australian National University, Research School of Pacific Studies, Dept. of Linguistics, Box 4, Canberra, A.C.T. 2600, Australia. Ed. S. A. Wurm. cum.index: 1963-1970 in Pacific Linguistics, Series D, no. 9.

495 AT ISSN 0078-9178
PAPERS IN SOUTH EAST ASIAN LINGUISTICS. (Subseries of Pacific Linguistics. Series A: Occasional Papers) 1967. irreg., no. 7, 1980. price varies. (Linguistic Circle of Canberra) Australian National University, Research School of Pacific Studies, Dept. of Linguistics, Box 4, Canberra, A.C.T. 2600, Australia. Ed. S. A. Wurm. cum.index: 1963-1970 in Pacific Linguistics, Series D, no. 9.

410 NE ISSN 0078-9194
PAPERS ON FORMAL LINGUISTICS. 1961. irreg. price varies. (University of Pennsylvania, Department of Linguistics, US) Mouton Publishers, Noordeinde 41, 2514 GC The Hague, Netherlands (U.S. addr.: Mouton Publishers, c/o Walter de Gruyter, Inc., 200 Saw Mill River Road, Hawthorne, NY 10532)

400 GW ISSN 0341-3195
PAPIERE ZUR TEXTLINGUISTIK/PAPERS IN TEXTLINGUISTICS. irreg., no. 28, 1980. price varies. (Universitaet Bielefeld) Verlag Helmut Buske, Schlueterstr. 14, 2000 Hamburg 13, W. Germany (B.R.D.) Eds. Jens Ihwe, Janos S. Petofi, Hannes Rieser.

439 NE
PDR PRESS PUBLICATIONS ON DUTCH. no. 2, 1977. irreg. Peter de Ridder Press, Box 168, 2160 AD Lisse, Netherlands.

491.86 CS
PEDAGOGICKA FAKULTA V USTI NAD LABEM. SBORNIK: RADA BOHEMISTICKA. (Text in Czech; summaries in English, German, Russian) irreg. 16 Kcs. Statni Pedagogicke Nakladatelstvi, Ostrovni 30, 113 01 Prague 1, Czechoslovakia.

410 370 PH ISSN 0076-3780
PHILIPPINE NORMAL COLLEGE. LANGUAGE STUDY CENTER. OCCASIONAL PAPER. 1967. irreg., no. 11, 1974. price varies. Philippine Normal College, Language Study Center, Manila 2801, Philippines. circ. 500.

410 GW ISSN 0079-1598
PHILOLOGEN-JAHRBUCH. a. DM.20. Verlag Jahrbuch der Lehrer der Hoeheren Schulen, Richard Wagner Str. 1, 5000 Cologne 10, W. Germany (B.R.D.) Ed. K. Mueller.

401 US ISSN 0079-1628
PHILOLOGICAL MONOGRAPHS. 1931. irreg., 1973, no. 31. (American Philological Association) Scholars Press, Box 5207, Missoula, MT 59806. Ed. John J. Keaney. circ. 3,000.

400 UK ISSN 0079-1636
PHILOLOGICAL SOCIETY TRANSACTIONS. 1842. a. £7($14) Basil Blackwell, Publisher, Ltd., 108 Cowley Road, Oxford OX4 1JF, England. index.

491 891 AU ISSN 0079-1644
PHILOLOGISCHE BEITRAEGE ZUR SUEDOST- UND OSTEUROPAFORSCHUNG. (Text in English, German) 1971. irreg. price varies. Wilhelm Braumueller, Universitaets-Verlagsbuchhandlung GmbH, Servitengasse 5, A-1092 Vienna, Austria. Ed. Ivan Galabov. index. circ. 900.

407 PL ISSN 0137-6349
POLITECHNIKA WROCLAWSKA. STUDIUM PRAKTYCZNEJ NAUKI JEZYKOW OBCYCH. PRACE NAUKOWE. STUDIA I MATERIALY. (Text in German, Polish, Russian; summaries in English) 1974. irreg., no. 11, 1979. price varies. Politechnika Wroclawska, Wybrzeze Wyspianskiego 27, 50-370 Wroclaw, Poland (Dist. by: Ars Polona-Ruch, Krakowskie Przedmiescie 7, Warsaw, Poland) Ed. Marian Kloza. circ. 380.

490 PL
POLONICA. (Text in Polish; summaries in English) 1975. irreg., 1976, vol. 2. 60 Zl. (Polska Akademia Nauk, Instytut Jezyka Polskiego) Ossolineum, Publishing House of the Polish Academy of Sciences, Rynek 9, 50-106 Wroclaw, Poland. Ed. S. Urbanczyk.

400 PL ISSN 0079-3272
POLSKA AKADEMIA NAUK. ODDZIAL W KRAKOWIE. KOMISJA FILOLOGII KLASYCZNEJ. PRACE. (Text in English, French, German, Latin and Polish; summaries in English and French) 1960. irreg., no. 17, 1978. price varies. Ossolineum, Publishing House of the Polish Academy of Sciences, Rynek 9, Wroclaw, Poland (Dist. by Ars Polona-Ruch, Krakowskie Przedmiescie 7, Warsaw, Poland)

400 PL ISSN 0079-3310
POLSKA AKADEMIA NAUK. ODDZIAL W KRAKOWIE. KOMISJA JEZYKOZNAWSTWA. PRACE. (Text in Polish, Latin and French) 1964. irreg., latest, 1979. price varies. Ossolineum, Publishing House of the Polish Academy of Sciences, Rynek 9, 50-106 Wroclaw, Poland (Dist. by Ars Polona-Ruch, Krakowskie Przedmiescie 7, Warsaw, Poland)

400 PL ISSN 0079-3329
POLSKA AKADEMIA NAUK. ODDZIAL W KRAKOWIE. KOMISJA JEZYKOZNAWSTWA. WYDAWNICTWA ZRODLOWE. (Text in Polish; summaries in English) irreg. price varies. Ossolineum, Publishing House of the Polish Academy of Sciences, Rynek 9, 50-106 Wroclaw, Poland (Dist. by Ars Polona-Ruch, Krakowskie Przedmiescie 7, Warsaw, Poland)

410 PL ISSN 0032-3802
POLSKIE TOWARZYSTWO JEZYKOZNAWCZE. BIULETYN. (Text in English, German and Polish) irreg., vol. 36, 1979. 45 Zl. Ossolineum, Publishing House of the Polish Academy of Sciences, Rynek 9, Wroclaw, Poland (Dist. by: Ars Polona-Ruch, Krakowskie Przedmiescie 7, Warsaw, Poland) Ed. A. Heinz.

410 PL ISSN 0079-4678
POZNANSKIE TOWARZYSTWO PRZYJACIOL NAUK. KOMISJA JEZYKOZNAWCZA. PRACE. (Text in English, German or Polish; summaries in English, French, German) 1962. irreg. price varies. Poznanskie Towarzystwo Przyjaciol Nauk, Mielzynskiego 27/29, 61-725 Poznan, Poland (Dist by Ars Polona-Ruch, Krakowskie Przedmiescie 7, Warsaw, Poland) Indexed: Lang.&Lang.Behav.Abstr.

400 PL ISSN 0079-3485
PRACE JEZYKOZNAWCZE. (Text in French and Polish) 1954. irreg., vol. 92, 1979. price varies. (Polska Akademia Nauk, Komitet Jezykoznawstwa) Ossolineum, Publishing House of the Polish Academy of Sciences, Rynek 9, 50-106 Wroclaw, Poland (Dist. by Ars Polona-Ruch, Krakowskie Przedmiescie 7,Warsaw, Poland)

491.8 PL ISSN 0079-4775
PRACE ONOMASTYCZNE. (Text in Polish; summaries in English, French and German) 1955. irreg., vol. 27, 1978. price varies. (Polska Akademia Nauk, Komitet Jezykoznawstwa) Ossolineum, Publishing House of the Polish Academy of Sciences, Rynek 9, 50-106 Wroclaw, Poland (Dist. by Ars Polona-Ruch, Krakowskie Przedmiescie 7, Warsaw, Poland)

PRAKRIT TEXT SOCIETY. PUBLICATIONS. see *LITERATURE*

491.86 CS ISSN 0079-4902
PRAMENY CESKE A SLOVENSKE LINGVISTIKY. RADA CESKA. 1970. irreg. price varies. (Ceskoslovenska Akademie Ved) Academia, Publishing House of the Czechoslovak Academy of Sciences, Vodickova 40, 112 29 Prague 1, Czechoslovakia. Ed. Josef Vachek.

400 UK
PRINCETON-CAMBRIDGE SERIES IN CHINESE LINGUISTICS. 1970. irreg., no. 6, 1976. $64 for latest vol. (Princeton University, Chinese Linguistics Project) Cambridge University Press, Box 110, Cambridge CB2 3RL, England (and 32 E. 57 St., New York, N.Y. 10022)
 Formerly: Princeton-Cambridge Studies in Chinese Linguistics (ISSN 0079-5178)

410 NE
PUBLICATIONS IN LANGUAGE SCIENCES. Short title: P L S. vol. 2, 1979. irreg. price varies. Foris Publications, Box 509, 3300 AM Dordrecht, Netherlands.

490 956 NE ISSN 0079-7715
PUBLICATIONS IN NEAR AND MIDDLE EAST STUDIES. SERIES B. irreg. price varies. (Columbia University, Department of Middle East Languages and Cultures, US) Mouton Publishers, Noordeinde 41, 2514 GC The Hague, Netherlands (U.S. addr.: Mouton Publishers, c/o Walter de Gruyter, Inc., 200 Saw Mill River Road, Hawthorne, NY 10532) (Co-sponsor: Middle East Institute)

PUBLICATIONS ROMANES ET FRANCAISES. see *LITERATURE*

410 840 NE ISSN 0165-8743
PURDUE UNIVERSITY MONOGRAPHS IN ROMANCE LANGUAGE. Short title: PUMRL. 1979. irreg., vol. 6, 1981. price varies. (Purdue University, US) John Benjamins B.V., Box 52519, 1007 HA Amsterdam, Netherlands. Eds. A. H. Pasco, W. M. Whithby.

440 CN ISSN 0079-8770
QUEBEC (PROVINCE) OFFICE DE LA LANGUE FRANCAISE. CAHIERS. 1965. irreg., no. 28, 1978. free. Office de la Langue Francaise, 700 Bd. Saint-Cyrille Est, 2e, Quebec, P.Q. G1R 5A9, Canada. illus.

420 SI
R E L C ANNUAL REPORT. (Text in English) 1968/69. a. $5($4) Southeast Asian Ministers of Education Organization, Regional Language Centre, 30 Orange Grove Road, Singapore 1025, Singapore. charts. stat. circ. 400. (back issues avail.; reprint service avail. from UMI)

418 CL ISSN 0033-698X
R L A; revista de linguistica teorica y aplicada. Title varies: Revista de Linguistica Aplicada. (Text in Spanish; occasionally in English & French; abstracts in English) 1963. a. $2.50 individuals; institutions $4. Universidad de Concepcion, Instituto Central de Lenguas, Casilla 1807, Concepcion, Chile. Eds. Nelson Cartagena, Max S. Echeverria. adv. bk. rev. charts. circ. 750. Indexed: Lang.&Lang.Behav.Abstr. Lang.Teach.&Ling.Abstr.

400 CN ISSN 0079-9335
R L S: REGIONAL LANGUAGE STUDIES... NEWFOUNDLAND. 1968. irreg. free. ‡ Memorial University of Newfoundland, Folklore and Language Archive, St. John's, Nfld. A1C 5S7, Canada. Ed. William Kirwin. bk. rev. circ. 250. Indexed: M.L.A.

RAJASTHAN UNIVERSITY STUDIES IN ENGLISH. see *LITERATURE*

439 NE
RANDGEBIEDEN; een interdisciplinaire serie. vol. 3, 1978. irreg. price varies. Dick Coutinho B.V., Badlaan 2, Muiderberg, Netherlands. Ed.B.P.F.A1. bibl.

410 PR
READINGS IN SPANISH-ENGLISH CONTRASTIVE LINGUISTICS. (Text in English, Spanish) 1973. irreg. Inter American University Press, Box 3255, San Juan, PR 00936. Ed. Rose Nash. (reprint service avail. from UMI)

418.02 FR
RECHERCHES EN LINGUISTIQUE ETRANGERE. Variant title: Universite de Besancon. Annales Litteraires. 1973. irreg. (Universite de Besancon, Faculte des Lettres et Sciences Humaines) Societe d'Edition les Belles Lettres, 95 Bd. Raspail, Paris 75006, France.

RECHERCHES GERMANIQUES. see *LITERATURE*

410 FR
RECHERCHES LINQUISTIQUES. 1975. irreg. 62 F. Universite de Metz, Centre d'Analyse Syntaxique, Metz, France (Subscr. to: Librairie Klincksieck, 11 rue de Lille, 75007 Paris, France)

400 US
REVERSE ACRONYMS, INITIALISMS AND ABBREVIATIONS DICTIONARY. 1972. biennial. $58. Gale Research Company, Book Tower, Detroit, MI 48226. Ed. Ellen T. Crowley.
Formerly (until 1976): Reverse Acronyms and Initialisms Dictionary.

REVIEW (CHARLOTTESVILLE) see *LITERATURE*

REVISTA IBERICA. see *LITERATURE*

469 PO ISSN 0080-2433
REVISTA PORTUGUESA DE FILOLOGIA. 1960. a (2nos./vol.) 380 esc. Universidade de Coimbra, Instituto de Estudos Romanicos, Casa do Castelo, Rua da Sofia 47, Coimbra, Portugal. Ed. Manuel de Paiva Boleo.

REVISTA SIGNOS DE VALPARAISO; estudios de lengua y literatura. see *LITERATURE*

REVUE DES ETUDES LATINES. see *CLASSICAL STUDIES*

REVUE DES ETUDES SLAVES. see *LITERATURE*

800 FR ISSN 0080-2603
REVUE HITTITE ET ASIATIQUE. 1930. a. price varies. Editions Klincksieck, 11 rue de Lille, Paris 7, France. Ed. E. LaRoche. bk. rev.

450 IT ISSN 0080-293X
RICERCHE DI STORIA DELLA LINGUA LATINA. 1967. irreg., no. 16, 1981. price varies. Edizioni dell' Ateneo S.p.A., P.O. Box 7216, 00100 Rome, Italy. Ed. Alfonso Traina. circ. 1,000.

491.8 PL ISSN 0080-3588
ROCZNIK SLAWISTYCZNY. (Text in French, German and Polish) 1908. a. 55 Zl. (Polska Akademia Nauk, Komitet Slowianoznawstwa) Ossolineum, Publishing House of the Polish Academy of Sciences, Rynek 9, 50-106 Wroclaw, Poland (Dist. by Ars Polona-Ruch, Krakowskie Przedmiescie 7, Warsaw, Poland) Ed. F. Slawski.

479.1 BE ISSN 0080-3855
ROMANICA GANDENSIA. 1953. irreg. price varies. ‡ Rijksuniversiteit te Gent, Section de Philologie Romane, Blandijnberg 2, B-9000 Ghent, Belgium.

430 830 SW ISSN 0080-3863
ROMANICA GOTHOBURGENSIA. (Subseries of Acta Universitatis Gothoburgensis) 1955. irreg., no. 16, 1978. price varies; also exchange basis. Acta Universitatis Gothoburgensis, Box 5096, S-402 22 Goeteborg 5, Sweden (Dist. in U. S., Canada, and Mexico by: Humanities Press, Inc., 171 First Ave., Atlantic Highlands, NJ 07716) Eds. H. Nilsson-Ehle, Gunnar von Proschwitz.

400 SZ ISSN 0080-3871
ROMANICA HELVETICA. (Text in German, French, or Italian) 1935. irreg., vol. 92, 1979. price varies. (Collegium Romanicium Helvetiorum a Curatoribus Vocis Romanicae) Francke Verlag, Postfach, CH-3000 Berne 26, Switzerland.

400 870 GW ISSN 0080-3898
ROMANISTISCHES JAHRBUCH. 1947. irreg., vol. 28, 1978. DM.108($60) (Universitaet Hamburg, Ibero-Amerikanisches Forschungsinstitut) Walter de Gruyter und Co., Genthiner Str. 13, 1000 Berlin 30, W. Germany (B.R.D.) adv. bk. rev.

491.7 891.7 CS
RUSSICA OLOMUCENSIA. (Text in Czech or Russian; summaries in Russian) 1968. irreg. free. Univerzita Palackeho, Filozoficka Fakulta, Katedra Rusistiky, Krizkovskeho 10, 771 80 Olomouc, Czechoslovakia.

439.31 839.31 NE
RUYGH-BEWERP. 1966. irreg., vol. 9, 1979. price varies. Rijksuniversiteit Te Utrecht, Instituut de Vooys voor Nederlandse Taal- en Letterkunde, Emmalaan 29, Utrecht, Netherlands.

410 572 US
S. I. L. MUSEUM OF ANTHROPOLOGY PUBLICATION. (Text in English; some vols. avail. in Spanish or Portuguese) 1976. irreg. price varies. Summer Institute of Linguistics, Museum of Anthropology, 7500 W. Camp Wisdom Rd., Dallas, TX 75236. Eds. George L. Huttar, William R. Merrifield. (also avail. in microfiche; back issues avail.)

400 US ISSN 0079-7669
S I L PUBLICATIONS IN LINGUISTICS AND RELATED FIELDS. Abbreviated title: S I L Series. 1958. irreg., no. 63, 1979. $5-18. (Summer Institute of Linguistics) Academic Publications, 7500 W. Camp Wisdom Rd., Dallas, TX 75211. Ed. George Huttar.

400 900 GE ISSN 0080-5297
SAECHSISCHE AKADEMIE DER WISSENSCHAFTEN, LEIPZIG. PHILOLOGISCH-HISTORISCHE KLASSE. ABHANDLUNGEN. 1896. irreg., vol, 67, 1977. price varies. (Philologisch-Historische Klasse) Akademie-Verlag, Leipziger Str. 3-4, 108 Berlin, E. Germany (D.D.R.)

410 900 GE ISSN 0080-5300
SAECHSISCHE AKADEMIE DER WISSENSCHAFTEN, LEIPZIG. PHILOLOGISCH-HISTORISCHE KLASSE. SITZUNGSBERICHTE. irreg., vol. 119, 1977. price varies. (Philologisch-Historische Klasse) Akademie-Verlag, Leipziger Str. 3-4, 108 Berlin, E. Germany (D.D.R.)

440 GW
SALZBURGER ROMANISTISCHE SCHRIFTEN. 1972. irreg. DM.25 per vol., approx. (Universitaet Salzburg, Institut fuer Romanische Philologie, AU) Wilhelm Fink Verlag, Nikolaistr 2, 8000 Munich 64, W. Germany (B.R.D.) Ed. Karin Rieser-Spriegel. bibl.

SAMMLUNG GROOS. see *EDUCATION — Higher Education*

491.8 891.8 DK ISSN 0080-6765
SCANDO-SLAVICA. (Supplements avail.) (Text in English, French, German, Italian and Russian) 1955. a. Kr.200. (Association of Scandinavian Slavicists and Baltologists) Munksgaard, 35 Noerre Soegade, DK-1370 Copenhogen K, Denmark. Ed. K. Rahbek Schmidt. bk. rev. index. circ. 800. (reprint service avail. from ISI) Indexed: Curr.Cont.

491.8 891.8 DK
SCANDO-SLAVICA. SUPPLEMENTUM. irreg. price varies. (Association of Scandinavian Slavicists and Baltologists) Munksgaard, 35 Noerre Soegade, DK-1370 Copenhagen K, Denmark. (reprint service avail. from ISI)

SCHATZKAMMER; der deutschen Sprachlehre, Dichtung und Geschichte. see *HISTORY — History Of North And South America*

400 800 SZ ISSN 0080-7214
SCHWEIZER ANGLISTISCHE ARBEITEN/SWISS STUDIES IN ENGLISH. (Text in German or English) 1935. irreg., vol. 99, 1979. price varies. ‡ Francke Verlag, Postfach, CH-3000 Berne 26, Switzerland. Eds. R. Fricker, E. Leisi, H. Straumann.

410 II
SEMINAR ON DRAVIDIAN LINGUISTICS. PROCEEDINGS. irreg., 5th, 1975. Annamalai University, Department of Linguistics, Annamalainagar P.O., Tamil Nadu, India. Eds. S. Agesthialingom, P.S. Subrahmanyam. bibl.

400 SP
SEMINARIO DE FILOLOGIA VASCA JULIO DE URQUIJO. ANUARIO. (Text in English, French, Spanish) a. 250 ptas. Seminario de Filologia Vasca Julio de Urquijo, Palacio de la Diputacion de Guipuzcoa, San Sebastian (Guipuzcoa), Spain.

410 PE
SERIE LINGUISTICA PERUANA. 1963. irreg. no. 15, 1976. price varies. Instituto Linguistico de Verano, Departamento de Estudios Etno-Linguisticos, Casilla 2492, Lima 100, Peru.

420 375.4 II
SERIES IN ENGLISH LANGUAGE AND LITERATURE. (Text in English) 1978. irreg. price varies. Bahri Publications Pvt. Ltd., 57 Santnagar, New Delhi 110065, India. Ed. Ujjal Singh Bahri.

407 II
SERIES IN INDIAN LANGUAGES AND LINGUISTICS. 1972. irreg. price varies. Bahri Publications Pvt. Ltd., 57 Santnagar, New Delhi 110065, India. Ed. Ujjal Shingh Bahri.

869 FR
SILLAGES. (Text in French and Portuguese; summaries in English) 1972. a. 15 F.($4.50) Universite de Poitiers, Departement d'Etudes Portugaises et Bresiliennes, 95 Avenue du Recteur Pineau, 86022 Poitiers, France. Ed. R.A. Lawton. circ. 750.
Portuguese language study and teaching

490 PL ISSN 0081-0002
SLAVIA OCCIDENTALIS. (Text in Czech, Polish, Russian; summaries in French) 1922. a. price varies. Poznanskie Towarzystwo Przyjaciol Nauk, Mielzynskiego 27/29, 61-725 Poznan, Poland (Dist. by Ars Polona-Ruch, Krakowskie Przedmiescie 7, Warsaw, Poland) Ed. Wladyslaw Kuraszkiewicz.

400 800 SW ISSN 0081-0010
SLAVICA GOTHOBURGENSIA. (Subseries of Acta Universitatis Gothoburgensis) 1958. irreg., no. 6, 1974. price varies; also exchange basis. (Goeteborgs Universitet, Department of Slavic Studies) Acta Universitatis Gothoburgensis, Box 5096, S-402 22 Goeteborg 5, Sweden (Dist. in U.S., Canada, and Mexico by: Humanities Press, Inc., 171 First Ave., Atlantic Highlands, NJ 07716) Ed. Gunnar Jacobson.

491.8 891.8 SW
SLAVICA LUNDENSIA. (Text in Slavic, English, German and Swedish; summaries in English and Russian) 1973. a. Kr.25. Lunds Universitet, Slaviska Institutionen, Finngatan 12, S-223 62 Lund, Sweden. Ed. Lubomir Durovic. circ. 400. (also avail. in microfilm from UMI; back issues avail.)

490 UR
SLAVYANSKAYA FILOLOGIYA. 1964. irreg. 0.72 Rub. Izdatel'stvo Leningradskii Universitet, Universitetskaya nab. 7/9, Leningrad B-164, U.S.S.R. bibl.

SLOVACI V ZAHRANICI. see *HISTORY — History Of Europe*

490 GW ISSN 0340-6423
SOCIETAS URALO-ALTAICA. VEROEFFENTLICHUNGEN. 1969. irreg., vol. 13, 1980. price varies. Verlag Otto Harrassowitz, Taunusstr. 6, Postfach 2929, 6200 Wiesbaden, W. Germany (B.R.D.) Ed. Bd.

410 301.2 FR
SOCIETE D'ETUDES LINGUISTIQUES ET ANTHROPOLOGIQUES DE FRANCE. NUMERO SPECIAL. no. 2, 1974. irreg. 250 F. Societe d'Etudes Linguistiques et Anthropologiques de France, 5 rue de Marseille, 75010 Paris, France.

SOCIETY FOR SLOVENE STUDIES. DOCUMENTATION SERIES. see *HISTORY — History Of Europe*

410 US
SOCIETY OF FEDERAL LINGUISTS. NEWSLETTER. 1946. irreg. (approx. 4/yr.) membership. Society of Federal Linguists, Inc., Box 7765, Washington, DC 20044. Ed. Deanna Hammond. circ. 150 (controlled)

491 BU ISSN 0081-1831
SOFIISKI UNIVERSITET. FAKULTET PO SLAVIANSKA FILOLOGIIA. GODISHNIK. (Text in various languages) irreg., vol. 63, 1970. 2.40 lv. price varies. Publishing House of the Bulgarian Academy of Sciences, Ul. Akad. G. Bonchev, 1113 Sofia, Bulgaria. Ed. I. Duridanov. bibl. circ. 1,000.

410 BU ISSN 0584-0252
SOFIISKI UNIVERSITET. FAKULTET PO ZAPADNI FILOLOGII. GODISHNIK/ L'UNIVERSITE DE SOFIA. FACULTE DES LETTRES. ANNUAIRE. (Text in various languages) irreg. vol. 70, 1975. 3.81 lv. price varies. Publishing House of the Bulgarian Academy of Sciences, Ul. Akad. G. Bonchev, 1113 Sofia, Bulgaria. bibl. circ. 1,000.

SPEECH COMMUNICATION DIRECTORY. see *EDUCATION — Special Education And Rehabilitation*

440 FR
SPICAE; cahiers de l'Atelier Vincent de Beauvais. 1978. irreg. (Universite de Nancy II, Centre de Recherches et d'Applications Linguistiques) Centre National de la Recherche Scientifique, 15 Quai Anatole France, 75700 Paris, France. (Co-sponsor: Institut de Recherche et d'Histoire des Textes) Eds. Helene Nais, Jean Schneider.

SPRACHE UND DATENVERARBEITUNG. see *COMPUTER TECHNOLOGY AND APPLICATIONS*

400 SZ ISSN 0081-3826
SPRACHE UND DICHTUNG. NEUE FOLGE. 1956. irreg., vol. 28, 1978. price varies. Paul Haupt AG, Falkenplatz 14, 3001 Berne, Switzerland. Eds. M. Bindschedler, W. Kohlschmidt, P. Zinsli.

400 943 GE
SPRACHE UND GESELLSCHAFT. 1974. irreg., vol. 9, 1976. price varies. (Akademie der Wissenschaften der DDR, Zentralinstitut fuer Sprachwissenschaft) Akademie-Verlag, Leipziger Str. 3-4, 108 Berlin, E. Germany (D.D.R.) adv.
Former title: Akademie der Wissenschaften, Berlin. Zentralinstitut fuer Sprachwissenschaft. Schriften (ISSN 0065-5260)

410 US
SPRINGER SERIES IN LANGUAGE AND COMMUNICATION. 1978. irreg., vol. 10, 1981. price varies. Springer-Verlag, 175 Fifth Ave., New York, NY 10010 (Also Berlin, Heidelberg, Vienna) Ed. W.J.M. Levelt. (reprint service avail. from ISI)

400 DK ISSN 0038-8645
SPROG OG KULTUR. 1932. irreg. Kr.15. Aarhus Universitet, Institut for Jysk Sprog- og Kulturforskning, Aarhus, Denmark. Ed. Bd.

400 891.1 II ISSN 0081-3915
SRI VENKATESWARA UNIVERSITY. DEPARTMENT OF SANSKRIT. SYMPOSIUM. (Text in Sanskrit and English) 1962. irreg., 1967, no. 4. Rs.4. Sri Venkateswara University, Department of Sanskrit, Tirupati, Andhra Pradesh, India. Ed. E. R. Sreekrishna Sarma.

SRI VENKATESWARA UNIVERSITY. ORIENTAL JOURNAL. see *HISTORY — History Of Asia*

SRPSKA AKADEMIJA NAUKA I UMETNOSTI. ODELJENJE JEZIKA I KNJIZEVNOSTI. POSEBNA IZDANJA. see *LITERATURE*

400 YU ISSN 0081-3958
SRPSKA AKADEMIJA NAUKA I UMETNOSTI. ODELJENJE JEZIKA I KNJIZEVNOSTI. GLAS. (Text in Serbo-Croatian; summaries in French, English, German or Russian) 1951, N.S. irreg. price varies. Srpska Akademija Nauka i Umetnosti, Knez Mihailova 35, 11001 Belgrade, Yugoslavia (Dist. by: Prosveta, Terazije 16, Belgrade, Yugoslavia) circ. 600.

410 US ISSN 0085-6673
STANFORD OCCASIONAL PAPERS IN LINGUISTICS. 1971. irreg. free. ‡ Stanford University, Committee on Linguistics, Stanford, CA 94305 (Available from: E R I C, National Institute of Education, U.S. Dept. of H.E.W., Washington DC 20208) Ed. Elizabeth Traugott. circ. controlled. (processed)

420 SW
STOCKHOLM STUDIES IN ENGLISH. (Subseries of Acta Universitatis Stockholmiensis) (Text in English) 1937. irreg., vol. 49, 1978. price varies. (Stockholms Universitet) Almqvist & Wiksell International, Box 62, S-101 20 Stockholm, Sweden. Eds. Alarik Rynell, Lennart A. Bjork. (back issues avail.)

410 890 SW
STOCKHOLM STUDIES IN FINNISH LANGUAGE AND LITERATURE. 1976. irreg. Stockholms Universitet, Fack, 104 05 Stockholm, Sweden.

410 IT ISSN 0391-1942
STRUMENTI LINGUISTICI. 1976. irreg., no. 11, 1978. price varies. Liguori Editore s.r.l., Via Mezzocannone 19, 80134 Naples, Italy. Ed. Gianfranco Folena.

491.9 891.9 IT ISSN 0081-6116
STUDI ALBANESI. STUDI E TESTI. 1965. irreg., 1972, no. 5. price varies. (Universita degli Studi di Roma, Istituto Studi Albanesi) Casa Editrice Leo S. Olschki, Casella Postale 66, 50100 Florence, Italy. Ed. Ernesto Koliqi. circ. 1,000.

410 IT ISSN 0085-6827
STUDI E SAGGI LINGUISTICI; supplemento alla rivista l'Italia Dialettale. (Text in Italian; summaries in English) 1961. a. L.10000. (Universita degli Studi di Pisa, Istituto di Glottologia) Giardini Editori e Stampatori, Via Santa Bibbiana 28, Pisa, Italy. Ed. Tristano Bolelli. index. circ. 350.

STUDI E TESTI DI LINGUA E LETTERATURA ITALIANA. see *LITERATURE*

450 IT
STUDI LINGUISTICI SALENTINI.* 1965. Associazione Linguistica Salentina, Villa Sebaste, Via per Campi, 73051, Novoli (Lecce), Italy. illus.

400 PL ISSN 0081-6272
STUDIA ANGLICA POSNANIENSIA; AN INTERNATIONAL REVIEW OF ENGLISH STUDIES. (Text in English) 1969. irreg., 1976, vol. 8. price varies. Uniwersytet im. Adama Mickiewicza w Poznaniu, Ul. Stalingradzka 1, 61-712 Poznan, Poland (Dist. by: Ars Polona, Krakowskie Przedmiescie 7, 00-068 Warsaw, Poland) Ed. Jacek Fisiak. adv. bk. rev. circ. 1,300.

420 SW ISSN 0562-2719
STUDIA ANGLISTICA UPSALIENSES. (Subseries of Acta Universitatis Upsaliensis) 1963. irreg. price varies. Almqvist & Wiksell International, Box 62, S-101 20 Stockholm, Sweden. Eds. Johannes Soderlind, Olov Fryckstedt, Gunnar Sorelius. (back issues avail.)

491 NE ISSN 0081-6345
STUDIA CAUCASICA. 1963. irreg. Peter de Ridder Press, Box 168, 2160-AD-Lisse, Netherlands (Dist. in the U.S. by Humanities Press, Inc., 171 Fifth Ave., Atlantic Highlands, NJ 07716) Ed. A. H. Kuipers. adv. bk. rev. illus. charts. circ. 150.

491.6 UK ISSN 0081-6353
STUDIA CELTICA. (Text in English and Welsh; occasionally in French and German) 1966. biennial. £8 per double vol. (University of Wales, Board of Celtic Studies) University of Wales Press, 6 Gwennyth St., Cathays, Cardiff CF2 4YD, Wales. Ed. J. E. Caerwyn Williams. bk. rev. circ. 400. (reprint service avail. from UMI)

STUDIA FENNICA: REVUE DE LINGUISTIQUE ET D'ETHNOLOGIE FINNOISES. see *ANTHROPOLOGY*

439 BE ISSN 0081-6442
STUDIA GERMANICA GANDENSIA. (Text in Dutch, English, German) 1959. a. 300 Fr. Rijksuniversiteit te Gent, Faculteit van Letteren en Wijsbegeerte, Blandijnberg 2, B-9000 Ghent, Belgium. Ed. G. A. R. De Smet. index.

430 GE ISSN 0081-6469
STUDIA GRAMMATICA. 1962. irreg., vol. 14, 1977. price varies. (Akademie der Wissenschaften der DDR, Zentralinstitut fuer Sprachwissenschaft) Akademie-Verlag, Leipziger Str. 3-4, 108 Berlin, E. Germany (D.D.R.)

400 IT
STUDIA HISTORICA ET PHILOGIA: SECTIO ROMANICA. 1974. irreg. Licosa S.p.A., Via Lamarmora 45, 50121 Florence, Italy. Ed. R. Picchio. circ. 2,000.

400
STUDIA HISTORICA ET PHILOGICA: SECTIO SLAVICA. irreg. Licosa S.p.A., Via Lamarmora 45, 50121 Florence, Italy.

400
STUDIA HISTORICA ET PHILOGICA: SECTIO SLAVO-ROMANICA. irreg. Licosa S.p.A., Via Lamarmora 45, 50121 Florence, Italy.

407 US
STUDIA LINGUISTICA ET PHILOLOGICA. 1975. irreg. $20 per vol. Anma Libri, Box 876, Saratoga, CA 95070.

410　　　　　　　　SW　ISSN 0081-6809
STUDIA PHILOLOGIAE SCANDINAVICAE
UPSALIENSIA. (Subseries of Acta Universitatis
Upsaliensis) 1961. irreg., vol. 15, 1979. price varies;
exchange avail. (Uppsala Universitet) Almqvist &
Wiksell International, 26 Gamla Brogatan, S-101 20
Stockholm, Sweden. Ed.Bd.

400　　　　　　　　FI　ISSN 0585-5462
STUDIA PHILOLOGICA JYVASKYLAENSIA.
(Text in English, Finnish, French, German and
Swedish) 1966. irreg. price varies. Jyvaskylan
Yliopisto, Kirjasto - University of Jyvaskyla,
Seminaarinkatu 15, 40100 Jyvaskyla 10, Finland.
Ed. Kalevi Tarvainen. circ. 400-500.

400　　　　　　　　JA　ISSN 0300-1067
STUDIA PHONOLOGICA/ONSEI KAGAKU
KENKYU. (Text in English, German or Japanese)
1961. annual. Kyoto University, Institution for
Phonetic Sciences - Kyoto Daigaku Onsei Kagaku
Sogo Kenkyu Bukai, Nihonmatsucho, Yoshida,
Sakyo-ku, Kyoto 606, Japan. Ed. Toshiyuki Sakai.
illus. circ. 1,000.

400　　　　　　　　PL
STUDIA POLONISTYCZNE. (Text in Polish;
summaries in English, French, German or Russian)
1973. irreg., 1977 vol. 4. price varies. Uniwersytet
im. Adama Mickiewicza w Poznaniu, Stalingradzka
1, 61-712 Poznan, Poland (Dist. by: Ars Polona,
Krakowskie Przedmiescie 7, 00-068 Warsaw,
Poland) Eds. Wladyslaw Kuraszkiewicz, Tadeusz
Witczak.

410　　　　　　　　PL　ISSN 0137-6608
STUDIA SEMIOTYCZNE. (Text in English, French
and Polish) irreg., vol. 7, 1977. 54 Zl. (Polskie
Towarzystwo Semiotyczne) Ossolineum, Publishing
House of the Polish Academy of Sciences, Rynek 9,
Wroclaw, Poland (Dist. by: Ars Polona-Ruch,
Krakowskie Przedmiescie 7, Warsaw, Poland) Ed.
Jerzy Pelc.

400 080　　　　　　NE　ISSN 0081-6957
STUDIA THEODISCA. (Summaries occasionally in
English, French and German) 1965. irreg., no. 13,
1974. price varies. Van Gorcum, P.O. Box 43,
Assen, Netherlands.

400　　　　　　　　RM　ISSN 0039-3444
STUDIA UNIVERSITATIS "BABES-BOLYAI".
PHILOLOGIA. (Text in Romanian; summaries in
English, French, German, Italian, Russian) 1956. s-
a. exchange basis. Universitatea "Babes Bolyai",
Biblioteca Centrala Universitara, Str. Clinicilor Nr.
2, Cluj-Napoca, Romania. bk. rev. charts. illus.
index.

410　　　　　　　　AU
STUDIA URALICA. 1978. a. price varies.
(Universitaet Wien, Institut fuer Finno-Ugristik)
Verband der Wissenschaftlichen Gesellschaften
Oesterreichs, Lindengasse 37, A-1010 Vienna,
Austria.

494　　　　　　　　SW　ISSN 0081-7015
STUDIA URALICA ET ALTAICA UPSALIENSIA.
(Subseries of Acta Universitatis Upsaliensis) (Text in
English and Swedish) 1964. irreg., vol. 11, 1976.
price varies. (Uppsala Universitet) Almqvist &
Wiksell International, Box 62, S-101 20 Stockholm,
Sweden. Ed. Bo Wickman. bibl. charts.

491.8　　　　　　　PL　ISSN 0081-7090
STUDIA Z FILOLOGII POLSKIEJ I
SLOWIANSKIEJ. (Text in Polish; papers and
summaries in Slavonic languages) 1955. irreg., 1976,
vol. 15. price varies. (Polska Akademia Nauk,
Komitet Slowianoznawstwa) Panstwowe
Wydawnictwo Naukowe, Miodowa 10, Warsaw,
Poland (Dist. by Ars Polona-Ruch, Krakowskie
Przedmiescie 7, Warsaw, Poland)) Ed. Zdzislaw
Stieber.

490　　　　　　　　GW　ISSN 0585-5853
STUDIEN ZU DEN BOGAZKOY-TEXTEN. 1965.
irreg., vol. 25, 1980. price varies. (Akademie der
Wissenschaften und der Literatur, Kommission fuer
den Alten Orient) Verlag Otto Harrassowitz,
Taunusstr. 6, Postfach 2929, 6200 Wiesbaden, W.
Germany (B.R.D.)

410　　　　　　　　GW　ISSN 0081-7244
STUDIEN ZUR ENGLISCHEN PHILOLOGIE,
NEUE FOLGE. (Text in English or German) 1963.
irreg., no. 21, 1981. price varies. Max Niemeyer
Verlag, Pfrondorfer Str. 4, 7400 Tuebingen, W.
Germany (B.R.D.) Eds. Gerhard Mueller-Schwefe,
Friedrich Schubel.

STUDIEN ZUR INDOLOGIE UND IRANISTIK.
see HISTORY — History Of Asia

410 150　　　　　　US
STUDIES IN APPLIED PSYCHOLINGUISTICS.
1979. irreg. price varies. Plenum Publishing Corp.,
233 Spring St., New York, NY 10013. Ed. R. W.
Rieber.

400　　　　　　　　SA
STUDIES IN BANTOETALE. 1974. a. R.2.50.
University of Pretoria, Department of Bantu
Languages, Pretoria, South Africa. circ. 150.

410
STUDIES IN CHINESE TERMINOLOGY. (Text in
Chinese, English) 1956. irreg., no. 18, 1980. $3.50.
University of California, Berkeley, Center for
Chinese Studies, Institute of East Asian Studies,
Berkeley, CA 94720. Eds. John Jamieson & Cyril
Birch. (reprint service avail. from UMI)
  Formerly: Studies in Chinese Communist
Terminology (ISSN 0081-7686)

430 375.4　　　　　GW
STUDIES IN DESCRIPTIVE LINGUISTICS. (Text
in English; summaries in French, German) 1978.
irreg. price varies. Julius Groos Verlag, Hertzstr. 6,
Postfach 102423, D-6900 Heidelberg 1, W.
Germany (B.R.D.) Ed. D. Nehls. circ. 1,000. (back
issues avail.)

410　　　　　　　　NE
STUDIES IN GENERATIVE GRAMMAR. vol. 8,
1979. irreg. price varies. Foris Publications, Box
509, 3300 AM Dordrecht, Netherlands.

485 475　　　　　　NE
STUDIES IN GREEK AND LATIN LINGUISTICS.
1980. irreg. price varies. Van Gorcum, Box 43,
Assen, Netherlands.

411　　　　　　　　II
STUDIES IN INDIAN EPIGRAPHY/BHARATIYA
PURABHILEKHA PATRIKA. 1975. a.
(Epigraphical Society of India) Geetha Book House,
New Statue Circle, Mysore, India. Eds. Z. A. Desai,
Ajay Mitra Shastri. illus.

400　　　　　　　　US
STUDIES IN LANGUAGE. irreg. price varies.
Harper and Row Publishers, Inc., 10 East 53rd St.,
New York, NY 10022.

400　　　　　　　　US　ISSN 0586-6928
STUDIES IN LANGUAGE AND LINGUISTICS.
biennial. price varies. Texas Western Press,
University of Texas at El Paso, El Paso, TX 79968.

410 800　　　　　　NE　ISSN 0165-7763
STUDIES IN LANGUAGE COMPANION SERIES.
Short title: SLCS. 1979. irreg. price varies. John
Benjamins B.V., Box 52519, 1007 HA Amsterdam,
Netherlands. Eds. John W. M. Verhaar, Werner
Abraham.

410 370　　　　　　UK　ISSN 0144-3127
STUDIES IN LANGUAGE DISABILITY AND
REMEDIATION. 1976. irreg. price varies. Edward
Arnold (Publishers) Ltd., 41 Bedford Square,
London WC1B 3DQ, England.

417 480　　　　　　UK　ISSN 0081-8275
STUDIES IN MYCENAEAN INSCRIPTIONS AND
DIALECT. 1956. a. British Association for
Mycenaean Studies, Laundress Lane, Faculty
Rooms, Cambridge CB2 1SD, London WC1H 0PY,
England.

410 890　　　　　　II
STUDIES IN SEMIOTICS AND LITERATURE.
1979. irreg. price varies. Bahri Publications Pvt.
Ltd., 57 Santnagar, New Delhi 110065, India. Ed.
Ujjal Singh Bahri.

492　　　　　　　　NE　ISSN 0081-8461
STUDIES IN SEMITIC LANGUAGES AND
LINGUISTICS. 1967. irreg., vol. 12, 1981. price
varies. E. J. Brill, Oude Rijn 33a-35, Leiden,
Netherlands.

491.7　　　　　　　UK　ISSN 0081-8631
STUDIES IN THE MODERN RUSSIAN
LANGUAGE. 1967. irreg., no. 8, 1970. $60 for
latest vol. Cambridge University Press, Box 110,
Cambridge CB2 3RL, England (and 32 E. 57 St.,
New York NY 10022) Ed. D. Ward.

491　　　　　　　　RM　ISSN 0081-8860
STUDII DE SLAVISTICA. 1969. irreg. (Academia
Republicii Socialiste Romania, Institutul de
Lingvistica) Editura Academiei Republicii Socialiste
Romania, Calea Victoriei 125, Bucharest, Romania
(Subscr. to: ILEXIM, Str. 13 Decembrie Nr. 3, P.O.
Box 136-137, Bucharest, Romania) bk. rev.

410.5　　　　　　　JA
SUMMER INSTITUTE IN LINGUISTICS.
DESCRIPTIVE AND APPLIED LINGUISTICS.
(Subseries of the University's Publication 6-A) (Text
in English) 1961. a. $5. International Christian
University - Kokusai Kirisutokyo Daigaku, 3-10-2
Osawa, Mitaka, Tokyo 181, Japan. Ed. Bd. bibl.
  Continues: Summer Institute in Linguistics.
Studies in Descriptive and Applied Linguistics.

418　　　　　　　　US
SUMMER INSTITUTE OF LINGUISTICS.
LANGUAGE DATA. AFRICAN SERIES. 1971.
irreg; no. 7, 1976. $2.60-5.25. Academic
Publications, 7500 W. Camp Wisdom Rd., Dallas,
TX 75211. Ed. Dr. John Bendor-Samuel. (also avail.
in microfiche)

410　　　　　　　　US
SUMMER INSTITUTE OF LINGUISTICS.
LANGUAGE DATA. AMERINDIAN SERIES.
1973. irreg., no. 7, 1979. $2.60-5. Academic
Publications, 7500 W. Camp Wisdom Rd., Dallas,
TX 75211. bibl. charts. (also avail. in microfiche)

418　　　　　　　　US
SUMMER INSTITUTE OF LINGUISTICS.
LANGUAGE DATA. ASIAN-PACIFIC SERIES.
1971. irreg; no. 11, 1976. price varies. Academic
Publications, 7500 W. Camp Wisdom Rd., Dallas,
TX 75236. (also avail. in microfiche)

498　　　　　　　　BL
SUMMER INSTITUTE OF LINGUISTICS. SERIE
LINGUISTICA. 1974. irreg. price varies. Summer
Institute of Linguistics, Departamento de Estudos
Tecnicos, C.P. 14-2221, Brasilia 70000, Brazil. circ.
300.

410　　　　　　　　US
SUMMER INSTITUTE OF LINGUISTICS. WORK
PAPERS. vol. 21, 1977. a. Summer Institute of
Linguistics, c/o University of North Dakota, Box
8217, University Sta., Grand Forks, ND 58201. Ed.
John P. Daly.

410 572　　　　　　FI　ISSN 0355-0214
SUOMALAIS-UGRILAISEN SEURA.
AIKAKAUSKIRJA/SOCIETE FINNO-
OUGRIENNE. JOURNAL. (Text in Finnish,
English and German) 1886. a. Suomalais-Ugrilainen
Seura, Snellmaninkatu 9-11, 00170 Helsinki 17,
Finland.

SVENSKA LITTERATURSAELLSKAPET I
FINLAND. SKRIFTER. see HISTORY

410　　　　　　　　US　ISSN 0092-4563
SYNTAX AND SEMANTICS. irreg. Academic Press,
Inc., 111-5th Ave., New York, NY 10003.

410　　　　　　　　FR　ISSN 0066-9776
T.A. DOCUMENTS. 1966. irreg. price varies.
Editions Klincksieck, 11 rue de Lille, Paris 7e,
France (Dist. by: University of Alabama Press,
Drawer 2877, University, AL 35486) Ed. A.
Deweze.

400 820　　　　　　US
T S E: TULANE STUDIES IN ENGLISH. 1949. a.
Tulane University, Department of English, New
Orleans, LA 70118. Ed. Huling E. Ussery. circ.
2,000. Indexed: Abstr.Engl.Stud. M.L.A.
  Formerly: Tulane Studies in English (ISSN 0082-
6758)

410　　　　　　　　NZ
TE REO. 1958. a. NZ.$5. Linguistic Society of New
Zealand, c/o University of Auckland, Private Bag,
Auckland 1, New Zealand. bibl. circ. 350.

439.5 SW ISSN 0081-573X
TEKNISKA NOMENKLATURCENTRALEN
PUBLIKATIONER. 1941. irreg., no. 72, 1978. price
varies. Tekniska Nomenklaturcentralen - Swedish
Centre of Technical Terminology, Box 5243, S-102
45 Stockholm, Sweden.

490 II
TELUGU AKADEMI LANGUAGE MONOGRAPH
SERIES. 1974. irreg. Rs.16.25($8) Telugu Akademi,
Hyderabad 500029, India.

808.5 US ISSN 0363-8782
TEXAS SPEECH COMMUNICATION JOURNAL.
1976. a. $2.50. Texas Speech Communication
Association, North Texas State University, Dept. of
Speech Communication, Denton, TX 78203. Ed.
Keith Erickson.

418.02 NE ISSN 0046-2837
TRANSLATION NEWS. 1971. irreg. International
Translations Centre, Doelenstraat 101, 2611 NS
Delft, Netherlands. Ed. D. Van Bergeijk. bibl. circ.
800.

400 BE ISSN 0082-6049
TRAVAUX DE LINGUISTIQUE. (Text in French)
1969. irreg. price varies. ‡ Rijksuniversiteit te Gent,
Dienst voor Franse Linguistiek - State University of
Ghent, Department of French Linguistics,
Blandijnberg 2, 9000 Ghent, Belgium.

400 FR ISSN 0082-6057
TRAVAUX DE LINGUISTIQUE ET DE
LITTERATURE. 1963. 2 vols. per yr. price varies.
(Universite de Strasbourg II, Centre de Philologie et
de Litteratures Romanes) Editions Klincksieck, 11
rue de Lille, 75007 Paris, France. Ed. George
Straka.

410 FR
TRAVAUX DE LINGUISTIQUE JAPONAISE.
1974. irreg. Universite de Paris VII, Groupe de
Linguistique Japonaise, 2 Place Jussieu, 75005 Paris,
France. Ed. Andre Wlodarczyk.
 Formerly: Universite de Paris VII. Groupe de
Linguistique Japonaise. Travaux (ISSN 0339-8811)

410 700 SP
TRAZA Y BAZA; cuadernos hispanos de simbologia,
arte y literatura. 1972. a. $9. Ediciones el Albir,
Calle de Los Angeles 8, Barcelona 1, Spain. bk. rev.

400 BE ISSN 0082-6847
TURCICA; REVUE D'ETUDES TURQUES. 1969. a.
Editions Peeters s.p.r.l., B.P. 41, 2B-3000 Louvain,
Belgium. Ed. Mrs. I. Melikoff. bk. rev.

TURUN YLIOPISTO. KLASSILLISEN
FILOLOGIAN LAITOS. OPERA EX INSTITUTO
PHILOLOGIAE CLASSICAE UNIVERSITATIS
TURKUENSIS EDITA. see CLASSICAL
STUDIES

810 410 SA
U C T STUDIES IN ENGLISH. 1970. a. exchange
basis. University of Cape Town, Department of
English, Rondebosch 7700, South Africa. Ed.Bd.
adv. bk. rev. circ. 450. Indexed: M.L.A.
 Formerly(1970-1972): Studies in English.

418.02 GW
DER UEBERSETZER. 1964. m. DM.18($8) Verband
Deutschsprachiger Ueebersetzer Literarischer und
Wissenschftlicher Werke e.V., Fuerststr. 17, 7400
Tuebingen, W. Germany (B.R.D.) Ed. Klaus
Birkenhauer, Eva Bornemann. bk. rev. bibl. stat.
circ. 700. (back issues avail.)

410 UY
UNIVERSIDAD DE LA REPUBLICA. FACULTAD
DE HUMANIDADES Y CIENCIAS. REVISTA.
SERIE LINGUISTICA. N.S. 1979. irreg.
Universidad de la Republica, Facultad de
Humanidades y Ciencias, Seccion Revista, Tristan
Narvaja 1674, Montevideo, Uruguay. Dir. Beatriz
Martinez Osorio.
 Supersedes in part: Universidad de la Republica.
Facultad de Humanidades y Ciencias. Revista.

410 BL
UNIVERSIDADE DE SAO PAULO. CENTRO DE
ESTUDOS PORTUGUESES. BOLETIM
INFORMATIVO. 1975. irreg. Universidade de Sao
Paulo, Centro de Estudos Portugueses, Cidade
Universitario "Armando de Salles Oliveira", C.P.
8191, Sao Paulo, Brazil. Ed. Massaud Moises. bk.
rev. circ. 1,500.

489 IT ISSN 0072-0852
UNIVERSITA DEGLI STUDI DI GENOVA.
ISTITUTO DI FILOLOGIA CLASSICA E
MEDIEVALE. PUBBLICAZIONI. 1952. irreg.
price varies. (Universita degli Studi di Genova,
Istituto di Filologia Classica e Medievale) Tilgher-
Genova s.a.s., Via Assarotti 52, 16122 Genoa, Italy.
Ed. T. Mantero. circ. 500-1,000.

480 IT ISSN 0078-8627
UNIVERSITA DEGLI STUDI DI PALERMO.
ISTITUTO DI FILOLOGIA GRECA.
QUADERNI. 1957. irreg., 1974, no. 6. price varies.
Istituto Siciliano di Studi Bizantini e Neoellenici,
Via Noto, 34, 90141 Palermo, Italy.

450 IT ISSN 0080-4029
UNIVERSITA DEGLI STUDI DI ROMA. SCUOLA
DI FILOLOGIA MODERNA. PUBBLICAZIONI.
1955. irreg., 1967, no. 12. price varies. Universita
degli Studi di Roma, Scuola di Filologia Moderna,
11-B via Ruggero Bonghi, 00184 Rome, Italy. circ.
1,000.

491.7 891.7 CS
UNIVERSITA PALACKEHO. PEDAGOGICKA
FAKULTA. SBORNIK PRACI: RUSKY JAZYK A
LITERATURA. (Text in Czech or Russian,
summaries in Czech, English, German, Russian)
1972. irreg. price varies. Statni Pedagogicke
Nakladatelstvi, Ostrovni 30, 113 01 Prague 1,
Czechoslovakia. Ed. Ljubov Ordeltova. bibl. circ.
300. Key Title: Rusky Jazyk a Literatura.

410 RM
UNIVERSITATEA "AL. I. CUZA" DIN IASI.
ANALELE STIINTIFICE. SECTIUNEA 3E:
LINGVISTICA. (Text in Romanian; Summaries in
Foreign Languages) 1955. a. $10. Universitatea "Al.
I. Cuza" din Iasi, Calea 23 August Nr.11, Jassy,
Romania (Subscr. to: ILEXIM, Str. 13 Decembrie
Nr. 3, P.O. Box 136-137, Bucharest, Romania) bk.
rev. abstr. charts. illus.

410 RM
UNIVERSITATEA BUCURESTI. ANALELE.
FILOLOGIE. (Text in Romanian, English, French,
Italian; summaries in Russian) a. $10. Universitatea
Bucuresti, Bd. Gh. Gheorghiu-Dej Nr. 64,
Bucharest, Romania.

400 RM ISSN 0082-4461
UNIVERSITATEA DIN TIMISOARA. ANALELE.
STIINTE FILOLOGICE.* a. Universitatea din
Timisoara, Bd. Vasile Pirvan Nr. 4, Timisoara,
Romania (Subscr. to: ILEXIM, Calea Grivitei 64-
66, P.O. Box 136-137, Bucharest, Romania)

410 BE ISSN 0577-1765
UNIVERSITE CATHOLIQUE DE LOUVAIN.
CENTRE INTERNATIONAL DE
DIALECTOLOGIE GENERALE. TRAVAUX.
1955. irreg. price varies. Universite Catholique de
Louvain, Centre International de Dialectologie
Generale, Blijde-Inkomststraat 22, 3000 Louvain,
Belgium.

400 900 BE ISSN 0076-1311
UNIVERSITE CATHOLIQUE DE LOUVAIN.
RECUEIL DE TRAVAUX D'HISTOIRE ET DE
PHILOLOGIE. (Text in English, Flemish, French)
1904. irreg., 6th series, no. 12, 1977. price varies.
Editions Peeters s.p.r.l., B.P. 41, B-3000 Louvain,
Belgium.

440 840 DK
UNIVERSITE D'ODENSE. ETUDES ROMANES.
(Text in French and English) 1971. irreg., no. 11,
1978. price varies. Odense University Press, 36,
Pjentedamsgade, DK-5000 Odense, Denmark. (back
issues avail.)

400 FR ISSN 0068-0273
UNIVERSITE DE BORDEAUX. COLLECTION
SINOLOGIQUE. 1969. irreg. 27 F. Universite de
Bordeaux, Societe Bordelaise de Diffusion de
Travaux des Lettres et Sciences Humaines, Domaine
Universitaire, 33405 Talence, France.

414 FR
UNIVERSITE DE GRENOBLE III. INSTITUT DE
PHONETIQUE. BULLETIN. 1972. a. 25 F. per
issue. Universite de Grenoble III (Universite des
Langues et Lettres), Institut de Phonetique,
Domaine Universitaire de Saint-Martin-d'Heres, B.
P. 25-X, 38040 Grenoble Cedex, France.

410 FR
UNIVERSITE DE GRENOBLE III. INSTITUT DE
PHONETIQUE. TRAVAUX: SERIE A:
MANUALS. irreg. price varies. Universite de
Grenoble III (Universite des Langues et Lettres),
Institut de Phonetique, Domaine Universitaire de
Saint-Martin-d'Heres, Boite Postale 25-X, 38040
Grenoble Cedex, France.
 Formerly: Universite de Grenoble. Institut de
Phonetique. Manuels. Serie A (ISSN 0085-1264)

410 FR ISSN 0085-1272
UNIVERSITE DE GRENOBLE III. INSTITUT DE
PHONETIQUE. TRAVAUX. SERIE B: ETUDES
LINGUISTIQUES. 1967. irreg. price varies.
Universite de Grenoble III (Universite des Langues
et Lettres), Institut de Phonetique, Domaine
Universitaire de Saint-Martin-d'Heres, B.P. 25-X,
38040 Grenoble Cedex, France.

UNIVERSITE DE NANCY II. CENTRE DE
RECHERCHES ET D'APPLICATIONS
PEDAGOGIQUES EN LANGUES. MELANGES.
see EDUCATION — Teaching Methods And
Curriculum

479 FR ISSN 0081-5918
UNIVERSITE DE STRASBOURG II. CENTRE DE
PHILOLOGIE ET LITTERATURES ROMANES.
ACTES ET COLLOQUES. 1963. irreg. price varies.
(Universite de Strasbourg II, Centre de Philologie et
de Litteratures Romanes) Editions Klincksieck, 11
rue de Lille, 75007 Paris, France.

400 FR ISSN 0081-5934
UNIVERSITE DE STRASBOURG II. INSTITUT DE
PHONETIQUE. TRAVAUX. 1970. a. exchange
basis. Universite de Strasbourg II, Institut de
Phonetique, 25 rue du Soleil, Strasbourg, France.

UNIVERSITE DE TUNIS. ECOLE NORMALE
SUPERIEURE. SECTION A: LETTRES ET
SCIENCES HUMAINES. SERIE 1: LANGUE ET
LITTERATURE. see LITERATURE

410 ZR
UNIVERSITE NATIONALE DU ZAIRE,
LUBUMBASHI. CENTRE DE LINGUISTIQUE
THEORIQUE ET APPLIQUEE. BULLETIN
D'INFORMATION. irreg., no. 23, 1978. Universite
Nationale du Zaire, Lubumbashi, Centre de
Linguistique Theorique et Appliquee, B.P. 1607,
Lubumbashi, Zaire.

UNIVERSITE SAINT-JOSEPH. FACULTE DES
LETTRES ET DES SCIENCES HUMAINES.
RECHERCHE. SERIE A: LANGUE ARABE ET
PENSEE ISLAMIQUE. see RELIGIONS AND
THEOLOGY — Islamic

400 US
UNIVERSITY OF CALIFORNIA, BERKELEY.
LANGUAGE BEHAVIOR RESEARCH
LABORATORY. MONOGRAPH SERIES. 1973,
no. 4. irreg. price varies. ‡ University of California,
Berkeley, Language Behavior Research Laboratory,
2220 Piedmont Ave., Berkeley, CA 94720.

400 US
UNIVERSITY OF CALIFORNIA, BERKELEY.
LANGUAGE BEHAVIOR RESEARCH
LABORATORY, WORKING PAPER SERIES.
1967. irreg., no. 47, 1977. price varies. University of
California, Berkeley, Language-Behavior Research
Laboratory, 2229 Piedmont Ave., Berkeley, CA
94720.

400 US ISSN 0068-6484
UNIVERSITY OF CALIFORNIA PUBLICATIONS
IN LINGUISTICS. 1945. irreg. price varies.
University of California Press, 2223 Fulton St.,
Berkeley, CA 94720.

400 US ISSN 0068-6492
UNIVERSITY OF CALIFORNIA PUBLICATIONS
IN MODERN PHILOLOGY. 1909. irreg. price
varies. University of California Press, 2223 Fulton
St., Berkeley, CA 94720.

410 GH
UNIVERSITY OF GHANA. INSTITUTE OF
AFRICAN STUDIES. COLLECTED
LANGUAGE NOTES. no. 13, 1972. irreg. price
varies. University of Ghana, Institute of African
Studies, Box 73, Legon, Ghana.

494 II
UNIVERSITY OF KERALA. DEPARTMENT OF TAMIL. RESEARCH PAPERS. (Text in English or Tamil) 1970. a. University of Kerala, Department of Tamil, Kariavattom, Trivandrum 685001, Kerala, India.
   Continues (vol. 5, 1974): University of Kerala. Department of Tamil. Journal.

490 II ISSN 0076-2237
UNIVERSITY OF MADRAS. KANNADA SERIES.* irreg. University of Madras, Chepauk, Triplicane, Madras 600005, Tamil Nadu, India.

490 II ISSN 0076-2245
UNIVERSITY OF MADRAS. MALAYALAM SERIES.* irreg. University of Madras, Chepauk, Triplicane, Madras 600005, Tamil Nadu, India.

490 II ISSN 0076-2261
UNIVERSITY OF MADRAS. SANSKRIT SERIES.* irreg. University of Madras, Chepauk, Triplicane, Madras 600005, Tamil Nadu, India.

490 II ISSN 0076-227X
UNIVERSITY OF MADRAS. TAMIL SERIES.* irreg. University of Madras, Chepauk, Triplicane, Madras 600005, Tamil Nadu, India.

490 II ISSN 0076-2288
UNIVERSITY OF MADRAS. TELUGU SERIES.* irreg. University of Madras, Chepauk, Triplicane, Madras 600005, Tamil Nadu, India.

490 II ISSN 0076-2296
UNIVERSITY OF MADRAS. URDU SERIES.* irreg. University of Madras, Chepauk, Triplicane, Madras 600005, Tamil Nadu, India.

495.1 MY ISSN 0553-0644
UNIVERSITY OF MALAYA. CHINESE LANGUAGE SOCIETY. JOURNAL/MAJALLAH PANTAI/PAN T'AI HSUEH PAO. (Text in Chinese, English, and Malay) irreg. University of Malaya, Chinese Language Society, Kuala Lumpur, Malaysia. illus.

UNIVERSITY OF MANITOBA ANTHROPOLOGY PAPERS see ANTHROPOLOGY

410 US ISSN 0085-123X
UNIVERSITY OF NORTHERN COLORADO. MUSEUM OF ANTHROPOLOGY. OCCASIONAL PUBLICATIONS IN ANTHROPOLOGY. LINGUISTICS SERIES. 1970. irreg. price varies. University of Northern Colorado, Museum of Anthropology, Attn. George E. Fay, Ed., Greeley, CO 80639. circ. 300. (processed)

400 US ISSN 0079-0672
UNIVERSITY OF PENNSYLVANIA. DEPARTMENT OF LINGUISTICS. TRANSFORMATIONS AND DISCOURSE ANALYSIS PAPERS. 1957. irreg., 1971, no. 87. free. University of Pennsylvania, Linguistics Research Project, Williams Hall, Philadelphia, PA 19174. Ed. Henry Hiz.

491.7 US
UNIVERSITY OF PITTSBURGH. DEPARTMENT OF SLAVIC LANGUAGES AND LITERATURES. SLAVIC SERIES. (Text in Russian; summaries in English) 1972. biennial. price varies. University of Pittsburgh, Department of Slavic Languages & Literatures, 119 LF, Pittsburgh, PA 15260. Ed. Nikolai P. Poltoratzky.

491.1 II ISSN 0079-3809
UNIVERSITY OF POONA. CENTRE OF ADVANCED STUDY IN SANSKRIT. PUBLICATIONS. (Text in English and Sanskrit) 1965. irreg. price varies. University of Poona, Centre of Advanced Study in Sanskrit, Ganeshkhind, Poona 411007, India.

UNIVERSITY OF RAJASTHAN. STUDIES IN SANSKRIT AND HINDI. see LITERATURE

410 SW
UNIVERSITY OF STOCKHOLM. INSTITUTE OF LINGUISTICS. MONOGRAPHS. Abbbreviated title: M I L U S. (Text in English) 1974. irreg., no. 5, 1979. Kr.25. Stockholms Universitet, Institute of Linguistics, Drottninggatan 116, Box 6801, S-106 91 Stockholm. Sweden. Eds. Benny Brodda, Bjoern Lindblom.

400 AT ISSN 0042-0093
UNIVERSITY OF SYDNEY. AUSTRALIAN LANGUAGE RESEARCH CENTRE. OCCASIONAL PAPERS. 1964. irreg. price varies. ‡ University of Sydney, Australian Language Research Centre, c/o Secretary, Dept. of English, Sydney, N.S.W. 2006, Australia. Ed. R. D. Eagleson. circ. 400. Indexed: Social. Abstr.

479 CN ISSN 0082-5336
UNIVERSITY OF TORONTO ROMANCE SERIES. (Text in English; occasionally in French) 1949. irreg. price varies. (Department of Romance Languages) University of Toronto Press, Front Campus, Toronto, Ont. M5S 1A6, Canada (and 33 East Tupper St., Buffalo, N.Y. 14203) (also avail. in microfiche)

410 CS ISSN 0083-4173
UNIVERZITA KOMENSKEHO. FILOZOFICKA FAKULTA. ZBORNIK: PHILOLOGICA. (Text and summaries in German, Slovak and several other languages) 1949. a. exchange basis. ‡ Univerzita Komenskeho, Filozoficka Fakulta, Gondova 2, 806 01 Bratislava, Czechoslovakia. Ed. Alexander Csanda. illus. maps. circ. 649.

491.86 891.86 CS
UNIVERZITA PALACKEHO. PEDAGOGICKA FAKULTA. SBORNIK PRACI: CESKY JAZYK A LITERATURA. (Text in Czech; summaries and contents page in Czech, German and Russian) irreg, vol. 2, 1973. 28 Kcs. price varies. Statni Pedagogicke Nakladatelstvi, Ostrovni 30, 113 01 Prague 1, Czechoslovakia. Eds. Eva Doupalova, Miloslav Krbec. charts.

410 PL ISSN 0083-4378
UNIWERSYTET JAGIELLONSKI. ZESZYTY NAUKOWE. PRACE JEZYKOZNAWCZE. (Vol. 3- called also vol. 6- , continuing the volume numbering of Seria Nauk Spolecznych, Filologia, which it supersedes) (Text in Polish; summaries in French) 1956. a. price varies. Panstwowe Wydawnictwo Naukowe, Miodowa 10, Warsaw, Poland (Dist. by Ars Polona-Ruch, Krakowskie Przedmiescie 7, Warsaw, Poland)

491.47 PL
UNIWERSYTET SLASKI W KATOWICACH. PRACE JEZYKOZNAWCZE. (Subseries of its: Prace Naukowe) (Summaries in English or French) 1969. irreg. available on exchange. Uniwersytet Slaski w Katowicach, Ul. Bankowa 14, 40-007 Katowice, Poland.

410 GW
UNTERSUCHUNGEN ZUR ROMANISCHEN PHILOLOGIE. 1967. irreg., no.13, 1979. price varies. Verlag Anton Hain GmbH, Adelheidstr. 2, Postfach 1220, 6240 Koenigstein, W. Germany (B.R.D.) Eds. W.T. Elwert, H. Kroell.

479 GW ISSN 0083-4580
UNTERSUCHUNGEN ZUR SPRACH- UND LITERATURGESCHICHTE DER ROMANISCHEN VOELKER. 1959. irreg., vol. 10, 1981. price varies. (Akademie der Wissenschaften und der Literatur, Mainz, Kommission fuer Romanische Philologie) Franz Steiner Verlag GmbH, Friedrichstr. 24, Postfach 5529, 6200 Wiesbaden, W. Germany (B.R.D.)

410 FR ISSN 0563-9786
VIA DOMITIA. 1954. a. Universite de Toulouse II (le Mirail), Service de Publications, 56 rue du Taur, 31000 Toulouse, France. illus.

410 NE ISSN 0165-7666
VICUS CUADERNOS: LINGUISTICA. (Text in Spanish and English) 1977. a. fl.60. John Benjamins B.V., Amsteldijk 44, Box 52519, 1007 HA Amsterdam, Netherlands. Ed. M.B. Fontanella de Weinberg. charts. illus. index. (back issues avail.)

410 US ISSN 0083-646X
VIRGINIA PLACE NAME SOCIETY. OCCASIONAL PAPERS. 1961. irreg. $4. ‡ Virginia Place Name Society, c/o Manuscripts Depatment, University of Virginia Library, Charlottesville, VA 22901. Ed. Vesta Lee Gordon. circ. 100.

491 954 II ISSN 0083-6621
VISHVESHVARANAND INDOLOGICAL SERIES. (Text in English and Sanskrit) 1950. irreg., vol. 68, 1976. price varies. Vishveshvaranand Vedic Research Institute, P. O. Sadhu Ashram, Hoshiarpur 146021, Punjab, India. Ed. Vishva Bandhu.

491.7 UR
VOPROSY RUSSKOGO YAZYKOZNANIYA. 1976. irreg. 1.21 Rub. per issue. Izdatel'stvo Moskovaskii Universitet, Leninskie Gory, Moscow V-234, U.S.S.R. Ed. K. Gorshkova. circ. 4,760.

410 NR ISSN 0331-0531
WEST AFRICAN JOURNAL OF MODERN LANGUAGES/REVUE OUEST AFRICAINE DES LANGUES VIVANTES. 1976. a. $20. West African Modern Languages Association, c/o University of Maiduguri, Department of Languages and Linguistics, Borno State, Nigeria. Ed. C.M.B. Brann. adv. bk. rev. circ. 1,000.

410 CN
WESTERN CONFERENCES ON LINGUISTICS. PROCEEDINGS OF THE ANNUAL MEETING. no. 8, 1979. a. Linguistic Research Inc., Box 5677, Sta. L, Edmonton, Alta. T6C 4G1, Canada.

WHERE TO LEARN ENGLISH IN GREAT BRITAIN. see EDUCATION — Guides To Schools And Colleges

420 820 AU ISSN 0083-9914
WIENER BEITRAEGE ZUR ENGLISCHEN PHILOLOGIE. (Text in English, German) 1895. irreg., vol. 77, 1977. price varies. Wilhelm Braumueller, Universitaets-Verlagsbuchhandlung GmbH, Servitengasse 5, A-1092 Vienna, Austria. Ed. Siegfried Korninger. index. circ. 600.

400 AU ISSN 0083-9922
WIENER BEITRAEGE ZUR KULTURGESCHICHTE UND LINGUISTIK. 1930. irreg., vol. 19, 1976. S.210. (Universitaet Wien, Institut fuer Voelkerkunde) Verlag Ferdinand Berger und Soehne OHG, Wienerstr. 21-23, A-3580 Horn, Austria.

400 800 AU ISSN 0084-0033
WIENER ROMANISTISCHE ARBEITEN. (Text in French, German) 1962. a. price varies. Wilhelm Braumueller, Universitaets-Verlagsbuchhandlung GmbH, Servitengasse 5, A-1092 Vienna, Austria. Ed. Georg Rabuse. index. circ. 600.

491.7 AU ISSN 0084-0041
WIENER SLAVISTISCHES JAHRBUCH/ VIENNESE SLAVONIC YEARBOOK. (Text in English, French, German, Polish and Russian) 1950. a. DM.98. (Universitaet Wien, Institut fuer Slavische Philologie) Hermann Boehlaus Nachf., Schmalzhofgasse 4, Postfach 167, A-1061 Vienna, Austria. Eds. J. Hamm, F.V. Mares, G. Wytrzens. adv. bk. rev. bibl. illus. circ. 500.

400 AU ISSN 0084-005X
WIENER STUDIEN. ZEITSCHRIFT FUER KLASSISCHE PHILOLOGIE UND PATRISTIK. (Text in Ancient Greek, English, German and Latin) 1897. a. DM.98. (Universitaet Wien, Institut fuer Klassische Philologie) Hermann Boehlaus Nachf., Schmalzhofgasse 4, Postfach 167, A-1061 Vienna, Austria. Ed.Bd. adv. bk. rev. bibl. illus. circ. 800.

410 US ISSN 0163-0016
WORKING PAPERS IN APPLIED LINGUISTICS. no. 6, 1979. irreg. (approx. 2/yr.) free exchange. Ohio University, Department of Linguistics, 204 Gondy Hall, Athens, OH 45701. Eds. James Coady, Elona K. Lucas. abstr. bibl. charts. illus. circ. 250.

491.85 PL ISSN 0084-2990
WROCLAWSKIE TOWARZYSTWO NAUKOWE. KOMISJA JEZYKOWA. ROZPRAWY. (Text in English, German and Polish) 1957. irreg., vol. 11, 1978. price varies. Ossolineum, Publishing House of the Polish Academy of Sciences, Rynek 9, Wroclaw, Poland (Dist. by Ars Polona-Ruch, Krakowskie Przedmiescie 7, Warsaw, Poland)

400 PL ISSN 0075-5281
WYZSZA SZKOLA PEDAGOGICZNA, KATOWICE. ZESZYTY NAUKOWE. SEKCJA JEZYKOZNAWSTWA.* 1959. a. price varies. Wyzsza Szkola Pedagogiczna, Katowice, Ul. Szkolna 9, Katowice, Poland.

490   PL
WYZSZA SZKOLA PEDAGOGICZNA, KRAKOW. PRACE JEZYKOZNAWCZE. 1970. irreg. 128.00 Zl. Wyzsza Szkola Pedagogiczna, Krakow, Podchorazych 2, 30-084 Krakow, Poland. Ed. Eugeniusz Pawlowski. illus.

400   PL   ISSN 0324-9050
WYZSZA SZKOLA PEDAGOGICZNA, OPOLE. ZESZYTY NAUKOWE. FILOLOGIA POLSKA. irreg., vol. 28, 1980. price varies; available on exchange. Wyzsza Szkola Pedagogiczna, Opole, Oleska 48, 45-052 Opole, Poland (Dist. by: Ars Polona-Ruch, Krakowskie Przedmiescie 7, Warsaw, Poland)

400   US   ISSN 0513-4412
YALE LINGUISTIC SERIES. 1963. irreg., latest, 1978. Yale University Press, 92A Yale Sta., New Haven, CT 06520.

492.49   US   ISSN 0044-0442
YIDISHE SHPRAKH/YIDDISH LANGUAGE. (Text in Yiddish) 1941. a. $15. Yivo Institute for Jewish Research, 1048 Fifth Avenue, New York, NY 10028. Ed. Mordkhe Schaechter. bk. rev. circ. 2,000. (also avail. in microform) Indexed: M.L.A.

410   UK   ISSN 0513-2762
YORKSHIRE DIALECT SOCIETY. SUMMER BULLETIN. 1953. a. £1. Yorkshire Dialect Society, c/o S. Ellis, School of English, University of Leeds, Leeds LS2 9JT, England. Ed. B. T. Dyson. bk. rev. circ. 750.

410   UK
YORKSHIRE DIALECT SOCIETY TRANSACTIONS. 1897. a. £1. Yorkshire Dialect Society, School of English, University of Leeds, Leeds LS2 9JT, England. Ed. Dr. P. Anderson. circ. 800. (also avail. in microfiche)

410   YU
YUGOSLAV SERBO-CROATIAN-ENGLISH CONTRASTIVE PROJECT. SERIES B: STUDIES. (Text in English) 1969. irreg. 50 din. Institute of Linguistics, Zagreb, Djure Salaja 3, 41000 Zagreb, Yugoslavia. Ed. Rudolf Filipovic. circ. 500. Indexed: Sociol.Abstr.

491   YU
ZBORNIK ZAGREBACKE SLAVISTICKE SKOLE. 1973. irreg. Medjunarodni Slavisticki Centar SR Hrvatske, Djure Salaja 3, Zagreb, Yugoslavia. (Co-sponsor: Sveucilista u Zagrebu, Filozofski Fakulteti) Eds. Franjo Grcevic and Mladen Kuzmanovic.

491.6   GW   ISSN 0084-5302
ZEITSCHRIFT FUER CELTISCHE PHILOLOGIE. (Text in English, French, German or Irish) 1904; no issues published between 1944 and 1952. irreg. DM.92. Max Niemeyer Verlag, Pfrondorfer Str. 4, 7400 Tuebingen, W. Germany (B.R.D.)

400   GW   ISSN 0341-0838
ZEITSCHRIFT FUER DIALEKTOLOGIE UND LINGUISTIK. BEIHEFTE. irreg., vol. 38, 1978. price varies. Franz Steiner Verlag GmbH, Friedrichstr. 24, Postfach 5529, 6200 Wiesbaden, W. Germany (B.R.D.)

440   GW   ISSN 0341-0811
ZEITSCHRIFT FUER FRANZOESISCHE SPRACHE UND LITERATUR. BEIHEFTE.NEUE FOLGE. irreg., vol. 7, 1981. price varies. Franz Steiner Verlag GmbH, Friedrichstr. 24, Postfach 5529, 6200 Wiesbaden, W. Germany (B.R.D.) Eds. H. Stimm, A. Noyer-Weidner.

400   GW   ISSN 0084-5396
ZEITSCHRIFT FUER ROMANISCHE PHILOLOGIE. BEIHEFTE. (Text in German or French) 1906. irreg., no. 182, 1981. Max Niemeyer Verlag, Pfrondorfer Str. 4, 7400 Tuebingen, W. Germany (B.R.D.) Ed. Kurt Baldinger.

LINGUISTICS — Abstracting, Bibliographies, Statistics

439.3 016   NE   ISSN 0045-186X
BIBLIOGRAFIE VAN DE NEDERLANDSE TAAL-EN LITERATUUR WETENSCHAP. 1970. a. fl.55. Nederlands Letterkundig Museum en Documentatiecentrum, Juffrouw Idastraat 11, The Hague, Netherlands. Ed.Bd. 5-yr cum. 1975.

BIBLIOGRAPHIE LINGUISTISCHER LITERATUR. see *LITERATURE* — *Abstracting, Bibliographies, Statistics*

418.02 011   GW   ISSN 0009-1944
CHARTOTHECA TRANSLATIONUM ALPHABETICA; international bibliography of translations on index cards, in 160 series. 1954. m, with annual and quinquennial compilations. DM.390. Hans W. Bentz Verlag, Wittkopstr. 16, D-4500 Osnabroeck, W. Germany (B.R.D.) Ed. Margret Bentz. bibl. circ. 660.

410 016   US
CURRENT ESPERANTO BOOK LIST. (Text in English, Esperanto) 1964. s-a. $1. Esperanto League for North America, Box 1129, El Cerrito, CA 94530. bk. rev. bibl. stat. circ. 2,000.

400 016   US
DICTIONARIES, ENCYCLOPEDIAS, AND OTHER WORD-RELATED BOOKS. irreg., latest 2nd edt. Gale Research Company, Book Tower, Detroit, MI 48226. Ed. Annie M. Brewer.

400 016   GW
FACHWOERTERBUECHER UND LEXIKA. EIN INTERNATIONALES VERZEICHNIS/INTERNATIONAL BIBLIOGRAPHY OF DICTIONARIES. irreg., 6th ed., 1977. K. G. Saur Verlag KG, Poessenbacherstr. 12 B, Postfach 711009, 8000 Munich 71, W. Germany (B.R.D.) adv.
Formerly: Internationale Bibliographie der Fachwoerterbuecher (ISSN 0074-9702)

410   CK
INSTITUTO LINGUISTICO DE VERANO EN COLOMBIA. BIBLIOGRAFIA. irreg. Instituto Linguistico de Verano en Colombia, Apartado Aereo 27744, Bogota, Colombia. Ed. Nancy L. Morse.

016 410   NE
LINGUISTIC BIBLIOGRAPHY. (Text in English and French) 1949. a. fl.195($102.65) (International Permanent Committee of Linguistics) Martinus Nijhoff, Box 566, 2501 CN The Hague, Netherlands (U.S. addr.: Kluwer Academic Publishers Group, 160 Old Derby St., Hingham, MA 02043) Eds. J. J. Beylsmit, J. C. Rijlaarsdam.

M L A DIRECTORY OF PERIODICALS; a guide to journals and series in languages and literatures. (Modern Language Association of America) see *LITERATURE* — *Abstracting, Bibliographies, Statistics*

479 016   GW   ISSN 0080-388X
ROMANISCHE BIBLIOGRAPHIE/BIBLIOGRAPHIE ROMANE/ROMANCE BIBLIOGRAPHY. (Supplement to: Zeitschrift fuer Romanische Philologie) (Text in German, French and English) 1965. irreg. price varies. Max Niemeyer Verlag, Pfrondorfer Str. 4, 7400 Tuebingen, W. Germany (B.R.D.) Ed. Gustav Ineichen.

808.5 371.9   US   ISSN 0081-3656
SPEECH INDEX; an index to 259 collections of orations and speeches for various occasions. 1935. irreg., 1966, 4th ed. price varies. Scarecrow Press, Inc., 52 Liberty St., Box 656, Metuchen, NJ 08840. Ed. Roberta B. Sutton. circ. 3,000.

400 016   US
SUMMER INSTITUTE OF LINGUISTICS. PUBLICATIONS CATALOG. 1968. a. Academic Publications, 7500 W. Camp Wisdom Rd., Dallas, TX 75236. circ. 7,000.

YEAR'S WORK IN MODERN LANGUAGE STUDIES. see *LITERATURE* — *Abstracting, Bibliographies, Statistics*

LITERARY AND POLITICAL REVIEWS

323.4   US
A IS A; writings on freedom and individualism. 1971. irreg. $4 for 12 issues. Mega, 9730 Hyne Rd., Brighton, MI 48116. Ed. Dale Haviland. adv. bk. rev. movie rev. play rev. illus. circ. 500. (back issues avail.)
Formerly: A Is A Newsletter (ISSN 0044-569X)

ABHANDLUNGEN ZUR KUNST-, MUSIK- UND LITERATURWISSENSCHAFT. see *ART*

061   CN
ACADEMIE DES SCIENCES MORALES ET POLITIQUES, MONTREAL. TRAVAUX ET COMMUNICATIONS. 1973. irreg. Editions Paulines, 250 Nord Bd. St. Francois, Sherbrooke, Quebec, Canada.

ACADEMIE ROYALE DE LANGUE ET DE LITTERATURE FRANCAISES. ANNUAIRES. see *LINGUISTICS*

056.1   VE
ACTUALIDADES. 1976. irreg. Bol.$4 per no. Centro de Estudios Latinoamericanos "Romulo Gallegos", Departamento de Documentacion e Intercambio de Informacion, Apdo. Postal 75667, Caracas 1062, Venezuela. bk. rev.

808.8   US
AIEEE. 1974. irreg. free to individuals. Alphaville Books, Box 3424, Charlottesville, VA 22903. Ed. Bd. adv. illus. circ. 900. (back issues avail.)

056.9   BL
ALMANAQUE; cadernos de literatura e ensaio. 1976. irreg. Editora Brasiliense, Rua Barao de Itapetininga 93, 01042 Sao Paulo, Brazil.

700   PE   ISSN 0570-4006
ANUARIO CULTURAL DEL PERU. (Publication suspended 1959-1977) 1954. a. Libreria-Editorial Juan Mejia Baca, Azangaro 722, Lima, Peru. Ed. Julio Vargas Prada.

800   AG
APUNTES DE LA LINEA. irreg. Diagonal Norte 1142, 2 Piso, Buenos Aires, Argentina. Ed. Julia Constenza. illus.

860   VE
ARAISA. 1975. irreg. Centro de Estudios Latinoamericanos Romulo Gallegos, Departamento de Documentacion e Intercambio de Informacion, Apdo. Postal 75667, Caracas 1062, Venezuela. bk. rev.

056.1   VE
ARTE Y VIDA; hacia un nuevo mundo. 1977. irreg. Arte y Vida Editorial, Apdo. 51494, Caracas, Zona 105, Venezuela.

056.9   BL
ATLANTICO; cadernos de cultura. (Text in Portuguese, Spanish) irreg. Rua Pires da Mota 954, Apdo 91, Ila Palam, 01529 Sao Paulo, Brazil. illus.

820   UK
BACONIANA. 1885. a. £1. ‡ Francis Bacon Society Inc., Canonbury Tower, Islington, London N.1, England. Ed. Bd. bk. rev. bibl. index in prep.

800   US   ISSN 0005-5859
BARAT REVIEW; a journal of literature and the arts. 1966. s-a. $8. Barat College, Lake Forest, IL 60045. Ed. Lauri S. Lee. bk. rev. film rev. play rev. illus. cum.index. circ. 2,000.

808.8   US   ISSN 0149-0354
BARATARIA. 1974. irreg. $5. New South Press, Box 15060, New Orleans, LA 70175. Ed. Bd. bk. rev. illus. circ. 1,000. (tabloid format)
Formerly: Barataria Review.

741.5 808.87   US   ISSN 0091-2220
BEST EDITORIAL CARTOONS OF THE YEAR. 1973. a. $11.95 hardcover; 5.95 paperback. (Association of American Editorial Cartoonists) Pelican Publishing Co., Inc., c/o Milburn Calhoun, Pub., 630 Burmaster St., Gretna, LA 70058. Ed. Charles Brooks. circ. 6,000.

LITERARY AND POLITICAL REVIEWS

051　　　　　US　ISSN 0092-5306
BEST OF NATIONAL LAMPOON. (No. 2 Not Published) 1971. irreg. $2.50 single issue. ‡ National Lampoon, Inc., 635 Madison Ave., New York, NY 10022. Ed. Henry Beard. illus. circ. 400,000.

059　　　　　NE
BIBLIOTEKA SAMIZDATA. no. 8, 1977. irreg. price varies. Alexander Herzen Foundation, Amstel 268, Amsterdam, Netherlands.

808.87　　　　　US
BIGGEST GREATEST CRACKED ANNUAL. a. $1.25. Major Magazines, Inc. (Subsidiary of: Candar Publishing Corp.) 235 Park Ave. South, New York, NY 10003. circ. 425,000.

808.8 910.03　　　　　US
BLACK FORUM. 1975. 1/yr. $3. Black Forum Magazine, Box 1090, Bronx, NY 10451. Ed. Rejish Windham. adv. bk. rev. illus. circ. 4,000. (back issues avail.)

814　　　　　US　ISSN 0006-8233
BOTH SIDES NOW. 1969. irreg., 6-12/yr. $2 for 10 issues. Free People Inc., Box 13079, 1232 Laura St., Jacksonville, FL 32206. adv. bk. rev. circ. 4,000. (also avail. in microform from BLH)

817.5　　　　　CN　ISSN 0707-7319
BREATHING. 1978. irreg. Can.$5. Breathing Enterprises, Box 55, Sta. Z, Toronto, Ont. M5N 2Z3, Canada. illus.
　Wit and humour

830　　　　　GW
BRECHT-JAHRBUCH. (Vol. 1-3 published by Athenaeum-Verlag GmbH) (Text in English, French, German) 1974. a. DM.7. (Internationale Brecht-Gesellschaft) Suhrkamp Verlag, Lindenstr. 29-35, 6000 Frankfurt 1, W. Germany (B.R.D.) (Subscr. to: John Fuegi, University of Wisconsin, Department of Comparative Literature, Milwaukee, WI 53201) Ed. John Fuegi. bk. rev. play rev. circ. 10,000.
　Formerly: Brecht Heute.

053.1　　　　　GW
BUNTE BLAETTER. 1975. a. DM.5. Literarische Union e V., Schulstr. 8, 6645 Beckingen 1, W. Germany (B.R.D.) Ed. Maria-Magdalena Durben. adv. bk. rev. bibl. circ. 1,000. (back issues avail.)

808.8　　　　　US
CHIMAERA; undergraduate literary magazine. 1971. irreg (3-4/yr) free. Seton Hall University, Student Center, South Orange, NJ 07079. Ed. Edward O'Toole. bk. rev. film rev. play rev. illus. circ. 2,000. (tabloid format)

059　　　　　GR
CHRONIKO; yearbook about Greek culture. 1970. a. Dr.300($10) Athens Cultural Center, 7 Xenofontos St., Athens 118, Greece. Ed. A. Baharian.

808.8　　　　　US
COASTLINE MAGAZINE. 1973. irreg. $5. New Horizons Communications Group Press, Box 914, Culver City, CA 90230 (Or 3718 Clarington Ave., Los Angeles, CA 90034) Ed. Bd. adv. bk. rev. illus. circ. 1,000. (back issues avail.)

056.9　　　　　BL
COLECAO TESTEMUNHOS. 1977. irreg. Editora Versus Ltda, Rua Capote Valente 376, CEP 05409, Sao Paulo, S.P., Brazil. Eds.Omar de Barros Filho, Rui Veiga.

COLECCAO N'GOLA. see HISTORY — History Of Africa

056.1　　　　　AG
COLECCION ENSAYOS. no. 16, 1976. irreg. Editorial Plus Ultra, Viamonte 1755, 1055 Buenos Aires, Argentina.

847　　　　　FR
COLLECTION "HUMOR D'AUJOURD'HUI". 1976. irreg. 18 F. Editions Seghers, 6 Place Saint Sulpice, 75006 Paris, France.

840　　　　　CN
COLLECTION LIGNES QUEBECIOSES. irreg. price varies. Presses de l'Universite de Montreal, C.P. 6128, Succ. A, Montreal, Que. H3C 3J7, Canada. (reprint service avail. from UMI)
　Formerly: Collection Lignes Quebecioses. Textuelles.

800 320　　　　　FR
CONTINENT. 1975. irreg. Editions Gallimard, 5 rue Sebastien-Bottin, 75007 Paris, France.
　Literary and political review of translations from Russian

056.1　　　　　UY
DESTABANDA. 1977. irreg. Mario A. Aiello, Ed. and Pub., Gaboto 1918, Montevideo, Uruguay.

800 700　　　　　US
DIRIGO: ME. Variant title: ME. 1980. irreg. (approx. q.) $10. Pittore Euferico, Box 1132, Peter Stuyvesant Sta., New York, NY 10009. Ed. Charles J. Stanley. illus. circ. 1,500.

051 614.7　　　　　CN　ISSN 0085-011X
EARTH AND YOU; vehicle of current ideas for modern men. 1970. a. Can.$2. T. Toth, Ed. & Pub., 1608 Eglinton Ave. W., Toronto, Ont. M6E 2G8., Canada. circ. 1,000. (back issues avail.)

056.9　　　　　BL
EDICOES CADERNOS CULTURAIS; uma revista de cultura do nordeste para o Brasil. irreg. Cr.$10 per no. (Universidade Federal de Pernambuco) Editora Universitaria, Recife, Brazil. illus.

056.1　　　　　UY
EN EL NUEVO URUGUAY/IN THE NEW URUGUAY. (Text in English, Spanish) 1978. irreg. free. Montysur S.A., Misiones 1361, Montevideo, Uruguay. Ed. Marco Zoboli. illus.

051　　　　　US
EQUALITY. 1965. irreg. contributions. Richard Fichter, Ed. & Pub., 28 E. Vine, Oxford, OH 45056 (and Postfach 2803, 6 Frankfurt/Main, W. Germany (B.R.D.)) bk. rev. circ. 500. (looseleaf format; also avail. in microform from BLH)

052　　　　　CH
EVENSONGS/YEH KO. (Text in Chinese or English) irreg., no. 12, 1975. (English Department Evening School) Tamkang College of Arts & Sciences, No. 5, Lane 199, Kinghua St., Taipei, Taiwan, Republic of China. Ed. po-hsin Kuo. adv. bk. rev. illus. circ. 3,000.

808.87　　　　　US
EXTRA SPECIAL CRACKED. a. $1.25 per issue. Major Magazines, Inc. (Subsidiary of: Candar Publishing Corp.) 235 Park Ave. South, New York, NY 10003. circ. 400,000.

808.8 052　　　　　UK
FANATIC; a paper of passion. 1977. irreg. price varies. Open Head Press, 2 Blenheim Cresc., London W11 1NN, England. (back issues avail.)

808.87　　　　　SP
FORGES. no. 2, 1974. irreg. 200. Sedmay Ediciones, Fleming 51, Madrid 16, Spain.

700　　　　　SP
FORMA ABIERTA; cuadernos de creacion e investigacion artistica. (Supplement of: Instituto de Estudios Alicantinos. Revista) no. 3, 1976. irreg. Instituto de Estudios Alicantinos, Diputacion Provincial, Alicante, Spain. Ed. Juan Orts Serrano.

030　　　　　FR　ISSN 0071-9633
FRONTERA OBERTA. (Text in Catalan) 1969. irreg. price varies. ‡ Ediciones Catalanes de Paris, 18 rue Jobbe-Duval, 75015 Paris, France.

056.1　　　　　CK
GACETA; revista internacional de cultura. 1976. irreg. $3 per no. Instituto Colombiano de Cultura, Carrera 3-A no. 18-24, Apdo. Aereo 29665, Bogota, Colombia. Ed. Gloria Zea de Uribe.

056.1　　　　　US　ISSN 0162-0029
GARCIA LORCA REVIEW. (Text in Various Languages) 1973. a. $3.50. State University of New York, College at Brockport, Department of Foreign Languages and Literatures, Brockport, NY 14420. Ed. Grace Alvarez-Altman. bk. rev. bibl. charts. circ. controlled. (back issues avail)

808.838　　　　　AT　ISSN 0310-9968
GEGENSCHEIN. 1971. irreg., no. 39, 1979. Aus.$1 for 4 nos.; US$1 for 3 nos. ‡ c/o Eric B. Lindsay, Ed., 6 Hillcrest Ave., Faulconbridge, N.S.W. 2776, Australia. bk. rev. circ. 245.

GESHER. see RELIGIONS AND THEOLOGY — Judaic

051　　　　　YE
AL-GHAD. 1975. irreg. 1.50 rials. General Union of Development Cooperatives, Ministry of Social Affairs, Labor and Youth, Sana'a, Yemen. Ed. Humud al-'Amudi. adv. charts. stat.

808.8　　　　　US　ISSN 0533-2869
GREYFRIAR/SIENA STUDIES IN LITERATURE. 1960. a. free. ‡ Siena College, Department of English, Loudonville, NY 12211. Ed. Peter A. Fiore. bibl. circ. 750. Indexed: M.L.A.

051　　　　　CN　ISSN 0017-453X
GRONK. 1967. irreg. Can.$12 for 6 nos. Ganglia Press, 310 Dupont St., Toronto, Ont. M5R 1V9, Canada. Ed. B. P. Nichol. circ. 200.
　Formerly: Ganglia.

059　　　　　MG
HAITENY, HAISORATA, HAIRAHA. 1978. irreg. Academie Malgache, Section 1, B.P. 6217, Tsimbazaza, Antananarivo, Malagasy Republic. circ. 300.

HARRISON STREET REVIEW. see LITERATURE

059　　　　　FR
HOR YEZH. (Text in Breton) 1954. irreg. 40 F. (for 4 nos.) c/o P. Denis, Le Ris, Ploare, 29100 Douarnenez, France. Ed. Arzel Even.

817　　　　　US　ISSN 0439-5794
HORSESHIT: THE OFFENSIVE REVIEW; a down to earth magazine. 1965. triennial. $10 for 4 nos. ‡ Equine Products Co., Box 361, Hermosa Beach, CA 90254. Eds. R. & T. Dunker. illus. circ. 150,000.

056.9　　　　　PO
IDEALEDA. 1976. irreg. Publicacoes Idealeda, Rua Bartolomeu Dias 43-2, Ermesinde, Lisbon, Portugal. adv. bibl. illus.

700　　　　　PO
INFORMACAO CULTURAL. 1976. irreg. Secretaria da Estado da Cultura, Av. da Republica 16, Lisboa 1, Portugal.

059　　　　　NE　ISSN 0167-3696
INS AND OUTS; a magazine of awareness. (Text in English) 1978. irreg. $20 for 6 issues. Ins & Outs Press, Box 3759, Amsterdam, Netherlands. Ed.Edward Woods. adv. bk. rev. circ. 2,500.

INTERNATIONAL DOSTOEVSKY SOCIETY BULLETIN. see LITERATURE

INVISIBLE CITY. see LITERATURE — Poetry

052　　　　　UK
IPSE. 1976. a. £3.50($6) (International Poetry Society) Hub Publications Ltd., Youlgrave, Bakewell, Derbyshire, England. Ed. Robin Gregory. bk. rev. circ. 500.

JOURNAL OF CROATIAN STUDIES; annual review of the Croatian Academy of America. see HISTORY — History Of Europe

700　　　　　TR
KAIRI. 1976. a. 22 Fitt St., Woodbrook, Port-of-Spain, Trinidad. Ed. Christopher Laird. bk. rev. bibl. illus.

051　　　　　YE
AL-KALIMA; majallat al-muthaqqafiyn al-yamaniyiyn. irreg. 2 rials. Box 1109, Sana'a, Yemen. Ed.Ibrahim al-Maqhafi. adv. bk. rev.

810　　　　　US　ISSN 0022-8990
KARAMU. 3. a. $1 for 2 nos. Karamu Association, English Department, Eastern Illinois University, Charleston, IL 61920. Ed.Bd. illus. cum.index. circ. 300. (processed)

808.87　　　　　US
KING SIZED CRACKED. a. $1.25 per issue. Major Magazines Inc. (Subsidiary of: Candar Publishing Corp.) 235 Park Ave. South, New York, NY 10003. circ. 500,000.

700　　　　　US
LEFT CURVE; art & revolution. 1974. irreg. $7 for 3 nos. to individuals; institutions $14. 1230 Grant Ave., Box 302, San Francisco, CA 94133. Ed. Csaba Polony. bk. rev. film rev. play rev. illus. circ. 1,000. (back issues avail.) Indexed: Alt.Press Ind.

LITERARY AND POLITICAL REVIEWS

051   FR
LIGNE CREATRICE. 1971. irreg., 14 nos. published through 1975. 20 F. per no. c/o J. Tarkieltaub, 69 rue d'Hauteville, Paris, France. Ed. Isidore Isou. bibl. illus.

800   US
LOST AND FOUND TIMES. 1975. irreg., no. 7, 1979. $5 for 5 nos. Luna Bisonte Prods, 137 Leland Ave., Columbus, OH 43214. Ed. John M. Bennett. circ. 500.

051   US
LUMEN/AVENUE A. 1979. s-a. $8 for 2 nos. Lumen Press, c/o Graham, Box 412, Stuyvesant Sta., New York, NY 10009. Ed. James Graham. bk. rev. film rev. play rev. circ. 50.

051   US   ISSN 0149-4902
M O T A; a counter-counter culture multi-media revue. 1975. irreg., no. 17, 1979. $3. (Museum of Temporary Art) MOTA Press, Box 28385, Washington, DC 20005. Ed. Janet Schmuckal. circ. 1,000.

MIDAMERICA (EAST LANSING) see *LITERATURE*

052   CN
MUSKEG REVIEW. (Text in English) 1974. a. Can.$1. Lakehead University, Art and Literary Society, c/o Keith Muncaster, Oliver Rd., Thunder Bay N, Ont., Canada. illus. circ. 500.

808.8   CN   ISSN 0547-0749
N R C - NOUVELLE REVUE CANADIENNE. (Text in English and French) 1956. irreg. N R C Publishing Co., Ottawa, Ont., Canada.
     Formerly: Nouvelle Revue Canadienne (ISSN 0383-2961)

320.5 800   CN   ISSN 0702-7532
NEW LITERATURE AND IDEOLOGY. French edition: Nouvelle Litterature et Ideologie (ISSN 0703-8011) 1969. irreg. Can.$6 for 4 nos. Norman Bethune Institute of Ideological Studies, Box 727, Adelaide Station, Toronto M5C 2J8 Ont., Canada (Subscr. to: National Publications Centre, P.O. Box 727, Adelaide Station, Toronto, Ont., Canada) bk. rev. circ. 5,000.
     Incorporating: Literature and Ideology (ISSN 0024-4740)

808.8   CN
NEW MITRE; students' literary magazine. (Text in English and French) 1893. a. Can.$2.50($2.50) Bishop's University, Student's Representative Council, Sec. Dir. of Finance, Lennoxville, Que., Canada. adv. bk. rev. illus. circ. controlled. (tabloid format)
     Formerly: Mitre.

028.1   SW
NEW SWEDISH BOOKS. (Text in English) irreg. Svenska Institutet - Swedish Institute, Box 7434, 103 91 Stockholm, Sweden. adv. bibl. illus.

800   IT
NUOVO 75. 1967. a. Centro Studi Metodologici, Via Senato 24, 20121 Milan, Italy. Ed. Bd. circ. 1,000.

700   US
OJITO. 1976. a. $6. New Mexico State University, Department of English, Las Cruces, NM 88003. adv. circ. 1,500. (back issues avail.)

051   UK   ISSN 0030-6568
OTHER SCENES; the international newspaper. 1967. irreg. $10. Other Scenes Inc., Bcm-Oscenes, London WC1V, England (U.S. address: Box 4137, Grand Central Station, New York, NY 10017) Ed. John Wilcock. bk. rev. illus. circ. 2,000. (also avail. in microform from UMI)
     Underground

051   US
OTTERBEIN MISCELLANY. (Text in English, French and German) 1965. a. $1. Otterbein College, Westerville, OH 43081. Ed. Norman Chaney. bk. rev. circ. 200 (controlled)

051   US
PARAMETERS; an occasional newsletter of critical issues. irreg. Circle Forum, Box 176, Portland, OR 97207.

056.9   BL
PARANA EM TRES DIMENSOES. 1973. irreg. Editora Mayo, Curitiba, Parana, Brazil. illus.

051   US
PASS-AGE: A FUTURES JOURNAL. 1976. a. $3.95. (Earth Metabolic Design, Inc.) Pass-Age: a Futures Journal, 431 S. 45th St., Philadelphia, PA 19104. Eds. Robert Kahn, Timothy Wessels. charts. illus. stat. tr.lit. circ. 100.

800   NE
PDR PRESS PUBLICATIONS ON WILLIAM BUTLER YEATS. 1977. irreg. Peter de Ridder Press, Box 168, 2160 AD Lisse, Netherlands.

810   US
PEMBROKE MAGAZINE. 1969. a. $3. (North Carolina Arts Council) Pembroke State University, P.O. Box 60, Pembroke, NC 28372. Ed. Shelby Stephenson. adv. bk. rev. illus. cum. index (1969-73) circ. 1,500. (also avail. in microfilm from UMI; back issues avail)

320   US
PEOPLE AND THE PURSUIT OF TRUTH. 1975. irreg. $9.50. Berkeley Enterprises, Inc., 815 Washington St., Newtonville, MA 02160. Ed. Edmund C. Berkeley. bk. rev. circ. 285.

053.1   GW   ISSN 0031-6784
DIE PFORTE; Zeitschrift und Schriften fuer wertidealistische Philosophie und Kultur. 1947. a. DM.12. Dr. Kurt Port Verlag GmbH, Dulkweg 9, 7300 Esslingen-Wiflingshausen, W. Germany (B.R.D.) bk. rev. index. circ. 3,000.

056.1   AG
PLUMA Y PINCEL; para la difusion del arte y la cultura latinoamericanos. 1976. irreg. Editorial Arte y Letras de America, Nicaragua 5925, Buenos Aires, Argentina. Ed. Romeo Medina.

800   IT
PUBBLICO; rassegna annuale di fatti letterari. 1977. a. L.3500. Saggiatore S.p.A., Via San Senatore 10, 20122 Milan, Italy. Ed. Vittorio Spinazzola.

051   US
PUBLIC OCCURRENCE. 1975. irreg. $5. Frayed Page Collective, 118 Pine Street, Burlington, VT 05401. Ed. Eugene Scribner. adv. bk. rev. illus. tr.lit. circ. 4,000. Indexed: Alt.Press Ind.

052   UK
REBECCA; a radical magazine for Wales. (Text in English and Welsh) 1973. irreg. £6($25) Hosts of Rebecca, 15 Windsor Esplanade, Docks, Caerdydd, Wales. Ed. Paddy French. (back issues avail.)

056.1   PE
RUNA. irreg. S.150 per no. Instituto Nacional de Cultura, Azangaro 235, Lima, Peru. Eds. Maruja Barrig, Luis Freire. illus.

810   US
SARAH LAWRENCE REVIEW. 1957. irreg. contr. free circ. Sarah Lawrence College, Bronxville, NY 10708.
     Former titles: Sarah Lawrence Literary Review; S.L. Literary Review (ISSN 0036-4746)

800   UK
SATURDAY MORNING. no. 2, 1976. irreg. Institute of U.S. Studies, 31 Tavistock Sq., London WC1, England. Ed. Simon Pettet.

811   US   ISSN 0037-5969
SEVENTIES; a magazine of poetry and opinion. (Text in Danish, French, German and Swedish) 1958. irreg. $4 for 4 nos. Seventies Press, Odin House, Madison, MN 56256 (Dist. by Book People, 2940 Seventh St., Berkeley, CA 94710) Ed. & Pub. Robert Bly. bk. rev. illus. circ. 3,000. (also avail. in microfilm from UMI)
     Formerly: Sixties.

800 700   PY
SIGNOS; revista de letras y artes. 1973. irreg. Estados Unidos 1120, Asuncion, Paraguay. illus.

808.87   GW
SLAPSTICK. 1978. DM.2.60 per no. Pardon Verlagsgesellschaft mbH, Oeder Weg 157, D-6000 Frankfurt 1, W. Germany (B.R.D.) Ed.Hans A. Nikel.
     Wit and humor

943.7   GW   ISSN 0037-7058
SLOWAKEI/SLOVAKIA; kulturpolitische Revue. 1963. a. DM.6. Matus-Cernak-Institut, Kulturelles Zentrum der Slowaken in Deutschland, Postfach 100924, 5000 Cologne 1, W. Germany (B.R.D.) Ed. Alba Greiner. bk. rev. circ. 1,500.

SNOECK'S; LITERATUUR KUNST FILM TONEEL MODE REIZEN. see *HUMANITIES: COMPREHENSIVE WORKS*

054.1   FR
SOCIETE J.K. HUYSMANS.BULLETIN. vol. 12, 1973. irreg (about twice a year) membership only. ‡ Societe J.K. Huysmans, 22 rue Guynemer, 75006 Paris, France. adv. bk. rev. circ. 600(controlled)

296.67   IS   ISSN 0082-4585
SOURCES OF CONTEMPORARY JEWISH THOUGHT/MEKEVOT. Title varies: To the Source/El Ha'ayin. (Text in English, French, Spanish, Hebrew) 1968. irreg., 1975, no. 6. price varies. World Zionist Organization, Department for Torah Education and Culture in the Diaspora, Box 92, Jerusalem, Israel (Subscr. to: Jewish Agency, Publication Service, 515 Park Ave., New York, N.Y. 10022) Ed.Bd.

059   LO
SPARK. 1977. bi-m. National University of Lesotho, Roma, Lesotho. Ed. N. Theko.

323.4 808.8   UK
SPEKTRUM; unperiodical journal of banned writers. (Text in Czech) 1978. irreg. (approx. 3/yr.) Writers & Scholars International Ltd., 21 Russell St., Covent Garden, London WC2B 5HP, England. illus. circ. 1,200.

808.87   US
STUDIES IN AMERICAN HUMOR. 1974. irreg., vol. 3, no. 1, 1976. $7 to individuals; institutions $12. American Humor Publications, Inc., Southwest Texas State University, Department of English, San Marcos, TX 78666. Ed. Jack Meathenia. adv. bk. rev. circ. 300. Indexed: M.L.A.
     Wit and humor

808.87   US   ISSN 0163-4143
STUDIES IN CONTEMPORARY SATIRE. 1973. a. $3. c/o C. Darrel Sheraw, Ed., Department of English, Clarion State College, Clarion, PA 16214 (Subscr. to D.R. Wilmes, Co-editor, Pennsylvania State University, Shenango Valley Campus, 147 Shenango Ave., Sharon, PA 16146) adv. bk. rev. circ. 300-400. (back issues avail.)

051   US
THOREAU SOCIETY BOOKLETS. 1942. irreg. free with subscr. to Thoreau Society Bulletins. Thoreau Society, Inc., State University College, Geneseo, NY 14454. Ed. Walter Harding. illus. circ. 1,200. (reprint service avail. from UMI)

808.8   AT   ISSN 0310-6217
TUBE. 1973. irreg. Aus.$1 for 3 issues. c/o Richard Coady, Ed., 32 Coventry Rd., Strathfield, NSW 2135, Australia.

800   US
U S 1 WORKSHEETS. 1973. 2-3/yr. $4 for 8 nos. U S 1 Poets' Cooperative, 21 Lake Dr., Roosevelt, NJ 08555. circ. 1,000. (tabloid format; back issues avail.) Indexed: Ind.Amer.Per.Verse.

UGANDA JOURNAL. see *HISTORY — History Of Africa*

850   AG
UNIVERSIDAD NACIONAL DE LA PLATA. FACULTAD DE HUMANIDADES Y CIENCIAS DE LA EDUCACION. DEPARTAMENTO DE LETRAS. SERIE TRABAJOS. COMUNICACIONES Y CONFERENCIAS.* irreg; 1972, no. 15. Universidad Nacional de la Plata, Facultad de Humanidades y Ciencias de la Educacion, Departamento de Letras, Calle 7 no. 776, La Plata, Argentina. bibl.

UNIVERSIDADE DE LISBOA. FACULDADE DE LETRAS. REVISTA. see *LITERATURE*

960 GH ISSN 0020-2703
UNIVERSITY OF GHANA. INSTITUTE OF AFRICAN STUDIES. RESEARCH REVIEW. (Text in English) 1965. 3/yr. price varies. University of Ghana, Institute of African Studies, Box 73, Legon, Ghana. Ed. J. K. Agovi. bk. rev. charts. illus. circ. 500.

322.4 UK ISSN 0305-8646
UNIVERSITY OF GLASGOW. INSTITUTE OF LATIN AMERICAN STUDIES. OCCASIONAL PAPERS. 1972. irreg., no. 29, 1979. £2. ‡ University of Glasgow, Institute of Latin American Studies, Glasgow G12 8QH, Scotland. Ed. S.E. Mitchell.

UNMUZZLED OX. see LITERATURE — Poetry

810 US
VILE INTERNATIONAL. 1974. a. $10. Banana Productions, 1183 Church St., San Francisco, CA 94114. adv. charts. illus. circ. 1,000(controlled) Formerly: Vile.

052 AT
WORONI. 1948. irreg. Aus.$2.50($10) Australian National University, Students' Association, Canberra, A. C. T. 2600, Australia.

LITERARY AND POLITICAL REVIEWS — Abstracting, Bibliographies, Statistics

ALTERNATIVES IN PRINT; an international catalog of books, pamphlets, periodicals and audiovisual materials. see SOCIAL SCIENCES: COMPREHENSIVE WORKS — Abstracting, Bibliographies, Statistics

NEW PAGES GUIDE TO ALTERNATIVE PERIODICALS. see SOCIAL SCIENCES: COMPREHENSIVE WORKS — Abstracting, Bibliographies, Statistics

051 301 US ISSN 0146-5716
NEW PERIODICALS INDEX. 1977. s-a. $45. Mediaworks Ltd., Box 4494, Boulder, CO 80306. Ed. Bd. circ. 300.
    Covers alternative and new age publications

016 800 US
SELECT BIBLIOGRAPHICAL GUIDES. irreg. price varies. Oxford University Press, 200 Madison Ave., New York, NY 10016 (And Ely House, 37 Dover St., London W1X 4AH, England)

808.8 016 CN
WINTERGREEN; a directory of progressive periodicals. 1979. a. Can.$5($6) Alternative Research, Box 1294, Kitchener, Ont. N2G 4G8, Canada. Ed.Bd. circ. 1,500.

LITERATURE

see also Literature—Poetry; Adventure and Romance; Publishing and Book Trade

A: A JOURNAL OF CONTEMPORARY LITERATURE. see LITERATURE — Poetry

808.5 US ISSN 0360-0939
A C A BULLETIN. 1972. q. $30 ($15 to libraries) Association for Communication Administration, 5105 Blacklick Rd., Annandale, VA 22003. (reprint service avail. from UMI)
    Continues: Association of Departments and Administrators in Speech Communication. Bulletin.

810 US
A M S OCCASIONAL. 1965. irreg. membership. Arthur Machen Society, Bob L. Mowey, Dir. of Libraries, Wittenberg University, Thomas Library, Springfield, OH 45501. illus. circ. 200.

A P U PRESS ALASKANA SERIES. (Alaska Pacific University Press) see HISTORY

A S C A P BIOGRAPHICAL DICTIONARY. (American Society of Composers, Authors and Publishers) see MUSIC

820 UK
A S L S NEWSLETTER. irreg. membership. Association for Scottish Literary Studies, c/o Tom Crawford, Ed., Dept. of English, University of Aberdeen, Old Aberdeen AB9 2UB, Scotland.

800 GW
AACHENER BEITRAEGE ZUR KOMPARATISTIK. 1977. irreg., no. 3, 1977. price varies. Bouvier Verlag Herbert Grundmann, Am Hof 32, Postfach 1268, 5300 Bonn 1, W. Germany (B.R.D.) Ed. Hugo Dyserinck.

ABOUT BOOKS FOR CHILDREN. see CHILDREN AND YOUTH — For

869 BL ISSN 0065-0447
ACADEMIA CAMPINENSE DE LETRAS. PUBLICACOES. 1958. irreg., no. 38, 1978. Cr.$40 available on exchange. Academia Campinense de Letras, Rua Marechal Deodoro, 525, 13100 Campinas SP, Brazil. Ed. Lycurgo de Castro Santos Filho. circ. 500(controlled)

800 SP ISSN 0065-0455
ACADEMIA ESPANOLA, MADRID. ANEJOS DEL BOLETIN. 1959. irreg.; latest issue, no. 38. price varies. Real Academia Espanola, Calle de Felipe IV no. 4, Madrid 14, Spain.

860 US
ACADEMIA NORTEAMERICANA DE LA LENGUA ESPANOLA. BOLETIN. (Text in Spanish) 1976. irreg. $8 to individuals; institutions $12. Academia Norteamericana de la Lengua Espanola, Box 7, F.D.R. Post Office, New York, NY 10022 (Subscr. to: Odon Betanzos, 125 Queen St., Staten Island, N.Y. 10314) Ed. Eugenio Chang-Rodriguez. bk. rev. illus. circ. 3,000.

800 BL ISSN 0001-3846
ACADEMIA PAULISTA DE LETRAS. REVISTA. 1937. irreg. free. Academia Paulista de Letras, Largo do Arouche 312, Sao Paulo, Brazil. Ed. Leonardo Arroyo. bibl. circ. 1,500.

860 BL
ACADEMIA PERNAMBUCANA DE LETRAS. REVISTA. 1901. irreg. Academia Pernambucana de Letras, Av. Rui Barbosa, 1596, Recife, Brazil. illus.

840 FR ISSN 0065-0587
ACADEMIE FRANCAISE. ANNUAIRE; documents et notices sur les membres de l'Academie. 1966. irreg. Academie Francaise, 23 Quai de Conti, Paris 6e, France.

ACCADEMIA MUSICALE CHIGIANA. QUADERNI. see ART

839.3 NE ISSN 0084-5892
ACHTER HET BOEK. 1962. irreg. (approx. 1-3 nos. per yr.) fl.35. Nederlands Letterkundig Museum en Documentatiecentrum, Juffrouw Idastraat 11, The Hague, Netherlands. Ed.Bd. bibl. illus.

ACOPEL; temas de linguistica y literatura. see LINGUISTICS

057 YU ISSN 0567-784X
ACTA NEOPHILOLOGICA. (Text in various languages) 1968. a. $2. Funiverza Edvarda Kardelja V Ljubljani, Filozofska Fakulteta, Askerceva 12, 61000 Ljubljana, Yugoslavia. Ed. Janez Stanonik. bk. rev. bibl. circ. 400.

800 US ISSN 0065-1877
ADAPTATIONS SERIES. 1970. irreg., no. 5, 1980. $1.50-$2.95. Proscenium Press, P.O. Box 361, Newark, DE 19711. Ed. Robert Hogan. (reprint service avail. from UMI)

ADVENTURES IN POETRY. see LITERATURE — Poetry

820 US ISSN 0065-4000
AFRICAN LITERATURE TODAY. 1968. a. $12.50. (University of Sierra Leone, Fourah Bay College, SL) Africana Publishing Co. (Subsidiary of Holmes & Meier Publishers, Inc.) 30 Irving Pl., New York, NY 10003. (Co-publisher: Heinemann Educational Books, London) Ed. Eldred Durosimi Jones. adv. bk. rev. index. (back issues avail.)

800 FR ISSN 0065-4787
AILLEURS ET DEMAIN; CLASSIQUES.* 1970. irreg. price varies. Editions R. Laffont, 6 Place Saint-Sulpice, Paris 6e, France.

889 GR
AIOLIKA GRAMMATA. 1971. irreg. $15. Hodos Nireos 41, Palaion Phaliron, Athens, Greece. circ. 2,000.

800 GW ISSN 0002-2985
AKADEMIE DER WISSENSCHAFTEN UND DER LITERATUR, MAINZ. KLASSE DER LITERATUR. ABHANDLUNGEN. 1950. irreg. price varies. Franz Steiner Verlag GmbH, Friedrichstr. 24, Postfach 5529, 6200 Wiesbaden, W. Germany (B.R.D.) index.

820 CN ISSN 0707-994X
ALBERTA AUTHORS BULLETIN. 1972. irreg. Cultural Development Division, Film and Literary Arts Branch, 12th Floor, CN Tower, 1004 104th Ave., Edmonton, Alta. T5J 0K5, Canada.

800 CN ISSN 0065-616X
ALEXANDER LECTURES. 1929. irreg. price varies. University of Toronto Press, Front Campus, Toronto, Ont. M5S 1A6, Canada (U.S. Address: 33 East Tupper St., Buffalo, NY 14203) (also avail. in microfiche)

ALFA. see LINGUISTICS

820 II
ALIGARH JOURNAL OF ENGLISH STUDIES. (Text in English) 1976. a. Rs.25($6) Aligarh Muslim University, Department of English, Aligarh, Uttar Pradesh, India. Ed. A. A. Ansari.

830 GW ISSN 0065-6607
ALTDEUTSCHE TEXTBIBLIOTHEK. ERGAENZUNGSREIHE. 1963. irreg. price varies. Max Niemeyer Verlag, Pfrondorfer Str. 4, 7400 Tuebingen, W. Germany (B.R.D.)

809 GW
ALTE ABENTEUERLICHE REISEBERICHTE. 1966. irreg. price varies. Horst Erdmann Verlag, Hartmeyerstr. 117, Postfach 1380, 7400 Tuebingen, W. Germany (B.R.D.) circ. 4,000.

709 UK
AMERICAN ARTS PAMPHLET SERIES. 1970. irreg., (1-2/yr.) £1($3.50) ‡ University of Exeter, American Arts Documentation Centre, Queens Building, Exeter EX 4QH, England. Ed. M. Gidley. circ. 1,000-1,300.

810 US ISSN 0516-9631
AMERICAN AUTHORS AND CRITICS SERIES. 1961. irreg. price varies. Holt, Rinehart and Winston, 383 Madison Ave., New York, NY 10017.

814.008 US ISSN 0065-9142
AMERICAN LITERARY SCHOLARSHIP. 1963. a. price varies. Duke University Press, Box 6697, College Sta., Durham, NC 27708. Eds. J. Albert Robbins, James L. Woodress. (reprint service avail. from ISI, UMI)

840 FR ISSN 0399-1121
AMITIE HENRI BOSCO. CAHIERS. 1973. a. 50 F.($12) Amitie Henri Bosco, c/o Monique Barea, Les Oliviers III, 76 A des Baumettes, 06000 Nice, France. cum.index:1973-1977(nos.1-14) (back issues avail.)

800 940 NE
AMSTERDAMER BEITRAEGE ZUR NEUEREN GERMANISTIK. 1972. irreg. price varies. ‡ Editions Rodopi N.V., Keizersgracht 302-304, 1016 EX Amsterdam, Netherlands. Ed. Gerd Labroisse. circ. 600.

830 NE
AMSTERDAMER PUBLIKATIONEN ZUR SPRACHE UND LITERATUR. 1972. irreg., approx. 20/yr. price varies. Editions Rodopi N.V., Keizersgracht 302-304, 1016 EX Amsterdam, Netherlands (Dist. in the U.S. by: Humanities Press, Inc., 171 First Ave., Atlantic Highlands, NJ 07718) Ed. Cola Minis. circ. 500.
    Germanic languages

ANALECTA CARTUSIANA; review for Carthusian history and spirituality. see RELIGIONS AND THEOLOGY

ANALECTA ROMANICA. see LINGUISTICS

860 SP
ANALES DE LITERATURA HISPANOAMERICANA. 1972. a. 900 ptas.($14) Universidad Complutense de Madrid, Catedra de Literatura Hispanoamericano, Ciudad Universitaria, Madrid 3, Spain. (Co-sponsor: Instituto de Cultura Hispanica) bk. rev. bibl.

860 US
ANALES GALDOSIANOS. (Text in Spanish and English) 1966. a. $4. Asociacion International de Galdosianos, Boston University, 2745 Commonwealth Ave., Boston, MA 02215. Ed. Rodolfo Cardona. bk. rev. circ. 375.

800 US ISSN 0066-152X
ANALYST. 1953. irreg. free; back numbers must be purchased. ‡ Northwestern University, Department of English, Evanston, IL 60201. Ed. Robert Mayo. circ. 200. (processed)

ANANDA ACHARYA UNIVERSAL SERIES. see PHILOSOPHY

809 IR ISSN 0517-8045
ANCIENT IRANIAN CULTURAL SOCIETY. PUBLICATION/ANSOMAN-E FARHANG-E IRAN-E BASTAN. NASHRIJEH. (Text in Farsi) 1962. irreg. Rs.30 per no. Ancient Iranian Cultural Society, Nadri Ave., Kuche-Ye Shahrowkh, Box 14-1262, Teheran, Iran. Ed. Farhang Mehr.

800 DK ISSN 0084-6465
ANDERSENIANA. (Text in Danish; occasionally in English and German; summaries in English, German, French, Danish) 1933. a. Kr.45. Hans Christian Andersen Museum, Hans Jensensstraede 39-43, DK-5000 Odense C, Denmark. Ed. Niels Oxenvad. adv. bk. rev. abstr. bibl. illus. cum.index. circ. 1,000.

840 FR
ANDRE GIDE; la revue des lettres modernes. 1970. a. price varies. Lettres Modernes, 73, rue du Cardinal Lemoine, 75005 Paris, France. Ed. Claude Martin. bk. rev. (back issues avail)

820 DK ISSN 0066-1805
ANGLISTICA. 1953. irreg., latest vol. 20, 1974. price varies. Rosenkilde og Bagger Forlag, 3 Kron-Prinsens-Gade, Copenhagen K, Denmark. Ed. T.J.B. Spencer.

809 GW
ANGLISTISCHE FORSCHUNGEN. 1901. irreg., vol. 134, 1978. price varies. Carl Winter Universitaetsverlag, Lutherstr. 59, 6900 Heidelberg, W. Germany (B.R.D.)

940 820 410 SZ
ANGLO-AMERICAN FORUM. (Text in English and German; summaries in English) 1975. irreg. price varies. Verlag Peter Lang AG, Muenzgraben 2, Postfach, CH-3000 Berne 7, Switzerland. Ed. Christoph Gutknecht. bk. rev. abstr. bibl. circ. 400 (controlled) (back issues avail)

ANGOL FILOLOGIAI TANULMANYOK/ HUNGARIAN STUDIES IN ENGLISH. see LINGUISTICS

843 FR ISSN 0084-6473
ANNEE BALZACIENNE. 1960. a. 85 F. (Groupe d'Etudes Balzaciennes) Editions Garnier Freres, 19,rue des Plantes, 75014 Paris, France.

840 FR ISSN 0066-3387
ANNUAIRE NATIONAL DES LETTRES. 1976/77. a. Editions Dany Thibaud, 52 rue Labrouste, 75015 Paris, France.

813 US
ANNUAL WORLD'S BEST SF. 1965. a. $1.95. Daw Books, Inc., 1633 Broadway, New York, NY 10019. Ed. Donald A. Wollheim. circ. 100,000.
Science fiction

879 US ISSN 0066-4456
ANNUALE MEDIAEVALE. 1960. a. $13.50. Humanities Press, Inc., 171 1st Ave., Atlantic Highlands, NJ 07716. Ed. Frank Zborny. adv.

860 SP
ANO LITERARIO ESPANOL. 1974. a. Editorial Castalia, Zurbano 39, Madrid 10, Spain. Ed.Bd.

810 US
ANON NINE. irreg. Street Fiction Press, 201 E. Liberty St., Ann Arbor, MI 48108.

800 821 UK
ANTHILL. 1977. q. £2. Sarum Press, 99 Wendell Rd., London W.12, England.

860 CR ISSN 0587-5196
ANUARIO DEL CUENTO COSTARICCENSE. 1967. a. $10. Editorial Costa Rica, Calles la y 3a, Apdo 2014, San Jose, Costa Rica.

891.7 UR
APPARAT UPRAVLENIYA SOTSIALISTICHESKOGO GOSUDARSTVA. IZDANIE V DVUKH CHASTYAKH. 1976. irreg. (Akademiya Nauk SSSR, Institut Gosudarstva i Prava) Izdatel'stvo Yuridicheskaya Literatura, Moscow, U.S.S.R. Ed. Bd.

860 UY ISSN 0066-5606
AQUI.* irreg. Editorial Arca, Colonia 1263, Montevideo, Uruguay.

AL-ARABIYYA. see LINGUISTICS

ARCHIVE FOR REFORMATION HISTORY. LITERATURE REVIEW/ARCHIV FUER REFORMATIONSGESCHICHTE. LITERATURBERICHT. see RELIGIONS AND THEOLOGY

840 FR ISSN 0066-6556
ARCHIVES CLAUDELIENNES. (Subseries Of: Archives des Lettres Modernes) 1958. irreg. price varies. Lettres Modernes, 73, rue du Cardinal-Lemoine, 75005 Paris, France.

800 CN ISSN 0066-6572
ARCHIVES DES LETTRES CANADIENNES. 1961. irreg. price varies. (University of Ottawa, Centre de Recherches de Litterature Canadienne-Francaise) Editions Fides, 235 E. Dorchester Blvd., Montreal H2X 1N9, Que., Canada.

809 FR ISSN 0003-9675
ARCHIVES DES LETTRES MODERNES; etudes de critique et d'histoire litteraire. 1957. 6-10/yr. 145 F. for 60 "cahiers". Lettres Modernes, 73 rue du Cardinal Lemoine, 75005 Paris, France. Ed. Michel J. Minard.

860 CK ISSN 0066-6734
ARCHIVO EPISTOLAR COLOMBIANO. 1965. irreg., latest issue, no. 14, 1980. Instituto Caro y Cuervo, Seccion de Publicaciones, Apdo. Aereo 20002, Bogota, Colombia.

800 PL ISSN 0066-6904
ARCHIWUM LITERACKIE. (Text in Polish) 1956. irreg., vol. 22, 1978. price varies. (Polska Akademia Nauk, Instytut Badan Literackich) Ossolineum, Publishing House of the Polish Academy of Sciences, Rynek 9, Wroclaw, Poland (Dist. by Ars Polona-Ruch, Krakowskie Przedmiescie 7, Warsaw, Poland) circ. 1,500.

ARCHIWUM TLUMACZEN Z TEORII LITERATURY I METODOLOGII BADAN LITERACKICH. see LINGUISTICS

820 PK
ARIEL. (Text in English) 1972. a. Rs.15. University of Sind, Department of English, Jamshoro, Hyderabad 6, Pakistan.

002 AT ISSN 0311-2926
ARK. 1973. Aus.$2 for 3 nos. c/o Susan & Ronald Clarke, 2-159 Herring Rd., North Ryde, N.S.W. 2113, Australia.
Formerly: Mentor.

810 US ISSN 0044-8885
ARK RIVER REVIEW. 1971. irreg., 1-3/yr. $5 for 4 nos. c/o English Department, Wichita State University, Wichita, KS 67208. Eds. Anthony Sobin, Jonathan Katz. circ. 1,000. Indexed: Ind.Amer.Per.Verse.

839 439 DK
ARNAMAGNAEAN INSTITUTE AND DICTIONARY. BULLETIN. 1964. irreg. free. Arnamagnaean Institute, Njalsgade 76, DK-2300 Copenhagen S, Denmark.
Formerly (until 1975): Arnamagnaean Institute. Bulletin (ISSN 0066-7765)

840 FR ISSN 0066-8893
ASSOCIATION DES AMIS D'ALFRED DE VIGNY. BULLETIN.* 1970, no. 3. irreg. price varies. Association des Amis d'Alfred de Vigny, 6 Av. Constant-Coquelin, Paris 7e, France.

944 FR ISSN 0004-6116
ASTRADO; revue bilingue de Provence. (Text in French & Provencal) 1965. s-a. 30 F.($30) for 2 nos. Astrado Prouvencalo, 2 rue Vincent Allegre, 83100 Toulon, France. Ed. L. Bayle. bk. rev. illus. circ. 1,000.

800 IT
ATALANTA. 1976. irreg.; no. 2, 1977. L.4900. Giardini Editori e Stampatori, Via Santa Bibbiana 28, 56100 Pisa, Italy. Eds. S. G. Mancini, M. Pagnini.

800 US ISSN 0044-9857
ATHANOR. 1971. 2/yr. $5 for 4 nos. Athanor Press, P. O. Box 582, Clarkson, NY 14430. Ed. Douglas Calhoun. bk. rev. circ. 500. (processed)

860 BL
ATRAVES. 1976. irreg. Livraria Duas Cidades, Rua Bento Freitas 158, 01220 Sao Paulo SP, Brazil. Ed.Bd. illus.

806 US
AUGUST DERLETH SOCIETY. NEWSLETTER. 1977. irreg. $1. August Derleth Society, 20 E. Delaware, Chicago, IL 60611. Ed. Richard H. Fawcett. adv. bk. rev. circ. 200.

830 709 GW ISSN 0341-1230
AURORA; Jahrbuch der Eichendorff-Gesellschaft. (Text in German; summaries in English) 1953. a. price varies. Eichendorff-Gesellschaft, Postfach 5503, 8700 Wuerzburg, W. Germany (B.R.D.) Eds. Wolfgang Fruehwald, Franz Heiduk, Helmut Koopmann. bk. rev. bibl. illus. index. circ. 1,000.

830 709 GW ISSN 0171-6530
AURORA-BUCHREIHE. 1974. irreg. price varies. Eichendorff-Gesellschaft, Postfach 5503, 8700 Wuerzburg, W. Germany (B.R.D.) Eds. Wolfgang Fruewald, Franz Heiduk, Helmut Koopmann. circ. 1,000.

808 920 US ISSN 0145-1499
AUTHORS IN THE NEWS; compilation of news stories and feature articles from American newspapers and magazines, covering prominent writers in all fields. 1975. irreg., 1976, vol. 2. $32 per vol. Gale Research Company, Book Tower, Detroit, MI 48226. Ed. Barbara Nykoruk.
Formerly: Contemporary Authors News.

840 FR ISSN 0067-2610
AVANT-SIECLE. 1967. irreg., no. 14, 1974. price varies. Lettres Modernes, 73, Rue du Cardinal-Lemoine, 75005 Paris, France. Ed. Louis Forestier.

800 UY ISSN 0067-2637
AVES DEL ARCA.* irreg. Editorial Arca, Colonia 1263, Montevideo, Uruguay.

800 700 CN ISSN 0382-5272
B. C. MONTHLY. 1972. 5/-6/yr. $15. Canada's National Magazine, Box 48884, Vancouver, B.C. V7X 1A8, Canada. Ed. Gerry Gilbert. bk. rev. circ. 250.

B L A C. (Black Literature and Arts Congress) see ETHNIC INTERESTS

800 US
BACK ROADS; an annual magazine of literature and art. 1973. a. $1.50. Monday Books, Box 543, Cotati, CA 94928. Ed. Stella Monday. adv. bk. rev. illus. circ. 2,000. (also avail. in microform from UMI)
Formerly: Paper Pudding.

813 US ISSN 0005-4070
BAKER STREET JOURNAL; an irregular quarterly of Sherlockiana. 1946. 4/yr. $10. Fordham University Press, University Box L, Bronx, NY 10458. Ed. John Linsenmeyer. adv. bk. rev. bibl. illus. index. circ. 1,800.

820 UK ISSN 0306-8404
BANDERSNATCH. 1973. irreg. membership. Lewis Carroll Society, 69 Ashby Rd., Woodville, Burton-on-Trent, Staffs, England (Subscr. to: Lindsay Fulcher, 20 Vincent Terrace, London N.1., England) Ed. Brian Sibley.

896　　　　　　　　SA　ISSN 0067-4044
BANTU TREASURY. 1957. irreg. price varies.
Witwatersrand University Press, Jan Smuts Ave.,
Johannesburg 2001, South Africa.

840　700　　　　　　　　　FR
BARBACANE; revue des pierres et des hommes. vol.
11, 1975. a. 40 F. Cercle Culturel et Artisanal de
Bonaguil, Chateau de Bonaguil, Saint Front sur
Lemance, 47500 Fumel, France. Ed. Max Pons. adv.
bk. rev. circ. 500.

840　　　　　　　　　　　FR
BARBEY D'AUREVILLY. Variant title: Series Barbey
d'Aurevilly. (Subseries of: Revue des Lettres
Modernes) 1966. a. price varies. Lettres Modernes,
73, rue du Cardinal Lemoine, 75005 Paris, France.
Ed. Jacques Petit. bk. rev. (back issues avail.)

371　023.5　　　　AU　ISSN 0067-4206
DIE BARKE; Lehrer-Jahrbuch. 1956. a.
Oesterreichischer Buchklub der Jugend,
Mayerhofgasse 6, A-1040 Vienna, Austria. Ed. R.
Bamberger.

800　　　　　　FR　ISSN 0067-4222
BAROQUE; revue internationale. 1963. irreg. price
varies. ‡ Centre International de Synthese du
Baroque, 30 rue de la Banque, Montauban, France.
Ed. Mostra del Larzac.
　　Former titles (until 1966): Journees
Internationales d'Etude du Baroque. Actes; 1963-
1965: Journees Internationales d'Etudes du Baroque.

830　　　　　　GW　ISSN 0067-446X
BASIS; Jahrbuch fuer deutsche Gegenwartsliteratur.
(Vol. 1-4 published by Athenaeum-Verlag GmbH)
1970. a. DM.7. Suhrkamp Verlag, Lindenstr. 29-35,
6000 Frankfurt 1, W. Germany (B.R.D.) Eds.
Reinhold Grimm, Jost Hermand. bk. rev. circ.
10,000.

080　　　　　　SZ　ISSN 0067-4494
BASLER DRUCKE. 1951. irreg. price varies.
Birkhaeuser Verlag, Elisabethenstr. 19, CH-4010
Basel, Switzerland.
　　Fiction with art illustrations

830　430　　　　SZ　ISSN 0067-4508
BASLER STUDIEN ZUR DEUTSCHEN SPRACHE
UND LITERATUR. 1954. irreg., vol. 56, 1979.
price varies. ‡ Francke Verlag, Postfach, CH-3000
Berne 26, Switzerland. Eds. E.E. Mueller, K.
Pestalozzi, H. Rupp, M. Stern & L. Wiesmann.

891.7　　　　　　CN　ISSN 0005-6952
BAYAVAYA USKALOS; Byelorussian literary
magazine. (Text in Byelorussian) 1950. a. Can.$3 or
donation. Byelorussian Literary Association, 24
Tarlton Rd., Toronto, Ont. M5P 2MC, Canada. Ed.
Siergey Khmara. bk. rev. illus. circ. 500.

800　　　　　　　　　US
BEAU FLEUVE SERIES. 1970. irreg., no. 9, 1976.
$1. Intrepid Press, Box 1423, Buffalo, NY 14214.
Ed. Allen De Loach.

BEBOP DRAWING CLUB BOOK. see *ART*

891.4　　　　　　II　ISSN 0005-769X
BEDUIN. (Text in Bengali) 1966. a. Rs.12. Rani
Suhasini Roy, Tamluk Raj House, Tamluk,
Midnapore, West Bengal, India. Ed. Bhabanee
Mukhopadhyay.

809　　　　　　GW　ISSN 0170-3315
BEITRAEGE ZUR LITERATUR DES 15-18.
JAHRHUNDERTS. (Text in English and German)
irreg., vol. 6, 1978. price varies. Franz Steiner
Verlag GmbH, Friedrichstr. 24, Postfach 5529, 6200
Wiesbaden, W. Germany (B.R.D.) Ed.Hans-Gert
Roloff.

800　　　　　　CN　ISSN 0067-5733
BENT. (Text in English) 1969. irreg., 1971, no. 7.
Can.$0.25. ‡ 1111 Bewdley Avenue, Victoria, B. C.,
Canada. Ed. Byrd Lukinuk. adv. circ. 300.

820　　　　　　　　　　UK
BERNARD SHAW SOCIETY JOURNAL. 1976. a.
£5. Bernard Shaw Society, High Orchard, 125
Markyate Rd., Dagenham, Essex RM8 2LB,
England. Ed. E. Ford. adv. bk. rev. film rev. play
rev. abstr. bibl. charts. illus. stat. tr.lit. index.
circ. 200. (looseleaf format)

813.08　　　　　　US　ISSN 0067-6233
BEST AMERICAN SHORT STORIES. 1915. a. $10.
Houghton Mifflin Co., One Beacon St., Boston, MA
02107. Ed. Martha Foley.

813.01　　　　　　CN　ISSN 0703-9476
BEST CANADIAN STORIES. 1971. a. $15.95
(clothbound); $7.95(paperback) Oberon Press, 401a
Inn of the Provinces, Ottawa, Ont. K1R 7S8,
Canada. Eds. John Metcalf, Leon Rooke. adv. bk.
rev. circ. 2,500.
　　Continues: New Canadian Stories (ISSN 0316-
7518)

813.5　　　　　　US　ISSN 0067-625X
BEST DETECTIVE STORIES OF THE YEAR. 1945.
a. $8.95. ‡ E. P. Dutton & Co., Inc., 201 Park Ave.
S., New York, NY 10003. Ed. Allen J. Hubin.

813　　　　　　US　ISSN 0095-7119
BEST SCIENCE FICTION OF THE YEAR. 1972. a.
$1.50. Ballantine Books., 201 East 50th St., New
York, NY 10022.

810　　　　　　US　ISSN 0092-8119
BEST SCIENCE FICTION STORIES OF THE
YEAR. 1972. a. $8.95. E. P. Dutton & Co., Inc.,
201 Park Ave. S., New York, NY 10003. Ed. Lester
del Rey.

812.5　　　　　　US　ISSN 0067-6284
BEST SHORT PLAYS. 1969. a. $10.50. Chilton Book
Co., Chilton Way, Radnor, PA 19089. Ed. Stanley
Richards.

840　016　　　　FR　ISSN 0067-6942
BIBLIOGRAPHIE DE LA LITTERATURE
FRANCAISE DU MOYEN AGE A NOS JOURS.
1966. a. price varies. Librairie Armand Colin, 103
Bd. St-Michel, Paris 5, France. Ed. Rene Rancoeur.

840　　　　　　　　　　FR
BIBLIOGRAPHIE DES AUTEURS MODERNES
DE LANGUE FRANCAISE. vol. 21, 1975. irreg.
$75.75. Chronique des Lettres Francaises, 33 rue de
Verneuil, Paris 7e, France.

860　　　　　　　　　　CK
BIBLIOTECA COLOMBIANA. 1970. irreg., no. 19,
1979. Instituto Caro y Cuervo, Seccion de
Publicaciones, Apdo. Aereo 20002, Bogota,
Colombia.

800　　　　　　　　　　IT
BIBLIOTECA DI LETTERATURA E ARTE. 1975.
irreg. price varies. Giardini Editori e Stampatori, Via
Santa Bibbiana 28, 56100 Pisa, Italy.

860　　　　　　　　　　SP
BIBLIOTECA ROMANICA HISPANICA. 1950.
irreg. Editorial Gredos, Sanchez Pacheco 81,
Madrid 2, Spain.
　　Formerly: Biblioteca Romanica Hispanica.
Estudios y Ensayos (ISSN 0519-7201)

891.85　　　　　　PL　ISSN 0519-8631
BIBLIOTEKA PISARZOW POLSKICH. SERIA A.
1953. irreg. price varies. (Polska Akademia Nauk,
Instytut Badan Literackich) Ossolineum, Publishing
House of the Polish Academy of Sciences, Rynek 9,
Wroclaw, Poland (Dist. by Ars Polona-Ruch,
Krakowskie Przedmiescie 7, Warsaw, Poland) Ed.
Jerzy Woronczak. circ. 1,000-2,000.
　　Formerly: Biblioteka Pisarzow Polskich (ISSN
0067-7736)

439　839　　　　DK　ISSN 0067-7841
BIBLIOTHECA ARNAMAGNAEANA; consilio et
auctoritate legati Arnamagnaeani. (Text in Danish,
English, German, Icelandic, Norwegian, and
Swedish) 1941. irreg. price varies. Arnamagnaean
Institute, Njalsgade 76, DK-2300 Copenhagen S,
Denmark (Dist. by: C. A. Reitzels Boghandel A-S,
Noerregade 20, DK-1165 Copenhagen K, Denmark)

839.6　439　　　　DK　ISSN 0067-785X
BIBLIOTHECA ARNAMAGNAEANA.
SUPPLEMENTUM. 1956. irreg. price varies.
Arnamagnaean Institute, Njalsgade 76, DK-2300
Copenhagen S, Denmark (Dist. by: C. A. Reitzels
Boghandel A-S, Noerregade 20, DK-1165
Copenhagen K, Denmark)

BIBLIOTHECA RUSSICA. see *LINGUISTICS*

BIBLIOTHEQUE D'ETUDES BALKANIQUES. see
LINGUISTICS

BIBLIOTHEQUE FRANCAISE ET ROMANE.
SERIE E: LANGUE ET LITTERATURE
FRANCAISES AU CANADA. see *LINGUISTICS*

840　　　　　　FR　ISSN 0067-835X
BIBLIOTHEQUE FRANCAISE ET ROMANE.
SERIE B: EDITIONS CRITIQUES DE TEXTES.
1962. irreg. price varies. (Universite de Strasbourg
II, Centre de Philologie et de Litteratures Romanes)
Editions Klincksieck, 11 rue de Lille, Paris 7,
France. Ed. Georges Straka.

840　　　　　　FR　ISSN 0067-8368
BIBLIOTHEQUE FRANCAISE ET ROMANE.
SERIE C: ETUDES LITTERAIRES. 1960. irreg.
price varies. (Universite de Strasbourg II, Centre de
Philologie et de Litteratures Romanes) Editions
Klincksieck, 11 rue de Lille, Paris 7, France. Ed.
Paul Vernois.

840　　　　　　FR　ISSN 0067-8376
BIBLIOTHEQUE FRANCAISE ET ROMANE.
SERIE D: INITIATION, TEXTES ET
DOCUMENTS. 1964. irreg. price varies.
(Universite de Strasbourg II, Centre de Philologie et
de Litteratures Romanes) Editions Klincksieck, 11
rue de Lille, Paris 7, France. Ed. Georges Straka.

840　　　　　　FR　ISSN 0067-8422
BIBLIOTHEQUE INTROUVABLE. 1966. irreg.
Lettres Modernes, 73 rue du Cardinal Lemoine,
75005 Paris, France.

800　　　　　　　　　　PO
BIBLOS. 1925. a. price varies. Universidade de
Coimbra, Faculdade de Letras, Paco das Escolas,
Coimbra, Portugal. bk. rev. circ. 500.

810　　　　　　　　　　US
BLACK JACK. 1973. irreg., no. 5, 1977. $3.50. c/o
Art Cuelho, Ed., Box 214, Big Timber, MT 59011.
circ. 350.

820　　　　　　　　　　IT
BLUE GUITAR; rivista annuale di letteratura inglese e
americana. (Text in English and Italian) 1975. a.
L.25000. (Universita degli Studi di Messina, Facolta
di Magistero) Herder Editrice e Libreria s.r.l.,
Piazza Montecitorio, 120, 00186 Rome, Italy. Ed.
Angela Giannitrapani.

806　　　　　　　　　　AG
BOLETIN DE LA S A D E. 1975. Sociedad
Argentina de Escritores, Uruguay 1371, Buenos
Aires 1016, Argentina. Ed. Horacio Esteban Ratti.

800　080　　　　UY　ISSN 0067-9909
BOLSILIBROS.* irreg. Editorial Arca, Colonia 1263,
Montevideo, Uruguay.

830　　　　　　GW　ISSN 0068-001X
BONNER ARBEITEN ZUR DEUTSCHEN
LITERATUR. 1961. irreg., no. 34, 1979. price
varies. Bouvier Verlag Herbert Grundmann, Am Hof
32, Postfach 1268, 5300 Bonn 1, W. Germany
(B.R.D.) Ed. Benno von Wiese.

810　　　　　　US　ISSN 0147-0787
BOOKS AT BROWN. 1938. irreg., vol. 25, 1977. $10.
Brown University Library, Friends of the Library,
Box A, Providence, RI 02912.

808.838　　　　　　CN　ISSN 0706-9014
BOREALIS; a Canadian magazine of science fiction &
fantasy. 1978. irreg. Can.$5. Northern Star Press,
Box 3174 South, Halifax, N.S. B3J 3H5, Canada.
Ed.John Bell. bk. rev. circ. 1,000. (back issues
avail.)
　　Science fiction

800　　　　　　　　　　FR
BOUTEILLE A LA MER. irreg. price varies. c/o Ed.
Marc Beigbeder, 8 rue Theo- Renaudot, 75015
Paris, France.

BRECHT-JAHRBUCH. see *LITERARY AND
POLITICAL REVIEWS*

800　　　　　　UK　ISSN 0068-1334
BRITISH AUTHORS SERIES. 1967. irreg. price
varies. Cambridge University Press, 100
Cambridge CB2 3RL, England (and 32 E. 57 St.,
New York, NY 10022) Ed. Robin Mayhead. index.

BRNO STUDIES IN ENGLISH. see *LINGUISTICS*

820　　　　　　　UK　ISSN 0309-7765
BRONTE SOCIETY TRANSACTIONS. 1895. a.
£2($6) Bronte Parsonage Museum, Haworth,
Keighley, Yorks., England (U.S. and Canadian
Orders to: Mrs. Diane McGuire, Long Pasture Rd.,
Little Compton, RI 02837) Ed. Charles H. Lemon.
bk. rev. bibl. illus. cum.index. circ. 2,000. Indexed:
Abstr. Engl. Stud.

821.8　　　　　　US　ISSN 0092-4725
BROWNING INSTITUTE STUDIES. 1973. a. $20 to
non-members. Browning Institute, Inc., Box 2983,
Grand Central Sta., New York, NY 10017. Ed.
William S. Peterson. adv. bk. rev. illus. index. circ.
1,000.

810　　　　　　　US
BROWNS MILLS REVIEW. 1980. irreg. $4. David
Vajda, Ed. & Pub., Box 6915-A, Press Ave., NJ
08015.

810　　　　　　　US　ISSN 0068-3035
BRYN MAWR-HAVERFORD REVIEW. irreg., latest
1976. price varies. Bryn Mawr College and
Haverford College, Haverford Student Council,
Student Government Association, Bryn Mawr, PA
19010. Ed. Vicki Weber. adv. bk. rev. circ. 2,000.
Formerly (1960-66): Bryn Mawr Review.

BULLETIN DES JEUNES ROMANISTES. see
LINGUISTICS

820　　　　　　　UK
BULWER LYTTON CIRCLE CHRONICLE. 1973. a.
$15. (Bulwer Lytton Circle) High Orchard Press,
High Orchard, 125 Markyate Rd., Dagenham, Essex
RM8 2LB, England. Eds. Eric F. J. Ford, Howard
Cooper-Brown. bk. rev. index. (also avail. in
microform from UMI) Indexed: Abstr.Engl.Stud.

813　　　　　　　US　ISSN 0007-6333
BURROUGHS BULLETIN. 1947. irreg. membership.
‡ (Burroughs Bibliophiles) House of Greystoke,
6657 Locust, Kansas City, MO 64131. Ed. Vernell
W. Coriell. bk. rev. bibl. film rev. illus. circ. 2,800.
(processed)
Covers the works of Edgar Rice Burroughs

800　　　　　　　US　ISSN 0068-4325
BURT FRANKLIN ESSAYS IN LITERATURE
AND CRITICISM. (Text in English and Romance
languages) 1968. irreg., 1973, no. 200. price varies.
Lenox Hill Publishing and Distributing Corporation,
235 E. 44th St., New York, NY 10003. (back issues
avail.)

BYDGOSKIE TOWARZYSTWO NAUKOWE.
WYDZIAL NAUK HUMANISTYCZNYCH.
PRACE. SERIA B (JEZYK I LITERATURA) see
LINGUISTICS

BYZANTINE AND MODERN GREEK STUDIES.
see *LINGUISTICS*

895.1　792　　　　US
C H I N O P E R L PAPERS. (Text in Chinese and
English) 1969. a. $5. (Conference on Chinese Oral
and Performing Literature) Cornell University,
China-Japan Program, 140 Uris Hall, Ithaca, NY
14853. Ed. Bd. bk. rev. bibl. circ. 200.
Formerly: C H I N O P E R L News.

800　　　　　　　CN　ISSN 0068-4961
CAHIERS CANADIENS CLAUDEL. 1963. irreg.
price varies. University of Ottawa Press, 65 Hastey
Ave., Ottawa, Ont. K1N 6N5, Canada. Ed. E.
Roberto.

CAHIERS CESAIRIENS. see *THEATER*

840　　　　　　　FR　ISSN 0575-0415
CAHIERS CHARLES DU BOS. 1955. a. Societe des
Amis de Charles Du Bos, 76 bis rue des Saints-
Peres, 75007 Paris, France. circ. 400. (back issues
avail)

CAHIERS CULTURELS. see *LINGUISTICS*

840　　　　　　　FR　ISSN 0575-0466
CAHIERS D'ANALYSE TEXTUELLE. 1959. a. 32
F. (Les Lettres Belges, BE) Societe d'Edition les
Belles Lettres, 95 Bd. Raspail, 75007 Paris, France.
Ed. Paul Delbouille. (back issues avail.) Indexed:
Sociol.Abstr.

CAHIERS DE CIVILISATION MEDIEVALE.
SUPPLEMENT. see *HISTORY — History Of
Europe*

840　　　　　　　SZ　ISSN 0007-9847
CAHIERS DE LA RENAISSANCE VAUDOISE.
1926. irreg.(2-4/yr.) price varies. 18 Petit-Chene,
1003 Lausanne, Switzerland. Ed. Olivier Delacretaz.
illus. circ. 1,500-10,000.

800　　　　　　　FR　ISSN 0068-5089
CAHIERS DE SAINT-MICHEL DE CUXA. 1970.
irreg. 25 F. Association Culturelle de Cuxa, Centre
Permanent de Recherches et d'Etudes Pre-Romanes
et Romanes, Abbaye de Saint-Michel de Cuxa,
Prades-Codalet, France (Subscr. Address: c/o Andre
Delteil, 4, rue Louis Esparre, 66000 Perpignan,
France) bk. rev.

800　　　　　　　FR　ISSN 0008-0365
CAHIERS NATURALISTES. 1955. a. 70 F.($18)
(Societe Litteraire des Amis d'Emile Zola) Editions
Grasset et Fasquelle, 61 rue Saints-Peres, Paris(6e),
France. Dir. Henri Mitterand. adv. bk. rev. bibl.
charts. cum.index. circ. 1,800.

840　　　　　　　SZ
CAHIERS SUISSES ROMAIN ROLLAND. 1977.
irreg. price varies. Editions de la Baconniere S.A.,
Box 185, 2017 Boudry, Switzerland. (reprint service
avail. from UMI)

820　　　　　　　FR　ISSN 0575-2124
CALIBAN; etudes anglaises et nord-americaines. (Text
in English or French; summaries in other languages)
1964. a. 17 F. (for single issue) Universite de
Toulouse II (le Mirail), Institut d'Etudes Anglaises
et Nord-Americaines, 109 bis, rue Vauquelin, 31081
Toulouse Cedex, France.

891.8　　　　　　US　ISSN 0068-5798
CALIFORNIA SLAVIC STUDIES. 1960. irreg. price
varies. University of California Press, 2223 Fulton
St., Berkeley, CA 94720.

870　880　　　　UK
CAMBRIDGE GREEK AND LATIN CLASSICS.
irreg. price varies. Cambridge University Press, Box
110, Cambridge CB2 3RL, England (And 32 E.
57th St., New York NY 10022) Eds. E. J. Kenney,
P. E. Easterling.

CAMBRIDGE LATIN TEXTS. see *LINGUISTICS*

800　　　　　　　UK　ISSN 0008-199X
CAMBRIDGE QUARTERLY. 1965. irreg. £9.60($21)
for 3 nos. 2 Summerfield, Cambridge CB3 9HE,
England. Ed.Bd. adv. bk. rev. index. circ. 1,000.
Indexed: Hum.Ind.

800　　　　　　　US
CAMELS COMING NEWSLETTER. 1972. a. $2.
Box 703, San Francisco, CA 94101. Ed. Richard
Morris. bk. rev. illus. circ. 600.

812　792　　　　CN
CANADIAN PLAY SERIES. irreg. price varies.
University of Toronto Press, Front Campus,
Toronto, Ont. M5S 1A6, Canada.

CANADIAN WRITERS AND CRITICS. see
JOURNALISM

830.9　　　　　　CN　ISSN 0317-7254
CARLETON GERMANIC PAPERS. 1973. a.
Can.$3. Carleton University, Department of
German, Ottawa K1S 5B6, Canada. Ed. Bd. circ.
140. (back issues avail.) Indexed: M.L.A.

800　　　　　　　UK　ISSN 0069-0961
CASSAL BEQUEST LECTURES. (Text in French)
1961 (1959 Lectures) irreg. price varies. Athlone
Press, 90-91 Great Russell St., London WC1B 3PY,
England.

700　800　　　　IT　ISSN 0008-8935
CENACOLO; arte e letteratura. 1949. a. Associazione
Cenacolo, Via Madama Cristina 90, 10126 Turin,
Italy. Ed. Dr. Giacomo Negri. adv. bk. rev. bibl.
illus.

820　　　　　　　UK　ISSN 0069-164X
CENTRAL LITERARY MAGAZINE. 1873. a. 25p.
45 Sandhills Lane, Barnt Green, Nr. Birmingham,
England. Ed. W. H. M. Sparks.

800　　　　　　　AE　ISSN 0069-1720
CENTRE CULTUREL FRANCAIS, ALGIERS.
RENCONTRES CULTURELLES.* 1970. irreg.
price varies. Centre Culturel Francais, 7 rue
Medecin-Capitaine Kassani Issad, Algiers, Algeria.

800　　　　　　　US
CHANEY CHRONICAL. (Companion to: What's
New About London, Jack) 1972. irreg. (1-2/yr)
$0.50 per no. London Northwest, 929 South Bay
Rd., Olympia, WA 98506. Ed. David H.
Schlottman. bk. rev. bibl. circ. 25. (processed)

800　　　　　　　FR　ISSN 0395-7845
CHANTS DES PEUPLES. no. 2, 1974. irreg. Editions
Caracteres, 7 rue de l'Arbalete, 75005 Paris, France.
Dir. Bruno Durocher. illus.

CHARIOTEER; an annual review of modern Greek
culture. see *HISTORY — History Of Europe*

800　770　　　　US
CHICAGO RENAISSANCE. 1976. a. $5.95.
(Chicago Renaissance Workshop) Natural Resources
Unlimited, 3531 Roesner Dr., Markham, IL 60426.
Ed. Joe H. Mitchell. circ. 3,000.

800　　　　　　　CN　ISSN 0315-467X
CHIEN D'OR/GOLDEN DOG. (Text in English and
French) 1972. irreg. c/o Editor, English
Department, Carleton University, Ottawa, Ont.,
Canada. Ed. Michael Gnarowski. illus.
Supersedes: Yes (ISSN 0044-0353)

808　　　　　　　US　ISSN 0092-8208
CHILDREN'S LITERATURE. a. $15 cloth; $5.95
paper. c/o Francelia Butler, Ed., Dept. of English,
Univ. of Connecticut, Storrs, CT 06268.

028.5　　　　　　US　ISSN 0092-8208
CHILDREN'S LITERATURE (NEW HAVEN) 1972.
a. $6.95. (Children's Literature Foundation) Yale
University Press, 92A Yale Sta., New Haven, CT
06520. Ed. Francelia Butler. bk. rev. illus.
cum.index, vols. 1-5. circ. 3,000.

891.43　　　　　　II
CHILDREN'S LITERATURE SERIES. (Text in
Hindi) 1951. irreg., vol. 29, 1963. price varies.
Vishveshvaranand Vedic Research Institute, P.O.
Sadhu Ashram, Hoshiarpur 146021, Punjab, India.

810　　　　　　　US　ISSN 0009-4285
CHIMES. a. free. Saint Mary's College, Notre Dame,
IN 46556. illus. circ. 1,600.

820　　　　　　　HK　ISSN 0069-3642
CHIMES.* 1961. irreg. free. Univ. of Hong Kong,
English Society, Hong Kong, Hong Kong.

818　　　　　　　US　ISSN 0069-3928
CHRISTMAS: AN AMERICAN ANNUAL OF
CHRISTMAS LITERATURE AND ART. 1931. a.
$6.50 hardbound; $3.25 paper. Augsburg Publishing
House, 426 S. Fifth St., Minneapolis, MN 55415.
Ed. R. E. Haugan. circ. 90,000.

CHRONIQUES DE PORT-ROYAL. see
RELIGIONS AND THEOLOGY

890　701　　　　II
CINMAY SMRTI PATHAGARA. (Text in Bengali)
1970. a. Rs.8. 26-8A Mahatma Gandhi Rd.,
Calcutta 9, India. adv.

700　100　　　　FR　ISSN 0069-4177
CIRCE. 1969. irreg. 215 F. Lettres Modernes, 73 rue
du Cardinal Lemoine, 75005 Paris, France. Ed. Jean
Burgos.

810　　　　　　　US
CITY LIGHTS ANTHOLOGY. irreg. City Lights
Books, 261 Columbus Ave., San Francisco, CA
94133.

860　　　　　　　CK　ISSN 0069-4444
CLASICOS COLOMBIANOS. 1954. irreg., no. 7,
1980. Instituto Caro y Cuervo, Apartado Aereo
20002, Bogota, Colombia.

850　　　　　　　IT
CLASSICI ITALIANI MINORI. irreg. Angelo Longo
Editore, Via Rocca Ai Fossi 6, Casella Postale 431,
48100 Ravenna, Italy. Ed. Enzo Esposito.

820　　　　　　　US　ISSN 0069-4509
CLASSICS OF BRITISH HISTORICAL
LITERATURE. 1970. irreg., no. 13, 1975. price
varies. University of Chicago Press, 5801 S. Ellis
Ave., Chicago, IL 60637. Ed. John L. Clive. (reprint
service avail. from UMI,ISI)

800 NE
CODICES MANUSCRIPTI, BIBLIOTHECA UNIVERSITATIS LEIDENSIS. 1910. irreg., vol. 19, 1977. price varies. Leiden University Press, c/o Martinus Nijhoff, Box 566, 2501 CN The Hague, Netherlands.

810 US ISSN 0084-8816
COLD-DRILL. 1970. a. $3. Boise State University, Department of English, 1910 College Blvd., Boise, ID 83707. Ed. A. Thomas Trusky. adv. charts. illus. circ. 750. (looseleaf format)

869 BL
COLECAO EDITORA DO ESCRITOR EM REVISTA. 1976. irreg. $5. Editora do Escritor Ltda, Rua Senador Vlaquer 133, 04744 Sao Paulo, Brazil.

800 IT ISSN 0069-5165
COLLANA DI CULTURA. 1963. irreg., no. 33, 1981. price varies. Edizioni dell' Ateneo S.p.A., P.O. Box 7216, 00100 Rome, Italy. circ. 1,000.

850 IT ISSN 0069-5203
COLLANA DI STUDI E SAGGI. 1959. irreg. price varies. Societa Accademica Romena, Foro Traiano 1a, 00187 Rome, Italy.

809 IT
COLLANA DI TESTI E DI CRITICA. 1964. irreg., no. 22, 1978. price varies. Liguori Editore s.r.l., Via Mezzocannone 19, 80134 Naples, Italy. Ed. Giorgio Petrocchi.

800 FR
COLLECTION "CHANTS DES PEUPLES". vol. 2, 1974. irreg. Editions Caracteres, 7 rue de l'Arbalete, 75005 Paris, France.

800 840 CN
COLLECTION LES ROUGES GORGES. 1971. irreg. price varies. Ecrits des Forges Inc., 2095 Sylvain, Trois-Rivieres, Quebec, Canada.

800 CN
COLLECTION LITTERATURE DU JOUR. no. 4, 1972. irreg. Can.$3.15. Editions du Jour, 6765 rue de Marseille, Montreal, Que. H1N 1M4, Canada.

840 CN
COLLECTION PRESENCE. irreg. price varies. University of Ottawa Press, 65 Hastey Ave., Ottawa, Ont., K1N 6N5, Canada.

810 US ISSN 0161-486X
COLUMBIA; a magazine of poetry and prose. 1977. irreg., 1-2/yr. $3. Columbia University School of the Arts, Writing Division, 404 Dodge, Columbia University, New York, NY 10027. Ed. John Plaskett. adv.

820 US ISSN 0069-6412
COMITATUS; A JOURNAL OF MEDIEVAL AND RENAISSANCE STUDIES. 1970. a. $3.50 to individuals; institutions $6. (University of California, Los Angeles, Center for Medieval and Renaissance Studies) Undena Publications, Box 97, Malibu, CA 90265. bk. rev. circ. 500.

800 US
COMPARATIST. 1977. a. $6. Southern Comparative Literature Association, c/o Department of English, North Carolina State University, Box 5308, Raleigh, NC 27607. Ed. Jean S. Smoot. bk. rev. circ. 300.

809 UK
COMPARATIVE CRITICISM; a yearbook. 1979. a. $39.50 for latest vol. (British Comparative Literature Association) Cambridge University Press, Box 110, Cambridge CB2 3RL, England (And 32 E. 57th St., New York, NY 10022) Ed. Elinor Shaffer.

808 MX
COMUNIDAD LATINOAMERICANA DE ESCRITORES. REVISTA. 1968. irreg; continues numbering under new title, with no. 15. $1. Comunidad Latinoamericana de Escritores, Calle Comunal 17 (San Angel), Mexico 20, DF, Mexico. adv. bk. rev. index. circ. 1,000.
Formerly (to no. 14: Comunidad Latinoamericana de Escritores. Boletin (ISSN 0069-8202)

800 US ISSN 0069-8407
CONFERENCE IN THE STUDY OF TWENTIETH-CENTURY LITERATURE, MICHIGAN STATE UNIVERSITY. PROCEEDINGS. 1961. irreg., 1966, no. 4. price varies. Michigan State University, Department of English, East Lansing, MI 48824.

800 BE ISSN 0010-5694
CONFINS. 1962. irreg. (7-8/yr.) 100 Fr.($2) ‡ Institut Catholique des Hautes Etudes Commerciales, Union des Etudiants, 2 Bd. Brand Whitlock, 1040 Brussels, Belgium. Ed. Jacques van der Moot. adv. bk. rev. film rev. illus. circ. 500. (processed)

890 FR ISSN 0589-3496
CONNAISSANCE DE L'ORIENT. COLLECTION UNESCO D'OEUVRES REPRESENTATIVES. 1956. (Unesco, UN) Editions Gallimard, 5, rue Sebastien-Bottin, Paris (7e), France.

809 860 US
CONSENSO: REVISTA DE LITERATURA. (Text in Spanish) 1977. a. $5. Publicaciones Consenso, Pennsylvania State Univ., 3550 Seventh St. Rd., New Kensington, PA 15068. Ed. Luis F. Gonzalez-Cruz. illus. circ. 250. (back issues avail.)

800 US ISSN 0069-9381
CONTEMPORARY DRAMA SERIES. 1971. irreg., no. 4, 1979. $2.95. Proscenium Press, P. O. Box 361, Newark, DE 19711. Ed. Robert Hogan. (reprint service avail. from UMI)

809 US ISSN 0091-3421
CONTEMPORARY LITERARY CRITICISM SERIES; excerpts from criticism of the works of today's novelists, poets, playwrights, and other creative writers. 1973. irreg., vol. 13, 1979. $48 per vol. Gale Research Company, Book Tower, Detroit, MI 48226. Ed. Dedria Bryfonski. cum.index.

810 US
CONTEMPORARY LITERARY SCENE. 1973. a. $8.95. c/o Department of English, Virginia Commonwealth University, VA 23284. Eds. Frank Magill, Walton Beacham.

001.3 808 US
CONTEMPORY ESSAY SERIES. irreg. price varies. Harper and Row Publishers, Inc., 10 East 53rd St., New York, NY 10022.

800 US
CONTRABAND. 1971. $5 for 5 nos. ‡ Contraband Press, Box 4073, Station A, Portland, ME 04101. Ed. Bd. bk. rev. illus. circ. 750. Indexed: ACCESS.

892.4 IS ISSN 0010-7948
CONTRAST. 1969. a. $1.50. Bar-Ilan University, English Department, Ramat Gan, Israel. Ed. Daniela Grunfeld. bk. rev. charts. illus.

800 US ISSN 0193-6875
CONTRIBUTIONS TO THE STUDY OF SCIENCE FICTION AND FANTASY. irreg. price varies. Greenwood Press, 8 Post Rd. W., Westport, CT 06881. Ed. Marshall Tymn.

800 AT ISSN 0311-1245
COR SERPENTIS. 1971. irreg. free. Monash University, Science Fiction Association, c/o Union, Monash University, Clayton, Vic. 3168, Australia.

801 100 US
CORONA. 1980. a. $6. Montana State University, Department of History and Philosophy, Bozeman, MT 59717. Eds. Lynda and Michael Sexson.

810 US
COSMIC CIRCUS. 1971. 1-2/yr. $5. c/o Regg King, Ed., 521 33rd St., Oakland, CA 94609. circ. 2,000.

840 US
CRITICAL BIBLIOGRAPHY OF FRENCH LITERATURE. 1951. irreg., vol. 6, 1980. price varies. Syracuse University Press, 1011 E. Water St., Syracuse, NY 13210. Ed. Richard A. Brooks.

800 US ISSN 0070-153X
CRITICAL ESSAYS IN MODERN LITERATURE. 1957. irreg. price varies. University of Pittsburgh Press, 127 N. Bellefield Ave., Pittsburgh, PA 15260.

800 UK
CRITICAL HERITAGE SERIES. irreg. price varies. Routledge & Kegan Paul Ltd., Broadway House, Newtown Rd., Henley-on-Thames, Oxon. RG9 1EN, England (U.S. address: Routledge Journals, 9 Park St., Boston, MA 02108)

899 820 AT
CRITICAL REVIEW. 1958. a. Aus.$2. Australian National University, Research School of Social Sciences, History of Ideas Unit, Box 4, Canberra, A.C.T. 2600, Australia. bk. rev. circ. 1,500-1,700. Indexed: Abstr.Engl.Stud. M.L.A.
Former titles: Critical Review Melbourne (ISSN 0070-1548); Critical Review. Melbourne-Sydney.

CRITICISM AND INTERPRETATION; journal for literature, linguistics. history and aesthetics. see HUMANITIES: COMPREHENSIVE WORKS

809 US
CRITICISM MONOGRAPHS. irreg. Wayne State University Press, 5959 Woodward Ave., Detroit, MI 48202. (back issues avail.)

800 FR ISSN 0070-1556
CRITIQUES DE NOTRE TEMPS ET... 1970. irreg. 18.50 F. Editions Garnier Freres, 19, rue des Plantes, 75014 Paris, France. circ. 10,000.

868 SP
CUADERNOS DE LA GAYA CIENCIA. 1975. irreg. Gaya Ciencia, Barcelona, Spain. illus.

807 860 AG
CUADERNOS PARA EL ESTUDIO DE LA ESTETICA Y LA LITERATURA. no. 8, 1974. irreg. Universidad Nacional del Nordeste, Instituto de Letras, Resistencia, Chaco, Argentina.

820 UK
CYFRES CLASURON YR ACADEMI. (Text in Welsh) 1980. irreg. price varies. (Welsh Academy) University of Wales Press, 6 Gwennyth St., Cathays, Cardiff CF2 4YD, Wales. Ed. P. J. Donovan. (reprint service avail. from UMI)

808.838 UK
CYPHER. irreg., approx. s-a. £1.50 for 5 issues; in U.S. $3 for 4. Plovers Barrow, School Road Nomansland, Salisbury, Wilts, England (Avail. in U.S. from Cy Giauvin, 17829 Peters, Roseville, MI 48066) Ed. James Goddard. adv. bk. rev. film rev. illus. circ. 500.
Science fiction reviews

DACOROMANIA; Jahrbuch fuer oestliche Latinitaet. see LINGUISTICS

800 US ISSN 0084-9537
DADA/SURREALISM. 1971. a. ‡ (Association for the Study of Dada & Surrealism) Queens College Press, Flushing, NY 11367. Ed. Mary Ann Caws. circ. 300.

891.7 UR
DALYAGLYADY LITARATURNY ZBORNIK. (Text in Belarussian) 1975. irreg. Vydavetstva Mastatskaya Litabatura, Minsk, U.S.S.R. Ed. Bd.

810 US
DAMASCUS ROAD. 1959. irreg. $2.25 per no. c/o C. S. Hanna, 6271 Hill Dr., Wacosville, PA 18106. circ. 500. (also avail. in microform from UMI)

800 FR ISSN 0070-279X
DANS LE FANTASTIQUE.* 1970. irreg. price varies. Christian Bourgois Editeur, 8 rue Garanciere, 75006 Paris, France.

850 US ISSN 0070-2862
DANTE STUDIES; with the Annual Report of the Dante Society. 1881/82. a. $15. State University of New York Press, State University Plaza, Albany, NY 12246. Ed. Anthony L. Pellegrini. circ. 600. (also avail. in microform from UMI)
Until 1967 (Vol. 85): Dante Society of America. Report, with Accompanying Papers.

410 NE
DE PROPRIETATIBUS LITTERARUM. SERIES DIDACTICA. 1972. irreg. price varies. Mouton Publishers, Noordeinde 41, 2514 GC The Hague, Netherlands (U.S. addr: Mouton Publishers, c/o Walter de Gruyter, Inc., 200 Saw Mill River Road, Hawthorne, NY 10532)

800 NE ISSN 0070-3060
DE PROPRIETATIBUS LITTERARUM. SERIES MAJOR. 1967. irreg. price varies. Mouton Publishers, Noordeinde 41, 2514 GC The Hague, Netherlands (U.S. addr: Mouton Publishers, c/o Walter de Gruyter, Inc., 200 Saw Mill River Road, Hawthorne, NY 10532)

800 NE ISSN 0070-3079
DE PROPRIETATIBUS LITTERARUM. SERIES MINOR. 1966. irreg. price varies. Mouton Publishers, Noordeinde 41, 2514 GC The Hague, Netherlands (U.S. addr: Mouton Publishers, c/o Walter de Gruyter, Inc., 200 Saw Mill River Road, Hawthorne, NY 10532)

800 NE ISSN 0070-3087
DE PROPRIETATIBUS LITTERARUM. SERIES PRACTICA. 1966. irreg. price varies. Mouton Publishers, Noordeinde 41, 2514 GC The Hague, Netherlands (U.S. addr: Mouton Publishers, c/o Walter de Gruyter, Inc., 200 Saw Mill River Road, Hawthorne, NY 10532)

810 705 US ISSN 0070-3141
DECEMBER; a magazine of the arts and opinion. 1958. irreg. $12.50 for 4 issues. December Press, 6232 N. Hoyne, No.1-C, 4343 N. Clarendon, Chicago, IL 60659. adv. bk. rev. film rev. illus. circ. 1,200. (also avail. in microform from UMI; back issues avail.) Indexed: Abstr.Engl.Stud. Ind.Little Mag.

810 US
DESPERADO. 1969. irreg. $1 per no. c/o Kell Robertson, Ed., 2429-A 24th St., San Francisco, CA 94110. circ. 500.

830 GW
DEUTSCHE AKADEMIE FUER SPRACHE UND DICHTUNG. SCHRIFTENREIHE. 1954. irreg., no. 51, 1977. price varies. Verlag Lambert Schneider, Hausackerweg 16, 6900 Heidelberg 1, W. Germany (B.R.D.)

830 GW ISSN 0070-4318
DEUTSCHE SCHILLER-GESELLSCHAFT. JAHRBUCH. 1957. a. price varies. Alfred Kroener Verlag, Reuchlinstr. 4, 7000 Stuttgart 1, W. Germany (B.R.D.) Eds. Fritz Martini, Walter Mueller-Seidel, Bernhard Zeller.

820 GW ISSN 0070-4326
DEUTSCHE SHAKESPEARE-GESELLSCHAFT WEST. JAHRBUCH. 1948. a. price varies (1978-79 double vol. DM. 74) Quelle und Meyer, Schloss-Wolfsbrunnen-Weg 29, Postfach 104480, 6900 Heidelberg 1, W. Germany (B.R.D.) Ed. Herman Heuer. bk. rev. circ. 2,000.

830 GW ISSN 0418-9140
DEUTSCHE STUDIEN. 1965. irreg., no. 30, 1976. price varies. Verlag Anton Hain KFg, Muehlgasse 3, Postfach 180, 6554 Meisenheim, W. Germany (B.R.D.) Eds. W. Flemming, W. J. Schroeder.

430 830 GE ISSN 0070-4334
DEUTSCHE TEXTE DES MITTELALTERS. 1948, vol. 42. irreg., vol. 69, 1976. price varies. Akademie-Verlag, Leipziger Str. 3-4, 108 Berlin, E. Germany (D.D.R.)

810 US
DEVON COUNTRY CHRONICLE. 1964. 5-6/yr. $2.50. Chicago B.S.I., 509 S. Atkins, Lombard, IL 60148. Ed. Robert W. Hahn. bk. rev. bibl. circ. 200.

820 SA
DIALOGUE; a literary annual for young writers. 1971. a. R.0.70. P.O. Box 102, Wynberg 7824, South Africa. Ed. Tim Peacock. bk. rev. circ. 4,500.

400 US ISSN 0360-215X
DICTIONARY OF CONTEMPORARY QUOTATIONS. 1976. biennial. $35. John Gordon Burke, Inc., Box 1492, Evanston, IL 60204.

813.01 CN ISSN 0702-8520
DIME BAG: FICTION ISSUE. 1977. irreg. Glendon College, Toronto, Ont., Canada.

050 810 820 US ISSN 0070-6094
DIRECTORY OF PERIODICALS PUBLISHING ARTICLES ON ENGLISH AND AMERICAN LITERATURE AND LANGUAGE. 1959. irreg., 4th ed. 1975. $10 $3.50 paper. Swallow Press, Inc., 811 W. Junior Terr., Chicago, IL 60613. Eds. Donna Gerstenberger and George Hendrick.

800 RM ISSN 0070-6892
DOCUMENTE SI MANUSCRISE LITERARE. 1967. irreg. (Academia de Stiinte Sociale si Politice, Institutul de Istorie si Teorie Literara "G. Calinescu") Editura Academiei Republicii Socialiste Romania, Calea Victoriei 125, Bucharest, Romania (Subscr. to: ILEXIM, Str. 13 Decembrie Nr. 3, P.O. Box 136-137, Bucharest, Romania) Ed. Paul Cornea.

057.87 891.87 CS
DOMOVA POKLADNICA. a. 20 Kcs. Priroda, Krizkova 7, 894 17 Bratislava, Czechoslovakia.

800 JA
DOSHISHA STUDIES IN FOREIGN LITERATURE.* (Text in Japanese, English, French or German) 1971. irreg. 1000 Yen. Doshisha University, Gaikoku Bungakukai, Karasuma Imadegawa, Kamikyo-ku, Kyoto 602, Japan.

378.1 UK ISSN 0012-589X
DRAGON. (Editions in English and Welsh) 1966. a. 10p. University College of Wales, Students' Union, Aberystwyth, Cardiganshire, Wales. Eds. G. J. Hill, Huw Jones. adv. bk. rev. film rev. illus. record rev. circ. 1,000.

822 UK ISSN 0070-7198
DRAMASCRIPTS SERIES. (Text in English or bilingual with English Translations) 1965. irreg., 1970, no. 4. price varies. Oleander Press, 17 Stansgate Ave., Cambridge CB2 2QZ, England (U.S. address: 210 Fifth Ave., New York, N.Y. 10010) Eds. Philip Ward And Wayne Schlepp.

830 SZ
DREHPUNKT. SONDERNUMMER. (Text in German) irreg. price varies. Z-Verlag, Postfach 794, CH-4002 Basel, Switzerland.

830 GW ISSN 0073-2885
E.T.A. HOFFMANN-GESELLSCHAFT. MITTEILUNGEN. 1939. a. DM.22. E.T.A. Hoffmann-Gesellschaft, Goennerstr. 2/II, 8600 Bamberg, W. Germany (B.R.D.) circ. 850.

820 US ISSN 0070-7864
EARLY ENGLISH TEXT SOCIETY. PUBLICATIONS. EXTRA SERIES. no. 34, 1966. irreg., latest issue no. 124. price varies. Oxford University Press, 200 Madison Ave., New York, NY 10016 (and Ely House, 37 Dover St., London W1X 4AH, England)

820 US ISSN 0070-7872
EARLY ENGLISH TEXT SOCIETY. PUBLICATIONS. ORIGINAL SERIES. 1970? irreg., latest no. 279. price varies. Oxford University Press, 200 Madison Ave., New York, NY 10016 (and Ely House, 37 Dover St., London W1X 4AH, England)

820 US ISSN 0070-7880
EARLY ENGLISH TEXT SOCIETY. PUBLICATIONS. SUPPLEMENTARY TEXTS. 1970. irreg., latest no. 5. price varies. Oxford University Press, 200 Madison Ave., New York, NY 10016 (and Ely House, 37 Dover St., London W1X 4AH, England)

840 SZ ISSN 0070-8879
ECRITURE; l'annnee litteraire en suisse romande. 1964. a. 20 Fr. Editions Bertil Galland, 29 rue du Lac, CH-1800 Vevey, Switzerland. Ed. Bertil Galland. circ. 2,000.

839 439 DK ISSN 0070-9069
EDITIONES ARNAMAGNAEANAE. SERIES A. (Text in Danish, English, Icelandic) 1958. irreg. price varies. Arnamagnaean Institute, Njalsgade 76, DK-2300 Copenhagen S, Denmark (Dist. by: C. A. Reitzels Boghandel A-S, Noerregade 20, DK-1165 Copenhagen K, Denmark)

839 439 DK ISSN 0070-9077
EDITIONES ARNAMAGNAEANAE. SERIES B. (Text in Danish, English, Icelandic) 1960. irreg. price varies. Arnamagnaean Institute, Njalsgade 76, DK-2300 Copenhagen S, Denmark (Dist. by: C. A. Reitzels Boghandel A-S, Noerregade 20, DK-1165 Copenhagen K, Denmark)

839 DK ISSN 0070-9085
EDITIONES ARNAMAGNAEANAE. SUPPLEMENTUM. 1963. irreg. Arnamagnaean Institute, Njalsgade 76, DK-2300 Copenhagen S, Denmark (Dist. by: C. A. Reitzels Boghandel A-S, Noerregade 20, DK-1165 Copenhagen K, Denmark)

820 792 UK
EDWARDIAN STUDIES. 1976. a. £5($15) (Edwardian Studies Association) High Orchard Press, High Orchard, 125 Markyate Rd., Dagenham, Essex RM8 2LB, England. adv. bk. rev. index.
Literature and drama of the Edwardian era

810 UK
EIGHTEEN NINETIES SOCIETY.JOURNAL. 1965. a. membership. Eighteen Nineties Society, 28 Carlingford Rd., Hampstead, London NW3 1RX, England. Ed. G. Krishnamurti. adv. bk. rev. circ. 750. (processed) Indexed: Abstr. Engl.Stud.
Formerly: Francis Thompson Society. Journal (ISSN 0532-5781)

820 AU
ELIZABETHAN AND RENAISSANCE STUDIES. (Text in English) 1972. irreg., no. 60, 1977. S.245. Universitaet Salzburg, Institut fuer Englische Sprache, Akademiestr. 24, A-5020 Salzburg, Austria. Ed. James Hogg. circ. 250.

809.02 US ISSN 0363-4841
ENCOMIA. 1975. irreg. $7.50. International Courtly Literature Society, Temple University, Humanities Building, Temple University, Philadelphia, PA 19122. Ed. F.R.P. Akehurst. adv. bk. rev. illus. circ. 600.

800 US ISSN 0071-0164
ENCORE. 1948. a. $2. National Association of Dramatic and Speech Arts, Shaw University, Box 124, Raleigh, NC 27611. Ed. H.B. Caple. adv. bk. rev. circ. 1,000. (also avail. in microform from UMI) Indexed: T.D.S.I.
Scholarly and creative writing about Black theatre and rhetoric

814 US ISSN 0071-0598
ENGLISH INSTITUTE. SELECTED ESSAYS. 1939. a. price varies. Johns Hopkins University Press, Baltimore, MD 21218 (Vols. before 1978 pub. by: Columbia University Press, 136 S. Broadway, Irvington-on-Hudson, NY 10533)

809 US
ENGLISH LITERARY RENAISSANCE SUPPLEMENTS. 1972. irreg., no. 3, 1977. price varies; free with subscription to English Literary Renaissance. University of Massachusetts, Department of English, Amherst, MA 01002. Ed. Arthur F. Kinney.
Formerly: English Literary Renaissance Monographs.

080 800 UK ISSN 0071-061X
ENGLISH LITTLE MAGAZINES. 1967. irreg., no. 16, 1971. price varies. Frank Cass & Co. Ltd., Gainsborough House, 11 Gainsborough Rd., London E11 1RS, England (Dist. in U.S. by: Biblio Distribution Center, 81 Adams Drive, Totowa, N.J. 07512)

808 IT ISSN 0425-0575
ENGLISH MISCELLANY; a symposium of history, literature and the arts. 1950. a. price varies. Edizioni di Storia e Letteratura, Via Lancellotti 18, 00186 Rome, Italy. Ed. Mario Praz.

860 UY ISSN 0071-0679
ENSAYO Y TESTIMONIO.* irreg. Editorial Arca, Colonia 1263, Montevideo, Uruguay.

800 GW
ENSEMBLE; international literary yearbook. (Text in English, French, German) 1969. a. DM.19.80. (Bayerische Akademie der Schoenen Kuenste) Verlagsgruppe Langen- Mueller, Hubertusstr. 4, 8000 Munich 19, W. Germany (B.R.D.) circ. 2,000.
Supersedes: Gestalt und Gedanke; Jahrbuch.

860 CK ISSN 0120-1263
ESCRITOS. 1974. irreg. $.50 per no. Universidad Pontificia Bolivariana, Facultad de Filosofia y Letras, Biblioteca Central - Seccion Canje, Aptdo 1178, Medellin, Colombia. Ed. Gonzolo Soto P. adv. bk. rev. bibl.

824 US ISSN 0071-1357
ESSAYS AND STUDIES. 1910. a. price varies. Humanities Press, Inc., 171 First Ave., Atlantic Highlands, NJ 07716.

ESSAYS IN FOREIGN LANGUAGES AND LITERATURES/GAIKOKUGO GAIKOKU BUNGAKU KENKYU. see *LINGUISTICS*

840 844 AT ISSN 0071-139X
ESSAYS IN FRENCH LITERATURE. (Text in English and French) 1964. irreg., vol. 12, 1977. $3. University of Western Australia, Nedlands, W. A. 6009, Australia.

800 US ISSN 0071-1470
ESSENTIAL ARTICLES. 1961. irreg., no. 9, 1979. price varies. Shoe String Press Inc., 995 Sherman Ave., Hamden, CT 06514. Ed. James Thorp III.
Anthologies of articles essential to the study of various periods and authors in the field of literature

809 UY
ESTUDIOS CRITICOS. 1977. irreg. price varies. A C A L I Editorial, Ituzaingo 1495-97, Montevideo, Uruguay. Dir. Jorge Arbeleche.

ESTUDIOS DE LINGUISTICA Y LITERATURA. see LINGUISTICS

860 MX ISSN 0071-1691
ESTUDIOS DE LITERATURA. 1958. irreg; latest issue, 1976. price varies. ‡ Universidad Nacional Autonoma de Mexico, Instituto de Investigaciones Esteticas, Torre de Humanidades, Ciudad Universitaria, Mexico 20, D.F., Mexico.

860 SP ISSN 0071-1705
ESTUDIOS DE LITERATURA CONTEMPORANEA. 1968. irreg. $3. to $5. Real Academia Espanola de la Lengua, c/o Alonso Vicente Zamora, Felipe IV no. 4, Madrid, Spain. circ. 2,000.

ESTUDIOS ROMANICAS. see LINGUISTICS

800 BL
ESTUDOS BAIANOS. 1970. irreg. Universidade Federal da Bahia, Centro Editorial e Didatico, Rua A. Viana s/n, Canela, Salvador, Bahia, Brazil. Ed. Bd. circ. 1,000.

ESTUDOS ITALIANOS EM PORTUGAL. see ART

840 SZ ISSN 0531-9455
ETUDES BAUDELAIRIENNES. 1970. irreg., no. 9, 1980. price varies. Editions de la Baconniere S.A., Box 185, CH-2017 Boudry, Switzerland.

840 FR ISSN 0425-4791
ETUDES BERNANOSIENNES. Variant title: Series Georges Bernanos. (Subseries of: Revue des Lettres Modernes) 1960. a. price varies. Lettres Modernes, 73, rue du Cardinal Lemoine, 75005 Paris, France. Ed. Michel Esteve. bk. rev. (back issues avail.)

400 900 SZ ISSN 0071-1934
ETUDES DE PHILOLOGIE ET D'HISTOIRE. (Text in French or English) 1967. irreg., no. 30, 1976. price varies. Librarie Droz, 11, rue Massot, 1211 Geneva 12, Switzerland.

800 FR ISSN 0071-2051
ETUDES FINNO-OUGRIENNES. 1964. irreg. price varies. (Universite de Paris X (Paris-Nanterre), Centre d'Etudes Finno-Ougriennes) Editions Klincksieck, 11 rue de Lille, Paris 7, France. bk. rev.

800 479 FR ISSN 0071-2078
ETUDES GOBINIENNES. (Text in French; occasionally in German) 1966. a. price varies. Editions Klincksieck, 11 rue de Lille, Paris 7, France. Eds. A. B. Duff, J. Gaulmier. bk. rev.

810 US ISSN 0094-2367
EVERYMAN. 1963. irreg.(approx. 2/yr.) $3 for 2 nos. Deciduous, 1456 W. 54th St., Cleveland, OH 44102. Ed. Christopher Franke. circ. 1,000.

810 US ISSN 0421-9090
EXILE; contemporary literature. vol. 23, 1976. irreg. Denison University, Granville, OH 43023. illus.

820 AT ISSN 0085-039X
EXPRESSION. 1964. a. free. Wollongong Teachers College, Literary Club, Wollongong, N.S.W. 2500, Australia. Ed. R.W. Colvin. bk. rev. circ. 400.

830 AU
FACETTEN. 1970. a. S.82. (Kulturamt) Jugend und Volk Verlagsgesellschaft, Tiefer Graben 7, A-1014 Vienna, Austria.

808.8 US ISSN 0094-5862
FAMILY ALBUM. 1966. a. $9.95. A. J. Holman Co. (Subsidiary of: J.B. Lippincott Co.) Box 956, E. Washington Sq., Philadelphia, PA 19105. Eds. Arthur and Nancy de Moss. illus.
Formerly: Gold Star Family Album.

810 US
FATHAR. 1970. irreg., 1-2/yr., vol. 7, 1975. $0.75 per no. c/o Duncan McNaughton, Ed., Box 355, Bolinas, CA 94924. circ. 500.

800 US
FAULT. 1971. irreg. $1. c/o Terence Ames, Ed., 41186 Alice Ave., Fremont, CA 94538. illus. circ. 500. (back issues and chapbooks avail.)

800 301.412 FR
FEMMES EN LITTERATURE. 1976. irreg. price varies. Librairie Klincksieck, 11, rue de Lille, Paris 7e, France. Dir. Patrice Laurent.

800 US
FIFTH SUN. 1979. irreg. Quincunx Press, 1134-B Chelsea Ave., Santa Monica, CA 90403. Ed. Max Benavidez.

991.4 US ISSN 0071-4852
FILIPINIANA BOOK GUILD. PUBLICATIONS. 1962. irreg., vol. 25, 1980. (Filipiniana Book Guild, PH) Cellar Book Shops (Dist.), 18090 Wyoming, Detroit, MI 48221. circ. 400.

FILOLOGIA BALTYCKA/BALTIC PHILOLOGY. see LINGUISTICS

810 US
FIRE EXIT. 1967. irreg. c/o William Corbett, Ed., 9 Columbus Square, Boston, MA 02116. circ. 500-1,000.

700.5 US
FIRELANDS REVIEW. 1973. a. $3. Rudinger Foundation, Firelands College, Huron, OH 44839. Ed. Joel Rudinger. illus. circ. 1,000.
Formerly: Firelands Arts Review (ISSN 0094-8012)

810 US ISSN 0071-5654
FITZGERALD/HEMINGWAY ANNUAL. 1969. a. $36. ‡ Gale Research Company, Book Tower, Detroit, MI 48226. Eds. Matthew J. Bruccoli, Richard Layman.
Interviews, reminiscences and book reviews

FLANNERY O'CONNOR BULLETIN. see BIOGRAPHY

810 US ISSN 0147-1686
FLOATING ISLAND. 1976. irreg., no. 3, 1979. Floating Island Publications, Box 516, Point Reyes Station, CA 94956. Ed. Michael Sykes. illus. circ. 500.

FOLGER SHAKESPEARE LIBRARY ANNUAL REPORT. see LIBRARY AND INFORMATION SCIENCES

890 296 US
FOLK LITERATURE OF THE SEPHARDIC JEWS. 1971. irreg. price varies. University of California Press, 2223 Fulton St., Berkeley, CA 94720.

810 US
FOR NOW. 1961. 2-3/yr. $0.50 per no. c/o Donald Phelps, Ed., 694 Chauncey St., Brooklyn, NY 11207. circ. 500.

809 IT ISSN 0390-2153
FORME DEL SIGNIFICATO. 1974. irreg., no. 25, 1979. price varies. Liguori Editore s.r.l., Via Mezzocannone 19, 80134 Naples, Italy. Ed.Bd.

830 NE
FORSCHUNGSBERICHTE ZUR D D R-LITERATUR. 1980. irreg. price varies. Editions Rodopi N.V., Keizersgracht 302-304, Amsterdam, Netherlands. Ed. Gerd Labroisse.

800 GW ISSN 0071-7703
FORSCHUNGSPROBLEME DER VERGLEICHENDEN LITERATURGESCHICHTE. 1951. irreg., no. 7, 1978. price varies. Max Niemeyer Verlag, Pfrondorfer Str. 2, 7400 Tuebingen, W. Germany (B.R.D.)

810 US ISSN 0015-9344
FRAGMENTS; a literary magazine. 1957. a. $1.50. Seattle University, College of Arts and Sciences, Department of English, 900 Broadway, Seattle, WA 98122. Eds. Edwin Weihe & Kenneth Maclean.

830 430 GW ISSN 0071-9226
FRANKFURTER BEITRAEGE ZUR GERMANISTIK. 1967. irreg., vol. 15, 1977. price varies. Carl Winter Universitaetsverlag, Lutherstr. 59, 6900 Heidelberg, W. Germany (B.R.D.)

491 891 GW ISSN 0067-592X
FREIE UNIVERSITAET BERLIN. OSTEUROPA-INSTITUT. SLAVISTISCHE VEROEFFENTLICHUNGEN. (Title Varies: Veroffentlichungen der Abteilung fuer Slavische Sprachen und Literaturen) 1953. irreg. price varies. Freie Universitaet Berlin, Osteuropa Institut, Garystr. 55, 1000 Berlin 33 (Dahlem), W. Germany (B.R.D.) Ed.Bd. circ. 500.

800 GW ISSN 0071-9463
FREIES DEUTSCHES HOCHSTIFT, FRANKFURT AM MAIN. JAHRBUCH. (Text in English and German) 1962. a. price varies. Max Niemeyer Verlag, Pfrondorfer Str. 4, 7400 Tuebingen, W. Germany (B.R.D.) Ed. Detlev Lueders.

840 SA
FRENCH STUDIES IN SOUTHERN AFRICA. Added title: Cahiers de l'A F S S A. (Text in French) 1972. a., latest no. 6, 1978. R.6. Association for French Studies in Southern Africa, University of Cape Town, Department of Romance Studies, Private Bag, Rondesbosch, Cape Town, South Africa. bibl.

810 US ISSN 0016-4275
GAMBIT. vol.3,1970. a. California State University, Long Beach, Department of English, Long Beach, CA 90801. circ. 450.

830 GW
GASOLIN 23. 1973. irreg., no. 7, 1979. Nova Press, Friedrichstr. 60, 6000 Frankfurt, W. Germany (B.R.D.) Eds. J. Ploog, W. Hartmann. adv. illus. circ. 2,000.

800 GW ISSN 0072-0550
GEISTIGE BEGEGNUNG; Moderne Erzaehler der Welt. 1962. irreg. DM.28. (Institut fuer Auslandsbeziehungen, Stuttgart) Horst Erdmann Verlag, Hartmeyerstr. 117, Postfach 1380, 7400 Tuebingen, W. Germany (B.R.D.) circ. 4,000.

800 GW
GESAMTHOCHSCHULE WUPPERTAL. SCHRIFTENREIHE LITERATURWISSENSCHAFT. 1976. irreg., vol. 9, 1979. price varies. Bouvier Verlag Herbert Grundmann, Am Hof 32, Postfach 1268, 5300 Bonn 1, W. Germany (B.R.D.) Ed. Bd.

GOETEBORGER GERMANISTISCHE FORSCHUNGEN. see LINGUISTICS

830 GE
GOETHE-JAHRBUCH. 1880. a, vol. 97, 1980. M.35. (Goethe-Gesellschaft, Weimar) Hermann Boehlaus Nachfolger, Meyerstr. 50a, 53 Weimar, E. Germany (D.D.R.) Ed. Karl-Heinz Hahn. bk. rev.
Formerly: Goethe-Gesellschaft. Jahrbuch (ISSN 0072-484X)

GOTHENBURG STUDIES IN ENGLISH. see LINGUISTICS

860 UY ISSN 0072-5439
GRANDES TODOS.* irreg. Editorial Arca, Colonia 1263, Montevideo, Uruguay.

800 US ISSN 0092-5268
GRANTS AND AWARDS AVAILABLE TO AMERICAN WRITERS. 1971. a. $3.50 to individuals; institutions $6.50. P. E. N. American Center, 47 Fifth Ave., New York, NY 10003. circ. 4,000.
Formerly: List of Grants and Awards Available to American Writers (ISSN 0075-983X)

800 US ISSN 0160-6565
GUEST AUTHOR; a directory of speakers. 1978. biennial. Hermes Press, 51 Lenox St., Brockton, MA 02401. Ed. Jane Manthorne, Rose Moorachian. circ. 2,000.

800 FR ISSN 0072-8020
GUIDE DES PRIX LITTERAIRES. 1951. irreg., 1965, 5th ed. 61.88 F. (Syndicat des Industries du Livres) Cercle de la Librairie, 117 Bd. Saint Germain, 75279 Paris Cedex 06, France.

840 FR ISSN 0072-8993
GUILLAUME APOLLINAIRE. (Issued as a subseries of Revue des Lettres Modernes. Cited also as Series Guillaume Apollinaire) 1962. a. Lettres Modernes, 73 rue du Cardinal-Lemoine, 75005 Paris, France. Ed. Michel Decaudin. bk. rev.

830 GW
HABELTS DISSERTATIONSDRUCKE. REIHE GERMANISTIK. 1973. irreg. price varies. Rudolf Habelt Verlag, Am Buchenhang 1, 5300 Bonn 1, W. Germany (B.R.D.)

800 700 US
HAND BOOK. 1976. irreg., approx. 2/yr. $8. c/o R. Ratner, 50 Spring St., New York, NY 10012. Eds. Susan Mernit and Rochelle Ratner. bk. rev. illus. circ. 1,000.

810 US
HARRISON STREET REVIEW. 1970. irreg. (approx. a.) 4438 Harrison St., Kansas City, MO 64111. Ed. Bd. adv. bibl. illus. circ. 2,000(controlled) (processed)

800 420 US ISSN 0073-0513
HARVARD ENGLISH STUDIES. 1970. irreg., 1972, no. 3. Harvard University Press, 79 Garden St., Cambridge, MA 02138.

HARVARD SLAVIC MONOGRAPHS. see HISTORY — History Of Europe

800 US ISSN 0073-0696
HARVARD STUDIES IN COMPARATIVE LITERATURE. 1910. irreg., 1972, nos. 31,32. price varies. Harvard University Press, 79 Garden St., Cambridge, MA 02138.

HARVARD-YENCHING INSTITUTE. MONOGRAPH SERIES. see HISTORY — History Of Asia

810 US ISSN 0073-0866
HARVEST. 1936. a. $1. University of Houston, Department of English, Cullen Blvd., Houston, TX 77004. index.

800 US ISSN 0362-7888
HARVEST. 1974. a. $2.95. Connecticut Writers League, Box 78, Farmington, CT 06032. Ed. Alfred B. Clark. circ. 1,000. (back issues avail.)

830 GW ISSN 0073-1560
HEBBEL-JAHRBUECHER. a. price varies. (Hebbel-Gesellschaft) Westholsteinische Verlagsanstalt Boyens und Co., Am Wulf-Isebrand-Platz, Postfach 1880, 2240 Heide, W. Germany (B.R.D.) Eds. H. Stolte, H. Grundmann, E. Oldenburg.

830 920 GW ISSN 0073-1692
HEINE-JAHRBUCH. 1962. a. DM.19.80. (Heinrich-Heine-Institut, Duesseldorf) Hoffmann und Campe Verlag, Harvestehuder Weg 45, 2000 Hamburg 13, W. Germany (B.R.D.) Ed. Joseph A. Kruse. bk. rev. circ. 1,300.

800 US ISSN 0017-9884
HEIRS. (Text in Chinese, English, Spanish) 1968. irreg. $9. Heirs, Inc., 657 Mission St., Rm. 205, San Francisco, CA 94105. Ed. Bd. adv. illus. circ. 4,000. (also avail. in microform from UMI; reprint service avail. from UMI)

880 480 GW ISSN 0018-0084
HELLENIKA; Zeitschrift fuer deutsch-griechische kulturelle und wirtschaftliche Zusammenarbeit. 1964. a. DM.9. (Vereinigung der Deutsch-Griechischen Gesellschaften) Verlag Ferdinand Kamp, Wildumestr. 6, 4630 Bochum, W. Germany (B.R.D.) Ed. Prof. Dr. Isidora Rosenthal-Kamarinea. adv. bk. rev. abstr. bibl. circ. 3,000.

820 UK ISSN 0073-1927
HERBERT READ SERIES. 1961. irreg. 52p.($1.25) Oleander Press, 17 Stansgate Ave., Cambridge CB2 2QZ, England (U.S. address: 210 Fifth Ave., New York, N.Y. 10010) Ed. Philip Ward.

809 400 JA ISSN 0387-9348
HERON; essays on language & literature. (Text in English and Japanese) 1966. a. Saitama University, 255 Simo-Okubo, Urawa-shi, Saitama-ken, Japan. Ed.Bd. circ. 200.

850 860 US ISSN 0160-3493
HISPANO-ITALIC STUDIES. 1976. irreg. price varies. (Georgetown University, School of Languages and Linguistics) Georgetown University Press, Washington, DC 20057. Eds. Bruno M. Damiani, F. Michael Gerli, Roberto Severino.

100 800 SZ ISSN 0073-2397
HISTOIRE DES IDEES ET CRITIQUE LITTERAIRE. 1954. irreg., no. 161, 1977. price varies. Librarie Droz, 11, rue Massot, 1211 Geneva 12, Switzerland. circ. 1,500.

810 793 US
HOB-NOB ANNUAL. 1969. a. $1. 715 Dorsea Rd., Lancaster, PA 17601. Ed. M. K. Henderson. bk. rev. circ. 150.
Formerly (until 1979): Hob-Nob Quarterly.

808 FR
HOMMES ET LES LETTRES. irreg., vol. 2, 1977. Editions l' Hermes, 31 rue Pasteur, 69007 Lyon, France. Ed. Jacques Goudet.

800 UK ISSN 0305-926X
HOUSMAN SOCIETY JOURNAL. 1974. a. £3. Housman Society, c/o Miss B. E. Barley, Area Library, Stratford Rd., Bromsgrove, Worcs. B60 1AP, England. Ed. R. P. Graves. adv. bk. rev. bibl. circ. 350. (back issues avail.)

800 US
HUERTA CHAPBOOK SERIES. 1973. irreg., 1-2/yr., no. 6, 1979. $2 per no. Huerta Press, Box 27b, Lakeville, NY 14480. Ed. Gerald McCarthy. bk. rev. circ. 600. (also avail. in microform from UMI)
Supersedes: Huerta.

894.51 HU ISSN 0439-9080
HUNGARIAN P.E.N/P.E.N. HONGROIS. (Text in English and French) 1961. a. free. Hungarian P.E.N. Club, Vorosmarty ter 1, 1051 Budapest, Hungary. Ed. Laszlo Kery. adv. bk. rev. bibl. circ. 1,000.

839.82 920 NO ISSN 0073-4365
IBSEN AARBOKEN/IBSEN YEARBOOK. 1951/52. a. price varies. Universitetsforlaget, Kolstadgt. 1, Box 2959-Toeyen, Oslo 6, Norway (U. S. address: Box 258, Irvington-on-Hudson)

820 IE ISSN 0019-1027
ICARUS.* 1950. irreg. 25p.($1.50) per no. University of Dublin, Trinity College, Dublin, Ireland. Eds. Ernest Bates & David Norris. adv. bk. rev. circ. 600.

809 BE
ICON. CAHIER. (Text in Dutch, English and French) 1970. a. 200 Fr. Icon, Lobergenbos 27, B-3200 Louvain, Belgium. Ed. Jozef Peeters. bk. rev. bibl. circ. 400.
Former titles: Icon-Werkgroep Jean Ray. Cahier; Cahier Jean Ray.

800 400 US ISSN 0073-5175
ILLINOIS STUDIES IN LANGUAGE AND LITERATURE. 1915. irreg. University of Illinois Press, 54 E. Gregory, Box 5081, Station A, Champaign, IL 61820. Ed. Bd. (reprint service avail. from UMI)

806 AT ISSN 0310-3048
IN PRINT. 1972. a. Aus.$0.40. Townsville Writers' Group, Flat 2, First St., Railway Estate, Townsville, Qld 4810, Australia.

830 NE
INDICES ZUM ALTDEUTSCHEN SCHRIFTTUM. 1976. irreg. price varies. Editions Rodopi N.V., Keizersgracht 302-304, 1016 EX Amsterdam, Netherlands. Ed. R. Ralph Anderson. circ. 300.

800 US ISSN 0190-0234
INKLINGS. 1979. irreg. Mudborn Press, 209 W. De la Guerra, Santa Barbara, CA 93101. Ed. Judyl Mudfoot. circ. 500.

800 GW ISSN 0443-2460
INSEL-ALMANACH. 1905. a. price varies. Insel-Verlag, Lindenstr. 29, 6000 Frankfurt, W. Germany (B.R.D.) bk. rev. circ. 5,000.

820 CN ISSN 0380-2957
INSIDE. 1975. irreg. Can.$0.25. Ursa Major Press, 302, 60 High St., Nelson, B.C. V1L 3Z4, Canada. Ed. E. Kluge.

891.7 947 FR ISSN 0078-9976
INSTITUT D'ETUDES SLAVES, PARIS. BIBLIOTHEQUE RUSSE. (Text and summaries in French and Russian) 1912. irreg., vol. 58, 1980. price varies. Institut d'Etudes Slaves, 9 rue Michelet, F - 75006 Paris, France.

891.8 FR ISSN 0079-001X
INSTITUT D'ETUDES SLAVES, PARIS. TEXTES. 1926. irreg., vol. 11, 1968. price varies. Institut d'Etudes Slaves, 9 rue Michelet, F-75006 Paris, France.

891 943 FR ISSN 0079-0028
INSTITUT D'ETUDES SLAVES, PARIS. TRAVAUX. 1923. irreg.; 1970, vol. 30. price varies. Institut d'Etudes Slaves, 9 rue Michelet, F-75006 Paris, France.

800 FR ISSN 0073-8212
INSTITUT DE RECHERCHE ET D'HISTOIRE DES TEXTES, PARIS. DOCUMENTS, ETUDES ET REPERTOIRES. 1958. irreg., 1974, no. 22. price varies. Institut de Recherche et d'Histoire des Textes, Paris, 15, Quai Anatole- France, 75700 Paris, France.

800 FR ISSN 0073-8263
INSTITUT DES ETUDES OCCITANES. PUBLICATIONS. 1970. irreg. price varies. Presses Universitaires de France, 108 Bd. Saint Germaine, 75279 Paris Cedex 6, France (Service des Periodiques, 12 rue Jean de Beauvais, 75005 Paris)

INSTITUT FRANCAIS D'INDOLOGIE. PUBLICATIONS. see HISTORY — History Of Asia

860 CK
INSTITUTO CARO Y CUERVO. SERIE GRANADA ENTREABIERTA. 1973. irreg., no. 27, 1980. Instituto Caro y Cuervo, Aptdo. Aereo 20002, Bogota, Colombia.

860 400 CK ISSN 0073-9928
INSTITUTO CARO Y CUERVO. SERIE MINOR. 1950. irreg., no. 22, 1980. Instituto Caro y Cuervo, Seccion de Publicaciones, Apdo. Aereo 20002, Bogota, Colombia.

800 MX ISSN 0077-1236
INSTITUTO TECNOLOGICO Y DE ESTUDIOS SUPERIORES. PUBLICACIONES. SERIE LETRAS. 1965. irreg., 1970, no. 4. Instituto Tecnologico y de Estudios Superiores de Monterrey, Sucursal de Correos "J", Monterrey, N.L., Mexico.

800 RM
INSTITUTUL PEDAGOGIC ORADEA. LUCRARI STIINTIFICE: SERIA LITERATURA. (Continues in part its Lucrari Stiintifice: Seria Filologie (1971-72), its Lucrari Stiintifice: Seria A and Seria B (1969-1970), and its Lucrari Stiintifice (1967-68).) (Text in Rumanian, occasionally in English or French; summaries in Rumanian, French, English or German) irreg. Institutul Pedagogic Oradea, Calea Armatei Rosii Nr. 5, Oradea, Romania.

INTERAUTEURS. see PATENTS, TRADEMARKS AND COPYRIGHTS

840 700 FR ISSN 0074-1140
INTERFERENCES, ARTS, LETTRES. 1968. irreg. price varies. Lettres Modernes, 73 rue du Cardinal-Lemoine, 75005 Paris, France.

820 UK ISSN 0074-1396
INTERNATIONAL ARTHURIAN SOCIETY. REPORT OF CONGRESS/SOCIETE INTERNATIONALE ARTHURIENNE. RAPPORTS DU CONGRES. 1949. a., 12th, 1979, Regensburg, W. Germany. £4 to members. International Arthurian Society, c/o Prof. Cedric Pickford, French Department, University of Hull, Hull HU6 7RX, Yorkshire, England. Ed. Prof. Charles Foulon. bk. rev. circ. 1,600.

840 FR ISSN 0571-5865
INTERNATIONAL ASSOCIATION OF FRENCH STUDIES. CAHIERS. 1951. a. 50 Fr. International Association of French Studies, 11 Place Marcelin-Berthelot, 75005 Paris, France. Ed. Robert Garapon.

INTERNATIONAL AUTHORS AND WRITERS WHO'S WHO. see *BIOGRAPHY*

800   GW ISSN 0074-2813
INTERNATIONAL COMPARATIVE LITERATURE ASSOCIATION. PROCEEDINGS OF THE CONGRESS. 1955. triennial, 1978, 7th Montreal, Canada. DM.213. (International Comparative Literature Association - Association Internationale de Litterature Comparee) Kunst und Wissen Erich Bieber OHG, Wilhelmstr. 4, Postfach 46, 7000 Stuttgart 1, W. Germany (B.R.D.)
1970, 6th, Bordeaux, France.
Proceedings published in host country

891.7   US ISSN 0047-0686
INTERNATIONAL DOSTOEVSKY SOCIETY BULLETIN. 1972. a. $8. International Dostoevsky Society, c/o Martin P. Rice, University of Tennessee, Department of Germanic and Slavic Languages, Knoxville, TN 37919. Ed. Rudolf Neuhaeuser. bk. rev. bibl. circ. 500.

INTERNATIONAL FEDERATION FOR MODERN LANGUAGES AND LITERATURE. CONGRESS REPORTS. see *LINGUISTICS*

800 860 US ISSN 0074-6495
INTERNATIONAL INSTITUTE OF IBERO-AMERICAN LITERATURE. CONGRESS PROCEEDINGS. MEMORIA. biennial, 19th, Pittsburgh, 1979. International Institute of Ibero-American Literature - Institute Internacional de Literatura Iberoamericana, c/o Bruce Stiehm, Sec.-Treas., 1312 C.L., University of Pittsburgh, Pittsburgh, PA 15260. circ. 2,000.
Proceedings published by sponsoring university

INTERNATIONAL JOURNAL OF SLAVIC LINGUISTICS AND POETICS. see *LINGUISTICS*

800   UK ISSN 0074-722X
INTERNATIONAL P. E. N. CONGRESS. REPORT. irreg., 39th, 1974, Jerusalem. International P.E.N., 7 Dilke St., London SW3 4JE, England.

830   GW ISSN 0340-4528
INTERNATIONALES ARCHIV FUER SOZIALGESCHICHTE DER DEUTSCHEN LITERATUR. (Text in English, French, German) 1976. a. DM.86. Max Niemeyer Verlag, Pfrondorfer Str. 4, Postfach 2140, 7400 Tuebingen, W. Germany (B.R.D.) Ed. Bd. adv. bk. rev. bibl.

800   US
INTERPRETATIONS; studies in language and literature. 1968. a. Memphis State University, Department of English, Memphis, TN 38152. Eds. J. Lasley Dameron, Charles Long, William Osborne.

IRISH DRAMA SELECTIONS. see *THEATER*

800   UK ISSN 0140-895X
IRISH LITERARY STUDIES. 1977. irreg. Colin Smythe, Ltd., Gerrards Cross, Buckinghamshire SL9 7AE, England (Dist. in U.S. by: Barnes & Noble Books, Littlefield Adams, Adams Drive, Totowa, N. J. 07511) circ. 1,500.

800   US ISSN 0075-0816
IRISH PLAY SERIES. 1968. irreg., no. 18, 1981. price varies. Proscenium Press, P.O. Box 361, Newark, DE 19711. Ed. Robert Hogan. (reprint service avail. from UMI)

820   US ISSN 0193-9777
IRISH RENAISSANCE ANNUAL. 1980. a. $12. University of Delaware Press, 4 Cornwall Dr., East Brunswick, NJ 08816. Ed. Zack Bower.

894   HU ISSN 0075-0824
IRODALOM - SZOCIALIZMUS. (Text in Hungarian; occasional summaries in German or Russian) 1959. irreg. price varies. (Magyar Tudomanyos Akademia) Akademiai Kiado, Publishing House of the Hungarian Academy of Sciences, P.O. Box 24, H-1363 Budapest, Hungary.

800   HU ISSN 0075-0832
IRODALOMELMELET KLASSZIKUSAI. 1963. irreg. price varies. (Magyar Tudomanyos Akademia) Akademiai Kiado, Publishing House of the Hungarian Academy of Sciences, P.O. Box 24, H-1363 Budapest, Hungary.

809   HU ISSN 0075-0840
IRODALOMTORTENETI FUZETEK. 1950. irreg. price varies. (Magyar Tudomanyos Akademia) Akademiai Kiado, Publishing House of the Hungarian Academy of Sciences, P.O. Box 24, H-1363 Budapest, Hungary.

809   HU ISSN 0075-0859
IRODALOMTORTENETI KONYVTAR. (Text in Hungarian; occasional summaries in French or German) 1957. irreg. price varies. (Magyar Tudomanyos Akademia) Akademiai Kiado, Publishing House of the Hungarian Academy of Sciences, P.O. Box 24, H-1363 Budapest, Hungary.

800   IT ISSN 0077-2763
ISTITUTO UNIVERSITARIO ORIENTALE DI NAPOLI. ANNALI. SEZIONE GERMANICA. 1958. 8/yr. L.24000. Herder Editrice e Libreria s.r.l., Piazza Montecitorio 117-121, 00186 Rome, Italy. Ed. Bd. bk. rev. bibl. circ. 1,000.

800   US
ITALIAN CULTURE. (Text in English, French, Italian) 1978. a. $12. American Association of University Professors of Italian, c/o Anthony K. Cassell, Department of Italian, University of Illinois, Urbana, IL 61801. Ed. Aldo Scaglione. bk. rev. bibl. circ. 1,000.

850   UK ISSN 0075-1634
ITALIAN STUDIES. 1937. a. £6.50($17.50) Society for Italian Studies, c/o Prof. G. H. McWilliam, Department of Italian, University of Leicester, Leicester LE1 7RH, England. Ed. Prof. T. G. Griffith. adv. bk. rev. bibl. circ. 750. (back issues avail.)

JACOBEAN DRAMA STUDIES. see *THEATER*

800   II ISSN 0448-1143
JADAVPUR JOURNAL OF COMPARATIVE LITERATURE. (Text mainly in English; occasionally in Bengali; summaries in English) 1961. a. Rs.12.50($3) Jadavpur University, Department of Comparative Literature, Calcutta 32, India. Ed. Naresh Guha. index. cum.index: vols. 1-10. circ. 500. Indexed: Abstr.Engl.Stud.

807   BG
JAHANGIRNAGAR UNIVERSITY. DEPARTMENT OF ENGLISH. BULLETIN. (Text in English) vol. 2, 1978. Tk.5. Jahangirnagar University, Department of English, Savar, Dacca, Bangladesh.

811   US ISSN 0362-8302
JAM TO-DAY. 1973. irreg. $3.75 for 2 nos. Jam To-Day, Box 249, Northfield, VT 05663. Eds. Don D. Stanford, Judith A. Stanford, Floyd Stuart. bk. rev. circ. 400.

054   FR
JEAN GIONO. Cited also as: Series Jean Giono. (Issued as a subseries of la Revue des Lettres Modernes) 1974. a. price varies. Lettres Modernes, 73, rue du Cardinal-Lemoine, 75005 Paris, France. (back issues avail.)

830   GW ISSN 0075-3580
JEAN-PAUL-GESELLSCHAFT. JAHRBUCH. 1966. a. price varies. C. H. Beck'sche Verlagsbuchhandlung, Wilhelmstr. 9, 8000 Munich 40, W. Germany (B.R.D.) Ed. Kurt Woelfel. bk. rev.

820   UK
JOHN CREASY'S MYSTERY BEDSIDE BOOK; the anthology of the Crime Writer's association. 1976. irreg. £4.50. Hodder and Stoughton, Warwick Lane, London EC4P 4AH, England. Ed. Herbert Harris.

812   US
JOHN GASSNER'S BEST AMERICAN PLAYS. 1939. irreg. $10.95. Crown Publishers, Inc., One Park Ave., New York, NY 10016. Ed. Clive Barnes.
Formerly: Best American Plays (ISSN 0067-6225)

800   US ISSN 0075-4099
JOURNAL FOR THE PROTECTION OF ALL BEINGS. 1960. irreg., no. 4, 1978. $3.50. City Lights Books, 261 Columbus Ave., San Francisco, CA 94133.
Poetry, prose, fiction

800 950 NE ISSN 0085-2376
JOURNAL OF ARABIC LITERATURE. 1970. a. fl.48. E. J. Brill, Oude Rijn 33a-35, Leiden, Netherlands. Indexed: M.L.A.

800   US
JOURNAL OF GERMAN-AMERICAN STUDIES. (Text and summaries in English and German) 1969. a. $6. Society for German-American Studies, 7204 Langerford Dr., Cleveland, OH 44129 (OR 21010 Mastick Rd., Cleveland, OH 44126) Ed. Dr. Robert E. Ward. adv. bk. rev. bibl. circ. 300. Indexed: M.L.A.
Formerly (until vol. 11, 1976): German-American Studies (ISSN 0046-5836)

800   CN ISSN 0381-6524
JOURNAL OF OUR TIME. 1977. irreg. Can.$3.95 per no. Traditional Studies Press, Box 984, Adelaide St. Sta., Toronto, Ont. M5C 2K4, Canada. bk. rev.

800   UK
JULES VERNE VOYAGES. 1978. a. £5($15) (Jules Verne Circle) High Orchard Press, High Orchard, 125 Markyate Rd., Dagenham, Essex RM8 2LB, England. Ed. F. James. circ. 100.
Works of Jules Verne

JYVASKYLA STUDIES IN THE ARTS. see *ART*

809   II
KAKATIYA JOURNAL OF ENGLISH STUDIES. Other title: K J E S. (Text in English) 1976. a. Rs.5($1) Osmania University, Post-Graduate Centre, Department of English, Vidyaranyapuri, Warangal 506009, India.

890 700 CE
KALAVA HA SAHITYAYA. (Text in Sinhalese) 1976. irreg. Rs.1. Nava Parapura, 26 Clifford Ave., Colombo 3, Sri Lanka.

808 301.2 MW
KALULU; bulletin of Malawian oral literature and cultural studies. 1976. irreg. Chancellor College, Writer's Group, Box 280, Limbe, Malawi.

860   PE
KANAN; revista anual de cultura. 1978. a. Instituto Nacional de Cultura, Filial Ancash, Plaza de Armas s/n, Huaras, Peru. Dir. Francisco Gonzales. bk. rev.

800 340 JA ISSN 0453-1981
KANAZAWA UNIVERSITY. FACULTY OF LAW AND LITERATURE. STUDIES AND ESSAYS. (Text in English and Japanese) 1953. a. Kanazawa University, Faculty of Law and Literature, 1-1 Marunouchi, Kanazawa 920, Japan. bibl.

833   GW
KARL-MAY-GESELLSCHAFT. JAHRBUCH. a. Karl-May-Gesellschaft, Erdkampsweg 33, Postfach 630225, 2000 Hamburg 63, W. Germany (B.R.D.)

800   US
KHATRU. 1975. irreg. $4 for 4 issues. Phantasmicom Press, 1339 Welden Ave., Baltimore, MD 21211. Ed. Jeffrey D. Smith. bk. rev. circ. 300. (processed)

KLAUS-GROTH-GESELLSCHAFT. JAHRESGABEN. see *LINGUISTICS*

830   GW ISSN 0075-6318
KLEINE DEUTSCHE PROSADENKMAELER DES MITTELALTERS; Erst und Neuausgaben der Forschungstelle fuer deutsche prosa des Mittelalters. 1965. irreg. price varies. (Universitaet Wuerzburg, Seminar fuer Deutsche Philologie) Wilhelm Fink Verlag, Nikolaistr. 2, 8000 Munich 40, W. Germany (B. R. D.) Ed. Kurt Ruh.

KONINKLIJKE ACADEMIE VOOR NEDERLANDSE TAAL- EN LETTERKUNDE. JAARBOEK. see *LINGUISTICS*

810   JA ISSN 0454-8132
KYUSHU AMERICAN LITERATURE STUDIES. (Text in English) no. 20, 1979. a. (Kyushu American Literature Society - Kyushu Amerika Bungaku-Kai) Kyushu University, College of General Education, 4-2-1 Ropponmatsu, Chuo-Ku, Fukuoka 810, Japan. bk. rev. bibl.

800   FR   ISSN 0335-9190
L.S.I. 1971. irreg. price varies. Jean Jachymiak, Pub., 6 Square de la Dordogne, Paris 17e, France. adv. bk. rev. circ. 2,000.
  Formerly: Litterature. Science. Ideologie. (ISSN 0075-9996)

LAMAR LECTURE SERIES. see *HISTORY*

800 400   FR   ISSN 0075-7985
LANGUES ET STYLES. 1959. irreg., no. 5, 1974. price varies. Lettres Modernes, 73, rue du Cardinal Lemoine, 75005 Paris, France.

LEA. see *BIBLIOGRAPHIES*

810 820   US   ISSN 0075-8396
LEBARON RUSSELL BRIGGS PRIZE HONORS ESSAYS IN ENGLISH. 1965. a. Harvard University Press, 79 Garden St., Cambridge, MA 02138.

850   IT   ISSN 0075-8426
LECTURA DANTIS ROMANA. 1965-66. a. price varies. (Casa di Dante in Roma) Casa Editrice Felice le Monnier, Via Scipione Ammirato, 100, C.P.455, 50136 Florence, Italy.

800 792 942   UK   ISSN 0140-8089
LEEDS MEDIEVAL STUDIES. 1975. irreg. University of Leeds, Graduate Centre for Medieval Studies, Leeds LS2 9JT, England. (back issues avail.)

820   UK   ISSN 0075-8566
LEEDS STUDIES IN ENGLISH. 1967 N.S. a. price varies. University of Leeds, School of English, Leeds LS2 9JT, England. Eds. P. Meredith, S. Ellis.
  Supersedes: Leeds Studies in English and Kindred Languages.

830   NE   ISSN 0458-9971
LEIDSE GERMANISTISCHE EN ANGLISTISCHE REEKS. 1962. irreg., vol. 17, 1978. price varies. Leiden University Press, c/o Martinus Nijhoff, Box 566, 2501 CN The Hague, Netherlands.

LEIDSE ROMANISTISCHE REEKS. see *LINGUISTICS*

892   IS
LEKET. (Text in Hebrew; English translation available) irreg. World Zionist Organization, P.O. Box 92, Jerusalem, Israel. Ed. David Hardan. illus.

830   GW   ISSN 0075-8833
LESSING YEARBOOK. (Text in English or German) 1969. a. price varies. (Lessing Society) Max Hueber Verlag, Max-Hueber-Str.4, 8045 Ismaning, W. Germany (B.R.D.) Ed. G. Hillen. bk. rev.

850   IT
LETTERATURA ITALIANA. STUDI E TESTI. 1977. irreg. L.11000. Bulzoni Editore, Via dei Liburni 14, 00185 Rome, Italy. Dir. Walter Binni.

850   IT   ISSN 0075-8892
LETTERE ITALIANE. BIBLIOTECA. 1962. irreg., vol. 22, 1978. price varies. Casa Editrice Leo S. Olschki, Casella Postale 66, 50100 Florence, Italy. Eds. Vittore Branca, Giovanni Getto. circ. 1,000.

839.5   US   ISSN 0075-9155
LIBRARY OF SCANDINAVIAN LITERATURE. 1967. irreg. price varies. (American-Scandinavian Foundation) Twayne Publishers, Inc. (Subsidiary of: G. K. Hall & Co.) 70 Lincoln St., Boston, MA 02111. Ed. Erik J. Friis.

830   GW
LICHTWARK-STIFTUNG. VEROEFFENTLICHUNG. irreg. price varies. Hans Christians Verlag, Kl. Theaterstr. 9, 2000 Hamburg 36, W. Germany (B.R.D.) bk. rev. bibl. circ. controlled.

LILI. BEIHEFTE. (Zeitschrift fuer Literaturwissenschaft und Linguistik) see *LINGUISTICS*

LIMI. see *LINGUISTICS*

LINGUA E LITERATURA. see *LINGUISTICS*

LINGUISTIC & LITERARY STUDIES IN EASTERN EUROPE. see *LINGUISTICS*

830   GW
LITERARISCHE HEFTE. vol. 11, 1972. irreg. DM.8.50. Raith Verlag, Herzog Heinrich Str. 21, 8000 Munich 2, W. Germany (B.R.D.) Ed.Bd. bk. rev. illus. circ. 1,200.

830   GW   ISSN 0340-7888
LITERARISCHER VEREIN IN STUTTGART. BIBLIOTHEK. Abbreviated title: B L V S. 1842. irreg., vol. 302, 1981. price varies. Anton Hiersemann Verlag, Rosenbergstr. 113, Postfach 723, 7000 Stuttgart 1, W. Germany (B.R.D.)

891.87   CS
LITERARNO-MUZEJNY LETOPIS. (Text in Slovak; summaries in German and Russian) 1967. a. price varies. Matica Slovenska, Mudronova 35, 036 52 Martin, Czechoslovakia. bk. rev.
  Continues: Letopis Pamatnika Slovenskej Literatury (ISSN 0075-8841)

891.87   CS   ISSN 0075-9872
LITERARNY ARCHIV. (Text in Slovak; summaries in German and Russian) 1964. approx 1-2/yr. price varies. Matica Slovenska, Mudronova 35, 036 52 Martin, Czechoslovakia. bk. rev.

891.87   CS
LITERARRIA. irreg, vol. 16, 1973. price varies. (Slovenska Akademia Vied, Literarnovedny Ustav) Veda, Publishing House of the Slovak Academy of Sciences, Klemensova 19, 895 30 Bratislava, Czechoslovakia. Ed. Karol Rosenbaum.

820 810   US   ISSN 0075-9902
LITERARY MONOGRAPHS. 1967. irreg. ‡ University of Wisconsin Press, 114 N. Murray St., Madison, WI 53715.

801   US   ISSN 0160-8703
LITERARY ONOMASTICS STUDIES. 1974. a. $5. State University of New York, College at Brockport, Department of Foreign Languages and Literatures, Brockport, NY 14420. Ed. Grace Alvarez-Altman. circ. controlled. (looseleaf format)

800 028   PK   ISSN 0075-9929
LITERARY PRIZES IN PAKISTAN. (Text in English) 1964. a. Rs.4.($1.) National Book Council of Pakistan, Theosophical Hall, M. A. Jinnah Rd., Karachi, Pakistan.
  Formerly: Incentives for Better Books in Pakistan.

830   GW   ISSN 0343-1657
LITERATUR FUER LESER; Zeitschrift fuer Interpretationpraxis und geschichtliche Texterkenntnis. 1968. 3/yr. DM.48. R. Oldenbourg Verlag GmbH, Rosenheimer Str. 145, 8000 Munich 80, W. Germany (B.R.D.) Eds. Rolf Geissler, Herbert Kaiser. adv.

800   GW   ISSN 0075-9937
LITERATUR UND WIRKLICHKEIT. 1967. irreg., vol. 20, 1978. price varies. Bouvier Verlag Herbert Grundmann, Am Hof 32, Postfach 1268, 5300 Bonn 1, W. Germany (B.R.D.) Ed. Karl Otto Conrady.

891.7   UR
LITERATURA DREVNEI RUSI. 1975. irreg. 1 Rub. Moskovskii Gosudarstvennyi Pedagogicheskii Institut, Kafedra Russkoi Literatury, Moscow, U.S.S.R. circ. 1,000.

891.7   UR
LITERATURA O VOLOGODSKOI OBLASTI, VOLOGADA, BIBLIOTEKA IM BABUSKINA. 1976. a. Vologodskaya Oblastnaya Biblioteka, Spravochno Bibliograficheskii Otdel, Zhdanova, i, 160000, Vologda, U.S.S.R.

891.7   UR
LITERATURA OB ARKHANGEL'SKOI OBLASTI. 1973. a. (Arkhangel'skaya Oblastnaya Biblioteka, Bibliograficheskii Otdel) Severo-Zapadnoe Knizhnoe Izdatel'stvo, Arkhangel'sk, U.S.S.R.

830   GW   ISSN 0075-997X
LITERATURWISSENSCHAFTLICHES JAHRBUCH. NEUE FOLGE. 1961. a. price varies. (Goerres-Gesellschaft) Duncker und Humblot, Dietrich-Schaefer-Weg 9, Postfach 410329, 1000 Berlin 41, W. Germany (B.R.D.) Ed. H. Kunisch. bk. rev.

800   GW
LITFASS; Berliner Zeitschrift fuer Literatur. 1976. q. DM.18.50. Wochenendweg 11, 1000 Berlin 47, W. Germany (B.R.D.) Ed.Assen Assenov. adv. bk. rev. bibl. illus. stat. tr.lit. index.

800   PL   ISSN 0084-3008
LITTERARIA; teoria literatury-metodologia-kultura-humanistyka. 1969. irreg., vol. 11, 1979. 30 Zl. (Wroclawskie Towarzystwo Naukowe) Ossolineum, Publishing House of the Polish Academy of Sciences, Rynek 9, Wroclaw, Poland (Dist. by Ars Polona-Ruch, Krakowskie Przedmiescie 7, Warsaw, Poland) (Co-Sponsor: Polska Akademia Nauk) Ed. Jan Trzynadlowski. bk. rev. circ. 700. (also avail. in microfilm)

840   FR   ISSN 0563-9751
LITTERATURES. 1952. 20 F. Universite de Toulouse II (le Mirail), Faculte des Lettres et Sciences Humaines, 109 bis, rue Vauquelin, 31081 Toulouse Cedex, France. (back issues avail)

800   FR   ISSN 0069-5459
LITTERATURES ANCIENNES. 1970. irreg. price varies. Presses Universitaires de France, 108 Bd. Saint Germaine, 75279 Paris Cedex 6, France (Service des Periodiques, 12 rue Jean de Beauvais, 75005 Paris)

800   CN   ISSN 0076-0153
LIVRES ET AUTEURS QUEBECOIS. 1936. a. Can.$12. Presses de l'Universite Laval, C.P. 2447, Quebec G1K 7R4, Montreal, 110 Que., Canada. Ed. Maximilien Laroche. bk. rev. circ. 2,000.
  Formerly: Livres et Auteurs Canadians.

800   UK   ISSN 0076-0188
LLEN CYMRU. (Text in Welsh) 1950. irreg. £3 per vol. (Board of Celtic Studies) University of Wales Press, 6 Gwennyth St., Cathays, Cardiff CF2 4YD, Wales. Ed. A. O. H. Jarman. bk. rev. circ. 500. (also avail. in microfilm from UMI; reprint service avail. from UMI)
  Welsh literature

800   PL   ISSN 0076-0404
LODZKIE TOWARZYSTWO NAUKOWE. WYDZIAL I. PRACE. (Text in Polish; summaries in English, French and Russian) 1947. irreg., no. 78, 1977. price varies. Ossolineum, Publishing House of the Polish Academy of Sciences, Rynek 9, 50-106 Wroclaw, Poland (Dist. by Ars Polona-Ruch, Krakowskie Przedmiescie 7, 00-068 Warsaw, Poland) (Co-sponsor: Polska Akademia Nauk)

800   US
LOEB CLASSICAL LIBRARY. irreg. price varies. Harvard University Press, 79 Garden St., Cambrdige, MA 02138.

296 950   US   ISSN 0364-068X
LOKA. irreg. Naropa Institute, 1441 Broadway, Boulder, CO 80302. Ed. Rick Fields. illus.

830   UK
LONDON GERMAN STUDIES. 1980. irreg. price varies. University of London, Institute of Germanic Studies, 29 Russell Square, London WC1B 5DP, England. circ. 500.

800   US   ISSN 0076-1001
LOST PLAY SERIES. 1965. irreg., no. 13,1979. $1.75-$2.95. Proscenium Press, P.O. Box 361, Newark, DE 19711. Ed. Robert Hogan. (reprint service avail. from UMI)

M L A INTERNATIONAL BIBLIOGRAPHY OF BOOKS AND ARTICLES ON THE MODERN LANGUAGES AND LITERATURES. (Modern Language Association of America) see *BIBLIOGRAPHIES*

800 700   YU   ISSN 0350-3089
MACEDONIAN REVIEW; history, culture, literature, arts. (Text in English) 1971. 3/yr. 300 din.($14) Kulturen Zivot - Cultural Life, Rabotnicki Dom 5, 91001 Skopje, Yugoslavia. Ed. Boris Visinski. bk. rev. illus.

829   CN
MCMASTER OLD ENGLISH STUDIES AND TEXTS. 1980. irreg. price varies. University of Toronto Press, Front Campus, Toronto, Ont. M5S 1A6, Canada. Ed. Alvin A. Lee.

800 398   GW   ISSN 0076-2326
MAERCHEN DER EUROPAEISCHEN VOELKER.
(Text in various languages; translations in German)
1961. irreg. price varies. (Gesellschaft zur Pflege der
Maerchengutes der Europaeischen Voelker)
Aschendorffsche Verlagsbuchhandlung, Soester Str.
13, 4400 Muenster, W. Germany (B.R.D.)

MAGAZIN POLOVNIKA. see *SPORTS AND GAMES — Outdoor Life*

810   CN   ISSN 0076-2350
MAGENTA FROG. 1970. irreg. Can.$3 per no.
Talonbooks, 201-1019 E. Cordova St., Vancouver 6,
B.C., Canada. Eds. Gordon Fidler, Arnold Saba.
circ. 2,000.

894.51   HU   ISSN 0076-2385
MAGYAR IRODALOMTORTENETIRAS
FORRASAI; FONTES AD HISTORIAM
LITTERARIAM HUNGARIAE SPECTANTES.
1960. irreg. price varies. (Magyar Tudomanyos
Akademia) Akademiai Kiado, Publishing House of
the Hungarian Academy of Sciences, P.O. Box 24,
H-1363 Budapest, Hungary.

810   US   ISSN 0076-2717
MAINE WRITERS' CONFERENCE CHAPBOOK.
1956. a. $2. Pejepscot Press, 10 Mason St.,
Brunswick, ME 04011. Ed. Sheldon Christian. circ.
500. (back issues avail.)

830   GW   ISSN 0076-2784
MAINZER REIHE. 1956. irreg. Akademie der
Wissenschaften und der Literatur, Mainz,
Geschwister-Scholl-Str. 2, 6500 Mainz, W. Germany
(B.R.D.)

800   UK
MAJOR EUROPEAN AUTHOR SERIES. irreg. price
varies. Cambridge University Press, Box 110,
Cambridge CB2 3RL, England (And 32 E. 57th St.,
New York NY 10022)

810.8   CN   ISSN 0702-7575
MAMASHEE. 1977. irreg. Can.$1.25 per no. c/o M.
Drage, R.R.1 Inwood, Ont. N0N 1K0, Canada.
(processed)
Formerly: Quest for a Common Denominator
(ISSN 0700-5482)

990   FJ   ISSN 0379-5268
MANA. (Text in English) 1973. 2/yr. f$4. South
Pacific Creative Arts Society, Box 5083, Suva, Fiji.
adv. bk. rev. illus. circ. 1,500.
Formerly: Mana Annual of Creative Writing.

810   US
MANASSAS REVIEW. 1977. irreg. Northern Virginia
Community College, Manassas Campus, Manassas,
VA 22110. Ed. Patrick Bizzaro.

820   UK   ISSN 0025-4711
MASQUE. 1918. a. 30p. University of Strathclyde,
Students' Association, S. R. C. Publications, 90
John St, Glasgow C. 1, Scotland. Ed. Graham
Brown. adv. bk. rev. film rev. play rev. illus. circ.
2,500(controlled)
Formerly: Mask.

890   UR
MASTERSKAYA; uroki literaturnogo masterstva.
1975. irreg. 0.28 Rub. Izdatel'stvo Molodaya
Gvardiya, Ul. Sushevskaya, 21, Moscow a-55,
U.S.S.R.

800 940   CN   ISSN 0316-0874
MEDIAEVAL SOURCES IN TRANSLATION.
1949. irreg. price varies. Pontifical Institute of
Mediaeval Studies, 59 Queen's Park Crescent E.,
Toronto, Ont. M5S 2C4, Canada. circ. 1,000.

MEDIAEVALIA. see *HISTORY*

MEDIEVAL ACADEMY BOOKS. see *HISTORY — History Of Europe*

MEDIEVAL ACADEMY REPRINTS FOR
TEACHING. see *HISTORY — History Of Europe*

MELBOURNE SLAVONIC STUDIES. see
LINGUISTICS

820   AT   ISSN 0085-3283
MELBOURNE UNIVERSITY MAGAZINE. a.
Aus.$1 per no. University of Melbourne, Students
Representative Council, Union House, Univ. of
Melbourne, Parkville, Vic. 3052, Australia.

056.1   PE
MELIBEA. 1975. irreg. Casimiro Ulloa, 125, Lima,
Peru. illus.

800   US
MIAM. 1977. irreg., latest no. 6. $5 to individuals;
institutions $15. Box 14083, San Francisco, CA
94114. Ed. Tom Mandel. circ. 350.

801   US   ISSN 0076-8103
MICHIGAN SLAVIC CONTRIBUTIONS. (Text in
English, Russian and Slavic Languages) 1968. $2.-
$3. University of Michigan, Department of Slavic
Languages and Literatures, 3040 Modern Language
Bldg., Ann Arbor, MI 48109. Ed. Ladislaw Matejka.

890 491.8 375.4   US   ISSN 0543-9930
MICHIGAN SLAVIC MATERIALS. 1961. irreg., no.
15, 1977. University of Michigan, Department of
Slavic Languages and Literatures, 3040 Modern
Language Bldg., Ann Arbor, MI 48109. Ed.
Ladislav Matejka.

891.7   US
MICHIGAN SLAVIC TRANSLATIONS. 1972.
irreg., no. 2, 1973. University of Michigan,
Department of Slavic Languages and Literatures,
3040 Modern Language Bldg., Ann Arbor, MI
48104. Ed. Ladislav Matejka.

810   US
MID-HUDSON LANGUAGE STUDIES. 1978. a. $3.
Mid-Hudson Modern Language Association, c/o
George J. Sommer, Ed., Marist College,
Poughkeepsie, NY 12601. circ. 400.

800   US   ISSN 0190-2911
MIDAMERICA (EAST LANSING) 1973. a. $7.50
per no. Society for the Study of Midwestern
Literature, Ernst Bessey Hall, Michigan State
University, East Lansing, MI 48824. Ed. David D.
Anderson. bk. rev. circ. 1,000. (back issues avail.)
Indexed: Abstr. Engl. Stud. M. L. A.
Formerly: Midwestern Annual.

810   US   ISSN 0076-8596
MIDWEST MONOGRAPHS. SERIES 1 (DRAMA)*
1967. irreg. $0.50. (University of Illinois at Urbana-
Champaign) Depot Press, Room 204, English Bldg.,
Urbana, IL 61801.

800   US   ISSN 0076-8618
MIDWEST MONOGRAPHS. SERIES 3 (GRAPHIC
WORKS)* irreg., 1969, no. 2. price varies.
(University of Illinois at Urbana-Champaign) Depot
Press, Room 204, English Bldg., Urbana, IL 61801.

800   US   ISSN 0076-8626
MIDWEST MONOGRAPHS. SERIES 4
(TRANSLATION)* 1969. irreg. price varies.
(University of Illinois at Urbana-Champaign) Depot
Press, Room 204, English Bldg., Urbana, IL 61801.

800   US   ISSN 0076-8634
MIDWEST MONOGRAPHS. SERIES 5 (CULTURE
AND CRITICISM)* 1969. irreg. $1. (University of
Illinois at Urbana-Champaign) Depot Press, Room
204, English Bldg., Urbana, IL 61801.

810   US
MIDWESTERN MISCELLANY. irreg. membership.
Society for the Study of Midwestern Literature, 240
Ernst Bassey Hall, Michigan State University, East
Lansing, MI 48824.

800   US   ISSN 0163-2469
MILFORD SERIES; popular writers of today. 1976.
irreg., 6-10/yr. $2.95 per no., paper; $3.95 cloth.
Borgo Press, Box 2845, San Bernardino, CA 92406.
Ed. R. Reginald. circ. 3,000.

810   US
MILL. no. 3, 1977. irreg. $6 to individuals, libraries
$8. White Ewe Press, Box 996, Adelphi, MD 20783.
Ed. Kevin Urick. adv. bk. rev. illus. circ. 250.

821.4   US   ISSN 0076-8820
MILTON STUDIES. 1969. a. price varies. University
of Pittsburgh Press, 127 N. Bellefield Ave.,
Pittsburgh, PA 15260. Ed. James Simmonds.

809 860   BL
MIMESIS. (Text in English, Portuguese & Spanish)
1975. irreg. Instituto de Biociencias, Letras e
Ciencias Exatas de Sao Jose do Rio Preto,
Faculdade de Filosofia, Ciencias e Letras, Rua
Cristovao Colombo 2265, 15000 Sao Jose do Rio
Preto, Sao Paulo, Brazil. illus.
Formerly: Etudos Anglo-Hispanico.

800 798   US   ISSN 0076-9142
MINNESOTA DRAMA EDITIONS. irreg., no. 9,
1975. price varies. (Guthrie Theater Co) University
of Minnesota Press, 2037 University Ave. S.E.,
Minneapolis, MN 55455. Ed. Michael Langham.

810   US
MIRROR NORTHWEST. 1971. a. $1.50. ‡ c/o
English Dept., Bellevue Community College,
Bellevue, WA 98007. Ed. Carl Waluconis. circ. 700.

MISCELLANEA BYZANTINA MONACENSIA. see
HISTORY — History Of Europe

810   US   ISSN 0076-9649
MISSOURI LITERARY FRONTIERS SERIES. 1967.
irreg. price varies. University of Missouri Press, 107
Swallow Hall, Columbia, MO 65201.

809   CN   ISSN 0316-5973
MODERNIST STUDIES: LITERATURE AND
CULTURE, 1920-1940. 1974. irreg. Can.$12($13)
per vol. c/o Eds. Shirley Rose and Ernest Griffin,
Dept. of English, University of Alberta, Edmonton,
Alta. T6G 2E1, Canada. adv. bk. rev. bibl. illus.
circ. 300. (back issues avail.) Indexed: M.L.A.

810   US   ISSN 0085-3534
MONMOUTH REVIEWS; JOURNAL OF THE
LITERARY ARTS.* 1972. a. Monmouth College,
Editorial Office, Cedar Ave., West Long Branch, NJ
07664. Ed. Harry A. Maxson, Jr. adv.

891.8 940   PL   ISSN 0077-0531
MONOGRAFIE SLAWISTYCZNE. 1959. irreg., vol.
41, 1979. price varies. (Polska Akademia Nauk,
Komitet Slowianoznawstwa) Ossolineum, Publishing
House of the Polish Academy of Sciences, Rynek 9,
50-106 Wroclaw, Poland (Dist. by Ars Polona-Ruch,
Krakowskie Przedmiescie 7, Warsaw, Poland)

810   US   ISSN 0027-0733
MONUMENT IN CANTOS AND ESSAYS. 1968.
irreg., approx. annual. $1 to individuals; institutions
$2. Monument Press, 4508 Mexico Gravel Rd.,
Columbia, MO 65201. Ed. Victor Myers. cum.index
every 3 yrs. circ. 300. (also avail. in microfilm from
UMI; back issues avail.)

830   NE
MONUMENTA LITERARIA NEERLANDICA.
1979. irreg. price varies. North-Holland Publishing
Co., Box 211, 1000 AE Amsterdam, Netherlands.

820   AT
MOONABOOLA QUILL. 1959. irreg. free. (Hervey
Bay Writers' Workshop) Maryborough Adult
Education Centre, P.O. Box 65, Maryborough, Qld
4650, Australia. Ed. A. Crawfoot.

430 830   GW   ISSN 0077-1872
MUENCHNER GERMANISTISCHE BEITRAEGE.
1968. irreg. price varies. Wilhelm Fink Verlag,
Nikolaistr 2, 8000 Munich 40, W. Germany (B. R.
D.) Eds. Werner Betz, Herman Kunisch.

830   GW   ISSN 0077-1996
MUENSTERSCHE BEITRAEGE ZUR
DEUTSCHEN LITERATURWISSENSCHAFT.
1966. irreg. price varies. Aschendorffsche
Verlagsbuchhandlung, Soester Str. 13, 4400
Muenster, W. Germany (B.R.D.) Ed. Wolfdietrich
Rasch.

810   GW
MUNICH ROUND UP. vol. 10, 1975. irreg. (3-4/yr.)
$5.30. Waldemar Kumming, Ed. & Pub.,
Herzogspitalstr. 5, 8000 Munich 2, W. Germany
(B.R.D.) (U.S. subscr. to: Andrew Porter, Box 4175,
New York, NY 10017) bk. rev. circ. 300.

800   NR   ISSN 0331-3468
MUSE; journal of creative and critical writing from
Nsukka. 1963. a. £N1 per no. University of Nigeria,
Department of English, Nsukka, Nigeria. Ed.
Okorie W. Okorie. adv. bk. rev. circ. 1,000.

809　　　　　　　　　IT
MUSEUM CRITICUM. vol. 10, 1975. irreg.; vol. 12, 1977. price varies. Giardini Editori e Stampatori, Via Santa Bibbiana 28, 56100 Pisa, Italy. Ed. Benedetto Marzullo.

813　　　　　　US　ISSN 0000-0302
MYSTERY & DETECTION ANNUAL. 1972. a. c/o Donald K. Adams, Ed. & Pub., Department of English, Occidental College, Los Angeles, CA 90041. bk. rev. circ. 1,200. Indexed: M.L.A.

806　　　　　　　　US
MYTHRIL. irreg. $2.50 for 4 nos. Mythopoeic Society, Box 4671, Whittier, CA 90607. illus. circ. 200. (reprint service avail. from UMI)

890　　　　　　　　AU
N R L/NEUE RUSSISCHE LITERATUR. (Text in German and Russian) 1978. a. $14. Institut fuer Slawistik, Akademiestrasse 24, A-5020, Salzburg, Austria.

860　　　　　　UY　ISSN 0077-2801
NARRADORES DE ARCA.* irreg. Editorial Arca, Colonia 1263, Montevideo, Uruguay.

NARRATIVA LATINOAMERICANA. see
HISTORY — History Of North And South America

810　　　　　　US　ISSN 0077-2879
NASSAU REVIEW. 1964. a. free. Nassau Community College, Department of English, Office of Community Relations, Garden City, NY 11530. Ed. Paul A. Doyle. circ. 1,500.

810　　　　　　US　ISSN 0073-1382
NATHANIEL HAWTHORNE JOURNAL. 1971. a. $24. Gale Research Company, Book Tower, Detroit, MI 48226. Ed. C. E. Frazer Clark Jr.
Previously unpublished letters

890　　　　　　CN　ISSN 0077-6300
NEAR AND MIDDLE EAST SERIES. 1949. irreg. price varies. University of Toronto Press, Front Campus, Toronto, Ont. M5S 1A6, Canada (and 33 Tupper St., Buffalo, N.Y. 14203) (also avail. in microfiche)

810　　　　　　US　ISSN 0162-3818
NEBULA WINNERS. 1965. a. price varies. Harper & Row Publishers, Inc., 10 E. 53rd St., New York, NY 10022. Ed. Clifford D. Simak.
Formerly: Nebula Award Stories (ISSN 0077-6408)

830　　　　　　GW　ISSN 0077-7668
NEUDRUCKE DEUTSCHER LITERATURWERKE. 1961, N.S. irreg. price varies. Max Niemeyer Verlag, Pfrondorfer Str. 4, 7400 Tuebingen, W. Germany (B.R.D.)
Continues: Neudrucke Deutscher Literaturwerke des XVI und XVII Jahrhunderts & Neudrucke des Deutscher Literaturwerke des XVIII und XIX Jahrhunderts.

830　　　　　　GW　ISSN 0077-7676
NEUDRUCKE DEUTSCHER LITERATURWERKE. SONDERREIHE. 1964. irreg. price varies. Max Niemeyer Verlag, Pfrondorfer Str. 4, 7400 Tuebingen, W. Germany (B.R.D.)

709　　　　　　US　ISSN 0077-7994
NEW AFRICAN LITERATURE AND THE ARTS.* (Text mainly in English; occasionally in French) 1966. irreg., vol. 3, 1973. $8.95. Thomas Y. Crowell Co. (Subsidiary of: Dun-Donnelley Publishing Co.) 10 E. 53rd St., New York, NY 10022. Ed. Joseph Okpaku.

NEW ART REVIEW. see MUSIC

810　　　　　　　　CN
NEW BRUNSWICK CHAPBOOKS. 1968. irreg; (approx 3-4/yr) Can.$0.85. ‡ Nancy Bauer, Ed. & Pub., 252 Stanley St., Fredericton, N.B. E3B 3A3, Canada. circ. 250.

810　　　　　　US　ISSN 0467-1872
NEW CADUCEAN; Downstate's literary magazine. vol. 14, 1974. a. free to medical students and hospital personnel. Downstate Medical Center, 450 Clarkson Ave., Brooklyn, NY 11203. Eds. Irwin Berlin & Arthur Sonberg. circ. 1,000.

800　410　　　　　　AT
NEW CEYLON WRITING; creative and critical writing of Sri Lanka. 1970. irreg. Aus.$5. (Macquarie University, School of English & Linguistics) Yasmine Gooneratne, Pub. & Ed., North Ryde, N.S.W. 2113, Australia. adv. bk. rev. play rev. abstr. bibl. circ. 250.

800　700　　　　　　UK
NEW DEPARTURES. 1959. irreg. price varies. c/o Michael Horovitz, Ed., Mullions, Piedmont, Bisley, Strond, Glos. GL6 7BU, England. adv. bk. rev. circ. 10,000.

813　　　　　　US　ISSN 0099-0906
NEW DIMENSIONS SCIENCE FICTION. 1971. irreg. Harper & Row Publishers, Inc., 10 E. 53rd St., New York, NY 10022. Key Title: New Dimensions (Garden City)

820　　　　　　UK　ISSN 0028-6540
NEW RAMBLER. 1941. a. $4. Johnson Society of London, Broadmead, Eynsford Rd., Farningham, Kent, Eng. Ed. James H. Leicester. adv. bk. rev. illus. play rev. circ. 300. (back issues avail.) Indexed: Abstr.Engl.Stud.

800　700　　　　　　US　ISSN 0028-6575
NEW RENAISSANCE; an internnational magazine of ideas and opinions, emphasizing literature & the arts. 1968. s-a. $7 for 3 issues. c/o Louise T. Reynolds, Ed., 9 Heath Rd., Arlington, MA 02174. adv. bk. rev. film rev. play rev. illus. index. circ. 1,500. Indexed: Abstr.Engl.Stud. Alt.Press Ind. Ind.Amer.Per.Verse.

800　　　　　　　　UK
NEW STORIES. 1976. irreg. £4. Arts Council, 105 Piccadilly, London W1V 0AU, England.

810
NEW VOICES. 1972. a. $3. c/o Don Fried, Ed., 102 Butterville, New Paltz, NY 12561. circ. 500.

809　820　　　　　　IE
NEW YEATS PAPERS. 1972. irreg. price varies. Dolemen Press Ltd., The Lodge, Mountrath, Portlaoise, Ireland. Ed. Liam Miller. circ. 2,000.
Formerly: Yeats Centenary Papers (ISSN 0084-4160)

810　375　　　　　　US　ISSN 0548-9040
NEW YORK STATE ENGLISH COUNCIL. MONOGRAPH SERIES. 1950. biennial. price varies. New York State English Council (Rochester), c/o David R. Wood, Exec. Sec., 131 W. Broad St., Rochester, NY 14608. Ed. Judy Schwartz. bibl. (also avail. in microform from EDR) Indexed: Sociol.Abstr.

809　808.8　　　　　US　ISSN 0077-9504
NEW YORK UNIVERSITY STUDIES IN COMPARATIVE LITERATURE. 1967. irreg. New York University Press, Washington Square, New York, NY 10003.

051　　　　　　　　US
NEWSNOVEL. 1970. irreg. $10. Alfred B. Glaser, Box 3232, Riverside, CA 92509. Ed. Darlene Wheeler. illus. charts. circ. 10,000(controlled)

800　　　　　　　　NP
NHU JAH. (Text in Newari) irreg. Rs.1.50. Gyan Jyoti Pustakalaya, Balakhu Tvah, Khwap 10, Nepal.

820　　　　　　AT　ISSN 0085-4204
NIMROD. 1963. a. $0.40 per no. ‡ University of Newcastle, Students Association, Shortland, N.S.W. 2308, Australia. adv. bk. rev. circ. 500.

NIVADAKA EKANKIKA. see THEATER

NORDISTICA GOTHOBURGENSIA. see
LINGUISTICS

839.82　　　　　　NO　ISSN 0078-1266
NORSK LITTERAER AARBOK. (Text mainly in Norwegian; partly Danish and Swedish) 1966. a. Kr.56. Norske Samlaget, Trondheimsvn. 15, Oslo 5, Norway. Ed. Leif Maehle. cum.index every 5 years.

840　　　　　　　　US
NORTH CAROLINA STUDIES IN THE ROMANCE LANGUAGES AND LITERATURES. (Text in English, French, Italian, Latin, Spanish) 1940. irreg., no. 179, 1976. price varies. University of North Carolina at Chapel Hill, Department of Romance Languages, Dey Hall 014A, Chapel Hill, NC 27514.
Formerly: Studies in the Romance Languages and Literatures (ISSN 0081-8666)

800　　　　　　US　ISSN 0190-3012
NORTHERN NEW ENGLAND REVIEW. 1973. a. $3. Box 825, Franklin Pierce College, Rindge, NH 03461. adv. bk. rev. circ. 1,000.

410　810　　　　　　NO　ISSN 0078-1991
NORWEGIAN STUDIES IN ENGLISH. 1953. irreg. no. 19, 1974. price varies. (Universitetet i Oslo, Britisk Institutt - University of Oslo, British Institute) Universitetsforlaget, Kolstadgt. 1, Box 2959-Toeyen, Oslo 6, Norway (U.S. address: Box 258, Irvington-on-Hudson, NY 10533) (Co-sponsor: Universitetet i Bergen; Universitet i Trondheim) Ed. Bd.
Formerly (vol.1): Oslo Studies in English.

840　920　　　　　　FR　ISSN 0078-2165
NOUVELLE BIBLIOTHEQUE NERVALIENNE. (Consists of two subdivisions: Textes and Etudes et Documents; subdivisions are numbered consecutively within the main series) 1959. irreg. Lettres Modernes, 73, rue du Cardinal Lemoine, 75005 Paris, France.

850　　　　　　　　IT
NUOVA UNIVERSALE STUDIUM. 1974. irreg., no. 34, 1979. price varies. Edizioni Studium-Vita Nova, Via Crescenzio 63, 00193 Rome, Italy.

891.7　　　　　　　　UR
O LITERATURE DLYA DETEI. vol. 20, 1976. irreg. 0.36 Rub. per issue. Izdatel'stvo Detskaya Literatura, Nab. Kutuzova 6, 192187 Leningrad, U.S.S.R. circ. 10,000.

890　　　　　　　　JA
OBELISK. 1973. a. 800 Yen. Kase Sadako, Ed. & Pub., 3-12-9 Taito, Taito-ku, Tokyo 110, Japan. circ. 800. Indexed: Jap.Per.Ind.

800　　　　　　　　US
OBRAS (VENICE) 1968. q. $15. Beyond Baroque Foundation, 681 Venice Blvd., Old Venice City Hall, Box 803, Venice, CA 90291. Ed. Manuel "Manazar" Gamboa. bk. rev. film rev. play rev. circ. 7,000.
Former titles (until 1980): Beyond Baroque (1976); Beyond Baroque/Newforms. Incorporating: New Magazine: Arts and Letters; which was formerly: NeWLetterS; Newbooks; Beyond Baroque (ISSN 0006-0445)

891.85　　　　　　PL　ISSN 0078-2963
OBRAZ LITERATURY POLSKIEJ. 1965. irreg. price varies. (Polska Akademia Nauk, Instytut Badan Literackich) Panstwowe Wydawnictwo Naukowe, Miodowa 10, Warsaw, Poland.

430　400　940　　　UK　ISSN 0307-7497
OCCASIONAL PAPERS IN GERMAN STUDIES. (Text in English with German quotations) 1972. irreg. 40p.($0.84) per. no. University of Warwick, Department of German Studies, Coventry CV4 4AL, England. (Co-sponsor: Volkswagen Foundation) Ed. Tony Phelan. circ. 200.

800　　　　　　UK　ISSN 0078-3099
OCCASIONAL PAPERS IN MODERN LANGUAGES. (Text in all modern languages except English) 1966. irreg. individually priced. University of Hull Publications Committee, Hull HU6 7RX, England. Ed. J.C.Ireson.
Contributions by members of modern language departments, University of Hull, and elsewhere

800　　　　　　DK　ISSN 0078-3323
ODENSE UNIVERSITY STUDIES IN LITERATURE. (Text in Danish; summaries in English) 1969. irreg., no. 7, 1979. price varies. Odense University Press, 36, Pjentedamsgade, DK-5000 Odense, Denmark.

ODENSE UNIVERSITY STUDIES IN SCANDINAVIAN LANGUAGES AND LITERATURES. see LINGUISTICS

838 AU
OESTERREICHISCHE AKADEMIE DER WISSENSCHAFTEN. KOMMISSION FUER LITERATURWISSENSCHAFT. VEROEFFENTLICHUNGEN. (Subseries of: Oesterreichische Akademie der Wissenschaften. Philosophisch-Historische Klasse. Sitzungsberichte) 1973. irreg. Verlag der Oesterreichischen Akademie der Wissenschaften, Dr. Ignaz Seipel Platz, A-1010 Vienna, Austria.

052   GH   ISSN 0048-1629
OKYEAME; Ghana's literary magazine. 1961. irreg. price varies. University of Ghana, Institute of African Studies, Box 73, Legon, Ghana. circ. 1,000.

810   US
OLD RED KIMONO. 1972. a. free contr. circ. Floyd Junior College, Humanities Division, Box 1864, Rome, GA 30161. Ed. Ken Anderson. index. circ. 750. (processed)

810   US
ONE SHOT. irreg; latest 1973-74. $0.89. Casper Publications, 618 Western Ave, Madison, WI 53711. illus. (back issues avail.)

810   US   ISSN 0474-3326
ORBIT (NEW YORK); a science fiction anthology. 1966. irreg., no. 18, 1976. Harper and Row Publishers, Inc., 10 E. 53rd St., New York, NY 10022. Ed. Damon Knight.

800   US   ISSN 0474-3369
ORCRIST: a journal of fantasy in the arts. 1967. a. (approx.) $1 per no. Tolkien Society, University of Wisconsin, c/o Ed. Richard C. West, 1922 Madison St., Madison, WI 53711. bk. rev. bibl. illus. circ. 200. (processed; also avail. in microfilm; back issues avail) Indexed: Abstr.Eng.Stud. M.L.A.

800   UK
ORDINARY LIVES. 1976. irreg. £6.95. Dennis Dobson Books Ltd., 80 Kensington Church St., London W8 4BZ, England.

800 410   US
OREGON STATE MONOGRAPHS. STUDIES IN LITERATURE AND LANGUAGE. irreg., latest no. 2. price varies. Oregon State University Press, 101 Waldo Hall, Corvallis, OR 97331.

810   US
OUT THERE. 1967. irreg. $1. Pedestrian Press, 552 25th Ave., San Francisco, CA 94121. Ed. Stephen M. H. Braitman. circ. 500-1,000.

820 000.3   US
OXFORD ENGLISH MONOGRAPHS. irreg. price varies. Oxford University Press, 200 Madison Ave., New York, NY 10016 (And Ely House, 37 Dover St., London W1X 4AH, England) Ed.Bd.

830 410   UK   ISSN 0078-7191
OXFORD GERMAN STUDIES. (Text and summaries in English and German) 1966. a. £5.95($15) Wightwick, Boars Hill, Oxford 0X1 5DR, England. Eds. P. F. Ganz, T. J. Reed. circ. 500. (back issues avail.)

820   US   ISSN 0078-7221
OXFORD HISTORY OF ENGLISH LITERATURE. irreg. Oxford University Press, 200 Madison Ave., New York, NY 10016 (and Ely House, 37 Dover St., London W1X 4AH, England) Eds. Bonamy Dobree, Norman Davis.

890   US
OXFORD IN ASIA; MODERN AUTHORS. irreg. price varies. Oxford University Press, 200 Madison Ave., New York, NY 10016 (And Ely House, 37 Dover St., London W1X 4AH, England)

800   US
OXFORD LIBRARY OF AFRICAN LITERATURE. irreg. price varies. Oxford University Press, 200 Madison Ave., New York, NY 10016 (And Ely House, 37 Dover St., London W1X 4AH, England) Ed.Bd.

800   US
OXFORD MODERN LANGUAGE AND LITERATURE MONOGRAPHS. irreg. price varies. Oxford University Press, 200 Madison Ave., New York, NY 10016 (And Ely House, 37 Dover St., London W1X 4AH, England) Ed.Bd.

OXFORD THEATRE TEXTS. see *THEATER*

OZIANA. see *CLUBS*

PACIFIC COAST COUNCIL ON LATIN AMERICAN STUDIES. PROCEEDINGS. see *HISTORY — History Of North And South America*

810   US
PANHANDLER. no. 6, 1978. a. University of West Florida, Writers Workshop, English Dept., Pensacola, FL 32504. Ed. Rawa K. McDaniels.

800   FR   ISSN 0078-9429
PARALOGUE. 1965. irreg. Lettres Modernes, 73, rue de Cardinal Lemoine, 75005 Paris, France.

800   US
PARMA ELDALAMBERON. 1972. irreg. $3.50 for 4 nos. Mythopoeic Society, Box 4671, Whittier, CA 90607. Ed.Bd. illus. circ. 200. (also avail. in microform from UMI; reprint service avail. from UMI)

848.9   FR
PAUL VALERY. (Subseries of: Revue des Lettres Modernes) 1974. irreg. Lettres Modernes, 73, rue du Cardinal-Lemoine, 75005 Paris, France. bibl.

800   NE
PDR PRESS PUBLICATIONS IN LITERARY SYSTEMS. (Text in English) 1976. irreg, no. 2, 1976. $8.50. Peter de Ridder Press, Box 168, Lisse 1660, Netherlands.

860   SP
PENSAMIENTO LITERARIO ESPANOL. 1976. irreg. Fundacion Juan March, Castello 71, Madrid 6, Spain.

800   UK
PEOPLE LIKE THAT. 1970. irreg. Central London Adult Education Institute, 6 Bolt Court, Fleet St., London E.C.4, England. Ed. Bernard Miller. illus.

800   US
PERSEA; an international review. 1977. a. $3.45. Persea Books, Inc., 225 Lafayette St., New York, NY 10012. Eds. Michael Braziller, Karen Braziller. circ. 1,000.

810   US
PERSONAL INJURY MAGAZINE. 1975. irreg. $7 for 3 issues. Michael Sappol, Ed. & Pub., 628 E. 14th St. Apt 3., New York, NY 10009. charts. illus.

810   US
PERSPECTIVES. 1973. irreg. $2 for 4 issues. State University of New York, College at Potsdam, Department of English, Potsdam, NY 13676. Eds. Krishna Baldev Vaid, Anthony Boyle. circ. 500.

800   US   ISSN 0079-1008
PERSPECTIVES IN CRITICISM. 1962. irreg. price varies. University of California Press, 2223 Fulton St., Berkeley, CA 94720.

PHILOLOGISCHE BEITRAEGE ZUR SUEDOST- UND OSTEUROPAFORSCHUNG. see *LINGUISTICS*

800   CN   ISSN 0079-1784
PHOENIX. SUPPLEMENTARY VOLUMES. 1952. irreg. price varies. University of Toronto Press, Front Campus, Toronto, Ont. M5S 1A6, Canada (and 33 East Tupper St., Buffalo, N.Y. 14203) Ed.Bd. (also avail. in microfiche)

800   US   ISSN 0192-8716
PIKESTAFF FORUM. 1978. irreg. $10 for 6 nos. Pikestaff Publications, Inc., Box 127, Normal, IL 61761. Eds. James R. Scrimgeour, Robert D. Sutherland. bk. rev. index. circ. 1,000. (tabloid format; back issues avail.) Indexed: Ind.Amer.Per.Verse.

800   US   ISSN 0192-8724
PIKESTAFF REVIEW. 1979. irreg. $10 for 3 nos. Pikestaff Publications, Inc., Box 127, Normal, IL 61761. Eds. James R. Scrimgeour, Robert D. Sutherland. circ. 500. (back issues avail.) Indexed: Ind.Amer.Per.Verse.

891.85   PL   ISSN 0079-211X
PISARZE SLASCY XIX I XX WIEKU.* 1965. irreg. price varies. Slaski Instytut Naukowy, Francuska 12, Katowice, Poland (Dist. by Ars Polona-Ruch, Krakowskie Przedmiescie 7, Warsaw, Poland)

806   AT   ISSN 0311-0753
PLAIN TURKEY. 1973. irreg. Mt. Isa Writers Workshop, 97 Trainor St., Mt. Isa, Qld. 4825, Australia. Ed. R. Algie.

800   US
PLANET DRUM. 1973. irreg. $10. Planet Drum Foundation, Box 31251, San Francisco, CA 94131. circ. 3,000.

800   IT
PLEIADI. irreg. Angelo Longo Editore, Via Rocca Ai Fossi 6, Casella Postale 431, 48100 Ravenna, Italy. Ed. Franco Mollia.

809   US
POE MESSENGER. 1969. a. membership. Poe Foundation, Inc., 1914-16 E. Main St., Richmond, VA 23223. bk. rev. play rev. illus. circ. 550. (back issues avail.)

POETES ET PROSATEURS DU PORTUGAL. see *LITERATURE — Poetry*

830   IT   ISSN 0079-2500
POETI E PROSATORI TEDESCHI. 1962. irreg., no. 6, 1972. price varies. Edizioni dell' Ateneo S.p.A., P.O. Box 7216, 00100 Rome, Italy. Ed. Paolo Chiarini. circ. 1,000.

POETIC DRAMA AND POETIC THEORY. see *LITERATURE — Poetry*

811   US
POETRY: PEOPLE. 1973. irreg. (1-2/yr) $6.50. ‡ R.V.K. Publishing Co, Box 264, Menomonee Falls, WI 53051. Ed. S.P. Stavrakis. adv. illus. circ. 1,000-3,000.

POLSKA AKADEMIA NAUK. ODDZIAL W KRAKOWIE. KOMISJA HISTORYCZNOLITERACKA. ROCZNIK. see *HISTORY*

809   PL   ISSN 0554-579X
POLSKA AKADEMIA NAUK. ODDZIAL W KRAKOWIE. KOMISJA HISTORYCZNOLITERACKA. PRACE. (Text in English, French and Polish) 1961. irreg., no. 40, 1979. price varies. Ossolineum, Publishing House of the Polish Academy of Sciences, Rynek 9, Wroclaw, Poland (Dist. by: Ars Polona-Ruch, Krakowskie Przedmiescie 7, Warsaw, Poland)

891.8   PL   ISSN 0079-3434
POLSKA AKADEMIA NAUK. ODDZIAL W KRAKOWIE. KOMISJA SLOWIANOZNAWSTWA. PRACE. (Text in Polish; summaries in English and Russian) 1962. irreg., no. 40, 1979. price varies. Ossolineum, Publishing House of the Polish Academy of Sciences, Rynek 9, 50-106 Wroclaw, Poland (Dist. by Ars Polona-Ruch, Krakowskie Przedmiescie 7, Warsaw, Poland)

839   NE
POPULAIRE LITERATUUR; en reeks teksten uit de late Middeleeuwen. 1979. irreg. price varies. Dick Coutinho B.V., Badlaan 2, Muiderberg, Netherlands.

800 850   IT
PORTICO. (In two parts: Letteratura Italiana; Letteratura Straniera) irreg. Angelo Longo Editore, Via Rocca Ai Fossi 6, Casella Postale 431, 48100 Ravenna, Italy. Ed. Antonio Piromalli.

820   US
POWYS NEWSLETTER. 1970. irreg., approx. a. $4 per no. (Colgate University) Colgate University Press, 303 Lawrence Hall, Hamilton, New York, NY 13346. Ed. R.L. Blackmore. bk. rev. bibl. circ. 300.

891.85   PL   ISSN 0079-4767
PRACE LITERACKIE. 1959. irreg., vol. 19, 1977. price varies. (Uniwersytet Wroclawski) Ossolineum, Publishing House of the Polish Academy of Sciences, Rynek 9, Wroclaw, Poland (Dist. by Ars Polona-Ruch, Krakowskie Przedmiescie 7, Warsaw, Poland) circ. 500. (also avail. in microfilm)

LITERATURE

891.85   PL   ISSN 0079-4791
PRACE POLONISTYCZNE. 1951. a. 50 Zl.($9)
(Lodzkie Towarzystwo Naukowe) Ossolineum,
Publishing House of the Polish Academy of
Sciences, Rynek 9, 50-106 Wroclaw, Poland (Dist.
by Ars Polona-Ruch, Krakowskie Przedmiescie 7,
00-068 Warsaw, Poland) (Co-sponsor: Polska
Akademia Nauk) bk. rev. circ. 800. (also avail. in
microfilm)

491 891   II
PRAKRIT TEXT SOCIETY. PUBLICATIONS. irreg.
price varies. Prakrit Text Society, c/o Lalbhai
Dalpatbhai Institute of Indology, Near Gujarat
University, P. O. Navarangpura, Ahmedabao
380009, India.

810   US
PRESIDIO. vol.39, 1972. bi-m. $2. Iowa State
Penitentiary at Fort Madison, Box 316, Fort
Madison, IA 52627. Ed. Danny Harris. illus.

891   UR
PRIAMUR'E MOE; literaturno-khudozhestvennyi
sbornik. irreg. 1.05 Rub. Khabarovskoe Knizhnoe
Izdatel'stvo, Ul. Lenina, 181, Blagoveshchensk,
U.S.S.R. illus.

PRIMAVERA. see *WOMEN'S INTERESTS*

800   US   ISSN 0079-5186
PRINCETON ESSAYS IN LITERATURE. 1964.
irreg. price varies. Princeton University Press,
Princeton, NJ 08540. (reprint service avail. from
UMI)

840   CN
PRIX DE LA REVUE ETUDES FRANCAISES.
irreg. price varies. Presses de l'Universite de
Montreal, C.P. 6128, Succ. A, Montreal, Que. H3C
3J7, Canada. (reprint service avail. from UMI)

813.5   US   ISSN 0079-5453
PRIZE STORIES; THE O. HENRY AWARDS. 1919.
a. $10.95. Doubleday & Company, Inc., 245 Park
Ave., New York, NY 10017. Ed. William
Abrahams. circ. 12,000.

820   II
PROBITAS. (Text in English) Rs.3($2) per no. Aruna
Printing Works, Berhampur 760002, India.
"devoted to literature and culture"

860   SP
PROSA GALEGA. 1976. irreg. Editorial Galaxia,
Reconquista 1, Vigo, Spain.

830.9   SZ
PROTHESE; Versuchszeitschrift fuer neue Literatur
und anderes. 1973. irreg. (2-3/yr.) Moser Zogg,
Chileweg 811, 8912 Obfelden, Switzerland.

810   US   ISSN 0048-5640
PROUD BLACK IMAGES. 1971. a. $1.25. New
World Arts Workshop, Rm. 414 Ohio Union, 1739
N. High St., Ohio State University, Columbus, OH
43210. Ed. Edie Kendall. illus. circ. 1,500.

840 440   SZ   ISSN 0079-7812
PUBLICATIONS ROMANES ET FRANCAISES.
1933, no. 9. irreg., no. 143, 1977. price varies.
Librarie Droz, 11, rue Massot, 1211 Geneva 12,
Switzerland. circ. 1,000.

860   AG
PUENTE: LECTURA PARA TODOS. no. 3, 1976.
irreg. Editorial Guadalupe, Mansilla 3865, Buenos
Aires, Argentina. Ed. Carlos A. Merlino.

800   US
PUERTO DEL SOL. 1961-1976; resumed 1980. a. $6.
New Mexico State University, Writing Center, Box
3E, Las Cruces, NM 88003. Ed. Joseph Tujo. bk.
rev. illus. circ. 1,500.

PURDUE UNIVERSITY MONOGRAPHS IN
ROMANCE LANGUAGE. see *LINGUISTICS*

810   US   ISSN 0149-7863
PUSHCART PRIZE: BEST OF THE SMALL
PRESSES. 1976. a. $17.95. Pushcart Press, Box
845, Yonkers, NY 10701. Ed. Bill Henderson. circ.
40,000. (back issues avail.)

808   IT
QUADERNI DI LETTERATURE AMERICANE.
1976. irreg. Cisalpino-Goliardica, Via Bassini 17-2,
20133 Milan, Italy.

820   SA
QUARRY; new South African writing. (Text in
English) 1976. a. c/o A. Donker, Craighall Mews,
Jan Smuts Ave., Craighall Park, Johannesburg 2196,
South Africa. illus.

800   US
QUARTERLY REVIEW OF LITERATURE
CONTEMPORARY POETRY SERIES. 1943.
irreg., 2 issues per vol. $10 paperback; $20
hardback. 26 Haslet Ave., Princeton, NJ 08540.
Eds. Theodore & Renee Weiss. adv. circ. 5,000.
Indexed: R.G. Ind.Little Mag.
    Formerly: Quarterly Review of Literature (ISSN
0033-5819)

830 920   GW   ISSN 0075-2371
RAABE- GESELLSCHAFT. JAHRBUCH. 1960. a.
DM.20. Waisenhaus Buchdruckerei und Verlag,
Waisenhausdamm 13, 3300 Braunschweig, W.
Germany (B. R. D.) bk. rev.

890   II
RABIBASARA. (Text in Bengali) vol. 10, 1978. a.
Rs.5. Bengala Buks, 7, Nabin Kundu Lane, Calcutta
700006, India.

800   US   ISSN 0360-7887
RACKHAM LITERARY STUDIES. (Text in English,
French & German) 1970. a. $1. University of
Michigan, 4024 Modern Language Bldg., Ann
Arbor, MI 48104. Ed. Rebecca E. Schrader. circ.
1,000.

820 420   II   ISSN 0448-1690
RAJASTHAN UNIVERSITY STUDIES IN
ENGLISH. (Text in English) 1963. a. University of
Rajasthan, Gandhi Nagar, Jaipur 302004, India. bk.
rev.

890   PK
RAVI. (Issued in 3 parts) (Text in English, Panjabi or
Urdu) a. price varies. Government College, Lahore,
Pakistan.

500 700 800   SP   ISSN 0034-060X
REAL ACADEMIA DE CORDOBA DE
CIENCIAS, BELLAS LETRAS Y NOBLES
ARTES. BOLETIN. 1922. a. 200 ptas. Real
Academia de Cordoba de Ciencias, Bellas Letras y
Nobles Artes, Ambrosia de Morales 9, Cordoba,
Spain. bk. rev. abstr. charts. illus. index. circ. 500.

830 430   FR   ISSN 0399-1989
RECHERCHES GERMANIQUES. (Text in French
and German) 1971. a. 28 F. Universite de
Strasbourg II, 22 rue Descartes, 67000 Strasbourg,
France. Eds. G. L. Fink & Marc Schweyer. bibl.
circ. 1,200. (back issues avail.)

822   CN
RECORDS OF EARLY ENGLISH DRAMA. 1979.
irreg. price varies. University of Toronto Press,
Front Campus, Toronto, Ont. M5S 1A6, Canada.
Ed. Alexander F. Johnson.

800   US
RED DUST; new writing. 1972. irreg., no. 3, 1979.
$4.95 cloth; $2.50 paper. Red Dust Inc., 218 East
81st St., New York, NY 10028. Ed. Joanna
Gunderson. circ. 1,000.

811   US   ISSN 0484-2650
REFLECTION (SPOKANE); Gonzaga's literary
magazine. 1960. a. free. Gonzaga University,
Spokane, WA 99258. circ. 600.

894   HU   ISSN 0080-0570
REGI MAGYAR PROZAI EMLEKEK. (Text in
Hungarian; occasional summaries in German) 1968.
irreg. price varies. (Magyar Tudomanyos Akademia)
Akademiai Kiado, Publishing House of the
Hungarian Academy of Sciences, P.O. Box 24, H-
1363 Budapest, Hungary.

860   AG
RELATOS INEDITOS ARGENTINOS. 1977. irreg.
Editorial Castor y Pollux, Sarmiento 640, Buenos
Aires, Argentina.

RENAISSANCE DRAMA. see *THEATER*

800   US   ISSN 0584-4207
RENAISSANCE PAPERS. 1956. a. $3. Southeastern
Renaissance Conference, Duke University, Editorial
Office, 402 Allen Bldg., Durham, NC 27706. Eds.
Dennis G. Donovan, A. Leigh DeNeef. illus. index.
circ. 450. (also avail. in microfilm from UMI)

809 420 375.4   US   ISSN 0190-3233
REVIEW (CHARLOTTESVILLE) 1979. a. $20.
(Virginia Polytechnic Institute and State University)
University Press of Virginia, Box 3608 University
Sta., Charlottesville, VA 22903. Eds. James O.
Hoge, James L.W. West III. circ. 1,500.

800   US   ISSN 0034-6640
REVIEW OF NATIONAL LITERATURES. 1970. a.
$14 per no. to non-members, $12 members. Council
on National Literatures, Box 81, Whitestone, NY
11357. Ed. Anne Paolucci. adv. bk. rev. bibl. circ.
1,200. (back issues avail.)

869   BL   ISSN 0080-2352
REVISTA DE LETRAS. (Text in English, French,
German, Italian, Portuguese and Spanish) 1960. a.
Cr.$120. Universidade Estadual Paulista "Julio de
Mesquita Filho", Instituto de Letras, Historia e
Psicologia de Assis, Assis, Sao Paulo, Brazil. bk. rev.
circ. 1,000.

850   SP
REVISTA HIPERION. 1978. irreg. 1000 ptas. (for 4
nos.) Peralta Ediciones, San Fermin 6, Pamplona,
Spain. Ed.Bd. illus.

860   US   ISSN 0482-6558
REVISTA IBERICA. (Text in Spanish, English, and
Portuguese) 1952. irreg. (2-4/yr.) price varies. ‡
Maria-Luisa De la Casa, Ed. & Pub., 2600 Walker
Lane, Salt Lake City, UT 84117. bk. rev.

850   IT   ISSN 0080-2441
REVISTA SCRIITORILOR ROMANI. (Text in
Rumanian) 1962. a. price varies. Societa
Accademica Romena, Foro Traiano 1a, 00187
Rome, Italy.

400 800   CL   ISSN 0035-0451
REVISTA SIGNOS DE VALPARAISO; estudios de
lengua y literatura. Variant title: Revista Signos.
(Text in Spanish; summaries in English, French and
Spanish) 1967. a. $6. (Universidad Catolica de
Valparaiso, Instituto de Literatura y Ciencias del
Languaje) Ediciones Universitarias de Valparaiso,
Monttsaavedra 44, Casilla 1415, Valparaiso, Chile.
Ed. Eduardo Godoy. bk. rev. circ. 500.

891 943   FR   ISSN 0080-2557
REVUE DES ETUDES SLAVES. 1921. a. 240 F.
Institut d'Etudes Slaves, 9 rue Michelet, F - 75006
Paris, France. bk. rev. circ. 800.

809   FR   ISSN 0035-2136
REVUE DES LETTRES MODERNES; histoire des
idees et des litteratures. 1954. irreg. Lettres
Modernes, 73 rue du Cardinal Lemoine, 75005
Paris, France. Ed. M. J. Minard. bk. rev. bibl.

801   UK   ISSN 0484-9035
REYNARD. 1954. irreg. (1-2/yr.) $5. ‡ Quaker
Fellowship of the Arts, c/o Ed. & Pub. Charles
Kohler, Overmist, Yew Tree Rd., Dorking, Surrey,
England (Subscr. to: 41 Ludlow Road, Guildford,
Surrey, England) circ. 500. (processed)

860   AG
RIO NEGRO, ARGENTINA. DIRECCION
PROVINCIAL DE CULTURA. MONOGRAFIAS.
1972. irreg. free. Direccion Provincial de Cultura,
Roca 250, Viedma, Rio Negro, Argentina.

820   UK
ROBERT BURNS CHRONICLE. 1892. a. £2.25 cloth
bound; £1 paper. Burns Federation, Dick Institute,
Elmbank Avenue, Kilmarnock KAI 3BU, Scotland.
adv. bk. rev. bibl. illus. cum.index. circ. 3,000.

800   GW   ISSN 0557-2614
ROMANFUEHRER; der Inhalt der Romane und
Novellen der Weltliteratur. 1952. irreg., vol. 16,
1979. DM.98 per vol. Anton Hiersemann Verlag,
Rosenbergstr. 113, Postfach 723, 7000 Stuttgart 1,
W. Germany (B.R.D.)

ROMANICA GOTHOBURGENSIA. see
LINGUISTICS

ROMANICA HELVETICA. see *LINGUISTICS*

820   AU
ROMANTIC REASSESSMENT. 1972. irreg., no. 65,
1977. Universitaet Salzburg, Institut fuer
Englische Sprache, Akademiestr. 24, A-5020
Salzburg, Austria. Ed. James Hogg. circ. 300.

LITERATURE

800   US   ISSN 0161-682X
ROMANTIST. 1977. a. $5.50. F. Marion Crawford Memorial Society, Saracinesca House, 3610 Meadowbrook Ave., Nashville, TN 37205. Ed.Bd. adv. bk. rev. circ. 300(controlled) Indexed: M.L.A.

800   UR
ROMANTIZM V RUSSKOI I SOVETSKOI LITERATURE. 1973. irreg. 68 Rub. Kazanskii Universitet, Ul. Lenina, 4/5, Kazan, U.S.S.R.

ROYAL IRISH ACADEMY. PROCEEDINGS. SECTION C: ARCHAEOLOGY, CELTIC STUDIES, HISTORY, LINGUISTICS AND LITERATURE. see *ARCHAEOLOGY*

RUSSICA OLOMUCENSIA. see *LINGUISTICS*

RUYGH-BEWERP. see *LINGUISTICS*

800   US
S L A NEWSLETTER. 1975. a. $5. Southern Comparative Literature Association, c/o Dept. of English, North Carolina State Univ., Box 5308, Raleigh, NC 27607. Ed. Jean J. Smoot. bibl. circ. 2,000.

891   UK   ISSN 0080-5122
S W A T H; yearly book of literature. (Text in Lithuanian) 1964. a. $3. Lithuanian House Ltd., Nida Press, 1-2, Ladbroke Gardens, London W11, England (Dist. in U.S. by Draugas, 4545 W. 63 St., Chicago, Ill. 60629) Ed. K. Barenas.

801   II
SAMBALPUR UNIVERSITY. POST-GRADUATE DEPARTMENT OF ORIYA. JOURNAL. (Text in Oriya) no. 2, 1976. a. Sambalpur University, Post Graduate Department of Oriya, Jotibihara, Sambalpur, India.

800   US
SANDS; a literary magazine. a. $6.50. c/o Joyce Meler, Ed., 7170 Briar Cove Dr., Dallas, TX 75240.
Formerly: Sand.

890   II
SARVOTKRUSHTA MARATHI KATHA. (Text in Marathi) vol. 9, 1974. a. Rs.16($2) c/o Mrs. Chhaya Kolarkar, Ed., 43/348 Sant Tukaram Nagar, Pimpri, Poona 411018, India. circ. 1,500. (back issues avail.)
Short stories

890   II   ISSN 0581-8532
SATAPITAKA. INDO-ASIAN LITERATURES. 1957. irreg. price varies. (International Academy of Indian Culture) Impex India, 2/18 Ansari Rd., New Delhi 110002, India. Ed. Lokesh Chandra. circ. 100.
Series of collectanea reproduced in original scripts and languages

SAVACOU; a journal of the Caribbean artists movement. see *ART*

840   UR
SBORNIK STATEI PO FRANTSUZSKOI LINGVISTIKE I METODIKE PREPODAVANIYA INOSTRANNOGO YAZIKA V VUZE. 1971, vol. 3. irreg. 0.35 Rub. Moskovskii Gosudarstvennyi Pedagogicheskii Institut Inostrannykh Yazykov, Rostokinskii pr., 13, Moscow B-14, U.S.S.R. bibl.

SCANDO-SLAVICA. see *LINGUISTICS*

SCANDO-SLAVICA. SUPPLEMENTUM. see *LINGUISTICS*

830   GW
SCHLESWIG-HOLSTEINISCHER HEIMATKALENDER. 1938. irreg. DM.6.90. (Schleswig-Holsteinischer Heimatbund) Heinrich Moeller Soehne GmbH, Bahnhofstr. 12-16, 2370 Rendsburg, W. Germany (B.R.D.). illus.

830   GW   ISSN 0085-5952
SCHMANKERL; literarische Blaetter fuer Bayerisch-Oesterreichische Mundarten. 1969. 4-6/yr. DM.3 per no. Verlag Friedl Brehm, Poeckinger Weg 10, 8133 Feldafing, W. Germany (B. R. D.) Ed. Friedl Brehm. adv. bk. rev.

SCHRIFTEN ZUR JUGENDLEKTUERE. see *CHILDREN AND YOUTH — For*

SCHRIFTENREIHE DES BUCHKLUBS DER JUGEND. see *CHILDREN AND YOUTH — For*

839   NE   ISSN 0080-7192
SCHRIJVERS PRENTENBOEK. 1958. irreg.(approx. 1 issue per year) fl.8. Nederlands Letterkundig Museum en Documentatiecentrum, Juffr. Idastraat 11, The Hague, Netherlands.

894.2 951.7   US   ISSN 0080-8377
SCRIPTA MONGOLICA. (Text in English, French; occasionally Mongolian) 1952. irreg., 1969, no. 4. price varies. (Harvard-Yenching Institute) Harvard University Press, 79 Garden St., Cambridge, MA 02138.

889 949.5   RM   ISSN 0080-8385
SCRIPTORES BYZANTINI. 1958. irreg. Editura Academiei Republicii Socialiste Romania, Calea Victoriei 125, Bucharest, Romania (Subscr. to: ILEXIM, Str. 13 Decembrie Nr. 3, P.O. Box 136-137, Bucharest, Romania)

895   MY
SEJAHTERA. (Text in English or Malay) a. Islamic Students' Union of the University of Malaya - Persatuan Mahasiswa Islam Universiti Malaya, Kuala Lumpur, Malaysia.

860   CR
SERIE ESTUDIOS LITERARIOS. 1975. irreg. exchange. Ministerio de Cultura, Juventud y Deportes, Dept. de Publicaciones, Apdo. 10227, San Jose, Costa Rica.

860   PR
SERIE LITERATURA HOY. 1976. irreg. $6. Instituto de Cultura Puertorriquena, Apdo. 4184, San Juan, PR 00905.

SERIES IN SIKH HISTORY AND CULTURE. see *HISTORY — History Of Asia*

800   GE   ISSN 0080-9128
SHAKESPEARE-JAHRBUCH. 1864. a. vol. 116, 1980. M.35. (Deutsche Shakespeare Gesellschaft) Hermann Boehlaus Nachfolger, Meyerstr. 50a, 53 Weimar, E. Germany (D.D.R.) Eds. A. Schloesser, A. G. Kuckhoff. bk. rev.

820 378.3   US   ISSN 0080-9144
SHAKESPEARE RESEARCH AND OPPORTUNITIES; REPORT OF THE MODERN LANGUAGE ASSOCIATION OF AMERICA CONFERENCE. 1955. a. individuals $5; libraries and institutions $10. Modern Language Association of America Conference, c/o Prof. W. R. Elton, City University of New York, 33 W. 42nd St., New York, NY 10036. circ. 1,000. (also avail. in microform from UMI)

820   JA   ISSN 0582-9402
SHAKESPEARE STUDIES. (Text in English) 1962. a. 3000 Yen($5) Shakespeare Society of Japan, 18 Naka-machi, Shinjuku-ku, Tokyo 162, Japan. Ed. Jiro Ozu. circ. 700. Indexed: M.L.A.

809   US   ISSN 0582-9399
SHAKESPEARE STUDIES; an annual gathering of research, criticism & review. 1965. a. $25. Burt Franklin & Co., Inc., 235 E. 44 St., New York, NY 10017.

822   UK   ISSN 0080-9152
SHAKESPEARE SURVEY. 1948. a. $39.50. Cambridge University Press, Box 110, Cambridge CB2 3RL, England (and 32 E. 57 St., New York NY 10022) Ed. Stanley Wells. index. Indexed: Hum.Ind.

810   US
SHANKPAINTER. 1970. 1-2/yr. free. Fine Arts Work Center in Provincetown, Inc., c/o Lyle Fox, Ed., Box 565, Provincetown, MA 02657. circ. 700.

820   US
SHAW ANNUAL. 1951. a. $15.95. Pennsylvania State University Press, 215 Wagner Bldg., University Park, PA 16802. Ed. Dr. Stanley Weintraub. bk. rev. bibl. illus. index,cum. ind. 1950-1975. circ. 600. (also avail. in microform from MIM,UMI; reprint service avail. from UMI) Indexed: Abstr.Engl.Stud. M.L.A.
Formerly: Shaw Review (ISSN 0037-3354)

SHILOACH CENTER FOR MIDDLE EASTERN & AFRICAN STUDIES. MONOGRAPH SERIES. see *HISTORY — History Of The Near East*

800   US   ISSN 0080-9403
SHORT PLAY SERIES. 1966. irreg., no. 8, 1979. $0.50-$2. Proscenium Press, P.O. Box 361, Newark, DE 19711. Ed. Robert Hogan. (reprint service avail. from UMI)

840   FR
SIECLE ECLATE: DADA, SURREALISME ET LES AVANT-GARDES. 1974. a. price varies. Lettres Modernes, 73 rue du Cardinal Lemoine, 75005 Paris, France. circ. 2,500.

SILLAGES. see *LINGUISTICS*

810   US   ISSN 0037-5306
SILO. 1962. a. $3 per no. Bennington College, Bennington, VT 05201. adv. bk. rev. circ. 500(approx.)

810   US
SKYWRITING. 1971. irreg. $7.50. Blue Mountain Press, 511 Campbell Ave., Kalamazoo, MI 49007. Ed. Martin Grossman. adv. bk. rev. circ. 500. Indexed: Ind.Amer.Per.Verse.

SLADE MAGAZINE; murals, poems, drawings, photography, other articles. see *ART*

SLAVICA LUNDENSIA. see *LINGUISTICS*

891   NE   ISSN 0081-0029
SLAVISTIC PRINTING AND REPRINTINGS. irreg. price varies. Mouton Publishers, Noordeinde 41, 2514 GC The Hague, Netherlands (U.S. addr.: Mouton Publishers, c/o Walter de Gruyter, Inc., 200 Saw Mill River Road, Hawthorne, NY 10532)

810   US
SLIT WRIST MAGAZINE. 1976. irreg. $3. 333 E. 30th St., 14F, No. 4-B, New York, NY 10016. Ed. Terry Swanson. circ. 400.

810   US
SLOUGH. 1975. irreg. $4. Altruistic Enterprises, English Dept., University of Utah, Salt Lake City, UT 84103 (Or: 184 Q St., No. 2, Salt Lake City, UT 84103) Eds. Charles B. & Pat Ellis Taylor. adv. bk. rev. circ. 500.
Formerly: Texas Slough.

860   SP
SOCIEDAD ESPANOLA DE LITERATURA GENERAL Y COMPARADA. ANUARIO. 1978. a. price varies. Ediciones Catedra, Don Ramon de la Cruz 67, Madrid, Spain. adv. circ. 2,000.

840   FR   ISSN 0081-0754
SOCIETE CHATEAUBRIAND. BULLETIN. NOUVELLE SERIES. 1930; N.S. 1957. a. 60 F. Societe Chateaubriand, 122 Bd. de Courcelles, Paris, France (Subscr. to: Librairie Pierre Chretien, 178 Faubourg St. Honore, Paris 8e, France)

800   FR   ISSN 0085-624X
SOCIETE D'ETUDE DU VINGTIEME SIECLE. BULLETIN. 1971. irreg. 20 F. Societe D'Etude du Vingtieme Siecle, 24 rue Emile Dubois, 75014 Paris, France. Ed. Marie-Claire Bancquart. adv. bibl.

800   FR
SOCIETE D'ETUDES DANTESQUES. BULLETIN. 1949. biennial. 20 F. Centre Universitaire Mediterraneen, Societe d'Etudes Dantesques, 65 Promenade des Anglais, 06000 Nice, France.

840   FR   ISSN 0037-9182
SOCIETE DES AMIS DE MONTAIGNE. BULLETIN. 1912. irreg. 70 F. Societe des Amis de Montaigne, 6, Villa Chanez, 75016 Paris, France. Ed. Pierre Michel. bk. rev. circ. 525. (back issues avail)

800 700 100   UK
SOCIETY FOR RENAISSANCE STUDIES. OCCASIONAL PAPERS. 1973. a. membership. Society for Renaissance Studies, Department of History, Westfield College (University of London), Kidderpore Ave., London NW3 7ST, England. Ed. David Wootton. circ. 500.

810   US
SOCIETY FOR THE STUDY OF SOUTHERN LITERATURE. NEWSLETTER. Short title: S.S.S.L. 1968. irreg. $2. Society for the Study of Southern Literature, c/o Robert L. Phillips, Ed., Box 2625, Mississippi State University, Mississippi State, MS 39762. circ. 500.

800   700   US
SOFT STONE; an international journal of the arts.
   1974. irreg., 1-2/yr. $1 per no. Karl Wang, Ed. &
   Pub, 102-40 62nd Ave., Apt. 6C, Forest Hills, NY
   11375. bk. rev.

810   US
SOME FRIENDS. 1972. irreg. (approx. annually)
   $1.50. c/o Terry J. Cooper, Ed., Box 6395, Tyler,
   TX 76701. circ. 500.

SOUNDINGS (SANTA BARBARA); collections of
   the University Library. see LIBRARY AND
   INFORMATION SCIENCES

891.7   UR
SOVETSKAYA LITERATURA, TRADITSII I
   NOVATORSTVO. 1976. irreg. 0.68 Rub. per issue.
   Izdatel'stvo Leningradskii Universitet,
   Universitetskaya Nab. 7/9, Leningrad B-164,
   U.S.S.R. Ed. L. Gladkovskaya. circ. 6,550.

891   FR   ISSN 0303-111X
SOVETSKIE LJUDI SEGODNJA/VIE
   QUOTIDIENNE EN U.R.S.S. PRISE SUR LE
   VIF. (In two series Textes Litteraires and Dossiers)
   (Text in Russian; notes and comments in French or
   Russian) 1969. irreg. price varies. Institut d'Etudes
   Slaves, 9 rue Michelet, 75006 Paris, France.

SPECULUM ANNIVERSARY MONOGRAPHS. see
   HISTORY — History Of Europe

800   IT
SPECULUM ARTIUM. (Text in English, French and
   Italian) irreg. Angelo Longo Editore, Via Rocca Ai
   Fossi 6, Casella Postale 431, 48100 Ravenna, Italy.
   Ed. Aldo Scaglione.

830   GW   ISSN 0085-6584
SPEKTRUM DES GEISTES; Literaturkalender. 1951.
   a. DM.19.80. Lesen Verlag GmbH, Friedrichstr. 13,
   8000 Munich 40, W. Germany (B.R.D.) Ed.
   Ehrhardt Heinold. circ. 10,000.

820.3   US
SPENSER STUDIES; a Renaissance poetry annual.
   1980. a. price varies. University of Pittsburgh Press,
   127 N. Bellefield Ave., Pittsburgh, PA 15260. Eds.
   Patrick Cullen, Thomas P. Roche, Jr.

800   PL   ISSN 0079-3183
SREDNIOWIECZE.STUDIA O KULTURZE/
   ETUDES SUR LA CULTURE MEDIEVALE/
   MIDDLE AGES STUDIES IN CULTURE.
   (Editions in Polish, French, English) 1961. a. price
   varies. Polska Akademia Nauk, Instytut Badan
   Literackich, Nowy Swiat 72, Palac Staszica, 00-330
   Warsaw, Poland.

891.92 491.92   YU   ISSN 0081-3990
SRPSKA AKADEMIJA NAUKA I UMETNOSTI.
   ODELJENJE JEZIKA I KNJIZEVNOSTI.
   POSEBNA IZDANJA. (Text in Serbo-Croatian;
   summaries in French, English, German or Russian)
   1950. irreg. price varies. Srpska Akademija Nauka i
   Umetnosti, Knez Mihailova 35, 11001 Belgrade,
   Yugoslavia (Dist. by: Prosveta, Terazije 16,
   Belgrade, Yugoslavia) circ. 600.

840   850   US
STANFORD FRENCH & ITALIAN STUDIES. 1975.
   irreg., approx. 4 vols./yr. $20 per vol. (Stanford
   University, Department of French and Italian)
   Anma Libri, Box 876, Saratoga, CA 95070. Ed.
   Alphonse Juilland.

810   US   ISSN 0085-6746
STEINBECK MONOGRAPH SERIES. 1971. a. until
   1982, irreg. thereafter. $2-6. John Steinbeck Society,
   English Dept., Ball State Univ., Muncie, IN 47306.
   Ed. Tetsumaro Hayashi. bk. rev. circ. 470.

STOCKHOLM STUDIES IN FINNISH
   LANGUAGE AND LITERATURE. see
   LINGUISTICS

809   SW   ISSN 0491-0869
STOCKHOLM STUDIES IN HISTORY OF
   LITERATURE. (Subseries of Acta Universitatis
   Stockholmiensis) (Text in English and Spanish)
   1956. irreg., latest no. 21. price varies. (Stockholms
   Universitet) Almqvist & Wiksell International, Box
   62, S-101 20 Stockholm, Sweden. Eds. O.
   Lindberger, I. Jonsson. (back issues avail.)

890   SW
STOCKHOLM STUDIES IN RUSSIAN
   LITERATURE. (Subseries of Acta Universitatis
   Stockholmiensis) (Text in Russian; summaries in
   English) irreg., latest no. 9. price varies.
   (Stockholms Universitet) Almqvist & Wiksell
   International, Box 62, S-101 20 Stockholm, Sweden.
   Ed. Nils Ake Nilsson.

STONY THURSDAY BOOK. see LITERATURE —
Poetry

820   US   ISSN 0081-5861
STORIES FROM THE HILLS. 1970. a. $4. Morris
   Harvey College Publications, Charleston, WV
   25304. Ed. William Plumley. circ. 2,000.
   Explores Appalachia motifs

818.005   CN
STORY SO FAR. 1971. irreg. price varies. Coach
   House Press, 401(Rear) Huron St., Toronto, Ont.
   M5S 2G5, Canada.

800   US
STORYQUARTERLY. 1975. irreg. $10 for 4 nos. to
   individuals; institutions $12. StoryQuarterly, Inc.,
   820 Ridge Rd., Highland Park, IL 60035. Ed.Bd.
   adv. bk. rev. illus. circ. 1,500. Indexed:
   Amer.Hum.Ind.

891.86   CS   ISSN 0081-5896
STRAHOVSKA KNIHOVNA. (Text in Czech;
   summaries in French and German) 1966. a. price
   varies. Pamatnik Narodniho Pisemnictvi, Strahovske
   nadv. 132, Prague 1, Czechoslovakia. Ed. Pravoslav
   Kneidl.

STUDI ALBANESI. STUDI E TESTI. see
LINGUISTICS

STUDI AMERICANI. see HISTORY — History Of
North And South America

850   IT
STUDI DANTESCHI. (Text and summaries in Italian;
   occasionally Text in English, French, German)
   1920. a. L.11000. Angelo Longo Editore, Via Rocca
   Ai Fossi 6, Casella Postale 431, 48100 Ravenna,
   Italy. adv. cum index.

840   IT   ISSN 0585-4768
STUDI DI LETTERATURA FRANCESE. (Text in
   language of authors) 1967. a. price varies.
   (Universita degli Studi di Padova, Istituto di
   Letterature Straniere) Casa Editrice Leo S. Olschki,
   Casella Postale 66, 50100 Florence, Italy. Ed. Bd.
   circ. 1,000.

809   IT
STUDI E TESTI DELL'ANTICHITA. 1975. irreg.,
   no. 10, 1978. price varies. Societa Editrice
   Napoletana s.r.l., Corso Umberto I 34, 80138
   Naples, Italy. Ed. Fabio Cupaiuolo.

809   850   IT
STUDI E TESTI DI LETTERATURA ITALIANA.
   1974. irreg., no. 14, 1978. price varies. Societa
   Editrice Napoletana s.r.l., Corso Umberto I 34,
   80138 Naples, Italy.

850   IT
STUDI E TESTI DI LINGUA E LETTERATURA
   ITALIANA. 1977. irreg. (Universita degli Studi di
   Ferrara, Istituto di Filologia Classica e Moderna)
   Casa Editrice Patron, Via Badini 12-14, 40127
   Bologna, Italy.

800   IT   ISSN 0585-492X
STUDI ISPANICI. 1962. a. L.5000. Giardini Editori e
   Stampatori, Via Santa Bibbiana 28, 56100 Pisa,
   Italy. Ed.Bd.

850   IT   ISSN 0081-6256
STUDI TASSIANI. 1951. a. L.4000. Centro di Studi
   Tassiani, Via Pignola 103, 24100 Bergamo, Italy.
   cum.index: vols. 1-10, 11-20.

800   US
STUDIA BIBLIOGICA. 1980. a. American
   Institute for Writing Research, Corp., Box 2129,
   Grand Central Sta., New York, NY 10163 (In
   Canada: Box 2697, Sta. B, Kitchener, Ont. N2H
   6M3) Ed. Dr. Cornelius Dima-Dragan.

830   PL
STUDIA GERMANICA POSNANIENSIA. (Text in
   German) 1971. irreg., no. 6, 1977. price varies.
   Uniwersytet im. Adama Mickiewicza w Poznaniu,
   Stalingradzka 1, 61-712 Poznan, Poland (Dist. by:
   Ars Polona, Krakowskie Przedmiescie 7, 00-068
   Warsaw, Poland) Ed. Stefan H. Kaszynski. bk. rev.
   bibl.

891   941.5   IE   ISSN 0081-6477
STUDIA HIBERNICA. 1961. a. £3. ‡ St. Patrick's
   College, Editorial Committee, Dublin 9, Ireland. Ed.
   D. F. Cregan. bk. rev. circ. 1,000. Indexed: M.L.A.
   Studies in Irish culture

809   PL   ISSN 0137-4389
STUDIA POLONO-SLAVICA ORIENTALIA.
   ACTA LITTERARIA. irreg., vol. 5, 1979. price
   varies. (Polska Akademia Nauk, Instytut
   Slowianoznawstwa, Pracownia Literatur
   Wschodnioslowianskich) Ossolineum, Publishing
   House of the Polish Academy of Sciences, Rynek 9,
   Wroclaw, Poland (Dist. by: Ars Polona-Ruch,
   Krakowskie Przedmiescie 7, Warsaw, Poland) Ed.
   Bazyli Bialokozowicz.

800   PL   ISSN 0081-6884
STUDIA ROSSICA POSNANIENSIA. (Text in
   Polish and Russian; summaries in English and
   Russian) 1970. irreg., 1976, vol. 7. price varies.
   Uniwersytet im. Adama Mickiewicza w Poznaniu,
   Stalingradzka 1, 61-712 Poznan, Poland (Dist. by:
   Ars Polona, Krakowskie Przedmiescie 7, 00-068
   Warsaw, Poland) Ed. Zbigniew Baranski, Leszek
   Ossowski. bk. rev. circ. 700.

800   PL   ISSN 0081-6949
STUDIA STAROPOLSKIE. 1953. irreg., vol. 47,
   1978. price varies. (Polska Akademia Nauk, Instytut
   Badan Literackich) Ossolineum, Publishing House of
   the Polish Academy of Sciences, Rynek 9, Wroclaw,
   Poland (Dist. by Ars Polona-Ruch, Krakowskie
   Przedmiescie 7, Warsaw, Poland)

800   PL   ISSN 0081-7112
STUDIA Z OKRESU OSWIECENIA. (Text in Polish;
   summaries in English and French) 1964. irreg., vol.
   17, 1979. price varies. (Polska Akademia Nauk,
   Instytut Badan Literackich) Ossolineum, Publishing
   House of the Polish Academy of Sciences, Rynek 9,
   Wroclaw, Poland (Dist. by Ars Polona-Ruch,
   Krakowskie Przedmiescie 7, Warsaw, Poland)
   Ed.Bd. bibl. circ. 500-1,500.

830   GW   ISSN 0081-7236
STUDIEN ZUR DEUTSCHEN LITERATUR. 1966.
   irreg., no. 63, 1981. price varies. Max Niemeyer
   Verlag, Pfrondorfer Str. 4, 7400 Tuebingen, W.
   Germany (B.R.D.) Eds. Richard Brinkmann,
   Friedrich Sengle, Klaus Ziegler.

820   GW
STUDIEN ZUR ENGLISCHEN LITERATUR. 1969.
   irreg., vol. 19, 1978. price varies. Bouvier Verlag
   Herbert Grundmann, Am Hof 32, Postfach 1268,
   5300 Bonn 1, W. Germany (B.R.D.) Ed. Johannes
   Kleinsteuck.

830   GW
STUDIEN ZUR GERMANISTIK, ANGLISTIK
   UND KOMPARATISTIK. 1970. irreg., latest vol.
   87, 1979. price varies. Bouvier Verlag Herbert
   Grundmann, Am Hof 32, Postfach 1268, 5300 Bonn
   1, W. Germany (B.R.D.) Eds. A. Arnold, A. Hass.

800   GW
STUDIEN ZUR LITERATUR DER MODERNE.
   1976. irreg., vol. 8, 1979. price varies. Bouvier
   Verlag Herbert Grundmann, Am Hof 32, Postfach
   1268, 5300 Bonn 1, W. Germany (B.R.D.) Ed.
   Helmut Koopmann.

860   301   GW
STUDIEN ZUR LITERATUR- UND
   SOZIALGESCHICHTE SPANIENS UND
   LATEINAMERIKAS. 1975. irreg., no. 2, 1979.
   price varies. Bouvier Verlag Herbert Grundmann,
   Am Hof 32, Postfach 1268, 5300 Bonn 1, W.
   Germany(B.R.D.) Ed. Martin Franzbach.

STUDIEN ZUR PHILOSOPHIE UND LITERATUR
   DES NEUNZEHNTEN JAHRHUNDERTS. see
   PHILOSOPHY

STUDIES IN AMERICAN JEWISH LITERATURE.
   see ETHNIC INTERESTS

810   NE   ISSN 0081-752X
STUDIES IN AMERICAN LITERATURE. 1964. irreg. price varies. Mouton Publishers, Noordeinde 41, 2514 GC The Hague, Netherlands (U.S. addr: Mouton Publishers, c/o Walter de Gruyter, Inc., 200 Saw Mill River Road, Hawthorne, NY 10532)

STUDIES IN CLASSICAL LITERATURE. see *CLASSICAL STUDIES*

800   US   ISSN 0081-7767
STUDIES IN COMPARATIVE RENAISSANCE. 1968. irreg. price varies. Hennessey & Ingalls, Inc., 8321 Campion Dr., Los Angeles, CA 90045. Ed. David H. Malone. adv.

809   US   ISSN 0081-7775
STUDIES IN COMPARATIVE LITERATURE. (Text in English, French, German, Italian, Latin, Spanish) 1950. irreg., no. 61, 1977. price varies. ‡ University of North Carolina Press, Box 2288, Chapel Hill, NC 27514. (reprint service avail. from UMI)

820   NE   ISSN 0081-7899
STUDIES IN ENGLISH LITERATURE. 1965. irreg. price varies. Mouton Publishers, Noordeinde 41, 2514 GC The Hague, Netherlands (U.S. addr: Mouton Publishers, c/o Walter de Gruyter, Inc., 200 Saw Mill River Road, Hawthorne, NY 10532)

840   NE   ISSN 0081-7937
STUDIES IN FRENCH LITERATURE. 1964. irreg. price varies. Mouton Publishers, Noordeinde 41, 2514 C The Hague, Netherlands (U.S. addr: Mouton Publishers, c/o Walter de Gruyter, Inc., 200 Saw Mill River Road, Hawthorne, NY 10532)

800   NE   ISSN 0081-7945
STUDIES IN GENERAL AND COMPARATIVE LITERATURE. 1965. irreg. price varies. Mouton Publishers, Noordeinde 41, 2514 GC The Hague, Netherlands (U.S. addr: Mouton Publishers, c/o Walter de Gruyter, Inc., 300 Saw Mill River Road, Hawthorne, NY 10532)

830   NE   ISSN 0081-797X
STUDIES IN GERMAN LITERATURE. 1964. irreg. price varies. Mouton Publishers, Noordeinde 41, 2514 GC The Hague, Netherlands (U.S. addr: Mouton Publishers, c/o Walter de Gruyter, Inc., 200 Saw Mill River Road, Hawthorne, NY 10532)

860   US
STUDIES IN HISPANIC LITERATURES. irreg. price varies. Phaeton Press, Inc., 85 Tompkins St., Staten Island, NY 10304.

850   NE   ISSN 0081-8119
STUDIES IN ITALIAN LITERATURE. 1966. irreg. price varies. Mouton Publishers, Noordeinde 41, 2514 GC The Hague, Netherlands (U.S. addr: Mouton Publishers, c/o Walter de Gruyter, Inc., 200 Saw Mill River Road, Hawthorne, NY 10532)

STUDIES IN LANGUAGE COMPANION SERIES. see *LINGUISTICS*

800   US
STUDIES IN LITERATURE AND CRITICISM. irreg. price varies. Burt Franklin & Co., Inc., 235 East 44th St., New York, NY 10017.

STUDIES IN MEDIEVAL CULTURE. see *HISTORY*

890   US
STUDIES IN MIDDLE EASTERN LITERATURES. 1972. irreg., no. 10, 1978. price varies. Bibliotheca Islamica, Inc., Box 1536, Chicago, IL 60690.

890   US
STUDIES IN MODERN HEBREW LITERATURE. irreg. price varies. Cornell University Press, 124 Roberts Place, Ithaca, NY 14850.

479   US   ISSN 0085-6894
STUDIES IN ROMANCE LANGUAGES. 1970. irreg. price varies. University Press of Kentucky, Lexington, KY 40506. Ed. John E. Keller.

820   US   ISSN 0039-3770
STUDIES IN SCOTTISH LITERATURE. 1963. a. $14.95. University of South Carolina Press, Columbia, SC 29208. Ed. G. Ross Roy. bk. rev. bibl. illus. index. circ. 525. Indexed: Abstr.Engl.Stud.

STUDIES IN SEMIOTICS AND LITERATURE. see *LINGUISTICS*

860   NE   ISSN 0081-8534
STUDIES IN SPANISH LITERATURE. 1971. irreg. Mouton Publishers, Noordeinde 41, 2514 GC The Hague, Netherlands (U.S. addr: Mouton Publishers, c/o Walter de Gruyter, Inc., 200 Saw Mill River Road, Hawthorne, NY 10532)

800   US   ISSN 0149-015X
STUDIES IN THE AMERICAN RENAISSANCE. 1978. a. $25. Twayne Publishers, Inc., 70 Lincoln St., Boston, MA 02111. Ed. Joel Myerson. bk. rev. bibl. illus. circ. 1,000.

830   US   ISSN 0081-8593
STUDIES IN THE GERMANIC LANGUAGES AND LITERATURES. 1949. irreg., no. 91, 1978. price varies. University of North Carolina Press, Box 2288, Chapel Hil, NC 27514. (reprint service avail. from UMI)

820   US
STUDIES IN TUDOR AND STUART LITERATURE. irreg. price varies. Oxford University Press, 200 Madison Ave., New York, NY 10016 (And Ely House, 37 Dover St., London W1X 4AH, England) Eds. Alan Brissenden, F. H. Mares.

800   RM   ISSN 0081-8852
STUDII DE LITERATURA UNIVERSALA SI COMPARATA.* irreg. Editura Academiei Republicii Socialiste Romania, Calea Victoriei 125, Bucharest, Romania (Subscr. to: ILEXIM, Str. 13 Decembrie Nr. 3, P.O. Box 136-137, Bucharest, Romania)

810   US
SUCTION. 1968. irreg. $1.50 per no. c/o Darrell Gray, Ed., 197 14th St., San Francisco, CA 94103. circ. 1,000.

SUEDOSTDEUTSCHES KULTURWERK, MUNICH. SCHRIFTENREIHEN. REIHE A. KULTUR UND DICHTUNG. see *HISTORY — History Of Europe*

SURREALIST TRANSFORMACTION. see *ART*

810   US
SURVIVING IN AMERICA. 1971. irreg. $3. c/o H. Samuel Hamod, Ed., Box 225, Princeton, NJ 08540. circ. 300.

806   SW
SVERIGES FOERFATTARFOERBUND. MEDLEMSFOERTECKNING. Sveriges Foerfattarfoerbund, Box 5252, 102 45 Stockholm 5, Sweden.

800   AT   ISSN 0082-0520
SYDNEY STUDIES IN LITERATURE. 1967. irreg., no. 8, 1979. price varies. ‡ Sydney University Press, Press Bldg., University of Sydney, New South Wales, Australia (Dist. by: International Scholarly Book Services, Inc., Box 555, Forest Grove, OR 97116) Eds. G. W. Wilkes, A. P. Riemer.

850   RM
SYNTHESIS; Bulletin du Comite National Roumain de Litterature Comparee. (Text in English, French, German, Italian, Spanish) 1972. a. $10. Editura Academiei Republicii Socialiste Romania, Calea Victoriri 125, Bucharest, Romania (Subscr. to: ILEXIM, Str. 13 Decembrie Nr. 3, P.O. Box 136-137, Bucharest, Romania) Ed. Zoe Dumitrescu Busulenga. bk. rev.

800   II   ISSN 0082-1454
TAGORE STUDIES. (Text in English) 1969. a. Rs.5.00,($2) Tagore Research Institute, c/o Ms. Pronoti Mukerji, 4 Elgin Rd., Calcutta 20, India. Ed. Somendra Nath Bose.

860   CL
TALLER DE LETRAS. (Some vols. accompanied by supplements) 1971. a. Universidad Catolica de Chile, Instituto de Letras, Av. Bernardo O'Higgins 340, Casilla 114-D, Santiago, Chile. Ed. Cedomil Goic. bk. rev. bibl. illus. index. circ. 1,000.

800   US   ISSN 0497-2384
TENNESSEE STUDIES IN LITERATURE. 1956. a. $$7.50 for cloth; paper $4. (University of Tennessee, Department of English) University of Tennessee Press, Knoxville, TN 37916. Eds. Allison R. Ensor, Thomas J. A. Heffernan. bk. rev. bibl. cum.index. circ. 1,000. (also avail. in microform from UMI; back issues avail.) Indexed: M.L.A.

820   UK   ISSN 0082-2841
TENNYSON RESEARCH BULLETIN. 1967. a. free to Society members. Tennyson Society, Tennyson Research Centre, Central Library, Free School Lane, Lincoln, England. Ed.Bd. bk. rev. index. cum.index every 5 years. circ. 500.

820   UK   ISSN 0082-285X
TENNYSON SOCIETY, LINCOLN, ENGLAND. MONOGRAPHS. 1969. irreg., no. 8, 1977. membership. Tennyson Society, Tennyson Research Centre, Central Library, Free School Lane, Lincoln, England. Ed.Bd. circ. 500.

820   UK   ISSN 0307-3572
TENNYSON SOCIETY, LINCOLN, ENGLAND. OCCASIONAL PAPERS. 1974. irreg. membership. Tennyson Society, Tennyson Research Centre, Central Library, Free School Lane, Lincoln, England.

820   UK   ISSN 0082-2868
TENNYSON SOCIETY, LINCOLN, ENGLAND. REPORT. 1961. a. free. Tennyson Society, Tennyson Research Centre, Central Library, Free School Lane, Lincoln, England. circ. 500.

808.8   US   ISSN 0084-9103
TEXAS TECH UNIVERSITY. INTERDEPARTMENTAL COMMITTEE ON COMPARATIVE LITERATURE. PROCEEDINGS OF THE COMPARATIVE LITERATURE SYMPOSIUM. 1968. a. price varies. Texas Tech University, Interdepartmental Committee on Comparative Literature, Box 4079, Lubbock, TX 79409 (Subscr. to: Gift and Exchange Dept., Tex. Tech U. Library, Box 4079, Lubbock, TX 79409) Eds. Wolodymyr T. Zyla, Wendell M. Aycock. illus. circ. 1,250. Indexed: Abstr.Engl.Stud. M.L.A.

800 320   GE   ISSN 0081-3257
TEXTAUSGABEN ZUR FRUEHEN SOZIALISTISCHEN LITERATUR IN DEUTSCHLAND. 1963. irreg., vol. 20, 1977. price varies. (Akademie der Wissenschaften der DDR, Zentralinstitut fuer Literaturgeschichte) Akademie-Verlag, Leipziger Str. 3-4, 108 Berlin, E. Germany (D.D.R.) Ed. Ursula Muenchow.

840   SZ
TEXTES LITTERAIRES FRANCAIS. 1895. irreg, no. 236, 1977. price varies. Librairie Droz, 11 rue Massot, 1211 Geneva 12, Switzerland.

830 920   GW   ISSN 0082-3880
THEODOR-STORM-GESELLSCHAFT. SCHRIFTEN. 1952. a. price varies. Westholsteinische Verlagsanstalt Boyens und Co., Am Wulf-Isebrand-Platz, Postfach 1880, 2240 Heide, W. Germany (B.R.D.) Eds. Karl Ernst Laage, V. Hand.

830   UK   ISSN 0082-4119
THESES IN GERMANIC STUDIES. 1962. quinquennial. price varies. ‡ University of London, Institute of Germanic Studies, 29 Russell Sq., London W.C.1B 5DP, England.

800   UK   ISSN 0307-1642
THOMAS HARDY SOCIETY. REVIEW. 1976. a. 50p.($1) Thomas Hardy Society Ltd., c/o John C. Pentney, Asst. Secy., 8 Brooklands Rd., Langport, Somerset TA10 9SZ, England. Ed. F. B. Pinion. bk. rev. circ. 2,900.

820   UI   ISSN 0082-416X
THOMAS HARDY YEAR BOOK. 1970. a. 1p.($3) Toucan Press, Birling, Mt. Durand, St. Peter Port, Guernsey, Channel Islands. Eds. J. Stevens Cox, G. Stevens Cox. adv. bk. rev. circ. 2,000-3,000. Indexed: Br.Hum.Ind.

800   SZ   ISSN 0082-4186
THOMAS MANN GESELLSCHAFT. BLAETTER. 1958. a. price varies. Raemistrasse 5, 8001 Zurich, Switzerland. bk. rev. circ. 1,000.

LITERATURE

820 UK ISSN 0040-6562
THRESHOLD. 1957. irreg., no. 31, 1980. price varies. Lyric Players Theatre, 55 Ridgeway St., Belfast 9, N. Ireland. Ed. John Boyd. bk. rev. circ. 1,000.

820 US ISSN 0082-4410
TIMES LITERARY SUPPLEMENT. T.L.S; ESSAYS AND REVIEWS. 1962. irreg. price varies. Oxford University Press, 200 Madison Ave., New York, NY 10016 (and Ely House, 37 Dover St., London W1X 4AH, England)

860 US
TLALOC. (Text in Spanish) 1971. a. $2 or on exchange. ‡ State University of New York at Stony Brook, Department of Hispanic Languages and Literatures, Stony Brook, NY 11790. Ed. Jane L. Hyland. bk. rev. film rev. play rev. illus. circ. 3,000.

810 US
TOOTH OF TIME REVIEW. 1974. 4-6/yr. $10. c/o John Brandi, Ed., Box 356, Guadalupita, NM 87722.

800 780 US
TOOTHPICK, LISBON & THE ORCAS ISLANDS. 1971. irreg. $5 per no. Toothpick, Lisbon & the Orcas Islands Press, 922 East Alder, Seattle, WA 98122. Ed. Michael Wiater. bk. rev. illus. circ. 500.

940 CN ISSN 0082-5050
TORONTO MEDIAEVAL LATIN TEXTS. 1972. irreg. $3.75. ‡ Pontifical Institute of Mediaeval Studies, 59 Queen's Park Crescent. E., Toronto, Ont. M5S 2C4. Ed.Bd.

891.85 PL ISSN 0067-7787
TOWARZYSTWO LITERACKIE IM. A. MICKIEWICZA. BIBLIOTEKA. 1960. irreg., vol. 11, 1979. price varies. Ossolineum, Publishing House of the Polish Academy of Sciences, Rynek 9, 50-106 Wroclaw, Poland.

800 US
TRANSIENT. 1973. irreg., no. 6, 1977. $5. ‡ Transient Press, Box 4662, Albuquerque, NM 87106. Ed. Ken Saville. circ. 250.
Formerly: Is.

810 US ISSN 0041-1299
TRANSPACIFIC. 1966. irreg. $4. c/o Nicholas Crome, Ed., Yellow Springs, OH 45387. illus.
Formerly: Colorado State Review.

TRAVAUX DE LINGUISTIQUE ET DE LITTERATURE. see LINGUISTICS

TRAZA Y BAZA; cuadernos hispanos de simbologia, arte y literatura. see LINGUISTICS

810 US ISSN 0041-2171
TREE. 1970. a. $4. Tree Books, Box 9005, Berkeley, CA 94709. Ed. David Meltzer. bk. rev. bibl. illus. circ. 1,300.

420.5 809 JA ISSN 0496-3547
TSUDA REVIEW. (Text in English) 1956. a. Tsuda-Juku Women's College - Tsuda-juku Daigaku, 11491 Tsuda-machi, Kodaira City, Tokyo, Japan.

809 US
TWENTIETH-CENTURY LITERARY CRITICISM; excerpts from criticism of the works of novelists, poets, playwrights, and other creative writers of the era 1900-1960. 1978. a. $48 per vol. Gale Research Company, Book Tower, Detroit, MI 48226. Eds. Dedria Bryfonski, Sharon Hall. bibl. index. (back issues avail.)

810 US
TYPEWRITER. 1971. 1-2/yr. $2 per no. Bird in the Bush, Box 409, Iowa City, IA 52240. Eds. R. Caldwell, Claire Maric. circ. 200.

810.8 CN ISSN 0226-3440
U. C. REVIEW. Variant title: University College Literary Review. a. University of Toronto, University College, Toronto, Ont. M5S 1A1, Canada. illus.

U C T STUDIES IN ENGLISH. (University of Cape Town) see LINGUISTICS

890 US
UKRAINIAN LITERARY LIBRARY. (Text in Ukrainian; summaries in English) no. 14, 1974. irreg. membership. Shevchenko Scientific Society, 302 W. 13 St., New York, NY 10014.

810 US
UMBRA. 1962. a. $3. c/o David Henderson, Ed., Box 4338 Sathergate Sta., Berkeley, CA 94704.

895 UN ISSN 0566-6201
UNESCO ASIAN FICTION SERIES. irreg. price varies. Unesco Press, 7 Place de Fontenoy, F-75700 Paris, France (Dist. in U.S. by: Unipub, 345 Park Ave. S., New York, NY 10010)

890 SW
UNGA DIKTARA. a. Bokfoerlaget Inferi, Box 167, 821 01 Bollnaes 1, Sweden.

UNICORN GERMAN SERIES. see HISTORY — History Of Europe

860 CK
UNIVERSIDAD DE ANTIOQUIA. EXTENSION CULTURAL. EDICIONES. 1975. irreg. Universidad de Antioquia, Extension Cultural, Medellin, Colombia.

860 UY
UNIVERSIDAD DE LA REPUBLICA. FACULTAD DE HUMANIDADES Y CIENCIAS. REVISTA. SERIE LETRAS. N.S. 1979. irreg. Universidad de la Republica, Facultad de Humanidades y Ciencias, Seccion Revista, Tristan Narvaja 1674, Montevideo, Uruguay. Dir. Beatriz Martinez Osorio.
Supersedes in part: Universidad de la Republica. Facultad de Humanidades y Ciencias. Revista.

860 VE
UNIVERSIDAD DE LOS ANDES. ESCUELA DE LETRAS. ANUARIO. 1975. a. exchange basis. Universidad de los Andes, Escuela de Letras, Merida, Venezuela. Ed. Bd.

860 SP
UNIVERSIDAD DE NAVARRA. DEPARTAMENTO DE LITERATURA ESPANOLA. PUBLICACIONES. 1974. irreg.; 1979, no. 4. price varies. Ediciones Universidad de Navarra S.A., Plaza de los Sauces 1 y 2, Baranain, Pamplona, Spain.

860 UY ISSN 0077-1252
UNIVERSIDAD DE URUGUAY. DEPARTAMENTO DE LITERATURA IBEROAMERICANA PUBLICACIONES.* irreg. Universidad de Uruguay, Departamento de Literatura Iberoamericana, Montevideo, Uruguay.

860 VE
UNIVERSIDAD DEL ZULIA. REVISTA. vol. 57, 1977. a. Universidad del Zulia, Direccion de Cultura, Maracaibo, Venezuela. bibl.

800 PO
UNIVERSIDADE DE LISBOA. FACULDADE DE LETRAS. REVISTA.* irreg.; 1971, 3rd series, no. 13. Esc.150. Universidade de Lisboa, Faculdade de Letras, Ciudade Universitaria, Lisbon 4, Portugal. Ed. Bd. bk. rev. bibl.

UNIVERSIDADE DE SAO PAULO. INSTITUTO DE ESTUDOS BRASILEIROS. REVISTA. see HISTORY — History Of North And South America

869 BL ISSN 0079-9327
UNIVERSIDADE FEDERAL DE MINAS GERAIS. CORPO DISCENTE. REVISTA LITERARIA.
Cover title: R L; Revista Literaria. 1966. a. free. Universidade Federal de Minas Gerais, Servico de Relacoes Universitarias, Rua Carangola 288, Caixa Postal 1621, 30000 Belo Horizonte, Minas Gerais, Brazil. Eds Plinio Carneiro, Ana Maria de Almeida, Ronald Claver Camargo. bk. rev. illus. circ. 2,000.

800 400 IT ISSN 0076-6623
UNIVERSITA DEGLI STUDI DI MESSINA. ISTITUTO DI FILOLOGIA MODERNA. BIBLIOTECA LETTERARIA. 1957. irreg. price varies. (Istituto di Filologia Moderna) Casa Editrice Felice le Monnier, Via Scipione Ammirato 100, C.P. 202, 50136 Florence, Italy.

UNIVERSITA DEGLI STUDI DI PADOVA. FACOLTA DI LETTERE E FILOSOFIA. OPUSCOLI ACCADEMICI. see ART

UNIVERSITA DEGLI STUDI DI PADOVA. FACOLTA DI LETTERE E FILOSOFIA. PUBBLICAZIONI. see ART

491 CS
UNIVERSITA PALACKEHO. FILOSOFICKA FAKULTA. SLAVICA.* (Subseries of its Philologica) (Text in Czech; summaries in French or German) 1971. irreg. 8.50 Kcs. Statni Pedagogicke Nakladatelstvi, Ostrovni 30, 113 01 Prague 1, Czechoslovakia. bibl. illus.
Continues its Series Slavica.

UNIVERSITA PALACKEHO. PEDAGOGICKA FAKULTA. SBORNIK PRACI: RUSKY JAZYK A LITERATURA. see LINGUISTICS

850 RM
UNIVERSITATEA "AL. I. CUZA" DIN IASI. ANALELE STIINTIFICE. SECTIUNEA 3F. : LITERATURA. (Text in Romanian: summaries in foreign languages) 1955. a. $10. Universitatea "Al. I. Cuza" Din Iasi, Calea 23 August Nr. 11, Jassy, Romania (Subscr. to: ILEXIM, Str. 13 Decembrie Nr. 3, P.O. Box 136-137, Bucharest, Romania) bk. rev. abstr. charts. illus.

880 FR ISSN 0065-4981
UNIVERSITE D'AIX-MARSEILLE I. CENTRE D'ETUDES ET DE RECHERCHES HELLENIQUES. PUBLICATIONS. 1958. irreg. Universite d'Aix-Marseille I (Universite de Provence), Centre d'Etudes et de Recherches Helleniques, Service des Publications, 13621 Aix en Provence, France.

UNIVERSITE D'ODENSE. ETUDES ROMANES. see LINGUISTICS

001.3 FR
UNIVERSITE DE DAKAR. FACULTE DES LETTRES ET SCIENCES HUMAINES. ANNALES. 1971? a. Presses Universitaires de France, 108 Bd. Saint Germaine, 75279 Paris Cedex 6, France (Service des Periodiques, 12 rue Jean de Beauvais, 75005 Paris) Ed. Jacques Gengoux. bibl. charts. illus.

800 FR ISSN 0080-0929
UNIVERSITE DE HAUTE BRETAGNE. CENTRE D'ETUDES HISPANIQUES, HISPANO-AMERICAINES ET LUSO-BRESILIENNES. TRAVAUX. 1965, no. 5. a. price varies. ‡ Universite de Rennes II (Universite de Haute Bretagne), 6 Avenue Gaston Berger, 35043 Rennes, France. Ed.Bd. adv. bk. rev. circ. 1,000.

840 FR ISSN 0181-561X
UNIVERSITE DE HAUTE BRETAGNE. CENTRE D'ETUDES IRLANDAISES. CAHIER. 1976. a. 23 F. Universite de Rennes II(Universite de Haute Bretagne), Centre d'Etudes Irlandaises, 6 Ave. Gaston Berger, 35043 Rennes, France. Ed. Jean Noel. circ. 500.
Formerly: Universite de Haute Bretagne. Centre d'Etudes Anglo-Irlandaises. Cahier.

800 700 SZ ISSN 0041-915X
UNIVERSITE DE LAUSANNE. FACULTE DES LETTRES. PUBLICATIONS. 1930. irreg. price varies. Librarie Droz, 11 rue Massot, 1211 Geneva 12, Switzerland.

800 SZ ISSN 0077-7633
UNIVERSITE DE NEUCHATEL. FACULTE DES LETTRES. RECUEIL DE TRAVAUX. 1905. irreg., no. 81, 1975. price varies. Librarie Droz, 11 rue Massot, 1211 Geneva 12, Switzerland. circ. 500-1,000.

UNIVERSITE DE STRASBOURG II. CENTRE DE PHILOLOGIE ET LITTERATURES ROMANES. ACTES ET COLLOQUES. see LINGUISTICS

UNIVERSITE DE STRASBOURG II. INSTITUT DE PHONETIQUE. TRAVAUX. see LINGUISTICS

890 410 TI
UNIVERSITE DE TUNIS. ECOLE NORMALE SUPERIEURE. SECTION A: LETTRES ET SCIENCES HUMAINES. SERIE 1: LANGUE ET LITTERATURE. 1977. irreg. Universite de Tunis, Ecole Normale Superieure, Tunis, Tunisia.

820   US   ISSN 0066-7536
UNIVERSITY OF ARIZONA. DEPARTMENT OF ENGLISH. GRADUATE ENGLISH PAPERS. 1966. a. or s-a. $1. ‡ University of Arizona, Department of English, Tucson, AZ 85721. (Affiliate: English Graduate Union) Dir. Oliver F. Sigworth. bk. rev. circ. 250.

830   UK   ISSN 0144-9850
UNIVERSITY OF LONDON. INSTITUTE OF GERMANIC STUDIES. BITHELL MEMORIAL LECTURES. 1975. a. £1.50. University of London, Institute of Germanic Studies, 29 Russell Square, London WC1B 5DP, England. Ed.Bd. circ. 1,000.

830   UK
UNIVERSITY OF LONDON. INSTITUTE OF GERMANIC STUDIES. BITHELL SERIES OF DISSERTATIONS. 1979. irreg. University of London, Institute of Germanic Studies, 29 Russell Square, London WC1B 5DP, England. Ed. Bd. circ. 500.

830   UK   ISSN 0076-0803
UNIVERSITY OF LONDON. INSTITUTE OF GERMANIC STUDIES. LIBRARY PUBLICATIONS. 1961. irreg. price varies. ‡ University of London, Institute of Germanic Studies, 29 Russell Sq., London WC1B 5DP, England. circ. 500.

891.8   CN   ISSN 0076-4035
UNIVERSITY OF MANITOBA. DEPARTMENT OF SLAVIC STUDIES. READINGS IN SLAVIC LITERATURE. (Text in English, Russian and Ukrainian) 1959. irreg. price varies. University of Manitoba, Department of Slavic Studies, Winnipeg, Man. R3T 2N2, Canada. Ed. J. B. Rudnyckyj.

820   US   ISSN 0081-7880
UNIVERSITY OF MISSISSIPPI STUDIES IN ENGLISH. 1960. a. $2. University of Mississippi, Department of English, University, Lafayette Co., MS 38677. Ed. Benjamin Fisher, IV. adv. bk. rev. circ. 450. Indexed: M.L.A.

491.1 891.1   II   ISSN 0448-1712
UNIVERSITY OF RAJASTHAN. STUDIES IN SANSKRIT AND HINDI. 1965. irreg. University of Rajasthan, Departments of Sanskrit and Hindi, Gandhi Nagar, Jaipur 302004, India.

UNIVERSITY OF TORONTO ROMANCE SERIES. see LINGUISTICS

820   US   ISSN 0082-6812
UNIVERSITY OF TULSA. DEPARTMENT OF ENGLISH. MONOGRAPH SERIES. 1966. irreg., 1972, no. 14. University of Tulsa, Department of English, 600 S. College Ave., Tulsa, OK 74104.

UNIVERZITA KOMENSKEHO. FILOZOFICKA FAKULTA. ZBORNIK: PHILOLOGICA. see LINGUISTICS

UNIVERZITA PALACKEHO. PEDAGOGICKA FAKULTA. SBORNIK PRACI: CESKY JAZYK A LITERATURA. see LINGUISTICS

891.85 943   PL   ISSN 0072-0488
UNIWERSYTET GDANSKI. WYDZIAL HUMANISTYCZNY. ZESZYTY NAUKOWE. PRACE HISTORYCZNO-LITERACKIE. 1965. irreg. Uniwersytet Gdanski, Ul. Czerwonej Armii 110, 81-824 Sopot, Poland (Dist. by Ars Polona-Ruch, Krakowskie Przedmiescie 7, Warsaw, Poland)

891.85   PL   ISSN 0083-436X
UNIWERSYTET JAGIELLONSKI. ZESZYTY NAUKOWE. PRACE HISTORYCZNOLITERACKIE. (Vol. 3- called also vol. 5-, continuing the volume numbering of Seria Nauk Spolecznych. Filologia, which it supersedes) (Text in Polish, rarely in English, French or Russian; summaries in English, French, German, Russian) 1955. a. price varies. Panstwowe Wydawnictwo Naukowe, Miodowa 10, Warsaw, Poland (Dist by Ars Polona-Ruch, Krakowskie Przedmiescie 7, Warsaw, Poland) Ed. Prof. Dr. Jozef Buszko.

809   PL
UNIWERSYTET SLASKI W KATOWICACH. PRACE HISTORYCZNOLITERACKIE. irreg., 1976, vol. 4. 41 Zl. Uniwersytet Slaski w Katowicach, Ul. Bankowa 14, 40-007 Katowice, Poland. Eds. Jana Zaremby, T. Klaka.

811   US   ISSN 0049-559X
UNSPEAKABLE VISIONS OF THE INDIVIDUAL. 1971. a. $9. Tuvoti Books, Box 439, California, PA 15419. Eds. Arthur W. Knight, Kit Knight. adv. bk. rev. illus. circ. 2,000.

830   GW   ISSN 0083-4564
UNTERSUCHUNGEN ZUR DEUTSCHEN LITERATURGESCHICHTE. 1962. irreg., no. 29, 1980. price varies. Man Niemeyer Verlag, Pfrondorferstr. 4, 7400 Tuebingen, W. Germany (B.R.D.)

800   US   ISSN 0163-3295
URTHKIN; prose/verse. 1978. a. $3.95. Box 67485, Los Angeles, CA 90067. Ed. Larry Ziman. circ. 1,000. (also avail. in magnetic tape; back issues avail.)

810   US
URTHONA. a. free. Boston University, 236 Bay State Rd., Boston, MA 02215. illus.

810   US
VALHALLA. 1971. a. price varies. Merging Media, 59 Sandra Circle, Westfield, NJ 07090. Ed. Rochelle H. Dubois. circ. 500.

800   US
VANCOUVER COMMUNITY PRESS. WRITING SERIES. no. 13, 1973. irreg. Vancouver Community Press, 2504 York St., Vancouver 9, B.C., Canada.

810   US
VELVET WINGS. 2-3/yr. $2 per no. Paradoxical Press, 1228 Oxford St., Berkeley, CA 94709. Ed. Sarah Kennedy.

860   AG
VENGA QUE LE CUENTO; publicacion periodica aleatoria de narradores argentinos. no. 1974. irreg. Prudan 1330, Buenos Aires, Argentina. adv. illus.

VER SACRUM; NEUE HEFTE FUER KUNST UND LITERATUR. see ART

800   GW   ISSN 0170-3633
VERSCHOLLENE UND VERGESSENE. irreg. price varies. (Akademie der Wissenschaften und der Literatur, Mainz) Franz Steiner Verlag GmbH, Friedrichstr. 24, Postfach 5529, 6200 Wiesbaden, W. Germany (B.R.D.)

820   CN   ISSN 0384-868X
VERSUS. irreg.; no. 2, 1976. Can.$5 for 4 nos. Villeneuve Publications, P.O. Box 503, Outremont Sta., Montreal, Que. H2V 1K0, Canada. Eds. Fred Louder, Robyn Sarah.

800   NE
VERZAMELING VAN MIDDELNEDERLANDSE BIJBELTEKSTEN. Added title page title: Corpus Sacrae Scripturae Neerlandicae Medii Aevii. 1970. irreg. E. J. Brill, Oude Rijn 33a-35, Leiden, Netherlands.

830   NE
VESTDIJK KRONIEK. no. 13, 1976. q. fl.25. (Vestdijkkring) Thespa Uitgeverij, Koninginneweg 164, Amsterdam, Netherlands. Ed. Bd.

890   UR
VETER STRANSTVII. vol. 11, 1976. irreg. 0.80 Rub. per no. Izdatel'stvo Fizkul'tura i Sport, Kalyaevska Ul., 27, Moscow K-6, U.S.S.R. Ed.Bd. illus. circ. 100,000.

809   US
VIKING CRITICAL LIBRARY. irreg. Viking Press, Inc., 625 Madison Ave., New York, NY 10022.

839   UK   ISSN 0083-6257
VIKING SOCIETY FOR NORTHERN RESEARCH. TEXT SERIES. 1953. irreg. Viking Society for Northern Research, University College, Gower St., London WC1E 6BT, England.

809   US   ISSN 0190-3233
VIRGINIA POLYTECHNIC INSTITUTE AND STATE UNIVERSITY. REVIEW. 1979. a. University Press of Virginia, Box 3608 University Sta., Charlottesville, VA 22903. circ. 2,000.

800   FR   ISSN 0083-6826
VOIX DANS LE MONDE. 1969. irreg. price varies. Editions B. Arthaud, 6 rue de Mezieres, Grenoble, France.

800   US
VOYAGER SERIES. vol. 115, 1973. irreg. Mirage Press (Baltimore), 5111 Liberty Heights Ave., Baltimore, MD 21207.

807   US
WADSWORTH GUIDES TO LITERARY STUDY. irreg. Wadsworth Publishing Co., 10 Davis Dr., Belmont, CA 94002.

809   US   ISSN 0083-7210
WARD-PHILLIPS LECTURES IN ENGLISH LANGUAGE AND LITERATURE. 1967. irreg., no. 10, 1979. price varies. ‡ (University of Notre Dame, Department of English) University of Notre Dame Press, Notre Dame, IN 46556. Indexed: Cath.Ind.

810   US   ISSN 0043-0455
WASHINGTON AND JEFFERSON LITERARY JOURNAL. 1966. a. free to students & faculty. Washington and Jefferson College, Washington, PA 15301. illus. circ. 600.
Formerly: Wall.

800   UK
WELLSIANA; world of H. G. Wells. 1908. a. £5($15) High Orchard Press, High Orchard, 125 Markyate Rd., Dagenham, Essex RM8 2LB, England. Eds. Royston King, E. Ford. adv. bk. rev. circ. 100. (looseleaf format)

810   US
WESTIGAN REVIEW CHAPBOOKS. irreg. Westigan Review Press, c/o John Knapp, 2nd, Swetman Hall, State University College, Oswego, NY 13126.

800   US
WHAT'S NEW ABOUT LONDON, JACK? (Companion to Chaney Chronical) 1971. irreg. $5 for 10 nos. London Northwest, 929 South Bay Rd., Olympia, WA 98506. Ed. David H. Schlottman. adv. bk. rev. bibl. film.rev. play rev. circ. 70. (processed)

830   AU   ISSN 0083-9906
WIENER ARBEITEN ZUR DEUTSCHEN LITERATUR. 1970. a. price varies. Wilhelm Braumueller, Universitaets-Verlagsbuchhandlung GmbH, Servitengasse 5, A-1092 Vienna, Austria. Eds. Herbert Seidler and Werner Welzig. index. circ. 600.

WIENER BEITRAEGE ZUR ENGLISCHEN PHILOLOGIE. see LINGUISTICS

830 831   AU
WIENER-GOETHE-VEREIN. JAHRBUCH. 1878. a. S.150. Wiener-Goethe-Verein, Reitschulgasse 2, A-1010 Vienna, Austria. Ed. Wolfgang Martens, Herbert Zeman. adv. bk. rev. circ. 550.

WIENER ROMANISTISCHE ARBEITEN. see LINGUISTICS

800   US   ISSN 0361-2481
WIND; literary journal. 1971. q. $5 to individuals; institutions $6. Wind Press, c/o Quentin R. Howard, R.F.D. Route No. 1, Box 809K, Pikeville, KY 41501. adv. bk. rev. circ. 600. Indexed: Ind.Amer.Per.Verse.

808   US
WINDHAVEN; feminist fantasy & science fiction. 1977. irreg., no. 5, 1979. $6. Atalanta Press, Box 5688, University Sta., Seattle, WA 98105. Ed. Jessica Amanda Salmonson. bk. rev. illus. circ. 1,200.
Supersedes: Literary Magazine of Fantasy and Terror.

810   US
WINDOW. no. 4, 1977. irreg. $6 for 4 issues. Window Press, 7005 Westmoreland Dr., Takoma Park, MD 20012. Ed. Bd.

808.83   UK   ISSN 0084-0394
WINTER'S TALES; an anthology of long short stories. 1955. a. £4.95($9.95) Macmillan Journals Ltd. (Subsidiary of: Macmillan Publishers Ltd.) 4 Little Essex St., London W.C.2, England. Ed. A. D. Maclean. circ. 4,000.

800   GW   ISSN 0084-0467
WIRKUNG DER LITERATUR. 1969. irreg., 1973, vol. 4. Athenaeum-Verlag GmbH, Falkensteiner Str. 75-77, 6000 Frankfurt 18, W. Germany (B.R.D.)

810   370   US
WISCONSIN COUNCIL OF TEACHERS OF ENGLISH. SERVICE BULLETIN SERIES. no. 24, 1979. irreg. $0.50-1 per no. c/o Nicholas J. Karolides, Ed., University of Wisconsin-River Falls, River Falls, WI 54022. (back issues avail.)

800   700   US
WITTENBERG REVIEW OF LITERATURE AND ART. 1977. a. Wittenberg University, Box 1, Recitation Hall, Springfield, OH 45501. Eds. Marty Lammon, Jill Gassaway. illus. circ. 900.

WOOLNER INDOLOGICAL SERIES. see *PHILOSOPHY*

818   CN   ISSN 0316-8670
WORDS FROM INSIDE. 1972. a. Can.$3. Prison Arts Foundation, 80 Chatham St., Brantford, Ont. N3T 2P1, Canada. Ed. Andreas Schroeder.

800   CN   ISSN 0316-3768
WRIT. 1970. irreg. Can.$7 for 2 nos. c/o Innis College, University of Toronto, Toronto, Ont. M5S 1J5, Canada. Ed. Roger Greenwald. bk. rev. index. circ. 800. (back issues avail.)

808   UK   ISSN 0260-2776
WRITER. 1963. a. £4.60. United Writers Publications, Trevail Mill, Zennor, St. Ives, Cornwall TR26 3BW, England. Ed. Sydney Sheppard. adv. bk. rev. illus. mkt. tr.lit. circ. 4,000.
Incorporating: Writer's Review (ISSN 0043-9568)

810   US
WRITERS FORUM. no. 5, 1978. a. University of Colorado at Colorado Springs, English Department, Colorado Springs, CO 80907. Ed. Alex Blackburn.

800   UK   ISSN 0141-5050
WRITERS OF WALES. 1970. irreg. price varies. (Welsh Arts Council) University of Wales Press, 6 Gwennyth St., Cathays, Cardiff CF2 4YD, Wales. Eds. Meic Stephens, R. Brinley Jones. (reprint service avail. from UMI)

828   II
WRITERS WORKSHOP LITERARY READER. (Text in English) 1972. irreg. Rs.60 hardback; Rs. 15 flexiback. Writers Workshop, 162-92 Lake Gardens, Calcutta 700045, India. Ed. P. Lal. circ. 1,000.

810   US   ISSN 0084-2745
WRITING. 1964. irreg., no. 40, 1980. price varies. Four Seasons Foundation, Box 31411, San Francisco, CA 94131 (Dist. by: Subco, Box 10233, Eugene, OR 97440) Ed. Donald Allen. circ. 3,000.

XANTHIPPE; feminist literary magazine. see *WOMEN'S INTERESTS*

820   CN   ISSN 0704-5697
Y E R MONOGRAPH SERIES. (Yeats Elliot Review) 1978. irreg. Can.$8. University of Alberta, Department of English, Edmonton, Alta. T6G 2E5, Canada.

830   US   ISSN 0084-3334
YALE GERMANIC STUDIES. 1964. irreg., no. 6, 1976. price varies. Yale University Press, 92A Yale Sta., New Haven, CT 06520. Indexed: M.L.A.

879.9   US   ISSN 0084-3423
YALE ROMANIC STUDIES. SECOND SERIES. 1951. irreg; no. 26, 1976. price varies. Yale University Press, 92A Yale Sta., New Haven, CT 06520.

891.8   US   ISSN 0084-3431
YALE RUSSIAN AND EAST EUROPEAN STUDIES. 1966. irreg., no. 14, 1978. Yale University Press, 92A Yale Sta., New Haven, CT 06520.

820   810   US   ISSN 0084-3482
YALE STUDIES IN ENGLISH. 1898. irreg., no. 189, 1978. price varies. Yale University Press, 92A Yale Sta., New Haven, CT 06520. Indexed: M.L.A.

800   US   ISSN 0084-3695
YEARBOOK OF COMPARATIVE AND GENERAL LITERATURE. (Issued 1952-60 as subseries of University of North Carolina, Studies in Comparative Literature) 1952. a. $5 per vol. Indiana University, Comparative Literature Program, Ballantine Hall 402, Bloomington, IN 47401 (Vols. 1-11 (1952-62) Available from Russell and Russell, Publishers, 122 E. 42 St., New York, N.Y. 10017) Ed. Horst Frenz. bk. rev. circ. 1,200.

809.915   US   ISSN 0084-3709
YEARBOOK OF COMPARATIVE CRITICISM. 1968. a. price varies. Pennsylvania State University Press, 215 Wagner Bldg., University Park, PA 16802. Ed. Joseph Strelka. (reprint service avail. from UMI)

YEARBOOK OF ENGLISH STUDIES. see *HUMANITIES: COMPREHENSIVE WORKS*

840   947   US
YEARBOOK OF ROMANIAN STUDIES. a. Romanian Studies Association of America, c/o Paul G. Teodorescu, Ed., 7 John Circle, No. 4, Salinas, CA 93901.

820.6   US   ISSN 0084-4144
YEAR'S WORK IN ENGLISH STUDIES. 1919. a. price varies. Humanities Press, Inc., 171 First Ave., Atlantic Highlands, NJ 07716. bk. rev. index.

296   830   IS
YERUSHOLAYMER ALMANAKH. (Text in Yiddish) 1974. a. Yidishe Shrayber Grupe in Yerusholaim., Shederot Eshkol 12/6, Jerusalem, Israel. illus.

810   US
YES! CAPRA CHAPBOOK SERIES. no. 20, 1974. irreg. Capra Press, c/o Book People, 2940 Seventh St., Berkeley, CA 94710.

891.85   PL   ISSN 0084-4411
Z DZIEJOW FORM ARTYSTYCZNYCH W LITERATURZE POLSKIEJ. (Text in Polish) 1963. irreg., vol. 53, 1979. price varies. (Polska Akademia Nauk, Instytut Badan Literackich) Ossolineum, Publishing House of the Polish Academy of Sciences, Rynek 9, 50-106 Wroclaw, Poland (Dist. by Ars Polona-Ruch, Krakowskie Przedmiescie 7, Warsaw, Poland)

891.82   YU   ISSN 0084-5183
ZBORNIK ISTORIJE KNJIZEVNOSTI/RECUEIL DES TRAVAUX DE L'HISTOIRE DE LA LITTERATURE. (Text in Serbo-Croatian; summaries in French, English, German or Russian) 1960. irreg. price varies. Srpska Akademija Nauka i Umetnosti, Odeljenje Literature i Jezika, Knez Mihailova 35, YU 11001 Belgrade, Yugoslavia (Dist. by: Prosveta, Terazije 16, Belgrade, Yugoslavia) Ed. Antonije Isakovic. circ. 1,000.

891.82   YU   ISSN 0084-5205
ZBORNIK ZA ISTORIJU, JEZIK I KNJIZEVNOST SRPSKOG NARODA. SPOMENICI NA SRPSKOM JEZIKU. (Text in Serbo-Croatian; summaries in French, English, German or Russian) 1902. irreg. price varies. Srpska Akademija Nauka i Umetnosti, Knez Mihailova 35, 11001 Belgrade, Yugoslavia (Dist. by Prosveta, Terazije 16, Belgrade, Yugoslavia) circ. 600.

ZEITSCHRIFT FUER CELTISCHE PHILOLOGIE. see *LINGUISTICS*

400   GW   ISSN 0084-5817
ZWEISPRACHIGE REIHE. (Text in German, English, Spanish and Portuguese) 1964. irreg. DM.7.80. Max Hueber Verlag, Max-Hueber-Str.4, 8045 Ismaning, W. Germany (B.R.D.) Ed. Klaus Zobel.

810   301.412   US   ISSN 0094-3320
13TH MOON; a feminist literary magazine. 1973. irreg. $12 per no. to individuals; institutions $4.50. 13th Moon, Inc., Drawer F, Inwood Sta., New York, NY 10034. Ed. Ellen Marie Bissert. adv. bk. rev. illus. circ. 3,000. Indexed: Abstr.Pop.Cult. Ind.Amer.Per.Verse.

843   CN   ISSN 0708-2495
36 MANIERES. 1978. irreg. Can.$2.50 per no. Editions Trente Six, C.P. 2114, succ. B, Hull, Que. J8X 3Z4, Canada.

LITERATURE — Abstracting, Bibliographies, Statistics

820   016   AT   ISSN 0084-7216
A. A. T. E. GUIDE TO ENGLISH BOOKS. 1970. a. Aus.$3 (or Aus.$12 for combined subscription with English in Australia) ‡ Australian Association for the Teaching of English, Box 203, Norwood, S.A. 5067, Australia. Ed. M. Gill. adv. bk. rev. index. circ. 4,000.

016   820   US
ANNOTATED SECONDARY BIBLIOGRAPHY SERIES ON ENGLISH LITERATURE IN TRANSITION, 1880-1920. irreg. price varies. Northern Illinois University Press, 515 Garden Road, Dekalb, IL 60115.

420   016   UK   ISSN 0066-3786
ANNUAL BIBLIOGRAPHY OF ENGLISH LANGUAGE AND LITERATURE. 1920. a. $80.50 for vol.s 40-52. Modern Humanities Research Association, Kings College, London WC2R 2LS, England (Vols. 1-39 avail. from: Wm. Dawson & Sons Ltd., Cannon House, Folkstone, Kent, England) Eds. M. Smith, Jim Misenheimer.

016   820   UK   ISSN 0307-9864
ANNUAL BIBLIOGRAPHY OF SCOTTISH LITERATURE. 1969. a. $6.75 to individuals; $8 to institutions. Scottish Group of the University, College and Research Section of the Library Association, National Library of Scotland, George IV Bridge, Edinburgh EH1 1EW, Scotland. Eds. J. Kidd, R.H. Carnie. adv. bk. rev. circ. 400.

860   016   SP
BIBLIOGRAFIA DE LA LITERATURA HISPANICA. 1960. irreg. Libreria Cientifica Medinaceli, Vitrubio 16, Madrid 6, Spain.

809   016   IT
BIBLIOGRAFIA E STORIA DELLA CRITICA. irreg. Angelo Longo Editore, Via Rocca Ai Fossi 6, Casella Postale 431, 48100 Ravenna, Italy. Ed. Enzo Esposito.

016   830   GW   ISSN 0523-2449
BIBLIOGRAPHIE DER DEUTSCHEN SPRACH- UND LITERATURWISSENSCHAFT. 1957. a. DM.170 (approx.) Vittorio Klostermann, Frauenlobstr. 22, Postfach 900601, 6000 Frankfurt 90, W. Germany (B. R. D.) Ed. Clemens Koettelwesch. circ. 2,000.
Formerly: Bibliographie der Deutschen Literaturwissenschaft.

016   840   GW   ISSN 0523-2465
BIBLIOGRAPHIE DER FRANZOESISCHEN LITERATURWISSENSCHAFT. 1960. a. DM.200 (approx.) Vittorio Klostermann, Frauenlobstr. 22, 6000 Frankfurt 90, W. Germany (B. R. D.) Ed. Otto Klapp. circ. 1,500.

830   430   016   GW
BIBLIOGRAPHIE LINGUISTISCHER LITERATUR. a. price varies. Vittorio Klostermann, Frauenlobstr. 22, Postfach 900601, D-6000 Frankfurt 90, W. Germany(B.R.D.)
Formerly (1976-1979): Bibliographie Unselbstaendiger Literatur-Linguistik.

800   016   DK   ISSN 0067-8473
BIDRAG TIL H. C. ANDERSENS BIBLIOGRAFI. 1966. irreg., vol. 8, 1975. price varies. Kongelige Bibliotek, Christians Brygge 8, DK-1219 Copenhagen K, Denmark.

016   US   ISSN 0524-0581
BOOK REVIEW INDEX: ANNUAL CLOTHBOUND CUMULATIONS. 1965. a. $72 per vol. Gale Research Company, Book Tower, Detroit, MI 48226. Ed. Gary Tarbert. (back issues avail.)

016   028.1   GW   ISSN 0068-3396
EIN BUECHERTAGEBUCH; Buchbesprechungen aus der Frankfurter Allgemeinen Zeitung. 1967. a. DM.12. Frankfurter Allgemeine Zeitung, Postfach 2901, Hellerhofstr. 2-4, 6000 Frankfurt am Main 1, W. Germany (B.R.D.) bk. rev. circ. 12,000.

800   016   CN   ISSN 0316-0696
CANADIAN ESSAY AND LITERATURE INDEX. 1973. a. University of Toronto Press, Front Campus, Toronto, Ont. M5S 1A6, Canada.

016 880   US   ISSN 0528-2594
CATALOGUS TRANSLATIONEM ET
COMMENTATORIUM; Medieval and Renaissance
Latin translations. 1960. irreg., latest issue, vol. 4.
$59.95 for vol. 4. Catholic University of America
Press, 620 Michigan Ave., N.E., Washington, DC
20064.

028.5 370   US   ISSN 0069-3480
CHILDREN'S BOOKS IN PRINT. 1962. a. $35. R.R.
Bowker Company, 1180 Ave. of the Americas, New
York, NY 10036 (Orders to P.O. Box 1807, Ann
Arbor, Mich. 48106)
    Formerly: Children's Books for Schools and
Libraries.

015   DK   ISSN 0070-2714
DANIA POLYGLOTTA; literature on Denmark in
languages other than Danish and books of Danish
interest published abroad. 1947; 1969, N.S. a. price
varies. Kongelige Bibliotek, Danish Department,
Christians Brygge 8, 1219 Copenhagen K, Denmark
(Avail. on exchange Rom: I.D.E., Danmarks Institut
for International Udveksling, Amaliegade 38, DK-
1256 Copenhagen K, Denmark) Eds. Sven C.
Jacobsen, Jan William Rasmussen.

DIRECTORY OF CANADIAN PLAYS AND
PLAYWRIGHTS. see *THEATER — Abstracting,
Bibliographies, Statistics*

800 011   US   ISSN 0160-4880
FICTION CATALOG. quinquennial w. annual
supplements. $45. ‡ H. W. Wilson Co., 950
University Ave., Bronx, NY 10452. Ed. Estelle A.
Fidell.

016   US   ISSN 0090-9130
INDEX OF AMERICAN PERIODICAL VERSE.
1971. a. Scarecrow Press, Inc., 52 Liberty St.,
Metuchen, NJ 08840. Comp. S. W. Zulauf, E. M.
Cifelli. circ. 3,000.

810 029   US   ISSN 0073-5914
INDEX TO EARLY AMERICAN PERIODICAL
LITERATURE, 1728-1870; a survey of American
literature. 1949. irreg. price varies. William-
Frederick Press, 308 E. 79th St., New York, NY
10021. Ed. T. Reed. bk. rev.

800   GW   ISSN 0073-7208
INDICES ZUR DEUTSCHEN LITERATUR. 1968.
irreg., vol. 7. price varies. Athenaeum-Verlag
GmbH, Falkensteiner Str. 75-77, 6000 Frankfurt 18,
W. Germany (B.R.D.)

820 398   US   ISSN 0074-1388
INTERNATIONAL ARTHURIAN SOCIETY.
BIBLIOGRAPHICAL BULLETIN. (Text in
English and French) 1949. a. $12.50 to non-
members; members $10. International Arthurian
Society, c/o Norris J. Lacy, Sec.-Treas., Department
of French and Italian, University of Kansas,
Lawrence, KS 66045. Ed. Charles Foulon. bk. rev.
circ. 1,400. (also avail. in microfilm)

800   US   ISSN 0075-9880
LITERARY AND LIBRARY PRIZES. 1935. irreg.
$24.95. R.R. Bowker Company, 1180 Ave. of the
Americas, New York, NY 10036 (Orders to P. O.
Box 1807, Ann Arbor, Mich. 48106) index. (reprint
service avail. from UMI)

800 400 016   US
M L A DIRECTORY OF PERIODICALS; a guide to
journals and series in languages and literatures.
1979. biennial. $65. Modern Language Association
of America, 62 Fifth Avenue, New York, NY
10011. Ed. Eileen M. Mackesy.

800 016   US   ISSN 0554-3037
PLAY INDEX. quinquennial. $28. H. W. Wilson Co.,
950 University Ave., Bronx, NY 10452. Ed. Estelle
A. Fidell.

891.85 016   PL   ISSN 0079-3590
POLSKA BIBLIOGRAFIA LITERACKA. 1944.
irreg., 1976 (for the year 1973) $41.25 per volume.
(Polska Akademia Nauk, Instytut Badan
Literackich) Panstwowe Wydawnictwo Naukowe,
Ul. Miodowa 10, Warsaw, Poland. Ed. K.
Witkowska.

029.5   US   ISSN 0085-5979
SCIENCE FICTION BOOK REVIEW INDEX. 1970.
a. price varies. c/o Ed. Hal Hall, 3608 Meadow
Oaks Lane, Bryan, TX 77801. bk. rev. circ. 750.
(back issues avail)

800 016   US
SHORT STORY INDEX; an index to stories in
collections and periodicals. 1974. a. plus 5 yr.
cumulation. $25. H. W. Wilson Co., 950 University
Ave., Bronx, NY 10452. Ed. Gary L. Bogart.

809   SW   ISSN 0345-0112
TEXT; Svensk tidskrift foer bibliografi. (Text in
English and Swedish) 1974. irreg.(approx. 1/yr.)
Kr.60 per vol.(4 issues) ‡ (Center for Bibliographical
Studies, Uppsala) Dahlia Books, International
Publishers and Booksellers, P.O. Box 23037, S-750
23 Uppsala, Sweden. Ed. Rolf E. du Rietz. adv. bk.
rev.

016 840   IT   ISSN 0072-7660
UNIVERSITE DE GRENOBLE. INSTITUT
FRANCAIS DE FLORENCE. PUBLICATION.
SERIE 2: COLLECTION D'ETUDES
BIBLIOGRAPHIQUES.* 1957. irreg., 1969, no. 10.
price varies. (Universite de Grenoble, FR) Casa
Editrice G. C. Sansoni Editore Nuova S.p.A., Via
Benedetto Varchi 47, 50132 Florence, Italy. (Co-
sponsor: Institut Francais de Florence)

405   UK   ISSN 0084-4152
YEAR'S WORK IN MODERN LANGUAGE
STUDIES. 1929-30. a. $85 for vols. 30-41. Modern
Humanities Research Association, King's College,
London WC2, England (Vols. 1-29 Avail. from:
Wm. Dawson & Sons Ltd., Cannon House,
Folkstone, Kent, England) Ed. G. Price. index. circ.
850.
    Critical bibliography of language and literature
(modern and Medieval) for all European languages
except English

LITERATURE — Poetry

811   US
A: A JOURNAL OF CONTEMPORARY
LITERATURE. 1976. s-a. $2 student, senior citizen;
$2.50 regular; $5 institutions. A Press Ltd., P.O.
Box 311, Laguna, NM 87026. Ed. William
Oandasan. bk. rev. circ. 500.

811   US
AB INTRA. 1972. irreg. $2.50 for 4 issues. Hellric
Publications, 39 Eliot St., Jamaica Plain, MA 02130.
Ed. Dolores Stewart. circ. 500.

810   US   ISSN 0515-2003
ACADEMY OF AMERICAN POETS. LAMONT
POETRY SELECTIONS. 1954. a. price varies.
Academy of American Poets, 1078 Madison Ave.,
New York, NY 10028.

811 810   US
ADVENTURES IN POETRY. 1967. 1-2/yr. $4. c/o
Larry Fagin, Ed., 437 E. 12th St., New York, NY
10009. circ. 500.

811   US
AEOLIAN-HARP. 1968. a. $5 per no. Geneva Alice
Verkennes, Ed. & Pub., 1395 James St., Burton, MI
48529. bk. rev. (back issues avail.)

821   UK   ISSN 0140-5136
ALEMBIC. 1973. a. £3($10) for 4 nos. 28 Holmdale
Rd., London N.W.6, England. Ed. Robert Hampson.
bk. rev. bibl. circ. 200. (back issues avail.)

811   US
AMERICAN POETRY SERIES. 1973. irreg., vol. 21,
1981. price varies. Ecco Press Ltd., 1 W. 30 St.,
New York, NY 10001.

ANTHILL. see *LITERATURE*

811   US   ISSN 0196-2221
ANTHOLOGY OF MAGAZINE VERSE AND
YEARBOOK OF AMERICAN POETRY. 1980. a.
Monitor Book Co., Inc., 195 S. Beverly Dr., Beverly
Hills, CA 90212. Ed. Alan F. Pater.

861   AG
ANTOLOGIA POETICA DEL PARTIDO DE
ESTEBAN ECHEVERRIA. 1979. a. Arg.$10000.
Asociacion de Artes y Letras de Esteban, c/o
Graciela B. de Fini, 462 Colon, Monte Grande,
Buenos Aires, Argentina.

861   AG
ANUARIO DE POETAS CONTEMPORANEOS.
1976. a. Club de Poetas, Casilla de Correo 881/CC,
1000 Buenos Aires, Argentina.

869.4   BL
ANUARIO DE POETAS DO BRASIL. 1976. a. $24.
Folha Carioca Editora S.A., Rua Joao Cardoso 23,
Cep 20000 Rio de Janeiro, Brazil.

861   CK
AQUARIMANTIMA. 1973. irreg. Apartado Aereo
3845, Medelin, Colombia.

861   AG
AQUARIO; revista internacional de poesia. 1977.
irreg. $2.50. Paraguay 647, Buenos Aires, Argentina.
Eds. Sergio Chaves, Sigfrido Radaelli.

811   US
AQUILA. vol. 2, 1977. irreg. $6. R O Q Press, 116
Old Mill Rd., Apt. 6, State College, PA 16801. Ed.
Bob Quarteroni. adv. bk. rev. circ. 450.

808.81   US
ARCHIVE FOR NEW POETRY NEWSLETTER.
1978. irreg. price varies. (Archive for New Poetry)
University of California, San Diego, Central
University Library, La Jolla, CA 92903. Ed.
Michael Davidson.

811   US
ARDIS NEW POETS SERIES. no. 7, 1977. irreg., no.
9, 1978. price varies. Ardis Publishers, 2901
Heatherway Dr., Ann Arbor, MI 48108.

808.1   FR   ISSN 0066-734X
ARGUS DE LA POESIE FRANCAISE.* 1971. irreg.
30 F. Association Poesie Vivante France, B.P.8,
01210 Ferney-Voltaire, France.

811   US
AVALON DISPATCH. irreg. membership. Avalon
Poets, c/o Vernon Payne, 212 W. First St., San
Angelo, TX 76901.

B. C. MONTHLY. see *LITERATURE*

810   US
BABY JOHN.* (Text mainly in English occasionally
in German, French & Italian) 1970. irreg (1-2/yr.)
$3 for 4 nos. 5406 Latona Ave NE, Seattle, WA
98105. Ed. James Evans. adv. bk. rev. illus. circ.
250.

811   US   ISSN 0067-5695
BELOIT POETRY JOURNAL. CHAPBOOK. 1951.
irreg., approx. biennial, no. 16, 1980. $2 included in
subscr. to Beloit Poetry Journal. ‡ Beloit Poetry
Journal, Box 2, Beloit, WI 53511.

811   US
BERKELEY POETS COOPERATIVE. (No. 13 not
published) 1969. 2/yr. $5. Berkeley Poets'
Workshop and Press, Box 459, Berkeley, CA 94701.
Ed. Charles Entrekin. illus. circ. 2,500.

861   AG
BIBLIOTECA DE POESIA. no. 181, 1976. irreg.
Ediciones Corregidor, Talcahuano 463, Buenos
Aires, Argentina.

BIRTHSTONE. see *ART*

273   US
BLACKBERRY. (Chapbook series) irreg., approx. 6/
yr. $1.75 per no. Gary Lawless, Ed. & Pub., Box
186, Brunswick, ME 04011.

811   US
BLUE MOUNTAIN PRESS CHAPBOOK. 1974.
irreg. $2 per no. Blue Mountain Press, 511
Campbell St., Kalamazoo, MI 49007.

811   CN
BOOK OF CANADIAN PROSE. irreg., vol. 2, 1973.
price varies. W. J. Gage, Ltd., 1500 Birchmount
Rd., Scharborough 4, Ont., Canada.

811   US
BRAINCHILD. vol. 3, 1976. irreg. c/o Janet
DiGirolamo, 1440 N. Fourth, Springfield, IL 62702.

811   US
BRAZILLER SERIES OF POETRY. irreg. price
varies. George Braziller, Inc., One Park Ave., New
York, NY 10016.

LITERATURE — POETRY

821　　　　CN　ISSN 0382-5272
BRITISH COLUMBIA MONTHLY. 1972. 1-7/yr. Can.$2. Gerry Gilbert, Ed. & Pub., Box 48884, Vancouver 5, B.C., Canada. adv. bk. rev. index. circ. 1,000.

890　　　　AT　ISSN 0310-2467
BRONZE SWAGMAN BOOK OF BUSH VERSE. 1973. a. Aus.$2. Winton Tourist Promotion Association, P.O. Box 44, Winton, Qld. 4735, Australia.

821　　　　UK　ISSN 0301-7257
BYRON JOURNAL. 1973. a. £1. Byron Society Journal Ltd., 6 Gertrude St., London SW10 0JN, England. Ed.Bd. adv. bk. rev. circ. 2,000. (back issues avail.)
　Life & work of Lord Byron

811　　　　US
C Q. (Contemporary Quarterly); poetry and art. 1976. irreg. $10. 1600 Campus Rd., Box 41110, Los Angeles, CA 90041. Ed. John D. Engle. adv. bk. rev. illus. circ. 1,000. (tabloid format)

811　　　　US
CAFETERIA. 1971. irreg. $3. Cafeteria Press, Box 4104, Modesto, CA 95352. Eds. Gordon Preston, Rick Robbins. bk. rev. circ. 300.

841　　　　FR
CAHIERS TRISTAN L'HERMIT. 1979. a. 24 F. Rougerie Editeur, Mortemart, 87330 Mezieres-sur-Issoire, France.

811　　　　US
CELEBRATION. 1975. irreg. $5 for 4 nos. c/o William J. Sullivan, Ed., 2707 Lawina Rd, Baltimore, MD 21216. circ. 300.

811　　　　US
CENTERING. 1973. irreg. $1. Years Press, ATL EBH, Michigan State University, East Lansing, MI 48824. Ed. F. Richard Thomas. circ. 300. (also avail. in microform from UMI)

811　760　US
CHOICE (BINGHAMTON); a magazine of poetry and graphics. 1961. a. $5. State University of New York at Binghamton, Box Z, Binghamton, NY 13901. Eds. Milton Kessler, John Logan. circ. 1,000.

811　　　　US
CIRCLE; a periodical of reversible poetry. 1973. biennial. $2 per no. ‡ Circle Forum, Box 176, Portland, OR 97207. Ed. Mrs. J. M. Gates. bk. rev. circ. controlled.

811　　　　US
CIRCLETS; an occasional newsletter of reversible poetry. no. 4, 1977. irreg. Circle Forum, Box 176, Portland, OR 97207.

861　　　　US
CIRCULO POETICO; cuadernos de poesia. (Text in English & Spanish) 1971. a. $4. Circulo de Cultura Panamericano, 16 Malvern Pl., Verona, NJ 07044 (Editorial address: 615 Lenox Ave., No. 1, Miami Beach, FL 33139) illus. circ. 500.

821　　　　UK
CIVIL SERVICE POETRY; Europe, Commonwealth & United States. 1968. a. 30p.($1) per no. ‡ Emma (Printers & Publishers), Arden House, Sunny Point, Walton-on-Naze, Essex CO14 8LD, England (U.S. subscr. to: Thomas Kell, Office of Personnel Management, Office of Public Affairs, Washington, D.C. 20415) Eds. Mabs Allen, Ernest Meadowcroft. bibl.

841　　　　FR
CLIVAGES. 1974. irreg., no. 7, 1981. Editions Clivages, 15 rue de Saint Senoch, Paris 75017, France. Ed. Jean P. Leger. illus.

811　　　　US　ISSN 0098-7093
COLDSPRING JOURNAL. 1974. irreg. $12. Cherry Valley Editions, Box 303, Cherry Valley, NY 13320. Ed. Charles Plymell. illus.

861　　　　SP
COLECCION "BAHIA". irreg; 1979, no. 10. Ediciones Bahia, Fray Bartolome Bloque 1, Algeciras, Spain. Ed. Manual Fernandez Mota. circ. 700.

861　　　　SP
COLECCION PENTESILEA. 1978. irreg. Ediciones Caballo Griego para la Poesia, Bolonia 3, Madrid 28, Spain. Ed. Maya Smerdou Altolaguirre.

861　　　　AG
COLECCION POESIA DEL NUEVO TIEMPO. no. 3, 1976. irreg. Ediciones Tres Tiempos, Av. Belgrano 225, Buenos Aires, Argentina. Ed. Sigfrido Radaelli. illus.

851　　　　IT
COLLANA DI POESIA. 1974; N.S. 1977. irreg., no. 5, 1977. price varies. Societa Editrice Napoletana s.r.l., Corso Umberto I 34, 80138 Naples, Italy. Ed. Domenico Rea.

CONFINS. see LITERATURE

811　　　　US
CONNECTIONS. 1972. a. $3.50. Connections Magazine, Bell Hollow Rd., Putnam Valley, NY 10579. Ed. Toni Ortner-Zimmerman. bk. rev. circ. 600.

821　　　　CN　ISSN 0384-0433
CONTEMPORARY POETRY OF BRITISH COLUMBIA. 1970. irreg. Sono Nis Press, c/o Dept. of Creative Writing, University of British Columbia, Vancouver, B.C., Canada. Ed. J. M. Yates.

CONTRAST. see LITERATURE

811　　　　US　ISSN 0011-0736
COYOTE'S JOURNAL. 1964. irreg. ‡ James Koller, Ed. & Pub., P.O. Box 629, Brunswick, ME 04011. circ. 1,000. (also avail. in microform from UMI)

811　　　　US　ISSN 0011-0841
CRAZY HORSE. no.4,1970. irreg. (approx. 2/yr.) $4 for 4 issues. Southwest Minnesota State College, American Language Skills Program, Marshall, MN 56258. Eds. Howard Mohr, Al Zolynas. bk. rev. circ. 500.

861　　　　VE　ISSN 0070-1785
CUADERNOS PARA ESTUDIANTES: LOS POETAS.* 1967. irreg. Bs.1. Instituto Nacional de Cultura y Bellas Artes, Box 6238, Caracas, Venezuela.
　Monographs in paper, issued primarily for "los estudiantes de Secundaria"

811　　　　US　ISSN 0011-4359
CYCLO-FLAME. (Supplement: Avalon Dispatch) 1963. biennial. $5. Avalon Poets, c/o Vernon Payne, 212 W. First St., San Angelo, TX 76901. bk. rev. index. circ. 500.
　Formerly: Cyclotron; Flame.

821　　　　UK
CYFRES BARDDONIAETH PWLLGOR CYFIEITHIADAU YR ACADEMI. (Text in Welsh) 1980. irreg. price varies. (Welsh Academy) University of Wales Press, 6 Gwennyth St., Cathays, Cardiff CF2 4YD, Wales. Ed. D. Myrddin Lloyd. (reprint service avail. from UMI)
　Translations of poetry into Welsh

808.1　　　US　ISSN 0084-9529
DACOTAH TERRITORY; a magazine of poetry. 1971. irreg., no. 17, 1980. $2.50. Territorial Press, Box 775, Moorhead, MN 56560. Ed. Mark Vinz. bk. rev. circ. 1,000.

811　　　　US
DESERT FIRST WORKS. 1976. irreg. $2.50 per no. Desert First Works Press, 4948 N. La Canada Dr., Tuscon, AZ 85705. Ed. Jacqueline Young.

DICHTER UND ZEICHNER. see ART

811　　　　US　ISSN 0162-8739
A DIFFERENT DRUMMER; the poet's journal. 1975. irreg. $25. Drummer Press, Box 487-U, 18 Union St., Toms River, NJ 08753. Ed. Samuel Evins Brown. adv. bk. rev. index. circ. 2,500.

808.81　　　II
DIPAVALI. (Text in Marathi) vol. 33, 1977. a. Rs.7. Ravindra Kesava Kothavale, 316 Prasad Chambers, Bombay 400004, India.

811　　　　US
DIRECTORY OF AMERICAN POETS AND FICTION WRITERS. 1973. irreg., latest, 1980-81 edt. $10 paperback; $18 hardbound. ‡ Poets & Writers, Inc., 201 W. 54 St., New York, NY 10019. (reprint service avail. from UMI)
　Formed by the merger of: Directory of American Poets & Directory of American Fiction Writers.

808.81　　　US
DOCUMENTS FOR NEW POETRY. 1978. irreg. $3.75 per no. University of California, San Diego, Archive for New Poetry, Mandeville Department of Special Collections, University Library, La Jolla, CA 92093.

811　　　　US
EGO. irreg. Rosary College, 7900 W. Division, River Forest, IL 60305.

890　　　　II
EK BACHARER SRESTHA KABITA. (Text in Bengali) 1973. a. Rs.4($1) c/o Mrs. Bhaswati Sinha, 36 Ballygunge Place, Calcutta 19, India. Eds. M. Manindra Gupta, Ranjit Sinha. adv. illus. stat. circ. 1,000.

ETUDES BAUDELAIRIENNES. see LITERATURE

EVERYMAN. see LITERATURE

811　　　　US　ISSN 0014-4770
EXPERIMENT; an international review of new poetry. 1944. irreg. $4.20. Experiment Press, 6565 N.E. Windermere Rd., Seattle, WA 98105. Ed. Carol Ely Harper. adv. bk. rev. illus. index. circ. 400.

821　　　　UK　ISSN 0015-7740
FORMAT. 1966. irreg. £0.50. ‡ Stilt Press, c/o Alan & Joan Tucker, The Bookshop, Stroud, Gloucestershire, Eng. Ed. Alan Tucker. circ. 150 (controlled) (processed)

821　　　　AT　ISSN 0310-639X
GENTLE FOLK AND OTHER CREATURES. 1972. irreg. c/o Jamie Griffen, Union Building, Australian National University, P.O. Box 4, Canberra City, A.C.T. 2601, Australia.

821　　　　UK
GETTING YOUR POETRY PUBLISHED. 1973. biennial. 50p. Association of Little Presses of Great Britain, 18 Clairview Rd., London S. W. 16, England. Ed. Peter Finch. circ. 25,000.

GIZEH; journal of philosophy & poetry. see PHILOSOPHY

811　　　　US
GLITCH. 1978. irreg., 2-3/yr. $3 per no. c/o Paul McDonough, Ed., 515 Lamar, Apt. 271, Arlington, TX 76011.

811　　　　US
GREENFIELD REVIEW CHAPBOOK. 1971. irreg., latest no. 47. $5 per no. Greenfield Review Press, Greenfield Center, NY 12833.

811　　　　US
GRIST. 1975. irreg. $50 per no. Grist Press, 195 Lakeview Avenue, Cambridge, MA 02130. Ed. Bd. illus. circ. 1,000. (tabloid format)

811　　　　US
GROUND ZERO. 1975. irreg. Box 91415, Cleveland, OH 44101. circ. 500-1,000.

821　　　　UK
GUILDHALL POETS. a. £0.35. 19 Rugwood Rd., Flackwell Heath, High Wycombe HP10 9HA, England.

811　　　　US
HAIKU. 1967. irreg. $6. William J. Higginson, Ed. & Pub., Box 2702, Paterson, NJ 07509. bk. rev. illus. circ. 300.

800　　　　US　ISSN 0085-1531
HIPPOCRENE. 1971. a. University of Houston, Department of English, Houston, TX 77004. illus.

861　　　　AG
HOJAS DE POESIA. irreg. $2.50. Aquario, Paraguay 647, Buenos Aires, Argentina. Ed. Sergio Chaves, Sigfrido Radaelli. (poster format)

811 US
HORBLY GNOME.* 1971. a. $2.50. Funch Press, 1100 West Samano, Edinburg, TX 78539. Ed. Seth Wade. circ. 300.

800 US
HOT WATER REVIEW. 1976. a. $3. Hot Water Review, Inc., Box 8396, Philadelphia, PA 19101. Eds. Peter Bushyeager, Joel Colten. circ. 1,000.

811 US
HUDSON RIVER ANTHOLOGY. 1972. a. $1. Vassar College, Poughkeepsie, NY 12601. illus. circ. 1,000.

821 AT
HUNTER VALLEY POETS. 1965. irreg. Aus.$1. Nimrod Publications, University of Newcastle, Dept. of English, Australia. Ed. Norman Talbot. bk. rev. circ. 1,750.

811 US
HYN ANTHOLOGY. 1969. irreg. (1/yr.) $1.25. Home Planet Publications, P.O. Box 415, Stuyvesant Station, New York, NY 10009. Ed. Donald Lev. adv. bk. rev. film rev. illus. circ. 300.

811 PE ISSN 0300-4031
IN TERRIS; revista de poesia. 1967. irreg. Livio Gomez Flores, Ed. & Pub., Francisco Cornejo 847, Tacna, Peru. adv. bk. rev. illus. circ. 1,000. (also avail. in microform; back issues avail.)

811 US
IN THE LIGHT. 1975. irreg $7 for 3 no. Jim Hanson, Ed. & Pub., 1249 W. Loyola, No.207, Chicago, IL 60626. bibl. circ. 250. (back issues avail.)

808.1 US ISSN 0085-1884
INLET. 1972. a. free. Virginia Wesleyan College, Department of English, Norfolk, VA 23502. Ed. Joseph Harkey. circ. 1,000.

811 US ISSN 0020-1774
INSCAPE. 1970. irreg $5 for 4 nos. Baleen Press, Box 13448, Phoenix, AZ 85002. Eds. Joy Harvey & Ramona Weeks. illus. circ. 300.

810.8 US ISSN 0094-2715
INSCAPE. vol. 33, 1977. a. $1. Pasadena City College, 1570 E. Colorado Blvd., Pasadena, CA 91106. illus. Key Title: Inscape (Pasadena)
Continues (since vol. 30): Pipes of Pan.

051 US ISSN 0147-4936
INVISIBLE CITY. 1971. irreg. (approx. 1/yr.) $2. Red Hill Press, 6 San Gabriel Drive, Fairfax, CA 94930. Eds. John McBride & Paul Vangelisti. circ. 3,000. (tabloid format; also avail. in microform) Indexed: Access.
Formerly: Red Hill Press (ISSN 0034-2009)

808.81 II
JAMINRAITU. (Text in Telugu) a. Zamin Ryot Press, 170 Thipparajuvari St, Nellore 524001, India.

890 KE ISSN 0449-0738
JOHARI ZA KISWAHILI. (Text in Swahili) 1960. irreg, vol. 13, 1975. Kenya Literature Bureau, Box 30022, Nairobi, Kenya.

JOURNAL OF OUR TIME. see LITERATURE

811 US
JUNCTION. 1973. a. $1.50. City University of New York, Brooklyn College, Graduate Student Association, La Guardia Hall, Room 237C, Brooklyn, NY 11210. Ed. Marshall Scott Grossman. bk. rev. bibl. circ. 600.

808.81 BG
KAGAJA. 1978. Tk.2. Shafiuddin Ahmad, 14 Bangabandhu Ave., Dacca 2, Bangladesh.

821 US ISSN 0453-4387
KEATS-SHELLEY JOURNAL; Keats, Shelley, Byron, Hunt, and their circles. 1952. a. $12.50 (includes Keats-Shelley Memorial Bulletin) Keats-Shelley Association of America, Inc., The Carl H. Pforzheimer Library, Room 815, 41 East 42nd St., New York, NY 10017. Ed. Rae Ann Nager. bk. rev. bibl. circ. 1,000. Indexed: Abstr.Engl.Stud. M.L.A.

821 UK
KEEPSAKE POEMS. 1972. irreg. £1($3.50) for 5 nos. ‡ Keepsake Press, 26 Sydney Rd., Richmond, Surrey TW9 1VB, England. Eds. R. Lewis, S. Toulson. illus. circ. 180.

811 CN
KILLALY CHAPBOOKS. 1972. irreg. Can.$6($6) for 4 nos. Killaly Press, 764 Dalkeith Ave., London, Ontario N5X 1R8, Canada. Ed. Clarke E. Leverette. circ. 100.

811 US
KITABU CHA JUA. 1966. irreg $6. Box 771, San Francisco, CA 94101. Ed. Joe Goncalves. bk. rev. circ. 500 (approx.) (tabloid format) Indexed: Hum.Ind.
Formerly (until vol. 1, no. 19, 1974): Journal of Black Poetry (ISSN 0021-9339)

811 US ISSN 0146-2377
KONGLOMERATI. 1972. irreg., approx. q. $20. Konglomerati Press, Box 5001, Gulfport, FL 33737. Eds. Richard Mathews, Barbara Russ. adv. bk. rev. illus. circ. 300.

800 US
KOSMOS; a journal of poetry. 1975. irreg $8 to individuals; institutions $12. Kosmos, 2580 Polk St., San Francisco, CA 94109. Ed. Kosrof Chantikian. circ. 750.

811 US
KUKSU; journal of backcountry writing. 1972. irreg. $5. Kuksu Press, Box 980, Alleghany Star Rt., Nevada City, CA 95959. Ed. Dale Pendell. bk. rev. circ. 1,500.
Formerly: Kyoi.

811 US ISSN 0023-8511
LARVAE DU GOLDEN GATE. 1971. irreg. included with subscription to Star West. Star West Publications, Box 731, Sausalito, CA 94965. Ed. Leon Spiro. illus. circ. 1,000. (also avail. in microfilm from UMI)

811 US ISSN 0363-2164
LAUGHING BEAR. 1976. irreg. $5 for 4 nos. Laughing Bear Press, Box 14, Woodinville, WA 98072. Ed. Tom Person. adv. bk. rev. circ. 1,000.

811 II
LAVA. 1975. irreg. Rs.24($10) for 12 issues. Lava Publications, 26/53 W.E.A., New Delhi 110005, India. Ed. G. P. Vimal. bk. rev.

811 US ISSN 0147-121X
LIGHT; a poetry review. 1973. q. $5 to individuals; institutions $6. Box 1298-B, Stuyvesant P.O., New York, NY 10009. Ed. Roberta C. Gould. adv. bk. rev. illus. circ. 1,000.

861 SP
LINDES - CUADERNOS DE POESIA. no. 9, 1977. irreg. Difusora de Cultura, S.A., Padre Vinas 60, Valencia, Spain. Eds. R. Arias, R. Bellveser, P. Besso.

800 UK
LITTLE WORD MACHINE. 1971. irreg (2-3/yr.) £2 for 4 nos. L. W. M. Publications, c/o Nick Toczek, Ed., Flat 3, 39 Queenswood Rd., Moseley, Birmingham B13 9AX, England. adv. bk. rev. circ. 2,000.

808.81 US
LOCKERT LIBRARY OF POETRY IN TRANSLATION. 1967. a. price varies. Princeton University Press, Princeton, NJ 08540. (reprint service avail. from UMI)

811 US
LOOK QUICK. 1975. irreg. $2.50. Quick Books, Box 4434, Boulder, CO 80306. Eds. Joel Scherzer, Robbie Rubinstein. circ. 500. (also avail. in microfilm; back issues avail.)

811 US
LUCKIAMUTE; contemporary northwest poetry. no. 4, 1975. irreg. $2.50. 224 N.W. 10th St., Corvallis, OR 97330. Eds. Phillip G. Hope, Richard Daniels.

811 US ISSN 0076-1699
LYRICAL IOWA; poetry by Iowa authors. 1946. a. $2.50. Iowa Poetry Association, c/o Virginia Blanck Moore, Ed., 1724 E. 22nd St., Des Moines, IA 50317. circ. 800.

811 US ISSN 0076-2334
MAGAZINE. Variant title: Mag. 1964. irreg., no. 5, 1973. $10. ‡ Interim Books, Box 35, Village Station, New York, NY 10014. Ed. Kirby Congdon. circ. 500. (also avail. in microform from UMI)

840 SZ ISSN 0076-3748
LA MANDRAGORE QUI CHANTE. 1961. irreg., latest vol. 36. price varies. Editions de la Baconniere S. A., Box 185, 2017 Boudry, Switzerland. (reprint service avail. from UMI)

811 US
MICKLE STREET REVIEW. 1979. a. $3 to individuals; institutions $5. Walt Whitman House Association, 330 Mickle St., Camden, NJ 08103. Eds. Frank McQuilkin, Geoffrey M. Sill.

810 US ISSN 0076-860X
MIDWEST MONOGRAPHS. SERIES 2 (POETRY)* 1968. irreg., 1969, no. 2. $50. (University of Illinois at Urbana-Champaign) Depot Press, Room 204, English Bldg., Urbana, IL 61801.

MIDWEST MONOGRAPHS. SERIES 4 (TRANSLATION) see LITERATURE

811 US
MILK QUARTERLY. 1972. irreg. $4. Yellow Press, Inc., 2394 Blue Island, Chicago, IL 60608. Ed. Bd.

821 US ISSN 0540-0961
MILTON SOCIETY OF AMERICA. PROCEEDINGS. a. $3. Milton Society of America, c/o Michael Lieb, Department of English, University of Illinois, Chicago Circle, Chicago, IL 60680.

MONUMENT IN CANTOS AND ESSAYS. see LITERATURE

811 US
MOUNTAIN SUMMER; a little magazine of verse. 1974. a. $1.75. Ex Libris, Tennessee Ave., Sewanee, TN 37375. Ed. Don Keck DuPree. circ. 700.

811 US
MOVING FINGER. vol. 4, 1974. biennial. $0.50. Indiana State University, Evansville, 8600 University Blvd., Evansville, IN 47712. Eds. Chuck Connor, Debbie Miller. illus.

821 IE
NEPTUNE'S KINGDOM; poetry review. (Text in English) 1972. irreg. 10p.($1) per issue. c/o Martin Gleeson, Ed., 5 Victoria Terrace, Kilkee, Co. Clare, Ireland. bk. rev. illus. circ. 500.

NEW BRUNSWICK CHAPBOOKS. see LITERATURE

NEW LITERATURE AND IDEOLOGY. see LITERARY AND POLITICAL REVIEWS

820 UK ISSN 0077-8621
NEW POETRY.* 1971. irreg., 1971, no. 4. L.1($3.) Atlantic Press, 9 Duke St. Mansions, Duke St., London W1M 6JQ, England (Represented by Atlantic Press International, 520 Fifth Ave., New York, NY 10036) Ed. Brian H. Wormald.

821 UK
NEW POETS. a. £4. Regency Press, 43 New Oxford St., London WCIA 1BH, England.

811 US
NEW POETS SERIES. vol. 4, 1976. a. $2.50 per no. 541 Piccadilly Rd., Baltimore, MD 21204. Ed. Clarinda Harriss Lott. circ. 750.

811 US ISSN 0028-7482
NEW YORK QUARTERLY. 1970. irreg. $9 individuals; $12 institutions. New York Quarterly Poetry Review Foundation Inc., Box 2415, Grand Central Station, New York, NY 10017. Ed. Marjorie Finnell. adv. bibl. cum.index every 10 issues. (back issues avail.)

811 US
OPENSPACES.* 1973. irreg. $2. ‡ Laurel Press, 1409 S. Saltair Ave., Los Angeles, CA 90025. Eds. Robert Edward Brown, Elizabeth Brown. illus. circ. 250.

821 UK ISSN 0030-459X
ORE. 1954. irreg. (1-2/yr.) price varies. c/o Ed. Eric Ratcliffe, 7 the Towers, Stevenage, Herts., SG1 1HE, England. bk. rev.

LITERATURE — POETRY

811 US ISSN 0030-7629
OX HEAD. 1967. irreg. $7 for 10 issues. Ox Head Press, 414 N. Sixth St., Marshall, MN 56258. Ed. Don Olsen. circ. 200-500.

869 BL
PALAVRA POETICA. no. 2, 1978. irreg. Summus Editorial Ltda., Rua Cardoso de Almeda 1287, C.P. 13814, 05013 Sao Paulo, SP, Brazil. Dir. Affonso Romano de Sant'Anna. circ. 3,000.

PAPER AIR. see *LINGUISTICS*

821 UK ISSN 0079-0087
PARKLANDS POETS SERIES. 1969. irreg; no. 15, 1975. £0.50. Akros Publications, 25 Johns Rd., Radcliffe-on-Trent, Nottingham NG12 2GW, England. Ed. Duncan Glen. circ. 300.

890 US ISSN 0160-5534
PEREKRESTKI; almanac. (Text in Russian, occasionally English) 1977. a. $5. Crossroads, 7738 Woodbine Ave., Philadelphia, PA 19151. Ed. Valentina Sinkevich. circ. 500-600.
Cyrillic alphabet

PERSONAL INJURY MAGAZINE. see *LITERATURE*

811 US ISSN 0079-2438
POCKET POETS SERIES. 1955. irreg., no. 37, 1978. price varies. City Lights Books, 261 Columbus Ave., San Francisco, CA 94133.

821 UK
POEM PAMPHLET. 1976. irreg. £0.50. Festival Office, Ilkley, West Yorkshire LS29 8HF, England. Ed. Michael Dawson. circ. 750-1,000.

861 US
POEMA CONVIDADO. (Text in Portuguese) 1973. irreg. c/o Teresinka Pereira, Ed., Department of Spanish and Portuguese, University of Colorado, Boulder, CO 80301. bk. rev. circ. 500.

861 UY ISSN 0079-2462
POESIA.* irreg. Editorial Arca, Colonia 1263, Montevideo, Uruguay.

861 SP
POESIA. (Text in Catalan, French, Spanish) irreg. Edicions Proa, Tuset 3, Barcelona, Spain. illus.

811 US
POET; peu a peu. 1973. a. $8.50. Fine Arts Society, 2314 W. Sixth St., Mishawaka, IN 46544. Ed. Doris Nemeth. illus. circ. 1,000 (controlled) (back issues avail.)

861 PY
POETAS. 1977. irreg. (Pen Club del Paraguay) Fondo Editor Paraguayo, Asuncion, Paraguay.

811 FR ISSN 0079-2470
POETES ET PROSATEURS DU PORTUGAL. 1970. irreg. price varies. (Fundacao Calouste Gulbenkian, PO) Presses Universitaires de France, 108 Bd. Saint Germaine, 75279 Paris Cedex 6, France (Service des Periodiques, 12 rue Jean de Beauvais, 75005 Paris)

820 AU
POETIC DRAMA AND POETIC THEORY. (Text in English) 1972. irreg., no. 32, 1976. S.245. Universitaet Salzburg, Institut fuer Englische Sprache, Akademiestr. 24, A-5020 Salzburg, Austria. Ed. James Hogg. circ. 200.

811 US ISSN 0032-2067
POETRY BAG; an annual journal of poems. 1966. a. $3 for 3 years. R. P. Dickey, Ed. & Pub., c/o Department of English, University of Arizona, Tucson, AZ 85721. circ. 550-600. (also avail. in microform from UMI)

811 US
POETRY CLEARINGHOUSE. irreg. Folger Shakespeare Library, Poetry Office, 201 E. Capitol St., S.E., Washington, DC 20003. Ed. Jean Nordhaus. circ. dist. only in Washington area.

821 UK ISSN 0032-2083
POETRY MARKET. 1965. irreg. 25p. per mo. Aubrey Bush Publications, 17 Balmoral Rd., Forest Rd., Nottingham NG1 4HX, England. Ed. Aubrey Bush. adv. bk. rev. mkt. play rev.

811 US ISSN 0048-4601
POETRY MISCELLANY. 1971. a. $3. University of Tennessee at Chattanooga, Department of English, c/o Richard Jackson, Ed., Chattanooga, TN 37402. bk. rev. circ. 600.

821 NZ
POETRY NEW ZEALAND. 1971. biennial, vol. 4, 1979. price varies. John McIndoe, c/o Dept. of English, Victoria University of Wellington, Wellington, New Zealand. Ed. Dr. Frank McKay. circ. 1,500.

821 UK
POETRY SUPPLEMENT. 1957. a. membership (nonmembers 75p per no.) Poetry Book Society Ltd., 9 Long Acre, London WC2E 9LH, England. circ. 1,500.
Formerly: New Poems.

821 AT ISSN 0311-2810
POETS OF AUSTRALIA. 1974. a. Queensland Writers' Workshop, P.O. Box 230, North Quay, Qld. 4000, Australia.

821 UK
POET'S YEARBOOK. 1975. a. £2.45. Poet's Yearbook Ltd., 1 Herbert Rd., London N11 2QN, England. Ed.S.T. Gardiner.

811 PL ISSN 0079-2527
POETYKA. ZARYS ENCYKLOPEDYCZNY. 1956. irreg., vol. 5, 1979. price varies. (Polska Akademia Nauk, Instytut Badan Literackich) Ossolineum, Publishing House of the Polish Academy of Sciences, Rynek 9, 50-106 Wroclaw, Poland (Dist. by Ars Polona-Ruch, Krakowskie Przedmiescie 7, Warsaw, Poland) Eds. Maria Renata Mayenowa and Lucylla Pszczolowska.

899 UR
POEZIYA(MOSCOW) vol. 20, 1977. irreg. 0.99 Rub. per issue. Izdatel'stvo Molodaya Gvardiya, Ul.Sushchevskaya, 21, 103030 Moscow, U.S.S.R. Ed. N. Starshinov. illus. circ. 65,000.

808.81 US ISSN 0196-822X
PRACTICES OF THE WIND; a magazine/anthology of poetry. 1980. irreg. $4 per no. Box 214, Kalamazoo, MI 49005. Eds. Nicolaus Waskowsky, David M. Marovich. circ. 500.

811 US
PRINCETON SERIES OF CONTEMPORARY POETS. 1975. a. price varies. Princeton University Press, Princeton, NJ 08540. (reprint service avail. from UMI)

861 SP
PROVINCIA; coleccion de poesia. 1974, no. 20. irreg. 400 ptas.($6) (for 6 nos.) Institucion "Fray Bernardino de Sahagun", Edificio Fierro, Puerta de la Reina, 1, Leon, Spain. circ. 1,000.

861 AG
PROVINCIA. vol. 8, 1976. irreg. $2. Rafael M. Altamirano, Ed. & Pub., Calle Libertad, Casa 16, Barrio los Olivos 5870, Villa Dolores, Argentina.

811 US
PTOLEMY. 1979. irreg. $2. David Vajda, Ed. & Pub., 455-1 Seneca Trail, Rt. 4, Browns Mills, NJ 08015.

851 IT ISSN 0391-3104
QUADERNI DEL VITTORIALE. 1977. irreg. L.10000($24) Fondazione del Vittoriale, Via Solferino 32, Milan, Italy. illus. tr.lit. circ. 5,000.

808 IT ISSN 0079-8274
QUADERNI DI POESIA NEOGRECA. 1967. irreg., no. 4, 1976. price varies. Istituto Siciliano di Studi Bizantini e Neoellenici, Via Noto, 34, 90141 Palermo, Italy.

811 CN
QUARTERBACKS. 1970. irreg. $2 for set of 8. Quarterbacks, Delta Canada, 351 Gerald Street, Lasalle, Quebec H8P 2A4, Canada. Ed. Glen Siebrasse. circ. 500. (all back issues (1-8) available)
Continuing series of 4-8 page chapbooks on Canadian poets.

QUARTERLY REVIEW OF LITERATURE CONTEMPORARY POETRY SERIES. see *LITERATURE*

811 US ISSN 0147-0396
REBIS CHAPBOOK SERIES. 1977. irreg. Allegany Mountain Press, 111 N. 10th St., Olean, NY 14760.

869 809 BL
REVISTA DE POESIA E CRITICA. 1976. irreg. CLS 415, Bloco B, Lote 2, Sobreloja, Brasilia, Brazil.

811 US
ROOM; a woman's literary journal. 1975. a. $3.50. Box 40610, San Francisco, CA 94110. Eds. Gail Newman, Kathy Barr. bk. rev. circ. 750. (back issues avail.)

821 UK
ROUTLEDGE HISTORY OF ENGLISH POETRY. 1977. irreg. price varies. Routledge and Kegan Paul Ltd., Broadway House, Newtown Rd., Henley -on-Thames, Oxon. RG9 1EN, England (U.S. orders to: Routledge Journals, 9 Park St., Boston, MA 02108) Ed. R. A. Foakes.

811 US
SAILING THE ROAD CLEAR. 1973. irreg. $5 (3 issues) c/o Jane Creighton, Box 238, Old Mystic, CT 06372. circ. 400.

811 US ISSN 0036-360X
SALT LICK. 1969. irreg. $5. Salt Lick Press, Box 1064, Quincy, IL 62301. Ed. James Haining. bk. rev. illus. circ. 1,200. (processed; also avail. in microform from UMI)

811 US
SALTED IN THE SHELL. 1971. a. $1.50. Gary Lawless, Ed. & Pub., Box 186, Brunswick, ME 04011. bk. rev. circ. 250-350. (processed)

811 US
SAN FRANCISCO GALLERY. 1973. a.; latest issue, 1973. $1. ‡ Coffee Gallery, 1353 Grant Ave., San Francisco, CA 94113. Eds. Tom Cuson & Jeanne Sirotkin. adv. illus. circ. 600.

808.1 CN ISSN 0080-6560
SASKATCHEWAN POETRY BOOK. 1936. biennial. price varies. Saskatchewan Poetry Society, 3104 College Avenue, Regina, Saskatchewan S4T 1V7, Canada. circ. 600. (back issues avail.)

841 FR
SENTIERS POESIE. no.2, 1973. irreg. 34 F. Editions Subervie, 21, rue de l'Embergue, F-12 Rodez, France.

811 US
SEVEN. 1958. irreg. $4 for 4 nos. 115 S. Hudson, Oklahoma City, OK 73102. Ed. James Neill Northe. circ. 1,000.

SEVENTIES; a magazine of poetry and opinion. see *LITERARY AND POLITICAL REVIEWS*

808.81 US ISSN 0037-329X
SHANTIH; new international writings. 1971. irreg. $8 for 4 issues. Box 125, Bay Ridge Station, Brooklyn, NY 11220. Eds. Irving Gottesman & John Friedman. adv. bk. rev. illus. circ. 1,000.

808.81 US
SMALL MOON. 1974. irreg., no. 7/8, 1979. $2 per no. Small Moon, Inc., 52 1/2 Dimick St., Somerville, MA 02143. adv. bk. rev. circ. 3,000. (back issues avail.)

700 US
SO AND SO MAGAZINE. 1973. a. $15. So and So Press, 2864 Folsom, San Francisco, CA 94110. Ed. John Marron. bk. rev. circ. 500. (back issues avail.)
Formerly: Bad Breath.

841 FR ISSN 0081-0908
SOCIETE DES POETES FRANCAIS, ANNUAIRE. 1958. a. Societe des Poetes Francais, Hotel de Massa, 38 rue du Faubourg Saint-Jacques, Paris 14e, France. Dir. Roland le Cordier.

811 US
SPRING (SYRACUSE) 1979. a. $1. Michael Chieco, Box 225, University Sta., Syracuse, NY 13210.

811 US
SPRING RAIN. 1971. 2-4/yr. $4. Spring Rain Press, Box 15319, Seattle, WA 98115. Ed. Karen Gates. circ. 500. (also avail. in microform from UMI)

582 LUMBER AND WOOD

821 UK
STARDANCE.* 1972. a. 10p. c/o Marek Urbanowicz, Ed., 49 Sheen Park, Richmond, Surrey, England.

811 US
STARWHISPERING. 1974. irreg. $0.25. Charlu Press, c/o Lewis Sanders and Charles G. Roach, 125 Taylor, Jackson, TN 38301. Ed. Lewis Sanders. circ. 500.

891 UR
STIKHI. (Subseries of: Repertuar Khudozhestvennoi Samodeyatelnosti. Seriya - Repertuarnye Sborniki) 1967. irreg. Izdatel'stvo Iskusstvo, Tsvetnoi bulvar, 25, Moscow K-51, U.S.S.R.

811 US ISSN 0039-176X
STONE. 1967. a. $2.50. Stone Press (San Francisco), 3978 26th St., San Francisco, CA 94131. Ed. Rich Joergensen. illus. circ. 500.

821 820 IE
STONY THURSDAY BOOK. (Text in English and Gaelic) 1975. irreg., no. 6, 1978. £2($4.50) 128 Sycamore Ave., Rath Bhan, Limerick, Ireland. Ed. John Liddy. bk. rev. play rev. bibl. illus. circ. 1,000. (back issues avail.)

821 CN
STORM WARNING. no. 2, 1976. irreg. McClelland and Steward Ltd., 25 Hollinger Rd., Toronto, Ont., Canada.

811 861 US
SULPHUR RIVER; poetry review. (Text in English and Spanish) 1979. irreg. $1.25 per no. Box 155, Bogata, TX 75417. Ed. Bd.

811 US
SUNBURY POETRY SERIES BY WOMEN. 1974. irreg. $1.50 per no. Sunbury Press, Box 274, Jerome Ave. Sta., Bronx, NY 10468. Ed. Virginia Scott.

808.81 HU ISSN 0586-3783
SZEP VERSEK. 1964. a. 26 Ft. ‡ Magveto Kiado, Vorosmarty ter 1, Budapest V, Hungary. Ed. G. Kardos.

811 US
TAR RIVER POETRY. 1960. 1-2/yr. $4. East Carolina University, Department of English, Greenville, NC 27834. Ed. Peter Makuck. bk. rev. illus. circ. 1,000. (tabloid format)
Formerly (until 1978): Tar River Poets (ISSN 0039-9639)

821
THROUGH CASA GUIDI WINDOWS; the bulletin of the Browning Institute. 1975. irreg. Browning Institute Inc., Box 2983, Grand Central Station, New York, NY 10017. Ed. Bd. adv. bibl.

811 CN
TITMOUSE ANNUAL. 1972. a. Can.$4. Intermedia Press Ltd, Box 3294, Vancouver, B.C., V6B 3X9, Canada (Editorial address: 720 W. 19th Ave., Vancouver, B.C., Canada) Eds. Avron and Linda Uyehara-Hoffman. illus. circ. 500.
Formerly: Titmouse Review (ISSN 0315-0720)

TRANSPACIFIC. see LITERATURE

808.1 US ISSN 0085-7378
TREEWELL. 1968. a. $1. Johnson C. Smith University, 100 Beatties Ford Rd, Charlotte, NC 28216. Ed. Carolyn McClair. bk. rev. illus. circ. 500.

811
TRELLIS. 1973. irreg. Trellis Press Association, Box 656, Morgantown, WV 26505. Ed. Bd. circ. 1,000. (also avail. in microform from UMI; reprint service avail. from UMI)

811 US
TWO FEET OF POETRY. 1970. irreg. $0.50. c/o Barry Targan, Ed., 46 Burgoyne St., Sschuylerville, NY 12871. illus. circ. 200. (looseleaf format)

U. C. REVIEW. see LITERATURE

811 HU ISSN 0082-7312
UJ MAGYAR NEPKOLTESI GYUJTEMENY. 1955. irreg. price varies. (Magyar Tudomanyos Akademia) Akademiai Kiado, Publishing House of the Hungarian Academy of Sciences, P.O. Box 24, H-1363 Budapest, Hungary.

861 CK
UNIVERSIDAD DE LOS ANDES. CUADERNOS DE LETRAS. (Text in Spanish) 1973. irreg. Universidad de los Andes, Comite de Publicaciones, Bogota, Colombia. bibl.

811 US ISSN 0049-5557
UNMUZZLED OX. 1971. irreg. $8. Unmuzzled Ox Foundation, Ltd., 105 Houston St., New York, NY 10013. Ed. Michael Andre. adv. bk. rev. bibl. illus. circ. 4,500. Indexed: Ind.Amer.Per.Verse.

811 US
UNREALIST. 1978. a. $3. Unrealist Press, Box 935, Morgantown, WV 26505. Ed. Bd. bk. rev. circ. 500.

890 BG
UTSABA. (Text in Bengali) a. Tk.5. Syed Zafar Ali, 113 Jagannath Saha Rd., Dacca 1, Bangladesh.

811 US
VAGABOND CHAPBOOK. vol. 6, 1976. irreg. $1 per no. Vagabond Press, 1610 N. Water St., Ellensburg, WA 98926.

821 SA
VEER. 1973? a. R.1. University of Port Elizabeth, Students' Representative Council, Post Box 1600, Port Elizabeth, South Africa. Eds. Dorien du Toit, Pierre Prevot van der Merwe. circ. 300.

861 SP
VERDE YERBA;* antologia Hispanoamericana de poesia. 1972, no. 10. irreg. Carabela, General Sanjuro 53, Dpto 50, Barcelona 12, Spain.

821 UK
VERMOUTH. irreg. 40p. Ver Poets, 61 & 63 Chiswell Green Lane, St. Albans, Herts, AL2 3AG, England. Eds. May Badman, Jeff Cloves.

821 IS
VOICES - ISRAEL; magazine of English poetry in Israel. (Text in English and Hebrew) 1972. a. $2. Israeli Poets in English Group, c/o R. Rose, 38 Nehemia St., Nave Sha'anan, Haifa, Israel. Eds. R. Rose, A. Aharoni and M. Levinson. adv. circ. 500.

810 US
VOYAGES TO THE INLAND SEA. 1971. a.(not published in 1978) $8. ‡ University of Wisconsin-La Crosse, Center for Contemporary Poetry, Murphy Library, La Crosse, WI 54601. Ed. John Judson. circ. 500.

WASHINGTON AND JEFFERSON LITERARY JOURNAL. see LITERATURE

811 US
WESTIGAN REVIEW OF POETRY. 1969. irreg. $4 for 4 nos. c/o Don Stap, English Department, University of Utah, Salt Lake City, UT 84112. Ed. John Knapp, 2nd. bk. rev. circ. 500. (also avail. in microform from UMI)

811 US ISSN 0511-8832
WHITTIER NEWSLETTER. 1966. a. free. Whittier Clubs of Haverhill and Amesbury, c/o Ed. John B. Pickard, Department of English, University of Florida, Gainesville, FL 32611. bk. rev. bibl. circ. 600. (looseleaf format; back issues avail)

WIENER-GOETHE-VEREIN. JAHRBUCH. see LITERATURE

800 US ISSN 0084-0238
WILLIAM-FREDERICK POETS SERIES. 1949. irreg., no. 187, 1979. price varies. William-Frederick Press, 308 E. 79th St., New York, NY 10021. Ed. Alvin Levin.

811 US
WISCONSIN POETRY. 1950. irreg. $5 per copy. A.M. Sterk, Ed. & Pub., P.O. Box 187, Milwaukee, WI 53201. bk. rev. illus. (back issues available)

811 301.412 US
WOMEN - POEMS. 1971. irreg. $1.50 per no. Women-Poems Press, 23 Meriam St., Lexington, MA 02173. Eds. Celia Gilbert, Pat Rabby. circ. 2,000.

811 US
WOMEN TALKING, WOMEN LISTENING. 1975. a. $3. Women Talking, Women Listening Press, Box 2414, Dublin, CA 94566. Ed. Sharon Lee. circ. 1,200.

811 US ISSN 0043-8154
WORLD. 1966. irreg. (1-2/yr.) $2 per no. Poetry Project, St. Marks Church In-The-Bowery, 10th St & Second Ave., New York, NY 10003. circ. 500. (processed)

811 US
XANADU. 1975. a. $3.50. Long Island Poetry Collective, Inc., Box 773, Huntington, NY 11743. Eds. Coco Gordon, Beverly Lawn. Mildred Jeffrey. bk. rev. circ. 1,000. (back issues avail.)

811 US ISSN 0084-3458
YALE SERIES OF YOUNGER POETS. 1919. a. price varies. Yale University Press, 92A Yale Sta., New Haven, CT 06520. Ed. Richard Hugo.

811 US
YEARBOOK OF WORKS RE APPALACHIA. 1969. a. $4 per yr. Morris Harvey College Publications, Charleston, WV 25304. Ed. William Plumley. circ. 5,000. (tabloid format; also avail. in record)

821 AT
YOUR FRIENDLY FASCIST. 1970. irreg. Aus.$0.20 per no. Pig's Arse Press, Box 164, Wentworth Bldg., City Rd., Darlington, N.S.W. 2008, Australia. Ed. Rae Desmond Jones. circ. 300.

LUMBER AND WOOD

see Forests and Forestry—Lumber and Wood

MACHINERY

see also Agriculture—Agricultural Equipment

621.9 FR
ANNUAIRE DE LA MECANIQUE. (Special Edition in French, English, German and Spanish) a. 176 F. (Federation des Industries Mecaniques et Transformatrices des Metaux) Union Francaise d'Annuaires Professionnels, 13 Avenue Vladimir Komarov, B.P. 36, 78190 Trappes, France.

621.9 FR
ANNUAIRE NATIONAL DES MATIERES PREMIERES DE RECUPERATION ET DU MATERIEL D'OCCASION. 1953. a. 52 F. S E P Edition, 194-196 rue Marcadet, 75018 Paris, France. adv.

ANNUAIRE REPERTOIRE DE LA MOTOCULTURE DE PLAISANCE. see GARDENING AND HORTICULTURE

621.9 FR
ANNUAIRE TECHNIQUE DE LA SOUS - TRAITANCE MECANIQUE. biennial. 93 F. (Federation des Industries Mecaniques et Transformatrices des Metaux) Union Francaise d'Annuaires Professionnels, 13 Avenue Vladimir Komarov, B.P. 36, 78190 Trappes, France.

ASSOCIATED EQUIPMENT DISTRIBUTORS. RENTAL RATES COMPILATION; nationally averaged rental rates for construction equipment including complete model specifications. see BUILDING AND CONSTRUCTION

621.9 671.3 US ISSN 0045-1983
BIG BOOK OF METALWORKING MACHINERY. 1970. irreg. $58. Zulch and Zulch, Inc., 16255 Ventura Blvd., Encino, CA 91436. Ed. William C. Zulch. adv. charts. illus. cum.index.

621.9 FR
CATALOGUE DES CONSTRUCTEURS FRANCAIS D'EQUIPEMENTS POUR LES INDUSTRIES ALIMENTAIRES. biennial? 375 F. Societe d'Edition et de Promotion Agricoles, Industrielles et Commerciales, 42 rue du Louvre, 75001 Paris, France.

CHINA (REPUBLIC). MACHINERY AND ELECTRICAL APPARATUS INDUSTRY YEARBOOK/CHUNG-HUA MIN KUO CHI CHI YU TIEN KUNG CHI TSAI NIEN CHIEN. see *ELECTRICITY AND ELECTRICAL ENGINEERING*

621.9   US
DESIGN NEWS ELECTRICAL/ELECTRONIC REFERENCE EDITION. 1970. a. $6. Cahners Publishing Co., Inc. (Boston), 221 Columbus Ave., Boston, MA 02116 (Subscr. to: 270 St. Paul St., Denver, CO 80206) Ed. Steven Kern. circ. controlled.

621.9   US
DESIGN NEWS FASTENING REFERENCE EDITION. 1970. a. $6. Cahners Publishing Co. Inc. (Boston), 221 Columbus Ave., Boston, MA 02116 (Subscr. to: 270 St. Paul St., Denver, CO 80206) Ed. Steven Kern. circ. controlled.

621.9   US
DESIGN NEWS FLUID POWER REFERENCE EDITION. 1970. a. $6. Cahners Publishing Co. Inc. (Boston), 221 Columbus Ave., Boston, MA 02116 (Subscr. to: 270 St. Paul St., Denver, CO 80206) Ed. Steven Kern. circ. controlled.

621.9   US
DESIGN NEWS MATERIALS REFERENCE EDITION. 1970. a. $6. Cahners Publishing Co. Inc. (Boston), 221 Columbus Ave., Boston, MA 02116 (Subscr. to: 270 St. Paul St., Denver, CO 80206) Ed. Steven Kern. circ. controlled.

621.9   US
DESIGN NEWS POWER TRANSMISSION REFERENCE EDITION. 1970. a. $6. Cahners Publishing Co., Inc. (Boston), 221 Columbus Ave., Boston, MA 02116 (Subscr. to: 270 St. Paul St., Denver, CO 80206) Ed. Steven Kern. circ. controlled.

338.4   621.9   US   ISSN 0070-8550
ECONOMIC HANDBOOK OF THE MACHINE TOOL INDUSTRY. 1967. a. $15. National Machine Tool Builders' Association, 7901 Westpark Dr., McLean, VA 22102. circ. 2,000.

621.9   MX
EQUIPO; materiales y servicio. 1962. a. 125($100) Editorial Innovacion, Espana 396, Mexico 13, D.F., Mexico. Ed. Cesar Macazaga. adv.

ERDBAU. see *BUILDING AND CONSTRUCTION*

621.9   SZ
FOERDERMITTELKATALOG; Foerdern-Lagern-Verteilen. 1969. a. 14 Fr. Verlag Binkert AG, CH-4335 Laufenburg, Switzerland. Ed. Max Binkert. adv. circ. 4,000.

338.4   US   ISSN 0091-8377
INDUSTRIAL MACHINERY AND EQUIPMENT PRICING GUIDE. 1972. a. $19.95. Litton Educational Publishing, 680 Kinderkamack Rd., Oradell, NJ 07675. Ed. W. Edgerton. Key Title: Machinery and Equipment Pricing Guide.

621.9   UK   ISSN 0074-6835
INTERNATIONAL MACHINE TOOL DESIGN AND RESEARCH CONFERENCE. PROCEEDINGS. 1960. a., 17th, 1977. £36.10. (University of Birmingham, Department of Mechanical Engineering) Macmillan Press Ltd., 4 Little Essex St., London WC2R 3LF, England. Ed. Prof. S.A. Tobias. circ. 550.

621   UK
INTERNATIONAL PRESSURE DIE CASTING CONFERENCES. PROCEEDINGS. triennial. (European Pressure Die Casting Committee) Zinc Development Association, 34 Berkeley Sq., London WlX 6AJ, England.
Formerly: International Pressure Die Casting Conferences. Report (ISSN 0074-7521)

INTERNATIONAL TEXTILE MACHINERY. see *TEXTILE INDUSTRIES AND FABRICS*

621.9   621.3   AU   ISSN 0025-4533
MASCHINENWELT-ELEKTROTECHNIK. 1946. a. S.425. Reinhold Schmidt Verlag, Mariahilferstr. 113, A-1060 Vienna, Austria. Ed. Ch. Schwestka. adv. bk. rev. charts. illus. pat. index. circ. 6,000.
Formerly: Maschinenwelt und Elektrotechnik.

621.86   US
MATERIAL HANDLING ENGINEERING HANDBOOK AND DIRECTORY. biennial. $27. Penton-IPC, 614 Superior Ave., W., Cleveland, OH 44113. Ed. Bernie Knill. circ. 24,000. (reprint service avail. from UMI)

MINING AND ALLIED MACHINERY CORPORATION. ANNUAL REPORT. see *MINES AND MINING INDUSTRY*

621.9   US
NATIONAL TOOL, DIE AND PRECISION MACHINING ASSOCIATION. BUYERS GUIDE. 1968. a. $15. National Tool Die and Precision Machining Association, 9300 Livingston Rd., Washington, DC 20022. adv.

621.8   HU   ISSN 0133-297X
NEHEZIPARI MUSZAKI EGYETEM, MISKOLC. PUBLICATIONS. SERIES C: MACHINERY. (Text in English, German, Russian) irreg., vol. 34, no. 1, 1978. Nehezipari Muszaki Egyetem, Miskolc, Hungary. Ed. Bd. bibl. index.

NORTH CAROLINA METALWORKING DIRECTORY. see *BUSINESS AND ECONOMICS — Trade And Industrial Directories*

621.9   PL   ISSN 0324-9646
POLITECHNIKA WROCLAWSKA. INSTYTUT KONSTRUKCJI I EKSPLOATACJI MASZYN. PRACE NAUKOWE. KONFERENCJE. 1973. irreg., no. 6, 1978. price varies. Politechnika Wroclawska, Wybrzeze Wyspianskiego 27, 50-370 Wroclaw, Poland (Dist. by: Ars Polona-Ruch, Krakowskie Przedmiescie 7, Warsaw, Poland) Ed. Marian Kloza. illus.

620   PL   ISSN 0324-962X
POLITECHNIKA WROCLAWSKA. INSTYTUT KONSTRUKCJI I EKSPLOATACJI MASZYN. PRACE NAUKOWE. MONOGRAFIE. (Text in Polish; summaries in English and Russian) 1969. irreg., no. 8, 1979. price varies. Politechnika Wroclawska, Wybrzeze Wyspianskiego 27, 50-370 Wroclaw, Poland (Dist. by: Ars Polona-Ruch, Krakowskie Przedmiescie 7, Warsaw, Poland) Ed. Marian Kloza.

620   PL   ISSN 0324-9638
POLITECHNIKA WROCLAWSKA. INSTYTUT KONSTRUKCJI I EKSPLOATACJI MASZYN. PRACE NAUKOWE. STUDIA I MATERIALY. (Text in Polish: summaries in English and Russian) 1970. irreg., no. 22, 1978. price varies. Politechnika Wroclawska, Wybrzeze Wyspianskiego 27, 50-370 Wroclaw, Poland (Dist. by: Ars Polona-Ruch, Krakowskie Przedmiescie 7, Warsaw, Poland) Ed. Marian Kloza.

621.9   UR
POLITEKHNICHNYI INSTYTUT KIEV. VESTNIK. SERIYA MASHINOSTROENIYA. (Summaries in English) irreg. 1.21 Rub. Politekhnichnyi Instytut, Kiev, Brest-Litovskii pr., 39, Kiev, U.S.S.R. illus.

621
PROBLEMY MASHINOSTROENIYA. 1975. irreg. 0.82 Rub. single issue. (Akademiya Nauk Ukrainskoi S.S.R., Institut Problem Mashinostroeniya) Izdatel'stvo Naukova Dumka, Ul. Repina 3, Kiev, U.S.S.R. illus.

621.9   669   US   ISSN 0074-4557
S D C E INTERNATIONAL DIE CASTING CONGRESS. TRANSACTIONS. 1960. biennial. $50 to members; non-members $65. Society of Die Casting Engineers, Inc., 455 State St., Des Plaines, IL 60016. Ed. William L. Sharp. cum.index, 1960-1979. (also avail. in microfilm from UMI; reprint service avail. from UMI)
Issued formerly as: National Die Casting Congress. Transactions.

621.9   US
SWEDISH MACHINE TOOLS/MACHINES OUTILS SUEDOISES/MACHINES UTILES SUEDOISES. (Text and summaries in English, French and German) 1953. a? free. (Foereningen Svenska Verktygsmaskintillverkare, SW) Chilton Co., Inc., Chilton Way, Radnor, PA 19089. circ. 8,000.

621.46   US   ISSN 0092-1661
SYMPOSIUM ON INCREMENTAL MOTION CONTROL SYSTEMS AND DEVICES. PROCEEDINGS. 1972. a. price varies; $35 for 1977. University of Illinois at Urbana-Champaign, Department of Electrical Engineering, Urbana, IL 61801. (Co-Sponsors: Warner Electric Brake & Clutch Co., (U.S.); Westool Ltd., (England)) Ed. B. C. Kuo. illus. Key Title: Proceedings. Annual Symposium. Incremental Motion Control Systems and Devices.

621.9   US
TURBOMACHINERY SYMPOSIUM. PROCEEDINGS. 1972. a. $25. Texas A & M University, Department of Mechanical Engineering, Gas Turbine Laboratories, College Station, TX 77843.

621.9   US   ISSN 0085-6916
UNIVERSITAET STUTTGART. INSTITUT FUER STEUERUNGSTECHNIK DER WERKZEUGMASCHINEN UND FERTIGUNGSEINRICHTUNGEN. I S W BERICHTE. 1972. irreg., vol. 31, 1981. price varies. Springer-Verlag, 175 Fifth Ave., New York, NY 10010 (also Berlin, Heidelberg, Vienna) (reprint service avail. from ISI)

MACROECONOMICS

see *Business and Economics — Macroeconomics*

MANAGEMENT

see *Business and Economics — Management*

MARKETING AND PURCHASING

see *Business and Economics — Marketing and Purchasing*

MATHEMATICS

510   DK   ISSN 0065-017X
AARHUS UNIVERSITET. MATEMATISK INSTITUT. LECTURE NOTES SERIES. 1963. irreg., no. 53, 1979. price varies. Aarhus Universitet, Matematisk Institut, Ny Munkegade, 8000 Aarhus C, Denmark.

510   DK
AARHUS UNIVERSITET. MATEMATISK INSTITUT. MEMOIRS. 1974. irreg. Aarhus Universitet, Matematisk Institut, Ny Munkegade, 8000 Aarhus C, Denmark.

510   DK   ISSN 0065-0188
AARHUS UNIVERSITET. MATEMATISK INSTITUT. VARIOUS PUBLICATIONS SERIES. 1962. irreg., no. 30, 1979. price varies. Aarhus Universitet, Matematisk Institut, Ny Munkegade, 8000 Aarhus C, Denmark.

510   500   600   FI   ISSN 0001-5105
ACADEMIAE ABOENSIS, SERIES B: MATHEMATICS, SCIENCE, ENGINEERING. (Text in English, German and Swedish) 1922. irreg., no. 37, 1977. price varies. Aabo Akademi, Domkyrkotorget 3, 20500 Aabo 50, Finland. charts. index. Indexed: Chem.Abstr. Math.R.
Formerly: Acta Academiae Aboensis. Series B: Mathematica et Physica.

510 PL ISSN 0065-1036
ACTA ARITHMETICA. (Text in English, Russian, French, German and Italian) 1935. irreg., 1976, vol. 29. $40 per volume. (Polska Akademia Nauk, Instytut Matematyczny) Panstwowe Wydawnictwo Naukowe, Ul. Miodowa 10, Warsaw, Poland (Dist. by Ars Polona-Ruch, Krakowskie Przedmiescie 7, Warsaw, Poland) Ed. A. Schinzel. bibl. charts.

510 621.381 FI ISSN 0355-2713
ACTA POLYTECHNICA SCANDINAVICA. MATHEMATICS AND COMPUTER SCIENCE SERIES. (Texts and summaries in English, French and German) irreg. (2-3/yr.) Fmk.60. Teknillisten Tieteiden Akatemia - Finnish Academy of Technical Sciences, Kansakoulukatu 10 A, SF-00100 Helsinki 10, Finland. Ed. Hans Andersin. index; cum. index (1958-1979) circ. 250. (also avail. in microfilm from UMI; back issues avail.; reprint service avail. from UMI)
 Formerly: Acta Polytechnica Scandinavica. Mathematics and Computing Machinery Series (ISSN 0001-6861)

510 US ISSN 0065-3217
ADVANCES IN PROBABILITY. 1971. irreg., vol. 5, 1979. price varies. Marcel Dekker, Inc., 270 Madison Ave., New York, NY 10016. Eds. Peter Ney, Sidney Port.

510 PL
AKADEMIA ROLNICZA, POZNAN. ROCZNIK. ALGORYTMY BIOMETRYCZNE I STATISTYCZNE. (Summaries in English and Russian) 1972. irreg. price varies. Akademia Rolnicza, Poznan, Ul. Wojska Polskiego 28, 60-637 Poznan, Poland. Indexed: Bibl.Agri.

510 530 GW ISSN 0065-5295
AKADEMIE DER WISSENSCHAFTEN, GOETTINGEN. NACHRICHTEN 2. MATHEMATISCH-PHYSIKALISCHE KLASSE. (Text in English, German; occasionally in French) 1893. irreg. price varies. Vandenhoeck und Ruprecht, Theaterstr. 13, Postfach 77, 3400 Goettingen, W. Germany (B.R.D.) index.

510 500 GW ISSN 0002-2993
AKADEMIE DER WISSENSCHAFTEN UND DER LITERATUR, MAINZ. MATHEMATISCH-NATURWISSENSCHAFTLICHE KLASSE. ABHANDLUNGEN. (Text in English, French and German) 1950. irreg. price varies. (Mathematisch-Naturwissenschaftliche Klasse) Franz Steiner Verlag GmbH, Friedrichstr. 24, Postfach 5529, 6200 Wiesbaden, W. Germany (B.R.D.) abstr. charts. illus. index. Indexed: Chem.Abstr.

510 CN ISSN 0317-8579
ALBERTA TEACHERS ASSOCIATION. MATHEMATICS MONOGRAPH. 1964. a. membership. Alberta Teachers' Association, 11010 - 142 Street, Edmonton, Alberta T5N 2R1, Canada. Ed. W.G. Cathcart.
 Supersedes: Mathematics Annual (ISSN 0085-3178)

510 US ISSN 0065-9258
AMERICAN MATHEMATICAL SOCIETY. COLLOQUIUM PUBLICATIONS. 1905. irreg. price varies. American Mathematical Society, P.O. Box 6248, Providence, RI 02940. index in each vol. Indexed: Math.R. Zent.Math. Zent.Math.

510 US ISSN 0065-9266
AMERICAN MATHEMATICAL SOCIETY. MEMOIRS. 1950; n.s. 1975; vol. 1, no. 154. irreg. price varies. American Mathematical Society, P.O. Box 6248, Providence, RI 02940. circ. 600. Indexed: Math.R. Zent.Math.

510 US ISSN 0065-9290
AMERICAN MATHEMATICAL SOCIETY. TRANSLATIONS. SERIES 2. (Supersedes Series 1) 1955. irreg., latest 1978. price varies. American Mathematical Society, P.O. Box 6248, Providence, RI 02940. Ed. Ben Silver. cum.index 1966-1973. circ. 700.

510 FI ISSN 0066-1953
ANNALES ACADEMIAE SCIENTIARUM FENNICAE. SERIES A, 1: MATHEMATICA. (Text in English, French, German) 1941. irreg. price varies. Suomalainen Tiedeakatemia - Academia Scientiarum Fennica, Snellmanink. 9-11, 00170 Helsinki 17, Finland. Ed. Olli Lehto. index, cum. index (1941-1967 in vol. 400) circ. 700-750. (also avail. in microform; back issues avail.; reprint service avail. from UMI) Indexed: Bull.Signal. Math.R. Psychol.Abstr. Ref.Zh. Zent.Math.

510 PL ISSN 0066-2216
ANNALES POLONICI MATHEMATICI. (Text in various languages) 1954. irreg., 1976, vol. 31, no. 3. $30 per volume. (Polska Akademia Nauk, Instytut Matematyczny) Panstwowe Wydawnictwo Naukowe, Ul. Miodowa 10, Warsaw, Poland (Dist. by Ars Polona-Ruch, Krakowskie Przedmiescie 7, Warsaw, Poland) Eds. Yozef Siciak, Jacek Szarski. bibl.

510 658 PL
ANNALES SOCIETATIS MATHEMATICAE POLONAE. SERIES 4: FUNDAMENTA INFORMATICAE. Cover title: Fundamenta Informaticae. (Text in English) 1977. q. 60 Zl.($12) per no. (Polskie Towarzystwo Matematyczne) Panstwowe Wydawnictwo Naukowe, Ul. Sniadeckich 8, 00-950 Warsaw, Poland (Dist. by Wiss. Buchhandlung Harry Munchberg, 33-94 Langelsheim 2 Postfach, W. Germany (B.R.D.)) Ed.Bd. circ. 500.

510 PL ISSN 0365-1029
ANNALES UNIVERSITATIS MARIAE CURIE-SKLODOWSKA. SECTIO A. MATHEMATICA. (Text in English, French) 1946. ir. Uniwersytet Marii Curie-Sklodowskiej, Plac Marii Curie-Sklodowskiej 5, 20-031 Lublin, Poland. Eds. J. Krzyz, A. Bielecki. Indexed: Math.R.

510 IT ISSN 0003-4622
ANNALI DI MATEMATICA; pura ed applicata. (Text in English, French, German and Italian) 1850. irreg. (approx. 3-4/yr.) L.25000 per no. Nicola Zanichelli Editore, Via Irnerio 34, Bologna 40126, Italy. Ed. Dir. Giovanni Sansone. bibl. charts. circ. 700. Indexed: Math.R.

510 US
ANNALS OF MATHEMATICS STUDIES. irreg., no. 94, 1980. price varies. Princeton University Press, 41 Williams Street, Princeton, NJ 08540. (reprint service avail. from UMI)

510 US
APPLICATIONS OF MATHEMATICS. 1975. irreg., vol. 16, 1981. price varies. Springer-Verlag, 175 Fifth Ave., New York, NY 10010 (Also Berlin, Heidelberg, Vienna) Eds. A.V. Balakrishnan, W. Hildenbrand. (reprint service avail. from ISI)

510 US ISSN 0066-5452
APPLIED MATHEMATICAL SCIENCES. (Text in English) 1972. irreg., vol. 35, 1981. price varies. Springer-Verlag, 175 Fifth Ave., New York, NY 10010 (Also Berlin, Heidelberg) (reprint service avail. from ISI) Indexed: Math.R.

510 531 US ISSN 0066-5479
APPLIED MATHEMATICS AND MECHANICS; An international series of monographs. 1957, no. 2. irreg., vol. 15, 1974. price varies. Academic Press Inc., 111 Fifth Ave., New York, NY 10003. Eds. F. N. Frenkiel, G. Temple. (also avail. in microfiche)

510 GW ISSN 0518-5378
ARISTO - MITTEILUNGEN FUER INGENIEUR- UND HOCHSCHULEN. (Editions also in English and Spanish) 1957. a. free. Aristo - Werke Dennert und Pape KG, Haferweg 46, 2000 Hamburg 50, W. Germany (B.R.D.) Ed. R. Jaeger. circ. 20,000.
 Information for teachers of mathematics about slide rules, drafting instruments and electronic calculators

510 UR
ASIMPTOTICHESKIE METODY V TEORII SISTEM. 1971. 1 Rub. Irkutskii Gosudarstvennyi Universitet im. A. A. Zhdanova, Ul. Karla Marksa, 1, Irkutsk, U.S.S.R. Ed. A. N. Panchenkov. circ. 600.

BALSKRISHNAN-NEUSTADT SERIES. see
TECHNOLOGY: COMPREHENSIVE WORKS

BAYERISCHE AKADEMIE DER WISSENSCHAFTEN. MATHEMATISCH-NATURWISSENSCHAFTLICHE KLASSE. SITZUNGBERICHTE. see *SCIENCES: COMPREHENSIVE WORKS*

510 US
BERKELEY SYMPOSIA ON MATHEMATICAL STATISTICS AND PROBABILITY. irreg., 6th, 1972. price varies. University of California Press, 2223 Fulton St., Berkeley, CA 94720.

510 PL
BIBLIOTEKA MATEMATYCZNA. irreg., t. 22, 1977. Panstwowe Wydawnictwo Naukowe, Miodowa 10, 00-251 Warsaw, Poland.

BIOMATHEMATICS. see *BIOLOGY*

510 BL
BOLETIM DE ANALISE E LOGICA MATEMATICA. 1969. irreg. Universidade Federal Fluminense, Instituto de Matematica, Niteroi, Brazil.

510 US
C R C HANDBOOK OF MATHEMATICAL SCIENCES. 1962. irreg., 5th edt.,1979. $49.95. C R C Press, Inc., 2000 N.W. 24th St., Boca Raton, FL 33431. Ed.William H. Beyer.
 Formerly: C R C Handbook of Tables for Mathematics (ISSN 0574-9700)

CAMBRIDGE MONOGRAPHS ON MATHEMATICAL PHYSICS. see *PHYSICS*

CAMBRIDGE MONOGRAPHS ON MECHANICS AND APPLIED MATHEMATICS. see *PHYSICS — Mechanics*

510 530.15 UK
CAMBRIDGE TRACTS IN MATHEMATICS. 1905. irreg.,no. 80, 1981. $34.50 for latest vol. Cambridge University Press, Box 110, Cambridge CB2 3RL, England (and 32 E. 57 St., New York, NY 10022) Ed.Bd.
 Formerly: Cambridge Tracts in Mathematics and Mathematical Physics (ISSN 0068-6824)

510.5 CN ISSN 0380-5921
CANADIAN MATHEMATICAL CONGRESS. RESEARCH COMMITTEE. REPORT. (Text in English; some French) 1950. a. Canadian Mathematical Congress, Research Committee, 3421 Drummond St., Montreal, Que. H3G 1X7, Canada. (processed)

510 AT
CANBERRA MATHEMATICAL ASSOCIATION. NEWSLETTER. 1963. irreg. Aus.$0.75. Canberra Mathematical Association, Institute of Advanced Studies, Australian National University, Box 4, Canberra City, A.C.T. 2601, Australia. Ed. E. Lee.

510 CN
CARLETON LECTURE NOTE SERIES. 1972. irreg. price varies. Carleton University, Department of Mathematics, Ottawa, Ont. K1S 5B6, Canada. Ed. L.E. May. circ. controlled. Indexed: Math.Rev.

510 CN ISSN 0069-0600
CARLETON MATHEMATICAL SERIES. (Text in English and French) 1971. irreg. price varies. Carleton University, Department of Mathematics, Ottawa, Ont. K1S 5B6, Canada. Ed. L.E. May. circ. controlled. Indexed: Math.Rev.

510 US ISSN 0069-0813
CARUS MATHEMATICAL MONOGRAPHS. irreg., 1968, vol. 15. $11. Mathematical Association of America, 1225 Connecticut Ave. N.W., Washington, DC 20036.

510 SZ
CENTRE DE RECHERCHES EN MATHEMATIQUES PURES. PUBLICATIONS. SERIE 1. 1958. irreg. price varies. Centre de Recherches en Mathematiques Pures, P.R. Gare 2, Ave. du Premier Mars 24, 2002 Neuchatel, Switzerland. Ed. S. Piccard. cum.index.
 Continues: Universite de Neuchatel. Seminaire de Geometrie. Publications. Serie 1. Courtes Publications (ISSN 0077-7641)

510   SZ
CENTRE DE RECHERCHES EN MATHEMATIQUES PURES. PUBLICATIONS. SERIE 2. MONOGRAPHIES. 1966. irreg. price varies. Centre de Recherches en Mathematiques Pures, P.R. Gare 2, Ave. du Premier Mars 24, 2002 Neuchatel, Switzerland. Ed. S. Piccard.
Continues: Universite de Neuchatel. Seminaire de Geometrie. Publications. Serie 2. Monographies (ISSN 0077-765X)

510   SZ
CENTRE DE RECHERCHES EN MATHEMATIQUES PURES. PUBLICATIONS. SERIE 3. OEUVRES. irreg. Centre de Recherches en Mathematiques Pures, P.R. Gares 2, 2002 Neuchatel, Switzerland.

510   SZ
CENTRE DE RECHERCHES EN MATHEMATIQUES PURES. PUBLICATIONS. SERIE 4. CONFERENCES COMMUNICATIONS. irreg. Centre de Recherches en Mathematiques Pures, P.R. Gares 2, 2002 Neuchatel, Switzerland.

CHANTIERS DE PEDAGOGIE MATHEMATIQUE. see *EDUCATION — Teaching Methods And Curriculum*

510   US   ISSN 0084-8719
CHAPEL HILL CONFERENCE ON COMBINATORIAL MATHEMATICS AND ITS APPLICATIONS. PROCEEDINGS. 1967. irreg., 1970 vol. 2. $5. ea. ‡ (U.S. Air Force Office of Scientific Research) University of North Carolina at Chapel Hill, Department of Statistics, Chapel Hill, NC 27514.

510   US   ISSN 0069-3286
CHICAGO LECTURES IN MATHEMATICS. 1964. irreg., latest 1976. price varies. University of Chicago Press, 5801 S. Ellis Ave., Chicago, IL 60637. Ed. Irving Kaplansky. (reprint service avail. from UMI,ISI)

510   FR
COLLECTION FORMATION DES ENSEIGNANTS ET FORMATION CONTINUE. 1973. irreg. Editions Hermann, 293 rue Lecourbe, 75015 Paris, France. illus.
Formerly: Collection Formation des Enseignants.

510   PL   ISSN 0010-1354
COLLOQUIUM MATHEMATICUM. (Text in various languages) 1947. irreg., 1975, vol. 34, no. 1. $30 per volume. (Polska Akademia Nauk, Instytut Matematyczny) Panstwowe Wydawnictwo Naukowe, Ul. Miodowa 10, Warsaw, Poland (Dist. by Ars Polona-Ruch, Krakowskie Przedmiescie 7, Warsaw, Poland) Ed. Edward Marczewski. Indexed: Math.R.

COMMENTATIONES PHYSICO-MATHEMATICAE. see *PHYSICS*

COMPUTER SCIENCE AND APPLIED MATHEMATICS. see *COMPUTER TECHNOLOGY AND APPLICATIONS*

CONFERENCE ON PROBABILITY AND STATISTICS IN ATMOSPHERIC SCIENCES. PREPRINTS. see *METEOROLOGY*

510   CN
CONGRESSUS NUMERANTIUM; a conference journal on numerical themes. 1970. 3/yr.(approx.) price varies. Utilitas Mathematica Publishing Inc., Box 7, University Centre, University of Manitoba, Winnipeg, Man. R3T 2N2, Canada. Ed. Ralph G. Stanton. Indexed: Math. R. Zent.Math.
Incorporating (since 1971): Maintoba Conference on Numerical Mathematics and Computing. Proceedings; (since 1970): Southeastern Conference on Combinatorics, Graph Theory and Computing Proceedings.

510 530   US
COURS ET DOCUMENTS DE MATHEMATIQUES ET DE PHYSIQUE. a. price varies. Gordon and Breach Science Publishers, One Park Ave., New York, NY 10016. Eds. Maurice Levy, E. Schatzman.

510   CS
CZECHOSLOVAK SYMPOSIUM ON GRAPH THEORY. (Text in English) irreg., 2d, 1974, Prague. $37.50 per no. (Ceskoslovenska Akademie Ved, Matematicky Ustav) Academia, Publishing House of the Czechoslovak Academy of Sciences, Vodickova 40, 112 29 Prague 1, Czechoslovakia. illus.

DEVELOPMENTS IN GEOMATHEMATICS. see *EARTH SCIENCES — Geophysics*

510   HU   ISSN 0070-671X
DISQUISITIONES MATHEMATICAE HUNGARIAE. (Text in English, French, German or Hungarian) 1970. irreg., vol. 8, 1977. price varies. (Magyar Tudomanyos Akademia) Akademiai Kiado, Publishing House of the Hungarian Academy of Sciences, P.O. Box 24, H-1363 Budapest, Hungary.

510   PL   ISSN 0012-3862
DISSERTATIONES MATHEMATICAE/ ROZPRAWY MATEMATYCZNE. (Text in English, French, Polish, German and Russian; summaries in English and Russian) 1952. irreg., 1976, vol. 130. price varies. (Polska Akademia Nauk, Instytut Matematyczny) Panstwowe Wydawnictwo Naukowe, Ul. Miodowa 10, Warsaw, Poland (Dist. by Ars Polona-Ruch, Krakowskie Przedmiescie 7, Warsaw, Poland) Ed. Karol Borsuk. index. Indexed: Math.R.

510   UK   ISSN 0309-8648
DOZENAL REVIEW. 1959. irreg. £3. Dozenal Society of Great Britain, 69 Scotby Road, Carlisle, Cumbria CA4 8BG, England. Ed. S. Ferguson. bk. rev. index. circ. 200. (tabloid format)
Formerly (until 1977): Duodecimal Review.

510   US   ISSN 0071-1136
ERGEBNISSE DER MATHEMATIK UND IHRER GRENZGEBIETE. (Text in German or English; occasionally French or Italian) 1955. irreg., no. 97, 1979. price varies. Springer-Verlag, 175 Fifth Ave., New York, NY 10010 (also Berlin, Heidelberg, Vienna) Ed. P. Z. Hilton. circ. 2,000. (reprint service avail. from ISI) Indexed: Math.R.

510   FR   ISSN 0071-7614
ETUDES MATHEMATIQUES EN VUE DES APPLICATIONS: FORMULAIRE DE MATHEMATIQUES A L'USAGE DES PHYSICIENS ET DES INGENIEURS. irreg., latest issue, 1964. price varies. (Centre d'Etudes Mathematiques en Vue des Applications, Paris) Centre National de la Recherche Scientifique, 15 Quai Anatole-France, 75700 Paris, France.

510 530.15   UK   ISSN 0071-2248
EUREKA; THE ARCHIMEDEAN'S JOURNAL. 1939. a. price varies. Cambridge University Mathematical Society, Junior Branch of the Mathematical Association, Cambridge, England. bk. rev. circ. 500.

029.7   US   ISSN 0361-0977
FORMAL LINGUISTICS. irreg. Harvard University, Department of Linguistics, Cambridge, MA 02138.
Continues: Mathematical Linguistics and Automatic Translation.

510   CS
FORMATOR SYMPOSIUM ON MATHEMATICAL METHODS FOR THE ANALYSIS OF LARGE-SCALE SYSTEMS. (Text in English) irreg., 2d, 1974, Prague. $28.75 per no. (Ceskoslovenska Akademie Ved, Matematicky Ustav) Academia, Publishing House of the Czechoslovak Academy of Sciences, Vodickova 40, 112 29 Prague 1, Czechoslovakia.

510   FR   ISSN 0071-8564
FRANCE. DELEGATION GENERALE A LA RECHERCHE SCIENTIFIQUE ET TECHNIQUE. REPERTOIRE NATIONAL DES LABORATOIRES; LA RECHERCHE UNIVERSITAIRE; SCIENCES EXACTES ET NATURELLES. TOME 4: MATHEMATIQUES, SCIENCES DE L'ESPACE ET DE LA TERRE. 1966. irreg. 20 F. Documentation Francaise, 29-31 Quai Voltaire, 75340 Paris 07, France.

510   PL
FUNCTIONES ET APPROXIMATIO COMMENTARII MATHEMATICI. (Text in English) 1974. irreg., vol. 7, 1979. price varies. Uniwersytet im. Adama Mickiewicza w Poznaniu, Instytut Matematyki, Matejki 48/49, 60-769 Poznan, Poland (Dist. by: Ars Polona, Krakowskie Przedmiescie 7, 00-068 Warsaw, Poland) Ed. J. Musielak and A. Alexiewicz. circ. 600.

510 500   PL   ISSN 0072-0445
GDANSKIE TOWARZYSTWO NAUKOWE. WYDZIAL III. NAUK MATEMATYCZNO-PRZYRODNICZYCH. ROZPRAWY. (Text in Polish; summaries in English and Russian) 1964. irreg. price varies. Ossolineum, Publishing House of the Polish Academy of Sciences, Rynek 9, 50-106 Wroclaw, Poland (Dist. by Ars Polona-Ruch, Krakowskie Przedmiescie 7, Warsaw, Poland) Ed. Ryszard Piekos.

510   US   ISSN 0072-5285
GRADUATE TEXTS IN MATHEMATICS. (Text in English) 1971. irreg., vol. 78, 1981. price varies. Springer-Verlag, 175 Fifth Ave., New York, NY 10010 (Also Berlin, Heidelberg) Eds. P. R. Halmos, F. W. Gehring, C. C. Moore. (reprint service avail. from ISI) Indexed: Math.R.

510   GR   ISSN 0072-7466
GREEK MATHEMATICAL SOCIETY. BULLETIN/ HELLENIKE MATHEMATIKE HETAIREIA. DELTION. (Text in Greek, English, French, German, and Italian) 1960. a. $20. Greek Mathematical Society, 34, E. Venizelou St., Athens 143, Greece. Ed.Bd. circ. 1,000.

510   US   ISSN 0072-7830
GRUNDLEHREN DER MATHEMATISCHEN WISSENSCHAFTEN IN EINZELDARSTELLUNGEN. (Text in English, occasionally in German and French) no. 229, 1979. irreg., no. 241, 1981. price varies. Springer-Verlag, 175 Fifth Ave., New York, NY 10010 (also Berlin, Heidelberg, Vienna) (reprint service avail. from ISI)

510   II   ISSN 0073-2281
HINDU ASTRONOMICAL AND MATHEMATICAL TEXT SERIES. (Text in English and Sanskrit; summaries in English) 1957. irreg. price varies. University of Lucknow, Department of Mathematics and Astronomy, Lucknow, Uttar Pradesh, India. Ed. R. P. Agarwala.

510   GE   ISSN 0073-2842
HOCHSCHULBUECHER FUER MATHEMATIK. 1955. irreg. price varies. VEB Deutscher Verlag der Wissenschaften, Postfach 1216, 108 Berlin, E. Germany (D.D.R.) Eds. H. Grell, R. Maruhn, W. Rinow.

I B M RESEARCH SYMPOSIA SERIES. see *PHYSICS*

510   AT   ISSN 0311-0621
I M U CANBERRA CIRCULAR. 1972. irreg (4/yr.-approx) free. (International Mathematical Union) B.H. Neumann, Ed. & Pub., Department of Mathematics, Australian National University, P.O. Box 4, Canberra A.C.T. 2600, Australia. circ. 200.

510   JA
IBARAKI UNIVERSITY. FACULTY OF SCIENCE. BULLETIN. SERIES A: MATHEMATICS. (Text in English; summaries in Japanese) 1968. a. exchange basis. Ibaraki University, Faculty of Science, 2-1-11 Bunkyo, Mito 310, Japan.

510   II   ISSN 0019-5839
INDIAN MATHEMATICAL SOCIETY. JOURNAL. (Text in English) 1909; N.S. 1934. a. $15. Indian Mathematical Society, Tata Institute of Fundamental Research, Homi Bhabha Rd., Bombay 400005, India. Ed. K.G. Ramanathan. bk. rev. bibl. pat. tr.lit. index. circ. 1,200(approx.) Indexed: Math.R.

510   II
INDIAN NATIONAL SCIENCE ACADEMY. MATHEMATICAL TABLES. 1956. irreg. Rs.15($5) Indian National Science Academy, Bahadur Shah Zafar Marg, New Delhi 110002, India. Eds. M. S. Cheema and H. Gupta.
Continues: National Institute of Sciences of India. Mathematical Tables (ISSN 0466-3276)

510　　　　　　　　　　FR
INSTITUT HENRI POINCARE. GROUPE
D'ETUDE D'ANALYSE ULTRAMETRIQUE.
EXPOSES. 1974. a. Universite de Paris VI, Groupe
d'Etude d'Analyse Ultrametrique, 11 rue Pierre et
Marie Curie, F-75231 Paris Cedex 05, France
(Subscr. address: Offilib, 48 rue Gay Lussac, F-
75240 Paris Cedex 05, France) Ed. Paul Belgodere.
(back issues avail) Indexed: Math.R. Ref.Zh. Zent.
Math.

510　　　　　　　　　　FR
INSTITUTE HENRI POINCARE. SEMINAIRE
PAUL KREE. EXPOSES. 1975. a. Universite de
Paris VI, Seminaire Paul Kree, 11 rue Pierre et
Marie Curie, F-75231 Paris Cedex 05, France
(Subscr. address: Ofilib, 48 rue Gay Lussac, F-
75240 Paris Cedex 05) Ed. Paul Belgodere. (back
issues avail.) Indexed: Math.R. Ref.Zh. Zent.Math.

510　　　　　　　　　　UK
INSTITUTE OF MATHEMATICS AND ITS
APPLICATIONS. PROCEEDINGS. irreg. price
varies. Institute of Mathematics and Its
Applications, Maitland House, Warrior Sq.,
Southend-on-Sea, Essex SS1 2JY, England.

510　　　　　　　　　　JA
INSTITUTE OF STATISTICAL MATHEMATICS.
ANNUAL REPORT/TOKEI SURI KENKYUSHO
NENPO. (Text in Japanese) 1967. a. Institute of
Statistical Mathematics - Tokei Suri Kenkyusho, 4-
6-7 Minami Azabu, Minato-ku, Tokyo 106, Japan.

510　　　　　　　　　　IT
INSTITUTIONES MATHEMATICAE. 1976. irreg.
Istituto Nazionale di Alta Matematica, Citta
Universitaria, 00100 Rome, Italy (Dist by:
Academic Press, Inc., 111 Fifth Ave., New York,
NY 10003; and 24-28 Oval Rd., London NW7
7DX, England)

510　　　　　　　　　　RM
INSTITUTUL PEDAGOGIC ORADEA. LUCRARI
STIINTIFICE: SERIA MATEMATICA. (Continues
in part its Lucrari Stiintfice: Seria Matematica,
Fizica, Chimie (1971-72), its Lucrari Stiintifice:
Seria A and Seria B (1969-1970), and its Lucrari
Stiintifice (1967-68).) (Text in Rumanian,
occasionally in English or French; summaries in
Rumanian, French, English or German) 1967. a.
Institutul Pedagogic Oradea, Calea Armatei Rosii
Nr. 5, Oradea, Romania.

515　　　　　　　　　　US
INTERNATIONAL CONFERENCE ON
COMPUTING FIXED POINTS WITH
APPLICATIONS. PROCEEDINGS. 1977. irreg.,
1st, 1974, Clemson University (pub. 1977)
Department of the Navy, Office of Naval Research,
Arlington, VA 22217. (Co-sponsor: U.S. Army
Research Office)

INTERNATIONAL CONFERENCE ON THE
THEORY AND APPLICATIONS OF
DIFFERENTIAL GAMES. PROCEEDINGS. see
*ELECTRICITY AND ELECTRICAL
ENGINEERING*

510　530　　　II　　ISSN 0074-705X
INTERNATIONAL MONOGRAPHS ON
ADVANCED MATHEMATICS AND PHYSICS.*
(Text in English) 1961. irreg., 1973, no. 44.
Hindustan Publishing Corp., 6-U.B. Jawahar Nagar,
Delhi 110007, India.

510　　　　　　　　　　US
INTERNATIONAL SERIES IN NONLINEAR
MATHEMATICS; theory, methods and
applications. 1980. irreg. Pergamon Press, Inc.,
Maxwell House, Fairview Park, Elmsford, NY
10523. Eds. V. Lakshmikantham, C. P. Tsokos.

510　　　　　US　　ISSN 0539-0125
INTERNATIONAL SERIES IN PURE AND
APPLIED MATHEMATICS. 1957. irreg., vol. 105,
1976. price varies. Pergamon Press, Inc., Maxwell
House, Fairview Park, Elmsford, NY 10523.
　　Formerly: International Series of Monographs in
Pure and Applied Mathematics.

ISSLEDOVANIA PO TEORII ALGORIFMOV I
MATEMATICHESKOI LOGIKE. see
PHILOSOPHY

510　　　　　　　　　　UR
ISTORIKO-MATEMATICHESKIE
ISSLEDOVANIYA. vol. 22, 1977. irreg. 1.94 Rub.
per no. (Akademiya Nauk S.S.S.R., Institut Istorii
Estestvoznaniya i Tekhniki) Izdatel'stvo Nauka,
Podsosenskii per., 21, Moscow K-62, U.S.S.R. Ed.
A. Yushkevich. abstr. bibl. illus. circ. 1,500.

510　　　　　　　　　　GW
JAHRBUCH UEBERBLICKE MATHEMATIK. 1975.
a. DM.28. Bibliographisches Institut AG, Dudenstr.
6, Postfach 311, 6800 Mannheim 1, W. Germany
(B.R.D.) Ed. Bd.

510　　　　　　　　　　US
JAMES K. WHITTEMORE LECTURES IN
MATHEMATICS GIVEN AT YALE
UNIVERSITY. irreg., no. 6, 1975. Yale University
Press, 92A Yale Sta., New Haven, CT 06520.

510　　　　　GW　　ISSN 0075-4102
JOURNAL FUER DIE REINE UND
ANGEWANDTE MATHEMATIK. (Text in
English, German, French) 1826. irreg., vol. 312,
1979. DM.136($68) per vol. Walter de Gruyter und
Co., Genthiner Str. 13, 1000 Berlin 30, W.
Germany (B.R.D.) Eds. Helmut Hasse, Hans
Rohrbach. adv. Indexed: Math.R.

510　　　　　JA　　ISSN 0075-4293
JOURNAL OF MATHEMATICS. (Text in English)
1967. a. available on exchange. Tokushima
University, Faculty of Education - Tokushima
Daigaku Kyoiku Gakubu, 1-4 Minamijosanjimi-cho,
Tokushima 770, Japan. Ed. I. Shimoda.

510　　　　　FI　　ISSN 0075-4641
JYVASKYLAN YLIOPISTO. MATEMATIIKAN
LAITOS. REPORT. 1967. irreg. exchange basis
only. ‡ Jyvaskylan Yliopisto, Matematiikan Laitos -
University of Jyvaskyla, Department of
Mathematics, Sammonkatu 6, SF-40100 Jyvaskyla
10, Finland. Ed. V. Nevanlinna.

510　　　　　　　　　　UR
KHAR'KOVSKII GOSUDARSTVENNYI
INVERSITET. MATEMATIKA I MEKHANIKA.
(Subseries of: Khar'kovskii Universitet.Vestnik) vol.
41, 1976. irreg. 0.56 Rub. per issue. Izdatel'stvo
Vysshaya Shkola-Khar'kov, Universitetskaya 16,
310000 Khar'kov, U.S.S.R. Ed. I. Tarapov. circ.
1,000.

KOEBENHAVNS UNIVERSITET. INSTITUT FOR
ANVENDT OG MATEMATISK LINGVISTIK.
SKRIFTER. see *LINGUISTICS*

510　530　　　DK　　ISSN 0023-3323
KONGELIGE DANSKE VIDENSKABERNES
SELSKAB. MATEMATISK-FYSISKE
MEDDELELSER. (Text in English, French and
German) 1919. irreg., vol. 40, no. 6, 1979. price
varies. Kongelige Danske Videnskabernes Selskab -
Royal Danish Academy of Sciences and Letters,
Dantes Plads 5, DK-1556 Copenhagen V, Denmark
(Orders to: Munksgaards Boghandel, Noerregade 6,
DK-1165 Copenhagen K, Denmark) bibl. charts.
illus. index. Indexed: Chem.Abstr. Math.R.
Met.Abstr. Sci.Abstr.

510　　　　　　　　　　UR
KRAEVYE ZADACHI DLYA
DIFFERENTSIAL'NYKH URAVNENII. 1971.
irreg. 1.10 Rub. Akademiya Nauk Uzbekskoi S.S.R.,
Institut Matematiki im V. I. Romanovskogo,
Astronomicheskii tup., 11, Tashkent, U. S. S. R.

510　500　　　JA　　ISSN 0454-8221
KYUSHU INSTITUTE OF TECHNOLOGY.
BULLETIN: MATHEMATICS, NATURAL
SCIENCE/KYUSHU KOGYO DAIGAKU
KENKYU HOKOKU, SHIZENKAGAKU. (Text in
European languages) 1955. a. on exchange basis.
Kyushu Institute of Technology - Kyushu Kogyo
Daigaku, 1-1 Sensui-cho, Kitakyushu 804, Japan.

510　　　　　RM　　ISSN 0075-8175
LATIN LANGUAGE MATHEMATICIANS
GROUP. ACTES ET TRAVAUX DU CONGRES.
1957. irreg. (Latin Language Mathematicians'
Group) Editura Academiei Republicii Socialiste
Romania, Calea Victoriei 125, Bucharest, Romania
(Subscr. to: Ilexim, Str. 13 Decembrie Nr. 3, P.O.
Box 136-137, Bucharest, Romania)

510　574　　　US　　ISSN 0341-633X
LECTURE NOTES IN BIOMATHEMATICS. 1974.
irreg., vol. 39, 1981. price varies. Springer-Verlag,
175 Fifth Ave., New York, NY 10010 (Also Berlin,
Heidelberg, Vienna) Ed. S. Levin. (reprint service
avail. from ISI)

510　330　　　US　　ISSN 0075-8442
LECTURE NOTES IN ECONOMICS AND
MATHEMATICAL SYSTEMS; Operations
Research, Computer Science, Social Science. 1968.
irreg., vol. 187, 1981. price varies. Springer-Verlag,
175 Fifth Ave., New York, NY 10010 (also Berlin,
Heidelberg, Vienna) (reprint service avail. from ISI)
　　Formerly: Lecture Notes in Operations Research
and Mathematical Systems.

510　　　　　US　　ISSN 0075-8434
LECTURE NOTES IN MATHEMATICS. (Text in
English; occasionally in German and French) 1964.
irreg., vol. 847, 1981. price varies. Springer-Verlag,
175 Fifth Ave., New York, NY 10010 (Also Berlin,
Heidelberg) Eds. A. Dold, B. Eckmann. (reprint
service avail. from ISI) Indexed: Math.R.

510　　　　　US　　ISSN 0075-8469
LECTURE NOTES IN PURE AND APPLIED
MATHEMATICS. 1971. irreg., vol. 53, 1980. price
varies. Marcel Dekker, Inc., 270 Madison Ave.,
New York, NY 10016. Eds. E. J. Taft, Edwin
Hewitt, S. Kobayashi.

510　　　　　US　　ISSN 0075-8485
LECTURES IN APPLIED MATHEMATICS. 1957.
irreg., vol. 16, 1977. price varies. American
Mathematical Society, Box 6248, Providence, RI
02940. Indexed: Math.R. Zent.Math.

510　570　　　US　　ISSN 0075-8523
LECTURES ON MATHEMATICS IN THE LIFE
SCIENCES. 1968. irreg. price varies. American
Mathematical Society, P.O.B. 6248, Providence, RI
02940. circ. 350. Indexed: Math.R. Zent.Math.

510　　　　　US　　ISSN 0146-9231
LENINGRAD UNIVERSITY. VESTNIK.
MATHEMATICS. (English translation of
mathematics section of Vestnk Leningradsko
Universiteta) irreg. $130 to non-members; members
$65. American Mathematical Society, Box 6248,
Providence, RI 02940. circ. 150.

510　500　　　PL　　ISSN 0076-0412
LODZKIE TOWARZYSTWO NAUKOWE.
WYDZIAL III. NAUK MATEMATYCZNO-
PRZYRODNICZYCH. PRACE. (Text in Polish;
summaries in English or French) 1947. irreg. price
varies. Panstwowe Wydawnictwo Naukowe, Ul.
Miodowa 10, Warsaw, Poland.

510　　　　　UK　　ISSN 0076-0552
LONDON MATHEMATICAL SOCIETY.
LECTURE NOTE SERIES. 1971. irreg., no. 46,
1980. $14.95 for latest vol. Cambridge University
Press, Box 110, Cambridge CB2 3RL, England (and
32 E. 57 St., New York NY 10022) Ed. I. M.
James. index.

510　　　　　US　　ISSN 0076-0560
LONDON MATHEMATICAL SOCIETY.
MONOGRAPHS. 1970. irreg., no. 13, 1978. price
varies. Academic Press Inc., 111 Fifth Ave., New
York, NY 10003. Eds. P.M. Cohn, G.E.H. Reuter.

510　　　　　　　　　　US
LOS ALAMOS SYMPOSIUM ON MATHEMATICS
IN THE NATURAL SCIENCES.
PROCEEDINGS. (Subseries of: Surveys in Applied
Mathematics) 1976. irreg., 1st, 1974 (pub. 1976)
Academic Press, Inc, 111 Fifth Ave., New York,
NY 10003 (And Berkeley Square House, London
W.1, England) Ed. N. Metropolis.

MATCH; informal communications in mathematical
chemistry. see *CHEMISTRY*

510　530　　　UR
MATEMATICHESKAYA FIZIKA I
FUNKTSIONALNYI ANALIZ. (Text in Russian;
summaries in English) irreg. 1 Rub. Akademiya
Nauk Ukrainskoi S.S.R., Fiziko- Tekhnicheskii
Institut Nizkikh Temperatur, Pr. Lenina 47,
Kharkov, U.S.S.R.

510 PL
MATEMATYKA. 1963. irreg., 1975, vol. 2. price varies. Uniwersytet im. Adama Mickiewicza w Poznaniu, Stalingradzka 1, 61-712 Poznan, Poland (Dist. by: Ars Polona, Krakowskie Przedmiescie 7, 00-068 Warsaw, Poland) Ed. Maria Zawiejska-Jankowska.
  Formerly: Uniwersytet im. Adama Mickiewicza w Poznaniu. Wydzial Matematyki, Fizyki i Chemii. Prace. Seria Matematyka (ISSN 0551-6625)

510 AG ISSN 0025-553X
MATHEMATICAE NOTAE. (Text in English, French, German, Italian & Spanish) vol.22, 1970/71. a. ‡ Instituto de Matematica Beppo Levi, Avenida Pellegrini 250, Rosario, Argentina. bk. rev. circ. 500. Indexed: Appl. Mech. Rev. Math.R.

510 NZ ISSN 0581-1155
MATHEMATICAL CHRONICLE. 1969. irreg., vol. 10, 1981. NZ.$13 to institutions; NZ $6.50 to individuals. University of Auckland, Department of Mathematics, Private Bag, Auckland, New Zealand. Ed. J. A. Kalman. bibl. charts.

510 CN ISSN 0076-5333
MATHEMATICAL EXPOSITIONS. 1946. irreg. price varies. University of Toronto Press, Front Campus, Toronto, Ont. M5S 1A6, Canada (and 33 East Tupper St., Buffalo, N. Y. 14203) (also avail. in microfiche)

510 US
MATHEMATICAL NOTES (PRINCETON) 1966. a. price varies. Princeton University Press, Princeton, NJ 08540. (Co-publisher: University of Tokyo Press) (reprint service avail. from UMI)

519 530.15 NE
MATHEMATICAL PHYSICS AND APPLIED MATHEMATICS. 1976. irreg. price varies. D. Reidel Publishing Co., Box 17, 3300 AA Dordrecht, Netherlands (And Lincoln Building, 160 Old Derby St., Hingham, MA 02043)

510 JA ISSN 0549-4540
MATHEMATICAL SOCIETY OF JAPAN. PUBLICATIONS. (Text in English and European languages) 1955. irreg. Mathematical Society of Japan - Nihon Sugakkai, c/o University of Tokyo, Faculty of Science, 7-3-1 Hongo, Bunkyo-ku, Tokyo 113, Japan.

510 US ISSN 0076-5376
MATHEMATICAL SURVEYS. 1950. irreg., no. 16, 1978. price varies. American Mathematical Society, P.O. Box 6248, Providence, RI 02940. circ. 450. Indexed: Math.R. Zent.Math.

MATHEMATICAL SYSTEMS IN ECONOMICS.
see BUSINESS AND ECONOMICS — Economic Systems And Theories, Economic History

510 US ISSN 0076-5384
MATHEMATICAL TABLE SERIES. 1954. irreg., 1966, vol. 40. price varies. Pergamon Press, Inc., Maxwell House, Fairview Park, Elmsford, NY 10523. index.

510 UK ISSN 0305-7259
MATHEMATICS IN SCHOOL. 1972. 5/yr. £11.50($30) (Mathematical Association) Longman Group Ltd., Journals Division, Fourth Ave., Harlow, Essex, England. Ed. Bd. adv. bk. rev. illus. index.
Study and teaching

510 620 US ISSN 0076-5392
MATHEMATICS IN SCIENCE AND ENGINEERING; series of monographs and textbooks. 1961. irreg., vol. 41, 1979. price varies. Academic Press Inc., 111 Fifth Ave., New York, NY 10003. Ed. Richard E. Bellman.

510.8 US ISSN 0091-7214
MATHEMATICS INTERNATIONAL. 1972. irreg. $36.50 per vol. Gordon and Breach Science Publishers, 1 Park Ave., New York, NY 10016. illus.
  Selected translations from international mathematics literature

510 FR ISSN 0076-5406
MATHEMATIQUES ET SCIENCES DE L'HOMME. 1965. irreg., 1969, no. 9. price varies. Editions de l'Ecole des Hautes Etudes en Sciences Sociales, 24-26 Blvd. de l'Hopital, F-75005 Paris, France.

510 GE ISSN 0076-5430
MATHEMATISCHE LEHRBUECHER UND MONOGRAPHIEN. ABTEILUNG: MATHEMATISCHE MONOGRAPHIEN. 1952. irreg., vol. 41, 1977. price varies. (Akademie der Wissenschaften der DDR, Zentralinstitut fuer Mathematik und Mechanik) Akademie-Verlag, Leipziger Str. 3-4, 108 Berlin, E. Germany (D.D.R.)

510 GE ISSN 0076-5449
MATHEMATISCHE SCHUELERBUECHEREI. 1956. irreg. price varies. VEB Deutscher Verlag der Wissenschaften, Postfach 1216, 108 Berlin, E. Germany (D.D.R.)

510 530 GW
METHODEN UND VERFAHREN DER MATHEMATISCHEN PHYSIK. 1969. irreg., vol. 16, 1976. price varies. Bibliographisches Institut AG, Dudenstr. 6, Postfach 311, 6800 Mannheim 1, W. Germany (B.R.D.) Eds. Bruno Brosowski, Erich Martensen. (back issues avail.)

510 NE
METHODS IN GEOMATHEMATICS. (Text in English) 1976. irreg. Elsevier Scientific Publishing Co., Box 211, 1000 AE Amsterdam, Netherlands. charts.

510.78 US ISSN 0076-9908
MODERN ANALYTIC AND COMPUTATIONAL METHODS IN SCIENCE AND MATHEMATICS. 1963. irreg., 1973, vol. 40. $19.50. Elsevier North-Holland, Inc., New York, 52 Vanderbilt Ave., New York, NY 10017. Ed. Richard Bellman.

510 BL
MONOGRAFIAS DE MATEMATICA. 1969. irreg. price varies. Instituto de Matematica Pura e Aplicada, Rua Luiz de Camoes 68, Rio de Janeiro RJ, Brazil. Ed. Cesar Camacho.

510 PL ISSN 0077-0507
MONOGRAFIE MATEMATYCZNE. (Text in English, French, German and Polish) 1932. irreg., 1976, vol. 57. price varies. (Polska Akademia Nauk, Instytut Matematyczny) Panstwowe Wydawnictwo Naukowe, Miodowa 10, Warsaw, Poland (Dist. by Ars Polona-Ruch, Krakowskie Przedmiescie 7, Warsaw, Poland)

510 RM
MONOGRAFII MATEMATICE. 1973. irreg. 30 lei. Universitatea din Timisoara, Facultatea de Stiinte ale Naturii, Bd. Vasile Pirvan Nr. 4, Timisoara, Romania. Ed. Dumitru Gaspar. circ. 150.

510 UK
MONOGRAPHS AND STUDIES IN MATHEMATICS. no. 2, 1976. irreg. Pitman Publishing Co., 39 Parker St., London WC2B 5PB, England. Ed. Bd.

510 US
MONOGRAPHS ON NUMERICAL ANALYSIS. irreg. price varies. Oxford University Press, 200 Madison Ave., New York, NY 10016 (And Ely House, 37 Dover St., London W1X 4AH, England) Eds. E. T. Goodwin, L. Fox.

510.8 US ISSN 0077-1554
MOSCOW MATHEMATICAL SOCIETY. TRANSACTIONS. English edition of: Moskovskoe Matematicheskoe Obshchestvo. Trudy. 1965. irreg., latest issue 1978. $120 to non-members. American Mathematical Society, Box 6248, Providence, RI 02940. (Co-sponsor: London Mathematical Society) Ed. Ben Silver. circ. 450.

510 UR
MOSKOVSKOE MATEMATICHESKOE OBSHCHESTVO. TRUDY. vol. 34, 1977. irreg. 2.90 Rub. per no. Izdatel'stvo Moskovskii Universitet, Universitetskii Prospekt, 13, Moscow V-234, U.S.S.R. Ed. O. Oleinik. bibl. illus. circ. 1,270.

510 500 NE
N A T O ADVANCED STUDY INSTITUTE SERIES. C: MATHEMATICAL AND PHYSICAL SCIENCES. (Text in English) irreg. price varies. (North Atlantic Treaty Organization, Scientific Affairs Division, BE) D. Reidel Publishing Co., P.O. Box 17, 3300 AA Dordrecht, Netherlands (And Lincoln Building, 160 Old Derby St., Hingham, MA 02043) charts. illus.

510 SI ISSN 0077-2739
NANTA MATHEMATICA. 1966. s-a. $30. Nanyang University, Lee Kong Chian Institute of Mathematics and Computer Science, Jurong Rd., Singapore 2263, Singapore. Ed.Bd. adv. (back issues avail.) Indexed: Math.R. Zent.Math.

510 370 US ISSN 0077-4103
NATIONAL COUNCIL OF TEACHERS OF MATHEMATICS. YEARBOOK. 1926. a. National Council of Teachers of Mathematics, 1906 Association Dr., Reston, VA 22091. circ. controlled. (reprint service avail. from UMI)

510 UN ISSN 0077-8893
NEW TRENDS IN MATHEMATICS TEACHING. (Editions in English, French and Spanish) 1966. irreg; latest issue, 1978. 14 F.($9.25) Unesco, 7-9 Place de Fontenoy, 75700 Paris, France (Dist. in U.S. by: Unipub, 345 Park Ave. S., New York, NY 10010)

511 JA
NIIGATA UNIVERSITY. FACULTY OF SCIENCE. SCIENCE REPORTS. SERIES A: MATHEMATICS. (Text in European languages) 1964. a. exchange basis. Niigata University, Faculty of Science - Niigata Daigaku Rigakubu, 8050 Igarashi Nino-cho, Niigata-shi 950-21, Japan.

510 NE
NORTH-HOLLAND MATHEMATICAL LIBRARY. 1971. irreg., vol. 22, 1979. price varies. North-Holland Publishing Co., Box 211, 1000 AE Amsterdam, Netherlands.

510 NE
NORTH-HOLLAND MATHEMATICS STUDIES. 1970. irreg., vol. 38, 1979. price varies. North-Holland Publishing Co., Box 211, 1000 AE Amsterdam, Netherlands.

620 510 NE ISSN 0066-5460
NORTH-HOLLAND SERIES IN APPLIED MATHEMATICS AND MECHANICS. 1967. irreg., vol. 25, 1979. price varies. North-Holland Publishing Co., Box 211, 1000 AE Amsterdam, Netherlands. Eds. H. A. Lauwerier & W. T. Koiter.

510 AG ISSN 0078-2009
NOTAS DE ALGEBRA Y ANALISIS. (Text in Spanish, French and English) 1966. irreg., 1978, no. 7. price varies. ‡ Universidad Nacional del Sur, Instituto de Matematica, Bahia Blanca, Argentina. circ. 1,000. Indexed: Math.R. Zent.Math.

510 AG ISSN 0078-2017
NOTAS DE LOGICA MATEMATICA. (Text in Spanish, French, English, Portuguese) 1963. irreg., no. 33, 1974. irreg. price varies. ‡ Universidad Nacional del Sur, Instituto de Matematica, Avda. Alem 1253, 8000 Bahia Blanca, Argentina. bibl. circ. 1,000. Indexed: Math.R. Zent.Math.

510 BL ISSN 0085-5413
NOTAS E COMMUNICACOES DE MATEMATICA. (Text in English, French, Portuguese and Spanish) 1965. irreg.; latest issue, no. 50, n.d. price varies. Universidade Federal de Pernambuco, Departamento de Matematica, Edf. dos Institutos Basicos, 50,000 Recife, PE, Brazil.

510 CL
NOTAS MATEMATICAS. English edition: Mathematical Notes. 1972. a. free. Universidad Catolica de Chile, Instituto de Matematicas, Casilla 114-D, Santiago, Chile (Subscr. to: Instituto de Matematica, Vicuna Mackenna 4860, Santiago, Chile) Ed. Alvaro Cofre. circ. 200.

510 AT
NOTES IN PURE MATHEMATICS. irreg. price varies. Australian National University, Department of Pure Mathematics, P.O. Box 4, Canberra, 2600, Australia.

510 US
NOTES ON MATHEMATICS AND ITS APPLICATIONS. a. price varies. Gordon and Breach Science Publishers, One Park Ave., New York, NY 10016. Ed. Jacob T. Schwartz, Maurice Levy.

519 UR
OPTIMIZATSIYA. irreg (approx 5-6/yr) 1 Rub. Akademiya Nauk S.S.S.R., Sibirskoe Otdelenie, Institut Matematiki, Novosibirsk, Akademgorodok, U. S. S. R. Ed. L. V. Vantorovich.

510   US   ISSN 0078-6330
ORGANIZATION OF AMERICAN STATES. DEPARTMENT OF SCIENTIFIC AFFAIRS. SERIE DE MATEMATICA: MONOGRAFIAS. 1965, no. 2. irreg., no. 22, 1979. price varies. Organization of American States, Department of Publications, Washington, DC 20006.

510   US
OXFORD APPLIED MATHEMATICS AND COMPUTING SCIENCE SERIES. irreg. price varies. Oxford University Press, 200 Madison Ave., New York, NY 10016 (And Ely House, 37 Dover St., London W1X 4AH, England) Ed.Bd.

510   US
OXFORD LOGIC GUIDES. irreg. price varies. Oxford University Press, 200 Madison Ave., New York, NY 10016 (And Ely House, 37 Dover St., London W1X 4AH, England) Ed. Dana Scott.

510   US
OXFORD MATHEMATICAL HANDBOOKS. irreg. price varies. Oxford University Press, 200 Madison Ave., New York, NY 10016 (And Ely House, 37 Dover St., London W1X 4AH, England) Eds. John Crank, C. C. Ritchie.

510   US
OXFORD MATHEMATICAL MONOGRAPHS. irreg. price varies. Oxford University Press, 200 Madison Ave., New York, NY 10016 (And Ely House, 37 Dover St., London W1X 4AH, England) Eds. G. Temple, G. Higman.

510   530   CS
PEDAGOGICKA FAKULTA V OSTRAVE. MATEMATIKA, FYZIKA.* (Subseries of its Sbornik Praci; Rada A) (Text in Czech; summaries in English, German, Russian) 1971. irreg. Statni Pedagogicke Nakladatelstvi, Ostrovni 30, 113 01 Prague 1, Czechoslovakia. illus.
    Supersedes in part its Prirodni Vedy a Matematika.

510   US   ISSN 0079-0826
PERGAMON MATHEMATICAL TABLES SERIES.* irreg. price varies. Pergamon Press, Inc., Maxwell House, Fairview Park, Elmsford, NY 10523 (And Headington Hill Hall, Oxford OX3 0BW, England)

160   510   US
PERSPECTIVES IN MATHEMATICAL LOGIC. irreg.; 4th, 1979. price varies. Springer Verlag, 175 Fifth Ave., New York, NY 10010 (And Berlin, Heidelberg, Vienna) Ed.Bd. (reprint service avail. from ISI)

510   US   ISSN 0031-8019
PHILOSOPHIA MATHEMATICA. (Text in English, French and German) 1964. irreg. $12 per yr. Paideia Press, c/o J. Fang, Ed., Philosophy Department, Old Dominion University, Norfolk, VA 23508. adv. bk. rev. circ. 600. Indexed: Phil.Ind.

PHILOSOPHICAL MEMOIRS OF SCIENCES & MATHS. see *SCIENCES: COMPREHENSIVE WORKS*

PHYSICA MATHEMATICA UNIVERSITATIS OSLOENSIS. see *PHYSICS*

510   US
POCKET MATHEMATICAL LIBRARY. 1967. irreg., approx. 1/yr. price varies. Gordon and Breach Science Publishers, One Park Ave., New York, NY 10016. Eds. J. T. Schwartz, R. A. Silverman. charts.

POLISH ACADEMY OF SCIENCES. INSTITUTE OF COMPUTER SCIENCE. REPORTS. see *COMPUTER TECHNOLOGY AND APPLICATIONS*

510   PL
POLISH ACADEMY OF SCIENCES. MATHEMATICAL INSTITUTE. BANACH CENTER PUBLICATIONS. (Text in various languages) 1976. irreg. price varies. Panstwowe Wydawnictwo Naukowe, Miodowa 10, Warsaw, Poland. Ed. Czeslaw Olech.

510   PL   ISSN 0072-0372
POLITECHNIKA GDANSKA. ZESZYTY NAUKOWE. MATEMATYKA. (Text in Polish; summaries in Russian and one West-European language) 1963. irreg. price varies. Politechnika Gdanska, Majakowskiego 11/12, 81-952 Gdansk 6, Poland (Dist. by: Osrodek Rozpowszechniania Wydawnictw Naukowych Pan, Palac Kultury i Nauki, 00-901 Warsaw, Poland)

510   PL
POLITECHNIKA LODZKA. ZESZYTY NAUKOWE. MATEMATYKA. (Text in Polish; summaries in English and Russian) 1961. irreg. price varies. Politechnika Lodzka, Ul. Zwirki 36, 90-924 Lodz, Poland (Dist. by: Ars Polona-Ruch, Krakowskie Przedmiescie 7, Warsaw, Poland) Ed. Izydor Dziubinski. circ. 383. Indexed: Math. R.

510   530   PL   ISSN 0072-470X
POLITECHNIKA SLASKA. ZESZYTY NAUKOWE. MATEMATYKA-FIZYKA. (Text in Polish; summaries in English and Russian) 1961. irreg. price varies. Politechnika Slaska, W. Pstrowskiego 7, 44-100 Gliwice, Poland (Dist. by: Ars Polona, Krakowskie Przedmiescie 7, 00-068 Warsaw, Poland) Ed. Stawomir Konczak. circ. 315.

510   PL   ISSN 0324-9603
POLITECHNIKA WROCLAWSKA. INSTYTUT MATEMATYKI. PRACE NAUKOWE. MONOGRAFIE. (Former Name of Institute: Instytut Matematyki i Fizyki Teoretycznej) (Text in Polish; summaries in English and Russian) 1974. irreg., 1977, no. 4. price varies. Politechnika Wroclawska, Wybrzeze Wyspianskiego 27, 50-370 Wroclaw, Poland (Dist. by: Ars Polona-Ruch, Krakowskie Przedmiescie 7, Warsaw, Poland) Ed. Marian Kloza. circ. 475.

510   530   PL   ISSN 0324-9611
POLITECHNIKA WROCLAWSKA. INSTYTUT MATEMATYKI. PRACE NAUKOWE. STUDIA I MATERIALY. (Former Name of Institute: Instytut Matematyki i Fizyki Teoretycznej) (Text in Polish; summaries in English and Russian) 1970. irreg., 1977, no. 13. price varies. Politechnika Wroclawska, Wybrzeze Wyspianskiego 27, 50-370 Wroclaw, Poland (Dist. by: Ars Polona-Ruch, Krakowskie Przedmiescie 7, Warsaw, Poland) Ed. Marian Kloza.

510   PL   ISSN 0079-368X
POLSKIE TOWARZYSTWO MATEMATYCZNE. ROCZNIKI. SERIA I: COMMENTATIONES MATHEMATICAE. PRACE MATEMATYCZNE. (Text in English, French, German, Polish or Russian; summaries in English, French or Russian) 1955. irreg., 1975, vol. 18, no. 2. $2.25 per no. Panstwowe Wydawnictwo Naukowe, Ul. Miodowa 10, Warsaw, Poland (Dist. by Ars Polona-Ruch, Krakowskie Przedmiescie 7, Warsaw, Poland) Ed. Wladyslaw Orlicz, Julian Musielak. bibl, index.

510   531   UR
POLUTEHNILINE INSTITUUT TALLINN. MATEMATIKA I TEORETICHESKAYA MEKHANIKA. (Subseries of its Toimetised. Seeria A) (Text in Russian; summaries in English or German) irreg. 0.55 Rub. Polutehniline Instituut, Ehitajate tee 5, Tallinn, U.S.S.R.

510   US   ISSN 0079-3841
POPULAR LECTURES IN MATHEMATICS SERIES. 1961. irreg; 1965, vol. 16. price varies. Pergamon Press, Inc., Maxwell House, Fairview Park, Elmsfor, NY 10523. Ed. Straszewicz.

POSTEPY CYBERNETYKI. see *COMPUTER TECHNOLOGY AND APPLICATIONS*

510   PL   ISSN 0079-4686
POZNANSKIE TOWARZYSTWO PRZYJACIOL NAUK. KOMISJA MATEMATYCZNO-PRZYRODNICZA. PRACE. (Text in Polish; summaries in English and French) 1921. irreg. price varies. Poznanskie Towarzystwo Przyjaciol Nauk, Mielzynskiego 27/29, 61-725 Poznan, Poland (Dist by Ars Polona-Ruch, Krakowskie Przedmiescie 7, Warsaw, Poland) Indexed: Chem.Abstr.

510   US   ISSN 0079-4821
PRACTICAL TABLE SERIES. 1958. irreg., 1966, vol. 7. price varies. Pergamon Press, Inc., Maxwell House, Fairview Park, Elmsford, NY 10523. Ed. Attwood. index.

510   US   ISSN 0079-5194
PRINCETON MATHEMATICAL SERIES. 1946. irreg., no. 33, 1971. price varies. Princeton University Press, Princeton, NJ 08540 (and University of Tokyo Press, Tokyo, Japan) (back issues avail.; reprint service avail. from UMI)

PRINCETON STUDIES IN MATHEMATICAL ECONOMICS. see *BUSINESS AND ECONOMICS*

510   US   ISSN 0079-5313
PRINDLE, WEBER AND SCHMIDT COMPLEMENTARY SERIES IN MATHEMATICS.* irreg., 1967, no. 6. Prindle Weber and Schmidt Inc., 20 Newbury St., Boston, MA 02116.

519   US   ISSN 0079-5607
PROBABILITY AND MATHEMATICAL STATISTICS; a series of monographs and textbooks. 1967. irreg., vol. 35, 1978. price varies. Academic Press Inc., 111 Fifth Ave., New York, NY 10003. Eds. Z. W. Birnbaum, E. Lukacs.

510   US
PROBLEM BOOKS IN MATHEMATICS. 1981. irreg., vol. 2, 1982. Springer-Verlag, 175 Fifth Ave., New York, NY 10010 (And Berlin, Heidelberg, Vienna) Ed. P. Halmos.

510   US   ISSN 0079-5739
PROBLEMS IN MATHEMATICAL ANALYSIS REPORT. 1968. irreg., 1971, vol. 2. price varies. Consultants Bureau, Special Research Report (Subsidiary of: Plenum Publishing Corp.) 227 W. 17th St., New York, NY 10011. Ed. V.I. Smirnov.

510   UR
PROBLEMY ISTORII MATEMATIKI I MEKHANIKI. 1972. irreg. 1 Rub. Moskovskii Universitet, Leninskie Gory, Moscow V-234, U.S.S.R. illus.

510   US   ISSN 0079-8169
PURE AND APPLIED MATHEMATICS; a series of monographs and textbooks. 1949. irreg., vol. 62, 1975. price varies. Academic Press Inc., 111 Fifth Ave., New York, NY 10003. Eds. Paul A. Smith, Samuel Eilenberg.

510   US
PURE AND APPLIED MATHEMATICS: A WILEY INTERSCIENCE SERIES OF TEXTS, MONOGRAPHS AND TRACTS. 1948. irreg., latest, 1980. price varies. John Wiley & Sons, Inc., 605 Third Ave., New York, NY 10016. Ed.Bd.
    Formed by the merger of: Interscience Tracts in Pure and Applied Mathematics (ISSN 0074-994X) & Pure and Applied Mathematics; a Series of Texts and Monographs (ISSN 0079-8185)

510   US   ISSN 0079-8177
PURE AND APPLIED MATHEMATICS SERIES. 1970. irreg., vol. 53, 1979. price varies. Marcel Dekker, Inc., 270 Madison Ave., New York, NY 10016. Ed. S. Kobayashi.

510   IT   ISSN 0391-3236
QUADERNI DI ANALISI MATEMATICA. 1977. irreg., no. 2, 1978. price varies. Liguori Editore s.r.l., Via Mezzocannone 19, 80134 Naples, Italy. Eds. Federico Cafiero, Antonio Zitarosa.

510   CN   ISSN 0079-8797
QUEEN'S PAPERS ON PURE AND APPLIED MATHEMATICS. (Text in English and French) 1966. irreg. price varies. ‡ Queen's University, Department of Mathematics, Kingston, Ont. K7L 3N6, Canada. Eds. P. Ribenboim, A. J. Coleman.
    Formerly: Queen's University at Kingston. Department of Mathematics. Research Report (ISSN 0075-6105)

R E C S A M NEWS. (Regional Centre for Education in Science and Mathematics) see *EDUCATION — Teaching Methods And Curriculum*

510   II   ISSN 0079-9602
RANCHI UNIVERSITY MATHEMATICAL JOURNAL. (Text in English) 1970. a. Rs.15($3) Ranchi University, Department of Mathematics, Ranchi 1, Bihar, India. Ed. K. M. Saksena. Indexed: Math.R.

MATHEMATICS

510 375 AT
RHOMBUS. 1973. 4/yr. Mathematical Association of Western Australia, Department of Mathematics, University of Western Australia, Nedlands, WA 6009, Australia. Ed. H. Mansfield.

510 UK
ROYAL IRISH ACADEMY. CONFERENCE ON NUMERICAL ANALYSIS. PROCEEDINGS. no.3,1977. biennial; 3rd 1976. (Royal Irish Academy, IE) Academic Press Inc. (London) Ltd., 24-28 Oval Rd., London NW1 7DX, England (And 111 Fifth Ave., New York, NY 10003) Ed. John H. Miller.

510 500 UK ISSN 0080-4614
ROYAL SOCIETY OF LONDON. PHILOSOPHICAL TRANSACTIONS. SERIES A. MATHEMATICAL AND PHYSICAL SCIENCES. 1665. irreg. £57 per vol. Royal Society of London, 6 Carlton House Terrace, London S.W.1, England. author index every 10 years. (reprint service avail. from ISI) Indexed: Appl.Mech.Rev. Chem.Abstr. Eng.Ind. Math.R. Met.Abstr. Sci.Abstr.

500 510 UK ISSN 0080-4630
ROYAL SOCIETY OF LONDON. PROCEEDINGS. SERIES A. MATHEMATICAL AND PHYSICAL SCIENCES. 1832. irreg. £27.50 per vol. Royal Society of London, 6 Carlton Terrace, London S.W.1, England. author index every 10 yrs. (reprint service avail. from ISI) Indexed: Chem.Abstr. Eng.Ind. Math.R. Met.Abstr. Sci.Abstr.

510 US ISSN 0080-5084
S I A M - A M S PROCEEDINGS. 1959. irreg.(approx. a.) price varies. (Society for Industrial and Applied Mathematics) American Mathematical Society, P.O. Box 6248, Providence, RI 02940. index in each vol. Indexed: Math.R. Zent.Math.
Formerly: American Mathematical Society. Proceedings of Symposia in Applied Mathematics.

SAECHSISCHE AKADEMIE DER WISSENSCHAFTEN, LEIPZIG. MATHEMATISCH-NATURWISSENSCHAFTLICHE KLASSE. ABHANDLUNGEN. see *SCIENCES: COMPREHENSIVE WORKS*

SAECHSISCHE AKADEMIE DER WISSENSCHAFTEN, LEIPZIG. MATHEMATISCH-NATURWISSENSCHAFTLICHE KLASSE. SITZUNGSBERICHTE. see *SCIENCES: COMPREHENSIVE WORKS*

510 530 540 JA ISSN 0558-2431
SAITAMA UNIVERSITY. SCIENCE REPORTS. SERIES A: MATHEMATICS. (Text in English) 1952. a. exchange basis. Saitama University, 255 Shimookubo, Urawa-shi 338, Japan.
Formerly: Saitama University. Science Reports. Series A: Mathematics, Physics and Chemistry (ISSN 0558-2431)

519.5 US ISSN 0094-8837
SELECTED TABLES IN MATHEMATICAL STATISTICS. 1973. irreg. American Mathematical Society, Box 6248, Providence, RI 02940.

510 519 US ISSN 0065-9274
SELECTED TRANSLATIONS IN MATHEMATICAL STATISTICS AND PROBABILITY. 1961. irreg. price varies. (Institute of Mathematical Statistics) American Mathematical Society, P.O. Box 6248, Providence, RI 02940. Ed. Ben Silver. cum.index 1966-1973.

510 RM
SEMINAR ARGHIRIADE. (Text in English, French, German, Romanian) 1974. irreg. 20 lei. Universitatea din Timisoara, Facultatea de Stiinte ale Naturii, Bd. Vasile Pirvan Nr. 4, Timisoara, Romania. Ed. Achim Dragomir. circ. 250. Indexed: Math.R. Zentr.Fur Math.

510 SP ISSN 0085-6029
SEMINARIO MATEMATICO GARCIA DE GALDEANO. PUBLICACIONES. (Text in Spanish and English; summaries in English) 1959. irreg. 300 ptas. Seminario Matematico Garcia de Galdeano, Facultad de Ciencias, Zaragoza, Spain.

510 530 IT ISSN 0391-3252
SERIE DI MATEMATICA E FISICA. 1974. irreg., no. 6, 1980. price varies. Liguori Editore s.r.l., Via Mezzocannone 19, 80134 Naples, Italy. Ed. G. Vidossich.

510 530 IT
SERIE DI MATEMATICA E FISICA. PROBLEMI RISOLTI. 1978. irreg., no. 3, 1979. price varies. Liguori Editore s.r.l., Via Mezzocannone 19, 80134 Naples, Italy. Ed. Livio C. Piccinini.

519 US ISSN 0080-8962
SERIES IN DECISION AND CONTROL. 1966. irreg., unnumbered, latest vol. 1972. price varies. John Wiley & Sons, Inc., 605 Third Ave., New York, NY 10016. Ed. R.A. Howard.

SHINSHU UNIVERSITY. FACULTY OF TEXTILE SCIENCE AND TECHNOLOGY. JOURNAL. SERIES F: PHYSICS AND MATHEMATICS. see *PHYSICS*

510 CE ISSN 0080-956X
SIGMA. (Text in English, Sinhala and Tamil; summaries in English) 1957-58. a. Rs.5. University of Sri Lanka, Senate House, Box 1406, Bauddhaloka Mawatha, Colombo 7, Sri Lanka. Ed.Bd. adv. bk. rev.

510 BU ISSN 0081-1858
SOFIISKI UNIVERSITET. FAKULTET PO MATEMATIKA I MEKHANIKA. GODISHNIK/ L'UNIVERSITE DE SOFIA. FACULTE DES MATHEMATIQUES ET DE MECANIQUE. ANNUAIRE. (Text in Bulgarian and English) irreg. vol. 67, 1972/73. 1.84 lv. price varies. Publishing House of the Bulgarian Academy of Sciences, Ul. Akad. G. Bonchev, 1113 Sofia, Bulgaria. Ed. M. Pecheva. circ. 578.

510 CH
SOOCHOW JOURNAL OF MATHEMATICAL & NATURAL SCIENCES. 1975. irreg. NT.$150($5) per no. Soochow University, Wai Shuang Hsi, Shih Lin, Taipei, Taiwan, Republic of China.

509 US
SOURCES IN THE HISTORY OF MATHEMATICS AND PHYSICAL SCIENCES. 1975. irreg.; vol. 2, 1979. price varies. Springer Verlag, 175 Fifth Ave., New York, NY 10010 (And Berlin, Heidelberg, Vienna) Eds. G. J. Toomer, M. J. Klein. (reprint service avail. from ISI)

510 530 GE ISSN 0081-4113
STAATLICHER MATHEMATISCH-PHYSIKALISCHER SALON, DRESDEN. VEROEFFENTLICHUNGEN. 1960. irreg. price varies. VEB Deutscher Verlag der Wissenschaften, Postfach 1216, E. Germany (D.D.R.), German Democratic Republic. Ed. H. Groetzsch.

510 CN ISSN 0085-6800
STUDENT MATHEMATICS. 1970. a. Can.$0.20. ‡ c/o S. K. Harburn, Ed., Faculty of Education, Rm. 373, University of Toronto, 371 Bloor St. West, Toronto M5S 2R7, Canada. bk. rev. circ. 3,000.

510 PL ISSN 0039-3223
STUDIA MATHEMATICA. (Text in various languages) 1929. irreg., 1975, vol. 54, no. 2. per volume. (Polska Akademia Nauk, Instytut Matematyczny) Panstwowe Wydawnictwo Naukowe, Ul. Miodowa 10, Warsaw, Poland (Dist. by: Ars Polona-Ruch, Krakowskie Przedmiescie 7, Warsaw, Poland) Ed. W. Orlicz. bibl. index. Indexed: Math.R.

511 NE ISSN 0049-237X
STUDIES IN LOGIC AND THE FOUNDATIONS OF MATHEMATICS. 1954. irreg., vol. 101, 1979. price varies. North-Holland Publishing Co., Box 211, 1000 AE Amsterdam, Netherlands. Ed. Bd.

510 US ISSN 0081-8208
STUDIES IN MATHEMATICS. 1962. irreg. $11. Mathematical Association of America, 1225 Connecticut Ave., N.W., Washington, DC 20036 (Dist. by) Prentice-Hall, Inc., Englewood Cliffs, NJ 07810) Ed. C. W. Curtis.

510 US ISSN 0081-8216
STUDIES IN MATHEMATICS. 1963. irreg., no. 7, 1976. (Tata Institute of Fundamental Research, II) Oxford University Press, 200 Madison Ave., New York, NY 10016 (and Ely House, 37 Dover St., London W1X 4AH, England) Ed. M.S. Narasimhan.

510 NE
STUDIES IN MATHEMATICS AND ITS APPLICATIONS. 1975. irreg., vol. 9, 1979. price varies. North-Holland Publishing Co., Box 211, Amsterdam, Netherlands (Dist. in the U.S. and Canada by: Elsevier North-Holland, Inc., New York, 52 Vanderbilt Ave., New York, NY 10017) Eds. J. L. Lions, G. Papanicolaou, R.T. Rockafellar. bibl.

509 US
STUDIES IN THE HISTORY OF MATHEMATICS AND PHYSICAL SCIENCES. 1975. irreg., vol. 5, 1980. price varies. Springer Verlag, 175 Fifth Ave., New York, NY 10010 (And Berlin, Heidelberg, Vienna) Eds. M. J. Klein, G. J. Toomer. (reprint service avail. from ISI)

510 IT ISSN 0082-0725
SYMPOSIA MATHEMATICA. (Contributions in English, French, German and Italian) 1969. irreg., 1972, vol. 9. price varies. Istituto Nazionale di Alta Matematica, Citta Universitaria, Rome, Italy (Dist. by: Academic Press, Inc., 111 Fifth Ave., New York, NY 10003; and 24-28 Oval Rd., London NW7 7DX, England)

510 530 II ISSN 0082-075X
SYMPOSIA ON THEORETICAL PHYSICS AND MATHEMATICS. (Title of Summer School Proceedings varies, Vols. 1 and 2 Called Matscience Summer School. Proceedings) (Text in English) 1963. irreg., 1970, vol. 10. $20. Institute of Mathematical Sciences, Adyar, Madras 20, India.
Represents: Institute of Mathematical Sciences, Madras, India. Proceedings of Symposia and Summer Schools.

519.5 US
SYMPOSIUM ON NONLINEAR ESTIMATION THEORY AND ITS APPLICATIONS. PROCEEDINGS.* 1970. irreg. Western Periodicals Co., 13000 Raymer St., North Hollywood, CA 91605.

510 PL ISSN 0082-1268
SZCZECINSKIE TOWARZYSTWO NAUKOWE. WYDZIAL NAUK MATEMATYCZNO TECHNICZNYCH. PRACE. 1959. irreg. price varies. Panstwowe Wydawnictwo Naukowe, Ul. Miodowa 10, Warsaw, Poland. Ed. H. Lesinski.

510 US
TATA INSTITUTE LECTURE NOTES. 1979. irreg. price varies. (Tata Institute of Fundamental Research, II) Springer-Verlag, 175 Fifth Ave., New York, NY 10010 (Also Berlin, Heidelberg, Vienna) Eds. K.G. Ramanathan, B.V. Sreekantan. (reprint service avail. from ISI)
Supersedes in part: Tata Institute of Fundamental Research. Lectures on Mathematics and Physics (ISSN 0496-9472) & Tata Institute of Fundamental Research. Lectures on Mathematics and Physics. Mathematics (ISSN 0406-6987)

510 US
TATA INSTITUTE STUDIES IN MATHEMATICS. 1978? irreg. price varies. (Tata Institute of Fundamental Research, II) Springer-Verlag, 175 Fifth Ave., New York, NY 10010 (Also Berlin, Heidelberg, Vienna) Ed. K. G. Ramanathan. (reprint service avail. from ISI)

510 UR ISSN 0082-2191
TBILISI UNIVERSITET. INSTITUT PRIKLADNOI MATEMATIKI. SEMINAR. ANNOTATSII DOKLADOV. (Text in Russian; summaries in English and Georgian) 1969. irreg., 1971, no. 4. price varies. Tbilisi Universitet, Chavchavadze Ave., Tbilisi, U.S.S.R. Eds. T. Gegelia, L. Magnaradze. circ. 400.

510 UR
TEORIYA FUNKTSII, FUNKTSIONAL'NYI ANALIZ I IKH PRILOZHENIYA. vol. 27, 1977. irreg. 0.60 Rub. per issue. (Khar'kovskii Gosudarstvennyi Universitet) Izdatel'stvo Vysshaya Shkola-Khar'kov, Universitetskaya 16, 310003 Khar'kov, U.S.S.R. Ed. I. Ostrovskii. abstr. charts. circ. 1,000.

510 UR
TEORIYA FUNKTSII KOMPLEKSNOGO PEREMENNOGO I KRAEVYE ZADACHI. 1972. irreg. 0.80 Rub. Chuvashskii Gosudarstvennyi Universitet, Moskovskii prospekt, 15, Cheboksary, U.S.S.R.

510 UR
TEORIYA SLUCHAINYKH PROTSESSOV. 1973. irreg., no. 3, 1975. 1.38 Rub. (Akademiya Nauk Ukrainskoi S.S.R., Institut Prikladnoi Matematiki i Mekhaniki) Izdatel'stvo Naukova Dumka, Ul. Repina 3, Kiev, U.S.S.R. Ed. I. I. Gikhman. circ. 1,400.

511 530 JA
TOKYO UNIVERSITY OF EDUCATION. FACULTY OF SCIENCE. SCIENCE REPORTS. SECTION A: MATHEMATICS AND PHYSICS/ TOKYO KYOKAI DAIGAKU RIGAKUBU KIYO A. (Text in European languages) 1930. a. exchange basis. Tokyo University of Education, Faculty of Science - Tokyo Kyoiku Daigaku Rigakubu, 3-29-1 Otsuka, Bunkyo-ku, Tokyo 112, Japan.

510 US ISSN 0065-9282
TRANSLATIONS OF MATHEMATICAL MONOGRAPHS. (Chiefly from Russian sources) 1962. irreg. price varies. American Mathematical Society, Box 6248, Providence, RI 02940. Ed. Ben Silver. circ. 400. Indexed: Math.R.

510 US ISSN 0083-1786
U.S. NATIONAL BUREAU OF STANDARDS. APPLIED MATHEMATICS SERIES. 1948. irreg. price varies. U. S. National Bureau of Standards, Washington, DC 20234 (Orders to: Supt. of Documents, Washington, DC 20402)

510 UY
UNIVERSIDAD DE LA REPUBLICA. FACULTAD DE HUMANIDADES Y CIENCIAS. REVISTA. SERIE CIENCIAS EXACTAS. N.S. 1978. irreg. Universidad de la Republica, Facultad de Humanidades y Ciencias, Seccion Revista, Tristan Narvaja 1674, Montevideo, Uruguay. Dir. Beatriz Martinez Osorio.
  Supersedes in part: Universidad de la Republica. Facultad de Humanidades y Ciencias. Revista.

510 UY ISSN 0077-1295
UNIVERSIDAD DE URUGUAY. INSTITUTO DE MATHEMATICA Y ESTADISTICA. PUBLICACIONES DIDACTICAS.* (Text in English or Spanish) 1956. irreg., 1969, no. 2. Universidad de Uruguay, Instituto de Matematica y Estadistica, J. Herrera y Reissig 565, Montevideo, Uruguay.

510 MX
UNIVERSIDAD NACIONAL AUTONOMA DE MEXICO. INSTITUTO DE MATEMATICAS. MONOGRAFIAS. irreg. $4. Universidad Nacional Autonoma de Mexico, Instituto de Matematicas, Nueva Area de la Investigacion Cientifica, Circuito Exterior, Ciudad Universitaria, Mexico 20, D.F., Mexico.

510 310 BL
UNIVERSIDADE FEDERAL DE RIO DE JANEIRO. INSTITUTO DE MATEMATICA. MEMORIAS DE MATEMATICA. (Text in English, French, Spanish, Portuguese; summaries in English) 1971. irreg; no. 104, 1978. $3 (institutions; free to individuals) Universidade Federal do Rio de Janeiro, Instituto de Matematica, C.P. 1835-ZC-00, 21910 Rio de Janeiro RJ, Brazil. Ed.Bd. circ. controlled.

510 BL
UNIVERSIDADE FEDERAL DO RIO DE JANEIRO. INSTITUTO DE MATEMATICA. TEXTOS DE METODOS MATEMATICOS. (Text in language of author) 1972. irreg; no. 14, 1977. $4 (insitutions; free to individuals) Universidade Federal do Rio de Janeiro, Instituto de Matematica, Caixa Postal 1835 ZC-00, 21910 Rio de Janeiro RJ, Brazil.
  Formerly: Universidade Federal do Rio de Janeiro. Instituto de Matematica. Notas de Matematica Fisica.

510 IT ISSN 0035-6298
UNIVERSITA DEGLI STUDI DI PARMA. RIVISTA DI MATEMATICA. (Text in English, French, German, Italian and Spanish) 1950. a. L.40000($50) Universita degli Studi di Parma, Istituto di Matematica, Via Universita 12, 43100 Parma, Italy. Dir. Bianca Manfredi. bk. rev. bibl. charts. index. circ. 500. Indexed: Appl. Mech. Rev. Math.R.

510 GW
UNIVERSITAET GIESSEN. MATEMATISCHES INSTITUT. VORLESUNGEN. (Text in English and German) 1974. irreg. price varies. Universitaet Giessen, Matematisches Institut, Arndt Str. 2, 6300 Giessen, W. Germany (B.R.D.) Ed. F. Timmesfeld.

510 AU
UNIVERSITAET INNSBRUCK. MATHEMATISCHE STUDIEN. (Subseries of: Universitaet Innsbruck. Veroefentlichungen) 1974. irreg. price varies. Oesterreichische Kommissionsbuchhandlung, Maximilian Str. 17, A-6020 Innsbruck, Austria. Ed. Roman Liedl.

510 530 570 RM
UNIVERSITATEA DIN BRASOV. BULETINUL SERIA C. STIINTE ALE NATURII SI PEDAGOGIE. (Text in Romanian; summaries in English, French, German) v. 18, 1976. a. price varies. Universitatea din Brasov, Bd. Gh. Gheorghiu-Dej Nr. 29, Brasov, Romania. bibl. illus.

514 516 RM
UNIVERSITATEA DIN TIMISOARA. FACULTATEA DE STIINTE ALE NATURII. LUCRARILE SEMINARULUI DE GEOMETRIE SI TOPOLOGIE. (Text in English, French, German, Romanian) 1972. irreg. 20 lei. Universitatea din Timisoara, Facultatea de Stiinte ale Naturii, Bd. Vasile Pirvan Nr.4, Timisoara, Romania. Ed. Prof. Dr. I. Papuc. circ. 250.

510 RM
UNIVERSITATEA DIN TIMISOARA. FACULTATEA DE STIINTE ALE NATURII. SEMINARUL DE TEORIA FUNCTIILOR SI MATEMATICI APLICATE. A: SPATII METRICE PROBABILISTE. (Text in English, French, German, Romanian) 1973. irreg. 20 lei. Universitatea din Timisoara, Facultatea de Stiinte ale Naturii, Bd. Vasile Pirvan Nr.4, Timisoara, Romania. Ed. Prof. Dr. Ioan Bitea. circ. 250.

510 RM
UNIVERSITATEA DIN TIMISOARA. FACULTATEA DE STIINTE ALE NATURII. SEMINARUL DE TEORIA FUNCTIILOR SI MATEMATICI APLICATE. B: ANALIZA NUMERICA. (Text in English, French, German, Romanian) 1975. irreg. 20 lei. Universitatea din Timisoara, Facultatea de Stiinte ale Naturii, Bd. Vasile Pirvan Nr.4, Timisoara, Romania. Ed. Prof. Dr. Ioan Bitea. circ. 250.

510 RM
UNIVERSITATEA DIN TIMISOARA. FACULTATEA DE STIINTE ALE NATURII. SEMINARUL DE TEORIA STRUCTURILOR. (Text in English, French, German, Romanian) 1971. irreg. 20 lei. Universitatea din Timisoara, Facultatea de Stiinte ale Naturii, Bd. Vasile Pirvan Nr. 4, Timisoara, Romania. Ed. Prof. Dr. Constantin Popa. circ. 250.

510 BE
UNIVERSITE CATHOLIQUE DE LOUVAIN. INSTITUT DE MATHEMATIQUE PURE ET APPLIQUEE. RAPPORT. (Text and summaries in French and English) 1978. irreg. free. Cabay Libraire-Conseil S.A., Place de l'Agora 11, 1348 Louvain-la-Neuve, Belgium. bibl. charts.

510 FR ISSN 0069-472X
UNIVERSITE DE CLERMONT-FERRAND II. ANNALES SCIENTIFIQUES. SERIE MATHEMATIQUE. 1962. irreg. price varies. Universite de Clermont-Ferrand II, Unite d'Enseignement et de Recherche de Sciences Exactes et Naturelles, B.P. 45, 63170 Aubiere, France. circ. 250. (back issues avail.)

510 FR ISSN 0373-0956
UNIVERSITE SCIENTIFIQUE ET MEDICALE DE GRENOBLE. INSTITUT FOURIER. ANNALES. (Text in English, French and German; Summaries in English and French) 1949. a. 430 F. Universite de Grenoble I (Universite Scientifique et Medicale de Grenoble), Institut Fourier, Boite Postale 116, 38402 Saint-Martin d'Heres, France. Ed. Bd. circ. 1,500. Indexed: Math.R. Zent.Math.

510 NE
UNIVERSITEIT VAN AMSTERDAM. MATHEMATISCH INSTITUUT. REPORT. (Text in English, French, or German) 1970. irreg. exchange basis. ‡ Universiteit van Amsterdam, Mathematisch Instituut, Roetersstraat 15, 1018 WB Amsterdam, Netherlands. Ed. P. van Emde Boas. circ. 250.

510 NZ
UNIVERSITY OF AUCKLAND. DEPARTMENT OF MATHEMATICS. REPORT SERIES. 1971. irreg., no. 168, 1980. free to individuals or on exchange. University of Auckland, Department of Mathematics, Private Bag, Auckland, New Zealand.

510 NO ISSN 0084-778X
UNIVERSITY OF BERGEN. DEPARTMENT OF APPLIED MATHEMATICS. REPORT. (Text in English) 1964. irreg. exchange basis. Universitetet i Bergen, Department of Applied Mathematics, Allegt. 53-55, 5014 Bergen-U, Norway. circ. 100. (processed)

510 CN
UNIVERSITY OF CALGARY. DEPARTMENT OF MATHEMATICS AND STATISTICS. RESEARCH PAPERS. 1966. irreg. University of Calgary, Department of Mathematics and Statistics, Calgary, Alta, Canada. Ed. Dr. K. Varadarajan.
  Formerly: University of Calgary. Department of Mathematics and Computing Science. Research Papers (ISSN 0575-206X)

519 DK
UNIVERSITY OF COPENHAGEN. INSTITUTE OF MATHEMATICAL STATISTICS. LECTURE NOTES. (Text in English) 1972. irreg., no. 3, 1979. price varies. Koebenhavns Universitet, Institut for Matematisk Statistik, 5 Universitetsparken, 2100 Copenhagen OE, Denmark.

UNIVERSITY OF MARYLAND. INSTITUTE FOR FLUID DYNAMICS AND APPLIED MATHEMATICS. PUBLIC LECTURE SERIES. see PHYSICS — Mechanics

510 US ISSN 0076-9665
UNIVERSITY OF MISSOURI, COLUMBIA. MATHEMATICAL SCIENCES TECHNICAL REPORTS. 1964. irreg. free. University of Missouri-Columbia, Columbia, MO 65201.

510 PK
UNIVERSITY OF THE PUNJAB. DEPARTMENT OF MATHEMATICS. JOURNAL OF MATHEMATICS. (Text in English) no. 6, 1973. a. University of the Punjab, Department of Mathematics, New Campus, Lahore, Pakistan. circ. 500.

510 US ISSN 0084-0890
UNIVERSITY OF WISCONSIN. MATHEMATICAL RESEARCH CENTER SERIES. (Published by Wiley since vol. 13; vols. 22 and 23 published by Academic Press) 1964, no. 13. irreg. latest vol. 27. price varies. John Wiley & Sons, Inc, 605 Third Ave., New York, NY 10016.

510 PL
UNIWERSYTET GDANSKI. WYDZIAL MATEMATYKI, FIZYKI, CHEMII. ZESZYTY NAUKOWE. MATEMATYKA. (Text in Polish; summaries in English) 1972. irreg. price varies. Uniwersytet Gdanski, Ul. Czerwonej Armii 110, 81-824 Sopot, Poland. illus.

510 PL ISSN 0083-4386
UNIWERSYTET JAGIELLONSKI. ZESZYTY NAUKOWE. PRACE MATEMATYCZNE.* (Supersedes in part Seria Nauk Matematyczno-Przyrodniczych. Matematyka, Fizyka, Chimia, continuing its volume numbering) (Text in Polish; summaries in French, English, Russian) 1959, no. 5. irreg. price varies. Panstwowe Wydawnictwo Naukowe, Miodowa 10, Warsaw, Poland (Dist. by Ars Polona-Ruch, Krakowskie Przedmiescie 7, Warsaw, Poland)

510 PL
UNIWERSYTET SLASKI W KATOWICACH. PRACE MATEMATYCZNE. (Subseries of its: Prace Naukowe) (Text in Polish; summaries in English) 1969. irreg. available on exchange. Uniwersytet Slaski w Katowicach, Ul. Bankowa 14, 40-007 Katowice, Poland. Ed. Mieczyslaw Kucharzewski. circ. 385.

510 CN ISSN 0382-0718
VECTOR. 1968. irreg. membership. (B.C. Association of Mathematics Teachers) B.C. Teachers' Federation, 105-2235 Burrard St., Vancouver, B. C. V6J 3H9, Canada. illus. Indexed: Can.Educ.Ind.
Formerly: British Columbia Association of Mathematics Teachers. Newsletter (ISSN 0382-0726)

VINCULUM. see EDUCATION — Teaching Methods And Curriculum

510 US
WADSWORTH DEVELOPMENTAL MATHEMATICS SERIES. irreg. Wadsworth Publishing Co., 10 Davis Dr., Belmont, CA 94002.

530 510 GE ISSN 0084-098X
WISSENSCHAFTLICHE TASCHENBUECHER. REIHE MATHEMATIK, PHYSIK. 1965. irreg. price varies. Akademie-Verlag, Leipziger Str. 3-4, 108 Berlin, E. Germany (D.D.R.)

510 CN ISSN 0315-1700
WORLD DIRECTORY OF HISTORIANS OF MATHEMATICS. 1972. irreg. Can.$4. University of Toronto, Department of Mathematics, Toronto, Ont., Canada.

510 JA ISSN 0512-2740
WORLD DIRECTORY OF MATHEMATICIANS. 1958. quadrennial, 6th edt., 1979. $20. Bureau of the World Directory of Mathematicians, c/o Mathematics Dept., Kyoto University, Kyoto 606, Japan.

510 US ISSN 0084-3377
YALE MATHEMATICAL MONOGRAPHS. 1971. irreg., no. 7, 1980. price varies. Yale University Press, 92A Yale Sta., New Haven, CT 06520.

510 531 GE
ZENTRALINSTITUT FUER MATHEMATIK UND MECHANIK. SCHRIFTENREIHE. 1972. irreg. price varies. (Akademie der Wissenschaften der DDR, Zentralinstitut fuer Mathematik und Mechanik) Akademie-Verlag, Leipziger Str. 3-4, 108 Berlin, E. Germany (D.D.R.) Ed. Bd.

MATHEMATICS — Abstracting, Bibliographies, Statistics

510 BL ISSN 0067-6667
BIBLIOGRAFIA BRASILEIRA DE MATEMATICA. 1970. irreg. Cr.$200($10) Instituto Brasileiro de Informacao em Ciencia e Tecnologia, Rio de Janeiro, Brazil. bk. rev. circ. 300.
Supersedes in part: Bibliografia Brasileira de Matematica e Fisica.

512 016 UR
KOLTSA; BIBLIOGRAFIYA. irreg. 0.45 Rub. single issue. Akademiya Nauk S. S. S. R., Sibirskoe Otdelenie, Institut Matematiki, Novosibirsk, Akademgorodok, U.S.S.R.

530 510 US
U S S R REPORT: PHYSICS AND MATHEMATICS. irreg. (approx. 9/yr.) $36. U.S. Joint Publications Research Service, 1000 N. Glebe Rd., Arlington, VA 22201 (Orders to: NTIS, Springfield, VA 22161)
Formerly: U S S R and Eastern Europe Scientific Abstracts: Physics and Mathematics; Which was formed by the merger of: U S S R Scientific Abstracts: Physics and Mathematics; East European Scientific Abstracts: Physics and Mathematics.

UNIVERSIDADE FEDERAL DE RIO DE JANEIRO. INSTITUTO DE MATEMATICA. MEMORIAS DE MATEMATICA. see MATHEMATICS

MECHANICAL ENGINEERING

see Engineering — Mechanical Engineering

MECHANICS

see Physics — Mechanics

MEDICAL SCIENCES

610.7 US ISSN 0092-0371
A. A. M. C. CURRICULUM DIRECTORY. a. Association of American Medical Colleges, One Dupont Circle, N.W., Washington, DC 20036.

A A M C DIRECTORY OF AMERICAN MEDICAL EDUCATION. (Association of American Medical Colleges) see EDUCATION — Higher Education

A.L.Z.A. CONFERENCE SERIES. see BIOLOGY

610 GE ISSN 0065-0315
ABHANDLUNGEN MODERNER MEDIZIN. 1971. irreg., vol. 8, 1976. price varies. Johann Ambrosius Barth Verlag, Salomonstr 18b, 701 Leipzig, E. Germany (D.D.R.) (back issues avail.)

610 US
ABRAHAM FLEXNER LECTURES IN MEDICINE. irreg. price varies. Vanderbilt University Press, Box 1813 Station B, Nashville, TN 37235.

610 IT ISSN 0390-7783
ACCADEMIA DELLE SCIENZE DI SIENA DETTA DE FISIOCRITICI. ATTI. 1760: currently series 14. a. L.15000. Accademia delle Scienze di Siena Detta de Fisiocritici, Piazza S. Agostino 4, 53100 Siena, Italy.
Formerly: Accademia dei Fisiocritici, Siena. Sezione Medico-Fisica (ISSN 0065-0722)

610 IT ISSN 0001-4427
ACCADEMIA MEDICA LOMBARDA. ATTI. (Issued in 4 Vols.) a. L.12000. Accademia Medica Lombarda, Ospedale Policlinico "Paciglione Beretta Est", Via Festa del Perdona 37, 20122 Milan, Italy. bibl. illus. index,cum.index. circ. 1,200. Indexed: Biol.Abstr. Chem.Abstr. Ind. Med.

610 IT
ACCADEMIA MEDICA PISTOIESE "FILIPPO PACINI". BOLLETINO. 1928. a. L.5000($20) ‡ Accademia Medica Pistoiese "Filippo Pacini", Via della Rosa, Pistoia, Italy. Ed. Collatino Cantieri. adv.

615 610 FR
ACCESSOIREX. (Medical accessories available in pharmacies) 1971. a.; with 11 supplements. 262 F. Societe d'Editions Medico-Pharmaceutiques, 26, rue le Brun, 75013 Paris, France. circ. 9,000 (controlled) (looseleaf format; also avail. in microfiche)

ACTA HISTORICA LEOPOLDINA. see SCIENCES: COMPREHENSIVE WORKS

610 IT ISSN 0065-1389
ACTA MEDICAE HISTORIAE PATAVINA. (Text in Italian or language of contributor; summaries in Italian, French, English, German) 1955. a. L.6,000($8.) Universita degli Studi di Padova, Istituto di Storia della Medicina, Via Fallopia 50, 35100 Padua, Italy. Ed. Loris Premuda. index in vol. 10. circ. 250.
History

ACTA PATHOLOGICA ET MICROBIOLOGICA SCANDINAVICA. SECTION A: PATHOLOGY. SUPPLEMENTUM. see BIOLOGY

ACTUALITES BIBLIOGRAPHIQUES EN MEDECINE, PHARMACIE ET SCIENCES BIOMEDICALES. see BIBLIOGRAPHIES

636.089 610 AT ISSN 0065-1907
ADELAIDE. INSTITUTE OF MEDICAL AND VETERINARY SCIENCE. ANNUAL REPORT OF THE COUNCIL. 1937/38. a. free. Institute of Medical and Veterinary Science, Frome Rd, Adelaide, S.A., Australia. Ed. Dr. R. G. Edwards.

ADVANCES IN BIOLOGICAL AND MEDICAL PHYSICS. see BIOLOGY — Biophysics

612.015 574.192 US ISSN 0065-2571
ADVANCES IN ENZYME REGULATION. 1963. a. $94. Pergamon Press, Inc., Journals Division, Maxwell House, Fairview Park, Elmsford, NY 10523. Ed. George Weber. adv. (also avail. in microform from MIM,UMI) Indexed: Ind.Med.

ADVANCES IN EXPERIMENTAL MEDICINE AND BIOLOGY. see BIOLOGY

610 US
ADVANCES IN INFLAMMATION RESEARCH. 1979. irreg. price varies. Raven Press, 1140 Ave. of the Americas, New York, NY 10036. Ed. Gerald Weissmann. Indexed: Curr.Cont.

616.026 US ISSN 0065-2822
ADVANCES IN INTERNAL MEDICINE. 1954. a. price varies. ‡ Year Book Medical Publishers, Inc., 35 E. Wacker Dr., Chicago, IL 60601. Indexed: Ind.Med.
Internal medicine

ADVANCES IN MEDICAL SOCIAL SCIENCE: HEALTH AND ILLNESS AS VIEWED BY ANTHROPOLOGY, GEOGRAPHY, HISTORY, PSYCHOLOGY AND SOCIOLOGY. see SOCIAL SCIENCES: COMPREHENSIVE WORKS

ADVANCES IN POLYAMINE RESEARCH. see BIOLOGY — Biological Chemistry

ADVANCES IN THE BIOSCIENCES. see BIOLOGY

616.98 US ISSN 0065-3683
AEROMEDICAL REVIEWS. 1958. irreg., latest issue, 1975. U.S. Air Force, School of Aerospace Medicine, Aeromedical Library (SUL-2), Brooks Air Force Base, TX 78235. (also avail. in microfiche) Indexed: Ind.Med.
Military

616.98 US ISSN 0065-3764
AEROSPACE MEDICAL ASSOCIATION. ANNUAL SCIENTIFIC MEETING; PREPRINTS. 1963. a. price varies. Aerospace Medical Association, Washington National Airport, Washington, DC 20001. Ed. Fred Stoffel.
Aerospace medicine

610 PL ISSN 0067-6489
AKADEMIA MEDYCZNA, BIALYSTOK. ROCZNIK. (Summaries in Russian and English) 1955. a. Panstwowy Zaklad Wydawnictw Lekarskich, Dluga 38-40, Warsaw, Poland.

610 YU ISSN 0350-0071
AKADEMIJA NAUKA I UMJETNOSTI BOSNE I HERCEGOVINE. ODELJENJE MEDICINSKIH NAUKA. RADOVI. vol. 57, 1975. irreg. Akademija Nauka i Umjetnosti Bosne i Hercegovine, Odeljenje Medicinskih Nauka, Obala Vojvode Stepe 42, Sarajevo, Yugoslavia.

610 GW ISSN 0340-1901
AKTUELLE PROBLEME DER INTENSIVMEDIZIN/CURRENT TOPICS IN INTENSIVE CARE MEDICINE. (Text in English, French, German) 1974. irreg. price varies. Dr. Dietrich Steinkopff Verlag, Saalbaustr. 12, Postfach 11 1008, 6100 Darmstadt 11, W. Germany (B.R.D.) Eds. K.-D. Grosser, E. Glaser.

612 574 DK ISSN 0065-6186
ALFRED BENZON SYMPOSIUM. PROCEEDINGS. 1969. irreg. price varies. Munksgaard, 35 Noerre Soegade, DK-1370 Copenhagen K, Denmark (Dist. in U.S. by: Academic Press Inc., 171 First Ave., Atlantic Highlands, NJ 07716) (reprint service avail. from ISI)

610 574 US ISSN 0589-1019
ALLIANCE FOR ENGINEERING IN MEDICINE AND BIOLOGY. PROCEEDINGS OF THE ANNUAL CONFERENCE. vol. 1, covering 12th conference, 1959. a. $15 to non-members; members $10. Alliance for Engineering in Medicine & Biology, c/o Susan Fletcher, 4405 East-West Hwy., Suite 404, Bethesda, MD 20014. circ. 3,000. Indexed: Chem.Abstr. Eng.Ind.

ALLIED HEALTH EDUCATION DIRECTORY. see EDUCATION — Guides To Schools And Colleges

MEDICAL SCIENCES

388.3 610   US   ISSN 0401-6351
AMERICAN ASSOCIATION FOR AUTOMOTIVE MEDICINE. PROCEEDINGS. 1959. a. American Association for Automotive Medicine, Box 222, Morton Grove, IL 60053. Ed. Norman E. McSwain, Jr., M.D.

616.07 574.2 589.9   US   ISSN 0065-7298
AMERICAN ASSOCIATION OF PATHOLOGISTS AND BACTERIOLOGISTS. SYMPOSIUM. MONOGRAPHS. Williams & Wilkins Co., 428 E. Preston St., Baltimore, MD 21202. Ed. Nathan Kaufman.

616.98   US   ISSN 0065-7778
AMERICAN CLINICAL AND CLIMATOLOGICAL ASSOCIATION. TRANSACTIONS. 1881. a. $20. American Clinical and Climatological Association, c/o Richard Johns, M.D., Sec-Treas., Johns Hopkins Medical School, 720 Rutland Ave., Baltimore, MD 21205. Ed. Dr. Theodore J. Abernethy. circ. 500. Indexed: Ind.Med.

    US
AMERICAN COLLEGE OF PHYSICIANS. DIRECTORY. 1929. biennial. per no. ‡ American College of Physicians, 4200 Pine St., Philadelphia, PA 19104.

610 534   US   ISSN 0065-8871
AMERICAN INSTITUTE OF ULTRASOUND IN MEDICINE. ANNUAL SCIENTIFIC CONFERENCE. PROGRAM. a. $7.50 to non-members. American Institute of Ultrasound in Medicine, Attn. Michael Meinerz, Executive Office, 4405 East-West Hwy., Suite 504, Washington, DC 20014. Ed. Robin Heydman. adv. bk. rev. circ. 6,500.

AMERICAN LECTURES IN ANATOMY. see BIOLOGY

AMERICAN LECTURES IN CLINICAL MICROBIOLOGY. see BIOLOGY — Microbiology

610   US
AMERICAN LECTURES IN MEDICAL WRITING AND COMMUNICATION. irreg. price varies. Charles C. Thomas, Publisher, 301-327 E. Lawrence Ave., Springfield, IL 62717.

610 500   US
AMERICAN LECTURES IN THE HISTORY OF MEDICINE AND SCIENCE. irreg. price varies. Charles C. Thomas, Publisher, 301-327 E. Lawrence Ave., Springfield, IL 62717.
History

610   US   ISSN 0147-2291
AMERICAN MEDICAL ASSOCIATION. DIRECTORY OF ACCREDITED RESIDENCIES. 1914. biennial. $3.50. American Medical Association, 535 N. Dearborn St., Chicago, IL 60611. Ed. Rose Tracy.
Former titles: American Medical Association. Directory of Approved Residencies; American Medical Association. Directory of Approved Internships and Residencies.

610   US   ISSN 0569-6534
AMERICAN MEDICAL ASSOCIATION. DIRECTORY OF OFFICIALS AND STAFF. 1960. a. American Medical Association, 535 N. Dearborn St., Chicago, IL 60610. circ. controlled.

610   US   ISSN 0065-9339
AMERICAN MEDICAL DIRECTORY. 1906. irreg., 27th ed., 1978. $210 for 4 vols. American Medical Association, 535 N. Dearborn St, Chicago, IL 60610.

610   SA   ISSN 0066-1279
AMOEBA.* 1952. irreg. University of Natal, Faculty of Medicine, P.O. Box 39, Congella, Durban, Natal, South Africa. Ed. O. M. Munyaradzi.

610   NE   ISSN 0066-1368
ANALECTA BOERHAAVIANA. 1959. irreg., no. 8, 1979. price varies. E. J. Brill, Oude-Rijn 33a-35, Leiden, Netherlands. Ed. G. A. Lindeboom.

610   SP
ANALES DE LA UNIVERSIDAD HISPALENSE. SERIE: MEDICINAS. irreg. price varies. Universidad de Sevilla, San Fernando 4, Seville, Spain. charts, illus.

610   SP   ISSN 0517-6832
ANALES DE MEDICINA. ESPECIALIDADES. 1907. Academia de Ciencies Mediques de Catalunya i de Balears, 551 Paseo de la Bonanova 47, Barcelona 6, Spain.
Supersedes in part (since 1953): Anales de Medicina (ISSN 0003-2514)

610   SP   ISSN 0517-6824
ANALES DE MEDICINA. MEDICINA. 1907. Academia de Ciencies Mediques de Catalunya i de Balears, Paseo de la Bonanova 47, Barcelona 6, Spain.
Supersedes in part (since 1953): Anales de Medicina (ISSN 0003-2514)

ANATOMISCHE GESELLSCHAFT. VERHANDLUNGEN. see *BIOLOGY*

610   PL   ISSN 0066-1945
ANNALES ACADEMIAE MEDICAE STETINENSIS.* 1951. a. Panstwowy Zaklad Wydawnictw Lekarskich, Ul. Dluga 38-40, Warsaw, Poland. Indexed: Ind.Med.

610   FI   ISSN 0066-1996
ANNALES ACADEMIAE SCIENTIARUM FENNICAE. SERIES A, 5: MEDICA. (Text in English, French, German) 1943. irreg. price varies. Suomalainen Tiedeakatemia - Academia Scientiarum Fennica, Snellmanink. 9-11, 00170 Helsinki 17, Finland. Ed. Osmo Jarvi. circ. 400. (also avail. in microform; back issues avail.; reprint service avail. from UMI) Indexed: Biol.Abstr. Bull.Signal. Chem.Abstr. Excerp.Med. Ind.Med. Ref.Zh.

610   PL   ISSN 0066-2240
ANNALES UNIVERSITATIS MARIAE CURIE-SKLODOWSKA. SECTIO D. MEDICINA. (Text in Polish; summaries in English, table of contents in English and Russian) 1946. a. price varies. Uniwersytet Marii Curie-Sklodowskiej, Plac Marii Curie-Sklodowskiej 5, 20-031 Lublin, Poland. Ed. Stanislaw Bryc. Indexed: Biol.Abstr. Chem.Abstr. Ind.Med. Int.Abstr.Biol.Sci.

ANNALS OF CLINICAL RESEARCH. SUPPLEMENTUM. see *MEDICAL SCIENCES — Experimental Medicine, Laboratory Technique*

610   FR
ANNUAIRE DES STATIONS THERMALES ET CLIMATIQUES ET DES ETABLISSEMENTS MEDICAUX FRANCAIS. 1854. a. Expansion Scientifique, 15 rue Saint Benoit, 75278 Paris Cedex 06, France. adv.
Formerly: Annuaire des Stations Hydro-Minerales, Climatiques, et Balneaires de France et des Etablissements Medicaux (ISSN 0066-2941)

610   FR   ISSN 0066-3298
ANNUAIRE MEDICAL DE L'HOSPITALISATION FRANCAISE. (Includes supplement: Vademecum) 1949. a. 200. Edi-Publi-France, 8 rue Blanche, 75009 Paris, France.

610   FR
ANNUAIRE MEDICAL DU DR. PORCHERON ET PROF. G. BELTRAMI. 1912. a. free to qualified personnel. SO-GE-CO-PRO S.A.R.L, 20-26 rue Caisserie, 13235 Marseille Cedex 1, France. adv.

615.8   FR   ISSN 0066-3301
ANNUAIRE NATIONAL DE LA KINESITHERAPIE. 1969. a. 70 F. Editions Louis Johanet, 68 rue Boursault, Paris 17e, France.
Physiotherapy

610   FR   ISSN 0337-5935
ANNUAIRE NATIONAL DES MASSEURS KINESITHERAPEUTES. vol. 2, 1975. a. Federation Francaise des Masseurs-Kinesitherapeutes Reeducateurs., 9 rue des Petits-Hotels, 75010 Paris, France.
Continues: Annuaire National M.K.D.E. France (ISSN 0337-5927)

ANNUAL EDITIONS: READINGS IN HUMAN DEVELOPMENT. see *BIOLOGY — Physiology*

610   US
ANNUAL REVIEW OF MEDICINE: SELECTED TOPICS IN THE CLINICAL SCIENCES. 1950. a. $20. Annual Reviews Inc., 4139 El Camino Way, Palo Alto, CA 94306. Ed. William P. Creger. cum.index. (back issues avail.; reprint service avail. from ISI) Indexed: Biol.Abstr. Chem.Abstr. Ind.Med. Psychol.Abstr. M.M.R.I.
Formerly: Annual Review of Medicine (ISSN 0066-4219)

610   IT
ANTHOLOGIA MEDICA SANTORIANA. a. price varies. Giardini Editori e Stampatori, Via Santa Bibbiana 28, 56100 Pisa, Italy. Ed. Marcello Comel.

610   CL
ANUARIO ENFERMEDADES DE NOTIFICACION OBLIGATORIA. a. Ministerio de Salud, Departamento de Planificacion, Santiago, Chile.

610   NE
APPLIED METHODS IN ONCOLOGY. 1978. irreg. price varies. Elsevier North-Holland Biomedical Press, Box 211, 1000 AE Amsterdam, Netherlands.

610 574   GW   ISSN 0066-5665
ARBEITEN AUS DEM PAUL-EHRLICH-INSTITUT, DEM GEORG-SPEYER-HAUS UND DEM FERDINAND-BLUM-INSTITUT. a. price varies. Gustav Fischer Verlag, Wollgrasweg 49, Postfach 720143, 7000 Stuttgart 70, W. Germany (B.R.D.) Indexed: Ind.Med.

616 331.822   GE   ISSN 0066-5843
ARBEITSMEDIZIN; Abhandlungen ueber Berufskrankheiten und deren Verhuetung. 1935. irreg., no. 34, 1968. price varies. Johann Ambrosius Barth Verlag, Salomonstr. 18b, 701 Leipzig, E. Germany (D.D.R.) Ed. E. Holstein.

610   GW   ISSN 0342-1694
ARCHIV FUER ARZNEITHERAPIE. (Text in English and German) 1976. 2-3/yr. price varies. Duncker und Humblot, Dietrich-Schaefer-Weg 9, 1000 Berlin 41, W. Germany (B.R.D.) Ed. Dr. Hans Braun. adv. bk. rev. charts. illus.

610   MX   ISSN 0066-6521
ARCHIVALIA MEDICA.* 1963. irreg. Mex.$15.($1.20) Universidad Nacional Autonoma de Mexico, Facultad de Medicina, Ciudad Universitaria, Villa Obregon, Mexico 20, D.F., Mexico.

616.07   IT   ISSN 0004-0061
ARCHIVIO DE VECCHI; per l'anatomia patologica e la medicina clinica. 1938. irreg. L.24000. Grafica Toscana, Via Mannelli 29R, 50132 Florence, Italy. Ed. Prof. Antonio Costa. bibl. charts. illus. index. circ. 1,000. Indexed: Biol.Abstr. Chem.Abstr. Ind.Med.
Pathology

ARKANSAS. DIVISION OF REHABILITATION SERVICES. ANNUAL REPORT. see *SOCIAL SERVICES AND WELFARE*

616.07   PO   ISSN 0066-7854
ARQUIVOS DE PATOLOGIA GERAL E ANATOMIA PATOLOGICA. (Text in Portuguese; summaries in English and French) 1913. a. available on exchange. Universidade de Coimbra, Instituto de Anatomia Patologica, 3049 Coimbra Codex, Portugal. Ed. Renato Trincao. circ. 400.
Pathology

610 572   SP   ISSN 0210-4466
ASCLEPIO; archivo iberoamericano de historia de la medicina. 1949. a. 480 ptas. (Instituto Arnau de Vilanova) Consejo Superior de Investigaciones Cientificas, Vitrubio 16, Madrid 6, Spain. Ed. Pedro Lain Entralgo. bk. rev. bibl. cum.index: 1949-1973.
History

610.7   MX   ISSN 0004-4857
ASOCIACION MEXICANA DE FACULTADES Y ESCUELAS DE MEDICINA. BOLETIN. 1962. irreg. free. Asociacion Mexicana de Facultades y Escuelas de Medicina, Av. V. Carranza 870 Despacho 15, Apdo. Postal 836, San Luis Potosi, Mexico. Ed. Dr. Miguel R. Barrios Zubiaga. bibl. charts. illus. index. circ. 750 (approx.)
Study and teaching

610 IS
ASSIA. (Text in Hebrew and English) vol. 4, 1976. irreg. $15. Shaare Zedek Hospital, Falk Schlesinger Institute for Medical Halachic Research, Box 293, Jerusalem, Israel. Ed. Dr. Avraham Steinberg. bk. rev. abstr. circ. 750.

610 FR
ASSISES DE MEDECINE. a. free. Expansion Scientifique, 15, rue St. Benoit, 75278 Paris Cedex 06, France.

610 US ISSN 0066-9458
ASSOCIATION OF AMERICAN PHYSICIANS. TRANSACTIONS. 1886. a. $20 domestic; $21 foreign. William J. Dornan, Inc., Willows Ave., Collingdale, PA 19023. Ed. Dr. K. Frank Austin. Indexed: Ind.Med.

ASSOCIATION OF LIFE INSURANCE MEDICAL DIRECTORS OF AMERICA. TRANSACTIONS. see INSURANCE

610 UK ISSN 0067-2130
AUSTRALIAN SOCIETY FOR MEDICAL RESEARCH. PROCEEDINGS. 1961. a. $1. Blackwell Scientific Publications Ltd., Osney Mead, Oxford OX2 OEL, England. Ed. Bd. adv. (back issues avail.; reprint service avail. from ISI)

AVIATION MEDICAL EDUCATION SERIES. see AERONAUTICS AND SPACE FLIGHT

610 IT
AVVENIRE MEDICO. a. price varies. Giardini Editori e Stampatori, Via Santa Bibbiana 28, 56100 Pisa, Italy.

610 574 SZ ISSN 0067-4524
BASLER VEROEFFENTLICHUNGEN ZUR GESCHICHTE DER MEDIZIN UND DER BIOLOGIE. 1953. irreg., no. 32, 1979. price varies. ‡ Schwabe und Co. AG, Steinentorstr. 13, 4010 Basel, Switzerland. Ed. Heinrich Buess. index.

610 US ISSN 0067-4672
BAYER-SYMPOSIEN. (Text in English) 1969. irreg., vol. 7, 1979. price varies. (Bayer AG, GW) Springer-Verlag, 175 Fifth Avenue, New York, NY 10010 (also Berlin, Heidelberg, Vienna) (reprint service avail. from ISI)

610 GW ISSN 0301-0457
BEHRING INSTITUT. MITTEILUNGEN. irreg. price varies. (Behring-Werke, Marburg) C. H. Beck'sche Verlagsbuchhandlung, Wilhelmstr. 9, 8000 Munich 40, W. Germany (B.R.D.)
Formerly: Behring-Werke. Mitteilungen (ISSN 0067-4885)

BEITRAEGE ZUR PSYCHOLOGIE UND SOZIOLOGIE DES KRANKEN MENSCHEN. see PSYCHOLOGY

BENCHMARK PAPERS IN HUMAN PHYSIOLOGY. see BIOLOGY — Physiology

611 574.4 SZ ISSN 0067-7833
BIBLIOTHECA ANATOMICA. (Text in English, French and German) 1961. irreg. (approx. 1/yr.) 100 Fr.($60) per vol. (1981 price) S. Karger AG, Allschwilerstrasse 10, P.O. Box, CH-4009 Basel, Switzerland. Ed. G. Wolf-Heidegger. (reprint service avail. from ISI) Indexed: Biol.Abstr. Chem.Abstr. Curr.Cont. Ind.Med.
Anatomy

BIOCHEMISTRY OF DISEASE. see BIOLOGY — Biological Chemistry

610 US
BIOMEDICAL COMPUTING SERIES. irreg. price varies. Research Studies Press, Box 92, 2130 Pacific Ave., Forest Grove, OR 97116. Ed. D.W. Hill.

610.28 614 US
BIOMEDICAL ENGINEERING AND HEALTH SYSTEMS: A WILEY-INTERSCIENCE SERIES. (Issues not published consecutively) 1968. irreg., unnumbered, latest, 1979. price varies. John Wiley & Sons, Inc., 605 Third Ave., New York, NY 10016. Ed. John H. Milsum.
Formerly: Biomedical Engineering Series of Monographs (ISSN 0067-8848)
Biomedical engineering

610 574 US
BIOMEDICAL MATERIALS RESEARCH SYMPOSIA. irreg., no. 7, 1976. price varies. John Wiley & Sons, Inc., 605 Third Ave., New York, NY 10016.

610.28 US ISSN 0067-8856
BIOMEDICAL SCIENCES INSTRUMENTATION. 1963. a. since 1974. price varies. Instrument Society of America, 400 Stanwix Street, Pittsburgh, PA 15222. Indexed: Appl.Mech.Rev. Ind.Med.
Medical instrumentation

616.043 US
BIRTH DEFECTS INSTITUTE. SYMPOSIA. 1972. a. price varies. Academic Press, Inc., 111 Fifth Ave., New York, NY 10003. Ed. Ernest B. Hook.
Congenital defects

616.043 US ISSN 0547-6844
BIRTH DEFECTS ORIGINAL ARTICLE SERIES. irreg., vol. 16, 1980. price varies. (March of Dimes Birth Defects Foundation) Alan R. Liss, Inc., 150 Fifth Ave., New York, NY 10011. Indexed: Ind.Med.
Congenital defects.

610 NE
BOERHAAVE SERIES FOR POSTGRADUATE MEDICAL EDUCATION. 1969. irreg., vol. 13, 1978. price varies. Leiden University Press, c/o Martinus Nijhoff, Box 566, 2501 CN The Hague, Netherlands.
Study and teaching

610 574 MX ISSN 0067-9666
BOLETIN DE ESTUDIOS MEDICOS Y BIOLOGICOS. (Some articles in English) irreg.; latest issue, 1974. $20. Universidad Nacional Autonoma de Mexico, Instituto de Investigaciones Bibliograficas, Apdo. Postal 29124, Mexico 1, D.F., Mexico. (Co-sponsor: Biblioteca Nacional) Ed. Dr. Alfonso Escobar. bk. rev. Indexed: Biol.Abstr. Excerp.Med. Ind.Med.

610 CN ISSN 0707-0462
BRITISH COLUMBIA. MEDICAL SERVICES PLAN. PHYSICIAN'S NEWSLETTER. 1977. Medical Services Plan, Box 1600, Victoria, B.C. V8V 2X9, Canada.

616.96 574.524 BU ISSN 0068-371X
BULGARSKA AKADEMIIA NA NAUKITE. TSENTRALNA KHELMINTOLOGICHNA LABORATORIIA. IZVESTIIA. (Summaries in various languages) 1955. a. 1.97 lv. Publishing House of the Bulgarian Academy of Sciences, Ul. Akad. G. Bonchev, 1113 Sofia, Bulgaria (Dist. by: Hemus, 6, Rouski Blvd., 1000 Sofia, Bulgaria) circ. 500.
Helminthology

610 US ISSN 0590-4129
C P T. (Physicians' Current Procedural Terminology) 1966. irreg., 4th ed., 1977. $12. American Medical Association, 535 N. Dearborn St, Chicago, IL 60610. (also avail. in microfiche)
Formerly (1st & 2nd eds.): Current Procedural Terminology (ISSN 0065-9312)

CALENDAR OF INTERNATIONAL AND REGIONAL CONGRESSES OF MEDICAL SCIENCES. see MEETINGS AND CONGRESSES

610 CN ISSN 0381-2561
CANADA HEALTH MANPOWER INVENTORY. (Text in English and French) 1969. a. free. Department of National Health and Welfare, Health Economics & Statistics Division, Jeanne Mance Bldg, Tunney's Pasture, Ottawa, Ont. K1A 1B4, Canada. stat. circ. 1,200.

610 CN ISSN 0068-9203
CANADIAN MEDICAL DIRECTORY. 1955. a. Can.$39. Southam Communications Ltd., 1450 Don Mills Rd., Don Mills, Ont. M3B 2X7, Canada.

CANADIAN REHABILITATION COUNCIL FOR THE DISABLED. ANNUAL REPORT. see EDUCATION — Special Education And Rehabilitation

362.1 CN
CATHOLIC HEALTH ASSOCIATION OF CANADA. DIRECTORY. (Text in English and French) 1968. a. Catholic Health Association of Canada, 312 Daly Ave., Ottawa K1N 6G7, Canada.
Formerly: Catholic Hospital Association of Canada. Directory (ISSN 0380-8475)

616 JA ISSN 0078-6632
CENTER FOR ADULT DISEASES, OSAKA. ANNUAL REPORT. (Text in English) 1961. a. free. Center for Adult Diseases, Osaka, 1-3-3 Nakanoshi, Higashinari-ku, Osaka 537, Japan. Ed. Nobuyuki Senda, M.D.

610 FR ISSN 0069-1879
CENTRE D'INFORMATION DES SERVICES MEDICAUX D'ENTREPRISES ET INTERENTREPRISES. ANNUAIRE. 1965. irreg. 30 F. Centre d'Information des Services Medicaux d' Entreprises et Interentreprises, 31 rue Mederic, 75821 Paris Cedex 17, France.

614 AG
CENTRO LATINOAMERICANO DE ADMINISTRACION MEDICA. TRADUCCIONES. 1973. irreg. (Organizacion Panamericana de la Salud, UN) Centro Latinoamericano de Administracion Medica, Av. Cordoba 2351, Buenos Aires, Argentina.

CHICAGO HISTORY OF SCIENCE AND MEDICINE. see HISTORY

CHINESE JOURNAL OF PHYSIOLOGY. see BIOLOGY — Physiology

610 US ISSN 0084-8786
CIBA COLLECTION OF MEDICAL ILLUSTRATIONS. 1953. irreg., vol. 7, 1979. price varies. CIBA Pharmaceutical Co., Medical Education Division, 556 Morris Ave., Summit, NJ 07901. illus. (avail. on slides)

610 SP
CIENCIAS MEDICAS BOLSILLO. 1977. irreg., no. 11, 1979. price varies. Ediciones Universidad de Navarra, S.A., Plaza de los Sauces 1 y 2, Baranain, Pamplona, Spain.

610 NE
CLINCAL THERAPEUTICS. 1978. irreg. $26 for 6 issues. Excerpta Medica, Box 211, 1000 AE Amsterdam, Netherlands.

CLINICAL AND BIOCHEMICAL ANALYSIS. see BIOLOGY — Biological Chemistry

610 US ISSN 0191-7870
CLINICAL BIOMECHANICS. 1971. irreg. Clinical Biomechanics Corp., Box 35185, Los Angeles, CA 90035.

610.28 US
CLINICAL ENGINEERING SERIES. irreg. Academic Press, Inc., 111 Fifth Ave., New York, NY 10003. Eds. Cesar A. Caceres.
Biomedical engineering

610 NE
CLINICAL STUDIES. 1971. irreg., vol. 5, 1974. Elsevier North-Holland Biomedical Press, Box 211, 1000 AE Amsterdam, Netherlands. Ed. Bd.

610 SP
COLECCION MEDICINA. 1974. irreg.; 1979, no. 9. price varies. (Universidad de Navarra, Facultad de Medicina) Ediciones Universidad de Navarra, S.A., Plaza de los Sauces, 1 y 2, Baranain, Pamplona, Spain.

610 CN
COLLEGE OF PHYSICIANS AND SURGEONS OF BRITISH COLUMBIA. ANNUAL REPORT. a. membership. College of Physicians and Surgeons of British Columbia, 1807 W. 10th Ave., Vancouver, B.C. V6J 2A9, Canada.

610 CN ISSN 0069-5726
COLLEGE OF PHYSICIANS AND SURGEONS OF BRITISH COLUMBIA. MEDICAL DIRECTORY. a. Can.$27.50. College of Physicians and Surgeons of British Columbia, 1807 W. 10th Ave., Vancouver, B.C. V6J 2A9, Canada.

MEDICAL SCIENCES

610   US
COLOR ATLAS SERIES. (All vols. originally published in UK series: Wolfe Medical Atlases) irreg., latest 1979. Year Book Medical Publishers, Inc., 35 Wacker Dr., Chicago, IL 60601.
Formerly: Year Book Color Atlas Series.

614   US   ISSN 0094-1336
COMPREHENSIVE HEALTH PLAN FOR NEW JERSEY. 1974. a. New Jersey Comprehensive Health Planning Agency, John Fitch Plaza, Box 1540, Trenton, NJ 08625. illus.

615.8   FR   ISSN 0071-2817
CONFEDERATION EUROPEENE POUR LA THERAPIE PHYSIQUE. CONGRESS REPORTS. irreg., 1971, 14th, Strasbourg. European Confederation for Physical Therapy, 11 rue des Petits - Hotels, 75010 Paris, France.
Physiotherapy

610   MQ   ISSN 0414-4406
CONGRESS INTERNATIONAL MEDICAL DE PAYS DE LANGUE FRANCAISE DE L'HEMISPHERE AMERICAIN. RAPPORTS ET COMMUNICATIONS. 1951. biennial. price varies. Societe Medicale des Antilles et Guyane Francaises, Section Martiniquaise, 35 rue Victor Severe, Fort de France, Martinique. circ. 1,000.

616.07   574.2   MZ
CONGRESSO NACIONAL DE ANATOMIA PATOLOGICAS. ACTAS. 1968. irreg. avail. on exchange. Universidade Eduardo Mondlane, Faculdade de Medicine, Caixa Postal 257, Maputo, Mozambique.
Pathology

610   US   ISSN 0147-1058
CONTRIBUTIONS IN MEDICAL HISTORY. irreg. price varies. Greenwood Press, 8 Post Rd. W., Westport, CT 06881. Ed. John Burnham.

612   SZ   ISSN 0301-4193
CONTRIBUTIONS TO HUMAN DEVELOPMENT. (Text in English) 1962. irreg. (approx. 1/yr.) 50 Fr.($30) per vol. (1981 price) S. Karger AG, Allschwilerstrasse 10, P.O. Box, CH-4009 Basel, Switzerland. Eds. J.A. Meacham, H. Thomae. (reprint service avail. from ISI) Indexed: Biol. Abstr. Chem. Abstr. Curr. Cont. Ind. Med.
Formerly: Bibliotheca Vita Humana.

CONTRIBUTIONS TO SENSORY PHYSIOLOGY. see *BIOLOGY — Physiology*

610   CN   ISSN 0315-226X
CORPORATION PROFESSIONNELLE DES MEDECINS DU QUEBEC. ANNUAIRE MEDICAL. a. Can.$30. Corporation Professionnelle des Medecins du Quebec, 1440 Ouest rue St. Catherine, Suite 914, Montreal, Que. H3G 1S5, Canada.

610   CN   ISSN 0315-2979
CORPORATION PROFESSIONNELLE DES MEDECINS DU QUEBEC. BULLETIN. 1961. irreg. (10-15/yr.) free. Corporation Professionnelle des Medecins du Quebec, 1440 Ouest rue St. Catherine, Suite 914, Montreal, Que H3G 1S5, Canada. Ed. Dr. Roger Beard.
Formerly: College des Medecins et Chirurgiens de la Province de Quebec. Bulletin (ISSN 0069-5599)

610   GE   ISSN 0070-0347
CORPUS MEDICORUM GRAECORUM. 1958. irreg., vol. 20, 1977. price varies. (Akademie der Wissenschaften der DDR) Akademie-Verlag, Leipziger Str. 3-4, 108 Berlin, E. Germany (D.D.R.) (Co-sponsors: Koenigliche Daenische Akademie; Saechsische Akademie der Wissenschaften, Leipzig)
History

610   US
COUNTWAY LIBRARY ASSOCIATES HISTORICAL PUBLICATIONS. 1972. irreg. price varies. Francis A. Countway Library of Medicine, 10 Shattuck St., Boston, MA 02115. illus.
History

610   US   ISSN 0145-4498
CURRENT CONCEPTS IN EMERGENCY MEDICINE. 1976. irreg. C.V. Mosby Co., 11830 Westline Industrial Dr., St. Louis, MO 63141. Ed. Ronald L. Krome. illus.

610   US   ISSN 0070-2005
CURRENT MEDICAL INFORMATION AND TERMINOLOGY. 1963. irreg., 4th ed., 1971. American Medical Association, 535 N. Dearborn St., Chicago, IL 60610. index. (also avail. in microfiche)
Formerly: Current Medical Terminology.

610   615   UK   ISSN 0300-7995
CURRENT MEDICAL RESEARCH AND OPINION. 1972. irreg., vol. 5, 1978. $35 for ten consecutive nos. Clayton-Wray Publications Ltd., 27 Sloane Square, London SW1W 8AB, England. Ed. N. B. Clayton. index. circ. 6,000. (back issues avail.) Indexed: Curr.Cont. Ind.Med.

CURRENT PROBLEMS IN CLINICAL BIOCHEMISTRY. see *BIOLOGY — Biological Chemistry*

616.07   574.2   US   ISSN 0090-8584
CURRENT TOPICS IN COMPARATIVE PATHOBIOLOGY. vol. 2, 1973. irreg. Academic Press, Inc., 111 Fifth Ave., New York, NY 10003. Ed. Thomas C. Cheng.
Pathology

614   SZ   ISSN 0376-4249
CURRENT TOPICS IN CRITICAL CARE MEDICINE. (Text in English) 1976. irreg. (approx. 1/yr.) 90 Fr.($54) per vol. (1981 price) S. Karger AG, Allschwilerstrasse 10, P.O. Box, CH-4009 Basel, Switzerland. Eds. W.C. Shoemaker, B.M. Tavares. (reprint service avail. from ISI)

610   UK
CURRENT TOPICS IN INFECTION. 1980. irreg. price varies. Edward Arnold (Publishers) Ltd., 41 Bedford Square, London WC1B 3DQ, England. Ed. I. Phillips.

616.07   574.2   US   ISSN 0070-2188
CURRENT TOPICS IN PATHOLOGY. irreg., vol. 69, 1980. price varies. Springer-Verlag, 175 Fifth Ave., New York, NY 10010 (also Berlin, Heidelberg, Vienna) (reprint service avail. from ISI) Indexed: Ind.Med.
Formerly: Ergebnisse der Allgemeinen Pathologie und Pathologischen Anatomie.
Pathology

610   GW   ISSN 0300-8096
D T. I. (Diagnostische und Therapeutische Informationen) 1966. irreg. price varies. Dr. Dietrich Steinkopff Verlag, Saalbaustr. 12, Postfach 11 108, 6100 Darmstadt 11, W. Germany (B.R.D.) Eds. D. Haan, C.W. Lorenz, L. Pippig. circ. 3,000.
Formerly: Diagnostische Informationen fuer die aerztliche Praxis (ISSN 0070-4660)

610   DK   ISSN 0011-6092
DANISH MEDICAL BULLETIN. (Summaries in Interlingua) 1954. irreg. (6-8/yr.) Kr.115 (free to medical institutions on request) Alminedelige Danske Laegeforening - Danish Medical Association, Kristianiagade 12 A, DK-2100 Copenhagen, Denmark (Subscr. to: Laegeforeningens Forlag, Esplanaden 8 A, DK-1263 Copenhagen K, Denmark) Ed. John Philip. adv. charts. illus. circ. 5,200. Indexed: Biol.Abstr. Chem.Abstr. Ind.Med. Nutr.Abstr.

610   DK   ISSN 0084-9588
DANSK MEDICINHISTORISK AARBOG/ YEARBOOK OF DANISH MEDICAL HISTORY. (Text in Danish; summaries in English) 1972. a. Kr.60. Koebenhavns Universitet, Medicinsk-Historiske Institut og Museum, Bredgade 62, DK-1260 Copenhagen, Denmark. Ed. Anna-Elisabeth Brade.
History

610   HU
DEBRECENI ORVOSTUDOMANYI EGYETEM. EVKONYV. 1966. a. free; exchange basis. ‡ Debreceni Orvostudomanyi Egyetem, Nagyerdei korut 98, 4012 Debrecen, Hungary. Ed. Alajos Bolodar. abstr. bibl. stat. index. circ. 650.

616.02   US
DEUTSCHE GESELLSCHAFT FUER INNERE MEDIZIN. VERHANDLUNGEN. 44th congress, 1932. irreg., 86th congress, 1980. price varies. Springer-Verlag, 175 Fifth Ave., New York, NY 10010 (Also Berlin, Heidelberg, Vienna) Ed. B. Schlegel. (reprint service avail. from ISI)

616.07   574.2   GW   ISSN 0070-4113
DEUTSCHE GESELLSCHAFT FUER PATHOLOGIE. VERHANDLUNGEN. a. price varies. Gustav Fischer Verlag, Wollgrasweg 49, Postfach 720143, 7000 Stuttgart 70, W. Germany (B.R.D.) Indexed: Ind.Med.
Pathology

DIARIO DE CONGRESOS MEDICOS. see *MEETINGS AND CONGRESSES*

DIRECTORY OF HEALTH SCIENCES LIBRARIES. see *LIBRARY AND INFORMATION SCIENCES*

610   MY
DIRECTORY OF INFORMATION ON MEDICAL PRACTITIONERS IN MALAYSIA. Cover title: Directory of Medical Practitioners Malaysia. (Supplement avail.) (Text in English) 1969. triennial, latest 1978. Malaysian Medical Association, MMA House, (4th Floor), 124 Jalan Pahang, Kuala Lumpur, Malaysia. Eds. Dr. Lim Say Wan, Dr. Yeoh Poh Hong. circ. 3,500(controlled) (back issues avail.)

610   US   ISSN 0070-5829
DIRECTORY OF MEDICAL SPECIALISTS. 1940. biennial. $99.50. Marquis Academic Media, 200 E. Ohio St., Chicago, IL 60611 (and 4300 W. 62nd St., Indianapolis, Ind. 46268)

616.07   574.2   US   ISSN 0070-6086
DIRECTORY OF PATHOLOGY TRAINING PROGRAMS. 1968. a. $25. ‡ Intersociety Committee on Pathology Information, 4733 Bethesda Ave., Suite 735, Bethesda, MD 20014. Ed. Judy Graves. circ. 2,500.
Pathology

610   US
DIRECTORY OF SELF-ASSESSMENT PROGRAMS FOR PHYSICIANS. irreg. $1.25. American Medical Association, 535 N. Dearborn St., Chicago, IL 60610.

610   US   ISSN 0094-5471
DIRECTORY OF WOMEN PHYSICIANS IN THE U.S. 1973. irreg., 2nd edt., 1979. $10. American Medical Association, 535 N. Dearborn St., Chicago, IL 60610. (Co-Sponsor: American Medical Women's Association)

610   US
DISASTER MEDICINE. 1979. irreg., vol. 3, 1981. price varies. Springer-Verlag, 175 Fifth Ave., New York, NY 10010 (Also Berlin, Heidelberg, Vienna) Eds. R. Frey, P. Safar. (reprint service avail. from ISI)

610   MY
DOCTOR'S COOP NEWSLETTER. 1971. irreg. M.0.50. Medical Practitioners Laboratory and Stores Cooperative Society, 643-1 Jalan Ipoh, Kuala Lumpur, Malaysia. Ed. Dr. S. Param Palam. charts. illus. stat.

610   JA   ISSN 0385-5023
DOKKYO JOURNAL OF MEDICAL SCIENCES. (Includes proceedings of the annual meetings of the Society) 1974. s-a. on exchange basis. Dokkyo Medical Society, Dokkyo University School of Medicine, Mibu, Tochigi 321-02, Japan. Ed. Akihiko Kajita. Indexed: Chem.Abstr.

610   NE   ISSN 0586-2779
DRUG-INDUCED DISEASES. Represents: Symposium on Drug-Induced Diseases. Proceedings. 1972. vol. 4. irreg. Excerpta Medica, P. O. Box 211, 1000 AE Amsterdam, Netherlands. Eds. L. Meyler, H.M. Peck.

610   UK
EARLY DIAGNOSIS PAPERS. 1967. irreg. price varies. Office of Health Economics, 162 Regent St., London W1R 6DD, England. Ed. J. C. McKenzie. charts.

352.3   US   ISSN 0145-2037
EDUCATIONAL COMMISSION FOR FOREIGN MEDICAL GRADUATES. ANNUAL REPORT. 1958. a. free. Educational Commission for Foreign Medical Graduates, 3624 Market St., Philadelphia, PA 19104. circ. 5,000.
Formerly: Educational Council for Foreign Medical Graduates. Annual Report (ISSN 0422-6690)

MEDICAL SCIENCES

610   US   ISSN 0070-959X
ELDRIDGE REEVES JOHNSON FOUNDATION FOR MEDICAL PHYSICS. COLLOQUIUM. PROCEEDINGS.* 1963. irreg., 1969, 5th (pub. 1971) $13.50, vol. 1; $14.50, vol. 2. (University of Pennsylvania) Academic Press, Inc., 111 Fifth Ave., New York, NY 10003.

610   UK
ELECTRO MEDICAL TRADE ASSOCIATION. PRODUCTS DIRECTORY. (Text in English; summaries in French, German and Spanish) 1965. irreg. free to qualified personnel. ‡ Electro Medical Trade Association Ltd., 276 High St., Guildford, Surrey GU1 3JU, England. circ. 500 (approx.)

610.28   629   US   ISSN 0360-7577
ENGINEERING IN MEDICINE. 1975. irreg., vol. 2, 1976. price varies. Springer Verlag, 175 Fifth Ave., New York, NY 10010 (And Berlin, Heidelberg, Vienna) Ed. M. Schaldach. (reprint service avail. from ISI)
Biomedical engineering

610.28   US   ISSN 0071-0334
ENGINEERING IN MEDICINE AND BIOLOGY CONFERENCE. RECORD. a. (Alliance for Engineering in Medicine and Biology) Institute of Electrical and Electronics Engineers, Inc., 445 Hoes Lane, Piscataway, NJ 08854.
Biomedical engineering

616.026   US   ISSN 0071-111X
ERGEBNISSE DER INNEREN MEDIZIN UND KINDERHEILKUNDE. NEW SERIES/ ADVANCES IN INTERNAL MEDICINE AND PEDIATRICS. (Text in German; occasionally in English) 1949. irreg., vol. 45, 1980. price varies. Springer-Verlag, 175 Fifth Ave., New York, NY 10010 (also Berlin, Heidelberg, Vienna) (reprint service avail. from ISI) Indexed: Ind.Med.
Internal medicine

610   GW   ISSN 0071-1853
ETHNOMEDIZIN. 1971. s-a. DM.60 for 2 yrs. Arbeitskreis Ethnomedizin, Curschmannstrasse 33, 2000 Hamburg 20, W. Germany (B.R.D.) Ed. J. Sterly. bk. rev.

EXPERIMENTAL BIOLOGY AND MEDICINE. see *BIOLOGY*

610   CN
F. M. O. Q. NOUVELLES. 1972. irreg. Federation des Medecins Omnipraticiens du Quebec, 1440 St. Catherine St. West, Suite 1100, Montreal, Que. H3G 1R8, Canada. circ. 5,000.

610   FI   ISSN 0355-4813
FINLAND. KANSANELAKELAITOS. JULKAISUJA. SARJA AL. (Text in Finnish; summaries in English) 1975. irreg., no. AL11, 1979. Kansanelakelaitos - Social Insurance Institution of Finland, Research Institute of Social Security, Olavinkato 1 A, SF-00100 Helsinki 10, Finland.

610   368   FI   ISSN 0355-4848
FINLAND. KANSANELAKELAITOS. JULKAISUJA. SARJA E. 1967. irreg., no. E99, 1978. Kansanelakelaitos - Social Insurance Institution of Finland, Research Institute of Social Security, Olavinkato 1 A, SF-00100 Helsinki 10, Finland.

616.39   FI   ISSN 0355-4856
FINLAND. KANSANELAKELAITOS. JULKAISUJA. SARJA EL. (Text in English and Finnish; summaries in English) 1973. irreg., no. EL13, 1978. Kansanelakelaitos - Social Insurance Institution of Finland, Research Institute of Social Security, Olavinkato 1 A, SF-00100 Helsinki 10, Finland.

610   368.4   FI   ISSN 0355-4821
FINLAND. KANSANELAKELAITOS. JULKAISUJA. SARJA M. 1967. irreg., no. M28, 1978. Kansanelakelaitos - Social Insurance Institution of Finland, Research Institute of Social Security, Olavinkato 1 A, SF-00100 Helsinki 10, Finland.

616.39   FI   ISSN 0355-483X
FINLAND. KANSANELAKELAITOS. JULKAISUJA. SARJA ML. (Text in Finnish; summaries in English) 1973. irreg., ML15, 1978. Kansanelakelaitos - Social Insurance Institution of Finland, Research Institute of Social Security, Olavinkato 1 A, SF-00100 Helsinki 10, Finland.

610   617.6   FI
FINLAND. LAAKINTOHALLITUS. LAAKARIT, HAMMASLAAKARIT/LAKARE, TANDLAEKARE. (Text in Finnish and Swedish) 1976. a. Valtion Painatuskeskus, Annankatu 44, 00100 Helsinki 10, Finland.
Formerly: Finland. Laakintohallitus. Laakarit, Hammaslaakarit, Sairaalat (ISSN 0430-5299)

610   YU   ISSN 0350-0233
FOLIA ANATOMICA IUGOSLAVICA. (Supplement accompanies each vol.) 1972. irreg. $10. (Udruzenje Anatoma Jugoslavije) Univerzitet u Sarajevu, Mose Pijade 6, Sarajevo, Yugoslavia. Ed. Hajrudin Hadziselimovic. bk. rev. circ. 600.

610   US   ISSN 0085-0829
FOREIGN MEDICAL SCHOOL CATALOGUE. 1971. a. $9.95. Foreign Medical School Information Center, One East Main Street, Bay Shore, NY 11706. Ed. Charles R. Modica. stat. circ. controlled.
Study and teaching

616.15   GE
FORTSCHRITTE DER HAEMATOLOGIE; Zytomorphologie - Seriologie - Immunologie - Haemostaseologie. 1970. irreg., vol. 4, 1977. price varies. Johann Ambrosius Barth Verlag, Salomonstr. 186, 701 Leipzig, E. Germany (D.D.R.) Ed.Bd.

610   FR
FRANCE. INSTITUT NATIONAL DE LA SANTE ET DE LA RECHERCHE MEDICALE. COLLOQUES. 1971. irreg. price varies. Institut National de la Sante et de la Recherche Medicale, 101 rue de Tolbiac, 75654 Paris Cedex 13, France.

FRANKLIN MCLEAN MEMORIAL RESEARCH INSTITUTE. ANNUAL REPORT. see *BIOLOGY — Biological Chemistry*

610   US   ISSN 0016-1160
FRESNO COUNTY MEDICAL SOCIETY. BULLETIN. 1949. a. $12. Fresno County Medical Society, 3425 N. First St., Fresno, CA 93726. Ed.Bd. adv. illus.
Organization news

610   NE
GENEESKUNDIG ADRESBOEK. Cover title: Geneeskundig Adresboek voor Nederland. a. H. W. Blok Uitgeverij B.V., Schiedamse Vest 59, Rotterdam, Netherlands.
Supersedes in part: Geneeskundig Jaarboekje.

610   NE
GENEESKUNDIG JAARBOEK MEDICIJNEN. Cover title: Geneeskundig Jaarboek. a. H. W. Blok Uitgeverij B. V., Schiedamse Vest 59, Rotterdam, Netherlands.
Supersedes in part: Geneeskundig Jaarboekje.

610   UK   ISSN 0072-0763
GENERAL MEDICAL COUNCIL, LONDON. MEDICAL REGISTER. 1859. a. £25. General Medical Council, 44 Hallam Street, London, W1N 6AE, England.

GEOGRAPHIA MEDICA. see *GEOGRAPHY*

610   US
GERMINAL IDEAS. 1970. irreg. $12. Montefiore Hospital & Medical Center, Residency Program in Social Medicine, 3329 Rochambeau Ave., Bronx, NY 10462. Ed. Dr. Jo Bouffond. circ. 200. (back issues avail.)

610   614   UN
GLOSSARY OF HEALTH CARE TERMINOLOGY. no. 4, 1975. a. free. World Health Organization, Regional Office for Europe, Scherfigsvej 8, 2100 Copenhagen 0, Denmark.

610   YU   ISSN 0065-1214
GODISEN ZBORNIK NA MEDICINSKIOT FAKULTET VO SKOPJE/ACTA FACULTATIS MEDICINAE SKOPIENSIS. (Text in French, German, Macedonian, Serbo-Croatian; summaries in English; Macedonian) 1954. a. Univerzitet vo Skoplje, Medicinski Fakultet, Karpos 11, Box 105, 91000 Skopje, Yugoslavia. Ed. Avram Sadikario. Indexed: Ind.Med.

GREAT BRITAIN. GENERAL REGISTER OFFICE. STUDIES ON MEDICAL AND POPULATION SUBJECTS. see *POPULATION STUDIES*

610   UK   ISSN 0309-0132
GREAT BRITAIN. MEDICAL RESEARCH COUNCIL. HANDBOOK. bienniel. price varies. Medical Research Council, 20 Park Crescent, London W1N 4AL, England.

610   UK
GREAT BRITAIN. MEDICAL RESEARCH COUNCIL. ANNUAL REPORT. a. price varies. Medical Research Council, 20 Park Crescent, London W1N 4AL, England (Avail. from H.M.S.O., c/o Liaison Officer, Atlantic House, Holborn Viaduct, London EC1P 1BN, England) illus.
Formerly (until 1965): Great Britain. Medical Research Council. Report (ISSN 0072-6567)

GUIDE MEDICAL ET HOSPITALIER. see *HOSPITALS*

610   PK
GUIDE PHARMA. (Text in English) 1975. a. Rs.25. Pasha & Pasha, Lahore, Pakistan.
Medical directory of the Lahore District

610   FR   ISSN 0072-8209
GUIDE ROSENWALD: ANNUAIRE MEDICAL ET PHARMACEUTIQUE. 1887. a. Expansion Scientifique, 15 rue Saint-Benoit, 75278 Paris Cedex 06, France.

610   US   ISSN 0085-1353
GUIDE TO BIOMEDICAL STANDARDS. 1971. a. $9. ‡ Quest Publishing Co., 1351 Titan Way, Brea, CA 92621. Ed. Allan F. Pacela. circ. 3,500.

610   IS   ISSN 0072-923X
HADASSAH MEDICAL ORGANIZATION. REPORT. (Text in English) irreg., latest issue, 1972/73. Hadassah Medical Organization, Jerusalem, Israel. Eds. Philip and Hadassah Gillon. adv.

610   US   ISSN 0073-0874
HARVEY LECTURES. 1953. irreg., series 72, 1979. price varies. Academic Press, Inc., 111 Fifth Ave., New York, NY 10003. cum. index: series 1-50 in series 50 (1956) Indexed: Ind.Med.

HEALTH CONSEQUENCES OF SMOKING. see *DRUG ABUSE AND ALCOHOLISM*

HEALTH LAW BULLETIN. see *PUBLIC HEALTH AND SAFETY*

HEALTH PHYSICS SOCIETY. NEWSLETTER. see *MEDICAL SCIENCES — Radiology And Nuclear Medicine*

610   US   ISSN 0190-2989
HEALTH SCIENCES AUDIOVISUAL RESOURCE LIST. a. University of Connecticut, Health Center, Farmington, CT 06032. index.

HISTORICAL STUDIES IN THE LIFE SCIENCES. see *SCIENCES: COMPREHENSIVE WORKS*

362   JA
HOKKAIDO REHABILITATION/HOKKAIDO RIHABIRTESHON GAKKAI ZASSHI. (Text in Japanese) 1964; publication suspended 1970-71. irreg. Hokkaido Rehabilitation Association - Hokkaido Rihabiriteshon Gakkai, c/o Sapporo Ika Daigaku Seik Geka, Minami Ichijo Nishi-16-chome, Sapporo 060, Japan.
Rehabilitation

610   HK
HONG KONG MEDICAL ASSOCIATION. BULLETIN. (Text in English) 1948. a. $5 for non-members; free to members. Hong Kong Medical Association, Duke of Windsor Building, 15 Hennessy Road, 5th Floor, Hong Kong, Hong Kong. Ed. Sr. Mary Aquinas. adv. circ. 2,000. (back issues avail) Indexed: Excerp.Med.

610   618.92   CN   ISSN 0082-5034
HOSPITAL FOR SICK CHILDREN, TORONTO. RESEARCH INSTITUTE. ANNUAL REPORT. 1969. a. Hospital for Sick Children, Toronto, Ont., Canada. Ed. Dr. A. Rothstein. circ. 500.

610   NE
HUMAN REPRODUCTIVE MEDICINE. 1977. irreg., vol. 4, 1980. price varies. Elsevier North-Holland Biomedical Press, Box 211, 1000 AE Amsterdam, Netherlands. Ed. E.S.E. Hafez.

MEDICAL SCIENCES

610 US ISSN 0536-1184
I B M MEDICAL SYMPOSIUM. PROCEEDINGS. 1959. triennial, 10th, 1971. price varies. International Business Machines Corp., Data Processing Division, 112 E. Post Rd., White Plains, NY 10601.

613.7 US
I C H P E R CONGRESS PROCEEDINGS. 1958. biennial. membership. International Council on Health, Physical Education and Recreation, 1201 16th St., N.W., Washington, DC 20036.
Formerly: I C H P E R Congress Reports (ISSN 0074-4417)
Physical fitness

615.845 UK ISSN 0305-9596
I E E MEDICAL ELECTRONICS MONOGRAPHS. 1971. irreg. price varies. (Institution of Electrical Engineers) Peter Peregrinus Ltd., Box 26, Hitchin, Herts. SG5 1SA, England (U.S. address: IEEE Service Center, 445 Hoes Lane, Piscataway, NJ 08854) Eds. B.W. Watson and D.W. Hill.

615.8 II
INDIAN ASSOCIATION OF PHYSIOTHERAPISTS. JOURNAL. 1965. a. membership. Indian Association of Physiotherapists, c/o Mrs. S. M. Sanghavi, 3rd Fl., 35 Chowpaty Sea Face, Bombay 400007, Iindia. adv. bk. rev. circ. 500.
Physiotherapy

610 II ISSN 0367-9012
INDIAN JOURNAL OF MEDICAL RESEARCH, SUPPLEMENT. (Text in English) 1922. irreg. Rs.200($70) Indian Council of Medical Research, Box 4508, Ansari Nagar, New Delhi 11016, India. Ed. Dr. G.V. Satyavati. bk. rev. bibl. charts. Indexed: Biol.Abstr. Chem.Abstr. Curr.Cont. Ind.Med. Nutr.Abstr. Sci.Cit.Ind. Trop.Dis.Bull.

INDUSTRIAL HEALTH FOUNDATION. MEDICAL SERIES. BULLETIN. see *INDUSTRIAL HEALTH AND SAFETY*

610 IT
INFORMOZIONI E ATTUALITA MONDIALI. vol.24,1970. irreg. included in subscr. to: Minerva Medica. Edizioni Minerva Medica, Corso Bramante 83-85, 10126 Turin, Italy. Ed. Dir. T. Oliaro. bibl. Indexed: Ind.Med.
Former titles: Attualita Mondiali (ISSN 0004-7333) & Lamiss.

INSTITUT FUER DEN WISSENSCHAFTLICHEN FILM. PUBLIKATIONEN ZU WISSENSCHAFTLICHEN FILMEN. SEKTION MEDIZIN. see *MOTION PICTURES*

610 US ISSN 0073-8638
INSTITUTE FOR CLINICAL SCIENCE. PROFICIENCY TEST SERVICE. REPORT. 1949. a (compilation of monthly reports) $110 (incl. also monthly samples) Institute for Clinical Science, 1833 Delancey Place, Philadelphia, PA 19103. Ed. F.W. Sunderman. circ. 1,000.

610 BL
INSTITUTO BUTANTAN. COLETANEA DE TRABALHOS. (Publication Suspended 1925-1950) 1901. irreg. Instituto Butantan, Caixa Postal 65, Sao Paulo, Brazil.

611 574.4 UR ISSN 0074-1353
INTERNATIONAL ANATOMICAL CONGRESS. PROCEEDINGS. (Text in English, French, German) 1st, 1905. quinquennial, 1970, 9th, Leningrad. International Anatomical Congress, C/O Prof. Dr. Shdanow, Karl Marx Prospekt 18, Moscow K-9, U.S.S.R.

610 FR ISSN 0074-1760
INTERNATIONAL ASSOCIATION OF THALASSOTHERAPY. CONGRESS REPORTS. (Proceedings published by organizing committee) 1954. triennial; 1975, 16th, Opatija, Yugoslavia. International Association of Thalasso-Therapy, c/o Professeur D. Leroy, 6, rue Lafayette, 35000 Rennes, France.
Marine medicine

616.043 NE ISSN 0074-3038
INTERNATIONAL CONFERENCE ON CONGENITAL MALFORMATIONS. PROCEEDINGS. irreg., 1969, 3rd, The Hague. fl.98($40.95) (National Foundation-March of Dimes) Excerpta Medica, P.O.B. 211, Amsterdam, Netherlands (Dist. in the U.S. and Canada by: Elsevier North-Holland, Inc., New York, 52 Vanderbilt Ave., New York, NY 10017)
Congenital defects

610 001.53 IT ISSN 0074-3615
INTERNATIONAL CONGRESS OF CYBERNETIC MEDICINE. PROCEEDINGS. 1960. biennial. International Society of Cybernetic Medicine, 348 via Roma, 80134 Naples, Italy. Ed. A. Masturzo. circ. 500.
Cybernetics

INTERNATIONAL CONGRESS OF LIFE ASSURANCE MEDICINE. PROCEEDINGS. see *INSURANCE*

615.8 SA ISSN 0074-3828
INTERNATIONAL CONGRESS OF OCCUPATIONAL THERAPY. PROCEEDINGS. 1974. irreg., 7th, 1978, Jerusalem. World Federation of Occupational Therapists, c/o Judith Farrell, Box 26445, Arcadia, Pretoria 0007, South Africa (Publisher of proceedings varies)
Physiotherapy

610 NE ISSN 0074-3887
INTERNATIONAL CONGRESS OF PHYSICAL MEDICINE. ABSTRACTS OF PAPERS PRESENTED. quadrennial. (International Federation of Physical Medicine and Rehabilitation) Excerpta Medica, P.O.B. 211, Amsterdam, Netherlands (Inquire: the Federation, c/o A.P.M. van Gestel, Rehabilitation Centre, Eindhoven, Kempense Baan 96, Eindhoven, Netherlands) 1976, 7th, Rio de Janiero

INTERNATIONAL CONGRESS ON MEDICAL LIBRARIANSHIP. PROCEEDINGS. see *LIBRARY AND INFORMATION SCIENCES*

616.7 NE
INTERNATIONAL CONGRESS ON MUSCLE DISEASES. ABSTRACTS. (Abstracts of 3rd Congress published in 1974) 1969. irreg., 1st, Milan, 1969. $18.75. Excerpta Medica, P.O.B. 211, 1000 AE Amsterdam, Netherlands.

619 NO
INTERNATIONAL COUNCIL FOR LABORATORY ANIMAL SCIENCE. PROCEEDINGS OF THE SYMPOSIUM. 1958. triennial, 7th, 1979, Utrecht. price varies (DM .85 for 6th) International Council for Laboratory Animal Science, c/o Dr. Stian Erichsen, Sec.-Gen., National Institute of Public Health, Postuttak, Oslo 1, Norway. (also avail. in microfiche from NTI)
Formerly: International Committee on Laboratory Animals. Proceedings of Symposium (ISSN 0074-2805)
Laboratory animals

610 FI ISSN 0074-6037
INTERNATIONAL FEDERATION OF MEDICAL STUDENTS' ASSOCIATIONS. REPORTS OF GENERAL ASSEMBLY. 1951. a. free. International Federation of Medical Students' Associations, Stenbaeckinkatu 9, SF-00290 Helsinki 29, Finland.

610 US ISSN 0074-6932
INTERNATIONAL MEDICAL CONGRESS. YEAR BOOK. 1966. q. $5. Association for International Medical Study, Inc., 1040 E. McDonald St., Lakeland, FL 33801. Ed. Ben H. McConnell, M.D. circ. 2,000.

610 FR
INTERNATIONAL MEDICAL DIRECTORY.* irreg. World Medical Association, 28 Av. des Alpes, F-01210 Ferney-Voltaire, France.

INTERNATIONAL MEDICAL WHO'S WHO. see *BIOGRAPHY*

610 GW
INTERNATIONAL ORGANIZATION FOR COOPERATION IN HEALTH CARE. GENERAL ASSEMBLY. REPORT. 1979. a. free. Medicus Mundi Internationalis, Mozartstr. 9, D-5100 Aachen, W. Germany (B.R.D.)
Supersedes: International Organization for Medical Cooperation. General Assembly. Report (ISSN 0579-3912)

616.07 US ISSN 0074-7718
INTERNATIONAL REVIEW OF EXPERIMENTAL PATHOLOGY. 1962. irreg., vol. 19, 1979. price varies. Academic Press, Inc., 111 Fifth Ave., New York, NY 10003. Eds. G. W. Richter, M. A. Epstein. index. Indexed: Ind.Med.
Pathology

610 US ISSN 0146-8197
INTERNATIONAL SERIES ON BIOMECHANICS. 1976. irreg. price varies. University Park Press, American Medical Publishers, Chamber of Commerce Bldg., Baltimore, MD 21202.

616.07 SZ ISSN 0074-8536
INTERNATIONAL SOCIETY OF GEOGRAPHICAL PATHOLOGY. PROCEEDINGS OF THE CONFERENCE. (Text in English, French, German) 1953. irreg., 1975, 12th, Zurich. International Society of Geographical Pathology, c/o J.R. Ruettner, Sec., Kantonsspital, Schmelzbergstr. 10, CH-8006 Zurich, Switzerland.
Pathology

616 SZ ISSN 0074-8544
INTERNATIONAL SOCIETY OF INTERNAL MEDICINE. CONGRESS PROCEEDINGS. 1950. biennial, 1974, 12th, Tel Aviv. International Society of Internal Medicine, c/o Dr. Philippe C. Frei, Hospital Nestle, 1011 Lausanne, Switzerland (Proceedings of 12th and 13th Congress published by: S. Karger AG, Arnold-Boecklin-Str. 25, 4011 Basel, Switzerland)
Internal medicine

INTERNATIONAL SYMPOSIUM ON GROWTH HORMONE. ABSTRACTS. see *BIOLOGY — Physiology*

610 SZ
INTERNATIONAL SYMPOSIUM ON THE PHARMACOLOGY OF THERMOREGULATION. 4th, 1979. irreg. $48.90. S. Karger AG, Allschwilerstrasse 10, P.O. Box, CH-4009 Basel, Switzerland. Ed. B. Cox. illus.

INTERNATIONAL UNION OF SCHOOL AND UNIVERSITY HEALTH AND MEDICINE. CONGRESS REPORTS. see *EDUCATION*

JACKSON LABORATORY ANNUAL REPORT. see *BIOLOGY — Genetics*

616.98 GW ISSN 0075-241X
JAHRBUCH DER WEHRMEDIZIN. 1967. biennial. DM.24.80. Wehr und Wissen Verlagsgesellschaft GmbH, Heilsbachstr., Postfach 87, 5300 Bonn-Duisdorf, W. Germany (B.R.D.) adv. circ. 3,500.
Military

JIWAJI UNIVERSITY. JOURNAL: SCIENCE, TECHNOLOGY & MEDICINE. see *SCIENCES: COMPREHENSIVE WORKS*

JOURNAL OF BIOMEDICAL MATERIALS RESEARCH. SYMPOSIA. see *BIOLOGY*

JOURNAL OF CYTOLOGY AND GENETICS. see *BIOLOGY — Genetics*

610 US ISSN 0161-5491
JOURNAL OF HOLISTIC HEALTH. 1976. a. $8.50. Association for Holistic Health, Box 33202, San Diego, CA 92103. Ed.Michael Gosney.

610 JA ISSN 0075-4579
JUNTENDO UNIVERSITY, TOKYO. MEDICAL ULTRASONICS RESEARCH CENTER. ANNUAL REPORT.* (Text in English) a. Juntendo University, School of Medicine, Medical Ultrasonics Research Center, 2-1-2 Hongo, Bunkyo-ku, Tokyo 113, Japan.

610 VE ISSN 0075-5222
KASMERA. irreg; vol. 5, 1974. Universidad del Zulia, Departamento de Medicina Tropical, Maracaibo, Venezuela. circ. 1,000. Indexed: Abstr. Hyg. Biol. Abstr. Trop. Dis. Bull.

MEDICAL SCIENCES

610 UK ISSN 0085-2546
KING'S GAZETTE; the journal of King's College Hospital. 1921. irreg. 1p. Kings College Hospital Medical School, Denmark Hill, London SE5 8RX, England. adv. bk. rev. illus. circ. 1,000.

610 JA ISSN 0075-6431
KOBE UNIVERSITY MEDICAL JOURNAL/KOBE DAIGAKU IGAKUBU KIYO. (Continues: Kobe Ika Daigaku. Kiyo) (Table of contents and abstracts in English) 1949. a. free. (Kobe University Medical Society - Kobe Daigaku Igakkai) Kobe University, School of Medicine, 7-12-1 Kusunoki-Cho, Ikuta-ku, Kobe 650, Japan. Ed. Hajimu Takeda. Indexed: Ind.Med.

610 HU ISSN 0075-6792
KORANYI SANDOR TARSASAG. TUDOMANYOS ULESEK. 1961. irreg. price varies. Akademiai Kiado, Publishing House of the Hungarian Academy of Sciences, P.O. Box 24, H-1363 Budapest, Hungary.

610 JA ISSN 0075-7217
KUMAMOTO UNIVERSITY. INSTITUTE OF CONSTITUTIONAL MEDICINE. BULLETIN. SUPPLEMENT. (Text in English or European languages; summaries in English) 1951. a. available on exchange. Kumamoto University, Institute of Constitutional Medicine - Kumamoto Daigaku Taishitsu Igaku Kenkyusho, 4-24-1 Kuhonzi, Kumamoto 862, Japan.

610 US
LECTURE NOTES IN MEDICAL INFORMATICS. 1978. irreg., vol. 10, 1981. Springer-Verlag, 175 Fifth Ave., New York, NY 10010 (Also Berlin, Heidelberg, Vienna) Eds. D. A. B. Lindberg, P. L. Reichertz. (reprint service avail. from ISI)

610 CS ISSN 0075-8736
LEKARSKE PRACE. (Articles mainly in Slovak, some in English, German or Russian; summaries in one or two of the other languages) 1961. irreg., approx. s-a; vol. 10, no. 2, 1973. (Slovenska Akademia Vied) Veda, Publishing House of the Slovak Academy of Sciences, Klemensova 19, 895 30 Bratislava, Czechoslovakia. Indexed: Ind.Med.

610 PL ISSN 0076-0420
LODZKIE TOWARZYSTWO NAUKOWE. WYDZIAL IV. NAUK LEKARSKICH. PRACE. (Text in Polish; summaries in French and Russian) 1951. irreg. price varies. Panstwowe Wydawnictwo Naukowe, Ul. Miodowa 10, Warsaw, Poland.

616.8 CN ISSN 0707-0934
M S ONTARIO. 1977. 4-6/yr. free. Multiple Sclerosis Society of Canada, Ontario Division, 130 Bloor St. W., Toronto, Ont. M5S 1N5, Canada. Ed. Deanna Groetzinger. bk. rev. circ. 7,000.

610 CN ISSN 0024-905X
MCGILL MEDICAL JOURNAL. 1931. 2-3/yr. Can.$5 for 4 nos. McGill Medical Undergraduate Society, McIntyre Medical Sciences Bldg., 3655 Drummond St., Montreal, Que. H3G 1Y6, Canada. Ed. D. K. Fast. adv. bk. rev. abstr. bibl. illus. index. circ. 5,000. Indexed: Chem.Abstr. Ind.Med.

610 UG ISSN 0025-1119
MAKERERE MEDICAL JOURNAL. 1957. a. $5.75. Makerere University Medical Students' Association, Box 7072, Kampala, Uganda. adv. bk. rev. charts. illus. circ. 1,000. Indexed: Biol. Abstr. Chem. Abstr.

MAKERERE UNIVERSITY. ALBERT COOK LIBRARY. LIBRARY BULLETIN AND ACCESSION LIST. see LIBRARY AND INFORMATION SCIENCES

610 BL
MANUAL DO INTERNO E RESIDENTE. a. Editora Medica Ltda., Rua Pinheiros 504, Sao Paulo, Brazil. adv. circ. 12,000.
Study and teaching

612 GE
MARTIN-LUTHER-UNIVERSITAET HALLE-WITTENBERG. WISSENSCHAFTLICHE BEITRAEGE. 1969. irreg. price varies. Johann Ambrosius Barth Verlag, Salomonstr. 186, 701 Leipzig, E. Germany (D.D.R.).

616.07 US
MASSON MONOGRAPHS IN DIAGNOSTIC PATHOLOGY. 1981. irreg., vol. 4, 1981. price varies. Masson Publishing U.S.A., Inc., 14 E. 60th St., New York, NY 10022. Ed. Stephen S. Sternberg, M.D.
Pathology

MEDICAID RECIPIENT CHARACTERISTICS AND UNITS OF SELECTED MEDICAL SERVICES. see SOCIAL SERVICES AND WELFARE

MEDICAID STATISTICS. see SOCIAL SERVICES AND WELFARE

610 UK ISSN 0076-5899
MEDICAL ANNUAL; A year book of treatment and practitioners' index. 1883. a. price varies. John Wright & Sons Ltd., 42-44 Triangle W., Bristol BS8 1EX, England. Eds. Ronald Bodley Scott, R. Milnes Walker. adv. index. circ. 7,000.

610 IR
MEDICAL COUNCIL OF IRAN. PUBLICATION/NEZAM PEZESHKI-YE IRAN. NASHRIYEH. (Text in Persian) 1970. irreg. free to physicians. Medical Council of Iran, 40 Shirin Ave., Hafez Ave., P.O.B. 3474, Teheran, Iran. Ed. Mohammad Ali Hafizi.

610 US
MEDICAL EDUCATION SOURCES. 1973. a. free. Professional Information Services, Inc., Box 533, Englewood, NJ 07631. adv. circ. 32,361 (controlled)

615.845 US
MEDICAL ELECTRONICS AND EQUIPMENT NEWS BUYERS' GUIDE. 1966. a. $5. Reilly Publishing Co., 532 Busse Highway, Park Ridge, IL 60068. adv. charts. circ. controlled.
Formerly: Medical Electronics and Equipment News Dictionary and Buyers' Guide.
Medical electronics

610 US ISSN 0094-9604
MEDICAL GROUP MANAGEMENT ASSOCIATION. INTERNATIONAL DIRECTORY. 1961. a. $50. ‡ Medical Group Management Association, 4101 E. Louisiana Ave., Denver, CO 80222. Ed. Barbara Hoagland. circ. 3,500.

610 530 US ISSN 0076-5953
MEDICAL PHYSICS SERIES. 1969. irreg. price varies. Academic Press Inc., 111 Fifth Ave., New York, NY 10003. Ed. J. M. A. Lenihan.
Medical physics

610 380.1 JA
MEDICAL PRODUCT OF JAPAN; directory of medical equipment. (Text in English) no. 5, 1979. biennial. 6000 Yen. Genyosha Publications, Inc, 3-18-2 Shibuya, Shibuya-ku, Tokyo 150, Japan. adv.

610 UK ISSN 0076-5961
MEDICAL PROTECTION SOCIETY. ANNUAL REPORT. 1892. a. free to members. ‡ Medical Protection Society Ltd., 50 Hallam Street, London W1N 6DE, England. Ed. Dr. P. G. T. Ford. adv. circ. 60,000.

616.98 AT ISSN 0025-7494
MEDICAL RESEARCH BULLETIN. 1965. irreg. free. ‡ Department of Veterans' Affairs, M. L. C. Tower, Woden, A.C.T. 2606, Australia. Ed. K. Fleming. bibl. stat. circ. 1,200.
General medical subjects with special reference to war-caused injuries and diseases

610 KE ISSN 0076-5988
MEDICAL RESEARCH CENTRE, NAIROBI. ANNUAL REPORT. 1966. a. free. ‡ Medical Research Centre, Nairobi, Box 20752, Nairobi, Kenya. (Affiliate: Koninklijk Instituut voor de Tropen, Netherlands)

610 GH
MEDICAL RESEARCH CENTRES IN GHANA: CURRENT RESEARCH PROJECTS. 1973. irreg. free. Council for Scientific and Industrial Research, Box M-32, Accra, Ghana. Ed. D.K. Opare-Sem. (back issues avail.)

610 IE ISSN 0076-5996
MEDICAL RESEARCH COUNCIL (IRELAND). REPORT. 1937. a. free. ‡ Medical Research Council of Ireland, 9 Clyde Rd., Dublin 4, Ireland. circ. controlled.

610 CN
MEDICAL RESEARCH COUNCIL OF CANADA. GRANTS AND AWARDS GUIDE/GUIDE DE SUBVENTIONS ET BOURSES. (Text and summaries in English and French) a. Medical Research Council, Ottawa K1A 0W9, Canada. charts. circ. 18,000.

610 CN
MEDICAL RESEARCH COUNCIL OF CANADA. REPORT OF THE PRESIDENT. (Text in English & French) 1960. a. free. Medical Research Council, Ottawa, Ont. K1A 0W9, Canada. charts. illus. stat. index. circ. 7,000(controlled)

616.98 US
MEDICAL RESEARCH IN THE V.A. 1957. a. $0.40. U.S. Veterans Administration, Medical Research Service, 810 Vermont Ave., N.W., Washington, DC 20420 (Orders to Supt. of Documents, U.S. Government Printing Office, Washington, DC 20402) Ed. Russell D. Bowman. Formerly: Highlights of V A Medical Research (ISSN 0073-2141)
Military

610.7 US ISSN 0066-9423
MEDICAL SCHOOL ADMISSION REQUIREMENTS, U. S. A. AND CANADA. 1950. a. $6.75. ‡ Association of American Medical Colleges, 1 Dupont Circle, N.W., Washington, DC 20036. circ. 32,000.

610 UK ISSN 0076-6011
MEDICAL SOCIETY OF LONDON. TRANSACTIONS. 1773. a. £2. Medical Society of London, 11 Chandos Street, Cavendish Square, London, W1N OEB, England. Ed. Ewart Jepson. Indexed: Ind.Med.

610 US ISSN 0565-811X
MEDICAL SUBJECT HEADINGS. (Issued as Pt. 2 of the January Index Medicus) 1960. a. $8 for 1980 edt. U. S. National Library of Medicine, U.S. National Institutes of Health, Bethesda, MD 20209 (Orders to: Supt. of Documents, Washington, DC 20402) circ. 8,000.

610 US ISSN 0076-6062
MEDICINAL RESEARCH: A SERIES OF MONOGRAPHS. 1967. irreg., vol. 9, 1978. price varies. Marcel Dekker, Inc., 270 Madison Ave., New York, NY 10016. Ed. Gary Grunewald.

610 US
MEDICINE (NEW YORK). a. John Wiley & Sons, Inc., 605 Third Ave., New York, NY 10016.

610 US
MEDIQUIZ ANNUAL. 1975. irreg., vol. 2 in prep. $25. Romaine Pierson Publishers, Inc., 80 Shore Rd., Port Washington, NY 11050. Eds. Charles A. Ragan, Jr., Frederick Coulston. charts. illus. circ. 3,600.

610 GW ISSN 0025-8431
MEDIZINHISTORISCHES JOURNAL. (Text in English, French and German) 1966. irreg. (previously quarterly), vol. 12, 1977. DM.78 per vol. (Akademie der Wissenschaften und der Literatur, Mainz, Kommission fuer Geschichte der Medizin und der Naturwissenschaften) Georg Olms Verlag GmbH, Hagentorwall 7, 3200 Hildesheim, W. Germany (B.R.D.) Ed.Bd. adv. index. circ. 1,000.
History

610 GE ISSN 0070-721X
MEDIZINISCHE AKADEMIE "CARL GUSTAV CARUS" DRESDEN. SCHRIFTEN. 1959. irreg., vol. 11, 1974. price varies. Medizinische Akademie "Carl Gustav Carus", Zentralbibliothek, Fiedlerstr. 27, 8019 Dresden, E. Germany (D.D.R.) circ. 800.

610 US
MEDIZINISCHE INFORMATIK UND STATISTIK. (Text Mainly in German) 1976. irreg., vol. 23, 1980. price varies. Springer-Verlag, 175 Fifth Ave., New York, NY 10010 (Also Berlin, Heidelberg, Vienna) Ed.Bd. (reprint service avail. from ISI)

MEDICAL SCIENCES

610   US   ISSN 0076-6151
MEDIZINISCHE LAENDERKUNDE. GEOMEDICAL MONOGRAPH SERIES. 1967. irreg., no. 6, 1979. Springer-Verlag, 175 Fifth Ave., New York, NY 10010 (also Berlin, Heidelberg, Vienna) (reprint service avail. from ISI)

610   GW   ISSN 0076-616X
MEDIZINISCHE PRAXIS; Sammlung fuer aerztliche Fortbildung. 1927. irreg., vol. 48, 1974. price varies. Dr. Dietrich Steinkopff Verlag, Saalbaustr. 12, Postfach 11 1008, 6100 Darmstadt 11, W. Germany (B.R.D.) Ed. Alexander Sturm, Jr. circ. 2,000.

MEMBRANE TRANSPORT PROCESSES. see
BIOLOGY — Biophysics

MEMBRANES: A SERIES OF ADVANCES. see
BIOLOGY

610   US   ISSN 0076-6526
MERCK MANUAL; A HANDBOOK OF DIAGNOSIS AND THERAPY. 1899. irreg., 13th edt., 1977. $14.50. Merck and Co., Inc., Box 2000, Rahway, NJ 07065. Ed. Dr. Robert Berkow.

616.07   SZ   ISSN 0076-681X
METHODS AND ACHIEVEMENTS IN EXPERIMENTAL PATHOLOGY. (Text in English) 1965. irreg. (approx. 1/yr.) 100 Fr.($60) per vol. (1981 price) S. Karger AG, Allschwilerstrasse 10, P.O. Box, CH-4009 Basel, Switzerland. Eds. G. Jasmin, M. Cantin. (reprint service avail. from ISI) Indexed: Biol.Abstr. Chem.Abstr. Curr.Cont. Ind.Med.
Pathology

410   GE
MIKROBIELLE UMWELT UND ANTIMIKROBIELLE MASSNAHMEN; Schriftenreihe fuer Theorie und Praxis in Medizin, Pharmazie und Wirtschaft. 1977. irreg., vol. 3, 1977. price varies. Johann Ambrosius Barth Verlag, Salomonstr. 186, 701 Leipzig, E. Germany (D.D.R.) Ed.Bd.

378   US   ISSN 0085-3488
MINORITY STUDENTS OPPORTUNITIES IN UNITED STATES MEDICAL SCHOOLS. 1970. a. Association of American Medical Colleges, One Dupont Circle, N.W., Ste. 200, Washington, DC 20036.

612   US
MODERN CONCEPTS IN MEDICAL PHYSIOLOGY. irreg. price varies. Macmillan Publishing Co., Inc., 866 Third Ave., New York, NY 10022.

610   US
MONOGRAPHS FOR STUDENTS OF MEDICINE. irreg., vol. 3, 1975. price varies. Academic Press, Inc., 111 Fifth Avenue, New York, NY 10003.

610 574.87   SZ   ISSN 0077-0809
MONOGRAPHS IN CLINICAL CYTOLOGY. (Text in English) 1965. irreg. (approx. 1/yr.) 100 Fr.($60) per vol. (1981 price) S. Karger AG, Allschwilerstrasse 10, P.O. Box, CH-4009 Basel, Switzerland. Ed.Bd. (reprint service avail. from ISI) Indexed: Biol.Abstr. Chem.Abstr. Curr.Cont. Ind.Med.
Embryology

616.07   US   ISSN 0077-0922
MONOGRAPHS IN PATHOLOGY. 1960. irreg. price varies. (International Academy of Pathology) Williams & Wilkins Co., 428 E. Preston St., Baltimore, MD 21202.
Pathology

610   JA   ISSN 0469-4759
NAGOYA UNIVERSITY. RESEARCH INSTITUTE OF ENVIRONMENTAL MEDICINE. ANNUAL REPORT/NAGOYA DAIGAKU KANKYO IGAKU KENKYUSHO NENPO. (Text in English) 1951. a. exchange basis. Nagoya University, Research Institute of Environmental Medicine - Nagoya Daigaku Kankyo Igaku Kenkyusho, Furo-cho, Chikusa-ku, Nagoya 464, Japan.

610   US   ISSN 0027-8785
NATIONAL BOARD EXAMINER. 1923. irreg. free. National Board of Medical Examiners, 3930 Chestnut St., Philadelphia, PA 19104. Ed. Edithe J. Levit. circ. 62,000.

610   UK   ISSN 0072-6567
NATIONAL INSTITUTE FOR MEDICAL RESEARCH. REPORT. 1973. a. National Institute for Medical Research, Mill Hill, London N.W.7, England.
Formerly: National Institute for Medical Research. Scientific Report (ISSN 0307-076X)

NATIONAL INSTITUTE OF POLAR RESEARCH. MEMOIRS. SERIES E. BIOLOGY AND MEDICAL SCIENCE. see *BIOLOGY*

610   GW   ISSN 0077-6173
NAUHEIMER FORTBILDUNGS-LEHRGAENGE. 1924. a. price varies. Dr. Dietrich Steinkopff Verlag, Saalbaustr. 12, Postfach 11 1008, 6100 Darmstadt 11, W. Germany (B.R.D.) Ed. O. Hammer. index. circ. 1,500.

610   GW   ISSN 0300-8371
NEUE MUENCHNER BEITRAEGE ZUR GESCHICHTE DER MEDIZIN UND NATURWISSENSCHAFTEN. MEDIZINHISTORISCHE SERIE. 1970. irreg., vol. 8, 1978. price varies. Werner Fritsch Verlag, Postfach 751, 8000 Munich 1, W. Germany (B.R.D.) Eds. Heinz Goerke, Joern Wolf. index. Indexed: Ind.Med.
History

610   US
NEW IMAGE OF MAN IN MEDICINE. 1977. irreg., vol. 3, 1979. Futura Publishing Co., 295 Main St., Mount Kisco, NY 10549. Ed. Karl E. Shaefer, M.D.

610   US   ISSN 0028-7911
NEW YORK UNIVERSITY POST-GRADUATE MEDICAL SCHOOL. INTER-CLINIC INFORMATION BULLETIN. 1961. irreg. free. ‡ New York University Post-Graduate Medical School, 317 E 34th St., New York, NY 10016. Ed. Charles J. Martin. bk. rev. abstr. bibl. charts. illus. stat. index. circ. 3,700. Indexed: Curr.Cont. Excerp.Med. Except.Child Educ.Abstr. Rehabil.Lit.

610   NZ
NEW ZEALAND REGISTER OF SPECIALISTS. a. NZ.$2. Medical Council of New Zealand., P.O. Box 5135, Wellington, New Zealand.

610   CN   ISSN 0078-0316
NEWFOUNDLAND MEDICAL DIRECTORY. 1961. a. free. Newfoundland Medical Board, Registrar, 47 Queen's Rd., St. John's Nfld., A1C 2A7, Canada. circ. 700.

610   NR   ISSN 0078-0782
NIGERIAN MEDICAL DIRECTORY. 1967. a. £N10. African Literary and Scientific Publications Ltd., 9 Kodesho St., Ikeja, Lagos, Nigeria. Ed. V. O. Awosika. adv. bk. rev. circ. 3,000.

NOBEL PRIZE LECTURES-PHYSIOLOGY OF MEDICINE. see *BIOLOGY — Physiology*

610   SW   ISSN 0078-1061
NORDISK MEDICINHISTORISK AARSBOK. (Text in Swedish; summaries in English) 1953. a. Kr.50. Medicinhistoriska Museet - Museum of Medical History, Aasoegatan 146, 116 32 Stockholm, Sweden. Ed. Wolfram Kock. adv. circ. 1,000.
Formerly: Medicinhistorisk Aarsbok.
History

610.6   US   ISSN 0361-5537
NORTH CAROLINA MEDICAL SOCIETY. TRANSACTIONS. a. North Carolina Medical Society, 222 N. Person St., Raleigh, NC 27611. Key Title: Transactions - North Carolina Medical Society.
Formerly: Medical Society of the State of North Carolina. Transactions.

610 574   JA   ISSN 0469-2071
NUKADA INSTITUTE FOR MEDICAL AND BIOLOGICAL RESEARCH. REPORTS. (Text in English) irreg. exchange basis. Nukada Institute for Medical and Biological Research - Nukada Igaku Seibutsugaku Kenkyusho, 5-18 Inage-cho, Chiba-shi 280, Japan.

610   US   ISSN 0078-2890
OAK RIDGE ASSOCIATED UNIVERSITIES. MEDICAL DIVISION. RESEARCH REPORT. 1951. a. free. ‡ Oak Ridge Associated Universities, Inc., Information Services Department, P.O. Box 117, Oak Ridge, TN 37830. Ed. Dr. Gould A. Andrews. circ. 3,000.

610 681   US
OXFORD MEDICAL ENGINEERING SERIES. irreg. price varies. Oxford University Press, 200 Madison Ave., New York, NY 10016 (And Ely House, 37 Dover St., London W1X 4AH, England) Eds. B. Sayers, P. Cliffe.

610 575   US
OXFORD MONOGRAPHS ON MEDICAL GENETICS. irreg. price varies. Oxford University Press, 200 Madison Ave., New York, NY 10016 (And Ely House, 37 Dover St., London W1X 4AH, England) Ed. J. A. Fraser Roberts.

610   US
P I N (PHYSICIANS INFORMATION NETWORK) 1977. irreg. free. New York University Medical Center, 550 First Ave., New York, NY 10016. Ed. Harold P. Burbage, Jr. circ. 2,000.

610   US   ISSN 0078-8864
PAN AMERICAN MEDICAL WOMEN'S ALLIANCE. NEWSLETTER.* 1956. irreg. price varies. Pan American Medical Women's Alliance, Ed. & Pub. Ruth Knubloch, M.D., 203 Court St., Little Valley, NY 14755.

610   PP
PAPUA NEW GUINEA INSTITUTE OF MEDICAL RESEARCH. MONOGRAPH SERIES. 1971. irreg. price varies. Papua New Guinea Institute of Medical Research, P.O. Box 60, Goroka, Papua New Guinea. bibl. charts. illus.

616.07 574.2   US   ISSN 0079-0184
PATHOLOGY ANNUAL. a. Appleton-Century-Crofts (Subsidiary of: Prentice-Hall) 292 Madison Ave., New York, NY 10017. Ed. Dr. Sheldon C. Sommers. bibl. charts. illus. circ. 4,000. Indexed: Ind.Med.
Pathology

616.07   GW   ISSN 0344-0338
PATHOLOGY, RESEARCH AND PRACTICE. (Text in German, English, or French; summaries in English and German) 1886. irreg., 4 nos. per vol. DM.230 per vol. (European Society of Pathology) Gustav Fischer Verlag, Wollgrasweg 49, Postfach 720143, 7000 Stuttgart 70, W. Germany (B.R.D.) Ed. Dr. W. Sandritter. adv. bk. rev. charts. illus. index. circ. 600. Indexed: Biol.Abstr. Chem.Abstr. Ind.Med. Nutr.Abstr.
Former titles: Pathology and Practice; Beitraege zur Pathologie (ISSN 0005-8165)
Pathology

610   US
PERSPECTIVES IN AUDIOLOGY. 1977. irreg. price varies. University Park Press (Subsidiary of: American Medical Publishers) Chamber of Commerce Bldg., Baltimore, MD 21202. Ed. L.L. Lloyd.

610   SZ   ISSN 0301-3014
PERSPECTIVES IN MEDICINE. (Text in English) 1972. irreg. (approx. 1/yr.) 30 Fr.($18) per vol. (1981 price) S. Karger AG, Allschwilerstrasse 10, P.O. Box, CH-4009 Basel, Switzerland. Ed. L. van der Reis. (reprint service avail. from ISI)

610 615   UK   ISSN 0142-1581
PHARMACEUTICAL MEDICINE. 1979. irreg. £5. Cambridge Medical Publications Ltd., 435 Wellingborough Rd., Northampton NN1 4EZ, England.

PHILOSOPHY AND MEDICINE. see
PHILOSOPHY

610   US
PHYSICIAN DISTRIBUTION & MEDICAL LICENSURE IN THE U. S. 1943. a. $12. American Medical Association, 535 N. Dearborn St., Chicago, IL 60610. Ed. G. A. Roback.
Former titles: Distribution of Physicians; Distribution of Physicians, Hospitals, Hospital Beds in the U. S. (ISSN 0419-4357)

610　　　US　　ISSN 0093-4461
PHYSICIANS' DESK REFERENCE. 1947. a. $13.50.
‡ Medical Economics Co., 680 Kinderkamack Road, Oradell, NJ 07649. circ. 330,000 (controlled)

610　　　US
PHYSICIANS' DESK REFERENCE FOR NONPRESCRIPTION DRUGS. 1980. a. Medical Economics Co., 680 Kinderkamack Rd., Oradell, NJ 07649.

615.8　　　CN　　ISSN 0708-1006
PHYSIOQUEBEC. (Text in English and French) 1975. irreg. membership. Professional Corporation of Physiotherapists of Quebec, Suite 816, 1440 St. Catherine St. W., Montreal, Que. H3G 1R8, Canada. illus.
Physical therapy

362　　　US
POLLING. 1974. irreg? free. ‡ United Cerebral Palsy of New York City, Inc., 122 E. 23rd St., New York, NY 10010. (Co-sponsor: Epilepsy Foundation of America) Ed. Daniel A. Poling, 2nd. adv. bk. rev. illus. circ. 10,000.
Rehabilitation

610　　　PL　　ISSN 0079-3558
POLSKA AKADEMIA NAUK. WYDZIAL NAUK MEDYCZNYCH. ROZPRAWY.* (Text in Polish; summaries in English, Russian) 1956. irreg. price varies. Panstwowy Zaklad Wydawnictw Lekarskich, Dluga 38/40, Warsaw, Poland (Dist. by Ars Polona-Ruch, Krakowskie Przedmiescie 7, Warsaw, Poland) Ed. Witold Orlowski.

610　　　US　　ISSN 0361-7742
PROGRESS IN CLINICAL AND BIOLOGICAL RESEARCH. 1975. irreg. price varies. Alan R. Liss Inc., 150 Fifth Ave., New York, NY 10011. (reprint service avail. from ISI) Indexed: Ind.Med.

616.075　　　US　　ISSN 0079-6174
PROGRESS IN CLINICAL PATHOLOGY. 1967. a. Grune and Stratton, Inc. (Subsidiary of: Harcourt Brace Jovanovich, Inc.) 111 Fifth Avenue, New York, NY 10003. Ed. Mario Stefanini. Indexed: Ind.Med.
Pathology

610　　　NE
PROGRESS IN MEDICAL ULTRASOUND; reviews and comments. 1980. a. Excerpta Medica, Box 211, 1000 AE Amsterdam, Netherlands. Ed. A. Kurjak.

PROGRESS IN MEDICINAL CHEMISTRY. see *CHEMISTRY*

612　　　US
PROGRESS IN SENSORY PHYSIOLOGY. 1981. irreg. Springer-Verlag, 175 Fifth Ave., New York, NY 10010 (Also Berlin, Heidelberg, Vienna) (reprint service avail. from ISI)
Physiology

QUANTITATIVE METHODS FOR BIOLOGISTS AND MEDICAL SCIENTISTS. see *BIOLOGY*

610　　　CN　　ISSN 0079-8789
QUEEN'S MEDICAL REVIEW. 1951. a. Queen's University, Aesculapian Society, Kingston, Ontario, Canada. Ed. R. B. Egerdie. adv. circ. 1,000.

613　　　US
RECENT ADVANCES IN OBESITY RESEARCH. 1977. irreg. price varies. Technomic Publishing Co., Inc., 265 Post Rd. W., Westport, CT 06880. Eds. Dr. Alan N. Howard, Dr. George A. Bray. illus.

610　　　US　　ISSN 0079-9939
RECENT ADVANCES IN PLASMA DIAGNOSTICS. (Translated from original Russian) 1971. irreg., 1971, vol. 3. price varies. Consultants Bureau, Special Research Report (Subsidiary of: Plenum Publishing Corp.) 227 W. 17th St., New York, NY 10011. Ed. V. T. Tolok.

610　　　US
REFERENCE DATA ON PROFILE OF MEDICAL PRACTICE. 1971. a. American Medical Association, Center for Health Services Research and Development, 535 N. Dearborn St., Chicago, IL 60610.

610　300　　US　　ISSN 0092-8836
REFERENCE DATA ON SOCIOECONOMIC ISSUES OF HEALTH. 1971. a. $1.50. American Medical Association, Center for Health Services Research and Development, 535 North Dearborn St., Chicago, IL 60610. illus. stat.

610　　　SA
REGISTER OF MEDICAL PRACTITIONERS, INTERNS AND DENTISTS FOR THE REPUBLIC OF SOUTH AFRICA. (Text and summaries in Afrikaans and English) a. with m. supplements. R.8.32 (plus R.3.12 for m. supplements) South African Medical & Dental Council, P.O. Box 205, Pretoria 0001, South Africa.

362　　　JA　　ISSN 0036-0538
REHABILITATION/RYOIKU. (Text in Japanese) 1960. a. $6.50. Japanese Society for Crippled Children - Nihon Shitai Fujiyuji Kyokai, 3-13-15 Higashi Ikebukuro, Toshima-ku, Tokyo 170, Japan. Ed. Bd. circ. 2,000.
Rehabilitation

REHABILITATION DER ENTWICKLUNGSGEHEMMTEN. see *EDUCATION — Special Education And Rehabilitation*

362　　　US
REHABILITATION UND PRAEVENTION. 1977. irreg., vol. 13, 1980. price varies. Springer-Verlag, 175 Fifth Ave., New York, NY 10010 (Also Berlin, Heidelberg, Vienna) (reprint service avail. from ISI)
Rehabilitation

610　　　UK　　ISSN 0143-3083
RESEARCH AND CLINICAL FORUMS. 1979. irreg. 33 Vale Rd., Tunbridge Wells, Kent TN1 1BP, England.

610　　　TH　　ISSN 0557-7330
RESEARCH INTO DISEASE.* 1967. irreg. South East Asia Treaty Organization, Sri Ayudhaya Road, P.O. Box 517, Bangkok, Thailand.

610　　　US
RHODES DIRECTORY OF BLACK PHYSICIANS IN THE UNITED STATES. 1976. triennial. Aqua Dynamics Ltd., 2624 Nevada Ave., Norfolk, VA 23513.

ROBERT WOOD JOHNSON FOUNDATION. ANNUAL REPORT. see *SOCIAL SERVICES AND WELFARE*

610　378　　US　　ISSN 0080-3359
ROCHESTER CONFERENCE ON PROGRAMMED INSTRUCTION IN MEDICAL EDUCATION. PROCEEDINGS.* 1965. irreg. $5. University of Rochester, Rochester, NY 14627. Ed. Jerome P. Lysaught. index. circ. 5,000.

610　　　US
ROCKEFELLER UNIVERSITY, NEW YORK. SCIENTIFIC AND EDUCATIONAL PROGRAMS. 1979. biennial. free. Rockefeller University Press, 1230 York Ave., New York, NY 10021. circ. 5,500. (reprint service avail. from ISI, UMI)
　　Supersedes (1955-1979): Rockefeller University, New York. Annual Report (ISSN 0080-3405)

610.69　　　CN　　ISSN 0707-3542
ROLLCALL. 1974. irreg. Can.$5. University of British Columbia, Division of Health Services Research and Development, Vancouver, B.C. V6T 1W5, Canada. illus.

610　　　UK
ROYAL COLLEGE OF GENERAL PRACTITIONERS. OCCASIONAL PAPERS. irreg. price varies. Royal College of General Practitioners, Alford House, 9 Marlborough Rd., Exeter EX2 4TJ, England.

616.07　574.2　　AT
ROYAL COLLEGE OF PATHOLOGISTS OF AUSTRALIA. BROADSHEETS. 1967. irreg. Aus.$1 membership. Royal College of Pathologists of Australia, 82 Windmill St., Sydney, N.S.W. 2000, Australia. Ed. Dr. A.K. Sewell. circ. 1,200.

610　　　UK
ROYAL COLLEGE OF PHYSICIANS OF EDINBURGH. DIRECTORY. 1910. irreg. Royal College of Physicians of Edinburgh, 9 Queen Street, Edinburgh EH2 1JQ, Scotland. circ. (controlled)
　　Formerly: Royal College of Physicians of Edinburgh. Yearbook and Calendar.

610　　　UK　　ISSN 0144-8676
ROYAL SOCIETY OF MEDICINE. ANNUAL REPORT OF THE COUNCIL. (Previously issued in the Society's Calendar) 1959/60. a. free. Royal Society of Medicine, 2 Queen Anne St., London W1M 0BR, England. circ. 17,500. (reprint service avail. from UMI, ISI)

610　　　AU　　ISSN 0080-4797
RUDOLF VIRCHOW MEDICAL SOCIETY IN THE CITY OF NEW YORK. PROCEEDINGS. 1942. irreg., 1972, no. 27. price varies. Verlag Ferdinand Berger und Soehne OHG, Wienerstr. 21-23, A-3580 Horn, Austria. Indexed: Ind.Med.

SAINT GEORGE'S HOSPITAL GAZETTE. see *HOSPITALS*

610　　　US　　ISSN 0095-5876
SAN DIEGO BIOMEDICAL SYMPOSIUM. PROCEEDINGS. a. price varies. Box 80543, San Diego, CA 92138. (back issues avail.) Key Title: Proceedings of the San Diego Biomedical Symposium.
　　Continues: San Diego Symposium for Biomedical Engineering. Proceedings.

SCANDINAVIAN JOURNAL OF CLINICAL AND LABORATORY INVESTIGATION. SUPPLEMENT. see *MEDICAL SCIENCES — Experimental Medicine, Laboratory Technique*

616.98　　　GW　　ISSN 0080-679X
SCHIFFAHRTMEDIZINISCHES INSTITUT DER MARINE, KIEL. VEROEFFENTLICHUNGEN. 1969. irreg. free. Schiffahrtmedizinisches Institut der Marine, Kopperpahler Allee 120, 2300 Kiel-Kronshagen, W. Germany (B.R.D.) Ed. A. Wandel. adv.
Military

610　　　SZ
SCHWEIZERISCHER MEDIZINALKALENDER. (Text in German) 1878. a. 32.50 Fr. Schwabe und Co. AG, Steinentorstr. 13, 4010 Basel, Switzerland. Ed. M. Soliva. adv. index. circ. 10,000.

610　　　SZ　　ISSN 0080-7400
SCHWEIZERISCHES MEDIZINISCHES JAHRBUCH. (Text in French, German) 1968. a. 72 Fr. ‡ (Schweizerische Aerzteorganisation - Federation of Swiss Physicians) Schwabe und Co. AG, Steinentorstr. 13, 4010 Basel, Switzerland. adv. index. circ. 5,000.

610　　　US　　ISSN 0361-3054
SCRIPPS CLINIC AND RESEARCH FOUNDATION. SCIENTIFIC REPORT. irreg. Scripps Clinic and Research Foundation, 10666 N. Torrey Pines Rd., La Jolla, CA 92037. Key Title: Scientific Report (La Jolla)

610　　　FR
SEMAINE DES HOPITAUX. 1925. w. 690 F. Semaine des Hopitaux (Subsidiary of: Expansion Scientifique) 15, rue Saint-Benoit, 75278 Paris Cedex 06, France. adv. circ. 16,808.

610　615　　KO
SEOUL NATIONAL UNIVERSITY. FACULTY PAPERS.* (Text in English; summaries in Korean) 1972. a. Seoul National University, Research Committee, Seoul, S.Korea. Ed. Byong Seol Seo.

SHEVCHENKO SCIENTIFIC SOCIETY. PROCEEDINGS OF THE SECTION OF CHEMISTRY, BIOLOGY AND MEDICINE. see *CHEMISTRY*

615.7　　　NE　　ISSN 0583-1881
SIDE EFFECTS OF DRUGS. 1972. a. Excerpta Medica, P.O. Box 211, 1000 AE Amsterdam, Netherlands. Ed. M.N.G. Dukes.

616.8　　　SZ　　ISSN 0302-5128
SLEEP. Represents: European Congress on Sleep Research. Proceedings. (Text in English) irreg. 190 Fr.($108) per vol. (1981 price) S. Karger AG, Allschwilerstrasse 10, P.O. Box, CH-4009 Basel, Switzerland. (reprint service avail. from ISI)

MEDICAL SCIENCES

610 SP ISSN 0583-7480
SOCIEDAD ESPANOLA DE HISTORIA DE LA MEDICINA. BOLETIN. vol 14, 1974. a. Sociedad Espanola de Historia de la Medicina, Duque de Medinaceli 4, Madrid-14, Spain. bibl.
History

610 LU ISSN 0037-9247
SOCIETE DES SCIENCES MEDICALES DU GRAND-DUCHE DE LUXEMBOURG. BULLETIN. (Text in English, French & German) 1863. 2-3/yr. free to institutions. Societe des Sciences Medicales du Grand-Duche de Luxembourg, 3 rue Conrad I, Luxembourg, Luxembourg. Ed. Dr. M. Dicato. adv. bk. rev. bibl. charts. illus. circ. 850. Indexed: Chem.Abstr. Ind.Med.

610 300 US
SOCIOMEDICAL SCIENCES SERIES. 1975. irreg. price varies. Spectrum Publications, Inc., 175-20 Wexford Terrace, Jamaica, NY 10032. Ed. Carl D. Chambers.

610 US
SONIC EXCHANGE. 1976. a. $5 to non-members. American Institute of Ultrasound in Medicine, 4405 East-West Hwy., Suite 504, Washington, DC 20014. Ed. Michael Meinerz. illus. circ. 6,500.

610 360 SA
SOUTH AFRICAN MEDICAL AND DENTAL COUNCIL. REGISTER OF SUPPLEMENTARY HEALTH SERVICE PROFESSIONS. a. R.5.20. South African Medical and Dental Council, Box 205, Pretoria 0001, South Africa.

610 SA ISSN 0081-248X
SOUTH AFRICAN MEDICAL RESEARCH COUNCIL. ANNUAL REPORT/SUID-AFRIKAANSE MEDIESE NAVORSINGSRAAD. JAARVERSLAG. (Text in Afrikaans and English) 1969-70. a, latest 1978. free. South African Medical Research Council, P.O. Box 70, Tygerberg 7505, South Africa. circ. 1,000.

613 SZ ISSN 0076-6186
SOZIALMEDIZINISCHE UND PAEDAGOGISCHE JUGENDKUNDE. (Text in German) 1965. irreg. (approx. 1/yr.) 50 Fr.($30) per vol. (1981 price) S. Karger AG, Allschwilerstrasse 10, P.O. Box, CH-4009 Basel, Switzerland. Ed. G. Ritzel. (reprint service avail. from ISI) Indexed: Biol.Abstr. Chem.Abstr. Curr.Cont. Ind.Med.
Formerly: Medizinische und Paedagogische Jugendkunde.

610 UK
SPECTACULAR DISEASES. no. 4, 1979. irreg. £0.75 per no. c/o Paul Green, 83b London Rd., Peterborough, Cambs, England.

616.07 US ISSN 0081-3699
SPEZIELLE PATHOLOGISCHE ANATOMIE. 1966. irreg., vol. 14, 1981. price varies. Springer-Verlag, 175 Fifth Ave., New York, NY 10010 (also Berlin, Heidelberg, Vienna) (reprint service avail. from ISI)
Pathology

610 YU ISSN 0081-3966
SRPSKA AKADEMIJA NAUKA I UMETNOSTI. ODELJENJE MEDICINSKIH NAUKA. GLAS. (Text in Serbo-Croatian; summaries in French, English, German or Russian) 1949, N.S. irreg. price varies. Srpska Akademija Nauka i Umetnosti, Knez Mihailova 35, 11001 Belgrade, Yugoslavia (Dist. by: Prosveta, Terazije 16, Belgrade, Yugoslavia) Ed. Vojislav Danilovic. circ. 1,000. Indexed: Excerp.Med. Ind.Med.

610 YU ISSN 0081-4016
SRPSKA AKADEMIJA NAUKA I UMETNOSTI. ODELJENJE MEDICINSKIH NAUKA. POSEBNA IZDANJA. (Text in Serbo-Croatian; summaries in French, English, German or Russian) 1950. irreg. price varies. Srpska Akademija Nauka i Umetnosti, Knez Mihailova 35, 11001 Belgrade, Yugoslavia (Dist. by: Prosveta, Terazije 16, Belgrade, Yugoslavia) Ed. Vojislav Danilovic. circ. 600. Indexed: Excerp.Med. Ind.Med.

STUDIA I MATERIALY Z DZIEJOW NAUKI POLSKIEJ. SERIA B. HISTORIA NAUK BIOLOGICZNYCH I MEDYCZNYCH. see *BIOLOGY*

610 GW ISSN 0081-7333
STUDIEN ZUR MEDIZINGESCHICHTE DES NEUNZEHNTEN JAHRUNDERTS. 1963. irreg., vol. 9, 1978. Vandenhoeck und Ruprecht, Theaterstr. 13, Postfach 77, 3400 Goettingen, W. Germany (B.R.D.)
History

610 614 UK ISSN 0473-8837
STUDIES ON CURRENT HEALTH PROBLEMS. 1962. irreg. price varies. (Association of the British Pharmaceutical Industry) Office of Health Economics, 162 Regent St., London W1R 6DD, England. Ed.Bd. charts.

610 500 GW ISSN 0341-0773
SUDHOFFS ARCHIV. BEIHEFTE. irreg., vol. 22, 1981. price varies. Franz Steiner Verlag GmbH, Friedrichstr. 24, Postfach 5529, 6200 Wiesbaden, W. Germany (B.R.D.)

610 SW ISSN 0346-6000
SWEDEN. SOCIALSTYRELSEN. FOERFATTNINGSSAMLING: MEDICAL. irreg. (approx. 122/yr.) Kr.90. Socialstyrelsen - National Board of Health and Welfare, 106 30 Stockholm, Sweden. index. circ. 8,000. (looseleaf format) Supersedes in part (1883-1976): Sweden. Medicinalvaesendet. Foerfattningssamling (ISSN 0346-5837)

610 SW
SWEDEN. SOCIALSTYRELSEN. LEGITIMERADE LAEKARE/AUTHORIZED PHYSICIANS. a. Kr.33. (National Board of Health and Welfare) Liber Foerlag, Fack, S-162 89 Vaellingby, Sweden. index. circ. 2,000.

SYMPOSIUM ON COMPUTER APPLICATIONS IN MEDICAL CARE. see *COMPUTER TECHNOLOGY AND APPLICATIONS*

610 011 US
SYMPOSIUM ON ETHICAL ISSUES IN HUMAN EXPERIMENTATION. PROCEEDINGS. 1972. irreg. free. New York University Medical Center, Urban Health Affairs Program, 550 First Ave., New York, NY 10016. bibl.

610 PL ISSN 0082-125X
SZCZECINSKIE TOWARZYSTWO NAUKOWE. WYDZIAL NAUK LEKARSKICH. PRACE. (Text in Polish; summaries in English, Polish and Russian) 1959. irreg. price varies. Panstwowy Zaklad Wydawnictw Lekarskich, Dluga 38/40, Warsaw, Poland (Dist. by Ars Polona-Ruch, Krakowskie Przedmiescie 7, Warsaw, Poland)

610 US ISSN 0098-1052
TEXAS FAMILY PHYSICIAN. 1975. bi-m. Texas Academy of Family Physicians, 1905 N. Lamar, Austin, TX 78705.

TEXAS REPORTS ON BIOLOGY AND MEDICINE. see *BIOLOGY*

610.28 JA ISSN 0082-4739
TOKYO MEDICAL AND DENTAL UNIVERSITY. INSTITUTE FOR MEDICAL AND DENTAL ENGINEERING. REPORTS/IYO KIZAI KENKYUSHO HOKOKU. (Table of contents and summaries also in English) 1967. a. free. Tokyo Medical and Dental University, Institute for Medical and Dental Engineering - Tokyo Ika Shika Daigaku Iyo Kizai Kenkyusho, 2-3-10 Surugadai, Kanda, Chiyoda-ku, Tokyo, Japan. Ed. Tatsuo Togawa. Indexed: Dent.Ind.

610 JA ISSN 0082-4771
TOKYO METROPOLITAN RESEARCH LABORATORY OF PUBLIC HEALTH, ANNUAL REPORT/TOKYO-TORITSU EISEI KENKYUSHO KENKYU NENPO. (Text in Japanese; summaries occasionally in English) 1949-50. a. exchange basis. Tokyo Metropolitan Research Laboratory of Public Health - Tokyo-toritsu Eisei Kenkyusho, 3-24-1 Hyakunin-cho, Shinjuk-ku, Tokyo 160, Japan.

610 FI ISSN 0355-9483
TURUN YLIOPISTO. JULKAISUJA. SARJA D. MEDICA-ODONTOLOGICA. (Latin title: Annales Universitatis Turkuensis) 1972. irreg. price varies. Turun Yliopisto - University of Turku, SF-20500 Turku 50, Finland.

610 US ISSN 0082-7134
U C L A FORUM IN MEDICAL SCIENCES. 1962. irreg. price varies. (University of California, Los Angeles) Academic Press, Inc., 111 Fifth Ave., New York, NY 10003. Indexed: Ind.Med.

610.25 US ISSN 0091-8393
U S MEDICAL DIRECTORY. irreg. U S Directory Service (Miami), 121 S. E. 1st St., Box 1565, Miami, FL 33101.

610 150 301.1 US
U S S R REPORT: BIOMEDICAL AND BEHAVIORAL SCIENCES. 1973. irreg. (approx. 14/yr.) $70. U.S. Joint Publications Research Service, 1000 N. Glebe Rd., Arlington, VA 22201 (Orders to: NTIS, Springfield, VA 22161)
Former titles: U S S R and Eastern Europe Scientific Abstracts: Biomedical and Behavioral Sciences; U S S R and Eastern Europe Scientific Abstracts: Biomedical Sciences.

574 616.9 US
U S S R REPORT: SPACE BIOLOGY AND AEROSPACE MEDICINE. English translation of: Kosmicheskaia Biologiia i Aviakosmicheskaia Meditsina. vol. 8, 1974. irreg. (approx. 7/yr.) $35. U.S. Joint Publications Research Service, 1000 N. Glebe Rd., Arlington, VA 22201 (Orders to NTIS, Springfield, VA 22161)
Former titles: Space Biology and Aerospace Medicine; Space Biology and Medicine.
Translations of reports on Soviet technology in aerospace medicine

610 US
ULTRASOUND IN BIOMEDICINE. irreg. price varies. Research Studies Press, Box 92, 2130 Pacific Ave, Forest Grove, OR 97116. Ed. Dr. D. N. White.

610 534 US ISSN 0098-0382
ULTRASOUND IN MEDICINE. 1975. a. price varies. Plenum Publishing Corp., 233 Spring St., New York, NY 10013. Ed. D. N. White.
Incorporating: American Institute of Ultrasound in Medicine. Proceedings of Annual Meeting (ISSN 0065-888X)

616.98 US ISSN 0083-355X
U. S. VETERANS ADMINISTRATION. MEDICAL RESEARCH PROGRAM. 1957. a. $0.40. U.S. Veterans Administration, Medical Research Service, 810 Vermont Ave., N.W., Washington, DC 20240 (Orders to: Supt. of Documents, U. S. Government Printing Office, Washington, DC 20402) Ed. Russell D. Bowman.
Military

610 VE ISSN 0542-6375
UNIVERSIDAD DEL ZULIA. FACULTAD DE MEDICINA. REVISTA. (Text in Spanish; summaries in English) 1968. irreg. Bs.32($9.50) (or exchange) Universidad del Zulia, Facultad de Medicina, Apartado 526, Maracaibo, Venezuela. Ed. G. Olivares. bibl. charts. illus. index. circ. 1,000. Indexed: Abstr. Hyg. Biol. Abstr. Excerp. Med. Trop. Dis. Bull.

UNIVERSIDAD INDUSTRIAL DE SANTANDER. REVISTA - INVESTIGACIONES. see *ENGINEERING*

610 CK ISSN 0120-0909
UNIVERSIDAD INDUSTRIAL DE SANTANDER. REVISTA - MEDICINA. (Text in Spanish; summaries in English, French, German and Spanish) 1969. irreg. $2 per no. or exchange basis. Universidad Industrial de Santander, Apartado Aereo 678, Bucaramanga, Colombia. adv. bk. rev. bibl. charts. illus. cum. index every 5 yrs.

610 BL ISSN 0301-7729
UNIVERSIDADE FEDERAL DE MINAS GERAIS. FACULDADE DE MEDICINA. ANAIS. 1943? a. Universidade Federal de Minas Gerais, Faculdade de Medicina, C.P. 1621, 30000 Belo Horizonte, Minas Gerais, Brazil. Ed.Bd.

610 BL ISSN 0085-042X
UNIVERSIDADE FEDERAL DO RIO GRANDE DO SUL. FACULDADE DE MEDICINA. ANAIS. (Text in Portuguese; summaries in English) 1938. irreg. free. ‡ Universidade Federal do Rio Grande do Sul, Faculdade de Medicina, Rua Sarmento Leite s/n, 90000 Porto Alegre, R.S, Brazil. Ed. Dr. Alaor Teixeira. circ. 1,000(approx.). Indexed: Biol.Abstr.

610 AU ISSN 0579-7772
UNIVERSITAET INNSBRUCK. MEDIZINISCHE FAKULTAET. ARBEITEN. 1970. irreg. price varies. Oesterreichische Kommissionsbuchhandlung, Maximilianstrasse 17, A-6020 Innsbruck, Austria. Ed. Hans Schroecksnadel.

610 LB
UNIVERSITY OF LIBERIA. A. M. DOGLIOTTI COLLEGE OF MEDICINE. ANNUAL REPORT OF THE DEAN. a. University of Liberia, A. .M. Dogliotti College of Medicine, Monrovia, Liberia.

610 010.7 UK ISSN 0076-0854
UNIVERSITY OF LONDON. ROYAL POSTGRADUATE MEDICAL SCHOOL. REPORT. 1936. a. free. ‡ University of London, Royal Postgraduate Medical School, Hammersmith Hospital, Du Cane Rd., London W12 0HS, England.

610 CN ISSN 0076-4108
UNIVERSITY OF MANITOBA. MEDICAL JOURNAL. 1929. 3-4/yr. Can.$8. University of Manitoba, Faculty of Medicine, 770 Bannatyne Ave., Winnipeg, Man. R3E 0W3, Canada. Ed.Bd. bk. rev. circ. 1,500. (back issues avail.)

UNIVERSITY OF NEW SOUTH WALES. BIOMEDICAL LIBRARY. NEWSLETTER. see LIBRARY AND INFORMATION SCIENCES

VITAMINS AND HORMONES: ADVANCES IN RESEARCH AND APPLICATIONS. see PHARMACY AND PHARMACOLOGY

610 UN ISSN 0512-3054
W H O TECHNICAL REPORT SERIES. (Edts. in English, French, Russian and Spanish) 1950. irreg., no. 638, 1979. $48. World Health Organization - Organisation Mondiale de la Sante, Distribution and Sales Service, 20 Avenue Appia, CH-1211 Geneva 27, Switzerland. circ. 15,000.

WAYNE STATE UNIVERSITY, DETROIT. MEDICAL SCHOOL LIBRARY. REPORT. see LIBRARY AND INFORMATION SCIENCES

619 US
WESLEY W. SPINK LECTURES ON COMPARATIVE MEDICINE. 1972. biennial. price varies. University of Minnesota Press, 2037 University Ave. S.E., Minneapolis, MN 55455.

WISSENSCHAFTLICHE FORSCHUNGSBERICHTE. REIHE 1. GRUNDLAGENFORSCHUNG UND GRUNDLEGENDE METHODIK. ABT. B. BIOLOGIE UND MEDIZIN/CURRENT TOPICS IN SCIENCE. REIHE 1. BASIC RESEARCH. ABT. B. BIOLOGY AND MEDICINE. see BIOLOGY

610 US
WOMEN IN CONTEXT: DEVELOPMENT AND STRESSES. 1978. irreg. price varies. Plenum Press, 233 Spring St., New York, NY 10013. Eds. Carol C. Nadelson, Malkah T. Notman.

610 NE
WORKSHOP CONFERENCE HOECHST. 1973. a. Excerpta Medica, Box 211, 1000 AE Amsterdam, Netherlands.

615.8 UK ISSN 0084-151X
WORLD CONFEDERATION FOR PHYSICAL THERAPY. PROCEEDINGS OF THE CONGRESS. 1953. irreg., 1967, 5th, Melbourne. World Confederation of Physical Therapy, 20-22 Mortimer St., London W1, England.
Physiotherapy

WORLD DIRECTORY OF MEDICAL SCHOOLS/ REPERTOIRE MONDIAL DES ECOLES DE MEDECINE. see EDUCATION — Guides To Schools And Colleges

610 FR ISSN 0084-1897
WORLD MEDICAL ASSOCIATION. GENERAL ASSEMBLY. PROCEEDINGS.* (Issued in Association's World Medical Journal) a, 1947, 29th, Sweden. World Medical Association, 28 Av. des Alpes, F-01210 Ferney-Voltaire, France.

YALE STUDIES IN THE HISTORY OF SCIENCE AND MEDICINE. see SCIENCES: COMPREHENSIVE WORKS

610 US ISSN 0147-1996
YEAR BOOK OF FAMILY PRACTICE. 1977. a. price varies. Year Book Medical Publishers, Inc., 35 E. Wacker Dr., Chicago, IL 60601. Ed. R. Rakel.

610 US ISSN 0084-3873
YEAR BOOK OF MEDICINE. 1933. a. price varies. ‡ Year Book Medical Publishers, Inc., 35 E. Wacker Dr., Chicago, IL 60601. Ed. Bd.

616.07 US ISSN 0084-3946
YEAR BOOK OF PATHOLOGY AND CLINICAL PATHOLOGY. 1940. a. price varies. ‡ Year Book Medical Publishers, Inc., 35 E. Wacker Dr., Chicago, IL 60601. Eds. F. A. Carone, R. B. Conn.
Pathology

610 790.1 US ISSN 0162-0908
YEAR BOOK OF SPORTS MEDICINE. 1979. a. price varies. Year Book Medical Publishers, Inc., 35 E. Wacker Dr., Chicago, IL 60601. Ed.Bd.

MEDICAL SCIENCES — Abstracting, Bibliographies, Statistics

301.2 016 US ISSN 0098-1850
ABSTRACTS OF DOCTORAL DISSERTATIONS IN ANTHROPOLOGY. (Subseries of: Eastern New Mexico University. Contributions in Anthropology) 1968. a. price varies. Eastern New Mexico University, Paleo-Indian Institute, Paleo-Indian Institute, Portales, NM 88130. Ed. R. G. Campbell. circ. 1,000.

610 016 GE ISSN 0070-3915
AKADEMIE FUER AERZTLICHE FORTBILDUNG DER DDR. BIBLIOGRAPHIE. (Subseries of its Wissenschaftliche Veroeffentlichungen und Vortraege) 1972. irreg. free. Akademie fuer Aerztliche Fortbildung der DDR, Noeldnerstr. 34-36, 1134 Berlin, W. Germany (B.R.D.)

610 013 PL ISSN 0066-1937
ANNALES ACADEMIAE MEDICAE CRACOVIENSIS. INDEX DISSERTATIONUM EDITARUM. (Text in English, Polish and Russian) 1955. a. price varies. Akademia Medyczna, Krakow, Botaniczna 3, Krakow, Poland (Dist. by Ars Polona-Ruch, Krakowskie Przedmiescie 7, Warsaw, Poland) Ed. Dr. Mieczyslaw Goldsztajn. circ. 1,000.

610 016 CS
ANNUAL OF CZECHOSLOVAK MEDICAL LITERATURE. (Text in English) 1956. a. free. Ustav Vedeckych Lekarskych Informaci, Sokolska 31, 121 32 Prague 2, Czechoslovakia. index. circ. 400. (microfiche)

617.6 US ISSN 0084-6554
ANNUAL REPORT ON DENTAL AUXILIARY EDUCATION. 1967. a. American Dental Association, Division of Educational Measurements, 211 E. Chicago Ave., Chicago, IL 60611. Ed. David R. DeMarais. (also avail. in microform from UMI)

617.6 US ISSN 0065-8030
ANNUAL REPORT ON DENTAL EDUCATION. 1967. a. American Dental Association, Division of Educational Measurements, 211 E. Chicago Ave., Chicago, IL 60611. Ed. David R. DeMarais. (also avail. in microform from UMI)
Formerly: Dental Students' Register (ISSN 0065-8049)

ASSOCIATION FRANCAISE POUR LA DIFFUSION DU LIVRE SCIENTIFIQUE, TECHNIQUE ET MEDICAL (BULLETINS COLLECTIFS) see SCIENCES: COMPREHENSIVE WORKS — Abstracting, Bibliographies, Statistics

610 016 BL ISSN 0067-6675
BIBLIOGRAFIA BRASILEIRA DE MEDICINA. 1939. irreg. Cr.$300($15) Instituto Brasileiro de Informacao em Ciencia e Tecnologia, Rio de Janeiro, Brazil. bk. rev. circ. 300.
Formerly (until 1958): Indice-Catalogo Medico Brasileiro.

617.643 BL ISSN 0100-6266
BIBLIOGRAFIA BRASILEIRA DE ODONTOLOGIA. (Text in Portuguese; introduction and information in English) 1966-67. biennial. $10 individuals; free to institutions. ‡ Universidade de Sao Paulo, Faculdade de Odontologia, Seccao de Documentacao Odontologica, Rua Tres Rios 363, Sao Paulo, Brazil. circ. 700.

610 016 YU ISSN 0067-6799
BIBLIOGRAFIJA MEDICINSKE PERIODIKE JUGOSLAVIJE/INDEX MEDICUS IUGOSLAVICUS. (Text in Serbo-Croatian; summaries in English, German, French and Russian) 1966. a. 150 din.($10) Opca Bolnica "Dr. Josip Kajfes", Miskine 64, Zagreb, Yugoslavia.

610 016 CS ISSN 0067-6802
BIBLIOGRAPHIA MEDICA CECHOSLOVACA. 1947. m. free. Ustav Vedeckych Lekarskych Informaci, Sokolska 31, 121 32 Prague 2, Czechoslovakia. Ed. Jan Peska. index. circ. 700.

610 016 US ISSN 0363-0161
BIBLIOGRAPHY OF BIOETHICS. 1975. a. $44 per vol. Gale Research Company, Book Tower, Detroit, MI 48226. Ed. LeRoy Walters.

616.8 016 UK ISSN 0067-7183
BIBLIOGRAPHY OF DEVELOPMENTAL MEDICINE AND CHILD NEUROLOGY. BOOKS AND ARTICLES RECEIVED. (Supplement to: Developmental Medicine and Child Neurology) 1963. a. price varies. Spastics International Medical Publications, 5A Netherhall Gardens, London NW3 5RN, England (Dist. in U.S. by: J.B. Lippincott Co., E. Washington Square, Philadelphia, PA 19105) Ed. Dr. M.C.O. Bax. circ. 5,200.

616.8 016 US ISSN 0084-7879
BIBLIOGRAPHY OF ELECTRICAL RECORDINGS IN THE CNS AND RELATED LITERATURE. 1970. a. $10. Brain Information Service-Brain Research Institute, University of California, Los Angeles, Center for Health Sciences, Los Angeles, CA 90024. (Co-sponsor: National Institute of Neurological and Communicative Disorders and Stroke) circ. 600. (also avail. in microform from UMI; back issues avail.)

539 616 JA
BIBLIOGRAPHY OF PUBLISHED PAPERS OF THE RADIATION EFFECTS RESEARCH FOUNDATION/HOSHASEN EIKYO KENKYUSHO HAPPYO ROMBUN MOKUROKU. (Text in English and Japanese) 1959. a. price varies. ‡ Radiation Effects Research Foundation - Hoshasen Eikyo Kenkyusho, 5-2 Hijiyama-Koen, Hiroshima 730, Japan (Avail. in U.S. from National Technical Informationn Service, Springfield, Va. 22151) circ. 1,000.
Formerly (until 1975): Bibliography of Published Papers of the Atomic Bomb Casualty Commission (ISSN 0067-7221)

617 US ISSN 0067-7264
BIBLIOGRAPHY OF SURGERY OF THE HAND. 1967. a. $15. American Society for Surgery of the Hand, c/o Gail M. Gorman, Three Parker Pl., Suite 132, 2600 S. Parker Rd., Aurora, CO 80014. Ed. Dr. John P. Adams. circ. 800. (back issues avail.) Indexed: Ind.Med.

610 016 US ISSN 0067-7280
BIBLIOGRAPHY OF THE HISTORY OF MEDICINE. 1965. a., quinquennial cumulation. price varies. U. S. National Library of Medicine, 8600 Rockville Pike, Bethesda, MD 20209 (Orders to: Supt. of Documents, Washington, DC 20402)
History

612 016 US ISSN 0084-7887
BIBLIOGRAPHY ON THE HYPOTHALAMIC-PITUITARY-GONADAL SYSTEM. 1969. a. $10 or with subscr. to Neuroendocrine Control Mechanism Bulletin. Brain Information Service-Brain Research Institute, University of California, Los Angeles, Center for Health Sciences, Los Angeles, CA 90024. Ed. Michael Fineman. circ. 1,000. (also avail. in microform from UMI; back issues avail.)

MEDICAL SCIENCES — ABSTRACTING, BIBLIOGRAPHIES, STATISTICS

614 617   CN   ISSN 0317-3720
CANADA. STATISTICS CANADA. SURGICAL PROCEDURES AND TREATMENTS/ INTERVENTIONS CHIRURGICALES ET TRAITEMENTS. (Catalog 82-208) (Text in English and French) 1969. a. Can.$10($12) Statistics Canada, Publications Distribution, Ottawa, Ont. K1A 0V7, Canada. (also avail. in microform from MML)

016 610   CN
CANADIAN LOCATIONS OF JOURNALS INDEXED FOR MEDLINE/DEPOTS CANADIENS DES REVUES INDEXEES POUR MEDLINE. 1970. a. Can.$12. National Research Council of Canada, Canada Institute for Scientific and Technical Information (CISTI), Publications Section, Ottawa, K1A 0S2, Canada. circ. 300.
    Formerly: Canadian Locations of Journals Indexed in Index Medicus (ISSN 0316-3938)

312.3   NZ   ISSN 0548-9415
CANCER DATA: DEATHS AND CASES REPORTED (WELLINGTON) a. price varies. National Health Statistics Centre, Box 6314, Te Aro, Wellington 1, New Zealand. stat. circ. controlled.

618   US   ISSN 0190-4981
COMBINED CUMULATIVE INDEX TO PEDIATRICS. 1979. triennial. $24.50. Numarc Book Corporation, 1280 Main St., Buffalo, NY 14209. Ed. Arnold C. Westphal. circ. 2,000. (back issues avail.)

610 016   US   ISSN 0090-1377
CUMULATED ABRIDGED INDEX MEDICUS. a. $28 for 1979 edt. U. S. National Library of Medicine, 8600 Rockville Pike, Bethesda, MD 20209 (Orders to: Supt. of Documents, Washington, DC 20402) circ. 1,500.

610 016   US   ISSN 0590-3408
CUMULATED INDEX MEDICUS. a. $160 for 1979 edt. U. S. National Library of Medicine, 8600 Rockville Pike, Bethesda, MD 20209 (Orders to: Supt. of Documents, Washington, DC 20402) circ. 5,000.

610.73 016   US   ISSN 0146-5554
CUMULATIVE INDEX TO NURSING & ALLIED HEALTH LITERATURE. 1961. a. cum. of Nursing and Allied Health Literature Index. $48. Glendale Adventist Medical Center Publications Service, Box 871, Glendale, CA 91209. Ed. Ferne Fannin Hubert. bk. rev. film rev. cum. index 1956 to date. circ. 4,750. (also avail. in microform from MIM,UMI)
    Formerly (until 1977): Cumulative Index to Nursing Literature (ISSN 0011-3018); Incorporating: C I N A H L'S List of Subject Headings; Which was formerly (until 1977): Cumulative Index to Nursing Literature, Nursing Subject Headings (ISSN 0070-1793)

616.994 016   US
CURRENT ARTICLES ON NEOPLASIA. 1958. irreg. free. University of Texas M. D. Anderson Hospital and Tumor Institute, Research Medical Library, Texas Medical Center, Houston, TX 77030. Ed. Marie Harvin. circ. 1,500.
    Formerly: Articles on Neoplasia (ISSN 0004-3664)

616.462 016   US   ISSN 0070-4652
DIABETES-RELATED LITERATURE INDEX BY AUTHORS AND KEY WORDS IN THE TITLE. (Supplement to Diabetes, Journal of the American Diabetes Association) 1960. a. distributed to membership and subscribers of Diabetes. U.S. National Institute of Arthritis Metabolism and Digestive Diseases, National Institutes of Health, Bethesda, MD 20014 (Orders to: Supt. of Documents, Washington, D.C 20402) Ed. Dr. Arnold Lazarow.
    Diabetes

016 610   GW   ISSN 0340-5559
DOKUMENTATION IMPFSCHAEDEN-IMPFERFOLGE. (Text in English, French, German) 1972. a. DM.5. Institut fuer Dokumentation und Information ueber Sozialmedizin und Oeffentliches Gesundheitswesen, Westerfeldstr. 15, Postfach 5408, 4800 Bielefeld 1, W. Germany (B.R.D.) Ed. O. Nacke. bk. rev.

610 310 574   GW   ISSN 0303-4577
I M B I S; Information fuer medizinisch-biologische Statistik und deren Grenzgebiete. 1973. irreg. free. Universitaet Marburg, Institut fuer Medizinisch-biologische Statistik, Coelber Str. 1, 3550 Marburg 1, W. Germany (B.R.D.)

ILLINOIS HEALTH SCIENCES LIBRARIES SERIALS HOLDINGS LIST. see *LIBRARY AND INFORMATION SCIENCES — Abstracting, Bibliographies, Statistics*

610 015   US   ISSN 0162-6639
INDEX OF N L M SERIAL TITLES. 1972. a. $35 for 1980 edt. National Library of Medicine, 8600 Rockville Pike, Bethesda, MD 20209 (Orders to: Supt. of Documents, Washington, DC 20402)

616.742 016   US   ISSN 0019-3933
INDEX OF RHEUMATOLOGY. Variant title: Annual Index of Rheumatology. 1965. a. $10. (American Rheumatism Association) Arthritis Foundation, American Rheumatism Association Section, 3400 Peachtree Rd. N.E., Atlanta, GA 30326. circ. 500.

610 016   CK   ISSN 0019-705X
INDICE MEDICO COLOMBIANO. 1961. a. Col.$250($8) Universidad de Antioquia, Escuela Interamericana de Bibliotecologia, Apdo. Aereo 1307, Medellin, Colombia. (Co-sponsor: Asociacion Colombiana de Facultades de Medicina) bibl. circ. 500.

011 610   GW   ISSN 0340-8094
INDICES NATURWISSENSCHAFTLICH-MEDIZINISCHER PERIODICA BIS 1850. 1971. irreg., vol. 3, 1981. price varies. Anton Hiersemann Verlag, Rosenbergstr. 113, Postfach 723, 7000 Stuttgart 1, W. Germany (B.R.D.) Ed. Armin Geus.

340.6 016   US
INTERNATIONAL BIBLIOGRAPHY OF THE FORENSIC SCIENCES. 1975. a. $20. International Reference Organization in Forensic Medicine and Sciences, c/o Wm. G. Eckert, M.D., Laboratory, St. Francis Hospital, Wichita, KS 67214.

617.11 016   US   ISSN 0090-0575
INTERNATIONAL BIBLIOGRAPHY ON BURNS. (Base volume covers 1950-1969) 1969. a. $10. National Institute for Burn Medicine, 909 E. Ann St., Ann Arbor, MI 48104. Ed. Irving Feller, M.D. circ. 1,000.
    Burns

610 016   IS   ISSN 0075-1251
ISRAEL MEDICAL BIBLIOGRAPHY. (Text in English) 1948. biennial. free. Ministry of Health, Jerusalem, Israel. Ed. Nadia Levenberger.

610 016   IS   ISSN 0449-4881
JERUSALEM HISTORICAL MEDICAL PUBLICATIONS. (Text in English) 1968. irreg. Hebrew University of Jerusalem, Hadassah Medical School, Division of the History of Medicine, Box 1172, Jerusalem, Israel.
    History

610 016   SW   ISSN 0075-9813
LIST BIO-MED; BIOMEDICAL SERIALS IN SCANDINAVIAN LIBRARIES. (Supplements Avail.) (Text in English) 1965. irreg., 4th edt., 1978 plus a. supplement. Kr.250 for base vol.; Kr. 90 for supplement. Karolinska Institutet, Bibliotek, Box 60201, S-104 01 Stockholm, Sweden. Ed. Erkki Hakulinen. adv. circ. 600.

011 610   PR
LIST OF CURRENT SERIAL PUBLICATIONS BEING RECEIVED AT THE UNIVERSITY OF PUERTO RICO MEDICAL SCIENCES CAMPUS LIBRARY. a; latest issue, 1972. free. Universidad de Puerto Rico, Medical Sciences Campus Library, G.P.O. Box 5067, San Juan, PR 00936. (processed)

610   US   ISSN 0093-3821
LIST OF JOURNALS INDEXED IN INDEX MEDICUS. 1974. a. $5 for 1980 edt. U. S. National Library of Medicine, 8600 Rockville Pike, Bethesda, MD 20209 (Orders to: Supt. of Documents, Washington, DC 20402) circ. 3,500.

610 015   US   ISSN 0196-755X
LIST OF SERIALS AND MONOGRAPHS INDEXED FOR ONLINE USERS. 1980. a. $6.50 for 1980 edt. U.S. National Library of Medicine, 8600 Rockville Pike, Bethesda, MD 20209 (Orders to: NTIS, Springfield, VA 22161)

610 016   US   ISSN 0000-0574
MEDICAL BOOKS AND SERIALS IN PRINT. 1972. a. $55. R.R. Bowker Company, 1180 Ave. of the Americas, New York, NY 10036 (Orders to: Box 1807, Ann Arbor, MI 48106)
    Formerly: Medical Books in Print (ISSN 0076-5929)

610   UK   ISSN 0076-6003
MEDICAL RESEARCH INDEX. irreg., 5th edt. 1979. ‡ Longman Group Ltd., Longman House, Burnt Mill, Harlow, Essex CM20 2JE, England (Dist. in U.S. and Canada by: Gale Research Co. Ltd., Book Tower, Detroit, MI 48226)

616.8   NZ   ISSN 0548-992X
MENTAL HEALTH DATA. a. price varies. National Health Statistics Centre, P.O. Box 6314 Te Aro, Wellington 1, New Zealand. circ. controlled.

016 610   US   ISSN 0083-2251
NATIONAL LIBRARY OF MEDICINE. LITERATURE SEARCH SERIES. 1966. irreg. free. ‡ U.S. National Library of Medicine, National Institutes of Health, 8600 Rockville Pike, Bethesda, MD 20209. Ed. Charlotte Kenton. circ. 1,000.

617.6   US
NORTHWESTERN UNIVERSITY. DENTAL SCHOOL LIBRARY. CURRENT SUBSCRIPTIONS LIST. 1970. a. free. Northwestern University, Dental School Library, 311 East Chicago Ave., Chicago, IL 60611. bibl. circ. 350. (processed)

610   NO
NORWAY. STATISTISK SENTRALBYRAA. HELSEPERSONELLSTATISTIKK. (Subseries of Norges Offisielle Statistikk) 1979. biennial. Statistisk Sentralbyraa, Box 8131-Dep., Oslo 1, Norway.
    Supersedes: Norway. Statistisk Sentralbyraa. Legestatistikk (ISSN 0377-8886)

610.73 016   US   ISSN 0146-5554
NURSING AND ALLIED HEALTH LITERATURE INDEX. 1977. bi-m. with a. cum. $48. Glendale Adventist Medical Center Publications Service, Box 871, Glendale, CA 91209. Ed. Ferne Fannin. circ. 4,750.
    Formerly (1956-1976): Nursing Literature Index.

016.61   US   ISSN 0093-2248
P.M.B.R. PHYSICIAN'S MEDICAL BOOK REFERENCE. 1974. a. $25.95. Medi-Facts Publishing Co., 2337 Lemoine Avenue, Fort Lee, NJ 17024. circ. 40,000.

616.8   US   ISSN 0079-0060
PARKINSON'S DISEASE AND RELATED DISORDERS. CUMULATIVE BIBLIOGRAPHY.* a. $13.75 per 3-vol set. U.S. National Institute of Neurological and Communicative Disorders and Stroke, Bethesda, Washington, MD 20014.

SOUTH DAKOTA. DEPARTMENT OF SOCIAL SERVICES. ANNUAL MEDICAL REPORT. see *SOCIAL SERVICES AND WELFARE — Abstracting, Bibliographies, Statistics*

617.6   FR   ISSN 0399-0656
THESINDEX DENTAIRE; index alphabetique des sujets traites dans les theses de sciences odontologiques et de chirurgie dentaire soutenues en France et dans certains pays de langue francaise. 1975. a. Bibliotheque Interuniversitaire, Section Medecine, Pharmacie, Odontologie-Clermont Ferrand, 28 Place Henri Dunant, F-63039 Clermont-Ferrand Cedex, France. Eds. Gisele Dufour, Raymond Perrin. cum.index.
    Formerly(1968-1974): Catalogue des Theses Francaises de Science Odontologiques et de Chirurgie Dentaire.

610 016　　　　　　FR　ISSN 0399-0648
THE INDEX MEDICAL. 1973. a. price varies.
Bibliotheque Interuniversitaire, Section Medecine, Pharmacie, Odontologie-Clermont Ferrand, 28 Place Henri Dunant, F-63039 Clermont Ferrand Cedex, France. Ed. Raymond Perrin. cum.index. circ. 500.
Formerly (until 1976): Index Alphabetique Annuel des Sujets Traites dans les Theses de Medecine.

612 016　　　　　　JA　ISSN 0082-4518
TISSUE CULTURE STUDIES IN JAPAN: THE ANNUAL BIBLIOGRAPHY/NIHON SOSHIKI BAIYO KENKYU NENPO. (Text in European languages) 1957. a. membership ($3 fee) Japanese Tissue Culture Association - Nihon Soshiki Baiyo Gakkai, c/o Tokyo Daigaku Igakubu Kaibogaku Kyoshito, 7-3-1 Hongo, Bunkyo-ku, Tokyo 113, Japan. Ed. M. Yamada.

614.84　　　　　　　UK
UNITED KINGDOM FIRE STATISTICS. 1960. a. price varies. Home Office, 50 Queen Anne's Gate, London SW1H 9AT, England.
Formerly: United Kingdom Fire and Loss Statistics (ISSN 0082-7959)

131.3　　　　　　US　ISSN 0098-972X
U.S. NATIONAL INSTITUTE OF MENTAL HEALTH. MENTAL HEALTH STATISTICAL NOTES. 1969. irreg. free. U. S. National Institute of Mental Health, Division of Biometry and Epidemiology, Survey and Reports Branch, 5600 Fishers Lane, Rockville, MD 20857. stat. charts. circ. 3,000-4,000. (processed; also avail. in microfiche) Indexed: Ind.Med.　Amer.Stat.Ind.

616.8　310　　　　　US
U.S. NATIONAL INSTITUTE OF MENTAL HEALTH. REPORT SERIES ON MENTAL HEALTH STATISTICS. SERIES A: MENTAL HEALTH FACILITIES REPORT. 1969. price varies. U. S. National Institute of Mental Health, Division of Biometry and Epidemiology, Survey and Reports Branch, 5600 Fishers Lane, Rockville, MD 20857. circ. 3,000-4,000. (also avail. in microfiche) Indexed: Amer.Stat.Ind.

618.8　310　　　　　US
U.S. NATIONAL INSTITUTE OF MENTAL HEALTH. REPORT SERIES ON MENTAL HEALTH STATISTICS. SERIES B: ANALYTICAL AND SPECIAL STUDY REPORTS. 1968. U. S. National Institute of Mental Health, Division of Biometry and Edidemiology, Survey and Reports Branch, 5600 Fishers Lane, Rockville, MD 20857. circ. 3,000-4,000. (also avail. in microfiche) Indexed: Amer.Stat.Ind.

618.8　310　　　　US　ISSN 0566-7038
U.S. NATIONAL INSTITUTE OF MENTAL HEALTH. REPORT SERIES ON MENTAL HEALTH STATISTICS. SERIES C: METHODOLOGY REPORTS. 1969. U.S. National Institute of Mental Health, Division of Biometry and Epidemiology, Survey and Reports Branch, 5600 Fishers Lane, Rockville, MD 20857. circ. 3,000-4,000. (also avail. in microfiche)

610 016　　　　　US　ISSN 0083-6540
VIRGINIA UNION LIST OF BIOMEDICAL SERIALS. 1970. a. free. University of Virginia, School of Medicine, Health Sciences Library, Box 234, Charlottesville, VA 22901. Ed. Frederick O'Bryant. circ. 600.

617.7　016　　　　US　ISSN 0049-6510
VISION INDEX. 1971. a. $24. Visual Science Information Center, Pacific Medical Center, Box 7999, San Francisco, CA 94120. Ed. Harold R. Gibson. bk. rev. circ. 700.

616.994　　　　　US　ISSN 0084-3679
YEAR BOOK OF CANCER. 1957. a. price varies. ‡ Year Book Medical Publishers, Inc., 35 E. Wacker Dr., Chicago, IL 60601. Eds. R. E. Clark, R. W. Cumley.

MEDICAL SCIENCES — Allergology And Immunology

576　615.37　　　　DK
ACTA PATHOLOGICA ET MICROBIOLOGICA SCANDINAVICA. SECTION C: IMMUNOLOGY. SUPPLEMENTUM. irreg. price varies. Munksgaard, 35 Noerre Soegade, DK-1370 Copenhagen K, Denmark. (reprint service avail. from ISI)

616.97　　　　　US　ISSN 0065-2776
ADVANCES IN IMMUNOLOGY. 1961. irreg., vol. 27, 1979. price varies. Academic Press, Inc., 111 Fifth Ave., New York, NY 10003. Eds. F. J. Dixon, Jr., Henry Kunkell. index. Indexed: Ind.Med.

616.97　　　　　SZ　ISSN 0065-6372
ALLERGOLOGICUM; TRANSACTIONS OF THE COLLEGIUM INTERNATIONALE. (Text in English) 1955. biennial, 12th, New Orleans. Collegium Internationale Allergologicum, c/o P. Dukor, Ciba-Geigy Ltd., CH-4002 Basel, Switzerland.

616.97　　　　　　US
AMERICAN ACADEMY OF ALLERGY. POLLEN AND MOLD COMMITTEE. STATISTICAL REPORT. 1973. a. free. Ross Laboratories, 625 Cleveland Ave., Columbus, OH 43216. Ed. Bill Rohn. circ. 100.

616.97　615.37　　　US
AMERICAN LECTURES IN ALLERGY AND IMMUNOLOGY. irreg. price varies. Charles C. Thomas, Publisher, 301-327 E. Lawrence Ave., Springfield, IL 62717.

616.97　　　　　US　ISSN 0090-1083
ANNUAL REVIEW OF ALLERGY. 1973. a. $18. ‡ Medical Examination Publishing Co., Inc., 65-36 Fresh Meadow Lane, Flushing, NY 11365. Ed. Claude Frazier. charts. illus.

615.37　　　　　SZ　ISSN 0301-3782
BASEL INSTITUTE FOR IMMUNOLOGY. ANNUAL REPORT. (Text in English) 1972. a. free to libraries and immunologists. Basel Institute for Immunology, Grenzacherstrasse 487, CH-4058 Basel, Switzerland. Ed. C.M. Steinberg. circ. 2,500.

615.37　　　　　CN　ISSN 0068-9653
CANADIAN SOCIETY FOR IMMUNOLOGY. BULLETIN. 1967. irreg. membership. ‡ Canadian Society for Immunology, c/o Dept. of Immunology, University of Manitoba, Basic Medical Sciences Bldg., Winnipeg, Man. R3E 0W3, Canada. Ed. Dr. B. Sabiston.

615.37　　　　　SZ　ISSN 0301-3146
CANADIAN SOCIETY FOR IMMUNOLOGY. INTERNATIONAL SYMPOSIUM. PROCEEDINGS. irreg. (CN) S. Karger AG, Allschwilerstrasse 10, P.O. Box, CH-4009 Basel, Switzerland. Ed. D. G. Ingram. bibl. (reprint service avail. from ISI)

615.37　574　　　　US
CLINICAL IMMUNOBIOLOGY. irreg. Academic Press, Inc., 111 Fifth Ave., New York, NY 10003. Eds. F. H. Bach, R. Good.

615.37　　　　　US　ISSN 0090-8800
CONTEMPORARY TOPICS IN MOLECULAR IMMUNOLOGY. 1972. irreg. price varies. Plenum Press, 233 Spring St., New York, NY 10013. Eds. F. P. Inman, Ralph A. Reisfeld. Indexed: Ind.Med.

615.37　576　　　　SZ　ISSN 0301-3081
CONTRIBUTIONS TO MICROBIOLOGY AND IMMUNOLOGY. (Text in English) 1973. irreg. (approx. 2/yr.) 100 Fr.($60) per vol. (1981 price) S. Karger AG, Allschwilerstrasse 10, P.O. Box, CH-4009 Basel, Switzerland. (reprint service avail. from ISI) Indexed: Biol.Abstr. Chem.Abstr. Curr.Cont. Ind.Med.
Supersedes: Bibliotheca Microbiologia (ISSN 0067-8058)

615.37　　　　　UK　ISSN 0141-3368
CURRENT TOPICS IN IMMUNOLOGY. 1975. irreg. price varies. Edward Arnold(Publishers) Ltd., 41 Bedford Square, London WC1B 3DQ, England. Ed. J. L. Turk.

616.7　　　　　SZ　ISSN 0301-5149
DEVELOPMENTS IN BIOLOGICAL STANDARDIZATION. (Text in English, French and German) 1964. irreg. (approx. 2/yr.) 100 Fr.($60) per vol. (1981 price) (International Association of Biological Standardization) S. Karger AG, Allschwilerstrasse 10, P.O. Box, CH-4009 Basel, Switzerland. (reprint service avail. from ISI) Indexed: Biol.Abstr.　Curr.Cont.　Ind.Med.
Continues: Progress in Immunobiological Standardization (ISSN 0079-6344) & Symposia Series in Immunobiological Standardization (ISSN 0082-0768)

616.07　　　　　UK　ISSN 0301-4703
ESSAYS IN FUNDAMENTAL IMMUNOLOGY. 1973. irreg. Blackwell Scientific Publications Ltd., Osney Mead, Oxford OX2 0EL, England. Ed. Ivan M. Roitt. Indexed: Chem.Abstr.

HOKKAIDO UNIVERSITY. INSTITUTE OF IMMUNOLOGICAL SCIENCE. BULLETIN. see MEDICAL SCIENCES — Respiratory Diseases

617　612　　　　DK　ISSN 0105-2896
IMMUNOLOGICAL REVIEWS. (Text in English) 1969. irreg. price varies. Munksgaard, 35 Noerre Soegade, DK-1370 Copenhagen K, Denmark. Goeran Moeller. adv. circ. 1,200. (reprint service avail. from ISI) Indexed: Chem.Abstr.　Curr.Cont.
Formerly: Transplantation Reviews (ISSN 0082-5948)

615.37　　　　　US　ISSN 0092-6019
IMMUNOLOGY: AN INTERNATIONAL SERIES OF MONOGRAPHS AND TREATISES. irreg. price varies. Academic Press, Inc., 111 Fifth Ave., New York, NY 10003. Eds. F. J. Dixon, H. G. Kunkel.

615.37　　　　　GW　ISSN 0071-7908
IMMUNOLOGY REPORTS AND REVIEWS/ FORTSCHRITTE DER IMMUNITAETSFORSCHUNG. (Text in English and German) 1959. irreg., vol. 7, 1979. price varies. Dr. Dietrich Steinkopff Verlag, Saalbaustr. 12, Postfach 11 1008, 6100 Darmstadt 11, W. Germany (B.R.D.) Ed. K. O. Vorlaender. index. circ. 2,000. Indexed: Curr.Cont.

615　　　　　US　ISSN 0073-5531
IMMUNOPATHOLOGY. Represents: International Symposium on Immunopathology. (Text in English, French, German) 1959. irreg., 7th, 1977. price varies. Grune and Stratton, Inc. (Subsidiary of: Harcourt Brace Jovanovich, Inc.) 111 Fifth Ave., New York, NY 10003. Eds. Dr. Pierre Grabar, Dr. Peter A. Miescher.

616.97　　　　　　SZ
INTERNATIONAL ASSOCIATION OF BIOLOGICAL STANDARDIZATION. (SYMPOSIUM PROCEEDINGS) (Supplement to: Developments in Biological Standardization) 36th, 1978. irreg. $80.60. S. Karger AG, Allschwilerstrasse 10, P.O. Box, CH-4009 Basel, Switzerland. Eds. W. Hennessen, C. Huygelen. illus.

616.97　　　　　NE　ISSN 0443-8604
INTERNATIONAL CONGRESS OF ALLERGOLOGY. ABSTRACTS OF REPORTS OF DISCUSSION AND OF COMMUNICATIONS. (Abstracts of 8th Congress published 1973) irreg. (International Association of Allergology) Excerpta Medica, P.O.B. 211, 1000 AE Amsterdam, Netherlands (Inquire: Dr. C. E. Arbesman, 50 High St., Buffalo, N.Y.)
Allergies

616.97　　　　　US　ISSN 0074-3453
INTERNATIONAL CONGRESS OF ALLERGOLOGY. PROCEEDINGS.* irreg., 1976, 9th, Buenos Aires. International Association of Allergology, c/o Dr. C. E. Arbesman, 50 High St, Buffalo, NY 14203.

616.97　　　　　SZ　ISSN 0074-4220
INTERNATIONAL CONVOCATION ON IMMUNOLOGY. PAPERS. 1968. irreg., 6th, 1978, Niagara Falls. 150 Fr.($90) per vol. (1981 price) (Center for Immunology) S. Karger AG, Allschwilerstrasse 10, P.O. Box, CH-4009 Basel, Switzerland. (reprint service avail. from ISI)

616.97 US
MENARINI SERIES ON IMMUNOPATHOLOGY. 1979. irreg., vol. 2, 1980. price varies. (Menarini Foundation) Springer-Verlag, 175 Fifth Ave., New York, NY 10010 (Also Berlin, Heidelberg, Vienna) (Co-sponsor: World Health Organization) (reprint service avail. from ISI)

615.1 616.9 US ISSN 0076-6917
METHODS IN IMMUNOLOGY AND IMMUNOCHEMISTRY. 1967. irreg., vol. 5, 1975. price varies. Academic Press, Inc, 111 Fifth Ave, New York, NY 10003. Eds. C. A. Williams, M. W. Chase.

616.97 SZ ISSN 0077-0760
MONOGRAPHS IN ALLERGY. (Text in English) 1966. irreg. (approx. 2/yr.) 90 Fr.($54) per vol. (1981 price) S. Karger AG, Allschwilerstrasse 10, P.O. Box, CH-4009 Basel, Switzerland. Ed.Bd. (reprint service avail. from ISI) Indexed: Biol.Abstr. Chem.Abstr. Curr.Cont. Ind.Med.

615.37 US
PERSPECTIVES IN IMMUNOLOGY; a series of publications based on symposia. 1969. irreg., latest 1978. Academic Press, Inc., 111 Fifth Ave., New York, NY 10003.

616.97 SZ ISSN 0079-6034
PROGRESS IN ALLERGY. (Text in English) 1939. irreg. (approx. 1/yr.) 150 Fr.($90) per vol. (1981 price) S. Karger AG, Allschwilerstrasse 10, P.O. Box, CH-4009 Basel, Switzerland. Eds. P. Kallos, B.H. Waksman, A.L. de Weck. (reprint service avail. from ISI) Indexed: Biol.Abstr. Chem.Abstr. Curr.Cont. Ind.Med.

615.37 GW ISSN 0340-904X
ZEITSCHRIFT FUER IMMUNITAETSFORSCHUNG-IMMUNOBIOLOGY. (Text and summaries in German and French) 1909. irreg., 5 nos per vol. DM.186 per vol. Gustav Fischer Verlag, Wollgrasweg 49, Postfach 720143, 7000 Stuttgart 70, W. Germany (B.R.D.) Ed. H. Brandis. circ. 900. Indexed: Biol.Abstr. Chem.Abstr. Ind.Med.
Former titles: Zeitschrift fuer Immunitaetsforschung - Immunologie; Zeitschrift fuer Immunitaetsforschung, Experimentelle und Klinische Immunologie (ISSN 0300-872X)

MEDICAL SCIENCES — Anaesthesiology

617.96 US ISSN 0093-7401
A S A REFRESHER COURSES IN ANESTHESIOLOGY. 1973. a. $10. (American Society of Anesthesiologists) J. B. Lippincott Co., E. Washington Square, Philadelphia, PA 19105. Ed. Dr. Solomon Hershey. charts. illus.

617.96 DK ISSN 0515-2720
ACTA ANAESTHESIOLOGICA SCANDINAVICA. SUPPLEMENTUM. irreg. free to subscribers. Munksgaard, 35 Noerre Soegade, DK-1370 Copenhagen K, Denmark. (reprint service avail. from ISI) Indexed: Biol.Abstr. Chem.Abstr. Curr.Cont. Ind.Med.

617.96 US
AMERICAN LECTURES IN ANESTHESIOLOGY. irreg. price varies. Charles C. Thomas, Publisher, 301-327 E. Lawrence Ave., Springfield, IL 62717.

617.96 US
ANAESTHESIOLOGIE UND INTENSIVMEDIZIN/ANAESTHESIOLOGY AND INTENSIVE CARE MEDICINE. (Contributions in German, English, French) 1963. irreg., vol. 134, 1981. price varies. Springer-Verlag, 175 Fifth Ave., New York, NY 10010 (also Berlin, Heidelberg, Vienna) (reprint service avail. from ISI)
Formerly: Anaesthesiology and Resuscitation (ISSN 0066-1341)

617.96 UK ISSN 0144-8684
CURRENT TOPICS IN ANAESTHESIA. 1979. irreg. price varies. Edward Arnold (Publishers) Ltd., 41 Bedford Square, London WC1B 3DQ, England.

DENTAL ANAESTHESIA AND SEDATION. see MEDICAL SCIENCES — Dentistry

617.96 SP ISSN 0071-2671
EUROPEAN CONGRESS OF ANAESTHESIOLOGY. PROCEEDINGS. (Proceedings published in host countries) 1962. quadrennial, 4th, Madrid, 1974. (World Federation of Societies of Anaesthesiologists) European Congress of Anaesthesiology, Inquire: Professor Arias, Arapiles 16, Madrid, Spain.

617.96 GW ISSN 0303-6200
INTENSIVMEDIZINISCHE PRAXIS. 1965. a. avail. only with subscr. to Chirurgische Praxis (DM.198) Hans Marseille Verlag, Buerkleinstr. 12, 8000 Munich 22, W. Germany (B.R.D.) Eds. H. E. Grewe, M. Schmid. adv. bk. rev. bibl. charts. illus. circ. 5,000. (also avail. in microform from UMI)
Formerly(until 1979): Anasthesiologische Praxis (ISSN 0044-8214)

617.96 US
KLINISCHE ANAESTHESIOLOGIE UND INTENSIVTHERAPIE. 1973. irreg., vol. 22, 1980. price varies. Springer-Verlag, 175 Fifth Ave., New York, NY 10010 (Also Berlin, Heidelberg, Vienna) Ed.Bd. (reprint service avail. from ISI)

617.96 NE ISSN 0303-254X
MONOGRAPHS IN ANAESTHESIOLOGY. 1974. irreg. $21 price varies. Excerpta Medica, Box 211, 1000 AE Amsterdam, Netherlands.

617.96 US ISSN 0099-1546
PROGRESS IN ANAESTHESIOLOGY. 1975. irreg. Raven Press, 1140 Ave. of the Americas, New York, NY 10036.

617 UK
ROYAL COLLEGE OF SURGEONS OF ENGLAND. FACULTY OF ANAESTHETISTS. NEWSLETTER. 1965. a. membership. ‡ Royal College of Surgeons of England, Faculty of Anaesthetists, 35-43 Lincoln's Inn Fields, London WC2A 3PN, England. circ. 4,750(controlled)

617.96 011 GE
SYMPOSIUM ANAESTHESIOLOGIAE INTERNATIONALE. BERICHTE. (Text in German, English, Russian) 1966. biennial. M.50. Society for Anesthesiology and Resuscitation of the GDR, Karowerstr. 11, Berlin , E. Germany (D.D.R.) Ed. E. Danzmann. adv. circ. 500.

617.95 NE ISSN 0084-1595
WORLD CONGRESS OF ANAESTHESIOLOGISTS. PROCEEDINGS. irreg., 6th, 1976, Mexico City. $56.25. (World Federation of Societies of Anaesthesiologists) Excerpta Medica, P.O.B. 211, 1000 AE Amsterdam, Netherlands.

617.96 US ISSN 0084-3652
YEAR BOOK OF ANESTHESIA. 1961. a. price varies. ‡ Year Book Medical Publishers, Inc., 35 E. Wacker Dr., Chicago, IL 60601. Ed. Bd.

MEDICAL SCIENCES — Cancer

616.994 US ISSN 0065-230X
ADVANCES IN CANCER RESEARCH. 1953. irreg., vol. 34, 1981. price varies. Academic Press, Inc. (Subsidiary of: Harcourt Brace Jovanovich) 111 Fifth Ave., New York, NY 10003. Eds. Jesse P. Greenstein, Alexander Haddow. Indexed: Ind.Med.

616.9 US ISSN 0066-1627
ANDERSON HOSPITAL AND TUMOR INSTITUTE, HOUSTON, TEXAS. GENERAL REPORT. 1965. biennial. free. University of Texas, M.D. Anderson Hospital and Tumor Institute, Texas Medical Center, Houston, TX 77030. circ. 5,000.

616.9 US ISSN 0066-1635
ANDERSON HOSPITAL AND TUMOR INSTITUTE, HOUSTON, TEXAS. RESEARCH REPORT. 1955. biennial. free. University of Texas, M.D. Anderson Hospital and Tumor Institute, Texas Medical Center, Houston, TX 77030. circ. 4,000.

616.99 SW
ANNUAL REPORT ON RESULTS OF TREATMENT IN GYNECOLOGICAL CANCER. 1937. triennial. Kr.60($15) International Federation of Gynecology and Obstetrics, Cancer Committee, Radiumhemmet, S-104 01 Stockholm, Sweden. Ed. Dr. H. L. Kottmeier. adv. circ. 1,400.
Formerly (1937-1979): Annual Report on the Results of Treatment in Carcinoma of the Uterus, Vagina, and Ovary.

616.9 SP
ASOCIACION ESPANOLA CONTRA EL CANCER. MEMORIA TECNICO-ADMINISTRATIVA. 1958. a. free. ‡ Asociacion Espanola Contra el Cancer, Amador de los Rios 5, Madrid 4, Spain. charts. stat.
Formerly: Asociacion Espanola Contra el Cancer. Memoria de la Assemblea General (ISSN 0066-8540)

616.992 CN ISSN 0068-1423
BRITISH COLUMBIA. CANCER FOUNDATION. ANNUAL REPORT. 1950. a. Cancer Foundation, 2656 Heather St., Vancouver, B.C. V5Z 3J3, Canada.

616.9 CN ISSN 0708-0999
CANADIAN CANCER SOCIETY. B. C. AND YUKON DIVISION. NEWSLETTER. 1978. irreg. membership. Canadian Cancer Society, B.C. and Yukon Division, 1926 West Broadway, Vancouver, B.C. V6T 1Z2, Canada. illus.
Formerly: Canadian Cancer Society. B.C. and Yukon Division. Provincial News (ISSN 0708-1030)

616.99 NE
CANCER CHEMOTHERAPY. 1979. a. Excerpta Medica, Box 211, 1000 AE Amsterdam, Netherlands. Ed. H. M. Pinedo.

616.994 US ISSN 0069-0147
CANCER FACTS AND FIGURES. 1951. a. free. ‡ American Cancer Society Inc., 777 Third Ave., New York, NY 10017. Ed. Gigi Marion. circ. 400,000.

615 619 US ISSN 0340-7004
CANCER IMMUNOLOGY AND IMMUNOTHERAPY. 1976. 2 vols. per yr., 3 nos. per vol. $185. Springer Verlag, 175 Fifth Ave., New York, NY 10010 (And Berlin, Heidelberg, Vienna) (reprint service avail. from ISI)

616.9 CN ISSN 0315-9884
CANCER IN ONTARIO. 1946. a. free. Ontario Cancer Treatment and Research Foundation, 7 Overlea Blvd., Toronto, Ont. M4H 1A8, Canada. Ed. J. O. Godden. circ. 16,000.
Formerly: Ontario Cancer Treatment and Research Foundation. Annual Report (ISSN 0078-4699)

616.9 PR
CANCER IN PUERTO RICO. (Text in English and Spanish) 1950. a. Department of Health, Cancer Control Program, Central Cancer Registry, Santurce, PR 00908. Ed. Dr. Isidro Martinez. circ. 1,000. Indexed: Excerp.Med.

616.9 SW ISSN 0069-0155
CANCER INCIDENCE IN SWEDEN. 1960. a. price varies. (Swedish Cancer Registry) Liber Foerlag, Fack, S-162 89 Vaellingby, Sweden. circ. 2,000.

616.994 JA
CANCER INSTITUTE SCIENTIFIC REPORT. 1976. a. free. Cancer Institute, 1-37-1 Kami-Ikebukuro, Toshima-ku, Tokyo 170, Japan. Ed. Dr. Tadashi Utakoji. circ. 1,500.

616.994 UK ISSN 0365-9623
CANCER RESEARCH CAMPAIGN. ANNUAL REPORT. 1924. a. free to medical & scientific institutions. Cancer Research Campaign, 2 Carlton House Terrace, London SW1Y 5AR, England. circ. controlled.

616.9 US ISSN 0069-0171
CANCER SEMINAR PROCEEDINGS. 1950-1974; N.S. 1975. irreg. $10. University of South Florida, College of Medicine, Tampa, FL 33620. Ed. J. A. del Regato, M.D.

616.994 CN
CANCER TREATMENT AND RESEARCH FOUNDATION. ANNUAL REPORT. 1950. a. British Columbia Cancer Treatment and Research Foundation, 2656 Heather St., Vancouver, B.C., Canada.

616 US ISSN 0147-4006
CARCINOGENESIS; a comprehensive survey. 1976. irreg., vol. 5, 1979. price varies. Raven Press, 1140 Ave. of the Americas, New York, NY 10036.

CURRENT PRACTICE IN ONCOLOGIC NURSING. see MEDICAL SCIENCES — Nurses And Nursing

362.1 US ISSN 0095-6775
DAMON RUNYON-WALTER WINCHELL CANCER FUND. ANNUAL REPORT. 1973. a. Damon Runyon Walter Winchell Cancer Fund, 33 W. 56th St., New York, NY 10019. Key Title: Annual Report - Damon Runyon-Walter Winchell Cancer Fund.
Continues: Damon Runyon Memorial Fund for Cancer Research. Report.

616.9 GW ISSN 0070-4229
DEUTSCHES KREBSFORSCHUNGSZENTRUM. VEROEFFENTLICHUNGEN. 1965. irreg. Deutsches Krebsforschungszentrum, Institut fuer Dokumentation, Information und Statistik, Im Neuenheimer Feld 280, 6900 Heidelberg 1, W. Germany (B.R.D.)

616 US
EUROPEAN ORGANIZATION FOR RESEARCH ON TREATMENT OF CANCER. MONOGRAPH SERIES. 1975. irreg., vol. 5, 1978. price varies. (BE) Raven Press, 1140 Ave. of the Americas, New York, NY 10036. Ed. M.J. Staquet. Indexed: Curr.Cont.

FRONTIERS OF RADIATION THERAPY AND ONCOLOGY. see MEDICAL SCIENCES — Radiology And Nuclear Medicine

616.9 US ISSN 0072-0151
GANN MONOGRAPHS. (Text mainly in English; occasionally in French or German) 1966. irreg.(approx. 2 issues per year); 1970, no. 9. price varies. (Japanese Cancer Association) University Park Press, Chamber of Commerce Bldg., Baltimore, MD 21202. Ed. Tomizo Yoshida M.D.
Proceedings of international conferences and symposia dealing with cancer or related fields

616.994 FR ISSN 0072-7806
GROUPEMENT DES ENTREPRISES FRANCAISES DANS LA LUTTE CONTRE LE CANCER. BULLETIN NATIONAL DE LIAISON.* (Title varies) irreg., 1970, no. 4. price varies. Federation Nationale des Groupements des Entreprises Francaises dans la Lutte Contre le Cancer, 4 rue Auber, Paris 8e, France.

616.9 JA
HYOGO CANCER HOSPITAL. BULLETIN/ HYOGO-KENRITSU BYOIN GAN SENTA KIYO. (Text in Japanese; table of contents also in English) 1962/63. a. Hyogo Cancer Hospital - Hyogo-kenritsu Byoin Gan Senta, Kobe, Japan.
Continues (vol. 7, 1973): Hyogo-ken Gan Senta Nenpo (ISSN 0441-537X)

616.994 UN
I A R C MONOGRAPHS ON THE EVALUATION OF THE CARCINOGENIC RISK OF CHEMICALS TO HUMANS. (Text in English) 1972. irreg. price varies. International Agency for Research on Cancer - Centre International de Recherche sur le Cancer, 150 cours Albert-Thomas, 69372 Lyon Cedex 2, France (U.S. subscr. addr.: World Health Organization, Box 5284, Church Street Station, New York, NY 10246) Indexed: Curr.Cont.
Formerly: I A R C Monographs on the Evaluation of Carcinogenic Risk of Chemicals to Man.

616.994 UN ISSN 0300-5038
I A R C SCIENTIFIC PUBLICATIONS. 1971. irreg. price varies. International Agency for Research on Cancer - Centre International de Recherche sur le Cancer, 150 cours Albert-Thomas, 69372 Lyon Cedex 2, France (U.S. subscr. addr.: World Health Organization, Box 5284, Church Street Station, New York, NY 10246) Ed. W. Davis. Indexed: Curr.Cont. Ind.Med.
Formerly: International Agency for Research on Cancer. I A R C Technical Publications.

616.994 UK
IMPERIAL CANCER RESEARCH FUND. SCIENTIFIC REPORT. 1973. a. private circulation to qualified personnel. Imperial Cancer Research Fund, Lincoln's Inn Fields, London, WC2A 3PX, England.

616.994 MX ISSN 0076-7131
INSTITUTO NACIONAL DE CANCEROLOGIA, MEXICO. REVISTA. 1954. irreg. free. Instituto Nacional de Cancerologia, Ninos Heroes 151, Mexico 7, D.F., Mexico. (Co-sponsor: Sociedad Mexicana de Estudios Oncologicos) Ed. Dr. Jose Noriega Limon. adv. circ. 5,000. Indexed: Ind.Med.

616.992 PE ISSN 0079-1083
INSTITUTO NACIONAL DE ENFERMEDADES NEOPLASICAS. TRABAJOS DE INVESTIGACION CLINICA Y EXPERIMENTAL. (Text in Castilian and English) 1952. a. free. Instituto Nacional de Enfermedades Neoplasicas, Av. Alfonso Ugarte 825, Lima, Peru. Ed. Eduardo Caceres, M.D. index.

616.99 US ISSN 0190-1575
INTERNATIONAL ADVANCES IN SURGICAL ONCOLOGY. 1979. irreg. price varies. Alan R. Liss, Inc., 150 Fifth Ave., New York, NY 10011. Ed. Gerald P. Murphy. charts. illus.

616.99 SZ
INTERNATIONAL CATALOGUE OF FILMS, FILMSTRIPS AND SLIDES ON PUBLIC EDUCATION ABOUT CANCER. Variant title: International Catalogue of Films for Public Education About Cancer. (Subseries of U I C C Technical Report Series) (Text in English; summaries in English, French and Spanish) 1977. irreg. 30 Fr. International Union Against Cancer - Union Internationale Contre le Cancer, 3 rue de Conseil-General, 1205 Geneva, Switzerland. circ. 1,000.

616.99 SZ
INTERNATIONAL DIRECTORY OF SPECIALIZED CANCER RESEARCH AND TREATMENT ESTABLISHMENTS. (Subseries of U I C C Technical Report Series) 1976. irreg. 100 Fr.($30) International Union Against Cancer - Union Internationale Contre le Cancer, 3 rue de Conseil-General, 1205 Geneva, Switzerland.

616.9 UN ISSN 0538-7736
INTERNATIONAL HISTOLOGICAL CLASSIFICATION OF TUMOURS. (Edts. in English, French, and Spanish) 1967. irreg. price varies. World Health Organization - Organisation Mondiale de la Sante, Distribution and Sales Service, 20 Avenue Appia, Ch-1211 Geneva 27, Switzerland. (slides in box accompany each text)

610 SZ ISSN 0074-9192
INTERNATIONAL UNION AGAINST CANCER. MANUAL/UNION INTERNATIONALE CONTRE LE CANCER. MANUELE. (Text in English and French) 1963. irreg., latest 1979. free. ‡ International Union Against Cancer - Union Internationale Contre le Cancer, 3 rue de Conseil-General, 1205 Geneva, Switzerland.

616.994 SZ ISSN 0074-9206
INTERNATIONAL UNION AGAINST CANCER. PROCEEDINGS OF CONGRESS. quadrennial, 12th, 1978, Buenos Aires. International Union Against Cancer - Union Internationale Contre le Cancer, 3 rue du Conseil General, 1205 Geneva, Switzerland.

616.9 JA ISSN 0075-3327
JAPAN SOCIETY FOR CANCER THERAPY. PROCEEDINGS OF THE CONGRESS. (Text in English) 1963. a. 5000 Yen. Japan Society for Cancer Therapy - Nihon Gan Chiryo Gakkai, Kyoto University Medical School, Second Surgical Division, Shogoin Kawara-cho, Sakyo-ku, Kyoto 606, Japan.

616.994 JA ISSN 0022-2119
JOURNAL OF KARYOPATHOLOGY/ SAIBOKAKU BYORIGAKU ZASSHI; tumor and tumor virus. (Text in Japanese; summaries in English) 1953. irreg. $2. Okayama University, School of Medicine, Department of Pathology - Okayama Daigaku Igakubu Byorigaku Kyoshitsu, 2-5-1 Shikata-cho, Okayama 700, Japan. Ed. Y. Hamazaki. adv. Indexed: Ind.Med.

616.99 SZ ISSN 0379-1998
KARGER HIGHLIGHTS: ONCOLOGY; reported selected top articles. 1979. a. 15 Fr.($9) (1981 price) S. Karger AG, Allschwilerstrasse 10, P.O. Box, CH-4009 Basel, Switzerland. Ed. F. Homburger. charts. illus. (reprint service avail. from ISI)

KAZAKHSKII NAUCHNO-ISSLEDOVATEL'SKII INSTITUT ONKOLOGII I RADIOLOGII. TRUDY. see MEDICAL SCIENCES — Radiology And Nuclear Medicine

616.99 US ISSN 0160-2454
M D ANDERSON CLINICAL CONFERENCES ON CANCER. 1978. a. (M D Anderson Hospital, Tumor Institute) Raven Press, 1140 Ave. of the Americas, New York, NY 10036.

616.99 US
M D ANDERSON SYMPOSIA IN FUNDAMENTAL CANCER RESEARCH. 1978. a. Raven Press, 1140 Ave. of Americas, New York, NY 10036.

616.99 US
M D ANDERSON SYMPOSIA ON THE DIAGNOSIS AND MANAGEMENT OF CANCER. 1979. irreg. price varies. Raven Press, 1140 Ave. of the Americas, New York, NY 10036.

616.9 US ISSN 0076-342X
MALIGNANT INTRIGUE. 1970. irreg., latest 1975, next 1981. $25. Julia M. Lampkin-Asam, Ed. & Pub., 433 Prince Ave., Tuscaloosa, AL 35401. circ. 100-300.

616.99 UK
MANAGEMENT OF MALIGNANT DISEASE SERIES. 1978. irreg. price varies. Edward Arnold (Publishers) Ltd., 41 Bedford Square, London WC1B 3DQ, England. Eds.M. J. Peckham, R. L. Carter.

616.9 CN ISSN 0076-3802
MANITOBA CANCER TREATMENT AND RESEARCH FOUNDATION. REPORT. 1957-58. a. free. Manitoba Cancer Treatment and Research Foundation, 700 Bannatyne Ave., Winnipeg, Man. R3E 0V9, Canada.

616.99 US
MASSON CANCER MANAGEMENT SERIES. 1977. irreg., vol. 8, 1981. price varies. Masson Publishing U.S.A., Inc., 14 E. 60th St., New York, NY 10022. Ed. Luther W. Brady, M.D.

MASSON MONOGRAPHS IN PEDIATRIC HEMATOLOGY/ONCOLOGY. see MEDICAL SCIENCES — Pediatrics

616.99 US ISSN 0076-6852
METHODS IN CANCER RESEARCH. 1967. irreg., vol. 17, 1979. price varies. Academic Press,Inc., 11 Fifth Ave., New York, NY 10003. Ed. Harris Busch.

616.9 JA
NATIONAL CANCER CENTER. ANNUAL REPORT/KOKURITSU GAN SENTA NENPO. (Text in Japanese) 1967. a. National Cancer Center - Kokuritsu Gan Senta, 5-1-1 Tsukiji, Chuo-ku, Tokyo 104, Japan.

616.9 JA ISSN 0077-3662
NATIONAL CANCER CENTER. COLLECTED PAPERS/KOKURITSU GAN SENTA, TOKYO. COLLECTED PAPERS. (Text in English) 1966. a. free to medical libraries and researchers. National Cancer Center - Kokuritsu Gan Senta, 5-1-1 Tsukiji, Chuo-ku, Tokyo 104, Japan. author index. circ. 225.

616.994 US ISSN 0077-3670
NATIONAL CANCER CONFERENCE. PROCEEDINGS; addresses and panel discussions sponsored by the American Cancer Society and the National Cancer Institute. irreg. 219 E. 42 St., New York, NY 10017.

616.9　　　　CN　ISSN 0077-3689
NATIONAL CANCER INSTITUTE OF CANADA. REPORT. a. free. National Cancer Institute of Canada, 77 Bloor St. W., Suite 401, Toronto, Ont. M5S 2V7, Canada. Ed. Dr. P. G. Scholefield. circ. 800.

661.994　　　　UK　ISSN 0307-6695
NEW ASPECTS OF BREAST CANCER. 1974. irreg. Heinemann Medical Books Ltd., 23 Bedford Square, London WC1B 3HH, England (Dist.in U.S. by: Yearbook Medical Publishers Inc., 35 E.Wacker Drive, Chicago, IL 60601) illus.

616　　　　JA
OSAKA UNIVERSITY. INSTITUTE FOR CANCER RESEARCH. ANNUAL REPORT. (Text in English) irreg. exchange basis. Osaka University, Institute for Cancer Research - Osaka Daigaku Igakubu Fuzoku Gankenku Shisetsu, 3-12 Dojimahama-dori, Fukushima-ku, Osaka-shi 553, Japan.

616.994　　　　IT　ISSN 0069-8520
PERUGIA QUADRENNIAL INTERNATIONAL CONFERENCES ON CANCER. PROCEEDINGS. 1957. quadrennial. price varies. Universita degli Studi di Perugia, Division of Cancer Research, P.O.Box 327, 06100 Perugia, Monteluce, Italy. Ed. Lucio Severi. index.

616.99　　　　US
PRINCESS TAKAMATSU CANCER RESEARCH SYMPOSIA. 1972. a. price varies. University Park Press, American Medical Publishers, Chamber of Commerce Bldg., Baltimore, MD 21202.

616　　　　US　ISSN 0145-3726
PROGRESS IN CANCER RESEARCH AND THERAPY. 1976. irreg., vol. 11, 1979. price varies. Raven Press, 1140 Ave. of the Americas, New York, NY 10036.

616.994　　　　US　ISSN 0079-6166
PROGRESS IN CLINICAL CANCER. 1965. irreg. price varies. Grune and Stratton, Inc. (Subsidiary of: Harcourt Brace Jovanovich, Inc.) 111 Fifth Avenue, New York, NY 10003. Ed. I. M. Ariel, M.D. Indexed: Ind.Med.

616.994　　　　SZ　ISSN 0079-6263
PROGRESS IN EXPERIMENTAL TUMOR RESEARCH. (Text in English) 1960. irreg. (approx. 1/yr.) 150 Fr.($90) per vol. (1981 price) S. Karger AG, Allschwilerstrasse 10, P.O. Box, CH-4009 Basel, Switzerland. Ed. F. Homburger. (reprint service avail. from ISI) Indexed: Biol.Abstr. Chem.Abstr. Curr.Cont. Ind.Med.

616.9　　　　YU　ISSN 0079-9580
RAK V SLOVENIJI. TABELE/CANCER IN SLOVENIA. TABLES. (Text in Slovenian) 1957. a. free. Onkoloski Institut, Zaloska C,2, 61005 Ljubljana, Yugoslavia. Ed. Bozena Ravnihar. index. circ. 900.

616.994　　　　US　ISSN 0080-0015
RECENT RESULTS IN CANCER RESEARCH/ FORTSCHRITTE DER KREBSFORSCHUNG. (Text in English; Occasionally in German or French) 1965. irreg., vol. 78, 1981. price varies. Springer-Verlag, 175 Fifth Ave., New York, NY 10010 (also Berlin, Heidelberg, Vienna) Ed. P. Rentchnick. (reprint service avail. from ISI) Indexed: Ind.Med.

616.9　　　　US　ISSN 0081-0045
SLOAN-KETTERING INSTITUTE FOR CANCER RESEARCH. PROGRESS REPORT. 1949. a. free. Sloan-Kettering Institute for Cancer Research, 410 E. 68 St., New York, NY 10021. Ed. Dr. Stacey B. Day.
Continues: Memorial Sloan-Kettering Cancer Center. New York. Report.

616.994　　　　US　ISSN 0082-0733
SYMPOSIA ON FUNDAMENTAL CANCER RESEARCH. PAPERS. 1947, no. 2; proceedings of first never published. a. price varies. Williams & Wilkins Co., 428 E. Preston St., Baltimore, MD 21202. (Co-sponsors: University of Texas M.D. Anderson Hospital and Tumor Institute, Houston; University of Texas Graduate School of Biomedical Sciences) Eds. R. W. Cumley & J. McCay.

TASK FORCE ON ENVIRONMENTAL CANCER AND HEART AND LUNG DISEASE. ANNUAL REPORT TO CONGRESS. see ENVIRONMENTAL STUDIES

616.9　　　　SZ　ISSN 0074-9222
U I C C TECHNICAL REPORT SERIES. 1968. irreg., latest vol. 48. price varies. ‡ International Union Against Cancer - Union Internationale Contre le Cancer, 3 rue de Conseil-General, 1205 Geneva, Switzerland.

616.994　　　　US　ISSN 0083-1921
U. S. NATIONAL CANCER INSTITUTE. MONOGRAPH. 1959. irreg., latest issue no. 47. price varies. U. S. National Cancer Institute, Department of Health, Education, and Welfare, Bethesda, MD 20205 (Orders to: Supt. of Documents, Washington, DC 20402) Indexed: Ind.Med.

616.9　　　　US　ISSN 0090-2403
U.S. NATIONAL CANCER INSTITUTE. REPORT OF THE CARCINOGENESIS PROGRAM. irreg. U.S. National Cancer Institute, Office of the Associate Director for Carcinogenesis, Building 37, Room 3a21, Bethesda, MD 20205. Key Title: Report of the Carcinogenesis Program.

616.9　　　　US　ISSN 0092-9468
U. S. NATIONAL CANCER PROGRAM. REPORT OF THE NATIONAL CANCER ADVISORY BOARD SUBMITTED TO THE PRESIDENT OF THE UNITED STATES FOR TRANSMITTAL TO THE CONGRESS OF THE UNITED STATES. (Subseries of U.S. Dept. of Health, Education, and Welfare. DHEW Publication) 1973. irreg. free. U.S. National Cancer Institute, Bethesda, MD 20205. circ. 20,000. Key Title: National Cancer Program; Report of the National Cancer Advisory Board Submitted to the President of the United States for Transmittal to the Congress of the United States.

WEST COAST CANCER SYMPOSIUM. PROCEEDINGS. see MEDICAL SCIENCES — Radiology And Nuclear Medicine

MEDICAL SCIENCES — Cardiovascular Diseases

616.1　　　　US
ACUTE MYOCARDIAL INFARCTION SYMPOSIUM. PROCEEDINGS. a. price varies. Williams and Wilkins Co., 428 E. Preston St, Baltimore, MD 21202.

616.1　　　　SZ　ISSN 0065-2326
ADVANCES IN CARDIOLOGY. (Text in English) 1956. irreg. (approx. 2/yr.) 120 Fr.($72) per vol. (1981 price) S. Karger AG, Allschwilerstrasse 10, P.O. Box, CH-4009 Basel, Switzerland. (reprint service avail. from ISI) Indexed: Biol.Abstr. Chem.Abstr. Curr.Cont. Ind.Med.

616.1　　　　SZ　ISSN 0378-6900
ADVANCES IN CARDIOVASCULAR PHYSICS. (Text in English) a. 100 Fr.($60) per vol. (1981 price) S. Karger AG, Allschwilerstrasse 10, P.O. Box, CH-4009 Basel, Switzerland. Ed. D.N. Ghista. charts. illus. index. circ. 1,000. (reprint service avail. from ISI) Indexed: Biol.Abstr. Chem.Abstr. Curr.Cont. Ind.Med.

612 591　　　　SZ　ISSN 0065-2938
ADVANCES IN MICROCIRCULATION. (Text in English) 1968. irreg. (approx. 1/yr.) 100 Fr.($60) (1981 price) S. Karger AG, Allschwilerstrasse 10, P.O. Box, CH-4009 Basel, Switzerland. Eds. H. Harders, E. Davis, B.M. Altura. (reprint service avail. from ISI) Indexed: Biol.Abstr. Chem.Abstr. Curr.Cont. Ind.Med.

616.1　　　　US　ISSN 0270-4056
ADVANCES IN MYOCARDIOLOGY. 1972. irreg., vol. 4, 1974 (approx. 2 vols. per yr.) $39.50. (International Study Group for Research in Cardiac Metabolism) University Park Press, Chamber of Commerce Bldg., Baltimore, MD 21202. Eds. G. Rona, N. S. Dhalla. Indexed: Ind.Med.
Formerly: Recent Advances in Studies on Cardiac Structure and Metabolism (ISSN 0363-5872)

616.1　　　　US
ADVANCES IN THE MANAGEMENT OF CARDIOVASCULAR DISEASE. 1980. a. price varies. Year Book Medical Publishers, Inc., 35 E. Wacker Dr., Chicago, IL 60601. Ed. William T. Foley.

616.1　　　　US　ISSN 0146-8790
ADVANCES IN THE MANAGEMENT OF CLINICAL HEART DISEASE. 1976. irreg.,vol. 4, 1980. Futura Publishing Co., 295 Main St., Box 330, Mount Kisco, NY 10549. Eds. Drs. Jacob I. Haft, Charles P. Bailey.

616.1　　　　US
AMERICAN COLLEGE OF CARDIOLOGY. SYMPOSIA. 1973. irreg. price varies. University Park Press, American Medical Publishers, Chamber of Commerce Bldg., Baltimore, MD 21202.

616.6　　　　US　ISSN 0065-8499
AMERICAN HEART ASSOCIATION. MONOGRAPHS. 1960. irreg., no. 44, 1974. price varies. American Heart Association, Inc., 7320 Greenville Ave., Dallas, TX 75231. Indexed: Ind.Med.

616.1　　　　US　ISSN 0065-8502
AMERICAN HEART ASSOCIATION. SCIENTIFIC SESSIONS. ABSTRACTS. 1927. a. $8. American Heart Association, Inc., Committee on Scientific Sessions Program, 7320 Greenville Ave., Dallas, TX 75231. adv. index. circ. 20,000.

616.1　　　　IO　ISSN 0587-5471
ASIAN PACIFIC CONGRESS OF CARDIOLOGY. SYMPOSIA.* irreg. Asian-Pacific Society of Cardiology, c/o Cardiac Centre, Jalan Diponegoro 69, Jakarta, Indonesia, NY 10003 (Symposia from 4th Congress, 1968, pub. by Academic Press, US)
Cardiology

616.136　　　　US　ISSN 0362-1650
ATHEROSCLEROSIS REVIEWS. 1975. irreg., vol. 6, 1979. price varies. Raven Press, 1140 Ave. of the Americas, New York, NY 10036. Eds. Rodolfo Paoletti, Antonio Gotto. Indexed: Curr.Cont. Sci.Cit.Ind.
Atherosclerosis

616.1　　　　GW　ISSN 0075-7101
BEITRAEGE ZUR KARDIOLOGIE UND ANGIOLOGIE. (Text in English, French, German) 1937. irreg. price varies. Dr. Dietrich Steinkopff Verlag, Saalbaustr. 12, Postfach 11 1008, 6100 Darmstadt 11, W. Germany (B.R.D.) Eds. F. Bender, W. Meesmann. circ. 1,500.
Formerly: Kreislauf Buecherei.
Cardiology and Angiology

616.1　　　　SZ　ISSN 0067-7906
BIBLIOTHECA CARDIOLOGICA. (Text in English) 1939. irreg. (approx. 1/yr.) 80 Fr.($48) per vol. (1981 price) S. Karger AG, Allschwilerstrasse 10, P.O. Box, CH-4009 Basel, Switzerland. (reprint service avail. from ISI) Indexed: Biol.Abstr. Chem.Abstr. Curr.Cont. Ind.Med.
Cardiology

616.1　　　　CN　ISSN 0068-8851
CANADIAN HEART FOUNDATION. ANNUAL REPORT. (Text in English, and French) a. free. Canadian Heart Foundation, Suite 1200, One Nicholas St., Ottawa, Ont. K1N 7B7, Canada.

616.1　　　　US　ISSN 0163-1675
CARDIOLOGY UPDATE; review for physicians. 1979. a. Elsevier North-Holland, Inc., New York, 52 Vanderbilt Ave., New York, NY 10017. Ed. E. Rapaport.

616.6　　　　US　ISSN 0069-0384
CARDIOVASCULAR CLINICS. 1969. 3 vols./yr., vol. 10, 1979. $37.50 per no. F. A. Davis Co., 1915 Arch St., Philadelphia, PA 19103. Ed.Bd. Indexed: Ind.Med.

617.41　　　　US　ISSN 0069-0406
CARDIOVASCULAR SURGERY. (Subseries of: American Heart Assn. Monographs) 1962. a. $6. American Heart Association, Inc., Council on Cardiovascular Surgery, 7320 Greenville Ave., Dallas, TX 75231. adv. circ. 20,000. Indexed: Ind.Med.

616.1　　　　　　US　　ISSN 0069-4193
CIRCULATION. SUPPLEMENT. 1964. irreg. price varies. American Heart Association, Inc., 7320 Greenville Ave., Dallas, TX 75231. Ed. Dr. Neal S. Bricker. adv. circ. 20,000. Indexed: Ind.Med.

616.1　　　　　　US　　ISSN 0069-4185
CIRCULATION RESEARCH. SUPPLEMENT. 1964. irreg. price varies. American Heart Association, Inc., 7320 Greenville Ave., Dallas, TX 75231. Ed. Neal S. Bricker. circ. 20,000. Indexed: Ind.Med.

616.1　　　　　　US
CLINICAL CARDIOLOGY MONOGRAPHS. 1972. irreg., latest 1978. price varies. Grune and Stratton, Inc. (Subsidiary of: Harcourt Brace Jovanovich, Inc.) 111 Fifth Ave., New York, NY 10003.
　　Formerly (vol. 1): Cardiovascular Diseases; Current Status and Advances.

616.2　　　　　　US　　ISSN 0069-5319
COLLECTED WORKS ON CARDIO-PULMONARY DISEASE. 1959. irreg.; latest issue, vol. 21, 1977. free. Heineman Medical Research Center, Box 4457, Charlotte, NC 28204. Indexed: Ind.Med.

COMPUTERS IN CARDIOLOGY. see COMPUTER TECHNOLOGY AND APPLICATIONS

616.1　　　　　　US　　ISSN 0093-5166
CONTEMPORARY PROBLEMS IN CARDIOLOGY. 1974. irreg., vol. 3, 1976. Futura Publishing Co., 295 Main St., Box 330, Mount Kisco, NY 10549. Ed. Robert S. Eliot, M.D. illus.
　　Cardiology

616.1　　　　　　US
CURRENT CARDIOLOGY. 1979. a. $30. Houghton Mifflin Professional Publishers, Medical Division, 2 Park St., Boston, MA 02107.

616.1　　　　　　US
CURRENT CARDIOVASCULAR TOPICS. 1975. irreg. price varies. Thieme-Stratton, Inc., 381 Park Ave. S., New York, NY 10016. Ed. E. Donoso.

616.1　　612.5　　GW　　ISSN 0070-4075
DEUTSCHE GESELLSCHAFT FUER KREISLAUFFORSCHUNG. VERHANDLUNGEN. (Text in English, French, German) 1928. a. price varies. Dr. Dietrich Steinkopff Verlag, Saalbaustr. 12, Postfach 11 1008, 6100 Darmstadt 11, W. Germany (B.R.D.) Ed. W. Schaper. index. circ. 2,000. Indexed: Ind.Med.

616.1　　　　　　US　　ISSN 0163-6065
DIRECTORY OF BLOOD ESTABLISHMENTS REGISTERED UNDER SECTION 510 OF THE FOOD, DRUG, AND COSMETIC ACT. 1976. a. U.S. Food and Drug Administration, Bureau of Biologics, Bethesda, MD 20014.

612.1　　　　　　SZ　　ISSN 0071-2655
EUROPEAN CONFERENCE ON MICROCIRCULATION. PROCEEDINGS. 1960. irreg., 10th, 1978, Cagliari. 150 Fr.($90) per vol. (1981 price) (European Society on Microcirculation) S. Karger AG, Allschwilerstrasse 10, P.O. Box, CH-4009 Basel, Switzerland. (reprint service avail. from ISI)

616.1　　　　　　BE　　ISSN 0421-7527
EUROPEAN CONGRESS OF CARDIOLOGY. ABSTRACTS OF PAPERS.* (Text in English, German & French) 1952. irreg., 1976, 7th, The Hague. European Society of Cardiology, c/o Prof. H. Denolin, 178 Av. Winston Churchill, 1180 Brussels, Belgium.
　　Cardiology

616.1　　　　　　BE　　ISSN 0423-7242
EUROPEAN CONGRESS OF CARDIOLOGY. (PROCEEDINGS)* 1952. irreg., 1976, 7th, The Hague. European Society of Cardiology, c/o Prof. H. Denolin, 178 Av. Winston Churchill, 1180 Brussels, Belgium.
　　Cardiology

616.1　　　　　　SZ　　ISSN 0302-511X
EUROPEAN CONGRESS ON BALLISTOCARDIOGRAPHY AND CARDIOVASCULAR DYNAMICS. PROCEEDINGS. (Subseries of: Bibliotheca Cardiologica) (Text in English) irreg. 140 Fr.($84) per vol. (1981 price) S. Karger AG, Allschwilerstrasse 10, P.O. Box, CH-4009 Basel, Switzerland. (reprint service avail. from ISI)

616.1　　　　　　US　　ISSN 0073-425X
HYPERTENSION SERIES. (Supplement to: Circulation Research) 1952. a. $5-6. American Heart Association, Inc., 7320 Greenville Ave., Dallas, TX 75231. circ. 4,500. Indexed: Ind.Med.
Represents: Council for High Blood Pressure Research. Proceedings.
　　Hypertension

616.13　　　　　　IT　　ISSN 0074-347X
INTERNATIONAL CONGRESS OF ANGIOLOGY. PROCEEDINGS. 1952. irreg., 1976, 10th, Tokyo. International Union of Angiology, c/o Marcello Tesi, Via Bonifacio Lupi 11, 20129 Florence, Italy. Proceedings published in host country

612.1　　615.65　　FR　　ISSN 0074-8528
INTERNATIONAL SOCIETY OF BLOOD TRANSFUSION. PROCEEDINGS OF THE CONGRESS. irreg., 1975, 14th, Helsinki. International Society of Blood Transfusion, c/o J. P. Soulier, 6 rue Alexandre Cabanel, 75015 Paris, France.
　　Blood transfusion

616.1　　　　　　SZ　　ISSN 0074-8765
INTERNATIONAL SYMPOSIUM ON ATHEROSCLEROSIS. PROCEEDINGS.* 1966. irreg., 1962, 2nd, Chicago. International Society of Cardiology, c/o Pierre Moret, Sec.-Gen., Box 127, CH-1211 Geneva 12, Switzerland.

616.12　　　　　　SZ　　ISSN 0378-9853
KARGER HIGHLIGHTS: CARDIOLOGY; reprinted selected top articles. (Text in English) 1978. a. 15 Fr.($9) (1981 price) S. Karger AG, Allschwilerstrasse 10, P.O. Box, CH-4009 Basel, Switzerland. Ed. J.J. Kellermann. charts. illus. circ. 6,600. (reprint service avail. from ISI) Indexed: Biol.Abstr. Curr. Cont.

616.1　　　　　　SZ　　ISSN 0077-099X
MONOGRAPHS ON ATHEROSCLEROSIS. (Text in English) 1969. irreg (approx. 1/yr.) 80 Fr.($48) per vol. (1981 price) S. Karger AG, Allschwilerstrasse 10, P.O. Box, CH-4009 Basel, Switzerland. Ed.Bd. (reprint service avail. from ISI) Indexed: Biol.Abstr. Chem.Abstr. Curr.Cont. Ind.Med.
　　Atherosclerosis

616.1　　　　　　SZ　　ISSN 0302-2293
MONOGRAPHS ON STANDARDIZATION OF CARDIOANGIOLOGICAL METHODS. Variant title: Standardization of Cardioangiological Methods. 1972. irreg. (International Committee for the Standardization of Angiological Methods) Verlag Hans Huber, Laenggassstr. 76 und Marktgasse 9, CH-3000 Berne 9, Switzerland. (Co-sponsor: Council on Clinical Science of the International Society of Cardiology)

616.1　　　　　　AT　　ISSN 0077-4685
NATIONAL HEART FOUNDATION OF AUSTRALIA. RESEARCH-IN-PROGRESS. 1962. a. free. National Heart Foundation of Australia, Box 2, Woden, A.C.T. 2605, Australia. Ed. Ralph Reader. circ. 500.

616.1　　　　　　US
NEW HORIZONS AND CARDIOVASCULAR DISEASES. BASIC SCIENCE AND DIAGNOSIS. 1980. irreg., vol. 2, 1980. price varies. Futura Publishing Co., 295 Main St., Box 330, Mount Kisco, NY 10549. Ed. Dr. Richard Kones. index.

616.1　　　　　　US　　ISSN 0361-0527
PERSPECTIVES IN CARDIOVASCULAR RESEARCH. 1976. irreg., vol. 4, 1979. Raven Press, 1140 Ave. of the Americas, New York, NY 10036.

PERSPECTIVES IN NEPHROLOGY AND HYPERTENSION. see MEDICAL SCIENCES — Urology And Nephrology

616.1　　　　　　US　　ISSN 0146-6917
PRINCETON CONFERENCE ON CEREBROVASCULAR DISEASES. 1976. irreg., vol. 11, 1979. price varies. Raven Press, 1140 Ave. of the Americas, New York, NY 10036. index. Key Title: Cerebrovascular Diseases.
　　Formerly (until 1976): Cerebral Vascular Diseases. Conference (ISSN 0069-2255)

616　　　　　　US
PROGRESS IN CARDIAC REHABILITATION. 1973. irreg. price varies. Thieme-Stratton, Inc., 381 Park Ave. South, New York, NY 10016. Ed. L. R. Zohman.

616.1　　　　　　US　　ISSN 0097-109X
PROGRESS IN CARDIOLOGY; a series. 1972. a. Lea & Febiger, 600 S. Washington Sq., Philadelphia, PA 19106. Eds. Paul Yu, John Goodwin. illus.
　　Cardiology

618　　　　　　US　　ISSN 0361-0233
PROGRESS IN CHEMICAL FIBRINOLYSIS AND THROMBOLYSIS. 1975. irreg., vol. 3, 1979. price varies. Raven Press, 1140 Avenue of the Americas, New York, NY 10036.
　　Formerly: International Conference on Synthetic Fibrinolytic--Thrombolytic Agents. Proceedings.

616.15　　　　　　US
PROGRESS IN HEMOSTASIS AND THROMBOSIS. 1972. irreg. price varies. Grune and Stratton, Inc. (Subsidiary of: Harcourt Brace Jovanovich, Inc.) 111 Fifth Ave., New York, NY 10003. Ed. Theodore H. Spaet, M.D.
　　Formerly: Progress in Hemostasis.

TASK FORCE ON ENVIRONMENTAL CANCER AND HEART AND LUNG DISEASE. ANNUAL REPORT TO CONGRESS. see ENVIRONMENTAL STUDIES

362.1　　　　　　US
U. S. NATIONAL HEART, LUNG, AND BLOOD ADVISORY COUNCIL. REPORT. (Subseries of: D H E W Publication) 1973. a. U.S. National Heart, Lung, and Blood Advisory Council, 9000 Rockville Pike, Bethesda, MD 20014.
　　Continues: U.S. National Heart and Lung Advisory Council. Annual Report (ISSN 0095-0262)

362.1　　　　　　US
U. S. NATIONAL HEART, LUNG, AND BLOOD INSTITUTE. REPORT OF THE DIRECTOR. 1974. a. U.S. National Heart, Lung, and Blood Institute, 900 Rockville Pike, Bethesda, MD 20014.
　　Continues: U.S. National Heart and Lung Institute. Annual Report of the Director of the National Heart and Lung Institute (ISSN 0095-0254)

616.1005　　　　　　US　　ISSN 0145-4145
YEAR BOOK OF CARDIOLOGY. 1968. a. price varies. ‡ Year Book Medical Publishers, Inc., 35 E. Wacker Dr., Chicago, IL 60601. Ed. Bd.
　　Former titles: Yearbook of Cardiovascular Medicine (ISSN 0360-6031) & Yearbook of Cardiovascular Medicine and Surgery (ISSN 0084-3687); Supersedes in part title issued 1962-67 as: Yearbook of Cardiovascular and Renal Disease.

MEDICAL SCIENCES — Chiropractics, Homeopathy, Osteopathy

615.533　　　　　　US
AMERICAN ACADEMY OF OSTEOPATHY YEARBOOK. Variant title: Yearbook of Selected Osteopathic Papers. 1943. a. $15. ‡ American Academy of Osteopathy, 2630 Airport Rd., Colorado Springs, CO 80910. illus. cum.index 1972. circ. 1,100 (controlled)
　　Osteopathy

615.533　　　　　　US　　ISSN 0084-358X
YEARBOOK AND DIRECTORY OF OSTEOPATHIC PHYSICIANS. 1908. a. $35. American Osteopathic Association, 212 E. Ohio St., Chicago, IL 60611. Ed. George W. Northup, D.O. adv. stat. index. circ. 17,000.
　　Osteopathy

MEDICAL SCIENCES — Communicable Diseases

574.5　　616.9　　YU　　ISSN 0350-3658
ACTA PARASITOLOGICA IUGOSLAVICA. 1970. irreg. 20 din. Drustvo Parazitologa Jugoslavije, Rockfelerova 7, Zagreb, Yugoslavia. Ed. Teodor Wikerhauser. adv. circ. 500.

ADVANCES IN VIRUS RESEARCH. see
BIOLOGY — Microbiology

616.96   AG
CENTRO PANAMERICANO DE ZOONOSIS.
BOLETIN INFORMATIVO. ENFERMEDADES
TRANSMITIDAS POR ALIMENTOS EN LAS
AMERICAS. (Editions in English and Spanish)
1974. a. free. Centro Panamericano de Zoonosis,
Casilla 3092 Correo Central, 1000 Buenos Aires,
Argentina. circ. 1,450(Spanish edt.); 750(English
edt.)
    Supersedes in part (since 1978): Centro
Panamericano de Zoonosis. Boletin Informativo.

616.998   AG
CENTRO PANAMERICANO DE ZOONOSIS.
BOLETIN INFORMATIVO. HIDATIDOSIS EN
LAS AMERICAS. (Editions in English and
Spanish) 1974. a. free. Centro Panamericano de
Zoonosis, Casilla 3092 Correo Central, 1000 Buenos
Aires, Argentina. circ. 1,450(Spanish edt.);
750(English edt.)
    Supersedes in part (since 1978): Centro
Panamericano de Zoonosis. Boletin Informativo.

616.998   AG
CENTRO PANAMERICANO DE ZOONOSIS.
BOLETIN INFORMATIVO. LEPTOSPIROSIS
EN LAS AMERICAS. (Editions in English and
Spanish) 1974. a. free. Centro Panamericano de
Zoonosis, Casilla 3092 Correo Central, 1000 Buenos
Aires, Argentina. circ. 1,450(Spanish edt.);
750(English edt.)
    Supersedes in part (since 1978): Centro
Panamericano de Zoonosis. Boletin Informativo.

616.96   AG
CENTRO PANAMERICANO DE ZOONOSIS.
BOLETIN INFORMATIVO. TUBERCULOSIS
EN LAS AMERICAS. (Editions in English and
Spanish) 1974. a. free. Centro Panamericano de
Zoonosis, Casilla 3092 Correo Central, 1000 Buenos
Aires, Argentina. circ. 1,450(Spanish edt.);
750(English edt.)
    Supersedes in part (since 1978): Centro
Panamericano de Zoonosis. Boletin Informativo.

616.998   BL
HANSENIASIS LETTER. (Text in English)
no.6,Jul.,1977. irreg. Instituto de Saude, Divisao de
Hansenologia e Dermatologia Sanitaria, Caixa Postal
8027, 01000 Sao Paulo, Brazil. bibl. (processed)

610   US   ISSN 0090-6549
INFECTIOUS DISEASE REVIEWS. Represents:
Annual Infectious Disease Symposia. Proceedings.
1971. irreg., vol. 6, 1981. price varies. Futura
Publishing Co., 295 Main Street, Box 330, Mount
Kisco, NY 10549. Ed. Dr. William J. Holloway.
illus. Indexed: Chem.Abstr.

616.01 576.64   AE   ISSN 0020-2460
INSTITUT PASTEUR D'ALGERIE. ARCHIVES.
(Text in French and English) 1921. a. 30 din.($6.)
Institut Pasteur d'Algerie, Rue Docteur Laveran,
Algiers, Algeria. bibl, charts, illus, stat. index. circ.
1,000. (also avail. in microfilm) Indexed: Ind.Med.
Virology

616.01 576   GR   ISSN 0004-6620
INSTITUT PASTEUR HELLENIQUE. ARCHIVES.
(Text in French; summaries in English and Greek)
1923. a. free. ‡ Institut Pasteur Hellenique, 127
Ave. de la Reine Sophie, Athens 618, Greece. adv.
circ. 1,500. Indexed: Bull.Inst.Pasteur.
Trop.Dis.Bull.

INSTITUTO DE HIGIENE E MEDICINA
TROPICAL. ANAIS. see PUBLIC HEALTH AND
SAFETY

616.96   PL   ISSN 0074-3356
INTERNATIONAL COMMISSION ON
TRICHINELLOSIS. PROCEEDINGS. (Published
as a No. of "Wiadomosci Parazytologiczne") 1962.
irreg. 20 Zl. Polskie Towarzystwo Parazytologiczne,
Norwida 29, 50-375 Wroclaw, Poland. Ed. Z.
Pawlowski. bk. rev.
Parasitology

616.9   GR   ISSN 0074-4212
INTERNATIONAL CONGRESSES ON TROPICAL
MEDICINE AND MALARIA. (PROCEEDINGS)
(Proceedings issued at discretion of host country;
none issued for 8th, Teheran.) quinquennial; 9th
Athens. International Congresses on Tropical
Medicine and Malaria, c/o Prof. J. Papa Vassilious,
University of Athens, Athens, Greece.
Tropical medicine

616.998   US
INTERNATIONAL LEPROSY CONGRESS.
TRANSACTIONS. 1933. quinquennial, 1973, 10th,
Bergen. $10 to non-members. ‡ International
Leprosy Association, International Journal of
Leprosy, Business Office, Box 1097, Bloomfield, NJ
07003 (Editorial Office: Leahi Hospital, 3675
Kilauea Ave., Honolulu, HI 96816) Ed. Dr. Olaf K.
Skinsnes.
    Formerly: International Leprosy Congress.
Abstracts and Papers (ISSN 0074-6762)
Leprosy

616.988   US   ISSN 0074-7777
INTERNATIONAL REVIEW OF TROPICAL
MEDICINE. 1961. irreg., 1971, vol. 4. price varies.
Academic Press, Inc., 111 Fifth Ave., New York,
NY 10003. Ed. David R. Lincicome. index.
Tropical medicine

616.96 576.64   US   ISSN 0076-6933
METHODS IN VIROLOGY. 1967. irreg., vol. 6,
1977. price varies. Academic Press, Inc, 111 Fifth
Ave., New York, NY 10003. Eds. Karl
Maramorosch, Hilary Koprowski.
Virology

616.96   AG   ISSN 0524-952X
MUSEO ARGENTINO DE CIENCIAS
NATURALES "BERNARDINO RIVADAVIA."
INSTITUTO NACIONAL DE INVESTIGACION
DE LAS CIENCIAS NATURALES. REVISTA.
PARASITOLOGIA. 1968. irreg.; latest issue 1980.
Museo Argentino de Ciencias Naturales "Bernardino
Rivadavia", Instituto Nacional de Investigacion de
las Ciencias Naturales, Avda. Angel Gallardo 470,
Casilla de Correo 220-Sucursal 5, Buenos Aires,
Argentina.

576.64   US   ISSN 0072-9086
PERSPECTIVES IN VIROLOGY. Title varies:
Gustav Stern Symposia on Perspectives in Virology.
1958. irreg., vol. 10, 1978. price varies. Raven Press,
1140 Ave. of the Americas, New York, NY 10036.
Ed. Morris Pollard. Indexed: Biol.Abstr.
Chem.Abstr.
Virology

610 576.64   SZ   ISSN 0079-645X
PROGRESS IN MEDICAL VIROLOGY. (Text in
English) 1958. irreg. (approx. 1/yr.) 100 Fr.($60)
per vol. (1981 price) S. Karger AG,
Allschwilerstrasse 10, P.O. Box, CH-4009 Basel,
Switzerland. Ed. J. L. Melnick. (reprint service
avail. from ISI) Indexed: Biol.Abstr. Chem.Abstr.
Curr.Cont. Ind.Med.
Virology

616.96   JA   ISSN 0555-4349
PROGRESS OF MEDICAL PARASITOLOGY IN
JAPAN. (Text in English) 1964. a. Meguro
Parasitological Museum - Meguro Kiseichu-kan, 4-1-
1 Shimomeguro, Meguro-ku, Tokyo 153, Japan
(Dist. by: Maruzen Co., Ltd., Box 5050 Tokyo
International, Tokyo 100-31, Japan)
Parasitology

616.988   UK   ISSN 0080-4711
ROYAL SOCIETY OF TROPICAL MEDICINE
AND HYGIENE, LONDON. YEARBOOK. 1908.
a. £6. Royal Society of Tropical Medicine and
Hygiene, Mansion House, 26 Portland Place,
London, W1N 4EY, England. adv. circ. 3,500.
Tropical medicine

616.9   US   ISSN 0162-5454
SEMINARS IN INFECTIOUS DISEASE. 1978. a.
price varies. Thieme-Stratton, Inc., 381 Park Ave.
S., New York, NY 10016. Eds. L. Weinstein, B.N.
Fields.

610   US   ISSN 0360-4977
TOPICS IN INFECTIOUS DISEASES. 1975. irreg.;
vol. 3, 1978. price varies. Springer Verlag, 175 Fifth
Ave., New York, NY 10010 (And Berlin,
Heidelberg, Vienna) (reprint service avail. from ISI)

616.9   SZ
TROPICAL DISEASES RESEARCH SERIES. 1979.
irreg., no. 3, 1980. price varies. (Special Programme
for Research and Training in Tropical Diseases,
UN) Schwabe und Co. AG, Steinentorstr. 13, 410
Basel, Switzerland. (Co-sponsors of program: United
Nations Development Programme; World Bank;
World Health Organization)

610   US
U.S. ARMY MEDICAL RESEARCH INSTITUTE
OF INFECTIOUS DISEASES. ANNUAL
PROGRESS REPORT. a. U.S. Army Medical
Research Institute of Infectious Diseases, Fort
Detrick, Frederick, MD 21701 (Orders to: NTIS,
Springfield, VA 22151) Key Title: Annual Progress
Report - U.S. Army Medical Research Institute of
Infectious Diseases.
Military

616.9   US
U. S. CENTER FOR DISEASE CONTROL.
DIPHTHERIA SURVEILLANCE REPORT. 1962.
irreg. U.S. Center for Disease Control, Dept. of
Health, Education and Welfare, Atlanta, GA 30333.
charts. stat. (looseleaf format)

616.998   US
U.S. CENTER FOR DISEASE CONTROL.
LEPROSY SURVEILLANCE REPORT. 1970.
irreg, no. 2, 1972. U.S. Center for Disease Control,
1600 Clifton Rd., N.E., Dept. of Health, Education
and Welfare, Atlanta, GA 30333. charts. stat.
Leprosy

616.9   US
U.S. CENTER FOR DISEASE CONTROL.
LISTERIOSIS SURVEILLANCE REPORT. irreg.
U.S. Center for Disease Control, 1600 Clifton Rd.,
N.E., Dept. of Health, Education and Welfare,
Atlanta, GA 30333. charts. stat.

616.9   US   ISSN 0501-8390
U.S. CENTER FOR DISEASE CONTROL.
MALARIA SURVEILLANCE REPORT. 1955. a.
free. U.S. Center for Disease Control, 1600 Clifton
Rd., N.E., Atlanta, GA 30333. Ed. Dr. Myron G.
Schultz. circ. 2,000.

VIROLOGY MONOGRAPHS/VIRUSFORSCHUNG
IN EINZELDARSTELLUNGEN. see
BIOLOGY — Microbiology

610   KO
YONSEI REPORTS ON TROPICAL MEDICINE.
(Text in English) 1970. a. available on exchange.
Yonsei University, College of Medicine, Box 71,
Seoul, S. Korea. Ed. Chin-Thack Soh. adv. abstr.
bibl. charts. stat. (tabloid format)
Tropical medicine

616.96 574.524   GW   ISSN 0172-5599
ZENTRALBLATT FUER BAKTERIOLOGIE,
PARASITENKUNDE,
INFEKTIONSKRANKHEITEN UND HYGIENE.
ORIGINALE REIHE A: MEDIZINISCHE
MIKROBIOLOGIE UND PARASITOLOGIE.
irreg., 4 nos. per vol. DM.178. Gustav Fischer
Verlag, Wollgrasweg 49, 7000 Stuttgart 70, 7000
Stuttgart 72, W. Germany (B.R.D.) Ed. G.
Henneberg. circ. 1,100. Indexed: Ind.Med.
Parasitology

MEDICAL SCIENCES — Dentistry

617.6   JA   ISSN 0571-2912
A.P.D.S.A. JOURNAL.* 1968. irreg. Asian Pacific
Dental Student Association, c/o Nihon University
School of Dentistry, 1-8 Surugadai, Chiyoda-ku,
Tokyo 101, Japan.

617.6   US   ISSN 0065-079X
ACCEPTED DENTAL THERAPEUTICS. 1934.
biennial. $11.50. American Dental Association, 211
E. Chicago Ave., Chicago, IL 60611. Ed. Gordon
H. Schrotenboer. index.
    Formerly: Accepted Dental Remedies.

MEDICAL SCIENCES — DENTISTRY

617.6 US ISSN 0091-729X
ADMISSION REQUIREMENTS OF U.S. AND CANADIAN DENTAL SCHOOLS. 1963. a. $7.50. American Association of Dental Schools, 1625 Massachusetts Ave, N.W., Washington, DC 20036. circ. 8,000.
  Formerly: Admission Requirements of American Dental Schools (ISSN 0065-1990)

617.6 US ISSN 0065-3020
ADVANCES IN ORAL BIOLOGY. 1964. irreg., 1970, vol. 4. price varies. Academic Press, Inc., 111 Fifth Ave., New York, NY 10003. Ed. Peter H. Staple. index.

617.6 US ISSN 0090-3329
AMERICAN DENTAL ASSOCIATION. ANNUAL REPORTS AND RESOLUTIONS. a. price varies. American Dental Association, 211 E. Chicago Ave., Chicago, IL 60611.

617.6 US ISSN 0065-8073
AMERICAN DENTAL DIRECTORY. 1947. a. $50. American Dental Association, 211 E. Chicago Ave., Chicago, IL 60611.

617.6 US
AMERICAN LECTURES IN DENTISTRY. irreg. price varies. Charles C. Thomas, Publisher, 301-327 E. Lawrence Ave., Springfield, IL 62717.

617.6 FR ISSN 0066-2194
ANNALES ODONTO-STOMATOLOGIQUES. 1944. irreg. (Societe Odonto-Stomatologique de Lyon) Union des Etudes et Recherches des Sciences Odontologiques, 6 Place Deperet, 69- Lyon 7E, France.

617.6 FR ISSN 0066-2712
ANNUAIRE DENTAIRE. 1936/37. a. 100 F.($20) Editions de Chabassol, 30 rue de Gramont, 75002 Paris, France. Ed. B. Laloup. adv. circ. 6,500.

618
ANNUAL REPORT ON ADVANCED DENTAL EDUCATION. 1972. a. free. American Dental Association, 211 E. Chicago Ave., Chicago, IL 60611. Ed. David R. DeMarais. (also avail. in microform from UMI)

617.6 AT ISSN 0066-5339
APOLLONIA. irreg. University of Sydney, Dental Alumni Society, Sydney, N. S. W., Australia.

353.9 US ISSN 0098-6824
ARIZONA. STATE DENTAL BOARD. REPORT. a. State Dental Board, Phoenix, AZ 85007. Key Title: Report - Arizona State Dental Board.

617.6 UK ISSN 0308-4922
BRITISH PAEDODONTIC SOCIETY. PROCEEDINGS. 1971. a. £2.40($3.00) British Paedodontic Society, c/o F. J. Hill, Hon. Sec., Eastman Dental Hospital, Gray's Inn Rd., London WC1X 8LD, England. adv. circ. 1,000(controlled) (back issues avail.)

617.6 CN ISSN 0068-8622
CANADIAN DENTAL ASSOCIATION. DIRECTORY. a. membership (non-members $35) Canadian Dental Association, 1815 Alta Vista Drive, Ottawa, Ont. K1G 3Y6, Canada.

617.6 CN ISSN 0068-8630
CANADIAN DENTAL ASSOCIATION. TRANSACTIONS. a. membership. Canadian Dental Association, 1815 Alta Vista Drive, Ottawa, Ont. K1G 3Y6, Canada.

617.6 US ISSN 0069-4096
CINCINNATI DENTAL SOCIETY BULLETIN. 1930. irreg. free. Cincinnati Dental Society, 3012 Glenmore Ave., Cincinnati, OH 45238. Ed. Leo G. Naber. adv. circ. 650.

617.6 AG ISSN 0069-9799
COOPERADOR DENTAL.* 1933. irreg. membership. Cooperativa Dental Argentina, M.T. de Alvear 2167, Buenos Aires, Argentina. Eds. H. B. Ferreri, Horacio Martinez. adv. bk. rev. circ. 6,000.

617.6 US ISSN 0070-2110
CURRENT THERAPY IN DENTISTRY. 1964. irreg., vol. 6, 1977. price varies. ‡ C. V. Mosby Co., 11830 Westline Industrial Dr., St. Louis, MO 63141. Ed.Bd. bk. rev.

617.6 CN
DALHOUSIE DENTAL JOURNAL. vol. 19, 1980. a. Dalhousie University, Dental Students Society, Halifax, N.S. B3H 4H8, Canada. circ. 1,000. (back issues avail.)

617.6 US
DENTAL ADMISSION TESTING PROGRAM. 1951. a. free. American Dental Association, Division of Educational Measurements, 211 E. Chicago Ave., Chicago, IL 60611. Ed. David R. DeMarais. circ. 175,000.

617.6 AT ISSN 0311-0699
DENTAL ANAESTHESIA AND SEDATION. 1972. irreg. Aus.$10. Australian Society for the Advancement of Anaesthesia and Sedation in Dentistry, 108 Longueville Rd., Land Cove, NSW 2066, Australia. Ed. Thomas A. Scahill. Indexed: Ind.Dent.Lit.

617.6 CN ISSN 0070-3656
DENTAL GUIDE. 1965. a. Southam Communications Ltd., 1450 Don Mills Rd., Don Mills, Ont., Canada. Ed. Sharon Sinclair. adv. circ. 11,956.

617.6 UK ISSN 0070-3699
DENTAL PRACTITIONER HANDBOOK. 1965. irreg. John Wright & Sons Ltd., 42-44 Triangle West, Bristol BS8 1EX, England.

617.6 US ISSN 0070-3702
DENTAL PRODUCTS ANNUAL REPORT; a compilation of new equipment, supplies, and preventive dentistry aids. 1970. a. $10. ‡ Irving-Cloud Publishing Co., 7300 N. Cicero Ave., Lincolnwood, Chicago, IL 60046. Ed. Jeanne K. Matson. adv. bk. rev. index. circ. 114,484.

617.6 IE ISSN 0084-9723
DENTAL REGISTER OF IRELAND. 1929. a. £1. Eason & Son, Ltd., 57 Merrion Sq., Dublin 2, Ireland.

617.6 US ISSN 0147-264X
DENTAL RESEARCH IN THE UNITED STATES AND OTHER COUNTRIES. 1970. a. free. U.S. National Institute of Dental Research, U.S. National Institutes of Health, Bldg. W, Rm. 551, Bethesda, MD 20014. circ. 1,800(controlled)
  Until 1976 edition issued as: Dental Research in the United States, Canada, and Great Britain (ISSN 0094-484X)

617.6 UK
DENTAL TECHNICIAN YEARBOOK. 1979. a. £4. A.E. Morgan Publications Ltd., 172 Kingston Rd., Ewell, Epsom, Surrey KT19 0SB, England. Ed. D. Ritchie. adv.

617.6 JA ISSN 0070-3737
DENTISTRY IN JAPAN/NIHON NO SHIKA IRYO. (Text in English) 1968. irreg., no. 14, 1974. not for sale. ‡ (Japanese Association for Dental Science - Nihon Shika Igakkai) Japan Dental Association, 4-1-20 Kudan Kita, Chiyoda-ku, Tokyo 102, Japan. Ed. S. Kikuchi. circ. 1,000.

617.6 US
DENTIST'S DESK REFERENCE; materials, instruments & equipment. 1962. irreg., every 2-3 yrs. $13.95. American Dental Association, 211 E. Chicago Ave., Chicago, IL 60611. Ed. J. W. Stanford. bibl, charts, illus. circ. 10,000.
  Formerly: Guide to Dental Materials and Devices (ISSN 0093-9706)

617.6 US
DETROIT MIRROR AND EXPLORER. 1961. irreg. (4 nos. per year) price varies. University of Detroit, School of Dentistry, Detroit, MI 48207. Ed. Dr. Dominick N. Shoha. adv.
  Formerly: Detroit Dental Spectrum (ISSN 0070-3877)

617.6 GW
DEUTSCHER ZAHNAERZTEKALENDER. 1941. a. DM.44. Carl Hanser Verlag, Kolbergerstr. 22, Postfach 860420, 8000 Munich 80, W. Germany (B.R.D.) Ed. Werner Ketterl. adv. circ. 7,200.

617.6 378 US ISSN 0090-0141
DIRECTORY OF DENTAL EDUCATORS. title changed with 1971-72 ed. from: Directory of Dental Educators in the United States and Canada. 1966. irreg. price varies. American Association of Dental Schools, 1625 Massachusetts Ave., N.W., Washington, DC 20036.

617.6 US ISSN 0517-1024
FACTS ABOUT STATES FOR THE DENTIST SEEKING A LOCATION. 1953. triennial. American Dental Association, Bureau of Economic Research & Statistics, 211 E. Chicago Ave., Chicago, IL 60611. Eds. Nancy Burkholder, Laurie Mankoski.

FINLAND. LAAKINTOHALLITUS. LAAKARIT, HAMMASLAAKARIT/LAKARE, TANDLAEKARE. see *MEDICAL SCIENCES*

614 US
FLUORIDATION CENSUS. 1954. irreg., 1977 ed. covers 1975. U.S. Center for Disease Control, Bureau of State Services, Dental Disease Prevention Activity, 1600 Clifton Rd., N.E., Atlanta, GA 30333.

617.643 SZ ISSN 0301-536X
FRONTIERS OF ORAL PHYSIOLOGY. (Text in English) 1974. irreg. (approx. 1/yr.) 130 Fr.($78) per vol. (1981 price) S. Karger AG, Allschwilerstrasse 10, P.O. Box, CH-4009 Basel, Switzerland. Ed. Y. Kawamura. (reprint service avail. from ISI) Indexed: Ind.Med.

617.6 UK ISSN 0072-0674
GENERAL DENTAL COUNCIL. DENTISTS REGISTER. 1878. a. £7.50. General Dental Council, 37 Wimpole St., London W1M 8DQ, England.

617.6 UK ISSN 0072-0682
GENERAL DENTAL COUNCIL. MINUTES OF THE PROCEEDINGS. 1956. a. £2. General Dental Council, 37 Wimpole St., London W1M 8DQ, England.

617.6 SW ISSN 0072-4831
GOETEBORGS TANDLAEKARE SAELLSKAP. AARSBOK. 1918. a. Kr.70. Goeteborgs Tandlaekare Saellskap, Erik Dahlbergsgatan 9, 411 26 Goeteborg, Sweden. Ed. Lars Ralph. adv.

617.6 US ISSN 0361-9273
GUIDEBOOK OF U.S. & CANADIAN POSTDOCTORAL DENTAL PROGRAMS. 1976. irreg. $3. American Association of Dental Schools, 1625 Massachusetts Ave., N.W., Washington, DC 20036.

617.6 US ISSN 0073-1021
HAWAII DENTAL ASSOCIATION. TRANSACTIONS. a. Hawaii Dental Association, 1000 Bishop St., Suite 805, Honolulu, HI 96813.

617.3 US ISSN 0073-1404
HAYES DIRECTORY OF DENTAL SUPPLY HOUSES. 1935. a. $45. Edward N. Hayes, Ed. & Pub., 4229 Birch St., Newport Beach, CA 92660.

617.6 CK ISSN 0073-1900
HERALDO DENTAL. 1949. irreg. free. Heraldo Dental, Carrera 18, No. 34-34, Bucaramanga, Colombia. Ed. Carlos Perez-Martinez. index, cum.index: 1960-1965.

617.6 JA ISSN 0073-2915
HOKKAIDO DENTAL ASSOCIATION. JOURNAL/HOKKAIDO SHIKA ISHIKAISHI, DOSHIKAI TSUSHIN. (Text in Japanese) 1948. a. Hokkaido Dental Association - Hokkaido Shika Ishikai, 7-2 Odori Nishi, Chuo-ku, Sapporo 060, Japan.

617.6 US ISSN 0074-1256
INTERNATIONAL ACADEMY OF ORAL PATHOLOGY. PROCEEDINGS. 1962. irreg., 1969, 4th, Johannesburg. $27.50. Gordon & Breach Science Publishers, 1 Park Avenue, New York, NY 10016.

617.6 UK
INTERNATIONAL COLLEGE OF DENTISTS. EUROPEAN SECTION. NEWSLETTER. a. International College of Dentists, European Section, 121 Palatine Rd., Manchester M20 9YA, England. Ed. Charlie Przetak. circ. 400.

617.6 II ISSN 0074-2600
INTERNATIONAL COLLEGE OF DENTISTS. INDIA SECTION. NEWSLETTER. a. International College of Dentists, India Section, c/o Indarjit Singh, D 11/43 Kidwai Nagar East, New Delhi, India. Indexed: Ind.Dent.Lit.

MEDICAL SCIENCES — DERMATOLOGY AND VENEREOLOGY

617.6 US ISSN 0074-3054
INTERNATIONAL CONFERENCE ON ENDODONTICS. TRANSACTIONS. 1953. quinquennial, 1973, 5th, Philadelphia. $5. University of Pennsylvania, School of Dental Medicine, 4001 Spruce St., Philadelphia, PA 19104. Ed. Louis J. Grossman. bk. rev. circ. 2,000.

617.6 US ISSN 0074-3216
INTERNATIONAL CONFERENCE ON ORAL BIOLOGY. PROCEEDINGS. (Special issue of Journal of Dental Research) irreg.; latest issue, 1974. (International Association for Dental Research) Professional Publication Producers, Box 25027, Houston, TX 77005. Ed. Barnet M. Levy. circ. 4,500. Indexed: Oral Res.Abstr.

617.6 JM
JAMAICA DENTAL ASSOCIATION. NEWSLETTER. irreg. Jamaica Dental Association, P.O. Box 19, Kingston 5, Jamaica.

617.632 DK ISSN 0075-4331
JOURNAL OF PERIODONTAL RESEARCH. SUPPLEMENTUM. (Text in English) 1966. irreg. free to subscribers. Munksgaard, 35 Noerre Soegade, DK-1370 Copenhagen K, Denmark. Ed. Harald Loe. adv. (reprint service avail. from ISI) Indexed: Biol.Abstr. Chem.Abstr. Ind.Med. Nutr.Abstr.

617.6 SZ ISSN 0379-2005
KARGER HIGHLIGHTS: ORAL SCIENCE; reprinted selected top articles. 1979. a. 15 Fr.($9) (1981 price) S. Karger AG, Allschwilerstrasse 10, P. O. Box, CH-4009 Basel, Switzerland. Ed. Howard M. Myers. charts. (reprint service avail. from ISI)

617.6 CN ISSN 0024-9025
MCGILL DENTAL REVIEW. 1934. irreg. McGill University, Dental Students' Society, Montreal, Quebec. Canada. illus. Indexed: Ind.Dent.Lit. Dent.Ind.

617.6 US
MASSON MONOGRAPHS IN DENTISTRY. 1979. irreg., vol. 3, 1981. price varies. Masson Publishing U.S.A., Inc., 14 E. 60th St., New York, NY 10022. Ed. Dr. Lester Burket.

618 US
MEHARRY MEDICAL COLLEGE. SCHOOL OF DENTISTRY. PROCEEDINGS OF AN ORAL RESEARCH SEMINAR. 1973. biennial. free. Meharry Medical College, School of Dentistry, 1005 18th Ave. N., Nashville, TN 37208. Ed. Theodore E. Bolden. (back issues avail)

617.6 US ISSN 0360-7232
MENTALIS. 1971. irreg. University of California, Los Angeles. School of Dentistry, Los Angeles, CA 90024. illus.

617.6 CE
MIRROR AND PROBE.* (Text in English; summaries in Sinhala and Tamil) 1963. a. Dental Students' Association, University of Sri Lanka, University Park, Peradeniya, Sri Lanka. adv. charts. illus. stat. circ. controlled.

617.6 SZ ISSN 0077-0892
MONOGRAPHS IN ORAL SCIENCE. (Text in English) 1972. irreg. (approx. 1/yr.) 100 Fr.($60) per vol. (1981 price) S. Karger AG, Allschwilerstrasse 10, P.O. Box, CH-4009 Basel, Switzerland. Ed. H. M. Myers. adv. (reprint service avail. from ISI) Indexed: Biol.Abstr. Chem.Abstr. Curr.Cont. Ind.Med.

617.6 CN
NOVA SCOTIA DENTAL ASSOCIATION. NEWSLETTER. irreg. membership. Nova Scotia Dental Association, 2745 Dutch Village Rd., Suite 205, Box 604, Halifax, N.S. B3J 2R7, Canada.

617.6 FI ISSN 0078-3358
ODONTOLOGISKA SAMFUNDET I FINLAND. AARSBOK. 1946. a. Fmk.50. Odontologiska Samfundets i Finland, Bergmansg. 11 D 11, SF-00140 Helsinki 14, Finland. adv. circ. 500.

617.6 FR ISSN 0078-6608
ORTHODONTIE FRANCAISE. (1921-1962 called also Comptes Rendus du Congres Annuel) 1921. a. 400 F. Julien Prelat, 17, rue du Petit-Pont, 75005 Paris, France. Indexed: Ind.Med.

617.6 US ISSN 0079-0125
PASSAIC COUNTY DENTAL SOCIETY. BULLETIN.* irreg. Passaic County Dental Society, c/o Dr. A. Rand, 1000 Clifton Ave., Clifton, NJ 07013. Indexed: Ind.Dent.Lit.

617.6 AT ISSN 0079-5631
PROBE. 1949. a. Aus.$3. University of Adelaide, Dental Students Society, School of Dentistry, Adelaide, Australia. adv. bk. rev. circ. 500.

617.6 US ISSN 0090-7995
RHODES DIRECTORY OF BLACK DENTISTS REGISTERED IN THE UNITED STATES. triennial with a. supplements. $25. Aqua Dynamics Ltd., 2624 Nevada Ave., Norfolk, VA 23513. Ed. Lord Cecil Rhodes. stat.

617.6 AT
ROYAL AUSTRALASIAN COLLEGE OF DENTAL SURGEONS. ANNALS. 1967. irreg. free to Fellows of the College. Royal Australasian College of Dental Surgeons, 229 Macquarie St., Sydney, N.S.W. 2000, Australia. Ed. Dr. Robert Harris. circ. 800.
Former titles: Royal Australian College of Dental Surgeons. Annals (ISSN 0312-7923); Australian College of Dental Surgeons. Annals. (ISSN 0004-8895)

617.6 US ISSN 0024-5968
S D A DENTIST. 1962. a. $7.50. Loma Linda University, School of Dentistry Alumni Association, Loma Linda, CA 92354. Ed. Hugh C. Love, D.D.S. adv. charts. illus. circ. 1,450.
Formerly: Loma Linda University Dentist.

617.6 GE ISSN 0080-584X
SAMMLUNG MEUSSER; Abhandlungen aus dem Gebiete der klinischen Zahnheilkunde. 1915. irreg., 1971, no. 43. price varies. Johann Ambrosius Barth Verlag, Salomonstr. 18b, 701 Leipzig, E. Germany (D.D.R.) Ed. Prof. Dr. E. Wannenmacher.

617.6 US ISSN 0080-598X
SAN MATEO COUNTY DENTAL SOCIETY. BULLETIN. m. free. ‡ San Mateo County Dental Society, 1941 O'Farrel St., San Mateo, CA 94403. Eds. Dr. Richard Fagin, Dr. Donald Hermansen. adv. circ. 425.

617.6 FR ISSN 0081-1203
SOCIETE ODONTO-STOMATOLOGIQUE DU NORD-EST. REVUE ANNUELLE.* Called also: Revue Odonto-Stomatologique du Nord-Est. 1969. a. Societe Odonto-Stomatologique du Nord-Est, 9 rue Saint-Nicolas, 54000 Nancy, France.

617.6 JA
SOCIETY OF NIPPON DENTAL COLLEGE. ANNUAL PUBLICATIONS. (Text in English) 1964. a. exchange basis. Society of Nippon Dental College - Nihon Shika Daigaku Shigakkai, 1-9-20 Fujimi, Chiyoda-ku, Tokyo 102, Japan.

617.6 FI ISSN 0355-4651
SUOMEN HAMMASLAAKARISEURA. TOIMITUKSIA. SUPPLEMENTA/FINNISH DENTAL SOCIETY. PROCEEDINGS. SUPPLEMENT. (Text in English; summaries in Finnish) irreg., no. 74, 1978. Fmk.30. Suomen Hammaslaakariseura - Finska Tandlaekaraellskapet (Finnish Dental Society), Akavatalo, Rautatielaisenkatu 6, SF-00520 Helsinki 52, Finland.

617.6 FI ISSN 0081-9433
SUOMEN NAISHAMMASLAAKARIT RYHMA. JULKAISU. (Summaries in English) 1963. a. Suomen Naishammaslaakarit Ryhma - Finnish Women Dentists' Association, Helsinki, Finland. adv.

SYNDICAT GENERAL DES INDUSTRIES MEDICO - CHIRURGICALES ET DENTAIRES. ANNUAIRE. see MEDICAL SCIENCES — Surgery

617.6 US
THIRTIETH DISTRICT DENTAL SOCIETY, FRESNO, CALIFORNIA. BULLETIN. 1953. irreg. ‡ Fresno-Madera Dental Socety, 3425 North First St., Fresno, CA 93726. adv. circ. 600.
Former titles: Thirteenth District Dental Society. Bulletin; Fifth District Dental Society. Bulletin (ISSN 0071-9544)

TOKYO MEDICAL AND DENTAL UNIVERSITY. INSTITUTE FOR MEDICAL AND DENTAL ENGINEERING. REPORTS/IYO KIZAI KENKYUSHO HOKOKU. see MEDICAL SCIENCES

617.6 CN
U W O/D S S JOURNAL. a. University of Western Ontario, Dental Students Society, London, Ont. N6A SK7, Canada. Ed. Bernard J. Adler. adv. circ. 4,000 (controlled) (back issues avail.)

617.6 UY ISSN 0083-4785
UNIVERSIDAD DE LA REPUBLICA. FACULTAD DE ODONTOLOGIA. ANALES. (Supplements accompany some numbers) 1955. irreg. exchange basis. Universidad de la Republica, Facultad de Odontologia, Gral. las Heras 1925, Montevideo, Uruguay. Indexed: Dent.Ind.

617.6 BL
UNIVERSIDADE FEDERAL DE PERNAMBUCO. FACULDADE DE ODONTOLOGIA. ANAIS. (Text in Portuguese; summaries in English) 1960. a. Universidade Federal de Pernambuco, Faculdade de Odontologia, Recife, Pernambuco, Brazil.
Continues (with vol. 5): Universidade do Recife. Faculdade de Odontologia. Anais.

617.6 SW ISSN 0076-3438
UNIVERSITY OF LUND. SCHOOL OF DENTISTRY. FACULTY OF ODONTOLOGY. ANNUAL PUBLICATIONS. Cover title: University of Lund. Faculty of Odontology. Annual Publications. (Text in English) 1958. a. free. Lunds Universitet, Odontologiska Fakulteten, School of Dentistry, 214 21 Malmoe, Sweden. Ed. Lars-Eric Granath.

617.6 US ISSN 0076-843X
UNIVERSITY OF MICHIGAN. SCHOOL OF DENTISTRY. ALUMNI BULLETIN. 1937. a. University of Michigan, School of Dentistry, Ann Arbor, MI 48104. Charles C. Kelsey. circ. 6,000. Indexed: Dent.Ind.

617.6 CN ISSN 0042-0255
UNIVERSITY OF TORONTO UNDERGRADUATE DENTAL JOURNAL. 1964. a. $4 for 2 yrs. McLean-Hunter Ltd., University Ave., Toronto, Ont. M5W 1A7, Canada. Ed. Bd. adv. bk. rev. abstr. charts. illus.

617.6 US ISSN 0083-7431
WASHINGTON STATE DENTAL JOURNAL. 1934. a. $3. Washington State Dental Association, Box 9824, Seattle, WA 98109. adv. circ. 3,000. Indexed: Dent.Ind.

WORLD DIRECTORY OF DENTAL SCHOOLS. see EDUCATION — Guides To Schools And Colleges

617.6 UK
YEAR BOOK AND DIRECTORY FOR THE DENTAL TECHNICIAN. 1972. a. £2.50. Dental Publications Ltd, 172 Kingston Rd., Ewell, Epsom, Surrey KT19 0SB, England. Ed. E.A. Dennison. adv. circ. controlled.

617.6058 US ISSN 0084-3717
YEAR BOOK OF DENTISTRY. 1936. a. price varies. ‡ Year Book Medical Publishers, Inc., 35 E. Wacker Dr., Chicago, IL 60601. Ed. Bd.

617.6 GE ISSN 0084-4462
ZAHNAERZTLICHE FORTBILDUNG. 1949. irreg., vol. 16, 1973. price varies. Johann Ambrosius Barth Verlag, Salomonstr. 18b, 701 Leipzig, E. Germany (D.D.R.) Ed. Erwin Reichenbach.

MEDICAL SCIENCES — Dermatology And Venereology

616.5 US ISSN 0065-2253
ADVANCES IN BIOLOGY OF SKIN. 1960. irreg. price varies. Plenum Press, 233 Spring St., New York, NY 10013. index.

616.5 US
AMERICAN LECTURES IN DERMATOLOGY. irreg. price varies. Charles C. Thomas, Publisher, 301-327 E. Lawrence Ave., Springfield, IL 62717.

616.5 616.95   FR   ISSN 0066-345X
ANNUAIRE NATIONAL DES SPECIALISTES
QUALIFIES EXCLUSIFS EN DERMATOLOGIE
ET VENEREOLOGIE. 1962. a. 20 F. Revue de
Medecine, 40, rue Paul- Valery, 75116 Paris,
France.

616.5   US   ISSN 0360-4020
ASSOCIATION OF MILITARY
DERMATOLOGISTS. JOURNAL. 1975. irreg.
free. Dome Laboratories, 400 Morgan Lane, West
Haven, CT 06516.
    Association of Military Dermatologists. Bulletin.

616.5   SZ   ISSN 0070-2064
CURRENT PROBLEMS IN DERMATOLOGY.
(Text in English) 1959. irreg. (approx. 1/yr.) 100
Fr.($60) per vol. (1981 price) S. Karger AG,
Allschwilerstrasse 10, P.O. Box, CH-4009 Basel,
Switzerland. Ed. J. W. H. Mali. (reprint service
avail. from ISI) Indexed: Biol.Abstr. Chem.Abstr.
Curr.Cont. Ind.Med.

616.5   US   ISSN 0163-1691
DERMATOLOGY UPDATE; review for physicians.
1979. a. Elsevier North-Holland, Inc., New York,
52 Vanderbilt Ave., New York, NY 10017. Ed. S.
Moschella.

616.5 616.95   US   ISSN 0071-7932
FORTSCHRITTE DER PRAKTISCHEN
DERMATOLOGIE UND VENEROLOGIE. 1952.
irreg., vol. 8, 1976. price varies. Springer-Verlag,
175 Fifth Ave., New York, NY 10010 (also Berlin,
Heidelberg, Vienna) (reprint service avail. from ISI)

HANSENIASIS LETTER. see *MEDICAL
SCIENCES — Communicable Diseases*

616.5   US
MASSON MONOGRAPHS IN
DERMATOPATHOLOGY. 1981. irreg. Masson
Publishing U.S.A., Inc., 14 E. 60th St., New York,
NY 10022. Ed. A. Bernard Ackerman, M.D.

PARAPHARMEX. see *PHARMACY AND
PHARMACOLOGY*

616 312.39   CN   ISSN 0319-0382
VENEREAL DISEASES IN CANADA. French
edition: Maladies Veneriennes au Canada (ISSN
0319-0390) 1972. a. free. Department of National
Health and Welfare, Brooke Claxton Bldg., Ottawa,
Ont. K1A OK9, Canada. illus.
    Formerly: Canada. Epidemiology Division.
Venereal Disease in Canada (ISSN 0319-0382)

616.505   US   ISSN 0093-3619
YEAR BOOK OF DERMATOLOGY. 1933. a. price
varies. ‡ Year Book Medical Publishers, Inc., 35 E.
Wacker Dr., Chicago, IL 60601. Ed. Richard L.
Dobson.
    Formerly: Yearbook of Dermatology and
Syphilology (ISSN 0093-3627)

MEDICAL SCIENCES — Endocrinology

616.4   DK   ISSN 0300-9750
ACTA ENDOCRINOLOGICA CONGRESS.
ADVANCE ABSTRACTS. 1971. irreg., latest edt.
1979. price varies; free to subscribers to Acta
Endocrinologica. Periodica, Skolegade 12, DK-2500
Valby Copenhagen, Denmark. Indexed: Biol.Abstr.
Curr.Cont. Ind.Med. Nutr.Abstr.

616.4   AG   ISSN 0065-1192
ACTA ENDOCRINOLOGICA PANAMERICANA.*
irreg. Panamerican Federation of Endocrine
Societies, c/o Dr. Noe Altschuler, 25 de Mayo no.
648, Vicente Lopez, Buenos Aires, Argentina.

616.4   US   ISSN 0065-2903
ADVANCES IN METABOLIC DISORDERS.
(Supplements avail.) 1964. irreg., vol. 10, 1977.
price varies. Academic Press, Inc., 111 Fifth Ave.,
New York, NY 10003. Eds. R. Levine, R. Luft.
index. (also avail. in microfiche) Indexed: Ind.Med.
Ind.Med.

616.4   US   ISSN 0587-4394
ADVANCES IN METABOLIC DISORDERS.
SUPPLEMENTS. 1970. irreg, vol. 2, 1973. price
varies. Academic Press, Inc., 111 Fifth Ave., New
York, NY 10003.

616.4   US
ADVANCES IN PROSTAGLANDIN AND
THROMBOXANE RESEARCH. 1976. irreg., vol.
6, 1980. price varies. Raven Press, 1140 Ave. of the
Americas, New York, NY 10036. Indexed:
Curr.Cont. Ind.Med.

616.4   US   ISSN 0098-0161
ADVANCES IN SEX HORMONE RESEARCH.
1974. irreg (approx 1 vol. per yr.) $32.50.
University Park Press (Subsidiary of: American
Medical Publishers) Chamber of Commerce Bldg.,
Baltimore, MD 21202. Eds. J. A. Thomas, R. L.
Singhal. Indexed: Ind.Med.

616.4   US
BIOCHEMICAL ACTIONS OF HORMONES. vol.
3, 1975. irreg., vol. 6, 1979. price varies. Academic
Press, Inc., 111 Fifth Ave., New York, NY 10003.
Ed. Gerald Litwack.

616.4   US   ISSN 0160-242X
COMPREHENSIVE ENDOCRINOLOGY. 1978.
irreg. Raven Press, 1140 Ave. of the Americas, New
York, NY 10036. Ed. Luciano Martini.

616.4   US
CONTEMPORARY METABOLISM; analytical
reviews of basic & clinical progress. 1976. a. Plenum
Publishing Corp., 233 Spring St., New York, NY
10013. Ed. Norbert Freinkel.

616.4   US   ISSN 0091-7397
CURRENT TOPICS IN EXPERIMENTAL
ENDOCRINOLOGY. 1971. irreg., vol. 3, 1978.
price varies. Academic Press, Inc., 111 Fifth
Avenue, New York, NY 10003. Ed. L. Martini,
V.H.T. James. Indexed: Ind.Med.

616.4   US   ISSN 0094-6761
CURRENT TOPICS IN MOLECULAR
ENDOCRINOLOGY. 1974. irreg. price varies.
Plenum Press, 233 Spring St., New York, NY
10013. Eds. Bert W. O'Malley, Anthony R. Means.

616.4   NE
DEVELOPMENTS IN ENDOCRINOLOGY. 1977.
irreg., vol. 6, 1980. price varies. Elsevier North-
Holland Biomedical Press, Box 211, 1000 AE
Amsterdam, Netherlands.

616.4   UA   ISSN 0070-9506
EGYPTIAN SOCIETY OF ENDOCRINOLOGY
AND METABOLISM. JOURNAL.* (Publication
suspended 1968-71) (Text in English) 1955. irreg.
Egyptian Society of Endocrinology and Metabolism,
42 Sharia Kasr el-Aini, Cairo, Egypt.

616.4   AT
ENDOCRINE SOCIETY OF AUSTRALIA.
PROCEEDINGS. 1958. a. Aus.$3. Endocrine
Society of Australia, c/o Endocrine Unit, Royal
Adelaide Hospital, Adelaide, S.A. 5000, Australia.
adv. circ. 650. Indexed: Excerp.Med.

616.4 616.8   US   ISSN 0532-7466
FRONTIERS IN NEUROENDOCRINOLOGY.
irreg; vol. 5, 1978. price varies. Raven Press, 1140
Ave. of the Americas, New York, NY 10036. Eds.
L. Martini and William F. Ganong. Indexed:
Curr.Cont. Sci.Cit.Ind.

616.4   SZ   ISSN 0301-3073
FRONTIERS OF HORMONE RESEARCH. (Text in
English) 1972. irreg. (approx. 1/yr.) 100 Fr.($60)
per vol. (1981 price) S. Karger AG,
Allschwilerstrasse 10, P.O. Box, CH-4009 Basel,
Switzerland. Ed. T.J.B. van Wimersma Greidanus.
(reprint service avail. from ISI) Indexed: Biol.Abstr.
Chem.Abstr. Curr.Cont. Ind.Med.
    Formerly: Monographs in Hormone Research
(ISSN 0077-0868)

616.4   JA   ISSN 0533-6724
GUMMA SYMPOSIA ON ENDOCRINOLOGY.
(Text in English) 1964. a. free or on exchange.
Gumma University, Institute of Endocrinology, 39-
15 Showa-machi, Maebashi, Gumma 371, Japan.

HORMONAL PROTEINS AND PEPTIDES. see
BIOLOGY — Biological Chemistry

616.4   SZ
INTERNATIONAL BEILINSON SYMPOSIUM
(PROCEEDINGS) (Supplement to: Pediatric and
Adolescent Endocrinology) 4th, 1978. irreg. $133.
S. Karger AG, Allschwilerstrasse 10, P.O. Box, CH-
4009 Basel, Switzerland. Eds. Z. Laron, M. Karp.
illus.

616.4   NE   ISSN 0538-6462
INTERNATIONAL CONGRESS OF
ENDOCRINOLOGY. PROCEEDINGS.*
(Subseries of International Congress Series) 1960.
irreg. (International Society of Endocrinology)
Excerpta Medica, P.O.B. 221, Amsterdam,
Netherlands (Inquire: Dr. John C. Beck, McIntyre
Medical Sciences Center, Montreal, Canada)
    1976, 4th, Hamburg

616.4   NE   ISSN 0074-4107
INTERNATIONAL CONGRESS ON HORMONAL
STEROIDS. ABSTRACTS OF PAPERS
PRESENTED.* 1962. irreg., 1970, 3rd, Hamburg.
fl.59.50($24.95) Excerpta Medica, P.O.B. 211,
Amsterdam, Netherlands (Dist. in the U.S. and
Canada by: Elsevier North-Holland, Inc., New
York, 52 Vanderbilt Ave., New York, NY 10017)
    1974, 4th, Mexico

616.462   NE   ISSN 0074-4522
INTERNATIONAL DIABETES FEDERATION.
PROCEEDINGS OF CONGRESS. (Abstracts of
8th Congress, 1973, available from Excerpta
Medica) 1952. triennial, 1970, 7th Buenos Aires.
fl.196($81.75) Excerpta Medica, P.O.B. 211, 1000
AE Amsterdam, Netherlands (Inquire: the
Federation, Dinkeziekenhuis, Losser, Netherlands)
    Diabetes

616.4 616.8   SZ   ISSN 0301-309X
INTERNATIONAL SYMPOSIUM ON BRAIN-
ENDOCRINE INTERACTION. PROCEEDINGS.
(Text in English) irreg., 3rd, 1977, Wuerzburg. 150
Fr.($90) (1981 price) S. Karger AG,
Allschwilerstrasse 10, P.O. Box, CH-4009 Basel,
Switzerland. (reprint service avail. from ISI)

616.4 612   US   ISSN 0539-0559
INTERNATIONAL SYMPOSIUM ON
COMPARATIVE ENDOCRINOLOGY.
PROCEEDINGS.* (Subseries of General and
Comparative Endocrinology. Supplement) a.
Academic Press, Inc, 111 Fifth Ave., New York,
NY 10003.

616.4   US   ISSN 0074-9095
INTERNATIONAL THYROID CONFERENCE.
PROCEEDINGS. irreg., 1965, 5th, Rome. $64.50.
Academic Press Inc., 111 Fifth Ave., New York,
NY 10003. C. Cassano, M. Andreoli.
    1970, 6th, Vienna

616.4   FR   ISSN 0075-4439
JOURNEES ANNUELLES DE DIABETOLOGIE
DE L'HOTEL DIEU. 1961. a. price varies. (Hotel-
Dieu, Clinique Medico-Sociale du Diabete et des
Maladies Metaboliques) Flammarion Medecine
Sciences, 20 rue de Vaugirard, 75006 Paris, France
(U.S. subscr. address: S.F.P.A., c/o M. Benech, 14
E. 60 St., NY 10022) Ed. Rathery, M.D. Indexed:
Ind.Med.
    Diabetes

616.4   US   ISSN 0077-1015
MONOGRAPHS ON ENDOCRINOLOGY. 1967.
irreg., vol. 19, 1981. price varies. Springer-Verlag,
175 Fifth Ave., New York, NY 10010 (also Berlin,
Heidelberg, Vienna) (reprint service avail. from ISI)
Indexed: Ind.Med.

616.4   SZ   ISSN 0304-4254
PEDIATRIC AND ADOLESCENT
ENDOCRINOLOGY. (Text in English) 1976. irreg.
(approx. 2/yr.) 190 Fr.($114) per 2 vols. (1981
price) S. Karger AG, Allschwilerstrasse 10, P.O.
Box, CH-4009 Basel, Switzerland. Ed. Z. Laron.
(reprint service avail. from ISI)

616.4   FR   ISSN 0079-5666
PROBLEMES ACTUELS D'ENDOCRINOLOGIE
ET DE NUTRITION. 1957. a. Expansion
Scientifique, 15 rue St. Benoit, 75278 Paris Cedex
06, France. Ed. H. P. Klotz. Indexed: Ind.Med.

616.4 574.192   US   ISSN 0079-9963
RECENT PROGRESS IN HORMONE RESEARCH. PROCEEDINGS OF THE LAURENTIAN HORMONE CONFERENCE. 1947. irreg., vol. 34, 1978. price varies. Academic Press, Inc, 111 Fifth Ave., New York, NY 10003. Ed. Gregory Pincus. index. cum.index: subject vols. 1-10 (1947-1954) in vol. 11 (1955) Indexed: Ind.Med.

616.4   CK   ISSN 0037-8445
SOCIEDAD COLOMBIANA DE ENDOCRINOLOGIA. REVISTA. (Text in Spanish; summaries in English and Spanish) 1958. s-a. $6. Sociedad Colombiana de Endocrinologia, Apdo. Aereo 29714, Bogota, D.E., Colombia. Ed. Alfredo F. Jacome, M.D. adv. index. circ. 2,000. Indexed: Biol. Abstr.

616.4 591   UK   ISSN 0081-136X
SOCIETY FOR ENDOCRINOLOGY (GREAT BRITAIN) MEMOIRS. 1959. irreg., no. 20, 1973. $42.50 for latest vol. Cambridge University Press, Box 110, Cambridge CB2 3RL, England (and 32 E. 57 St., New York NY 10022)

616.4   US   ISSN 0193-0982
SPECIAL TOPICS IN ENDOCRINOLOGY AND METABOLISM. 1979. irreg. price varies. Alan R. Liss, Inc., 150 Fifth Ave., New York, NY 10011. Eds. Margo P. Cohen, Piero P. Foa. charts. illus.

616.46   US   ISSN 0163-9609
U.S. NATIONAL DIABETES ADVISORY BOARD. ANNUAL REPORT. 1978. a. U.S. National Diabetes Advisory Board, Box 30174, Bethesda, MD 20014.
Diabetes

616.4053   US   ISSN 0084-3741
YEAR BOOK OF ENDOCRINOLOGY. 1950. a. price varies. ‡ Year Book Medical Publishers, Inc., 35 E. Wacker Dr., Chicago, IL 60601. Eds. T.B. Schwartz, Will G. Ryan.

MEDICAL SCIENCES — Experimental Medicine, Laboratory Technique

A I CH E EQUIPMENT TESTING PROCEDURES. (American Institute of Chemical Engineers) see *ENGINEERING — Chemical Engineering*

ANLEITUNG FUER DIE CHEMISCHE LABORATORIUMSPRAXIS. see *CHEMISTRY*

616   FI   ISSN 0066-2291
ANNALS OF CLINICAL RESEARCH. SUPPLEMENTUM. (Text in English) 1969. irreg. Fmk.40($20) free with subscription. Finnish Medical Society Duodecim, Runeberginkatu 47 A, SF-00260 Helsinki 26, Finland. Ed. M. H. Frick. adv. index. (also avail. in microform from UMI) Indexed: Biol.Abstr. Curr.Cont. Ind.Med.
Incorporating since 1969: Annales Paediatriae Fenniae. Supplementum & Annales Medicinae Internae.

616   FR
ANNUAIRE DES LABORATOIRES D'ANALYSES DE BIOLOGIE MEDICALE DE FRANCE. a. Labo-France, 7 rue Godot de Mauroy, 75009 Paris, France. adv.
Formerly: Annuaire des Laboratoires d'Analyses de France.

ARCHIVOS DE BIOLOGIA Y MEDICINA EXPERIMENTALES. see *BIOLOGY*

616   UR
BIOLOGIYA LABORATORNYKH ZHIVOTNYKH. irreg. 2 Rub. Akademiya Meditsinskikh Nauk S.S.S.R., Nauchno- Issledovatel'skaya Laboratoriya Eksperimental'no- Biologicheskikh Modelei, Moskovskaya Oblast', G. Khimki, Pos. Svetlie Gory, U.S.S.R. bibl.
Laboratory animals

610.28   US   ISSN 0090-5488
BIOMATERIALS, MEDICAL DEVICES AND ARTIFICIAL ORGANS. 1973. irreg., 4 nos. per vol.; vol. 8, 1980. $72 per vol. Marcel Dekker Journals, 270 Madison Ave., New York, NY 10016 (Prepaid subscr. to: Box 11305, Church St. Sta., New York NY 10049) Ed. T. F. Yen. illus. Indexed: Ind.Med.
Medical instrumentation

616   US
BIOPSY INTERPRETATION SERIES. irreg. price varies. Raven Press, 1140 Ave. of the Americas, New York, NY 10036. Ed. Dr. Ancel Blaustein. Indexed: Curr.Cont.

542   US
CLINICAL LAB PRODUCTS ANNUAL GUIDE.* 1975. a. Clinical Lab Products, Inc., Box 166, Amherst, MA 03031. Ed. David J. Premo. adv. circ. 48,000.

542 681.2   US   ISSN 0093-8076
CLINICAL LABORATORY REFERENCE. Abbreviated title: C L R. 1974. a. $6. (Medical Laboratory Observer) Medical Economics Co., 680 Kinderkamack Rd., Oradell, NJ 07649. Ed. S. Raymond Gambino. circ. 55,000(controlled)

DECHEMA MONOGRAPHIEN. see *CHEMISTRY — Analytical Chemistry*

616   US
GUIDE FOR THE CARE AND USE OF LABORATORY ANIMALS. 1963. irreg. $2.20 (single copies free) U.S. National Institutes of Health, Bethesda, MD 20205 (Orders to: Supt. Doc., Washington, DC 20402)
Until 1972: Guide for Laboratory Animal Facilities and Care (ISSN 0072-8098)
Laboratory animals

HUMAN GENE MAPPING. see *BIOLOGY — Genetics*

616   UK
INSTITUTE OF MEDICAL LABORATORY SCIENCES. LONDON, ANNUAL REPORT. 1943. a. free. ‡ Institute of Medical Laboratory Sciences, 12 Queen Anne St., London W1M OAU, England. circ. 15,500.
Formerly: Institute of Medical Laboratory Technology. London. Annual Report (ISSN 0073-9448)

619   SZ
INTERNATIONAL COLLOQUIUM ON PROSPECTIVE BIOLOGY (PROCEEDINGS) 4th, 1978. irreg. $100. S. Karger AG, Allschwilerstrasse 10, P.O. Box, CH-4009 Basel, Switzerland. Eds. G. Siest, D.S. Young. illus.

INTERNATIONAL COUNCIL FOR LABORATORY ANIMAL SCIENCE. PROCEEDINGS OF THE SYMPOSIUM. see *MEDICAL SCIENCES*

619   NO
INTERNATIONAL WORKSHOP ON NUDE MICE. PROCEEDINGS. 1974. irreg., no. 2, 1977. International Council for Laboratory Animal Science, c/o Dr. S. Erichsen, Secretary-General, National Institute of Public Health, Postuttak, Oslo 1, Norway (Publisher varies; 2nd avail. from: University of Tokyo Press, 7-3-1 Hongo, Bunkyo-ku, Tokyo 113, Japan)
Laboratory animals

542   MX
LABORATORIOS DE ESPECIALIDADES Y CONTROL. 1963. a. 125 ptas.($90) Editorial Innovacion, Espana 396, Mexico 13, D.F., Mexico. Ed. Cesar Macazaga. adv.

606   US
LABORATORY AND RESEARCH METHODS IN BIOLOGY AND MEDICINE. 1978. irreg. price varies. Alan R. Liss, Inc., 150 Fifth Ave., New York, NY 10011.

616   UK   ISSN 0458-5933
LABORATORY ANIMAL HANDBOOKS. 1968. irreg. price varies. (Laboratory Animal Science Association) Laboratory Animals Ltd., 7 Warwick Court, London WC1R 5DP, England. circ. 750-1,500. Indexed: Biol.Abstr. Excerp.Med.
Laboratory animals

LABORATORY TECHNIQUES IN BIOCHEMISTRY AND MOLECULAR BIOLOGY. see *BIOLOGY — Biological Chemistry*

619.98 610   SZ   ISSN 0079-5119
PRIMATES IN MEDICINE. (Text in English) 1968. irreg. (approx. 1/yr.) 140 Fr.($84) per vol. (1981 price) S. Karger AG, Allschwilerstrasse 10, P.O. Box, CH-4009 Basel, Switzerland. Ed. J. Moor-Jankowski. (reprint service avail. from ISI) Indexed: Biol.Abstr. Chem.Abstr. Curr.Cont. Ind.Med.

619.98 610   SZ   ISSN 0079-5127
PRIMATOLOGIA. (Text in English, French and German) 1956. irreg. (approx. 1/yr.) 150 Fr.($90) per vol. (1981 price) S. Karger AG, Allschwilerstrasse 10, P.O. Box, CH-4009 Basel, Switzerland. Eds. H.O. Hofer, A.H. Schultz, D. Starck. circ. 1,000. (reprint service avail. from ISI) Indexed: Biol.Abstr. Chem.Abstr. Curr.Cont. Ind.Med.

RAVEN PRESS SERIES IN EXPERIMENTAL PHYSIOLOGY. see *BIOLOGY — Physiology*

616   UK   ISSN 0085-591X
SCANDINAVIAN JOURNAL OF CLINICAL AND LABORATORY INVESTIGATION. SUPPLEMENT. (Text in English) 1951. irreg. (Scandinavian Society for Clinical Chemistry and Clinical Physiology) Blackwell Scientific Publications Ltd., Osney Mead, Oxford OX2 0EL, England. Eds. Lorentz Eldjarn, F. Kiil, M.D. adv. circ. 2,057. (back issues avail.; reprint service avail. from ISI) Indexed: Curr.Cont.

616   US
STANFORD SERIES ON METHODS AND TECHNIQUES IN THE CLINICAL LABORATORY. 1972. irreg., 1975 latest vol. price varies. John Wiley & Sons, Inc., 605 Third Ave., New York, NY 10016. Ed. Paul Wolf.

TECHNIQUES OF CHEMISTRY. see *CHEMISTRY*

616   FI   ISSN 0355-9076
VALTION TEKNILLINEN TUTKIMUSKESKUS. SAIRAALATEKNIIKAN LABORATORIO. TIEDONANTO/TECHNICAL RESEARCH CENTRE OF FINLAND. BIOMEDICAL ENGINEERING LABORATORY. REPORT. (Text mainly in Finnish, some in English or Swedish) 1977. irreg. price varies. Valtion Teknillinen Tutkimuskeskus - Technical Research Centre of Finland, Vuorimiehentie 5, 02150 Espoo 15, Finland.

610 591   GW   ISSN 0300-1016
VERSUCHSTIERKUNDE. 1972. irreg. price varies. Verlag Paul Parey (Berlin), Lindenstr. 44-47, 1000 Berlin 61, W. Germany (B.R.D.) Eds. M. Merkenschlager, K. Gaertner. bibl. illus. index.

MEDICAL SCIENCES — Forensic Sciences

340.6   BE   ISSN 0065-1397
ACTA MEDICINAE LEGALIS ET SOCIALIS. (Represents proceedings of its triennial world congress and its annual international meetings; not published 1969-1971) (Text in English and French) 1948. a. International Academy of Legal Medicine and Social Medicine, 39 rue Dos Fanchon, 4020 Liege, Belgium. circ. 400. Indexed: Chem.Abstr. Ind.Med.

614.19   GW   ISSN 0570-5886
ARBEITSMETHODEN DER MEDIZINISCHEN UND NATURWISSENSCHAFTLICHEN KRIMINALISTIK. 1962. irreg., vol. 15,1977. price varies. Max Schmidt-Roemhild Verlag, Mengstr. 16, 2400 Luebeck 1, W. Germany (B.R.D.)

340.6   AU   ISSN 0067-5016
BEITRAEGE ZUR GERICHTLICHEN MEDIZIN. 1911. a, vol. 37, 1979. price varies. Franz Deuticke, Helferstorfer Strasse 4, A-1010 Vienna, Austria. Ed. Wilhelm Holczabek. cum. index(vols. 1-20 in vol. 20; vols. 21-30 in vol. 31) circ. 250. (back issues avail.) Indexed: Chem.Abstr. Ind.Med.

340.6 610   FR   ISSN 0075-9473
INSTITUT DE MEDECINE LEGALE ET DE MEDECINE SOCIALE. ARCHIVES. 1935. irreg; latest 1966. Institut de Medecine Legale et de Medecine Sociale, Place Theo Varlet, 59000 Lille, France.

614.19   CK
INSTITUTO NACIONAL DE MEDICINA LEGAL DE COLOMBIA. REVISTA. 1975. irreg. Instituto Nacional de Medicina Legal de Colombia, Carrera 13, no. 7-46, Bogota, Colombia.

340.6   IT   ISSN 0074-1248
INTERNATIONAL ACADEMY OF LEGAL MEDICINE AND OF SOCIAL MEDICINE. (CONGRESS REPORTS)* triennial, 1973, 9th, Rome. International Academy of Legal Medicine and Social Medicine, c/o Prof. Ferdinando Antoniotti, Viale Regina, Elena 336, 00161 Rome, Italy.

340.6   US   ISSN 0075-8590
LEGAL MEDICINE ANNUAL. 1969. a. price varies. Appleton-Century-Crofts (Subsidiary of: Prentice-Hall) 292 Madison Ave., New York, NY 10017. Ed. Cyril H. Wecht. Indexed: Ind.Med.

340.6   CE
MEDICO-LEGAL SOCIETY OF SRI LANKA. PROCEEDINGS. Medico-Legal Society of Sri Lanka, 111 Francis Rd., Colombo 10, Sri Lanka.

340.6   US
NATIONAL MEDICO-LEGAL SYMPOSIUM. 1971. biennial. $7. American Medical Association, 535 N. Dearborn St., Chicago, IL 60610. (Co-sponsor: American Bar Association)

614   US   ISSN 0363-2679
OKLAHOMA JOURNAL OF FORENSIC MEDICINE. 1972. irreg. Board of Medicolegal Investigations, Office of the Chief Medical Examiner, Box 26901, 800 Northeast 13th St., Oklahoma City, OK 73190. Ed. Fred B. Jordan, M.D. illus. circ. 1,000.

340   614.19   US   ISSN 0511-8662
WHAT'S NEW IN FORENSIC SCIENCES.* Cover title: Forensic Sciences. Official Publication of the American Academy of Forensic Sciences. a. American Academy of Forensic Sciences, 11400 Rockville Pike, Suite 515, Rockville, MD 20852.

MEDICAL SCIENCES — Gastroenterology

616   FR   ISSN 0066-3425
ANNUAIRE NATIONAL DES SPECIALISTES QUALIFIES EXCLUSIFS DES MALADIES DE L'APPAREIL DIGESTIF. 1964, 2nd ed. a. 23 F. Revue de Medecine, 40, rue Paul-Valery, 75116 Paris, France.

616.3   SZ   ISSN 0302-0665
FRONTIERS OF GASTROINTESTINAL RESEARCH. (Text in English) 1960. irreg. (approx. 1/yr.) 110 Fr.($66) per vol. (1981 price) S. Karger AG, Allschwilerstrasse 10, P.O. Box, CH-4009 Basel, Switzerland. Ed. L. van der Reis. (reprint service avail. from ISI) Indexed: Biol.Abstr. Chem.Abstr. Curr.Cont. Ind.Med.
    Formerly: Bibliotheca Gastroenterologica (ISSN 0302-0665)

616.3   FR   ISSN 0072-0291
GASTER; L'ANNUAIRE DE GASTRO-ENTEROLOGIE.* 1966. biennial. Laboratoires Biotherax, 58 rue du Landy, La Plaine-Saint-Denis, France.

616.3   II
INDIAN SOCIETY OF GASTROENTEROLOGY. PROCEEDINGS OF THE ANNUAL CONFERENCE. a. Indian Society of Gastroenterology, c/o Christian Medical College Hospital, Vellore 632004, Tamil Nadu, India.

616.3   US   ISSN 0079-6271
PROGRESS IN GASTROENTEROLOGY. 1968. irreg., vol. 3, 1977. Grune and Stratton, Inc. (Subsidiary of: Harcourt Brace Jovanovich, Inc.) 111 Fifth Avenue, New York, NY 10003. Ed. George B. Jerzy Glass.

616.362   US   ISSN 0079-6409
PROGRESS IN LIVER DISEASES. 1961. irreg., vol. 6, 1979. price varies. Grune & Stratton, Inc., (Subsidiary of: Harcourt Brace Jovanovich, Inc.) 111 5th Ave, New York, NY 10003. Eds. H. Popper and F. Schaffner. index. Indexed: Ind.Med.

616.3   NO   ISSN 0085-5928
SCANDINAVIAN JOURNAL OF GASTROENTEROLOGY. SUPPLEMENT. (Text in English) 1968. irreg. Kr.625($125) for Journal and its Supplements. Universitetsforlaget, Kolstadgt. 1, Box 2959-Toeyen, Oslo 6, Norway (U.S. address: Box 258, Irvington-on-Hudson, NY 10533) Ed. Johannes Myren. circ. 1,500. (back issues avail.) Indexed: Ind.Med.

MEDICAL SCIENCES — Hematology

616.15   US
AMERICAN LECTURES IN HEMATOLOGY. irreg. price varies. Charles C. Thomas, Publisher, 301-327 E. Lawrence Ave., Springfield, IL 62717.

616.1   SZ   ISSN 0067-7957
BIBLIOTHECA HAEMATOLOGICA. (Text in English) 1955. irreg. (approx. 1/yr.) 100 Fr.($60) per vol. (1981 price) (European Society of Hematology) S. Karger AG, Allschwilerstrasse 10, P.O. Box, CH-4009 Basel, Switzerland. Ed. A. Haessig. (reprint service avail. from ISI) Indexed: Biol.Abstr. Chem.Abstr. Curr.Cont. Ind.Med.

616.15   YU   ISSN 0523-6150
BILTEN ZA HEMATOLOGIJU I TRANSFUZIJU. 1973. a. Zavod za Transfuziju Krvi, Belgrade, Svetosavska 39, Belgrade, Yugoslavia. (Co-sponsor: Udruzenje Hematologa i Transfuziologa Jugoslavije) Ed. Budimir Dinic. Indexed: Ind.Med.

616.15   US
CLINICAL MONOGRAPHS IN HEMATOLOGY. 1979. irreg. price varies. Thieme-Stratton, Inc., 381 Park Ave. S., New York, NY 10016. Ed. T.F. Necheles.

616.15   US
CONTEMPORARY HEMATOLOGY/ONCOLOGY. 1977. a. Plenum Publishing Corp., 233 Spring St., New York, NY 10013. Ed.Bd.
    Formerly: Year in Hematology.

616.15   US
CURRENT TOPICS IN HEMATOLOGY. 1978. irreg. price varies. Alan R. Liss, Inc., 150 Fifth Ave., New York, NY 10011. bibl. illus. Indexed: Biol.Abstr.

616.15   US   ISSN 0440-0607
HAEMATOLOGIE UND BLUTTRANSFUSION. (Supplement to Blut) (Text in English or German) 1962. irreg., vol. 24, 1979. price varies. Springer-Verlag, 175 Fifth Ave., New York, NY 10010 (Also Berlin, Heidelberg, Vienna) Eds. W. Stich, G. Ruhenstroth-Bauer. (reprint service avail. from ISI)

616.15   GW
INTERNATIONAL COMMITTEE FOR STANDARDIZATION IN HEMATOLOGY. SYMPOSIA. irreg., 13th, 1972. price varies. Institut fuer Standardisierung und Dokumentation im Med Laboratorium, Hugstetter Str. 55, D-7800 Freiburg im Breisgau, W. Germany (B.R.D.)

612.1   US   ISSN 0074-3682
INTERNATIONAL CONGRESS OF HEMATOLOGY. PROCEEDINGS.* biennial since 1958; 1974, 15th, Jerusalem. International Society of Hematology, c/o Dr. J. L. Tullis, 110 Francis St., Boston, MA 02215.
    Proceedings published in host country

616.1   US   ISSN 0093-9404
OVERVIEW OF BLOOD. 1971. irreg., approx. biennial. $10. Blood Information Service, 508 Getzville Rd., Buffalo, NY 14226. Ed. Charles Bishop.

616.1508   US   ISSN 0079-6301
PROGRESS IN HAEMATOLOGY. 1956. irreg., vol. 10, 1977. $38.50. Grune and Stratton, Inc. (Subsidiary of: Harcourt Brace Jovanovich, Inc.) 111 Fifth Avenue, New York, NY 10003. Ed. E. B. Brown. Indexed: Ind.Med.

616.15   DK   ISSN 0080-6722
SCANDINAVIAN JOURNAL OF HAEMATOLOGY. SUPPLEMENTUM. (Text in English) 1964. irreg. free to subscribers. Munksgaard, 35 Noerre Soegade, Dk-1370 Copenhagen K, Denmark. Ed. Aage Videbaek. adv. (reprint service avail. from ISI) Indexed: Biol.Abstr. Chem.Abstr. Curr.Cont. Ind.Med.

MEDICAL SCIENCES — Hypnosis

159.7   616.891   US   ISSN 0517-5178
AMERICAN SOCIETY OF CLINICAL HYPNOSIS. DIRECTORY. irreg. price varies. American Society of Clinical Hypnosis, 401 Peachtree St. N.E., Suite 804, Atlanta, GA 30308.

MEDICAL SCIENCES — Nurses And Nursing

see also Gerontology and Geriatrics; Hospitals

610.73   US   ISSN 0065-9509
AMERICAN NURSES' ASSOCIATION. CONFERENCE FOR MEMBERS AND PROFESSIONAL EMPLOYEES OF STATE BOARDS OF NURSING AND A N A ADVISORY COUNCIL. PROCEEDINGS. a. American Nurses Association, Council for State Boards of Nursing, 2420 Pershing Rd., Kansas City, MO 64108.

610.73   US   ISSN 0065-9517
AMERICAN NURSES' ASSOCIATION. HOUSE OF DELEGATES. REPORTS. biennial. price varies. American Nurses Association, 2420 Pershing Rd., Kansas City, MO 64108.

610.73   US   ISSN 0361-0772
AMERICAN NURSES' ASSOCIATION. HOUSE OF DELEGATES. SUMMARY PROCEEDINGS. irreg. American Nurses' Association, 2420 Pershing Rd., Kansas City, MO 64108. Key Title: Summary Proceedings, A N A House of Delegates.

610.73   VE   ISSN 0066-8613
ASOCIACION VENEZOLANA DE ENFERMERAS PROFESIONALES. BOLETIN.* irreg. Asociacion Venezolana de Enfermeras Profesionales, Edificio Sur, 4 Piso, Oficina 412, el Silencio, Caracas, Venezuela.

610.73   378   US   ISSN 0069-5602
BACCALAUREATE EDUCATION IN NURSING: KEY TO A PROFESSIONAL CAREER IN NURSING. Title varies: College Education: Key to a Professional Career in Nursing. 1964. a. $1 (back issues not available) National League for Nursing, 10 Columbus Circle, New York, NY 10019.

610.73   BB   ISSN 0572-6042
BARBADOS NURSING JOURNAL. a. membership. Barbados Registered Nurses Association, Gibson House, Spry Street, Bridgetown, Barbados, W. I.

610.73   CN   ISSN 0068-9386
CANADIAN NURSES ASSOCIATION. BIENNIAL MEETING. FOLIO OF REPORTS. (Title Varies) (Text in English and French) 1940. biennial. membership only. Canadian Nurses Association - Association des infirmieres et infirmiers du Canada, c/o 50 The Driveway, Ottawa, Ont. K2P 1E2, Canada. circ. controlled.

610.73   CN   ISSN 0383-0101
CANADIAN NURSES ASSOCIATION. LIBRARY. PERIODICAL HOLDINGS. a. Canadian Nurses Association - Association des infirmieres et infirmiers du Canada, 50 The Driveway, Ottawa, Ont. K2P 1E2, Canada.

610.73   US
CONTEMPORARY NURSING SERIES. irreg., vol. 7, 1973. price varies. (American Nurses Association) American Journal of Nursing Co., 10 Columbus Circle, New York, NY 10019.

610.73 US ISSN 0070-1890
CURRENT CONCEPTS IN CLINICAL NURSING. 1967. irreg., vol. 4, 1973. $15.50. C. V. Mosby Co., 11830 Westline Industrial Dr., St. Louis, MO 63141. Ed.Bd.

610.73 301.4 US
CURRENT PRACTICE IN FAMILY CENTERED COMMUNITY NURSING; a sociocultural framework. biennial. C.V. Mosby Co., 11830 Westline Industrial Dr., St. Louis, MO 63141. Ed. Nancy Evans.

610.73 618 US ISSN 0361-9249
CURRENT PRACTICE IN OBSTETRIC AND GYNECOLOGICAL NURSING. 1976. irreg. C.V. Mosby Co., 11830 Westline Industrial Dr., St. Louis, MD 63141.

610.73 616.99 US
CURRENT PRACTICE IN ONCOLOGIC NURSING. 1976. irreg. C.V. Mosby Co., 11830 Westline Industrial Dr., St. Louis, MO 63141.

610.73 618.92 US ISSN 0361-9257
CURRENT PRACTICE IN PEDIATRIC NURSING. irreg. C.V. Mosby Co., 1130 Westline Industrial Dr., St. Louis, MO 63141.

610.73 378 US ISSN 0070-9166
EDUCATION FOR NURSING: THE DIPLOMA WAY. 1966. a. $1
National League for Nursing, 10 Columbus Circle, New York, NY 10019.

610.73 US
FACHSCHWESTER - FACHPFLEGER. 1975. irreg.; latest, 1978. price varies. Springer-Verlag, 175 Fifth Ave., New York, NY 10010 (Also Berlin, Heidelberg, Vienna) (reprint service avail. from ISI)

610.73 US ISSN 0071-3651
FACTS ABOUT NURSING; a statistical summary. 1935. a. $6.50. (American Nurses Association, Statistics Department) American Journal of Nursing Co., 10 Columbus Circle, New York, NY 10019. Ed. Aleda Roth.

610.73 AU ISSN 0073-0181
HANDBUCH FUER DIE SANITAETSBERUFE OESTERREICH. 1950. a. S.295. Dieter Goeschl Buch- und Zeitschriftenverlag, Klopstockgasse 34, A-1170 Vienna, Austria. Ed. Walter Urbarz. adv. index. circ. 5,500.

HOME CARE SERVICES IN NEW YORK STATE. see SOCIAL SERVICES AND WELFARE

HOSPITAL AND NURSING YEARBOOK OF SOUTHERN AFRICA. see HOSPITALS

INDUSTRIAL HEALTH FOUNDATION. NURSING SERIES. BULLETINS. see INDUSTRIAL HEALTH AND SAFETY

610.7 US ISSN 0075-0387
IOWA NURSES' ASSOCIATION. BULLETIN. 1957, vol. 11. a. $3. Iowa Nurses' Association, 308 Shops Bldg., Des Moines, IA 50309. Indexed: C.I.N.L.
Continues: Iowa State Nurses' Association. Bulletin.

610.73 SP
LIBROS DE ENFERMERIA. 1975. irreg.; 1979. no. 10. Ediciones Universidad de Navarra, S.A., Plaza de los Sauces 1 y 2, Baranain, Pamplona, Spain.

610.73 UK
LONDON HOSPITAL LEAGUE OF NURSES REVIEW. 1921. a. membership. London Hospital League of Nurses, London Hospital, Whitechapel, London E1, England. Ed. D.J. Dolman. adv. circ. 2,400(controlled)

610.73 US ISSN 0095-5884
LOUISIANA. STATE BOARD OF NURSE EXAMINERS. REPORT. a. State Board of Nurse Examiners, 150 Baronne St., New Orleans, LA 70112. Key Title: Report - Louisiana State Board of Nurse Examiners.

610.73 378 US
MASTERS EDUCATION: ROUTE TO OPPORTUNITIES IN CONTEMPORARY NURSING. 1966. a. $1. National League for Nursing, 10 Columbus Circle, New York, NY 10019.
Formerly: Masters Education; Route to Opportunities in Modern Nursing (ISSN 0076-5104)

610.73 US
N L N NURSING DATA BOOK: STATISTICAL INFORMATION ON NURSING EDUCATION & NEWLY LICENSED NURSES. a. $9.95. National League for Nursing, 10 Columbus Circle, New York, NY 10019.
Supersedes: Some Statistics on Baccaluareate and Higher Degree Programs in Nursing (ISSN 0081-203X)

610.73 378 US ISSN 0077-5118
NATIONAL LEAGUE FOR NURSING. ASSOCIATE DEGREE EDUCATION FOR NURSING. 1972. a. $0.75. National League for Nursing, 10 Columbus Circle, New York, NY 10019.

610.73 US
NATIONAL LEAGUE FOR NURSING. BACCALAUREATE PROGRAMS ACCREDITED FOR PUBLIC HEALTH NURSING PREPARATION. a. $1.50. National League for Nursing, Council of Baccalaureate and Higher Degree Programs, 10 Columbus Circle, NY 10019.

610.73 US
NATIONAL LEAGUE FOR NURSING. DIRECTORY OF CAREER MOBILITY PROGRAMS IN NURSING EDUCATION. 1973. irreg., 2nd edt., 1975-1976. $7.95. National League for Nursing, 10 Columbus Circle, New York, NY 10019.

610.73 US ISSN 0077-5134
NATIONAL LEAGUE FOR NURSING. LEAGUE EXCHANGE. 1952. irreg., no. 107, 1975. price varies. National League for Nursing, 10 Columbus Circle, New York, NY 10019.

610.73 US ISSN 0028-730X
NEW YORK L P N. vol.34, 1973. irreg., formerly q. membership (non-members $3) Licensed Practical Nurses and Technicians of New York, Inc., 250 W. 57th St., New York, NY 10019. adv. charts. illus. circ. 4,500.

610.73 US
NURSING(YEAR) CAREER DIRECTORY. 1979. a. free. Intermed Communications, Inc., Springhouse, PA 19477. Ed. June F. Gomez. adv. charts. illus. tr.lit. index. circ. 100,000(controlled)

NURSING AND ALLIED HEALTH LITERATURE INDEX. see MEDICAL SCIENCES — Abstracting, Bibliographies, Statistics

610.73 US ISSN 0162-9069
NURSING JOB NEWS: NURSING JOB GUIDE TO OVER 7000 HOSPITALS. Short title: Nursing Job Guide to over 7000 Hospitals. 1979. a. $15. Prime National Publishing Corp., 470 Boston Post Rd., Weston, MA 02193. Ed. Ira Alterman. adv. charts. illus. stat. circ. 10,000. (back issues avail.)

610.73 CE
NURSING JOURNAL. a. Sri Lanka Nurses Association, Post Basic School of Nursing, Regent St., Colombo 10, Sri Lanka.

610.73 US
NURSING OPPORTUNITIES. 1970. a. $8.95. R N Publications (Subsidiary of: Medical Economics Co.) 680 Kinderkamack Rd., Oradell, NJ 07649. adv. circ. 200,000.

610.7 AU
OESTERREICHISCHER KRANKENPFLEGERVERBAND. FORTBILDUNGSPROGRAMM. 1969. a. free. Oesterreichischer Krankenpflegeverband, Mollgasse 3a, A-1180 Vienna, Austria. Ed. Irmgard Kappelmueller. circ. 6,000.

610.73 AU
OESTERREICHISCHER SCHWESTERNKALENDER. 1948. a. S.25. Oesterreichischer Krankenpflegeverband, Mollgasse 3a, A-1180 Vienna, Austria. Ed. Hannelore Kriegner. circ. 5,500.

610.73 US
PRACTICAL NURSING CAREER. 1968. a. $0.75. National League for Nursing, 10 Columbus Circle, New York, NY 10019.

371.7 US ISSN 0569-230X
SCHOOL NURSING MONOGRAPHS. 1969. irreg. price varies. American Alliance for Health, Physical Education, Recreation, and Dance, National Council for School Nurses, 1900 Association Dr., Reston, VA 22091.

610.73 GW
SPRACHFUEHRER FUER DIE KRANKENPFLEGE. (Text in English, French, German and Spanish) 1968. irreg. DM.11.50. Deutscher Berufsverband fuer Krankenpflege, Arndt Str. 15, 6000 Frankfurt 1, W. Germany (B.R.D.)

610.73 US ISSN 0081-4423
STATE-APPROVED SCHOOLS OF NURSING - L. P. N./L. V. N. 1958. a. $4.95. National League for Nursing, 10 Columbus Circle, New York, NY 10019.

610.73 US ISSN 0081-4431
STATE-APPROVED SCHOOLS OF NURSING - R. N. a. $4.95. National League for Nursing, 10 Columbus Circle, New York, NY 10019.

610.73 UK ISSN 0302-1440
STUDY OF NURSING CARE: RESEARCH PROJECT SERIES. irreg. £1. Royal College of Nursing, Henrietta Place, Cavendish Square, London W1M 0AB, England. bibl.

610.73 US ISSN 0095-2141
U.S. BUREAU OF HEALTH RESOURCES DEVELOPMENT. DIVISION OF NURSING. SPECIAL PROJECT GRANTS AND CONTRACTS AWARDED FOR IMPROVEMENT IN NURSE TRAINING. irreg. U.S. Bureau of Health Planning and Resources Development, Division of Nursing, U.S. Health Resources Administration, Bethesda, MD 20014. Key Title: Special Project Grants and Contracts Awarded for Improvement in Nurse Training.

610.73 US
WASHINGTON NURSE. 1977. irreg.(approx. 7/yr.) included in subscription to Washington State Journal of Nursing. Washington State Nurses Association, 1109 Second Ave., Seattle, WA 98101. Ed. Beverly M. Smith. adv. circ. 8,500 (controlled) Indexed: C.I.N.L.
Supersedes (1929-1977): W S N A Mini Journal.

WORLD DIRECTORY OF POST-BASIC AND POST-GRADUATE SCHOOLS OF NURSING. see EDUCATION — Guides To Schools And Colleges

610.73 US
WYOMING NURSE. irreg., approx. m. $1. Wyoming Nurses Association, Seminoe Dam Route, Sinclair, WY 82334. Ed. Carolyn M. Haygood. circ. 900. (processed)
Formerly: Wyoming Nurses Newsletter (ISSN 0084-3164)

MEDICAL SCIENCES — Obstetrics And Gynecology

618.1 618.2 US ISSN 0065-728X
AMERICAN ASSOCIATION OF OBSTETRICIANS AND GYNECOLOGISTS. TRANSACTIONS. 1888. a. American Association of Obstetricians and Gynecologists, c/o Edgar L. Makowski, Sec., 4200 E. 9th Ave., Denver, CO 80262. Ed. Dr. R. Mattingly. circ. 250.

618.1 618.2 US ISSN 0065-8480
AMERICAN GYNECOLOGICAL SOCIETY. TRANSACTIONS OF THE A G S. 1878. a. price varies. C. V. Mosby Co., 11830 Westline Industrial Dr., St. Louis, MO 63141. circ. 200. (reprint service avail. from UMI,ISI)

618   US
AMERICAN LECTURES IN GYNECOLOGY AND OBSTETRICS. irreg. price varies. Charles C. Thomas, Publisher, 301-327 E. Lawrence Ave., Springfield, IL 62717.

618.1 618.2   FR   ISSN 0066-3395
ANNUAIRE NATIONAL DES SPECIALISTES EN GYNECOLOGIE-OBSTETRIQUE ET DES COMPETENTS EXLUSIFS EN GYNECOLOGIE ET OBSTETRIQUE. 1969, 2nd ed. irreg. 36 F. Revue de Medecine, 40, rue Paul-Valery, 75116 Paris, France.

AUSTRALIA. BUREAU OF STATISTICS. PERINATAL DEATHS. see POPULATION STUDIES

618   SP
AVANCES EN OBSTETRICIA Y GINECOLOGIA. 1975. a. 875 ptas. Salvat Editores, S.A., Mallorca 41-49, Barcelona 15, Spain. Ed. J. Gonzalez-Merlo. charts. illus. circ. 2,000.

618.2   AG
B.I.M. BOLETIN DEL INSTITUTO DE MATERNIDAD "ALBERTO PERALTA RAMOS". (Text and summaries in Spanish; occasionally in English) 1941. irreg. Instituto de Maternidad "Alberto Peralta Ramos", Asociacion Medica, Buenos Aires, Argentina.

618.1   GW   ISSN 0068-337X
BUECHEREI DES FRAUENARZTES. (Beginning 1972, supplements Zeitschrift fuer Geburtshilfe und Perinatologie) 1956. irreg., vol. 10, 1980. price varies. Ferdinand Enke Verlag, Herdweg 63, 7000 Stuttgart 1, W. Germany (B.R.D.) Eds. H. Jung, F. Kubli, H. Wulf.

618   US
CLINICAL MONOGRAPHS IN OBSTETRICS AND GYNECOLOGY. 1975. irreg. John Wiley & Sons, Inc., 605 Third Ave., New York, NY 10016.

618.1 618.2   SZ   ISSN 0304-4246
CONTRIBUTIONS TO GYNECOLOGY AND OBSTETRICS. (Text in English) 1950. irreg. (approx. 1/yr.) 80 Fr.($48) per vol.(1981 price) S. Karger AG, Allschwilerstrasse 10, P.O. Box, CH-4009 Basel, Switzerland. Ed. P.J. Keller. (reprint service avail. from ISI) Indexed: Biol.Abstr. Chem.Abstr. Curr.Cont. Ind.Med.
Formerly: Advances in Obstetrics and Gynaecology (ISSN 0065-2997)

CURRENT PRACTICE IN OBSTETRIC AND GYNECOLOGICAL NURSING. see MEDICAL SCIENCES — Nurses And Nursing

618.2   AU   ISSN 0071-2698
EUROPEAN CONGRESS OF PERINATAL MEDICINE. PROCEEDINGS. biennial, 5th, 1976, Uppsala. European Association of Perinatal Medicine, c/o Arnold Pollack, Postfach 35, A-1095 Vienna, Austria.

HAROLD C. MACK SYMPOSIUM. PROCEEDINGS. see BIOLOGY — Physiology

618   NE   ISSN 0074-3135
INTERNATIONAL CONFERENCE ON INTRA-UTERINE CONTRACEPTION. PROCEEDINGS.* 1962. irreg., 1964, 2nd, New York. (Population Council, US) Excerpta Medica, P.O.B. 211, Amsterdam, Netherlands (Dist. in the U.S. and Canada by: Elsevier North-Holland, Inc., 245 Vanderbilt Ave., New York, NY 10017)

618.2   SZ   ISSN 0302-5152
INTERNATIONAL CONGRESS OF PSYCHOSOMATIC MEDICINE IN OBSTETRICS AND GYNAECOLOGY. PROCEEDINGS. (Text in English) irreg. 190 Fr.($114) per vol. (1981 price) S. Karger AG, Allschwilerstrasse 10, P.O. Box, CH-4009 Basel, Switzerland. Ed. H. Hirsch. bibl. illus. (reprint service avail. from ISI)

JOURNAL OF POPULATION STUDIES. see BIRTH CONTROL

610   PO   ISSN 0302-4326
MATERNIDADE DR. ALFREDO DA COSTA, LISBON. ARQUIVO CLINICO. 1973. a. Esc.40. Centro de Documentacao e Informacao da Maternidade Dr. Alfredo da Costa, Imprensa Nacional, Rua Viriato, Lisbon, Portugal. Dir. Armendo Jorge Santos Carvalho Da Fonseca.
Supersedes: Instituto Maternal, Lisbon. Revista Clinica (ISSN 0024-4279)

MONTHLY EXTRACT. see WOMEN'S INTERESTS

618.1 618.2   US   ISSN 0078-7442
PACIFIC COAST OBSTETRICAL AND GYNECOLOGICAL SOCIETY. TRANSACTIONS. 1944-46, vol. 14. a. (Pacific Coast Obstetrical and Gynecological Society) C. V. Mosby Co., 11830 Westline Industrial Dr., St. Louis, MO 63141. Indexed: Ind.Med.
Continues: Pacific Coast Society of Obstetrics and Gynecology. Transactions.

618   US
PERINATAL MEDICINE: REVIEW AND COMMENTS. 1976. biennial. C. V. Mosby Co., 11830 Westline Industrial Dr., St. Louis, MO 63141. Eds. Drs. Frederick C. Battaglia, Giacomo Meschia, E. J. Quilligan. bibl. charts. illus.

618.1   US   ISSN 0079-6298
PROGRESS IN GYNECOLOGY. irreg., vol. 6, 1975. $64.25. Grune & Stratton, Inc., (Subsidiary of: Harcourt Brace Jovanovich, Inc.) 111 Fifth Ave., New York, NY 10003. Eds. Melvin Taylor, Thomas H. Green. index.

618.3   US   ISSN 0362-5699
REVIEWS IN PERINATAL MEDICINE. 1976. a. price varies. Raven Press, 1140 Ave. of the Americas, New York, NY 10036. Eds. Emile M. Scarpelli, Ermelando V. Cosmi.

618   UK
SOCIETY FOR THE PROTECTION OF UNBORN CHILDREN. BULLETIN. 1968. irreg (2-3/yr) membership. Society for the Protection of Unborn Children, 9A Brechin Place, London SW7 4QB, England. Ed. Phyllis Bowman. stat. circ. 15,000. (tabloid format)

618.1   SA
UNIVERSITY OF CAPE TOWN. DEPARTMENT OF OBSTETRICS AND GYNAECOLOGY. ANNUAL REPORT. (Text in English) 1952. a. free. University of Cape Town, Department of Obstetrics and Gynaecology, Medical School, Anzio Road, Observatory, Cape Town 7925, South Africa. (Co-sponsor: Cape Provincial Administration) Ed. Herman A. van Coeverden de Groot. circ. 250.
Formerly: University of Cape Town. Department of Gynaecology. Annual Report (ISSN 0069-0228)

618.1 618.2   US   ISSN 0084-3911
YEAR BOOK OF OBSTETRICS AND GYNECOLOGY. 1933. a. price varies. ‡ Year Book Medical Publishers, Inc., 35 E. Wacker Dr., Chicago, IL 60601. Eds. R.M. Pitkin, Frank J. Zlatnik.

MEDICAL SCIENCES — Ophthalmology And Optometry

617.7   FR   ISSN 0065-115X
ACTA CONCILIUM OPHTHALMOLOGICUM. (Text in English, French, German, Spanish) quadrennial, 1974, 22nd, Paris. International Federation of Ophthalmological Societies, 8 Av. Daniel Leseur, 75007 Paris, France. (reprint service avail. from ISI) Indexed: Curr.Cont.
Represents: International Congress of Ophthalmology.

617.7   DK   ISSN 0065-1451
ACTA OPHTHALMOLOGICA. SUPPLEMENTUM. (Text in English) 1922. irreg. price varies. Scriptor Publisher A-S, Gasvaerksvej 15, 1656 Copenhagen K, Denmark. Ed. Poul Bradenstrup. adv. Indexed: Curr.Cont. Ind.Med.

617   II
ALL INDIA OPHTHALMOLOGICAL SOCIETY. PROCEEDINGS. (Text in English) a. All India Ophthalmological Society, Sarojini Sadan, Congress House, V. Patel Rd., Bombay 400004, India.

617.7   US   ISSN 0065-9533
AMERICAN OPHTHALMOLOGICAL SOCIETY. TRANSACTIONS. 1864. a. $40 per vol. ‡ Whiting Press, Inc., Rochester, MN 55901 (Subscr. to: Dr. Robert W. Hollenhorst, Sec.-Treas., American Ophthalmological Society, 420 5th Ave. S.W., Rochester, MN 55901) Ed. Dr. Thomas P. Kearns. index. circ. 700. (back issues avail.) Indexed: Ind.Med.

617.7 616.21   US   ISSN 0066-0655
AMERICAN SOCIETY OF OPHTHALMOLOGIC AND OTOLARYNGOLOGIC ALLERGY. TRANSACTIONS. 1941. a. $6. American Society of Ophthalmologic and Otolaryngologic Allergy, c/o Dr. David A. Dolowitz, Ed., 2000 S. Ninth East, Salt Lake City, UT 84105.

617.7   FR   ISSN 0301-4495
ANNEE THERAPEUTIQUE ET CLINIQUE EN OPHTHALMOLOGIE. 1950. a. Fueri-Lamy, 21 rue Paradis, 13001 Marseille, France. Indexed: Ind.Med.
Formerly: Annee Therapeutique en Ophtalmologie (ISSN 0066-2402)

617.7   US   ISSN 0067-0308
ATLAS OF EXTERNAL DISEASES OF THE EYE. 1966. irreg., vol. 5, 1976. price varies. C. V. Mosby Co., 11830 Westline Industrial Dr., St. Louis, MO 63141. Ed. David D. Donaldson M.D.

617.3   US   ISSN 0067-9283
BLUE BOOK OF OPTOMETRISTS. 1912. biennial. $18. Professional Press, Inc., 101 E. Ontario St., Chicago, IL 60611. index.

617.7   UK   ISSN 0068-2314
BRITISH ORTHOPTIC JOURNAL. 1939. a. £3.45. British Orthoptic Society, Tavistock House North, Tavistock Sq., London W.C.1, England. Ed. N. K. Bullock. adv. bk. rev. cum.index every 5 yrs.

617.7   GW   ISSN 0068-3361
BUECHEREI DES AUGENARZTES. 1938. irreg., no. 83, 1981. price varies. Ferdinand Enke Verlag, Herdweg 63, 7000 Stuttgart 1, W. Germany (B.R.D.) Ed. F. Hollwich. Indexed: Ind.Med.

617.7   US   ISSN 0096-2716
CONTACT LENS JOURNAL. 1966. a. $6. (Contact Lens Society of America) Woodbine Publishers, Inc., 90 Bagby Rd., Suite 222, Birmingham, AL 35209. Ed. Kenneth Swanson. adv. bk. rev. abstr, charts, illus. circ. 11,000.
Formerly: Contact Lens Society of America Journal (ISSN 0589-5065)
Contact lenses

617.7   US   ISSN 0097-8353
CURRENT CONCEPTS IN OPHTHALMOLOGY. 1967. irreg., vol. 6, 1979. C. V. Mosby Co., 3301 Washington Blvd., St. Louis, MO 63103. illus.

617.7   US   ISSN 0190-2970
CURRENT TOPICS IN EYE RESEARCH. 1979. irreg. Academic Press, Inc., 111 Fifth Ave., New York, NY 10003. illus.

618   DK
DANISH OPHTHALMOLOGICAL SOCIETY. TRANSACTIONS. Issued with: Acta Ophthalmologica (ISSN 0001-639X) (Text in English) a. (Danish Ophthalmological Society) Scriptor Publisher A-S, Gasvaerksvej 15, DK-1656 Copenhagen K, Denmark.

617.7   US   ISSN 0070-427X
DEUTSCHE OPHTHALMOLOGISCHE GESELLSCHAFT. ZUSAMMENKUNFT. BERICHT. 1949. irreg., 77th, 1980. price varies. Springer-Verlag, 175 Fifth Ave., New York, NY 10010 (also Berlin, Heidelberg, Vienna) (reprint service avail. from ISI) Indexed: Ind.Med.

617.7   SZ   ISSN 0250-3751
DEVELOPMENTS IN OPHTHALMOLOGY. (Text in English, French and German) 1980. irreg (approx. 2/yr.) 100 Fr.($60) per vol. (1981 price) S. Karger AG, Allschwilerstrasse 10, P.O. Box, CH-4009 Basel, Switzerland. Ed. W. Straub. charts. (reprint service avail. from ISI) Indexed: Biol.Abstr. Chem.Abstr. Curr.Cont. Ind.Med.
Incorporates: Advances in Ophthalmology (ISSN 0065-3004) & Bibliotheca Ophthalmologica (ISSN 0067-8090) & Modern Problems in Ophthalmology (ISSN 0077-0078)

617.7 NE
DOCUMENTA OPHTHALMOLOGICA
PROCEEDINGS SERIES. (Text in English, French, and German; summaries in English) 1973. irreg., vol. 32, 1980. price varies. Dr. W. Junk Publishers, Box 13713, 2501 ES The Hague, Netherlands. Ed. H. E. Henkes. circ. 600.

617.7 NE ISSN 0071-2965
EUROPEAN OPHTHALMOLOGICAL SOCIETY. CONGRESS. ABSTRACTS.* 1960. quadrennial, 1968, 3rd, Amsterdam. Excerpta Medica, Box 211, Amsterdam, Netherlands (Inquire: Jules Francois, De Smet de Naeyerpl. 15, 9000 Ghent, Belgium) 1976, Hamburg

617.7 NE ISSN 0301-326X
EUROPEAN OPHTHALMOLOGICAL SOCIETY. CONGRESS ACTA. (Text in English, French and German) quinquennial, 6th, 1980, Brighton. 180 Fr.($76) per vol. (approx.) European Ophthalmological Society, c/o Harold E. Henkes, Eye Clinic, Schiedamse Vest 180, 3001 Rotterdam, Netherlands.

617.7 US ISSN 0072-8977
GUILD OF PRESCRIPTION OPTICIANS OF AMERICA. REFERENCE LIST. 1954. irreg., approx. biennial. $20. Guild of Prescription Opticians of America, 1250 Connecticut Ave. N.W., Washington, DC 20036. (Affiliate: Opticians Association of America) Ed. J. A. Miller. circ. 10,000.

617.7 UK
INTERNATIONAL OPTICAL YEAR BOOK. 1903. a. I P C Business Press Ltd., 40 Bowling Green Lane, London E.C.1, England. Ed. Philip Mullins.

617.7 US
MAJOR PROBLEMS IN OPHTHALMOLOGY. 1975. irreg. W.B. Saunders Co., West Washington Square, Philadelphia, PA 19105. (reprint service avail. from UMI, ISI)

617.7 US ISSN 0077-7803
NEURO-OPHTHALMOLOGY. (Proceedings of symposium sponsored by University of Miami and the Bascom Palmer Eye Institute) 1964. irreg., vol. 9, 1977. $39.50. C. V. Mosby Co., 11830 Westline Industrial Dr., St. Louis, MO 63141. Ed. Joel S. Glaser, M.D.

617.7 NE
NEURO-OPHTHALMOLOGY. 1980. every 18 months. Excerpta Medica, Box 211, 1000 AE Amsterdam, Netherlands. Eds. S. Lessell, J.T.W. van Dalen.

617.7 US ISSN 0077-8605
NEW ORLEANS ACADEMY OF OPHTHAMOLOGY. TRANSACTIONS. a. price varies. C. V. Mosby Co., 11830 Westline Industrial Dr., St. Louis, MO 63141. Ed.Bd.

617.7 US
OCULAR THERAPEUTICS AND PHARMACOLOGY. 4th edt., 1973. irreg., 5th edt., 1977. $22.50. C. V. Mosby Co., 11830 Westline Industrial Dr., St. Louis, MO 63141. Eds. Philip P. Ellis, Donn L. Smith.
Formerly: Handbook of Ocular Therapeutics and Pharmacology (ISSN 0072-985X)

617.7 UK ISSN 0078-5334
OPHTHALMOLOGICAL SOCIETIES OF THE UNITED KINGDOM. TRANSACTIONS. 1880. a. L.4($25) J. & A. Churchill, 104 Gloucester Place, London, W1, England. Indexed: Ind. Med.

617.7 UA ISSN 0078-5342
OPHTHALMOLOGICAL SOCIETY OF EGYPT. BULLETIN. (Text in French, English, Arabic) 1902. a. $10. Ophthalmological Society of Egypt, Dar el Hekma, 42 Kasr el-Aini St., Cairo, Egypt. Indexed: Ind.Med. Ophthal.Lit.

617.7 CH
OPHTHALMOLOGICAL SOCIETY OF THE REPUBLIC OF CHINA. TRANSACTIONS. (Text and summaries occasionally in English) 1962. a. NT.$200($5) c/o National Taiwan University Hospital, Department of Ophthalmology, 1 Chan-Teh St., Taipei 100, Taiwan, Republic of China. Ed. Dr. Jung-Mao Chang. adv. cum.index. circ. 400. Indexed: Ophthal.Lit.

617.7 US ISSN 0146-4582
RED BOOK OF OPHTHALMOLOGY. biennial. $19. Professional Press, Inc., 101 East Ontario St., Chicago, IL 60611. adv.
Formerly: Red Book of Eye, Ear, Nose and Throat Specialists.

617.7 BE ISSN 0081-0746
SOCIETE BELGE D'OPHTALMOLOGIE. BULLETIN. 1896. q. 3500 Fr. Societe Belge d'Ophtamologie, c/o Mme. Gillis, 24 Ave. des Jardins, 1030 Brussels, Belgium. adv. circ. 900. Indexed: Ind.Med.

617.7 FR ISSN 0081-1270
SOCIETE D'OPHTALMOLOGIE DE FRANCE. BULLETIN. 1949. irreg. 290 F.($59) Publicite Stephane Batard, 21 Rue Saint-Fiacre, Paris 2e, France. Indexed: Chem.Abstr. Ind.Med.

617.7 UK ISSN 0082-1195
SYSTEM OF OPHTHALMOLOGY. 1958. irreg. price varies. Henry Kimpton Ltd., 205 Great Portland St., London W1N 6LR, England (Dist. in U.S. by C. V. Mosby Co., 3207 Washington Blvd., St. Louis, Mo. 63103) Ed. Stewart Duke-Elder, M.D.

617.705 US ISSN 0084-392X
YEAR BOOK OF OPHTHALMOLOGY. 1900. a. price varies. ‡ Year Book Medical Publishers, Inc., 35 E. Wacker Dr., Chicago, IL 60601. Ed. W. F. Hughes.

MEDICAL SCIENCES — Orthopedics And Traumatology

617.3 DK ISSN 0300-8827
ACTA ORTHOPAEDICA SCANDINAVICA. SUPPLEMENTUM. irreg. free to subscribers. (Scandinavian Orthopaedic Association) Munksgaard, Noerre Soegade 35, DK-1370 Copenhagen K, Denmark. (reprint service avail. from ISI) Indexed: Curr.Cont. Ind.Med.

617 SZ
AKTUELLE PROBLEME IN CHIRURGIE ORTHOPADIE. 1966. irreg. price varies. Verlag Hans Huber, Laenggassstr. 76 und Marktgasse 9, CH-3000 Berne 9, Switzerland (Dist. by Williams & Wilkins Company, 428 E. Preston St., Baltimore, MD 21202) Ed. M. Saegesser. Indexed: Ind.Med.
Formerly: Aktuelle Probleme in der Chirurgie (ISSN 0065-5589)

617.3 US ISSN 0065-6895
AMERICAN ACADEMY OF ORTHOPAEDIC SURGEONS. COMMITTEE ON INSTRUCTIONAL COURSES. INSTRUCTIONAL COURSE LECTURES. 1944. irreg., vol. 28, 1979. price varies. (American Academy of Orthopaedic Surgeons) C. V. Mosby Co., 11830 Westline Industrial Dr., St. Louis, MO 63141.
From 1961 to the present, lectures published monthly in Journal of Bone and Joint Surgery

617.3 US ISSN 0516-8856
AMERICAN ACADEMY OF ORTHOPAEDIC SURGEONS. DIRECTORY. a. price varies. American Academy of Orthopaedic Surgeons, Box 7195, Chicago, IL 60680 (Or 10 Shattuck St., Boston, MA 02115)

617.3 US
AMERICAN LECTURES IN ORTHOPAEDIC SURGERY. irreg. price varies. Charles C. Thomas, Publisher, 301-327 E. Lawrence Ave., Springfield, IL 62717.

617.3 GW ISSN 0068-3388
BUECHEREI DES ORTHOPAEDEN. 1969. irreg., no. 27, 1980. price varies. Ferdinand Enke Verlag, Herdweg 63, 7000 Stuttgart 1, W. Germany (B.R.D.) Eds. P. Otte, K.-F. Schlegel.

617.3 US ISSN 0070-203X
CURRENT PRACTICE IN ORTHOPAEDIC SURGERY. 1963. irreg., vol. 8, 1979. $32.50. C. V. Mosby Co., 11830 Westline Industrial Dr., St. Louis, MO 63141. Ed. James P. Ahstrom, Jr., M.D. Indexed: Ind.Med.

610 US ISSN 0085-1469
HEFTE ZUR UNFALLHEILKUNDE. irreg., no. 149, 1981. price varies. Springer Verlag, 175 Fifth Ave., New York, NY 10010 (also Berlin, Heidelberg, Vienna) (reprint service avail. from ISI) Indexed: Ind.Med.

617.58 US ISSN 0095-7216
HIP; proceedings of the Open Scientific Meeting of the Hip Society. 1973. a. price varies. (Hip Society) C. V. Mosby Co., 11830 Westline Industrial Dr., St. Louis, MO 63141. illus. (back issues avail.)

617.3 BE ISSN 0074-8552
INTERNATIONAL SOCIETY OF ORTHOPAEDIC SURGERY AND TRAUMATOLOGY. PROCEEDINGS OF CONGRESSES. (Text in English, French, German, Italian, Spanish) 1929. triennial; 12th, Israel, 1972. International Society of Orthopaedic Surgery and Traumatology, c/o Secretary General, 43 rue des Champs Elysees, 1050 Brussels, Belgium.

617.11 NE
INTERNATIONAL SYMPOSIUM ON PHARMACOLOGICAL TREATMENT IN BURNS. PROCEEDINGS.* (Published in International Congress Series) irreg., 1st, Milan, 1968. (International Society for Burn Injuries) Excerpta Medica, P.O.B. 211, Amsterdam, Netherlands (Inquire: A. B. Wallace, Royal College of Surgeons, 18 Nicolson St., Edinburgh EH8 9DW, Scotland)

617.3 UK ISSN 0077-0159
MODERN TRENDS IN ORTHOPAEDICS. (Title varies slightly) 1950. irreg., latest vol. 6, 1972. £10.80 for latest vol. Butterworth & Co. (Publishers) Ltd., 88 Kingsway, London WC2B 6AB, England. Indexed: Ind.Med.

617.3 GW
ORTHOPAEDIC PRACTITIONER. (Consists of selected articles from Orthopaedische Praxis) (Text in English) 1978. a. DM.32. Medizinisch-Literarische Verlagsgesellschaft mbH, Ringstr. 4, Postfach 120/140, 3110 Uelzen 1, W. Germany(B.R.D.)

617.3 US
PROGRESS IN ORTHOPAEDIC SURGERY. 1977. irreg., vol. 4, 1980. Springer-Verlag, 175 Fifth Ave., New York, NY 10010 (And Berlin, Heidelberg, Vienna) (reprint service avail. from ISI)

RECONSTRUCTION SURGERY AND TRAUMATOLOGY. see MEDICAL SCIENCES — Surgery

617.3 US ISSN 0080-0686
REGISTRY OF ACCREDITED FACILITIES AND CERTIFIED INDIVIDUALS IN ORTHOTICS AND PROSTHETICS. a. $15. ‡ American Board for Certification in Orthotics and Prosthetics, 1444 N. St., N.W., Washington, DC 20005. circ. 2,500.
Formerly: Registry of Certified Prosthetic and Orthopedic Appliance Facilities.

617.3 FR ISSN 0081-1033
SOCIETE FRANCAISE DE CHIRURGIE ORTHOPEDIQUE ET TRAUMATOLOGIQUE. CONFERENCES D'ENSEIGNEMENT. 1967. irreg., latest 1973. price varies. Expansion Scientifique, 15 rue Saint-Benoit, 75278 Paris Cedex 06, France. Ed. J. Duparc.

617.3 UK ISSN 0260-9320
STUDIES IN JOINT DISEASE. 1980. a. Pitman Medical Ltd., 57 High St., Tunbridge Wells, Kent TN1 1XH, England. illus.

617 GW ISSN 0510-5315
DIE WIRBELSAEULE IN FORSCHUNG UND PRAXIS. 1956. irreg., vol. 92, 1980. price varies. Hippokrates Verlag GmbH, Neckarstr. 121, Postfach 593, 7000 Stuttgart 1, W. Germany (B.R.D.) Ed. Herbert Junghanns.

617.305 US ISSN 0084-3938
YEAR BOOK OF ORTHOPEDICS AND TRAUMATIC SURGERY. 1940. a. price varies. ‡ Year Book Medical Publishers, Inc., 35 E. Wacker Dr., Chicago, IL 60601. Ed. Mark B. Coventry.

MEDICAL SCIENCES — Otorhinolaryngology

616.855 612.85 US ISSN 0569-8561
A S H A DIRECTORY. a. price varies. American Speech-Language-Hearing Association, 10801 Rockville Pike, Rockville, MD 20852.

371.9 617.8 612.85 US ISSN 0569-8553
A S H A REPORTS. no. 7, 1972. irreg., no. 9, 1974. American Speech-Language-Hearing Association, 10801 Rockville Pike, Rockville, MD 20852. Ed. Robert T. Wertz.

616.21 SZ ISSN 0065-3071
ADVANCES IN OTO-RHINO-LARYNGOLOGY. (Text in English) 1953. irreg. (approx. 1/yr) 100 Fr.($60) (1981 price) S. Karger AG, Allschwilerstrasse 10, P.O. Box, CH-4009 Basel, Switzerland. Ed. C.R. Pfaltz. (reprint service avail. from ISI) Indexed: Biol.Abstr. Chem.Abstr. Curr.Cont. Ind.Med.

616.21 US ISSN 0065-7603
AMERICAN BRONCHO-ESOPHAGOLOGICAL ASSOCIATION. TRANSACTIONS. 1921. a. $20. ‡ American Broncho-Esophagological Association, c/o James B. Snow, Jr., M.D., 3400 Spruce St., Philadelphia, PA 19140. Ed. Dr. James B. Snow, Jr. circ. 356.

616.21 US ISSN 0065-9037
AMERICAN LARYNGOLOGICAL, RHINOLOGICAL AND OTOLOGICAL SOCIETY. TRANSACTIONS. a. $12.75. (American Laryngological Rhinological and Otological Society) Laryngoscope Co., 9216 Clayton Road, Ste. 18, St. Louis, MO 63124.

617.8 371.912 US
AMERICAN LECTURES IN SPEECH AND HEARING. irreg. price varies. Charles C. Thomas, Publisher, 301-327 E. Lawrence Ave., Springfield, IL 62717.

617.8 US
AMERICAN OTOLOGICAL SOCIETY. TRANSACTIONS. a. price varies. American Otological Society, 1100 E. Genesee St., Syracuse, NY 13210.

AMERICAN SOCIETY OF OPHTHALMOLOGIC AND OTOLARYNGOLOGIC ALLERGY. TRANSACTIONS. see MEDICAL SCIENCES — Ophthalmology And Optometry

616.21 IT ISSN 0066-2267
ANNALI DI LARINGOLOGIA, OTOLOGIA, RINOLOGIA, FARINGOLOGIA. (Publication suspended 1930, 1944) 1900. irreg. (Gruppo Otologi Ospedalieri Italiani) Vita Farmaceutici, Via Cernaia 20, Turin, Italy. Indexed: Ind.Med.

616.2 IT ISSN 0066-9865
ASSOCIAZIONE ITALIANA LARINGECTOMIZZATI. ATTI (DEL) CONVEGNO NAZIONALE. 1957. a. Associazione Italiana Laringectomizzati, Piazza Bertarelli, 4, Milan, Italy.

617.89 US ISSN 0197-3657
EAR RESEARCH INSTITUTE. PROGRESS REPORT. 1973. a. (Los Angeles Foundation of Otology) Ear Research Institute, 256 S. Lake St., Los Angeles, CA 90057. Key Title: Progress Report - Ear Research Institute.
Formerly: Los Angeles Foundation of Otology. Progress Report.

616.21 GE ISSN 0072-9418
HALS-, NASEN- UND OHRENHEILKUNDE; zwangslose Schriftenreihe. 1938. irreg., no. 27, 1977. price varies. Johann Ambrosius Barth Verlag, Salomonstr. 18b, 701 Leipzig, E. Germany (D.D.R.) Eds. A. Herrmann, H. Jacobi. (back issues avail.)

M S H A. (Michigan Speech and Hearing Association) see DEAF

616.21 US ISSN 0077-8516
NEW JERSEY SPEECH AND HEARING ASSOCIATION. NEWSLETTER. 1969. irreg. (approx. 4/yr.) $5. New Jersey Speech and Hearing Association (Neptune), c/o Natalie B. Lubinsky, Ed., Box 1166, Neptune, NJ 07753. circ. 1,400.

616.21 AT ISSN 0030-6614
OTO-LARYNGOLOGICAL SOCIETY OF AUSTRALIA. JOURNAL. 1962. a. Aus.$10. ‡ Oto-Laryngological Society of Australia, 33-35 Atchison St., St. Leonards, N.S.W. 2065, Australia. Ed. Dr. Rory Willis. adv. bk. rev. circ. 1,000. (also avail. in microform from UMI) Indexed: DSH Abstr. Excerp.Med.

616.21 371 SA
SOUTH AFRICAN JOURNAL OF COMMUNICATION DISORDERS/SUID-AFRIKAANSE TYDSKRIF VIR KOMMUNIKASIEAFWYKINGS. (Text in English and Afrikaans; summaries in English) 1948. a. R.2.50. South African Speech & Hearing Association - Suid-Afrikaanse Vereniging vir Spraak- en Gehoorheelkunde, Box 31782, Braamfontein 2017, South Africa. Ed. M. Aron. adv. bk. rev. circ. 1,400. Indexed: Ind.Med. DSH Abstr.
Former titles: South African Speech and Hearing Association. Journal (ISSN 0081-2471); South African Logopedic Society. Journal.

616.21 US
YEAR BOOK OF OTOLARYNGOLOGY. 1900. a. price varies. ‡ Year Book Medical Publishers, Inc., 35 E. Wacker Dr., Chicago, IL 60601. Eds. M. M. Paparella, M. S. Strong.
Formerly (1958-1975): Year Book of the Ear, Nose and Throat (ISSN 0084-4055); Supersedes in part: Yearbook of the Eye, Ear, Nose and Throat.

MEDICAL SCIENCES — Pediatrics

618.92 US
ADVANCES IN BEHAVIORAL PEDIATRICS. 1980. a. J A I Press, Box 1285, 165 W. Putnam Ave., Greenwich, CT 06830. Ed. Bonnie W. Camp.

ADVANCES IN CHILD DEVELOPMENT AND BEHAVIOR. see PSYCHOLOGY

618.92 US ISSN 0065-3101
ADVANCES IN PEDIATRICS. 1942. a. price varies. Year Book Medical Publishers, Inc., 35 E. Wacker Dr., Chicago, IL 60601. Indexed: Ind.Med.

618.92 US ISSN 0065-6909
AMERICAN ACADEMY OF PEDIATRICS. COMMITTEE ON INFECTIOUS DISEASES. REPORT. 1938. irreg., 1974, 17th ed. $6. American Academy of Pediatrics, Committee on Infectious Diseases, 1801 Hinman Ave., Evanston, IL 60204.

618.92 US
AMERICAN PEDIATRIC SOCIETY AND SOCIETY FOR PEDIATRIC RESEARCH. PROGRAM AND ABSTRACTS; abstracts of the annual meeting. 1930. a. $7. Williams & Wilkins Co., 428 E. Preston St., Baltimore, MD 21202. Ed. Joanne Brasel, M.D. index.
Formerly: Society for Pediatric Research. Program and Abstracts (ISSN 0081-1459)

618.92 FR ISSN 0066-3514
ANNUAIRE NATIONAL DES SPECIALISTES QUALIFIES EXCLUSIFS EN PEDIATRIE. 1965, 3rd ed. a. 35 F. Revue de Pediatrie, 40, rue Paul-Valery, 75116 Paris, France.

616.8 367 GW ISSN 0067-5105
BEITRAEGE ZUR KINDERPSYCHOTHERAPIE. 1965. irreg. no. 28, 1978. price varies. Ernst Reinhardt, GmbH und Co., Verlag, Kemnatenstr. 46, 8000 Munich 19, W. Germany (B.R.D.) Ed. Gerd Biermann. index. (reprint service avail. from ISI and UMI)

618.92 PL
BIBLIOTEKA PEDIATRY. 1974. irreg. Panstwowy Zaklad Wydawnictw Lekarskich, Ul. Dluga 38-40, Warsaw, Poland. Ed. Krystyna Bozkowa.

BOSTON CHILDREN'S MEDICAL CENTER. PUBLICATIONS FOR PARENTS. see CHILDREN AND YOUTH — About

618.92 GW ISSN 0373-3165
BUECHEREI DES PAEDIATERS. 1972. irreg., no. 82, 1980. price varies. Ferdinand Enke Verlag, Herdweg 63, 7000 Stuttgart 1, W. Germany (B.R.D.) Eds. O. Vivell, W. Burmeister.
Continues: Archiv fuer Kinderheilkunde. Beihefte (ISSN 0066-6378)

618.92 155.4 US
CHILD BEHAVIOR AND DEVELOPMENT. 1975. irreg. Spectrum Publications, Inc., 175-20 Wexford Terrace, Jamaica, NY 10032.

618.92 IS ISSN 0069-3413
CHILD HEALTH IN ISRAEL/BERI'UT HA-YELED BE-YISRAEL.* (Text in Hebrew and English) 1965. a. Israel Clinical Pediatric Society, Meretz, P.O.B. 344, Tel Aviv, Israel.

612 UK ISSN 0069-4835
CLINICS IN DEVELOPMENTAL MEDICINE. 1959. irreg.(approx. 4 per year) £22($50) Spastics International Medical Publications, 5A Netherhall Gardens, London NW3 5RN, England (Dist. in U.S. by J.B. Lippincott Company, E. Washington Square, Philadelphia, PA 19105)

COMBINED CUMULATIVE INDEX TO PEDIATRICS. see MEDICAL SCIENCES — Abstracting, Bibliographies, Statistics

618.92 US
CURRENT DIAGNOSTIC PEDIATRICS. 1977. irreg., vol. 3, 1980. $25. Springer-Verlag, 175 Fifth Ave., New York, NY 10010 (Also Berlin, Heidelberg, Vienna) Ed. A. Chrispin. (reprint service avail. from ISI)

CURRENT PRACTICE IN PEDIATRIC NURSING. see MEDICAL SCIENCES — Nurses And Nursing

EARLY CHILDHOOD DEVELOPMENT IN TEXAS. see CHILDREN AND YOUTH — About

ERGEBNISSE DER INNEREN MEDIZIN UND KINDERHEILKUNDE. NEW SERIES/ADVANCES IN INTERNAL MEDICINE AND PEDIATRICS. see MEDICAL SCIENCES

HAWAII. FAMILY HEALTH SERVICES DIVISION. CRIPPLED CHILDREN SERVICES BRANCH. REPORT. see SOCIAL SERVICES AND WELFARE

618.92 SZ ISSN 0073-1811
HELVETICA PAEDIATRICA ACTA. SUPPLEMENTUM. (Text in French, German; summaries in English, German, Italian) 1945. irreg. price varies. (Swiss Society of Paediatrics) Schwabe und Co. AG, Steinentorstr. 13, 4010 Basel, Switzerland.

HOSPITAL FOR SICK CHILDREN, TORONTO. RESEARCH INSTITUTE. ANNUAL REPORT. see MEDICAL SCIENCES

618.92 FR ISSN 0075-4471
JOURNEES PARISIENNES DE PEDIATRIE. 1966. a. price varies. (Hopital des Enfants Malades, Centre d'Etudes sur les Maladies du Metabolisme Chez l'Enfant) Flammarion Medecine-Sciences, 20 rue de Vaugirard, 75006 Paris, France (U.S. subscr. address: S.F.P.A., c/o M. Benech, 14 E. 60t St., NY 10022) Ed. P. Royer.

618.92 US
MASSON MONOGRAPHS IN PEDIATRIC HEMATOLOGY/ONCOLOGY. 1980. irreg., vol. 4, 1981. price varies. Masson Publishing U.S.A., Inc., 14 E. 60th St., New York, NY 10022. Eds. Drs. Carl Pochedly, Denis R. Miller.

618.92 SZ ISSN 0077-0086
MODERN PROBLEMS IN PAEDIATRICS. (Text in English) 1954. irreg. (approx. 2/yr.) 100 Fr.($60) per vol. (1981 price) S. Karger AG, Allschwilerstrasse 10, P.O. Box, CH-4009 Basel, Switzerland. Ed.Bd. (reprint service avail. from ISI) Indexed: Biol.Abstr. Chem.Abstr. Curr.Cont. Ind.Med.

618.92 US ISSN 0162-6906
MONOGRAPHS IN DEVELOPMENTAL PEDIATRICS. 1978. irreg. University Park Press, 233 E. Redwood St., Baltimore, MD 21202.

618.92 SZ ISSN 0077-0914
MONOGRAPHS IN PAEDIATRICS. (Text in English) 1971. irreg. (approx. 1/yr.) 70 Fr.($42) per vol. (1981 price) S. Karger AG, Allschwilerstrasse 10, P.O. Box, CH-4009 Basel, Switzerland. Ed.Bd. (reprint service avail. from ISI) Indexed: Biol.Abstr. Chem.Abstr. Curr.Cont. Ind.Med.
Supersedes title issued 1924-70: Bibliotheca Paediatrica.

MEDICAL SCIENCES — PSYCHIATRY AND NEUROLOGY

616.8   GW   ISSN 0174-304X
NEUROPEDIATRICS; journal of pediatric neurobiology, neurology and neurosurgery. (Text in English) 1969. q. DM.166 per vol. Hippokrates Verlag GmbH, Neckarstr. 121, Postfach 593, 7000 Stuttgart 1, W. Germany (B.R.D.) Ed. F. J. Schulte. adv. circ. 1,200. Indexed: Ind.Med.
     Formerly: Neuropaediatrie (ISSN 0028-3797)

618.92   US
PAEDIATRIE UND PAEDOLOGIE. SUPPLEMENT. 1972. irreg., vol. 6, 1980. price varies. Springer-Verlag, 175 Fifth Ave., New York, NY 10010 (Also Berlin, Heidelberg, Vienna) (reprint service avail. from ISI)

618.92   US
PAEDIATRIE: WEITER- UND FORTBILDUNG. (Text in German) 1981. irreg. Springer-Verlag, 175 Fifth Ave., New York, NY 10010 (Also Berlin, Heidelberg, Vienna) Ed. H. Ewerbeck. (reprint service avail. from ISI)

618.92   PL   ISSN 0079-4279
POSTEPY PEDIATRII.* (Text in Polish; summaries in English, Polish, and Russian) 1955. a. Panstwowy Zaklad Wydawnictw Lekarskich, Dluga 38-40, Warsaw, Poland. Ed. Jana Raszka, M.D.

618.92   SZ   ISSN 0079-6646
PROGRESS IN PEDIATRIC RADIOLOGY. (Text in English) 1967. irreg. (approx. 1/yr.) 160 Fr.($96) per vol.(1981 price) S. Karger AG, Allschwilerstrasse 10, P.O. Box, CH-4009 Basel, Switzerland. Ed. H. J. Kaufmann. (reprint service avail. from ISI) Indexed: Biol.Abstr. Chem.Abstr. Curr.Cont. Ind.Med.

618.92   GW   ISSN 0079-6654
PROGRESS IN PEDIATRIC SURGERY. (Text in German; summaries in French) 1971. a. price varies. Urban and Schwarzenberg, Pettenkoferstr. 18, Postfach 202440, 8000 Munich 2, W. Germany (B.R.D.) Indexed: Ind.Med.

618.92   136.7   FR   ISSN 0079-726X
PSYCHIATRIE DE L'ENFANT. 1958. a.(in 2 issues) 190 F Presses Universitaires de France, Service des Periodiques, 12 rue Jean-de-Beauvais, 75005 Paris, France. Eds. J. Ajuriaguerra, R. Diatkine, S. Lebovici. cum.index. Indexed: Ind.Med. Psychol.Abstr.

STANDARDS AND RECOMMENDATIONS FOR HOSPITAL CARE OF NEWBORN INFANTS. see *HOSPITALS*

618.92   US   ISSN 0084-3954
YEAR BOOK OF PEDIATRICS. 1933. a. price varies. ‡ Year Book Medical Publishers, Inc., 35 E. Wacker Dr., Chicago, IL 60601. Eds. Frank A. Oski, James A. Stockman, III.

MEDICAL SCIENCES — Psychiatry And Neurology

616.8   US   ISSN 0065-1419
ACTA NEUROCHIRURGICA. SUPPLEMENT. (Text in English or German) 1950. irreg., vol. 30, 1981. price varies. Springer-Verlag, 175 Fifth Ave., New York, NY 10010 (Also Berlin, Heidelberg, Vienna) (reprint service avail. from ISI)

616.8   DK   ISSN 0065-1427
ACTA NEUROLOGICA SCANDINAVICA. SUPPLEMENTUM. (Text in English) 1932. irreg. free to subscribers. Munksgaard, 35 Noerre Soegade, DK-1370 Copenhagen, Denmark. Ed. Dr. H. Pakkenberg. adv. (reprint service avail. from ISI) Indexed: Curr.Cont. Ind.Med.

616.8   US   ISSN 0065-1435
ACTA NEUROPATHOLOGICA. SUPPLEMENT. 1962. irreg., no. 6, 1975. price varies. Springer-Verlag, 175 Fifth Ave., New York, NY 10010 (also Berlin, Heidelberg, Vienna) (reprint service avail. from ISI) Indexed: Ind.Med.

616.8   DK   ISSN 0065-1591
ACTA PSYCHIATRICA SCANDINAVICA. SUPPLEMENTUM. (Text in English) 1932. irreg. free to subscribers. Munksgaard, 35 Noerre Soegade, DK-1370 Copenhagen K, Denmark. Ed. Erik Stroemgren. adv. (reprint service avail. from ISI) Indexed: Curr.Cont. Ind.Med.

616.8   US   ISSN 0065-2008
ADOLESCENT PSYCHIATRY. 1971. a. $25. University of Chicago Press, 5801 S. Ellis Ave., Chicago, IL 60637 (Orders to: 11030 Langley Ave., Chicago, IL 60628) (reprint service avail. from UMI,ISI)

616.8   US
ADVANCES AND TECHNICAL STANDARDS IN NEUROSURGERY. 1974. irreg., vol. 7, 1980. price varies. Springer-Verlag, 175 Fifth Ave., New York, NY 10010 (Also Berlin, Heidelberg, Vienna) Ed.Bd. (reprint service avail. from ISI)

ADVANCES IN BIOCHEMICAL PSYCHOPHARMACOLOGY. see *PHARMACY AND PHARMACOLOGY*

616.8   SZ   ISSN 0378-7354
ADVANCES IN BIOLOGICAL PSYCHIATRY. 1978. irreg. (approx. 2/yr.) 45 Fr.($27) (1981 price) S. Karger AG, Allschwilerstrasse 10, P.O. Box, CH-4009 Basel, Switzerland. Eds. H.M. van Praag, J. Mendlewicz. illus. circ. 1,000. (reprint service avail. from ISI) Indexed: Biol.Abstr. Curr.Cont.

616.8   370.15   UK
ADVANCES IN MENTAL HANDICAP RESEARCH. 1979. irreg. £13.70. John Wiley & Sons Ltd., Baffins Lane, Chichester, Sussex PO19 1UD, England. (reprint service avail. from UMI, ISI) *Mental retardation*

ADVANCES IN NEUROCHEMISTRY. see *BIOLOGY — Biological Chemistry*

616.8   US   ISSN 0091-3952
ADVANCES IN NEUROLOGY. 1973. irreg., vol. 27, 1979. price varies. Raven Press, 1140 Ave. of the Americas, New York, NY 10036. Indexed: Curr.Cont. Ind.Med.

616.8   US   ISSN 0302-2366
ADVANCES IN NEUROSURGERY. 1973. irreg., vol. 9, 1981. price varies. Springer-Verlag, 175 Fifth Ave., New York, NY 10010 (And Berlin, Heidelberg, Vienna) (reprint service avail. from ISI)

616.8   US   ISSN 0146-0722
ADVANCES IN PAIN RESEARCH AND THERAPY. 1976. irreg., vol. 3, 1979. price varies. Raven Press, 1140 Ave. of the Americas, New York, NY 10036. Ed. John J. Bonica. index. Indexed: Curr.Cont.

616.8   SZ   ISSN 0065-3268
ADVANCES IN PSYCHOSOMATIC MEDICINE. (Text in English) 1960. irreg. (approx. 1/yr.) 100 Fr.($60) per vol. (1981 price) S. Karger AG, Allschwilerstrasse 10, P.O. Box, CH-4009 Basel, Switzerland. Ed.Bd. (reprint service avail. from ISI) Indexed: Biol.Abstr. Chem.Abstr. Curr.Cont. Ind.Med. SSCI.

ADVANCES IN SLEEP RESEARCH. see *BIOLOGY — Physiology*

616.8   SZ   ISSN 0065-3381
ADVANCES IN STEREOENCEPHALOTOMY. (Text in English) irreg. (approx. 1/yr.) 160 Fr.($96) per vol. (1981 price) S. Karger AG, Allschwilerstrasse 10, P.O. Box, CH-4009 Basel, Switzerland. (reprint service avail. from ISI) Indexed: Biol.Abstr. Chem.Abstr. Curr.Cont. Ind.Med.

616.8   SZ   ISSN 0065-5600
AKTUELLE PROBLEME IN DER PSYCHIATRIE, NEUROLOGIE, NEUROCHIRURGIE. 1968. irreg. price varies. Verlag Hans Huber, Laenggassstr. 76 und Marktgasse 9, CH-3000 Berne 9, Switzerland (Dist. by Williams & Wilkins Company, 428 E. Preston St., Baltimore, MD 21202) Ed.Bd.

616.89   US
AMERICAN COLLEGE OF PSYCHIATRISTS. PAPERS PRESENTED AT THE ANNUAL MEETING. a. $22 to individuals; institutions $36. Brunner-Mazel, Inc., 19 Union Sq. W., New York, NY 10003.

616.89   US
AMERICAN JOURNAL OF VIDEOLOGY. 1977? a. $12 to individuals; institutions $20. (American Society of Videology) World Journal Press, Box 859, E. Lansing, MI 48823. Ed. Bd. (also avail. in microfilm from UMI; reprint service avail. from UMI)
     Formerly: American Journal of Videotherapy.

616.836   US
AMERICAN LECTURES IN CEREBRAL PALSY. irreg. price varies. Charles C. Thomas, Publisher, 301-327 E. Lawrence Ave., Springfield, IL 62717. *Cerebral palsy*

616.8   US
AMERICAN LECTURES IN CLINICAL PSYCHIATRY. irreg. price varies. Charles C. Thomas, Publisher, 301-327 E. Lawrence Ave., Springfield, IL 62717.

616.8   US
AMERICAN LECTURES IN OBJECTIVE PSYCHIATRY. irreg. price varies. Charles C. Thomas, Publisher, 301-327 E. Lawrence Ave., Springfield, IL 62717.

616.808   US   ISSN 0065-9479
AMERICAN NEUROLOGICAL ASSOCIATION. TRANSACTIONS. 1875. a. price varies. Springer Publishing Co., Inc., 200 Park Ave. S., New York, NY 10003. Ed. Peritz Scheinberg, M.D. Indexed: Ind.Med.

616.89   US
AMERICAN ORTHOPSYCHIATRIC ASSOCIATION. PAPERS PRESENTED AT THE ANNUAL CONVENTION. a. price varies. Wayne State University Press, 5959 Woodward Ave., Detroit, MI 48202.

920   616.89   US   ISSN 0065-9827
AMERICAN PSYCHIATRIC ASSOCIATION. BIOGRAPHICAL DIRECTORY. 1958, 3rd ed. triennial. $49.50. (Jaques Cattell Press) R. R. Bowker Company, 1180 Ave. of the Americas, New York, NY 10036 (Orders to P.O. Box 1807, Ann Arbor, Mich. 48106) (reprint service avail. from UMI)

616.89   US   ISSN 0090-4988
AMERICAN PSYCHIATRIC ASSOCIATION. MEMBERSHIP DIRECTORY. irreg. $8 to non-members; $5 to members. American Psychiatric Association, 1700 18 St., N.W., Washington, DC 20009.

616.89   US   ISSN 0090-1881
AMERICAN PSYCHIATRIC ASSOCIATION. SCIENTIFIC PROCEEDINGS IN SUMMARY FORM. a. $7 for latest no. American Psychiatric Association, 1700 18 St., N.W., Washington, DC 20009.

616.89   US
AMERICAN PSYCHIATRIC ASSOCIATION. TASK FORCE REPORTS. irreg., no. 11, 1976. $3 for latest no. American Psychiatric Association, 1700 18 St., N.W., Washington, DC 20036.

AMERICAN PSYCHOPATHOLOGICAL ASSOCIATION. PUBLICATIONS. see *PSYCHOLOGY*

616.89   US   ISSN 0091-7389
AMERICAN PSYCHOPATHOLOGICAL ASSOCIATION. PROCEEDINGS OF THE ANNUAL MEETING. a. price varies. Johns Hopkins University Press, Baltimore, MD 21218.

616.8   US   ISSN 0066-0132
AMERICAN SOCIETY FOR NEUROCHEMISTRY. TRANSACTIONS. 1970. a. $6. ‡ American Society for Neurochemistry, c/o Dr. Claude Baxter, Chief, Neurochemical Labs (151 F), V. A. Hospital, Sepulveda, CA 91343.

616.8   FR   ISSN 0066-3476
ANNUAIRE NATIONAL DES SPECIALISTES QUALIFIES EXCLUSIFS EN NEUROPSYCHIATRIE. 1965. irreg. 35 F. Revue de Medecine, 40, rue Paul- Valery, 75116 Paris, France.

MEDICAL SCIENCES — PSYCHIATRY AND NEUROLOGY

618.928 US ISSN 0066-4030
ANNUAL PROGRESS IN CHILD PSYCHIATRY AND CHILD DEVELOPMENT. 1968. a. price varies. Brunner-Mazel, Inc., 19 Union Sq. W., New York, NY 10003. Eds. S. Chess, A. Thomas. bk. rev.

616.8 US ISSN 0147-006X
ANNUAL REVIEW OF NEUROSCIENCE. 1978. a. $20. Annual Reviews Inc., 4139 El Camino Way, Palo Alto, CA 94306. Ed. W. Maxwell Cowan. bibl. index; cum. index. (back issues avail.; reprint service avail. from ISI) Indexed: Chem.Abstr. Psychol.Abstr. Sci.Cit.Ind.

616.8 US ISSN 0090-287X
ANNUAL REVIEW OF THE SCHIZOPHRENIC SYNDROME. 1971-1977(vol. 5) biennial. price varies. Brunner-Mazel Inc., 19 Union Sq. W., New York, NY 10003. Ed. Robert Cancro. illus.

353.9 616.858 US ISSN 0093-7452
ARKANSAS. DEPARTMENT OF MENTAL RETARDATION. ANNUAL REPORT. a. Department of Mental Retardation, Conway, AR 72032. illus. stat. Key Title: Annual Report - Arkansas. Department of Mental Retardation.

610 US ISSN 0091-7443
ASSOCIATION FOR RESEARCH IN NERVOUS AND MENTAL DISEASE. RESEARCH PUBLICATIONS. a. price varies. Raven Press, 1140 Ave. of the Americas, New York, NY 10036. Indexed: Curr.Cont. Ind.Med.

616.8 US ISSN 0092-4334
B I S CONFERENCE REPORT. 1971. 3-4/yr. $5 per no. Brain Information Service-Brain Research Institute, University of California, Los Angeles, Center for the Health Sciences, Los Angeles, CA 90024. (Co-sponsor: National Institute of Neurological and Communicative Disorders and Stroke) (back issues avail.)

616.8 GE ISSN 0067-5156
BEITRAEGE ZUR NEUROCHIRURGIE. 1959. irreg., no. 16, 1970. price varies. Johann Ambrosius Barth Verlag, Salomonstr. 18b, 701 Leipzig, E. Germany (D.D.R.) (back issues avail.) Indexed: Ind.Med.

616.8 SZ ISSN 0067-8147
BIBLIOTHECA PSYCHIATRICA. (Text in English and German) 1917. irreg. (approx. 1/yr.) 80 Fr.($48) per vol. (1981 price) S. Karger AG, Allschwilerstrasse 10, P.O. Box, CH-4009 Basel, Switzerland. Ed. P. Berner. (reprint service avail. from ISI) Indexed: Biol.Abstr. Chem.Abstr. Curr.Cont. Ind.Med. SSCI.

BIOFEEDBACK SOCIETY OF AMERICA. PROCEEDINGS OF THE ANNUAL MEETING. see *PSYCHOLOGY*

612.8 US ISSN 0092-6930
CAJAL CLUB. PROCEEDINGS. irreg., vol. 2, 1977. ‡ Cajal Club, c/o Glenn V. Russell, Ed., Department of Anatomy, University of Texas Medical Branch, Galveston, TX 77550. circ. 500(controlled) Key Title: Proceedings of the Cajal Club.

CANADIAN PARAPLEGIC ASSOCIATION. ANNUAL REPORT. see *SOCIAL SERVICES AND WELFARE*

616.8 US
CEREBRAL FUNCTION SYMPOSIUM. PROCEEDINGS. 1970. irreg., 2nd, 1972. price varies. Charles C. Thomas, Publisher, 301-327 E. Lawrence Ave., Springfield, IL 62717.

616.8 CN
CLARENCE M. HINCKS MEMORIAL LECTURES. a. University of Toronto Press, Front Campus, Toronto, Ontario M5S 1A6, Canada (U.S. Address: 33 E. Tupper St., Buffalo, NY 14203)

616.8 CN ISSN 0069-441X
CLARKE INSTITUTE OF PSYCHIATRY. MONOGRAPH SERIES. 1967. irreg. price varies. University of Toronto Press, Front Campus, Toronto, Ont. M5S 1A6, Canada. (also avail. in microfiche)

616.8 IT
CLINICA NEUROPSICHIATRICA. (Text in Italian; summaries in English, French, German, Italian) 1965. Ospedale Neuropsichiatrico, Teramo, Italy.

616.8 AT ISSN 0158-1597
CLINICAL AND EXPERIMENTAL NEUROLOGY. 1963. a. Aus.$11.10. (Australian Association of Neurologists) Adis Press Australasia Pty. Ltd., 404 Sydney Rd., Balgowlah, N.S.W. 2093, Australia. Eds. T. H. Tyrer and M. J. Eadie. circ. 300. (also avail. in microfilm from UMI) Indexed: Ind.Med.
Formerly: Australian Association of Neurologists Proceedings (ISSN 0084-7224)

617.48 US ISSN 0069-4827
CLINICAL NEUROSURGERY; PROCEEDINGS. 1953. a. price varies. (Congress of Neurological Surgeons) Williams and Wilkins Co., 428 E. Preston St., Baltimore, MD 21202. index, cum. index 1953-62. Indexed: Ind.Med.

CLINICS IN DEVELOPMENTAL MEDICINE. see *MEDICAL SCIENCES — Pediatrics*

616.8 US
COMMITTEE TO COMBAT HUNTINGTONS DISEASE NEWSLETTER. 1967. 3-4/yr. free. Committee to Combat Huntington's Disease, Inc., 250 W. 57th St., New York, NY 10019. Ed. Marjorie Guthrie. circ. 8,000. (processed)

616.8 US ISSN 0069-9446
CONTEMPORARY NEUROLOGY SERIES. 1966. 3 vols/yr. $35 per no. F. A. Davis Co., 1915 Arch St., Philadelphia, PA 19103. Ed.Bd. Indexed: Ind.Med.

CONTRIBUICOES EM PSICOLOGIA, PSIQUIATRIA E PSICANALISE. see *PSYCHOLOGY*

616.8 BL ISSN 0080-6404
COORDENADORIA DE SAUDE MENTAL, SAO PAULO. ARQUIVOS. (Text in Portuguese; summaries in English) 1924. irreg. free. Hospital de Juqueri, Franco da Rocha, Estado de Sao Paulo, Brazil. Ed. Dr. Paulo Fraleits. bk. rev.

616.8 US ISSN 0590-3955
CURRENT ISSUES IN PSYCHIATRY. 1967. price varies. Science House Publishers, 59 Fourth Ave., New York, NY 10003.

616.8 US ISSN 0161-780X
CURRENT NEUROLOGY. 1978. a. Houghton Mifflin Professional Publishers, 2 Park St., Boston, MA 02107. illus.

616.891 US ISSN 0070-2080
CURRENT PSYCHIATRIC THERAPIES. 1961. a. price varies. Grune and Stratton, Inc. (Subsidiary of: Harcourt Brace Jovanovich, Inc.) 111 Fifth Avenue, New York, NY 10003. Ed. Jules H. Masserman, M.D. Indexed: Ind.Med.

616.8 NE
DEVELOPMENTS IN NEUROSCIENCE. 1977. irreg., vol. 9, 1980. price varies. Elsevier North-Holland Biomedical Press, Box 211, 1000 AE Amsterdam, Netherlands.

362.2 US ISSN 0095-4888
DIRECTORY OF MINNESOTA'S AREA MENTAL HEALTH, MENTAL RETARDATION, INEBRIETY PROGRAMS. 1973. irreg. Department of Public Welfare, Public Information, Education Section, 658 Cedar St., St. Paul, MN 55155.
Continues: Directory of Minnesota's Area Mental Health - Mental Retardation Programs.

ENCOUNTERER. see *PSYCHOLOGY*

616.853 UK
EPILEPSY (YEAR) 1978. a. British Epilepsy Association, Crowthorne House, New Wokingham Rd., Wokingham, Berks, England.
Epilepsy

616.8 GW ISSN 0071-8025
FORUM DER PSYCHIATRIE. 1961; Neue Folge, 1977. irreg., vol. 10, 1980. price varies. Ferdinand Enke Verlag, Herdweg 63, 7000 Stuttgart 1, W. Germany (B.R.D.) Ed. Bd.

616.8 AG ISSN 0016-271X
FUNDACION ROUX-OCEFA. ARCHIVOS. (Text in Spanish; summaries in English) 1966. irreg. $10. (Sociedad Argentina de Neuropatologia) Fundacion Roux-Ocefa, Montevideo 81, Buenos Aires, Argentina. Ed. Moises Polak. bk. rev. bibl. charts. index. cum.index. Indexed: Ind.Med.

616.89 US
GROUP FOR THE ADVANCEMENT OF PSYCHIATRY. PUBLICATION. 1947. irreg., approx. 12 in 3 yrs. $30 for 3 yrs. Group for the Advancement of Psychiatry, 419 Park Ave. S., New York, NY 10016. Dir. Alex Sareyan. cum.index. circ. 5,000. Indexed: Ind.Med.
Supersedes (after 1977, vol. 9): Group for the Advancement of Psychiatry. Report (ISSN 0072-775X) & Group for the Advancement of Psychiatry. Symposium.

616.89 GW ISSN 0017-4947
GRUPPENPSYCHOTHERAPIE UND GRUPPENDYNAMIK. (Summaries in English and German) 1968. irreg. (4 nos. per vol.) DM.68. Vandenhoeck und Ruprecht, Theaterstr 13., Postfach 77, 3400 Goettingen, W. Germany (B.R.D.) Ed. Dr. Annelise Heigl-Evers. circ. 1,200. Indexed: SSCI.

HAWAII. DEPARTMENT OF HEALTH. MENTAL HEALTH STATISTICAL SECTION. PSYCHIATRIC OUTPATIENT, INPATIENT AND COMMUNITY PROGRAMS. see *SOCIAL SERVICES AND WELFARE*

616.8 US ISSN 0271-521X
IBRO NEUROSCIENCE CALENDAR. 1980. a. $6. Pergamon Press, Inc., Journals Division, Maxwell House, Fairview Park, Elmsford, NY 10523 (And Headington Hill Hall, Oxford OX3 0BW, England) (also avail. in microform from MIM,UMI)

ILLINOIS. DEPARTMENT OF MENTAL HEALTH AND DEVELOPMENTAL DISABILIITIES. ANNUAL REPORT. see *SOCIAL SERVICES AND WELFARE*

362.2 CN ISSN 0380-2892
IN A NUTSHELL. 1971. irreg. Mental Patients Association, 2146 Yew St., Vancouver, British Columbia V6K 3G7, Canada. illus.
Formerly: M P A News (ISSN 0380-2906)

362.2 II ISSN 0302-1610
INDIAN JOURNAL OF PSYCHIATRIC SOCIAL WORK. (Text in English) 1972. a. $3. Indian Society of Psychiatric Social Work, Hospital for Mental Diseases, Kanke, Ranchi 6, India. Ed. R. K. Upadhyay. adv. bk. rev. circ. 1,000. Indexed: Psychol.Abstr.

616.8 618.928 US ISSN 0074-963X
INTERNATIONAL ASSOCIATION FOR CHILD PSYCHIATRY AND ALLIED PROFESSIONS. YEARBOOK. Added title: Child in His Family. 1970. irreg., vol. 5, 1978. price varies. John Wiley & Sons, Inc., 605 Third Ave., New York, NY 10016. Eds. E. James Anthony, Cyrille Koupernik.
Formerly: International Yearbook for Child Psychiatry and Allied Disciplines.

616.89 UK ISSN 0085-2007
INTERNATIONAL ASSOCIATION FOR SCIENTIFIC STUDY OF MENTAL DEFICIENCY. PROCEEDINGS OF INTERNATIONAL CONGRESS. 1967. triennial, 4th, 1976, Washington, D.C. International Association for Scientific Study of Mental Deficiency, c/o Dr. D. A. Primrose, Royal Scottish National Hospital, Larbert, Scotland.

616.855 SZ ISSN 0074-1655
INTERNATIONAL ASSOCIATION OF LOGOPEDICS AND PHONIATRICS. REPORTS OF CONGRESS. triennial, 18th, 1980,Washington. International Association of Logopedics and Phoniatrics, c/o Dr. A. Muller,Gen.Sec., Av. de la Gare 6, CH-1003 Lausanne, Switzerland.

610 US ISSN 0361-0462
INTERNATIONAL BRAIN RESEARCH ORGANIZATION MONOGRAPH SERIES. 1975. irreg., vol. 6, 1979. price varies. Raven Press, 1140 Ave. of the Americas, New York, NY 10036. M. A. B. Brazier. Indexed: Curr.Cont. Sci.Cit.Ind.

MEDICAL SCIENCES — PSYCHIATRY AND NEUROLOGY

616.8   SZ   ISSN 0302-5136
INTERNATIONAL COLLEGE OF PSYCHOSOMATIC MEDICINE. PROCEEDINGS OF THE CONGRESS. (Text in English) irreg. 110 Fr.($66) per vol. (1981 price) S. Karger AG, Allschwilerstrasse 10, P.O. Box, CH-4009 Basel, Switzerland. (reprint service avail. from ISI)

616.89   NE   ISSN 0074-3372
INTERNATIONAL CONGRESS FOR CHILD PSYCHIATRY. PROCEEDINGS.* quadrennial, 1970, 7th, Jerusalem. Excerpta Medica, P.O. Box 211, Amsterdam, Netherlands (Inquire: Prof. D. J. Duche, 54 Blvd. Emile Dugier, 75-Paris, France)

616.8   IE   ISSN 0074-3631
INTERNATIONAL CONGRESS OF ELECTROENCEPHALOGRAPHY AND CLINICAL NEUROPHYSIOLOGY (PROCEEDINGS) (Supplement to: Electroencephalography and Clinical Neurophysiology) irreg., 1969, 8th, Marseilles, France. (International Federation of Societies for Electroencephalography and Clinical Neurophysiology) Elsevier-North Holland Scientific Publishers Ltd., Box 85, Limerick, Ireland.

616.8   NE   ISSN 0534-9109
INTERNATIONAL CONGRESS OF NEUROLOGICAL SCIENCES. ABSTRACTS AND DESCRIPTIONS OF CONTRIBUTIONS OF THE SCIENTIFIC PROGRAM. irreg. Excerpta Medica, P.O.B. 211, 1000 AE Amsterdam, Netherlands.

617.48   NE   ISSN 0074-3801
INTERNATIONAL CONGRESS OF NEUROLOGICAL SURGERY. ABSTRACTS OF PAPERS. 1957. irreg, 5th, published in 1973. fl.37($15.50) (World Federation of Neurological Societies) Excerpta Medica, P.O.B. 211, 1000 AE Amsterdam, Netherlands.

617.481   US
INTERNATIONAL CONGRESS OF PSYCHOSURGERY. PROCEEDING. irreg. price varies. University Park Press, Chamber of Commerce Bldg, Baltimore, MD 21202.

616.89   SZ   ISSN 0074-3917
INTERNATIONAL CONGRESS OF PSYCHOTHERAPY. PROCEEDINGS/VERHANDLUNGEN/COMPTES RENDUS. (Text in English, French and German) triennial since 1964; 1976, 10th, Paris. 100 Fr.($60) per vol. (1981 price) (International Federation for Medical Psychotherapy) S. Karger AG, Allschwilerstrasse 10, P.O. Box, CH-4009 Basel, Switzerland. (reprint service avail. from ISI)

616.8   SZ   ISSN 0074-5847
INTERNATIONAL FEDERATION FOR MEDICAL PSYCHOTHERAPY. CONGRESS REPORTS. 1972. triennale, 8th, 1970, Milan: 10th, 1976, Paris. International Federation for Medical Psychotherapy, 11-bis rue Caroline, CH-1000 Lausanne, Switzerland (Order 8th report from: S. Karger AG, Arnold-Boecklin-Str. 25, CH-4011 Basel, Switzerland) Eds. H. K. Fierz, T. Spoerri.

616.8   US   ISSN 0091-0600
INTERNATIONAL JOURNAL OF PSYCHOANALYTIC PSYCHOTHERAPY. 1972. q. $27.50. Jason Aronson, Inc., 111 Eighth Ave., New York, NY 10011. Ed. Dr. Robert J. Langs. bk. rev. bibl. circ. 3,000. Indexed: Ind.Med. Psychol.Abstr. SSCI.
Incorporating (as of 1974): International Journal of Psychiatry.

INTERNATIONAL LEAGUE OF SOCIETIES FOR THE MENTALLY HANDICAPPED. WORLD CONGRESS PROCEEDINGS. see *PSYCHOLOGY*

616.8   US   ISSN 0074-7742
INTERNATIONAL REVIEW OF NEUROBIOLOGY. 1959. irreg., vol. 19, 1976. price varies. Academic Press, Inc., 111 Fifth Ave., New York, NY 10003. Eds. Carl C. Pfeiffer, John R. Smythies. index. Indexed: Ind.Med.

157 616.858   US   ISSN 0074-7750
INTERNATIONAL REVIEW OF RESEARCH IN MENTAL RETARDATION. 1966. irreg., vol. 9, 1978. price varies. Academic Press, Inc., 111 Fifth Ave, New York, NY 10003. Ed. Norman R. Ellis.
Mental retardation

INTERNATIONAL SYMPOSIUM ON BRAIN-ENDOCRINE INTERACTION. PROCEEDINGS. see MEDICAL SCIENCES — Endocrinology

616.8   JA
JAPANESE NEUROCHEMICAL SOCIETY. BULLETIN/SHINKEI KAGAKU. (Text in Japanese) 1962. a. price varies. Japanese Neurochemical Society, c/o Dept. of Physiology, Keio University School of Medicine, Shinanomachi, Shinjuku-ku, Tokyo 160, Japan. Ed. Prof. Yasuzo Tsukada. bk. rev. bibl. (processed)
Formerly: Nerve Chemistry (ISSN 0037-3796)

616.8   US   ISSN 0303-6995
JOURNAL OF NEURAL TRANSMISSION. SUPPLEMENT. no. 11, 1974. irreg., no. 16, 1981. Springer-Verlag, 175 Fifth Ave., New York, NY 10010 (also Berlin, Heidelberg, Vienna) (reprint service avail. from ISI)
Formerly: Journal of Neuro-Visceral Relations. Supplement (ISSN 0075-4323); Continues: Acta Neurovegetativa. Supplement.

616.8   US   ISSN 0075-7608
LAFAYETTE CLINIC HANDBOOKS IN PSYCHIATRY. 1967. irreg. price varies. Wayne State University Press, 5959 Woodward Ave., Detroit, MI 48202. Ed. Robert Tennenhouse.

616.8   US   ISSN 0075-7616
LAFAYETTE CLINIC MONOGRAPHS IN PSYCHIATRY. 1965. irreg. price varies. Wayne State University Press, 5959 Woodward Ave., Detroit, MI 48202.

618.9   US   ISSN 0091-6315
MENTAL RETARDATION AND DEVELOPMENTAL DISABILITIES. 1970. a. Brunner-Mazel, Inc., 19 Union Sq. W., New York, NY 10003. Ed. J. Wortis.
Continues: Mental Retardation.

616.8   US   ISSN 0077-0043
MODERN PERSPECTIVES IN PSYCHIATRY. 1965. irreg. price varies. Brunner-Mazel, Inc., 19 Union Sq. W., New York, NY 10003. Ed. John G. Howells.

616.8   SZ   ISSN 0077-0094
MODERN PROBLEMS OF PHARMACOPSYCHIATRY. (Text in English) 1968. irreg. (approx. 1/yr.) 80 Fr.($48) per vol. (1981 price) S. Karger AG, Allschwilerstrasse 10, P.O. Box, CH-4009 Basel, Switzerland. Ed.Bd. (reprint service avail. from ISI) Indexed: Biol.Abstr. Chem.Abstr. Curr.Cont. Ind.Med.

616.894   US   ISSN 0077-0620
MONOGRAPH SERIES ON SCHIZOPHRENIA. 1950. irreg., 1969, no. 8. price varies. International Universities Press, Inc., Fifth Ave., New York, NY 10016.

616.8   US   ISSN 0077-0671
MONOGRAPHIEN AUS DEM GESAMTGEBIETE DER PSYCHIATRIE - PSYCHIATRY SERIES. 1970. irreg., no. 25, 1981. price varies. Springer-Verlag, 175 Fifth Ave., New York, NY 10010 (also Berlin, Heidelberg, Vienna) (reprint service avail. from ISI) Indexed: Ind.Med. Psychol.Abstr.
Supersedes in part: Monographien aus dem Gesamtgebiete der Neurologie und Psychiatrie.

MONOGRAPHS IN MODERN NEUROBIOLOGY. see *BIOLOGY*

616.8   SZ   ISSN 0300-5186
MONOGRAPHS IN NEURAL SCIENCES. (Text in English) 1972. irreg. (approx. 1/yr.) 80 Fr.($48) per vol. (1981 price) S. Karger AG, Allschwilerstrasse 10, P.O. Box, CH-4009 Basel, Switzerland. Ed. M. M. Cohen. (reprint service avail. from ISI) Indexed: Biol.Abstr. Chem.Abstr. Curr.Cont. Ind.Med.
Formerly: Monographs in Basic Neurology.

616.8   US   ISSN 0090-4074
NATIONAL DIRECTORY OF PROVIDERS OF PSYCHIATRIC SERVICES TO RELIGIOUS INSTITUTIONS. 1973. irreg. $1. American Psychiatric Association, Task Force on Religion and Psychiatry, 1700 18th St. N.W., Washington, DC 20009. (processed)

616 301   US   ISSN 0547-7115
NATIONAL GUILD OF CATHOLIC PSYCHIATRISTS. BULLETIN. a. $12. National Guild of Catholic Psychiatrists, c/o Marie Kraus, 120 Hill St., Whitinsville, MA 01588. Ed. Thomas K. Ciesla, M.D. bk. rev. circ. 400. (back issues avail.)

616.834   US
NATIONAL MULTIPLE SCLEROSIS SOCIETY. ANNUAL REPORT. a. membership. National Multiple Sclerosis Society, 205 E. 42nd St., New York, NY 10017.

612.78   NE   ISSN 0301-6412
NEUROLINGUISTICS; international series devoted to speech physiology and speech pathology. 1973. irreg. price varies. Swets Publishing Service (Subsidiary of: Swets en Zeitlinger B.V.) Heereweg 347B, 2161 CA Lisse, Netherlands (Dist. in the U.S. and Canada by: Swets North America, Inc. Box 517, Berwyn, PA 19312) Eds. Yvan Lebrun, Richard Hoops.

618   JA   ISSN 0470-8105
NEUROLOGIA MEDICO-CHIRURGICA. (Text in European languages) 1959. a. Japan Neurosurgical Society - Nihon Noshinkei Geka Gakkai, Department of Neurosurgery, Faculty of Medicine, University of Tokyo, 7-3-1 Hongo, Bunkyo-ku, Tokyo 113, Japan. Indexed: Ind.Med.

616.8   US   ISSN 0077-7838
NEURORADIOLOGY WORKSHOP. 1961. irreg. Grune & Stratton, Inc., (Subsidiary of: Harcourt Brace Jovanovich, Inc.) 111 5th Ave, New York, NY 10003. Eds. L. M. Davidoff, H. Jacobson and H. M. Zimmerman. index.

616.8   US   ISSN 0077-7846
NEUROSCIENCE RESEARCH. 1968. irreg., vol. 5, 1973. $18.50, Academic Press Inc., 111 Fifth Ave., New York, NY 10003. Eds. S. Ehrenpreis, O. Solnitsky.

616.8   US
NEUROSCIENCE SYMPOSIA. 1975. a. price varies. Society for Neuroscience, 9650 Rockville Pike, Bethesda, MD 20014.

616.8   US   ISSN 0028-3975
NEUROSPORA NEWSLETTER. 1962. a. $4. Yale University School of Medicine, Department of Microbiology, 310 Cedar St., New Haven, CT 06510. Ed. Barbara J. Bachmann. circ. 500.

615.9   US   ISSN 0160-2748
NEUROTOXICOLOGY. 1977. irreg. Raven Press, 1140 Ave. of the Americas, New York, NY 10036.

616.89 150   DK
ODENSE UNIVERSITY STUDIES IN PSYCHIATRY AND MEDICAL PSYCHOLOGY. (Text in Danish and English) 1973. irreg., no. 2, 1975. price varies. Odense University Press, 36, Pjentedamsgade, DK-5000 Odense, Denmark. (back issues avail.)

616.8   US
OXFORD NEUROLOGICAL MONOGRAPHS. irreg. price varies. Oxford University Press, 200 Madison Ave., New York, NY 10016 (And Ely House, 37 Dover St., London W1X 4AH, England) Ed. W. Ritchie Russell.

PRAXIS DER KINDERPSYCHOLOGIE UND KINDERPSYCHIATRIE. BEIHEFTE. see *PSYCHOLOGY*

616.8 612.821   NE   ISSN 0079-6123
PROGRESS IN BRAIN RESEARCH. 1963. irreg., vol. 52, 1980. price varies. Elsevier North-Holland Biomedical Press, Box 211, 1000 AE Amsterdam, Netherlands. Indexed: Ind.Med.

616.8 612　　　　　SZ　ISSN 0378-4045
PROGRESS IN CLINICAL NEUROPHYSIOLOGY.
(Text in English) 1977. irreg. 120 Fr.($72) (1981 price) S. Karger AG, Allschwilerstrasse 10, P.O. Box, CH-4009 Basel, Switzerland. Ed. J.E. Desmedt. charts. illus. index. circ. 2,000. (also avail. in microfilm; microfiche; back issues avail.; reprint service avail. from ISI) Indexed: Biol.Abstr. Chem.Abstr. Curr.Cont. Ind.Med.

617.48　　　　　SZ　ISSN 0079-6492
PROGRESS IN NEUROLOGICAL SURGERY.
(Text in English) 1966. irreg. (approx. 1/yr.) 100 Fr.($60) per vol. (1981 price) S. Karger AG, Allschwilerstrasse 10, P.O. Box, CH-4009 Basel, Switzerland. Eds. H. Krayenbuehl, P.E. Maspes, W.H. Sweet. (reprint service avail. from ISI) Indexed: Biol.Abstr. Chem.Abstr. Curr.Cont. Ind.Med.

616.8　　　　　　US
PROGRESS IN NEUROPATHOLOGY. 1971. irreg., vol. 4, 1979. price varies. Raven Press, 1140 Ave. of the Americas, New York, NY 10036. Ed.H. M. Zimmerman, M.D.

616.8　　　　　　FI　ISSN 0079-7227
PSYCHIATRIA FENNICA/FINNISH PSYCHIATRY. (Text mainly in English; occasionally in German) 1970. a. Fmk.90. (Foundation for Psychiatric Research in Finland) Psychiatria Fennica, Arkadiankatu 35 B 37, 00100 Helsinki 10, Finland. Ed. K. A. Achte. adv. bk. rev. circ. 2,000. Indexed: Excerp.Med. Psychol.Abstr.

616.8　　　　　　FI　ISSN 0355-7693
PSYCHIATRIA FENNICA. JULKAISUSERJA/ PSYCHIATRIA FENNICA. REPORTS. (Text mainly in English) 1970. irreg., no. 31, 1978. Fmk.25. ‡ (Foundation for Psychiatric Research in Finland) Psychiatria Fennica, Arkadiankatu 35 B 37, 00100 Helsinki 10, Finland. Ed. K. A. Achte. circ. 150-300. Indexed: Excerp.Med. Psychol.Abstr.
Formerly: Helsingin Yliopisto Keskussairaala. Psykiatria Klinika. Julkaisusarja (ISSN 0073-1730)

616.8　　　　　　FI　ISSN 0355-7707
PSYCHIATRIA FENNICA. MONOGRAFIASARJA/PSYCHIATRIA FENNICA. MONOGRAPHS. (Text mainly in English) 1970. irreg., no. 8, 1977. Fmk.35. (Foundation for Psychiatric Research in Finland) Psychiatria Fennica, Arkadiankatu 35 B 37, 00100 Helsinki 10, Finland. Ed. K. A. Achte. circ. 1,000. Indexed: Excerp.Med. Psychol.Abstr.

616.8　　　　　　SZ　ISSN 0079-7286
PSYCHIATRY AND ART. (Text in English) 1968. irreg. (approx. 1/yr) 120 Fr.($72) per vol. (1981 price) (International Congress of Psychopathology of Expression) S. Karger AG, Allschwilerstrasse 10, P.O. Box, CH-4009 Basel, Switzerland. Ed. Irene Jakab. (reprint service avail. from ISI) Indexed: Biol.Abstr. Chem.Abstr. Curr.Cont. Ind.Med.

616.8 001.3　　　US　ISSN 0363-8952
PSYCHIATRY AND THE HUMANITIES. 1976. a. price varies. (Washington School of Psychiatry, Forum on Psychiatry and the Humanities) Yale University Press, 92A Yale Sta., New Haven, CT 06520. Ed. Joseph H. Smith.

616.857 616.8　　SZ　ISSN 0080-1453
RESEARCH AND CLINICAL STUDIES IN HEADACHE. (Text in English) 1967. irreg. (approx. 1/yr.) 80 Fr.($48) per vol. (1981 price) S. Karger AG, Allschwilerstrasse 10, P.O. Box, CH-4009 Basel, Switzerland. Eds. A.P. Friedman, Mary E. Granger. (reprint service avail. from ISI) Indexed: Biol.Abstr. Chem.Abstr. Curr.Cont. Ind.Med.
　Migraine

RESEARCH METHODS IN NEUROCHEMISTRY. see BIOLOGY — Biological Chemistry

616.8　　　　　　US
REVIEWS OF NEUROSCIENCE. 1974. irreg., vol. 4, 1979. price varies. Raven Press, 1140 Avenue of the Americas, New York, NY 10036.

616.8　　　　　　US　ISSN 0080-715X
SCHRIFTENREIHE NEUROLOGIE/NEUROLOGY SERIES. (Partly supersedes: Monographien aus dem Gesamtgebiete der Neurologie und Psychiatrie) (Text in German; occasionally in English) 1959. irreg.; vol. 21, 1978. price varies. Springer-Verlag, 175 Fifth Ave., New York, NY 10010 (also Berlin, Heidelberg, Vienna) (reprint service avail. from ISI) Indexed: Ind.Med.

616.8　　　　　　JA　ISSN 0080-8547
SEISHIN-IGAKU INSTITUTE OF PSYCHIATRY, TOKYO. BULLETIN/SEISHIN IGAKU KENKYUSHO, TOKYO. GYOSEKI SHU. (Text in Japanese; table of contents and summaries in English) 1954. a. free to qualified personnel. Seishin Igaku Institute of Psychiatry - Seishin Igaku Kenkyusho, 4-11-11 Komone, Itabashi-ku, Tokyo 173, Japan.

SEMINARS IN NEUROLOGICAL SURGERY. see MEDICAL SCIENCES — Surgery

616.89　　　　　US　ISSN 0094-6184
SERIAL HANDBOOK OF MODERN PSYCHIATRY. 1974. irreg. price varies. Thieme-Stratton, Inc., 381 Park Ave. South, New York, NY 10016. Eds. J. H. Masserman, J. J. Schwab.

616.8　　　　　　SZ　ISSN 0080-9012
SERIES PAEDOPSYCHIATRICA. (Supplements of the Acta Paedopsychiatrica) (Text in English, French, German) 1965. irreg., vol. 5, 1978. price varies. Schwabe und Co. AG, Steinentorstr. 13, 4010 Basel, Switzerland. Ed. Jakob Lutz. index. Indexed: Ind.Med.

616.8　　　　　　US　ISSN 0093-0407
SLEEP RESEARCH. 1972. a. $20. Brain Information Service-Brain Research Institute, University of California, Los Angeles, Center for the Health Sciences, Los Angeles, CA 90024. Ed. Bd. bk. rev. bibl. circ. 800. (back issues avail)

362.2 616.8　　　US　ISSN 0095-0858
SOCIAL PSYCHIATRY. 1974. a. (American Association for Social Psychiatry) Grune & Stratton, Inc. (Subsidiary of: Harcourt Brace Jovanovich, Inc.) 111 Fifth Ave., New York, NY 10003. Key Title: Social Psychiatry (New York. 1974)

616.8　　　　　　US　ISSN 0091-6528
SOCIETY FOR NEUROSCIENCE. ANNUAL MEETING. CONFERENCE REPORT. (Subseries of B I S Conference Reports) 1971. a. $5. Brain Information Service-Brain Research Institute, Univeristy of California, Los Angeles, School of Medicine, Los Angeles, CA 90024.

616.8　　　　　　US
SOVIET RESEARCH REPORTS. irreg. $6 per vol. Brain Information Service-Brain Research Institute, University of California, Los Angeles, Center for the Health Sciences, Los Angeles, CA 90024.

616.8　　　　　　US
STUDIES OF BRAIN FUNCTION. 1977. irreg., vol. 5, 1981. price varies. Springer-Verlag, 175 Fifth Ave., New York, NY 10010 (Also Berlin, Heidelberg, Vienna) Ed.Bd. (reprint service avail. from ISI)

616.8　　　　　　US　ISSN 0093-3317
STUDIES ON THE DEVELOPMENT OF BEHAVIOR AND THE NERVOUS SYSTEM. 1973. irreg. price varies. Academic Press, Inc., 111 Fifth Avenue, New York, NY 10003. Ed. Gilbert Gottlieb.

616.8　　　　　　NE
SUPPLEMENTS TO ELECTROENCEPHALOGRAPHY AND CLINICAL NEUROPHYSIOLOGY. 1950. irreg., no. 34, 1978. price varies. Elsevier North-Holland Biomedical Press, Box 211, 1000 AE Amsterdam, Netherlands.

616.8　　　　　　JA
TOKYO METROPOLITAN INSTITUTE OF NEUROSCIENCES. ANNUAL REPORT/ TOKYO-TO SHINKEI KAGAKU SOGO KENKYUJO NEMPO. (Text in Japanese) 1972. a. Tokyo Metropolitan Institute of Neurosciences, 2-6 Musashidai, Fuchu-shi, Tokyo 183, Japan.

618.9　　　　　　SW
UNION OF EUROPEAN PEDOPSYCHIATRISTS. PROCEEDINGS.* (Text in English, French or German) irreg., 4th, Stockholm, 1971. $39.50. Halsted Press, 605 Third Ave., New York, NY 10016. Ed. Arna-Lisa Annell. bibl.

616.82　　　　　　US
U.S. CENTER FOR DISEASE CONTROL. NEUROTROPIC VIRAL DISEASES SURVEILLANCE: ASEPTIC MENINGITIS. a. free. U.S. Center for Disease Control, 1600 Clifton Rd., Atlanta, GA 30333.

616.832　　　　　US
U.S. CENTER FOR DISEASE CONTROL. NEUROTROPIC VIRAL DISEASES SURVEILLANCE: ENCEPHALITIS. a. free. U.S. Center for Disease Control, 1600 Clifton Rd., Atlanta, GA 30333.

616.8　　　　　　US
U.S. CENTER FOR DISEASE CONTROL. NEUROTROPIC VIRAL DISEASES SURVEILLANCE: ENTEROVIRUS. a. U.S. Center for Disease Control, 1600 Clifton Rd, Atlanta, GA 30333.

616.835　　　　　US
U.S. CENTER FOR DISEASE CONTROL. NEUROTROPIC VIRAL DISEASES SURVEILLANCE: POLIOMYELITIS. a. free. U.S. Center for Disease Control, 1600 Clifton Rd., Atlanta, GA 30333.

616.8　　　　　　US　ISSN 0094-9582
U.S. NATIONAL INSTITUTE OF NEUROLOGICAL DISEASES AND STROKE. RESEARCH PROGRAM REPORTS. irreg. $1.45. U.S. National Institute of Neurological and Communicative Disorders and Stroke, Bethesda, Washington, MD 20014 (Orders to: U.S. Supt. of Documents, Washington, DC 20402) Key Title: Research Program Reports.

616.8　　　　　　US　ISSN 0083-3568
U. S. VETERAN'S ADMINISTRATION. SPINAL CORD INJURY CONFERENCE. CONFERENCE PROCEEDINGS. (Proceedings of 1st not published) 1953, 2nd. biennial. U.S. Veterans Administration, 810 Vermont Ave., N.W., Washington, DC 20420. Indexed: Ind.Med.
Continues: Clinical Spinal Cord Injury Conference. Proceedings.

616.8　　　　　　CN　ISSN 0083-5196
VANCOUVER NEUROLOGICAL CENTRE. ANNUAL REPORTS. a. free. Vancouver Neurological Centre, 1195 W. 8th Ave., Vancouver, B.C. V6H 1C5, Canada.

616.8　　　　　　GW　ISSN 0340-0905
WAKING AND SLEEPING; international journal for wakefulness, fatigue, sleep and dreams. (Text in English) 1976. q. DM.103($45) Gesellschaft zur Erforschung und Bekaempfung von Schlafstoerungen e.V.) Editio Asklepion, Im Hause Gebs, Theaterstrasse 24, D-8700 Wuerzburg, W. Germany (B.R.D.) Ed. Dr. U.J. Jovanovic. adv. bk. rev. abstr. bibl. charts. illus. index. circ. 1,000. (back issues avail.)

616.8　　　　　　US　ISSN 0084-0092
WIENER ZEITSCHRIFT FUER NERVENHEILKUNDE UND DEREN GRENZGEBIETE. SUPPLEMENT. 1966. irreg. 1969, no. 2. Springer-Verlag, 175 Fifth Ave., New York, NY 10010 (also Berlin, Heidelberg, Vienna) (reprint service avail. from ISI)

616.89　　　　　　AU　ISSN 0084-1609
WORLD CONGRESS OF PSYCHIATRY. PROCEEDINGS. 1950. irreg., 1971, 5th, Mexico. $100. World Psychiatric Association, c/o Prof. P. Berner, Psychiatrische Universitaetsklinik, Lazarettgasse 14, A-1097 Vienna, Austria (Proceedings of 5th, 1971 avail. from: Excerpta Medica, Box 211, Amsterdam, Netherlands)

616.8 617　　　　US
YEAR BOOK OF NEUROLOGY & NEUROSURGERY. 1969. a. price varies. Year Book Medical Publishers, Inc., 35 E. Wacker Dr., Chicago, IL 60601. Ed.Bd.
Supersedes in part: Year Book of Neurology, Psychiatry and Neurosurgery.

616.89　　　　　US　ISSN 0084-3970
YEAR BOOK OF PSYCHIATRY AND APPLIED
MENTAL HEALTH. 1970. a. Yearbook Medical
Publishers, Inc., 35 E. Wacker Dr., Chicago, IL
60601. Ed. Bd.
　　Supersedes in Part: Yearbook of Neurology,
Psychiatry and Neurosurgery.

150　616.89　　GW　ISSN 0085-8412
ZEITSCHRIFT FUER PSYCHOSOMATISCHE
MEDIZIN UND PSYCHOANALYSE.
BEIHEFTE. 1970. irreg., no. 8, 1980. price varies.
Vandenhoeck und Ruprecht, Theaterstr. 13, 3400
Goettingen, W. Germany (B.R.D.) Indexed:
Psychol.Abstr.　SSCI.

MEDICAL SCIENCES — Radiology And Nuclear Medicine

610　　　　　　　US
AMERICAN LECTURES IN NUCLEAR
MEDICINE. irreg. price varies. Charles C. Thomas,
Publisher, 301-327 E. Lawrence Ave., Springfield,
IL 62717.

615.842　　　　　US
AMERICAN LECTURES IN RADIATION
THERAPY. irreg. price varies. Charles C. Thomas,
Publisher, 301-327 E. Lawrence Ave., Springfield,
IL 62717.

616　　　　　　　US
AMERICAN LECTURES IN ROENTGEN
DIAGNOSIS. irreg. price varies. Charles C.
Thomas, Publisher, 301-327 E. Lawrence Ave.,
Springfield, IL 62717.

615.84　　　　　FR　ISSN 0066-3468
ANNUAIRE NATIONAL DES SPECIALISTES
QUALIFIES EXCLUSIFS EN
ELECTRORADIOLOGIE. 1967. irreg. 22 F.
Revue de Medecine, 40, rue Paul- Valery, 75116
Paris, France.

615.84　　　　　SZ　ISSN 0067-8155
BIBLIOTHECA RADIOLOGICA. (Text in English)
1959. irreg. (approx. 1/yr) 80 Fr.($48) per vol.
(1981 price) S. Karger AG, Allschwilerstrasse 10,
P.O. Box, CH-4009 Basel, Switzerland. (reprint
service avail. from ISI) Indexed: Biol.Abstr.
Chem.Abstr.　Curr.Cont.　Ind.Med.

615.8　　　　　　IT
C.I.R.M. a. Centro Internazionale Radio-Medico, Via
Architettura 41, 00144 Rome, Italy.

615.842　　　　　US
CONFERENCE ON COMPUTERS IN
RADIOLOGY. PROCEEDINGS. 1973? a. Institute
of Electrical and Electronics Engineers, Inc.,
Computer Society, 5855 Naples Plaza, No. 301,
Long Beach, CA 90803.

615.8　　　　　　US　ISSN 0149-2454
CURRENT CONCEPTS IN RADIOLOGY. 1972.
irreg., vol. 3, 1977. price varies. C. V. Mosby Co.,
11830 Westline Industrial Dr., St. Louis, MO
63140.

615.8　　　　　　US　ISSN 0161-7818
CURRENT RADIOLOGY. 1978. a. Houghton Mifflin
Professional Publishers, 2 Park St., Boston, MA
02107. illus.

ENVIRONMENTAL HEALTH SERIES:
RADIOLOGICAL HEALTH. see PUBLIC
HEALTH AND SAFETY

618　619　　　　US　ISSN 0340-6997
EUROPEAN JOURNAL OF NUCLEAR
MEDICINE. 1976. m. $129. (European Nuclear
Medicine Society) Springer Verlag, 175 Fifth Ave.,
New York, NY 10010 (And Berlin, Heidelberg,
Vienna) Eds. H. Hundeshagen, G. Thiessen. (reprint
service avail. from ISI)

615　616.9　　　SZ　ISSN 0071-9676
FRONTIERS OF RADIATION THERAPY AND
ONCOLOGY. (Text in English) 1967. irreg.
(approx. 1/yr) 30 Fr.($78) per vol. (1981 price) S.
Karger AG, Allschwilerstrasse 10, P.O. Box, CH-
4009 Basel, Switzerland. Ed. J. M. Vaeth. (reprint
service avail. from ISI) Indexed: Biol.Abstr.
Chem.Abstr.　Curr.Cont.　Ind.Med.

612.014　　　　　US　ISSN 0073-1498
HEALTH PHYSICS SOCIETY. NEWSLETTER.
1959. irreg. free to members. Health Physics
Society, c/o R. J. Burk, Jr., Exec. Secretary, 4720
Montgomery Lane, Bethesda, MD 20014. Ed. O. L.
Cordes. circ. 3,500.

612.014　　　　　JA　ISSN 0073-232X
HIROSHIMA UNIVERSITY. RESEARCH
INSTITUTE FOR NUCLEAR MEDICINE AND
BIOLOGY. PROCEEDINGS/HIROSHIMA
DAIGAKU GENBAKU HOSHANO IGAKU
KENKYUSHO NENPO. (Text in English and
Japanese) 1960. a. not for sale. Hiroshima
University, Research Institute for Nuclear Medicine
and Biology - Hiroshima Daigaku Genbaku
Hoshano Kenkyusho, Kasumi, Hiroshima 734,
Japan. Ed.Bd.

615.8　　　　　　US　ISSN 0074-0543
INSTRUMENTATION IN NUCLEAR MEDICINE.
1967. irreg. price varies. Academic Press, Inc., 111
Fifth Ave., New York, NY 10003. Ed. G. J. Hine.

574.191　　　　　PL　ISSN 0074-0640
INSTYTUT BADAN JADROWYCH. ZAKLAD
RADIOBIOLOGII I OCHRONY ZDROWIA.
PRACE DOSWIADCZAINE. (Text in English,
Polish, German or French; summaries in English)
1960. irreg., vol. 4, 1973. free. (Institute of Nuclear
Research) Osrodek Informacji o Energii Jadrowej,
Palac Kultury i Nauki, Warsaw, Poland. Ed. Maria
Kopec. author index.

616.8　　　　　　US　ISSN 0074-2759
INTERNATIONAL COMMISSION ON
RADIOLOGICAL PROTECTION. REPORT.
1960. irreg., vol. 23, 1975. price varies. Pergamon
Press, Inc., Maxwell House, Fairview Park,
Elmsford, NY 10523.

615.84　612.014　　SZ　ISSN 0074-3933
INTERNATIONAL CONGRESS OF RADIOLOGY.
(REPORTS) irreg., 1973, 13th, Madrid; 1977, 14th,
Rio de Janeiro. International Society of Radiology,
c/o Prof. Dr. W. A. Fuchs, University Hospital,
Department of Diagnostic Radiology, Inselspital,
CH-3010 Berne, Switzerland. Ed. Gomez Lopez
Bonmati. circ. 10,000. Indexed: Excerp.Med.

615.842　　　　　UA　ISSN 0021-1907
ISOTOPE AND RADIATION RESEARCH. 1968. a.
$5. Middle Eastern Regional Radioisotope Centre
for the Arab Countries, Sh. Malaeb el Gamaa,
Dokki, Cairo, Egypt. bk. rev.

615.842　　　　　SZ　ISSN 0379-4474
KARGER HIGHLIGHTS: MEDICAL IMAGING;
reprinted selected top articles. 1979. a. 15 Fr.($9)
(1981 price) S. Karger AG, Allschwilerstrasse 10, P.
O. Box, CH-4009 Basel. Ed. H. J. Kaufman. charts.
illus. (reprint service avail. from ISI)

615.8　　　　　　UR　ISSN 0075-529X
KAZAKHSKII NAUCHNO-ISSLEDOVATEL'SKII
INSTITUT ONKOLOGII I RADIOLOGII.
TRUDY. (Text in Russian; summaries in English)
1965. a. price varies. Kazakhskii Nauchno-
Issledovatel'skii Institut Onkologii i Radiologii,
Alma-Ata, U.S.S.R.

615.842　　　　　US
N C R P STATEMENTS. 1954. irreg. free. National
Council on Radiation Protection and Measurements,
7910 Woodmont Avenue, Suite 1016, Washington,
DC 20014. Ed. W. Roger Ney.

NEURORADIOLOGY WORKSHOP. see MEDICAL
SCIENCES — Psychiatry And Neurology

574.191　　　　　UK　ISSN 0550-8398
NON-IONIZING RADIATION; r.f., microwaves,
infra-red, lasers. 1969. irreg. £14.50($39) Kendervic
Ltd., 3 Erpingham Rd., London SW15 1BE,
England. bk. rev. abstr. charts. illus. index.

615.842　　　　　US
NUCLEAR MEDICINE ANNUAL. a. Raven Press,
1140 Ave. of the Americas, New York, NY 10036.
Eds. Leonard Freeman, Heidi S. Weissman.

615.8　　　　　　US　ISSN 0273-0278
POSTGRADUATE RADIOLOGY; a journal of
continuing education. 1981. q. $40. Futura
Publishing, 295 Main St., Box 330, Mt. Kisco, NY
10549. Ed. Herbert L. Abrams, M.D. adv. bk. rev.
abstr. illus. index. circ. 3,600.

615.842　　　　　SZ　ISSN 0079-6573
PROGRESS IN NUCLEAR MEDICINE. (Text in
English) 1972. irreg. (approx. 1/yr.) 120 Fr.($72)
per vol. (1981 price) S. Karger AG,
Allschwilerstrasse 10, P.O. Box, CH-4009 Basel,
Switzerland. Eds. A. Donath, A.N. Serafini. (reprint
service avail. from ISI)

PROGRESS IN PEDIATRIC RADIOLOGY. see
MEDICAL SCIENCES — Pediatrics

615.8　　　　　　US　ISSN 0079-6735
PROGRESS IN RADIATION THERAPY. 1958.
irreg., 1965, vol. 3. $34.75. Grune & Stratton, Inc.,
(Subsidiary of: Harcourt Brace Jovanovich, Inc.) 111
5th Ave., New York, NY 10003. Ed. Franz
Buschke. index.

615　　　　　　　UN
RADIATION DOSIMETRY DATA; CATALOGUE.
1964. irreg. free. International Atomic Energy
Agency - Agence Internationale de l'Energie
Atomique, Wagramer Str. 5, Box 100, A-1400
Vienna, Austria. circ. 3,000.
　　Until 1969: International Atomic Energy Agency.
Radiation Data for Medical Use; Catalogue (ISSN
0538-4850)

539.1　616　　　　JA
RADIATION EFFECTS RESEARCH
FOUNDATION. ANNUAL REPORT/
HOSHASEN EIKYO KENKYUSHO NENPO.
(Text in English and Japanese) 1958. a. price varies.
‡ Radiation Effects Research Foundation -
Hoshasen Eikyo Kenkyusho, 5-2 Hijiyama-Koen,
Hiroshima 730, Japan (Avail. in U.S. from National
Technical Information Service, Springfield, Va.
22151) circ. 1,000. Indexed: Nucl.Sci.Abstr.
　　Formerly (until 1974/75): Atomic Bomb Casualty
Commission, Hiroshima. Annual Report.

615.842　　　　　US
RADIOLOGY TODAY. 1981. irreg. Springer-Verlag,
175 Fifth Ave., New York, NY 10010 (Also Berlin,
Heidelberg, Vienna) (reprint service avail. from ISI)

616.9　　　　　　US　ISSN 0163-6170
RECENT ADVANCES IN NUCLEAR MEDICINE.
1965. irreg., vol. 5, 1978. price varies. Grune &
Stratton Inc., (Subsidiary of: Harcourt Brace
Jovanovich, Inc.) 111 Fifth Ave., New York, NY
10003.
　　Former titles: Progress in Nuclear Medicine
(ISSN 0079-6581); Progress in Atomic Medicine
(ISSN 0085-5189)

618　　　　　　　US　ISSN 0364-2348
SKELETAL RADIOLOGY; including computed
tomography. 1976. q. $60. (International Skeletal
Society) Springer Verlag, 175 Fifth Ave., New
York, NY 10010 (And Berlin, Heidelberg, Vienna)
Ed.Bd. adv. bk. rev. charts. illus. index. circ. 650.
(also avail. in microfilm; reprint service avail. from
ISI) Indexed: Curr.Cont.

615.842　　　　　UK　ISSN 0260-4043
ULTRASOUND PATENTS & PAPERS. 1980. irreg.
Scientific and Medical Information Services,
Kingsbourne House, 229 High Holborn, London
WC1V 7DA, England. illus.

618　574　　　　UR
VOPROSY RADIOBIOLOGII I
BIOLOGICHESKOGO DEISTVIYA
TSITOSTATICHESKIKH PREPARATOV. 1969.
irreg. (Tomskii Meditsinskii Institut, Tsentralnaya
Nauchno-Issledovatelskaya Laboratoriya) Izdatel'svo
Tomskii Universitet, Prospekt Lenina, 36, Tomsk-
10, U.S.S.R. bibl. illus.

615.842　　　　　US
WEST COAST CANCER SYMPOSIUM.
PROCEEDINGS. (Subseries of: Frontiers of
Radiation Therapy and Oncology) vol. 8, 1973. a.
University Park Press, Chamber of Commerce Bldg.,
Baltimore, MD 21202.
　　Formerly (until 1972): San Francisco Cancer
Symposium. Proceedings.

615.84　　　　　US　ISSN 0098-1672
YEAR BOOK OF DIAGNOSTIC RADIOLOGY.
1932. a. price varies. ‡ Year Book Medical
Publishers, Inc., 35 E. Wacker Dr., Chicago, IL
60601. Ed. Bd.
　　Formerly (until 1975): Year Book of Radiology
(ISSN 0084-3989)

615.8 US ISSN 0084-3903
YEAR BOOK OF NUCLEAR MEDICINE. 1966. a. price varies. ‡ Year Book Medical Publishers, Inc., 35 E. Wacker Dr., Chicago, IL 60601. Ed. J. L. Quinn.

MEDICAL SCIENCES — Respiratory Diseases

616.2 SZ ISSN 0065-3500
ADVANCES IN TUBERCULOSIS RESEARCH. (Text in English, French, and German) 1948. irreg. (approx. 1/yr.) 100 Fr.($60) per vol (1981 price) S. Karger AG, Allschwilerstrasse 10, P.O. Box, CH-4009 Basel, Switzerland. Ed. G. Urbanczik. (reprint service avail. from ISI) Indexed: Biol.Abstr. Chem.Abstr. Curr.Cont. Ind.Med.

616.2 US ISSN 0361-5006
ANNUAL SYMPOSIUM ON PULMONARY DISEASES. a. U.S. Army, Fitzsimons Army Medical Center, Denver, CO 80200.

616.2 GE ISSN 0067-8228
BIBLIOTHEK FUER DAS GESAMTGEBIET DER LUNGENKRANKHEITEN. 1921. irreg., no. 104, 1972. price varies. Johann Ambrosius Barth Verlag, Salomonstr. 18b, 701 Leipzig, E. Germany (D.D.R.) Eds. W. Lindig, H. Rink. (back issues avail.)
Formerly: Tuberkulose-Bibliothek.

616.2 PE ISSN 0069-2166
CENTRO DE SALUD "MAX ARIAS SCHREIBER", LIMA. CONGRESO NACIONAL DE TUBERCULOSIS Y ENFERMEDADES RESPIRATORIAS.* irreg., 1970, 9th. Dispensario Antituberculoso "Max Arias Schreiber", Raymondi 2da Cuadra (La Victoria), Lima, Peru.

616.2 US
CYSTIC FIBROSIS G A P CONFERENCE REPORTS. 1969. irreg., vol. 3, 1979. Cystic Fibrosis Foundation (Rockville), 6000 Executive Blvd., Suite 309, Rockville, MD 20852. Eds. Robert E. Wood, M.D., and Philip M. Farrell, M.D. bibl. charts. illus. stat. circ. 2,800.

616.2 DK
EUROPEAN JOURNAL OF RESPIRATORY DISEASES. SUPPLEMENTUM. (Text in English) 1920. irreg. free to subscribers. Munksgaard, 35 Noerre Soegade, DK-1370 Copenhagen K, Denmark. Eds. E. Berglund, J. Georg. adv. (reprint service avail. from ISI) Indexed: Curr.Cont. Ind.Med.
Formerly (until 1980): Scandinavian Journal of Respiratory Diseases. Supplementum (ISSN 0080-6730)

616.2 JA
HOKKAIDO UNIVERSITY. INSTITUTE OF IMMUNOLOGICAL SCIENCE. BULLETIN. (Text in Japanese; summaries in English and Japanese) 1953. a. exchange basis. Hokkaido University, Institute of Immunological Science, North 15, West 7, Sapporo 060, Japan. Ed. Shichiro Kakimoto. circ. 300.
Until 1975: Kekkaku No Kenkyu. (ISSN 0075-5354)

616.2 SP ISSN 0302-7406
INSTITUTO ANTITUBERCULOSO FRANCISCO MORAGAS. PUBLICACIONES. (Supplements issued in alternate years) (Text in Spanish; summaries in English) 1933. biennial. exchange basis. Instituto Antituberculoso Francisco Moragas, Paseo de San Juan 20, Barcelona, Spain. circ. controlled. (back issues avail)

616.26 FR ISSN 0074-9249
INTERNATIONAL UNION AGAINST TUBERCULOSIS. BULLETIN. (Publication suspended 1940-46) (Text in English, French,and Spanish) 1924. q. International Union Against Tuberculosis, 3, rue Georges Ville, 3, 75116 Paris, France. Indexed: Ind.Med.
With vol. 24 includes: International Tuberculosis Yearbook.

616.246 NE
INTERNATIONAL UNION AGAINST TUBERCULOSIS. CONFERENCE PROCEEDINGS. (Format varies; some reports also issued in Union's Bulletin) biennial, 23th, Tokyo. (FR) Excerpta Medica, P.O. Box 211, 1000 AE Amsterdam, Netherlands (Inquire: International Union Against Tuberculosis, 20 rue Greuze, 75-Paris 16e, France)

616.2 JA ISSN 0075-3165
JAPAN ANTI-TUBERCULOSIS ASSOCIATION. REPORTS ON MEDICAL RESEARCH PROBLEMS/KEKKAKU YOBOKAI KENKYU GYOSEKI. (Text in English) 1951. a. exchange basis. Japan Anti-Tuberculosis Association - Nihon Kekkaku Yobokai, 1-3-12 Misaki-cho, Chiyoda-ku, Tokyo 101, Japan. Ed. Tadao Shimao, M.D. circ. 800.

616.2 CN ISSN 0075-9465
LIGUE ANTITUBERCULEUSE DE QUEBEC. RAPPORT. 1947. a. free. Ligue Antituberculeuse de Quebec, 261 W. Rue St-Vallier, Quebec 8, Canada.

616.2 SZ ISSN 0079-6751
PROGRESS IN RESPIRATION RESEARCH. (Text in English) 1963. irreg. (approx. 1/yr.) 120 Fr.($72) per vol. (1981 price) S. Karger AG, Allschwilerstrasse 10, P.O. Box, CH-4009 Basel, Switzerland. Ed. H. Herzog. (reprint service avail. from ISI) Indexed: Biol.Abstr. Chem.Abstr. Curr.Cont. Ind.Med.

616.2 SA ISSN 0081-2501
S A N T A ANNUAL REPORT/S A N T A JAARLIKSE VERSLAG. (Text in Afrikaans and English) 1949. a. free. South African National Tuberculosis Association, 621 Leisk House, 195 Bree St., Johannesburg 2001, South Africa. Ed. Evelyn Stubbs. circ. 2,000.

TASK FORCE ON ENVIRONMENTAL CANCER AND HEART AND LUNG DISEASE. ANNUAL REPORT TO CONGRESS. see ENVIRONMENTAL STUDIES

616.246 614 US
U.S. CENTER FOR DISEASE CONTROL. TUBERCULOSIS IN THE UNITED STATES. 1974. a. free. U.S. Center for Disease Control, Tuberculosis Control Division, 1600 Clifton Rd. N.E., Atlanta, GA 30333. charts. illus. stat. circ. 7,000.
Formed by the merger of: U.S. Center for Disease Control. Reported Tuberculosis Data & U.S. Center for Disease Control. Tuberculosis Program Reports.

616.246 614 US
U.S. CENTER FOR DISEASE CONTROL. TUBERCULOSIS STATISTICS: STATES AND CITIES. a. U.S. Center for Disease Control, Tuberculosis Control Division, 1600 Clifton Rd., N.E., Atlanta, GA 30333. circ. 7,000.
Formerly: U.S. Center for Disease Control. Tuberculosis: States and Cities.

U. S. NATIONAL HEART, LUNG, AND BLOOD ADVISORY COUNCIL. REPORT. see MEDICAL SCIENCES — Cardiovascular Diseases

U. S. NATIONAL HEART, LUNG, AND BLOOD INSTITUTE. REPORT OF THE DIRECTOR. see MEDICAL SCIENCES — Cardiovascular Diseases

616.995 AG
UNIVERSIDAD DE BUENOS AIRES. CATEDRA DE PATOLOGIA Y CLINICA DE LA TUBERCULOSIS. ANALES. vol. 29, 1970. irreg. Universidad de Buenos Aires, Catedra de Patologia y Clinica de la Tuberculosis, Avda. Velez Sarsfield 405, Buenos Aires, Argentina.

616.2 ZA ISSN 0084-5000
ZAMBIA. PNEUMOCONIOSIS MEDICAL AND RESEARCH BUREAU AND PNEUMOCONIOSIS COMPENSATION BOARD. ANNUAL REPORTS. 1964. a. 25 n. Government Printer, P.O. Box 136, Lusaka, Zambia.

MEDICAL SCIENCES — Rheumatology

616.742 FR ISSN 0065-1818
ACTUALITE RHUMATOLOGIQUE, PRESENTEE AU PRATICIEN; cahier annuel d'informations et de renseignements. a. price varies. Expansion Scientifique, 15 rue Saint Benoit, 75278 Paris Cedex 06, France.

616.742 US
AMERICAN RHEUMATISM ASSOCIATION. DIRECTORY. biennial. price varies. Arthritis Foundation, American Rheumatism Association Section, 3400 Peachtree Road, N.E., Atlanta, GA 30326.

616.7 FR ISSN 0066-3522
ANNUAIRE NATIONAL DES SPECIALISTES QUALIFIES EXCLUSIFS EN RHUMATOLOGIE. 1962. a. 28 F. Revue de Medecine, 40, rue Paul-Valery, 75116 Paris, France.

616.7 US ISSN 0191-2836
ARTHRITIS FOUNDATION. ANNUAL REPORT. 1965? a. Arthritis Foundation, 3400 Peachtree Rd. N.E., Ste. 1101, Atlanta, GA 30326.

616.7 US ISSN 0518-794X
ARTHRITIS FOUNDATION. CONFERENCE SERIES. irreg.; no. 21, 1977. price varies. Arthritis Foundation, 3400 Peachtree Rd., N.E., Atlanta, GA 30326.

616.742 GE ISSN 0067-5199
BEITRAEGE ZUR RHEUMATOLOGIE. 1958. irreg. price varies. VEB Verlag Volk und Gesundheit, Neue Gruenstr. 18, 102 Berlin, German Democratic Republic. Ed. Kurt Seidel.

616.7 SW
BERTINE KOPERBERG CONFERENCE (PROCEEDINGS) (Supplement to: Scandinavian Journal of Rheumatology) 2nd, 1978. irreg. $28.50. Almqvist & Wiksell International, Box 62, S-101 20 Stockholm, Sweden. Ed. T. W. Feltkamp. illus.

616.742 CN ISSN 0068-8258
C.A.R. SCOPE. 5-6/yr. membership. Canadian Arthritis and Rheumatism Society, 45 Charles St., East, Toronto Ont. M4Y 1S3, Canada.

616.742 GW ISSN 0070-4121
DEUTSCHE GESELLSCHAFT FUER RHEUMATOLOGIE. VERHANDLUNGEN. (Supplement to: Zeitschrift fuer Rheumatologie) (Text in German; summaries in English and French) 1969. irreg., vol. 5, 1978. price varies. Dr. Dietrich Steinkopff Verlag, Saalbaustr. 12, Postfach 11 1008, 6100 Darmstadt 11, W. Germany (B.R.D.) adv. index. circ. 2,000. Indexed: Curr.Cont. Ind.Med.

616.742 SZ ISSN 0071-7851
FORTBILDUNGSKURSE FUER RHEUMATOLOGIE. (Text in German) 1971. irreg. (approx. 1/yr.) 90 Fr.($54) per vol. (1981 price) S. Karger AG, Allschwilerstrasse 10, P.O. Box, CH-4009 Basel, Switzerland. Eds. G. Kaganas, W. Mueller, F. Wagenhaeuser. (reprint service avail. from ISI) Indexed: Biol.Abstr. Chem.Abstr. Curr.Cont. Ind.Med.

616.742 UK
MATHILDA AND TERENCE KENNEDY INSTITUTE OF RHEUMATOLOGY. ANNUAL REPORT. a., 10th 1976. free. Mathilda and Terence Kennedy Institute of Rheumatology, Bute Gardens, Hammersmith, London W6 7DW, England. circ. 2,000(controlled)

616.742 IT ISSN 0048-7449
REUMATISMO. (Supplements accompany some vols) 1949. irreg. L.12000. (Societa Italiana per lo Studio del Reumatismo e per la Lotta Contro le Malattie Reumatiche) Longanesi & C., Sezione Redi, Via Borghetto 5, 20122 Milan, Italy. Ed. Elisa Cirla. adv. bk. rev. illus. Indexed: Biol.Abstr. Chem.Abstr. Ind.Med.

616.742 US ISSN 0080-2700
RHEUMATISM REVIEW. 1935. biennial, 23rd, 1978. price varies. ‡ Arthritis Foundation, 3400 Peachtree Rd., N.E., Atlanta, GA 30326. Ed. Dr. William Mikkelsen.

616.742   GW   ISSN 0080-2719
RHEUMATISMUS. (Text in English, French, German) 1938. irreg., vol. 44, 1979. price varies. Dr. Dietrich Steinkopff Verlag, Saalbaustr. 12, Postfach 11 1008, 6100 Darmstadt 11, W. Germany (B.R.D.) Ed. Rudolf Schoen. index. circ. 1,500.

616.742   SZ   ISSN 0080-2727
RHEUMATOLOGY. (Text in English) 1966. irreg. (approx. 1/yr.) 120 Fr.($72) per vol. (1981 price) S. Karger AG, Allschwilerstrasse 10, P.O. Box, CH-4009 Basel, Switzerland. Ed. J. Rotstein. (reprint service avail. from ISI) Indexed: Biol.Abstr. Chem.Abstr. Curr.Cont. Ind.Med.

616.7   UK
TOPICAL REVIEWS IN RHEUMATIC DISORDERS. 1980. biennial. £12.50. John Wright & Sons Ltd., 42-44 Triangle West, Bristol BS8 1EX, England.

616.7   US   ISSN 0190-5422
U.S. NATIONAL ARTHRITIS ADVISORY BOARD. ANNUAL REPORT. a. U.S. National Arthritis Advisory Board, Box 30286, Bethesda, MD 20014. Key Title: Annual Report - National Arthritis Advisory Board.

MEDICAL SCIENCES — Surgery

617   GE
ACTA CHIRURGIAE MAXILLO-FACIALIS. 1975. irreg., vol. 5, 1979. price varies. (Internationale Gesellschaft fuer Kiefer-Gesichts-Chirurgie) Johann Ambrosius Barth Verlag, Salomonstr. 18b, 701 Leipzig, E. Germany (D.D.R.)

ACTA NEUROCHIRURGICA. SUPPLEMENT. see MEDICAL SCIENCES — Psychiatry And Neurology

ADVANCES AND TECHNICAL STANDARDS IN NEUROSURGERY. see MEDICAL SCIENCES — Psychiatry And Neurology

ADVANCES IN NEUROSURGERY. see MEDICAL SCIENCES — Psychiatry And Neurology

617.082   US   ISSN 0065-3411
ADVANCES IN SURGERY. 1966. a. price varies. Year Book Medical Publishers, Inc., 35 E. Wacker Dr., Chicago, IL 60601. Indexed: Ind.Med.

617.585   US   ISSN 0065-7190
AMERICAN ASSOCIATION OF FOOT SPECIALISTS. PROGRAM JOURNAL.* 1958. a. $35. American Association of Foot Specialists, Inc., P.O. Box 54, 1801 Vauxhall Rd., Union, NJ 02083.
Podiatry

617.5   US   ISSN 0065-7204
AMERICAN ASSOCIATION OF GENITO-URINARY SURGEONS. TRANSACTIONS. a. American Association of Genito-Urinary Surgeons, 22 W. Greene St., Baltimore, MD 21201. (also avail. in microform from UMI) Indexed: Ind.Med.

610   US
AMERICAN LECTURES IN SPORTSMEDICINE, PHYSICAL EDUCATION AND RECREATION. irreg. price varies. Charles C. Thomas, Publisher, 301-327 E. Lawrence Ave., Springfield, IL 62717.

617.585   US   ISSN 0065-9770
AMERICAN PODIATRY ASSOCIATION. DESK REFERENCE AND DIRECTORY WITH CATALOGUE OF AUDIO-VISUAL, INFORMATIONAL AND EDUCATIONAL MATERIALS AND STANDARD PODIATRIC NOMENCLATURE. 1948. a. $20. American Podiatry Association, 20 Chevy Chase Circle, N.W., Washington, DC 20015. circ. controlled.
Podiatry

617   US   ISSN 0066-0078
AMERICAN SOCIETY FOR ARTIFICIAL INTERNAL ORGANS. TRANSACTIONS. 1955. a. American Society for Artificial Organs, Inc., c/o Dr. George E. Schreiner, Department of Medicine, Georgetown University Hospital, Washington, DC 20007. Indexed: Ind.Med.

617   US
AMERICAN SOCIETY OF PLASTIC AND RECONSTRUCTIVE SURGEONS. SYMPOSIA. vol. 5, 1973. irreg., vol. 19, 1978. price varies. C. V. Mosby Co., 11830 Westline Industrial Dr., St. Louis, MO 63140.

617   US   ISSN 0066-0833
AMERICAN SURGICAL ASSOCIATION. TRANSACTIONS. 1882. a. J. B. Lippincott Co., E. Washington Sq., Philadelphia, PA 19105. circ. controlled.

617   AG   ISSN 0066-1465
ANALES DE CIRUGIA. 1935. irreg. Calle Paraguay 40, Rosario, Prov. de Santa Fe, Argentina.

617   FR   ISSN 0066-3417
ANNUAIRE NATIONAL DES SPECIALISTES QUALIFIES EN CHIRURGIE. 1967. irreg. 26 F. Revue de Medecine, 40, rue Paul- Valery, 75116 Paris, France.

617   IT   ISSN 0066-670X
ARCHIVIO PUTTI DI CHIRURGIA DEGLI ORGANI DI MOVIMENTO. (Text in Italian; summaries in English, French, German and Italian) 1951. a. L.30000($30) Aulo Gaggi Editore, Via Andrea Costa 131/5, 40134 Bologna, Italy. Ed. O. Scaglietti. bk. rev. circ. 1,500. Indexed: Ind.Med.

617   BL   ISSN 0066-7846
ARQUIVOS DE CIRURGIA CLINICA E EXPERIMENTAL.* (Supplements accompany some issues) (Some summaries in English) 1937. irreg. Universidade de Sao Paulo, Hospital das Clinicas, Caixa Postal 4066, Sao Paulo, Brazil.

617   IT   ISSN 0066-9873
ASSOCIAZIONE MEDICA CHIRURGICA DI TIVOLI E DELLA VAL D'ANIENE. ATTI E MEMORIE.* 1961. biennial. free. Associazione Medica Chirurgica di Tivoli e della Val d'Aniene, Tivoli, Italy. index.

BEITRAEGE ZUR NEUROCHIRURGIE. see MEDICAL SCIENCES — Psychiatry And Neurology

CARDIOVASCULAR SURGERY. see MEDICAL SCIENCES — Cardiovascular Diseases

CLINICAL NEUROSURGERY; PROCEEDINGS. see MEDICAL SCIENCES — Psychiatry And Neurology

CURRENT TOPICS IN CRITICAL CARE MEDICINE. see MEDICAL SCIENCES

617   US   ISSN 0070-2196
CURRENT TOPICS IN SURGICAL RESEARCH. 1969. irreg., 1971, vol. 3. price varies. Academic Press, Inc., 111 Fifth Ave., New York, NY 10003. Eds. G. D. Zuidema, D. B. Skinner.

617   SZ
EUROPEAN SOCIETY FOR SURGICAL RESEARCH. CONGRESS PROCEEDINGS. (Supplement to: European Surgical Research) 14th, 1979. irreg. $30.10. S. Karger AG, Allschwilerstrasse 10, P.O. Box, CH-4009 Basel, Switzerland. Ed. R. Camprodon.

617   GW   ISSN 0071-7916
FORTSCHRITTE DER KIEFER- UND GESICHTS-CHIRURGIE. (Some summaries in English, French and Spanish) 1955. irreg., vol. 25, 1980. price varies. Georg Thieme Verlag, Herdweg 63, Postfach 732, 7000 Stuttgart 1, W. Germany (B.R.D.) Indexed: Ind.Med.

617   US   ISSN 0071-8041
FORUM ON FUNDAMENTAL SURGICAL PROBLEMS. Variant title: Surgical Forum. 1950. a. $9. American College of Surgeons, 55 E. Erie St., Chicago, IL 60611. Ed. Marilyn Lux. circ. 6,000.

INTERNATIONAL CONGRESS OF NEUROLOGICAL SURGERY. ABSTRACTS OF PAPERS. see MEDICAL SCIENCES — Psychiatry And Neurology

617.95   NE   ISSN 0579-3785
INTERNATIONAL CONGRESS OF PLASTIC AND RECONSTRUCTIVE SURGERY. TRANSACTIONS.* (Subseries of International Congress Series) 1959. irreg. Excerpta Medica, P.O.B. 211, Amsterdam, Netherland (Inquire: John Watson, 122 Harley St., London WIN 1AN, England)
Plastic surgery

INTERNATIONAL CONGRESS OF PSYCHOSURGERY. PROCEEDING. see MEDICAL SCIENCES — Psychiatry And Neurology

617   US
INTERNATIONAL SYMPOSIUM ON PLASTIC AND RECONSTRUCTIVE SURGERY OF THE FACE AND NECK. PROCEEDINGS. 1972. irreg., latest, 1977. Grune and Stratton, Inc. (Subsidiary of: Harcourt Brace Jovanovich, Inc.) 111 Fifth Ave., New York, NY 10003. Eds. John Conley, John T. Dickinson. bibl. illus.
Plastic surgery

617   US   ISSN 0075-3815
JOHN ALEXANDER MONOGRAPH SERIES ON VARIOUS PHASES OF THORACIC SURGERY. irreg. price varies. Charles C. Thomas, Publisher, 301-327 E. Lawrence Ave., Springfield, IL 62717.
Thoracic surgery

607   IT
JOURNAL OF CARDIOVASCULAR SURGERY. CONGRESS PROCEEDINGS. irreg. price varies. (International Cardiovascular Society) Edizioni Minerva Medica, Corso Bramante 83-85, 10126 Turin, Italy.
Cardiovascular surgery

617   US   ISSN 0023-8236
LANGENBECKS ARCHIV FUER CHIRURGIE. (Text in German; summaries in English & German) 1860. 2 vols. per yr., 4 nos. per vol. $278. (Deutsche Gesellschaft fuer Chirurgie, GW) Springer-Verlag, 175 Fifth Ave., New York, NY 10010. (Also Berlin, Heidelberg, Vienna) Ed.Bd. (also avail. in microform; back issues avail.; reprint service avail. from ISI) Indexed: Biol.Abstr. Chem.Abstr. Ind.Med.
Incorporating: Burns Beitraege fuer Klinische Chirurgie (ISSN 0007-2680)

617.102   SZ   ISSN 0076-6070
MEDICINE AND SPORT. (Text in English) 1966. irreg. (approx. 1/yr.) 100 Fr.($60) per vol. (1981 price) S. Karger AG, Allschwilerstrasse 10, P.O. Box, CH-4009 Basel, Switzerland. Eds. E. Jokl, M. Hebbelinck. (reprint service avail. from ISI) Indexed: Biol.Abstr. Chem.Abstr. Curr.Cont. Ind.Med.
Sports medicine

617   US   ISSN 0540-5556
MODERN SURGICAL MONOGRAPHS. 1959. irreg. price varies. Grune and Stratton, Inc. (Subsidiary of: Harcourt Brace Jovanovich, Inc.) 111 Fifth Ave., New York, NY 10003. Ed. Richard H. Egdahl, M.D.

617   US   ISSN 0196-1918
MODERN TECHNICS IN SURGERY. ABDOMINAL SURGERY. 1980. irreg., approx. a. price varies. Futura Publishing Co., 295 Main St., Box 330, Mount Kisco, NY 10549. Ed. Dr. Seymour I. Schwartz. index.

617.54   US   ISSN 0163-7029
MODERN TECHNICS IN SURGERY. CARDIAC/THORACIC SURGERY. 1979. irreg., approx. a. price varies. Futura Publishing Co., 295 Main St., Box 330, Mount Kisco, NY 10549. Ed. Dr. Lawrence H. Cohn. index.

617   US   ISSN 0271-8219
MODERN TECHNICS IN SURGERY. HEAD AND NECK SURGERY. 1981. irreg., approx. a. price varies. Futura Publishing Co., 295 Main St., Box 330, Mount Kisco, NY 10549. Ed. Dr. Moses Nussbaum. index.

617   US   ISSN 0163-7037
MODERN TECHNICS IN SURGERY. NEUROSURGERY. 1979. irreg., approx. a. price varies. Futura Publishing Co., 295 Main St., Box 330, Mount Kisco, NY 10549. Ed. Dr. Joseph Ransohoff. index.

617 US
MODERN TECHNICS IN SURGERY. UROLOGIC SURGERY. 1980. irreg., approx. a. price varies. Futura Publishing Co., 295 Main St., Box 330, Mount Kisco, NY 10549.

617.95 US
MONOGRAPHS ON PLASTIC SURGERY. 1973. irreg. price varies. Oxford University Press, 200 Madison Ave., New York, NY 10016 (And Ely House, 37 Dover St., London W1X 4AH, England)
Plastic surgery

NEUROLOGIA MEDICO-CHIRURGICA. see MEDICAL SCIENCES — Psychiatry And Neurology

NEUROPEDIATRICS; journal of pediatric neurobiology, neurology and neurosurgery. see MEDICAL SCIENCES — Pediatrics

617.96 GW ISSN 0079-4899
PRAKTISCHE CHIRURGIE. 1936. irreg., no. 92, 1980. price varies. Ferdinand Enke Verlag, Herdweg 63, 7000 Stuttgart 1, W. Germany (B.R.D.) Ed. H. Buerkle De La Camp.
Continues: Vortraege aus der Praktischen Chirurgie (ISSN 0083-6931)

PROGRESS IN NEUROLOGICAL SURGERY. see MEDICAL SCIENCES — Psychiatry And Neurology

PROGRESS IN PEDIATRIC SURGERY. see MEDICAL SCIENCES — Pediatrics

617 SZ ISSN 0079-6824
PROGRESS IN SURGERY. (Text in English) 1961. irreg. (approx. 1/yr.) 100 Fr.($60) per vol.(1981 price) S. Karger AG, Allschwilerstrasse 10, P.O. Box, CH-4009 Basel, Switzerland. Ed. Bd. (reprint service avail. from ISI) Indexed: Biol.Abstr. Chem.Abstr. Curr.Cont. Ind.Med.

617.95 SZ ISSN 0080-0260
RECONSTRUCTION SURGERY AND TRAUMATOLOGY. (Text in English) 1953. irreg. (approx. 1/yr.) 80 Fr.($80) per vol. (1981 price) S. Karger AG, Allschwilerstrasse 10, P.O. Box, CH-4009 Basel, Switzerland. Ed. G. Chapchal. (reprint service avail. from ISI) Indexed: Biol.Abstr. Chem.Abstr. Curr.Cont. Ind.Med.

610 UK
ROYAL COLLEGE OF SURGEONS OF ENGLAND. HANDBOOK. quinquennial. Royal College of Surgeons of England, Lincoln's Inn Fields, London WC2A 3PN, England.

616 US ISSN 0160-2489
SEMINARS IN NEUROLOGICAL SURGERY. 1978. irreg., no. 5, 1979. Raven Press, 1140 Ave. of the Americas, New York, NY 10036.

617 US
SOUTHERN SURGICAL ASSOCIATION. TRANSACTIONS. a. $25. J. B. Lippincott Co., E. Washington Sq., Philadelphia, PA 19105. (reprint service avail. from UMI,ISI)

617.102 GE ISSN 0075-8655
SPORTMEDIZINISCHE SCHRIFTENREIHE. 1967. irreg., vol. 16, 1978. price varies. (Deutsche Hochschule fuer Koerperkultur Leipzig) Johann Ambrosius Barth Verlag, Salomonstr. 18b, 701 Leipzig, E. Germany (D.D.R.) Eds. K. Tittel, L. Pickenheim, H. Doebler. (back issues avail.)
Sports medicine

617.102 US ISSN 0081-427X
STANDARD NOMENCLATURE OF ATHLETIC INJURIES. 1966. irreg. $2. American Medical Association, Committee on Sports Injuries, 535 N. Dearborn St., Chicago, IL 60610. index.
Sports medicine

616 US ISSN 0081-9638
SURGERY ANNUAL. a. price varies. Appleton-Century-Crofts, 292 Madison Ave., New York, NY 10017.

617 MX
SURGERY YEARBOOK. (Text in Spanish) a. Mex.$30. Academia Mexicana de Cirugia, Calles Brasil y Venezuela, Apdo. Postal 7994, Mexico 1 D.F., Mexico.

617 US ISSN 0081-9646
SURGICAL PATHOLOGY. 4th edt., 1968. irreg; 5th edt., 1974. $59.50. C. V. Mosby Co., 11830 Westline Industrial Dr., St. Louis, MO 63141. Ed. Lauren V. Ackerman, M.D.

617 US ISSN 0081-9654
SURGICAL TRADE BUYERS GUIDE. 1940. a. $18 $24 foreign. Cassak Publications, Inc., 2009 Morris Ave., Union, NJ 07083. Ed. Laurie N. Cassak. adv. circ. 5,000.

617.95 NE ISSN 0082-0482
SWISS SOCIETY OF PLASTIC AND RECONSTRUCTIVE SURGEONS. PROCEEDINGS (OF) ANNUAL MEETING.* 1965. a. Excerpta Medica, P.O. Box 211, Amsterdam, Netherlands (And New York Academy of Medicine, 2 E. 103 St., New York, N.Y. 10029)
Plastic surgery

617 617.6 FR ISSN 0396-0382
SYNDICAT GENERAL DES INDUSTRIES MEDICO - CHIRURGICALES ET DENTAIRES. ANNUAIRE. vol. 2, 1975. a. Editions de Chabassol, 30 rue de Gramont, 75002 Paris, France.

617 US ISSN 0074-3984
TRANSPLANTATION TODAY. Represents: International Congress of the Transplantation Society. Proceedings. 1967. biennial, vol. 5, 1979. Grune and Stratton, Inc. (Subsidiary of: Harcourt Brace Jovanovich, Inc.) 111 Fifth Avenue, New York, NY 10003. Ed. Dr. Felix T. Rapaport.

YEAR BOOK OF NEUROLOGY & NEUROSURGERY. see MEDICAL SCIENCES — Psychiatry And Neurology

617.95 US ISSN 0084-3962
YEAR BOOK OF PLASTIC AND RECONSTRUCTIVE SURGERY. 1970. a. Year Book Medical Publishers, Inc., 35 E. Wacker Dr., Chicago, IL 60601. Ed. Bd.
Plastic surgery

617.005 US ISSN 0090-3671
YEAR BOOK OF SURGERY. 1971. a. ‡ Year Book Medical Publishers, Inc., 35 East Wacker Drive, Chicago, IL 60601. Ed. Bd. illus.
Formerly: Year Book of General Surgery.

MEDICAL SCIENCES — Urology And Nephrology

616.6 FR ISSN 0073-3326
ACTUALITES NEPHROLOGIQUES. 1960. a. price varies. (Hopital Necker, Clinique Nephrologique) Flammarion Medecine Sciences, 20 rue de Vaugirard, 75006 Paris, France (U.S. subscr. address: S.F.P.A., c/o Mr. Benech, 14 E. 60th St., New York, NY 10022) Ed. J. P. Grunfeld. cum.index: 1960-69.

616.6 US ISSN 0084-5957
ADVANCES IN NEPHROLOGY FROM THE NECKER HOSPITAL. 1971. a. ‡ Yearbook Medical Publishers, Inc., 35 E. Wacker Dr., Chicago, IL 60601. Indexed: Ind.Med.

AMERICAN ASSOCIATION OF GENITO-URINARY SURGEONS. TRANSACTIONS. see MEDICAL SCIENCES — Surgery

616.6 UK ISSN 0007-1331
BRITISH JOURNAL OF UROLOGY. 1929. 6/yr. £25($60) (British Association of Urological Surgeons) Longman Group Ltd., Journals Division, Fourth Ave., Harlow, Essex, England (Dist. in U.S. by: Williams & Wilkins Co., 428 E. Preston St., Baltimore, MD 21202) Ed. G.D. Chisholm. adv. bk. rev. abstr. bibl. illus. index; cum.index. (also avail. in microform from UMI) Indexed: Biol.Abstr. Chem.Abstr. Ind.Med. Nutr.Abstr.

616.6 US ISSN 0270-2088
CONTROVERSIES IN NEPHROLOGY. 1979. a. Georgetown University Hospital, Nephrology Division, 3800 Reservoir Rd., N.W., Washington, DC 20007.

610 US ISSN 0148-4265
CURRENT NEPHROLOGY. 1977. a. $28. Houghton Mifflin Professional Publishers, Medical Division, 2 Park St., Boston, MA 02107. Ed. Harvey C. Gonick, M.D. circ. 1,300.

616.6 US ISSN 0070-413X
DEUTSCHE GESELLSCHAFT FUER UROLOGIE. VERHANDLUNGSBERICHT. 1962, session 19. irreg., 31st session, 1980. price varies. Springer-Verlag, 175 Fifth Ave., New York, NY 10010 (also Berlin, Heidelberg, Vienna) (reprint service avail. from ISI)

616.6 SW
EUROPEAN COLLOQUIUM ON RENAL PHYSIOLOGY (PROCEEDINGS) (Supplement to: Uppsala Journal of Medical Sciences) 3rd, 1979. irreg. $23.80. Almqvist & Wiksell International, Box 62, S-101 20 Stockholm, Sweden. Ed. Hans R. Ulfendahl.

616.6 GW ISSN 0071-7975
FORTSCHRITTE DER UROLOGIE UND NEPHROLOGIE. (Text in German and English) 1970. irreg., vol. 12, 1979. price varies. Dr. Dietrich Steinkopff Verlag, Saalbaustr. 12, Postfach 11 1008, 6100 Darmstadt 11, W. Germany (B.R.D.) Ed. W. Vahlensieck. index. circ. 2,000.

616.6 SZ ISSN 0074-378X
INTERNATIONAL CONGRESS OF NEPHROLOGY. PROCEEDINGS. (Text in English) 1960. irreg., 7th, 1978, Montreal. 150 Fr.($90) per vol. (1981 price) (International Society of Nephrology) S. Karger AG, Allschwilerstrasse 10, P.O. Box, CH-4009 Basel, Switzerland. Ed. M. Bergeron. (reprint service avail. from ISI)

616.6 FR ISSN 0074-8579
INTERNATIONAL SOCIETY OF UROLOGY. REPORTS OF CONGRESS. (Reports published in host country) irreg., 1975, 17th, Madrid. International Society of Urology, c/o Prof. Rene Kuess, 63 Ave. Niel, 75017 Paris, France.

616.6 SZ ISSN 0378-8490
KARGER HIGHLIGHTS: NEPHROLOGY; reprinted selected top articles. (Text in English) 1978. a. 15 Fr.($9) (1981 price) S. Karger AG, Allschwilerstrasse 10, P.O. Box, CH-4009 Basel, Switzerland. Ed. G.M. Berlyne. circ. 6,600. (reprint service avail. from ISI) Indexed: Biol.Abstr. Curr.Cont.

616.6 US
KIDNEY INTERNATIONAL. SUPPLEMENT. 1974. irreg.; vol. 8, 1977. price varies (free to subscribers of Kidney International) Springer-Verlag, 175 Fifth Ave., New York, NY 10010 (Also Berlin, Heidelberg, Vienna) (reprint service avail. from ISI)

MODERN TECHNICS IN SURGERY. UROLOGIC SURGERY. see MEDICAL SCIENCES — Surgery

616.6 US ISSN 0077-5096
NATIONAL KIDNEY FOUNDATION. ANNUAL REPORT. 1957/58. a. free. National Kidney Foundation, 2 Park Ave., New York, NY 10016.

616.6 616.132 US ISSN 0092-2900
PERSPECTIVES IN NEPHROLOGY AND HYPERTENSION. 1973. irreg., unnumbered, latest 1979. price varies. John Wiley & Sons, Inc., 605 Third Ave., New York, NY 10016. Ed. E.L. Becker. Indexed: Ind.Med.
Nephrology and Hypertension

616.6 FR ISSN 0083-4769
URO-NEPHRO; ANNUAIRE DE L'UROLOGIE ET DE LA NEPHROLOGIE.* 1969. irreg. price varies. Laboratoires Winthrop, 92-98 Bld. Victor-Hugo, Clichy, France.

616.6 US ISSN 0084-4071
YEAR BOOK OF UROLOGY. 1933. a. price varies. ‡ Year Book Medical Publishers, Inc., 35 E. Wacker Dr., Chicago, IL 60601. Eds. Jay Y. Gillenwater, Stuart S. Howards.

MEETINGS AND CONGRESSES

578 011 US ISSN 0569-2628
A A F M PROCEEDINGS OF ANNUAL MEETING. 1952. a. $8. American Association of Feed Microscopists, c/o Mrs. Wilma J. Hill, Secy-Treas, Box 586, Quincy, IL 62301. circ. 200.

AMERICAN LIBRARY ASSOCIATION. ANNUAL CONFERENCE PROGRAM. see *LIBRARY AND INFORMATION SCIENCES*

011 BE
ANNUAL INTERNATIONAL CONGRESS CALENDAR. (Text in English) 1961. a. 900 Fr. Union of International Associations, 1, rue aux Laines, 1000 Brussels, Belgium. Ed. G. de Coninck. adv. index. cum.index.

610 011 SZ ISSN 0301-2891
CALENDAR OF INTERNATIONAL AND REGIONAL CONGRESSES OF MEDICAL SCIENCES. (Text in English and French) 1949. a. 14 Fr.($5.50). Council for International Organizations of Medical Sciences - Conseil des Organisations Internationales des Sciences Medicales, c/o World Health Organization, 20 Ave. Appia, CH-1211 Geneva 27, Switzerland. Ed. Dr. Louis J. Verhoestraete. adv.
Formed by the merger of, and assuming the numbering of the former: Calendar of International Congresses of Medical Sciences (ISSN 0589-915X) & Calendar of Regional Congresses of Medical Sciences (ISSN 0574-248X)

011 338 CN ISSN 0068-8967
CANADIAN INDUSTRY SHOWS AND EXHIBITIONS. 1964. a. Can.$16. Maclean-Hunter Ltd., 481 University Ave., Toronto, Ont. M5W 1A7, Canada. Ed. Betty Gay.

CONFERENCE PAPERS ANNUAL INDEX. see *ABSTRACTING AND INDEXING SERVICES*

011 910.2 UK
CONFERENCES MEETINGS & EXHIBITIONS WELCOME. 1979. a. free to qualified personnel. Lewis Publications Ltd., 31 Castle St., Kingston upon Thames, Surrey KT1 1ST, England. Ed. David Jacobson. adv. circ. 25,000.

711 UK
CONGRESS IN PARK AND RECREATION ADMINISTRATION. PROGRAMME. triennial; 1983, Barcelona. International Federation of Park and Recreation Administration, c/o Kenneth L. Morgan, Sec. Gen., The Grotto, Lower Basildon, Reading, Berks. RG8 9NE, England.
Formerly: World Congress in Public Park Administration. Programme (ISSN 0510-8233)

060 BE ISSN 0573-5661
CONGRESS OF INTERNATIONAL CONGRESS ORGANIZERS AND TECHNICIANS. PROCEEDING. (Subseries of International Congress Sciences Series) irreg., 6th, 1977, Kyoto. 600 Fr. Union of International Associations, 1, rue aux Laines, 1000 Brussels, Belgium.

011 CN ISSN 0315-100X
CONVENTIONS & MEETINGS-CANADA. 1971. a. Can.$25. Effective Communications Ltd., 505 Consumers Rd., Suite 303, Willowdale, Ont. M2J 4V8, Canada. Ed. J. W. Nuttall. adv. circ. 10,174(controlled) (back issues avail.)

COUNCIL OF LEGAL EDUCATION. CALENDAR. see *LAW*

610 011 SP ISSN 0210-5578
DIARIO DE CONGRESOS MEDICOS. irreg. Ediciones Doyma S.A., Travesera de Gracia 17-21, Barcelona 21, Spain. adv. circ. 30,000.

011 US ISSN 0417-5751
DIRECTORY OF CONVENTIONS. (Includes Mid-Year Supplements) 1952. a. plus supplement. $60. Successful Meetings, Directory Department, 633 Third Ave., New York, NY 10017. Ed. Toula de Prince. circ. 3,000.

DOMOVA POKLADNICA. see *LITERATURE*

011 EI
EUROPEAN PARLIAMENT. SELECTED DOCUMENTS. 1967. irreg. Office for Official Publications of the European Communities, Case Postal 1003, Luxembourg (Dist. in the U.S. by: European Community Information Service, 2100 M St., NW, Suite 707, Washington, DC 20037) Ed. Bd. charts.

FRANCE. INSTITUT NATIONAL DE LA SANTE ET DE LA RECHERCHE MEDICALE. COLLOQUES. see *MEDICAL SCIENCES*

011 AG ISSN 0301-7567
GUIA DE REUNIONES CIENTIFICAS Y TECNICAS EN LA ARGENTINA. 1959. a. free. Secretaria de Estado de Ciencia y Tecnologia, Ministerio de Cultura y Educacion, Av. Cordoba 831, 1054 Buenos Aires, Argentina. circ. 4,000.

011 363.6 US
INTERNATIONAL ASSOCIATION OF CORONERS AND MEDICAL EXAMINERS. PROCEEDINGS. 1970. a. $20. International Association of Coroners and Medical Examiners, 2121 Adelbert Road, Cleveland, OH 44106. Ed. Dr. S. R. Gerber. circ. 300.

011 BE ISSN 0538-6772
INTERNATIONAL CONGRESS SCIENCE SERIES. 1961. irreg. price varies. Union of International Associations, 1,rue aux Laines, 1000 Brussels, Belgium.

011 NE ISSN 0531-5131
INTERNATIONAL CONGRESS SERIES. irreg., no. 360, 1975. price varies. Excerpta Medica, Box 211, 1000 AE Amsterdam, Netherlands.

658.8 US
INTERNATIONAL CONVENTION FACILITIES DIRECTORY. a. $10. Bill Communications, Inc., 633 Third Ave, New York, NY 10017.

KALENDAR ODBORARA. see *LABOR UNIONS*

057.87 CS
KULTURNOPOLITICKY KALENDAR. a. 30 Kcs. Obzor, Ceskoslovenskej Armady 29, 893 36 Bratislava, Czechoslovakia. illus.

MEETINGS, CONFERENCES & CONVENTIONS: A FINANCIAL POST GUIDE. see *BUSINESS AND ECONOMICS*

627 011 US
NATIONAL CONFERENCE ON FLUID POWER. PROCEEDINGS. Title varies: National Conference on Industrial Hydraulics. Proceedings. 1947. a. $30. (Illinois Institute of Technology) National Conference on Fluid Power, 10 W. 32nd St., Rm. 232, Chicago, IL 60616. Ed. Mrs. Marian Walker, Sec. circ. 500.

647 US ISSN 0094-5242
OFFICIAL MEETING FACILITIES GUIDE. 1974. $15. Ziff-Davis Publishing Co., Public Transportation & Travel Division, Box 606, Neptune, NJ 07753. illus.

011 UK
SCOTLAND: CONFERENCES, MEETINGS, SEMINARS. irreg. free. Scottish Tourist Board, 23 Ravelston Terrace, Edinburgh EH4 3EU, Scotland.

SVETOVY KONGRES SLOVAKOV. BULLETIN. see *ETHNIC INTERESTS*

SYMPOSIUM ON ETHICAL ISSUES IN HUMAN EXPERIMENTATION. PROCEEDINGS. see *MEDICAL SCIENCES*

METALLURGY

see also Metallurgy—Welding

669 US
A I S E YEARBOOK. 1907. a. $30 to non-members; members $25. Association of Iron and Steel Engineers, Suite 2350, Three Gateway Center, Pittsburgh, PA 15222. Ed. John A. Kotsch. index. circ. 1,600.
Formerly: Association of Iron and Steel Engineers. A I S E Proceedings.

ACTA POLYTECHNICA SCANDINAVICA. CHEMISTRY INCLUDING METALLURGY SERIES. see *CHEMISTRY*

669 620.1 US ISSN 0069-8490
ADVANCES IN X-RAY ANALYSIS. Represents: Annual Conference on Applications of X-Ray Analysis. Proceedings. 1960. a. price varies. (University of Denver, Denver Research Institute) Plenum Press, 233 Spring St., New York, NY 10013.

669 FR ISSN 0065-4256
AGENDA DE LA QUINCAILLERIE; fers et metaux. 1956. a. free to members of the Syndicate. Regie Publicite Industrielle, 36 rue du Fer-a-Moulin, 75005 Paris, France.

669 629.8 PL
AKADEMIA GORNICZO-HUTNICZA IM. STANISLAWA STASZICA. INSTYTUT MASZYN HUTNICZYCH I AUTOMATYKI. PRACE. (Subseries of its Zeszyty Naukowe) (Summaries in German and Russian) 1972. 2/yr. 19 Zl. single issue. Panstwowe Wydawnictwo Naukowe, Miodowa 10, Warsaw, Poland (Dist. by: Ars Polona-Ruch, Krakowskie Przedmiescie 7, Warsaw, Poland) illus. circ. 300-500. Indexed: Appl.Mech.Rev. Ref.Zh.

671 PL ISSN 0075-7004
AKADEMIA GORNICZO-HUTNICZA IM. STANISLAWA STASZICA. ZESZYTY NAUKOWE. HUTNICTWO.* (Text in Polish; summaries in English and Russian) 1959. irreg. price varies. Panstwowe Wydawnictwo Naukowe, Miodowa 10, Warsaw, Poland (Dist. by Ars Polona-Ruch, Krakowskie Przedmiescie 7, Warsaw, Poland) Ed. Michal Odlanicki-Poczobutt.

669 UR
AKADEMIYA NAUK KAZAKHSKOI S.S.R. INSTITUT METALLURGII I OBOGASHCHENIYA. TRUDY. vol. 52, 1977. irreg. 1.80 Rub. per no. Izdatel'stvo Nauka Kazakhskoi S.S.R., Ul.Shevchenko 28, 480021 Alma-Ata, U.S.S.R. Ed. A. Kunaev. abstr. bibl. illus. circ. 1,000.

669.722 AT ISSN 0084-6279
ALUMINIUM DEVELOPMENT COUNCIL OF AUSTRALIA. TECHNICAL PAPERS. 1967. irreg. Aluminium Development Council of Australia, 99 Elizabeth St., Sydney, N.S.W. 2000, Australia.
Aluminum

669.722 GW
ALUMINIUM INTERN: ALUMINIUM UND AUTOMOBIL. irreg. (approx. 4/yr.) DM.38. (Aluminium-Zentrale e.V.) Aluminium-Verlag GmbH, Koenigsallee 30, Postfach 1207, 4000 Duesseldorf 1, W. Germany(B.R.D.)

673 US ISSN 0065-6658
ALUMINUM STANDARDS AND DATA. 1968. biennial. $3. Aluminum Association, Inc., 818 Connecticut Ave., Washington, DC 20006. circ. 40,000. (also avail. in microform)

673 US
ALUMINUM STANDARDS AND DATA-METRIC. biennial. $3. Aluminum Association, Inc., 818 Connecticut Ave., N.W., Washington, DC 20006. circ. 40,000. (also avail. in microform)

673 338.4 US ISSN 0065-6666
ALUMINUM STATISTICAL REVIEW. (Title varies: Aluminum Industry Annual Statistical Review) 1962. a. $5. Aluminum Association, Inc., Statistical & Marketing Research Committee, 818 Connecticut Ave., N.W., Washington, DC 20006. circ. 15,000.

669.722 UK ISSN 0141-531X
ALUMINUM WORLD SURVEY. 1969. irreg., latest edt., 1977. £15($33) Metal Bulletin Ltd., Park House, 3 Park Terrace, Worcester Park, Surrey, England.
Aluminum

669.028 671.2 US ISSN 0065-8375
AMERICAN FOUNDRYMEN'S SOCIETY. TRANSACTIONS. 1896. a. $100 to non-members. American Foundrymen's Society, Inc, Golf & Wolf Rds, Des Plaines, IL 60016. cum.index: 10 years. (also avail. in microform from UMI; reprint service avail. from UMI)

METALLURGY

AMERICAN INSTITUTE OF MINING, METALLURGICAL AND PETROLEUM ENGINEERS. NATIONAL OPEN HEARTH AND BASIC OXYGEN STEEL DIVISION. PROCEEDINGS OF THE CONFERENCE. see *MINES AND MINING INDUSTRY*

ANNUAL BOOK OF A S T M STANDARDS. PART 1. STEEL PIPING, TUBING, AND FITTINGS. (American Society for Testing and Materials) see *ENGINEERING — Engineering Mechanics And Materials*

ANNUAL BOOK OF A S T M STANDARDS. PART 2. FERROUS CASTINGS, FERRO-ALLOYS. see *ENGINEERING — Engineering Mechanics And Materials*

ANNUAL BOOK OF A S T M STANDARDS. PART 3. STEEL PLATE, SHEET, STRIP AND WIRE; METALLIC COATED PRODUCTS. see *ENGINEERING — Engineering Mechanics And Materials*

ANNUAL BOOK OF A S T M STANDARDS. PART 4. STRUCTURAL STEEL; CONCRETE REINFORCING STEEL; PRESSURE VESSEL PLATE AND FORGINGS; STEEL RAILS, WHEELS, AND TIRES; STEEL FASTENERS. see *ENGINEERING — Engineering Mechanics And Materials*

ANNUAL BOOK OF A S T M STANDARDS. PART 5. STEEL BARS, CHAIN, AND SPRINGS; BEARING STEEL; STEEL FORGINGS. see *ENGINEERING — Engineering Mechanics And Materials*

ANNUAL BOOK OF A S T M STANDARDS. PART 6. COPPER AND COPPER ALLOYS (INCLUDING ELECTRICAL CONDUCTORS) see *ENGINEERING — Engineering Mechanics And Materials*

ANNUAL BOOK OF A S T M STANDARDS. PART 7. DIE-CAST METALS; LIGHT METALS AND ALLOYS (INCLUDING ELECTRICAL CONDUCTORS) see *ENGINEERING — Engineering Mechanics And Materials*

ANNUAL BOOK OF A S T M STANDARDS. PART 8. NONFERROUS METALS--NICKEL, LEAD, AND TIN ALLOYS, PRECIOUS METALS, PRIMARY METALS; REACTIVE METALS. see *ENGINEERING — Engineering Mechanics And Materials*

ANNUAL BOOK OF A S T M STANDARDS. PART 9. ELECTRODEPOSITED METALLIC COATINGS; METAL POWDERS, SINTERED P/M STRUCTURAL PARTS. see *ENGINEERING — Engineering Mechanics And Materials*

ANNUAL BOOK OF A S T M STANDARDS. PART 10. METALS - MECHANICAL, FRACTURE, AND CORROSION TESTING; FATIGUE; EROSION; EFFECT OF TEMPERATURE. see *ENGINEERING — Engineering Mechanics And Materials*

ANNUAL BOOK OF A S T M STANDARDS. PART 11. METALLOGRAPHY; NONDESTRUCTIVE TESTING. see *ENGINEERING — Engineering Mechanics And Materials*

ANNUAL BOOK OF A S T M STANDARDS. PART 12. CHEMICAL ANALYSIS OF METALS; SAMPLING AND ANALYSIS OF METAL BEARING ORES. see *ENGINEERING — Engineering Mechanics And Materials*

669   CL
AREA METALURGIA. Short title: Metalurgia. (Text in Spanish; summaries in English) irreg. Universidad Tecnica del Estado, Departamento de Investigaciones Cientificas y Tecnologicas, Avda. Ecuador 3469, Santiago, Chile. illus.

671.2   FR
ASSOCIATION TECHNIQUE DE FONDERIE. ANNUAIRE; ingenieurs et techniciens. 1911. biennial. Agence de Diffusion et de Publicite, 24 Place du General Catroux, 75017 Paris, France. adv.
Founding

669   AT
AUSTRALASIAN INSTITUTE OF METALS. PROCEEDINGS OF THE ANNUAL CONFERENCE. 1947. a. price varies. Australian Institute of Metals, 191 Royal Parade, Parkville, Vic. 3052, Australia. bibl, charts, illus. (also avail. in microfiche)
Formerly: Australian Institute of Metals. Proceedings of the Annual Conference.

AUSTRALASIAN INSTITUTE OF MINING AND METALLURGY. SYMPOSIA SERIES. see *MINES AND MINING INDUSTRY*

669 622   US   ISSN 0067-5768
BERG- UND HUETTENMAENNISCHE MONATSHEFTE. SUPPLEMENT. 1967. irreg.; no. 3, 1973. Springer-Verlag, 175 Fifth Ave, New York, NY 10010 (also Berlin, Heidelberg, Vienna) (reprint service avail. from ISI)

669   UK   ISSN 0308-7778
BRANDS AND ALLOYS. 1975. irreg. £12($27) Metal Bulletin Books Ltd., Park House, 3 Park Terrace, Worcester Park, Surrey, England.

669   UK
BRITISH INDEPENDENT STEEL COMPANIES AND THEIR PRODUCTS. 1969. irreg. free. British Independent Steel Producers Association, 5 Cromwell Rd, London S.W. 7 2HX, England. Ed. G. Knott. circ. 5,000.

669   UK   ISSN 0068-2586
BRITISH STEEL CORPORATION. ANNUAL REPORT AND ACCOUNTS. a. £1. British Steel Corp., 12 Addiscombe Rd., Croydon CR9 3JH, England (Avail. from: H.M.S.O., c/o Liaison Officer, Atlantic House, London EC1P 1BW, England) illus.

C. I. M. DIRECTORY. (Canadian Institute of Mining and Metallurgy) see *MINES AND MINING INDUSTRY*

669.1   MX
CAMARA NACIONAL DE LA INDUSTRIA DEL HIERRO Y DEL ACERO. INFORME DEL PRESIDENTE. a. $5. Camara Nacional de la Industria del Hierro y del Acero, Amores 338, Apdo. Postal 12783, Mexico 12, D.F., Mexico.

CANADA. STATISTICS CANADA. MANUFACTURERS OF ELECTRIC WIRE AND CABLE/FABRICANTS DE FILS ET DE CABLES ELECTRIQUES. see *ELECTRICITY AND ELECTRICAL ENGINEERING*

669   CN   ISSN 0527-5717
CANADA. STATISTICS CANADA. SMELTING AND REFINING/FONTE ET AFFINAGE. (Catalogue 41-214) (Text in English and French) 1927. a. Can.$4.50($5.40) Statistics Canada, Publications Distribution, Ottawa, Ont. K1A 0V7, Canada. (also avail. in microform from MML)

669.1   FR
CHAMBRE SYNDICALE DE LA SIDERUGIE FRANCAISE. BULLETIN STATISQUE. SERIE BLEUE. COMMERCE EXTERIEUR. a. 110 F. Societe d'Editions de la Siderurgie, B.P. 707-08, 75367 Paris Cedex 08, France.
Iron and steel

669.1   FR
CHAMBRE SYNDICALE DE LA SIDERUGIE FRANCAISE. BULLETIN STATISQUE. SERIE ROUGE. PRODUCTION. a. Societe d'Editions de la Siderurgie, B.P. 707-08, 75367 Paris Cedex 08, France.
Iron and steel

COKE OVEN MANAGERS' ASSOCIATION. YEAR BOOK. see *MINES AND MINING INDUSTRY*

669   FR   ISSN 0069-5807
COLLOQUE DE METALLURGIE. a. Presses Universitaires de France, 108 Bd. Saint Germaine, 75279 Paris Cedex 6, France (Service des Periodiques, 12 rue Jean de Beauvais, 75005 Paris)

COMMISSION OF THE EUROPEAN COMMUNITIES. COLLECTION OBJECTIFS GENERAUX ACIER. see *MINES AND MINING INDUSTRY*

669   UK
COPPER SURVEY. 1980. irreg £18($43.20) Metal Bulletin Ltd., Park House, 3 Park Terrace, Worcester Park, Surrey, England. adv.
Copper

620.112   US
CORROSION MONOGRAPH SERIES. 1966. irreg., unnumbered, latest, 1980. price varies. John Wiley & Sons, Inc., 605 Third Ave., New York, NY 10016. Ed. Bd.

669 530   SZ
DIFFUSION AND DEFECT MONOGRAPH SERIES. (Text in English) 1972. irreg.(approx. 1/yr.) price varies. Trans Tech S.A., Trans Tech House, 4711 Aedermannsdorf, Switzerland. Ed. F.H. Wohlbier. circ. 500. Indexed: Chem.Abstr. Met.Abstr. Sci.Abstr.
Formerly: Diffusion Monograph Series.

669   US   ISSN 0070-5039
DIRECTORY IRON AND STEEL PLANTS. 1916. a. $25. Association of Iron and Steel Engineers, Suite 2350, Three Gateway Center, Pittsburgh, PA 15222. Ed. John A. Kotsch. adv. circ. 5,000.

669.14   US
DIRECTORY OF IRON AND STEEL WORKS OF THE UNITED STATES AND CANADA. triennial. price varies. American Iron and Steel Institute, 1000 16th St., N.W., Washington, DC 20036.

DIRECTORY OF STEEL FOUNDRIES IN THE UNITED STATES, CANADA AND MEXICO. see *BUSINESS AND ECONOMICS — Trade And Industrial Directories*

671.25   US
DUCTILE IRON PIPE NEWS. a. Cast Iron Pipe Association, 1301 West 22nd Street, Suite 509, Oak Brook, IL 60521. Ed. C.J. Mower. charts. illus.

669 380   US   ISSN 0070-7597
DUN AND BRADSTREET METALWORKING DIRECTORY. (Published in one national and 5 regional editions) 1961. a. Dun's Marketing Services (Subsidiary of: Dun & Bradstreet, Inc.) Three Century Drive, Parsippany, NJ 07054. (also avail. in magnetic tape)

669   US
E/M J INTERNATIONAL DIRECTORY OF MINING AND MINERAL PROCESSING OPERATIONS. 1968. a. $55. McGraw-Hill Publications Co., 1221 Ave. of the Americas, New York, NY 10020. Ed. Elaine Romano.

ELEKTRYFIKACJA I MECHANIZACJA GORNICTWA I HUTNICTWA/ ELECTRIFICATION AND MECHANIZATION IN MINING AND METALLURGY. see *MINES AND MINING INDUSTRY*

671   FR
ESTAMPAGE, FORGE, EXTRUSION ET TECHNIQUES CONNEXES. a. irreg. (Federation des Industries Mecaniques et Transformatrices des Metaux, Syndicat National de l'Estampage et de la Forge) Union Francaise d'Annuaires Professionnels, 13 Avenue Vladimir Komarov, B.P. 36, 78190 Trappes, France.

338.4   UK   ISSN 0306-204X
EUROPEAN GLASS DIRECTORY AND BUYER'S GUIDE. 1970/71. a. £13.50. (Glass Manufacturers Federation) Fuel & Metallurgical Journals Ltd., Queensway House, 2 Queensway, Redhill, Surrey RH1 1QS, England. Ed. K. Murrell. adv. bk. rev.
Formerly: Glass Directory and Buyer's Guide.

669   UK   ISSN 0308-7786
EUROPEAN SCRAP DIRECTORY. 1976. irreg. £15($33.75) Metal Bulletin Books Ltd., Park House, 3 Park Terrace, Worcester Park, Surrey, England.

671   UK   ISSN 0014-5785
F E & Z N. (Editions in English, French, German, Italian and Spanish) 1960. a. free. Zinc Development Association, 34 Berkeley Square, W1X 6AJ, London, England. charts. illus.

METALLURGY

671.2   BE
FEDERATION DES ENTREPRISES DE L'INDUSTRIE DES FABRICATIONS METALLIQUES, MECANIQUES, ELECTRIQUES ET DE LA TRANSFORMATION DES MATIERES PLASTIQUES. CENTRE DE RECHERCHES SCIENTIFIQUES ET TECHNIQUES. SECTION: FONDERIE (FD). RESEARCH REPORTS. 1965. irreg. Federation des Entreprises de l'Industrie des Fabrications Metalliques, Mecaniques, Electriques et de la Transformation des Matieres Plastiques, 21 rue des Drapiers, 1050 Brussels, Belgium.
Founding

669.6   FR   ISSN 0085-0519
FER-BLANC EN FRANCE ET DANS LE MONDE. 1956. a. free. Chambre Syndicale des Producteurs de Fer-Blanc et de Fer-Noir, 5 rue Paul Cezanne, 75008 Paris, France. charts. stat. circ. 800.
Tin

669   UK   ISSN 0141-4690
FERRO-ALLOYS SURVEY. 1979. irreg. £15($36) Metal Bulletin Ltd., Park House, 3 Park Terrace, Worcester Park, Surrey, England. adv.

671   UK   ISSN 0071-5182
FINISHING HANDBOOK AND DIRECTORY. 1950. a. free to subscribers of monthly Product Finishing. Sawell Publications Ltd., 127, Stanstead Road, London SE23 1JE, England. Ed. R. S. Capp. adv. circ. 4,192.

FONTES ET ACIERS/GHISE ED ACCIAI/ ROHEISEN UND STAHLERZEUGNISSE/ RUWIJER EN STALLPRODUKTEN. see *MINES AND MINING INDUSTRY*

669   UK   ISSN 0071-8130
FOUNDRY DIRECTORY AND REGISTER OF FORGES. 1959. biennial. £10. Standard Catalogue Information Services Ltd., Medway Wharf Rd., Tonbridge, Kent TN9 1QR, England.

671.2   UK   ISSN 0306-4212
FOUNDRY YEARBOOK. 1972. a. £13.50. Fuel and Metallurgical Journals Ltd., Queensway House, 2 Queensway, Redhill, Surrey RH1 1QS, England. Ed. C. McCombe. adv. charts. tr. lit. circ. 3,000.
Founding

669   GE
FREIBERGER FORSCHUNGSHEFTE. MONTANWISSENSCHAFTEN: REIHE B. METALLURGIE UND WERBSTOFFTECHNIK. 1951. irreg. price varies. (Bergakademie Freiberg) VEB Deutscher Verlag fuer Grundstoffindustrie, Karl-Heine-Str. 27, 7031 Leipzig, E. Germany (D.D.R.)
    Formerly: Freiberger Forschungshefte. Montanwissenschaften: Reihe B. Metallurgie (ISSN 0071-9420)

GENERAL COMMISSION ON SAFETY AND HEALTH IN THE IRON AND STEEL INDUSTRY. REPORT. see *INDUSTRIAL HEALTH AND SAFETY*

669   US
I L Z R O ANNUAL RESEARCH REPORT. 1963. a. free. International Lead Zinc Research Organization, Inc., 292 Madison Ave., New York, NY 10017. Ed. A. L. Ponikvar. bibl. charts. illus. pat. stat. circ. 1,500.

669   US   ISSN 0146-7980
I L Z R O LEAD RESEARCH DIGEST. (Editions in French, Spanish, Japanese) 1963. a. free. International Lead Zinc Research Organization, Inc., 292 Madison Ave., New York, NY 10017. Ed. A. L. Ponikvar. bibl. charts. illus. pat. stat. circ. 3,500.

669   US   ISSN 0146-7999
I L Z R O ZINC RESEARCH DIGEST. 1963. a. free. International Lead Zinc Research Organization, Inc., 292 Madison Ave., New York, NY 10017. Ed. A. L. Ponikvar. bibl. charts. illus. pat. stat. circ. 4,500.

669 331.88   SZ
I M F STUDIES. 1972. irreg. free. International Metalworkers Federation, 54 bis, Rte. des Acacias, CH-1227 Geneva, Switzerland. Ed. Bd. charts. illus.

669   US
I S A MINING AND METALLURGY INSTRUMENTATION SYMPOSIUM. PROCEEDINGS. 3rd, 1975. irreg. $10. Instrument Society of America, 400 Stanwix St., Pittsburgh, PA 15222.

669   II
INDIAN INSTITUTE OF METALS. PROCEEDINGS. Indian Institute of Metals, 2 Sambhunath Pandit St., Calcutta 700020, India.

669   SW   ISSN 0015-7953
INSTITUTET FOER METALLFORSKNING. FORSKNINGSVERKSAMHETEN. 1952. a. free. Institutet foer Metallforskning - Swedish Institute for Metals Research, Drottning Kristinas Vaeg 48, S-114 28 Stockholm, Sweden. Ed. Rune Lagneborg. bibl. illus. circ. 2,400.

669   UK
INTERNATIONAL CADMIUM CONFERENCE. PROCEEDINGS. irreg., 1st 1978, San Francisco. (Cadmium Association) Metal Bulletin Ltd., Park House Park Terrace, Worcester Park, Surrey KT4 7HY, England. (Co-sponsors: Cadmium Council, New York; International Lead Zinc Research Organization)

669.4   UK   ISSN 0074-316X
INTERNATIONAL CONFERENCE ON LEAD. PROCEEDINGS. 1962. triennial, 7th 1980, Madrid. £15. Lead Development Association, 34 Berkeley Sq., London W1X 6AJ, England. circ. 1,000.

669   UK
INTERNATIONAL CONFERENCE ON THE PROTECTION OF PIPES. PROCEEDINGS. 1975. irreg., 3rd, 1979. price varies. British Hydromechanics Research Association, Cranfield, Bedford MK43 0AJ, England (Dist. in U.S. by: Air Science Co., Box 143, Corning, N.Y. 14830)

620.112   GW   ISSN 0074-4123
INTERNATIONAL CONGRESS ON METALLIC CORROSION. (PROCEEDINGS) 1961. quadrennial. European Federation of Corrosion, c/o DECHEMA, Postfach 97-01-46, D-6000 Frankfurt/ Main 97, W. Germany (B.R.D.)
    8th, 1981, Mainz, W. Germany

671.3   SZ   ISSN 0074-6983
INTERNATIONAL METALWORKERS' CONGRESS. REPORTS. triennial, 24th, 1977, Munich. free. International Metalworkers' Federation, 54 bis, Rte. des Acacias, 1227 Geneva, Switzerland.

671.37   US   ISSN 0074-7513
INTERNATIONAL POWDER METALLURGY CONFERENCE. PROCEEDINGS-MODERN DEVELOPMENTS IN POWDER METALLURGY. 1960. triennial since 1973; 5th, Chicago. price varies. Metal Powder Industries Federation, 105 College Road East, Princeton, NJ 08540. circ. 1,000.

669.142   US
INTERNATIONAL SPECIALTY CONFERENCE ON COLD-FORMED STEEL STRUCTURES. (PROCEEDINGS) 3rd, 1975. irreg. $30. University of Missouri-Rolla, Department of Civil Engineering, Rolla, MO 65401.
Steel

669.6   UK   ISSN 0074-9125
INTERNATIONAL TIN RESEARCH COUNCIL. ANNUAL REPORT. 1938. a. free. International Tin Research Institute, Fraser Rd., Perivale, Greenford, Middlesex, UB6 7AQ, England (and Tin Research Institute, Inc., 483 W. Sixth Ave., Columbus, Ohio 43201) Ed. C. J. Evans. circ. 5,000.
Tin

669   UK   ISSN 0141-5271
INTERNATIONAL ZINC & GALVANIZING DIRECTORY. irreg., latest edt., 1976. £10($22.50) Metal Bulletin Ltd., Park House, 3 Park Terrace, Worcester Park, Surrey, England.
Zinc

669   UK   ISSN 0140-8402
IRON & MANGANESE ORES SURVEY. 1978. irreg. £15($36) Metal Bulletin Ltd., Park House, 3 Park Terrace, Worcester Park, Surrey, England.
Iron

669.1 338.4   UK   ISSN 0075-0867
IRON AND STEEL. ANNUAL STATISTICS FOR THE UNITED KINGDOM. 1918. a. £15. Iron and Steel Statistics Bureau, P.O. Box No. 230, 12, Addiscombe Rd., Croydon CR9 6BS, England.

669.1   UK   ISSN 0075-0875
IRON AND STEEL WORKS OF THE WORLD. 1952. irreg., latest edt., 1978. £35($78.75) Metal Bulletin Books Ltd., Park House, 3 Park Terr., Worcester Park, Surrey, England. Eds. R. P. Cordero, R. Serjeantson. adv.

669.142   BG
ISPATA. (Text in English or Bengali) no. 4, 1977. a. Tk.25. Chittagong Steel Mills, Patenga, Chittagong, Bangladesh.

669   GW   ISSN 0075-2819
JAHRBUCH OBERFLAECHENTECHNIK. a. DM.56. Metall-Verlag GmbH, Hubertusallee 18, 1000 Berlin 33, W. Germany (B.R.D.) Ed.Bd. adv. circ. 4,200.

669   JA
JAPAN STEEL WORKS TECHNICAL NEWS. (Text in European languages) 1961. irreg. exchange basis. Japan Steel Works, Ltd. - Nihon Seikosho, 1-12 Yuraku-cho, Chiyoda-ku, Tokyo 100, Japan.

669.2   JA   ISSN 0075-3475
JAPAN'S IRON AND STEEL INDUSTRY. (Text in English) 1951. a. $19. Kawata Publicity Inc. - Kawata Paburishiti K. K., Central P.O. Box 1157, Tokyo 100-91, Japan. Ed Sukeyuki Kawata. adv. circ. 7,500.

669   GW
KORROSIONSVERHALTEN VON ZINK. irreg., vol. 4, 1977. price varies. (Zinkberatung e.V.) Metall-Verlag GmbH, Hubertusallee 18, 1000 Berlin 33, W. Germany (B.R.D.)

669   UR   ISSN 0302-9069
LITEINOE PROIZVODSTVO, METALLOVEDENIE I OBRABOTKA METALLOV DAVLENIEM. irreg. 0.47 Rub. (Krasnoyarskii Institut Tsvetnykh Metallov) Krasnoyarskoe Knizhnoe Izdatel'stvo, Prospekt Mira, 89, Krasnoyarsk, U.S.S.R. illus.

M. T. I. A. ANNUAL REPORT. (Metal Trades Industry Association of Australia) see *BUSINESS AND ECONOMICS — Labor And Industrial Relations*

671 382   AT
M T I A N E G'S EXPORT NOTE PAD. 1969. irreg. Aus.$1. Metal Trades Industry Association National Export Group, National Office, 105 Walker St., North Sydney, NSW 2060, Australia. Ed. H. S. Wells.
    Formerly: Australian Metal Trades Export Group's Export Note Pad.

338.4   US   ISSN 0095-7976
MATERIALS PERFORMANCE BUYER'S GUIDE; the corrosion control products/services purchasing directory. irreg. $10. National Association of Corrosion Engineers, Box 218340, Houston, TX 77218.

669   US
MATERIALS RESEARCH AND ENGINEERING/ WERKSTOFF- FORSCHUNG UND -TECHNIK. 1980. irreg. price varies. Springer-Verlag, 175 Fifth Ave, New York, NY 10010 (also Berlin, Heidelberg, Vienna) Ed. B. Ilschner. (reprint service avail. from ISI)
    Supersedes (1948-1976): Reine und Angewandte Metallkunde in Einzeldarstellungen (ISSN 0080-0791)

669 338.2   UK   ISSN 0076-664X
METAL BULLETIN HANDBOOK. 1968. a. £16($36) Metal Bulletin Ltd., Park House, 3 Park Terr., Worcester Park, Surrey, England. Ed. R. Packard. adv. circ. 3,000. (back issues avail.)
    Supersedes: Quin's Metal Handbook.

381   US   ISSN 0098-2210
METAL DISTRIBUTION. 1975. a. Metal Center News, 7 E. 12th St., New York, NY 10003. illus.

669 US
METAL FINISHING GUIDEBOOK & DIRECTORY. 1932. a. $5.95. Metals and Plastics Publications, Inc., One University Plaza, Hackensack, NJ 07601. Ed. Joseph Mazia. adv. circ. 15,000.

669 US
METAL STAMPING BUYER'S GUIDE. 1962. a. American Metal Stamping Association, 27027 Chardon Rd., Richmond Heights, OH 44143. adv. circ. 14,500.

669 671 US ISSN 0076-6658
METAL STATISTICS. 1904. a. $25. Fairchild Publications, Inc., (Subsidiary of: Capital Cities Media, Inc.) 7 East 12th St., New York, NY 10003. adv. circ. 19,000.

669 UK ISSN 0143-7607
METAL TRADERS OF THE WORLD. 1980. irreg. £30($72) Metal Bulletin Books Ltd., Park House, 3 Park Terrace, Worcester Park, Surrey, England. adv.

669 GW ISSN 0026-0770
METALLGESELLSCHAFT AKTIENGESELLSCHAFT. REVIEW OF THE ACTIVITIES. (Text in English and German) 1929, N.S. 1959. a. Metallgesellschaft AG, Reuterweg 14, 6000 Frankfurt 1, W. Germany (B.R.D.) Eds. Hans Schreiber, Sylvia Noske. bibl. charts. illus. circ. 10,000. Indexed: Chem.Abstr. Eng.Ind. Met.Abstr.

669 II
METALLURGICAL ENGINEER. (Text in English) 1969. a. free or on exchange basis. (Metallurgical Engineering Association, Department of Metallurgical Engineering) Indian Institute of Technology, Bombay, Powai, Bombay, India. Ed. Dr.P.Ramakrishnan. adv. Indexed: Chem.Abstr. Eng.Ind. Met.Abstr.

669 UK ISSN 0308-7794
METALLURGICAL PLANTMAKERS OF THE WORLD. 1973. irreg. £10($22.50) Metal Bulletin Books Ltd., Park House, 3 Park Terr., Worcester Park, Surrey, England. Ed. R. Serjeantson. adv.

669 UK
METALLURGY AND MATERIAL SCIENCE. 1981. irreg. price varies. Edward Arnold (Publishers) Ltd., 41 Bedford Square, London WC1B 3DQ, England.

669 US ISSN 0094-5447
METALLURGY-MATERIALS EDUCATION YEARBOOK. irreg. American Society for Metals, Metals Park, OH 44073.

669 621.38 MX
METALMECANICA; metalurgia, electricidad y electronica. 1967. a. 125($60) Editorial Innovacion, Espana 396, Mexico 13, D.F., Mexico. Ed. Cesar Macazaga. adv.

METALURGIA. see ANTHROPOLOGY

669 US ISSN 0361-1213
MICROSTRUCTURAL SCIENCE. 1974. irreg., vol. 4, 1976. (International Metallographic Society, Inc.) Elsevier North-Holland, Inc., New York, 52 Vanderbilt Ave., New York, NY 10017. illus.
Supersedes: International Microstructural Analysis Society. Proceedings: Annual Technical Meeting.

MINERAL INDUSTRIES NEWSLETTER. see EARTH SCIENCES — Geology

669 UK ISSN 0140-8399
MINOR METALS SURVEY. 1978. irreg. £15($36) Metal Bulletin Ltd., Park House, 3 Park Terrace, Worcester Park, Surrey, England. adv.

669 US
MOLYSULFIDE NEWSLETTER. 1956. irreg. free. Climax Molybdenum Co. Technical Information Department, 1 Greenwich Plaza, Greenwich, CT 06830. Ed. Kurt Miska. circ. 10,000.

MONOGRAPH SERIES ON METALLURGY IN NUCLEAR TECHNOLOGY. see
ENGINEERING — Engineering Mechanics And Materials

672 UR
MOSKOVSKII INSTITUT STALI I SPLAVOV. NAUCHNYE TRUDY. 1972. irreg. 0.85 Rub. Izdatel'stvo Metallurgiya, 2-i Obydenskii Per., 14, Moscow G-34, U.S.S.R. illus.

669 658.5 US ISSN 0077-3379
N A M F MANAGEMENT MANUAL. 1960. irreg. $100 to non-members; members $25. National Association of Metal Finishers, 111 E. Wacker Dr., Chicago, IL 60601. Ed. J. D. Carey. index.

669 SA
N I M REPORTS. 1966. irreg. free. National Institute for Metallurgy, Private Bag X3015, Randburg 2125, South Africa. bibl. illus. Indexed: Chem.Abstr. Met.Abstr. Mineral.Abstr. Nucl.Sci.Abstr.

338.4 US ISSN 0363-1737
NATIONAL METALWORKING BLUE BOOK. Variant title: Metal Working Blue Book. irreg. National Blue Books, Inc., 20929-3 Roscoe Blvd., Canoga Park, CA 91304.

669 HU ISSN 0324-4679
NEHEZIPARI MUSZAKI EGYETEM, MISKOLC. PUBLICATIONS. SERIES B: METALLURGY. (Text in English, German, Russian) irreg., vol. 33, no. 4, 1978. Nehezipari Muszaki Egyetem, Miskolc, Hungary. Ed. Bd. bibl. index.

671.37 US
NEW PERSPECTIVES IN POWDER METALLURGY. 1966. irreg., vol. 7, 1980. price varies. Metal Powder Industries Federation, 105 College Road East, Princeton, NJ 08540. circ. 1,000.
Formerly: Perspectives in Powder Metallurgy (ISSN 0079-1032)

669.1 JA
NIPPON STEEL REPORT. a. Nippon Steel Corporation, 2-6-3 Otemachi, Chiyoda-ku, Tokyo 100, Japan (U.S. Address: 345 Park Ave., 41st Floor, New York, NY 10022)

669 US ISSN 0360-9553
NON-FERROUS METAL DATA. 1920. a. $25. American Bureau of Metal Statistics Inc., 420 Lexington Ave., New York, NY 10017. Ed. William J. Lambert. cum.index. circ. 5,000.
Formerly (until 1974): American Bureau of Metal Statistics. Year Book (ISSN 0065-7611)

673 UK ISSN 0078-0987
NON-FERROUS METAL WORKS OF THE WORLD. 1967. irreg., latest edt., 1974. £16($36) Metal Bulletin Books Ltd., Park House, 3 Park Terr., Worcester Park, Surrey, England. Ed. T.J. Tarring. adv.

NORTH CAROLINA METALWORKING DIRECTORY. see BUSINESS AND ECONOMICS — Trade And Industrial Directories

669 UR
NOVYE ISSLEDOVANIYA V KHIMII, METALLURGII I OBOGASHCHENII. (Subseries of: Gornyi Instituti, Leningrad. Nauchnye Trudy) irreg. 0.75 Rub. Leningradskii Gornyi Institut, Leningrad, U.S.S.R. illus.

671 UR
OCHISTKA VODNOGO I VOZDUSHNOGO BASSEINOV NA PREDPRIYATIYAKH CHERNOI METALLURGII. irreg. 1.12 Rub.($18.60) (Ministerstvo Chernoi Metallurgii) Izdatel'stvo Metallurgiya, 2-i Obydenskii Per., 14, Moscow G-34, U.S.S.R. illus.

669 GW ISSN 0078-3420
OERLIKON SCHWEISSMITTEILUNGEN. 1955. irreg. free. Oerlikon Elektrodenfabrik Eisenberg GmbH, 6719 Eisenberg/Pfalz, W. Germany (B.R.D.) (Co-sponsor: Schweissindustrie Oerlikon Buehrle AG, Zurich) Ed. K. Weigel.

338.47 672 FR ISSN 0474-5973
ORGANIZATION FOR ECONOMIC COOPERATION AND DEVELOPMENT. SPECIAL COMMITTEE FOR IRON AND STEEL. IRON AND STEEL INDUSTRY. 1953-54. irreg. $4.50. Organization for Economic Cooperation and Development, 2 rue Andre Pascal, 75 Paris 16-e, France (U. S. orders to: O.E.C.D. Publications and Information Center; 1750 Pennsylvania Ave., N.W., Washington, D. C. 20006) (also avail. in microfiche)

669 PL ISSN 0372-9699
POLITECHNIKA CZESTOCHOWSKA. ZESZYTY NAUKOWE. NAUKI TECHNICZNE. HUTNICTWO. (Text in Polish; summaries in English and Russian) 1969. irreg. Politechnika Czestochowska, Ul. Deglera 31, 42-200 Czestochowa, Poland (Dist. by: Ars Polona-Ruch, Krakowskie Przedmiescie 7, Warsaw, Poland) Ed. Boleslaw Paczula.

669 PL ISSN 0324-802X
POLITECHNIKA SLASKA. ZESZYTY NAUKOWE. HUTNICTWO. (Text in Polish; summaries in English and Russian) 1971. irreg. price varies. Politechnika Slaska, W. Pstrowskiego 7, 44-100 Gliwice, Poland (Dist. by: Ars Polona, Krakowskie Przedmiescie 7, 00-068 Warsaw, Poland) Ed. Izabella Hyla.

669 PL ISSN 0079-3345
POLSKA AKADEMIA NAUK. ODDZIAL W KRAKOWIE. KOMISJA METALURGICZNO-ODLEWNICZA. PRACE: METALURGIA. (Text in English and Polish; summaries in English and Russian) 1965. irreg., no. 27, 1979. price varies. Ossolineum, Publishing House of the Polish Academy of Sciences, Rynek 9, Wroclaw, Poland (Dist. by Ars Polona-Ruch, Krakowskie Przedmiescie 7, Warsaw, Poland) Eds. Stanislaw Gorczyca and Czeslaw Podrzucki. circ. 500. Indexed: Chem.Abstr. Eng.Ind.
Formerly: Polska Akademia Nauk. Komisja Metalurjaodlewnienia. Metalurgia.

669 NE
PROCESS METALLURGY. 1978. irreg. price varies. Elsevier Scientific Publishing Co., Box 211, 1000 AE Amsterdam, Netherlands.

669.05 US ISSN 0091-6145
PROGRESS IN EXTRACTIVE METALLURGY. 1973. irreg. $29.50. Gordon and Breach Science Publishers, 1 Park Ave., New York, NY 10016. illus.

671 US ISSN 0079-6719
PROGRESS IN POWDER METALLURGY; P-M Technical Conference proceedings. 1947. a. Metal Powder Industries Federation, 105 College Road East, Princeton, NJ 08540.

669 IT ISSN 0080-1216
REPERTORIO DELLE INDUSTRIE SIDERURGICHE ITALIANE. 1949. every 5 years. L.19000. Associazione Industrie Siderurgiche Italiane, Piazza Velasca 8, 20122 Milan, Italy.

671 669 UK ISSN 0080-505X
RYLAND'S DIRECTORY. a. £17. Fuel and Metallurgical Journals Ltd., Queensway House, 2 Queensway, Redhill, Surrey RH1 1QS, England. Ed. A. Palmer. adv.

620.1 DK ISSN 0581-9431
SCANDINAVIAN CORROSION CONGRESS. PROCEEDINGS. (Text in English) 1954. irreg. (approx. triennial) $20. Korrosionscentralen, ATV, Park Alle 345, DK-2600 Glostrup, Denmark.
Corrosion

669 UK ISSN 0143-7844
SHEET METAL INDUSTRIES INTERNATIONAL. (Supplement to: Sheet Metal Industries) (Text in English, French, German and Spanish) 1979. a. £7. Fuel and Metallurgical Journals Ltd., Queensway House, 2 Queensway, Redhill, Surrey RH1 1QS, England.

669 UK ISSN 0305-7798
SHEET METAL INDUSTRIES YEAR BOOK. a. £13.50. Fuel and Metallurgical Journals Ltd., Queensway House, 2 Queensway, Redhill, Surrey RH1 1QS, England. Ed. E. H. Lloyd. adv. bibl. index.

669.142 BL
SIDERURGIA BRASILEIRA S.A. RELATORIO DE DIRETORIA. 1973. a. Siderurgia Brasileira S.A., Setor de Autarquias Sul, Quadra 2, Bloco K, 70070 Brasilia, Brazil. illus. circ. 5,000.
Steel

669.23 336 US ISSN 0066-4332
SILVER MARKET. 1916. a. free. ‡ Handy and Harman, 850 Third Ave, New York, NY 10022. Ed. Susan L. Dunn. circ. 20,000.

669   SP   ISSN 0085-6096
SINDICATO NACIONAL DEL METAL, MADRID. INFORME-ECONOMICO Y SOCIAL. 1963. a; latest issue, 1975. free. Sindicato Nacional del Metal, C. Diego de Leon 50, Madrid 6, Spain.

669 622   SA
SOUTH AFRICAN INSTITUTE OF MINING AND METALLURGY. MONOGRAPH SERIES. 1978. irreg. price varies. South African Institute of Mining and Metallurgy, Box 61019, Marshalltown 2107, South Africa.

669   SA
SOUTH AFRICAN METAL INDUSTRIES DIRECTORY & HANDBOOK. a. R.15. Cupola Publications (Pty) Ltd., Metal Industries House, 84 Marshall St., Box 1338, Johannesburg, South Africa. adv.

338.9   US   ISSN 0363-5090
SOUTH CAROLINA METALWORKING DIRECTORY. irreg. free. State Development Board, Box 927, Columbia, SC 29202.

672   GW   ISSN 0081-4172
STAHL UND FORM. 1964. irreg. DM.3.30. (Beratungsstelle fuer Stahlverwendung) Verlag Stahleisen mbH, Breite Str. 27, Postfach 8229, 4000 Duesseldorf 1, W. Germany (B.R.D.)

672   GW   ISSN 0081-4180
STAHLEISEN KALENDER. 1951. a. DM.17. (Verein Deutscher Eisenhuettenleute) Verlag Stahleisen mbH, Breite Str. 27, Postfach 8229, 4000 Duesseldorf 1, W. Germany (B.R.D.)

669.142   UK
STAINLESS STEEL DIRECTORY. 1975. biennial. £5.25. Modern Metals Publications Ltd., 39 Hillside Gardens, Brockham, Betchworth, Surrey RH3 7ER, England. Ed. K. T. Rowland.
    Formerly: Directory of the Stainless Steel Industry.

669.142   UK   ISSN 0141-5298
STAINLESS STEEL WORLD GUIDE. 1964. irreg., latest edt., 1979. £15($33.75) Metal Bulletin Ltd., Park House, 3 Park Terrace, Worcester Park, Surrey, England.
    Steel

669   AT   ISSN 0085-6657
STANDARDS FOR AUSTRALIAN ALUMINIUM MILL PRODUCTS. (Metric Edition) irreg. Aus.$1. Aluminium Development Council of Australia, 99 Elizabeth St., Sydney, N.S.W. 2000, Australia.

338.4 669   EI   ISSN 0081-4954
STATISTICAL OFFICE OF THE EUROPEAN COMMUNITIES. SIDERURGIE ANNUAIRE. (Text in French, German, Italian, Dutch) 1964. a. B.P. 1907, Luxembourg, Luxembourg (Dist. in the U.S. by: European Community Information Service, 2100 M St., NW, Suite 707, Washington, DC 20037)

669.1   II   ISSN 0081-511X
STATISTICS FOR IRON AND STEEL INDUSTRY IN INDIA. (Text in English) 1964. irreg., 1973, 4th ed. price varies. Hindustan Steel Limited, Ranchi 834002, India. Ed S. Subramu. index.

669   UN   ISSN 0081-5195
STATISTICS OF WORLD TRADE IN STEEL. 1962. a.; latest 1973. price varies. United Nations Publications, Room LX-2300, New York, NY 10017 (Or Distribution and Sales Section. Palais des Nations, CH-1211 Geneva 10, Switzerland)

669   GW   ISSN 0081-5365
STATISTISCHES JAHRBUCH DER EISEN- UND STAHLINDUSTRIE. 1929. a. DM.42.50. (Wirtschaftsvereinigung Eisen- und Stahlindustrie) Verlag Stahleisen mbH, Breite Str. 27, Postfach 8229, 4000 Duesseldorf 1, W. Germany (B.R.D.)

669.142   SA
STEEL FABRICATIONS. 1979. biennial. R.30. Thomson Publications S.A. (Pty) Ltd., Box 8308, Johannesburg 2000, South Africa. Ed. Carola Tonetti. adv.

338.4   UK
STEEL TIMES ANNUAL REVIEW OF THE STEEL INDUSTRY. (Title varies slightly) 1965. a. £20 combined subscription with Steel Times. Fuel & Metallurgical Journals Ltd., Queensway House, 2 Queensway, Surrey RH1 1QS, England. Ed. Gordon Garbett. adv. illus. circ. 2,500.

669   UK   ISSN 0308-8006
STEEL TRADERS OF THE WORLD. 1976. irreg. £20($45) Metal Bulletin Books Ltd., Park House, 3 Park Terrace, Worcester Park, Surrey, England.
    Steel

669   GW
SVETSAREN; Schweisstechnische Erfahrungsberichte. irreg. free. Kjellberg-ESAB GmbH, Postfach 100763, 5650 Solingen, W. Germany (B.R.D.) Ed. M. Puschner.
    Formerly: Kjelberg-e SAB-Schriften; Erfahrungsberichte ueber Lichtbogen-Schweisstechnik (ISSN 0075-6261)

669.1   SW
SWEDISH STEEL MANUAL. (Text and summaries in English) 1962. irreg. Jernkontoret - Swedish Ironmasters' Association, Box 1721, S-111 87 Stockholm, Sweden. Ed. Hans von Delwig.

669   GW   ISSN 0082-1772
TASCHENBUCH DER GIESSEREI-PRAXIS. 1952. a. DM.32. Fachverlag Schiele und Schoen GmbH, Markgrafenstr. 11, 1000 Berlin 61, W. Germany (B.R.D.) Ed. E. Brunhuber. adv. circ. 5,000.

669   GW   ISSN 0340-5060
THYSSEN TECHNISCHE BERICHTE. (Text in German; contents page in English, French and German) 1969. irreg. free. Thyssen AG, Postfach 11067, 4100 Duisburg 11, W. Germany (B.R.D.) Eds. Alfred Altgeld, Carl-Friedrich Baumann. bibl. charts. illus. Indexed: Chem.Abstr. Eng.Ind. Met.Abstr.
    Formerly: Thyssenforschung (ISSN 0040-666X)

669   UK
TIN STATISTICS. 1973. a. £10. International Tin Council, Haymarket House, 1 Oxendon St., London SW1Y 4EQ, England.
    Supersedes in part: International Tin Council. Statistical Yearbook (ISSN 0074-9117); International Tin Council. Statistical Supplement. Tin, Tinplate Canning (ISSN 0074-9109)

669.6   UK   ISSN 0141-5301
TINPLATE WORLD SURVEY. 1967. irreg., latest edt., 1976. £7.50($16.88) Metal Bulletin Ltd., Park House, 3 Park Terrace, Worcester Park, Surrey, England.
    Tinplate

U. S. ENVIRONMENTAL PROTECTION AGENCY. UPGRADING METAL-FINISHING FACILITIES TO REDUCE POLLUTION. see ENVIRONMENTAL STUDIES

669   AT   ISSN 0085-4018
UNIVERSITY OF NEW SOUTH WALES. METALLURGICAL SOCIETY. METALLURGICAL REVIEW. 1956/57. a. free. ‡ University of New South Wales, Metallurgical Society, Box 1, Kensington, N.S.W. 2033, Australia. Ed. B. J. Gale. adv. circ. 1,500. Indexed: Aus.P.A.I.S.

669   UK   ISSN 0080-9209
UNIVERSITY OF SHEFFIELD. METALLURGICAL SOCIETY. JOURNAL. 1962. a. 75p. Sheffield University Metallurgical Society, Dept. of Metallurgy, Portobello St, Sheffield S1 3JD, England. Ed. J. H. Beynon. adv. circ. 1,000. Indexed: Met.Abstr.

621.5 669   US
VACUUM METALLURGY CONFERENCE. PROCEEDINGS. 1959. irreg. price varies. American Vacuum Society, 335 E. 45th St., New York, NY 10017. (Affiliate: American Institute of Physics)
    Supersedes: Vacuum Metallurgy Conference. Transactions (ISSN 0083-5056)

620.112 671.2 549   FI   ISSN 0357-1831
VALTION TEKNILLINEN TUTKIMUSKESKUS. METALLURGIAN JA MINERAALITEKNIIKAN LABORATORIO. TIEDONANTO/TECHNICAL RESEARCH CENTRE OF FINLAND. LABORATORY OF METALLURGY AND MINERAL ENGINEERING. REPORT. (Text mainly in Finnish, some in English or Swedish) 1970. irreg. price varies. Valtion Teknillinen Tutkimuskeskus - Technical Research Centre of Finland, Vuorimiehentie 5, 02150 Espoo 15, Finland.
    Corrosion; founding

669   CS   ISSN 0042-3726
VYSOKA SKOLA BANSKA. SBORNIK VEDECKYCH PRACI: RADA HUTNICKA/INSTITUTE OF MINING AND METALLURGY. TRANSACTIONS: METALLURGICAL SERIES. (Text in Czech; summaries in English, German, Russian) 1955. 2-8/yr. 25 Kcs.($1) per issue. Statni Pedagogicke Nakladatelstvi, Ostrovni 30, 113 01 Prague 1, Czechoslovakia. bk. rev. abstr. bibl. charts. illus. stat. index.

669   GW
W E M A BEZUGSQUELLENVERZEICHNIS. (Text in German; index in English, French, Spanish and Russian) 1950. irreg. DM.20. Wirtschaftsverband Eisen-Maschinen-und Apparatebau e. V.(WEMA), Karolingerplatz 10-11, 1000 Berlin 19, W. Germany (B.R.D.) circ. 3,000.

671.2   JA   ISSN 0511-1927
WASEDA UNIVERSITY. CASTING RESEARCH LABORATORY. REPORT. (Text in English) 1950. a. exchange basis. Waseda University, Casting Research Laboratory - Waseda Daigaku Imono Kenkyushitsu, 1-500 Totsuka-cho, Shinjuku-ku, Tokyo 160, Japan.

669   US
WESTERN MACHINERY & STEEL WORLD BUYER'S DIRECTORY. 1921. a. $30. Cardinal Publishing Co., 1098 Harrison St., San Francisco, CA 94103. adv.

669   UK
WHERE TO BUY NON-FERROUS METALS IN THE UNITED KINGDOM. 1976. irreg. £2.95. Modern Metals Publications Ltd., 39 Hillside Gardens, Brockham, Betchworth, Surrey, England.

671.3   US   ISSN 0361-6304
WHO'S WHO IN P/M. a. $25. American Powder Metallurgy Institute, Box 2054, Princeton, NJ 08540. adv.
    Formerly: American Powder Metallurgy Institute. Membership Directory and Yearbook.

669   UK   ISSN 0143-6872
WHO'S WHO IN STEEL. (2 volumes) 1979. a. £7($16.80) Metal Bulletin Books Ltd., Park House, 3 Park Terrace, Worcester Park, Surrey, England. Ed. R. Cordero.
    Steel

671.8   UK
WIRE INDUSTRY MACHINERY GUIDE; international wire machinery review. (Text in English, French, German, Spanish) 1956. a. £5. Magnum Publications Ltd., 110-112 Station Rd. E., Oxted, Surrey RH8 0QA, England. circ. 5,202.
    Formerly: Wire Review (ISSN 0084-0432)

671.8   UK   ISSN 0084-0424
WIRE INDUSTRY YEARBOOK; international buyers guide. (Text in English, French, German, Italian and Spanish) 1951. a. £8. Magnum Publications Ltd., 110-112 Station Rd. E., Oxted, Surrey RH8 0QA, England. adv. circ. 5,202.

669.6   UK
WORLD CONFERENCE ON TIN. PROCEEDINGS. irreg., 4th, 1974 Kuala Lumpur. £30. International Tin Council, Haymarket House, 1 Oxenden St., London SW1Y 4EQ, England.
    Tin

METALLURGY — Abstracting, Bibliographies, Statistics

669 016   US   ISSN 0001-2556
A S M. BIBLIOGRAPHY SERIES. 1967. a. (80 topics avail.). $35 per topic to non-members; members $30. American Society for Metals, Metals Park, OH 44073.

338.4   CN   ISSN 0575-884X
CANADA. STATISTICS CANADA. IRON AND STEEL MILLS/SIDERURGIE. (Catalog 41-203) (Text in English and French) 1927. a. Can.$4.50($5.40) Statistics Canada, Publications Distribution, Ottawa, Ont. K1A 0V7, Canada. (also avail. in microform from MML)

CANADA. STATISTICS CANADA. MANUFACTURERS OF ELECTRIC WIRE AND CABLE/FABRICANTS DE FILS ET DE CABLES ELECTRIQUES. see *ELECTRICITY AND ELECTRICAL ENGINEERING*

338.4   CN   ISSN 0527-5997
CANADA. STATISTICS CANADA. ORNAMENTAL AND ARCHITECTURAL METAL INDUSTRY/INDUSTRIE DES PRODUITS METALLIQUES D'ARCHITECTURE ET D'ORNEMENT. (Catalogue 41-221) (Text in English and French) 1960. a. Can.$4.50($5.40) Statistics Canada, Publications Distribution, Ottawa, Ont. K1A 0V7, Canada. (also avail. in microform from MML)

310 671   UK
INTERNATIONAL STEEL STATISTICS - WORLD TABLES. a. price varies. British Steel Corp., 12 Addiscombe Rd., Croydon CR9 3JH, England.

669   JA   ISSN 0451-6001
LIGHT METAL STATISTICS IN JAPAN/ KEIKINZOKU KOGYO TOKEI NENPO. (Text mainly in Japanese) irreg. 1000 Yen. Japan Light Metal Association - Keikinzoku Kyokai, c/o Nihonbashi Asahi Seimeikan, 2-1-3 Nihonbashi, Chuo-ku, Tokyo 102, Japan. stat.

U S S R REPORT: MATERIALS SCIENCE AND METALLURGY. see *ENGINEERING — Abstracting, Bibliographies, Statistics*

669   UK
WORLD BUREAU OF METAL STATISTICS. ANNUAL REPORT. a. World Bureau of Metal Statistics, 41 Doughty St., London WC1N 2LF, England.

METALLURGY — Welding

671.5   AT   ISSN 0084-7631
AUSTRALIAN WELDING RESEARCH ASSOCIATION. BULLETIN.* 1966. irreg. $1 per no. Australian Welding Research Association, 307 Pitt St., Sydney, N.S.W. 2000, Australia.

671.52   UK
INTERNATIONAL CONFERENCE ON ADVANCES IN WELDING PROCESSES. PROCEEDINGS. vol. 4, 1979. irreg. £21. Welding Institute, Abington Hall, Abington, Cambridge CB1 6AL, England.

671.52   US
INTERNATIONAL THERMAL SPRAYING CONFERENCE. PREPRINT OF PAPERS. irreg., 8th, 1976, Miami Beach. $25. American Welding Society, 2501 N.W. 7th St., Miami, FL 33125.

671.5   AT   ISSN 0085-5065
PRACTICAL WELDER. 1970. q. $0.60 per no. Commonwealth Industrial Gases Ltd., Box 2244, Sydney, N.S.W. 2001, Australia.

SHEET METAL INDUSTRIES INTERNATIONAL. see *METALLURGY*

SHEET METAL INDUSTRIES YEAR BOOK. see *METALLURGY*

671.52   FI   ISSN 0355-6395
VALTION TEKNILLINEN TUTKIMUSKESKUS. METALLILABORATORIO. TIEDONANTO/ TECHNICAL RESEARCH CENTRE OF FINLAND. METALS LABORATORY. REPORT. (Text mainly in Finnish, some in English or Swedish) 1976. irreg. price varies. Valtion Teknillinen Tutkimuskeskus - Technical Research Centre of Finland, Vuorimiehentie 5, 02150 Espoo 15, Finland.

671.52   UK
WELDING; a buyers guide to welding equipment, consumables and services. vol. 5, 1977. a. Welding Institute, Abington Hall, Abington, Cambridge CB1 6AL, England. Ed. C. Humphries. adv.

671.5   US   ISSN 0511-4365
WELDING DATA BOOK. 1958. biennial. $27. Penton-IPC, 614 Superior Ave. W., Cleveland, OH 44113. Ed. Rosalie Brosilow. adv. charts. illus. circ. 24,000. (reprint service avail. from UMI)

METEOROLOGY

ACTA GEOGRAPHICA DEDRECINA. see *GEOGRAPHY*

551.5   SG   ISSN 0065-4248
AGENCE POUR LA SECURITE DE LA NAVIGATION AERIENNE EN AFRIQUE ET A MADAGASCAR. DIRECTION DE L'EXPLOITATION METEOROLOGIQUE. PUBLICATIONS. SERIE 1. 1966. irreg., no. 42, 1978. price varies. ‡ Agence pour la Securite de la Navigation Aerienne en Afrique et a Madagascar, Direction de l'Exploitation Meteorologique, B.P. 3144, Dakar, Senegal.

551.5   SG   ISSN 0084-6015
AGENCE POUR LA SECURITE DE LA NAVIGATION AERIENNE EN AFRIQUE ET A MADAGASCAR. DIRECTION DE L'EXPLOITATION METEOROLOGIQUE. PUBLICATIONS. SERIE 2. 1965. irreg., no. 60, 1978. price varies. ‡ Agence pour la Securite de la Navigation Aerienne en Afrique et a Madagascar, Direction de l'Exploitation Meteorologique, B.P. 3144, Dakar, Senegal.

551.5   ES   ISSN 0084-6236
ALMANAQUE SALVADORENO. 1945. a. $.60. Direccion General de Recursos Naturales Renovables, Servicio Meteorologico, Final la Avda. Norte, Santa Tecla, El Salvador. adv. circ. 2,000.

551.5   US   ISSN 0065-9401
AMERICAN METEOROLOGICAL SOCIETY. METEOROLOGICAL MONOGRAPHS. 1947. irreg., no. 38 (vol. 16) 1977. price varies. ‡ American Meteorological Society, 45 Beacon St., Boston, MA 02108. Ed. E. W. Bierly. Indexed: Biol.Abstr. Chem.Abstr. Sci.Abstr. Meteor. & Geoastrophys.Abstr.

551.5   GW   ISSN 0072-4122
ANNALEN DER METEOROLOGIE. NEUE FOLGE. 1948; 1963 N.S. irreg., no. 16, 1980. Deutscher Wetterdienst, Frankfurter Str. 135, Postfach 185, 6050 Offenbach (Main) 1, W. Germany (B.R.D.)

551.5   PK
ANNUAL GEOMAGNETIC BULLETIN OF PAKISTAN. vol. 9-10, 1963/64. a. Meteorological Department, Headquarters Office, 34-J Block No. 6, P.E.C.H.S., Karachi 29, Pakistan.

551.5 551   US   ISSN 0066-6394
ARCHIV FUER METEOROLOGIE, GEOPHYSIK UND BIOKLIMATOLOGIE. SERIES A. METEOROLOGY AND GEOPHYSICS. SUPPLEMENT. 1966. irreg. Springer-Verlag, 175 Fifth Ave., New York, NY 10010 (also Berlin, Heidelberg, Vienna) (reprint service avail. from ISI) Indexed: Biol.Abstr. Chem.Abstr. Meteor.& Geoastrophys.Abstr.

551.6   FR   ISSN 0373-7349
ASSOCIATION NATIONALE D'ETUDE ET DE LUTTE CONTRE LES FLEAUX ATMOSPHERIQUES. RAPPORT DE CAMPAGNE. 1951. a. free. Association Nationale de Lutte Contre les Fleaux Atmospheriques, 52, rue Alfred-Dumeril, 31400 Toulouse, France. illus.
 Formerly: Association Nationale de Lutte Contre les Fleaux Atmospheriques. Rapport de Campagne. Continues the Rapport sur la Campagne issued by the association under its earlier name: Association d'Etudes des Moyens de Lutte Contre les Fleaux Atmospheriques.

551.5   US   ISSN 0091-2026
ATMOSPHERIC TECHNOLOGY. 1966. a. free. (University Corporation for Atmospheric Research) National Center for Atmospheric Research, Boulder, CO 80307. Ed. Marie Boyko. illus. stat. circ. 2,000(approx.) (back issues avail)
 Formerly: Facilities for Atmospheric Research (ISSN 0014-6420)

551.5   US   ISSN 0094-4696
ATMOSPHERIC TURBIDITY AND PRECIPITATION CHEMISTRY DATA FOR THE WORLD. irreg. $5.25. U.S. National Climatic Center, Federal Building, Asheville, NC 28801. (Co-Sponsor: World Meteorological Organization)

551.5   AT   ISSN 0067-1312
AUSTRALIA. BUREAU OF METEOROLOGY. BULLETIN. 1908. irreg., no. 49, 1974. price varies. Bureau of Meteorology, Publications Section, Box 1289 K, Melbourne, Vic. 3001, Australia. Indexed: Meteor. & Geoastrophys.Abstr.

551.5   AT   ISSN 0067-1320
AUSTRALIA. BUREAU OF METEOROLOGY. METEOROLOGICAL STUDY. 1954. irreg., no. 30, 1979. available on exchange. Bureau of Meteorology, Publications Section, Box 1289 K, Melbourne, Vic. 3001, Australia. Indexed: Meteor. & Geoastrophys.Abstr.

551.5 551   AU   ISSN 0067-2351
AUSTRIA. ZENTRALANSTALT FUER METEOROLOGIE UND GEODYNAMIK. JAHRBUCH. 1854. irreg. price varies. Zentralanstalt fuer Meteorologie und Geodynamik, Hohe Warte 38, A-1190 Vienna, Austria.

551.5 551   BE   ISSN 0020-255X
BELGIUM. INSTITUT ROYAL METEOROLOGIQUE. PUBLICATIONS. (Text in Dutch, English and French) 1952. irreg.(15-20/yr.) Institut Royal Meteorologique, 3 Av. Circulaire, 1180 Brussels, Belgium. circ. 290.

BIOMETEOROLOGY; PROCEEDINGS. see *BIOLOGY*

551.5   BL   ISSN 0067-9585
BOLETIM CLIMATOLOGICO. 1962. irreg.; no. 4, 1980. price varies; avail. on exchange. ‡ Universidade de Sao Paulo, Instituto Oceanografico, Cidade Universitaria, Butanta, 05508 Sao Paulo, SP, Brazil. circ. 250.

551.5   GW   ISSN 0006-7156
BONNER METEOROLOGISCHE ABHANDLUNGEN. (Text in English and German) 1962. irreg. price varies. (Universitaet Bonn, Meteorologisches Institut) Ferd. Duemmlers Verlag, Kaiserstr. 31, 5300 Bonn 1, W. Germany (B.R.D.) Ed. Prof.Dr. H. Flohn. abstr. charts. illus. Indexed: Meteor. & Geoastrophys.Abstr.

551.5   BU   ISSN 0068-3876
BULGARSKA AKADEMIIA NA NAUKITE. INSTITUT PO KHIDROLOGIIA I METEOROLOGIIA. IZVESTIIA. (Summaries in various languages) 1964. irreg. price varies. Publishing House of the Bulgarian Academy of Sciences, Ul. Akad. G. Bonchev, 1113 Sofia, Bulgaria (Dist. by: Hemus, 6, Rouski Blvd., 1000 Sofia, Bulgaria) Ed. I. Marinov. circ. 500.

551.5   CM
CAMEROON. SERVICE D'HYDROMETEOROLOGIE. PLUVIOMETRIE MENSUELLE ET ANNUELLE. a. $17.75. Service d'Hydrometeorologie, Yaounde, Cameroon. charts. stat.

METEOROLOGY

551.6　　　　CN　ISSN 0068-7715
CANADA. ATMOSPHERIC ENVIRONMENT SERVICE. CLIMATOLOGICAL STUDIES. 1965. irreg. price varies. Atmospheric Environment Service, 4905 Dufferin St., Downsview, Ont. M3H 5T4, Canada (Subscr. to: Supply & Services Canada, Printing & Publishing, Ottawa, Ont. K1A 0S9, Canada)
Climatology

551.5　　　　CN　ISSN 0068-7782
CANADA. ATMOSPHERIC ENVIRONMENT SERVICE. METEOROLOGICAL TRANSLATIONS. 1959. irreg., no. 33, 1979. Can.$1.50. ‡ Atmospheric Environment Service, 4905 Dufferin St., Downsview, Ont M3H 5T4, Canada (Subscr. to Supply & Services Canada, Printing & Publishing, Ottawa, Ont. K1A 0S9, Canada) circ. 500.

551.538　　　　CN　ISSN 0068-7790
CANADA. ATMOSPHERIC ENVIRONMENT SERVICE. SNOW COVER DATA. CANADA. 1954-55. a. Can.$1. Atmospheric Environment Service, 4905 Dufferin St, Downsview, Ont. M3H 5T4 Canada. Canada (Subscr. to: Supply & Services Canada, Printing & Publishing, Ottawa, Ont. K1A 0S9, Canada) Ed. B.J. Yorke. circ. 800.

551.5　　　　CN　ISSN 0068-7804
CANADA. ATMOSPHERIC ENVIRONMENT SERVICE. TECHNICAL MEMORANDA. (Text in English; summaries in English and French) 1954. irreg., TEC 871, 1979. $0.50. Atmospheric Environment Service, 4905 Dufferin St., Downsview, Ont., M3H 5T4, Canada (Subscr. to: Supply & Services Canada, Printing & Publishing, Ottawa, Ont. K1A 0S9, Canada)

551.5　　　　CN　ISSN 0068-9246
CANADIAN METEOROLOGICAL MEMOIRS. 1935. irreg., no. 31, 1977. Can.$2.50. Atmospheric Environment Service, 4905 Dufferin St., Downsview, Ont., M3H 5T4, Canada.

551.5　　　　CN
CANADIAN METEOROLOGICAL RESEARCH REPORTS. (Text in English; summaries in English and French) 1968. irreg. Can.$1.50 per no. Atmospheric Environment Service, 4905 Dufferin St., Downsview, Ont. M3H 5T4, Canada.

551.5　　　　CN　ISSN 0068-9254
CANADIAN METEOROLOGICAL SOCIETY. ANNUAL CONGRESS. 1967. a. $2.50. Canadian Meteorological Society, Dept. of Meteorology, McGill University, Box 6070, Montreal, Que. H3C 3G1, Canada. Ed. I. D. Rutherford. circ. 1,000. Indexed: Meteor. & Geoastrophys.Abstr.

551.5　　　　US　ISSN 0148-5628
CLIMATOLOGICAL DATA FOR AMUNDSEN-SCOTT, ANTARCTICA. 1958. irreg., approx. biennial. free. U.S. National Climatic Center, Federal Building, Asheville, NC 28801. (tabloid format; also avail. in processed)
Former titles (1970-1972): Climatological Data for Selected U.S. Antarctic Stations; (until 1970): Climatological Data for Antarctic Stations.

551.5　　　　IO　ISSN 0009-8957
CLIMATOLOGICAL DATA FOR JAKARTA OBSERVATORY. (Text in English) 1956. a. exchange basis. Meteorological and Geophysical Institute - Pusat Meteorologi dan Geofisika, Jalan Arief Rakhman Hakim 3, Jakarta, Indonesia.

COLOMBO OBSERVATORY. REPORT. see *ASTROLOGY*

551.5　　　　US　ISSN 0067-0340
COLORADO STATE UNIVERSITY. ATMOSPHERIC SCIENCE PAPER. 1959. irreg. available on exchange. ‡ Colorado State University, Department of Atmospheric Science, College of Engineering, Fort Collins, CO 80523. (also avail. in microfiche) Indexed: Meteor. & Geoastrophys.Abstr.
Supersedes: Atmospheric Science Technical Paper & Atmospheric Science Research Report.

551.51　　　　AT　ISSN 0310-1908
COMMONWEALTH SCIENTIFIC AND INDUSTRIAL RESEARCH ORGANIZATION. DIVISION OF ATMOSPHERIC PHYSICS. ANNUAL REPORT. biennial. free. C. S. I. R. O., Division of Atmospheric Physics, 314 Albert St., East Melbourne, Vic. 3002, Australia. illus.

551.51　　　　AT
COMMONWEALTH SCIENTIFIC AND INDUSTRIAL RESEARCH ORGANIZATION. DIVISION OF ATMOSPHERIC PHYSICS. TECHNICAL PAPER. 1972. irreg. (approx. 1-3/yr.) free. C. S. I. R. O., Division of Atmospheric Physics, 314 Albert Street, East Melbourne, Vic. 3002, Australia. circ. 750. (tabloid format)

551.5　　　　US
CONFERENCE ON ATMOSPHERIC ENVIRONMENT OF AEROSPACE SYSTEMS AND APPLIED METEOROLOGY. PREPRINTS. 1968, 3rd. irreg., latest 1978. $20. ‡ American Meteorological Society, 45 Beacon St., Boston, MA 02108. adv. Indexed: Meteor. & Geoastrophys.Abstr.
Former titles: Conference on Aerospace and Aeronautical Meteorology. Preprints; National Conference on Aerospace Meteorology. Proceedings (ISSN 0077-3913)

551.5　　　　US
CONFERENCE ON COASTAL METEOROLOGY. (PREPRINTS) irreg.; 1976, Virginia Beach, VA. $20. American Meteorological Society, 45 Beacon St., Boston, MA 02108.

551.68　　　　US
CONFERENCE ON PLANNED AND INADVERTENT WEATHER MODIFICATION. PREPRINTS. 1968. irreg., 6th, 1977. $20. ‡ American Meteorological Society, 45 Beacon St., Boston, MA 02108. adv. Indexed: Meteor. & Geoastrophys.Abstr.
Former titles: Conference on Weather Modification. Preprints; National Conference on Weather Modification. Preprints (ISSN 0077-3956); National Conference on Weather Modification. Proceedings.

551.5　519.5　US
CONFERENCE ON PROBABILITY AND STATISTICS IN ATMOSPHERIC SCIENCES. PREPRINTS. 1968. irreg., 5th, 1977. $20. ‡ American Meteorological Society, 45 Beacon St., Boston, MA 02108. adv. Indexed: Meteor. & Geoastrophys.Abstr.
Formerly: Statistical Meteorological Conference. Proceedings.

551.635　　　　US　ISSN 0069-8636
CONFERENCE ON RADAR METEOROLOGY. PREPRINTS. 1951. biennial. $20. ‡ American Meteorological Society, 45 Beacon St., Boston, MA 02108. adv. Indexed: Meteor. & Geoastrophys.Abstr.

551.55　　　　US　ISSN 0069-8679
CONFERENCE ON SEVERE LOCAL STORMS. PREPRINTS. 7th, 1971. irreg., 10th, 1977. $20. ‡ American Meteorological Society, 45 Beacon St., Boston, MA 02108. adv. Indexed: Meteor. & Geoastrophys.Abstr.

551.63　　　　US
CONFERENCE ON WEATHER FORECASTING AND ANALYSIS AND AVIATION METEOROLOGY. PREPRINTS. 6th, 1976. irreg., latest 1978. $20. American Meteorological Society, 45 Beacon St., Boston, MA 02108.
Formerly: Conference on Weather Forecasting and Analysis. Preprints.

551.5　370　US
CURRICULA IN THE ATMOSPHERIC AND OCEANOGRAPHIC SCIENCES. Variant title: Curricula in the Atmospheric Sciences. biennial. $5. American Meteorological Society, 45 Beacon St., Boston, MA 02108.

551.5　　　　IO
DATA-DATA IKLIM DI INDONESIA. (Text in English and Indonesian) 1973. a. Meteorological and Geophysical Institute - Pusat Meteorologi dan Geofisika, Jalan Arif Rachman Hakim 3, Jakarta, Indonesia.

551.5　　　　GW　ISSN 0072-4130
DEUTSCHER WETTERDIENST. BERICHTE. 1953. irreg., no. 153, 1980. price varies. Deutscher Wetterdienst, Frankfurter Str. 135, Postfach 185, 6050 Offenbach (Main) 1, W. Germany (B.R.D.)

551.5　　　　GW　ISSN 0072-1603
DEUTSCHER WETTERDIENST. SEEWETTERAMT. EINZELVEROEFFENTLICHUNGEN. 1953. irreg., no. 98, 1979. price varies. Deutscher Wetterdienst, Seewetteramt, Bernhard Nocht-Str. 76, Postfach 180, 2000 Hamburg 4, W. Germany (B.R.D.) bk. rev. circ. 250.

551.5　　　　NE
DEVELOPMENTS IN ATMOSPHERIC SCIENCE. 1974. irreg., vol. 12, 1980. price varies. Elsevier Scientific Publishing Co., Box 211, 1000 AE Amsterdam, Netherlands.

551.5　　　　EC
ECUADOR. INSTITUTO NACIONAL DE METEOROLOGIA E HIDROLOGIA. ANUARIO METEOROLOGICO. 1959. a. available on exchange. Instituto Nacional de Meteorologia e Hidrologia, Daniel Hidalgo No. 132 y 10 de Agosto, Quito, Ecuador. index.
Supersedes: Ecuador. Servicio Nacional de Meteorologia e Hidrologia. Anuario Meteorologico (ISSN 0070-8941)

551.5　　　　UA
EGYPT. METEOROLOGICAL AUTHORITY. ANNUAL METEOROLOGICAL REPORT. a, latest 1972. $1.50. Meteorological Authority, Kubri-el-Qubbeh, Cairo, Egypt.

551.5　318　PN　ISSN 0378-6757
ESTADISTICA PANAMENA. SITUACION FISICA. SECCION 121-CLIMA. METEOROLOGIA. 1952-57. a. Bl..30. Direccion de Estadistica y Censo, Contraloria General, Apartado 5213, Panama 5, Panama. circ. 800.

551.5　　　　FI　ISSN 0358-2671
FINLAND. ILMATIETEEN LAITOS. ILMASAHKOHAVAINTOJA/FINNISH METEOROLOGICAL INSTITUTE. OBSERVATIONS OF ATMOSPHERIC ELECTRICITY. 1980. a. price varies. Ilmatieteen Laitos - Finnish Meteorological Institute, Box 503, SF-00101 Helsinki 10, Finland.

551.5　　　　FI　ISSN 0071-5204
FINLAND. ILMATIETEEN LAITOS. TIEDONANTOJA. (Text in Finnish) 1961. irreg., no. 34, 1980. price varies. ‡ Ilmatieteen Laitos - Finnish Meteorological Institute, Box 503, SF-00101 Helsinki 10, Finland.

551.4　　　　FI　ISSN 0355-1717
FINLAND. ILMATIETEEN LAITOS. TUTKIMUSSELOSTE; ilmansuojelu, ilmatiede, geomagnetismi ja aeronomia. (Text in Finnish) 1968. irreg., no. 81, 1979. Ilmatieteen Laitos - Finnish Meteorological Institute, Box 503, SF-00101 Helsinki 10, Finland.

551.5　　　　FI　ISSN 0071-5190
FINNISH METEOROLOGICAL INSTITUTE. CONTRIBUTIONS. (Text in English) 1925. irreg., no. 84, 1976. price varies. ‡ Ilmatieteen Laitos - Finnish Meteorological Institute, Box 503, SF-00101 Helsinki 10, Finland.

551.5　　　　FI　ISSN 0071-5220
FINNISH METEOROLOGICAL INSTITUTE. OBSERVATIONS OF RADIOACTIVITY. (Text in English) 1962. a. price varies. ‡ Ilmatieteen Laitos - Finnish Meteorological Institute, Box 503, SF-00101 Helsinki 10, Finland.

FINNISH METEOROLOGICAL INSTITUTE. OBSERVATIONS OF SATELLITES. VISUAL OBSERVATIONS OF ARTIFICIAL EARTH SATELLITES IN FINLAND. see *AERONAUTICS AND SPACE FLIGHT*

551.5　　　　FI　ISSN 0071-5239
FINNISH METEOROLOGICAL INSTITUTE. SOIL TEMPERATURE MEASUREMENTS. (Text in English) 1968. irreg., no. 3, 1979. price varies. ‡ Ilmatieteen Laitos - Finnish Meteorological Institute, Box 503, SF-00101 Helsinki 10, Finland.

551.41　　　　FI　ISSN 0355-1733
FINNISH METEOROLOGICAL INSTITUTE. TECHNICAL REPORT. (Text in English) 1971. irreg., no. 21, 1979. price varies. Ilmatieteen Laitos - Finnish Meteorological Institute, Box 503, SF-00100 Helsinki 10, Finland.

METEOROLOGY

550 UR
FIZIKA AERODISPERSNYKH SISTEM. (Text in Russian; summaries in English) 1969. irreg. Izdatel'stvo Kievskii Universitet, Bul'var Tarasa Shevchenko, 14, Kiev, U.S.S.R. (Subscr. to: Mezhdunarodnaya Kniga, Moscow, G-200, U. S. S. R.) illus.

550 UR
FIZIKA NIZHNEI ATMOSFERY. (Subseries of: Institut Eksperimentalnoi Meteorologii. Trudy) 1972. irreg. (Institut Eksperimentalnoi Meteorologii) Gidrometeoizdat, Vasilevskii ostrov, 3, Leningrad V-53, U.S.S.R. illus.

551.5 AT
FLINDERS INSTITUTE FOR ATMOSPHERIC AND MARINE SCIENCES. COMPUTING REPORTS. 1972. irreg., no. 11, 1978. Flinders Institute for Atmospheric and Marine Sciences, Bedford Park, S.A. 5042, Australia. Ed. Peter Schwerdtfeger. circ. 150.

551.5 AT
FLINDERS INSTITUTE FOR ATMOSPHERIC AND MARINE SCIENCES. RESEARCH REPORTS. 1972. irreg., no. 33, 1980. Flinders Institute for Atmospheric and Marine Sciences, Bedford Park, S.A. 5042, Australia. Ed. Peter Schwerdtfeger. circ. 200.

551.5 AT
FLINDERS INSTITUTE FOR ATMOSPHERIC AND MARINE SCIENCES. TECHNICAL REPORTS. 1973. irreg., no. 4, 1980. Aus.$20. Flinders Institute for Atmospheric and Marine Sciences, Bedford Park, S.A. 5042, Australia. Ed. Peter Schwerdtfeger. circ. 150.

551.5 GE ISSN 0072-1506
GERMANY (DEMOCRATIC REPUBLIC, 1949-) METEOROLOGISCHER DIENST. ABHANDLUNGEN. 1964. irreg., no. 118, 1976. price varies. Akademie-Verlag, Leipziger Strasse 3-4, 108 Berlin, E. Germany (D.D.R.)

551.5 GH
GHANA. METEOROLOGICAL DEPARTMENT. CLIMATOLOGICAL NOTES. irreg., latest no. 5. price varies. Meteorological Department, Box 87, Legon, Accra, Ghana.

551.5 GH
GHANA. METEOROLOGICAL DEPARTMENT. PROFESSIONAL NOTES. irreg., latest no. 23. price varies. Meteorological Department, Box 87, Legon, Accra, Ghana.

551.5 GH
GHANA. METEOROLOGICAL DEPARTMENT. SUN AND MOON TABLES FOR GHANA. Short title: Sun and Moon Tables for Ghana. 1954. a. NC.1. Meteorological Department, Box 87, Legon, Accra, Ghana.

551.5 UN ISSN 0084-1986
GLOBAL ATMOSPHERIC RESEARCH PROGRAMME. G A R P SPECIAL REPORTS. irreg. World Meteorological Organization, 41 Ave. Giuseppe Motta, CH-1211 Geneva 20, Switzerland (Dist. in U.S. by: Unipub, 345 Park Ave. S., New York, NY 10010)

551.5 UN ISSN 0084-1978
GLOBAL ATMOSPHERIC RESEARCH PROGRAMME. PUBLICATION SERIES. irreg. World Meteorological Organization, 41 Ave. Giuseppe Motta, CH-1211 Geneva 20, Switzerland (Dist. in U.S. by: Unipub, 345 Park Ave. S., New York, NY 10010)

551.5 UK ISSN 0072-6605
GREAT BRITAIN. METEOROLOGICAL OFFICE. ANNUAL REPORT. a. price varies. H. M. S. O., P. O. Box 569, London SE1 9NH, England.

551.5 UK ISSN 0072-6621
GREAT BRITAIN. METEOROLOGICAL OFFICE. SCIENTIFIC PAPER. 1960. irreg. price varies. H. M. S. O., P. O. Box 569, London SE1 9NH, England.

551.6 GY
GUYANA. HYDROMETEOROLOGICAL SERVICE. ANNUAL CLIMATOLOGICAL DATA SUMMARY. (Subseries of: Guyana. Hydrometeorological Service) a. Hydrometeorological Service, Georgetown, Guyana. illus.

551.5 IS
HEBREW UNIVERSITY OF JERUSALEM. DEPARTMENT OF ATMOSPHERIC SCIENCES. LIST OF CONTRIBUTIONS. 1970. a. Hebrew University of Jerusalem, Department of Atmospheric Sciences, Terra Santa College Building, Jerusalem, Israel.

HOERBIGER INSTITUT. MITTEILUNGEN. see *ASTRONOMY*

551.5 HK
HONG KONG. ROYAL OBSERVATORY. CLIMATOLOGICAL NOTE. 1976. a. Royal Observatory, Nathan Road, Kowloon, Hong Kong, Hong Kong.

551.5 HK
HONG KONG. ROYAL OBSERVATORY. OCCASIONAL PAPER. irreg., no. 33, 1976. Royal Observatory, Nathan Rd., Kowloon, Hong Kong, Hong Kong.

551.5 CS
HYDROMETEOROLOGICKY USTAV. SBORNIK PREDPISU. irreg. price varies. Holeckova 8, 151 29 Prague 5, Czechoslovakia.

551.5 CS
HYDROMETEOROLOGICKY USTAV. VYROCNI ZPRAVA. a. price varies. Statni Nakladatelstvi Technicke Literatury, Spalena 51, 113 02 Prague 1, Czechoslovakia.

551.57 CS
HYDROMETEOROLOGICKY USTAV, BRATISLAVA. ZBORNIK PRAC. (Text in Russian; summaries in Czech or Slovak, and in German) 1972. irreg., approx. biennial. 30 Kcs. Slovenske Pedagogicke Nakladatelstvo, Sasinkova 5, 891 12 Bratislava, Czechoslovakia. illus.

551.5 US
I A M P NEWS BULLETIN. irreg. International Association of Meteorology and Atmospheric Physics, c/o Stanley Ruttenberg, Sec.-Gen., National Center for Atmospheric Research, Box 3000, Boulder, CO 80307.

ICEFIELD RANGES RESEARCH PROJECT SCIENTIFIC RESULTS. see *EARTH SCIENCES*

551.5 II ISSN 0250-6017
INDIAN INSTITUTE OF TROPICAL METEOROLOGY. ANNUAL REPORT. 1971/72. a. contr.circ. Indian Institute of Tropical Meteorology, Ramdurg House, University Rd., Poona 411005, India. circ. controlled.

551.5 II ISSN 0250-6009
INDIAN INSTITUTE OF TROPICAL METEOROLOGY. RESEARCH REPORT. 1971. irreg. Indian Institute of Tropical Meteorology, Ramdurg House, University Rd., Poona 411005, India. circ. controlled.

551.5 UR
INSTITUT EKSPERIMENTAL'NOI METEOROLOGII. TRUDY. vol. 16, 1977. irreg. price varies. Izdatel'stvo Gidrometeoizdat, Moskovskoe Otdelenie, Ul. Buzheninovskaya, 42-1, Moscow 107061, U.S.S.R. abstr. circ. 400.

551.5 AO
INSTITUTO DE INVESTIGACAO AGRONOMICA DE ANGOLA. DIVISAO DE METEOROLOGIA AGRICOLA. ANUARIO. 1972. a. free. Instituto de Investigacao Agronomica de Angola, C.P. 406, Nova Lisboa, Angola. Indexed: Trop.Abstr.

505 RM
INSTITUTUL DE METEOROLOGIE SI HIDROLOGIE. STUDII DE CLIMATOLOGIE. (Text in Romanian; summaries in English, French, Russian) 1974. irreg. Institutul de Meteorologie si Hidrologie, Soseaua Bucuresti-Ploiesti 97, Bucharest, Romania. illus.

551.5 PL
INSTYTUT METEOROLOGII I GOSPODARKI WODNEJ. PRACE. (Text in Polish; summaries in English and Russian) 1974. irreg., 1976, no. 4. 140 Zl. single issue. Instytut Meteorologii i Gospodarki Wodnej, Ul. Podlesna 61, 00-967 Warsaw, Poland.

551.576 CN ISSN 0074-3011
INTERNATIONAL CONFERENCE ON CLOUD PHYSICS. PROCEEDINGS. 1968. irreg., 1968, 14th, Toronto. Can.$20. (International Association of Meteorology and Atmospheric Physics) International Commission on Cloud Physics, Inquire: Prof. W. Hitschfeld, Sec., Dept. of Meteorology, McGill University, Montreal 110, Que, Canada. Ed. R. List. circ. 1,500.
Proceedings published in host country

551.5 SW
INTERNATIONAL METEOROLOGICAL INSTITUTE IN STOCKHOLM. ANNUAL REPORT. (Report year ends June 30) 1973. a. free. International Meteorological Institute in Stockholm, Arrhenius Laboratory, S-106 91 Stockholm, Sweden. Ed. Marianne Skaarman. circ. 600.

551.5 IS ISSN 0075-126X
ISRAEL. METEOROLOGICAL SERVICE. ANNUAL RAINFALL SUMMARY. SERIES B (OBSERVATIONAL DATA) (Text and summaries in English and Hebrew) 1947/48. a. $0.40. Meteorological Service, Box 25, Bet Dagan, Israel.

551.5 IS ISSN 0075-1286
ISRAEL. METEOROLOGICAL SERVICE. ANNUAL WEATHER REPORT. SERIES B (OBSERVATIONAL DATA) (Text and summaries in Hebrew and English) 1949. a. $0.40. Meteorological Service, Box 25, Bet Dagan, Israel.

551.5 IS ISSN 0075-1278
ISRAEL. METEOROLOGICAL SERVICE. SERIES A (METEOROLOGICAL NOTES) (Text in English and Hebrew) 1951. irreg. Meteorological Service, Box 25, Bet Dagan, Israel.

551.5 IS ISSN 0444-6801
ISRAEL. METEOROLOGICAL SERVICE. SERIES C (MISCELLANEOUS PAPERS) (Text in Hebrew and English) 1949. irreg. Meteorological Service, Box 25, Bet Dagan, Israel.

551.5 IS
ISRAEL. METEOROLOGICAL SERVICE. SOLAR RADIATION AND RADIATION BALANCE AT BET DAGAN, ISRAEL. SERIES B (OBSERVATIONAL DATA) (Text in Hebrew or English) 1969. a. $1.20. Meteorological Service, Box 25, Bet Dagan, Israel.

551.51 IT ISSN 0075-1952
ISTITUTO DI FISICA DELL'ATMOSFERA, ROME. RAPPORTI INTERNI PROVVISORI ADIFFUSIONE LIMITATA. (Contribution in Italian and English) 1966. irreg. Istituto di Fisica dell'Atmosfera, Piazzale Luigi Sturzo 31, 00144 Rome, Italy. Indexed: Meteor. & Geoastrophys.Abstr.

551.51 IT ISSN 0075-1960
ISTITUTO DI FISICA DELL'ATMOSFERA, ROME. RAPPORTI SCIENTIFICI. (Contributions in Italian and English) 1962. irreg. Istituto di Fisica dell'Atmosfera, Piazzale Luigi Sturzo 31, 00144 Rome, Italy. Indexed: Meteor. & Geoastrophys.Abstr.

551.51 IT ISSN 0075-1979
ISTITUTO DI FISICA DELL'ATMOSFERA, ROME. RAPPORTI TECNICI. (Contributions in Italian, English and French) 1961. irreg. Istituto di Fisica dell'Atmosfera, Piazzale Luigi Sturzo 31, 00144 Rome, Italy. Indexed: Meteor. & Geoastrophys.Abstr.

METEOROLOGY

551.51   IT   ISSN 0075-191X
ISTITUTO DI FISICA DELL'ATMOSFERA, ROME. CONTRIBUTI SCIENTIFICI: PUBBLICAZIONI DI FISICA DELL'ATMOSFERA E DI METTEOROLOGIA. (Contributions in Italian, English and German) 1964. irreg. Istituto di Fisica dell'Atmosfera, Piazzale Luigi Sturzo 31, 00144 Rome, Italy. Indexed: Meteor. & Geoastrophys.Abstr.

551.51   IT   ISSN 0075-1928
ISTITUTO DI FISICA DELL' ATMOSFERA, ROME. PUBBLICAZIONI DIDATTICHE. 1962. irreg. $10. Istituto di Fisica dell'Atmosfera, Piazzale Luigi Sturzo 31, 00144 Rome, Italy. Indexed: Meteor. & Geoastrophys.Abstr.

551.51   IT   ISSN 0075-1936
ISTITUTO DI FISICA DELL'ATMOSFERA, ROME. PUBBLICAZIONI SCIENTIFICHE. (Contributions in Italian and English) 1962. irreg. Istituto di Fisica dell'Atmosfera, Piazzale Luigi Sturzo 31, 00144 Rome, Italy. Indexed: Meteor. & Geoastrophys.Abstr.

551.51   IT   ISSN 0075-1944
ISTITUTO DI FISICA DELL'ATMOSFERA, ROME. PUBBLICAZIONI VARIE. (Contributions in Italian and English) 1962. irreg. Istituto di Fisica dell'Atmosfera, Piazzale Luigi Sturzo 31, 00144 Rome, Italy. Indexed: Meteor. & Geoastrophys.Abstr.

551.4   IT   ISSN 0082-6448
ISTITUTO SPERIMENTALE TALASSOGRAFICO, TRIESTE. ANNUARIO. 1954. a. L.2000. Istituto Sperimentale Talassografico, Viale R. Gessi, 2, 34123 Trieste, Italy.

551.65   IT   ISSN 0075-1731
ITALY. ISTITUTO CENTRALE DI STATISTICA. ANNUARIO DI STATISTICHE METEOROLOGICHE. a. L.12000. Istituto Centrale di Statistica, Via C. Balbo, 16, 00100 Rome, Italy. circ. 800.

551.65   JA   ISSN 0448-3758
JAPAN. METEOROLOGICAL AGENCY. ANNUAL REPORT/KISHO-CHO NENPO ZENKOKU KISHOHYO. (Issued in two parts) 1886/1887. a. $12. Japan Weather Association, c/o Japan Meteorological Agency, 1-3-4 Otemachi, Chiyoda-ku, Tokyo 100, Japan.

551.6   JA   ISSN 0075-3467
JAPANESE PROGRESS IN CLIMATOLOGY/ NIPPON NO KIKOGAKU NO SHINPO. (Text in English) 1964. a. $5 also available on exchange. (Japanese Climatological Seminar - Kikogaku Danwakai) Tokyo University of Education, Laboratory of Climatology, 3-29-1 Otsuka, Bunkyo-ku, Tokyo 112, Japan. Ed. Dr. T. Sekiguti. circ. 1,050.
Climatology

551.63   US
JOURNAL OF WEATHER MODIFICATION. 1969. a. $30. Weather Modification Association, Box 8116, Fresno, CA 93727. Ed. Thomas J. Henderson. adv. cum index 1969-1976. circ. 500. (back issues avail.)

551.5   UR
KLIMAT I GIDROGRAFIYA ZABAIKAL'YA. 1972. irreg. 0.40 Rub. Geograficheskoe Obshchestvo S.S.S.R. Zabaikal'skii Filial, Chita, U. S. S. R. illus.

551.5   KO
KOREA (REPUBLIC). CENTRAL METEOROLOGICAL OFFICE. ANNUAL REPORT. a. 1000 Won($2) Central Meteorological Office, Seoul, S. Korea.

551.5   CN   ISSN 0076-1877
MCGILL UNIVERSITY, MONTREAL. BRACE RESEARCH INSTITUTE. ANNUAL REPORT. 1958. a. Can.$1.50. McGill University, Brace Research Institute, Ste. Anne de Bellevue, Que. H0A 1C0, Canada.

551.6   CN   ISSN 0076-1931
MCGILL UNIVERSITY, MONTREAL. DEPARTMENT OF GEOGRAPHY. CLIMATOLOGICAL RESEARCH SERIES. 1966. irreg. price varies. McGill University, Department of Geography, C.P. 6070, Station A, Montreal, H3C 3G1, Que., Canada. Ed. Prof. B. J. Garnier. circ. 15.
Climatology

551.5   CN   ISSN 0076-1842
MCGILL UNIVERSITY, MONTREAL. DEPARTMENT OF METEOROLOGY. PUBLICATION IN METEOROLOGY. (Text in English and French) 1955. irreg. free. McGill University, Department of Meteorology, 805 Sherbrooke St. W., Montreal, Que., Canada. bibl. illus. circ. 150. Indexed: Arct.Bibl.

551.5   MW
MALAWI. METEOROLOGICAL SERVICES. TOTALS OF MONTHLY AND ANNUAL RAINFALL. (Text and summaries in English) 1969/70. a, latest issue 1976-77. K.0.50. Meteorological Services, Box2, Chileka, Malawi (Avail. from: Government Printer, Box 37, Zomba, Malawi) stat.

551.5   MY   ISSN 0126-8864
MALAYSIA. METEOROLOGICAL SERVICE. SUMMARY OF OBSERVATIONS FOR MALAYSIA. (Text and summaries in English) 1930. a. $30. ‡ Meteorological Service - Perkhidmatan Kujicuaca Malaysia, Jalan Sultan, Petaling Jaya, Selangor, Malaysia.
Formerly: Malaysia. Meterological Service. Summary of Observations for Malaya, Sabah and Sarawak.

551.5   MF   ISSN 0076-5511
MAURITIUS. METEOROLOGICAL SERVICES. REPORT. a, latest issue 1973-74. price varies. Government Printing Office, Elizabeth II Ave., Port Louis, Mauritius.

530   US   ISSN 0076-5643
MAX-PLANCK-INSTITUT FUER AERONOMIE. MITTEILUNGEN. 1959. irreg.; vol. 55, 1977. price varies. Springer-Verlag, 175 Fifth Ave., New York, NY 10010 (Also Berlin, Heidelberg, Vienna) (reprint service avail. from ISI)

551   GW   ISSN 0543-5919
"METEOR" FORSCHUNGSERGEBNISSE. REIHE B. METEOROLOGIE UND AERONOMIE. (Text in German; summaries in English) 1967. irreg., no. 13, 1978. price varies. (Deutsche Forschungsgemeinschaft) Gebrueder Borntraeger Verlagsbuchhandlung, Johannesstr. 3A, 7000 Stuttgart 1, W. Germany (B.R.D.) Eds. L. Hasse, H.U. Roll. charts. illus.

551.5   FI   ISSN 0076-6747
METEOROLOGICAL YEARBOOK OF FINLAND. PART 1A: CLIMATOLOGICAL DATA. (Text in English and Finnish) 1962. a. price varies. ‡ Ilmatieteen Laitos - Finnish Meteorological Institute, Box 503, SF-00101 Helsinki 10, Finland.

551.5   FI   ISSN 0076-6739
METEOROLOGICAL YEARBOOK OF FINLAND. PART 1B: CLIMATOLOGICAL DATA FROM JOKIOINEN AND SODANKYLA OBSERVATORIES. (Text in Finnish and English) 1961. a. price varies. ‡ Ilmatieteen Laitos - Finnish Meteorological Institute, Box 503, SF-00101 Helsinki 10, Finland.

551.5   FI   ISSN 0076-6755
METEOROLOGICAL YEARBOOK OF FINLAND. PART 2: PRECIPITATION AND SNOW COVER DATA. (Text in Finnish and English) 1960. a. price varies. ‡ Ilmatieteen Laitos - Finnish Meteorological Institute, Box 503, SF-00101 Helsinki 10, Finland.

551.5   FI   ISSN 0076-6763
METEOROLOGICAL YEARBOOK OF FINLAND. PART 4: MEASUREMENTS OF RADIATION AND BRIGHT SUNSHINE. (Text in English and Finnish) 1966. a. price varies. ‡ Ilmatieteen Laitos, Box 503, SF-00101 Helsinki 10, Finland.

551.5   NO
METEOROLOGISKE ANNALER. (Text in English) vol. 6, 1974. m. Norske Meteorologiske Instituti, Blindern, Oslo 3, Norway. Ed. O. Haug. charts.

551.51   JA   ISSN 0077-264X
NAGOYA UNIVERSITY. RESEARCH INSTITUTE OF ATMOSPHERICS. PROCEEDINGS/ NAGOYA DAIGAKU KUDEN KENKYUSHO HOKOKU. (Text in English) 1953. a. Nagoya University, Research Institute of Atmospherics - Nagoya Daigaku Kuden Kenkyusho, 3-13 Honohara, Toyokawa 442, Aichi-ken, Japan.

551.65   JA   ISSN 0386-5525
NATIONAL INSTITUTE OF POLAR RESEARCH. MEMOIRS. SERIES B: METEOROLOGY. (Text in English) 1969. irreg., No. 2, 1974. exchange basis. National Institute of Polar Research - Kokuritsu Kyokuchi Kenkyujo, 9-10 Kaga, 1-chome, Itabashi-ku, Tokyo 174, Japan. Ed Takesi Nagata. circ. 1,000. Indexed: Curr.Antarc.Lit.
Supersedes: Japanese Antarctic Research Expedition, 1956-1962. Scientific Reports. Series B: Meteorology (ISSN 0075-336X)

551.5   II
NATIONAL REPORT FOR INDIA: METEOROLOGY AND ATMOSPHERIC ANALYSIS. (Text in English) triennial. Meteorological Department, Lodi Road, New Delhi 110003, India.

551.5   II
NATIONAL REPORT FOR INDIA: SEISMOLOGY AND PHYSICS OF THE EARTH'S INTERIOR. (Text in English) triennial. Meteorological Department, Lodi Rd., New Delhi 110003, India.
Continues: India (Republic). Meteorological Department Report on Seismology (ISSN 0536-9029)

551.5   NA   ISSN 0077-667X
NETHERLANDS ANTILLES. BUREAU VOOR DE STATISTIEK. STATISTIEK VAN DE METEOROLOGISCHE WAARNEMINGEN IN DE NEDERLANDSE ANTILLEN.* irreg. fl.2. Bureau voor de Statistiek, Fort Amsterdam, Netherlands Antilles.

551.5 630   IT
OSSERVAZIONI DI METEOROLOGIA AGRARIA DELLA PUGLIA E BASILICATA; dati meteorologici della Puglia e Lucania. (Subseries of: Istuto Sperimentale Agronomico. Annali) 1953,N.S. 1969. a. exchange basis. Istituto Sperimentale Agronomico, Via Celso Ulpiani 5, Bari, Italy. Ed. V. Rizzo. charts.
Formerly: Bollettino Meteorologico Agrario & Dati Meteorologico della Puglia e Luciania (ISSN 0006-6834)

551.5   US
OXFORD MONOGRAPHS ON METEOROLOGY. irreg. price varies. Oxford University Press, 200 Madison Ave., New York, NY 10016 (And Ely House, 37 Dover St., London W1X 4AH, England) Ed. P. A. Sheppard.

551.5   PN   ISSN 0078-8899
PANAMA CANAL COMPANY. METEOROLOGICAL AND HYDROGRAPHIC BRANCH. CLIMATOLOGICAL DATA: CANAL ZONE AND PANAMA. 1908. irreg., latest 1971. free. Panama Canal Company, Meteorological and Hydrographic Branch, Box M, Balboa Heights, Panama.

551.5   PH
PHILIPPINE AGRICULTURAL METEOROLOGY BULLETIN. 1970. irreg., latest Jan.-Mar. 1974. 3p.($0.50) Philippine Atmospheric, Geophysical and Astronomical Services Administration, Agricultural Meteorological Division, Weather Bureau, Quezon City, Philippines. charts. stat. circ. 130.

551.5 551   PO
PORTUGAL. INSTITUTO NACIONAL DE METEOROLOGIA E GEOFISICA. REVISTA. 1978. a. Esc.300. Instituto Nacional de Meteorologia e Geofisica, Rua C do Aeroporto, 1700 Lisbon, Portugal. charts. illus. stat.

PROBLEMY FIZIKI ATMOSFERY. see *PHYSICS*

610 551.5   NE
PROGRESS IN BIOMETEOROLOGY. (Issued in three parts: Division A: Progress in Human Biometeorology, Division B: Progress in Animal Biometeorology, and Division C: Progress in Plant Biometeorology) (Text in English) 1972. irreg. price varies. Swets Publishing Service (Subsidiary of: Swets en Zeitlinger B.V.) Heereweg 347B, 2161 CA Lisse, Netherlands (Dist. in the U.S. and Canada by: Swets North America, Inc. Box 517, Berwyn, PA 19312) circ. 600. Indexed: Biol.Abstr. Chem.Abstr.

METEOROLOGY

551.6 US
PUBLICATIONS IN CLIMATOLOGY. 1948. irreg., 1 vol. of 3-4 nos. per yr. price varies. (Laboratory of Climatology, Centerton, N.J.) C. W. Thornthwaite Associates, Rt. 1, Centerton, Elmer, NJ 08318. circ. 500.
Climatology

551.527 NO
RADIATION OBSERVATIONS IN BERGEN; radiation yearbook. 1965. a. free. Universitetet i Bergen, Radiation Observatory, Geophysical Institute, Bergen, Norway. Ed. H. Schieldrup Paulsen.

551.5 551 BE ISSN 0072-4440
RIJKSUNIVERSITEIT TE GENT. STERRENKUNDIG OBSERVATORIUM. MEDEDELINGEN: METEOROLOGIE EN GEOFYSICA. (Text and summaries in Dutch, English or French) 1961. irreg. free. Rijksuniversiteit te Gent, Sterrenkundig Observatorium, Krijgslaan 271, B-9000 Ghent, Belgium.

551.5 CS ISSN 0554-9221
ROCENKA POVETRNOSTNICH POZOROVANI OBSERVATORE KARLOV. a. 10 Kcs. Holeckova 8, 151 29 Prague 5, Czechoslovakia.

551.5 614.71 CS
ROCENKA ZNECISTENI OVZDUSI NA UZEMI C S R. a. 92.50 Kcs. Holeckova 8, 151 29 Prague 5, Czechoslovakia.

551.5 PL ISSN 0080-3448
ROCZNIK ELEKTRYCZNOSCI ATMOSFERYCZNEJ I METEOROLOGII. (Subseries of Prace Obserwatorium Geofizycznego Im. St. Kalinowskiego w Swidrze) (Text in French and Polish; summaries in French) 1961. irreg. 25 Zl. (Polska Akademia Nauk, Instytut Geofizyki) Panstwowe Wydawnictwo Naukowe, Miodowa 10, Warsaw, Poland (Dist. by Ars Polona-Ruch, Krakowskie Przedmiescie 7, Warsaw, Poland) Ed. Roman Teisseyre.

551.527 FR
S B A R M O. BULLETIN. (Text in English) vol. 6, 1974. irreg (4/yr) 130 F.($20) per volume (4 issues) Scientific Ballooning and Radiations Monitoring Organization, Observatoire de Parc Saint-Marie, 4 Avenue Neptune, 94 Saint-Maur des Fosses, France. bibl. charts.

551.6 CN ISSN 0706-9391
SASKATCHEWAN RESEARCH COUNCIL. PHYSICS DIVISION. ANNUAL CLIMATIC SUMMARY. 1975. Saskatchewan Research Council., Physics Division, 30 Campus Drive, Saskatoon, Sask. S7N 0X1, Canada.

551.6 SZ ISSN 0080-7338
SCHWEIZERISCHE METEOROLOGISCHE ZENTRALANSTALT. ANNALEN. 1864. a. 54 Fr. Schweizerische Meteorologische Zentralanstalt - Swiss Meteorological Institute, Kraehbuehlstrasse 58, CH-8044 Zurich, Switzerland. index.

551.5 SZ ISSN 0080-7346
SCHWEIZERISCHE METEOROLOGISCHE ZENTRALANSTALT. VEROEFFENTLICHUNGEN. (Text in German, French and Italian; summaries in German, French, Italian and English) 1962. irreg., no. 37, 1976. price varies. Schweizerische Meteorologische Zentralanstalt - Swiss Meteorological Institute, Kraehbuehlstr. 58, 8044 Zurich, Switzerland.

551.527 SA
SOUTH AFRICA. WEATHER BUREAU. ANNUAL RADIATION BULLETIN/JAARLIKSE STRALINGSBULLETIN. a. R.2.65. Weather Bureau, Department of Transport, Private Bag X193, Pretoria 0001, South Africa.

551.5 SA ISSN 0081-2315
SOUTH AFRICA. WEATHER BUREAU. RADIOSONDE RAWIN DATA. 1956. irreg., latest issue 1974. R.1.10. Weather Bureau, Department of Transport, Private Bag 193, Pretoria 0001, South Africa.

551.65 SA ISSN 0081-2323
SOUTH AFRICA. WEATHER BUREAU. REPORT ON METEOROLOGICAL DATA OF THE YEAR/VERSLAG OOR WEERKUNDIGE DATA VAN DIE JAAR. 1926. irreg., latest issue 1973. R.1.80. Weather Bureau, Department of Transport, Private Bag 193, Pretoria 0001, South Africa. circ. 900.

551.6 SA
SOUTH AFRICA. WEATHER BUREAU. TECHNICAL PAPER/TEGNIESE VERHANDELINGE. 1974. irreg., no. 4, 1976. R.0.40. Weather Bureau, Department of Transport, Private Bag X193, Pretoria 0001, South Africa.

551.5 SA ISSN 0081-2331
SOUTH AFRICA. WEATHER BUREAU. W.B. SERIES. 1971. irreg. no. 38, 1975. price varies. Weather Bureau, Department of Transport, Private Bag X193, Pretoria 0001, South Africa. circ. 1,500.

551.5 US
SYMPOSIUM ON METEOROLOGICAL OBSERVATION AND INSTRUMENTATION. PREPRINTS. irreg., 4th, 1978. $20. American Meteorological Society, 45 Beacon St., Boston, MA 02108.

551.5 US
SYMPOSIUM ON TURBULENCE, DIFFUSION AND AIR POLLUTION. PREPRINTS. irreg., 4th, 1979. $25. American Meteorological Society, 45 Beacon St., Boston, MA 02108.
Formerly: Symposium on Atmospheric Turbulence, Diffusion and Air Quality. Preprints.

551.5 TG
TOGO. DIRECTION DE LA METEOROLOGIE NATIONALE. RESUME ANNUEL DU TEMPS. a. Direction de la Meteorologie Nationale, B.P. 1505, Lome, Togo.

551.6 US
U.S. NATIONAL OCEANIC AND ATMOSPHERIC ADMINISTRATION. ANNUAL CLIMATE DIAGNOSTIC WORKSHOP. PROCEEDINGS. 1976. a. U.S. National Oceanic and Atmospheric Administration, 6010 Executive Blvd., Rockville, MD 20852.
Climatology

551.6 551.46 US ISSN 0091-8512
U.S. NATIONAL OCEANIC AND ATMOSPHERIC ADMINISTRATION. NATIONAL CLIMATIC CENTER. MARINE CLIMATOLOGICAL SUMMARIES. 1961. irreg. $7.45. U.S. National Climatic Center, Federal Building, Asheville, NC 28801. (Co-Sponsor: World Meteorological Organization)
Climatology

551.6 551.46 US ISSN 0091-8725
U. S. NATIONAL WEATHER SERVICE. DATA ACQUISITION DIVISION. MARINE SURFACE OBSERVATIONS. (Subseries of United States National Weather Service. Weather Service Observing Handbook) irreg., latest edt. 1974. free. ‡ U.S. National Weather Service, U.S. National Oceanic and Atmospheric Administration, Washington, DC 20233. circ. 3,000. Key Title: Marine Surface Observations.
Supersedes: Manual of Marine Meteorological Observations, Circular M.

551.552 US ISSN 0092-2056
U. S. OFFICE OF FEDERAL COORDINATOR FOR METEOROLOGICAL SERVICES AND SUPPORTING RESEARCH. NATIONAL HURRICANE OPERATIONS PLAN. (Subseries of its F C M) 1962. irreg. U.S. National Oceanic and Atmospheric Administration, Federal Coordinator for Meteorological Services and Supporting Research, Rockville, MD 20852. illus. circ. 1,000. Key Title: National Hurricane Operations Plan.

UNIVERSITAET ZU KOELN. INSTITUT FUER GEOPHYSIK UND METEOROLOGIE. MITTEILUNGEN. see *EARTH SCIENCES — Geophysics*

551.6 UK
UNIVERSITY OF EAST ANGLIA. CLIMATIC RESEARCH UNIT. RESEARCH PUBLICATION. no. 3, 1974. irreg. price varies. University of East Anglia, Climatic Research Unit, School of Environmental Sciences, Norwich NR4 7TJ, England.

551.5271 US ISSN 0193-9629
UNIVERSITY OF WISCONSIN, MADISON. ENGINEERING EXPERIMENT STATION. ANNUAL REPORT. a. free. University of Wisconsin-Madison, Engineering Experiment Station, Informational Resources Office, 1500 Johnson Dr., Madison, WI 53706. Ed. Ann Bitter. charts. illus. Key Title: Annual Report - Engineering Experiment Station (Madison)

551.5 PL ISSN 0083-7334
UNIWERSYTET WARSZAWSKI. KATEDRA KLIMATOLOGII. PRACE I STUDIA.* (Text in Polish; summaries in English) 1964. a. available on exchange. Uniwersytet Warszawski, Krakowskie Przedmiescie 26/28, Warsaw, Poland.

551.5 SW
UPPSALA IONOSPHERIC OBSERVATORY. RAPPORTER AR. 1977. irreg. price varies. Uppsala Ionospheric Observatory, S-755 90 Uppsala, Sweden.

551.5 SW
UPPSALA IONOSPHERIC OBSERVATORY. RAPPORTER SR. 1977. irreg. price varies. Uppsala Ionospheric Observatory, S-755 90 Uppsala, Sweden.

551.5 SW
UPPSALA IONOSPHERIC OBSERVATORY. RAPPORTER TR. 1978. irreg. price varies. Uppsala Ionospheric Observatory, S-755 90 Uppsala, Sweden.

551.65 JA
WAKAYAMA PREFECTURE. ANNUAL REPORT OF METEOROLOGY/WAKAYAMA-KEN KISHO NENPO. (Text in Japanese) a. Wakayama Local Meteorological Observatory - Wakayama Chiho Kishodai, 4 Onoshiba-cho, Wakayama 640, Japan. charts. stat.

551.6 US
WEATHER ALMANAC. 1974. irreg.; 2nd edt. 1977. $35. Gale Research Company, Book Tower, Detroit, MI 48226. Eds. James A. Ruffner, Frank Bair.

551.65 US
WEATHER GUIDE CALENDAR. Short title: Weatherguide. 1975. a. $4.95. Freshwater Biological Research Foundation, Box 90, Navarre, MN 55392. Ed. Bruce Watson.
Former titles: Weather Guide Calendar Almanac; (until 1977): Minnesota and Environs Weather Almanac (ISSN 0095-7348)

551.6 US
WESTERN SNOW CONFERENCE. PROCEEDINGS. 1948. a. $7.50. Western Snow Conference, Room 360, U.S. Court House, Spokane, WA 99201. circ. 800.

551.5 UN ISSN 0084-1927
WORLD METEOROLOGICAL CONGRESS. ABRIDGED REPORT WITH RESOLUTIONS. (Text in English, French, Russian, Spanish) 1952. irreg. price varies. World Meteorological Organization, 41 Ave. Giuseppe Motta, CH-1211 Geneva 20, Switzerland (Dist. in U.S. by: Unipub, 345 Park Ave. S., New York, NY 10010)

551.5 UN ISSN 0084-1935
WORLD METEOROLOGICAL CONGRESS. PROCEEDINGS. (Text in English and French) 1952. irreg. World Meteorological Organization, 41 Ave. Giuseppe Motta, CH-1211 Geneva 20, Switzerland (Dist. in U.S. by: Unipub, Box 433, Murray Hill Station)

551.5 UN ISSN 0084-1994
WORLD METEOROLOGICAL ORGANIZATION. ANNUAL REPORTS. 1953. a. price varies. World Meteorological Organization, 41 Ave. Giuseppe Motta, CH-1211 Geneva 20, Switzerland (Dist. in U.S. by: Unipub, 345 Park Ave. S., New York, NY 10010)

551.5 UN
WORLD METEOROLOGICAL ORGANIZATION. BASIC DOCUMENTS AND OFFICIAL REPORTS. irreg. World Meteorological Organization, 41 Ave. Giuseppe Motta, CH-1211 Geneva 20, Switzerland (Dist. in U.S. by: Unipub, 345 Park Ave. S., New York, NY 10010)
Formerly: World Meteorological Organization. Basic Documents, Records and Reports (ISSN 0084-1943)

551.5   UN
WORLD METEOROLOGICAL ORGANIZATION.
EXECUTIVE COMMITTEE REPORTS:
ABRIDGED REPORTS WITH RESOLUTIONS.
irreg. price varies. World Meteorological
Organization, 41 Ave. Giuseppe Motta, CH-1211
Geneva 20, Switzerland (Dist. in U.S. by: Unipub,
345 Park Ave. S., New York, NY 10010)
    Formerly: World Meteorological Organization.
Executive Committee Sessions: Abridged Reports
with Resolutions (ISSN 0084-196X)

551.5   UN
WORLD METEOROLOGICAL ORGANIZATION.
REPORTS OF SESSIONS OF REGIONAL
ASSOCIATIONS. irreg. price varies. World
Meteorological Organization, 41 Ave. Giuseppe
Motta, CH-1211 Geneva 20, Switzerland (Dist. in
U.S. by: Unipub, 345 Park Ave. S., New York, NY
10010)
    Formerly: World Meteorological Association.
Regional Associations. Abridged Final Reports
(ISSN 0084-1900)

551.5   UN
WORLD METEOROLOGICAL ORGANIZATION.
REPORTS OF SESSIONS OF TECHNICAL
COMMISSIONS. irreg. price varies. World
Meteorological Organization, 41 Ave. Giuseppe
Motta, CH-1211 Geneva 20, Switzerland (Dist. in
U.S. by: Unipub, 345 Park Ave. S., New York, NY
10010)
    Formerly: World Meteorological Association.
Technical Commissions Abridged Final Reports
(ISSN 0084-1919)

WORLD METEOROLOGICAL ORGANIZATION.
SPECIAL ENVIRONMENTAL REPORTS. see
ENVIRONMENTAL STUDIES

551.5   UN   ISSN 0084-201X
WORLD METEOROLOGICAL ORGANIZATION.
TECHNICAL NOTES. 1954. irreg. price varies.
World Meteorological Organization, 41 Ave.
Giuseppe Motta, CH-1211 Geneva 20, Switzerland
(Dist. in U.S. by: Unipub, 345 Park Ave. S., New
York, NY 10010)

551.6   NE   ISSN 0084-2265
WORLD SURVEY OF CLIMATOLOGY. 1969.
irreg., vol. 7, 1977. price varies. Elsevier Scientific
Publishing Co., Box 211, 1000 AE Amsterdam,
Netherlands. Ed. H.E. Landsberg.
    Climatology

551.63   UN   ISSN 0084-2451
WORLD WEATHER WATCH PLANNING
REPORTS. 1966. irreg. price varies. World
Meteorological Organization, 41 Ave. Giuseppe
Motta, CH-1211 Geneva 20, Switzerland (Dist. in
U.S. by: Unipub, 345 Park Ave. S., New York, NY
10010)

551.5   RH   ISSN 0085-5693
ZIMBABWE. DEPARTMENT OF
METEOROLOGICAL SERVICES. RAINFALL
REPORT. a. ‡ Department of Meteorological
Services, Box BE 150, Belvedere, Salisbury,
Zimbabwe.

551.5   RH   ISSN 0085-5707
ZIMBABWE. DEPARTMENT OF
METEOROLOGICAL SERVICES. REPORT. a. ‡
Department of Meteorological Services, Box BE
150, Belvedere, Salisbury, Zimbabwe.

METEOROLOGY — Abstracting, Bibliographies, Statistics

551.5 016   GW   ISSN 0072-4149
DEUTSCHER WETTERDIENST.
BIBLIOGRAPHIEN. 1955. irreg., no.35, 1980.
price varies. Deutscher Wetterdienst, Frankfurter
Str. 135, Postfach 185, 6050 Offenbach (Main) 1,
W. Germany (B.R.D.)

551.5 016   IT   ISSN 0075-1901
ISTITUTO DI FISICA DELL'ATMOSFERA,
ROME. BIBLIOGRAFIA GENERALE. (Text in
Italian; occasionally English or French Editions
Available) 1963. irreg. Istituto di Fisica
dell'Atmosfera, Piazzale Luigi Sturzo 31, 00144
Rome, Italy. Indexed: Meteor. &
Geoastrophys.Abstr.

METROLOGY AND STANDARDIZATION

681 389   HU
ACTS IMEKO. 1958. irreg., 9th, 1982, Berlin (West)
International Measurement Confederation, IMEKO
Secretariat, P.O.B. 457, 1371 Budapest, Hungary
(Dist. in U.S. by Plenum Press, 227 W. 17 St., New
York, N.Y. 10011) (Co-publisher: North-Holland
Publishing Co.) Indexed: Chem.Abstr.
    Formerly: International Measurement
Conference. Proceedings. Acta IMEKO (ISSN
0074-6916)

681 530.7   US   ISSN 0568-0204
ADVANCES IN TEST MEASUREMENT; with
Instrumentation in the Aerospace Industry. 1963? a.
price varies. Instrument Society of America, Test
Measurement Division, 400 Stanwix St, Pittsburgh,
PA 15222.

389   US   ISSN 0363-5260
AMERICAN NATIONAL METRIC COUNCIL.
ANNUAL REPORT. a. American National Metric
Council, 1625 Massachusetts Ave., N.W.,
Washington, DC 20036. Key Title: Annual Report -
American National Metric Council.

389 658.5   US   ISSN 0360-6929
AMERICAN SOCIETY FOR QUALITY
CONTROL. ANNUAL TECHNICAL
CONFERENCE TRANSACTIONS. 1946. a. $17.
American Society for Quality Control, 161 W.
Wisconsin Ave, Milwaukee, WI 53203. index by
category, author and title. circ. 4,500. (also avail. in
microfiche from UMI) Indexed: Eng.Ind.
    Formerly: American Society for Quality Control.
Transactions of Annual Technical Conferences
(ISSN 0066-0159)

328.94 354.94   AT
AUSTRALIA. METRIC CONVERSION BOARD.
ANNUAL REPORT.* (Subseries of: Australia.
Parliament. Parliamentary Papers) a. Aus.$1.
Australian Government Publishing Service, Box 84,
Canberra, A.C.T. 2600, Australia.

389.6   AT
AUSTRALIAN ANTI-METRIC ASSOCIATION.
NEWSLETTER. irreg. Australian Anti-Metric
Association, 50 Cardigan St., Carlton, Vic. 3053,
Australia.

389   AU
AUSTRIA. BUNDESAMT FUER EICH- UND
VERMESSUNGSWESEN. AMTSBLATT FUER
DAS EICHWESEN. 1952. irreg (8/yr.) S.370.
Kommissionsverlag der Oesterreichischen
Staatsdruckerei, Rennweg 12a, A-1037 Vienna,
Austria. index. circ. 500.

389   UK   ISSN 0068-2578
BRITISH STANDARDS YEAR BOOK. a. £4 to non-
members. British Standards Institution, British
Standards House, 2 Park Street, London, W1,
England. circ. 40,000.

389.6   CN
CANADIAN STANDARDS ASSOCIATION.
ANNUAL REPORT. (Editions in English and
French) 1919. a. free. ‡ Canadian Standards
Association, 178 Rexdale Blvd., Rexdale, Ontario
M9W 1R3, Canada. circ. 15,000.

389.6   CN
CANADIAN STANDARDS ASSOCIATION.
STANDARDS CATALOGUE. 1930. a. free. ‡
Canadian Standards Association, 178 Rexdale Blvd,
Rexdale, Ont. M9W 1R3, Ont., M9W 1R3. circ.
250,000.
    Supersedes: Canadian Standards Association. List
of Publications.

389   FR
CATALOGUE DES NORMES FRANCAISES.
vol.32,1976. a. 120 F. Association Francaise de
Normalisation, Tour Europe - Cedex, 92080 Paris la
Defense, France. Ed. J. Abecassis. adv. circ. 15,000.

621.3   FR
COMITE INTERNATIONAL DES POIDS ET
MESURES. COMITE CONSULTATIF
D'ELECTRICITE. (RAPPORT ET ANNEXES)
(Travaux of sessions 1-8(1928-57) issued in Proces-
Verbaux du Comite International des Poids et
Mesures) 1961, 9th. irreg.; 15th session, 1978.
Bureau International des Poids et Mesures, Pavillon
de Breteuil, 92310 Sevres, France.

535   FR   ISSN 0588-621X
COMITE INTERNATIONAL DES POIDS ET
MESURES. COMITE CONSULTATIF DE
PHOTOMETRIE ET RADIOMETRIE.(RAPPORT
ET ANNEXES) (Sessions 1-4, 1937-1957 issued in
Proces-Verbaux du Comite International des Poids
et Mesures)) irreg; 1977, 9th session. Bureau
International des Poids et Mesures, Pavillon de
Breteuil, 92310 Sevres, France. charts, illus.

536.5   FR
COMITE INTERNATIONAL DES POIDS ET
MESURES. COMITE CONSULTATIF DE
THERMOMETRIE. RAPPORTS ET ANNEXES.
(Sessions 1-5 (1939-1958) issued in Proces-Verbaux
du Comite International des Poids et Mesures)) 6th
session, 1962. biennial. Bureau International des
Poids et Mesures, Pavillon de Breteuil, 92310
Sevres, France. bibl. charts. stat.

389   FR
COMITE INTERNATIONAL DES POIDS ET
MESURES. COMITE CONSULTATIF DES
UNITES (RAPPORT ET ANNEXES) 1967. irreg.;
7th session 1980. Bureau International des Poids et
Mesures, Pavillon de Breteuil, 92310 Sevres, France.

389   FR   ISSN 0588-6228
COMITE INTERNATIONAL DES POIDS ET
MESURES. COMITE CONSULTATIF POUR LA
DEFINITION DE LA SECONDE. (RAPPORT
ET ANNEXES) (First session issued in Proces-
Verbaux du Comite International des Poids et
Mesures) 1957. irreg; 8th session, 1977. Bureau
International des Poids et Mesures, Pavillon de
Breteuil, 92310 Sevres, France.

389   FR   ISSN 0588-6236
COMITE INTERNATIONAL DES POIDS ET
MESURES. COMITE CONSULTATIF POUR LA
DEFINITION DU METRE (RAPPORT ET
ANNEXES) (Sessions 1-2 (1953-1957) Issued in
Proces-Verbaux du Comite International des Poids
et Mesures) 1962, 3rd. irreg.; 6th session, 1979.
Bureau International des Poids et Mesures, Pavillon
de Breteuil, 92310 Sevres, France.

389   FR
COMITE INTERNATIONAL DES POIDS ET
MESURES. COMITE CONSULTATIF POUR LES
ETALONS DES MESURE DES
RAYONNEMENTS IONISANTS (RAPPORT ET
ANNEXES) (First session issued in Proces-Verbaux
du Comite International des Poids et Mesures)
1959. irreg.; 8th session, 1979. Bureau International
des Poids et Mesures, Pavillon de Breteuil, 92310
Sevres, France.
    Formerly: Comite International des Poids et
Mesures. Comite Consultatif pour les Etalons de
Mesure des Radiations Ionisantes(Rapport et
Annexes) (ISSN 0588-6244)

389   FR
COMITE INTERNATIONAL DES POIDS ET
MESURES. PROCES-VERBAUX DES SEANCES.
1875. irreg.; 69th session, 1979. Bureau
International des Poids et Mesures - International
Bureau of Weights and Measures, Pavillon de
Breteuil, 92300 Sevres, France. charts. illus. stat.
index.

389.6   AT
COMMONWEALTH SCIENTIFIC AND
INDUSTRIAL RESEARCH ORGANIZATION.
DIVISION OF APPLIED PHYSICS. BIENNIAL
REPORT. biennial. free. C. S. I. R. O., Division of
Applied Physics, P.O. Box 218, Lindfield, N.S.W.
2070, Australia. circ. 2,000.
    Former titles: Commonwealth Scientific and
Industrial Research Organization. National
Measurement Laboratory. Biennial Report;
Commonwealth Scientific and Industrial Research
Organization. National Standards Laboratory.
Biennial Report; C. S. I. R. O. Division of Physics &
Applied Physics. Annual Reports.

389.6 FR
CONFERENCE GENERALE DES POIDS ET MESURES. COMPTES RENDUS DES SEANCES. 1889. irreg., 16th, 1979. Bureau International des Poids et Mesures, 92310 Sevres, France.

389.6 MX
CONGRESO MEXICANO DE CONTROL DE CALIDAD. ANUAL. (In 2 vols.) 1973. a. $20. Instituto Mexicano de Control de Calidad, Thiers 251, Mexico 5, D.F., Mexico.

621.38 US ISSN 0070-6639
D I S A INFORMATION. MEASUREMENT AND ANALYSIS. (Editions appear in English and German) 1965. irreg., latest no. 24. free. D I S A Electronics, 779 Susquehanna Ave., Franklin Lakes, NJ 07417. Ed. N. J. Madsen. circ. 25,000.
  Formerly: D I S A Information. Electronic Measurement of Mechanic Events.

350.821 DK
DENMARK. JUSTERVAESENET. AARSBERETNING. 1977. a? Justervaesenet, Amager Blvd. 115, 2300 Copenhagen S, Denmark.

389.1 GW ISSN 0070-4261
DIN-TASCHENBUECHER. 1963. irreg. price varies. (Deutsches Institut fuer Normung e.V.) Beuth Verlag GmbH, Burggrafenstr. 4-7, 1000 Berlin 30, W. Germany (B.R.D.) circ. 2,000.

389 US ISSN 0070-6558
DIRECTORY OF UNITED STATES STANDARDIZATION ACTIVITIES. (Subseries of its Special Publication Series) irreg. U. S. National Bureau of Standards, Washington, DC 20234 (Orders to: Supt of Documents, Washington, DC 20402)

389 EI
E U R O N O R M. (Editions in French, German, Italian and Dutch) irreg. price varies. Office for Official Publications of the European Communities, C.P. 1003, Luxembourg 1, Luxembourg (Avail. also from: Association Francaise de Normalisation, Paris-La Defense; Institut Belge de Normalisation, Brussels; Beuth-Vertries, Berlin; Ente Nazionale Italiano di Unificazione, Milan; and Nederlands Normalistie-Instituut, The Hague)

389.1 GW ISSN 0071-0660
ENGLISH TRANSLATIONS OF GERMAN STANDARDS. 1952. irreg. (Deutsches Institut fuer Normung e.V.) Beuth Verlag GmbH, Burggrafenstr. 4-7, 1000 Berlin 30, W. Germany (B.R.D.) circ. 10,000.

620 SZ ISSN 0071-2981
EUROPEAN ORGANIZATION FOR QUALITY CONTROL. CONFERENCE PROCEEDINGS. 1970. a, 21st, 1977, Varna. European Organization for Quality Control, Box 2613, CH-3001 Berne, Switzerland.

389.152 UK ISSN 0072-6869
GREAT BRITAIN. DEPARTMENT OF THE ENVIRONMENT. METRICATION IN THE CONSTRUCTION INDUSTRY. irreg., 1971, no. 3. Department of the Environment, 2 Marsham St., London SW1P 3EB, England (Avail. from H.M.S.O., c/o Liaison Officer, Atlantic House, Holborn Viaduct, London EC1P 1BN, England)

389 FR ISSN 0335-394X
GUIDE DE L'ACHETEUR NF; equipement menager. 1962. a. 12 F. Association Francaise de Normalisation, Tour Europe - Cedex 7, 92080 Paris la Defense, France. abstr. illus. index. circ. 40,000.

389.6 US
HANDBOOK FOR METRIC USAGE. 1977. irreg. $6. American Home Economics Association, 2010 Massachusetts Ave. N.W., Washington, DC 20036.

389.6 IR
I S I R I YEARBOOK. (Text in English) 1975. a. free. Institute of Standards and Industrial Research of Iran, Box 2937, Teheran, Iran. Ed. F. Hazegh. circ. 1,000.

389.6 SZ ISSN 0303-3317
I S O ANNUAL REVIEW. (Text in English and French) 1972. a. International Organization for Standardization, 1 rue de Varembe, 1211 Geneva 20, Switzerland (Dist. in U.S. by: American National Standards Institute, 1430 Broadway, New York, NY 10018)

389.6 SZ ISSN 0303-3309
I S O CATALOGUE. (Text in English and French) a. International Organization for Standardization, 1 rue de Varembe, 1211 Geneva 20, Switzerland (Dist. in U.S. by: American National Standards Institute, 1430 Broadway, New York, NY 10018)

389 SZ
I S O INTERNATIONAL STANDARDS. (Body of existing I S O Recommendations and I S O International Standards called I S O Standards) 1954. irreg. price varies. International Organization for Standardization, 1 rue de Varembe, 1211 Geneva 20, Switzerland (Dist. in the U.S. by: American National Standards Institute, 1430 Broadway, New York, NY 10018)

389 SZ ISSN 0536-2067
I S O MEMENTO. (Text in English and French) a. International Organization for Standardization, 1 rue de Varembe, 1211 Geneva 20, Switzerland (Dist. in the U.S. by: American National Standards Institute, 1430 Broadway, New York, NY 10018)

389.6 US
IDENTIFIED SOURCES OF SUPPLY. 1960. a. $145. National Standards Association, Inc., 5116 River Rd., Washington, DC 20016. Ed. C. Miller. (also avail. in microfiche)
  Formerly: Source (Washington)

389 AT
M. C. B. NEWS. 1971. irreg. free. Metric Conversion Board, Box 587, Crows Nest, N.S.W. 2065, Australia. Ed. Dennis Blewett. circ. 14,000.
  Formerly: M. C. B. Newsletter (ISSN 0310-6462)

MARINE STANDARDIZATION IN JAPAN. see TRANSPORTATION — Ships And Shipping

389.6 CN ISSN 0383-9184
METRIC FACT SHEETS. 1973. irreg. $7 (subscription includes Metric Message) Canadian Metric Association, Box 35, Fonthill, Ont. L0S 1E0, Canada.

389.6 US
METRIC YEARBOOK. 1975. a. $25. J. J. Keller & Associates, Inc., 145 W. Wisconsin Ave., Neenah, WI 54956. Ed. Patricia Lauxx.

389 US ISSN 0081-4318
NATIONAL CONFERENCE OF STANDARDS LABORATORIES. PROCEEDINGS. 1962. irreg. U.S. National Bureau of Standards, Washington, DC 20234 (Orders to: NCSL Secretariat, NBS, Boulder, CO 80303)

389.1 US ISSN 0077-3964
NATIONAL CONFERENCE ON WEIGHTS AND MEASURES. REPORT. 1905. a. approx. $6. U.S. National Bureau of Standards, Washington, DC 20234. cum. index: 1905-60.

389 PK ISSN 0078-8457
PAKISTAN STANDARDS INSTITUTION. REPORT.* (Text in English) 1959-60. a. Pakistan Standards Institution, 39 Garden Road, Karachi 3, Pakistan.

POLITECHNIKA WROCLAWSKA. INSTYTUT METROLOGII ELEKTRYCZNEJ. PRACE NAUKOWE. KONFERENCJE. see ELECTRICITY AND ELECTRICAL ENGINEERING

POLITECHNIKA WROCLAWSKA. INSTYTUT METROLOGII ELEKTRYCZNEJ. PRACE NAUKOWE. MONOGRAFIE. see ELECTRICITY AND ELECTRICAL ENGINEERING

POLITECHNIKA WROCLAWSKA. INSTYTUT METROLOGII ELEKTRYCZNEJ. PRACE NAUKOWE. PRZEMYSL. see ELECTRICITY AND ELECTRICAL ENGINEERING

POLITECHNIKA WROCLAWSKA. INSTYTUT METROLOGII ELEKTRYCZNEJ. PRACE NAUKOWE. STUDIA I MATERIALY. see ELECTRICITY AND ELECTRICAL ENGINEERING

389 690 FR ISSN 0335-3559
REPERTOIRE DE MATERIAUX ET ELEMENTS CONTROLES DU BATIMENT. 1965. a. 12 F. Association Francaise de Normalisation, Tour Europe - Cedex 7, 92080 Paris la Defense, France. adv. bibl. index. circ. 7,500.

389.6 620 FI ISSN 0357-0312
S F S CATALOGUE; catalogue of Finnish national standards. (Text and summaries in English and Finnish) 1924. a. Fmk.25. Suomen Standardisoimisliitto, Bulevardi 5, 00120 Helsinki 12, Finland.

623.82 389 GW ISSN 0036-6048
SCHIFFBAU-NORMUNG. 1961. 1-2/yr. free. Deutsches Institut fuer Normung e.V., Normenausschuss Schiffbau, Kirchenallee 57, 2000 Hamburg 1, W. Germany (B.R.D.) circ. 480. (processed)

389.6 CS
SEZNAM PLATNYCH CESKOSLOVENSKYCH STATNICH A OBOROVYCH NOREM.* 1953. irreg. 63 Kcs. Urad pro Normalizaci a Mereni, Vaclavske nam. 19, 113 47 Prague 1, Czechoslovakia. Ed. Irena Murova. circ. 17,000.

350.821 SI
SINGAPORE. METRICATION BOARD. ANNUAL REPORT. (Text in English) 1971. a. free to qualified personnel. Metrication Board, 15 Grange Rd., Singapore 0923, Singapore. circ. controlled.

350.821 SI
SINGAPORE. METRICATION BOARD. METRIC GUIDE FOR CONSUMERS. irreg. Metrication Board, 15 Grange Rd., Singapore 0923, Singapore.

389 SA ISSN 0081-2137
SOUTH AFRICA. BUREAU OF STANDARDS. S A B S YEARBOOK. (Text in Afrikaans or English) 1963. a. price varies. Bureau of Standards, Private Bag X191, Pretoria 0001, South Africa. (looseleaf format)

STANDARDS FOR AUSTRALIAN ALUMINIUM MILL PRODUCTS. see METALLURGY

620.1 TZ
TANZANIA. BUREAU OF STANDARDS. DIRECTOR'S ANNUAL REPORT. 1976/77. a. Bureau of Standards, Box 9524, Dar es Salaam, Tanzania.

389 US
U.S. NATIONAL BUREAU OF STANDARDS. ANNUAL REPORT. 1902. a. price varies. U. S. National Bureau of Standards, Washington, DC 20234 (Orders to: Supt. Doc., Washington, DC 20402)
  Formerly: Technical Highlights of the National Bureau of Standards (ISSN 0083-1905)

389 US
U.S. NATIONAL BUREAU OF STANDARDS. FEDERAL INFORMATION PROCESSING STANDARDS. irreg. price varies. U.S. National Bureau of Standards, Washington, DC 20234 (Orders to: NTIS, Springfield, VA 22161)

389 US
U.S. NATIONAL BUREAU OF STANDARDS. MONOGRAPHS. irreg. price varies. U.S. National Bureau of Standards, Washington, DC 20234 (Orders to: Supt. of Documents, Washington, DC 20402)

389 US ISSN 0083-1840
U.S. NATIONAL BUREAU OF STANDARDS. NATIONAL STANDARD REFERENCE DATA SERIES. irreg. price varies. U. S. National Bureau of Standards, Washington, DC 20234 (Orders to: Supt. of Documents, Washington, DC 20402)

389.608 621.3   US
U.S. NATIONAL BUREAU OF STANDARDS. SEMICONDUCTOR MEASUREMENT TECHNOLOGY. irreg. U.S. National Bureau of Standards, Washington, DC 20234. illus.
Former titles: U.S. National Bureau of Standards. Semiconductor Measurement Technology. Quarterly Report (ISSN 0145-4676); Continues: U.S. National Bureau of Standards. Methods of Measurement for Semiconductor Materials, Process Control, and Devices; Quarterly Report (ISSN 0090-8541)

389   US   ISSN 0083-1913
U. S. NATIONAL BUREAU OF STANDARDS. TECHNICAL NOTES. 1959. irreg. price varies. U. S. National Bureau of Standards, Washington, DC 20234 (Orders to: Supt. of Documents, Washington, DC 20402)

389   US
U.S. NATIONAL BUREAU OF STANDARDS. VOLUNTARY PRODUCT STANDARDS. irreg. U. S. National Bureau of Standards, Washington, DC 20234 (Orders to: Supt. of Documents, Washington, DC 20402)
Former titles: U.S. National Bureau of Standards. Commercial Standards (ISSN 0083-1808) & U.S. National Bureau of Standards. Product Standards (ISSN 0083-1859)

MICROBIOLOGY

see Biology—Microbiology

MICROSCOPY

see Biology—Microscopy

MILITARY

see also Civil Defense

355.31   FR
AGENDA DES ARMEES. 1977. a. Editions Charles Lavauzelle et Cie, B.P. 8, 87350 Panazol, France.

358.41   US   ISSN 0065-4825
AIR OFFICER'S GUIDE. 1948. irreg., 24th edt., 1975. $8.95. Stackpole Books, Cameron and Kelker Sts., Harrisburg, PA 17105.

355   US   ISSN 0065-647X
ALMANAC OF WORLD MILITARY POWER. 1970. biennial. $45. Presidio Press, Box 3515, San Rafael, CA 94902. index. circ. 3,000.

355   FR
ANNUAIRE DEFENSE D'AFRIQUE ET DU MOYEN ORIENT. (Supplement to: Jeune Afrique) 1980. a. 150 F. Groupe J.A., 51 Av des Ternes, 75017 Paris, France. charts. illus. (reprint service avail from UMI)

359   AG   ISSN 0066-703X
ARGENTINA. DEPARTAMENTO DE ESTUDIOS HISTORICOS NAVALES. SERIE A: CULTURA NAUTICA. 1961. irreg. Departamento de Estudios Historicos Navales, Instituto de Publicaciones Navales, Av. Cordoba 547, Buenos Aires, Argentina.

359   AG   ISSN 0066-7048
ARGENTINA. DEPARTAMENTO DE ESTUDIOS HISTORICOS NAVALES. SERIE B: HISTORIA NAVAL ARGENTINA. 1960. irreg; no. 18, 1975. price varies. Departamento de Estudios Historicos Navales, Instituto de Publicaciones Navales, Av. Cordoba 547, Buenos Aires, Argentina.

359 920   AG   ISSN 0066-7056
ARGENTINA. DEPARTAMENTO DE ESTUDIOS HISTORICOS NAVALES. SERIE C: BIOGRAFIAS NAVALES ARGENTINAS. irreg. Departamento de Estudios Historicos Navales, Instituto de Publicaciones Navales, Av. Cordoba 547, Buenos Aires, Argentina.

359 980   AG
ARGENTINA. DEPARTAMENTO DE ESTUDIOS HISTORICOS NAVALES. SERIE E: DOCUMENTOS. 1977. irreg. Departamento de Estudios Historicos Navales, Instituto de Publicaciones Navales, Av. Cordoba 547, Buenos Aires, Argentina.

ARGENTINA. SECRETARIA DE GUERRA. DIRECCION DE ESTUDIOS HISTORICOS. BOLETIN BIBLIOGRAFICO. see *HISTORY — History Of North And South America*

399 739.7   CN
ARMS STUDY SERIES. 1975. irreg., no. 8, 1975. Museum Restoration Service, Box 390, Bloomfield, Ont. K0K 1G0, Canada.

355   US   ISSN 0148-6799
ARMY OFFICER'S GUIDE. 1930. irreg., 40th edt., 1975. $8.95. Stackpole Books, Cameron and Kelker Sts., Harrisburg, PA 17105. Ed. L. P. Crocker. circ. 10,000.
Formerly: Officer's Guide (ISSN 0078-3811)

355   II   ISSN 0004-3826
ARTILLERY JOURNAL. 1948. a. Artillery Association, School of Artillery, Deolali, India. adv. bk. rev. circ. 5,000.

355.115   AT
AUSTRALIA. DEPARTMENT OF VETERANS AFFAIRS. DIRECTORY OF EX-SERVICE ORGANISATIONS. 1971. a. free. Department of Veterans Affairs, Central Office, P.O. Box 21, Woden, A.C.T. 2606, Australia. Ed. Russell A. Faull.
Formerly: Australia. Repatriation Department. Directory of Ex-Service Organisations (ISSN 0310-2173)

335   AT
AUSTRALIAN DEFENSE EQUIPMENT CATALOGUE. 1975. a. Aus.$300. (Department of Productivity) Peter Isaacson Publications, 46-49 Porter St., Prahran, Vic. 3181, Australia. adv. illus.

355   GW   ISSN 0067-5253
BEITRAEGE ZUR WEHRFORSCHUNG. 1963. irreg. price varies. (Arbeitskreis fuer Wehrforschung) Wehr und Wissen Verlagsgesellschaft GmbH, Heilsbachstr., Postfach 87, 5300 Bonn-Duisdorf, W. Germany (B.R.D.)

355   GW
BERNARD UND GRAEFE AKTUELL. 1967. irreg., no. 18, 1976. price varies. (Arbeitskreis fuer Wehrforschung) Bernard und Graefe Verlag, Hubertusstr. 5, 8000 Munich 19, W. Germany (B.R.D.)
Incorporating: Wehrwissenschaftliche Berichte (ISSN 0083-7822); Wehrforschung Aktuell; Beitraege zur Wehrforschung.

355   UK
BIBLIOTHECA HISTORICO MILITARIS. (Text in German) 1976. irreg. £3.50. Carl Slienger, Box 4ST, London W1P 1AA, England.
History

355   US
BUILDING NATIONAL SECURITY; disarmament action guide. 1976. a. $10. Coalition for a New Foreign and Military Policy, 120 Maryland Ave. NE, Washington, DC 20002. Eds. Cynthia Washington, Tom Wenger. circ. 100,000.

354   CN   ISSN 0383-4638
CANADA. DEPARTMENT OF NATIONAL DEFENCE. DEFENCE. a. Can.$3($3.60) Department of National Defence, Ottawa, Ont., Canada. illus.

355   CN
CANADA. DEPARTMENT OF NATIONAL DEFENCE. DIRECTORATE OF HISTORY. OCCASIONAL PAPER. 1976. irreg. Can.$5.95($7.15) per no. Department of National Defence, Ottawa, Ont. K1A 0K2, Canada.

355   CN   ISSN 0316-1919
CANADA. NATIONAL MUSEUM OF MAN. MERCURY SERIES. CANADIAN WAR MUSEUM. PAPERS/CANADA. MUSEE NATIONAL DE L'HOMME. COLLECTION MERCURE. MUSEE CANADIEN DE LA GUERRE. DOSSIERS. (Text in English or French) 1972. irreg. free. (National Museum of Man) National Museums of Canada, Ottawa, Ontario K1A 0M8, Canada.
History

358   CN   ISSN 0068-8843
CANADIAN GUNNER. 1965. a. Can.$3. (Royal Regiment of Canadian Artillery) Leech Printing Ltd., Brandon, Man., Canada. (back issues avail)

971   CN
CANADIAN WAR MUSEUM. HISTORICAL PUBLICATIONS. irreg, no. 8, 1973. price varies. University of Toronto Press, Front Campus, Toronto, Ont. M5S 1A6, Canada.

355   II   ISSN 0069-2654
CHANAKYA DEFENCE ANNUAL. (Text in English) 1969. a. $10. ‡ Chanakya Publishing House, 3 Thornhill Rd., Allahabad 1, India. Ed. Ravi Kaul. adv. bk. rev. circ. 5,200. (back issues avail.)

CIVIL WAR COLLECTORS' DEALER DIRECTORY. see *HOBBIES — Antiques*

359   US   ISSN 0364-3263
COMBAT FLEETS OF THE WORLD. 1897. biennial. (U.S. Naval Institute) Naval Institute Press, Annapolis, MD 21402. Ed. Jean Labayle Couhat.

355.64   US   ISSN 0091-2905
COMMANDERS' CONFERENCE INFORMATION EXCHANGE PROGRAM. REPORT. (Conference for 1972- sponsored by various departments of the U.S. Armed Forces) a. Commanders' Conference Information Exchange Program, Governors Island, New York, NY 10004. illus. Key Title: Report on Annual Commanders' Conference Information Exchange Program.

909   US   ISSN 0084-9251
CONTRIBUTIONS IN MILITARY HISTORY. 1969. irreg. price varies. Greenwood Press, 88 Post Rd. W., Westport, CT 06881. Ed. Thomas E. Griess.

355   SZ
DEFENCE MARKET PROFILES. a. updates (plus base vol.) Interavia S.A., 86 Ave. Louis Casai, Case Postale 162, CH-1216 Cointrin/Geneva, Switzerland.

355 327   US
DEFENSE FOREIGN AFFAIRS HANDBOOK; political, economic & defense data on every country in the world. 1976. a. $97. Copley Associates, 2030 M St N.W. No. 602, Washington, DC 20036. Ed. Gregory R. Copley. circ. 2,500. (back issues avail.)

355   GW   ISSN 0417-3635
DEUTSCHES SOLDATENJAHRBUCH. 1953. a. DM.45. Schild-Verlag GmbH, Federseestr. 1, 8000 Munich 60, W. Germany (B.R.D.) Ed. Helmut Damerau. adv. bk. rev. bibl. charts. illus. stat. circ. 9,000(controlled)

EASTERN EUROPE REPORT: POLITICAL, SOCIOLOGICAL AND MILITARY AFFAIRS. see *POLITICAL SCIENCE*

355   SZ
ELECTRONIC WARFARE. a. updates plus base vol. Interavia S.A., 86 Ave. Louis Casai, Case Postale 162, CH-1216 Cointrin/Geneva, Switzerland.

366 940   FR
ETUDES MILITAIRES. 1973. irreg. 80 F. Centre d'Histoire Militaire, Montpellier, France. charts. stat.

FOERENINGEN ARMEMUSEI VAENNER. MEDDELANDEN: KUNGLIGA ARMEMUSEUM. see *MUSEUMS AND ART GALLERIES*

355 973   US   ISSN 0071-9641
FRONTIER MILITARY SERIES. 1951. irreg. price varies. Arthur H. Clark Co., 1264 S. Central Ave., Glendale, CA 91204. index.

MILITARY 639

DAS GELTENDE SEEVOELKERRECHT IN EINZELDARSTELLUNGEN. see *LAW — International Law*

GLADIUS; etudes sur les armes anciennes, l'armement, l'art militaire et la vie culturelle en Orient et Occident. see *HOBBIES — Antiques*

355 US
GOVERNMENT BUSINESSS WORLDWIDE REPORTS. 1969. irreg. price varies or free with subscr. to Defense Business. J. H. Wagner, Ed. & Pub., Box 5651, Washington, DC 20016. charts. illus. stat.

355 NQ ISSN 0017-5005
GUARDIA NACIONAL. 1933. irreg. free. Guardia Nacional de Nicaragua, Oficina del Encargado General de Abastos, Loma de Tiscapa, Managua, Nicaragua.

GUIDE TO GOVERNMENT-LOAN FILMS. see *MOTION PICTURES*

335 US
HANDBOOK OF SERVICE MEMBERS' AND VETERANS' BENEFITS. 1956. irreg. $1.25. Research and Review Service of America, Inc., P.O. Box 1727, Indianapolis, IN 46206.
Formerly: Handbook of Servicemen's and Veterans' Benefits (ISSN 0072-9914)

355 GW
HANDBUCH ZUR DEUTSCHEN MILITAERGESCHICHTE. 1964. irreg., vol. 6, 1970. price varies. (Militaergeschichtliches Forschungsamt) Bernard und Graefe Verlag, Hubertusstr. 5, 8000 Munich 19, W. Germany (B.R.D.)

355 US ISSN 0073-0394
HARMON MEMORIAL LECTURES IN MILITARY HISTORY. 1959. a. free. United States Air Force Academy, Dept. of History, Colorado Springs, CO 80840. circ. 1,000.

HIGH FLIGHT. see *AERONAUTICS AND SPACE FLIGHT*

399 739.7 CN ISSN 0440-9221
HISTORICAL ARMS SERIES. 1963. irreg. Museum Restoration Service, Box 390, Bloomfield, Ont. K0K 1G0, Canada.

355 UK ISSN 0305-0440
HISTORICAL BREECHLOADING SMALLARMS ASSOCIATION. JOURNAL. 1973. a. £4. Historical Breechloading Smallarms Association, c/o Imperial War Museum, Lambeth Road, London SE1 6HZ, England. Ed. C. Owen. bk. rev. bibl. charts. illus. circ. 2,000.
History

INCOME TAX GUIDE FOR MILITARY PERSONNEL. see *BUSINESS AND ECONOMICS — Public Finance, Taxation*

355 US ISSN 0073-8654
INSTITUTE FOR DEFENSE ANALYSES. PAPERS.* irreg. Institute for Defense Analyses, 400 Army - Navy Dr., Arlington, VA 22202 (Avail. from: National Technical Information Service, Springfield, VA 22151)

355 US ISSN 0073-8662
INSTITUTE FOR DEFENSE ANALYSES. REPORTS.* irreg. Institute for Defense Analyses, 400 Army-Navy Drive, Arlington, VA 22202 (Avail. from: National Technical Information Service, Springfield, VA 22151)

355 US ISSN 0073-8670
INSTITUTE FOR DEFENSE ANALYSES. STUDIES.* irreg. Institute for Defense Analyses, 400 Army - Navy Dr., Arlington, VA 22202 (Avail. from: National Technical Information Service, Springfield, VA 22151)

INTERNATIONAL ASSOCIATION OF MUSEUMS OF ARMS AND MILITARY HISTORY. CONGRESS REPORTS. see *MUSEUMS AND ART GALLERIES*

355 US ISSN 0145-2584
INTERNATIONAL COUNTERMEASURES HANDBOOK. 1975. a. $40. E W Communications, Inc., 1170 E. Meadow Dr., Palo Alto, CA 94303. Ed. Harry F. Eustace. adv. bibl. charts. illus. stat. (back issues avail.)

355 796 BE
INTERNATIONAL MILITARY SPORTS COUNCIL. TECHNICAL BROCHURE/ CONSEIL INTERNATIONAL DU SPORT MILITAIRE. BROCHURE TECHNIQUE. 1964. irreg., no. 21, 1977. International Military Sports Council, Ave. des Abeilles 2, B-1050 Brussels, Belgium.
Formerly: International Military Sports Council Academy. Technical Brochure (ISSN 0538-8732)

359 IT ISSN 0075-1588
ISTITUTO UNIVERSITARIO NAVALE, NAPLES. ANNALI. (Text in Italian; summaries in English) 1920. a. Istituto Universitario Navale, Via Acton 38, Naples 80100, Italy.

J A G JOURNAL. (U.S. Department of the Navy) see *LAW*

358.4 GW ISSN 0075-2320
JAHRBUCH DER LUFTWAFFE. 1966. a. DM.32. Wehr und Wissen Verlagsgesellschaft GmbH, Heilsbachstr., Postfach 87, 5300 Bonn-Duisdorf, W. Germany (B.R.D.) Eds. Wolfgang Flume, Manfred Sadlowski. adv. circ. 7,000.

358 623 GW ISSN 0075-2428
JAHRBUCH DER WEHRTECHNIK. 1966. a. DM.32. Wehr und Wissen Verlagsgesellschaft GmbH, Heilsbachstr., Postfach 87, 5300 Bonn-Duisdorf, W. Germany (B. R. D.) Ed. Wolfgang Flume. adv. circ. 5,000.

355 GW ISSN 0075-2282
JAHRBUCH DES HEERES. 1967. biennial. DM.32. Wehr und Wissen Verlagsgesellschaft GmbH, Heilsbachstr., Postfach 87, 5300 Bonn-Duisdorf, W. Germany (B.R.D.) Ed. R. Hausschild. adv. circ. 7,000.

355 UK
JANE'S ARMOUR AND ARTILLERY. biennial. £35. Jane's Publishing Co., Paulton House, 8 Shepherdess Walk, London N.1., England. Ed. Christopher F. Foss.

355 UK
JANE'S COMBAT SUPPORT EQUIPMENT. biennial. £37.50. Jane's Publishing Co., Paulton House, 8 Shepherdess Walk, London N.1., England. Ed. Christopher F. Foss.

359 UK ISSN 0075-3025
JANE'S FIGHTING SHIPS. a. £40. Jane's Publishing Co., Paulton House, 8 Shepherdess Walk, London N.1., England. Ed. Capt. John E. Moore.

355 UK ISSN 0306-3410
JANE'S INFANTRY WEAPONS. a. £40. Jane's Publishing Co., Paulton House, 8 Shepherdess Walk, London N.1., England. Ed. Col. John Weeks.

355 UK
JANE'S MILITARY COMMUNICATIONS. biennial. £35. Jane's Publishing Co., Paulton House, 8 Shepherdess Walk, London N.1., England. Ed. R. J. Raggett.

355 UK ISSN 0075-3068
JANE'S WEAPON SYSTEMS. a. £40. Jane's Publishing Co., Paulton House, 8 Shepherdess Walk, London N.1., England. Ed. Ronald T. Pretty.

970.04 US
KENTUCKY. ADJUTANT-GENERAL'S OFFICE. REPORT. a. Adjutant-General's Office, Frankfort, KY 40601.

KOEHLERS FLOTTENKALENDER. JAHRBUCH FUER SCHIFFAHRT UND HAEFEN. see *TRANSPORTATION — Ships And Shipping*

355 US ISSN 0163-1373
L A M P OCCASIONAL NEWSLETTER. 1970. irreg., no. 12, 1979. free. American Bar Association, Standing Committee on Legal Assistance for Military Personnel, 1155 E. 60 St., Chicago, IL 60637. Ed. Connie Berg. circ. 4,000.
Formerly: American Bar Association. Standing Committee on Legal Assistance for Servicemen. Occasional Newsletter (ISSN 0065-7522)

354 LB
LIBERIA. MINISTRY OF NATIONAL DEFENSE. ANNUAL REPORT. a. Ministry of National Defense, Monrovia, Liberia.

MCGRAW-HILL SERIES IN MISSILE AND SPACE TECHNOLOGY. see *AERONAUTICS AND SPACE FLIGHT*

MILITAERHISTORISK TIDSKRIFT. see *HISTORY — History Of Europe*

355 NO ISSN 0026-3842
MILITAERPSYKOLOGISKE MEDDELELSER. 1955. irreg. free. ‡ Forsvarets Psykologitjeneste, Oslo Mil, Oslo 1, Norway.

355 UK ISSN 0459-7222
MILITARY BALANCE. 1959. a. £5($11) International Institute for Strategic Studies, 23 Tavistock St, London WC2E 7NQ, England. charts. stat. circ. 19,500.

355.27 SZ
MILITARY COMMUNICATIONS. a. updates to base vol. Interavia S.A., 86 Ave. Louis Casai, Case Postale 162, CH-1216 Cointrin/Geneva, Switzerland.

355 UK
MILITARY INTELLIGENCE CRITICAL ATTRIBUTES. 1981. irreg. $250. Aviation Studies International, Sussex House, Parkside, Wimbledon, London SW19 5NB, England.

355 US ISSN 0160-0311
MILITARY JOURNAL. 1977. irreg. $6 for 4 issues. International Graphics Corp., 218 Beech St., Bennington, VT 05201. Ed. Ray Merriam. adv. bk. rev. illus. circ. 2,700.

355 II ISSN 0076-8782
MILITARY YEAR BOOK. (Text in English) 1965. a. Rs.65($25) Guide Publications, 60-20 Prabhat Rd., New Delhi 110005, India (Dist. in U.S. by International Publications Service, 114 E. 32 St., New York, N.Y 10016) Ed. S.P. Baranwal. adv. circ. 5,800.

355 UK
N A A F I REPORTS. 1956. a. contr. circ. ‡ Navy, Army and Air Force Institutes, Kennington, London SE11, England. Ed. Ronald Walker. illus. circ. 200,000.

355 FR
NATION ARMEE. irreg., vol. 2, 1977. Editions Copernic, B.P. 129, 75326 Paris Cedex 07, France. Dir. Philippe Conrad.

355 UK ISSN 0021-7336
NATIONAL DEFENCE COLLEGE GAZETTE. 1949. a. ‡ National Defence College, Latimer, Chesham, Bucks County, England. Ed. Wg. Cdr. J. H. Constable. adv. circ. controlled.
Formerly: Joint Services Staff College Gazette.

355 US ISSN 0363-8618
NATIONAL GUARD ALMANAC. 1975. a. $2.50. Uniformed Services Almanac, Inc., Box 76, Washington, DC 20044 (Subscr. to, Dept. G)
Formerly: Uniformed Services Almanac. National Guard Edition (ISSN 0363-8588)

355 US
NATIONAL STRATEGY INFORMATION CENTER. STRATEGY PAPERS. 1969. irreg. (2-3/ yr.) $2.25-2.95. National Strategy Information Center, 111 E. 58th St., New York, NY 10022. Eds. Frank N. Trager, William Henderson. bibl. stat. circ. 7,500.

MILITARY

353.9   US   ISSN 0094-7326
NEW MEXICO. VETERANS' SERVICE COMMISSION. REPORT. a. Veterans' Service Commission, Villagra Bldg., 408 Galisteo St., Box 2324, Santa Fe, NM 87503. charts. stat. Key Title: Report of the New Mexico Veteran's Service Commission.

355   NZ
NEW ZEALAND. MINISTRY OF DEFENCE. REPORT. a. Government Printing Office, Private Bag, Wellington, New Zealand.

355   NZ
NEW ZEALAND. MINISTRY OF DEFENCE. REVIEW OF DEFENCE POLICY. 1957. irreg. price varies. Ministry of Defence, Wellington, New Zealand

355.12   GW
OFF DUTY - PACIFIC. (Text in English) m. Rios Group, Inc., Eschersheimer Landstr. 69, 6000 Frankfurt 1, W. Germany (B.R.D.) Ed.James Shaw. adv. bk. rev. film rev. tr.lit. index. circ. 80,000.
U.S. personnel and their families

355.12   GW
OFF DUTY - WEST. (Text in English) m. Rios Group, Inc., Eschersheimer Landstr. 69, 6000 Frankfurt 1, W. Germany (B.R.D.) Ed.James Shaw. adv. bk. rev. film rev. tr.lit. index. circ. 190,000.
Service personnel in western U.S., Alaska, Hawaii

355.31   BE
PALLAS. (Text in Dutch and French) q. 250 Fr. Association des Officiers en Service Actif, 77 Avenue Milcamps, 1040 Brussels, Belgium.

355.115   US   ISSN 0190-4930
PLANS FOR THE IMPLEMENTATION OF THE POST-VIETNAM ERA VETERANS' EDUCATIONAL ASSISTANCE ACT OF 1977. a. U.S. Veterans Administration, 810 Vermont Ave., N.W., Washington, DC 20420 (Orders to: Supt. Doc., Washington, DC 20402)
Veterans

R. M. C. HISTORICAL JOURNAL. (Royal Military College of Australia) see *HISTORY — History Of Australasia And Other Areas*

355.058   US   ISSN 0305-6155
R. U. S. I. AND BRASSEY'S DEFENCE YEARBOOK. 1890. a. $20. (Royal United Services Institute) Westview Press, 5500 Central Ave., Boulder, CO 80301.
Formerly: Brassey's Annual - the Armed Forces Year-Book (ISSN 0068-0702)

355.3   US   ISSN 0363-860X
RESERVE FORCES ALMANAC. 1975. a. $2.50. Uniformed Services Almanac, Inc., Box 76, Washington, DC 20044 (Subscr. to:, Dept. R)
Formerly: Uniformed Services Almanac. Special Reserve Forces Edition (ISSN 0360-554X)

355   US   ISSN 0149-7197
RETIRED MILITARY ALMANAC. a. $2.50. Uniformed Services Almanac, Inc., Box 76, Washington, DC 20044 (Subscr. to, Dept M)

SAGE RESEARCH PROGRESS SERIES ON WAR, REVOLUTION AND PEACEKEEPING. see *POLITICAL SCIENCE — International Relations*

SAGE SERIES ON ARMED FORCES AND SOCIETY. see *POLITICAL SCIENCE*

359   US   ISSN 0080-9292
SHIPS AND AIRCRAFT OF THE UNITED STATES FLEET. 1939. irreg., 12 edt., 1981. $24.95. Naval Institute Press, Annapolis, MD 21402. Ed. Norman Polmar. index.

SOCIETY OF COLONIAL WARS. BULLETIN. see *HISTORY — History Of North And South America*

SOLDIER SHOP ANNUAL. see *HOBBIES*

355.03   SA
SOUTH AFRICA. DEPARTMENT OF DEFENSE. WHITE PAPER ON DEFENSE AND ARMAMENT PRODUCTION. (Text in: Afrikaans and English) irreg. Department of Defense, Cape Town, South Africa.

355 310   US
SOVIET ARMED FORCES REVIEW ANNUAL. Abbreviated title: S A F R A. 1977. a. $31.50 (vol. 1); $35(vol. 2); $36(vol. 3) Academic International Press, Box 555, Gulf Breeze, FL 32561. Ed. David R. Jones. bibl. charts. illus. stat. (back issues avail.)

355 320   US
STUDIES IN DEFENSE POLICY. 1971. irreg., no. 15, 1975. price varies. Brookings Institution, 1775 Massachusetts Ave. N.W., Washington, DC 20036.

355   NE
STUDIES IN U.S. NATIONAL SECURITY. 1977. irreg. (U.S. Army War College, Strategic Studies Institute, US) Sijthoff & Noordhoff International Publishers b.v., Box 4, 2400 MA Alphen aan den Rijn, Netherlands (U.S. address: 20010 Century Blvd., Germantown, MD 20767) Ed. James A.Kuhlman.

355   FI   ISSN 0039-5633
SUOMI MERELLA. 1934. biennial. Fmk.25. Meriupseeriyhdistys, Merivoimien Esikunta, 00160 Helsinki 16, Finland. Ed. S. Kanerva. adv. bk. rev. abstr. illus. circ. 800.

355.155   UK   ISSN 0491-6204
SURMACH. (Text in Ukrainian) 1955. a. £.50($1.30) Association of Ukranian Former Combatants in Great Britain, 49 Linden Gardens, London W2 4HG, England. Ed. S. M. Fostun. bk. rev. circ. 1,000.

384 355   GW   ISSN 0082-1861
TASCHENBUCH FUER DEN FERNMELDEDIENST. 1960. a. DM.14.80. Wehr und Wissen Verlagsgesellschaft GmbH, Heilsbachstr., Postfach 87, 5300 Bonn-Duisdorf, W. Germany (B.R.D.) Ed. Gunter Seeck. adv. illus. circ. 3,500.

355   GW   ISSN 0082-1942
TASCHENBUCH FUER LOGISTIK. 1961. a. DM.14.80. Wehr und Wissen Verlagsgesellschaft GmbH, Heilsbachstr., Postfach 87, 5300 Bonn-Duisdorf, W. Germany (B.R.D.) Eds. J. Gerber, H. Stein. illus.

TEMPORARY MILITARY LODGING AROUND THE WORLD. see *TRAVEL AND TOURISM*

355   FR   ISSN 0036-2794
TRIOMPHE SAINT-CYR; plaquette annuelle des promotions de l'Ecole Special Militaire de St. Cyr et de l'Ecole Militaire Interarmes. 1949. a. 43 F. Ecole Speciale Militaire de Saint-Cyr, 56210 Coetquidan, France. (Co-sponsor: Ecole Militaire Interarmes) adv. circ. 1,000.
Formerly: Triomphe.

U S M A LIBRARY BULLETIN. see *LIBRARY AND INFORMATION SCIENCES*

355.1   US
U S S R REPORT: MILITARY AFFAIRS. irreg. (approx. 86/yr.) $301. U.S. Joint Publications Research Service, 1000 N. Glebe Rd., Arlington, VA 22201 (Orders to: NTIS, Springfield, VA 22161)
Formerly: Translations on U S S R Military Affairs.

355   UN   ISSN 0082-8076
UNITED NATIONS. DISARMAMENT COMMISSION. OFFICIAL RECORDS. irreg. price varies. United Nations Publications, Room LX-2300, New York, NY 10017 (Or Distribution and Sales Section, Palais des Nations, CH-1211 Geneva 10, Switzerland)

358 600   US
U.S. AIR FORCE GEOPHYSICS LABORATORY. AFGL (SERIES) 1960? irreg. no subscriptions. U.S. Air Force Geophysics Laboratory, Hanscom Air Force Base, Bedford, MA 01730 (Order from: National Technical Information Service, Springfield, VA 22151) (also avail. in microform)
Supersedes: U.S. Air Force Cambridge Research Laboratories. AFCRL (Series) (ISSN 0082-870X)

356.1   US   ISSN 0091-2271
U. S. ARMY INFANTRY CENTER. HISTORY; ANNUAL SUPPLEMENT. a. free to qualified military agencies. U.S. Army Infantry School, Attn: ATSH-SE, Fort Benning, GA 31905. Key Title: History. Annual Supplement.

355   US   ISSN 0082-9862
U. S. DEPARTMENT OF DEFENSE. DEFENSE PROGRAM AND DEFENSE BUDGET. (Also called: Defense Budget and Defense Program) a. U.S. Department of Defense., The Pentagon, Washington, DC 20301 (Orders to: Supt. of Documents, Washington, Dc 20402)

355.6   US   ISSN 0098-3888
U. S. DEPARTMENT OF DEFENSE. REPORT OF SECRETARY OF DEFENSE TO THE CONGRESS. a. $4.00. U. S. Department of Defense, The Pentagon, Washington, DC 20301 (Orders to: Supt. of Documents, Washington, Dc 20402) Key Title: Report of Secretary of Defense to the Congress.

355   US   ISSN 0083-1328
U. S. INDUSTRIAL COLLEGE OF THE ARMED FORCES. MONOGRAPH SERIES.* 1944. irreg. U.S. Industrial College of the Armed Forces., Fort Lesley J. McNair, Washington, DC 20319.

359   US   ISSN 0077-6238
U. S. NAVAL INSTITUTE. NAVAL REVIEW; annual review of world seapower. (May issue of U.S. Naval Institute, Proceedings) 1962. a. $11. Naval Institute Press, Annapolis, MD 21402. Ed. Frank Uhlig, Jr. adv. bk. rev. circ. 76,000.

355.11   US   ISSN 0083-3576
U. S. VETERANS ADMINISTRATION. V A FACT SHEETS. 1961. a. $0.20. U. S. Veterans Administration, 810 Vermont Ave., N.W., Washington, DC 20420.

355.11   US   ISSN 0083-3533
U. S. VETERANS ADMINISTRATION. ANNUAL REPORT. 1931. a. price varies. U. S. Veterans Administration, 810 Vermont Ave., N.W., Washington, DC 20420 (Orders to: Supt. Doc., Washington, DC 20402)

355   FR
VIVAT HUSSAR. 1966. a. Association des Amis du Musee International des Hussards, Musee Massey, 65000 Tarbes, France. Ed. Bd. adv. bibl. illus. circ. 1,500.

355   YU   ISSN 0067-5660
VOJNI MUZEJ, BELGRADE. VESNIK/MILITARY MUSEUM, BELGRADE. BULLETIN. (Text in Serbocroatian; summaries in French and English) 1954. irreg. 20 din. each. Vojnoizdavacki Zavod, Balkanska 53, 11002 Belgrade, Yugoslavia. Ed. Momir Vujovic. bk. rev. circ. 1,000.

355.02   US   ISSN 0361-0373
WAR AND SOCIETY; a yearbook of military history. 1975. a. $24.50. Holmes & Meier Publishers, Inc., 30 Irving Pl., New York, NY 10003.

350   GW
WEISSBUCH ZUR SICHERHEIT DER BUNDESREPUBLIK DEUTSCHLAND UND ZUR LAGE DER BUNDESWEHR. 1970. irreg. $10. Bundesministerium der Verteidigung, Postfach 1328, 5300 Bonn, W. Germany (B.R.D.)

355   GW   ISSN 0083-9078
WEYERS FLOTTENTASCHENBUCH. 1900. a. DM.84. Bernard und Graefe Verlag, Hubertus Str. 5, 8000 Munich 19, W. Germany (B.R.D.)

355.115   US   ISSN 0083-9108
WHAT EVERY VETERAN SHOULD KNOW. 1937. a (with m. supplements) $5 (with supplements $16) Veterans Information Service, P.O. Box 111, East Moline, IL 61244. Ed. Patrick L. Murphy. index.

355   US
WORLD MILITARY EXPENDITURES AND ARMS TRANSFERS. a. U.S. Arms Control and Disarmament Agency, Dept. of State Bldg., Washington, DC 20451 (Also avail. from: Supt. of Documents, Washington, DC 20402)
Formerly: World Military Expenditures; Which supersedes: World Military Expenditures and Related Data (ISSN 0082-8793)

WUERZBURGER WEHRWISSENSCHAFTLICHE ABHANDLUNGEN. see *LAW*

MILITARY — Abstracting, Bibliographies, Statistics

359 090 AG ISSN 0066-7080
ARGENTINA. DEPARTAMENTO DE ESTUDIOS HISTORICOS NAVALES. SERIE J: LIBROS Y IMPRESOS RAROS. 1962. irreg.; no. 2, 1970. Departamento de Estudios Historicos Navales, Instituto de Publicaciones Navales, Av. Cordoba 547, Buenos Aires, Argentina.

359 AG ISSN 0066-7331
ARGENTINA. SERVICIO DE INTELIGENCIA NAVAL. BIBLIOTECAS DE LA ARMADA. BOLETIN BIBLIOGRAFICO. 1943. a. Servicio de Inteligencia Naval, Bibliotecas de la Armada, Edificio Libertad, Comodoro Py y Corbeta Uruguay, Buenos Aires, Argentina. Ed. Juan A. Manon.

016 355 US ISSN 0083-1336
U. S. INDUSTRIAL COLLEGE OF THE ARMED FORCES. RESEARCH PROJECT ABSTRACTS.*
a. U.S. Industrial College of the Armed Forces., Fort Lesley J. McNair, Washington, DC 20319.

VIRGINIA MILITARY INSTITUTE, LEXINGTON. PUBLICATIONS, THESES, AND DISSERTATIONS OF THE STAFF AND FACULTY. see EDUCATION — Abstracting, Bibliographies, Statistics

355.115 310 US
WISCONSIN. DEPARTMENT OF VETERANS AFFAIRS. BIENNIAL REPORT. 1977. biennial. Department of Veterans Affairs, 77 N. Dickinson St., Madison, WI 53702.
Veterans

MINES AND MINING INDUSTRY

see also Metallurgy

A M D E L BULLETIN. (Australia Mineral Development Laboratories) see EARTH SCIENCES — Geology

622 CM ISSN 0575-7258
ACTIVITES MINERES AU CAMEROUN. 1962. a, latest 1975. Direction des Mines et de la Geologie, Ministere des Mines et de l'Energie, Yaounde, Cameroon.

622 PL
AKADEMIA GORNICZO-HUTNICZA IM. STANISLAWA STASZICA. INSTYTUT GORNICTWA PODZIEMNEGO. PRACE. (Subseries of its Zeszyty Naukowe. Gornictwo) (Summaries in English and Russian) 1971. irreg. 120 Zl. single issue. Panstwowe Wydawnictwo Naukowe, Miodowa 10, Warsaw, Poland (Dist. by: Ars Polona-Ruch, Krakowskie Przedmiescie 7, Warsaw, Poland) illus.

622 PL ISSN 0075-6997
AKADEMIA GORNICZO-HUTNICZA IM. STANISLAWA STASZICA. ZESZYTY NAUKOWE. GORNICTWO. (Text in Polish; summaries in English and Russian) 1959. irreg., no. 44, 1972. price varies. Panstwowe Wydawnictwo Naukowe, Miodowa 10, Warsaw, Poland (Dist. by Ars Polona-Ruch, Krakowskie Przedmiescie 7, Warsaw, Poland) Ed. Michal Odlanicki-Poczobutt.

338.4 GW
ALUMINUM SMELTERS; Europe, Japan, USA. (Edts. in English, French, German) 1965. a. free. Organisation of European Aluminium Smelters, Graf-Adolf-Str. 18, 4100 Duesseldorf, W. Germany (B.R.D.) Ed. Dr. Gottfried Uhlig.
Formerly: Organisation of European Aluminum Smelters. Economic Situation of the Aluminum Smelters in Europe (ISSN 0474-4829)

622 US
AMERICAN INSTITUTE OF MINING, METALLURGICAL AND PETROLEUM ENGINEERS. COUNCIL OF ECONOMICS. PROCEEDINGS OF THE ANNUAL MEETING. 1967. a. price varies. American Institute of Mining, Metallurgical and Petroleum Engineers, Inc., Council of Economics, 345 E. 47 St., New York, NY 10017. Indexed: Eng.Ind.

669 622 665.5 US
AMERICAN INSTITUTE OF MINING, METALLURGICAL AND PETROLEUM ENGINEERS. NATIONAL OPEN HEARTH AND BASIC OXYGEN STEEL DIVISION. PROCEEDINGS OF THE CONFERENCE. Cover title: Steelmaking Proceedings. 1917? a. $25 to non-members; members $10.50. American Institute of Mining, Metallurgical and Petroleum Engineers, Inc., National Open Hearth Steel Committee, Iron and Steel Society, New York, NY 10017.

ANGOLA. DIRECCAO PROVINCIAL DOS SERVICOS DE GEOLOGIA E MINAS. BOLETIM. see EARTH SCIENCES — Geology

622 BE ISSN 0003-4290
ANNALES DES MINES DE BELGIQUE/ ANNALEN DER MIJNEN VAN BELGIE. (Text in Dutch and French; summaries in Dutch, English, French and German) 1896. a. 1995 Fr. (Institut National des Industries Extractives - Nationaal Instituut voor de Extractiebedrijven) Editions Techniques et Scientifiques, Rue Borrens 35-43, 1050 Brussels, Belgium. Ed. G. Lonis. adv. bk. rev. abstr. charts. illus. circ. 900. Indexed: Chem.Abstr. Eng.Ind.

622 FR ISSN 0071-822X
ANNUAIRE DE L'ADMINISTRATION ET DU CORPS DES MINES. (Compiled from Information Contained in les Annales des Mines) 1852. a. 50 F.($11) Bureau de Documentation Miniere, Division de Documentation, 4, rue las Cases, 75700 Paris, France (Orders to G. E. D. I. M; 19, rue du Grand-Moulin, 42 Saint-Etienne, France) Ed. Francois Callot. adv. circ. 1,500. (back issues available)

ANNUAL BOOK OF A S T M STANDARDS. PART 26. GASEOUS FUELS; COAL AND COKE; ATMOSPHERIC ANALYSIS. see ENGINEERING — Engineering Mechanics And Materials

622 UN ISSN 0066-3808
ANNUAL BULLETIN OF COAL STATISTICS FOR EUROPE. 1968. a; vol. 13, 1978. price varies. United Nations Economic Commission for Europe, Palais des Nations, 1200 Geneva 10, Switzerland (Or United Nations Publications, Room LX-2300, New York, NY 10017)

338.7 II
ANNUAL REPORT OF THE WORKING AND AFFAIRS OF MYSORE MINERALS LIMITED. (Text in English) a. Mysore Minerals Ltd., Bangalore, Karnataka, India.

338.2 BL
ANUARIO MINERAL BRASILEIRO. 1972. a. Cr.$140. Departamento Nacional da Producao Mineral, Setor Autarquia Norte, Quadra 1 Bloco B, 70000 Brasilia D.F., Brazil. illus. stat.

549 US ISSN 0066-5487
APPLIED MINERALOGY. TECHNISCHE MINEROLOGIE. 1971. irreg., vol. 11, 1977. price varies. Springer-Verlag, 175 Fifth Ave., New York, NY 10010 (also Berlin, Heidelberg, Vienna) (reprint service avail. from ISI)

ARGENTINA. SERVICIO NACIONAL MINERO GEOLOGICO. ANALES. see EARTH SCIENCES — Geology

ARGENTINA. SERVICIO NACIONAL MINERO GEOLOGICO. BOLETIN. see EARTH SCIENCES — Geology

553 AG ISSN 0066-7161
ARGENTINA. SERVICIO NACIONAL MINERO GEOLOGICO. ESTADISTICA MINERA. 1909. irreg. price varies. Servicio Nacional Minero Geologico, Biblioteca, Av. Santa Fe 1548, Buenos Aires, Argentina.
Formerly: Argentine Republic. Direccion Nacional de Geologia y Mineria. Estadistica Minera.

ARIZONA LANDMARKS. see AGRICULTURE

ASBESTOS PRODUCER/PRODUCTEUR D'AMIANTE. see BUILDING AND CONSTRUCTION

622 669 AT
AUSTRALASIAN INSTITUTE OF MINING AND METALLURGY. SYMPOSIA SERIES. 1972. irreg., no. 14, 1976. Australasian Institute of Mining and Metallurgy, Clunies Ross House, 191 Royal Parade, Parkville, Vic. 3052, Australia.

338.2 AT ISSN 0311-8975
AUSTRALIA. BUREAU OF STATISTICS. MINERAL PRODUCTION. 1971. a. free. Australian Bureau of Statistics, P.O. Box 10, Belconnen, A.C.T. 2616, Australia. circ. 2,200.

338.2 AT ISSN 0067-1762
AUSTRALIAN COAL INDUSTRY RESEARCH LABORATORIES. ANNUAL REPORT. 1966. a. free. Australian Coal Industry Research Laboratories Ltd, Box 83, Northryde, N.S.W. 2113, Australia. Ed. A. Robertson. Indexed: Chem.Abstr.

622 620.1 AT
AUSTRALIAN GEOMECHANICS JOURNAL. 1971. Aus.$8($10.50) Institution of Engineers, Australia, 11 National Circuit, Barton, A.C.T. 2600, Australia. (Co-sponsor: Australasian Institute of Mining and Metallurgy) (back issues avail.)

622 AT
AUSTRALIAN MINERAL INDUSTRIES RESEARCH ASSOCIATION. BULLETIN. irreg., no. 6, 1976. Aus.$2. Australian Mineral Industries Research Association, Clunies Ross House, 191 Royal Parade, Parkville, Victoria 3052, Australia. Ed. Bd. illus.

549 AT
AUSTRALIAN MINERAL INDUSTRIES RESEARCH ASSOCIATION. NON-CONFIDENTIAL RESEARCH INFORMATION. 1967. a. Aus.$2. Clunies Ross House, 191 Royal Parade, Parkville, Vic. 3052, Australia.

622 AT ISSN 0084-7488
AUSTRALIAN MINERAL INDUSTRY. ANNUAL REVIEW. 1948. a. price on application. Bureau of Mineral Resources, Geology and Geophysics, Box 378, Canberra City, A.C.T. 2061, Australia.
Formerly: Australia Mineral Industry Review (ISSN 0067-1509)

622 AT
AUSTRALIAN MINING YEARBOOK. a. Aus.$10. Thomson Publications (Australia) Pty. Ltd., 47 Chippen St., Chippendale, N.S.W. 2008, Australia. Ed. Mike Dunne. (also avail. in microfiche)

622 CS
BANICKE LISTY/FOLIA MONTANA. (Text in slovak; summaries in English, French, Russian) 1974. irreg. 9. (Slovenska Akademia Vied, Banicky Ustav Sav) Veda, Publishing House of the Slovak Academy of Sciences, Klemensova 19, 895 30 Bratislava, Czechoslovakia. illus.

622 BE
BELGIUM. ADMINISTRATION DES MINES. STATISTIQUES: HOUILLE, COKES, AGGLOMERES METALLURGIE, CARRIERES/ STATISTIEKEN: STEENKOLEN, COKES, AGGLOMERATEN, METALLNIJVERHEID, GROEVEN. irreg. Administration des Mines, 30 rue de Mot, 1040 Brussels, Belgium. illus. free.
Formerly: Belgium. Administration des Mines. Service: Statistiques. Siderurgie, Houille, Agglomeres, Cokes (ISSN 0525-4752)

BERG- UND HUETTENMAENNISCHE MONATSHEFTE. SUPPLEMENT. see METALLURGY

BERGBAU-BERUFSGENOSSENSCHAFT. GESCHAEFTSBERICHT. see LABOR UNIONS

622 BO ISSN 0067-9852
BOLIVIA. SERVICIO GEOLOGICO. SERIE MINERALOGICA. CONTRIBUCIONE. 1968. irreg. Servicio Geologico, Casilla 2729, La Paz, Bolivia.

662 UR
BOR'BA S GAZOM V UGOL'NYKH SHAKHTAKH. irreg. 0.61 Rub. (Nauchno-Issledovatelski Institut po Bezopasnosti Rabot V Gornoi Promyshlennosti, Makeevka) Izdatel'stvo Nedra, Tretyakovskii proezd, 1, Moscow K-12, U.S.S.R. illus.

622 BL
BRAZIL. DEPARTAMENTO NACIONAL DA PRODUCAO MINERAL. AVULSO. 1974. irreg. free. Departamento Nacional da Producao Mineral, Setor Autarcuia Norte, Quadra 1, Bloco B, Brasilia, D.F., Brazil.

622 BL
BRAZIL. DEPARTAMENTO NACIONAL DA PRODUCAO MINERAL. BOLETIM. 1973. irreg. price varies. Departamento Nacional da Producao Mineral, Setor Autarcuia Norte, Quadra 1, Bloco B, Brasilia, D.F., Brazil. (back issues avail)

622 665.5 CN ISSN 0365-9356
BRITISH COLUMBIA. MINISTRY OF ENERGY, MINES AND PETROLEUM RESOURCES. ANNUAL REPORT. a. Ministry of Energy, Mines and Petroleum Resources, Victoria, B. C. V8V 1X4, Canada.

622.33 333.7 CN ISSN 0707-3739
BRITISH COLUMBIA. MINISTRY OF THE ENVIRONMENT. NORTHEAST COAL STUDY PRELIMINARY ENVIRONMENTAL REPORT. 1977. a. Ministry of the Environment, Resource Analysis Branch, Parliament Bldgs., Victoria, B.C. V8V 1X5, Canada. illus. Key Title: Northeast Coal Study. Preliminary Environmental Report.

622 CN ISSN 0705-5196
C A N M E T REPORT. irreg. price varies. Canada Centre for Mineral and Energy Technology, 555 Booth St., Ottawa, Ont. K1A 0G1, Canada.
Incerporating(as of 1977): C A N M E T Review.

C.I.E. SERVICIO INFORMATIVO. (Centro de Investigaciones Energeticas) see *PETROLEUM AND GAS*

622 669 CN ISSN 0068-9009
C. I. M. DIRECTORY. 1967. a. Can.$75. Canadian Institute of Mining and Metallurgy, 400-1130 Sherbrooke West, Montreal, Que. H3A 2M8, Canada. Ed. J. I. McGerrigle. adv. circ. 12,000.

CALIFORNIA. DIVISION OF MINES AND GEOLOGY. BULLETIN. see *EARTH SCIENCES — Geology*

622 CN
CANADA. MINERAL POLICY SECTOR. MINERAL INFORMATION BULLETIN. 1953. irreg. price varies. Department of Energy, Mines and Resources, Mineral Policy Sector, Ottawa, Ont. K1A 0E4, Canada (Orders to: Supply and Services Canada, Publishing Centre, Hull, Que. K1A OS5, Canada)
Former titles: Canada. Mineral Development Sector. Mineral Information Bulletin; Canada. Mineral Resources Branch. Mineral Information Bulletin. (ISSN 0068-7812)

622 CN
CANADA. MINERAL POLICY SECTOR. MINERAL REPORT. 1956. irreg. price varies. Department of Energy, Mines and Resources, Mineral Policy Sector, Ottawa Ontario K1A 0E4, Canada (Orders to: Supply and Services Canada, Publishing Centre, Hull, Que K1A OS5, Canada)
Former titles: Canada. Mineral Development Sector. Mineral Report; Canada. Mineral Resources Branch. Mineral Report (ISSN 0068-7820)

622 CN
CANADA. MINERAL POLICY SECTOR. MINERAL SURVEY. 1962, no. 2. irreg. price varies. Department of Energy, Mines and Resources, Mineral Policy Sector, Ottawa, Ontario K1A 0E4, Canada (Orders to: Supply and Services Canada, Publishing Centre, Hull, Que. K1A OS5, Canada)
Former titles: Canada. Mineral Development Center. Mineral Survey; Canada. Mineral Resources Branch. Mineral Survey (ISSN 0068-7839)

338.2 CN ISSN 0590-580X
CANADA. NORTHERN NATURAL RESOURCES AND ENVIRONMENT BRANCH. MINING SECTION. NORTH OF 60: MINES AND MINERALS, ACTIVITIES. 1972. a. free. Department of Indian and Northern Affairs, Public Information Branch, 400 Laurier Ave. West, Ottawa, Ont. K1A 0H4, Canada.
Continues: Canada. Department of Indian Affairs and Northern Development. Mines and Minerals, Activities.

622 CN ISSN 0068-9270
CANADIAN MINERALS YEARBOOK/ ANNUAIRE DES MINERAUX DU CANADA. 1962. a. price varies. Department of Energy, Mines and Resources, Mineral Policy Sector, Publication Distribution Office, Ottawa, Ontario K1A OE4, Canada (Orders to: Supply and Services Canada, Publishing Centre, Hull, Que. K1A OS5, Canada)

622 CN ISSN 0068-9289
CANADIAN MINES HANDBOOK. 1931. a. Can.$17 (paper); Can.$20(hardcover) Northern Miner Press Ltd., 7 Labatt Ave, Toronto, Ont. M5A 3P2, Canada. Ed. A. Worobec. circ. 18,500. (also avail. in microfilm)

338.2 622 CN ISSN 0068-9297
CANADIAN MINES REGISTER OF DORMANT AND DEFUNCT COMPANIES. 1960. irreg. Can.$35 including supplements. Northern Miner Press Ltd, 7 Labatt Ave, Toronto, Ont. M5A 3P2, Canada. Ed. A. Worobec.

338.2 622 CN ISSN 0068-9300
CANADIAN MINES REGISTER OF DORMANT AND DEFUNCT COMPANIES. SUPPLEMENT. 1966. irreg., 3rd. 1976. Can.$15. Northern Miner Press Ltd, 7 Labatt Ave., Toronto, Ont. M5A 3P2, Canada. Ed. A. Worobec.

622 CN ISSN 0315-9140
CANADIAN MINING JOURNAL'S REFERENCE MANUAL & BUYERS' GUIDE. 1891. a. Can.$22($32) National Business Publications, Ltd. (Subsidiary of: Southam Business Publications, Ltd.) 310 Victoria Ave., Westmount, P.Q. H3Z 2M9. Ed. Richard Fish. adv. circ. 2,970.
Formerly: Canadian Mining Manual (ISSN 0068-9319)

622 665.5 CN
CANADIAN OIL & GAS HANDBOOK. a. Northern Miner Press Ltd., 7 Labatt Ave., Toronto, Ont. M5A 3P2, Canada. Ed. Alexandra Wordbec.

624 CN ISSN 0375-605X
CANADIAN ROCK MECHANICS SYMPOSIUM. PROCEEDINGS. (Text mainly in English; occasionally in French) 1962. irreg. Department of Energy, Mines and Resources, Mines Branch, Ottawa, Ont. K1A 0E4, Canada. illus.

622 II
CENTRAL MINE PLANNING & DESIGN INSTITUTE. MANUALS. (Text in English) 1976. irreg. free. Central Mine Planning & Design Institute Ltd. (Subsidiary of: Coal India Limited) Publications Wing, Gondwana Place, Kanke Rd., Ranchi 834008, Bihar, India.

622 II ISSN 0070-4628
CENTRAL MINING RESEARCH STATION, DHANBAD. PROGRESS REPORT. (Also called Annual Report) 1961. a. price varies. Central Mining Research Station, Barwa Rd., Dhanbad 826001, Bihar, India. (Affiliate: Council of Scientific and Industrial Research) Ed. A. Dhar. circ. 8,000.

338.2 CM ISSN 0069-2530
CHAMBRE DE COMMERCE, D'INDUSTRIE ET DES MINES DU CAMEROUN. RAPPORT ANNUEL. a. EAs.1000. Chambre de Commerce, d'Industrie et des Mines du Cameroun, B.P. 4011, Douala, Cameroon. circ. 350.

CHAMBRE SYNDICALE DE LA SIDERUGIE FRANCAISE. BULLETIN STATISQUE. SERIE BLEUE. COMMERCE EXTERIEUR. see *METALLURGY*

CHAMBRE SYNDICALE DE LA SIDERUGIE FRANCAISE. BULLETIN STATISQUE. SERIE ROUGE. PRODUCTION. see *METALLURGY*

338 FR ISSN 0069-259X
CHAMBRE SYNDICALE DES MINES DE FER DE FRANCE. RAPPORT D'ACTIVITE. a. Chambre Syndicale des Mines de Fer de France, 15 bis rue de Marignan, 75008 Paris, France. charts. stat.

338 622 FR
CHARBONNAGES DE FRANCE. RAPPORT D'ACTIVITE. 1947. a. Centre d'Etudes et Recherches des Charbonnages de France, 33, rue de la Baume, 75008 Paris, France.
Formerly: Charbonnages de France. Rapport (ISSN 0069-2697)

622.33 CH
CHINA, REPUBLIC. MINING RESEARCH AND SERVICE ORGANISATION. M R S O SPECIAL REPORT. 1977. irreg. Mining Research and Service Organization, Industrial Technology Research Institute, Taipei, Taiwan, Republic of China.

533.61 US ISSN 0069-4592
CLAY RESOURCES BULLETIN. 1967. irreg., 1972, no. 3. $3. Geological Survey, Box G, University Station, Baton Rouge, LA 70893.

622 US ISSN 0145-417X
COAL DATA. a. $15. National Coal Association, Coal Bldg., 1130 17 St. N.W., Washington, DC 20036. Ed. King Lin.
Formerly: Bituminous Coal Data (ISSN 0067-897X)

338.2 622 US
COAL FACTS. 1948. biennial. free to libraries, educators, non-profit institutions; $5 to others. National Coal Association, 1130 17th St. N.W., Washington, DC 20036. Ed. Thomas B. Johnson. index.
Formerly (until 1972): Bituminous Coal Facts (ISSN 0067-8988)

338.2 CN ISSN 0700-284X
COAL IN CANADA, SUPPLY AND DEMAND. 1971. irreg. Department of Energy, Mines and Resources, Energy Policy Sector, Ottawa, Ontario, Canada. stat.

622 CN ISSN 0069-4894
COAL MINES IN CANADA. a. price varies. Department of Energy, Mines and Resources, Mineral Policy Sector, Ottawa, Ontario K1A OE4, Canada (Orders to: Supply and Services Canada, Publishing Centre, Hull, Que. K1A OS5, Canada) charts. stat.

553 US ISSN 0069-4916
COAL TRAFFIC ANNUAL. a. $50. National Coal Association, Coal Bldg., 1130 17 St., N.W., Washington, DC 20036. Ed. King Lin.

553 UK ISSN 0069-4991
COKE OVEN MANAGERS' ASSOCIATION. YEAR BOOK. 1917. a. £10. C O M A (Year Book) Ltd., Waveney House, Adwick Road, Mexborough, Yorks S64 0BS, England. Ed. A. J. Johnston. adv. circ. 750.

622 531.64 CK
COLOMBIA. MINISTERIO DE MINAS Y ENERGIA. BOLETIN DE MINAS Y ENERGIA. 1977 n.s. irreg. Ministerio de Minas y Energia, Bogota, Colombia. illus.
Former titles: Colombia. Ministerio de Minas y Energia. Boletin de Minas & Colombia. Ministerio de Minas y Energia. Boletin de Petroleos.

622 US ISSN 0069-6056
COLORADO SCHOOL OF MINES. PROFESSIONAL CONTRIBUTIONS. 1965. irreg., no. 10, 1980. $12. (Colorado School of Mines) Colorado School of Mines Press, Golden, CO 80401. Ed. Jon W. Raese. bibl. charts. illus. stat. cum.index 1953-1973. (reprint service avail. from UMI) Indexed: Chem.Abstr.

622 US ISSN 0069-6064
COLORADO SCHOOL OF MINES. RESEARCH; annual report of the research activities of the faculty and graduate school. a. Colorado School of Mines, Graduate School and Research Services, Golden, CO 80401. Ed. William A. Mattingly.

622 EI
COMMISSION OF THE EUROPEAN COMMUNITIES. RECUEILS DE RECHERCHES CHARBON. (Editions usually in French and German and occasionally in Italian or Dutch) 1966. irreg; 1971, no. 40. 75 Fr. Office for Official Publications of the European Communities, C.P. 1003, Luxembourg 1, Luxembourg (Dist. in the U.S. by: European Community Information Service, 2100 M St., NW, Suite 707, Washington, DC 20037)

MINES AND MINING INDUSTRY

338.9   EI   ISSN 0069-6757
COMMISSION OF THE EUROPEAN COMMUNITIES. INVESTMENTS IN THE COMMUNITY COALMINING AND IRON AND STEEL INDUSTRIES. REPORT ON THE SURVEY. (Editions also in French, German, Italian, and Dutch) 1956. a. price varies. Office for Official Publications of the European Communities, C.P. 1003, Luxembourg 1, Luxembourg (Dist. in U.S. by European Community Information Service, 2100 M St., N.W., 707, Washington, DC 20037)

338.2   EI   ISSN 0531-3198
COMMISSION OF THE EUROPEAN COMMUNITIES. COLLECTION OBJECTIFS GENERAUX ACIER. (Editions in French, German, Italian and Dutch) 1962. irreg.; 1971, no. 4. price varies. Office for Official Publications of the European Communities, C.P. 1003, Luxembourg 1, Luxembourg (Dist. in the U.S. by: European Community Information Service, 2100 M St., NW, Suite 707, Washington, DC 20037)
     Includes issues of Memorandum sur les Objectifs de..., which appear in appropriate language ed. of the Journal Officiel

COMMONWEALTH SCIENTIFIC AND INDUSTRIAL RESEARCH ORGANIZATION. INSTITUTE OF EARTH RESOURCES. ANNUAL REPORT. see *ENGINEERING — Civil Engineering*

622.33   AT
COMMONWEALTH SCIENTIFIC AND INDUSTRIAL RESEARCH ORGANIZATION. DIVISION OF APPLIED GEOMECHANICS. GEOMECHANICS OF COAL MINING REPORT. 1978. irreg. Aus.$2 per no. C. S. I. R. O., Division of Applied Geomechanics, Box 54, Mt. Waverley, Vic. 3149, Australia.
Coal

624.176   AT   ISSN 0069-7257
COMMONWEALTH SCIENTIFIC AND INDUSTRIAL RESEARCH ORGANIZATION. DIVISION OF APPLIED GEOMECHANICS. TECHNICAL PAPER. 1965. irreg. C. S. I. R. O., Division of Applied Geomechanics, P.O. Box 54, Mt. Waverley 3149, Victoria, Australia.

624.176   AT   ISSN 0069-7249
COMMONWEALTH SCIENTIFIC AND INDUSTRIAL RESEARCH ORGANIZATION. DIVISION OF APPLIED GEOMECHANICS. TECHNICAL REPORT. 1963. irreg. Aus.$20. C. S. I. R. O., Division of Applied Geomechanics, P.O. Box 54, Mt. Waverley 3149, Victoria, Australia.
     Formerly: Commonwealth Scientific and Industrial Research Organization. Division of Soil Mechanics. Technical Report.

549   AT   ISSN 0156-9953
COMMONWEALTH SCIENTIFIC AND INDUSTRIAL RESEARCH ORGANIZATION. INSTITUTE OF EARTH RESOURCES. INVESTIGATION REPORT. 1954. irreg. free. ‡ C.S.I.R.O., Institute of Earth Resources, Box 136, North Ryde. N.S.W.2113, Australia. Ed. J. Thomson. circ. 300-1,000(controlled) Indexed: Chem.Abstr.
     Former titles: Commonwealth Scientific and Industrial Research Organization. Minerals Research Laboratories. Investigation Report (ISSN 0084-8999); Commonwealth Scientific and Industrial Research Organization. Division of Coal Research. Investigation Report.

549   AT   ISSN 0156-9945
COMMONWEALTH SCIENTIFIC AND INDUSTRIAL RESEARCH ORGANIZATION. INSTITUTE OF EARTH RESOURCES. TECHNICAL COMMUNICATION. 1953. irreg., approx. 2/yr. free. ‡ C. S. I. R. O., Institute of Earth Resources, P.O. Box 136, North Ryde, N.S.W. 2113, Australia. Ed. J. Thomson. circ. controlled. Indexed: Chem.Abstr.
     Former titles: Commonwealth Scientific and Industrial Research Organization. Minerals Research Laboratories. Technical Communication; Commonwealth Scientific and Industrial Research Organization. Division of Mineral Chemistry. Technical Communication.

333.7   338.2   CN
CUMULATIVE ANNUAL STATISTICS: ALBERTA COAL INDUSTRY. (Subseries of Its ERCB) 1973. a. Can.$10. ‡ Energy Resources Conservation Board, 603 6th Ave., S.W., Calgary, T2P 0T4, Alta, Canada. illus. stat.

622   BL
DESTAQUES. 1974. irreg. free. Ministerio das Minas e Energia, Centro de Documentacao, Esplanada dos Minosterios, Bloco V, Brasilia DF, Brazil. circ. 2,000.

E/M J INTERNATIONAL DIRECTORY OF MINING AND MINERAL PROCESSING OPERATIONS. see *METALLURGY*

E N I ANNUAL REPORT. (Ente Nazionale Idrocarburi) see *ENERGY*

622   671   PL   ISSN 0070-9964
ELEKTRYFIKACJA I MECHANIZACJA GORNICTWA I HUTNICTWA/ ELECTRIFICATION AND MECHANIZATION IN MINING AND METALLURGY. (Subseries of: Akademia Gorniczo-Hutnicza im. Stanislawa Staszica. Zeszyty Naukowe) (Text and summaries in English) 1954. irreg. (Akademia Gorniczo-Hutnicza im. Stanislawa Staszica) Panstwowe Wydawnictwo Naukowe, Miodowa 10, Warsaw, Poland (Dist. by Ars Polona-Ruch, Krakowskie Przedmiescie 7, Warsaw, Poland)

622   338   SP   ISSN 0071-156X
ESTADISTICAS MINERA Y METALURGICA DE ESPANA. a. 500 ptas. Ministerio de Industria, Direccion General de Minas y Combusitbles, Servicio de Publicaciones, Claudio Coello 44, Madrid 1, Spain.

EXPLORATION IN BRITISH COLUMBIA. see *EARTH SCIENCES — Geology*

338.2   665.5   CN   ISSN 0227-1656
FINANCIAL POST SURVEY OF MINES AND ENERGY RESOURCES. 1980. a. Can.$23. Maclean-Hunter Ltd., 481 University Ave., Toronto M5W 1A7, Canada. Ed. John Byrne. adv. circ. 17,000.
     Formed by the merger of: Financial Post Survey of Mines (ISSN 0071-5085) & Financial Post Survey of Energy Resources (ISSN 0705-7091)
     Investment and financial information on publicly owned mining and resource companies in Canada

622   UK   ISSN 0141-3244
FINANCIAL TIMES MINING INTERNATIONAL YEAR BOOK. 1887. a. £30. Longman Group Ltd., Longman House, Burnt Mill, Harlow, Essex CM20 2JE, England. Ed. William G. Nightingale. adv. index. circ. 4,000.
     Formerly: Mining Year Book.

338.2   EI   ISSN 0531-3120
FONTES ET ACIERS/GHISE ED ACCIAI/ ROHEISEN UND STAHLERZEUGNISSE/ RUWIJER EN STALLPRODUKTEN. a. (incl. 7-11 inserts per yr.) 83.50 F. (annual subscription incl. inserts) Office for Official Publications of the European Communities, C.P. 1003, Luxembourg 1, Luxembourg (Dist. in U.S. by European Community Information Service, 2100 M St., N.W. Suite 707, Washington, D.C. 20037) (looseleaf format)

FRANCE. BUREAU DE RECHERCHES GEOLOGIQUES ET MINIERES. MEMOIRES. see *EARTH SCIENCES — Geology*

FREIBERGER FORSCHUNGSHEFTE. MONTANWISSENSCHAFTEN: REIHE A. BERGBAU UND GEOTECHNIK, ARBEITSSCHUTZ UND SICHERHEITSTECHNIK, GRUNDSTOFF-VERFAHRENSTECHNIK, MASCHINEN- UND ENERGIETECHNIK. see *EARTH SCIENCES — Geology*

FUNDACION BARILOCHE. INSTITUTO DE ECONOMIA DE LA ENERGIA. PUBLICACIONES. see *ENERGY*

338.7   ZR
GECAMINES ANNUAL REPORT/GECAMINES RAPPORT ANNUEL. (English edition not published in 1978) (Editions in English and French) a. Generale des Carrieres et des Mines, Division des Relations Publiques, B.P. 450, Lubumbashi, Zaire. illus.

622   ZR
GENERALE DES CARRIERES ET DES MINES. MONOGRAPHIE. irreg (approx. 4/yr.) Generale des Carrieres et des Mines, Division des Relations Publiques, B.P. 450, Lubumbashi, Zaire.
     Formerly: Generale des Carrieres et Mines du Zaire. Monographie.

338.2   US
GEORGIA. GEOLOGICAL SURVEY. CIRCULAR 2. MINING DIRECTORY OF GEORGIA. irreg. 1972, 17th ed. free. ‡ Department of Natural Resources, Geologic and Water Resources Division, 19 Hunter St., Rm 400, Atlanta, GA 30334. Ed. L. P. Stafford.

338.2   US   ISSN 0433-5473
GEORGIA. GEOLOGICAL SURVEY. INFORMATION CIRCULAR. 1933. irreg. $1.50. ‡ Department of Natural Resources, Geologic and Water Resources Division, 19 Hunter St., Rm. 400, Atlanta, GA 30334. Ed. L.P. Stafford.

339   UK
GREAT BRITAIN. DOMESTIC COAL CONSUMERS' COUNCIL. ANNUAL REPORT. a. H.M.S.O., P.O.B. 569, London SE1 9NH, England.
     Formerly: Great Britain. Industrial Coal Consumers' Council. Report (ISSN 0072-646X)

GREAT BRITAIN. INSTITUTE OF GEOLOGICAL SCIENCES. MINERAL ASSESSMENT REPORT. see *EARTH SCIENCES — Geology*

GREAT BRITAIN. INSTITUTE OF GEOLOGICAL SCIENCES. OVERSEAS GEOLOGY AND MINERAL RESOURCES. see *EARTH SCIENCES — Geology*

338.2   BL
GUIA ECONOMICO E INDUSTRIAL DO ESTADO DE MINAS GERAIS. a. free. Federacao das Industrias do Estado de Minas Gerais, Av. Carandai 1115, 30000 Belo Horizonte, Brazil. Ed. Paulo A.S. Passos. adv. charts. stat.
     Supersedes (since 1979): Anuario Industrial de Minas Gerais (ISSN 0066-5231)

553   UK   ISSN 0072-8713
GUIDE TO THE COALFIELDS. 1948. a. £8.50. Fuel and Metallurgical Journals Ltd., Queensway House, 2 Queensway, Redhill, Surrey RH1 1QS, England. Ed. E. G. Corbin. adv.

HIROSHIMA UNIVERSITY. JOURNAL OF SCIENCE. SERIES C. GEOLOGY AND MINERALOGY. see *EARTH SCIENCES — Geology*

549   622.342   CN   ISSN 0382-0734
HOLLINGER MINES LIMITED. ANNUAL REPORT. (Text in English and French) 1968. a. Hollinger Mines Ltd., Suite 601, Commerce Court E., Box 221, Toronto, Ont. M5L 1E8, Canada. illus.

338.2   II   ISSN 0073-6597
I M E DIRECTORY: MINES, MINERALS, EQUIPMENT. (Indian Mining and Engineering) (Text in English) 1965. a. $5. Mining Engineers Association, Esperanca Ground Floor, Colaba Causeway, Bombay 1, India. Ed. J. F. de Souza.

622   557   US   ISSN 0073-442X
IDAHO. BUREAU OF MINES AND GEOLOGY. BULLETIN. 1920. irreg., 1969, no. 23. price varies. Bureau of Mines and Geology, Moscow, ID 83843.

622   517   US   ISSN 0073-4446
IDAHO. BUREAU OF MINES AND GEOLOGY. INFORMATION CIRCULAR. 1957. irreg., no. 34, 1980. price varies. Bureau of Mines and Geology, Moscow, ID 83843.

338.2   553   US   ISSN 0094-9442
ILLINOIS MINERALS NOTES. 1954. irreg., no. 76, 1980. free. ‡ State Geological Survey, Natural Resources Bldg., 615 E. Peabody Dr., Champaign, IL 61820. circ. 2,000.
     Formed by the merger of: Illinois. State Geological Survey. Industrial Mineral Notes (ISSN 0073-4853) & Illinois. State Geological Survey. Mineral Economic Briefs (ISSN 0073-5116)

MINES AND MINING INDUSTRY

622 US
ILLINOIS MINING INSTITUTE. PROCEEDINGS. 1892. a. $5 (free to members, mining schools and technical libraries) Illinois Mining Institute, 203 Natural Resources Building, Urbana, IL 61801. Ed. Dr. M.E. Hopkins. adv. circ. 1,400.

622 II ISSN 0445-7897
INDIAN MINERALS YEAR BOOK. (Text in English) a. $39.78. Indian Bureau of Mines, New Sectretariat Bldg., Nagpur 440001, India (Order from; Controller of Publications, Civil Lines, Delhi 110054, India)

622.07 II ISSN 0304-1158
INDIAN SCHOOL OF MINES. ANNUAL REPORT. (Text in English) a. Indian School of Mines, Dhanbad 826004, Bihar, India. illus. Key Title: Annual Report-Indian School of Mines.

338.2 660 UK ISSN 0141-5263
INDUSTRIAL MINERALS DIRECTORY. 1977. irreg. £25($56.25) Metal Bulletin Books Ltd., Park House, 3 Park Terrace, Worcester Park, Surrey KT4 7HY, England. Ed. Brian Coope.

622 BE
INSTITUT NATIONAL DES INDUSTRIES EXTRACTIVES. RAPPORT ANNUEL. Dutch edition: Nationaal Instituut voor de Extractiebedrijven. Jaarbericht. (Editions in French and Dutch) 1968. a. free. Editions Techniques et Scientifiques, Rue Borrens 35-43, 1050 Brussels, Belgium. circ. 3,200 (both edts.) (back issues avail.)

622.8 US
INSTITUTE ON COAL MINE HEALTH AND SAFETY. (PROCEEDINGS) 1976. a. $12. (Colorado School of Mines) Colorado School of Mines Press, Golden, CO 80401. (reprint service avail. from UMI)

622 US
INSTRUMENTATION IN THE MINING AND METALLURGY INDUSTRIES. 1973. a. price varies. Instrument Society of America, 400 Stanwix St., Pittsburgh, PA 15222.

622 382 US
INTERNATIONAL COAL. a. $100. National Coal Association, Coal Bldg., 1130 17th St. N.W., Washington, DC 20036. Ed. King Lin.
Formerly: World Coal Trade (ISSN 0084-148X)

622.33 US
INTERNATIONAL COAL EXPLORATION SYMPOSIUM. PROCEEDINGS. Variant title: Coal Exploration Proceedings. 1976. irreg. $25. (World Coal Magazine) Miller Freeman Publications, Inc., 500 Howard St., San Francisco, CA 94105. Ed. William L. G. Muir. charts. illus. index.
Coal

549 US ISSN 0074-7017
INTERNATIONAL MINERALOGICAL ASSOCIATION. PROCEEDINGS OF MEETINGS. (Proceedings usually published in host country) 1959. biennial. price varies. International Mineralogical Association, c/o Marjorie Hooker, Secretary, 2018 Luzerne Ave, Silver Spring, MD 20910. Indexed: Mineral.Abstr.

622 IR ISSN 0075-0514
IRANIAN MINERAL STATISTICS.* (Text in English and Persian) 1962. a. free. Ministry of Finance and Economic Affairs, Bureau of Statistics, Tehran, Iran.

622.33 IT
ITALY. ENTE NAZIONALE IDROCARBURI. ENERGIA ED IDROCARBURI. SOMMARIO STATISTICO. (Text in Italian; summaries in English) irreg. (Ente Nazionale Idrocarburi) Staderini S.p.A., Pomezia, Italy. charts.

556 338.2 IV
IVORY COAST. DIRECTION DES MINES ET DE LA GEOLOGIE. RAPPORT PROVISOIRE SUR LES ACTIVITIES DU SECTEUR. irreg. Direction des Mines et de la Geologie, B.P. 1368, Abidjan, Ivory Coast.

622 GW ISSN 0075-255X
JAHRBUCH FUER BERGBAU, ENERGIE, MINERALOEL UND CHEMIE. 1893. a. DM.54. Verlag Glueckauf GmbH, Franz-Fischer-Weg 61, Postfach 1794, 4300 Essen 1, W. Germany (B. R. D.) adv. circ. 4,500.
Formerly: Jahrbuch des Deutschen Bergbaus.

338.7 II ISSN 0304-7164
JAMMU & KASHMIR MINERALS LIMITED. ANNUAL REPORT. (Text in English) a. Jammu & Kashmir Minerals Limited, Srinagar, India. Key Title: Annual Report-Jammu & Kashmir Minerals Limited.

622 AT ISSN 0075-3777
JOBSON'S MINING YEAR BOOK. 1957. a. Aus.$45. Jobson's Publications (Subsidiary of: Dun & Bradstreet (Australia) Pty. Ltd.) G.P.O. Box 425G, Melbourne, Vic. 3001, Australia. Ed. H.J. Rijnhart. adv.

622 KE ISSN 0075-580X
KENYA. MINES AND GEOLOGICAL DEPARTMENT. ANNUAL REPORT.* a. Mines and Geological Department, Box 30009, Nairobi, Kenya (Orders to: Government Printing and Stationery Department, Box 30128, Nairobi, Kenya)

KONINKLIJK NEDERLANDS GEOLOGISCH MIJNBOUWKUNDIG GENOOTSCHAP. VERHANDELINGEN. see EARTH SCIENCES — Geology

LANDESMUSEUM JOANNEUM. ABTEILUNG FUER GEOLOGIE, PALAEONTOLOGIE UND BERGBAU. MITTEILUNGEN. see PALEONTOLOGY

LIBERIA. MINISTRY OF LANDS AND MINES. ANNUAL REPORT. see ENGINEERING — Civil Engineering

LOUISIANA STATE UNIVERSITY. LAW SCHOOL. INSTITUTE ON MINERAL LAW. PROCEEDINGS. see LAW

622 551 CN
MANITOBA. MINERAL RESOURCES DIVISION. GEOLOGICAL PAPER. 1968. irreg. free. Mineral Resources Division, Box 12, 989 Century St., Winnipeg, Man. R3H OW4, Canada.
Formerly: Manitoba. Mining Engineering Division. Geological Paper (ISSN 0076-387X)

MANITOBA. MINERAL RESOURCES DIVISION. PUBLICATION. see EARTH SCIENCES — Geology

622 FR
MEMENTO DES MINES ET CARRIERES. 1958. a. 219 F. Regie Publicite Industrielle, 36 rue du Fer a Moulin, 75005 Paris, France. bk. rev.

MEMOIRES POUR SERVIR A L'EXPLICATION DES CARTES GEOLOGIQUES ET MINIERES DE LA BELGIQUE. see EARTH SCIENCES — Geology

622 CK
METAL. a. Fedemetal, Av. Caracas No. 37-15, Bogota, Colombia.

673 IT
METALLI NON FERROSI IN ITALIA: STATISTICHE. 1954. a. L.24000. Associazione Nazionale Industrie Metalli Non Ferrosi, Via Leopardi, 18, Milan, Italy. illus.

622 CN ISSN 0076-6704
METALLURGICAL WORKS IN CANADA, NONFERROUS AND PRECIOUS METALS. a. price varies. Department of Energy, Mines and Resources, Mineral Policy Sector, Ottawa, Ontario K1A OE4, Canada (Orders to: Supply and Services Canada, Publishing Centre, Hull, Que. K1A 0S5, Canada)

622 CN ISSN 0076-6712
METALLURGICAL WORKS IN CANADA, PRIMARY IRON AND STEEL. a. price varies. Department of Energy, Mines and Resources, Mineral Policy Sector, Ottawa, Ontario K1A OE4, Canada (Orders to: Supply and Services Canada, Publishing Centre, Hull, Que. K1A 0S5, Canada)

622 MX
MEXICO. DIRECCION GENERAL DE ESTADISTICA. ESTADISTICA MINEROMETALURGICA: PRODUCCION Y EXPORTACION. irreg.; latest 1972. free. Direccion General de Estadistica, Secretaria de Programacion y Presupuestro, Balderas 71, Agencia de Correos 245, Mexico 1, D. F., Mexico. stat. circ. controlled.

622 US ISSN 0085-3372
MICHIGAN MINERAL PRODUCERS ANNUAL DIRECTORY: 1971. a. one copy free; $0.25 each additional. Department of Natural Resources, Geological Survey Division, Information Services Center, Box 30028, Lansing, MI 48909. Eds. B.L. Champion, S.E. Wilson.
Supersedes: Directory of Michigan Mineral Operators.

622 AT ISSN 0085-3453
MINE AND QUARRY MECHANISATION. 1960. a. Aus.$24. Magazine Associates, Box 714, Potts Point, N.S.W. 2011, Australia. Ed. Neville Fortescue. adv. circ. 1,250. (back issues avail.)

338.2 US ISSN 0085-3445
MINERAL INDUSTRY OF MICHIGAN ANNUAL STATISTICAL SUMMARY: 1963. a. $0.25. Department of Natural Resources, Geological Survey Division, Information Services Center, Box 30028, Lansing, MI 48909. Eds. B.L. Champion, S.E. Wilson.
Supersedes: Michigan's Mineral Industries.

MINERALS AND ROCKS; monograph series of theoretical and experimental studies. see EARTH SCIENCES — Geology

622 US
MINES DIRECTORY. 1910. a. $10. Colorado School of Mines, Alumni Association, Guggenheim Hall, Golden, CO 80401. Ed. Patricia C. Petty. adv. circ. 5,200.

622 613.62 EI ISSN 0588-702X
MINES SAFETY AND HEALTH COMMISSION. REPORT/ORGANE PERMANENT POUR LA SECURITE DANS LES MINES E HOUILLE. RAPPORT. 1967. a. free. Commission of the European Communities, 200 rue de la Loi, 1049 Brussels, Belgium.
Issued 1959-1966 as: European Coal and Steel Community. Organe Permanent pour la Securite dans les Mines de Houille. Rapport (ISSN 0531-2922)

338.7 II
MINING AND ALLIED MACHINERY CORPORATION. ANNUAL REPORT. (Text in English) a. Mining and Allied Machinery Corporation, Durgapur, India. illus.

622 AT
MINING & CONSTRUCTION METHODS AND EQUIPMENT. 1973. irreg. Finecraft Publishing Co., Box 260, Neutral Bay Junction, N.S.W. 2089, Australia. Ed. Fiona Stewart.

622 UK ISSN 0076-8995
MINING ANNUAL REVIEW. 1935. a. £20($46) Mining Journal Ltd., 15 Wilson Street, London EC2M 2TR, England. Ed. Michael West. adv. circ. 11,000. (also avail. in microfilm) Indexed: Ref.Zh.

622 CN ISSN 0316-2281
MINING IN CANADA - FACTS & FIGURES. French edition: Mines au Canada-Renseignements et Statistiques (ISSN 0316-2311) (Text in English or French) 1964. a. free. Mining Association of Canada, 36 Toronto St., Suite 409, Toronto, Ont. M5C 2C2, Canada. charts. stat. circ. 24,000. (back issues avail.)

622 RH
MINING IN ZIMBABWE. 1950. a. $13. Thomson Publications Zimbabwe, Box 1683, Salisbury, Zimbabwe. Ed. J. Cockbill. adv. circ. controlled.
Formerly: Mining in Rhodesia (ISSN 0076-8987)

622 II
MINING INDUSTRY & TRADE ANNUAL. (Text in English) 1962. a. $15. Praveen Corp, Sayajiganj, Baroda 390005, India. Ed. C. M. Pandit.
Formerly: Mining Industry & Trade Journal (ISSN 0026-5217)

MINES AND MINING INDUSTRY

622   US
MINING INDUSTRY OF IDAHO. ANNUAL REPORT. 1899. a. Department of Labor and Industrial Services, Mine Safety Bureau, 317 Main St., Rm. 4000, Statehouse, Boise, ID 83720. stat. index. circ. controlled. (processed)

622   CN   ISSN 0317-9508
MINING-WHAT MINING MEANS TO CANADA. (Editions in English and French) 1964. biennial. free. Mining Association of Canada, 36 Toronto St., Suite 409, Toronto, Ont., Canada. circ. 100,000.

622   US
MINING YEARBOOK. 1969. a. $10. ‡ Colorado Mining Association, 330 Denver Hilton Office Bldg., 1515 Cleveland Place, Denver, CO 80202. Ed. David R. Cole. adv. cum.index (1969-1975) circ. 2,500.

338   JA
MINING YEARBOOK OF JAPAN/HONPO KOGYO NO SUSEI. (Text in Japanese; captions in English or Japanese) 1906. a. Ministry of International Trade and Industry, Research and Statistics Division - Tsusho Sangyo Chosakai, Minister's Secretariat, 6-15-1 Ginza, Chuo-ku, Tokyo 104, Japan. stat.

MONTANA. BUREAU OF MINES AND GEOLOGY. BULLETIN. see *EARTH SCIENCES — Geology*

622   US   ISSN 0077-1104
MONTANA. BUREAU OF MINES AND GEOLOGY. DIRECTORY OF MINING ENTERPRISES. (Subseries of Bulletins) a. Bureau of Mines and Geology, Montana College of Mineral Science and Technology, Butte, MT 59701.

MONTANA. BUREAU OF MINES AND GEOLOGY. MEMOIR. see *EARTH SCIENCES — Geology*

MONTANA. BUREAU OF MINES AND GEOLOGY. SPECIAL PUBLICATIONS. see *EARTH SCIENCES — Geology*

553   UK   ISSN 0077-3786
NATIONAL COAL BOARD. REPORT AND ACCOUNTS. a. H.M.S.O., P.O.B. 569, London SE1 9NH, England.

622 338   UK   ISSN 0307-7691
NATIONAL COAL BOARD STATISTICAL TABLES. 1947. a. £1.50. National Coal Board, Hobart House, Grosvenor Place, London SW1X 7AE, England.
    Formerly: National Coal Board (Great Britain). Annual Report and Accounts. Vol. 2, Accounts and Statistical Tables (ISSN 0077-376X)

NATIONAL RESEARCH INSTITUTE FOR POLLUTION AND RESOURCES. ANNUAL REPORT/KOGAI SHIGEN KENKYUSHO NENPO. see *ENVIRONMENTAL STUDIES*

NATIONAL RESEARCH INSTITUTE FOR POLLUTION AND RESOURCES. SCIENCE REPORT/KOGAI SHIGEN KENKYUSHO HOKOKU. see *ENVIRONMENTAL STUDIES*

622   HU   ISSN 0324-4628
NEHEZIPARI MUSZAKI EGYETEM, MISKOLC. PUBLICATIONS. SERIES A: MINING. (Text in English, German, Russian) irreg., vol. 35, no. 1, 1978. Nehezipari Muszaki Egyetem, Miskolc, Hungary. Ed. Bd. bibl. index.

NEVADA. BUREAU OF MINES AND GEOLOGY. BULLETIN. see *EARTH SCIENCES — Geology*

NEVADA. BUREAU OF MINES AND GEOLOGY. REPORT. see *EARTH SCIENCES — Geology*

622   CN
NEW BRUNSWICK. BEACH RESOURCES-EASTERN NEW BRUNSWICK. irreg. price varies. Department of Natural Resources, Mines Division, Fredericton, N.B., Canada.

622   CN   ISSN 0077-8109
NEW BRUNSWICK. MINERAL RESOURCES BRANCH. REPORT OF INVESTIGATIONS. 1966. irreg. price varies. Department of Natural Resources, Geology Division, Fredericton, N.B., Canada.

622   CN
NEW BRUNSWICK. WETLANDS-PEATLANDS RESOURCES. irreg. price varies. Department of Natural Resources, Mines Division, Fredericton, N.B., Canada.

622   NL
NEW CALDEONIA. SERVICE DES MINES ET DE LA GEOLOGIA. RAPPORT ANNUEL. a. Service des Mines, Noumea, New Caledonia. illus.

622   US
NEW MEXICO. BUREAU OF MINES AND MINERAL RESOURCES. BULLETIN. 1915. irreg., no. 107, 1976. price varies. Bureau of Mines and Mineral Resources, Socorro, NM 87801.

622   US
NEW MEXICO. BUREAU OF MINES AND MINERAL RESOURCES. CIRCULAR. 1930. irreg., no. 169, 1979. price varies. Bureau of Mines and Mineral Resources, Socorro, NM 87801.

622   US   ISSN 0548-5975
NEW MEXICO. BUREAU OF MINES AND MINERAL RESOURCES. MEMOIR. 1956. irreg., no. 37, 1979. price varies. Bureau of Mines and Mineral Resources, Socorro, NM 87801.

622   US   ISSN 0098-7077
NEW MEXICO. BUREAU OF MINES AND MINERAL RESOURCES. PROGRESS REPORT. 1972. irreg., no. 10, 1978. price varies. Bureau of Mines and Mineral Resources, Socorro, NM 87801. Key Title: Progress Report - New Mexico Bureau of Mines & Mineral Resources.

622   AT
NEW SOUTH WALES. DEPARTMENT OF MINERAL RESOURCES AND DEVELOPMENT. ANNUAL REPORT. 1875. a. price varies. Department of Mineral Resources and Development, G.P.O. Box 5288, Sydney, N.S.W. 2001, Australia. index. circ. 500.
    Formerly: New South Wales. Department of Mines. Annual Report (ISSN 0077-8664)

622   AT
NEW SOUTH WALES. DEPARTMENT OF MINERAL RESOURCES AND DEVELOPMENT. ANNUAL REPORT. STATISTICAL SUPPLEMENT. 1972. a. price varies. Department of Mineral Resources and Development, G.P.O. Box 5288, Sydney, N.S.W. 2001, Australia. circ. 500.
    Formerly: New South Wales. Department of Mines. Annual Report. Statistical Supplement.

622 660   AT   ISSN 0077-8672
NEW SOUTH WALES. DEPARTMENT OF MINES. CHEMICAL LABORATORY. REPORT. 1961. irreg. Department of Mineral Resources & Development, Box 5288, Sydney, N.S.W. 2001, Australia.

622 559   AT   ISSN 0077-8680
NEW SOUTH WALES. DEPARTMENT OF MINES. COALFIELDS BRANCH. REPORTS. 1962. irreg. Department of Mineral Resources & Development, Box 5288, Sydney, N.S.W. 2001, Australia.

622 559   AT   ISSN 0077-8729
NEW SOUTH WALES. GEOLOGICAL SURVEY. MINERAL INDUSTRY SERIES. 1967, no. 3. irreg., nos. 40, 44 & 38 1979. price varies. Department of Mineral Resources & Development, Box 5288, Sydney, N.S.W. 2001, Australia. Ed. H. Basden. circ. 400. Indexed: Bibl.&Ind.Geol.

622 559   AT   ISSN 0077-8737
NEW SOUTH WALES. GEOLOGICAL SURVEY. MINERAL RESOURCES SERIES. 1898. irreg., no. 43, 1978. price varies. Department of Mineral Resources and Development, G.P.O. Box 5288, Sydney, N.S.W. 2001, Australia. Ed. H. Basden. index. circ. 400. Indexed: Bibl.&Ind.Geol.

338.2   NZ
NEW ZEALAND. MINISTRY OF ENERGY. MINES DIVISION. ANNUAL REPORT. a. Ministry of Energy, Mines Division, Box 6342, Wellington, New Zealand.
    Formerly: New Zealand. Mines Department. Mines Statement.

622   CN   ISSN 0078-0340
NEWFOUNDLAND. MINERAL DEVELOPMENT DIVISION. INFORMATION. 1934. irreg. $0.50 price varies. Mineral Development Division, St. John's, Nfld., Canada.

622   CN   ISSN 0078-0359
NEWFOUNDLAND. MINERAL DEVELOPMENT DIVISION. INFORMATION CIRCULAR. 1959. irreg. price varies. Mineral Development Division, St. John's, Nfld., Canada.

622   CN   ISSN 0078-0367
NEWFOUNDLAND. MINES BRANCH. ANNUAL REPORT SERIES. 1964. a. price varies. Mineral Development Division, Confederation Bldg., St. Johns, Newfoundland, Canada.

622   CN
NEWFOUNDLAND AND LABRADOR. BULLETIN. irreg. price varies. Mineral Development Division, St. Johns, Nfld., Canada. bibl. charts. illus. circ. controlled.

622   CN
NEWFOUNDLAND AND LABRADOR. MINERAL RESOURCES REPORT. irreg. price varies. Mineral Development Division, St. Johns, Nfld., Canada. bibl. charts. illus. stat. circ. controlled.

338.2 622   NR   ISSN 0078-0707
NIGERIAN CHAMBER OF MINES. ANNUAL REVIEW.* (Title Varies: Chairman's Annual Report, President's Annual Report) 1951. a. free. Nigerian Chamber of Mines, P.O. Box 454, Jos, Benue-Plateau State, Nigeria. Ed. G. Griffin.

NIIGATA UNIVERSITY. FACULTY OF SCIENCE. SCIENCE REPORTS. SERIES E: GEOLOGY AND MINERALOGY. see *EARTH SCIENCES — Geology*

553   US
NORTH CAROLINA. GEOLOGICAL SURVEY SECTION. BULLETIN. 1893. irreg., no. 86, 1979. price varies. Department of Natural Resources and Community Development, Geological Survey Section, Box 27687, Raleigh, NC 27611.
    Formerly: North Carolina. Division of Mineral Resources. Bulletin.

553   US
NORTH CAROLINA. GEOLOGICAL SURVEY SECTION. ECONOMIC PAPER. no. 3, 1900. irreg., no. 68, 1970. Department of Natural Resources and Community Development, Geological Survey Section, Box 27687, Raleigh, NC 27611.
    Formerly: North Carolina. Division of Mineral Resources. Economic Paper.

553   US
NORTH CAROLINA. GEOLOGICAL SURVEY SECTION. INFORMATION CIRCULAR. 1940. irreg., no. 24, 1978. price varies. Department of Natural Resources and Community Development, Geological Survey Section, Box 27687, Raleigh, NC 27611.
    Formerly: North Carolina. Division of Mineral Resources. Information Circular.

553   US
NORTH CAROLINA. GEOLOGICAL SURVEY SECTION. SPECIAL PUBLICATION. 1965. irreg., no. 7, 1977. price varies. ‡ Department of Natural Resources and Community Development, Geological Survey Section, P.O. Box 27687, Raleigh, NC 27611.
    Formerly: North Carolina . Division of Mineral Resources. Special Publication (ISSN 0078-1398)

338.2   US   ISSN 0078-401X
OHIO. DIVISION OF MINES. REPORT; with coal and industrial mineral directories of reporting firms. 1872. a. free. ‡ Department of Industrial Relations, Division of Mines, 2323 W. Fifth Ave., Box 825, Columbus, OH 43216. Ed. Ellen Stringer. index.
    Formerly: Ohio. Division of Mines. Annual Report with Coal and Industrial Mineral Directories of Reporting Firms.

622   US
OIL SHALE SYMPOSIUM PROCEEDINGS. 1964. a. $16. (Colorado School of Mines) Colorado School of Mines Press, Golden, CO 80401. (reprint service avail. from UMI)

MINES AND MINING INDUSTRY

622 551   CN   ISSN 0704-2752
ONTARIO. GEOLOGICAL SURVEY. ANNUAL REPORT OF THE REGIONAL AND RESIDENT GEOLOGIST. 1967. a. Can.$2. Geological Survey, Queens Park, Toronto, Ont., Canada. Ed. C. R. Kusbia. circ. 1,000. (back issues avail.)

ONTARIO. GEOLOGICAL SURVEY. GUIDE BOOKS. see *EARTH SCIENCES — Geology*

549   CN
ONTARIO. GEOLOGICAL SURVEY. MINERAL DEPOSIT CIRCULARS. 1950. irreg., 1-2/yr. price varies. Geological Survey, 77 Grenville St., Parliament Bldgs., Toronto, Ont., Canada.
    Formerly: Ontario. Division of Mines. Mineral Resource Circulars.

622   CN
ONTARIO. GEOLOGICAL SURVEY. MISCELLANEOUS PAPERS. 1960. irreg., 3-4/yr. price varies. Geological Survey, 77 Grenville St., Parliament Bldgs., Toronto, Ont., Canada.
    Formerly: Ontario. Division of Mines. Miscellaneous Papers.

622 557   CN
ONTARIO. GEOLOGICAL SURVEY. REPORT. 1960. irreg. price varies. Geological Survey, 77 Grenville St., Parliament Bldgs., Toronto, Ont., Canada. Indexed: Can.Ind.Geo.Sci.Data.
    Formerly: Ontario. Division of Mines. Geological Reports; Incorporating: Ontario. Division of Mines. Geochemical Reports.

OREGON. STATE DEPARTMENT OF GEOLOGY AND MINERAL INDUSTRIES. BULLETIN. see *EARTH SCIENCES — Geology*

OREGON. STATE DEPARTMENT OF GEOLOGY AND MINERAL INDUSTRIES. G M I SHORT PAPERS. see *EARTH SCIENCES — Geology*

OREGON. STATE DEPARTMENT OF GEOLOGY AND MINERAL INDUSTRIES. MISCELLANEOUS PAPERS. see *EARTH SCIENCES — Geology*

OREGON. STATE DEPARTMENT OF GEOLOGY AND MINERAL INDUSTRIES. MISCELLANEOUS PUBLICATIONS. see *EARTH SCIENCES — Geology*

PACIFIC NORTHWEST METALS AND MINERALS CONFERENCE. PROCEEDINGS OF GOLD AND MONEY SESSION AND GOLD TECHNICAL SESSION. see *BUSINESS AND ECONOMICS*

622   AT
PANGUNA. 1971. irreg. Bougainville Copper Pty. Ltd., 95 Collins St., Melbourne, Vic. 3000, Australia.

338.2   US
PENNSYLVANIA. OFFICE OF MINES AND LAND PROTECTION. ANNUAL REPORT. Cover title: Pennsylvania. Department of Environmental Resources. Annual Report on Mining, Oil and Gas and Land Reclamation and Conservaion Activities. 1870. a. $5. Department of Environmental Resources, Harrisburg, PA 17120 (Orders to: Pennsylvania State Bookstore, Tenth & Market Sts., Harrisburg, PA 17120) Ed. Catherine Miles. stat.
    Formerly (until 1973): Pennsylvania. Anthracite, Bituminous Coal and Oil and Gas Divisions. Annual Report.

338.2 622   US   ISSN 0079-0591
PENNSYLVANIA STATE UNIVERSITY. EARTH AND MINERAL SCIENCES EXPERIMENT STATION. BULLETIN. 1929. irreg. price varies. Pennsylvania State University, College of Earth and Mineral Sciences, Earth and Mineral Sciences Experiment Sta., 415 Walker Bldg., University Park, PA 16802. Ed. Arnulf Muan. circ. 200-2,000. Indexed: Chem.Abstr.

549   US   ISSN 0079-0605
PENNSYLVANIA STATE UNIVERSITY. EARTH AND MINERAL SCIENCES EXPERIMENT STATION. BULLETIN. MINERAL CONSERVATION SERIES. PAPER. 1957. irreg. price varies. Pennsylvania State University, College of Earth and Mineral Sciences, Earth and Mineral Sciences Experiment Sta., 415 Walker Bldg., University Park, PA 16802. Ed. Arnulf Muan. circ. 200-2,000. Indexed: Chem.Abstr.

622 338.2   US   ISSN 0079-0613
PENNSYLVANIA STATE UNIVERSITY. EARTH AND MINERAL SCIENCES EXPERIMENT STATION. CIRCULAR. 1929. irreg. price varies. Pennsylvania State University, College of Earth & Mineral Sciences, Earth and Mineral Sciences Experiment Station, 415 Walker Bldg., University Park, PA 16802. Ed. Arnulf Muan. circ. 225.

PETRO QUIMICA; petroleo y mineria. see *PETROLEUM AND GAS*

622   PH   ISSN 0085-4875
PHILIPPINE MINING AND ENGINEERING JOURNAL. MINING ANNUAL AND DIRECTORY. Included as July issue of Phillipine Mining and Engineering Journal. 1971. a. P.3($15) Business Masters International, 55 U.E. Tech. Avenue, University Hills, Subdivision Malabon, Rizal, Philippines. Ed. Luciano B. Quitlong. adv. circ. 10,000.

622 333.7   PH
PHILIPPINES. BUREAU OF MINES. ANNUAL REPORT. 1973. a. $3. Bureau of Mines, Manila, Philippines.

622   US
PIT & QUARRY HANDBOOK AND BUYERS GUIDE; equipment and technical reference manual for nonmetallic industry. 1907. a. $75. Pit and Quarry Publications, Inc., 105 W. Adams St., Chicago, IL 60603. Ed. B. C. Herod. adv. index. circ. 8,700.
    Formerly: Pit and Quarry Handbook and Purchasing Guide (ISSN 0079-2128)

622   PL   ISSN 0372-9508
POLITECHNIKA SLASKA. ZESZYTY NAUKOWE. GORNICTWO. (Text in Polish; summaries in English and Russian) 1959. irreg. price varies. Politechnika Slaska, W. Pstrowskiego 7, 44-100 Gliwice, Poland (Dist. by: Ars Polona, Krakowskie Przedmiescie 7, 00-068 Warsaw, Poland) Ed. Miroslaw Chudek.

622   PL   ISSN 0324-9670
POLITECHNIKA WROCLAWSKA. INSTYTUT GORNICTWA. PRACE NAUKOWE. KONFERENCJE. (Text in Polish; summaries in English and Russian) 1971. irreg., no. 4, 1978. price varies. Politechnika Wroclawska, Wybrzeze Wyspianskiego 27, 50-370 Wroclaw, Poland (Dist, by: Ars Polona-Ruch, Krakowskie, Przedmiescie 7, Warsaw, Poland) Ed. Marian Kloza.

622   PL   ISSN 0324-9689
POLITECHNIKA WROCLAWSKA. INSTYTUT GORNICTWA. PRACE NAUKOWE. MONOGRAFIE. (Text in Polish; summaries in English and Russian) 1973. irreg., no. 13, 1979. price varies. Politechnika Wroclawska, Wybrzeze Wyspianskiego 27, 50-370 Wroclaw, Poland (Dist. by: Ars Polona-Ruch, Krakowskie Przediescie 7, Warsaw, Poland) Ed. Marian Kloza. illus.

622   PL
POLITECHNIKA WROCLAWSKA. INSTYTUT GORNICTWA. PRACE NAUKOWE. STUDIA I MATERIALY. (Text in Polish; summaries in English and Russian) 1970. irreg., no. 15, 1978. price varies. Politechnika Wroclawska, Wybrzeze Wyspianskiego 27, 50-370 Wroclaw, Poland (Dist. by: Ars Polona-Ruch, Krakowskie Przedmiescie 7, Warsaw, Poland) Ed. Marian Kloza.

622   PL   ISSN 0079-3280
POLSKA AKADEMIA NAUK. ODDZIAL W KRAKOWIE. KOMISJA GORNICZO-GEODEZYJNA. PRACE: GORNICTWO. (Text in Polish; summaries in English and Russian) 1965. irreg., no. 20, 1979. price varies. Ossolineum, Publishing House of the Polish Academy of Sciences, Rynek 9, Krakow, Poland (Dist. by Ars Polona-Ruch, Krakowskie Przedmiescie 7, Warsaw, Poland) Ed. Zbigniew Strzelecki.

622   PL
PROJEKTY-PROBLEMY. BUDOWNICTWO WEGLOWE. (Text in Polish; table of contents in English and Russian) irreg., 1976, vol. 21, no. 5. Glowne Biuro Studiow i Projektow Gorniczych, Plac Grunwaldzki 8-10, 40-950 Katowice, Poland. Ed. Mieczyslaw Glanowski. charts. illus. circ. 824.

622   JA
REPORT OF OVERSEAS MINING INVESTIGATION: MADAGASCAR, SWAZILAND/KAIGAI KOGYO JIJO CHOSA HOKOKUSHO: MADAGASUKARU, SUWAJIRANDO. (Text in Japanese) irreg. Metal Mining Agency, Data Center - Kinzoku Kogy Jigyodan. Shiryo Senta, 6-3 Shiba Nishikubo Saguragawa-cho, Shiba, Minato-ku, Tokyo 105, Japan. charts, illus.

622   JA
REPORT OF OVERSEAS MINING INVESTIGATION: INDIA, PAKISTAN, BANGLADESH/KAIGAI KOGYO JIJO CHOSA HOKOKUSHO: INDO, PAKISUTAN, BANGURADISSHU. (Text in Japanese) irreg. Metal Mining Agency, Data Center - Kinzoku Kogyo Jigyodan. Shiryo Senta, 6-3 Shiba Nishikubo Saguragawa-cho, Shiba, Minato-ku, Tokyo 105, Japan. charts, illus.

RESERVES OF COAL, PROVINCE OF ALBERTA. see *ENERGY*

338.2   TZ   ISSN 0082-1659
REVIEW OF THE MINERAL INDUSTRY IN TANZANIA. Title varies: Tanzania. Geology and Mines Division. Review of the Mineral Industry. (Former name of issuing body: Mineral Resources Division) 1965. a. free. Geology and Mines Division, Box 903, Dodoma, Tanzania. circ. 400.

622   US   ISSN 0080-3375
ROCK MECHANICS/FELSMECHANIK/MECHANIQUE DES ROCHES. SUPPLEMENT. 1970. irreg., no. 10, 1981. Springer-Verlag, 175 Fifth Ave., New York, NY 10010 (also Berlin, Heidelberg, Vienna) (reprint service avail. from ISI)
    Continues: Felsmechanik und Ingenieurgeologie. Rock Mechanics and Engineering Geology. Supplement.

622   UK   ISSN 0080-4495
ROYAL SCHOOL OF MINES, LONDON. JOURNAL. 1951. a. £1. Royal School of Mines Association, Prince Consort Road, London SW7 2BP, England. Ed. A. J. Carr. adv. bk. rev. circ. 1,600.

622.33   CN   ISSN 0581-8109
SASKATCHEWAN. DEPARTMENT OF MINERAL RESOURCES. ANNUAL REPORT. 1974. a. Department of Mineral Resources, 1915 Hamilton St., Regina, Sask. S4P 4V4, Canada. charts. illus.

338.2   CN   ISSN 0707-2570
SASKATCHEWAN. DEPARTMENT OF MINERAL RESOURCES. STATISTICAL YEARBOOK. 1964. a. Can.$10. ‡ Department of Mineral Resources, Publications Office, 1914 Hamilton St., Regina, Sask. S4P 4V4, Canada.

338.2   FR   ISSN 0081-0797
SOCIETE DE L'INDUSTRIE MINERALE. ANNUAIRE. 1855. a. 125 F. Societe de l'Industrie Minerale, 19, rue du Grand Moulin, 42029 St.-Etienne Cedex, France. adv. index.

338.7   IV   ISSN 0250-3697
SOCIETE POUR LE DEVELOPPEMENT MINIER DE LA COTE D'IVOIRE. RAPPORT ANNUEL. 1962. a. free. Societe pour le Developpement Minier de la Cote d'Ivoire, B.P. 2816, Abidjan, Ivory Coast. illus.

622 551   SA
SOUTH AFRICA. DEPARTMENT OF MINES. ANNUAL REPORT. (Text in Afrikaans and English) N.S. 1947. a. R.2.70. Department of Mines, Private Bag 112, Pretoria 0001, South Africa (Orders to: Government Printer, Bosman St., Private Bag X85, Pretoria 0001, South Africa)
    Includes: South Africa. Geological Survey. Report of the Director of the Geological Survey.

SOUTH AFRICAN INSTITUTE OF MINING AND METALLURGY. MONOGRAPH SERIES. see *METALLURGY*

MINES AND MINING INDUSTRY

622 620   SA   ISSN 0081-2498
SOUTH AFRICAN MINING AND ENGINEERING YEARBOOK. Variant title: S.A. Mining and Engineering Yearbook. 1915. a. R.45. Thomson Publications S. A. (Pty) Ltd., P.O. Box 8308, Johannesburg 2000, South Africa. Ed. H. Engelhardt. adv. index.

622   SP
SPAIN. INSTITUTO GEOLOGICO Y MINERO. COLLECCION MEMORIAS. 1854. irreg. 300 ptas. (Instituto Geologico y Minero) Spain. Ministerio de Industria, Servicio de Publicaciones, Claudio Coello 44, Madrid 1, Spain.

338.2   MY   ISSN 0302-6620
STATES OF MALAYA CHAMBER OF MINES. COUNCIL REPORT. (Text in English) a. States of Malaya Chamber of Mines, Wisma Doshi, 1st Fl., 12, Jalan Tuanku Abdul Rahman, Box 2560, Kuala Lumpur, Malaysia.

338.2   MY
STATES OF MALAYA CHAMBER OF MINES. YEARBOOK. 1966. a. M.$7.50. States of Malaya Chamber of Mines, Wisma Doshi, 1st Fl., 12, Jalan Tuanku Abdul Rahman, Box 2560, Kuala Lumpur, Malaysia. stat.

622 665.5   US
STEAM-ELECTRIC PLANT FACTORS (1978) a. $100. National Coal Association, Coal Bldg., 1130 17 St., N.W., Washington, DC 20036. Ed. King Lin.
Former titles: Steam Electric Fuels (ISSN 0090-3884); Steam-Electric Plant Factors (ISSN 0081-5411)

338.2   US
SUMMARY OF MINERAL INDUSTRY ACTIVITIES IN COLORADO. (Part 2) 1897. a. $2. Division of Mines, 1313 Sherman St., Denver, CO 80203. stat. circ. controlled.

622   SW   ISSN 0039-6435
SVENSK BERGS- OCH BRUKSTIDNING.* 1922. irreg. (10-12/yr.) Kr.40. Kungsbroplan 1, 112 27 Stockholm, Sweden. Ed. Magnus Edlund.

622   US   ISSN 0085-7068
SYMPOSIUM ON COAL MINE DRAINAGE RESEARCH. PAPERS. 1965. a. or biennial. $10. ‡ (Coal Industry Advisory Committee to the Ohio River Valley Water Sanitation Commission) Bituminous Coal Research, Inc., 350 Hochberg Rd., Monroeville, PA 15146 (Or National Coal Association, 1130 17th St. N.W., Washington, DC 20036)

622   US
SYMPOSIUM ON SURFACE MINING AND RECLAMATION. 1973. a., latest 1977. $10. (National Coal Association) Bituminous Coal Research, Inc., 350 Hochberg Rd., Monroeville, PA 15146.

622   US
TAILING DISPOSAL TODAY; proceedings. 1973. irreg. price varies. (Tailing Symposium) Miller Freeman Publications, Inc., 500 Howard St., San Francisco, CA 94105. illus.

TASMANIA. DEPARTMENT OF MINES. TECHNICAL REPORTS. see EARTH SCIENCES — Geology

TOKYO UNIVERSITY OF EDUCATION. FACULTY OF SCIENCE. SCIENCE REPORTS. SECTION C: GEOGRAPHY, GEOLOGY AND MINERALOGY. see EARTH SCIENCES — Geology

622   US   ISSN 0586-3031
U S SYMPOSIUM ON ROCK MECHANICS. PROCEEDINGS. irreg., 18th, 1977. $35. (Colorado School of Mines) Colorado School of Mines, Golden, CO 80401. (reprint service avail. from UMI)

338.2   UK   ISSN 0308-5090
UNITED KINGDOM MINERAL STATISTICS. 1973. a. price varies. Institute of Geological Sciences, Exhibition Rd., South Kensington, London SW7 2DE, England (Avail. from H.M.S.O., c/o Liaison Officer, Atlantic House, Holborn Viaduct, London EC1P 1BN, England) stat.

550   UN   ISSN 0082-8114
UNITED NATIONS ECONOMIC AND SOCIAL COMMISSION FOR ASIA AND THE PACIFIC. MINERAL RESOURCES DEVELOPMENT SERIES. 1952. irreg., no. 44, 1978. price varies. United Nations Economic and Social Commission for Asia and the Pacific, United Nations Bldg., Rajamnern Ave., Bangkok 2, Thailand (Dist. by: United Nations Publications, Room LX-2300, New York, NY 10017; or Distribution and Sales Section, Palais des Nations, CH-1211 Geneva 10, Switzerland)

622   US   ISSN 0082-9129
U. S. BUREAU OF MINES. BULLETIN. 1910. irreg. price varies. U. S. Bureau of Mines, Dept. of the Interior, Washington, DC 20240. (also avail. in microfiche from NTI)

622   US   ISSN 0082-9137
U. S. BUREAU OF MINES. COMMODITY DATA SUMMARIES. 1957. a. free. ‡ U. S. Bureau of Mines, Dept. of the Interior, Washington, DC 20240. Ed. Albert E. Schreck. circ. 5,000.

622   US   ISSN 0498-7845
U.S. BUREAU OF MINES. MINERAL INDUSTRY SURVEYS. a. free. U.S. Bureau of Mines, U.S. Dept. of the Interior, Washington, DC 20240 (Orders to: 4800 Forbes Ave., Pittsburgh, PA 15213)

549   US   ISSN 0076-8952
U.S. BUREAU OF MINES. MINERALS YEARBOOK. 1932. a. U.S. Bureau of Mines, Dept. of the Interior, Washington, DC 20402 (Orders to: Supt. Doc., Washington, DC 20402)

622   US
U. S. BUREAU OF MINES. TECHNICAL PROGRESS REPORT. 1968. irreg. free. U.S. Bureau of Mines, Department of the Interior, 2401 E St., N.W., Washington, DC 20241. index.cum index every 5 years. circ. 2,500(controlled) Indexed: Chem.Abstr.

622 338.2   US   ISSN 0082-9382
U. S. BUREAU OF THE CENSUS. CENSUS OF MINERAL INDUSTRIES. 1840. quinquennial. price varies. U.S. Bureau of the Census, Dept. of Commerce, Washington, DC 20233 (Orders to: Supt. Doc., Washington, DC 20402)

622.8   US   ISSN 0097-9376
U.S. MINING ENFORCEMENT AND SAFETY ADMINISTRATION. INFORMATIONAL REPORT. irreg. U.S. Mining Enforcement and Safety Administration, 2401 Wilson Blvd., Arlington, VA 22203. Key Title: Informational Report- United States Department of the Interior, Mining Enforcement and Safety Administration.

549   IT
UNIVERSITA DEGLI STUDI DI FERRARA. ISTITUTO DI MINERALOGIA. ANNALI. NUOVA SERIE. SEZIONE 17: SCIENZE MINERALOGICHE E PETROGRAFICHE. (Text in Italian; summaries in English, French and Italian) vol. 1, no. 7, 1973. irreg. Universita degli Studi di Ferrara, Istituto di Mineralogia, Ferrara, Italy. bibl. charts.

UNIVERSITE DE CLERMONT-FERRAND II. ANNALES SCIENTIFIQUES. SERIE GEOLOGIE ET MINERALOGIE. see EARTH SCIENCES — Geology

338.2 622   US   ISSN 0065-5961
UNIVERSITY OF ALASKA. MINERAL INDUSTRY RESEARCH LABORATORY. REPORT. 1964. irreg., no. 40, 1978. price varies. University of Alaska, Mineral Industry Research Laboratory, Box 95303, Fairbanks, AK 99701.

UNIVERSITY OF TEXAS, AUSTIN. BUREAU OF ECONOMIC GEOLOGY. MINERAL RESOURCE CIRCULARS. see EARTH SCIENCES — Geology

UTAH GEOLOGICAL AND MINERAL SURVEY. BULLETIN. see EARTH SCIENCES — Geology

622   II
UTTAR PRADESH. STATE MINERAL DEVELOPMENT CORPORATION. ANNUAL REPORT AND ACCOUNTS. (Text in English and Hindi) a. State Mineral Development Corporation, B-52 Mandir Marg, Lucknow 226006, India.

VALTION TEKNILLINEN TUTKIMUSKESKUS. METALLURGIAN JA MINERAALITEKNIIKAN LABORATORIO. TIEDONANTO/TECHNICAL RESEARCH CENTRE OF FINLAND. LABORATORY OF METALLURGY AND MINERAL ENGINEERING. REPORT. see METALLURGY

622 665   VE
VENEZUELA. MINISTERIO DE ENERGIA Y MINAS. MEMORIA Y CUENTA. 1952. a. free. Ministerio de Energia y Minas, Torre Norte, Centro Simon Bolivar, Caracas, Venezuela. charts. stat.
Formerly: Venezuela. Ministerio de Minas e Hidrocarburos. Memoria y Cuenta (ISSN 0083-5374)

553 622   US
VIRGINIA. DIVISION OF MINERAL RESOURCES. PUBLICATIONS. 1959. irreg. price varies. Department of Conservation and Economic Development, Division of Mineral Resources, Box 3667, Charlottesville, VA 22903.
As of 1977 incorporating: Virginia. Division of Mineral Resources. Bulletin; Virginia. Division of Mineral Resources. Information Circular (ISSN 0083-632X); Virginia. Division of Mineral Resources. Resources Report (ISSN 0083-6338); Virginia. Division of Mineral Resources. Report of Investigations (ISSN 0083-6346)

557.97   US   ISSN 0147-1783
WASHINGTON (STATE) DIVISION OF GEOLOGY AND EARTH RESOURCES. INFORMATION CIRCULAR. 1939. irreg., no. 68, 1979. Department of Natural Resources, Division of Geology and Earth Resources, Olympia, WA 98501. Key Title: Information Circular - State of Washington, Department of Natural Resources, Division of Geology and Earth Resources.

338.2   US
WEST VIRGINIA. DEPARTMENT OF MINES. ANNUAL REPORT. a. free. Department of Mines, Charleston, WV 25305.

338.2   ISSN 0083-8462
WEST VIRGINIA. DEPARTMENT OF MINES. DIRECTORY OF MINES. 1895. a. free. Department of Mines, State Capitol Bldg., Rm. 151-E, Charleston, WV 25305.

338.2   US   ISSN 0091-5513
WEST VIRGINIA COAL FACTS. 1971. a. $3. West Virginia Coal Association, One Valley Sq., Suite 1340, Charleston, WV 25301. Ed. Dan R. Fields. stat. illus. circ. 5,000.

WEST VIRGINIA COAL-GEOLOGY BULLETINS. see EARTH SCIENCES — Geology

622   US   ISSN 0083-842X
WEST VIRGINIA COAL MINING INSTITUTE. PROCEEDINGS. 1919. irreg. $7.50. West Virginia Coal Mining Institute, 213 White Hall, Morgantown, WV 26506. Ed. Jay Hilary Kelley.

622   US
WEST VIRGINIA MINERAL RESOURCES SERIES. 1971. irreg. Geological and Economic Survey, Box 879, Morgantown, WV 26505.
Formerly: West Virginia Geological Survey. Mineral Resources Series.

338.2   US   ISSN 0095-4322
WORLD MINES REGISTER. 1976. biennial. Miller Freeman Publications, Inc., 500 Howard St., San Francisco, CA 94105. Ed. James R. Ledbetter.

622   US
WORLD MINING. LATIN AMERICAN EDITION. 1974. a. $3. Miller Freeman Publications, Inc., 500 Howard St., San Francisco, CA 94105. Ed. R. J. M. Wyllie. circ. 6,400.

622   PL
WORLD MINING CONGRESS. REPORT. (Published in Host Country) 1958. triennial since 1976; 10th, 1979, Istanbul. ‡ World Mining Congress, National Organizing Committee, c/o Ing. M. Najberg, Secretary-General, Al. Ujazdowskie 1-3, Warsaw, Poland (Order 10th Report from: MTA, Ankara, Turkey) circ. 2,000-2,500.
Formerly: International Organizing Committee of World Mining Congresses. Report (ISSN 0074-2775)

MINES AND MINING INDUSTRY — ABSTRACTING, BIBLIOGRAPHIES, STATISTICS

338.2   ZA   ISSN 0076-9010
ZAMBIA MINING YEARBOOK. 1955. a. free.
Copper Industry Service Bureau, Kitwe, Zambia
(Dist. by American Metal Climax, Inc., 1270 Ave.
of the Americas, New York, N.Y. 10026)
    Formerly: Copperbelt of Zambia Mining Industry
Year Book.

ZIMBABWE. MINISTRY OF LANDS AND
NATURAL RESOURCES. REPORT OF THE
SECRETARY FOR LANDS AND NATURAL
RESOURCES. see CONSERVATION

MINES AND MINING INDUSTRY —
Abstracting, Bibliographies, Statistics

553 551 016   AT
AUSTRALIA. BUREAU OF MINERAL
RESOURCES, GEOLOGY AND GEOPHYSICS.
OPEN FILE CIRCULAR. 1964. irreg. Bureau of
Mineral Resources, Geology and Geophysics, P. O.
Box 378, Canberra City, A.C.T. 2601, Australia.
Lists unpublished reports

622 319.4   AT
AUSTRALIA. BUREAU OF STATISTICS.
MINERAL EXPLORATION. 1974. a. free.
Australian Bureau of Statistics, Box 10, Belconnen,
A.C.T. 2616, Australia. circ. 1,900.

622   AT
AUSTRALIA. BUREAU OF STATISTICS.
VICTORIAN OFFICE. MINERAL
PRODUCTION - VICTORIA. 1966. a. free.
Australian Bureau of Statistics, Victorian Office,
Box 2796Y, G.P.O., Melbourne, Vic. 3001,
Australia. Ed. H. L. Speagle. circ. 400.

622.33   CN   ISSN 0705-436X
CANADA. STATISTICS CANADA. COAL MINES/
MINES DE CHARBON. (Catalog 26-206) (Text in
English and French) 1917. a. Can.$6($7.20)
Statistics Canada, Publications Distribution, Ottawa,
Ont. K1A 0V7, Canada. (also avail. in microform
from MML)

338.2   CN   ISSN 0575-8645
CANADA. STATISTICS CANADA. GENERAL
REVIEW OF THE MINERAL INDUSTRIES/
REVUE GENERALE SUR LES INDUSTRIES
MINERALES; mines, quarries and oil wells/mines,
carrieres et puits de petrole. (Catalog 26-201) (Text
in English and French) 1949. a. Can.$4.50($5.40)
Statistics Canada, Publications Distribution, Ottawa,
Ont. K1A 0V7, Canada. (also avail. in microform
from MML)

338.2   CN   ISSN 0381-9256
CANADA. STATISTICS CANADA.
MISCELLANEOUS NON-METALLIC
MINERAL PRODUCTS INDUSTRIES/
INDUSTRIES DES PRODUITS MINERAUX
NON-METALLIQUES DIVERS. (Catalogue 44-
210) (Text in English and French) 1927. a.
Can.$4.50($5.40) Statistics Canada, Publications
Distribution, Ottawa, Ont. K1A 0V7, Canada. (also
avail. in microform from MML)

549   CN   ISSN 0380-7797
CANADA'S MINERAL PRODUCTION,
PRELIMINARY ESTIMATE/PRODUCTION
MINERALE DU CANADA, CALCUL
PRELIMINAIRE. (Catalogue 26-202) (Text in
English and French) 1927. a. Can.$4.50($5.40)
Statistics Canada, Publications Distribution, Ottawa,
Ont. K1A 0V7, Canada. (also avail. in microform
from MML)

016 622   UR
EKONOMIKA UGOL'NOI PROMYSHLENNOSTI.
irreg. 0.76 Rub. Ministerstvo Ugol'noi
Promyshlennosti, Moscow, U.S.S.R. bibl.

622.3   US   ISSN 0071-6235
FLOTATION INDEX. a. Dow Chemical Co., 1703 S.
Saginaw Rd., Midland, MI 48640.

338.2   GR   ISSN 0072-7415
GREECE. NATIONAL STATISTICAL SERVICE.
ANNUAL STATISTICAL SURVEY OF MINES,
QUARRIES AND SALTERNS. (Text in English
and Greek) a., latest 1977. $1.50. National
Statistical Service, Publications and Information
Division, 14-16 Lycourgou St., Athenss 112,
Greece.

622   VE
HIERRO; y otros datos estadisticos. 1965. a. free.
Ministerio de Energia y Minas, Oficina de
Economia Minera, Piso 24, Torre Norte, Centro
Simon Bolivar, Caracas, Venezuela.
    Formerly: Venezuela. Ministerio de Minas e
Hidrocarburos. Oficina de Economia Minera. Hierro
y Otros Datos Estadisticos (ISSN 0083-5382)

622   FR
INTERGOVERNMENTAL COUNCIL OF COPPER
EXPORTING COUNTRIES. STATISTICAL
BULLETIN. (Text in English, French, and Spanish)
irreg. Intergovernmental Council of Copper
Exporting Countries, 177 Av. du Roule, 92200
Neuilly sur Seine, France.

338.2 315   KO   ISSN 0075-6849
KOREA (REPUBLIC) BUREAU OF STATISTICS.
REPORT ON MINING AND
MANUFACTURING SURVEY/
KWANGGONGUP TONGGYE ZO SA BOGO
SEO. (Text in Korean and English) 1963. a. 3210
Won. Bureau of Statistics, Economic Planning
Board, Gyeongun-Dong, Jongro-Gu, Seoul, S.
Korea. Ed. Heung-Koo Kang. circ. 1,000.

338.2   NZ
NEW ZEALAND. MINISTRY OF ENERGY.
MINES DIVISION. ANNUAL RETURNS OF
PRODUCTION FROM QUARRIES AND
MINERAL PRODUCTION STATISTICS. a.
Ministry of Energy, Mines Division, Box 6342,
Wellington, New Zealand. illus.
    Formerly: New Zealand. Mines Department.
Annual Returns of Production from Quarries and
Mineral Production Statistics.

314 622   PL   ISSN 0079-2675
POLAND. GLOWNY URZAD STATYSTYCZNY.
ROCZNIK STATYSTYCZNY GORNICTWA.
YEARBOOK OF MINING STATISTICS.* (Issued
in its Seria Roczniki Branzowe. Branch Yearbooks)
irreg. Glowny Urzad Statystyczny, Al.
Niepodleglosci 208, 00-925 Warsaw, Poland.

622 338.2   SA
SOUTH AFRICA. DEPARTMENT OF
STATISTICS. MINING: FINANCIAL
STATISTICS. (Report No. 16-01) a, latest 1975.
R.3.50. Department of Statistics, Private Bag X44,
Pretoria 0001, South Africa (Orders to: Government
Printer, Bosman St., Private Bag X85, Pretoria 0001,
South Africa)

622 338.2   SA
SOUTH AFRICA. DEPARTMENT OF
STATISTICS. SURVEY OF THE ACCOUNTS OF
MINING COMPANIES. (Report No. 09-02) a,
latest 1976/77. R.2. Department of Statistics,
Private Bag X44, Pretoria 0001, South Africa
(Orders to: Government Printer, Bosman St.,
Private Bag X85, Pretoria 0001, South Africa)

312 622   GW
STATISTISCHE MITTEILUNGEN DER
BERGBEHOERDEN DER BUNDESREPUBLIK.
a. DM.39.50. Ed. Piepersche Buchdruckerei und
Verlagsanstalt, Osteroeder Str. 8, Postfach 10, 3392
Clausthal-Zellerfeld, W. Germany (B.R.D.) stat.
(tabloid format)

VENEZUELA. MINISTERIO DE ENERGIA Y
MINAS. APENDICE ESTADISTICO. see
ENERGY — Abstracting, Bibliographies, Statistics

VENEZUELA. MINISTERO DE ENERGIA Y
MINAS. MEMORIA. see ENERGY —
Abstracting, Bibliographies, Statistics

338.2 310   UK
WORLD MINERAL STATISTICS; world production,
exports and imports. 1977. a. price varies. Institute
of Geological Sciences, Exhibition Rd., London
SW7 2DE, England (Avail. from H.M.S.O., c/o
Liaison Officer, Atlantic House, Holborn Viaduct,
London EC1P 1BN, England) circ. 1,000.
    Supersedes: Institute of Geological Sciences,
London. Statistical Summary of the Mineral
Industry (ISSN 0073-9367)

MOTION PICTURES

791.43   US   ISSN 0092-5675
ACADEMY AWARDS OSCAR ANNUAL. (Special
1978 issue: Academy Awards 50th Anniversary
Issue) 1971. a. $9.95 softcover; $14.95 hardcover. E
S E California, 509 N. Harbor Rd., La Habra, CA
90631. Ed. Robert A. Osborne. illus.

790   RM
ALMANAHUL CINEMA. a. 15 lei. Arhiva Nationala
de Filme, Bd. Gh. Gheorghiu-Dej Nr. 65, Bucharest,
Romania. illus.

778.534   SZ
AMATEURFILM JOURNAL. a. Alma-Verlag,
Postfach 1020, 8953 Dietikon, Switzerland. Ed.
Albert Haeusermann.
    Formerly: Super-8 Journal.

791.43   US
AMERICAN FILM FESTIVAL GUIDE. 1959. a. $5.
Educational Film Library Association, Inc., 43 W.
61 St., New York, NY 10023. Ed. Nadine Covert.
adv. index. cum. index: 1959-1963. circ. 5,000.
    Formerly: Festival Film Guide (ISSN 0071-4658)

791.4   US   ISSN 0065-8308
AMERICAN FILM REVIEW. 1962. a. free. ‡
American Educational and Historical Film Center,
Eastern College, St. Davids, PA 19087. Ed. John A.
Baird, Jr. circ. 30,000.

778.5   FR
ANNEE DU CINEMA. a. price varies. Editions
Calmann-Levy, 3 rue Auber, 75009 Paris, France.
illus.

ANNUAIRE BIOGRAPHIQUE DU CINEMA ET
DE LA TELEVISION EN FRANCE ET EN
BELGIQUE. see COMMUNICATIONS — Radio
And Television

791.43   FR   ISSN 0066-2968
ANNUAIRE DU CINEMA ET TELEVISION. 1948.
a. 120 F.($25) Editions Bellefaye, 1 Av. de l'Abbe
Roussel, 75016 Paris, France. Ed. Gisele Bellefaye.
adv.

778.5   US   ISSN 0163-5123
ANNUAL INDEX TO MOTION PICTURE
CREDITS. 1978. a. Academy of Motion Picture
Arts and Sciences, 8949 Wilshire Blvd., Beverly
Hills, CA 90211. Ed. Sallyroll.

778.5   US   ISSN 0163-5123
ANNUAL INDEX TO MOTION PICTURE
CREDITS. 1979. a. $150. (Academy of Motion
Picture Arts and Sciences) Greenwood Press, 88
Post Rd. W., Westport, CT 06881.
    Formerly: Screen Achievement Records Bulletin
(ISSN 0147-2313)

791.4   US
ANTHOLOGY FILM ARCHIVES SERIES. 1975.
irreg. price varies. New York University Press,
Washington Square, New York, NY 10003.

791.43   BL   ISSN 0066-5053
ANUARIO DE CINEMA.* a. Livraria Kosmos
Editora, Rua do Rosario 135-137, C P 3481, Rio de
Janeiro, Brazil. Ed. Roberto Bandeira.

791.4   RM
ANUL CINEMATOGRAFIC. 1966. a. free. Arhiva
Nationala de Filme, Bd. Gh. Gheorgiu Dej, Nr. 65,
Bucharest, Romania. Ed. Isabela Cionis.

011   US
ASSOCIATION FILMS. FREE LOAN FILMS.
Caption title, 1973/74: Free Loan 16 mm. Sound
Motion Pictures. a. free. Association-Sterling Films,
866 Third Ave., New York, NY 10022. illus.
    Former titles: Association-Sterling Films. Free
Loan Films (ISSN 0093-0881); Association Films.
16mm. Sound Free Loan Films, Sales and Rental
Subjects.

791   IT
ATTUALITA CINEMATOGRAFICHE. 1964. a.
Edizioni Letture, Piazza San Fedele 4, 20121 Milan,
Italy.

MOTION PICTURES

384.1 791.4   US   ISSN 0098-5481
BACKSTAGE TV FILM/TAPE & SYNDICATION
DIRECTORY. a. $10. Backstage Publications, Inc.,
165 W. 46th St., New York, NY 10036.

791.43   GW   ISSN 0067-6209
BESONDERS WERTVOLL. KURZFILME. 1956. a.
DM.19.80. Filmbewertungsstelle Wiesbaden,
Schloss, 6200 Wiesbaden 12, W. Germany (B.R.D.)
circ. 1,000.

791.43   GW   ISSN 0067-6217
BESONDERS WERTVOLL. LANGFILME. 1958. a.
DM.19.80. Filmbewertungsstelle Wiesbaden,
Schloss, 6200 Wiesbaden 12, W. Germany (B.R.D.)
circ. 1,000(approx.)

778.5   US   ISSN 0147-4049
BRIGHT LIGHTS. 1974. irreg. $7 for 4 nos. c/o Gary
Morris, Ed., Box 26081, Los Angeles, CA 90026.
bk. rev. film rev. illus. circ. 2,500. Indexed:
Int.Ind.Film Per.
    For the film director

791.43   UK   ISSN 0068-2004
BRITISH FILM FUND AGENCY. ANNUAL
REPORT. a. price varies. British Film Fund
Agency, P.O.B. 569, London S.E.1, England (Avail.
from: H.M.S.O., c/o Liaison Officer, Atlantic
House, London EC1P 1BW, England)

778   UK   ISSN 0068-4449
BUSINESS MONITOR: MISCELLANEOUS
SERIES. M2 CINEMAS. a. price varies.
Department of Industry, 1 Victoria St., London
S.W.1., England (Avail. from H.M.S.O., c/o Liaison
Officer, Atlantic House, Holborn Viaduct, London
EC1P 1BN, England)

778.5   CN   ISSN 0382-2273
C F D C ANNUAL REPORT. 1968. a. free.
Canadian Film Development Corporation, 800 Place
Victoria, Suite 2220, Montreal, Que. H4Z 1A8,
Canada.

011   CN   ISSN 0316-5019
C F F S INDEX OF FEATURE LENGTH FILMS.
Variant title: C F F S Index of 16 MM & 35 MM
Feature Length Films Available in Canada. (Text
mainly in English; summaries in French) 1947.
irreg. Can.$30. Canadian Federation of Film
Societies, Index Committee, Box 484, Sta. A,
Toronto, Ont. M5W 1E4, Canada. Ed.Bd. adv.
circ. 500.

791   FR   ISSN 0526-6513
C.I.C.A.E. BULLETIN D'INFORMATION.
(Confederation Internationale des Cinemas d'Art et
d'Essai) irreg. International Experimental and Art
Film Theatres Confederation, c/o Jean Leseure,
Secretary General, 22 rue d'Artois, 75008 Paris,
France.

791.4   US   ISSN 0007-9219
C T V D: CINEMA-TV-DIGEST; a quarterly review
of the serious, foreign-language cinema-TV-press.
winter 1961/62. irreg. $3 for 4 nos. Hampton
Books, Route 1, Box 76, Newberry, SC 29108. Ed.
Ben Hamilton. adv. bk. rev. film rev. illus. circ.
500-600. (back issues avail.)

CANADA COUNCIL ANNUAL REPORT AND
SUPPLEMENT. see ART

792.93   CN   ISSN 0316-5515
CANADIAN FILM DIGEST YEARBOOK. 1951. a.
Can.$12 per no. Film Publications of Canada
Limited, 175 Bloor St. E., Toronto, Ont. M4W 1E1,
Canada. Ed. Patricia Thompson. adv.

791.43   CN   ISSN 0705-548X
CANADIAN FILM SERIES. 1976. irreg., no. 6,
1981. price varies. Canadian Film Institute, 75
Albert St., Suite 611, Ottawa, Ont. K1P 5E7,
Canada.

778.5   IT
CATALOGO BOLAFFI DEL CINEMA ITALIANO.
1967. irreg.; no. 5, 1978. $9000. Giulio Bolaffi
Editore s.p.a., Via Cavour 17F, 10123 Turin, Italy.
Ed. Umberto Allemandi. illus. circ. 5,000.

CELEBRITY SERVICE INTERNATIONAL
CONTACT BOOK; trade directory / entertainment
industry. see THEATER

CENTRE INTERNATIONAL DE LIAISON DES
ECOLES DE CINEMA ET DE TELEVISION.
BULLETIN D'INFORMATIONS. see
COMMUNICATIONS — Radio And Television

791.43   UY   ISSN 0069-4118
CINE CLUB DEL URUGUAY. CUADERNOS.*
1962. irreg.(approx. 1 issue per year) Cine Club del
Uruguay, Rincon 567, Montevideo, Uruguay.

791.43   PO   ISSN 0704-061X
CINECLUBE. 1968. irreg. Esc.30. Cineclube do
Porto, Rua do Rosario, 5-10, Oporto, Portugal. Ed.
Fernando Saraiva. bk. rev. film rev. play rev. abstr.
bibl. illus. cum.index. circ. 3,000.
    Formerly: Cineclube do Porto. Boletim Circular
(ISSN 0009-7012)

778.5   US
CINEFAN. 1974. biennial. $2. Fandom Unlimited
Enterprises, c/o Randall D. Larson, 774 Vista
Grande Ave., Los Altos, CA 94022. film rev.

778.5   US   ISSN 0145-3483
CINEGRAM. vol. 2, 1977. irreg. Cinegram, Inc., 512
S. Main, Ann Arbor, MI 45104. Ed. Peter F.
Kuchnicki. adv.

791.43   SP   ISSN 0069-4134
CINEGUIA; directorio Espanol de cine, teatro y
television. 1960. a. 1600 ptas. Jose Luis Barbero,
Ed. & Pub., Antonio Acuna, 13, Madrid 9, Spain.
adv. circ. 3,000.

791.43 792   UK
CINEMA AND SOCIETY. irreg. price varies.
Routledge & Kegan Paul Ltd., Broadway House,
Newtown Rd., Henley-on-Thames, Oxon. RG9
1EN, England (U.S. address: Routledge Journals, 9
Park St., Boston MA 02108)

791.43   IT   ISSN 0009-7152
CINEMA E SOCIETA. 1966. irreg. L.1000 per no.
Giorgio Trentin, Ed. & Pub., Via Monte Cervialto
102, 00139 Rome, Italy. film rev. illus. circ. 2,500.
(tabloid format)

791.43   US   ISSN 0069-4150
CINEMA STUDIES.* 1967. irreg., 1970, no. 3. $2.
Art and Nature, 10 Harborside Park, Dennisport,
MA 02639. Ed. Gerald Noxon.

778.5   US   ISSN 0162-0126
CINEMONKEY; a serious film journal. 1976. irreg.
$7. Cinemonkey Inc,., Box 8502, Portland, OR
97207. Ed. Douglas Holm. adv. bk. rev. film rev.
    Formerly: Scintilation.

778.5   FR
COLLECTION CA-CINEMA. irreg; no. 8, 1978.
Editions Albatros, 14 rue de l'Armorique, 75015
Paris, France. Eds. Francois Barat et Joel Farges.

778.5   CN
COMITE D'ACTOR CINEMATOGRAPHIQUE.
CAHIERS. (Text in English, French, Spanish) irreg.
Can.$1 per no. Comite d'Actor Cinematographique,
360 rue McGill, C.H. 212 Montreal, Quebec H2Y
2E9, Canada. bibl. illus.

791   FR   ISSN 0589-9591
COUNCIL OF EUROPE FILM WEEKS. a. Council
of Europe, Film and Television Division,
Publications Section, 67006 Strasbourg, France
(Dist. in U. S. by Manhattan Publishing Co., 225
Lafayette St., New York, N. Y. 10012)

778.5   US
COUNCIL ON INTERNATIONAL
NONTHEATRICAL EVENTS. YEARBOOK;
Golden Eagle film awards. 1962. a. $6. Council on
International Nontheatrical Events, Inc., 1201
Sixteenth Street, N.W., Washington, DC 20036.
film rev. illus. stat. circ. 1,200.

791.43   GE
D D R FILM INFORMATION.* (Text in English,
French and German) 1974. irreg. D E E A Studio
for Shortfilms, Milastr. 2, 1058 Berlin, E. Germany
(D.D.R.)

778.5   DK   ISSN 0418-3304
DANISH FILMS. (Text in English, French, and
German) a. Danske Filminstitut, Store
Soendervoldstraede, DK-1419 Copenhagen,
Denmark. illus.

791.43   DK   ISSN 0070-3621
DENMARK. STATENS FILMCENTRAL. S F C
FILM. 1950. biennial (w. supplements) free. Statens
Filmcentral - Danish Government Film Office, 27
Vestergade, 1456 Copenhagen K, Denmark. Eds.
Axel Jepsen, Mogens Elvius.

791.43   FR   ISSN 0070-7155
DOSSIERS DU CINEMA. (Series includes 2
publications: Cineastes & Films) 1971. irreg., latest
issues--1974(Cineastes); 1975(Films) price varies. ‡
Editions Casterman, 66 rue Bonaparte, Paris 6e,
France. Ed. Claude Michel Cluny. adv. bk. rev.
index. circ. 5,000.

DRAGON. see LITERATURE

ENTERTAINMENT INDUSTRY DIRECTORY. see
BUSINESS AND ECONOMICS — Trade And
Industrial Directories

791.43   FR   ISSN 0014-1992
ETUDES CINEMATOGRAPHIQUES. 1960. irreg.
85 F. Lettres Modernes, 73 rue du Cardinal-
Lemoine, 75005 Paris, France. Ed. Michel Esteve.
bibl. illus.

778.5   GW   ISSN 0427-8186
F B W-INFORMATION. 1962. a. DM.7.
Filmbewertungsstelle Wiesbaden, Schloss, 6200
Wiesbaden 12, W. Germany(B.R.D.) Ed. Theo
Fuerstenau.
    Motion picture awards and ratings

778.5   US
FACTFILE. no. 11, 1977. irreg. American Film
Institute, National Education Services, John F.
Kennedy Center for Performing Arts, Washington,
DC 20566. bibl.

778.5   SZ
FILM & TV GRAPHICS; an international survey of
the art of film animation. a. $37.50. Walter Herdeg
Graphis Press, 107 Dufourstrasse, 8008 Zurich,
Switzerland (Dist. by Hastings House Publishers,
Inc., 10 East 40th St., New York, NY 10016)

FILM ANGELS. see BUSINESS AND
ECONOMICS — Investments

791.43   CN   ISSN 0015-1173
FILM CANADIANA: THE CANADIAN FILM
INSTITUTE YEARBOOK OF CANADIAN
CINEMA. (Text in English and French) 1971. a.
price varies. Canadian Film Institute, 75 Albert St.,
Suite 611, Ottawa, Ont. K1P 5E7, Canada.

791.43   GW   ISSN 0071-4879
FILM-ECHO FILMWOCHE. VERLEIH-KATALOG.
1949. a. DM.153. Axtmann-Verlag, Wilhelmstr. 42,
6200 Wiesbaden 1, W. Germany (B.R.D.) Ed. Horst
Axtmann. adv. bk. rev. circ. 45,000.

778.5   CN   ISSN 0704-9536
FILM EDMONTON. 1977. irreg. Can.$0.50 per no.
Edmonton Film Society, 501, 10015-119 St.,
Edmonton, Alta. T5K 1Y7, Canada.

778.5 780   US
FILM MUSIC BUYER'S GUIDE. 1977. a. $4.50. R T
S, Box 687, Dept. BW, Costa Mesa, CA 92627.

791.43   US
FILM NEWS OMNIBUS. 1974. triennial. $15. Film
News Co., 250 W. 57th St., New York, NY 10019.
Ed. Rohama Lee. film rev. illus.

791.43   US   ISSN 0361-722X
FILM READER. 1975. a. $7.50 to individuals;
libraries $10. c/o Film Division, Northwestern
University, Evanston, IL 60201. Ed. Bd. adv. circ.
1,000.

791.43   UK   ISSN 0071-4917
FILM REVIEW. 1970. a. £5.95. W. H. Allen & Co.
Ltd., 44 Hill St., London W1X 8LB, England.

791.43   SW   ISSN 0071-4925
FILMAARSBOKEN/SWEDISH FILM ANNUAL.
1967-68. a. Proprius, Vaertavaegen 35, S-115 29
Stockholm, Sweden. Ed. Bertil Wredlund. adv. circ.
1,500.

778.5   IS
FILMMAKERS AND FILM PRODUCTION
SERVICES OF ISRAEL. (Text in English) 1976. a.
Israel Film Centre, Box 299, Jerusalem, Israel. adv.

791 IS
FILMMAKING IN ISRAEL. (Brochure of Locations Available for Filming) (Text in English) 1970. irreg. free. ‡ Israel Film Centre, Box 299, Jerusalem, Israel. circ. 2,500.
Former titles: Israel Film-Making Plus (ISSN 0075-1162); Film.

791.43 GW ISSN 0071-4941
FILMSTATISTISCHES TASCHENBUCH. 1957. a. DM.18. Spitzenorganisation der Filmwirtschaft e.V., Langenbeckstr. 9, 6200 Wiesbaden, W. Germany (B.R.D.) Ed. Reinhard Knierim. circ. 700.

778.5 DK
FILMVIDENSKABELIGT ARBOG. 1973. a. Kr.18.50. (Koebenhavns Universitet, Filmvidenskabeligt Institut) C. A. Reitzels Forlag, 35 Noerre Soegade, DK-1370 Copenhagen K, Denmark. illus. circ. 500.
Supersedes in part (as of 1978): Koebenhavns Universitet. Institut for Filmvidenskab. Skrifter.

778.5 AG
FOTO CINE GUIA. a. $2.50. Editorial Fotografia Universal, Muniz 1327/49, Buenos Aires, Argentina.

778.5 770 384.5 US
GADNEY'S GUIDE TO 1800 INTERNATIONAL CONTESTS, FESTIVALS & GRANTS IN FILM & VIDEO, PHOTOGRAPHY, TV-RADIO BROADCASTING, WRITING, POETRY, PLAYWRITING & JOURNALISM. 1979. biennial. $15.95. Festival Publications, Box 10180, Glendale, CA 91209. Ed. Alan Gadney.

778 UK ISSN 0072-5773
GREAT BRITAIN. CINEMATOGRAPH FILMS COUNCIL. ANNUAL REPORT. a. H.M.S.O., P.O.B. 569, London SE1 9NH, England.

778 UK ISSN 0072-6958
GREAT BRITAIN. NATIONAL FILM FINANCE CORPORATION. ANNUAL REPORT. a. H.M.S.O., P.O.B. 569, London SE1 9NH, England.

791.43 US ISSN 0072-8284
GUIDE TO COLLEGE COURSES IN FILM AND TELEVISION. 1969. biennial from 1970/71. price varies. American Film Institute, Kennedy Center, Washington, DC 20566. Ed. Peter Bukalski.

791 CN ISSN 0383-0187
GUIDE TO FILM AND TELEVISION COURSES IN CANADA. (Text in English and French) 1971. biennial price varies. Canadian Film Institute, 75 Albert St., Suite 611, Ottawa, Ont. K1P 5E7, Canada.

791 370 US ISSN 0072-8438
GUIDE TO FREE-LOAN TRAINING FILMS (16 MM) 1970. irreg., 2nd edt., 1975. $7.95. Serina Press, 70 Kennedy St., Alexandria, VA 22305. Ed. Daniel Sprecher.

791 355 US
GUIDE TO GOVERNMENT-LOAN FILMS. irreg. $9.95. Serina Press, 70 Kennedy St., Alexandria, VA 22305.
Formerly: Guide to Military-Loan Films (ISSN 0072-8536)

792 US
I F I D A FILM DIRECTORY. a. $1. International Film Importers and Distributors of America, 40 West 57th Street, New York, NY 10019.

770 US
IMPACT FILMS CATALOG. a. free. Impact Films Inc., 144 Bleecker St., New York, NY 10012. circ. 10,000.

015 II
INDIAN FILMS. (Text in English) 1972. a. Rs.40. Motion Picture Enterprises, Alaka Talkies, Poona 411030, India. Ed. B. V. Dharap. adv. illus. index. circ. 1,200.

791 II
INDIAN MOTION PICTURE ALMANAC. (Text in English) a. Rs.40. Shot Publications, 3-B Madan St., Calcutta 700013, India. illus.
Incorporating: Bengal Motion Picture Diary & General Information.

778.5 BL
INFORMACOES SOBRE A INDUSTRIA CINEMATOGRAFICA BRASILEIRA. ANUARIO. a. Empresa Brasileira de Filmes, Departamento de Ingressos Padronizados, Av. 13 de Maio no. 41, Rio de Janeiro, Brazil.

574 610 GW ISSN 0073-8417
INSTITUT FUER DEN WISSENSCHAFTLICHEN FILM. PUBLIKATIONEN ZU WISSENSCHAFTLICHEN FILMEN. SEKTION BIOLOGIE. (Text and summaries in English, French or German) 1963. irreg., series 12, 1979. DM.7 per issue. Institut fuer den Wissenschaftlichen Film, Nonnenstieg 72, 3400 Goettingen, W. Germany (B.R.D.) Ed.H.-K. Galle.

791.43 GW ISSN 0341-5910
INSTITUT FUER DEN WISSENSCHAFTLICHEN FILM. PUBLIKATIONEN ZU WISSENSCHAFTLICHEN FILMEN. SEKTION ETHNOLOGIE. (Text and summaries in English, French, German) 1963. irreg., series 9, 1979. DM.7. Institut fuer den Wissenschaftlichen Film, Nonnenstieg 72, 3400 Goettingen, W. Germany (B.R.D.) Ed. H.-K. Galle.
Formerly: Institut fuer den Wissenschaftlichen Film. Publikationen zu Wissenschaftlichen Filmen. Sektion Voelkerkunde.

791.43 900 GW ISSN 0341-5937
INSTITUT FUER DEN WISSENSCHAFTLICHEN FILM. PUBLIKATIONEN ZU WISSENSCHAFTLICHEN FILMEN. SEKTION GESCHICHTE, PUBLIZISTIK. (Text in German; summaries in English, French and German) 1963. irreg., ser. 4, 1977/1979. DM.7. Institut fuer den Wissenschaftlichen Film, Nonnenstieg 72, 34 Goettingen, W. Germany (B.R.D.) Ed. H.-K. Galle.
Formerly: Publikationen zu Wissenschaftlichen Filmen. Sektion Geschichte, Paedagogik (ISSN 0073-8441)

610 791.43 GW ISSN 0341-5929
INSTITUT FUER DEN WISSENSCHAFTLICHEN FILM. PUBLIKATIONEN ZU WISSENSCHAFTLICHEN FILMEN. SEKTION MEDIZIN. (Text in English, French and German, Summaries in German) 1970. irreg., series 4 1977/1979. DM.7 per issue. Institut fuer den Wissenschaftlichen Film, Nonnenstieg 72, 3400 Goettingen, W. Germany (B.R.D.) Ed. H.-K. Galle.

500 791.43 GW ISSN 0073-8433
INSTITUT FUER DEN WISSENSCHAFTLICHEN FILM. PUBLIKATIONEN ZU WISSENSCHAFTLICHEN FILMEN. SEKTION TECHNISCHE WISSENSCHAFTEN, NATURWISSENSCHAFTEN. (Text and summaries in English, French or German) 1963. irreg., series 5 and 6, 1979. DM.7. Institut fuer den Wissenschaftlichen Film, Nonnenstieg 72, 3400 Goettingen, W. Germany (B.R.D.) Ed. H.-K. Galle.

791 RM ISSN 0538-4281
INTERNATIONAL ANIMATED FILM ASSOCIATION. BULLETIN. 1967, no. 15. irreg. International Animated Film Association - Association Internationale du Film d'Animation, c/o Marin Paraianu, 45 Strada Olteni, Bucuresti 4, Romania.

791 US ISSN 0074-462X
INTERNATIONAL DIRECTORY OF 16MM FILM COLLECTORS. 1971. irreg.(approx. biennial) $15. (16mm Filmland) Evan H. Foreman, Ed. & Pub., P.O. Drawer F, Mobile, AL 36601. circ. 1,000. (tabloid format)

791.43 UK ISSN 0074-6053
INTERNATIONAL FILM GUIDE. 1964. a. $9.95. Tantivy Press, 136-148 Tooley St., London SE1 2TT, England (Dist. in U.S. by: A.S. Barnes & Co., 11175 Flintkote Ave., San Diego, CA 92121) Ed. Peter Cowie. adv. bk. rev. (also avail. in microfilm from UMI; reprint service avail. from UMI)

791.43 US ISSN 0074-7084
INTERNATIONAL MOTION PICTURE ALMANAC; reference tool of the film industry. 1930. a. $35. Quigley Publishing Co., 159 W. 53 St., New York, NY 10019. Ed. Richard Gertner. adv.

770 US ISSN 0075-2509
JAHRBUCH DES KAMERAMANNS. 1959. a. DM.20.70. D D K-Verlag Ingeborg Weber, Rotbuchstr. 21, 8000 Munich 90, W. Germany (B.R.D.) adv.

791.43 UK
KEMPS INTERNATIONAL FILM AND TELEVISION YEAR BOOK. 1956. a. $55. Kemp's Group (Printers & Publishers) Ltd., 1-5 Bath St., London EC1V 9QA, England. adv.
Formerly: Kemps Film and Television Year Book (International) (ISSN 0075-5427)

791.43 YU
KINEMATOGRAFIJA U SRBIJI - UPOREDO SFRJ. (Subseries of Biblioteka Dokumentacije) 1969. a. 120 din.($15) Institut za Film, Belgrade, Cika Ljubina 15, Belgrade, Yugoslavia. Ed. M. Ilic. stat. circ. 1,000.
Formerly: Kinematografija u Srbiji (ISSN 0350-2651)

778.5 KO
KOREA FILM CATALOG. a. International Cultural Society of Korea, P.O. Box 2147, Seoul, S. Korea. illus.

778.5 US
M E R C DIRECTORY. 1977. a. $1.50 (free to New York State residents) (Media Equipment Resource Center) Publishing Center for Cultural Resources, 152 W. 442nd St., New York, NY 10036.

MINI-IMAGES. see *ADVERTISING AND PUBLIC RELATIONS*

791.43 US
MODERN FILM SCRIPTS. irreg. price varies. Simon and Schuster, Inc., 630 Fifth Ave., New York, NY 10020 (Orders from: 1 W. 39th St., New York, N.Y. 10018)

791.43 US
MOVIE LIFE YEARBOOK. s-a. $1. Ideal Publishing Corp., 2 Park Ave., New York, NY 10016. adv.

791 JA ISSN 0085-3577
MOVIE/TV MARKETING GLOBAL MOTION PICTURE YEAR BOOK. (Text in English) 1955. a. $36. Movie-TV Marketing, Box 30, Central Post Office, Tokyo 100-91, Japan. Ed. Glenn F. Ireton. adv. circ. 100,000. (also avail. in microform from UMI)

791.43 CN ISSN 0548-4162
NEW CANADIAN FILM. French edition: Nouveau Cinema Canadien (ISSN 0550-1318) 1968. irreg. Cinematheque Quebecoise, 360 McGill St., Montreal, Que. H2Y 2E9, Canada. illus.

778.5 US ISSN 0163-1276
NEW YORK PRODUCTION MANUAL; for motion pictures, television commercials and videotape industries. 1980. a? $35. New York Production Manual, Inc., One Washington Square Village, New York, NY 10012. Ed. Shmuel Bension.

791.43 US ISSN 0362-3688
NEW YORK TIMES FILM REVIEWS. 1968. biennial. New York Times Co., 229 W. 43rd St, New York, NY 10036. illus.

384.8 CN
OFFICE DES COMMUNICATIONS SOCIALES, MONTREAL. SELECTION DE FILMS IN 16 MM. 1966. irreg. Can.$12. ‡ Office des Communications Sociales, 4005 rue de Bellechasse, Montreal, Que. H1X 1J6, Canada. circ. 1,500.
Formerly: Office des Communications Sociales, Montreal. Selection de Films pour Cine Clubs. (ISSN 0078-3730)

778.5 322.4 BL
PARTO. 1979. irreg. Indicato dos Empregados em Estabelecimentos Bancarios de Sao Paulo, Comissao de Cinema dos Bancarios, Rua Sao Bento 365, C.E.P. 01011, Sao Paulo, Brazil. film rev. charts.

791.43 US ISSN 0031-8833
PHOTON. 1963. irreg. $4. Mark Frank, Ed. & Pub., 801 Ave. C, Brooklyn, NY 11218. adv. bk. rev. film rev. illus. circ. 40,000. (back issues avail)

791.43 FR ISSN 0079-2535
POINTS. FILMS. 1971. irreg. price varies. Editions du Seuil, 27 rue Jacob, 75261 Paris Cedex 06, Paris 6e, France.

778.5 BG
PRAKSHEPANA. (Text in Bengali) 1978. irreg. Tk.5. Arganta International Film Society, 112 Dhanmondi R.A., Road No. 3, Dacca 5, Bangladesh.

778.5 US
PYRAMID FILM AND VIDEO CATALOG. 1960.
biennial. free. Pyramid Film & Video, Box 1048,
Santa Monica, CA 90406. Ed. Jean Phillips. film
rev. circ. 60,000.

791 CN ISSN 0085-543X
RECUEIL DES FILMS. 1955. a. Can.$10. ‡ Office
des Communications Sociales, 4005 rue de
Bellechasse, Montreal, Que. H1X 1J6, Canada. adv.
film rev. circ. 1,500.

791.43 SP
RESUMEN CINEMATOGRAFICO. 1951. a. 150
ptas. Cine-Asesor, Plaza Marina Espanola, 6,
Madrid, Spain. Ed. Manuel Olivera Garrido. circ.
5,000.

778.5 NE
S F W SCIENTIFIC FILMS-HOLLAND. (Text in
English, French, German, Spanish) 1968. irreg. free.
Stichting Film en Wetenschap, Box 9550, 3506 GN
Utrecht, Netherlands.

778.5 DK
SAERRAKKE. 1978. irreg (approx 1/yr) Kr.18.50.
(Koebenhavns Universitet, Filmvidenskabeligt
Institut) C.A. Reitzels Forlag, 35 Noerre Soegade,
DK-1370 Copenhagen K, Denmark.
Supersedes in part (as of 1978): Koebenhavns
Universitet, Institut for Filmvidenskab Skrifter.

791 UK
SCREEN INTERNATIONAL FILM AND T.V.
YEARBOOK. 1945. a. $50. King Publications Ltd.,
Film House, 142 Wardour Street, London W1V
4BR, England. Ed. Peter Noble. adv. circ. 4,000.
Former titles: International Film and T.V.
Yearbook; British Film and T.V. Yearbook (ISSN
0068-1997)

791.43 US ISSN 0080-8288
SCREEN WORLD. 1949. a. $12.95. Crown
Publishers, Inc., One Park Ave., New York, NY
10016.

371.3 UN ISSN 0503-440X
SELECTED LIST OF CATALOGUES FOR SHORT
FILMS AND FILMSTRIPS. (Issued in Unesco's
Reports and Papers on Mass Communication) 1955.
irreg. Unesco Press, 7 Place de Fontenoy, F-75700
Paris, France (Dist. in U.S. by: Unipub, 345 Park
Ave. S., New York, NY 10010)
Title in 1955: Catalogues of Short Films and
Filmstrips.

791.43 GW ISSN 0071-4933
SPIELFILMLISTE. 1958. a. DM.5. Institut Jugent,
Film, Fernsehen, Waltherstr. 23, 8000 Munich 2, W.
Germany (B.R.D.) Ed. Hans Strobel. adv.
Formerly: Filmliste.

778.5 AT
SPROCKET. 1966. irreg. membership. International
Film Theatre, P.O. Box 90, Subiaco, W.A. 6008,
Australia. (Co-sponsor: Perth Film Society) Ed. A.
Dean. circ. 300.

778.5 CE
SRI LANKA FILM ANNUAL. (Text in Sinhalese)
no. 28, 1975. a. Rs.6.95. National Catholic Film
Office, St. Phillip Neri's Church, Katukurunda,
Kalutara, Sri Lanka. film rev.

STAGECAST-IRISH STAGE AND SCREEN
DIRECTORY. see THEATER

STELLE FILANTI. see BIOGRAPHY

778.5 NE
STICHTING FILM EN WETENSCHAP.
CATALOGUE 16MM FILMS. a. Stichting Film en
Wetenschap, Box 9550, 3506 GN Utrecht,
Netherlands.

STUDII SI CERCETARI DE ISTORIA ARTEI.
SERIA TEATRU-MUZICA-CINEMATOGRAFIE.
see THEATER

791.43 SW ISSN 0081-9867
SVENSKA FILMINSTITUTET.
DOKUMENTATIONSAVDELNINGEN.
SKRIFTER. 1967. irreg. Svenska Filminstitutet,
Filmhuset Borgvaegen, Box 27 126, 102 52
Stockholm, Sweden.

TELEVISION NETWORK MOVIES. see
COMMUNICATIONS — Radio And Television

778.5 US
THOUSAND EYES. irreg., nos. 2-3, 1977. $3 per no.
Thousand Eyes Film Book Shop, 144 Bleecker St.,
New York, NY 10012. adv. film rev. charts. illus.
tr.lit.

778.5 AT
VICTORIA. STATE FILM CENTRE. NEW FILMS.
1954. irreg. price varies. Victoria State Film Centre,
1 McArthur St., East Melbourne, Vic. 3002,
Australia. circ. 2,000.

VIDEO REGISTER. see BUSINESS AND
ECONOMICS — Trade And Industrial Directories

778.5 FR
VIVRE LE CINEMA. 1977. irreg. Editions Jacques
Glenat, 6 rue Lieutenant Chanaron, 38000
Grenoble, France. Ed. Gilbert Hus.

791 US ISSN 0083-9639
WHO'S WHO IN MOVIES.* 1965. a. $0.50. Sterling
Publishing Co., Inc., 419 Park Ave. S., New York,
NY 10016. Ed. Janice Coughlan.

778.5 NE
3 D FILM GIDS; catalogus korte films (16mm) irreg.
Verenigde Filmdiensten, Postbus 515, Hilversum,
Netherlands. illus.

MOTION PICTURES — Abstracting, Bibliographies, Statistics

016 791.43 RM ISSN 0084-7828
BIBLIOGRAFIA INTERNATIONALA CINEMA/
BIBLIOGRAPHIE INTERNATIONALE
CINEMA. 1967. a. $3. Arhiva Nationala de Filme,
Bd. Gh. Gheorghiu-Dej, Nr. 65, Bucharest,
Romania. Ed. Cristina Corciovescu. index.

791.43 CN ISSN 0380-6294
CANADA. STATISTICS CANADA. MOTION
PICTURE THEATRES AND FILM
DISTRIBUTORS/CINEMAS ET
DISTRIBUTEURS DE FILMS. (Catalogue 63-207)
(Text in English and French) 1930. a.
Can.$4.50($5.40) Statistics Canada, Publications
Distribution, Ottawa, Ont. K1A 0V7, Canada. (also
avail. in microform from MML)

EDUCATIONAL FILMS. see EDUCATION —
Abstracting, Bibliographies, Statistics

FILMS: THE VISUALIZATION OF
ANTHROPOLOGY. see ANTHROPOLOGY —
Abstracting, Bibliographies, Statistics

011 US
FLORIDA STATE UNIVERSITY.
INSTRUCTIONAL SUPPORT CENTER. FILM.
Cover title: Film Catalog. Florida State University.
1954. biennial. free. Florida State University,
Instructional Support Center, Tallahassee, FL
32306. Ed. Carolyn B. Peterson. circ. 3,000.
Formerly: Florida State University. Media
Services. Motion Pictures; Florida State University.
Educational Media Center. Educational Motion
Pictures (ISSN 0430-7313)

791 US
GUIDE TO FREE LOAN FILMS ABOUT
FOREIGN LANDS. irreg., latest issue 1975. $9.95.
Serina Press, 70 Kennedy St., Alexandria, VA
22305. Ed. Daniel Sprecher.
Formerly: Guide to Foreign Government-Loan
Film (16 MM) (ISSN 0072-8411)

791 US ISSN 0072-8462
GUIDE TO GOVERNMENT-LOAN FILMS
VOLUME 1: THE CIVILIAN AGENCIES. 1969.
irreg., 5th edt., 1978. $9.95. Serina Press, 70
Kennedy St., Alexandria, VA 22305. Ed. Daniel
Sprecher.

016.791 791.43 US ISSN 0000-0388
INTERNATIONAL INDEX TO FILM
PERIODICALS. (Vols. for 1972- prepared by the
International Federation of Film Archives) 1972. a.
St. Martins Press, 175 Fifth Ave., New York, NY
10010 (And St. James's Press, 3 Percy St., London
W1P 9FA, England)

778.5 016 US ISSN 0363-7778
MEDIA REVIEW DIGEST; the only complete guide
to reviews of non-book media. 1970. q. with annual
cum. $150. Pierian Press, 5000 Washtenaw Ave.,
Ann Arbor, MI 48104. Ed. C. Edward Wall.
cum.index.
Formerly: Multi Media Reviews Index (ISSN
0091-5858)
Films, film strips, records, tapes, slides,
transparencies, overlays, games, kits

778.5 MX
MEXICO. CENTRO DE INFORMACION
TECNICA Y DOCUMENTACION. INDICE DE
PELICULAS. a. (Centro de Informacion Tecnica y
Documentacion) Mexico. Servicio Nacional de
Adiestramiento Rapido de la Mano de Obra en la
Industria, Calzada Atzcapotzalco-la Villa 209,
Mexico 16, D.F., Mexico.

338 016 US
N I C E M INDEX TO PRODUCERS AND
DISTRIBUTORS. vol. 4, 1976. biennial. $24.
National Information Center for Educational Media,
University of Southern California, University Park,
Los Angeles, CA 90007. (also avail. in microfiche)

791.4 016 DK
NYE BOEGER OM FILM/TV/NEW BOOKS ON
FILM/TV. (Text in Danish and English) 1967. a.
free. Danske Filmmuseum, Store
Soendervoldstraede, 1419 Copenhagen K, Denmark.
Ed. Karen Jones. circ. 1,000.
Formerly: Nye Boeger om Film (ISSN 0048-
1238)

PSYCHOLOGICAL CINEMA REGISTER; films and
video in the behavioral sciences. see
PSYCHOLOGY — Abstracting, Bibliographies,
Statistics

016 791.4 CN ISSN 0315-7326
SIXTEEN MM FILMS AVAILABLE IN THE
PUBLIC LIBRARIES OF METROPOLITAN
TORONTO. 1969. a. Can.$20. Metropolitan
Toronto Library Board, 789 Yonge St., Toronto,
Ontario M4W 2G8, Canada.

016 371.42 DK
UDDANNELSE OG ERHVERV KATALOG. 1967.
a. free. Faellesudvalget mellem
Erhvervsvejledningsraadet, Vester Voldgade 113,
1503 Copenhagen V, Denmark. (Co-sponsor:
Uddannelsesraadet for Grundskolen) Ed. Bodit
Sneslev.

MUNICIPAL GOVERNMENT

see Public Administration—Municipal
Government

MUSEUMS AND ART GALLERIES

ACHTER HET BOEK. see LITERATURE

069 500 JA
AKIYOSHI-DAI MUSEUM OF NATURAL
HISTORY. BULLETIN. (Text in English or
Japanese; summaries in English) 1961. irreg., 1969,
no. 6. Akiyoshi-dai Museum of Natural History,
Akiyoshi-dai, Akiyoshi-cho Miya-gun, Yamaguchi
754-05, Japan. Ed. M. Ota.
Formerly: Akiyoshi-dai Science Museum. Bulletin
(ISSN 0065-5554)

707.4 US
ALLIED ARTISTS OF AMERICA. ANNUAL
EXHIBITION (BULLETIN) 1914. a. Allied Artists
of America, 15 Gramercy Park South, New York,
NY 10003. Ed. Bd. circ. 3,000.

708.1 US ISSN 0065-6410
ALLIED ARTISTS OF AMERICA. EXHIBITION
CATALOG. 1914. a. $2.50. ‡ Allied Artists of
America, 15 Gramercy Park South, New York, NY
10003. adv. circ. 1,600.

MUSEUMS AND ART GALLERIES

945   IT   ISSN 0569-1346
ALTAMURA. a. L.5000 membership. Museo Civico, Biblioteca, Palazzo degli Studi, Altamura, Italy. Ed. Celio Sabini. bibl. illus.

069   500   US
AMERICAN MUSEUM OF NATURAL HISTORY. ANNUAL REPORT. 1870. a. American Museum of Natural History, 79th St. and Central Park West, New York, NY 10024. Ed. Ann Breen. bibl. charts. illus. circ. 5,000.

069.5   GR
ANNALES MUSEI GOULANDRIS; contributiones ad historiam naturalem graeciae et regionis mediterraneae. (Text in English, German, French; summaries in English and Greek) 1973. a. Dr.450(S15) Goulandris Natural History Museum, 13, Levidou Str., Kifissia, Greece.

574   500.907   US
ARIZONA-SONORA DESERT MUSEUM. ANNUAL REPORT. 1957. a. free. ‡ Arizona-Sonora Desert Museum, Inc., Rt. 9, Box 900, Tucson, AZ 85704.

700   HU   ISSN 0133-6673
ARS DECORATIVA; annuaire du Musee des Arts Decoratifs et du Musee d'Art d'Extreme Orient Ferenc Hopp. (Text in German, French, English) 1973. a. exchange basis. Iparmuveszeti Muzeum, Ulloi ut 33, 1091 Budapest 9, Hungary. Ed. Imre Jakabffy.
Supersedes: Iparmuveszeti Muzeum. Evkonyv.

708   AT   ISSN 0066-7935
ART BULLETIN OF VICTORIA. (Supersedes its Annual Bulletin, 1959-1966) 1967/68. a. price varies. National Gallery of Victoria, c/o Mr. R.P. Nolan, 180 St. Kilda Rd., Melbourne, Vic. 3004, Australia.

708   CN
ART GALLERY OF HAMILTON. ANNUAL WINTER EXHIBITION. 1948. a. Can.$5. ‡ Art Gallery of Hamilton, 123 King St. W., Hamilton, Ont. L8P 4S8, Canada. Ed. Glen E. Cumming.
Formerly (until 1974): Art Gallery of Hamilton. Annual Exhibition (ISSN 0072-9639)

708   CN   ISSN 0082-5018
ART GALLERY OF ONTARIO. ANNUAL REPORT. 1966-67. a. Art Gallery of Ontario, 317 Dundas St. W., Toronto, Ont. M5T 1G4, Canada. circ. 2,500.

708   AT   ISSN 0066-796X
ART GALLERY OF SOUTH AUSTRALIA. SPECIAL EXHIBITIONS. irreg. ‡ Art Gallery of South Australia, North Terrace, Adelaide, S.A. 5000, Australia.

708   US   ISSN 0069-3235
ART INSTITUTE OF CHICAGO. MUSEUM STUDIES. 1966. irreg., vol. 8, 1976. price varies. ‡ Art Institute of Chicago, Museum Store, Michigan at Adams St., Chicago, IL 60603. (back issues avail.)

ARTISTS IN CANADA. see ART

069.950   KO
ASIAN AND PACIFIC COUNCIL. MUSEUM CONFERENCE. PROCEEDINGS. (Text in English) irreg. Asian and Pacific Council, Cultural and Social Centre, C.P.O. Box 3129, Seoul, S. Korea. illus.

591   594   NZ   ISSN 0067-0456
AUCKLAND INSTITUTE AND MUSEUM. BULLETIN. 1941. irreg.; no. 11, 1977. price varies. Auckland Institute and Museum, Private Bag, Auckland 1, New Zealand. Ed. K. A. J. Wise. (back issues avail.)

069.7   NZ   ISSN 0067-0464
AUCKLAND INSTITUTE AND MUSEUM. RECORDS. 1930. a. NZ.$17. Auckland Institute and Museum, Private Bag, Auckland 1, New Zealand. Ed. K. A. J. Wise. index. circ. 300. (back issues avail.) Indexed: Ind.N.Z.Per.

708   SZ   ISSN 0067-0618
AUS DEM SCHWEIZERISCHEN LANDESMUSEUM. 1953. irreg., no. 41, 1978. price varies. Paul Haupt AG, Falkenplatz 14, CH-3001 Berne, Switzerland.

069   AT   ISSN 0067-1967
AUSTRALIAN MUSEUM, SYDNEY. MEMOIRS. 1851. irreg., 1966, no. 12. price varies. Australian Museum, 6-8 College St., Sydney, N.S.W. 2000, Australia. Ed. F. H. Talbot.

069.7   AT   ISSN 0067-1975
AUSTRALIAN MUSEUM, SYDNEY. RECORDS. 1890. irreg. price varies. Australian Museum, 6-8 College St., Sydney, N.S.W., Australia. Ed. D. J. G. Griffin.

708.1   US   ISSN 0045-3242
B.A.C.A. CALENDAR OF CULTURAL EVENTS. 1971. a. $5. Brooklyn Arts and Cultural Association, Brooklyn Institute of Arts & Sciences, 200 Eastern Parkway, Brooklyn, NY 11238. Ed. Charles Reichenthal.

BILDUNG IM GESCHICHTSMUSEUM. see HISTORY — History Of Europe

069   GE   ISSN 0067-9461
BODENDENKMALPFLEGE IN MECKLENBURG. 1964. a. price varies. (Museum fuer Ur- und Fruehgeschichte, Schwerin) VEB Deutscher Verlag der Wissenschaften, Postfach 1216, 108 Berlin, E. Germany (D.D.R.) Ed. E. Schuldt.

069   US   ISSN 0084-7992
BOWDOIN COLLEGE. MUSEUM OF ART. OCCASIONAL PAPERS. 1972. irreg., no. 2, 1975. price varies. ‡ Bowdoin College, Museum of Art, Brunswick, ME 04011. Ed. R. Peter Mooz.
Formerly: Walker Art Museum. Bulletin.

708   BX   ISSN 0084-8131
BRUNEI MUSEUM. SPECIAL PUBLICATION/ MUZIUM BRUNEI. PENERBITAN KHAS. (Text in English and Malay) 1972. irreg., latest no.10. price varies. Brunei Museum, Kota Batu, Bandar Seri Begawan, Brunei. Ed. P.M. Dato Shariffiddin. circ. 1,000.

708   BX   ISSN 0068-2918
BRUNEI MUSEUM JOURNAL. (Text in English) 1969. a. B.$10. Brunei Museum, Kota Batu, Bandar Seri Begawan, Brunei. Ed. P.M. Dato Shariffiddin. circ. 3,000.

C C I JOURNAL. (Canadian Conservation Institute) see CONSERVATION

063   BE
CAHIERS DE MARIEMONT. 1970. a. 200 Fr. Musee Royal de Mariemont, Service de Documentation, B-6510 Morlanelz-Mariemont, B-6510 Morlanwelz-Mariemont. Ed. Pierre-Jean Foulon. circ. 1,000.

CANADIAN DIRECTORY OF RAILWAY MUSEUMS AND DISPLAYS. see TRANSPORTATION — Railroads

069   UK
CARMARTHEN COUNTY MUSEUM. PUBLICATION. 1975. irreg. £0.50. Carmarthen County Museum, County Hall, Carmarthen, England. Ed. J. H. Little. illus.

708   US   ISSN 0069-4061
CINCINNATI ART MUSEUM. BULLETIN. (Some issues are Annual Reports.) 1930; N.S. 1950. irreg., 1977, vol. 11. $4 per no. Cincinnati Art Museum, Publications Clerk, Eden Park, Cincinnati, OH 45202. Dir. Millard F. Rogers, Jr. circ. 3,000. (also avail. in microform from UMI) Indexed: Art Ind.

708   IT   ISSN 0070-0479
CORPUS VASORUM ANTIQUORUM. ITALIA. 1927. irreg., no. 58, 1980. price varies. Erma di "Bretschneider", Via Cassiodoro 19, 00193 Rome, Italy.

069   SW   ISSN 0070-2528
DAEDALUS. (Text in Swedish; occasional paper in English) 1931. a. Kr.75. Tekniska Museet - National Museum of Science and Technology, S-115 27 Stockholm, Sweden. adv. cum.index. circ. 5,000. Indexed: SSCI.

069   DK
DANSK KULTURHISTORISK MUSEUMSFORENING. MUSEUMSREGISTER. a. Dansk Kulturhistorisk Museumsforening, Postbox 26, DK-4000 Roskilde, Denmark.

708   US   ISSN 0070-3028
DAYTON ART INSTITUTE. ANNUAL REPORT. 1931. a. $2.50. Dayton Art Institute, Box 941, Dayton, OH 45401. circ. 3,000.

069   DK   ISSN 0084-9308
DENMARK. NATIONALMUSEET. ARBEJDSMARKT. 1928. a. Nationalmuseet, Oplysningsafdelingen, Ny Vestergade 10, 1471 Copenhagen K, Denmark.

708.8   DK
DENMARK. NATIONALMUSEET. WORKING PAPERS. irreg. Nationalmuseet, Oplysningsafdelingen, Ny Vestergade 10, 1471 Copenhagen K, Denmark.

069   355   SW
FOERENINGEN ARMEMUSEI VAENNER. MEDDELANDEN: KUNGLIGA ARMEMUSEUM. 1938. a. Kr.45. Foereningen Armemusei Vaenner, Riddargatan 13, Box 14095, 104 41 Stockholm, Sweden (Dist. by Esher Foerlag, Fack, S-162 89 Vaellingby, Sweden) Ed. Bengt M. Holmquist.
Formerly (1938-1977, no. 37): Foereningen Armemusei Vaenner. Meddelanden: Armemuseum.

069   IT   ISSN 0072-0070
GABINETTO DISEGNI E STAMPE DEGLI UFFIZI. CATALOGHI. 1951. irreg., no. 53, 1979. price varies. Casa Editrice Leo S. Olschki, Casella Postale 66, 50100 Florence, Italy. circ. 1,500.

708   GW   ISSN 0072-0089
GALERIE NIERENDORF, BERLIN. KUNSTBLAETTER. 1963. irreg., no. 32, 1974. price varies. ‡ Galerie Nierendorf, Hardenbergstr. 19, 1000 Berlin 12, W. Germany (B.R.D.) Ed. Florian Karsch. circ. 2,000.

708   AU
GALERIE SANCT LUCAS. GEMAELDE ALTER MEISTER. 1959. a. S.50. Galerie Sanct Lucas, Josefsplatz 5, Palais Pallavicini, A-1010 Vienna, Austria. illus.

708.5   IT
GALLERIA DEL CAVALLINO. MOSTRE. 1956. a. $2. Edizioni del Cavallino, San Marco 1725, 30124 Venice, Italy. illus. circ. 1,500.

760   UR   ISSN 0077-1562
GOSUDARSTVENNYI MUZEI IZOBRAZITEL'NYKH ISKUSSTV IM. PUSHKINA. SOOBSHCHENIYA. (Text in Russian; summaries in French) 1960. irreg. Gosudarstvennyi Muzei Izobrazitel'nykh Iskusstv im. Pushkina, Volkhonka 12, 121019 Moscow, U.S.S.R.

708   UK   ISSN 0083-5900
GREAT BRITAIN. VICTORIA AND ALBERT MUSEUM. ILLUSTRATED BOOKLETS. 1951. irreg. price varies. Victoria and Albert Museum, South Kensington, London S.W.7, England (Avail. from H.M.S.O., c/o Liaison Officer, Atlantic House, Holborn Viaduct, London EC1P 1BN, England)

708   UK   ISSN 0083-5919
GREAT BRITAIN. VICTORIA AND ALBERT MUSEUM. MONOGRAPHS. irreg. price varies. Victoria and Albert Museum, South Kensington, London S.W. 7, England (Avail. from H.M.S.O., c/o Liaison Officer, Atlantic House, Holborn Viaduct, London EC1P 1BN, England)

GUIA DE LATINOAMERICA. see EDUCATION — Guides To Schools And Colleges

016.9173   US   ISSN 0093-1047
HARRIS AUCTION GALLERIES. COLLECTORS' AUCTION. 1962. irreg., approx. 8/yr. $14. Harris Auction Galleries, Inc., 873-875 N. Howard St., Baltimore, MD 21201. Eds. Barr Harris, Allen Atwood. circ. 1,000. Key Title: Collectors' Auction (Baltimore)

708.1   US   ISSN 0018-6708
HOUSTON, TEXAS. MUSEUM OF FINE ARTS BULLETIN. 1970-1971. irreg. $0.75 per no. Museum of Fine Arts, Houston, Box 6826, 1001 Bissonnet, Houston, TX 77005. Ed. Anne Feltus. charts. illus. circ. 8,000.

069 979.6 US
IDAHO MUSEUM OF NATURAL HISTORY.
OCCASIONAL PAPERS. 1958. irreg. price varies.
‡ Idaho Museum of Natural History, Idaho State
University, Pocatello, ID 83209. circ. 400. (reprint
service avail. from UMI)
Formerly: Idaho State University Museum.
Occasional Papers (ISSN 0073-4551)

069 708 US ISSN 0073-7038
INDIANA UNIVERSITY ART MUSEUM.
PUBLICATIONS. 1962. irreg., no. 5, 1965. price
varies. Indiana University Art Museum,
Bloomington, IN 47401.

355 UK ISSN 0074-168X
INTERNATIONAL ASSOCIATION OF MUSEUMS
OF ARMS AND MILITARY HISTORY.
CONGRESS REPORTS. 1957. triennial., 1969, 5th,
Rome, Naples, Brescia. membership. International
Association of Museums of Arms and Military
History, c/o William Reid, National Army Museum,
London S.W.3, England. circ. controlled.
1972, 6th, Zurich

INVENTAIRE GENERAL DES MONUMENTS ET
DES RICHESSES ARTISTIQUES DE LA
FRANCE. see ARCHITECTURE

708.1 069.7 US ISSN 0021-356X
J. B. SPEED ART MUSEUM BULLETIN. 1940.
irreg. (2-3/yr.) $4.50. ‡ J. B. Speed Art Museum,
2035 S. Third St., Box 8345, Louisville, KY 40208.
Ed. Addison Page. illus. circ. 2,500.

655.5 GW ISSN 0075-2193
JAHRBUCH DER AUKTIONSPREISE; fuer
Buecher, Handschriften und Autographen. 1950. a.
DM.184. Dr. Ernst Hauswedell and Co. Verlag,
Magdalenenstr. 8, 2000 Hamburg 13, W. Germany
(B.R.D.) Ed. Ernst Hauswedell. adv. circ. 1,300.

069 708 GW ISSN 0075-2207
JAHRBUCH DER BERLINER MUSEEN. 1959. a.
price varies. (Staatliche Museen Preussischer
Kulturbesitz Berlin) Gebr. Mann Verlag, Lindenstr.
76, Postfach 110303, 1000 Berlin 61, W. Germany
(B.R.D.)

708 700 GW ISSN 0075-2274
JAHRBUCH DER HAMBURGER
KUNSTSAMMLUNGEN. 1948. a. DM.48.
(Hamburger Kunsthalle) Dr. Ernst Hauswedell und
Co. Verlag, Magdalenenstr. 8, 2000 Hamburg 13,
W. Germany (B.R.D.) (Co-sponsor: Museum fuer
Kunst und Gewerbe, Hamburg) adv.

069.7 700 GW
JAHRBUCH DER WERBUNG. 1964. a. price varies.
Econ-Verlag GmbH, Grupellostr. 28, Postfach 9229,
4000 Duesseldorf 1, W. Germany (B.R.D.) Ed.
Walter Scheele. adv.
Formerly (until 1975): Werbung in Deutschland
(ISSN 0083-8012)

JOURNAL OF ASIAN ART. see ART

069 II
JOURNAL OF INDIAN MUSEUMS. (Text in
English) a. Museums Association of India, c/o
Crafts Museum, Thapar House, 124 Janpath, New
Delhi 110001, India.

KAERNTNER MUSEUMSSCHRIFTEN. see ART

708 GW ISSN 0075-6326
KLEINE MUSEUMSHEFTE. 1967. irreg. price
varies. Rheinland-Verlag, Kennedy-Ufer 2, 5000
Cologne 21, W. Germany (B.R.D.) (Distr. by:
Rudolf Habelt Verlag, Am Buchenhang 1, 5300
Bonn, W. Germany (B.R.D.))

913 930 069 GW
KOELNER ROEMER-ILLUSTRIERTE. Portion of
title: Roemer-Illustrierte. 1974. irreg. Roemisch-
Germanisches Museum, Columbastr. 5, 5000
Cologne 1, W. Germany (B. R. D.) illus.

708 BE ISSN 0066-4979
KUNSTHISTORISCHE MUSEA, ANTWERP.
SCHONE KUNSTEN.* 1953. a. price varies.
Kunsthistorische Musea, Antwerp, Rubenshuis,
Rubensstraat 9-11, Antwerp 1, Belgium.

069 FR
LABORATOIRE DE RECHERCHE DES MUSEES
DE FRANCE. ANNALES. 1970. a. 50 F.($12.50)
Services Techniques et Commerciaux de la Reunion
des Musees Nationaux, 10, rue de l'Abbaye, Paris
75006, France. Ed. Madeleine Hours.

708 940 GE ISSN 0070-7201
LANDESMUSEUM FUER VORGESCHICHTE,
DRESDEN. VEROEFFENTLICHUNGEN. 1952.
irreg. price varies. VEB Deutscher Verlag der
Wissenschaften, Postfach 1216, 108 Berlin, E.
Germany (D.D.R.)

708 940 GE ISSN 0072-940X
LANDESMUSEUM FUER VORGESCHICHTE,
HALLE. VEROEFFENTLICHUNGEN. 1964.
irreg. price varies. (Landesmuseum fuer
Vorgeschichte, Halle) VEB Deutscher Verlag der
Wissenschaften, Postfach 1216, 108 Berlin, E.
Germany (D.D.R.)

708 069 UK ISSN 0075-899X
LIBRARIES, MUSEUMS AND ART GALLERIES
YEAR BOOK. 1897. irreg. £15($16.50) ‡ James
Clarke & Co. Ltd., 7 All Saints Passage, Cambridge
CB2 3LS, England (Dist. in U.S. and Canada by R.
R. Bowker Co., Box 1807, Ann Arbor, MI 48106)
Eds. Adrian Brink, Derry Watkins. adv. index. circ.
3,500.

LOCUS SELECT. see ART

LOS ANGELES COUNTY MUSEUM OF ART.
BULLETIN. see ART

708.1 US
M F A BULLETIN. 1903. a. $4. Boston Museum of
Fine Arts, Huntington Ave., Boston, MA 02115.
Ed. Margaret Jupe. illus. index. circ.
13,000(approx.) Indexed: Art Ind.
Former titles, until 1978: Boston Museum
Bulletin (ISSN 0006-7997); Museum of Fine Arts.
Bulletin.

069 II
MAHARAJA SAWAI MAN SINGH II MEMORIAL
SERIES. irreg., no. 3, 1978. Rs.40. Maharaja Sawai
Man Singh II Museum, City Palace, Jaipur 302002,
India. Ed. Gopal Narayan Bahura.

069 II
MANIPUR STATE MUSEUM. BULLETIN. (Text in
English) 1972. a. Rs.3. Manipur State Museum,
Publications Sub-Committee, Imphal 759001,
Manipur, India.

069 CN ISSN 0076-3888
MANITOBA MUSEUM OF MAN AND NATURE.
BIENNIAL REPORT. 1966. irreg. Manitoba
Museum of Man and Nature, 190 Rupert Ave.,
Winnipeg, Man. R3B ON2, Canada.
Formerly: Manitoba Museum of Man and
Nature. Annual Report.

708 US ISSN 0077-8958
METROPOLITAN MUSEUM JOURNAL. 1968. a.,
latest vol. 14, 1979. $22.50. Metropolitan Museum
of Art, Fifth Ave. & 82nd St., New York, NY
10028. Ed. M.E.D. Laing. illus. (back issues avail.)

069 977.4 US ISSN 0076-8235
MICHIGAN STATE UNIVERSITY. MUSEUM
PUBLICATIONS. CULTURAL SERIES. 1961.
irreg., 1967, vol. 1, no. 3. price varies. ‡ Michigan
State University, Museum, East Lansing, MI 48824
(And Exchange Dept., MSU Library, East Lansing,
MI 48824) Ed. Rollin H. Baker. index at end of ea.
completed vol. circ. 1,850.

960 FR ISSN 0553-2507
MUSEE DE L'HOMME, PARIS. CATALOGUES.
SERIE B: AFRIQUE BLANCHE ET LEVANT.
(Supplement to: Objets et Mondes) 1965. irreg.
price varies. Museum Nationale d'Histoire
Naturelle, Musee de l'Homme, Palais de Chaillot,
Place du Trocadero, 75116 Paris, France.

960 FR
MUSEE DE L'HOMME, PARIS. CATALOGUES.
SERIE C: AFRIQUE NOIRE. (Supplement to:
Objets et Mondes) 1970. irreg. price varies.
Museum Nationale d'Histoire Naturelle, Musee de
l'Homme, Palais de Chaillot, Place du Trocadero,
75116 Paris, France.

900 FR
MUSEE DE L'HOMME, PARIS. CATALOGUES.
SERIE E: OCEANIE. (Supplement to Objets et
Mondes) 1967. irreg. price varies. Museum
Nationale d'Histoire Naturelle, Musee de l'Homme,
Palais de Chaillot, Place du Trocadero, 75116 Paris,
France.
Formerly: Musee de l'Homme, Paris. Catologues.
Serie E: Polynesie.

950 FR
MUSEE DE L'HOMME, PARIS. CATALOGUES.
SERIE F: MADAGASCAR. (Supplement to: Objets
et Mondes) 1971. irreg. price varies. Museum
Nationale d'Histoire Naturelle, Musee de l'Homme,
Palais de Chaillot, Place du Trocadero, 75116 Paris,
France.

970 FR ISSN 0553-2515
MUSEE DE L'HOMME, PARIS. CATALOGUES.
SERIE G: ARCTIQUES. (Supplement to: Objets et
Mondes) 1963. irreg. price varies. Museum
Nationale d'Histoire Naturelle, Musee de l'Homme,
Palais de Chaillot, Place du Trocadero, 75116 Paris,
France.

900 FR
MUSEE DE L'HOMME, PARIS. CATALOGUES.
SERIE H: AMERIQUE. (Supplement to: Objets et
Mondes) 1963. irreg. price varies. Museum
Nationale d'Histoire Naturelle, Musee de l'Homme,
Palais de Chaillot, Place du Trocadero, 75116 Paris,
France.

950 FR
MUSEE DE L'HOMME, PARIS. CATALOGUES.
SERIE K: ASIE. (Supplement to: Objets et
Mondes) 1969. irreg. price varies. Museum
Nationale d'Histoire Naturelle, Musee de l'Homme,
Palais de Chaillot, Place du Trocadero, 75116 Paris,
France.

708.5 IT
MUSEO BODONIANO. BOLLETINO. 1972. irreg.
Museo Bodoniano, Biblioteca Palatina, Palazzo della
Pilotta, 43100 Parma, Italy. bk. rev. circ. 8,000.
(also avail. in microfilm)

301.2 DR
MUSEO DEL HOMBRE DOMINICANO. SERIE
CATALOGOS Y MEMORIAS. 1976. irreg., no.
11, 1979. Museo del Hombre Dominicano, Calle
Pedro Henriquez Urena, Plaza de la Cultura, Santo
Domingo, Dominican Republica. illus.

301.2 DR
MUSEO DEL HOMBRE DOMINICANO. SERIE
MESAS REDONDAS. 1978. irreg. price varies.
Museo del Hombre Dominicano, Calle Pedro
Henriquez Urena, Plaza de la Cultura, Santo
Domingo, Dominican Republic. illus.

708 IT ISSN 0080-3936
MUSEO DELL'IMPERO ROMANO. STUDI E
MATERIALI. 1938. irreg., no. 10, 1981. price
varies. Erma di "Bretschneider", Via Cassiodoro, 19,
00193 Rome, Italy.

069 CR
MUSEO NACIONAL DE COSTA RICA.
INFORME RENDIDO AL MINSTERIO DE
EDUCACION PUBLICA. 1941. a. free. Museo
Nacional de Costa Rica, P.O. Box 749, San Jose,
Costa Rica. circ. controlled. (tabloid format)

MUSEO NACIONAL DE HISTORIA NATURAL.
ANALES. see SCIENCES: COMPREHENSIVE
WORKS

069 PE
MUSEO NACIONAL DE LA CULTURAL
PERUANA. REVISTA. 1932. a. $20. Museo
Nacional de la Cultura Peruana, Apartado 3048,
Lima 1, Peru. Ed. Rosalia Avalos de Matos. circ.
1,000.

709.5 IT
MUSEO NAZIONALE D'ARTE ORIENTALE.
SCHEDE. no. 6, 1974. irreg. Museo Nazionale
d'Arte Orientale, Via Merulana 248, Rome 00185,
Italy. bibl.

069 IT
MUSEO NAZIONALE DI CASTEL SAN
ANGELO. QUADERNI. 1976. a. (Associazione
Amici di Castel San Angelo) De Luca Editore, Via
S. Anna 11, 00186 Rome, Italy. illus.

MUSEUMS AND ART GALLERIES

069   IT
MUSEOLOGIA. 1972. a. L.15000. Universita Internazionale dell'Arte, Centro di Studi per la Museologia, Via Incontri, 3, 50139 Florence, Italy. (Co-sponsor: Societa di Museologia) Ed. Carlo L. Ragghianti. adv. bk. rev.

MUSEU DO INDIO. DOCUMENTACAO. see HISTORY — History Of North And South America

708   BL   ISSN 0080-3111
MUSEU NACIONAL, RIO DE JANEIRO. ARQUIVOS. (Text in Portuguese; summaries in English) 1876. irreg., latest issue 1975. exchange only. Museu Nacional, Quinta da Boa Vista, 20940 Rio de Janeiro, RJ, Brazil. charts. bibl. illus. Indexed: Biol.Abstr.

708   NE   ISSN 0077-2275
MUSEUM BOYMANS-VAN BEUNINGEN. AGENDA-DIARY. (Text in Dutch and English) 1956. a. Museum Boymans-van Beuningen, Mathenesserlaan 18-20, P.O. Box 2277, Rotterdam, Netherlands.

MUSEUM FUER UR- UND FRUEHGESCHICHTE DES BEZIRKES POTSDAM, FRANKFURT/ODER UND COTTBUS. VEROEFFENTLICHUNGEN. see HISTORY

MUSEUM FUER VOELKERKUNDE IN HAMBURG. MITTEILUNGEN. see FOLKLORE

069   398   GE   ISSN 0075-8663
MUSEUM FUER VOELKERKUNDE, LEIPZIG. JAHRBUCH. irreg., vol. 30, 1975. price varies. Akademie-Verlag, Leipziger Str. 3-4, 108 Berlin, E. Germany (D.D.R.)

708   390   GE   ISSN 0075-8671
MUSEUM FUER VOELKERKUNDE, LEIPZIG. VEROEFFENTLICHUNGEN. irreg., vol. 30, 1976. price varies. Akademie-Verlag, Leipziger Str. 3-4, 108 Berlin, E. Germany (D.D.R.)

708.1   US   ISSN 0027-4097
MUSEUM NOTES. Represents: Rhode Island School of Design. Museum of Art. Bulletin. 1943. a. $5. Rhode Island School of Design, Museum of Art, Providence, RI 02903. Ed. Stephen E. Ostrow. bibl. illus. circ. 3,600. Indexed: Art Ind.

708   SW   ISSN 0081-5691
MUSEUM OF FAR EASTERN ANTIQUITIES. BULLETIN. 1929. a. Kr.100. Oestasiatiska Museet - Museum of Far Eastern Antiquities, Skeppsholmen, Box 16381, 103 27 Stockholm, Sweden. Ed. Bernard Karlgren. circ. 800.

069   US   ISSN 0430-635X
MUSEUM OF NORTHERN ARIZONA CERAMIC SERIES. 1952. irreg. price varies. ‡ Museum of Northern Arizona, Route 4, Box 720, Flagstaff, AZ 86001. Ed. Bd. bibl. charts. illus. circ. controlled.

708   059   UK   ISSN 0141-6723
MUSEUMS AND GALLERIES IN GREAT BRITAIN AND IRELAND. 1955. a. £1.05. A B C Historic Publications, Oldhill, London Rd., Dunstable, Bedfordshire LU6 3EB, England. adv. circ. 20,000.
Formerly: Museums and Galleries (ISSN 0077-2267)

708   UN   ISSN 0077-233X
MUSEUMS AND MONUMENTS SERIES. (English, French and Spanish editions) 1952. irreg.; vol. 15, 1973. price varies. Unesco, 7-9 Place de Fontenoy, 75700 Paris, France (Dist. in U.S. by: Unipub, 345 Park Ave. S., New York, NY 10010)

069   UK   ISSN 0306-5332
MUSEUMS ASSOCIATION INFORMATION SHEETS. 1970. irreg. Museums Association, 34 Bloomsbury Way, London WC1A 2SF, England. Ed. Jane Jenkins.

708   PK   ISSN 0077-2348
MUSEUMS JOURNAL OF PAKISTAN. (Text in English) a. Museums Association of Pakistan, Victoria Memorial Hall, Peshawar, Pakistan.

069   II
MUSEUMS NEWSLETTER. irreg. Museums Association of India, c/o Crafts Museum, Thapar House, 124 Janpath, New Delhi 110001, India.

069   708   GW
MUSEUMS OF THE WORLD/MUSEEN DER WELT. (Text in English) 1973. irreg., 3rd edt., 1981. DM.148. K.G. Saur Verlag KG, Poessenbacherstr. 12 B, Postfach 711009, 8000 Munich 71, W. Germany (B.D.R.) adv.

069   UK   ISSN 0307-7675
MUSEUMS YEARBOOK. (Including a Directory of Museums and Art Galleries of the British Isles) 1956. a. £16 to non-members. Museums Association, 34 Bloomsbury Way, London WC1A 2SF, England. Ed. Jane Jenkins. circ. 1,800.
Formerly: Museums Calendar (ISSN 0580-2652)

708   RM
MUZEUL NATIONAL. (Text in Romanian; summaries in English, French, German, Russian) 1974. a. Muzeul de Istorie al Republicii Socialiste Romania, Calea Victoriei Nr.12, Bucharest, Romania. Ed. Florian Georgescu. illus.

600   069   CS
NARODNI TECHNICKE MUZEUM. CATALOGUES OF COLLECTIONS. irreg. price varies. Narodni Technicke Muzeum, Kostelni 42, 170 78 Prague 7, Czechoslovakia.

069   SA
NATAL MUSEUM. OCCASIONAL PUBLICATONS. irreg., no. 2, 1976. Natal Museum, Loop St., Pietermaritzburg 3201, South Africa.

NATIONAL GALLERY, LONDON. TECHNICAL BULLETIN. see ART

708   069   CN
NATIONAL GALLERY OF CANADA. ANNUAL BULLETIN/GALERIE NATIONALE DU CANADA. BULLETIN ANNUELLE. (Text in English and French) 1979. a. Can.$10. National Gallery of Canada, Ottawa, Ont. K1A 0M8, Canada. Eds. Jean-Rene Ostiguy, Myron Laskin. illus. circ. 5,000.
Formed by the merger of: National Gallery of Canada. Annual Review (ISSN 0078-6977) & National Gallery of Canada. Bulletin (ISSN 0027-9323)

NATIONAL GALLERY OF CANADA. JOURNAL/GALERIE NATIONALE DU CANADA. JOURNAL. see ART

NATIONAL GALLERY OF CANADA. LIBRARY. CANADIANA IN THE LIBRARY OF THE NATIONAL GALLERY OF CANADA: SUPPLEMENT. see ART

354.689   RH
NATIONAL GALLERY OF ZIMBABWE-RHODESIA. ANNUAL REPORT AND BALANCE SHEET AND INCOME AND EXPENDITURE ACCOUNT. 1953. a. free. National Gallery of Zimbabwe-Rhodesia, Box 8155, Causeway, Salisbury, Zimbabwe. illus. circ. 250.
Formerly: National Gallery of Rhodesia. Annual Report and Balance Sheet and Income and Expenditure Account.

069   387   UK   ISSN 0141-1268
NATIONAL MARITIME MUSEUM. OCCASIONAL LECTURE SERIES. 1978. irreg. price varies. National Maritime Museum, Romney Rd., Greenwich SE10 9NF, England. illus.

708   TZ   ISSN 0082-1675
NATIONAL MUSEUM OF TANZANIA. ANNUAL REPORT. 1966. a. 2s. National Museum of Tanzania, P.O. Box 511, Dar es Salaam, Tanzania. circ. 1,100.

708   PH   ISSN 0076-3756
NATIONAL MUSEUM OF THE PHILIPPINES. ANNUAL REPORT. (Text in English) 1966/67. irreg. free. National Museum of the Philippines, Rizal Park, Manila, Philippines. Ed. Rosario B. Tantoco. circ. controlled. (processed)

069   UK
NATIONAL MUSEUM OF WALES. ANNUAL REPORT. (Text in English, Welsh) 1907. a. 25p. plus postage. National Museum of Wales, Cathays Park, Cardiff CF1 3NP, Wales. Ed. Dr. D. A. Bassett. circ. 1,000.

NATURKUNDLICHES MUSEUM "MAURITIANUM" ALTENBURG. ABHANDLUNGEN UND BERICHTE. see SCIENCES: COMPREHENSIVE WORKS

708   US   ISSN 0077-6513
NELSON GALLERY AND ATKINS MUSEUM. BULLETIN. 1956. irreg, 3 issues annually. ‡ Nelson Gallery-Atkins Museum, 4525 Oak St., Kansas City, MO 64111. Ed. Ross E. Taggart. circ. 6,500.

708   US   ISSN 0077-7919
NEVADA. STATE MUSEUM, CARSON CITY. OCCASIONAL PAPERS. 1968. irreg., no. 3, 1978. price varies. Nevada State Museum, Carson City, NV 89701. circ. 1,000.

708   US   ISSN 0077-7927
NEVADA. STATE MUSEUM, CARSON CITY. POPULAR SERIES. 1965. irreg., 1972, no. 4. price varies. Nevada State Museum, Carson City, NV 89701. Ed. Bd. circ. 1,000.

069   CN   ISSN 0703-0606
NEW BRUNSWICK MUSEUM. JOURNAL. 1977. a. free to members. New Brunswick Museum, 277 Douglas Ave., Saint John, N.B. E2K 1E5, Canada.
Supersedes: New Brunswick Museum. Memo (ISSN 0027-4062)

708.1   US   ISSN 0029-2567
NORTH CAROLINA MUSEUM OF ART. BULLETIN. 1957. irreg. $4. North Carolina Museum of Art, Raleigh, NC 27611. Ed.Bd. illus. circ. 4,000.

708   SZ   ISSN 0067-4311
OEFFENTLICHE KUNSTSAMMLUNG. JAHRESBERICHT. 1904. irreg., latest 1977. price varies. ‡ Oeffentliche Kunstsammlung, Kunstmuseum Basel, St. Albangraben 16, CH-4010 Basel, Switzerland. Ed. Paul H. Boerlin.

708.1   AU   ISSN 0029-909X
OESTERREICHISCHE GALERIE. MITTEILUNGEN. 1957. a. S.140. Oesterreichische Galerie, Postfach 12, A-1037 Vienna, Austria. Dir. Dr. Hans Aurenhammer. illus. circ. 700. (tabloid format)

069   US   ISSN 0090-6700
OFFICIAL MUSEUM DIRECTORY. 1961. a. $53.35 to non-members; $48.40 to members. (American Association of Museums) National Register Publishing Co. Inc., 5201 Old Orchard Rd., Skokie, IL 60077. Ed. Bob Weicherding. adv. abstr. circ. 4,000.

069   500   US   ISSN 0079-0354
PEARCE-SELLARDS SERIES. 1963. irreg., no. 32, 1980. price varies. Texas Memorial Museum, University of Texas at Austin, 24 and Trinity, Austin, TX 78705. Ed. Jane C. Sullivan. (reprint service avail. from UMI)

708.1   US   ISSN 0031-7160
PHAROS. 1963. irreg., approx. s-a. membership. Museum of Fine Arts, St. Petersburg, 255 Beach Drive N., St. Petersburg, FL 33701. illus. circ. 2,400.

069.7   AT   ISSN 0079-8835
QUEENSLAND MUSEUM, BRISBANE. MEMOIRS. 1912. a. since 1966. price varies. ‡ Queensland Museum, Gregory Terrace, Fortitude Valley, Brisbane 4006, Australia. Ed. B.M. Campbell. circ. 650. Indexed: Biol.Abstr. Aus.Sci.Ind. Zoo.Rec.

708   CN   ISSN 0035-7154
R. L. C.'S MUSEUM GAZETTE. 1966. irreg. Richard L. Coulton, Ed. & Pub., Bentley, Alberta T0C 0J0, Canada. adv. bk. rev. abstr. charts. tr.lit. cum.index. circ. 400. (processed)

708   CN   ISSN 0082-5115
ROYAL ONTARIO MUSEUM. ANNUAL REPORT. 1949-50. a. free. Royal Ontario Museum, 100 Queen's Park, Toronto M5S 2C6, Ont., Canada. Ed. John Campsie.

069   913   CN   ISSN 0316-1285
ROYAL ONTARIO MUSEUM. ARCHAEOLOGY MONOGRAPHS. 1973. irreg. price varies. Royal Ontario Museum, 100 Queen's Park, Toronto, Ont. M5S 2C6, Canada. Ed. Bd. bibl. illus.

SAALBURG-JAHRBUCH. see *ARCHAEOLOGY*

069   II
SALAR JUNG MUSEUM. ANNUAL REPORT.
(Text in English or Hindi) a. Salar Jung Museum, Hyderabad 500002, Andhra Pradesh, India.

069   AT   ISSN 0076-6240
SCIENCE MUSEUM OF VICTORIA. REPORT OF ACTIVITIES. 1947. a. Science Museum of Victoria, 304-328 Swanston St., Melbourne, Vic. 3000, Australia. Ed. F. J. Kendall. illus.

SEFUNIM. see *ARCHAEOLOGY*

069   BP
SOLOMON ISLANDS MUSEUM ASSOCIATION. JOURNAL. 1975. a. Solomon Islands Museum Association, Box 313, Honiara, British Solomon Islands.

069   US   ISSN 0073-4985
SOUTHERN ILLINOIS UNIVERSITY. UNIVERSITY MUSEUM STUDIES. 1968. irreg., no. 11, 1977. price varies. ‡ Southern Illinois University, Carbondale, University Museum, Carbondale, IL 62901. Ed. B. C. Hedrick.

709   GW   ISSN 0075-5133
STAATLICHE KUNSTHALLE KARLSRUHE. BILDHEFTE. 1958. irreg. price varies. Staatliche Kunsthalle Karlsruhe, Hans-Thoma-Str. 2, 7500 Karlsruhe, W. Germany (B.R.D.)

709   GW   ISSN 0075-5141
STAATLICHE KUNSTHALLE KARLSRUHE. GRAPHIK-SCHRIFTENREIHE. 1933. irreg. price varies. Staatliche Kunsthalle Karlsruhe, Hans Thoma-Str. 2, 7500 Karlsruhe, W. Germany (B.R.D.)

709   GW   ISSN 0067-284X
STAATLICHE KUNSTSAMMLUNGEN IN BADEN-WUERTTEMBERG. JAHRBUCH. 1964. a. DM.45. Deutscher Kunstverlag GmbH, Vohburger Str. 1, 8000 Munich 21, W. Germany (B.R.D.) circ. 600.

STAATLICHE MUSEEN ZU BERLIN. JAHRBUCH. FORSCHUNGEN UND BERICHTE. see *ART*

708   301.2   GE   ISSN 0070-7295
STAATLICHES MUSEUM FUER VOELKERKUNDE DRESDEN. ABHANDLUNGEN UND BERICHTE. 1881. irreg., vol. 37, 1975. price varies. Akademie-Verlag, Leipzger Str. 3-4, 108 Berlin, E. Germany (D.D.R.) bk. rev. circ. 1,250.
     Supersedes (from vol. 21, 1962): Staatliches Museum fuer Voelkerkunde und Tierkunde. Abhandlungen und Berichte.

069   GW   ISSN 0078-2777
STADTBIBLIOTHEK NUERNBERG. AUSSTELLUNGSKATALOG. 1955. irreg., vol. 87, 1976. Stadtbibliothek, Egidienplatz 23, 8500 Nuernberg 2, W. Germany (B.R.D.)

708   US   ISSN 0085-6665
STANFORD MUSEUM. 1971. biennial. $3. Stanford University, Stanford Museum, Stanford, CA 94305. Eds. Betsy G. Fryberger, Carol M. Osborne. circ. 2,500.

069   NO   ISSN 0333-0656
STAVANGER MUSEUM. AARBOK. (Summaries in English) 1890. a. Kr.50. Stavanger Museum, 4000 Stavanger, Norway.

069   NO   ISSN 0333-0664
STAVANGER MUSEUM. SKRIFTER. (Text in Norwegian; summaries in English) 1920. irreg., vol. 10, 1981. Stavanger Museum, 4000 Stavanger, Norway. illus.

069   HU   ISSN 0133-3046
STUDIA COMITATENSIA. (Text in Hungarian; summaries in English, French, German, Russian) 1972. a. exchange basis. Pest Megyei Muzeumok Igazgatosaga, Marx ter 6, 2001 Szentendre, Hungary. Ed. Nandor Ikvai. illus.

069   II   ISSN 0081-8259
STUDIES IN MUSEOLOGY. (Text in English) 1965. a. Rs.10($2.) Maharaja Sayajirao University of Baroda, Department of Museology, Sayaji Park, Baroda 390002, Gujarat, India. Ed. V. H. Bedekar. bk. rev. circ. 400.

708   069   SW   ISSN 0081-5683
SWEDEN. NATIONALMUSEUM. SKRIFTSERIE. 1954. irreg., no. 18, 1979. price varies. Nationalmuseum, Box 16176, 103 24 Stockholm, Sweden.

708.9   MG
TALOHA. (Text in French and Malagasy) 1965. irreg., latest no. 7, 1976. FMG.1200. Universite de Madagascar, Musee d'Art et d'Archeologie, B.P. 564 Isoraka, Antananarivo, Malagasy Republic.

060   US   ISSN 0082-3074
TEXAS MEMORIAL MUSEUM. BULLETIN. 1960. irreg., no. 30, 1978. price varies. Texas Memorial Museum, University of Texas at Austin, 24 and Trinity Sts., Austin, TX 78705. Ed. Jane C. Sullivan. (reprint service avail. from UMI)

069   500   US   ISSN 0082-3082
TEXAS MEMORIAL MUSEUM. MISCELLANEOUS PAPERS. 1968. irreg., no. 7, 1980. price varies. Texas Memorial Museum, University of Texas at Austin, 24 and Trinity, Austin, TX 78705. Ed. Jane C. Sullivan. (reprint service avail. from UMI)
     Reprint series

060   US
TEXAS MEMORIAL MUSEUM. MUSEUM NOTES. 1938. irreg., no. 13, 1980. price varies. Texas Memorial Museum, University of Texas at Austin, 24th and Trinity, Austin, TX 78705. Ed. Jane C. Sullivan. (reprint service avail. from UMI)

709   DK   ISSN 0085-7262
THORVALDSEN MUSEUM. MEDDELELSER. (Text in Danish; summaries in English, French, German) 1917. irreg., latest 1978. price varies. Thorvaldsen Museum, Porthusgade 2, 1213 Copenhagen K, Denmark. illus. index. circ. 1,200.

069   SZ
THURGAUISCHE MUSEUM. MITTEILUNGEN. 1946. irreg., latest 1974. 3 Fr. Thurgauische Museumsgesellschaft, CH-8500 Frauenfeld, Switzerland. Ed. Albert Schoop.

069   AU
TIROLER LANDESMUSEUM FERDINANDEUM, INNSBRUCK. VEROEFFENTLICHUNGEN. 1825. a. S.250. Tiroler Landesmuseum Ferdinandeum, Innsbruck, Museumstr. 15, A-6010 Innsbruck, Austria. Ed. Dr. Josef Ladurner. circ. 280.

069   SA   ISSN 0496-1102
TRANSVAAL MUSEUM. BULLETIN. 1955. irreg., vol. 31, 1978. price varies. Transvaal Museum, Box 413, Pretoria, Transvaal, South Africa.

069   SA
TRANSVAAL MUSEUM. MEMOIRS. 1951. irreg., no. 20, 1975. Transvaal Museum, Box 413, Pretoria, South Africa.

069   NO   ISSN 0085-7394
TROMSOE MUSEUM. SKRIFTER. (Text in English & Norwegian) 1925. irreg., 1968, vol. 13. price varies. Universitetsforlaget, Kolstadtg. 1, Box 2959-Toeyen, Oslo 6, Norway (U.S. address: Box 258, Irvington-on-Hudson, NY 10533)

069.9   BL
UNIVERSIDADE DE SAO PAULO. MUSEU PAULISTA. COLECAO. SERIE DE MOBILIARIO. irreg. Universidade de Sao Paulo, Museu Paulista, Caixa Posta 42503, Parque da Independencia, 04263 Sao Paulo, Brazil. Ed Setembrino Petri.
     Supersedes in part (since 1975): Museu Paulista. Colecao (ISSN 0080-6382)

069   US   ISSN 0093-7436
UNIVERSITY OF ALASKA MUSEUM. ANNUAL REPORT. a. University of Alaska Museum, Fairbanks, AK 99701. circ. controlled.

708   700   US
UNIVERSITY OF KANSAS. SPENCER MUSEUM OF ART. MISCELLANEOUS PUBLICATIONS. 1952. irreg., no. 98, 1975. price varies. University of Kansas, Spenser Museum of Art, Lawrence, KS 66045. Ed. Ruth Lawner. circ. 1,200-2,500.
     Formerly: University of Kansas. Museum of Art. Miscellaneous Publications (ISSN 0075-501X)

709   US
UNIVERSITY OF MASSACHUSETTS. ART ACQUISITIONS. 1963. irreg. free. University of Massachusetts, Fine Arts Council, 125 Herter Hall, Amherst, MA 01002. illus. circ. 350 (controlled)

708   US   ISSN 0270-1642
UNIVERSITY OF MICHIGAN. MUSEUMS OF ART AND ARCHAEOLOGY. BULLETIN. 1978. a. $5. University of Michigan Museum of Art, Alumni Memorial Hall, Ann Arbor, MI 48109. (Co-sponsors: Kelsey Museum of Archaeology, Department of the History of Art) Eds. Marvin Eisenberg, Jacquelynn Baas Slee. circ. 500.
     Supersedes (N.S. 1965-1977): University of Michigan. Museum of Art. Bulletin (ISSN 0076-8391)

708   US   ISSN 0077-8583
UNIVERSITY OF NEW MEXICO ART MUSEUM. BULLETIN. 1965-66. a. $3. University of New Mexico, Art Museum, Albuquerque, NM 87131. Dir. Van Deren Coke. circ. 1,000.

090   CS
USTREDNA SPRAVA MUZEI A GALERII. VYROCNE SPRAVY O CINNOSTI SLOVENSKYCH MUZEI. 1966. a. free. Ustredna Sprava Muzei a Galerii, Lodna 2, 891 29 Bratislava, Czechoslovakia. Ed. Milan Rybecky. stat.
     Formerly: Slovenske Narodne Muzeum. Muzeologicky Kabinet. Vyrocne Spravy o Cinnosti Slovenskych Muzei.

708   CN   ISSN 0083-5161
VANCOUVER ART GALLERY. ANNUAL REPORT. 1932. a. free. Vancouver Art Gallery, 1145 Georgia St., Vancouver, B. C. V6E 3H2, Canada. circ. 3,500.

069   SW   ISSN 0083-5536
VARBERGS MUSEUM. AARSBOK. 1950. a. Kr.25. Varbergs Museum, 432 00 Varberg, Sweden. Ed. Bengt-Arne Person. adv. bk. rev.

954.9   069   BG
VARENDRA RESEARCH MUSEUM. JOURNAL. (Text in English) 1972. a. Tk.15($3) Varendra Research Museum, University of Rajshahi, Rajshahi, Bangladesh.

069   AT   ISSN 0083-5986
VICTORIA, AUSTRALIA. NATIONAL MUSEUM OF VICTORIA. MEMOIRS. 1906. a. plus special issues. Aus.$5. National Museum of Victoria Council, 285-321 Russell St., Melbourne 3000, Victoria, Australia. Eds. D. Stone, T.A. Darragh. circ. 1,500. Indexed: Bull.Signal. Zoo.Rec.

600   NO   ISSN 0048-2277
VOLUND. Represents: Norsk Teknisk Museum. Yearbook. (Text in Norwegian; summaries in English) 1953. a. Kr.25. ‡ Norsk Teknisk Museum - Norwegian Museum of Science and Technology, Fyrstikkalleen 1, Oslo 6, Norway. Ed. Torleif Lindtveit. adv. illus. circ. 2,000.

069   708   AT
WESTERN AUSTRALIA. PUBLIC LIBRARY, MUSEUM AND ART GALLERY. RECORD. 1974. irreg. Public Library, Museum and Art Gallery, Perth, W. A., Australia.

069   AT
WESTERN AUSTRALIAN MUSEUM, PERTH. ANNUAL REPORT. a. Western Australian Museum, Perth, W.A., Australia.
     Formerly: Western Australia Museum, Perth. Report of the Museum Board (ISSN 0083-8721)

069   AT   ISSN 0312-3162
WESTERN AUSTRALIAN MUSEUM, PERTH. RECORDS. 1910. irreg. Aus.$2.50. Western Australian Museum, Francis St., Perth, W. A. 6000, Australia. Indexed: Aus.Sci.Ind.

069   AT   ISSN 0313-122X
WESTERN AUSTRALIAN MUSEUM, PERTH. RECORDS. SUPPLEMENT. 1975. irreg. Aus.$2.50. Western Australian Museum, Francis St., Perth, W.A. 6000, Australia. Indexed: Aus.Sci.Ind.

069.7   AT   ISSN 0083-873X
WESTERN AUSTRALIAN MUSEUM, PERTH. SPECIAL PUBLICATION. 1948. irreg. price varies. Western Australian Museum, Francis St., Perth, W.A. 6000, Australia.

708　　　　US　ISSN 0511-8824
WHITNEY REVIEW. 1960/61. a. $2. Whitney Museum of American Art, 945 Madison Ave. at 75 St., New York, NY 10021.

WHO'S WHO IN AMERICAN ART. see *BIOGRAPHY*

708.1　　　　US
WORCESTER ART MUSEUM. JOURNAL. 1979. a. $3. Worcester Art Museum, 55 Salisbury St., Worcester, MA 01608. Ed. Gaye L. Brown. illus. circ. 5,000.
  Supersedes (1935-1979): Worcester Art Museum Bulletin; Which was formerly titled: Worcester Art Museum. News Bulletin and Calendar (ISSN 0043-7891)

900　700　　　　UN
WORLD CULTURAL HERITAGE. (Editions in English, French and Spanish) 1973. irreg.; latest issue, 1974. free on request. Unesco, Department for Cultural Heritage, 7-9 Place de Fontenoy, 75700 Paris, France. Ed. N. Chauveau.

708　　　　US　ISSN 0084-3539
YALE UNIVERSITY ART GALLERY. BULLETIN. 1926. irreg., 2-3/yr. $2 per no. Yale University Art Gallery, 2006 Yale Sta., New Haven, CT 06520. Ed. Caroline Rollins. circ. 2,100. (also avail. in microform from UMI) Key Title: Bulletin - Yale University Art Gallery.

708　　　　ZA　ISSN 0084-4977
ZAMBIA NATIONAL MUSEUMS BOARD. REPORT. a. 20 n. National Museums Board, Livingstone Museum, Box 498, Livingstone, Zambia.

069　　　　ZA
ZAMBIA MUSEUMS JOURNAL. 1970. a. K.5. National Museums Board, Livingstone Museum, Box 498, Livingstone, Zambia. Eds. N.M. Katanekwa, P.M. Simbotwe. circ. 1,500.

MUSEUMS AND ART GALLERIES — Abstracting, Bibliographies, Statistics

060　　　　US
CATALOG OF MUSEUM PUBLICATIONS AND MEDIA; a directory and index of publications and audiovisuals available from U.S. and Canadian institutions. 1972. irreg., latest edt. 1980. $92. Gale Research Company, Book Tower, Detroit, MI 48226. Eds. Paul Wasserman, Esther Herman. index.
  Former titles: Museum Catalog of Publications and Media; Museum Media.

069.5　011　　　　II
CATALOGUE OF ARABIC MANUSCRIPTS IN SALAR JUNG MUSEUM. (Text in English) 1957. irreg., vol. 2, 1962. Rs.3($1.50) Salar Jung Museum, Hyderabad 500002, Andhra Pradesh, India.

069.5　011　　　　II
CATALOGUE OF PERSIAN MANUSCRIPTS IN SALAR JUNG MUSEUM. (Text in English) 1965. irreg.; vol. 6, 1975. Rs.4($1.50) Salar Jung Museum, Hyderabad 500002, Andhra Pradesh, India. illus.

069.5　011　　　　II
CATALOGUE OF URDU MANUSCRIPTS IN SALAR JUNG MUSEUM. (Text in Urdu) 1957. irreg. Rs.3($1.50) Salar Jung Museum, Hyderabad 500002, Andhra Pradesh, India. illus.

708　010　　　　AU
OESTERREICHISCHES MUSEUM FUER VOLKSKUNDE. KATALOGE. 1946. irreg. price varies. Verlag Ferdinand Berger und Soehne OHG, Wiener Str. 21-23, A-3580 Horn, Austria.

069　016　　　　CS
SELECTED BIBLIOGRAPHY OF MUSEOLOGICAL LITERATURE. (Text in English) 1970. a. exchange basis. Ustredna Sprava Muzei a Galerii, Lodna 2, 891 29 Bratislava, Czechoslovakia. Eds. Milan Rybecky, Viera Schnappova. index.
  Formerly: Bibliographical Selection of Museological Literature (ISSN 0067-6861)

016　　　　CS
VYBEROVA BIBLIOGRAFIA MUZEOLOGICKEJ LITERATURY. 1962. a. exchange basis. Ustredna Sprava Muzei a Galerii, Lodna 2, 891 29 Bratislava, Czechoslovakia. Eds. Milan Rybecky, Viera Schnappova.

MUSIC

see also Dance; Sound Recording and Reproduction

780.42　　　　CN　ISSN 0704-6138
A C M E NEWSLETTER. 1976. irreg. free. Academy of Country Music Entertainment, 9312 150 Ave., Edmonton, Alta. T5E 2N8, Canada. illus.

789.91　　　　US　ISSN 0587-1956
A R S C BULLETIN. 1968. a. Association for Recorded Sound Collections, c/o Les Waffen, Exec. Sec., Box 1643, Manassas, VA 22110.

780　800　070.5　920　US
A S C A P BIOGRAPHICAL DICTIONARY. irreg. $5.25. American Society of Composers, Authors and Publishers, 1 Lincoln Plaza, New York, NY 10023.

ABHANDLUNGEN ZUR KUNST-, MUSIK- UND LITERATURWISSENSCHAFT. see *ART*

780　　　　IT
ACCADEMIA DEI CONCORDI ROVIGO. COLLANA DI MUSICHE. no. 12, 1977. irreg. price varies. Giardini Editori e Stampatori, Via Santa Bibbiana 28, 56100 Pisa, Italy.

786.5　　　　GW　ISSN 0567-7874
ACTA ORGANOLOGICA. 1967. a. (Gesellschaft der Orgelfreunde e.V.) Verlag Merseburger Berlin GmbH, Motz Str. 13, 3500 Kassel, W. Germany (B.R.D.) illus.

780　　　　GW　ISSN 0001-6942
ACTA SAGITTARIANA. (Text in English, French and German) 1963. a. membership. Internationale Heinrich Schuetz-Gesellschaft e.V., Heinrich-Schuetz-Allee 35, 3500 Kassel-Wilhelmshoehe, W. Germany (B.R.D.) Ed. Sieglinde Froehlich-Spillner. adv. bk. rev. illus. circ. 2,000.

780　　　　SA　ISSN 0065-4019
AFRICAN MUSIC. (Text in English and French) 1954. irreg. (approx. a.) R.10($15) International Library of African Music, Rhodes University, Institute of Social and Economic Research, Grahamstown 6140, South Africa. Ed. Andrew Tracey. bk. rev. cum. index with each vol. (covers 4 nos.) (back issues avail.) Indexed: RILM.
  Supersedes (1948-1953): African Music Society. Newsletter.

780　　　　US
AFRO-AMERICAN MUSIC OPPORTUNITIES ASSOCIATION. RESOURCE PAPERS. irreg. price varies. Afro-American Music Opportunities Association, 2909 Wayzata Blvd., Minneapolis, MN 55440.

780　　　　UR
AKADEMIYA NAUK AZERBAIDZHANSKOI S.S.R. MUZEI ISTORII. TRUDY. (Text in Azerbaijani and Russian) vol. 9, 1973. irreg. 1.50 Rub. per no. Izdatel'stvo Elm, Ul. Narimanova, 31, Baku 370073, U.S.S.R. Ed. P. Azizbekova. illus. circ. 500.

783　282　　　　GW
ALLGEMEINER CAECILIEN-VERBAND. SCHRIFTENREIHE. irreg., latest no. 13. price varies. Allgemeiner Caecilien-Verband, Koelnstr. 415, 5300 Bonn, W. Germany (B.R.D.)

780　　　　US　ISSN 0065-6704
AMATEUR CHAMBER MUSIC PLAYERS. DIRECTORY. (Overseas Directory or North American Directory published in alternate years) 1948. a. free. Amateur Chamber Music Players, Inc., Box 547, Vienna, VA 22180 (Orders to: Helen Rice, Sec., 15 W. 67th St., New York, NY 10023) circ. 6,200.

AMERICAN ARTS PAMPHLET SERIES. see *LITERATURE*

789.5　　　　US　ISSN 0093-1330
AMERICAN BELL ASSOCIATION. DIRECTORY. a. (some vols. accompanied by supplemental directory) $7 to members. American Bell Association, Route 1, Box 286, Natrona Heights, PA 15065. Key Title: Directory - American Bell Association.

780　　　　US　ISSN 0065-8316
AMERICAN FOLK MUSIC OCCASIONAL. 1970. irreg. $2.95. Oak Publications, 33 W. 60 St., New York, NY 10023. Eds. Chris Strachwitz, Pete Welding.

780　　　　GW　ISSN 0065-8855
AMERICAN INSTITUTE OF MUSICOLOGY. MISCELLANEA. 1951. irreg. (American Institute of Musicology, US) Haenssler-Verlag, Postfach 1220, Bismarckstrasse 4, 7303 Neuhausen-Stuttgart, W. Germany (B.R.D.) Ed. Armen Carapetyan.

781.9　　　　US
AMERICAN MUSICAL INSTRUMENT SOCIETY. JOURNAL. 1975. a. membership. American Musical Instrument Society, U S D Box 194, Vermillion, SD 57069. Ed. William Hettrick. adv. bk. rev. bibl. charts. illus.

780　　　　US　ISSN 0569-6666
AMERICAN MUSICOLOGICAL SOCIETY. GREATER NEW YORK CHAPTER. PUBLICATIONS. 1965. irreg. price varies. American Musicological Society, Greater New York Chapter, City University of New York Graduate Center, 535 E. 80 St., New York, NY 10021.

780　　　　US
AMERICAN MUSICOLOGICAL SOCIETY. STUDIES AND DOCUMENTS. irreg., no. 6, 1972. price varies. Galaxy Music Corp, 2121 Broadway, New York, NY 10023.

780　　　　US　ISSN 0066-0701
AMERICAN SOCIETY OF UNIVERSITY COMPOSERS. PROCEEDINGS. 1966. biennial. $8. American Society of University Composers, 250 W. 57 St., Rm. 626-7, New York, NY 10019. Ed. Warner Hutchison. circ. 1,000. (also avail. in microform from UMI) Indexed: Music Ind.

780　　　　IS　ISSN 0066-1260
AMLI STUDIES IN MUSIC BIBLIOGRAPHY. (Text in English and other languages) 1970. irreg. $5 per no. Haifa Music Museum and Amli Library, P.O. Box 5111, Haifa, Israel. Ed. Moshe Gorali. circ. 750. Indexed: RILM.

780　　　　GW　ISSN 0569-9827
ANALECTA MUSICOLOGIA. (Vol. 1-11 Published by Boehlau-Verlag) 1963. irreg., vol. 18, 1978. price varies. (Deutsches Historisches Institut in Rom, Musikgeschichtliche Abteilung, IT) Arno Volk Verlag Hans Gerig KG, Drususgasse 7-11, 5000 Cologne 1, W. Germany (B.R.D.) illus.

780　　　　SZ
ANNALES PADEREWSKI. 1979. irreg., at least 1/yr. Societe Paderewski a Morges, c/o Hugues Faesi, Chemin de Lallex, 1603 Grandvaux, Switzerland.

782.1　792.8　　　　FR
ANNEE DE L'OPERA ET DE LA DANSE. a. Editions Calmann-Levy, 3 rue Auber, 75009 Paris, France. Eds. Sylvie de Nussac, Sergio Segalini & Simone Dupuis.

780　　　　US
ANNOTATED REFERENCE TOOLS IN MUSIC SERIES. (Text in English, French and German) 1978. irreg., vol. 2, 1979. Pendragon Press, 162 W. 13th St., New York, NY 10011. (back issues avail.)

780.904　　　　IT
ANNUARIO MUSICALE. 1976. a. L.3900($7) Gruppo Editoriale Suono, Via del Casaletto 380, 00151 Rome, Italy. adv. illus. circ. 80,000.

786　　　　GW
ARCHIV FUER MUSIKORGANOLOGIE. vol. 2, 1977. irreg. (1-2/yr) DM.25 per no. Institut fuer Musikorganologie, D-8911 Unterdiessen, Angerweg 6, Munich, W. Germany (B.R.D.) Ed. Leopold Vorreiter.

780 GW ISSN 0570-6769
ARCHIV FUER MUSIKWISSENSCHAFT.
BEIHEFTE. (Text in English and German) irreg.,
vol. 18, 1978. price varies. Franz Steiner Verlag
GmbH, Friedrichstr. 24, Postfach 5529, 6200
Wiesbaden, W. Germany (B.R.D.)

780.903 IT
ARCHIVUM MUSICUM; collana di testi rari. 1978.
irreg. price varies. Studio per Edizioni Scelte,
Lungarno Guicciardini 9, 50125 Florence, Italy.
Ed.Bd.

780 SA ISSN 0379-6485
ARS NOVA. 1969. a. R.2.10. University of South
Africa, Department of Musicology, Box 392,
Pretoria, South Africa. adv. bk. rev. circ. 450.

780 YU ISSN 0587-5455
ARTI MUSICES/MUSICOLOGICAL YEARBOOK.
(Text in Croatian; summaries in English) 1969. a.
50 din.($4.50) ‡ Muzicka Akademija u Zagrebu,
Muzikoloski Zavod - Zagreb Academy of Music,
Gunduliceva 6, 41001 Zagreb, Yugoslavia. Ed. Bd.
adv. bibl. illus.

780 US ISSN 0081-1319
ASIAN MUSIC PUBLICATIONS. SERIES A:
BIBLIOGRAPHIC AND RESEARCH AIDS.
1970. irreg.; latest issue, 1974. (Society for Asian
Music) Asian Music Publications, c/o School of
Music, University of Washington, Seattle, WA
98195. Ed. Fredric Lieberman. circ. 400. (back
issues avail.) Indexed: RILM.
Formerly: Society for Asian Music. Publication
Series. Series A: Bibliographic and Research Aids.

780 US ISSN 0081-1327
ASIAN MUSIC PUBLICATIONS. SERIES B.
TRANSLATIONS. irreg. (Society for Asian Music)
Asian Music Publications, c/o School of Music,
University of Washington, Seattle, WA 98195. Ed.
Fredric Lieberman. Indexed: RILM.
Formerly: Society for Asian Music. Publication
Series. Series B: Translations.

780 US ISSN 0081-1335
ASIAN MUSIC PUBLICATIONS. SERIES C:
REPRINTS. irreg. (Society for Asian Music) Asian
Music Publications, c/o School of Music, University
of Washington, Seattle, WA 98195. Ed. Fredric
Lieberman. Indexed: RILM.
Formerly: Society for Asian Music. Publication
Series. Series C: Reprints.

780 US ISSN 0081-1343
ASIAN MUSIC PUBLICATIONS. SERIES D:
MONOGRAPHS. 1969. irreg.,latest issue 1977.
(Society for Asian Music) Asian Music Publications,
c/o School of Music, University of Washington,
Seattle, WA 98195. Ed. Fredric Lieberman. circ.
400(approx.) Indexed: RILM.
Formerly: Society for Asian Music. Publications
Series. Series D: Monographs.

780 AT ISSN 0311-2764
AUSTRALIAN COMPOSER. 1972. irreg. free to
members. Fellowship of Australian Composers, P.O.
Box 522, Strathfield, NSW 2135, Australia.
Formerly: Fellowship of Australian Composers.
Newsletter.

781.7 AT
AUSTRALIAN COUNTRY MUSIC ANNUAL.
1973. a. 2. Country Music Australia, Box 497,
Tamworth, N.S.W. 2340, Australia. Ed. Max Ellis.
adv. bk. rev. circ. 5,000.
Country

780.7 AT
AUSTRALIAN SOCIETY FOR MUSIC
EDUCATION. REPORT OF PROCEEDINGS OF
THE NATIONAL CONFERENCE. 3rd, 1977. a.
Australian Society for Music Education, School of
Music, Canberra, A.C.T., Australia.

780 US
B A MAGAZINE. vol. 6, 1977. irreg. Brooklyn
Academy of Music, 30 Lafayette Ave., Brooklyn,
NY 11217. illus.

780 US ISSN 0084-8018
B B C MUSIC GUIDES. 1969. irreg., no. 39, 1978.
price varies. University of Washington Press,
Seattle, WA 98105. Ed. Gerald Abraham.

780 GE ISSN 0084-7682
BACH-JAHRBUCH. 1904. a. price varies.
(International Union of the New Bach Society)
Evangelische Verlagsanstalt GmbH, Krautstr. 52,
1017 Berlin, E. Germany (D.D.R.) Eds. H.-J.
Schulze, C. Wolff. bibl. charts. illus.

785 US ISSN 0084-7704
BAND MUSIC GUIDE. 1959. irreg. $14.50.
Instrumentalist Co., 1418 Lake Street, Evanston, IL
60204.

782.1 US
BAROQUE OPERATIC ARIAS. irreg., book 2, 1973.
price varies. Oxford University Press, 200 Madison
Ave., New York, NY 10016 (And Ely House, 37
Dover St., London W1X 4AH, England) Ed. Denis
Arnold.

787 US
BASS WORLD. 1972. a. membership. International
Society of Bassists, University of Cincinnati,
College-Conservatory of Music, Cincinnati, OH
45221. Ed. Lucas Drew. adv. bk. rev. circ. 1,000.
Formerly: Probas.

780.42 UK
BAY CITY ROLLERS ANNUAL. 1978. a. £1.30.
Stafford Pemberton Publishing Co. Ltd., Ruskin
Chambers, Drury Lane, Knutsford, Cheshire WA16
6HA, England.

780 US ISSN 0084-7763
BEECHAM SOCIETY BULLETIN. 1972. irreg. $6
includes subscription to Le Grand Baton. ‡ Sir
Thomas Beecham Society (Redondo Beach), 664
South Irena Ave., Redondo Beach, CA 93401. Ed.
Stanley H. Mayes.
Formerly: Beecham Society Newsletter.

780 GW ISSN 0522-5949
BEETHOVEN-JAHRBUCH. 1954. biennial. price
varies. Verein Beethoven-Haus Bonn, Postfach 73,
5300 Bonn 1, W. Germany (B.R.D.) Eds. Paul
Mies, Joseph Schmidt-Goerg. bibl.

780 AU ISSN 0067-5067
BEITRAEGE ZUR HARMONIKALEN
GRUNDLAGENFORSCHUNG. 1968. irreg., no.
11, 1980. price varies. Musikverlag Elisabeth Lafite,
Hegelgasse 13/22, A-1010 Vienna, Austria.

780 AU
BEITRAEGE ZUR JAZZFORSCHUNG/STUDIES
IN JAZZ RESEARCH. (Text in German) 1969.
irreg., vol. 5, 1975. S.350 to non-members.
(International Society for Jazz Research)
Akademische Druck- und Verlagsanstalt,
Auersperggasse 12, 8010 Graz, Austria (Subscr. to:
Leonhardstr. 15, 8010 Graz, Austria) Eds. Alfons
M. Dauer, Franz Kerschbaumer. (back issues avail.)
Indexed: RILM.

789 US ISSN 0092-8666
BELL TOWER. 9/yr. $7 membership. American Bell
Association, Box 286, RD 1, Natrona Heights, PA
15065. illus. circ. 2,600.

780 PL ISSN 0067-7779
BIBLIOTEKA SLUCHACZA KONCERTOWEGO.
SERIA WPROWADZAJACA. 1956. irreg. price
varies. Polskie Wydawnictwo Muzyczne, Al.
Krasinskiego 11, Krakow, Poland (Dist. by Ars
Polona-Ruch, Krakowskie Przedmiescie 7, Warsaw,
Poland)

781.57 GW
BIELEFELDER KATALOG - JAZZ. a. DM.10.80.
Bielefelder Verlagsanstalt KG, Niederwall 53,
Postfach 1140, 4800 Bielefeld, W. Germany
(B.R.D.)

780 US ISSN 0067-8600
BILLBOARD'S INTERNATIONAL BUYER'S
GUIDE OF THE MUSIC-RECORD-TAPE
INDUSTRY. 1958. a. $35. Billboard Directories,
2160 Patterson St., Cincinnati, OH 45214 (And
9000 Sunset Blvd., Los Angeles, CA 90069) circ.
45,000. (also avail. in microfilm from KTO)
Formerly (until 1960): Billboard. International
Buyer's Guide of the Music-Record Industry.

780.42 US
BILLBOARD'S INTERNATIONAL CLUB AND
DISCO EQUIPMENT SOURCEBOOK. Variant
title: International Disco Sourcebook. 1976. a. $10.
Billboard Directories, 2160 Patterson St., Cincinnati,
OH 45214 (And 9000 Sunset Blvd., Los Angeles,
CA 90069) circ. 45,000.
Formerly: Billboard's International Disco
Sourcebook (ISSN 0147-5533)

792 US
BILLBOARD'S TALENT IN ACTION. 1970. a. $5.
Billboard Directories, 2160 Patterson St., Cincinnati,
OH 45214 (And 9000 Sunset Blvd., Los Angeles,
CA 90069) circ. 45,000. (also avail. in microfilm
from KTO)

781.57 US
BIXIANA. no.12, 1976. irreg. Bix Beiderbecke
Memorial Society, 2225 West 17th St., Davenport,
IA 52804. (processed)

784 BE
BLUES.* (Text in French) 1970. irreg. $3. 39 rue
Chanbery, 1040 Brussels, Belgium. illus.

781.57 US
BLUES RESEARCH. 1959. irreg., no. 17, 1975. $0.50
per no. Record Research, 65 Grand Ave., Brooklyn,
NY 11205. Eds. Anthony Rotante & Paul Sheatsley.
charts. illus.

780 920 GW
BRAHMS-GESELLSCHAFT HAMBURG.
JAHRESGABE. a. membership. Brahms-
Gesellschaft Hamburg, Hamburg, W. Germany
(B.R.D.) illus.

780 US
BRASS PLAYERS' GUIDE. a. $1. Robert King Music
Co., 112A Main St., North Easton, MA 02356. Ed.

780 US ISSN 0363-454X
BRASS RESEARCH SERIES. irreg. Brass Press, 136
Eighth Ave., Nashville, TN 37203. Ed. Stephen L.
Glover.

781.7 UK
BRISTOL FOLK NEWS. Cover title: Folk News.
1970. irreg. 15p. English Folk Dance and Song
Society, Bristol District, c/o John Maher, Shanboe,
Claremont Ave., Bishopston, 7, Bristol, England.
Ed. John Maher. bk. rev. illus. circ. 600-800.

781.97 016 UK ISSN 0068-1407
BRITISH CATALOGUE OF MUSIC. 1957. a, with 2
interim issues. £24. British Library, Bibliographic
Services Division, 2 Sheraton St., London W1V
4BH, England. Ed. Patrick Mills. bibl. index.
circ. 1,000.

780.7 CN ISSN 0007-0564
BRITISH COLUMBIA MUSIC EDUCATOR.
vol.13,1970. irreg. membership. ‡ (B.C. Music
Educators' Association) B.C. Teachers'
Federation, 105-2235 Burrard St., Vancouver, B.C. V6J 3H9,
Canada. adv. bk. rev. illus. stat. circ. 700.
(processed) Indexed: Can.Educ.Ind.
Study and teaching

784 UK ISSN 0308-4698
BRITISH COUNTRY MUSIC ASSOCIATION.
YEARBOOK. a. membership. British Country
Music Association, P.O. Box 2, Newton Abbot
TQ12 4HT, England. illus.

780 UK ISSN 0306-5928
BRITISH MUSIC YEARBOOK. 1972. a. £7.50. A. &
C. Black (Publishers) Ltd., 35 Bedford Row,
London WC1R 4JH, England. Ed. Arthur Jacobs.
adv. stat. index. circ. 5,000.
Formerly: Music Yearbook.

780 BU ISSN 0068-3965
BULGARSKA AKADEMIIA NA NAUKITE.
INSTITUT ZA MUZIKOZNANIE. IZVESTIIA.
(Summaries in various languages) 1952. 3.51 lv. per
issue. Publishing House of the Bulgarian Academy
of Sciences, Ul. Akad. G. Bonchev, 1113 Sofia,
Bulgaria (Dist. by: Hemus, 6, Rouski Blvd., 1000
Sofia, Bulgaria) Ed. Petko Stainov. circ. 500.

780　　　　　　　　　　US
BULLETIN OF RESEARCH IN MUSIC
  EDUCATION. Cover title, fall 1970- : P M E A.
  1969. a. free to qualified personnel. Pennsylvania
  Music Educators Association, Inc., Swope Hall,
  West Chester State College, West Chester, PA
  19380. Ed. Ira Singleton. circ. 4,000. Indexed:
  Music Artic.Guide.

780 026　　　　　CN　　ISSN 0383-1299
C A M L NEWSLETTER/A C B M NOUVELLES.
  (Text in English and French) 1972. q. Can.$20 to
  individuals; Can. $35 to institutions. Canadian
  Association of Music Libraries, c/o National
  Library of Canada, 395 Wellington St., Ottawa, Ont.
  K1A 0N4, Canada. Ed. Mervin Lewis. adv. bk. rev.
  circ. 150.
    Supersedes: Canadian Music Library Association.
  Newsletter (ISSN 0383-1280)

780　　　　　　UK　　ISSN 0574-9468
C.I.A. REVUE.* 1953. irreg. Confederation
  Internationale des Accordeonistes, c/o J. J. Black,
  Secretary, Somerset House, Cranleigh, Surrey,
  England.

780.92　　　　　FR
CAHIERS DEBUSSY. 1974. irreg. Centre de
  Documentation Claude Debussy, 11 rue d'Alsace,
  Saint Germain-en-Laye, France. illus.

780　　　　　　　CN
CANADIAN COMPOSERS SERIES. 1975. irreg.
  price varies. University of Toronto Press, Front
  Campus, Toronto, Ont. M5S 1A6, Canada.

780　　　　　CN　　ISSN 0068-8746
CANADIAN FOLK MUSIC JOURNAL. (Text in
  English and French) 1973. a. Can.$5 individuals;
  $10 institutions (subscribers receive both Journal
  and Newsletter) Canadian Folk Music Society, 134
  Shelborne St. S.W., Calgary, Alta. T3C 2K8,
  Canada. Ed. Edith Fowke. bk. rev. circ. 400.

780　　　　　CN　　ISSN 0381-5730
CANADIAN MUSIC DIRECTORY. 1926. a.
  Can.$14($25) Lloyd Publications of Canada, Box
  262, West Hill, Ont. M1E 4R5, Canada. Ed. J.
  Lloyd. adv. index. circ. 5,300.

780　　　　　CN　　ISSN 0068-9335
CANADIAN MUSIC INDUSTRY DIRECTORY.
  1965. a. Can.$10. R P M Music Publications Ltd., 6
  Brentcliffe Road, Toronto, M4G 3Y2, Ont., Canada.

CANTO LIBRE; a bilingual trimester of Latin
  American people's art. see ETHNIC INTERESTS

781.7 398　　　　UK
CANU GWERIN/FOLK SONG. 1909. a.
  membership. Welsh Folk-Song Society, c/o Mrs. B.
  L. Roberts, Hafan, Cricieth, Gwynedd, Wales. circ.
  250. (back issues avail.)
    Formerly(until 1978): Welsh Folk-Song Society.
  Journal.
  Folk

780　　　　　GW　　ISSN 0069-116X
CATALOGUS MUSICUS. 1963. irreg., no. 7, 1975.
  price varies. (International Association of Music
  Libraries) Baerenreiter Verlag, Heinrich-Schuetz-
  Allee 31-37, 3500 Kassel-Wilhelmshoehe, W.
  Germany (B.R.D.) (Co-sponsor: International
  Musicological Society) Bd. Bd.

781.7　　　　　IE　　ISSN 0009-0174
CEOL; a journal of Irish music. (Text in English and
  Irish) 1963. irreg. $3. Breandan Breathnach, Ed. &
  Pub., 47 Frascati Park, Blackrock, Dublin, Ireland.
  adv. bk. rev. record rev. illus. cum.index. circ.
  1,000. (also avail. in microfilm) Indexed: RILM.
  Folk music

780　　　　　　　　RM
CERCETARI DE MUZICOLOGIE. 1967. irreg.
  Conservatorul "Ciprian Porumbescu", Str. Stirbei
  Voda Nr. 33, Bucharest, Romania.

780　　　　　　　　UK
CHELYS; journal of the Viola da Gamba Society.
  1969. a. £2.10. Viola da Gamba Society, c/o G. D.
  Davidson, 2 Northfield, Braughing, Ware,
  Hertfordshire, England. Ed. M.J. Hobbs. bk. rev.
  illus. circ. 250. Indexed: RILM.

380.1　　　　　　　IT
CHI E DOV E. (Special issue of Musica e Dischi)
  1971. a. L.4000. Musica e Dischi, Via Giannone 2,
  20149 Milan, Italy. Ed. Mario de Luigi Jr.

780　　　　　　IT　　ISSN 0069-3391
CHIGIANA. 1964. a. price varies. (Accademia
  Musicale Chigiana, Siena) Casa Editrice Leo S.
  Olschki, Casella Postale 66, 50100 Florence, Italy.
  Ed. Luciano Alberti. bk. rev. circ. 1,000.

780.01　　　　　　　HK
CHINESE UNIVERSITY OF HONG KONG.
  CHUNG CHI COLLEGE. MUSIC
  DEPARTMENT. HOLDINGS OF THE CHINESE
  MUSIC ARCHIVES. (Text in English and Chinese)
  1974. a. Chinese University of Hong Kong, Chung
  Chi College, Music Department, Shatin N.T., Hong
  Kong, Hong Kong. illus.

780　　　　　　US　　ISSN 0069-3758
CHORD AND DISCORD. 1933. irreg. (every 3-4
  years) free. Bruckner Society of America Inc., Box
  2570, Iowa City, IA 52244. Ed. Jack Diether. circ.
  750.

784　　　　　　GW　　ISSN 0009-5036
DER CHORDIRIGENT; Nachrichtenblatt fuer
  Chorleiter. 1951. a. free. B. Schott's Soehne,
  Weihergarten 5, Postfach 3640, 6500 Mainz 1, W
  Germany (B.R.D.) Ed. Hilger Schallehn. circ.
  20,000.

780　　　　　　　　UK
CITY OF BIRMINGHAM SYMPHONY
  ORCHESTRA. ANNUAL PROSPECTUS. a. 40p.
  plus postage. City of Birmingham Symphony
  Orchestra, 9 Margaret St., Birmingham B3 3RP,
  England. circ. 10,000. (tabloid format)

780　　　　　　　　UK
CITY OF BIRMINGHAM SYMPHONY
  ORCHESTRA. PROM PROSPECTUS. a. 20p. plus
  postage. City of Birmingham Symphony Orchestra,
  9 Margaret St., Birmingham B3 3RP, England. circ.
  8,000. (tabloid format)

789.91　　　　　　　US
CLASSICAL RECORD REFERENCE BOOK. 1970.
  a. Andre Perrault Classical Record Mail Order
  Center, The Old Stone House, Winooski, VT 05404.
  Ed. Jacques J. Gosselin.

780.9　　　　　　IT　　ISSN 0069-5270
COLLECTANEA HISTORIAE MUSICAE. 1953.
  irreg., 1966, vol. 4. price varies. Casa Editrice Leo
  S. Olschki, Casella Postale 66, 50100 Florence,
  Italy. circ. 500.

781.7　　　　　　　　UK
COMPLETE CATALOGUE OF CONTEMPORARY
  WELSH MUSIC. irreg; latest no.6. 60p. per no.
  Guild for the Promotion of Welsh Music, 94 Walter
  Rd., Swansea SA1 5QA, Wales. Ed. Robert Smith.

780 927　　　　US　　ISSN 0069-8016
COMPOSERS OF THE AMERICAS/
  COMPOSITORES DE AMERICA. 1955. a. $7.
  Organization of American States, Department of
  Publications, Washington, DC 20006. circ. 2,000.

780　　　　　　　　UK
COMPOSERS OF WALES SERIES. 1978. irreg.
  price varies. (Welsh Arts Council) University of
  Wales Press, 6 Gwennyth St., Cathays, Cardiff CF2
  4YD, Wales. Ed. Roy Bohana. (reprint service avail.
  from UMI)

789.91　　　　　　　NE
COMPOSERS' VOICE; Dutch contemporary music
  on records. a. Donemus Foundation, Paulus
  Potterstraat 14, 1071 CZ Amsterdam, Netherlands
  (Dist. in the U.S. and Canada by: C.F. Peters Corp.,
  373 Park Ave. South, New York, NY 10016)

780.904　　　　　　　US
COMPOSIUM DIRECTORY OF NEW MUSIC.
  1970. a. $8.95. Crystal Record Co., 2235 Willida
  Lane, Sedro Woolley, WA 98284. Ed. Carol
  Cunning. circ. 2,000. (back issues avail.)

780.01　　　　　US　　ISSN 0093-0253
COMPUTATIONAL MUSICOLOGY
  NEWSLETTER. 1973. irreg. free. c/o J. Wenker,
  1998 Pacific Ave. Unit 105, San Francisco, CA
  94109. circ. 500.

780　　　　　　　　GW
CONCENTUS MUSICUS. 1973. irreg., vol. 4, 1978.
  price varies. (Deutsches Historisches Institut in
  Rom, Musikgeschichtliche Abteilung, IT) Arno
  Volk Verlag Hans Gerig KG, Drususgasse 7-11,
  5000 Cologne 1, W. Germany (B.R.D.). illus.

780　　　　　　　　UK
CONSORT; journal of the Dolmetsch foundation.
  1929. a. £6. Dolmetsch Foundation, 14 Chestnut
  Way, Godalming, Surrey GU7 1TS, England. Ed.
  Mrs. Shelagh M. Godwin. adv. bk. rev. charts. illus.
  cum.index: 1929-1972. circ. 900. (also avail. in
  microfilm) Indexed: RILM.

CONTACTS & FACILITIES; in the entertainment
  industry. see THEATER

780　　　　　　US　　ISSN 0162-0088
CONTRIBUTIONS TO MUSIC EDUCATION. 1972.
  a. free. Ohio Music Education Association, c/o
  Peter R. Webster, Ed., Department of Music, Case
  Western Reserve University, Cleveland, OH 44106.
  circ. 1,100. (back issues avail.) Indexed: Music Ind.

786　　　　　　　　SA
CONTRIBUTIONS TO THE DEVELOPMENT OF
  THE PIANO SONATA. 1967. irreg., latest no. 2,
  1970. price varies. A. A. Balkema Ltd., P.O. Box
  3117, Cape Town 8000, South Africa (And Box
  1675, Rotterdam, Netherlands; in the U.S. and
  Canada, 99 Main St., Salem, NH 03079)

780　　　　　　US　　ISSN 0193-6891
CONTRIBUTIONS TO THE STUDY OF MUSIC
  AND DANCE. irreg. price varies. Greenwood
  Press, 8 Post Rd. W., Westport, CT 06881.

780　　　　　　GW　　ISSN 0070-0363
CORPUS MENSURABILIS MUSICAE. irreg.
  (American Institute of Musicology, US) Haenssler-
  Verlag, Postfach 1220, Bismarckstrasse 4, 7303
  Neuhausen-Stuttgart, W. Germany (B.R.D.)
  Medieval and Renaissance

780　　　　　　GW　　ISSN 0070-0460
CORPUS SCRIPTORUM DE MUSICA. (Text mainly
  in Latin) 1950. irreg. (American Institute of
  Musicology, US) Haenssler-Verlag, Postfach 1220,
  Bismarckstrasse 4, 7303 Neuhausen-Stuttgart, W.
  Germany (B.R.D.)

780　　　　　　US　　ISSN 0070-1262
COUNTRY DANCE AND SONG. 1968. a. $6 to
  institutions. Country Dance and Song Society of
  America, 55 Christopher St., New York, NY 10014.
  Ed. Anthony Barrand. bk. rev. circ. 800. (also avail.
  in microfilm from UMI)

780　　　　　　　　US
COUNTRY MUSIC SOURCEBOOK. a. $10.
  Billboard Publications, Inc., 9000 Sunset Blvd., Los
  Angeles, CA 90069. adv. circ. 47,000. (also avail. in
  microfilm from KTO)

784　　　　　　US　　ISSN 0092-5454
COUNTRYWIDE ANNUAL YEAR BOOK.* 1973/
  74. a. $2. Country Publishing Co., Box 186, Fairfax,
  VA 22030. illus.

CURRENT ISSUES IN MUSIC EDUCATION. see
  EDUCATION — Teaching Methods And
  Curriculum

780　　　　　　　　US
DETROIT MONOGRAPHS IN MUSICOLOGY.
  1971. irreg. price varies. Information Coordinators,
  Inc., 1435-37 Randolph St., Detroit, MI 48226. Ed.
  Bruno Nettl.

780　　　　　　GW　　ISSN 0417-2051
DEUTSCHE GESELLSCHAFT FUER MUSIK DES
  ORIENTS. MITTEILUNGEN. (Text in English
  and German) 1962. irreg. DM.28. (Deutsche
  Gesellschaft fuer Musik des Orients) Verlag der
  Musikalienhandlung Karl Dieter Wagner,
  Rothenbaumchaussee 1, 2000 Hamburg 13, W.
  Germany (B.R.D.) illus. (back issues avail.)

785　　　　　　　　UK
DIRECTORY OF BRITISH BRASS BANDS. irreg.
  £1. British Federation of Brass Bands, 28 Marigold
  St., Rochdale, Lancs., England.

785 CN ISSN 0705-6249
DIRECTORY OF CANADIAN ORCHESTRAS
AND YOUTH ORCHESTRAS/ANNUAIRE DES
ORCHESTRES ET ORCHESTRES DES JEUNES
CANADIENS. (Text in English and French) 1976.
a. Can.$3.50. Association of Canadian Orchestras,
56 The Esplanade, Suite 311, Toronto, Ont. M5E
1A7, Canada. (Co-sponsor: Ontario Federation of
Symphony Orchestras)

780 US
DIRECTORY OF MUSIC FACULTIES IN
COLLEGES & UNIVERSITIES U.S. AND
CANADA. 1967. biennial. $15. ‡ College Music
Society, Regent Box 44, University of Colorado,
Boulder, CO 80309. Ed. Craig Short. circ. 3,000.
Indexed: Music Ind. RILM.
 Continues: Directory of Music Faculties in
American Colleges and Universities (ISSN 0419-
3040)

780 US ISSN 0360-8700
DISC COLLECTOR NEWSLETTER. 1950. irreg. $3
for 10 issues. Disc Collector Publications, Box 169,
Cheswold, DE 19936. cum.index: in preparation.
circ. 1,200.
 Formerly: Disc Collector (ISSN 0070-6655)

780.1 US ISSN 0095-8115
DISCOGRAPHY SERIES. 1969. irreg. 1978. nos. 18-
19. $2 price varies. J. F. Weber, Ed. & Pub., 310
Genesee St., Utica, NY 13502. bibl. circ. 300.
(processed)

780 BE
DOCUMENTA MUSICAE NOVAE; critical edition
of contemporary music sources. (Text in Dutch,
English and French) 1968. irreg. $12.
Rijksuniversiteit te Gent, Seminarie voor
Musicologie, Muinkkaai, 45, B-9000 Ghent,
Belgium. Ed. Herman Sabbe. circ. 200. Indexed:
RILM.

782.1 UK ISSN 0307-1448
DONIZETTI SOCIETY. JOURNAL. 1974. a. $15.
Donizetti Society, 56 Harbut Rd., London SW11
2RB, England. illus.

DRAGON. see LITERATURE

785.0671 CS
DYCHOVA HUDBA. irreg, vol. 17, 1976. 8 Kcs. per
no. Opus, Bratislava, Czechoslovakia.

780 US
E A M ACCENTS. 1977. irreg. European American
Music Distributors Corporation, 195 Allwood Rd.,
Clifton, NJ 07012. illus. circ. 8,000.

780 US
EARLY MUSIC LABORATORY. BULLETINS
AND TAPES. 1967. a. $15. Early Music
Laboratory, Box 2552, Hollywood, CA 90028. Ed.
Sol Babitz. (back issues avail)

780 US ISSN 0363-4558
EDWARD H. TARR SERIES. irreg. Brass Press, 136
Eighth Ave., Nashville, TN 37203.

ENJOYING THE ARTS. see DANCE

780 US ISSN 0071-1195
ERNEST BLOCH SOCIETY. BULLETIN. 1967. a.
membership. Ernest Bloch Society, 171 Marguerite
Ave., Mill Valley, CA 94941 (Or Star Route 2,
Gualala, CA 95445) Eds. Lucienne B. Dimitroff,
Suzanne Bloch, Ivan Bloch. circ. 3,000.

ESSAYS ON ASIAN THEATER, MUSIC AND
DANCE. see THEATER

780 US ISSN 0364-9210
ETHNODISC JOURNAL OF RECORDED SOUND.
1972. irreg. $50 for 5 vols., cassette ed.; $140 for 5
vols., open reel ed. Pachart Publishing House, 1130
San Lucas Cir., Tucson, AZ 85733 (Subscr. to: Box
35549, Tucson, AZ 85740) Ed. Dr. Joseph M.
Pacholczyk. charts. illus. (magazine plus cassettes
or open reel tape)
 Formerly: Ethnodisc Recordings.

783 FR ISSN 0071-2086
ETUDES GREGORIENNES. (Text in English,
French and Italian) 1954. irreg. price varies. ‡
Editions Abbaye Saint-Pierre de Solesmes, F-72300
Sable sur Sarthe, France. Dir. D. Jean Claire. bk.
rev. circ. 500. Indexed: RILM.

780 GE ISSN 0073-0025
EUROPAEISCHE VOLKSMUSIKINSTRUMENTE.
HANDBUCH. 1967. irreg. price varies. VEB
Deutscher Verlag fuer Musik, Karlstr. 10, 701
Leipzig, E. Germany (D.D.R.) Eds. Ernst
Emsheimer, Erich Stockmann.

780.1 US
FESTSCHRIFT SERIES. 1977. irreg., vol. 2, 1978.
Pendragon Press, 162 W. 13th St., New York, NY
10011. (back issues avail.) Indexed: RILM.

FILM MUSIC BUYER'S GUIDE. see MOTION
PICTURES

FLORIDA FESTIVAL ARTS DIRECTORY. see
ART

781.7 793.31 UK ISSN 0531-9684
FOLK MUSIC JOURNAL. 1965. a. included with
subscr. to English Dance and Song. English Folk
Dance and Song Society, Cecil Sharp House, 2
Regents Park Rd., London NW1 7AY England. Ed.
Mike Yates. adv. bk. rev. cum.index. circ. 11,000.
(also avail. in microform from UMI)

780.01 AU
FORSCHUNGEN ZUR AELTEREN
MUSIKGESCHICHTE. 1976. irreg. (Universitaet
Wien, Musikwissenschaftliches Institut) Verband der
Wissenschaftlichen Gesellschaften Oesterreichs,
Lindengasse 37, A-1070 Vienna, Austria. Eds. Franz
Foedermayr, Othmar Wessely.

780.01 UK ISSN 0072-0127
GALPIN SOCIETY JOURNAL; for the Study of
Musical Instruments. 1948. a. £5 to non-members.
Galpin Society, c/o Mrs. M. Cranmer, 116 Tenison
Rd., Cambridge, CB1 2DW, England. Ed. Anthony
Baines. adv. bk. rev. index. circ. 1,600. (also avail.
in microfilm from UMI)

782.1 UK ISSN 0434-1066
GLYNDEBOURNE FESTIVAL PROGRAMME
BOOK. 1952. a. £2. ‡ (Glyndebourne Festival
Opera) Glyndebourne Productions Ltd.,
Glyndebourne, Lewes, Sussex BN8 5UU, England.
Ed. Moran Caplat. adv. circ. 26,000.

783.7 US
GOSPEL MUSIC ASSOCIATION. ANNUAL
DIRECTORY. a. $5. Gospel Music Association,
Box 1201, Nashville, TN 37202. adv. illus. circ.
15,000.
 Former titles: Gospel Music Association. Annual
Directory and Yearbook (ISSN 0362-7330); Gospel
Music Directory and Yearbook.

784 US ISSN 0092-0592
GRAPEVINE (SARATOGA)* 1972. irreg. $3.20 for 5
issues. c/o L. Ransil, 19801 Braemar Dr., Saratoga,
CA 95070. illus.

780.6 UK
HALLE PROSPECTUS. 1858. a. 75p. Halle Concerts
Society, 30 Cross St., Manchester M2 7BA,
England. Ed. Clive F. Smart. adv. circ. 13,000.

780 GW
HAMBURGER JAHRBUCH FUER
MUSIKWISSENSCHAFT. 1974. a. DM.82. Verlag
der Musikalienhandlung Karl Dieter Wagner,
Rothenbaumchaussee 1, 2000 Hamburg 13, W.
Germany (B.R.D.)

780 US ISSN 0073-0629
HARVARD PUBLICATIONS IN MUSIC. 1967.
irreg., no. 7, 1975. price varies. Harvard University
Press, 79 Garden St., Cambridge, MA 02138.

780 920 GW ISSN 0440-5323
HAYDN-STUDIEN. (Text in German and English)
1965. irreg., 1-2/yr. price varies. (Joseph-Haydn-
Institut e.V.) G. Henle Verlag, Forstenrieder Allee
122, Postfach 710466, 8000 Munich 71, W.
Germany (B.R.D.) Ed. Georg Feder. adv. illus.
index. circ. 750. Indexed: RILM.

780 US ISSN 0073-1390
HAYDN YEARBOOK. HAYDN JAHRBUCH. (Text
and summaries in English and German) 1962. irreg.,
vol. 10, 1978. price varies. (Verein Internationale
Joseph Haydn Institut, Eisenstadt, AU) Universal
Edition Sales, Inc., 195 Allwood Rd., Clifton, NJ
07012 (In Association with Universal Edition,
Vienna, London, Zurich, Mainz, Milan) Ed.Bd. bk.
rev.

780 DK ISSN 0441-5833
HI FI AARBOGEN. 1973. a. Kr.67.50. Forlaget
Audio A-S, St. Kongensgade 72, DK-1264
Copenhagen K, Denmark. Ed. Bd. adv. illus. tr.lit.
circ. 16,000. (back issues avail.)

HI FI NEWS & RECORD REVIEW ANNUAL. see
SOUND RECORDING AND REPRODUCTION

HI-FI REPORT; Text-Handbuch der Zeitschrift
Fonoforum. see SOUND RECORDING AND
REPRODUCTION

HIGH FIDELITY'S BUYING GUIDE TO TAPE
SYSTEMS. see SOUND RECORDING AND
REPRODUCTION

780.904 GW
HINDEMITH-JAHRBUCH/ANNALES
HINDEMITH. 1971. a. DM.18 (single copy, DM,
24) (Paul-Hindemith-Institut) B. Schott's Soehne,
Weihergarten 5, Postfach 3640, 6500 Mainz 1, W.
Germany (B.R.D.) Ed. Dieter Rexroth. bk. rev. circ.
1,200.

780 IT ISSN 0073-2516
HISTORIAE MUSICAE CULTORES BIBLIOTECA.
1952. irreg., vol. 31, 1978. price varies. Casa
Editrice Leo S. Olschki, Casella Postale 66, 50100
Florence, Italy. circ. 1,000.

HONKY TONKIN': A TRAVEL GUIDE TO
AMERICAN MUSIC. see TRAVEL AND
TOURISM

780 CS
HUDOBNY ARCHIV. (Text in Slovak; summaries
also in German and Russian) 1974. irreg. price
varies. Matica Slovenska, Mudronova 35, 036 52
Martin, Czechoslovakia.

780 HU ISSN 0441-4446
HUNGARIAN MUSICAL GUIDE. (Editions in
English, French, German) 1966. 2/yr. free.
Nemzetkozi Zenei Versenyek es Fesztivalok Irodaja,
Vorosmarty ter 1, P.O.B. 80, 1366 Budapest 5,
Hungary. Ed. Edith Galambos. circ. 10,000.

781.7 US ISSN 0091-9764
HUNTSVILLE ASSOCIATION OF FOLK
MUSICIANS. NEWSLETTER. 1968. irreg. $2.
Huntsville Association of Folk Musicians, P.O. Box
1444, Huntsville, AL 35807. Ed. T. W. Burcham.
bk. rev. illus. circ. 250. Key Title: Newsletter -
Huntsville Association of Folk Musicians.

780 US ISSN 0097-6539
HYPE. 1970. irreg. $2.75 for 4 issues. Box 14001,
Washington, DC 20044. Ed. Mark Jenkins. adv. bk.
rev.
 Rock music

780 GW
I S M E YEARBOOK. (Text in English) 1973. a.
DM.20. (International Society for Music Education)
B. Schott's Soehne, Weihergarten 5, Postfach 3640,
6500 Mainz 1, W. Germany (B.R.D.) Ed. Egon
Kraus. bk. rev.

780 UK
INCORPORATED SOCIETY OF MUSICIANS
HANDBOOK & REGISTER OF MEMBERS.
1882. a. Incorporated Society of Musicians, 10
Stratford Place, London W1N 9AE, England. adv.
circ. 8,000(controlled)

INDIAN RECORDS. see SOUND RECORDING
AND REPRODUCTION

780 US
INDIANA DIRECTORY OF MUSIC TEACHERS.
1941. a. $7. ‡ Indiana University, School of Music,
Music Education Department, Bloomington, IN
47401. Ed. Miriam Gelvin. index. circ. 220.

780 AU
INNSBRUCKER BEITRAEGE ZUR
MUSIKWISSENSCHAFT. 1977. irreg. price varies.
Musikverlag Helbling, Hunoldstr. 14, 6021
Innsbruck, Austria. Ed. Walter Salmen. charts. illus.
index.

MUSIC

780   IT   ISSN 0073-8611
INSTITUTA ET MONUMENTA. SERIES I: MONUMENTA. 1954. irreg. price varies. (Universita degli Studi di Pavia, Scuola di Paleografia e Filologia Musicale) Fondazione "Claudio Monteverdi", Corso Garibaldi 178, 26100 Cremona, Italy.

780   IT
INSTITUTA ET MONUMENTA. SERIES II. INSTITUTA. 1969. irreg. price varies. (Universita degli Studi di Pavia, Scuola di Paleografia e Filologia Musicale) Fondazione "Claudio Monteverdi", Corso Garibaldi 178, 26100 Cremona, Italy. circ. controlled.

781.5   US
INSTITUTE FOR STUDIES IN AMERICAN MUSIC. MONOGRAPHS. 1973. irreg., no. 15, 1981. Institute for Studies in American Music, City University of New York, Brooklyn College, Department of Music, Brooklyn, NY 11210.

780   US   ISSN 0538-4257
INTERNATIONAL ALBAN BERG SOCIETY. NEWSLETTER.* 1968. irreg. University of New Hampshire, Department of Music, Durham, NH 03824. Ed. Mark Devoto.

780   IT
INTERNATIONAL CONGRESS OF VERDI STUDIES. PROCEEDINGS. (Text in Italian, English, German, French and Spanish) irreg. L.10600. Istituto di Studi Verdiani, Strada della Repubblica 57, 43100 Parma, Italy.

780   CN   ISSN 0074-6096
INTERNATIONAL FOLK MUSIC COUNCIL. YEARBOOK. 1969. a. membership. International Folk Music Council, Department of Music, Queen's University, Kingston, Ont. K7L 3N6, Canada. bk. rev. circ. 1,200.
    Formerly: International Folk Music Council Journal.

780   UK
INTERNATIONAL MUSIC GUIDE. a. $8.95. Tantivy Press, 136-148 Tooley St., London SE1 2TT, England (Dist. in U.S. by A.S. Barnes & Co., 11175 Flintkote Ave., San Diego, CA 92121) (reprint service avail. from UMI)

016 780   US   ISSN 0085-218X
INTERNATIONAL PERCUSSION REFERENCE LIBRARY. CATALOG. 1962. biennial, no. 7, 1979. $3.50. Arizona State University, Department of Music, Tempe, AZ 85281. Ed. Mervin W. Britton. circ. 400.

780   US
INTERNATIONAL TALENT AND TOURING DIRECTORY. 1978. a. $25. Billboard Directories, 2160 Patterson St., Cincinnati, OH 45214 (And 9000 Sunset Blvd., Los Angeles, CA 90069) circ. 45,000. (also avail. in microfilm from KTO)
    Formerly: International Talent Directory; Incorporating: Billboard's on Tour (ISSN 0361-5383) & Campus Attractions (ISSN 0067-8597); Which was formerly (1964-1968): Billboard. Music on Campus.

780   US   ISSN 0363-5708
INTERNATIONAL TROMBONE ASSOCIATION SERIES. irreg. Brass Press, 136 Eighth Ave., Nashville, TN 37203. Ed. Stephen L. Glover.

780   US   ISSN 0363-2849
INTERNATIONAL TRUMPET GUILD. JOURNAL. Cover title: I T G Journal. 1976. a. $15. International Trumpet Guild, Box 50183, Columbia, SC 29250 (Orders to: Gordon Mathie, Crane School of Music, SUC, Potsdam, NY 13676) Ed. Linda Anne Farr.

780   UK   ISSN 0307-2894
INTERNATIONAL WHO'S WHO IN MUSIC AND MUSICIANS' DIRECTORY. 1935. triennial. price varies. Melrose Press Ltd., 17-21 Churchgate St., Soham, Ely, Cambridgeshire CB7 5DS, England (Dist. in U.S. by: Gale Research Co., Detroit, MI 48226)
    Formerly: Who's Who in Music and Musicians' International Directory (ISSN 0083-9647)

780   IE
IRISH FOLK MUSIC STUDIES. 1972. a. £1. Folk Music Society of Ireland, c/o Hugh Shields, Ed., 3 Syderham Road, Dundrum, Dublin 14, Ireland. adv. bk. rev. bibl.

781.7   IS
ISRAEL STUDIES IN MUSICOLOGY. 1978. a. price varies. Israel Musicological Society, Box 503, Jerusalem, Israel. Ed. Eliyahu Schleifer.

780   IT   ISSN 0075-1596
ISTITUZIONI E MONUMENTI DELL' ARTE MUSICALE ITALIANA NUOVA SERIE. 1957. irreg., 1964, no. 3. Casa Editrice Leo S. Olschki, Casella Postale 66, 50100 Florence, Italy. circ. 500.

JAHRBUCH FUER LITURGIK UND HYMNOLOGIE. see *RELIGIONS AND THEOLOGY*

780   398   GW   ISSN 0075-2703
JAHRBUCH FUER MUSIKALISCHE VOLKS- UND VOELKERKUNDE. 1968. a. price varies. Staatliches Institut fuer Musikforschung, 14 Stauffenbergstr., 1000 Berlin 30, W. Germany (B.R.D.)

784.4   398   GW   ISSN 0075-2789
JAHRBUCH FUER VOLKSLIEDFORSCHUNG. 1928. a. price varies. (Deutsches Volksliederarchiv) Erich Schmidt Verlag (Bielefeld), Viktoriastr. 44A, Postfach 7330, 4800 Bielefeld 1, W. Germany (B.R.D.) Ed. Rolf Wilhelm Brednich. adv. bk. rev. index.

780   GW
JAHRBUCH PETERS. 1980. a. Verlag C. F. Peters, Kennedyallee 101, Postfach 700906, 6000 Frankfurt 70, W. Germany (B. R. D.) (Dist. by: C. F. Peters Corp., 373 Park Ave. S., New York, NY 10016) Ed. Rudolf Eller.
    Supersedes (1973-1977): Deutsches Jahrbuch der Musikwissenschaft (ISSN 0070-4504)

780   JA   ISSN 0075-3459
JAPANESE PHONOGRAPH RECORDS OF FOLK SONGS, CLASSICAL AND POPULAR MUSIC. (Text in Japanese) a. Japan Phonograph Record Association, 8-9 Tsukiji, Chuo-ku, Tokyo, Japan.

780   AU   ISSN 0075-3572
JAZZFORSCHUNG/JAZZ RESEARCH. (Text and summaries in English, German) 1969. a. price varies; free to members. (International Society for Jazz Research) Universal Edition AG, Karlsplatz 6, Postfach 130, Vienna A-1015, Austria (U.S. Orders to: EAMC, 195 Allwood Rd., Clifton NJ 07012) (Co-Sponsors: Hochschule fuer Musik und Institut fuer Jazz Darstellende Kunst.) Eds. Friedrich Koerner and Dieter Glawischnig.

781.57   US
JAZZOLOGIST. 1963. 4-6/yr. $6.75. New Orleans Jazz Club of California, Box 1225, Kerrville, TX 78028. Ed. Mort Enob. adv. bk. rev. rec.rev. bibl. circ. 5,000.

780   GW   ISSN 0446-9577
JOSEPH HAAS GESELLSCHAFT. MITTEILUNGENSBLATT. 1950. a. membership. Joseph Haas Gesellschaft e.V., Veroneserstr. 4, 8000 Munich 90, W. Germany (B.R.D.) Ed. Philipp Mohler. bk. rev. bibl. cum. index. circ. 300.

783   US
JOURNAL OF JEWISH MUSIC AND LITURGY. 1976. a. $4. Cantorial Council of America, c/o Yeshiva University, 500 W. 185th St., New York, NY 10033. Ed. Macy Nulman. circ. 300.

780   US   ISSN 0364-2216
JOURNAL OF THE GRADUATE MUSIC STUDENTS AT THE OHIO STATE UNIVERSITY. 1969. irreg., no. 6, 1977. Ohio State University, School of Music, 1899 N. College Rd., Columbus, OH 43210.

789.91   US
KASTLEMUSICK DIRECTORY FOR COLLECTORS OF RECORDINGS. a. $12.95. Kastlemusick, Inc., 901 Washington St., Wilmington, DE 19801.

780   UR
KAZANSKII GOSUDARSTVENNYI PEDAGOGICHESKII INSTITUT. VOPROSY ISTORII, TEORII MUZYKI I MUZYKAL'NOGO VOSPYTANIYA. SBORNIK. 1970. biennial. 70-80 Kop. Kazanskii Gosudarstvennyi Pedagogicheskii Institut, Ul. Mezjlauk, 1, 420021 Kazan, U.S.S.R. circ. 600.

780   UK
KEMPS INTERNATIONAL MUSIC AND RECORD YEARBOOK. 1965. a. $30. Kemp's Group (Printers & Publishers) Ltd., 1-5 Bath St., London EC1V 9QA, England. adv.
    Former titles: Kemps Music and Record Industry Year Book International (ISSN 0305-7100); Kemps Music and Record Industry Year Book (ISSN 0075-5451)

780   NE
KIJKBOEKJES. (Text in Dutch and English) 1976. irreg., no. 5, 1977. fl.30 per no. (Gemeentemuseum) Uitgeverij Frits Knuf B.V., Box 720, 4116 ZJ Buren, Netherlands. illus.

780   GW   ISSN 0075-6199
KIRCHENMUSIKALISCHES JAHRBUCH. 1876. a. price varies. Allgemeiner Caecilien-Verband, Koelnstr. 415, 5300 Bonn, W. Germany (B.R.D.) Ed. Karl Gustav Fellerer. bk. rev.

780   GW
KOELNER BEITRAEGE ZUR MUSIKFORSCHUNG. irreg., vol. 96, 1978. price varies. Gustav Bosse Verlag, Von-der-Tann-Str. 38, Postfach 417, 8400 Regensburg 1, W. Germany (B.R.D.) Ed. Michael Trapp.

780   JA
KUNITACHI COLLEGE OF MUSIC. MEMOIRS/ KUNITACHI ONGAKU DAIGAKU KENKYU KIYO. (Text in Japanese) 1966. a. 2500 Yen. Kunitachi College of Music - Kunitachi Ongaku Daigaku, 5-5-1 Kashiwa-cho, Tachikawa-shi, Tokyo 190, Japan. Ed.Bd. illus. circ. 800.

781.97 016   US   ISSN 0075-9864
LISTENING LIBRARY OF LP RECORDINGS. 1957? a. free. Listening Library, Inc., 1 Park Ave., Old Greenwich, CT 06870.

786   AU
LISZT INFORMATION-COMMUNICATION; Mitteilungsblatt. 1972. a. 15. Prugg-Verlag Eisenstaedter Graphische GmbH, Joseph Haydngasse 10, A-7000 Eisenstadt, Austria. Ed. Emmerich Karl Horvath. bibl. illus. circ. 1,000-1,500. (looseleaf format; back issues avail)

780   UK   ISSN 0141-0792
LISZT SOCIETY. JOURNAL. 1976. a. membership. Liszt Society Ltd., 32 Chivelston, 78 Wimbledon Park Side, Wimbledon, London SW19 5LH, England. Ed. Adrian Williams. bk. rev. bibl. circ. 300.
    Formerly: Liszt Society, London. Newsletter (ISSN 0459-5084)

LITERARNO-MUZEJNY LETOPIS. see *LITERATURE*

780   RM
LUCRARI DE MUZICOLOGIE. (Text in Romanian; summaries in Russian, English, German, French) a. free. Conservatorul "George Dima", Str. 23 August Nr. 25, Cluj-Napoca, Romania. Indexed: RILM.

780   UK   ISSN 0460-007X
LUTE SOCIETY JOURNAL. 1959. a. £3($8) Lute Society, 71 Priory Rd., Kew Gardens, Richmond, Surrey TW9 3DH, England. Ed. Ian Harwood. (back issues avail.)

780   US   ISSN 0076-1524
LUTE SOCIETY OF AMERICA. JOURNAL. 1968. a. membership. Lute Society of America, c/o Beedle White, Mountain View Farm, Rt. 5, Lexington, VA 24450. Ed. Peter Danner. adv. bk. rev. index. circ. 600.

781.7 UK
MANCHESTER FOLK DIRECTORY. a. £0.20. T. & C. Hicks, 12 Winster Ave., Stretford M32 95E, England. illus.

MASQUE. see *LITERATURE*

784.3 787.61 CS
MELODIE PRE VAS. irreg, vol. 7, 1974. 7 Kcs. per no. Opus, Bratislava, Czechoslovakia.

780 CS ISSN 0544-4136
MISCELLANEA MUSICOLOGICA. (Text in Czech; summaries in German) 1956. approx. a. 24.50 Kcs. Universita Karlova, Filosoficka Fakulta, Katedra Dejin Hudby, Divadla a Filmu, Nam. Krasnoarmejcu 1, 116 38 Prague 1, Czechoslovakia. Ed. Frantisek Muzik. illus. circ. 700. Indexed: RILM.

780.01 AT ISSN 0076-9355
MISCELLANEA MUSICOLOGICA; Adelaide studies in musicology. 1966. irreg. price varies. (University of Adelaide) Libraries Board of South Australia, Box 419 G.P.O., Adelaide, S. 5001, Australia. Ed. Andrew D. McCredie. circ. 500. Indexed: Aus.P.A.I.S.

780 US ISSN 0085-350X
MISSOURI JOURNAL OF RESEARCH IN MUSIC EDUCATION. 1962. a. $2. ‡ Missouri Music Educators Association, c/o Jack Stephenson, Ed., Conservatory of Music, University of Missouri-Kansas City, 4420 Warwick Blvd., Kansas City, MO 64111. circ. 800.

781.57 IT
MODERN JAZZ. (Text in English) irreg. Ruggero Stiassi, Ed. & Pub., Via Putti 3, Bologna, Italy. adv. rec.rev. (processed)

789.9 US
MODERN RECORDING'S BUYER'S GUIDE. a. Cowan Publishing Corp., 14 Vanderventer Ave., Port Washington, NY 11050.

MONOGRAPHS ON MUSIC, DANCE AND THEATER IN ASIA. see *DANCE*

780 PL ISSN 0077-1465
MONUMENTA MUSICAE IN POLONIA. (Text mainly in Latin; occasionally in Polish and other languages) 1966. irreg. price varies. (Polska Akademia Nauk, Instytut Sztuki) Panstwowe Wydawnictwo Naukowe, Miodowa 10, Warsaw, Poland (Dist. by Ars Polona-Ruch, Krakowskie Przedmiescie 7, Warsaw, Poland) Ed. Jozef M. Chominski.

780 SW ISSN 0077-1473
MONUMENTA MUSICAE SUECICAE. (Text in English, German & Swedish) 1958. irreg., vol. 9, 1979. price varies. Svenska Samfundet foer Musikforskning - Swedish Society for Musicology, Strandvaegen 82, 115 27 Stockholm, Sweden.

780 US ISSN 0077-1503
MONUMENTS OF RENAISSANCE MUSIC. 1964. irreg., vol. 6, 1975. price varies. University of Chicago Press, 5801 S. Ellis Ave., Chicago, IL 60637. Ed. Edward E. Lowinsky. (reprint service avail. from UMI,ISI)

780 GW ISSN 0077-1805
MOZART-JAHRBUCH. (Text in English, French and German) 1950. a. price varies. (Internationale Stiftung Mozarteum, AU) Baerenreiter-Verlag, Heinrich-Schuetz-Allee 29-37, 3500 Kassel-Wilhelmshoehe, W. Germany (B.R.D.) Ed.Bd. adv. index. circ. 1,000.

780 US
MUGWUMPS' INSTRUMENT HERALD. CATALOG REPRINT SERIES. 1972. irreg. Mugwumps' Instrument, 12704 Barbara Rd., Silver Spring, MD 20906.

780 II
MUSIC ACADEMY. CONFERENCE SOUVENIR. (Text in English, Sanskrit or Tamil) 1940. a. Music Academy, 306 Mowbray's Rd., Royapettah, Madras 600014, India.

780 II
MUSIC ACADEMY. JOURNAL. (Text in English, Tamil and Sanskrit) 1929. a. Rs.12($3) Music Academy, Royapettah, 306 Mowbray's Rd., Madras 600014, India.

780 UK ISSN 0085-3607
MUSIC AND LIFE. ca. 1950. 3-4/yr. £1.20. Music Group of the Communist Party, c/o George Burn, Ed., 17 Huntingdon Rd., London N.2, England. circ. 300. (processed)

780 UK
MUSIC & VIDEO WEEK YEARBOOK. no. 7, 1976. a. Spotlight Publications Ltd., 40 Long Acre, London WC2 9JT, England.
Formerly: Music Week Industry Year Book.

780 IE
MUSIC ASSOCIATION OF IRELAND. ANNUAL REPORT. 1975. a. Music Association of Ireland, 11 Suffolk St., Dublin 2, Ireland. stat.

780 JA
MUSIC CULTURES/KANSAI ONGAKU BUNKA SHIRYO. 1979. a. 1500 Yen. Osaka College of Music - Osaka Ongaku Daigaku, 1-1-8 Shonai-saiwaicho, Toyonaka, Osaka, Japan. Ed. Nobuo Nishioka. adv. illus. circ. 1,000.
Former titles (1976-1978): Date of Music in Western Japan; (1972-1975): Date of Music in Kansai District.

788 US ISSN 0077-2402
MUSIC EDUCATORS NATIONAL CONFERENCE. SELECTIVE MUSIC LIST: VOCAL SOLOS AND ENSEMBLES. 1968. irreg., latest edt. 1974. $4.50. ‡ Music Educators National Conference, Center for Educational Associations, 1902 Association Dr., Reston, VA 22091.

780.7 US
MUSIC EDUCATORS NATIONAL CONFERENCE. SELECTIVE MUSIC LISTS: FULL ORCHESTRA, STRING ORCHESTRA. 1971. irreg., latest edt. 1978. $2. ‡ Music Educators National Conference, Center for Educational Associations, 1902 Association Dr., Reston, VA 22091.
Formerly: Music Educators National Conference. Selective Music Lists: Band, Orchestra, and String Orchestra.

785 US
MUSIC EDUCATORS NATIONAL CONFERENCE. SELECTIVE MUSIC LISTS: INSTRUMENTAL SOLOS AND ENSEMBLES. 1972. irreg., latest edt. 1979. $5. ‡ Music Educators National Conference, Center for Educational Associations, 1902 Association Dr., Reston, VA 22091.

780.1 US
MUSIC FORUM. 1967. irreg., 1977, vol. 4. price varies. Columbia University Press, 136 South Broadway, Irvington-on-Hudson, NY 10533. Ed. Felix Salzer. illus.

780 US ISSN 0077-2372
MUSIC HANDBOOK. 1956. a. $1.95. Maher Publications, Inc., 222 W. Adams St., Chicago, IL 60606. Ed. Jack Maher.

780 US
MUSIC IN AMERICAN LIFE. irreg. price varies. University of Illinois Press, Urbana, IL 61801. (reprint service avail. from UMI)

780 US ISSN 0077-2410
MUSIC IN HIGHER EDUCATION. 1967. a. $5. National Association of Schools of Music, 11250 Roger Bacon Dr., No. 5, Reston, VA 22090. circ. 1,000.

MUSIC LIBRARY ASSOCIATION. TECHNICAL REPORTS; information for music media specialists. see *LIBRARY AND INFORMATION SCIENCES*

789.91 UK ISSN 0308-9347
MUSIC MASTER. 1974. a (with monthly supplements) £30. John Humphries, Ed. & Pub., Music House, 1 De Cham Ave., Hastings, Sussex, England. Ed. Michael Preston.
Incorporating: Singles Master & Record Prices.

780 US
MUSIC NOTES. vol. 9, 1976. irreg. Yamaha International Corp., 6600 Orangethorpe Ave., Buena Park, CA 90620. Ed.Jaclyn Marquart. illus.

MUSIC O C L C USERS GROUP. NEWSLETTER. see *LIBRARY AND INFORMATION SCIENCES*

780 US
MUSIC THEORY SPECTRUM. 1979. a. $18. Society for Music Theory, School of Music, Indiana University, Bloomington, IN 47405. Ed. Bryan R. Simms.

380.1 UK ISSN 0307-8523
MUSIC TRADES DIRECTORY. irreg. £6.45. Trade Papers Ltd., 46-47 Chancery Lane, London WC2A 1JB, England. adv.
Former titles: Music Trades International Directory; Music Trades International Yearbook; Piano World and Music Trades Review Yearbook.

780 950 US ISSN 0140-6078
MUSICA ASIATICA. 1978. irreg (approx. a) price varies. Oxford University Press, 200 Madison Ave., New York, NY 10016 (And Ely House, 37 Dover St., London W1X 4AH, England) Ed. Laurence Picken.

780 UK ISSN 0580-2954
MUSICA BRITANNICA; a national collection of music. 1951. irreg. price varies. (Royal Musical Association) Stainer and Bell Ltd., 82 High Rd., London N2 9PW, England.

780.9 GW ISSN 0077-2461
MUSICA DISCIPLINA; yearbook of the history of music, Medieval and Renaissance. (Text in English, French, German) 1946. a. (American Institute of Musicology, US) Haenssler-Verlag, Postfach 1220, Bismarckstrasse 4, 7303 Neuhausen-Stuttgart, W. Germany (B.R.D.)

781.7 US
MUSICA JUDAICA. (Text in English and Hebrew) 1976. a. $5 to individuals; institutions $10. American Society for Jewish Music, 155 Fifth Ave., New York, NY 10010. Eds. Israel J. Katz, Albert Weisser.

780 PL ISSN 0077-247X
MUSICA MEDII AEVI. (Text in Polish; summaries in English) 1965. irreg. price varies. (Polska Akademia Nauk, Instytut Sztuki) Polskie Wydawnictwo Muzyczne, Al. Krasinskiego 11, Krakow, Poland (Dist. by: Ars Polona-Ruch, Krakowskie Przedmiescie 7, Warsaw, Poland) Ed. Jerzy Morawski.

790 US
MUSICAL AMERICA INTERNATIONAL DIRECTORY OF THE PERFORMING ARTS. 1968/69. a. $25. A B C Leisure Magazines Inc., 825 Seventh Ave., New York, NY 10019. Ed. Shirley Fleming. adv. circ. 21,000.
Formerly: Musical America Annual Directory Issue (ISSN 0580-308X)

781.7 KE
MUSICAL INSTRUMENTS OF EAST AFRICA. 1975. irreg. EAs.0.80. Nelson Africa Ltd., Box 73146, Nairobi, Kenya.

780.1 781.7 SP
MUSICOLOGIA ESPANOLA. 1975. irreg. Ministerio de Educacion y Ciencia, Comisaria Nacional de la Musica, Madrid 3, Spain.

780 HU ISSN 0077-2488
MUSICOLOGICA HUNGARICA. NEUE FOLGE. (Text in German) 1967. irreg., vol. 6, 1976. price varies. (Magyar Tudomanyos Akademia) Akademiai Kiado, Publishing House of the Hungarian Academy of Sciences, P.O. Box 24, H-1363 Budapest, Hungary.

780 CS ISSN 0581-0558
MUSICOLOGICA SLOVACA. 1969. irreg. price varies. (Slovenska Akademia Vied, Umenovedny Ustav) Veda, Publishing House of the Slovak Academy of Sciences, Klemensova 19, 895 30 Bratislava, Czechoslovakia.

780 GW ISSN 0077-2496
MUSICOLOGICAL STUDIES AND DOCUMENTS. (Text in English; occasionally in French) 1948. irreg. (American Institute of Musicology, US) Haenssler-Verlag, Postfach 1220, Bismarckstrasse 4, 7303 Neuhausen-Stuttgart, W. Germany (B.R.D.) Ed. Armen Carapetyan.

MUSIC

780   AT   ISSN 0077-250X
MUSICOLOGY. 1965. a. Aus.$20($25) to non-members. Musicological Society of Australia, Union Box 300, University of New South Wales, Box 1, Kensington, N.S.W. 2033, Australia. Ed. Francis Cameron.

780   GW
MUSIK AUS DER STEIERMARK. 1959. 4-6/yr. (Steirischer Tonkuenstlerbund, AU) Fritz Schulz Verlag (Freiburg-Tiengen), Am Maerzengraben 6, 7800 Freiburg-Tiengen, W. Germany (B.R.D.) Eds. Konrad Stekl, Wolfgang Suppan.

780   SW   ISSN 0077-2518
MUSIK I SVERIGE. (Text in Swedish; occasional English summary) 1969. irreg. price varies. Svenskt Musikhistoriskt Arkiv, Sibyllegatan 2, S-114 51 Stockholm, Sweden. (Co-sponsor: Svenska Samfundet foer Musikforskning) Indexed: RILM.

780   DK
MUSIK OG FORSKNING. 1975. irreg. (Koebenhavns Universitet, Musikvidenskabeligt Institut) Akademisk Forlag, St. Kannikestraede 8, DK-1169 Copenhagen K, Denmark.

780   GW   ISSN 0077-2526
MUSIKALISCHE DENKMAELER. 1955. irreg. Akademie der Wissenschaften und der Literatur, Mainz, Geschwister-Scholl-Str. 2, 6500 Mainz, W. Germany (B.R.D.).

780   SW   ISSN 0081-5675
MUSIKHISTORISKA MUSEET, STOCKHOLM. SKRIFTER. 1964. irreg., no. 8, 1979. price varies. Musikhistoriska Museet, Sibyllegatan 2, S-114 51 Stockholm, Sweden. Indexed: RILM.

780   GW
MUSIKPAEDAGOGISCHE BIBLIOTHEK. 1962. irreg., vol. 24, 1981. DM.16.80. Heinrichshofen's Verlag, Liebigstr. 16, 2940 Wilhelmshaven, W. Germany (B.R.D.) (Dist. in U.S. by C.F. Peters Corp., 373 Park Ave., S., New York, N.Y. 10016) Ed. Walter Kolneder.

780   YU   ISSN 0580-373X
MUZIKOLOSKI ZBORNIK/MUSICOLOGICAL ANNUAL. (Text in Slovene, English, German, Italian; summaries in English and Slovene) 1965. a. price varies. Univerza Edvarda Kardelja v Ljubljani, Filozofska Fakulteta, Oddelek za Muzikologijo, Askerceva 12, 61000 Ljubljana, Yugoslavia. Ed. Dragotin Cvetko. illus. index. circ. 500. Indexed: RILM

780   398   UR
MUZYKAL'NAYA FOLKLORISTIKA. (Text in Russian; summaries in English and German) 1973. irreg. 0.79 Rub. (Soyuz Kompozitorov Rossiiskoi S.F.S.R., Folklornaya Komissiya) Izdatel'stvo Sovetskii Kompozitor, Naberezhnaya Morisa Toreza, 30, Moscow W-35, U.S.S.R. illus.

371   780   UR   ISSN 0302-847X
MUZYKAL'NOE VOSPITANIE V SHKOLE. irreg. 0.57 Rub. Izdatel'stvo Muzyka, Neglinnaya ul., 14, Moscow K-45, U.S.S.R.

780   US   ISSN 0547-4175
NATIONAL ASSOCIATION OF SCHOOLS OF MUSIC. DIRECTORY. 1950. a. $5. National Association of Schools of Music, 11250 Roger Bacon Dr., No. 5, Reston, VA 22090.

780.7   US   ISSN 0077-3409
NATIONAL ASSOCIATION OF SCHOOLS OF MUSIC. PROCEEDING OF THE ANNUAL MEETING. 1934. a. $4. National Association of Schools of Music, 11250 Roger Bacon Dr., Reston, VA 22090.

782   US   ISSN 0085-381X
NATIONAL OPERA ASSOCIATION. MEMBERSHIP DIRECTORY. 1955. a. $15. National Opera Association, Inc., c/o Constance Eberhart, Hotel Wellington, 7Th Ave. at 55th St., New York, NY 10019.

780   GW   ISSN 0077-7714
NEUE MUSIKGESCHICHTLICHE FORSCHUNGEN. 1968. irreg. price varies. ‡ Breitkopf und Haertel, Walkmuehlstr. 52, Postfach 1707, 6200 Wiesbaden, W. Germany (B.R.D.) Ed. Lothar Hoffman-Erbrecht.

780   700   810   US
NEW ART REVIEW. vol. 2, 1976. irreg. Contemporary Music Foundation, 4105 Devon Dr., Indianapolis, IN 46226. Ed. A. Paul Johnson. illus.

781.7   UK
NEW CITY SONGSTER. 1968. a. 50p. per no. 35 Stanley Ave., Beckenham, Kent BR3 2PU, England. Eds. Ewan MacColl, Peggy Seeger. adv. illus. index. circ. 4,000.

780.7   US
NEW OXFORD HISTORY OF MUSIC. irreg. price varies. Oxford University Press, 200 Madison Ave., New York, NY 10016 (And Ely House, 37 Dover St., London W1X 4AH, England) Ed.Bd.

780   US   ISSN 0085-4042
NEW YORK PRO MUSICA INSTRUMENTAL SERIES. 1967. irreg., 1970, no. 6. $3.50. ‡ Associated Music Publishers, Inc., 866 Third Ave., New York, NY 10022.

780   GW   ISSN 0078-3471
OESTERREICHISCHE GESELLSCHAFT FUER MUSIK. BEITRAEGE. 1967. irreg. price varies. (AU) Baerenreiter Verlag, Heinrich-Schuetz-Allee 31-37, 3500 Kassel-Wilhelmshoehe, W. Germany (B.R.D.) Eds. R. Klein, K. Roschitz.

780   AU
OESTERREICHISCHE GESELLSCHAFT FUER MUSIKWISSENSCHAFT. MITTEILUNGEN. 1973. irreg. Oesterreichische Gesellschaft fuer Musikwissenschaft, Postfach 1461, A-1011 Vienna, Austria. Ed. Theophil Antonicek.

780   920   AU   ISSN 0078-3501
OESTERREICHISCHE KOMPONISTEN DES XX. JAHRHUNDERTS. 1964. irreg. price varies. Musikverlag Elisabeth Lafite, Hegelgasse 13/22, A-1010 Vienna, Austria (and Oesterreichischer Bundesverlag, Schwarzenbergstr. 5, 1015 Vienna 1, Austria)

784   AU   ISSN 0473-8624
OESTERREICHISCHES VOLKSLIEDWERK. JAHRBUCH. 1952. a. S.120. Oesterreichischer Bundersverlag, Schwarzenbergstr. 5, A-1010 Vienna, Austria. Ed. Gerlinde Haid. bk. rev. index. circ. 600. Indexed: RILM.
Supersedes: Volkslied, Volkstanz, Volksmusik.

780.65   US   ISSN 0078-3889
OFFICIAL TALENT & BOOKING DIRECTORY. 1970. a. $50. Specialty Publications, Inc., 7033 Sunset Blvd., No. 222, Los Angeles, CA 90028. Ed. Steve Tolin. index. circ. 10,000(controlled) (back issues avail.)

780.7   CN   ISSN 0700-5318
OPUS. irreg. University of Western Ontario, Faculty of Music, London, Ont. N6A 3K7, Canada. illus.

780   GW
ORGAN BUILDING PERIODICAL/ZEITSCHRIFT FUER ORGELBAU; I S O information. (Text in English and German) 1969. irreg. DM.34 for 3 issues. (International Society of Organbuilders - Internationale Orgelbauer-Vereinigung) Orgelbau-Fachverlag I S O Information, Postfach 234, 7128 Lauffen, W. Germany (B.R.D.) Ed. Richard Rensch. adv. bk. rev. circ. 2,000.
Formerly: I S O Information (ISSN 0579-5613)

786   US
ORGAN HISTORICAL SOCIETY. NATIONAL CONVENTION (PROCEEDINGS) 7th, 1962. a. Organ Historical Society, Inc., Box 209, Wilmington, OH 45177. adv. illus.

780   NE   ISSN 0078-6098
ORGAN YEARBOOK; a journal for the players and historians of keyboard instruments. (Text in English, French and German) 1970. a. fl.40. Uitgeverij Frits Knuf B. V., Box 720, 4116 ZJ Buren, Netherlands. Ed. Peter Williams. adv. bk. rev. circ. 3,000. (back issues avail)

788   789   US   ISSN 0078-6586
ORIGINAL MANUSCRIPT MUSIC FOR WIND AND PERCUSSION INSTRUMENTS. 1964. irreg. $1.50. ‡ Music Educators National Conference, Center for Educational Associations, 1902 Association Dr., Reston, VA 22091. Ed. Richard K. Weerts.

780   US   ISSN 0078-7264
OXFORD STUDIES OF COMPOSERS. irreg., no. 16, 1979. price varies. Oxford University Press, 200 Madison Ave., New York, NY 10016 (and Ely House, 37 Dover St., London W1X 4AH, England) Ed. Colin Mason.

789.9   US   ISSN 0360-2109
PAUL'S RECORD MAGAZINE. 1975. irreg. $2 per no. Paul E. Bezanker, Ed. & Pub., 180 Benton St., Box 14241, Hartford, CT 06114. adv. bk. rev. rec.rev. illus. stat. index, cum.index. circ. 1,500. Indexed: Pop.Mus.Per.Ind.

780   UK   ISSN 0309-0019
PERFORMING RIGHT NEWS. 1976. irreg. membership. Performing Right Society Ltd., 29-33 Berners St., London W1P 4AA, England. circ. 12,000. Indexed: Mus.Ind.
Replaces: Performing Right (ISSN 0031-5257)

780   UK   ISSN 0309-0884
PERFORMING RIGHT YEAR BOOK. a. membership. Performing Right Society Ltd., 29-33 Berners St., London W1P 4AA, England.

780   US   ISSN 0191-1554
PERFORMING WOMAN; a national directory of professional women musicians. 1978. a. $5. J. D. Dinneen, Ed. & Pub., 26910 Grand View Ave., Hayward, CA 94542. circ. 4,000.

780   UK
PLAINSONG & MEDIAEVAL MUSIC SOCIETY. JOURNAL. 1978. irreg. Plainsong & Mediaeval Music Society, The Church Lodge, Giles, Wimborne, Dorset, England. bk. rev.

780   PL   ISSN 0079-3612
POLSKA PIESN I MUZYKA LUDOWA. ZRODLA I MATERIALY. 1974. irreg. price varies. (Polska Akademia Nauk, Instytut Sztuki) Polskie Wydawnictwo Muzyczne, Al. Krasinskiego 11, Krakow, Poland (Dist. by Ars Polona-Ruch, Krakowskie Przedmiescie 7, Warsaw, Poland)

780   US   ISSN 0095-4101
POPULAR MUSIC PERIODICALS INDEX. 1973. a. Scarecrow Press, Inc., 52 Liberty St., Metuchen, NJ 08840. Comp. Dean Tudor, Linda Biesenthal.

781.7   PL
PRACE ARCHIWUM SLASKIE KULTURY MUZYCZNEJ. (Text in Polish; summaries in English, German and Russian) 1972. irreg. price varies. Panstwowa Wyzsza Szkola Muzyczna, Ul. 27 Stycznia 33, 40-025 Katowice, Poland. Ed. Karol Musiol. bibl. illus. Indexed: RILM.
Formerly: Archiwum Slaskie Kultury Muzycznej.

780   US   ISSN 0079-5259
PRINCETON STUDIES IN MUSIC. 1964. irreg., no. 7, 1973. price varies. Princeton University Press, Princeton, NJ 08540. (reprint service avail. from UMI)

780   US
PURCHASER'S GUIDE TO THE MUSIC INDUSTRIES. 1897. a. free with subscription to Music Trades. Music Trades Corporation, c/o George Magliola, Box 432, 80 West St., Englewood, NJ 07631. Ed. John F. Majeski. circ. 8,000. (reprint service avail. from UMI)

780   GW   ISSN 0079-905X
QUELLENKATALOGE ZUR MUSIKGESCHICHTE. 1966. irreg., vol. 19, 1981. DM.90. Heinrichshofen's Verlag, Liebigstr. 16, 2940 Wilhelmshaven, W. Germany (B.R.D.) (Dist. in U.S. by C. F. Peters Corp., 373 Park Ave. S., New York, N.Y. 10016) Ed. Richard Schaal.

780   SP   ISSN 0076-2318
REAL CONSERVATORIO SUPERIOR DE MUSICA. ANUARIO.* a. Real Conservatorio Superior de Musica, Plaza de Isabel II, Madrid 13, Spain.

780   FR   ISSN 0080-0139
RECHERCHES SUR LA MUSIQUE FRANCAISE CLASSIQUE. 1960. a. price varies. Editions A. et J. Picard, 82, rue Bonaparte, 75006 Paris, France.

RECORDING IN GREAT BRITAIN. see *SOUND RECORDING AND REPRODUCTION*

MUSIC

780 US
RECORDS IN REVIEW. 1956. a. $15.95. A B C Leisure Magazines, Wyeth Press, Box 550, Great Barrington, MA 01230. Ed.Edith Carter. circ. 3,500. (also avail. in microform from UMI)

780 GW
REGER-STUDIEN. 1978. irreg. price varies. (Max-Reger-Institut, Bonn) Breitkopf und Haertel, Walkmuehlstr. 52, Postfach 1707, 6200 Wiesbaden, W. Germany(B.R.D.) Eds., Guenter Massenkeil, Susanne Popp.

780 HU ISSN 0080-0562
REGI MAGYAR DALLAMOK TARA/CORPUS MUSICAE POPULARIS HUNGARICAE. (Text in Hungarian; occasional summaries in German) 1958. irreg. price varies. (Magyar Tudomanyos Akademia, Nepzenekutato Csoport) Akademiai Kiado, Publishing House of the Hungarian Academy of Sciences, P.O. Box 24, H-1363 Budapest, Hungary.

780.92 UK
REGISTER OF EARLY MUSIC. irreg. Oxford University Press, Press Rd., Neasden, London NW10 0DD, England.

780 GW
RENAISSANCE MANUSCRIPT STUDIES. 1973. irreg., latest vol. 2. (American Institute of Musicology, US) Haenssler-Verlag, Postfach 1220, Bismarckstrasse 4, 7303 Neuhausen-Stuttgart, W. Germany (B.R.D.)

780 UK ISSN 0080-1828
RESOURCES OF MUSIC. 1969. irreg., no. 18, 1978. $5.95 for latest vol. Cambridge University Press, Box 110, Cambridge CB2 3RL, England (and 32 E. 57 St., New York NY 10022) Ed. John Paynter.

781.7 398 VE
REVISTA INSTITUTO INTERAMERICANO DE ETNOMUSICOLOGIA Y FOLKLORE. Short title: Revista I N I D E F. 1975. irreg. Instituto Interamericano de Etnomusicologia y Folklore, Instituto Nacional de Cultura y Bella Artes, Apartado 6238, Caracas, Venezuela. illus.

781.7 JM
ROOTS NEWS. 1976. irreg. B & J Production Ltd., 1 Annette Crescent, Kingston 10, Jamaica.

780 UK ISSN 0080-4320
ROYAL COLLEGE OF ORGANISTS. YEAR BOOK. 1864-5. a. £1.35. ‡ Royal College of Organists, Kensington Gore, London SW7 2QS, England. adv. circ. 4,000.

780 IE
ROYAL IRISH ACADEMY OF MUSIC. PROSPECTUS. (Text in English and Irish) 1973. a. 50p. ‡ Royal Irish Academy of Music, 36/38 Westland Row, Dublin, 2, Ireland. circ. 1,000.

780 UK ISSN 0080-4452
ROYAL MUSICAL ASSOCIATION, LONDON. PROCEEDINGS. 1874-75. a. £6.50 to non-members. Royal Musical Association, c/o Hugh Cobbe, British Library, Great Russell St., London WC1B 3DG, England. Ed. David Greer. cum.index: vols. 1-90. circ. 1,200. Indexed: RILM.

780 UK ISSN 0080-4460
ROYAL MUSICAL ASSOCIATION, LONDON. R. M. A. RESEARCH CHRONICLE. 1961. a. £4 to non-members. Royal Musical Association, c/o Hugh Cobbe, British Library, Great Russell St., London WC1B 3DG, England. Ed. Geoffrey Chew. circ. 600. Indexed: RILM.

780 GW ISSN 0080-519X
SAARBRUECKER STUDIEN ZUR MUSIKWISSENSCHAFT. 1966. irreg. price varies. (Universitaet des Saarlandes, Musikwissenschaftliches Institut) Baerenreiter Verlag, Heinrich-Schuetz-Allee 31-37, 3500 Kassel-Wilhelmshoehe, W. Germany (B.R.D.) Ed. Walter Wiora.

784 GW
SAENGER-TASCHENKALENDER. 1955. a. price varies. (Deutscher Saengerbund e.V.) Verlag Deutsche Saengerzeitung GmbH, Luepertzender Str. 157-163, 4050 Moenchengladbach, W. Germany (B.R.D.) adv. circ. 12,000.

780 GW ISSN 0085-588X
SAMMLUNG MUSIKWISSENSCHAFTLICHER ABHANDLUNGEN/COLLECTION D'ETUDES MUSICOLOGIQUES. (Text in German, French, and English) 1932. irreg., no. 66, 1981. price varies. Verlag Valentin Koerner, H.-Sielcken-Str. 36, Postfach 304, D-7570 Baden-Baden 1, W. Germany (B.R.D.)

791 GW
SCHOTT AKTUELL. (Text in German) 1961. irreg. free. B. Schott's Soehne, Weihergarten 5, Postfach 3640, 6500 Mainz 1, W. Germany (B. R. D.) Ed. Bd. music rev. circ. 2,800. (tabloid format)
Formerly: Schott-Kurier (ISSN 0036-6919)

780 GW
SCHUETZ-JAHRBUCH. 1980. a. price varies. (Internationale Heinrich Schuetz-Gesellschaft e.V.) Baerenreiter Verlag, Heinrich-Schuetz-Allee 31-37, 3500 Kassel-Wilhelmshoehe, W. Germany (B.R.D.)
Supersedes(1966-197?): Sagittarius (ISSN 0080-5408)

789.91 028.5 US
SCHWANN CHILDREN'S & CHRISTMAS RECORD & TAPE GUIDE. 1964. a. $1.25. A B C Schwann Publications, Inc., 137 Newbury St., Boston, MA 02116. Ed. Richard Blackham. adv. circ. 18,300.

780 SZ ISSN 0080-7354
SCHWEIZERISCHE MUSIKFORSCHENDE GESELLSCHAFT. PUBLIKATIONEN. SERIE II. 1952. irreg., no. 30, 1977. price varies. Paul Haupt AG, Falkenplatz 14, CH-3001 Berne, Switzerland.

781.7 UK
SCOTTISH FOLK DIRECTORY. 1973. a. 40p. ‡ c/o Sheila Douglas, Ed., 12 Mansfield Rd., Perth, Scotland. adv. bk. rev. circ. 500-800.

781.7 US ISSN 0361-6622
SELECTED REPORTS IN ETHNOMUSICOLOGY. 1966. irreg. (Council on Ethnomusicology.) University of California, Los Angeles, Department of Music, Los Angeles, CA 90024. illus. circ. 800.

780.01 IT
SEMINARIO DI STUDI E RICERCHE SUL LINGUAGGIO MUSICALE. ATTI. 1971. a. Istituto Musicale F. Canneti, Villa Cordellina-Lombardi, Montecchio Maggiore, Vincenza, Italy. illus.

783 US
SHALSHELET: THE CHAIN. vol. 11, 1976. irreg. Hebrew Union College-Jewish Institute of Religion, School of Sacred Music Cantorial Alumni Association, 40 W. 68th St., New York, NY 10023. Ed. C.Herman.

780 790 UK
SHOWCALL. 1973. a. £5.50 for 2 parts. Carson and Comerford Ltd., Stage House, 47 Bermondsley St., London SE1 3XT, England. adv. illus. index.

SILO. see *LITERATURE*

784.7691 786.97 CS
SLOVENSKE LUDOVE PIESNE PRE AKORDEON. irreg., vol. 3, 1974. 8 Kcs. per no. Opus, Bratislava, Czechoslovakia.

781.7 US ISSN 0145-210X
SONGSMITH'S JOURNAL. 1976. irreg. $3. PhoeniXongs, Box 622, Northbrook, IL 60062. Ed. James Durst. adv. illus. tr.lit. circ. 3,000.

784.61 US ISSN 0560-8325
SONGWRITER'S ANNUAL DIRECTORY. a. $4. Songwriter's Review, 1697 Broadway, New York, NY 10019. Ed. Sydney Berman.

780.65 US ISSN 0161-5971
SONGWRITER'S MARKET. 1979. a. $9.95. Writer's Digest, 9933 Alliance Rd., Cincinnati, OH 45242. Ed. William Brohaugh.

784 US ISSN 0098-0730
SOUL IN REVIEW. 1975. irreg. $1. Soul in Review Publications, 572 W. 125 St., New York, NY 10027. illus.

780 UK ISSN 0081-2080
SOUNDINGS: A MUSIC JOURNAL. 1970. a. £1($6) University College of Wales, Department of Music, Cardiff, Wales. (Co-sponsor: Welsh Arts Council) Ed. Stephen Walsh. bk. rev. circ. 200. Indexed: RILM.

780 SA
SOURCE GUIDE FOR MUSIC/BRONNEGIDS VIR MUSIEK. 1970. a (1971 pub. 1975) price varies. Human Sciences Research Council, Private Bag X41, Pretoria 0001, South Africa.

780 SP
SPAIN. DIRECCION GENERAL DE BELLAS ARTES. SEMANA DE MUSICA EN LA NAVIDAD. irreg. Direccion General de Bellas Artes, Murcia, Spain. illus.

780 YU ISSN 0490-6659
SRPSKA AKADEMIJA NAUKA I UMETNOSTI. ODELJENJE LIKOVNE I MUZICKE UMETNOSTI. MUZICKA IZDANJA. 1953. irreg. available on exchange. Srpska Akademija Nauka i Umetnosti, Odeljenje Likovne i Muzicke Umetnosti, Knez Mihailova 35, 11001 Belgrade, Yugoslavia (Dist. by: Prosveta export import Terazije 16, 11001 Belgrade)

SRPSKA AKADEMIJA NAUKA I UMETNOSTI. ODELJENJE LIKOVNE I MUZICKE UMETNOSTI. POSEBNA IZDANJA. see *ART*

780 IT ISSN 0081-6388
STUDIA ET DOCUMENTA HISTORIAE MUSICAE: BIBLIOTHECA.* 1964. irreg. price varies. Giacomo A. Caula, Ed. & Pub., Corso Fiume 16, Turin, Italy.

780.01 NO ISSN 0332-5024
STUDIA MUSICOLOGICA NORVEGICA. (Text in English and Norwegian) 1968. irreg., no. 5, 1979. price varies. Universitetsforlaget, Kolstadgt. 1, Box 2959-Toeyen, Oslo 6, Norway (U. S. address: Box 258, Irvington-on-Hudson, NY 10533)

780 SW ISSN 0081-6744
STUDIA MUSICOLOGICA UPSALIENSIA. NOVA SERIES. (1952-58, vols. 1-8; 1965 designated as Nova Series and issued in Acta Universitatis Upsaliensis) irreg., vol. 6, 1979. price varies. (Uppsala Universitet) Almqvist and Wiksell International, Box 62, S-101 20 Stockholm, Sweden. Ed. Ingmar Bengtsson.

780 GW ISSN 0081-7341
STUDIEN ZUR MUSIKGESCHICHTE DES NEUNZEHNTEN JAHRHUNDERTS. irreg. price varies. Baerenreiter Verlag, Heinrich-Schuetz-Allee 29-37, 3500 Kassel-Wilhelmshoehe, W. Germany (B.R.D.)

780 US ISSN 0081-7902
STUDIES IN ETHNOMUSICOLOGY. irreg., 1965, no. 2. $3.95. Oak Publications, 33 W. 60 St., New York, NY 10023. Ed. M. Kolinski.

780 AT ISSN 0081-8267
STUDIES IN MUSIC. 1967. a. Aus.$6. University of Western Australia, Nedlands, 6009 W.A., Australia (Dist. in U.S. by: Theodore Front Musical Literature, 131 N. Robertson Blvd., Beverly Hills, CA 90211; Dist. in U.K. by: Alfred A. Kalmus, Ltd., 2-3 Fareham St., London W. 1., England) Ed. Frank Callaway. circ. 950. Indexed: RILM.

STUDII SI CERCETARI DE ISTORIA ARTEI. SERIA TEATRU-MUZICA-CINEMATOGRAFIE. see *THEATER*

780 SW ISSN 0081-9816
SVENSK TIDSKRIFT FOER MUSIKFORSKNING/ SWEDISH JOURNAL OF MUSICOLOGY. (Text in Swedish, English and German; summaries in English) 1919. s-a. Kr.55. Svenska Samfundet foer Musikforskning - Swedish Society for Musicology, Strandvaegen 82, 115 27 Stockholm, Sweden. Ed. Anders Loenn. adv. bk. rev. index, cum.index: 1919-68 (vols. 1-50) circ. 600. Indexed: RILM.

780 016 SW ISSN 0586-0709
SVENSKT MUSIKHISTORISKT ARKIV. BULLETIN. 1966. irreg (approx. 1/yr.) Kr.10. Svenskt Musikhistoriskt Arkiv, Sibyllegatan 2, S-114 51 Stockholm, Sweden. circ. 300. Indexed: RILM.

784 US
SYMPOSIUM ON CARE OF THE
PROFESSIONAL VOICE. TRANSCRIPTS.
(Published in 3 parts) 1978. a., 8th symposium,
1979. $25. Voice Foundation, 320 Park Ave, New
York, NY 10022. Ed. Van Lawrence. charts. illus.
(back issues avail.)
Singing

780 PL
SZKICE O KULTURZE MUZYCZNEJ XIX WIEKU.
STUDIA I MATERIALY. (Text in Polish;
summaries in English) irreg., 1976, vol. 3. $9.40.
(Polska Akademia Nauk, Instytut Sztuki)
Panstwowe Wydawnictwo Naukowe, Miodowa 10,
Warsaw, Poland (Dist. by: Ars Polona-Ruch,
Krakowskie Przedmiescie 7, Warsaw, Poland) Ed. Z.
Chechlinska. charts. illus.

T R U K-P A C T. (Transvaalse Raad vir die
Uitvoerende Kunste-Performing Arts Council
Transvaal) see *THEATER*

780 US
T.U.B.A. SERIES. 1975. irreg. price varies. (Tubists
Universal Brotherhood Association) Brass Press, 136
Eighth Ave., Nashville, TN 37203. Ed. Stephen L.
Glover.

780 II
TAMIL ICAIC CANKAM MATURAI. ANTU VILA
MALAR. (Text in Tamil) 1978. a. Rs.7.50. Tamil
Icaic Cankam Maturai, Tamil Isai Sangam Madurai,
7 Vallabai Rd, Madurai 600002, India.

780 GW ISSN 0082-187X
TASCHENBUCH FUER LITURGIE UND
KIRCHENMUSIK. (Will Not Appear in 1978 but
Resume with 1979 Volume) 1958. a. price varies.
Verlag Friedrich Pustet, Gutenbergstr. 8, 8400
Regensburg 1, W. Germany (B.R.D.) Ed. Franz
Johann Loeffler. adv. bk. rev. circ. 2,500.
Formerly: Taschenbuch fuer den Kirchenmusiker.

780 GW ISSN 0082-1969
TASCHENBUECHER ZUR
MUSIKWISSENSCHAFT. 1969. irreg., vol. 80,
1981. DM.14.80. Heinrichshofen's Verlag, Liebigstr.
16, 2940 Wilhelmshaven, W. Germany (B.R.D.) -
(Dist. in U.S. by C. F. Peters Corp., 373 Park Ave.
S., New York, N.Y. 10016) Ed. Richard Schaal.

780.58 IS ISSN 0082-2132
TATZLIL/CHORD; forum for music research and
bibliography. (Text in Hebrew; summaries in
Fnglish) 1960. a. $4. Haifa Music Museum and
Amli Library, P.O.B. 5111, Haifa, Israel. Ed. Moshe
Gorali. bk. rev. bibl. rec.rev. index;cum.index:
1960-70. circ. 1,000. Indexed: RILM.

780 US
THEMATIC CATALOGUE SERIES. (Text in
English, French and German) 1977. irreg., vol. 7,
1980. Pendragon Press, 162 W. 13th St., New York,
NY 10011. (back issues avail.)

TOOTHPICK, LISBON & THE ORCAS ISLANDS.
see *LITERATURE*

780.904 US
TOP TENS AND TRIVIA OF ROCK AND ROLL
AND RHYTHM AND BLUES. ANNUAL
SUPPLEMENT. vol. 2, 1975. a. $4.50. Blueberry
Hill Publishing Co., Box 24170, St. Louis, MO
63130. Ed. Joe Edwards.

781.7 US ISSN 0161-3081
TUNE UP. irreg. $6. Philadelphia Folksong Society,
Box 215, Philadelphia, PA 19105.
Folk

780 UK
TUTOR & TEXTBOOK - ELEMENTARY PIPING &
DRUMMING. 1963. 80p.($1.50) ‡ Scottish Pipe
Band Association, 45, Washington Street, Glasgow,
G3 8AZ, Scotland. adv.

789.91 US
U C L A MUSIC LIBRARY DISCOGRAPHY
SERIES. 1977. irreg. free. University of California,
Los Angeles, Ethnomusicology Archive, Los
Angeles, CA 90024. Ed. Stephen M. Fry. circ. 200.

780 CN
UKULELE YES! 1976. a. Can.$15. Doane Musical
Enterprise Ltd., Box 125, Armdale, Halifax, N.S.
B3L 4J9, Canada. Ed. Cam Trowsdale. adv. illus.

780.01 UY
UNIVERSIDAD DE LA REPUBLICA. FACULTAD
DE HUMANIDADES Y CIENCIAS. REVISTA.
SERIE MUSICOLOGIA. N.S. 1979. irreg.
Universidad de la Republica, Facultad de
Humanidades y Ciencias, Seccion Revista, Tristan
Narvaja 1674, Montevideo, Uruguay. Dir. Beatriz
Martinez Osorio.
Supersedes in part: Universidad de la Republica.
Facultad de Humanidades y Ciencias. Revista.

UNIVERSIDAD NACIONAL DE COLOMBIA.
CENTRO DE ESTUDIOS FOLKLORICOS.
MONOGRAFIAS. see *FOLKLORE*

780 US ISSN 0068-6409
UNIVERSITY OF CALIFORNIA PUBLICATIONS
IN CONTEMPORARY MUSIC. 1966. irreg. price
varies. University of California Press, 2223 Fulton
St., Berkeley, CA 94720.

780 AT
UNIVERSITY OF WESTERN AUSTRALIA.
DEPARTMENT OF MUSIC. MUSIC
MONOGRAPH. no. 2; 1975. irreg. $12.50 per no.
University of Western Australia, Department of
Music, Nedlands, W. A. 6009, Australia. Ed. Frank
Calloway.

UNIVERZITA KOMENSKEHO. FILOZOFICKA
FAKULTA. ZBORNIK: MUSAICA. see *ART*

780 UR
V MIRE MUZYKI; Kalendar'. a. 1.07 Rub. Izdatel'stvo
Sovetskii Kompozitor, Naberezhnaya Morisa Toreza
30, Moscow W-35, U.S.S.R. illus.

780 IT ISSN 0042-3734
VERDI. (Text in English, German & Italian) 1960.
irreg. L.10600 for 3 nos. Istituto di Studi Verdiani,
Strada della Repubblica 57, 43100 Parma, Italy.
illus. index; cum.index every 3 nos.

780 GW ISSN 0543-1735
VEROEFFENTLICHUNGEN DES MAX-REGER-
INSTITUTES. 1966. irreg. price varies. (Max-
Reger-Institut) Ferd. Duemmlers Verlag, Kaiserstr.
32, D-5300, Bonn 1, W. Germany (B.R.D.)

780 GW
VEROEFFENTLICHUNGEN ZUR
MUSIKFORSCHUNG. 1973. irreg., vol. 5, 1981.
DM.28. Heinrichshofen's Verlag, Liebigstr. 16, 2940
Wilhelmshaven, W. Germany (B.R.D.) (Dist. in U.S.
by C.F. Peters Corp., 373 Park Ave. S., New York,
NY 10016) Ed.Richard Schaal.

780 FR ISSN 0083-6109
VIE MUSICALE EN FRANCE SOUS LES ROIS
BOURBONS. SERIE 1: ETUDES. (Text in English
and French: summaries in French) 1954. irreg. price
varies. Editions A. et J. Picard, 82 rue Bonaparte,
75006 Paris, France. Ed. Norbert Dufourcq.

780 FR ISSN 0083-6117
VIE MUSICALE EN FRANCE SOUS LES ROIS
BOURBONS. SERIE 2: RECHERCHES SUR LA
MUSIQUE CLASSIQUE FRANCAISE. (Text in
English and French; summaries in French) 1960. a.
price varies. Editions A. et J. Picard, 82 rue
Bonaparte, 75006 Paris, France. Ed. Nobert
Dufourcq.

780 US ISSN 0507-0252
VIOLA DA GAMBA SOCIETY OF AMERICA
JOURNAL. 1964. a. membership. Viola da Gamba
Society of America, Inc., c/o John A. Whisler, Pub.
Mgr., 178 S. McLean, Apt. 4, Memphis, TN 38104.
adv. bk. rev. bibl. illus. circ. 300.

780 DK
VIVALDI INFORMATIONS. (Text in English,
French and German) 1971. a. $8. International
Antonio Vivaldi Society, c/o Istituto Italiano de
Cultura, Gjoeringlisvej 11, DK-2900 Hellerup,
Denmark. Eds. P. Ryom & P. Augustinus. bk. rev.
bibl, illus. index. circ. 800(controlled) (back issues
avail.)
Formerly: International Antonio Vivaldi Society.
Informations.

784 UR
VOPROSY UCHEBNO-VOSPITATEL'NOI
RABOTY V SAMODEYATEL'NYKH
KOLLEKTIVAKH. (Subseries of the Institute's
Trudy) 1972. irreg. 0.33 Rub. (Nauchno-
Issledovatel'skii Institut Kul'tury, Otdel' Narodnogo
Tvorchestva) Izdatel'stvo Sovetskaya Rossiya,
Proezd Sapunova 13/15, Moscow K-12, U.S.S.R.

780 US
WADSWORTH MUSIC SERIES. irreg. Wadsworth
Publishing Co., 10 Davis Dr., Belmont, CA 94002.

784.4 US ISSN 0091-9020
WASHINGTON FOLK STRUMS. 1964. irreg. 9937
Cottrell Terrace, Silver Spring, MD 20903. illus.

780 US ISSN 0083-7881
WELLESLEY EDITION. 1952. irreg. $5. Wellesley
College, Department of Music, Wellesley, MA
02181. Ed. Owen Jander. circ. 110.

780 US ISSN 0083-7873
WELLESLEY EDITION CANTATA INDEX
SERIES. 1964. irreg. $3-$5. ‡ Wellesley College,
Department of Music, Wellesley, MA 02181. Ed.
Owen Jander. circ. 110.

WHO'S WHO AMONG MUSIC STUDENTS IN
AMERICAN HIGH SCHOOLS; a biographical
dictionary of outstanding music students in
American high schools. see *BIOGRAPHY*

780 AU
WIENER FIGARO. irreg. (at least once a year)
Mozartgemeinde Wien, Metternichgasse 8, A-1030
Vienna, Austria. Ed. Otto Schneider.

780 AU ISSN 0084-0017
WIENER MUSIKHOCHSCHULE.
PUBLIKATIONEN. 1967. irreg., no. 7, 1978. price
varies. Musikverlag Elisabeth Lafite, Hegelgasse 13/
22, A-1010 Vienna, Austria.

783 UK
WORLD OF CHURCH MUSIC. 1963. a. £2.50.
Royal School of Church Music, Addington Palace,
Croydon CR9 5AD, England. Ed. Lionel Dakers.
adv. bk. rev. (also avail. in microform from UMI;
reprint service avail. from UMI)
Formerly(until 1980): English Church Music
(ISSN 0071-0555)

780.42 NE
WORLD POP NEWS. (Text in English) no. 2, 1976.
bi-m. Phonogram International B.V., Postbus 23,
Baarn, Netherlands. illus.

780 UK
WORLD RECORD MARKETS. 3rd ed., 1976. a. £3.
Henry Melland Ltd., 23 Ridgmount St., London
WC1E 7AH, England.

780 US ISSN 0084-3504
YALE STUDIES IN THE HISTORY OF MUSIC.
1947. irreg., 1969, no. 5. price varies. Yale
University Press, 92A Yale Sta., New Haven, CT
06520.

780 IS ISSN 0084-439X
YUVAL. (Text in English, French, Hebrew; summaries
in English and Hebrew) 1968. irreg. price varies.
(Jewish Music Research Centre) Magnes Press, The
Hebrew University, Jerusalem, Israel. Ed. Israel
Adler.

780 PL ISSN 0084-442X
Z DZIEJOW MUZYKI POLSKIEJ. 1960. irreg.
Bydgoskie Towarzystwo Naukowe, Jezuicka 4,
Bydgoszcz, Poland (Dist. by Ars Polona-Ruch,
Krakowskie Przedmiescie 7, Warsaw, Poland)

780 PL ISSN 0084-571X
ZRODLA DO HISTORII MUZYKI POLSKIEJ.
1960. irreg. price varies. Polskie Wydawnictwo
Muzyczne, Al. Krasinskiego 11, Krakow, Poland.

016.78 US ISSN 0093-0288
1810 OVERTURE. 1972. 4-6/yr. free. Northwestern
University, Music Library, Evanston, IL 60201. Ed.
Patricia Felch Monokoski. bk. rev. bibl. circ. 300.

MUSIC — Abstracting, Bibliographies, Statistics

016 780   NE   ISSN 0084-7844
BIBLIOGRAPHIA MUSICOLOGICA; a bibliography of musical literature. (Text in various languages) 1970. a. fl.225($110) Joachimsthal Publishers, Box 2238, 3500 GE Utrecht, Netherlands. Ed. A.M. Joachimsthal. (back issues avail.)

016.78   US   ISSN 0360-2753
BIBLIOGRAPHIC GUIDE TO MUSIC. (Text in English and French) a. $60. G. K. Hall and Co., 70 Lincoln St., Boston, MA 02111.
    Formerly: Music Book Guide (ISSN 0360-1943)

780 016   US
BIBLIOGRAPHIES IN AMERICAN MUSIC. 1974. irreg. price varies. (College Music Society) Information Coordinators Inc., 1435-37 Randolph St., Detroit, MI 48226.

015 789.91   BU
BULGARSKI GRAMOFONNI PLOCHI. 1974. a. 0.30 lv. Narodna Biblioteka Kiril i Metodii, 11, Tolbukhin Blvd., Sofia, Bulgaria. bibl. circ. 350.

010 780   CN   ISSN 0381-9507
CANADIAN L P & TAPE CATALOGUE. 1975. irreg. Can.$3.50. M. J. Mac Arthur Wrightman, Ed. & Pub., 33 Seguin St., Ottawa, Ont., Canada (U.S. Address: 930 Mary St., Ann Arbor, MI 48104) circ. 1,000.

780 016   US   ISSN 0070-3885
DETROIT STUDIES IN MUSIC BIBLIOGRAPHY. 1961. irreg., no. 40, 1979. price varies. Information Coordinators, Inc., 1435-37 Randolph St., Detroit, MI 48226. Ed. Bruno Nettl.

780 016   GE   ISSN 0075-2959
JAHRESVERZEICHNIS DER MUSIKALIEN UND MUSIKSCHRIFTEN; Veroeffentlichungen der DDR. der BRD und Westberlins sowie deutschsprachige Werke anderer Laender. (In 2 Vols: Teil 1 Alphabetischer Teil; Teil 2 Systematischer Teil und Registerteil) a. M.128 for both vols. VEB Friedrich Hofmeister Musikverlag, Karlstr. 10, 701 Leipzig, E. Germany (D.D.R.)
    Formerly: Jahresverzeichnis der Musikalien und Musikschriften.

780 016   JA
JAPAN FEDERATION OF COMPOSERS. CATALOGUE OF PUBLICATIONS. (Text in Japanese & English) 1970. a. free. Japan Federation of Composers, Shinanomachi Bldg., 602 33-Shinanomachi, Shinjuku-ku, Tokyo 160, Japan. Ed.Bd.

780 371.3 016   CN
KODALY INSTITUTE OF CANADA. MONOGRAPH; a selected bibliography of the Kodaly concept of music education. vol. 2, 1979. irreg. Can.$8.50. Avondale Press, Box 451, Willowdale, Ont. M2N 5T1, Canada. Ed.Bd.

MEDIA REVIEW DIGEST; the only complete guide to reviews of non-book media. see MOTION PICTURES — Abstracting, Bibliographies, Statistics

MUSIC & MUSICIANS: BRAILLE SCORES CATALOG - CHORAL. see BLIND — Abstracting, Bibliographies, Statistics

MUSIC & MUSICIANS: BRAILLE SCORES CATALOG - ORGAN. see BLIND — Abstracting, Bibliographies, Statistics

MUSIC & MUSICIANS: BRAILLE SCORES CATALOG - PIANO. see BLIND — Abstracting, Bibliographies, Statistics

MUSIC & MUSICIANS: BRAILLE SCORES CATALOG - VOICE. see BLIND — Abstracting, Bibliographies, Statistics

MUSIC & MUSICIANS: INSTRUCTIONAL CASSETTE RECORDINGS CATALOG. see BLIND — Abstracting, Bibliographies, Statistics

MUSIC & MUSICIANS: INSTRUCTIONAL DISC RECORDINGS CATALOG. see BLIND — Abstracting, Bibliographies, Statistics

MUSIC & MUSICIANS: LARGE-PRINT SCORES AND BOOKS CATALOG. see BLIND — Abstracting, Bibliographies, Statistics

780   US
MUSIC-IN-PRINT ANNUAL SUPPLEMENT. 1979. a. $40. Musicdata, Inc., 18 W. Chelten Ave., Philadelphia, PA 19144.

780 016   US   ISSN 0077-2429
MUSIC INDEXES AND BIBLIOGRAPHIES. 1970. irreg., no. 11, 1974. price varies. (European American Music Corporation) Universal Edition Sales, Inc., 195 Allwood Rd., Clifton, NJ 07012. Ed. Carolyn H. Hunter. Indexed: RILM.

780 029.5   US   ISSN 0094-6478
MUSIC LIBRARY ASSOCIATION. INDEX AND BIBLIOGRAPHY SERIES. 1964. irreg. price varies. Music Library Association, 2017 Walnut St., Philadelphia, PA 19103. circ. 250.
    Formerly: Music Library Association. Index Series (ISSN 0077-2445)
    Analytical indexes to various serial publications of music and bibliographies of musical material

016 780.7 371.9   US
MUSIC THERAPY INDEX. 1976. irreg. $19.95 per no. to individuals; institutions $29.95. National Association for Music Therapy, Inc., Box 610, Lawrence, KS 66044. Ed. Charles T. Eagle.

780 016   DK   ISSN 0085-3623
MUSIKALIER I DANSKE BIBLIOTEKER/MUSIC IN DANISH LIBRARIES; accesionskatalog/union catalogue. (Text in Danish and English) 1970. a. price varies. Kongelige Bibliotek, Christians Brygge 8, DK-1219 Copenhagen K, Denmark. Ed. Inge Henriksen.

016   DK
ODENSE UNIVERSITET. UNIVERSITETSBIBLIOTEK. MUSIKLITTERATUR OG MUSIKALIER. NYANSKAFFELSER. 1972. irreg. (2-4/yr.) free. ‡ Odense Universitet, Universitetsbibliotek, Campusvej 55, 5230 Odense M, Denmark.

780 016   JA
ONGAKU BUNKEN YOSHI MOKUROKU. (Text in Japanese, English, French, German) 1973. a. 500 Yen. (Japanese Committee of RILM) Academia Music Co., Ltd., 3-16-5 Hongo, Bunkyo-ku, Tokyo 113, Japan. (Affiliate: International Repertory of Music Literature) bk. rev.
    Formerly: Nihon Ongaku Bunken Yoshi Mokuroku.

780 016   US   ISSN 0582-1487
SCHWANN ARTIST CATALOG. triennial. price varies. A B C Schwann Publications, Inc., 137 Newbury Rd., Boston, MA 02116. Ed. Donna Hieken. circ. 50,000.

780 016   US
U C L A MUSIC LIBRARY BIBLIOGRAPHY SERIES. 1977. irreg. free. University of California, Los Angeles, Music Library, Schoenberg Hall, Los Angeles, CA 90024. Ed. Stephen M. Fry. circ. 300. (back issues avail.)

NEEDLEWORK

see Hobbies — Needlework

NUCLEAR ENERGY

see Physics — Nuclear Energy

NUMISMATICS

see Hobbies — Numismatics

NURSES AND NURSING

see Medical Sciences — Nurses and Nursing

NUTRITION AND DIETETICS

613.2   US   ISSN 0149-9483
ADVANCES IN NUTRITIONAL RESEARCH. 1977. a. Plenum Publishing Corp., 233 Spring St., New York, NY 10013. Ed. Harold H. Draper.

641.1   US
AMERICAN DIETETIC ASSOCIATION. ANNUAL REPORT AND PROCEEDINGS. a. price varies. American Dietetic Association, 430 N. Michigan Ave., Chicago, IL 60611.

613.2   US   ISSN 0199-9885
ANNUAL REVIEW OF NUTRITION. 1981. a. Annual Reviews, Inc., 4139 El Camino Way, Palo Alto, CA 94306.

613.2   BL   ISSN 0084-6775
ARQUIVOS BRASILEIROS DE NUTRICAO. (Text in Portuguese; summaries in English) 1947. irreg. Instituto de Nutricao, Largo da Misericordia, 24, Rio de Janeiro, Brazil.

641.1   SZ   ISSN 0067-8198
BIBLIOTHECA NUTRITIO ET DIETA. (Text in English, German, and French) 1960. irreg. (approx. 1/yr.) 95 Fr.($60) per vol. (1981 price) S. Karger AG, Allschwilerstrasse 10, P.O. Box, CH-4009 Basel, Switzerland. Ed.Bd. (reprint service avail. from ISI) Indexed: Biol.Abstr. Chem.Abstr. Curr.Cont. Ind.Med.

664   GW   ISSN 0340-2002
C.I.I.A. SYMPOSIA. (Commission Internationale des Industries Agricole et Alimentaires) (Text in English, French, German) 1974. irreg. price varies. Dr. Dietrich Steinkopff Verlag, Saalbaustr. 12, Postfach 11 1008, 6100 Darmstadt 11, W. Germany (B.R.D.) Ed. R. Ammon.

612.3   UK   ISSN 0069-6943
COMMONWEALTH BUREAU OF NUTRITION. TECHNICAL COMMUNICATIONS. 1939, no. 11. irreg. price varies. Commonwealth Agricultural Bureaux, Farnham House, Farnham Royal, Slough SL2 3BN, England.

641.1   US   ISSN 0090-0443
CURRENT CONCEPTS IN NUTRITION. 1972. irreg., vol. 8, 1980. price varies. John Wiley & Sons, Inc., 605 Third Ave., New York, NY 10016. Ed. M. Winick. Indexed: Ind.Med.

616.39   US
CURRENT TOPICS IN NUTRITION AND DISEASE. 1977. irreg. price varies. Alan R. Liss, Inc., 150 Fifth Ave., New York, NY 10011. bibl. illus. index.

641.1 612   GW   ISSN 0067-4982
CURRENT TOPICS IN NUTRITIONAL SCIENCES/BEITRAEGE ZUR ERNAEHRUNGSWISSENSCHAFT. (Text in English and German) 1957. irreg., vol. 7, 1979. price varies. Dr. Dietrich Steinkopff Verlag, Saalbaustr. 12, Postfach 11 1008, 6100 Darmstadt 11, W. Germany (B.R.D.) Ed. Dr. Konrad Lang. index. circ. 2,000.

641.1   US
EAT WELL-LIVE WELL. irreg. University of Alaska, Cooperative Extension Service, Fairbanks, AK 99701.

613.2   FR
ECOLE NATIONALE SUPERIEURE DE BIOLOGIE APPLIQUEE A LA NUTRITION ET A L'ALIMENTATION. CAHIERS. Cover title: E N S B A N A Cahiers. 1966. 2/yr. 100 F. ‡ Ecole Nationale Superieure de Biologie Appliquee a la Nutrition et a l'Alimentation, Association des Amis, Eleves et Anciens Eleves, Bd. Gabriel 21, Dijon, France. adv. bibl. charts, illus. circ. 3,000.
    Former titles: Amis de l'E.N.S.B.A.N.A & Amis de l'I.B.A.N.A.(Publication) (ISSN 0003-1801)

613.2   UN   ISSN 0071-707X
F A O NUTRITION MEETINGS REPORT SERIES. 1951. irreg., 1970, no. 46. Food and Agriculture Organization of the United Nations, Distribution and Sales Section, Via delle Terme di Caracalla, 00100 Rome, Italy (Dist. in U.S. by: Unipub, 345 Park Ave. S., New York, NY 10010) Indexed: Ind.Med.

613.2   UN   ISSN 0071-7088
F A O NUTRITIONAL STUDY. (Text in English, French and Spanish) irreg., 1970, no. 24. price varies. Food and Agriculture Organization of the United Nations, Distribution and Sales Section, Via delle Terme di Caracalla, 00100 Rome, Italy (Dist. in U.S. by: Unipub, 345 Park Ave. S., New York, NY 10010) Indexed: Ind.Med.

FINLAND. KANSANELAKELAITOS. JULKAISUJA. SARJA EL. see *MEDICAL SCIENCES*

FINLAND. KANSANELAKELAITOS. JULKAISUJA. SARJA ML. see *MEDICAL SCIENCES*

640   FR   ISSN 0071-8297
FRANCE. CENTRE NATIONAL DE COORDINATION DES ETUDES ET RECHERCHES SUR LA NUTRITION ET L'ALIMENTATION. CAHIERS TECHNIQUES. 1958. irreg., 1972, no. 16. price varies. Centre National de la Recherche Scientifique, 15 Quai Anatole-France, 75700 Paris, France.

641   UN   ISSN 0533-4179
INSTITUTO DE NUTRICION DE CENTRO AMERICA Y PANAMA. INFORME ANUAL. 1950. a. exchange basis. United Nations, Institute of Nutrition of Central America and Panama - Instituto de Nutricion de Centro America y Panama, Carretera Roosevelt, Zona 11, Aptdo Postal 11-88, Guatemala City, Guatemala. circ. 450.

INSTITUTO DE TECNOLOGIA DE ALIMENTOS. COLETANEA. see *FOOD AND FOOD INDUSTRIES*

641   BL   ISSN 0074-0144
INSTITUTO DE TECNOLOGIA DE ALIMENTOS. INSTRUCOES PRATICAS. 1968. irreg.; no. 4, 1974. Cr.$20. ‡ Instituto de Tecnologia de Alimentos, C.P. 139, Campinas, S.P., Brazil. Ed. Julio Cesar Medina.

641   BL   ISSN 0074-0152
INSTITUTO DE TECNOLOGIA DE ALIMENTOS. INSTRUCOES TECNICAS. 1968. irreg. Cr.$20. ‡ Instituto de Tecnologia de Alimentos, C.P. 139, Campinas, S.P., Brazil.

631.26   UK
INTERNATIONAL VEGETARIAN HEALTH FOOD HANDBOOK. 1974. biennial. £1.75. Vegetarian Society, c/o Bronwen Humphreys, Ed., Parkdale, Dunham Rd., Altrincham, Cheshire WA14 4QG, England. cum.index. circ. 20,000.
Former titles: Vegetarian Health Food Handbook; Vegetarian Handbook (ISSN 0083-5315); Food Reformers' Yearbook.
Vegetarianism

613.2   UN   ISSN 0075-3971
JOINT F A O/W H O EXPERT COMMITTEE ON NUTRITION. REPORT. (Issued in F A O Nutrition Meetings Report Series) irreg., 1966, 7th Report (pub. 1967) Food and Agriculture Organization of the United Nations, Distribution and Sales Section, Via delle Terme di Caracalla, 00100 Rome, Italy (Dist. in U.S. by: Unipub, 345 Park Ave. S., New York, NY 10010)

574.13   JA
NATIONAL INSTITUTE OF NUTRITION. ANNUAL REPORT/KOKURITSU EIYO KENKYUSHO HOKOKU. (Text in Japanese) 1949. a. exchange basis. National Institute of Nutrition - Kosei-sho Kokuritsu Eiyo Kenkyusho, 1 Toyama-cho, Shinjuku-ku, Tokyo 162, Japan.

641.1   II
NATIONAL INSTITUTE OF NUTRITION. REPORT. (Text in English) a. free. National Institute of Nutrition, c/o Indian Council of Medical Research, Jamia-Osmania, Hyderabad-500 007, India.
Continues: Nutrition Research Laboratories. Annual Report.

641.1   NO
NORWAY. FISKERIDIREKTORATET. SKRIFTER. SERIE ERNAERING. (Text in English and Norwegian) 1976. irreg. price varies. Fiskeridirektoratet - Directorate of Fisheries, Box 185, 5001 Bergen, Norway. Ed. Georg Lambertsen. Indexed: Chem.Abstr. Nutr.Abstr.

613.2   CN   ISSN 0078-236X
NOVA SCOTIA. DEPARTMENT OF PUBLIC HEALTH. NUTRITION DIVISION. ANNUAL REPORT. a. free to qualifield personnel. Department of Public Health, Halifax, N.S., Canada. Ed. Jessie Rae.

618   US
NUTRITION AND THE BRAIN. 1975. irreg., vol. 5, 1979. price varies. Raven Press, 1140 Ave. of the Americas, New York, NY 10036. Eds. Richard J. and Judith J. Wurtman. Indexed: Curr.Cont. Sci.Cit.Ind.

613.2   US   ISSN 0160-2470
NUTRITION IN HEALTH AND DISEASE. 1978. irreg., vol. 2, 1980. Raven Press, 1140 Ave. of the Americas, New York, NY 10036.

NUTRITION NEWS IN ZAMBIA. see *FOOD AND FOOD INDUSTRIES*

641   JM
NYAM NEWS. irreg. free. Caribbean Food and Nutrition Institute, Jamaica Centre, Box 140, Mona, Kingston 7, Jamaica.

641.1   PH
PHILIPPINES. FOOD AND NUTRITION RESEARCH INSTITUTE. ANNUAL REPORT. 1950. a. free. Food and Nutrition Research Institute, 727 Pedro Gil St., Box 774, Ermita, Manila, Philippines. circ. controlled.
Formerly: Philippines. Food and Nutrition Center. Annual Report (ISSN 0071-7142)

PROBLEMES ACTUELS D'ENDOCRINOLOGIE ET DE NUTRITION. see *MEDICAL SCIENCES — Endocrinology*

616   US
PROGRESS IN HUMAN NUTRITION. 1971. irreg., vol. 2, 1978. $23.50. AVI Publishing Company, 250 Post Rd. East, Box 831, Westport, CT 06881.

613.2   US
SOURCEBOOK ON FOOD AND NUTRITION. 2nd ed., 1980. irreg. $39.50. Marquis Academic Media (Subsidiary of: Marquis Who's Who, Inc.) 200 E. Ohio St., Chicago, IL 60611.

641   SW   ISSN 0082-0415
SWEDISH NUTRITION FOUNDATION. SYMPOSIA. (Text in English) 1962. a. price varies. Almqvist & Wiksell International, Box 62, S-101 20 Stockholm, Sweden. Ed. Gunnar Blix, M.D.

613.2   US
WESTERN HEMISPHERE NUTRITION CONGRESS. PROCEEDINGS. 1965. triennial. $15. American Medical Association, Department of Foods & Nutrition, 535 N. Dearborn St., Chicago, IL 60610. (Co-sponsors: American Institute of Nutrition; Nutrition Society of Canada: Sociedad Latinoamericano de Nutricion; American Society for Clinical Nutrition) Eds. P. L. White, N. Selvey. circ. 1,200.

613.2   US
WOMAN'S DAY 101 WAYS TO LOSE WEIGHT AND STAY HEALTHY. 1973. a. Fawcett Publications, Inc. (Subsidiary of: C B S Publications) 1515 Broadway, New York, NY 10036. Ed. Ellene Saunders. adv. illus.

641.1   SZ   ISSN 0084-2230
WORLD REVIEW OF NUTRITION AND DIETETICS. (Text in English) 1964. irreg. (approx. 1/yr.) 160 Fr.($96) per vol. (1981 price) S. Karger AG, Allschwilerstrasse 10, P.O. Box, CH-4009 Basel, Switzerland. Ed. G. H. Bourne. (reprint service avail. from ISI) Indexed: Biol.Abstr. Chem.Abstr. Curr.Cont. Ind.Med.

ZAMBIA. NATIONAL FOOD AND NUTRITION COMMISSION. ANNUAL REPORT. see *FOOD AND FOOD INDUSTRIES*

641   GW   ISSN 0084-5337
ZEITSCHRIFT FUER ERNAEHRUNGSWISSENSCHAFT. SUPPLEMENTA. (Text in English, French and German) 1961. irreg., no. 22, 1979. price varies. Dr. Dietrich Steinkopff Verlag, Saalbaustr. 12, Postfach 11 1008, 6100 Darmstadt 11, W. Germany (B.R.D.) Ed. Konrad Lang. index. circ. 2,000.

NUTRITION AND DIETETICS — Abstracting, Bibliographies, Statistics

612.3 016   UK   ISSN 0069-6935
COMMONWEALTH BUREAU OF NUTRITION. ANNOTATED BIBLIOGRAPHIES. 1967, no. 2. irreg. price varies. (Commonwealth Bureau of Nutrition) Commonwealth Agricultural Bureaux, Farnham House, Farnham Royal, Slough SL2 3BN, England. bk. rev. Indexed: Nutr.Abstr.

OBSTETRICS AND GYNECOLOGY

see *Medical Sciences—Obstetrics and Gynecology*

OCCUPATIONS AND CAREERS

see also *Business and Economics—Labor and Industrial Relations*

331.7   US   ISSN 0361-5057
ABBOTT, LANGER & ASSOCIATES. COLLEGE RECRUITING REPORT. 1972. a. $40. Abbott, Langer & Associates, Box 275, Park Forest, IL 60466. Ed. Steven Langer. circ. 500. Key Title: College Recruiting Report.

371.42 387.7   US   ISSN 0065-4914
AIRLINE GUIDE TO STEWARDESS & STEWARDS CAREER. 1968. a. $4.95. International Publishing Co. of America, 665 La Villa Dr., Miami Springs, FL 33166 (Distributed by: Arco Publishing Co., 219 Park Ave. South, New York, N.Y. 10003) Ed. Marjorie R. Tingley. circ. 2,000,0000.
Formerly: Annual Guide to Stewardess Career.

378.3   GW   ISSN 0568-7276
DER AKADEMIKER IN WIRTSCHAFT UND VERWALTUNG; Wegweiser fuer den Fuehrungsnachwuchs aus Universitaeten, Hochschulen und Fachhochschulen in Industrie, Handel und Behoerden. 1962. a. free. Ingeborg Wallenwein, Ed. & Pub., Frankfurter Landstr. 6a, 6370 Oberursel, W. Germany (B.R.D.) circ. 35,000.

371.4   US   ISSN 0065-9622
AMERICAN PERSONNEL AND GUIDANCE ASSOCIATION. CONVENTION ABSTRACTS. 1968. a. $5.50. ‡ American Personnel and Guidance Association, Two Skyline Pl., Ste. 400, 5203 Leesburg Pike, Falls Church, VA 22041. circ. controlled. (reprint service avail. from UMI)

371.42   AT
AUSTRALIAN CAREERS GUIDE; for school leavers, parents and careers advisers. a. David Boyce Publishing & Associates, 44 Regent St., Redfern, N.S.W. 2016, Australia. adv. circ. 10,000.

371.42   US
CALIFORNIA PERSONNEL & GUIDANCE ASSOCIATION. MONOGRAPHS. 1960. irreg., no. 11, 1977. price varies. California Personnel & Guidance Association, 654 E. Commonwealth Ave., Fullerton, CA 92631.

371.42   UK
CAREERS AND VOCATIONAL TRAINING. irreg. £4.95. Arlington Books (Publishers) Ltd., 3 Clifford St., Mayfair, London W1X 1RA, England. Ed. Margaret Grainger. adv. index. circ. 5,000.

OCCUPATIONS AND CAREERS

371.42   CN   ISSN 0318-6229
CAREERS FOR GRADUATES/CARRIERES POUR DIPLOMES. (Text in English and French) 1973. a. free to Canadian University graduates; others Can. $2. Development Publications Ltd., Box 84, Sta. A., Willowdale, Ont. M2N 5S7, Canada.

371.42   UK   ISSN 0069-0422
CAREERS FOR SCHOOL LEAVERS. 1970. a. £13. VNU Business Publications BV, 53-55 Frith St., London W1A 2HG, England. Ed. Iris Rosier.
     Formerly: Directory of Opportunities for School Leavers.

371.42   US   ISSN 0069-0449
CAREERS IN DEPTH. 1960. irreg. $4.98. Richards Rosen Press, 29 E. 21 St., New York, NY 10010. Ed. Ruth C. Rosen.

371.42   II
CAREERS INFORMATION SERIES. irreg. price varies. Central Institute for Research and Training in Employment Service, New Delhi, India (Order from: Controller, Department of Publications, Civil Lines, Delhi 110054, India)

371.42   331.1   US   ISSN 0190-4663
CHRONICLE CAREER INDEX ANNUAL. a. $10.50. Chronicle Guidance Publications, Inc., Aurora St., Moravia, NY 13118.
     Formerly: Career Index (ISSN 0576-7296)

331.7   US   ISSN 0069-5734
COLLEGE PLACEMENT ANNUAL. 1957. a. $3 members; $5 non-members. College Placement Council, Inc., Box 2263, Bethlehem, PA 18001. Ed. Joan M. Bowser. adv. illus. circ. 400,000.

331   US
COLLEGIATE SUMMER EMPLOYMENT GUIDE. a. American Collegiate Employment Institute, Summer Employment Division, 3223 Ernst St., Franklin Park, IL 60131.

920   CK
DIRECTORIO NACIONAL DE PROFESIONALES. irreg. E C O C Ltda., Calle 17 no. 5-43, Apdo. Aereo 30969, Bogota, Colombia. illus.

371.42   US
DIRECTORY OF CAREER PLANNING AND PLACEMENT OFFICES. 1960. a. $10 to non-members; $8 to members. College Placement Council, Inc., Box 2263, Bethlehem, PA 18001. Ed. M. Virginia Pee. circ. 6,500.
     Formerly (until 1977): Directory of College Placement Offices (ISSN 0070-5284)

371.42   US   ISSN 0272-2135
DIRECTORY OF COLLEGE RECRUITING PERSONNEL. 1979. a. $10 to non-members, $8 to members. College Placement Council, Inc., Box 2263, Bethlehem, PA 18001. Ed. Joan M. Bowser. circ. 4,500.

DIRECTORY OF COURSES. TOURISM-HOSPITALITY-RECREATION. see EDUCATION — Higher Education

371.42   UK   ISSN 0070-6019
DIRECTORY OF OPPORTUNITIES FOR GRADUATES. 1957. a. £13. VNU Business Publications BV, 53-55 Frith St., London W1A 2HG, England. Ed. Iris Rosier.

331.1   UK   ISSN 0070-6051
DIRECTORY OF OVERSEAS SUMMER JOBS. 1969. a. $6.95. Vacation-Work, 9 Park End St., Oxford, England (Dist. in U.S. by: Writer's Digest Books, 9933 Alliance Rd., Cincinnati, OH 45242) Ed. Charles James.

371.42   US
DIRECTORY OF PUBLIC SERVICE INTERNSHIPS; opportunities for the graduate, post graduate and mid-career professional. biennial. $7. National Center for Public Service Internship Programs, 1735 Eye St., N.W., Suite 601, Washington, DC 20006.

DIRECTORY OF SPECIAL PROGRAMS FOR MINORITY GROUP MEMBERS; CAREER INFORMATION SERVICES, EMPLOYMENT SKILLS, BANKS, FINANCIAL AID SOURCES. see EDUCATION — Guides To Schools And Colleges

371.4   UK
DIRECTORY OF SUMMER JOBS IN BRITAIN. 1970. a. $5.95. Vacation-Work, 9 Park End St., Oxford, England (Dist. in U.S. by: Writer's Digest Books, 9933 Alliance Rd., Cincinnati, OH 45242) Ed. David Stevens.

371.4   600   UK   ISSN 0309-5290
DIRECTORY OF TECHNICAL AND FURTHER EDUCATION. 1956. biennial. George Godwin Ltd., 1-3 Pemberton Row, Fleet St., London EC4P 4HL, England. index.
     Former titles: Yearbook of Technical and Further Education; Yearbook of Technical Education and Training for Industry (ISSN 0084-4020)

EDUCATION & CAREERS IN SOUTH AFRICA. see EDUCATION

371.2   US
EMERITI FOR EMPLOYMENT. 1956. a. ‡ National Committee on the Emeriti Inc., Box 24451, Los Angeles, CA 90024. Ed. Albert Gordon. circ. controlled.

331.7   CN   ISSN 0381-3711
EMPLOYERS OF NEW COMMUNITY COLLEGE GRADUATES: DIRECTORY. (Text in English and French) 1971. a. Can.$5. Department of Manpower and Immigration, Economic Analysis and Forecasts Branch, Ottawa, Ont. K1A 0J9, Canada. illus.

331.7   370.7   CN   ISSN 0381-372X
EMPLOYERS OF NEW UNIVERSITY GRADUATES: DIRECTORY. French edition: Annuaire des Employeurs des Nouveaux Diplomes de College. (Text in English and French) 1971. a. Can.$5. Department of Manpower and Immigration, Economic Analysis and Forecasts Branch, Ottawa, Ont. K1A 0J9, Canada. illus.
     Formerly: Directory of Employers Offering Employment to New University Graduates (ISSN 0381-3738)

371.42   UK   ISSN 0071-0148
EMPLOYMENT OPPORTUNITIES FOR ADVANCED POST-GRADUATE SCIENTISTS AND ENGINEERS. 1966. a. £1. Classic Publications Ltd., Recorder House, Church St., London, N12, England.

371.42   US
FEDERAL EMPLOYMENT DIRECTORY. 1978. a. $12.50. Kent-Harbridge, Inc., Box 477, Fairfax, VA 22030. Ed. Robert M. Dias. circ. 6,000.

371.42   US   ISSN 0434-8850
GUIDE TO EMPLOYMENT ABROAD. 1958. a. $3. ‡ Hill International Publications, P.O. Box 79, East Islip, NY 11730.

371.42   IS   ISSN 0072-9248
HADASSAH VOCATIONAL GUIDANCE INSTITUTE. REPORT. (Editions in English & Hebrew) 1948. a. free. ‡ Hadassah Vocational Guidance Institute, P.O. Box 1406, Jerusalem, Israel. (Co-sponsor: Hadassah Women Zionist Organization of America) Ed. Z. Sardi. circ. 400 (English edt.) 800 (Hebrew edt.)

371.42   658.2   HK
HONG KONG TRAINING COUNCIL. REPORT. (Text in English and Chinese) a. (Hong Kong Training Council) Government Publications Centre, Connaught Place, Hong Kong, Hong Kong. Ed. Bd.

371.42   US
JOB CATALOG; where to find that creative job in Washington, DC. 1979. a. $6. Mail Order USA, Box 19083, Washington, DC 20036. Ed. Dorothy O'Callaghan. circ. 2,000.

371.42   US
LOOKING FOR EMPLOYMENT IN FOREIGN COUNTRIES REFERENCE HANDBOOK. 1968. biennial. $50. World Trade Academy Press, Inc., 50 East 42nd St., New York, NY 10017. Ed. J. L. Angel. circ. 10,000.

331   US
MASSACHUSETTS. DIVISION OF EMPLOYMENT SECURITY. SURVEY OF UNFILLED JOB OPENINGS - BOSTON. a. free. Division of Employment Security, Government Center, Boston, MA 02114. charts. stat.
     Formerly: Massachusetts. Division of Employment Security. Quarterly Survey of Unfilled Job Openings - Boston (ISSN 0580-7727)

371.42   UK   ISSN 0066-3972
N U T GUIDE TO CAREERS WORK. 1957. a. 75p. (National Union of Teachers) Teacher Publishing Co. Ltd., Derbyshire House, Lower Street, Kettering, Northants, NN16 8BB, England. Ed. Sheila Hart. adv. circ. 70,000.
     Formerly: Annual Guide to Careers for Young People.

NATIONAL EMPLOYMENT LISTING SERVICE FOR THE CRIMINAL JUSTICE SYSTEM. FEDERAL EMPLOYMENT INFORMATION DIRECTORY. see CRIMINOLOGY AND LAW ENFORCEMENT

NATIONAL EMPLOYMENT LISTING SERVICE FOR THE CRIMINAL JUSTICE SYSTEM. POLICE EMPLOYMENT GUIDE. see CRIMINOLOGY AND LAW ENFORCEMENT

NATIONAL EMPLOYMENT LISTING SERVICE FOR THE CRIMINAL JUSTICE SYSTEM. SPECIAL EDITION: EDUCATION OPPORTUNITIES. see CRIMINOLOGY AND LAW ENFORCEMENT

371.42   NE
NETHERLANDS. RAAD VOOR DE BEROEPSKEUZEVOORLICHTING. VERSLAG VAN DE WERKZAAMHEDEN. 1965. a. free. Raad voor de Beroepskeuzevoorlichting, Volmerlaan 1, Rijswijk, Netherlands.

371.42   NN
NEW HEBRIDES. BUREAU OF STATISTICS. MANPOWER AND EMPLOYMENT SURVEY. FINAL RESULTS/ENQUETE SUR L'EMPLOI ET LA MAIN D'OEUVRE. DEFINITIFS. (Text in English, French) 1973 ed., 1978. irreg. free. Bureau of Statistics, Port Vila, New Hebrides. stat. circ. 500.

371.42   NN
NEW HEBRIDES. BUREAU OF STATISTICS. MANPOWER AND EMPLOYMENT SURVEY. PRELIMINARY RESULTS/ENQUETE SUR L'EMPLOI ET LA MAIN D'OEUVRE. (Text in English, French) 1973 ed., 1978. irreg. free. Bureau of Statistics, Port Vila, New Hebrides. stat. circ. 300.

331.1   US
OFFICIAL GUIDE TO AIRLINE CAREERS. 1977. a. $5.95. International Publishing Co. of America, 665 La Villa Dr., Miami Springs, FL 33166. Ed. Marjorie Tingley. adv. circ. 10,000.

371.42   SA
OPPORTUNITIES FOR GRADUATES IN SOUTHERN AFRICA. (Text in Afrikaans and English) 1964. a. R.3 (free to students) Management Development Publishers (Pty) Ltd., Box 10061, Johannesburg 2000, South Africa. Ed. M. A. Ogilvy. adv. index; cum.index. circ. 25,000.

331.11   FR   ISSN 0474-5892
ORGANIZATION FOR ECONOMIC COOPERATION AND DEVELOPMENT. SOCIAL AFFAIRS DIVISION. DEVELOPING JOB OPPORTUNITIES. 1965. irreg. Organization for Economic Cooperation and Development, 2 rue Andre Pascal, 75775 Paris 16, France (U. S. orders to: O.E.C.D. Publications and Information Center, 1750 Pennsylvania Ave., N. W., Washington, D. C. 20006) (also avail. in microfiche)

371.42   US
PROFESSIONAL WOMEN AND MINORITIES; a manpower data resource service. 1975. triennial plus annual supplements. $75 ($30 for annual supplement) Scientific Manpower Commission, 1776 Massachusetts Ave., N.W., Washington, DC 20036. Ed.Bd. bibl. charts. index. circ. 2,500. (looseleaf format; reprint service avail. from UMI)

RESOURCES FOR TOURISM/HOSPITALITY/RECREATION. see EDUCATION — Higher Education

331.1 US ISSN 0146-5015
SALARIES OF SCIENTISTS, ENGINEERS AND TECHNICIANS; a summary of salary surveys. 1965. biennial. $20. Scientific Manpower Commission, 1776 Massachusetts Avenue, N.W., Washington, DC 20036. Ed. Eleanor L. Babco. charts. illus. stat. circ. 2,500. (reprint service avail. from UMI)

331.1 US
SCIENCE, ENGINEERING, AND HUMANITIES DOCTORATES IN THE UNITED STATES: PROFILE. 1973. biennial. free. National Research Council, Commission on Human Resources, 2101 Constitution Ave., Washington, DC 20418. Ed. Betty D. Maxfield. charts. stat. tr.lit.
Formerly (until 1977): Doctoral Scientists and Engineers in the United States. Profile (ISSN 0095-0750)

371.42 UK ISSN 0080-8032
SCOTTISH GRADUATE.* 1959. a. (Scottish Union of Students) J.E.P. and Associates, Suite 23, 107-111 Fleet Street, London, EC4, England.

371.42 SA
SOUTH AFRICAN CAREERS GUIDE. a. R.2 to individuals; free to students. Management Development Publishers (Pty) Ltd., Glencairn, 6th Fl., 73 Market St., Box 10061, Johannesburg 2000, South Africa. Ed. M. A. Ogilvy. adv.

331.1 US ISSN 0081-9352
SUMMER EMPLOYMENT DIRECTORY OF THE UNITED STATES. 1952. a. $8.95 cloth; $6.95 paper. Writer's Digest Books, 9933 Alliance Rd., Cincinnati, OH 45242. Ed. Lynne Lapin. adv. bk. rev. circ. 25,000.
Lists names and addresses of employers and the summer and part-time jobs they have available to high school seniors, college students, and teachers

331.71 FR ISSN 0082-2442
TECHNIQUES ARTISANALES MODERNES.* 1970. irreg. price varies. Editions C. Massin et Cie, 2 rue de l'Echelle, 75001 Paris, France.

371.42 UK
TEMPORARY OCCUPATIONS AND EMPLOYMENT. biennial, 4th ed. 1976. 70p. Independent Schools Careers Organization, 12a-18a Princess Way, Camberely, Surrey GU15 3SP, England. Ed. Joan Hills.

U N I T A R NEWS. (United Nations Institute for Training and Research) see BUSINESS AND ECONOMICS — Labor And Industrial Relations

331.1 US
U.S. DEPARTMENT OF LABOR. EMPLOYMENT AND TRAINING ADMINISTRATION. GUIDE TO LOCAL OCCUPATIONAL INFORMATION. irreg., 5th edt., 1976. U.S. Employment and Training Administration, Washington, DC 20210.
Directory of selected State employment service publications

371.4 340 US
WASHINGTON WANT ADS; a guide to legal careers in the federal government. 1952. irreg., approx. biennial. $7.50 to non-members; members $5. ‡ American Bar Association, Law Student Division, 1155 E. 60th St., Chicago, IL 60637. Ed. David Martin. circ. 7,000.
Formerly: Federal Government Legal Career Opportunities (ISSN 0065-7476)

375 SW
YRKE OCH FRAMTID. 1972. a. (Yrksev Agledningsenheten) Liber Foerlag, Fack, 162 89 Vaellingby. illus.

354.689 ZA ISSN 0514-5457
ZAMBIA. EDUCATIONAL AND OCCUPATIONAL ASSESSMENT SERVICE. ANNUAL REPORT. a. 20 n. Government Printer, P.O. Box 2186, Lusaka, Zambia. stat.

OCCUPATIONS AND CAREERS — Abstracting, Bibliographies, Statistics

371.42 016 US ISSN 0195-4156
CAREERS (SARATOGA) 1979. a. $5. Vitality Associates, Box 154, Saratoga, CA 95070.

371.42 016 UY ISSN 0069-1046
CATALOGO DE PUBLICACIONES LATINOAMERICANAS SOBRE FORMACION PROFESIONAL. 1964. a. price varies. Centro Interamericano de Investigacion y Documentacion Sobre Formacion Profesional, Rio Negro 1241, Casilla de Correo 1761, Montevideo, Uruguay (Dist. in U.S. by International Labour Office, Washington Branch Office, 666 11th St., N.W., Washington, D.C. 20001) Indexed: CIRF Abstr.

371.42 US ISSN 0161-0562
CURRENT CAREER AND OCCUPATIONAL LITERATURE. biennial. H.W. Wilson Co., 950 University Ave., Bronx, NY 10452.

NETHERLANDS. CENTRAAL BUREAU VOOR DE STATISTIEK. STATISTIEK VAN DE VOORLICHTING BIJ SCHOLEN EN BEROEPSKEUZE. STATISTICS OF VOCATIONAL GUIDANCE. see EDUCATION — Abstracting, Bibliographies, Statistics

NETHERLANDS. CENTRAAL BUREAU VOOR DE STATISTIEK. STATISTIEK VAN HET BEROEPSONDERWIJS: AGRARISCH ONDERWIJS. see EDUCATION — Abstracting, Bibliographies, Statistics

NETHERLANDS. CENTRAAL BUREAU VOOR DE STATISTIEK. STATISTIEK VAN HET BEROEPSONDERWIJS: TECHNISCH EN NAUTISCH ONDERWIJS. STATISTICS ON VOCATIONAL TRAINING. see EDUCATION — Abstracting, Bibliographies, Statistics

331.1 016 US
SCIENCE & ENGINEERING CAREERS - A BIBLIOGRAPHY. 1964. irreg. $2. Scientific Manpower Commission, 1776 Massachusetts Avenue N.W., Washington, DC 20036. Ed. Eleanor L. Babco. bibl. circ. 3,000. (back issues avail.; reprint service avail. from UMI)
Formerly: Science, Engineering and Related Career Hints (SEARCH) - Bibliography of Career Information.

371.42 317 US
U.S. BUREAU OF LABOR STATISTICS. OCCUPATIONAL OUTLOOK HANDBOOK. 1946. biennial. price varies. U.S. Bureau of Labor Statistics, 441 G. St., N.W., Washington, DC 20212 (Orders to: Supt. of Documents, Washington, DC 20402)

OCEANOGRAPHY

see Earth Sciences—Oceanography

OFFICE EQUIPMENT AND SERVICES

see Business and Economics—Office Equipment and Services

OPHTHALMOLOGY AND OPTOMETRY

see Medical Sciences—Ophthalmology and Optometry

OPTICS

see Physics—Optics

ORGANIC CHEMISTRY

see Chemistry—Organic Chemistry

ORIENTAL RELIGIONS

see Religions and Theology—Oriental

ORIENTAL STUDIES

see also History—History of Asia; Linguistics

950 GW ISSN 0567-4980
ABHANDLUNGEN FUER DIE KUNDE DES MORGENLANDES. (Text in English, French, and German) irreg., vol. 46, no. 2, 1981. price varies. (Deutsche Morgenlaendische Gesellschaft) Franz Steiner Verlag GmbH, Friedrichstr. 24, Postfach 5529, 6200 Wiesbaden, W. Germany (B.R.D.) Ed.Ewald Wagner.

950 NE ISSN 0065-0382
ABR-NAHRAIN. 1959/60. a. price varies. (University of Melbourne, Department of Middle Eastern Studies, AT) E. J. Brill, Oude Rijn 33a-35, Leiden, Netherlands. Indexed: Old Test.Abstr.

950 NE ISSN 0065-0390
ABR-NAHRAIN. SUPPLEMENTS. 1964. irreg. price varies. (University of Melbourne, Department of Middle Eastern Studies, AT) E. J. Brill, Oude Rijn 33a-35, Leiden, Netherlands.

950 DK ISSN 0001-6438
ACTA ORIENTALIA. (Text in English, French or German) a. Kr.260. Munksgaard, 35 Noerre Soegade, DK-1370 Copenhagen K, Denmark. Ed. Soeren Egerod. bk. rev. circ. 500. (reprint service avail. from ISI) Indexed: Curr.Cont.

950 GW ISSN 0170-3196
AETHIOPISTISCHE FORSCHUNGEN. (Text in English and German) irreg., vol. 9, 1981. price varies. Franz Steiner Verlag GmbH, Friedrichstr. 24, Postfach 5529, 6200 Wiesbaden, W. Germany (B.R.D.) Ed.E. Hammerschmidt.

AFRO-ASIA. see HISTORY

950 GW ISSN 0568-4447
AKADEMIE DER WISSENSCHAFTEN UND DER LITERATUR, MAINZ. ORIENTALISCHE KOMMISSION. VEROEFFENTLICHUNGEN. (Text in French and German) irreg., vol. 33, 1981. price varies. Franz Steiner Verlag GmbH, Friedrichstr. 24, Postfach 5529, 6200 Wiesbaden, W. Germany (B.R.D.)

954 II
ALL-INDIA ORIENTAL CONFERENCE. SUMMARIES OF PAPERS. (Text in English, Hindi or Sanskrit) irreg., 27th 1974. Kurukshetra University, Kurukshettra, India. Ed. Gopikamohan Bhattacharya.

950 NE ISSN 0065-6593
ALTBABYLONISCHE BRIEFE IM UMSCHRIFT UND UEBERSETZUNG. 1964. irreg., vol. 9, 1981. price varies. E. J. Brill, Oude Rijn 33a-35, Leiden, Netherlands.

ALTORIENTALISCHE FORSCHUNGEN. see HISTORY — History Of The Near East

950 VC
ANALECTA ORIENTALIA. 1931. irreg; no. 50, 1975. price varies. (Pontificio Istituto Biblico) Biblical Institute Press, Piazza della Pilotta 35, 00187 Rome, Italy.

ANNUAIRE DE L'EGYPTOLOGIE. see ARCHAEOLOGY

ORIENTAL STUDIES

068.549 954   BG
ANNUAL GENERAL MEETING OF THE ASIATIC SOCIETY OF BANGLADESH; REPORT OF THE GENERAL SECRETARY. (Text in English) a. Asiatic Society of Bangladesh, Dacca Museum Bldgs., Ramna, Dacca 2, Bangladesh.

ARS ORIENTALIS; the arts of Islam and the East. see *ART*

950   IT
ARTE ORIENTALE IN ITALIA. (Subseries of Rome (City). Museo Nazionale d'Arte Orientale. Pubblicazione) 1971. irreg. L.700-1000. ‡ Museo Nazionale d'Arte Orientale, Via Merulana 248, Rome 00185, Italy. Ed. Giovanni Poncini. illus. circ. 1,000.

ARTIBUS ASIAE SUPPLEMENTA. see *ART*

ARTS ASIATIQUES. see *ART*

950 960 490 890   CS   ISSN 0571-2742
ASIAN AND AFRICAN STUDIES. (Text in English) 1965. irreg. price varies. (Slovenska Akademia Vied, Kabinet Orientalistiky) Veda, Publishing House of the Slovak Academy of Sciences, Klemensova 19, 895 30 Bratislava, Czechoslovakia. Ed. I. Dolezal. bk. rev. index.

950   JA
ASIAN CULTURAL CENTRE FOR UNESCO. ORGANIZATION AND ACTIVITIES. (Text in English) a. Asian Cultural Centre for Unesco - Yunesuko Ajia Bunka Senta, No.6 Fukuro-machi, Shinjuku-ku, Tokyo 162, Japan. illus.

ASIAN CULTURAL STUDIES. see *HISTORY — History Of Asia*

ASIAN STUDIES MONOGRAPHS SERIES. see *HISTORY — History Of Asia*

ASIAN STUDIES SERIES. see *HISTORY — History Of Asia*

ASIAN THEATRE REPORTS. see *THEATER*

950   II   ISSN 0004-4709
ASIATIC SOCIETY, BOMBAY. JOURNAL. N.S. 1925. a. price varies. Asiatic Society, Bombay, Town Hall, Bombay 1, India (Subscr. to: Arthur Probsthain, 41 Great Russell St., London, W.C. 1, England) Ed.Bd. bk. rev. llus. circ. 1,000.

950   II   ISSN 0571-3161
ASIATIC SOCIETY, CALCUTTA. JOURNAL. (Text in English) vol. 18, 1976. a. $9. Asiatic Society, Calcutta, 1 Park St., Calcutta 16, India. bk. rev. bibl. charts. illus.

950   II
ASIATIC SOCIETY, CALCUTTA. MONOGRAPH SERIES. irreg. price varies. Asiatic Society, Calcutta, 1 Park St., Calcutta 16, India.

950   II
ASIATIC SOCIETY, CALCUTTA. SEMINAR SERIES. irreg. Asiatic Society, Calcutta, 1 Park St., Calcutta 16, India.

950   SP   ISSN 0571-3692
ASOCIACION ESPANOLA DE ORIENTALISTAS. BOLETIN. (Text in European languages) 1965. a. 600 ptas.($14) (Asociacion Espanola de Orientalistas) F. M. Pareja, Ed. & Pub., Limite 5, Madrid 3, Spain. bk. rev. charts. illus. circ. 500. (back issues avail.)

ASSOCIATION FOR ASIAN STUDIES. MONOGRAPHS. see *HISTORY — History Of Asia*

952   AU   ISSN 0522-6759
BEITRAEGE ZUR JAPANOLOGIE. (Text in German & English; summaries in English & Japanese) 1955. irreg., vol. 16, 1979. price varies. Universitaet Wien, Institut fuer Japanologie, Universitaetsstr. 7/4, A-1010 Vienna, Austria. Eds. Alexander Slawik, Sepp Linhart. circ. 200.

950   VC
BIBLICA ET ORIENTALIA. no. 31, 1976. irreg. price varies. (Pontificio Istituto Biblico) Biblical Institute Press, Piazza della Pilotta 35, 00187 Rome, Italy.

BIBLIOTECA DEGLI STUDI CLASSICI E ORIENTALI. see *CLASSICAL STUDIES*

BIBLIOTHECA ISLAMICA. see *RELIGIONS AND THEOLOGY — Islamic*

950 490   HU   ISSN 0067-8104
BIBLIOTHECA ORIENTALIS HUNGARICA. (Text in English, French, German) 1955. irreg., vol. 24, 1979. price varies. (Magyar Tudomanyos Akademia) Akademiai Kiado, Publishing House of the Hungarian Academy of Sciences, P.O. Box 24, H-1363 Budapest, Hungary.

890   FR
BIBLIOTHEQUE IRANIENNE. (Text in Persian, Arabic or French) 1949. irreg., vol.. 22, 1975. (Institut Franco-Iranien, Departement d'Iranologie) Adrien Maisonneuve, 11 rue Saint-Sulpice, 75006 Paris, France. (Co-Sponsor: Institut d'Etudes Iraniennes de l'Universite de Paris)

954   II   ISSN 0001-902X
BRAHMAVIDYA. Variant title: Adyar Library Bulletin. (Text in English and Sanskrit; sometimes German and French) 1937. a. $6. Adyar Library and Research Centre, Adyar, Madras 600020, India. Ed.Bd. adv. bk. rev. cum. index (vols.1-41) circ. 300. (back issues avail)

950   UK
BRITISH ASSOCIATION OF ORIENTALISTS. BULLETIN. 1963. biennial. £2. British Association of Orientalists, c/o Dept. of Oriental Manuscripts, British Library, Great Russell St., London WC1, England. Ed. Dr. G. D. Gupta. bibl. circ. 350(controlled)

951   US   ISSN 0049-254X
BULLETIN OF SUNG AND YUAN STUDIES. (Text in Chinese and English) 1970. a. $5 to individuals; institutions $8. c/o Charles A. Peterson, Ed., Department of History, McGraw Hall, Cornell University, Ithaca, NY 14853. bk. rev. bibl. illus. circ. 300.
Formerly (until vol. 14, 1978): Sung Studies Newsletter.

950   II
CHAUKHAMBHA ORIENTAL RESEARCH STUDIES. 1976. irreg. price varies. Chaukhambha Orientalia, Gokul Bhawan, K 37/39 Gwaldas Shah Lane, Varanasi 221001, India.

CHINESE SCIENCE; an informal and irregular journal dedicated to the study of traditional Chinese science, technology, and medicine. see *SCIENCES: COMPREHENSIVE WORKS*

951   HK
CHINESE UNIVERSITY OF HONG KONG. INSTITUTE OF CHINESE STUDIES. JOURNAL. a. HK.$50($8.70) Chinese University of Hong Kong, Institute of Chinese Studies, 677 Nathan Road., 12th Floor, Kowtoon, Hong Kong. bibl. charts. illus.

950   AG
COLECCION ORIENTE-OCCIDENTE. 1976. irreg. price varies. Universidad del Salvador, Instituto Latinoamericano de Investigaciones Comparadas Oriente-Occidente, Collao 966, 1022 Buenos Aires, Argentina. Eds. F. Garcia Bazan, P. Matin. circ. 2,000.

951   FR
COLLEGE DE FRANCE. INSTITUT DES HAUTES ETUDES CHINOISES. MEMOIRS. 1975. irreg. Presses Universitaires de France, 108 Bd. Saint Germaine, 75279 Paris Cedex 6, France (Service des Periodiques, 12 rue Jean de Beauvais, 75005 Paris) illus.

950   US   ISSN 0010-2016
COLUMBIA UNIVERSITY. ANCIENT NEAR EASTERN SOCIETY. JOURNAL. Short title: A N E S. 1968. a. $10. Columbia University, Ancient Near Eastern Society, 602 Kent Hall, New York, NY 10027. Ed. Edward L. Greenstein. adv. illus. circ. 400. (also avail. in microfilm) Indexed: Old Test.Abstr.

950   US
COLUMBIA UNIVERSITY. EAST ASIAN INSTITUTE. STUDIES. 1962. irreg., latest 1980. price varies. Columbia University Press, 136 South Broadway, Irvington-on-Hudson, NY 10533.

959   US   ISSN 0589-7300
CORNELL UNIVERSITY. MODERN INDONESIA PROJECT. MONOGRAPHS. 1958. irreg., no. 58, 1978. price varies. Cornell University, Southeast Asia Program, Ithaca, NY 14853.

950   GW
DEUTSCHE GESELLSCHAFT FUER OSTASIENKUNDE. KOORDINIERUNGSSTELLE FUER GEGENWARTSBEZOGENE OST- UND SUEDOSTASIENFORSCHUNG. MITTEILUNGEN. 1966. irreg. (2-3 per year) DM.15 per year. Deutsche Gesellschaft fuer Ostasienkunde, Rothenbaumchaussee 32, 2000 Hamburg 13, W. Germany (B.R.D.) Ed. Bernhard Dahm. adv. bk. rev. circ. 900.
Formerly: Deutsche Gesellschaft fuer Ostasienkunde. Koordinierungstelle fuer Gegenwartsbezogene Ostasienforschung Mitteilungen (ISSN 0070-4105)

950   GW   ISSN 0341-0803
DEUTSCHE MORGENLAENDISCHE GESELLSCHAFT. ZEITSCHRIFT. SUPPLEMENTA. irreg., vol. 4, 1980. price varies. Franz Steiner Verlag GmbH, Friedrichstr. 24, Postfach 5529, 6200 Wiesbaden, W. Germany (B.R.D.)

954   II
DHANIRAM BHALLA GRANTHAMALA. (Text in Hindi and Sanskrit) irreg., vol. 19, 1972. price varies. Vishveshvaranand Vedic Research Institute, P.O. Sadhu Ashram, Hoshiarpur 146021, Punjab, India. Ed. Vishva Bandhu.

915   II
DIRECTORY OF INSTITUTIONS OF ORIENTAL STUDIES IN OVERSEAS COUNTRIES. (Text in English) 1974. irreg. $3. Lord International, 2/6 Canal Road, Vijay Nagar, Delhi 110009, India.

950 895 495   CS
DISSERTATIONES ORIENTALES. (Text in Chinese and English) vol. 35, 1975. irreg. price varies. (Ceskoslovenska Akademie Ved, Orientalni Ustav) Academia, Publishing House of the Czechoslovak Academy of Sciences, Vodickova 40, 112 29 Prague 1, Czechoslovakia. Ed. Jaroslav Cesar.

950   FR
DOCUMENTS D'HISTOIRE MAGHREBINE. irreg. Librairie Orientaliste Paul Geuthner, 12, rue Vavin, 75006 Paris, France. Ed. Ch. de la Veronne.

950   FR
ECOLE FRANCAISE D'EXTREME-ORIENT.BULLETIN. 1901. irreg., vol. 67, 1980. price varies. Librairie Adrien Maisonneuve, 11 rue St. Sulpice, 75006 Paris, France.

959   BE   ISSN 0531-1926
ETUDES ORIENTALES. 1963. irreg., no. 9, 1981. price varies. Librairie-Editions Thanh-Long, 34 rue Dekens, 1040 Brussels, Belgium. (back issues avail.)

950   AT   ISSN 0085-0586
FLINDERS ASIAN STUDIES LECTURE. 1970. a. free. ‡ Flinders University of South Australia, School of Social Sciences, Director of Asian Studies, Bedford Park, S. A. 5042, Australia. Ed. Dr. H. S. Leng.

950   PL   ISSN 0015-5675
FOLIA ORIENTALIA. (Text in English, French and German) 1959. a. 80 Zl. (Polska Akademia Nauk, Oddzial w Krakowie, Komisja Orientalistyczna) Ossolineum, Publishing House of the Polish Academy of Sciences, Rynek 9, Wroclaw, Poland. Ed. Tadeusz Lewicki. bk. rev. abstr. bibl. circ. 590.

956.1   GW   ISSN 0342-1082
FRANKFURTER TURKOLOGISCHE ARBEITSMITTEL. 1977. irreg., vol. 2, 1979. price varies. Verlag Otto Harrassowitz, Taunusstr. 6, Postfach 2929, 6200 Wiesbaden, W. Germany (B.R.D.) Ed. Horst Wilfrid Brands.

950   GW   ISSN 0170-3307
FREIBURGER ALTORIENTALISCHE STUDIEN. irreg., vol. 4, 1981. price varies. Franz Steiner Verlag GmbH, Friedrichstr. 24, Postfach 5529, 6200 Wiesbaden, W. Germany (B.R.D.) Ed.Burkhart Kienast.

956 297 GW ISSN 0170-3285
FREIBURGER ISLAMSTUDIEN. irreg., vol. 8, 1981. price varies. Franz Steiner Verlag GmbH, Friedrichstr. 24, Postfach 5529, 6200 Wiesbaden, W. Germany (B.R.D.) Ed. Hans Robert Roemer.

950 GW ISSN 0170-3455
GLASENAPP-STIFTUNG. irreg., vol. 22, 1981. price varies. (Glasenap-Stiftung) Franz Steiner Verlag GmbH, Friedrichstr. 24, Postfach 5529, 6200 Wiesbaden, W. Germany (B.R.D.)

950 GW ISSN 0171-4910
GOETTINGER ORIENTFORSCHUNGEN. REIHE: GRUNDLAGEN UND ERGEBNISSE. 1978. irreg. price varies. Verlag Otto Harrassowitz, Taunusstr.6, Postfach 2929, 6200 Wiesbaden, W. Germany (B.R.D.)

935 950 GW ISSN 0340-6326
GOETTINGER ORIENTFORSCHUNGEN. REIHE I: SYRIACA. irreg., vol. 19, 1979. price varies. Verlag Otto Harrassowitz, Taunusstr. 6, Postfach 2929, 6200 Wiesbaden, W. Germany (B.R.D.)

935 950 GW ISSN 0340-6334
GOETTINGER ORIENTFORSCHUNGEN. REIHE III: IRANICA. 1973. irreg., vol. 4, 1977. price varies. Verlag Otto Harrassowitz, Taunusstr. 6, Postfach 2929, 6200 Wiesbaden, W. Germany (B.R.D.)

932 GW ISSN 0340-6342
GOETTINGER ORIENTFORSCHUNGEN. REIHE IV: AEGYPTEN. 1973. irreg., vol. 10, 1979. price varies. Verlag Otto Harrassowitz, Taunusstr. 6, Postfach 2929, 6200 Wiesbaden, W. Germany (B.R.D.)

938 GW ISSN 0340-6350
GOETTINGER ORIENTFORSCHUNGEN. REIHE VI: HELLENISTICA. 1974. irreg., vol. 7, 1975. price varies. Verlag Otto Harrassowitz, Taunusstr. 6, Postfach 2929, 6200 Wiesbaden, W. Germany (B.R.D.)

GOVERNMENT ORIENTAL MANUSCRIPTS LIBRARY. BULLETIN. see *LIBRARY AND INFORMATION SCIENCES*

950 US ISSN 0073-0548
HARVARD JOURNAL OF ASIATIC STUDIES. 1936. s-a. from 1977, previously a. $15. Harvard-Yenching Institute, 2 Divinity Ave., Cambridge, MA 02138. Ed. Donald H. Shively. bk. rev. cum. index: 1936-57, also non-cum every 5 years. circ. 1,200. (also avail. in microform from BLH,MIM,UMI) Indexed: Bk.Rev.Index. Hum.Ind. Soc.Sci.Ind. Arts & Hum.Cit.Ind.

410 SZ ISSN 0073-0971
HAUTES ETUDES ORIENTALES. 1968. irreg. (Ecole Pratique des Hautes Etudes, Centre de Recherches d'Histoire et de Philologie, FR) Librarie Droz, 11, rue Massot, 1211 Geneva 12, Switzerland. circ. 1,000.

INDICES VERBORUM LINGUAE MONGOLIAE MONUMENTIS TRADITORUM. see *LINGUISTICS*

954 IT
INDOLOGICA TAURINENSIA. (Text in various languages) 1973. a. L.20000. (International Association of Sanscrit Studies) Herder Editrice e Libreria s.r.l., Piazza Montecitorio 120, 00186 Rome, Italy. Ed. Oscar Botto. (back issues avail.)

950 913 FR ISSN 0537-779X
INSTITUT FRANCAIS D'ARCHEOLOGIE D'ISTANBUL. BIBLIOTHEQUE ARCHEOLOGIQUE ET HISTORIQUE. 1959. irreg., vol. 28, 1980. Librairie Adrien Maisonneuve, 11 rue Saint-Sulpice, Paris 6e, France.

950 BE
INSTITUT ORIENTALISTE DE LOUVAIN. PUBLICATIONS. Abbreviated title: P.I.O.L. 1970. irreg., no. 17, 1977. Editions Peeters s.p.r.l., B.P. 41, B-3000 Louvain, Belgium.
  Supersedes (1932-1968): Bibliotheque de Museon.

IRANICA ANTIQUA; dealing with archaeology, history, religion, art and literature of ancient Persia. see *ARCHAEOLOGY*

492 IS
ISRAEL ORIENTAL STUDIES. (Text in English, French & German) 1971. a. Tel-Aviv University, Faculty of Humanities, Department of Arabic Studies, Ramat-Aviv, Tel-Aviv, Israel (U. S. dist.: Transaction, Inc., Rutgers-The State University, New Brunswick, NJ 08903)

ISTITUTO UNIVERSITARIO ORIENTALE DI NAPOLI. SEMINARIO DI STUDI DEL MONDO CLASSICO. ANNALI. SEZIONE LINGUISTICA. see *CLASSICAL STUDIES*

JAPAN-AMERICA SOCIETY OF WASHINGTON. BULLETIN. see *POLITICAL SCIENCE — International Relations*

JOURNAL OF ARABIC LITERATURE. see *LITERATURE*

950 II ISSN 0022-3301
JOURNAL OF ORIENTAL RESEARCH. (Text in English and Sanskrit) 1927. irreg. $3. Kuppuswami Sastri Research Institute, 66 Royapettah High Rd., Madras 4, India. Ed. Dr. V. Raghavan. bk. rev. illus. index.

KEILSCHRIFTTEXTE AUS BOGHAZKOI. see *ARCHAEOLOGY*

KUNST DES ORIENTS/ART OF THE ORIENT. see *ART*

950 895 II
LALBHAI DALPATBHAI INSTITUTE OF INDOLOGY. PUBLICATIONS. (Text in various languages) irreg. price varies. Lalbhai Dalpatbhai Institute of Indology, Near Gujarat University, P.O. Navarangpura, Ahmedabad 380009, India.

954 UK ISSN 0142-601X
LONDON STUDIES ON SOUTH ASIA. 1980. irreg. £5.50. Curzon Press, 42 Gray's Inn Rd., London W.C.1., England. bibl. index.

954 II
MADHYA PRADESH ITIHASA PARISHAD. JOURNAL. (Text in English or Hindi) 1959. irreg. (approx. a.) Rs.20. Madhya Pradesh Itihasa Parishad, 34/14, South T. T. Nagar, Bhopal 462003, India. Ed. S. D. Guru. bk. rev. circ. 500. (also avail. in microfilm)
  History, art, archaeology, and civilization of Madhya Pradesh

327 FR ISSN 0495-7725
MAISON FRANCO-JAPONAISE. BULLETIN. (Text in French and Japanese) N.S. 1951. irreg. (approx. every 2-3 yrs.) Presses Universitaires de France, 108 Bd. Saint Germaine, 75279 Paris Cedex 6, France (Service des Periodiques, 12 rue Jean de Beauvais, 75005 Paris) Ed. Bd. bibl.

951 UK ISSN 0305-7429
MODERN CHINA STUDIES. INTERNATIONAL BULLETIN. 1970. a. £4($15) to institutions: £2 ($7.50) to individuals. Contemporary China Institute, School of Oriental and African Studies, Malet St., London WC1E 7HP, England.

MODERN MIDDLE EAST SERIES. see *HISTORY — History Of Asia*

950 US
MONGOLIAN STUDIES. a. $15. Mongolia Society, Inc., Drawer 606, Bloomington, IN 47402. Eds. L. W. Moses, S. A. Halkovic. adv. bk. rev. abstr. bibl. charts. stat. circ. 400.
  Formerly: Mongolia Society Newsletter;
  Supersedes: Mongolia Society Bulletin (ISSN 0026-9654)

894.2 HU
MONUMENTA LINGUAE MONGOLICAE COLLECTA. (Text in Mongolian with transcriptions in Roman letters and introduction in French) 1971. irreg. price varies. (Magyar Tudomanyos Akademia) Akademiai Kiado, Publishing House of the Hungarian Academy of Sciences, P.O. Box 24, H-1363 Budapest, Hungary. Ed. L. Ligeti.
  Supersedes: Mongol Nyelvemlektar (ISSN 0540-6471)

950 SZ ISSN 0077-149X
MONUMENTA SERICA; journal of oriental studies. (Text in English, French, German) 1934. irreg. 82 Fr. Editions Saint-Paul, Perolles 36, CH-1700 Fribourg, Switzerland. Ed. Heinrich Busch, S.V.D. bk. rev. circ. 500. (also avail. in microfilm) Indexed: Hist.Abstr.

950 GW ISSN 0170-3668
MUENCHENER OSTASIATISCHE STUDIEN. (Text in English and German) irreg., vol. 26, 1981. price varies. Franz Steiner Verlag GmbH, Friedrichstr. 24, Postfach 5529, 6200 Wiesbaden, W. Germany (B.R.D.) Eds.W. Bauer, H. Franke.

950 GW ISSN 0170-3676
MUENCHENER OSTASIATISCHE STUDIEN. SONDERREIHE. (Text in English and German) irreg., vol. 3, 1978. price varies. Franz Steiner Verlag GmbH, Friedrichstr. 24, Postfach 5529, 6200 Wiesbaden, W. Germany (B.R.D.) Eds.W. Bauer, H. Franke.

MUSEO NAZIONALE D'ARTE ORIENTALE. SCHEDE. see *MUSEUMS AND ART GALLERIES*

950 BE
MUSEON; revue d'etudes orientales. 1881. a. 1500 Fr.($50) Editions Peeters s.p.r.l., B.P. 41, B-3000 Louvain, Belgium.

MUSEUM OF FAR EASTERN ANTIQUITIES. BULLETIN. see *MUSEUMS AND ART GALLERIES*

MUSICA ASIATICA. see *MUSIC*

954 II ISSN 0580-4396
MYSORE ORIENTALIST. (Text in English or Sanskrit) 1967. a. $5. Oriental Research Institute, University of Mysore, P.O.B. 14, Mysore 5, Karnataka, India. Ed. G. Marulasiddaiah.
  Indological studies

951 NP
NEPAL-ANTIQUARY. BIBLIOGRAPHICAL SERIES. 1976. irreg. Rs.50. Office of Nepal-Antiquary, 20/401 Naxal, Kathmandu, Nepal.

950 NE ISSN 0078-6527
ORIENS. (Text in German, English, French) 1948. irreg. price varies. (Internationale Gesellschaft fuer Orientforschung) E. J. Brill, Oude Rijn 33a-35, Leiden, Netherlands. Ed. R. Sellheim. bk. rev. cum.index:vol.1-10.

950 AT ISSN 0030-5340
ORIENTAL SOCIETY OF AUSTRALIA. JOURNAL. 1961. a. Aus.$7.50. University of Sydney, Department of Oriental Studies, Sydney 2006, Australia. Ed. Prof. A.R. Davis. bk. rev. charts. circ. 500. Indexed: Aus.P.A.I.S.

950 297 JA
ORIENTAL STUDIES/TOHO GAKUHO. (Text in Japanese; table of contents in English) 1931. a. Kyoto University, Research Institute for Humanistic Studies - Kyoto Daigaku Jimbun Kagata Kenkyusyo, 50 Kitashurakawa, Ogura-machi, Sagyo-ku, Kyoto, Japan. illus.

950 HU
ORIENTAL STUDIES/KELETI TANULMANYOK. (Text in Hungarian, English, French, German, Russian and languages of the East) 1976. irreg. exchange basis. Magyar Tudomanyos Akademia, Konyvtar, Akademia u.2, P.O.B. 7, 1361 Budapest 5, Hungary. Ed. Eva Apor. circ. 800.

950 200 VC
ORIENTALIA CHRISTIANA ANALECTA. 1923. irreg. price varies. Pontificio Istituto Orientale, Piazza S. Maria Maggiore 7, 00185 Rome, Italy.
  Continues (since 1935): Orientalia Christiana.

950 SW ISSN 0078-656X
ORIENTALIA GOTHOBURGENSIA. (Subseries of Acta Universitatis Gothoburgensis) 1969. irreg., vol. 4, 1980. price varies. Acta Universitatis Gothoburgensis, Box 5096, S-402 22 Goeteborg 5, Sweden (Dist. in U.S., Canada and Mexico by: Humanities Press, Inc., 171 First Ave., Atlantic Highlands, NJ 07716) Ed. Heikki Palva.

950 BE ISSN 0085-4522
ORIENTALIA LOVANIENSIA PERIODICA. (Text in English, French, German and Dutch; summaries in English) 1970. a. 900 Fr. Katholieke Universiteit te Leuven, Departement Orientalistiek, Blijde Inkomststraat 21, B-3000 Louvain, Belgium. Ed. P. Naster. abstr. charts. illus. cum.index. Indexed: Old Test. Abstr.

950 NE
ORIENTALIA RHENO-TRAIECTINA. 1949. irreg., vol. 25, 1980. price varies. E.J. Brill, Oude Rijn 33a-35, Leiden, Netherlands. Eds. J. Gonda, H.W. Obbink.

950 SW ISSN 0078-6578
ORIENTALIA SUECANA. 1952. a. Kr.75($15) (Uppsala Universitet) Almqvist & Wiksell International, Box 62, S-101 20 Stockholm, Sweden. Ed. Frithiof Rundgren. circ. 600.

954 II
PANJAB UNIVERSITY INDOLOGICAL SERIES. irreg. price varies. Vishveshvaranand Vedic Research Institute, P.O. Sadhu Ashram, Hoshiarpur 146021, Punjab, India.

894 494 947.87 US ISSN 0031-5508
PERMANENT INTERNATIONAL ALTAISTIC CONFERENCE (PIAC). NEWSLETTER. 1966. 2-3/yr. free. (Permanent International Altaistic Conference) Indiana University, Department of Uralic and Altaic Studies, 101 Goodbody Hall, Goodbody Hall, Bloomington, IN 47405. Ed. Prof. Denis Sinor. adv. bibl. circ. 750. (processed)
Organization news

950 PL ISSN 0079-3426
POLSKA AKADEMIA NAUK. ODDZIAL W KRAKOWIE. KOMISJA ORIENTALISTYCZNA. PRACE. (Text in English, French, German, Polish) 1962. irreg., no. 15, 1977. price varies. Ossolineum, Publishing House of the Polish Academy of Sciences, Rynek 9, 50-106 Wroclaw, Poland (Dist. by Ars Polona-Ruch, Krakowskie Przedmiescie 7, Warsaw, Poland) circ. 700.

950 PL ISSN 0079-4783
PRACE ORIENTALISTYCZNE. (Text in English, French, German, Polish, and Russian) 1954. irreg. price varies. (Polska Akademia Nauk, Zaklad Orientalistyki) Panstwowe Wydawnictwo Naukowe, Ul. Miodowa 10, Warsaw, Poland.

RECORDS OF CIVILIZATION. SOURCES AND STUDIES. see *HISTORY*

REVUE D'EGYPTOLOGIE. see *ARCHAEOLOGY*

950 PL ISSN 0080-3545
ROCZNIK ORIENTALISTYCZNY. (Text in English, French, German or Russian and Polish) 1914. irreg., 1976, vol. 38. price varies. (Polska Akademia Nauk, Komitet Nauk Orientalistycznych) Panstwowe Wydawnictwo Naukowe, Ul. Miodowa 10, Warsaw, Poland (Dist by Ars Polona-Ruch, Krakowskie Przedmiescie 7, Warsaw, Poland) Ed. J. Reychman.

950 HK ISSN 0085-5774
ROYAL ASIATIC SOCIETY. HONG KONG BRANCH. JOURNAL. 1961. a. HK.$25. Royal Asiatic Society, Hong Kong Branch, Box 13864, Hong Kong, Hong Kong. Ed. James W. Hayes. bk. rev. cum. index: vols. 1-10 (1961-1970) circ. 700. Indexed: Hist.Abstr.

954 CE
ROYAL ASIATIC SOCIETY. SRI LANKA BRANCH. JOURNAL. (Text in English) N.S., vol. 16, 1972. a. Rs.10. Royal Asiatic Society, Sri Lanka Branch, Reid Avenue, Colombo 7, Sri Lanka.
Supersedes: Royal Asiatic Society. Ceylon Branch. Journal.

960 DK ISSN 0069-1704
SCANDINAVIAN INSTITUTE OF ASIAN STUDIES. ANNUAL NEWSLETTER. 1968. a. free. Scandinavian Institute of Asian Studies - Centralinstitut for Nordisk Asienforskning, 2 Kejsergade, DK-1155 Copenhagen K, Denmark. Ed. Soren Egerod. circ. 3,000.

930 950 DK ISSN 0069-1712
SCANDINAVIAN INSTITUTE OF ASIAN STUDIES. MONOGRAPH SERIES. (Text in English) 1969. irreg., no. 40, 1979. price varies. Scandinavian Institute of Asian Studies - Centralinstitut for Nordisk Asienforskning, 2 Kejsergade, DK-1155 Copenhagen K, Denmark (Outside Scandinavia, orders to: Curzon Press, 88 Gray's Inn Rd., London W.C.1., England) circ. 700-1,500.

SCHRIFTEN ZUR GESCHICHTE UND KULTUR DES ALTEN ORIENT. see *HISTORY — History Of Asia*

950 296 NE
SEMITIC STUDY SERIES. (Text in English) 1902. irreg. E. J. Brill, Oude Rijn 33a-35, Leiden, Netherlands.
Jewish interests

951 GW ISSN 0170-3706
SINOLOGICA COLONIENSIA; Ostasiatische Beitraege der Universitaet zu Koeln. irreg., vol. 10, 1981. price varies. (Universitaet zu Koeln) Franz Steiner Verlag GmbH, Friedrichstr. 24, Postfach 5529, 6200 Wiesbaden, W. Germany (B.R.D.) Ed. Martin Grimm.

954 GW ISSN 0584-3170
SOUTH ASIAN STUDIES. (Text in English) irreg., vol.10, 1981. price varies. (Universitaet Heidelberg, Suedasien Institut (New Delhi), II) Franz Steiner Verlag GmbH, Friedrichstr. 24, Postfach 5529, 6200 Wiesbaden, W. Germany (B.R.D.)

SOUTH EAST ASIA LIBRARY GROUP NEWSLETTER. see *LIBRARY AND INFORMATION SCIENCES*

SOUTHERN ILLINOIS UNIVERSITY, EDWARDSVILLE. ASIAN STUDIES. OCCASIONAL PAPER SERIES. see *POLITICAL SCIENCE — International Relations*

950 FI ISSN 0039-3282
STUDIA ORIENTALIA. (Text in English, French and German) 1925. irreg. price varies. Suomen Itamainen Seura - Finnish Oriental Society, Snellmaninkatu 9-11, 00170 Helsinki 17, Finland. Ed. Tapani Harviainen. bk. rev. charts. illus. cum.index.

950 VC
STUDIA POHL. (Text in language of author) 1967. irreg; no. 11, 1976. price varies. (Pontificio Istituto Biblico) Biblical Institute Press, Piazza della Pilotta 35, 00187 Rome, Italy.

950 VC
STUDIA POHL: SERIES MAIOR. 1969. irreg; no. 5, 1976. price varies. (Pontificio Istituto Biblico) Biblical Institute Press, Piazza della Pilotta 35, 00187 Rome, Italy. charts. illus.

STUDIEN ZUR OSTASIATISCHEN SCHRIFTKUNST. see *ART*

954 UK ISSN 0142-6028
STUDIES ON ASIAN TOPICS. irreg. £4. (Scandinavian Institute of Asian Studies) Curzon Press Ltd., 42 Gray's Inn Rd., London WC1, England.

950 US
STUDIES ON EAST ASIA. (Text in English or Oriental languages) 1971. irreg. price varies per no. ‡ Western Washington University, Center for East Asian Studies, Bellingham, WA 98225. Ed. Henry G. Schwarz.
Formerly (until vol. 13): Western Washington State College. Program in East Asian Studies. Occasional Papers.

951 CH
SUI YUAN WEN HSIEN. (Text in Chinese) 1977. a. free. Association of Fellow Provincials of Sui Yuan, 101 4th St., Chung Yang Hsin Ts'un, Hsin Tien, Taipei 231, Taiwan, Republic of China. Ed. Chi-Yuan Lee. circ. 1,500. (back issues avail)

951 CH
TAMKANG COLLEGE. INSTITUTE OF AREA STUDIES. AREA STUDIES. (Text in English) 1977. Tamkang College, Institute of Area Studies, King-Hau St., Taipei, Taiwan 106, Republic of China. Ed. Robert J. Clarke.

950 BL
UNIVERSIDADE DE SAO PAULO. FACULDADE DE FILOSOFIA, LETRAS E CIENCIAS HUMANAS. DEPARTAMENTO DE LINGUISTICA E LINGUAS ORIENTAIS. BOLETIM. no. 8, 1977 (n.s.) irreg. exchange requested. Universidade de Sao Paulo, Faculdade de Filosofia, Letras e Ciencias Humanas, Departamento de Linguistica e Linguas Orientais, Caixa Postal 8.105, 0.1000 Sao Paulo, Brazil.

UNIVERSITE CATHOLIQUE DE LOUVAIN. INSTITUT ORIENTALISTE. PUBLICATIONS. see *HISTORY — History Of Asia*

950 BE
UNIVERSITE LIBRE DE BRUXELLES. INSTITUT DE PHILOLOGIE ET D'HISTOIRE ORIENTALES ET SLAVES. ANNUAIRE. 1957? a. Editions de l'Universite de Bruxelles, Parc Leopold, 1040 Brussels, Belgium.

955 200 LE
UNIVERSITE SAINT-JOSEPH. FACULTE DES LETTRES ET DES SCIENCES HUMAINES. RECHERCHE. SERIE B: ORIENT CHRETIEN. (Previously published by its Institut des Lettres Orientales in 4 series) 1956; NS. 1971. irreg., latest no. 6. price varies. Dar el-Mashreq, Imprimerie Catholique, 2 rue Huvelin, Box 946, Beirut, Lebanon (Subscr. to: Librairie Orientale, c/o Maroun Nehme, 106-108 Blvd. de Grenelle, 75015 Paris, France)

950 HK ISSN 0378-2689
UNIVERSITY OF HONG KONG. CENTRE OF ASIAN STUDIES. OCCASIONAL PAPERS AND MONOGRAPHS. (Text in English or Chinese; summaries in English) 1970. irreg., nos. 27-41, 1979-1980. price varies. University of Hong Kong, Centre of Asian Studies, Pokfulam Road, Hong Kong, Hong Kong. Ed. Edward K. Y. Chen. (processed)

951 UK ISSN 0085-2856
UNIVERSITY OF LONDON. SCHOOL OF ORIENTAL AND AFRICAN STUDIES. CONTEMPORARY CHINA INSTITUTE. PUBLICATIONS. 1970. irreg. price varies. Cambridge University Press, Box 110, Cambridge CB2 3RL, England (And 32 E. 57th St., New York NY 10022) Ed. Bd.

915.4 II
UNIVERSITY OF RAJASTHAN. SOUTH ASIAN STUDIES CENTRE. ANNUAL REPORT. (Text in English) 1966. irreg., latest issue, 1973. University of Rajasthan, South Asian Studies Centre, Gandhi Nagar, Jaipur 302004, India.

UNIVERZITA KOMENSKEHO. FILOZOFICKA FAKULTA. ZBORNIK: GRAECOLATINA ET ORIENTALIA. see *CLASSICAL STUDIES*

VARENDRA RESEARCH MUSEUM. JOURNAL. see *MUSEUMS AND ART GALLERIES*

950 GW ISSN 0506-7936
VERZEICHNIS DER ORIENTALISCHEN HANDSCHRIFTEN IN DEUTSCHLAND. Short title: V O H D. irreg., vol. 32, 1978. price varies. (Deutsche Morgenlaendische Gesellschaft) Franz Steiner Verlag GmbH, Friedrichstr. 24, Postfach 5529, 6200 Wiesbaden, W. Germany (B.R.D.) Ed. Wolfgang Voigt.

950 GW ISSN 0506-7944
VERZEICHNIS DER ORIENTALISCHEN HANDSCHRIFTEN IN DEUTSCHLAND. SUPPLEMENTBAENDE. Short title: V O H D Supplementbaende. (Text in English and German) irreg., vol. 24, 1981. price varies. (Deutsche Morgenlaendische Gesellschaft) Franz Steiner Verlag GmbH, Friedrichstr. 24, Postfach 5529, 6200 Wiesbaden, W. Germany (B.R.D.) Ed. Wolfgang Voigt.

950 956 IT
VICINO ORIENTE. 1978. a. L.8000. Universita degli Studi di Roma, Istituto di Studi del Vicino Oriente, Rome, Italy. Ed. Mario Liverani.

954 II
VISHVA VICHARAMALA. (Text in Hindi and Sanskrit) irreg. price varies. Vishveshvaranand Vedic Research Institute, P.O. Sadhu Ashram, Hoshiarpur 146021, Punjab, India. Ed. Vishva Bandhu.

954 II
VISHVESHVARANAND VEDIC RESEARCH INSTITUTE. RESEARCH AND GENERAL PUBLICATIONS. (Text in English, Hindi, and Sanskrit) 1921. irreg. price varies. Vishveshvaranand Vedic Research Institute, P.O. Sadhu Ashram, Hoshiarpur 146021, Punjab, India.

956 AU ISSN 0084-0076
WIENER ZEITSCHRIFT FUER DIE KUNDE DES MORGENLANDES. (Text in English, French, German and Italian) 1887. irreg. price varies. Universitaet Wien, Institut fuer Orientalistik, Universitaets Str. 7/V, A-1010 Vienna, Austria. Ed. Andreas Tietze. adv. bk. rev. circ. 250.

WISCONSIN CHINA SERIES. see *HISTORY — History Of Asia*

ORIENTAL STUDIES — Abstracting, Bibliographies, Statistics

S F W SCIENTIFIC FILMS-HOLLAND. see *MOTION PICTURES*

950 016 HK ISSN 0441-1900
UNIVERSITY OF HONG KONG. CENTRE OF ASIAN STUDIES. BIBLIOGRAPHIES AND RESEARCH GUIDES. (Text in English and Chinese; summaries in English) 1970. irreg., nos. 14-18, 1979-1980. price varies. ‡ University of Hong Kong, Centre of Asian Studies, Pokfulam Road, Hong Kong, Hong Kong. Ed. Edward K. Y. Chen. (processed)

ORNITHOLOGY

see *Biology — Ornithology*

ORTHOPEDICS AND TRAUMATOLOGY

see *Medical Sciences — Orthopedics and Traumatology*

OTORHINOLARYNGOLOGY

see *Medical Sciences — Otorhinolaryngology*

OUTDOOR LIFE

see *Sports and Games — Outdoor Life*

PACKAGING

ANNUAL BOOK OF A S T M STANDARDS. PART 20. PAPER; PACKAGING; BUSINESS COPY PRODUCTS. see *ENGINEERING — Engineering Mechanics And Materials*

658 AT
AUSTRALIAN PACKAGING BUYERS GUIDE. (Includes subscription to Australian Packaging) 1965. a. Aus.$10($15) (National Packaging Association of Australia) I P C Business Press (Australia) Pty. Ltd., 3-13 Queen St., Chippendale, N.S.W. 2008, Australia. Ed. N. M. MacLeod. circ. 1,200.
Formerly: Australian Packaging and Materials Handling Yearbook and Buyers Guide (ISSN 0084-7526)

658.788 FR
B I C-CODE. (Text in English and French) 1972. a. 80 Fr. per no. Bureau International des Containers - International Container Bureau, 38, Cours Albert 1er, Paris (8e), France. charts.

621 US ISSN 0360-8689
BEST IN PACKAGING. (Subseries of: Print Casebooks) 1975. a. $13.95. R C Publications, Inc., 355 Lexington Ave., New York, NY 10017 (Or 6400 Goldsboro Rd., Washington, DC 20034) illus.

658.7884 US ISSN 0068-7014
CAN MANUFACTURERS INSTITUTE. ANNUAL METAL CANS SHIPMENT REPORT. a. $50. Can Manufacturers Institute, 1625 Massachusetts Ave., N.W., Washington, DC 20036.

CANADA'S MEAT INDUSTRY. see *FOOD AND FOOD INDUSTRIES*

380.5 CN
CONTAINERIZATION AND MATERIAL HANDLING ANNUAL. a. Anchor Press, 1434 St. Catherine St. W., Suite 504, Montreal, Que. H3G 1R4, Canada. Ed. O. J. Silva. adv. illus.

658.788 FR
CONTAINERS. 1933. q. 65 F. Bureau International des Containers - International Container Bureau, 38 Cours Albert 1er, 75008 Paris, France.

DIRECTORY OF RESEARCH REPORTS RELATING TO PRODUCE PACKAGING AND MARKETING. see *FOOD AND FOOD INDUSTRIES*

ELECTRONIC PACKAGING AND PRODUCTION VENDOR SELECTION ISSUE. see *ENGINEERING*

670 MX
ENVASE Y EMBALAJE. 1975. a. 125($50) Editorial Innovacion, Espana 396, Mexico 13, D.F., Mexico. Ed. Cesar Macazaga. adv.

614.7 670 AT
ENVIROFACTS. 1975. irreg. free. Packaging Council of Australia, 370 St. Kilda Rd., Melbourne, Vic. 3004, Australia.
Supersedes: Packaging Council of Australia. Environment Newsletter.

670 SA
FASTENERS AND ADHESIVES. 1979. a. R.35. Thomson Publications S.A. (Pty) Ltd., Box 8308, Johannesburg 2000, South Africa. Eds. Chris Emery, Henry Snow. adv.

658.7884 663.19 US ISSN 0072-4637
GLASS CONTAINERS. 1957. a. free. Glass Containers Manufacturers Institute, 1800 K St., N.W., Washington, DC 20006.

659.12 SZ ISSN 0072-5536
GRAPHIS PACKAGING; an international survey of package design. (Text in English, German, French) 1959. irreg., 3rd. edt. 1977. $49.50. Walter Herdeg Graphis Press, 107 Dufourstrasse, 8008 Zurich, Switzerland (Dist. by Hastings House Publishers, Inc., 10 East 40 St., New York, NY 10016) Ed. Walter Herdeg. circ. 14,000.

338.4 US ISSN 0553-1454
GROCERS BAGS AND GROCERS SACKS; a graphic and tabular review. irreg. not for sale. Paper Bag Institute, 41 East 42nd Street, New York, NY 10017. illus. stat.

670 AU
INFORMATIONSDIENST VERPACKUNG. 1973. irreg. price varies. Oesterreichisches Institut fuer Verpackungswesen, Hochschule fuer Welthandel, Franz Klein-Gasse 1, A-1190 Vienna, Austria. Ed. Erich F. Ketzler. circ. 250.
Formerly: Oesterreichisches Institut fuer Verpackung. Mitteilungen.

621.7 670 GW ISSN 0074-5766
INTERNATIONAL ENCYCLOPEDIA ON PACKAGING MACHINES/CATALOGUE INTERNATIONAL DES MACHINES D' EMBALLAGE/CATALOGO INTERNAZIONALE DELLE MACCHINE PER L' IMBALLAGGIO/INTERNATIONALER VERPACKUNGSMASCHINEN- KATALOG FUER DIE ABPACKENDE INDUSTRIE. 1966. s-a. price varies. B. Behr's Verlag GmbH, Averhoffstr. 10, 2000 Hamburg 76, W. Germany (B.R.D.)

700 FR
J'EMBALLE. 1965. a. 160.80 F. Societe des Editions de l' Imprimerie Nouvelle, 89 rue Barrault, 75013 Paris, France. adv. bk. rev. tr.lit. circ. 6,000. (tabloid format)
Formerly: Graphiq'emballage.

658.83 US
KLINE GUIDE TO THE PACKAGING INDUSTRY. 1968. triennial. $100. Charles H. Kline & Co., Inc., 330 Passaic Ave, Fairfield, NJ 07006. Ed. Marlon Deitsch.
Formerly: Marketing Guide to the Packaging Industries (ISSN 0076-4590)

MATERIAL HANDLING ENGINEERING HANDBOOK AND DIRECTORY. see *MACHINERY*

658.7884 US ISSN 0077-0035
MODERN PACKAGING ENCYCLOPEDIA. 1929. a. $20 (includes Subscription to Modern Packaging Magazine) Morgan-Grampian, Inc., 205 E. 42nd St., New York, NY 10017. index.

658.7884 UK ISSN 0078-768X
PACKAGING DIRECTORY. 1946. a. £22.50. Wheatland Journals Ltd., Penn House, Penn Place, Rickmansworth, Herts WD3 1SN, England. Ed. A. J. LaRoche.

658.7884 US ISSN 0078-7698
PACKAGING MACHINERY MANUFACTURERS INSTITUTE. OFFICIAL PACKAGING MACHINERY DIRECTORY. Cover title: Packaging Machinery Directory. 1954. biennial. $2. Packaging Machinery Manufacturers Institute, 2000 K St. N. W., Washington, DC 20006. Ed. Claude S. Breeden, Jr. index. circ. 35,000.

658.788 US
PACKAGING MARKETPLACE; the practical guide to packaging sources. 1978. irreg. $45. Gale Research Company, Book Tower, Detroit, MI 48226. Ed. Joseph F. Hanlon.

658.7 II
PACKAGING UPDATE. (Text in English) 1975. a. Rs.35. Indian Institute of Packaging, E-2 Marol Industrial Estate, MIDC, Andheri East, Bombay 400093, India. abstr.

PRODUCE MARKETING ALMANAC. see *FOOD AND FOOD INDUSTRIES*

670 SZ
SCHWEIZER VERPACKUNGSKATALOG. (Text in French and German) 1947. a. 19 Fr. Verlag Binkert AG, CH-4335 Lauferburg, Switzerland. Ed. Max Binkert. adv. circ. 4,100.

670 FR
TECH-EMBAL; annuaire des fournisseurs de l'emballage. 1966. a. 200 F. Editions Technorama, 31 Place Saint Ferdinand, 75017 Paris, France. Ed. R. Baschet. circ. 2,000.

PACKAGING — Abstracting, Bibliographies, Statistics

674.82 CN ISSN 0576-0070
CANADA. STATISTICS CANADA. WOODEN BOX FACTORIES/FABRIQUES DE BOITES EN BOIS. (Catalog 35-209) (Text in English and French) 1960. a. Can.$4.50($5.40) Statistics Canada, Publications Distribution, Ottawa, Ont. K1A 0V7, Canada. (also avail. in microform from MML)

PAINTS AND PROTECTIVE COATINGS

ANNUAL BOOK OF A S T M STANDARDS. PART 27. PAINT - TESTS FOR FORMULATED PRODUCTS AND APPLIED COATINGS. see ENGINEERING — Engineering Mechanics And Materials

ANNUAL BOOK OF A S T M STANDARDS. PART 28. PAINT - PIGMENTS, RESINS AND POLYMERS. see ENGINEERING — Engineering Mechanics And Materials

ANNUAL BOOK OF A S T M STANDARDS. PART 29. PAINT - FATTY OILS AND ACIDS, SOLVENTS, MISCELLANEOUS; AROMATIC HYDROCARBONS; NAVAL STORES. see ENGINEERING — Engineering Mechanics And Materials

698   UK
BRITISH DECORATORS ASSOCIATION. MEMBERS REFERENCE HANDBOOK. 1932. a. British Decorators Association, 6 Haywra Street, Harrogate, North Yorkshire, HG1 5BL, England. Ed. Kenneth A.C. Blease. adv. abstr. charts. circ. 3,000.

667.6   FR   ISSN 0396-1214
CATALOGUE NATIONAL DU TRAITEMENT DES SURFACES DE L'ANTICORROSION ET DES TRAITEMENTS THERMIQUES. 1963. a. 36 F. Editions du Cartel, 2 rue de Florence, 75008 Paris, France. Ed. A. L. Savu. adv. circ. 10,000.

338.4   UK
CHATFIELD'S EUROPEAN DIRECTORY OF PAINTS AND ALLIED PRODUCTS/ ANNUAIRE CHATFIELD EUROPEAN DE PEINTURES ET PRODUITS ASSIMILES/ CHATFIELDS EUROPAEISCHES ADRESSBUCH FUER ANSTRICHMITTEL-UND VERWANDTE PRODUKTE. Short title: European Directory of Paints and Allied Products. (Text in English, French, or German) irreg. price varies. Chatfield Applied Research Laboratories Ltd., Croydon, England.

667.6   667.7   FR   ISSN 0071-416X
FEDERATION D'ASSOCIATIONS DE TECHNICIENS DES INDUSTRIES DES PEINTURES, VERNIS, EMAUX ET ENCRES D'IMPRIMERIE DE L'EUROPE CONTINENTALE. ANNUAIRE OFFICIEL. OFFICIAL YEARBOOK. AMTLICHES JAHRBUCH. (Text in English, French, German) 1955. biennial. Federation d'Associations de Techniciens des Industries des Peintures, Vernis, Emaux et Encres d'Imprimerie de l'Europe Continentale., Maison de la Chimie, 28 rue Saint Dominique, 75007 Paris, France. adv. circ. 3,000.

667.6   US
FEDERATION OF SOCIETIES FOR COATINGS TECHNOLOGY. YEARBOOK AND ANNUAL MEMBERSHIP DIRECTORY.* 1928. a. $5. Federation of Societies for Coatings Technology, 1315 S. Walnut St., Suite 830, Philadelphia, PA 19107. Ed. Rosemary Falvey. adv. circ. 6,100.
Formerly: Federation of Societies for Paint Technology. Yearbook (ISSN 0071-4437)

698   UK
FINISHING DIARY. 1950. a. Wheatland Journals Ltd., Penn House, Penn Place, Rickmansworth, Herts WD3 1SN, England. Ed. Tom Tebbatt. adv. circ. 2,000.
Former titles: International Finishing Industries Manual (ISSN 0073-747X); Industrial Finishing Year Book.

667.6   FR   ISSN 0071-9048
FRANCE-PEINTURE. 1953. biennial. 96 F. Creations, Editions et Productions Publicitaires, 1 Place d'Estienne d'Orves, 75009 Paris, France. Ed. Georges Prieux. adv. circ. 9,100.
Directory of painting, varnishes and annexed industries

667.6   US
KLINE GUIDE TO THE PAINT INDUSTRY. 1965. triennial. $65. Charles H. Kline & Co., Inc., 330 Passaic Ave., Fairfield, NJ 07006. Ed. Joan Huber.
Formerly: Marketing Guide to the Paint Industry (ISSN 0076-4604)

667   US   ISSN 0095-2729
NATIONAL PAINT AND COATINGS ASSOCIATION. ANNUAL REPORT. a. National Paint & Coatings Association, 1500 Rhode Island Ave. N.W., Washington, DC 20005. Ed. Donna Kordoski. illus. Key Title: Annual Report - National Paint & Coatings Association.

667.6   380.1   US   ISSN 0090-5402
PAINT RED BOOK; directory of the paint and coatings industry. 1968. a. $29.50. Communication Channels, Inc., 6285 Barfield Rd., Atlanta, GA 30328. Ed. Art Swenn.

698   US
PAINTING AND DECORATING CRAFTSMAN MANUAL AND TEXTBOOK. irreg., 5th edt., 1975. $7.50. Painting and Decorating Contractors of America, 7223 Lee Highway, Falls Church, VA 22046. charts. illus.

667.6   UK   ISSN 0078-7817
POLYMERS PAINT AND COLOUR YEAR BOOK. 1961. a. £11.50. Fuel and Metallurgical Journals Ltd., Queensway House, 2 Queensway, Redhill, Surrey RH1 1QS, England. Ed. D. E. Eddowes. adv.
Formerly: Paint, Oil Colour Year Book.

698   FR
QUI FABRIQUE ET FOURNIT QUOI. 1973. irreg. 60 F. Editions Ampere, 46 rue Ampere, 75017 Paris, France.

382   II
SHELLAC EXPORT PROMOTION COUNCIL. ANNUAL REPORT. (Text in English) a. Shellac Export Promotion Council, 14/1-B Ezra St., Calcutta 1, India. stat.

667.6   DK   ISSN 0085-6126
SKANDINAVISK TIDSKRIFT FOR FAERG OCH LACK. AARSBOK. (Text in Scandinavian languages; summaries in English) a. free to members. (Federation of Scandinavian Paint and Varnish Technicians) Dansk Bladforlag K-S, Holbergsgade 20, DK-1057 Copenhagen K, Denmark.

698   US
STEEL STRUCTURES PAINTING BULLETIN. 1955. biennial. free. Steel Structures Painting Council, 4400 Fifth Ave., Pittsburgh, PA 15213. Ed. John D. Keane. circ. 20,000.

PAINTS AND PROTECTIVE COATINGS — Abstracting, Bibliographies, Statistics

698   016   UK   ISSN 0067-7094
BIBLIOGRAPHIES IN PAINT TECHNOLOGY. no. 15, 1967. irreg. R. H. Chandler Ltd., P.O. Box 55, Braintree, Essex CM7 6JT, England. (reprint service avail. from UMI)

PALEONTOLOGY

560   UR
AKADEMIYA NAUK S.S.S.R. INSTITUT PALEONTOLOGII. TRUDY. vol. 154, 1976. irreg. price aries. Izdatel'stvo Nauka, Podsosenskii Per., 21, Moscow K-62, U.S.S.R. Ed. A. Gamayunova. circ. 850.

560   572   GW   ISSN 0066-4723
ANTHROPOS; studie z oboru anthropologie, paleoethnologie, paleontologie a kvarterni geologie. (Text in German and Czech) 1959 N.S. irreg. price varies. (Moravske Museum, Brno, CS) Rudolf Habelt Verlag, Am Buchenhang 1, 5300 Bonn 1, W. Germany (B.R.D.)

560   551   GW   ISSN 0077-2070
BAYERISCHE STAATSSAMMLUNG FUER PALAEONTOLOGIE UND HISTORISCHE GEOLOGIE. MITTEILUNGEN. (Text and summaries in English and German) 1961. a. price varies. Bayerische Staatssammlung fuer Palaeontologie und Historische Geologie, Richard-Wagner-Strasse 10, 8000 Munich 2, W. Germany (B.R.D.) Ed. Dietrich Herm.

BULLETIN SCIENTIFIQUE DE BOURGOGNE. see SCIENCES: COMPREHENSIVE WORKS

560   FR   ISSN 0068-5054
CAHIERS DE MICROPALEONTOLOGIE. 1965. irreg. (Ecole Pratique des Hautes Etudes, Laboratoire de Micropaleontologie) Centre National de la Recherche Scientifique, 15 Quai Anatole France, 75700 Paris, France.

563   US   ISSN 0070-2242
CUSHMAN FOUNDATION FOR FORAMINIFERAL RESEARCH. SPECIAL PUBLICATION. 1952. irreg., no. 20, 1981. price varies. Cushman Foundation for Foraminiferal Research, E501 U.S. National Museum, Washington, DC 20560. Ed. R. V. Poore. circ. 600.

560   560.17   NE
DEVELOPMENTS IN PALAEONTOLOGY AND STRATIGRAPHY. irreg., vol. 6, 1977. Elsevier Scientific Publishing Co., Box 211, 1000 AE Amsterdam, Netherlands.

560   PL   ISSN 0015-573X
FOLIA QUATERNARIA. (Text in English and German) 1960. 1-2/yr., no. 37, 1978. price varies. (Polska Akademia Nauk, Oddzial w Krakowie) Ossolineum, Publishing House of the Polish Academy of Sciences, Rynek 9, Wroclaw, Poland. Ed. Kazimierz Kowalski.

560   NO
FOSSILS AND STRATA; a monograph series in palaeontology and stratigraphy. (Text in English) 1972. irreg. price varies. Universitetsforlaget, Kolstadgt. 1, Box 2959-Toeyen, Oslo 6, Norway (U. S. address: Box 258, Irvington-on-Hudson, NY 10533) Ed. Anders Martinsson.

FREIBERGER FORSCHUNGSHEFTE. MONTANWISSENSCHAFTEN: REIHE C. GEOWISSENSCHAFTEN. see EARTH SCIENCES

GEOLOGICA ET PALAEONTOLOGICA. see EARTH SCIENCES — Geology

560   UR
ITOGI NAUKI I TEKHNIKI: STRATIGRAFIYA, PALEONTOLOGIYA. 1970. a. 0.64 Rub. Vsesoyuznyi Institut Nauchno-Tekhnicheskoi Informatsii (Viniti), Ul. Baltiiskaya, 14, Moscow, U.S.S.R.
Continues: Itogi Nauki: Stratigrafiya. Paleontologiya (ISSN 0579-174X)

560   622   551   AU
LANDESMUSEUM JOANNEUM. ABTEILUNG FUER GEOLOGIE, PALAEONTOLOGIE UND BERGBAU. MITTEILUNGEN. vol. 32, 1972. irreg. price varies. Landesmuseum Joanneum, Abteilung fuer Geologie, Palaeontologie und Bergbau, Raubergasse 10, A-8010 Graz, Austria. illus.
Formerly: (until 1972): Joanneum. Museum fuer Bergbau, Geologie und Technik. Mitteilungen.

560.172   US   ISSN 0076-1389
LOWER PALAEOZIC ROCKS OF THE NEW WORLD. 1971. irreg., vol. 2, 1974. price varies. John Wiley & Sons, Inc., 605 Third Ave., New York, NY 10016. Ed. C. H. Holland.

MAN & ENVIRONMENT. see ANTHROPOLOGY

560   US
MICHIGAN STATE UNIVERSITY. MUSEUM PUBLICATIONS. PALEONTOLOGICAL SERIES. 1972. irreg. price varies. ‡ Michigan State University Museum, East Lansing, MI 48824. Ed. Bd. bibl. charts. illus. circ. 1,500.

563   US   ISSN 0160-2071
MICROPALEONTOLOGY SPECIAL PUBLICATIONS. 1976. irreg., no. 4, 1980. Micropaleontology Press, c/o American Museum of Natural History, Central Park West at 79th St., New York, NY 10024. Ed. John A. van Couvering. (reprint service avail. from UMI)

560   NE
MODERN QUATERNARY RESEARCH IN SOUTHEAST ASIA. 1975. a. $12.50. A.A. Balkema, Box 1675, 3000 BR Rotterdam, Netherlands (And 99 Main St., Salem, NH 03079) Eds. G.-J. Bartstra, W.A. Casparie.

MONOGRAPHS IN GEOLOGY AND PALEONTOLOGY. see *EARTH SCIENCES — Geology*

560   AG   ISSN 0524-9511
MUSEO ARGENTINO DE CIENCIAS NATURALES "BERNARDINO RIVADAVIA." INSTITUTO NACIONAL DE INVESTIGACION DE LAS CIENCIAS NATURALES. REVISTA. PALEONTOLOGIA. 1964. irreg.; latest issue 1980. Museo Argentino de Ciencias Naturales "Bernardino Rivadavia, Instituto Nacional de Investigacion de las Ciencias Naturales, Avda. Angel Gallardo 470, Casilla de Correo 220-Sucursal 5, Bueno Aires, Argentina.

560   UY
MUSEO NACIONAL DE HISTORIA NATURAL. COMMUNICACIONES PALEONTOLOGICAS. (Summaries in English, Spanish) 1970. irreg. exchange basis. Museo Nacional de Historia Natural, Casilla de Correos 399, Montevideo, Uruguay. Ed. Miguel A. Klappenbach.

NEUES JAHRBUCH FUER GEOLOGIE UND PALAEONTOLOGIE. ABHANDLUNGEN. see *EARTH SCIENCES — Geology*

560   AT   ISSN 0077-8699
NEW SOUTH WALES. GEOLOGICAL SURVEY. MEMOIRS: PALAEONTOLOGY. 1888. irreg., no. 17, 1975. price varies. Department of Mineral Resources & Development, Box 5288, Sydney, N.S.W. 2001, Australia. Ed. H. Basden. circ. 400. Indexed: Bibl.&Ind.Geol.
Formerly: New South Wales. Department of Mines. Memoirs: Palaeontology (ISSN 0077-8699)

560   US
NEW YORK PALEONTOLOGICAL SOCIETY. NOTES. irreg. $0.25 per no. New York Paleontological Society, 127 W. 83d St., Box 287, Planetarium Station, New York, NY 10024.

560   IS   ISSN 0085-4573
OSTRACODOLOGIST. 1964. irreg. free to scientific institutions and ostracode workers. Israel Institute of Energy and Petroleum, P.O.B. 17081, Tel Aviv 61170, Israel. Ed. E. Gerry. bibl. illus. circ. 500.

560   PK   ISSN 0078-8155
PAKISTAN. GEOLOGICAL SURVEY. MEMOIRS; PALEONTOLOGIA PAKISTANICA. (Text in English) 1956. irreg. price varies. ‡ Geological Survey of Pakistan, c/o Chief Librarian, Box 15, Quetta, Pakistan. circ. 1,500.

560   NE   ISSN 0078-8538
PALAEOECOLOGY OF AFRICA AND THE SURROUNDING ISLANDS AND ANTARCTICA. 1965. a. fl.45($22.50) per no. A. A. Balkema, Box 1675, 3000 BR Rotterdam, Netherlands (And 99 Main St., Salem, NH 03079) Eds. E. M. van Zinderen Bakker, A. Coetzee.

560   GW   ISSN 0085-4611
PALAEONTOGRAPHICA. SUPPLEMENTBAENDE. irreg., vol.8, part 2B, 1980. price varies. E. Schweizerbart'sche Verlagsbuchhandlung, Johannesstr. 3A, 7000 Stuttgart 1, W. Germany (B.R.D.) Ed. H.K. Erben.

560   US   ISSN 0078-8546
PALAEONTOGRAPHICA AMERICANA. 1917. irreg; latest issue no. 51. price varies. Paleontological Research Institution, 1259 Trumansburg Road, Ithaca, NY 14850. Ed. Dr. Peter R. Hoover.

560   SA   ISSN 0078-8554
PALAEONTOLOGIA AFRICANA. Represents: University of the Witwatersrand, Johannesburg. Bernard Price Institute for Palaeontological Research. Annals. 1953. a. price varies. University of the Witwatersrand, Johannesburg, Bernard Price Institute for Palaeontological Research, 1 Jan Smuts Ave., Johannesburg, South Africa. Ed. Dr. S. H. Haughton. bk. rev. circ. 600(approx.) Indexed: Biol.Abstr. Bull.Signal.

560   PL   ISSN 0078-8562
PALAEONTOLOGIA POLONICA. (Text in English or French) 1929. irreg., 1973, no. 29. price varies. (Polska Akademia Nauk, Zaklad Paleozoologii) Panstwowe Wydawnictwo Naukowe, Miodowa 10, Warsaw, Poland (Dist. by: Ars Polona-Ruch, Krakowskie Przedmiescie 7, Warsaw, Poland) Ed. Zofia Kielan-Jawdrowska. index.

560   NZ   ISSN 0078-8589
PALEONTOLOGICAL BULLETINS. 1913. irreg., no. 46, 1975. price varies. (Department of Scientific and Industrial Research) New Zealand Geological Survey, P.O. Box 30368, Lower Hutt, New Zealand. circ. 1,100. Indexed: Biol.Abstr.

560   US   ISSN 0078-8597
PALEONTOLOGICAL SOCIETY. MEMOIR. 1968. irreg. $8 per no. Paleontological Society, Dept. of Geological Sciences, University of Chicago, 5734 S. Ellis Ave., Chicago, IL 60637. Ed. Kenneth Caster. circ. 3,200.

560 557   US
PALEONTOLOGY AND GEOLOGY OF THE BADWATER CREEK AREA, CENTRAL WYOMING. (Subseries of the Annals of Carnegie Museum) irreg., latest issue no. 9. Carnegie Museum of Natural History, 4400 Forbes Ave, Pittsburgh, PA 15213. Indexed: Biol.Abstr. Zoo.Rec.

PRIRODNJACKI MUZEJ U BEOGRADU. GLASNIK. SERIJA A: MINEROLOGIJA, GEOLOGIJA, PALEONTOLOGIJA. see *EARTH SCIENCES — Geology*

560   IT   ISSN 0085-5235
QUATERNARIA. (Text and summaries in English, French, Italian, German and Spanish) 1954. a. price varies. Elena Aguet Blanc, Ed. & Pub., Via Giulio Caccini No. 1, 00198 Rome, Italy. adv. bk. rev. bibl. charts. illus. cum.index. circ. 800.

560   CS   ISSN 0036-5297
SBORNIK GEOLOGICKYCH VED: PALEONTOLOGIE/JOURNAL OF GEOLOGICAL SCIENCES: PALEONTOLOGY. (Text in English, French or German; summaries also in Russian) 1949. irreg. 25-40 Kcs. per no. Ustredni Ustav Geologicky, Malostranske nam. 19, 118 21 Prague 1, Czechoslovakia (Subscr. to: Artia, Ve Smeckach 30, 111 27 Prague 1) Ed. Vladimir Havlicek. charts. illus. circ. 600. (back issues avail.) Indexed: Bull.Signal. Ref.Zh. Bibl.& Ind.Geol.

560   SZ   ISSN 0080-7389
SCHWEIZERISCHE PALAEONTOLOGISCHE ABHANDLUNGEN/MEMOIRES SUISSE DE PALEONTOLOGIE. (Text in French and German) 1874. irreg. price varies. (Schweizerische Naturforschende Gesellschaft) Birkhaeuser Verlag, Elisabethenstr. 19, CH-4010 Basel, Switzerland. Ed. Hans Schaub. index.

560   US   ISSN 0081-0266
SMITHSONIAN CONTRIBUTIONS TO PALEOBIOLOGY. 1969. irreg. Smithsonian Institution Press, Washington, DC 20560. Ed. Albert L. Ruffin Jr. circ. 2,500. (reprint service avail. from UMI) Indexed: Biol.Abstr.

TERTIARY RESEARCH GROUP. SPECIAL PAPERS. see *EARTH SCIENCES — Geology*

TOHOKU UNIVERSITY. INSTITUTE OF GEOLOGY AND PALEONTOLOGY. CONTRIBUTIONS/TOHOKU DAIGAKU RIGAKUBU CHISHITSUGAKU KOSEIBUTSUGAKU KYOSHITSU KENKYU HOBUN HOKOKU. see *EARTH SCIENCES — Geology*

TOHOKU UNIVERSITY. INSTITUTE OF GEOLOGY AND PALEONTOLOGY. SCIENCE REPORTS. SECOND SERIES. see *EARTH SCIENCES — Geology*

565   NO   ISSN 0085-7386
TRILOBITE NEWS. (Text in English) 1971. a, latest 1976. free. Universitet i Oslo, Paleontologiska Museum, Sarsgate 1, Oslo 5, Norway. Ed. D.L. Bruton. bk. rev. abstr. bibl. index. circ. 250.

UNIVERSITA DEGLI STUDI DI FERRARA. ISTITUTO DI GEOLOGIA. PUBBLICAZIONI. see *EARTH SCIENCES — Geology*

560   IT
UNIVERSITA DEGLI STUDI DI FERRARA. ISTITUTO DI GEOLOGIA. ANNALI. SEZIONE 15. PALEONTOLOGIA UMANA E PALETNOLOGIA. (Text and summaries in Italian, English and French) 1959. irreg.; vol. 2, no. 12, 1976. exchange basis. Universita degli Studi di Ferrara, Istituto di Geologia, C.So Ercole 1 d'Este 32, Ferrara, Italy. circ. 450.
Formerly: Universita degli Studi di Ferrara. Istituto di Geologia, Paleontologia e Paleontologia Umana. Annali. Sezione 15. Paleontologia Umana e Paleontologia (ISSN 0071-4542)

UNIVERSITAET HAMBURG. GEOLOGISCH-PALAEONTOLOGISCHES INSTITUT. MITTEILUNGEN. see *EARTH SCIENCES — Geology*

UNIVERSITAET STUTTGART. INSTITUT FUER GEOLOGIE UND PALAEONTOLOGIE ARBEITEN NEUE FOLGE. see *EARTH SCIENCES*

560   US   ISSN 0075-5044
UNIVERSITY OF KANSAS. PALEONTOLOGICAL CONTRIBUTIONS. ARTICLES. 1947. irreg., no. 65, 1979. price varies. University of Kansas, Paleontological Institute, c/o Exchange and Gifts Dept., Library Sales Section, Lawrence, KS 66045. Ed. R. A. Robison. circ. 1,500. Indexed: Geo.Abstr.

560   US   ISSN 0075-5052
UNIVERSITY OF KANSAS. PALEONTOLOGICAL CONTRIBUTIONS. PAPERS. 1947. irreg., no. 92, 1978. price varies. University of Kansas, Paleontological Institute, c/o Exchange and Gifts Dept., Library Sales Section, Lawrence, KS 66045. Ed. R. A. Robison. circ. 1,500. Indexed: Bibl. & Ind.Geol.

560   US   ISSN 0041-9834
UNIVERSITY OF MICHIGAN. MUSEUM OF PALEONTOLOGY. CONTRIBUTIONS. 1924. irreg., vol. 24, nos. 18-23, 1977. price varies. University of Michigan, Museum of Paleontology, Museums Bldg., Ann Arbor, MI 48109. Ed. Robert V. Kesling. circ. 500. Indexed: Biol.Abstr.

560   US
UNIVERSITY OF MICHIGAN. MUSEUM OF PALEONTOLOGY. PAPERS ON PALEONTOLOGY. 1972. irreg., no. 17, 1976. University of Michigan, Museum of Paleontology, Ann Arbor, MI 48109.

560   SA
UNIVERSITY OF THE WITWATERSRAND, JOHANNESBURG. BERNARD PRICE INSTITUTE FOR PALAEONTOLOGICAL RESEARCH. MEMOIR. irreg. University of the Witwatersrand, Johannesburg, Bernard Price Institute for Palaeontological Research, 1 Jan Smuts Ave., Johannesburg 2001, South Africa.

550   CS
USTREDNI USTAV GEOLOGICKY. ROZPRAVY. (Text in English or German; summaries in Czech and English) 1926. irreg. 25-65 Kcs. per no. Ustredni Ustav Geologicky, Malostranske nam. 19, 118 21 Prague 1, Czechoslovakia (Subscr. to: Artia, Ve Smeckach 30, 111 27 Prague 1) charts. illus. circ. 650. (back issues avail.) Indexed: Bull.Signal. Ref.Zh. Bibl. & Ind.Geol.

560   NE   ISSN 0083-4963
UTRECHT MICROPALEONTOLOGICAL BULLETINS. (Text in English) 1969. irreg., no. 16, 1977. price varies. Rijksuniversiteit te Utrecht, Department of Stratigraphy and Paleontology, c/o T. van Schaik, Singel 105, Odijk, Netherlands. Ed. C. W. Drooger.

560   GE   ISSN 0078-8600
ZENTRALES GEOLOGISCHES INSTITUT. PALAEONTOLOGISCHE ABHANDLUNGEN. 1961 (Neue Folge, 1974) irreg., no. 26, 1976. price varies. Akademie-Verlag, Leipziger Str. 3-4, 108 Berlin, E. Germany (D.D.R.) Ed. Bd.

560 551   GW   ISSN 0373-9627
ZITTELIANA; Abhandlungen der Bayerischen Staatssammlung fuer Palaeontologie und Historische Geologie. 1969. irreg. price varies. Bayerische Staatssammlung fuer Palaeontologie und Historische Geologie, Richard-Wagner-Strasse 10, 8000 Munich 2, W. Germany (B.R.D.) Ed. Dietrich Herm.

PAPER AND PULP

see also Packaging

AGENDA MEMENTO DES PROTES. see *PRINTING*

676   FR
ANNUAIRE DE LA PAPETERIE; France, Allemagne, Belgique, Espagne Italie et Pays-bas. 1879. biennial. 200 F. (Ancienne Maison D l'Homme et Argy) S. I. A. C., 30 rue de Turbigo, F 75003 Paris, France.
     Formerly: Annuaire de la Papeterie Francaise (ISSN 0066-2577)

ANNUAL BOOK OF A S T M STANDARDS. PART 20. PAPER; PACKAGING; BUSINESS COPY PRODUCTS. see *ENGINEERING — Engineering Mechanics And Materials*

676   UK   ISSN 0068-2322
BRITISH PAPER AND BOARD INDUSTRY FEDERATION. TECHNICAL DIVISION. FUNDAMENTAL RESEARCH INTERNATIONAL SYMPOSIA. 1958. quadrennial. price varies. British Paper and Board Industry Federation, Plough Place, Fetter Lane, London EC4A 1AL, England. Ed. Francis M. Bolam. Indexed: Abstr.Bull.Inst.Pap.Chem.

676.2   UK   ISSN 0068-2330
BRITISH PAPER AND BOARD INDUSTRY FEDERATION. TECHNICAL SECTION. TECHNICAL PAPERS. 1960. a. price varies. British Paper and Board Industry Federation, Plough Place, Fetter Lane, London EC4A 1AL, England. Ed. Robert L. Ballard. index.

676.2   UK   ISSN 0068-2349
BRITISH PAPER AND BOARD INDUSTRY FEDERATION. TECHNICAL SECTION. YEARBOOK. 1960. a. price varies. British Paper and Board Industry Federation, Plough Place, Fetter Lane, London EC4A 1AL, England. Ed. Robert L. Ballard.

676   CN   ISSN 0068-9491
CANADIAN PULP AND PAPER ASSOCIATION. NEWSPRINT DATA; statistics of world demand and supply. 1935. a. free. ‡ Canadian Pulp and Paper Association, 2300 Sun Life Building, Montreal, H3B 2X9 Que., Canada. Ed. N. L. M. Boultbee. stat. circ. controlled.
     Until 1970 issued by: Newsprint Association of Canada. Newsprint Data.

676   CN   ISSN 0068-9505
CANADIAN PULP AND PAPER ASSOCIATION. PULP AND PAPER REPORT. a. free. Canadian Pulp and Paper Association, 2300 Sun Life Bldg., Montreal, Que. H3B 2X9, Canada. circ. 5,000.

676.1   CN   ISSN 0068-9521
CANADIAN PULP AND PAPER ASSOCIATION. TECHNICAL SECTION. PROCEEDINGS. 1915. a. Can.$40 to non-members. Canadian Pulp and Paper Association, 2300 Sun Life Bldg., Montreal, P.Q. H3B 2X9, Canada. index. circ. 4,000. Indexed: Abstr.Bull.Inst.Pap.Chem.

676   CN   ISSN 0068-9548
CANADIAN PULP AND PAPER ASSOCIATION. WOODLANDS SECTION. PUBLICATIONS. 1927. irreg. membership. ‡ Canadian Pulp and Paper Association, Woodlands Section, 2300 Sun Life Bldg., Montreal H3B 2X9, Que., Canada. Indexed: Abstr.Bull.Inst.Pap.Chem.

676   US   ISSN 0190-2172
I E E E ANNUAL PULP AND PAPER INDUSTRY TECHNICAL CONFERENCE. CONFERENCE RECORD. a. Institute of Electrical and Electronics Engineers, Inc., 445 Hoes Lane, Piscataway, NJ 08854.
     Formerly: Pulp and Paper Industry Technical Conference. Record (ISSN 0079-7944)

INDUSTRIEGEWERKSCHAFT DRUCK UND PAPIER. SCHRIFTENREIHE FUER BETRIEBSRATE. see *PRINTING*

676   US
INSTRUMENTATION IN THE PULP AND PAPER INDUSTRY. Includes: International I S A Pulp and Paper Instrumentation Symposium Proceedings. 1960. a. price varies. Instrument Society of America, 400 Stanwix St., Pittsburgh, PA 15222.

676   670   US   ISSN 0097-2509
INTERNATIONAL PULP & PAPER DIRECTORY. 1974. biennial. Miller Freeman Publications, Inc., 500 Howard St., San Francisco, CA 94105. Ed. James R. Ledbetter.

676   US
KLINE GUIDE TO THE PAPER AND PULP INDUSTRY. 1968. triennial. $10. Charles H. Kline & Co., Inc., 330 Passaic Ave, Fairfield, NJ 07006. Ed. Joan Huber.
     Formerly: Marketing Guide to the Paper and Pulp Industry (ISSN 0076-4612)

676   US   ISSN 0076-0277
LOCKWOOD'S DIRECTORY OF THE PAPER AND ALLIED TRADES. 1873. a. $55 (abridged edt. $40.) Vance Publishing Corporation (New York), 133 E. 58th St., New York, NY 10022. Ed. S. Coopersmith. adv. index. circ. 3,800.

676   NE   ISSN 0077-1414
MONUMENTA CHARTAE PAPYRACEAE HISTORIAM ILLUSTRANTIA/COLLECTION OF WORKS AND DOCUMENTS ILLUSTRATING THE HISTORY OF PAPER. (Text mainly in English; occasionally in other languages) 1950. irreg., vol. 14, 1977. price varies. (Universiteitsbibliotheek van Amsterdam) Paper Publications Society, Nieuwe Prinsengracht 57, 1018 EG Amsterdam, Netherlands. Ed. J. S. G. Simmons. circ. 500.

676   US
PAPER, PAPERBOARD, WOODPULP CAPACITY; fiber consumption. 1958. a. American Paper Institute, Inc., 260 Madison Ave., New York, NY 10016.

676   UK   ISSN 0302-4180
PAPER REVIEW OF THE YEAR. 1973. a. £8. Benn Publications Ltd., 25 New Street Square, London EC4A 3JA, England. Ed. Eric Haylock. index. circ. 4,386.

676   US
PAPER YEAR BOOK. 1943. a. $35. Harcourt Brace Jovanovich, Inc., 757 Third Ave., New York, NY 10017. Ed. Roy Wirtzfeld. adv. circ. 2,500.

676   UK   ISSN 0079-158X
PHILLIPS' PAPER TRADE DIRECTORY-EUROPE-MILLS OF THE WORLD. 1904. a. £25. Benn Publications Ltd., 25 New Street Square, London EC4A 3JA, England. Ed. Eric Haylock. adv. index. circ. 3,277.
     Incorporating: Papermakers' and Merchants' Directory of All Nations (ISSN 0078-9038)

676   US
PULP & PAPER BUYERS GUIDE. a. $10. Miller Freeman Publications, Inc., 500 Howard St., San Francisco, CA 94105. circ. 20,000. (also avail. in microfilm)

676   CN   ISSN 0317-3550
PULP & PAPER CANADA'S BUSINESS DIRECTORY. 1907. a. Can.$25($32) National Business Publications, Ltd. (Subsidiary of: Southam Business Publications, Ltd.) 310 Victoria Ave., Westmount, P. Q. H3Z 2M9, Canada. Ed. Fred Stevens. adv. index. circ. 1,816.
     Formerly: Canada's Pulp and Paper Business Directory (ISSN 0079-7936)

676   CN
PULP AND PAPER, CANADA'S REFERENCE MANUAL & BUYERS' GUIDE. 1930. a. Can.$20($30) National Business Publications, Ltd. (Subsidiary of: Southam Business Publications, Ltd.) 310 Victoria Ave., Westmount, P. Q. H3Z 2M9, Canada. Ed. Fred Stevens. adv. index. circ. 2,441.
     Formerly: Pulp & Paper Magazine of Canada's Reference Manual & Buyers' Guide (ISSN 0079-7952)

338.47   FR   ISSN 0474-5485
PULP AND PAPER INDUSTRY IN THE O E C D MEMBER COUNTRIES AND FINLAND/ INDUSTRIE DES PATES ET PAPIERS DANS LES PAYS MEMBRES DE L'OCDE ET LA FINLANDE. (Text in English and French) 1954. irreg. Organization for Economic Cooperation and Development, 2 rue Andre Pascal, 75775 Paris 16, France (U. S. Orders to: O.E.C.D. Publications Center, 1750 Pennsylvania Ave., N. W., Washington, D. C. 20006) (also avail. in microfiche)

676   CN   ISSN 0079-7960
PULP AND PAPER RESEARCH INSTITUTE OF CANADA. ANNUAL REPORT. 1968. a. free. ‡ Pulp and Paper Research Institute of Canada, 570 St. John's Road, Pointe Claire, Que. H9R 3J9, Canada. circ. 2,500.

676   AT   ISSN 0310-4389
SOMETHING ON PAPER. 1973. irreg. free. Associated Pulp and Paper Mills Ltd., G.P.O. Box 509H, Melbourne, Vic. 3001, Australia.

676   US   ISSN 0081-2129
SOURCES OF SUPPLY/BUYERS GUIDE. 1924. a. $30. Advertisers and Publishers Service, Inc., Drawer 795, Park Ridge, IL 60068. Ed. L. B. Cowan. adv. circ. 1,200.
     Formerly: Source of Supply Directory.

676   US
T A P P I TEST METHODS. 1926. irreg. $549.95 to non-members; members $366.63. ‡ Technical Association of the Pulp and Paper Industry, One Dunwoody Park, Atlanta, GA 30338. index. (looseleaf format)
     Former titles: T A P P I Standards and Provisional Methods; T A P P I Standards and Suggested Methods.

676   US   ISSN 0091-7737
TECHNICAL ASSOCIATION OF THE PULP AND PAPER INDUSTRY. DIRECTORY. Running title: T A P P I Directory. 1931. a. membership. ‡ Technical Association of the Pulp and Paper Industry, One Dunwoody Park, Atlanta, GA 30338. adv. circ. 22,000. Key Title: Directory - Technical Association of the Pulp and Paper Industry.

676   US
TECHNICAL ASSOCIATION OF THE PULP AND PAPER INDUSTRY. PROCEEDINGS. 9/yr. $404.95. Technical Association of the Pulp & Paper Industry, One Dunwoody Park, Atlanta, GA 30338.
     Former titles, 1978-1979: Conference Proceedings; 1976-1977: Conference Papers; 1967-1975: Conference Preprints.

676   US
TRANSPORT AND HANDLING IN THE PULP AND PAPER INDUSTRY; proceedings. 1975. irreg. (Pulp & Paper International Symposium) Miller Freeman Publications, Inc., 500 Howard St., San Francisco, CA 94105. illus.

676   US   ISSN 0083-7024
WALDEN'S A B C GUIDE AND PAPER PRODUCTION YEARBOOK. 1887. a. $50. Walden - Mott Corporation, 466 Kinderkamack Rd., Oradell, NJ 07649. Ed. Michael Balbian. index.

676   UK
WHO'S WHO IN CORRUGATED. a. £7. International Paper Board Industry, Binsted House, Devonshire Close, Devonshire St., London W1N 2DL, England. Ed. Kenneth C. Binsted.

338.4   JA   ISSN 0453-1515
YEARBOOK OF PULP AND PAPER STATISTICS/ KAMI PARUPU TOKEI NENPO. (Editions in English and Japanese) 1947. a. (Ministry of International Trade and Industry, Research and Statistics Division - Tsusho Sangyo-sho Daijin Kanbo Chosa Tokei-bu) Research Institute of International Trade and Industry (Tsusho Sangiyo Chosakai), Kobikikan Bekkan, 6-15-2 Ginza, Chuo-ku, Tokyo 104, Japan.

PAPER AND PULP — Abstracting, Bibliographies, Statistics

676.2　　　　　CN　ISSN 0384-465X
CANADA. STATISTICS CANADA.
CORRUGATED BOX MANUFACTURERS/
FABRICANTS DE BOITES EN CARTON
ONDULE. (Catalog 36-213) (Text in English and
French) 1961. a. Can.$4.50($5.40) Statistics Canada,
Publications Distribution, Ottawa, Ont. K1A 0V7,
Canada. (also avail. in microform from
MML)

338.4　　　　　CN　ISSN 0316-4241
CANADIAN PULP AND PAPER ASSOCIATION.
ANNUAL NEWSPRINT SUPPLEMENT. a. free.
Canadian Pulp and Paper Association, 2300 Sun
Life Building, Montreal, Que. H3B 2X9, Canada.
stat.

676　016　　　　US　ISSN 0073-9480
INSTITUTE OF PAPER CHEMISTRY.
BIBLIOGRAPHIC SERIES. 1929. irreg., no. 289,
1981. price varies. Institute of Paper Chemistry,
1043 E. South River St., Appleton, WI 54912. Ed.
Lillian Roth. bk. rev. author, subject and patent
index. circ. 600.

676　　　　　　NE
NETHERLANDS. CENTRAAL BUREAU VOOR
DE STATISTIEK. PRODUKTIESTATISTIEKEN:
PAPIER- EN KARTONINDUSTRIE. a. fl.7.85.
Centraal Bureau voor de Statistiek, Prinses
Beatrixlaan 428, Voorburg, Netherlands (Orders to:
Staatsuitgeverij, Christoffel Plantijnstraat, The
Hague, Netherlands)
Formed by the merger of: Netherlands. Centraal
Bureau voor de Statistiek. Produktiestatistiek van de
Papierindustries & Netherlands. Centraal Bureau
voor de Statistiek. Produktiestatistiek
Strokartonindustrie.

676　310　　　　FR
STATISTIQUES DE L'INDUSTRIE FRANCAISE
DES PATES. PAPIERS ET CARTONS. irreg.
Centre d'Etudes et de Productivite des Industries
des Papiers, Cartons et Celluloses, 154, Boulevard
Haussmann, 75008 Paris, France. illus.
Continues: Quelques Donnees Statistiques sur
l'Industrie Francaise des Pates, Papiers, Cartons
(ISSN 0481-0112)

PARAPSYCHOLOGY AND OCCULTISM

133　　　　　　US
ADVANCES IN PARAPSYCHOLOGICAL
RESEARCH. 1977. irreg. price varies. Plenum
Press, 233 Spring St., New York, NY 10013. Ed.
Bd.

133　　　　　　CN　ISSN 0409-7734
CACTUS. 1951. irreg. Cactus Inc., 873 St.-Jean,
Quebec City, Canada. illus.

130　　　　　　II
I I S T BULLETINS; human electricity and
experiments on soul. (Text in English and Telugu)
1969. m. $7. Indian Institute of Soul Technology,
Azamabad, Hyderabad 50020, India. Ed. N.
Lashminarayana. adv. bk. rev. circ. 1,000.
Formerly(until Dec. 1976): Auto-Writing (ISSN
0005-089X)

132　　　　　　FR　ISSN 0534-9168
INTERNATIONAL CONGRESS OF
PSYCHOPATHOLOGICAL ART. PROGRAM.
PROGRAMME. (Text in English, French and
German) irreg. International Society of Art and
Psychopathology, c/o Dr. C. Wiart, Clinique de la
Faculte, 100 rue de la Sante, 75 Paris 14, France.

133　　　　　　US　ISSN 0147-782X
INTERNATIONAL PSYCHIC REGISTER; a
directory of practitioners of the psychic arts in the
United States, Canada & Great Britain. 1977. a. $4.
Ornion Press, Box 1816, Erie, PA 16507. Ed.
Donald A. McQuaid.

133　　　　　　US
NEWS NOVEL. 1969. irreg. Box 3232, Riverside, CA
92519. Ed. Darlene Wheeler.

133.91　　　　　US
NUERUOLOG; the journal of reality frontiers. 1975.
irreg. $1.50. Network Publishing, Box 317, Berkeley,
CA 94701. Ed. Ted Schultz. bk. rev. abstr. bibl.
charts. illus. tr.lit. circ. 1,500. (back issues avail.)

133　　　　　　US
OCCULTISM UPDATE. (Supplement to the
Encyclopedia of Occultism and Parapsychology)
1978. irreg. $35 for 4 nos. Gale Research Company,
Book Tower, Detroit, MI 48226. Ed. Leslie
Shepard.

133　　　　　　US　ISSN 0078-9437
PARAPSYCHOLOGICAL MONOGRAPHS. 1958.
irreg., latest no. 17. price varies. Parapsychology
Foundation, 228 E. 71st St., New York, NY 10012.
Indexed: Psychol.Abstr.

133　　　　　　US
PARAPSYCHOLOGY FOUNDATION.
PROCEEDINGS OF INTERNATIONAL
CONFERENCES. 1953. a. price varies.
Parapsychology Foundation, 228 E. 71st St., New
York, NY 10021.

133.324　　　　　UK　ISSN 0079-4953
PREDICTION ANNUAL. a. 85p. Link House
Publications Ltd., Link House, Dingwall Ave.,
Croydon CR9 2TA, England. Ed. Jo Logan. adv.
bk. rev. circ. 45,000.

133.91　　　　　US
PSYCHIC STUDIES. a. price varies. Gordon and
Breach Science Publishers, One Park Ave., New
York, NY 10016. Ed. Stanley Krippner, Irene Hall.

133　　　　　　US　ISSN 0094-7172
RESEARCH IN PARAPSYCHOLOGY. 1972. a. $10.
(Parapsychological Association) Scarecrow Press,
Inc., 52 Liberty St., Metuchen, NJ 08840.
Continues: Parapsychological Association.
Proceedings.

133　　　　　　FR　ISSN 0484-8934
REVUE METAPSYCHIQUE. irreg. 30 F. per no.
Institut Metaphysique International, 1 Place
Wagram, 75017 Paris, France.

133　　　　　　FR　ISSN 0080-7672
SCIENCES SECRETES. 1970. irreg. price varies.
Editions Pierre Belfond, 3 bis Passage de la
Boucherie, 75006 Paris, France.

133　　　　　　UK　ISSN 0081-1475
SOCIETY FOR PSYCHICAL RESEARCH.
PROCEEDINGS. 1882. irreg. membership. Society
for Psychical Research, 1 Adam and Eve Mews,
London, W8 6VQ, England. Ed. Renee Haynes.
Indexed: Br.Hum.Ind. Psychol.Abstr.

133.4　　　　　US　ISSN 0085-8250
WITCHCRAFT DIGEST. (Supplement to W I C A
Newsletter) 1970. a. $1.40 per no. (Witches
International Craft Associates; Witches Liberation
Movement) Hero Press, Suite 1B, 153 West 80 St.,
New York, NY 10024. Ed. Leo Louis Martello. adv.
bk. rev. circ. 3,000.
Formerly: Witchcraft (ISSN 0014-2840)

133　　　　　　US
WITCHES ALMANAC. 1971-72. a. $1.95 per no. ‡
Grosset & Dunlap, 51 Madison Ave., New York,
NY 10010 (Mailing Address: Box 740, Newport, RI
02840) Eds. Elizabeth Pepper and John Wilcock.
adv. charts. illus. circ. 100,000.

PATENTS, TRADEMARKS AND COPYRIGHTS

346.73　608.7　　US　ISSN 0361-3844
ATTORNEYS AND AGENTS REGISTERED TO
PRACTICE BEFORE THE U.S. PATENT AND
TRADEMARK OFFICE. irreg. $3.70. U.S. Patent
and Trademark Office, Washington, DC 20231
(Orders to: Supt. of Documents, Washington, DC
20402)
Former titles: Attorneys and Agents Registered
to Practice Before the U.S. Patent Office (ISSN
0092-5934); Roster of Attorneys and Agents
Registered to Practice Before the U.S. Patent Office;
Directory of Registered Patent Attorneys and
Agents (ISSN 0565-9582)

608.7　　　　　AT
AUSTRALIA. DESIGNS OFFICE. REGISTERED
OWNERS OF DESIGNS AND ARTICLES IN
RESPECT OF WHICH DESIGNS HAVE BEEN
REGISTERED UNDER THE DESIGNS ACT.
1973. irreg. Designs Office, Canberra, A.C.T. 2600,
Australia.

608.7　　　　　AT
AUSTRALIA. PATENT OFFICE. REPORT. 1972/
73. a. Aus.$0.45. Patent Office, Canberra, A.C.T.
2600, Australia. illus.

340　　　　　　AT　ISSN 0311-2934
AUSTRALIAN COPYRIGHT COUNCIL.
BULLETIN. 1973. irreg. Australian Copyright
Council, 252 George St, Sydney, N.S.W. 2000,
Australia. Eds. David Catterns; Peter Banki.

347.7　　　　　US　ISSN 0069-9950
COPYRIGHT LAW SYMPOSIUM. 1950. irreg., no
25, 1980. price varies. (American Society of
Composers, Authors, and Publishers) Columbia
University Press, 136 South Broadway, Irvington-
On-Hudson, NY 10533.

340　　　　　　UN　ISSN 0069-9969
COPYRIGHT LAWS AND TREATIES OF THE
WORLD. SUPPLEMENTS. a. Unesco, 7-9 Place de
Fontenoy, 75700 Paris, France. (Co sponsor: World
Intellectual Property Organization) (also avail. in
looseleaf format)

340　　　　　　US　ISSN 0070-3176
DECISIONS OF THE UNITED STATES COURTS
INVOLVING COPYRIGHTS. (Subseries of U.S.
Copyright Office. Bulletin) 1910. biennial. price
varies. U.S. Library of Congress, Copyright Office,
The Library of Congress, Washington, DC 20559
(Orders to: Supt. of Documents, Washington, DC
20402) cum. index.

608.7　　　　　DK
DENMARK. DIREKTORATET FOR PATENT- OG
VAREMAERKEVAESENET.
AARSBERETNING. 1975. a. Direktoratet for
Patent- og Varemaerkevaesenet - Patents and
Trademarks Authority, Nyropsgade 45, DK-1602
Copenhagen V, Denmark.

608.7　　　　　US　ISSN 0083-3029
GENERAL INFORMATION CONCERNING
TRADEMARKS. irreg. $0.95. U.S. Patent and
Trademark Office, Washington, DC 20231 (Orders
to: Supt. of Documents, Washington, DC 20402)

608.7　　　　　UK　ISSN 0072-5706
GREAT BRITAIN. DEPARTMENT OF TRADE.
PATENTS, DESIGN AND TRADE
MARKS(ANNUAL REPORT) a. H.M.S.O., P.O.
Box 569, London SE1 9NH, England.

608　　　　　　US　ISSN 0073-5043
ILLINOIS STATE BAR ASSOCIATION. PATENT,
TRADEMARK, AND COPYRIGHT
NEWSLETTER. 1961. irreg., 1970, vol. 11, no. 1.
membership. Illinois State Bar Association, Illinois
Bar Center, Springfield, IL 62701. Ed. Edmund A.
Godula. (back issues avail.)

608.7　　　　　US　ISSN 0362-0719
INDEX OF PATENTS ISSUED FROM THE
UNITED STATES PATENT AND TRADEMARK
OFFICE. 1920. a. price varies. U.S. Patent and
Trademark Office, Washington, DC 20231 (Orders
to: Supt. of Documents, Washington, DC 20402)
Formerly: U. S. Patent Office. Index of Patents
Issued from the United States Patent Office (ISSN
0083-3037)

608.7　　　　　US　ISSN 0099-0809
INDEX OF TRADEMARKS ISSUED FROM THE
U.S. PATENT AND TRADEMARK OFFICE. a.
price varies. U.S. Patent and Trademark Office,
Washington, DC 20231 (Orders to: Supt. of
Documents, Washington, DC 20402)
Formerly: Index of Trademarks Issued from the
United States Patent Office (ISSN 0083-3045)

INDUSTRIAL PROPERTY LAW. ANNUAL. see
LAW

340　　　　　　AT
INSTITUTE OF PATENT ATTORNEYS OF
AUSTRALIA. ANNUAL PROCEEDINGS. a.
membership. Institute of Patent Attorneys of
Australia, 414 Collins St., Melbourne, Vic. 3000,
Australia.

608.7 US
INTELLECTUAL PROPERTY LAW REVIEW. 1969. a. $47.50. Clark Boardman Co., Ltd., 435 Hudson St., New York, NY 10014. Ed. Thomas E. Costner. index. circ. 1,100.
Formerly: Patent Law Review (ISSN 0079-0168)

608.7 FR ISSN 0020-515X
INTERAUTEURS. 1930. a. 25 F. International Confederation of Societies of Authors and Composers, 11 rue Keppler, 75116 Paris, France. abstr. bibl. index. circ. 500.

341.758 FR ISSN 0074-2899
INTERNATIONAL CONFEDERATION OF SOCIETIES OF AUTHORS AND COMPOSERS. irreg., no. 186, 1976. International Confederation of Societies of Authors and Composers, 11 rue Keppler, 75116 Paris, France.

340 UN ISSN 0336-3686
INTERNATIONAL COPYRIGHT INFORMATION CENTRE. INFORMATION BULLETIN. French edition: Centre International d'Information sur le Droit d'Auteur. Bulletin d'Information. Spanish edition: Centro Internacional de Informaciones sobre el Derecho de Autor. Bulletin de Informacion. 1973. irreg. free. Unesco, International Copyright Information Centre, 7-9 Place de Fontenoy, 75700 Paris, France. Ed. Jose Miguel de Azaola. circ. 2,300 (English edt.); 1,300 (French edt.); 600 (Spanish edt.)

340 GW ISSN 0539-1512
INTERNATIONALE GESELLSCHAFT FUER URHEBERRECHT. YEARBOOK. (Text in English, French, German, Italian and Spanish) irreg., vol. 3, 1976. International Copyright Society, Herzog-Wilhelm-Str. 28, 8000 Munich 2, W. Germany (B.R.D.)

340 NE
MONOGRAPHS ON INDUSTRIAL PROPERTY AND COPYRIGHT LAW. (Text in English) 1976. irreg. Sijthoff & Noordhoff International Publishers b.v., Box 4, MA Alphen aan den Rijn, Netherlands (U.S. address: 20010 Century Blvd., Germantown, MD 20767)

602.7 US
NEW TRADE NAMES. (Supplement to: Trade Names Dictionary) 1976. a., between edts. of Trade Names Dictionary. $65 for 2 yrs. Gale Research Company, Book Tower, Detroit, MI 48226. Ed. Ellen T. Crowley.

608.7 CN ISSN 0079-015X
PATENT AND TRADEMARK INSTITUTE OF CANADA. ANNUAL PROCEEDINGS. 1928. a. membership. Patent and Trademark Institute of Canada, Box 1298, Sta. B, Ottawa, Ont. K1P 5R3, Canada, Canada.

608.7 US ISSN 0553-3864
PATENT LAW ANNUAL-SOUTHWESTERN LEGAL FOUNDATION. a. $28.50. Matthew Bender & Co., Inc., 235 E. 45th St., New York, NY 10017. Ed. Virginia S. Cameron.

608.7 II
PATENT OFFICE TECHNICAL SOCIETY. JOURNAL. (Text in English) vol. 10. 1976. irreg. Patent Office Technical Society, Calcutta, India. patents. stat.

608.7 UK
REGISTER OF PATENT AGENTS. 1889. a. 50p.($0.50) Chartered Institute of Patent Agents, Staple Inn Bldgs., High Holborn, London WC1V 7PZ, England. circ. 2,500.

REPERTOIRE GENERAL DE LA PRODUCTION FRANCAISE. see *BUSINESS AND ECONOMICS — Trade And Industrial Directories*

608.7 UK ISSN 0080-1364
REPORTS OF PATENT, DESIGN, TRADE MARK AND OTHER CASES. 1884. irreg. £36. Patent Office, St. Mary Cray, Orpington, Kent, BR5 3RD, England. Ed. Michael Fysh. circ. 1,800.

602.7 BL
SINAL; registro de marcas e simbolos. irreg. Editora de Guias Ltda., Av. Paulista 1776, 01310 Sao Paulo, Brazil. illus.

602.7 SW
SVENSKT VARUMAERKESARKIV/SWEDISH TRADEMARK ARCHIVE; computer-indexed microfiche archive including full information about registered trademarks and pending applications. 1976. a (with updates weekly) Kr.3500 (minimum 2 yrs.); pending applications only Kr.650/yr. Patent- och Registreringsverket - Royal Patent and Registration Office, Box 5055, S-102 42 Stockholm, Sweden.

608 SW
SWEDEN. PATENT- OCH REGISTERERINGSVERKET. AARSBERAETTELSE/SWEDEN. ROYAL PATENT AND REGISTRATION OFFICE. ANNUAL REPORT. (Text in English & Swedish) 1965. a. Kr.20. Patent- och Registreringsverket - Royal Patent and Registration Office, Box 5055, S-102 42 Stockholm, Sweden. pat. stat. circ. 3,000.

TAXATION OF PATENTS, TRADEMARKS, COPYRIGHTS AND KNOW-HOW (SUPPLEMENT) see *BUSINESS AND ECONOMICS — Public Finance, Taxation*

602.7 IT
TOP TRADEMARKS ANNUAL. Cover title: Top Symbols & Trademarks of the World. no. 8, 1977. a. Deco Press (Subsidiary of: Franco Maria Ricci Editore) Via Santa Sofia 8, 20122 Milan, Italy. Eds. Franco M. Ricci, Corinna Ferrari.

608.7 US ISSN 0082-5786
TRADE-MARK REGISTER OF THE UNITED STATES. 1958. a. $89. ‡ Patent Searching Service, 454 Washington Bldg., Washington, DC 20005. Ed. Cyril W. Sernak. cum.index 1881-1980.

602.7 US
TRADE NAMES DICTIONARY. (Supplement: New Trade Names) 1976. irreg., 2nd ed., 1979. $85 (2 vols.) Gale Research Company, Book Tower, Detroit, MI 48226. Ed. Ellen T. Crowley.

340 US ISSN 0090-2845
U. S. COPYRIGHT OFFICE. ANNUAL REPORT OF THE REGISTER OF COPYRIGHTS. 1910. a. free. U. S. Library of Congress, Copyright Office, Library of Congress, Washington, DC 20559. Key Title: Annual Report of the Register of Copyrights.

608.7 US ISSN 0083-3002
U.S. PATENT AND TRADEMARK OFFICE. ANNUAL REPORT OF THE COMMISSIONER OF PATENTS. 1837. a. price varies. U.S. Patent and Trademark Office, Washington, DC 20231 (Orders to: Supt. of Documents, Washington, DC 20402)

608.7 US ISSN 0083-3010
U.S. PATENT AND TRADEMARK OFFICE. CLASSIFICATION BULLETINS. irreg. price varies. U.S. Patent and Trademark Office, Washington, DC 20231 (Orders to: Supt. of Documents, Washington, DC 20402)

608.7 US
U.S. PATENT AND TRADEMARK OFFICE. TRADEMARK RULES OF PRACTICE OF THE PATENT AND TRADEMARK OFFICE WITH FORMS AND STATUTES. irreg. $3.50. U.S. Patent and Trademark Office, Washington, DC 20231 (Orders to: Supt. of Documents, Washington, DC 20402)
Formerly: U.S. Patent Office. Trademark Rules of Practice of the Patent Office with Forms and Statutes (ISSN 0083-307X)

PEDIATRICS

see *Medical Sciences — Pediatrics*

PERFUMES AND COSMETICS

see *Beauty Culture — Perfumes and Cosmetics*

PERSONNEL MANAGEMENT

see *Business and Economics — Personnel Management*

PETROLEUM AND GAS

553 AT ISSN 0084-7534
A. P. E. A. JOURNAL. 1961. a. Aus.$10. ‡ Australian Petroleum Exploration Association, Box 3974, Sydney, N.S.W. 2001, Australia. Ed. K. M. Horler. circ. 1,500. Indexed: Aus.Sci.Ind.

665.5 US
AFRICA-MIDDLE EAST PETROLEUM DIRECTORY. 1979. a. $25. PennWell Publishing Co., Box 1260, Tulsa, OK 74101.
Supersedes in part: Eastern Hemisphere Petroleum Directory (ISSN 0070-8224)

338.2 665.5 US ISSN 0065-5813
ALASKA PETROLEUM AND INDUSTRIAL DIRECTORY. 1958. a. $20. Alaska Directory Corp., 409 W. Northern Lights Blvd., Anchorage, AK 99503. Ed. Kristen Nelson. circ. 200.
Before 1970: Alaska Petroleum Directory.

ALBERTA. DEPARTMENT OF ENERGY AND NATURAL RESOURCES, ANNUAL REPORT. see *ENERGY*

665.5 CN ISSN 0703-2358
ALBERTA PETROLEUM MARKETING COMMISSION. ANNUAL REPORT. 1974. a. Alberta Petroleum Marketing Commission, 1000 Bow Valley Square 11, 205 5th Ave. S.W., Box 9084, Edmonton, Alta., Canada. illus.

620 CN ISSN 0034-5180
ALBERTA RESEARCH COUNCIL. INFORMATION SERIES. 1947. irreg. price varies (Can.$0.50-$7) Alberta Research Council, Publications Dept., 11315-87th Ave., Edmonton T6G 2C2, Alta., Canada. Indexed: Eng.Ind.

665.5 GW
ALLGEMEINE GASTARIFE IN DER BUNDESREPUBLIK DEUTSCHLAND. 1970. a. price varies. (Verband des Deutschen Gas- und Wasserwerke) ZfGW-Verlag GmbH, Voltastr. 79, 6000 Frankfurt 90, W. Germany (B.R.D.) stat. circ. (controlled) (looseleaf format)

665.5 US ISSN 0065-731X
AMERICAN ASSOCIATION OF PETROLEUM GEOLOGISTS. MEMOIR. 1962. irreg., no. 27, 1978. price varies. American Association of Petroleum Geologists, Box 979, Tulsa, OK 74101. cum.index: 1946-55, 1956-65, each memoir is indexed.

665.7 US ISSN 0362-4994
AMERICAN GAS ASSOCIATION. OPERATING SECTION. PROCEEDINGS. 1965. a. price varies. American Gas Association, 1515 Wilson Blvd., Arlington, VA 22209. illus. Key Title: Operating Section Proceedings.

665.7 US ISSN 0091-2786
AMERICAN GAS ASSOCIATION. RESEARCH AND DEVELOPMENT. 1944. a. $0.10. American Gas Association, Department of Research & Engineering, 1515 Wilson Blvd., Arlington, VA 22209. illus. circ. 2,500. Key Title: Research and Development - American Gas Association.

AMERICAN INSTITUTE OF MINING, METALLURGICAL AND PETROLEUM ENGINEERS. NATIONAL OPEN HEARTH AND BASIC OXYGEN STEEL DIVISION. PROCEEDINGS OF THE CONFERENCE. see *MINES AND MINING INDUSTRY*

PETROLEUM AND GAS

025.3 665.5   US   ISSN 0193-5151
AMERICAN PETROLEUM INSTITUTE.
CENTRAL ABSTRACTING AND INDEXING
SERVICE. THESAURUS. 1964. a. $150. American
Petroleum Institute, Central Abstracting and
Indexing Service, 156 William St., New York, NY
10038. Key Title: Thesaurus - American Petroleum
Institute.
  Continues: American Petroleum Institute.
Information Retrieval System, Subject Authority
List.

AMERICAN PETROLEUM INSTITUTE.
COMMITTEE ON MEDICINE AND
ENVIRONMENTAL HEALTH. MEDICAL
RESEARCH REPORTS. see *PUBLIC HEALTH
AND SAFETY*

665.5   US   ISSN 0569-6909
AMERICAN PETROLEUM INSTITUTE. DIVISION
OF REFINING. PROCEEDINGS. a. price varies.
American Petroleum Institute, Division of Refining,
1801 K St., N.W., Washington, DC 20006.

665.7   US   ISSN 0066-149X
ANALYSES OF NATURAL GASES OF THE
UNITED STATES. 1917. a. price varies. U. S.
Bureau of Mines, Dept. of the Interior, Washington,
DC 20240.

ANNUAL BOOK OF A S T M STANDARDS.
PART 23. PETROLEUM PRODUCTS AND
LUBRICANTS (1) see *ENGINEERING —
Engineering Mechanics And Materials*

ANNUAL BOOK OF A S T M STANDARDS.
PART 24. PETROLEUM PRODUCTS AND
LUBRICANTS (2) see *ENGINEERING —
Engineering Mechanics And Materials*

ANNUAL BOOK OF A S T M STANDARDS.
PART 25. PETROLEUM PRODUCTS AND
LUBRICANTS (3); AEROSPACE MATERIALS.
see *ENGINEERING — Engineering Mechanics
And Materials*

ANNUAL BOOK OF A S T M STANDARDS.
PART 26. GASEOUS FUELS; COAL AND
COKE; ATMOSPHERIC ANALYSIS. see
*ENGINEERING — Engineering Mechanics And
Materials*

665.7   UN   ISSN 0066-3824
ANNUAL BULLETIN OF GAS STATISTICS FOR
EUROPE/BULLETIN ANNUEL DU
STATISTIQUES DE GAZ POUR L'EUROPE.
(Text in English, French and Russian) 1961. a; vol.
XXIV, 1978. price varies. United Nations Economic
Commission for Europe, Palais des Nations, 1200
Geneva 10, Switzerland (Or United Nations
Publications, Room LX-2300, New York, NY
10017).

665.5   US
ANNUAL REVIEW OF CALIFORNIA OIL & GAS
EXPLORATION. 1952? a. $30. Munger Oilgram,
9800 S. Sepulveda Blvd., Ste. 723, Box 45738, Los
Angeles, CA 90045. Ed. Averill H. Munger.

665.7   US   ISSN 0066-5371
APPALACHIAN GAS MEASUREMENT SHORT
COURSE, WEST VIRGINIA UNIVERSITY.
PROCEEDINGS. (Issued as subseries in its Bulletin
series) 1939. a. $15. West Virginia University,
Engineering Experiment Station, College of
Engineering, Morgantown, WV 26506. Ed. Donald
M. Bondurant. circ. 1,000.

338.2   FR
ARAB OIL & GAS DIRECTORY. (Text in English)
1974. a. $160. Arab Petroleum Research Center, 7
Av. Ingres, 75781 Paris Cedex 16, France. adv.
illus. stat. circ. 4,355.

665   US
ARMSTRONG OIL DIRECTORY: CENTRAL
UNITED STATES. 1961. a. $30. Oil Men's
Association of America, c/o Alan Armstrong, Ed.,
1606 South Jackson St., Amarillo, TX 79102.
  Formerly: Hank Seale Oil Directory: Central
United States (ISSN 0073-0238)

665   US
ARMSTRONG OIL DIRECTORY: LOUISIANA,
MISSISSIPPI, ARKANSAS, TEXAS GULF
COAST AND EAST TEXAS. 1958. a. $30. Oil
Men's Association of America, c/o Alan Armstrong,
Ed., 1606 South Jackson St., Amarillo, TX 79102.
  Formerly: Hank Seale Oil Directory: Louisiana,
Mississippi, Arkansas, Texas Gulf Coast and East
Texas (ISSN 0073-0254)

665   US
ARMSTRONG OIL DIRECTORY: TEXAS
INCLUDING SOUTHEAST NEW MEXICO.
1957. a. $30. Oil Men's Association of America, c/o
Alan Armstrong, Ed., 1606 South Jackson St.,
Amarillo, TX 79102.
  Formerly: Hank Seale Oil Directory: Texas
Including Southeast New Mexico (ISSN 0073-0262)

665.5   US
ASIA-PACIFIC PETROLEUM DIRECTORY. 1979.
a. $30. PennWell Publishing Co., Box 1260, Tulsa,
OK 74101.
  Supersedes in part: Eastern Hemisphere
Petroleum Directory (ISSN 0070-8224)

665.7   FR   ISSN 0066-9806
ASSOCIATION TECHNIQUE DE L'INDUSTRIE
DU GAZ EN FRANCE. COMPTE RENDU DU
CONGRES. (Text in French; summaries in English,
French, German) 1874. irreg. Association Technique
de l'Industrie du Gaz en France, 62, rue de
Courcelles, 75008 Paris, France.

AUSTRALIA. BUREAU OF STATISTICS.
ECONOMIC CENSUSES: ELECTRICITY AND
GAS ESTABLISHMENTS, DETAILS OF
OPERATIONS. see *ELECTRICITY AND
ELECTRICAL ENGINEERING*

AUSTRALIAN CONFERENCE ON CHEMICAL
ENGINEERING. PROCEEDINGS. see
ENGINEERING — Chemical Engineering

696   AT
AUSTRALIAN GAS INDUSTRY DIRECTORY. a.
Australian Gas Association, Box 323, Canberra
City, A.C.T. 2601, Australia. Ed. Ruth Booth.
  Former titles: Directory of the Australian Gas
Industry; Australian Gas Association. Directory.

553   AT   ISSN 0314-3171
AUSTRALIAN INSTITUTE OF PETROLEUM.
ANNUAL REPORT. 1977. a. free. Australian
Institute of Petroleum, Ltd., 227 Collins St.,
Melbourne, Vic. 3000, Australia.

BRITISH COLUMBIA. MINISTRY OF ENERGY,
MINES AND PETROLEUM RESOURCES.
ANNUAL REPORT. see *MINES AND MINING
INDUSTRY*

BRITISH COLUMBIA. MINISTRY OF ENERGY,
MINES AND PETROLEUM RESOURCES.
BULLETIN. see *EARTH SCIENCES — Geology*

665.7   UK   ISSN 0072-0216
BRITISH GAS CORPORATION. REPORT AND
ACCOUNTS. 1948/50. a. £1.50. British Gas
Corporation, 59 Bryanston Street, Marble Arch,
London W1A 2AZ, England. circ. 9,000. (also avail.
in microfilm)
  Formerly: Gas Council (Great Britain) Report
and Accounts.

665.7   US   ISSN 0197-8098
BROWN'S DIRECTORY OF NORTH AMERICAN
AND INTERNATIONAL GAS COMPANIES.
1887. a. $95. Harcourt Brace Jovanovich, Inc., 757
Third Ave., New York, NY 10017 (Subscr. to: One
E. First St., Duluth, MN 55802) Ed. Zane Chastain.
adv. circ. 948.
  Formerly (until 1978): Brown's Directory of
North American Gas Companies (ISSN 0068-2888)

662   AG
C.I.E. SERVICIO INFORMATIVO. no. 10, 1974.
irreg. (3-4/yr) Centro de Investigaciones
Energeticas, Av. Belgrano 748, Buenos Aires,
Argentina. charts. stat.

665.5 553   CN
C S P G MEMOIRS. no. 6, 1980. irreg. Can.$40. ‡
Canadian Society of Petroleum Geologists, 612
Lougheed Bldg., Calgary, Alta., Canada. Ed. Don
Glass. adv. bk. rev. charts. stat. circ. 2,200.

665.5   US   ISSN 0362-1243
CALIFORNIA. DIVISION OF OIL AND GAS.
ANNUAL REPORT OF THE STATE OIL AND
GAS SUPERVISOR. 1915. a. free. Divison of Oil
and Gas, 1416 9th St., Sacramento, CA 95814. illus.
circ. 2,200.

338.2   CN
CANADA. DEPARTMENT OF INDIAN AND
NORTHERN AFFAIRS. OIL AND GAS LAND
AND EXPLORATION SECTION. OIL AND
GAS ACTIVITIES. NORTH OF 60. (Editons in
English and French) 1965. a. free. Department of
Indian and Northern Affairs, Oil and Minerals
Division, 400 Laurier Ave. W., Ottawa, Ont. K1A
OH4, Canada. bibl. charts. illus. stat. circ. 4,000.
(tabloid format)

622.33   CN   ISSN 0317-4085
CANADA. NORTHERN NATURAL RESOURCES
AND ENVIRONMENT BRANCH. OIL AND
MINERAL DIVISION. NORTH OF 60: OIL
AND GAS TECHNICAL REPORTS. irreg. free.
Department of Indian and Northern Affairs, Public
Information Branch, 400 Laurier Ave. West,
Ottawa, Ont. K1A OH4, Canada.
  Continues: Canada. Northern Economic
Development Branch. Oil and Gas Technical
Reports- North of 60.

665.5   CN   ISSN 0068-8800
CANADIAN GAS ASSOCIATION. STATISTICAL
SUMMARY OF THE CANADIAN GAS
INDUSTRY. 1961. a. free. ‡ Canadian Gas
Association, 55 Scarsdale Rd., Don Mills, Ont.,
Canada.

CANADIAN GAS FACTS. see *ENERGY*

CANADIAN GAS UTILITIES DIRECTORY. see
ENERGY

CANADIAN OIL & GAS HANDBOOK. see *MINES
AND MINING INDUSTRY*

665.5   US
CANADIAN OIL INDUSTRY DIRECTORY. 1979.
a. $35. PennWell Publishing Co., Box 1260, Tulsa,
OK 74101.

665   CN   ISSN 0068-9394
CANADIAN OIL REGISTER. 1951. a. Can.$55. C.
O. Nickle Publications, (Subsidiary of: Southam
Communications Ltd.) Suite 110, 330 Ninth Ave.
S.W., Calgary. Alta. T2P 1K8, Canada. Ed. Jean
Omelusik. adv. circ. 5,500.

665.5   VE
COLECCION LA ALQUITRANA. 1975. irreg; no. 5,
1976. Ministerio de Energia y Minas, Torre Norte,
Centro Simon Bolivar, Venezuela. bibl.

338.2   CK
COLOMBIA. MINISTERIO DE MINAS Y
ENERGIA. OFICINA DE PLANEACION.
INDICADORES DE LA INDUSTRIA DEL
PETROLEO. irreg. Ministerio de Minas y Energia,
Oficina de Planeacion, Seccion de Investigaciones
Economicas, Bogota, Colombia. stat.

665.5 333.91   UY
COMISION DE INTEGRACION ELECTRICA
REGIONAL. RECURSOS ENERGETICOS DE
LOS PAISES DE LA C I E R. (Text in Castilian,
Portuguese) 1968. irreg. Comision de Integracion
Electrica Regional, Bulevar Artigas 996,
Montevideo, Uruguay. index.

COMITE DE CONTROLE DE L'ELECTRICITE ET
DU GAZ. RAPPORT ANNUEL. see
*ELECTRICITY AND ELECTRICAL
ENGINEERING*

665.5   US
COMPOSITE CATALOG OF OIL FIELD
EQUIPMENT & SERVICES. 1929. biennial. Gulf
Publishing Co., 3301 Allen Parkway, Box 2608,
Houston, TX 77001. Ed. Robert Rust. adv. tr.lit.
index. circ. 22,000.

CRUDE-OIL AND PRODUCTS PIPELINES. see
ENERGY

622   IS
DELEK. ANNUAL REPORT. (Text in English and
Hebrew) a. free. Delek, Israel Fuel Corporation, 6
Ahuzat Bayit St, Tel Aviv, Israel.

PETROLEUM AND GAS

665.5   NE
DEVELOPMENTS IN PETROLEUM SCIENCE. irreg., vol. 11, 1980. Elsevier Scientific Publishing Co., Box 211, 1000 AE Amsterdam, Netherlands.

662   UR
DINAMIKA IZLUCHAYUSCHEGO GAZA. 1974. irreg. 0.51 Rub. Akademiya Nauk S. S. S. R., Vychislitel'nyi Tsentr, Ul. Vavilova, 40, Moscow V-333, U.S.S.R.

DIRECTORY OF ELECTRIC LIGHT AND POWER COMPANIES. see *ELECTRICITY AND ELECTRICAL ENGINEERING*

665.5   US
DIRECTORY OF GAS UTILITY COMPANIES. a. $18. Midwest Oil Register, Inc., Drawer 7248, Tulsa, OK 74105.

665.5   US   ISSN 0417-5905
DIRECTORY OF GEOPHYSICAL AND OIL COMPANIES WHO USE GEOPHYSICAL SERVICE. a. $18. Midwest Oil Register, Inc., Drawer 7248, Tulsa, OK 74105.

665.5   US
DIRECTORY OF LAND DRILLING AND OILWELL SERVICING CONTRACTORS. 1974. a. $30. PennWell Publishing Co., Box 1260, 1421 S. Sheridan, Tulsa, OK 74101. Ed. Robert M. Wilkerson.
     Formerly: Land Drilling and Oilwell Servicing Contractors Directory.

665.7   US
DIRECTORY OF MUNICIPAL NATURAL GAS SYSTEMS. a. $10. American Public Gas Association, 301 Maple Ave., W., Vienna, VA 22180. Ed. Betty L.Verrips. adv. circ. 750.

655.5   658.8   US   ISSN 0070-5993
DIRECTORY OF OIL MARKETING AND WHOLESALE DISTRIBUTORS. 1945. a. $20. Midwest Oil Register, Inc., Drawer 7248, 1381 E. 51 St., Tulsa, OK 74105.

665.5   US   ISSN 0415-9764
DIRECTORY OF OIL WELL DRILLING CONTRACTORS. a. $30. Midwest Oil Register, Inc., Drawer 7248, Tulsa, OK 74105.

665.5   US   ISSN 0415-9772
DIRECTORY OF OIL WELL SUPPLY COMPANIES. a. $25. Midwest Oil Register, Inc., Drawer 7248, Tulsa, OK 74105.

665.5   SP
ENCICLOPEDIA NACIONAL DEL PETROLEO PETROLQUIMICA Y GAS. 1970. a. 3000 ptas.($84) Oilgas S. A., Paseo de la Habana, 48, Madrid 16, Spain. Ed. Carlos Martin. circ. 5,000.

665.7   IT   ISSN 0071-0687
ENTE NAZIONALE IDROCARBURI. REPORT AND STATEMENT OF ACCOUNTS.* a. Ente Nazionale Idrocarburi, Piazzale Enrico Mattei 1, 00144 Rome, Italy.

665.5   US
EUROPEAN PETROLEUM DIRECTORY. 1979. a. $40. Pennwell Publishing Co., Box 1260, Tulsa, OK 74101. adv.
     Supersedes in part: Eastern Hemisphere Petroleum Directory (ISSN 0070-8224)

665.5   GW   ISSN 0342-6947
EUROPEAN PETROLEUM YEARBOOK/ JAHRBUCH DER EUROPAEISCHEN ERDOELINDUSTRIE/ANNUAIRE EUROPEEN DU PETROLE. Variant title: A N E P. 1963. a. DM.120. Verlag and Werbung Otto Vieth, Alfredstr. 1, 2000 Hamburg 76, W. Germany (B.R.D.) Ed. Otto Vieth. adv. circ. 3,000.

665.5   US
FEDERAL COAL MANAGEMENT REPORT. 1976. irreg. U.S. Department of the Interior, Washington, DC 20240 (Orders to: Supt. of Documents, Washington, DC 20402)

665.5   UK   ISSN 0141-3228
FINANCIAL TIMES OIL AND GAS INTERNATIONAL YEAR BOOK. 1910. a. £35. Longman Group Ltd., Longman House, Burnt Mill, Harlow, Essex CM20 2JE, England. adv. index. circ. 6,000.
     Formerly: Oil and Petroleum Year Book.

668   UK   ISSN 0141-3236
FINANCIAL TIMES WHO'S WHO IN WORLD OIL AND GAS. a. £24. Longman Group Ltd., Longman House, Burnt Mill, Harlow, Essex CM20 2JE, England.

FOREIGN TRADE REPORTS. BUNKER FUELS. see *BUSINESS AND ECONOMICS — International Commerce*

665.5   VE
FRENTE NACIONAL PRO-DEFENSA DEL PETROLEO VENEZOLANO. ACTUACIONES. 1970. irreg. $5 per no. Frente Nacional Pro Defensa del Petroleo Venezolano, Apto. 50514, Caracas 105, Venezuela. circ. 3,000.

FUEL OIL SALES. see *ENERGY*

665.5   US
FUTURE GAS CONSUMPTION OF THE UNITED STATES. vol. 5, 1973. biennial. $3. University of Denver, Denver Research Institute, Denver, CO 80210.

662   AT   ISSN 0072-0208
GAS AND FUEL CORPORATION OF VICTORIA. ANNUAL REPORT. a. free. ‡ Gas and Fuel Corporation of Victoria, 171 Flinders St., Melbourne 3000, Australia. circ. 9,500.

665.7   UK   ISSN 0307-3084
GAS DIRECTORY AND WHO'S WHO. 1896. a. £15.50. Benn Publications Ltd., 25 New Street Sq., London EC4A 3JA, England. Ed. G. Battison. adv. index. circ. 1,187.
     Formerly: Gas Directory and Undertakings of the World; Incorporating: Gas Journal Directory (ISSN 0072-0240) & Gas Industry Directory (ISSN 0072-0232) & Who's Who in the Gas Industry (ISSN 0083-9779)

665   US
GAS FACTS; a statistical record of the gas utility industry. 1946. a. $15. American Gas Association, Department of Statistics, 1515 Wilson Blvd, Arlington, VA 22209. circ. 3,000.

665.7   UK   ISSN 0072-0259
GAS MARKETING POCKET BOOK AND DIARY. 1972. a. £3. Benn Publications Ltd., 25 New Street Sq., London EC4A 3JA, England. Ed. G. Battison. circ. 8,500.
     Formerly: Gas Services Pocket Book.

665.5   US   ISSN 0096-8870
GAS PROCESSORS ASSOCIATION. ANNUAL CONVENTION. PROCEEDINGS. Title varies: Natural Gas Processors Association. Annual Convention. Proceedings. 1921. a. price varies. Gas Processors Association, 1812 First Pl., Tulsa, OK 74103. Indexed: Chem.Abstr.

665.5   531.64
GAS RESOURCE STUDIES. 1977. irreg. (Colorado School of Mines) Colorado School of Mines Press, Golden, CO 80401. (reprint service avail. from UMI)

662   FR   ISSN 0072-0321
GAZ DE FRANCE. SECRETARIAT GENERAL. SCHEMA D'ORGANISATION PROFOR.* 1966. a. Gaz de France, Departement Profor, 5 Av. de Friedland, Paris (8e), France.

665.7   FR
GUIDE DU PETROLE, GAZ, PETROCHIMIE. 1931. a. 430 F. Editions Lesourd, 66 rue de la Rochefoucauld, 75009 Paris, France. adv.
     Formerly: Guide du Petrole, Gaz, Chimie (ISSN 0072-8055)

665.5   FR
GUIDE OFFSHORE. a. 180 F. Editions Olivier Lesourd, 66 rue de la Rochefoucauld, 75009 Paris, France. circ. 2,000.

665.5   UK   ISSN 0306-9192
GUIDE TO BRITISH OFFSHORE SUPPLIERS. 1974. a. £6. I. P. C. Business Press Ltd., 33-40 Bowling Green Lane, London EC1R 0NE, England. adv. circ. 10,000.

338.2   US   ISSN 0073-2656
HISTORICAL STATISTICS OF THE GAS INDUSTRY. 1956. irreg. $15. American Gas Association, Department of Statistics, 1515 Wilson Blvd., Arlington, VA 22209. circ. 1,000.

665.5   US
HYDROCARBON PROCESSING CATALOG. 43rd, 1976. a. Gulf Publishing Co., 3301 Allen Parkway, Box 2608, Houston, TX 77001.

665   CN   ISSN 0073-5760
I P A C PETROLEUM NEWS. 1963. irreg. membership. Independent Petroleum Association of Canada, 1610 Norcen Tower, 715 5Th Ave. S.W., Calgary, Alta. T2P 2X6, Canada. Ed. G. W. Cameron. circ. 600.
     Formerly: I P A C Newsletter.

665.5   US
ILLINOIS PETROLEUM. 1926. irreg., no. 119, 1980. free. ‡ State Geological Survey, 118 Natural Resources Bldg., 615 E. Peabody Dr., Champaign, IL 61820. circ. 2,000-4,200.

338.7   II
INDO-BURMA PETROLEUM COMPANY. ANNUAL REPORT. (Text in English) a. Indo-Burma Petroleum Company, Gillander House, Netaji Subhas Rd., Box 952, Calcutta 700 001, India. stat.

665.5   IT   ISSN 0073-7275
INDUSTRIA DEL PETROLIO IN ITALIA. a. Direzione Generale delle Fonti di Energia e Industrie di Base, Via Molise 2, 00187 Rome, Italy. charts. stat.

665.5   FR   ISSN 0073-8360
INSTITUT FRANCAIS DU PETROLE. COLLECTION COLLOQUES ET SEMINAIRES. 1964. irreg., 1979, vol. 32. price varies. Editions Technip, 27 rue Ginoux, 75737 Paris 15, France. circ. 1,000-1,500. Indexed: Bull.Signal. Chem.Abstr. Geophys.Abstr. Petrol.Abstr.

665.5   FR   ISSN 0073-8379
INSTITUT FRANCAIS DU PETROLE. RAPPORT ANNUEL. 1963. a. free. Institut Francais du Petrole, 1 et 4 Avenue de Bois-Preau, B.P. No. 311, 92506 Rueil-Malmaison Cedex, France. circ. 6,000. Indexed: Ocean.Abstr. Petrol.Abstr.

665.5   551   IS   ISSN 0073-8832
INSTITUTE FOR PETROLEUM RESEARCH AND GEOPHYSICS, HOLON, ISRAEL. REPORT. irreg. Institute for Petroleum Research and Geophysics, Box 1717, Holon, Israel.

665.5   UK
INSTITUTE OF ENERGY. NORTHERN IRELAND SECTION. YEAR BOOK. 1970. a. £2. Institute of Fuel, Northern Ireland Section, 3 Clarence St. W., Belfast, N. Ireland. Ed. F. R. McBride. circ. 1,200.
     Formerly: Institute of Fuel. Northern Ireland Section. Year Book.

665.5   UK
INSTITUTE OF ENERGY. PAPERS OF THE NATIONAL CONVENTION. 1972. a. £12($29.50) Institute of Energy, 18 Devonshire St., London W1N 2AU, England.
     Formerly: Institute of Fuel. Papers of the National Convention.

662   US
INSTITUTE OF GAS TECHNOLOGY. ANNUAL REPORT. a. free. Institute of Gas Technology, 3424 S. State St., Chicago, IL 60616. Ed. J. White. stat.
     Formerly: Institute of Gas Technology. Director's Report.

665.7   US
INTERNATIONAL CONFERENCE ON LIQUEFIED NATURAL GAS. PAPERS. (Papers in English, some in French; abstracts in English and French) 1968. irreg. $43 for 1977 edt. ‡ Institute of Gas Technology, 3424 South State St., Chicago, IL 60616. (Co-Sponsors: International Gas Union & International Institute of Refrigeration) Ed. Jack White. Indexed: Chem.Abstr. Gas Abstr.
     Formerly: International Conference on Liquefied Natural Gas. Proceedings (ISSN 0538-611X)

665.5   621   UK
INTERNATIONAL GAS BEARING SYMPOSIUM. PROCEEDINGS. irreg., 8th, 1981. price varies. British Hydromechanics Research Association, Cranfield, Bedford MK43 0AJ, England (Dist. in U.S. by: Air Service Co., Box 143, Corning, N.Y. 14830)

338.39 UK ISSN 0074-6126
INTERNATIONAL GAS UNION. PROCEEDINGS
OF CONFERENCES. (Text in English and French)
1931. triennial, 1973, 12th Nice. International Gas
Union, Inquire: A. G. Higgins, Gen. Sec., 17
Grosvenor Crescent, London SW1, England (For
Abstracts of Proceedings: Institute of Gas
Technology, 3424 South State St., Chicago, IL
60616)
    1976, 13th, London

665.5 US
INTERNATIONAL OIL AND GAS
DEVELOPMENT. 1930. a. $100. International Oil
Scouts Association, Box 2121, Austin, TX 78768.
Ed. Arthur Viohl, Jr. circ. 2,000.

665.5 US ISSN 0148-0375
INTERNATIONAL PETROLEUM
ENCYCLOPEDIA. 1968. a. $52.50. PennWell
Publishing Co., P.O. Box 1260, Tulsa, OK 74101.
Ed. John C. McCaslin.

338.47 US
INTERSTATE OIL COMPACT COMMISSION
ANNUAL REPORT. 1974. a. Interstate Oil
Compact Commission, Box 53127, Oklahoma City,
OK 73152.

665.5 IS ISSN 0075-1367
ISRAEL PETROLEUM AND ENERGY YEAR
BOOK.* (Text in English) 1968. a. David Kraft
Publishing Company, 26 Ficus St., P. O. B. 28117,
Tel Aviv, Israel.

665.5 NE
JAARBOEK VAN DE OPENBARE
GASVOORZIENING. 1971. a. fl.30. Vereniging
van Exploitanten van Gasbedrijven in Nederland,
Postbus 137, 7300 AC Apeldoorn, Netherlands.
(Co-sponsor: VEG-Gasinstituut N.V.) circ. 2,000.

665.5 JA
JAPAN PETROLEUM AND ENERGY
YEARBOOK. (Text in English) 1975. a. 100000
Yen($125) Japan Petroleum Consultants Ltd. -
Nihon Sekiyu Konsarutanto K. K., Box 1185, Tokyo
Central, Tokyo 100-91, Japan. Ed. K. Kurokawa.
stat. circ. 1,000.

547 YU
JUGOPETROL, TRGOVINSKO PREDUZECE ZA
PROMET NAFTE I NAFTINIH DERIVATA.
BILTEN. 1972. irreg. Jugopetrol, 23. Oktobar 27,
Novi Sad, Yugoslavia. Ed. Sava Vrbaski.

622 US
KANSAS OIL LIFTING SHORT COURSE
SELECTED PAPERS. 1972. biennial (approx.) $7.
University of Kansas Southwest Center, 222 Fulton
Terrace, P.O. Box 653, Garden City, KS 67846.
(Co-sponsor: Petroleum Industry Educational
Steering Committee of the Southwest) Ed. C.N.
Francis. charts. illus. stat. circ. 150-400
(controlled) (looseleaf format) Indexed: Chem.Abstr.

533 UR
KATALITICHESKAYA KONVERSIYA
UGLEVODORODOV. 1974. irreg. 1.37 Rub.
(Akademiya Nauk Ukrainskoi S.S.R., Institut Gaza)
Izdatel'stvo Naukova Dumka, Ul. Repina 3, Kiev,
U.S.S.R. illus.

662 HU ISSN 0075-6962
KOSZEN ES KOOLAJ ANYAGISMERETI
MONOGRAFIAK. 1964. irreg. price varies.
(Magyar Tudomanyos Akademia) Akademiai Kiado,
Publishing House of the Hungarian Academy of
Sciences, P.O. Box 24, H-1363 Budapest, Hungary.

665.7 338.39 US ISSN 0075-9759
L P-GAS MARKET FACTS; statistical handbook of
the LP-gas industry. 1950. a. $10. ‡ National L P-
Gas Association, 1301 W. 22nd St., Oak Brook, IL
60521. Ed. M. A. Spear. index.

665.5 US ISSN 0075-8116
LATIN AMERICAN PETROLEUM DIRECTORY.
1971. a. $35. PennWell Publishing Co., Box 1260,
Tulsa, OK 74101. Ed. Robert M. Wilkerson.

338.47 US ISSN 0539-2063
LEGAL REPORT OF OIL AND GAS
CONSERVATION ACTIVITIES. a. Interstate Oil
Compact Commission, Box 53127, Oklahoma City,
OK 73152.

LIQUIFIED PETROLEUM GAS SALES. see
ENERGY

665 HU
MAGYAR OLAJIPARI MUZEUM. EVKONYV.
1974. a. Magyar Olajipari Muzeum, Zalaegerszeg,
Hungary. illus.

665.7 US ISSN 0085-3429
MICHIGAN'S OIL AND GAS FIELDS: ANNUAL
STATISTICAL SUMMARY. 1964. a. $2.
Department of Natural Resources, Geological
Survey Division, Information Services Center, Box
30028, Lansing, MI 48909.

353.9 US ISSN 0095-3024
MINNESOTA. DEPARTMENT OF REVENUE.
PETROLEUM DIVISION. ANNUAL REPORT.
1973. a. Department of Revenue, Petroleum
Division, Centennial Office Bldg., St. Paul, MN
55145. Key Title: Annual Report - Petroleum
Division.

665.5 MR
MOROCCO. DIRECTION DES MINES ET DE LA
GEOLOGIE. ACTIVITE DU SECTEUR
PETROLIER. (Text in French) irreg. Direction des
Mines et de la Geologie, Rabat, Morocco. stat.

655.5 US
N P N FACTBOOK. (National Petroleum News) a.
$13. McGraw-Hill Publications Co., 1221 Ave. of
the Americas, New York, NY 10020 (Subscr.
address: National Petroleum News, Box 520
Hightstown, NJ 08520) stat.

NATIONAL STRIPPER WELL SURVEY. see
ENERGY

NATURAL GAS (ANNUAL) see ENERGY

665.5 CN ISSN 0077-6041
NATURAL GAS PROCESSING PLANTS IN
CANADA. a. price varies. Department of Energy,
Mines and Resources, Mineral Policy Sector,
Ottawa, Ontario K1A OE4, Canada (Orders to:
Supply and Services Canada, Publishing Centre,
Hull, Que. K1A 0S5, Canada)

665.5 UR
NEFTEGAZONOSNYE I PERSPEKTIVNYE
KOMPLEKSY TSENTRALNYKH I
VOSTOCHNYKH OBLASTEI RUSSKOI
PLATFORMY. (Subseries of: Vsesoyuznyi Nauchno
- Issledovatel'skii Geologorazvedochnyi Neftyanoi
Institut. Trudy) irreg. 1.65 Rub. per issue.
(Vsesoyuznyi Nauchno - Issledovatel'skii
Geologorazvedochnyi Neftyanoi Institut)
Izdatel'stvo Nedra, Tretyakovskii proezd, 1,
Moscow K-12, U. S. S. R. illus.

NEFTENA I VUGLISHTNA GEOLOGIIA/
PETROLEUM AND COAL GEOLOGY. see
EARTH SCIENCES — Geology

338.4 NO
NORWEGIAN OFFSHORE INDEX. (Text in
English) 1974. a. contr. free circ. (Export Council of
Norway) Selvig Publishing A-S, Box 9070
Vaterland, Oslo 1, Norway. (Co-sponsor: Federation
of Norwegian Industries)

665.7 US ISSN 0475-1310
OFFSHORE CONTRACTORS AND EQUIPMENT
DIRECTORY. 1969. a. $45. PennWell Publishing
Co., Box 1260, Tulsa, OK 74101. Ed. Robert M.
Wilkerson.
    Formerly: Worldwide Offshore Contractors
Directory (ISSN 0084-2575)

665 UK ISSN 0260-6437
OFFSHORE OIL & GAS YEARBOOK. 1975. a. £42.
Kogan Page Ltd., 120 Pentonville Rd., London N1
9JN, England. adv. illus. index.
    Former titles: European Offshore Oil and Gas
Yearbook; U.K. Offshore Oil and Gas Yearbook.

330.9 665.5 KU
OIL AND ARAB COOPERATION. ANNUAL
REVIEW. a. $10. Organization of Arab Petroleum
Exporting Countries, Box 20501, Kuwait.
    Formerly: Petroleum and Arab Economic
Development.

338.2 US ISSN 0471-380X
OIL & GAS DIRECTORY. 1970/71. a. $20. ‡
Geophysical Directory, Inc., 2200 Welch Ave.,
Houston, TX 77019 (Subscr. to: Box 13508,
Houston, TX 77019) Ed. Jack Weyand. adv. circ.
4,600.

665.5 665.74 II
OIL AND NATURAL GAS COMMISSION.
BULLETIN. (Text in English) 1964. 2/yr.
Rs.10($2) Institute of Petroleum Exploration, Oil
and Natural Gas Commission, 9 Kaulagarh Rd.,
Dehadun, U.P., India. Ed. Atr Raju. circ. 1,400.
(back issues avail.)

338.2 665.5 US ISSN 0471-3850
OIL DIRECTORY OF ALASKA. a. $10. Midwest
Oil Register, Inc., Drawer 7248, Tulsa, OK 74105.

665.5 US ISSN 0474-0114
OIL DIRECTORY OF CANADA. a. $15. Midwest
Oil Register, Inc., Drawer 7248, Tulsa, OK 74105.

665.5 US ISSN 0472-7711
OIL DIRECTORY OF COMPANIES OUTSIDE
THE U.S. AND CANADA. Title varies: Oil
Directories of Foreign Companies Outside the
U.S.A. and Canada. a. $15. Midwest Oil Register,
Inc., Drawer 7248, Tulsa, OK 74105.

665.5 338.2 US ISSN 0471-3877
OIL DIRECTORY OF HOUSTON, TEXAS. a. $10.
Midwest Oil Register, Inc., Drawer 7248, Tulsa, OK
74105.

662 US
OIL PRICE DATABOOK. irreg. $125. Oil Buyers'
Guide, Box 998, Lakewood, NJ 08701.

338.47 US
OIL PRODUCING INDUSTRY IN YOUR STATE.
1939. a. single copies free. ‡ Independent Petroleum
Association of America, 1101 16th St. N.W.,
Washington, DC 20036. Ed. M. L. Mesnard. adv.
charts. illus. stat. circ. 17,000-20,000.

665.538 FI ISSN 0472-8874
OLJYPOSTI. irreg. Neste Oy, PL 432, 00100 Helsinki
10, Finland. illus.

338.2 CN ISSN 0078-5059
ONTARIO. MINISTRY OF NATURAL
RESOURCES. PETROLEUM RESOURCES
BRANCH. DRILLING AND PRODUCTION
REPORT, OIL AND NATURAL GAS. 1965. a.
price varies. Ministry of Natural Resources,
Petroleum Resources Branch, Parliament Bldgs.,
Toronto, Ont. M7A 1W3, Canada. circ. 650.

665.5 CN ISSN 0078-5040
ONTARIO PETROLEUM INSTITUTE. ANNUAL
CONFERENCE PROCEEDINGS. 1962. a. $15.
Ontario Petroleum Institute Inc., Box 396,
Chatham, Ont., Canada.

553 US ISSN 0078-5741
OREGON. STATE DEPARTMENT OF GEOLOGY
AND MINERAL INDUSTRIES. OIL AND GAS
INVESTIGATIONS. 1963. irreg., no. 5, 1976. price
varies. Department of Geology and Mineral
Industries, 1069 State Office Building, Portland, OR
97201.

338.2 665.5 FR ISSN 0474-6007
ORGANIZATION FOR ECONOMIC
COOPERATION AND DEVELOPMENT.
SPECIAL COMMITTEE FOR OIL. OIL
STATISTICS. SUPPLY AND DISPOSAL. (Text in
English and French) 1961. irreg. $13. Organization
for Economic Cooperation and Development, 2 rue
Andre Pascal, 75775 Paris 16, France (U. S. orders
to: O.E.C.D. Publications and Information Center;
1750 Pennsylvania Ave., N. W., Washington, D. C.
20006) (also avail. in microfiche)

665.5 KU
ORGANIZATION OF ARAB PETROLEUM
EXPORTING COUNTRIES. ANNUAL ENERGY
REPORT. a. $4. Organization of Arab Petroleum
Exporting Countries, Box 20501, Kuwait.

665.2 338.2 KU
ORGANIZATION OF ARAB PETROLEUM
EXPORTING COUNTRIES. ANNUAL
STATISTICAL REPORT. a. $8. Organization of
Arab Petroleum Exporting Countries, Box 20501,
Kuwait.

PETROLEUM AND GAS

341.7   KU
ORGANIZATION OF ARAB PETROLEUM EXPORTING COUNTRIES. SECRETARY GENERAL'S ANNUAL REPORT. 1974. a. Organization of Arab Petroleum Exporting Countries, Box 20501, Kuwait. charts. stat.

338.2   665.5   AU   ISSN 0474-6317
ORGANIZATION OF THE PETROLEUM EXPORTING COUNTRIES. ANNUAL REVIEW AND RECORD. 1967. a. Organization of the Petroleum Exporting Countries, Obere-Donaustr. 93, A-1020 Vienna, Austria.

338.2   665.5   AU   ISSN 0475-0608
ORGANIZATION OF THE PETROLEUM EXPORTING COUNTRIES. ANNUAL STATISTICAL BULLETIN. 1966. a. Organization of the Petroleum Exporting Countries, Obere-Donaustr. 93, A-1020 Vienna, Austria.

665   PK   ISSN 0552-9115
PAKISTAN PETROLEUM LIMITED. ANNUAL REPORT. (Text in English) a. Pakistan Petroleum Ltd., PIDC House, Dr. Ziauddin Ahmad Rd., Karachi 4, Pakistan.

665.5   622   MX
PETRO QUIMICA; petroleo y mineria. 1970. a. 125($50) Editorial Innovacion, Espana 396, Mexico 13, D.F., Mexico. Ed. Cesar Macazaga. adv.

665.5   BL
PETROBRAS. CONSOLIDATED REPORT. (Text in English) a. Petroleo Brasileiro S.A., Servico de Relacoes Publicas, Av. Chile 65, Rio de Janeiro RJ, Brazil. Dir. Araken de Oliveira. charts. illus. stat.

665.5   FR   ISSN 0069-6552
PETROLE(YEAR); activite de l'industrie petroliere. 1950. a. 275 F. Comite Professionnel du Petrole, 51 Bld. de Courcelles, Paris 8e, France.

665.5   BL
PETROLEO E GAS. irreg. Shell Brasil, S.A., Av. Rio Branco 109, Rio de Janeiro, Brazil. illus.

PETROLEUM AND CHEMICAL INDUSTRY TECHNICAL CONFERENCE. RECORD. see ENGINEERING — Chemical Engineering

665.5   US
PETROLEUM EQUIPMENT DIRECTORY. 1955. a. $10. Petroleum Equipment Institute, Box 2380, Tulsa, OK 74101. Ed. Martha Siddons. adv. circ. 3,000.

665.5   552   CH
PETROLEUM GEOLOGY OF TAIWAN/T'AIWAN SHIH YU TI CHIH. (Text in English) 1962. a. Chinese Petroleum Corporation, Exploration Division, 46 Chung Cheng Rd., Miaoli, Taiwan, Republic of China.

665.5   JA
PETROLEUM INDUSTRY IN JAPAN. (Text in English) 1955. a. membership. World Petroleum Congress, Japanese National Committee - Sekai Sekiyu Kaigi Nihon Kokunai Iinkai, Kasahara Bldg., 1-6-10 Uchi Kanda, Chiyoda-ku, Tokyo 101, Japan. stat.

662   US
PETROLEUM MARKETER'S HANDBOOK. irreg. $59. Oil Buyer's Guide, Box 998, Lakewood, NJ 08701.

665.5   CN   ISSN 0079-1296
PETROLEUM REFINERIES IN CANADA. a. price varies. Department of Energy, Mines and Resources, Mineral Policy Sector, Ottawa, Ontario K1A OE4, Canada (Orders to: Supply and Services Canada, Publishing Centre, Hull, Que K1A 0S5, Canada)

PETROLEUM STATEMENT (ANNUAL) see ENERGY

665.54   US
PIPE LINE & PIPE LINE CONTRACTORS. a. $18. Midwest Oil Register, Inc., Drawer 7248, Tulsa, OK 74105.

665.5   US
PIPE LINE ANNUAL DIRECTORY OF PIPELINES. 1928. a. $30. Oildom Publishing Co., 3314 Mercer St., Box 22267, Houston, TX 77027. Ed. Oliver Klinger, Jr. adv. stat. circ. 14,000.

553   UR
PRIRODNYI GAZ SIBIRI. 1969. irreg. Vsesoyuznyi Nauchno-Issledovatelskii Institut Prirodnykh Gazov, Tyumenskii Filial, Tyumen, U.S.S.R. illus.

665.53   US
REFINING, CONSTRUCTION, PETROCHEMICAL & NATURAL GAS PROCESSING PLANTS OF THE WORLD. a. $22. Midwest Oil Register, Inc., Drawer 7248, Tulsa, OK 74105.

665.5   US
REPORTS OF RESEARCH SUPPORTED BY THE PETROLEUM RESEARCH FUND. 1957. a. free. American Chemical Society, 1155 Sixteenth Street, N.W., Washington, DC 20036. illus. circ. 3,500.

553   665   CN
SASKATCHEWAN. DEPARTMENT OF MINERAL RESOURCES. PETROLEUM AND NATURAL GAS RESERVOIR ANNUAL. 1963. a. Can.$35. ‡ Department of Mineral Resources, Publications Office, Toronto-Dominion Bank Bldg., 1914 Hamilton St., Regina, Sask. S4P 4V4, Canada.

338.7   CN
SASKATCHEWAN OIL AND GAS CORPORATION. ANNUAL REPORT. 1974. a. free. Saskatchewan Oil and Gas Corporation, 1500 Chateau Tower, 1920 Broad St., Regina, Sask. S4P 3V2, Canada. charts. illus.

SCHEDULE OF WELLS DRILLED FOR OIL AND GAS, PROVINCE OF ALBERTA. see ENERGY

622.338   665.7   CN   ISSN 0524-5508
SCHEDULE OF WELLS DRILLED FOR OIL AND NATURAL GAS IN BRITISH COLUMBIA. 1976. a. Petroleum and Natural Gas Branch, Victoria, B.C., Canada. illus.

665.5   AU   ISSN 0080-858X
SELECTED DOCUMENTS OF THE INTERNATIONAL PETROLEUM INDUSTRY. 1967. a. price varies. Organization of the Petroleum Exporting Countries, Obere-Donaustr. 93, A-1020 Vienna, Austria.

665.5   FR
SOCIETE NATIONALE ELF AQUITAINE. RAPPORT ANNUEL. a. free. Societe Nationale Elf Aquitaine, Direction des Relations Publiques de la Communication, 7 rue Nelaton, 75739 Paris Cedex 15, France. charts. illus. stat.

665.5   622   US   ISSN 0081-1688
SOCIETY OF PETROLEUM ENGINEERS OF AMERICAN INSTITUTE OF MINING, METALLURGICAL AND PETROLEUM ENGINEERS. PETROLEUM TRANSACTIONS REPRINT SERIES. 1958. irreg. $25. American Institute of Mining, Metallurgical and Petroleum Engineers, Inc., Society of Petroleum Engineers, 6200 N. Central Expressway, Dallas, TX 75206. Ed. Jim McInnis.

665.5   US   ISSN 0081-1696
SOCIETY OF PETROLEUM ENGINEERS OF AMERICAN INSTITUTE OF MINING, METALLURGICAL AND PETROLEUM ENGINEERS. TRANSACTIONS. 1925. a. $25 to non-members. American Institute of Mining, Metallurgical and Petroleum Engineers, Inc., Society of Petroleum Engineers, 6200 N. Central Expressway, Dallas, TX 75206. Ed. Jim McInnis. adv. charts. illus. index. circ. 5,000. (back issues avail.) Indexed: Chem.Abstr. Eng.Ind. Gas Abstr. Petrol.Abstr.

622.338   US   ISSN 0081-1718
SOCIETY OF PROFESSIONAL WELL LOGGING ANALYSTS. S P W L A ANNUAL LOGGING SYMPOSIUM TRANSACTIONS. 1960. a. price varies. Society of Professional Well Log Analysts, 806 Main St., Suite B-1, Houston, TX 77002. adv. bibl. charts. illus. circ. 2,500. Indexed: Petrol.Abstr.

665.5   SP
SPAIN. MINISTERIO DE HACIENDA. DELEGACION DEL GOBIERNO EN CAMPSA. MEMORIA. irreg. Ministerio de Hacienda, Delegacion del Gobierno en Campsa, Madrid, Spain. illus.
Petroleum industry and trade

338.2   UK   ISSN 0081-5039
STATISTICAL REVIEW OF THE WORLD OIL INDUSTRY. a. free. British Petroleum Co., Ltd., London, England (U.S. Dist. BP North America Inc., 620 Fifth Ave., New York, NY 10020) circ. 40,000.

665.7   NE   ISSN 0081-5225
STATISTIEK VAN DE GASVOORZIENING IN NEDERLAND. 1953. a. fl.7.85. Centraal Bureau voor de Statistiek, Prinses Beatrixlaan 428, Voorburg, Netherlands (Orders to: Staatsuitgeverij, Christoffel Plantijnstraat, The Hague, Netherlands) circ. 375.

338.4   FR
STATISTIQUES DE L'INDUSTRIE GAZIERE EN FRANCE. irreg. Direction du Gaz, de l'Electricite et du Charbon, 3-5 Rud Barbet de Jouy, 75700 Paris, France. illus.
Continues: France. Direction du Gaz et de l'Electricite. Statistiques Officielles de l'Industrie Gaziere en France (ISSN 0429-3843)

STEAM-ELECTRIC PLANT FACTORS (1978) see MINES AND MINING INDUSTRY

665.54   US
SYNTHETIC PIPELINE GAS SYMPOSIUM. PROCEEDINGS. vol. 7, 1975. irreg. $50 for latest issue. American Gas Association, 1515 Wilson Blvd., Arlington, VA 22209. (Co-sponsors: U.S. Energy Research & Development Administration; International Gas Union)
Pipes

665.538   US
TEXAS. RAILROAD COMMISSION. OIL AND GAS DIVISION. ANNUAL REPORT. a. $4.20. Railroad Commission, Oil and Gas Division, Drawer 12967, Capitol Station, Austin, TX 78711. (back issues avail.)
Fuel

665.5   US   ISSN 0092-7996
TEXAS YEARBOOK. 1973. a. $40. International Oil Scouts Association, Box 2121, Austin, TX 78768. Ed. Arthur Viohl, Jr. circ. 500.

665.53   US   ISSN 0082-6324
TRENDS IN THE INTERNATIONAL PETROLEUM-REFINING INDUSTRY. 1964. triennial. free; limited distribution. ‡ Ethyl Corporation, Research Laboratories, 1600 W. Eight Mile Rd., Ferndale, MI 48220. Ed. John C. Lane. circ. 2,500.

354   TR
TRINIDAD AND TOBAGO. MINISTRY OF ENERGY AND ENERGY-BASED INDUSTRIES. ANNUAL REPORT. a. free. Ministry of Energy and Energy-Based Industries, Box 96, Port-of-Spain, Trinidad. illus. stat.
Continues: Trinidad and Tobago. Ministry of Petroleum and Mines. Annual Report.

665.5   US   ISSN 0082-8599
U S A OIL INDUSTRY DIRECTORY. 1962. a. $50. PennWell Publishing Co., Box 1260, Tulsa, OK 74101. Ed. Robert M. Wilkerson.

552   TS
UNITED ARAB EMIRATES. MINISTRY OF PETROLEUM AND INDUSTRY. AKHBAR AL-PETROL WALL SINAA. irreg. Ministry of Petroleum and Industry, Abu Dhabi, United Arab Emirates. Ed. Muhammad al-Sitri.

665.538   US
U.S. DEPARTMENT OF ENERGY. STRATEGIC PETROLEUM RESERVE OFFICE. ANNUAL REPORT. a. U.S. Department of Energy, Strategic Petroleum Reserve Office, Washington, DC 20545.
Fuel

665.5   FR   ISSN 0396-2644
UNITES PETROCHIMIQUES DANS LES PAYS DE L'OPEP ET DE L'OPAEP/ PETROCHEMICAL UNITS IN THE OPEC AND OAPEC COUNTRIES. (Text in English, French) 1976. a. (Institut Francais du Petrole) Editions Technip, 27 rue Ginoux, 75737 Paris Cedex 15, France.

665.5   FR   ISSN 0339-5081
UNITES PETROCHIMIQUES EN EUROPE DE L'OUEST/PETROCHEMICAL UNITS IN WESTERN EUROPE. (Text in English, French) a. (Institut Francais du Petrole) Editions Technip, 27 rue Ginoux, 75737 Paris Cedex 15, France.

665.538   FI   ISSN 0355-3590
VALTION TEKNILLINEN TUTKIMUSKESKUS. POLTTL- JA VOITELUAINELABORATORIO. TIEDONANTO/TECHNICAL RESEARCH CENTRE OF FINLAND. FUEL AND LUBRICANT RESEARCH LABORATORY. REPORT. (Text mainly in Finnish, some in English or Swedish) 1972. irreg. price varies. Valtion Teknillinen Tutkimuskeskus - Technical Research Centre of Finland, Vuorimiehentie 5, 02150 Espoo 15, Finland.
Fuel; lubrication

VENEZUELA. MINISTERIO DE ENERGIA Y MINAS. MEMORIA Y CUENTA. see MINES AND MINING INDUSTRY

338.2   VE
VENEZUELA. MINISTERIO DE ENERGIA Y MINAS. PETROLEO Y OTROS DATOS ESTADISTICOS. English edition: Venezuelan Petroleum Industry. Statistical Data. a. free. Ministerio de Energia y Minas, Oficina de Estudios Economicos Energeticos, Torre Norte, Caracas, Venezuela.
Formerly: Venezuela. Ministerio de Minas e Hidrocarburos. Oficina de Economia Petrolera. Petroleo y Otros Datos Estadisticos (ISSN 0083-5390)

665   AT   ISSN 0310-7787
W A P E T JOURNAL. 1971. a. free. West Australian Petroleum Pty. Ltd., Wapet House, 12 St. George's Terrace, Perth, W.A. 6000, Australia.

665.5   US
WORLDWIDE DIRECTORY OF PIPELINES AND CONTRACTORS. 1976. a. $30. Pennwell Publishing Co., Box 1260, 1421 S. Sheridan, Tulsa, OK 74101. Ed. Robert M. Wilkerson.

665.5   US   ISSN 0084-2583
WORLDWIDE PETROCHEMICAL DIRECTORY. 1962. a. $40. PennWell Publishing Co., Box 1260, Tulsa, OK 74101. Ed. Robert M. Wilkerson.

665.73   US   ISSN 0084-2591
WORLDWIDE REFINING AND GAS PROCESSING. 1942. a. $50. PennWell Publishing Co., Box 1260, Tulsa, OK 74101. Ed. Robert M. Wilkerson.

PETROLEUM AND GAS — Abstracting, Bibliographies, Statistics

622.33   US
ALASKA. OIL AND GAS CONSERVATION COMMISSION. STATISTICAL REPORT. a. Oil and Gas Conservation Commission, 3001 Porcupine Dr., Anchorage, AK 99501. illus.
Former titles: Alaska. Division of Oil and Gas Conservation. Statistical Report; Alaska. Department of Natural Resources. Division of Oil and Gas. Statistical Report (ISSN 0360-5558)

665.7   CN   ISSN 0068-7103
CANADA. STATISTICS CANADA. CRUDE PETROLEUM AND NATURAL GAS INDUSTRY/INDUSTRIE DU PETROLE BRUT ET DU GAZ NATUREL. (Catalog 26-213) (Text in English and French) 1926. a. Can.$6($7.20) Statistics Canada, Publications Distribution, Ottawa, Ont. K1A 0V7, Canada. (also avail. in microform from MML)

665.5   CN   ISSN 0527-5318
CANADA. STATISTICS CANADA. GAS UTILITIES (TRANSPORT AND DISTRIBUTION SYSTEMS) /SERVICES DE GAZ (RESEAUX DE TRANSPORT ET DE DISTRIBUTION) (Catalog 57-205) (Text in English and French) 1959. a. Can.$7($8.440) Statistics Canada, Publications Distribution, Ottawa, Ont. K1A 0V7, Canada. stat. (also avail. in microform from MML)

665.5   CN   ISSN 0068-7162
CANADA. STATISTICS CANADA. PETROLEUM REFINERIES/RAFFINERIES DE PETROLE. (Catalog 45-205) (Text in English and French) 1918. a. Can.$4.50($5.40) Statistics Canada, Publications Distribution, Ottawa, Ont. K1A 0V7, Canada. (also avail. in microform from MML)

FINLAND. TILASTOKESKUS. ASUNTOTUOTANTO/FINLAND. STATISTIKCENTRALEN. BOSTADSPRODUKTIONEN/FINLAND. CENTRAL STATISTICAL OFFICE. PRODUCTION OF DWELLINGS. see HOUSING AND URBAN PLANNING — Abstracting, Bibliographies, Statistics

360   FI   ISSN 0430-5604
FINLAND. TILASTOKESKUS. TALONRAKENNUSTILASTO/FINLAND. STATISTIKCENTRALEN. HUSBYGGNADSSTATISTIK/FINLAND. CENTRAL STATISTICAL OFFICE. HOUSE CONSTRUCTION STATISTICS. (Section XVIII C of Official Statistics of Finland) (Text in Finnish, Swedish and English) 1961. a. Fmk.15. Tilastokeskus, Annankatu 44, SF-00100 Helsinki 10, Finland (Subscr. to: Government Printing Centre, Box 516, SF-00100 Helsinki 10, Finland)

665.5   II
INDIAN PETROLEUM AND PETROCHEMICALS STATISTICS. (Text in English) 1976. a. free. Ministry of Petroleum, Economics and Statistics Division, New Delhi 110001, India. stat. circ. controlled.
Formerly: Indian Petroleum and Chemicals Statistics.

665.5   LY   ISSN 0075-9260
LIBYA. CENSUS AND STATISTICAL OFFICE. REPORT OF THE ANNUAL SURVEY OF PETROLEUM MINING INDUSTRY. (Text in Arabic and English) 1965. a. free. Census and Statistical Department, Ministry of Planning, Tripoli, Libya.

665.5 338.2   FR
ORGANIZATION FOR ECONOMIC COOPERATION AND DEVELOPMENT. OIL STATISTICS/STATISTIQUES PETROLIERES. (Text in English & French) 1970. irreg. $13. Organization for Economic Cooperation and Development, 2 rue Andre-Pascal, 75775 Paris Cedex 16, France (U.S. orders to: O.E.C.D. Publications and Information Center, 1750 Pennsylvania Ave., N.W., Washington, DC 20006) charts. stat. (also avail. in microfiche; back issues avail.)
Formerly: Organization for Economic Cooperation and Development. Provisional Oil Statistics/Statistiques Petrolieres Provisoires (ISSN 0029-7062)

338.4   US   ISSN 0095-4128
PROPYLENE ANNUAL. 1974. a. $35 for participating companies; full service is $4300. DeWitt & Co., 3650 Dresser Tower, 601 Jefferson St., Houston, TX 77002. ill.

310   US
STATISTICS FOR GAS UTILITIES IN PENNSYLVANIA. 1956. a. free. Department of Commerce, Bureau of Statistics, Research and Planning, 630B Health & Welfare Bldg., Harrisburg, PA 17120. charts. stat. circ. controlled.

665.5 338.2   US
TWENTIETH CENTURY PETROLEUM STATISTICS. 1945. a. $15. DeGolyer and MacNaughton, One Energy Square, Dallas, TX 75206. stat.

338.2   AT
VICTORIA, AUSTRALIA. DEPARTMENT OF MINERALS AND ENERGY. THE PETROLEUM AND GAS INDUSTRIES IN VICTORIA. STATISTICAL REVIEW. 1970. a. Aus.$10. Department of Minerals and Energy, 151 Flinders St., Victoria, Australia. Ed. W.L. Doran. circ. 1,000.
Formerly: Victoria. Ministry of Fuel and Power. the Petroleum and Gas Industries in Victoria: Statistical Review.

PETS

636.8   AT
A C I YEAR BOOK. 1978. a. Aus.$2.50 per no. Australian Cat Federation, Inc., Box 135, Claremont, W.A. 6010, Australia. Ed.L. M. Thomas. (back issues avail)

179.3   SA
ANIMAL ANTI-CRUELTY LEAGUE. CHAIRMAN'S REPORT. 1972. vol. 1/3. a. free. Animal Anti-Cruelty League, P.O. Box 49007, Rosettenville, Transvaal, South Africa. Ed. Angus O. McLaren.

636.8   US   ISSN 0069-1003
CAT FANCIERS ASSOCIATION. YEAR BOOK. 1958. a. $19.95. Cat Fanciers Association, P.O. Box 430, Red Bank, NJ 07701. Ed. Marna Fogarty. adv. circ. 6,000.

636.8   AT
CAT FANCIERS' MAGAZINE. 1971. irreg. Aus.$2. Cat Fanciers' Club of Tasmania, P.O. Box 114, North Hobart, Tas. 7002, Australia.

636.7   AT   ISSN 0311-0761
DANE DIGEST. 1973. irreg. Aus.$0.20 each. Great Dane Club of Victoria, 74 Rankin Rd., Frentree Gully, Vic. 3156, Australia. Ed. Ernest Yarra.

636.8   UK   ISSN 0070-7015
DOG WORLD ANNUAL. 1930. a. $15. A. R. Gallant, Clergy House, Churchyard, Kent TN23 1QW, England. index.

636.7   CN
DOGS IN CANADA ANNUAL. a. Apex Publishers & Publicity Ltd., Suite 500, 3 Church St., Toronto, Ont. M5E 1M2, Canada. Ed. Elizabeth M. Dunn. adv.

636.7   US   ISSN 0164-4289
KENNEL REVIEW. 1898. irreg. $18. B & E Publications, 828 N. La Brea Ave., Hollywood, CA 90038.

636.1   UK   ISSN 0077-4448
NATIONAL EQUINE (AND SMALLER ANIMALS) DEFENCE LEAGUE. ANNUAL REPORT. 1909. a. membership. National Equine Defence League, 138 Blackwell Rd., Carlisle CA2 4DL, England. Ed. Frank E. Tebbutt. circ. 3,000.

PETS WELCOME. see TRAVEL AND TOURISM

574   UK   ISSN 0080-8210
SCOTTISH SOCIETY FOR PREVENTION OF VIVISECTION. ANNUAL PICTORIAL REVIEW. 1912. a. free. ‡ Scottish Society for Prevention of Vivisection, 10 Queensferry St., Edinburgh EH2 4PG, Scotland. Ed. Clive Hollands. circ. 10,000.

636   US
SHIH TZU BULLETIN. irreg. $6. American Shih Tzu Club, Box 1016, Tryon, NC 28782. illus. (tabloid format)
Dogs

636.7   US   ISSN 0082-5441
TOURING WITH TOWSER. 1948. biennial. $1. Gaines Dog Research Center, 250 North St., White Plains, NY 10625 (Orders to: Box 1007, Kankakee, IL 60901) Ed. Tom O'Shea. circ. 22,500.

636.7   US
WHERE TO BUY, BOARD OR TRAIN A DOG. biennial. $1. Gaines Dog Research Center, 250 North St., White Plains, NY 10625 (Subscr. to: Gaines Kennel Directory, Box 1007, Kankakee, IL 60901)

PHARMACY AND PHARMACOLOGY

636.7   AT
WORKING KELPIE COUNCIL. NATIONAL STUD BOOK. 1967. irreg. Aus.$4 to non members. Working Kelpie Council, P.O. Box E31, Castle Hill, N.S.W. 2154, Australia.

PHARMACY AND PHARMACOLOGY

see also Drug Abuse and Alcoholism

615.1   US   ISSN 0065-9304
A M A DRUG EVALUATIONS. 1971. triennial. $37.50. (American Medical Association) P S G Publishing Company, Inc., 545 Great Rd., Littleton, MA 01460. charts. illus.

ACCESSOIREX. see *MEDICAL SCIENCES*

615.1   370.58   US   ISSN 0065-7980
ACCREDITED COLLEGES OF PHARMACY. 1940. a. free. American Council on Pharmaceutical Education, One E. Wacker Dr., Chicago, IL 60601. Ed. Dr. Daniel A. Nona. circ. 10,000(approx.)

615   GW   ISSN 0341-0854
ACTA PHARMACEUTICA TECHNOLOGICA. SUPPLEMENTA. irreg. price varies. (Arbeitsgemeinschaft fuer Pharmazeutische Verfahrenstechnik e. V.) Deutscher Apotheker Verlag, Postfach 40, 7000 Stuttgart 1, W. Germany (B.R.D.)

615.1   DK   ISSN 0065-1508
ACTA PHARMACOLOGICA ET TOXICOLOGICA. SUPPLEMENTUM. (Text in English) 1947. irreg. free to subscribers. Munksgaard, Noerre Soegade 35, DK-1370 Copenhagen K, Denmark. Ed. Jens Schou. (reprint service avail. from ISI) Indexed: Biol.Abstr. Chem.Abstr. Curr. Cont. Ind.Med.

615.78   US   ISSN 0147-071X
ADVANCES IN BEHAVIORAL PHARMACOLOGY. 1977. irreg. Academic Press, Inc., 111 Fifth Ave., New York, NY 10003. illus.

615   616.8   US   ISSN 0065-2229
ADVANCES IN BIOCHEMICAL PSYCHOPHARMACOLOGY. 1969. irreg., vol. 21, 1979. price varies. Raven Press, 1140 Ave. of the Americas, New York, NY 10036. Eds. E. Costa, P. Greengard. Indexed: Curr.Cont. Ind.Med. Sci.Cit.Ind.

410   US   ISSN 0190-4817
ADVANCES IN CANCER CHEMOTHERAPY. 1979. irreg. $29.75. Marcel Dekker, Inc., 270 Madison Ave., New York, NY 10016. Ed. Andre Rosowsky.

ADVANCES IN CLINICAL CHEMISTRY. see *BIOLOGY — Biological Chemistry*

ADVANCES IN CYTOPHARMACOLOGY. see *BIOLOGY — Cytology And Histology*

615.1   UK   ISSN 0065-2490
ADVANCES IN DRUG RESEARCH. 1964. irreg., vol. 12, 1978. price varies. Academic Press Inc. (London) Ltd., 24-28 Oval Rd, London NW1 7DX, England (and 111 Fifth Ave., New York, N.Y. 10003) Ed. A. B. Simonds. index. Indexed: Ind.Med.

615   US   ISSN 0146-3810
ADVANCES IN GENERAL AND CELLULAR PHARMACOLOGY. 1976. irreg. price varies. Plenum Press, 233 Spring St., New York, NY 10013. Eds. Toshio Narahashi, C. Paul Bianchi.

615   US   ISSN 0065-3136
ADVANCES IN PHARMACEUTICAL SCIENCES. 1964. irreg., vol. 4, 1975. price varies. Academic Press, Inc., 111 Fifth Ave., New York, NY 10003 (and Berkeley Square House, London W.1, England) Eds. H. S. Bean, A. H. Beckett, J. E. Carless. index. Indexed: Ind.Med.

615.1   US   ISSN 0065-3144
ADVANCES IN PHARMACOLOGY AND CHEMOTHERAPY. 1962. irreg., vol. 16, 1979. price varies. Academic Press, Inc., 111 Fifth Ave., New York, NY 10003. Ed. S. Garattini. index. (also avail. in microfiche) Indexed: Ind.Med.
Former titles: Advances in Pharmacology; Advances in Chemotherapy.

ADVANCES IN STEROID BIOCHEMISTRY AND PHARMACOLOGY (1978) see *BIOLOGY — Biological Chemistry*

615.1   US   ISSN 0065-8111
AMERICAN DRUG INDEX. 1950. a. $16. J. B. Lippincott Co., E. Washington Sq., Philadelphia, PA 19105. Ed. Norman F. Billups. (reprint service avail. from UMI)

615.1   US   ISSN 0364-7471
AMERICAN DRUGGIST BLUE BOOK. a. price varies. Hearst Magazines, 224 W. 57th St., New York, NY 10019.

615   US
AMERICAN HOSPITAL FORMULARY SERVICE. 1959. 2 base vols. plus 4-6 supplements per yr. $50 first yr, $20 thereafter. American Society of Hospital Pharmacists, 4630 Montgomery Ave., Washington, DC 20014. Ed. Judith A. Kepler.

615   US
AMERICAN LECTURES IN PHARMACOLOGY. irreg. price varies. Charles C. Thomas, Publisher, 301-327 E. Lawrence Ave., Springfield, IL 62717.

615.19   US
ANALYTICAL PROFILES OF DRUG SUBSTANCES. 1972. irreg., vol. 8, 1979. price varies. Academic Press, Inc., 111 Fifth Ave., New York, NY 10003. Ed. Klaus Florey.

615.1   FR   ISSN 0066-2186
ANNALES MOREAU DE TOURS. 1962. irreg. price varies. Presses Universitaires de France, 108 Bd. Saint Germaine, 75279 Paris Cedex 6, France (Service des Periodiques, 12 rue Jean de Beauvais, 75005 Paris)

615   FR   ISSN 0396-0625
ANNUAIRE DES FOURNISSEURS DE LABORATOIRES PHARMACEUTIQUES ET COSMETIQUES. vol. 2, 1976. a. Agence de Diffusion et de Publicite, 24 Place du General Catroux, 75017 Paris, France.
Continues: Annuaire des Fournisseurs de Laboratoires Pharmaceutiques (ISSN 0517-8991)

615   FR   ISSN 0066-3158
ANNUAIRE GENERAL DE LA PHARMACIE FRANCAISE. 1932. a. 115 F. Association Generale des Syndicats Pharmaceutiques, c/o Mme. Boiscourt, Ed., 47 rue de la Victoire, Paris 9e, France. adv. circ. 6,000.

615   SP   ISSN 0379-4121
ANNUAL DRUG DATA REPORT. (Text in English) 1979. latest vol. 3, 1981. $85. J.R. Prous, S.A. International Publishers, Provenza 385-387, Apdo. 540, Barcelona, Spain. bibl. charts.

615.1   US   ISSN 0065-7743
ANNUAL REPORTS IN MEDICINAL CHEMISTRY. 1965. irreg., vol. 13, 1978. price varies. (American Chemical Society, Division of Medicinal Chemistry) Academic Press, Inc., 111 Fifth Ave., New York, NY 10003. Ed. Frank H. Clarke. Indexed: Chem.Abstr. Curr.Cont.

615.1   US   ISSN 0362-1642
ANNUAL REVIEW OF PHARMACOLOGY AND TOXICOLOGY. 1961. a. $20. Annual Reviews Inc., 4139 El Camino Way, Palo Alto, CA 94306. Eds. Robert George, Ronald Okun. bibl. index; cum.ind. (also avail. in microfilm; microfiche; back issues avail.; reprint service avail. from ISI) Indexed: Biol.Abstr. Chem.Abstr. Ind.Med. Psychol.Abstr. Sci.Cit.Ind. M.M.R.I.
Formerly: Annual Review of Pharmacology (ISSN 0066-4251)

615.329   576   US
ANTIBIOTICS. 1967. irreg., vol. 5A, 1979. price varies. Springer-Verlag, 175 Fifth Ave., New York, NY 10010 (Also Berlin, Heidelberg, Vienna) (reprint service avail. from ISI)

615.1   SZ   ISSN 0066-4758
ANTIBIOTICS AND CHEMOTHERAPY. (Text in English) 1954. irreg. (approx. 1/yr.) 100 Fr.($60) per vol. (1981 price) S. Karger AG, Allschwilerstrasse 10, P.O. Box, CH-4009 Basel, Switzerland. Eds. H. Schoenfeld, R.W. Brockman, F.E. Hahn. (reprint service avail. from ISI) Indexed: Biol.Abstr. Chem.Abstr. Curr.Cont. Ind.Med.

615   GW   ISSN 0066-5347
APOTHEKER-JAHRBUCH. 1915. a. price varies. (Deutscher Apotheker Verein) Wissenschaftliche Verlagsgesellschaft mbH, Postfach 40, 7000 Stuttgart 1, W. Germany (B.R.D.) Ed. Herbert Huegel. adv. index. cum.index.

615.1   SP
ARCHIVAS DE FARMACOLOGIA Y TOXICOLOGIA. 1949. irreg. Universidad Complutense de Madrid, Facultad de Medicina, Pabellon, Madrid 3, Spain.
Formerly (1949-1975): Spain. Consejo Superior de Investigaciones Cientificas. Instituto de Farmacologia Experimental. Archivos (ISSN 0024-9629)

615.9   US
ARCHIVES OF TOXICOLOGY. SUPPLEMENT. 1978. irreg., vol. 2, 1979. price varies. Springer-Verlag, 175 Fifth Ave., New York, NY 10010 (Also Berlin, Heidelberg, Vienna) (reprint service avail. from ISI)

615   SP
ARCHIVOS DE FARMACOLOGIA Y TOXICOLOGIA. 1975. irreg. Universidad Complutense de Madrid, Departamento Coordinado de Farmacologia, Ciudad Universitaria, Madrid, Spain.

615.1   PH   ISSN 0066-8419
ASIAN JOURNAL OF PHARMACY. (Text in English) 1967. a. membership. Federation of Asian Pharmaceutical Associations, Hizon Building, 29 Quezon Blvd., Quezon City, Philippines. Ed. Jesusa A. Concha. circ. 1,000. Indexed: I.P.A.

615   BL
ASSOCIACAO BRASILEIRA DA INDUSTRIA FARMACEUTICA. PESQUISA. 1976. irreg. Associacao Brasileira da Industria Farmaceutica, Av. Beira Mar 262, CEP 20000 Rio de Janeiro R J, Brazil. Ed.Bd. charts.

615.1   CN   ISSN 0066-9555
ASSOCIATION OF FACULTIES OF PHARMACY OF CANADA. PROCEEDINGS. 1970. a. membership. ‡ Association of Faculties of Pharmacy of Canada, c/o Dr. A. M. Goodeve, Faculty of Pharmaceutical Sciences, University of British Columbia, Vancouver 8, B.C., Canada. circ. 200.
Before 1969, Vol. 26: Canadian Conference of Pharmaceutical Faculties. Proceedings.

615   SP
AVANCES EN TERAPEUTICA. 1969. a. 450 ptas. (Universidad Autonoma de Barcelona) Salvat Editores, S.A., Mallorca 41-49, Barcelona 15, Spain. Ed. J. Laporte; J. A. Salva. charts. illus. circ. 2,000.

615   BL
BRAZIL. CONSELHO FEDERAL DE FARMACIA. RELATORIO. irreg. Conselho Federal de Farmacia, Brasilia, Brazil. illus.

615   US
BRITISH PHARMACOLOGICAL SOCIETY. SYMPOSIA. 1973. irreg (1-2/yr.) price varies. University Park Press, American Medical Publishers, Chamber of Commerce Bldg., Baltimore, MD 21202.

615.1   UK   ISSN 0068-2519
BRITISH SOCIETY FOR THE HISTORY OF PHARMACY. TRANSACTIONS. 1970. irreg. price varies. British Society for the History of Pharmacy, 36 York Place, Edinburgh EH1 3HU, Scotland. Ed. M. P. Earles.
History

615   BL   ISSN 0068-4775
CADASTRO BRASILEIRO DE MATERIAS-PRIMAS FARMACEUTICAS, POR PRODUTO, POR FABRICANTE. 1966. a. free. Associacao Brasileira da Industria Farmaceutica, Av. Beira Mar 262, Rio de Janeiro, Brazil. adv.

PHARMACY AND PHARMACOLOGY

615   CN   ISSN 0068-8452
CANADIAN CHEMICAL, PHARMACEUTICAL AND PRODUCT DIRECTORY. 1948. a. Can.$20($30) Lloyd Publications of Canada, Box 262, West Hill, Ont. M1E 4R5, Canada. Ed. J. Lloyd. adv. index. circ. 7,000.
Formerly: Canadian Chemical Directory.

615.1   FR   ISSN 0069-4665
CATALOGUE DES THESES DE PHARMACIE SOUTENUES EN FRANCE. QUINQUENNIAL CUMULATION. 1960. quinquennial. price varies. (Bibliotheque Interuniversitaire, Section Medecine, Pharmacie, Odontologie-Clermont Ferrand) Editions de Sante, 19 rue Louis le Grand, 75002 Paris, France. Eds. J. Archimbaud, R. Perrin, M. Sarazin.

615.1   UK
CHEMIST AND DRUGGIST DIRECTORY. 1868. a. £18. Benn Publications Ltd., 25 New Street Square, London EC4A 3JA, England. Ed. A. Wright. adv. circ. 3,000.

615   US   ISSN 0362-5664
CLINICAL NEUROPHARMACOLOGY. 1976. irreg., vol. 4, 1979. price varies. Raven Press, 1140 Ave. of the Americas, New York, NY 10036. Ed. Harold L. Klawans. charts, illus. index. (back issues avail) Indexed: Curr.Cont.

615   NE
CLINICAL PHARMACOLOGY AND DRUG EPIDEMIOLOGY. 1977. irreg. price varies. Elsevier North-Holland Biomedical Press, Box 211, 1000 AE Amsterdam, Netherlands.

615   CN   ISSN 0069-7966
COMPENDIUM OF PHARMACEUTICALS AND SPECIALTIES. (Text in English and French) 1960. a. Can.$32. Canadian Pharmaceutical Association, 1101-1815 Alta Vista Drive, Ottawa, Ont. K1G 3Y6, Canada. Ed. D. L. Thompson. bk. rev. circ. 60,000 (English edt.); 16,000 (French edt.)

615   SP
CUADERNOS DE FARMACOLOGIA. 1948. irreg. 50 ptas. Universidad de Granada, Secretariado de Publicaciones e Intercambio Cientifico, Granada, Spain.

615   SP
CUADERNOS DE HISTORIA DE LA FARMACIA. 1971. irreg. price varies. Universidad de Granada, Secretariado de Publicaciones, Hospital Real, Granada, Spain. Ed. Jose L. Valverde.

CURRENT TOPICS IN ENVIRONMENTAL AND TOXICOLOGICAL CHEMISTRY. see *CHEMISTRY*

615   MX
DICCIONARIO DE ESPECIALIDADES FARMACEUTICAS. 1944. a. Mex.$300. Medellin 184, Mexico 7 D.F., Mexico. Ed. Dr. Emilio Rosenstein. adv. circ. 42,000.

615   BL
DICIONARIO DE ESPECIALIDADES FARMACEUTICAS. a. free. Associacao Editora de Publicacoes Medicas Ltda, Editora de Publicacoes Cientificas Ltda, Rua do Russel 404, Rio de Janeiro, Brazil. adv. circ 55,000.

615   FR   ISSN 0419-1153
DICTIONNAIRE VIDAL. a. 87 F.($16) Office de Vulgarisation Pharmaceutique, 11 rue Quentin Bauchart, 75008-Paris, France.
Supersedes: Dictionnaire de Specialites Pharmaceutiques.

615   BL   ISSN 0070-6612
DIRETORIO BRASILEIRO DE INDUSTRIA FARMACEUTICA. 1968. a. free. Associacao Brasileira da Industria Farmaceutica, 262 Av. Beira Mar, 7 andar, Rio de Janeiro, Brazil. adv.

615   JA
DRUG APPROVAL AND LICENSING PROCEDURES IN JAPAN. (Text in English) 1973. biennial, 3rd edt., 1978. 50000 Yen. Yakugyo Jiho Co., Ltd., 2-36 Kanda Jinbo-cho, Chiyoda-ku, Tokyo 101, Japan.

615   US   ISSN 0095-599X
DRUG INTERACTIONS. a. $26. University Park Press, Chamber of Commerce Bldg., Baltimore, MD 21202.

330   US
DRUG STORE MARKET GUIDE; a detailed distribution analysis. 1981. a. $119. 1739 Horton Ave., Mohegan Lake, NY 10547. Ed. Melanie R. Buse.

615   US   ISSN 0419-764X
DRUG TOPICS HEALTH & BEAUTY AIDS DIRECTORY; the pink book. 1960. biennial. $16. Medical Economics Co., 680 Kinderkamack Rd., Oradell, NJ 07649. Ed. Jerry Levine. circ. 2,000.
Formerly: Pink Book.
Classifies over 20,000 non-prescription drugstore products

615.1   US   ISSN 0070-7376
DRUG TOPICS REDBOOK. 1897. a. $15 (Including 2 supplements) Medical Economics Co., 680 Kinderkamack Rd., Oradell, NJ 07649. Ed. Jerry Levine. circ. 75,000. (also avail. in magnetic tape)

615   US   ISSN 0070-7392
DRUGS IN CURRENT USE AND NEW DRUGS. 1955. a. price varies. Springer Publishing Co., Inc., 200 Park Ave. S., New York, NY 10003. Ed. Walter Modell, M.D. (also avail. in microform from UMI)

615   US   ISSN 0070-7406
DRUGS OF CHOICE. 1958. biennial. $33.50. C. V. Mosby Co., 11830 Westline Industrial Dr., St. Louis, MO 63141. Ed. Walter Modell, M.D.

615   US   ISSN 0071-1446
ESSAYS IN TOXICOLOGY. 1969. irreg., vol. 7, 1976. price varies. Academic Press, Inc., 111 Fifth Ave., New York, NY 10003. Ed. F. R. Blood. (also avail. in microfiche).

614.35   614.28   UN   ISSN 0082-8335
ESTIMATED WORLD REQUIREMENTS OF NARCOTIC DRUGS. (Text in English, French and Spanish) 1946. a.; latest, 1975. price varies. International Narcotics Control Board - Organe Internationale de Controle des Stupefiants, Distributions and Sales Section, Palais des Nations, CH-1211 Geneva 10, Switzerland (Or United Nations Publications, Room LX-2300, New York, NY 10017)

614.35   614.28   UN   ISSN 0082-8327
ESTIMATED WORLD REQUIREMENTS OF NARCOTIC DRUGS, SUPPLEMENT. (Text in English, French and Spanish) irreg.; latest, supp. 5, 1975. price varies. International Narcotics Control Board - Organe Internationale de Controle des Stupefiants, Distribution and Sales Section, Palais des Nations, CH-1211 Geneva 10, Switzerland (Or United Nations Publications, Room LX-2300, New York, NY)

615.7   NE
EUROPEAN SOCIETY OF TOXICITY. PROCEEDINGS.* irreg. Excerpta Medica, P.O.B. 211, Amsterdam, Netherlands (Inquire: Dr. E. Eichenberger, Wander AG, 3001 Berne, Switzerland)
Formerly: European Society for the Study of Drug Toxicity. Proceedings (ISSN 0071-3090) 1974, 19th, Carlsbad, CSSR

615   US   ISSN 0090-6654
EVALUATIONS OF DRUG INTERACTIONS. a. $15. American Pharmaceutical Association, 2215 Constitution Ave., N.W., Washington, DC 20037.

615   US   ISSN 0094-8640
EVALUATIONS OF DRUG INTERACTIONS. SUPPLEMENT. 1974. a. $7. American Pharmaceutical Association, 2215 Constitution Ave., N.W., Washington, DC 20037. bibl.

EXECUTIVE DIRECTORY OF THE U.S. PHARMACEUTICAL INDUSTRY. see *BUSINESS AND ECONOMICS — Trade And Industrial Directories*

614   016   US   ISSN 0429-9442
F D A CLINICAL EXPERIENCE ABSTRACTS. irreg., approx. m. U. S. Food and Drug Administration, 5600 Fisher's Lane, Rockville, MD 20857.

F D A COMPLIANCE POLICY GUIDE. see *FOOD AND FOOD INDUSTRIES*

615   FR   ISSN 0071-7622
FORMULAIRE THERA. 1944. a. 60 F. Societe d'Editions Medico- Pharmaceutiques, 26, rue le Brun, 75013 Paris, France.

615.1   SZ   ISSN 0071-786X
FORTSCHRITTE DER ARZNEIMITTELFORSCHUNG/PROGRESS IN DRUG RESEARCH/PROGRES DES RECHERCHES PHARMACEUTIQUES. (Text in English, French and German) 1959. irreg.(1-2/yr.) Birkhaeuser Verlag, Elisabethenstr. 19, CH 4010 Basel, Switzerland. Ed. Ernst Jucker. Indexed: I.P.A.

015.1   FR   ISSN 0072-7954
GUIDE ANALYTIQUE DU PHARMACIEN D'OFFICINE.* 1968, 4th ed. irreg. price varies. Synthese Editeur, 51 rue Vivienne, Paris 2e, France.

615   US
HANDBOOK OF NON PRESCRIPTION DRUGS. biennial. price varies. American Pharmaceutical Association, 2215 Constitution Ave., N.W., Washington, DC 20037.

615   US   ISSN 0073-0033
HANDBUCH DER EXPERIMENTELLEN PHARMAKOLOGIE/HANDBOOK OF EXPERIMENTAL PHARMACOLOGY. (Contributions in German and English) 1950. irreg., vol. 57, 1981. price varies. Springer-Verlag, 175 Fifth Ave., New York, NY 10010 (also Berlin, Heidelberg, Vienna) (reprint service avail. from ISI)

615.1   US   ISSN 0073-1420
HAYES DRUGGIST DIRECTORY. 1912. a. $120. Edward N. Hayes, Ed. & Pub., 4229 Birch St, Newport Beach, CA 92660.

615   SZ
INDEX NOMINUM. (Text in German, French, English) 1956. irreg., 10th edt., 1980. 185 Fr. Societe Suisse de Pharmacie, Marktgasse 52, 3011 Berne, Switzerland.

615.1   II   ISSN 0073-6635
INDIAN PHARMACEUTICAL GUIDE. (Text in English) 1963. a. $30. Pamposh Publications, E-38 Hauz Khas, New Delhi 110016, India. Ed. Mohan C. Bazaz.

615   SP
INDICE DE ACTUALIDAD FARMACOLOGICA. 1971. a. $150. Julio Garcia Peri Editor, Sanchez Pacheco 81-83, Madrid 2, Spain. adv. circ. 4,000.

615   US   ISSN 0093-3589
INDUSTRIAL PHARMACOLOGY. 1973. irreg., vol. 3, 1979. Futura Publishing Co., 295 Main St., Box 330, Mount Kisco, NY 10549. Eds. Stuart Fielding, Harbans Lal. bibl. charts. illus.

615   IT   ISSN 0073-7984
INFORMATORE FARMACEUTICO. 1940. a. $103 includes subscr. to Notiziario Medico Farmaceutico. Organizzazione Editoriale Medico-Farmaceutica, Via Edolo 42, Box 10434, 20125 Milan, Italy. Ed. Dr. Lucio Marini.

615.5   GW   ISSN 0074-3577
INTERNATIONAL CONGRESS OF CHEMOTHERAPY. PROCEEDINGS.* irreg., 1971, 7th, Prague. (International Society of Chemotherapy) Dustri Verlag Dr. Karl Feistle, Bahnhofstr. 5, D-8024 Deisenhofen, W. Germany (B.R.D.) (Dist. in U.S. and Canada by: University Park Press, Chamber of Commerce Bldg., Baltimore, MD 21202)

INTERNATIONAL CONGRESS ON CLINICAL CHEMISTRY. ABSTRACTS. see *BIOLOGY — Biological Chemistry*

INTERNATIONAL CONGRESS ON CLINICAL CHEMISTRY. PAPERS. see *BIOLOGY — Biological Chemistry*

INTERNATIONAL CONGRESS ON CLINICAL CHEMISTRY. PROCEEDINGS. see *BIOLOGY — Biological Chemistry*

615 US
INTERNATIONAL DIRECTORY OF INVESTIGATORS IN PSYCHOPHARMACOLOGY. 1973. irreg. U.S. National Institute of Mental Health, 5600 Fishers Lane, Rm. 9-105, Rockville, MD 20852. (Co-sponsor: World Health Organization) Ed. Alice A. Leeds. circ. 6,000.

615.19 GW
INTERNATIONAL SYMPOSIUM ON CAPTOPRIL. (Supplement to: Drug Development and Evaluation) 1979. irreg. $22. Gustav Fischer Verlag, Wollgraweg 49, Postfach 720143, 7000 Stuttgart 70, W. Germany (B.R.D.) Eds. Franz Gross, Rainer K. Liedtke. illus.

INTERNATIONAL SYMPOSIUM ON PHARMACOLOGICAL TREATMENT IN BURNS. PROCEEDINGS. see *MEDICAL SCIENCES — Orthopedics And Traumatology*

INTERNATIONAL SYMPOSIUM ON QUANTUM BIOLOGY AND QUANTUM PHARMACOLOGY. PROCEEDINGS. see *BIOLOGY*

615.1 GW ISSN 0074-9729
INTERNATIONALE GESELLSCHAFT FUER GESCHICHTE DER PHARMAZIE. VEROEFFENTLICHUNGEN. NEUE FOLGE. (Text in English and German) 1953 N.S. irreg., vol. 48, 1980. price varies. Wissenschaftliche Verlagsgesellschaft mbH, Postfach 40, 7000 Stuttgart 1, W. Germany (B.R.D.) Ed. Wolfgang-Hagen Hein.
History

615.11 JA
J A P T A LIST: JAPANESE DRUG DIRECTORY. (Supplements issued separately) 1968. irreg. latest edition 1973, supplement 1976. $65. (Japan Pharmaceutical Traders' Association) Yakuji Nippo Ltd., 1 Kanda Izumicho, Chiyoda-ku, Tokyo 101, Japan. Key Title: Japanese Drug Directory.

615 JA
JAPAN DRUG INDUSTRY REVIEW. (Text in English) biennial. 8000 Yen. Yakugyo Jiho Co., Ltd., 2-36 Kanda Jinbo-Cho, Chiyoda-ku, Tokyo 101, Japan.
Formerly (until 1976): Handbook of the Japan Drug Industry.

615.1 UA ISSN 0085-2406
JOURNAL OF DRUG RESEARCH OF EGYPT. Cover title: Journal of Drug Research. (Text in English; summaries in English & Arabic) 1968. a. $12. National Organisation for Drug Control and Research, Drug Research and Control Center, 6, Abou-Hazem St., Pyramids Ave., Box 29, Cairo, Egypt. Ed. A. W. el-Borolossy. bk. rev. illus. Indexed: Biol.Abstr. Chem.Abstr. I.P.A.

615 BE
JOURNEE SCIENTIFIQUE DE MARS. CONFERENCES ET COMMUNICATIONS. 1956. a. price varies. Universite de Liege, Cercle Scientifiques des Anciens Aleves de l'Institut de Pharmacie A. Gilkinet, 4000 Liege, Liege, Belgium. circ. 250-300.
Formerly: Universite de Liege. Institut de Pharmacie. Recueil des Conferences Organisees Par le Cercle A. Gilkinet (ISSN 0075-9341)

615 SA ISSN 0076-8847
M I M S DESK REFERENCE. 1965. a. M. I. M. S. (Pty) Ltd., P.O. Box 2059, Pretoria 0001, South Africa. Ed. Deo Botha. adv. index.
Formerly: M I M S Reference Manual.

615 US ISSN 0085-3100
MARIO NEGRI INSTITUTE FOR PHARMACOLOGICAL RESEARCH. MONOGRAPHS. 1970. irreg., no. 13, 1979. price varies. Raven Press, 1140 Ave. of the Americas, New Yor, NY 10036. Ed. Silvio Garattini. Indexed: Biol.Abstr. Chem.Abstr. Curr.Cont.
Proceedings of international biomedical symposia covering pharmacological problems

MARKETING GUIDE. see *BUSINESS AND ECONOMICS — Marketing And Purchasing*

615 UK
MARTINDALE: THE EXTRA PHARMACOPOEIA. 1883. biennial; latest 1977. £30($60) per copy. Pharmaceutical Society of Great Britain, 1 Lambeth High St., London SE1 7JN, England (Dist. in U.S. by: Rittenhouse Book Distributors, Philadelphia, PA 19104) Ed. Ainley Wade. index.
Incorporating: Squires Companion.

615 US ISSN 0076-6054
MEDICINAL CHEMISTRY; series of monographs. 1963. irreg., vol. 14, 1977. price varies. Academic Press Inc., 111 Fifth Ave., New York, NY 10003. Ed. George deStevens.

615 US ISSN 0076-6518
MERCK INDEX; AN ENCYCLOPEDIA OF CHEMICALS AND DRUGS. 1889. irreg., 9th ed., 1976. $18. Merck and Co. Inc, Box 2000, Rahway, NJ 07065. Ed. Martha Windholz.

615 US ISSN 0076-9959
MODERN DRUG ENCYCLOPEDIA AND THERAPEUTIC INDEX. 1934. biennial. $40. Yorke Medical Group, Yorke Medical Books (Subsidiary of: Technical Publishing Co.(New York)) 666 Fifth Ave., New York, NY 10103. Ed. Arthur J. Lewis, M.D.

615 US ISSN 0098-6925
MODERN PHARMACOLOGY-TOXICOLOGY. 1973. irreg., vol. 16, 1979. Marcel Dekker, Inc., 270 Madison Ave., New York, NY 10016. Eds. W. Bousquet, R.F. Palmer. illus. Indexed: Chem.Abstr.
Formerly: Modern Pharmacology (ISSN 0092-0150)

MODERN PROBLEMS OF PHARMACOPSYCHIATRY. see *MEDICAL SCIENCES — Psychiatry And Neurology*

615 574.1 US ISSN 0364-2569
MONOGRAPHS IN PHARMACOLOGY AND PHYSIOLOGY. 1976. irreg. Spectrum Publications, Inc., 175-20 Wexford Terrace, Jamaica, NY 10032. Eds. Elliot S. Vesell, Sivio Garattini.

N. A. C. D. S. LILLY DIGEST. (National Association of Chain Drug Stores) see *BUSINESS AND ECONOMICS — Marketing And Purchasing*

N A R D ALMANAC. (National Association of Retail Druggists) see *ENCYCLOPEDIAS AND GENERAL ALMANACS*

615 US ISSN 0077-3263
NATIONAL ASSOCIATION OF BOARDS OF PHARMACY. PROCEEDINGS. 1904. a. $25. National Association of Boards of Pharmacy, One E. Wacker Dr., Chicago, IL 60601. Ed. Fred T. Mahaffey. index. circ. 500.

NEPAL. DEPARTMENT OF MEDICINAL PLANTS. ANNUAL REPORT. see *BIOLOGY — Botany*

OCULAR THERAPEUTICS AND PHARMACOLOGY. see *MEDICAL SCIENCES — Ophthalmology And Optometry*

615 JA ISSN 0387-480X
OSAKA UNIVERSITY. FACULTY OF PHARMACEUTICAL SCIENCES. MEMOIRS/OSAKA DAIGAKU YAKUGAKUBU KIYO. (Text in Japanese and English) 1950. a. exchange basis. Osaka University, Faculty of Pharmaceutical Sciences - Osaka Daigaku Yakugakubu, 133-1 Yamadakami, Suita, Osaka, Japan. abstr. circ. 300.

615 616.5 FR
PARAPHARMEX. a; with 16 supplements. 210 F. Societe d'Editions Medico-Pharmaceutiques, 26, rue le Brun, 75013 Paris, France. circ. 12,000 (controlled) (looseleaf format; also avail. in microfiche)

615.9 US
PERSPECTIVES IN TOXICOLOGY. irreg. Raven Press, 1140 Ave. of the Americas, New York, NY 10036. Ed. Robert L. Dixon.
Toxicology

615 US ISSN 0569-6917
PHARMACEUTICAL DIRECTORY. 1961. a. price varies. American Pharmaceutical Association, 2215 Constitution Ave., N.W., Washington, DC 20037.

615.1 UK ISSN 0079-1393
PHARMACEUTICAL HISTORIAN. 1967. irreg. (approx. 3/yr.) £2.25. British Society for the History of Pharmacy, 36 York Place, Edinburgh EH1 3HU, Scotland. Ed. A. Wright.
History

PHARMACEUTICAL MEDICINE. see *MEDICAL SCIENCES*

615 US
PHARMACOLOGY OF ANAESTHETIC DRUGS. irreg. price varies. Research Studies Press, Box 92, 2130 Pacific Ave., Forest Grove, OR 97116. Ed. J.P. Payne.

615 UN ISSN 0553-9382
PHARMACOPOEIA INTERNATIONALIS/INTERNATIONAL PHARMACOPOEIA. 1951. irreg., 3rd, 1979. World Health Organization - Organisation Mondiale de la Sante, Distribution and Sales Service, 20 Avenue Appia, Ch-1211 Geneva 27, Switzerland.

615 UK
PHARMATHERAPEUTICA. (Text and summaries in various languages) 1976. irreg. £17.50($35) Clayton-Wray Publications Ltd., 27 Sloane Sq., London SW1W 8A8, England (Subscriptions to:, 516 Wandsworth Rd., London SW8 3JX, England) Ed. Nigel Clayton. circ. 5,500. Indexed: Chem.Abstr. Curr.Cont.

615.19 US
PRESCRIPTION DRUG INDUSTRY FACT BOOK; pharmaceuticals, medical devices and diagnostic products. irreg., once every 3 or 4 yrs. Pharmaceutical Manufacturers Association, 1155 15th St. N.W., Washington, DC 20005. Ed.Bd. charts. stat. circ. 5,000.

615 SZ ISSN 0079-6085
PROGRESS IN BIOCHEMICAL PHARMACOLOGY. (Text in English) 1965. irreg. (approx. 1/yr.) 150 Fr.($90) per vol. (1981 price) S. Karger AG, Allschwilerstrasse 10, P.O. Box, CH-4009 Basel, Switzerland. Ed. R. Paoletti. (reprint service avail. from ISI) Indexed: Biol.Abstr. Chem.Abstr. Curr.Cont. Ind.Med.

615.9 US ISSN 0079-6158
PROGRESS IN CHEMICAL TOXICOLOGY. 1963. irreg., vol. 5, 1974. price varies. Academic Press, Inc, 111 Fifth Ave, New York, NY 10003. Ed. A. Stolman. index. Indexed: Ind.Med.

615 US
QUALITY CONTROL IN THE PHARMACEUTICAL INDUSTRY. irreg. Academic Press, Inc., 111 Fifth Ave., New York, NY 10003.

615.1 GW ISSN 0085-5367
QUELLEN UND STUDIEN ZUR GESCHICHTE DER PHARMAZIE. 1960. irreg. price varies. Jal-Verlag, Postfach 1136, 8700 Wuerzburg 2, W. Germany (B.R.D.) Ed. Rudolf Schmitz.

615.1 GW ISSN 0080-0899
REMEDIA HOECHST. (Text in English, French and German) 1900. irreg. Hoechst AG, Postfach 800320, 6230 Frankfurt 80, W. Germany (B.R.D.)

615 IT
REPERTORIO TERAPEUTICO; medicamenta-drugs international index. (Text in English, Italian) 1963. irreg., 6th ed., 1979. $75. Organizzazione Editoriale Medico-Farmaceutica, Via Edolo 42, Box 10434, 20125 Milan, Italy. Ed. Dr. Lucio Marini.

REVIEWS OF PHYSIOLOGY, BIOCHEMISTRY AND EXPERIMENTAL PHARMACOLOGY. see *BIOLOGY — Physiology*

615 CR
REVISTA CIENCIAS FARMACEUTICAS. (Text in Spanish; summaries in English & Spanish) 1976. a. Col.10($2) Colegio de Farmaceuticos de Costa Rica, Aptdo 396, San Jose, Costa Rica.

615 IT
RIVISTA DI FARMACOLOGIA E TERAPIA. irreg. L.25000. (Universita degli Studi di Modena, Societa di Medicina Sperimentale) Società Tipografica Editrice Modenese, Via Tabboni 4, 41100 Modena, Italy. Ed. W. Ferrari.

615   IT   ISSN 0081-0703
S.I.S.F. DOCUMENTI. 1965. irreg. price varies. Societa Italiana di Scienze Farmaceutiche, Via Giorgio Jan 18, 20129 Milan, Italy.

615 368.4   CN   ISSN 0707-0152
SASKATCHEWAN. PRESCRIPTION DRUG PLAN. ANNUAL REPORT. 1976. a. Prescription Drug Plan, Dept. of Health, 3211 Albert St., Regina. Sask, Canada.

615   US
SCHOOLS IN THE UNITED STATES AND CANADA OFFERING GRADUATE EDUCATION IN PHARMACOLOGY. 1963. a. free. American Society for Pharmacology and Experimental Therapeutics, 9650 Rockville Pike, Bethesda, MD 20014.

SIDE EFFECTS OF DRUGS. see *MEDICAL SCIENCES*

615   US   ISSN 0585-2471
STEPHEN WILSON ANNUAL PHARMACY SEMINAR. REPORT. a. free. Wayne State University, College of Pharmacy, Detroit, MI 48202. circ. controlled.

615.19   SZ
SYMPOSIA ON THE PHARMACOLOGY OF THERMOREGULATION. (Text in English) irreg. 100 Fr.($60) (1981 price) S. Karger AG, Allschwilerstr. 10, P. O. Box, CH-4009 Basel, Switzerland. (reprint service avail. from ISI) Indexed: Biol.Abstr. Curr.Cont. Ind.Med.

615.9   US
TARGET ORGAN TOXICITY. irreg. Raven Press, 1140 Ave. of the Americas, New York, NY 10036. Ed. Robert L. Dixon.
Toxicology

615   GW   ISSN 0068-0729
TECHNISCHE UNIVERSITAET BRAUNSCHWEIG. PHARMAZIEGESCHICHTLICHEN SEMINAR. VEROEFFENTLICHUNGEN. 1957. irreg., vol. 22, 1980. price varies. Deutscher Apotheker Verlag, Postfach 40, 7000 Stuttgart 1, W. Germany (B.R.D.) Ed. Wolfgang Schneider.
History

615   DK   ISSN 0082-4003
THERIACA; samlinger til farmaciens og medicinens historie. (Text in Danish; summaries in English) 1956. irreg., no. 19, 1978. price varies. Dansk Farmacihistorisk Selskab - Danish Society of the History of Pharmacy, Farmacilaboratorium, Universistetsparken 2, DK-2100 Copenhagen, Denmark.
History

615.9   US   ISSN 0361-3410
TOXICOLOGY ANNUAL. 1975. irreg., vol. 3, 1978. Marcel Dekker, Inc., 270 Madison Ave., New York, NY 10016. Ed. C. Winek.

615   US   ISSN 0090-6816
U S A N AND THE U S P DICTIONARY OF DRUG NAMES. 1963. a. $19.50. ‡ United States Pharmacopeial Convention, Inc., 12601 Twinbrook Pkwy., Rockville, MD 20852. Ed. Mary C. Griffiths.

615.11   US   ISSN 0091-3839
U S P GUIDE TO SELECT DRUGS. 1973. irreg., latest 1976. United States Pharmacopeial Convention, Inc., 12601 Twinbrook Parkway, Rockville, MD 20852. Ed. William M. Heller.

615.1   US   ISSN 0077-4235
U.S. FOOD AND DRUG ADMINISTRATION. NATIONAL DRUG CODE DIRECTORY. 1969. a. $18.75. U.S. Food and Drug Administration, Bureau of Drugs, 5600 Fisher's Lane, Rockville, MD 20857 (Orders to: Supt. Doc., Washington, DC 20402)

615.12   US
UNITED STATES DISPENSATORY. irreg., 1973, 27th ed. $35. J. B. Lippincott Co., E. Washington Sq., Philadelphia, PA 19105. Eds. Arthur Osol, Robertson Pratt & Alfonso Gennaro. index.
Formerly: United States Dispensatory and Physicians Pharmacology (ISSN 0083-0429)

615.11   US
UNITED STATES PHARMACOPEIA-NATIONAL FORMULARY. 1820. irreg.; USP vol. 20, 1980; NF vol. 15, 1980. $90 includes annual supplements. United States Pharmacopeial Convention, Inc, 12601 Twinbrook Parkway, Rockville, MD 20852.
Formed by the 1980 merger of: National Formulary (ISSN 0084-6414) & United States Pharmacopeia; Which was formerly titled: Pharmacopeia of the United States of America (ISSN 0079-1407)

615   SP   ISSN 0067-4176
UNIVERSIDAD DE BARCELONA. FACULTAD DE FARMACIA. MEMORIA.* biennial. price varies. Universidad de Barcelona, Facultad de Farmacia, Av. Jose Antonio 585, Barcelona 7, Spain.

615.329 547   BL   ISSN 0080-0228
UNIVERSIDADE FEDERAL DE PERNAMBUCO. INSTITUTO DE ANTIBIOTICOS. REVISTA. (Text in Portuguese; summaries in English, Portuguese) 1958. irreg. latest issue vol. 15, 1975. available on exchange. ‡ Universidade Federal de Pernambuco, Instituto de Antibioticos, Recife, Pernambuco, Brazil. bibl. charts. illus. circ. 800. Indexed: Chem.Abstr.

615.1   CS   ISSN 0041-9087
UNIVERSITAS COMENIANA. ACTA PHARMACEUTICAE. (Text in English, German, Russian) 1958. 1-2 nos. per yr. exchange basis. (Univerzita Komenskeho, Farmaceuticka Fakulta) Slovenske Pedagogicke Nakladatelstvo, Sasinkova 5, 891 12 Bratislava, Czechoslovakia (Subscr. to: Univerzita Komenskeho, Farmaceuticka Fakulta, Ustredna Kniznica, Odbojarov 12, 880 34 Bratislava) Ed. M. Chalabala. charts. illus. index. Indexed: Chem.Abstr. I.P.A.
Formerly: Acta Facultatis Pharmaceuticae Bohemoslovenicae.

615   BE   ISSN 0075-935X
UNIVERSITE DE LIEGE. INSTITUT DE PHARMACIE. TRAVAUX PUBLIES. 1921. triennial. exchange basis. Universite de Liege, Institut de Pharmacie, 5 rue Fusch, 4000 Liege, Belgium.

615.9   US   ISSN 0094-7962
UNIVERSITY OF CALIFORNIA, DAVIS. FOOD PROTECTION AND TOXICOLOGY CENTER. SUMMARY REPORT. a. University of California, Davis, Food Protection and Toxicology Center, Davis, CA 95616. illus. Key Title: Summary Report - Food Protection and Toxicology Center, University of California, Davis.

615   US   ISSN 0072-1344
UNIVERSITY OF GEORGIA. SCHOOL OF PHARMACY. PHARMACEUTICAL SERVICES FOR SMALL HOSPITALS AND NURSING HOMES. 1967. irreg. $3. University of Georgia, Center for Continuing Education, Athens, GA 30602.

615.328 612.405   US   ISSN 0083-6729
VITAMINS AND HORMONES: ADVANCES IN RESEARCH AND APPLICATIONS. 1943. irreg., vol. 38, 1980. price varies. Academic Press, Inc (Subsidiary of: Harcourt Brace Jovanovich) 111 Fifth Ave, New York, NY 10003. Eds. R. Harris, K. Thimann. index.cum.index: vols. 1-5 (1943-1947) in vol. 6(1948); vols. 6-10(1948-1952) in vol. 11 (1953); vols. 11-15 (1953-1957) in vol. 16 (1958) Indexed: Ind.Med.
Vitamins

615   JA   ISSN 0509-5832
WAKSMAN FOUNDATION OF JAPAN. REPORT. (Text in English) 1962. a. exchange basis. Waksman Foundation of Japan - Nihon Wakkusuman Zaidan, c/o Keio Daigaku Igakubu, 30-8 Daikyo-machi, Shinjuku-ku, Tokyo 106, Japan.

615.19   NR   ISSN 0303-691X
WEST AFRICAN JOURNAL OF PHARMACOLOGY AND DRUG RESEARCH. 1974. biennial. $10.60. (West African Society for Pharmacology) Literamed Publications Nigeria, Ltd., Oregun Village, P.M.B. 1068, Ikeja, Nigeria. Indexed: Ind.Med.

615.1   US   ISSN 0083-8969
WESTERN PHARMACOLOGY SOCIETY. PROCEEDINGS. 1958. a. $10. Western Pharmacology Society, c/o Peter Lomax, Ed., Dept. of Pharmacology, U.C.L.A. School of Medicine, Los Angeles, CA 90024. circ. 800. (also avail. in microform from UMI) Indexed: Curr.Cont. Ind.Med.

615.1   US   ISSN 0043-6593
WISCONSIN PHARMACY EXTENSION BULLETIN. (Insert in Wisconsin Pharmacist) 1957? irreg.(published m. until vol. 24, no. 3, Mar. 1980) University of Wisconsin-Madison, Extension Services in Pharmacy, 425 N. Chapter St., Rm 155 Pharmacy Bldg., Madison, WI 53706. Ed. Melvin H. Weinswig. stat. circ. 1,500. Indexed: Chem.Abstr.

615   UK
WORLD DIRECTORY OF PHARMACEUTICAL MANUFACTURERS. 1977. irreg., 3rd ed. 1980. $145. IMSWORLD Publications Ltd., York House, 37 Queen Square, London WC1N 3BL, England.

WORLD DIRECTORY OF SCHOOLS OF PHARMACY. see *EDUCATION — Guides To Schools And Colleges*

615   UK
WORLD LICENSE REVIEW. 1980. a. $750. IMSWORLD Publications Ltd., 37 Queen Square, London WC1N 3BL, England.

615.1058   US   ISSN 0084-3733
YEAR BOOK OF DRUG THERAPY. 1933. a. price varies. ‡ Year Book Medical Publishers, Inc., 35 E. Wacker Dr., Chicago, IL 60601. Ed.Bd.

PHARMACY AND PHARMACOLOGY — Abstracting, Bibliographies, Statistics

615 016   US   ISSN 0069-4770
CLIN-ALERT. 1962. 24/yr. $57. Science Editors, Inc., 149 Thierman Lane, P.O. Box 7185, Louisville, KY 40207. Ed.Bd. (back issues avail.)
Consists of numbered abstracts of current reports dealing with drug reactions and inter-reactions

016 615   US   ISSN 0098-2806
FATE OF DRUGS IN THE ORGANISM; A BIBLIOGRAPHIC SURVEY. 1974. irreg., vol. 4, 1977. (Societe Francaise des Sciences et Techniques Pharmaceutiques, FR) Marcel Dekker, Inc., 270 Madison Ave., New York, NY 10016. Ed. J. L. Hirtz. Key Title: Fate of Drugs in the Organism. Supersedes: Sort des Medicaments dans l'Organisme.

610 016   BE   ISSN 0018-8948
I C I A INFORMATION BULLETIN. 1964. irreg. $5 per no. International Center of Information on Antibiotics, 32 Bd. Constitution, B-4020 Liege, Belgium. (Co-sponsor: World Health Organization) Ed. L. Delcambe. abstr. bibl. circ. 2,000. Indexed: Microbiol.Abstr.

615.19   II
INDIAN CHEMICALS AND PHARMACEUTICALS STATISTICS. (Text in English) 1967. a. free. Ministry of Chemicals and Fertilizers, Economics and Statistics Division, New Delhi, India. stat. circ. controlled.

615.1   US   ISSN 0031-7152
PHARMINDEX. 1958. m. $65. Skyline Publishers, Inc., Box 1029 Federal Sta., Portland, OR 97207. Ed. Frank D. Portash. mkt. tr.lit. index monthly and annually. Indexed: Chem.Abstr. I.P.A.

PHILATELY

see *Hobbies — Philately*

PHILOSOPHY

see also *Religions and Theology*

100 370 GW ISSN 0065-0366
ABHANDLUNGEN ZUR PHILOSOPHIE,
PSYCHOLOGIE UND PAEDAGOGIK. 1954.
irreg., vol. 144, 1979/80. price varies. Bouvier
Verlag Herbert Grundmann, Am Hof 32, Postfach
1268, 5300 Bonn 1, W. Germany (B.R.D.)

100 HU ISSN 0324-6957
ACTA MARXISTICA LENINISTICA. FILOZOFIAI
TANULMANYOK. (Text in Hungarian,
occasionally German, Russian) vol. 24, 1978. irreg.
Kossuth Lajos Tudomanyegyetem, Egyetem Ter 1,
4010 Debrecen, Hungary. Ed. Istvan Konya.

140 HU ISSN 0324-6957
ACTA MARXISTICA LENINISTICA.
TUDOMANYOS SZOCIALIZMUS
TANULMANYOK. (Text in Hungarian,
occasionally German, Russian) vol.24,1978. irreg.
Kossuth Lajos Tudomanyegyetem, Egyetem Ter 1,
4010 Debrecen, Hungary. Ed. Dezso Farkas.

100 200 IT ISSN 0065-1540
ACTA PHILOSOPHICA ET THEOLOGICA. (Text
in English, French, German, Italian, Rumanian,
Spanish) 1958. irreg. price varies. Societa
Accademica Romena, Foro Traiano 1a, 00187
Rome, Italy.

100 PL ISSN 0208-564X
ACTA UNIVERSITATIS NICOLAI COPERNICI.
FILOZOFIA. 1960. irreg. price varies. Uniwersytet
Mikolaja Kopernika, Fosa Staromiejska 3, Torun,
Poland (Dist.by Osrodek Rozpowszechniania
Wydawnictw Naukowych PAN, Palac Kultury i
Nauki, 00-901 Warsaw, Poland)
  Formerly: Uniwersytet Mikolaja Kopernika,
Torun. Nauki Humanistyczno-Spoleczne. Filozofia
(ISSN 0083-4475)

100 301 IT
AGORA (RAVENNA) irreg. Angelo Longo Editore,
Via Rocca Ai Fossi 6, Casella Postale 431, 48100
Ravenna, Italy. Ed. Enrico De Mas.

100 CL ISSN 0568-3939
AISTHESIS; revista chilena de investigaciones
esteticas. 1966. a. $6.50. Universidad Catolica de
Chile, Instituto de Estetica, Diagonal Oriente 3.300,
Santiago, Chile. Ed. Radoslav Ivelic. bibl. cum.
index. circ. 1,000.

100 US ISSN 0149-2004
ALETHEIA; an international journal of philosophy.
(Text in English & German) 1977. a. $14.
University of Dallas Press, Box 477, University of
Dallas, Irving, TX 75061. Ed. Josef Seifert.

282 206 US ISSN 0065-7638
AMERICAN CATHOLIC PHILOSOPHICAL
ASSOCIATION. PROCEEDINGS. 1926. a. $8.
American Catholic Philosophical Association, The
Catholic University of America, Washington, DC
20064. Ed. Rev. George F. McLean. adv. cum.
index: vol. 1-39 (1926-65) (also avail. in microfilm)
Indexed: Cath.Ind.

100 US
AMERICAN LECTURES IN PHILOSOPHY. irreg.
price varies. Charles C. Thomas, Publisher, 301-327
E. Lawrence Ave., Springfield, IL 62717.

106 US ISSN 0065-9738
AMERICAN PHILOSOPHICAL SOCIETY.
MEMOIRS. 1935. irreg. price varies. American
Philosophical Society, 104 S. Fifth St, Philadelphia,
PA 19106. Ed. Whitfield J. Bell, Jr. index to each
vol. (reprint service avail. from UMI,ISI)

106 US ISSN 0065-9746
AMERICAN PHILOSOPHICAL SOCIETY.
TRANSACTIONS. 1769. 1 vol./yr. containing 1-10
parts published irregularly. $40. American
Philosophical Society, 104 S. Fifth St, Philadelphia,
PA 19106. Ed. Whitfield J. Bell, Jr. index in some
volumes; cum.index: 1769-1960. (reprint service
avail. from UMI,ISI) Indexed: SSCI.

106 US ISSN 0065-9762
AMERICAN PHILOSOPHICAL SOCIETY.
YEARBOOK. 1937. a. $5. American Philosophical
Society, 104 S. Fifth St., Philadelphia, PA 19106.
Ed. Whitfield J. Bell, Jr. index. (also avail. in
microform from UMI; reprint service avail. from
UMI,ISI)

100 NE
ANALECTA HUSSERLIANA; yearbook of
phenomenological research. (Text in English) 1971.
irreg. price varies. D. Reidel Publishing Co., Box 17,
3300 AA Dordrecht, Netherlands (And Lincoln
Building, 160 Old Derby St., Hingham, MA 02043)
Ed. Anna-Teresa Tymieniecka.

891 II
ANANDA ACHARYA UNIVERSAL SERIES. (Text
in English) 1971. irreg. price varies.
Vishveshvaranand Vedic Research Institute, P.O.
Sadhu Ashram, Hoshiarpur 146021, Punjab, India.

ANNALES D'ESTHETIQUE/CHRONIKA
AISTHETIKES. see ART

100 301 PL ISSN 0137-2025
ANNALES UNIVERSITATIS MARIAE CURIE-
SKLODOWSKA. SECTIO I. PHILOSOPHIA-
SOCIOLOGIA. (Text in English or Polish;
summaries in English, French, German, Russian)
1976. a. Uniwersytet Marii Curie-Sklodowskiej, Plac
Marii Curie-Sklodowskiej 5, 20-031 Lublin, Poland.
Ed. Z. Cackowski.

100 SP ISSN 0066-5215
ANUARIO FILOSOFICO. 1968. s-a. 1000 ptas.($18)
(Universidad de Navarra, Facultad de Filosofia y
Letras) Ediciones Universidad de Navarra, S.A.,
Plaza de los Sauces, 1 y 2, Baranain, Pamplona,
Spain. Ed. Juan J. Rodriguez Rosado. adv.

104 US ISSN 0066-5614
AQUINAS LECTURE SERIES. 1937. a. $6.95.
(Marquette University, Aristotelean Society)
Marquette University Press, 1324 W. Wisconsin
Ave., Milwaukee, WI 53233. (back issues avail.)

170 300 340 GW ISSN 0341-079X
ARCHIV FUER RECHTS- UND
SOZIALPHILOSOPHIE. BEIHEFTE. NEUE
FOLGE. (Text in English, French, German) irreg.,
vol. 15, 1981. price varies. (Internationale
Vereinigung fuer Rechts- und Sozialphilosophie)
Franz Steiner Verlag GmbH, Friedrichstr. 24,
Postfach 5529, 6200 Wiesbaden, W. Germany
(B.R.D.)

180 FR
ARCHIVES D'HISTOIRE DOCTRINALE ET
LITTERAIRE DU MOYEN AGE. (Text in French,
English, German, Latin) 1926. a. price varies.
Librairie Philosophique J. Vrin, 6 Place de la
Sorbonne, 75005 Paris, France. Eds. Etienne Gilson,
Marie Therese d'Alverny, Marie-Dominique Chenu,
O.P. index. circ. 750.

100 NE ISSN 0066-6610
ARCHIVES INTERNATIONALES D'HISTOIRE
DES IDEES/INTERNATIONAL ARCHIVES OF
THE HISTORY OF IDEAS. (Text in English and
French) 1963. irreg. price varies. Martinus Nijhoff,
Box 566, 2501 CN The Hague, Netherlands. Eds. P.
Dibon, R. Popkin.

109 309 PL ISSN 0066-6874
ARCHIWUM HISTORII FILOZOFII I MYSLI
SPOLECZNEJ. (Text in Polish; summaries in
French, German, or Russian) 1954. a. 75 Zl. per
volume. (Polska Akademia Nauk, Instytut Filozofii i
Socjologii) Ossolineum, Publishing House of the
Polish Academy of Sciences, Rynek 9, Wroclaw,
Poland. Ed. Andrzej Walicki.

100 UK
ARGUMENTS OF THE PHILOSOPHERS. irreg.
price varies. Routledge & Kegan Paul Ltd.,
Broadway House, Newtown Rd., Henley-on-
Thames, Oxon. RG9 1EN, England (U.S. address:
Routledge Journals, 9 Park St., Boston, MA 02108)

149 US ISSN 0304-1409
ATHEIST. 1946. irreg. membership. ‡ (Atheist
Association) Truth Seeker Co., Inc., Box 2832, San
Diego, CA 92112. Ed. James Hervey Johnson. circ.
500. (back issues available)

100 230 GW ISSN 0067-5024
BEITRAEGE ZUR GESCHICHTE DER
PHILOSOPHIE UND THEOLOGIE DES
MITTELALTERS NEUE FOLGE. 1891. irreg.
price varies. Aschendorffsche Verlagsbuchhandlung,
Soester Str. 13, 4400 Muenster, W. Germany
(B.R.D.) Eds. Ludwig Hoedl, Wolfgang Kluxen.

BEITRAEGE ZUR GESCHICHTE DES
RELIGIOESEN UND WISSENSCHAFTLICHEN
DENKENS. see RELIGIONS AND THEOLOGY

105 FR ISSN 0339-8498
BELISANE; bulletin de philosophie et d'histoire
traditionnelles. 1977. q. 24 F. Claude Boumendil,
Repro 2000, 11, rue Gutenberg, 06000 Nice,
France. Eds. Claude Passet, Daniel Robert.

100 GW
BOEHLAU PHILOSOPHICA. 1976. irreg. price
varies. Boehlau-Verlag GmbH, Niehler Str. 272-274,
5000 Cologne 60, W. Germany (B. R. D.)

100 GW
BONNER AKADEMISCHE REDEN. no. 16, 1951.
irreg., no. 49, 1979. price varies. Bouvier Verlag
Herbert Grundmann, Am Hof 32, Postfach 1268,
5300 Bonn 1, W. Germany (B.R.D.)

100 GW
BOUVIER DISPUTANDA; ein interdisziplinaeres
Diskussionsforum. 1959. irreg., no. 12, 1978. price
varies. Bouvier Verlag Herbert Grundmann, Am Hof
32, Postfach 1268, 5300 Bonn 1, W. Germany
(B.R.D.)

100 BU ISSN 0068-3973
BULGARSKA AKADEMIIA NA NAUKITE.
INSTITUT PO FILOSOFIIA. IZVESTIIA.
(Summaries in various languages) 1954. irreg. 2.85
lv. per issue. Publishing House of the Bulgarian
Academy of Sciences, Ul. Akad. G. Bonchev, 1113
Sofia, Bulgaria (Dist. by: Hemus, 6, Rouski Blvd.,
1000 Sofia, Bulgaria) Ed. A. Polikarpov. circ. 550.

180 BE ISSN 0068-4023
BULLETIN DE PHILOSOPHIE MEDIEVALE. (Text
mainly in French; contributions in English, German,
Italian and Spanish) 1959. a. 500 Fr.($20)
International Society for the Study of Medieval
Philosophy - Societe Internationale pour l'Etude de
la Philosophie Medievale, College Thomas More
(SH3), Chemin d'Aristote 1, B-1348 Louvain-la-
Neuve, Belgium. Ed. C. Wenin. adv. circ. 1,000.
(back issues avail.) Indexed: Phil.Ind.
  Formerly (1959-1963): Societe Internationale
pour l'Etude de la Philosophie Medievale. Bulletin.

100 BE ISSN 0008-0284
CAHIERS INTERNATIONAUX DE
SYMBOLISME. 1962. irreg. (3-4/yr.) 500 Fr. to
individuals; Fr. 1000 to institutions and libraries.
Universite de l'Etat a Mons, Centre
Interdisciplinaire d'Etudes Philosophiques, 17 Place
Warocque, 7000 Mons, Belgium. bk. rev. circ. 1,200.

100 ZR
CAHIERS PHILOSOPHIQUES AFRICAINS/
AFRICAN PHILOSOPHICAL JOURNAL. (Text
in French) 1972. irreg. Universite Nationale du
Zaire, Lubumbashi, Department de Philosophie, B.
P. 1825, Lubumbashi, Zaire.

100 US
CENTRAL ISSUES IN PHILOSOPHY SERIES.
1970. irreg. price varies. Prentice-Hall, Inc., Box
500, Englewood Cliffs, NJ 07632. Ed. B. Brody.

160 IT
CENTRO SUPERIORE DI LOGICA E SCIENZE
COMPARATE. QUADERNI. 1971. irreg., no. 8,
1976. Centro Superiore di Logica e Scienze
Comparate, Via Belmeloro 3, 40126 Bologna, Italy.

100 CE ISSN 0577-4772
CEYLON RATIONALIST AMBASSADOR. (Text in
English) 1967? a. Rs.5($1) Ceylon Rationalist
Association, 89 Pamankada Lane, Colombo 6, Sri
Lanka. Ed. Abraham T. Kovoor. circ. 3,000. (back
issues avail.)

160 US
CLARENDON LIBRARY OF LOGIC AND
PHILOSOPHY. irreg. price varies. Oxford
University Press, 200 Madison Ave., New York,
NY 10016 (And Ely House, 37 Dover St., London
W1X 4AH, England) Ed. L. Jonathan Cohen.

100 SP ISSN 0069-5076
COLECCION FILOSOFICA. 1963. irreg.; 1979, no.
32. price varies. (Universidad de Navarra, Facultad
de Filosofia y Letras) Ediciones Universidad de
Navarra, S.A., Plaza de los Sauces, 1 y 2 Baranain,
Pamplona, Spain.

100　　　　　　　AG　ISSN 0069-5149
COLECCION PENSAMIENTO ARGENTINO.*
1966. irreg. price varies. Universidad Nacional de la
Plata, Facultad de Humanidades y Ciencias de la
Educacion, Calle 7 no. 776, La Plata, Argentina.

100　　　　　　　NE
COLLECTANEA CARTESIANA. (Text in French)
1981. irreg. price varies. Quadratures, Postbus 6463,
1005 EL Amsterdam, Netherlands. Ed.Bd.

COLLECTED WORKS OF ERASMUS. see
HUMANITIES: COMPREHENSIVE WORKS

100　　　　　　　CN
COLLECTION PHILOSOPHICA. 1972. irreg. price
varies. University of Ottawa Press, 65 Hastey Ave.,
Ottawa, Ont., K1N 6N5, Canada.

100　　　　　　　FR　ISSN 0069-5440
COLLECTION PSI. 1969. irreg. price varies. Librairie
Bloud et Gay, 3 rue Garanciere, Paris 6e, France.

100　　　　　　　GE
COLLEGIUM PHILOSOPHICUM JENENSE. 1977.
irreg., vol. 3, 1980. price varies. (Friedrich-Schiller-
Universitaet, Sektion Marxistisch-Leninistische
Philosophie) Hermann Boehlaus Nachfolger,
Meyerstr. 50a, 53 Weimar, E. Germany (D.D.R.)
(back issues avail.)

100　　　　　　　IT　ISSN 0069-5777
COLLEZIONE DI FILOSOFIA. irreg. price varies.
Casa Editrice Taylor, Corso Stati Uniti, 53, 10129
Torino, Italy.

100　　　　　　　GW
CONSCIENTA. 1968. irreg., vol. 9, 1979. price varies.
Bouvier Verlag Herbert Grundmann, Am Hof 32,
Postfach 1268, 5300 Bonn 1, W. Germany (B.R.D.)
Ed. Gerhard Funke.

100　　　　　　　US
CONSCIOUSNESS AND SELF-REGULATION:
ADVANCES IN RESEARCH. 1976. a. price
varies. Plenum Publishing Corp., 233 Spring St.,
New York, NY 10013. Eds. Gary Schwartz, David
Shapiro.

100　　　　　　　US　ISSN 0414-7790
CONTEMPORARY PHILOSOPHY SERIES. irreg.
price varies. Cornell University Press, 124 Roberts
Place, Ithaca, NY 14850.

CONTEMPORARY RELIGIOUS MOVEMENTS: A
WILEY-INTERSCIENCE SERIES. see
RELIGIONS AND THEOLOGY

100　　　　　　　US　ISSN 0084-926X
CONTRIBUTIONS IN PHILOSOPHY. 1968. irreg.
price varies. Greenwood Press, 88 Post Rd. W.,
Westport, CT 06881.

CORONA. see *LITERATURE*

100　　　　　　　AG
CUADERNOS DE FILOSOFIA. no. 23, 1975. irreg.
price varies. Universidad de Buenos Aires, Facultad
de Filosofia y Letras, Instituto de Filosofia, Av. 25
de Mayo no. 217, Buenos Aires, Argentina. Ed.
Eugenie Pucciarelli. bk. rev. abstr. bibl. index. circ.
1,500.

100　　　　　　　CK
CUADERNOS DE FILOSOFIA. (Text in Spanish,
Portuguese) irreg. Universidad de Concepcion,
Instituto Central de Filosofia, Casilla 2092,
Concepcion, Chile.

100　　　　　　　SP
CUADERNOS SALMANTINOS DE FILOSOFIA.
1974. a. 600 ptas.($13) Universidad Pontificia de
Salamanca, Compania 1, Salamanca, Spain. Ed.
Saturnino Alvarez Turienzo.

100　　　　　　　UY　ISSN 0590-2568
CUADERNOS URUGUAYOS DE FILOSOFIA.
1961. irreg. Universidad de la Republica, Facultad
de Humanidades y Ciencias, Cerrito 75,
Montevideo, Uruguay.

100　　　　　　　DK　ISSN 0070-2749
DANISH YEARBOOK OF PHILOSOPHY. (Text in
English, French and German) 1964. a. price varies.
Munksgaard, 35 Noerre Soegade, DK-1370
Copenhagen K, Denmark (Dist. in U.S. by:
Humanities Press, Inc., 171 First Ave., Atlantic
Highlands, NJ 07716) index. circ. 400. (reprint
service avail. from ISI) Indexed: Curr.Cont.

DANS LE FANTASTIQUE. see *LITERATURE*

100　　　　　　　GW　ISSN 0070-3419
DENKEN, SCHAUEN, SINNEN. 1962. irreg. 38.
Verlag Freies Geistesleben GmbH, Haussmannstr.
76, 7000 Stuttgart, W. Germany (B. R. D.) Indexed:
Dm.

100　　　　　　　AT　ISSN 0084-9804
DIALECTIC. 1967. a. $0.50 ea. ‡ Newcastle
University Philosophy Club, Department of
Philosophy, Univ. of Newcastle, Shortland, N.S.W.
2308, Australia. Ed.Bd. circ. 150-300.

160　　　　　　　IT
DIALETTICA. irreg. price varies. Edizioni Studium-
Vita Nova, Via Crescenzio 63, 00193 Rome, Italy.

100　　　　　　　MX　ISSN 0419-0890
DIANOIA; anuario de filosofia. 1955. a.
Mex.$180($8) Universidad Nacional Autonoma de
Mexico, Instituto de Investigaciones Filosoficas,
Villa Obregon, Ciudad Universitaria, Mexico 20,
D.F., Mexico. circ. 1,200. (back issues avail.)

100　　　　　　　SZ　ISSN 0070-4806
DIDEROT STUDIES. (Text in English and French)
1949. a. price varies. Librarie Droz, 11, rue Massot,
1211 Geneva 12, Switzerland. Eds. Otis Fellows,
Diana Guiragossian. bk. rev.

105　　　　　　　GR
DIOTIMA; epitheoresis philosophikes ereunes/revue
de recherche philosophique/review of philosophical
research. (Text in English, French, or Greek) 1973.
irreg. $10. (Hellenic Society for Philosophical
Studies) Grigoris Publications, 71 Solonos St.,
Athens 143, Greece. Ed. L. Bargeliotes. adv. bk.
rev.

100　　　　　　　US　ISSN 0070-508X
DIRECTORY OF AMERICAN PHILOSOPHERS.
1962. biennial. price varies. Bowling Green State
University, Philosophy Documentation Center,
Bowling Green, OH 43403. Ed. Archie J. Bahm.
circ. 1,100.

181.45　294.54　　　SA
DIVINE PATH. 1967. irreg., latest 1977. free.
Sivananda School of Yoga, Embassy Place, 240 Bree
St., 3rd Fl., Johannesburg 2001, South Africa. illus.
circ. 500.
　　Former titles (1967-1976): Sivananda School of
Yoga. News Bulletin & Illumination Annual (ISSN
0019-235X)
Yoga

100　　　　　　　US　ISSN 0070-7708
DUQUESNE STUDIES. PHILOSOPHICAL SERIES.
1952. irreg. price varies. Duquesne University Press,
600 Forbes Ave., Pittsburgh, PA 15219 (Dist. by
Humanities Press, Inc., Atlantic Highlands, NJ
07716) Eds. Andre Schuwer, John Sallis.

100　　　　　　　UK　ISSN 0142-3371
EFRYDIAU ATHRONYDDOL. (Text in Welsh)
1938. a. £1. University of Wales Press, 6 Gwennyth
St., Cathays, Cardiff CF2 4YD, Wales. Ed. Prof.
T.A. Roberts. bk. rev. circ. 500. (reprint service
avail. from UMI)

110　　　　　　　US
EMISSARY. 1975. irreg. q. until 1979. $3.50. Eden
Valley Press, Box 328, Loveland, CO 80537. Ed.
Robert H. Moore. bk. rev. circ. 2,000.
　　Supersedes: Ontological Thought (ISSN 0030-
3151)

100　　　　　　　VE
ESTUDIOS FILOSOFICOS. 1974. irreg. Bs.10 per no.
Universidad Simon Bolivar, Departamento de
Filosofia, Apdo. 5354, Caracas, Venezuela. (Co-
sponsor: Sociedad Venezolana de Filosofia) Ed.
Alberto Rosales. bibl.

100　　　　　　　AG　ISSN 0325-5387
ETHOS; revista de filosofia practica. 1973. a. $10.
Instituto de Filosofia Practica, Av. de Mayo 1437,
Buenos Aires, Argentina. Ed. Julio Guido Soaje
Ramos. bk. rev. bibl. circ. 500.

100　　　　　　　CN　ISSN 0708-319X
ETIENNE GILSON SERIES. 1979. a. price varies.
Pontifical Institute of Mediaeval Studies, 59 Queen's
Park Crescent E., Toronto, Ont. M5S 2C4, Canada.
circ. 500.

189　　　　　　　BE　ISSN 0071-1926
ETUDES DE PHILOLOGIE, D'ARCHEOLOGIE
ET D'HISTOIRE ANCIENNE. 1934. irreg. price
varies. Institut Historique Belge de Rome, c/o
Archives Generales du Royaume, 2-6 Rue de
Ruysbroeck, B-1000 Brussels, Belgium. circ.
controlled.

170　　　　　　　PL　ISSN 0014-2263
ETYKA. (Text in Polish; summaries in English and
Russian) 1966. a. $6.50. (Polska Akademia Nauk,
Instytut Filozofii i Socjologii) Panstwowe
Wydawnictwo Naukowe, Miodowa 10, 00-251
Warsaw, Poland. Ed. Marek Fritzhand. bk. rev.
abstr. illus. circ. 1,000.

EXPLORATIONS. see *PSYCHOLOGY*

197　　　　　　　UR
FILOSOFSKIE NAUKI. 1971. irreg. 0.95 Rub.
Kazakhskii Gosudarstvennyi Universitet, Ul. Lenina
18, Alma-Ata, U.S.S.R. bibl

100　　　　　　　PL
FILOZOFIA-LOGIKA. 1961. irreg. price varies.
Uniwersytet im. Adama Mickiewicza w Poznaniu,
Stalingradzka 1, 61-712 Poznan, Poland (Dist. by:
Ars Polona, Krakowskie Przedmiescie 7, 00-068
Warsaw, Poland) bk. rev.
　　Formerly: Uniwersytet im. Adama Mickiewicza w
Poznaniu. Wydzial Filozoficzno-Historyczny. Prace.
Seria Filozofia-Logika (ISSN 0083-4246)

100　　　　　　　HU　ISSN 0071-4984
FILOZOFIAI IROK TARA. 1950. irreg. price varies.
(Magyar Tudomanyos Akademia) Akademiai Kiado,
Publishing House of the Hungarian Academy of
Sciences, P.O. Box 24, H-1363 Budapest, Hungary.

100　　　　　　　HU　ISSN 0071-4992
FILOZOFIAI TANULMANYOK. 1964. irreg. price
varies. (Magyar Tudomanyos Akademia) Akademiai
Kiado, Publishing House of the Hungarian Academy
of Sciences, P.O. Box 24, H-1363 Budapest,
Hungary.

100　301　335　　GW　ISSN 0067-5911
FREIE UNIVERSITAET BERLIN. OSTEUROPA-
INSTITUT. PHILOSOPHISCHE UND
SOZIOLOGISCHE VEROEFFENTLICHUNGEN.
1959. irreg. price varies. Freie Universitaet Berlin,
Osteuropa-Institut, Garystr. 55, 1000 Berlin 33
(Dahlem), W. Germany (B.R.D.) Ed.Bd. circ. 500.

294　　　　　　　US　ISSN 0072-0577
GEMEINSCHAFT DER SELBST-
VERWIRKLICHUNG. JAHRESHEFT. (Text in
German) 1959. a. $0.95. Self-Realization Fellowship,
Inc., 3880 San Rafael Ave, Los Angeles, CA 90065.
Ed. Jane Brush. circ. 2,000.

GESHER. see *RELIGIONS AND THEOLOGY —
Judaic*

110　121　801　　US　ISSN 0270-3580
GIZEH; journal of philosophy & poetry. (Text in
English, French and Italian) 1980. a. $6.95. Out of
London Press, 12 W. 17th St., New York, NY
10011. Eds. Luigi Ballerini, Richard Milazzo. circ.
1,500.

100　　　　　　　II
GOKULDAS SANSKRIT SERIES. (Text in English
and Sanskrit) no. 4, 1975. irreg. Rs.25($4)
Chaukhambha Orientalia, Gokul Bhawan, K 37/109
Gwaldas Shah Lane, Varanasi 221001, India.

100　　　　　　　UK
GOLDEN BLADE. 1949. a. £1.50($4)
(Anthroposophical Society in Great Britain) Rudolf
Steiner Press, 35 Park Rd., London NW1 6XT,
England (Dist. in U.S. by: St. George Book Service,
Box 225, Spring Valley, N.Y. 10977) Eds. Jonathan
Westphal, Adam Bittleston. adv. bk. rev. illus. circ.
2,500.

100 GW ISSN 0072-9604
HAMBURGER STUDIEN ZUR PHILOSOPHIE.
1970. irreg., no. 7, 1979. price varies. Verlag
Helmut Buske, Schlueterstr. 14, 2000 Hamburg 13,
W. Germany (B.R.D.)

182 GW ISSN 0073-1579
HEGEL-JAHRBUCH. 1961. a. (Hegel-Gesellschaft)
Pahl-Rugenstein Verlag, Gottesweg 54, 5000
Cologne 51, W. Germany (B.R.D.) Ed. W.R. Beyer.

100 US
HEGEL SOCIETY OF AMERICA.
PROCEEDINGS. 1968. biennial. $17.50.
Humanities Press, Inc., 171 First Ave., Atlantic
Highlands, NJ 07716.

190 GW ISSN 0073-1587
HEGEL-STUDIEN. 1955. irreg., vol. 17, 1977; latest
no. 19. price varies. (Deutsche
Forschungsgemeinschaft, Hegel Kommission)
Bouvier Verlag Herbert Grundmann, Am Hof 32,
Postfach 1268, 5300 Bonn 1, W. Germany (B.R.D.)
Eds. F. Nicolin, O. Poeggeler.

100 GW
HESTIA. 1961? biennial. price varies. Bouvier Verlag
Herbert Grundmann, Am Hof 32, Postfach 1268,
5300 Bonn 1, W. Germany (B.R.D.)

100 UK
HISTORY AND PHILOSOPHY OF LOGIC. 1980.
irreg. £18. Abacus Press, Abacus House, Speldhurst
Rd., Tunbridge Wells, Kent TN4 0HU, England.
Ed. Dr. I. Grattan-Guinness. bk. rev.

170 300 IT ISSN 0018-4292
HOMINE. (Summaries in Italian and English) 1962.
irreg., latest issue, no. 38-40. L.4500($8.50) (Centro
di Ricerca per le Scienze Morali e Sociali) Casa
Editrice G. C. Sansoni Editore Nuova S.p.A., Via
Benedetto Varchi 47, 50132 Florence, Italy. Ed.
Franco Lombardi. bk. rev. bibl. charts. illus.
index. cum.ind. circ. 1,500.

HYPOMNEMATA; Untersuchungen zur Antike und
zu ihrem Nachleben. see CLASSICAL STUDIES

I I S T BULLETINS; human electricity and
experiments on soul. (Indian Institute of Soul
Technology) see PARAPSYCHOLOGY AND
OCCULTISM

100 CK ISSN 0019-140X
IDEAS Y VALORES. 1951. irreg. exchange basis.
Universidad Nacional de Colombia, Facultad de
Ciencias Humanas, Apartado Aereo 14490,
Departamento de Filosofia, Bogota, Colombia. Dir.
Ramon Perez Mantilla. bk. rev. circ. 1,000.

100 II
INDIAN PHILOSOPHICAL ANNUAL. 1967. a.
Rs.10 plus postage. University of Madras, Centre
for Advanced Study in Philosophy, Chepauk,
Triplicane P.O., Madras 600005, Tamil Nadu, India.
Ed. T.M.P. Mahadevan. circ. 300.

100 GE
INFORMATIONSBULLETIN. AUS DEM
PHILOSOPHISCHEM LEBEN DER DDR. 1965.
irreg. M.3 per no. Zentralstelle fuer Philosophische
Information und Dokumentation, J.-Dieckmann-Str.
19-23, 108 Berlin, E. Germany (D.D.R.) Ed. Ch.
Neumann. circ. 600.
Formerly: Informationen aus dem
Philosophischen Leben in der DDR (ISSN 0020-
0328)

100 UN
INTERNATIONAL COUNCIL FOR PHILOSOPHY
AND HUMANISTIC STUDIES. BULLETIN.
(Edts. in English and French) 1949. biennial. free. ‡
International Council for Philosophy and
Humanistic Studies, c/o Maison de l'Unesco, 1 rue
Miollis, 75732 Paris Cedex 15, France. circ. 3,200.
(back issues avail.)
Formerly: International Council for Philosophy
and Humanistic Studies. General Assembly. Compte
Rendu (ISSN 0074-4298)

100 US ISSN 0074-4603
INTERNATIONAL DIRECTORY OF
PHILOSOPHY AND PHILOSOPHERS. 1965.
biennial until 1974; quadrennial from 1978. price
varies. Bowling Green State University, Philosophy
Documentation Center, Bowling Green, OH 43403.
Ed. Ramona Cormier et al. circ. 1,050.

190 NE ISSN 0074-6258
INTERNATIONAL HUMANIST AND ETHICAL
UNION. PROCEEDINGS OF THE CONGRESS.
1952. irreg., 7th, 1978, Amsterdam. price varies.
International Humanist and Ethical Union,
Oudegracht 152, Utrecht, Netherlands.

100 FR ISSN 0074-6525
INTERNATIONAL INSTITUTE OF PHILOSOPHY.
ACTES. (Proceedings of annual meeting) (Text in
English, French or German) 1955. a; 22nd, Berne,
1976. International Institute of Philosophy, 173
Boulevard St. Germain, 75272 Paris, France.
Proceedings published in host country

500 US ISSN 0074-8064
INTERNATIONAL SERIES IN NATURAL
PHILOSOPHY. 1965. irreg., vol. 92, 1978. price
varies. Pergamon Press, Inc., Maxwell House,
Fairview Park, Elmsford, NY 10523. index.
Formerly: International Series of Monographs in
Natural Philosophy.

INTERNATIONAL SIVANANDA YOGA LIFE
AND YOGA VACATIONS. see PHYSICAL
FITNESS AND HYGIENE

140 GW
INTERNATIONALE VEREINIGUNG ZUR
FOERDERUNG DES STUDIUMS DER
HEGELSCHEN PHILOSOPHIE.
VEROEFFENTLICHUNG. (Subseries of Hegel-
Studien. Beihefte) 1964. irreg., latest no. 9. free.
Bouvier Verlag Herbert Grundmann, Am Hof 32,
Postfach 1268, 5300 Bonn 1, W. Germany (B.R.D.)
Ed. Dieter Henrich. adv. bk. rev. circ. 1,000.

100 NE ISSN 0075-0395
IOWA PUBLICATIONS IN PHILOSOPHY. 1963.
irreg. price varies. (University of Iowa, US)
Martinus Nijhoff, Box 566, 2501 CN The Hague,
Netherlands.

160 510 UR ISSN 0302-9085
ISSLEDOVANIA PO TEORII ALGORIFMOV I
MATEMATICHESKOI LOGIKE. 1973. irreg. 1.12
Rub. Akademiya Nauk S. S. S. R., Vychislitel'nyi
Tsentr, Ul. Vavilova, 40, Moscow V-333, U. S. S. R.

100 IT
ISTITUTO ITALIANO PER GLI STUDI
FILOSOFICI. SERIE STUDI. 1977. irreg.
Bibliopolis, Via Arangio Ruiz 83, Naples, Italy.

100 GW ISSN 0075-2916
JAHRESKATALOG PHILOSOPHIE. 1965. biennial.
DM.26.20. Werbegemeinschaft Elwert und Meurer,
Hauptstr. 101, 1000 Berlin 62, W. Germany
(B.R.D.) adv.

JAPAN ASSOCIATION FOR PHILOSOPHY OF
SCIENCE. ANNALS. see SCIENCES:
COMPREHENSIVE WORKS

JOURNAL OF PHILOSOPHY OF SPORT. see
SPORTS AND GAMES

JOURNAL OF THE PHILOSOPHY OF SPORT. see
SPORTS AND GAMES

100 PL
KATOLICKI UNIWERSYTET LUBELSKI.
WYDZIAL FILOZOFICZNY. ROZPRAWY. (Text
in Polish; summaries in English, French or German)
1957. irreg. price varies. Katolicki Uniwersytet
Lubelski, Towarzystwo Naukowe, Chopina 29, 20-
023 Lublin, Poland. index. circ. 3,150.

100 US
KIERKEGAARD'S WRITINGS. 1978. a. price varies.
Princeton University Press, Princeton, NJ 08540.
(reprint service avail. from UMI)

100 GW ISSN 0454-448X
KOSMOSOPHIE. irreg., vol. 4, 1978. price varies.
(Paracelsus-Kommission) Franz Steiner Verlag
GmbH, Friedrichstr. 24, Postfach 5529, 6200
Wiesbaden, W. Germany (B.R.D.) Ed. Kurt
Goldammer.

KUNGLIGA VITTERHETS- , HISTORIE- OCH
ANTIKVITETS AKADEMIEN. HANDLINGAR.
FILOLOGISK-FILOSOFISKA SERIEN/ROYAL
ACADEMY OF LETTERS, HISTORY AND
ANTIQUITIES. PROCEEDINGS.
PHILOLOGICAL-PHILOSOPHICAL SERIES. see
LINGUISTICS

100 NE ISSN 0459-0007
LEIDSE WIJSGERIGE REEKS. 1966. irreg., vol. 2,
1971. price varies. Leiden University Press, c/o
Martinus Nijhoff, Box 566, 2501 CN The Hague,
Netherlands.

100 200 UK
LIBRARY OF PHILOSOPHY AND RELIGION.
irreg. price varies. Macmillan Press Ltd., 4 Little
Essex St., London WC2R 3LF, England. Ed. Prof.
John Hick.

100 US ISSN 0075-9554
LINDLEY LECTURE. 1961. irreg. price varies:
$0.75-$1. University of Kansas, Department of
Philosophy, Lawrence, KS 66045. Ed. John Bricke.
circ. 600.

100 UK ISSN 0307-2606
LOCKE NEWSLETTER. (Text in English, French,
German and Italian) 1970. a. £3.50($6) c/o Roland
Hall, Editor, Dept. of Philosophy, University of
York, Heslington, York Y0L 5DD, England.
Indexed: Phil.Ind.

LOKA. see LITERATURE

100 GW ISSN 0076-2776
MAINZER PHILOSOPHISCHE FORSCHUNGEN.
1966. irreg., vol. 19, 1978. price varies. Bouvier
Verlag Herbert Grundmann, Am Hof 32, Postfach
1268, 5300 Bonn 1, W. Germany (B.R.D.) Ed.
Gerhard Funke.

106 806 UK ISSN 0076-3721
MANCHESTER LITERARY AND
PHILOSOPHICAL SOCIETY. MEMOIRS AND
PROCEEDINGS. 1785. a. £4. Manchester Literary
and Philosophical Society, 36 George St.,
Manchester, England. Ed. D.S.L. Cardwell. circ.
600. Indexed: Br.Hum.Ind.

100 US
MATERIAL FOR THOUGHT. no. 7, 1977. irreg. Far
West Press, Box 549, San Francisco, CA 94101.

180 US ISSN 0076-5856
MEDIAEVAL PHILOSOPHICAL TEXTS IN
TRANSLATION. 1942. a. $5.95. Marquette
University Press, 1324 W. Wisconsin Ave.,
Milwaukee, WI 53233.

100 PL ISSN 0076-5880
MEDIAEVALIA PHILOSOPHICA POLONORUM.
(Text in French or German) 1957. a. 45 Zl. (Polska
Akademia Nauk, Instytut Filozofii i Socjologii)
Ossolineum, Publishing House of the Polish
Academy of Sciences, Rynek 9, 50-106 Wroclaw,
Poland (Dist. by Ars Polona-Ruch, Krakowskie
Przedmiescie 7, Warsaw, Poland) Ed. W. Senko.

109 IT
MEDIOEVO; rivista di storia della filosofia medievale.
1975. irreg. L.18000. (Universita degli Studi di
Padova, Centro per Ricerche di Filosofia Medievale)
Editrice Antenore, Via Rusca 15, Padua 35100,
Italy. Ed. Bd.

100 NE
MELBOURNE INTERNATIONAL PHILOSOPHY
SERIES. (Text in English) 1976. irreg. price varies.
(University of Melbourne, Philosophy Department,
AT) Martinus Nijhoff, Box 566, 2501 CN The
Hague, Netherlands. Ed. Jan T. J. Srzednicki.

100 AU ISSN 0076-6720
METAPHYSISCHE RUNDSCHAU. irreg.
Fuchtshallergasse 4/25, A-1090 Vienna, Austria.

100 US ISSN 0363-6550
MIDWEST STUDIES IN PHILOSOPHY. 1976. a.
University of Minnesota, 2037 University
Ave., S.E., Minneapolis, MN 55455. Ed. Bd.

100 500 US ISSN 0076-9258
MINNESOTA STUDIES IN THE PHILOSOPHY
OF SCIENCE. 1956. irreg., vol. 9, 1978. price
varies. (Minnesota Center for Philosophy of
Science) University of Minnesota Press, 2037
University Ave. S.E., Minneapolis, MN 55455. Eds.
Herbert Feigl et al. index.

180 930 GW
MISCELLANEA MEDIAEVALIA. 1962. irreg., vol.
13, 1980. DM.188($105) (Universitaet zu Koeln,
Thomas-Institut) Walter de Gruyter und Co.,
Genthiner Str.13, 1000 Berlin 30, W. Germany
(B.R.D.) Ed. Albert Zimmermann.

PHILOSOPHY

MITZION TETZEH TORAH. M.T.T. see
RELIGIONS AND THEOLOGY — Judaic

100   GW
MODERN GERMAN STUDIES. no. 2, 1978. irreg., no. 3, 1978. price varies. Bouvier Verlag Herbert Grundmann, Am Hof 32, Postfach 1268, 5300 Bonn 1, W. Germany (B.R.D.)

108   GW
MONOGRAPHIEN ZUR PHILOSOPHISCHEN FORSCHUNG. 1974. irreg., no. 194, 1980. price varies. Verlag Anton Hain GmbH und Co., Adelheidstr. 2, Postfach 1220, 6240 Koenigstein, W. Germany (B.R.D) Ed. Georgi Schischkoff.

100   US   ISSN 0068-4333
MONOGRAPHS IN PHILOSOPHY AND RELIGIOUS HISTORY. (Text in various languages) 1966. irreg. (approx. 25/yr); 1973, no. 129. price varies. Lenox Hill Publishing and Distributing Corporation, 235 E. 44th St., New York, NY 10017. (back issues avail.)
Formerly: Burt Franklin Philosophy Monograph Series.

100   500   UR
NEKOTORYE FILOSOFSKIE VOPROSY SOVREMENNOGO ESTESTVOZNANIYA. 1973. irreg. 0.66 Rub. Lenizdat, Fontanka 59, Leningrad, U.S.S.R.

100   GW   ISSN 0085-3917
NEUE HEFTE FUER PHILOSOPHIE. 1971. irreg., no. 20, 1980. price varies. Vandenhoeck und Ruprecht, Theaterstr. 13, Postfach 77, 3400 Goettingen, W. Germany (B.R.D.) Ed.Bd. circ. 2,200.

120   US
NEW STUDIES IN PRACTICAL PHILOSOPHY. irreg. price varies. University of California Press, 2223 Fulton St., Berkeley, CA 94720.

100   GW
NIETZSCHE-STUDIEN; internationales Jahrbuch fuer die Nietzsche-Forschung. (Text in English and German) irreg., vol. 9, 1980. price varies. Walter de Gruyter und Co., Genthiner Str. 13, 1000 Berlin 30, W. Germany (B.R.D.)

NORSKE VIDENSKAPS-AKADEMI. HISTORISK-FILOSOFISK KLASSE. AVHANDLINGER TWO. see *HISTORY*

NUOVA UNIVERSALE STUDIUM. see *LITERATURE*

100   US
OBJECTIVIST CALENDAR. 1976. irreg. $9 for 8 nos. Barbara Weiss, Ed. & Pub., Box 95, Murray Hill Sta., New York, NY 10016. bk. rev. circ. 3,500. (looseleaf format; back issues avail.)

100   DK
ODENSE UNIVERSITY STUDIES IN PHILOSOPHY. (Text in English) 1972. irreg., no. 4, 1978. price varies. Odense University Press, 36, Pjentedamsgade, DK-5000 Odense, Denmark. (back issues avail.)

OESTERREICHISCHE AKADEMIE DER WISSENSCHAFTEN. PHILOSOPHISCH-HISTORISCHE KLASSE. ANZEIGER. see *HISTORY — History Of Europe*

190   900   US   ISSN 0078-608X
ORESTES BROWNSON SERIES ON CONTEMPORARY THOUGHT AND AFFAIRS. 1958. irreg., 1973, no. 8. price varies. Fordham University Press, University Box L, Bronx, NY 10458.

100   US
OXFORD READINGS IN PHILOSOPHY. irreg. price varies. Oxford University Press, 200 Madison Ave., New York, NY 10016 (And Ely House, 37 Dover St., London W1X 4AH, England) Ed. G. J. Warnock.

100   PK   ISSN 0078-8406
PAKISTAN PHILOSOPHICAL CONGRESS. PROCEEDINGS. (Text in English) 1954. a. Rs.15. Pakistan Philosophical Congress, Department of Philosophy, University of the Punjab, New Campus, Lahore, Pakistan. Ed. B. A. Dar. circ. 900.

170   US   ISSN 0079-0249
PAUL ANTHONY BRICK LECTURES. 1960. irreg., 1973, no. 9. price varies. University of Missouri Press, 107 Swallow Hall, Columbia, MO 65201.

104   US   ISSN 0079-0257
PAUL CARUS LECTURES. 1925. irreg., no. 14, 1973. price varies. (American Philosophical Association) Open Court Publishing Co., Box 599, La Salle, IL 61301. Ed. Eugene Freeman. index in each volume. (reprint service avail. from UMI)

100   GW
PERSPEKTIVEN DER PHILOSOPHIE. NEUES JAHRBUCH. (Text in German) 1975. a. price varies. Verlag Dr. H.A. Gerstenberg, Rathausstr. 18, Postfach 390, 3200 Hildesheim, W. Germany (B.R.D.) Eds. R. Berlinger, F. Kaulbach, W. Schrader. adv. bk. rev.

DIE PFORTE; Zeitschrift und Schriften fuer wertidealistische Philosophie und Kultur. see *LITERARY AND POLITICAL REVIEWS*

100   NE   ISSN 0079-1350
PHAENOMENOLOGICA. (Text in English, French, German) 1958. irreg. price varies. (Centre d'Archives Husserl, BE) Martinus Nijhoff, Box 566, 2501 CN The Hague, Netherlands. Ed. S. Ysseling.

100   US
PHENOMENOLOGY INFORMATION BULLETIN. 1977. a. $5. World Institute for Advanced Phenomenological Research and Learning, 348 Payson Rd., Belmont, MA 02178. Ed. Bd. adv. bk. rev. circ. 1,000.

100   US   ISSN 0162-234X
PHILOSOPHER'S ANNUAL. 1978. a. Rowman and Littlefield, 81 Adams Dr., Totowa, NJ 07512.

105   GR
PHILOSOPHIA. (Text in English, French, German, or Greek) 1971. a. $12. Research Center for Greek Philosophy - Kentron Erevnis tes Hellenikes Philosophias, 14 Anagnostopoulou St., Athens 136, Greece. bk. rev. circ. 600. Indexed: Bull.Signal. Phil.Ind.

180   NE   ISSN 0079-1687
PHILOSOPHIA ANTIQUA. 1946. irreg., vol. 38, 1981. price varies. E. J. Brill, Oude Rijn 33a-35, Leiden, Netherlands.

PHILOSOPHIA MATHEMATICA. see *MATHEMATICS*

100   CL
PHILOSOPHICA. 1978. a. $10. (Universidad Catolica de Valparaiso, Instituto de Filosofia) Ediciones Universitarias de Valparaiso, Valparaiso, Chile. Ed. Juan Antonio Widow. bk. rev. circ. 500.

100   SJ   ISSN 0079-1695
PHILOSOPHICAL SOCIETY OF THE SUDAN. PROCEEDINGS OF THE ANNUAL CONFERENCE. (Text and summaries in English and Arabic) 1952. a. price varies. Philosophical Society of the Sudan, P.O. Box 526, Khartoum, Sudan.

100   NE
PHILOSOPHICAL STUDIES SERIES IN PHILOSOPHY. 1974. irreg. price varies. D. Reidel Publishing Co., Box 17, 3300 AA Dordrecht, Netherlands (And Lincoln Building, 160 Old Derby St., Hingham, MA 02043) Eds. Wilfrid Sellars, Keith Lehrer.

105   FR
PHILOSOPHIE. 1972. a. 17.00 F. Universite de Toulouse II (le Mirail), 109 bis, rue Vauquelin, 31081 Toulouse Cedex, France.

100   GW
PHILOSOPHISCHE ABHANDLUNGEN. irreg., vol. 50, 1981. price varies. Vittorio Klostermann, Frauenlobstr. 22, Postfach 900601, 6000 Frankfurt 90, W. Germany (B.R.D)

181   GE   ISSN 0079-1717
PHILOSOPHISCHE STUDIENTEXTE. 1955. irreg. price varies. Akademie-Verlag, Leipziger Str. 3-4, 108 Berlin, E. Germany (D.D.R.)

100   GW   ISSN 0031-8183
PHILOSOPHISCHES JAHRBUCH. 1888. a. DM.52. (Goerres-Gesellschaft) Karl Alber GmbH, Hermann-Herder-Str.4, 7800 Freiburg, W. Germany (B.R.D.) Ed.Bd. bk. rev. abstr. bibl. circ. 800.

100   610   NE
PHILOSOPHY AND MEDICINE. (Text in English) 1975. irreg. price varies. D. Reidel Publishing Co., P.O. Box 17, 3300 AA Dordrecht, Netherlands (And Lincoln Building, 160 Old Derby St., Hingham, MA 02043) Eds. H. Tristram Engelhardt Jr., Stuart F. Spicker.

100   US   ISSN 0164-0771
PHILOSOPHY RESEARCH ARCHIVES; a bilingual microfilm journal of philosophy. (Text in English & French; summaries in English & French) 1976. a. $25 to institutions; $12.50 to individuals. Bowling Green State University, Philosophy Documentation Center, Bowling Green, OH 43403. (Co-sponsor: American Philosophical Association; Canadian Philosophical Association) Ed. A.I. Melden. (microfiche) Indexed: Phil.Ind.

100   PL   ISSN 0079-4635
POZNANSKIE TOWARZYSTWO PRZYJACIOL NAUK. KOMISJA FILOZOFICZNA. PRACE. (Text in Polish; summaries in English, French, German, Russian) 1921. irreg., 1970, vol. 12, no.2. price varies. Panstwowe Wydawnictwo Naukowe, Miodowa 10, Warsaw, Poland (Dist. by Ars Polona-Ruch, Krakowskie Przedmiescie 7, Warsaw, Poland)

105   BL
PRESENCA FILOSOFICA. 1974. irreg. $10. Sociedade Brasileira de Filosofos Catolicos, Rua Mandel Vitorino 625, ZC-13, 20000 Rio de Janeiro, Brazil. bibl.

100   FR
PRESENCE DE GABRIEL MARCEL. CAHIER. a. 50 F. (Presence de Gabriel Marcel) Fondation Europeenne de la Culture, 9 Ave. Franklin-Roosevelt, 75008 Paris, France.

100   001.3   GW
PROBLEMATA. 1971. irreg. price varies. Friedrich Frommann Verlag Guenther Holzboog GmbH und Co., Postfach 500460, Koenig-Karl-Str., 7000 Stuttgart 50, W. Germany (B.R.D.) Ed. Guenther Holzboog.

100   IT
PUBBLICAZIONI DI VERIFICHE. irreg. price varies. Verifiche, Casella Postale 269, Trento, Italy.

100   IT
QUADERNI DI VERIFICHE. irreg. price varies. Verifiche, Casella Postale 269, Trento, Italy. bibl.

QUAKER ENCOUNTERS. see *RELIGIONS AND THEOLOGY — Other Denominations And Sects*

294.54   IT
RASSEGNA DI LETTERATURA TOMISTICA. (Text mainly in French and Italian) 1969. a. price varies. Edizioni Domenicane Italiane, Via L. Palmieri 19, 80133 Naples, Italy. Ed. P. Clementte Vansteenkiste OP. bk. rev. (back issues avail.)
Formerly: Bulletin Thomiste.

RENCONTRES INTERNATIONALES DE GENEVE. see *SOCIAL SCIENCES: COMPREHENSIVE WORKS*

100   US   ISSN 0085-5553
RESEARCH IN PHENOMENOLOGY. 1971. a. $7.50 individuals; $10 libraries. Humanities Press, Inc., 171 First Avenue, Atlantic Highlands, NJ 07716. Ed. John Sallis. adv. bk. rev. circ. 1,000.

100   600   US   ISSN 0161-7249
RESEARCH IN PHILOSOPHY AND TECHNOLOGY. 1977. a. $21.25 to individuals; institutions $42.50. J A I Press, Box 1678, 165 W. Putnam Ave., Greenwich, CT 06830. Eds. Paul T. Durbin, Carl Mitcham. bibl.

330   II
REVIEW JOURNAL OF PHILOSOPHY AND SOCIAL SCIENCE. (Text in English) biennial. Rs.50($6) Anu Prakashan, Shivaji Rd, Meerut 25001, India (Editorial office: Dr. Michael V. Belok, College of Education, Arizona State University, Tempe, AZ 85211) Ed. Michael V. Belok.

199.8 AG
REVISTA DE FILOSOFIA LATINOAMERICANA. 1975. irreg. Arg.$1000($10) Ediciones Castaneda, Centenario 1399, 1718 San Antonio de Padua, Buenos Aires, Argentina.

100 335.4 NE ISSN 0303-3856
REVOLUTIONARY WORLD; an international journal of philosophy. (Text in English) 1973. irreg., approx. 5/yr. fl.110. B. R. Gruener B. V., P.O. Box 70020, Nieuwe Herengracht 31, Amsterdam, Netherlands. Ed. David H. DeGrood. adv. bk. rev. bibl. circ. 200.

REVUE DE THEOLOGIE ET DE PHILOSOPHIE. CAHIERS. see *RELIGIONS AND THEOLOGY*

100 UK ISSN 0080-4436
ROYAL INSTITUTE OF PHILOSOPHY. LECTURES. 1968. a; latest vol. 8, 1973-1973. price varies. Macmillan Press Ltd., Little Essex St., London W. C. 2, England.

100 IT
SAGGI FILOSOFICI. 1979. irreg., vol. 2, 1979. price varies. Casa Editrice Leo S. Olschki, Casella Postale 66, 50100 Florence, Italy.

100 920 AU ISSN 0558-3489
SALZBURGER BEITRAEGE ZUR PARACELSUSFORSCHUNG. 1960. irreg., vol. 19, 1978. price varies. (Internationale Paracelsus-Gesellschaft) Verband der Wissenschaftlichen Gesellschaften Oesterreichs, Lindengasse 37, A-1010 Vienna, Austria.

100 AU ISSN 0080-5696
SALZBURGER JAHRBUCH FUER PHILOSOPHIE. 1957. a. price varies. Universitaetsverlag Anton Pustet, Bergstr. 12, Postfach 144, A-5021 Salzburg, Austria.

100 AU ISSN 0080-5726
SALZBURGER STUDIEN ZUR PHILOSOPHIE. 1962. irreg. price varies. Universitaetsverlag Anton Pustet, Bergstr. 12, Postschliessfach 144, 5021 Salzburg, Austria.

100 GW ISSN 0080-6935
SCHOPENHAUER-JAHRBUCH. a. price varies. (Schopenhauer Gesellschaft e.V.) Verlag Dr. Waldemar Kramer, Bornheimer Landwehr 57a, 6000 Frankfurt 60, W. Germany (B.R.D.) Ed. Arthur Huebscher. bk. rev. circ. 1,912.

SERIES IN THE PHILOSOPHY OF SCIENCE. see *SCIENCES: COMPREHENSIVE WORKS*

SHAW ANNUAL. see *LITERATURE*

SOCIETY FOR RENAISSANCE STUDIES. OCCASIONAL PAPERS. see *LITERATURE*

100 GW
SPECULA. 1978. irreg. price varies. Friedrich Frommann Verlag Guenther Holzboog GmbH und Co., Postfach 500460, Koenig-Karl-Str. 27, 7000 Stuttgart 50, W. Germany (B.R.D.) Ed. Guenther Holzboog.

181.45 CE
SRI AUROBINDO CENTENARY ANNUAL.* 1972. a. Rs.3. Sri Aurobindo Centenary Committee, 47 Galle Face Court, Galle Rd., Colombo 3, Sri Lanka. illus.

101 SW ISSN 0491-0877
STOCKHOLM STUDIES IN PHILOSOPHY. (Subseries of Acta Universitatis Stockholmiensis) (Text in English) 1957. irreg., latest no. 6. price varies. (Stockholms Universitet) Almqvist & Wiksell International, Box 62, S-101 20 Stockholm, Sweden. Eds. Harald Ofstad, Anders Wedberg. (back issues avail.)

100 IT ISSN 0081-6310
STUDIA ARISTOTELICA. 1958. irreg.; 1977, no. 8. price varies. (Universita degli Studi di Padova) Editrice Antenore, Via G. Rusca 15, 35100 Padua, Italy.

100 NE
STUDIA CARTESIANA. (Text in English and French) 1979. a. price varies. Quadratures, Postbus 6463, 1005 EL Amsterdam, Netherlands. Ed.Bd. bk. rev.

111.85 PL ISSN 0081-637X
STUDIA ESTETYCZNE. (Text in Polish; summaries in English and Russian) 1964. irreg., 1975, vol. 12. price varies. (Polska Akademia Nauk, Instytut Filozofii i Socjologii) Panstwowe Wydawnictwo Naukowe, Ul. Miodowa 10, Warsaw, Poland. Ed. Slaw Krzemien-Ojak. bk. rev.

100 GW ISSN 0341-0765
STUDIA LEIBNITIANA. SONDERHEFTE. (Text in English and German) irreg., vol. 9, 1981. price varies. (Gottfried Wilhelm Leibniz Gesellschaft, Hannover) Franz Steiner Verlag GmbH, Friedrichstr. 24, Postfach 5529, 6200 Wiesbaden, W. Germany (B.R.D.) Ed.Bd.

100 GW ISSN 0303-5980
STUDIA LEIBNITIANA. SUPPLEMENTA. (Text in English, French, and German) irreg., vol. 21, 1981. price varies. (Gottfried Wilhelm Leibniz Gesellschaft, Hannover) Franz Steiner Verlag GmbH, Friedrichstr. 24, Postfach 5529, 6200 Wiesbaden, W. Germany (B.R.D.) Ed.Bd.

189 PL ISSN 0039-3231
STUDIA MEDIEWISTYCZNE/MEDIAEVISTIC STUDIES. (Summaries in French) 1959. irreg. $7.50 exchange basis. Polska Akademia Nauk, Instytut Filozofii i Socjologii, Nowy Swiat 72, Warsaw, Poland (Dist. by: Ars Polona-Ruch, Krakowskie Przedmiescie 7, 00-068 Warsaw, Poland)

100 HU ISSN 0076-2466
STUDIA PHILOSOPHICA ACADEMIAE SCIENTIARUM HUNGARICAE. (Text in English, French, German, Russian) 1961. irreg. price varies. (Magyar Tudomanyos Akademia) Akademiai Kiado, Publishing House of the Hungarian Academy of Sciences, P.O. Box 24, H-1363 Budapest, Hungary.

100 RM ISSN 0578-5480
STUDIA UNIVERSITATIS "BABES-BOLYAI". PHILOSOPHIA. (Text in Romanian; summaries in French, English, German, Russian) 1958. s-a. exchange basis. Universitatea "Babes-Bolyai", Biblioteca Centrala Universitara, Str. Clinicilor 2, Cluj-Napoca, Romania. bk. rev. cum.index:(1956-1963) (1964-1970)
  Incorporates (since 1975): Studia Universitatis Babes-Bolyai. Psychologia-Pedagogia (ISSN 0578-5502) & Studia Universitatis Babes-Bolyai. Sociologia.

100 NE
STUDIEN ZUR ANTIKEN PHILOSOPHIE. 1971. irreg. price varies. B. R. Gruener B.V., Box 70020, Amsterdam, Netherlands. (back issues avail.)

100 GW ISSN 0340-5958
STUDIEN ZUR FRANZOESISCHEN PHILOSOPHIE DES ZWANZIGSTEN JAHRHUNDERTS. irreg., vol. 8, 1979. price varies. Bouvier Verlag Herbert Grundmann, Am Hof 32, Postfach 1268, 5300 Bonn 1, W. Germany (B.R.D.) Eds. V. v. Berning, H. R. Schlette.

109 SZ
STUDIEN ZUR PHILOSOPHIE DES 18. JAHRHUNDERTS. 1976. irreg. price varies. Verlag Peter Lang AG, Muenzgraben 2, Postfach, CH-3000 Berne 7, Switzerland.

100 800 GW ISSN 0081-735X
STUDIEN ZUR PHILOSOPHIE UND LITERATUR DES NEUNZEHNTEN JAHRHUNDERTS. 1968. irreg., vol. 36, 1979. price varies. Vittorio Klostermann, Frauenlobstr. 22, 6000 Frankfurt 90, W. Germany (B.R.D.)

STUDIES IN HISTORY AND PHILOSOPHY. PAMPHLET SERIES. see *HISTORY*

100 JA ISSN 0081-8380
STUDIES IN PHILOSOPHY.* (Text in English, French and German) irreg. available on exchange only. Fukuoka University, Faculty of Literature, 11 Nanakuma, Fukuoka City, Japan.

100 NE ISSN 0081-8399
STUDIES IN PHILOSOPHY. 1963. irreg. price varies. Mouton Publishers, Noordeinde 41, 2514 GC The Hague, Netherlands (U.S. addr: Mouton Publishers, c/o Walter de Gruyter, Inc., 200 Saw Mill River Road, Hawthorne, NY 10532)

100 US ISSN 0585-6965
STUDIES IN PHILOSOPHY & THE HISTORY OF PHILOSOPHY. 1961. irreg., vol. 8, 1980. price varies. ‡ Catholic University of America Press, 620 Michigan Ave. N.E., Washington, DC 20064. Ed. Jude P. Dougherty.

STUDIES IN THE LOGIC OF SCIENCE. see *SCIENCES: COMPREHENSIVE WORKS*

100 320 RM
STUDII DE FILOZOFIE SI SOCIALISM STIINTIFIC. 1974. irreg. Universitatea din Timisoara, Bd. Vasile Pirvan Nr.4, Timisoara, Romania.

100 FR
SURFACES (PARIS, 1978) 1978. irreg. Editions Jean-Michel Place, 12 rue Pierre et Marie Curie, 75005 Paris, France. Dir. Peter Hoy.

160 GW ISSN 0082-0660
SYMBOLON; Jahrbuch fuer Symbolforschung. (Vol. 1-7 published by Schwabe-Verlag, Basel) 1955. a. DM.36.80. (Gesellschaft fuer Wissenschaftliche Symbolforschung) Wienand Verlag KG, Postfach 410948, 5000 Cologne 41, W. Germany (B.R.D.) Ed. Julius Schwabe. index. circ. 1,000.

109 160 NE ISSN 0082-111X
SYNTHESE HISTORICAL LIBRARY; texts and studies in the history of logic and philosophy. 1969. irreg., no. 15, 1975. price varies. D. Reidel Publishing Co., P.O. Box 17, 3300 AA Dordrecht, Netherlands (And Lincoln Building, 160 Old Derby St., Hingham, MA 02043) Eds. N. Kretzmann, G. Nuchelmans, and L.M. De Rijk.

109 NE ISSN 0082-1128
SYNTHESE LIBRARY; monographs on epistemology, logic. methodology, philosophy of science and of knowledge, and the mathematical methods of social and behavioral sciences. 1959. irreg. price varies. D. Reidel Publishing Co., P.O. Box 17, 3300 AA Dordrecht, Netherlands (And Lincoln Building, 160 Old Derby St., Hingham, MA 02043) Ed. Bd.

100 GE
THEMATISCHE INFORMATION PHILOSOPHIE. 1977. irreg. price varies. Zentralstelle fuer Philosophische Information und Dokumentation, J.-Dieckmann-Str. 19-23, 108 Berlin, E. Germany (D.D.R.) Ed. Ch. Neumann. circ. 150.
  Formerly (1974-76): Sonderinformation Philosophie; 1965-1970: Informationen Philosophie.

105 US
TOPICS IN PHILOSOPHY. 1975. irreg. price varies. University of California Press, 2223 Fulton St., Berkeley, CA 94720.

100 GW
TOTOK: HANDBUCH DER GESCHICHTE DER PHILOSOPHIE. irreg., vol. 4, 1981. price varies. Vittorio Klostermann, Frauenlobstr. 22, D-6000 Frankfurt 90, W. Germany(B.R.D.)

100 NE ISSN 0082-6766
TULANE STUDIES IN PHILOSOPHY. (Text in English) 1950. irreg. fl.21. (Tulane University, Department of Philosophy, US) Martinus Nijhoff, Box 566, 2501 CN The Hague, Netherlands. Ed. Robert C. Whittemore. circ. 1,500. (back issues avail.) Indexed: Phil.Ind.

100 SP
UNIVERSIDAD DE DEUSTO. PUBLICACIONES. FILOSOFIA. 1977. irreg. Universidad Comercial de Deusto, Bilbao, Spain.

100 SP ISSN 0008-7750
UNIVERSIDAD DE GRANADA. CATEDRA FRANCISCO SUAREZ. ANALES. (Text planned in English, French, German; summaries in Spanish) 1961. a. 400 ptas. Universidad de Granada, Catedra Francisco Suarez, Secretariado de Publicaciones, Hospital Real, Granada, Spain. Dir. Nicolas M. Lopez Calera.

100 UY
UNIVERSIDAD DE LA REPUBLICA. FACULTAD DE HUMANIDADES Y CIENCIAS. REVISTA. SERIE FILOSOFIA. N.S. 1979. irreg. Universidad de la Republica, Facultad de Humanidades y Ciencias, Seccion Revista, Tristan Narvaja 1674, Montevideo, Uruguay. Dir. Beatriz Martinez Osorio.
  Supersedes in part: Universidad de la Republica. Facultad de Humanidades y Ciencias. Revista.

PHILOSOPHY — ABSTRACTING, BIBLIOGRAPHIES, STATISTICS

110   SP   ISSN 0580-8650
UNIVERSIDAD DE MADRID. SEMINARIO DE METAFISICA. ANALES. no. 11, 1976. a. 200 ptas. Universidad Complutense de Madrid, Catedra de Metafisica (Critica), Madrid, Spain. Ed. Sergio Rabade Romeo. bk. rev. bibl. circ. 500. Indexed: Phil.Ind.

100   IT
UNIVERSITA DEGLI STUDI DI FIRENZE. ISTITUTO DI FILOSOFIA. ANNALI. 1979. a. Casa Editrice Leo S. Olschki, Casella Postale 66, 50100 Florence, Italy.

100   IT   ISSN 0078-7779
UNIVERSITA DEGLI STUDI DI PADOVA. SCUOLA DI PERFEZIONAMENTO IN FILOSOFIA. PUBBLICAZIONI. 1963. irreg. L.1000.($1.60) Casa Editrice Dott. Antonio Milani, Via Jappelli 5, 35100 Padua, Italy.

100   RM   ISSN 0075-353X
UNIVERSITATEA "AL. I. CUZA" DIN IASI. ANALELE STIINTIFICE. SECTIUNEA 3B: STIINTE FILOZOFICE. (Text in Romanian; summaries in foreign languages) a. $10. Universitatea "Al. I. Cuza" din Iasi, Calea 23 August, Nr. 11, Jassy, Romania (Subscr. to: ILEXIM, Str. 13 Decembrie Nr. 3, P.O. Box 136-137, Bucharest, Romania)

100 940 340   RM
UNIVERSITATEA BUCURESTI. ANALELE. FILOZOFIE. ISTORIE. DREPT. (Text in various languages with summaries) a. $10. Universitatea Bucuresti, Bd. Gh. Gheorghiu-Dej Nr. G4, Bucharest, Romania.

160   RM   ISSN 0068-3116
UNIVERSITATEA BUCURESTI. ANALELF. ACTA LOGICA.* (Supersedes its Analele. Seria Acta Logica) (Text in various languages with summaries) 1958-19?? a. Universitatea Bucuresti, Bulevardul Gh. Gheorghiu Dej 64, Bucharest, Rumania (Dist. by Cartimex, Str. 13 Decemvrie 3-5, P.O. Box 134-145, Bucharest, Rumania)

084   FR
UNIVERSITE DE BESANCON. CENTRE DE DOCUMENTATION ET DE BIBLIOGRAPHIE PHILOSOPHIQUES. TRAVAUX. 1973. irreg. (Universite de Besancon, Centre de Documentation et de Bibliographie Philosophiques) Societe d'Edition "les Belles Lettres", 95, Boulevard Raspail, 75006 Paris, France. illus.

100   BE
UNIVERSITE LIBRE DE BRUXELLES. INSTITUT DE PHILOSOPHIE. ANNALES. 1969. a. 300 Fr. Editions de l'Universite de Bruxelles, Parc Leopold, 1040 Brussels, Belgium. Ed. Chaim Perelman. bk. rev. bibl. circ. 1,000.

100   II
UNIVERSITY OF CALCUTTA. DEPARTMENT OF PHILOSOPHY. JOURNAL. (Text in English) 1975. a. Rs.5. University of Calcutta, Department of Philosophy, Asutosh Bldg., Calcutta 700073, India.

180   II   ISSN 0076-2253
UNIVERSITY OF MADRAS. PHILOSOPHICAL SERIES.* irreg. University of Madras, Chepauk, Triplicane, Madras 600005, Tamil Nadu, India.

700 500   UK   ISSN 0078-0251
UNIVERSITY OF NEWCASTLE-UPON-TYNE. PHILOSOPHICAL SOCIETY. PROCEEDINGS.* 1964. irreg., 1969, vol. 1, no. 15. 5s.($0.60) University of Newcastle-Upon-Tyne, Philosophical Society, Armstrong Bldg., Queen Victoria Rd., Newcastle-Upon-Tyne NE1 7RU, England. Ed. J. A. Richardson.

105   SL
UNIVERSITY OF SIERRA LEONE. FOURAH BAY COLLEGE. PHILOSOPHICAL SOCIETY. JOURNAL. 1977. a. University of Sierra Leone, Fourah Bay College, Philosophical Society, Freetown, Sierra Leone.

501   NE
UNIVERSITY OF WESTERN ONTARIO SERIES IN PHILOSOPHY OF SCIENCE. Variant title: Western Ontario Series. (Text in English) 1972. irreg. price varies. (University of Western Ontario, CN) D. Reidel Publishing Co., P.O. Box 17, 3300 AA Dordrecht, Netherlands (And Lincoln Building, 160 Old Derby St., Hingham, MA 02043) Ed. J. J. Leach.

UNIVERZITA KOMENSKEHO. FILOZOFICKA FAKULTA. ZBORNIK: MARXIZMUS-LENINIZMUS. see *POLITICAL SCIENCE*

100   CS
UNIVERZITA KOMENSKEHO. FILOZOFICKA FAKULTA. ZBORNIK: INFORMATIKA. (Text in Slovak; summaries in English, German and Russian) 1973. a. exchange basis. Slovenske Pedagogicke Nakladatelstvo, Sasinkova 5, 891 12 Bratislava, Czechoslovakia. Ed. Emilia Chura.

100   CS   ISSN 0083-4181
UNIVERZITA KOMENSKEHO. FILOZOFICKA FAKULTA. ZBORNIK: PHILOSOPHICA. (Text in Czech or Slovak; summaries in German and Russian) 1960. a. exchange basis. (Univerzita Komenskeho, Filozoficka Fakulta) Slovenske Pedagogicke Nakladatelstvo, Sasinkova 5, 891-12 Bratislava, Czechoslovakia. Ed. Lev Hanzel. circ. 700.

146.3 320.53   CS
UNIVERZITA KOMENSKEHO. USTAV MARXIZMU-LENINIZMU. ZBORNIK: MARXISTICKA FILOZOFIA. (Text in Slovak; summaries in English, German, Russian) 1970. irreg. price varies. Univerzita Komenskeho, Ustav Marxizmu-Leninizmu, Safarikovo nam. 12, Bratislava, Czechoslovakia.
Supersedes in part the Institute's Zbornik and continues its vol. numbering.

100 301   PL   ISSN 0072-0453
UNIWERSYTET GDANSKI. WYDZIAL HUMANISTYCZNY. ZESZYTY NAUKOWE. FILOZOFIA I SOCJOLOGIA. 1965. irreg. 20 Zl. Uniwersytet Gdanski, Ul. Czerwonej Armii 110, 81-824 Sopot, Poland (Dist. by Ars Polona-Ruch, Krakowskie Przedmiescie 7, Warsaw, Poland)

100   US
VAN LEER JERUSALEM FOUNDATION SERIES. irreg. Humanities Press, Inc., 171 First Ave., Atlantic Highlands, NJ 07716.

100   US
WADSWORTH STUDIES IN PHILOSOPHICAL CRITICISM. irreg. Wadsworth Publishing Co., 10 Davis Dr., Belmont, CA 94002.

100   AU   ISSN 0083-999X
WIENER JAHRBUCH FUER PHILOSOPHIE. 1968. a. price varies. Wilhelm Braumueller, Universitaets-Verlagsbuchhandlung GmbH, Servitengasse 5, A-1092 Vienna, Austria. Ed. Erich Heintel. bk. rev. index. circ. 700.

181.4 954   AU   ISSN 0084-0084
WIENER ZEITSCHRIFT FUER DIE KUNDE SUEDASIENS UND ARCHIV FUER INDISCHE PHILOSPHIE. 1957. a. S.210. (Oesterreichische Akademie der Wissenschaften, Kommission fuer Sprachen und Kulturen Sued- und Ostasiens) Gerold und Co., Graben 31, A-1011 Vienna, Austria (and E. J. Brill, Antwerpener Str. 6-12, Leiden, Netherlands) (Co-sponsor: Universitaet Wien. Indologisches Institut) Eds. E. Frauwallner and G. Oberhammer.
Until 1969: Wiener Zeitschrift fuer Die Kunde Sued- und Ostasiens & Archiv fuer Indische Philosophie.

100   NE   ISSN 0084-0106
WIJSGERIGE TEKSTEN EN STUDIES/ PHILOSOPHICAL TEXTS AND STUDIES. 1956. irreg., no. 23, 1975. price varies. ‡ (Rijksuniversiteit te Utrecht - University of Utrecht) Van Gorcum, Box 43, Assen, Netherlands (Dist. by Humanities Press, Inc., 171 First Ave, Atlantic Highlands, N.J. 07716) Ed. C. J. de Vogel, K. Kuypers.

100   GW
WISSENSCHAFT UND GEGENWART. GEISTESWISSENSCHAFTLICHE REIHE. irreg., no. 61, 1978. price varies. Vittorio Klostermann, Frauenlobstr. 22, Postfach 900601, 6000 Frankfurt 90, W. Germany (B.R.D.)

574   US
WOODBRIDGE LECTURES, COLUMBIA UNIVERSITY. no. 4, 1972. irreg. Columbia University Press, 136 S. Broadway, Irvington-on-Hudson, NY 10533.

181 891   II   ISSN 0084-1242
WOOLNER INDOLOGICAL SERIES. (Text in English, Hindi, and Sanskrit) 1960. irreg., vol. 21, 1976. price varies. Vishveshvaranand Vedic Research Institute, P. O. Sadhu Ashram, Hoshiarpur 146021, Punjab, India. Ed. Vishvu Bandhu.

100   II
WORLD'S WISDOM SERIES. (Text in English) 1976. irreg. Oriental Publishers and Distributors, 1488, Pataudi House, Darya Ganj, New Delhi 110002, India.

WORLD'S WOMAN'S CHRISTIAN TEMPERANCE UNION. CONVENTION REPORT. see *SOCIOLOGY*

YOKOHAMA NATIONAL UNIVERSITY. HUMANITIES. SECTION 1: PHILOSOPHY AND SOCIAL SCIENCES/YOKOHAMA KOKURITSU DAIGAKU JIMBUN KIYO DAI-1-RUI, TETSUGAKU, SHAKAI KAGAKU. see *SOCIAL SCIENCES: COMPREHENSIVE WORKS*

101   GW   ISSN 0514-2733
ZEITSCHRIFT FUER PHILOSOPHISCHE FORSCHUNG. BEIHEFTE. 1951. irreg., no. 36, 1976. price varies. Verlag Anton Hain GmbH, Adelheidstr. 2, Postfach 1220, 6240 Koenigstein, W. Germany (B.R.D.) Eds. H. M. Baumgartner, O. Hoeffe.

PHILOSOPHY — Abstracting, Bibliographies, Statistics

100 016   VC   ISSN 0084-7836
BIBLIOGRAPHIA INTERNATIONALIS SPIRITUALITATIS. (Text in various languages; summaries in Latin) 1966. a. L.4600($57) (Pontificio Istituto di Spiritualita) Edizioni del Padri Carmelitani Scalzi, Piazza S. Pancrazio 5-A, 00152 Rome, Italy. circ. 570.

BIBLIOGRAPHIE DER SOZIALETHIK. see *SOCIAL SCIENCES: COMPREHENSIVE WORKS — Abstracting, Bibliographies, Statistics*

BIBLIOGRAPHY OF SOCIETY, ETHICS AND THE LIFE SCIENCES. see *BIOLOGY — Abstracting, Bibliographies, Statistics*

100   FR   ISSN 0080-4789
RUDOLF STEINER PUBLICATIONS. 1963. irreg. 42 F. (Rudolf Steiner Nachlassverwaltung) Librairie Fischbacher, 33 Rue de Seine, 75-Paris 6, France. Ed. V. Rivierez.

PHOTOGRAPHY

see also *Motion Pictures*

ACOUSTICAL IMAGING: RECENT ADVANCES IN VISUALIZATION AND CHARACTERIZATION. see *PHYSICS — Sound*

ADVANCES IN HOLOGRAPHY. see *PHYSICS*

770   FR   ISSN 0084-6481
ANNUAIRE DE LA PHOTOGRAPHIE PROFESSIONNELLE. 1966. a. 78 F. Confederation Francaise de la Photographie, 16 Pl. Vendome, 75001 Paris, France. Ed. Antoine de Saisset.

770   II
ANNUAL OF INDIAN PHOTOGRAPHY. 1978. a. Rs.12. Sooriya Publishing House, 52 Thaiyappa Mudali St, V.O.C. Nagar, Madras 600001, India.

770   AG
ANUARIO DE LA FOTOGRAFIA ARTISTICA ARGENTINA. 1976. a. Editorial Foco s.r.l., Monroe 5117, Buenos Aires, Argentina. Dir. Hector Zampaglione. illus.

770　　　　　AT　ISSN 0067-2076
AUSTRALIAN PHOTOGRAPHY DIRECTORY. 1951. a. Aus.$21 with 12 copies of Australian Photography. Globe Publishing Co. Pty. Ltd., 381 Pitt St., Sydney, N.S.W. 2001, Australia. Ed. Terry Swan. adv. bk. rev. circ. 30,000.

779　　　　　US　ISSN 0090-7197
BLACK PHOTOGRAPHERS ANNUAL.* 1973. a. $5.95 softcover; $10.95 hardcover. Black Photographers Annual Inc., 55 Hicks St., Brooklyn, NY 11201 (Subscr. to: Light Impressions Corp., P.O. Box 3012, Rochester, NY 14614) Ed. Joe Crawford.

770　　　　　UK　ISSN 0068-2217
BRITISH JOURNAL OF PHOTOGRAPHY ANNUAL. 1860. a. £6. Henry Greenwood & Co. Ltd., 28 Great James St., London WC1N 3HL, England (Dist. in U.S. by: Focal Press Inc., 10 E. 40th St., New York, N.Y. 10016) Ed. G. W. Crawley. adv. index. circ. 12,000.

778.3　　　　US　ISSN 0362-0131
BUYER'S GUIDE TO MICROGRAPHIC EQUIPMENT, PRODUCTS, AND SERVICES. 1971. a. free. National Micrographics Association, 8728 Colesville Road, Suite 1101, Silver Spring, MD 20910. Ed. Denise L. Harlow. adv. charts. index. circ. controlled.
　　Formerly: Buyer's Guide to Microfilm Equipment, Products, and Services (ISSN 0084-8204)

CAMERART PHOTO TRADE DIRECTORY. see BUSINESS AND ECONOMICS — Trade And Industrial Directories

779　　　　　US
CENTER FOR CREATIVE PHOTOGRAPHY. 1976. irreg. $15 for 5 nos. (University of Arizona, Center for Creative Photography) University of Arizona Library, Tucson, AZ 85721. circ. 800.

CHICAGO RENAISSANCE. see LITERATURE

770　　　　　US　ISSN 0069-5998
COLOR PHOTOGRAPHY. 1959. a. $1.95. Ziff-Davis Publishing Co., One Park Ave., New York, NY 10016. Ed. H. M. Kinzer. adv. circ. 170,000.

771　　　　　US
CONSUMER GUIDE PHOTO ANNUAL. 1973. a. $2.95. Consumer Guide Magazine, 3841 W.Oakton, Skokie, IL 60076. bk. rev. illus. circ. 90,000.
　　Supersedes: Consumer Guide Photographic Equipment Test Reports Quarterly (ISSN 0091-4576)

770　　　　　UK
CREATIVE CAMERA COLLECTION. 1975. irreg. $27.50. Coo Press, Ltd., 19 Doughty St., London WC1N 2PT, England. Ed. Colin Osman. adv. circ. 10,000.
　　Formerly: Creative Camera International Year Book (ISSN 0306-3909)

DIRECTORY OF LIBRARY REPROGRAPHIC SERVICES. see LIBRARY AND INFORMATION SCIENCES

770　　　　　US　ISSN 0070-6140
DIRECTORY OF PROFESSIONAL PHOTOGRAPHY. 1938. a. $12.50. ‡ (Professional Photographers of America) P P A Publications and Events, Inc., 1090 Executive Way, Des Plaines, IL 60018. Ed. Scott F. Schwar. adv. circ. 15,000.

770　　　　　SP
EVERFOTO. (Suspended 1959-72) 1958. a. Editorial Everest, Carretera Leon-La Coruna Km.5, 4500 Leon, Spain. illus.
　　Formerly: Anuario de la Fotografia Espanola.

770　　　　　BE
FEDERATION NATIONALE DE LA PHOTOGRAPHIE PROFESIONELLE. ANNUAIRE. Short title: F.N.P.P. Annuaire. (Text in French and Flemish) a. (Nationale Federatie van Beroepsfotografie) Editions Publi-Contact, Ave. Hansen-Soulie 98, 1040 Brussels, Belgium. adv.

770　　　　　SP
FOTO GALAXIS. (Text in English & Spanish) irreg. Galaxis, S.A., Zamora 46-48, Barcelona, Spain. illus.

526.982　　　MX
FOTOGRAMETRIA, FOTOINTERPRETACION Y GEODESIA.* irreg. Sociedad Mexicana de Fotogrametria, Fotointerpretacion y Geodesia, Tacuba No. 5, Corredores Entrada No. 4, Salon No. 39, Mexico-1, Mexico. illus.

778.3　910　　PL　ISSN 0071-8076
FOTOINTERPRETACJA W GEOGRAFII. (Text in Polish; summaries in English) 1964. irreg., 1976, vol. 11. price varies. Uniwersytet Warszawski, Krakowskie Przedmiescie 26/28, 00-325 Warsaw, Poland. (Co-sponsors: Uniwersytet Gdanski, Uniwersytet Slaski)

770　　　　　US　ISSN 0190-1567
FREE STOCK PHOTOGRAPHY DIRECTORY. a. $10. Infosource Business Publications, 1600 Lehigh Parkway E., Allentown, PA 18103.

GADNEY'S GUIDE TO 1800 INTERNATIONAL CONTESTS, FESTIVALS & GRANTS IN FILM & VIDEO, PHOTOGRAPHY, TV-RADIO BROADCASTING, WRITING, POETRY, PLAYWRITING & JOURNALISM. see MOTION PICTURES

GRAPHIS POSTERS; international annual of poster art. see ART

770　　　　　FR
GUIDE D'ACHAT DE LA PHOTOGRAPHIE: 160 OBJECTIFS POUR APPAREILS REFLEX 24 X 36. 1981. a. Editions V. M., 16 Bd. Malesherbes, 75017 Paris, France. Ed. Robert Monnier. adv. illus. circ. 25,000.

770　　　　　FR
GUIDE D'ACHAT DE LA PHOTOGRAPHIE: 50 APPAREILS REFLEX 24 X 36. 1981. a. Editions V. M., 116 Bd. Malesherbes, 75017 Paris, France. Ed. Robert Monnier. adv. illus. circ. 25,000.

778.3　　　　US　ISSN 0360-8654
GUIDE TO MICROGRAPHIC EQUIPMENT. 1959. triennial. $32 to non-members; members $22. National Micrographics Association, 8728 Colesville Rd., Silver Spring, MD 20910. Ed. Hubbard W. Ballou.
　　Formerly (until 1975): Guide to Microreproduction Equipment (ISSN 0533-5388)

HEIRS. see LITERATURE

INTERNATIONAL FILE OF MICROGRAPHICS EQUIPMENT & ACCESSORIES. see BUSINESS AND ECONOMICS — Trade And Industrial Directories

686　778.1　　GW
INTERNATIONALER KONGRESS FUER REPROGRAPHIE UND INFORMATION. FACHREFERATE UND PLENARVORTRAEGE. irreg., 4th, 1975. DM.180. K.G. Saur Verlag KG, Poessenbacherstr. 12 B, Postfach 711009, 8000 Munich 71, W. Germany (B.R.D.)
　　Reprography

771.3　　　　US　ISSN 0093-9374
LEICA MANUAL. irreg., 15th edt., 1979. $23. Morgan & Morgan, Inc., 145 Palisade St., Dobbs Ferry, NY 10522. illus.

770　　　　　US　ISSN 0024-063X
LEICA PHOTOGRAPHY. 1932. irreg. free to Leica owners. E. Leitz, Inc., Rockleigh, NJ 07647. Ed. Helen Wright. bk. rev. charts. illus. index. circ. 55,000.

700　　　　　US　ISSN 0161-4223
LIGHTWORKS. 1975. irreg. $15 to individuals; institutions $20. Lightworks Magazine, Box 434, Brookline, MA 02146. Ed. Charlton Burch. adv. bk. rev. illus. circ. 3,000.

778.35　　　　FR　ISSN 0076-6364
MEMOIRES DE PHOTO-INTERPRETATION. 1963. irreg 1970, no. 7. price varies. (Ecole Pratique des Hautes Etudes) Librairie Touzot, 38 rue Saint Sulpice, 75006 Paris, France.

779.05　　　　US　ISSN 0580-8162
MODERN PHOTOGRAPHY ANNUAL.* (Text in English, French or German) 1970. a. $1.50. A B C Leisure Magazines, Inc., 130 E. 59th St., New York, NY 10022. illus.

770　　　　　US　ISSN 0197-5986
MODERN PHOTOGRAPHY'S GUIDE TO THE WORLD'S BEST CAMERAS. a. $2.95. Modern Photography, 130 E. 59 St., New York, NY 10022.

779.05　　　　US
MODERN PHOTOGRAPHY'S PHOTO BUYING GUIDE. 1969. a. $3.95. A B C Leisure Magazines, Inc, 825 Seventh Ave., New York, NY 10019. Ed. Harold Martin. adv. illus. circ. 125,000.

029.7　778.315　US
NATIONAL MICROGRAPHICS ASSOCIATION. PROCEEDINGS OF THE ANNUAL CONFERENCE. 1952. a. $10. National Micrographics Association, 8728 Colesville Rd., Silver Spring, MD 20910. Ed. Ellen Meyer. circ. 200. (also avail. in microform from UMI)
　　Formerly: National Microfilm Association. Proceedings of the Annual Convention (ISSN 0077-5223)
　　Microphotography

770　　　　　UK　ISSN 0143-036X
NEW MAGIC LANTERN JOURNAL. 1978. irreg. Magic Lantern Society of Great Britain, Newlyn, Nether Lane, Nutley, Sussex, England. illus.

770　　　　　US　ISSN 0029-0513
NIKON WORLD. 1967. a. $6. Ehrenreich Photo-Optical Industries, Inc., 623 Stewart Ave., Garden City, NY 11530. Ed. Robert G. Norwick. bk. rev. illus. tr.lit. circ. 120,000.

770　　　　　US　ISSN 0078-2971
OBSERVATION.* 1966. a. State University of New York at Albany, Department of Art, Albany, NY 12203.
　　Record of works done by students and faculty over a one year period"

770.5　　　　US　ISSN 0093-1365
PHOTO INFORMATION ALMANAC. irreg. $1.50. Billboard Publications, Inc. (New York), 1515 Broadway, New York, NY 10036. illus.

771　　　　　US
PHOTO-LAB INDEX; cumulative formulary of standard recommended photographic procedures. 1939. a. (q.updates) $39.95 ($12.50 for Supplements) ‡ Morgan & Morgan, Inc., 145 Palisade St, Dobbs Ferry, NY 10522. Ed. Ernest M. Pittaro. charts. index. cum.index. circ. 8,000. (looseleaf format)

770　　　　　US　ISSN 0147-247X
PHOTOGRAPHER'S MARKET. 1978. a. $12.95. Writer's Digest, 9933 Alliance Rd., Cincinnati, OH 45242.
　　Supersedes in part: Artists & Photographer's Market (ISSN 0146-8294)

770.62　　　　US　ISSN 0093-254X
PHOTOGRAPHIC HISTORICAL SOCIETY OF NEW YORK. MEMBERSHIP DIRECTORY. 1973. a. membership. Photographic Historical Society of New York, Box 1839, Radio City Sta., New York, NY 10101. illus. circ. 600. Key Title: Membership Directory of the Photographic Historical Society of N.Y.

778.3　　　　US　ISSN 0302-4210
PHOTOGRAPHIC TECHNIQUES IN SCIENTIFIC RESEARCH. 1973. irreg. $21.50. Academic Press, Inc, 111 Fifth Ave., New York, NY 10003. Eds. J. Cruise, A. Newman. illus.

770　　　　　US
PHOTOGRAPHIC TRADE NEWS MASTER BUYING GUIDE. no. 38, 1975. a. included with subscr. to Photographic Trade News. P T N Publishing Corp., 250 Fulton Ave., Hempstead, NY 11550. Eds. Edward C. Wagner, Rudolf Maschke. illus.

770　　　　　AT
PHOTOGRAPHIC WORLD ANNUAL. 1979. a. Australian Hi-Fi Publications Pty. Ltd., Box 341, Mona Vale, N.S.W. 2103, Australia. Ed. Peter Bramwell.

770　　　　　AT
PHOTOGRAPHIC WORLD BUYER'S GUIDE. CAMERAS. 1979. a. Australian Hi-Fi Publications Pty. Ltd., Box 341, Mona Vale, N.S.W. 2103, Australia. Ed. Richard Lachlan.

770   AT
PHOTOGRAPHIC WORLD BUYER'S GUIDE.
CINE. 1979. a. Australia Hi-Fi Publications Pty.
Ltd., Box 341, Mona Vale, N.S.W. 2103, Australia.
Ed. Richard Lachlan.

770   AT
PHOTOGRAPHIC WORLD BUYER'S GUIDE.
DARKROOMS. 1979. a. Australia Hi-Fi
Publications Pty. Ltd., Box 341, Mona Vale, N.S.W.
2103, Australia. Ed. Richard Lachlan.

770   AT
PHOTOGRAPHIC WORLD BUYER'S GUIDE.
INDEX. 1979. a. Australian Hi-Fi Publications Pty.
Ltd., Box 341, Mona Vale, N.S.W. 2103, Australia.
Ed. Richard Lachlan.

770   AT
PHOTOGRAPHIC WORLD BUYER'S GUIDE.
LENSES. 1979. a. Australian Hi-Fi Publications
Pty. Ltd., Box 341, Mona Vale, N.S.W. 2103,
Australia. Ed. Richard Lachlan.

770   AT
PHOTOGRAPHIC WORLD BUYER'S GUIDE.
PROJECTORS. 1979. a. Australian Hi-Fi
Publications Pty. Ltd., Box 341, Mona Vale, N.S.W.
2103, Australia. Ed. Richard Lachlan.

770   659   SZ   ISSN 0079-1830
PHOTOGRAPHIS; international annual of advertising
and editorial photography. (Text in English, French,
German) 1966. a. 105 Fr.($49.50) Walter Herdeg
Graphis Press, 107 Dufourstrasse, 8008 Zurich,
Switzerland (Dist. by Hastings House Publishers,
Inc., 10 E. 40 St., New York NY 10016) Ed.
Walter Herdeg. index. circ. 12,500.

770   US   ISSN 0079-1849
PHOTOGRAPHY ANNUAL. 1950. a. $1.95. Ziff-
Davis Publishing Co., 1 Park Ave., New York, NY
10016. Ed. H. M. Kinzer. adv. circ. 305,000.

770   US   ISSN 0079-1857
PHOTOGRAPHY DIRECTORY AND BUYING
GUIDE. 1957. a. $2.95. Ziff-Davis Publishing Co., 1
Park Ave., New York, NY 10016. Ed. Jim Hughes.
adv. charts, illus. circ. 205,000. (back issues avail.)

770   UK   ISSN 0142-7865
PHOTOGRAPHY/POLITICS. a. £6. Photography
Workshop, 152 Upper St., London N1, England.
illus.

770.5   US   ISSN 0090-4406
PHOTOGRAPHY YEAR. 1973. a. Time-Life Books,
Inc. (Subsidiary of: Time Inc.) 777 Duke Street,
Alexandria, VA 22314. Ed. Edward Brash. illus.

770   UK   ISSN 0079-1865
PHOTOGRAPHY YEAR BOOK. 1937. a. £6.50.
Argus Books Ltd. (Subsidiary of: Fountain Press)
Station Road, Kings Langley, Hertfordshire,
England. Ed. John Sanders. adv.

770   US
PROFESSIONAL PHOTOGRAPHIC EQUIPMENT
DIRECTORY AND BUYING GUIDE. 1975. a.
$10. P T N Publishing Corp., 250 Fulton Ave.,
Hempstead, NY 11550. Eds. Rudolf Maschke,
Edward C. Wagner. illus.

770   US
STILL: YALE PHOTOGRAPHY ANNUAL. 1970.
irreg., latest no. 3, 1973. price varies. Yale
University, School of Art and Architecture,
Department of Graphic Design, 180 York St., New
Haven, CT 06520 (Dist. by George Wittenborn,
Inc., 1018 Madison Ave., New York, N.Y. 10021)

770   UK
SYMPOSIUM ON PHOTOGRAPHIC GELATIN.
PROCEEDINGS. no. 3 1974. irreg. (Royal
Photographic Society of Great Britain, Scientific and
Technical Group) Academic Press Inc. (London)
Ltd., 24-28 Oval Rd., London NW 1 7DX,
England. Ed. R.J. Cox.

770   FI   ISSN 0356-8075
VALOKUVAUKSEN VUOSIKIRJA/FINNISH
PHOTOGRAPHIC YEARBOOK/FINSK
FOTOGRAFISK ARSBOK. (Text in English,
Finnish or Swedish) 1972. irreg. Fmk.50($13)
Suomen Valokuvataiteen Museon Saatio, Box 596,
SF-00101 Helsinki 10, Finland. Ed. Ritva Keski-
Korhonen. adv. illus. circ. 5,000.

770   US   ISSN 0084-0998
WISSENSCHAFTLICHE UND ANGEWANDTE
PHOTOGRAPHIE. (Issues Not Published
Consecutively) 1955. irreg. Springer-Verlag, 175
Fifth Ave., New York, NY 10010 (also Berlin,
Heidelberg, Vienna) Ed. J. Stueper. (reprint service
avail. from ISI)

770   US   ISSN 0084-103X
WOLFMAN REPORT ON THE PHOTOGRAPHIC
INDUSTRY IN THE UNITED STATES. 1958. a.
$75. A B C Leisure Magazines, Inc., 825 7th Ave.,
New York, NY 10019. Ed. Lydia Wolfman. adv.
circ. 9,000.

WRITERS' AND PHOTOGRAPHERS'
MARKETING GUIDE; DIRECTORY OF
AUSTRALIAN AND NEW ZEALAND
LITERARY AND PHOTO MARKETS. see
PUBLISHING AND BOOK TRADE

PHOTOGRAPHY — Abstracting, Bibliographies, Statistics

770   016   US   ISSN 0193-2810
PHOTOGRAPHY INDEX. 1979. a. $8.95.
Photographic Research Publications, Box 333,
Detroit, MI 48235.

PHYSICAL CHEMISTRY

see *Chemistry—Physical Chemistry*

PHYSICAL FITNESS AND HYGIENE

see also *Medical Sciences; Nutrition and Dietetics; Public Health and Safety; Sports and Games*

ACTA MEDICA ET SOCIOLOGICA. see
SOCIOLOGY

330   613   US
ADVANCES IN HEALTH ECONOMICS AND
HEALTH SERVICES RESEARCH. 1979. a.
$17.25 to individuals; institutions $34.50. J A I
Press, Box 1678, 165 W. Putnam Ave., Greenwich,
CT 06830. Ed. Richard M. Scheffler.
Formerly (until 1981): Research in Health
Economics (ISSN 0197-0690)

613   CN   ISSN 0708-2673
ALBERTA HEALTH EDUCATION PROGRAMS.
1978. a. Manpower Services Division, Career
Resources Branch, Devonian Bldg., 5th Floor,
11160 Jasper Ave., Edmonton, Alta. T5K 0L1,
Canada.

AMERICAN LECTURES IN SPORTSMEDICINE,
PHYSICAL EDUCATION AND RECREATION.
see *MEDICAL SCIENCES — Surgery*

ANGOLA. SECRETARIA PROVINCIAL DE
SAUDE, TRABALHO. PREVIDENCIA E
ASSISTENCIA. SINTESE DA ACTIVIDADE
DOS SERVICOS E ORGANISMOS. see *PUBLIC
ADMINISTRATION*

179   AT   ISSN 0310-8228
CONSEQUENCES. 1971. irreg. Education
Department, Parliament Place, West Perth, WA
6005, Australia.

CURRENT TOPICS IN BIOENERGETICS. see
BIOLOGY — Biophysics

613.2   US
DIET & EXERCISE. 1978. a. $2 per. no. Meredith
Corporation, 1716 Locust St., Des Moines, IA
50336.

362.1   CN   ISSN 0707-0047
DIRECTORY OF LIFESTYLE CHANGE
SERVICES. 1978. a. free. Health Department,
Healthful Lifestyle Program, 1060 W. 8th Ave,
Vancouver, B.C. V6H 1C4, Canada.

613.7   US   ISSN 0091-6331
EXERCISE AND SPORT SCIENCES REVIEWS.
1973. irreg. Academic Press, Inc., 111 Fifth Ave.,
New York, NY 10003. Ed. Jack H. Wilmore.
Indexed: Ind.Med.

613.7   SZ
FORSCHUNGSINSTITUT DER
EIDGENOESSISCHEN TURN- UND
SPORTSCHULE MAGGLINGEN.
WISSENSCHAFTLICHE SCHRIFTENREIHE. no.
7, 1976. irreg. Birkhaeuser Verlag, Elisabethenstr.
19, CH-4010 Basel, Switzerland.

HAWAII. DEPARTMENT OF HEALTH.
RESEARCH AND STATISTICS OFFICE. R & S
REPORT. see *POPULATION STUDIES*

HEALTH MEDIA BUYER'S GUIDE. see
ADVERTISING AND PUBLIC RELATIONS

I C H P E R CONGRESS PROCEEDINGS.
(International Council on Health, Physical
Education and Recreation) see *MEDICAL
SCIENCES*

IMPACT (SYRACUSE) see *BIRTH CONTROL*

613   SZ   ISSN 0074-3100
INTERNATIONAL CONFERENCE ON HEALTH
AND HEALTH EDUCATION. PROCEEDINGS.
(Text in English, French, Spanish) triennial. price
varies. International Union for Health Education, 3
rue Viollier, 1207 Geneva, Switzerland. Ed. Annette
le Meitour-Kaplun. Indexed: Curr.Cont.

613   614   IT
INTERNATIONAL CONGRESS ON HYGIENE
AND PREVENTIVE MEDICINE.
PROCEEDINGS. (Text in English, French,
German, Italian and Spanish) irreg., 8th, 1978,
Mexico City. price varies. International Federation
for Preventive and Social Medicine, Via Salaria 237,
00199 Rome, Italy. Ed. G. A. Canaperia.

613.7   181.45   CN   ISSN 0708-076X
INTERNATIONAL SIVANANDA YOGA LIFE
AND YOGA VACATIONS. 1977. irreg. donations.
Sivananda Yoga Vedanta Centre, Headquarters,
Sivananda Ashram Yoga Camp, 8Th Ave., Val
Morin, Que. J0T 2R0, Canada. illus.
Formerly: International Yoga Life and Yoga
Vacations (ISSN 0381-9043)

613   US   ISSN 0163-0253
LIFE LINES. 1976. irreg. membership. (Committee
for an Extended Lifespan) Dominion Press, Box
696, San Marcos, CA 92069. Ed. Sid Ryan. bk. rev.
circ. 5,000. (also avail. in microform from UMI)
Formerly (until 1978): Chairman's Chat (ISSN
0145-949X)

613.7   FI   ISSN 0355-7073
LIIKUNTAKASVATUS. 1939. 5-6/yr. Fmk.20($5)
Suomen Liikunnanopettajain Liitto,
Mannerheimintie 87 B, 00270 Helsinki 27, Finland
(Subscr. to: Vesalantie 51, 00940 Helsinki 94,
Finland) (Co-sponsor: Koululiikuntaliitto) Ed. Kalevi
Salo. adv. bk. rev. circ. 3,200.

613   US   ISSN 0363-0366
MEDICAL AND HEALTH ANNUAL. 1976. a.
$14.95. Encyclopaedia Britannica, Inc., 425 N.
Michigan Ave., Chicago, IL 60611. Ed. Ellen
Bernstein.

613   US
MEDICAL & HEALTH INFORMATION
DIRECTORY. 1978. biennial. $62. Gale Research
Company, Book Tower, Detroit, MI 48226. Ed.
Anthony T. Kruzas.

613   II
N I H A E TECHNICAL REPORT. irreg. Rs.2.
National Institute of Health Administration and
Education, R-55 Greater Kailish 1, New Delhi
110048, India.

613   AU   ISSN 0028-9620
NEYDHARTINGER MOORPOST. 1950. irreg.
S.10($1.) Moorbad Neydharting, Pfarrplatz 3-4, A-
4010 Linz, Austria. Ed. Prof. Otto Stoeber. charts.
illus. mkt. pat. stat. tr.mk. (looseleaf format)

PLAYGIRL HEALTH AND BEAUTY GUIDE. see
BEAUTY CULTURE

RECENT ADVANCES IN OBESITY RESEARCH.
see MEDICAL SCIENCES

613 UK
ROYAL SOCIETY OF HEALTH. PAPERS. irreg.
Royal Society of Health, 13 Grosvenor Place,
London SW1X 7EN, England. Ed. J. Audrey
Ellison.

SELECTIVE GUIDE TO AUDIOVISUALS FOR
MENTAL HEALTH AND FAMILY LIFE
EDUCATION. see PSYCHOLOGY

SELECTIVE GUIDE TO PUBLICATIONS FOR
MENTAL HEALTH AND FAMILY LIFE
EDUCATION. see PSYCHOLOGY —
Abstracting, Bibliographies, Statistics

SOZIALMEDIZINISCHE UND PAEDAGOGISCHE
JUGENDKUNDE. see MEDICAL SCIENCES

613.7 790.1 FI
STUDIES IN SPORT, PHYSICAL EDUCATION
AND HEALTH. (Text in English and Finnish)
1971. irreg., no. 9, 1976. exchange basis. Jyvaskylan
Yliopisto, Kirjasto - University of Jyvaskyla,
Seminaarinkatu 15, 40100 Jyvaskyla 10, Finland.
Ed. Paavo V. Komi. circ. 400-500.

SUMITOMO BULLETIN OF INDUSTRIAL
HEALTH/SUMITOMO SANGYO EISEI. see
INDUSTRIAL HEALTH AND SAFETY

VOGUE BEAUTY & HEALTH GUIDE. see
BEAUTY CULTURE

WOMAN'S DAY 101 WAYS TO LOSE WEIGHT
AND STAY HEALTHY. see NUTRITION AND
DIETETICS

PHYSICAL FITNESS AND HYGIENE — Abstracting, Bibliographies, Statistics

016 613.85 US ISSN 0067-7361
BIBLIOGRAPHY ON SMOKING AND HEALTH.
(Subseries of: Public Health Service Bibliography
Series) 1967. a. price varies. U.S. Office on Smoking
and Health, Technical Information Center, Park
Bldg., Rm. 116, 5600 Fisheries Lane, Rockville, MD
20857. Ed. Donald R. Shopland. index.

016 613.85 US ISSN 0070-6000
DIRECTORY OF ON-GOING RESEARCH IN
SMOKING AND HEALTH. 1967. biennial. $2.
U.S. Office on Smoking and Health, Technical
Information Center, Park Blg., Rm. 116, 5600
Fisheries Lane, Rockville, MD 20857. Ed. Donald
R. Shopland. index.

614 UK ISSN 0140-3273
HEALTH EDUCATION INDEX; and Guide to
Voluntary Social Welfare Organisations. 1970. 2/yr.
B. Edsall & Co. Ltd., 36 Eccleston Square, London
SW1V 1PF, England. Ed. B. Edsall. adv. illus. pat.
circ. 4,000.

613 016 US
N I C E M INDEX TO HEALTH AND SAFETY
EDUCATION-MULTIMEDIA. vol. 3, 1976.
biennial. $55. National Information Center for
Educational Media, University of Southern
California, University Park, Los Angeles, CA 90007.
(also avail. in microfiche)

613.85 US ISSN 0081-0363
SMOKING AND HEALTH BULLETIN. 1967.
irreg.(approx. 10 issues per year) free; limited
distribution. U.S. Office on Smoking and Health,
Technical Information Center, Park Bldg., Rm. 116,
5600 Fisheries Lane, Rockville, MD 20857. Ed.
Donald R. Shopland. index. circ. 4,000.
Formerly: Smoking and Health Bibliographical
Bulletin.

613.7 015 UK
SPORTS DOCUMENTATION CENTRE. LIST OF
PERIODICAL HOLDINGS. (Text in English and
other languages) 1974. irreg. free. Sports
Documentation Centre, Main Library, Box 363,
University of Birmingham, Birmingham B15 2TT,
England. Ed. Bd.
Formerly: National Documentation Center for
Sport, Physical Education and Recreation. List of
Periodical Holdings.

616.863 016 US
U.S. NATIONAL CLEARINGHOUSE FOR DRUG
ABUSE INFORMATION. SELECTED
REFERENCE SERIES. 1973. series 7. irreg. free. ‡
U.S. National Clearinghouse for Drug Abuse
Information, 5600 Fishers Lane, Rockville, MD
20852. circ. 10,000 (approx.)

PHYSICS

see also Physics—Heat; Physics—
Mechanics; Physics—Nuclear Energy;
Physics—Optics; Physics—Sound

530 US ISSN 0094-243X
A I P CONFERENCE PROCEEDINGS. 1970. irreg.,
no. 67, 1981. American Institute of Physics, 335 E.
45th St., New York, NY 10017. Ed. Hugh C.
Wolfe. bibl, charts, illus, stat. (back issues avail.)
Indexed: C.P.I. Chem.Abstr. Phys.Abstr.

530 CH
ACADEMIA SINICA. INSTITUTE OF PHYSICS.
ANNUAL REPORT. vol. 7, 1977. a. exchange
basis. Academia Sinica, Institute of Physics,
Nankang, Taipei, Taiwan, Republic of China. Ed.
E.K. Lin. circ. 500.

530 US ISSN 0065-1559
ACTA PHYSICA AUSTRIACA. SUPPLEMENT.
1965. irreg., no. 21, 1980. price varies. Springer-
Verlag, 175 Fifth Ave., New York, NY 10010 (also
Berlin, Heidelberg, Vienna) (reprint service avail.
from ISI)

530 540 HU ISSN 0567-7947
ACTA PHYSICA ET CHIMICA DEBRECINA.
(Text in English, German, Russian) 1954. a.
Kossuth Lajos Tudomanyegyetem, P.O. Box 5, H-
4010 Debrecen 10, Hungary. Eds. R. Gaspar, S.
Makleit.

530 US
ADVANCES IN AEROSOL PHYSICS. irreg., vol. 7,
1973. price varies. Halsted Press (Subsidiary of:
John Wiley & Sons, Inc.) 605 Third Ave., New
York, NY 10016. Ed. V. A. Fedoseev.

530 541.3 US ISSN 0065-2385
ADVANCES IN CHEMICAL PHYSICS. 1958. irreg.,
vol. 43, 1980. price varies. John Wiley & Sons, Inc.,
605 Third Ave., New York, NY 10016. Ed. I.
Prigogine.

ADVANCES IN ELECTRONICS AND
ELECTRON PHYSICS. see ELECTRICITY AND
ELECTRICAL ENGINEERING

ADVANCES IN ELECTRONICS AND
ELECTRON PHYSICS. SUPPLEMENT. see
ELECTRICITY AND ELECTRICAL
ENGINEERING

535 774 US ISSN 0361-2961
ADVANCES IN HOLOGRAPHY. 1975. irreg., vol.
3, 1976. Marcel Dekker, Inc., 270 Madison Ave.,
New York, NY 10016. Ed. N. Farhat. illus.

538 US ISSN 0065-2873
ADVANCES IN MAGNETIC RESONANCE. 1965.
irreg., vol. 9, 1978. price varies. Academic Press,
Inc., 111 Fifth Ave., New York, NY 10003. Ed. J.
S. Waugh. index. (also avail. in microfiche)

ADVANCES IN MICROWAVES. see
ELECTRICITY AND ELECTRICAL
ENGINEERING

ADVANCES IN MICROWAVES. SUPPLEMENTS.
see ELECTRICITY AND ELECTRICAL
ENGINEERING

530.41 US ISSN 0065-3357
ADVANCES IN SOLID STATE PHYSICS.* irreg.
price varies. Pergamon Press, Inc., Maxwell House,
Fairview Park, Elmsford, NY 10523 (And
Headington Hill Hall, Oxford OX3 0BW, England)

530.08 US ISSN 0065-3470
ADVANCES IN THEORETICAL PHYSICS. 1965.
irreg., 1968, vol. 2. price varies. Academic Press,
Inc., 111 Fifth Ave., New York, NY 10003. Ed.
Keith A. Brueckner. index.

AKADEMIE DER WISSENSCHAFTEN,
GOETTINGEN. NACHRICHTEN 2.
MATHEMATISCH-PHYSIKALISCHE KLASSE.
see MATHEMATICS

AMERICAN CRYSTALLOGRAPHIC
ASSOCIATION. PROGRAM & ABSTRACTS. see
CHEMISTRY — Crystallography

530 FI ISSN 0066-2003
ANNALES ACADEMIAE SCIENTIARUM
FENNICAE. SERIES A, 6: PHYSICA. (Text in
English, French, German) 1957. irreg. price varies.
Suomalainen Tiedeakatemla - Academia Scientiarum
Fennica, Snellmanink. 9-11, 00170 Helsinki 17,
Finland. Ed. V. Hovi. cum.index (1957-1972 in vol.
400) circ. 600. (also avail. in microform; back issues
avail.; reprint service avail. from UMI) Indexed:
Appl.Mech.Rev. Bull.Signal. Chem.Abstr.
Psychol.Abstr. Ref.Zn. Int.Aerosp.Abstr.
Nucl.Sci.Abstr. Phys.Ber.

ANNUAL REVIEW OF ASTRONOMY AND
ASTROPHYSICS. see ASTRONOMY

531.14 US
ANNUAL SUMMARY OF PROGRESS IN
GRAVITATION SCIENCES. 1974. a. membership.
‡ Ensanian Physicochemical Institute, Box 98,
Eldred, PA 16731. Ed. Minas Ensanian. bk. rev.
abstr. bibl. charts. illus. pat. stat. circ.
100(controlled)

530 620 US ISSN 0066-5509
APPLIED PHYSICS AND ENGINEERING. (Text
in English) 1967. irreg., 1976, no. 12. price varies.
Springer-Verlag, 175 Fifth Ave., New York, NY
10010 (also Berlin, Heidelberg, Vienna) (reprint
service avail. from ISI)

ASTROPHYSICA NORVEGICA/NORWEGIAN
JOURNAL OF THEORETICAL
ASTROPHYSICS. see ASTRONOMY

ASTROPHYSICS AND SPACE SCIENCE
LIBRARY; a series of books on the developments
of space science and of general geophysics and
astrophysics published in connection with the
journal Space Science Reviews. see ASTRONOMY

530 NE
ATOMIC ENERGY LEVELS AND GROTRIAN
DIAGRAMS. 1976. irreg., latest 1978. price varies.
North-Holland Publishing Co., Box 211, 1000 AE
Amsterdam, Netherlands.

AURORAL OBSERVATORY. MAGNETIC
OBSERVATIONS. see ASTRONOMY

AUSTRALIAN NATIONAL UNIVERSITY,
CANBERRA. DEPARTMENT OF
ENGINEERING PHYSICS. PUBLICATION EP-
RR. see ENGINEERING

530 AT ISSN 0084-7518
AUSTRALIAN NATIONAL UNIVERSITY,
CANBERRA. RESEARCH SCHOOL OF
PHYSICAL SCIENCES. RESEARCH PAPER.
irreg. free to qualified personnel. ‡ Australian
National University, Research School of Physical
Sciences, Box 4, Canberra, A.C.T. 2600, Australia.

539 621.48 SZ ISSN 0304-2901
C E R N ANNUAL REPORT. French edition: C E R
N Rapport Annuel (ISSN 0304-291X) (Former
name of body: Conseil Europeen pour la Recherche
Nucleaire) (Edts. in English and French) 1955. a.
free. European Organization for Nuclear Research,
CH-1211 Geneva 23, Switzerland. circ. 6,072
combined. Indexed: INIS. Nucl.Sci.Abstr.

539.7 SZ ISSN 0366-5690
C E R N-H E R A REPORTS. (Former name of
body: Conseil Europeen pour la Recherche
Nucleaire) 1969. irreg. free. European Organization
for Nuclear Research, CH-1211 Geneva 23,
Switzerland. (also avail. in microfiche) Indexed: IIS.

539　　　　　　SZ　ISSN 0007-8328
C E R N REPORTS. (Former name of body: Conseil Europeen pour la Recherche Nucleaire) 1955. irreg. free. European Organization for Nuclear Research, CH-1211 Geneva 23, Switzerland. (also avail. in microfiche) Indexed: INIS Atomind.

001.6 539.7　　　SZ　ISSN 0304-2898
C E R N SCHOOL OF COMPUTING. PROCEEDINGS. (Former name of body: Conseil Europeen pour la Recherche Nucleaire) 1970. biennial. European Organization for Nuclear Research, CH-1211 Geneva 23, Switzerland. (also avail. in microfiche) Indexed: INIS Atomind.

539　　　　　　SZ　ISSN 0531-4283
C E R N SCHOOL OF PHYSICS. PROCEEDINGS. (Former name of body: Conseil Europeen pour la Recherche Nucleaire) 1966. irreg. free. European Organization for Nuclear Research, CH-1211 Geneva 23, Switzerland. (also avail. in microfiche) Indexed: INIS Atomind.

530 510　　　　UK
CAMBRIDGE MONOGRAPHS ON MATHEMATICAL PHYSICS. irreg., no. 5, 1980. $29.95 for latest vol. Cambridge University Press, Box 110, Cambridge CB2 3RL, England (And 32 E. 57th St., New York NY 10022) Ed.Bd.

530　　　　　　UK
CAMBRIDGE MONOGRAPHS ON PHYSICS. irreg. price varies. Cambridge University Press, Box 110, Cambridge CB2 3RL, England (And 32 E. 57th St., New York NY 10022) Eds. M. W. Berry, C. Jordan.

530　　　　　　UK
CAMBRIDGE SOLID STATE SCIENCE SERIES. irreg. price varies. Cambridge University Press, Box 110, Cambridge CB2 3RL, England (And 32 E. 57th St., New York NY 10022) Ed. Bd.

530　　　　　　CN　ISSN 0068-8339
CANADIAN ASSOCIATION OF PHYSICISTS. ANNUAL REPORT/ASSOCIATION CANADIENNE DES PHYSICIENS. a. Canadian Association of Physicists, 151 Slater St., Suite 903, Ottawa, Ont. K1P 5H3, Canada. circ. 2,200.

530　　　　　　US
CENTER FOR HISTORY OF PHYSICS. NEWSLETTER. 1964. irreg. free. American Institute of Physics, Center for History of Physics, 335 E. 45th St., New York, NY 10017. Ed. Spencer Weart. circ. 4,000.

CENTRO DE RADIO ASTRONOMIA E ASTROFISICA MACKENZIE. OBSERVATORIA NACIONAL. RELATORIO ANUAL. see *ASTRONOMY*

530　　　　　　US　ISSN 0069-3294
CHICAGO LECTURES IN PHYSICS. 1963. irreg., vol. 6, 1973. price varies. University of Chicago Press, 5801 S. Ellis Ave., Chicago, IL 60637. (reprint service avail. from UMI,ISI)

530 510　　　　FI　ISSN 0069-6609
COMMENTATIONES PHYSICO-MATHEMATICAE. (Text in English, French, German) 1924. irreg. price varies. Societas Scientiarum Fennica, Snellmansgatan 9-11, SF-00170 Helsinki, Finland. Ed. Lennart Simons. charts. illus. index. circ. 1,000 (approx.) (also avail. in microfilm) Indexed: Bull.Signal. Chem.Abstr. Ref.Zh. Sci.Abstr. Phys.Ber. Zent.Math.

COMMONWEALTH SCIENTIFIC AND INDUSTRIAL RESEARCH ORGANIZATION. DIVISION OF RADIOPHYSICS. REPORT. see *ASTRONOMY*

COMMONWEALTH SCIENTIFIC AND INDUSTRIAL RESEARCH ORGANIZATION. DIVISION OF TEXTILE PHYSICS. ANNUAL REPORT. see *TEXTILE INDUSTRIES AND FABRICS*

COURS ET DOCUMENTS DE MATHEMATIQUES ET DE PHYSIQUE. see *MATHEMATICS*

530　　　　　　NE
CURRENT TOPICS IN MATERIALS SCIENCE. 1977. irreg. price varies. North-Holland Publishing Co., Box 211, 1006 AE Amsterdam, Netherlands. Ed. E. Kaldis.

530 548　　　　NE
DEFECTS IN SOLIDS. 1968. irreg., vol. 11, 1979. price varies. North-Holland Publishing Co., Box 211, 1000 AE Amsterdam, Netherlands.
　　Formerly: Defects in Cristalline Solids (ISSN 0070-3230)

DIFFUSION AND DEFECT MONOGRAPH SERIES. see *METALLURGY*

DIRECTORY OF PHYSICS & ASTRONOMY STAFF MEMBERS. see *EDUCATION — Higher Education*

DIRECTORY OF THE SOLAR INDUSTRY. see *BUSINESS AND ECONOMICS — Trade And Industrial Directories*

530　　　　　　NE
DISLOCATIONS IN SOLIDS. 1978. irreg., vol. 5, 1979. price varies. North-Holland Publishing Co., Box 211, 1000 AE Amsterdam, Netherlands. Ed. F.R.N. Nabarro.

530　　　　　　US
DOCUMENTS ON MODERN PHYSICS. a. price varies. Gordon and Breach Science Publishers, One Park Ave., New York, NY 10016. Ed.Bd.

530　　　　　　IE　ISSN 0070-7414
DUBLIN INSTITUTE FOR ADVANCED STUDIES. COMMUNICATIONS. SERIES A. 1943. irreg., no. 23, 1975. price varies. ‡ Dublin Institute for Advanced Studies, 10 Burlington Rd., Dublin 4, Ireland.

530　　　　　　NE
ENRICO FERMI INTERNATIONAL SUMMER SCHOOL OF PHYSICS. 1976. irreg., vol. 72, 1979. price varies. North-Holland Publishing Co., Box 211, 1000 AE Amsterdam, Netherlands.

530　　　　　　US　ISSN 0071-1438
ESSAYS IN PHYSICS. 1970. irreg., vol. 6, 1976. price varies. Academic Press Inc., 111 Fifth Ave., New York, NY 10003. Eds. G. K. T. Conn, G. N. Fowler. Indexed: CA. Nucl.Sci.Abstr.

530　　　　　　SZ
EUROPHYSICS CONFERENCE ABSTRACTS. a. 200 Fr. European Physical Society, Box 69, CH-1213 Petit-Lancy 2, Switzerland.

530　　　　　　PL
FIZYKA. 1961. irreg., no. 24, 1976. price varies. Uniwersytet im. Adama Mickiewicza w Poznaniu, Stalingradzka 1, 61-712 Poznan, Poland (Dist. by: Ars Polona, Krakowskie Przedmiescie 7, 00-068 Warsaw, Poland)
　　Formerly: Uniwersytet im. Adama Mickiewicza w Poznaniu. Wydzial Matematyki, Fizyki i Chemii. Seria Fizyka.

530　　　　　　CS
FOLIA FACULTATIS SCIENTIARUM NATURALIUM UNIVERSITATIS PURKYNIANAE BRUNENSIS: PHYSICA. irreg (7-1/yr.) price varies. Universita J. E. Purkyne, Prirodovedecka Fakulta, Kotlarska 2, 611 37 Brno, Czechoslovakia.

530　　　　　　FR　ISSN 0080-1062
FRANCE. DELEGATION GENERALE A LA RECHERCHE SCIENTIFIQUE ET TECHNIQUE. REPERTOIRE DES SCIENTIFIQUES FRANCAIS. TOME 5: PHYSIQUE. 1967. irreg. 25 F. Documentation Francaise, 29-31 Quai Voltaire, 75340 Paris 07, France.

530　　　　　　FR　ISSN 0071-8572
FRANCE. DELEGATION GENERALE A LA RECHERCHE SCIENTIFIQUE ET TECHNIQUE. REPERTOIRE NATIONAL DES LABORATOIRES; LA RECHERCHE UNIVERSITAIRE; SCIENCES EXACTES ET NATURELLES. TOME 1: PHYSIQUE. 1964. irreg. 35 F. Documentation Francaise, 29-31 Quai Voltaire, 75340 Paris 07, France.

530　　　　　　US　ISSN 0429-7725
FRONTIERS IN PHYSICS. 1961. irreg. price varies. Benjamin-Cummings Publishing Co., c/o Addison-Wesley, Reading, MA 01867.

530　　　　　　IT
GIORNALE DI FISICA. QUADERNI. 1976. irreg. (Societa Italiana di Fisica) Editrice Compositori s.r.l., Viale 12 Giugno 1, Bologna 40124, Italy.

530 378　　　　US　ISSN 0147-1821
GRADUATE PROGRAMS: PHYSICS, ASTRONOMY, AND RELATED FIELDS. 1980. a. $12.50. American Institute of Physics, 335 E. 45th St., New York, NY 10017. Ed. Dion W. J. Shea.

535 540　　　　US　ISSN 0072-8403
GUIDE TO FLUORESCENCE LITERATURE. 1967. irreg., 1974, vol. 3. price varies. Plenum Publishing Corp., I.F.I.--Plenum Data Co., 233 Spring St., New York, NY 10013. Ed. R. A. Passwater.

530　　　　　　GE　ISSN 0073-2850
HOCHSCHULBUECHER FUER PHYSIK. 1953. irreg. price varies. VEB Deutscher Verlag der Wissenschaften, Postfach 1216, 108 Berlin, E. Germany (D.D.R.) Eds. Robert Rompe, Ernst Schmutzer.

530　　　　　　NE
LES HOUCHES SUMMER SCHOOL PROCEEDINGS. (Text in English and French) 1951. irreg., vol. 31,1979. price varies. (FR) North-Holland Publishing Co., Box 211, 1000 AE Amsterdam, Netherlands.
　　Formerly: Ecole d'Ete de Physique Theorique. Les Houches.

530　　　　　　HU　ISSN 0133-5502
HUNGARIAN ACADEMY OF SCIENCES. CENTRAL RESEARCH INSTITUTE FOR PHYSICS. YEARBOOK/MAGYAR TUDOMANYOS AKADEMIA.KOZPONTI FIZIKAI KUTATO INTEZET. EVKONYV. (Text in English) 1973. a. Magyar Tudomanyos Akademia, Kozponti Fizikai Kutato Intezet, Box 49, 1525 Budapest, Hungary. Ed. T. Dolinszky.

510.78　　　　　US　ISSN 0085-2082
I B M RESEARCH SYMPOSIA SERIES. 1971. irreg. price varies. Plenum Press, 233 Spring St., New York, NY 10013.

539.7　　　　　NE
I K O NEWSLETTER. (Text in English) irreg. (National Institute for Nuclear Physics and High Energy Physics. Section K - Institute for Physics Research) Colorado School of Mines, Box 4395, 1009 AJ Amsterdam, Netherlands. illus.

530　　　　　　UK　ISSN 0305-2346
INSTITUTE OF PHYSICS, LONDON. CONFERENCE SERIES. PROCEEDINGS. 1967. irreg., no. 59, 1981. price varies. Institute of Physics, Techno House, Redcliffe Way, Bristol BS1 6NX, England (U.S. Address: American Institute of Physics, Dept. N/M, 335 E. 45th St., New York, NY 10017)

530　　　　　　RM
INSTITUTUL PEDAGOGIC ORADEA. LUCRARI STIINTIFICE: SERIA FIZICA. (Continues in part its Lucrari Stiintifice: Seria Matematica, Fizica, Chimie (1971-72), its Lucrari Stiintifice: Seria A and Seria B (1969-1970), and its Lucrari Stiintifice (1967-68)) (Text in Rumanian, occasionally in English or French; summaries in Rumanian, French or German) 1967. a. Institutul Pedagogic Oradea, Calea Armatei Rosii Nr. 5, Oradea, Romania.

530　　　　　　NE
INSTITUUT VOOR KERNPHYSISCH ONDERZOEK. ANNUAL REPORT. a. Instituut voor Kernphysisch Onderzoek - Institute for Nuclear Physics Research, Ooster Ringdijk 18, Postbus 4395, 1009 AJ Amsterdam, Netherlands.

530　　　　　　UN　ISSN 0304-7091
INTERNATIONAL CENTRE FOR THEORETICAL PHYSICS. ANNUAL REPORT. 1964. a. free. International Atomic Energy Agency, International Centre for Theoretical Physics, Piazza Oberdan 6, Trieste 34100, Italy.
　　Formerly (until 1965): International Centre for Theoretical Physics. Report (ISSN 0538-5415)

530　　　　　　CN
INTERNATIONAL CONFERENCE ON FINITE ELEMENTS IN FLOW PROBLEMS. PROCEEDINGS. 1980. irreg. International Conference on Finite Elements in Flow Problems, Banff, Alta., Canada.

537.532　　　　UK　ISSN 0074-3143
INTERNATIONAL CONFERENCE ON PHENOMENA IN IONIZED GASES. PROCEEDINGS. (Title Varies: International Conference on Ionization Phenomena in Gases. Proceedings) (Text in English, French, German) 1953. biennial; 1971, 10th, London. £24. (International Union of Pure and Applied Physics) Donald Parsons & Co. Ltd., 6 Brewer St., Oxford, England.
Proceedings published in host country

538　　　　US　ISSN 0074-6843
INTERNATIONAL MAGNETICS CONFERENCE. DIGEST. a. $12. Institute of Electrical and Electronics Engineers Inc, 445 Hoes Lane, Piscataway, NJ 08854.

INTERNATIONAL MONOGRAPHS ON ADVANCED MATHEMATICS AND PHYSICS. see *MATHEMATICS*

530　　　　US　ISSN 0074-784X
INTERNATIONAL SCHOOL OF PHYSICS "ENRICO FERMI." PROCEEDINGS. 1959. irreg. price varies. (Societa Italiana di Fisica, IT) Academic Press, Inc., 111 Fifth Ave., New York, NY 10003.

530 531　　　US　ISSN 0539-0133
INTERNATIONAL SERIES IN SOLID STATE PHYSICS. 1963. irreg., 1970, vol. 7. price varies. Pergamon Press, Inc., Maxwell House, Fairview Park, Elmsford, NY 10523. index.
Formerly: International Series of Monographs on Solid State Physics.

530　　　　US
INTERNATIONAL SERIES OF MONOGRAPHS ON PHYSICS. irreg. price varies. Oxford University Press, 200 Madison Ave., New York, NY 10016 (And Ely House, 37 Dover St., London W1X 4AH England) Eds. W. Marshall, D. H. Wilkinson.

537　　　　US　ISSN 0074-8129
INTERNATIONAL SERIES ON ELECTRONICS AND INSTRUMENTATION. 1953. irreg., vol. 24, 1964. price varies. Pergamon Press, Inc., Maxwell House, Fairview Park, Elmsford, NY 10523. index.
Formerly: International Series of Monographs on Electronics and Instrumentation.

530 520　　US　ISSN 0074-9931
INTERSCIENCE MONOGRAPHS AND TEXTS IN PHYSICS AND ASTRONOMY. 1957. irreg., vol. 29, 1978. price varies. (Wiley-Interscience) John Wiley & Sons, Inc., 605 Third Ave., New York, NY 10016. Ed. R. E. Marshak.

530 520　　US　ISSN 0074-9958
INTERSCIENCE TRACTS ON PHYSICS AND ASTRONOMY. 1954. irreg., 1972, vol. 29. John Wiley & Sons, Inc., 605 Third Ave., New York, NY 10016. Ed. R. E. Marshak. index.

IOWA STATE UNIVERSITY. IOWA AGRICULTURE AND HOME ECONOMICS EXPERIMENT STATION. RESEARCH BULLETIN SERIES. see *AGRICULTURE*

530　　　　IS
ISRAEL PHYSICAL SOCIETY. ANNALS; conference proceedings. (Text in English) 1977. irreg., Haifa, 1976. price varies. Israel Physical Society, c/o Department of Physics, Hebrew University, Jerusalem, Israel (U.S. Distributor: American Institute of Physics, Marketing Services, 335 E. 45 St., New York, N Y 10017)

530　　　　FI　ISSN 0075-465X
JYVASKYLAN YLIOPISTO. DEPARTMENT OF PHYSICS. RESEARCH REPORT. 1969. irreg., no. 6, 1977 (5-6/yr.) exchange basis. Jyvaskylan Yliopisto, Department of Physics - University of Jyvaskyla, Nisulankatu 78, SF-40720 Jyraskyla 72, Finland. circ. 100. (processed)

KONGELIGE DANSKE VIDENSKABERNES SELSKAB. MATEMATISK-FYSISKE MEDDELELSER. see *MATHEMATICS*

530　　　　JA
KUMAMOTO UNIVERSITY. DEPARTMENT OF PHYSICS. PHYSICS REPORTS. 1973. a. free. Kumamoto University, Department of Physics - Kumamoto Daigaku Rigakubu Butsurikyoshitsu, Faculty of Science, 2-39-1 Kurokami, Kumamoto 860, Japan. circ. 400.

530　　　　JA　ISSN 0085-2627
KYUSHU UNIVERSITY. FACULTY OF SCIENCE. MEMOIRS SERIES B: PHYSICS/KYUSHU DAIGAKU RIGAKUBU KIYO, B, BUTSURIGAKU. (Text in English) 1951. a. exchange basis. Kyushu University, Faculty of Science, Department of Physics - Kyushu Daigaku Rigakubu, 6-10-1 Hakozaki, Higashi-ku, Fukuoka 812, Japan. circ. 600.

530 548　　US　ISSN 0075-787X
LANDOLT-BOERNSTEIN, ZAHLENWERTE UND FUNKTIONEN AUS NATURWISSENSCHAFTEN UND TECHNIK. NEUE SERIE. GROUP 3: CRYSTAL PHYSICS. 1966. irreg., vol. 16, 1981. price varies. Springer-Verlag, 175 Fifth Ave., New York, NY 10010 (also Berlin, Heidelberg, Vienna) (reprint service avail. from ISI)

539　　　　US　ISSN 0091-9489
LAWRENCE BERKELEY LABORATORY. RESEARCH HIGHLIGHTS. 1967. a. free. University of California, Berkeley, Lawrence Berkeley Laboratory, Public Information Department, Berkeley, CA 94720. circ. 12,500. (some back issues available)

530　　　　US　ISSN 0075-8450
LECTURE NOTES IN PHYSICS. 1969. irreg., vol. 137, 1981. price varies. Springer-Verlag, 175 Fifth Ave., New York, NY 10010 (also Berlin, Heidelberg, Vienna) (reprint service avail. from ISI)

530　　　　US
MCGRAW-HILL ADVANCED PHYSICS MONOGRAPH SERIES. irreg. price varies. McGraw-Hill Book Co., 8171 Redwood Highway, Novato, CA 94947.

MASS SPECTROMETRY. see *CHEMISTRY*

MATEMATICHESKAYA FIZIKA I FUNKTSIONALNYI ANALIZ. see *MATHEMATICS*

530　　　　NE
MATERIALS PROCESSING: THEORY AND PRACTICES. 1980. irreg. price varies. North-Holland Publishing Co., Box 211, 1000 AE Amsterdam, Netherlands.

MATHEMATICAL PHYSICS AND APPLIED MATHEMATICS. see *MATHEMATICS*

MEDICAL PHYSICS SERIES. see *MEDICAL SCIENCES*

METHODEN UND VERFAHREN DER MATHEMATISCHEN PHYSIK. see *MATHEMATICS*

530　　　　US　ISSN 0076-6860
METHODS IN COMPUTATIONAL PHYSICS: ADVANCES IN RESEARCH AND APPLICATIONS. 1963. irreg., vol. 17, 1972. price varies. Academic Press, Inc, 111 Fifth Ave., New York, NY 10003. Eds. B. Adler, S. Fernbach, M. Rotenberg. index. (also avail. in microfiche)
Indexed: Appl. Mech. Rev.

530　　　　US　ISSN 0076-695X
METHODS OF EXPERIMENTAL PHYSICS. 1956. irreg., vol. 14, 1979. Academic Press, Inc, 111 Fifth Ave., New York, NY 10003. Ed. L. Marton.

530　　　　US
MIDLAND MACROMOLECULAR MONOGRAPHS. vol. 3, 1977. irreg., vol. 4 in prep. price varies. Gordon and Breach Science Publishers, One Park Ave., New York, NY 10016. Ed. Hans-Georg Elias.

530　　　　GE
MONOGRAPHIEN ZUR TERRESTRISCHEN, SOLAREN UND KOSMISCHEN PHYSIK. 1973. irreg. price varies. Akademische Verlagsgesellschaft Geest und Portig K.G., Sternwartenstr. 8, 701 Leipzig, E. Germany (D.D.R.) bibl. charts.

MONOGRAPHS IN PHYSICAL MEASUREMENT. see *ENGINEERING*

530 540　　US
MONOGRAPHS ON THE PHYSICS AND CHEMISTRY OF MATERIALS. irreg. price varies. Oxford University Press, 200 Madison Ave., New York, NY 10016 (And Ely House, 37 Dover St., London W1X 4AH, England) Ed. Willis Jackson.

530 541　　FR　ISSN 0078-9771
MUSEUM NATIONAL D'HISTOIRE NATURELLE, PARIS. MEMOIRES. NOUVELLE SERIE. SERIE D. SCIENCES PHYSICO-CHIMIQUES. 1950. irreg. price varies. Museum National d'Histoire Naturelle, 38, rue Geoffroy-Saint-Hilaire, Paris 5, France.

530.44　　　JA　ISSN 0547-1567
NAGOYA UNIVERSITY. INSTITUTE OF PLASMA PHYSICS. ANNUAL REVIEW/NAGOYA DAIGAKU PURAZUMA KENKYUSHO NENPO. (Text in English) 1960/61. a. exchange basis. Nagoya University, Institute of Plasma Physics - Nagoya Daigaku Purazuma Kenkyusho, Furo-cho, Chikusa-ku, Nagoya-shi 464, Japan.
Plasma physics

530.44　　　JA
NAGOYA UNIVERSITY. INSTITUTE OF PLASMA PHYSICS. TECHNICAL REPORTS. (Text in English) 1969. irreg. exchange basis. Nagoya University, Institute of Plasma Physics - Nagoya Daigaku Purazuma Kenkyusho, Furo-cho, Chikusa-ku, Nagoya-shi 464, Japan.
Plasma physics

530.07　　　NE
NEDERLANDSE CENTRALE ORGANISATIE VOOR TOEGEPAST-NATUURWETENSCHAPPELIJK ONDERZOEK. TECHNISCH-PHYSISCHE DIENST. ANNUAL REPORT. (Text in English) a. Nederlandse Centrale Organisatie voor Toegepast-Natuurwetenschappelijk Onderzoek, Technisch-Physische Dienst, Stieltjesweg 1, Delft, Netherlands.

530　　　　UN　ISSN 0077-8907
NEW TRENDS IN PHYSICS TEACHING. (Text in English and French) 1968. irreg. price varies. Unesco, 7-9 Place de Fontenoy, 75700 Paris, France (Dist. in U.S. by: Unipub, 345 Park Ave. S., New York, NY 10010)

539　　　　JA
NIIGATA AIRGLOW OBSERVATORY. BULLETIN. (Text in English) 1972. a. on exchange basis. (Niigata Airglow Observatory) Niigata University, Faculty of Science, 8050 Igarashi Nino-cho, Niigata-shi 950-21, Japan.

530　　　　JA
NIIGATA UNIVERSITY. FACULTY OF SCIENCE. SCIENCE REPORTS. SERIES B: PHYSICS. (Text in European languages) 1964. irreg. exchange basis. Niigata University, Faculty of Science - Niigata Daigaku Rigakubu, 8050 Igarashi Nino-cho, Niigata-shi 950-21, Japan.

530　　　　NE
NOBEL PRIZE LECTURES - PHYSICS. (Text in English) irreg., ca. every 3 yrs. price varies. Elsevier Scientific Publishing Co., P.O. Box 211, 1000 AE Amsterdam, Netherlands.

530.4　　　US　ISSN 0078-0995
NON-METALLIC SOLIDS; a series of monographs. 1964. irreg. price varies. Academic Press Inc., 111 Fifth Ave., New York, NY 10003. Ed. H. Rawson.

548　　　　NE
NORTH-HOLLAND SERIES IN CRYSTAL GROWTH. irreg., vol. 2, 1979. North-Holland Publishing Co., Box 211, 1000 AE Amsterdam, Netherlands.

530　　　　AT　ISSN 0085-4409
NUCLEUS. 1954. a. free. Science Foundation for Physics, Sydney, N.S.W. 2006, Australia. (Co-sponsor: University of Sydney, School of Physics) Ed. Prof. H. Messel. circ. 1,000.

530　　　　US　ISSN 0078-6322
ORGANIZATION OF AMERICAN STATES. DEPARTMENT OF SCIENTIFIC AFFAIRS. SERIE DE FISICA: MONOGRAFIAS. (Subseries of Coleccion de Monografias Cientificas) (Text in Spanish) 1965. irreg., no. 13, 1979. price varies. Organization of American States, Department of Publications, Washington, DC 20006. circ. 3,000.

530 US ISSN 0472-3325
OXFORD LIBRARY OF THE PHYSICAL
SCIENCES. 1957. irreg. price varies. Oxford
University Press, 200 Madison Ave., New York,
NY 10016 (And Ely House, 37 Dover St., London
W1X 4AH, England) Ed.Bd.

530 US
OXFORD PHYSICS SERIES. 1973. irreg., vol. 10,
1975. price varies. Oxford University Press, 200
Madison Ave., New York, NY 10016 (And Ely
House, 37 Dover St., London W1X 4AH, England)
Ed.Bd.

530 US
OXFORD STUDIES IN PHYSICS. irreg. price varies.
Oxford University Press, 200 Madison Ave., New
York, NY 10016 (And Ely House, 37 Dover St.,
London W1X 4AH, England) Ed.Bd.

538.3 UR
PARAMAGNITNYI REZONANS. irreg. 0.58 Rub.
single issue. Kazanskii Universitet, Ul. Lenina, 4/5,
Kazan, U.S.S.R. illus.

PEDAGOGICKA FAKULTA V OSTRAVE.
MATEMATIKA, FYZIKA. see *MATHEMATICS*

510 530 NO ISSN 0078-6780
PHYSICA MATHEMATICA UNIVERSITATIS
OSLOENSIS. (Text in English: occasionally in
German) 1959. irreg. Universitetet i Oslo, Institutt
for Teoretisk Fysikk, Blindern, Oslo 3, Norway.

530 NE
PHYSICAL COMMUNICATIONS. 1973. irreg. on
exchange basis. Technische Hogeschool Twente,
Department of Physics - Twente Technological
University, P.O. 217, Enschede, Netherlands.

530.07 II
PHYSICAL RESEARCH LABORATORY,
AHMEDABAD: ANNUAL REPORT. (Text in
English) 1954. a. ‡ Physical Research Laboratory,
Ahmedabad-9, India. illus. circ. 250.

530 US ISSN 0092-8437
PHYSICS. a. $1. American Institute of Physics, 335
East 45 St., New York, NY 10017. Ed. Phil Shewe.
(back issues avail.)

530 CS
PHYSICS AND APPLICATIONS. (Text in English)
a. price varies. (Slovenska Akademia Vied) Veda,
Publishing House of the Slovak Academy of
Sciences, Klemensova 19, 895 30 Bratislava,
Czechoslovakia. Ed. Mikulas Blazek.
Formerly: High Energy Particle Physics.

530 574 US
PHYSICS AND BIOLOGY. irreg. University
Publications, Box 47, Blackburg, VA 24060.

PHYSICS AND CHEMISTRY IN SPACE. see
CHEMISTRY

530.41 547.1 US ISSN 0079-1954
PHYSICS AND CHEMISTRY OF THE ORGANIC
SOLID STATE. 1963. irreg., latest, 1979. price
varies. John Wiley & Sons, Inc., 605 Third Ave,
New York, NY 10016. Eds. D. Fox, M. M. Labes,
A. Weissberger.

530 US
PHYSICS AND CONTEMPORARY NEEDS. a.
Plenum Publishing Corp., 233 Spring St., New
York, NY 10013. Ed. R. Azuddin.

PHYSICS MANPOWER - EDUCATION AND
EMPLOYMENT STATISTICS. see
EDUCATION — Higher Education

530 US ISSN 0079-1970
PHYSICS OF THIN FILMS; ADVANCES IN
RESEARCH AND DEVELOPMENT. 1963. irreg.,
vol. 10, 1978. price varies. Academic Press, Inc, 111
Fifth Ave., New York, NY 10003. Eds. George
Haas, R. E. Thun. index. (also avail. in microfiche)

530 GE ISSN 0079-1997
PHYSIKALISCH-CHEMISCHE TRENN- UND
MESSMETHODEN. 1960. irreg. price varies. VEB
Deutscher Verlag der Wissenschaften, Postfach
1216, 108 Berlin, E. Germany (D.D.R.) Ed. Erich
Krell.

530 621 UK ISSN 0079-208X
PION APPLIED PHYSICS SERIES. 1970. irreg.
price varies. Pion Ltd., 207 Brondesbury Park,
London NW2 5JN, England (Dist. by Academic
Press Inc.(London) Ltd., 24-28 Oval Rd., London
NW1 7DX, England) Ed. H.J. Goldsmid.

530.44 US
PLASMA PHYSICS. a. price varies. Gordon and
Breach Science Publishers, One Park Ave., New
York, NY 10016. Ed. A. Kolb.
Plasma physics

530 PL ISSN 0072-0364
POLITECHNIKA GDANSKA. ZESZYTY
NAUKOWE. FIZYKA. 1967. irreg. price varies.
Politechnika Gdanska, Majakowskiego 11/12, 81-
952 Gdansk 6, Poland (Dist. by: Osrodek
Rozpowszechniania Wydawnictw Naukowych Pan,
Palac Kultury i Nauki, 00-901 Warsaw, Poland)

530 PL
POLITECHNIKA LODZKA. ZESZYTY
NAUKOWE. FIZYKA. (Text in Polish; summaries
in English and Russian) 1973. irreg. price varies.
Politechnika Lodzka, Ul. Zwirki 36, 90-924 Lodz,
Poland (Dist. by: Ars Polona-Ruch, Krakowskie
Przedmiescie 7, Warsaw, Poland) Ed. Jan
Karniewicz. circ. 383. Indexed: Chem.Abstr.

530 PL ISSN 0079-4511
POLITECHNIKA POZNANSKA. ZESZYTY
NAUKOWE. FIZYKA. (Text in Polish; summaries
in English and Russian) 1964. irreg. price varies.
Politechnika Poznanska, Pl. Curie-Sklodowskiej 5,
Poznan, Poland. circ. 150.

POLITECHNIKA SLASKA. ZESZYTY NAUKOWE.
MATEMATYKA-FIZYKA. see *MATHEMATICS*

530 PL
POLITECHNIKA WARSZAWSKA. INSTYTUT
FIZYKI. PRACE. (Text in English, Polish and
Russian) irreg., 1975, no. 13. price varies.
Politechnika Warszawska, Instytut Fizyki, Plac
Jednosci Robotniczej 1, 00-661 Warsaw, Poland.
Ed. Wlodzimierz Scislowski.

621 530 PL ISSN 0370-0828
POLITECHNIKA WROCLAWSKA. INSTYTUT
FIZYKI. PRACE NAUKOWE. MONOGRAFIE.
(Text in Polish; summaries in English and Russian)
1972. irreg., no. 9, 1979. price varies. Politechnika
Wroclawska, Wybrzeze Wyspianskiego 27, 50-370
Wroclaw, Poland (Dist. by: Ars Polona-Ruch,
Krakowskie Przedmiescie 7, Warsaw, Poland) Ed.
Marian Kloza.

621 PL ISSN 0324-9697
POLITECHNIKA WROCLAWSKA. INSTYTUT
FIZYKI. PRACE NAUKOWE. STUDIA I
MATERIALY. (Text in Polish; summaries in
English and Russian) 1969. irreg., 1976, no. 7. price
varies. Politechnika Wroclawska, Wybrzeze
Wyspianskiego 27, 50-370 Wroclaw, Poland (Dist.
by: Ars Polona-Ruch, Krakowskie Przedmiescie 7,
Warsaw, Poland) Ed. Marian Kloza.

POLITECHNIKA WROCLAWSKA. INSTYTUT
MATEMATYKI. PRACE NAUKOWE. STUDIA I
MATERIALY. see *MATHEMATICS*

530 US
POLYMER PHYSICS. vol. 2, 1977. irreg. Academic
Press, Inc., 111 Fifth Ave., New York, NY 10003
(And: Berkeley Square House, London W.1,
England) Ed. R. S. Stein.

530 US ISSN 0079-5216
PRINCETON SERIES IN PHYSICS. 1971. irreg.
price varies. Princeton University Press, Princeton,
NJ 08540. Eds. A.S. Wightman, J.J. Hopfield.
(reprint service avail. from UMI)

530 551.5 UR
PROBLEMY FIZIKI ATMOSFERY. vol. 15, 1978.
irreg. 1.50 Rub. per no. Izdatel'stvo Leningradskii
Universitet, Universitetskaya Nab. 7/9, Leningrad
B-164, U.S.S.R. circ. 1,000.

PROGRESS IN NUCLEAR ENERGY(NEW
SERIES) see *CHEMISTRY*

530 US ISSN 0079-6816
PROGRESS IN SURFACE SCIENCE. 1971. 4/yr.
$80. Pergamon Press, Inc., Journals Division,
Maxwell House, Fairview Park, Elmsford, NY
10523 (And Headington Hill Hall, Oxford OX3
0BW, England) Ed. S. G. Davison. (also avail. in
microform from MIM,UMI) Indexed: Chem.Abstr.

530 621 US ISSN 0079-8193
PURE AND APPLIED PHYSICS; a series of
monographs and textbooks. irreg., vol. 41, 1975.
price varies. Academic Press Inc., 111 Fifth Ave.,
New York, NY 10003. Eds. H. S. W. Massey, Keith
A. Brueckner.

536 US ISSN 0481-1275
QUANTUM PHYSICS AND ITS APPLICATIONS.
1964. a. price varies. Gordon and Breach Science
Publishers, One Park Ave., New York, NY 10016.
Ed. R. Smoluchowski.

530 378 UK ISSN 0308-9290
RESEARCH FIELDS IN PHYSICS AT UNITED
KINGDOM UNIVERSITIES AND
POLYTECHNICS. vol. 5, 1978. a. £11. (Institute of
Physics) Physics Trust Publications, Blackhorse
Road, Letchworth, Herts SG6 1HN, England (Dist.
in U.S. by: American Institute of Physics, 335 E.
45th St., New York, NY 10017)

RESEARCH IN SURFACE FORCES. see
CHEMISTRY — Physical Chemistry

530 US
REVIEWS OF MODERN PHYSICS
MONOGRAPHS. irreg. price varies. Academic
Press, Inc., 111 Fifth Ave., New York, NY 10003.

530.44 US ISSN 0080-2050
REVIEWS OF PLASMA PHYSICS. (English
translation of original Russian text) 1965. irreg.,
1974, vol. 6. price varies. Consultants Bureau, 233
Spring St., New York, NY 10013. Ed. M. A.
Leontovich.

530.15 AG ISSN 0080-2360
REVISTA DE MATEMATICA Y FISICA
TEORICA. SERIE A. (Text in Spanish, French,
German, Italian and English; summaries in English)
1940. a. $15. ‡ Universidad Nacional de Tucuman,
Facultad de Ciencias Exactas y Tecnologia, Avda.
Independencia 1700, Tucuman, Argentina. Eds.
Felix E. Herrera, Arturo Battig. index. circ. 1,000.
Indexed: Math.R. Zent.Math.

S T P NOTES. (Inter-Union Commission of Solar
Terrestrial Physics) see *ASTRONOMY*

SAITAMA UNIVERSITY. SCIENCE REPORTS.
SERIES A: MATHEMATICS. see
MATHEMATICS

SCIENZE DELLA MATERIA. see *CHEMISTRY*

530 UK ISSN 0080-8253
SCOTTISH UNIVERSITIES' SUMMER SCHOOL
IN PHYSICS. PROCEEDINGS. 1961. a. Academic
Press Inc. (London) Ltd., 24-28 Oval Rd., London
NW1 7DX, England (and 111 Fifth Ave., New
York, N.Y. 10003)

530 NE ISSN 0080-8636
SELECTED TOPICS IN SOLID STATE PHYSICS.
(Text in English) 1962. irreg., vol. 15, 1977. price
varies. North-Holland Publishing Co., P.O. Box 211,
1000 AE Amsterdam, Netherlands. Ed. E. P.
Wohlfarth.

530 RM ISSN 0080-8806
SEMINAR DE FIZICA TEORETICA. 1969. irreg.
(Institutul de Fizica, Bucharest) Editura Academiei
Republicii Socialiste Romania, Calea Victoriei 125,
Bucharest, Romania (Subscr. to: ILEXIM, Str. 13
Decembrie Nr. 3, P.O. Box 136-137, Bucharest,
Romania) Ed. V. Novacu.

SERIE DI MATEMATICA E FISICA. see
MATHEMATICS

SERIE DI MATEMATICA E FISICA. PROBLEMI
RISOLTI. see *MATHEMATICS*

530 510 JA
SHINSHU UNIVERSITY. FACULTY OF TEXTILE SCIENCE AND TECHNOLOGY. JOURNAL. SERIES F: PHYSICS AND MATHEMATICS. (Text in European languages; summaries in English) 1962. irreg. exchange basis. Shinshu University, Faculty of Textile Science and Technology - Shinshu Daigaku Sen'i Gakubu, 3-15-1 Tokida, Ueda, Nagano 386, Japan.

SMITHSONIAN CONTRIBUTIONS TO ASTROPHYSICS. see *ASTRONOMY*

SMITHSONIAN INSTITUTION. ASTROPHYSICAL OBSERVATORY. S A O SPECIAL REPORT. see *ASTRONOMY*

530 IT ISSN 0037-8801
SOCIETA ITALIANA DI FISICA. BOLLETTINO. 1958. irreg. $13 to non-members. Editrice Compositori s.r.l., Viale XII Guigno 1, Bologna, Italy.

530 FR ISSN 0081-1076
SOCIETE FRANCAISE DE PHYSIQUE. ANNUAIRE. 1913. triennial. 35 F. Societe Francaise de Physique, 33 rue Croulebarbe, 75013 Paris, France.

533.5 FR
SOCIETE FRANCAISE DU VIDE. COMPTES RENDUS DES TRAVAUX DES CONGRES ET COLLOQUES. irreg. price varies. Societe Francaise du Vide, 19 rue du Renard, 75004 Paris, France. *Vacuum techniques*

SOLAR TERRESTRIAL ENVIRONMENTAL RESEARCH IN JAPAN. see *EARTH SCIENCES — Geophysics*

530 US ISSN 0081-1947
SOLID STATE PHYSICS; ADVANCES IN RESEARCH AND APPLICATIONS. 1955. irreg., vol. 33, 1978. price varies. Academic Press, Inc, 111 Fifth Ave., New York, NY 10003. Eds. Frederick Seitz, David Turnbull, Henry Ehrenreich. index. cum.index: subject, vol. 1-10 (1955-1960) in vol. 11 (1960)

530 US ISSN 0081-1955
SOLID STATE PHYSICS; ADVANCES IN RESEARCH AND APPLICATIONS. SUPPLEMENT. 1958. irreg., suppl. 15, 1979. price varies. Academic Press, Inc, 111 Fifth Ave., New York, NY 10003. Ed.Bd.

537 US ISSN 0081-1971
SOLID STATE SURFACE SCIENCE. 1969. irreg., vol. 3, 1973. price varies. Marcel Dekker, Inc., 270 Madison Ave., New York, NY 10016. Ed. M. Green.

SOURCES IN THE HISTORY OF MATHEMATICS AND PHYSICAL SCIENCES. see *MATHEMATICS*

530 540 US
SPRINGER SERIES IN CHEMICAL PHYSICS. 1978. irreg., vol. 15, 1981. price varies. Springer-Verlag, 175 Fifth Ave., New York, NY 10010 (Also Berlin, Heidelberg, Vienna) Ed.Bd. (reprint service avail. from ISI)

530 US
SPRINGER SERIES IN COMPUTATIONAL PHYSICS. 1977. irreg. price varies. Springer-Verlag, 175 Fifth Ave., New York, NY 10010 (Also Berlin, Heidelberg, Vienna) Ed. H. Cabannes. (reprint service avail. from ISI)

SPRINGER SERIES IN ELECTROPHYSICS. see *ELECTRICITY AND ELECTRICAL ENGINEERING*

539 US ISSN 0081-3869
SPRINGER TRACTS IN MODERN PHYSICS. (Text in English) 1964. irreg., vol. 90, 1981. price varies. Springer-Verlag, 175 Fifth Ave, New York, NY 10010 (also Berlin, Heidelberg, Vienna) (reprint service avail. from ISI)
Continues: Ergebnisse der Exacten Naturwissenschaften.

STAATLICHER MATHEMATISCH-PHYSIKALISCHER SALON, DRESDEN. VEROEFFENTLICHUNGEN. see *MATHEMATICS*

531 UK ISSN 0305-9960
STATISTICAL MECHANICS. 1973. biennial. Chemical Society, Burlington House, London W1V OBN, England (Subscr to: Blackhorse Road, Letchworth, Herts SG6 1HN, Eng) Ed. Prof. K. Singer. charts. illus. index. Indexed: Chem.Abstr.

530 RM
STUDIA UNIVERSITATIS "BABES-BOLYAI". PHYSICA. (Text in Romanian; summaries in English, French, German, Russian) 1959. s-a. exchange basis. Universitatea "Babes-Bolyai", Biblioteca Centrala Universitara, Str. Clinicilor Nr. 2, Cluj-Napoca, Romania.

530 NE ISSN 0081-8542
STUDIES IN STATISTICAL MECHANICS. 1962. irreg., vol. 7, 1979. price varies. North-Holland Publishing Co., Box 211, 1000 AE Amsterdam, Netherlands. Eds. E. W. Montroll, J. L. Lebowitz.

STUDIES IN THE HISTORY OF MATHEMATICS AND PHYSICAL SCIENCES. see *MATHEMATICS*

SURVEY OF THE EMERGING SOLAR ENERGY INDUSTRY. see *ENERGY*

SYMPOSIA ON THEORETICAL PHYSICS AND MATHEMATICS. see *MATHEMATICS*

530 NE
TECHNISCH FYSISCHE DIENST TNO-TH. JAARVERSLAG. (Text in Dutch; summaries in English) a. Technisch Fysische Dienst TNO-TH - Institute of Applied Physics TNO-TH, Stieltjesweg 1, Box 155, Delft, Netherlands. illus.

530 US ISSN 0082-2590
TECHNISCHE PHYSIK IN EINZELDARSTELLUNGEN. 1948. irreg., vol. 18, 1973. price varies. Springer-Verlag, 175 Fifth Ave., New York, NY 10010 (also Berlin, Heidelberg, Vienna) (reprint service avail. from ISI)

530 US
TEXTS AND MONOGRAPHS IN PHYSICS. 1976. irreg. Springer Verlag, 175 Fifth Ave., New York, NY 10010 (And Berlin, Heidelberg, Vienna) Ed. W. Beiglboeck. (reprint service avail. from ISI)

TOKYO UNIVERSITY OF EDUCATION. FACULTY OF SCIENCE. SCIENCE REPORTS. SECTION A: MATHEMATICS AND PHYSICS/ TOKYO KYOKAI DAIGAKU RIGAKUBU KIYO A. see *MATHEMATICS*

530 621 US
TOPICS IN APPLIED PHYSICS. 1974. irreg., vol. 48, 1981. Springer-Verlag, 175 Fifth Ave., New York, NY 10010 (Also Berlin, Heidelberg, Vienna) (reprint service avail. from ISI)

TOPICS IN ASTROPHYSICS AND SPACE PHYSICS. see *AERONAUTICS AND SPACE FLIGHT*

530 US
TOPICS IN CURRENT PHYSICS. 1976. irreg., vol. 27, 1981. price varies. Springer-Verlag, 175 Fifth Ave., New York, NY 10010 (Also Berlin, Heidelberg, Vienna) (reprint service avail. from ISI)

530 IT ISSN 0533-0386
UNIVERSITA DEGLI STUDI DI FERRARA. ANNALI. SEZIONE 14. FISICA SPERIMENTALE E TEORICA. (Text in Italian & English) irreg. free or on exchange basis. Universita degli Studi di Ferrara, Via de Pisis 24, 44100 Ferrara, Italy.

UNIVERSITATEA DIN BRASOV. BULETINUL SERIA C. STIINTE ALE NATURII SI PEDAGOGIE. see *MATHEMATICS*

530 540 RM ISSN 0082-4453
UNIVERSITATEA DIN TIMISOARA. ANALELE. STIINTE FIZICO-CHIMICE. 1963. s-a. $10. Universitatea din Timisoara, Bd. Vasile Pirvan Nr. 4, Timisoara, Romania (Subscr. to: ILIXIM, Str. 13 Decembrie Nr. 3, P.O. Box 136-137, Bucharest, Romania)

530 FR ISSN 0069-4738
UNIVERSITE DE CLERMONT-FERRAND II. ANNALES SCIENTIFIQUES. SERIE PHYSIQUE. 1963. irreg. price varies. Universite de Clermont-Ferrand II, Unite d'Enseignement et de Recherche de Sciences Exactes et Naturelles, B.P. 45, 63170 Aubiere, France. circ. 250. (back issues avail.)

UNIVERSITY OF CALIFORNIA ENGINEERING AND PHYSICAL SCIENCES EXTENSION SERIES. see *ENGINEERING*

530 NE ISSN 0022-8141
UNIVERSITY OF LEIDEN. KAMERLINGH ONNES LABORATORY. COMMUNICATIONS. (Text in English; occasionally in French and German) 1885. 10-12/yr. price varies; fl.0.12 per page. Rijksuniversiteit te Leiden, Kamerlingh Onnes Laboratory, Nieuwsteeg 18, Leiden, Netherlands. charts. illus. circ. 400-500. Indexed: Chem.Abstr.

530 PP ISSN 0085-4735
UNIVERSITY OF PAPUA NEW GUINEA. DEPARTMENT OF PHYSICS. TECHNICAL PAPER. 1968. irreg. free. ‡ University of Papua New Guinea, Department of Physics, Box 4820, University P.O., Papua New Guinea. circ. 50-100.

530 JA ISSN 0082-4801
UNIVERSITY OF TOKYO. INSTITUTE FOR SOLID STATE PHYSICS. TECHNICAL REPORT. SERIES B. (Text in English) 1960. irreg. (approx. 1 no. per year), 1973, no. 15. University of Tokyo, Institute for Solid State Physics - Tokyo Daigaku Bussei Kenkyusho, 7-22-1 Roppongi, Minato-ku, Tokyo 106, Japan.

530 PL
UNIWERSYTET GDANSKI. WYDZIAL MATEMATYKI, FIZYKI, CHEMII. ZESZYTY NAUKOWE. FIZYKA. (Text in Polish; summaries in English) 1972. irreg. 15 Zl. Uniwersytet Gdanski, Ul. Czerwonej Armii 110, 81-824 Sopot, Poland. illus.

530 PL ISSN 0083-4335
UNIWERSYTET JAGIELLONSKI. ZESZYTY NAUKOWE. PRACE FIZYCZNE. (Text in English and Polish; summaries in English and Russian) 1963. irreg., 1972, vol. 10. price varies. Panstwowe Wydawnictwo Naukowe, Miodowa 10, Warsaw, Poland (Dist by Ars Polona-Ruch, Krakowskie Przedmiescie 7, Warsaw, Poland) Ed. Bronislaw Sredniawa. circ. 600.

530 PL
UNIWERSYTET SLASKI W KATOWICACH. PHYSICS PAPERS. (Subseries of its: Prace Naukowe) (Text in English) 1973. irreg. available on exchange. Uniwersytet Slaski w Katowicach, Ul. Bankowa 14, 40-007 Katowice, Poland.

VICTORIA, BRITISH COLUMBIA. DOMINION ASTROPHYSICAL OBSERVATORY. PUBLICATIONS. see *ASTRONOMY*

530 UR ISSN 0301-6919
VOPROSY FIZIKI TVERDOGO TELA. 1974. irreg. 2.30 Rub. Chelyabinskii Gosudarstvennyi Pedagogicheskii Institut, Chelyabinsk, U.S.S.R. illus.

WESTERN REGIONAL SOLAR ENERGY DIRECTORY. see *ENERGY*

WISSENSCHAFTLICHE FORSCHUNGSBERICHTE. REIHE 1. GRUNDLAGENFORSCHUNG UND GRUNDLEGENDE METHODIK. ABT. A. CHEMIE UND PHYSIK/CURRENT TOPICS IN SCIENCE. REIHE 1. BASIC RESEARCH. ABT. A. CHEMISTRY AND PHYSICS. see *CHEMISTRY*

WISSENSCHAFTLICHE TASCHENBUECHER. REIHE MATHEMATIK, PHYSIK. see *MATHEMATICS*

539.7 GE ISSN 0323-8776
Z F I-MITTEILUNGEN. 1974. irreg., no. 18, 1979. Akademie der Wissenschaften der DDR, Zentralinstitut fuer Isotopen- und Strahlenforschung, Permoserstr. 15, 705 Leipzig, E. Germany(D.D.R.) Ed. R. Schroeter. (also avail. in microfiche) Indexed: INIS Atomind.

530   PL   ISSN 0044-1597
ZAGADNIENIA DRGAN NIELINIOWYCH. 1960. irreg. price varies. (Polska Akademia Nauk, Instytut Podstawowych Problemow Techniki) Panstwowe Wydawnictwo Naukowe, Ul. Miodowa 10, Warsaw, Poland. abstr. bibl. charts. illus. index.
Nonlinear vibration problems

PHYSICS — Abstracting, Bibliographies, Statistics

520 523.01 016   US   ISSN 0067-0022
ASTRONOMY AND ASTROPHYSICS ABSTRACTS. 1969. irreg., vol. 29, 1981. price varies. Springer-Verlag, 175 Fifth Ave., New York, NY 10010 (also Berlin, Heidelberg, Vienna) (reprint service avail. from ISI)

539 016   CN   ISSN 0067-0405
ATOMIC ENERGY OF CANADA. LIST OF PUBLICATIONS. 1952. irreg. free. Atomic Energy of Canada Ltd., Technical Information Branch, S.D.D.O., Station 14, Chalk River, Ont. K0J 1J0, Canada.

539.7 016   AT
AUSTRALIA. ATOMIC ENERGY COMMISSION. RESEARCH ESTABLISHMENT. LIST OF REPORT PUBLICATIONS. irreg. Atomic Energy Commission, Research Establishment, Private Mail Bag, Sutherland N.S.W. 2232, Australia. illus.

530 016   BL   ISSN 0067-6640
BIBLIOGRAFIA BRASILEIRA DE FISICA. 1961. irreg. Cr.$200($10) Instituto Brasileiro de Informacao em Ciencia e Tecnologia, Rio de Janeiro, Brazil. bk. rev. circ. 300.
Supersedes in part: Bibliografia Brasileira de Matematica e Fisica.

539.7 016   UN
C I N D A; an index to the literature on microscopic neutron data. (Text in English; foreword in English, French, Russian & Spanish) 1965. a. price varies. International Atomic Energy Agency, Nuclear Data Section, Division of Publications, Wagramer Str. 5, Box 100, A-1400 Vienna, Austria (Dist. in U.S. by: Unipub, 345 Park Ave. S., New York, NY 10010) (Co-sponsors: U.S.A. National Neutron Cross-Section Center; U.S.S.R. Nuclear Data Centre; N.E.A. Neutron Data Compilation Centre) circ. 1,500.

539.7 011   US
CUMULATIVE BIBLIOGRAPHY OF LITERATURE EXAMINED BY THE RADIATION SHIELDING INFORMATION CENTER. 1965. irreg. Oak Ridge National Laboratory, Radiation Shielding Information Center, Box X, Oak Ridge, TN 37830. Ed. D. K. Trubey. (also avail. in microfiche; magnetic tape; back issues avail.)

532 016   GW   ISSN 0340-8388
DOKUMENTATION RHEOLOGIE/ DOCUMENTATION RHEOLOGY. (Text in English) 1954. a. $60. Bundesanstalt fuer Materialpruefung, Unter den Eichen 87, 1000 Berlin 45, W. Germany (B.R.D.) (Co-sponsor: Deutsche Rheologische Gesellschaft) Ed. Edith Rudolph. bibl. index. circ. 500. (back issues avail.)
Formerly: Deutsche Rheologische Gesellschaft. Berichte (ISSN 0012-0626)
Rheology

530 540 016   UK
EIGHT PEAK INDEX OF MASS SPECTRA. (In two editions: printed version & computer readable version) vol. 2, 1975. irreg. Chemical Society, Burlington House, London W1V 0BN, England. (also avail. in magnetic tape)

539.7 016   SZ   ISSN 0304-2871
EUROPEAN ORGANIZATION FOR NUCLEAR RESEARCH. LISTE DES PUBLICATIONS SCIENTIFIQUES/LIST OF SCIENTIFIC PUBLICATIONS. (Former name of body: Conseil Europeen pour la Recherche Nucleaire) 1955. a. free. European Organization for Nuclear Research, CH-1211 Geneva 23, Switzerland.
Former titles: European Organization for Nuclear Research. Repertoire des Communications Scientifiques. Index of Scientific Publications (ISSN 0423-7781); European Organization for Nuclear Research. Repertoire des Publications Scientifiques. Index of Scientific Publications.

016 621.48   UN   ISSN 0534-7319
I A E A LIBRARY FILM CATALOG. 1962. a. free.
‡ International Atomic Energy Agency, Kaertner Ring 11, Wagramer Str. 5, Box 100, A-1400 Vienna. index. circ. 2,500 (approx.)

539.7 016   IS
ISRAEL. ATOMIC ENERGY COMMISSION. TECHNICAL INFORMATION DEPARTMENT. LITERATURE SURVEYS. (Text in English) 1960. irreg. free. Atomic Energy Commission, Technical Information Department, Soreg Nuclear Research Centre, Yavne, Israel.

530 016   US   ISSN 0094-0003
PHYSICAL REVIEW INDEX. a. $12 to non-members. American Institute of Physics, 335 E. 45th St., New York, NY 10017. Ed. Bd. circ. 5,400.

530 016   US   ISSN 0080-0821
RELIABILITY PHYSICS SYMPOSIUM ABSTRACTS.* a. Institute of Electrical and Electronics Engineers, Inc., 445 Hoes Lane, Piscataway, NJ 08854.

530.41 016   US   ISSN 0081-1963
SOLID STATE PHYSICS LITERATURE GUIDES. 1970. irreg., vol. 7, 1975. price varies. Plenum Publishing Corp., I.F.I.--Plenum Data Co., 233 Spring St., New York, NY 10013.

311   DK
UNIVERSITY OF COPENHAGEN. INSTITUTE OF MATHEMATICAL STATISTICS. ANNUAL REPORT. (Text in English) a. Koebenhavns Universitet, Institut for Matematisk Statistik, 5 Universitetsparken, 2100 Copenhagen OE, Denmark.

ZIDIS. see *BUSINESS AND ECONOMICS — Abstracting, Bibliographies, Statistics*

PHYSICS — Heat

621.59 536.56   US   ISSN 0065-2482
ADVANCES IN CRYOGENIC ENGINEERING. Represents: Cryogenic Engineering Conference Proceedings. 1960. irreg. price varies. Plenum Press, 233 Spring St., New York, NY 10013. Ed. K.D. Timmerhaus.

536.2   US   ISSN 0065-2717
ADVANCES IN HEAT TRANSFER. (Supplements avail.) 1964. irreg., vol. 14, 1979. price varies. Academic Press, Inc., 111 Fifth Ave., New York, NY 10003. Eds. Thomas F. Irvine, Jr., James P. Harnett. index. (also avail. in microfiche)

536 621   US   ISSN 0066-1538
ANALYTICAL CALORIMETRY. Represents: American Chemical Society Symposium on Analytical Calorimetry. 1968. irreg. price varies. Plenum Press, 233 Spring St., New York, NY 10013. Eds. R. S. Porter, J. F. Johnson.

536.56
APPLICATIONS OF CRYOGENIC TECHNOLOGY. 1969. irreg., vol. 9, 1979. price varies. Scholium International, Inc., 130-30 31st Ave., Flushing, NY 11354.
Cryogenics

536   US
BIENNIAL SYMPOSIUM ON CRYOGENIC INSTRUMENTATION. PROCEEDINGS. 1976. biennial. Instrument Society of America, 400 Stanwix St., Pittsburgh, PA 15222.

COMITE INTERNATIONAL DES POIDS ET MESURES. COMITE CONSULTATIF DE THERMOMETRIE. RAPPORTS ET ANNEXES. see *METROLOGY AND STANDARDIZATION*

536 697   US
H M T: THE SCIENCE AND APPLICATION OF HEAT MASS TRANSFER; reports,reviews & computer programs. 1977. irreg. Pergamon Press, Inc., Maxwell House, Fairview Park, Elmsford, NY 10523 (And Headington Hill Hall, Oxford OX3 0BW, England) Ed. D.Brian Spalding.

536   JA   ISSN 0073-2931
HOKKAIDO UNIVERSITY. INSTITUTE OF LOW TEMPERATURE SCIENCE. SERIES A. PHYSICAL SCIENCE. (From No. 1-10 (1952-1956) Series A and B issued in one Vol.) (Text in English) 1952. irreg. exchange basis. Hokkaido University, Institute of Low Temperature Science, North 19, West 8, Kita-ku, Sapporo 060, Japan. Ed. Seiiti Kinosita. circ. 600.

536   PL
INTERNATIONAL CONFERENCE ON CALORIMETRY AND THERMODYNAMICS. PROCEEDINGS. 1969. irreg., 1st, Warsaw, 1969. $20. Polska Akademia Nauk, Instytut Chemii Fizycznej, Kasprzaka 44/52, 01-224 Warsaw, Poland. Ed. Prof. M. Smialawski.

536.56   US   ISSN 0538-7051
INTERNATIONAL CRYOGENICS MONOGRAPH SERIES. 1964. irreg. price varies. Plenum Press, 233 Spring St., New York, NY 10013. Eds. K. Timmerhaus, K. Mendelssohn.
Cryogenics

536.56 530.4   US
MONOGRAPHS IN LOW TEMPERATURE PHYSICS. 1972. irreg. price varies. Plenum Press, 233 Spring St., New York, NY 10013. Eds. John G. Daunt, K. Mendelssohn.
Cryogenics

536.56   NE   ISSN 0079-6417
PROGRESS IN LOW TEMPERATURE PHYSICS. 1955. irreg., vol. 7B, 1979. price varies. North-Holland Publishing Co., P.O. Box 211, 1000 AE Amsterdam, Netherlands. Ed. C. J. Gorter.
Cryogenics

536.56   UR   ISSN 0082-4089
SILUMINE FIZIKA/TEPLOFIZIKA. (Text in Russian; summaries in English and Lithuanian) 1968. irreg., no. 7, 1975. price varies. Akademiya Nauk Litovskoi S.S.R, Institut Fiziko-Tekhnicheskikh Problem Energetiki, Metalo 4, 233684 Kaunas, U. S. S. R. Ed. A. Zukauskas. circ. 2,000. Indexed: Ref.Zh.

536   US
TEMPERATURE: ITS MEASUREMENT AND CONTROL IN SCIENCE AND INDUSTRY. Variant title: American Institute of Physics. Symposium on Temperature. Proceedings. approx. every ten years. price varies. Instrument Society of America, 400 Stanwix St., Pittsburgh, PA 15222.

536   UR
TEPLOPROVODNOST' I DIFFUZIYA. 1969. irreg. 0.54 Rub. Politekniskais Instituts, Riga, Ul. Lenina, 1, Riga, U.S.S.R. illus.

532 016   UR
VOPROSY GIDRODINAMIKI I TEPLOOBMENA V KRIOGENNYKH SISTEMAKH. 1970. irreg. 0.85 Rub. Akademiya Nauk Ukrainskoi S.S.R., Fiziko- Tekhnicheskii Institut Nizkikh Temperatur, Pr. Lenina 47, Kharkov, U.S.S.R. ill.

PHYSICS — Mechanics

530 620.1   US   ISSN 0065-2156
ADVANCES IN APPLIED MECHANICS. (Supplements avail: Rarefied Gas Dynamics) 1948. irreg., vol. 19, 1979. price varies. Academic Press, Inc., 111 Fifth Ave., New York, NY 10003. Eds. Richard von Mises, Theodore von Karman. index. (also avail. in microfiche)

532   US   ISSN 0066-4189
ANNUAL REVIEW OF FLUID MECHANICS.
1969. a. $20. Annual Reviews Inc., 4139 El Camino Way, Palo Alto, CA 94306. Eds. Milton Van Dyke, J. V. Wehausen. bibl. index; cum.index. (back issues avail.; reprint service avail. from ISI) Indexed: Biol.Abstr. Chem.Abstr. Ocean.Abstr. Sci.Abstr. Int.Aerosp.Abstr. M.M.R.I. Nucl.Sci.Abstr. T.C.E.A.
Rheology

APPLIED MATHEMATICS AND MECHANICS; An international series of monographs. see *MATHEMATICS*

531   BU
BIOMEKHANIKA/BIOMECHANICS. (Text in Bulgarian and Russian; summaries in English and Russian) 1974. irreg. 2 lv. per no. (Bulgarska Akademiia na Naukite, Tsentralna Laboratoriia po Biomekhanika) Publishing House of the Bulgarian Academy of Sciences, Ul. Akad. G. Bonchev, 1113 Sofia, Bulgaria (Dist. by: Hemus, 6, Rouski Blvd., 1000 Sofia, Bulgaria) Ed. G. Brankov. bibl. illus. circ. 600.

531 510   UK
CAMBRIDGE MONOGRAPHS ON MECHANICS AND APPLIED MATHEMATICS. irreg. price varies. Cambridge University Press, Box 110, Cambridge CB2 3RL, England (And 32 E. 57th St., New York NY 10022) Eds. G. K. Batchelor, J. W. Miles.

533   UR
CHISLENNYE METODY V DINAMIKE RAZREZHENNYKH GAZOV. 1973. irreg. 0.73 Rub. Akademiya Nauk S.S.S.R., Laboratoriya Teorii Protsessov Perenosa, Leninskii prospekt, 14, Moscow V-71, U.S.S.R. illus.

532.1   UK   ISSN 0070-1424
CRANFIELD FLUIDICS CONFERENCE. PROCEEDINGS. irreg., 7th, 1977. price varies. British Hydromechanics Research Association, Cranfield, Bedford MK 43 0AJ, England (Dist. in U.S. by: Air Science Co., Box 143, Corning, N.Y. 14830)

533   SZ   ISSN 0084-5744
EIDGENOESSISCHE TECHNISCHE HOCHSCHULE ZUERICH. MITTEILUNGEN. AERODYNAMIK. (Text in German, French or English) 1949, no. 9. irreg., 1963, no. 32. price varies. (Swiss Federal Institute of Technology) Buchdruckerei und Verlag Leemann AG, Arbenzstr. 20, 8034 Zurich, Switzerland.

531   UR
FIZICHESKAYA MEKHANIKA. 1974. irreg. vol. 3, 1978. 1.80 Rub. per no. Izdatel'stvo Leningradskii Universitet, Universitetskaya Nab. 7/9, Leningrad B-164, U.S.S.R. abstr. bibl. charts. circ. 2,000.

FIZIKO-KHIMICHESKA MEKHANIKA/PHYSICO-CHEMICAL MECHANICS. see *CHEMISTRY — Physical Chemistry*

532   PL
FLUID DYNAMICS TRANSACTIONS. (Text in English) irreg., 1976, vol. 8, pt. 2. price varies. (Polska Akademia Nauk, Instytut Podstawowych Problemow Techniki) Panstwowe Wydawnictwo Naukowe, Miodowa 10, Warsaw, Poland.

GREAT BRITAIN. HYDRAULICS RESEARCH STATION. REPORTS. see *ENGINEERING — Hydraulic Engineering*

531   NE
MECHANICS: DYNAMICAL SYSTEMS. (Text in English) 1974. irreg. price varies. Sijthoff & Noordhoff International Publishers b.v., Box 4, 2400 MA Alphen aan den Rijn, Netherlands (9700 AB Groningen, Netherlands; U.S. address: 20010 Century Blvd., Germantown, MD 20767) bibl.

533   GW   ISSN 0374-1257
MITTEILUNGEN AUS DEM MAX-PLANCK-INSTITUT FUER STROEMUNGSFORSCHUNG. 1950. irreg no. 69, 1979. price varies. Max-Planck-Institut fuer Stroemungsforschung, Boettingerstr. 4-8, 3400 Goettingen, W. Germany (B.R.D.) Ed. E.-A. Mueller. circ. 300. Indexed: Appl.Mech.Rev.
Formerly: Mitteilungen aus dem Max-Planck-Institut fuer Stroemungsforschung und der Aerodynamischen Versuchsanstalt (ISSN 0076-5678)

530 540   NE
PHYSICS AND CHEMISTRY OF MATERIALS WITH LAYERED STRUCTURES. (Text in English) 1976. irreg. D. Reidel Publishing Co., P.O. Box 17, 3300 AA Dordrecht, Netherlands (And Lincoln Building, 160 Old Derby St., Hingham, MA 02043) Ed. E. Mooser.

531   PL   ISSN 0079-4538
POLITECHNIKA POZNANSKA. ZESZYTY NAUKOWE. MECHANIKA. (Text in Polish; summaries in English and Russian) 1958. irreg. price varies. Politechnika Poznanska, Pl. Curie-Sklodowskiej 5, Poznan, Poland. Ed. Zbigniew Glowacki. circ. 150.

POLITECHNIKA WROCLAWSKA. INSTYTUT MATERIALOZNAWSTWA I MECHANIKI TECHNICZNEJ. PRACE NAUKOWE. KONFERENCJE. see *ENGINEERING — Mechanical Engineering*

531   PL   ISSN 0324-9565
POLITECHNIKA WROCLAWSKA. INSTYTUT MATERIALOZNAWSTWA I MECHANIKI TECHNICZNEJ. PRACE NAUKOWE. MONOGRAFIE. (Text in Polish; summaries in English and Russian) 1969. irreg., no. 13, 1979. price varies. Politechnika Wroclawska, Wybrzeze Wyspianskiego 27, 50-370 Wroclaw, Poland (Dist. by: Ars Polona-Ruch, Krakowskie Przedmiescie 7, Warsaw, Poland) Ed. Marian Kloza.

531   PL   ISSN 0370-0917
POLITECHNIKA WROCLAWSKA. INSTYTUT MATERIALOZNAWSTWA I MECHANIKI TECHNICZNEJ. PRACE NAUKOWE. STUDIA I MATERIALY. (Text in Polish; summaries in English and Russian) 1970. irreg., 1978, no. 25. price varies. Politechnika Wroclawska, Wybrzeze Wyspianskiego 27, 50-370 Wroclaw, Poland (Dist. by: Ars Polona-Ruch, Krakowskie Przedmiescie 7, Warsaw, Poland) Ed. Marian Kloza.

621.3   PL   ISSN 0324-9395
POLITECHNIKA WROCLAWSKA. INSTYTUT TECHNIKI CIEPLNEJ I MECHANIKI PLYNOW. PRACE NAUKOWE. KONFERENCJE. (Text in Polish and English) 1974. irreg., 1978, no. 3. price varies. Politechnika Wroclawska, Wybrzeze Wyspianskiego 27, 50-370 Wroclaw, Poland (Dist. by: Ars Polona-Ruch, Krakowskie Przedmiescie 7, Warsaw, Poland) Ed. Marian Kloza. circ. 575.

621.3   PL   ISSN 0324-9387
POLITECHNIKA WROCLAWSKA. INSTYTUT TECHNIKI CIEPLNEJ I MECHANIKI PLYNOW. PRACE NAUKOWE. MONOGRAFIE. (Text in Polish; summaries in English and Russian) 1970. irreg., no. 5, 1978. price varies. Politechnika Wroclawska, Wybrzeze Wyspianskiego 27, 50-370 Wroclaw, Poland (Dist. by: Ars Polona-Ruch, Krakowskie Przedmiescie 7, Warsaw, Poland) Ed. Marian Kloza.

621.3   PL   ISSN 0324-9409
POLITECHNIKA WROCLAWSKA. INSTYTUT TECHNIKI CIEPLNEJ I MECHANIKI PLYNOW. PRACE NAUKOWE. STUDIA I MATERIALY. (Text in Polish; summaries in English and Russian) 1970. irreg., 1978, no. 12. price varies. Politechnika Wroclawska, Wybrzeze Wyspianskiego 27, 50-370 Wroclaw, Poland (Dist. by: Ars Polona-Ruch, Krakowskie Przedmiescie 7, Warsaw, Poland) Ed. Marian Kloza.

531 620.1   PL   ISSN 0079-3337
POLSKA AKADEMIA NAUK. ODDZIAL W KRAKOWIE. KOMISJA MECHANIKI STOSOWANEJ. PRACE: MECHANIKA. (Text in English and Polish; summaries in English and Russian) 1966. irreg., no. 10, 1979. price varies. Ossolineum, Publishing House of the Polish Academy of Sciences, Rynek 9, Wroclaw, Poland (Dist. by Ars Polona-Ruch, Krakowskie Przedmiescie 7, Warsaw, Poland) Ed. Roman Ciesielski.
Formerly: Polska Akademia Nauk. Komisja Nauk Technicznych. Prace.

POLUTEHNILINE INSTITUUT TALLINN. MATEMATIKA I TEORETICHESKAYA MEKHANIKA. see *MATHEMATICS*

605   US   ISSN 0360-2273
POPULAR MECHANICS DO-IT-YOURSELF YEARBOOK. a. Hearst Magazines, 224 W. 57th St., New York, NY 10019. illus.

671   UR
PRIKLADNAYA MEKHANIKA I PRIBOROSTROENIE. 1973. irreg. 1.07 Rub. Lenizdat, Fontanka, 59, Leningrad, U. S. S. R. illus.

PROBLEMY ISTORII MATEMATIKI I MEKHANIKI. see *MATHEMATICS*

532   US   ISSN 0035-4538
RHEOLOGY BULLETIN. 1937. irreg. membership. (Society of Rheology) American Institute of Physics, 335 East 45th St., New York, NY 10017. Ed. Raymond R. Myers.
Rheology

531   FR   ISSN 0081-0835
SOCIETE D'ERGONOMIE DE LANGUE FRANCAISE. ACTES DU CONGRES. 1963. irreg. Societe d'Ergonomie de la Langue Francaise, Centre d'Etudes Bioclimatiques, 21 rue Becquerel, F-67087 Strasbourg, France.

531   NE
STUDIES IN APPLIED MECHANICS. 1979. irreg., vol. 4, 1980. price varies. Elsevier Scientific Publishing Co., Box 211, 1000 AE Amsterdam, Netherlands.

532   US   ISSN 0082-0849
SYMPOSIUM ON NAVAL HYDRODYNAMICS. PROCEEDINGS. 1956. biennial. price varies. U.S. Department of the Navy, Office of Naval Research, 800 North Quincy, Arlington, VA 22217.

T & A M REPORT. (Department of Theoretical and Applied Mechanics) see *ENGINEERING — Engineering Mechanics And Materials*

532 510   US   ISSN 0076-4825
UNIVERSITY OF MARYLAND. INSTITUTE FOR FLUID DYNAMICS AND APPLIED MATHEMATICS. PUBLIC LECTURE SERIES. 1951. irreg., no. 52, 1973. price varies. University of Maryland, Institute for Fluid Dynamics and Applied Mathematics, College Park, MD 20742.

VOPROSY GIDRODINAMIKI I TEPLOOBMENA V KRIOGENNYKH SISTEMAKH. see *PHYSICS — Heat*

ZENTRALINSTITUT FUER MATHEMATIK UND MECHANIK. SCHRIFTENREIHE. see *MATHEMATICS*

PHYSICS — Nuclear Energy

A E. see *ENERGY*

539   CN   ISSN 0067-0367
A E C L REPORT SERIES. (Text in English; abstracts in English and French) 1952. irreg. price varies. Atomic Energy of Canada, Ltd., Technical Information Branch, S.D.D.O., Station 14, Chalk River, Ont. K0J 1J0, Canada. cum.index. Indexed: INIS Atomind.

539.7   FI   ISSN 0355-2721
ACTA POLYTECHNICA SCANDINAVICA. APPLIED PHYSICS SERIES. (Text and summaries in English, German and French) irreg.(2-3/yr.) Fmk.60. Teknillisten Tieteiden Akatemia - Finnish Academy of Technical Sciences, Kansakoulukatu 10 A, SF-00100 Helsinki 10, Finland. Ed. Mauri Luukkala. index; cum. index(1958-1979) circ. 250. (also avail. in microfilm from UMI; back issues avail.; reprint service avail. from UMI)
Formerly: Acta Polytechnica Scandinavica. Physics Including Nucleonics Series (ISSN 0001-6888)

539   US   ISSN 0065-2199
ADVANCES IN ATOMIC AND MOLECULAR PHYSICS. 1965. irreg., vol. 15, 1979. price varies. Academic Press, Inc., 111 Fifth Ave., New York, NY 10003. Ed. D.R. Bates. index. (also avail. in microfiche)

PHYSICS — NUCLEAR ENERGY

539   US   ISSN 0065-2970
ADVANCES IN NUCLEAR PHYSICS. 1968. irreg. price varies. Plenum Press, 233 Spring St., New York, NY 10013. Eds. M. Baranger, E. Vogt.

539 621.48   US   ISSN 0065-2989
ADVANCES IN NUCLEAR SCIENCE AND TECHNOLOGY. 1962. irreg., vol. 9, 1976. price varies. Academic Press, Inc., 111 Fifth Ave., New York, NY 10003. Eds. E. J. Henley, H. Kouts. index.

539   US
AMERICAN NUCLEAR SOCIETY. PROCEEDINGS OF THE EXECUTIVE CONFERENCE. irreg., latest 1980. price varies. American Nuclear Society, 555 N. Kensington Ave, La Grange Park, IL 60525.

539   US
AMERICAN NUCLEAR SOCIETY. PROCEEDINGS OF THE NATIONAL TOPICAL MEETING. irreg. price varies. American Nuclear Society, 555 N. Kensington Ave., La Grange Park, IL 60525.

539   US
AMERICAN NUCLEAR SOCIETY. PROCEEDINGS OF THE PACIFIC BASIN CONFERENCE ON NUCLEAR POWER DEVELOPMENT. 1976. irreg., 3rd, 1981. $48. American Nuclear Society, 555 N. Kensington Ave., La Grange Park, IL 60525.

621.48   FR   ISSN 0066-2593
ANNUAIRE DE L'ACTIVITE NUCLEAIRE FRANCAISE. 1962. irreg. 35 F. Groupe Intersyndical de l'Industrie Nucleaire, Forum Atomique Francais, 15, rue Beaujon, Paris 8e, France. circ. 2,500.
Formerly: Annuaire Bilingue de l'Industrie Nucleaire Francaise.

539   US   ISSN 0163-8998
ANNUAL REVIEW OF NUCLEAR AND PARTICLE SCIENCE. 1952. a. $22.50. Annual Reviews Inc., 4139 El Camino Way, Palo Alto, CA 94306. Ed. J.D. Jackson. bibl. index; cum.index. (back issues avail.; reprint service avail. from ISI) Indexed: Chem.Abstr. Sci.Abstr. M.M.R.I. Nucl.Sci.Abstr.
Formerly: Annual Review of Nuclear Science (ISSN 0066-4243)

539.7   PH   ISSN 0115-3757
ATOMEDIA. 1975. a. Philippine Atomic Energy Commission, Don Marianos Marcas Ave., Diliman, Quezon City, Philippines. Ed. Remedios A. Savellano. circ. 1,000.

539.7   US
ATOMIC AND NUCLEAR DATA REPRINTS. 1973. irreg., vol. 2, 1973. price varies. Academic Press, Inc., 111 Fifth Ave., New York, NY 10003.

539   CN   ISSN 0067-0383
ATOMIC ENERGY OF CANADA. ANNUAL REPORT. 1952-53. a. free. Atomic Energy of Canada Ltd., Technical Information Branch, S. D. D.O., Station 14, Chalk River, Ont. K0J 1J0, Canada. Indexed: INIS Atomind.

539.7   US   ISSN 0090-6360
ATOMIC PHYSICS. Represents: International Conference on Atomic Physics. Proceedings. 1969. irreg. price varies. Plenum Press, 233 Spring St., New York, NY 10013. illus.

539 621.48   AT   ISSN 0067-1657
AUSTRALIA.ATOMIC ENERGY COMMISSION. RESEARCH ESTABLISHMENT. A A E C/E. 1958. irreg., 1970, no. 208. $2.20 restricted distribution. Atomic Energy Commission, Research Establishment, Private Mail Bag, Sutherland N.S.W. 2232, Australia. index. cum.index: 1958-1970. (also avail. in microfiche) Indexed: INIS Atomind. Nucl.Sci.Abstr.

539 621.48   AT
AUSTRALIA. ATOMIC ENERGY COMMISSION. RESEARCH ESTABLISHMENT. A A E C/IP. 1975. irreg. Aus.$2. Atomic Energy Commission, Research Establishment, Private Mail Bag, Sutherland, N.S.W. 2232, Australia. circ. controlled. (also avail. in microfiche) Indexed: INIS Atomind.

539 621.48   AT   ISSN 0067-1665
AUSTRALIA.ATOMIC ENERGY COMMISSION. RESEARCH ESTABLISHMENT. A A E C/M. 1959. irreg. $2.20 restricted distribution. Atomic Energy Commission, Research Establishment, Private Mail Bag, Sutherland N.S.W. 2232, Australia. index. cum.index: 1959-1970. Indexed: INIS Atomind. Nucl.Sci.Abstr.

539.7   US
BENCHMARK PAPERS IN NUCLEAR PHYSICS. 1976. irreg., vol. 2, 1976. Dowden, Hutchinson & Ross, Inc., 523 Sarah St., Stroudsburg, PA 18360 (Dist. by Academic Press, Inc., 111 Fifth Ave., New York, NY 10003) Ed. Stanley Hanna.

539   II
BHABHA ATOMIC RESEARCH CENTRE. NUCLEAR PHYSICS DIVISION. ANNUAL REPORT. 1971. a. $5. Bhabha Atomic Research Centre, Trombay, Bombay 400085, India. circ. controlled. Indexed: Chem.Abstr. Nucl.Sci.Abstr.

539.7   US   ISSN 0092-1548
BROOKHAVEN HIGHLIGHTS. 1971. biennial. $11. Brookhaven National Laboratory, Upton, NY 11973 (Orders to: National Technical Information Service, 5285 Port Royal Rd., Springfield, VA 22151) illus. (also avail. in microfiche)

539.7   US
BROOKHAVEN LECTURE SERIES. no. 83, 1969. irreg., no. 145, 1977. Brookhaven National Laboratory, Upton, NY 11973 (Orders to: National Technical Information Service, 5285 Port Royal Rd., Springfield, VA 22151) (back issues avail.)

539.7   EI
BUREAU EURISTOP. CAHIERS D'INFORMATION. (Texts available in English, French, German, Italian or Dutch) 1963. irreg.; latest issue, 1975. free. ‡ Bureau Euristop, Rue de la Loi 200, 1049 Brussels, Belgium. circ. controlled. Indexed: INIS Atomind. Nucl.Sci.Abstr.

539.7   EI
BUREAU EURISTOP. INFORMATIONS TECHNICO-ECONOMIQUES. (Texts available in English, French, German, Italian or Dutch) 1963. irreg.; latest issue, 1975. free. ‡ Bureau Euristop, Rue de la Loi 200, 1049 Brussels, Belgium. circ. controlled. Indexed: INIS Atomind. Nucl. Sci. Abstr.

C E R N ANNUAL REPORT. (European Organization for Nuclear Research) see *PHYSICS*

C E R N-H E R A REPORTS. (European Organization for Nuclear Research) see *PHYSICS*

C E R N REPORTS. (European Organization for Nuclear Research) see *PHYSICS*

C E R N SCHOOL OF COMPUTING. PROCEEDINGS. (European Organization for Nuclear Research) see *PHYSICS*

C E R N SCHOOL OF PHYSICS. PROCEEDINGS. (European Organization for Nuclear Research) see *PHYSICS*

539   CN   ISSN 0706-1293
CANADIAN NUCLEAR ASSOCIATION. ANNUAL INTERNATIONAL CONFERENCE PROCEEDINGS. French edition (ISSN 0706-1900) (Editions in English and French) 1961. a. membership. Canadian Nuclear Association, 111 Elizabeth St., 11th Floor, Toronto, Ont. M5G 1P7, Canada.
Former titles: Canadian Nuclear Association. Annual Meeting; Canadian Conference on Uranium and Atomic Energy. Proceedings (ISSN 0068-8517)

539   CN   ISSN 0227-1907
CANADIAN NUCLEAR SOCIETY. ANNUAL CONFERENCE PROCEEDINGS. 1980. a. Canadian Nuclear Association, 111 Elizabeth St., 11th Floor, Toronto, Ont. M5G 1P7, Canada.

539   CN   ISSN 0226-7470
CANADIAN NUCLEAR SOCIETY. TRANSACTIONS. French edition: Societe Nucleaire Canadienne. Sommaire des Communications (ISSN 0226-7489) (Editions in English and French) irreg. Canadian Nuclear Association, 111 Elizabeth St., 11th Floor, Toronto, Ont. M5G 1P7, Canada.

621.48 539.7   EI
CENTRAL NUCLEAIRE ARDENNES. (Text in French only) 1964. a. 6.65 F. 1970. (European Atomic Energy Community) Office for Official Publications of the European Communities, C.P. 1003, Luxembourg, Luxembourg (Dist. in U.S. by European Community Information Service, 2100 M St., N.W., Suite 707, Washington, D.C. 20037)

621.48 539.7   EI   ISSN 0591-1044
CENTRALE ELLETRONUCLEARE LATINA. RELAZIONE ANNUALE. (Text in Italian only) 1963. a. 6.65 F. (European Atomic Energy Community) Office for Official Publications of the European Communities, C.P. 1003, Luxembourg 1, Luxembourg (Dist. in U.S. by European Community Information Service, 2100 M St., N.W., Suite 707, Washington, D.C. 20037) (Affiliate: Co-sponsor: Ente Nazionale per l'Energia Elletrica)

621.48 539.7   EI   ISSN 0591-1036
CENTRALE NUCLEARE GARIGLIANO. RELAZIONE ANNUALE. (Text in Italian only) 1962/63. price varies. (European Atomic Energy Community) Office for Official Publications of the European Communities, C.P. 1003, Luxembourg 1, Luxembourg (Dist. in U.S. by European Community Information Service, 2100 M St., N.W., Suite 707, Washington, D.C. 20037) (Affiliate: Co-sponsor: Ente Nazionale per l'Energia Elletrica)

539 621   US   ISSN 0069-8644
CONFERENCE ON REMOTE SYSTEMS TECHNOLOGY. PROCEEDINGS. 1951. a. $32. American Nuclear Society, 555 N. Kensington Ave., La Grange Park, IL 60525. circ. 1,000. Indexed: Chem.Abstr. Pollut.Abstr. Sci.Abstr.

539.76   US   ISSN 0069-9977
CORAL GABLES CONFERENCE ON FUNDAMENTAL INTERACTIONS AT HIGH ENERGY. (PROCEEDINGS) 1969. a. $62 (5 vol. set) (University of Miami, Center for Theoretical Studies) Gordon and Breach Science Publishers, One Park Ave., New York, NY 10016.

CUMULATIVE BIBLIOGRAPHY OF LITERATURE EXAMINED BY THE RADIATION SHIELDING INFORMATION CENTER. see *PHYSICS — Abstracting, Bibliographies, Statistics*

539.7   DK
DENMARK. ATOMENERGIKOMMISSIONENS FORSOEGSANSLAEG, RISOE. (ANNUAL REPORT) a. Atomenergikommissionens Forsoegsanslaeg Risoe - Atomic Energy Commission Research Establishment Risoe, DK-4000 Roskilde, Denmark.

539 621.48   DK   ISSN 0418-6443
DENMARK. ATOMENERGIKOMMISSIONENS FORSOEGSANSLAEG, RISOE. RISOE REPORT. (Text in English) 1967. irreg., no. 366, 1977. Atomenergikommissionens Forsoegsanslaeg Risoe - Atomic Energy Commission Research Establishment Risoe, DK-4000 Roskilde, Denmark.

539.7   US   ISSN 0092-8518
DIRECTORY: WHO'S WHO IN NUCLEAR ENERGY. 1967. irreg, latest 1976. $28 to non-members; $5 to members. American Nuclear Society, 555 N. Kensington Ave., La Grange Park, IL 60525. Ed. S. H. Krapp, Prod. Mgr. circ. 3,000. Key Title: Directory - American Nuclear Society.

539 621.48   FR   ISSN 0071-8467
FRANCE. COMMISSARIAT A L'ENERGIE ATOMIQUE. ANNUAL REPORT. 1945. a. free. Commissariat a l'Energie Atomique, 29-33 rue de la Federation, Paris 15e, France. circ. 20,000.

539 016   US   ISSN 0072-0712
GENERAL ATOMIC COMPANY. LIBRARY. JOURNAL OF HOLDINGS OF THE LIBRARY.*
Formerly issued as: General Dynamic Corporation. General Atomic Division. Library. Journal of Holdings. 1962. a. free. Gulf General Atomic Inc., P.O. Box 81608, San Diego, CA 92138. Ed. Richard J. Tommey. subject index.

PHYSICS — NUCLEAR ENERGY

539   FR   ISSN 0337-2219
GUIDE INTERNATIONAL DE L'ENERGIE NUCLEARE. (Text in English, French) 1960. a. 370 F.($34) Editions Lesourd, 66 rue de la Rochefoucauld, 75009 Paris, France. adv. circ. 3,000.
Former titles: Guide International de l'Energie Atomique et des Etudes Spatiales (ISSN 0072-8128) & Annuaire-Guide International de l'Energie Atomique et des Autres Energies (ISSN 0066-3212)

539   GW
HAHN-MEITNER-INSTITUT FUER KERNFORSCHUNG BERLIN. JAHRESBERICHT. 1958. a. free. Hahn-Meitner-Institut fuer Kernforschung Berlin, Glienicker St. 100, 1000 Berlin 39, W. Germany (B.R.D.). index. cum.index. Indexed: INIS Atomind.
Formerly: Hahn-Meitner-Institut fuer Kernforschung Berlin. Bericht (ISSN 0072-9280)

539.721   US   ISSN 0073-1153
HAWAII TOPICAL CONFERENCE IN PARTICLE PHYSICS. PROCEEDINGS. 4th, 1971. biennial. price varies. University Press of Hawaii, 2840 Kolowalu St., Honolulu, HI 96822. (reprint service avail. from UMI,ISI)

539   GW
I F F BULLETIN. (Text in English or German) 1972. irreg. free. ‡ Institut fuer Festkoerperforschung, Kernforschungsanlage Juelich, Postfach 365, Juelich, W. Germany (B.R.D.) illus.

I N I S REFERENCE SERIES. see *LIBRARY AND INFORMATION SCIENCES*

539   JA
I P C R CYCLOTRON PROGRESS REPORT. (Text in English) 1967. a. 3000 Yen. Institute of Physical and Chemical Research - Rikagaku Kenkyusho Saikurotoron Kenkyushitsu, 2-1 Hirosawa, Wako 351, Japan.

539   JA
I P C R CYCLOTRON REPORT. (Text in European languages) 1970. irreg. Institute of Physical and Chemical Research - Rikagaku Kenkyusho Saikurotoron Kenkyushitsu, 2-1 Hirosawa, Wako 351, Japan.

539   JA
I P C R CYCLOTRON TECHNICAL REPORT. (Text in English) 1971. irreg. price varies. Institute of Physical and Chemical Research - Rikagaku Kenkyusho Saikurotoron Kenkyushitsu, 2-1 Hirosawa, Wako 351, Japan.

539   GW
IMPULSTECHNIKEN. irreg., vol. 6, 1976. price varies. R. Oldenbourg Verlag GmbH, Rosenheimer Str. 145, Postfach 801360, 8000 Munich 80, W. Germany (B.R.D.) charts.

539   II   ISSN 0073-618X
INDIA. DEPARTMENT OF ATOMIC ENERGY. ANNUAL REPORT. (Text in English and Hindi) a. free. Department of Atomic Energy, Publications Officer, Chhatrapati Shivaji Maharaj Marg, Bombay 400039, India.

539.7   SP   ISSN 0081-3397
INFORMES J. E. N. (Text in Spanish; summaries in Spanish and English) 1956. irreg., 40-50/yr. price varies. Junta de Energia Nuclear, Ciudad Universitaria, Avda. Complutense 22, Madrid 3, Spain. bk. rev. circ. 300. (back issues avail.) Indexed: Nucl.Sci.Abstr.

539 621.48   US   ISSN 0073-9472
INSTITUTE OF NUCLEAR MATERIALS MANAGEMENT. PROCEEDINGS OF ANNUAL MEETING. (Included in Nuclear Materials Management) 1960. a. $20. Institute of Nuclear Materials Management, Inc., Box 6247, Louisville, KY 40207.

539   MX   ISSN 0076-7476
INSTITUTO NACIONAL DE ENERGIA NUCLEAR. PUBLICATION. (Text in English and Spanish) 1957. irreg. free. Instituto Nacional de Energia Nuclear, Department of Libraries and Documentation Services, Insurgentes sur 1079, Mexico, D.F., Mexico. index for numbers 1-47 in no.48. Index for nos. 1-150 in no. 178. Index for nos. 151-200 in Suppl. no. 221. circ. 300. Indexed: Nucl.Sci.Abstr. Phys.Abstr.

530   RM
INSTITUTUL DE FIZICA ATOMICA. SESIUNEA STIINTIFICA ANUALA DE COMUNICARI; PROGRAM SI REZUMATE. a. Institutul de Fizica Atomica, Soseaua Magurele, Bucharest, Romania.

539 621.48   US   ISSN 0074-0942
INTER-AMERICAN NUCLEAR ENERGY COMMISSION. FINAL REPORT. 1959. a. $1. Organization of American States, General Secretariat, Department of Publications, 17th and Constitution Ave. N.W., Washington, DC 20006. circ. 1,000.

539.7 621.48   UN   ISSN 0085-2023
INTERNATIONAL ATOMIC ENERGY AGENCY. ANNUAL REPORT. (Report of Board of Governors to General Conference) (Editions in English, French, Russian, Spanish) 1958. a. free. International Atomic Energy Agency - Agence Internationale de l'Energie Atomique, Wagramer Str. 5, Box 100, A-1400 Vienna, Austria.

INTERNATIONAL ATOMIC ENERGY AGENCY. LEGAL SERIES. see *LAW*

539 621.48   UN   ISSN 0074-1876
INTERNATIONAL ATOMIC ENERGY AGENCY. PANEL PROCEEDINGS SERIES. (Text in English, French or Spanish) 1960. irreg. price varies. International Atomic Energy Agency - Agence Internationale de l'Energie Atomique, Wagramer Str. 5, Box 100, A-1400 Vienna, Austria (Dist. in U.S. by: Unipub, 345 Park Ave. S., New York, NY 10010)

539 621.48   UN
INTERNATIONAL ATOMIC ENERGY AGENCY. POWER REACTORS IN MEMBER STATES. (Text in English) a. price varies. International Atomic Energy Agency - Agence Internationale de l'Energie Atomique, Wagramer Str.5, Box 100, A-1400 Vienna, Austria (Dist. in U.S. by: Unipub, 345 Park Ave. S., New York, NY 10010)

539 621.48   UN   ISSN 0074-1884
INTERNATIONAL ATOMIC ENERGY AGENCY. PROCEEDINGS SERIES. (Text in English, French, Russian and Spanish) 1959. irreg. price varies. International Atomic Energy Agency, Division of Publications, Wagramer Str. 5, Box 100, A-1400 Vienna, Austria (Dist. in U.S. by: Unipub, 345 Park Ave. S., New York, NY 10010)

539 621.48   UN   ISSN 0074-1906
INTERNATIONAL ATOMIC ENERGY AGENCY. TECHNICAL DIRECTORIES. (Text in English) 1959. irreg. price varies. International Atomic Energy Agency - Agence Internationale de l'Energie Atomique, Wagramer Str. 5, Box 100, A-1400 Vienna, Austria (Dist. in U.S. by: Unipub, 345 Park Ave. S., New York, NY 10010)

539 621.48   UN   ISSN 0074-1914
INTERNATIONAL ATOMIC ENERGY AGENCY. TECHNICAL REPORT SERIES. (Text mainly in English; some in French, Russian or Spanish) 1960. irreg. price varies. International Atomic Energy Agency - Agence Internationale de l'Energie Atomique, Wagramer Str. 5, Box 100, A-1400 Vienna, Austria (Dist. in U.S. by: Unipub, 345 Park Ave. S., New York, NY 10010) Indexed: Ocean.Abstr. Pollut.Abstr.

539.7   US
INTERNATIONAL CONFERENCE IN PARTICLE TECHNOLOGY. PROCEEDINGS. 1973. irreg. $22. I I T Research Institute, 10 West 35th St., Chicago, IL 60616.

INTERNATIONAL CONFERENCE ON EXPERIMENTAL MESON SPECTROSCOPY. PROCEEDINGS. see *PHYSICS — Optics*

539   CN
INTERNATIONAL CONFERENCE ON HIGH ENERGY PHYSICS AND NUCLEAR STRUCTURE. PROCEEDINGS. irreg., 3rd, 1970. price varies. International Union of Pure and Applied Physics, c/o Prof. L. Kerwin, Sec.-Gen., Universite Laval, Quebec, P.Q. G1K 7P4, Canada.

621.48   FR   ISSN 0534-8811
INTERNATIONAL CONFERENCE ON SHIELDING AROUND HIGH ENERGY ACCELERATORS. PAPERS. (Text in English and French) 1962. irreg. Presses Universitaires de France, 108 Bd. Saint Germaine, 75279 Paris Cedex 6, France (Service des Periodiques, 12 rue Jean de Beauvais, 75005 Paris)

539.75   JA   ISSN 0074-333X
INTERNATIONAL CONFERENCE ON THE PHYSICS OF ELECTRONIC AND ATOMIC COLLISIONS. PAPERS. (Publisher varies for each conference) 1958. irreg. International Union of Pure and Applied Physics, Commission on Atomic and Molecular Physics and Spectroscopy, c/o Prof. K. Talzayanagi, Institute of Space and Aeronautical Science, University of Tokyo, Konaba, Meguro-ku, Japan.

539   US   ISSN 0538-6586
INTERNATIONAL CONGRESS OF RADIATION RESEARCH. PROCEEDINGS.* 1958. irreg. Academic Press Inc., 111 5th Ave., New York, NY 10003.

539.733   US
INTERNATIONAL CYCLOTRON CONFERENCE. PROCEEDINGS. (Published in A I P Conference Proceedings) irreg., 6th, 1972. price varies. American Institute of Physics, 335 E. 45th St., New York, NY 10017.

539.721   US   ISSN 0074-7858
INTERNATIONAL SCHOOL OF PHYSICS "ETTORE MAJORANA," ERICE, ITALY. PROCEEDINGS.* 1963. a. Academic Press, Inc, 111 Fifth Ave., New York, NY 10003.

539.7   US   ISSN 0579-5664
INTERSOCIETY ENERGY CONVERSION CONFERENCE. PROCEEDINGS. (In 3 vols.) 13th, 1978. irreg. $97. American Nuclear Society, 555 N. Kensington Ave., La Grange Park, IL 60525.

621.48   IS   ISSN 0075-0980
ISRAEL. ATOMIC ENERGY COMMISSION. IA-REPORTS. (Text in English or Hebrew with English abstracts) 1958. irreg., latest issue, 1978. exchange basis. ‡ Atomic Energy Commission, Soreg Nuclear Research Centre, Yavne, Israel. circ. exchange basis.

539 621.48   JA   ISSN 0449-4830
JAPAN ATOMIC ENERGY COMMISSION. ANNUAL REPORT/GENSHIRYOKU NENPO. (Text in English) 1961. a. exchange basis. Japan Atomic Energy Commission - Genshiryoku Iinkai, 2-2-1 Kasumigaseki, Chiyoda-ku, Tokyo 100, Japan.

539.7   EI
JOINT NUCLEAR RESEARCH CENTER, ISPRA, ITALY. ANNUAL REPORT. a. Commission of the European Communities, Luxembourg, Luxembourg (Dist. in the U.S. by: European Community Information Service, 2100 M St. NW, Suite 707 Washington, DC 20037)

539 621.48   GW
KERNFORSCHUNGSZENTRUM KARLSRUHE. ERGEBNISBERICHT UEBER FORSCHUNG UND ENTWICKLUNG. 1970. irreg. Kernforschungszentrum Karlsruhe GmbH, Weberstr. 5, Postfach 3640, 7500 Karlsruhe, W. Germany (B.R.D.) illus. circ. 1,000.
Formerly: Gesellschaft fuer Kernforschung. Bericht ueber Forschungs- und Entwicklungsarbeiten.

621.48   EI
KERNKRAFT LINGEN. JAHRESBERICHT. (Text in German only) 1967. a. 7.75 F. (European Atomic Energy Community) Office for Official Publications of the European Communities, C.P. 1003, Luxembourg, Luxembourg (Dist. in U.S. by European Community Information Service, 2100 M St., N.W., Washington, D.C. 20037)

621.48   EI   ISSN 0453-767X
KERNKRAFT ZENTRALE, GUNDREMMINGEN. JAHRESBERICHTE. (Text in German only) 1967. a. 9.45 F. (European Atomic Energy Community) Office for Official Publications of the European Communities, C.P. 1003, Luxembourg 1, Luxembourg (Dist. in the U.S. by: European Community Information Service, 2100 M St. NW, Suite 707, Washington, DC 20037)

PHYSICS — NUCLEAR ENERGY

621.48   EI
KERNKRAFTWERK OBRIGHEIM. JAHRESBERICHT. (Text in German only) 1967. a. price varies. (European Atomic Energy Community) Office for Official Publications of the European Communities, C.P. 1003, Luxembourg 1, Luxembourg (Dist. in U.S. by European Community Information Service, 2100 M St., N.W., Suite 707, Washington, D.C. 20037)

621.48   539.7   NO   ISSN 0534-4050
KJELLER REPORT. Abbreviated title: K R. (Text in English) 1959. irreg. exchange basis. Institutt for Atomenergi, P.O. Box 40, N-2007 Kjeller, Norway. Indexed: INIS Atomind. Nucl.Sci.Abstr.

539.7   JA   ISSN 0386-0752
KYOTO UNIVERSITY. INSTITUTE OF ATOMIC ENERGY. RESEARCH ACTIVITIES. (Text in English) 1968. a. Kyoto University, Institute of Atomic Energy - Kyoto Daigaku Genshi Enerugi Kenkyusho, Gokasho, Uji 611, Japan. Ed. Bd.

539.7   JA
KYOTO UNIVERSITY. INSTITUTE OF ATOMIC ENERGY. TECHNICAL REPORTS/KYOTO DAIGAKU GENSHI ENERUGI KENKYUSHO KENKYU HOKOKU. (Text in English) 1951. irreg. Kyoto University, Institute of Atomic Energy - Kyoto Daigaku Genshi Enerugi Kenkyusho, Gokasho, Uji 611, Japan.

539   US   ISSN 0075-7888
LANDOLT-BOERNSTEIN, ZAHLENWERTE UND FUNKTIONEN AUS NATURWISSENSCHAFTEN UND TECHNIK. NEUE SERIE. GROUP 1: NUCLEAR PHYSICS/ LANDOLT-BOERNSTEIN NUMERICAL DATA AND FUNCTIONAL RELATIONSHIPS IN SCIENCE AND TECHNOLOGY. NEW SERIES. 1961. irreg., vol. 9, 1981. price varies. Springer-Verlag, 175 Fifth Ave., New York, NY 10010 (also Berlin, Heidelberg, Vienna) (reprint service avail. from ISI)

539   US   ISSN 0075-7918
LANDOLT-BOERNSTEIN, ZAHLENWERTE UND FUNKTIONEN AUS NATURWISSENSCHAFTEN UND TECHNIK. NEUE SERIE. GROUP 2: ATOMIC PHYSICS. 1965. irreg., vol. 11, 1981. $147.60. Springer-Verlag, 175 Fifth Ave., New York, NY 10010 (also Berlin, Heidelberg, Vienna) (reprint service avail. from ISI)

539.733   US   ISSN 0076-8146
MICHIGAN STATE UNIVERSITY. DEPARTMENT OF PHYSICS. CYCLOTRON PROJECT.* irreg., 1964, no. 21. Michigan State University, Department of Physics, East Lansing, MI 48824.

539.7   US   ISSN 0078-088X
N M R. (Nuclear Magnetic Resonance); basic principles and progress. (Text mainly in English, occasionally in German) 1969. irreg., vol. 20, 1981. price varies. Springer - Verlag, 175 Fifth Ave., New York, NY 10010 (And Berlin, Heidelberg, Vienna) Ed. E. Fluck. illus. (reprint service avail. from ISI)

539   JA
N S R A MEMO. (Text in Japanese) 1966. irreg. exchange basis. Nuclear Safety Research Association - Genshiryoku Anzen Kenkyu Kyokai, 1-2-2 Uchisaiwai-cho, Chiyoda-ku, Tokyo 100, Japan. abstr.

539   621.48   JA
NIHON UNIVERSITY. ATOMIC ENERGY RESEARCH INSTITUTE. ANNUAL REPORT. (Text in English) a. exchange basis. Nihon University, Atomic Energy Research Institute, 1-8 Kanda Surugadai, Chiyoda-ku, Tokyo 101, Japan.

539   DK
NORDISK INSTITUT FOR TEORETISK ATOMFYSIK. VIRKSOMHEDSBERETNING/ NORDITA REPORT. (Text in Danish and English) irreg. contr. free circ. Nordisk Institut for Teoretisk Atomfysik, Blegdamsvej 17, DK-2100 Copenhagen OE, Denmark. circ. controlled.

539   CN
NUCLEAR CANADA. YEARBOOK. 1976. a. Canadian Nuclear Association, 111 Elizabeth St., 11th Floor, Toronto, Ont. M5G 1P7, Canada.

621.48   US   ISSN 0078-2599
NUCLEAR ENGINEERING. (Subseries of A I Ch E Symposium Series) irreg., approx. a. $20. American Institute of Chemical Engineers, 345 E. 47 St., New York, NY 10017. Ed. S. Fourdrinier.

539.7   FR
NUCLEAR FUEL CYCLE REQUIREMENTS. (Text in English and French) irreg. price varies. Organization for Economic Cooperation and Development, Nuclear Energy Agency, 38 Bd. Suchet, 75016 Paris, France (U.S. orders to: O.E.C.D. Publications and Information Center, Suite 1207, 1750 Pennsylvania Ave. N.W., Washington, DC 20006)

621.48   US   ISSN 0078-2610
NUCLEAR NEWS BUYERS GUIDE. Variant title: Nuclear News Industry Report. 1969. a. $41.50 or with subscr. to Nuclear News. American Nuclear Society, 555 N. Kensington Ave., La Grange Park, IL 60525. Ed. M. William Diekman. adv. circ. 14,000.

539.7   US   ISSN 0550-3205
NUCLEAR PHYSICS. 1963. a. price varies. Gordon and Breach Science Publishers, One Park Ave., New York, NY 10016. Eds. L. Lederman, J. Weneser.

539.7   US
NUCLEAR PHYSICS MONOGRAPHS. 1978. irreg. price varies. Plenum Press, 233 Spring St., New York, NY 10013. Eds.Erich W. Vogt, John W.Negele.

539.7   621   US   ISSN 0078-2637
NUCLEAR SCIENCE AND APPLICATIONS. 1965. s-a. Harwood Academic Publishers GmbH, Box 786, Cooper Sta., New York, NY 10276. Indexed: Chem.Abstr. Nucl.Sci.Abstr.

539.7   US
NUCLEAR SCIENCE APPLICATIONS-SECTION B-IN DEPTH REVIEWS. irreg. included with Section A. Harwood Academic Publisher GmbH, Box 786 Cooper Station, New York, NY 10276.

539   621
NUCLEAR SCIENCE TECHNOLOGY MONOGRAPH SERIES. 1966. irreg., latest 1980. American Nuclear Society, 555 N. Kensington Ave., La Grange Park, IL 60525. (Co-sponsor: U.S. Department of Energy) bk. rev. circ. 1,000. Formerly: A E C/A N S Monographs (ISSN 0065-9487)

539   621.48   FR   ISSN 0078-6284
O E C D HALDEN REACTOR PROJECT. (English and French Editions) 1960. a. no report in 1963. free. Organization for Economic Cooperation and Development, Nuclear Energy Agency, 2, rue Andre-Pascal, 75775 Paris, Cedex 16, France (U.S. orders to: O.E.C.D. Publications and Information Center, Suite 1207, 1750 Pennsylvania Ave. N.W., Washington, DC 20006) charts, illus. stat. circ. 4,300. (also avail. in microfiche) Indexed: INIS Atomind.

539   621.48   FR   ISSN 0078-625X
ORGANIZATION FOR ECONOMIC COOPERATION AND DEVELOPMENT. NUCLEAR ENERGY AGENCY. ACTIVITY REPORT. (Was European Nuclear Energy Agency until 1972 when Japan became first non-European member.) (English and French Editions) 1958. a. free. Organization for Economic Cooperation and Development, Nuclear Energy Agency, 38 Bd. Suchet, 75016 Paris, France (U.S. subscr. to: O.E.C.D. Publications and Information Center, 1750 Pennsylvania Ave. N.W., Washington, DC 20006) Ed. J. de la Ferte. charts. illus. stat. circ. 3,500. (also avail. in microfiche)

539   JA   ISSN 0473-4580
OSAKA UNIVERSITY. LABORATORY OF NUCLEAR STUDIES. REPORT. (Text in English) 1962. irreg. exchange basis. Osaka University, Laboratory of Nuclear Studies, 1-1 Machikanayama-cho, Toyonaka, Osaka 560, Japan.

539.7   US
OXFORD STUDIES IN NUCLEAR PHYSICS. irreg. price varies. Oxford University Press, 200 Madison Ave., New York, NY 10016 (And Ely House, 37 Dover St., London W1X 4AH, England) Ed. P.E. Hodgson.

539.7   US
PARTICLES AND NUCLEI SERIES. 1972. irreg., vol. 2, 1972-1973. price varies. Consultants Bureau, Special Research Report (Subsidiary of: Plenum Publishing Corp.) 227 W. 17 St., New York, NY 10011. Ed. N.N. Bogolyubov.

539.7   PH   ISSN 0553-9978
PHILIPPINE ATOMIC ENERGY COMMISSION. ANNUAL REPORT. a. free. ‡ Philippine Atomic Energy Commission, Don Mariano Marcos Ave., Diliman, Quezon City, Phillipines. illus. circ. 1,000.

539   PH   ISSN 0079-1490
PHILIPPINES NUCLEAR JOURNAL. 1966. irreg. $10. ‡ Philippine Atomic Energy Commission, Don Mariano Marcos Ave., Diliman, Quezon City, Philippines. Ed. Carlito R. Aleta. circ. 2,000.

539.7   544.6   US   ISSN 0079-6565
PROGRESS IN NUCLEAR MAGNETIC RESONANCE SPECTROSCOPY. Variant title: Progress in Nuclear Magnetic Resonance Spectrosopy of Cyclopentadienyl Compounds. 1966. 4/yr. $75. Pergamon Press, Inc., Journals Division, Maxwell House, Fairview Park, Elmsford, NY 10523 (And Headington Hill Hall, Oxford OX3 0BW, England) Ed. J. W. Emsley. index. (also avail. in microform from MIM,UMI) Indexed: Chem.Abstr.

539   621.48   JA
RIKKYO UNIVERSITY. INSTITUTE FOR ATOMIC ENERGY. REPORT. (Text in Japanese and English) 1966. irreg. exchange basis. Rikkyo University, Institute for Atomic Energy, 10 Matsukoshi, Sajima, Yokosuka-shi 240-01, Japan.

539.7   SZ
SCHWEIZERISCHES INSTITUT FUER NUKLEARFORSCHUNG. JAHRESBERICHT. a. Schweizerisches Institut fuer Nuklearforschung, CH-5234 Villigen, Switzerland.

539.7   SA
SOUTHERN UNIVERSITIES NUCLEAR INSTITUTE. ANNUAL RESEARCH REPORT. a. Southern Universities Nuclear Institute, P.O. Box 17, Faure 7131, South Africa.

381   US   ISSN 0094-7482
STATUS OF THE MARKET NUCLEAR FUEL FABRICATION. a. Nuclear Assurance Corporation, 24 Executive Park West, Atlanta, GA 30329. stat.

539   621.48   BE   ISSN 0081-7155
STUDIECENTRUM VOOR KERNENERGIE. ANNUAL SCIENTIFIC REPORT. 1962. a. exchange basis. Centre d'Etude de l'Energie Nucleaire - Studiecentrum voor Kernenergie, Boeretang 200, B-2400 MOL, Belgium. Ed. R. Billiau. illus. circ. 1,300. Indexed: INIS Atomind.

539.7   US
STUDIES IN RADIATION EFFECTS IN SOLIDS. a. price varies. Gordon and Breach Science Publishers, One Park Ave., New York, NY 10016. Ed. G. J. Dienes, L. T. Chadderton.

539   CN   ISSN 0082-6367
T R I U M F, VANCOUVER, BRITISH COLUMBIA. REPORT.* (Tri-University Meson Facility) 1967. a. free. University of British Columbia, Vancouver, B.C. V6T 1W5, Canada. Indexed: Nucl.Sci.Abstr.

539   621.48   UK   ISSN 0082-7940
UNITED KINGDOM ATOMIC ENERGY AUTHORITY. ANNUAL REPORT. 1954. a. price varies. H.M.S.O., P.O.B. 569, London SE1 9NH, England.

539.7   621.48   US
U.S. ATOMIC ENERGY COMMISSION. MONOGRAPHS. a. price varies. Gordon and Breach Science Publishers, One Park Ave., New York, NY 10016. Ed. George Klir.

539   BL   ISSN 0067-5687
UNIVERSIDADE FEDERAL DE MINAS GERAIS. INSTITUTO DE PESQUISAS RADIOATIVAS. RELATORIOS ANUAIS.* (Text and summaries in English and Portuguese) 1968. a. free. Universidade Federal de Minas Gerais, Instituto de Pesquisas Radiativas, Belo Horizonte, MG, Brazil.

539.7 540 CN
UNIVERSITE LAVAL. CENTRE DE RECHERCHES SUR LES ATOMES ET LES MOLECULES. RAPPORT ANNUEL; physics and chemistry of atoms and molecules. (Text in French) 1968. a. free. Universite Laval, Centre de Recherches sur les Atomes et les Molecules, Quebec, Que. G1K 7P4, Canada. circ. controlled.

539.7 FR ISSN 0399-127X
UNIVERSITE SCIENTIFIQUE ET MEDICALE DE GRENOBLE. INSTITUT DES SCIENCES NUCLEAIRES. RAPPORT ANNUEL. (Text in French; summaries in English) 1970. a. free. Universite de Grenoble I (Universite Scientifique et Medicale de Grenoble), Institut des Sciences Nucleaires, 53 Ave. des Martyrs, 38026 Grenoble CEDEX, France. circ. 700. (back issues avail) Indexed: INIS Atomind.

539.7 CN
UNIVERSITY OF ALBERTA. NUCLEAR RESEARCH CENTRE. PROGRESS REPORT. 1969. a. free. University of Alberta, Nuclear Research Centre, Edmonton, Alta. T6G 2N5, Canada. circ. 300. (back issues avail.)

539 JA
UNIVERSITY OF TOKYO. INSTITUTE FOR NUCLEAR STUDY. ANNUAL REPORT. (Text in English) 1960. a. exchange basis. University of Tokyo, Institute for Nuclear Study - Tokyo Daigaku Genshikaku Kenkyusho, 3-2-1 Midori-cho Tanashi-shi, Tokyo 188, Japan. abstr.

539 JA ISSN 0495-7814
UNIVERSITY OF TOKYO. INSTITUTE FOR NUCLEAR STUDY. INS-J. (Text in English) 1957. irreg. exchange basis. University of Tokyo, Institute for Nuclear Study - Tokyo Daigaku Genshikaku Kenkyusho, 3-2-1 Midori-cho Tanashi-shi, Tokyo 188, Japan.

539 JA
UNIVERSITY OF TOKYO. INSTITUTE FOR NUCLEAR STUDY. INS-PH. (Text in Japanese) 1969. irreg. exchange basis. University of Tokyo, Institute for Nuclear Study - Tokyo Daigaku Genshikaku Kenkyusho, 3-2-1 Midori-cho Tanashi-shi, Tokyo 188, Japan.

539 JA ISSN 0563-7848
UNIVERSITY OF TOKYO. INSTITUTE FOR NUCLEAR STUDY. INS-PT. (Text in Japanese; summaries in English) 1957. irreg. exchange basis. University of Tokyo, Institute for Nuclear Study - Tokyo Daigaku Genshikaku Kenkyusho, 3-2-1 Midori-cho Tanashi-shi, Tokyo 188, Japan.

539 JA
UNIVERSITY OF TOKYO. INSTITUTE FOR NUCLEAR STUDY. INS-TCH. (Text in Japanese; summaries in English) 1967. irreg. exchange basis. University of Tokyo, Institute for Nuclear Study - Tokyo Daigaku Genshikaku Kenkyusho, 3-2-1 Midori-cho Tanashi-shi, Tokyo 188, Japan.

539 JA
UNIVERSITY OF TOKYO. INSTITUTE FOR NUCLEAR STUDY. INS-TEC. (Text in Japanese; summaries in English) 1971. irreg. exchange basis. University of Tokyo, Institute for Nuclear Study - Tokyo Daigaku Genshikaku Kenkyusho, 3-2-1 Midori-cho Tanashi-shi, Tokyo 188, Japan.

539 JA ISSN 0563-7872
UNIVERSITY OF TOKYO. INSTITUTE FOR NUCLEAR STUDY. INS-TH. (Text in Japanese; summaries in English) 1954. irreg. exchange basis. University of Tokyo, Institute for Nuclear Study - Tokyo Daigaku Genshikaku Kenkyusho, 3-2-1 Midori-cho Tanashi-shi, Tokyo 188, Japan.

539 JA ISSN 0563-7880
UNIVERSITY OF TOKYO. INSTITUTE FOR NUCLEAR STUDY. INS-TL. (Text in Japanese; summaries in English) 1954. irreg. exchange basis. University of Tokyo, Institute for Nuclear Study - Tokyo Daigaku Genshikaku Kenkyusho, 3-2-1 Midori-cho Tanashi-shi, Tokyo 188, Japan.

539 JA
UNIVERSITY OF TOKYO. INSTITUTE FOR NUCLEAR STUDY. INS-TS. (Text in Japanese; summaries in English) 1967. irreg. exchange basis. University of Tokyo, Institute for Nuclear Study - Tokyo Daigaku Genshikaku Kenkyusho, 3-2-1 Midori-cho Tanashi-shi, Tokyo 188, Japan.

539 JA ISSN 0495-7822
UNIVERSITY OF TOKYO. INSTITUTE FOR NUCLEAR STUDY. REPORT. (Text in English) 1959. irreg. exchange basis. University of Tokyo, Institute for Nuclear Study - Tokyo Daigaku Genshikaku Kenkyusho, 3-2-1 Midori-cho Tanashi-shi, Tokyo 188, Japan.

539.7 FI ISSN 0355-3663
VALTION TEKNILLINEN TUTKIMUSKESKUS. REAKTORILABORATORIO. TIEDONANTO/ TECHNICAL RESEARCH CENTRE OF FINLAND. REACTOR LABORATORY. REPORT. (Text mainly in Finnish, some in English or Swedish) 1971. irreg. price varies. Valtion Teknillinen Tutkimuskeskus - Technical Research Centre of Finland, Vuorimiehentie 5, 02150 Espoo 15, Finland.

539.7 621.3 FI
VALTION TEKNILLINEN TUTKIMUSKESKUS. SAHKO- JA ATOMITEKNIIKKA. JULKAISU. (Text in Finnish or Swedish) 1977. irreg. price varies. Valtion Teknillinen Tutkimuskeskus - Technical Research Centre of Finland, Vuorimiehentie 5, 02150 Espoo 15, Finland. circ. 200.

539.7 FI ISSN 0355-3698
VALTION TEKNILLINEN TUTKIMUSKESKUS. YDINVOIMATEKNIIKAN LABORATORIO. TIEDONANTO/TECHNICAL RESEARCH CENTRE OF FINLAND. NUCLEAR ENGINEERING LABORATORY. REPORT. (Text mainly in Finnish, some in English or Swedish) 1973. irreg. price varies. Valtion Teknillinen Tutkimuskeskus - Technical Research Centre of Finland, Vuorimiehentie 5, 02150 Espoo 15, Finland.

539.7 UK
WORLD NUCLEAR DIRECTORY. 1981. irreg. £70. Longman Group Ltd., Longman House, Burnt Mill, Harlow, Essex CM20 2JE, England (Dist. in U.S. and Canada by Gale Research Co. Ltd., Book Tower, Detroit, MI 48226)

PHYSICS — Optics

535.8 541 HU ISSN 0065-0412
ABSORPTION SPECTRA IN THE ULTRAVIOLET AND VISIBLE REGION. (Text in English) 1959. irreg., vol. 22, 1978. price varies. (Magyar Tudomanyos Akademia) Akademiai Kiado, Publishing House of the Hungarian Academy of Sciences, P.O. Box 24, H-1363 Budapest, Hungary (Distr. in U.S. by Robert E. Krieger Publishing Co. Inc., 645 New York Ave., Huntington, N.Y. 11743) Ed. Laszlo Lang.

ANNUAIRE ET STATISTIQUE DE L'ENSEIGNEMENT CATHOLIQUE. see *EDUCATION*

535.84 UK ISSN 0306-1353
ANNUAL REPORTS ON ANALYTICAL ATOMIC SPECTROSCOPY. no. 7, 1978. a. price varies. Chemical Society, Burlington House, London W1V 0BN, England. Ed. J. B. Dawson. bibl. charts. illus.
Spectroscopy

535.84 US ISSN 0066-4103
ANNUAL REPORTS ON N M R SPECTROSCOPY. 1968. a. price varies. Academic Press Inc., 111 Fifth Ave., New York, NY 10003. Ed. E. F. Mooney. Indexed: Chem.Abstr.
Spectroscopy

535 UK ISSN 0066-4235
ANNUAL REVIEW OF N M R SPECTROSCOPY. 1968. a. price varies. Academic Press Inc. (London) Ltd., 24-28 Oval Rd, London NW1 7DX, England (And 111 Fifth Ave., New York, NY 10003) Ed. G. A. Webb.
Spectroscopy

535 681 US ISSN 0066-5495
APPLIED OPTICS. SUPPLEMENT. 1962. irreg., 1969, no.3. price varies. (Optical Society of America, Inc.) American Institute of Physics, 335 E. 45th St., New York, NY 10017. Eds. K. E. Shuler, W. R. Bennet, Jr. (also avail. in microfiche) Indexed: Phys.Abstr.

535.84 US ISSN 0570-4928
APPLIED SPECTROSCOPY REVIEWS. 1968. 2/yr. $42. Marcel Dekker Journals, 270 Madison Ave., New York, NY 10016 (Prepaid subscr. to: Box 11305, Church St. Sta., New York NY 10049) Ed. E.G. Brame, Jr. Indexed: Chem.Abstr.
Spectroscopy

535 US
ATMOSPHERIC OPTICS. 1970. irreg., vol. 2, 1972. price varies. Consultants Bureau, Special Research Report, 227 W. 17 St., New York, NY 10011. Ed. Nikolai B. Divari.

535 US
BENCHMARK PAPERS IN OPTICS. 1975. irreg., vol. 3, 1977. price varies. Dowden, Hutchinson and Ross, Inc., 523 Sarah St., Stroudsburg, PA 18360 (Dist. by Academic Press, Inc., 111 Fifth Ave., New York, NY 10003) Ed. S. S. Ballard.

COMITE INTERNATIONAL DES POIDS ET MESURES. COMITE CONSULTATIF DE PHOTOMETRIE ET RADIOMETRIE.(RAPPORT ET ANNEXES) see *METROLOGY AND STANDARDIZATION*

535 SZ ISSN 0084-5752
EIDGENOESSISCHE TECHNISCHE HOCHSCHULE ZUERICH. MITTEILUNGEN. PHOTOELASTIZITAET. 1943. irreg., 1965, no. 10. (Swiss Federal Institute of Technology) Buchdruckerei und Verlag Leemann AG, Arbenzstr. 20, 8034 Zurich, Switzerland.

539.7 US
INTERNATIONAL CONFERENCE ON EXPERIMENTAL MESON SPECTROSCOPY. PROCEEDINGS. (Published in A I P Conference Proceedings, Particles and Fields subseries) irreg., 5th, 1978. $19. American Institute of Physics, 335 E. 45 St., New York, NY 10017. Eds.M.D. Fiske, W.W. Havens, Jr. bibl. illus.

535.58 US ISSN 0190-4132
INTERNATIONAL CONFERENCE ON LASERS. PROCEEDINGS. irreg. (Society for Optical & Quantum Electronics) S T S Press, Box 245, McLean, VA 22101. Ed. Vincent J. Corcoran.
Lasers

535 681.1 GW ISSN 0075-272X
JAHRBUCH FUER OPTIK UND FEINMECHANIK. 1954. a. DM.27. Fachverlag Schiele und Schoen GmbH, Markgrafenstr. 11, 1000 Berlin 61, W. Germany (B.R.D.) Ed. Dionys Hacman. adv. circ. 5,000.

535 658.8 US ISSN 0075-8027
LASER FOCUS BUYERS' GUIDE. 1966. a. $22. Advanced Technology Publications, Inc., 1001 Watertown St., Newton, MA 02165. Ed. Herb Brody. adv. bk. rev. circ. 20,000.
Until 1970: Laser Marketers' and Buyers' Guide.

535 US ISSN 0075-8035
LASERS: A SERIES OF ADVANCES. 1966. irreg., vol. 4, 1976. price varies. Marcel Dekker, Inc., 270 Madison Ave., New York, NY 10016. Ed. A.K. Levine. Indexed: Chem.Abstr.

535 338.47 US ISSN 0078-5474
OPTICAL INDUSTRY AND SYSTEMS DIRECTORY. 1954. a. $38.50. Optical Publishing Co., Inc, Box 1146, Berkshire Common, Pittsfield, MA 01201. Ed. T.C. Laurin. adv. circ. 12,000. (reprint service avail. from UMI)

535 US
OPTICAL INFORMATION PROCESSING. a. Plenum Publishing Corp., 233 Spring St., New York, NY 10013.

535 621 US ISSN 0078-5482
OPTICAL PHYSICS AND ENGINEERING. 1968? irreg. price varies. Plenum Press, 233 Spring St., New York, NY 10013. Ed. William L. Wolfe.

535 US ISSN 0078-5504
OPTICS AND SPECTROSCOPY. SUPPLEMENT. (English translation of Russian language editions) 1966. irreg., 1970, no. 4. $20. (Optical Society of America, Inc.) American Institute of Physics, 335 E. 45th St., New York, NY 10017.

PROGRESS IN NUCLEAR MAGNETIC RESONANCE SPECTROSCOPY. see *PHYSICS — Nuclear Energy*

535　　　　　　　　　NE　ISSN 0079-6638
PROGRESS IN OPTICS. 1961. irreg., vol. 18, 1980.
price varies. North-Holland Publishing Co., P.O.
Box 211, 1000 AE Amsterdam, Netherlands. Ed. E.
Wolf. index, cum index vols.1-15.

SCANNING ELECTRON MICROSCOPY; an
internaional review of advances in techniques and
applications of the scanning electron microscope.
see *BIOLOGY — Microscopy*

535　　　　　　　　　US　ISSN 0361-0748
SOCIETY OF PHOTO-OPTICAL
INSTRUMENTATION ENGINEERS.
PROCEEDINGS. 1963. 50/yr. $36 per no.
(approx.) Society of Photo-Optical Instrumentation
Engineers, Box 10, 405 Fieldston Rd., Bellingham,
WA 98225. (reprint service avail. from UMI, ISI)
　　Formerly: S P I E Seminar Proceedings (ISSN
0583-9572)

SPECTROSCOPIC PROPERTIES OF INORGANIC
& ORGANOMETALLIC COMPOUNDS; specialist
periodical reports. see *CHEMISTRY*

535　　　　　　　　　US
SPRINGER SERIES IN OPTICAL SCIENCES.
1976. irreg., vol. 26, 1981. price varies. Springer
Verlag, 175 Fifth Ave., New York, NY 10010 (And
Berlin, Heidelberg, Vienna) (reprint service avail.
from ISI)

535　　　　　　　　　UK
U.V. SPECTROMETRY GROUP. BULLETIN. 1973.
a. £3. U.V. Spectrometry Group, c/o D. Irish, Pye
Unicam Ltd., York St., Cambridge CB1 2PX,
England. Ed. Dr. A. Knowles. cum.index. circ. 450.
(back issues avail) Indexed: Chem.Abstr.
　　From 1949-1972: Photoelectric Spectrometry
Group Bulletin (ISSN 0079-1814)
　　Spectroscopy

535　　　　　　　　　UR
USPEKHI FORONIKI. vol. 6, 1977. irreg. 1.83 Rub.
per no. (Leningradskii Universitet) Izdatel'stvo
Leningradskii Universitet, Universitetskaya Nab. 7/
9, Leningrad B-164, U.S.S.R. abstr. bibl. circ. 705.

617.7　　　　　　　　GW
WISSENSCHAFTLICHE VEREINIGUNG FUER
AUGENOPTIK UND OPTOMETRIE.
FACHVORTRAEGE DES WVAO -
JAHRESKONGRESSES. 1952. a. price varies.
Median-Verlag, Hauptstr. 64, Postfach 103964, 6900
Heidelberg 1, W. Germany (B.R.D.) adv.
　　Formerly: Wissenschaftliche Vereinigung der
Augenoptiker. Fachvortraege der Jahrestagungen
(ISSN 0084-1005)

535　　　　　　　　　GW　ISSN 0044-2054
ZEISS INFORMATION. (German and English
editions) 1953. irreg. free. Carl Zeiss, Postfach
1369/1380, 7082 Oberkochen, W. Germany
(B.R.D.) Ed. Wolfgang Pfeiffer. charts. illus. index.
circ. 105,000. Indexed: Chem.Abstr.

PHYSICS — Sound

see also *Sound Recording and Reproduction*

A.C.A. INDUSTRY GUIDE TO HEARING AIDS.
INTERNATIONAL EDITION. (Acoustic
Corporation of America) see *DEAF*

534　774　　　　　　US
ACOUSTICAL IMAGING: RECENT ADVANCES
IN VISUALIZATION AND
CHARACTERIZATION. Represents: International
Symposium on Acoustical Holography. Proceedings.
1969. irreg. price varies. Plenum Press, 233 Spring
St., New York, NY 10013.
　　Formerly (until 1977): Acoustical Holography
(ISSN 0065-0870)

534　　　　　　　　　PL
AKUSTYKA. 1972. irreg., no. 2, 1976. price varies.
Uniwersytet im. Adama Mickiewicza w Poznaniu,
Stalingradzka 1, 61-712 Poznan, Poland (Dist. by:
Ars Polona, Krakowskie Przedmiescie 7, 00-068
Warsaw, Poland)
　　Formerly: Uniwersytet im. Adama Mickiewicza w
Poznaniu. Wydzial Matematyki, Fizyki i Chemii.
Prace. Seria Akustyka.

AMERICAN INSTITUTE OF ULTRASOUND IN
MEDICINE. ANNUAL SCIENTIFIC
CONFERENCE. PROGRAM. see *MEDICAL
SCIENCES*

534　　　　　　　　　US
BENCHMARK PAPERS IN ACOUSTICS. 1972.
irreg., vol. 13, 1979. Dowden, Hutchinson & Ross,
Inc., 523 Sarah St., Stroudsburg, PA 18360 (Dist. by
Academic Press, Inc., 111 Fifth Ave., New York,
NY 10003) Ed. R. B. Lindsay. illus. index.

534　　　　　　　　　CN　ISSN 0074-400X
INTERNATIONAL CONFERENCE ON
ACOUSTICS. REPORTS. 1963. irreg., 9th. 1977,
Spain. International Commission on Acoustics, c/o
Dr. E. A. W. Shaw, Division de Physique, Conseil
National de Recherches, Ottawa, Ont. K1A 0R6,
Canada.

534　　　　　　　　　US
INTERNATIONAL SYMPOSIUM ON
NONLINEAR ACOUSTICS. ABSTRACTS OF
PAPERS. irreg., 7th, 1976. Virginia Polytechnic
Institute and State University, Blacksburg, VA
24061.

534.4　614.7　　　　CN
MUSIC OF THE ENVIRONMENT SERIES. 1977.
irreg. World Soundscape Project, Sonic Research
Studio, Dept. of Communication Studies, Simon
Fraser University, Burnaby, B.C. V5A 1S6, Canada.
Ed. R. Murray Schafer.

534　　　　　　　　　US　ISSN 0079-1873
PHYSICAL ACOUSTICS: PRINCIPLES AND
METHODS. 1964. irreg., vol. 13, 1977. price varies.
Academic Press Inc., 111 Fifth Ave., New York,
NY 10003. Ed. W. P. Mason.

534　　　　　　　　　UR
PROBLEMY DIFRAKTSII I RASPROSTRANENIIA
VOLN/PROBLEMS OF DIFFRACTION AND
SPREADING OF WAVES. vol. 15, 1977. irreg.
1.69 Rub. per no. Izdatel'stvo Leningradskii
Universitet, Universitetskaya Nab. 7/9, Leningrad
B-164, U.S.S.R. abstr. bibl. circ. 900.

534　　　　　　　　　UR
RADIOTEKHNIKA. vol. 42, 1977. irreg. 0.67 Rub.
per issue. (Khar'kovskii Institut Radioelektroniki)
Izdatel'stvo Vysshaya Shkola-Khar'kov,
Universitetskaya 16, 310003 Khar'kov, U.S.S.R. Ed.
A. Tereshchenko. abstr. charts. circ. 1,000.

620.2　534　　　　　US　ISSN 0090-5607
ULTRASONICS SYMPOSIUM. PROCEEDINGS.
(Symposia for (1972-) sponsored by the IEEE
Group on Sonics and Ultrasonics) a. $10. Institute
of Electrical and Electronics Engineers, Inc, 445
Hoes Lane, Piscataway, NJ 08854. Key Title:
Proceedings - Ultrasonics Symposium.

ULTRASOUND IN MEDICINE. see *MEDICAL
SCIENCES*

PHYSIOLOGY

see *Biology—Physiology*

PLASTICS

668　　　　　　　　　US　ISSN 0065-1931
ADHESIVES RED BOOK. 1968. a. $29.50.
Communication Channels, Inc., 6285 Barfield Rd.,
Atlanta, GA 30328. Ed. Art Sweun.

ANNUAL BOOK OF A S T M STANDARDS.
PART 22. WOOD; ADHESIVES. see
*ENGINEERING — Engineering Mechanics And
Materials*

ANNUAL BOOK OF A S T M STANDARDS.
PART 34. PLASTIC PIPE. see
*ENGINEERING — Engineering Mechanics And
Materials*

ANNUAL BOOK OF A S T M STANDARDS.
PART 35. PLASTICS - GENERAL TEST
METHODS; NOMENCLATURE. see
*ENGINEERING — Engineering Mechanics And
Materials*

ANNUAL BOOK OF A S T M STANDARDS.
PART 36. PLASTICS--MATERIALS, FILM,
REINFORCED AND CELLULAR PLASTICS;
HIGH MODULUS FIBERS AND THEIR
COMPOSITES. see *ENGINEERING —
Engineering Mechanics And Materials*

ASSOCIATION FRANCAISE DES INGENIEURS
DU CAOUTCHOUC ET DES PLASTIQUES.
ANNUAIRE. see *RUBBER*

BENCHMARK PAPERS IN POLYMER
CHEMISTRY. see *CHEMISTRY*

668.4　　　　　　　　CN　ISSN 0068-9459
CANADIAN PLASTICS DIRECTORY AND
BUYER'S GUIDE. 1959. a. Can.$25. Southam
Communications Ltd., 1450 Don Mills Rd., Don
Mills, Ont. M3B 2X7, Canada.

668.4　　　　　　　　UK　ISSN 0306-5502
EUROPEAN PLASTICS BUYERS GUIDE. 1931. a.
£15. I P C Business Press Ltd., 33-40 Bowling
Green Lane, London EC1R ONE, England. adv.
circ. 5,000.
　　Former titles: Europlastics Year Book (ISSN
0068-2381); British Plastics Year Book.

668.4　　　　　　　　FR　ISSN 0071-9056
FRANCE PLASTIQUES. 1949. a. 145 F. Creations,
Editions et Productions Publicitaires, 1 Place
d'Estienne d'Orves, 75009 Paris, France. Ed.
Georges Prieux. adv. circ. 5,000.

668.4　　　　　　　　SZ　ISSN 0073-0084
HANDBUCH DER INTERNATIONALEN
KUNSTOFFINDUSTRIE/INTERNATIONAL
PLASTICS DIRECTORY/MANUEL
INTERNATIONAL DES PLASTIQUES. (Text and
index in English, German, French) 1958. every 10
yrs. 250 Fr. Verlag fuer Internationale
Wirtschaftsliteratur GmbH, P.O. Box 108, CH-8047
Zurich, Switzerland. Ed. Walter Hirt. index.

668.4　　　　　　　　II
HINDUSTAN LATEX. VARSHIKA RIPORTA/
HINDUSTAN LATEX. ANNUAL REPORTS.
(Text in Hindi and English) 11 edt, 1976/77. a.
Varikkat House, TC 4/485, Kowdiar, Trivandrum
695003, India. stat.

668.4　　　　　　　　GW
INFORMATIONEN UEBER VERSTAERKTE
KUNSTSTOFFE. 1961. irreg., approx. 4/yr.
membership. Arbeitsgemeinschaft Verstarkte
Kunstsoffe e. V., Niddastr. 44, 6000 Frankfurt 1, W.
Germany (B.R.D.) bk. rev. abstr. stat. tr.lit.

668.4　　　　　　　　US
INTERNATIONAL PROGRESS IN URETHANES.
1976. irreg. price varies. Technomic Publishing Co.,
Inc., 265 Post Rd. W., Westport, CT 06880. Ed.Bd.

KLINE GUIDE TO THE PLASTICS INDUSTRY.
see *BUSINESS AND ECONOMICS — Trade And
Industrial Directories*

668.4　　　　　　　　GW　ISSN 0075-7276
KUNSTSTOFF-INDUSTRIE UND IHRE HELFER.
a. DM.38. Industrieschau-Verlagsgesellschaft,
Berliner Allee 8, 6100 Darmstadt, W. Germany
(B.R.D.)

668.4　　　　　　　　GW　ISSN 0075-7292
KUNSTSTOFFE IM LEBENSMITTELVERKEHR.
1962. irreg., no. 25, 1978. DM.118.
(Bundesgesundheitsamt, Kunststoff-Kommission)
Carl Heymanns Verlag KG, Gereonstr. 18-32, 5000
Cologne 1, W. Germany (B.R.D.)

668.4　338.47　　　　AU
KUNSTSTOFFE IN OESTERREICH. irreg.
(Fachverband der Chemischen Industrie
Oesterreichs, Gruppe Kunststoffverarbeitende
Industrie) Julius Dressler Buch- und
Zeitschriftenverlag, Schwindgasse 5, A-1041 Vienna,
Austria. (Co-sponsor: Arbeitsgemeinschaft der
Kunstoffverarbeitenden Gewerbebetriebe)

660.2 US ISSN 0085-3518
MODERN PLASTICS ENCYCLOPEDIA. (Special October issue of: Modern Plastics) 1925. a. McGraw-Hill Publications Co., 1221 Ave. of the Americas, New York, NY 10020. Ed. Joan Agranoff. adv. circ. 56,000.

668.4 US
MONOGRAPHS ON PLASTICS. 1972. irreg., vol. 1, pt. 2., 1973. price varies. Marcel Dekker, Inc., 270 Madison Avenue, New York, NY 10016.

NEW TRADE NAMES IN THE RUBBER AND PLASTICS INDUSTRIES. see *RUBBER*

668.4 SW
P K L PLASTER. 1969. biennial. Kr.75. Plast- och Kemikalieleverantoerers Foerening, Box 5512, S-114 85 Stockholm, Sweden.

PLASTICHEM. see *ENGINEERING — Chemical Engineering*

668.4 MX
PLASTICOS Y RESINAS (ANNUAL) 1964. a. 125($100) Editorial Innovacion, Espana 396, Mexico 13, D.F., Mexico. Ed. Cesar Macazaga. adv.

668.4 667.6 SA
PLASTICS AND RUBBER YEARBOOK AND BUYERS' GUIDE OF S.A. 1959. a. R.25. Thomson Publications S. A. (Pty) Ltd., Box 3808, Johannesburg 2000, South Africa. Ed. H Engelhardt. index.
Former titles: Plastics, Rubber and Paint Buyers' Guide and Yearbook for Southern Africa; Plastics, Paint and Rubber Buyers' Guide for S.A. (ISSN 0079-2306)

668.4 US ISSN 0099-0450
PLASTICS MANUFACTURING CAPABILITIES IN MISSISSIPPI. biennial. Mississippi Research and Development Center, Drawer 2470, Jackson, MS 39205.

668.4 US
PLASTICS TECHNOLOGY. PLASTICS MANUFACTURING HANDBOOK AND BUYERS GUIDE. 1967. a. included in subscr. to Plastics Technology. Bill Communications, Inc., 633 Third Ave., New York, NY 10017. Ed. Malcolm Riley. adv. charts. illus. tr lit. index. circ. 38,000. (reprint service avail. from UMI)

668.4 PL ISSN 0370-0879
POLITECHNIKA WROCLAWSKA. INSTYTUT TECHNOLOGIII ORGANICZNEJ I TWORZYW SZTUCZNYCH. PRACE NAUKOWE. STUDIA I MATERIALY. (Text in Polish; summaries in English and Russian) 1971. irreg., 1977, no. 17. price varies. Politechnika Wroclawska, Wybrzeze Wyspianskiego 27, 50-370 Wroclaw, Poland (Dist. by: Ars Polona-Ruch, Krakowskie Przedmiescie 7, Warsaw, Poland) Ed. Marian Kloza.

668.4 US
POLYMERS-PROPERTIES AND APPLICATIONS. 1977. irreg., vol. 4, 1981. price varies. Springer-Verlag, 175 Fifth Ave, New York, NY 10010 (also Berlin, Heidelberg, Vienna) (reprint service avail. from ISI)
Supersedes(1952-1970): Chemie, Physik und Technologie der Kunststoffe in Einzeldarstellungen (ISSN 0069-3073)

R A P R A RECENT LITERATURE ON HAZARDOUS ENVIRONMENTS IN INDUSTRY. (Rubber and Plastics Research Association of Great Britain) see *RUBBER*

668.4 UK ISSN 0306-3607
REINFORCED PLASTICS CONGRESS. 1958. biennial. £20. ‡ British Plastics Federation, 5 Belgrave Square, London SW1X 8PH, England.
Formerly: International Reinforced Plastics Conference. Papers and Proceedings. (ISSN 0074-7661)

668 FR
REPERTOIRE TECHNIQUE DE LA SOUS-TRAITANCE DES INDUSTRIES PLASTIQUES. biennial. 100 F. (Federation Francaise des Industries Transformatrices des Plastiques) Union Francaise d'Annuaires Professionnels, 13 Avenue Vladimir Komarov, B.P. 36, 78190 Trappes, France.

RUBBER AND PLASTICS INDUSTRY TECHNICAL CONFERENCE. RECORD. see *RUBBER*

RUBBER RESEARCH INSTITUTE OF SRI LANKA. JOURNAL. see *RUBBER*

660
SOCIETY OF PLASTICS ENGINEERS MONOGRAPHS. 1973. irreg., unnumbered, latest 1980. price varies. John Wiley & Sons, Inc., 605 Third Ave., New York, NY 10016.

668.4 US
SOCIETY OF THE PLASTICS INDUSTRY. CELLULAR PLASTICS DIVISION. CONFERENCE PROCEEDINGS. irreg. price varies. Technomic Publishing Co., Inc., 265 Post Rd. W., Westport, CT 06880.

668.4 US
SOCIETY OF THE PLASTICS INDUSTRY. URETHANE DIVISION. CONFERENCE PROCEEDINGS. 1979. irreg. price varies. Technomic Publishing Co., Inc., 265 Post Rd. W., Westport, CT 06880.

668.4 US ISSN 0049-1764
SOVIET PROGRESS IN POLYURETHANES. 1973. irreg., latest issue 1975. $35 per no. Technomic Publishing Co., Inc., 265 Post Rd. W., Westport, CT 06880. Ed. Dr. Kurt Gingold.

668.4
STRUCTURAL FOAM CONFERENCE. PROCEEDINGS. vol. 3, 1975. irreg. (Society of the Plastics Industry) Technomic Publishing Co. Inc., 265 W. State St., Westport, CT 06880.

SYNDICAT GENERAL DES COMMERCES ET INDUSTRIES DU CAOUTCHOUC ET DES PLASTIQUES. GUIDE. see *BUSINESS AND ECONOMICS — Trade And Industrial Directories*

668.4 658.78 US ISSN 0083-0968
UNITED STATES FOAMED PLASTIC MARKETS AND DIRECTORY. 1963. a. $25. Technomic Publishing Co. Inc., 265 Post Rd. W., Westport, CT 06880. Ed. M. Kohudic. circ. 8,000.
Title Varies: International Foamed Plastic Markets and Directory.

668.4 CN ISSN 0382-0424
VISION. (Text in English and French) 1969. irreg. Association des Professeurs d'Arts Plastiques du Quebec, Box 424, Station Youville, Montreal,Que. H2P 2V6, Canada. illus.

668.4 US
WORLD PLASTICS. 1979. a. $3500. S R I International, World Petrochemicals Program, 333 Ravenswood Ave., Menlo Park, CA 94025.

POETRY

see *Literature — Poetry*

POLITICAL SCIENCE

see also *Political Science — Civil Rights; Political Science — International Relations; Public Administration*

321 US ISSN 0066-1228
A C A INDEX; analysis of voting records of members of U. S. Congress. 1960. a. contributions of $15 or more. Americans for Constitutional Action, 955 l'Enfant Plaza North, S.W., Washington, DC 20024. cum.index: 1955 (Senate); 1957(House of Representatives) circ. 5,000.

320 327 US
A E I HOOVER POLICY STUDIES. (Subseries of: Hoover Institution Studies) 1971. irreg. price varies. American Enterprise Institute for Public Policy Research, 1150 - 17th St. N.W., Washington, DC 20036. (Co-sponsor: Hoover Institution on War, Revolution and Peace)

350 US
A I RECOMMENDS. irreg. Associated Industries of New York State, Inc., 150 State St., Albany, NY 12207.

320 US ISSN 0094-7954
A P S A DEPARTMENTAL SERVICES PROGRAM SURVEY OF DEPARTMENTS. 1971-72. a. $20. American Political Science Association, 1527 New Hampshire Ave., N.W., Washington, DC 20036. stat. circ. 500.

320.07 US ISSN 0092-8658
A.P.S.A. DIRECTORY OF DEPARTMENT CHAIRPERSONS. 1972. a. $20. American Political Science Association, 1527 New Hampshire Ave., N.W., Washington, DC 20036. circ. 500.
Formerly: A.P.S.A. Directory of Department Chairmen (ISSN 0092-8658)

320 US ISSN 0195-914X
ABRAHAM LINCOLN ASSOCIATION. PAPERS. 1979. a. $15. Abraham Lincoln Association, Old State Capitol, Springfield, IL 62706. Eds. Mary Ellen McElligott, Janice Petterchak.

320 300 VE
ACADEMIA DE CIENCIAS POLITICAS Y SOCIALES. BOLETIN. 1937. irreg. Academia de Ciencias Politicas y Sociales, Ciudad Universitaria, Caracas, Venezuela. bibl.

320 AG
ACADEMIA NACIONAL DE CIENCIAS MORALES Y POLITICAS. ANALES. 1972. a. Academia Nacional de Ciencias Morales y Politicas, Avda. Corrientes, 1723, Buenos Aires, Argentina.

320 US ISSN 0065-0684
ACADEMY OF POLITICAL SCIENCE. PROCEEDINGS. 1910. irreg., 2/yr. membership. Academy of Political Science, 619 W. 114th St., Ste. 500, New York, NY 10025. index. circ. 11,000. (also avail. in microform from UMI) Indexed: SSCI. Soc.Sci.Ind.

ACTA FACULTATIS POLITICO-JURIDICAE UNIVERSITATIS SCIENTIARUM BUDAPESTIENSIS DE ROLANDO EOTVOS NOMINATAE. see *LAW*

350 338 CK ISSN 0001-8309
ADMINISTRACION Y DESARROLLO. 1962. irreg. Col.200($5) Escuela Superior de Administracion Publica, Centro de Investigaciones en Administracion Publica, Diagonal 40 No. 46A-37, Apdo. Aereo 29745, Bogota, Colombia. Ed. Luis O. Beltran Jara. adv. bk. rev. bibl. charts. stat. circ. 2,000.

328 973 US
ADVANCE LOCATOR FOR CAPITOL HILL. 1963. a. Congressional Staff Directory, Box 62, Mt. Vernon, VA 22121.

320 338 UK ISSN 0308-678X
AFRICA GUIDE. 1977. a. £12.50($30) World of Information, 21 Gold St., Saffron Walden, Essex CB10 1EJ, England. Ed. Graham Hancock. adv. illus. stat.

320 960 SA
AFRICAN FREEDOM. ANNUAL. 1977. a. Southern African Freedom Foundation, Box 781112, Sandton 2146, South Africa. Ed. F. R. Metrowich.

320 350 SA ISSN 0304-615X
AFRICANUS. (Text in English and Afrikaans) 1972. a. R.1.55. University of South Africa, Department of Development Administration and Politics, P.O. Box 392, Pretoria 0001, South Africa. Ed. P. J. Hugo. adv. bk. rev. charts. stat. circ. 330. (back issues avail.)

949.65 US ISSN 0002-4651
ALBANIA REPORT. 1970. q. contributions. (Albanian Affairs Study Group) Gamma Publishing Co., Box 206, New York, NY 10008. Ed.Bd. circ. 3,000.

POLITICAL SCIENCE

320   SZ
ALMANACH WISSENSCHAFTS- UND BILDUNGSPOLITISCHER ORGANISATIONEN DER SCHWEIZ/ALMANACH DES ORGANISATIONS SUISSES DE LA POLITIQUE DE LA SCIENCE ET DE L'ENSEIGNEMENT. 1976. triennial. (Gesellschaft fuer Hochschule und Forschung, Zurich - Societe Universite et Recherche, Zurich) Schwabe und Co. AG, Steinentorstr. 13, 4010 Basel, Switzerland.

324   US   ISSN 0065-678X
AMERICA VOTES; handbook of contemporary American election statistics. 1956. biennial. $41.50. Congressional Quarterly Inc., 1414 22nd St., N.W., Washington, DC 20037. Ed. Richard M. Scammon.

322.4   US
AMERICAN ENTERPRISE INSTITUTE FOR PUBLIC POLICY RESEARCH. A E I FORUMS. 1977. irreg. American Enterprise Institute for Public Policy Research, 1150 Seventeenth St. N.W., Washington, DC 20036.
     Supersedes (1967-1976): American Enterprise Institute for Public Policy Research. Debates, Meetings and Symposia.

320   US
AMERICAN ENTERPRISE INSTITUTE FOR PUBLIC POLICY RESEARCH. LEGISLATIVE ANALYSES. 1943. irreg. (approx 20/yr.) $3.75 per copy. American Enterprise Institute for Public Policy Research, 1150 17th St. N.W., Washington, DC 20007.
     Formerly: American Enterprise Institute for Public Policy Research. Legislative and Special Analyses (ISSN 0065-8146)

322.4   US
AMERICAN ENTERPRISE INSTITUTE FOR PUBLIC POLICY RESEARCH. REPRINTS. 1972. irreg. $0.75 per copy. American Enterprise Institute for Public Policy Research, 1150 Seventeenth St. N.W., Washington, DC 20036. Ed. Bd. bibl.

335   US   ISSN 0084-6368
AMERICAN INSTITUTE FOR MARXIST STUDIES. OCCASIONAL PAPERS. 1966. irreg., no. 33, 1979. American Institute for Marxist Studies, 20 E. 30th St., New York, NY 10016.

335   US   ISSN 0065-8677
AMERICAN INSTITUTE FOR MARXIST STUDIES. MONOGRAPH SERIES. 1965. irreg., no. 4, 1973. price varies. (American Institute for Marxist Studies) Humanities Press, Inc., 171 First Avenue, Atlantic Highlands, NJ 07716.

320   US
AMERICAN JEWISH COMMITTEE. DOMESTIC AFFAIRS DEPARTMENT. PERTINENT PAPERS. At head of title: Our Stake in the Urban Condition. 1978. irreg., approx. 2/yr. $0.25 per no. American Jewish Committee, Domestic Affairs Department, 165 E. 56th St., New York, NY 10022. circ. 3,000.

323   US   ISSN 0066-1236
AMERICANS FOR CONSTITUTIONAL ACTION. REPORT. 1961. a. contributions of $15 or more. Americans for Constitutional Action, 955 l'Enfant Plaza N. S.W., Washington, DC 20024. circ. 5,000.

355.224   CN   ISSN 0382-6295
AMNESTY INTERNATIONAL (TORONTO GROUP) NEWSLETTER. 1969. irreg. Amnesty International (Toronto Group), Toronto, Ont., Canada.

320   GW   ISSN 0072-9426
ANALYSEN. irreg. price varies. (Hochschule fuer Wirtschaft und Politik, Hamburg) Leske Verlag und Budrich GmbH, Fuerstenbergstr.23, Postfach 300406, 5090 Leverkusen 3, W. Germany (B.R.D.)

328   BE   ISSN 0066-1589
ANCIENS PAY ET ASSEMBLEES D'ETATS.* (Text in language of contributor) 1950. irreg. price varies. (International Committee of Historical Sciences, Commission for the History of State Assemblies) Editions Nauwelaerts, Muntstraat 10, B-3000 Louvain, Belgium.

320 960   SG   ISSN 0066-2364
ANNEE POLITIQUE AFRICAINE. 1964. a. 10000 Fr.CFA. Societe Africaine d'Edition, 16 bis, rue de Thiong, Dakar, Senegal (And 32, rue de l'Echiquier, Paris, France) Ed.Bd.

320   SZ   ISSN 0066-2372
ANNEE POLITIQUE SUISSE/SCHWEIZERISCHE POLITIK IN JAHRE. (Text in German and French) 1965. a. 24 Fr. Universitaet Bern, Forschungszentrum fuer Schweizerische Politik - Universite de Berne, Centre de Recherche de Politique Suisse, Neubrueck Str. 10, 3012 Berne, Switzerland. index. circ. 1,500.

320   SZ   ISSN 0066-3727
ANNUAIRE SUISSE DE SCIENCE POLITIQUE/ SCHWEIZERISCHES JAHRBUCH FUER POLITISCHE WISSENSCHAFT/SWISS POLITICAL SCIENCE YEARBOOK. (Text in German, French, English) 1961. a. 30 Fr. (Forschungsstelle fuer Politische Wissenschaft) Paul Haupt AG, Falkenplatz 14, CH-3001 Berne, Switzerland. Ed. R. E. Germann.

320.4   US   ISSN 0090-547X
ANNUAL EDITIONS: READINGS IN AMERICAN GOVERNMENT. 1973/74. a. price varies. Dushkin Publishing Group, Sluice Dock, Guilford, CT 06437. illus. Key Title: American Government. Text.

320   UK   ISSN 0066-4057
ANNUAL REGISTER WORLD EVENTS. 1758. a. £12. ‡ Longman Group Ltd., Longman House, Burnt Mill, Harlow, Essex CM20 2JE, England. Ed. H. V. Hodson. index.

320   VE   ISSN 0066-4936
ANTOLOGIAS DEL PENSAMIENTO POLITICO. 1961. irreg. price varies. Universidad Central de Venezuela, Instituto de Estudios Politicos, Caracas, Venezuela.

320   CR   ISSN 0377-7316
ANUARIO DE ESTUDIOS CENTROAMERICANOS. 1974. a. Col.40($8) Editorial Universidad de Costa Rica, Ciudad Universitaria, Costa Rica. Ed. Mario Flores Macal.

320   MX
ANUARIO POLITICO DE AMERICA LATINA. 1974. a. Universidad Nacional Autonoma de Mexico, Facultad de Ciencias Politicas y Sociales, Ciudad Universitaria, Mexico 20, D.F., Mexico.

ARABIAN STUDIES. see *HISTORY — History Of The Near East*

979.1 320   US   ISSN 0571-0111
ARIZONA POLITICAL ALMANAC. 1952. biennial. price varies. Secretary of the State, Capitol Bldg., F1700 W. Washington, Phoenix, AZ 85007.

320   US
ARIZONA STATE UNIVERSITY. CENTER FOR PUBLIC AFFAIRS. MONOGRAPH. 1962. irreg., latest issue 1977. price varies. ‡ Arizona State University, Center for Public Affairs, Tempe, AZ 85281. Ed. John Hall. index. circ. 500.
     Formerly: Arizona State University, Tempe. Institute of Public Administration. Monograph. (ISSN 0066-748X)

320   US
ARKANSAS STATE DIRECTORY. 1973. biennial. $2. Heritage Publishing Co. (North Little Rock), 4Th & Poplar, North Little Rock, AR 72201. Ed. Pat McNeill. adv. circ. 5,000.

ASIA & PACIFIC. see *BUSINESS AND ECONOMICS — Economic Situation And Conditions*

ASIA SERIALS: VIETNAM REPORT. see *BUSINESS AND ECONOMICS — Economic Situation And Conditions*

320   CH   ISSN 0571-2920
ASIAN PEOPLES' ANTI-COMMUNIST LEAGUE. CHINA. PAMPHLET. (Text in English) 1955. irreg. (10-12/yr) $1-2. ‡ Asian Peoples' Anti-Communist League - Republic of China, 1, Tsiangtao E. Road, Sec. 1, Taipei, Taiwan, Republic of China. Ed. Bd. bibl. circ. 10,000.

320   BG
ASIAN STUDIES. (Text in English) 1979. irreg. Tk.10($2) Center for Asian Studies, Department of Government and Politics, Jahangirnagar University, Dacca, Bangladesh.

350   US
ASSOCIATED INDUSTRIES OF NEW YORK STATE. BULLETIN. irreg. Associated Industries of New York State, Inc., 150 State St., Albany, NY 12207.

329   AT   ISSN 0310-785X
AUSTRALIAN LABOR PARTY. A. C. T. BRANCH. NEWSLETTER. 1973. irreg. free. Australian Labor Party, Australian Capital Territory Branch, Box 918, Civic Square, Canberra City, A. C. T. 2608, Australia. Ed. Peter Vallee.

320.531   AT   ISSN 0310-8252
AUSTRALIAN MARXIST REVIEW. 1972. 3-4/yr. Aus.$4. Socialist Party of Australia, 392 Sussex St., Sydney, N.S.W. 2000, Australia. bibl.
     Marxism

320   AT
AUSTRALIAN NATIONAL UNIVERSITY, CANBERRA. RESEARCH SCHOOL OF SOCIAL SCIENCES. DEPARTMENT OF POLITICAL SCIENCE. OCCASIONAL PAPERS. 1965. irreg., no. 14, 1978. price varies. Australian National University, Department of Political Science, Box 4, Canberra, A.C.T. 2600, Australia (Dist. in U.S. by International Scholarly Book Services, P.O. Box 4347, Portland, Ore. 97208)
     Formerly: Australian National University, Canberra. Department of Political Science. Occasional Paper. (ISSN 0067-2033)

322   AT
AUSTRALIAN PARLIAMENTARY HANDBOOK. 1915. irreg.; (approx every 3 years) price varies. Australian Government Publishing Service, P.O. Box 84, Canberra. A.C.T. 2600, Australia. illus. circ. 2,000.
     Formerly: Parliamentary Handbook of the Commonwealth of Australia.

320   BG
BANGLADESH POLITICAL STUDIES. (Text in English or Bengali) 1978. a. Tk.35. University of Chittagong, Department of Political Science, Chittagong, Bangladesh.

320   GW   ISSN 0522-6643
BEITRAEGE ZUR GESCHICHTE DES PARLEMENTARISMUS UND DER POLITISCHEN PARTEIEN. 1952. irreg., vol. 65, 1978. price varies. Droste-Verlag GmbH, Pressehaus Am Martin-Luther-Platz, Postfach 1122, 4000 Duesseldorf 1, W. Germany (B.R.D.)

320   GW   ISSN 0582-0421
BEITRAEGE ZUR POLITISCHEN WISSENSCHAFT. 1967. irreg., vol. 30, 1978. price varies. Duncker und Humblot, Dietrich-Schaefer-Weg 9, 1000 Berlin 41, W. Germany (B.R.D.) Ed. G.T.W. Dietzel.

320   US   ISSN 0067-5717
BENJAMIN F. FAIRLESS LECTURES. 1964. a. (Carnegie-Mellon University) Columbia University Press, 36 South Broadway, Irvington-On-Hudson, NY 10533.

320   AG
BIBLIOTECA DE SECRETOS POLITICOS. no. 2, 1976. irreg. Ediciones Gota de Agua, Sarmiento 1983, Buenos Aires, Argentina.

320   US
BOBBS-MERRILL POLITICAL SCIENCE ANNUAL. 1966. a. Bobbs-Merrill Co., Inc., 4300 W. 62nd St., Indianapolis, IN 46206. Ed. Cornelius P. Cotter.

320 301   US
BRITISH POLITICAL SOCIOLOGY YEARBOOK. 1974. a. Halsted Press (Subsidiary of: John Wiley & Sons, Inc.) 605 Third Ave., New York, NY 10016. Ed. Ivor Crewe.

BUDESHTE/AVENIR. see *ETHNIC INTERESTS*

322.4   PO
CADERNOS POLITICOS DE EDUCACAO POPULAR. no. 4, 1975. irreg. $15. Iniciativas Editoriais, Av. Rio de Janeiro 6, Lisbon, Lisbon 5.

320   BE   ISSN 0575-0571
CAHIERS DE BRUGES/BRUGES QUARTERLY. (Text in French or English; summary in other language) 1951. irreg. (College d'Europe) Uitgeverij de Tempel, 37 Tempelhof, Bruges, Belgium.

320   FR   ISSN 0068-5038
CAHIERS DE LA QUATRIEME
INTERNATIONALE. 1971. irreg. price varies.
S.I.E., 10, Impasse Guemenee, 75004 Paris, France.

320   FR   ISSN 0068-5194
CAHIERS NEPALAIS. 1969. irreg. price varies.
Centre National de la Recherche Scientifique, 15
Quai Anatole-France, 75700 Paris, France.

353.9   US   ISSN 0084-8271
CALIFORNIA GOVERNMENT & POLITICS
ANNUAL. 1970. a. ‡ California Center, 1617 10th
St., Sacramento, CA 95814. Ed.Bd. circ. 7,000. (also
avail. in microfilm)

320   US
CALIFORNIA JOURNAL ALMANAC OF STATE
GOVERNMENT AND POLITICS. 1975. biennial.
California Center, 1617 10th St., Sacramento, CA
95814. Ed. Ed Salzman. charts.illus.stat.

328 920   US   ISSN 0068-6530
CALIFORNIANS IN CONGRESS. 1955. biennial.
free. (California Congressional Recognition Project,
Inc.) Claremont Men's College, Department of
Political Science, Pitzer Hall, Claremont, CA 91711.
Eds. Alfred Balitzer, Benjamin Waldman. (back
issues avail)

320   UK   ISSN 0575-6871
CAMBRIDGE STUDIES IN THE HISTORY AND
THEORY OF POLITICS. 1967. irreg. price varies.
Cambridge University Press, Box 110, Cambridge
CB2 3RL, England (And 32 E. 57th St., New York
NY 10022) Ed.Bd.

320   US
CAMPAIGN PRACTICES REFERENCE SERVICE.
1974. irreg., approx. m. $131 (or $211 including
Campaign Practices Reports) Plus Publications, Inc.,
2626 Pennsylvania Ave., N.W., Washington, DC
20037.

320.971   CN
CANADIAN CRITICAL ISSUES SERIES. irreg.
price varies. Paper Jacks Ltd., 330 Steelcase Rd. E.,
Markham, Ont. L3R 2M1, Canada.

320   CN   ISSN 0068-8835
CANADIAN GOVERNMENT SERIES. 1947. irreg.
price varies. University of Toronto Press, Front
Campus, Toronto, Ont. M5S 1A6, Canada (and 33
East Tupper St., Buffalo, N.Y. 14203) Ed. C. B.
Macpherson. (also avail. in microfiche)

320   CN   ISSN 0380-9420
CANADIAN JOURNAL OF POLITICAL &
SOCIAL THEORY. (Revue Canadienne de Theorie
Politique et Sociale) (Text in English & French)
1977. triennial. Can.$10($12) individuals;
Can.$15($17) libraries; Can. $7 ($9) students.
University of Winnipeg, 515 Portage Ave.,
Winnipeg, Man. R3B 2E9, Canada. Ed. A. Kroker.
adv. bk. rev. index. circ. 800. (back issues avail.)
Indexed: Int.Polit.Sci.Abstr.

328   CN   ISSN 0315-6168
CANADIAN PARLIAMENTARY GUIDE. a. price
varies. P. G. Normandin, P.O. Box 3453, Station C,
Ottawa, Ont. K1Y 4J6, Canada.

320   CN
CANADIAN POLITICAL SCIENCE
ASSOCIATION. UPDATING THESES IN
CANADIAL POLITICAL STUDIES,
COMPLETED AND IN PROGRESS. (Includes
Biennial Supplements) 1970. biennial. Can.$20 (or
free with subscr. to Journal of Political Science)
Canadian Political Science Association, c/o
Carleton University, Ottawa, Ont. K1S 5B6,
Canada. circ. 2,000.

CANADIAN STUDIES IN HISTORY AND
GOVERNMENT. see *HISTORY — History Of
North And South America*

330.122 320.531   IT   ISSN 0391-1934
CAPITALISMO E SOCIALISMO. (Numbers not
published consecutively) 1976. irreg., no. 10, 1980.
price varies. Liguori Editore s.r.l., Via
Mezzocannone 19, 80134 Naples, Italy. Ed. Bruno
Jossa.

320   US   ISSN 0528-2187
CASES IN PRACTICAL POLITICS. 1960. irreg.
price varies. McGraw Hill Book Co., 1221 Avenue
of the Americas, New York, NY 10020.

320   US
CATHOLIC UNIVERSITY OF AMERICA.
SCHOOL OF LAW. CENTER FOR NATIONAL
POLICY REVIEW. ANNUAL REPORT. a.
Catholic University of America School of Law,
Center for National Policy Review, Washington,
DC 20017.

320   US
CENTER FOR THE STUDY OF THE
PRESIDENCY. PROCEEDINGS. 1973. irreg., vol.
3, 1980. $8 cloth; $5 paper. Center for the Study of
the Presidency, 926 Fifth Ave., New York, NY
10021. (also avail. in microform from UMI; reprint
service avail. from UMI)

320   PR
CENTRO DE ESTUDIOS DE LA REALIDAD
PUERTORRIQUENA. CUADERNOS. no. 2,
1974. irreg. Ediciones Huracan, Avda. Gonzalez
1003, Santa Rica, Rio Piedras, PR 00925.

951   US
CHINA FACTS AND FIGURES ANNUAL. 1978. a.
$37. Academic International Press, Box 555, Gulf
Breeze, FL 32561. Ed. John L. Scherer.

320   IT
CHRISTIAN DEMOCRATIC STUDY AND
DOCUMENTATION CENTER. CAHIERS
D'ETUDES. 1968. irreg. Christian Democratic
World Union, 107 via del Plebiscito, Rome 00186,
Italy.
   Formerly: International Christian Democratic
Study and Documentation Center. Cahiers d'Etudes
(ISSN 0538-5539)

329   IT
CHRISTIAN DEMOCRATIC WORLD UNION.
INFORMATION BULLETIN. 1964. irreg.
Christian Democratic World Union, 107 via del
Plebiscito, Rome 00186, Italy.
   Formerly (until 1972): International Christian
Democratic Study and Documentation Center.
Bulletin International (ISSN 0538-5520)

320   SZ
CHRONICLE OF PARLIAMENTARY ELECTIONS
AND DEVELOPMENTS. (Editions in French and
English) 1967. a. 30 Fr. Inter-Parliamentary Union,
International Center for Parliamentary
Documentation - Union Interparlementaire, Place
du Petit-Saconnex, 1209 Geneva, Switzerland.
   Formerly (until vol. 12, 1978): Chronicle of
Parliamentary Elections (ISSN 0074-1043)

320   SZ   ISSN 0069-4533
CLASSIQUES DE LA PENSEE POLITIQUE. 1965.
irreg., 1968, no. 5. price varies. Librarie Droz, 11
rue Massot, 1211 Geneva 12, Switzerland. circ.
1,000.

320   BL
COLECAO CAMINHOS BRASILEIROS. irreg.
Edicoes Tiempo Brasileiro Ltda, Rua Gago
Coutinho 61, C.P. 16099, ZC-01 Laranjeiras, Rio de
Janeiro, Brazil. Dir. Carlos Chagas Filho.

323 946   AG   ISSN 0069-5025
COLECCION ABERRI TA AZKATASUNA. (Text
in Basque and Spanish) 1954. irreg., latest issue,
1972. Editorial Vasca Ekin s.r.l., Belgrano 1144,
Buenos Aires 1092, Argentina.

320   UY
COLECCION CIEN TEMAS BASICOS. no. 18,
1976. irreg. Editorial Medina s.r.l., Montevideo,
Uruguay.

320   CR
COLECCION CUADERNOS CEDAL. 1974. irreg.
Centro de Estudios CEDAL, Apartado 874, San
Jose, Costa Rica. Ed. Alberto Baeza Flores.

320   SP
COLECCION IBERICA. 1976. irreg. Editorial
Anagrama, Calle de la Cruz 44, Barcelona 17,
Spain.

320   VE
COLECCION MONOGRAFIAS POLITICAS. 1978.
irreg. Editorial Juridica Venezolana, Edificio E X A,
Av. Liberator, Apdo. 62616, Chacao, Caracas 106,
Venezuela.

320   SP
COLECCION PUYAL. no. 4, 1976. irreg. 100 ptas.
Publicaciones Porvivir Independiente, Luesia
(Zaragoza), Spain.

320   SP
COLECCION TESTIGO DIRECTO. no. 2, 1976.
irreg. Sedmay Ediciones, Fleming 51, Madrid 16,
Spain. Ed. Jose Maya. illus.

320   FR   ISSN 0069-5483
COLLECTION U. SERIE ETUDES
ALLEMANDES. 1970. irreg. price varies. Librairie
Armand Colin, 103 Bld. Saint-Michel, Paris 5e,
France.

320.531   FR
COMBAT CULTUREL. 1975. irreg. price varies.
Editions Syros, 1 rue de Varenne, 75006 Paris,
France. illus.

322.4   CK
COMITE DE ACCION INTERAMERICANA DE
COLOMBIA. BOLETIN. irreg. Comite de Accion
Interamericana de Colombia, Calle 38 no. 8-28,
Apdo. Aereo 10598, Bogota, Colombia.

330 320   EI   ISSN 0069-6730
COMMISSION OF THE EUROPEAN
COMMUNITIES. ETUDES: SERIE POLITIQUE
SOCIALE. (Text in Dutch, French, German,
Italian) 1963. irreg. Office for Official Publications
of the European Communities, Case Postale 1003,
Luxembourg 1, Luxembourg (Dist. in the U.S. by
European Community Information Service, 2100 M
St. N.W., Suite No. 707, Washington, DC 20037)

329.9   FR
COMMUNIST PROGRAM. (Text in English) 1975.
irreg. 24 F.($4) (International Communist Party)
Editions Programme, 20, rue Jean Bouton, 75012
Paris, France. Ed. Saro. bk. rev. bibl. charts. circ.
2,400.
   Communism

320.532   FR
COMMUNISTES FRANCAIS ET L'EUROPE. 1978.
irreg. Parti Communiste Francais, 2 Place du
Colonel Fabien, 75019 Paris, France.

COMPARATIVE POLITICAL ECONOMY AND
PUBLIC POLICY SERIES. see *BUSINESS AND
ECONOMICS — Economic Systems And
Theories, Economic History*

329.9   II
CONGRESS MARCHES AHEAD. (Text in English)
1970. irreg. price varies. All India Congress
Committee, Publications Department, 5 Dr.
Rajendra Prasad Rd., New Delhi 110001, India.

328 973   US   ISSN 0069-8938
CONGRESSIONAL STAFF DIRECTORY. 1959. a.
$22. Congressional Staff Directory, Box 62, Mount
Vernon, VA 22121. Ed. Charles Brownson.

320   US
CONNECTIONS TWO. 1974. irreg. $3. National
American Studies Connections Collective, c/o Doris
Friedersohn, Exec. Sec'y, 209 Hillcrest Ave.,
Leonia, NJ 07605. bibl. circ. 500.
   Formerly (until 1973): Connections.

322.4   HO
CONSEJO CENTRAL EJECUTIVO DEL PARTIDO
LIBERAL DE HONDURAS. MEMORIA. irreg.
Partido Liberal, Consejo Central Ejecutivo,
Tegucigalpa, Honduras.

320   US   ISSN 0147-1066
CONTRIBUTIONS IN POLITICAL SCIENCE.
1978. irreg. Greenwood Press, 88 Post Rd. W.,
Westport, CT 06881. Ed. Bernard K. Johnpoll.

320   IT
CONTROCAMPO. 1977. irreg. Casa Editrice
Armando Armando, Via della Gensola 60-61, 00153
Rome, Italy.

320   US
COUNTRIES OF THE WORLD; and their leaders
yearbook. 1974. a. $40. Gale Research Company,
Book Tower, Detroit, MI 48226.

POLITICAL SCIENCE

320   US
CROATIAN INFORMATION SERIES. 1975. irreg. (2-3/yr) Croatian Information Service, P.O. Box 3025, Arcadia, CA 91006. Ed. C. Michael McAdams. bibl.

320   AG
CUADERNOS DE ESTUDIOS LATINOAMERICANOS. no. 2, 1974. irreg. Universidad Nacional del Nordeste, Instituto de Letras, Resistencia, Chaco, Argentina. Dir. Alfredo Veirave.

320   PE
DEBATE SOCIALISTA. 1977. irreg. Mosca Azul Editores, La Paz 651, Lima 18, Peru. Ed. Mirko Lauer. circ. 2,000.

321   GW   ISSN 0070-3389
DEMOKRATISCHE EXISTENZ HEUTE. 1961. irreg., vol. 20, 1973. price varies. (Universitaet zu Koeln, Forschungsinstitut fuer Politische Wissenschaften und Europaeische Fragen) Carl Heymanns Verlag KG, Gereonstr. 18-32, 5 Cologne 1, W. Germany (B.R.D.) adv. bk. rev.

328   DK   ISSN 0084-9707
DENMARK. FOLKETINGET. FOLKETINGSAARBOG. a. price varies. J. H. Schultz Forlag, Vognmagergade 2, 1120 Copenhagen K, Denmark. Ed. Arne Marquard. circ. 1,500.

354   BU
DIRECTORY OF KEY BULGARIAN GOVERNMENT AND PARTY OFFICIALS. American Embassy (in Bulgaria), 1, Aleksandur Stamboliiski Blvd., Sofia, Bulgaria.

328.38   US   ISSN 0146-0323
DIRECTORY OF REGISTERED LOBBYISTS AND LOBBYIST LEGISLATION. 1973. irreg., 2nd 1975. $44.50. Marquis Academic Media, 200 E. Ohio St., Chicago, IL 60611.
Formerly: Directory of Registered Federal and State Lobbyists (ISSN 0092-1874)

320.5   US
DIRECTORY OF THE AMERICAN LEFT; an intelligence report. 1979. a. $12.95. Editorial Research Service, Box 1832, Kansas City, MO 64141. Ed. Laird M. Wilcox. bibl. circ. 500. Indexed: P.A.I.S.
Supersedes (1969-1970): Guide to the American Left (ISSN 0017-5315)

320   US
DIRECTORY OF THE AMERICAN RIGHT; an intelligence report. 1978. a. $12.95. Editorial Research Service, Box 1832, Kansas City, MO 64141. Ed. Laird M. Wilcox. Indexed: P.A.I.S.

320.532   IT
DOCUMENTARIA. 1976. irreg. Iskra Edizioni, Via Adige 3, 20135 Milan, Italy.

320.531   UK
DOCUMENTS IN SOCIALIST HISTORY. no. 2, 1974. irreg. (Bertrand Russell Peace Foundation) Spokesman Books, Bertrand Russell House, Gamble St., Nottingham, England.

320 900   US
DOCUMENTS OF REVOLUTION. irreg. price varies. Cornell University Press, 124 Roberts Place, Ithaca, NY 14850.

320   UK   ISSN 0070-7007
DOD'S PARLIAMENTARY COMPANION. 1832. a. £14.50. Dod's Parliamentary Companion Ltd., Elm Cottage, Chilsham Lane, Herstmonceux, Hailsham, East Sussex, England. Ed. J. B. Smith. adv. bk. rev. index. circ. 3,700. (also avail. in microform from UMI)

320 940   GW   ISSN 0070-7031
DOKUMENTE ZUR DEUTSCHLANDPOLITIK. (In five series) 1961. irreg., reihe 4, no.11, 1976. price varies. (Bundesminister fuer Innerdeutsche Beziehungen) Alfred Metzner Verlag GmbH, Zeppelinallee 43, Postfach 970148, 6000 Frankfurt 97, W. Germany (B.R.D.) Eds. Karl Dietrich Bracher, Hans-Adolf Jacobsen.

320 940   GW   ISSN 0341-3276
DOKUMENTE ZUR DEUTSCHLANDPOLITIK. BEIHEFTE. 1975. irreg. price varies. (Bundesministerium fuer Innerdeutsche Beziehungen) Alfred Metzner Verlag GmbH, Zeppelinallee 43, Postfach 970148, 6000 Frankfurt 97, W. Germany (B.R.D.) Eds. K. D. Bracher, H.-A. Jacobsen.

DOMOVA POKLADNICA. see *LITERATURE*

320.253 301 355   US
EASTERN EUROPE REPORT: POLITICAL, SOCIOLOGICAL AND MILITARY AFFAIRS. 1968. irreg. (approx. 138/yr.) $414. U.S. Joint Publications Research Service, 1000 N. Glebe Rd., Arlington, VA 22201 (Orders to: NTIS, Springfield, VA 22161)
Formerly: Translations on Eastern Europe. Political, Sociological and Military Affairs.

320   PE
EDICIONES RIKCHAY PERU. 1976. irreg. Editorial I N A P, Avda. 28 de Julio 878, Miraflores, Lima, Peru.

328.73   US   ISSN 0095-7186
ELECTION INDEX. 1966. biennial. $8. Congressional Staff Directory, Box 62, Mount Vernon, VA 22121.
Biographical briefs on the members and the candidates; lists the cities and towns in their districts; list of campaign managers; election statistics going back four elections

341.7   SP   ISSN 0464-3755
ESCUELA DIPLOMATICA. CUADERNOS. 1960. irreg. price varies. Escuela Diplomatica, Paseo de Juan 23, No. 5, Madrid 3, Spain. bibl. charts. illus. stat. circ. 1,000. (back issues avail)

328   PN   ISSN 0078-897X
ESTADISTICA PANAMENA. ESTADISTICA ELECTORAL. 1960. quadriennial. free. Direccion de Estadistica y Censo, Contraloria General, Apartado 5213, Panama 5, Panama. circ. 2,000.

320   BL
EX. 1973. irreg. Cr.$70. Ex-Editora, Rua Santo Antonio 1043, CP 01314, Sao Paulo, Brazil. illus.

320   UK   ISSN 0071-3570
FABIAN SOCIETY. ANNUAL REPORT. 1891. a. 30p. Fabian Society, 11 Dartmouth St., London, SW1H 9BN, England.
Formerly: Annual Report on Work of Fabian Society.

320   US
FACT PAPER ON SOUTHERN AFRICA. 1976. irreg. International Defense and Aid Fund for Southern Africa, North American Committee, Box 17, Cambridge, MA 02138. Ed. Kenneth N. Carstens.

FACTS ON FILE. YEARBOOK. see *HISTORY — Abstracting, Bibliographies, Statistics*

FINLAND; books and publications in politics, political history and international relations. see *HISTORY — History Of Europe*

FLINDERS JOURNAL OF HISTORY AND POLITICS. see *HISTORY — History Of Australasia And Other Areas*

FOCUS ON POLITICS. see *HISTORY*

320   AU
FOEDERALISMUS-STUDIEN. 1977. irreg., vol. 2, 1978. price varies. Hermann Boehlaus Nachf., Schmalzhofgasse 4, Postfach 167, A-1061 Vienna, Austria. Eds. R. Novak, B. Sutter, G. D. Hasiba. circ. 650.

320   FR
FORCES NOUVELLES INFO. 1977. m. 12 F. Societe Occidentale d'Edition, 7 Bd. de Sebastopol, 75001 Paris, France.

320   FR
FRANCE. MINISTERE DE LA COOPERATION. SERVICE DES ETUDES ET QUESTIONS INTERNATIONALES. DONNEES STATISTIQUES SUR LES ACTIVITES ECONOMIQUES, CULTURELLES ET SOCIALES. irreg. Ministere de la Cooperation, Service des Etudes et Questions Internationales, 20 rue Monsieur, 75700 Paris, France. charts.
Formerly: Cooperation entre la France et les Etats Francophones d'Afrique Noire et de l'Ocean Indien.

320.531   FR
FRANCE DES POINTS CHAUDS. Short title: Points Chauds. irreg. price varies. Editions Syros, 1 rue de Varenne, 75006 Paris, France.

327   FR   ISSN 0082-5409
FRANCE-IBERIE RECHERCHE. ETUDES ET DOCUMENTS. 1970. irreg. price varies. Universite de Toulouse II (le Mirail), Institut d'Etudes Hispaniques, Hispanoamericaines, 109 bis, rue Vauquelin, 31081 Toulouse Cedex, France.

327   US   ISSN 0488-728X
FREE ALBANIAN/SHQIPTARI I LIRE. (Text in English and Albanian) 1957. 1-2/yr. donation. Free Albania Committee, 150 Fifth Ave., New York, NY 10011. Ed.Bd. bk. rev. illus. circ. 1,000. (tabloid format)

FREIE UNIVERSITAET BERLIN. OSTEUROPA-INSTITUT. BERICHTE. see *HUMANITIES: COMPREHENSIVE WORKS*

FREIE UNIVERSITAET BERLIN. OSTEUROPA-INSTITUT. ERZIEHUNGSWISSENSCHAFTLICHE VEROEFFENTLICHUNGEN. see *EDUCATION*

FREIE UNIVERSITAET BERLIN. OSTEUROPA-INSTITUT. PHILOSOPHISCHE UND SOZIOLOGISCHE VEROEFFENTLICHUNGEN. see *PHILOSOPHY*

320   US
GEORGETOWN UNIVERSITY CENTER FOR STRATEGIC AND INTERNATIONAL STUDIES. SIGNIFICANT ISSUES SERIES. 1979. irreg., vol. 2, 1980. $5.95 per no. Georgetown University, Center for Strategic and International Studies, 1800 K St. N.W., Suite 400, Washington, DC 20006. Ed. Robert G. Neumann.

320   US
GERMAN POLITICAL STUDIES. 1974. a. $18.95 for hardbound; softbound $8.95. Sage Publications, Inc., 275 S. Beverly Dr., Beverly Hills, CA 90212 (And Sage Publications, Ltd., 28 Banner St., London EC1Y 8QE, England) (back issues avail.)

320   SW
GOETEBORG STUDIES IN POLITICS. irreg., no. 7, 1977. price varies. C.W.K. Gleerup (Subsidiary of: LiberLaeromedel) Box 1205, S-221 05 Lund, Sweden. Ed. Joergen Westerstaahl.
Formerly: Studier i Politik/Studies in Politics.

320 327   GW
GOETTINGER QUELLENHEFTE. irreg. price varies. Vandenhoeck und Ruprecht, Theaterstr. 13, Postfach 77, 3400 Goettingen, W. Germany (B.R.D.)

300   II   ISSN 0436-1326
GOKHALE INSTITUTE MIMEOGRAPH SERIES. 1967. irreg. price varies. Gokhale Institute of Politics and Economics, Pune 411004, India.

320 330   II   ISSN 0072-4912
GOKHALE INSTITUTE OF POLITICS AND ECONOMICS. STUDIES. (Text in English) irreg., 1975, no. 64. price varies. Gokhale Institute of Politics and Economics, Pune 411004, India (Dist. by: Orient Longman Ltd., Nicol Rd., Ballard Estate, Bombay 400038, India)

322.4   US
GRASS ROOTS GUIDES; on democracy and practical politics. irreg. latest no. 59, 1978. $9 for 10 issues. Center for Information on America, Washington, CT 06793.

GUIA DEL TERCER MUNDO. see *ENCYCLOPEDIAS AND GENERAL ALMANACS*

POLITICAL SCIENCE

320   US   ISSN 0091-9632
GUIDE TO GRADUATE STUDY IN POLITICAL SCIENCE. 1972. biennial. $10. American Political Science Association, 1527 New Hampshire Ave. N.W., Washington, DC 20036. circ. 2,500.

320.4   US   ISSN 0095-2842
HANDBOOK OF ILLINOIS GOVERNMENT. (Supplement to Illinois Blue Book in alternate years) irreg. Secretary of State, Springfield, IL 62700. illus.

320   US
HARVARD POLITICAL CLASSICS. irreg. price varies. Harvard University Press, 79 Garden St., Cambridge, MA 02138.

320   US
HARVARD POLITICAL STUDIES. irreg. price varies. Harvard University Press, 79 Garden St., Cambridge, MA 02138.

320   GW
HEIDELBERGER POLITISCHE SCHRIFTEN. 1969. irreg., no. 9, 1977. price varies. Verlag Anton Hain GmbH, Adelheidstr. 2, Postfach 1220, 6240 Koenigstein, W. Germany (B.R.D.) Ed. Dolf Sternberger.

320   301   SZ   ISSN 0073-182X
HELVETIA POLITICA; Schriften des Forschungszentrums fuer Geschichte und Soziologie der schweizerischen Politik. (Text in German, French or Italian) 1966. irreg. price varies. ‡ Francke Verlag, Postfach, CH-3000 Berne 26, Switzerland. Eds. Erich Gruner, Peter Gilg, Beat Junker.

HISTORIC DOCUMENTS. see *HISTORY — History Of North And South America*

943.7   320   301   CS   ISSN 0441-8026
HISTORICA CARPATICA. irreg., vol. 6, 1975. price varies. (Vychodoslovenske Muzeum) Vychodoslovenske Krajske Vydavatelstvo, Orlai Ul., 11, 040 01 Kosice, Czechoslovakia.

HITOTSUBASHI JOURNAL OF LAW AND POLITICS. see *LAW*

920   320   US   ISSN 0085-1582
HOOVER INSTITUTION BIBLIOGRAPHIES SERIES. 1960, no. 8. irreg., no. 58, 1977. (Stanford University, Hoover Institution on War, Revolution and Peace) Hoover Institution Press, Publications Dept., Stanford, CA 94305.

320   US
HOOVER INSTITUTION ON WAR, REVOLUTION AND PEACE. FOREIGN LANGUAGE PUBLICATIONS SERIES. 1967. irreg. price varies. (Stanford University, Hoover Institution on War, Revolution and Peace) Hoover Institution Press, Stanford, CA 94305.

320   US   ISSN 0085-1590
HOOVER INSTITUTION ON WAR, REVOLUTION AND PEACE. LIBRARY SURVEYS. 1970. irreg. price varies. (Stanford University, Hoover Institution on War, Revolution and Peace) Hoover Institution Press, Stanford, CA 94305.

320   US   ISSN 0073-3296
HOOVER INSTITUTION ON WAR, REVOLUTION, AND PEACE. PUBLICATIONS SERIES. 1932. irreg., latest, no. 191. (Stanford University, Hoover Institution on War, Revolution and Peace) Hoover Institution Press, Stanford, CA 94305.

320   US   ISSN 0073-330X
HOOVER INSTITUTION STUDIES SERIES. 1963. irreg., no. 56, 1977. (Stanford University, Hoover Institution on War, Revolution and Peace) Hoover Institution Press, Stanford, CA 94305.

320   SZ
I P Z INFORMATION. REIHE S: SUBVERSION. 1971. irreg., no. 17, 1978. price varies. Institut fuer Politologische Zeitfragen, Postfach 2720, 8023 Zurich, Switzerland.

320.531   AU
I U S Y BULLETIN. 1971. irreg. free. International Union of Socialist Youth, Neustiftgasse, A-1070 Vienna, Austria. Ed. Htun Aung. illus.
    Formerly: I U S Y Survey (ISSN 0019-0888)
Socialism

ILLINOIS GOVERNMENT RESEARCH. see *PUBLIC ADMINISTRATION*

320   US
IN PURSUIT OF LIBERTY. 1976. irreg.(2-4/yr.) $6. Center for Libertarian Studies, 200 Park Ave. S., New York, NY 10003. Ed. Peter J. Ferrara. circ. 1,200.
    Formerly: Center for Libertarian Studies. Newsletter.

300   AU   ISSN 0083-6125
INFORMATIONEN ZU AKTUELLEN FRAGEN DER SOZIAL- UND WIRTSCHAFTPOLITIK. 1962. irreg. price varies. ‡ Verein fuer Sozial- und Wirtschaftsforschung, Renngasse 12, A-1010 Vienna, Austria. circ. 1,000.

320   FR   ISSN 0073-7925
INFORMATIONS ET ETUDES SOCIALISTES.* 1971. irreg. 20 F. Institut d'Etudes Socialistes, Paris, 25 rue du Louvre, Paris 1er, France.

329   AT
INSIGHT. 1968. irreg. Aus.$2. Young Labor Association of South Australia, Trades Hall, 11-16 South Terrace, Adelaide, S.A. 5000, Australia. Ed. Doug Lorimer.

320   BE   ISSN 0073-8131
INSTITUT BELGE DE SCIENCE POLITIQUE. BIBLIOTHEQUE. NOUVELLE SERIE. 1959. irreg. Institut Belge de Science Politique, 43 rue des Champs-Elysees, 1050 Brussels, Belgium.

320   BE   ISSN 0073-814X
INSTITUT BELGE DE SCIENCE POLITIQUE. BIBLIOTHEQUE. SERIE DOCUMENTS. 1967. irreg. Institut Belge de Science Politique, 43 rue des Champs-Elysees, 1050 Brussels, Belgium.

320   BE   ISSN 0073-8158
INSTITUT BELGE DE SCIENCE POLITIQUE. DOCUMENTS. (Text in French and Dutch) 1967. a. 200 Fr. Institut Belge de Science Politique, 43 rue des Champs-Elysees, 1050 Brussels, Belgium.

320   FR   ISSN 0078-995X
INSTITUT D'ETUDES POLITIQUES DE PARIS. LIVRET. 1954-55. biennial. 20 F. Librarie Vuibert, 63 Bld. Saint- Germain, 75005 Paris, France.

INSTITUT DES HAUTES ETUDES DE L'AMERIQUE LATINE. CENTRE D'ETUDES POLITIQUES, ECONOMIQUES ET SOCIALES. PUBLICATIONS MULTIGRAPHIEES. see *HISTORY — History Of North And South America*

INSTITUT DES HAUTES ETUDES DE L'AMERIQUE LATINE. TRAVAUX ET MEMOIRES. see *HISTORY — History Of North And South America*

INSTITUT FUER ASIENKUNDE. SCHRIFTEN. see *HISTORY — History Of Asia*

320   AG   ISSN 0074-0063
INSTITUTO DE CIENCIA POLITICA RAFAEL BIELSA. ANUARIO. 1968. a. Arg.$75($8) Universidad Nacional de Rosario, Instituto de Ciencia Politica Rafael Bielsa, Facultad de Ciencia Politica y Relaciones Internacionales, Division Publicaciones, Cordoba 2020, Rosario, Argentina. Ed. Alberto Dominguez.

320.9   UK
INTELLIGENCE DIGEST SPECIAL BRIEFS. irreg. $62. Intelligence International Ltd., 17 Rodney Rd., Chetenham, Glos. GL50 1JQ, England.

323.44   US   ISSN 0579-6695
INTER-AMERICAN PRESS ASSOCIATION. COMMITTEE ON FREEDOM OF THE PRESS. REPORT. a. membership. Inter-American Press Association, 2911 N.W. 39th St., Miami, FL 33142.

320.532   UK   ISSN 0140-0649
INTERNATIONAL COMMUNIST. 1976. irreg. 30p. International Communist League, 98 Gifford St., London N1 ODE, England. Ed. Martin Thomas. bk. rev. circ. 1,000. (also avail. in microfilm from HPL)

341.2   US   ISSN 0363-7123
INTERNATIONAL ORGANISATIONS IN WORLD POLITICS YEARBOOK. a. $27.50. Westview Press, 5500 Central Ave., Boulder, CO 80301.

320   CN
INTERNATIONAL POLITICAL SCIENCE ASSOCIATION. WORLD CONGRESS. 1951. triennial, 11th, 1979, Moscow. price varies. International Political Science Association, c/o University of Ottawa, Ottawa, Ont. K1N 6N5, Canada.
    Formerly: International Political Science Association. World Conference. Proceedings (ISSN 0074-7467)

INTERNATIONAL YEAR BOOK AND STATESMEN'S WHO'S WHO. see *SOCIAL SCIENCES: COMPREHENSIVE WORKS*

320   US
INTERNATIONAL YEARBOOK OF ORGANIZATIONAL DEMOCRACY. 1982. a? John Wiley & Sons, Inc., 605 Third Ave., New York, NY 10016. Ed. Frank A. Heller.

320   SZ   ISSN 0579-8337
INTER-PARLIAMENTARY UNION. SERIES: "REPORTS AND DOCUMENTS". 1965. irreg., no. 8, 1978. price varies. Inter-Parliamentary Union, Place du Petit-Saconnex, 1209 Geneva, Switzerland.

320   US   ISSN 0074-1078
INTER-UNIVERSITY CONSORTIUM FOR POLITICAL AND SOCIAL RESEARCH. ANNUAL REPORT. 1963. a. free. Inter-University Consortium for Political and Social Research, Box 1248, Ann Arbor, MI 48106.

320   AT   ISSN 0311-1989
INTERVENTION. 1972. irreg. institutions Aus. $15; individuals Aus. $6. Intervention Collective, P.O. Box 104, Carleton, Vic. 3053, Australia. Ed.Bd. adv. bk. rev. circ. 1,200. Indexed: Aus. P.A.I.S.

320.531   UK
IRELAND SOCIALIST REVIEW. 1977/78. irreg., no. 6, 1979/80. £2 for individuals; £4 for institutions (for 4 nos.) c/o 60 Loughborough Rd., London SW9, England. bk. rev.
Socialism

IRODALOM - SZOCIALIZMUS. see *LITERATURE*

320   NE
ISSUES IN CONTEMPORARY POLITICS. (Text in English) 1975. irreg. price varies. Martinus Nijhoff, Box 442, The Hague, Netherlands (U.S. addr.: Mouton Publishers, c/o Walter de Gruyter, Inc., 200 Saw Mill River Road, Hawthorne, NY 10532)

320   IT
ISTITUTO GRAMSCI PIEMONTESE. MATERIALI. vol. 2, 1976. irreg. (Istituto Gramsci Piemontese) T. Musolini Editore, Via Pianezza 14, 10149 Turin, Italy.

320   IT
ISTITUTO PER LA STORIA DEL MOVIMENTO LIBERALE. QUADERNO. 1977. irreg. Arnaldo Forni Editore, Via Gramsci 164, 40010 Bologna, Italy.

320.9   IT
ITALIA NELLA POLITICA INTERNAZIONALE. 1973. a. (Istituto Affari Internazionali) Edizioni di Comunita, Via Manzoni 12, 20121 Milan, Italy.

320   956   US   ISSN 0075-3009
JAMES TERRY DUCE MEMORIAL SERIES. 1966. irreg., vol. 3, 1975. price varies. Middle East Institute, 1761 N St. N.W., Washington, DC 20036. (reprint service avail. from UMI)

328.54   II   ISSN 0448-2433
JAMMU AND KASHMIR. LEGISLATIVE COUNCIL. COMMITTEE ON PRIVILEGES. REPORT. (Text in English) irreg. Legislative Council, Committee on Privileges, Srinagar, Jammu and Kashmir, India.

JAPAN ANNUAL OF LAW AND POLITICS. see *LAW*

JAPAN REPORT. see *BUSINESS AND ECONOMICS — Economic Situation And Conditions*

POLITICAL SCIENCE

320.532   JA   ISSN 0007-4683
JAPANESE COMMUNIST PARTY. CENTRAL COMMITTEE. BULLETIN: INFORMATION FOR ABROAD. (Text in English) 1961. irreg. $28. Japanese Communist Party, Sendagaya 4-26-7, Shibuya-ku, Tokyo, Japan. adv. illus.

320   JA   ISSN 0549-4192
JAPANESE POLITICAL SCIENCE ASSOCIATION. YEARBOOK/NIHON SEIJI GAKKAI NENPO: SEIJIGAKU. Short title: Seijigaku. (Text in Japanese; summaries in English) 1950. a. Japanese Political Science Association - Nihon Seiji Gakkai, c/o Faculty of Law, University of Tokyo, 7-3-1 Hongo. Bunkyo-ku, Tokyo 113, Japan. bk. rev.

JOHNS HOPKINS UNIVERSITY STUDIES IN HISTORICAL AND POLITICAL SCIENCE. see *HISTORY*

320   CN   ISSN 0705-0852
JOURNAL DE LA MAJORITE. vol. 3, 1977. irreg. Association Nationale des Etudiants du Quebec, 2336 Chemin Ste-Foy, Quebec G1V 1S8, Canada. circ. 25,000. (tabloid format)

JOURNAL OF HISTORY AND POLITICAL SCIENCE. see *HISTORY — History Of Asia*

320   US
JOURNAL OF SOCIAL AND POLITICAL STUDIES MONOGRAPH SERIES. irreg., unnumbered. $8 per no. Institute for the Study of Man, Inc., 1629 K St., N.W., Suite 520, Washington, DC 20006.

328   US   ISSN 0270-4331
KANSAS. LEGISLATIVE RESEARCH DEPARTMENT. REPORT ON KANSAS LEGISLATIVE INTERIM STUDIES. 1971. a. free. ‡ Legislative Research Department, Topeka, KS 66612. circ. controlled.

KAPITALISTATE. see *BUSINESS AND ECONOMICS*

KNOW YOUR CONGRESS. see *PUBLIC ADMINISTRATION*

320.532   UR
KOMMUNISTICHESKAYA PARTIYA SOVETSKOGO SOYUZA. VYSSHAYA PARTIINAYA SHKOLA. UCHENYE ZAPISKI. 1973. irreg. 1.14 Rub. Izdatel'stvo Mysl, Leninskii Prospekt: 15, 117071 Moscow B-71, U.S.S.R.

320   KO
KOREA (REPUBLIC). TONGIL CHUCHE KUNGMIN HOEUI. KUNGMIN HOEUI BO/ NATIONAL CONFERENCE REVIEW.* (Text in Korean) 1973. irreg. Tongil Chuche Kungmin Hoeui Samucho, 88 Kyongun-Dong, Chongno-Gu, Seoul, S. Korea. illus.

320 330   KO
KOREA POLICY SERIES.* no. 16, 1973. irreg. Korean Overseas Information Service, Seoul, S. Korea.

KOREAN AFFAIRS REPORT. see *BUSINESS AND ECONOMICS — Economic Situation And Conditions*

LATIN AMERICA & CARIBBEAN. see *BUSINESS AND ECONOMICS — Economic Situation And Conditions*

LATIN AMERICA REPORT. see *BUSINESS AND ECONOMICS — Economic Situation And Conditions*

LAW AND POLITICAL REVIEW. see *LAW*

320   UK
LIBERAL FOCUS. 1973, no. 8. irreg. per no. Liberal Publication Department, 9 Poland St., London W1V 3DG, England. stat. circ. 5,000.

320   UK
LIBERAL PUBLICATION DEPARTMENT. STUDY PAPER. 1976. irreg. 25p. per no. Liberal Publication Department, 9 Poland St., London W1V 3DG, England. charts. stat.
     Formerly: Liberal Party Organisation. Study Paper (ISSN 0308-9657)

320   LH
LIECHTENSTEIN. POLITISCHE SCHRIFTEN. 1972. irreg. $18. Liechsteinsteinische Akademische Gesellschaft, Vaduz, Liechtenstein.

320   FR
LUTTES SOCIALES. 1979. irreg. Librairie Francois Maspero, 1 Place Paul Painleve, 75005 Paris, France. Ed. Gerard Althabe. circ. 4,000.

320   US   ISSN 0076-1729
M.L. SEIDMAN MEMORIAL TOWN HALL LECTURE SERIES. 1967. a. $5. Southwestern at Memphis, 2000 North Pky., Memphis, TN 38110. Ed. Phineas J. Sparer. circ. 300.

335   HU   ISSN 0076-2415
MAGYAR MUNKASMOZGALMI MUZEUM. EVKONYV. 1967/68. biennial. 90 Ft. Nepmuvelesi Propaganda Iroda, Gorkij Fasor 45, Budapest VII, Hungary. Eds. Bela Esti, Tibor Hetes, Emil Horn.

320   UG
MAKERERE POLITICAL REVIEW.* 1971. irreg. Makerere Political Society, Political Science Department, Makerere University, Kampala, Uganda. Ed. Amos Danson Twino. bibl.

320.531   CE
MAKSVADAYA. (Text in Sinhalese) vol. 3, 1977. irreg. Sarat Vidana Patirana, 17 Barracks Lane, Kew Rd., Colombo 2, Sri Lanka.

320   MW
MALAWI. DEPARTMENT OF INFORMATION. PARLIAMENTARY BIOGRAPHIES. (Text in English) 1971. a. free. Department of Information, Box 494, Blantyre, Malawi. circ. 2,000.

320   MW   ISSN 0076-3225
MALAWI. MINISTRY OF LOCAL GOVERNMENT. ANNUAL REPORT. a, latest 1970. K.0.50. Government Printer, P.O. Box 37, Zomba, Malawi.

320 914   UK
MALTA YEARBOOK. a. $10. Publishing and Distributing Co. Ltd., 177 Regent St., London W.1., England.

320   IT
MANIFESTO. QUADERNO. irreg. no. 5, 1976. L.2000. Alfani Editore, Via Tomacelli 146, Rome, Italy.

320   GW   ISSN 0542-6480
MARBURGER ABHANDLUNGEN ZUR POLITISCHEN WISSENSCHAFT. 1964. irreg., vol. 23, 1978. price varies. Verlag Anton Hain GmbH, Adelheidstr. 2, Postfach 1220, 6240 Koenigstein, W. Germany (B.R.D.) Ed. Wolfgang Abendroth.

320   US
MARINE AFFAIRS JOURNAL. 1973. a. $1. University of Rhode Island, Marine Advisory Service, Marine Affairs Program, Narragansett Bay Campus, Narragansett, RI 02882. charts. circ. 300. (back issues avail.)

016.3354   US   ISSN 0098-9509
MARXISM AND THE MASS MEDIA; towards a basic bibliography. 1972. irreg., latest 1980. price varies. (International Mass Media Research Center, FR) International General, Box 350, New York, NY 10013 (And 173 Ave. de la Dhuys, 93170 Bagnolet, France) Ed. Seth Siegelaub. circ. 1,500-3,000.

320.531   IT
MARXISTA EUROPEA. 1967. a. with supplements. L.10000. Fourth International - Posadist, International Secretariat, C.P. 5059, 00153 Rome, Italy. Ed. Agostino Bozano. bk. rev. circ. 500.
Communism

320.532   CN   ISSN 0047-6110
MASS LINE. 1970. irreg. price varies. Communist Party of Canada (Marxist- Leninist), Box 666, Station C, Montreal, Que., Canada (Subscr. to: National Publications Centre, P.O. Box 727, Adelaide Station, Toronto, Ont., Canada) Ed. Hardial S. Bains. charts. illus.
Communism

320   IT
MATERIALIMARSILIO. 1977. irreg. Marsilio Editori S.p.A., Fondamenta Santa Chiara, Santa Croce 518-A, 30125 Venice, Italy.

320   AT   ISSN 0085-3224
MELBOURNE JOURNAL OF POLITICS. 1968. a. Aus.$3. ‡ University of Melbourne, Political Science Society, Parkville, Vic. 3052, Australia. Ed. E. N. Vandeloo. adv. bk. rev. circ. 1,000. Indexed: Aus.P.A.I.S.

320   AT
MELBOURNE POLITICS MONOGRAPHS. 1973. a. Aus.$6. ‡ University of Melbourne, Department of Political Science, Parkville 3052, Victoria, Australia. Ed.Bd. adv. bk. rev. bibl.

949.3   BE   ISSN 0025-908X
MEMO FROM BELGIUM. (English ed. issued in 2 series, "Facts and Comments" and "Views and Surveys"; numbering is continuous) (Editions in Dutch,English,French,German,Italian and Spanish) 1960. 4-6/yr. free. Ministere des Affaires Etrangeres, 2 rue des Quatre Bras, 1000 Brussels, Belgium (For English edition, inquire: Consulate General de Belgique, Information Officer, 50 Rockefeller Plaza, Suite 1104, New York, New York) charts. illus. circ. 3,000(each) Indexed: P.A.I.S.

327   US
MIDDLE EAST INSTITUTE NEWSLETTER. irreg. Middle East Institute, 1761 N St. N.W., Washington, DC 20036. bibl. (reprint service avail. from UMI)

320 330   UK
MIDDLE EAST YEARBOOK. 1977. a. £12.45($25) International Communications Ltd., 63 Long Acre, London WC2E 9JH, England. Ed. Gill Garb. bk. rev. illus. stat. circ. 10,000. (also avail. in microfilm; back issues avail.)

322.4   UK
MILITANT PAMPHLETS. 1975? irreg. price varies. Militant, 1 Mentmore Terrace, London E8 3PN, England.

335.83   UK   ISSN 0026-5721
MINUS ONE; an individualist review. 1963. irreg. £1.50 for six nos. S. E. Parker, Ed. & Pub., Basement Flat, 91 Talbot Rd., London W. 2., England. adv. bk. rev. circ. 250. (processed)

320   US
MISSOURI POLITICAL SCIENCE ASSOCIATION. PROCEEDINGS OF THE ANNUAL MEETING. 1972. a. $1 to non-members. ‡ Missouri Political Science Association, University of Missouri, 118 Middlebush Hall, Columbia, MO 65201. Ed. Robert F. Karsch. circ. 200.

320   US
MODERN COMPARATIVE POLITICS SERIES. irreg. price varies. Holt, Rinehart and Winston, 383 Madison Ave., New York, NY 10017.

MONASH PAPERS ON SOUTHEAST ASIA. see *HISTORY — History Of Asia*

323.4   GW   ISSN 0026-9239
MONATSBLAETTER FUER FREIHEITLICHE WIRTSCHAFTSPOLITIK. 1955. a. DM.15. Fritz Knapp Verlag GmbH, Neue Mainzer Str. 60, 6000 Frankfurt 1, W. Germany (B.R.D.) Ed. Peter Muthesius. adv. bk. rev. index. circ. 2,000.

MONGOLIA REPORT. see *BUSINESS AND ECONOMICS — Economic Situation And Conditions*

320   AT   ISSN 0077-2143
MUNICIPAL ASSOCIATION OF VICTORIA. MINUTES OF PROCEEDINGS OF ANNUAL SESSION. 1879. a. free; available to member councils. ‡ Municipal Association of Victoria, 15 Queens Rd., Melbourne, Vic. 3004, Australia. Ed. Ian R. Pawsey. index. circ. 4,000.

808.8   UK
NATIONAL AWAMI PARTY OF BANGLA DESH (IN GREAT BRITAIN). BULLETIN.* irreg., 1973, no. 5. National Awami Party of Bangla Desh, 86 Oakleigh Road, London N.11, England. Ed. Fazlul Huq.

352   AT   ISSN 0085-3682
NATIONAL CIVIC COUNCIL. FACTS. 1959. irreg.
Aus.$8. National Civic Council, 5 Riversdale Rd.,
Hawthorn, Vic. 3122, Australia. Ed. Peter W.
Taylor. adv. circ. 7,000.

NATIONAL DIRECTORY OF STATE AGENCIES.
see BUSINESS AND ECONOMICS — Trade And
Industrial Directories

329.9   CN   ISSN 0707-0349
NATIONAL P C PRESIDENT. (Text in English and
French) 1976. Progressive Conservative Party of
Canada, 178 Queen St., Ottawa, Ont. K1P 5E1,
Canada.

329   US   ISSN 0077-5282
NATIONAL PARTY PLATFORMS.
SUPPLEMENT. 1961. irreg., 6th edt., 1977. price
varies. University of Illinois Press, 54 E. Gregory,
Box 5081, Station A, Champaign, IL 61820. Eds.
Kirk H. Porter, Donald B. Johnson. (reprint service
avail. from UMI)
Sixth edition covers 1840-1976

353.002   US   ISSN 0092-2935
NATIONAL ROSTER OF BLACK ELECTED
OFFICIALS. 1970. a. $17.50. Joint Center for
Political Studies, 1301 Pennsylvania Ave., N.W.,
Suite 400, 1426 H St., N.W., Washington, DC
20004. circ. 5,000.

329   PL
NAUKI POLITYCZNE. 1974. irreg. price varies.
Uniwersytet im. Adama Mickiewicza w Poznaniu,
Stalingradzka 1, 61-712 Poznan, Poland (Dist. by:
Ars Polona, Krakowskie Przedmiescie 7, 00-068
Warsaw, Poland)

NEAR EAST AND NORTH AFRICA REPORT. see
BUSINESS AND ECONOMICS — Economic
Situation And Conditions

320   NE
NETHERLANDS.
RIJKSVOORLICHTINGSDIENST.
HOOFPUNTEN VAN HET
REGERINGSBELEID. irreg.
Rijksvoorlichtingsdienst, The Hague, Netherlands.

320   330   UK
NEW AFRICAN YEARBOOK. 1977. a. £12.45($25)
International Communications Ltd., 63 Long Acre,
London WC2E 9JH, England. Ed. Gill Garb. bk.
rev. illus. stat. (also avail. in microfilm; back issues
avail.)

320   NZ
NEW ZEALAND. DEPARTMENT OF INTERNAL
AFFAIRS. REPORT. a. Department of Internal
Affairs, Wellington, New Zealand.

900   US
NEWS DICTIONARY. 1977. a. $14.95 clothbound;
$9.95 paperbound. Facts on File, Inc., 119 W. 57
St., NY 10019.

952   US
NEWSLETTER OF RESEARCH ON JAPANESE
POLITICS. 1969. a. $2.25. ‡ Brigham Young
University, Asian Studies Program, Center for
International and Area Studies, Provo, UT 84602.
Ed. Lee W. Farnsworth. bk. rev. bibl. circ. 200.
(tabloid format; back issues avail.)

320   US   ISSN 0078-0979
NOMOS. 1958. a. $17.50. (American Society for
Political and Legal Philosophy) New York
University Press, Washington Square, New York,
NY 10003. Eds. J. Roland Pennock, John W.
Chapman.

320   US
NORTH CAROLINA MANUAL. 1901. biennial. $8.
Secretary of State, 101 Administration Bldg.,
Raleigh, NC 27611. Ed. John L. Cheney, Jr. circ.
4,500(controlled)

320   SP
NUESTROMUNDO. 1979. irreg. Ediciones de la
Torre, Calle de Augusto Figueroa 17, Madrid,
Spain.

320   949.2   UK   ISSN 0144-3070
OCCASIONAL PAPERS IN MODERN DUTCH
STUDIES. 1980. irreg. University of Hull
Publications Committee, Hull HU6 7RX, England.
Ed. P. K. King.

320   AU   ISSN 0170-0847
OESTERREICHISCHES JAHRBUCH FUER
POLITIK. a. price varies. Verlag fuer Geschichte
und Politik, Neulinggasse 26, A-1030 Vienna,
Austria. Eds. Andreas Khol, Alfred Stirnemann.

OMBUDSMAN AND OTHER COMPLAINT-
HANDLING SYSTEMS SURVEY. see LAW

324   US   ISSN 0078-530X
OPERATIONS AND POLICY RESEARCH.
INSTITUTE FOR THE COMPARATIVE STUDY
OF POLITICAL SYSTEMS. ELECTION
ANALYSIS SERIES.* 1963. irreg., 1968, no. 6.
price varies. Institute for the Comparative Study of
Political Systems, 4000 Albemarle St. N.W.,
Washington, DC 20016.

324   US   ISSN 0078-5288
OPERATIONS AND POLICY RESEARCH.
INSTITUTE FOR THE COMPARATIVE STUDY
OF POLITICAL SYSTEMS. POLITICAL STUDY
SERIES.* (No. 1 called Special Article Series)
1964. irreg. $2. Institute for the Comparative Study
of Political Systems, 4000 Albemarle St. N.W.,
Washington, DC 20016.

320   US
OREGON STATE MONOGRAPHS. STUDIES IN
POLITICAL SCIENCE. irreg., latest no. 2. price
varies. Oregon State University Press, 101 Waldo
Hall, Corvallis, OR 97331.

320   338   UK
P S I: BROADSHEET SERIES AND MAJOR
REPORTS. 1933. irreg. £50. Policy Studies
Institute, 1/2 Castle Lane, London SW1E 6DR,
England.
Formerly: P E P (ISSN 0030-7947)

320   338   UK
P S I DISCUSSION PAPERS. 1978. irreg. Policy
Studies Institute, 1/2 Castle Lane, London SW1E
6DR, England.

PAKISTAN. NATIONAL ASSEMBLY. DEBATES.
OFFICIAL REPORT. see PUBLIC
ADMINISTRATION

956.94   320   US
PALESTINE! 1976. irreg. (4-5/yr.) $5 for 10 nos.
Palestine Solidarity Committee, Box 1757,
Manhattanville Sta., New York, NY 10027. Ed.Bd.
bk. rev. illus. circ. 2,500.

329   IT
PANORAMA DEMOCRATE CHRETIEN. (Text in
French) 1968. irreg. Christian Democratic World
Union, 107 via del Plebiscito, Rome 00186, Italy.
Formerly: International Christian Democratic
Study and Documentation Center. Informations
(ISSN 0538-5555)

323   US   ISSN 0085-4751
PARDON ME, BUT. 1965. irreg. $0.50. Nord Davis,
Jr., Ed. & Pub., Box 29, Topton, NC 28781. circ.
30,000. (looseleaf format)

320   CN
PARTICIPATION. (Text in English and French)
1977. 3/yr. (plus annual supplement) $50 non-
members. International Political Science
Association, c/o University of Ottawa, Ottawa, Ont.
K1N 6N5, Canada. circ. controlled.
Formerly: International Political Science
Association. Circular (ISSN 0074-7459)

329.9   CK
PARTIDO COMUNISTA DE COLOMBIA.
DOCUMENTOS. 1975. irreg. Editorial 8 de Junio,
Apdo. 51694, Medellin, Colombia.

329.9   SP
PARTIDO SOCIALISTA POPULAR. CONGRESO.
(ACTAS) no. 3, 1976. irreg. Tucar Ediciones S.A.,
Almagro 44, Madrid 4, Spain.

320   PE
PARTIDO SOCIALISTA REVOLUCIONARIO.
INFORMES. 1977. irreg. Partido Socialista
Revolucionario, Pontevedra 173 - Surco, Lima,
Peru. Ed. Francisco Moncloa.

PARTO. see MOTION PICTURES

320   CN
PAST & PRESENT. irreg. University of Waterloo,
Department of Political Science, Waterloo, Ont.,
Canada. Ed. T. H. Qualter.

320   CN   ISSN 0553-4283
PEACE RESEARCH REVIEWS. 1967. irreg.
Can.$20($20) for 6 nos. Peace Research Institute-
Dundas, 25 Dundana Ave., Dundas, Ont. L9H 4E5,
Canada. Eds. Dr. Alan Newcombe, Dr. Hanna
Newcombe. circ. 500.

320   US   ISSN 0094-8055
PEACE SCIENCE SOCIETY (INTERNATIONAL).
PAPERS. 1963. a. $8 per vol. Peace Science Society
(International), School of Management, State
University of New York at Binghamton,
Binghamton, NY 13901. Ed. Manus Chatterji. adv.
circ. 1,000. Key Title: Papers - Peace Science
Society International.
Formerly: Peace Research Society (International).
Papers.

PEOPLE AND THE PURSUIT OF TRUTH. see
LITERARY AND POLITICAL REVIEWS

001.45   960   US
PERSPECTIVES ON SOUTHERN AFRICA. irreg.
price varies. University of California Press, 2233
Fulton St., Berkeley, CA 94720.

329   FR
LE POING ET LA ROSE. 1970. irreg. Parti
Socialiste, 7 bis Place du Palais Bourbon, 75007
Paris, France. Ed. Lionel Jospin.
Formerly: Bulletin Socialiste (ISSN 0068-4155)

320   080   NE   ISSN 0079-2926
POLEMOLOGISCHE STUDIEN. (Text in Dutch and
English) 1963. irreg., vol. 16, 1972. price varies.
(Rijksuniversiteit te Groningen, Polemologisch
Instituut - State University at Groningen) Van
Gorcum, Box 43, Assen, Netherlands.

320   US   ISSN 0160-2675
POLICY GRANTS DIRECTORY. 1977. irreg. $3 to
individuals; institutions $5. Policy Studies
Organization, University of Illinois, 361 Lincoln
Hall, Urbana, IL 61801. Eds. Stuart Nagel, Marian
Neef. bibl. charts. stat. index. circ. 2,400. (reprint
service avail. from ISI)

320   070.5   US
POLICY PUBLISHERS AND ASSOCIATIONS
DIRECTORY. 1980. irreg. $3 to individuals;
institutions $5. Policy Studies Organization,
University of Illinois at Urbana-Champaign, 361
Lincoln Hall, Urbana, IL 61801. Eds. Stuart Nagel,
Kathleen Burkholder. (reprint service avail. from
ISI)

320   US
POLICY RESEARCH CENTERS DIRECTORY.
1978. irreg. $3 to individuals; institutions $5. Policy
Studies Organization, University of Illinois, 361
Lincoln Hall, Urbana, IL 61801. Eds. Stuart Nagel,
Marian Neef. bibl. charts. stat. index. circ. 2,400.
(reprint service avail. from ISI)

309.2   US   ISSN 0362-6016
POLICY STUDIES DIRECTORY. 1974. irreg. $3 to
individuals; institutions $5. Policy Studies
Organization, University of Illinois at Urbana-
Champaign, 361 Lincoln Hall, Urbana, IL 61801.
Eds. Stuart Nagel, Marian Neef. bibl. charts. stat.
index. circ. 2,400. (reprint service avail. from ISI)

309.2   US
POLICY STUDIES PERSONNEL DIRECTORY.
1979. irreg. $3 to individuals; institutions $5. Policy
Studies Organization, 361 Lincoln Hall, University
of Illinois, Urbana, IL 61801. Eds. Stuart Nagel,
Nancy Munshaw. bibl. charts. stat. index. circ.
2,400. (reprint service avail. from ISI)

320   PL   ISSN 0079-3000
POLISH ROUND TABLE. (Text in English) 1967. a.
110 Zl. (Polskie Towarzystwo Nauk Politycznych)
Ossolineum, Publishing House of the Polish
Academy of Sciences, Rynek 9, Wroclaw, Poland
(Dist. by Ars Polona-Ruch, Krakowskie
Przedmiescie 7, Warsaw, Poland) Ed. Longin
Pastusiak. circ. 700.

320 VE
POLITEIA. 1972. a. price varies. Universidad Central de Venezuela, Instituto de Estudios Politicos, Caracas, Venezuela (Subscr. to: Servicio de Distribucion y Venta, Biblioteca Central, Universidad Central, Caracas, Venezuela) bk. rev. circ. 2,000.

320 UY ISSN 0079-3027
POLITICA.* irreg. Editorial Arca, Colonia 1263, Montevideo, Uruguay.

320 GE
POLITICAL DOCUMENTS OF THE GERMAN DEMOCRATIC REPUBLIC. (Text in English) 1974. irreg. Panorama D.D.R. - Auslandspresseagentur, Wilhelm-Pieck-Str. 49, 1054 Berlin, E. Germany (D.D.R.)

POLITICAL ECONOMY OF WORLD-SYSTEMS ANNUALS. see *BUSINESS AND ECONOMICS — Economic Systems And Theories, Economic History*

320.9 II
POLITICAL EVENTS ANNUAL. (Text in English) 1975. a. price varies. Sterling Publishers Pvt. Ltd., AB/9, Safdarjang Enclave, New Delhi 110016, India. Ed. S. L. Sheakdher. circ. 1,100.

320 309 US
POLITICAL HANDBOOK OF THE WORLD. 1928. a. $19.95. (State University of New York at Binghamton, Center for Social Analysis) McGraw-Hill Book Co., 1221 Ave. of the Americas, New York, NY 10020. Ed. Arthur S. Banks. circ. 7,000.
Formerley: Political Handbook and Atlas of the World (ISSN 0079-3035)

320 UK
POLITICAL PARTIES OF THE WORLD. irreg. Longman Group Ltd., Longman House, Burnt Mill, Harlow, Essex CM20 2JE, England (Dist. in U.S. and Canada by: Gale Research Co. Ltd., Book Tower, Detroit, MI 48226)

320 301 US
POLITICAL POWER AND SOCIAL THEORY; a research annual. 1980. a. J A I Press, 165 W. Putnam Ave., Greenwich, CT 06830. Ed. Maurice Zeitlin.

320 US ISSN 0091-3715
POLITICAL SCIENCE REVIEWER. 1971. a. $8. Intercollegiate Studies Institute, Inc., 14 S. Bryn Mawr Ave., Bryn Mawr, PA 19010. Ed. George W. Carey. adv. bk. rev. circ. 2,000. (also avail. in microform from UMI)

320 UK ISSN 0144-7440
POLITICAL STUDIES ASSOCIATION OF THE UNITED KINGDOM. NEWSLETTER. 1975. irreg. membership. Political Studies Association of the United Kingdom, c/o J. Lovenduski, Dept. of European Studies, Loughborough University, Loughborough, Leics. LE11 3TU, England.

322.44 US
POLITICAL TERRORISM. 1975. irreg., vol. 2, 1978. $15.75. Facts on File, Inc., 119 W. 57th St., New York, NY 10019. Ed. Lester Sobel. index.

320 NE
POLITIEK AKTUEEL. vol. 4, 1976. irreg. price varies. Xeno, Groningen, Netherlands.

320 GW
POLITIK UND WAEHLER. 1970. irreg., no. 20, 1978. price varies. Verlag Anton Hain GmbH, Adelheidstr. 2, Postfach 1220, 6240 Koenigstein, W. Germany (B.R.D.) Ed. Bd.

320 GW ISSN 0340-9244
POLITIKWISSENSCHAFTLICHE FORSCHUNG. a. price varies. (Freie Universitaet Berlin, Leitstelle Politische Dokumentation) K.G. Saur Verlag KG, Poessenbacherstr. 12 B, Postfach 711009, 8000 Munich 71, W. Germany (B.R.D.)

320 SZ ISSN 0085-4980
POLITIQUE DE LA SCIENCE. German edition: Wissenschaftspolitik. 1972. irreg (5/yr) free. ‡ Office de la Science et de la Recherche, P.O. Box 2732, Wildhainweg 9, 3001 Berne, Switzerland. bibl. index. circ. 4,000.

320 AU
POLITISCHE BILDUNG. irreg. S.16 per no. (Bundesministerium fuer Unterricht und Kunst) Verlag fuer Geschichte und Politik, Neulinggasse 26, A-1030 Vienna, Austria. Ed.Bd.

324.2 US ISSN 0085-5081
PRECINCT RETURNS FOR MAJOR ELECTIONS IN SOUTH DAKOTA. (Subseries of the Bureau's Special Project) 1962. biennial. $3. University of South Dakota, Governmental Research Bureau, Vermillion, SD 57069. Ed. Alan L. Clem. stat. circ. 200 (controlled)

325 CN
PRINCE EDWARD ISLAND. CIVIL SERVICE COMMISSION. ANNUAL REPORT. 1963. a. free. ‡ Civil Service Commission, Charlottetown, Canada. circ. 100-150.

335 II
PROBLEMS OF NATIONAL LIBERATION. (Text in English) 1974. irreg. Rs.3. Ranadhir Dasgupta, 10 Bondel Rd., Calcutta 700019, India. Eds. Satyendra Narayan Mazumdar, Narahari Kaviraj.
Communism

320 SW ISSN 0552-2005
PROBLEMS OF THE BALTIC.* (Text in English) irreg., 1973, no. 3. Estonian Information Centre, Box 450, S104 30 Stockholm 45, Sweden. Ed. Endel Krepp. bibl. charts.

320 943.8 PL ISSN 0079-5798
PROBLEMY POLONII ZAGRANICZNEJ. 1960. irreg., vol. 9, 1975. price varies. (Polska Akademia Nauk, Komitet Badania Polonii Zagranicznej) Ossolineum, Publishing House of the Polish Academy of Sciences, Rynek 9, Wroclaw, Poland. Ed. Wiktor Szczerba.

320 VE
PROCESO POLITICO. 1976. irreg. Bs.5.30($10) Apartado 70850, Caracas 107, Venezuela.

329.9 CN ISSN 0702-7222
PROGRESSIVE CONSERVATIVE PARTY OF CANADA. LEADER'S REPORT. 1976. irreg. free. Progressive Conservative Party of Canada, 178 Queen St., Ottawa, Ont. K1P 5E1, Canada.

320.531 US
PROLETARIAN INTERNATIONALISM. 1979. irreg., 4-6/yr. $11. (Marxist-Leninist Party of the U.S.A.) Marxist-Leninist Publications, Box 11972, Ft. Dearborn Sta., Chicago, IL 60611.

PUBLIC ADMINISTRATION AND DEMOCRACY. see *PUBLIC ADMINISTRATION*

320 US
PUBLIC CITIZEN. 1976. irreg. 1346 Connecticut Ave N.W., Washington, DC 20036. Ed. Tim Dlugos. illus. (tabloid format)

320 US ISSN 0079-7790
PUBLICATIONS ON RUSSIA AND EASTERN EUROPE. 1969. irreg., no. 8, 1977. price varies. (University of Washington, School for International Studies) University of Washington Press, Seattle, WA 98105.

320 UY
PURIFICACION. 1977. irreg. Instituto Nacional de Investigaciones Historicas y Geopoliticas, Avda. 18 de Julio 2226, Montevideo, Uruguay. Dir. J.J. Scapusio.

320 IT
QUADERNI DEL SALVEMINI. vol 16/17, 1975. irreg. price varies. Movimento Gaetano Salvemini, Via di Torre Argentina 18, 00186 Rome, Italy. Ed.Bd.

320 IT
QUADERNI SICILIANI. 1973. irreg. L.300. (Partito Comunista Italiano) Di Modica, Via M. Stabile 216, 90141 Sicily, Italy. ill.

320 330 II
R.B.R.R. KALE MEMORIAL LECTURES. 1937. a; none published 1947 or 1970. price varies. Gokhale Institute of Politics and Economics, Pune 411004, India (Dist. by: Orient Longman, Ltd., Nicol Rd., Ballard Estate, Bombay 400038, India)

RADICAL SCIENCE JOURNAL. see *SCIENCES: COMPREHENSIVE WORKS*

320 327 US ISSN 0079-9491
RADNER LECTURES. 1964, no. 2. irreg., 1976, no. 7. Columbia University Press, 136 South Broadway, Irvington-On-Hudson, NY 10533.

RECHTS- UND STAATSWISSENSCHAFTEN. see *LAW*

RECHTSWISSENSCHAFT UND SOZIALPOLITIK. see *LAW*

320.531 UK
RED LETTERS; Communist Party literature journal. 1978. irreg. 80p. per no. Central Books Ltd., 37 Gray's Inn Rd., London W.C.1., England.

320.531 301.412 CN
RED MENACE; a libertarian socialist newsletter. 1976. irreg., no. 5, 1980. Can.$3. Box 171, Station D, Toronto, Ont., Canada. bk. rev. circ. 1,000. (tabloid format; back issues avail.)
Socialism

320 362.971 CN
REPERTOIRE ADMINISTRATIF. no. 2, 1975. irreg. Can.$6. Editeur Officiel du Quebec, 1283 Bd. Charest ouest, Quebec G1N 2C9, Canada. adv. circ. 3,000.
Formerly: Collection l'Etat et le Citoyen.

320 IE
REPSOL PAMPHLETS. 1971, no. 7. irreg. Republican Educational Department, 30 Gardiner Place, Dublin 1, Ireland. Ed. Bd. charts.

329 US ISSN 0363-9290
REPUBLICAN ALMANAC. irreg. Republican National Committee, Political/Research Division, 310 First St., S.E., Washington, DC 20003. illus.

RESEARCH IN POLITICAL ECONOMY; an annual compilation of research. see *BUSINESS AND ECONOMICS — Economic Systems And Theories, Economic History*

RESEARCH IN SOCIAL PROBLEMS AND PUBLIC POLICY; a research annual. see *SOCIOLOGY*

320 US
RESEARCH INSTITUTE ON INTERNATIONAL CHANGE. STUDIES. irreg. price varies. Westview Press, 5500 Central Ave., Boulder, CO 80301. Ed. Zbigniew Brzezinski.

320 AG
REVISTA ARGENTINA DE POLITICA. 1958. irreg. Editorial Norte, Cuenca 1818, Buenos Aires, Argentina. Ed. S. W. Medraho.

320 350 II
ROLE OF STATE LEGISLATURES IN THE FREEDOM STRUGGLE. 1976. irreg. Rs.30. Indian Council of Historical Research, 35 Ferozeshah Rd., New Delhi 110001, India (Distributed by: People's Publishing House Ltd., Rani Jhansi Rd., New Delhi 110005, India)

320 US
ROSTER OF WOMEN IN POLITICAL SCIENCE. 4th edt. 1976. biennial. $5. American Political Science Association, Committee on the Status of Women in the Profession, 1527 New Hampshire., NW, Washington, DC 20036.

320 US
S C A FREE SPEECH YEARBOOK. c.1960. a. $5. Speech Communication Association, 5105 Blacklick Rd., No. E, Annandale, VA 22003. (reprint service avail. from UMI)
Formerly: Freedom of Speech Yearbook (ISSN 0071-9366)

329 AT
S. Y. A. INTERNAL BULLETIN. 1970. irreg. Socialist Youth Alliance, c/o Col. Moynard, 6 Uther St., Surry Hills, N.S.W. 2010, Australia.

320 US
SAGE ELECTORAL STUDIES YEARBOOK. 1975. a. $18.50 for hardcover; softcover $8.95. Sage Publications, Inc., 275 S. Beverly Dr., Beverly Hills, CA 90212 (And Sage Publications Ltd., 28 Banner St., London EC1Y 8QE, England) Eds. Louis Maisel, Paul Sacks. (back issues avail.)

POLITICAL SCIENCE

SAGE SERIES ON AFRICAN MODERNIZATION AND DEVELOPMENT. see *BUSINESS AND ECONOMICS — International Development And Assistance*

327 US ISSN 0080-5378
SAGE SERIES ON ARMED FORCES AND SOCIETY. 1971. irreg., vol. 12, 1977. $10-$25 per vol. (Inter-University Seminar on Armed Forces and Society) Sage Publications, Inc., 275 S. Beverly Drive, Beverly Hills, CA 90212 (And Sage Publications, Ltd., 28 Banner St., London EC1Y 8QE, England) Eds. Charles C. Moskos, Jr., and Morris Janowitz. (back issues avail.)

320 US
SAGE YEARBOOKS IN POLITICS AND PUBLIC POLICY. 1975. a. $8.95 softcover; hardcover $18.50. (Policy Studies Organization) Sage Publications, Inc., 275 South Beverly Dr, Beverly Hills, CA 90212 (And Sage Publications, Ltd., 28 Banner St., London EC1Y 8QE, England) Ed. Stuart S. Nagel. bibl, charts, illus, stat. (back issues avail.)

SAMISDAT; stimmen aus den "anderen Russland". see *HISTORY — History Of Europe*

320 SZ
ST. GALLER STUDIEN ZUR POLITIKWISSENSCHAFT. 1975. irreg., no. 5, 1979. price varies. Paul Haupt AG, Falkenplatz 14, CH-3001 Berne, Switzerland.

SCHOULER LECTURES IN HISTORY AND POLITICAL SCIENCE. see *HISTORY*

320 GW
SCHRIFTEN ZUR POLITISCHEN WISSENSCHAFT. 1956. irreg., no. 10, 1976. price varies. Verlag Anton Hain GmbH, Adelheidstr. 2, Postfach 1220, 6240 Koenigstein, W. Germany (B.R.D.)

320 SZ
SCHRIFTENRIEHE RISIKOPOLITIK. 1975. irreg. Verlag Peter Lang AG, Muenzgraben 2, Postfach, CH-3000 Berne 7, Switzerland.

320 UK
SCOTTISH GOVERNMENT YEARBOOK. 1976. a. £10. Paul Harris Publishing, 25 London St., Edinburgh EH3 6LY, Scotland. Eds. Dr. H. M. Drucker, N. Drucker. adv. bibl. stat. circ. 1,200. (back issues avail.)

320 FR ISSN 0080-8938
SERIE AFRIQUE NOIRE. 1970. irreg. price varies. (Institut d'Etudes Politiques de Bordeaux) Editions A. Pedone, 13 rue Soufflot, 75005 Paris, France.

320 FR ISSN 0586-9889
SERIE VIE LOCALE. 1969. irreg. price varies. (Institut d'Etudes Politiques de Bordeaux, Centre d'Etude et de Recherche sur la Vie Locale) Editions A. Pedone, 13, rue Soufflot, 75005 Paris, France.

SHVUT; Jewish problems in the USSR and Eastern Europe. see *ETHNIC INTERESTS*

SIR GEORGE EARLE MEMORIAL LECTURE ON INDUSTRY AND GOVERNMENT. see *BUSINESS AND ECONOMICS*

SLOVAK PRESS DIGEST. see *ETHNIC INTERESTS*

SLOVANSKE STUDIE. see *HISTORY — History Of Europe*

320.531 IT
SOCIALISMO OGGI. no. 6, 1976. irreg. price varies. Marsilio Editori S.p.A., Fondamenta Santa Chiara, San Croce 518-A, 30125 Venice, Italy.

335 UK ISSN 0081-0606
SOCIALIST REGISTER; a survey of movements and ideas. 1964. a. price varies. Merlin Press, 3 Manchester Rd, London E.14, England. Eds. Ralph Miliband, John Saville.

SOOCHOW JOURNAL OF SOCIAL & POLITICAL SCIENCES. see *SOCIAL SCIENCES: COMPREHENSIVE WORKS*

320 US ISSN 0560-8996
SOURCES IN WESTERN POLITICAL THOUGHT. irreg. price varies. Macmillan Publishing Co., Inc., 866 Third Ave., New York, NY 10022.

SOUTH AND EAST ASIA REPORT. see *BUSINESS AND ECONOMICS — Economic Situation And Conditions*

320 NL ISSN 0081-2811
SOUTH PACIFIC COMMISSION. HANDBOOK. (Text in English or French) 1968. irreg., no. 20, 1980. price varies. South Pacific Commission, B.P. D5, Noumea, Cedex, New Caledonia.

320 NL ISSN 0081-282X
SOUTH PACIFIC COMMISSION. INFORMATION CIRCULAR. (Text in English or French) 1968. irreg., no. 85, 1980. free. South Pacific Commission, B.P. D5, Noumea, Cedex, New Caledonia.

320 NL ISSN 0081-2838
SOUTH PACIFIC COMMISSION. INFORMATION DOCUMENT. (Text in English or French) 1967. irreg., no. 48, 1979. free. South Pacific Commission, B.P. D5, Noumea, Cedex, New Caledonia.

320 NL
SOUTH PACIFIC COMMISSION. OCCASIONAL PAPER. 1977. irreg., no. 17, 1980. South Pacific Commission, B.P. D5, Noumea, Cedex, New Caledonia. bibl.

320 NL ISSN 0081-2846
SOUTH PACIFIC COMMISSION. REPORT OF S P C TECHNICAL MEETINGS. (Text in English or French) irreg. price varies. South Pacific Commission, B.P. D5, Noumea, Cedex, New Caledonia.

320 NL ISSN 0081-2862
SOUTH PACIFIC COMMISSION. TECHNICAL PAPER. (Text in English or French) 1949. irreg., no. 178, 1979. price varies. South Pacific Commission, B.P. D5, Noumea, Cedex, New Caledonia.

300 320 GW
SOZIALWISSENSCHAFTLICHES JAHRBUCH FUER POLITIK. 1969. a. price varies. Guenter Olzog Verlag, Thierschstr. 11, 8000 Munich 22, W. Germany (B.R.D.) Ed. R. Wildermann. index.

320 SZ ISSN 0081-4105
STAAT UND POLITIK. 1966. irreg., vol. 23, 1978. price varies. Paul Haupt AG, Falkenplatz 14, 3001 Berne, Switzerland. Ed. Richard Reich.

STAT A PRAVO. see *LAW*

320 NR
STATESMAN. 1973. a. £N1($3.40) Political Science Student Association, Political Science Students Association, University of Ibadan, Department of Political Science, Ibadan, Nigeria. Ed. Theo Adebowale. adv. bk. rev. bibl.

320 UK ISSN 0081-4601
STATESMAN'S YEAR BOOK; statistical and historical annual of the states of the world. 1864. a. £13.75. Macmillan Press Ltd. (Subsidiary of: Macmillan Publishers Ltd.) Little Essex St., London WC2R 3LF, England. Ed. John Paxton. index. circ. 35,000.

320 GW
STICHWOERTER ZUR ENTWICKLUNGSPOLITIK. 1970. Laetare-Verlag Stein, Herzbachweg 2, 6460 Gelnhausen, W. Germany (B.R.D.)

320 SW ISSN 0085-6762
STOCKHOLM STUDIES IN POLITICS. (Text in Swedish or English; summaries in English) 1971. irreg. price varies. Stockholms Universitet, Department of Political Science, Fack, S-104 05 Stockholm 5, Sweden.

320 GW
STUDIEN ZUM POLITISCHEN SYSTEM DER BUNDESREPUBLIK DEUTSCHLAND. 1973. irreg., no. 26, 1981. price varies. Verlag Anton Hain GmbH, Adelheidstr. 2, Postfach 1220, 6240 Koenigstein, W. Germany (B.R.D.) Ed. Heino Kaack.

320 US
STUDIES IN BEHAVIORAL POLITICAL SCIENCE. irreg. price varies. Oxford University Press, 200 Madison Ave., New York, NY 10016 (And Ely House, 37 Dover St., London W1X 4AH, England) Ed. Robert Presthus.

320 US
STUDIES IN CONTEMPORARY POLITICS. irreg. price varies. New Viewpoints, c/o Franklin Watts, Inc., 730 Fifth Ave., New York, NY 10019.

STUDIES IN DEFENSE POLICY. see *MILITARY*

STUDIES IN EAST EUROPEAN AND SOVIET PLANNING, DEVELOPMENT AND TRADE. see *BUSINESS AND ECONOMICS — Production Of Goods And Services*

320 II
STUDIES IN ELECTORAL POLITICS IN THE INDIAN STATES. (Text in English) irreg. Manohar Book Service, 2 Daryaganj, Ansari Rd., Panna Bhawan, Delhi 110006, India. Eds. Myron Weiner, John Osgood Field. charts, stat.

320 338 UK
STUDIES IN EUROPEAN POLITICS. 1978. irreg. Policy Studies Institute, 1/2 Castle Lane, London SW1E 6DR, England.

320 US ISSN 0081-7996
STUDIES IN HISTORICAL AND POLITICAL SCIENCE. EXTRA VOLUMES. irreg., 1968, vol. 15. (Johns Hopkins University) Bergman Publishers, Inc., 224 W. 20th St., New York, NY 10011.

320 US
STUDIES IN IMPERIALISM. 1973. irreg., latest 1977. University of Chicago Press, 5801 S. Ellis Ave., Chicago, IL 60637. Ed. Robin W. Winks. adv. bk. rev. (reprint service avail. from UMI,ISI)

320 US ISSN 0081-802X
STUDIES IN INTERNATIONAL AFFAIRS. 1967. irreg; no. 26, 1975. price varies. (Washington Center of Foreign Policy Research) Johns Hopkins University Press, Baltimore, MD 21218.

320 US
STUDIES IN INTERNATIONAL AND COMPARATIVE POLITICS. Variant title: Studies in Comparative Politics Series. 1973. irreg., no. 15, 1980. price varies. American Bibliographical Center-Clio Press, 2040 Alameda Padre Serra, Box 4397, Santa Barbara, CA 93103. Ed. Peter H. Merkl.

320 US ISSN 0081-8054
STUDIES IN INTERNATIONAL COMMUNISM. 1963. irreg; no. 21, 1975. price varies. Massachusetts Institute of Technology, Center for International Studies, Cambridge, MA 02139.

320 355 CN ISSN 0081-8690
STUDIES IN THE STRUCTURE OF POWER: DECISION MAKING IN CANADA. 1964. irreg. price varies. (Social Science Research Council of Canada) University of Toronto Press, Front Campus, Toronto, Ont. M5S 1A6, Canada (and 33 East Tupper St., Buffalo, N.Y. 14023) Ed. John Meisel. (also avail. in microfiche)

947 320 GW
STUDIES ON THE SOVIET UNION. (Text in English) 1957. irreg. Institute for the Study of the USSR, Mannhardtstr. 6, 8000 Munich, W. Germany (B.R.D.)

STUDII DE FILOZOFIE SI SOCIALISM STIINTIFIC. see *PHILOSOPHY*

320 UK ISSN 0585-7694
STUDY CENTRE FOR YUGOSLAV AFFAIRS. REVIEW. 1960. biennial. price varies. Study Centre for Yugoslav Affairs, 4 Audley Square, S. Audley St., London W1Y 5DR, England. Ed. Desimir Tochitch. adv. bk. rev. bibl. circ. 3,000.

SUBSAHARAN AFRICA REPORT. see *BUSINESS AND ECONOMICS — Economic Situation And Conditions*

320 IT
SUL FILO DEL TEMPO. 1976. irreg. Iskra Edizioni, Via Adige 3, 20135 Milan, Italy.

POLITICAL SCIENCE

320 US ISSN 0146-2156
SUMMARY OF CONGRESS. biennial. Political Research, Inc., Tagoland at Bent Tree, 16850 Dallas Parkway, Dallas, TX 75248.

SURMACH. see *MILITARY*

328 SW
SWEDEN. RIKSDAGEN. FOERTECKNING OEVER RIKSDAGENS LEDAMOETER. a. Kr.3.55. Riksdagen, Riksdagens Tryckeriexpedition, S-100 12 Stockholm, Sweden.

320 SW
SWEDEN. RIKSDAGEN. RIKSDAGEN AARSBOK. a. Riksdagen, Riksdagens Tryckeriexpedition, S-100 12 Stockholm, Sweden.
  Continues: Sweden. Riksdagen. Riksdag.

320 GW
SYSTEMATISCHE POLITIKWISSENSCHAFT. 1976. irreg. price varies. Akademische Verlagsgesellschaft, Bahnhofstr. 39, Postfach 1107, 6200 Wiesbaden, W. Germany (B.R.D.)

320 AU
TANGENTE. bi-m. S.45. Ring Freiheitlicher Jugend, Kaerntnerstrasse 28, Mezzanin, A-1010 Vienna, Austria. Ed. Karl Sevelda. adv.

320 MX
TEMAS NACIONALES. 1975. irreg. Mex.$25($2.50) Instituto de Estudios Politicos Economicos y Sociales, Insurgentes Norte, 59, Mexico, D.F., Mexico. charts.

320 US
TEMPLE UNIVERSITY. CENTER FOR THE STUDY OF FEDERALISM. CENTER REPORT. no. 11, 1976. irreg. Temple University, Center for the Study of Federalism, Philadelphia, PA 19122.

320 IT
TEORIE E OGGETTI. 1978. irreg., no. 6, 1980. price varies. Liguori Editore s.r.l., Via Mezzocannone 19, 80134 Naples, Italy. Eds. Roberto Esposito, Giancarlo Mazzacurati.

328 US
TEXAS LEGISLATIVE ISSUES: REPORT OF THE TEXAS LEGISLATURE PRE-SESSION CONFERENCE; judicial reorganization, revenue sharing, property taxation and school finance. 1971. biennial. $3.50. University of Texas at Austin, Lyndon B. Johnson School of Public Affairs, Drawer Y, University Station, Austin, TX 78712. circ. 1,200.
  Formerly: Texas Legislature Pre-Session Conference. Proceedings and Report.

320 GW
THEORIE UND ORGANISATION. 1976. irreg. DM.5. Verlag 2000 GmbH, Ludwigstr. 33, Postfach 591, 6050 Offenbach, W. Germany (B.R.D.)

320 920 UK ISSN 0082-4399
TIMES GUIDE TO THE HOUSE OF COMMONS; complete survey of Parliament after a General Election. 1880. irreg. £12.50. Times Books Ltd., 16 Golden Square, London W1R 4BN, England. Ed. Alan Wood. index. circ. 5,000.

320 US
TSUSHIN 1971. irreg. $4. Anti-Stalinism Study Group, Box 8724, Emeryville, CA 94608. abstr. (processed)

320 US ISSN 0082-6774
TULANE STUDIES IN POLITICAL SCIENCE. 1954. irreg., vol. 15, 1975. price varies per vol. Tulane University, Department of Political Science, New Orleans, LA 70118.

320.253 301 US
U S S R REPORT: POLITICAL AND SOCIOLOGICAL AFFAIRS. 1969. irreg. approx. 84/yr.) $336. U.S. Joint Publications Research Service, 1000 N. Glebe Rd., Arlington, VA 22201 (Orders to: NTIS, Springfield, VA 22161)
  Formerly: Translations on U S S R Political and Sociological Affairs.

U S S R REPORT: PROBLEMS OF THE FAR EAST. see *POLITICAL SCIENCE — International Relations*

320.253 US
U S S R REPORT: TRANSLATIONS FROM "KOMMUNIST". 1966. irreg. (approx. 9/yr.) $57. U.S. Joint Publications Research Service, 1000 N. Glebe Rd., Arlington, VA 22201 (Orders to: NTIS, Springfield, VA 22161)
  Formerly: Translations from "Kommunist".

UNION DEMOCRACY REVIEW. see *LABOR UNIONS*

320 MY
UNITED MALAYS NATIONAL ORGANISATION. PENVATA. irreg. United Malays National Organisation, Jl. T. Ab. Rahman, Bangunan UMNO, Kuala Lumpur, Malaysia.

320 US ISSN 0082-9447
U. S. BUREAU OF THE CENSUS. CONGRESSIONAL DISTRICT DATA BOOK. 1961. irreg. price varies. U.S. Bureau of the Census, Dept. of Commerce, Washington, DC 20233 (Orders to: Supt. of Documents, Washington, DC 20402)

320 US
U.S. CONGRESS. CONGRESSIONAL DIRECTORY. 1857. a. $8.50 avail. in 4 different edts. ranging in price from $3.50 to $13. U.S. Government Printing Office, Public Documents Department, Washington, DC 20402. Ed. Larry Kennedy. circ. 100,000. (also avail. in microform from UMI)

320 US
U.S. FEDERAL ELECTION COMMISSION. ANNUAL REPORT. 1976. a. U.S. Federal Election Commission, 325 K St., N.W., Washington, DC 20463 (Orders to: Supt. of Documents, Washington, DC 20463) Ed. Louise D. Wides. charts. illus. stat. circ. 1,800. (back issues avail.)

UNITED STATES GOVERNMENT MANUAL (1973) see *PUBLIC ADMINISTRATION*

320 US
UNITED STATES POLITICAL SCIENCE DOCUMENTS. 1975. a. $75. University of Pittsburgh, University Center for International Studies, G-6 Mervis Hall, Pittsburgh, PA 15260. (Co-sponsor: American Poltical Science Association)

320 VE ISSN 0083-5420
UNIVERSIDAD CENTRAL DE VENEZUELA. INSTITUTO DE ESTUDIOS POLITICOS. CUADERNOS. 1959. irreg.; latest issue, 1974. price varies. Universidad Central de Venezuela, Instituto de Estudios Politicos, Instituto de Estudios Politicos, Venezuela. circ. 400.

320 CK
UNIVERSIDAD DE LOS ANDES. CUADERNOS DE CIENCIA POLITICA. no. 4, Jul, 1974. irreg. Universidad de los Andes, Calle 18 A Carrera 1E, Apdo. Aereo 4976, Bogota, Colombia.

320 IT
UNIVERSITA DEGLI STUDI DI TRIESTE. FACOLTA DI SCIENZE POLITICHE. PUBBLICAZIONI. 1975. irreg., no. 20, 1981. L.2500 per copy. Casa Editrice Dott. A. Giuffre, Via Statuto 2, 20121 Milan, Italy. bibl.

320 970 FR ISSN 0399-0443
UNIVERSITE DE BORDEAUX III. CENTRE DE RECHERCHES SUR L'AMERIQUE ANGLOPHONE. ANNALES. N.S. 1976. a. 40 F.($7) (for 2 nos.) Maison des Sciences de l'Homme d'Aquitaine, Esplanade des Antilles, Domaine Universitaire, 33405 Talence Cedex, France. Ed. J. F. Beranger. adv. circ. 200.

327 SZ
UNIVERSITE DE GENEVE. INSTITUT UNIVERSITAIRE DE HAUTES ETUDES INTERNATIONALES. DISCUSSION PAPER. irreg., no. 9, 1976. Universite de Geneve, Institut Universitaire de Hautes Etudes Internationales, 132 rue de Lausanne, Box 53, CH-1211 Geneva, Switzerland.

327 SZ ISSN 0073-859X
UNIVERSITE DE GENEVE. INSTITUT UNIVERSITAIRE DE HAUTES ETUDES INTERNATIONALES. ETUDES ET TRAVAUX. (Text in English, French, German) 1960. irreg., no. 14, 1973. price varies. Librarie Droz, 11 rue Massot, CH-1211 Geneva 12, Switzerland. circ. 1,000.

327 SZ ISSN 0073-8603
UNIVERSITE DE GENEVE. INSTITUT UNIVERSITAIRE DE HAUTES ETUDES INTERNATIONALES. PUBLICATION. (Text in English, French, German) 1931. irreg., no. 51, 1973. price varies. Librarie Droz, 11 rue Massot, CH-1211 Geneva 12, Switzerland. circ. 800-1,000.

320 060 FR ISSN 0077-2720
UNIVERSITE DE NANCY II. CENTRE EUROPEEN UNIVERSITAIRE. MEMOIRES. 1962. irreg. price varies. Universite de Nancy II, Centre Europeen Universitaire, 25 rue Baron Louis, 54001 Nancy Cedex, 54 Nancy.

320 FR
UNIVERSITE DE NANCY II. FACULTE DE DROIT ET DES SCIENCES ECONOMIQUES. ETUDES ET TRAVAUX. SERIE ECONOMIE REGIONALE. 1973. irreg. price varies. Universite de Nancy II, Faculte de Droit et des Sciences Economiques, Service des Publications, B.P. 454, 54001 Nancy, France. adv. circ. 200.

320 FR
UNIVERSITE DE NANCY II. FACULTE DE DROIT ET DES SCIENCES ECONOMIQUES. ETUDES ET TRAVAUX. SERIE SCIENCE POLITIQUE. 1972. irreg. price varies. Universite de Nancy II, Faculte de Droit et des Sciences Economiques, Service des Publications, B.P. 454, 54001 Nancy, France. adv.

330 BE
UNIVERSITE LIBRE DE BRUXELLES. INSTITUT D'ETUDES EUROPEENS. THESES ET TRAVAUX POLITIQUES. 1971. irreg., unnumbered, latest 1973. Editions de l'Universite de Bruxelles, Parc Leopold, 1040 Brussels, Belgium.

327 US ISSN 0068-6093
UNIVERSITY OF CALIFORNIA, BERKELEY. INSTITUTE OF INTERNATIONAL STUDIES. RESEARCH SERIES. 1961. 2-3/yr. price varies. University of California, Berkeley, Institute of International Studies, Berkeley, CA 94720. Ed. Paul M. Gilchrist.

UNIVERSITY OF GLASGOW. INSTITUTE OF LATIN AMERICAN STUDIES. OCCASIONAL PAPERS. see *LITERARY AND POLITICAL REVIEWS*

320 UK
UNIVERSITY OF GLASGOW. INSTITUTE OF LATIN AMERICAN STUDIES. OCCASIONAL PAPERS. (Text in English) 1971. irreg. University of Glasgow, Institute of Latin American Studies, Glasgow GL2 8QH, Scotland. Ed.Bd. bibl.

320 355 US ISSN 0080-2794
UNIVERSITY OF RHODE ISLAND. BUREAU OF GOVERNMENT RESEARCH. RESEARCH SERIES. 1960. irreg., latest 1976. price varies. University of Rhode Island, Bureau of Government Research, Kingston, RI 02881. index. circ. controlled.

320 SI
UNIVERSITY OF SINGAPORE POLITICAL SCIENCE SOCIETY. JOURNAL. (Text in English) 1971. irreg. S.$2. University of Singapore Political Science Society, University of Singapore, Bukit Timah Rd, Singapore 10, Singapore. adv. bk. rev. circ. 2,000.

320 US
UNIVERSITY OF TEXAS, AUSTIN. LYNDON B. JOHNSON SCHOOL OF PUBLIC AFFAIRS. POLICY RESEARCH PROJECT REPORT. 1971. irreg. University of Texas at Austin, Lyndon B. Johnson School of Public Affairs, Drawer Y, Austin, TX 78712. charts. stat.
  Formerly: University of Texas, Austin. Lyndon B. Johnson School of Public Affairs. Seminar Research Report.

320.5322 335.43 CS
UNIVERZITA KOMENSKEHO. FILOZOFICKA FAKULTA. ZBORNIK: MARXIZMUS-LENINIZMUS. (Text in Slovak. contents page and summaries in English and Russian) 1962. irreg., approx. a. exchange basis. Slovenske Pedagogicke Nakladatelstvo, Sasinkova 5, 891 12 Bratislava, Czechoslovakia.

UNIVERZITA KOMENSKEHO. USTAV MARXIZMU-LENINIZMU. ZBORNIK: MARXISTICKA FILOZOFIA. see *PHILOSOPHY*

320.53   CS
UNIVERZITA KOMENSKEHO. USTAV MARXIZMU-LENINIZMU. ZBORNIK: DEJINY ROBOTNICKEHO HNUTIA. (Text in Slovak; summaries in English, German, Russian) 1972. irreg. price varies. Univerzita Komenskeho, Ustav Marxizmu-Leninizmu, Safarikovo nam. 12, Bratislava, Czechoslovakia.

320   PL
UNIWERSYTET JAGIELLONSKI. ZESZYTY NAUKOWE. PRACE Z NAUK POLITYCZNYCH. (Text in Polish; summaries English or Russian) 1971. irreg., 1972, vol. 3. price varies. Panstwowe Wydawnictwo Naukowe, Miodowa 10, Warsaw, Poland (Subscr. address: Ars Polona, Centrala Handlu Zagranicznego, Krakowskie Przedmiescie 7, Warsaw, Poland) Ed. Jan Wolenski.

350   US
UPDATE (ALBANY) irreg. Associated Industries of New York State Inc., 150 State St., Albany, NY 12207.

322.4   US
URBAN GUERILLA. Short title: T U G. no. 4, 1977. irreg. 423 Oak St., San Francisco, CA 94102.

320   FR
VAINCRE; journal du G U D, Front de la Jeunesse. 1977. 10/yr. 20 F. (Groupe, Union, Defense) Societe Occidentale d'Edition, 7 Bd. de Sebastopol, 75001 Paris, France. illus.

320 340   GW   ISSN 0083-5676
VERFASSUNG UND VERFASSUNGSWIRKLICHKEIT. 1966. irreg., vol. 8, 1973. price varies. Duncker und Humblot, Dietrich-Schaefer-Weg 9, 1000 Berlin 41, W. Germany (B.R.D.) Eds. Ferdinand A. Hermens, Werner Kaltefleiter. adv. bk. rev.

320   UR
VOPROSY KRITIKI BURZHUAZNOI POLITIKI I IDEOLOGII. SBORNIK NAUCHNYKH TRUDOV. (Text in Russian) vol. 3, 1977. a. 0.42 Rub. per issue. Latviiskii Gosudarstvennyi Universitet, Kafedra Nauchnogo Kommunizma, Bulvar Raynisa, 19, Riga, U.S.S.R.
Marxism

329   US
WADSWORTH SERIES IN AMERICAN POLITICS. irreg. Wadsworth Publishing Co., 10 Davis Dr., Belmont, CA 94002.

320   JA   ISSN 0511-196X
WASEDA POLITICAL STUDIES. (Text in English) 1957. irreg. Waseda University, Graduate Division of Political Science, Totsuka-machi, Shinjuku-ku, Tokyo 160, Japan.

320 296   US
WASHINGTON LETTER. irreg. American Jewish Committee, Washington Representative, c/o Hyman Bookbinder, 818 18th St. N.W., Washington, DC 20006.

320   US
WASHINGTON REPRESENTATIVES. 1977. a. $35. Columbia Books, Inc., Suite 1336, 777 14th St. N.W., Washington, DC 20005. Eds. Craig Colgate, Arthur Close.
Formerly: Directory of Washington Representatives of American Associations & Industry.

WESTERN EUROPE REPORT. see *BUSINESS AND ECONOMICS — Economic Situation And Conditions*

328.54   II
WHO IS WHO. (Text in English) 1961. biennial. Rs.5. Legislative Council, Fort St. George, Madras 600009, India. illus. circ. controlled.

WHO'S WHO IN AMERICAN POLITICS. see *BIOGRAPHY*

320 920   GW   ISSN 0000-0256
WHO'S WHO IN DER POLITIK/WHO'S WHO IN GERMAN POLITICS. 1971. irreg., 2nd ed., 1981. K.G. Saur Verlag KG, Poessenbacherstr. 12 B, Postfach 711009, 8000 Munich 71, W. Germany (B.R.D.)

WHO'S WHO IN GOVERNMENT. see *BIOGRAPHY*

320   US
WISCONSIN. STATE ELECTIONS BOARD. ANNUAL REPORT. a. State Elections Board, 121 S. Pinckney St., Madison, WI 53703.

WORLD CHRONOLOGIES SERIES. see *HISTORY*

320   IS
WORLD ZIONIST ORGANIZATION. ZIONIST CONGRESS. KONGRES HA-TSIYONI. HAHLATOT. (Text in Hebrew) irreg. World Zionist Organization, Jerusalem, Israel.

WOYTINSKY LECTURES. see *PUBLIC ADMINISTRATION*

320   US
WRITINGS OF THE LEFT. irreg. Grove Press, c/o Random House, 201 E. 50 St., New York, NY 10022.

320   US   ISSN 0513-1405
YALE LAW SCHOOL STUDIES. 1950. irreg. Yale University, School of Law, New Haven, CT 06520.

320   US   ISSN 0084-3490
YALE STUDIES IN POLITICAL SCIENCE. 1954. irreg., no. 30, 1979. price varies. Yale University Press, 92A Yale Sta., New Haven, CT 06520.

369.4   UK   ISSN 0513-5982
YOUNG FABIAN PAMPHLET. 1961. irreg., no. 49, 1981. 40-70p. Fabian Society, 11 Dartmouth St., London SW1H 9BN, England. Ed. Bd. charts, stat. circ. 5,000-10,000.

320.531   CN   ISSN 0044-0884
YOUNG SOCIALIST. 1970. irreg. Box 517, Station a, Toronto, Ont., Canada. illus.
Formerly: Young Socialist Forum (ISSN 0513-6121)

320.532   CN   ISSN 0382-4047
YOUNG WORKER. 1970. irreg. Young Worker Publishing Co., 24 Cecil St., Toronto, Ont., Canada.
Formerly: Young Communist (ISSN 0382-4039)

956.940   UK   ISSN 0084-5531
ZIONIST YEAR BOOK. 1951/52. a. £4($12) Zionist Federation of Great Britain and Northern Ireland, Rex House, 4-12 Regent St., London S.W.1, England. Ed. Jane Moarman. adv. index. circ. 1,200-1,500.
Zionism

320   US   ISSN 0164-0356
50 STATE LEGISLATIVE REVIEW. biennial. Political Research, Inc., Tagoland at Bent Tree, 16850 Dallas Parkway, Dallas, TX 75248.

POLITICAL SCIENCE — Abstracting, Bibliographies, Statistics

335 016   US   ISSN 0065-8650
AMERICAN INSTITUTE FOR MARXIST STUDIES. BIBLIOGRAPHIC SERIES. 1965. irreg., latest no. 15. American Institute for Marxist Studies, 20 E. 30th St., New York, NY 10016.

320 016   PO
BIBLIOGRAFIA CIENTIFICA DA JUNTA DE INVESTIGACOES DO ULTRAMAR. 1960. a. Junta de Investigacoes Cientificas do Ultramar, Centro de Documentacao e Informacao, Rua Jau 47, 1300 Lisbon, Portugal. bibl.

320 016   GW   ISSN 0067-8015
BIBLIOTHECA IBERO-AMERICANA. 1959. irreg. price varies. (Ibero-Amerikanisches Institut) Colloquium Verlag, Unter den Eichen 93, 1000 Berlin 45, W. Germany (B.R.D.) Ed. Wilhelm Stegmann. circ. 1,000.

341.1 355 016   US
CALIFORNIA STATE UNIVERSITY, LOS ANGELES. CENTER FOR THE STUDY OF ARMAMENT AND DISARMAMENT. POLITICAL ISSUES BIBLIOGRAPHY SERIES. 1972. irreg. (approx. 6-10/yr.) $2.50-$3.00 per issue. California State University, Los Angeles, Center for the Study of Armament and Disarmament, 5151 State University Dr., Los Angeles, CA 90032. Ed. Susan Hoffman Hutson. circ. 1-300. (processed)
Formerly: California State University, Los Angeles. Center for the Study of Armament and Disarmament. Classroom Study Series.

011 320   GE
D D R-PUBLIKATIONEN ZUR IMPERIALISMUSFORSCHUNG, AUSWAHLBIBLIOGRAPHIE. a. Institut fuer Internationale Politik und Wirtschaft, Breite Str. 11, 102 Berlin, E. Germany (D.D.R.) bibl.

320 070.5   US   ISSN 0149-7847
DIRECTORY OF CONSERVATIVE AND LIBERTARIAN SERIALS, PUBLISHERS, AND FREELANCE MARKETS. 1977. irreg., 2nd edt. 1979. $5.45. Dennis D. Murphy, Ed. & Pub., Box B-26, Box B, Tucson, AZ 85705.

015 327   II
DOCUMENTATION ON ASIA. 1960. a. Rs.100($30) Indian Council of World Affairs, Library, Sapru House, Barakhamba Rd., New Delhi 110001, India. Eds. Mrs. V. Machwe, Ashok Jambhakar.

314 320   FI   ISSN 0355-2209
FINLAND. TILASTOKESKUS. KANSANEDUSTAJAIN VAALIT/FINLAND. STATISTIKCENTRALEN. RIDSDAGSMANNAVALEN/FINLAND. CENTRAL STATISTICAL OFFICE. PARLIAMENTARY ELECTIONS. (Section XXIX A of Official Statistics of Finland) (Text in Finnish, Swedish and English) 1909. irreg. Fmk.16. Tilastokeskus, Annankatu 44, SF-00100 Helsinki 10, Finland (Subscr. to: Government Printing Centre, Box 516, SF-00100 Helsinki 10, Finland)

327 015   UN   ISSN 0072-0658
GENERAL CATALOGUE OF UNESCO AND UNESCO-SPONSORED PUBLICATIONS. (Text in English and French) 1964. irreg., 1969, 2nd supp. 8 F. Unesco, 7-9 Place de Fontenoy, 75700 Paris, France (Dist. in U.S. by: Unipub, 345 Park Ave. S., New York, NY 10010)

INDIA AND WORLD AFFAIRS: AN ANNUAL BIBLIOGRAPHY. see *HISTORY — Abstracting, Bibliographies, Statistics*

327 016   YU
INSTITUTE OF INTERNATIONAL POLITICS AND ECONOMICS. DOCUMENTATION BULLETIN.* (Text in English) 1972. irreg. Institut za Medjunarodnu Politiku i Privredu u Beogradu - Institute of International Politics and Economics, Makedonska 25, Box 750, Belgrade, Yugoslavia. bibl.

320 016.32   UK   ISSN 0085-2058
INTERNATIONAL BIBLIOGRAPHY OF THE SOCIAL SCIENCES. POLITICAL SCIENCE. 1953. irreg., vol. 28, 1979. £32.50. Tavistock Publications Ltd., 11 New Fetter La., London C4P 4EE, England (Dist. in U.S. by: Methuen Inc., 733 Third Ave., New York, N.Y. 10017)
Title page also reads: International Bibliography of Political Science.

JOURNALS OF DISSENT AND SOCIAL CHANGE; a bibliography of titles in the California State University, Sacramento, library. see *SOCIOLOGY — Abstracting, Bibliographies, Statistics*

324   NE   ISSN 0077-7013
NETHERLANDS. CENTRAAL BUREAU VOOR DE STATISTIEK. STATISTIEK DER VERKIEZINGEN. GEMEENTERADEN. ELECTION STATISTICS. MUNICIPAL COUNCILS. (Text in Dutch and English) 1946. irreg. fl.25. Centraal Bureau voor de Statistiek, Prinses Beatrixlaan 428, Voorburg, Netherlands (Orders to: Staatsuitgeverij, Christoffel Plantijnstraat, The Hague, Netherlands)

POLITICAL SCIENCE — CIVIL RIGHTS

324   NE   ISSN 0077-703X
NETHERLANDS. CENTRAAL BUREAU VOOR DE STATISTIEK. STATISTIEK DER VERKIEZINGEN. TWEEDE KAMER DER STATEN-GENERAAL. ELECTION STATISTICS. SECOND CHAMBER OF THE STATES-GENERAL. (Text in Dutch and English) 1946. irreg. fl.21.50. Centraal Bureau voor de Statistiek, Prinses Beatrixlaan 428, Voorburg, Netherlands (Orders to: Staatsuitgeverij, Christoffel Plantijnstraat, The Hague, Netherlands)

320 016   JA
PUBLICATIONS ON POLITICAL SCIENCE IN JAPAN. (Text in English and Japanese) 1965. a. Japanese Political Science Association - Nihon Seiji Gakkai, c/o Faculty of Law, University of Tokyo, 7-3-1 Hongo, Bunkyo-ku, Tokyo 113, Japan.

015   SI
SINGAPORE NATIONAL PRINTERS. PUBLICATIONS CATALOGUE. (Text in English) 1973. irreg. free. Singapore National Printers Ltd., 303 Upper Serangoon Road, Box 485, Singapore 13, Singapore. circ. 600.
Supersedes: Singapore. Catalogue of Government Publications.

327 011   SA
SOUTH AFRICAN INSTITUTE OF INTERNATIONAL AFFAIRS. BIBLIOGRAPHICAL SERIES/SUID-AFRIKAANSE INSTITUUT VAN INTERNASIONALE AANGELEENTHEDE. BIBLIOGRAFIESE REEKS. 1976. irreg., no. 3, 1978. price varies. South African Institute of International Affairs, Box 31596, Braamfontein, Transvaal 2017, South Africa.

327 016   US
WAR PEACE BIBLIOGRAPHY SERIES. 1973. irreg., no. 14, 1980. price varies. (California State University, Los Angeles, Center for the Study of Armament and Disarmanent) American Bibliographical Center-Clio Press, 2040 Alameda Padre Serra, Box 4397, Santa Barbara, CA 93103. Ed. Richard Dean Burns.

POLITICAL SCIENCE — Civil Rights

323.4   US
ACCESS REFERENCE SERVICE. 1976. irreg. $182 (or $257 including Access Reports) Plus Publications, Inc., 2626 Pennsylvania Ave., N.W., Washington, DC 20037.

323.4   UK
ANTI-APARTHEID MOVEMENT. ANNUAL REPORT OF ACTIVITIES AND DEVELOPMENTS. a. Anti-Apartheid Movement, 89 Charlotte St., London W1P 2DQ, England.

323.4   NE
CASE STUDIES ON HUMAN RIGHTS AND FUNDAMENTAL FREEDOMS. 1975. irreg. fl.75 per no. Martinus Nijhoff, Box 566, 2501 CN The Hague, Netherlands. Ed. Willem A. Veenhoven.

323.4   UK   ISSN 0144-8285
CATHOLIC COMMISSION FOR RACIAL JUSTICE. NOTES & REPORTS. 1978. irreg. free. Catholic Commission for Racial Justice, Church Hall, 1 Amwell St., London EC1R 1UL, England.

320   AT
CIVIL LIBERTY. 1968. irreg. Aus.$3. Council for Civil Liberties, P.O. Box 201, Glebe, NSW 2037, Australia. circ. 1,600.

341.48   FR
COUNCIL OF EUROPE. STANDING COMMITTEE ON THE EUROPEAN CONVENTION ON ESTABLISHMENT (INDIVIDUALS). PERIODICAL REPORT. 1971. irreg. Council of Europe, Publication Section, 67006 Strasbourg, France (Dist. in U. S. by Manhattan Publishing Co., 225 Lafayette St., New York, N. Y. 10012)

341.48   FR
EUROPEAN COMMISSION OF HUMAN RIGHTS. REPORT. (Text in English) a. European Commission of Human Rights, 67006 Strasbourg, France.

323.4   GW   ISSN 0073-3903
EUROPEAN COURT OF HUMAN RIGHTS. PUBLICATIONS. SERIES A: JUDGMENTS AND DECISIONS/COUR EUROPEENNE DES DROITS DE L'HOMME. PUBLICATIONS. SERIE A: ARRETS ET DECISIONS. (Text in English and French) 1961. irreg., vol. 27, 1979. Carl Heymanns Verlag KG, Gereonst. 18-32, 5000 Cologne 1, W. Germany (B.R.D.)

323   GW   ISSN 0073-3911
EUROPEAN COURT OF HUMAN RIGHTS. PUBLICATIONS. SERIES B: PLEADINGS, ORAL ARGUMENTS AND DOCUMENTS/COUR EUROPEENNE DES DROITS DE L'HOMME. PUBLICATIONS. SERIE B: MEMOIRES, PLAIDOIRIES ET DOCUMENTS. (Text in English and French) 1961. irreg., vol. 20, 1978. price varies. Carl Heymanns Verlag KG, Gereonstr. 18-32, 5000 Cologne 1, W. Germany (B.R.D.)

GRAY PANTHER NEWS. see *GERONTOLOGY AND GERIATRICS*

323.4   US   ISSN 0046-8207
H R W NEWSLETTER. 1971. irreg. free to contributors. Human Rights for Women, Inc., 1128 National Press Building, Washington, DC 20045. Ed. Mary Eastwood. circ. 1,000. (also avail. in microform from BLH)

323   US   ISSN 0085-1434
HARD CORE NEWS;* newsletter of the Texas libertarian movement. 1969. irreg. free. Hard Core News Printing Co-Op, P.O. Box 66321, Houston, TX 77006. adv. bk. rev. film rev. play rev. tr.lit. circ. 700. (processed)

323   US   ISSN 0073-1137
HAWAII. OFFICE OF THE OMBUDSMAN. REPORT. 1971. a. free. Office of the Ombudsman, Kekuanaoa Bldg., 4th Fl., 465 S. King St., Honolulu, HI 96813. Ed. Herman S. Doi. circ. controlled.

HOMOSEXUAL INFORMATION CENTER. NEWSLETTER. see *HOMOSEXUALITY*

323.4   CN   ISSN 0441-4128
HUMAN RELATIONS. 1958. a. free. ‡ Ontario Human Rights Commission, Ministry of Labour, 400 University Ave., Toronto, Ont. M7A 1T7, Canada. Ed. Harold B. Attin. circ. 50,000. (back issues avail)

323.4   US   ISSN 0098-0579
HUMAN RIGHTS ORGANIZATIONS & PERIODICALS DIRECTORY. 1973. biennial. $10. Meiklejohn Civil Liberties Institute, 1715 Francisco St., Berkeley, CA 94703. Ed. David Christiano. bibl. circ. 1,000.

323.4   UK   ISSN 0260-7522
I C S A BULLETIN. no. 9, Oct. 1980. irreg. International Committee against Apartheid, Racism and Colonialism in Southern Africa, 30a Danbury St., London N1 8JV, England.

I W G I A DOCUMENTS; documentation of oppression of ethnic groups in various countries. (International Work Group for Indigenous Affairs) see *ANTHROPOLOGY*

I W G I A NEWSLETTER. (International Work Group for Indigenous Affairs) see *ANTHROPOLOGY*

347   US   ISSN 0093-8939
ILLINOIS. JUDICIAL INQUIRY BOARD. REPORT. 1973. irreg. free. Judicial Inquiry Board, 205 W. Wacker Dr., Suite 1515, Chicago, IL 60606. Key Title: Report - Judicial Inquiry Board (Chicago)

323.4   US
INDIANA. CIVIL RIGHTS COMMISSION. TRIENNIAL REPORT. 1962. triennial. Civil Rights Commission, 311 W. Washington St., Suite 319, Indianapolis, IN 46204.
Formerly: Indiana. Civil Rights Commission. Annual Report (ISSN 0073-6856)

323   US   ISSN 0074-0764
INTER-AMERICAN COMMISSION OF WOMEN. SPECIAL ASSEMBLY. FINAL ACT/COMISION INTERAMERICANA DE MUJERES. ASAMBLEA EXTRAORDINARIA. ACTA FINAL. 1963, 3rd. biennial. price varies. Organization of American States, 17th and Constitution Aves. N.W., Washington, DC 20006. circ. 3,000.

323.4   CN   ISSN 0226-661X
INTER-CHURCH COMMITTEE ON HUMAN RIGHTS IN LATIN AMERICA. NEWSLETTER. 1977. irreg. free contr. circ. Inter-Church Committee on Human Rights in Latin America, Suite 201, 40 St. Clair Ave. E., Toronto, Ont. M4T 1M9, Canada.

301.45 968   UN   ISSN 0538-8333
INTERNATIONAL LABOUR OFFICE. SPECIAL REPORT OF THE DIRECTOR-GENERAL ON THE APPLICATION OF THE DECLARATION CONCERNING THE POLICY OF APARTHEID OF THE REPUBLIC OF SOUTH AFRICA. 1965. a. price varies. International Labour Office - Bureau International du Travail, Publications Sales Service, CH-1211 Geneva 20, Switzerland (U.S. Distributor: I L O Branch Office, 1750 New York Ave. N.W., Washington, DC 20006) (also avail. in microform)

323.4   US   ISSN 0363-9347
INTERNATIONAL LEAGUE FOR HUMAN RIGHTS. ANNUAL REPORT. 1950. a., latest issue, 1977. $10 includes subscription to Human Rights Bulletin. ‡ International League for Human Rights, 236 E. 46th St., New York, NY 10017. circ. controlled.
Formerly: International League for the Rights of Man. Annual Report.

320.56 331.88   CS
INTERNATIONAL TRADE UNION CONFERENCE FOR ACTION AGAINST APARTHEID. RESOLUTION. (Text in English) irreg., 2nd 1977, Geneva. free. World Federation of Trade Unions, Nam Curieovych 1, 116 88 Prague 1, Czechoslovakia. illus.

320   US
IOWA CIVIL RIGHTS COMMISSION. ANNUAL REPORT. no. 8, 1975. a. Civil Rights Commission, 1209 E. Court Ave., Des Moines, IA 50319.

323 341   IS
ISRAEL YEARBOOK ON HUMAN RIGHTS. (Text in English) 1971. a. I£80($10) ‡ Tel Aviv University, Faculty of Law, Ramat Aviv, Tel Aviv, Israel. Ed. Dr. Yoram Dinstein. bk. rev. circ. 1,500.

323.4 340   US
JUSTICE DEPARTMENT WATCH. 1977. 4-5/yr. Committee for Public Justice, 22 E. 40th St., New York, NY 10016. circ. 10,000.

KATALLAGETE. see *RELIGIONS AND THEOLOGY*

323.4   CN   ISSN 0383-5588
MANITOBA. HUMAN RIGHTS COMMISSION. ANNUAL REPORT. 1974. a. Human Rights Commission, 430 Edmonton St., Winnipeg, Man. R3B 2M3, Canada. illus.

323.4   US
MICHIGAN. CIVIL RIGHTS COMMISSION. ANNUAL REPORT. 1964. a. free. Department of Civil Rights, 125 W. Allegan St., Lansing, MI 48933.
Former titles (1970-1972): Civil Rights in Michigan; Michigan. Civil Rights Commission. Report (ISSN 0076-7875)

323   US   ISSN 0076-9118
MINNESOTA. DEPARTMENT OF HUMAN RIGHTS. BIENNIAL REPORT. 1967-68. biennial. free. Department of Human Rights, 200 Capitol Square Bldg., St. Paul, MN 55101. Ed. Jack C. Kraywinkle. circ. 2,000.

MINORITY RIGHTS GROUP. REPORTS. see *SOCIOLOGY*

MORGONBRIS. see *WOMEN'S INTERESTS*

N G T F ACTION REPORT. (National Gay Task Force) see *HOMOSEXUALITY*

323.4 US
NEW YORK (STATE). DIVISION OF HUMAN RIGHTS. ANNUAL REPORT. a. Division of Human Rights, 2 World Trade Center, New York, NY 10047.

NO MORE FUN AND GAMES; a journal of female liberation. see WOMEN'S INTERESTS

323.4 US ISSN 0270-2282
NORTH AMERICAN HUMAN RIGHTS DIRECTORY. 1980. irreg. $11. Garrett Park Press, Garrett Park, MD 20766. Eds. Laurie S. Wiseberg, Harry M. Scoble.

323.4 CN
OPERATION LIBERTE. 1978. irreg. Ligue des Droites et Libertes, 1825 de Champlain, Montreal, Que. H2L 2S9, Canada. (back issues avail.)

323.4 US ISSN 0032-9177
PROBE (SANTA BARBARA) 1968. irreg. donations. ‡ Box 13390 UCSB, Santa Barbara, CA 93107. Ed. Perry Adams. adv. bk. rev. illus. circ. 15,000. (tabloid format)
Formerly: Argo.

323.4 US
RACE AND NATIONS SERIES. irreg. price varies. (Center on International Race Relations) D.C. Heath & Company, 125 Spring St., Lexington, MA 02173.

RAZON MESTIZA. see WOMEN'S INTERESTS

SEQUEL. see HOMOSEXUALITY

354.68 SA ISSN 0584-2166
SOUTH AFRICA. DEPARTMENT OF COLOURED RELATIONS AND REHOBOTH AFFAIRS. ANNUAL REPORT. a. Government Printer, Bosman St., Private Bag X85, Pretoria 0001, South Africa.

SPEKTRUM; unperiodical journal of banned writers. see LITERARY AND POLITICAL REVIEWS

323 US
STATE OF BLACK AMERICA. 1975. a. $12.50. National Urban League, 500 E. 62 St., New York, NY 10021.

STUDIES IN HUMAN RIGHTS. see POLITICAL SCIENCE — International Relations

301.45 SA ISSN 0081-9778
SURVEY OF RACE RELATIONS IN SOUTH AFRICA. 1948. a. R.6($8.05) South African Institute of Race Relations, P.O. Box 97, Johannesburg, South Africa. Ed. M. Horrell. circ. 6,000.

323 FR ISSN 0082-7770
UNION PROFESSIONNELLE FEMININE. ANNUAIRE.* 1964. a. Federation Francaise des Clubs de Femmes de Carrieres Liberales et Commerciales et de Professions Diverses, c/o Mme. Kraemer-Bach, 75 rue de Longchamp, Paris 16e, France.

323.4 US ISSN 0082-9641
U.S. COMMISSION ON CIVIL RIGHTS. CLEARINGHOUSE PUBLICATIONS. 1965. irreg. limited numbers of copies available free from the Commission. U.S. Commission on Civil Rights, 1121 Vermont Ave. N.W., Washington, DC 20425 (Orders to: Supt. of Documents, Washington, DC 20402;, Or up to 50 copies available Free from U.S. Commission on Civil Rights)

U.S. EQUAL EMPLOYMENT OPPORTUNITY COMMISSION. ANNUAL REPORT. see BUSINESS AND ECONOMICS — Labor And Industrial Relations

323.4 US
VIEWPOINT; minority outlook on current issues. 1970. irreg. (approx. 1-2/yr) price varies. ‡ Council on Interracial Books for Children, Inc., 1841 Broadway, Rm. 300, New York, NY 10023. bibl. illus.

323.4 US ISSN 0083-8594
WEST VIRGINIA. HUMAN RIGHTS COMMISSION. REPORT. 1961. biennial. free. Human Rights Commission, P. & G. Bldg., 2019 E. Washington St., Charleston, WV 25305. circ. 1,000.

323.4 US ISSN 0085-8242
WISCONSIN WOMEN NEWSLETTER. 1971. irreg., vol. 9, 1979. free. University of Wisconsin-Extension, Family Living Education and Women's Education Resources, 430 & 433 Lowell Hall, 610 Langdon St., Madison, WI 53706. Ed. Marian Thompson. circ. 4,000. (processed)
Formerly: Women's Education Newsletter.

956.940 296 SA ISSN 0043-7603
WOMEN'S ZIONIST COUNCIL OF SOUTH AFRICA. NEWS AND VIEWS. 1949. 4-5/yr. membership. Women's Zionist Council of South Africa, Zionist Centre, Box 18, Johannesburg 2000, South Africa. Ed. Hetty Schwartz. adv. bk. rev. charts. illus. play rev. circ. 18,500.
Zionism

323.4 NE
YEARBOOK OF HUMAN RIGHTS. 1959. a., except 1964. price varies. (Council of Europe, FR) Martinus Nijhoff, Box 566, 2501 CN The Hague, Netherlands.
Formerly: European Convention on Human Rights. Yearbook (ISSN 0071-2701)

323.4 UN ISSN 0084-4098
YEARBOOK ON HUMAN RIGHTS. (Editions in English and French) 1946. irreg. price varies. United Nations Publications, LX 2300, New York, NY 10017 (Or Distribution and Sales Section, CH-1211 Geneva 10, Switzerland)

POLITICAL SCIENCE — International Relations

see also Law — International Law

320 FR
A D U K. (Adresar Ukraintsiv u Vilnomu Sviti) 1973. irreg. Premiere Imprimerie Ukrainienne en France, 3, rue du Sabot, 75006 Paris, France. illus.

300 US
AFRICAN COLONIAL STUDIES. 1974. irreg. (Stanford University, Hoover Institution on War, Revolution and Peace) Hoover Institution Press, Stanford, CA 94305.

327 US
AMERICAN FOREIGN RELATIONS-A DOCUMENTARY RECORD. 1939. irreg., latest edt. 1977. $28.50. Council on Foreign Relations, Inc., 58 East 68th St., New York, NY 10021 (Subscr. to: New York University Press, 113 University Pl., New York, NY 10003) Ed. Elaine P. Adam. index. (reprint service avail. from UMI)
Formerly: Documents on American Foreign Relations (ISSN 0070-6973); Incorporates: United States in World Affairs (ISSN 0083-128X)

327 JA
AMERICAN REVIEW. (Text in Japanese and English; summaries in English) irreg; 1973, no. 7. $3.40 per no. (Japanese Association of American Studies) University of Tokyo, Center for American Studies, 153 Komaba, Meguro-ku, Tokyo 153, Japan. bibl.

AMERICAN UNIVERSITIES FIELD STAFF. ANNUAL REPORT OF THE EXECUTIVE DIRECTOR. see EDUCATION — Higher Education

323 UK
AMNESTY INTERNATIONAL REPORT. 1962. a. £2.50. Amnesty International, 10 Southampton St., London WC2E 7HF, England.
Formerly: Amnesty International Annual Report (ISSN 0569-9495)

327 FR ISSN 0066-295X
ANNUAIRE DIPLOMATIQUE ET CONSULAIRE DE LA REPUBLIQUE FRANCAISE. 1879. a. 78 F. Ministere des Affaires Etrangeres, Direction du Personnel et de l'Administration Generale, 37 Quai d'Orsay, 75700 Paris, France (Subs to: l'Imprimerie Nationale, 27, rue de la Convention, 75015 Paris, France) adv.

327 FR
ANNUAIRE ECONOMIQUE D'AFRIQUE ET DU MOYEN-ORIENT. (Supplement to Jeune Afrique) a. 150 F. Groupe J.A., 51 Av. des Ternes, 75017 Paris, France. charts. illus. (reprint service avail from UMI)
Formerly: Afrique et Moyen-Orient.

327 UK
ANNUAL POWER AND CONFLICT; a survey of political violence and international pressures. a. £10($22.50) Institute for the Study of Conflict, 12-12a Golden Square, London W1R 3AF, England. (Co-sponsor: National Strategy Information Center, New York)

341.13 327 US ISSN 0066-4340
ANNUAL REVIEW OF UNITED NATIONS AFFAIRS. 1949. a. price varies. Oceana Publications, Inc., Dobbs Ferry, NY 10522. index. cum.index in 1965-66 vol.

327 IT
ANNUARIO DIPLOMATICO DELLA REPUBBLICA ITALIANA. 1963. a. Ministero degli Affari Esteri, Rome, Italy.
Formerly: Annuario Diplomatico del Regno d'Italia.

320.9 JA
ASIAN PARLIAMENTARIANS' UNION. CENTRAL SECRETARIAT. REPORT ON MEETING OF APU SECRETARIES-GENERAL IN TOKYO.* 1972. a. Asian Parliamentarians' Union, TBR Bldg., Room 807, 2-10-2 Nagata-cho, Chiyoda-ku, Tokyo, Japan.

327 UK ISSN 0067-0065
AT THE COURT OF ST. JAMES'S. 1954. a. £2.50. Diplomatist Associates Ltd., Shooter's Lodge, Windsor Forest, Berks, England. Ed. B. Millan.

327 AT ISSN 0084-7135
AUSTRALIA. DEPARTMENT OF FOREIGN AFFAIRS. INTERNATIONAL TREATIES AND CONVENTIONS. (Included in its Select Documents on International Affairs) 1966. a. price varies. Department of Foreign Affairs, Canberra, A.C.T. 2600, Australia.

327 AT ISSN 0519-5950
AUSTRALIA. DEPARTMENT OF FOREIGN AFFAIRS. SELECT DOCUMENTS ON INTERNATIONAL AFFAIRS. irreg. price varies. Department of Foreign Affairs, Canberra, A.C.T. 2600, Australia.
An annual series of international treaties and conventions

327 AT
AUSTRALIAN-AMERICAN NEWS N.S.W. ANNUAL EDITION. Aus.$50 per no. Australian-American Association, N.S.W. Division, 39-41 Lower Fort St., Sydney, N.S.W. 2000, Australia. Ed. T. Padley. adv. illus.

327 AT
AUSTRALIAN MISSION TO THE UNITED NATIONS. UNITED NATIONS GENERAL ASSEMBLY. AUSTRALIAN DELEGATION. REPORT. 1946. a. price varies. Australian Government Publishing Service, P.O. Box 84, Canberra City, A.C.T. 2601, Australia.

327 AT ISSN 0312-9217
AUSTRALIA'S OVERSEAS DEVELOPMENT ASSISTANCE. 1973. a. Aus.$0.25. Department of the Treasury, P.O. Box 84, Canberra, A.C.T. 2600, Australia.
Formerly: Australia's External Aid (ISSN 0310-6152)

327 CN ISSN 0708-0859
B. C. PEACE NEWS. 1978. irreg. B. C. Peace Council, 712-207 West Hastings St., Vancouver, B.C. V6B 1H7, Canada.
Formerly: B. C. News (ISSN 0708-0840)

341.13 UN ISSN 0067-4419
BASIC FACTS ABOUT THE UNITED NATIONS. irreg. $1. United Nations Publications, Room LX-2300, New York, NY 10017 (Or Distribution and Sales Section, Palais des Nations, CH-1211 Geneva 10, Switzerland)

POLITICAL SCIENCE — INTERNATIONAL RELATIONS

338.9   GW   ISSN 0170-1916
BOCHUMER MATERIALEN ZUR ENTWICKLUNGSFORSCHUNG UND ENTWICKLUNGSPOLITIK. 1976. irreg. price varies. (Ruhr-Universitaet, Bochum, Institut fuer Entwicklungsforschung und Entwicklungspolitik) Horst Erdmann Verlag, Hartmeyerstr. 117, Postfach 1380, 7400 Tuebingen, W. Germany (B.R.D.)

327   338.9   GW   ISSN 0572-6654
BOCHUMER SCHRIFTEN ZUR ENTWICKLUNGSFORSCHUNG UND ENTWICKLUNGSPOLITIK. 1968. irreg. price varies. (Ruhr-Universitaet, Bochum, Institut fuer Entwicklungsforschung und Entwicklungspolitik) Horst Erdmann Verlag, Hartmeyerstr. 117, Postfach 1380, 7400 Tuebingen, W. Germany (B.R.D.) circ. 1,000.

327   UK   ISSN 0307-2061
BRITISH NATIONAL ASSOCIATION FOR SOVIET AND EAST EUROPEAN STUDIES. INFORMATION BULLETIN. 1975. a. membership. British National Association for Soviet and East European Studies, University of Glasgow, 10 South Park Terrace, Glasgow GL2 8LQ, Scotland. Ed. D. Matko. bk. rev. bibl. circ. 2,000.

327   GW   ISSN 0435-7183
BUNDESINSTITUT FUER OSTWISSENSCHAFTLICHE UND INTERNATIONALE STUDIEN. BERICHTE. 1967. irreg. Bundesinstitut fuer Ostwissenschaftliche und Internationale Studien, Lindenborn Str. 22, 5000 Cologne, W. Germany (B.R.D.) bibl.

327   US
C W/P S SPECIAL STUDIES. 1977. irreg. $2 per no. Center for War-Peace Studies, 218 E. 18th St., New York, NY 10003.
    Formerly: C W/P S Study.

327   FR   ISSN 0084-8220
CAHIERS AMITIE FRANCO-VIETNAMIENNE.* a. Association d'Amitie Franco-Vietnamienne, 37, rue Ballu, 75009 Paris, France. bibl. charts. illus.

CAHIERS DE BRUGES/BRUGES QUARTERLY. see POLITICAL SCIENCE

327   FR   ISSN 0068-5224
CAHIERS ROUGE. NOUVELLE SERIE INTERNATIONALE. 1970. irreg. price varies. S.I.E., 10, Impasse Guemenee, 75004 Paris, France.

327   US
CALIFORNIA STATE UNIVERSITY, LOS ANGELES. CENTER FOR THE STUDY OF ARMAMENT AND DISARMAMENT. OCCASIONAL PAPERS SERIES. 1972. irreg., no. 7, 1979. $2 per no. California State University, Los Angeles, Center for the Study of Armament and Disarmament, 5151 State University Dr., Los Angeles, CA 90032. Ed. R. D. Burns. circ. 300.

327   CN
CANADA. DEPARTMENT OF EXTERNAL AFFAIRS. REFERENCE PAPERS. irreg. Department of External Affairs, Information Division, Ottawa, Ont. K1A 0G2, Canada.

327   CN
CANADA. DEPARTMENT OF EXTERNAL AFFAIRS. STATEMENTS AND SPEECHES. 1945. irreg. free. Department of External Affairs, Information Division, Ottawa, Ont. K1A 0G2, Canada. circ. 4,000.

327   CN   ISSN 0068-7685
CANADA IN WORLD AFFAIRS. irreg. Canadian Institute of International Affairs, 15 King's College Circle, Toronto, Ont. M5S 2V9, Canada. (reprint service avail. from UMI)

327   CN   ISSN 0317-5693
CANADIAN COMMISSION FOR UNESCO. ANNUAL REPORT. (Text in English and French) 1958. a. free. ‡ Canadian Commission for Unesco, 255 Albert St., Box 1047, Ottawa, Ont. K1P 5V8, Canada. Ed. Louise Beaulne. circ. 3,500.

327   CN
CANADIAN FOREIGN RELATIONS. French edition: Relations Etrangeres du Canada. a. Department of External Affairs, Information Division, Ottawa, Ont. K1A 0G2, Canada. illus.

327   NE
CARIBBEAN YEARBOOK OF INTERNATIONAL RELATIONS. 1975. a. fl.125. (University of the West Indies, Institute of International Relations, TR) Sijthoff & Noordhoff International Publishers B.V., Box 4, 2400 MA Alphen aan den Rijn, Netherlands. Ed. Leslie F. Manigat.

327   CN   ISSN 0383-2848
CARLETON UNIVERSITY, OTTAWA. NORMAN PATERSON SCHOOL OF INTERNATIONAL AFFAIRS. BIBLIOGRAPHY SERIES. 1975. irreg. (1-2/yr) Can.$1.50 per no. Carleton University, Norman Paterson School of International Affairs, Ottawa, Ont. K1S 5B6, Canada. Ed. Jane Beaumont.

327.172   US   ISSN 0094-3029
CARNEGIE ENDOWMENT FOR INTERNATIONAL PEACE. FINANCIAL REPORT. irreg. Carnegie Endowment for International Peace, 11 Dupont Circle, N.W., Washington, DC 20036 (Or 30 Rockefeller Plaza, New York, NY 10020) (reprint service avail. from UMI) Key Title: Financial Report - Carnegie Endowment for International Peace.

327   US   ISSN 0069-0643
CARNEGIE ENDOWMENT FOR INTERNATIONAL PEACE IN THE 1970'S. 1979. irreg. free. Carnegie Endowment for International Peace, 11 Dupont Circle N.W., Washington, DC 20036 (Or 30 Rockefeller Plaza, New York, NY 10020) circ. controlled. (reprint service avail. from UMI)
    Supersedes (1911-1979): Carnegie Endowment for International Peace Report (ISSN 0069-0643); Which was formerly: Carnegie Endowment for International Peace. Annual Report.

327   US
CASES IN INTERNATIONAL POLITICS. irreg. price varies. Holt, Rinehart and Winston, 383 Madison Ave., New York, NY 10017.

327   UK   ISSN 0144-7149
CHRONICLE (LONDON) 1979. irreg. free. Dag Hammarskjold Information Centre on the Study of Violence and Peace, 68 Eton Place, Eton College Rd., London NW3 2DS, England.

327   US   ISSN 0145-9686
CLEMENTS' ENCYCLOPEDIA OF WORLD GOVERNMENTS. 1974. biennial. $195 (includes Clements' International Report) Political Research, Inc., Tegoland at Bent Tree, 16850 Dallas Parkway, Dallas, TX 75248. Ed. John Clements.

327   FR   ISSN 0069-5475
COLLECTION U. SERIE DROIT DES COMMUNAUTES EUROPEENNES. 1970. irreg. price varies. Librairie Armand Colin, 103 Bld. Saint-Michel, Paris 5e, France.

327   FR   ISSN 0069-5505
COLLECTION U. SERIE RELATIONS ET INSTITUTIONS INTERNATIONALES. 1970. irreg. price varies. Librairie Armand Colin, 103 Bld. Saint-Michel, Paris 5e, France.

327   BE
COLLOQUES EUROPEENS. 1968? irreg., unnumbered, latest 1978. (Universite Libre de Bruxelles, Institut d'Etudes Europeennes) Editions de l'Universite de Bruxelles, Parc Leopold, 1040 Brussels, Belgium.

COMMONWEALTH INSTITUTE, LONDON. ANNUAL REPORT. see GEOGRAPHY

341.13   US   ISSN 0069-8601
CONFERENCE ON UNITED NATIONS PROCEDURES. REPORT. 1970. a. free. Stanley Foundation, 420 E. Third St., Muscatine, IA 52761. circ. 5,000. (also avail. in microfilm)
    Formerly: Conference on Organization and Procedures of the United Nations. Report.

COUNCIL OF EUROPE. COMMITTEE OF INDEPENDENT EXPERTS ON THE EUROPEAN SOCIAL CHARTER. CONCLUSIONS. see SOCIAL SERVICES AND WELFARE

341.18   FR   ISSN 0589-9478
COUNCIL OF EUROPE. COUNCIL FOR CULTURAL COOPERATION. ANNUAL REPORT. (Edts. in English and French) 1959. a. $4. Council of Europe, Council for Cultural Co-Operation, Publications Section, 67006 Strasbourg, France (Dist. in U. S. by Manhattan Publishing Co., 225 Lafayette St., New York, N. Y. 10012) (Co-sponsor: Cultural Fund) circ. 4,000 combined.

327.73   US
COUNCIL ON FOREIGN RELATIONS. ANNUAL REPORT. a. Council on Foreign Relations, Inc., 58 E. 68th St., New York, NY 10021. (reprint service avail. from UMI)
    Formerly: Council on Foreign Relations. President's Report (ISSN 0093-4615)

327   US
COUNCIL ON FOREIGN RELATIONS. COUNCIL PAPERS ON INTERNATIONAL AFFAIRS. 1973. irreg. price varies. Council on Foreign Relations, Inc., 58 E. 68th St., New York, NY 10021. bibl. charts. (reprint service avail. from UMI)

327   CN
CURRENT COMMENT; comments of controversial topics in international affairs. 1970. irreg. (approx. 5/yr.) Carleton University, Norman Paterson School of International Affairs, Ottawa, Ont. K1S 5B6, Canada. Dr. J. Geo. Neuspiel. charts. cum.index. circ. controlled. (processed)

327   US
CURRENT ISSUES. 1979. irreg. $15. Center for International Policy, 120 Maryland Ave. N.E., Washington, DC 20002. Ed. Donald L. Ranard. charts. illus. stat. circ. 5,000. (back issues avail.)

327   UK   ISSN 0070-2900
DAVID DAVIES MEMORIAL INSTITUTE OF INTERNATIONAL STUDIES, LONDON. ANNUAL MEMORIAL LECTURE. 1954. a. £1. David Davies Memorial Institute of International Studies, Thorney House, 34 Smith Square, London SW1, England. Ed. M. M. Sibthorp.

DEFENSE FOREIGN AFFAIRS HANDBOOK; political, economic & defense data on every country in the world. see MILITARY

341.13   UN   ISSN 0070-3303
DELEGATIONS TO THE UNITED NATIONS. 1946. biennial; 29th session, General Assembly; 1974. price varies. United Nations Publications, Room LX-2300, New York, NY 10017 (Or Distribution and Sales Section, Palais des Nations, CH-1211 Geneva 10, Switzerland)

327   GW   ISSN 0080-7125
DEUTSCH-AUSLAENDISCHE BEZIEHUNGEN. SCHRIFTENREIHE. 1961. irreg. price varies. (Institut fuer Auslandsbeziehungen, Stuttgart) Horst Erdmann Verlag, Hartmeyerstr. 117, Postfach 1380, 7400 Tuebingen, W. Germany (B.R.D.) circ. 3,000.

DIGEST OF WORLD EVENTS. see HISTORY

327   US
DIMENSIONS OF NATIONS. 1972. irreg., vol. 3, 1978. price varies. Sage Publications, Inc., 275 S. Beverly Dr., Beverly Hills, CA 90212 (And Sage Publications, Ltd., 28 Banner St., London EC1Y 8QE, England) Ed. R. J. Rummel. (back issues avail.)

327   943   HU   ISSN 0070-492X
DIPLOMACIAI IRATOK MAGYARORSZAG KULPOLITIKAJAHOZ. (Text in Hungarian; summaries in German) 1962. irreg. price varies. (Magyar Tudomanyos Akademia) Akademiai Kiado, Publishing House of the Hungarian Academy of Sciences, P.O. Box 24, H-1363 Budapest, Hungary.

327   CN   ISSN 0486-4514
DIPLOMATIC CORPS AND CONSULAR AND OTHER REPRESENTATIVES IN CANADA. CORPS DIPLOMATIQUE ET REPRESENTANTS CONSULAIRES ET AUTRES AU CANADA. (Text in English and French) 1969. irreg. Can.$2.75. Department of External Affairs, Information Division, Ottawa, Ont. K1A 0G2, Canada. illus.

341.7　　　　　　　　YU　ISSN 0070-4946
DIPLOMATIC CORPS OF BELGRADE.* (Text in English, French) 1969. a. 70 din.($6) Medjunarodna Politika, Nemanjina 34, 11000 Belgrade, Yugoslavia. Ed. R. Petkovic.

327　　　　　　　　　NP
DIPLOMATIC LIST AND LIST OF REPRESENTATIVES OF UNITED NATIONS AND ITS SPECIALIZED AGENCIES AND OTHER MISSIONS. (Text in English) a. Protocol Division, Ministry of Foreign Affairs, Kathmandu, Nepal.

327　100　　　　　　　US
DIRECTORY FOR A NEW WORLD; worldwide guide of organizations fostering a new universal person and civilization based on unity-in-diversity among all peoples. 1966. a. $3. Unity-in-Diversity Council, 7433 Madora Ave., Canoga Park, CA 91306. Ed. Leland P. Stewart. circ. 1,000.
  Formerly: International Cooperation Council. Directory (ISSN 0074-4239)

327　　　　　　　　　GE
DOCUMENTS ON THE POLICY OF THE GERMAN DEMOCRATIC REPUBLIC. 1966. irreg. Verlag Zeit im Bild, Julian T--Grimau--Allee, 8010 Dresden, E. Germany (D.D.R.)
  Formerly: Documents of the National and International Policy of the G D R.

327　　　　　　　US　ISSN 0070-7473
DUKE UNIVERSITY. COMMONWEALTH-STUDIES CENTER. PUBLICATIONS. 1956. irreg., 1973, no. 44. price varies. 6697 College Station, Durham, NC 27708.

327　　　　　　　US　ISSN 0070-8100
EAST EUROPE MONOGRAPHS. 1969. irreg., no. 4, 1974. price varies. (Studiengesellschaft fuer Fragen Mittel - und Osteuropaeischer Partnerschaft, GW) Park College, Governmental Research Bureau, Kansas City, MO 64152. Eds. Jerzy Hauptmann, Gotthold Rhode.

327　　　　　　　　　NE
EAST-WEST PERSPECTIVES. (Text in English) 1976. irreg. price varies. (East-West Foundation) Sijthoff & Noordhoff International Publishers b.v., Box 4, 2400 MA Alphen aan den Rijn, Netherlands. Ed.Bd. charts. stat.

327　　　　　　　　　NE
ENVIRONMENTAL PROGRAMMES OF INTERGOVERNMENTAL ORGANIZATIONS. 1977. irreg. fl.200($102) updating service fl.0.30 ($0.12) per page. Martinus Nijhoff, Box 566, 2501 CN The Hague, Netherlands. Ed. P. L. de Reeder. (looseleaf format)

327　　　　　　　BE　ISSN 0071-1896
ETUDES DE CAS DE CONFLITS INTERNATIONAUX. 1959. irreg. (Carnegie Endowment for International Peace, European Center) Editions de l'Universite de Bruxelles, Parc Leopold, 1040 Brussels, Belgium.

327　016　　　　　EI　ISSN 0071-2213
ETUDES UNIVERSITAIRES SUR L'INTEGRATION EUROPEENNE/UNIVERSITY STUDIES ON EUROPEAN INTEGRATION. (Editions in English and French) 1963. irreg. $8-$10. (European Community Institute for University Studies) Commission of the European Communities, 200, rue de la Loi, B-1049 Brussels, Belgium. Ed. Anne-Marie Nantermoz. circ. 4,000.

327　341　　　　　GW　ISSN 0071-2329
EUROPAEISCHE SCHRIFTEN. 1963. irreg. DM.8.50. (Institut fuer Europaeische Politik, Bonn) Europa Union Verlag GmbH, Stockenstr. 1-5, 5300 Bonn 1, W. Germany (B.R.D.) Ed. Wolfgang Wessels.

341.13　　　　　　UN　ISSN 0071-3244
EVERYMAN'S UNITED NATIONS. 1948. quinquennial. price varies. United Nations Publications, Room LX 2300, New York, NY 10017 (Or Distribution and Sales Section, Palais des Nations, CH-1211 Geneva 10, Switzerland)

FILMOTECA ULTRAMARINA PORTUGUESA. BOLETIM. see *HISTORY*

FIRST HAND INFORMATION. see *HISTORY — History Of Europe*

327　　　　　　　US　ISSN 0071-7320
FOREIGN CONSULAR OFFICES IN THE UNITED STATES. (Subseries of U. S. Dept. of State. Department and Foreign Service Series) 1932. a. U.S. Department of State, Bureau of Public Affairs, 2201 C St. N.W., Washington, DC 20520 (Orders to Supt. of Documents, Washington, DC 20402)

327　　　　　　　　　US
FOREIGN POLICY RESEARCH INSTITUTE. MONOGRAPH SERIES. 1964. irreg. price varies. ‡ Foreign Policy Research Institute, 3508 Market St., Suite 350, Philadelphia, PA 19104. Dir. William R. Kintner. circ. 500.
  Formerly: Foreign Policy Research Institute. Research Monograph Series (ISSN 0553-5743)

327　　　　　　　US　ISSN 0071-7355
FOREIGN RELATIONS OF THE UNITED STATES. 1861. irreg. price varies. U.S. Department of State, Bureau of Public Affairs, Office of the Historian, Washington, DC 20250 (Orders to Supt. of Documents, Washington, DC 20402)

329　　　　　　　NO　ISSN 0332-8244
FORUM FOR UTVIKLINGSSTUDIER/FORUM FOR DEVELOPMENT STUDIES. irreg. (10-12/yr.) Kr.45. Norsk Utenrikspolitisk Institutt - Norwegian Institute of International Affairs, Postboks 8159, Dep., Oslo 1, Norway. Ed. Olav Stokke.

354　　　　　　　　　FR
FRANCE. MEDIATEUR. RAPPORT ANNUEL DU MEDIATEUR. 1973. a. Direction des Journaux Officiels, 26 rue Desaix, 75015 Paris, France.

327　　　　　　　　　FR
FRANCE. MINISTERE DE LA COOPERATION. SERVICE DES ETUDES ET QUESTIONS INTERNATIONALES. ETUDES ET DOCUMENTS. irreg. Ministere de la Cooperation, Service des Etudes et Questions Internationales, 20 rue Monsieur, 75700 Paris, France.

327　　　　　　　FR　ISSN 0071-8181
FRANCE-ALLEMAGNE. 1967. irreg., approximately 3/yr. free. Internationale Union of Mayors, Mairie de Paris, 75196 Paris, France.

327　　　　　　　　　II
GANDHI PEACE FOUNDATION LECTURES. irreg. Radakrishna Indraprastha Estate, Nehru House, 221/3 Deen Royal Upadhyaya Marg, New Delhi 110002, India.

327　　　　　　　　　CN
GATT-FLY; an inter-church initiative for an alternate trade policy. 1973. irreg. Can.$7.50($10) 600 Jarvis St., Toronto, Ont. M4Y 2J6, Canada. illus.

909　　　　　　　US　ISSN 0072-4742
GLOBAL FOCUS SERIES. 1961. irreg., approx. every 18 mos., no. 17, 1977. $2. ‡ University of Wisconsin-Milwaukee, Institute of World Affairs, Box 413, Milwaukee, WI 53201. Ed. Gary J. Topp. circ. controlled.

327　　　　　　　UK　ISSN 0072-6397
GREAT BRITAIN. FOREIGN AND COMMONWEALTH OFFICE. TREATY SERIES. 1892. irreg. H.M.S.O., P.O. Box 569, London SE1 9NH, England.

327　　　　　　　　　US
HARVARD STUDIES IN INTERNATIONAL AFFAIRS. 1961. irreg., no. 40, 1978. price varies. ‡ Harvard University, Center for International Affairs, 1737 Cambridge St., Cambridge, MA 02138. Ed. Peter Jacobsohn. circ. 2,000. Indexed: SSCI.
  Until sept. 1974: Occasional Papers in International Affairs (ISSN 0078-3072)

341　327　　　　　US　ISSN 0073-0734
HARVARD UNIVERSITY. CENTER FOR INTERNATIONAL AFFAIRS. ANNUAL REPORT. 1961 (1958-1960) a. free. Harvard University, Center for International Affairs, 1737 Cambridge St., Cambridge, MA 02138. Ed. Peter Jacobsohn. circ. 3,000.

300　　　　　　　　　US
HISTORIES OF THE RULING COMMUNIST PARTIES SERIES. 1977. irreg. (Stanford University, Hoover Institution on War, Revolution and Peace) Hoover Institution Press, Stanford, CA 94305.

300　　　　　　　　　US
HOOVER INSTITUTION ON WAR, REVOLUTION AND PEACE. ARCHIVAL DOCUMENTARY. 1977. irreg. (Stanford University, Hoover Institution on War, Revolution and Peace) Hoover Institution Press, Stanford, CA 94305.

300　　　　　　　　　US
HOOVER INSTITUTION ON WAR, REVOLUTION AND PEACE. INTERNATIONAL STUDIES SERIES. 1977. irreg. (Stanford University, Hoover Institution on War, Revolution and Peace) Hoover Institution Press, Stanford, CA 94305.

300　　　　　　　　　US
HOOVER INSTITUTION ON WAR, REVOLUTION AND PEACE. LECTURE SERIES. 1977. irreg. (Stanford University, Hoover Institution on War, Revolution and Peace) Hoover Institution Press, Stanford, CA 94305.

300.6　　　　　　　US　ISSN 0091-6293
HOOVER INSTITUTION ON WAR, REVOLUTION, AND PEACE. REPORT. a. (Stanford University, Hoover Institution on War, Revolution, and Peace) Hoover Institution Press, Stanford, CA 94305. illus. circ. controlled. Key Title: Report - Hoover Institution on War, Revolution and Peace.

327　　　　　　　US　ISSN 0073-3776
HUDSON INSTITUTE. REPORT TO THE MEMBERS. 1962. a. Hudson Institute, Quaker Ridge Rd., Croton-on-Hudson, NY 10520.

327　　　　　　　　　US
HUMAN RIGHTS ACTION GUIDE. 1977. a. $10. Coalition for a New Foreign and Military Policy, 120 Maryland Ave. NE, Washington, DC 20002. Ed. Cindy Buhl. circ. 100,000.

341.1　　　　　　FI　ISSN 0074-7289
I P R A STUDIES IN PEACE RESEARCH. (Text in English) 1966. irreg., no. 7, 1979. price varies. International Peace Research Association, Box 70, 33101 Tampere 10, Finland. Ed. Bert V. A. Rolings.

327　　　　　　　US　ISSN 0193-905X
INDEX TO INTERNATIONAL PUBLIC OPINION. 1980. a. $75. (Macmillan Press Ltd.) Greenwood Press, 88 Post Rd. W., Westport, CT 06881 (Orders in Eastern Hemisphere to: Macmillan, 4 Little Essex St., London WC2R 3LF, England) Eds. Elizabeth Hann Hastings, Philip K. Hastings.

327　954　　　　　II　ISSN 0537-2704
INDIAN YEARBOOK OF INTERNATIONAL AFFAIRS. 1952-1968; 1973- a. Indian Study Group of International Affairs, University of Madras, Chepauk, Triplicane P.O., Madras 600005, Tamil Nadu, India. bk. rev. index.
  Law and international relations

980　　　　　　　GW　ISSN 0073-8948
INSTITUT FUER IBEROAMERIKA-KUNDE. SCHRIFTENREIHE. (Text in German; occasionally Spanish) 1963. irreg., no.28, 1977. price varies. Horst Erdmann Verlag, Hartmeyerstr. 117, Postfach 1380, 7400 Tuebingen, W. Germany (B.R.D.)

327　　　　　　　　　BL
INSTITUTO CULTURAL ITALO-BRASILEIRO. CADERNO. no. 8, 1972. irreg. Instituto Cultural Italo-Brasileiro, Rua Frei Caneca 1071, Sao Paulo, Brazil.

327　300　　　　　BE　ISSN 0074-6487
INTERNATIONAL INSTITUTE OF DIFFERING CIVILIZATIONS. (SESSION PAPERS) 1894. irreg.; 35th, Brussels, 1973. price varies. International Institute of Differing Civilizations, 11 Blvd. Waterloo, 1000 Brussels, Belgium. circ. 1,000.

327　　　　　　　FR　ISSN 0308-762X
INTERNATIONAL NEWSLETTER. 1977. irreg. 30 F. (International Information Center for Soviet and East European Studies) Institut National d'Etudes Slaves, 9 rue Michelet, 75006 Paris, France. Ed. Mrs. M. M. Bonnard. adv. circ. 100.

POLITICAL SCIENCE — INTERNATIONAL RELATIONS

341.7   FI   ISSN 0074-7297
INTERNATIONAL PEACE RESEARCH ASSOCIATION. PROCEEDINGS OF THE CONFERENCE. (Incl. in I P R A Studies in Peace Research) (Text in English) 1965. biennial, 7th, 1977, Oaxtepec, Mexico. price varies. International Peace Research Association, Box 70, 33101 Tampere 10, Finland.

327   US
INTERNATIONAL POLICY REPORT. vol. 2, 1976. irreg., latest no. 9? $1.50 per no. Center for International Policy, 120 Maryland Ave. N.E., Washington, DC 20002.

327 900   NE
INTERNATIONAL STRAITS OF THE WORLD. 1978. irreg. price varies. Sijthoff & Noordhoff International Publishers b.v., Box 4, 2400 MA Alphen Aan den Rijn, Netherlands (Subscr. to: Box 66, 9700 AB Groningen, Netherlands; U.S. address: 20010 Century Blvd., Germantown, MD 20767)

327 331.88   CS
INTERNATIONAL TRADE UNION COMMITTEE OF SOLIDARITY WITH THE WORKERS AND PEOPLE OF CHILE. BULLETIN. (Text in English) no. 5, June 1977. irreg., approx. 1-2/yr. free. World Federation of Trade Unions, International Trade Union Committee of Solidarity with the Workers and People of Chile, Nam. Curieovych 1, 116 88 Prague 1, Czechoslovakia. illus.

301.412   UK   ISSN 0020-9120
INTERNATIONAL WOMEN'S NEWS. vol.58,1963. 5/yr. £3 membership. International Alliance of Women, 47 Victoria St., 3Rd Floor, London SW1H 0EQ, England. Ed. Mrs. H. Whittick. bk. rev. circ. 1,200.

327   GW
INTERNATIONALE POLITIK UND WIRTSCHAFT. irreg., vol. 40, 1976. price varies. (Deutsche Gesellschaft fuer Auswaertige Politik und Wirtschaft) R. Oldenbourg Verlag GmbH, Rosenheimer Str. 145, 8000 Munich 80, W. Germany (B.R.D.)

INTERNATIONALES RECHT UND DIPLOMATIE. see LAW — International Law

320   SZ   ISSN 0074-1051
INTER-PARLIAMENTARY UNION. CONFERENCE PROCEEDINGS/UNION INTERPARLEMENTAIRE. COMPTES RENDUS DES CONFERENCES. (Text in English and French) 1897. a. 20 Fr. for vol. 1; 45 francs for vol. 2. Inter-Parliamentary Union - Union Interparlementaire, Place du Petit Saconnex, 1209 Geneva, Switzerland. circ. 800(approx.)

327   IT
ISTITUTO SUPERIORE EUROPEO DI STUDI POLITICI. COLLANA DI STUDI. 1974. irreg. Editori Meridionali Riuniti, Reggio Calabria, Italy.

327   US   ISSN 0075-2142
JACOB BLAUSTEIN LECTURES IN INTERNATIONAL AFFAIRS. 1967. irreg., 1971, no. 2. Columbia University Press, 136 South Broadway, Irvington-On-Hudson, NY 10533.

327 952 970   US   ISSN 0021-4299
JAPAN-AMERICA SOCIETY OF WASHINGTON. BULLETIN. 1957. 6-8/yr. free. Japan-America Society of Washington Inc., 1302 18th St., N.W., Suite 704, Washington, DC 20036. adv. bk. rev. illus. circ. 700.

327   EI   ISSN 0447-8452
JOINT MEETING OF THE MEMBERS OF THE CONSULTATIVE ASSEMBLY OF THE COUNCIL OF EUROPE AND OF THE MEMBERS OF THE EUROPEAN PARLIAMENTARY ASSEMBLY. OFFICIAL REPORT OF DEBATES. French edition: Reunions Jointes des Membres de l'Assemblee Consultative du Conseil de l'Europe et des Membres du Parlement Europeen. Compte Rendu in Extenso des Debats (ISSN 0447-8444) (Editions also in German, Italian and Dutch) 1953. a. 75 Fr. Office for Official Publications of the European Communities, C.P. 1003, Luxembourg 1, Luxembourg (Dist. in U.S. by European Community Information Service, 2100 M St., N.W., Suite 707, Washington D.C. 20037)

327   TZ
JOURNAL OF INTERNATIONAL RELATIONS. 1976. irreg. (3-4/yr.) $1.50 per no. International Relations Association, University of Dar es Salaam, Dar es Salaam, Tanzania. Ed. Mzirai Kangero. circ. 300.
Formerly (until no. 2, 1978): International Relations Association. Journal.

327   AT   ISSN 0311-0419
KABAR. 1969. irreg. Aus.$3 $4 to non-members; $1 each. Australia Indonesia Association of New South Wales, Box 802, G.P.O. Sydney, NSW 2001, Australia. Eds. P. Wallace and Max Lane.
Formerly: Australia Indonesia Association of New South Wales. Bulletin.

327   KO
KOREAN JOURNAL OF INTERNATIONAL RELATIONS. 1963. irreg. Korean Association of International Relations, c/oGraduate School of Public Administration, Seoul National University, 119 Tongsung-Dong, Chongno-Ku, Seoul, S. Korea.

327 980   US
LATIN AMERICAN INTERNATIONAL AFFAIRS. 1975. irreg., vol. 2, 1978. price varies. (Center for Inter-American Relations) Sage Publications, Inc., 275 S. Beverly Dr., Beverly Hills, CA 90212 (And Sage Publications, Ltd., 28 Banner St., London EC1Y 8QE, England)

327   LO   ISSN 0460-2099
LESOTHO. MINISTRY OF FOREIGN AFFAIRS. DIPLOMATIC AND CONSULAR LIST. a. Ministry of Foreign Affairs, Maseru, Lesotho.

354   LB
LIBERIA. MINISTRY OF FOREIGN AFFAIRS. ANNUAL REPORT. a. Ministry of Foreign Affairs, Monrovia, Liberia.

327   HU   ISSN 0541-9220
MAGYAR KULPOLITIKAI EVKONYV. 1968. a. $7.20. Kulugymininiszterium, Steindl u., Budapest 5, Hungary.

327   IT
MANUALI DI POLITICA INTERNAZIONALE. irreg. price varies. Istituto per gli Studi di Politica Internazionale, Via Clerica, 5, 20100 Milan, Italy.

327   MF   ISSN 0085-3194
MAURITIUS DIRECTORY OF THE DIPLOMATIC CORPS. a. Ministry of External Affairs, Tourism and Immigration, Port Louis, Mauritius (Subscr. to: Government Printing Office, Elizabeth II Ave., Port Louis, Mauritius)

327   US   ISSN 0077-0582
MONOGRAPH SERIES IN WORLD AFFAIRS. 1963. 4/yr. $12 to individuals; institutions $16. University of Denver, Graduate School of International Studies, University Park, Denver, CO 80208. (Affiliate: Social Science Foundation) Ed. Karen A. Feste. adv. circ. 1,000. Indexed: SSCI.

355   BE   ISSN 0549-7175
N A T O HANDBOOK. French edt.: Manuel de l' O T A N. (Editions in various languages) 1952. a (English and French editions); irreg (other languages) free. North Atlantic Treaty Organization, Information Service, Distribution Unit, 1110 Brussels, Belgium (U.S. address: Distribution Services Staff, Bureau of Public Affairs (PA/M), Dept. of State, Washington, DC 20520) (reprint service avail. from UMI)

327   NO
N U P I NOTAT. irreg. no. 160, 1979. Kr.120 incl. N U P I Rapport. Norsk Utenrikspolitisk Institutt - Norwegian Institute of International Affairs, Postboks 8159, Dep., Oslo 1, Norway.

327   NO
N U P I RAPPORT. (Text in English and Norwegian) irreg., no. 43, 1980. Kr.120 incl. N U P I Notat. Norsk Utenrikspolitisk Institutt - Norwegian Institute of International Affairs, Postboks 8159, Dep., Oslo 1, Norway.

NEAR EAST FOUNDATION. ANNUAL REPORT. see BUSINESS AND ECONOMICS — International Development And Assistance

354   NZ
NEW ZEALAND. MINISTRY OF FOREIGN AFFAIRS. PUBLICATION. irreg. Ministry of Foreign Affairs, Wellington, New Zealand.
Continues: New Zealand. Department of External Affairs. Publicatiion.

327.931   NZ
NEW ZEALAND. MINISTRY OF FOREIGN AFFAIRS. REPORT. (Subseries of: New Zealand. Ministry of Foreign Affairs. Publication) a. NZ.$0.35. Ministry of Foreign Affairs, Wellington, New Zealand.

341.23   NZ
NEW ZEALAND. MINISTRY OF FOREIGN AFFAIRS. UNITED NATIONS HANDBOOK. (Subseries of: New Zealand. Ministry of Foreign Affairs. Publication) irreg. NZ.$3.60. Ministry of Foreign Affairs, Wellington, New Zealand.
Continues: New Zealand. Department of External Affiars. United Nations and Specialised Agencies Handbook.

916.69   NR   ISSN 0078-0685
NIGERIA YEAR BOOK. 1952. a. Daily Times of Nigeria Ltd., Box 139, Lagos, Nigeria.

327   NR   ISSN 0078-0731
NIGERIAN INSTITUTE OF INTERNATIONAL AFFAIRS. LECTURE SERIES. (Text in English) 1969. irreg. price varies. Nigerian Institute of International Affairs, G.P.O. 1727, Lagos, Nigeria.

327   NR   ISSN 0331-6254
NIGERIAN INSTITUTE OF INTERNATIONAL AFFAIRS. MONOGRAPH SERIES. (Text in English) 1979. irreg. Nigerian Institute of International Affairs, G.P.O. Box 1727, Kofo Aboyomi Rd., Victoria Island, Lagos, Nigeria (U.S. dist.: First Western Corp., 6323 Beachway Dr., Falls Church, VA 22044). charts. stat. (back issues avail.)

323.4   NR
NIGERIAN INSTITUTE OF INTERNATIONAL AFFAIRS. SEMINAR SERIES. irreg. price varies. Nigerian Institute of International Affairs, Box 1727, Lagos, Nigeria.

327.05   NR   ISSN 0331-3646
NIGERIAN JOURNAL OF INTERNATIONAL AFFAIRS. 1975. s-a. £N20. Nigerian Institute of International Affairs, Box 1727, Kofo Abayomi Rd., Victoria Island, Lagos, Nigeria. bibl.

327.172   NE
NOBEL PRIZE LECTURES - PEACE. (Text in English) 1972. irreg., approx. every 3 yrs. fl.82. Elsevier Scientific Publishing Co., P.O. Box 211, 1000 AE Amsterdam, Netherlands. Ed. F. W. Haberman.

327.025   US   ISSN 0078-1002
NONALIGNED THIRD WORLD ANNUAL;* the politics of ideas. 1970. a. with irregular supplements. $14 cloth; $8.50 pap. Books International of DH-TE International, Inc., P.O. Box 14487, St. Louis, MO 63178 (and P.O. Box 7403, Washington, D.C. 20044) Ed. Andrew Carvely. index.

301.29   NO
NORGE-AMERIKA FORENINGEN. YEARBOOK. 1945. a. free. Norway-America Association, Drammensvn. 20C, Oslo 2, Norway. Ed. Erling Christophersen. bk. rev. illus. circ. 2,000.
Continues: Norge-Amerika Foreningen. Report.

327   NO   ISSN 0332-7299
NORSK UTENRIKSPOLITISK AARBOK. (Subseries of: Utenrikspolitiske Skrifter) 1974. a. Norsk Utenrikspolitisk Institutt - Norwegian Institute of International Affairs, Postboks 8159, Dep., Oslo 1, Norway. stat.

327 917.106   CN
NORTH-SOUTH; Canadian journal of Latin American studies. (Text in English, French, Portuguese and Spanish) 1976. a. Can.$19. Canadian Association of Latin American Studies, c/o Prof. Antonio Urrello, University of British Columbia, Department of Hispanic and Italian Studies, Vancouver, B.C. V6T 1W5, Canada. bk. rev. circ. 500.

POLITICAL SCIENCE — INTERNATIONAL RELATIONS

329   BE
ORGANISATION INTERNATIONALE ET RELATIONS INTERNATIONALES. 1975. a. 2809 Fr. (Centre de Recherches sur les Institutions Internationales) Etablissements Emile Bruylant, 67 rue de la Regence, 1000 Brussels, Belgium.

341.18   US
ORGANIZATION OF AMERICAN STATES. GENERAL ASSEMBLY. ACTAS Y DOCUMENTOS. irreg. price varies. Organization of American States, Department of Publications, Washington, DC 20006. circ. 2,000.

327   FI   ISSN 0355-1849
PAASIKIVI-SOCIETY. MIMEOGRAPH SERIES. (Text mostly in Finnish) irreg., no. 17, 1978. (Finnish Institute of International Affairs) Ulkopoliittinen Instituutti, Dagmarinkatu 8 C 40, SF-00100 Helsinki 10, Finland. (processed)

327   UK
PAKISTAN SOCIETY BULLETIN. 1951. a. 50p. ‡ Pakistan Society, 37 Sloane St., London S.W. 1, England. Ed. L. V. Deane. adv. bk. rev. circ. 700.

341.1   AT   ISSN 0031-3564
PEACE PLANS. 1964. irreg., nos. 16-18, 1975. Aus.$1. ‡ J. M. Zube, Ed. & Pub., 7 Oxley St, Berrima, N.S.W. 2577, Australia. bk. rev. bibl. index. cum.index. circ. 500-1,000. (also avail. in microfiche)

327   US   ISSN 0085-4808
PEACE RESEARCH LABORATORY. ANNUAL REPORT. 1955. irreg. free. Peace Research Laboratory, Character Research Association, 6251 San Bonita, St. Louis, MO 63105. Ed. Theo. F. Lentz. circ. 500.

327   950   PH
PHILIPPINES CHINESE HISTORICAL ASSOCIATION. ANNALS. (Text in English) vol. 5, 1975. a. P.25($6) Philippine Chinese Historical Association, Box 3131, Manila, Philippines. Ed. Gideon Hsu. bibl.

PRINCETON UNIVERSITY. CENTER OF INTERNATIONAL STUDIES POLICY MEMORANDUM. see *LAW — International Law*

341   327   US   ISSN 0555-1501
PRINCETON UNIVERSITY. CENTER OF INTERNATIONAL STUDIES. RESEARCH MONOGRAPH SERIES. 1959. irreg., no. 45, 1980. price varies. Princeton University, Center of International Studies, Corwin Hall, Princeton, NJ 08544. (back issues avail.)

327   US
PRINCETON UNIVERSITY. CENTER OF INTERNATIONAL STUDIES. WORLD ORDER STUDIES PROGRAM: OCCASIONAL PAPER. 1975. irreg., no. 8, 1980. price varies. Princeton University, Center of International Studies, Corwin Hall, Princeton, NJ 08544.

RADNER LECTURES. see *POLITICAL SCIENCE*

327   FR   ISSN 0080-0333
RECUEIL DES INSTRUCTIONS DONNEES AUX AMBASSADEURS ET MINISTRES DE FRANCE. irreg., 1970, vol. 29. price varies. Centre National de la Recherche Scientifique, 15 Quai Anatole-France, 75700 Paris, France.

341.13   UN   ISSN 0082-8211
RESOLUTIONS OF THE GENERAL ASSEMBLY OF THE UNITED NATIONS. (Issued as subseries of Official Records. Supplements) irreg. price varies. (United Nations, General Assembly) United Nations Publications, Room LX-2300, New York, NY 10017 (Or Distribution and Sales Section, Palais des Nations, CH-1211 Geneva 10, Switzerland)

327   SW
S I D A DEVELOPMENT STUDIES. (Text in English) 1972. 2-3/yr. Styrelsen foer Internationell Utveckling - Swedish International Development Authority, S-105 25 Stockholm, Sweden. bibl. illus.

327   US   ISSN 0094-0658
SAGE INTERNATIONAL YEARBOOK OF FOREIGN POLICY STUDIES. 1973. a. $18.50 for hardcover; softcover $8.95. Sage Publications, Inc., 275 S. Beverly Dr., Beverly Hills, CA 90212 (And Sage Publications, Ltd., 28 Banner St., London EC1Y 8QE, England) Ed. Patrick McGowan. (back issues avail.)

327   US   ISSN 0080-536X
SAGE RESEARCH PROGRESS SERIES ON WAR, REVOLUTION AND PEACEKEEPING. 1971. a. $18.50 cloth; $8.95 paper. (Inter-University Seminar on Armed Forces and Society) Sage Publications, Inc., 275 S. Beverly Drive, Beverly Hills, CA 90212 (And Sage Publications, Ltd., 28 Banner St., London EC1Y 8QE, England) (back issues avail.)

327   SZ
SCHWEIZERISCHE GESELLSCHAFT FUER AUSSENPOLITIK. SCHRIFTENREIHE. 1972. irreg., no. 6, 1979. price varies. Paul Haupt AG, Falkenplatz 14, CH-3001 Berne, Switzerland.

327   CN   ISSN 0080-8814
SEMINAR ON CANADIAN-AMERICAN RELATIONS (PAPERS) 1965. a. Can.$10. University of Windsor, Windsor, Ont. N9B 3P4, Canada. Ed. Dr. J. Alex Murray. circ. 2,000.

351   SG
SENEGAL. LISTE DU CORPS DIPLOMATIQUE. irreg. Imprimerie Nationale, Rufisque, Senegal.
    Continues: Senegal. Service du Protocole. Liste Diplomatique et Consulaire.

327   FR   ISSN 0080-8903
SENNACIECA REVUO. 1952. a. $4. Sennacieca Asocio Tutmonda, 67 Avenue Gambetta, 75020 Paris, France. bk. rev.

SOCIETY FOR INTERNATIONAL DEVELOPMENT. WORLD CONFERENCE PROCEEDINGS. see *BUSINESS AND ECONOMICS — International Development And Assistance*

327   SA
SOUTH AFRICAN INSTITUTE OF INTERNATIONAL AFFAIRS. ANNUAL REPORT. 1966. a. R.1. South African Institute of International Affairs, Box 31596, Braamfontein, Transvaal 2017, South Africa.

327   SA
SOUTH AFRICAN INSTITUTE OF INTERNATIONAL AFFAIRS. OCCASIONAL PAPERS. irreg. (approx. 10/yr.) R.10. South African Institute of International Affairs, Box 31596, Braamfontein, Transvaal 2017, South Africa.

327   NL
SOUTH PACIFIC COMMISSION. ANNUAL REPORT. (Text in English and French) 1948. a. free. South Pacific Commission, B.P. D5, Noumea, Cedex, New Caledonia.
    Formerly: South Pacific Commission. South Pacific Report (ISSN 0081-2854)

327   US
SOUTHERN ILLINOIS UNIVERSITY, EDWARDSVILLE. ASIAN STUDIES. OCCASIONAL PAPER SERIES. irreg. Southern Illinois University, Edwardsville, University Graphics and Publications, Edwardsville, IL 62025. Ed. Gene T. Hsiao. bibl.

327   US   ISSN 0163-6057
SOVIET UNION; domestic, economic and foreign policies. 1973. a. $24.50. Holmes & Meier Publishers, Inc., 30 Irving Pl., New York, NY 10003 (U.K. address: 131 Trafalgar Rd., Greenwich, London SE10 9TX, England) Ed. Wolfgang Berner. (back issues avail.)

327   060   US   ISSN 0081-3516
SPANISH INSTITUTE. ANNUAL REPORT. 1958. a. free. Spanish Institute, Inc., 684 Park Ave., New York, NY 10021.

320   US   ISSN 0145-8841
STANLEY FOUNDATION. OCCASIONAL PAPER. 1972. irreg., no. 25, 1981. free. Stanley Foundation, 420 E. Third St., Muscatine, IA 52761. bibl. circ. 5,000. (also avail. in microfilm) Key Title: Occasional Paper - Stanley Foundation.

327   UK   ISSN 0459-7230
STRATEGIC SURVEY. 1967. a. £4($9) International Institute for Strategic Studies, 23 Tavistock St., London WC2E 7NQ, England. charts. circ. 15,000.

327   US
STRATEGY FOR PEACE U.S. FOREIGN POLICY CONFERENCE. REPORT. 1959. a. free. ‡ Stanley Foundation, 420 E. Third St., Muscatine, IA 52761. Dir. Jack Smith. circ. 16,000.
    Formerly: Strategy for Peace Conference. Report (ISSN 0081-5942)

323.4   US   ISSN 0146-3586
STUDIES IN HUMAN RIGHTS. 1975. irreg. Greenwood Press, 88 Post Rd. W., Westport, CT 06881. Ed. George W. Shepherd.

327   341   US   ISSN 0081-8046
STUDIES IN INTERNATIONAL AFFAIRS. 1961. irreg. price varies. (Institute of International Studies) Westview Press, 1898 Flatiron Ct., Boulder, CO 80301.

327   BE
STUDIES IN INTERNATIONAL RELATIONS. 1973. irreg., no. 4, 1979. Leuven University Press, Krakenstraat 3, B-3000 Louvain, Belgium.

327   FI   ISSN 0081-9441
SUOMEN OSALLISTUMINEN YHDISTYNEIDEN KANSAKUNTIEN TOIMINTAAN. (Text in Finnish; occasionally in English) 1957. a. Fmk.49. Ulkoasiainministerio - Ministry for Foreign Affairs, Aleksi 3, Helsinki 17, Finland. circ. 1,500.

327   US
SURVEY OF INTERNATIONAL AFFAIRS. irreg. price varies. (Royal Institute of International Affairs, UK) Oxford University Press, 200 Madison Ave., New York, NY 10016 (And Ely House, 37 Dover St., London W1X 4AH, England)

327   SW
SVERIGE-EG. Variant title: Sverige-Europeiska Gemenskaperna. 1973. a. (Utrikesdepartementet - Ministry of Foreign Affairs) Liber Foerlag, Fack, S-162 89 Vaellingby, Sweden. (Co-sponsor: Handelsdepartementet)

327   IS
TEL-AVIV UNIVERSITY. DAVID HOROWITZ INSTITUTE FOR THE RESEARCH OF DEVELOPING COUNTRIES. RESEARCH REPORTS AND PAPERS. (Text in Hebrew & English) 1972. irreg. Tel-Aviv University, David Horowitz Institute for the Research of Developing Countries, Tel-Aviv, Israel. circ. 250. (looseleaf format)

327   TH
THAILAND. MINISTRY OF FOREIGN AFFAIRS. NEWS BULLETIN. no. 9, 1977. irreg. Ministry of Foreign Affairs, Department of Information, Bangkok, Thailand.

327   US
TRANSATLANTIC PERSPECTIVES. 1978. irreg. German Marshall Fund of the U.S., 11 Dupont Circle, N.W., Washington, DC 20036. Ed. Joseph Foote.

327   US
TRIANGLE PAPERS. 1973. irreg., approx. 3/yr. price varies. (Trilateral Commission) New York University Press, Washington Square, New York, NY 10003. Ed. Bd. circ. 3,000. (back issues avail.)

341.1   UN   ISSN 0041-5308
U N H C R REPORT. (Editions in English and French) 1968. irreg. $2-2.50. United Nations High Commissioner for Refugees, Palais des Nations, CH-1211 Geneva 10, Switzerland (Or United Nations Publications, Room LX-2300 New York, NY 10017) charts. illus. circ. 26,000.
    Refugees

327   UN
U N I T A R-P S SERIES. (Peaceful Settlement) (Edts. in English and French) 1971. irreg; latest issue, 1974. price varies. United Nations Institute for Training and Research, Publications Office, 801 United Nations Plaza, New York, NY 10017 (Order from: United Nations Publications, Room LX-2300, New York, NY 10017; or Distribution and Sales Section, Palais des Nations, CH 1211 Geneva 10, Switzerland) bk. rev.

POLITICAL SCIENCE — INTERNATIONAL RELATIONS

327 UN
U N I T A R REGIONAL STUDIES. 1972. irreg. price varies. United Nations Institute for Training and Research, Publications Office, 801 United Nations Plaza, New York, NY 10017 (Order from: United Nations Publications, Room LX-2300, New York, NY 10017; or Distribution and Sales Section, Palais des Nations, CH 1211 Geneva 10, Switzerland) bk. rev.

327 330.9 320 US
U S S R REPORT: PROBLEMS OF THE FAR EAST. irreg. (approx. 3/yr.) $18. U.S. Joint Publications Research Service, 1000 N. Glebe Rd., Arlington, VA 22201 (Orders to: NTIS, Springfield, VA 22161)
Formerly: Problems of the Far East.
Translations of articles by Soviet writers on Soviet relations with China and other Asian countries, and on economic and political conditions in China and Asia

327 301.1 150 US
UNDERSTANDING CONFLICT AND WAR. 1975. irreg., vol. 3, 1978. price varies. Sage Publications, Inc., 275 S. Beverly Dr., Beverly Hills, CA 90212 (And Sage Publications, Ltd., 28 Banner St., London EC1Y 8QE, England) Ed. R. J. Rummel. (back issues avail.)

327 UN ISSN 0082-7509
UNESCO. RECORDS OF THE GENERAL CONFERENCE. PROCEEDINGS. (Text in English, French, Russian and Spanish) irreg.; seventeenth session, 1972, pub. 1974. price varies. Unesco, 7-9 Place de Fontenoy, 75700 Paris, France (Dist. in U.S. by: Unipub, 345 Park Ave. S., New York NY 10010)

327 UN ISSN 0082-7517
UNESCO. RECORDS OF THE GENERAL CONFERENCE. RESOLUTIONS. (Text in English, French, Spanish, Russian and Arabic) irreg.; seventeenth session, 1972, pub. 1974. price varies. Unesco, 7-9 Place de Fontenoy, 75700 Paris, France (Dist. in U.S. by: Unipub, 345 Park Ave. S., New York NY 10010)

327 UN ISSN 0082-7525
UNESCO. REPORT OF THE DIRECTOR-GENERAL ON THE ACTIVITIES OF THE ORGANIZATION. (Text in English, French, Spanish, Russian and Arabic) 1959. a. price varies. Unesco, 7-9 Place de Fontenoy, 75700 Paris, France (Dist. in U.S. by: Unipub, 345 Park Ave. S., New York NY 10010)

341.13 UN ISSN 0082-8084
UNITED NATIONS. ECONOMIC AND SOCIAL COUNCIL. INDEX TO PROCEEDINGS. 1953. a.; 29th session, 1974. price varies. United Nations Publications, Room LX-2300, New York, NY 10017 (Or Distribution and Sales Section, Palais des Nations, CH-1211 Geneva 10, Switzerland)

341.13 UN ISSN 0082-8092
UNITED NATIONS. ECONOMIC AND SOCIAL COUNCIL. OFFICIAL RECORDS. irreg. price varies. United Nations Publications, Room LX-2300, New York, NY 10017 (Or Distribution and Sales Section, Palais des Nations, CH-1211 Geneva 10, Switzerland)

341.13 UN ISSN 0082-8157
UNITED NATIONS. GENERAL ASSEMBLY. INDEX TO PROCEEDINGS. 1953. a.; 29th session, 1974. price varies. United Nations Publications, Room LX-2300, New York, NY 10017 (Or Sales and Distribution Center, Palais des Nations, CH-1211 Geneva 10, Switzerland)

341.13 UN ISSN 0082-8408
UNITED NATIONS. SECURITY COUNCIL. INDEX TO PROCEEDINGS. 1953. a.; 29th yr., 1974 (pub. 1975) price varies. (United Nations Security Council) United Nations Publications, Room LX-2300, New York, NY 10017 (Or Distribution and Sales Section, Palais des Nations, CH-1211 Geneva 10, Switzerland)

341.13 UN ISSN 0082-8416
UNITED NATIONS. SECURITY COUNCIL. OFFICIAL RECORDS. irreg. price varies. United Nations Publications, Room LX-2300, New York, NY 10017 (Or Distribution and Sales Section, Palais des Nations, CH-1211 Geneva 10, Switzerland)

341.13 UN ISSN 0082-8483
UNITED NATIONS. TRADE AND DEVELOPMENT BOARD. OFFICIAL RECORDS. SUPPLEMENTS. irreg. price varies. United Nations Trade and Development Board, Palais des Nations, 1211 Geneva 10, Switzerland (Or United Nations Publications, Room LX-2300, New York, NY 10017)

341.13 UN ISSN 0082-8491
UNITED NATIONS. TRUSTEESHIP COUNCIL. INDEX TO PROCEEDINGS. 1953. a.; 41st session, 1974. $1. United Nations Publications, Room LX 2300, New York, NY 10017 (Or Distribution and Sales Section, Palais des Nations, CH-1211 Geneva 10, Switzerland)

341.13 UN ISSN 0082-8505
UNITED NATIONS. TRUSTEESHIP COUNCIL. OFFICIAL RECORDS. (Meetings not yet published) irreg.; 39th session, 1972. price varies. United Nations Publications, Room LX-2300, New York, NY 10017 (Or Distribution and Sales Section, Palais des Nations, CH-1211 Geneva 10, Switzerland) (also avail. in microfiche)

341.13 UN ISSN 0082-8513
UNITED NATIONS. TRUSTEESHIP COUNCIL. OFFICIAL RECORDS. SUPPLEMENTS. irreg. price varies. United Nations Publications, Room LX-2300, New York, NY 10017 (Or Distribution and Sales Section, Palais des Nations, CH-1211 Geneva 10, Switzerland) (also avail. in microfiche)

341.13 UN ISSN 0082-8521
UNITED NATIONS. YEARBOOK. 1947. a. price varies. United Nations Publications, Room LX-2300, New York, NY 10017 (Or Distribution and Sales Section, Palais des Nations, CH-1200 Geneva 10, Switzerland) index.

341.13 UN ISSN 0082-8009
UNITED NATIONS AND WHAT YOU SHOULD KNOW ABOUT IT. irreg. $1. United Nations Publications, Room LX 2300, New York, NY 10017 (Or Distribution and Sales Section, Palais des Nations, CH-1211 Geneva 10, Switzerland)

327 AT ISSN 0085-7475
UNITED NATIONS ASSOCIATION OF AUSTRALIA. UNITED NATIONS REPORTER.* 1962. irreg. United Nations Association of Australia, N.S.W. Division, 11 Loftus Street, Sydney, N.S.W. 2000, Australia.

327 US ISSN 0250-779X
UNITED NATIONS EDUCATIONAL, SCIENTIFIC AND CULTURAL ORGANIZATION. 1981. a. $30. Greenwood Press, 88 Post Rd. W., Westport, CT 06881. Ed. Hylke Tromp.

327 UN
UNITED NATIONS INSTITUTE FOR TRAINING AND RESEARCH. REPORT OF THE EXECUTIVE DIRECTOR. a.; latest, 1974. $1.50 (1972) United Nations Institute for Training and Research, Publications Office, 801 United Nations Plaza, New York, NY 10017 (Order from: United Nations Publications, Room LX-2300, New York, NY 10017; or Distribution and Sales Section, Palais des Nations, CH 1211 Geneva 10, Switzerland)

341.13 US
UNITED NATIONS OF THE NEXT DECADE CONFERENCE. REPORT. 1965. a. free. Stanley Foundation, 420 E. Third St., Muscatine, IA 52761. circ. 16,000. (also avail. in microfilm)
Formerly: Conference on the United Nations of the Next Decade. Report (ISSN 0069-8733)

327 UN
UNITED NATIONS SOCIAL DEFENSE RESEARCH INSTITUTE. PUBLICATION. no. 12, Feb., 1976. irreg. United Nations Social Defense Research Institute, Via Giulia 52, 00186 Rome, Italy.

358 US ISSN 0082-8688
U.S. AIR FORCE ACADEMY ASSEMBLY. PROCEEDINGS. 1959. a. free to qualified personnel. United States Air Force Academy, Dept. of Political Science, Colorado Springs, CO 80840 (Orders to: Supt. of Documents, Washington, DC 20402) (Co-Sponsor: Columbia University American Assembly Program)

327 US ISSN 0083-0038
U. S. DEPARTMENT OF STATE. DEPARTMENT AND FOREIGN SERVICE SERIES. 1948. irreg. price varies. U.S. Department of State, Bureau of Public Affairs, Washington, DC 20250 (Orders to Supt. of Documents, Washington, DC 20402)

327 US ISSN 0083-0054
U. S. DEPARTMENT OF STATE. EAST ASIAN AND PACIFIC SERIES. 1932. irreg., no. 214, 1975. U.S. Department of State, Bureau of Public Affairs, Washington, DC 20250 (Orders to: Supt. of Documents, Washington, DC 20402)
Formerly: Far Eastern Series (ISSN 0083-0089)

327 382 US ISSN 0083-0097
U. S. DEPARTMENT OF STATE. GENERAL FOREIGN POLICY SERIES. 1948. irreg. price varies. U.S. Department of State, Bureau of Public Affairs, Washington, DC 20250 (Orders to Supt. of Documents, Washington, DC 20402)

327 US
U.S. DEPARTMENT OF STATE. HISTORICAL STUDIES DIVISION. MAJOR PUBLICATIONS: AN ANNOTATED BIBLIOGRAPHY. 1961. irreg. free. ‡ U. S. Department of State, Washington, DC 20520.

327 US ISSN 0083-0143
U. S. DEPARTMENT OF STATE. INTER-AMERICAN SERIES. 1929. irreg. price varies. U.S. Department of State, Bureau of Public Affairs, Washington, DC 20250 (Orders to Supt. of Documents, Washington, DC 20402)

327 US ISSN 0083-0119
U. S. DEPARTMENT OF STATE. INTERNATIONAL INFORMATION AND CULTURAL SERIES. 1948. irreg. price varies. U.S. Department of State, Bureau of Public Affairs, Washington, DC 20250 (Orders to Supt. of Documents, Washington, DC 20402)

327 US ISSN 0083-0127
U. S. DEPARTMENT OF STATE. INTERNATIONAL ORGANIZATION AND CONFERENCE SERIES. 1959. irreg. price varies. U.S. Department of State, Bureau of Public Affairs, Washington, DC 20250 (Orders to Supt. of Documents, Washington, DC 20402)

327 US ISSN 0083-0135
U. S. DEPARTMENT OF STATE. INTERNATIONAL ORGANIZATION SERIES. 1968. irreg. $0.10. U.S. Department of State, Bureau of Public Affairs, Washington, DC 20250 (Orders to Supt. of Documents, Washington, DC 20402)

327 US ISSN 0083-3088
U. S. PEACE CORPS. ANNUAL REPORT.* 1962. a. free. U. S. Peace Corps, ACTION, 806 Connecticut Ave., N.W., Washington, DC 20525 (Orders to: Supt. Doc., Washington, DC 20402)

327 US
UNITED STATES & THE WORLD: FOREIGN PERSPECTIVES. 1975. irreg., latest 1978. price varies. University of Chicago Press, 5801 S. Ellis Ave., Chicago, IL 60637. Ed. Akira Iriye. adv. bk. rev. (reprint service avail. from UMI,ISI)

327 US ISSN 0083-0208
UNITED STATES PARTICIPATION IN THE UNITED NATIONS.* (Subseries of its International Organization and Conference Series) a. U.S. Department of State, Bureau of Public Affairs, Washington, DC 20250 (Orders to: Supt. of Documents, Washington, DC 20402)

327.2 EC
UNIVERSIDAD DE GUAYAQUIL. ESCUELA DE DIPLOMACIA. REVISTA. 1973. irreg. Universidad de Guayaquil, Escuela de Diplomacia, Calle Chile 900, Apdo. 471, Guayaquil, Chile.

UNIVERSIDAD DE PANAMA. FACULTAD DE DERECHO Y CIENCIAS POLITICAS. CUADERNOS. see LAW

UNIVERSITAET HAMBURG. INSTITUT FUER INTERNATIONALE ANGELEGENHEITEN. WERKHEFTE. see LAW — International Law

327 GW ISSN 0341-3233
UNIVERSITAET HAMBURG. INSTITUT FUER INTERNATIONALE ANGELEGENHEITEN. VEROEFFENTLICHUNGEN. 1975. irreg., vol. 7, 1976. price varies. Alfred Metzner Verlag GmbH, Zeppelinallee 43, 6000 Frankfurt 97, W. Germany (B.R.D.)

327 GW
UNIVERSITAET HAMBURG. INSTITUT FUER INTERNATIONALE ANGELEGENHEITEN. VEROEFFENTLICHUNGEN. 1975. irreg. price varies. Institut fuer Internationale Angelegenheiten, Edmund-Siemers-Allee 1, 2000 Hamburg 13, W. Germany (B.R.D.)

327.73 BE ISSN 0076-1206
UNIVERSITE CATHOLIQUE DE LOUVAIN. CENTRE D'ETUDES POLITIQUES. WORKING GROUP "AMERICAN FOREIGN POLICY." CAHIER.* 1969. irreg. Universite Catholique de Louvain, Centre d'Etudes Politiques, 2, Place Mgr. Ladeuze, Louvain, Belgium (Dist. in U.S. by: Humanities Press, Inc., 171 First Ave., Atlantic Highlands, NJ 07716)

327 FR
UNIVERSITE DE METZ. CENTRE DE RECHERCHES RELATIONS INTERNATIONALES. TRAVAUX ET RECHERCHES. (Text in French and German) irreg. price varies. Universite de Metz, Centre de Recherches Relations Internationales, Faculte des Lettres et Sciences Humaines, Ile du Saulcy, 57000 Metz, France.

341 US ISSN 0076-9657
UNIVERSITY OF MISSOURI, ST. LOUIS. CENTER FOR INTERNATIONAL STUDIES. MONOGRAPH. 1970. irreg; no. 3, 1971. price varies. ‡ University of Missouri- St. Louis, Center for International Studies, St. Louis, MO 63121. Ed. Edwin H. Fedder.

323.4 US
UNIVERSITY OF NEW MEXICO. WOMEN'S CENTER NEWSLETTER. 1972. irreg. free. University of New Mexico, Women's Center, 1824 Las Lomas, N.E., Albuquerque, NM 87131. Ed. Jean Frakes. illus. circ. 3,000. (processed) Formerly: Joyous Struggle: a Women's Newsletter (ISSN 0085-2422)

327 US ISSN 0085-6452
UNIVERSITY OF SOUTH CAROLINA. INSTITUTE OF INTERNATIONAL STUDIES. ESSAY SERIES. 1967. irreg., no. 9, 1979. $2 per no. ‡ University of South Carolina, Institute of International Studies, Columbia, SC 29208. circ. 200. (back issues avail.)

327 NO
UTENRIKSPOLITISKE SKRIFTER/NORWEGIAN FOREIGN POLICY STUDIES. (Text in English and Norwegian) irreg. Norsk Utenrikspolitisk Institutt - Norwegian Institute of International Affairs, Postboks 8159, Dep., Oslo 1, Norway.

327 US ISSN 0145-8833
VANTAGE CONFERENCE REPORT. 1973. irreg., no. 8, 1980. free. Stanley Foundation, 420 E. Third St., Muscatine, IA 52761. (also avail. in microfilm)

320 US
WADSWORTH SERIES IN WORLD POLITICS. irreg. Wadsworth Publishing Co., 10 Davis Dr., Belmont, CA 94002.

327 CN
WELLESLEY PAPERS. 1973. irreg. price varies. ‡ Canadian Institute of International Affairs, 15 King's College Circle, Toronto, Ont. M5S 2V9, Canada. Ed. Bd. bibl. (reprint service avail. from UMI)

327 UK ISSN 0347-2205
WORLD ARMAMENTS AND DISARMAMENT: S I P R I YEARBOOK. 1969. a. (Stockholm International Peace Research Institute, SW) Taylor & Francis Ltd., 4 John St., London WC1N 2ET, England.

341.37 US
WORLD TREATY INDEX. 1975. irreg., 2nd edt., 1981. ‡ American Bibliographical Center-Clio Press, 2040 Alameda Padre Serra, Box 4397, Santa Barbara, CA 93103. Ed. Peter H. Rohn.

327.471 FI ISSN 0355-0079
YEARBOOK OF FINNISH FOREIGN POLICY. (Text in English) 1973. a. Fmk.20($5) Ulkopoliittinen Instituutti - Finnish Institute of International Affairs, Dagmarinkatu 8 C 40, SF-00100 Helsinki 10, Finland. Ed. Kari Mottola. Indexed: A.B.C.Pol.Sci.

327 BE ISSN 0084-3806
YEARBOOK OF INTERNATIONAL CONGRESS PROCEEDINGS. (Text in English; Index in French) 1969. irreg. 960 Fr. Union of International Associations, 1 rue aux Laines, 1000 Bruxelles, Belgium.

327 BE ISSN 0084-3814
YEARBOOK OF INTERNATIONAL ORGANIZATIONS. French edition: Annuaire des Organisations Internationales. (Text in English; index in English and French) 1949. biennial. 2300 Fr. Union of International Associations, 1 rue aux Laines, 1000 Bruxelles, Belgium.

341.058 UK ISSN 0084-408X
YEARBOOK OF WORLD AFFAIRS. 1947. a. price varies. (London Institute of World Affairs) Sweet & Maxwell Stevens Journals, 11 New Fetter Lane, London, E.C.4, England (Dist. in U.S. by: West View Press, 1898 Flatiron Ct., Boulder, CO 80301) Eds. G. W. Keeton, G. Schwarzenberger.

327 301 BE ISSN 0304-0089
YEARBOOK OF WORLD PROBLEMS AND HUMAN POTENTIAL. 1976. irreg. 2300 Fr. Union of International Associations, 1 rue aux Laines, 1000 Brussels, Belgium. (Co-sponsor: Mankind 2000) bibl.

327 335 US ISSN 0084-4101
YEARBOOK ON INTERNATIONAL COMMUNIST AFFAIRS. 1966. a. $35. (Stanford University, Hoover Institution on War Revolution and Peace) Hoover Institution Press, Stanford, CA 94305. Ed. Richard F. Staar. index.

YOUR UNITED NATIONS. see *HISTORY*

POPULATION STUDIES

see also Birth Control

301.32 US ISSN 0091-5610
AMERICAN UNIVERSITIES FIELD STAFF. POPULATION: PERSPECTIVE. 1971. irreg. $5.95. ‡ Freeman, Cooper & Co., 1736 Stockton St., San Francisco, CA 94133. (Co-Sponsor: Caltech Population Program) illus. stat. Key Title: Population. Perspective.

312 NE ISSN 0066-2062
ANNALES DE DEMOGRAPHIE HISTORIQUE. (Text in English and French) 1970. a. $35. (Societe de Demographie Historique) Mouton Publishers, Noordeinde 41, 2514 GC The Hague, Netherlands (U.S. addr: Mouton Publishers, c/o Walter de Gruyter, Inc., 200 Saw Mill River Road, Hawthorne, NY 10532)

312 FR
ANNUAIRE DES CENTRES DE RECHERCHE DEMOGRAPHIQUE/DIRECTORY OF DEMOGRAPHIC RESEARCH CENTERS. 1974. irreg. free. Committee for International Cooperation in National Research in Demography, 27 rue du Commandeur, 75675 Paris Cedex 14, France.

312 UK ISSN 0066-3964
ANNUAL ESTIMATES OF THE POPULATION OF SCOTLAND. 1958. a. 60p. General Register Office, Scotland, New Register House, Edinburgh 1, Scotland.

312 AG
ARGENTINA. INSTITUTO NACIONAL DE ESTADISTICA Y CENSOS. SERIE INFORMACION DEMOGRAFICA. a. Instituto Nacional de Estadistica y Censos, Hippolito Yrigoyen 250, Buenos Aires, Argentina.

312 US ISSN 0094-3576
ARKANSAS. BUREAU OF VITAL STATISTICS. ANNUAL REPORT OF BIRTHS, DEATHS, MARRIAGES AND DIVORCES AS REPORTED TO THE BUREAU OF VITAL STATISTICS. Variant title: Arkansas Vital Statistics Report. a. free. Bureau of Vital Statistics, Little Rock, AR 72201. illus. stat. Key Title: Annual Report of Births, Deaths, Marriages and Divorces as Reported to the Bureau of Vital Statistics (Little Rock)

312.097 US ISSN 0364-0728
ARKANSAS VITAL STATISTICS. a. Division of Health Statistics, 4815 W. Markham St., Little Rock, AR 72201.

301.32 UN ISSN 0084-6821
ASIAN POPULATION PROGRAMME NEWS. (Text in English) 1971. irreg.; 3-4 issues/yr. free upon request. ‡ United Nations Economic and Social Commission for Asia and the Pacific, Population Division, United Nations Bldg., Rajadamnern Ave, Bangkok 2, Thailand. charts. illus. circ. 5,000. (also avail. in microfiche)

301.3 UN ISSN 0066-8451
ASIAN POPULATION STUDIES SERIES. 1967. irreg.; no. 6, 1972. price varies. United Nations Economic and Social Commission for Asia and the Pacific, United Nations Bldg., Rajadamnern Ave., Bangkok 2, Thailand (Dist. by: United Nations Publications, Room LX-2300, New York, NY 10017; or Distribution and Sales Section, Palais des Nations, CH-1 211 Geneva 10, Switzerland)

301.426 CR
ASOCIACION DEMOGRAFICA COSTARRICENSE. INFORME DE LABORES. irreg. Asociacion Demografica Costarricense, San Jose, Costa Rica. stat.

312.2 AT
AUSTRALIA. BUREAU OF STATISTICS. DEATHS. a. free. Australian Bureau of Statistics, P.O. Box 10, Belconnen, A.C.T. 2616, Australia. illus. circ. 2,000.

312.5 AT
AUSTRALIA. BUREAU OF STATISTICS. MARRIAGES. 1973. a. free. Australian Bureau of Statistics, P.O. Box 10, Belconnen, A.C.T. 2616, Australia. illus. circ. 2,000.

312 618 AT
AUSTRALIA. BUREAU OF STATISTICS. PERINATAL DEATHS. 1973. a. free. Australian Bureau of Statistics, P.O. Box 10, Belconnen, A.C.T. 2616, Australia. stat. circ. 2,000.

312 AT ISSN 0067-088X
AUSTRALIA. BUREAU OF STATISTICS. SOUTH AUSTRALIAN OFFICE. BIRTHS. 1969. a. free. Australian Bureau of Statistics, South Australian Office, Box 2272, G.P.O., Adelaide, S.A. 5001, Australia.

312 AT ISSN 0067-0898
AUSTRALIA. BUREAU OF STATISTICS. SOUTH AUSTRALIAN OFFICE. DEATHS. 1969. a. free. Australian Bureau of Statistics, South Australian Office, Box 2272, G.P.O., Adelaide, S.A. 5001, Australia.

312 AT ISSN 0067-0901
AUSTRALIA. BUREAU OF STATISTICS. SOUTH AUSTRALIAN OFFICE. DIVORCE. 1947. a. free. Australian Bureau of Statistics, South Australian Office, Box 2272, G.P.O., Adelaide, S.A. 5001, Australia.

312 AT ISSN 0067-0952
AUSTRALIA. BUREAU OF STATISTICS. SOUTH AUSTRALIAN OFFICE. MARRIAGES. 1969. a. free. Australian Bureau of Statistics, South Australian Office, Box 2272 G.P.O., Adelaide, S.A. 5001, Australia.

312 AT ISSN 0067-1029
AUSTRALIA. BUREAU OF STATISTICS. TASMANIAN OFFICE. DEMOGRAPHY. 1949-50. a. free. Australian Bureau of Statistics, Tasmanian Office, Box 66A, G.P.O., Hobart, Tasmania 7001, Australia. circ. 550.

312 994   AT ISSN 0067-1088
AUSTRALIA. BUREAU OF STATISTICS.
VICTORIAN OFFICE. CAUSES OF DEATH.
1968. a. free. Australian Bureau of Statistics,
Victorian Office, Box 2796Y, G.P.O. Melbourne,
Victoria 3001, Australia. circ. 500.

312   AT ISSN 0067-1096
AUSTRALIA. BUREAU OF STATISTICS.
VICTORIAN OFFICE. DEMOGRAPHY. 1961. a.
free. Australian Bureau of Statistics, Victorian
Office, Box 2796Y, G.P.O. Melbourne, Victoria
3001, Australia. circ. 1,000.

AUSTRALIAN NATIONAL UNIVERSITY.
CANBERRA. DEPARTMENT OF
DEMOGRAPHY. FAMILY AND FERTILITY
CHANGE. see *SOCIOLOGY*

301.32   AT
AUSTRALIAN NATIONAL UNIVERSITY,
CANBERRA. DEPARTMENT OF
DEMOGRAPHY. STUDIES IN MIGRATION
AND URBANIZATION. 1975. irreg. Australian
National University, Department of Demography,
Canberra, A.C.T. 2600, Australia.

312   AU ISSN 0067-2335
AUSTRIA. STATISTISCHES ZENTRALAMT. DIE
NATUERLICHE
BEVOELKERUNGSBEWEGUNG. (Subseries of:
Beitraege zur Oesterreichischen Statistik) 1951. a.
S.180. ‡ (Oesterreichisches Statistisches Zentralamt)
Oesterreichische Staatsdruckerei, Vienna, Austria.
circ. 450.

312   II
BARODA REPORTER. (Text in English) 1960. a.
free. Demographic Research Centre, Baroda,
Maharajah Sayajirao University of Baroda, Faculty
of Science, Baroda 2, India. Ed. M.M. Gandotra.
adv. bk. rev. abstr. bibl. charts. illus. stat. circ.
500. (record)

312   GE
BEVOELKERUNGSSTATISTISCHES JAHRBUCH
DER DEUTSCHEN DEMOKRATISCHEN
REPUBLIK. a. (Staatliche Zentralverwaltung fuer
Statistik) Staatsverlag der DDR, Otto-Grotewohl-
Str. 17, 108 Berlin, E. Germany (D.D.R.)
  Continues: Germany (Democratic Republic,
1949-). Staatliche Zentralverwaltung fuer Statistik.
Abteilung Bevoelkerung und Kulturell-Soziale
Bereiche der Volkswirtschaft.

312   GW ISSN 0072-1867
BEVOELKERUNGSSTRUKTUR UND
WIRTSCHAFTSKRAFT DER
BUNDESLAENDER. a. DM.15.30. (Statistisches
Bundesamt) W. Kohlhammer-Verlag GmbH, Abt.
Veroeffentlichungen des Statistischen Bundesamtes,
Philipp-Reis-Str. 3, Postfach 421120, 6500 Mainz
42, W. Germany (B.R.D.)

312   FR
C I C R E D BULLETIN. irreg. controlled free circ.
Committee for International Cooperation in
National Research in Demography, 27 rue du
Commandeur, 75675 Paris Cedex 14, France.

301.3   US ISSN 0069-0724
CAROLINA POPULATION CENTER.
MONOGRAPH. 1969. irreg., latest issue no. 21.
price varies $1.50-$7.50. Carolina Population
Center, University Square 300 A, University of
North Carolina, Chapel Hill, NC 27514. Ed. Lynn
Igoe. circ. 1,000. Indexed: SSCi.

312   UN
CENTRO LATINOAMERICANO DE
DEMOGRAFIA. PUBLICACIONES P I S P A L.
irreg. price varies. United Nations, Centro
Latinoamericano de Demografia, Programa de
Investigaciones Sociales Sobre Problemas de
Poblacion Relevantes para Politicas de Poblacion en
America Latina, J. M. Infante 9, Casilla 91,
Santiago, Chile.

312   UN
CENTRO LATINOAMERICANO DE
DEMOGRAFIA. TEXTOS DE DIVULGACION.
1976. irreg. $2 per no. United Nations, Centro
Latinoamericano de Demografia - Regional Center
for Demographic Training and Research in Latin
America, Casilla 91, Santiago, Chile. stat.

312   CK
COLOMBIA. DEPARTAMENTO
ADMINISTRATIVO NACIONAL DE
ESTADISTICA. ANUARIO DEMOGRAFICO. a.
Departamento Administrativo Nacional de
Estadistica, Banco Nacional de Datos, Apdo
Nacional 80043, Bogota D.E., Colombia.

312   FR
COMITE INTERNATIONAL DE COOPERATION
DANS LES RECHERCHES NATIONALES EN
DEMOGRAPHIE. ACTES DES SEMINAIRES.
1973. irreg. Committee for International
Cooperation in National Research in Demography,
27 rue du Commandeur, 75675 Paris Cedex 14,
France.

312   AG
CONSEJO LATINOAMERICANO DE CIENCIAS
SOCIALES. SERIE POBLACION. INFORME DE
INVESTIGACION. 1973. irreg. price varies.
Consejo Latinoamericano de Ciencias Sociales,
Buenos Aires, Argentina.

312   CR
COSTA RICA. REVISTA DE ESTUDIOS Y
ESTADISTICAS. SERIE DEMOGRAFICA.
(Suspended Publication with No. 10, 1971; Resumed
Publication with No. 11, 1975) 1961. irreg., no. 12,
1980. Direccion General de Estadistica y Censos,
Apdo. 10163, San Jose, Costa Rica. charts. stat.

312   US ISSN 0082-9471
CURRENT POPULATION REPORTS. 1947. irreg.
$56 annual subscription includes P-20, P-23, P-25,
P-26, P-27, P-28, P-60, P-65. U. S. Bureau of the
Census, Subscriber's Services, Washington, DC
20233 (Orders to: Supt. of Documents, Washington,
DC 20402)

312 339   US
CURRENT POPULATION REPORTS: CONSUMER
BUYING INDICATORS. (Series P-65) 1963. irreg.
$56.00 including P-20, P-23, P-25, P-26, P-27, P-28,
P-60. U.S. Bureau of the Census, Washington, DC
20402 (Orders to: Supt. of Documents, Washington,
DC 20402)

312 339   US
CURRENT POPULATION REPORTS: CONSUMER
INCOME. (Series P-60) 1948. irreg. $56.00
including P-20, P-23, P-25, P-26, P-27, P-28, P-65.
U.S. Bureau of the Census, Washington, DC 20402
(Orders to: Supt. of Documents, Washington, DC
20402)

312   US
CURRENT POPULATION REPORTS: FARM
POPULATION. (Series P-27) 1945. irreg. $56.00
including P-20, P-23, P-25, P-26, P-28, P-60, P-65.
U.S. Bureau of the Census, Washington, DC 20402
(Orders to: Supt. of Documents, Washington, DC
20402)

312   US ISSN 0565-0917
CURRENT POPULATION REPORTS: FEDERAL-
STATE COOPERATIVE PROGRAM FOR
POPULATION ESTIMATES. (Series P-26) 1969.
irreg. $56.00 including P-20, P-23, P-25, P-27, P-28,
P-60, P-65. U.S. Bureau of the Census, Washington,
DC 20402 (Orders to: Supt. of Documents,
Washington, DC 20402)

312   US ISSN 0082-9498
CURRENT POPULATION REPORTS:
INTERNATIONAL POPULATION REPORTS.
(Series P-91) irreg. U.S. Bureau of the Census,
Washington, DC 20233 (Orders to: Supt. of
Documents, Washington, DC 20402)

312   US ISSN 0363-6836
CURRENT POPULATION REPORTS:
POPULATION CHARACTERISTICS. (Series P-
20) 1946. irreg. $56.00 including P-23, P-25, P-26,
P-27, P-28, P-60, P-65. U.S. Bureau of the Census,
Washington, DC 20233 (Subscriptions to: Supt. of
Documents, Washington, DC 20402)

312   US
CURRENT POPULATION REPORTS:
POPULATION CHARACTERISTICS.
GEOGRAPHIC MOBILITY. (Series P-20) 1948. a.
price varies. U. S. Bureau of the Census, Subscribers
Services, Washington, DC 20233 (Orders to: Supt.
of Documents, Washington, DC 20402)
  Formerly: Current Population Reports, P-20:
Population Characteristics. Mobility of the
Population of the United States (ISSN 0076-986X)

312   US ISSN 0082-948X
CURRENT POPULATION REPORTS:
POPULATION CHARACTERISTICS.
HOUSEHOLD AND FAMILY
CHARACTERISTICS. (Series P-20) a. price varies.
U. S. Bureau of the Census, Subscribers Services,
Washington, DC 20233 (Orders to: Supt. of
Documents, Washington, DC 20402)

312   US
CURRENT POPULATION REPORTS:
POPULATION CHARACTERISTICS. MARITAL
STATUS AND LIVING ARRANGEMENTS.
(Series P-20) a. price varies. U. S. Bureau of the
Census, Subscribers Services, Washington, DC
20233 (Orders to: Supt. of Docs., Wash., DC 20402)
  Formerly: Current Population Reports, P-20:
Population Characteristics. Marital Status and
Family Status (ISSN 0082-9501)

312   US
CURRENT POPULATION REPORTS:
POPULATION CHARACTERISTICS. SCHOOL
ENROLLMENT: SOCIAL AND ECONOMIC
CHARACTERISTICS OF STUDENTS. (Series P-
20) a. price varies. U. S. Bureau of the Census,
Subscribers Services, Washington, DC 20233
(Orders to: Supt. of Documents, Washington, DC
20402)
  Formerly: U. S. Bureau of the Census. Current
Population Reports: School Enrollment: October
(Year) (ISSN 0082-9528)

312   US
CURRENT POPULATION REPORTS:
POPULATION CHARACTERISTICS. SOCIAL
AND ECONOMIC CHARACTERISTICS OF
THE BLACK POPULATION. (Series P-20) a. price
varies. U. S. Bureau of the Census, Subscribers
Services, Washington, DC 20233 (Orders to: Supt.
of Documents, Washington, DC 20402)
  Formerly: U. S. Bureau of the Census. Current
Population Reports: Negro Population (ISSN 0082-
951X)

312   US
CURRENT POPULATION REPORTS:
POPULATION ESTIMATES AND
PROJECTIONS. (Series P-25) 1947. m. $56.00
including P-20, P-23, P-26, P-27, P-28, P-60, P-65.
U.S. Bureau of the Census, Washington, DC 20402
(Orders to: Supt. of Documents, Washington, DC
20402)

312   US ISSN 0071-1616
CURRENT POPULATION REPORTS;
POPULATION ESTIMATES AND
PROJECTIONS. ESTIMATES OF THE
POPULATION OF THE UNITED STATES AND
COMPONENTS OF POPULATION CHANGE.
(Series P-25) a. price varies. U. S. Bureau of the
Census, Subscribers Services, Washington, DC
20233 (Orders to: Supt. of Documents, Washington,
DC 20402)

312   US
CURRENT POPULATION REPORTS:
POPULATION ESTIMATES AND
PROJECTIONS. ESTIMATES OF THE
POPULATION OF THE UNITED STATES BY
AGE, SEX AND RACE. (Series P-25) a. price
varies. U. S. Bureau of the Census, Subscribers
Services, Washington, DC 20233 (Orders to: Supt.
of Documents, Washington, DC 20402)
  Formerly: Current Population Reports, P-25:
Population Estimates and Projections. Estimates of
the Population of the United States by Age, Color,
and Sex (ISSN 0071-1624)

312   US
CURRENT POPULATION REPORTS: SPECIAL
CENSUSES. (Series P-28) no. 102, 1942. irreg.
$56.00 including P-20, P-23, P-25, P-26, P-27, P-60,
P-65. U.S. Bureau of the Census, Washington, DC
20402 (Biannual summaries available from: Supt. of
Documents, Washington, DC 20402, Other P-28
reports available from Bureau's Subscriber Services
Section)

312   US   ISSN 0498-8485
CURRENT POPULATION REPORTS: SPECIAL STUDIES. (Series P-23) 1949. irreg. $56.00 including P-20, P-25, P-26, P-27, P-28, P-60, P-65. U.S. Bureau of the Census, Washington, DC 20233 (Orders to: Supt. of Documents, Washington, DC 20402)

312   YU   ISSN 0084-4357
DEMOGRAFSKA STATISTIKA. 1956. a. 200 din.($11.11) Savezni Zavod za Statistiku, Uzun Mirkova 1, Belgrade, Yugoslavia. circ. 600.
    Formerly: Yugoslavia. Savezni Zavod za Statistuku. Vitalna Statistika.

910   US
DEMOGRAPHIC MONOGRAPHS. a. price varies. Gordon and Breach Science Publishers, One Park Ave., New York, NY 10016. Ed.Bd.

312   UN   ISSN 0082-8041
DEMOGRAPHIC YEARBOOK. (Text in English and French) 1949. a. $17.50 price varies. United Nations, Department of Economic and Social Affairs, Secretariat, New York, NY 10017 (Dist. by: United Nations Publications, Room LX-2300, New York, NY 10017; or Distribution and Sales Section, Palais des Nations, CH-1211 Geneva 10, Switzerland)

312   FR
DEMOGRAPHIE AFRICAINE: BULLETIN DE LIAISON. (Includes special number) a. Groupe de Demographie Africaine, Departement de la Cooperation, 18, Bd. Adolphe Pinard, 75014 Paris, France.
    Demographie en Afrique d'Expression Francaise; Bulletin de Liaison.

312   FR   ISSN 0070-3354
DEMOGRAPHIE ET SCIENCES HUMAINES. 1970. irreg. (Institut National d'Etudes Demographiques) Presses Universitaires de France, 108 Bd. Saint Germaine, 75279 Paris Cedex 6, France (Service des Periodiques, 12 rue Jean de Beauvais, 75005 Paris)

312   FR   ISSN 0070-3362
DEMOGRAPHIE ET SOCIETES. 1960. irreg. price varies. (Ecole Pratique des Hautes Etudes, Centre de Recherches Historiques) Librairie Touzot, 38 rue Saint Sulpice, 75006 Paris, France.

312   DK   ISSN 0070-3478
DENMARK. DANMARKS STATISTIK. BEFOLKNINGENS BEVAEGELSER. (Subseries of its Statistiske Meddelelser) (Text in Danish; notes in English) 1931-33. a. Kr.15.83. Danmarks Statistik, Sejroegade 11, 2100 Copenhagen OE, Denmark.

DENMARK. DANMARKS STATISTIK. FAERDSELSUHELD. see *PUBLIC HEALTH AND SAFETY*

312   BE
DOSSIERS DE DEMOGRAPHIE DE LA BELGIQUE. 1975. irreg. 325 Fr. (Societe Belge de Demographie) Editions Derouaux, 10, Place St.-Jacques, Liege, Belgium. (looseleaf format)

301.32   UN
E S C A P COUNTRY MONOGRAPH SERIES. 1974. irreg. United Nations Economic and Social Commission for Asia and the Pacific, Population Division, United Nations Bldg., Rajadamnern Ave., Bangkok 2, Thailand (Dist. by: United Nations Publications, Room LX-2300, New York, NY 10017; or Distribution and Sales Section, Palais des Nations, CH-1211 Geneva 10, Switzerland) (also avail. in microfiche)

312   PN   ISSN 0378-6749
ESTADISTICA PANAMENA. SITUACION DEMOGRAFICA. SECCION 221. ESTADISTICAS VITALES - CIFRAS PRELIMINARES. 1957. s-a. Bl..30. Direccion de Estadistica y Censo, Contraloria General, Apartado 5213, Panama 6, Panama. circ. 1,800.
    Formerly: Estadistica Panamena. Seccion 221. Movimento de Problacion (ISSN 0078-8902)

310   FR   ISSN 0071-8823
FRANCE. INSTITUT NATIONAL D'ETUDES DEMOGRAPHIQUES. CAHIERS DE TRAVAUX ET DOCUMENTS. 1946. irreg., no. 89, 1980. price varies. Institut National d'Etudes Demographiques, 27 rue du Commandeur, 75675 Paris Cedex 14, France. Ed. G. Calot.

312 331   FR
FRANCE. INSTITUT NATIONAL DE LA STATISTIQUE ET DES ETUDES ECONOMIQUES. COLLECTIONS. SERIE D, DEMOGRAPHIE ET EMPLOI. (Text in French; summaries in English and Spanish) 1969. irreg. 220 F. for 10 nos. Institut National de la Statistique et des Etudes Economiques, 18, Bd. A. Pinard, F 75675 Paris, France. circ. 3,000.

330.08 331.1   FR
FRANCE. INSTITUT NATIONAL DE LA STATISTIQUE ET DES ETUDES ECONOMIQUES. ENQUETE SUR L'EMPLOI. (Subseries of Institut National de la Statistique et des Etudes Economiques. Serie D, Demographie et Emploi) 1968. a. Institut National de la Statistique et des Etudes Economiques, 18, Bd A. Pinard, F 75675 Paris 14, France. illus. stat. circ. 3,000.

312   US   ISSN 0362-0662
GEORGIA VITAL AND HEALTH STATISTICS. 1947. a. free. ‡ Department of Human Resources, Division of Physical Health, 47 Trinity Ave. S.W., Rm. 542-H, Atlanta, GA 30334. (also avail. in microfiche)
    Formerly: Georgia Vital and Morbidity Statistics (ISSN 0072-1379)

312   GH
GHANA POPULATION STUDIES. 1969. irreg., no. 7, 1976. price varies. University of Ghana, Institute of Statistical, Social and Economic Research, Legon, Ghana.

301.426   SW
GOETEBORGS UNIVERSITET. DEMOGRAPHIC RESEARCH INSTITUTE. REPORTS. no. 14, 1974. irreg. Goeteborgs Universitet, Demographic Research Institute, Viktoriagatan 13, S-411 25 Goeteborg, Sweden (Dist. by: Almqvist & Wiksell International, 26 Gamla Brogatan, S-111 20 Stockholm, Sweden)

312 610   UK   ISSN 0072-6400
GREAT BRITAIN. GENERAL REGISTER OFFICE. STUDIES ON MEDICAL AND POPULATION SUBJECTS. 1948. irreg. price varies. H.M.S.O., P.O. Box 569, London SE1 9NH, England.

312   US   ISSN 0093-3481
HAWAII. DEPARTMENT OF HEALTH. RESEARCH AND STATISTICS OFFICE. R & S REPORT. 1973. irreg., no. 19, 1977. free. Department of Health, Research and Statistics Office, P.O. Box 3378, Honolulu, HI 96801. stat. Key Title: R & S Report (Honolulu)

312   HU
HISTORISCH-DEMOGRAPHISCHE MITTEILUNGEN/COMMUNICATIONS DE DEMOGRAPHIE HISTORIQUE. (Text in French and German) irreg; no. 3, 1976. Eotvos Lorand Tudomanyegyetem, Allam es Jogtudomanyi Kar, Statisztikai Tanszek, Egyetem ter 1-3, Budapest 5, Hungary. Ed. Jozef Kovacsics.

312   HU   ISSN 0073-4020
HUNGARY. KOZPONTI STATISZTIKAI HIVATAL. DEMOGRAFIAI EVKONYV. 1965. a. 180 Ft. Statisztikai Kiado Vallalat, Kaszas U.10-12, P.O.B.99, 1300 Budapest 3, Hungary.

312   BE
I U S S P PAPERS. Variant title: International Union for the Scientific Study of Population. Documents du l'Union. 1974. irreg., no. 18, 1981. 180 Fr.($6) International Union for the Scientific Study of Population, 5 rue Forgeur, 4000 Liege, Belgium. bibl. (reprint service avail. from UMI)

312.2   II
INDIA. MINISTRY OF HOME AFFAIRS. VITAL STATISTICS DIVISION. CAUSES OF DEATH; A SURVEY. (Text in English) a. Ministry of Home Affairs, Vital Statistics Division, Registrar General, West Block No. 1, R. K. Puram, New Delhi 110022, India. stat.

POPULATION STUDIES   727

INDIAN HEALTH TRENDS AND SERVICES. see *PUBLIC HEALTH AND SAFETY*

312   II   ISSN 0070-3311
INSTITUTE OF ECONOMIC GROWTH, DELHI. CENSUS STUDIES.* (Text in English) 1969. irreg., 1969, no. 1. Rs.30. Institute of Economic Growth, Delhi, Univeristy of Delhi, Delhi 110007, India.

312   II
INSTITUTE OF ECONOMIC RESEARCH. PUBLICATIONS ON DEMOGRAPHY. (Text in English) irreg. price varies. Institute of Economic Research, Deputy Director, Vidyagiri, Dharwar 580004, Karnataka, India.

325   SZ
INTERGOVERNMENTAL COMMITTEE FOR EUROPEAN MIGRATION. REVIEW OF ACHIEVEMENTS. (Editions in English, French and Spanish) 1969. a. free. Intergovernmental Committee for European Migration, 16 Ave. Jean Trembley, Case Postale 100, CH-1211 Geneva 19, Switzerland. circ. 5,000.

301.32   II
INTERNATIONAL INSTITUTE FOR POPULATION STUDIES. DIRECTOR'S REPORT. (Text in English) 1956/57. a. International Institute for Population Studies, Govandi Station Rd., Deonar, Bombay 400088, India. Dir. K. Srinivasan.
    Former titles: International Institute for Population Studies. Annual Report & Demographic Training and Research Centre. Annual Report.

325   CN   ISSN 0383-2767
INTERNATIONAL NEWSLETTER ON MIGRATION. 1971. irreg. University of Waterloo, Waterloo, Ont. N2L 3GI, Canada.
    Formerly: International Migration Newsletter (ISSN 0383-2759)

312   BE   ISSN 0074-9338
INTERNATIONAL POPULATION CONFERENCE. PROCEEDINGS. quadrennial, 18th, 1977, Mexico City. 2200 Fr.($60) International Union for the Scientific Study of Population, 5 rue Forgeur, 4000 Liege, Belgium. (reprint service avail. from UMI)

312   US
INTERNATIONAL PROGRAM OF LABORATORIES FOR POPULATION STATISTICS. OCCASIONAL PUBLICATIONS. 1974. irreg. University of North Carolina at Chapel Hill, School of Public Health, Department of Biostatistics, Chapel Hill, NC 27514.

312   US
INTERNATIONAL PROGRAM OF LABORATORIES FOR POPULATION STATISTICS. SCIENTIFIC REPORT SERIES. (Text in English; summaries in French and Spanish) no. 20, 1975. irreg. University of North Carolina at Chapel Hill, School of Public Health, Department of Biostatistics, Chapel Hill, NC 27514.

312   BE
INTERNATIONAL UNION FOR THE SCIENTIFIC STUDY OF POPULATION. NEWSLETTER. (Text in English and French) a. 80 Fr.($2.50) International Union for the Scientific Study of Population, Rue Forgeur 5, 4000 Liege, Belgium. (reprint service avail. from UMI)

312   IS   ISSN 0075-0999
ISRAEL. CENTRAL BUREAU OF STATISTICS. CAUSES OF DEATH. (Subseries of its Special Series) (Text in Hebrew and English) 1950. a. I£90. Central Bureau of Statistics, Box 13015, Jerusalem, Israel.

312   IS
ISRAEL. CENTRAL BUREAU OF STATISTICS. SUICIDES AND ATTEMPTED SUICIDES. (Text in Hebrew and English) 1968? irreg., latest issue, 1976. I£90. Central Bureau of Statistics, Box 13015, Jerusalem, Israel.

312   IT   ISSN 0075-1685
ITALY. ISTITUTO CENTRALE DI STATISTICA. ANNUARIO DI STATISTICHE DEMOGRAFICHE. a. L.7500. Istituto Centrale di Statistica, Via Cesare Balbo 16, 00100 Rome, Italy. circ. 1,000.

314 IT ISSN 0075-1863
ITALY. ISTITUTO CENTRALE DI STATISTICA. POPOLAZIONE E MOVIMENTO ANAGRAFICO DEI COMUNI. a. L.75000. Istituto Centrale di Statistica, Via C. Balbo, 16, 00100 Rome, Italy. circ. 11,000.

301 US
JOHNS HOPKINS UNIVERSITY. POPULATION INFORMATION PROGRAM. POPULATION REPORT. SERIES L. ISSUES IN WORLD HEALTH. 1979. irreg. Johns Hopkins University, Population Information Program, 624 N. Broadway, Baltimore, MD 21205.

312 US
KANSAS. DEPARTMENT OF HEALTH AND ENVIRONMENT. ANNUAL SUMMARY OF VITAL STATISTICS. a. Department of Health and Environment, Topeka, KS 66603. stat.

312 KO
KOREA (REPUBLIC) ECONOMIC PLANNING BOARD. YEARBOOK OF MIGRATION STATISTICS. (Text in Korean & English) 1971. a. Bureau of Statistics, Economic Planning Board, Gyeongun-Dong, Jongo-Gu, Seoul, S. Korea. Ed. Heung-Koo Kang. circ. 200.

301.426 IO
LEMBAGA KELUARGA BERENTJANA NASIONAL.* 1969/1970. a. Sekretariat Pemerintah Daerah, Propinsi Djawa Tengah, Lamporan, Indonesia. charts. stat.

312 LY ISSN 0075-9236
LIBYA. CENSUS AND STATISTICAL OFFICE. GENERAL POPULATION CENSUS. (Text in Arabic and English) 1954. decennial. free. Census and Statistical Department, Ministry of Planning, Tripoli, Libya.

312 MM ISSN 0076-3470
MALTA. CENTRAL OFFICE OF STATISTICS. DEMOGRAPHIC REVIEW. a. £0.25. Central Office of Statistics, Auberge de Castille, Valletta, Malta (Subscr. to: Department of Information, Auberge de Castille, Valletta, Malta)

325 FI
MIGRATION INSTITUTE. MIGRATION STUDIES. (Includes three series: A (Finnish); B(Swedish); C (English)) 1974. irreg. price varies. Migration Institute, Kasarmialue, rak. 46, 20500 Turku 50, Finland. Dir. Olavi Koivukangas. bk. rev. charts. stat. circ. 1,000.
 Formerly: Institute for Migration, Turku. Migration Studies (ISSN 0356-780X)

301.3 SZ ISSN 0544-1188
MIGRATION TODAY. (Editions in English, French and Spanish) 1963. irreg. (approx. 3/yr.) free. World Council of Churches, Migration Desk, 150 Route de Ferney, 1211 Geneva 20, Switzerland. Ed. Alan Matheson. bk. rev. circ. 4,000.

312 US ISSN 0077-0930
MONOGRAPHS IN POPULATION BIOLOGY. 1967. irreg., latest, no. 15. price varies. Princeton University Press, Box 231, Princeton, NJ 08540. Ed. R.M. May. (reprint service avail. from UMI) Indexed: Ind.Med.

312 GR ISSN 0077-6114
MOUVEMENT NATUREL DE LA POPULATION DE LA GRECE. (Text in Greek and French) 1956. a., latest 1975. $5. National Statistical Service, Publications and Information Division, 14-16 Lycourgou St, Athens 112, Greece.

325 SP ISSN 0077-1767
MOVIMENTO NATURAL DE LA POBLACION DE ESPANA. 1961. irreg. price varies. Instituto Nacional de Estadistica, Avda. Generalisimo 91, Madrid 16, Spain.

312 NE
N I D I PUBLIKATIES. no. 2, 1978. irreg. price varies. (Nederlands Interuniversitair Demografish Instituut) Van Loghum Slaterus, Postbus 23, Deventer, Netherlands. Ed. E. W. Hofstee.

312 NE
NEDERLANDS INTERUNIVERSITAIR DEMOGRAFISCH INSTITUUT. PUBLICATIONS. (Text in English) 1976. irreg. price varies. (Nederlands Interuniversitair Demografisch Instituut - Netherlands Interuniversity Demographic Institute) Martinus Nijhoff, Box 566, 2501 CN The Hague, Netherlands. (Co-sponsor: Population and Family Study Centre)

312 NE
NEDERLANDS INTERUNIVERSITAIR DEMOGRAFISCH INSTITUUT. WORKING PAPERS. (Text in English) 1973. irreg. free. Nederlands Interuniversitair Demografisch Instituut - Netherlands Interuniversity Demographic Institute, Prinses Beatrixlaan 428, Voorburg, Netherlands. circ. 100-150.

312 614 NE
NETHERLANDS. CENTRAAL BUREAU VOOR DE STATISTIEK. JAAROVERZICHT BEVOLKING EN VOLKSGEZONDHEID. POPULATION AND HEALTH STATISTICS. (Supplement to Maandstatistiek van Bevolking en Volksgezonheid) 1971. a. fl.25. Centraal Bureau voor de Statistiek, Prinses Beatrixlaan 428, Voorburg, Netherlands (Orders to: Staatsuitgeverij, Christoffel Plantijnstraat, The Hague, Netherlands) circ. 1,000.

312 NN
NEW HEBRIDES. BUREAU OF STATISTICS. CENSUS OF POPULATION AND HOUSING, VILA AND SANTO, FINAL RESULTS: PART 1: HOUSING DATA/RECENSEMENT DE LA POPULATION ET DE L'HABITATION, VILA ET LUGANVILLE, RESULTATS DEFINITIFS: 1ERE PARTIE: DONNES SUR L'HABITAT. (Text in English, French) irreg. free. Bureau of Statistics, Port Vila, New Hebrides. stat. circ. 400.

312 NN
NEW HEBRIDES. BUREAU OF STATISTICS. CENSUS OF POPULATION AND HOUSING, VILA AND SANTO, FINAL RESULTS: PART 2: POPULATION DATA/RECENSEMENT DE LA POPULATION ET DE L'HABITAT, VILA ET LUGANVILLE, RESULTATS DEFINITIFS: 2EME PARTI: DONNEES SUR LA POPULATION. (Text in English, French) 1972 ed., 1978. irreg. free. Condominium Bureau of Statistics, Port Vila, New Hebrides. stat. circ. 400.

312 NN
NEW HEBRIDES. CONDOMINIUM BUREAU OF STATISTICS CENSUS OF POPULATION AND HOUSING, VILA AND SANTO, PRELIMINARY RESULTS/RECENSEMENT DE LA POPULATION ET DE L'HABITAT, PORT VILA ET LUGANVILLE, RESULTATS PRELIMINAIRES. (Text in English, French) 1972. irreg. free. Condominium Bureau of Statistics, Port Vila, New Hebrides. stat.

NEW YORK STATE BUSINESS FACT BOOK. PART 2: POPULATION AND HOUSING. see BUSINESS AND ECONOMICS — Economic Situation And Conditions

312 NZ ISSN 0110-375X
NEW ZEALAND. DEPARTMENT OF STATISTICS. POPULATION AND MIGRATION PART A: POPULATION. a. NZ.$1.20. Department of Statistics, Private Bag, Wellington, New Zealand (Subscr. to: Government Printing Office, Publications, Private Bag, Wellington, New Zealand)
 Supersedes in part: New Zealand. Department of Statistics. Population and Migration; New Zealand. Department of Statistics. Statistical Report of Population, Migration and Building. (ISSN 0077-9903)

312 NZ ISSN 0110-3768
NEW ZEALAND. DEPARTMENT OF STATISTICS. POPULATION AND MIGRATION. PART B: EXTERNAL MIGRATION. a. NZ.$1.20. Department of Statistics, Private Bag, Wellington, New Zealand (Subscr to: Government Printing Office, Publications, Private Bag, Wellington, New Zealand)
 Supersedes in part: New Zealand. Department of Statistics. Population and Migration.

312 NZ ISSN 0077-9687
NEW ZEALAND. DEPARTMENT OF STATISTICS. POPULATION CENSUS: AGES AND MARITAL STATUS. quinquennial, vol. 2, 1971, pub. 1974. NZ.$1.35. Department of Statistics, Private Bag, Wellington, New Zealand (Subscr. to: Government Printing Office, Publications, Private Bag, Wellington, New Zealand)

312 NZ
NEW ZEALAND. DEPARTMENT OF STATISTICS. POPULATION CENSUS: BIRTHPLACES AND ETHNIC ORIGIN. quinquennial, 1971, issued 1975. NZ.$3.15. Department of Statistics, Private Bag, Wellington, New Zealand (Subscr. to: Government Printing Office Publications, Private Bag, Wellington, New Zealand)
 Formerly: New Zealand. Department of Statistics. Population Census: Race (ISSN 0077-9776)

312 NZ ISSN 0077-9695
NEW ZEALAND. DEPARTMENT OF STATISTICS. POPULATION CENSUS: DWELLINGS. quinquennial, 1971 issued 1976. NZ.$1.85. Department of Statistics, Private Bag, Wellington, New Zealand (Subscr. to: Government Printing Office, Publications, Private Bag, Wellington, New Zealand)

312 NZ ISSN 0077-9709
NEW ZEALAND. DEPARTMENT OF STATISTICS. POPULATION CENSUS: EDUCATION. quinquennial, 1971 issued 1976. NZ.$2.10. Department of Statistics, Private Bag, Wellington, New Zealand (Subscr. to: Government Printing Office, Publications, Private Bag, Wellington, New Zealand)

312 NZ ISSN 0077-9717
NEW ZEALAND. DEPARTMENT OF STATISTICS. POPULATION CENSUS: GENERAL REPORT. quinquennial, 1971 issued 1977. NZ.$4.50. Department of Statistics, Private Bag, Wellington, New Zealand (Subscr. to: Government Printing Office, Publications, Private Bag, Wellington, New Zealand)

312 NZ
NEW ZEALAND. DEPARTMENT OF STATISTICS. POPULATION CENSUS: HOUSEHOLDS, FAMILIES & FERTILITY. quinquennial, 1971, issued 1976. NZ.$2.10. Department of Statistics, Private Bag, Wellington, New Zealand (Subscr. to: Government Printing Office, Publications, Private Bag, Wellington, New Zealand)
 Formerly: New Zealand. Department of Statistics. Population Census: Households (ISSN 0077-9725)

312 NZ ISSN 0077-9733
NEW ZEALAND. DEPARTMENT OF STATISTICS. POPULATION CENSUS: INCOMES. quinquennial, 1971, issued 1975. NZ.$1.60. Department of Statistics, Private Bag, Wellington, New Zealand (Subscr. to: Government Printing Office, Publications, Private Bag, Wellington, New Zealand)

312 NZ ISSN 0077-9741
NEW ZEALAND. DEPARTMENT OF STATISTICS. POPULATION CENSUS: INDUSTRIES AND OCCUPATIONS. quinquennial, 1971 issued 1975. NZ.$2.60. Department of Statistics, Private Bag, Wellington, New Zealand (Subscr. to: Government Printing Office, Publications, Private Bag. Wellington, New Zealand)

312 NZ ISSN 0077-975X
NEW ZEALAND. DEPARTMENT OF STATISTICS. POPULATION CENSUS: MAORI POPULATION AND DWELLINGS. quinquennial, vol. 8, 1971, pub. 1975. NZ.$3.10. Department of Statistics, Private Bag, Wellington, New Zealand (Subscr. to: Government Printing Office, Publications, Private Bag, Wellington, New Zealand)

312   NZ
NEW ZEALAND. DEPARTMENT OF
STATISTICS. POPULATION CENSUS:
PROVISIONAL POPULATION AND
DWELLING STATISTICS. quinquennial. NZ.$1.
Department of Statistics, Private Bag, Wellington,
New Zealand (Subscr. to: Government Printing
Office, Publications, Private Bag, Wellington, New
Zealand)
Formerly: New Zealand. Department of Statistics.
Population Census: Provisional Report on
Population and Dwellings (ISSN 0077-9768)

312   NZ   ISSN 0077-9784
NEW ZEALAND. DEPARTMENT OF
STATISTICS. POPULATION CENSUS:
RELIGIOUS PROFESSIONS. quinquennial, 1971
issued 1974. NZ.$3.15. Department of Statistics,
Private Bag, Wellington, New Zealand (Subscr. to:
Government Printing Office, Publications, Private
Bag, Wellington, New Zealand)

312   NQ
NICARAGUA. OFICINA EJECTIVA DE
ENCUESTOS Y CENSOS. BOLETIN
DEMOGRAFICO. no. 2, Feb. 1978. irreg.
C.$15($4) per no. Oficina Ejecutiva de Encuestas y
Censos, Apdo. Postal 4031, Managua, Nicaragua.
stat.

301.3   US
NOTES (NEW YORK) 1979. irreg. free. Ford
Foundation and Rockefeller Foundation, Research
Program on Population and Development Policy,
320 E. 43 St., New York, NY 10017. Eds. Marge
Horn, Mary Kritz. circ. 8,500.

301.32   MG
NY MPONIN'I MADAGASIKARA. (Text in French
or Malagasy) 1975. irreg. Direction de la Recherche
Scientifique et Technique, Section de Demographie,
B.P. 4096, Antananarivo, Malagasy Republic.

300   US
OTHER SIDE (WASHINGTON) 1973. irreg, no. 17,
1979. free. Environmental Fund, Inc., 1302 18th St.,
Washington, DC 20036. Ed. Wendy Butler. circ.
28,000.

312   PH
PHILIPPINES. NATIONAL CENSUS AND
STATISTICS OFFICE. SOCIAL INDICATOR.
Short title: Social Indicators of the Philippines. a,
latest 1974. P.7($3) National Census and Statistics
Office, Ramon Magsaysay Blvd., Manila,
Philippines. Ed. Tito A. Mijares. charts. stat.

301.32 312   CS
POPULACNI ZPRAVY. 1976. irreg (4-5/yr) price
varies. Federalni Ministerstvo Prace a Socialnich
Veci, Palackemo nam. 4, 12007 Prague 2,
Czechoslovakia. Ed. Jaroslav Havelka.

301.426 312   US
POPULATION: AN INTERNATIONAL
DIRECTORY OF ORGANIZATIONS AND
INFORMATION RESOURCES. (Subseries of
Who's Doing What Series) 1976. irreg. $18.75.
California Institute of Public Affairs, Box 10,
Claremont, CA 91711. Eds. Thaddeus C. Trzyna,
Joan Dickson Smith. bibl. stat.

301.426 613.9   US
POPULATION AND FAMILY PLANNING
PROGRAMS. 1969. irreg. $4.50. Population
Council, One Dag Hammarskjold Plaza, New York,
NY 10017.
Planned parenthood

312   PP   ISSN 0079-3868
POPULATION CENSUS OF PAPUA NEW
GUINEA. POPULATION CHARACTERISTICS
BULLETIN SERIES. 1966. irreg., latest issue, 1971.
free. Bureau of Statistics, P.O. Wards Strip, Papua
New Guinea. Ed. J. J. Shadlow. circ. 842.

312   US   ISSN 0079-3906
POPULATION ESTIMATES OF ARIZONA. Also
known as: Arizona. Department of Economic
Security. Report. 1968. a. free. ‡ Department of
Economic Security, Population Statistics Unit, Box
6123, Phoenix, AZ 85005. Ed. Jack Kronenfeld.
circ. 2,000.

312   IR
POPULATION GROWTH OF IRAN. 1974. irreg.
Statistical Centre, Iran Novin Ave, Teheran, Iran.
charts. stat.

301.32   US   ISSN 0094-0348
POPULATION MOBILITY IN HAWAII. 1971. irreg.
free. Department of Health, Box 3378, Honolulu, HI
96801. stat.

301.32   TH
POPULATION NEWSLETTER. 1969. irreg. (3-4/yr.)
free. Chulalongkorn University, Institute of
Population Studies, Bangkok 5, Thailand. circ.
1,000. (tabloid format)

312   NE   ISSN 0079-3930
POPULATION OF THE MUNICIPALITIES OF
THE NETHERLANDS. (Text in Dutch and
English) 1944-46. a. fl.10. Centraal Bureau voor de
Statistiek, Prinses Beatrixlaan 428, Voorburg,
Netherlands (Orders to: Staatsuitgeverij, Christoffel
Plantijnstraat, The Hague, Netherlands)

312   US
POPULATION PROFILES. vol. 14, 1975. irreg.,
latest vol. 17. $0.50 per no. Center for Information
on America, Washington, CT 06793. (Co-sponsor:
Council of State Social Studies Specialists) Ed.
Townsend Scudder. bibl. charts. stat. (also avail. in
microform from UMI)

312   UN   ISSN 0082-805X
POPULATION STUDIES. (Editions in English,
French and Spanish) 1948. irreg., no. 56, 1974.
price varies. (United Nations, Department of
Economic and Social Affairs) United Nations
Publications, LX 2300, New York, NY 10017.

312   PO
PORTUGAL. INSTITUTO NACIONAL DE
ESTATISTICA. CENTRO DE ESTUDOS
DEMOGRAFICOS. CADERNO. no. 2, 1976.
irreg. Instituto Nacional de Estatistica, Lisbon,
Portugal (Orders to: Imprensa Nacional, Casa da
Moeda, Direccao Comercial, rua D. Francisco
Manuel de Melo 5, Lisbon 1, Portugal) charts.

312   PO   ISSN 0079-4082
PORTUGAL. INSTITUTO NACIONAL DE
ESTATISTICA. CENTRO DE ESTUDOS
DEMOGRAFICOS. REVISTA. 1945. irreg.
Instituto Nacional de Estatistica, Lisbon, Portugal
(Orders to: Imprensa Nacional, Casa da Moeda,
Direccao Comercial, rua D. Francisco Manuel de
Melo 5, Lisbon 1, Portugal)

312   PO
PORTUGAL. INSTITUTO NACIONAL DE
ESTATISTICA. ESTATISTICAS
DEMOGRAFICAS. 1887. a. $100. Instituto
Nacional de Estatistica, Av. Antonio Jose de
Almeida, Lisbon 1, Portugal (Orders to: Imprensa
Nacional, Casa da Moeda, Direccao Comercial, rua
D. Francisco Manuel de Melo 5, Lisbon 1, Portugal)
Formerly: Portugal. Instituto Nacional de
Estatistica. Anuario Demografico. (ISSN 0079-4104)

312 301.32   PL   ISSN 0079-7189
PRZESZLOSC DEMOGRAFICZNA POLSKI.
MATERIALY I STUDIA. (Text in Polish;
summaries in English) 1967. irreg., 1974, no. 6.
price varies. (Polska Akademia Nauk, Komitet Nauk
Demograficznych) Panstwowe Wydawnictwo
Naukowe, Ul. Miodowa 10, Warsaw, Poland (Dist.
by Ars Polona-Ruch, Krakowskie Przedmiescie 7,
Warsaw, Poland) Ed. A. Szczypiorski.

312   FR
RAPPORT SUR LA SITUATION
DEMOGRAPHIQUE DE LA FRANCE. 1970. a.
Institut National d'Etudes Demographiques, 27 rue
du Commandeur, 75675 Paris Cedex 14, France. bk.
rev. stat. circ. 2,000.

REPRODUCTIONS. see *BIOLOGY*

325   NE   ISSN 0080-1623
RESEARCH GROUP FOR EUROPEAN
MIGRATION PROBLEMS. PUBLICATIONS.
1951. irreg. price varies. Martinus Nijhoff, Box 566,
2501 CN The Hague, Netherlands. Ed. G. Beyer.

312 330   US   ISSN 0163-7878
RESEARCH IN POPULATION ECONOMICS; an
annual compilation of research. 1978. a. $18.75 to
individuals; institutions $37.50. J A I Press, Box
1678, 165 W. Putnam Ave., Greenwich, CT 06830.
Ed. Julian L. Simon.

301.426   US
RESEARCH MONOGRAPHS ON HUMAN
POPULATION. irreg. price varies. Oxford
University Press, 200 Madison Ave., New York,
NY 10016 (And Ely House, 37 Dover St., London
W1X 4AH, England) Ed. G. Aimsworth Harrison.

312   US
RHODE ISLAND. DEPARTMENT OF HEALTH.
VITAL STATISTICS. a. free. Department of
Health, 101 Health Bldg., Davis St., Providence, RI
02908.

312 325   KO
SEOUL NATIONAL UNIVERSITY. POPULATION
AND DEVELOPMENT STUDIES CENTER.
BULLETIN. (Text in English; summaries in
Korean) 1972. a. 1000 Won($3) Seoul National
University, Population and Development Studies
Center, Gwan-ak Gu, Seoul, S. Korea. bibl.

312   US   ISSN 0094-6338
SOUTH CAROLINA VITAL AND MORBIDITY
STATISTICS. 1972. a. Department of Health and
Environmental Control, Office of Vital Records and
Public Health Statistics, 2600 Bull St., Columbia, SC
29201.

325   US
SPECTRUM (ST. PAUL) 1975. irreg. free. University
of Minnesota, Immigration History Research
Center, 826 Berry St., St. Paul, MI 55114. bk. rev.
illus. circ. 2,300. (back issues avail.)

301.3   PL
STUDIA POLONIJNE. (Text in Polish; summaries in
English) 1976. irreg. price varies. Katolicki
Uniwersytet Lubelski, Towarzystwo Naukowe,
Chopina 29, 20-023 Lublin, Poland. index. circ.
3,125.

312 301.32   US
STUDIES IN POPULATION. irreg. price varies.
Academic Press, Inc., 111 Fifth Ave., New York,
NY 10003. Ed. H. H. Winsborough.

312   US   ISSN 0147-1104
STUDIES IN POPULATION AND URBAN
DEMOGRAPHY. 1975. irreg. Greenwood Press, 88
Post Rd. W., Westport, CT 06881. Ed. Kingsley
Davis.

312   US
STUDIES IN SOCIAL AND ECONOMIC
DEMOGRAPHY. 1978. irreg. Duke University
Press, College Sta., Durham, NC 27708.

312   SW   ISSN 0082-0156
SWEDEN. STATISTISKA CENTRALBYRAAN.
BEFOLKNINGSFOERAENDRINGAR. (Text in
Swedish; summaries in English) 1911. a. price
varies. Liber Foerlag, Fack, S-162 89 Vaellingby,
Sweden. circ. 1,600.

312   SW   ISSN 0082-0164
SWEDEN. STATISTISKA CENTRALBYRAAN.
FOLKMAENGD. (Text in English; summaries in
English) 1910. a. Kr.63. Liber Foerlag, Fack, S-162
89 Vaellingby, Sweden. circ. 1,500-3,200.

312   US   ISSN 0495-257X
TEXAS VITAL STATISTICS. 1973. a. Department of
Health, 1100 W. 49th St., Austin, TX 78756.

312 317.29   TR   ISSN 0564-2612
TRINIDAD AND TOBAGO. CENTRAL
STATISTICAL OFFICE. CONTINUOUS
SAMPLE SURVEY OF POPULATION. 1964.
irreg. Central Statistical Office, Textel Building, 1,
Edward Street, Port of Spain, Trinidad (Orders to:
Government Printing Office, 2 Victoria Ave., Port
of Spain, Trinidad)

312   UN   ISSN 0503-3934
UNITED NATIONS. REGIONAL CENTRE FOR
DEMOGRAPHIC TRAINING AND RESEARCH
IN LATIN AMERICA. SERIE A/CENTRO
LATINOAMERICANO DE DEMOGRAFIA.
SERIE A: INFORMES SOBRE
INVESTIGACIONES REALIZADAS. (1974
Catalog Available) 1962. irreg. $2 per no. United
Nations, Centro Latinoamericano de Demografia -
United Nations. Regional Center for Demographic
Training and Research in Latin America, Casilla 91,
Santiago, Chile. stat. circ. 1,500.

312 UN ISSN 0503-3942
UNITED NATIONS. REGIONAL CENTRE FOR DEMOGRAPHIC TRAINING AND RESEARCH IN LATIN AMERICA. SERIE C/CENTRO LATINOAMERICANO DE DEMOGRAFIA. SERIE C: INFORMES SOBRE INVESTIGACIONES REALIZADAS POR LOS ALUMNOS DEL CENTRO. (1974 Catolog available) 1963. irreg. $2 per no. United Nations, Centro Latinoamericano de Demografia, Casilla 91, Santiago, Chile. stat. circ. 1,500.

312 UN ISSN 0503-3950
UNITED NATIONS. REGIONAL CENTRE FOR DEMOGRAPHIC TRAINING AND RESEARCH IN LATIN AMERICA. SERIE D. (1974 Catalog available) 1962. irreg. $2 per no. United Nations, Centro Latinoamericano de Demografia, Casilla 91, Santiago, Chile. circ. 1,000.

312 UN
UNITED NATIONS. REGIONAL CENTRE FOR DEMOGRAPHIC TRAINING AND RESEARCH IN LATIN AMERICA. SERIE I/CENTRO LATINOAMERICANO DE DEMOGRAFIA. SERIE I: RECOPILACION DE TRABAJOS SOBRES PAISES. 1972. irreg. $4. United Nations, Centro Latinoamericano de Demografia - United Nations. Regional Office for Demographic Training and Research in Latin America, Casilla 91, Santiago, Chile. stat.

312 US ISSN 0082-9390
U. S. BUREAU OF THE CENSUS. CENSUS OF POPULATION. 1790. decennial. price varies. U.S. Bureau of the Census, Dept. of Commerce, Washington, DC 20233 (Orders to: Supt. of Documents, Washington, DC 20402)

312 US ISSN 0082-9412
U. S. BUREAU OF THE CENSUS. CENSUS TRACT MANUAL.* irreg. $0.35. U.S. Bureau of the Census, Dept. of Commerce, Washington, DC 20233 (Orders to: Supt. Doc., Washington, DC 20402)

312 US
U.S. BUREAU OF THE CENSUS. RESEARCH DOCUMENT SERIES. irreg. controlled circulation. U.S. Bureau of the Census, International Demographic Statistics Center, Washington, DC 20233.

301.32 US
U.S. CENTER FOR POPULATION RESEARCH. INVENTORY OF FEDERAL POPULATION RESEARCH. 1970/71. a. Department of Health, Education, and Welfare, U.S. Center for Population Research, 7910 Woodmont Ave., Bethesda, MD 20205.
 Continues: U. S. National Institute of Child Health and Human Development. Center for Population Research. Federal Program in Population Research.

325 US ISSN 0083-1220
U. S. IMMIGRATION AND NATURALIZATION SERVICE. ADMINISTRATIVE DECISIONS UNDER IMMIGRATION AND NATIONALITY LAWS. 1940. irreg. price varies. U.S. Immigration and Naturalization Service, c/o Charles J. Gentry, Board of Immigration Appeals, Washington, DC 20530 (Orders to: Supt. of Documents, Washington, DC 20402)

325 US ISSN 0083-1239
U. S. IMMIGRATION AND NATURALIZATION SERVICE. ADMINISTRATIVE DECISIONS UNDER IMMIGRATION AND NATIONALITY LAWS. INTERIM DECISIONS OF THE DEPARTMENT OF JUSTICE. irreg. $4.25 per year. U.S. Immigration and Naturalization Service, c/o Charles J. Gentry, Board of Immigration Appeals, Washington, DC 20530 (Orders to: Supt. of Documents, Washington, DC 20402)

325 US ISSN 0083-1247
U. S. IMMIGRATION AND NATURALIZATION SERVICE. ANNUAL REPORT. 1892. a. price varies. U.S. Immigration and Naturalization Service., 425 I St. N.W., Washington, DC 20536 (Orders to: Supt. of Documents, Washington, DC 20402)

U. S. NATIONAL CENTER FOR HEALTH STATISTICS. VITAL AND HEALTH STATISTICS. SERIES 1. PROGRAMS AND COLLECTION PROCEDURES. see *PUBLIC HEALTH AND SAFETY*

U. S. NATIONAL CENTER FOR HEALTH STATISTICS. VITAL AND HEALTH STATISTICS. SERIES 2. DATA EVALUATION AND METHODS RESEARCH. see *PUBLIC HEALTH AND SAFETY*

U.S. NATIONAL CENTER FOR HEALTH STATISTICS. VITAL AND HEALTH STATISTICS. SERIES 3. ANALYTICAL STUDIES. see *PUBLIC HEALTH AND SAFETY*

U.S. NATIONAL CENTER FOR HEALTH STATISTICS. VITAL AND HEALTH STATISTICS. SERIES 4. DOCUMENTS AND COMMITTEE REPORT. see *PUBLIC HEALTH AND SAFETY*

U. S. NATIONAL CENTER FOR HEALTH STATISTICS. VITAL AND HEALTH STATISTICS. SERIES 20. DATA ON MORTALITY. see *PUBLIC HEALTH AND SAFETY*

U. S. NATIONAL CENTER FOR HEALTH STATISTICS. VITAL AND HEALTH STATISTICS. SERIES 21. DATA ON NATALITY, MARRIAGE, AND DIVORCE. see *PUBLIC HEALTH AND SAFETY*

312 US
U.S. NATIONAL CENTER FOR HEALTH STATISTICS. VITAL AND HEALTH STATISTICS. SERIES 23: DATA FROM THE NATIONAL SURVEY OF FAMILY GROWTH. 1976. irreg. U.S. National Center for Health Statistics, 3700 East-West Highway, Hyattsville, MD 20782.

UNIVERSITY OF ALBERTA. DEPARTMENT OF SOCIOLOGY. POPULATION RESEARCH LABORATORY. ALBERTA SERIES REPORT. see *SOCIOLOGY*

UNIVERSITY OF DAR ES SALAAM. BUREAU OF RESOURCE ASSESSMENT AND LAND USE PLANNING. ANNUAL REPORT. see *ENVIRONMENTAL STUDIES*

UNIVERSITY OF DAR ES SALAAM. BUREAU OF RESOURCE ASSESSMENT AND LAND USE PLANNING. RESEARCH PAPER. see *ENVIRONMENTAL STUDIES*

UNIVERSITY OF DAR ES SALAAM. BUREAU OF RESOURCE ASSESSMENT AND LAND USE PLANNING. RESEARCH REPORT. see *ENVIRONMENTAL STUDIES*

312 301.2 NR
UNIVERSITY OF LAGOS. HUMAN RESOURCES RESEARCH UNIT. MONOGRAPH. no. 2, 1974. irreg. University of Lagos, Human Resources Research Unit, Yaba, Lagos, Nigeria.

301.426 US
UNIVERSITY OF MICHIGAN. CENTER FOR POPULATION PLANNING. ANNUAL REPORT. 9th, 1974. a. University of Michigan, Center for Population Planning, Ann Arbor, MI 48104. circ. 1,000.
 Formerly: University of Michigan. Department of Population Planning. Annual Report.

301.32 US
UNIVERSITY OF MICHIGAN. POPULATION STUDIES CENTER. ANNUAL REPORT. a. University of Michigan, Population Studies Center, Ann Arbor, MI 48104. Key Title: Annual Report of the Population Studies Center, the University of Michigan.

312 US ISSN 0553-5816
UNIVERSITY OF PENNSYLVANIA. POPULATION STUDIES CENTER. ANALYTICAL AND TECHNICAL REPORT. 1961. irreg., no. 11 in prep. University of Pennsylvania, Population Studies Center, 3718 Locust Walk/CR, Philadelphia, PA 19104. charts. stat.

301.3 US ISSN 0084-0734
UNIVERSITY OF WISCONSIN, MADISON. APPLIED POPULATION LABORATORY. POPULATION NOTES. 1961. irreg. University of Wisconsin-Madison, Applied Population Laboratory, Department of Rural Sociology, 240 Agricultural Hall, Madison, WI 53706. circ. 800.

301.3 US ISSN 0084-0742
UNIVERSITY OF WISCONSIN, MADISON. APPLIED POPULATION LABORATORY. POPULATION SERIES. 1961. irreg. price varies. University of Wisconsin-Madison, Applied Population Laboratory, Department of Rural Sociology, 240 Agricultural Hall, Madison, WI 53706. circ. 500.

312 US
UNIVERSITY OF WISCONSIN-MADISON. APPLIED POPULATION LABORATORY. TECHNICAL SERIES. 1977. irreg. University of Wisconsin-Madison, Applied Population Laboratory, Madison, WI 53706.

312 UY
URUGUAY. DIRECCION GENERAL DE ESTADISTICA Y CENSOS. ESTADISTICAS VITALES. (Suspended 1974-1977; volume for 1978 contains 1975 statistics) 1961; N.S. 1978. irreg. Direccion General de Estadistica y Censos, Montevideo, Uruguay.

614 US ISSN 0500-7720
UTAH VITAL STATISTICS ANNUAL REPORT. a. $5. Department of Social Services, Bureau of Health Statistics, 150 West North Temple, Suite 158, Box 2500, Salt Lake City, UT 84110. stat.

VITAL STATISTICS OF THE UNITED STATES. see *PUBLIC HEALTH AND SAFETY*

312 US
WASHINGTON (STATE) OFFICE OF FINANCIAL MANAGEMENT. FORECASTING AND SUPPORT DIVISION. POPULATION TRENDS. 1968. a. State Office of Financial Management, Forecasting and Support Division, House Office Bldg., Olympia, WA 98501 (Dist. by: State Library, Olympia WA 98504)
 Former titles: Washington (State) Office of Program Planning and Fiscal Management. Population and Enrollment Section. Population Trends (ISSN 0083-7482); Before 1970: Washington (State) Planning and Community Affairs Agency. Population Series.

325 WS
WESTERN SAMOA. DEPARTMENT OF STATISTICS. MIGRATION REPORT. (Text in English) 1976. irreg. Department of Statistics, Box 1151, Apia, Western Samoa. circ. 300.

317 US
WHERE TO WRITE FOR BIRTH AND DEATH RECORDS: U.S. AND OUTLYING AREAS. irreg. free. U.S. Department of Health, Education & Welfare, U.S. National Center for Health Statistics, 3700 East-West Highway, Hyattsville, MD 20782 (Orders to: Superintendent of Documents, U.S. Government Printing Office, Washington, DC 20402)

312 US
WHERE TO WRITE FOR BIRTH AND DEATH RECORDS: U.S. CITIZENS WHO WERE BORN OR DIED OUTSIDE THE UNITED STATES. irreg. free. U.S. Department of Health, Education & Welfare, U.S. National Center for Health Statistics, 3700 East-West Highway, Hyattsville, MD 20782 (Orders to: Superintendent of Documents, U.S. Government Printing Office, Washington, DC 20402)

312 317 US ISSN 0565-8454
WHERE TO WRITE FOR DIVORCE RECORDS: U.S. AND OUTLYING AREAS. irreg. free. U.S. Department of Health, Education & Welfare, U.S. National Center for Health Statistics, 3700 East-West Highway, Hyattsville, MD 20782 (Orders to: Superintendent of Documents, U.S. Government Printing Office Washington, D.C. 20402)

317 US ISSN 0162-0916
WHERE TO WRITE FOR MARRIAGE RECORDS: UNITED STATES AND OUTLYING AREAS. irreg. free. U.S. Department of Health, Education & Welfare, U.S. National Center for Health Statistics, 3700 East-West Highway, Hyattsville, MD 20782 (Orders to: Superintendent of Documents, U.S. Government Printing Office, Washington, DC 20402)
 Formerly: Where to Write for Marriage Records (ISSN 0565-8462)

312 US ISSN 0091-5254
WISCONSIN POPULATION PROJECTIONS. 1969. irreg., 3rd edt., 1975. $5. Department of Administration, Bureau of Program Management, Madison, WI 53702 (Order from: Document Sales Unit, 202 S. Thornton Ave., Madison, WI 53702) stat.

312 NE
WORLD FERTILITY SURVEY. BASIC DOCUMENTATION. (Editions in English, French, Spanish and Arabic) irreg. (6-8/yr) free. International Statistical Institute, Prinses Beatrixlaan 428, Box 950, 2270 AZ Voorburg, Netherlands.

321 NE
WORLD FERTILITY SURVEY. COUNTRY REPORTS. 1976. irreg. price varies. International Statistical Institute, Prinses Beatrixlaan 428, Box 950, 2270 AZ Voorburg, Netherlands. stat.

312 NE
WORLD FERTILITY SURVEY. OCCASIONAL PAPERS. 1973. irreg. free. International Statistical Institute, Prinses Beatrixlaan 428, Box 950, 2270 AZ Voorburg, Netherlands.

312 NE
WORLD FERTILITY SURVEY. PROGRESS REPORTS. 1975. a. International Statistical Institute, 428 Prinses Beatrixlaan Box 950, 2270 AZ Voorburg, Netherlands.
Formerly: World Fertility Survey. Report.

312 NE
WORLD FERTILITY SURVEY. SCIENTIFIC REPORTS. 1977. irreg. free. International Statistical Institute, Prinses Beatrixlaan 428, Box 950, 2270 AZ Voorburg, Netherlands.

312 NE
WORLD FERTILITY SURVEY. TECHNICAL BULLETINS. 1977. irreg. free. International Statistical Institute, Prinses Beatrixlaan 428, Box 950, 2270 AZ Voorburg, Netherlands. stat.

312 US ISSN 0085-8315
WORLD POPULATION DATA SHEET. 1962. a. $1. Population Reference Bureau, Inc., 1337 Conn. Ave. N.W., Washington, DC 20036. Ed. Carl Haub. stat. circ. 8,500. (wall chart format)

312 FI ISSN 0506-3590
YEARBOOK OF POPULATION RESEARCH IN FINLAND/VAESTOENTUTKIMUKEN VUOSIKIRJA. (Text in English) 1946. a. Fmk.40. Vaestontutkimuslaitos - Population Research Institute, Helsinki, Kalevankatu 16, 00100 Helsinki 10, Finland. Ed. Jarl Lindgren. bk. rev. bibl. circ. 1,200.

316 325 ZA ISSN 0084-4543
ZAMBIA. CENTRAL STATISTICAL OFFICE. MIGRATION STATISTICS. Title varies: Zambia. Central Statistical Office. Migration Statistics: Immigrants and Visitors. 1965. a, latest 1977. K.0.30. Central Statistical Office, P.O. Box 1908, Lusaka, Zambia.

325 ZA ISSN 0084-4802
ZAMBIA. IMMIGRATION DEPARTMENT. REPORT. 1964. a. 10 n. Government Printer, P.O. Box 136, Lusaka, Zambia.

312.96 RH ISSN 0085-5685
ZIMBABWE. CENTRAL STATISTICAL OFFICE. CENSUS OF POPULATION. a. Rhod.$7.50. ‡ Central Statistical Office, P.O. Box 8063, Causeway, Salisbury, Zimbabwe. stat.

POPULATION STUDIES —
Abstracting, Bibliographies, Statistcs

312 US ISSN 0066-0752
AMERICAN STATISTICAL ASSOCIATION. SOCIAL STATISTICS SECTION. PROCEEDINGS. 1958. a. American Statistical Association, 806 15th St., N.W., Suite 640, Washington, DC 20005. (also avail. in microform from UMI)

312 016 MX
ANGLO AMERICAN DIRECTORY OF MEXICO. (Text in English and Spanish) 1932. a. Mex.$250($16) Monclova 2-A, Mexico 7, D. F., Mexico. Ed. Ruth Poyo. adv. circ. 6,500.

312 AT ISSN 0067-0766
AUSTRALIA. BUREAU OF STATISTICS. CAUSES OF DEATH. a. Aus.$3.15. Australian Bureau of Statistics, P.O. Box 10, Belconnen, A.C.T. 2616, Australia. circ. 976.

312 AT
AUSTRALIA. BUREAU OF STATISTICS. VICTORIAN OFFICE. ESTIMATED POPULATION IN LOCAL GOVERNMENT AREAS. 1955. a. free. Australian Bureau of Statistics, Victorian Office, Box 2796Y, G.P.O., Melbourne, Vic. 3001, Australia. circ. 3,000.
Formerly: Australia. Bureau of Statistics. Victorian Office. Estimated Population and Dwellings by Local Government Areas.

312 AT ISSN 0067-1290
AUSTRALIA. BUREAU OF STATISTICS. WESTERN AUSTRALIAN OFFICE. POPULATION, DWELLINGS AND VITAL STATISTICS. 1950. a. free. Australian Bureau of Statistics, Western Australian Office, 1-3 St. George's Terrace, Perth, W.A. 6000, Australia. Ed. E. Binns. circ. 800. (processed)

309 BE
BELGIUM. INSTITUT NATIONAL DE STATISTIQUE. BEVOLKINGSSTATISTIEKEN. irreg. 320 Fr. Institut National de Statistique - Nationaal Instituut voor de Statistiek, Leuvenseweg 44, 1000 Brussels, Belgium.

312 BE ISSN 0067-5490
BELGIUM. INSTITUT NATIONAL DE STATISTIQUE. STATISTIQUES DEMOGRAPHIQUES. (Text in Dutch and French) 1969. irreg. (2-4/yr.) 200 Fr. Institut National de Statistique, 44 rue de Louvain, 1000 Brussels, Belgium.
Absorbed: Belgium. Institut National de Statistique. Mouvement de la Population des Communes.

312.2 BE
BELGIUM. INSTITUT NATIONAL DE STATISTIQUE. STATISTIQUES DES CAUSES DE DECES. irreg. 300 Fr. per no. Institut National de Statistique, 44 rue de Louvain, 1000 Brussels, Belgium.

312 PL ISSN 0067-7795
BIBLIOTEKA WIADOMOSCI STATYSTYCZNYCH.* 1967. irreg., no. 31, 1979. Glowny Urzad Statystyczny, Al. Niepodleglosci 208, Warsaw, Poland.

312 CN ISSN 0380-7533
CANADA. STATISTICS CANADA. CAUSES OF DEATH, PROVINCES BY SEX AND CANADA BY SEX AND AGE/CAUSES DE DECES, PAR PROVINCES SELON LE SEXE ET LE CANADA SELON LE SEXE ET L'AGE. (Catalogue 84-203) (Text in English and French) 1965. a. Can.$10($12) Statistics Canada, Publications Distribution, Ottawa, Ont. K1A 0V7, Canada. (also avail. in microform from MML)

312 CN ISSN 0708-7012
CANADA. STATISTICS CANADA. ESTIMATES OF POPULATION FOR CANADA AND THE PROVINCES/ESTIMATIONS DE LA POPULATION DU CANADA ET DES PROVINCES. (Catalog 91-201) (Text in English & French) 1922. a. Can.$3($3.60) Statistics Canada, Publications Distribution, Ottawa, Ont. K1A 0V7, Canada. (also avail. in microform from MML)

312 CN ISSN 0227-1796
CANADA. STATISTICS CANADA. ESTIMATION OF POPULATION BY MARITAL STATUS, AGE AND SEX, CANADA AND PROVINCES/ ESTIMATIONS DE LA POPULATION SUIVANT L'ETAT MATRIMONIAL, L'AGE ET LE SEXE, CANADA ET PROVINCES. (Catalog 91-203) (Text in English and French) 1931. a. Can.$6($7.20) Statistics Canada, Publications Distribution, Ottawa, Ont. K1A 0V7, Canada. (also avail. in microform from MML)
Formerly: Population Estimates by Marital Status, Age & Sex, Canada and Provinces/ Estimations de la Population Suivant l'Etat Matrimonial, l'Age et le Sexe, Canada et Provinces (ISSN 0575-934X)

CANADA. STATISTICS CANADA. FAMILY INCOMES(CENSUS FAMILIES) /REVENUS DES FAMILLE (FAMILLES DE RECENSEMENT) see *BUSINESS AND ECONOMICS — Abstracting, Bibliographies, Statistics*

314 IT ISSN 0010-4957
COMUNE DI ROMA. UFFICIO DI STATISTICA E CENSIMENTO. BOLLETTINO STATISTICO. 1877. irreg; latest 1968, no. 8. L.1500. Comune di Roma, Ufficio di Statistica e Censimento, Via della Greca 5, 00186 Rome, Italy. circ. 650.

CYPRUS. DEPARTMENT OF STATISTICS AND RESEARCH. TOURISM, MIGRATION AND TRAVEL STATISTICS. see *TRAVEL AND TOURISM — Abstracting, Bibliographies, Statistics*

312.8 CY ISSN 0590-4846
CYPRUS. DEPARTMENT OF STATISTICS AND RESEARCH. DEMOGRAPHIC REPORT. 1963. a. Mils.750. Department of Statistics and Research, Ministry of Finance, Nicosia, Cyprus.

312 BE
DEMOGRAFIE. (Text in Dutch; summaries in French) 1975. irreg. 270 Fr. Vrije Universiteit Brussel, Dienst Uitgaven, Waaglaan 13, 1050 Brussels, Belgium. bibl. charts. stat.

325.7287 PN ISSN 0378-4975
ESTADISTICA PANAMENA. SITUACION DEMOGRAFICA. SECCION 231. MIGRACION INTERNACIONAL. 1970. a. Bol.$.30. Direccion de Estadistica y Censo, Apartado 5213, Panama 5, Panama. circ. 800.

312 FI ISSN 0355-2128
FINLAND. TILASTOKESKUS. KUOLLEISUUS- JA ELOONJAAMISTAULUJA/FINLAND. STATISTIKCENTRALEN. DOEDLIGHETS- OCH LIVSLAENGDSTABELLER/FINLAND. CENTRAL STATISTICAL OFFICE. LIFE TABLES. (Section VI A of Official Statistics of Finland) (Text in Finnish, Swedish and English) 1924. irreg. Tilastokeskus, Annankatu 44, SF-00100 Helsinki 10, Finland (Subscr. to: Government Printing Centre, Box 516, SF-00100 Helsinki 10, Finland)

312 FI
FINLAND. TILASTOKESKUS. VAESTO/ FINLAND. STATISTIKCENTRALEN. BEFOLKNING/FINLAND. CENTRAL STATISTICAL OFFICE. POPULATION. (Text in Finnish, Swedish and English) 1871. a. price varies. Tilastokeskus, Annankatu 44, SF-00100 Helsinki 10, Finland (Subscr. to: Government Printing Centre, Box 516, SF-00100 Helsinki 10, Finland)
Formerly: Finland. Tilastokeskus. Vaestonmuutokset (ISSN 0430-5612)

312 FI ISSN 0355-2136
FINLAND. TILASTOKESKUS. VAESTOLASKENTA/FINLAND. STATISTIKCENTRALEN. FOLKRAEKNINGEN/FINLAND. CENTRAL STATISTICAL OFFICE. POPULATION CENSUS. (Section VI C of Official Statistics of Finland) (Text in Finnish, Swedish and English) 1950. irreg (every 10 years) price varies. Tilastokeskus, Annankatu 44, SF-00100 Helsinki 10, Finland (Subscr. to: Government Printing Centre, Box 516, SF-00100 Helsinki 10, Finland)

325   FR   ISSN 0071-903X
FRANCE. OFFICE NATIONAL D'IMMIGRATION. STATISTIQUES DE L'IMMIGRATION. 1967. a. Office National d'Immigration, Section Documentation-Statistiques, 44 rue Bargue, 75732 Paris Cedex 15, France.

312   GW   ISSN 0072-1786
GERMANY (FEDERAL REPUBLIC, 1949-) STATISTISCHES BUNDESAMT. FACHSERIE 1, REIHE 1: GEBIET UND BEVOELKERUNG. (Consists of several subseries) 1960. a. price varies. W. Kohlhammer-Verlag GmbH, Abt. Veroeffentlichungen des Statistischen Bundesamtes, Philipp-Reis-Str. 3, Postfach 421120, 6500 Mainz 42, W. Germany (B.R.D.)

312   GW   ISSN 0072-1794
GERMANY (FEDERAL REPUBLIC, 1949-) STATISTISCHES BUNDESAMT. FACHSERIE 1, REIHE 2: BEVOELKERUNGSBEWEGUNG. 1959. a. price varies. W. Kohlhammer-Verlag GmbH, Abt. Veroeffentlichungen des Statistischen Bundesamtes, Philipp-Reis-Str. 3, Postfach 421120, 6500 Mainz 42, W. Germany (B.R.D.)

312   GW   ISSN 0072-1808
GERMANY (FEDERAL REPUBLIC, 1949-) STATISTISCHES BUNDESAMT. FACHSERIE 1, REIHE 2.3: WANDERUNGEN. 1959. a. price varies. W. Kohlhammer-Verlag GmbH, Abt. Veroeffentlichungen des Statistischen Bundesamtes, Philipp-Reis-Str. 3, Postfach 421120, 6500 Mainz 42, W. Germany (B.R.D.)

312   GW
GERMANY (FEDERAL REPUBLIC, 1949-) STATISTISCHES BUNDESAMT. FACHSERIE 1, REIHE 3: HAUSHAELTE UND FAMILIEN. 1969. irreg. DM.13. W. Kohlhammer-Verlag GmbH, Abt. Veroeffentlichungen des Statistischen Bundesamtes, Philipp-Reis-Str. 3, Postfach 421120, 6500 Mainz 42, W. Germany (B.R.D.)

016   BE
GEZINSSOCIOLOGISCHE DOCUMENTATIE; Jaarboek. 1976. a. (Katholieke Universiteit Te Leuven, Sociologisch Onderzoeksinstituut) Uitgeverij Acco, Tiensestraat 134-136, B-3000 Leuven, Belgium. circ. 800.

325 331   IT   ISSN 0390-6450
ITALY. ISTITUTO CENTRALE DI STATISTICA. ANNUARIO DI STATISTICHE DEL LAVORO. 1959. a. L.6000. Istituto Centrale di Statistica, Via Cesare Balbo 16, 00100 Rome, Italy. circ. 1,100.
    Formerly: Annuario di Statistiche del Lavoro e dell'Emigrazione (ISSN 0075-1693)

312   LU   ISSN 0076-1613
LUXEMBOURG. SERVICE CENTRAL DE LA STATISTIQUE ET DES ETUDES ECONOMIQUES. COLLECTION RP: RECENSEMENTS DE LA POPULATION. 1962. irreg. price varies. Service Central de la Statistique et des Etudes Economiques, B.P. 304, Luxembourg, Luxembourg.

312   MW   ISSN 0076-3306
MALAWI. NATIONAL STATISTICAL OFFICE. POPULATION CENSUS FINAL REPORT. 1966. irreg. (probably every 10 yrs) K.8.50($10.20) ‡ National Statistical Office, P.O. Box 333, Zomba, Malawi.

312   MY
MALAYSIA. DEPARTMENT OF STATISTICS. VITAL STATISTICS: PENINSULAR MALAYSIA. (Text in English & Malay) 1964. a, latest 1976. M.$3. Department of Statistics - Jabatan Perangkaan, Jalan Young, Kuala Lumpur 10-01, Malaysia. stat. circ. 800. (processed)

312.097   US   ISSN 0091-9187
NEW JERSEY. OFFICE OF DEMOGRAPHIC AND ECONOMIC ANALYSIS. POPULATION ESTIMATES FOR NEW JERSEY. (Report year ends July 1) a. Department of Labor and Industry, Division of Planning & Research, Office of Demographic and Economic Analysis, Box 845, Trenton, NJ 08625.

312   NZ
NEW ZEALAND. DEPARTMENT OF STATISTICS. POPULATION CENSUS. LOCATION AND INCREASE OF POPULATION. PART A: POPULATION SIZE AND DISTRIBUTION. quinquennial, 1976 issued 1977. NZ.$1.10. Department of Statistics, Private Bag, Wellington, New Zealand (Subscr. to: Government Printing Office, Publications, Private Bag. Wellington, New Zealand)
    Supersedes in part: New Zealand. Department of Statistics. Population Census: Increase and Location of Population (ISSN 0077-9792)

312   NZ
NEW ZEALAND. DEPARTMENT OF STATISTICS. POPULATION CENSUS. LOCATION AND INCREASE OF POPULATION. PART B: POPULATION DENSITY. quinquennial, 1976 issued 1977. NZ.$2.20. Department of Statistics, Private Bag, Wellington, New Zealand (Subscr. to: Government Printing Office, Publications, Private Bag, Wellington, New Zealand)
    Supersedes in part: New Zealand. Department of Statistics. Population Census: Increase and Location of Populaion (ISSN 0077-9792)

312   US   ISSN 0078-1371
NORTH CAROLINA. DIVISION OF HEALTH SERVICES. PUBLIC HEALTH STATISTICS BRANCH. NORTH CAROLINA VITAL STATISTICS. 1916. a. free. ‡ Department of Human Resources, Division of Health Services, P.O. Box 2091, Raleigh, NC 27602.

301.4   NO
NORWAY. STATISTISK SENTRALBYRAA. FAMILIE STATISTIKK/FAMILY STATISTICS. (Subseries of its Norges Offisielle Statistikk) (Text in English and Norwegian) 1974. irreg. Kr.11. Statistisk Sentralbyraa, Box 8131 Dep., Oslo 1, Norway.

312   NO   ISSN 0550-7170
NORWAY. STATISTISK SENTRALBYRAA. FOLKEMENGDEN ETTER ALDER OG EKTESKAPELIG STATUS/POPULATION BY AGE AND MARITAL STATUS. (Subseries of its Norges Offisielle Statistikk) (Text in Norwegian and English) a. Kr.15. Statistisk Sentralbyraa, Box 8131 Dep., Oslo 1, Norway.

312   NO
NORWAY. STATISTISK SENTRALBYRAA. FRAMSKRIVING AV FOLKEMENGDEN: REGIONALE TALL/POPULATION PROJECTIONS: REGIONAL FIGURES. (Subseries of its Norges Offisielle Statistikk) irreg. Kr.11. Statistisk Sentralbyraa, Box 8131 Dep., Oslo 1, Norway.

312   US
OKLAHOMA POPULATION ESTIMATES. 1966. a. free. Employment Security Commission, Research & Planning Division, 310 Will Rogers Bldg., Oklahoma City, OK 73105. Ed. Roger Jacks. charts. stat. circ. 850.

315 312   PH
PHILIPPINES. NATIONAL CENSUS AND STATISTICS OFFICE. YEARBOOK. Short title: Philippine Yearbook. (Text in English) 1940. biennial. P.100($35) National Census and Statistics Office, Ramon Magsaysay Blvd., Box 779, Manila, Philippines. Ed. Bd.

317.3   US   ISSN 0079-2403
POCKET DATA BOOK, USA. 1967. biennial. price varies. U.S. Bureau of the Census, Dept. of Commerce, Washington, DC 20233 (Orders to: Supt. of Documents, Washington, DC 20402)

312   PL   ISSN 0079-2616
POLAND. GLOWNY URZAD STATYSTYCZNY. ROCZNIK DEMOGRAFICZNY. (Subseries of its: Statystyka Polski) (Text in Polish; summaries in English and Russian) 1968. a. 85 Zl. Glowny Urzad Statystyczny, Al. Niepodlegosci 208, 00-925 Warsaw, Poland.

312   SE
POPULATION GROWTH IN SEYCHELLES. irreg. President's Office, Statistics Division, Box 206, Mahe, Seychelles (Subscr. to: Government Printer, Box 205, Union Vale, Mahe, Seychelles)

312   UK   ISSN 0080-7869
SCOTLAND. REGISTRAR GENERAL. ANNUAL REPORT. 1855. a. price varies. H.M.S.O., P.O. Box 569, London SE1 9NH, England.

016 312   NE   ISSN 0167-4757
SELECTED ANNOTATED BIBLIOGRAPHY OF POPULATION STUDIES IN THE NETHERLANDS. (Text in English) 1975. a. fl.4.50 in the Netherlands; other countries free. Nederlands Interuniversitair Demografisch Instituut - Netherlands Interuniversity Demographic Institute, Prinses Beatrixlaan 428, Voorburg, Netherlands. (Co-sponsor: Netherlands Demographic Society) Ed. R.B.H. van der Heijde. circ. 750.

312   SA
SOUTH AFRICA. DEPARTMENT OF STATISTICS. REPORT ON BIRTHS: WHITE, COLOURED AND ASIANS. (Report No. 07-01) a., latest 1977. R.5.60. Department of Statistics, Private Bag X44, Pretoria 0001, South Africa (Orders to: Government Printer, Bosman St., Private Bag X85, Pretoria 0001, South Africa)
    Formerly: South Africa. Department of Statistics. Report on Births.

312.5   SA
SOUTH AFRICA. DEPARTMENT OF STATISTICS. REPORT ON MARRIAGES AND DIVORCES: SOUTH AFRICA. (Roport No. 07-02) 1972. a., latest 1977. R.5.50. Department of Statistics, Private Bag X44, Pretoria 0001, South Africa (Orders to: Government Printer, Bosman St., Private Bag X85, Pretoria 0001,South Africa)

301.32 916.804   SA
SOUTH AFRICA. DEPARTMENT OF STATISTICS. TOURISM AND MIGRATION. (Report No. 19-01) a., latest 1977. R.5.60. Department of Statistics, Private Bag X44, Pretoria 0001, South Africa (Orders to: Government Printer, Bosman St., Private Bag X85, Pretoria 0001, South Africa)

315 312   TH
SURVEY OF MIGRATION IN BANGKOK METROPOLIS. (Text in English and Thai) 1974. a. National Statistical Office, Lan Luang Rd., Bangkok, Thailand. charts. stat.

312   SW   ISSN 0082-0245
SWEDEN. STATISTISKA CENTRALBYRAAN. STATISTISKA MEDDELANDEN. SUBGROUP BE (POPULATION) (Text in Swedish; table heads and summaries in English) 1963 N.S. irreg. Kr.40. Liber Foerlag, Fack, S-162 89 Vaellingby, Sweden. circ. 1,700.

312   TU
TURKIYE OZETLI NUFUS BIBLIYOGRAFYASI. 1970. a. TL.40. University of Hacettepe, Institute of Population Studies - Hacettepe Universitesi, Nufus Etutleri Enstitusu, Ankara, Turkey. Ed. Behire Balkan.

U.S. NATIONAL CENTER FOR HEALTH STATISTICS. CURRENT LISTING AND TOPICAL INDEX TO THE VITAL AND HEALTH STATISTICS SERIES. see *PUBLIC HEALTH AND SAFETY — Abstracting, Bibliographies, Statistics*

314 312   IT
UNIVERSITA DEGLI STUDI DI PADOVA. FACOLTA DI SCIENZE STATISTICHE, DEMOGRAFICHE ED ATTUARIALI. SERIE ESTRATTI. 1969. irreg., no. 172, 1979. Universita degli Studi di Padova, Facolta di Scienze Statistiche, Demografiche ed Attuariali, Via VIII Febbraio 1, 35100 Padua, Italy. bibl.

314 312   IT
UNIVERSITA DEGLI STUDI DI PADOVA. FACOLTA DI SCIENZE STATISTICHE, DEMOGRAFICHE ED ATTUARIALI. SERIE PUBBLICAZIONI. 1971. irreg., no. 11, 1978. Universita degli Studi di Padova, Facolta di Scienze Statistiche, Demografiche ed Attuariali, Via VIII Febbraio 1, 35100 Padua, Italy.

POSTAL AFFAIRS

see Communications — Postal Affairs

POULTRY AND LIVESTOCK

see Agriculture—Poultry and Livestock

PRINTING

655 760   FR
AGENDA MEMENTO DES PROTES. 1948. a. 100 F. (Federation des Syndicats des Industries Polygraphiques et de la Communication) France Lafayette, 10 rue Bleue, 75009 Paris, France.
Formerly: Agenda Memento des Cadres et Maitrises de l'Imprimerie, de l'Edition et des Industries Graphiques (ISSN 0084-6023)

BIBLIOTHECA HUNGARICA ANTIQUA. see *PUBLISHING AND BOOK TRADE*

052   UK   ISSN 0307-434X
BRITISH DIRECTORY OF LITTLE MAGAZINES AND SMALL PRESSES. 1975. irreg. $2.50. Dustbooks, 56 Blakes Lane, New Malden KT3 6NX, England.

686.2   UK
BRITISH PRINTER DATAGUIDE. 1978. a. £12.50($22) Maclean-Hunter Ltd., 30 Old Burlington St., London, W1X 2AE, England. Ed. Frances Helby.
Supersedes in part: British Printer Specification Manual (ISSN 0068-239X)

686.2   FR   ISSN 0572-7529
BUREAU INTERNATIONAL DES SOCIETES GERANT LES DROITS D'ENREGISTREMENT ET DE REPRODUCTION MECANIQUE. BULLETIN. irreg. International Bureau of the Societies Administering the Rights of Mechanical Recording and Reproduction, 12 rue Ballu, 75009 Paris, France.

CAMBRIDGE AUTHORS' AND PUBLISHERS' GUIDES. see *PUBLISHING AND BOOK TRADE*

CATALOGO NAZIONALE BOLAFFI DELLA GRAFICA. see *ART*

CENTRE NATIONAL D'ARCHEOLOGIE ET D'HISTOIRE DU LIVRE. PUBLICATION. see *ARCHAEOLOGY*

760   FR
COURRIER TECHNIQUE ARTS GRAPHIQUES. irreg., no. 26, 1975. Kodak-Pathe, Division Marches et Graphiques, 8 et 14 rue Villiot, 75580 Paris Cedex 12, France. Ed. Claude Vimeux.

655   FR
FACONNAGE DE L'IMPRIME. a. 69.50 F. Societe des Editions de l'Imprimerie Nouvelle, 89 rue Barrault, 75013 Paris, France. Ed. E. Mauduit. adv. circ. 6,000.

655.255   US   ISSN 0015-2803
FIRST TO FINAL. 1957. irreg. ‡ Proofreaders Club of New York, 38-15 149 St, Flushing, NY 11354. Ed. Allan Treshan. circ. 700. (back issues avail.)

686.2   GW
FOGRA-LITERATUR-PROFIL. 1975. irreg. (4-6/yr) DM.500 to individuals; members DM. 150. Deutsche Forschungsgesellschaft fuer Druck- und Reproduktionstechnik e.V. (FOGRA), Postfach 800469, Streitfeldstr. 19, 8000 Munich 80, W. Germany(B.R.D.)

331.88   US   ISSN 0094-4211
G.A.I.U. HANDBOOK OF WAGES, HOURS AND FRINGE BENEFITS. irreg. Graphic Arts International Union, Contract & Research Department, 1900 L St. N.W., Washington, DC 20036.

686.232   US   ISSN 0534-0489
G R I NEWSLETTER. 1962. irreg. (approx. 3-4/yr.) membership only. ‡ Gravure Research Institute, 22 Manhasset Avenue, Port Washington, NY 11050. Ed. Harvey F. George. bk. rev. charts. illus. pat. stat. cum.index. circ. 600 (controlled) (back issues avail)

655   US   ISSN 0147-1651
GRAPHIC ARTS GREEN BOOK; directory of graphic arts operating firms in Illinois, Indiana, Michigan and Wisconsin. 1970. a. $51.85. A.F. Lewis & Co., Inc., 15 Spinning Wheel Rd., Hinsdale, IL 60521 (And 853 Broadway, New York, NY 10003) Ed. L. Bauer. adv. circ. 10,000.
Formerly: Graphic Arts Trade Directory and Register (ISSN 0072-5498)

760   US   ISSN 0096-1159
GRAPHIC ARTS TECHNICAL FOUNDATION. RESEARCH PROJECT REPORT. 1947. irreg (approx. 6-8/yr.) $0.60 to members; $3.75 to non-members. ‡ Graphic Arts Technical Foundation, 4615 Forbes Ave, Pittsburgh, PA 15213. Ed. Mary Pat David.
Formerly (to April 1974, no. 101): Graphic Arts Technical Foundation. Research Progress Report.

760   US   ISSN 0160-0303
GRAPHIC COMMUNICATIONS MARKETPLACE. a. $15. Technical Information, Inc., Box 775, S. Lake Tahoe, CA 95705.

GRAPHIS ANNUAL; international annual of advertising and editorial graphics. see *ART*

763   AU   ISSN 0075-2266
GRAPHISCHE UNTERNEHMUNGEN OESTERREICHS. JAHRBUCH. 1930. a. S.150. Hauptverband der Graphischen Unternehmungen Oesterreichs, Gruenangergasse 4, A-1010 Vienna, Austria. adv. circ. 950.

686.2   US   ISSN 0091-5203
GRAVURE ENVIRONMENTAL AND O S H A NEWSLETTER. (Occupational Safety and Health Act) 1972. irreg. (approx. 3-4 yr.) membership. ‡ Gravure Research Institute, Environmental and O S H A Committee, 22 Manhasset Ave., Port Washington, NY 11050. (Co-sponsor: Gravure Technical Association) Ed. Harvey F. George. bk. rev. charts. illus. pat. stat. circ. 1,000 (controlled) (back issues available)

686.2   FR
GUTENBERG; annuaire des industries graphiques. 1936. a. 200 F. Editions Technorama, 31 Place Saint Ferdinand, 75017 Paris, France. Ed. R. Baschet. circ. 2,500.

943 655   GW   ISSN 0072-9094
GUTENBERG-JAHRBUCH. 1926. a. DM.40. Gutenberg-Gesellschaft, Liebfrauenplatz 5, 6500 Mainz, W. Germany (B.R.D.) Ed. Hans-Joachim Koppitz. adv. circ. 2,500.

686.2   GW   ISSN 0073-0173
HANDBUCH FUER DIE DRUCKINDUSTRIE BERLIN. 1946. a. DM.10. Kupijai und Prochnow, Verlag und Druckerei, Bluecherstr. 22, 1000 Berlin 61, W. Germany (B. R. D.)

686.2   GW
HANDSATZLETTER; Monografien der modernen Typographie. 1967. irreg. free. Johannes Wagner Schriftgiesserei und Messinglinienfabrik, Theodor-Heuss-Strasse 49, Postfach 227, 8070 Ingolstadt, W. Germany (B.R.D.) Ed. A. Droese. circ. 7,000.

760   GW   ISSN 0073-5620
IMPRIMATUR; JAHRBUCH FUER BUECHERFREUNDE. NEUE FOLGE. a. price varies. Gesellschaft der Bibliophilen, Merckstr. 32, 6100 Darmstadt, W. Germany (B.R.D.)

INDIAN & EASTERN NEWSPAPER SOCIETY PRESS HANDBOOK. see *JOURNALISM*

686.2   GW   ISSN 0170-3463
INDUSTRIEGEWERKSCHAFT DRUCK UND PAPIER. SCHRIFTENREIHE FUER BETRIEBSRATE. 1969. irreg. exchange basis. Industriegewerkschaft Druck und Papier, Friedrichstr. 15, Postfach 1282, 7000 Stuttgart 1, W. Germany (B.R.D.) Ed. Bd. charts. illus.

ISRAEL BOOK TRADE DIRECTORY; a guide to publishers, printers and a book trade services in Israel. see *PUBLISHING AND BOOK TRADE*

655   JA   ISSN 0546-0719
JAPAN PRINTING ART ANNUAL/NIHON INSATSU NENKAN. a. Japan Printing News Co., Ltd. - Nippon Insatsu Shinbunsha, 1-16-8 Shintomi, Chuo-ku, Tokyo 104, Japan. circ. 4,500.

686.221   JA
JAPAN TYPOGRAPHY ANNUAL/NIHON TAIPOGURAFI NENKAN. (Text in Japanese; title and captions for plates in English) 1974. a. $30. (Japan Typography Association - Nihon Tapogurafi Kyokai) Gurafikkusha, Box 102, 1-9-12 Kudan Kita, Chiyoda-ku, Tokyo, Japan (Overseas Distributor: Orion Books, Export Dept., 1-58 Kanda Jimbocho, Chiyoda-ku, Tokyo 101, Japan) illus.
Continues: Nihon Retaringu Nenkan.

760   FR
MATERIEL GRAPHIQUE. 1958. a. 180 F. Societe des Editions de l' Imprimerie Nouvelle, 89 rue Barrault, F-75013 Paris, France. Ed. M. Mauduit. circ. 6,000.

760   UK   ISSN 0079-0710
PENROSE ANNUAL; international review of the graphic arts. 1895. a. £12.50. Northwood Publications Ltd, Elm House, 10-16 Elm St., London WC1X OBP, England (Dist. in U.S. by: Hastings House Publishers, Inc., 10 E. 40th St., New York, NY 10016)

POLONIA TYPOGRAPHICA SAECULI SEDECIMI. see *ART*

760   NE   ISSN 0032-7476
PRENT 190; new circle of collectors of modern graphic art. 1965. a. fl.550. Gerlach en Co. B. V., Art Section, Schiphol-Center, Amsterdam, Netherlands.

665.1   UK   ISSN 0079-5321
PRINTING HISTORICAL SOCIETY. JOURNAL. 1965. £8 to members. Printing Historical Society, St. Bride Institute, Bride Lane, Fleet St, London E.C.4, England. Ed. James Mosley. circ. 1,000.

686.2   UK   ISSN 0308-1443
PRINTING INDUSTRIES ANNUAL. 1919. a. £30. ‡ British Printing Industries Federation, 11 Bedford Row, London, WC1R 4DX, England. adv. index. circ. 1,200.
Formerly: British Federation of Master Printers. Master Printers Annual (ISSN 0068-1989)

655   US   ISSN 0193-3949
PRINTING TRADES BLUE BOOK. DELAWARE VALLEY-OHIO EDITION; directory of graphic arts operating firms in Ohio, Pennsylvania, Delaware, Maryland, District of Columbia, and its Virginia suburbs. 1979. biennial. $51.85. A.F. Lewis & Co., Inc. (New York), c/o Harrie F. Lewis, 79 Madison Ave., New York, NY 10016. adv. circ. 5,250.

655   US   ISSN 0079-5348
PRINTING TRADES BLUE BOOK. NEW YORK EDITION; directory of graphic arts operating firms in metropolitan New York and New Jersey. 1910. a. $51.85. A.F. Lewis and Co., Inc. (New York), c/o Harrie F. Lewis, 79 Madison Ave., New York, NY 10016. adv. index. circ. 5,250.

655   US   ISSN 0079-5356
PRINTING TRADES BLUE BOOK. NORTHEASTERN EDITION; directory of graphic arts operating firms in New England and upstate New York. 1962/63. biennial. $51.85. A.F. Lewis and Co., Inc. (New York), c/o Harrie F. Lewis, 79 Madison Ave., New York, NY 10016. adv. index. circ. 5,250.

655   US   ISSN 0079-5364
PRINTING TRADES BLUE BOOK. SOUTHEASTERN EDITION; in Virginia (except D.C. suburbs), W. Virginia, North Carolina, South Carolina, Georgia, Florida, Kentucky, Tennessee, Alabama, Mississippi, and Louisiana. 1961-62. biennial. $51.85. A. F.Lewis and Co., Inc. (New York), 79 Madison Ave., 853 Broadway, New York, NY 10016. adv. index. circ. 5,250.

655   UK   ISSN 0079-5372
PRINTING TRADES DIRECTORY. 1960. a. £22. Benn Publications Ltd., 25 New Street Square, London EC4A 3JA, England. Ed. John Hedges. adv. index. circ. 2,500.

655   FR   ISSN 0066-3638
QUATRE MILLE IMPRIMERIES FRANCAISES.
1960. a. 248.30 F. Societe des Editions de l' Imprimerie Nouvelle, 89 rue Barrault, 75013 Paris, France.
Before 1966: Quatre Mille Imprimeries.

760   US   ISSN 0082-2299
T A G A PROCEEDINGS; technical papers presented at annual meeting. 1949. a. $40. Technical Association of the Graphic Arts, Box 3064 Federal Station, Rochester, NY 14614. index.cum.index: 1949-1966. (back issues avail.)

760   FI   ISSN 0355-3566
VALTION TEKNILLINEN TUTKIMUSKESKUS. GRAAFINEN LABBORATORIO. TIEDONANTO/TECHNICAL RESEARCH CENTRE OF FINLAND. GRAPHIC ARTS LABORATORY. REPORT. (Text mainly in Finnish, some in English or Swedish) 1972. irreg. price varies. Valtion Teknillinen Tutkimuskeskus - Technical Research Centre of Finland, Vuorimiehentie 5, 02150 Espoo 15, Finland.

PRODUCTION OF GOODS AND SERVICES

see Business and Economics—Production of Goods and Services

PROTESTANTISM

see Religions and Theology—Protestant

PSYCHIATRY AND NEUROLOGY

see Medical Sciences—Psychiatry and Neurology

PSYCHOLOGY

see also Medical Sciences—Psychiatry and Neurology

150   US
ACADEMIC PRESS SERIES IN COGNITION AND PERCEPTION. irreg., unnumbered, latest 1979. price varies. Academic Press, Inc. (Subsidiary of: Harcourt Brace Jovanovich) 111 Fifth Ave., New York, NY 10003. Eds. Edward C. Carterette, Morton P. Friedman.

155   SW   ISSN 0065-1605
ACTA PSYCHOLOGICA-GOTHOBURGENSIA.* (Text in English) 1956. irreg. price varies. Goeteborgs Universitet, Department of Psychology, Fack, S-400 20 Goeteborg 14, Sweden. Ed. John Elmgren.

150   130   CH   ISSN 0065-1613
ACTA PSYCHOLOGICA TAIWANICA. (Text in Chinese and English) 1958. a. $5. Chinese Psychological Association, c/o Department of Psychology, National Taiwan University, Taipei, Taiwan, Republic of China. Ed. Dr. Chao-Ming Cheng. adv. circ. 200. (back issues avail.) Indexed: Psychol.Abstr. SSCI.

155   618.92   US   ISSN 0065-2407
ADVANCES IN CHILD DEVELOPMENT AND BEHAVIOR. 1963. irreg., vol. 14, 1979. price varies. Academic Press, Inc., 111 Fifth Ave, New York, NY 10003. Eds. Hanye W. Reese. L. P. Lipsitt. index. (also avail. in microfiche) Indexed: Ind.Med.

155.4   US   ISSN 0149-4732
ADVANCES IN CLINICAL CHILD PSYCHOLOGY. 1977. a. Plenum Publishing Corp., 233 Spring St., New York, NY 10013. Eds. Benjamin Lahey, Alan Kazdin.
Child

ADVANCES IN EXPERIMENTAL SOCIAL PSYCHOLOGY. see SOCIOLOGY

301.1   US
ADVANCES IN FAMILY INTERVENTION ASSESSMENT AND THEORY. 1980. a. J A I Press, Box 1285, 165 W. Putnam Ave., Greenwich, CT 06830. Ed. John P. Vincent.

150   US   ISSN 0163-5379
ADVANCES IN INSTRUCTIONAL PSYCHOLOGY. 1978. irreg. Lawrence Erlbaum Associates, Publishers, 62 Maria Dr., Hillsdale, NJ 07642.

ADVANCES IN MENTAL HANDICAP RESEARCH. see MEDICAL SCIENCES — Psychiatry And Neurology

150   US   ISSN 0065-3241
ADVANCES IN PSYCHOBIOLOGY. 1972. irreg., vol. 3, 1976. John Wiley & Sons, Inc., 605 Third Ave., New York, NY 10016. Eds. G. Newton, A. Riesen. Indexed: Ind.Med.

150   US   ISSN 0065-325X
ADVANCES IN PSYCHOLOGICAL ASSESSMENT. 1968. irreg, vol. 4, 1978. $25. Jossey-Bass, Inc., Publishers, 433 California St., San Francisco, CA 94104. Ed. Paul McReynolds. (reprint service avail. from UMI)

150   US   ISSN 0065-3454
ADVANCES IN THE STUDY OF BEHAVIOR. 1965. irreg., vol. 10, 1979. price varies. Academic Press, Inc., 111 Fifth Ave, New York, NY 10003. Eds. D.S. Lehrman, R. Hinde, E. Shaw. index.

150   301.16   US
ADVANCES IN THE STUDY OF COMMUNICATION AND AFFECT. 1974. irreg. price varies. Plenum Press, 233 Spring St., New York, NY 10013. Ed.Bd.

157   US
AMERICAN ASSOCIATION OF SUICIDOLOGY. PROCEEDINGS OF THE ANNUAL MEETING. 1975, 8th. a. price varies. American Association of Suicidology, Box 3264, Houston, TX 77001. Ed. Pamela Cantor. circ. 500-1,000. (looseleaf format; back issues avail.)

150   US
AMERICAN BOARD OF PROFESSIONAL PSYCHOLOGY. POLICIES AND PROCEDURES FOR THE CREATION OF DIPLOMATES IN PROFESSIONAL PSYCHOLOGY.* 1947. a. American Board of Professional Psychology, c/o Dr. Margaret Ives, 2025 I St. N.W., Suite 405, Washington, DC 20006.

150   340   US
AMERICAN LECTURES IN BEHAVIORAL SCIENCE AND LAW. irreg. price varies. Charles C. Thomas, Publisher, 301-327 E. Lawrence Ave., Springfield, IL 62717.

150   US
AMERICAN LECTURES IN PSYCHOLOGY. irreg. price varies. Charles C. Thomas, Publisher, 301-327 E. Lawrence Ave., Springfield, IL 62717.

150   301   US
AMERICAN LECTURES IN SOCIAL AND REHABILITATION PSYCHOLOGY. irreg. price varies. Charles C. Thomas, Publisher, 301-327 E. Lawrence Ave., Springfield, IL 62717.

150   US   ISSN 0065-9843
AMERICAN PSYCHOANALYTIC ASSOCIATION. JOURNAL. MONOGRAPH. 1953. irreg., 1971, no. 4. International Universities Press, Inc., 315 Fifth Ave., New York, NY 10016. Indexed: SSCI.

616.89   US
AMERICAN PSYCHOANALYTIC ASSOCIATION. ROSTER. a. $7. American Psychoanalytic Association, 1 E. 57th St., New York, NY 10027. circ. 3,000.

AMERICAN PSYCHOLOGICAL ASSOCIATION. DIRECTORY. see BIOGRAPHY

AMERICAN PSYCHOLOGICAL ASSOCIATION. MEMBERSHIP REGISTER. see BIOGRAPHY

157.72   616.855   US   ISSN 0065-9886
AMERICAN PSYCHOPATHOLOGICAL ASSOCIATION. PUBLICATIONS. irreg., 1970, vol. 26, 59th meeting. Johns Hopkins University Press, Baltimore, MD 21218. Eds. J. Zubin, A. Freedman. index.

301.1   150   IO
ANDA; majalah psikologi populer. irreg. Yayasan Bina Psikologi, c/o Mulyono & Associates, Gedung Pant Trisula, Jalan Menteng Raya 35, Box 3216, Jakarta, Indonesia.

ANNUAL EDITIONS: READINGS IN HUMAN SEXUALITY. see BIOLOGY

155.2   US   ISSN 0198-912X
ANNUAL EDITIONS: READINGS IN PERSONAL GROWTH AND ADJUSTMENT. Short title: Readings in Personal Growth and Adjustment. a. $5.75. Dushkin Publishing Group, Sluice Dock, Guilford, CT 06437. illus.
Formerly: Annual Editions: Readings in Personality and Adjustment (ISSN 0361-3836)

150   US
ANNUAL EDITIONS: READINGS IN PSYCHOLOGY. a. price varies. Dushkin Publishing Group, Sluice Dock, Guilford, CT 06437.

150   US   ISSN 0092-5055
ANNUAL OF PSYCHOANALYSIS. 1973. a. $22.50. (Chicago Institute for Psychoanalysis) International Universities Press, Inc., 315 Fifth Ave., New York, NY 10016. Indexed: Psychol.Abstr.

370   JA   ISSN 0452-9650
ANNUAL REPORT OF EDUCATIONAL PSYCHOLOGY IN JAPAN/KYOIKU SHINRIGAKU NEMPO. 1961. a. Japanese Association of Educational Psychology - Nihon Kyoiku-shinri Gakkai, c/o Faculty of Education, University of Tokyo, 7-3-1 Hongo, Bunkyo-ku, Tokyo 113, Japan.

616.8   US   ISSN 0091-6595
ANNUAL REVIEW OF BEHAVIOR THERAPY THEORY & PRACTICE. 1973. a. price varies. Guilford Press, 200 Park Av. S., New York, NY 10003. Eds. Cyril M. Franks, G. Terrence Wilson.

150   US   ISSN 0066-4308
ANNUAL REVIEW OF PSYCHOLOGY. 1950. a. $20. Annual Reviews Inc., 4139 El Camino Way, Palo Alto, CA 94306. Eds. Lyman W. Porter, Mark R. Rosenzweig. bibl. index cum.index. (back issues avail.; reprint service avail. from ISI) Indexed: Biol.Abstr. Chem.Abstr. Ind.Med. Psychol.Abstr. SSCI. Child Devel.Abstr. DSH Abstr. Lang. & Lang.Behav.Abstr. M.M.R.I.

150   SP   ISSN 0066-5126
ANUARIO DE PSICOLOGIA. (Text in Spanish; summaries in English and French) 1969. a.(in 2 pts) $6. ‡ Universidad de Barcelona, Departmento de Psicologia, Nucleo Universitario, Barcelona 14, Barcelona, Spain. Ed. Miguel Siguan. bk. rev. circ. 250. Indexed: Psychol.Abstr.

ANUARIO DE SOCIOLOGIA Y PSICOLOGIA JURIDICAS. see LAW

ARCHIV FUER RELIGIONSPSYCHOLOGIE. see RELIGIONS AND THEOLOGY

BASIC CONCEPTS IN EDUCATIONAL PSYCHOLOGY SERIES. see EDUCATION

150   US
BASIC CONCEPTS IN PSYCHOLOGY SERIES. irreg. price varies. Brooks-Cole Publishing Co., 555 Abrego St., Monterey, CA 93940.

616.89   US   ISSN 0191-5681
BEHAVIORAL GROUP THERAPY. 1979. a. Research Press Co., 2612 N. Mattis Ave., Champaign, IL 61820.

150 SZ ISSN 0067-5075
BEITRAEGE ZUR HEILPAEDAGOGIK UND
HEILPAEDAGOGISCHEN PSYCHOLOGIE.
1963. irreg. price varies. Verlag Hans Huber,
Laenggassstr. 76 und Marktgasse 9, CH-3000 Berne
9, Switzerland (Dist. by Williams & Wilkins
Company, 428 E. Preston St., Baltimore, MD
21202) Ed. P. Moor.

157 GW
BEITRAEGE ZUR INDIVIDUALPSYCHOLOGIE.
1978. irreg. price varies. Ernst Reinhardt GmbH
und Co., Verlag, Kemnatenstr. 46, 8000 Munich 19,
W. Germany (B.R.D.)

155.4 GW
BEITRAEGE ZUR PSYCHODIAGNOSTIK DES
KINDES. 1972. irreg., no. 3, 1978. price varies.
Ernst Reinhardt GmbH und Co., Verlag,
Kemnatenstr. 46, 8000 Munich 19, W. Germany
(B.R.D.) Eds. G. Biermann, M. Kos.

614.58 GW
BEITRAEGE ZUR PSYCHOLOGIE UND
SOZIOLOGIE DES KRANKEN MENSCHEN.
1974. irreg., no. 4, 1978. price varies. Ernst
Reinhardt GmbH und Co., Verlag, Kemnatenstr. 46,
8000 Munich 19, W. Germany (B.R.D.) Eds. G.
Biermann, J.von Troschke.

155.2 GW ISSN 0067-5210
BEITRAEGE ZUR SEXUALFORSCHUNG. 1952.
irreg., vol. 57, 1978. price varies. (Deutsche
Gesellschaft fuer Sexualforschung) Ferdinand Enke
Verlag, Herdweg 63, 7000 Stuttgart 1, W. Germany
(B.R.D.) Ed.Bd. Indexed: Ind.Med.

150 610 US ISSN 0094-0895
BIOFEEDBACK SOCIETY OF AMERICA.
PROCEEDINGS OF THE ANNUAL MEETING.
(Former name of organization: Biofeedback
Research Society) 1972. a. $12 to non-members;
members $10. Biofeedback Society of America,
U.C.M.C. C268, 4200 E. 9th Ave., Denver, CO
80262. Ed. Francine Butler. circ. 2,000. (looseleaf
format)

BIRD BEHAVIOUR; an international and
multidisciplinary journal. see *BIOLOGY —
Ornithology*

150 AT
BULLETIN FOR PSYCHOLOGISTS. 1965. irreg.
Australian Council for Educational Research, P.O.
Box 210, Hawthorn, Vic. 3122, Australia.

150 CN ISSN 0068-9211
CANADIAN MENTAL HEALTH ASSOCIATION.
ANNUAL REPORT/ASSOCIATION
CANADIENNE POUR LA SANTE MENTALE.
RAPPORT ANNUEL. 1926. a. free. Canadian
Mental Health Association, 2160 Yonge Street,
Toronto, Ont. M4S 2Z3, Canada.

CASE ANALYSIS IN SOCIAL SCIENCE N
SOCIAL THERAPY. see *SOCIAL SCIENCES:
COMPREHENSIVE WORKS*

155.2 US ISSN 0009-1669
CHARACTER POTENTIAL; a record of research.
1962. irreg. $10 per vol. of 4 issues. Union College
(Schenectady), Character Research Project, 207
State St., Schenectady, NY 12305. Ed. John H.
Peatling. bibl. charts. cum.index: vols. 1-8. circ.
1,000. (also avail. in microform from UMI; reprint
service avail. from UMI) Indexed: Curr.Cont.
Psychol.Abstr. Psychol.R.G.

CHILD BEHAVIOR AND DEVELOPMENT. see
MEDICAL SCIENCES — Pediatrics

614.7 150 155.4 US
CHILDHOOD CITY NEWSLETTER. 1975. irreg. (4-
6/yr.) $3 domestic; $4 foreign. City University of
New York, Graduate Center, Environmental
Psychology Program, 33 West 42nd St., New York,
NY 10036. Ed. Bd. bk. rev. bibl. circ. 650.

COGNITION AND LANGUAGE; a series in
psycholinguistics. see *LINGUISTICS*

COMMISSION OF THE EUROPEAN
COMMUNITIES. COLLECTION PHYSIOLOGIE
ET PSYCHOLOGIE DU TRAVAIL. see
*BUSINESS AND ECONOMICS — Labor And
Industrial Relations*

370.15 157 US ISSN 0090-693X
COMMUNITY-CLINICAL PSYCHOLOGY SERIES.
Variant title: Community Psychology Series. 1973.
irreg., vol. 4, 1977. price varies per vol. (American
Psychological Association, Division of Community
Psychology) Human Sciences Press, 72 Fifth Ave.,
New York, NY 10011. Ed. Daniel Adelson. (reprint
service avail. from ISI,UMI) Key Title: Continuing
Series in Community Clinical Psychology.

150 301 US
COMMUNITY PSYCHOLOGY SERIES. 1972.
irreg., vol. 4, 1977. (American Psychological
Association, Division of Community Psychology)
Human Sciences Press, 72 Fifth Ave., New York,
NY 10011. Ed. Daniel Adelson. (reprint service
avail. from ISI,UMI)

150 US
COMPARATIVE STUDIES IN BEHAVIORAL
SCIENCE: A WILEY SERIES. 1970. irreg., latest
vol. 1975. John Wiley & Sons, Inc., 605 Third Ave.,
New York, NY 10016. Eds. R.T. Holt, J.E. Turner.

CONFERENCE ON EMPIRICAL RESEARCH IN
BLACK PSYCHOLOGY. see *EDUCATION —
Higher Education*

150 US ISSN 0069-8768
CONFERENCE ON VETERANS
ADMINISTRATION STUDIES IN MENTAL
HEALTH AND BEHAVIORAL SCIENCES.
HIGHLIGHTS. 1958. a. free. ‡ U. S. Veterans
Administration, Dept. of Medicine and Surgery, 810
Vermont Avenue, N.W., Washington, DC 20420.
Ed. C. James Klett.
  Formerly: Conference on Veterans
Administartion Cooperative Studies in Mental
Health and Behavioral Sciences Highlights.

616.89 BL
CONTRIBUICOES EM PSICOLOGIA,
PSIQUIATRIA E PSICANALISE. irreg. Editora
Campus Ltda (Subsidiary of: Elsevier North-
Holland, Inc) Rua Japeri 35, 20000 Rio de Janeiro
RJ, Brazil.

150 301.2 US
CROSS CULTURAL RESEARCH AND
METHODOLOGY SERIES. 1975. irreg., vol. 4,
1978. price varies. Sage Publications, Inc., 275 S.
Beverly Dr., Beverly Hills, CA 90212 (And Sage
Publications, Ltd., 28 Banner St., London EC1Y
8QE, England) Ed. Walter J. Lonner, John W.
Berry.

150 CL
CUADERNOS DE PSICOLOGIA.* 1972.
Universidad de Chile, Departamento de Psicologia,
Av. Bernardo O'Higgins 1058, Casilla 10-D,
Santiago, Chile. illus.

150 CK
CUADERNOS DE PSICOLOGIA. 1976. a. $3.
Universidad del Valle, Departmento de Psicologia,
Apdo Aereo 2188, Cali, Colombia. bk. rev. circ.
500.

155 US
CURRENT AUDIOVISUALS FOR MENTAL
HEALTH EDUCATION. irreg., 2nd edt., 1979.
$8.50. (Mental Health Materials Center) Marquis
Academic Media, 200 E. Ohio St., Chicago, IL
60611.

150 US ISSN 0070-2145
CURRENT TOPICS IN CLINICAL AND
COMMUNITY PSYCHOLOGY. 1969. irreg., vol.
3, 1971. price varies. Academic Press, Inc., 111
Fifth Ave, New York, NY 10003. Ed. C.D.
Spielberger.

155.937 US ISSN 0275-3510
DEATH EDUCATION AND THANATOLOGY.
1979. irreg., unnumbered. price varies. Hemisphere
Publishing Corporation, 1025 Vermont Ave., N.W.,
Washington, DC 20005 (Subscr. to: 19 W.44th St.,
New York, NY 10036) Ed. Hannelore Wass.

DIRECTORY FOR EXCEPTIONAL CHILDREN; a
listing of educational and training facilities. see
*EDUCATION — Special Education And
Rehabilitation*

150 301 370 US
DIRECTORY OF UNPUBLISHED
EXPERIMENTAL MENTAL MEASURES. 1973.
irreg. Human Sciences Press, 72 Fifth Ave., New
York, NY 10011. (reprint service avail. from
ISI,UMI)

150 US ISSN 0070-7716
DUQUESNE STUDIES. PSYCHOLOGICAL
SERIES. 1963. irreg. price varies. Duquesne
University Press, 600 Forbes Ave, Pittsburgh, PA
15219 (Dist. by Humanities Press, Inc., Atlantic
Highlands, NJ 07716) Ed. Amedeo Giorgi.

140 US
DUQUESNE STUDIES IN
PHENOMENOLOGICAL PSYCHOLOGY. 1971.
triennial. price varies. Duquesne University Press,
600 Forbes Avenue, Pittsburgh, PA 15219. Ed. A.
Giorgi.

E R I C CLEARINGHOUSE ON TESTS,
MEASUREMENT, AND EVALUATION. T M
REPORT SERIES. see *EDUCATION*

370 150 SW ISSN 0070-9263
EDUCATIONAL AND PSYCHOLOGICAL
INTERACTIONS. (Text in English) 1964. irreg.
free. Laerarhoegskolan i Malmoe, Pedagogisk-
Psykologiska Institutionen, Box 23501, S-200 45
Malmoe, Sweden. Ed. Aake Bjerstedt. Indexed:
Child Devel.Abstr. Psychol.Abstr. Sociol.Abstr.

158 UR
EKSPERIMENTAL'NAYA I PRIKLADNAYA
PSIKHOLOGIYA. vyp. 8, 1977. irreg. 0.80 Rub.
per issue. Izdatel'stvo Leningradskii Universitet,
Universitetskaya Nab. 7/9, Leningrad B-164,
U.S.S.R. circ. 5,150.

150 UR
EKSPERIMENTAL'NOE ISSLEDOVANIE
LICHNOSTI I TEMPERAMENTA. (Subseries of:
Permskii Gosudarstvennyi Pedagogicheskii Institut.
Uchenye Zapiski) irreg. 0.50 Rub. Permskii
Gosudarstvennyi Pedagogicheskii Institut, Perm,
U.S.S.R. illus.

616.89 US
ENCOUNTERER. 1971. irreg. $5 for 20 nos. Golden
Gate Foundation for Group Treatment, Box 1141,
Vallejo, CA 94590. Ed. Dr. F. H. Ernst.

616.891 BL ISSN 0014-1593
ESTUDOS DE PSICANALISE. (Text in Portuguese;
summaries in English & Portuguese) 1969. a.
cr.24($10) Universidade Estadual de Londrina,
Centro de Ciencias Humanas, Circulo de Estudos
Linguisticos, C.P. 2111, 86100 Londrina, Parana,
Brazil. Ed. Elias Hadad. abstr. circ. controlled.
Indexed: Psychol.Abstr. SSCI.
Psychoanalysis

301.15 US
EUROPEAN MONOGRAPHS IN SOCIAL
PSYCHOLOGY. 1971. irreg., vol. 14, 1978. price
varies. (European Association of Experimental
Social Psychology) Academic Press, Inc., 111 Fifth
Avenue, New York, NY 10003. Ed. Henri Tajfel.

150 US ISSN 0071-3295
EXCEPTIONAL INFANT. 1967. irreg., vol. 4, 1980.
price varies. Brunner-Mazel, Inc., 19 Union Sq. W.,
New York, NY 10003. Ed. Jerome Hellmuth.

150 US ISSN 0014-4967
EXPLORATIONS. 1964. irreg. free. Explorations
Institute, Box 1254, Berkeley, CA 94701. Ed. James
Elliott. adv. bk. rev. film rev. circ. 1,500. (back
issues avail.)

301.1 150 FR
FACTUELLES. 1977. irreg. Editions Copernic, B.P.
129, 75326 Paris Cedex 07, France. Dir. Alain de
Benoist.

614.58 US
FLORIDA. MENTAL HEALTH PROGRAM
OFFICE. STATISTICAL REPORT OF
COMMUNITY MENTAL HEALTH
PROGRAMS. a. Division of Mental Health, 1323
Winewood Blvd., Tallahassee, FL 32301. Ed.
Christiane J. Guignard.

157 US ISSN 0160-9807
FOCUS: UNEXPLORED DEVIANCE; an annual
editions reader. 1958. a. Dushkin Publishing Group,
Sluice Dock, Guilford, CT 06437.

PSYCHOLOGY

150　　　　　　　GW　ISSN 0071-7940
FORTSCHRITTE DER PSYCHOANALYSE; internationales Jahrbuch zur Weiterentwicklung der Psychoanalyse. 1964. a. DM.38. Verlag fuer Psychologie Dr. C. J. Hogrefe, Rohnsweg 25, Postfach 414, 3400 Goettingen, W. Germany (B. R. D.) circ. 500-1,000.

150.5　　　　　　IT
GIORNALE ITALIANO DI PSICOLOGIA. QUADERNI. no. 2, 1977. irreg. Societa Editrice il Mulino, Via Santo Stefano 6, 40125 Bologna, Italy.

150　378　　　　　US　ISSN 0072-5277
GRADUATE STUDY IN PSYCHOLOGY. a. $6. American Psychological Association, Educational Affairs Office, 1200 Seventeenth St. N.W., Washington, DC 20036. circ. 15,000.

150　　　　　　　US
GROUP THERAPY - AN OVERVIEW. 1973. a. price varies. Thieme-Stratton, Inc., 381 Park Ave. So., New York, NY 10016. Eds. L.R. Wolberg, M.L. Aronson.

150　　　　　　　US　ISSN 0093-4763
GROUPS: A JOURNAL OF GROUP DYNAMICS AND PSYCHOTHERAPY. vol. 5, 1974. a. $7. Association of Medical Group Psychoanalysts, c/o David Weisselberger, M.D., Ed., 185 E. 85 St., New York, NY 10028. circ. controlled. Indexed: Psychol.Abstr.
　　Formerly: Journal of Psychoanalysis in Groups (ISSN 0022-3964)

150　　　　　　　GW　ISSN 0085-1302
GRUPPENPSYCHOTHERAPIE UND GRUPPENDYNAMIK. BEIHEFTE. 1972. irreg., no. 7, 1978. price varies. Vandenhoeck und Ruprecht, Theaterstr. 13, Postfach 77, 3400 Goettingen, W. Germany (B. R. D.) Ed. A. Heigl-Evers. circ. 1,900.

150　　　　　　　CN　ISSN 0085-1493
HERE AND NOW; a brief of news from the IPR. (Text and summaries in French) 1969. irreg. contr. free circ. Institute of Psychological Research, Inc., 34 Fleury Street West, Montreal 357, P.Q., Canada. Ed. Jean-Marc Chevrier. circ. 2,000.

150.016　　　　　US　ISSN 0073-3822
HUMAN BASICS LIBRARY. 1965. irreg., 1966, no. 3. $3. Western Psychological Services, 12031 Wilshire Blvd, Los Angeles, CA 90025.

HUMAN FACTORS SOCIETY ANNUAL MEETING. PROCEEDINGS. see *SOCIOLOGY*

HYMAN BLUMBERG SYMPOSIUM SERIES. see *EDUCATION*

150　　　　　　　IT
INCONSCIO E CULTURA. (Numbers not published consecutively) 1978. irreg, a, 2, 1980. price varies. Liguori Editore s.r.l., Via Mezzocannone 19, 80134 Naples, Italy. Ed. Aldo Carotenuto.

INSTITUT FUER KONFLIKTFORSCHUNG. SCHRIFTENREIHE. see *SOCIOLOGY*

150　　　　　　　US
INSTITUTE FOR PSYCHOANALYSIS. NEWSLETTER. 1932. irreg. (approx. 3/yr.) free. Institute for Psychoanalysis, 180 N. Michigan Ave, Chicago, IL 60601. Ed. Jacqueline Miller. circ. 5,000.
　　Formerly: Institute for Psychoanalysis. Report (ISSN 0073-8875)

150　　　　　　　UK　ISSN 0073-9561
INSTITUTE OF PSYCHOPHYSICAL RESEARCH. PROCEEDINGS. 1968. irreg. £5.95. Institute of Psychophysical Research, 118 Banbury Rd., Oxford, England. Ed. C. E. Green. circ. 2,000-3,000.

370　150　　　　　RM
INSTITUTUL PEDAGOGIC ORADEA. LUCRARI STIINTIFICE: SERIA PEDAGOGIE, PSIHOLOGIE, METODICA. (Continues in part its Lucrari Stiintifice: Seria Istorie, Stiinte Sociale, Pedagogie (1971-72), its Lucrari Stiintifice: Seria A and Seria B (1969-70), and its Lucrari Stiintifice (1967-68).) (Text in Rumanian, occasionally in English or French; summaries in Rumanian, French, English or German) 1967. irreg. Institutul Pedagogic Oradea, Calea Armatei Rosii Nr. 5, Oradea, Romania.

150　　　　　　　NE
INTERNATIONAL ASSOCIATION FOR CROSS-CULTURAL PSYCHOLOGY. INTERNATIONAL CONFERENCE. SELECTED PAPERS. irreg., 4th, 1978, Munich. Swets Publishing Service (Subsidiary of: Swets en Zeitlinger B.V.) Heereweg 347B, 2161 CA Lisse, Netherlands (Dist. in the U.S. and Canada by: Swets North America, Inc. Box 517, Berwyn, PA 19312)

150　　　　　　　BE　ISSN 0074-1574
INTERNATIONAL ASSOCIATION OF APPLIED PSYCHOLOGY. PROCEEDINGS OF CONGRESS. 1920. irreg., 1971, 17th, Liege. Editest, 94 rue General Capiaumont, 1040 Brussels, Belgium (Inquire: Prof. R. Piret, 47 rue Cesar Franck, 4000 Liege, Belgium)
　　Proceedings published in host country

137　　　　　　　US　ISSN 0534-9044
INTERNATIONAL CONGRESS OF GRAPHOANALYSTS. PROCEEDINGS. a. International Graphoanalysis Society, 111 N. Canal St., Chicago, IL 60606. Ed. V. Peter Ferrara.

150　　　　　　　US　ISSN 0085-2112
INTERNATIONAL CONGRESS OF PSYCHOLOGY. PROCEEDINGS. (Text in English and French) quadrennial; 1976, 21st, Paris. International Union of Psychological Science, c/o Prof. Wayne H.Holtzman, Hogg Foundation for Mental Health, Univ. of Texas, Austin, TX 78712 (Inquire: Mme. H. Gratiot Alphadery, 28 rue Serpente, F-75066 Paris, France)
　　Published by host national organization: Great Britain, 1969; Japan, 1972; France, 1976.

INTERNATIONAL DIRECTORY OF BEHAVIOR AND DESIGN RESEARCH. see *ARCHITECTURE*

INTERNATIONAL JOURNAL OF PSYCHOANALYTIC PSYCHOTHERAPY. see *MEDICAL SCIENCES — Psychiatry And Neurology*

150　　　　　　　BE　ISSN 0074-6754
INTERNATIONAL LEAGUE OF SOCIETIES FOR THE MENTALLY HANDICAPPED. WORLD CONGRESS PROCEEDINGS. (Text in English, French, German, Spanish) 6th, 1975. irreg.; 7th, 1978, Vienna. International League of Societies for the Mentally Handicapped, 12 rue Forestiere, B-1050 Brussels, Belgium. Eds. Dr. R. F. Dybwad, P. J. Renoir.

616.8　618　　　　UK　ISSN 0074-7548
INTERNATIONAL PSYCHO-ANALYTICAL LIBRARY. 1921. irreg. price varies. (Institute of Psychoanalysis) Hogarth Press Ltd., 40-42 William IV St., London WC2N 4DF, England. Ed. Clifford Yorke.

150　　　　　　　US　ISSN 0074-8137
INTERNATIONAL SERIES OF MONOGRAPHS ON EXPERIMENTAL PSYCHOLOGY.* 1964. irreg. price varies. Pergamon Press, Inc., Maxwell House, Fairview Park, Elmsford, NY 10523 (And Headington Hill Hall, Oxford OX3 0BW, England)

150　　　　　　　US　ISSN 0538-9968
INTERNATIONAL SERIES ON CEREBROVISCERAL AND BEHAVIORAL PSYCHOLOGY AND CONDITIONED REFLEXES. 1965. irreg., vol. 3, 1974. price varies. Pergamon Press, Inc., Maxwell House, Fairview Park, Elmsford, NY 10523. index.
　　Formerly: International Series of Monographs in Cerebrovisceral and Behavioral Psychology and Conditioned Reflexes.

152　　　　　　　US
INTERNATIONAL SERIES ON EXPERIMENTAL PSYCHOLOGY. 1964. irreg., vol. 24, 1980. price varies. Pergamon Press, Inc., Maxwell House, Fairview Park, Elmsford, NY 10523 (And Headington Hill Hall, Oxford OX3 0B3, England) *Experimental*

152　　　　　　　US
J A B A MONOGRAPH SERIES. (Journal of Applied Behavior Analysis) 1968. irreg. $1 per no. Society for the Experimental Analysis of Behavior, Inc. (Lawrence), Department of Human Development, University of Kansas, Lawrence, KS 66044.

150　　　　　　　SZ　ISSN 0075-2363
JAHRBUCH DER PSYCHOANALYSE. 1964. irreg., latest 1974. price varies. Verlag Hans Huber, Laenggassstr. 76 und Marktgasse 9, Postfach, CH-3000 Berne 9, Switzerland (Dist. by Williams & Wilkins Company, 428 E. Preston St., Baltimore, MD 21202) Ed.Bd.

150　　　　　　　GW　ISSN 0075-2924
JAHRESKATALOG PSYCHOLOGIE. a. DM.24. Werbegemeinschaft Elwert und Meurer, Hauptstr. 101, 1000 Berlin 62, W. Germany (B.R.D.) adv.

JAPANESE BULLETIN OF ART THERAPY. see *ART*

150　　　　　　　UK　ISSN 0143-1218
JOURNAL OF BIODYNAMIC PSYCHOLOGY. 1980. a. £3. Biodynamic Psychology Publications, Boyesen Institute for Biodynamic Psychology, Centre Ave., Acton, London W.3, England.

155.4　616.8　　　UK　ISSN 0075-417X
JOURNAL OF CHILD PSYCHOTHERAPY. 1963. a. £3.50($8.50) Association of Child Psychotherapists, Burgh House, New End Sq, London NW3 1LT, England. Ed. Anne Hurry. adv. bk. rev. circ. 800. Indexed: Psychol.Abstr. Abstr.Soc.Work. Child Devel.Abstr.

JYVASKYLA STUDIES IN EDUCATION, PSYCHOLOGY AND SOCIAL RESEARCH. see *EDUCATION*

LAW AND PSYCHOLOGY REVIEW. see *LAW*

150　　　　　　　US　ISSN 0077-5908
LEARNING RESOURCES CORPORATION. SELECTED READING SERVICES.* 1961. irreg., 1969, no. 9. price varies. Learning Resources Corporation, (Subsidiary of: Whitman Associates) 10573 Assembly Dr., Fairfax, VA 22030.
　　Formerly: National Training Laboratories. Institute of Applied Behavioural Science. Selected Readings Series.

156　　　　　　　UK
LIBRARY OF ANALYTICAL PSYCHOLOGY. no. 2, 1974. a. £2.95. Society of Analytical Psychology, 30 Devonshire Place, London W1N 1PE, England.

150　016　　　　　US
MENTAL HEALTH MEDIA CENTER FILM CATALOG. 1973. a. free. ‡ National Association for Mental Health, 1800 N. Kent St., Rosslyn, VA 22209. circ. 5,000.
　　Formerly: Catalog of Selected Films for Mental Health Education (ISSN 0069-1038)

151.22　371.26　　US　ISSN 0076-6461
MENTAL MEASUREMENTS YEARBOOK. 1938. irreg.(every 3-5 yrs.), 8th, 1978. $120 (2 vols.) (Buros Institute of Mental Measurements) University of Nebraska Press, 901 N. 17th St., Lincoln, NE 68588.

155.4　　　　　　US　ISSN 0076-9266
MINNESOTA SYMPOSIA ON CHILD PSYCHOLOGY. 1966. a. price varies. (University of Minnesota, Institute of Child Development) Thomas Y. Crowell Co., 10 E. 53rd St., New York, NY 10022. Ed. John P. Hill.

150　130　　　　　SP　ISSN 0077-0469
MONOGRAFIAS DE PSICOLOGIA, NORMAL Y PATOLOGICA. 1945. irreg. price varies. Espasa-Calpe, S. A., Carretera de Irun 12200, Apartado 547, Madrid 34, Spain. Ed. Jose Germain.

150　　　　　　　PL　ISSN 0077-0515
MONOGRAFIE PSYCHOLOGICZNE. (Text in Polish; summaries in English and Russian) 1968. irreg., vol. 27, 1979. price varies. (Polska Akademia Nauk, Komitet Nauk Psychologicznych) Ossolineum, Publishing House of the Polish Academy of Sciences, Rynek 9, 50-106 Wroclaw, Poland (Dist. by Ars Polona-Ruch, Krakowskie Przedmiescie 7, Warsaw, Poland) Ed. Tadeusz Tomaszewski.

150　　　　　　　FR　ISSN 0077-071X
MONOGRAPHIES FRANCAISES DE PSYCHOLOGIE. 1959. irreg., 1974, no. 27. price varies. Centre National de la Recherche Scientifique, 15 Quai Anatole-France, 75700 Paris, France. Indexed: Psychol.Abstr.

150 US
MONOGRAPHS IN PSYCHOLOGY: AN INTERNATIONAL SERIES. 1972. irreg. price varies. Plenum Publishing Corp., 233 Spring St., New York, NY 10013. Ed.Bd.

150 371.33 US
N I C E M INDEX TO PSYCHOLOGY-MULTIMEDIA. biennial. $55. National Information Center for Educational Media, University of Southern California, University Park, Los Angeles, CA 90007. cum.index. circ. controlled. (also avail. in microfiche)

150 US
NAROPA INSTITUTE JOURNAL OF PSYCHOLOGY. 1980. a. $7.50. Nalanda Press, 1111 Pearl St., Boulder, CO 80302. Ed. Dr. Edward M. Poduall. circ. 1,000. (back issues avail.)

NATIONAL GUILD OF CATHOLIC PSYCHIATRISTS. BULLETIN. see *MEDICAL SCIENCES — Psychiatry And Neurology*

NATIONAL INSTITUTE FOR PERSONNEL RESEARCH. ANNUAL REPORT. see *BUSINESS AND ECONOMICS — Personnel Management*

158 US ISSN 0077-5339
NATIONAL PSYCHOLOGICAL ASSOCIATION FOR PSYCHOANALYSIS. BULLETIN. 1950. a. National Psychological Association for Psychoanalysis, Inc., 150 W. 13 St, New York, NY 10011. circ. 7,000.

159 US ISSN 0070-2099
NEBRASKA SYMPOSIUM ON MOTIVATION (PUBLICATION) (Subseries of Research in Motivation Series) 1953. a. price varies. University of Nebraska Press, 901 N. 17 St., Lincoln, NE 68588. index, cum.index: 1953-1958. Indexed: Ind.Med. Psychol.Abstr.

150 300 NE ISSN 0077-801X
NEW BABYLON: STUDIES IN THE SOCIAL SCIENCES. irreg. price varies. Mouton Publishers, Noordeinde 41, 2514 GC The Hague, Netherlands (U.S. addr.: Mouton Publishers, c/o Walter de Gruyter, Inc., 200 Saw Mill River Road, Hawthorne, NY 10532)

150 US ISSN 0077-9008
NEW YORK PSYCHOANALYTIC INSTITUTE. KRIS STUDY GROUP. MONOGRAPH. 1965. irreg., no. 6, 1975. price varies. International Universities Press, Inc., 315 Fifth Ave., New York, NY 10016. Eds. Bernard D. Fine, Edward D. Joseph, Herbert F. Waldhorn.

ODENSE UNIVERSITY STUDIES IN PSYCHIATRY AND MEDICAL PSYCHOLOGY. see *MEDICAL SCIENCES — Psychiatry And Neurology*

616.8 155 US ISSN 0094-6206
ORIGINS OF BEHAVIOR SERIES. 1974. irreg., latest 1980. price varies. John Wiley & Sons, Inc., 605 Third Ave., New York, NY 10016. Eds. Michael Lewis, L.A. Rosenblum.

150 II
OSMANIA UNIVERSITY. DEPARTMENT OF PSYCHOLOGY. RESEARCH BULLETIN. (Text in English) 1965. irreg. Osmania University, Department of Psychology, Hyderabad 500007, Andhra Pradesh, India. Ed. Shalini Bhogle. bk. rev. bibl. charts. stat. circ. controlled. Indexed: Psychol. Abstr.

150 US
P S C P TIMES. 1971. irreg., 6-8/yr. $5. Philadelphia Society of Clinical Psychologists, Box 27014, Philadelphia, PA 19118. Eds. Lita L. Schwartz, Frank A. Melone. circ. 200.

150 US ISSN 0079-0141
PASTORAL PSYCHOLOGY SERIES. 1962. irreg., 1980, no. 10. price varies. (Institute of Pastoral Psychology) Fordham University Press, University Box L, Bronx, NY 10458.
Includes: Institute of Pastoral Psychology. Proceedings (ISSN 0073-9502)

150 US ISSN 0079-0818
PERGAMON GENERAL PSYCHOLOGY SERIES. irreg. price varies. Pergamon Press, Inc., Maxwell House, Fairview Park, Elmsford, NY 10523 (And Headington Hill Hall, Oxford OX3 0BW, England) Eds. A. P. Goldstein, L. Krasner.

150 US ISSN 0079-0931
PERSONALITY AND PSYCHOPATHOLOGY; a series of texts, monographs and treatises. 1967. irreg., latest 1978. price varies. Academic Press Inc., 111 Fifth Ave., New York, NY 10003.

PERSPECTIVES IN LAW AND PSYCHOLOGY. see *LAW*

616.8 US ISSN 0094-1476
PHILADELPHIA ASSOCIATION FOR PSYCHOANALYSIS. JOURNAL. 1974. irreg. $16. Philadelphia Association for Psychoanalysis, 15 St. Asaph's Rd., Box 36, Bala Cynwyd, PA 19004. Ed. David M. Sachs, M.D. bk. rev. circ. 1,000. Key Title: Journal of the Philadelphia Association for Psychoanalysis.
Supersedes: Philadelphia Association for Psychoanalysis. Bulletin (ISSN 0480-2780)

150 616.89 GW ISSN 0085-5073
PRAXIS DER KINDERPSYCHOLOGIE UND KINDERPSYCHIATRIE. BEIHEFTE. 1958. irreg. price varies. Vandenhoeck und Ruprecht, Theaterstr. 13, 3400 Goettingen, W. Germany (B. R. D.) Ed. Annemarie Duehrssen. Indexed: Psychol.Abstr.

150 616 GW ISSN 0079-4945
PRAXIS DER KLINISCHEN PSYCHOLOGIE. 1969. irreg., 1971, no. 2. Verlag fuer Psychologie Dr. C. J. Hogrefe, Rohnsweg 25, Postfach 414, 3400 Goettingen, W. Germany (B. R. D.) Ed. Erna Duhm. circ. 1,000.

301.1 GW ISSN 0340-2150
PRAXIS DER SOZIALPSYCHOLOGIE. 1974. irreg., vol. 11, 1979. price varies. Dr. Dietrich Steinkopff Verlag, Saalbaustr. 12, Postfach 111008, 6100 Darmstadt 11, W. Germany (B.R.D.) Ed. G. Rudinger.

370.15 US ISSN 0079-5933
PROFESSIONAL SCHOOL PSYCHOLOGY. 1960. irreg., 1969, vol. 3. price varies. Grune & Stratton, Inc., (Subsidiary of: Harcourt Brace Jovanovich, Inc.) 111 5th Ave, New York, NY 10003. Eds. Monroe B. Gottsegen and Gloria B. Gottsegen. index.

616.8 US ISSN 0099-037X
PROGRESS IN BEHAVIOR MODIFICATION. 1975. a. Academic Press, Inc., 111 Fifth Ave., New York, NY 10003. Ed. M. Hersen. (also avail. in microfiche)

150 US ISSN 0079-6182
PROGRESS IN CLINICAL PSYCHOLOGY. 1952. irreg., 1971, vol. IX. price varies. Grune and Stratton, Inc. (Subsidiary of: Harcourt Brace Jovanovich, Inc.) 111 Fifth Avenue, New York, NY 10003.

155 US ISSN 0079-6255
PROGRESS IN EXPERIMENTAL PERSONALITY RESEARCH. 1964. irreg., vol. 8, 1978. price varies. Academic Press, Inc, 111 Fifth Ave, New York, NY 10003. Ed. B. Maher. Indexed: Ind.Med.

155 US
PROGRESS IN PSYCHOBIOLOGY AND PHYSIOLOGICAL PSYCHOLOGY. vol. 8, 1979. irreg. Academic Press, Inc., 111 Fifth Ave., New York, NY 10003.

158 UR
PSIKHOLOGICHESKIE ISSLEDOVANIYA. no. 6, 1976. irreg. Izdatel'stvo Moskovskii Universitet, Leninskie Gory, Moscow V-234, U.S.S.R. circ. 5,500.

150 US ISSN 0079-7294
PSYCHOANALYTIC STUDY OF SOCIETY. irreg., no. 7, 1976. price varies. Yale University Press, 92A Yale Sta., New Haven, CT 06511.

155.4 US ISSN 0079-7308
PSYCHOANALYTIC STUDY OF THE CHILD. 1945. a. price varies. Yale University Press, 92A Yale Sta., New Haven, CT 06520. Eds. Ruth E. Eisler, M.D., Albert J. Solnit, M.D. Indexed: Ind.Med. Psychol.Abstr.

131 US
PSYCHOBIOLOGY AND PHYSIOLOGICAL PSYCHOLOGY. 1967. irreg. price varies. Academic Press, Inc, 111 Fifth Ave, New York, NY 10003. Eds. Eliot Stellar, James M. Sprague.
Formerly (until vol. 6): Progress in Physiological Psychology (ISSN 0079-6670)

150 NE ISSN 0079-7324
PSYCHOLOGEN ADRESBOEK. 1960. a. fl.12.50. Nederlands Instituut van Psychologen - Netherlands Psychological Association, Nicolaas Maesstraat 122, 1071 RH Amsterdam, Netherlands. adv. circ. 8,000.

370.15 CS
PSYCHOLOGIA A SKOLA. 1972. irreg., approx. s-a. price varies. Slovenske Pedagogicke Nakladatelstvo, Sasinkova 5, 891 12 Bratislava, Czechoslovakia.

150 SA ISSN 0079-7332
PSYCHOLOGIA AFRICANA. (Text in English and Afrikaans; summaries in English) 1948. a. R.10 (for bound volume); R. 10(for preprints); R. 12.50(for bound volume and preprints) National Institute for Personnel Research - Nasionale Instituut vir Personeelnavorsing, P.O. Box 10319, Johannesburg 2000, South Africa. Ed. G. K. Nelson. bk. rev. index. circ. 400(approx.) Indexed: Curr.Cont. Psychol.Abstr. SSCI. Ind.S.A.Per. Psychol.R.G.

150 370 PL
PSYCHOLOGIA-PEDAGOGIKA. 1961. irreg. price varies. Uniwersytet im. Adama Mickiewicza w Poznaniu, Stlaingradzka 1, 61-712 Poznan, Poland (Dist. by: Ars Polona, Krakowskie Przedmiescie 7, 00-068 Warsaw, Poland) bk. rev.
Formerly: Uniwersytet im. Adama Mickiewicza w Poznaniu. Wydzial Historyczny. Prace. Seria Psychologia-Pedagogika (ISSN 0083-4254)

150 GW
PSYCHOLOGIA UNIVERSALIS FORSCHUNGSERGEBNISSE AUS DEM GESAMTGEBIET DER PSYCHOLOGIE. 1952. irreg., no. 49, 1979. price varies. Verlag Anton Hain GmbH, Adelheidstr. 2, Postfach 1220, 6240 Koenigstein, W. Germany (B.R.D.) Ed. Bd.

150 SA
PSYCHOLOGICAL INSTITUTE OF THE REPUBLIC OF SOUTH AFRICA. PROCEEDINGS/SIELKUNDIGE INSTITUUT VAN DIE REPUBLIEK VAN SUID-AFRIKA. VERRIGTINGS. (Text in Afrikaans and English) 1962. a. Psychological Institute of the Republic of South Africa, Box 2729, Pretoria, South Africa.

150 US ISSN 0079-7359
PSYCHOLOGICAL ISSUES. MONOGRAPH. irreg., no. 51, 1980. $12. International Universities Press, Inc, 315 Fifth Ave., New York, NY 10016. Ed. Herbert J. Schlesinger.

150 SW ISSN 0555-5620
PSYCHOLOGICAL RESEARCH BULLETIN. (Text in English) 1961. irreg. $8 incl. irreg. Monograph Series. Lunds Universitet, Department of Psychology, Paradisgatan 223, Lund, Sweden. Ed. G. Smith. bibl. charts. circ. 600. Indexed: Psychol.Abstr.

150 NE
PSYCHOLOGICAL STUDIES. irreg. price varies. Mouton Publishers, Noordeinde 41, 2514 GC The Hague, Netherlands (U.S. addr.: Mouton Publishers, c/o Walter de Gruyter, Inc., 200 Saw Mill River Road, Hawthorne, NY 10532) Ed.Bd.
Formerly: Psychological Studies. Major Series (ISSN 0079-7383)

301.1 150 GW ISSN 0341-938X
PSYCHOLOGIE UND GESELLSCHAFT. 1977. irreg., vol. 8, 1979. price varies. Dr. Dietrich Steinkopff Verlag, Saalbauster. 12, Postfach 11 1008, 6100 Darmstadt 11, W. Germany(B.R.D.) Ed. M. Stadler.

150 GW ISSN 0079-7405
PSYCHOLOGIE UND PERSON. 1961. irreg., no. 24, 1979. price varies. Ernst Reinhardt, GmbH und Co., Verlag, Kemnatenstr. 46, 8000 Munich 19, W. Germany (B.R.D.) (reprint service avail. from ISI and UMI)

150   SZ   ISSN 0079-7413
PSYCHOLOGISCHE PRAXIS. (Text in German) 1949. irreg. (approx. 2/yr.) 25 Fr.($15) per vol. (1981 price) S. Karger AG, Allschwilerstrasse 10, P.O. Box, CH-4009 Basel, Switzerland. Ed. R. Schmitz-Scherzer. (reprint service avail. from ISI) Indexed: Biol.Abstr. Chem.Abstr. Curr.Cont. Ind.Med. Psychol.Abstr. SSCI.

152.5   US   ISSN 0079-7421
PSYCHOLOGY OF LEARNING AND MOTIVATION: ADVANCES IN RESEARCH AND THEORY. 1967. irreg., latest vol. 12. price varies. Academic Press, Inc, 111 Fifth Ave, New York, NY 10003. Ed. G. H. Bower.

150   HU   ISSN 0079-7456
PSZICHOLOGIA A GYAKORLATBAN. 1963. irreg. price varies. (Magyar Tudomanyos Akademia) Akademiai Kiado, Publishing House of the Hungarian Academy of Sciences, P.O. Box 24, H-1363 Budapest, Hungary.

150   HU   ISSN 0079-7464
PSZICHOLOGIAI TANULMANYOK. (Text in Hungarian; summaries in English and German) 1958. irreg. price varies. (Magyar Tudomanyos Akademia) Akademiai Kiado, Publishing House of the Hungarian Academy of Sciences, P.O. Box 24, H-1363 Budapest, Hungary. Indexed: Psychol.Abstr.

150   NZ   ISSN 0079-7731
PUBLICATIONS IN PSYCHOLOGY. 1952. irreg., 1972, no. 26. exchange basis. ‡ Victoria University of Wellington, Department of Psychology, Private Bag, P.O. Box 196, Wellington, New Zealand. Indexed: Psychol.Abstr.

RESEARCH IN COMMUNITY AND MENTAL HEALTH; an annual compilation of research. see PUBLIC HEALTH AND SAFETY

150   US   ISSN 0191-3085
RESEARCH IN ORGANIZATIONAL BEHAVIOR; an annual series of analytical essays and critical reviews. 1979. a. $18.75 to individuals; institutions $37.50. J A I Press, Box 1678, 165 W. Putnam Ave., Greenwich, CT 06830. Ed. Barry M. Staw.

157   BL   ISSN 0048-7740
REVISTA DE PSICOLOGIA NORMAL E PATOLOGICA. (Suspended publication 1976-1979) N.S. 1979. irreg. Pontificia Universidade Catolica de Sao Paulo, Faculdade de Psicologia, Rua Monte Alegre 984, Sao Paulo, Brazil.

150   BE   ISSN 0085-1078
RIJKSUNIVERSITEIT TE GENT. LABORATORIUM VOOR EXPERIMENTELE, DIFFERENTIELE EN GENETISCHE PSYCHOLOGIE. MEDEDLINGEN EN WERKDOCUMENTEN. (Text in Dutch, English or French) 1961. irreg. price varies. ‡ Rijksuniversiteit te Gent, Laboratorium voor Experimentele, Differentiele en Genetische Psychologie, Blandijnberg, 2, 9000 Ghent, Belgium. (Co-sponsor: Centrum voor Ontwikkelingspsychologie) Ed. W. De Coster. circ. 500.

150   SZ   ISSN 0080-7079
SCHRIFTEN ZUR SOZIALPSYCHOLOGIE. 1962. irreg. price varies. Verlag Hans Huber, Laenggassstr. 76 und Marktgasse 9, CH-3000 Berne 9, Switzerland (Dist. by Williams & Wilkins Company, 428 E. Preston St., Baltimore, MD 21202) Ed. H. Fischer.

613.07   US
SELECTIVE GUIDE TO AUDIOVISUALS FOR MENTAL HEALTH AND FAMILY LIFE EDUCATION. 1973. biennial. $35. (Mental Health Materials Center) Marquis Academic Media, 200 E. Ohio St., Chicago, IL 60611. bk. rev. film rev. play rev. abstr. bibl. illus, annual index. circ. 3,000.
Supersedes in part: Selective Guide to Materials on Mental Health and Family Life Education; Which was formerly titled: Information Resources Center for Mental Health and Family Hygiene. I R C Recommends.

SELECTIVE GUIDE TO PUBLICATIONS FOR MENTAL HEALTH AND FAMILY LIFE EDUCATION. see PSYCHOLOGY — Abstracting, Bibliographies, Statistics

616.89   IT
SEMIOTICA & PSICANALISI. 1976. irreg. Marsilio Editori S.p.A., Fondamenta Santa Chiara, Santa Croce 518-A, Venice, Italy.

150 361   US   ISSN 0146-0846
SERIES IN CLINICAL AND COMMUNITY PSYCHOLOGY. 1974. irreg., unnumbered, latest 1980. price varies. Hemisphere Publishing Corporation, 1025 Vermont Ave. N.W., Washington, DC 20005. Eds. Charles D. Spielberger, Irwin G. Sarason. bibl. charts, illus. (back issues avail.; reprint service avail. from UMI)
Formerly: Series in Clinical Psychology.

150   US
SPRING; an annual of archetypal psychology and Jungian thought. 1940. a. $10. Spring Publications, Box 1, Univ. of Dallas Station, Irving, TX 75061. Ed. James Hillman. adv. bk. rev. circ. 4,000. (back issues avail) Indexed: Psychol.Abstr.

150   US   ISSN 0161-1089
STATE AND MIND. 1970. irreg. (approx. 4/yr.) $6 to individuals; institutions $12 for 6 nos. New Directions in Psychology, Inc., Box 89, W . Somerville, MA 02144. adv. bk. rev. circ. 4,000. Indexed: Alt.Press Ind.
Former titles: R T ; a Journal of Radical Therapy; Rough Times; Radical Therapist.

150   SW   ISSN 0081-5756
STOCKHOLMS UNIVERSITET. PSYKOLOGISKA INSTITUTIONEN. REPORT SERIES. (Text in English) 1954. irreg. (approx. 30/yr.) $1. Stockholms Universitet, Psykologiska Institutionen, Box 6706, S-113 85 Stockholm, Sweden. Ed. T. Kuennapas. index. circ. 500. Indexed: Psychol.Abstr.

152   SW   ISSN 0345-021X
STOCKHOLMS UNIVERSITET. PSYKOLOGISKA INSTITUTIONEN. REPORTS. SUPPLEMENT SERIES. (Text in English) 1970. irreg. (approx. 5/yr.) $2. Stockholms Universitet, Psykologiska Institutionen, Box 6706, S-113 85 Stockholm, Sweden. Ed. T. Kuennapas. index. circ. 400. Indexed: Psychol.Abstr.

150   US   ISSN 0364-1112
STRESS AND ANXIETY. (Subseries of: Series in Clinical and Community Psychology) 1975. irreg., vol. 7, 1980. price varies. Hemisphere Publishing Corporation, 1025 Vermont Ave. N.W., Washington, DC 20005 (Subscr. to 19 W.44 St., New York, NY 10036) Eds. C.D. Spielberger, I.G. Sarason.

STUDIENHEFTE PSYCHOLOGIE IN ERZIEHUNG UND UNTERRICHT. see EDUCATION — Higher Education

370.15   GW
STUDIENREIHE PAEDAGOGISCHE PSYCHOLOGIE. 1978. irreg. price varies. Ernst Reinhardt GmbH und Co., Verlag, Kemnatenstr. 46, 8000 Munich 19, W. Germany (B.R.D.) Eds. R. Dieterich, H.-R. Lueckert, H. Walter.
Educational

STUDIES IN APPLIED PSYCHOLINGUISTICS. see LINGUISTICS

150   US
STUDIES IN PHILOSOPHICAL PSYCHOLOGY. irreg. price varies. Humanities Press, Inc., 171 First Ave., Atlantic Highlands, NJ 07716.

STUDIES IN THE LEARNING SCIENCES. see EDUCATION

301.1   US   ISSN 0162-7171
SYNOPSIS OF FAMILY THERAPY PRACTICE. (Represents: Proceedings of the annual Antioch University/Maryland Symposium on Family Therapy Practice) a. $7.95. Family Therapy Practice Network Inc., 18114 Hillcrest Ave., Olney, MD 20832.

TESTS IN PRINT. see PSYCHOLOGY

375   US   ISSN 0361-025X
TESTS IN PRINT. 1961. irreg., no. 2, 1974. $70. University of Nebraska Press, 901 N. 17th St., Lincoln, NE 68588.

150   JA   ISSN 0040-8743
TOHOKU PSYCHOLOGICA FOLIA. (Text in European languages) 1933. a. exchange basis. ‡ Tohoku University, Department of Psychology, Faculty of Arts & Letters, 2-1-1 Katahira, Sendai 980, Japan. Ed. Junkichi Abe. charts. illus. index. circ. 800. Indexed: Biol.Abstr. Psychol.Abstr.

155   US
TOPICS IN COGNITIVE DEVELOPMENT. 1977. irreg. price varies. (Jean Piaget Society) Plenum Press, 233 Spring St., New York, NY 10013. Ed. Marilyn H. Appel.

150   FI
TURUN YLIOPISTO PSYKOLOGIAN TUTKIMUKSIA. irreg. price varies. Turun Yliopisto, Psykologian Laitos, Yliopistonk. 23 A, SF-20500 Turku 50, Finland.
Supersedes in part: Turun Yliopisto. Psykologian Laitos. Reports (ISSN 0082-7037)

301.1 150 SA
U N I S A PSYCHOLOGIA. (Text in Afrikaans and English) 1974. a. R.1.05. University of South Africa, Department of Psychology, Box 392, Pretoria 0001, South Africa. Ed. W. J. Jordan. adv. bk. rev. circ. 8,000.

U S S R REPORT: BIOMEDICAL AND BEHAVIORAL SCIENCES. see MEDICAL SCIENCES

UNDERSTANDING CONFLICT AND WAR. see POLITICAL SCIENCE — International Relations

150 200   US
UNION COLLEGE. CHARACTER RESEARCH PROJECT. NEWSLETTER. 1968. irreg. free. Union College (Schenectady), Character Research Project, 207 State Street, Schenectady, NY 12305. bk. rev. bibl. illus.

150   NO
UNIVERSITY OF BERGEN. INSTITUTE OF PSYCHOLOGY. REPORT. (Text in English) 1968. irreg. (6-10/yr.) Universitetet i Bergen, Psykologisk Instituut, Box 25, 5014 Bergen-U, Norway. charts. stat.

150 301   NZ   ISSN 0069-3774
UNIVERSITY OF CANTERBURY. DEPARTMENT OF PSYCHOLOGY AND SOCIOLOGY. RESEARCH PROJECTS. 1956 (approx) irreg. (2-3/yr); no, 24, 1975. price varies. University of Canterbury, Department of Psychology, Christchurch, New Zealand. Ed. R. A. M. Gregson. circ. 250(approx.)

616.8   US
UNIVERSITY OF MICHIGAN. MENTAL HEALTH RESEARCH INSTITUTE. ANNUAL REPORT. 1957. a. free. ‡ University of Michigan, Mental Health Research Institute, 205 Washtenaw Pl., Ann Arbor, MI 48109. Ed. Cathy Sniderman. circ. 2,000.

150   FI
UNIVERSITY OF TURKU PSYCHOLOGICAL REPORTS. (Text in English) 1963. irreg., no. 22, 1976. price varies. Turun Yliopisto, Psykologian Laitos - University of Turku, Institute of Psychology, Yliopistonk. 23 A, SF-20500 Turku 50, Finland.
Supersedes in part: Turun Yliopisto. Psykologian Laitos. Reports (ISSN 0082-7037)

150   CN   ISSN 0316-4675
UNIVERSITY OF WESTERN ONTARIO. DEPARTMENT OF PSYCHOLOGY. RESEARCH BULLETIN. 1965. irreg. University of Western Ontario, Department of Psychology, London, Ont., Canada. bibl, illus. (processed)

150   CS   ISSN 0083-419X
UNIVERZITA KOMENSKEHO. FILOZOFICKA FAKULTA. ZBORNIK: PSYCHOLOGICA. (Text in Slovak; summaries in English and Russian) 1961. a. exchange basis. Univerzita Komenskeho, Filozoficka Fakulta, Gondova 2, 806 01 Bratislava, Czechoslovakia. Ed. Tomas Pardel. circ. 700.

150 370   PL   ISSN 0083-4408
UNIWERSYTET JAGIELLONSKI. ZESZYTY
NAUKOWE. PRACE PSYCHOLOGICZNO-
PEDAGOGICZNE. 1957. irreg., 1972, vol. 18.
price varies. Panstwowe Wydawnictwo Naukowe,
Miodowa 10, Warsaw, Poland (Dist. by Ars Polona-
Ruch, Krakowskie Przedmiescie 7, Warsaw, Poland)
Ed. Maria Susulowska.

UNIWERSYTET SLASKI W KATOWICACH.
PRACE PSYCHOLOGICZNE. see *EDUCATION*

150 616.8   US   ISSN 0083-8977
W P S PROFESSIONAL HANDBOOK SERIES.
1965. irreg. $5.-$8. Western Psychological Services,
12031 Wilshire Blvd, Los Angeles, CA 90025.

153   US   ISSN 0083-7741
WAYNE STATE UNIVERSITY. CENTER FOR
THE STUDY OF COGNITIVE PROCESSES.
DISSERTATIONS IN COGNITIVE
PROCESSES.* 1962. a. free. Wayne State
University, Center for the Study of Cognitive
Processes, 768 Mackenzie Hall, Detroit, MI 48202.
Ed. Eli Salz.

150   US
WILEY SERIES IN BEHAVIOR. irreg., latest 1976.
John Wiley & Sons, Inc., 605 Third Ave., New
York, NY 10016. Ed. Kenneth MacCorquodale.

150 301.1   US
WILEY SERIES IN HUMAN FACTORS. 1971.
irreg., unnumbered, latest vol. 1976. price varies.
John Wiley & Sons, Inc., 605 Third Ave., New
York, NY 10016. Ed. D. Meister.

152   GW   ISSN 0340-031X
WISSENSCHAFTLICHE
FORSCHUNGSBERICHTE. REIHE 1.
GRUNDLAGENFORSCHUNG UND
GRUNDLEGENDE METHODIK. ABT. C.
PSYCHOLOGIE/CURRENT TOPICS IN
SCIENCE. REIHE 1. BASIC RESEARCH ABT.
C. PSYCHOLOGY. 1921. irreg. price varies. Dr.
Dietrich Steinkopff Verlag, Saalbaustr. 12, Postfach
11 1008, 6100 Darmstadt 11, W. Germany(B.R.D.)
Ed. S. Ertel. circ. 2,000.

616.89 614.582   CN   ISSN 0084-1757
WORLD FEDERATION FOR MENTAL HEALTH.
PROCEEDINGS OF ANNUAL MEETINGS.
(Since 1969, Federation incorporates activities of
the International Assn. of Social Psychiatry) 1948.
a. price varies. World Federation for Mental Health,
Dept. of Psychiatry, University of British Columbia,
Vancouver, B.C. V6O 1W5, Canada.

ZEITSCHRIFT FUER PSYCHOSOMATISCHE
MEDIZIN UND PSYCHOANALYSE.
BEIHEFTE. see *MEDICAL SCIENCES —
Psychiatry And Neurology*

PSYCHOLOGY — Abstracting, Bibliographies, Statistics

310 150   JA
BEHAVIORMETRIKA. (Text mainly in English)
1974. a. price varies. (Behaviormetric Society of
Japan) Japan Publications Trading Co., Ltd., Box
5030, Tokyo International, Tokyo 100-31, Japan (Or
1255 Howard St., San Francisco, CA 94103) Ed.
Chikio Hayashi.

BENCHMARK PAPERS IN BEHAVIOR. see
BIOLOGY — Zoology

016 150   AG   ISSN 0523-1698
BIBLIOGRAFIA ARGENTINA DE PSICOLOGIA.*
irreg., 1970, no. 5-6. Ministerio de Cultura y
Educacion, Direccion de Bibliotecos, 538 Calle 7,
La Plata, Argentina.

150 011   US   ISSN 0360-277X
BIBLIOGRAPHIC GUIDE TO PSYCHOLOGY.
(Text in various languages) a. $60. G. K. Hall &
Co., 70 Lincoln St., Boston, Ma 02111.
  Formerly: Psychology Book Guide.

301.1 016   GW
BIBLIOGRAPHIE DER DEUTSCHSPRACHIGEN
PSYCHOLOGISCHEN LITERATUR. a. DM.200
(approx.) Vittorio Klostermann, Frauenlobstr. 22,
Postfach 900601, D-6000 Frankfurt 90, W.
Germany (B.R.D.) Ed. J. Dambauer.

150 016   IR
BIBLIOGRAPHY OF PSYCHOLOGY/
KETABNAME-YE RAVANSHENASI. (Text in
Persian & English) 1971. irreg. Rs.20. University of
Teheran, Institute of Psychology, 21 Daneshkadeh
Ave., Baharestan Square, Teheran, Iran.

150   US   ISSN 0073-5884
INDEX OF PSYCHOANALYTIC WRITINGS. 1966,
no. 9. irreg., 1975, no. 14. International Universities
Press, Inc., 315 Fifth Ave., New York, NY 10016.
Ed. Alexander Grinstein.

152 573   US   ISSN 0272-0582
PSYCHOLOGICAL CINEMA REGISTER; films and
video in the behavioral sciences. Abbreviated title: P
C R. 1944. Pennsylvania State University, Audio-
Visual Services, University Park, PA 16802. Ed.
Lori A. Baldwin. circ. 7,000.

150 016   US
PSYCHOLOGY INFORMATION GUIDE SERIES.
1979. irreg., vol. 6, 1980. $30. Gale Research
Company, Book Tower, Detroit, MI 48226. Eds.
Sydney Schultz, Duane Schultz.

155   US
SELECTIVE GUIDE TO PUBLICATIONS FOR
MENTAL HEALTH AND FAMILY LIFE
EDUCATION. irreg., 4th edt. 1979. $34.50.
(Mental Health Materials Center) Marquis
Academic Media, 200 E. Ohio St., Chicago, IL
60611.
  Supersedes in part: Selective Guide to Materials
for Mental Health and Family Life Education.

PUBLIC ADMINISTRATION

see also *Public Administration — Municipal
Government; Housing and Urban
Planning; Social Services and Welfare*

350   TS
ABU DHABI. DEPARTMENT OF PLANNING.
STATISTICAL ABSTRACT AND YEARBOOK. a.
Department of Planning, Abu Dhabi, United Arab
Emirates.

350   TS
ABU DHABI OFFICAL GAZETTE. (Text in Arabic
and English) irreg. Council of Ministers Secretariat,
Box 516, Abu Dhabi, United Arab Emirates.

350   CR   ISSN 0044-6262
ADMINISTRACION, DESARROLLO,
INTEGRACION. Variant title: Instituto
Centroamericano de Administracion Publica.
Administracion, Desarrollo, Integracion. 1970. irreg.
free. Instituto Centroamericano de Administracion
Publica, Apartado 10025, San Jose, Costa Rica.
illus. charts.

ADMINISTRACION Y DESARROLLO. see
POLITICAL SCIENCE

350   CN   ISSN 0065-1974
ADMINISTRATOR. 1969. irreg. York University,
Faculty of Administrative Studies, Rm 111,
Administrative Studies Bldg., 4700 Keele St.,
Downsview, Ontario M3J 2R6, Canada. Ed. Robert
Wilson. circ. 1,200.

AFRICANUS. see *POLITICAL SCIENCE*

350   US
ALABAMA COUNTY DATA BOOK. a. $2.
Development Office, State Capitol, Montgomery,
AL 36130. charts, stat.

353.9   US   ISSN 0095-3865
ALASKA. LEGISLATURE. BUDGET AND AUDIT
COMMITTEE. ANNUAL REPORT. a. free.
Legislative Budget and Audit Committee, Pouch W,
Juneau, AK 99811. Key Title: Annual Report -
State of Alaska, Legislative Budget and Audit
Committee.

353.9   US   ISSN 0363-5376
ALASKA. OFFICE OF OMBUDSMAN. REPORT
OF THE OMBUDSMAN. 1975. a. Office of
Ombudsman, Juneau, AK 99801. circ. 2,000. Key
Title: Report of the Ombudsman (Juneau)

353.9   US   ISSN 0092-1858
ALASKA BLUE BOOK. 1973. biennial. $7.50. ‡
Department of Education, Division of State
Libraries and Museums, Pouch G, Juneau, AK
99811. illus. stat. circ. controlled.

363.6   CN   ISSN 0381-2294
ALBERTA. UTILITIES DIVISION. ANNUAL
REPORT. 1974. a. Utilties Division, 415 Petroleum
Plaza, 9945 108 St., Edmonton, Alta. T5K 2G6,
Canada.

348   US   ISSN 0360-165X
AMERICAN ENTERPRISE INSTITUTE FOR
PUBLIC POLICY RESEARCH. REVIEW,
SESSION OF THE CONGRESS. a. $3.75.
American Enterprise Institute for Public Policy
Research, 1150 17th St. N.W., Washington, DC
20036.
  Formerly: A E I Review, Session of the Congress
and Index of A E I Publications.

AMERICAN PUBLIC WORKS ASSOCIATION.
DIRECTORY. see *TECHNOLOGY:
COMPREHENSIVE WORKS*

350   US
AMERICAN SOCIETY FOR PUBLIC
ADMINISTRATION. SECTION ON
INTERNATIONAL AND COMPARATIVE
ADMINISTRATION. OCCASIONAL PAPERS.
1974. irreg., latest 1975. $3 per no. American
Society for Public Administration, Section on
International and Comparative Administration, 1225
Connecticut Ave. N. W., Washington, DC 20036.

354   AO
ANGOLA. SECRETARIA PROVINCIAL DE
SAUDE, TRABALHO. PREVIDENCIA E
ASSISTENCIA. SINTESE DA ACTIVIDADE
DOS SERVICOS E ORGANISMOS.* 1963. irreg;
(approx 1/yr) free. Secretaria Provincial de Saude,
Trabalho, Previdencia e Assistencia, Luanda,
Angola. circ. controlled. (tabloid format)

351   ML   ISSN 0066-2453
ANNUAIRE ADMINISTRATIF DE LA
REPUBLIQUE DU MALI. 1964. a. ‡ Chambre de
Commerce et d'Industrie du Mali, B.P. 46, Bamako,
Mali. circ. 100.

350   BE   ISSN 0066-2461
ANNUAIRE ADMINISTRATIF ET JUDICIAIRE
DE BELGIQUE/ADMINISTRATIEF EN
GERECHTELIJK JAARBOEK VOOR BELGIE.
1869. a. 3170 Fr. Etablissements Emile Bruylant, 67
rue de la Regence, 1000 Brussels, Belgium. circ.
5,500.

916.7   GO
ANNUAIRE NATIONAL OFFICIEL DE LA
REPUBLIQUE GABONAISE. 1973. a. 5000
Fr.CFA. Agence Havas Gabon, B.P. 213, Libreville,
Gabon. adv. illus. stat. circ. 5,000.

350.6   FR
ANNUAIRES CHATEAUDUN. 1971. a. 22 rue de
Chateaudun, 75009 Paris, France.

350   IT   ISSN 0084-6619
ANNUARIO AMMINISTRATIVO ITALIANO. a.
Guida Monaci, Via Francesco Crispi 10, 00187
Rome, Italy.

350   UK
ARABIAN GOVERNMENT AND PUBLIC
SERVICES DIRECTORY. a. Parrish-Rogers
International Ltd., Jubilee House, Billing Brook Rd.,
Weston Favell, Northampton NN3 4NW, England.

333.7   AG   ISSN 0302-5705
ARGENTINA. SERVICIO NACIONAL DE
PARQUES NACIONAL. ANALES. 1945. irreg.
25000p. Servicio Nacional de Parques Nacionales,
Santa Fe 690, Buenos Aires, Argentina. illus. circ.
4,000.
  Continues: Argentina. Direccion General de
Parques Nacionales. Anales de Parques Nacionales
(ISSN 0518-4614)

353.9   US   ISSN 0094-0712
ARIZONA. DEPARTMENT OF ECONOMIC
SECURITY. ANNUAL REPORT. 1973. a.
Department of Economic Security, 1717 W.
Jefferson, Box 6123, Phoenix, AZ 85005. illus. Key
Title: Annual Report - Arizona. Department of
Economic Security.

PUBLIC ADMINISTRATION

350   US
ARIZONA DIRECTORY OF STATE REGULATORY AGENCIES FOR BUSINESSES AND OCCUPATIONS. a. Office of Economic Planning and Development, 1645 W. Jefferson St., Rm. 428, Phoenix, AZ 85007.

ASSOCIATION OF HIGHWAY OFFICIALS OF THE NORTH ATLANTIC STATES. PROCEEDINGS. see *TRANSPORTATION — Roads And Traffic*

336.94   AT
AUSTRALIA. BUREAU OF STATISTICS. PUBLIC AUTHORITY FINANCE: FEDERAL AUTHORITIES. a. Australian Bureau of Statistics, P.O. Box 10, Belconnen, A.C.T. 2616, Australia. illus. stat. circ. 695.
    Formerly: Australia. Bureau of Statistics. Public Authority Finance: Authorities of the Australian Government.

350   AT   ISSN 0313-9948
AUSTRALIA. NATIONAL CAPITAL DEVELOPMENT COMMISSION. TECHNICAL PAPERS. 1974. irreg. price varies. National Capital Development Commission, 220 Northbourne Ave., Canberra, A.C.T. 2601, Australia.

350   AT
AUSTRALIA. PUBLIC SERVICE BOARD. ANNUAL REPORT. 1924. a. price varies. Australian Government Publishing Service, Box 84, Canberra, A.C.T. 2600, Australia. circ. 4,500.

348   US   ISSN 0092-0959
BALDWIN'S OHIO LEGISLATIVE SERVICE. 1971. 9-10/yr. $110. Banks-Baldwin Law Publishing Co., University Center, Box 1974, Cleveland, OH 44106. circ. 5,000.

351   BG
BANGLADESH. MINISTRY OF FOREIGN AFFAIRS. LIST OF THE DIPLOMATIC CORPS AND OTHER FOREIGN REPRESENTATIVES. (Text in English) Tk.5.75. Ministry of Foreign Affairs, Dacca, Bangladesh.

350   SZ   ISSN 0067-4540
BASLER ZEITSCHRIFT FUER GESCHICHTE UND ALTERTUMSKUNDE. (Text in German, French) 1902. a. 63 Fr. ‡ Historische und Antiquarische Gesellschaft zu Basel, Universitaetsbibliothek, Schoenbeinstr. 18-20, CH-4056 Basel, Switzerland. Eds. A. Staehelim, Martin Steinmann. circ. 1,200.

352   GW   ISSN 0067-4702
BAYERISCHES BEAMTEN-JAHRBUCH. 1968. a. DM.49.95. (Bayerischer Beamtenbund) Walhalla- und Praetoria-Verlag Georg Zwichenpflug, Dolomitenstr. 1, Postfach 301, 8400 Regensburg 1, W. Germany (B. R. D.) Ed. Dieter Kattenbeck.

354   NR
BENDEL STATE. MINISTRY OF INFORMATION, SOCIAL DEVELOPMENT AND SPORTS. ESTIMATE. a. £N5. Ministry of Information, Social Development and Sports, Printing and Stationery Division, P.M.B. 1099, Benin City, Nigeria (Orders to Bendel State Government Printer, Government Press, Benin City, Nigeria)
    Formerly: Bendel State. Ministry of Home Affairs and Information. Mid-Western State Estimates.

350   BE   ISSN 0005-8777
BENELUX PUBLIKATIEBLAD/BULLETIN BENELUX. (Supplement to Textes de Base Benelux) (Text in Dutch & French) 1958. irreg. (approx. 8/yr.) B E N E L U X Economic Union, Rue de la Regence 39, 1000 Brussels, Belgium. (looseleaf format)

310 350   BO
BOLIVIA. INSTITUTO NACIONAL DE ESTADISTICA. ESTADISTICAS REGIONALES DEPARTAMENTALES. a. $1.70. Instituto Nacional de Estadistica, Av. 6 de Agosto no. 2507, La Paz, Bolivia.

351   US   ISSN 0068-0125
BOOK OF THE STATES. 1935. biennial. $28. Council of State Governments, Box 11910, Iron Works Pike, Lexington, KY 40578. Ed. Jack Gardner. index. circ. 11,000.

350   FR
BOTTIN ADMINISTRATIF. 1943. a. $47. Societe Didot Bottin, 28 rue du Docteur Finlay, 75738 Paris Cedex 15, France.

353.002   US   ISSN 0363-6275
BRADDOCK'S FEDERAL-STATE-LOCAL GOVERNMENT DIRECTORY. 1975. a. $19.95. Braddock Publications, Inc., 1001 Connecticut Ave., N.W., Suite 210, Suite 905, Washington, DC 20036. Ed. Bonnie Stern.

631.6   BL
BRAZIL. DEPARTAMENTO NACIONAL DE OBRAS CONTRAS AS SECAS. RELATORIO. Cover title: Relatoria D N O C S. 1945. a. free. Departamento Nacional de Obras Contras as Secas, Rua Senador Pompeu No 713, Fortaleza-Ceara 60000, Brazil. bk. rev. charts, illus, stat. circ. controlled. (processed)

352 657   BL
BRAZIL. INSPETORIA-GERAL DE FINANCAS. BALANCOS GERAIS DA UNIAO.* 1972. a. free. Inspetoria-Geral de Financas, Esplanada dos Ministerios, Brasilia D.F., Brazil.

350   BL
BRAZIL. MINISTERIO DO INTERIOR. RELATORIO DE ATIVIDADES. irreg. Ministerio do Interior, Secretaria Geral, Brasilia, Brazil. illus. Regional planning

363.6   AU   ISSN 0520-9048
BRENNSTOFFSTATISTIK DER WAERMEKRAFTWERKE FUER DIE OEFFENTLICHE ELEKTRIZITAETSVERSORGUNG IN OESTERREICH. (Issued in cooperation with Osterreichische Elektrizitaetswirtschafts-A.G.) a. Bundesministerium fuer Handel, Gewerbe und Industrie, Am Hof 6a, A-1010 Vienna, Austria.

350   BX   ISSN 0084-8123
BRUNEI ANNUAL REPORT. 1958. a. B.$10. Department of Information, Bandar Seri Begawan, Brunei. circ. 1,500.

354.666   LB
BUDGET OF THE GOVERNMENT OF LIBERIA.* 1960. a. Bureau of the Budget, Monrovia, Liberia.

350   TI
LE BUDGET TUNISIEN. 1978. a. 1500 din. Dar el Amal d'Edition, de Diffusion, et de Presse, Rue 2 Mars 1934, Tunis, Tunisia. circ. 10,000.

363.6   FR   ISSN 0154-0033
BULLETIN OFFICIEL DU MINISTERE DE L'ENVIRONNEMENT ET DU CADRE DE VIE ET DU MINISTERE DES TRANSPORTS. irreg. 288 F. France. Direction des Journaux Officiels, 26 rue Desaix, 75732 Paris, France. (Co-sponsor: Ministere des Transports)

331.795   CE
BUREAUCRAT. Cover title: Da Biyurokrat. (Text in English or Sinhalese) 1974. irreg. Rs.4. Sri Lanka Administrative Service Association, Box 1520, Colombo, Sri Lanka.

353.9   US
CALIFORNIA JOB CREATION PROGRAM BOARD. ANNUAL REPORT. 1970. a. free. California Job Creation Program Board, 1125 10th St., Sacramento, CA 95814. Ed. P. Blair Jackson, Robert S. Barton. stat. circ. 1,000.
    Formerly: California Job Development Corporation Law Executive Board. Annual Report (ISSN 0092-4253)

350   US
CALIFORNIA POLICY SEMINAR. MONOGRAPH. 1978. irreg., no. 3, 1978. University of California, Berkeley, Institute of Governmental Studies, Berkeley, CA 94720. (reprint service avail. from UMI)

350   CN   ISSN 0382-1161
CANADA. COMMISSIONER OF OFFICIAL LANGUAGES. ANNUAL REPORT. (Text in English and French) 1971. a. Commissioner of Official Languages, Ottawa, Ont. K1A OT8, Canada.

350   CN
CANADA. DEPARTMENT OF CONSUMER & CORPORATE AFFAIRS. ANNUAL REPORT. (Text in English & French) 1968. a. free. ‡ Department of Consumer & Corporate Affairs, Place du Portage, Ottawa-Hull K1A OC9, Canada. Ed. Claude Jarry. charts. stat. circ. 2,000.

354   CN   ISSN 0383-5154
CANADA. DEPARTMENT OF INDUSTRY, TRADE AND COMMERCE. ANNUAL REPORT. 1970. a. Department of Industry, Trade and Commerce, Ottawa, Ont., Canada. stat.

CANADA. LAW REFORM COMMISSION. ANNUAL REPORT. see *LAW*

350   CN
CANADA. NATIONAL ENERGY BOARD. REPORTS TO THE GOVERNOR IN COUNCIL. 1960. irreg. price varies. ‡ National Energy Board, 473 Albert St., Ottawa, Ont. K1A 0E5, Canada. circ. controlled.

537   CN   ISSN 0068-791X
CANADA. NATIONAL ENERGY BOARD. STAFF PAPERS. 1960. irreg. ‡ National Energy Board, Ottawa, Ont., Canada. circ. controlled.

354   CN
CANADA. TREASURY BOARD SECRETARIAT. ESTIMATES/BUDGET DES DEPENSES. a. Can.$6. Treasury Board, Place Bell Canada, 19th Floor, Ottawa, Ont. K1A OR5, Canada. stat.

350.722   CN   ISSN 0706-6007
CANADA. TREASURY BOARD SECRETARIAT. FEDERAL EXPENDITURE PLAN. (Text in English and French) 1977. a. Treasury Board, Communications Division, Place Bell Canada, 19th Floor, Ottawa, K1A OR5, Canada. charts. stat.

309.1   SG
CARTE D'IDENTITE DU SENEGAL. 1971. a. free. Ministere de l'Information et de Telecommunications, Direction de l'Information, 58 Bd. de la Republique, Dakar, Senegal. illus. stat.

328   CJ   ISSN 0300-4740
CAYMAN ISLANDS. LEGISLATIVE ASSEMBLY. MINUTES. 1966. irreg. price varies. Legislative Assembly, Box 243, Georgetown, Grand Cayman, Cayman Islands, B.W.I. (processed)

350   AG
CENTRO DE ESTUDIOS DE ESTADO Y SOCIEDAD. DOCUMENTOS DE TRABAJO. 1970. irreg. Instituto Torcuato di Tella, Av. Cordoba 939, Buenos Aires, Argentina.
    Supersedes in part: Centro de Investigaciones en Administracion Publica. Documentos de Trabajo (ISSN 0069-214X)

350   JA
CHINA DIRECTORY. (Text in English and Japanese) 1971. irreg. 8000 Yen($40) Radiopress, Inc, Fuji Television Bldg, 7 Ichigaya Kawada- cho, Shinjuku-ku, Tokyo 162, Japan. Ed. Jiro Inagawa. bk. rev. circ. 2,000.

352.16   CN
CIVIC PUBLIC WORKS REFERENCE MANUAL AND BUYER'S GUIDE. 1954. a. Can.$15. Maclean-Hunter, Ltd, 481 University Ave, Toronto M5W 1A7, Canada. Ed. Walter Jones.
    Former titles: Civic Municipal Reference Manual and Purchasing Guide (ISSN 0069-4258); Civic Administration's Municipal Reference Manual and Purchasing Guide.

350   US
CIVIL SERVICE NEWS. irreg. free. ‡ U.S. Office of Personnel Management, News Unit, 1900 E St., Room 5F10, Washington, DC 20415. (processed)
    Formerly: Civil Service News Releases (ISSN 0009-8019)
    Civil service

350   UK   ISSN 0302-329X
CIVIL SERVICE YEAR BOOK. a. £4. Civil Service Department, Whitehall, London S.W.1, England (Avail. from H.M.S.O., c/o Liaison Officer, Atlantic House, Holborn Viaduct, London EC1P 1BN, England)
    Formerly: British Imperial Calendar and Civil Service List.

350   CK
COLOMBIA. DEPARTAMENTO ADMINISTRATIVO NACIONAL DE ESTADISTICA. DIVISION POLITICO-ADMINISTRATIVA. 1953. irreg. Departamento Administrativo Nacional de Estadistica, Banco Nacional de Datos, Centro Administrativo Nacional, Apdo. Aereo 80043, Avenida Eldorado, Bogota, Colombia. illus.

354.94   AT
COMMONWEALTH GOVERNMENT DIRECTORY. 1973. irreg. price varies. Australian Government Publishing Service, P.O. Box 84, Canberra, A.C.T. 2600, Australia.
   Formerly: Australian Government Directory.

354   CN
COMMUNICATOR. 1976. irreg. Newfoundland Association of Public Employees, Box 1085, St. John's, Nfld. A1C 5M5, Canada. Ed. Brenda M. Murphy. illus. circ. 12,500.
   Former titles: N A P E Journal (ISSN 0381-6826); N A P E News (ISSN 0318-1723)

350   336   TT
CONGRESS OF MICRONESIA. JOINT COMMITTEE ON PROGRAM AND BUDGET PLANNING. PUBLIC HEARINGS ON HIGH COMMISSIONER'S PRELIMINARY BUDGET. (Text in English) a. Congress of Micronesia, Joint Committee on Program and Budget Planning, Capitol Hill, Saipan 96950, Mariana Islands.

CONGRESS OF MICRONESIA. SENATE. JOURNAL. see *LAW*

350   US   ISSN 0149-9130
CONTEMPORARY ECONOMIC PROBLEMS. 1976. a. American Enterprise Institute for Public Policy Research, 1150 17th St. N. W., Washington, DC 20036.
   Formerly: A E I Studies on Contemporary Economic Problems (ISSN 0149-922X); Incorporating: American Enterprise Institute for Public Policy Research. Long-Range Studies (ISSN 0065-8154) & Foreign Affairs Studies & National Energy Studies; Supersedes: American Enterprise Institute for Public Policy Research. Evaluative Studies Series.

350   US
CONTEMPORARY GOVERNMENT SERIES. irreg. price varies. Houghton Mifflin Co., One Beacon St., Boston, MA 02107.

350   US   ISSN 0099-006X
COUNCIL OF STATE GOVERNMENTS. SOUTHERN LEGISLATIVE CONFERENCE. SUMMARY, ANNUAL MEETING. a. $3. Council of State Governments, Southern Legislative Conference, 3384 Peachtree Rd. N.E., Room 610, Atlanta, GA 30326. Key Title: Summary, Annual Meeting of the Southern Legislative Conference of the Council of State Governments.

011   UK   ISSN 0070-1211
COUNCILS, COMMITTEES AND BOARDS; a handbook of advisory, consultative, executive and similar bodies in British public life. 1970. biennial, 4th, 1980. £32.50($100) ‡ C.B.D. Research Ltd., 154 High St., Beckenham, Kent BR3 1EA, England (Dist. in U.S. by: Gale Research Co., Book Tower, Detroit, MI 48226) Ed. I. G. Anderson. index. circ. 2,000.

350   US
CURRENT GOVERNMENTS REPORTS. quarterly and annual. $20.50 annual subscription for GE, GF, GR, GT series; single copies available. U.S. Bureau of the Census, Subscriber Services Section, Washington, DC 20233 (Series GE, GF, GR, GT available from Bureau's Subscriber Services Section, Other series available from: Supt. of Documents, Washington, DC 20402)

350   331   US
CURRENT GOVERNMENTS REPORTS: COUNTY EMPLOYMENT. (Series GE-4) a. U.S. Bureau of the Census, Subscriber Services Section, Washington, DC 20233.

CURRENT GOVERNMENTS REPORTS: FINANCES OF EMPLOYEE RETIREMENT SYSTEMS OF STATE AND LOCAL GOVERNMENTS. see *BUSINESS AND ECONOMICS — Public Finance, Taxation*

350   331   US
CURRENT GOVERNMENTS REPORTS, GE-GOVERNMENT EMPLOYMENT. annual. $20.50 with GF, GR, GT series. U.S. Bureau of the Census, Subscriber Services Section, DC 20233.

CURRENT GOVERNMENTS REPORTS, GR FINANCES OF SELECTED PUBLIC EMPLOYEE RETIREMENT SYSTEMS. see *BUSINESS AND ECONOMICS — Public Finance, Taxation*

362   US   ISSN 0360-4357
D.P.I. YELLOW PAGES. a. Department of Public Institutions, Box 94728, Lincoln, NE 68509.

350   US   ISSN 0094-7911
DELAWARE STATISTICAL ABSTRACT. biennial. $5. Office of Management, Budget & Planning, Thomas Collins Bldg., Dover, DE 19901. stat.

352   GW   ISSN 0070-4423
DEUTSCHES BEAMTEN-JAHRBUCH; BUNDESAUSGABE. 1968. a. DM.49.95. Walhalla- und Praetoria-Verlag Georg Zwichenpflug, Dolomitenstr. 1, Postf. 301, 8400 Regensburg 1, W. Germany (B.R.D.) Eds. Erich Sayn, Karl-August Weber. bk. rev.

350   GT
DIARIO DE CENTRO AMERICO. irreg. 18 Calle No. 6-72, Zona 1, Guatemala, Guatemala.
   Formerly: Guatemalteco.
   Official organ of the Republic of Guatemala

034   350   FR
DICTIONNAIRE DES COMMUNES (LAVAUZELLE ET CIE) quadrenially. 133 F. per no. Editions Charles Lavauzelle et Cie, 25 Quai des Grands Augustins, 75006 Paris, France.

352   US   ISSN 0070-5888
DIRECTORY OF MUNICIPAL OFFICIALS OF NEW MEXICO. a. $10 to governments; others $13. ‡ New Mexico Municipal League, 1229 Paseo de Peralta, Box 846, Santa Fe, NM 87501.

353.9   US   ISSN 0094-6346
DIRECTORY OF SELECTED ILLINOIS STATE AGENCIES. irreg. State Library, Centennial Bldg., Springfield, IL 62756. (Co-sponsor: Illinois Secretary of State)

353.9   US   ISSN 0440-4947
DIRECTORY OF STATE, COUNTY , AND FEDERAL OFFICIALS. 1964. a. price varies. Legislative Reference Bureau, State Capitol, Honolulu, HI 96813.

354.729   DR
DOMINICAN REPUBLIC. OFICINA NACIONAL DE PRESUPUESTO. EJECUCION PRESUPUESTARIA. INFORME. a. Oficina Nacional de Presupuesto, Santo Domingo, Dominican Republic. Dir. Rafael F.Nunez Llano. charts, stat.
   Formerly: Dominican Republic. Oficina Nacional de Presupuesto. Ejecucion del Presupuesto.

354   DR
DOMINICAN REPUBLIC SECRETARIA DE ESTADO DE OBRAS PUBLICAS Y COMUNICACIONES. OPC. 1972. irreg. free. ‡ Secretaria de Estado de Obras Publicas y Comunicaciones, c/o Director General de Programacion y Proyectos, Santo Domingo, Dominican Republic. adv. index. circ. 1,000.
   Formerly: Dominican Republic. Secretaria de Obras Publicas y Comunicaciones. Estadistica (ISSN 0070-7066)

351   US   ISSN 0092-8380
ENCYCLOPEDIA OF GOVERNMENTAL ADVISORY ORGANIZATIONS. 1973. irreg., 2nd ed, 1975. $94. Gale Research Company, Book Tower, Detroit, MI 48226. Ed. Linda E. Sullivan, Anthony T. Kruzas.

350   US
ESSAYS IN PUBLIC WORKS HISTORY. 1976. irreg., no. 9, 1980. Public Works Historical Society, 1313 E. 60th St., Chicago, IL 60637.

354   PN   ISSN 0378-2603
ESTADISTICA PANAMENA. SITUACION ECONOMICA. SECCION 342. CUENTAS NACIONALES. 1950. a. Bl..30. Direccion de Estadistica y Censo, Contraloria General, Apartado 5213, Panama 5, Panama. circ. 2,200.

352   FR
EUROPEAN CONFERENCE OF LOCAL AND REGIONAL AUTHORITIES. DOCUMENTS. (For 1st and 2nd Sessions, Documents and Texts Adopted issued in one vol) 1957. irreg. price varies. European Conference of Local and Regional Authorities, Publications Section, Strasbourg, France (Dist. in U.S. by Manhattan Publishing Co., 225 Lafayette St., New York, N.Y. 10012) (Affiliate: Council of Europe) bk. rev.
   Formerly: European Conference of Local Authorities. Documents (ISSN 0071-2612)

352   FR
EUROPEAN CONFERENCE OF LOCAL AND REGIONAL AUTHORITIES. OFFICIAL REPORTS OF DEBATES. (Reports of 1st-3rd Sessions never published) 1962. a. price varies. European Conference of Local and Regional Authorities, Publications Section, Strasbourg, France (Dist. in U.S. by Manhattan Publishing Co., 225 Lafayette St., New York, N.Y. 10012) (Affiliate: Council of Europe) bk. rev.
   Formerly: European Conference of Local Authorities. Official Reports of Debates (ISSN 0071-2620)

352   FR
EUROPEAN CONFERENCE OF LOCAL AND REGIONAL AUTHORITIES. TEXTS ADOPTED. (For 1st and 2nd Sessions, Documents and Texts Adopted issued in one vol) 1957. a. price varies. European Conference of Local and Regional Authorities, Publications Section, Strasbourg, France (Dist. in U.S. by Manhattan Publishing Co., 225 Lafayette St., New York, N.Y. 10012) bk. rev.
   Formerly: European Conference of Local Authorities. Texts Adopted (ISSN 0071-2639)

350   II   ISSN 0085-1795
F M U OCCASIONAL LECTURES. no. 2, 1971. irreg. price varies. Indian Institute of Public Administration, Financial Management Unit, Indraprastha Estate, Ring Rd., New Delhi 110002, India.

FEDERAL ART PATRONAGE NOTES. see *ART*

353.007   US   ISSN 0363-5422
FEDERAL BUDGET: FOCUS AND PERSPECTIVES. irreg. Tax Foundation, Inc., 1875 Connecticut Ave., N.W., Washington, DC 20009. stat.

353   331.2   US
FEDERAL CIVILIAN WORK FORCE STATISTICS. ANNUAL REPORT OF EMPLOYMENT BY GEOGRAPHIC AREA. 1966. a. ‡ U.S. Office of Personnel Management, Agency Compliance and Evaluation, Work Force Analysis and Statistics Branch, 1900 E St. N.W., Washington, DC 20415 (Orders to: Supt. of Documents, Washington, DC 20402) stat. circ. 1,200. (also avail. in microform) Indexed: C.I.S.Ind.
   Former titles: Annual Report of Federal Civilian Employment by Geographic Area (ISSN 0090-6263); Annual Report of Federal Civilian Employment in the United States by Geographic Area.

351   US   ISSN 0071-4127
FEDERAL EMPLOYEES ALMANAC. 1954. a. $2.75. Federal Employees News Digest, Inc., P.O. Box 457, Merrifield, VA 22116. Ed. Joseph Young.

FEDERAL REPORTER. see *AERONAUTICS AND SPACE FLIGHT*

350   CN   ISSN 0708-9511
FEDERATION OF CANADIAN MUNICIPALITIES. ANNUAL CONFERENCE PROCEEDINGS. (Text in English and French) 1937. a. price varies. Federation of Canadian Municipalities, Suite 600, 220 Laurier Ave. W., Ottawa, Ont. K1P 5Z9, Canada. circ. 500.
   Formerly (until 1976): Canadian Federation and Municipalities. Annual Conference and Proceedings (ISSN 0068-8711)

350   FJ
FIJI INFORMATION. a. free. Ministry of Information, Government Bldgs., Suva, Fiji.

PUBLIC ADMINISTRATION

353.9   US   ISSN 0095-5175
FLORIDA. DEPARTMENT OF
ADMINISTRATION. BUDGET IN BRIEF. a.
Department of Administration, Tallahassee, FL
32301. Key Title: Budget in Brief - State of Florida.

362.6   US
FLORIDA'S LOCAL RETIREMENT SYSTEMS: A
SURVEY. 1973. triennial. free. Department of
Administration, Division of Retirement, Room 530,
Carlton Building, Tallahassee, FL 32304. Ed.
Douglas M. Mann. stat. index. circ. 800.

944 338.9   FR   ISSN 0071-8491
FRANCE. COMMISSION NATIONALE DE
L'AMENAGEMENT DU TERRITOIRE.
RAPPORT. 1964. irreg., 1971, no. 2.
Documentation Francaise, 29/31 Quai Voltaire,
75340 Paris Cedex 07, France.

350   FR   ISSN 0071-8513
FRANCE. CONSEIL NATIONAL DE LA
COMPTABILITE. RAPPORT D'ACTIVITE. 1962.
irreg., 1975, no. 8. price varies. Conseil National de
la Comptabilite, c/o Imprimerie Nationale,
Etablissement de Douai. Route d'Auby, 59128
Flers-en-Escrebieux, France.

350   FR   ISSN 0080-1186
FRANCE. DELEGATION GENERALE A LA
RECHERCHE SCIENTIFIQUE ET TECHNIQUE.
REPERTOIRE PERMANENT DE
L'ADMINISTRATION FRANCAISE. 1945. a. 38
F. Documentation Francaise, 29-31 Quai Voltaire,
75340 Paris, France.

353.9   US   ISSN 0091-3448
GEORGIA. STATE ECONOMIC OPPORTUNITY
OFFICE. ANNUAL REPORT. a. free. State
Economic Opportunity Office, 618 Ponce de Leon
Ave. N.E., Atlanta, GA 30308. stat. Key Title:
Annual Report - State Economic Opportunity Office
(Atlanta)

001.4   GW
GERMANY (FEDERAL REPUBLIC, 1949-).
BUNDESMINISTERIUM FUER BILDUNG AND
WISSENSCHAFT. FORSCHUNGSBERICHT
DER BUNDESREGIERUNG.* irreg. Verlag Dr.
Heger, Goethestrasse 54, 53 Bonn-Bad Godesberg,
W. Germany (B.R.D.)

354   GW
GERMANY (FEDERAL REPUBLIC, 1949-)
PRESSE- UND INFORMATIONSAMT
BULLETIN ARCHIVE SUPPLEMENT. (Text in
English) 1974. irreg. Presse und Informationsamt -
Press and Information Office, Welckerstr. 11, 5300
Bonn, W. Germany (B.R.D.)

350   UK   ISSN 0140-5764
GOVERNMENT AND MUNICIPAL
CONTRACTORS. 1935. a. £12. Sell's Publications
Ltd., Sell's House, 39 East St., Epsom KT17 1BQ,
Surrey, England. adv. bk. rev. circ. 5,000.
    Former titles: Sell's Government and Municipal
Contractors Register (ISSN 0072-5129);
Government and Municipal Contractors Register.

350   SI
GOVERNMENT AND PUBLIC
ADMINISTRATION SOCIETY. JOURNAL. (Text
in English & Chinese) a. not for sale. Government
and Public Administration Society, Nanyang
University, Singapore, Singapore.

353   US   ISSN 0072-5153
GOVERNMENT CONTRACTS MONOGRAPHS.
1961. irreg., no. 12, 1979. price varies. ‡ George
Washington University, Government Contracts
Program, 2000 H St. N.W., Rm. 308, Washington,
DC 20052.

350   US   ISSN 0072-517X
GOVERNMENT IN HAWAII; a handbook of
financial statistics. 1954. a. $1. Tax Foundation of
Hawaii, 680 Alexander Young Bldg, Honolulu, HI
96813.

354.54   II
GOVERNMENT OF ANDHRA PRADESH.
REPORT.* (Text in English) a. Office of the
Comptroller and Auditor-General, Director of
Printing and Stationery, Hyderabad, Andhra
Pradesh, India.
    Continues: Government of Andhra Pradesh.
Audit Report.

350   US   ISSN 0094-6648
GRADUATE SCHOOL PROGRAMS IN PUBLIC
AFFAIRS AND PUBLIC ADMINISTRATION.
Variant titles: N A S P A A Roster. Programs in
Public Affairs and Administration. irreg., latest
1978. $10. National Association of Schools of
Public Affairs and Administration, 1225
Connecticut Ave., N.W., Suite 306, Washington,
DC 20036.

351.1   UK   ISSN 0307-9589
GREAT BRITAIN. CIVIL SERVICE
DEPARTMENT. REPORT. 1969. irreg., 3rd
report, 1973. price varies. Civil Service Department,
Whitehall, London SW1A 2AZ, London EC1P
1BN, England (Avail. from H.M.S.O., c/o Liaison
Officer, Atlantic House, Holborn Viaduct, London
EC1P 1BN, England) stat.

GREAT BRITAIN. DEPARTMENT OF THE
ENVIRONMENT. STATISTICS FOR TOWN
AND COUNTRY PLANNING. SERIES 1. see
HOUSING AND URBAN PLANNING

GREAT BRITAIN. DEPARTMENT OF THE
ENVIRONMENT. STATISTICS FOR TOWN
AND COUNTRY PLANNING. SERIES 2. see
HOUSING AND URBAN PLANNING

350   UK   ISSN 0072-7032
GREAT BRITAIN. PUBLIC WORKS LOAN
BOARD. REPORT. a. 70p. Public Works Loan
Board, Royex House, Aldermanbury Square,
London EC2V 7LT, England (Avail. from
H.M.S.O., c/o Liaison Officer, Atlantic House,
Holborn Viaduct, London EC1P 1BN, England)

352 300   UK   ISSN 0072-7350
GREATER LONDON PAPERS; problems of
government of greater London. 1961. irreg., latest
1976. price varies. London School of Economics
and Political Science, Houghton St., Aldwych,
London W.C.2, England.

353.9   US   ISSN 0072-8454
GUIDE TO GOVERNMENT IN HAWAII. 1961.
irreg., 6th edt., 1978. $3. Legislative Reference
Bureau, State Capitol, Honolulu, HI 96813. Ed. Jon
T. Okudara.

353.9   US   ISSN 0091-0716
GUIDE TO NEBRASKA STATE AGENCIES.
(Supplement to: Nebraska State Publications
Checklist) 1973. a. inculded in subscr. to Nebraska
State Publications Checklist. Nebraska Publications
Clearinghouse, 1420 P St., NE, Lincoln, NE 68508.
Ed. Vern Buis. circ. 500. (also avail. in microfiche)

350   US
GUIDE TO TEXAS STATE AGENCIES. irreg; 5th
ed., 1977. $12.50. University of Texas at Austin,
Lyndon B. Johnson School of Public Affairs, Austin,
TX 78712.

HANDAKTEN FUER DIE STANDESAMTLICHE
ARBEIT. see LAW

350   US
HARVARD UNIVERSITY. PROGRAM ON
INFORMATION TECHNOLOGIES AND
PUBLIC POLICY. WORKING PAPER. irreg.
Harvard University, Program on Information
Technologies and Public Policy, Cambridge, MA
02138.

350 336   US
HAWAII. LEGISLATIVE AUDITOR. SPECIAL
REPORTS. 1965. irreg.(3-5/yr) free. ‡ Office of the
Auditor, State Capitol, Honolulu, HI 96813. charts.
stat.

350   US   ISSN 0073-1277
HAWAII. LEGISLATIVE REFERENCE BUREAU.
REPORT. 1951. irreg. price varies. Legislative
Reference Bureau, State Capitol, Honolulu, HI
96813.

350   US   ISSN 0073-3865
HUMAN RESOURCES RESEARCH
ORGANIZATION. BIBLIOGRAPHY OF
PUBLICATIONS. 1953. a. free. Human Resources
Research Organization, 300 North Washington St.,
Alexandria, VA 22314. Ed. Lola M. Zook. circ.
5,000. (also avail. in microform from NTI)

350   US   ISSN 0073-3873
HUMAN RESOURCES RESEARCH
ORGANIZATION. PROFESSIONAL PAPERS.
1966. irreg. free. Human Resources Research
Organization, 300 North Washington St,
Alexandria, VA 22314. (also avail. in microform
from NTI) Indexed: Psychol.Abstr.

350   US   ISSN 0073-389X
HUMAN RESOURCES RESEARCH
ORGANIZATION. TECHNICAL REPORT. 1953.
irreg. price varies. Human Resources Research
Organization, 300 North Washington St.,
Alexandria, VA 22314. (also avail. in microform
from NTI) Indexed: Psychol.Abstr.

352.7   NE   ISSN 0539-1083
I U L A (PUBLICATION) (Text in French and
English) 1967. irreg., no. 109, 1976. International
Union of Local Authorities, Wassenaarseweg 45,
2596 CG The Hague, Netherlands.

353   US   ISSN 0195-7783
ILLINOIS GOVERNMENT RESEARCH. 1959.
irreg. (approx. 3-4/yr.) free to qualified personnel.
University of Illinois at Urbana-Champaign, Institute
of Government & Public Affairs, 1201 W. Nevada
St., Urbana, IL 61801.
    Formerly: Illinois Government. (ISSN 0073-4837)

350   US   ISSN 0149-3752
ILLINOIS ISSUES ANNUAL. 1976. a. $3.75.
Sangamon State University, Springfield, IL 62708.
Ed. Caroline Gherardini. circ. 1,500.

354   II
INDIA. CARDAMOM BOARD. ANNUAL
REPORT. (Text in English) a. Cardamom Board,
Chittoor Rd., Cochin 682018, India.

350   II   ISSN 0073-6171
INDIA. CENTRAL VIGILANCE COMMISSION.
REPORT. (Text in English and Hindi) 1965. a. free.
Central Vigilance Commission, 3 Dr. Rajendra
Prasad Rd., New Delhi, India. circ. controlled.

354   II
INDIA. DEPARTMENT OF ECONOMIC
AFFAIRS. BUDGET DIVISION. KEY TO THE
BUDGET DOCUMENTS. (Text in English) a.
Department of Economic Affairs, Budget Division,
New Delhi, India.

INDIA. DEPARTMENT OF POWER. REPORT. see
ENERGY

354   II   ISSN 0445-6831
INDIA. PARLIAMENT. PUBLIC ACCOUNTS
COMMITTEE. REPORT ON THE ACCOUNTS.
(Each report covers various agencies of the
government.) (Text in English) 1947/48. a.
Parliament, Public Accounts Committee, Lok Sabha
Secretariat, New Delhi, India.

351.1   II   ISSN 0073-6236
INDIA. UNION PUBLIC SERVICE COMMISSION
REPORT. (Report year ends Mar. 31) (Text in
English) 1951. a. Union Public Service Commission,
Minto Rd., New Delhi, India.

350   US   ISSN 0148-9232
INDIANA. OFFICE OF COMMUNITY SERVICES
ADMINISTRATION. ANNUAL REPORT. 1976.
a. free. Office of Community Services
Administration, 20 N. Meridian St., Indianapolis,
IN 46204. Ed. Donald Henry. circ. 2,000.

INDIANA UNIVERSITY. SCHOOL OF PUBLIC
AND ENVIRONMENTAL AFFAIRS.
OCCASIONAL PAPERS. see
ENVIRONMENTAL STUDIES

350   IO
INDONESIA. DEPARTEMEN PENERANGAN.
SIARAN UMUM. irreg. Department of
Information, Direktorat Publikasi, Jl. Merdeka Barat
7, Jakarta, Indonesia.

INFORMATIQUE DANS LES
ADMINISTRATIONS FRANCAISES. see
COMPUTER TECHNOLOGY AND
APPLICATIONS

350   CN
INSTITUTE FOR RESEARCH ON PUBLIC
POLICY. OCCASIONAL PAPERS. no.13, 1980.
irreg. Institute for Research on Public Policy, 2149
Mackay St., Montreal, Que. H3G 2J2, Canada.

350 IE ISSN 0073-9596
INSTITUTE OF PUBLIC ADMINISTRATION, DUBLIN. ADMINISTRATION YEARBOOK AND DIARY. (Text mainly in English; some Irish) 1967. a. £15. Institute of Public Administration, 57-61 Lansdowne Rd, Dublin 4, Ireland. Ed. A. Farmar. adv. circ. 8,500.

350 IE ISSN 0073-9588
INSTITUTE OF PUBLIC ADMINISTRATION, DUBLIN. ANNUAL REPORT. (Text mainly in English; some Irish) 1958. a. free. Institute of Public Administration, 57-61 Lansdowne Road, Dublin 4, Ireland. Ed. Tess Higgins. circ. 2,000.

354 SJ ISSN 0073-9618
INSTITUTE OF PUBLIC ADMINISTRATION, KHARTOUM. OCCASIONAL PAPERS. 1964. irreg. Institute of Public Administration, P.O. Box 1492, Khartoum, Sudan.

354 SJ ISSN 0073-9626
INSTITUTE OF PUBLIC ADMINISTRATION, KHARTOUM. PROCEEDINGS OF THE ANNUAL ROUND TABLE CONFERENCE. (Text in English or Arabic) 1959. irreg. Institute of Public Administration, P.O. Box 1492, Khartoum, Sudan.

354.7 CN ISSN 0380-3988
INSTITUTE OF PUBLIC ADMINISTRATION OF CANADA. BULLETIN. (Text in English and French) 1979. irreg. Institute of Public Administration of Canada, 897 Bay St., Toronto, Ont. M5S 1Z7, Canada.

350 CR ISSN 0073-9944
INSTITUTO CENTROAMERICANO DE ADMINISTRACION PUBLICA. SERIE 100. ASPECTOS HUMANOS DE LA ADMINISTRACION. 1965. irreg. price varies. Instituto Centroamericano de Administracion Publica, Apartado 10025, San Jose, Costa Rica.

350 CR ISSN 0073-9952
INSTITUTO CENTROAMERICANO DE ADMINISTRACION PUBLICA. SERIE 200. CIENCIA DE LA ADMINISTRACION. 1960. irreg. price varies. Instituto Centroamericano de Administracion Publica, Apartado 10025, San Jose, Costa Rica.

350 CR ISSN 0073-9960
INSTITUTO CENTROAMERICANO DE ADMINISTRACION PUBLICA. SERIE 300: INVESTIGACION. 1968. irreg. price varies. Instituto Centroamericano de Administracion Publica, Apartado 10025, San Jose, Costa Rica.

350 CR ISSN 0073-9979
INSTITUTO CENTROAMERICANO DE ADMINISTRACION PUBLICA. SERIE 400: ECONOMIA Y FINANZAS. 1968. irreg. price varies. Instituto Centroamericano de Administracion Publica, Apartado 10025, San Jose, Costa Rica.

350 CR ISSN 0073-9995
INSTITUTO CENTROAMERICANO DE ADMINISTRACION PUBLICA. SERIE 600: INFORMES DE SEMINARIOS. 1964. irreg. price varies. Instituto Centroamericano de Administracion Publica, Apartado 10025, San Jose, Costa Rica.

350 CR ISSN 0074-0004
INSTITUTO CENTROAMERICANO DE ADMINISTRACION PUBLICA. SERIE 700: MATERIALES DE INFORMACION. 1966. irreg. free. Instituto Centroamericano de Administracion Publica, Apartado 10025, San Jose, Costa Rica.

350 CR ISSN 0074-0012
INSTITUTO CENTROAMERICANO DE ADMINISTRACION PUBLICA. SERIE 800: METODOLOGIA DE LA ADMINISTRACION. 1964. irreg. price varies. Instituto Centroamericano de Administracion Publica, Apartado 10025, San Jose, Costa Rica.

350 CR ISSN 0074-0020
INSTITUTO CENTROAMERICANO DE ADMINISTRACION PUBLICA. SERIE 900: MISCELANEAS. 1965. irreg. price varies. Instituto Centroamericano de Administracion Publica, Apartado 10025, San Jose, Costa Rica.

INTERNATIONAL ASSOCIATION OF CORONERS AND MEDICAL EXAMINERS. PROCEEDINGS. see *MEETINGS AND CONGRESSES*

350 BE ISSN 0074-6479
INTERNATIONAL INSTITUTE OF ADMINISTRATIVE SCIENCES. REPORTS OF THE INTERNATIONAL CONGRESS. 1910. triennial since 1947; 18th, 1980, Madrid. price varies. International Institute of Administrative Sciences, 25 rue de la Charite, 1040 Brussels, Belgium.

351.7 614.84 UK ISSN 0074-7890
INTERNATIONAL SECURITY DIRECTORY; world police, fire and security forces, services, products and supplies. 1963. a. £14.50($35) Court & Judicial Publishing Co. Ltd., Box 39, Henley-on-Thames, Oxfordshire RG9 5UA, England. Ed. C.G.A. Parker. adv. index.

350 US ISSN 0074-106X
INTER-UNIVERSITY CASE PROGRAM. CASE STUDY. (Title varies: I C P Case Series; at head of title: Cases in Public Administration and Policy Information) 1951. irreg. price varies. Inter-University Case Program, Box 229, Syracuse, NY 13210. Ed. E. A. Bock.

350 IQ
IRAQ. MINISTRY OF INFORMATION. INFORMATION SERIES. irreg., no.72, 1977. Ministry of Information, Baghdad, Iraq.

350 IE
IRELAND. PUBLIC SERVICE ADVISORY COUNCIL. REPORT. 1974. a. price varies. Government Publications Sales Office, G.P.O. Arcade, Dublin, Ireland.

350 IS
ISRAEL. COMMISSIONER FOR COMPLAINTS FROM THE PUBLIC (OMBUDSMAN) ANNUAL REPORT. (Editions in English and Hebrew) 1972. a. free. Commissioner for Complaints from the Public, Jerusalem, Israel. circ. 2,000.

354 IV
IVORY COAST. DIRECTION DU BUDGET SPECIAL D'INVESTISSEMENT ET D'EQUIPMENT. RAPPORT DE PRESENTATION DU BUDGET SPECIAL D'INVESTISSEMENT ET D'EQUIPMENT. irreg. Direction du Budget Special d'Investissement et d'Equipment, Abidjan, Ivory Coast. stat.

350 JA
JAPANESE SOCIETY FOR PUBLIC ADMINISTRATION. ANNALS/NIPPON GYOSEI KENKYU NENPO. (Text in Japanese) a. Japanese Society for Public Administration - Nippon Gyosei Gakkai, c/o Faculty of Law, University of Tokyo, Motofuji-cho, Bunkyo-ku, Tokyo 113, Japan. bibl.

350 KE ISSN 0075-5761
K I A OCCASIONAL PAPERS. 1968. irreg., latest no. 4. price varies. Kenya Institute of Administration, P.O. Lower Kabete, Nairobi, Kenya. Ed. H. K. M. Wacirah.

352 NR
KADUNA STATE. MINISTRY OF WORKS. REPORT.* 1960-61. a. price varies. Ministry of Works, Kaduna, Nigeria.
Formerly: North-Central State. Ministry of Works. Report (ISSN 0078-1762)

354.669 NR
KANO STATE OF NIGERIA GAZETTE. 1967. irreg. Government Printer, Kano, Nigeria.
Continues: Northern Nigeria Gazette.

354 II
KARNATAKA. DEPARTMENT OF TOURISM. ANNUAL REPORT. (Text in English) 1975. a. Department of Information and Tourism, 5 Infantry Rd., Bangalore, India.

338.9 KE
KENYA. MINISTRY OF FINANCE AND PLANNING. BUDGET SPEECH BY MINISTER FOR FINANCE AND PLANNING. (Text in English) a. Ministry of Finance and Planning, Box 30007, Nairobi, Kenya (Orders to: Government Printing and Stationery Department, Box 30128, Nairobi, Kenya)
Former titles: Kenya. Ministry of Finance and Economic Planning. Budget Speech; Kenya. Ministry of Finance. Speech Delivered to the National Assembly, Presenting the Budget.

354 KE
KENYA. MINISTRY OF FINANCE AND PLANNING. PLAN IMPLEMENTATION REPORT. 1973. irreg. Ministry of Finance and Planning, Box 30007, Nairobi, Kenya (Orders to: Government Printing and Stationery Department, Box 30128, Nairobi, Kenya)

350 KE ISSN 0075-5931
KENYA. PUBLIC ACCOUNTS COMMITTEE. ANNUAL REPORT. a., latest 1974-75. Government Printing and Stationery Department, Box 30128, Nairobi, Kenya.

354 KE ISSN 0065-1966
KENYA INSTITUTE OF ADMINISTRATION. JOURNAL. 1965. a. EAs.7.50. Kenya Institute of Administration, P.O. Lower Kabete, Nairobi, Kenya. Ed. H. K. M. Wacirah.
Formerly: Administration in Kenya.

350 US
KNOW YOUR CONGRESS. 1943. new edition each session. $4.95. Capital Publishers, Inc., P.O. Box 6235, 5306 Belt Rd., N.W., Washington, DC 20015. Ed. Diosdado M. Yap. circ. 100,000. (also avail. in microform)

350 DK ISSN 0085-2589
KONGELIG DANSK HOF- OG STATSKALENDER; STATSHAANDBOG FOR KONGERIGET DANMARK. 1771. a. price varies. J. H. Schultz Forlag, Vognmagergade 2, 1120 Copenhagen K, Denmark. Ed. Herluf Nielsen. circ. 23,000.

350 US
LANE STUDIES IN REGIONAL GOVERNMENT. irreg. price varies. University of California Press, 2223 Fulton St., Berkeley, CA 94720.

350 LB
LIBERIA. INSTITUTE OF PUBLIC ADMINISTRATION. ANNUAL REPORT. a. Institute of Public Administration, Monrovia, Liberia.

354 LB
LIBERIA. MINISTRY OF ACTION FOR DEVELOPMENT AND PROGRESS ANNUAL REPORT. a. Ministry of Action for Development and Progress, Monrovia, Liberia.

354 LB ISSN 0304-7326
LIBERIA. MINISTRY OF PUBLIC WORKS. ANNUAL REPORT. (Text in English) a. Ministry of Public Works, Monrovia, Liberia.

350 LB
LIBERIA. OFFICE OF NATIONAL PLANNING. ANNUAL REPORT TO THE PRESIDENT ON THE OPERATION AND ACTIVITIES. 1961. a. Office of National Planning, Monrovia, Liberia.
Formerly: Liberia. Bureau of Economic Research and Statistics. Annual Report to the President on the Operation and Activities.

340 352 AT ISSN 0076-0242
LOCAL GOVERNMENT REPORTS OF AUSTRALIA. 1911. irreg. Aus.$61.50. Law Book Co. Ltd., 31 Market St., Sydney, N.S.W. 2000, Australia. Ed. Kenneth Gifford.

350 UK ISSN 0307-0441
LOCAL GOVERNMENT TRENDS. 1974. a. £10. Chartered Institute of Public Finance and Accountancy, 1 Buckingham Place, London SW1E 6HS, England. (back issues avail.)

352 US ISSN 0076-1397
LOYOLA UNIVERSITY. CENTER FOR URBAN POLICY. STUDIES. 1965. irreg., no. 15, 1976. $1. Loyola University of Chicago, Center for Urban Policy, 820 North Michigan Avenue, Chicago, IL 60611.

350 US
M A P A ANNUAL REPORT. a. free. Omaha-Council Bluffs Metropolitan Area Planning Agency, 7000 W. Center Rd., Suite 200, Omaha, NE 68106. circ. 1,000.

353.9 US ISSN 0091-0678
MAINE. STATE PLANNING OFFICE. ANNUAL REPORT. 1972. a. free. State Planning Office, 189 State Street, Augusta, ME 04330. illus. circ. 1,000. Key Title: Annual Report - State Planning Office. Executive Department. State of Maine.

353.9 US ISSN 0098-8766
MARYLAND. COMMISSION ON INTERGOVERNMENTAL COOPERATION. ANNUAL REPORT. a. Commission on Intergovernmental Cooperation, Old Armory Bldg., Box 231, Annapolis, MD 21404. Key Title: Annual Report - Maryland Commission on Intergovernmental Cooperation.

353.9 975.2 US ISSN 0076-4752
MARYLAND. DEPARTMENT OF STATE PLANNING. ACTIVITIES REPORT. Cover title: State Planning in Maryland. 1959/60. a. free; $0.12 postage. Department of State Planning, 301 W. Preston St, Baltimore, MD 21201. circ. 300.

141 310 US ISSN 0094-4491
MARYLAND MANUAL. Title varies: Manual-State of Maryland. 1898. biennial. $6. Hall of Records Commission, P.O. Box 828, Annapolis, MD 21404. Ed. Gregory A. Stiverson. charts. illus. stat. index. circ. 9,500. (back issues avail)

353.9 US ISSN 0362-1898
MASSACHUSETTS. BOARD OF PUBLIC ACCOUNTANCY. ANNUAL REPORT. a. Department of Civil Service and Registration, Board of Public Accountancy, Leverett Saltonstall Bldg., Government Center, 100 Cambridge St., MA 02202. Key Title: Annual Report - Board of Public Accountancy.

MATERIALIEN ZUR SOZIAL- UND WIRTSCHAFTSPOLITIK. see *SOCIOLOGY*

350 MF ISSN 0076-5503
MAURITIUS. LEGISLATIVE ASSEMBLY. SESSIONAL PAPER. irreg., latest 1972. price varies. Government Printing Office, Elizabeth II Ave., Port Louis, Mauritius.

MAURITIUS. MINISTRY OF WORKS AND INTERNAL COMMUNICATIONS. REPORT. see *TRANSPORTATION*

352 US ISSN 0076-7107
METROPOLITAN WASHINGTON COUNCIL OF GOVERNMENTS. ANNUAL REPORT. Issue for 1979-1980 titled: Next Year, Next Decade, Next Century. 1961. a. free. Metropolitan Washington Council of Governments, 1875 Eye St., Washington, DC 20006.

352 US ISSN 0076-7115
METROPOLITAN WASHINGTON COUNCIL OF GOVERNMENTS. REGIONAL DIRECTORY. 1962. a. free. Metropolitan Washington Council of Governments, 1875 Eye St. N.W., Washington, DC 20006.

350 MX ISSN 0076-7530
MEXICO. DIRECCION GENERAL DE PRENSA, MEMORIAS, BIBLIOTECAS Y PUBLICACIONES. COLECCION: DOCUMENTOS ECONOMICOS DE LA ADMINISTRACION PUBLICA. 1970. irreg., 1971, no 7. Secretaria de Hacienda Credito Publico, Direccion General de la Prensa, Memorias, Bibliotecas y Publicaciones, Departmento de Asuntos Internacionales, Mexico, D.F., Mexico.

353.9 US ISSN 0095-733X
MICHIGAN. DEPARTMENT OF MANAGEMENT AND BUDGET. ANNUAL REPORT. 1973. a. Department of Management and Budget, Stevens T. Mason Bldg., 2nd Fl., West Wing, Lansing, MI 48933. illus. stat. Key Title: Annual Report - Department of Management and Budget.
Continues: Michigan. Department of Administration. Report.

350 US ISSN 0076-7956
MICHIGAN GOVERNMENTAL STUDIES. irreg.; 1968, no. 50. price varies. ‡ University of Michigan, Institute of Public Policy Studies, 1516 Rackham Bldg., Ann Arbor, MI 48104.

MICHIGAN STATE EMPLOYEES' RETIREMENT SYSTEM FINANCIAL AND STATISTICAL REPORT. see *BUSINESS AND ECONOMICS — Labor And Industrial Relations*

351 US ISSN 0076-8243
MICHIGAN STATE UNIVERSITY. PUBLIC ADMINISTRATION PROGRAM. RESEARCH REPORT.* 1959-1960; discontinued after no. 3. irreg. Michigan State University, Public Administration Program, East Lansing, MI 48823.

350 US ISSN 0093-8246
MONTANA. DEPARTMENT OF BUSINESS REGULATION. ANNUAL REPORT. a. Department of Business Regulation, 805 N. Main, Helena, MT 59601. Key Title: Annual Report of the Department of Business Regulation (Helena)

350 US ISSN 0085-3550
MONTANA. GOVERNOR'S ANNUAL REPORT. 1971. a. free to qualified personnel. Office of Budget & Program Planning, Capitol Building, Helena, MT 59601.

353.9 US ISSN 0090-4325
MONTANA. OFFICE OF THE LEGISLATIVE AUDITOR. DEPARTMENT OF INSTITUTIONS REIMBURSEMENTS PROGRAM; REPORT ON AUDIT. (Report year ends June 30) a. Office of the Legislative Auditor, Department of Institutions Reimbursements Program, State Capitol, Helena, MT 59601.

MONTANA. OFFICE OF THE LEGISLATIVE AUDITOR. STATE OF MONTANA BOARD OF INVESTMENTS. REPORT ON EXAMINATION OF FINANCIAL STATEMENTS. see *BUSINESS AND ECONOMICS — Investments*

350 MR
MOROCCO. DIRECTION DE LA STATISTIQUE. COMPTES DE LA NATION. a. DH.10. Direction de la Statistique, B.P. 178, Rabat, Morocco.

350 UK ISSN 0077-4456
N A L G O ANNUAL REPORT. a. National and Local Government Officiers Association, Nalgo House, 1 Mabledon Place, London WC1H 9AJ, England.

352 US ISSN 0095-1455
NATIONAL ASSOCIATION OF REGIONAL COUNCILS. DIRECTORY. 1969. a. membership. ‡ National Association of Regional Councils, 1700 K St. N.W., Washington, DC 20006. adv. circ. 2,000.
Former titles: Regional Council Directory (ISSN 0190-2334) & Directory of Regional Councils (ISSN 0070-6205)

353.008 US
NATIONAL ASSOCIATION OF REGULATORY UTILITY COMMISSIONERS. ANNUAL REPORT ON UTILITY AND CARRIER REGULATION. a. $25. National Association of Regulatory Utility Commissioners, 1102 Interstate Commerce Commission Bldg., Box 684, Washington, DC 20044.

353.9 US ISSN 0191-3441
NATIONAL GOVERNORS' ASSOCIATION. ANNUAL MEETING. PROCEEDINGS. 1908. a. $8.50. National Governors' Conference, 444 N. Capitol St., Washington, DC 20001.
Formerly: National Governors' Conference. Proceedings of the Annual Meeting (ISSN 0077-4634)

350 JA ISSN 0453-0675
NATIONAL RESEARCH INSTITUTE OF POLICE SCIENCE. DATA/KAGAKU KEISATSU KENKYUSHO SHIRYO. (Text in Japanese) irreg. National Research Institute of Police Science - Kagaku Keisatsu Kenkyusho, 6 Sanban-cho, Chiyoda-ku, Tokyo 102, Japan.

336.782 US ISSN 0090-628X
NEBRASKA. ACCOUNTING DIVISION. ANNUAL REPORT OF RECEIPTS AND DISBURSEMENTS STATE OF NEBRASKA. Cover title. 1967/68-1970/71: State of Nebraska Annual Fiscal Report. 1966. a. free. ‡ State Accounting Division, Lincoln, NE 68509. illus. stat. circ. 300-350. Key Title: Annual Report of Receipts and Disbursements. State of Nebraska.

353.9 US ISSN 0092-6841
NEVADA. OFFICE OF LEGISLATIVE AUDITOR. BIENNIAL REPORT. (Subseries of Nevada. Legislative Counsel Bureau. Bulletin) 1974. biennial. Office of Legislative Auditor, Carson City, NV 89701. stat.
Formerly: Nevada. Office of Fiscal Analyst. Annual Report (ISSN 0092-6841)

352 US
NEW YORK (STATE) DEPARTMENT OF STATE. MANUAL FOR THE USE OF THE LEGISLATURE OF THE STATE OF NEW YORK; New York State Legislative manual. 1827. biennial. $10. Department of State, Publications Bureau, 162 Washington Ave., Albany, NY 12231. Dir. Irene Stone. circ. 15,500.

353.9 015 US ISSN 0077-9296
NEW YORK. STATE LIBRARY, ALBANY. CHECKLIST OF OFFICIAL PUBLICATIONS OF THE STATE OF NEW YORK. (Title varies: Vols. 1-15 as Official Publications of the State of New York) 1947. m., cumulated every year, every 5 years, every 15 years. $1 or exchange. State Library, Gift and Exchange Section, Albany, NY 12224. author index for vols. 1-23. circ. 1,500.

350 US
NEW YORK RED BOOK. biennial. $35. Williams Press, Patroon Station, Albany, NY 12204. Ed. George A. Mitchell.

353.9 US
NEW YORK SEA GRANT INSTITUTE. ANNUAL REPORT. a. State University of New York, 411 State St., Albany, NY 12246. (Co-publisher: Cornell University) illus.
Formerly: New York State Sea Grant Program. Annual Report (ISSN 0360-3326)

338.9 US ISSN 0077-9423
NEW YORK STATE URBAN DEVELOPMENT CORPORATION. ANNUAL REPORT. 1969. a. (not published 1975-1976) free. Urban Development Corporation, 1345 Ave. of the Americas, New York, NY 10019. circ. controlled.

354 NZ
NEW ZEALAND. DEPARTMENT OF MAORI AFFAIRS. REPORT. irreg. price varies. Department of Maori Affairs, Wellington, New Zealand.

352 NZ ISSN 0110-3466
NEW ZEALAND. DEPARTMENT OF STATISTICS. LOCAL AUTHORITY STATISTICS. a. NZ.$4.40. Department of Statistics, Private Bag, Wellington, New Zealand (Subscr. to: Government Printing Office, Publications, Private Bag, Wellington, New Zealand)

350 NZ ISSN 0111-0470
NEW ZEALAND PLANNING COUNCIL. PLANNING PAPER. no.5, 1980. irreg. New Zealand Planning Council, Box 5066, Wellington, New Zealand.

324.2 US ISSN 0092-1726
NORTH CAROLINA. SECRETARY OF STATE. NORTH CAROLINA ELECTIONS. 1972. irreg. Secretary of State, Administration Bldg., Raleigh, NC 27611. Ed. John L. Cheney, Jr. illus. stat. Key Title: North Carolina Elections.

353.9 US
NORTH CAROLINA. STATE GOALS AND POLICY BOARD. ANNUAL REPORT. 1972. a. Department of Administration, State Goals and Policy Board, 116 W. Jones St., Raleigh, NC 27603. Ed. Elaine H. Matthews. stat. circ. 3,000.
Formerly: North Carolina. Council on State Goals and Policy. Annual Report (ISSN 0093-9730)

323 UK
NORTHERN IRELAND. COMMISSIONER FOR COMPLAINTS. ANNUAL REPORT. 1970. a. price varies. Office of the Northern Ireland Commissioner for Complaints, River House, 48 High St., Belfast BT1 2JT, N. Ireland (Orders to H.M. Stationery Office, Chichester House, Chichester St., Belfast, Northern Ireland) circ. 170.

PUBLIC ADMINISTRATION

354   CN
NOVA SCOTIA. DEPARTMENT OF DEVELOPMENT. ANNUAL REPORT. 1971. a. free. Department of Development, Box 519, Halifax, N.S. B3J 2R7, Canada. Ed. Seymour C. Hamilton. circ. 300(controlled)

354.716   CN
NOVA SCOTIA. OFFICE OF THE OMBUDSMAN. ANNUAL REPORT. 1971. a. free. Office of the Ombudsman, Halifax, Nova Scotia, Canada. Ed. Dr. Harry D. Smith. circ. 2,000.

350   CN   ISSN 0078-2300
NOVA SCOTIA COMMUNITY PLANNING CONFERENCE PROCEEDINGS. 1963. irreg. Dalhousie University, Institute of Public Affairs, Halifax, N.S. B3H 3J5, Canada. circ. 200.

350   IT   ISSN 0078-2750
NUOVA DIRIGENZA; richerche esperienze e commenti sulla funzione pubblica. 1967. irreg., 1969, no. 11. L.200($2.10) Giovanni Mammucari, Ed. & Pub., Casella Postal 306, 00100 Rome, Italy.

350   FR
O E C D STUDIES IN RESOURCE ALLOCATION. 1974. irreg. Organization for Economic Cooperation and Development, 2 rue Andre Pascal, 75775 Paris Cedex 16, France (U.S. orders to: O.E.C.D. Publications Center, 1750 Pennsylvania Ave. N.W., Washington, D.C. 20006) (also avail. in microfiche)

350   SP
O Y M. irreg. 60 ptas. (Servicio Central de Organizacion y Metodos) Spain. Boletin Oficial del Estado, Eloy Gonzalo, 19, Madrid 10, Spain.

DER OEFFENTLICHE HAUSHALT; Archiv fuer das oeffentliche Haushaltswesen. see *BUSINESS AND ECONOMICS — Public Finance, Taxation*

350   US
OHIO STATE UNIVERSITY. SCHOOL OF PUBLIC ADMINISTRATION. WORKING PAPER SERIES. 1972. irreg. free. Ohio State University, School of Public Administration, 1775 College Rd., Columbus, OH 42310. circ. controlled

OMBUDSMAN AND OTHER COMPLAINT-HANDLING SYSTEMS SURVEY. see *LAW*

ON S I T E. (Sculpture in the Environment) see *ART*

350   US
OREGON BLUE BOOK. biennial. $3 per no. Secretary of State, 136 State Capitol, Salem, OR 97310. Ed. Sonya Lindly Smith.

350   CN
ORGANIZATION OF THE GOVERNMENT OF CANADA/ADMINISTRATION FEDERALE DU CANADA. (Text in English and French) 1958. irreg., latest 13th, 1980. price varies. Supply and Services Canada, Publishing Centre, Hull, Que. K1A 0S5, Canada. Eds. Karen Laughlin (Eng.); Fernand Bourret (Fr.)

354   TH   ISSN 0475-2015
ORGANIZATIONAL DIRECTORY OF THE GOVERNMENT OF THAILAND. (Text in English and Thai) irreg. Translation & Secretarial Office, 56 Suan Luang I Street, Pathum Wan, Bangkok, Thailand.

354.669   NR
OYO STATE. ESTIMATES INCLUDING BUDGET SPEECH AND MEMORANDUM. Short title: Oyo State of Nigeria Estimates. a. £N40. Government Printer, Ibadan, Nigeria.
Formerly: Western State. Estimates Including Budget Speech and Memorandum.

340.05   NR
OYO STATE OF NIGERIA GAZETTE. (Supplements accompany some numbers) irreg. £N12. Government Printer, Ibadan, Nigeria.
Formerly: Western State. Gazette.

350   PK   ISSN 0078-8333
PAKISTAN. NATIONAL ASSEMBLY. DEBATES. OFFICIAL REPORT. (Text in English) 1962. irreg. Rs.0.50. National Assembly, Islamabad, Pakistan (Order from: Manager of Publications, Government of Pakistan, 2nd Floor, Ahmad Chamber, Tariq Rd., P.E.C.H.S., Karachi 29, Pakistan)

350   PN
PANAMA. TRIBUNAL ELECTORAL. MEMORIA. irreg. Tribunal Electoral, Panama, Panama.

350   US   ISSN 0078-9151
PAPERS IN PUBLIC ADMINISTRATION. 1962. irreg., no. 33, 1977. price varies. ‡ Arizona State University, Center for Public Affairs, Tempe, AZ 85281. Ed. John Hall. index. circ. 500-1,000.
Supersedes (as of 1970): Arizona State University. Governmental Finance Institute. Proceedings (ISSN 0072-5196)

350   US   ISSN 0078-916X
PAPERS IN PUBLIC ADMINISTRATION.* 1948. irreg., 1965, no. 47. price varies. ‡ University of Michigan, Institute of Public Policy Studies, 1516 Rackham Bldg., Ann Arbor, MI 48104.

354   PP   ISSN 0078-9399
PAPUA NEW GUINEA. PUBLIC SERVICE BOARD. REPORT.* a. price varies. Government Printer, Box 2150, Konedobu, Papua New Guinea.

350 920   BL
PERFIS PARLAMENTARES. 1977. irreg. Camara dos Deputados, Brasilia, Brazil.

350   PH
PHILIPPINES. DEPARTMENT OF PUBLIC INFORMATION. POLICY STATEMENTS. irreg., no. 13, 1977. Department of Public Information, c/o Bureau of National and Foreign Information, U P L Building, Box 3396, Intramuros, Manila, Philippines.

350 020.6   PH
PHILIPPINES. GOVERNMENT PRINTING OFFICE. ITEMIZATION OF PERSONAL SERVICES AND ORGANIZATIONAL CHARTS. a. Government Printing Office, Boston St., Port Area, Manila, Philippines.

PLANO NACIONAL DE EDUCACAO ESPECIAL. see *EDUCATION — Special Education And Rehabilitation*

350   US
POLICY STUDIES REVIEW ANNUAL. 1977. a. $29.95. Sage Publications, Inc., 275 S. Beverly Drive, Beverly Hills, CA 90212 (And Sage Publications, Ltd., 28 Banner St., London EC1Y 8QE, England) Ed.Bd.

353   US   ISSN 0362-4765
POLITICAL SCIENCE UTILIZATION DIRECTORY. 1975. irreg. $3 to individuals; institutions $5. Policy Studies Organization, University of Illinois, 361 Lincoln Hall, Urbana, IL 61801. Ds. Stuart Nagel, Marian Neef. bibl. charts. stat. index. circ. 2,400. (reprint service avail. from ISI)

350.6   PO
PORTUGAL. MINISTERIO DO ULTRAMAR. RELATORIO DAS ACTIVIDADES. 1969. a. Ministerio do Ultramar, Agencia-Geral do Ultramar, Lisbon 3, Portugal.

354.717   CN
PRINCE EDWARD ISLAND. DEPARTMENT OF DEVELOPMENT. ANNUAL REPORT. 1971. a. free. ‡ Department of Development, Charlottetown, Prince Edward Island, Canada.

330   CN
PRINCE EDWARD ISLAND. DEPARTMENT OF INDUSTRY AND COMMERCE. ANNUAL REPORT. 1950. a. free. Department of Industry and Commerce, P.O. Box 2000, Charlottetown, P.E.I. C1A 7N8, Canada. stat. circ. 200.

PRINCE EDWARD ISLAND. DEPARTMENT OF THE ENVIRONMENT. ANNUAL REPORT. see *ENVIRONMENTAL STUDIES*

338.9 380   CN   ISSN 0079-5151
PRINCE EDWARD ISLAND. PUBLIC UTILITIES COMMISSION. ANNUAL REPORT. 1961. a. free. Public Utilities Commission, Box 577, Charlottetown, P.E.I. C1A 7L1, Canada. circ. 325.

352   PL   ISSN 0079-5801
PROBLEMY RAD NARODOWYCH. STUDIA I MATERIALY. (Text in Polish; summaries in English and Russian) 1964. irreg., vol. 44, 1979. price varies. (Polska Akademia Nauk, Instytut Panstwa i Prawa) Ossolineum, Publishing House of the Polish Academy of Sciences, Rynek 9, Wroclaw, Poland (Dist. by Ars Polona-Ruch, Krakowskie Przedmiescie 7, Warsaw, Poland) Ed. Stanislaw Gebert. circ. 1,600. (also avail. in microfilm)

350 329.3   US
PUBLIC ADMINISTRATION AND DEMOCRACY. irreg. price varies. Oxford University Press, 200 Madison Ave., New York, NY 10016 (And Ely House, 37 Dover St., London W1X 4AH, England) Ed. Dwight Waldo.

350   UN
PUBLIC ADMINISTRATION AND FINANCE NEWSLETTER. (Text in English, French or Spanish) 1966. irreg. contr. free circ. United Nations, Department of Economic and Social Affairs, Division of Public Administration and Finance, Secretariat, New York, NY 10017. bibl.
Formerly (until Apr.-June 1975): Public Administration (ISSN 0048-5799)

352   CN   ISSN 0381-7962
PUBLIC EMPLOYEES JOURNAL/JOURNAL DES EMPLOYES PUBLICS. 1969. a. New Brunswick Public Employees Association, Box 95, 238 King St., Fredericton, N.B., Canada. illus.
Supersedes: Civil Service Digest (ISSN 0578-3828)

353.03 973   US   ISSN 0079-7626
PUBLIC PAPERS OF THE PRESIDENTS OF THE UNITED STATES. a. price varies. U. S. Office of the Federal Register, National Archives and Records Service, Washington, DC 20408 (Orders to: Supt. of Documents, Washington, DC 20402)

388.4   US
PUBLIC POLICY STUDIES. vol. 10, 1975. irreg. Heritage Foundation, Inc., 513 C St. N.E., Washington, DC 20002. Indexed: N.

PUBLIC UTILITIES LAW ANTHOLOGY. see *LAW*

350   SZ   ISSN 0080-7249
PUBLICUS; Schweizer Jahrbuch des Oeffentlichen Lebens. (Text in French, German) 1958. a. 37 Fr. ‡ Schwabe und Co. AG, Steinentorstr. 13, 4010 Basel, Switzerland. Ed. Hans Reimann. adv. index. circ. 4,000.

350   PR
PUERTO RICO. NEGOCIADO DEL PRESUPUESTO. BOLETIN DE GERENCIA ADMINISTRATIVA. 1952. irreg. (approx. 4-6/yr.) free. Negociado del Presupuesto - Puerto Rico. Bureau of the Budget, Box 3228, San Juan, PR 00904. bk. rev. bibl. illus. stat. circ. 3,000.

354   AT
QUEENSLAND. LAND ADMINISTRATION COMMISSION. ANNUAL REPORT. a. Queensland. Government Printer, Brisbane, Australia. illus. stat.

350   SP
RENTA NACIONAL DE ESPANA; y su distribucion provincial (year) no. 10, 1976. irreg. Banco de Bilbao, Servicio de Estudios, Apartado 21, Bilbao, Spain. charts. stat.

350 658   US
RESEARCH IN PUBLIC POLICY AND MANAGEMENT. 1978. a. $17.25 to individuals; institutions $34.50. J A I Press, Box 1678, 165 W. Putnam Ave., Greenwich, CT 06830. Ed. John Crecine.

ROLE OF STATE LEGISLATURES IN THE FREEDOM STRUGGLE. see *POLITICAL SCIENCE*

351   RW
RWANDA. DIRECTION GENERALE DE LA STATISTIQUE. RAPPORT ANNUEL. a. Direction Generale de la Statistique, B.P. 46, Kigali, Rwanda.
Formerly: Rwanda. Direction Generale de la Documentation et de la Statistique. Rapport Annuel (ISSN 0080-5033)

PUBLIC ADMINISTRATION

350   BL
SAO PAULO, BRAZIL (STATE).
DEPARTAMENTO DE EDIFICIOS E OBRAS
PUBLICAS. RELATORIO DE ATIVIDADES.
irreg. Departamento de Edificios e Obras Publicas,
Sao Paulo, Brazil. stat.

338 381   CN   ISSN 0080-6498
SASKATCHEWAN. DEPARTMENT OF
INDUSTRY AND COMMERCE. REPORT FOR
THE FISCAL YEAR. 1957. a. free. Department of
Industry and Commerce, 7Th Floor, Saskatchewan
Power Bldg., Regina, Sask. S4P 2Y9, Canada.

350   GW
SCHRIFTEN ZUR OEFFENTLICHEN
VERWALTUNG UND OEFFENTLICHEN
WIRTSCHAFT. (Text in German; summaries in
English, French, and Russian) 1974. irreg. price
varies. Nomos Verlagsgesellschaft mbH und Co.
Kg., Postfach 610, 7570 Baden-Baden, W. Germany
(B.R.D.) Eds. P. Eichhorn, P. Friedrich.

350   UK   ISSN 0305-6562
SCOTLANDS REGIONS. 1933. a. £2. William
Culross & Son Ltd., Queen Street, Coupar Angus,
Perthshire, Scotland.
    Incorporating: County and Municipal Year Book
for Scotland (ISSN 0070-1300)

SEYCHELLES. OFFICE OF THE PRESIDENT.
BUDGET ADDRESS. see *BUSINESS AND
ECONOMICS — Public Finance, Taxation*

350   YU   ISSN 0037-7147
SLUZBEN VESNIK NA SOCIJALISTICKA
REPUBLIKA MAKEDONIJA. (Text in
Macedonian) 1945. irreg. 380 din. Socijalisticki
Savez Radnog Naroda SR Makedonije, 29 Noemvri
10a, Skopje, Yugoslavia. Ed. Petar Janevski.

350   US   ISSN 0362-3475
SOUTHEAST MICHIGAN COUNCIL OF
GOVERNMENTS. ANNUAL REPORT. a.
Southeast Michigan Council of Governments, 800
Book Bldg., Detroit, MI 48226. illus. Key Title:
Annual Report - Southeast Michigan Council of
Governments.

350   SX
SOUTH WEST AFRICA ADMINISTRATION:
WHITE PAPER ON THE ACTIVITIES OF THE
DIFFERENT BRANCHES. 1974. irreg. $0.75.
Administration, Private Bag 13186, Windhoek,
South West Africa.

350   SA
SOUTH WEST AFRICA SURVEY. a. R.5.30.
Government Printer, Bosman St., Private Bag X85,
Pretoria 0001, South Africa. (Prepared by:
Department of Foreign Affairs) illus. stat.

711   US   ISSN 0095-4810
SOUTHWEST NEW MEXICO COUNCIL OF
GOVERNMENTS. ANNUAL WORK
PROGRAM. a. Southwest New Mexico Council of
Governments, 211 1/2 N. Bullard, Box 1211, Silver
City, NM 88061. Key Title: Annual Work Program
- Southwest New Mexico Council of Governments.

354   SP
SPAIN. MINISTERIO DE HACIENDA.
SUBDIRECCION GENERAL DE
ORGANIZACION E INFORMACION.
ESTADISTICA DE LA INFORMACION AL
PUBLICO.* (Text in English, French, German and
Spanish) 1971/73. irreg. free. Ministerio de
Hacienda, Servicio de Publicaciones, Madrid (8),
Spain.

363.6   SP
SPAIN. MINISTERIO DE LA VIVIENDA. SERIE 3:
VIVIENDA. no. 1010, 1974. irreg. Ministerio de la
Vivienda, Secretaria General Tecnica, Madrid,
Spain.

350   SP
SPAIN. SERVICIO CENTRAL DE
PUBLICACIONES DE LA PRESIDENCIA DEL
GOBIERNO. COLECCION INFORME. irreg.
price varies. (Presidencia del Gobierno, Servicio
Central de Publicaciones) Spain. Boletin Oficial del
Estado, Eloy Gonzalo, 19, Madrid 10, Spain.

350   US   ISSN 0561-8630
STATE ADMINISTRATIVE OFFICIALS
(CLASSIFIED BY FUNCTIONS) 1957. biennial. $12. Council of
State Governments, Box 11910, Iron Works Pike,
Lexington, KY 40578.

350   US
STATE ELECTIVE OFFICIALS AND THE
LEGISLATURES. (Supplements Book of the States)
biennial. $12. Council of State Governments, Box
11910, Iron Works Pike, Lexington, KY 40578.

350   II   ISSN 0081-4504
STATE GOVERNMENT UNDERTAKINGS IN
GUJARAT. (Editions in English and Gujarati)
1960-61. a. Bureau of Economics and Statistics,
Sector No. 18, Gandhinagar, India.

350   US
STATE INFORMATION BOOK. 1973. biennial.
$18.50. Potomac Books, Inc., Publishers, Box 40604,
Palisades Sta., Washington, DC 20016. Eds. Susan
Lukowski, Cary T. Grayson, Jr.

350   US
STATE LEGISLATIVE LEADERSHIP,
COMMITTEES AND STAFF. (Supplements Book
of States) a. $12. Council of State Governments,
Box 11910 Iron Works Pike, Lexington, KY 40578.

309.2   US   ISSN 0092-8488
STATE PLANNING ISSUES. 1970. a. $3. National
Governors' Association, 444 N. Capitol St.,
Washington, DC 20001. Ed. H. Milton Patton. circ.
2,000. Key Title: State Planning Issues (Lexington)

354.624   SJ
SUDAN. MINISTRY OF FINANCE AND
NATIONAL ECONOMY. ANNUAL BUDGET
SPEECH, PROPOSALS FOR THE GENERAL
BUDGET AND THE DEVELOPMENT
BUDGET. a. Ministry of Finance and National
Economy, Box 298, Khartoum, Sudan.

354.624   SJ
SUDAN. MINISTRY OF FINANCE AND
NATIONAL ECONOMY. GENERAL BUDGET:
REVIEW, PRESENTATION AND ANALYSIS.
irreg. Ministry of Finance and National Economy,
Box 298, Khartoum, Sudan.

353.9   US   ISSN 0070-1157
SUGGESTED STATE LEGISLATION. 1941. a. $12.
Council of State Governments, Box 11910, Iron
Works Pike, Lexington, KY 40578. cum.index. circ.
4,000.

354   SQ
SWAZILAND. CENTRAL STATISTICAL OFFICE.
RECURRENT ESTIMATES OF PUBLIC
EXPENDITURE. (Report year ends Mar. 31.) a.
Central Statistical Office, Box 456, Mbabane,
Swaziland.

350   II   ISSN 0082-1594
TAMIL NADU. LEGISLATIVE COUNCIL.
QUINQUENNIAL REVIEW. (Text in English)
1952-57. quinquennial. Legislative Council, Fort St.
George, Madras 600009, India.

350   GW   ISSN 0082-1888
TASCHENBUCH FUER DEN OEFFENTLICHEN
DIENST. 1965. a. DM.39.95. Walhalla- und
Praetoria-Verlag Georg Zwichenpflug, Dolomitenstr.
1, Postfach 301, 8400 Regensburg 1, W. Germany
(B.R.D.) bk. rev.

350   US   ISSN 0082-2183
TAYLOR'S ENCYCLOPEDIA OF GOVERNMENT
OFFICIALS. FEDERAL AND STATE. 1967.
biennial. $295 (includes World Politics plus full
service) Political Research, Inc., Tegoland at Bent
Tree, 16850 Dallas Parkway, Dallas, TX 75248. Ed.
John Clements. index.

353.9   US   ISSN 0082-2752
TENNESSEE. STATE PLANNING OFFICE.
STATE PLANNING OFFICE PUBLICATION.
1965. irreg. price varies. State Planning Office, 660
Capitol Hill Bldg., 201 7th Ave No., Nashville, TN
37219.

353.9   US
TEXAS. LEGISLATIVE REFERENCE LIBRARY.
CHIEF ELECTED AND ADMINISTRATIVE
OFFICIALS. 1971/73. biennial. free. Legislative
Reference Library, P.O. Box 12488-Capitol Station,
Austin, TX 78711. Ed. Sally Reynolds.

TEXAS LEGISLATIVE ISSUES: REPORT OF THE
TEXAS LEGISLATURE PRE-SESSION
CONFERENCE; judicial reorganization, revenue
sharing, property taxation and school finance. see
POLITICAL SCIENCE

354   NZ
TOTALISATOR AGENCY BOARD. ANNUAL
REPORT. a. free. Totalisator Agency Board, 304
Lambton Quay, Wellington, New Zealand. illus.

350   CN   ISSN 0082-7746
UNION OF BRITISH COLUMBIA
MUNICIPALITIES. MINUTES OF ANNUAL
CONVENTION. 1904. a. free. Union of British
Columbia Municipalities, No. 204, 604 Blackford
St., New Westminster, B.C. V3M 1R6, Canada.

350   CN   ISSN 0082-7762
UNION OF NOVA SCOTIA MUNICIPALITIES.
PROCEEDINGS OF THE ANNUAL
CONVENTION. 1906. biennial. free. ‡ Union of
Nova Scotia Municipalities, Suite 132, 136 Roy
Bldg., 1657 Barrington St., Halifax, N.S. B3J 2A1,
Canada. circ. 1,200.

333   US   ISSN 0082-9110
U. S. BUREAU OF LAND MANAGEMENT.
PUBLIC LAND STATISTICS. 1962. a. U. S.
Bureau of Land Management, Division of Record
Systems, U.S. Dept. of the Interior, Washington,
DC 20240 (Orders to: Supt. of Documents,
Washington, DC 20402) Key Title: Public Land
Statistics.

352   US   ISSN 0082-9358
U. S. BUREAU OF THE CENSUS. CENSUS OF
GOVERNMENTS. 1850. quinquennial since 1957.
price varies. U.S. Bureau of the Census, Dept. of
Commerce, Washington, DC 20233 (Orders to:
Supt. of Documents, Washington, DC 20402)

350   US
U.S. CIVIL SERVICE COMMISSION. ANNUAL
REPORT. 1884. a. U.S. Office of Personnel
Management, 1900 E Street, N.W., Washington,
DC 20415 (Orders to Supt. of Documents,
Government Printing Office, Washington, DC
20402) charts. illus. stat. circ. 3,000(controlled)

355.03   US   ISSN 0091-6919
U. S. DEPARTMENT OF DEFENSE. DEFENSE
DEPARTMENT REPORT; a statement by the
Secretary of Defense to the Congress on the budget
and defense programs. 1968. a. price varies. U. S.
Department of Defense, The Pentagon, Washington,
DC 20301 (Orders to: Supt. of Documents,
Washington, DC 20402) (also avail. in microfiche)
Indexed: C.I.S.Ind. Key Title: Statement of
Secretary of Defense Before the House Armed
Services Committee on the Defense Budget and
Program.

353.007   US   ISSN 0566-5655
U.S. GENERAL SERVICES ADMINISTRATION.
MANAGEMENT IMPROVEMENT AND COST
REDUCTION GOALS. (Report year ends June 30.
Reports for 1969/70 and 1970/71 Issued in
Combined Form) irreg. $0.75 per no. U. S. General
Services Administration, General Services Bldg.,
Eighteenth and F Sts. N.W., Washington, DC
20405 (Orders to Supt. of Documents, U. S.
Government Printing Office, Washington, DC
20402)

328.73   US   ISSN 0095-2109
U.S. OFFICE OF TECHNOLOGY ASSESSMENT
ANNUAL REPORT TO THE CONGRESS. 1974.
a. U.S. Office of Technology Assessment, 119 D
Street N.E., Washington, DC 20510 (Avail. from
Supt. of Documents, U.S. Government Printing
Office, Washington, DC 20402) Key Title: Annual
Report to the Congress by the Office of Technology
Assessment.

353.008   US   ISSN 0360-9464
U.S. VETERANS ADMINISTRATION. ANNUAL REPORT ON RELIEF FROM ADMINISTRATIVE ERROR. a. U.S. Veterans Administration, 810 Vermont Ave. N.W., Washington, DC 20420 (Orders to: Supt. Doc., Washington, D.C. 20402)

350   US
UNITED STATES DIRECTORY OF FEDERAL REGIONAL STRUCTURE. 1972. a. $3.75. U.S. Office of the Federal Register, National Archives & Records Service, Washington, DC 20408 (Orders to: Supt. of Documents, Washington, DC 20402) circ. 3,000.

353   US   ISSN 0092-1904
UNITED STATES GOVERNMENT MANUAL (1973) 1934. a. $8.50. U. S. Office of the Federal Register, National Archives and Records Service, Washington, DC 20408 (Orders to: Supt. of Documents, Washington, DC 20402) (also avail. in microform from UMI)
Former titles (1948-1973): United States Government Organization Manual (ISSN 0083-1174); (1934-1948): United States Government Manual.

UNIVERSIDAD DE SEVILLA. INSTITUTO GARCIA OVIEDO. PUBLICACIONES. see *LAW*

350   AG
UNIVERSIDAD NACIONAL DEL LITORAL. FACULTAD DE CIENCIAS DE LA ADMINISTRACION. REVISTA. 1969. a. Universidad Nacional del Litoral, Facultad de Ciencias de la Administracion, 25 de Mayo, 1783, Santa Fe, Argentina.

350   US
UNIVERSITY OF ARIZONA. COLLEGE OF BUSINESS AND PUBLIC ADMINISTRATION. DEPARTMENT OF PUBLIC ADMINISTRATION. PUBLICATION P W. irreg. University of Arizona, College of Business and Public Administration, Department of Public Administration, Tucson, AZ 85721.

350   US
UNIVERSITY OF CALIFORNIA, SANTA BARBARA. URBAN ECONOMICS PROGRAM. RESEARCH REPORTS IN PUBLIC POLICY. no. 2, 1975. irreg. University of California, Santa Barbara, Urban Economics Program, Santa Barbara, CA 93106.

350   320   US
UNIVERSITY OF GEORGIA. INSTITUTE OF GOVERNMENT. RESEARCH PAPERS. 1973. irreg. $1 per no. University of Georgia, Institute of Government, Terrell Hall, Athens, GA 30602.

352   US   ISSN 0078-5970
UNIVERSITY OF OREGON. BUREAU OF GOVERNMENTAL RESEARCH AND SERVICE. INFORMATION BULLETIN. 1933. irreg;no.170,1975. price varies. ‡ University of Oregon, Bureau of Governmental Research and Service, Box 3177, Eugene, OR 97403. Ed. Kenneth C. Tollenaar.

352   US   ISSN 0078-5989
UNIVERSITY OF OREGON. BUREAU OF GOVERNMENTAL RESEARCH AND SERVICE. LEGAL BULLETIN. 1936. irreg., 1970, no. 14. price varies. University of Oregon, Bureau of Governmental Research and Service, Box 3177, Eugene, OR 97403. Ed. Kenneth C. Tollenaar.

352   US   ISSN 0078-5997
UNIVERSITY OF OREGON. BUREAU OF GOVERNMENTAL RESEARCH AND SERVICE. LOCAL GOVERNMENT NOTES AND INFORMATION: POLICY AND PRACTICE SERIES. 1966. irreg; no. 38, 1975. $1. University of Oregon, Bureau of Governmental Research and Service, Box 3177, Eugene, OR 97403. Ed. Kenneth C. Tollenaar. (looseleaf format)

352   US
UNIVERSITY OF OREGON. BUREAU OF GOVERNMENTAL RESEARCH AND SERVICE. PLANNING BULLETIN. 1947. irreg; no. 8, 1975. price varies. University of Oregon, Bureau of Governmental Research and Service, Box 3177, Eugene, OR 97403. Ed. Kenneth C. Tollenaar.

350   II
UNIVERSITY OF RAJASTHAN. STUDIES IN PUBLIC ADMINISTRATION. (Text in English) no. 2, 1973. irreg. University of Rajasthan, Department of Public Administration, Gandhi Nagar, Jaipur 302004, India.

350   351   US   ISSN 0080-2778
UNIVERSITY OF RHODE ISLAND. BUREAU OF GOVERNMENT RESEARCH. INFORMATION SERIES. 1961. irreg. no. 65, 1976. free. University of Rhode Island, Bureau of Government Research, Kingston, RI 02881. Ed. Anna G. Haggarty. (back issues avail.)

350   AT
UNIVERSITY OF SYDNEY. DEPARTMENT OF GOVERNMENT AND PUBLIC ADMINISTRATION. OCCASIONAL MONOGRAPH. 1969. irreg. price varies. University of Sydney, Department of Government and Public Administration, Sydney, New South Wales 2006, Australia. Ed. Henry Mayer. circ. 600.

350   US
UNIVERSITY OF TENNESSEE. INSTITUTE FOR PUBLIC SERVICE. MTAS MUNICIPAL TECHNICAL REPORT. 1973. irreg. $1. University of Tennessee, Institute for Public Service, Municipal Technical Advisory Service, Knoxville, TN 37916.

350   US
UNIVERSITY OF TEXAS AT AUSTIN. INSTITUTE OF LATIN AMERICAN STUDIES. TECHNICAL PAPERS SERIES. 1976. irreg. University of Texas at Austin, Institute of Latin American Studies, Sid W. Richardson Hall, Room 1.310, Austin, TX 78712. stat. circ. 450(controlled) (back issues avail.)

350   US
UNIVERSITY OF TEXAS, AUSTIN. LYNDON B. JOHNSON SCHOOL OF PUBLIC AFFAIRS. WORKING PAPER SERIES. vol. 5, 1976. irreg. University of Texas at Austin, Lyndon B. Johnson School of Public Affairs, Austin, TX 78712.

350   PH
UNIVERSITY OF THE PHILIPPINES. COLLEGE OF PUBLIC ADMINISTRATION. PUBLIC ADMINISTRATION AND SPECIAL STUDIES SERIES. (Text in English) a. price varies. University of the Philippines, College of Public Administration, Box 474, Manila, Philippines.

350   PH   ISSN 0079-9254
UNIVERSITY OF THE PHILIPPINES. INSTITUTE OF PUBLIC ADMINISTRATION. (PUBLICATION) 1959. irreg. University of the Philippines, Institute of Public Administration, Rizal Hall, P. Faura, Manila, Philippines.

350   UY
URUGUAY. CONSEJO DE ESTADO. DIARIO DE SESSIONES. 1974. irreg. Consejo de Estado, Montevideo, Uruguay.

VERMONT RESOURCES RESEARCH CENTER SERIES. see *ENVIRONMENTAL STUDIES*

363.6   AG
VIALIDAD ARGENTINA. 1974. irreg. Arg.$8. Direccion Nacional de Vialidad, Avenida Maipu 3, Buenos Aires, Argentina. stat.

350   AT   ISSN 0158-1589
VICTORIAN GOVERNMENT DIRECTORY. 1971. a. Aus.$3. Department of the Premier, 1 Treasury Place, Melbourne, Vic. 3000, Australia.
Formerly: Victoria, Australia. Directory of Government Departments and Authorities (ISSN 0310-8546)

VIE DES AFFAIRES; bulletin consacre a l'analyse des avis emis par les dirigeants d'entreprise a l'egard du droit economique et des politiques gouvernementales. see *BUSINESS AND ECONOMICS — Management*

340   US   ISSN 0092-1270
VIRGIN ISLANDS REGISTER. 1960. irreg., latest 1974. $18. ‡ Equity Publishing Corp., Orford, NH 03777. (looseleaf format)

350   CN   ISSN 0509-5166
W. C. J. MEREDITH MEMORIAL LECTURES. 1961. irreg. (McGill University, Faculty of Law) Richard de Boo Ltd., 70 Richmond St. E., Toronto, Ont. M5C 2M8, Canada.
Formerly: Lectures Bar Extension.

353.9   US   ISSN 0099-0671
W.V.O.E.S. ANNUAL REPORT. 1974. a. Office of Emergency Services, 806 Greenbrier St., Charleston, WV 25311.

328.797   US   ISSN 0091-8253
WASHINGTON (STATE) LEGISLATURE. PICTORIAL DIRECTORY. 1909. irreg., published each distinct legislation session. free. Legislature, Olympia, WA 98504. illus. Key Title: Pictorial Directory - Washington State Legislature.

350   US
WEST VIRGINIA. LEGISLATURE. PURCHASING PRACTICES AND PROCEDURES COMMISSION. REPORT TO THE WEST VIRGINIA LEGISLATURE. a. free. Legislature, Purchasing Practices and Procedures Commission, Charleston, WV 25305. Ed. Henry F. Bernhards. circ. 300.

350   US
WEST VIRGINIA PUBLIC AFFAIRS REPORTER. 1976. irreg. West Virginia University, Bureau for Government Research, Morgantown, WV 26506. Ed. David A. Bingham. circ. 3,500.

336   US   ISSN 0085-8226
WISCONSIN. DEPARTMENT OF ADMINISTRATION. ANNUAL FISCAL REPORT. 1960. a. free. Department of Administration, Bureau of Financial Operations, Madison, WI 53702.

350   US
WISCONSIN BLUE BOOK. biennial. $1 softcover; $2 hardcover. Department of Administration, Document Sales, 202 S. Thornton Ave., Madison, WI 53702.

350   US   ISSN 0084-263X
WOYTINSKY LECTURES. 1967. irreg., 1972, no. 3. price varies. ‡ University of Michigan, Institute of Public Policy Studies, 1516 Rackham Bldg., Ann Arbor, MI 48104.

350   US   ISSN 0094-3924
WYOMING. STATE OF WYOMING ANNUAL REPORT. 1973. a. Department of Administration and Fiscal Control, Research and Statistics Division, 302 Emerson Building, Cheyenne, WY 82002. stat. circ. controlled.

350   US
WYOMING DATA HANDBOOK. biennial. Department of Administration and Fiscal Control, Research and Statistics Division, 302 Emerson Building, Cheyenne, WY 82002. charts. stat. circ. 1,300.

ZAMBIA. CENTRAL STATISTICAL OFFICE. NATIONAL ACCOUNTS. see *BUSINESS AND ECONOMICS — Public Finance, Taxation*

342   ZA
ZAMBIA. COMMISSION FOR INVESTIGATIONS. ANNUAL REPORT. 1975. a. K.70. Commission for Investigations, Old Bank of Zambia Building. 3rd Floor, Box RW 494, Ridgeway, Lusaka, Zambia (Orders to: Government Printer, Box 136, Lusaka, Zambia)

354   RH
ZIMBABWE. DEPARTMENT OF WORKS. REPORT OF THE CONTROLLER OF WORKS. a; latest issue, 1973. Rhod.$0.50. Government Printer, Box 8062, Causeway, Zimbabwe. stat.

PUBLIC ADMINISTRATION —
Abstracting, Bibliographies, Statistics

350   SW   ISSN 0065-020X
AARSBOK FOER SVERIGES KUMMUNER. (Text in Swedish; summaries in English) 1918. a. Kr.27. (Statistiska Centralbyraan) Liber Foerlag, Fack, S-162 89 Vaellingby, Sweden. circ. 3,500.
Statistical yearbook of administrative districts of Sweden

PUBLIC ADMINISTRATION — MUNICIPAL GOVERNMENT

350   US   ISSN 0568-8442
ALASKA STATE LIBRARY, JUNEAU. STATE AND LOCAL PUBLICATIONS RECEIVED-ALASKA. (Limited Edt.) 1965. irreg. $5. ‡ Department of Education, Division of State Libraries and Museums, Juneau, AK 99811. (Affiliate: Alaska State Library) Ed. Louis Coatney. illus. index. circ. controlled.

350 016   US   ISSN 0091-5319
C I S ANNUAL. a. price varies. Congressional Information Service, 4520 East-West Hwy., Washington, DC 20014. stat. cum.index.

351 317   CN   ISSN 0527-5148
CANADA. STATISTICS CANADA. FEDERAL GOVERNMENT EMPLOYMENT IN METROPOLITAN AREAS/EMPLOI DANS L'ADMINISTRATION FEDERALE REGIONS METROPOLITAINES. (Catalogue 72-205) (Text in English and French) 1968. a. Can.$6($7.20) Statistics Canada, Publications Distribution, Ottawa, Ont. K1A 0V7, Canada. (also avail. in microform from MML)

336.71   CN   ISSN 0703-2749
CANADA. STATISTICS CANADA. LOCAL GOVERNMENT FINANCE: REVENUE AND EXPENDITURE, ASSETS AND LIABILITIES, ACTUAL/FINANCES PUBLIQUES LOCALES: REVENUS ET DEPENSES, ACTIF ET PASSIF, CHIFFRES REELS. (Catalogue 68-204) (Text in English and French) 1944. a. Can.$6($7.20) Statistics Canada, Publications Distribution, Ottawa, Ont. K1A 0V7, Canada. (also avail. in microform from MML)

350   UK   ISSN 0260-8642
CHARTERED INSTITUTE OF PUBLIC FINANCE AND ACCOUNTANCY. PLANNING AND DEVELOPMENT STATISTICS. ACTUALS. 1978. a. £10. Chartered Institute of Public Finance and Accountancy, 1 Buckingham Place, London SW1E 6HS, England. (back issues avail.)
     Formerly: Chartered Institute of Public Finance and Accountancy. Planning Estimates Statistics. Actuals (ISSN 0307-8329)

350   UK   ISSN 0260-7603
CHARTERED INSTITUTE OF PUBLIC FINANCE AND ACCOUNTANCY. WASTE COLLECTION STATISTICS. ACTUALS. 1977. a. £5. Chartered Institute of Public Finance and Accountancy, 1 Buckingham Place, London SW1E 6HS, England. (back issues avail.)

015   US
CHECKLIST OF AVAILABLE VERMONT STATE PUBLICATIONS. 1970. a. free. Department of Libraries, Law and Documents Unit, 111 State St., Montpelier, VT 05602. Ed. Vivian Bryan. circ. 350.

331 353 317   US   ISSN 0098-3497
CURRENT GOVERNMENTS REPORTS: LOCAL GOVERNMENT EMPLOYMENT IN SELECTED METROPOLITAN AREAS AND LARGE COUNTIES. (Series GE-3) 1970. a. price varies. U. S. Bureau of the Census, Dept. of Commerce, Washington, DC 20233. Ed. Alan V. Stevens. Key Title: Local Government Employment in Selected Metropolitan Areas and Large Counties.

015 350   GW
DEUTSCHE BIBLIOGRAPHIE. VERZEICHNIS AMTLICHER DRUCKSCHRIFTEN; Veroeffentlichungen der Behoerden, Koerperschaften, Anstalten und Stiftungen des oeffentlichen Rechts sowie der wichtigsten halbamtlichen Institutionen in der Bundesrepublik Deutschland und West-Berlin. 1957/1958 (1963) irreg. price varies. (Deutsche Bibliothek) Buchhaendler-Vereinigung GmbH, Gr. Hirschgraben 17-21, 6000 Frankfurt 1, W. Germany (B.R.D.) bibl. index. circ. 500.

350 016   US
FEDERAL INDEX. ANNUAL. a. $175. Capitol Services, Inc., 415 Second St., N.E., Washington, DC 20002.

314 352   FI   ISSN 0355-2217
FINLAND. TILASTOKESKUS. KUNNALLISVAALIT/FINLAND. STATISTIKCENTRALEN. KOMMUNALVALEN/FINLAND. CENTRAL STATISTICAL OFFICE. MUNICIPAL ELECTIONS. (Text in Finnish, Swedish and English) 1931. irreg. Fmk.18. Tilastokeskus, Annankatu 44, SF-00100 Helsinki 10, Finland (Subscr. to: Government Printing Centre, Box 516, SF-00100 Helsinki 10, Finland)

324   NE   ISSN 0077-7021
NETHERLANDS. CENTRAAL BUREAU VOOR DE STATISTIEK. STATISTIEK DER VERKIEZINGEN. PROVINCIALE STATEN. ELECTION STATISTICS. PROVINCIAL COUNCILS. (Text in Dutch and English) 1946. irreg. fl.17. Centraal Bureau voor de Statistiek, Prinses Beatrixlaan 428, Voorburg, Netherlands (Orders to: Staatsuitgeverij, Christoffel Plantijnstraat, The Hague, Netherlands)

328   NO
NORWAY. STATISTISK SENTRALBYRAA. KOMMUNE OG FYLKESTINGS VALGET/ MUNICIPAL AND COUNTY ELECTIONS. (Subseries of its Norges Offisielle Statistikk) (Text in English and Norwegian) 1902. quadrennial. Kr.15. Statistisk Sentralbyraa, Box 8131 Dep., Oslo 1, Norway. circ. 2,400.
     Formerly: Norway. Statistisk Sentralbyraa. Kommunevalget/Municipal Elections.

350   NO
NORWAY. STATISTISK SENTRALBYRAA. STORTINGSVALG/PARLIAMENTARY ELECTIONS. (Subseries of its Norges Offisiele Statistikk) 1894. quadrennial. price varies. Statistisk Sentralbyraa, Box 8131-Dep., Oslo 1, Norway. circ. 2,500.

380   US   ISSN 0091-0546
OREGON. PUBLIC UTILITY COMMISSIONER. STATISTICS OF ELECTRIC, GAS, STEAM HEAT, TELEPHONE, TELEGRAPH AND WATER COMPANIES. 1970. a. free. Public Utility Commissioner, Labor & Industries Bldg., Salem, OR 97310. stat. circ. 350.

352 310   CN   ISSN 0706-4403
PRINCE EDWARD ISLAND. DEPARTMENT OF MUNICIPAL AFFAIRS. ANNUAL REPORT. 1966. a. free. Department of Municipal Affairs, Box 2000, Charlottetow, P.E.I. C1A 7N8, Canada. stat. circ. 300. (back issues avail.)
     Formerly: Prince Edward. Department of Community Services. Annual Report.

350 016   US   ISSN 0193-970X
PUBLIC ADMINISTRATION SERIES: BIBLIOGRAPHY. 1978. irreg., approx. 20/month. $450. Vance Bibliographies, Box 229, Monticello, Il 61856. Ed. Mary Vance. s-a index. (back issues avail.) Indexed: P.A.I.S. Bibl.Ind.
     Supersedes in part: Council of Planning Librarians. Exchange Bibliography (ISSN 0010-9959)

RHODE ISLAND. STATE LIBRARY. CHECK-LIST OF PUBLICATIONS OF STATE AGENCIES. see LIBRARY AND INFORMATION SCIENCES — Abstracting, Bibliographies, Statistics

352 628 016   US
SOLID WASTE MANAGEMENT; AVAILABLE INFORMATION MATERIALS. 1968. irreg. U.S. Environmental Protection Agency, Office of Solid Waste Management Programs, Washington, DC 20460. circ. 15,000.

352   SA
SOUTH AFRICA. DEPARTMENT OF STATISTICS. LOCAL GOVERNMENT STATISTICS. (Report No. 13-03) a., latest 1977. R.5.60. Department of Statistics, Private Bag X44, Pretoria 0001, South Africa (Orders to: Government Printer, Bosman St., Private Bag X85, Pretoria 0001, South Africa)

352   SA
SOUTH AFRICA. DEPARTMENT OF STATISTICS. STATISTICS OF ADMINISTRATION BOARDS. (Report No. 13-13) a., latest 1978. R.3.50. Department of Statistics, Private Bag X44, Pretoria 0001, South Africa (Orders to: Government Printer, Bosman St., Private Bag X85, Pretoria 0001, South Africa)
     Formerly (until 1977): South Africa. Department of Statistics. Statistics of Bantu Affairs Administration Boards.

312 350   US   ISSN 0511-6775
WEST VIRGINIA STATISTICAL HANDBOOK. 1955. irreg. $4.50 per no. West Virginia University, Bureau of Business Research, Morgantown, WV 26506. Ed. Stanley J. Kloc. stat. Indexed: P.A.I.S.

350 314   YU
YUGOSLAVIA. SAVEZNI ZAVOD ZA STATISTIKU. KOMUNALNI FONDOVI U GRADSKIM NASELJIMA. (Subseries of: Yugoslavia. Savezni Zavod za Statistiku. Statisticki Bilten) irreg. 4 din. Savezni Zavod za Statistiku, Uzun Mirkova 1, Belgrade, Yugoslavia.

350 316   ZA
ZAMBIA. CENTRAL STATISTICAL OFFICE. FINANCIAL STATISTICS OF GOVERNMENT SECTOR (ECONOMIC AND FUNCTIONAL ANALYSIS) 1964. a, latest 1973. K.1. Central Statistical Office, P.O. Box 1908, Lusaka, Zambia.
     Formerly: Zambia. Central Statistical Office. Government Sector Accounts (Economic and Functional Analysis) (ISSN 0084-4527)

PUBLIC ADMINISTRATION — Municipal Government

see also Housing and Urban Planning

352   AT
ADELAIDE CITY COUNCIL MUNICIPAL REFERENCE BOOK. 1911. a. free. ‡ Adelaide City Council, Town Hall, King William St., Adelaide, S.A. 5000, Australia.
     Formerly: Adelaide City Council Municipal Yearbook (ISSN 0084-5922)

352.008   MF   ISSN 0304-6451
ASSOCIATION OF URBAN AUTHORITIES. ANNUAL BULLETIN. Added title: Local Government in Mauritius. (Text in English and French) 1962. a. Association of Urban Authorities, City Hall, Port Louis, Mauritius. circ. 200.

352   AT
BETTER BRISBANE. 1961. irreg. Aus.$3. Brisbane Development Association, 250 Edward St., Brisbane, Qld. 4000, Australia. Ed. Miss T.M. Rowatt. circ. 250.

352   CN
BRITISH COLUMBIA MUNICIPAL YEAR BOOK. 1949. a. Can.$8.50. JSB Productions Ltd., Box 46475, Station G, Vancouver, B.C. V6R 4G7, Canada. adv.

352 370   US
C G R B BULLETIN. 1913. 8-18/yr. $60. Citizens' Governmental Research Bureau, 125 East Wells St., Milwaukee, WI 53202. Ed. Norman N. Gill. charts. stat.
     Milwaukee region

330   US   ISSN 0009-756X
CITIZEN'S BUSINESS. 1910. irreg. $4 for 2 yrs. to non-members. Pennsylvania Economy League, Eastern Division, 215 South Broad Street, Philadelphia, PA 19107. Ed. M. Jacob. stat. circ. 3,557. (processed)

352   US
CITIZENS UNION RESEARCH FOUNDATION. OCCASIONAL PAPER SERIES. 1977. irreg. Citizens Union Research Foundation, Inc., 15 Park Row, New York, NY 10038.

352   AT
CITY OF PERTH. ANNUAL REPORT. a. City of Perth, Perth, W.A., Australia. Ed. E. H. Lee Steere. illus. stat.

PUBLIC ADMINISTRATION — MUNICIPAL GOVERNMENT

309.1　　　　US
COMMUNITY DEVELOPMENT FOCUS; reports on programs in Bolivia, Guyana, Nepal, Tanzania. 1970. irreg. $2. ‡ University of Missouri-Columbia, Department of Regional & Community Affairs, 726 Clark Hill, Columbia, MO 65201. Ed. Boyd Faulkner. circ. controlled.

352　　　　IT
CONFEDERAZIONE ITALIANA DEI SERVIZI PUBBLICI DEGLI ENTI LOCALI. ANNUARIO. 1961? a. L.25000. Confederazione Italiana dei Servizi Pubblici degli Enti Locali, Piazza Cola di Rienzo, 80, 00192 Rome, Italy. stat.

350　　　　FR
COUNCIL OF EUROPE. STEERING COMMITTEE ON REGIONAL AND MUNICIPAL MATTERS. STUDY SERIES: LOCAL AND REGIONAL AUTHORITIES IN EUROPE. 1972. irreg. free. Council of Europe, Steering Committee on Regional and Municipal Matters, Publications Section, 67006 Strasbourg, France (Dist. in U. S. by Manhattan Publishing Co., 225 Lafayette St., New York, N. Y. 10012) Ed. Bd. charts. stat.
  Formerly: Council of Europe. Committee on Cooperation in Municipal and Regional Matters. Study Series: Local and Regional Authorities in Europe.

352　　　　US
COUNCIL ON MUNICIPAL PERFORMANCE. ANNUAL REPORT. 1973. a. free to members. Council on Municipal Performance, 84 Fifth Ave., New York, NY 10011. Ed. John Tepper Marlin. illus. circ. 2,000.

352　　　　US　ISSN 0011-3727
CURRENT MUNICIPAL PROBLEMS. Annual cumulation (ISSN 0161-5122) 1959. q. plus a. cum. $98.50. Callaghan & Co., 3201 Old Grenview Rd., Wilmette, IL 60091. Eds. Paul A. Reaume & Robert H. Goodin. bk. rev. charts. cum.index. circ. 895. Indexed: SSCI.

352　　　　US　ISSN 0090-1989
DIRECTORY: NORTH DAKOTA CITY OFFICIALS. 27th edt. 1978. biennial. $6. North Dakota League of Cities, Box 2235, Bismarck, ND 58501. Ed. Arne Boyum. adv.

917.63　　　　US　ISSN 0092-0614
DIRECTORY OF LOUISIANA CITIES, TOWNS AND VILLAGES. irreg. free. Department of Transportation and Development, P.O. Box 44155, Capitol Station, Baton Rouge, LA 70804.

352　　　　US
DIRECTORY OF NORTH CAROLINA MUNICIPAL OFFICIALS. biennial. $15. ‡ North Carolina League of Municipalities, 214 N. Dawson St., Box 3069, Raleigh, NC 27602. Ed. Benjamin W. Taylor. circ. 675.

352　　　　US　ISSN 0092-8364
DISTRICT OF COLUMBIA. CITY COUNCIL. ANNUAL REPORT. 1967/69. a. City Council, Room 509, City Hall, 14th & E Sts. N.W., Washington, DC 20004. illus. Key Title: Annual Report of the District of Columbia City Council.

352　　　　US
FLORIDA. DIVISION OF LOCAL RESOURCE MANAGEMENT. MISCELLANEOUS SERIES. 1976? irreg, latest 1980. free. Department of Veteran and Community Affairs, Division of Local Resource Management, 2571 Executive Center Circle East, Tallahassee, FL 32301.

350　　　　US
FLORIDA. DIVISION OF LOCAL RESOURCE MANAGEMENT. PERSONNEL ASSISTANCE SERIES. 1979. irreg. free. Department of Veteran and Community Affairs, Division of Local Resource Management, 2571 Executive Center Circle East, Tallahassee, FL 32301.

352　　　　BL
FUNDACAO DE ASSISTENCIA AOS MUNICIPIOS DO ESTADO DE PARANA. BOLETIM INFORMATIVO. 1975. irreg. free. Fundacao de Assistencia aos Municipios, Rua Voluntarios da Patria 547, Curitiba, Parana, Brazil.

352　　　　GW　ISSN 0016-6200
GEMEINSAMES AMTSBLATT DES LANDES BADEN-WUERTTEMBERG. 1953. irreg., a. 40/yr. DM.66. Innenministerium, Dorotheenstr. 6, Postfach 277, 7000 Stuttgart 1, W. Germany (B.R.D.) Ed. H. Luetze. bk. rev. index.

352　　　　GW　ISSN 0342-3557
GESETZ UND VERORDNUNGSBLATT FUER DAS LAND HESSEN. DM.65. (Staatskanzlei) Verlag Dr. Max Gehlen GmbH und Co. KG, Daimlerstr. 12, Postfach 2247, 6380 Bad Homburg, W. Germany (B. R. D.) index. circ. 8,000.

352　　　　US
GLOUCESTER COUNTY NEWSLETTER. 1968. m. $3. 1223 Glen Terrace, Glassboro, NJ 08028. Ed. Rinehart S. Potts. bk. rev. circ. 1,000.

352　　　　US
GOVERNANCE OF METROPOLITAN REGIONS. SERIES. 1972. irreg. price varies. (Resources for the Future Inc.) Johns Hopkins University Press, Baltimore, MD 21218. Ed. Lowdon Wingo. bibl.

352　336　　　　UK　ISSN 0308-1745
GREAT BRITAIN. DEPARTMENT OF THE ENVIRONMENT. LOCAL GOVERNMENT FINANCIAL STATISTICS: ENGLAND AND WALES. (Joint publication with the Welsh Office) a. price varies. Department of the Environment, 2 Marsham St., London SW1P 3EB, England (Avail. from H.M.S.O., c/o Liaison Officer, Atlantic House, Holborn Viaduct, London EC1P 1BN, England) stat.

352.044　　　　FR
GUIDE PRATIQUE DE L'USAGER DES PREFECTURES. irreg. free to qualified personnel. Centre de Diffusion et d'Informations Administratives, 10, Boulevard Bonne Nouvelle, Paris 10, France. illus.

353.9　　　　US　ISSN 0094-5978
ILLINOIS. CITIES AND VILLAGES MUNICIPAL PROBLEMS COMMISSION. ANNUAL REPORT TO THE SESSION OF THE GENERAL ASSEMBLY. 1972. a. Cities and Villages Municipal Problems Commission, Springfield, IL 62706. Key Title: Annual Report to the Session of the General Assembly (Springfield)

352　　　　UK
INSTITUTE OF MARKET OFFICERS. LIST OF MEMBERS AND PROCEEDINGS OF THE ANNUAL GENERAL MEETINGS. 1943. a. free to members. ‡ Institute of Market Officers, Markets Dept., The Abattoir, Cricket Inn Road, Sheffield S2 5BD, England. Ed. S. R. Gee. circ. 240.

352　　　　SP　ISSN 0210-0975
INSTITUTO DE ESTUDIOS DE ADMINISTRACION LOCAL. SECRETARIADO IBEROAMERICANO DE MUNICIPIOS. BOLETIN DE INFORMACION. 1968. q. free. Instituto de Estudios de Administracion Local, Secretariado Iberoamericano de Municipios, Joaquin Garcia Morato, 7, Madrid 10, Spain. Ed. Jesualdo Dominguez-Alcahud y Monge. adv. illus. bibl.

352　　　　SP
INSTITUTO DE ESTUDIOS DE ADMINISTRACION LOCAL. SEMINARIOS Y SIMPOSIOS DE INVESTIGACION, CONCLUSIONES. 1971. a. Instituto de Estudios de Administracion Local, Centro de Estudios Urbanos, Joaquin Garcia Morato 7, Madrid 10, Spain.

352　　　　NE　ISSN 0074-9443
INTERNATIONAL UNION OF LOCAL AUTHORITIES. REPORTS OF CONGRESS. 1913. irreg., 24th, 1979, Manila. fl.30. International Union of Local Authorities, Wassenaarseweg 45, 2596 CG The Hague, Netherlands.
  20th, 1971, Vienna

336　　　　IS
ISRAEL. KNESSET. HAVA'ADA LEINYANEI BIKORET HAMEDINA. SIKUMEHA VE-HATSA 'OTEHA SHEL HAVA'ADA LEINYANEI BIKORET HAMEDINA LE-DIN VE-HESBON SHEL MEVAKER HA-MEDINA. 1973. a. Knesset, State Control Committee, Jerusalem, Israel. Ed. Aharon Berkner. circ. controlled. (processed)

352.008　　　　UK　ISSN 0305-1137
L B A HANDBOOK. 1970. quadrennial. free. ‡ London Boroughs Association, Westminster City Hall, Victoria St., London SW1E 6QW, England. Ed. Alan Blakemore. illus. circ. 12,000.

354　　　　LB　ISSN 0304-730X
LIBERIA. MINISTRY OF LOCAL GOVERNMENT, RURAL DEVELOPMENT & URBAN RECONSTRUCTION. ANNUAL REPORT. (Report year ends Sept. 30) 1972. a. Ministry of Local Government, Rural Development & Urban Reconstruction, Monrovia, Liberia.
  Continues the publication with the same title issued by the Ministry under its earlier name: Dept. of Internal Affairs.

352　　　　UK
LOCAL GOVERNMENT COMPANION. 1974. a. £9. Parliamentary Research Services, 18 Lincoln Green, Chichester, West Sussex PO19 4DN, England. Eds. F.W.S. & E. P. Craig.

342　　　　US　ISSN 0362-5729
LOCAL GOVERNMENT LAW BULLETIN. 1975. irreg., no. 10, 1977. University of North Carolina at Chapel Hill, Institute of Government, Chapel Hill, NC 27514.

352　　　　JA　ISSN 0449-0193
LOCAL GOVERNMENT REVIEW. (Text in English) 1973. a. 1200 Yen. Local Government Research and Data Center, 4-6-2 Minami Azabu, Minato-ku, Tokyo 106, Japan. Ed. Tomiko Kato. circ. 500.

351　　　　CN　ISSN 0076-7093
METROPOLITAN TORONTO. 1954. irreg., latest 1975. free. Municipality of Metropolitan Toronto, Clerk's Dept., Toronto, Ont., Canada.

352　　　　US　ISSN 0076-8014
MICHIGAN MUNICIPAL LEAGUE. MUNICIPAL LEGAL BRIEFS. 1961. irreg. $12. Michigan Municipal League, 1675 Green Rd., Box 1487, Ann Arbor, MI 48106. Ed. Louis Andrews. circ. 700.

352　　　　US　ISSN 0077-216X
MICHIGAN MUNICIPAL LEAGUE. SALARIES, WAGES AND FRINGE BENEFITS FOR MICHIGAN VILLAGES AND CITIES 1000-4000 POPULATION. 1943. a. $10. Michigan Municipal League, 1675 Green Rd., Box 1487, Ann Arbor, MI 48106.

352　　　　US　ISSN 0080-5548
MICHIGAN MUNICIPAL LEAGUE. SALARIES, WAGES, AND FRINGE BENEFITS IN MICHIGAN MUNICIPALITIES OVER 4,000 POPULATION. 1942. a. $20. Michigan Municipal League, 1675 Green Rd., Box 1487, Ann Arbor, MI 48106.

352　　　　AT　ISSN 0085-3585
MUNICIPAL ASSOCIATION OF TASMANIA. SESSION. MINUTES OF PROCEEDINGS. 1916. a. free. ‡ Municipal Association of Tasmania, 57 Collins St., Hobart, Tas. 7000, Australia. Ed. B.R. Johnson. index. circ. 200(controlled)

352.16　　　　US　ISSN 0077-2151
MUNICIPAL INDEX; purchasing guide for city officials and consulting engineers. 1924. a. $30. Morgan-Grampian, Inc., Berkshire Common, Pittsfield, MA 01201. Ed. Gary Lopenzina. adv. circ. 28,000.

352　340　　　　US　ISSN 0090-1768
MUNICIPAL RESEARCH AND SERVICES CENTER OF WASHINGTON. INFORMATION BULLETINS. irreg., nos. 377-382, 1977. Municipal Research and Services Center of Washington, 4719 Brooklyn Ave., N.E., Seattle, WA 98105.

352　　　　US　ISSN 0077-2186
MUNICIPAL YEAR BOOK. 1922. a. $42. ‡ International City Management Association, 1140 Connecticut Ave. N.W., Washington, DC 20036. Ed. Stanley Wolfson. bk. rev. circ. 14,000.
  Formerly: City Manager Yearbook.

352　　　　US
NATIONAL MUNICIPAL POLICY. 1951. a. $10 to non-members; members ‡ National League of Cities, 1620 Eye St., N.W., Washington, DC 20006. index.

PUBLIC FINANCE, TAXATION

352   CN   ISSN 0077-8060
NEW BRUNSWICK. DEPARTMENT OF MUNICIPAL AFFAIRS. REPORT. (Text in English and French) 1955. a. free. Department of Municipal Affairs, Box 6000, Fredericton, N.B. E3B 5H1, Canada. Ed. H. G. Irwin. circ. 1,000.

352   CN   ISSN 0381-7970
NEW BRUNSWICK PUBLIC EMPLOYEES ASSOCIATION. NEWS LETTER. 1970. irreg. New Brunswick Public Employees Association, Box 95, 238 King St., Fredericton, N.B., Canada. Key Title: News Letter - New Brunswick Public Employees Association.

352   UK
NEW LOCAL GOVERNMENT SERIES. no. 13, 1975. irreg. George Allen & Unwin (Publishers) Ltd., 40 Museum St., London W.C.1, England.

352.12   US   ISSN 0094-7547
NEW YORK (CITY) MAYOR. SCHEDULES SUPPORTING THE EXECUTIVE BUDGET. irreg. Office of the Mayor, City Hall, New York, NY 10007. Key Title: Schedules Supporting the Executive Budget.

PLANNING, PROGRAMMING, BUDGETING FOR CITY, STATE, COUNTY OBJECTIVES. P P B NOTE SERIES. see *BUSINESS AND ECONOMICS — Public Finance, Taxation*

350 320   US
PUBLIC AFFAIRS BULLETIN. 1978. a. free. ‡ University of South Carolina, Bureau of Governmental Research and Service, Columbia, SC 29208. Ed. Charlie B. Tyer. circ. 4,500.
     Supersedes (1959-1978): University of South Carolina Governmental Review (ISSN 0042-0050)

628   US   ISSN 0163-9730
PUBLIC WORKS MANUAL; and catalog file. a. $5. Public Works Journal Corporation, 200 South Broad St., Ridgewood, NJ 07451. Ed. E. B. Rodie. (reprint service avail. from UMI)
     Formed by the merger of: Environmental Wastes Control Manual (ISSN 0071-0946) & Street and Highway Manual (ISSN 0081-5977) & Water Works Manual (ISSN 0083-7717)

352   SP
REVISTA DE CIENCIA URBANA. no. 4, 1972. 4/yr. 200 ptas. Instituto de Estudios de Administracion Local, Centro de Estudios Urbanos, Joaquin Garcia Morato, 7, Madrid 10, Spain. Dir. Fernando Teran Troyano.

352   YU   ISSN 0037-7104
SLUZBENE NOVINE OPCINE KARLOVAC. 1964. irreg. 150 din. Skupstina Opcine Karlovac, Banjavciceva 9, Karlovac, Yugoslavia. Ed. Vladimir Funduk.

352   YU   ISSN 0037-7120
SLUZBENI GLASNIK OPCINE ROVINJ. (Text in Italian and Serbocroatian) 1964. irreg. 30 din. Skupstina Opcine Rovinj, Ul. Matteotti 1/1, Rovinj, Yugoslavia. Ed. Marija Matosovic.

352   US
STATE MUNICIPAL LEAGUE DIRECTORY. irreg., latest 1975. National League of Cities, 1620 Eye St. N.W., Washington, DC 20006.

352 336   US
UNIVERSITY OF OREGON. BUREAU OF GOVERNMENTAL RESEARCH AND SERVICE. LOCAL GOVERNMENT FINANCE. 1966. irreg. $1. University of Oregon, Bureau of Governmental Research and Service, Box 3177, Eugene. OR 97403. Ed. Kenneth C. Tollenaar. (looseleaf format)

352   US
UNIVERSITY OF RHODE ISLAND. BUREAU OF GOVERNMENT RESEARCH. LOCAL GOVERNMENT SERIES. no. 3, 1975. irreg. University of Rhode Island, Bureau of Government Research, Kingston, RI 02881.

352   PH
UNIVERSITY OF THE PHILIPPINES. COLLEGE OF PUBLIC ADMINISTRATION. LOCAL GOVERNMENT STUDIES. (Text in English) 1962. irreg. University of the Philippines, College of Public Administration, Local Government Center, Box 474, Manila, Philippines.

352   NE
VERENIGING VAN NEDERLANDSE GEMEENTEN. BLAUWE REEKS. irreg. Vereniging van Nederlandse Gemeenten, Postbus 30435, 2500 GK The Hague, Netherlands.

352   NE
VERENIGING VAN NEDERLANDSE GEMEENTEN. GROENE REEKS. irreg. Vereniging van Nederlandse Gemeenten, Postbus 30435, 2500 GK The Hague, Netherlands.

352   SP
VIDA LOCAL. BOLETIN DE INFORMACION. bi-m. 150 ptas. Instituto de Estudios de Administracion Local, Centro de Estudios Urbanos, Joaquin Garcia Morato, 7, Madrid 10, Spain.

PUBLIC FINANCE, TAXATION

see *Business and Economics — Public Finance, Taxation*

PUBLIC HEALTH AND SAFETY

see also *Birth Control; Fire Prevention; Funerals*

614   UN
A F R O TECHNICAL PAPERS. 1970. irreg.; 2-4/yr. World Health Organization, Regional Office for Africa - Organisation Mondiale de la Sante. Bureau Regionale de l'Afrique, B.P. No.6, Brazzaville, People's Republic of the Congo.

614.8   US   ISSN 0148-6039
ACCIDENT FACTS. a. $7. National Safety Council, 444 N. Michigan Ave., Chicago, IL 60611.

614   GW
AKADEMIE FUER OEFFENTLICHES GESUNDHEITSWESEN. SCHRIFTENREIHE. 1973. irreg. free. Akademie fuer Oeffentliches Gesundheitswesen, Auf'm Hennekamp 70, 4000 Duesseldorf 1, W. Germany (B.R.D.)
     Formerly: Akademie fuer Staatsmedizin, Duesseldorf. Jahrbuch (ISSN 0065-5392)

ALBANY BULLETIN ON HEALTH AND WELFARE LEGISLATION. see *SOCIAL SERVICES AND WELFARE*

ALBERTA. DEPARTMENT OF SOCIAL SERVICES AND COMMUNITY HEALTH. ANNUAL REPORT. see *SOCIAL SERVICES AND WELFARE*

614 360   CN   ISSN 0707-1434
ALBERTA. HEALTH AND SOCIAL SERVICES DISCIPLINES COMMITTEE. ANNUAL REPORT. 1977. a. free. Health and Social Services Disciplines Committee, 424 Legislative Bldg., Edmonton, Alta. T5K 2B6, Canada.

614.4   US
AMERICAN LECTURES IN EPIDEMIOLOGY. irreg. price varies. Charles C. Thomas, Publisher, 301-327 E. Lawrence Ave., Springfield, IL 62717.

614   US
AMERICAN LECTURES IN PUBLIC PROTECTION. irreg. price varies. Charles C. Thomas, Publisher, 301-327 E. Lawrence Ave., Springfield, IL 62717.

614 600   US
AMERICAN PETROLEUM INSTITUTE. COMMITTEE ON MEDICINE AND ENVIRONMENTAL HEALTH. MEDICAL RESEARCH REPORTS. irreg. price varies. American Petroleum Institute, Committee on Medicine and Environmental Health, 1801 K St., N.W., Washington, DC 20006.

614   US   ISSN 0003-0813
AMERICAN REVIEW OF WORLD HEALTH. 1964. irreg. membership. American Association for World Health, 2121 Virginia Ave. N.W., Washington, DC 20037. Ed. Philip E. Nelbach. adv. bk. rev. bibl. charts. illus. stat. circ. 3,000.

628   US   ISSN 0066-068X
AMERICAN SOCIETY OF SANITARY ENGINEERING. YEAR BOOK. 1906. a. $5. American Society of Sanitary Engineering, c/o Gael H. Dunn, Ed., Box 9712, Bay Village, OH 44140. adv. cum.index:1906-1950. 1951-1963. 1963-1970. circ. 2,700.
     Sanitary engineering

614   IT
ANNALI DI STUDI GIURIDICI E SOCIO-ECONOMICI SUL SERVIZIO SANITARI NAZIONALE E REGIONALE. 1975. irreg. Maria Ragno, Via Crescenzio 42, Rome, Italy.

312   BE   ISSN 0522-7690
ANNUAIRE STATISTIQUE DE LA SANTE PUBLIQUE/STATISTISCH JAARBOEK VAN VOLKSGEZONDHEID. (Text in Flemish and French) 1950. a. 170 Fr. Ministere de la Sante Publique et de la Famille, Centre de Traitement de l'Information - Ministerie van Volksgezondheid en van Het Gezin, Cite Administrative de l'Etat, Quartier Vesale, 1010 Brussels, Belgium. illus. stat.

628   IT
ANNUARIO SANITARIO. a. Guida Monaci, Via F. Crispi 10, 00187 Rome, Italy (And: via V. Monti 86, 20145 Milan, Italy) Ed. Alberto Zapponini.

353.9   US   ISSN 0362-1421
ARIZONA. DEPARTMENT OF HEALTH SERVICES. ANNUAL REPORT. 1974. a. Department of Health Services, 1740 W. Adams St., Phoenix, AZ 85007. illus. Key Title: Annual Report of the Arizona Department of Health Services.

614   AT
AUSTRALIA. DEPARTMENT OF HEALTH. ANNUAL REPORT. 1954. a. Department of Health, Box 100, Woden, A.C.T. 2606, Australia. illus. circ. 2,500.

614   AT   ISSN 0067-2165
AUSTRALIAN STUDIES IN HEALTH SERVICE ADMINISTRATION. 1968. irreg., nos. 24-25, 1974. Aus.$15. University of New South Wales, School of Health Administration, P.O. Box 1, Kensington, N.S.W. 2033, Australia. circ. 300.

610   BB
BARBADOS. MINISTRY OF HEALTH AND NATIONAL INSURANCE. CHIEF MEDICAL OFFICER. ANNUAL REPORT. 1972. a. Ministry of Health and National Insurance, Bridgetown, Barbados. charts. illus. stat. circ. 300.
     Formerly: Barbados. Ministry of Health and Welfare. Chief Medical Officer. Annual Report.

614   US
BASIC CONCEPTS IN HEALTH SCIENCE SERIES. irreg. price varies. Wadsworth Publishing Co., 10 Davis Drive, Belmont, CA 94002.

614   SA
BE SAFE AT HOME/WEES VEILIG TUIS. (Text in Afrikaans and English) a. Medical Association of South Africa, Medical House, Central Square, Pinelands 7405, South Africa. Ed. H. Ackermann. adv.

614 613   GE   ISSN 0067-5083
BEITRAEGE ZUR HYGIENE UND EPIDEMIOLOGIE. 1943. irreg., vol. 24, 1978. price varies. Johann Ambrosius Barth Verlag, Salomonstr. 18b, 701 Leipzig, E. Germany (D.D.R.) Eds. H. Habs, H. Rische. (back issues avail.) Indexed: Ind.Med.

BELGIUM. MINISTERE DE LA SANTE PUBLIQUE ET DE LA FAMILLE. CENTRUM VOOR BEVOLKINGS- EN GEZINSSTUDIEN. TECHNISCH RAPPORT. see *SOCIAL SERVICES AND WELFARE*

BELGIUM. MINISTERE DE LA SANTE PUBLIQUE ET DE LA FAMILLE. RAPPORT ANNUEL. see *SOCIAL SERVICES AND WELFARE*

BICYCLE RESOURCE GUIDE. see *SPORTS AND GAMES — Abstracting, Bibliographies, Statistics*

BIOMEDICAL ENGINEERING AND HEALTH SYSTEMS: A WILEY-INTERSCIENCE SERIES. see *MEDICAL SCIENCES*

PUBLIC HEALTH AND SAFETY

614 US
BLUE PRINT FOR HEALTH. 1946/47. a. free. ‡
Blue Cross Association, 840 N. Lake Shore Dr.,
Chicago, IL 60611. Ed. Eddie Miller.

614 MX
BOLETIN EPIDEMIOLOGICO ANUAL. a. Instituto
Mexicano del Seguro Social, Subdireccion General
Medica, Jefatura de Servicios de Medicina
Preventiva, San Jeronimo Lidice, Mexico 20, D.F.,
Mexico. stat.
Epidemiology

614 BS
BOTSWANA. MINISTRY OF HEALTH. REPORT.
1973. a. Ministry of Health, Gaborone, Botswana.
Formerly: Botswana. Department of Health.
Report.

BRITISH COLUMBIA. MEDICAL SERVICES
PLAN. PHYSICIAN'S NEWSLETTER. see
MEDICAL SCIENCES

614 US
CALIFORNIA. HEALTH AND WELFARE
AGENCY. PROPOSED COMPREHENSIVE
ANNUAL SERVICES PROGRAM PLAN. a.
Health and Welfare Agency, State Office Building 9,
744 P St., Sacramento, CA 95814. charts. stat.

614 US
CALIFORNIA MOSQUITO AND VECTOR
CONTROL ASSOCIATION. PROCEEDINGS
AND PAPERS OF THE ANNUAL MEETING.
1930. a. $10 per vol. California Mosquito Control
Association, 1737 W. Houston Ave., Visalia, CA
93277. (Co-sponsor: American Mosquito Control
Association) Ed. Thomas D. Mulhern. circ. 800.
(back issues avail)
Formerly(until vol. 45, 1977): California
Mosquito Control Association. Proceedings and
Papers of the Annual Meeting (ISSN 0091-6501)

614 360 CN ISSN 0068-7456
CANADA. DEPARTMENT OF NATIONAL
HEALTH AND WELFARE. ANNUAL REPORT.
(Text in English and French) 1944. a. free.
Department of National Health and Welfare,
Ottawa, Ont. K1A 0K9, Canada. circ. 10,000.

CANADIAN MENTAL HEALTH ASSOCIATION.
ANNUAL REPORT/ASSOCIATION
CANADIENNE POUR LA SANTE MENTALE.
RAPPORT ANNUEL. see *PSYCHOLOGY*

614 CN ISSN 0319-2644
CANADIAN PUBLIC HEALTH ASSOCIATION.
PROCEEDINGS OF THE ANNUAL MEETING.
(Text in English and French) 1974. irreg. Canadian
Public Health Association, 1335 Carling Ave., Suite
210, Ottawa, Ont. K1Z 1E5, Canada. illus.

614 FR ISSN 0069-2603
CHAMBRE SYNDICALE NATIONALE DES
ENTREPRISES ET INDUSTRIES DE
L'HYGIENE PUBLIQUE. ANNUAIRE. 1963.
biennial. 50 F. Chambre Syndicale Nationale des
Entreprises et Industries de l'Hygiene Publique, 10
rue Washington, 75008 Paris, France.

614 UK ISSN 0534-2104
CHARTERED INSTITUTE OF PUBLIC FINANCE
AND ACCOUNTANCY. CREMATORIA
STATISTICS. ACTUALS. 1956. a. £5. Chartered
Institute of Public Finance and Accountancy, 1
Buckingham Place, London SW1E 6HS, England.
(back issues avail.)

614 UN ISSN 0587-5943
CODEX COMMITTEE ON PESTICIDE
RESIDUES. REPORT OF THE MEETING.*
(Issued by FAO in Its Alinorm Series) 1966. Food
and Agriculture Organization of the United Nations,
Distribution and Sales Section, Via delle Terme di
Caracalla, I-00100 Rome, Italy.

COLORADO. STATE DEPARTMENT OF PUBLIC
HEALTH. ANNUAL PROGRESS REPORT.
STATE MIGRANT PLAN FOR PUBLIC
HEALTH SERVICES. see *SOCIAL SERVICES
AND WELFARE*

613.62 EI
COMMISSION OF THE EUROPEAN
COMMUNITIES. ANNUAL REPORTS ON THE
PROGRESS OF RESEARCH WORK
PROMOTED BY THE ECSC. French ed:
Commission des Communautes Europeennes.
Rapports Annuels sur l'Etat des Travaux de
Recherches Encouragees Par la CECA. 1967. a.
Commission of the European Communities, Service
de Renseignment et de Diffusion des Documents,
Rue de la Loi 200, 1049 Brussels, Belgium. circ.
controlled.

614 BL
COMPANHIA ESTADUAL DE TECNOLOGIA DE
SANEAMENTO BASICO E DE DEFESA DO
MEIO AMBIENTE. DIRECTORIA RELATORIA
ANUAL. a. Companhia Estadual de Tecnologia de
Saneamento Basico e Defesa do Meio Ambiente,
Avda. Prof. Frederico Hermann Filho 345, CEP
05459, Sao Paulo, Brazil. illus.

COMPREHENSIVE HEALTH PLAN FOR NEW
JERSEY. see *MEDICAL SCIENCES*

628 US ISSN 0069-8474
CONFERENCE OF STATE SANITARY
ENGINEERS. REPORT OF PROCEEDINGS.*
1920. a. U.S. Public Health Service, 5600 Fishers
Lane, Rockville, MD 20852.
Sanitary engineering

CONFERENCE ON TRACE SUBSTANCES IN
ENVIRONMENTAL HEALTH. PROCEEDINGS.
see *ENVIRONMENTAL STUDIES*

614 AG
CONGRESO ARGENTINO DE SANEAMIENTO.
TRABAJOS. vol. 4, 1974. irreg. Congreso
Argentino de Saneamiento, San Miguel de
Tucuman, Argentina.

614 US
CONNECTICUT HEALTH SERVICES RESEARCH
SERIES. 1971. a. price varies; $3-5. ‡ Connecticut
Hospital Research and Education Foundation, Inc.,
P.O. Box 504, North Haven, CT 06473. Eds.
Donald C. Riedel, Dr. James E.C. Walker. bibl.
charts. circ. 1,500-2,000.

614 US
CONTEMPORARY COMMUNITY HEALTH
SERIES. irreg. price varies. University of Pittsburgh
Press, 127 N. Bellefield Ave., Pittsburgh, PA 15260.

614.49 SZ ISSN 0377-3574
CONTRIBUTIONS TO EPIDEMIOLOGY AND
BIOSTATISTICS. (Text in English) 1977. irreg.
(approx. 1/yr.) 100 Fr.($60) per vol. (1981 price) S.
Karger AG, Allschwilerstrasse 10, P.O. Box, CH-
4009 Basel, Switzerland. Ed. M. A. Klingberg.
(reprint service avail. from ISI)

353.9 US ISSN 0095-6422
DELAWARE. DEPARTMENT OF HEALTH AND
SOCIAL SERVICE. ANNUAL REPORT. a.
Department of Health and Social Services, Dover,
DE 19901. illus. Key Title: Annual Report -
Department of Health and Social Services.

614 388.312 314 DK ISSN 0070-3516
DENMARK. DANMARKS STATISTIK.
FAERDSELSUHELD. (Subseries of its Statistiske
Meddelelser) (Text in Danish, notes in English)
1930. a. Kr.6.90. Danmarks Statistik, Sejroegade 11,
2100 Copenhagen OE, Denmark.

DIRECTORY OF JEWISH HEALTH AND
WELFARE AGENCIES. see *SOCIAL SERVICES
AND WELFARE*

614 US
DIRECTORY OF NATIONAL ORGANIZATIONS
CONCERNED WITH SCHOOL HEALTH. 8th
edt., 1974. biennial. $3.50 to non-members.
American School Health Association, Box 708,
Kent, OH 44240.

DIRECTORY OF SOCIAL AND HEALTH
AGENCIES OF NEW YORK CITY. see *SOCIAL
SERVICES AND WELFARE*

614 FR
ECONOMIE ET SANTE. (Supplement to: Revue
Francaise des Affaires Sociales) 1972. irreg. 12 F.
per no. (Ministere de la Sante et de la Securite
Sociale) Documentation Francaise, 29-31 Quai
Voltaire, 75340 Paris Cedex 07, France. (Co-
sponsor: Ministere du Travail) circ. 3,000.

614 HU ISSN 0073-4012
EGESZSEGNEVELES SZAKKONYVTARA. 1967.
irreg. price varies. Medicina Kiado, Beloiannisz u. 8,
1054 Budapest, Hungary.

614 US ISSN 0071-0873
ENVIRONMENTAL HEALTH ENGINEERING
SERIES. 1969. irreg., vol. 2-B, 1974. price varies.
Marcel Dekker, Inc., 270 Madison Ave., New York,
NY 10016. Eds. F. E. Gloyna, J. O. Ledbetter.

ENVIRONMENTAL HEALTH SERIES: AIR
POLLUTION. see *ENVIRONMENTAL STUDIES*

614 US ISSN 0071-0911
ENVIRONMENTAL HEALTH SERIES:
RADIOLOGICAL HEALTH.* 1962. irreg. U.S.
Public Health Service, 5600 Fishers Lane, Rockville,
MD 20852.

ENVIRONMENTAL MANAGEMENT FOR THE
PUBLIC HEALTH INSPECTOR. see
ENVIRONMENTAL STUDIES

ENVIRONMENTAL RADIATION
SURVEILLANCE IN WASHINGTON STATE;
ANNUAL REPORT. see *ENVIRONMENTAL
STUDIES*

614.7 EI
EUROPEAN ATOMIC ENERGY COMMUNITY.
CONTAMINATION RADIOACTIVE DES
DENREES ALIMENTAIRES DANS LES PAYS
DE LA COMMUNAUTE. (Multilingual text in
French, German, Italian and Dutch) 1965. a. price
varies. Office for Official Publications of the
European Communities, C.P. 1003, Luxembourg 1,
Luxembourg (Dist. in U.S. by European Community
Information Service, 2100 M St., N.W., Suite 707,
Washington, D.C. 20037)

614.7 EI
EUROPEAN ATOMIC ENERGY COMMUNITY.
RESULTATS DES MESURES DE LA
RADIOACTIVITE AMBIANTE DANS LES
PAYS DE LA COMMUNAUTE: AIR-
RETOMBEE-EAUX. (Editions also in German,
Italian and Dutch) 1965. a. 11.00 F. Office for
Official Publications of the European Communities,
C.P. 1003, Luxembourg 1, Luxembourg (Dist. in
U.S. by European Community Information Service,
2100 M St., N.W., Suite 707, Washington, D.C.
20037)

FLORIDA. MENTAL HEALTH PROGRAM
OFFICE. STATISTICAL REPORT OF
COMMUNITY MENTAL HEALTH
PROGRAMS. see *PSYCHOLOGY*

614 FR
FRANCE. MINISTERE DE LA SANTE ET DE LA
SECURITE SOCIALE. NOTES
D'INFORMATION. 1969. irreg., no. 145, 1980.
free. Ministere de la Sante et de la Securite Sociale,
Service de Press, 8 Ave. de Segur, 75700 Paris,
France.
Former titles: France. Ministere de la Sante.
Note d'Information (ISSN 0071-8882); Before 1969:
France. Ministere des Affaires Sociales. Information
Actualites.

614 FR
FRANCE. MINISTERE DE LA SANTE ET DE LA
SECURITE SOCIALE. TABLEAUX
STATISTIQUES "SANTE ET SECURITE
SOCIALE". 1971. a. price varies. Documentation
Francaise, 29-31 Quai Voltaire, 75340 Paris, France.
(Co-sponsor: Ministere du Travail)
Former titles: France. Ministere de la Sante.
Tableaux Sante et Securite Sociale & France.
Ministere de la Sante Publique et de la Securite
Sociale. Annuaire Statistique de la Sante et de
l'Action Sociale (ISSN 0071-8866)

GLOSSARY OF HEALTH CARE TERMINOLOGY.
see *MEDICAL SCIENCES*

PUBLIC HEALTH AND SAFETY

614   UK   ISSN 0072-5714
GREAT BRITAIN. CENTRAL HEALTH SERVICES COUNCIL. REPORT. a. Central Health Services Council, 10 John Adam St., London WC2N 6HD, England (Avail. from H.M.S.O., c/o Liaison Officer, Atlantic House, Holborn Viaduct, London EC1P 1BN, England)

614.3   UK
GREAT BRITAIN. COMMITTEE ON SAFETY OF MEDICINES. REPORT. 1971. a. price varies. Department of Health and Social Security, Committee on Safety of Medicines, Finsbury Square House, 33-37a Finsbury Square, London EC2A 1pP, England (Avail. from H.M.S.O., c/o Liaison Officer, Atlantic House, Holborn Viaduct, London EC1P 1BN, England)

614   UK   ISSN 0072-596X
GREAT BRITAIN. DEPARTMENT OF HEALTH AND SOCIAL SECURITY. ANNUAL REPORT. 1969. a. price varies. H.M.S.O., P.O. Box 569, London SE1 9NH, England.

614   362.11   UK   ISSN 0072-6036
GREAT BRITAIN. DEPARTMENT OF HEALTH AND SOCIAL SECURITY. HOSPITAL IN-PATIENT INQUIRY. 1960. irreg. price varies. H.M.S.O., P.O. Box 569, London SE1 9NH, England.

614   UK   ISSN 0072-6087
GREAT BRITAIN. DEPARTMENT OF HEALTH AND SOCIAL SECURITY. ON THE STATE OF THE PUBLIC HEALTH. (Annual Report of the Chief Medical Officer of the Department of Health and Social Security) 1921. a. price varies. H.M.S.O., P.O. Box 569, London SE1 9NH, England.

GUIDE TO THE HEALTH CARE FIELD. see *HOSPITALS*

HAWAII. DEPARTMENT OF HEALTH. MENTAL HEALTH SERVICES FOR CHILDREN AND YOUTH; children's MH services branch. see *SOCIAL SERVICES AND WELFARE*

614   UK
HEALTH AND PERSONAL SOCIAL SERVICES STATISTICS. a. H.M.S.O., P.O. Box 569, London SE1 9NH, England.
    Formerly: Digest of Health Statistics for England and Wales (ISSN 0070-4849)

614   AT   ISSN 0046-7073
HEALTH IN NEW SOUTH WALES. 1960. irreg. (approx. 3/yr.) free. ‡ Health Commission of N.S.W., Box K. 110, Haymarket, Sydney, N.S.W. 2000, Australia. Ed. Megan Wintle. bk. rev. circ. 30,000. Indexed: Aus.P.A.I.S.

614   610   340   US
HEALTH LAW BULLETIN. 1974. irreg. University of North Carolina at Chapel Hill, Institute of Government, Box 990, Chapel Hill, NC 27514. Ed. M. Patrice Solberg. bibl.

658   US   ISSN 0361-0195
HEALTH SYSTEMS MANAGEMENT. 1974. irreg., no. 10, 1977. Spectrum Publications, Inc., 175-20 Wexford Terrace, Jamaica, NY 10032. Eds. Drs. Samuel Levey, Alan Sheldon.

610.6   IT
I.F.P.S.M. NEWS. (Text in English, French, Italian) irreg. International Federation for Preventive and Social Medicine, Via Salaria 237, 00199 Rome, Italy.
    Formerly: I.F.H.P.M. News.

ILLINOIS. DEPARTMENT OF MENTAL HEALTH. DRUG ABUSE PROGRAM. PROGRESS REPORT. see *DRUG ABUSE AND ALCOHOLISM*

614   US
ILLINOIS. DEPARTMENT OF PUBLIC HEALTH. DIVISION OF HEALTH FACILITIES. DIRECTORY OF HEALTH CARE FACILITIES. a. free. Department of Public Health, 525 West Jefferson, Springfield, IL 62761.

613 310   US
INDIAN HEALTH TRENDS AND SERVICES. irreg. U.S. Indian Health Service, Office of Program Statistics, 5600 Fishers La., Rockville, MD 20852 (Orders to: Supt. of Documents, Washington, DC 20402) stat.

614   JA
INSTITUTE OF PUBLIC HEALTH. ANNUAL REPORT/KOKURITSU KOSHU EISEI-IN NENPO. (Text in Japanese) 1948. a. Institute of Public Health - Kokuritsu Koshu Eisei-in, 4-6-1 Shiroganedai, Minato-ku, Tokyo 108, Japan.

616.988   PO   ISSN 0075-9767
INSTITUTO DE HIGIENE E MEDICINA TROPICAL. ANAIS. (Text and summaries in French, Portuguese, and English) 1943. irreg. price varies. Instituto de Higiene e Medicina Tropical, Rua da Junqueira, 96, Lisbon 3, Portugal. bk. rev. circ. 1,000. Indexed: Ind.Med.
    Formerly: Lisbon. Escola Nacional de Saude Publica de Medicina Tropical. Anais.
    Tropical medicine

INSTYTUT BADAN JADROWYCH. ZAKLAD RADIOBIOLOGII I OCHRONY ZDROWIA. PRACE DOSWIADCZAINE. see *MEDICAL SCIENCES — Radiology And Nuclear Medicine*

614   UN   ISSN 0074-1892
INTERNATIONAL ATOMIC ENERGY AGENCY. SAFETY SERIES. (Text in English, French, Russian or Spanish) 1960. irreg. price varies. International Atomic Energy Agency - Agence Internationale de l'Energie Atomique, Wagramer Str. 5, Box 100, A-1400 Vienna, Austria (Dist. in U.S. by: Unipub, 345 Park Ave. S., New York, NY 10010)

INTERNATIONAL BANFF CONFERENCE ON MAN AND HIS ENVIRONMENT. PROCEEDINGS. see *ENVIRONMENTAL STUDIES*

INTERNATIONAL CONGRESS ON HYGIENE AND PREVENTIVE MEDICINE. PROCEEDINGS. see *PHYSICAL FITNESS AND HYGIENE*

INTERNATIONAL PROGRAM OF LABORATORIES FOR POPULATION STATISTICS. OCCASIONAL PUBLICATIONS. see *POPULATION STUDIES*

INTERNATIONAL PROGRAM OF LABORATORIES FOR POPULATION STATISTICS. SCIENTIFIC REPORT SERIES. see *POPULATION STUDIES*

INTERNATIONAL SECURITY DIRECTORY; world police, fire and security forces, services, products and supplies. see *PUBLIC ADMINISTRATION*

614.4   UK   ISSN 0074-8757
INTERNATIONAL SYMPOSIUM ON AEROBIOLOGY. PROCEEDINGS. irreg. Academic Press Inc. (London) Ltd., 24-28 Oval Rd., London NW1 7DX, England (And 111 Fifth Ave., New York, NY 10003)

INTERNATIONAL UNION OF SCHOOL AND UNIVERSITY HEALTH AND MEDICINE. CONGRESS REPORTS. see *EDUCATION*

614   IT   ISSN 0075-1758
ITALY. ISTITUTO CENTRALE DI STATISTICA. ANNUARIO DI STATISTICHE SANITARIE. 1962. a. L.13000. Istituto Centrale di Statistica, Via Cesare Balbo 16, 00100 Rome, Italy. circ. 950.

614   UN   ISSN 0449-122X
JOINT F A O/W H O CODEX ALIMENTARIUS COMMISSION. REPORT OF THE SESSION. 1963. irreg.; 1972, 9th. price varies. Food and Agriculture Organization of the United Nations, Distribution and Sales Section, Via delle Terme di Caracalla, I-00100 Rome, Italy (Dist. in U.S. by: Unipub, 345 Park Ave. S., New York, Ny 10010)

614   US   ISSN 0075-4668
KAISER FOUNDATION MEDICAL CARE PROGRAM. ANNUAL REPORT. 1960. a. free. ‡ Kaiser Foundation Medical Care Program, Public Affairs, 27th Floor, Ordway Building, Kaiser Center, Oakland, CA 94666. Ed. D. A. Scannell. circ. 24,000.

614   NE
KONINKLIJK INSTITUUT VOOR DE TROPEN. DEPARTMENT OF TROPICAL HYGIENE. ANNUAL REPORT. (Text in English) a. Koninklijk Instituut voor de Tropen, Department of Tropical Hygiene, Mauritskade 63, 1092 AD Amsterdam, Netherlands. Eds. J.W.L. Kleevens, A.van Amerongen-Woudstra.

614   NE   ISSN 0075-6954
KOSTEN EN FINANCIERING VAN DE GEZONDHEIDZORG IN NEDERLAND/COST OF HEALTH CARE IN THE NETHERLANDS. (Text in Dutch and English) 1953. irreg. fl.13.75. Centraal Bureau voor de Statistiek, Prinses Beatrixlaan 428, Voorburg, Netherlands (Orders to: Staatsuitgeverij, Christoffel Plantijnstraat, The Hague, Netherlands)

614   IS   ISSN 0301-4843
KUPAT-HOLIM YEARBOOK. (Editions in Hebrew and English) 1971. a. free. Histadrut, 93 Arlosoroff St., Tel Aviv, Israel.

614.83   US
LAURISTON S. TAYLOR LECTURE SERIES. 1977. a. $7. National Council on Radiation Protection and Measurements, 7910 Woodmont Ave., Ste. 1016, Washington, DC 20014. Ed. W. Roger Ney.

614   LB
LIBERIA. MINISTRY OF HEALTH AND SOCIAL WELFARE. ANNUAL REPORT. a, latest 1975. Ministry of Health and Social Welfare, Monrovia, Liberia.

614   FI
LIIKENNETURVA. REPORTS. irreg., no. 19, 1977. Liikenneturva - Central Organization for Traffic Safety in Finland, Iso Robertinkatu 20, 00120 Helsinki 12, Finland.

362.1   ZA
LUSAKA. MEDICAL OFFICER OF HEALTH. ANNUAL REPORT. a. free. Health and Welfare Department, Medical Officer of Health, Public Health Department, Box 789, Lusaka, Zambia. stat.

MAISONS D'ENFANTS ET D'ADOLESCENTS DE FRANCE. ALBUM-ANNUAIRE NATIONAL; publication documentaire illustree des etablissements de vacances, de repos, de soins, de cure et de prevention pour enfants et adolescents. see *CHILDREN AND YOUTH — About*

614   CN   ISSN 0383-3925
MANITOBA. HEALTH SERVICES COMMISSION. ANNUAL REPORT. 1971. a. free. Health Services Commission, Box 925, 599 Empress St., Winnipeg, Man. R3C 2T6, Canada.

614   CN   ISSN 0383-3933
MANITOBA. HEALTH SERVICES COMMISSION. STATISTICAL SUPPLEMENT TO THE ANNUAL REPORT. 1971. a. free. Health Services Commission, Box 925, 599 Empress St., Winnipeg, Man. R3C 2T6, Canada.

353.9   US
MASSACHUSETTS. DEPARTMENT OF PUBLIC HEALTH. ANNUAL REPORT. (Each issue has distinctive title) a. Department of Public Health, 600 Washington St., Boston, MA 02111. illus.

614   US
MENTAL HEALTH DIRECTORY. 1971. a. $5. U. S. National Institute of Mental Health, Rockville, MD 20852 (Orders to: Supt. of Documents, Washington, DC 20402)

MENTAL HEALTH MEDIA CENTER FILM CATALOG. see *PSYCHOLOGY*

MENTAL HEALTH STATISTICS FOR ILLINOIS. see *SOCIAL SERVICES AND WELFARE*

614   US   ISSN 0090-6425
MINNESOTA. STATE BOARD OF HEALTH. BIENNIAL REPORT. 1872. biennial. free. State Board of Health, 717 Delaware St. S.E., Minneapolis, MN 55440.

353.9 US
MISSOURI. DEPARTMENT OF MENTAL
HEALTH. ANNUAL REPORT. (Report year ends
June 30) 1968/69. a. free. Department of Mental
Health, 2002 Missouri Blvd., Box 687, Jefferson
City, MO 65101. illus. stat.
Former titles: Missouri. Division of Mental
Health. Annual Report (ISSN 0091-231X);
Missouri. Division of Mental Diseases. Report.

MISSOURI. DIVISION OF HIGHWAY SAFETY.
HIGHWAY SAFETY PLAN. see
TRANSPORTATION — Roads And Traffic

614 US
MODERN HEALTH CARE FORMS
(SUPPLEMENT) supplements issued periodically to
update base volume. $39.50 for base volume.
Warren, Gorham and Lamont, Inc., 210 South St.,
Boston, MA 02111.

614 UY
MORBILIDAD. irreg. Ministerio de Salud Publica,
Departamento de Estadistica, Montevideo, Uruguay.
stat.

614.862 US
MOTOR VEHICLE SAFETY; a report on activities
under the National Traffic and Motor Vehicle
Safety Act of 1966. 1966. a. U.S. National Highway
Traffic Safety Administration, 400 Seventh St.
N.W., Washington, DC 20590. (Prepared with: U.S.
Federal Highway Administration)

614.83 355.23 US ISSN 0083-209X
N C R P REPORT. 1931. irreg., no. 66, 1980. $4-14.
National Council on Radiation Protection and
Measurements, 7910 Woodmont Ave., Washington,
DC 20014. Ed. W. Roger Ney.

614 US
N I H FACTBOOK. 1976. irreg. $44.50. (U.S.
National Institutes of Health) Marquis Academic
Media, 200 E. Ohio St., Chicago, IL 60611.

628 380.1 UK
NATIONAL ASSOCIATION OF WASTE
DISPOSAL CONTRACTORS. TRADE
DIRECTORY. 1979. a. £5.50 to non-members.
National Association of Waste Disposal Contractors,
Suite 26/29, Wheatsheaf House, 4 Carmelite St.,
London EC4Y 0BM, England.
Sanitary engineering

614.8 II
NATIONAL CONFERENCE ON SAFETY.
PROCEEDINGS. 1970. a. Rs.10. National Safety
Council, Central Labour Institute Bldg., Sion,
Bombay 22, India. Ed. A. A. Krishnan. charts. circ.
2,000.

628 US ISSN 0077-4146
NATIONAL COUNCIL OF THE PAPER
INDUSTRY FOR AIR AND STREAM
IMPROVEMENT. REPORT TO MEMBERS. a. ‡
National Council of the Paper Industry for Air and
Stream Improvement, Inc., 260 Madison Ave., New
York, NY 10016.

614.83 355.23 US ISSN 0195-7740
NATIONAL COUNCIL ON RADIATION
PROTECTION AND MEASUREMENTS.
PROCEEDINGS OF THE ANNUAL MEETING.
15th, 1979. a. National Council on Radiation
Protection and Measurements, 7910 Woodmont
Ave., Washington, DC 20014.

614 US ISSN 0085-3755
NATIONAL HEALTH COUNCIL. ANNUAL
REPORT. 1920. a. free. National Health Council,
1740 Broadway, New York, NY 10019. (processed)

614 JA ISSN 0077-5002
NATIONAL INSTITUTE OF HYGIENIC
SCIENCES. BULLETIN/EISEI SHIKENJO
HOKOKU. (Text in Japanese; summaries in
English) 1886. a. National Institute of Hygienic
Sciences - Kokuritsu Eisei Shikenjo, 1-18-1
Kamiyoga, Setagaya-ku, Tokyo 158, Japan. Ed.
Akio Ishii. Indexed: Ind.Med.

628 614 US
NATIONAL WASTE PROCESSING
CONFERENCE. PROCEEDINGS; with
discussions. 1972. biennial. $28. American Society
of Mechanical Engineers, Incinerator Division, 345
E. 47th St., New York, NY 10017. (also avail. in
microfilm; microfiche)
Supersedes (as of 1976): National Incinerator
Conference. Proceedings (ISSN 0085-3763)

NETHERLANDS. CENTRAAL BUREAU VOOR
DE STATISTIEK. JAAROVERZICHT
BEVOLKING EN VOLKSGEZONDHEID.
POPULATION AND HEALTH STATISTICS. see
POPULATION STUDIES

614 CN
NEW BRUNSWICK. DEPARTMENT OF HEALTH.
ANNUAL REPORT. (Text in English and French)
a. free. Department of Health, Box 6000,
Fredericton, N.B. E3B 5H1, Canada. stat. circ. 700.

614 CN
NEW BRUNSWICK. HEALTH SERVICES
ADVISORY COUNCIL. ANNUAL REPORT/
RAPPORT ANNUEL. 1971. a. free. Health
Services Advisory Council, Fredericton, N.B.,
Canada.

NEW JERSEY. DEPARTMENT OF HUMAN
SERVICES. COMMUNITY MENTAL HEALTH
PROJECTS SUMMARY STATISTICS. see
SOCIAL SERVICES AND WELFARE

614 US
NEW YORK(STATE). DEPARTMENT OF
HEALTH. MONOGRAPH. 1969. irreg., no. 12,
1977. Department of Health, Public Inquiry Section,
Office of Health Communications & Education,
Albany, NY 12237. (back issues avail.)

614 US
NEW YORK (STATE). HEALTH PLANNING
COMMISSION, ADMINISTRATIVE PROGRAM
FOR HEALTH PLANNING AND
DEVELOPMENT. a. Health Planning Commission,
Empire State Plaza, Tower Bldg. Rm. 1683, Albany,
NY 12237.

353.9 US ISSN 0361-4018
NEW YORK STATE MEDICAL CARE
FACILITIES FINANCE AGENCY. ANNUAL
REPORT. 1974. a. Medical Care Facilities Finance
Agency, 3 Park Ave., New York, NY 10016. illus.
Key Title: Annual Report-New York State Medical
Care Facilities Finance Agency.

614 NZ
NEW ZEALAND HEALTH STATISTICS REPORT.
a. Department of Health, National Health Statistics
Centre, P.O. Box 6314, Wellington, New Zealand.

614.7 EI
NIVEAUX DE CONTAMINATION
RADIOACTIVE DU MILIEU AMBIANT ET DE
LA CHAINE ALIMENTAIRE. 1965. a. price
varies. (European Atomic Energy Community)
Office for Official Publications of the European
Communities, C.P. 1003, Luxembourg 1,
Luxembourg (Dist. in U.S. by European Community
Information Service, 2100 M St., N.W., Suite 707,
Washington, D.C. 20037)

362.1 US ISSN 0094-1816
NORTH DAKOTA. STATE DEPARTMENT OF
HEALTH. REPORT. Cover title: Health in North
Dakota. irreg. Department of Health, Bismarck, ND
58501. illus. stat. Key Title: Report - North Dakota
State Department of Health.

NORTHEASTERN REGIONAL ANTIPOLLUTION
CONFERENCE. PROCEEDINGS. see
ENVIRONMENTAL STUDIES

NOVA SCOTIA. DEPARTMENT OF PUBLIC
HEALTH. NUTRITION DIVISION. ANNUAL
REPORT. see *NUTRITION AND DIETETICS*

NOVA SCOTIA. EMERGENCY MEASURES
ORGANIZATION. REPORT. see *CIVIL
DEFENSE*

OHIO. DEPARTMENT OF MENTAL HEALTH
AND MENTAL RETARDATION. ANNUAL
FINANCIAL AND STATISTICAL REPORT. see
SOCIAL SERVICES AND WELFARE

OHIO STATE UNIVERSITY. DISASTER
RESEARCH CENTER. REPORT SERIES. see
SOCIAL SERVICES AND WELFARE

614.8 NE
OPERATIE VEILIGHEID. m (11/yr.) fl.7.50.
Veiligheidsinstituut - Dutch Foundation for the
Prevention of Accidents, Hobbemastraat 22, 1007
AR Amsterdam, Netherlands.

362.1 US ISSN 0092-3060
OREGON. OFFICE OF COMMUNITY HEALTH
SERVICES. LOCAL HEALTH SERVICES
ANNUAL SUMMARY. a. Office of Community
Health Services, Box 231, Portland, OR 97207. illus.
Key Title: Local Health Services Annual Summary
(Portland)

614 ET ISSN 0473-3657
ORGANIZATION OF AFRICAN UNITY.
HEALTH, SANITATION AND NUTRITION
COMMISSION. PROCEEDINGS AND
REPORT.* 1964. a. Organization of African Unity,
Health, Sanitation and Nutrition Commission, Box
3243, Addis Ababa, Ethiopia.

628 PL ISSN 0072-4696
POLITECHNIKA SLASKA. ZESZYTY NAUKOWE.
INZYNIERIA SANITARNA. (Text in Polish;
summaries in English and Russian) 1960. irreg. price
varies. Politechnika Slaska, W. Pstrowskiego 7, 44-
100 Gliwice, Poland (Dist. by: Ars Polona,
Krakowskie Przedmiescie 7, 00-068 Warsaw,
Poland) Ed. Stanislaw Mierzwinski.

627 628 PL ISSN 0084-2869
POLITECHNIKA WROCLAWSKA. INSTYTUT
INZYNIERI OCHRONY SRODOWSKA. PRACE
NAUKOWE. MONOGRAFIE. (Text in Polish;
summaries in English, French, German, Russian)
1969. irreg., no. 16, 1979. price varies. Politechnika
Wroclawska, Wybrzeze Wyspianskiego 27, 50-370
Wroclaw, Poland (Dist. by: Ars Polona-Ruch,
Krakowskie Przedmiescie 7, Warsaw, Poland) Ed.
Marian Kloza.

628 US ISSN 0079-3116
POLLUTION TECHNOLOGY REVIEW. 1973.
irreg., no. 72, 1981. $32-64. Noyes Data
Corporation, Noyes Bldg., Mill Road at Grand
Ave., Park Ridge, NJ 07656.
Formerly: Pollution Control Review.

628 PL ISSN 0079-3477
POLSKA AKADEMIA NAUK. KOMITET
GOSPODARKI WODNEJ. PRACE I STUDIA.
1956. irreg., vol. 11, 1972. price varies. Panstwowe
Wydawnictwo Naukowe, Ul, Miodowa 10, Warsaw,
Poland.

354 614 CN ISSN 0317-4530
PRINCE EDWARD ISLAND. DEPARTMENT OF
HEALTH. ANNUAL REPORT. a. Department of
Health, Box 3000, Charlottetown, P.E.I. C1A 7P1,
Canada. Ed. Burton Howatt.

614.8 US ISSN 0094-8470
PROGRESS IN RADIATION PROTECTION. 1973.
a. U.S. Bureau of Radiological Health, 5600 Fishers
Lane, Rockville, MD 20850. circ. 5,000.

614 US ISSN 0079-7006
PROPRIETARY ASSOCIATION. COMMITTEE ON
SCIENTIFIC DEVELOPMENT. ANNUAL
RESEARCH AND SCIENTIFIC
DEVELOPMENT CONFERENCE.
PROCEEDINGS. 1966. a. membership. Proprietary
Association, 1700 Pennsylvania Ave. N.W.,
Washington, DC 20006. circ. 1,000.

614 JA
PUBLIC CLEANSING SERVICE IN TOKYO/
SEISO JIGYO GAIYO. (Text in English) 1965. a.
exchange basis. Bureau of Public Cleansing - Tokyo-
to Seiso-kyoku Kikaku-bu, 3-8-1 Marunouchi,
Chiyoda-ku, Tokyo 100, Japan.

614 UG
PUBLIC HEALTH AND HYGIENE.* 1972, vol. 4.
a. Public Health Inspectors' Association, Box 46,
Kampala, Uganda. Ed. Wazarwahi Bwengye. adv.
bibl. illus.

PUBLIC HEALTH AND SAFETY

614   US   ISSN 0079-7596
PUBLIC HEALTH MONOGRAPH. 1951, no. 3. irreg. U. S. Public Health Service, Dept. of Health Education and Welfare, Bethesda, MD 20014. Indexed: Ind.Med.
Continues: Public Health Technical Monograph.

614   UN   ISSN 0555-6015
PUBLIC HEALTH PAPERS. French edition: Cahiers de Sante Publique. Russian edition: Tetradi Obshchestvennogo Zdravookhranenia. Spanish edition: Cuadernos de Salud Publica. 1959. irreg., no. 70, 1978. price varies. World Health Organization - Organisation Mondiale de la Sante, Distribution and Sales Service, 20 Avenue Appia, CH-1211 Geneva 27, Switzerland. circ. 1,100 (comb. circ.)

RAUMPLANUNG UND UMWELTSCHUTZ IM KANTON ZURICH. see *HOUSING AND URBAN PLANNING*

614   CK
REGISTRO DE ORGANISMOS DE SALUD. 1976. a. Departamento Administrativo Nacional de Estadistica, Banco Nacional de Datos, Apdo. Aereo 80043, Bogota, D.E., Colombia.

REPERTORIO TECNICHE AMBIENTALI. see *ENVIRONMENTAL STUDIES*

614   UN   ISSN 0085-5529
REPORT ON THE WORLD HEALTH SITUATION. (Editions in Arabic, English, French, Russian & Spanish) 1959. every 6 yrs. price varies. World Health Organization - Organisation Mondiale de la Sante, Distribution and Sales Service, 20 Avenue Appia, CH-1211 Geneva 27, Switzerland. circ. 6,200.

614   150   US   ISSN 0192-0812
RESEARCH IN COMMUNITY AND MENTAL HEALTH; an annual compilation of research. 1979. a. $18.75 ato individuals; institutions $37.50. J A I Press, Box 1678, 165 W. Putnam Ave., Greenwich, CT 06830. Ed. Roberta G. Simmons.

362.2   US   ISSN 0094-291X
RHODE ISLAND. DEPARTMENT OF MENTAL HEALTH, RETARDATION AND HOSPITALS. MENTAL HEALTH, RETARDATION AND HOSPITALS. 1971. a. free. Department of Mental Health, Retardation and Hospitals, Aime J. Forand Bldgs., 600 New London Ave., Cranston, RI 02920. Key Title: Mental Health, Retardation and Hospitals (Cranston)

ROBOT. see *TRANSPORTATION — Roads And Traffic*

ROCENKA ZNECISTENI OVZDUSI NA UZEMI C S R. see *METEOROLOGY*

628   US   ISSN 0080-6021
SANITATION INDUSTRY YEARBOOK. 1963. a. $12. (Solid Waste Management Magazine) Communication Channels, Inc., 6285 Barfield Rd., Atlanta, GA 30328. Ed. Shirley Kii. adv. circ. 21,000. (also avail. in microform from UMI) Indexed: Eng.Ind.

362.1   UK
SCOTTISH HEALTH SERVICES. irreg. H.M.S.O. (Edinburgh), 13a Castle St., Edinburgh EH2 3AR, Scotland.

352.94   SI
SINGAPORE. MINISTRY OF THE ENVIRONMENT. ANNUAL REPORT. (Text in English) 1972. a. Ministry of the Environment, Princess House, Alexandra Rd., Singapore 3, Singapore. illus.

614   SI
SINGAPORE PUBLIC HEALTH BULLETIN. (Text in English) 1967. a. cont. free circ. Ministry of Health, Palmer Road, Singapore 2, Singapore. (Co-sponsor: Singapore Ministry of Environment) circ. controlled.

016.628   US   ISSN 0092-0541
SOLID WASTE MANAGEMENT: ABSTRACTS FROM THE LITERATURE. (Supplement to U.S. Public Health Service. Publication No. 91) 1964. a. price varies. U.S. Environmental Protection Agency, M St. N.W., Washington, DC 20460 (Orders to: Supt. Doc., Washington, DC 20402) circ. 2,000.

614   SP
SPAIN. DIRECCION GENERAL DE SANIDAD. RESUMEN CRONOLOGICO DE LA LEGISLACION DEL ESTADO QUE AFECTA A SERVICOS DE SANIDAD. (Subseries of its Revista de Sanidad e Higiene Publica) 1970. irreg. Direccion General de Sanidad, Plaza de Espana 17, Madrid 13, Spain.

STUDIES ON CURRENT HEALTH PROBLEMS. see *MEDICAL SCIENCES*

614.77   EI
STUDIES ON THE RADIOACTIVE CONTAMINATION OF THE SEA. ANNUAL REPORT. a. 125.00 Fr. (1971 ed.) (European Atomic Energy Community) Office for Official Publications of the European Communities, C.P. 1003, Luxembourg 1, Luxembourg (Dist. in U.S. by European Community Information Service, 2100 M St., N.W., Suite 707, Washington, D.C. 20037)

614   SW   ISSN 0346-8445
SWEDEN. SJUKVAARDENS OCH SOCIALVAARDENS PLANERINGS- OCH RATIONALISERINGSINSTITUT. S P R I INFORMERAR. Short title: S P R I Informerar. 1968. irreg. (8-10/yr) free. Sjukvaardens och Socialvaardens Planerings- och Rationaliseringsinstitut - Swedish Planning and Rationalization Institute of the Health and Social Services, Box 27310, S-102 54 Stockholm, Sweden.

614   SW   ISSN 0082-0113
SWEDEN. SJUKVAARDENS OCH SOCIALVAARDENS PLANERINGS- OCH RATIONALISERINGSINSTITUT. S P R I RAAD. Short title: S P R I Raad. (Text in Swedish; summaries in English) 1968. irreg. price varies. Sjukvaardens och Socialvaardens Planerings- och Rationaliseringsinstitut - Swedish Planning and Rationalization Institute of the Health and Social Services, Box 27310, S-102 54 Stockholm, Sweden.

614   SW   ISSN 0586-1691
SWEDEN. SJUKVAARDENS OCH SOCIALVAARDENS PLANERINGS- OCH RATIONALISERINGSINSTITUT. S P R I RAPPORT. Short title: S P R I Rapport. (Text in Swedish; summaries in English) 1968. irreg. price varies. Sjukvaardens och Socialvaardens Planerings- och Rationaliseringsinstitut - Swedish Planning and Rationalization Institute of the Health and Social Services, Box 27310, S-102 54 Stockholm, Sweden.

614   SW   ISSN 0082-0105
SWEDEN. SJUKVAARDENS OCH SOCIALVAARDENS PLANERINGS- OCH RATIONALISERINGSINSTITUT. S P R I SPECIFIKATIONER. Short title: S P R I Specifikationer. (Text in Swedish; titles in English) 1968. irreg. price varies. Sjukvaardens och Socialvaardens Planerings- och Rationaliseringsinstitut - Swedish Planning and Rationalization Institute of the Health and Social Services, Box 27310, S-102 54 Stockholm, Sweden.

614   US   ISSN 0163-1667
TEXAS. DEPARTMENT OF HEALTH RESOURCES. BIENNIAL REPORT. biennial. Department of Health Resources, 1100 W. 49th St., Austin, TX 78756. Key Title: Biennial Report - Texas Department of Health Resources.

TOKYO METROPOLITAN RESEARCH LABORATORY OF PUBLIC HEALTH, ANNUAL REPORT/TOKYO-TORITSU EISEI KENKYUSHO KENKYU NENPO. see *MEDICAL SCIENCES*

614   TO   ISSN 0082-4895
TONGA. MINISTER OF HEALTH. REPORT. (Text in English and Tongan) 1951. a. price varies. ‡ Government Printer, Nuku-Alofa, Tongatapu, Tonga Islands.

614   JA
TOYAMA PREFECTURE. ANNUAL REPORT OF PUBLIC HEALTH/TOYAMA-KEN EISEI TOKEI NENPO. (Text in Japanese) 1949. a. free. Welfare Department - Toyama-ken Kosei-bu, 1-7 Shinsogawa, Toyama 930, Japan. circ. 400.

614   UN   ISSN 0566-7658
UNITED NATIONS. INTERNATIONAL NARCOTICS CONTROL BOARD. STATISTICS ON NARCOTIC DRUGS FURNISHED BY GOVERNMENTS IN ACCORDANCE WITH THE INTERNATIONAL TREATIES AND MAXIMUM LEVELS OF OPIUM STOCKS. (Editions in English, French, Spanish and Russian) 1968. a.; latest issue, 1973 (pub. 1975) $2 (1971) International Narcotics Control Board - Organe Internationale de Controle des Stupefiants, Distribution and Sales Section, Palais des Nations, CH-1200 Geneva 10, Switzerland (Or United Nations Publications, Room LX-2300, New York, NY 10017)

615   UN
UNITED NATIONS. PERMANENT CENTRAL NARCOTICS (OPIUM) BOARD. REPORT OF THE INTERNATIONAL NARCOTICS CONTROL BOARD ON ITS WORK. irreg. price varies. International Narcotics Control Board - Organe International de Controle des Stupefiants, Distribution and Sales Section, Palais des Nations, CH-1211 Geneva 10, Switzerland (Or United Nations Publications, Room LX-2300, New York, NY 10017)
Formerly: United Nations. Permanent Central Narcotics Board. Report to the Economic and Social Council on the Work of the Permanent Central Narcotics (Opium) Board (ISSN 0082-8343)

U.S. CENTER FOR DISEASE CONTROL. ABORTION SURVEILLANCE. ANNUAL SUMMARY. see *BIRTH CONTROL*

U. S. CENTER FOR DISEASE CONTROL. DIPHTHERIA SURVEILLANCE REPORT. see *MEDICAL SCIENCES — Communicable Diseases*

U.S. CENTER FOR DISEASE CONTROL. LEPROSY SURVEILLANCE REPORT. see *MEDICAL SCIENCES — Communicable Diseases*

U.S. CENTER FOR DISEASE CONTROL. LISTERIOSIS SURVEILLANCE REPORT. see *MEDICAL SCIENCES — Communicable Diseases*

U.S. CENTER FOR DISEASE CONTROL. MALARIA SURVEILLANCE REPORT. see *MEDICAL SCIENCES — Communicable Diseases*

312   US   ISSN 0090-1156
U.S. CENTER FOR DISEASE CONTROL. BRUCELLOSIS SURVEILLANCE: ANNUAL SUMMARY. a. U. S. Center for Disease Control, Atlanta, GA 30333. illus. Key Title: Brucellosis Surveillance; Annual Summary.

615.9   US   ISSN 0098-6623
U.S. CENTER FOR DISEASE CONTROL. FOODBORNE & WATERBORNE DISEASE OUTBREAKS. ANNUAL SUMMARY. a. U.S. Center for Disease Control, Atlanta, GA 30333. Key Title: Foodborne & Waterborne Disease Outbreaks. Annual Summary.
Continues: U.S. Center for Disease Control. Foodborne Outbreaks; Annual Summary.

614   US
U.S. CENTER FOR DISEASE CONTROL. SALMONELLA SURVEILLANCE. ANNUAL SUMMARY. 1962. a. free. ‡ U.S. Center for Disease Control, Bureau of Epidemiology. Bacterial Disease Division, 1600 Clifton Road, Atlanta, GA 30333. charts. stat. circ. 3,000.

614.5   US   ISSN 0094-6605
U.S. CENTER FOR DISEASE CONTROL. TETANUS SURVEILLANCE; REPORT. 1968. irreg. U.S. Center for Disease Control, Bureau of Epidemiology, Atlanta, GA 30333. Key Title: Tetanus Surveillance; Report.

614   US   ISSN 0361-9087
U.S. ENVIRONMENTAL PROTECTION AGENCY. EASTERN ENVIRONMENTAL RADIATION FACILITY. ANNUAL REPORT. 1959. a. controlled circ. U.S. Environmental Protection Agency, Office of Radiation Programs, Box 3009, Montgomery, AL 36109. Ed. Ellery D. Sauage. bibl. charts. illus. circ. (controlled)

664.07　　　　　　US　ISSN 0361-4522
U.S. FOOD AND DRUG ADMINISTRATION. PESTICIDE-P C B IN FOODS PROGRAM. EVALUATION REPORT. a. Food and Drug Administration, Bureau of Foods, 200 C St. S.W., Washington, DC 20204.

312　　　　　　US
U.S. NATIONAL CENTER FOR HEALTH STATISTICS. ADVANCE DATA FROM VITAL AND HEALTH STATISTICS. no. 47, 1979. irreg., no. 52, 1979. U.S. National Center for Health Statistics, 3700 East-West Highway, Hyattsville, MD 20782.

614　　　　　　US　ISSN 0083-1956
U. S. NATIONAL CENTER FOR HEALTH STATISTICS. HEALTH RESOURCES STATISTICS. 1965. a. U. S. National Center for Health Statistics, 3700 East-West Highway, Hyattsville, MD 20782.

312　　　　　　US　ISSN 0083-2014
U. S. NATIONAL CENTER FOR HEALTH STATISTICS. VITAL AND HEALTH STATISTICS. SERIES 1. PROGRAMS AND COLLECTION PROCEDURES. 1963. irreg. price varies. U. S. National Center for Health Statistics, Scientific and Technical Information Branch, 3700 East-West Highway, Hyattsville, MD 20782. Indexed: Excerp.Med.

312　　　　　　US　ISSN 0083-2057
U. S. NATIONAL CENTER FOR HEALTH STATISTICS. VITAL AND HEALTH STATISTICS. SERIES 2. DATA EVALUATION AND METHODS RESEARCH. 1963. irreg. price varies. U. S. National Center for Health Statistics, Scientific and Technical Information Branch, 3700 East-West Highway, Hyattsville, MD 20782. Indexed: Excerp.Med.

312　　　　　　US　ISSN 0083-2065
U.S. NATIONAL CENTER FOR HEALTH STATISTICS. VITAL AND HEALTH STATISTICS. SERIES 3. ANALYTICAL STUDIES. 1964. irreg. price varies. U. S. National Center for Health Statistics, Scientific and Technical Information Branch, 3700 East-West Highway, Hyattsville, MD 20782. Indexed: Excerp.Med.

312　　　　　　US　ISSN 0083-2073
U.S. NATIONAL CENTER FOR HEALTH STATISTICS. VITAL AND HEALTH STATISTICS. SERIES 4. DOCUMENTS AND COMMITTEE REPORT. 1965. irreg. price varies. U. S. National Center for Health Statistics, Scientific and Technical Information Branch, 3700 East-West Highway, Hyattsville, MD 20782. Indexed: Excerp.Med.

614　　　　　　US　ISSN 0083-1972
U. S. NATIONAL CENTER FOR HEALTH STATISTICS. VITAL AND HEALTH STATISTICS. SERIES 10. DATA FROM THE HEALTH INTERVIEW SURVEY. 1963. irreg. price varies. U. S. National Center for Health Statistics, Scientific and Technical Information Branch, 3700 East-West Highway, Hyattsville, MD 20782. Indexed: Excerp.Med.

614　　　　　　US
U.S. NATIONAL CENTER FOR HEALTH STATISTICS. VITAL AND HEALTH STATISTICS. SERIES 11. DATA FROM THE HEALTH AND NUTRITION EXAMINATION SURVEY. 1964. irreg. price varies. U. S. National Center for Health Statistics, Scientific and Technical Information Branch, 3700 East-West Highway, Hyattsville, MD 20782. Indexed: Excerp.Med.
　Formerly: U.S. National Center for Health Statistics. Vital and Health Statistics. Series 11. Data from the Health Examination Survey (ISSN 0083-1980)

362　　　　　　US
U.S. NATIONAL CENTER FOR HEALTH STATISTICS. VITAL AND HEALTH STATISTICS. SERIES 13. DATA ON HEALTH RESOURCES UTILIZATION. 1966. irreg. price varies. U. S. National Center for Health Statistics, Scientific and Technical Information Branch, 3700 East-West Highway, Hyattsville, MD 20782. Indexed: Excerp.Med.
　Incorporating: U.S. National Center for Health Care Statistics. Vital and Health Statistics. Series 12. Data from the Institutional Population Surveys (ISSN 0083-1964); Formerly: U.S. National Center for Health Care Statistics. Vital and Health Statistics. Series 13. Data from the Hospital Discharge Survey (ISSN 0083-2006)

614　　　　　　US　ISSN 0083-1999
U. S. NATIONAL CENTER FOR HEALTH STATISTICS. VITAL AND HEALTH STATISTICS. SERIES 14. DATA ON HEALTH RESOURCES: MANPOWER AND FACILITIES. 1968. irreg. price varies. U. S. National Center for Health Statistics, Scientific and Technical Information Branch, 3700 East-West Highway, Hyattsville, MD 20782. Indexed: Excerp.Med.

312　　　　　　US　ISSN 0083-2022
U. S. NATIONAL CENTER FOR HEALTH STATISTICS. VITAL AND HEALTH STATISTICS. SERIES 20. DATA ON MORTALITY. 1965. irreg. price varies. U. S. National Center for Health Statistics, Scientific and Technical Information Branch, 3700 East-West Highway, Hyattsville, MD 20782. Indexed: Excerp.Med.
　Incorporating in part: U.S. National Center for Health Statistics. Vital and Health Statistics. Series 22. Data on Natality and Mortality Surveys (ISSN 0083-2049)

312　　　　　　US　ISSN 0083-2030
U. S. NATIONAL CENTER FOR HEALTH STATISTICS. VITAL AND HEALTH STATISTICS. SERIES 21. DATA ON NATALITY, MARRIAGE, AND DIVORCE. 1964. irreg. price varies. U. S. National Center for Health Statistics, Scientific and Technical Information Branch, 3700 East-West Highway, Hyattsville, MD 20782. Indexed: Excerp.Med.
　Incorporating in part: U.S. National Center for Health Statistics. Vital and Health Statistics. Series 22. Date on Natality and Mortality Surveys (ISSN 0083-2049)

628　　　　　　GT
UNIVERSIDAD DE SAN CARLOS. FACULTAD DE INGENERIA. ESCUELA REGIONAL DE INGENIERIA SANITARIA. CARTA PERIODICA. 1966. irreg. Universidad de San Carlos de Guatemala, Escuela Regional de Ingenieria Sanitaria, Ciudad Universitaria, Zona 12, Guatemala. Ed. Arturo Acajabon Mendoza. bibl. charts. illus.
　Formerly: Brujula.

UNIVERSITY OF IOWA. GRADUATE PROGRAM IN HOSPITAL AND HEALTH ADMINISTRATION. HEALTH CARE RESEARCH SERIES. see HOSPITALS

UNIVERSITY OF MICHIGAN. MENTAL HEALTH RESEARCH INSTITUTE. ANNUAL REPORT. see PSYCHOLOGY

614.6　　　　　　US
V D ALERT. q? $25. American Social Health Association, 260 Sheridan Ave., Palo Alto, CA 94306.

614　　　　　　UN　ISSN 0512-3011
VACCINATION CERTIFICATE REQUIREMENTS FOR INTERNATIONAL TRAVEL/ CERTIFICATS DE VACCINATION EXIGES DANS LES VOYAGES INTERNATIONAUX. a. World Health Organization - Organisation Mondiale de la Sante, Distribution and Sales Service, 20 Avenue Appia, CH-1211 Geneva 27, Switzerland. circ. 13,000.

VERKEHRSPSYCHOLOGISCHER INFORMATIONSDIENST. see TRANSPORTATION — Roads And Traffic

614　　　　　　US
VITAL AND HEALTH STATISTICS MONOGRAPHS. irreg. American Public Health Association, 1015 15th St., N.W., Washington, DC 20005 (Dist. by: Harvard University Press, 79 Garden St., Cambridge, MA 02138)

614.109　　　　　　US　ISSN 0083-6710
VITAL STATISTICS OF THE UNITED STATES. 1937. a. price varies. U. S. National Center for Health Statistics, 3700 East-West Highway, Hyattsville, MD 20782.

W H O OFFSET PUBLICATIONS. (World Health Organization) see PUBLIC HEALTH AND SAFETY — Abstracting, Bibliographies, Statistics

W H O TECHNICAL REPORT SERIES. (World Health Organization) see MEDICAL SCIENCES

354　　　　　　AT
WESTERN AUSTRALIA. STATE HEALTH LABORATORY SERVICES. ANNUAL REPORT. a. State Health Laboratory Services, Perth, Australia. stat.

WISCONSIN. DEPARTMENT OF NATURAL RESOURCES. ANNUAL WATER QUALITY REPORT TO CONGRESS. see ENVIRONMENTAL STUDIES

614.8　388.1　　　　　　US
WISCONSIN ACCIDENT FACTS.* a. Department of Transportation, Madison, WI 53702. charts. stat.

WORLD DIRECTORY OF SCHOOLS OF PUBLIC HEALTH. see EDUCATION — Guides To Schools And Colleges

WORLD FEDERATION FOR MENTAL HEALTH. PROCEEDINGS OF ANNUAL MEETINGS. see PSYCHOLOGY

614　　　　　　UN　ISSN 0512-3038
WORLD HEALTH ORGANIZATION. MONOGRAPH SERIES. 1951. irreg. price varies. World Health Organization - Organisation Mondiale de la Sante, Distribution and Sales Service, 20 Avenue Appia, CH-1211 Geneva 27, Switzerland. circ. 9,000. Indexed: Ind.Med.

WORLD HEALTH ORGANIZATION. REGIONAL OFFICE FOR THE WESTERN PACIFIC. REPORT ON THE REGIONAL SEMINAR ON THE ROLE OF THE HOSPITAL IN THE PUBLIC HEALTH PROGRAMME. see HOSPITALS

614　　　　　　UN
WORLD HEALTH ORGANIZATION. REGIONAL OFFICE FOR AFRICA. REPORT OF THE REGIONAL COMMITTEE. 1959. a. not for sale. ‡ World Health Organization, Regional Office for Africa - Organisation Mondiale de la Sante. Bureau Regional de l'Afrique, B.P. No. 6, Brazzaville, People's Republic of the Congo.
　Formerly: World Health Organization. Regional Office for Africa. Report of the Regional Committee. Minutes of the Plenary Session (ISSN 0512-3070)

614　　　　　　UN　ISSN 0510-8837
WORLD HEALTH ORGANIZATION. REGIONAL OFFICE FOR AFRICA. REPORT OF THE REGIONAL DIRECTOR. 1951. a. not for sale. World Health Organization, Regional Office for Africa - Organisation Mondiale de la Sante. Bureau Regional de l'Afrique, B.P. No. 6, Brazzaville, People's Republic of the Congo.

614　　　　　　UN
WORLD HEALTH ORGANIZATION. REGIONAL OFFICE FOR THE EASTERN MEDITERRANEAN. BIENNIAL REPORT OF THE REGIONAL DIRECTOR. 1950. a.; latest 1973-1974. free. World Health Organization, Regional Office for the Eastern Mediterranean, P.O. Box 1517, Alexandria, Egypt. circ. 3,000.
　Formerly: World Health Organization. Regional Office for the Eastern Mediterranean. Annual Report of the Regional Director (ISSN 0512-3089)

614 UN ISSN 0512-4921
WORLD HEALTH ORGANIZATION. REGIONAL OFFICE FOR THE WESTERN PACIFIC. ANNUAL REPORT OF THE REGIONAL DIRECTOR TO THE REGIONAL COMMITTEE FOR THE WESTERN PACIFIC.* a. World Health Organization, Regional Office for the Western Pacific, P.O. Box 2932, Manila, Philippines.

614 UN ISSN 0085-8285
WORLD HEALTH ORGANIZATION. WORK OF W H O; biennial report of the director-general to the World Health Assembly and to the United Nations. (Editions in Arabic, English, French, Russian, Spanish) 1948. biennial. price varies. World Health Organization - Organisation Mondiale de la Sante, Distribution and Sales Service, 20 Avenue Appia, CH-1211 Geneva 27, Switzerland. circ. 8,000.

614 UN ISSN 0301-0740
WORLD HEALTH ORGANIZATION. WORLD HEALTH ASSEMBLY AND THE EXECUTIVE BOARD. HANDBOOK OF RESOLUTIONS AND DECISIONS. (Editions in Arabic, English, French, Russian & Spanish) 1948. a. World Health Organization - Organisation Mondiale de la Sante, Distribution and Sales Service, 20 Avenue Appia, CH-1211 Geneva 27, Switzerland. circ. 8,000.

614.4 US
WORLDWIDE REPORT: EPIDEMIOLOGY. irreg. (approx. 31/yr.) $155. U.S. Joint Publications Research Service, 1000 N. Glebe Rd., Arlington, VA 22201 (Orders to: NTIS, Springfield, VA 22161)
Former titles: World Epidemiology Review; Epidemiology Reports from the World Press.

WYOMING. DEPARTMENT OF HEALTH AND SOCIAL SERVICES. ANNUAL REPORT. see SOCIAL SERVICES AND WELFARE

614.44 610 GW ISSN 0172-5602
ZENTRALBLATT FUER BAKTERIOLOGIE, PARASITENKUNNDE, INFEKTIONSKRANKHEITEN UND HYGIENE-KRANKENHAUSHYGIENE-PRAEVENTIVE MEDIZIN-BETRIEBSHYGIENE. irreg., 4 nos. per vol. DM.196 separately; DM 164 with Originale Reihe A. Gustav Fischer Verlag, Wollgrasweg 49, Postfach 720143, 7000 Stuttgart 70, W. Germany (B.R.D.) Ed. M. Knorr. circ. 1,200. Indexed: Ind.Med.
Formerly: Zentralblatt fuer Bakteriologie, Parasitenkunde, Infektionskrankheiten und Hygiene. Orginale Reihe B: Hygiene - Praventive Medizin.

PUBLIC HEALTH AND SAFETY — Abstracting, Bibliographies, Statistics

614 318 AG
ARGENTINA. SECRETARIA DE ESTADO DE SALUD PUBLICA. PROGRAMA NACIONAL DE ESTADISTICAS DE SALUD. vol. 6, 1976. irreg. Secretaria de Estado de Salud Publica, Alsina 301, Buenos Aires, Argentina.

610 AT
AUSTRALIA. BUREAU OF STATISTICS. CHRONIC ILLNESSES, INJURIES AND IMPAIRMENTS. irreg. free. Australian Bureau of Statistics, P.O. Box 10, Belconnen, A.C.T. 2616, Australia. stat. circ. 1,000. (back issues avail.)

614.86 BE ISSN 0067-5504
BELGIUM. INSTITUT NATIONAL DE STATISTIQUE. STATISTIQUE DES ACCIDENTS DE LA CIRCULATION SUR LA VOIE PUBLIQUE. (Text in Dutch and French) 1954. a. 150 Fr. Institut National de Statistique, 44 rue de Louvain, 1000 Brussels, Belgium.
Formerly: Belgium. Institut National de Statistique. Statistique des Accidents de Roulage (ISSN 0067-5512)

900 016 SZ ISSN 0067-7000
BIBLIOGRAPHIE INTERNATIONALE DE L'HUMANISME ET DE LA RENAISSANCE. 1965. a. price varies. (International Federation of Societies and Institutes for the Study of the Renaissance) Librarie Droz, 11, rue Massot, 1211 Geneva 12, Switzerland. circ. 1,200.

361.6 016 CN
CANADA. DEPARTMENT OF NATIONAL HEALTH AND WELFARE. LIBRARY. ACQUISITIONS. (Text in English and French) 1947. irreg. Department of National Health and Welfare., Library, Ottawa, Ont., Canada.

628 310 UK ISSN 0142-1468
CHARTERED INSTITUTE OF PUBLIC FINANCE AND ACCOUNTANCY. WATER AND SEWAGE TREATMENT AND DISPOSAL STATISTICS. ACTUALS. 1978. a. £5. Chartered Institute of Public Finance and Accountancy, 1 Buckingham Place, London SW1E 6HS, England. (back issues avail.)

614 CL
CHILE. INSTITUTO NACIONAL DE ESTADISTICAS. ESTADISTICAS DE SALUD. 1965. irreg; latest 1973. Esc.60($18) Instituto Nacional de Estadisticas, Santiago, Chile.

614 NE
COMPENDIUM GEZONDHEIDSSTATISTIEK NEDERLAND/COMPENDIUM HEALTH STATISTICS OF THE NETHERLANDS. (Text in Dutch and English) 1974. irreg. fl.55. Centraal Bureau voor de Statistiek, Prinses Beatrixlaan 428, Voorburg, Netherlands (Orders to: Staatsuitgeverij, Christoffel Plantijnstraat, The Hague, Netherlands) (Co-sponsor: Ministry of Public Health and Environmental Hygiene) circ. 4,000.

DOKUMENTATION IMPFSCHAEDEN-IMPFERFOLGE. see MEDICAL SCIENCES — Abstracting, Bibliographies, Statistics

614 312 GW ISSN 0072-1840
GERMANY (FEDERAL REPUBLIC, 1949-) STATISTISCHES BUNDESAMT. FACHSERIE 12, REIHE 1: AUSGEWAEHLTE ZAHLEN FUER DAS GESUNDHEITSWESEN. 1959. a. DM.9.50. W. Kohlhammer-Verlag GmbH, Abt. Veroeffentlichungen des Statistischen Bundesamtes, Philipp-Reis-Str. 3, Postfach 421120, 6500 Mainz 42, W. Germany (B.R.D.)

GREECE. NATIONAL STATISTICAL SERVICE. SOCIAL WELFARE AND HEALTH STATISTICS. see SOCIAL SERVICES AND WELFARE — Abstracting, Bibliographies, Statistics

614 UN ISSN 0085-1450
HEALTH PHYSICS RESEARCH ABSTRACTS. (Text in English) 1967. irreg., no. 8, 1978. free. International Atomic Energy Agency - Agence Internationale de l'Energie Atomique, Division of Nuclear Safety & Environmental Protection, Wagramer Str. 5, Box 100, A-1400 Vienna, Austria.

615.9 US ISSN 0094-6494
ILLINOIS. DEPARTMENT OF PUBLIC HEALTH. POISON CONTROL PROGRAM REPORT. a. free. Department of Public Health, Springfield, IL 62706. Key Title: Poison Control Program Report.

614.1 US ISSN 0145-5990
KENTUCKY. DEPARTMENT FOR HUMAN RESOURCES. SELECTED VITAL STATISTICS AND PLANNING DATA. 1911. a. free. Department for Human Resources, Center for Comprehensive Health Systems Development, 275 E. Main St., Frankfort, KY 40621. circ. 3,000. Key Title: Selected Vital Statistics and Planning Data.
Former titles: Kentucky Vital Statistics (ISSN 0098-6739); Kentucky Vital Statistics Report.

614 310 US ISSN 0539-7413
MICHIGAN HEALTH STATISTICS. 1970. a. free. Department of Public Health, 3500 N. Logan St., Lansing, MI 98914. illus.
Continues: Michigan Public Health Statistics.

312 US ISSN 0094-5641
MINNESOTA HEALTH STATISTICS. 1950. a. free. Department of Health, Center for Health Statistics, 717 Delaware St. S. E., Minneapolis, MN 55440. circ. 900.

312 US ISSN 0098-1974
MISSOURI VITAL STATISTICS. a. Division of Health, Center for Health Statistics, Box 570, Jefferson City, MO 65102. (also avail. in microfiche)

614 US ISSN 0077-1198
MONTANA VITAL STATISTICS. 1954. a. free. ‡ Department of Health and Environmental Sciences, Helena, MT 59620. Ed. John C. Wilson. circ. 850. (also avail. in microform from UMI)
Continues: Montana. State Department of Health. Annual Statistical Supplement.

362.2 US
NEBRASKA. DEPARTMENT OF PUBLIC INSTITUTIONS. MENTAL HEALTH AND MENTAL RETARDATION SERVICES ANNUAL STATISTICAL REPORT. a. Department of Public Institutions, Medical Services Division, Box 94728, Lincoln, NE 68509. illus.

NORTH CAROLINA. DIVISION OF HEALTH SERVICES. PUBLIC HEALTH STATISTICS BRANCH. NORTH CAROLINA VITAL STATISTICS. see POPULATION STUDIES — Abstracting, Bibliographies, Statistcs

312.267 US ISSN 0085-428X
NORTH CAROLINA COMMUNICABLE DISEASE MORBIDITY STATISTICS. 1918. a. free. ‡ Department of Human Resources, Division of Health Services, P.O. Box 2091, Raleigh, NC 27602. stat.

373 NO
NORWAY. STATISTISK SENTRALBYRAA. HELSESTATISTIKK/HEALTH STATISTICS. (Subseries of its Norges Offisielle Statistikk) (Text in Norwegian; summaries in English) a. price varies. Statistisk Sentralbyraa, Box 8131-Dep., Oslo 1, Norway. circ. 2,100.

312 US ISSN 0098-5651
OKLAHOMA HEALTH STATISTICS. a. free. Department of Health, Public Health Statistics Division, Box 53551, Oklahoma City, OK 73105. illus.

614 314 PL ISSN 0079-2748
POLAND. GLOWNY URZAD STATYSTYCZNY. ROCZNIK STATYSTYCZNY OCHRONY ZDROWIA. YEARBOOK OF PUBLIC HEALTH STATISTICS.* (Issued in its Seria Roczniki Branzowe. Branch Yearbooks) irreg. Glowny Urzad Statystyczny, Al. Niepodleglosci 208, 00-925 Warsaw, Poland.

614.8 314 PL ISSN 0079-287X
POLAND. GLOWNY URZAD STATYSTYCZNY. WYPADKI DROGOWE.* a. Glowny Urzad Statystyczny, Al. Niepodleglosci 208, 00-925 Warsaw, Poland.

614.8 314 PL ISSN 0079-2888
POLAND. GLOWNY URZAD STATYSTYCZNY. WYPADKI PRZY PRACY. ACCIDENTS AT WORK.* a. Glowny Urzad Statystyczny, Al. Niepodleglosci 208, 00-925 Warsaw, Poland.

614 US ISSN 0079-7588
PUBLIC HEALTH CONFERENCE ON RECORDS AND STATISTICS. PROCEEDINGS. 1950, 2nd. a. U. S. National Center for Health Statistics, 3700 East-West Highway, Hyattsville, MD 20782.

614 016 US ISSN 0080-0341
RECURRING BIBLIOGRAPHY, EDUCATION IN THE ALLIED HEALTH PROFESSIONS. 1969. a. $1.25. ‡ Ohio State University, School of Allied Medical Professions, 1583 Perry St., Columbus, OH 43210. Ed. John E. Burke. index. circ. 450.

628 310 US ISSN 0162-6256
SANITARY SERVICES IN TENNESSEE. (Subseries of: Tennessee. State Planning Office. Publication) biennial. State Planning Office, 660 Capitol Hill Bldg., Nashville, TN 37219. stat.
Sanitary engineering

SOLID WASTE MANAGEMENT; AVAILABLE INFORMATION MATERIALS. see PUBLIC ADMINISTRATION — Abstracting, Bibliographies, Statistics

614 NZ ISSN 0550-824X
TRENDS IN HEALTH AND HEALTH SERVICES. biennial. price varies. National Health Statistics Centre, P.O. Box 6314 Te Aro, Wellington 1, New Zealand. circ. controlled.

317 016　　　　　US　ISSN 0092-7287
U.S. NATIONAL CENTER FOR HEALTH STATISTICS. CURRENT LISTING AND TOPICAL INDEX TO THE VITAL AND HEALTH STATISTICS SERIES. biennial. free. U.S. Department of Health, Education and Welfare, U.S. National Center for Health Statistics, 3700 East-West Highway, Hyattsville, MD 20782.

614　　　　　　　　　　UN
W H O OFFSET PUBLICATIONS. (Text in English and French; if required Arabic, Russian and Spanish) 1973. irreg. price varries. World Health Organization - Organisation Mondiale de la Sante, Distribution and Sales Service, 20 Ave Appi'a, CH-1211 Geneva 27, Switzerland. bibl. circ. 10,000.

628 016　　　　UN　ISSN 0083-761X
WASTE MANAGEMENT RESEARCH ABSTRACTS. (Text in English, French, Spanish, Russian) 1965. a. free. International Atomic Energy Agency - Agence Internationale de l'Energie Atomique, Division of Nuclear Safety and Environmental Protection, Wagramer Str. 5, Box 100, A-1400 Vienna, Austria.

614　　　　　　　　　　UN
WORLD HEALTH STATISTICS ANNUAL. 1951. a. price varies. World Health Organization - Organisation Mondiale de la Sante, Distribution and Sales Service, 20 Avenue Appia, CH-1211 Geneva 27, Switzerland. circ. 3,600.
Before 1965: Annual Epidemiological and Vital Statistics.

PUBLISHING AND BOOK TRADE

see also Bibliographies; Journalism; Patents, Trademarks and Copyrights; Printing

070.5　　　　　　US　ISSN 0065-0005
A B BOOKMAN'S YEARBOOK; specialist book trade annual. 1949. a. $7.50. Antiquarian Bookman, Box AB, Clifton, NJ 07015. Ed. Jacob L. Chernofsky. adv. bk. rev. index. cum.index: 10 year periods. circ. 10,000.

070.5　　　　　　US　ISSN 0065-0048
A B C OF BOOK TRADE. 1966. quinquennial. $5. Antiquarian Bookman, Box AB, Clifton, NJ 07015. Ed.Jacob L.Chernofsky.

658.8　　　　　　GW　ISSN 0065-2032
ADRESSBUCH FUER DEN DEUTSCHSPRACHIGEN BUCHHANDELS. 1839. a. Buchhaendler-Vereinigung GmbH, Grosser Hirschgraben 17-21, Postfach 2404, 6000 Frankfurt 1, W. Germany (B.R.D.) adv. circ. 4,000.

ADVERTISER'S GUIDE TO SCHOLARLY PERIODICALS. see *ADVERTISING AND PUBLIC RELATIONS*

070.5　　　　　　　　　UK
AFRICAN BOOK WORLD AND PRESS: A DIRECTORY. 1977. triennial. £30. Hans Zell Publishers Ltd. (Subsidiary of: K. G. Saur Verlag) Box 56, 14a St. Giles, Oxford OX1 3EL, England (Dist. in U.S.by: Gale Research Co., Book Tower, Detroit, MI 48226)

070.5　　　　　　US　ISSN 0065-759X
AMERICAN BOOK TRADE DIRECTORY. 1915. a. $59.95. (Jaques Cattell Press) R. R. Bowker Company, 1180 Ave. of the Americas, New York, NY 10036. (Orders to P.O. Box 1807, Ann Arbor, Mich. 48106) index. (reprint service avail. from UMI)

AMERICAN SOCIETY OF BOOKPLATE COLLECTORS AND DESIGNERS. YEAR BOOK. see *HOBBIES*

070.5　　　　　　　　　BE
ANNUAIRE DES EDITEURS BELGES. (Text in French and Dutch) 1968. biennial. free. Federation des Editeurs Belges, 111 Ave. du Parc, 1060 Brussels, Belgium. Ed. J. de Raeymaeker. circ. 8,000.

655.5　　　　　　UK　ISSN 0066-3913
ANNUAL DIRECTORY OF BOOKSELLERS IN THE BRITISH ISLES SPECIALISING IN ANTIQUARIAN AND OUT-OF-PRINT BOOKS. 1970. a. £3($9) Clique Ltd., 75 World's End Rd., Handsworth Wood, Birmingham B20 2NS, England.

070.5　　　　　　GW　ISSN 0066-4596
ANSCHRIFTEN DEUTSCHER VERLAGE UND AUSLAENDISCHER VERLAGE MIT DEUTSCHEN AUSLIEFERUNGEN. 1952. a. DM.38. Verlag der Schillerbuchhandlung Hans Banger, Alte Neusser Landstr. 302, 5000 Cologne 71, W. Germany (B. R. D.)

070.5　　　　　　II　ISSN 0066-8362
ASIAN BOOK TRADE DIRECTORY.* (Prepared with the assistance of UNESCO) (Text in English) 1964. irreg., 1967, 2nd ed. Rs.25($4) Nirmala Sadanand Publishers, 35 C Tardeo Rd., Bombay 400034, India. Ed. Sadanand Bhatkal.
Formerly: Directory of Asian Book Trade.

070　　　　　　　US　ISSN 0161-8318
ASSEMBLING; a collection of otherwise unpublishable creative work. 1970. a. $6.95. (Participation Projects Foundation) Assembling Press, Box 1967, Brooklyn, NY 11202. illus. circ. 1,000. (back issues avail.)

071　　　　　　　US　ISSN 0147-0310
ASSOCIATION OF AMERICAN PUBLISHERS. EXHIBITS DIRECTORY. 1967. a. $20 to nonmembers; $10 to members. Association of American Publishers, One Park Ave., New York, NY 10016. Ed. Ellen Bonn. circ. 1,000.
Continues: Directory of Exhibit Opportunities.

070.5　　　　　　US　ISSN 0571-6098
ASSOCIATION OF AMERICAN UNIVERSITY PRESSES DIRECTORY. 1960/61. a. $5. Association of American University Presses, Inc., One Park Ave., Rm. 1102, New York, NY 10016. Ed. Rita Ann Black. index. circ. (controlled)

070.5　　　　　　CN　ISSN 0381-727X
AUTHOR-PUBLISHER NEWS & VIEWS. 1975. a. McGraw-Hill Ryerson Ltd., 330 Progress Ave., Scarborough, Ont. M1P 2Z5, Canada.

070.5　　　　　　　　　UK
B. A. I. E. MEMBERSHIP DIRECTORY. biennial. £46. British Association of Industrial Editors, 3 Locks Yard., High St, Sevenoaks, Kent TN13 1LT, England. adv. circ. 1,200.
Former titles: Who's Who in Industrial Editing (ISSN 0068-1296) & British Association of Industrial Editors. B A I E Directory of Members.

020 940 090　　GE　ISSN 0067-5091
BEITRAEGE ZUR INKUNABELKUNDE. DRITTE FOLGE. 1965. irreg., vol. 6, 1979. M.30. (Deutsche Staatsbibliothek) Akademie-Verlag, Leipziger Strasse 3-4, 108 Berlin, E. Germany (D.D.R.)

070.5 658　　　　　　　US
BENCO REPORT; news of business-building book programs. 1964. irreg. free. Benjamin Company, 485 Madison Ave., New York, NY 10022. Ed. Roy Benjamin. circ. 25,000(controlled) (tabloid format)

741.6　　　　　　　　　US
BEST IN COVERS AND POSTERS. 1975. a. $13.95. R C Publications, Inc., 355 Lexington Ave., New York, NY 10017 (Or 6400 Goldsboro Rd., Washington, DC 20034) illus.
Formed by the 1977 merger of: Best in Covers (ISSN 0361-2066) & Best in Posters (ISSN 0360-8085)

070.5　　　　　　US　ISSN 0275-0945
BEST SELLERS & BEST CHOICES (YEAR); list of best sellers, "editors' choice," and recommended/prize-awarded books, with hardcovers and softcovers. 1981. a. $3.50. Ad Digest, 9302 Parkside, Box 165, Morton Grove, IL 60053. Ed. Chung I. Park.

090 070.5 686　　HU　ISSN 0067-8007
BIBLIOTHECA HUNGARICA ANTIQUA. 1960. irreg. price varies. (Magyar Tudomanyos Akademia) Akademiai Kiado, Publishing House of the Hungarian Academy of Sciences, P.O. Box 24, H-1363 Budapest, Hungary.

070.5　　　　　　UK　ISSN 0068-0095
BOOK AUCTION RECORDS. 1902. a. L.40. Wm. Dawson & Sons Ltd., Cannon House, Folkestone, Kent CT19 5EE, England. Ed. Wendy Y. Heath. adv. cum.index every 4 years. circ. 2,500.
A priced and annotated annual record of books auctioned world wide

020.75　　　　　　　　　US
BOOK COLLECTORS' HANDBOOK OF VALUES. irreg. price varies. G. P. Putnam's Sons, 200 Madison Ave., New York, NY 10016.

070.5　　　　　　UK　ISSN 0142-9523
BOOK DEALERS' AND COLLECTORS' YEARBOOK AND DIARY. 1978. a. £4.20. Sheppard Press Ltd., Box 42, Russell Chambers, Covent Garden, London WC2E 8AX, England.

070.5　　　　　　UK　ISSN 0068-0109
BOOK DEALERS IN NORTH AMERICA. 1956. triennial. £9. Sheppard Press, Ltd., P.O. Box 42, Russell Chambers, Covent Garden, London WC2E 8AX, England. index.

658.8　　　　　　US　ISSN 0160-970X
BOOK INDUSTRY TRENDS. Represents: Book Industry Study Group. Research Report. 1977. a. Book Industry Study Group, Inc., Box 2062, Darien, CT 06820. Ed. John P. Dessauer.

070.025　　　　　CN　ISSN 0700-5296
BOOK TRADE IN CANADA/INDUSTRIE DU LIVRE AU CANADA. (Text in English and French) 1975. a. $20. Ampersand Publishing Services, R.R.1, Caledon, Ont. L0N 1C0, Canada. circ. 2,000.
Formerly (until 1976): Book Publishers in Canada.

070.5　　　　　　UK　ISSN 0143-0270
BOOKDEALERS IN INDIA, PAKISTAN AND SRI LANKA. 1977. triennial. £3.50($7) Sheppard Press Ltd., P.O. Box 42, Russell Chambers, Covent Garden, London WC2E 8AX, England.

070.5　　　　　　　　　US
BOOKHUNTER'S GUIDE TO THE WEST AND SOUTHWEST. 1978. biennial. $6. Ephemera and Books, Box 19681, San Diego, CA 92119. Ed. Ray P. Reynolds.

070.5　　　　　　US　ISSN 0068-0133
BOOKMAN'S GUIDE TO AMERICANA. 1960. irreg; 7th ed., 1977. price varies. Scarecrow Press, Inc., 52 Liberty St., Metuchen, NJ 08840. circ. 3,000.

070.5　　　　　　US　ISSN 0068-0141
BOOKMAN'S PRICE INDEX; guide to the values of rare and other out-of-print books. 1964. irreg., vol. 14, 1978. $74 per vol. Gale Research Company, Book Tower, Detroit, MI 48226. Ed. Daniel F. McGrath.

BOOKMARK. see *LIBRARY AND INFORMATION SCIENCES*

BOOKS AND LIBRARIES AT THE UNIVERSITY OF KANSAS. see *LIBRARY AND INFORMATION SCIENCES*

070.5　　　　　　UK　ISSN 0068-0249
BOOKSELLERS ASSOCIATION OF GREAT BRITAIN AND IRELAND. LIST OF MEMBERS. a. ‡ Booksellers Association of Great Britain & Ireland, 154 Buckingham Palace Rd., London SW1W 9TZ, England. index.

655　　　　　　　UK　ISSN 0068-0257
BOOKSELLERS ASSOCIATION OF GREAT BRITAIN AND IRELAND. TRADE REFERENCE BOOK. 1969. irreg. £3. ‡ Booksellers Association of Great Britain & Ireland, 154 Buckingham Palace Rd., London SW1W 9TZ, England.

BOWKER ANNUAL; of library and book trade information. see *LIBRARY AND INFORMATION SCIENCES*

070.5　　　　　　US　ISSN 0068-0672
BRANDEIS UNIVERSITY. SOCIETY OF BIBLIOPHILES. PUBLICATIONS.* irreg., 1968, no. 3. Brandeis University Press, Waltham, MA 02154.

PUBLISHING AND BOOK TRADE

070.5   UK   ISSN 0302-2846
BRITISH BOOK DESIGN & PRODUCTION. 1973.
a. National Book League, Book House, 45 East Hill,
Wandsworth, London S.W. 18, England. illus.
Continues: British Book Production.

070.5   GW   ISSN 0068-3051
BUCH UND BUCHHANDEL IN ZAHLEN. 1952. a.
DM.9.35. Boersenverein des Deutschen
Buchhandels, Gr. Hirschgraben 17-21, 6000
Frankfurt, W. Germany (B.R.D.) Ed. Dr. Horst
Machill.

070   GW
BUCH UND ZEITSCHRIFT IN
GEISTESGESCHICHTE UND WISSENSCHAFT.
1976. irreg., no. 2, 1979. price varies. K.G. Saur
Verlag KG, Poessenbacherstr. 12 B, Postfach
711009, 8000 Munich 71, W.Germany (B.R.D.) Ed.
Bd.

070.5   GW   ISSN 0170-5105
BUCHHANDELSGESCHICHTE. ZWEITE FOLGE.
1979. irreg. (approx 4/yr.) DM.30. (Historische
Kommission des Boersenvereins des Deutschen
Buchhandles e.V.) Buchhaendler-Vereinigung
GmbH, Gr. Hirschgraben 17-21, D-6000 Frankfurt
1, W. Germany (B.R.D.) bk. rev.

091   ET
BULLETIN OF ETHIOPIAN MANUSCRIPTS. (Text
in English or Ethiopian) a. Ethiopian Manuscript
Microfilm Library, Box 30274, Addis Ababa,
Ethicpia.

BUREAU INTERNATIONAL DES SOCIETES
GERANT LES DROITS D'ENREGISTREMENT
ET DE REPRODUCTION MECANIQUE.
BULLETIN. see *PRINTING*

070   CN   ISSN 0045-3676
BUST. 1968. irreg. Bust Press, Box 367, Sta. F,
Toronto, Ont., Canada. illus.

658.8   US
BUY BOOKS WHERE, SELL BOOKS WHERE; a
directory of out of print booksellers and their
specialties. 1978. a. $17.50. Ruth E. Robinson,
Books, Rt. 7, Box 162A, Morgantown, WV 26505.
Eds. Ruth E. Robinson, Daryush Farudi. adv. circ.
3,000.
    Booksellers

070.5   686   UK
CAMBRIDGE AUTHORS' AND PUBLISHERS'
GUIDES. 1951. irreg. price varies. Cambridge
University Press, Box 110, Cambridge CB2 3RL,
England (and 32 E. 57 St., New York NY 10022)
    Formerly: Cambridge Authors' and Printers'
Guides (ISSN 0068-6603)

070.5   CN   ISSN 0576-470X
CANADIAN BOOK PRICES CURRENT. 1955.
irreg. price varies. McLelland & Stewart, Toronto,
Ont., Canada.

028.1   CN   ISSN 0383-770X
CANADIAN BOOK REVIEW ANNUAL. a.
Can.$29.50. Peter Martin Associates, 280 Bloor St.
W., Toronto, Ont. M5S 1W1, Canada. Ed.Bd.

070.5   UK
CASSELL AND PUBLISHERS ASSOCIATION
DIRECTORY OF PUBLISHING IN GREAT
BRITAIN, THE COMMONWEALTH, IRELAND,
SOUTH AFRICA AND PAKISTAN. 1960. a.
£9.95. Cassell Ltd., 35 Red Lion Sq., London
WC:R 4SG, England. Ed. Jane Deam. adv. index.
    Former titles: Cassell's Directory of Publishing in
Great Britain, The Commonwealth, Ireland, South
Africa and Pakistan (ISSN 0308-7018); Cassell's
Directory of Publishing in Great Britain, The
Commonwealth, Ireland and South Africa (ISSN
0069-097X)

CATHOLIC TRUTH. see *RELIGIONS AND
THEOLOGY* — Roman Catholic

070.5   BE
CERCLE BELGE DE LA LIBRAIRIE. ANNUAIRE.
1926. a. 900 Fr. Cercle Belge de la Librairie, Rue
du Luxembourg 5, Bte. 1, 1040 Brussels, Belgium.

070.5   FR
CEUX QUI FONT L'EDITION. 1977. biennial. 447
F. Societe d'Etudes et de Publications Industrielles,
15 Square de Vergennes, 75015 Paris, France.
(Affiliate: France Expansion)

070.5   US   ISSN 0069-3472
CHILDREN'S BOOKS: AWARDS AND PRIZES.
biennial. price varies. ‡ Children's Book Council,
Inc., 67 Irving Pl., New York, NY 10003. index.
circ. 6,000(approx.)

028.5   UK
CHILDREN'S BOOKS OF THE YEAR. a. National
Book League, Book House, 45 East Hill,
Wandsworth, London S.W. 18, England.

070.5   US
CHILDREN'S BOOKS: ONE HUNDRED TITLES
FOR READING AND SHARING. 1911. a. $1.50.
New York Public Library, Office of Branch
Libraries, 8 E. 40 St., New York, NY 10016.
    Former titles: Children's Books and Recordings:
Suggested as Holiday Gifts; Children's Books:
Suggested as Holiday Gifts (ISSN 0069-3502)

CITY & REGIONAL MAGAZINE DIRECTORY.
see *ADVERTISING AND PUBLIC RELATIONS*

070.5   UK   ISSN 0069-4614
CLEGG'S INTERNATIONAL DIRECTORY OF
THE WORLD'S BOOK TRADE. 1885. irreg. 50s.
James Clarke & Co. Ltd., 7 All Saints Passage,
Cambridge CB2 3LS, England.

090   DK   ISSN 0070-2811
DANSKE BOGAUKTIONER MED EN OVERSIGT
OVER BOGPRISERNE/DANISH BOOK
AUCTIONS WITH AN OUTLINE OF THE
BOOK PRICES. 1931. irreg. price varies.
Foreningen for Boghaandvaerk, Noerre
Farimagsgade 74, DK-1364 Copenhagen K,
Denmark. Eds. Volmer Rosenkilde, Hans Bagger.

070.5   GE   ISSN 0459-004X
DEUTSCHE BUECHEREI. JAHRBUCH. 1965. a.
M.20. Deutsche Buecherei, Deutscher Platz, 701
Leipzig, E. Germany(D.D.R.) bibl. illus. index.

DEUTSCHES BUECHERVERZEICHNIS. see
LIBRARY AND INFORMATION SCIENCES

070.5   UK
DIRECTORY OF BRITISH PUBLISHERS AND
THEIR TERMS. a. Booksellers Association of
Great Britain & Ireland, 154 Buckingham Palace
Rd., London SW1W 9TZ, England.

070.5   UK   ISSN 0070-5411
DIRECTORY OF DEALERS IN SECONDHAND
AND ANTIQUARIAN BOOKS IN THE BRITISH
ISLES. 1951. triennial. £9. Sheppard Press Ltd.,
P.O. Box 42, Russell Chambers, Covent Garden,
London WC2E 8AX, England.

070.5   US
DIRECTORY OF PUBLISHING OPPORTUNITIES
IN JOURNALS AND PERIODICALS. 1971.
irreg., 4th edt., 1979. $44.50. Marquis Academic
Media, 200 E. Ohio St., Chicago, IL 60611. index.
    Former titles: Directory of Publishing
Opportunities; Directory of Scholarly and Research
Publishing Opportunities (ISSN 0070-623X)

686   GW
DOKUMENTATION DEUTSCHSPRACHIGER
VERLAGE. 1962. triennial. price varies. Guenter
Olzog Verlag, Thierschstr. 11, 8000 Munich 22, W.
Germany (B.R.D.) Eds. C. Vinz, G. Olzog.

051
DONNELLEY-DIRECTORY RECORD. 1970. irreg.
free. Reuben H. Donnelley (New York), 825 Third
Ave., New York, NY 10022. Ed. T. Taraba. circ.
3,000.
    House organ

070.5   US   ISSN 0193-7383
EDITORIAL EYE; focusing on publications standards
and practices. 1978. irreg. (15-20/yr.) $45 for 20
nos. Editorial Experts, Inc., 5905 Pratt St.,
Alexandria, VA 22310. Ed. Peggy Smith. index;
cum.index. circ. 1,500. (looseleaf format; back issues
avail.)

070.5   UK   ISSN 0071-2523
EUROPEAN BOOKDEALERS; a directory of dealers
in secondhand and antiquarian books on the
continent of Europe. (Text in English, French and
German) 1966. triennial. £9. Sheppard Press Ltd.,
P.O. Box 42, Russell Chambers, Covent Garden,
London WC2E 8AX, England.

FACHLITERATUR ZUM BUCH- UND
BIBLIOTHEKSWESEN/INTERNATIONAL
BIBLIOGRAPHY OF THE BOOK TRADE AND
LIBRARIANSHIP. see *LIBRARY AND
INFORMATION SCIENCES*

070.5   AG
FEDERACION ARGENTINA DE PERIODISTAS.
GACETA.* 1970. a. Federacion Argentina de
Periodistas, Lavalle 1464, Buenos Aires, Argentina.
illus.

655   FR   ISSN 0078-9666
FRANCE. IMPRIMERIE NATIONALE.
ANNUAIRE. 1962. a. Imprimerie Nationale,
S.E.V.P.O., 39 rue de la Convention, 75732 Paris
Cedex 15, France.

FRIENDS OF THE NATIONAL LIBRARIES.
ANNUAL REPORT. see *LIBRARY AND
INFORMATION SCIENCES*

655   SY   ISSN 0072-0690
GENERAL DIRECTORY OF THE PRESS AND
PERIODICALS IN JORDAN AND KUWAIT.* a.
$15. Syrian Documentation Papers, P.O. Box 2712,
Damascus, Syria.

655   SY   ISSN 0072-0704
GENERAL DIRECTORY OF THE PRESS AND
PERIODICALS IN SYRIA.* a. $15. Syrian
Documentation Papers, P.O. Box 2712, Damascus,
Syria.

070.5   GE   ISSN 0067-5040
GESCHICHTE DES BUCHWESENS. BEITRAEGE.
1965. irreg. price varies. (Boersenverein der
Deutschen Buchhaendler, Historische Kommission)
VEB Fachbuchverlag, Karl-Heine-Str. 16, 7031
Leipzig, E. Germany (D.D.R.)

070.5   BL
GUIA DAS EDITORAS BRASILEIRAS. 1978. irreg.
Sindicato Nacional dos Editores de Livros, Av. Rio
Branco 37, s/1503/06, 20097 Rio de Janeiro R.J.,
Brazil.

658.8   BL
GUIA DAS LIVRARIAS E PONTOS DE VENDA
DE LIVROS NO BRASIL. 1976. irreg. Sindicato
Nacional dos Editores de Livros, Av. Rio Branca
37, s/1503/06, 20097 Rio de Janeiro R.J., Brazil.

070.5   SP   ISSN 0072-7903
GUIA DE EDITORES Y DE LIBREROS DE
ESPANA. 1950. irreg. price varies. Instituto
Nacional del Libro Espanol, Santiago Rusinol 8,
Madrid 3, Spain.

070.5   FR
GUIDE A L'USAGE DES AMATEURS DE
LIVRES. 1930. a. price varies. Syndicat National de
la Librairie Ancienne et Moderne, Hotel du Cercle
de la Librairie, 117 Boulevard Saint-Germain, 75006
Paris, France.
    Former titles: Guide du Livre Ancien et du Livre
d'Occasion & Syndicat National de la Librairie
Ancienne et Moderne. Repertoire (ISSN 0080-1100)

070.5   JA
GUIDE TO PUBLISHERS AND RELATED
INDUSTRIES IN JAPAN. (Text in English) 1970.
biennial. free. Publishers Association for Cultural
Exchange, 1-2-1 Sarugaku-cho, Chiyoda-ku, Tokyo
101, Japan. Ed. Shoichi Nakajima.

090.75   BE
GULDEN PASSER/COMPAS D'OR. (Text in Dutch,
English, French, and German) 1923. a. 500 Fr.($13)
Vereeniging der Antwerpsche Bibliophielen -
Antwerp Bibliophile Society, Museum Plantin-
Moretus, Vrijdammarkt 22, B-2000 Antwerp,
Belgium.

655   GW   ISSN 0073-0165
HANDBUCH FUER DEN WERBENDEN BUCH-
UND ZEITSCHRIFTENHANDEL. 1939. a.
DM.20. Bundesverband des Werbenden Buch- und,
Zeitschriftenhandels e.V., Akazienstr. 10, 5000
Cologne 71, W. Germany (B.R.D.)

HANDSATZLETTER; Monografien der modernen
Typographie. see *PRINTING*

PUBLISHING AND BOOK TRADE

029 070.5 GW ISSN 0342-4634
I S B N REVIEW. (International Standard Book Number) (Text in English, French and German) 1977. irreg. price varies. International I S B N Agency, Staatsbibliothek Preussischer Kulturbesitz, Postfach 1407, D-1000 Berlin 30, W. Germany (B.R.D.) Ed.K. W. Neubauer. adv.

028.1 970.1 CN
INDIAN BOOK REVIEW DIGEST. irreg. University of Alberta, Department of English, Edmonton, Alta. T6G 2E5, Canada.

020 027.7 US ISSN 0019-6800
INDIANA UNIVERSITY BOOKMAN. 1956. irreg. Indiana University Library, Bloomington, IN 47401. Eds. Cecil K. Byrd & William R. Cagle. circ. 500(controlled) (also avail. in microform from UMI)

070.5 BE ISSN 0073-8166
INSTITUT BELGE D'INFORMATION ET DE DOCUMENTATION. REPERTOIRE DE L'INFORMATION. Flemish edition: Belgisch Instituut voor Voorlichting en Documentatie. Repertorium van de Voorlichting. (Editions in French and Flemish) 1965. a. 100 Fr. ‡ Institut Belge d'Information et de Documentation - Belgian Information and Documentation Institute, Rue Montoyer, 3, B-1040 Brussels, Belgium. circ. 4,500.

070.5 US
INTERNAL PUBLICATIONS DIRECTORY. 1946. a. $71. National Research Bureau, Inc., 424 North Third St., Burlington, IA 52601. Ed. Milton Paule. bk. rev. index. circ. 3,000.
Formerly: Gebbie House Magazine Directory (ISSN 0072-0526)

070.5 UK
INTERNATIONAL BOOK DESIGN & PRODUCTION. biennial. National Book League, Book House, 45 East Hill, Wandsworth, London S.W. 18, England.

070.5 UK
INTERNATIONAL BOOK TRADE DIRECTORY. 1980. irreg. $47. Bowker Publishing Company Ltd., Box 5, Epping, Essex CM16 4BU, England.

655.5 070.5 DK ISSN 0538-7159
INTERNATIONAL DIRECTORY OF ANTIQUARIAN BOOKSELLERS/REPERTOIRE INTERNATIONAL DE LA LIBRAIRIE ANCIENNE. (Text in English and French) 1951-52. irreg., latest 1979. $20. International League of Antiquarian Booksellers, c/o Rosenkilde og Bagger Forlag, Box 2184, DK-1017 Copenhagen K, Denmark. Ed. Hans Bagger, Heinz Pummer. adv. circ. 1,800.

070.5 US ISSN 0074-6827
INTERNATIONAL LITERARY MARKET PLACE. Variant title (1975-76, 1977-78): European Literary Market Place. 1966. a. $27.50. R.R. Bowker Company, 1180 Ave. of the Americas, New York, NY 10036 (Orders to P.O. Box 1807, Ann Arbor, Mich. 48106) index. (reprint service avail. from UMI)

070.5 SZ ISSN 0074-7556
INTERNATIONAL PUBLISHERS ASSOCIATION. PROCEEDINGS OF CONGRESS. 1896. quadrennial, 21st, 1980, Stockholm. 20 Fr. International Publishers Association - Union Internationale des Editeurs (Internationale Verleger-Union), Ave. Miremont 3, 1206 Geneva, Switzerland.

070.5 IS
ISRAEL BOOK TRADE DIRECTORY; a guide to publishers, printers and a book trade services in Israel. (Text in English) 1967. biennial. Israel Export Institute, Book and Printing Center, 29, Hamered St., P.O. Box 29732, Tel Aviv, Israel. Ed. Asher Weill. circ. 3,000.
Former titles: Israel Book Trades Directory: a Select List; Publishers and Printers of Israel; a Select List (ISSN 0079-7820)

070.5 IT ISSN 0075-1677
ITALY. ISTITUTO CENTRALE DI STATISTICA. ANNUARIO DELLE STATISTICHE CULTURALI. a. L.6000. Istituto Centrale di Statistica, Via C. Balbo, 16, 00100 Rome, Italy. circ. 850.

JAHRBUCH DER AUKTIONSPREISE; fuer Buecher, Handschriften und Autographen. see *MUSEUMS AND ART GALLERIES*

658.8 JA ISSN 0387-3935
JAPAN ENGLISH MAGAZINE DIRECTORY. (Text in English) triennial. $60. Intercontinental Marketing Corp., P.O. 5056 Tokyo International, Tokyo 100-31, Japan. bibl.

070.5 IS
KATALOG SEFARIM KELALI. (Text in Hebrew) biennial. Book Publishers Association of Israel, 29 Carlebach St, P.O. Box 20123, Tel-Aviv, Israel. Ed. Zwi Steiner. adv.

KLEIO. see *HISTORY*

070.5 015 KO ISSN 0075-6881
KOREAN PUBLICATIONS YEARBOOK/ HAN'QUK CH'ULP; AN YON'GAM. 1963. a. $11. Korean Publishers Association, 105-2 Sagan-Dong, Chongno-Ku, Seoul, S. Korea. circ. 2,500. (back issues avail.)

LIBRARY INNOVATOR. see *LIBRARY AND INFORMATION SCIENCES*

070.5 BE
LIJSTENBOEK. 1929. a. 400 Fr.($8) Vereniging ter Bevordering van het Vlaamse Boekwezen - Association of Publishers of Dutch Language Books, Frankrijklei 93, Box 3, B-2000 Antwerp, Belgium. index. circ. 2,500.

070.5 US ISSN 0075-9899
LITERARY MARKET PLACE; with names and numbers. 1940. a. $32.50. R.R. Bowker Company, 1180 Ave. of the Americas, New York, NY 10036 (Orders to P.O. Box 1807, Ann Arbor, MI 48106) index. (reprint service avail. from UMI)

070.5 PO
LIVRARIA FIGUEIRINHAS CATALOGO.* 1898. a. free. Livraria Editora Figueirinhas, Praca da Liberdade 66-68, Porto, Portugal.

070.5 US ISSN 0000-0434
MAGAZINE INDUSTRY MARKET PLACE; the directory of American periodical publishing. Short title: M I M P. 1980. a. $40. R.R. Bowker Company, 1180 Ave. of the Americas, New York, NY 10036 (Orders to Box 1807, Ann Arbor, MI 48106) Ed. Olga S. Weber. adv.

028.1 US ISSN 0163-3058
MAGILL'S LITERARY ANNUAL. a. Salem Press, Englewood Cliffs, NJ 07632. Ed. F. N. Magill.
Formerly: Masterplots Annual.
Book reviews

MEDIA PERSONNEL DIRECTORY. see *JOURNALISM*

MICROFORM REVIEW. see *LIBRARY AND INFORMATION SCIENCES*

070.5 US
NATIONAL DIRECTORY OF NEWSLETTERS AND REPORTING SERVICES; a reference guide to national and international services, financial services, association bulletins, and training and educational services. (In 4 parts) 1966. irreg., 2nd edt. 1978. $58. Gale Research Company, Book Tower, Detroit, MI 48226. Ed. Robert C. Thomas.

070.5 CN ISSN 0077-5347
NATIONAL PUBLISHING DIRECTORY.* 1964-65. biennial. Prestige Books of Canada, 99 Vaugham Rd., Toronto, Ont., Canada.

070.5 US ISSN 0078-2882
O. P. MARKET. 1948. a. $5. Antiquarian Bookman, Box AB, Clifton, NJ 07015. Ed. Jacob L. Chernofsky. adv. circ. 10,000.
Out-of-print market

070.5 AU ISSN 0078-3455
DAS OESTERREICHISCHE BUCH. 1947. a. Hauptverband des Oesterreichischen Buchhandels, Gruenangergasse 4, A-1010 Vienna, Austria.

070 AU ISSN 0030-0004
OESTERREICHS PRESSE, WERBUNG, GRAPHIK. 1953. a. S.465. Verband Oesterreichischer Zeitungsherausgeber und Zeitungsverleger, Schreyvogelgasse 3, A-1010 Vienna, Austria. adv. bk. rev. mkt. tr.lit. index.

070.5 UK ISSN 0078-7159
OVERSEAS NEWSPAPERS AND PERIODICALS. (Issued in 2 vols., Vol. 1: Markets in Europe; Vol. 2: Markets outside Europe) 1952. biennial. £17($30) per vol. Publishing and Distributing Co. Ltd., 177 Regent St., London W.1, England. Ed. H. R. Vaughan. adv. circ. 5,000. (also avail. in microfilm from UMI)

PERIODICAL PERIODICAL. see *LIBRARY AND INFORMATION SCIENCES*

070.5 US
PERIODICAL TITLE ABBREVIATIONS; covering periodical title abbreviations in science, the social sciences, the humanities, law, medicine, religion, library science, engineering, education, business, art, and many other fields. 1969. irreg., 2nd edt. 1977. $42. Gale Research Company, Book Tower, Detroit, MI 48226. Ed. Leland G. Alkire.

POLICY PUBLISHERS AND ASSOCIATIONS DIRECTORY. see *POLITICAL SCIENCE*

091 BE
PUBLICATION DE SCRIPTORIUM. 1947. irreg. price varies. E. Story-Scientia, Prudens van Duyseplein 8, B-9000 Ghent, Belgium.

070.5 CH
PUBLICATIONS YEARBOOK, REPUBLIC OF CHINA; including catalogs of books and records. 1977. a. China Publishing Company, Box 337, Taipei, Taiwan, Republic of China.

PUBLISHERS, DISTRIBUTORS AND WHOLESALERS OF THE UNITED STATES. see *BUSINESS AND ECONOMICS — Trade And Industrial Directories*

070.5 UK ISSN 0079-7839
PUBLISHERS IN THE UNITED KINGDOM AND THEIR ADDRESSES. 1946. a. £2. J. Whitaker & Sons Ltd., 12 Dyott St., London WC1A 1DF, England. (reprint service avail. from UMI)

655 FR
REPERTOIRE INTERNATIONAL DES EDITEURS ET DIFFUSEURS DE LANGUE FRANCAISE. a. 140 F. Cercle de la Librairie, Service Documentation, 117 Bd. Saint-Germain, 75279 Paris Cedex 06, France. circ. 5,000.
Formerly: Livre de Langue Francaise-Repertoire des Editeurs (ISSN 0076-0110)

070.5 740 SZ ISSN 0080-6838
SCHOENSTE SCHWEIZER BUECHER. (Text in English, French and German) 1943. a. free. Schweizerischer Buchhaendler- und Verleger-Verband, Box 408, CH-8034 Zurich, Switzerland. (Co-sponsor: Eidgenoessisches Departement des Innern) bk. rev.

070.5 GE
DIE SCHOENSTEN BUECHER DER DEUTSCHEN DEMOKRATISCHEN REPUBLIK. 1963. a. M.5. VEB Fachbuchverlag, Karl-Heine-Str. 16, 7031 Leipzig, E. Germany (D.D.R.).
Formerly: Spiegel Deutscher Buchkunst (ISSN 0081-3702)
Report on the year's best books

070.5 SZ ISSN 0080-7230
SCHWEIZER BUCHHANDELS-ADRESSBUCH. 1965-66. biennial. price varies. Schweizerischer Buchhaendler- und Verleger-Verband, P.O.B. 408, CH-8034 Zurich, Switzerland.

011 UK ISSN 0306-0861
SCOTTISH SMALL PRESSES. irreg. National Book League, Scottish Office, 112k Paisley Road, Glasgow G52 1EQ, Scotland.
An annotated catalogue of books in print

070.5 SI ISSN 0080-9659
SINGAPORE BOOK WORLD. (Text in Chinese, English & Malay) 1970. a. S.$5. National Book Development Council of Singapore, c/o National Library, Stamford Road, Singapore 0617, Singapore (Subscr. to: Chopmen Enterprises, 428-429 Katong Shopping Center, Singapore 1543) Ed.Bd. adv. bk. rev. circ. 5,000. (back issues avail) Indexed: Lib.Sci.Abstr.

655 090 FR ISSN 0081-0878
SOCIETE DES FRANCS-BIBLIOPHILES. ANNUAIRE. 1948. a. membership. 39 rue Raynouard, 75016 Paris, France.

STREUDATEN DER SCHWEIZER PRESSE. see
ADVERTISING AND PUBLIC RELATIONS

090　　　　　　　IT　　ISSN 0081-6183
STUDI E TESTI DI PAPIROLOGIA. 1966. irreg.
price varies. (Universita degli Studi di Firenze,
Istituto Papirologico "G. Vitelli") Casa Editrice
Felice le Monnier, Via Scipione Ammirato 100, C.P.
455, 50136 Florence, Italy.

070.5　　　　　SW　　ISSN 0081-9859
SVENSKA
BOKFOERLAEGGAREFOERENINGEN.
MATRIKEL. a. Kr.35. Svenska
Bokfoerlaeggarefoereningen - Swedish Publishers
Association, Sveavaegen 52, S-111 34 Stockholm,
Sweden.

079.7　　　　　　CU
U P E C. irreg. Union de Periodistas de Cuba, Calle
23, No. 452, Havana, Cuba. illus.

070.5 016　　　　US　　ISSN 0083-4807
USED BOOK PRICE GUIDE. 1962. quinquennial
supplement. $39 for supplement. ‡ Price Guide
Publishers, 525 Kenmore Station, Kenmore, WA
98028. Ed. Mildred S. Mandeville.

070.5　　　　　　GW
WHO'S WHO AT THE FRANKFURT BOOK FAIR;
an International Publishers' Guide. 1969. a. DM.34.
(Frankfurt Book Fair) K.G. Saur Verlag KG,
Poessenbacherstr. 12 B, Postfach 711009, 8000
Munich 71, W. Germany (B.R.D.) adv.

029　　　　　　GW　　ISSN 0084-0955
WISSENSCHAFTLICHE REDAKTION. 1965. irreg.
DM.24. Bibliographisches Institut AG, Dudenstr. 6,
Postfach 311, 6800 Mannheim 41, W. Germany
(B.R.D.) Ed. O. Mittelstaedt, M. Wegner.

810　　　　　　US　　ISSN 0512-5472
WORKS IN PROGRESS. 1970. irreg. Literary Guild,
501 Franklin Ave., Garden City, NY 11531 (Dist.
by: Doubleday and Co., Inc., 245 Park Ave., New
York, NY 10017).

070.5　　　　　　UK　　ISSN 0084-2664
WRITERS' AND ARTISTS' YEARBOOK; a
directory for writers, artists, playwrights, writers for
film, radio and television, photographers and
composers. 1907. a. £2.95. A. & C. Black
(Publishers) Ltd., 35 Bedford Row, London WC1R
4JH, England. index.

070.5　　　　　AT　　ISSN 0084-2680
WRITERS' AND PHOTOGRAPHERS'
MARKETING GUIDE; DIRECTORY OF
AUSTRALIAN AND NEW ZEALAND
LITERARY AND PHOTO MARKETS. 1945.
biennial. Aus.$30. Australian Writers' Professional
Service, Box 28, Collins St. P.O., Melbourne, Vic.
3001, Australia. Ed. G. R. Pittaway.

070.5　　　　　　UK　　ISSN 0084-2699
WRITERS DIRECTORY. 1970. biennial. $30. St.
James Press, 3 Percy St., London W.1, England
(and St. Martin's Press, 175 Fifth Ave., New York,
NY 10010).

070.5　　　　　　US　　ISSN 0084-2710
WRITER'S HANDBOOK. 1936. a. $16.95. Writer,
Inc, 8 Arlington St., Boston, MA 02116. Ed. A. S.
Burack.

070.5　　　　　　US　　ISSN 0084-2729
WRITER'S MARKET. 1929. a. $15.95. (Writer's
Digest) F & W Publishing Corp., 9933 Alliance Rd.,
Cincinnati, OH 45242. Eds. John Brady, P.J.
Schemenaur. index.

070.5　800　　　US　　ISSN 0084-2737
WRITER'S YEARBOOK. 1930. a. $2.95. (Writer's
Digest) F & W Publishing Corp., 9933 Alliance Rd.,
Cincinnati, OH 45242. Ed. John Brady. adv. circ.
85,000. (also avail. in microform from UMI)

PUBLISHING AND BOOK TRADE —
Abstracting, Bibliographies, Statistics

070 015　　　　US　　ISSN 0091-9357
AMERICAN BOOK PRICES CURRENT. a. price
varies. Bancroft-Parkman, Inc., 121 E. 78 St., New
York, NY 10021.

070 015　　　　US
AMERICAN BOOK PRICES CURRENT. FIVE
YEAR INDEX. quinquennial. price varies.
Bancroft-Parkman, Inc., 121 E. 78 St., New York,
NY 10021.

655 011　　　　US　　ISSN 0002-7707
AMERICAN BOOK PUBLISHING RECORD/B P
R; arranged by subject according to the Dewey
Decimal Classification and indexed by author and
title. 1960. m. with a. & 5-yr. cumulations. $27.50
($59 for a. cum., $175 for 5-yr. cum.) R.R. Bowker
Company, 1180 Avenue of the Americas, New
York, NY 10036 (Orders to: Subscription Service
Dept., Box 13746, Philadelphia, PA 19101) tr.bibl.
index. cum.index. circ. 7,345. (also avail. in
microform from UMI)

070.5 010　　　　UA　　ISSN 0066-5630
ARAB BOOK ANNUAL/AL-KITAB AL-ARABI FI
AAM.* (Text in Arabic; summary in English) 1961.
a. el1,800; $8.70. Arab Book Information Centre,
P.O. Box 1509, Cairo, Egypt. Ed. S. H. Salama.

015　　　　　AT　　ISSN 0067-172X
AUSTRALIAN BOOKS IN PRINT; including
bookbuyers reference book. 1956. a(biennial until
1968) Aus.$30. D.W. Thorpe Pty. Ltd., 384 Spencer
St., Melbourne, Vic. 3003, Australia. Ed. Joyce
Nicholson. bk. rev. bibl. index.

020 011　　　　US　　ISSN 0145-3084
BIBLIOGRAPHY NEWSLETTER. Abbreviated title:
BiN. 1973. irreg. (approx.m.) $11. c/o Terry
Belanger, Ed., 21 Claremont Ave, New York, NY
10027. bk. rev. index. circ. 700. (back issues avail)

028.5 016　　　US
BIBLIOGRAPHY OF BOOKS FOR CHILDREN.
1935. triennial. $5.95. ‡ Association for Childhood
Education International, 3615 Wisconsin Ave. N.
W., Washington, DC 20016. Ed. Sylvia Sunderlin.
adv. bk. rev. circ. 6,000. (also avail. in microfiche
from UMI)
　Incorporating: Excellent Paperbacks for Children;
Which was formerly titled: Good and Inexpensive
Books for Children (ISSN 0360-537X)

070.5　　　　　IS
BOOKS FROM ISRAEL. a. Israel Export Institute,
Book and Printing Center, 29, Hamered St., Tel-
Aviv, Israel. adv. bk. rev. index.

070.5 015　　　AU
BUECHER; Das Lesemazin fuer Sie. 1949. a.
Hauptverband des Oesterreichischen Buchhandels,
Gruenangergasse 4, A-1010 Vienna, Austria. adv.
bk. rev.
　Former titles: Buecher fuer Alle (ISSN 0067-
0634) & Aus der Schatzkammer der Buecher.

015　　　　　　IT
CATALOGO DEI LIBRI IN COMMERCIO/
ITALIAN BOOKS IN PRINT. 1970. biennial. price
varies. (Associazione Italiana Editori) Editrice
Bibliografica s.r.l., Viale Vittorio Veneto 24, 20124
Milan, Italy (Dist. in U.S., Canada and Latin
America by R. R. Bowker Co., P.O. Box 1807, Ann
Arbor, Mich. 48106) circ. 3,000.
　Formerly: Catalogo dei Libri Italiani in
Commercio (ISSN 0069-1054)

070.5 016　　　US　　ISSN 0093-0431
CHILDREN'S LITERARY ALMANAC. 1973.
biennial. $6.95. George Kurian Reference Books,
Box 361, Tuckahoe, NY 10707. Ed. George Kurian.
bk. rev. circ. 3,500.

070.5 015　　　GW
DEUTSCHE BIBLIOGRAPHIE. FUENFJAHRES-
VERZEICHNIS. 1945/1950. irreg. price varies.
(Deutsche Bibliothek) Buchhaendler-Vereinigung
GmbH, Gr. Hirschbraben 17-21, 6000 Frankfurt 1,
W. Germany (B.R.D.) bibl. index. circ. 1,700.

DIRECTORY OF CONSERVATIVE AND
LIBERTARIAN SERIALS, PUBLISHERS, AND
FREELANCE MARKETS. see *POLITICAL
SCIENCE — Abstracting, Bibliographies, Statistics*

808　　　　　　US
DIRECTORY OF SMALL MAGAZINE/PRESS
EDITORS AND PUBLISHERS. 1970. a. $8.95.
Dustbooks, Box 100, Paradise, CA 95969. Ed. Len
Fulton.

016 028　　　GW
FREUDE MIT BUECHERN. 1951. a. DM.3. Verlag
Buecherschiff Walter Reutin, Rheinstr. 122,
Postfach 210947, 7500 Karlsruhe 21, W. Germany
(B.R.D.) Ed. H. Bode. bk. rev. circ. 5,000.

070.5 016　　　CH
GUIDE TO CHINESE PERIODICALS. 1972. irreg.
$4. Jeng Heing-Shorng, Ed. & Pub., 27, No. 10,
Lane 41, Paotai Rd., Shih Lin (III), Taipei, Taiwan,
Republic of China. Ed. Jeng Herng-Shorng. index.
circ. 500.

015　　　　　　PK
ILMI A'INO. (Text in Sindhi) a. Rs.2. University of
Sind, Institute of Sindhology, Jamshoro, Hyderabad
6, Pakistan.
　List of books and periodicals, publishers, cultural
and literary organizations in Sind

070.5 011　　　SA
INDEX TO SOUTH AFRICAN PERIODICALS/
REPERTORIUM VAN SUID-AFRIKAANSE
TYDSKRIFARTIKELS. (Text in Afrikaans and
English) 1940. a. R.10. Johannesburg Public Library,
Market Square, Johannesburg 2001, South Africa.
circ. 300. (back issues avail.)

028.1　　　　　II
INDIAN BOOK REVIEW INDEX. (Text in English)
1975/76. a. Rs.80($16) Indian Documentation
Service, Nai Subzi Mandi, Gurgaon 122001, India.
bk. rev.

070.5 016　　　GW
INTERNATIONAL BOOKS IN PRINT; English-
language titles published outside the USA and Great
Britain. 1979. biennial. £85. K. G. Saur Verlag KG,
Poessenbacherstr. 12 B, Postfach 711009, 8000
Munich 71, W. Germany(B.R.D.)

070　　　　　US　　ISSN 0092-3974
INTERNATIONAL DIRECTORY OF LITTLE
MAGAZINES AND SMALL PRESSES. 1965. a.
$13.95. Dustbooks, Box 100, Paradise, CA 95969.
Ed. Len Fulton. adv. circ. 10,000.
　Formerly: Directory of Little Magazines, Small
Presses and Underground Newspapers (ISSN 0084-
9979)

070.5　　　　　GW　　ISSN 0074-9877
INTERNATIONALES VERLAGSADRESSBUCH/
PUBLISHERS' INTERNATIONAL DIRECTORY.
1962. irreg., 8th ed., 1979. $85. K. G. Saur Verlag
KG, Poessenbacherstr. 12 B, Postfach 711009, 8000
Munich 71, W. Germany (B.R.D.) Ed. Michael Zils.
adv.

655 020 011　　　IT
ISTITUTO CENTRALE PER LA PATOLOGIA
DEL LIBRO "ALFONSO GALLO."
BOLLETTINO. (Suspended with 1972, Vol. 31,
resumed in 1978, with Vol. 32, 1973/74) (Text in
Italian; summaries in English) 1939. a. L.15000.
Istituto Centrale per la Patologia del Libro "Alfonso
Gallo.", Via Milano 76, 00184 Rome, Italy. Ed.Bd.
adv. bk. rev. bibl. charts. illus. cum.index. circ.
500. Indexed: Lib.Lit. Lib.Sci.Abstr.
　Formerly: Istituto di Patologia del Libro "Alfonso
Gallo." Bollettino (ISSN 0020-403X)

655.5　　　　HU　　ISSN 0076-2393
MAGYAR KONYV. (Text in Hungarian, German,
Russian) 1961. irreg. price varies. Magyar
Konyvkiadok es Konyvterjesztok Egyesulese,
Vorosmarty ter 1, 1051 Budapest 5, Hungary
(Subscr. to: Kultura, Box 149, H-1389 Budapest,
Hungary)

977.4 015　　　US　　ISSN 0026-2218
MICHIGAN IN BOOKS. 1958. irreg. free.
Department of Education, State Library Services,
Box 30007, Lansing, MI 48909. Ed. Richard J.
Hathaway. bk. rev. bibl. circ. 3,000.

015　　　　　　AT
NEW ZEALAND BOOKS IN PRINT. 1964. a.
Aus.$20. D.W. Thorpe Pty. Ltd., 384 Spencer St.,
Melbourne, Vic. 3003, Australia. Ed. Joyce
Nicholson. circ. 2,000.

655 011　　　UK　　ISSN 0031-1219
PAPERBACKS IN PRINT. 1960. a. £21. J. Whitaker
& Sons Ltd., 12 Dyott St., London WC1A 1DF,
England. adv. bibl. circ. 4,000. (reprint service avail.
from UMI)

REAL ESTATE 761

028.1 016 US
REFERENCE BOOK REVIEW INDEX. 1973. triennial. $42.50. Pierian Press, 5000 Washtenaw Ave., Ann Arbor, MI 48104.

070.5 016 CN ISSN 0315-5943
REPERTOIRE DE L'EDITION AU QUEBEC. 1972. biennial. Can.$50. (Association des Editeurs Canadiens) Edi-Quebec Inc., 1151 Alexandre DeSeve, Montreal, Que H2L 2T7, Canada. (Co-sponsors: Societe des Editeurs de Manuals Scolaires du Quebec; Conseil Superieur du Livre) index. circ. 1,200.

808 016 US
SMALL PRESS RECORD OF BOOKS IN PRINT. 1969. a. $17.95. Dustbooks, Box 100, Paradise, CA 95969. Ed. Len Fulton. adv.

020 296 016 US ISSN 0039-3568
STUDIES IN BIBLIOGRAPHY AND BOOKLORE; devoted to research in the field of Jewish bibliography. (Text in English, Hebrew & other languages) 1953. irreg. $7.50 per vol. Hebrew Union College, Jewish Institute of Religion. Library, 3101 Clifton Ave., Cincinnati, OH 45220. Ed.Bd. bk. rev. bibl. cum.index vols. 1-11. circ. 1,100. Indexed: Ind.Jew.Per.

015 CN
SUBJECT GUIDE TO CANADIAN BOOKS IN PRINT. 1973. a. University of Toronto Press., Toronto, Ont., Canada.

070.5 015 SQ
SWAZILAND NATIONAL BIBLIOGRAPHY. (Volume published in 1977 covers 1973-1976) 1977. a. University College of Swaziland, Private Bag, Kwaluseni, Swaziland.

070.5 015 SP ISSN 0067-4141
UNIVERSIDAD DE BARCELONA. BIBLIOTECA CENTRAL. CATALOGOS DE LA PRODUCCION EDITORIAL BARCELONA.* 1949-1950. a. Universidad de Barcelona, Biblioteca Central, Barcelona 7, Spain.

010 UK
WHITAKER'S THREE-YEAR CUMULATIVE BOOK LIST. 1968. triennial. £15. J. Whitaker & Sons Ltd., 12 Dyott St., London WC1A 1DF, England (Dist. in U.S. by: R. R. Bowker Co., P.O. Box 1807, Ann Arbor, MI 48106) (reprint service avail. from UMI)
　Formerly: Whitaker's Five-Year Cumulative Book List (ISSN 0000-0183)

RADIO AND TELEVISION

see Communications—Radio and Television

RADIOLOGY AND NUCLEAR MEDICINE

see Medical Sciences—Radiology and Nuclear Medicine

RAILROADS

see Transportation—Railroads

REAL ESTATE

see also Architecture; Building and Construction; Business and Economics—Investments; Housing and Urban Planning

333 US ISSN 0569-7840
A S A MONOGRAPH. 1969. irreg., no. 7, 1976. $5. American Society of Appraisers, Dulles International Airport, Box 17265, Washington, DC 20041.

333.33 630 CN ISSN 0701-7502
AGRICULTURAL REAL ESTATE VALUES IN ALBERTA. 1976. a. Department of Agriculture, Resource Economics Branch, Edmonton, Alta. T5K 2C8, Canada.
　Formerly: Rural Real Estate Values in Alberta (ISSN 0383-3585)

ALBERTA. OFFICE OF THE SUPERINTENDENT OF INSURANCE AND REAL ESTATE. ANNUAL REPORT. see INSURANCE

333.33 US ISSN 0065-8642
AMERICAN INDUSTRIAL REAL ESTATE ASSOCIATION. JOURNAL. 1961. a. $2 per no. ‡ American Industrial Real Estate Association, 5670 Wilshire Blvd., Los Angeles, CA 90036. Ed. B.J. Nolan. adv. circ. 15,000.

338.5 US ISSN 0569-7859
AMERICAN SOCIETY OF APPRAISERS. APPRAISAL AND VALUATION MANUAL. 1955/56. irreg. $15. American Society of Appraisers, Dulles International Airport, Box 17265, Washington, DC 20041.

526.9 CN ISSN 0318-2126
ASSOCIATION OF NEW BRUNSWICK LAND SURVEYORS.ANNUAL REPORT. 1955. a. Association of New Brunswick Land Surveyors, P.O. Box 22, Fredericton, New Brunswick E3B 4Y2, Canada. circ. 150 (controlled)

333.33 US
BETTER HOMES AND GARDENS HOW TO BUY A HOME. 1978. a. $1.95. Meredith Corporation, 1716 Locust St., Des Moines, IA 50336. adv. illus. circ. 400,000.

333.33 US
BLACK'S GUIDE TO THE OFFICE SPACE MARKET. 1976. a. $25. Black's Guide, Inc., Box 2090, Red Bank, NJ 07701. adv. circ. 15,000.
　Covers New York, Philadelphia, and Washington areas

333.33 690 UK
C A L U S RESEARCH REPORTS. 1975. irreg., no. 4, 1979. price varies. Centre for Advanced Land Use Studies, College of Estate Management, Whiteknights, Reading RG6 2AW, England.

333.33 DK
DENMARK. JORDFORDELINGSSEKRETARIATET. AARSBERETNING. 1951. a. Jordfordelingssekretariatet, Sankt Annae Plads 19, 1250 Copenhagen K, Denmark. illus.

DIRECTORY OF PROPERTY INVESTORS AND DEVELOPERS. see BUSINESS AND ECONOMICS — Investments

333.33 US
E-R-C DIRECTORY; employee relocation real estate services. 1964. a. $8 to non-members. Employee Relocation Council, 1627 K St. N.W., Washington, DC 20006. Ed. Cathryn M. Boles. circ. 7,500.
　Formerly: E R E A C Directory (ISSN 0071-0113)

333 US
EXPENSE ANALYSIS: CONDOMINIUMS, COOPERATIVES AND PLANNED UNIT DEVELOPMENTS. a. $20. National Association of Realtors, 155 E. Superior St., Chicago, IL 60611.
　Supersedes in part: Income-Expense Analysis Apartments, Condominiums and Cooperatives.

690 333 US
INCOME-EXPENSE ANALYSIS: APARTMENTS. 1954. a. $45. (Institute of Real Estate Management) National Association of Realtors, 155 E. Superior St., Chicago, IL 60611.
　Supersedes in part: Income-Expense Analysis Apartments, Condominiums and Cooperatives; Until 1973: Apartment Building Income-Expense Analysis (ISSN 0084-6651)

333 US
INCOME-EXPENSE ANALYSIS: SUBURBAN OFFICE BUILDINGS. a. $20. National Association of Realtors, 155 E. Superior St., Chicago, IL 60611.

333.33 JA ISSN 0073-7186
INDICES OF URBAN LAND PRICES AND CONSTRUCTION COST OF WOODEN HOUSES IN JAPAN. (Text in Japanese) s-a. price varies. Japan Real Estate Institute - Nippon Fudosan Kenkyusho, Kangin-Fujiya Bldg., 1-3-2 Toranomon, Minato-ku, Tokyo, Japan.

333.33 FR ISSN 0074-7637
INTERNATIONAL REAL ESTATE FEDERATION. REPORTS OF CONGRESS.* a, 1976, 27th, San Francisco. International Real Estate Federation, 68, rue des Archives, 75003 Paris, France.

333.33 UK
KEMPS PROPERTY INDUSTRY YEARBOOK. 1974. a. $45. Kemp's Group(Printers & Publishers) Ltd., 1-5 Bath St., London EC1V 9QA, England.
　Formerly: Kemps Estate Agents Yearbook and Directory.

332 340 AT ISSN 0085-266X
LAND LAWS SERVICE. 1938. irreg. Aus.$28. Law Book Co. Ltd., 31 Market St., Sydney, N.S.W. 2000, Australia.

333.33 FR ISSN 0024-5674
LOCATIONS VACANCES. a. 25 F. Editions Indicateur Bertrand, 11 et 13 rue du Louvre, 75003 Paris, France. adv. bk. rev.
　Advertisements for the renting of vacation homes, etc. in France and elsewhere

333.33 917.13 CN ISSN 0226-7837
MOVING TO OTTAWA/HULL. (Text in English and French) 1978. a. Moving to Publications, Box 272, Station C, Winnipeg, Man. R3M 3S7, Canada. illus.
　Formerly: Emmenager a Ottawa/Hull (ISSN 0702-9063)

333.33 917.124 CN ISSN 0225-5383
MOVING TO SASKATCHEWAN. 1981. a. Can.$3.50. Moving to Publications, Box 272, Station C, Winnipeg, Man. R3M 3S7, Canada. illus.

333.33 917.13 CN ISSN 0226-7829
MOVING TO TORONTO & AREA. 1980. a. Moving to Publications, Box 272, Station C, Winnipeg, Man. R3M 3S7, Canada.
　Formerly: Moving to Toronto (ISSN 0702-9179)

333.33 917.11 CN ISSN 0226-7276
MOVING TO VANCOUVER & B.C. 1980. a. Moving to Publications, Box 272, Station C, Winnipeg, Man. R3M 3S7, Canada. illus.
　Formerly: Moving to Vancouver/Victoria (ISSN 0702-9187)

333 US ISSN 0161-5882
NATIONAL ASSOCIATION OF REALTORS. EXISTING HOME SALES. 1976. a. $36 to non-members; members $24. National Association of Realtors, Department of Economics and Research, 430 N. Michigan Ave., Chicago, IL 60611. Key Title: Existing Home Sales.
　Formerly: National Association of Realtors. Department of Economics and Research. Existing Home Sales Series, Annual Report.

333.33 US
NATIONAL REAL ESTATE DIRECTORY. a. $9 included in $38 subscr. to National Real Estate Investor. Communication Channels, Inc., 6285 Barfield Rd., Atlanta, GA 30328. Ed. Stephen Lewis. adv. circ. 28,000. (also avail. in microfilm)

333.3 US ISSN 0090-1741
NATIONAL ROSTER OF REALTORS. a. $35. ‡ (National Association of Realtors) Stamats Publishing Co., 427 Sixth Ave. S.E., Cedar Rapids, IA 52406. Ed. Shirley Boyce. adv. illus. circ. 14,000.

333.33 UK ISSN 0078-3048
OCCASIONAL PAPERS IN ESTATE MANAGEMENT.1966. irreg., no. 11, 1978. price varies. Centre for Advanced Land Use Studies, College of Estate Management, Whiteknights, Reading RG6 2AW, England.

OLD-HOUSE JOURNAL CATALOG. see BUILDING AND CONSTRUCTION

REAL ESTATE — ABSTRACTING, BIBLIOGRAPHIES, STATISTICS

333.33   US
PREVIEWS GUIDE TO THE WORLD'S FINE REAL ESTATE. 1935. a. plus mid-yr. supp. $12. Previews Inc. (Subsidiary of: Allstate Enterprises, Inc.) 51 Weaver St., Greenwich, CT 06830. Ed. Ann Wilder. circ. 36,000.

333.33   CN
PRINCE EDWARD ISLAND. LAND DEVELOPMENT CORPORATION. ANNUAL REPORT. 1971. a. Land Development Corporation, Charlottetown, P.E.1., Canada. illus.

333.33   US
PRIVATE ISLAND "INVENTORY". 1975. a (plus irreg. supplements) $10. Private Islands Unlimited, 17538 Tulsa St., Granada Hills, CA 91344. Ed. Donald C. Ward. adv. circ. 5,000.

333.33   UK   ISSN 0305-5752
PROPERTY STUDIES IN THE U.K. AND OVERSEAS. 1974. irreg., no. 8, 1976. price varies. Centre for Advanced Land Use Studies, College of Estate Management, Whiteknights, Reading RG6 2AW, England. Eds. A. W. Davidson, J. E. Leonard.

332.6   333.33   US   ISSN 0095-1374
R.E.I.T. FACT BOOK. 1974. a. National Association of Real Estate Investment Trusts, 1101 17th St., N.W., Washington, DC 20036. illus.

347.2   CN
REAL ESTATE DEVELOPMENT ANNUAL. 1965. a. Can.$30. Maclean-Hunter Ltd., 481 University Ave., Toronto, Ont. M5W 1A7, Canada. Ed. Bill Lurz. adv. circ. 10,206.
     Formerly: Canadian Real Estate Annual (ISSN 0068-9564)

333.3   US   ISSN 0098-8936
REAL ESTATE DIRECTORY OF MANHATTAN. a. $210. Sanborn Map Company, Inc., 12 E. 41st St., New York, NY 10017.
     Continues: Real Estate Directory of the Borough of Manhattan.

333.33   US
REAL ESTATE FOR PROFESSIONAL PRACTITIONERS: A WILEY SERIES. 1973. irreg., latest, 1979. price varies. John Wiley & Sons, Inc., 605 Third Ave., New York, NY 10016. Ed. D. Clurman.

REAL ESTATE LAW DIGEST (SUPPLEMENT) see *LAW*

333.33   US   ISSN 0079-9890
REAL ESTATE REPORTS. 1966. irreg., no. 34, 1981. price varies. University of Connecticut, Center for Real Estate & Urban Economic Studies, Storrs, CT 06268. Ed. Judith B. Paesani. circ. 500. (also avail. in microfiche; Braille)

333.33   CN   ISSN 0085-5405
REAL ESTATE TRENDS IN METROPOLITAN VANCOUVER. 1958. a. Can.$10. Real Estate Board of Greater Vancouver, 1101 W. Broadway, Vancouver, B.C. V6H 1G2, Canada. Ed. N. G. Thompson. stat. circ. 2,000.

333   US   ISSN 0090-399X
REALTY BLUEBOOK. 1966. a. $14. Professional Publishing Corp., P.O. Box 4187, San Rafael, CA 94903. circ. 90,000.

333.33   UK   ISSN 0308-1451
ROYAL INSTITUTION OF CHARTERED SURVEYORS YEAR BOOK. 1975. a. £22. Kelly's Directories, Ltd., Windsor Court, East Grinstead House, East Grinstead, West Sussex RH19 1XB, England. adv. circ. 4,000.

333.33   BL
SAO PAULO, BRAZIL (STATE) DEPARTAMENTO DE ESTATISTICA. TRANSCRICAO DE TRANSMISSOES DE IMOVEIS POR COMARCA, SEGUNDO A NATUREZ DAS ESCRITURAS. irreg. Departamento de Estatistica, Divisao de Estatisticas Economicas, Secao de Estatisticas da Distribuicao e Consumc de Titulos, Bancos e Imoveis, Sao Paulo, Brazil.

STATE OF FLORIDA LAND DEVELOPMENT GUIDE. see *HOUSING AND URBAN PLANNING*

333.33   690   UK
STUDIES IN CONSTRUCTION ECONOMY. 1978. irreg., no. 2, 1979. price varies. Centre for Advanced Land Use Studies, College of Estate Management, Whiteknights, Reading RG6 2AW, England.

U. S. FEDERAL HOME LOAN BANK BOARD. REPORT. see *BUSINESS AND ECONOMICS — Banking And Finance*

U. S. FEDERAL HOME LOAN BANK BOARD. TRENDS IN THE SAVINGS AND LOAN FIELD. see *BUSINESS AND ECONOMICS — Banking And Finance*

333.3   US   ISSN 0068-5976
UNIVERSITY OF CALIFORNIA, BERKELEY. CENTER FOR REAL ESTATE AND URBAN ECONOMICS. RESEARCH REPORT. 1950. irreg., no. 37, 1972. price varies. ‡ University of California, Berkeley, Center for Real Estate and Urban Economics, 2420 Bowditch St., Berkeley, CA 94720. (also avail. in microfilm)

333.33   US   ISSN 0068-5968
UNIVERSITY OF CALIFORNIA, BERKELEY. CENTER FOR REAL ESTATE AND URBAN ECONOMICS. REPRINT SERIES. 1948. irreg., latest, no. 98. price varies. ‡ Univ. of California, Berkeley, Center for Real Estate and Urban Economics, 2420 Bowditch St., Berkeley, CA 94720. (also avail. in microfilm)

333.33   US   ISSN 0068-5984
UNIVERSITY OF CALIFORNIA, BERKELEY. CENTER FOR REAL ESTATE AND URBAN ECONOMICS. SPECIAL REPORT. 1963. irreg., no. 12, 1975. price varies. ‡ University of California, Berkeley, Center for Real Estate and Urban Economics, 2420 Bowditch St., Berkeley, CA 94720. (also avail. in microfilm)

333.7   US   ISSN 0068-5992
UNIVERSITY OF CALIFORNIA, BERKELEY. CENTER FOR REAL ESTATE AND URBAN ECONOMICS. TECHNICAL REPORT. 1966. irreg., 1972, no. 4. price varies. ‡ University of California, Berkeley, Center for Real Estate and Urban Economics, 2420 Bowditch St, Berkeley, CA 94720. (also avail. in microfilm)

333.33   US
UNIVERSITY OF CONNECTICUT. CENTER FOR REAL ESTATE AND URBAN ECONOMIC STUDIES. ANNUAL REPORT. 1965. a. University of Connecticut, Center for Real Estate and Urban Economic Studies, Storrs, CT 06268.

333.33   US   ISSN 0069-9047
UNIVERSITY OF CONNECTICUT. CENTER FOR REAL ESTATE AND URBAN ECONOMIC STUDIES. GENERAL SERIES. 1968. irreg., no. 14, 1979. price varies. ‡ University of Connecticut, Center for Real Estate and Urban Economic Studies, Storrs, CT 06268. Ed. Judith B. Paesani.

333   US
UNIVERSITY OF CONNECTICUT. CENTER FOR REAL ESTATE AND URBAN ECONOMIC STUDIES. WORKING PAPER. 1970. irreg., no. 4, 1977. free. University of Connecticut, Center for Real Estate and Urban Economic Studies, Storrs, CT 06268. Ed. Judith B. Paesani.

333.33   US   ISSN 0511-8719
WHERE TO RETIRE ON A SMALL INCOME. biennial. $4.95. Harian Publications, One Vernon Ave., Floral Park, NY 11001. Ed. Norman D. Ford. charts. illus.

REAL ESTATE — Abstracting, Bibliographies, Statistics

333   010   US
BIBLIOGRAPHY OF APPRAISAL LITERATURE. 1974. supplements every 2 yrs. $30. American Society of Appraisers, Dulles International Airport, Box 17265, Washington, DC 20041. Ed. Dexter D. MacBride.

333.33   314   DK   ISSN 0070-3508
DENMARK. DANMARKS STATISTIK. EJENDOMSSALG/SALES OF REAL PROPERTY. (Subseries of its Statistiske Meddelelser) (Text in Danish; notes in English) 1845-49. a. Kr.6.90. Danmarks Statistik, Sejroegade, 2100 Copenhagen OE, Denmark.

333.33   SA
SOUTH AFRICA. DEPARTMENT OF STATISTICS. TRANSFERS OF RURAL IMMOVABLE PROPERTY. (Report No. 06-02) a., latest 1978. R.2.40. Department of Statistics, Private Bag X44, Pretoria 0001, South Africa (Orders to: Government Printer, Bosman St., Private Bag X85, Pretoria 0001, South Africa)

333.34   314   SP   ISSN 0081-3370
SPAIN. INSTITUTO NACIONAL DE ESTADISTICA. INFORME SOBRE LA DISTRIBUCION DE LAS RENTAS. a. Instituto Nacional de Estadistica, Avda. Generalisimo 91, Madrid 16, Spain.

RELIGIONS AND THEOLOGY

see also Religions and Theology—Islamic; Religions and Theology—Judaic; Religions and Theology—Oriental; Religions and Theology—Protestant; Religions and Theology—Roman Catholic; Religions and Theology—Other Denominations and Sects

268   US
A A R DISSERTATION SERIES. 1974. irreg. $4.20 per vol. (American Academy of Religion) Scholar's Press, University of Montana, Missoula, MT 59801 (Or: 101 Salem St., Box 2268, Chic, CA 95926) Ed. Carl Rasehke.

200   US   ISSN 0084-6287
A A R STUDIES IN RELIGION. 1970. irreg. (American Academy of Religion) Scholar's Press, University of Montana, Missoula, MT 59801 (Or: California State University, Dept. of Religious Studies, Chico, CA 95926) Ed. Thomas J. Attizer.

268   US
A A R TEXTS AND TRANSLATIONS. 1976. irreg. (American Academy of Religion) Scholar's Press, University of Montana, Missoula, MT 59801 (Or: California State University, Dept. of Religion Studies, Chico, CA 95926) Ed. James Massey.

200   US
A T L A BIBLIOGRAPHY SERIES. irreg. price varies. (American Theological Library Association) Scarecrow Press, Inc., 52 Liberty St., Box 656, Metuchen, NJ 08840. Ed. Kenneth E. Rowe.

200   US
A T L A MONOGRAPH SERIES. irreg. (American Theological Library Association) Scarecrow Press, Inc., 52 Liberty St., Metuchen, NJ 08840. Ed. Dr. Kenneth E. Rowe.

255   NO   ISSN 0400-227X
AARBOK FOR DEN NORSKE KIRKE. 1951. a. Kr.25. (Bispedoemmeraadenes Fellesraad-- Kirkeraadet) Andaktsbokselskapet, Underhaugsveien 15, Oslo 3, Norway. Ed. Gunnar Roedahl. stat, index. circ. 3,500.

200   US   ISSN 0361-686X
ABBA; a journal of prayer. 1976. irreg., approx. a. $5 per issue. 3913 Wilbert Rd., Austin, TX 78751. Ed. Eutychus Peterson. adv. bk. rev. illus. circ. 333.

ABINGDON CLERGY INCOME TAX GUIDE. see *BUSINESS AND ECONOMICS — Public Finance, Taxation*

ACTA PHILOSOPHICA ET THEOLOGICA. see *PHILOSOPHY*

200   NE   ISSN 0065-1672
ACTA THEOLOGICA DANICA. (Text in English, German) 1958. irreg., vol. 14, 1980. price varies. E. J. Brill, Oude Rijn 33a-35, Leiden, Netherlands.

266 US
AFRICA PULSE. 1970. 2-3/yr. $4.
(Interdenominational Foreign Mission Association) Evangelical Missions Information Service, Box 794, Wheaton, IL 60187. (Co-sponsor: Evangelical Foreign Missions Association) Ed. David A. Hoffer. circ. 1,100.
Missions

268 US
AIDS TO THE STUDY OF RELIGION. 1976. irreg. (American Academy of Religion) Scholar's Press, University of Montana, Missoula, MT 59801 (Or: California State University, Dept. of Religion Studies, Chico, CA 95926) Ed. Charley Hardwide.

266 KE
ALL AFRICA CONFERENCE OF CHURCHES. REFUGEE DEPARTMENT. PROGRESS REPORT. a, latest 1974. All Africa Conference of Churches, Refugee Department, Pioneer House, Government Rd., Box 20301, Nairobi, Kenya.

266 KE
ALL AFRICA CONFERENCE OF CHURCHES. REFUGEE DEPARTMENT. PROJECT LIST. a, latest 1977. All Africa Conference of Churches, Refugee Department, Pioneer House, Government Rd., Box 20301, Nairobi, Kenya.

ALLIANCE REVIEW. see *EDUCATION*

240 SP
ALMANAQUE MISAL. a. $1.50. Editorial Sal Terrae, Guevara 20, Santander, Spain.

200 NE
AMSTERDAM STUDIES IN THEOLOGY. 1979. irreg. Editions Rodopi N.V., Keizersgracht 302-304, Amsterdam, Netherlands.

220 VC ISSN 0066-135X
ANALECTA BIBLICA. INVESTIGATIONES SCIENTIFICAE IN RES BIBLICAS. (Texts in various languages) 1952. irreg. Biblical Institute Press, Piazza della Pilotta 35, I-00187 Rome, Italy.

809 AU
ANALECTA CARTUSIANA; review for Carthusian history and spirituality. (Text in various languages) 1970. irreg., no. 63, 1979. DM.65 per no. Universitaet Salzburg, Institut fuer Englische Sprache, Akademiestr. 24, A-5020 Salzburg, Austria. Ed. James Hogg. circ. 300. (back issues avail)

200 FR ISSN 0066-2860
ANNUAIRE DES INSTITUTS DE RELIGIEUSES EN FRANCE. 1959. irreg., latest 1980. Service National des Vocations Francais, 106 rue du Bac, 75341 Paris, France.

200 US
ANNUAL REVIEW OF RESEARCH IN RELIGIOUS EDUCATION. 1980. a. $5. Union College (Schenectady), Character Research Project, 207 State St., Schenectady, NY 12305. Ed. John H. Peatling. circ. 1,000.

200 SZ
ANTICIPATION; Christian social thought in a future perspective. 1970. irreg (2-3/yr) 4 Fr.($2) per no. World Council of Churches, Department on Church and Society, 150 Route de Ferney, Box 66, 1211 Geneva 20, Switzerland. Ed. Paul Abrecht. circ. 5,000.
Supersedes: Background Information for Church and Society.

220 NE ISSN 0066-5320
APOCRYPHA NOVI TESTAMENTI. 1965. irreg., latest 1965. Van Gorcum, Box 43, 9400 AA Assen, Netherlands.

200 GW ISSN 0066-5711
ARBEITEN ZUR THEOLOGIE. REIHE 1. 1960. irreg., vol. 61, 1975. price varies. Calwer Verlag, Schwanhauser Str.44, 7000 Stuttgart 70, W. Germany (B.R.D.)

243 GW ISSN 0066-6386
ARCHIV FUER LITURGIEWISSENSCHAFT. 1950. a. price varies. (Abt-Herwegen-Institut fuer Liturgische und Monastische Forschung) Verlag Friedrich Pustet, Gutenbergstr. 8, 8400 Regensburg 1, W. Germany (B.R.D.) Ed. Emmanuel v. Severus. bk. rev. circ. 800.

209 GW ISSN 0066-6432
ARCHIV FUER MITTELRHEINISCHE KIRCHENGESCHICHTE. 1949. a. DM.48. Gesellschaft fuer Mittelrheinische Kirchengeschichte, Jesuitenstr. 13, 5500 Trier, W. Germany (B.R.D.)

200 150 GW ISSN 0084-6724
ARCHIV FUER RELIGIONSPSYCHOLOGIE. vol. 4, 1929. irreg., vol. 14, 1980. price varies. (Internationale Gesellschaft fuer Religionspsychologie) Vandenhoeck und Ruprecht, Theaterstr. 13, Postfach 77, 3400 Goettingen, W. Germany (B.R.D.) Eds. K. Krenn, Wilhelm Keilbach.

209 GW ISSN 0066-6491
ARCHIV FUER SCHLESISCHE KIRCHENGESCHICHTE. 1936. a. DM.22. (Institut fuer Ostdeutsche Kirchen- und Kulturgeschichte) Verlag August Lax, Postfach 8847, 3200 Hildesheim, W. Germany (B.R.D.) circ. 900.

291.64 US
ARCHIVE FOR REFORMATION HISTORY. LITERATURE REVIEW/ARCHIV FUER REFORMATIONSGESCHICHTE. LITERATURBERICHT. 1972. a. $17. American Society for Reformation Research, 6477 San Bonita, St. Louis, MO 63105.

260 IT ISSN 0066-6688
ARCHIVIO ITALIANO PER LA STORIA DELLA PIETA. (Text in language of contributor) 1951. irreg., 1970, no. 6. price varies. Edizioni di Storia e Letteratura, Via Lancellotti 18, 00186 Rome, Italy. Ed. Romana Guarnieri. cum.index in prep.

266 US
ASIA PULSE. 1970. 2-3/yr. $4. (Interdenominational Foreign Mission Association) Evangelical Missions Information Service, Box 794, Wheaton, IL 60187. (Co-sponsor: Evangelical Foreign Missions Association) Ed. David A. Hoffer. circ. 1,100.
Missions

200 060 FR ISSN 0066-8907
ASSOCIATION DES AMIS DE PIERRE TEILHARD DE CHARDIN. BULLETIN. 1966. a. 10 F. membership. Association des Amis de Pierre Teilhard de Chardin, 38 rue Geoffroy-Saint-Hilaire, 75005 Paris, France. bibl.

378 US
ASSOCIATION FOR PROFESSIONAL EDUCATION FOR MINISTRY. REPORT OF THE BIENNIAL MEETING. 1950. biennial. $10. Association for Professional Education for Ministry, c/o Oliver Williams, Pres., University of Notre Dame, Notre Dame, IN 46556 (Orders to: Joseph Kelly, Treas., St. Bernard's Seminary, 2260 Lake Ave., Rochester, NY 14612) Ed. Gaylord Noyce. circ. 400.
Missions

266 US ISSN 0519-153X
ASSOCIATION OF PROFESSORS OF MISSIONS. BIENNIAL MEETING. PROCEEDINGS. vol. 12, 1974. biennial. $3. Association of Professors of Missions, c/o Ed. John T. Boberg, 5401 S. Cornell Ave., Chicago, IL 60615. circ. 125. (processed)

268 US ISSN 0362-1472
ASSOCIATION OF THEOLOGICAL SCHOOLS IN THE UNITED STATES AND CANADA. BULLETIN. 1937. biennial. $3. Association of Theological Schools, Box 130, Vandalia, OH 45377. Ed. Leon Pacala. circ. 800.
Formerly: American Association of Theological Schools in the United States and Canada. Bulletin (ISSN 0065-7360)

268 US
ASSOCIATION OF THEOLOGICAL SCHOOLS IN THE UNITED STATES AND CANADA. DIRECTORY. 1918. a. $1.50. ‡ Association of Theological Schools, Box 130, Vandalia, OH 45377. Ed. Charlotte M. Thompson.
Formerly: American Association of Theological Schools in the United States and Canada. Directory (ISSN 0065-7379)

ATHEIST. see *PHILOSOPHY*

220 AT ISSN 0045-0308
AUSTRALIAN BIBLICAL REVIEW. 1951. a. Aus.$3.50($4.50) Fellowship for Biblical Studies, c/o Queen's College, University of Melbourne, Parkville, Vic. 3052, Australia. Eds. E. F. Osborn & N. M. Watson. bk. rev. circ. 300-400. Indexed: New Test.Abstr.

297.89 CN ISSN 0708-5052
BAHA'I STUDIES. 1976. irreg. Can.$2 per no. Canadian Association for Studies on the Baha'i Faith, 224 Fourth Ave., Ottawa, Ont. K1S 2L8, Canada.

297.89 IS ISSN 0045-1320
BAHA'I WORLD. (Text primarily in English; occasional articles in French, German, Persian) 1925. irreg., vol. 16, 1978. price varies. Baha'i World Centre, Box 155, Haifa 31-000, Israel (U.S. dist.: Baha'i Publishing Trust, 415 Linden Ave., Wilmette, Illinois 60091) circ. 15,000.

970 001 US ISSN 0067-3129
BAMPTON LECTURES IN AMERICA. 1949. irreg., 1978, no. 20. price varies. Columbia University Press, 136 South Broadway, Irvington-On-Hudson, NY 10533.

BEITRAEGE ZUR GESCHICHTE DER PHILOSOPHIE UND THEOLOGIE DES MITTELALTERS NEUE FOLGE. see *PHILOSOPHY*

266 GW ISSN 0067-5032
BEITRAEGE ZUR GESCHICHTE DES ALTEN MOENCHTUMS UND DES BENEDIKTINERORDENS. 1912. irreg. price varies. Aschendorffsche Verlagsbuchhandlung, Soester Str. 13, 4400 Muenster, W. Germany (B.R.D.) Ed. Emmanuel v. Severus.

200 100 GE ISSN 0067-5059
BEITRAEGE ZUR GESCHICHTE DES RELIGIOESEN UND WISSENSCHAFTLICHEN DENKENS. irreg., vol. 9, 1971. price varies. Akademie-Verlag, Leipziger Str. 3-4, 108 Berlin, E. Germany (D.D.R.)

230 GW ISSN 0067-5172
BEITRAEGE ZUR OEKUMENISCHEN THEOLOGIE. 1967. irreg., vol. 18, 1978. price varies. Ferdinand Schoeningh, Juehenplatz 1, 4790 Paderborn, W. Germany (B.R.D.) Ed. Heinrich Fries.

260 GW
BERCKERS TASCHENKALENDER. 1955. a. DM.7.50. Verlag Butzon und Bercker, Hoogeweg 71, Postfach 215, 4178 Kevelaer, W. Germany (B.R.D.)
Former title: Berckers Katholischer Taschenkalender.

BIBLIOGRAFIA TEOLOGICA COMENTADA DEL AREA IBEROAMERICANA. see *BIBLIOGRAPHIES*

200 SP ISSN 0067-740X
BIBLIOTECA DE TEOLOGIA. 1964. irreg.; 1979, no. 14. price varies. (Universidad de Navarra) Ediciones Universidad de Navarra, S.A., Plaza de los Sauces, 1 y 2 Barainain, Pamplona, Spain.

200 PL ISSN 0067-754X
BIBLIOTECZKA ATEISTY.* irreg. Stowarzyszenie Ateistow i Wolnomyslicieli, Oddzial Wojewod w Krakowie, Krakow, Poland.

209 PL ISSN 0519-8658
BIBLIOTEKA PISARZY REFORMACYJNYCH. (Text in Latin, Polish) 1958. irreg. price varies. (Polska Akademia Nauk, Instytut Filozofii i Socjologii) Panstwowe Wydawnictwo Naukowe, Ul. Miodowa 10, Warsaw, Poland (Subscr. address: Ars Polona-Ruch, Krakowskie Przedmiescie 7 ,00-068 Warsaw, Poland) Ed. L. Szczucki.

230 UK ISSN 0067-7752
BIBLIOTEKA POLSKA. SERIA TOMISTYCZNA. 1962. irreg. Veritas Foundation Publication Centre, 12 Praed Mews, London W2 1QZ, England. Ed. Very Rev. Msgr. Dr. Stanislaw Belch.

200 BE
BIBLIOTHECA EPHEMERIDUM THEOLOGICARUM LOVANIENSIUM. vol. 31, 1972. irreg., vol. 52, 1979. Leuven University Press, Krakenstraat 3, B-3000 Louvain, Belgium.

220	SZ	ISSN 0582-1673
BIBLISCHE BEITRAEGE. 1961. irreg. (1-2/yr.), no. 13, 1977. price varies. (Schweizerisches Katholische Bibelbewegung) Verlag S K B, Universite Misericorde 4219, CH-1700 Fribourg, Switzerland. Ed. Pierre Casetti. illus.

220	GW	ISSN 0523-5154
BIBLISCHE UNTERSUCHUNGEN. 1967. irreg. price varies. Verlag Friedrich Pustet, Gutenbergstr. 8, 8400 Regensburg 1, W. Germany (B. R. D.) Ed. Otto Kuss. circ. 800.

220	GW
BIBLISCHES SEMINAR. 1967. irreg. price varies. Calwer Verlag, Schwarnhauser Str. 44, 7000 Stuttgart 70, W. Germany (B.R.D.)

270 940	GW
BLAETTER FUER WUERTTEMBERGISCHE KIRCHENGESCHICHTE. 1895. a. DM.25. Verein fuer Wuerttembergische Kirchengeschichte, Gaensheidestr. 4, Postfach 92, 7000 Stuttgart 1, W. Germany (B.R.D.) Ed. Gerhard Schaefer. bk. rev. Indexed: Hist.Abstr. Amer.Hist. & Life.

200	GW	ISSN 0068-0443
BOTSCHAFT DES ALTEN TESTAMENTS; Erlauterungen Alttestamentlicher Schriften. 1958. irreg., vol. 7/8, 1980. price varies. Calwer Verlag, Schwarnhauser Str. 44, 7000 Stuttgart 70, W. Germany (B.R.D.)

207 268.8	US	ISSN 0068-2721
BROADMAN COMMENTS; INTERNATIONAL SUNDAY SCHOOL LESSONS. 1945. a. or q. $4.75. Broadman Press, 127 Ninth Ave. N., Nashville, TN 37234. Ed. Donald F. Ackland. circ. 18,000.

200	CN
CAHIERS DE RECHERCHE ETHIQUE. (Text in French) 1977. irreg. price varies. Editions Fides, 235 Est, Blvd. Dorchester, Montreal, Que. H2X 1N9, Canada.

220	GW
CALWER THEOLOGISCHE MONOGRAPHIEN. REIHE A: BIBELWISSENSCHAFT. 1972. irreg., no. 4, 1974. price varies. Calwer Verlag, Schwarnhauser Str. 44, 7000 Stuttgart 70, W. Germany (B.R.D.) Eds. Peter Stuhlmacher, Claus Westermann.

200	GW
CALWER THEOLOGISCHE MONOGRAPHIEN. REIHE C: PRAKTISCHE THEOLOGIE UND MISSIONSWISSENSCHAFT. 1973. irreg., vol. 5, 1980. price varies. Calwer Verlag, Schwarnhauser Str. 44, 7000 Stuttgart 70, W. Germany (B.R.D.) Ed. S. H. Bueckle, M. Seitz.

230	GW
CALWER THEOLOGISCHE MONOGRAPHIEN. REIHE B: SYSTEMATISCHE THEOLOGIE UND KIRCHENGESCHICHTE. 1973. irreg., no. 2, 1974. price varies. Calwer Verlag, Schwarnhauser Str. 44, 7000 Stuttgart 70, W. Germany (B.R.D.) Eds. J. Baur, M. Brecht, G. Kretschmar.

270	CN	ISSN 0008-3208
CANADIAN CHURCH HISTORICAL SOCIETY JOURNAL. 1950. irreg. Can.$8. Canadian Church Historical Society, 67 Victoria Ave. S., Hamilton, Ont. L8N 2S8, Canada. Ed. Dr. Christopher Headon. bk. rev. cum.index. circ. 450. (also avail. in microfilm) Indexed: Amer.Hist. & Life. Hist.Abstr. Rel.Per.
Church history

277.1	CN	ISSN 0701-4309
CANADIAN COUNCIL OF CHURCHES. RECORD OF PROCEEDINGS. 1944. triennial. Canadian Council of Churches - Conseil Canadien des Eglises, 40 St. Clair Ave., East, Toronto. Ont. M4T 1M9, Canada.

220	CN	ISSN 0068-970X
CANADIAN SOCIETY OF BIBLICAL STUDIES. BULLETIN/SOCIETE CANADIENNE DES ETUDES BIBLIQUES. BULLETIN. (Bulletin not issued 1960-63) 1935. a. included in membership fee. Canadian Society of Biblical Studies, Religious Studies, University of Calgary, Calgary, Alta, T2N 1N4, Canada. Ed. Dr. P. C. Craigie. circ. 220.

267	IT	ISSN 0069-0554
CARITAS INTERNATIONALIS. INTERNATIONAL YEARBOOKS. (Text in English) 1965. a. ‡ Caritas Internationalis, Piazza San Calisto 16, 00153 Rome, Italy.

267	IT	ISSN 0069-0562
CARITAS INTERNATIONALIS. REPORTS OF GENERAL ASSEMBLIES. (Text in English, French, and Spanish) quadrennial. ‡ Caritas Internationalis, Piazza San Calisto 16, 00153 Rome, Italy.

260	GW
CARITAS-KALENDER. 1924. a. DM.380. (Deutscher Caritasverband) Lambertus-Verlag GmbH, Sternwaldstr. 4, Postfach 1026, 7800 Freiburg, W. Germany (B.R.D.) Ed. Peter Gralla. circ. 72,000.

CARL NEWELL JACKSON LECTURES. see *FOLKLORE*

200	MW
CHANCELLOR COLLEGE. DEPARTMENT OF RELIGIOUS STUDIES. STAFF SEMINAR PAPER. irreg., no. 4, 1979. Chancellor College, Department of Religious Studies, Box 280, Zomba, Malawi.

200	US
CHICAGO HISTORY OF AMERICAN RELIGION. 1973. irreg., latest 1978. price varies. University of Chicago Press, 5801 S. Ellis Ave., Chicago, IL 60637. Ed. Martin E. Marty. adv. bk. rev. (reprint service avail. from UMI,ISI)

266	US
CHINESE WORLD PULSE. 1977. 2-3/yr. $4. (Interdenominational Foreign Mission Association) Evangelical Missions Information Service, Box 794, Wheaton, IL 60187. (Co-sponsor: Evangelical Foreign Missims Association) Ed. David A. Hoffer. circ. 1,100.
Missions

268	US	ISSN 0069-388X
CHRISTIAN SCHOOL DIRECTORY. 1920. a. $4.95. ‡ Christian Schools International, 3350 E. Paris Ave., Grand Rapids, MI 49508. Ed. LaVerne Triezenberg. circ. 3,500.

840	FR	ISSN 0529-4975
CHRONIQUES DE PORT-ROYAL. 1950. 20 F. Societe des Amis de Port-Royal, 23 Quai de Conti, 75006 Paris, France.

268	UK
CHURCH AND SCHOOL HANDBOOK. 1963. triennial. £9. Trade and Technical Press Ltd., Crown House, Morden, Surrey SM4 5EW, England. Ed. M. Carter. adv. illus. index.

268	UK
CHURCH POCKET BOOK AND DIARY. a. price varies. Society for Promoting Christian Knowledge, Holy Trinity Church, Marylebone Rd., London NW1 4DU, England.
Formerly: Churchman's Pocket Book and Diary (ISSN 0069-4029)

252	UK	ISSN 0069-4002
CHURCH PULPIT YEAR BOOK; sermon outlines. 1903. a. £1.75. ‡ Chansitor Publications, 46 Bedford Row, London WC1R 4LR, England. adv. index. circ. 3,000.

200	AG
COLECCION AMANECE. no. 4, 1976. irreg. Editora Patria Grande, Casilla de Correo 5, Buenos Aires 1408, Argentina.

200	SP	ISSN 0069-505X
COLECCION CANONICA. 1959. irreg.; 1979, no. 69. price varies. (Universidad de Navarra, Facultad de Derecho Canonico) Ediciones Universidad de Navarra, S.A., Plaza de los Sauces, 1 y 2 Baranain, Pamplona, Spain.
Canon law

200	CK
COLECCION COMUNICACION. 1977. irreg. Ediciones Paulinas, Calle 12 No. 6-11, Bogota, Colombia.

262.9	SP
COLECTANEA DE JURISPRUDENCIA CANONICA. 1974. a. 850 ptas.($22) Universidad Pontificia de Salamanca, Calle Compania 1, Salamanca, Spain.
Canon law

200	US
COLLEGE THEOLOGY SOCIETY. ANNUAL PUBLICATION. 1968. a. price varies. College Theology Society, c/o Villanova University, Villanova, PA 19085. Ed. Dr. Thomas M. McFadden. bibl. circ. 3,500.

369.4	UY
CONFEDERACION LATINOAMERICANA DE ASOCIACIONES CRISTIANAS DE JOVENES. CARTA. (Editions in English and Spanish) irreg. free. Confederacion Latinoamericana de Asociaciones Cristianas de Jovenes, Casilla 172, Montevideo, Uruguay.
Formerly: Federacion Sudamericana de Asociaciones Cristianas de Jovenes. Noticias (ISSN 0428-1039)

200	SW	ISSN 0069-8946
CONIECTANEA BIBLICA. NEW TESTAMENT SERIES. (Text in English and French) 1966. irreg., no. 9, 1977. price varies. C.W.K. Gleerup (Subsidiary of: LiberLaeromedel) Box 1205, S-221 05 Lund, Sweden. Eds. Birger Gerhardsson, Harald Riesenfeld.
Continues: Acta Seminarii Neotestamentici Upsaliensis & Coniectanea Neotestamentica.

200	SW	ISSN 0069-8954
CONIECTANEA BIBLICA. OLD TESTAMENT SERIES. 1967. irreg., no. 10, 1977. price varies. C.W.K. Gleerup (Subsidiary of: LiberLaeromedel) Box 1205, S-221 05 Lund, Sweden. Eds. Gillis Gerleman.

200	US	ISSN 0589-4867
CONSULTATION ON CHURCH UNION. DIGEST. 1962. irreg., approx. every 18 mos., latest issue, 1980. price varies. Consultation on Church Union, 228 Alexander St., Princeton, NJ 08540. Ed. Gerald F. Moede.

200	US
CONTEMPORARY RELIGIOUS MOVEMENTS: A WILEY-INTERSCIENCE SERIES. 1974. irreg., unnumbered, 8 vols. to date. John Wiley & Sons, Inc., 605 Third Ave., New York, NY 10016. Ed. I. Zaretsky.

200	US	ISSN 0147-1066
CONTRIBUTIONS TO THE STUDY OF RELIGION. 1981. irreg. Greenwood Press, 88 Post Rd. W., Westport, CT 06881. Ed. Henry W. Bowden.

COURTENAY LIBRARY OF REFORMATION CLASSICS. see *HISTORY — History Of Europe*

COURTENAY REFORMATION FACSIMILES. see *HISTORY — History Of Europe*

COURTENAY STUDIES IN REFORMATION THEOLOGY. see *HISTORY — History Of Europe*

200	PE
CUADERNOS DE TEOLOGIA ACTUAL, CIENCIAS SOCIALES Y REALIDAD NACIONAL. 1977. irreg. Centro de Proyeccion Cristiana, Avda. Horacio Urteaga 452, Lima, Peru.

270	GW	ISSN 0070-2234
CUSANUS-GESELLSCHAFT. BUCHREIHE. 1964. irreg. price varies. Aschendorffsche Verlagsbuchhandlung, Soester Str. 13, 4400 Muenster, W. Germany (B.R.D.) Eds. Rudolf Haubst, Erich Meuthen, Josef Stallmach.

200	US	ISSN 0193-6883
DENOMINATIONS IN AMERICA. irreg. price varies. Greenwood Press, 8 Post Rd. W., Westport, CT 06881. Ed. Harry Bowden.

221	GW
DIELHEIMER BLAETTER ZUM ALTEN TESTAMENT. 1972. irreg. price varies. Dr. H. Schult, Ed. & Pub., Am Hummelberg 11, 6909 Dielheim, W. Germany (B.R.D.) Eds. H Schult, B. Diebner. circ. 200.

200   CN
DIRECTORY OF DEPARTMENTS AND PROGRAMS OF RELIGIOUS STUDIES IN NORTH AMERICA. 1973. triennial. $5. Council on the Study of Religion, Wilfrid Laurier University, Waterloo, Ont. N2L 3C5, Canada. Ed. Harold Remus.

200   CN   ISSN 0318-0123
DONUM DEI. French edition (ISSN 0318-0131) (Editions in English and French) 1958. a. price varies. ‡ Canadian Religious Conference, 324 Laurier E, Ottawa, Ont. K1N 6P6, Canada. Ed. John Malo. circ. 4,500 (French edt.); 6,000 (English edt.)

200   US   ISSN 0070-7732
DUQUESNE STUDIES. THEOLOGICAL SERIES. 1963. irreg. price varies. Duquesne University Press, 600 Forbes Ave, Pittsburgh, PA 15219 (Dist. by Humanities Press, Inc., 171 First Ave., Atlantic Highlands, NJ 07716) Eds. Henry J. Koren, Charles Fenner.

266   US
E M I SSARY. 1970. 3-4/yr. $5. (Interdenominational Foreign Mission Association) Evangelical Missions Information Service, Box 794, Wheaton, IL 60187. (Co-sponsor: Evangelical Foreign Missions Association) Ed. David A. Hoffer. circ. 1,100.
Missions

200   FR   ISSN 0070-8860
ECRITS LIBRES. 1955. irreg., 1973, no. 16. 42 F. Librairie Fischbacher, 33 rue de Seine, 75-Paris 6, France.

220   VC
ELENCHUS BIBLIOGRAPHICUS BIBLICUS. a. L.21600($27) Pontificio Istituto Biblico, Piazza della Pilotta 35, 00187 Rome, Italy. Ed. Peter Nober S. J.
Bible

ETUDES GREGORIENNES. see *MUSIC*

200 060   FR   ISSN 0082-2612
ETUDES TEILHARDIENNES/TEILHARDIAN STUDIES. 1969. irreg. price varies. Editions du Seuil, 27 rue Jacob, 75261 Paris Cedex 06, France. Ed. J. P. DeMoulin.

266   US
EUROPE PULSE. 1970. irreg., 2-3/yr. $4. (Interdenominational Foreign Mission Association) Evangelical Missions Information Service, Box 794, Wheaton, IL 60187. (Co-sponsor: Evangelical Foreign Missions Association) Ed. David A. Hoffer. circ. 1,100.
Missions

260   GW   ISSN 0531-4798
EVANGELISCHE MISSION JAHRBUCH. 1969. a. DM.5.80. (Verband Evangelischer Missionskonferenzen) Missionshilfe Verlag, Mittelweg 143, 2000 Hamburg 13, W. Germany (B. R. D.) Ed. Lothar Engel. bk. rev. circ. 10,000.
Missions

200   US
FACT BOOK ON THEOLOGICAL EDUCATION. 1971. a. $10. Association of Theological Schools, Box 130, Vendalia, OH 45377. Ed. Marvin J. Taylor. circ. 700.

200   SZ   ISSN 0512-2589
FAITH AND ORDER PAPERS. 1949 N.S. irreg., no. 93, 1979. price varies. World Council of Churches, 150 Route de Ferney, CH-1211 Geneva 20, Switzerland (Dist. in the U.S. by: Friendship Press, 475 Riverside Dr., Room 1062, New York, NY 10027) cum.index (1910-48); (1910-1970)

200   CL
FE DE UN PUEBLO. 1975. irreg. $10. Universidad Catolica de Chile, Seminario Latinoamericano de Documentacion, Casilla 114 D, Santiago, Chile. circ. 1,000.

200   IT
FILOSOFIA DELLA RELIGIONE. TESTI E STUDI. 1977. irreg. Paideia Editrice, Via Corsica 58 - M, Brescia, Italy.

200   FR
FOI AUJOURD'HUI. 1977. m. 50 F. Bayard Presse, 5, rue Bayard, 75380 Paris Cedex 08, France. circ. 100,000.

200   US
GENERAL CONVENTION OF THE NEW JERUSALEM. JOURNAL. 1817. a. General Convention of the New Jerusalem in the United States of America, 48 Sargent St., Newton, MA 02158.

271   IT   ISSN 0072-4548
GIOVENTU PASSIONISTA/PASSIONIST YOUTH; rivista di formazione e d'informazione passionista. (Text in various languages; summaries in English) 1955. irreg., 1960, no. 3. $3. Edizioni E C O, 64048 S. Gabriele (Teramo), Italy. Ed. P. Natale Cavatassi.

268 260   US
GUIDE TO CHRISTIAN CAMPS. biennial. $6.95. Christian Camping International, Box 400, Somonauk, IL 60552.
Former titles: Christian Camping Internatioal Directory (ISSN 0069-3855); Before 1969: Christian Camp and Conference Association. International Directory.

268   US   ISSN 0072-9787
HANDBOOK OF DENOMINATIONS IN THE U.S. quinquennial. $7.95. Abingdon, 201 8th Ave. S, Nashville, TN 37202.

266   UK
HAPPY DAY DIARY. 1928. a. 10p. ‡ Lord's Day Observance Society, 47 Parish Lane, London SE2O 7LU, England. Ed. J. G. Roberts. circ. 45,000.

HARVARD SEMITIC MONOGRAPHS. see *LINGUISTICS*

200   US   ISSN 0440-3509
HARVARD STUDIES IN WORLD RELIGIONS. 1964. irreg. price varies. Harvard University Press, 79 Garden St., Cambridge, MA 02138.

201   US   ISSN 0073-0726
HARVARD THEOLOGICAL STUDIES. 1916. irreg., 1970, no. 25. price varies. (Harvard University) Scholars Press, University of Montana, Missoula, MT 59801.

200   US
HERMENEUTICS: STUDIES IN THE HISTORY OF RELIGION. irreg. price varies. University of California Press, 2223 Fulton St., Berkeley, CA 94720.

HISTORIANS OF EARLY MODERN EUROPE. NEWSLETTER. see *HISTORY — History Of Europe*

200   US
HOLIDAY BOOK. 1973. $1.50. Snibbe Publications, Inc., 523 Lakeview Rd., Clearwater, FL 33516. Ed. M.R. Bennett.
Former titles: All About Christmas & Christmas Guide.

200 933   IS
HOLY PLACES OF PALESTINE. (Text in various languages) 1970. irreg. Franciscan Printing Press, Box 14064, Jerusalem 91140, Israel.

200   FR
HOMMES ET EGLISE; ANNUAIRE DU CERDIC. 1970. a. 65 F. Universite de Strasbourg II, Centre de Recherche et de Documentation des Institutions Chretiennes, 9 Place de l'Universite, 67084 Strasbourg Cedex, France. Eds. Jean Schlick & Marie Zimmermann. bk. rev. circ. 2,000.

200   JA   ISSN 0073-3938
HUMANITIES, CHRISTIANITY AND CULTURE. (Text in Japanese, English, French, German; summaries in English and Japanese) 1964. approx. a. 400 Yen per no. International Christian University, Institute for the Study of Christianity and Culture - Kokusai Kirisutokyo Daigaku Kirisutokyo to Bunka Kenkyujo, 3-10-2 Osawa, Mitaka, Tokyo 181, Japan.
Formerly: International Christian University. Publications IV-B. Christianity and Culture.

200   US   ISSN 0422-4108
I. E. (CHICAGO) 1964. irreg. Ecumenical Institute, 3444 W. Congress Parkway, Chicago, IL 60624. illus.

200   US   ISSN 0363-5058
IN COMMON. 1971. irreg. $2. ‡ Consultation on Church Union, 228 Alexander St., Princeton, NJ 08540. Ed. Janet G. Penfield. circ. 10,000.

200   US   ISSN 0092-9018
INSPIRATION THREE. (Issued as subseries of a Pivot Family Reader) irreg. Keats Publishing Inc., 36 Grove St., Box 876, New Canaan, CT 06840.

INSTITUT FUER EUROPAEISCHE GESCHICHTE, MAINZ. VORTRAEGE. ABTEILUNG UNIVERSALGESSCHICHTE UND ABTEILUNG RELIGIONSGESCHICHTE. see *HISTORY*

INSTITUT FUER EUROPAEISCHE GESICHTE, MAINZ. VEROEFFENTLICHUNGEN. ABTEILUNG UNIVERSALGESCHICHTE UND ABTEILUNG RELIGIONSGESCHICHTE. see *HISTORY*

200   MX
INSTITUTO SUPERIOR DE ESTUDIOS ECLESIASTICOS. LIBRO ANUAL. (Volume for 1978-79 delayed) vol. 6, 1977. irreg. Instituto Superior de Estudios Eclesiasticos, Victoria 21, Mexico 22, D.F., Mexico. bk. rev.

200   UY
INSTITUTO TEOLOGICO DEL URUGUAY. CUADERNOS. no. 4, 1978. irreg. Instituto Teologico del Uruguay, Av. de Octubre 3060, Montevideo, Uruguay.

367   GW
INTERNATIONAL ASSOCIATION OF LIBERAL RELIGIOUS WOMEN. NEWSLETTER. 1949. a. membership. International Association of Liberal Religious Women, c/o Dr. Jutta Reich, Pres., Triefenbergweg 1, 6229 Schlangenbad 5, W. Germany (Edit. address: Havikhorst 17hs, Amsterdam 1083 TM, Netherlands) Ed. Gusta Greve.
Former titles: International Union of Liberal Christian Women. Newsletter; International League of Liberal Christian Women. Newsletter (ISSN 0074-6746)

200   FR   ISSN 0074-297X
INTERNATIONAL CONFERENCE OF SOCIOLOGY OF RELIGION.* 1948. biennial, 1972, 12th, The Hague. International Conference of Sociology of Religion, 39 rue de la Monnaie, 59042 Lille, France.

268   US   ISSN 0074-6770
INTERNATIONAL LESSON ANNUAL; commentary and teaching suggestions on the International Sunday School lessons. a. $4.50. Abingdon, 201 Eighth Ave. S., Nashville, TN 37203. Ed.. Horace R. Weaver.

221   NE   ISSN 0074-719X
INTERNATIONAL ORGANIZATION FOR THE STUDY OF THE OLD TESTAMENT. PROCEEDINGS OF THE INTERNATIONAL CONGRESS. (Proceedings published in organization's series: Vetus Testamentum) 1953. triennial, 8th, 1974, Edinburgh. E. J. Brill, Oude Rijn 33a-35, Leiden, Netherlands.

200 301   GW   ISSN 0074-9850
INTERNATIONALES JAHRBUCH FUER RELIGIONSSOZIOLOGIE. 1965. a. Westdeutscher Verlag GmbH, Faulbrunnenstr. 13, 6200 Wiesbaden, W. Germany (B.R.D.)

270   GW   ISSN 0075-2541
JAHRBUCH FUER ANTIKE UND CHRISTENTUM. 1958. a. price varies. (Universitaet Bonn, Franz Joseph Doelger-Institut) Aschendorffsche Verlagsbuchhandlung, Soester Str. 13, Postfach 1124, 4400 Muenster, W. Germany (B. R. D.) bk. rev.

270   GW   ISSN 0075-2568
JAHRBUCH FUER BERLIN-BRANDENBURGISCHE KIRCHENGESCHICHTE. a., vol.51, 1979. DM.16.50. (Arbeitsgemeinschaft fuer Berlin-Brandenburgische Kirchengeschichte) Christlicher Zeitschriftenverlag, Fregestr. 71, 1000 Berlin 41, W. Germany (B.R.D.) Ed. Joachim Foerster. circ. 850.
Supersedes: Jahrbuch fuer Brandenburgische Kirchengeschichte.

JAHRBUCH FUER CHRISTLICHE SOZIALWISSENSCHAFTEN. see *SOCIOLOGY*

RELIGIONS AND THEOLOGY

264 245   GW   ISSN 0075-2681
JAHRBUCH FUER LITURGIK UND
HYMNOLOGIE. 1955. a. price varies.
(International Fellowship of Research in Hymnology
- Internationale Arbeitsgemeinschaft fuer
Hymnologie) Johannes Stauda Verlag GmbH,
Heinrich-Schuetz-Allee 33, 3500 Kassel-
Wilhelmshoehe, W. Germany (B.R.D.) Eds. Konrad
Ameln, Christhard Mahrenholz, Alexander Voelker.
bk. rev.

270   GW   ISSN 0075-2762
JAHRBUCH FUER SCHLESISCHE
KIRCHENGESCHICHTE. 1882. a. DM.34.
(Verein fuer Schlesische Kirchengeschichte e.V.)
Verlag Unser Weg, Meesenring 15, 2400 Luebeck 1,
W. Germany (B.R.D.) Ed. Gerhard Hultsch. bk. rev.

268   FR
J'AIME LIRE. 1977. m. 115 F. Bayard Presse, 5, rue
Bayard, 75380 Paris Cedex 08, France.
     For children 7 to 9 years

200   UK   ISSN 0449-1602
JORDAN LECTURES IN COMPARATIVE
RELIGION. 1953. irreg., 12th series, 1978. price
varies. Athlone Press, 90-91 Great Russell St.,
London WC1B 3PY, England (Dist. in U.S. by:
Humanities Press Inc., 171 First Ave., Atlantic
Highlands, NJ 07716)

200   UK   ISSN 0143-5108
JOURNAL FOR THE STUDY OF THE NEW
TESTAMENT. SUPPLEMENT SERIES. irreg.
price varies. J S O T Press, Department of Biblical
Studies, University of Sheffield, Sheffield S10 2TN,
England.

221   UK   ISSN 0309-0787
JOURNAL FOR THE STUDY OF THE OLD
TESTAMENT. SUPPLEMENT SERIES. irreg.
price varies. J S O T Press, Department of Biblical
Studies, University of Sheffield, Sheffield S10 2TN,
England. Ed.Bd.

377.8   US   ISSN 0160-7774
JOURNAL OF SUPERVISION AND TRAINING
IN MINISTRY. 1978. a. $6.50. Association for
Clinical Pastoral Education, North Central Region,
950 E. 59th St., Box 215, Chicago, IL 60637. (Co-
sponsor: American Association of Pastoral
Counselors. Central Region)

261   US   ISSN 0022-9288
KATALLAGETE. 1965. irreg. $10 for 4 issues.
Committee of Southern Churchmen Inc., Box 2307,
College Sta., Berea, KY 40404. Ed. James Y.
Holloway. bk. rev. illus. circ. 4,500. (also avail. in
microform from UMI) Indexed: Rel.Per.

200   SW   ISSN 0085-2619
KYRKOHISTORISK AARSSKRIFT. (Text in Swedish
and English; summaries in English, German,
French) 1900. a. Kr.45. Svenska Kyrkohistoriska
Foereningen, Box 2006, 750 02 Uppsala, Sweden.
Ed. Ingun Montgomery. adv. bk. rev. circ. 1,000.

266   US
LATIN AMERICA PULSE. 1967. 2-3/yr. $4.
(Interdenominational Foreign Mission Association)
Evangelical Missions Information Service, Box 794,
Wheaton, IL 60187. (Co-sponsor: Evangelical
Foreign Missions Association) Ed. David A. Hoffer.
circ. 1,100.
     Missions

200   US   ISSN 0075-8531
LECTURES ON THE HISTORY OF RELIGIONS.
NEW SERIES. 1971, no. 9. irreg., 1977, no. 11.
Columbia University Press, 136 South Broadway,
Irvington-On-Hudson, NY 10533.

266.025   UK   ISSN 0075-8809
LEPROSY MISSION, LONDON. ANNUAL
REPORT. 1874. a. free. ‡ Leprosy Mission, 50
Portland Place, London W1N 3DG, England. Ed.
W. R Edgar. circ. 5,600.
     Formerly: Mission to Lepers, London. Annual
Report.
     Missions

LIBRARY OF PHILOSOPHY AND RELIGION. see
PHILOSOPHY

200   GW   ISSN 0076-0048
LITURGIEWISSENSCHAFTLICHE QUELLEN
UND FORSCHUNGEN. 1919. irreg. price varies.
Aschendorffsche Verlagsbuchhandlung, Soester Str.
13, 4400 Muenster, W. Germany (B.R.D.) Ed. W.
Heckenbach.

200 060   PH   ISSN 0076-0471
LOGOS; a series of monographs in scripture, theology,
philosophy. (Text in English) 1966. irreg., no. 13,
1979. price varies. Ateneo de Manila University,
Loyola School of Theology, Box 4082, Manila,
Philippines. Ed. Philip J. Calderone. circ. 500.
Indexed: Chr. Per. Ind.

200   UK   ISSN 0076-0536
LONDON DIVINITY SERIES. NEW TESTAMENT.
1959. irreg. price varies. James Clarke & Co. Ltd., 7
All Saints Passage, Cambridge CB2 3LS, England.

274   PO   ISSN 0076-1508
LUSITANIA SACRA. 1956. a. 140 esc. Centro de
Estudos de Historia Eclesiastica, Campo dos
Martires da Patria, 45, Lisbon-1, Portugal. Ed. Isaias
da Rosa Pereira.

200 020   US   ISSN 0076-4434
MARIAN LIBRARY STUDIES. NEW SERIES.
1953; 1969 N.S. a. $10. University of Dayton,
Marian Library, Dayton, OH 45469. Ed. Theodore
Koehler. circ. 200. Indexed: Cath.Ind.

200   MM
MELITA THEOLOGICA. (Text in English and
Italian) 1946. a. $5. Royal University Students'
Theological Association, Tal-Qroqq, Msida, Malta.
Ed. Alfred Camilleri. adv. bk. rev. index. circ.
1,000. Indexed: Old Test. Abstr.

200   IT
MEMORIE DOMENICANE. 1884, N.S. 1970. a.
price varies. Frati Predicatori, Provincia Romana,
Piazza S. Domenico 1, 51100 Pistoia, Italy. Ed.
Eugenio Marino. bk. rev. bibl. circ. 700. (tabloid
format)

200 230   AT   ISSN 0076-8790
MILLA WA-MILLA; the Australian bulletin of
comparative religion. 1961. a. Aus.$2. University of
Melbourne, Department of Middle Eastern Studies,
Parkville 3052, Victoria, Australia. Ed. John
Bowman. bk. rev. (back issues avail.)

267 270   ZA   ISSN 0076-8901
MINDOLO NEWS LETTER. 1961. irreg., 1970, no.
33. free; donation appreciated. Mindolo Ecumenical
Foundation, P.O. Box 1493, Kitwe, Zambia. Ed.
Jonathan C. Phiri. adv. circ. 4,000 (approx.)

266   UK
MISSIONS TO SEAMEN ANNUAL REPORT.
1856. a. free. Missions to Seamen, St. Michael
Paternoster Royal, College Hill, London EC4R
2RL, England. Ed. Gillian Ennis. index.
     Formerly: Missions to Seamen Handbook (ISSN
0076-9401)
     Missions

266   GW   ISSN 0076-941X
MISSIONSWISSENSCHAFTLICHE
ABHANDLUNGEN UND TEXTE/ETUDES ET
DOCUMENTS MISSIONNAIRES/MISSION
STUDIES AND DOCUMENTS. 1917. irreg. price
varies. (Internationales Institut fuer
Missionswissenschaftliche Forschungen)
Aschendorffsche Verlagsbuchhandlung, Soester Str.
13, 4400 Muenster, W. Germany (B.R.D.) Eds.
Josef Glazik, Bernward H. Willeke.
     Missions

266   GW   ISSN 0076-9428
MISSIONSWISSENSCHAFTLICHE
FORSCHUNGEN. 1962. irreg. price varies.
Guetersloher Verlagshaus Gerd Mohn, Koenigstr.
23, Postfach 2368, 4830 Guetersloh, W. Germany
(B.R.D.)
     Missions

201   US   ISSN 0076-9517
MISSISSIPPI STATE UNIVERSITY. CHRISTIAN
STUDENT CENTER. ANNUAL LECTURESHIP.
a. Mississippi State University, Christian Student
Center, Mississippi State, MS 39762.

200   GW
MODELLE FUER DEN
RELIGIONSUNTERRICHT. Short title: M. R. U.
1975. irreg., no. 7, 1976. price varies.
(Religionspaedagogische Projektentwicklung in
Baden und Wuerttemberg) Calwer Verlag,
Schwarnhauser Str. 44, 7000 Stuttgart 70, W.
Germany (B.R.D.) (Co-publisher: Koesel-Verlag)
Eds. Klaus Dessecker, Gerhard Martin.

NATIONAL DIRECTORY OF PROVIDERS OF
PSYCHIATRIC SERVICES TO RELIGIOUS
INSTITUTIONS. see *MEDICAL SCIENCES —
Psychiatry And Neurology*

NATIONAL GUILD OF CATHOLIC
PSYCHIATRISTS. BULLETIN. see *MEDICAL
SCIENCES — Psychiatry And Neurology*

225   SA
NEOTESTAMENTICA. 1967. a. R.3.30($3.79) New
Testament Society of South Africa, c/o Secretary,
Department of New Testament, Section B,
University of Pretoria, Pretoria 0002, South Africa.
Ed. A.B. du Toit. circ. 400. Indexed: New
Test.Abstr.

220   NE   ISSN 0077-8842
NEW TESTAMENT TOOLS AND STUDIES. 1960.
irreg., vol. 10, 1980. price varies. E. J. Brill, Oude
Rijn 33a-35, Leiden, Netherlands. Ed. Bruce M.
Metzger.

200   SW   ISSN 0085-4212
NORDISK EKUMENISK AARSBOK. (Text in
Danish, Norwegian and Swedish) 1972. a. Kr.50.
Nordiska Ekumeniska Institutet - Nordic
Ecumenical Institute, Box 68, S-193 00 Sigtuna,
Sweden. Ed. Bo Wirmark. adv. bk. rev. illus. index.
circ. 1,000.

200   GW   ISSN 0340-6407
ORIENS CHRISTIANUS; Hefte fuer die Kunde des
christlichen Orients. 1911. a. DM.68 (approx.)
Verlag Otto Harrassowitz, Taunusstr. 6, Postfach
2929, 6200 Wiesbaden, W. Germany (B.R.D.) Ed.
Julius Assfalg. adv. bk. rev. circ. 400. (back issues
avail.)

OXBRIDGE DIRECTORY OF RELIGIOUS
PERIODICALS. see *BIBLIOGRAPHIES*

266   US
OXFORD EARLY CHRISTIAN TEXTS. irreg. price
varies. Oxford University Press, 200 Madison Ave.,
New York, NY 10016 (And Ely House, 37 Dover
St., London W1X 4AH, England) Ed. Henry
Chadwick.

201   US   ISSN 0078-7272
OXFORD THEOLOGICAL MONOGRAPHS. irreg.
Oxford University Press, 200 Madison Ave., New
York, NY 10016 (and Ely House, 37 Dover St.,
London W1X 4AH, England) Ed. P. W. Bide.

200   SZ
P C R INFORMATION. 2-3/yr. World Council of
Churches, Programme to Combat Racism, 150
Route de Ferney, Box 66, 1211 Geneva 20,
Switzerland.

205   FR
PANORAMA AUJOURD'HUI; revue de reflexion
chretienne. 1968. m. 59 F. Bayard Presse, 5, rue
Bayard, 75380 Paris Cedex 08, France. circ.
140,500.

206   PP   ISSN 0078-9356
PAPUA NEW GUINEA. BUREAU OF
STATISTICS. STATISTICS OF RELIGIOUS
ORGANISATIONS. 1966. a. free. Bureau of
Statistics, P.O. Wards Strip, Papua New Guinea.
Ed. J. J. Shadlow. circ. 434.

200   US
PERE MARQUETTE THEOLOGY LECTURE
SERIES. 1969. a. $6.95. Marquette University
Press, 1324 W. Wisconsin Ave., Milwaukee, WI
53233.

267.6 369.4   FI   ISSN 0356-794X
PISTIS.* 1918. m. (10/yr.) Fmk.20. Nuorten Keskus r.
y., Liisankatu 27 A 5, 00170 Helsinki 17, Finland.
Ed. Pentti Kivimaki. circ. 6,000. (tabloid format)
     Formerly: Kirkon Nuoriso-Pistis (ISSN 0085-
2554)

207 268.8 US ISSN 0079-2543
POINTS FOR EMPHASIS; INTERNATIONAL SUNDAY SCHOOL LESSONS IN POCKET SIZE. (Large type edition also avail.) 1917. a. $1.95. Broadman Press, 127 Ninth Ave. N., Nashville, TN 37234. Ed. William J. Fallis. circ. 51,000.

281 CS ISSN 0079-4937
PRAVOSLAVNY THEOLOGICKY SBORNIK. (Text in Czech or Slovak) 1967. irreg., no. 4, 1974. 52 Kcs.($7) Pravoslavna Cirkev Ceskoslovenska, V jame 6, 110 00 Prague 1, Czechoslovakia. adv. circ. 3,000.

200 CN ISSN 0079-4996
PRESBYTERIAN CHURCH IN CANADA. GENERAL ASSEMBLY. ACTS AND PROCEEDINGS. a. Can.$5.50. Presbyterian Church in Canada, General Assembly, 50 Wynford Dr., Don Mills M3C IJ7, Ont., Canada.

220 NE ISSN 0079-7197
PSEUDEPIGRAPHA VETERIS TESTAMENTI GRAECE. 1964. irreg. price varies. (Rijksuniversiteit te Leiden) E. J. Brill, Oude Rijn 33a-35, Leiden, Netherlands.

200 933 IS
QUADERNI DE "LA TERRA SANTA". (Text in various languages) 1963. irreg. Franciscan Printing Press, Box 14064, Jerusalem 91140, Israel.

260 GW ISSN 0079-9084
QUELLEN UND FORSCHUNGEN ZUR WUERTTEMBERGISCHEN KIRCHENGESCHICHTE. 1967. irreg., vol. 6, 1975. price varies. Calwer Verlag, Schwanhauser Str. 44, 7000 Stuttgart 70, W. Germany (B.R.D.) Eds. Martin Brecht, Gerhard Schaefer.

240 CN ISSN 0079-9343
R. M. BUCKE MEMORIAL SOCIETY FOR THE STUDY OF RELIGIOUS EXPERIENCE. NEWSLETTER-REVIEW. 1966. irreg. Can.$4. R. M. Bucke Memorial Society, 4453 Maisonneuve Blvd. W., Montreal, Que. H3Z 1L8, Canada. Ed. Dr. Raymond H. Prince. bk. rev. circ. 300. (also avail. in processed)

240 CN ISSN 0079-9351
R. M. BUCKE MEMORIAL SOCIETY FOR THE STUDY OF RELIGIOUS EXPERIENCE. PROCEEDINGS OF THE CONFERENCE. 1965. irreg., vol. 7, 1974. price varies. R.M. Bucke Memorial Society, 4453 Maisonneuve Blvd., Montreal, Que. H3Z 1L8, Canada. Ed. Raymond H. Prince. circ. 300. (back issues avail.)

RECHERCHES INSTITUTIONNELLES. see *BIBLIOGRAPHIES*

200 GW
REGULAE BENEDICTI STUDIA. ANNUARIUM INTERNATIONALE. (Text in German, English and French) 1972. a. price varies. Verlag Dr. H. A. Gerstenberg, Rathausstr. 18, Postfach 390, 3200 Hildesheim, W. Germany (B.R.D.) Eds. B. Jaspert, E. Manning.

RELIGIOESE GRAPHIK; Blaetter fuer Freunde Christlicher Gebrauchsgraphik. see *ART*

290 200 NE ISSN 0080-0848
RELIGION AND REASON; METHOD AND THEORY IN THE STUDY AND INTERPRETATION OF RELIGION. 1972. irreg. price varies. Mouton Publishers, Noordeinde 41, 2514 GC The Hague, Netherlands (U.S. addr.: Mouton Publishers, c/o Walter de Gruyter, Inc., 200 Saw Mill River Road, Hawthorne, NY 10532) Ed. J.D.J. Waardenburg.

200 FR ISSN 0080-0864
RELIGION ET SCIENCES DE L'HOMME. 1971. irreg. price varies. Editions du Centurion, 17 rue du Babylone, Paris 7e, France.

200 060 AU ISSN 0080-0872
RELIGION, WISSENSCHAFT, KULTUR. JAHRBUCH. 1950. a. Wiener Katholische Akademie, Freyung 6, A-1010 Vienna, Austria.

200 301 IT
RELIGIONE E SOCIETA. no. 5, 1979. irreg. price varies. Edizioni Studium-Vita Nova, Via Crescenzio 63, 00193 Rome, Italy.

200 GW
RELIGIONSPAEDAGOGISCHE PRAXIS. Short title: R P P. 1971. irreg., vol. 20, 1977. price varies. Calwer Verlag, Schwanhauser Str. 44, 7000 Stuttgart 70, W. Germany (B.R.D.) (Co-publisher: Koesel-Verlag) Eds. Horst Klaus Berg, Wolfgang Lerner. (back issues avail.)

RELIGIOUS BOOKS AND SERIALS IN PRINT. see *BIBLIOGRAPHIES*

230 100 SZ
REVUE DE THEOLOGIE ET DE PHILOSOPHIE. CAHIERS. 1977. irreg. (approx. 1/yr.) Revue de Theologie et de Philosophie, 7 Chemin des Cedres, Lausanne, Switzerland.

266 US ISSN 0080-3367
ROCK MAGAZINE. (Text in Chinese and English) 1957. irreg. $10. Rev. Peter P.S. Ching, Ed. & Pub., 144-25 Roosevelt Ave., Flushing, NY 11354. adv. bk. rev.
Formerly: Evangel Refugee.
Comprehensive works report of American Mission to the Chinese, World Council of Clergymen and U.S. Naturalized Citizen Welfare Association

ROEMISCHE HISTORISCHE MITTEILUNGEN. see *HISTORY — History Of Europe*

220 SP
SAGRADA BIBLIA. 1976. irreg., no. 3, 1979. price varies. Ediciones Universidad de Navarra, S.A., Plaza de los Sauces 1 y 2, Baranain, Pamplona, Spain.
Bible

200 US ISSN 0082-4208
ST. THOMAS MORE LECTURES. 1964. irreg., 1969, no. 3. price varies. Yale University Press, 92A Yale Station, New Haven, CT 06520.

220 UK ISSN 0080-7206
SCHWEICH LECTURES. irreg. (British Academy) Oxford University Press, Press Rd., Neasden, London NW10 0DD, England.

200 FR ISSN 0075-4544
SIR MOSES MONTEFIORE COLLECTIONS DES JUIFS CELEBRES. Title varies: Juifs Celebres. 1969. irreg. 26 F. Librairie du Centre Communautaire, 19 Bd. Poissonniere, 75002 Paris, France.

200 CN ISSN 0537-6211
SOCIETE SAINT-JEAN-BAPTISTE DE MONTREAL. INFORMATION NATIONALE. 1962. irreg. Societe Saint-Jean-Baptiste de Montreal, 1182 rue Saint-Laurent, Montreal 18,Que., Canada. illus.
Formerly: Societe Saint-Jean-Baptiste de Montreal Bulletin.

266 UK ISSN 0081-1297
SOCIETY FOR AFRICAN CHURCH HISTORY. BULLETIN. (Text in English; summaries in French) 1963. a. £1.05. Society for African Church History, c/o Dept. of Religious Studies, Kings College, University of Aberdeen, Aberdeen AB9 2UB, 3cotland. Ed. A. F. Walls. circ. 400. Indexed: Afr.Abstr.

225 UK ISSN 0081-1432
SOCIETY FOR NEW TESTAMENT STUDIES. MONOGRAPH SERIES. 1965. irreg., no. 41, 1980. $24.50 for latest vol. Cambridge University Press, Box 110, Cambridge CB2 3RL, England (and 32 E. 57 St., New York NY 10022) Ed.R. McL. Wilson. index.

220 US
SOCIETY OF BIBLICAL LITERATURE. TEXTS AND TRANSLATIONS. (Text in English and Hebrew) vol. 3, 1974. irreg. $2. (Society of Biblical Literature) Scholars Press, University of Montana, Missoula, MT 59801.

230 SZ ISSN 0067-4907
SONDERBAENDE ZUR THEOLOGISCHEN ZEITSCHRIFT. 1966. irreg., no. 8, 1977. price varies. Friedrich Reinhardt Verlag, Missionsstr. 36, CH-4012 Basel, Switzerland (Dist. by: Albert J. Phiebig Books, Box 352, White Plains, NY 10602) Ed. Bo Reicke. circ. 1,000.
Formerly: Beihefte zur Theologischen Zeitschrift.

266 UK
SOUTH ASIA CHURCH AID ASSOCIATION. ANNUAL. 1970. a. £1. South Asia Church Aid Association, 2 Eaton Gate, London SW1W 9BL, England. circ. 1,500.
Former titles: South Asia Church Aid Newsletter (ISSN 0081-2595); Indian Church Aid Newsletter.

200 KE
SPEARHEAD. (Text in English) 1969. irreg. (4-5/yr.) EAs.60. (Amecea Pastoral Institute) Gaba Publications, Box 908, Eldoret, Kenya. Ed. Brian Hearne. circ. 2,700.
Formerly (until 1977): Gaba Pastoral Papers.

268.8 US ISSN 0081-4245
STANDARD LESSON COMMENTARY; International Sunday School lessons. 1954. a. $6.50 casebound; £5.50 kivar. ‡ Standard Publishing, 8121 Hamilton Ave., Cincinnati, OH 45231. Ed. James Fehl. circ. 100,000.

220 NE
STUDIA AD CORPUS HELLENISTICUM NOVI TESTAMENTI. (Text in English, French and German) 1970. irreg., vol. 6, 1980. price varies. E. J. Brill, Oude Rijn 33a-35, Leiden, Netherlands. Eds. H.D. Betz, G. Delling, W.C. van Unnik.

268 IT
STUDIA EPHEMERIDIS AUGUSTINIANUM. vol. 11, 1974. irreg. Institutum Patristicum Augustinianum, Via S. Uffizio, 25, 00193 Rome, Italy. (back issues avail)

100 GW ISSN 0081-6663
STUDIA IRENICA. (Text in German and English) 1968. irreg., 1971, no. 19. Verlag Dr. H. A. Gerstenberg, Rathausstr. 18, Postfach 390, 3200 Hildesheim, W. Germany (B. R. D.) Ed. Axel Hilmar Swinne.
Before 1971: Frankfurt Am Main. Universitaet. Institut fuer Wissenschaftliche Irenik. Schriften.

266 SP
STUDIA SILENSIA. (Text in English, French, German, Spanish and Portuguese) 1975. a. price varies. Abadia de Santo Domingo de Silos, Libreria de la Abadia, Burgos, Spain. Ed. Clemente de la Serna. ill. stat. tr lit. index,cum.index. circ. 1,500. (back issues avail)

200 NE ISSN 0585-6914
STUDIES IN MEDIEVAL AND REFORMATION THOUGHT. 1966. irreg., vol.. 28, 1981. price varies. E. J. Brill, Oude Rijn 33a-35, Leiden, Netherlands. Ed. H. A. Oberman. (back issues avail.)

230 NE ISSN 0081-8607
STUDIES IN THE HISTORY OF CHRISTIAN THOUGHT. 1966. irreg., vol. 23, 1980. price varies. E. J. Brill, Oude Rijn 33a-35, Leiden, Netherlands. Ed. Heiko A. Oberman.

220 IS ISSN 0081-8909
STUDIUM BIBLICUM FRANCISCANUM. ANALECTA. (Language of text varies) 1962. irreg., no. 14, 1980. price varies. Franciscan Printing Press, Box 14064, 91140 Jerusalem, Israel. circ. 1,000.

220 IS ISSN 0081-8917
STUDIUM BIBLICUM FRANCISCANUM. COLLECTIO MAJOR. (Text in various languages) 1941. irreg., no. 25, 1979. price varies. Franciscan Printing Press, P.O.B. 14064, 91140 Jerusalem, Israel. circ. 1,000.

220 IS ISSN 0081-8925
STUDIUM BIBLICUM FRANCISCANUM. COLLECTIO MINOR. (Text in various languages) 1961. irreg., no. 26, 1979. price varies. Franciscan Printing Press, P.O.B. 14064, 91140 Jerusalem, Israel. circ. 1,000.

220 IS ISSN 0081-8933
STUDIUM BIBLICUM FRANCISCANUM. LIBER ANNUUS. (Text in various Languages) 1951. a. price varies. Franciscan Printing Press, Box 14064, 91140 Jerusalem, Israel. circ. 600.

209 BE
SUBSIDA HAGIOGRAPHICA. irreg., no. 62, 1978 (1-2/yr.) Societe des Bollandistes, 24 Bd. Saint-Michel, 1040 Brussels, Belgium.

260 US
SUCCESSFUL WRITERS AND EDITORS GUIDEBOOK. 1977. irreg. $10.95. ‡ (Christian Writers Institute) Creation House, 396 E. St. Charles Rd., Carol Stream, IL 60187.
 Formerly: Handbook for Christian Writers (ISSN 0069-391X)

220 SW
SVENSK EXEGETISK AARSBOK. (Text in English or Swedish) 1936. a. (Uppsala Exegetiska Saellskap) C.W.K. Gleerup (Subsidiary of: LiberLaeromedel) Box 1205, 221 05 Lund, Sweden. bk. rev. illus.

200 SW ISSN 0082-0423
SWEDISH THEOLOGICAL INSTITUTE, JERUSALEM. ANNUAL. (Text in English and German) 1962. a. price varies. Swedish Theological Institute, c/o Prof. Goesta Lindeskog, Walleinsvaegen 4, 25236 Uppsala, Sweden. Ed. Hans Kosmala. Indexed: Old Test.Abstr.

268.8 US ISSN 0082-1713
TARBELL'S TEACHER'S GUIDE; to the International Bible Lessons for Christian teaching of the uniform course. 1905. a. $6.95. Fleming H. Revell Co., Old Tappan, NJ 07675. Ed. Frank S. Mead.

TASCHENBUCH FUER LITURGIE UND KIRCHENMUSIK. see MUSIC

TEAMWORK. see LIBRARY AND INFORMATION SCIENCES

200 465 GE ISSN 0082-3589
TEXTE UND UNTERSUCHUNGEN ZUR GESCHICHTE DER ALTCHRISTLICHEN LITERATUR. 1952. irreg., vol. 119, 1976. price varies. (Akademie der Wissenschaften der DDR, Zentralinstitut fuer Alte Geschichte und Archaeologie) Akademie-Verlag, Leipziger Str. 3-4, 108 Berlin, E. Germany (D.D.R.)

260 GW ISSN 0082-3597
TEXTE ZUR KIRCHEN- UND THEOLOGIEGESCHICHTE. 1966. irreg. price varies. Guetersloher Verlagshaus Gerd Mohn, Koenigstr. 23, Postfach 2368, 4830 Guetersloh, W. Germany (B.R.D.)

220 IS ISSN 0082-3767
TEXTUS. (Text in English; summaries in Hebrew) 1960. approx. a. $6. (Hebrew University of Jerusalem, Bible Project) Magnes Press, The Hebrew University, Jerusalem, Israel. cum. index: 1960-1966.

200 GW ISSN 0082-3775
TEXTUS PATRISTICI ET LITURGICI. 1964. irreg. price varies. (Institutum Liturgicum Ratisbonense) Verlag Friedrich Pustet, Gutenbergstr. 8, 8400 Regensburg 1, W. Germany (B. R. D.) Ed. Klaus Gamber. circ. 1,000.

200 US ISSN 0362-0603
THEOLOGICAL MARKINGS. 1971. irreg. United Theological Seminary of the Twin Cities, 3000 Fifth St. N.W., New Brighton, MN 55112.

230 GW
THEOLOGIE UND DIENST. 1973. irreg., latest no. 14. price varies. (Prediger- und Missionsseminar St. Chrischona) Brunnen-Verlag GmbH, Pestalozzistr. 1, Postfach 5205, 6300 Giessen 1, W. Germany (B.R.D.) Ed.Bd. circ. 3,000.

230 SZ ISSN 0082-3902
THEOLOGISCHE DISSERTATIONEN. (Editions in German and English; summaries in English or German) 1969. irreg., no. 15, 1980. price varies. (Universitaet Basel, Theologische Fakultaet) Friedrich Reinhardt Verlag, Missionsstr. 36, CH-4012 Basel, Switzerland (Dist. by Albert J. Phiebig Books, Box 352, White Plains, NY 10602) Ed. Bo Reicke.

200 US
THREE MINUTES A DAY; reflections for each day of the year. 1981. irreg. Christophers, Inc., 12 E. 48th St., New York, NY 10017. Ed. Joseph R. Thomas.

200 IT ISSN 0040-960X
TORRE DAVIDICA. 1957. irreg. free. Chiesa Universale Giuris-Davidica, Via Tevere 21, 00198 Rome, Italy. Ed. Elvira Giro. illus. circ. 2,000.

TREE. see LITERATURE

200 US
TRINITY UNIVERSITY MONOGRAPH SERIES IN RELIGION. 1972. irreg. (approx every 18 mos.) Trinity University Press, Trinity University, San Antonio, TX 78284. Ed. John H. Hayes.

200 US ISSN 0082-6596
TRINITY UNIVERSITY STUDIES IN RELIGION; papers by members of Trinity University Studies in Religion Seminar. 1951. irreg., vol. 10, 1975. price varies. Trinity University, Department of Religion, 715 Stadium Dr., San Antonio, TX 78284. circ. 110. (also avail. in microfilm from UMI) Indexed: New Test.Abstr. Rel.&Theol.Abstr.

207 UK ISSN 0082-7118
TYNDALE BULLETIN. 1956. a. £5. (Tyndale Fellowship for Biblical and Theological Research) Inter-Varsity Press, Norton St, Nottingham NG7 3HR, England. Ed. A. R. Millard. bk. rev. circ. 600. (back issues avail.) Indexed: New Test.Abstr.

UNION COLLEGE. CHARACTER RESEARCH PROJECT. NEWSLETTER. see PSYCHOLOGY

200 FR ISSN 0396-2393
UNION DES SUPERIEURES MAJEURS DE FRANCE. ANNUAIRE. 1975. a. Union des Superieures Majeures des Instituts Religieux de France, 10 rue Jean-Bart, 75006 Paris, France.

266 UK ISSN 0144-9508
UNITED SOCIETY FOR THE PROPAGATION OF THE GOSPEL. ANNUAL REPORT/REVIEW. 1704. a. 25p. United Society for the Propagation of the Gospel, 15 Tufton St., London SW1P 3QQ, England.
Missions

200 SP ISSN 0078-8759
UNIVERSIDAD DE NAVARRA. DEPARTAMENTO DE DERECHO CANONICO. MANUALES: DERECHO CANONICO. irreg.; 1979, no. 4. Ediciones Universidad de Navarra, S.A., Plaza de los Sauces, 1 y 2 Baranain, Pamplona, Spain.
Canon law

200 CK
UNIVERSIDAD JAVERIANA. FACULTAD DE TEOLOGIA. COLECCION PROFESORES. irreg. price varies. Universidad Javeriana, Facultad de Teologia, Carrera 10, No. 65-48, Bogota 2, D.E., Colombia.

230 AU ISSN 0579-7780
UNIVERSITAET INNSBRUCK. THEOLOGISCHE FAKULTAET. STUDIEN UND ARBEITEN. (Subseries of: Universitaet Innsbruck. Veroeffentlichungen) 1968. irreg., vol. 10, 1974. price varies. Oesterreichische Kommissionsbuchhandlung, Maximilianstrasse 17, A-6020 Innsbruck, Austria. Ed. Hans Bernhard Meyer.

266 GW ISSN 0077-197X
UNIVERSITAET MUENSTER. INSTITUT FUER MISSIONSWISSENSCHAFT. VEROEFFENTLICHUNGEN. 1949. irreg. price varies. Aschendorffsche Verlagsbuchhandlung, Soester Str. 13, 4400 Muenster, W. Germany (B.R.D.) Ed. Josef Glazik.
Missions

UNIVERSITE SAINT-JOSEPH. FACULTE DES LETTRES ET DES SCIENCES HUMAINES. RECHERCHE. SERIE B: ORIENT CHRETIEN. see ORIENTAL STUDIES

200 930 IT
VERBA SENIORUM. irreg. price varies. Edizioni Studium-Vita Nova, Via Crescenzio 63, 00193 Rome, Italy.

221 NE ISSN 0083-5889
VETUS TESTAMENTUM. SUPPLEMENTS. 1953. irreg., vol. 31, 1981. price varies. (International Organization for the Study of the Old Testament) E. J. Brill, Oude Rijn 33a-35, Leiden, Netherlands.

200 CN ISSN 0382-4926
VIE MONTANTE. EDITION CANADIENNE. 1973. irreg. 21, rue Ste-Elisabeth, Longueuil, Que., J4H 1J3, Canada. (newspaper)

200 CN ISSN 0507-1690
VITA EVANGELICA. French edition (ISSN 0315-5048) (Editions in English and French) 1965. irreg., no. 11, 1979. price varies. ‡ Canadian Religious Conference, 324 Laurier E., Ottawa, Ont. K1N 6P6, Canada. Ed. John Malo. circ. 3,500 (French edt.); 3,500 (English edt.)

200 FR
VIVANTE EGLISE. 1919. 10/yr. 48 F. Bayard Presse, 5, rue Bayard, 75380 Paris Cedex 08, France. circ. 10,250.

200 GW ISSN 0083-6923
VORREFORMATIONSGESCHICHTLICHE FORSCHUNGEN. 1902. irreg. price varies. Aschendorffsche Verlagsbuchhandlung, Soester Str. 13, 4400 Muenster, W. Germany (B.R.D.) Ed. Erwin Iserloh.

230 GW
WESTFALIA SACRA; Quellen und Forschungen zur Kirchengeschichte Westfalens. 1948. irreg. price varies. Aschendorffsche Verlagsbuchhandlung, Soester Str. 13, 4400 Muenster, W. Germany (B.R.D.) Ed. Alois Schroeer.

WHO'S WHO IN RELIGION. see BIOGRAPHY

200 SZ ISSN 0084-1676
WORLD COUNCIL OF CHURCHES. GENERAL ASSEMBLY. ASSEMBLY-REPORTS. (Text in English) 1948. irreg., 5th, 1975, 6th(expected 1983) price varies. World Council of Churches, 150 Route de Ferney, CH-1211 Geneva 20, Switzerland (Dist. in the U.S. by: Friendship Press, 475 Riverside Dr., Rm. 772, New York, NY 10027)

200 SZ ISSN 0084-1684
WORLD COUNCIL OF CHURCHES. MINUTES AND REPORTS OF THE CENTRAL COMMITTEE MEETING. (Text in English, French, German) 1948. approx. a, latest issue 1977. price varies. World Council of Churches, 150 Route de Ferney, CH-1211 Geneva 20, Switzerland (Dist. in the U.S. by: Friendship Press, 475 Riverside Dr., Rm. 772, New York, NY 10027)

200 SZ
WORLD STUDENT CHRISTIAN FEDERATION. DOSSIER. 1973. irreg. no. 10, 1975. price varies. World Student Christian Federation, 37, Quai Wilson, 1201 Geneva, Switzerland.

WORLD'S WISDOM SERIES. see PHILOSOPHY

200 US ISSN 0084-3407
YALE PUBLICATIONS IN RELIGION. irreg., no. 18, 1974. price varies. Yale University Press, 92A Yale Sta., New Haven, CT 06520.

200 US ISSN 0084-3644
YEARBOOK OF AMERICAN AND CANADIAN CHURCHES. 1916. a. $12.95. Abingdon, 201 Eighth Ave., So., Nashville, TN 37202. Ed. Constant H. Jacquet, Jr.
 Formerly: Yearbook of American Churches.

260 US ISSN 0084-4128
YEARBOOKS IN CHRISTIAN EDUCATION. 1969. a. price varies. (Lutheran Church in America, Board of Publication) Fortress Press, 2900 Queen Lane, Philadelphia, PA 19129.

200 UK ISSN 0085-8374
YORK JOURNAL OF CONVOCATION. 1856. irreg. £1.50. (Convocation of York) Church Information Office, Church House, Westminster, London S.W.1, England. Ed. Canon R. J. Graham. circ. 700 (controlled)

267.5 US ISSN 0084-4306
YOUNG WOMEN'S CHRISTIAN ASSOCIATION OF THE UNITED STATES OF AMERICA. THE PRINTOUT. a. membership. Young Women's Christian Association of the United States of America, National Board, 600 Lexington Ave., New York, NY 10022. Ed.Bd.

266 SA
YOUNG WORKER. (Natal, Cape and Transvaal editions avail.) 1976. irreg. R.1. (Young Christian Workers) Thrust Publications, Box 47160, Greyville 4023, South Africa. Ed. J. A. Boniaszczuk. circ. 10,000.

200   GW
ZEITSCHRIFT FUER DIE
ALTTESTAMENTLICHE WISSENSCHAFT.
BEIHEFTE. (Text in English and German) irreg.,
no. 153, 1980. DM.62($34.50) Walter de Gruyter
und Co., Genthiner Str. 13, 1000 Berlin 30, W.
Germany (B.R.D.) Ed. Georg Fohrer. bibl.

250   US   ISSN 0084-5558
ZONDERVAN PASTOR'S ANNUAL. a. $7.95.
Zondervan Publishing House, 1415 Lake Dr. S.E.,
Grand Rapids, MI 49506. Ed. Edward Viening. circ.
14,000. (reprint service avail. from UMI)

RELIGIONS AND THEOLOGY —
Abstracting, Bibliographies, Statistics

297 016   US   ISSN 0065-8847
AMERICAN INSTITUTE OF ISLAMIC STUDIES.
BIBLIOGRAPHIC SERIES. 1969. irreg. American
Institute of Islamic Studies, Box 10191, Denver, CO
80210.

200 314   VC
ANNUARIUM STATISTICUM ECCLESIAE/
STATISTIQUE DE L'EGLISE/STATISTICAL
YEARBOOK OF THE CHURCH. (Text in Latin,
English, French) 1969. a. L.16000. (Segretaria di
Stato, Ufficio Centrale di Statistica della Chiesa)
Libreria Editrice Vaticana, Vatican City, Italy.
charts. stat.
Formerly: Raccolta di Tavole Statistiche.

271   VC   ISSN 0570-7242
ARCHIVUM BIBLIOGRAPHICUM
CARMELITANUM. (Text in Latin and modern
languages) 1956. a. L.8000($10) Edizioni dei Padri
Carmelitani Scalzi, Piazza S. Pancrazio 5-A, 00152
Rome, Italy. Ed. Father Simeon de la Sagrada
Familia, O.C.D. circ. 700.

280.4 016   US   ISSN 0066-8710
ASSOCIATED CHURCH PRESS. DIRECTORY.
1947. a. $20 ($6 to libraries) Associated Church
Press, Box 306, Geneva, IL 60134. Ed. Donald F.
Hetzler. adv.
    Listing of Protestant publications in the United
States and Canada

255 011 920   IT
BIBLIOGRAPHIA FRANCISCANA. (Annual
supplement to Collectanea Franciscana) (Text in
Latin) 1931. a. price varies. Frati Minori
Cappuccini, Istituto Storico, Casella Postale 9091,
G.R.A. Km. 68,800, 00163 Rome, Italy. circ. 800.

296 016   US   ISSN 0067-6853
BIBLIOGRAPHICA JUDAICA. 1969. irreg., no. 8,
1977. Hebrew Union College-Jewish Institute of
Religion, 3101 Clifton Ave., Cincinnati, OH 45220.
Ed. Herbert C. Zafren.

282 011   US   ISSN 0008-8285
CATHOLIC PERIODICAL AND LITERATURE
INDEX. 1930. bi-m. with biennial cum. service
basis. Catholic Library Association, 461 W.
Lancaster Ave., Haverford, PA 19041. Ed.
Catherine M. Pilley. bk. rev. abstr. bibl. circ. 1,500.
(also avail. in microfilm from UMI)
    Former titles: Catholic Periodical Index (ISSN
0363-6895); Guide to Catholic Literature (ISSN
0145-191X)

282 011   US   ISSN 0008-8307
CATHOLIC PRESS DIRECTORY; official media
reference guide to Catholic newspapers and
magazines of the United States and Canada. 1923.
a. $10. Catholic Press Association, 119 North Park
Ave., Rockville Centre, NY 11570. Ed. Msgr. John
S. Randall. adv. index. circ. 2,000.

016.2
CURRENT CHRISTIAN BOOKS. a. Christian
Booksellers Association, Box 200, Colorado Springs,
CO 80901.
    Incorporating: Current Christian Books. Authors
and Titles (ISSN 0098-5554) & Current Christian
Books. Titles, Authors, and Publishers (ISSN 0098-
5562)

296 016   IS   ISSN 0073-5817
INDEX OF ARTICLES ON JEWISH STUDIES/
RESHIMAT MA'AMARIM BE-MADA'E HA-
YAHADUT. (Text in various languages) 1969.
biennial. I£80($10) single issue; IL£100 ($15)
double issue. ‡ Jewish National and University
Library, P.O. Box 503, Jerusalem, Israel. Ed. Dr.I.
Joel. circ. 1,200.

289 016   US   ISSN 0073-5981
INDEX TO PERIODICALS OF THE CHURCH OF
JESUS CHRIST OF LATTER-DAY SAINTS.
CUMULATIVE EDITION. 1966. a. $2 yearly;
$10.00 cum. 1961-1970. Church of Jesus Christ of
Latter-day Saints, 50 E. North Temple St., Salt
Lake City, UT 84150. circ. 3,000.

016 282   NE
KATHOLIEK DOCUMENTATIE CENTRUM.
BIBLIOGRAFIEEN. irreg. price varies. Katholiek
Documentatie Centrum, Erasmuslaan 36, 6525 GG
Nijmegen, Netherlands.

016 260   FR
OECUMENE; international bibliography indexed by
computer. (Text and summaries in English, French,
German & Italian) 1977. a. 80 F.($20) Universite de
Strasbourg II, Centre de Recherche et de
Documentation des Institutions Chretiennes, 9 Place
de l'Universite, 67084 Strasbourg Cedex, France. bk.
rev. circ. 1,000. (back issues avail.)

250   US
PASTORAL CARE AND COUNSELING
ABSTRACTS. 1972. a. $10. Virginia Institute of
Pastoral Care, Inc., c/o John L. Florell, 507 N.
Lombardy St., Richmond, VA 23220. bk. rev. circ.
400. (back issues avail.)

200   US   ISSN 0149-8436
RELIGION INDEX TWO: MULTI-AUTHOR
WORKS. 1978. a. $98. American Theological
Library Association, Religion Index Office, 600 S.
Woodlawn Ave., Chicago, IL 60637.

200 016   US   ISSN 0034-4044
RELIGIOUS & THEOLOGICAL ABSTRACTS.
1958. q. $32.50 to individuals; institutions $29.25.
Religious & Theological Abstracts Inc., Myerstown,
PA 17067. Ed. J. C. Christman. abstr. index. circ.
1,100. (also avail. in microfiche)

294.6   US   ISSN 0193-1466
SIKH RELIGIOUS STUDIES INFORMATION.
1979. irreg. $2 per no. Institute for Advanced
Studies of World Religions, Melville Memorial
Library, 5th Fl., State University of New York at
Stony Brook, Stony Brook, NY 11794. Ed. Richard
A. Gard.

200   UK   ISSN 0081-1440
SOCIETY FOR OLD TESTAMENT STUDY. BOOK
LIST. 1946. a. £2.75($6) ‡ Society for Old
Testament Study, c/o Rev. J. R. Duckworth, 109
Main Rd., Sidcup, Kent, England. Ed. R.N.
Whybray. index. circ. 1,800.

286 016   US   ISSN 0081-3028
SOUTHERN BAPTIST PERIODICAL INDEX. 1966.
a. $16.95. Southern Baptist Convention, Historical
Commission, 127 Ninth Ave. No., Nashville, TN
37234. circ. 350.

STUDIES IN BIBLIOGRAPHY AND BOOKLORE;
devoted to research in the field of Jewish
bibliography. see *PUBLISHING AND BOOK
TRADE — Abstracting, Bibliographies, Statistics*

296   US
STUDIES IN BIBLIOGRAPHY AND BOOKLORE.
1953. irreg., vol. 13, 1981. Hebrew Union College-
Jewish Institute of Religion, 3101 Clifton Ave.,
Cincinnati, OH 45220. Ed. Herbert C. Zafren.
Indexed: Amer.Hist. & Life. Hist.Abstr.
Ind.Jew.Per.

200 016   UK   ISSN 0306-087X
THEOLOGICAL AND RELIGIOUS INDEX. 1972.
irreg. £2. Theological Abstracting and
Bibliographical Services, 33 Mayfield Grove,
Harrogate, North Yorkshire HG1 5HD, England.
Ed. C.P. Cornish. bk. rev. circ. 150. (also avail. in
microfilm)

296 016   US
TZADDIKIM; a catalogue of Chassidic, Kabbalistic
and selected Judaic books. 1973. irreg. $2. ‡ Judaic
Book Service, 3726 Virden Ave., Oakland, CA
94619. adv. bk. rev. bibl. tr.lit. circ. 1,500.
(processed)

RELIGIONS AND THEOLOGY —
Islamic

268   NR   ISSN 0065-468X
AHMADU BELLO UNIVERSITY. CENTRE OF
ISLAMIC LEGAL STUDIES. JOURNAL. 1966.
irreg., vol. 5, 1974. Ahmadu Bello University,
Centre of Islamic Legal Studies, P.M.B. 1013, Zaria,
Nigeria (Overseas orders to: Wildy & Sons Ltd.,
Lincoln's Inn Archway, Carey St., London W.C. 2,
England)

297   NE
ASFAR. 1977. irreg. price varies. Rijksuniversiteit te
Leiden, Documentatiebureau Islam-Christendom,
Theologisch Instituut, Rapenburg 59, Leiden,
Netherlands.

956 297   GW   ISSN 0170-3102
BIBLIOTHECA ISLAMICA. (Text in English and
German) irreg., vol. 30, 1981. price varies.
(Deutsche Morgenlaendische Gesellschaft) Franz
Steiner Verlag GmbH, Friedrichstr. 24, Postfach
5529, 6200 Wiesbaden, W. Germany (B.R.D.) Ed.
Bd.

297.65   CN   ISSN 0707-2945
CANADIAN MUSLIM. (Text in English and Arabic)
1977. free contr. circ. Ottawa Muslim Association,
Box 2952, Sta. D, Ottawa, Ont. 51P 5W9, Canada.

CENTRE POUR L'ETUDE DES PROBLEMES DE
MONDE MUSULMAN CONTEMPORAIN.
INITIATIONS. see *HISTORY — History Of Asia*

CORRESPONDANCE D'ORIENT. see
HISTORY — History Of Asia

297   SP
CUADERNOS DE HISTORIA DEL ISLAM. 1967.
irreg. price varies. Universidad de Granada,
Facultad de Filosofia y Letras, Departamento de
Historia del Islam, Campus Universitario de Cartuja,
Granada, Spain. Ed. J. Bosch-Vila. adv. bk. rev. circ.
500.
    Formerly: Cuadernos de Historia del Islam. Serie
Monografica Islamica Occidentalia (ISSN 0070-
1696)

297   PK   ISSN 0002-399X
AL-DIRASAT AL-ISLAMIYAH. (Text in Arabic)
1965. q. $10. Islamic Research Institute, Box 1035,
Islamabad, Pakistan. Ed. M.A.R. Tahir Surti. bk.
rev. circ. 750. (back issues avail.)
Islamic studies

FREIBURGER ISLAMSTUDIEN. see *ORIENTAL
STUDIES*

297   US   ISSN 0075-0921
ISLAM IN PAPERBACK. (Subseries of the Institute's
Bibliographic Series) 1969. irreg. American Institute
of Islamic Studies, Box 10191, Denver, CO 80210.

297   US   ISSN 0362-1480
ISLAMIC STUDIES. 1973. irreg. American Institute
of Islamic Studies, Box 10191, Denver, CO 80210.

297   PK   ISSN 0541-5462
M.I.I. SERIES.* 1966. irreg. Muslim Intellectuals'
International, Box 5294, Karachi, Pakistan.

297   SI   ISSN 0559-2674
SEDAR; journal of Islamic studies. 1968. biennial.
S.$2. ‡ University of Singapore, Muslim Society,
Yusof Ishak House, Clementi Rd., Kent Ridge,
Singapore 5, Singapore. Ed. M. Dzulfighar Mohd.
adv. bibl.

297 400 LE
UNIVERSITE SAINT-JOSEPH. FACULTE DES LETTRES ET DES SCIENCES HUMAINES. RECHERCHE. SERIE A: LANGUE ARABE ET PENSEE ISLAMIQUE. (Previously published by its Institut des Lettres Orientales in 4 series) 1956; N.S. 1971. irreg., latest no. 11. price varies. Dar el-Mashreq, Imprimerie Catholique, 2 rue Huvelin, Box 946, Beirut, Lebanon (Subscr. to: Librairie Orientale, c/o Maroun Nehme, 106-108 Blvd. de Grenelle, 75015 Paris, France)

200 PK ISSN 0084-2052
WORLD MUSLIM CONFERENCE. PROCEEDINGS. (Published in: Muslim World) (Text in English) biennial. World Muslim Congress - Motamar al-Alam al-Islami, 224, Sharafabad, Karachi 0511, Pakistan.

297 PK ISSN 0084-2060
WORLD MUSLIM GAZETTEER. (Text in English) 1954. quinquennial. Rs.15. World Muslim Congress - Mozamar Al-Alam al-Islami, 224, Sharafabad, Karachi 0511, Pakistan. Ed. Inamullah Khan.

297 GW ISSN 0040-8646
WUDD; dedicated to the cause of Islam. 1970. a. DM.2. Hadayatullah Huebsch, Wickerer Str. 12, 6000 Frankfurt 1, W. Germany (B.R.D.) adv. bk. rev. charts.
Formerly: Toern.

ZIONISM; STUDIES IN THE HISTORY OF THE ZIONIST MOVEMENT AND OF THE JEWS IN PALESTINE/HA-TSIYONUT. see *RELIGIONS AND THEOLOGY — Judaic*

RELIGIONS AND THEOLOGY — Judaic

see also Ethnic Interests

A J S REVIEW. (Association for Jewish Studies) see *ETHNIC INTERESTS*

296 US ISSN 0065-6798
AMERICAN ACADEMY FOR JEWISH RESEARCH. PROCEEDINGS OF THE A A J R. 1939. a. $12.50 free to members. American Academy for Jewish Research, 3080 Broadway, New York, NY 10027 (Dist. by Kraus Reprint Corp., 16 E. 46 St., New York, N.Y. 10017) Ed. Isaac E. Barzilay.

296.67 US
AMERICAN JEWISH HISTORICAL SOCIETY. REPORT. 1968. irreg. $20 to members. ‡ American Jewish Historical Society, 2 Thornton Rd., Waltham, MA 02154. Ed. Bernard Wax. circ. 3,600.
Formerly (until 1976): American Jewish Historical Society. News (ISSN 0065-8944)

296 US ISSN 0065-8979
AMERICAN JEWISH ORGANIZATIONS DIRECTORY. 1957. biennial. $12. Frenkel Mailing Service, 24 Rutgers St., New York, NY 10002. Ed. Margaret Goldstein. adv. circ. 6,000.

296 US ISSN 0065-8987
AMERICAN JEWISH YEARBOOK. 1899. a. $15. (American Jewish Committee) Jewish Publication Society of America, 117 S. 17th St., Philadelphia, PA 19103. Eds. Morris Fine, Milton Himmelfarb. index.

296 NE ISSN 0066-5681
ARBEITEN ZUR GESCHICHTE DES ANTIKEN JUDENTUMS UND DES URCHRISTENTUMS. 1961. irreg., no. 15, 1978. price varies. (Institutum Iudaicum, Tuebingen, GW) E. J. Brill, Oude Rijn 33a-35, Leiden, Netherlands.

296 NE
ARBEITEN ZUR LITERATUR UND GESCHICHTE DES HELLENISTISCHEN JUDENTUMS. (Text in German) irreg., vol. 15, 1981. price varies. E. J. Brill, Oude Rijn 33a-35, Leiden, Netherlands.

296 US ISSN 0067-2742
B. G. RUDOLPH LECTURES IN JUDAIC STUDIES. 1963. a. free. ‡ Syracuse University, Department of Religion, Syracuse, NY 13210. Ed. A. Leland Jamison. circ. 7,500.

296 300 IS ISSN 0067-4109
BAR-ILAN: ANNUAL OF BAR-ILAN UNIVERSITY. (Text in Hebrew; summaries in English) 1963. a. $8. Bar-Ilan University, Ramat-Gan, Israel. Ed.Bd.

296 IS
BEER-SHEVA. (Text in Hebrew; summaries in English) 1973. a. Ben-Gurion University of the Negev, Box 2053, Beersheva, Israel. Eds. G. Blidstein, R. Bonfil and Y. Salmon. illus.

CANADIAN JEWISH ARCHIVES (NEW SERIES) see *ETHNIC INTERESTS*

296 US ISSN 0069-1607
CENTRAL CONFERENCE OF AMERICAN RABBIS. YEARBOOK. 1890. a. $15. ‡ Central Conference of American Rabbis, 790 Madison Ave., New York, NY 10021. Ed. Elliot L. Stevens. cum.index (1951-1970) circ. 1,500.

296 SP
COLECCION SENDA ABIERTA. SERIE II (AZUL): JUDAISMO. 1974. irreg. 150 ptas. (Centro de Estudios Judeo-Cristianos) Studium Ediciones, Bailen 19, Madrid 13, Spain.

CONFERENCE OF PRESIDENTS OF MAJOR AMERICAN JEWISH ORGANIZATIONS. REPORT. see *ETHNIC INTERESTS*

296 IS
ENCYCLOPAEDIA JUDAICA YEAR BOOK. (Text in English) 1973. a. Keter Publishing House Ltd., Givat Shaul Industrial Area, P.O.B. 7145, Jerusalem, Israel. Ed. Rabbi Professor L.I. Rabinowitz.

FOLK LITERATURE OF THE SEPHARDIC JEWS. see *LITERATURE*

296 US ISSN 0016-9145
GESHER. (Text in English and Hebrew) a. $5. Yeshiva University, Student Organization of Yeshiva, 500 W. 185th St., New York, NY 10033. Ed. Bd.

GRATZ COLLEGE ANNUAL OF JEWISH STUDIES. see *ETHNIC INTERESTS*

HARVARD JUDAIC MONOGRAPHS. see *ETHNIC INTERESTS*

HEBREW UNION COLLEGE ANNUAL. see *ETHNIC INTERESTS*

HEBREW UNION COLLEGE ANNUAL SUPPLEMENTS. see *ETHNIC INTERESTS*

268 US
HOLY BEGGARS' GAZETTE; journal of Chassidic Judaism. 1971. irreg. Judaic Book Service, 3726 Virden Ave., Oakland, CA 94619. Ed. Steven Maimes. bk. rev. bibl.

296 US ISSN 0075-3726
JEWISH BOOK ANNUAL. (Text in English, Hebrew and Yiddish) 1942. a. $15. National Jewish Welfare Board, Jewish Book Council, 15 E. 26th St., New York, NY 10010. Ed. Jacob Kabakoff. bk. rev. circ. 1,200.

296 US
JEWISH HISTORICAL SOCIETY OF DELAWARE. NEWSLETTER. 1975. irreg. membership. Jewish Historical Society of Delaware, 701 Brandywine Blvd., Wilmington, DE 19801.

909 UK ISSN 0306-7998
JEWISH HISTORICAL SOCIETY OF ENGLAND. ANNUAL REPORT AND ACCOUNTS FOR THE SESSION. 1964. a. membership. Jewish Historical Society of England, Mocatta Library & Museum, University College, 33 Seymour Place, London W1H 5AP, England.
Continues: Jewish Historical Society of England. Report and Balance Sheet.

296 NE
JEWISH LAW ANNUAL. 1978. a. fl.84. E.J. Brill, Oude Rijn 33a-35, Leiden, Netherlands. Ed.Bernard S. Jackson.

296 UK ISSN 0075-3769
JEWISH YEAR BOOK. 1896. a. £2($15.50) Jewish Chronicle Publications, 25 Furnival St, London EC4A 1JT, England. Ed. Michael Wallach. adv. bk. rev. circ. 5,000. (also avail. in microform)

JOURNAL OF JEWISH ART. see *ART*

JOURNAL OF JEWISH MUSIC AND LITURGY. see *MUSIC*

296 UK ISSN 0075-8744
LEO BAECK INSTITUTE. YEAR BOOK. (Text in English; occasionally German) 1956. a. £7.50. Secker & Warburg, 14 Carlisle Street, Soho Square, London W. 1, England (Dist. by Kraus-Thomson, Route 100, Millwood, N Y 10546 and Kraus-Thomson, Nendeln, Liechtenstein) Ed. Robert Weltsch. bk. rev. index. cum. index in preparation. circ. 2,500. Indexed: Hist.Abstr. Amer.Hist.& Life.

296 US
LIBRARY OF JEWISH LAW AND ETHICS. vol. 4, 1977. irreg. $12.50. Ktav Publishing House, 75 Varick St., New York, NY 10013.

HA-MESIVTA. see *LAW*

296 IS ISSN 0541-5632
MITZION TETZEH TORAH. M.T.T. 1968. irreg.; (approx. 2/yr.) price varies. Mitzion Tetzeh Torah, Ltd., P.O.B. 29435, 9 Derech Haifa Rd., Tel-Aviv, Israel. Ed. G. Rachaman. adv. bk. rev. circ. 1,000.

MUSICA JUDAICA. see *MUSIC*

296 IS ISSN 0048-0460
NIV HAMIDRASHIA. (Text in Hebrew and English) 1963. irreg. I£20. Friends of the Midrashia, Israel, A25 Lilienblum Str., Tel Aviv, Israel. Eds. Israel Sadan, Alexander Carlebach. circ. 5,000.

296 UK ISSN 0079-0052
PARKES LIBRARY PAMPHLETS. 1954. irreg. price varies. ‡ University of Southampton, Library, Highfield, Southampton, Hants SO9 5NH, England.

296 US ISSN 0079-936X
RABBINICAL ASSEMBLY, NEW YORK. PROCEEDINGS. (Text in English with some Hebrew and Yiddish) 1927. a (suspended 1970-1973) $6.50. Rabbinical Assembly, 3080 Broadway, New York, NY 10027. Ed. J. Harlow. cum.index: 1927-1968. circ. 1,400.

296 US
RECONSTRUCTIONIST RABBINICAL COLLEGE. PUBLICATIONS. 1977. irreg. price varies. Ktav Publishing House, 75 Varick St., New York, NY 10013.

SEMITIC STUDY SERIES. see *ORIENTAL STUDIES*

296 NE ISSN 0080-8881
SEMITIC TEXTS WITH TRANSLATIONS. (Titles in English and Dutch) 1965. irreg. price varies. Van Gorcum, Box 43, Assen, Netherlands.

SHVUT; Jewish problems in the USSR and Eastern Europe. see *ETHNIC INTERESTS*

296 US
SOLOMON GOLDMAN LECTURES; perspectives in Jewish learning. 1977. irreg. $5 paperback; $7 hardback. Spertus College of Judaica Press, 618 S. Michigan Avenue, Chicago, IL 60605. circ. 500.
Supersedes: Perspectives in Jewish Learning (ISSN 0079-1016)

SOURCES OF CONTEMPORARY JEWISH THOUGHT/MEKEVOT. see *LITERARY AND POLITICAL REVIEWS*

296 NE ISSN 0081-6914
STUDIA SEMITICA NEERLANDICA. 1956. irreg., no. 16, 1974. price varies. Van Gorcum, Box 43, Assen, Netherlands (Dist. by ISBS, P.O. Box 4347, Portland, OR 97208)

296 US ISSN 0081-7511
STUDIES IN AMERICAN JEWISH HISTORY. 1951. irreg., 1968, no.5. price varies. ‡ American Jewish Historical Society, 2 Thornton Rd., Waltham, MA 02154. index. circ. 1,000.

296　　　US　ISSN 0585-6833
STUDIES IN JUDAICA. 1963. irreg., vol. 6, 1975. price varies. Yeshiva University, 186 St. and Amsterdam Avenue, New York, NY 10033.

SURVEY OF CURRENT JEWISH RESEARCH. see EDUCATION — Higher Education

296　　　NE　ISSN 0082-3899
THEOKRATIA; JAHRBUCH DES INSTITUTUM JUDAICUM DELITZSCHIANUM. 1967-69. a. price varies. (Institutum Judaicum Delitzschianum) E. J. Brill, Oude Rijn 33a-35, Leiden, Netherlands.

TZADDIKIM REVIEW. see ETHNIC INTERESTS

296.8　　　US　ISSN 0363-3810
UNION OF AMERICAN HEBREW CONGREGATIONS. STATE OF OUR UNION. biennial. Union of American Hebrew Congregations, 838 Fifth Ave., New York, NY 10021.

WOMEN'S ZIONIST COUNCIL OF SOUTH AFRICA. NEWS AND VIEWS. see POLITICAL SCIENCE — Civil Rights

956.940　　　IS
WORD AND DEED. (Text in English) irreg. World Zionist Organization, Youth and Hechalutz Department, Box 92, Jerusalem, Israel.

WORKING PAPERS IN YIDDISH AND EAST EUROPEAN JEWISH STUDIES/IN GANG FUN ARBET: YIDISH UN MIZRAKH EYROPEISHE YIDISHE SHTUDIES. see ETHNIC INTERESTS

296　　　IS　ISSN 0084-2516
WORLD ZIONIST ORGANIZATION. GENERAL COUNCIL. ADDRESSES, DEBATES, RESOLUTIONS.* (Text in English) a. World Zionist Organization, P.O.B. 92, Jerusalem, Israel.

296　　　IS
YAD VASHEM STUDIES. (Text in English and Hebrew) 1957. irreg., vol. 13. 1979. price varies. Yad Vashem Martyr's and Heroes Remembrance Authority, P.O.B. 3477, Jerusalem, Israel. Ed. Livia Rothkirchen. bk. rev. index. cum.index: 1957-67. circ. 1,500.
　　Formerly (until 1976): Yad Vashem Studies on the European Jewish Catastrophe and Resistance (ISSN 0084-3296)

296　　　US　ISSN 0084-3369
YALE JUDAICA SERIES. 1948. irreg., no. 22, 1980. price varies. Yale University Press, 92A Yale Sta., New Haven, CT 06520.

296　　　IS　ISSN 0084-5523
ZIONISM; STUDIES IN THE HISTORY OF THE ZIONIST MOVEMENT AND OF THE JEWS IN PALESTINE/HA-TSIYONUT. (Text in Hebrew; occasionally in English) 1970. a. Tel Aviv University, Institute for Zionist Research, Tel Aviv, Israel. Ed. Daniel Carpi. circ. 1,000.

RELIGIONS AND THEOLOGY — Oriental

BRAHMAVIDYA. see ORIENTAL STUDIES

294.3　　　II
BUDDHIST STUDIES. (Text in English, Hindi and Sanskrit) 1974. a. Rs.10. University of Delhi, Department of Buddhist Studies, Delhi 110007, India.

200　　　US
BUTSUMON. 1976. irreg. Buddhist Bookstore, 1710 Octavia St., San Francisco, CA 94109. illus. (tabloid format)

294.3　　　US　ISSN 0097-7209
CRYSTAL MIRROR. 1971. a. (Tibetan Nyingma Meditation Center) Dharma Publishing, 2425 Hillside Ave., Berkeley, CA 94704. illus.

DIVINE PATH. see PHILOSOPHY

294.3　　　US　ISSN 0046-5445
GARUDA. 1971. a. ‡ Vajradhatu, 1345 Spruce St., Boulder, CO 80302. Ed.Bd. illus. circ. 10,000.

294.3　　　JA
INSTITUTE FOR THE COMPREHENSIVE STUDY OF LOTUS SUTRA. JOURNAL/HOKKE BUNKA KENKYU. (Text in English or Japanese) 1975. a. Rissho University, Institute for the Comprehensive Study of Lotus Sutra - Rissho Daigaku Hokekyo Bunka Kenkyujo, 4-2-16 Osaki, Shinagawa-ku, Tokyo 141, Japan. illus.

294　　　II　ISSN 0554-9906
PRAKIT JAIN INSTITUTE RESEARCH PUBLICATION SERIES. (Text in English and Hindi) 1964. irreg. price varies. Bihar Research Institute of Prakit, Jainology, and Ahimsa, Vaishali, India. Ed. G. C. Choudhary.

294.5　　　II
SIDDHA VANI. (Text in English or Hindi) 1972. a. Rs.6($1.50) Siddha Yoga Dham, S-174 Panch Shila Park, New Delhi 110017, India. Ed. Janak Nanda. adv. illus. circ. 2,000.

290　　　GW　ISSN 0340-6792
STUDIES IN ORIENTAL RELIGIONS. (Text in English and German) 1976. irreg., vol. 5, 1979. price varies. Verlag Otto Harrassowitz, Taunusstr. 6, Postfach 2929, 6200 Wiesbaden, W. Germany (B.R.D.) Eds. W. Heissig, H.-J. Klimkeit.

294　　　TH　ISSN 0084-1781
WORLD FELLOWSHIP OF BUDDHISTS. BOOK SERIES. 1965. irreg., latest issue, 1977. price varies. World Fellowship of Buddhists, 33 Sukhumvit Rd., Bangkok-11, Thailand.

294.3　　　SI
YOUNG BUDDHIST. (Text in English and Chinese) a. Singapore Buddhist Youth Organisations Joint Celebrations Committee, 83 Silat Road, Singapore 3, Singapore. illus.

294.3　　　US
ZEN WRITINGS. 1977. irreg., approx. 2/yr. Zen Center of Los Angeles, 927 S. Normandie Ave., Los Angeles, CA 90006. illus.
　　Supersedes (after 1975): Z.C.L.A. Journal (ISSN 0360-991X)

RELIGIONS AND THEOLOGY — Protestant

268　　　US　ISSN 0001-9674
AFFIRMATION. 1967. irreg. free. Union Theological Seminary in Virginia, 3401 Brook Road, Richmond, VA 23227. Ed. Kenneth Hood. bibl. illus. circ. 4,000.

264.03　　　UK
ALCUIN. 1974. a. Alcuin Club, 5 St. Andrew St., London EC4A 3AB, England.

286　　　US　ISSN 0092-3478
AMERICAN BAPTIST CHURCHES IN THE U. S. A. YEARBOOK. 1907. a. $4. American Baptist Churches in the U.S.A., Valley Forge, PA 19481. Ed. Robert C. Campbell. illus. circ. 3,500. Key Title: Yearbook of the American Baptist Churches in the U. S. A.

286　　　US　ISSN 0091-9381
AMERICAN BAPTIST CHURCHES IN THE U.S.A. DIRECTORY. 1971. a. $4. ‡ American Baptist Churches in the U.S.A., Valley Forge, PA 19481. Ed. Robert C. Campbell. circ. 6,000.
　　Supersedes in part: American Baptist Convention. Yearbook.

284　　　US　ISSN 0569-6348
AMERICAN LUTHERAN CHURCH. YEARBOOK. 1960. a. $3. Augsburg Publishing House, 426 S. 5th St., Minneapolis, MN 55415. Ed. Arnold R. Mickelson. adv.

286　　　US　ISSN 0066-1708
ANDREWS UNIVERSITY. MONOGRAPHS. 1966. irreg., 1973, vol. 7. $5.95. ‡ Andrews University Press, Berrien Springs, MI 49104. Ed. Dr. James J. C. Cox. adv. bk. rev.

283　　　CN　ISSN 0380-2469
ANGLICAN CHURCH OF CANADA. GENERAL SYNOD. JOURNAL OF PROCEEDINGS. 1894. triennial. Anglican Church of Canada, General Synod, 600 Jarvis Street, Toronto, Ont. M4Y 2J6, Canada. adv. bk. rev. circ. 450.

266　　　CN　ISSN 0317-8765
ANGLICAN YEAR BOOK. 1900. a. Can.$10.50. Anglican Church of Canada, General Synod, 600 Jarvis St., Toronto, Ont. M4Y 2J6, Canada. adv. charts. stat. circ. 1,000.

284　　　FR　ISSN 0066-362X
ANNUAIRE PROTESTANT; LA FRANCE PROTESTANTE ET LES EGLISES DE LANGUE FRANCAISE. 1922, 40th ed. a. 45 F. (Centrale du Livre Protestant) Librairie Fischbacher, 33 rue de Seine, 75 Paris 6, France.

266　　　US　ISSN 0091-2743
BAPTIST MISSIONARY ASSOCIATION OF AMERICA. DIRECTORY AND HANDBOOK. 1961. a. ‡ Baptist News Service, P.O. Box 97, Jacksonville, TX 75766. Ed. Leon Gaylor. circ. 5,000. Key Title: Directory and Handbook - Baptist Missionary Association of America.
Missions

266　　　UK　ISSN 0067-4060
BAPTIST MISSIONARY SOCIETY, LONDON. ANNUAL REPORT. 1792. a. 10p. Baptist Missionary Society, 93 Gloucester Place, London, W1H 4AA, England. circ. 7,000.
Missions

266.6　　　UK　ISSN 0067-4079
BAPTIST MISSIONARY SOCIETY, LONDON. OFFICIAL REPORT AND DIRECTORY OF MISSIONARIES. 1793. a. 15p. Baptist Missionary Society, 93 Gloucester Place, London W1H 4AA, England. circ. 6,000.
Missions

286.1　　　UK　ISSN 0302-3184
BAPTIST UNION DIRECTORY. 1861. a. Baptist Union of Great Britain and Ireland, 4, Southampton Row, London WC1B 4AB, England. Ed. Dr. D. S. Russell. adv. circ. 2,500.

286　　　CN　ISSN 0067-4087
BAPTIST UNION OF WESTERN CANADA. YEAR BOOK. 1907. a. Can.$4.75. Baptist Union of Western Canada, 4404 16 St. S.W., Calgary, Alta. T2T 4H9, Canada. Ed. Rev. H.A. Renfree. circ. 600 (controlled) (also avail. in microfilm)

286　　　US　ISSN 0067-4095
BAPTIST WORLD ALLIANCE. CONGRESS REPORTS. 1905. quinquennial; 13th, Stockholm, 1975 (published in 1976) $7.50. ‡ Baptist World Alliance, 1628 Sixteenth St., N.W., Washington, DC 20009. Ed. Cyril E. Bryant. circ. 8,000.

267　　　UK
C W M REPORT. 1795. biennial. 20p. Council for World Mission (Congregational and Reformed), 11 Carteret St., London SW1H 9DL, England. Ed. Brian H. Bailey. circ. 26,000.
　　Formerly: Congregational Council for World Mission. Annual Report (ISSN 0069-8857)
Missions

200　　　UK
CALENDARS AND INDEXES TO THE LETTERS AND PAPERS OF THE ARCHBISHOPS OF CANTERBURY IN LAMBETH PALACE LIBRARY. 1975. irreg. price varies. Mansell Publishing, 3 Bloomsbury Place, London WC1A 2QA, England (Dist. in U.S. by: Mansell, Merrimack Book Service, 99 Main St., Salem, NH 03079)

283　　　UK　ISSN 0069-3987
CHURCH OF ENGLAND YEARBOOK. 1882. a. £9 (includes statistical supplement) C I O Publishing, Church House, Dean's Yard, London SW1P 3NZ, England. adv. bk. rev. circ. 3,000.

285.241　　　UK　ISSN 0069-3995
CHURCH OF SCOTLAND. YEARBOOK. 1885. a. £4. Church of Scotland, Department of Publicity and Publication, 121 George St., Edinburgh EH2 4YN, Scotland. Ed. Rev. Andrew Herron. adv. index. circ. 3,000.

283　　　CN　ISSN 0382-4314
CRUSADER (TORONTO) vol. 44, 1973. irreg. Church Army in Canada, 397 Brunswick Ave., Toronto, Ont. M5R 2Z2, Canada. illus.
　　Continues: Anglican Crusader (ISSN 0382-4306)

DEUTSCHER HUGENOTTEN-VEREIN E.V. GESCHICHTSBLAETTER. see HISTORY — History Of Europe

284 CN ISSN 0702-844X
END-TIME NEWS. 1970. irreg. Solbrekken Evangelistic Association, Box 2424, Edmonton, Alta., Canada. illus.
Formerly: Edmonton Revival Centre. News (ISSN 0702-8458)

280 FR ISSN 0071-1330
ESPRIT ET LIBERTE; Protestantisme liberal. 1956. irreg., 1973, no. 24. 24 F. Librairie Fischbacher, 33 rue de Seine, 75-Paris 6, France.

286.1 CN ISSN 0317-266X
EVANGELICAL BAPTIST CHURCHES IN CANADA. FELLOWSHIP YEARBOOK. 1959. a. Fellowship of Evangelical Baptist Churches in Canada, 74 Sheppard Ave. W, Willowdale, Ont. M2N 1M3, Canada. illus. Key Title: Fellowship Yearbook.
Formerly: Missions Digest and Year Book (ISSN 0544-439X)

284 FR ISSN 0071-9064
FRANCE PROTESTANTE. 1952. a. 25 F. c/o Pasteur F. Delforge, Ed., 47 rue de Clichy, Paris (9e), France.

266 285 AT ISSN 0016-2108
FRONTIER NEWS. 1930. a. free. Australian Inland Mission Frontier Service, Australian Inland Mission, 123 Clarence St., Sydney, N.S.W. 2000, Australia. Ed. Rev. Max Griffiths. charts. illus. stat. circ. 17,500. (tabloid format)
Missions

200 CK
GUIA ECLESIASTICA LATINOAMERICANA. 1977. irreg. Consejo Episcopal Latinoamericano, Secretariado General, Apdo. Aereo 1931, Bogota, Colombia.

200 UK
HISTORICAL SOCIETY OF THE CHURCH IN WALES. JOURNAL. 1946. a. £2. Historical Society of the Church in Wales, c/o Owen W. Jones, The Vicarage, Builth Wells, Brec, Wales. Ed. Canon David Walker. charts. stat.

940 200 UK
HISTORICAL SOCIETY OF THE PRESBYTERIAN CHURCH OF WALES. JOURNAL. (Text in English and Welsh) 1916. a. 50p. Historical Society of the Presbyterian Church of Wales, The Manse, Caradog Rd., Aberystwyth, Dyfed, Wales. Ed. Rev. Gomer M. Roberts. bk. rev. circ. 600.

286 016 US ISSN 0073-5825
INDEX OF GRADUATE THESES IN BAPTIST THEOLOGICAL SEMINARIES. 1963. triennial. $5. Southern Baptist Convention, Historical Commission, 127 Ninth Ave. N., Nashville, TN 37234. Ed. Lynn E. May, Jr. circ. 200. (also avail. in microfilm)

284 IO
INDONESIA. DIRECTORATE GENERAL OF PROTESTANT AFFAIRS. ANNUAL REPORT/ INDONESIA. DIREKTORAT JENDERAL BIMBINGAN MASYARAKAT KRISTEN/ PROTESTAN LAPORAN TAHUNAN. (Text in Indonesian) a. Directorate General of Protestant Affairs, Jalan Moh. Husni Thamrin, Jakarta, Indonesia.

286 CN ISSN 0383-6061
INTERCOM. 1968. irreg. Fellowship of Evangelical Baptist Churches in Canada, 74 Sheppard Ave. W., Willowdale, Ont. M2N 1M3, Canada.

286.0415 UK ISSN 0075-0727
IRISH BAPTIST HISTORICAL SOCIETY. JOURNAL. 1969. a. £1. Baptist Union of Ireland, 3 Fitzwilliam St., Belfast BT9 6AW, Northern Ireland. Ed. Maurice Dowling. circ. 200.

274 GW ISSN 0075-6210
KIRCHLICHES JAHRBUCH FUER DIE EVANGELISCHE KIRCHE IN DEUTSCHLAND. a. price varies. Guetersloher Verlagshaus Gerd Mohn, Koenigstr. 23, Postfach 2368, 4830 Guetersloh, W. Germany (B.R.D.)

268 284.1 US ISSN 0076-1532
L E A YEARBOOK. a. Lutheran Education Association, 7400 Augusta Blvd., River Forest, IL 60305.

266.6 LB
LIBERIA BAPTIST MISSIONARY AND EDUCATIONAL CONVENTION. YEARBOOK. (Text in English) a. Liberia Baptist Missionary and Educational Convention, Bentol City, Liberia. illus.

266 US
LIBRARY OF PROTESTANT THOUGHT. irreg. price varies. Oxford University Press, 200 Madison Ave., New York, NY 10016 (And Ely House, 37 Dover St., London W1X 4AH, England)

284 US
LUTHERAN ANNUAL. 1910. a. $3.50 paper, $5.95 hardcover. ‡ (Lutheran Church-Missouri Synod) Concordia Publishing House, 3558 S. Jefferson Ave., St. Louis, MO 63118. Ed. Dr. Ralph R. Reinke. adv. circ. 30,000.

284 CN ISSN 0460-024X
LUTHERAN CHURCH IN AMERICA. WESTERN CANADA SYNOD. MINUTES OF THE ANNUAL CONVENTION. 1962. a. Lutheran Church in America, Western Canada Synod, 9901 107th Street, Edmonton, Alberta T5K 1G4, Canada.

284 AT
LUTHERAN CHURCH OF AUSTRALIA. YEARBOOK. 1967. a. Aus.$3. Lutheran Publishing House, 205 Halifax Street, Adelaide, S.A. 5000, Australia. Ed. E. W. Wiebusch.
Formed by the merger of: Australian Lutheran Almanac & Lutheran Almanac.

284 CN ISSN 0316-800X
LUTHERAN CHURCHES IN CANADA. DIRECTORY. 1954. a. Can.$2. ‡ Lutheran Council in Canada, 500-365 Hargrave St., Winnipeg, Man. R3B 2K3, Canada. Ed. Walter A. Schultz. adv. circ. 1,300.

284.1 US ISSN 0076-1540
LUTHERAN WORLD FEDERATION. PROCEEDINGS OF THE ASSEMBLY. irreg., 1970, 5th, Evian-Les-Bains, France. Augsburg Publishing House, 426 South 5th St., Minneapolis, MN 55415.

288 US ISSN 0360-7046
M S U U NEWSLETTER. 1974. irreg. membership. Ministerial Sisterhood Unitarian Universalist, c/o Rev. Marjorie N. Leaming, 438 View Dr., Santa Paula, CA 93060. circ. 100.

287 SW ISSN 0543-6206
METODISTKYRKANS I SVERIGE. AARSBOK. 1967. a. Kr.10. Foerlaget Sanctus, Box 5020, 102 41 Stockholm, Sweden. stat.

266 284 US ISSN 0093-8130
MISSION HANDBOOK: NORTH AMERICAN PROTESTANT MINISTRIES OVERSEAS. 1951. triennial. $15. Missions Advanced Research and Communication Center, 919 W. Huntington Dr., Monrovia, CA 91016. Ed. Edward R. Dayton. index.
Formerly: North American Protestant Ministries Overseas (ISSN 0078-1339)
Missions

266 UK ISSN 0077-3557
NATIONAL BIBLE SOCIETY OF SCOTLAND. ANNUAL REPORT. 1860. a. free. National Bible Society of Scotland, 7-8 Hampton Terrace, Edinburgh EH12 5XU, Scotland. circ. 20,000.

260 US
NATIONAL COUNCIL OF THE CHURCHES OF CHRIST IN THE U.S.A. TRIENNIAL REPORT. 1946. triennial. $3.50. National Council of the Churches of Christ in the U.S.A., 475 Riverside Dr, New York, NY 10027. Ed. Joseph P. Schmelter. circ. 10-15,000.
Formerly: National Council of the Churches of Christ in the United States of America. Church World Service. Annual Report (ISSN 0077-4111)

260 US ISSN 0077-412X
NATIONAL COUNCIL OF THE CHURCHES OF CHRIST IN THE UNITED STATES OF AMERICA. DIVISION OF OVERSEAS MINISTRIES. OVERSEAS MINISTRIES. 1965. triennial. $1. National Council of the Churches of Christ in the U.S.A., Division of Overseas Ministries, Rm. 656, 475 Riverside Dr., New York, NY 10115. circ. 5,000.

268 UK ISSN 0079-0117
PARTNERS IN LEARNING. 1968. a. £2.50. Methodist Church, Division of Education and Youth, 2 Chester House, Pages Lane, London N10 1PR, England (and National Christian Education Council, Robert Denholm House, Nutfield, Redhill RH1 4HW Surrey, England) Ed. Brian J. Sharp. circ. 28,000.

205 US
R E S WORLD DIACONAL BULLETIN. irreg. Reformed Ecumenical Synod, 1677 Gentian Dr. S.E., Grand Rapids, MI 49508.

284 GW ISSN 0080-0473
REFORMATIONSGESCHICHTLICHE STUDIEN UND TEXTE. 1906. irreg., vol. 116, 1978. price varies. Aschendorffsche Verlagsbuchhandlung, Soester Str. 13, 4400 Muenster, W. Germany (B.R.D.) Ed. Erwin Iserloh.

280 US ISSN 0080-0481
REFORMED CHURCH OF AMERICA. HISTORICAL SERIES. irreg., 1970, no. 2. Wm. B. Eerdmans Publishing Co., 255 Jefferson Ave., S.E., Grand Rapids, MI 49503.

267 UK ISSN 0080-8016
SCOTTISH EPISCOPAL CHURCH YEARBOOK. 1879. a. £2.50. ‡ Scottish Episcopal Church, 21 Grosvenor Crescent, Edinburgh EH12 5EE, Scotland. Ed. Rev. Canon F. F. Laming. index. circ. 800.

286 016 US ISSN 0081-3001
SOUTHERN BAPTIST CONVENTION. ANNUAL. 1845. a. $7.50. Southern Baptist Convention, 460 James Robertson Parkway, Nashville, TN 37219. Ed. Clifton J. Allen. subject index cumulated irregularly, 1953 (1845-1953), 1965 (1954-1965) circ. 35,000. (also avail. in microfilm)

286 016 US ISSN 0081-301X
SOUTHERN BAPTIST CONVENTION. HISTORICAL COMMISSION. MICROFILM CATALOGUE. 1954. a. $1.50. Southern Baptist Convention, Historical Commission, 127 Ninth Ave. No., Nashville, TN 37234. Ed. Lynn E. May, Jr. circ. 1,500.

284 AU
STUDIEN UND TEXTE ZUR KIRCHENGESCHICHTE UND GESCHICHTE. (Consists of two series) 1975. irreg., vol. 4 (series 1), vol. 3 (series 2), 1979. price varies. Hermann Boehlaus Nachf., Schmalzhofgasse 4, Postfach 167, A-1061 Vienna, Austria. Ed. Peter Barton. circ. 800. (back issues avail.)

251 SZ ISSN 0081-7406
STUDIENTAGE FUER DIE PFARRER; eine Sammlung von Vortraegen. 1962. irreg., 1968, no. 6. price varies. (Synodalrat der Evangelisch-Reformierten Landeskirche des Kantons Bern) Paul Haupt AG, Falkenplatz 14, 3001 Berne, Switzerland.

267 UK
UNITARIAN AND FREE CHRISTIAN CHURCHES. HANDBOOK AND DIRECTORY OF THE GENERAL ASSEMBLY. 1890. a(directory; quinquennial(handbook) £1. General Assembly of Unitarian Free Christian Churches, Essex Hall, 1-6 Essex St., Strand, London, WC2R 3HY, England. Ed. Christine Hayhurst. circ. 850.
Formerly: Unitarian and Free Christian Churches. Yearbook of the General Assembly (ISSN 0082-7797)

288 900 US ISSN 0082-7819
UNITARIAN HISTORICAL SOCIETY. PROCEEDINGS. 1925. a. or biennal; latest vol. 18. $5 per part (2 parts per vol.) Unitarian Historical Society, c/o Conrad Wright, Harvard Divinity School, Andover Hall, Cambridge, MA 02138. Ed. Harold F. Worthley. bk. rev. circ. 250.

288 UK ISSN 0082-7800
UNITARIAN HISTORICAL SOCIETY, LONDON. TRANSACTIONS. 1917. a. £3 to institutions. c/o Miss H. M. Summerskill, 4 Allerton Drive, Liverpool 18, England. Ed. Rev. Dr. H.J. McLachlan. bk. rev. index every 4 years. circ. 325. (also avail. in microform from UMI)

266 US ISSN 0082-7827
UNITARIAN UNIVERSALIST DIRECTORY. 1961. a. $10. Unitarian Universalist Association, 25 Beacon St., Boston, MA 02108. Ed. Rev. Carl Seaburg. adv. circ. 2,500. (also avail. in microform from UMI)

286 CN ISSN 0082-7843
UNITED BAPTIST CONVENTION OF THE ATLANTIC PROVINCES. YEARBOOK. 1963. a. price varies. United Baptist Convention of the Atlantic Provinces, Box 7053, Sta. A, Saint John, N.B. E2L 4S5, Canada. Ed. Dr. Keith R. Hobson. index. circ. 2,200.

200 CN ISSN 0082-786X
UNITED CHURCH OF CANADA. COMMITTEE ON ARCHIVES. BULLETIN. RECORDS AND PROCEEDINGS. 1948. a. Can.$3.50. United Church of Canada, Committee on Archives, Victoria University, 73 Queen's Park Cres., Toronto, Ont. M5S 2C4, Canada. Ed. Rev. C. G. Lucas. circ. 1,200.

200 CN ISSN 0082-7878
UNITED CHURCH OF CANADA. GENERAL COUNCIL. RECORD OF PROCEEDINGS. 1925. biennial. United Church of Canada, General Council, 85 St. Clair Ave. E., Toronto, Ont. M47 1M8, Canada. circ. 4,000.

200 CN ISSN 0082-7886
UNITED CHURCH OF CANADA. YEAR BOOK. 1925. a. United Church of Canada, 85 St. Clair Ave. E., Toronto, Ont. M4T 1M8, Canada. circ. 4,000.

285.241 UK ISSN 0082-7908
UNITED FREE CHURCH OF SCOTLAND. HANDBOOK. 1930. a. (Communications Board) United Free Church of Scotland, 11 Newton Place, Glasgow G3 7PR, Scotland.

287 US ISSN 0160-0885
UNITED METHODIST CHURCH. CURRICULUM PLANS. a. $3. United Methodist Church, Board of Discipleship, Curriculum Resources Committee, 201 8th Ave. S., Nashville, TN 37202. Key Title: Curriculum Plans.

287 US ISSN 0503-3551
UNITED METHODIST CHURCH. GENERAL MINUTES OF THE ANNUAL CONFERENCES. 1968. a. $9 paperbound; $13 clothbound. United Methodist Church, Department of Statistics, 1200 Davis St., Evanston, IL 60201. illus. Key Title: General Minutes of the Annual Conferences of the United Methodist Church.

268 US ISSN 0082-7983
UNITED METHODIST CHURCH (UNITED STATES) DIVISION OF EDUCATION. ADULT PLANBOOK. 1959. a. free. (United Methodist Church, Division of Education. Department of Adult Publications) United Methodist Publishing House, Graded Press, 201 Eighth Ave. S., Nashville, TN 37203. Ed. Ewart G. Watts. bk. rev. circ. 200,000.

287.6 US ISSN 0503-356X
UNITED METHODIST DIRECTORY. irreg. $4.95. United Methodist Publishing House, 201 8th Ave. S., Nashville, TN 37203.

285 US ISSN 0082-8548
UNITED PRESBYTERIAN CHURCH IN THE UNITED STATES OF AMERICA. MINUTES OF THE GENERAL ASSEMBLY. a. $4. United Presbyterian Church in the U.S.A., 475 Riverside Drive, Room 1201, New York, NY 10027. circ. 16,000.

285 UK ISSN 0069-8849
UNITED REFORMED CHURCH IN ENGLAND AND WALES. UNITED REFORMED CHURCH YEAR BOOK. 1973. a. £5.20. ‡ United Reformed Church in England and Wales, 86 Tavistock Pl., London WC1H 9RT, England. Ed. Rev. Ernest W. Todd. adv. circ. 2,000.

284 GW ISSN 0083-5633
VEREINIGTE EVANGELISCH-LUTHERISCHE KIRCHE DEUTSCHLANDS. AMTSBLATT. 1948. irreg. Lutherisches Verlagshaus GmbH, Mittelweg 111, 2000 Hamburg 13, W. Germany (B. R. D.) circ. 5,100.

286 US ISSN 0083-6311
VIRGINIA BAPTIST REGISTER. 1962. a. $2.50 to non-members. Virginia Baptist Historical Society, Box 34, University of Richmond, VA 23173. Ed. John S. Moore. index. circ. 500.
Early Virginia Baptist history

RELIGIONS AND THEOLOGY — Roman Catholic

271 US ISSN 0567-6630
ACADEMY OF AMERICAN FRANCISCAN HISTORY. BIBLIOGRAPHICAL SERIES. 1953. irreg., no. 4, vol. 1, 1978. $17.50. Academy of American Franciscan History, 9901 Carmelita Dr., Box 34440, Washington, DC 20034.

271 US ISSN 0065-0633
ACADEMY OF AMERICAN FRANCISCAN HISTORY. DOCUMENTARY SERIES. 1951. irreg., vol. 11, 1979. price varies. Academy of American Franciscan History, Box 34440, 9901 Carmelita Dr., Washington, DC 20034.
History

271 US ISSN 0065-0641
ACADEMY OF AMERICAN FRANCISCAN HISTORY. MONOGRAPH SERIES. 1953. irreg., vol. 12, 1977. price varies. Academy of American Franciscan History, Box 34440, Washington, DC 20034.
History

271 US ISSN 0065-065X
ACADEMY OF AMERICAN FRANCISCAN HISTORY. PROPAGANDA FIDE SERIES. 1966. irreg., vol. 8, 1980. $40. Academy of American Franciscan History, Box 34440, Washington, DC 20034. Eds. Mathias Kiemen, Alexander Wyse. index.
History

ACTA MEDIAEVALIA. see HISTORY — History Of Europe

270 VC ISSN 0065-1443
ACTA NUNTIATURAE GALLICAE. 1961. irreg. price varies. (Pontificia Universita Gregoriana, Facolta di Storia Ecclesiastica) Gregorian University Press, Piazza della Filotta, 4, 00187 Rome, Italy. (Co-sponsor Ecole Francaise de Rome) Ed. Pierre Blet, S.J. circ. 1,000.

282 IT ISSN 0001-642X
ACTA ORDINIS SANCTI AUGUSTINI; commentarium officiale. (Text in Latin & various languages) 1956. a. L.5500. Order of Saint Augustine, Economato Generale, Via S. Uffizio 25, 00193 Rome, Italy. circ. 500. (back issues avail.)

ALLGEMEINER CAECILIEN-VERBAND. SCHRIFTENREIHE. see MUSIC

200 PE
AMERICA LATINA. BOLETIN. no. 15, Feb., 1978. irreg. Movimiento Internacional de Estudiantes Catolicos, Centro de Documentacion, Apartado 3564, Lima 100, Peru. illus.

AMERICAN CATHOLIC PHILOSOPHICAL ASSOCIATION. PROCEEDINGS. see PHILOSOPHY

270 282 VC ISSN 0066-1376
ANALECTA GREGORIANA. (Text in various languages) 1930. irreg., latest, vol. 225. price varies. (Pontificia Universita Gregoriana) Gregorian University Press, Piazza della Filotta, 4, 00187 Rome, Italy. Ed. Gilles Pelland, S.J.

282 BE ISSN 0066-1414
ANALECTA VATICANO-BELGICA. DEUXIEME SERIE. SECTION A: NONCIATURE DE FLANDRE. 1924. irreg. price varies. Institut Historique Belge de Rome, c/oArchives Generales du Royaume, 2-6 rue de Ruysbroeck, B-1000 Brussels, Belgium. circ. controlled.

274 BE ISSN 0066-1422
ANALECTA VATICANO-BELGICA. DEUXIEME SERIE. SECTION B: NONCIATURE DE COLOGNE. 1956. irreg. price varies. Institut Historique Belge de Rome, c/oArchives Generales du Royaume, 2-6 rue de Ruysbroeck, B-1000 Brussels, Belgium. circ. controlled.

282 BE ISSN 0066-1430
ANALECTA VATICANO-BELGICA. DEUXIEME SERIE. SECTION C: NONCIATURE DE BRUXELLES. 1956. irreg. price varies. Institut Historique Belge de Rome, c/o Archives Generales du Royaume, 2-6 rue de Ruysbroeck, B-1000 Brussels, Belgium. circ. controlled.

282 BE ISSN 0066-1449
ANALECTA VATICANO-BELGICA. PREMIERE SERIE: DOCUMENTS RELATIFS AUX ANCIENS DIOCESES DE CAMBRAI, LIEGE, THEROUANNE ET TOURNAI. 1906. irreg. price varies. Institut Historique Belge de Rome, c/o Archives Generales du Royaume, 2-6 Rue de Ruysbroeck, B-1000 Brussels, Belgium. circ. controlled.

282 FR ISSN 0066-2488
ANNUAIRE CATHOLIQUE DE FRANCE. 1950. biennial. 140 F. Publicat, 17 Bd. Poissonniere, 75002 Paris, France. adv.

282.675 ZR
ANNUAIRE DE L'EGLISE CATHOLIQUE AU ZAIRE. a. Edition du Secretariat-General, Kinshasa-Combe, Zaire. illus.

282 CN ISSN 0706-8328
ANNUAIRE DE L'EGLISE DU QUEBEC. 1976. a. price varies. Publicite B. M. Inc., 450 Beaumont Ave, Montreal, Que. H3N 1T8, Canada. Ed. Raymond Bertrand. adv. circ. 3,600.
Formerly: Catholic Directory of Canada.

282 FR
ANNUAIRE DU DIOCESE DE LYON. (Supplement, from 1978, to: Eglise a Lyon et a Saint-Etienne) 1826. a. 50 F. Archeveche de Lyon, 1 Place de Fourviere, 69321 Lyon, France.
Formerly (until 1972): Ordo et Annuaire de l'Archdiocese de Lyon.

266 IT ISSN 0066-4464
ANNUARIO CATTOLICO D'ITALIA. 1956. biennial. L.50000. Editoriale Italiana, Via Vigliena 10, Rome, Italy. index. circ. 8,000.

282 VC ISSN 0066-6785
ARCHIVUM HISTORIAE PONTIFICAE. (Text in English, Latin, German, French, Italian, Spanish; summaries in Latin) 1963. a. $50. (Pontificia Universita Gregoriana, Facolta di Storia Ecclesiastica) Gregorian University Press, Piazza della Filotta, 4, 00187 Rome, Italy. Ed. Paulius Rabikauskas, S.J. adv. bk. rev. bibl. circ. 750. (back issues avail.)

282 CL
ARZOBISPADO DE SANTIAGO. VICARIA DE LA SOLIDARIDAD. ESTUDIOS. 1978. irreg. Arzobispado de Santiago, Vicaria de la Solidaridad, Plaza de Armas 444, Casilla 30D, Santiago, Chile.

282 US ISSN 0094-5323
AUGUSTINIAN STUDIES. (Text in various languages) 1970. a. $10. Augustinian Institute at Villanova University, c/o R. B. B. Paparella, Augustinian Institute, Villanova University, Villanova, PA 19085. Ed. Robert P. Russell, OSA. bk. rev. circ. 300. Indexed: Cath.Ind.

271 UK ISSN 0522-8883
BENEDICTINE YEARBOOK. 1863. a. 55p.($1) ‡ English Congregation of the Order of Saint Benedict, St. Mary's Priory, Leyland, Preston PR5 1PD, England. Ed. Rev. J. Gordon Beattle. adv. circ. 4,000. (tabloid format)
Supersedes: Benedictine Almanac.

282 VC
BIBLIOTECA APOSTOLICA VATICANA. CATALOGHI DI MANOSCRITTI. 1902. irreg., no. 42, 1978. price varies. Biblioteca Apostolica Vaticana, 00120 Citta del Vaticano, Italy.

282 VC
BIBLIOTECA APOSTOLICA VATICANA.
CATALOGHI DI MOSTRE. 1904. irreg., no. 18,
1977. price varies. Biblioteca Apostolica Vaticana,
00120 Citta del Vaticano, Italy.

282 VC
BIBLIOTECA APOSTOLICA VATICANA.
ILLUSTRAZIONI DI CODICI. CODICI
VATICANI. SERIES MAJOR. 1902. irreg., no. 37,
1975. price varies. Biblioteca Apostolica Vaticana,
0120 Citta del Vaticano, Italy.

282 VC
BIBLIOTECA APOSTOLICA VATICANA.
ILLUSTRAZIONI DI CODICI. CODICI
VATICANI. SERIES MINOR. 1910. irreg., no. 4,
1978. price varies. Biblioteca Apostolica Vaticana,
00120 Citta del Vaticano, Italy.

282 VC
BIBLIOTECA APOSTOLICA VATICANA. STUDI
E TESTI. 1900. irreg., no. 283, 1979. price varies.
Biblioteca Apostolica Vaticana, 00120 Citta del
Vaticano, Italy.

282 IT
BIBLIOTHECA INSTITUTI HISTORICI
SOCIETATIS IESU. 1941. irreg., no.41,1980.
Institutum Historicum Societatis Iesu - Jesuit
Historical Institute, Via dei Penitenzieri 20, 00193
Rome, Italy. (back issues avail.)

200 IT ISSN 0067-8163
BIBLIOTHECA SERAPHICO-CAPUCCINA.
(Multilingual text) 1932. irreg., no. 28, 1980. price
varies. Frati Minori Cappuccini, Istituto Storico,
Cas. Post. 9091, G.R.A. Km. 68,800, 00163 Rome,
Italy. index. circ. 500.

200 BE ISSN 0067-8279
BIBLIOTHEQUE DE LA REVUE D'HISTOIRE
ECCLESIASTIQUE.* (Text in Dutch, English,
French and Italian) 1928. irreg. Universite
Catholique de Louvain, Bureau de la Revue
d'Histoire Ecclesiastique, Bibliotheque, Mgr.
Ladeuzeplein, Louvain, Belgium.

282 BO
BOLIVIA: GUIA ECLESIASTICA. 1977. irreg.
Conferencia Episcopal Boliviana, Secretaria General,
Casilla 2309, La Paz, Bolivia. illus.
Formerly: Guia de la Iglesia.

200 366 CN ISSN 0381-596X
BRASIER. 1941. irreg. Can.$5. Association des
Guides Catholiques du Canada, 3827, rue St.-
Hubert, Montreal, Que. H2L 4A4, Canada. Ed.
Mireille Jodoin. illus.

282 CN
CANADIAN CATHOLIC HISTORICAL
ASSOCIATION. ANNUAL REPORT. 1975. irreg.
membership. Canadian Catholic Historical
Association, c/o P. Bolger, St. Dunstan's University,
Charlottetown, P. E. I., Canada.

282 US ISSN 0069-1208
CATHOLIC ALMANAC. 1904. a. $8.95 paper;
$12.95 cloth. Our Sunday Visitor, Inc., Noll Plaza,
Huntington, IN 46750. Ed. Rev. Felician A. Foy.
index.
Formerly: National Catholic Almanac.

220 US
CATHOLIC BIBLE QUARTERLY MONOGRAPH
SERIES. 1971. irreg. price varies. Catholic Biblical
Association of America, Catholic University of
America, Washington, DC 20064. Ed.Bd. circ.
1,000. Indexed: Cath.Ind. Old Test.Abstr. Rel.Per.
New Test.Abstr.

282 US ISSN 0069-1216
CATHOLIC CENTRAL UNION OF AMERICA.
PROCEEDINGS. 1855. a. $3. Catholic Central
Union of America, 3835 Westminster Place, St.
Louis, MO 63108. Ed. Harvey J. Johnson. circ.
2,000. (also avail. in microfilm)

267 UK ISSN 0069-1224
CATHOLIC DIRECTORY. 1837. a. £8.95.
Associated Catholic Publications (1912) Ltd., 33-39
Bowling Green Lane, London EC1R 0AB, England.
Ed.Rt.Rev.Mgr. David Morris. adv.

267 UK ISSN 0306-5677
CATHOLIC DIRECTORY FOR SCOTLAND. 1828.
a. £4.75. John S. Burns and Sons, 25 Finlas Street,
Possilpark, Glasgow, G22 5DS, Scotland.
Formerly: Catholic Directory for the Clergy and
Laity in Scotland (ISSN 0069-1232)

282 TZ ISSN 0069-1240
CATHOLIC DIRECTORY OF EASTERN AFRICA.
1965. triennial. EAs.16. ‡ T.M.P. Book Department,
P.O. Box 399, Tabora, Tanzania (Dist. by: White
Fathers, 777 Belvidere Ave., Plainfield, NJ 07062)

CATHOLIC HEALTH ASSOCIATION OF
CANADA. DIRECTORY. see *MEDICAL
SCIENCES*

282 US ISSN 0069-1267
CATHOLIC THEOLOGICAL SOCIETY OF
AMERICA. PROCEEDINGS. 1946. a. $7.50. ‡
Catholic Theological Society of America, Darlington
Seminary, Mahwah, NJ 07430. Ed. Brother Luke
Salm. index; cum. index. Indexed: Cath.Ind.

282 UK ISSN 0411-275X
CATHOLIC TRUTH. 1896. a. £1($2.40) ‡
Incorporated Catholic Truth Society, 38/40
Eccleston Square, London SW1V 1PD, England.
Ed. David Murphy. adv. bk. rev. bibl. circ.
35,000(controlled)
Incorporating: Catholic Book Notes.

282 FR
CATHOLICISME HIER, AUJOURD'HUI,
DEMAIN. 1935. approx. 3/yr. 95 F.($22) per vol.
Letouzey et Ane, 87 Bd. Raspail, 75006 Paris,
France.

282 VC ISSN 0578-4182
CLARETIANUM; commentaria theologica opera et
studio. (Text in various European languages and
Latin) 1961. a. L.10000($15) Pontificia Universitas
Lateranensis, Institutum Theologiae Vitae
Religiosae, Via Aurelia 617, 00165 Rome, Italy. Ed.
Bruno Proietti. bk. rev. bibl.
Formerly: Theologica.

282 BL
COLECAO FE E REALIDADE. no. 3, 1977. irreg.
Edicoes Loyola, Rua 1822 no. 347, C.P. 42335, Sao
Paulo, Brazil.

282 SP
COLECCION TEOLOGICA. 1970. irreg., no. 24,
1979. price varies. (Universidad de Navarra)
Ediciones Universidad de Navarra, S.A., Plaza de
los Sauces 1 y 2, Baranain, Pamplona, Spain.

282 SP
COLEGIO MAYOR P. FELIPE SCIO.
PUBLICACIONES. 1975. irreg. price varies.
Ediciones Calasancias, Paseo de Canalejas 75,
Apdo. 206, Salamanca, Spain.

282 IT
COLLANA DI TESTI PATRISTICI. no. 11, 1978.
irreg. price varies. Citta Nuova Editrice, Viale Carso
71, 00195 Rome, Italy. Ed. Antonio Quacquarelli.

282 IT ISSN 0069-5254
COLLANA RICCIANA. FONTI. 1963. irreg., no. 12,
1975. price varies. Casa Editrice Leo S. Olschki,
Casella Postale 66, 50100 Florence, Italy. Ed. P. di
Agresti. circ. 1,000.

200 US ISSN 0069-5750
COLLEGE THEOLOGY SOCIETY.
PROCEEDINGS. 1955. a. $5. College Theology
Society, c/o Villanova University, Villanova, PA
19085. Ed. Thomas McFadden. circ. 3,000. Indexed:
Cath.Ind.
Before 1968: Society of Catholic College
Teachers of Sacred Doctrine. Proceedings.

282 CN ISSN 0384-5087
CONFERENCE CATHOLIQUE CANADIENNE.
BULLETIN NATIONAL DE LITURGIE. (Text in
French) 1965. irreg. Conference Catholique
Canadienne, Office National de Liturgie, 1225 Est.
Boul St. Joseph, Montreal, Que. H2J 1L7, Canada.
illus.

282 GW ISSN 0070-0320
CORPUS CATHOLICORUM. 1919. irreg. price
varies. Aschendorffsche Verlagsbuchhandlung,
Soester Str. 13, 4400 Muenster, W. Germany
(B.R.D.) Ed. Erwin Iserloh.

200 BE
CORPUS CHRISTIANORUM. SERIES GRAECA.
1977. irreg. (2-3/yr.) N.V. Brepols I.G.P., Rue
Baron Francois du Four 8, B-2300 Turnhout,
Belgium. (Co-publisher: Leuven University Press)

282 PE
CUADERNOS DE ESTUDIO. 1979. irreg. $40
(includes subscr. to: Testimonios (en Historieta),
Cuadernos de Capacitacion and Cuadernos
Populares) Comision Evangelica Latinoamericana de
Educacion Cristiana, Av. General Garzon 2267,
Lima 11, Peru.

282 CK
CUADERNOS DE TEOLOGIA Y PASTORAL.
irreg. Ediciones Paulinas, Calle 12 no. 6-11, Bogota,
Colombia.

266 VC ISSN 0080-3995
DOCUMENTA MISSIONALIA. (Multi-language
text) 1943. irreg. price varies. Pontificia Universita
Gregoriana, Faculty of Missiology, Piazza della
Pilotta 4, 00187 Rome, Italy. Ed. Mariasusai
Dhavamony. circ. 800. Indexed: Bull.Signal.

200 DR
EME EME; estudios Dominicanos. 1972. irreg.
RD.$0.50 single issue. Universidad Catolica Madre
y Maestra, Centro de Estudios Dominicanos,
Santiago de los Caballeros, Dominican Republic.
Ed. Frank Moya Pons. index. circ. 2,000.

282 US ISSN 0014-8814
FATHERS OF THE CHURCH. 1947. irreg., vol. 67,
1979. price varies. Catholic University of America
Press, 620 Michigan Ave. N.E., Washington, DC
20064. Ed. Rev. Hermigild Dressler.

282 IT
FONTI E STUDI PER LA STORIA DEL SANTO A
PADOVA. (Text in Italian or English) 1976. irreg.
L.40000. Neri Pozza Editore, Via Gazzolle 6, 36100
Vicenza, Italy. Ed. Antonino Poppi. bibl. illus.

271.3 US ISSN 0080-5459
FRANCISCAN STUDIES. 1941; N.S, 1977. a. $10.
Franciscan Institute, St. Bonaventure University, St.
Bonaventure, NY 14778. Ed. Rev. Conrad L.
Harkins. Indexed: Cath.Ind.

282 SP
HISTORIA DE LA IGLESIA. 1971. irreg.; 1979, no.
12. price varies. Ediciones Universidad de Navarra,
S.A., Plaza de los Sauces, 1 y 2, Baranain,
Pamplona, Spain.

282 HK ISSN 0073-3210
HONG KONG CATHOLIC DIRECTORY AND
YEAR BOOK/HSIANG-KANG T'IEN CHU
CHIAO SHOU T'SE. (Text in Chinese and English)
1954. a. HK.$5($2.30) Catholic Truth Society,
Grand Bldg, P.O. Box 2984, Hong Kong, Hong
Kong. Ed. Louis Lee. adv. circ. 2,000.

200 230 FR
INSTITUT CATHOLIQUE DE PARIS. ANNUAIRE.
a. Institut Catholique de Paris, 21, rue d'Assas,
75270 Paris Cedex 06, France.

282 UK ISSN 0075-0735
IRISH CATHOLIC DIRECTORY. 1838. a. £7.95.
(Roman Catholic Church in All Ireland) Associated
Catholic Publications (1912) Ltd., 33-39 Bowling
Green Lane, London EC1R 0AB, England. adv.
index.

200 US
JEDNOTA KALENDAR. (Text in Slovak) 1897. a.
First Catholic Slovak Union, 3289 E. 55th St.,
Cleveland, OH 44127 (Subscr. address: Jednota
Printery, Box 150, Middletown, PA 17057) Ed.
Joseph C. Krajsa.

282 NE
KATHOLIEK DOCUMENTATIE CENTRUM.
ARCHIEVEN. 1973. irreg. price varies. Katholiek
Documentatie Centrum, Erasmuslaan 36, 6525 GG
Nijmegen, Netherlands.

282 NE
KATHOLIEK DOCUMENTATIE CENTRUM.
JAARBOEK. (Summaries in English and French)
1971. a. price varies. Dekker en Van de Vegt,
Fransestraat 30, Nijmegen, Netherlands. (Co-
sponsor: Archief voor de Geschiedenis van de
Katholieke Kerk in Nederland)

RELIGIONS AND THEOLOGY — ROMAN CATHOLIC

282 NE
KATHOLIEK DOCUMENTATIE CENTRUM. PUBLICATIES. 1971. irreg., vol. 9, 1979. price varies. Katholiek Documentatie Centrum, Erasmuslaan 36, 6525 GG Nijmegen, Netherlands. (back issues avail.)

200 GW ISSN 0075-5273
KATHOLISCHES LEBEN UND KIRCHENREFORM IM ZEITALTER DER GLAUBENSSPALTUNG. 1927. irreg. price varies. Aschendorffsche Verlagsbuchhandlung, Soester Str. 13, 4400 Muenster, W. Germany (B.R.D.) Ed. Erwin Iserloh.

201 PL
KATOLICKI UNIWERSYTET LUBELSKI. WYDZIAL TEOLOGICZNO-KANONICZNY. ROZPRAWY. (Text in Polish; summaries in English or French) 1947. irreg. price varies. Katolicki Uniwersytet Lubelski, Towarzystwo Naukowe, Chopina 29, 20-023 Lublin, Poland. index. circ. 3,150.

282 PL ISSN 0076-5244
MATERIALY ZRODLOWE DO DZIEJOW KOSCIOLA W POLSCE. 1965. irreg. price varies. Materialy Zrodlowe do Dziejow Kosciola w Polsce, Al. Raclawickie 14, Lublin, Poland (Dist. by Ars Polona-Ruch, Krakowskie Przedmiecie 7, Warsaw, Poland)

200 IT ISSN 0077-1449
MONUMENTA HISTORICA ORDINIS MINORUM CAPUCCINORUM. (Text in Latin and Italian) 1937. irreg., 1971, no. 14. price varies. Frati Minori Cappuccini, Istituto Storico, Cas. Post. 9091, G.R.A. Km. 68,800, 00163 Rome, Italy. Ed. Mariano d'Alatri. index. circ. 500.

282 IT
MONUMENTA HISTORICA SOCIETATIS IESU. irreg.; latest, vol. 118. Institutum Historicum Societatis Iesu - Jesuit Historical Institute, Via dei Penitenzieri 20, 00193 Rome, Italy. (back issues avail.)

282 VC ISSN 0077-1457
MONUMENTA IURIS CANONICI. (Series A: Corpus Glossatorum; Series B: Corpus Collectionum; Series C: Subsidia) 1969. irreg. price varies. Biblioteca Apostolica Vaticana, c/o F. Werlen, Economo, 00120 Citta del Vaticano, Italy.

282 GW ISSN 0077-2011
MUENSTERSCHWARZACHER STUDIEN. 1965. irreg. price varies. (Benediktinerabtei Muensterschwarzach) Vier-Tuerme-Verlag, 8711 Muensterschwarzach, W. Germany (B.R.D.) Ed. Edgar Friedmann.

NATIONAL CATHOLIC EDUCATIONAL ASSOCIATION. OCCASIONAL PAPERS. see *EDUCATION*

282 US
NATIONAL CATHOLIC WOMEN'S UNION. PROCEEDINGS. (Special issue of Social Justice Review) 1916. a. $3. National Catholic Women's Union, 3835 Westminster Pl., St. Louis, MO 63108. Ed. Harvey J. Johnson. circ. 2,100. (also avail. in microfilm)

282 UK ISSN 0048-0207
NEWMAN. 1950, N.S. 1972. a. £1.50($3.) Newman Association, 30 Baker St., London W1M 2DS, England. Ed. Martin Ward. circ. 3,000.

282 US
NOTRE DAME STUDIES IN AMERICAN CATHOLICISM. 1979. irreg. University of Notre Dame Press, Notre Dame, IN 46556. bibl.

282 IT ISSN 0078-253X
NOVARIEN. 1967. irreg. price varies. Associazione di Storia Ecclesiastica Novarese, Presso Archivio Storico Diocesano, Palazzo Vescovile, I-28100 Novara, Italy. Ed. Angelo L. Stoppa. bk. rev. circ. 1,000.

270 239 AU
OESTERREICHISCHE AKADEMIE DER WISSENSCHAFTEN. KOMMISSION ZUR HERAUSGABE DES CORPUS DER LATEINISCHEN KIRCHENVAETER. VEROEFFENTLICHUNGEN. irreg. Verlag der Oesterreichischen Akademie der Wissenschaften, Ignaz Seipel-Platz 2, A-1010 Vienna, Austria.

282 US ISSN 0078-3854
OFFICIAL CATHOLIC DIRECTORY; official directory of the Catholic Church in the United States and its possessions. 1817. a. P. J. Kenedy & Sons, P.O. Box 729, New York, NY 10022. Ed. A.J. Corbo. circ. controlled.

282 US
OFFICIAL WISCONSIN PASTORAL HANDBOOK. 1962. a. $7 to qualified personnel. ‡ Catholic Family Life Program, c/o Rev. John A. Furtmann, 2021 North 60th St., Milwaukee, WI 53208. adv. circ. 2,300(controlled)

282 CN ISSN 0078-4702
ONTARIO CATHOLIC DIRECTORY. 1915. a. Can.$3.25. ‡ Newman Foundation of Toronto, 771 Yonge St., Toronto, Ont. M4W 2G4, Canada. Rev. J.F. Mallon. adv. circ. 8,210.

ORIENTALIA CHRISTIANA ANALECTA. see *ORIENTAL STUDIES*

200 SP
PANORAMA DE LA TEOLOGIA LATINOAMERICANA. 1974. a. $8. (Universidad Catolica de Chile, Seminario Latinoamericano de Documentacion, Centro de Documentacion, CL) Ediciones Sigueme, Garcia Tejado 3, Apdo. 332, Salamanca, Spain. circ. 3,000.

267 SZ ISSN 0079-0281
PAX ROMANA. Represents: International Catholic Movement for Intellectual Cultural Affairs. Proceedings of the Plenary Assembly. irreg., 22nd, 1975. $4. International Catholic Movement for Intellectual and Cultural Affairs, General Secretariat, B.P. 1062, 1 Route du Jura, 1701 Fribourg, Switzerland. circ. 600.

255 IT
PICENUM SERAPHICUM. (Text in Italian) irreg. L.3500. Biblioteca Francescana, Conto Corrente Postale 15/27009, Falconara M. 60015, Italy.

282 FR
POINT THEOLOGIQUE. no. 17, 1976. irreg. Editions Beauchesne, 72 rue des Saints Peres, 75007 Paris, France. Ed.Charles Kannengiesser.

270 VC
PONTIFICIA UNIVERSITA GREGORIANA. DOCUMENTA MISSIONALIA. (Multi-Language text) 1964. irreg. price varies. Gregorian University Press, Piazza della Pilotta 4, Italy. Ed. Mariasusai Dhavamony.

270 VC ISSN 0080-3979
PONTIFICIA UNIVERSITA GREGORIANA. MISCELLANEA HISTORIAE PONTIFICIAE. (Multi-language text) 1939. irreg., latest, vol. 47. price varies. Gregorian University Press, Piazza della Pilotta, 4, 00187 Rome, Italy. Ed. Vincenzo Monachino.

266 VC ISSN 0080-3987
PONTIFICIA UNIVERSITA GREGORIANA. STUDIA MISSIONALIA. (Multi-language text) 1943. a. price varies. Gregorian University Press, Piazza della Pilotta, 4, 00187 Rome, Italy. Ed. Mariasusai Dhavamony.

282 GW
PRIESTERJAHRHEFT. 1926. a. free. Bonifatiuswerk der Deutschen Katholiken e.V., Kamp 22, 4790 Paderborn, W. Germany (B.R.D.) Ed. Anton Koetter. circ. 22,000 (controlled)

282 BE
PROBLEMES D'HISTOIRE DU CHRISTIANISM. (Text in French) 1970/71. a. price varies. (Universite Libre de Bruxelles, Institut d'Histoire du Christianisme) Editions de l'Universite de Bruxelles, Parc Leopold, B-1040 Brussels, Belgium.

282 IT ISSN 0079-824X
QUADERNI DEI PADRI BENEDETTINI DI SAN GIORGIO MAGGIORE. 1961. irreg., 1964, no. 3. price varies. (Fondazione Giorgio Cini) Casa Editrice Leo S. Olschki, Casella Postale 66, 50100 Florence, Italy. circ. 500.

200 US ISSN 0080-5432
SAINT BONAVENTURE UNIVERSITY. FRANCISCAN INSTITUTE. PHILOSOPHY SERIES. 1944. irreg., no. 16, 1972. price varies. Franciscan Institute, St. Bonaventure University, St. Bonaventure, NY 14778. Ed. Rev. Conrad L. Harkins.

200 US ISSN 0080-5440
SAINT BONAVENTURE UNIVERSITY. FRANCISCAN INSTITUTE. TEXT SERIES. 1951. irreg., no. 16, 1972. price varies. Franciscan Institute, St. Bonaventure University, St. Bonaventure, NY 14778. Ed. Rev. Conrad L. Harkins.

200 CN ISSN 0085-6134
SLOVENSKI JEZUITI V KANADE. YEAR BOOK. (Text in Slovak and English; summaries in English) 1957. a. contr. free circ. Slovak Jesuit Fathers in Canada, Box 600, Cambridge, Ont. N1R 5W3, Canada. Ed. Rev. Vincent Danco. adv. bk. rev. illus. stat. circ. 10,000.

940 AU ISSN 0081-5594
STILLE SCHAR. 1953. a. S.35. Gebetsliga, Wickenburggasse 5/10, A-1080 Vienna, Austria. circ. 10,000.

282 VC
STUDIA MISSIONALIA. (Multi-language text) 1943. a. price varies. Pontificia Universita Gregoriana, Faculty of Missiology, Piazza della Pilotta 4, 00187 Rome, Italy. Ed. Mariasusai Dhavamony. bk. rev. circ. 1,000. Indexed: Bull.Signal.

230 GW ISSN 0081-7295
STUDIEN ZUR GESCHICHTE DER KATHOLISCHEN MORALTHEOLOGIE. 1955, vol. 3. irreg., vol. 23, 1977. price varies. Verlag Friedrich Pustet, Gutenbergstr. 8, 8400 Regensburg 1, W. Germany (B. R. D.) Eds. Josef Rief, Johannes Gruendel. circ. 500.

255 IT ISSN 0562-4649
SUBSIDIA SCIENTIFICA FRANCISCALIA. (Text in French, German, Italian, Latin) 1962. irreg., no. 6, 1978. price varies. Frati Minori Cappuccini, Istituto Storico, Casella Postale 9091, G.R.A. Km. 68,800, 00163 Rome, Italy. index. circ. 500.

266 282 US
UNITED STATES CATHOLIC MISSION COUNCIL. HANDBOOK. 1950. a. $1.50. United States Catholic Mission Council, 11302 18th St., N.W., Washington, DC 20036. circ. 2,400.
Formerly: United States Catholic Missionary Personnel Overseas (ISSN 0082-9560)
Missions

200 CL ISSN 0069-3596
UNIVERSIDAD CATOLICA DE CHILE. FACULTAD DE TEOLOGIA. ANALES. 1940. irreg.; vol. 29, 1978. $8. Universidad Catolica de Chile, Facultad de Teologia, Casilla 114-D, Santiago, Chile. cum.index (1940-1969) circ. 500.

282 BE
UNIVERSITE CATHOLIQUE DE LOUVAIN. FACULTES DE THEOLOGIE ET DE DROIT CANONIQUE. COLLECTION DES DISSERTATIONS PRESENTEES POUR L'OBTENTION DU GRADE DE MAITRE A LA FACULTE DE THEOLOGIE OU A LA FACULTE DE DROIT CANONIQUE. 1841. irreg. (series quarto, vols. 2-3, 1978) Universite Catholique de Louvain, Facultes de Theologie et de Droit Canonique, Grand-Place 45, 1348 Louvain-la-Neuve, Belgium.
Formerly: Universite Catholique de Louvain. Facultes de Theologie et de Droit Canonique. Dissertations ad Gradum Magistri in Facultate Theologica Vel in Facultate Iuris Canonici Consequendum Conscriptae.

200 BE ISSN 0076-1230
UNIVERSITE CATHOLIQUE DE LOUVAIN. FACULTES DE THEOLOGIE ET DE DROIT CANONIQUE. TRAVAUX DE DOCTORAT EN THEOLOGIE ET EN DROIT CANONIQUE. NOUVELLE SERIE. 1969. irreg., vol. 4, 1974. exchange basis. Universite Catholique de Louvain, Facultes de Theologie et de Droit Canonique, Grand-Place 45, 1348 Louvain-la-Neuve, Belgium. circ. 200.

268 US ISSN 0070-3052
UNIVERSITY OF DAYTON. SCHOOL OF
EDUCATION. WORKSHOP PROCEEDINGS.
1970. irreg., latest issue, 1971. $3.25. University of
Dayton, School of Education, Dayton, OH 45469.
Ed. Louis J. Faerber.
Catholic education: elementary and secondary

264 US ISSN 0076-003X
UNIVERSITY OF NOTRE DAME. DEPARTMENT
OF THEOLOGY. LITURGICAL STUDIES. 1955.
irreg., no. 11, 1977. $9.95. ‡ University of Notre
Dame Press, Notre Dame, IN 46556. Indexed:
Cath.Ind.

282 AU ISSN 0083-9930
WIENER BEITRAEGE ZUR THEOLOGIE. 1963.
irreg., vol. 52, 1976. price varies. (Universitaet
Wien, Katholisch-Theologische Fakultaet) Wiener
Dom Verlag, Postfach 668, A-1011 Vienna, Austria.

200 AU ISSN 0084-0009
WIENER KATHOLISCHE AKADEMIE. STUDIEN.
irreg. Wiener Katholische Akademie, Freyung 6, A-
1010 Vienna, Austria.

RELIGIONS AND THEOLOGY —
Other Denominations And Sects

200 GW
ALT-KATHOLISCHES JAHRBUCH. a. DM.6.
Katholisches Bistum der Alt-Katholiken in
Deutschland, Gregor-Mendel-Str. 28, 5300 Bonn 1,
W. Germany (B.R.D.)

200 FR ISSN 0083-6184
ASSEMELEES DE DIEU DE FRANCE.
ANNUAIRE. 1958. a. 8 F. Viens et Vois, 9, rue
Claude Boyet, 69007 Lyon, France.

275.93 TH
CHRISTIAN DIRECTORY. (Text in English and
Thai) ε. B.75. Suthep Chaviwan, Box 1405,
Bangkok, Thailand. illus.

267 UK
CHRISTIAN ENDEAVOUR TOPIC BOOK. 1896. a.
95p. for each edt. ‡ Christian Endeavour Union of
Great Britain and Ireland, 18 Leam Terrace, Royal
Leamington Spa, Warwickshire CV31 1BB, England.
Eds. Brenda Eaton (General edt.); Oliver Woodham
(Junior edt.). circ. 1,700.
Formerly: Christian Endeavour Year Book (ISSN
0069-3363)
Missions

268 US ISSN 0069-3898
CHRISTIAN SERVICE TRAINING SERIES. 1963.
a. $2. for pupil book; $0.75 for leader's guide. ‡
(Mennonite Church, General Conference,
Commission on Education) Faith and Life Press,
724 Main St., Box 347, Newton, KS 67114. Eds.
Elizabeth Yoder, Laurence Martin. index.

261 US ISSN 0069-3979
CHURCH AND SOCIETY SERIES. 1962. irreg.
price varies. ‡ (Mennonite Church, General
Conference) Faith and Life Press, 724 Main St, Box
347, Newton, KS 67114. Ed. Elizabeth Yoder.

281.9 BE ISSN 0070-0398
CORPUS SCRIPTORUM CHRISTIANORUM
ORIENTALIUM: AETHIOPICA. 1904. irreg.,
latest no. 74, 1979. price varies. (Universite
Catholique de Louvain) Editions Peeters s.p.r.l., B.P.
41, B-3000 Louvain, Belgium. (Co-sponsor: Catholic
University of America) bk. rev.

281.9 BE ISSN 0070-0401
CORPUS SCRIPTORUM CHRISTIANORUM
ORIENTALIUM: ARABICA. 1903. irreg., latest
no. 35, 1978. price varies. (Universite Catholique de
Louvain) Editions Peeters s.p.r.l., B.P. 41, B-3000
Louvain, Belgium. (Co-sponsor: Catholic University
of America) bk. rev.

281.9 BE ISSN 0070-041X
CORPUS SCRIPTORUM CHRISTIANORUM
ORIENTALIUM: ARMENIACA. 1953. irreg., no.
12, 1980. price varies. (Universite Catholique de
Louvain) Editions Peeters s.p.r.l., B.P. 41, B-3000
Louvain, Belgium. (Co-sponsor: Catholic University
of America) bk. rev.

281.9 BE ISSN 0070-0428
CORPUS SCRIPTORUM CHRISTIANORUM
ORIENTALIUM: COPTICA. 1906. irreg., no. 42,
1980. price varies. (Universite Catholique de
Louvain) Editions Peeters s.p.r.l., B.P. 41, B-3000
Louvain, Belgium. (Co-sponsor: Catholic University
of America) bk. rev.

281.9 BE ISSN 0070-0436
CORPUS SCRIPTORUM CHRISTIANORUM
ORIENTALIUM: IBERICA. 1950. irreg., latest no.
18, 1968. price varies. (Universite Catholique de
Louvain) Editions Peeters s.p.r.l., B.P. 41, B-300
Louvain, Belgium. (Co-sponsor: Catholic University
of America) bk. rev.

281.9 BE ISSN 0070-0444
CORPUS SCRIPTORUM CHRISTIANORUM
ORIENTALIUM: SUBSIDIA. 1950. irreg., no. 61,
1980. price varies. (Universite Catholique de
Louvain) Editions Peeters s.p.r.l., B.P.41, B-3000
Louvain, Belgium. (Co-sponsor: Catholic University
of America) bk. rev.

281.9 BE ISSN 0070-0452
CORPUS SCRIPTORUM CHRISTIANORUM
ORIENTALIUM: SYRIACA. 1903. irreg., no. 184,
1980. price varies. (Universite Catholique de
Louvain) Editions Peeters s. p.r.l., B.P. 41, B-3000
Louvain, Belgium. (Co-sponsor: Catholic University
of America) bk. rev.

242.2 US ISSN 0092-7147
DAILY BREAD. 1969. a. $5. (Reorganized Church of
Jesus Christ of Latter Day Saints) Herald Publishing
House, 3225 S. Noland Rd., Drawer HH,
Independence, MO 64055. Ed. Barbara Howard.
circ. 12,000.
"a devotional guide for every day of the year."

268 UK
DAILY WATCHWORDS; the Moravian textbook
with almanack. 1722. a. 65p. Moravian Church in
Great Britain, Moravian Book Room, 5 Muswell
Hill, London N.10 3TJ, England. Ed. Mr. & Mrs. S.
W. Twine. circ. 4,500.

289.3 US ISSN 0093-786X
DESERET NEWS CHURCH ALMANAC. 1974. a.
$1.95. Deseret News, Box 1257, Salt Lake City, UT
84110. (Co-sponsor: Church of Jesus Christ of
Latter-Day Saints) illus.

267 UK ISSN 0071-9587
FRIENDS HISTORICAL SOCIETY. JOURNAL.
1903. a. Friends Historical Society, Friends House,
Euston Rd., London NW1 2BJ, England. Eds.Alfred
W. Braithwaite & Russell S. Mortimer.

200 UK ISSN 0072-0666
GENERAL CONFERENCE OF THE NEW
CHURCH. YEARBOOK. 1937. a. 25p. ‡ New
Church Press, 20 Bloomsbury Way, London WC1A
2TH, England. circ. 750.

I I S T BULLETINS; human electricity and
experiments on soul. (Indian Institute of Soul
Technology) see *PARAPSYCHOLOGY AND
OCCULTISM*

INDEX TO MORMONISM IN PERIODICAL
LITERATURE. see *ABSTRACTING AND
INDEXING SERVICES*

261 US ISSN 0073-9456
INSTITUTE OF MENNONITE STUDIES SERIES.
1961. irreg. price varies. ‡ (Associated Mennonite
Biblical Seminaries) Faith and Life Press, 724 Main
St, Box 347, Newton, KS 67114. Ed. Elizabeth
Yoder.

200 CN
ISSUE. 1974? irreg. free. United Church of Canada, 85
St. Clair Ave. E., Toronto, Ont. M4T 1M8, Canada.
Ed. Bd. illus.

289.9 US ISSN 0075-3602
JEHOVAH'S WITNESSES YEARBOOK. (Text in
various European languages) 1927. a. $1. ‡
(Jehovah's Witnesses, Governing Body) Watchtower
Bible & Tract Society, Inc., 25 Columbia Hts.,
Brooklyn, NY 11201. index.
Report of international preaching; also daily Bible
texts and comments

289.3 US ISSN 0094-7342
JOURNAL OF MORMON HISTORY. 1974. a. $4.
Mormon History Association, 1302 Edvalson St.,
Ogden, UT 84403.

289.3 US ISSN 0094-5633
MEASURING MORMONISM. 1974. a. $3.
Association for the Study of Sociology, Inc., 3646
East 3580 South, Salt Lake City, UT 84109 (Or
Glenn M. Vernon, Ed., University of Utah,
Department of Sociology, Salt Lake City, UT
84112)

290 US ISSN 0076-6429
MENNONITE HISTORY SERIES. 1966, vol. 2.
irreg. ‡ (Mennonite Church, General Conference,
Commission on Education) Faith and Life Press,
724 Main St, Newton, KS 67114. Ed. Elizabeth
Yoder.

289.7 US
MENNONITE YEARBOOK AND DIRECTORY.
vol. 71, 1980. a. $4.75. Mennonite Publishing
House, 616 Walnut Ave., Scottdale, PA 15683. Ed.
James E. Horsch.

281 US
MODERN ORTHODOX SAINTS. 1971. irreg., vol.
6, 1978. price varies. Institute for Byzantine and
Modern Greek Studies, 115 Gilbert Rd., Belmont,
MA 02178. Ed. Constantine Cavarnos. bibl. illus.
index. circ. 1,000.

200 BG
NATIONAL COUNCIL OF CHURCHES,
BANGLADESH. ANNUAL REPORT. (Text in
English and Bengali) a. National Council of
Churches, Bangladesh, 395, New Eskaton Rd.,
Dacca 2, Bangladesh. stat.

200 US ISSN 0145-7950
ORTHODOX CHURCH IN AMERICA.
YEARBOOK AND CHURCH DIRECTORY. a.
$6. Orthodox Church in America, Box 675, Syosset,
NY 11791. charts. illus. stat. circ. 3,000. Key
Title: Yearbook and Church Directory of the
Orthodox Church in America.
Supersedes: Russian Orthodox Greek Catholic
Church of America. Yearbook and Church
Directory (ISSN 0557-532X)

289.6 100
QUAKER ENCOUNTERS. irreg. William Sessions
Ltd., c/o Ebor Press, York YO3 9HS, England.

QUAKER PEACE AND SERVICE. ANNUAL
REPORT. see *SOCIAL SERVICES AND
WELFARE*

289.6 US ISSN 0033-5088
QUAKER RELIGIOUS THOUGHT. 1959. irreg., 2
or more/yr. $5 for 4 nos. Quaker Theological
Discussion Group, Route 1, Box 549, Alburtis, PA
18011. Eds. T. Vail Palmer, Jr., Dean Freiday. bk.
rev. circ. 500.

289 US ISSN 0586-7282
SALT LAKE CITY MESSENGER. 1964. irreg., no.
40, 1979. free. Modern Microfilm Co., 1350 South
West Temple St., Salt Lake, UT 84115 (Subscr. to:
P.O. Box 1884, Salt Lake City, UT 84110) Ed.
Jerald Tanner. circ. 8,000. (looseleaf format)

267.15 UK ISSN 0080-567X
SALVATION ARMY YEAR BOOK. 1906. a. 95p.
paperback; £1.50 hardback. ‡ (Salvation Army)
Salvationist Publishing and Supplies, Ltd., Judd St.,
Kings Cross, London WC1H 9NN, England. index.
circ. 11,000.

290 US
SAT NAM SERIES. irreg., vol. 2, 1973. price varies.
Spiritual Community Publications, Box 1080, San
Rafael, CA 94902.

261 US ISSN 0080-6943
SCHOWALTER MEMORIAL LECTURE SERIES.
1969. irreg. price varies. ‡ (Mennonite Church,
General Conference) Faith and Life Press, 724
Main St., Box 347, Newton, KS 67114. Ed.
Elizabeth Yoder.

200 US ISSN 0160-0354
SPIRITUAL COMMUNITY GUIDE; the new
consciousness source book. 1972. irreg; no. 4, 1978/
79. $5.95. Spiritual Community Publications, Box
1080, San Rafael, CA 94902. Ed. Parmatma Singh
Khalsa. circ. 20,000.

280　　　　　　US　ISSN 0081-7538
STUDIES IN ANABAPTIST AND MENNONITE
HISTORY. 1929. irreg., no. 17, 1974. price varies.
(Mennonite Historical Society) Mennonite
Publishing House, Herald Press, 616 Walnut Ave.,
Scottdale, PA 15683.

267　　　　　　UK　ISSN 0082-6588
TRINITARIAN BIBLE SOCIETY. ANNUAL
REPORT. 1831. a. 50p. ‡ Trinitarian Bible Society,
217 Kingston Rd., London SW19 3NN, England.
Ed. Rev. Terence H. Brown.

658.32　　　　US　ISSN 0360-9782
UNITED CHURCH OF CHRIST. PENSION
BOARDS (ANNUAL REPORT) 1967. a. free.
United Church of Christ, 132 W. 31st St., New
York, NY 10001. circ. 15,000. Key Title: Pension
Boards.

294.37　　　　　US
WHEEL SERIES. 1973. irreg. Four Seasons
Foundation, Box 31411, San Francisco, CA 94131
(Dist. by: Subco, Box 10233, Eugene, OR 97440)
Ed. Donald Allen. circ. 3,000.

RESPIRATORY DISEASES

see *Medical Sciences — Respiratory Diseases*

RHEUMATOLOGY

see *Medical Sciences — Rheumatology*

ROADS AND TRAFFIC

see *Transportation — Roads and Traffic*

ROMAN CATHOLICISM

see *Religions and Theology — Roman Catholic*

RUBBER

678　　　　　　FR　ISSN 0066-2674
ANNUAIRE DE L'INDUSTRIE DU
CAOUTCHOUC ET DE SES DERIVES. 1948.
biennial. 81 F. Michel Bongrand S.A., 17 Av.
Hoche, 75008 Paris, France. index in English.

ANNUAL BOOK OF A S T M STANDARDS.
PART 37. RUBBER, NATURAL AND
SYNTHETIC--GENERAL TEST METHODS;
CARBON BLACK. see *ENGINEERING —
Engineering Mechanics And Materials*

ANNUAL BOOK OF A S T M STANDARDS.
PART 38. RUBBER PRODUCTS, INDUSTRIAL--
SPECIFICATIONS AND RELATED TEST
METHODS; GASKETS; TIRES. see
*ENGINEERING — Engineering Mechanics And
Materials*

678　　　　　　IT　ISSN 0066-4499
ANNUARIO DELL' INDUSTRIA ITALIANA
DELLA GOMMA/YEARBOOK OF THE
ITALIAN RUBBER INDUSTRY. (Text in Italian,
French, German, English, Spanish) 1962. a.
L.30000. (Associazione Nazionale fra le Industrie
della Gomma) Gesto s.r.l., Via C. Battisti, 21, 20122
Milan, Italy. Ed. Enzo Belli-Nicoletti. adv. circ.
6,000.

678　668　　　　FR　ISSN 0066-9229
ASSOCIATION FRANCAISE DES INGENIEURS
DU CAOUTCHOUC ET DES PLASTIQUES.
ANNUAIRE. 1956. irreg. Association Francaise des
Ingenieurs du Caoutchouc et des Plastiques, 9 Av.
Hoche, Paris (8e), France. adv.

678　　　　　　GW　ISSN 0005-6987
BAYER-MITTEILUNGEN FUER DIE GUMMI-
INDUSTRIE. (English Edition: Technical Notes for
the Rubber Industry; French Edition: Informations
Bayer pour l'Industrie du Caoutchouc; Spanish
Edition: Informaciones Bayer para la Industria del
Caucho) 1955. irreg. (1-2/yr) Bayer AG, 5090
Leverkusen-Bayerwerk, W. Germany (B.R.D.) Ed.
Sigrid Koch. cum.index. circ. 4,000.

678.2　　　　　UK
BRITISH RUBBER INDUSTRY DIRECTORY. (Text
in English, French, German and Spanish) 1967.
triennial. £5.50. British Rubber Manufacturers'
Association Ltd., 90-91 Tottenham Court Rd.,
London W1P 0BR, England.

678　　　　　　UK　ISSN 0306-414X
EUROPEAN RUBBER DIRECTORY. 1950. biennial.
Maclaren Publishers Ltd., Davis House, 69-77 High
St., Croydon CR9 1QH, England. Ed. A. Clark.
adv. index. circ. 4,000.
　Formerly: Rubber Directory of Great Britain
(ISSN 0080-4770)

338.476　　　　AG　ISSN 0533-4500
GUIA DE LA INDUSTRIA DEL CAUCHO. 1969.
biennial. Arg.$3000. Federacion Argentina de la
Industria del Caucho, Av. Leandro N. Alem 1067,
1001 Buenos Aires, Argentina.

678　　　　　　SZ　ISSN 0073-0076
HANDBUCH DER INTERNATIONALEN
KAUTSCHUKINDUSTRIE/INTERNATIONAL
RUBBER DIRECTORY/MANUEL
INTERNATIONAL DE CAOUTCHOUC. (Text in
English, French, German) 1955. every 5 yrs. 172.80
Fr. Verlag fuer Internationale Wirtschaftsliteratur
GmbH, P.O.Box 108, CH-8047 Zurich, Switzerland.
Ed. Walter Hirt.

678　　　　　　II　ISSN 0073-6651
INDIAN RUBBER STATISTICS. (Text in English)
1958. a. price varies. Rubber Board, Kottayam
686009, Kerala, India.

678　028　　　　GW
INFORMACIONES BAYER PARA LA
INDUSTRIA DEL CAUCHO. English edition:
Technical Notes for the Rubber Industry. French
edition: Informations Bayer pour l'Industrie du
Caoutchouc. German edition: Bayer-Mitteilungen
fuer die Gummi-Industrie. 1955. irreg. (1-2/yr)
Bayer AG, 5090 Leverkusen-Bayerwerk, W.
Germany (B.R.D.) Ed. Sigrid Koch. cum.ind. circ.
1,000.

678　　　　　　GW
INFORMATIONS BAYER POUR L'INDUSTRIE
DU CAOUTCHOUC. English edition: Technical
Notes for the Rubber Industry. German edition:
Bayer-Mitteilungen fuer die Gummi-Industrie (ISSN
0005-6987); Spanish edition: Informaciones Bayer
para la Industria del Caucho. 1922. irreg. (1-2/yr)
Bayer AG, 5090 Leverkusen-Bayerwerk, W.
Germany (B.R.D.) Ed. Sigrid Koch. cum. index.
circ. 1,000.

678　　　　　　UK　ISSN 0074-7823
INTERNATIONAL RUBBER STUDY GROUP.
SUMMARY OF PROCEEDINGS OF THE
GROUP MEETINGS AND ASSEMBLIES. 92nd
Group Meeting 1979; 26th Assembly 1979.
International Rubber Study Group, Brettenham
House, 5-6 Lancaster Place, London WC2E 7ET,
England.

MODERN TIRE DEALER PRODUCTS
CATALOG. see *TRANSPORTATION*

678　　　　　　UK　ISSN 0077-8869
NEW TRADE NAMES IN THE RUBBER AND
PLASTICS INDUSTRIES. 1926. a. £15. Rubber
and Plastics Research Association of Great Britain,
Shawbury, Shrewsbury, Shropshire, England. circ.
500.

PLASTICS AND RUBBER YEARBOOK AND
BUYERS' GUIDE OF S.A. see *PLASTICS*

678　668　　　　UK　ISSN 0140-4156
R A P R A RECENT LITERATURE ON
HAZARDOUS ENVIRONMENTS IN
INDUSTRY. vol. 4, 1979. irreg. £100($240) Rubber
and Plastics Research Association of Great Britain,
Shawbury, Shrewsbury 5Y4 4NR, England. Ed. C.
Painter. abstr.

678　668.4　　　US　ISSN 0080-4762
RUBBER AND PLASTICS INDUSTRY
TECHNICAL CONFERENCE. RECORD. a.
Institute of Electrical and Electronics Engineers,
Inc., 445 Hoes Lane, Piscataway, NJ 08854.

678.2　　　　　MY
RUBBER PRODUCERS' COUNCIL OF
MALAYSIA. ANNUAL REPORT/MAJLIS
PENGELUAR-PENGELUAR GETAH TANAH
MELAYU. LAPURAN TAHUNAN. (Text in
Malay and English) 1951. a. M.$3. Rubber
Producers' Council of Malaysia - Majtis Penguluar-
Pengeluar Getah Tanah Melaya, Peti Surat 272,
Bangunan Getah Asli, Jalan Ampang, Kuala
Lumpur, Malaysia. stat.

678　　　　　　US　ISSN 0361-0640
RUBBER RED BOOK; directory of the rubber
industry. 1936. a. $45. Communication Channels,
Inc., 6285 Barfield Rd., Atlanta, GA 30328. Ed. Art
Swenn. circ. 5,600.

633.895　　　　MY　ISSN 0126-5849
RUBBER RESEARCH INSTITUTE OF MALAYSIA.
PLANTERS CONFERENCE PROCEEDINGS.
biennial. $21. Rubber Research Institute of Malaysia
- Pusat Penyelidikan Getah Tanah Melayu, Box
150, Kuala Lumpur 16-03, Malaysia. Eds. Ng Siew
Kee, J.C. Rajaro. charts. illus. circ. 2,000.

678　　　　　　CE
RUBBER RESEARCH
INSTITUTE OF SRI
LANKA. ANNUAL REVIEW. (Text in English) a.
Rubber Research Institute of Sri Lanka, Dartonfield,
Agalawatta, Sri Lanka.
　Supersedes: Rubber Research Institute of Ceylon.
Annual Review.

678　668.4　　　CE
RUBBER RESEARCH INSTITUTE OF SRI
LANKA. JOURNAL. (Text in English) vol. 53,
1976. irreg. Rs.15($3) ‡ Rubber Research Institute
of Sri Lanka, Dartonfield, Agalawatta, Sri Lanka.
Ed. Dr. O. S. Peries. adv. bk. rev. charts. illus. circ.
2,500. Indexed: Biol.Abstr. Chem.Abstr.
Abstr.Trop.Agri. Hort.Abstr. Plant Breed.Abstr.
RAPRA. Soils & Fert. Trop.Abstr.
　Formerly (until 1976): Rubber Research Institute
of Sri Lanka. Quarterly Journal (ISSN 0035-9521)

678　　　　　　US
RUBBER WORLD BLUE BOOK. 1977. a. $37.50.
Bill Communications, Inc., 633 Third Ave., New
York, NY 10017. (reprint service avail. from UMI)

SYNDICAT GENERAL DES COMMERCES ET
INDUSTRIES DU CAOUTCHOUC ET DES
PLASTIQUES. GUIDE. see *BUSINESS AND
ECONOMICS — Trade And Industrial Directories*

678　　　　　　GW
TECHNICAL NOTES FOR THE RUBBER
INDUSTRY. French edition: Informations Bayer
pour l'Industrie du Caoutchouc. German Edition
Bayer-Mitteilungen fuer die Gummi-Industrie (ISSN
0005-6987); Spanish edition: Informaciones Bayer
para la Industria del Caucho. 1955. irreg. (1-2/yr)
Bayer AG, 5090 Leverkusen-Bayerwerk, W.
Germany (B.R.D.) Ed. Sigrid Koch. cum. index.
circ. 2,000.

678.32　　　　　US　ISSN 0082-4496
TIRE AND RIM ASSOCIATION. STANDARDS
YEAR BOOK. 1927. a. price varies. ‡ Tire and Rim
Association, Inc., 3200 W. Market St., Akron, OH
44313. circ. 6,300.

678.2　　　　　US　ISSN 0083-5218
VANDERBILT RUBBER HANDBOOK. 1968. irreg.
R.T. Vanderbilt Co., Inc., 30 Winfield St., Norwalk,
CT 06855. Ed. Robert O. Babbit. index.
　A source of technical information for those
directly connected with the compounding and
processing of rubber and synthetic elastomers in
their dry form

778 RUBBER — ABSTRACTING, BIBLIOGRAPHIES, STATISTICS

678   GW   ISSN 0083-694X
VULKANISEUR-JAHRBUCH. 1952. a. DM.5.
Bielefelder Verlagsanstalt KG, Niederwall 53,
Postfach 1140, 4800 Bielefeld, W. Germany
(B.R.D.) adv. circ. 5,000.

RUBBER — Abstracting, Bibliographies, Statistics

678 016   US
BIBLIOGRAPHY OF RUBBER LITERATURE
INCLUDING PATENTS. 1942. a.; 1972 edt. publ.
1978. $30. American Chemical Society, Rubber
Division, University of Akron, Akron, OH 44325.

382 318   BL   ISSN 0572-5534
BRAZIL. SUPERINTENDENCIA DA BORRACHA.
ANNUARIO ESTATISTICO. MERCADO
ESTRANGEIRO. 1966? a. Superintendencia da
Borracha, Avda. Almirante Barroso 81, Caixa Postal
610, Rio de Janeiro RJ, Brazil. charts.

SCHOOL ORGANIZATION AND ADMINISTRATION

see *Education — School Organization and Administration*

SCIENCES: COMPREHENSIVE WORKS

500   US
A A A S SELECTED SYMPOSIA SERIES. 1978.
irreg. (American Association for the Advancement
of Science) Westview Press, 5500 Central Ave.,
Boulder, CO 80301. Ed. Frederick A. Praeger.

500   GW   ISSN 0343-7051
ABHANDLUNGEN AUS DEM GEBIET DER
AUSLANDSKUNDE. SERIES B & C. (Text in
English and German) irreg., vol. 74, 1978. price
varies. (Universitaet Hamburg, Seminar fuer Kultur
und Geschichte Indiens) Franz Steiner Verlag
GmbH, Friedrichstr. 24, Postfach 5529, 6200
Wiesbaden, W. Germany (B.R.D.)

500   US
ABSTRACT SYSTEM THEORY MONOGRAPHS.
1977. irreg. price varies. Science Monograph
Publishers, Box 71, South Dartmouth, MA 02748.

500   FI   ISSN 0356-6927
ACADEMIA SCIENTIARUM FENNICA.
YEARBOOK/SUOMALAINEN
TIEDEAKATEMIA. VUOSIKIRJA. (Text in
Finnish or English; summaries in English) 1977. a.
Suomalainen Tiedeakatemia - Academia Scientiarum
Fennica, Snellmaninkatu 9-11, 00170 Helsinki 17,
Finland. Ed. Lauri A. Vuorela. index. circ. 500.
(back issues avail.; reprint service avail. from UMI)
Indexed: Biol.Abstr. Ref.Zh.
  Supersedes (from 1977): Academia Scientiarum
Fennica. Proceedings/Sitzungsberichte (ISSN 0065-0501)

ACADEMIAE ABOENSIS, SERIES B:
MATHEMATICS, SCIENCE, ENGINEERING.
see *MATHEMATICS*

500   FR   ISSN 0065-0552
ACADEMIE DES SCIENCES. ANNUAIRE. 1917.
a. Centrale des Revues, Gauthier-Villars, B. P. 119,
93104 Montreuil Cedex, France.

500   FR   ISSN 0065-0560
ACADEMIE DES SCIENCES. INDEX
BIOGRAPHIQUE DES MEMBRES ET
CORRESPONDANTS. 1939. irreg. Centrale des
Revues, Gauthier-Villars, B. P. 119, 93104
Montreuil Cedex, France.

509   GW   ISSN 0366-8258
ACADEMIE INTERNATIONALE D'HISTOIRE
DES SCIENCES. COLLECTION DES
TRAVAUX. (Text in English, French, German)
irreg., vol. 23, 1978. price varies. Franz Steiner
Verlag GmbH, Friedrichstr. 24, Postfach 5529, 6200
Wiesbaden, W. Germany (B.R.D.)

500 060   PL   ISSN 0079-3159
ACADEMIE POLONAISE DES SCIENCES.
CENTRE SCIENTIFIQUE, PARIS.
CONFERENCES. (Text in French) 1953. irreg.
price varies. (Polska Akademia Nauk, Centre
Scientifique, Paris, FR) Panstwowe Wydawnictwo
Naukowe, Ul. Miodowa 10, Warsaw, Poland
(Editorial address: 74 rue Lauriston, Paris 16e,
France) Ed. Pawel Jan Nowacki.

ACADEMIE ROYALE DES SCIENCES, DES
LETTRES ET DES BEAUX-ARTS DE
BELGIQUE. ANNUAIRE. see *HUMANITIES: COMPREHENSIVE WORKS*

500   BE
ACADEMIE ROYALE DES SCIENCES, DES
LETTRES ET DES BEAUX ARTS DE
BELGIQUE. CLASSE DES SCIENCES.
MEMOIRES. irreg. price varies. Academie Royale
des Sciences, des Lettres et des Beaux Arts de
Belgique., Classe des Sciences, 43 Av. des Arts, B-1040 Brussels, Belgium (Subscr. to: Office
International de Librairie, 30 Av. Marnix, 1050
Brussels, Belgium)

500   US   ISSN 0096-7750
ACADEMY OF NATURAL SCIENCES OF
PHILADELPHIA. MONOGRAPHS. 1935. irreg.,
no.21,1980. price varies. Academy of Natural
Sciences of Philadelphia, 19th St. and the Parkway,
Philadelphia, PA 19103.

500   US   ISSN 0097-3157
ACADEMY OF NATURAL SCIENCES OF
PHILADELPHIA. PROCEEDINGS. 1842. a. price
varies. Academy of Natural Sciences of
Philadelphia, 19th St. and the Parkway,
Philadelphia, PA 19103. Ed. J. E. Bohlke.

500   US   ISSN 0097-3254
ACADEMY OF NATURAL SCIENCES OF
PHILADELPHIA. SPECIAL PUBLICATIONS.
1922. irreg., no. 13. price varies. Academy of
Natural Sciences of Philadelphia, 19th St. and the
Parkway, Philadelphia, PA 19103.

500   IT
ACCADEMIA LIGURE DI SCIENZE E LETTERE.
ATTI. (Text in Italian, English, French) 1890. a.
L.7000($12) Accademia Ligure di Scienze e Lettere,
Via Balbi 10, Palazzo Reale, 16126 Genoa, Italy.
Ed. Pietro Scotti. circ. 500. Indexed: Biol.Abstr.
Chem.Abstr.

ACCADEMIA LUCCHESE DI SCIENZE,
LETTERE ED ARTI. ATTI. NUOVA SERIE. see
ART

500   IT   ISSN 0065-0765
ACCADEMIA PATAVINA DI SCIENZE LETTERE
ED ARTI. COLLANA ACCADEMICA. 1966.
irreg., 1975, no. 6. price varies. Accademia Patavina
di Scienze Lettere ed Arti, Via Accademia 7, 35100
Padua, Italy.

500 060   IT   ISSN 0065-0781
ACCADEMIA TOSCANA DI SCIENZE E
LETTERE LA COLOMBARIA. STUDI. 1952.
irreg., vol. 51, 1978. price varies. Casa Editrice Leo
S. Olschki, Casella Postale 66, 50100 Florence,
Italy. circ. 1,000.

500 919 998   DK   ISSN 0065-1028
ACTA ARCTICA. (Text in English, German and
French) 1943. irreg. (every 3-5/yr.) price varies.
(Arktisk Institut) C. A. Reitzels Forlag, 35 Noerre
Soegade, DK-1370 Copenhagen K, Denmark. Ed.
Helge Larsen. (back issues avail.)

500.9 610   GE   ISSN 0001-5857
ACTA HISTORICA LEOPOLDINA. (Supplements
avail.) 1963. irreg., vol. 10, 1977. price varies.
(Deutsche Akademie der Naturforscher Leopoldina,
Archiv fuer Geschichte der Naturforschung und
Medizin) Johann Ambrosius Barth Verlag,
Salomonstr. 18b, 701 Leipzig, E. Germany (D.D.R.)
Ed. Prof. Dr. G. Uschmann. bibl. charts. illus. circ.
1,200.
  History

500 600   DK   ISSN 0065-1311
ACTA HISTORICA SCIENTIARUM
NATURALIUM ET MEDICINALIUM. (Text in
Danish, English, or German) 1942. irreg., no. 32,
1979. price varies. Odense University Press, 36,
Pjentedamsgade, DK-5000 Odense, Denmark.
Indexed: Ind.Med.

500 600   MX   ISSN 0567-7785
ACTA MEXICANA DE CIENCIA Y
TECNOLOGIA. (Suspended 1975-1978) (Text in
English or Spanish) 1967. irreg.; vols. 9-10, 1978,
cover 1975-76. Instituto Politecnico Nacional,
Comision de Operacion y Fomento de Actividades
Academicas, Apdo. Postal 42-161, Mexico 17, D.F.,
Mexico. bibl. charts. illus. index. circ. 1,000.

ACTA REGIAE SOCIETATIS SCIENTIARUM ET
LITTERARUM GOTHOBURGENSIS.
INTERDISCIPLINARIA. see *HUMANITIES: COMPREHENSIVE WORKS*

500   GE   ISSN 0304-2154
AKADEMIE DER WISSENSCHAFTEN DER DDR.
JAHRBUCH. 1950. a. price varies. Akademie-Verlag, Leipziger Strasse 3-4, 108 Berlin, E.
Germany (D.D.R.) Ed. Hermann Klare.
  Formerly: Akademie der Wissenschaften. Berlin.
Jahrbuch (ISSN 0065-5066)

500   GW   ISSN 0084-6082
AKADEMIE DER WISSENSCHAFTEN,
GOETTINGEN. JAHRBUCH. 1939. a. price
varies. Vandenhoeck und Ruprecht, Theaterstr. 13,
Postfach 77, 3400 Goettingen, W. Germany
(B.R.D.)

001.3 500   GW   ISSN 0084-6104
AKADEMIE DER WISSENSCHAFTEN UND DER
LITERATUR, MAINZ. JAHRBUCH. a. price
varies. Franz Steiner Verlag GmbH, Friedrichstr. 24,
Postfach 5529, 6200 Wiesbaden, W. Germany
(B.R.D.)

500   GW   ISSN 0065-5538
AKADEMISCHE VORTRAEGE UND
ABHANDLUNGEN. 1946. irreg., no. 46, 1979.
price varies. Bouvier Verlag Herbert Grundmann,
Am Hof 32, Postfach 1268, 5300 Bonn 1, W.
Germany (B.R.D.)

500   UR
AKADEMIYA NAUK LATVIISKOI S. S. R.
ELEKTRONIKAS UN SKAITLOSANAS
TEHNIKAS INSTITUTS. RASPOZNAVANIE
OBRAZOV. 1974. irreg. .71 Rub. Akademiya Nauk
Latviiskoi S. S. R., Elektronikas un Skaitlosanas
Tehnikas Instituts, Ul. Turgeneva, 19, Riga, U.S.S.R.
illus.

500   US   ISSN 0084-6120
ALASKA SCIENCE CONFERENCE.
PROCEEDINGS. Variant title: Science in Alaska.
1950. a. price varies. American Association for the
Advancement of Science, Alaska Division, P. O.
Box 80271, Fairbanks, AK 99708. circ. 500.

ALBERTA RESEARCH COUNCIL. ANNUAL
REPORT. see *TECHNOLOGY: COMPREHENSIVE WORKS*

500   CN
ALBERTA RESEARCH COUNCIL.
ATMOSPHERIC SCIENCES REPORTS. irreg.
price varies. Alberta Research Council, Publications
Department, 11315-87 Avenue, Edmonton, Alberta
T6G 2C2, Canada.
  Formerly: Alberta Research Council. Hail Studies
Reports (ISSN 0080-1542)

500   CN   ISSN 0080-1577
ALBERTA RESEARCH COUNCIL. MEMOIRS.
1959. irreg. price varies. Alberta Research Council,
11315-87 Avenue, Edmonton, Alta. T6G 2C2,
Canada.

ALBERTA RESEARCH COUNCIL. REPORTS. see
TECHNOLOGY: COMPREHENSIVE WORKS

500   AU
ALMANACH DER OESTERREICHISCHEN
FORSCHUNG. 1978. a. price varies. Verband der
Wissenschaftlichen Gesellschaften Oesterreichs,
Lindengasse 37, A-1070 Vienna, Austria.

SCIENCES: COMPREHENSIVE WORKS

500.9   GW
ALPENINSTITUT. SCHRIFTENREIHE. (Text in German, French, Italian) 1974. irreg. price varies. (Alpeninstitut fuer Umweltforschung und Entwicklungsplanung in der GFL) Geographische Buchhandlung R. Michels, Rosental 6, 8000 Munich 2, W. Germany (B.R.D.) Ed. Walter Danz.
Natural history

AMERICAN ACADEMY OF ARTS AND SCIENCES. RECORDS OF THE ACADEMY. see *ART*

500   US   ISSN 0361-7874
AMERICAN ASSOCIATION FOR THE ADVANCEMENT OF SCIENCE. HANDBOOK; OFFICERS, ORGANIZATION, ACTIVITIES. a. $2.50. American Association for the Advancement of Science, 1515 Massachusetts Ave., N.W., Washington, DC 20005.

500   US   ISSN 0361-1833
AMERICAN ASSOCIATION FOR THE ADVANCEMENT OF SCIENCE. MEETING PROGRAM. 1972. a. $7. American Association for the Advancement of Science, 1515 Massachusetts Ave. N.W., Washington, DC 20005. Ed. Arthur Herschman. adv. index. circ. 8,000 (approx.) Key Title: Annual Meeting - American Association for the Advancement of Science.

620   616   US   ISSN 0065-7964
AMERICAN COUNCIL OF INDEPENDENT LABORATORIES. DIRECTORY. 1937. biennial. $5. American Council of Independent Laboratories, Inc., 1725 K St. N.W., Washington, DC 20006. circ. 7,000.

AMERICAN LECTURES IN THE HISTORY OF MEDICINE AND SCIENCE. see *MEDICAL SCIENCES*

AMERICAN MEN AND WOMEN OF SCIENCE. PHYSICAL AND BIOLOGICAL SCIENCES. see *BIOGRAPHY*

500.9   US   ISSN 0003-0082
AMERICAN MUSEUM NOVITATES. 1921. irreg. price varies. American Museum of Natural History, Central Park West at 79th St, New York, NY 10024. Ed. Florence Brauner. circ. 2,500. Indexed: Biol.Abstr. Bull.Signal. Key Word Ind.Wildl.Res. Zoo.Rec.

AMERICAN MUSEUM OF NATURAL HISTORY. ANNUAL REPORT. see *MUSEUMS AND ART GALLERIES*

500   SP
ANALES DE LA UNIVERSIDAD HISPALENSE. SERIE: CIENCIAS. irreg. price varies. Universidad de Sevilla, San Fernando 4, Seville, Spain. charts, illus.

300   500   610   SP
ANALES DE LA UNIVERSIDAD HISPALENSE. SERIE: FILOSOFIA Y LETRAS. 3-4yr. price varies per no. Universidad de Sevilla, San Fernando 4, Seville, Spain.
Formerly: Universidad Hispalense. Anales. Series: Filosofia y Letras, Derecho, Medicina, Ciencias y Veterinaria (ISSN 0041-8552)

500   600   FI   ISSN 0066-2011
ANNALES ACADEMIAE SCIENTIARUM FENNICAE. SERIES B. (Text in English, French, German) 1909. irreg. price varies. Suomalainen Tiedeakatemia - Academia Scientiarum Fennica, Snellmanink. 9-11, 00170 Helsinki 17, Finland. Ed. Yrjo Blomstedt. cum.index (1909-1968 in vol. 150) circ. 500. (back issues avail.; reprint service avail. from UMI) Indexed: Abstr.Engl.Stud. Bull.Signal. Hist.Abstr. Psychol.Abstr. Lang. & Lang.Behav.Abstr.

500   GW   ISSN 0080-5165
ANNALES UNIVERSITATIS SARAVIENSIS. REIHE: MATHEMATISCH-NATURWISSENSCHAFTLICHE FAKULTAET. 1963. a. price varies. (Universitaet des Saarlandes) Gebrueder Borntraeger Verlagsbuchhandlung, Johannsstr. 3A, 7000 Stuttgart 1, W. Germany (B.R.D.) Ed. F. Firtion.

500   FR
ANNUAIRE DES FOURNISSEURS DE LABORATOIRES DE RECHERCHES. 1967. a. Agence de Diffusion et de Publicite, 24 Place du General Catroux, 75017 Paris, France. Ed. Raymond Mery. adv. circ. 3,500.

500   ISSN 0084-6600
ANNUAL REVIEW OF MATERIALS SCIENCE. 1971. a. $20. Annual Reviews Inc., 4139 El Camino Way, Palo Alto, CA 94306. Ed. Robert A. Huggins. bibl. index; cum.index. (back issues avail.; reprint service avail. from ISI) Indexed: Chem.Abstr. Sci.Abstr. Int.Aerosp.Abstr. M.M.R.I. Nucl.Sci.Abstr.

500   IC
ARBOK VISINDAFELAGS ISLENDINGA. 1975. a., next edt. 1980 (covering 1975-1979) Visindafelag Islendinga - Societas Scientiarum Islandica (Icelandic Scientific Society), Haskolabokasafn, 101 Reykjavik, Iceland. Ed Bjoern Sigfusson.

ARCTIC INSTITUTE OF NORTH AMERICA. RESEARCH PAPER. see *GEOGRAPHY*

919.8   500   CN   ISSN 0066-698X
ARCTIC INSTITUTE OF NORTH AMERICA. TECHNICAL PAPER. 1956. irreg., no. 27, 1974. price varies. Arctic Institute of North America, University Library Tower, 2920 24th Ave. N.W., Calgary, Alta. T2N 1N4, Canada. (also avail. in microform from UMI; reprint service avail. from UMI) Indexed: Biol.Abstr. Arct.Bibl.

500   US
ARCTINURUS NEWSLETTER. irreg. price varies. Arctinurus Co., Box 275, Bellmawr, NJ 08031.
New papers in science

950   II   ISSN 0066-8265
ASIA MONOGRAPH SERIES. (Text in English) irreg., no. 26, 1975. price varies. Asia Publishing House, Calicut St., Ballard Estate, Bombay 400038, India (And 440 Park Ave. S., New York NY 10016)

500   CN
ASSOCIATION CANADIENNE-FRANCAISE POUR L'AVANCEMENT DES SCIENCES. A C F A S; RESUMES DES COMMUNICATIONS. 1935. a. Can.$4 to non-members. Association Canadienne-Francaise pour l'Avancement des Sciences, C.P. 6060, Montreal H3C 3A7, Que., Canada.

500   CN   ISSN 0066-8842
ASSOCIATION CANADIENNE-FRANCAISE POUR L'AVANCEMENT DES SCIENCES. ANNALES. 1935. a. Association Canadienne-Francaise pour l'Avancement des Sciences, C. P. 6060, Montreal 101, Quebec, Canada. Indexed: Biol.Abstr. Arct.Bibl.

500   CN   ISSN 0066-8850
ASSOCIATION CANADIENNE-FRANCAISE POUR L'AVANCEMENT DES SCIENCES. BULLETIN. (Text in French) irreg. $2, annual membership. Association Canadienne-Francaise pour l'Avancement des Sciences, 2730 Ct Ste Catherine, Montreal, Canada.

500.9   ML
ASSOCIATION DES NATURALISTES DU MALI. BULLETIN. a. Association des Naturalistes du Mali, B.P. 1746, Bamako, Mali.

500   CN   ISSN 0067-0197
ATLANTIC PROVINCES INTER-UNIVERSITY COMMITTEE ON THE SCIENCES. ANNUAL REPORT. 1963. irreg. ‡ Atlantic Provinces Inter-University Committee on the Sciences, Box 24, Halifax, N. S., Canada. Ed. John E. Caryi. circ. 300.

375   500   CN   ISSN 0004-6825
ATLANTIC PROVINCES INTER-UNIVERSITY COMMITTEE ON THE SCIENCES. NEWSLETTER. 1965. irreg. free. ‡ Atlantic Provinces Inter-University Committee on the Sciences, Box 24, Halifax, N.S., Canada. Ed. John E. Caryi. circ. 1,200. (processed)

500.9   DK   ISSN 0067-0227
ATLANTIDE REPORT. SCIENTIFIC RESULTS OF THE DANISH EXPEDITION TO THE COASTS OF TROPICAL WEST AFRICA. (Text in English and French) 1950. irreg. price varies. (Koebenhavns Universitet) Scandinavian Science Press Ltd., Christiansholms Parallelvej 2, DK-2930 Klampenborg, Denmark. (Co-sponsor: British Museum) Eds. Joergen Knudsen & Torben Wolff.

500   US   ISSN 0077-5630
ATOLL RESEARCH BULLETIN. 1951. irreg. Smithsonian Institution Press, Washington, DC 20560. Ed. F. R. Fosberg. (reprint service avail. from UMI)

500   AU
AUS OESTERREICHS WISSENSCHAFT. 1973. a. price varies. Verband der Wissenschaftlichen Gesellschaften Oesterreichs, Lindgengasse 37, A-1070 Vienna, Austria.

500   AT   ISSN 0067-155X
AUSTRALIAN ACADEMY OF SCIENCE. RECORDS. 1966. a. Aus.$10. Australian Academy of Science, Box 783, Canberra City, A.C.T. 2601, Australia. index. circ. 500.

500   AT   ISSN 0067-1568
AUSTRALIAN ACADEMY OF SCIENCE. REPORTS. 1957. irreg., no. 24, 1980. Aus.$5.95 per no. Australian Academy of Science, Box 783, Canberra City, A.C.T. 2601, Australia. circ. 1,500.

500   AT   ISSN 0067-1584
AUSTRALIAN ACADEMY OF SCIENCE. YEAR BOOK. 1956. a. Aus.$10. Australian Academy of Science, Box 783, Canberra City, A.C.T. 2601, Australia. index. circ. 1,500.

500   AU   ISSN 0300-2772
AUSTRIA. BUNDESMINISTERIUM FUER WISSENSCHAFT UND FORSCHUNG. BERICHT DER BUNDESREGIERUNG AN DEN NATIONALRAT. 1968. a. free. Bundesministerium fuer Wissenschaft und Forschung, Minoritenplatz 5, A-1014 Vienna, Austria. stat. Key Title: Bericht der Bundesregierung an den Nationalrat.

500   CN
B. C. RESEARCH. ANNUAL REPORT. 1944-45. a. free. British Columbia Research Council, 3650 Wesbrook Mall, Vancouver, B. C. V6S 2L2, Canada. circ. 2,000.
Formerly: British Columbia Research Council. Annual Report (ISSN 0068-1652)

500.9   US   ISSN 0067-2866
BADLANDS NATURAL HISTORY ASSOCIATION. BULLETIN. 1968. irreg. price varies. ‡ Badlands Natural History Association, Box 72, Interior, SD 57750.

500.9   IQ
BASRAH NATURAL HISTORY MUSEUM. BULLETIN. (Text in English; summaries in Arabic and English) 1974. irreg. available on exchange basis. Basrah Natural History Museum, University of Basrah, Basrah, Iraq. Eds. Khalaf al-Robaae & P. V. George. abstr. bibl. index.

500.9   IQ
BASRAH NATURAL HISTORY MUSEUM. PUBLICATION. 1976. irreg. exchange basis. Basrah Natural History Museum, University of Basrah, Basrah, Iraq.

500   GW   ISSN 0084-6090
BAYERISCHE AKADEMIE DER WISSENSCHAFTEN. JAHRBUCH. 1912. a. price varies. C. H. Beck'sche Verlagsbuchhandlung, Wilhelmstr. 9, 8000 Munich 40, W. Germany (B.R.D.) index.

500   510   GW
BAYERISCHE AKADEMIE DER WISSENSCHAFTEN. MATHEMATISCH-NATURWISSENSCHAFTLICHE KLASSE. SITZUNGSBERICHTE. 1871. a, plus offprints. price varies. Bayerische Akademie der Wissenschaften, Marstallplatz 8, 8000 Munich 22, W. Germany (B.R.D.)

SCIENCES: COMPREHENSIVE WORKS

900 GW ISSN 0342-5991
BAYERISCHE AKADEMIE DER WISSENSCHAFTEN. PHILOSOPHISCH-HISTORISCHE KLASSE. SITZUNGSBERICHTE. a, plus offprints. Bayerische Akademie der Wissenschaften, Marstallplatz 8, 8000 Munich 22, W. Germany(B.R.D.)

500 GW ISSN 0522-6570
BEITRAEGE ZUR GESCHICHTE DER WISSENSCHAFT UND DER TECHNIK. 1961. irreg., vol. 16, 1981. price varies. (Deutsche Gesellschaft fuer Geschichte der Medizin, Naturwissenschaft und Technik e.V.) Franz Steiner Verlag GmbH, Friedrichstr. 24, Postfach 5529, 6200 Wiesbaden, W. Germany (B.R.D.) illus.
History

507 BE
BELGIUM. FONDS NATIONAL DE LA RECHERCHE SCIENTIFIQUE. LISTE DES BENEFICIAIRES D'UNE SUBVENTION. (Text in English, Flemish or French) 1928. a. Fonds National de la Recherche Scientifique, Rue d'Egmont 5, B-1050 Brussels, Belgium. circ. 2,100.

500 BE ISSN 0067-5407
BELGIUM. FONDS NATIONAL DE LA RECHERCHE SCIENTIFIQUE. RAPPORT ANNUEL. 1928. a. Fonds National de la Recherche Scientifique, Rue d'Egmont 5, B-1050 Brussels, Belgium. circ. 2,100.

500 IS
BEN-GURION UNIVERSITY OF THE NEGEV. RESEARCH AND DEVELOPMENT AUTHORITY. SCIENTIFIC ACTIVITIES. (Text in English) 1973/74. a. Ben-Gurion University of the Negev, Applied Research Institute, P.O. Box 1025, Beer-Sheva, Israel.
Supersedes: Negev Institute for Arid Zone Research, Beer-Sheva, Israel. Report for Year (ISSN 0077-6467)

500.9 GW ISSN 0067-5806
BERICHTE DES VEREINS NATUR UND HEIMAT UND DES NATURHISTORISCHEN MUSEUMS ZU LUEBECK. 1959. a. DM.6. Naturhistorisches Museum zu Luebeck, Muehlendamm 1, 2400 Luebeck, W. Germany (B.R.D.) Ed. G. von Studnik.

500.9 US ISSN 0005-9439
BERNICE P. BISHOP MUSEUM BULLETIN. 1922. irreg. Bishop Museum Press, Box 19000-A, Honolulu, HI 96819.

BERNICE PAUAHI BISHOP MUSEUM, HONOLULU. OCCASIONAL PAPERS. see *ANTHROPOLOGY*

BERNICE PAUAHI BISHOP MUSEUM, HONOLULU. SPECIAL PUBLICATIONS. see *ANTHROPOLOGY*

500 FR ISSN 0072-7520
BIBLIOTHEQUE UNIVERSITAIRE, GRENOBLE. PUBLICATIONS. 1969. irreg. price varies. Bibliotheque Universitaire, Grenoble, Saint-Martin-d'Heres, 38401 Grenoble, France.

500 GW ISSN 0523-8226
BOETHIUS; Texte und Abhandlungen zur Geschichte der exakten. 1962. irreg., vol. 11, 1978. price varies. Franz Steiner Verlag GmbH, Friedrichstr. 24, Postfach 5529, 6200 Wiesbaden, W. Germany (B.R.D.) Eds. J. E. Hofmann, F. Klemm, B. Sticker. illus.
History

500 TU
BOGAZICI UNIVERSITY JOURNAL: SCIENCES. (Text in English or Turkish) 1973. a. $3. Bogazici Universitesi, Box 2, Istanbul, Turkey.

500 501 NE ISSN 0068-0346
BOSTON STUDIES IN THE PHILOSOPHY OF SCIENCE; Boston colloquium for the philosophy of science. (Text in English) 1963. irreg. price varies. D. Reidel Publishing Co., Box 17, 3300 AA Dordrecht, Netherlands (And Lincoln Building, 160 Old Derby St., Hingham, MA 02043) Ed. Robert S. Cohen and Marx W. Wartofsky.

500.9 910 UK ISSN 0306-8838
BRADWELL ABBEY FIELD CENTRE FOR THE STUDY OF ARCHAEOLOGY, NATURAL HISTORY & ENVIRONMENTAL STUDIES. OCCASIONAL PAPERS. no. 4, 1980. irreg. 75p. Bradwell Abbey Field Centre Trust, Abbey Rd., Bradwell, Milton Keynes MK13 9AP, England. Ed. T. R. Slater. bibl.

500 GW
BRAUNSCHWEIGISCHE WISSENSCHAFTLICHE GESELLSCHAFT. ABHANDLUNGEN. 1949. irreg. price varies. Verlag Erich Goltze GmbH und Co. KG, Stresemannstr. 28, 3400 Goettingen, W. Germany (B.R.D.) Ed. K. H. Olsen.

500 600 BL
BRAZIL. CONSELHO NACIONAL DE DESENVOLVIMENTO CIENTIFICO E TECNOLOGICO. BOLETIM. vol. 2, 1977. irreg. Conselho Nacional de Desenvolvimento Cientifico e Tecnologico, Rua Capote Valente 376, CEP 05409, Sao Paulo, SP, Brazil.

500 BL
BRAZIL. CONSELHO NACIONAL DE DESENVOLVIMENTO CIENTIFICO E TECNOLOGICO. PROGRAMA DO TROPICA SEMI-ARIDO(PUBLICACION) irreg. Conselho Nacional de Desenvolvimento Cientifico e Tecnologico, Programa do Tropico Semi-Arido, Av. W-3 Norte Q-509-D, Brasilia, Brazil. Ed. Domingos Carvalho da Silva. charts. stat.

500 BL
BRAZIL. CONSELHO NACIONAL DE DESENVOLVIMENTO CIENTIFICO E TECNOLOGICO. RELATORIO DE ATIVIDADES. 1975. irreg. Conselho Nacional de Desenvolvimento Cientifico e Tecnologico, Av. W-3 Norte Q-509-D, Brasilia, Brazil.

500 CR
BRENESIA. (Text in various languages; summaries in Spanish; abstracts in English) 1972. irreg., approx. s-a. $6. ‡ Museo Nacional de Costa Rica, Departamento de Historia Natural, P.O. Box 749, San Jose, Costa Rica. Ed. Luis Diego Gomez P. circ. 1,000. (tabloid format) Indexed: Biol.Abstr. Zoo.Rec.

502 UK ISSN 0068-1040
BRISTOL NATURALISTS' SOCIETY. PROCEEDINGS. 1862. a. £1. Bristol Naturalists' Society, City Museum, Bristol 8, England. Ed. Dr. R. A. Avery. circ. 750. (also avail. in microform from UMI)

509 UK
BRITISH ANTARCTIC SURVEY. ANNUAL REPORT. a. British Antarctic Survey, Maddingley Rd., Cambridge CB3 0ET, England.

509 UK
BRITISH ANTARCTIC SURVEY. SCIENTIFIC REPORTS. irreg. British Antarctic Survey, Madingley Rd., Cambridge CB3 0ET, England.

500.1 560 FR
BULLETIN SCIENTIFIQUE DE BOURGOGNE. 1931. biennial. 30 F. Societe des Sciences Naturelles de Dijon, Faculte de Sciences, 6 Bd Gabriel, F 21000-Dijon, France (Subscr.address: Librairie de l'Universite, 17 rue de la Liberte, 21014 Dijon, France) Dir. N. Leneuf. circ. 300.

500 600 UK
C L A I M REPORT TO THE BRITISH LIBRARY AND DEVELOPMENT DEPARTMENT. 1969? irreg. Centre for Library and Information Management, Loughborough University, Loughborough, Leics. LE11 3TU, England.
Formerly: Cambridge University. Library Management Research Unit. Report to the Office for Scientific and Technical Information.

500 600 BE ISSN 0069-2026
C R I C RAPPORT DE RECHERCHE. (Text in French, Dutch, English) 1962. irreg. 125 Fr. Centre National de Recherches Scientifiques et Techniques pour l'Industrie Cimentiere, 46 rue Cesar Franck, B-1050 Brussels, Belgium.

500 SA ISSN 0081-2382
C S I R ANNUAL REPORT. 1945. a. free. Council for Scientific and Industrial Research, Publishing Division, Box 395, Pretoria 0001, South Africa. circ. 3,000 English edt.; 2,000 Afrikaans edt.

500 GH
C S I R ANNUAL REPORT. 1968. a. Council for Scientific and Industrial Research, Box M-32, Accra, Ghana. circ. controlled. (back issues avail.)

500 GH
C S I R HANDBOOK. 1970. a. Council for Scientific and Industrial Research, Box M-32, Accra, Ghana. (back issues avail.)

068 AT
C. S. I. R. O. DIRECTORY. 1951. a. Aus.$1.20. C. S. I. R. O., 314 Albert St., East Melbourne, Vic. 3002, Australia. circ. controlled.

500 600 AT ISSN 0069-7192
C. S. I. R. O. FILM CATALOGUE. irreg. free. C. S. I. R. O., 314 Albert St., E. Melbourne 3002, Victoria, Australia.

500 600 SA ISSN 0081-2390
C S I R ORGANIZATION AND ACTIVITIES. irreg. free. Council for Scientific and Industrial Research, Publishing Division, Box 395, Pretoria 0001, South Africa. circ. 3,000 English edt.; 2,000 Afrikaans edt.

574 550 US ISSN 0068-5461
CALIFORNIA ACADEMY OF SCIENCES. OCCASIONAL PAPERS. 1890. irreg.(4-9yr.) no. 135, 1980. price varies per no., annual subscr. with proceedings $10. ‡ California Academy of Sciences, Golden Gate Park, San Francisco, CA 94118. Ed. Tomio Iwamoto. index in each vol. circ. 1,000. (also avail. in microform from UMI) Indexed: Biol.Abstr.

500 060 US ISSN 0068-547X
CALIFORNIA ACADEMY OF SCIENCES. PROCEEDINGS. 1954; vol. 42, 4th series, 1980-81. irreg. (12-15 issues per year) price varies per no.; annual subscr. with Occasional Papers $10. ‡ California Academy of Sciences, Golden Gate Park, San Francisco, CA 94118. Ed. Tomio Iwamoto. index in each vol. circ. 1,000. (also avail. in microform from UMI) Indexed: Biol.Abstr. Key Word Ind.Wildl.Res.

354 CN
CANADA. MINISTRY OF STATE FOR SCIENCE AND TECHNOLOGY. ANNUAL REPORT/RAPPORT ANNUEL. 1971/72. a. ‡ Ministry of State for Science and Technology, Ottawa, Canada. circ. 2,000.

500 CN ISSN 0701-7391
CANADA. MINISTRY OF STATE FOR SCIENCE AND TECHNOLOGY. FEDERAL SCIENCE PROGRAMS. irreg. Ministry of State for Science and Technology, Ottawa, Ont., Canada.

500 026 CN ISSN 0703-0320
CANADA INSTITUTE FOR SCIENTIFIC AND TECHNICAL INFORMATION. ANNUAL REPORT/INSTITUT CANADIEN DE L'INFORMATION SCIENTIFIQUE ET TECHNIQUE. RAPPORT ANNUEL. a. free. National Research Council of Canada, Canada Institute for Scientific and Technical Information (CISTI), Ottawa, Ont. K1A OS2, Canada. circ. 3,000.
Formerly: National Science Library of Canada. Annual Report (ISSN 0077-5576)

500 US ISSN 0069-066X
CARNEGIE INSTITUTION OF WASHINGTON. YEAR BOOK. 1902. a. $10. Carnegie Institution of Washington, 1530 P St., Washington, DC 20005. Ed. Sheila A. McGough.

500.9 US ISSN 0097-4463
CARNEGIE MUSEUM OF NATURAL HISTORY. ANNALS OF (THE) CARNEGIE MUSEUM. 1901. irreg., vol. 45, 1974. price varies. ‡ Carnegie Museum of Natural History, 4400 Forbes Ave., Pittsburgh, PA 15213. Ed. Robert E. Porteous. charts. illus. index. circ. 800. Indexed: Biol.Abstr. Zoo.Rec. Key Title: Annals of the Carnegie Museum.
Natural history

500.9 US ISSN 0145-9031
CARNEGIE MUSEUM OF NATURAL HISTORY. SPECIAL PUBLICATION. no. 2, 1976. irreg. $14 per no. Carnegie Museum of Natural History, 4400 Forbes Ave., Pittsburgh, PA 15213.

SCIENCES: COMPREHENSIVE WORKS

500 UK ISSN 0069-0945
CASS LIBRARY OF SCIENCE CLASSICS. 1967. irreg., no. 23, 1971. price varies. Frank Cass & Co. Ltd., Gainsborough House, 11 Gainsborough Rd., London E11 1RS, England (Dist. in U.S. by: Biblio Distribution Center, 81 Adams Drive, Totowa, N.J. 07512)

CENTRE NATIONAL DE DOCUMENTATION SCIENTIFIQUE ET TECHNIQUE. RAPPORT D'ACTIVITE. see *TECHNOLOGY: COMPREHENSIVE WORKS*

500 FR
CENTRE NATIONAL DE LA RECHERCHE SCIENTIFIQUE. COLLOQUES INTERNATIONAUX. SCIENCES MATHEMATIQUES, PHYSIQUES, CHIMIQUES, BIOLOGIQUES ET MEDICALES. 1949, no.8. irreg. price varies. Centre National de la Recherche Scientifique, 15 Quai Anatole-France, 75700 Paris, France.
Formerly: Centre National de la Recherche Scientifique. Colloques Internationaux. Sciences Mathematiques, Physico-Chimiques, Biologiques et Naturelles (ISSN 0071-8300)

500 FR ISSN 0071-8327
CENTRE NATIONAL DE LA RECHERCHE SCIENTIFIQUE. RAPPORT D'ACTIVITE. 1958/59. a. price varies. Centre National de la Recherche Scientifique, 15 Quai Anatole-France, 75700 Paris, France.

500 FR ISSN 0071-8335
CENTRE NATIONAL DE LA RECHERCHE SCIENTIFIQUE. RAPPORT NATIONAL DE CONJONCTURE SCIENTIFIQUE. a. price varies. Centre National de la Recherche Scientifique, 15 Quai Anatole-France, 75700 Paris, France.

500 FR ISSN 0071-8351
CENTRE NATIONAL DE LA RECHERCHE SCIENTIFIQUE. TABLEAU DE CLASSEMENT DES CHERCHEURS. 1958. irreg. Centre National de la Recherche Scientifique, 15 Quai Anatole France, 75700 Paris, France.

500 CS ISSN 0069-228X
CESKOSLOVENSKA AKADEMIE VED. ROZPRAVY. MPV: RADA MATEMATICKYCH A PRIRODNICH VED. 1891. irreg., vol. 85, 1975. price varies. Academia, Publishing House of the Czechoslovak Academy of Sciences, Vodickova 40, 112 29 Prague 1, Czechoslovakia. circ. 1,000.

500 US ISSN 0009-3491
CHICAGO ACADEMY OF SCIENCES. BULLETIN. 1883. irreg., latest vol. 11, no. 7, 1972. price varies. Chicago Academy of Sciences, 2001 N. Clark St., Chicago, IL 60614. Ed. Dir. William J. Beecher. charts, illus, bibl. circ. 1,019. (also avail. in microform from UMI)

951 500 US ISSN 0361-9001
CHINESE SCIENCE; an informal and irregular journal dedicated to the study of traditional Chinese science, technology, and medicine. 1975. irreg(1-2/yr) $8 for 4 nos. 856 Williams Hall/CU, University of Pennsylvania, Philadelphia, PA 19104. Ed. N. Sivin. circ. 300.

500 600 JA ISSN 0578-2228
CHUO UNIVERSITY. FACULTY OF SCIENCE AND ENGINEERING. BULLETIN/CHUO DAIGAKU RIKOGAKUBU KIYO. (Summaries and some articles in English) a. Chuo University, Faculty of Science and Engineering, 1-13-27 Kasuga, Bunkyo-ku, Tokyo 112, Japan. illus.

500 600 BL ISSN 0084-8794
CIENCIA. (Text in Portuguese; summaries in English) 1970, vol. 1, no. 2. irreg. avail. on exchange. Centro Academico Piraja da Silva, Faculdade de Ciencias Medicas e Biologicas de Botucatu, C.P. 102, Rubiao-Junior, Botucatu, S.P., Brazil.

580 590 579 AT
CLEMATIS. 1962. a. Aus.$0.50. Bairnsdale Field Naturalists' Club, 13 Turnbull St., Bairnsdale, Vic. 3550, Australia. Ed. Ronald S. Yeates. circ. controlled.

500 FR ISSN 0366-757X
CODATA BULLETIN. (Includes Proceedings of the Codata Conference) 1967. irreg(3-5/yr) 100 F.($20) (for institutions; $8 for qualified individuals) International Council of Scientific Unions, Committee on Data for Science and Technology, 51 Bd. de Montmorency, 75016 Paris, France. Ed. Phyllis Glaeser. circ. 700.
Energy

500 FR ISSN 0538-6918
CODATA NEWSLETTER. (Text in English) 1968. irreg. International Council of Scientific Unions, Committee on Data for Science and Technology, CODATA Secretariat, 51 Bd de Montmorency, 75016 Paris, France. Dir. Bertrand Dreyfus. bk. rev. bibl.

500 SP
COLECCION CIENCIAS, HUMANIDADES E INGENIERIA. irreg. price varies. Colegio de Ingenieros de Caminos, Canales y Puertos, Almagro, 42, Madrid 4, Spain.

500 CK
COLECCION: DOCUMENTOS E HISTORIA DE LA CIENCIA EN COLOMBIA. irreg. Fondo Colombiano de Investigaciones Cientificas, Apdo. Aereo 29828, Bogota, Colombia.

500 US
COLORADO STATE UNIVERSITY RESEARCH. 1950. irreg. free. Colorado State University Experiment Station, Office of University Communications, Colorado State University, Fort Collins, CO 80523. Ed. James G. Bolick. circ. 5,000.
Formerly: Colorado Farm and Home Research.

500 US ISSN 0096-2279
COLORADO-WYOMING ACADEMY OF SCIENCES JOURNAL.* 1929. a. $5. Colorado-Wyoming Academy of Science., c/o Dept. of Environmental, Populations and Organismic Biology, University of Colorado, Boulder, CO 80302. Ed. Bd. abstr. circ. 300.

500 UK ISSN 0069-6277
COLSTON RESEARCH SOCIETY, BRISTOL, ENGLAND. PROCEEDINGS OF THE SYMPOSIUM. COLSTON RESEARCH PAPERS. 1948. a. price varies. John Wright & Sons Ltd., 42-44 Triangle West, Bristol BS8 1EX, England.

500 600 UK ISSN 0074-9540
CONGRES INTERNATIONAL D'HISTOIRE DES SCIENCES. ACTES. 1947. irreg., 13th, 1971, Moscow. International Union of the History & Philosophy of Science, c/o L. J. Cohe, Queen's College, Oxford, England.

CONNECTICUT ACADEMY OF ARTS AND SCIENCES. TRANSACTIONS. see *HUMANITIES: COMPREHENSIVE WORKS*

001.3 500 US ISSN 0069-8970
CONNECTICUT ACADEMY OF ARTS AND SCIENCES. MEMOIRS. 1801. irreg., 1969, vol. 18. Archon Books (Subsidiary of: Shoe String Press) 995 Sherman Ave., Hamden, CT 06514. Ed. Dorothea Rudnick. illus. Indexed: Biol.Abstr.

506 CN ISSN 0705-8292
CONSEIL DE LA JEUNESSE SCIENTIFIQUE. BOTTIN. (Text in French) 1977. a. $1 per. no. Conseil de la Jeunesse Scientifique, 1415 Est, rue Jarry, Montreal, Que. H2E 2Z7, Canada.

001 502 AG
CONSEJO NACIONAL DE INVESTIGACIONES CIENTIFICAS Y TECNICAS. INFORME SOBRE UN ANO DE LABOR. irreg. Consejo Nacional de Investigaciones Cientificas y Tecnicas, Rivadavia 1917, 1033 Buenos Aires, Argentina. illus.

500 600 UR ISSN 0069-9713
CONTRIBUTIONS TO THE HISTORY OF SCIENCE AND TECHNOLOGY IN BALTICS/ IZ ISTORII ESTESTVOZNANIYA I TEKHNIKI PRIBALTIKI. (Text in Russian; summaries in English) 1959. a or biennial. 1.50 Rub. (Akademiya Nauk Latviiskoi S. S. R.) Izdevnieciba Zinatne, Turgeneva iela, 19, Riga, U. S. S. R. Ed.Bd. bk. rev. circ. 1,000. Indexed: Bull.Signal. Chem.Abstr. Ref.Zh.

500 US ISSN 0070-1416
CRANBROOK INSTITUTE OF SCIENCE, BLOOMFIELD HILLS, MICHIGAN. BULLETIN. (Each Bulletin Has a Distinctive Title) 1931. irreg., no. 58, 1980. price varies. ‡ Cranbrook Institute of Science, Box 801, Bloomfield Hills, MI 48013. Dir. Robert N. Bowen. adv. bk. rev.

500.9 UK ISSN 0309-8656
CROYDON NATURAL HISTORY & SCIENTIFIC SOCIETY. PROCEEDINGS AND TRANSACTIONS. 1871. irreg. (approx. 3-4/yr.) £4 (includes the Society's Bulletin) Croydon Natural History and Scientific Society Ltd., 96A Brighton Rd., South Croydon, Surrey CR2 6AD, England. Ed. F.G. Peake. charts. illus. cum.index. circ. 1,000.
Natural history

500 US
CURRENT BIBLIOGRAPHIC DIRECTORY FOR THE ARTS & SCIENCES. Abbreviated title: C B D. 1979. a. $200. Institute for Scientific Information, 3501 Market St., University City Science Center, Philadelphia, PA 19104 (and 132 High St., Uxbridge, Middlesex, England) Ed. E. Garfield.
Former titles, 1969-1978: I S I's Who Is Publishing in Science (ISSN 0360-8174); 1966-1970: International Directory of Research and Development Scientists (ISSN 0538-7205)

500 600 IS ISSN 0301-4657
CURRENT RESEARCH AND DEVELOPMENT PROJECTS IN ISRAEL: NATURAL SCIENCES AND TECHNOLOGY. irreg. $60. (National Council for Research and Development) National Center of Scientific and Technological Information, P.O.B. 20125, Tel-Aviv, Israel.
Formerly: Directory of Current Research in Israel: Physical and Life Sciences (ISSN 0070-539X)

500 US
CURRENT TOPICS OF CONTEMPORARY THOUGHT. a. price varies. Gordon and Breach Science Publishers, One Park Ave., New York, NY 10016. Ed. Rubin Gotesky, Ervin Laszlo.

DAEDALUS. see *MUSEUMS AND ART GALLERIES*

500.9 US ISSN 0084-9650
DELAWARE MUSEUM OF NATURAL HISTORY. MONOGRAPH SERIES. 1970. irreg., latest, no. 3. price varies. Delaware Museum of Natural History, Box 3937, Greenville, DE 19807. Indexed: Biol.Abstr.
Natural history

500.9 US ISSN 0084-9669
DELAWARE MUSEUM OF NATURAL HISTORY. REPRODUCTION SERIES. 1968. irreg. price varies. Delaware Museum of Natural History, Box 3937, Greenville, DE 19807. Indexed: Biol.Abstr.
Natural history

500.9 US ISSN 0084-9677
DELAWARE MUSEUM OF NATURAL HISTORY. SPECIAL PUBLICATIONS. 1971. irreg. price varies. Delaware Museum of Natural History, Box 3937, Greenville, DE 19807. Indexed: Biol.Abstr.
Natural history

500 DK
DENMARK. PLANLAEGNINGSRAADET FOR FORSKNINGEN. BERETNING. 1974. a. Planlaegningsraadet, Forskningssekretariatet, Copenhagen, Denmark.

DESTERREICHISCHE AKADEMIE DER WISSENSCHAFTEN, VIENNA. MATHEMATISCH' NATURWISSENSCHAFTLICHE KLASSE. DENKSCHRIFTEN. see *MATHEMATICS*

500 GW ISSN 0070-3974
DEUTSCHE FORSCHUNGSGEMEINSCHAFT. DENKSCHRIFTEN ZUR LAGE DER DEUTSCHEN WISSENSCHAFT. 1957. irreg. price varies. Boldt Verlag, Postfach 110, 5407 Boppard, W. Germany (B.R.D.) bk. rev.

500 GW ISSN 0070-3982
DEUTSCHE FORSCHUNGSGEMEINSCHAFT. FORSCHUNGSBERICHTE. 1957. irreg. price varies. Boldt Verlag, Postfach 110, 5407 Boppard, W. Germany (B.R.D.)

SCIENCES: COMPREHENSIVE WORKS

500   GW   ISSN 0070-3990
DEUTSCHE FORSCHUNGSGEMEINSCHAFT. KOMMISSIONEN. MITTEILUNGEN. 1964. irreg. price varies. Boldt Verlag, Postfach 110, 5407 Boppard, W. Germany (B.R.D.) bk. rev.

500   GW   ISSN 0418-842X
DEUTSCHE FORSCHUNGSGEMEINSCHAFT. MEXIKO-PROJEKT; eine deutsch-mexikanische interdisziplinaere Regionalforschung im Becken von Puebla-Tlaxcala. (Text in German and Spanish) irreg., vol. 17, 1981. price varies. Franz Steiner Verlag GmbH, Friedrichstr. 24, Postfach 5529, 6200 Wiesbaden, W. Germany (B.R.D.) Ed.Wichelm Lauer.

500 600   US   ISSN 0070-5330
DIRECTORY OF COMPUTERIZED INFORMATION IN SCIENCE AND TECHNOLOGY. 1968. irreg. Science Associates International Inc., 1841 Broadway, New York, NY 10023.

500   UK   ISSN 0309-5339
DIRECTORY OF EUROPEAN ASSOCIATIONS. PART 2: NATIONAL LEARNED, SCIENTIFIC & TECHNICAL SOCIETIES. 1975. irreg., 2nd, 1979. £31.50($95) C B D Research Ltd., 154 High St., Beckenham, Kent BR3 1EA, England (Dist. in U.S. by: Gale Research Co., Book Tower, Detroit, MI 48226) Ed. I. G. Anderson. circ. 4,000.

500   CN   ISSN 0316-0297
DIRECTORY OF FEDERALLY SUPPORTED RESEARCH IN UNIVERSITIES/REPERTOIRE DE LA RECHERCHE DANS LES UNIVERSITES SUBVENTIONNEE PAR LE GOUVERNEMENT FEDERAL. 1972-73. a. Can.$50($50) National Research Council of Canada, Canada Institute for Scientific and Technical Information (CISTI), Ottawa, Ont. K1A 0S2, Canada. circ. 300.

500   RH
DIRECTORY OF ORGANIZATIONS CONCERNED WITH SCIENTIFIC RESEARCH AND TECHNICAL SERVICES IN RHODESIA. 1959. triennial,latest 1975. Scientific Liaison Office, Box 8510, Causeway, Zimbabwe.

500   IS
DIRECTORY OF RESEARCH INSTITUTES AND INDUSTRIAL LABORATORIES IN ISRAEL. (Text in Hebrew and English) 1962. irreg., 3rd edt., 1979. I£150($35) (National Council for Research and Development) National Center of Scientific and Technological Information, P.O. Box 20125, Tel-Aviv, Israel. index.
Formerly: Directory of Research Institutes and Industrial Research Units in Israel (ISSN 0334-2875)

500   US   ISSN 0070-6256
DIRECTORY OF SCIENCE RESOURCES FOR MARYLAND. 1963. biennial. $6. Department of Economic and Community Development, Business Directories, 2525 Riva Rd., Annapolis, MD 21401. Ed. Fred E. Ziegenhorn. adv.

500 060   IS   ISSN 0334-2824
DIRECTORY OF SCIENTIFIC AND TECHNICAL ASSOCIATIONS IN ISRAEL. (Guides to Sources of Information Series, No. 2) (Text in Hebrew and English) 1962. irreg. I£150($25) (National Council for Research and Development) National Center of Scientific and Technological Information, P.O.B. 20125, Tel-Aviv, Israel. 3 indexes.
Formerly: Directory of Scientific and Technical Associations and Institutes in Israel (ISSN 0070-6264)

500   UK   ISSN 0070-6272
DIRECTORY OF SCIENTIFIC DIRECTORIES. irreg., 3rd edt 1979. ‡ Longman Group Ltd., Longman House, Burnt Mill, Harlow, Essex CM20 2JE, England (Dist. in U.S. and Canada by: Gale Research Co. Ltd., Book Tower, Detroit, MI 48226)

500   NR   ISSN 0070-6280
DIRECTORY OF SCIENTIFIC RESEARCH IN NIGERIA. 1968. a. Science Association of Nigeria, Box 4039, Ibadan, Nigeria.

507   CE
DIRECTORY OF SCIENTIFIC RESEARCH PROJECTS IN SRI LANKA(CEYLON) (Text in English) 1970. irreg. $15. (Ceylon Institute of Scientific and Industrial Research) National Science Council of Sri Lanka, 47/5 Maitland Place, Colombo 7, Sri Lanka.

500   PK
DIRECTORY OF THE RESEARCH ESTABLISHMENTS IN PAKISTAN. (Text in English) 1975. a. Rs.20. National Science Council of Pakistan, P.O.B. 2001, Drigh Rd., Karachi 8, Pakistan.

500 600   PK
DIRECTORY OF THE SCIENTISTS, TECHNOLOGISTS, AND ENGINEERS OF THE P C S I R. (Text in English) 1975. irreg. Rs.10. Pakistan Council of Scientific and Industrial Research, Publications Branch, 39 Garden Rd., Karachi 0310, Pakistan.

500.9   US
DISCOVERY (NEW HAVEN) SUPPLEMENT. 1977. irreg., no. 2, 1978. price varies. Peabody Museum of Natural History, Yale University, New Haven, CT 06511. Ed. Zelda Edelson. circ. 1,000.
Natural history

500   SW   ISSN 0347-5719
DOCUMENTA. 1972. irreg. (3-5/yr.) Kungliga Svenska Vetenskapsakademien - Royal Swedish Academy of Sciences, Box 50005, S-104 05 Stockholm, Sweden. Ed. Lennart Daleus. bibl. illus.

500.9 913   UK   ISSN 0070-7112
DORSET NATURAL HISTORY AND ARCHAEOLOGICAL SOCIETY. PROCEEDINGS. 1877. a. £5. Dorset County Museum, Dorchester, Dorset, England. Ed. W. G. Putnam. bk. rev. circ. 2,000.

500   US   ISSN 0085-0071
DREXEL RESEARCH CONFERENCE. SUMMARY REPORT. 1971. a. free. ‡ Drexel University, 32nd & Chestnut Sts., Philadelphia, PA 19104.

500 600   US   ISSN 0085-008X
DREXEL UNIVERSITY RESEARCH REVIEW. 1970/71. a. free. ‡ Drexel University, 32nd & Chestnut Sts, Philadelphia, PA 19104. bibl. charts. illus. stat. circ. 2,000.

500   US
EASTERN EUROPE REPORT: SCIENTIFIC AFFAIRS. 1968. irreg. (approx. 53/yr.) $318. U.S. Joint Publications Research Service, 1000 N. Glebe Rd., Arlington, VA 22201 (Orders to: NTIS, Springfield, VA 22161)
Formerly: Translations on Eastern Europe. Scientific Affairs.

500   SZ
ECOLE POLYTECHNIQUE FEDERALE DE LAUSANNE. PUBLICATION. no. 120, 1971. irreg. Ecole Polytechnique Federale de Lausanne, 33 Ave. de Cour, 1007 Lausanne, Switzerland.

500 060   US
ENCYCLIA. 1924. a. $10. Utah Academy of Sciences, Arts, and Letters, c/o Levi S. Peterson, Ed., Department of English, Weber State College, Ogden, UT 84408. circ. 1,000. Indexed: Chem.Abstr.
Formerly (until vol. 54, 1977): Utah Academy of Science, Arts and Letters. Proceedings (ISSN 0083-4823)

500 600   NE
EPISTEME; a series in the foundational methodological, philosophical, psychological, sociological and political aspects of the sciences, pure and applied. (Text in English) 1975. irreg. price varies. D. Reidel Publishing Co., Box 17, 3300 AA Dordrecht, Netherlands (And Lincoln Building, 160 Old Derby St., Hingham, MA 02043) Ed. Mario Bunge.

500   GW   ISSN 0340-8833
ERNST-MACH-INSTITUT, FREIBURG. BERICHT. irreg. Ernst-Mach Institut, Eckerstr. 4, 7800 Freiburg, W. Germany (B.R.D.)
Formerly: Ernst-Mach-Institut, Freiburg. Wissenschaftlicher Bericht (ISSN 0071-1217)

500 600   SZ   ISSN 0071-335X
EXPERIENTIA. SUPPLEMENTUM. (Text in English, French and German) 1953. irreg., latest 1972. price varies. Birkhaeuser Verlag, Elisabethenstr. 19, CH-4010 Basel, Switzerland.

910   CS
FOLIA FACULTATIS SCIENTIARUM NATURALIUM UNIVERSITATIS PURKYNIANAE BRUNENSIS: GEOGRAPHIA. irreg (7-12/yr.) price varies. Universita J. E. Purkyne, Prirodovedecka Fakulta, Kotlarska 2, 611 37 Brno, Czechoslovakia.

500   FR   ISSN 0071-8319
FRANCE. CENTRE NATIONAL DE LA RECHERCHE SCIENTIFIQUE. COLLOQUES NATIONAUX. irreg., 1975, no. 933. Centre National de la Recherche Scientifique, 15 Quai Anatole-France, 75700 Paris, France.

500 949.3   BE
DE FRANSE NEDERLANDEN/PAYS-BAS FRANCAIS. 1976. a. 700 Fr. Stichting Ons Erfdeel, Murissonstraat 160, B-8530 Rekkem, Belgium. Ed. Jozef Deleu. circ. 2,000.

629.13   FA   ISSN 0085-0896
FRODSKAPARRIT; ANNALES SOCIETATIS SCIENTIARUM FAEROENSIS. (Text mainly in Faroese: summaries in English and occasionally in other languages) 1952. a. price varies. (Mentunargrunner Foeroya Loegtings) Foeroya Frodskaparfelag, DK-3800 Torshavn, Faeroe Islands. Ed.Bd. index. circ. 1,000.

500   FA   ISSN 0429-7539
FRODSKAPARRIT; ANNALES SOCIETATIS SCIENTIARUM FAERONSIS. SUPPLEMENTA. (Text and summaries in Danish, Faeroe or English) 1954. irreg. (Mentunargrunner Foeroya Loegtings) Foeroya Frodskaparfelag, DK-3800 Torshavn, Faeroe Islands. index.

500.9   US   ISSN 0016-2159
FRONTIERS; a magazine of natural history. 1936. a. (q. before 1979) membership (non-members $5) Academy of Natural Sciences of Philadelphia, 19th St., and the Parkway, Philadelphia, PA 19103. Ed. Robert Peck. adv. bk. rev. illus. index. circ. 5,500.

500   JA   ISSN 0071-9781
FUKUI UNIVERSITY. FACULTY OF EDUCATION. MEMOIRS. SERIES 2: NATURAL SCIENCE. (Text in English or Japanese) 1961. irreg. Fukui University, Faculty of Education - Fukui Daigaku Kyoikugakubu, 3-9-1 Bunkyo, Fukui-shi 910, Japan.

060   AG
FUNDACION BARILOCHE. MEMORIA ANUAL. a. Fundacion Bariloche, Casilla de Correo 138, San Carlos de Bariloche - Rio Negro, Argentina.

500   US
FUTURIST LIBRARY. a. price varies. Gordon and Breach Science Publishers, One Park Ave., New York, NY 10016.

GDANSKIE TOWARZYSTWO NAUKOWE. WYDZIAL III. NAUK MATEMATYCZNO-PRZYRODNICZYCH. ROZPRAWY. see *MATHEMATICS*

500 001.4   US   ISSN 0072-0798
GENERAL SYSTEMS YEARBOOK. 1956. a. $17.50 to non-members. Society for General Systems Research, Systems Science Institute, University of Louisville, Louisville, KY 40208. Ed. Anatol Rapoport. bk. rev. circ. 2,000. (back issues avail.)

007   GW
GERMANY (FEDERAL REPUBLIC,1949-) BUNDESMINISTERIUM FUER FORSCHUNG UND TECHNOLOGIE. BMFT FOERDERUNGSKATALOG. 1971. a. DM.30. Bundesministerium fuer Forschung und Technologie, Stresemann Str. 2, 5300 Bonn-Bad Godesberg, W. Germany (B.R.D.) circ. 4,000.

SCIENCES: COMPREHENSIVE WORKS

500.9 GE ISSN 0036-6978
GESCHICHTE DER NATURWISSENSCHAFTEN, TECHNIK UND MEDIZIN. SCHRIFTENREIHE. 1960. a. M.30 per vol. Akademische Verlagsgesellschaft Geest und Portig K.G., Sternwartenstr. 8, 701 Leipzig, E. Germany (D.D.R.) adv. bk. rev. bibl. charts. illus. index.
Formerly: Zeitschrift fuer Geschichte der Naturwissenschaften, der Technik und der Medizin.

500 SW ISSN 0348-6788
GOTHENBURG STUDIES IN THE HISTORY OF SCIENCE AND IDEAS. (Subseries of Acta Universitatis Gothoburgensis) 1979. irreg., vol. 2, 1979. price varies. Acta Universitatis Gothoburgensis, Box 5096, S-402 22 Goeteborg 5, Sweden (Dist. in U.S., Canada, and Mexico by: Humanities Press, Inc., 171 First Ave., Atlantic Highlands, NJ 07716) Eds. Sven-Eric Liedman, Henrik Sandblad.

007 US ISSN 0072-520X
GOVERNMENTAL RESEARCH ASSOCIATION DIRECTORY; directory of organizations and individuals professionally engaged in governmental research and related activities. 1938. biennial. $20. Governmental Research Association, Inc., P.O. Box 387, Ocean Gate, NJ 08740. index. circ. 700.

500.9 FR ISSN 0434-3581
GRANDS NATURALISTES FRANCAIS. 1952. irreg. price varies. Musee National d'Histoire Naturelle, 38 rue Geoffroy Saint Hilaire, 75005 Paris, France.

500 UK ISSN 0072-5919
GREAT BRITAIN. DEPARTMENT OF EDUCATION AND SCIENCE. SCIENCE POLICY STUDIES. 1967. irreg. price varies. Department of Education and Science, Elizabeth House, York Rd., London SE1 7PH, England (Avail. from H.M.S.O., c/o Liaison Officer, Atlantic House, Holborn Viaduct, London EC1P 1BN, England)

500 600 UK ISSN 0072-7148
GREAT BRITAIN. SCIENCE RESEARCH COUNCIL. REPORT. 1965-66. a. price varies. Science Research Council, State House, High Holborn, London WC1R 4TA, England (Avail. from H.M.S.O., c/o Liaison Officer, Atlantic House, Holborn Viaduct, London EC1P 1BN, England) illus.

500 IC
GREINAR; collection of miscellaneous papers. 1935. irreg., latest no. 6, 1977. price varies. Visindafelag Islendinga - Societas Scientiarum Islandica (Icelandic Scientific Society), Haskolabokasafn, 101 Reykjavik, Iceland. circ. 1,000.

500 100 200 GW
GRENZFRAGEN. 1972. irreg., vol. 7, 1978. (Goerres-Gesellschaft) Karl Alber GmbH, Hermann Herder Str. 4, 7800 Freiburg, W. Germany (B.R.D.) Ed. Norbert A. Luyten.

500 AG
GUIA DE INVESTIGACIONES EN CURSO DE LA UNIVERSIDAD DE BUENOS AIRES. 1968. irreg. price varies. Universidad de Buenos Aires, Instituto Bibliotecologico, Departamento de Registros Cientificos, Casilla de Correo 901, 1000 Buenos Aires, Argentina. Ed. Hans Gravenhorst.

500 600 UK
GUIDE TO SCIENCE AND TECHNOLOGY IN EASTERN EUROPE. 1979. irreg. Longman Group Ltd., Longman House, Burnt Mill, Harlow, Essex CM20 2JE, England (Dist. in U.S. and Canada by: Gale Research Co. Ltd., Book Tower, Detroit, MI 48226)

500 600 UK
GUIDE TO SCIENCE AND TECHNOLOGY IN THE ASIA/PACIFIC AREA. 1979. irreg. Longman Group Ltd., Longman House, Burnt Mill, Harlow, Essex CM20 2JE, England (Dist. in U.S. and Canada by: Gale Research Co. Ltd., Book Tower, Detroit, MI 48226)

500 600 TU ISSN 0072-9221
HACETTEPE FEN VE MUHENDISLIK BILIMLERI DERGISI. (Text in Turkish; summaries in English, French and German) 1971. a. TL.10($0.75) (University of Hacettepe) Hacettepe University Press, Ankara, Turkey. Ed. Alaattin Kutsal.

509 US
HARVARD MONOGRAPHS IN THE HISTORY OF SCIENCE. irreg. price varies. Harvard University Press, 79 Garden St., Cambridge, MA 02138.

500 US ISSN 0073-1595
HEIDELBERG SCIENCE LIBRARY. 1967. irreg.; unnumbered after vol. 22; latest 1979. Springer-Verlag, 175 Fifth Ave, New York, NY 10010 (also Berlin, Heidelberg, Vienna) (reprint service avail. from ISI)

500 US ISSN 0073-1625
HEIDELBERGER AKADEMIE DER WISSENSCHAFTEN. MATHEMATISCH-NATURWISSENSCHAFTLICHE KLASSE. SITZUNGSBERICHTE. 1948. irreg. price varies. Springer-Verlag, 175 Fifth Ave, New York, NY 10010 (also Berlin, Heidelberg, Vienna) (reprint service avail. from ISI)

500 US ISSN 0073-1633
HEIDELBERGER ARBEITSBUECHER. 1971. irreg., no. 10, 1976. price varies. Springer-Verlag, 175 Fifth Ave, New York, NY 10010 (also Berlin, Heidelberg, Vienna) (reprint service avail. from ISI)

500 US ISSN 0073-1641
HEIDELBERGER JAHRBUECHER. 1957. a. price varies. Springer-Verlag, 175 Fifth Ave, New York, NY 10010 (also Berlin, Heidelberg, Vienna) (reprint service avail. from ISI)

500 US ISSN 0073-1684
HEIDELBERGER TASCHENBUECHER. 1964. irreg., no. 208, 1981. price varies. Springer-Verlag, 175 Fifth Ave, New York, NY 10010 (also Berlin, Heidelberg, Vienna) (reprint service avail. from ISI)

500 JA
HIROSHIMA UNIVERSITY. FACULTY OF GENERAL EDUCATION. MEMOIRS: STUDIES IN NATURAL SCIENCES. (Text in English and Japanese) a. Hiroshima University, Faculty of General Education, 1-89 1-chome Higashisenda, Hiroshima 730, Japan. illus.

500 FR ISSN 0073-2362
HISTOIRE DE LA PENSEE. 1960. irreg., 1972, no. 17. price varies. Editions Hermann, 293 rue Lecourbe, 75015 Paris, France.

500 SP ISSN 0073-2494
HISTORIA Y FILOSOFIA DE LA CIENCIA. SERIE MAYOR. ENCUADERNADA. 1938. irreg. price varies. Espasa-Calpe, S.A., Carretera de Irun 12200, Apartado 547, Madrid 34, Spain.

500 SP ISSN 0073-2508
HISTORIA Y FILOSOFIA DE LA CIENCIA. SERIE MENOR. RUSTICA. 1938. irreg. price varies. Espasa-Calpe, S.A., Carretera de Irun 12200, Apartado 547, Madrid 34, Spain.

500 GW ISSN 0073-2532
HISTORIAE SCIENTIARUM ELEMENTA. (Text in German, English and Latin) 1962. irreg., 1973, vol. 5. price varies. Werner Fritsch Verlag, Postfach 751, 8000 Munich 1, W. Germany (B. R. D.) Ed. Werner Fritsch.

500 610 US
HISTORICAL STUDIES IN THE LIFE SCIENCES. 1977. a. price varies. Johns Hopkins University Press, Baltimore, MD 21218.

500 US
HISTORICAL STUDIES IN THE PHYSICAL SCIENCES. 1977. irreg. price varies. Johns Hopkins University Press, Baltimore, MD 21218.

700 500 JA ISSN 0073-2788
HITOTSUBASHI JOURNAL OF ARTS AND SCIENCES. (Text in English or French) 1960. a. 1500 Yen($12) Hitotsubashi University, Hitotsubashi Academy, 2-1 Naka, Kunitachi, Tokyo 186, Japan. Ed. T. Yamada. cum.index. circ. 940.

500 FR ISSN 0073-3180
HOMME FACE A LA NATURE.* 1970. irreg. price varies. Editions France-Empire, 68 rue Jean-Jacques Rousseau, 75001 Paris, France.

500 US ISSN 0075-0344
I A S BULLETIN. 1967. irreg. Iowa Academy of Science, University of Northern Iowa, Cedar Falls, IA 50613.

I A T U L PROCEEDINGS. (International Association of Technological Universities Libraries) see *LIBRARY AND INFORMATION SCIENCES*

500 US
I S I JOURNAL CITATION REPORTS. (Includes Journal Ranking, Reference Data, and Source Data Packages) 1973. a. $250 (incl. in subscr. to Science Citation Index and Social Science Citation Index) Institute for Scientific Information, 3501 Market St., University City Science Center, Philadelphia, PA 19104 (and 132 High St., Uxbridge, Middlesex, England)

500.9 US ISSN 0073-4918
ILLINOIS. NATURAL HISTORY SURVEY. BULLETIN. 1876. irreg., vol. 32, no. 2, 1980. single free copy. ‡ Illinois Natural History Survey, Natural Resources Bldg., Urbana, IL 61801. Ed. Robert M. Zewadski. Indexed: Biol.Abstr. Wild Life Rev. Zoo.Rec.

500.9 US ISSN 0073-4926
ILLINOIS. NATURAL HISTORY SURVEY. CIRCULAR. 1918. irreg., no. 55, 1980. free. ‡ Illinois Natural History Survey, Natural Resources Building, Urbana, IL 61801. Ed. Robert M. Zewadski. Indexed: Biol.Abstr. Zoo.Rec.

500 US ISSN 0162-1939
ILLINOIS. STATE MUSEUM. GUIDEBOOKLET SERIES. 1977. irreg., no. 4, 1980. Illinois State Museum, Springfield, IL 62706.

500 US ISSN 0095-2893
ILLINOIS. STATE MUSEUM. INVENTORY OF THE COLLECTIONS. 1969. irreg., no.1, pt. 3, 1980. free. Illinois State Museum, Springfield, IL 62706.

500 US ISSN 0360-0297
ILLINOIS. STATE MUSEUM. POPULAR SCIENCE SERIES. 1939. irreg., vol. 9, 1978. price varies. Illinois State Museum, Spring and Edwards Streets, Springfield, IL 62706. illus. Key Title: Popular Science Series.

500 US ISSN 0360-0289
ILLINOIS. STATE MUSEUM. STORY OF ILLINOIS SERIES. 1943. irreg., no.14, 1980. Illinois State Museum, Springfield, IL 62706.

500 SA
IMPULSE. (Not published 1974-76) 1971. irreg. free. University of Cape Town, Science Students' Council, Rondebosch 7700, South Africa. Eds. T. Warner, C. Millward. adv. bk. rev. bibl. charts. illus. circ. 900.

500 600 II ISSN 0085-1779
INDIA. COMMITTEE ON SCIENCE AND TECHNOLOGY. ANNUAL REPORT.* (Text in English) 1969. a. Committee on Science and Technology, Cabinet Secretariat, Department of Cabinet Affairs, New Delhi, India. charts. stat.

INDIAN NATIONAL SCIENCE ACADEMY. BIOGRAPHICAL MEMOIRS OF FELLOWS. see *BIOGRAPHY*

500 II
INDIAN NATIONAL SCIENCE ACADEMY. BULLETIN. 1952. irreg. price varies per issue. Indian National Science Academy, Bahadur Shah Zafar Marg, New Delhi 110002, India. abstr. charts. illus. circ. 600(approx.). Indexed: Sci.Abstr.
Continues: National Institute of Sciences of India. Bulletin (ISSN 0027-9528)

500 II
INDIAN NATIONAL SCIENCE ACADEMY. MONOGRAPHS. 1960. irreg. price varies. Indian National Science Academy, Bahadur Zafar Marg, New Delhi 110002, India.
Continues: National Institute of Sciences of India. N I S I Monographs (ISSN 0470-1380)

500 II ISSN 0073-6600
INDIAN NATIONAL SCIENCE ACADEMY.
PROCEEDINGS. (Text in English) 1935; in
separate pts. since 1955. parts A (Physical Sciences)
and B (biological Sciences) published in alternate
months. Rs.120($40) Indian National Science
Academy, Bahadur Shah Zafar Marg, New Delhi
110002, India. index. circ. 1,000. Indexed:
Biol.Abstr. Chem.Abstr. Met.Abstr. Sci.Abstr.
Sci.Abstr.
　　Formerly: National Institute of Sciences of India.
Proceedings.

500 II
INDIAN NATIONAL SCIENCE ACADEMY.
TRANSACTIONS. irreg. price varies. Indian
National Science Academy, Bahadur Shah Zafar
Marg, New Delhi 110002, India.

500 II ISSN 0073-6619
INDIAN NATIONAL SCIENCE ACADEMY.
YEAR BOOK. (Text in English) 1960. a. Rs.15($5)
Indian National Science Academy, Bahadur Shah
Zafar Marg, New Delhi 110002, India. circ. 1,000.
　　Formerly: National Institute of Sciences of India,
Calcutta. Year Book; Continues: National Institute
of Sciences of India. Yearbook (ISSN 0547-7573)

500 600 II ISSN 0085-1817
INDIAN SCIENCE CONGRESS ASSOCIATION.
PROCEEDINGS. (Text in English) 1914. a. in 4
pts. Rs.51. Indian Science Congress Association, 14
Dr. Biresh Guha St., Calcutta 700017, India. index.
circ. 5,000.

500 US ISSN 0073-6759
INDIANA ACADEMY OF SCIENCE.
MONOGRAPH. 1969. irreg., 1969, no. 1. price
varies. Indiana Academy of Science, 140 N. Senate
Ave., Indianapolis, IN 46204. Ed. William R.
Eberly. Indexed: Biol.Abstr.

500 US ISSN 0073-6767
INDIANA ACADEMY OF SCIENCE.
PROCEEDINGS. 1890. a. $7. Indiana Academy of
Science, 140 N. Senate Ave., Indianapolis, IN
46204. cum.index: vols. 1-80 (1890-1960)

500 IO
INDONESIA. NATIONAL SCIENTIFIC
DOCUMENTATION CENTRE. ANNUAL
REPORT/INDONESIA. PUSAT
DOKUMENTASI ILMIAH NASIONAL.
LAPORAN TAHUNAN. a. National Scientific
Documentation Centre, Jl. Jenderal Gatot Subroto,
Box 3065/Jkt., Jakarta, Indonesia.

605 IR
INFORMATIONS ET NOUVEAUTES
TECHNIQUES/ETTELA'AT VA TAZEHA-YE
FANNI. (Text in Persian & French) 1961. irreg.
free. Centre Francais d'Information Technique et
Industrielle, 62 Forsat Ave., Shahreza Ave., Box 11-
1555, Teheran, Iran. Eds. Aleksandr Gerigoriyans &
Bahman Shahparast. circ. 800.

060 PL ISSN 0537-667X
INFORMATOR NAUKI POLSKIEJ. 1958. a. $12.50.
Panstwowe Wydawnictwo Naukowe, Miodowa 10,
Warsaw, Poland (Dist. by: Ars Polona-Ruch,
Krakowskie Przedmiescie 7, Warsaw, Poland)

001.3 500 FR ISSN 0073-8190
INSTITUT DE FRANCE. ANNUAIRE. 1796. a.
membership. Institut de France, 23 Quai de Conti,
Paris 6e, France.

500 II ISSN 0073-8336
INSTITUT FRANCAIS DE PONDICHERY.
SECTION SCIENTIFIQUE ET TECHNIQUE.
TRAVAUX. (Text in French; summaries in English)
1957. irreg. price varies. Institut Francais de
Pondichery, Box 33, Pondichery 605001, India. Ed.
P. Legris. index. circ. 1,000. Indexed: Biol.Abstr.
Bull.Signal.

500 060 II ISSN 0073-8344
INSTITUT FRANCAIS DE PONDICHERY.
SECTION SCIENTIFIQUE ET TECHNIQUE.
TRAVAUX. HORS SERIE. (Text in English and
French) 1957. irreg. price varies. Institut Francais
de Pondichery, Box 33, Pondichery 605001, India.
Ed. P. Legris. index. circ. 1,200-1,500. Indexed:
Biol.Abstr. Bull.Signal.

500 600 AO ISSN 0074-0098
INSTITUTO DE INVESTIGACAO CIENTIFICA
DE ANGOLA. MEMORIAS E TRABALHOS.
(Text in Portuguese; summaries in English, French,
German) 1960. irreg., 1971, no. 8. price varies.
Instituto de Investigacao Cientifica de Angola,
Departamento de Documentacao e Informacao, P.O.
Box 3244, Luanda, Angola. abstr. (also avail. in
microform)

500 600 AO ISSN 0003-343X
INSTITUTO DE INVESTIGACAO CIENTIFICA
DE ANGOLA. RELATORIOS E
COMMUNICACOES. 1962. 1973, no. 25. Instituto
de Investigacao Cientifica de Angola, Departamento
de Documentacao e Informacao, P.O. Box 3244,
Luanda, Angola.

INTER-AMERICAN COUNCIL FOR
EDUCATION, SCIENCE, AND CULTURE.
FINAL REPORT. see *EDUCATION*

500 NE ISSN 0074-3402
INTERNATIONAL CONGRESS FOR LOGIC,
METHODOLOGY AND PHILOSOPHY OF
SCIENCE. PROCEEDINGS. 1960. quadrennial,
6th, 1980, Hannover. North Holland Publishing Co.,
P.O. Box 211, 1000 AE Amsterdam, Netherlands.

500 FR ISSN 0074-4387
INTERNATIONAL COUNCIL OF SCIENTIFIC
UNIONS. YEAR BOOK. 1954. a. $5. International
Council of Scientific Unions - Conseil International
des Unions Scientifiques, 51 Bld. de Montmorency,
Paris 75016, France. Ed. F.W.G. Baker. index. circ.
4,000.

500 US ISSN 0074-7866
INTERNATIONAL SCIENCE REVIEW SERIES.
1961. irreg., 1972, vol. 13. price varies. Gordon and
Breach Science Publishers, 1 Park Avenue, New
York, NY 10016.

500 AU ISSN 0074-980X
INTERNATIONALES FORSCHUNGSZENTRUM
FUER GRUNDFRAGEN DER
WISSENSCHAFTEN, SALZBURG.
FORSCHUNGSGESPRAECHE. 1963. irreg. price
varies. (Internationales Forschungszentrum fuer
Grundfragen der Wissenschaften, Salzburg)
Universitaetsverlag Anton Pustet, Bergstr. 12,
Postschliessfach 144, A-5021 Salzburg, Austria. Ed.
Thomas Michels.

500.9 IQ
IRAQ NATURAL HISTORY RESEARCH CENTER
AND MUSEUM. BULLETIN. (Text in English;
summaries in Arabic and English) 1961. irreg.
ID.2500 per no. Iraq Natural History Research
Centre and Museum, University of Baghdad, Bab al-
Muadham, Baghdad, Iraq. Ed. Munir K. Bunni.
Indexed: Biol.Abstr. Zoo.Rec.
　　Former titles: Iraq Natural History Research
Centre. Bulletin; Iraq Natural History Museum.
Bulletin (ISSN 0021-0897)

574 IQ
IRAQ NATURAL HISTORY RESEARCH CENTRE
AND MUSEUM. PUBLICATION. (Text in
English; summaries in English and Arabic) 1950.
irreg. ID.2 per no. Iraq Natural History Research
Centre and Museum., University of Baghdad, Bab
al-Muadham, Baghdad, Iraq. Ed. Munir K. Bunni.
Indexed: Zoo.Rec.
　　Former titles: Iraq Natural History Research
Centre. Publication (ISSN 0085-2260); Iraq Natural
History Museum. Publication.

ISLE OF MAN NATURAL HISTORY AND
ANTIQUARIAN SOCIETY. PROCEEDINGS. see
HISTORY

500 IS ISSN 0080-7753
ISRAEL. NATIONAL COUNCIL FOR RESEARCH
AND DEVELOPMENT. SCIENTIFIC
RESEARCH IN ISRAEL. 1968. irreg., 4th edt.,
1979. $10. National Council for Research and
Development, Kiryat Ben Gurian, Bldg. 3,
Jerusalem, Israel. circ. 2,000.

500 IT
ISTITUTO COMELIANA DI LUGANO.
COLLECTIO MONOGRAPHICA MINOR. 1976.
irreg.; vol. 4, 1978. L.10000. Giardini Editori e
Stampatori, Via Santa Bibbiana 28, 56100 Pisa,
Italy.

500 IT ISSN 0075-1499
ISTITUTO E MUSEO DI STORIA DELLA
SCIENZA. BIBLIOTECA. 1957. irreg., 1970, no. 8.
price varies. Casa Editrice Leo S. Olschki, Casella
Postale 66, 50100 Florence, Italy. Ed. M. L. Bonelli
Righini. circ. 1,000.

500 IT ISSN 0021-2504
ISTITUTO LOMBARDO ACCADEMIA DI
SCIENZE E LETTERE. RENDICONTI. A.
vol.107,1973. a. price varies. Istituto Lombardo
Accademia di Scienze e Lettere, Via Borgonuovo
25, 20121 Milan, Italy. Indexed: Appl.Mech.Rev.
Chem.Abstr. Math.R.

500 GW ISSN 0447-2624
JAHRBUCH DER WITTHEIT ZU BREMEN. 1957.
a. price varies. Verlag Roever, Muehlenweg 67,
2820 Leuchtenburg, W. Germany (B.R.D.)

501 JA ISSN 0453-0691
JAPAN ASSOCIATION FOR PHILOSOPHY OF
SCIENCE. ANNALS. (Text in English) 1954. a.
1800 Yen. Japan Association for Philosophy of
Science - Kagaku Kisoron Gakkai, c/o Institute of
Statistical Mathematics, 4-6-7 Minami Azabu,
Minato-ku, Tokyo 106, Japan.

509 JA ISSN 0090-0176
JAPANESE STUDIES IN THE HISTORY OF
SCIENCE. (Text in English) 1962. a. 3,000 Yen.
History of Science Society of Japan - Nippon
Kagakushi Gakkai, c/o Tokyo Institute of
Technology, O-okayama, Meguro-ku, Tokyo 152,
Japan.

505 605 610 II
JIWAJI UNIVERSITY. JOURNAL: SCIENCE,
TECHNOLOGY & MEDICINE. (Text in English)
1973. a. Rs.10. Jiwaji University, Vidhya Vihar,
Gwalior 2, Madhya Pradesh, India. illus.

500 AU
JOHANNES-KEPLER-UNIVERSITAET LINZ.
DISSERTATIONEN. 1974. irreg., no. 13, 1978.
price varies. (Johannes-Kepler-Universitaet Linz)
Verband der Wissenschaftlichen Gesellschaften
Oesterreichs, Lindengasse 37, A-1070 Vienna,
Austria.
　　Formerly: Johannes-Kepler-Hochschule Linz.
Dissertationen.

500 JA ISSN 0075-4307
JOURNAL OF NATURAL SCIENCE. (Text in
English or Japanese) 1952, vol. 2. a. available on
exchange. Tokushima University, Faculty of
Education - Tokushima Daigaku Kyoiku Gakubu, 1-
4 Minamijosanjima-cho, Tokushima 770, Japan. Ed.
M. Shimoizumi.

500 JA ISSN 0302-0479
KANAZAWA UNIVERSITY. COLLEGE OF
LIBERAL ARTS. ANNALS OF SCIENCE/
KANAZAWA DAIGAKU KYOYOBU RONSHU,
SHIZENKAGAKU- HEN. (Text in English or
Japanese) 1965. a. Kanazawa University, College of
Liberal Arts - Kanazawa Daigaku Kyoyobu,
Kanazawa 920, Japan. illus.

500 JA
KANAZAWA UNIVERSITY. FACULTY OF
EDUCATION. BULLETIN: NATURAL
SCIENCE/KANAZAWA DAIGAKU
KYOIKUGAKUBU KIYO, SHIZENKAGAKU-
HEN. (Text in Japanese; summaries and some
articles in English) 1952. irreg. Kanazawa
University, Faculty of Education - Kanazawa
Daigaku Kyoikugakubu, 1-1 Marunouchi, Kanazawa
920, Japan.

500 II ISSN 0075-5168
KARNATAK UNIVERSITY, DHARWAD, INDIA. JOURNAL. SCIENCE. (Text in English) 1956. a. Rs.8($4) Karnatak University, C. S. Kanavi, Director, Prasaranga, Dharwad 580003, Karnataka, India. Ed. M. S. Chennaveeraiah. circ. 500. Indexed: Biol.Abstr. Chem.Abstr. Math.R. Entomol.Abstr.

500.9 US ISSN 0075-5524
KENTUCKY NATURE STUDIES. 1971. irreg., latest issue, 1974. price varies. University Press of Kentucky, Lexington, KY 40506. Ed. Roger W. Barbour.

500 600 KE
KENYA NATIONAL ACADEMY FOR ADVANCEMENT OF ARTS AND SCIENCES. NEWSLETTER. Short title: K N A A S News. 1977. a. Kenya National Academy for Advancement of Arts and Sciences, Box 47288, Nairobi, Kenya. Ed. Francis Inganji.

KENYA PAST AND PRESENT. see *HISTORY — History Of Africa*

500.9 913 US ISSN 0075-6245
KIRTLANDIA. 1967. irreg.; no. 23, 1976. $2. ‡ Cleveland Museum of Natural History, Wade Oval, University Circle, Cleveland, OH 44106. Ed. David Brose. circ. 400. Indexed: Biol.Abstr.

500 JA
KOBE UNIVERSITY OF MERCANTILE MARINE. REVIEW. PART 2. NAVIGATION, MARINE ENGINEERING, NUCLEAR ENGINEERING AND SCIENTIFIC SECTION. (Text in Japanese, Abstracts in English) 1953. a. Kobe University of Mercantile Marine, 5-1-1 Fukae-Minami-machi, Higashinada-ku, Kobe 658, Japan.

001.3 500 NO
KONGELIGE NORSKE VIDENSKABERS SELSKAB. FORHANDLINGER. 1926. a. Kr.18. (Royal Norwegian Society of Sciences) Universitetsforlaget, Kolstadgt. 1, Box 2959-Toeyen, Oslo 6, Norway (U. S. address: Box 258, Irvington-on-Hudson, NY, 10533) Ed. Olaf I. Roenning.

001.3 500 NO
KONGELIGE NORSKE VIDENSKABERS SELSKAB. SKRIFTER/ROYAL NORWEGIAN SOCIETY OF SCIENCES. PUBLICATIONS. (Text in English) 1791. irreg. price varies. (Royal Norwegian Society of Sciences) Universitetsforlaget, Kolstadgt. 1, Box 2959-Toeyen, Oslo 6, Norway (U. S. address: Box 258, Irvington-on-Hudson, NY 10533) Ed. Olaf I. Roenning. charts. illus. stat.

500 NE ISSN 0065-5503
KONINKLIJKE NEDERLANDSE AKADEMIE VAN WETENSCHAPEN. AFDELING NATUURKUNDE, VERHANDELINGEN. EERSTE REEKS. (Text in Dutch, English, French and German) 1893. irreg., vol. 69, 1978. price varies. ‡ North-Holland Publishing Co., Box 211, 1000 AE Amsterdam, Netherlands. Ed. A.M. Verheggen. adv. bk. rev. circ. 1,000.

500 NE ISSN 0065-552X
KONINKLIJKE NEDERLANDSE AKADEMIE VAN WETENSCHAPPEN. AFDELING NATUURKUNDE. VERHANDELINGEN. TWEEDE REEKS. (Text in English, French, German and Dutch) 1893. irreg., vol. 72, 1979. price varies. ‡ North-Holland Publishing Co., Box 211, 1000 AE Amsterdam, Netherlands. Ed. A. M. Verheggen. adv. bk. rev. circ. 1,000.

500 HU ISSN 0075-6946
KORUNK TUDOMANYA. 1964. irreg. price varies. (Magyar Tudomanyos Akademia) Akademiai Kiado, Publishing House of the Hungarian Academy of Sciences, P.O. Box 24, H-1363 Budapest, Hungary.

500 BE
KTEMATA. 1974. irreg. price varies. E. Story-Scientia, Prudens van Duyseplein 8, B-9000 Ghent, Belgium.

500 060 SW ISSN 0081-9956
KUNGLIGA SVENSKA VETENSKAPSAKADEMIEN. BIDRAG TILL KUNGLIGA VETENSKAPSAKADEMIENS HISTORIA. 1963. irreg., vol. 15, 1979. Kungliga Svenska Vetenskapsakademien - Royal Swedish Academy of Sciences, Box 50005, S-104 05 Stockholm, Sweden.

500 JA
KYOTO PREFECTURAL UNIVERSITY. SCIENTIFIC REPORTS: NATURAL SCIENCE AND LIVING SCIENCE/KYOTO-FURITSU DAIGAKU GAKUJUTSU HOKOKU RIGAKU SEIKATSUKAGAKU. (Text in Japanese; summaries in English) 1952. irreg., no. 27, 1976. available on exchange. Kyoto Prefectural University - Kyoto-furitsu Daigaku, Shimogamo Hangi-cho, Sakyo-ku, Kyoto 606, Japan. Ed. Z. Hayashino.
Formerly: Kyoto Prefectural University. Scientific Reports: Natural Science, Domestic Science and Social Welfare (ISSN 0075-739X)

505 605 JA ISSN 0453-0047
KYOTO TECHNICAL UNIVERSITY. FACULTY OF INDUSTRIAL ARTS. MEMOIRS: SCIENCE AND TECHNOLOGY/KYOTO KOGEI SEN'I DAIGAKU KOGEIGAKUBU KIYO RIKO-HEN. (Text in English and European languages) 1952. a. exchange basis. Kyoto University of Industrial and Textile Fibers, Faculty of Industrial Arts - Kyoto Kogei Sen'i Daigaku, Kogeigakubu, Matsugasaki, Sakyoku, Kyoto 606, Japan.

KYUSHU INSTITUTE OF TECHNOLOGY. BULLETIN: MATHEMATICS, NATURAL SCIENCE/KYUSHU KOGYO DAIGAKU KENKYU HOKOKU, SHIZENKAGAKU. see *MATHEMATICS*

LASER. see *TECHNOLOGY: COMPREHENSIVE WORKS*

500 US
LEADING EDGE. irreg. free. S R I International, 333 Ravenswood Ave., Menlo Park, CA 94025. Ed. Lois M. Miller. charts. illus. Indexed: Int.Manage.Inform.
Formerly: Investments in Tomorrow.

500 UK
LEEDS PHILOSOPHICAL AND LITERARY SOCIETY. PROCEEDINGS. SCIENTIFIC. 1925. a. price varies. Leeds Philosophical and Literary Society, Central Museum, Calverley St., Leeds 2, England. Ed. P. R. J. Burch. charts. index. circ. 300-1,000.

500 GE
LEOPOLDINA; Mitteilungen aus der Deutschen Akademie der Naturforscher Leopoldina, Reihe 3. (Reihe 1: 1859-1922; Reihe 2: 1926-1930) 1955. a. exchange basis. Deutsche Akademie der Naturforscher Leopoldina, August-Bebel-Str. 50a, 01 Halle/S, E. Germany (D.D.R.) Ed. Georg Uschmann.

500 US ISSN 0075-9104
LIBRARY OF EXACT PHILOSOPHY. 1970. irreg., no. 12, 1981. Springer-Verlag, 175 Fifth Ave., New York, NY 10010 (also Berlin, Heidelberg, Vienna) Ed. M. Bunge. (reprint service avail. from ISI)

500 LY
LIBYAN JOURNAL OF SCIENCES; an international journal. (Text in English; summaries in Arabic) 1971. a. $3 (individuals) $4.50 (institutions) Alfateh University, Faculty of Science, Box 656, Tripoli, Libya. Ed. Dawd S. Dawd.

LOS ANGELES COUNCIL OF ENGINEERS & SCIENTISTS. PROCEEDINGS SERIES. see *ENGINEERING*

LOUISBURG COLLEGE JOURNAL OF ARTS AND SCIENCES. see *ART*

500 US
LOUISIANA ACADEMY OF SCIENCES. PROCEEDINGS. 1932. a. $7. Louisiana Academy of Sciences, c/o Dr. Bruce Boudreaux, Department of Entomology, Louisiana State University, Baton Rouge, LA 70803. Ed. Charles Faust. circ. 400. (back issues avail) Indexed: Biol.Abstr. Chem.Abstr.

509 016 SW ISSN 0076-163X
LYCHNOS-BIBLIOTEK. STUDIES OCH KAELLSKRIFTER UDGIVNA AV LAERDOMSHISTORISKA SAMFUNDET. STUDIES AND SOURCES PUBLISHED BY THE SWEDISH HISTORY OF SCIENCE SOCIETY. 1936. irreg. price varies. (Laerdomshistoriska Samfundet - Swedish History of Science Society) Almqvist & Wiksell International, Box 62, S-101 20 Stockholm, Sweden. Ed. Sten Lindroth. index.

509 SW ISSN 0076-1648
LYCHNOS-LAERDOMSHISTORISKA SAMFUNDETS AARSBOK. ANNUAL OF THE SWEDISH HISTORY OF SCIENCE SOCIETY. 1936. a. price varies. (Laerdomshistoriska Samfundet) Almqvist & Wiksell International, Box 62, S-101 20 Stockholm, Sweden. Ed. Sten Lindroth. bk. rev. index.

500 US ISSN 0024-8347
M R I QUARTERLY. 1967. irreg. Midwest Research Institute, 425 Volker Blvd., Kansas City, MO 64110. Ed. Mary Louise Lillis. circ. 10,000.
Formerly: M R I Report.

505.8 US ISSN 0076-2016
MCGRAW-HILL YEARBOOK OF SCIENCE AND TECHNOLOGY. 1962. a. $31.50. McGraw-Hill Book Co., 1221 Ave. of the Americas, New York, NY 10020. Ed. Daniel Lapedes.

500 SX
MADOQUA. (Text in English and Afrikaans; summaries in German, Afrikaans and French) 1969. irreg. (3-4/yr.) R.15. Administration, Nature, Conservation and Tourism Branch, Private Bag 13186, Windhoek 9100, South West Africa. Ed. B.J.G. de la Bat.
Replaces (as of vol. 9, no. 1, Jan. 1975): Madoqua. Series I & Madoqua. Series II & Namib Desert Research Station. Scientific Papers.

500 II ISSN 0085-2945
MADRAS. GOVERNMENT MUSEUM. BULLETIN. NEW SERIES. (Text in English) 1931. irreg. price varies. Government Museum, Madras, Director of Museums, Pantheon Road, Egmore, Madras 600008, India.

507 UG
MAKERERE UNIVERSITY. SCIENCE FACULTY. HANDBOOK. irreg. Makerere University, Science Faculty, Box 7062, Kampala, Uganda. circ. 1,000.

500 MW
MALAWI JOURNAL OF SCIENCE. 1972. a. 25p. Association for the Advancement of Science of Malawi, Box 280, Zomba, Malawi. adv. bk. rev. circ. 1,000.

500 MY ISSN 0301-0554
MALAYSIAN JOURNAL OF SCIENCE/JERNAL SAINS MALAYSIA. (Text in English) 1971. a. $6. University of Malaya, Faculty of Science, Lembah Pantai, Kuala Lumpur 22-11, Malaysia. Ed. Dr. Yong Hoi Sen. adv. bk. rev. circ. 1,000. Indexed: Biol.Abstr. Chem.Abstr.

500 GW ISSN 0076-5635
MAX-PLANCK-GESELLSCHAFT ZUR FOERDERUNG DER WISSENSCHAFTEN. JAHRBUCH. 1952. a. DM.64. Max-Planck-Gesellschaft zur Foerderung der Wissenschaften, Residenzstr. 1A, 8000 Munich 2, W. Germany (B.R.D.) Eds. R. Gerwin, G. Girod.

500 GW
MAX-PLANCK-GESELLSCHAFT ZUR FOERDERUNG DER WISSENSCHAFTEN BERICHTE UND MITTEILUNGEN. 1952. irreg. price not given. ‡ Max-Planck-Gesellschaft zur Foerderung der Wissenschaften., Residenzstr. 1a, Postfach 647, 8000 Munich 2, W. Germany (B.R.D.) Ed.Bd. bibl. charts. illus. circ. 6,000.
Formerly: Max-Planck-Gesellschaft zur Foerderung der Wissenschaften Mitteilungen (ISSN 0025-6102)

METODICKY ZPRAVODAJ CS. SOUSTAVY VEDECKYCH, TECHNICKYCH A EKONOMICKYCH INFORMACI. see *LIBRARY AND INFORMATION SCIENCES*

MINNESOTA STUDIES IN THE PHILOSOPHY OF SCIENCE. see *PHILOSOPHY*

500 600 CN
MIRRORED SPECTRUM; a collection of reports for the non-scientist and non-engineer about achievements in Canadian science and technology. vol. 2, 1978. a. price varies. Ministry of State for Science and Technology, Ottawa, Ont., Canada (Order from: Information Canada, Ottawa, Ont. K1A 0S9, Canada) Ed. Bd.

SCIENCES: COMPREHENSIVE WORKS

500 600 PL ISSN 0077-054X
MONOGRAFIE Z DZIEJOW NAUKI I TECHNIKI. (Text in Polish and French; summaries in English, French, German and Russian) 1957. irreg., vol. 94, 1979. price varies. (Polska Akademia Nauk, Zaklad Historii Nauki i Techniki) Ossolineum, Publishing House of the Polish Academy of Sciences, Rynek 9, 50-106 Wroclaw, Poland (Dist. by Ars Polona-Ruch, Krakowskie Przedmiescie 7, Warsaw, Poland) Ed. B. Suchodolski.

MUNICH ROUND UP. see *LITERATURE*

500 AG ISSN 0027-3880
MUSEO ARGENTINO DE CIENCIAS NATURALES "BERNARDINO RIVADAVIA" E INSTITUTO NACIONAL DE INVESTIGACIONES DE LA CIENCIAS NATURALES. REVISTA Y COMMUNICACIONES. 1964. irreg. free. Museo Argentino de Ciencias Naturales "Bernardino Rivadavia", Avda. Angel Gallardo 470, Casilla de Correo 220-Sucursal 5, Buenos Aires, Argentina. (Co-sponsor: Instituto Naconal de Investigaciones de la Ciencias Naturales) charts. illus.

500.9 IT
MUSEO CIVICO DI STORIA NATURALE "GIACOMO DORIA," GENOA. ANNALI. (Text in Italian, French, English, German) 1870. irreg. exchange only. Museo Civico di Storia Naturale "G. Doria", Via Brigata Liguria 9, 16121 Genova, Italy.

500 IT ISSN 0085-767X
MUSEO CIVICO DI STORIA NATURALE, VERONA. MEMORIE. (Issued in 3 Parts: Biologica, Abiologica & Preistorica) (Text in Italian, German, French and English; summaries in French, German and English) 1946-1972 N. S. 1974 (2nd series) a. L.7000. Museo Civico di Storia Naturale, Verona, Lungadige Porta Vittoria Nr. 9, 37100 Verona, Italy. circ. 600. Indexed: Biol.Abstr. Zoo.Rec.

500.9 IT
MUSEO CIVICO DI STORIA NATURALE, VERONA. BOLLETINO. 1974. a. exchange basis. Museo Civico di Storia Naturale, Verona, Lungadige Porta Vittoria 9, 37100 Verona, Italy.
 Supersedes in part (since 1974): Museo Civico di Storia Naturale di Verona. Memorie.

500.9 AG
MUSEO DE HISTORIA NATURAL DE SAN RAFAEL. REVISTA. 1956. irreg. price varies. Museo de Historia Natural de San Rafael, Avda.San Martin y Francis, 5600 San Rafael, Mendoza, Argentina. Ed. Humberto A. Lagiglia. bk. rev. charts. illus. index. circ. 1,500.
 Formerly: Museo de Historia Natural de San Rafael. Revista Cientifica de Investigaciones (ISSN 0027-3902)

500.9 069 UY
MUSEO NACIONAL DE HISTORIA NATURAL. ANALES. 1894, O.S.; 1925, N.S. irreg; latest issue, 1974. free on exchange. Museo Nacional de Historia Natural, Casilla de Correo 399, Montevideo, Uruguay. Ed. Miguel A. Klappenbach. circ. 1,200.
 Formerly: Montevideo. Museo de Historia Natural. Anales.

500 BL ISSN 0077-2240
MUSEU PARAENSE EMILIO GOELDI. PUBLICACOES AVULSAS. 1964. irreg., no. 28, 1975. Instituto Nacional de Pesquisas da Amazonia, Museu Paraense Emilio Goeldi, C.P. 399, Belem, Para, Brazil. bibl. illus.

500.9 FR ISSN 0078-9720
MUSEUM NATIONAL D'HISTOIRE NATURELLE, PARIS. ANNUAIRE. 1939. a. Museum National d'Histoire Naturelle, 38 rue Geoffroy-Saint-Hilaire, Paris 5e, France.

500.9 FR ISSN 0078-9739
MUSEUM NATIONAL D'HISTOIRE NATURELLE, PARIS. ARCHIVES. (Text in French and English) 1802. irreg. price varies. Museum National d'Histoire Naturelle, 38 rue Geoffroy-Saint-Hilaire, Paris 5, France.

500.9 FR
MUSEUM NATIONAL D'HISTOIRE NATURELLE, PARIS. LES GRANDS NATURALISTES FRANCAIS. 1952. irreg. price varies. Museum National d'Histoire Naturelle, 38 rue Geoffroy Saint-Hilaire, 75005 Paris, France. Dir. Roger Heim. illus.

500.9 US ISSN 0428-5395
MUSEUM OF NORTHERN ARIZONA TECHNICAL SERIES. 1953. irreg. ‡ Museum of Northern Arizona, Route 4, Box 720, Flagstaff, AZ 86001.
 Natural history of northern Arizona. Scientific reports.

N A T O ADVANCED STUDY INSTITUTE SERIES. C: MATHEMATICAL AND PHYSICAL SCIENCES. see *MATHEMATICS*

505 PH
N R C P RESEARCH BULLETIN. (Text in English) irreg. National Research Council of the Philippines, Quezon City, Philippines. illus.

500 CH
N S C REVIEW. (Text in English) 1965. a. free. National Science Council of the Republic of China, 2 Canton St., Taipei, Taiwan 107, Republic of China.

500 CH
N S C SPECIAL PUBLICATION. 1978. irreg. National Science Council of the Republic of China, 2 Canton St., Taipei, Taiwan 107, Republic of China.

500 CH
N S C SYMPOSIUM SERIES. 1979. irreg. National Science Council of the Republic of China, 2 Canton St, Taipei, Taiwan 107, Republic of China.

500 US
NANTUCKET MARIA MITCHELL ASSOCIATION. ANNUAL REPORT. 1912. a. membership. ‡ Nantucket Maria Mitchell Association, 1 Vestal Street, Nantucket, MA 02554. Ed. Merle T. Orleans. circ. 1,000. (back issues avail.)

500 US ISSN 0077-2925
NATIONAL ACADEMY OF SCIENCES. ANNUAL REPORT. 1863. a. National Academy of Sciences, 2101 Constitution Ave., Washington, DC 20418.

NATIONAL ACADEMY OF SCIENCES. BIOGRAPHICAL MEMOIRS. see *BIOGRAPHY*

500 US
NATIONAL ASSOCIATION OF ACADEMIES OF SCIENCE. DIRECTORY AND PROCEEDINGS. 1977. a. $5. National Association of Academies of Science, Department of Physics, University of Mississippi, University, MS 38677. (Affiliate: American Association for the Advancement of Science) Ed. Lee Bolen. circ. 400. (back issues avail.)
 Formerly: Association of Academies of Science. Directory and Proceedings.

500 910 US ISSN 0077-4626
NATIONAL GEOGRAPHIC SOCIETY RESEARCH REPORTS. irreg. no. 10, 1978. irreg., no. 9, 1976. $5. National Geographic Society, 17th & M Sts. N.W., Washington, DC 20036. Ed. John S. Lea.

500 JA ISSN 0386-555X
NATIONAL INSTITUTE OF POLAR RESEARCH. MEMOIRS. SERIES F: LOGISTICS. (Text in English) 1964. irreg., no. 3, 1979. exchange basis. National Institute of Polar Research - Kokuritsu Kyokuchi Kenkyujyo, 9-10 Kaga, 1-chome, Itabashi-ku, Tokyo 173, Japan. Ed. Takesi Nagata. circ. 1,000. Indexed: Curr.Antarc.Lit.
 Supersedes: Japanese Antarctic Research Expedition, 1956-1962. Scientific Reports. Series F: Logistic (ISSN 0075-3408)

500 SA ISSN 0067-9194
NATIONAL MUSEUM, BLOEMFONTEIN. MEMOIRS. (Text in Afrikaans and English) 1952. irreg., no. 12, 1979. price varies; dist. to institutions usually on exchange basis. National Museum, Bloemfontein, Box 266, Bloemfontein 9300, South Africa.

500 SA ISSN 0067-9208
NATIONAL MUSEUM, BLOEMFONTEIN. NAVORSINGE/RESEARCHES. (Text in Afrikaans or English) 1952. irreg., vol.4, part 2, 1979. price varies; dist. to institutions usually on exchange basis. National Museum, Bloemfontein, Box 266, Bloemfontein 9300, South Africa.

500.9 CN ISSN 0703-4660
NATIONAL MUSEUM OF NATURAL SCIENCES. NATURAL HISTORY NOTEBOOK SERIES. 1977. irreg. Can.$2.50 per no. National Museums of Canada, Ottawa, Ont. K1A 0M8, Canada.

500.9 CN ISSN 0704-576X
NATIONAL MUSEUM OF NATURAL SCIENCES. SYLLOGEUS. (Text in English and French) 1972. irreg. free. National Museums of Canada, Ottawa, Ont. K1A 0M8, Canada.

507 US ISSN 0093-8572
NATIONAL PATTERNS OF R. & D. RESOURCES; FUNDS & MANPOWER IN THE UNITED STATES. a. U.S. National Science Foundation, 1800 G St. N.W., Washington, DC 20550 (Orders to: Supt. of Documents, Washington, DC 20402)

500 SA
NATIONAL REGISTER OF RESEARCH PROJECTS: NATURAL AND HUMAN SCIENCES. (Text in Afrikaans and English) 1971. irreg. (approx. biennial) free. Office of the Scientific Adviser to the Prime Minister, P.B. X420, Pretoria 0001, South Africa. Ed. F.A. van Niererk. cum.index. circ. 6,000. (back issues avail.)
 Formerly: National Register of Research Projects: Natural Sciences.

NATIONAL RESEARCH COUNCIL, CANADA. ANNUAL REPORT ON SCHOLARSHIPS AND GRANTS IN AID OF RESEARCH/CONSEIL NATIONAL DE RECHERCHES DU CANADA. COMPTE RENDU ANNUEL DES BOURSES ET SUBVENTIONS D'AIDE A LA RECHERCHE. see *EDUCATION*

NATIONAL RESEARCH COUNCIL, CANADA. PUBLICATIONS. see *TECHNOLOGY: COMPREHENSIVE WORKS*

NATIONAL RESEARCH COUNCIL, CANADA. TECHNICAL TRANSLATION. see *TECHNOLOGY: COMPREHENSIVE WORKS*

500 CN
NATIONAL RESEARCH COUNCIL OF CANADA. REPORT OF THE PRESIDENT/RAPPORT DU PRESIDENT. (Text in English & French) 1916. a. free. ‡ National Research Council of Canada, Montreal Road, Ottawa K1A 0R6, Ontario, Canada. Ed. Wayne Campbell. circ. 9,000.

354.415 IE
NATIONAL SCIENCE COUNCIL (IRELAND). PROGRESS REPORT. 1972. irreg., latest 1969-71. £0.15. Government Publications Sales Office, G.P.O. Arade, Dublin 1, Ireland. circ. 1,200.

500 IE ISSN 0085-3836
NATIONAL SCIENCE COUNCIL (IRELAND). REGISTER OF SCIENTIFIC RESEARCH PERSONNEL. 1968. irreg. 32.5p. Government Publications Sales Office, G.P.O. Arcade, Dublin 1, Ireland. Eds. Diarmuid Murphy, Donal O. Brolchain. circ. 800. (tabloid format)

500 CH
NATIONAL SCIENCE COUNCIL, REPUBLIC OF CHINA. ANNUAL REPORT. (Text in Chinese) 1963. a. free. National Science Council of the Republic of China, 2 Canton St., Taipei, Taiwan 107, Republic of China.

500 JA ISSN 0082-4755
NATIONAL SCIENCE MUSEUM. MEMOIRS. (Text in English and Japanese; summaries in English) 1968. a. avail. on exchange basis only. National Science Museum - Kokuritsu Kagaku Hakubutsukan, 7-20 Ueno Park, Daito-ku, Tokyo 110, Japan. Ed. Bd. circ. 1,000(controlled)

500.9 SZ
NATUR HISTORISCHES MUSEUM DER STADT BERN. JAHRBUCH. 1966. triennial. 54.60 Fr. Naturhistorisches Museum, Brunnadernstr. 65, CH-3006 Berne, Switzerland. Ed. Walter Huber-Roth. illus.

SCIENCES: COMPREHENSIVE WORKS

500.9 AU ISSN 0028-0607
NATUR UND LAND. vol.56,1970. irreg. (4-6/yr.) S.140. Oesterreichischer Naturschutzbund, Postfach 910, A-6040 Innsbruck, Austria. (Co-sponsor: Oesterreichische Gesellschaft fuer Natur- und Umweltschutz) Ed. Walter Kofler. bk. rev. charts. illus. stat. index. circ. 3,500. Indexed: Biol.Abstr. Ecol.Abstr. Environ.Abstr.

500 US ISSN 0076-0900
NATURAL HISTORY MUSEUM OF LOS ANGELES COUNTY. CONTRIBUTIONS IN SCIENCE. (Text in English; summaries in Spanish) 1957. irreg. no. 301, 1979. Natural History Museum of Los Angeles County, 900 Exposition Blvd., Los Angeles, CA 90007. Ed. R. Edward Ostermeyer. cum.index, author: 1957-59, 1960-62, 1963-64, 1965-66, 1967-68. circ. 2,000. Indexed: Zoo.Rec.

505 US ISSN 0076-0943
NATURAL HISTORY MUSEUM OF LOS ANGELES COUNTY. SCIENCE SERIES. 1930. irreg. no. 30, 1978. Natural History Museum of Los Angeles County, 900 Exposition Blvd., Los Angeles, CA 90007. Ed. R. Edward Ostermeyer. bk. rev. circ. 5,000.

500 US
NATURAL SCIENCE NEWS. irreg. donation. Natural Science Research, Box 545, Winona Lake, IN 46590.

500 SZ ISSN 0077-6122
NATURFORSCHENDE GESELLSCHAFT IN BASEL. VERHANDLUNGEN/SOCIETY FOR NATURAL SCIENCES, BASEL. PROCEEDINGS. 1854. irreg. (approx. 2/yr.) Birkhaeuser Verlag, Elisabethenstr. 19, CH-4010 Basel, Switzerland. Ed. H. Schaefer.

500 SZ ISSN 0077-6130
NATURFORSCHENDE GESELLSCHAFT IN BERN. MITTEILUNGEN. (Text in German; summaries in French, English) 1843. a. 30 Fr. Naturforschende Gesellschaft in Bern, Stadt-und Universitaetsbibliothek, Muenstergasse 61, CH-3000 Berne 7, Switzerland. Ed. A. Bretscher. adv. cum.index: 1944-1968 in no. 26(1969)

500.9 GW ISSN 0077-6149
NATURHISTORISCHE GESELLSCHAFT NUERNBERG. ABHANDLUNGEN. 1851. irreg. price varies. Naturhistorische Gesellschaft Nuernberg, Gewerbemuseumsplatz 4, Luitpoldhaus, 8500 Nuernberg, W. Germany (B.R.D.) circ. 2,500.

500.9 AU ISSN 0083-6133
NATURHISTORISCHES MUSEUM IN WIEN. ANNALEN. (Text in English, French & German; summaries in English, French, German, Italian & Spanish) 1886. a. price varies. Naturhistorisches Museum in Wien, Burgring 7, P.F.417, A-1014 Vienna, Austria. bk. rev. index. circ. 1,100. (back issues avail.)

509 AU
NATURHISTORISCHES MUSEUM IN WIEN. NEUE DENKSCHRIFTEN. 1976. irreg. price varies. Naturhistorisches Museum in Wien, Burgring 7, Postfach 417, A-1014 Vienna, Austria. Eds. Ortwin Schultz & Friedrich Bachmayer.

500.9 AU ISSN 0505-5164
NATURHISTORISCHES MUSEUM IN WIEN. VEROEFFENTLICHUNGEN. NEUE FOLGE. 1958. irreg. price varies. Naturhistorisches Museum in Wien, Burgring 7, P.F. 417, A-1014 Vienna, Austria.

500 AU ISSN 0470-3901
NATURKUNDLICHES JAHRBUCH DER STADT LINZ. 1955. a. S.150. Stadtmuseum Linz, Bethlehemstrasse 7, A-4020 Linz/Donau, Austria. Ed. Aemilian Kloiber. illus. circ. 500.

500 GE ISSN 0065-6631
NATURKUNDLICHES MUSEUM "MAURITIANUM" ALTENBURG. ABHANDLUNGEN UND BERICHTE. 1958 (previous series were begun in 1837 and 1880) biennial. price varies. Naturkundliches Museum "Mauritianum", Postfach 128, 74 Altenburg, E. Germany (D.D.R.) Ed. Horst Grosse. circ. 800.

500 GW ISSN 0077-6157
NATURWISSENSCHAFTLICHE RUNDSCHAU. BUECHER DER ZEITSCHRIFT. 1966. irreg. price varies; special rate for subscribers of "Naturwissenschaftliche Rundschau". Wissenschaftliche Verlagsgesellschaft mbH, Postfach 40, 7000 Stuttgart 1, W. Germany (B.R.D.)

500 GW ISSN 0077-6165
NATURWISSENSCHAFTLICHER VEREIN FUER SCHLESWIG-HOLSTEIN. SCHRIFTEN. 1870. irreg. price varies. Lipsius & Tischer, Holstenstr. 80, 2300 Kiel, W. Germany (B.R.D.) Ed. Ekke W. Guenther. bk. rev.

500.9 AU
NATURWISSENSCHAFTLICHER VEREIN FUER STEIERMARK. MITTEILUNGEN. 1863. a. S.200. Naturwissenschaftlicher Verein fuer Steiermark, Universitaetsbibliothek, Universitaetsplatz 3, A-8010 Graz, Austria. Eds. Fritz Ebner, Stefan Plank. bk. rev. charts, illus. index, cum. index. (back issues avail.)

500 PL ISSN 0077-6181
NAUKA DLA WSZYSTKICH. 1966. irreg. price varies. (Polska Akademia Nauk, Oddzial w Krakowie) Panstwowe Wydawnictwo Naukowe, Miodowa 10, Warsaw, Poland (Dist. by Ars Polona-Ruch, Krakowskie Przedmiescie 7, Warsaw, Poland) Ed. Zygmunt Czerny.

500 UR
NAUKA SEGODNYA. 1973. a. 0.59 Rub. Izdatel'stvo Znanie, Novaya pl., 3-4, 101835 Moscow, U.S.S.R.

500 US ISSN 0077-6343
NEBRASKA ACADEMY OF SCIENCES. PROCEEDINGS. a. $1.50. Nebraska Academy of Sciences, 306 Morrill Hall, 14th & U Sts., Lincoln, NE 68588. Ed. A.W. Zechmann.

500 US ISSN 0077-6351
NEBRASKA ACADEMY OF SCIENCES. TRANSACTIONS. 1970-71. a. to be announced. Nebraska Academy of Sciences, 306 Morrill Hall, 14th & U Sts., Lincoln, NE 68588. Eds. Brent B. Nickal, T. Mylan Stout.

500 HU ISSN 0133-2929
NEHEZIPARI MUSZAKI EGYETEM, MISKOLC. PUBLICATIONS. SERIES D: NATURAL SCIENCES. (Text in English, German, Russian) irreg., vol. 33, no. 2, 1978. Nehezipari Muszaki Egyetem, Miskolc, Hungary. Ed. Endre Vincze. bibl. index. circ. 550.

NEKOTORYE FILOSOFSKIE VOPROSY SOVREMENNOGO ESTESTVOZNANIYA. see *PHILOSOPHY*

500 US ISSN 0085-3887
NEMOURIA; OCCASIONAL PAPERS OF THE DELAWARE MUSEUM OF NATURAL HISTORY. 1970. irreg., no. 22, 1979. $2. Delaware Museum of Natural History, Box 3937, Greenville, DE 19807. Indexed: Biol.Abstr.

500 GW
NEUE MUENCHNER BEITRAEGE ZUR GESCHICHTE DER MEDIZIN UND NATURWISSENSCHAFTEN. NATURWISSENSCHAFTSHISTORISCHE REIHE. 1969. irreg., vol. 6, 1979. price varies. Werner Fritsch Verlag, Postfach 751, 8000 Munich 1, W. Germany (B.R.D.) Eds. Friedrich Klemm, Christa Habrich. index.

500.9 US ISSN 0077-7900
NEVADA. STATE MUSEUM, CARSON CITY. NATURAL HISTORY PUBLICATIONS. 1962. irreg., 1969, no. 2. price varies. Nevada State Museum, Carson City, NV 89701. Ed. J. Scott Miller. circ. 1,000.

500 US
NEW PRIORITIES LIBRARY. a. price varies. Gordon and Breach Science Publishers, One Park Ave., New York, NY 10016. Ed. William Meyers.

500 US
NEW YORK ACADEMY OF SCIENCES. ANNALS. 1877. irreg. price varies. New York Academy of Sciences, 2 E. 63rd St., New York, NY 10021. Ed. Bill Boland. bibl. charts. illus. index. cum.index 1960-74. (also avail. in microfilm) Indexed: Biol.Abstr. Chem.Abstr. Math.R. Psychol.Abstr.

500 US ISSN 0028-7113
NEW YORK ACADEMY OF SCIENCES. TRANSACTIONS. vol. 38, 1977, N.S. irreg. New York Academy of Sciences, Two E. 63rd St., New York, NY 10021. Ed. Bill Boland. (also avail. in microform; back issues avail.)

NEW ZEALAND. NATIONAL RESEARCH ADVISORY COUNCIL. SENIOR AND POST DOCTORAL RESEARCH FELLOWSHIP AWARDS FOR RESEARCH IN NEW ZEALAND GOVERNMENT DEPARTMENTS. see *TECHNOLOGY: COMPREHENSIVE WORKS*

500.2 UK
NIGERIAN FIELD MONOGRAPHS. 1979. irreg. Nigerian Field Society, 54 Palmer Park Ave., Reading 4G6 1DN, England.

500 JA ISSN 0078-0944
NODA INSTITUTE FOR SCIENTIFIC RESEARCH. REPORT/NODA SANGYO KAGAKU KENKYUSHO KENKYU HOKOKU. (Text in English) 1957. a. free or exchange. Noda Institute for Scientific Research - Noda Sangyo Kagaku Kenkyusho, 399 Noda, Noda-shi, Chiba-ken 278, Japan. Ed. Michitaro Nagasawa. circ. 1,000. Indexed: Biol.Abstr. Chem.Abstr.

500 NO ISSN 0078-1231
NORGES TEKNISK-NATURVITENSKAPELIGE FORSKNINGSRAAD. AARSBERETNING. 1947/48. a. free. Norges Teknisk-Naturvitenskapelige Forskningsraad - Royal Norwegian Council for Scientific and Industrial Research, Sagnsveien 72, Taasen, Oslo 8, Norway.

500 510 NO
NORSKE VIDENSKAPS-AKADEMI. NATURVIDENSKAPELIG KLASSE. SKRIFTER. (Text in several Languages) 1925. irreg. price varies. (Norwegian Academy of Sciences and Letters) Universitetsforlaget, Kolstadgt. 1, Box 2959-Toeyen, Oslo 6, Norway (U. S. address: Box 258, Irvington-on-Hudson, NY 10533) abstr. bibl. circ. 1,000. Indexed: Appl.Mech.Rev. Biol.Abstr. Chem.Abstr. Math.R. Sci.Abstr.
Formerly: Norske Videnskaps-Akademi. Matematisk-Naturvidenkapelig Klasse. Skrifter (ISSN 0029-2338)

500 US
NORTH DAKOTA ACADEMY OF SCIENCE. PROCEEDINGS. 1947. a. $5 per vol. North Dakota Academy of Science, Box 8123, University Station, Grand Forks, ND 58202. Ed. A. William Johnson. circ. 900.

500 UK
NORTHAMPTONSHIRE NATURAL HISTORY SOCIETY AND FIELD CLUB JOURNAL. 1880. a. £1. Northamptonshire Natural History Society and Field Club, c/o S.V.F. Leleux, Treas., 7 Langham Pl., Northampton, England. Ed. H. Blackburn. bk. rev. charts. illus. circ. 500. (back issues avail.)

500 NO ISSN 0085-4301
NORWAY. FORSVARETS FORSKNINGSINSTITUTT. N D R E REPORT. (Text and summaries in English) 1953. irreg., no. 70, 1978. Forsvarets Forskningsinstitutt - Norwegian Defence Research Establishment, Box 25, N-2007 Kjeller, Norway. circ. (controlled)

500 001.3 NO
NORWEGIAN RESEARCH COUNCIL FOR SCIENCE AND THE HUMANITIES. ANNUAL REPORT. (Text in Norwegian; summary in English) a. Norges Almenvitenskapelige Forskningsraad, Munthesgate 29, Oslo 2, Norway.

500.9 US ISSN 0029-4608
NOTULAE NATURAE. 1939. irreg., no. 458, 1980. $1.25 ea.; or $36 for set of 100. Academy of Natural Sciences of Philadelphia, 19th and the Parkway, Philadelphia, PA 19103. Ed. F. B. Gill. abstr. charts. illus. Indexed: Biol.Abstr. Chem.Abstr.

510 GE
NOVA ACTA LEOPOLDINA. (Text in English and German) 1670. irreg., no. 232, 1978. price varies. (Deutsche Akademie der Naturforscher Leopoldina) Johann Ambrosius Barth Verlag, Salomonstr. 18b, Postfach 109, 701 Leipzig, E. Germany (D.D.R.) Ed. J.-H. Scharf. charts. illus. stat. (back issues avail.)

500 SW ISSN 0029-5000
NOVA ACTA REGIAE SOCIETATIS SCIENTIARUM UPSALIENSIS. (Text in several languages) 1773. irreg. price varies. (Kungliga Vetenskaps-Societeten - Royal Society of Sciences of Uppsala) Almqvist & Wiksell International, Box 62, S-101 20 Stockholm, Sweden. bibl. charts. illus. index.

NOVA SCOTIA RESEARCH FOUNDATION CORPORATION. ANNUAL REPORT. see *TECHNOLOGY: COMPREHENSIVE WORKS*

500 CN ISSN 0078-2521
NOVA SCOTIAN INSTITUTE OF SCIENCE. PROCEEDINGS. 1862. irreg. Can.$15. Nova Scotian Institute of Science, Science Library, Dalhousie University, Halifax, N.S. B3H 4J3, Canada. Ed. J.McLachlan. circ. 400. (also avail. in microfilm from CLA) Indexed: Biol.Abstr.

500 GW ISSN 0078-2920
OBERHESSISCHE GESELLSCHAFT FUER NATUR- UND HEILKUNDE, GIESSEN. BERICHTE. a. Wilhelm Schmitz Verlag, Kattenbachstr. 5, 6300 Giessen, W. Germany (B. R. D.) Ed. Ruediger Knapp. circ. 600.

001.3 500 AU ISSN 0078-3447
OESTERREICHISCHE AKADEMIE DER WISSENSCHAFTEN. ALMANACH. 1851. a. price varies. Verlag der Oesterreichischen Akademie der Wissenschaften, Dr. Ignaz Seipel-Platz 2, A-1010 Vienna, Austria. index. circ. 1,500.

500 600 FR ISSN 0071-9013
OFFICE DE LA RECHERCHE SCIENTIFIQUE ET TECHNIQUE OUTRE-MER. RAPPORT D'ACTIVITE. irreg. Office de la Recherche Scientifique et Technique Outre-Mer, 70/74 Route d'Aulnay, 93140 Bondy, France.

500 US ISSN 0078-4303
OKLAHOMA ACADEMY OF SCIENCE. PROCEEDINGS. 1920. a. $12.50. Oklahoma Academy of Science, c/o Donald E. Kizer, Route 3, Box 14-N, Ardmore, OK 73401. Ed. Glenn W. Todd. cum.index every 10 yrs. circ. 1,250. Indexed: Chem.Abstr. Biol.Abstr.

500 FR ISSN 0078-5601
ORDRE DES GEOMETRES-EXPERTS. ANNUAIRE. 1956. a. 25 F. Ordre des Geometres-Experts, 40 Av. Hoche, Paris 8e, France. circ. 3,000.

500 600 NG ISSN 0474-6171
ORGANIZATION OF AFRICAN UNITY. SCIENTIFIC TECHNICAL AND RESEARCH COMMISSION. PUBLICATION.* 1951. irreg. Organization of African Unity, Scientific Technical and Research Commission, Publications Bureau, Maison de l'Afrique, B.P. 878, Niamey, Niger.

500 US
ORGANIZATION OF AMERICAN STATES. DEPARTMENT OF SCIENTIFIC AFFAIRS. REPORT OF ACTIVITIES. 1963. irreg. Organization of American States, Department of Publications, Washington, DC 20006.
Formerly: Pan American Union. Department of Scientific Affairs. Report of Activities. (ISSN 0553-0334)

500 600 US ISSN 0250-7536
ORGANIZATION OF AMERICAN STATES. REGIONAL SCIENTIFIC AND TECHNOLOGICAL PROGRAM. NEWSLETTER. 1972. irreg. Organization of American States, Department of Scientific Affairs, Dept. of Publications, Washington, DC 20006. bibl.

500 PL ISSN 0078-6500
ORGANON. (Text in English, French, Russian, German) 1963. a. (Polska Akademia Nauk, Zaklad Historii Nauki i Techniki) Panstwowe Wydawnictwo Naukowe, Middowa 10, Warsaw, Poland (Dist. by Ars Polona-Ruch, Krakowskie Przedmiescie 7, Warsaw, Poland) Ed. Bogdan Suchodolski.

500.9 JA ISSN 0078-6675
OSAKA MUSEUM OF NATURAL HISTORY. BULLETIN/OSAKA-SHIRITSU SHIZENSHI HAKUBUTSUKAN KENKYU HOKOKU. (Text in English or Japanese; summaries of Japanese articles in English) 1954. a. avail. on exchange basis only. Osaka Museum of Natural History - Osaka-shiritsu Shizenshi Hakubutsukan, Nagai Park, Higashinagai-cho, Higashisumiyoshi-ku, Osaka 546, Japan. Ed. Isamu Hiura. circ. 1,300. Indexed: Biol.Abstr.

500.9 JA ISSN 0078-6683
OSAKA MUSEUM OF NATURAL HISTORY. OCCASIONAL PAPERS/SHIZENSHI KENKYU. (Text in Japanese or English; summaries in English) 1968. irreg.(1-3 per year) avail. on exchange basis only. Osaka Museum of Natural History - Osaka-shiritsu Shizenshi Hakubutsukan, Nagai Park, Higashinagai-cho, Higashisumiyoshi-ku, Osaka 546, Japan. Ed. Isamu Hiura. circ. 1,000. Indexed: Biol.Abstr.

500 GW ISSN 0340-4781
OSNABRUECKER NATURWISSENSCHAFTLICHE MITTEILUNGEN. (Text in German; summaries in English and German) 1873. a. DM.15. Naturwissenschaftlicher Verein Osnabrueck, Heger-Tor-Wall 27, 4500 Osnabrueck, W. Germany (B.R.D.) (Co-sponsor: Naturwissentschaftliches Museum Osnabrueck) Eds. Horst Klassen, Rainer Ehrnsberger. illus. stat.

500 BE
OUT OF SCHOOL SCIENTIFIC AND TECHNICAL EDUCATION. 1973. irreg (2-4/yrs.) 200 Fr.($5) International Coordinating Committee for the Presentation of Science and the Development of out-of-School Scientific Activities, 125 rue de Veeweyde, B-1070 Brussels, Belgium.

500 600 US ISSN 0078-7248
OXFORD SCIENCE RESEARCH PAPERS. 1967. irreg. Oxford University Press, 200 Madison Ave., New York, NY 10016 (and Ely House, 37 Dover St., London W1X 4AH, England)

500 US
PACIFIC SCIENCE ASSOCIATION. CONGRESS AND INTER-CONGRESS PROCEEDINGS. 1920. quadrennial; 13th, Vancouver, 1975. ‡ Pacific Science Association, Box 17801, Honolulu, HI 96817.
Formerly: Pacific Science Association. Congress Proceedings (ISSN 0078-7647)

500 PK
PAKISTAN ASSOCIATION FOR THE ADVANCEMENT OF SCIENCE. ANNUAL REPORT. (Text in English) a. Rs.4($1) Pakistan Association for the Advancement of Science, 14 Shah Jamal Scheme, Lahore 12, Pakistan.

500 607 PK ISSN 0078-804X
PAKISTAN COUNCIL OF SCIENTIFIC AND INDUSTRIAL RESEARCH. REPORT. (Text in English) 1953-58. a. price varies. Pakistan Council of Scientific and Industrial Research, 39 Garden Rd., Karachi 0310, Pakistan. Ed. M.A. Haleem. circ. 1,000.

500 PK ISSN 0078-8430
PAKISTAN SCIENCE CONFERENCE. PROCEEDINGS. (Text in English) a. Rs.60($15) Pakistan Association for the Advancement of Science, 14 Shah Jamal Scheme, Lahore 12, Pakistan. index.

500 PP ISSN 0085-4697
PAPUA AND NEW GUINEA SCIENTIFIC SOCIETY. ANNUAL REPORT AND PROCEEDINGS. 1949. a. Papua & New Guinea Scientific Society, c/o Geological Survey of Papua New Guinea, P.O. Box 778, Port Moresby, Papua New Guinea. Ed. Dorothy Shaw.

500 PP ISSN 0085-4700
PAPUA AND NEW GUINEA SCIENTIFIC SOCIETY. TRANSACTIONS. 1960. a. Papua & New Guinea Scientific Society, c/o Geological Survey of Papua New Guinea, P.O. Box 778, Port Moresby, Papua New Guinea.

500.9 FR
PARC NATIONAL DE LA VANOISE. TRAVAUX SCIENTIFIQUES. (Text in English; summaries in English, German and Italian) 1970. irreg. Direction Generale de la Protection de la Nature, 15, rue du Docteur-Juliand, Chambery. 73000, France.

500.9 US ISSN 0079-032X
PEABODY MUSEUM OF NATURAL HISTORY. BULLETIN. (Incorporates Bulletin of Bingham Oceanographic Collection which ceased 1967) 1926. irreg., no. 41, 1978. price varies. Peabody Museum of Natural History, Yale University, New Haven, CT 06511. Eds. John H. Ostrom, Zelda Edelson. circ. 500. Indexed: Biol.Abstr. Key Title: Bulletin - Peabody Museum of Natural History.

500.9 US ISSN 0079-0338
PEABODY MUSEUM OF NATURAL HISTORY. SPECIAL PUBLICATION. 1961. irreg., no. 14, 1974. price varies. Peabody Museum of Natural History, Yale University, New Haven, CT 06511.

500 US ISSN 0079-0745
PEORIA ACADEMY OF SCIENCE. PROCEEDINGS. 1968. a. $1. Peoria Academy of Science, Lakeview Center for the Arts and Sciences, 1125 W. Lake Ave., Peoria, IL 61614 (And 677 E. High Pt. Terrace, Peoria IL 61614) Ed. Bd. circ. 500.

PERIODICALS THAT PROGRESSIVE SCIENTISTS SHOULD KNOW ABOUT. see *BIBLIOGRAPHIES*

PETERSON'S GUIDES. ANNUAL GUIDES TO GRADUATE STUDY. BOOK 4: PHYSICAL SCIENCES. see *EDUCATION — Guides To Schools And Colleges*

500 PH ISSN 0079-1466
PHILIPPINE SCIENTIST. (Text in English) 1964. a. P.25($7) (University of San Carlos) San Carlos Publications, Cebu City 6401, Philippines. Ed. Joseph Baumgartner. circ. 180. (back issues avail.)

500 510 CN
PHILOSOPHICAL MEMOIRS OF SCIENCES & MATHS. 1974. a. Institute of Sciences & Maths, Box 1574, Guelph, Ont. N1H 6N7, Canada.

500 FR ISSN 0079-2373
POCHE-COULEURS LAROUSSE. 1970. irreg. price varies. Larousse, Library, 17 rue du Montparnase, 75280 Paris Cexex 06, France.

500 PL ISSN 0137-6217
POLITECHNIKA WROCLAWSKA. BIBLIOTEKA GLOWNA I OSRODEK INFORMACJI NAUKOWO-TECHNICZNEJ. PRACE NAUKOWE. KONFERENCJE. (Text in Polish; summaries in English and Russian) 1975. irreg. price varies. Politechnika Wroclawska, Wybrzeze Wyspianskiego 27, 50-370 Wroclaw, Poland (Dist. by; Ars Polona-Ruch, Krakowskie Przedmiescie 7, Warsaw, Poland) Ed. Marian Kloza. circ. 675.

500 PL ISSN 0137-6225
POLITECHNIKA WROCLAWSKA. BIBLIOTEKA GLOWNA I OSRODEK INFORMACJI NAUKOWO-TECHNICZNEJ. PRACE NAUKOWE. STUDIA I MATERIALY. (Text in Polish; summaries in English and Russian) 1974. irreg., no. 2, 1977. price varies. Politechnika Wroclawska, Wybrzeze Wyspianskiego 27, 50-370 Wroclaw, Poland (Dist. by: Ars Polona-Ruch, Krakowskie Przedmiescie 7, Warsaw, Poland) Ed. Marian Kloza. circ. 965.

POLITECNICA; revista de informacion tecnico - cientifica. see *ENGINEERING*

POLLUTION RESEARCH INDEX. see *ENVIRONMENTAL STUDIES*

SCIENCES: COMPREHENSIVE WORKS

500 060   PL   ISSN 0079-354X
POLSKA AKADEMIA NAUK. ODDZIAL W KRAKOWIE. KOMISJA NAUKOWYCH. SPRAWOZDANIA Z POSIEDZEN. (Text in Polish; summaries in English and Polish) 1957. s-a. price varies. Ossolineum, Publishing House of the Polish Academy of Sciences, Rynek 9, Wroclaw, Poland.

001.3 500   UK   ISSN 0079-371X
POLSKIE TOWARZYSTWO NAUKOWE NA OBCZYZNIE. ROCZNIK. 1951. a. £2. ‡ Polish Society of Arts and Sciences Abroad, 20 Princes Gate, London, S.W.7, England. Ed. B. Helczynski. circ. 600.

500.9   US   ISSN 0079-4295
POSTILLA. 1950. irreg., no. 183, 1980. price varies. Peabody Museum of Natural History, Yale University, New Haven, CT 06511. Eds. John M. Ostrom, Zelda Edelson. index. circ. 500. Indexed: Biol.Abstr.

500   SA   ISSN 0079-4341
POTCHEFSTROOM UNIVERSITY FOR CHRISTIAN HIGHER EDUCATION. WETENSKAPLIKE BYDRAES. REEKS B: NATUURWETENSKAPPE. SERIES. irreg. free. Potchefstroom University for Christian Higher Education, Potchefstroom, South Africa.

060 500   PL   ISSN 0079-4805
PRACE POPULARNONAUKOWE. 1961. irreg. price varies. (Towarzystwo Naukowe w Toruniu) Panstwowe Wydawnictwo Naukowe, Miodowa 10, Warsaw, Poland (Dist. by Ars Polona-Ruch, Krakowskie Przedmiescie 7, Warsaw, Poland) Ed. Artur Hutnikiewicz.

507   II   ISSN 0032-6690
PRAJNAN. (Text in English) 1967. a. price varies. Technical Teachers' Training Institute, 7 Mourbhanj Rd., Calcutta 700023, India. Ed. K. M. Ghosh. bk. rev. abstr. bibl. illus. stat.
Study and teaching

PROBABLE LEVELS OF R & D EXPENDITURES: FORECAST AND ANALYSIS. see *TECHNOLOGY: COMPREHENSIVE WORKS*

500   II   ISSN 0556-1906
PROGRESS OF SCIENCE IN INDIA. 1951. irreg. price varies. Indian National Science Academy, Bahadur Zafar Marg, New Delhi 110002, India.

500   US   ISSN 0191-5630
PROJECT (ELMSFORD); the science journal. 1974. a. $6. (World College of the Atlantic) Pergamon Press, Inc., Journals Division, Maxwell House, Fairview Park, Elmsford, NY 10523 (And Headington Hill Hall, Oxford OX3 0BW, England) Ed.C. D. O. Jenkins. adv. circ. 2,000. (also avail. in microform from MIM,UMI)

500 300   AO
PUBLICACOES CULTURAIS DA COMPANHIA. (Alternating series: biology, geology, climatology, history, archaeology and ethnology) (Text in Portuguese, French and English) irreg. Museu de Dundo, Dundo, Luanda, Angola.

500   US   ISSN 0079-7685
PUBLICATIONS IN MEDIEVAL SCIENCE. 1952. irreg. price varies. ‡ University of Wisconsin Press, 114 N. Murray St., Madison, WI 53715.

500   US
PUBLICATONS GRAMMA. a. price varies. Gordon and Breach Science Publishers, One Park Ave., New York, NY 10016.

500   IT
QUADERNI DI SCIENZA. 1959. irreg.; no. 5, 1976. Giardini Editori e Stampatori, Via Santa Bibbiana 28, 56100 Pisa, Italy.

500   AT   ISSN 0085-5278
QUEEN VICTORIA MUSEUM AND ART GALLERY. LAUNCESTON, TASMANIA. RECORDS. 1942. irreg., no. 67, 1979. price varies. Queen Victoria Museum, Wellington St., Launceston, Tasmania 7250, Australia. Ed. C.B. Tassell. circ. 500. Indexed: Biol.Abstr.

R E C S A M NEWS. (Regional Centre for Education in Science and Mathematics) see *EDUCATION — Teaching Methods And Curriculum*

500 320   UK   ISSN 0305-0963
RADICAL SCIENCE JOURNAL. 1974. irreg(1-2/yr) individuals £4; institutions £10.80 for 3 nos. Radical Science Journal Collective, 9 Poland St., London W1V 3DG, England. Ed.Bd. bk. rev. circ. 2,500. Indexed: Sociol.Abstr. Alt. Press Ind.

081 500 600   US   ISSN 0092-2803
RAND REPORT SERIES. irreg. Rand Corporation, 1700 Main St., Santa Monica, CA 90406.
Continues: Rand Corporation. Paper; Formerly: Rand Paper Series (ISSN 0092-2803)

500   FR
RAPPORT NATIONAL DE CONJONCTURE SCIENTIFIQUE. RAPPORT DE SYNTHESE. irreg. Centre National de la Recherche Scientifique, Comite National de la Recherche Scientifique, 15 Quai Anatole France, 75700 Paris, France.

500   US
RECENT ARTICLES AND RESEARCH IN PROGRESS.* irreg. price varies. M.S.S. Information Corporation, 133 E. 58th St., Ste. 807, New York, NY 10021.

500   JA
RECENT PROGRESS OF NATURAL SCIENCE IN JAPAN. (Text in English) irreg. Science Council of Japan - Nihon Gakujutsu Kaigi, 7-22-34 Roppongi, Minato-ku, Tokyo 106, Japan.

507 370   IS   ISSN 0034-3609
REHOVOT. (Text in English) 1959. a. free. Weizmann Institute of Science, Rehovot, Israel. Ed. Rinna Samuel. illus. circ. 19,000.

500   US
REIMPRESSIONS G & B. a. price varies. Gordon and Breach Science Publishers, One Park Ave., New York, NY 10016.

500 600   SA   ISSN 0081-2412
REPORT TO S C A R ON SOUTH AFRICAN ANTARCTIC RESEARCH ACTIVITIES. (Scientific Committee for Antarctic Research) a. free. Council for Scientific and Industrial Research, Co-operative Scientific Programmes Group, Box 395, Pretoria 0001, South Africa. circ. 300.

500   IE   ISSN 0085-5545
RESEARCH AND DEVELOPMENT IN IRELAND. 1967. irreg. Government Publications Sales Office, G.P.O. Arcade, Dublin 1, Ireland. Ed. Diarmuid Murphy.

500 007   US   ISSN 0080-1518
RESEARCH CENTERS DIRECTORY. 1960. irreg., 6th edt., 1979. $90. Gale Research Company, Book Tower, Detroit, MI 48226. Ed. Archie M. Palmer. index.

001 500   NO
RESEARCH IN NORWAY. 1973. a. free. Norges Almenvitenskapelige Forskningsraad - Norwegian Research Council for Science and the Humanities, Munthesgate 29, Oslo 2, Norway. (Co-sponsors: Ministry of Foreign Affairs: Central Committee for Norwegian Research) circ. 5,000.

500 600   US
RESEARCHER'S GUIDE TO WASHINGTON. 1978. biennial. $95. Washington Researchers, 918 16th St., N.W., Washington, DC 20006. Ed. Margaret Jennings.

001.3 500 600   GW   ISSN 0066-5754
RHEINISCH-WESTFAELISCHE AKADEMIE DER WISSENSCHAFTEN. VEROEFFENTLICHUNGEN. 1950. irreg. Westdeutscher Verlag GmbH (Opladen), Reuschenberger Str. 55, Postfach 300620, 5090 Leverkusen 3 - Opladen, W. Germany (B.R.D.)
Formerly (1950-1970): Arbeitsgemeinschaft fuer Forschung des Landes Nordrhein-Westfalen. Veroeffentlichungen.

500   RH
RHODESIA SCIENTIFIC ASSOCIATION. TRANSACTION. irreg. Rhodesia Scientific Association, Box 978, Salisbury, Zimbabwe.

500   IC
RIT OCCASIONAL PAPERS. (Text usually in English) 1923. irreg., latest no. 42, 1976. price varies. Visindafelag Islendinga - Societas Scientiarum Islandica (Icelandic Scientific Society), Haskolabokasafn, 101 Reykjavik, Iceland. circ. 1,000.

500   CN   ISSN 0080-4304
ROYAL CANADIAN INSTITUTE. PROCEEDINGS.* 1879. a. $1. Royal Canadian Institute, 191 College Street, Toronto 2b, Ontario, Canada.

500   CN   ISSN 0080-4312
ROYAL CANADIAN INSTITUTE. TRANSACTIONS. 1889. irreg. $2. Royal Canadian Institute, 191 College Street, Toronto 2b, Ontario, Canada.

500   IE   ISSN 0080-4339
ROYAL DUBLIN SOCIETY. SCIENTIFIC PROCEEDINGS SERIES A. 1959. irreg. price varies. Royal Dublin Society, Ballsbridge, Dublin 4, Ireland. circ. 750. Indexed: Chem.Abstr.

500   IE   ISSN 0080-4347
ROYAL DUBLIN SOCIETY. SCIENTIFIC PROCEEDINGS. SERIES B. 1960. irreg. price varies. Royal Dublin Society, Ballsbridge, Dublin 4, Ireland. circ. 750. Indexed: Chem.Abstr.

500   UK
ROYAL INSTITUTION OF GREAT BRITAIN. RECORD. 1799. a. £2.25. Royal Institution of Great Britain, 21 Albemarle St., London W1X 4BS, England. circ. 3,000(controlled)
Formerly: Royal Institution of Great Britain. Annual Report.

500   CN   ISSN 0080-4517
ROYAL SOCIETY OF CANADA. PROCEEDINGS. (Bound volume available: Proceedings and Transactions (ISSN 0316-4616)) (Text in English and French) 1882. N.S. vol. 17, 1979. a. Can.$6. Royal Society of Canada, 344 Wellington St., Ottawa, Ont. K1A ON4, Canada. Ed. Prof. Alexander G. McKay. (back issues avail.)

500   CN   ISSN 0316-4616
ROYAL SOCIETY OF CANADA. PROCEEDINGS AND TRANSACTIONS. (Bound volume includes Proceedings (ISSN 0080-4517) and Transactions (ISSN 0035-9122)) 1882. N.S. vol. 17, 1979. a. Can.$25. Royal Society of Canada, 344 Wellington St., Ottawa, Ont. K1A ON4, Canada. Ed. Prof. Alexander G. McKay.

500   CN   ISSN 0035-9122
ROYAL SOCIETY OF CANADA. TRANSACTIONS. (Bound volume available: Proceedings and Transactions (ISSN 0316-4616)) (Text in English and French) 1882. N.S. vol. 17, 1979. a. Can.$12.50. Royal Society of Canada, 344 Wellington St., Ottawa, Ont. K1A ON4, Canada. Ed. Prof. Alexander G. McKay. bibl. charts. illus. cum.index: 1882-1957 (in several vols) circ. 1,400. (also avail. in microform from MML) Indexed: Biol.Abstr. Chem.Abstr. Eng.Ind. Met.Abstr. Can.Ind.

500.2   UK   ISSN 0308-129X
ROYAL SOCIETY OF EDINBURGH. COMMUNICATIONS, PHYSICAL SCIENCES. irreg. Royal Society of Edinburgh, 22 George St., Edinburgh EH2 2PQ, Scotland. illus.

500   UK   ISSN 0080-4576
ROYAL SOCIETY OF EDINBURGH. YEAR BOOK. 1941. a. £5($15) Royal Society of Edinburgh, 22-24 George St., Edinburgh EH2 2PQ, Scotland. Ed. W. H. Rutherford. circ. 1,500.

ROYAL SOCIETY OF LONDON. PHILOSOPHICAL TRANSACTIONS. SERIES A. MATHEMATICAL AND PHYSICAL SCIENCES. see *MATHEMATICS*

ROYAL SOCIETY OF LONDON. PROCEEDINGS. SERIES A. MATHEMATICAL AND PHYSICAL SCIENCES. see *MATHEMATICS*

506   UK   ISSN 0080-4673
ROYAL SOCIETY OF LONDON. YEAR BOOK. 1898. a. £6.75. Royal Society of London, 6 Carlton House Terrace, London SW1Y 5AG, England. circ. 1,400. (reprint service avail. from ISI)

506 AT ISSN 0080-469X
ROYAL SOCIETY OF QUEENSLAND, ST. LUCIA. PROCEEDINGS. 1884. a. Aus.$10. Royal Society of Queensland, Box 50, St. Lucia, Queensland 4067, Australia. Eds. N.C. Stevens, A. Bailey. circ. 640.

500 SA ISSN 0035-919X
ROYAL SOCIETY OF SOUTH AFRICA. TRANSACTIONS. 1877. irreg (1-4/yr.) price varies. Royal Society of South Africa, University of Cape Town, Rondebosch 7700, South Africa. Ed. A. C. Brown. bibl. charts. illus. cum.index: 1878-1909; 1909-1955. circ. 700. (also avail. in microfilm from UMI) Indexed: Biol.Abstr. Chem.Abstr. Math.R. Sci.Abstr. S.A.Waterabstr.

500 AT ISSN 0085-5812
ROYAL SOCIETY OF SOUTH AUSTRALIA. TRANSACTIONS. 1878. a. Aus.$22. Royal Society of South Australia Inc., State Library Bldg, North Terrace, Adelaide, S.A. 5000, Australia. Ed. M.J. Tyler. index. circ. 800. Indexed: Biol.Abstr. Abstr.Anthropol.

506 AT ISSN 0080-4703
ROYAL SOCIETY OF TASMANIA, HOBART. PAPERS AND PROCEEDINGS. 1848. a. Aus.$7.50. Royal Society of Tasmania, G.P.O. Box 1166M, Hobart, Tasmania 7001, Australia. Ed. M.R. Banks. circ. 600(approx.)

500 AT ISSN 0035-9211
ROYAL SOCIETY OF VICTORIA. PROCEEDINGS. 1860. a. Aus.$16. Royal Society of Victoria, 9 Victoria St., Melbourne 3000, Australia. Ed. Prof. J. W. Warren. charts. illus. index. circ. 1,000. Indexed: Chem.Abstr. Sci.Abstr.

500 US
RUSSIAN MONOGRAPHS AND TEXTS ON THE PHYSICAL SCIENCES. a. price varies. Gordon and Breach Science Publishers, One Park Ave., New York, NY 10016.

500 US
RUSSIAN TRACTS ON THE PHYSICAL SCIENCES. a. price varies. Gordon and Breach Science Publishers, One Park Ave., New York, NY 10016.

S C I S NEWSLETTER. (Science Curriculum Improvement Study) see *EDUCATION — Teaching Methods And Curriculum*

991.1 570 MY ISSN 0036-2131
SABAH SOCIETY. JOURNAL. 1961. irreg. M.11 per no. Sabah Society - Pertubuhan Sabah, Box 547, Kota Kinabalu, Sabah, Malaysia. Ed. A. J. Yee. circ. 130-400. (tabloid format)
Natural history

500 GE ISSN 0080-5262
SAECHSISCHE AKADEMIE DER WISSENSCHAFTEN, LEIPZIG. JAHRBUCH. 1955 (covering 1949-53) irreg., vol. for 1973-74, 1976. price varies. Akademie-Verlag, Leipziger Str. 3-4, 108 Berlin, E. Germany (D.D.R.) Ed. Gerald Wiemers.

500 510 GE ISSN 0080-5289
SAECHSISCHE AKADEMIE DER WISSENSCHAFTEN, LEIPZIG. MATHEMATISCH-NATURWISSENSCHAFTLICHE KLASSE. ABHANDLUNGEN. 1896. irreg., vol. 52, 1974. price varies. Akademie-Verlag, Leipziger Str. 3-4, 108 Berlin, E. Germany (D.D.R.)

510 500 GE ISSN 0080-5270
SAECHSISCHE AKADEMIE DER WISSENSCHAFTEN, LEIPZIG. MATHEMATISCH-NATURWISSENSCHAFTLICHE KLASSE. SITZUNGSBERICHTE. 1896. irreg., vol. 112, 1977. price varies. Akademie-Verlag, Leipziger Str. 3-4, 108 Berlin, E. Germany (D.D.R.)

500 600 II
SAMBALPUR UNIVERSITY JOURNAL: SCIENCE AND TECHNOLOGY. (Text in English or Oriya) vol. 5, 1972. a. Rs.5. Sambalpur University, Budharaja Hills, Sambalpur 768001, Orissa, India.

500.9 500 US ISSN 0080-5920
SAN DIEGO SOCIETY OF NATURAL HISTORY. MEMOIRS. 1931. irreg. price varies. San Diego Society of Natural History, Balboa Park, Box 1390, San Diego, CA 92112. index. circ. 750. Indexed: Biol.Abstr. Ecol.Abstr.

500.9 US ISSN 0080-5939
SAN DIEGO SOCIETY OF NATURAL HISTORY. OCCASIONAL PAPERS. 1936. irreg. price varies. San Diego Society of Natural History, Balboa Park, Box 1390, San Diego, CA 92112.

500.9 US ISSN 0080-5947
SAN DIEGO SOCIETY OF NATURAL HISTORY. TRANSACTIONS. 1905. irreg. price varies. San Diego Society of Natural History, Balboa Park, Box 1390, San Diego, CA 92112. Indexed: Biol.Abstr. Ecol.Abstr.

500 SZ ISSN 0080-6056
SANKT GALLISCHE NATURWISSENSCHAFTLICHE GESELLSCHAFT. BERICHT UEBER DIE TAETIGKEIT.* 1860. irreg., 1969, vol. 79. approx. $4. Sankt Gallische Naturwissenschaftliche Gesellschaft, St. Gallen, Switzerland.

500.9 CN ISSN 0080-6552
SASKATCHEWAN NATURAL HISTORY SOCIETY. SPECIAL PUBLICATIONS. 1958. irreg. price varies. Saskatchewan Natural History Society, Box 1784, Saskatoon, Sask. S7K 3S1, Canada. Ed. Dr. C. Stuart Houston.

500 CN ISSN 0080-6587
SASKATCHEWAN RESEARCH COUNCIL. ANNUAL REPORT. 1947. a. free. Saskatchewan Research Council Library, 30 Campus Drive, Saskatoon Sask S7N 0X1, Canada.

500 SZ
SCHWEIZERISCHE NATURFORSCHENDE GESELLSCHAFT. JAHRBUCH/SOCIETE HELVETIQUE DES SCIENCES NATURELLES. ANNUAIRE. 1815. a. Birkhaeuser Verlag, Elisabethenstr. 19, CH-4010 Basel, Switzerland.
Formerly: Schweizerische Naturforschende Gesellschaft. Verhandlungen (ISSN 0080-7362)

500 SZ
SCHWEIZERISCHER WISSENSCHAFTSRAT. JAHRESBERICHT/CONSEIL SUISSE DE LA SCIENCE. RAPPORT ANNUEL. (Text in French & German) 1965. a. Schweizerischer Wissenschaftsrat, Wildhainweg 9, Postfach 2732, 3001 Berne, Switzerland.

500 600 US
SCIENCE AND ENGINEERING POLICY SERIES. irreg. price varies. Oxford University Press, 200 Madison Ave., New York, NY 10016 (And Ely House, 37 Dovver St., London W1X 4AH, England) Eds. Harrie Massey, Frederick Dainton.

500 301 US
SCIENCE AND SOCIETY SERIES. 1975. irreg. Science Resource Center, Inc., 897 Main St., Cambridge, MA 02139.

SCIENCE AND TECHNOLOGY; a purchase guide for branch and public libraries. see *LIBRARY AND INFORMATION SCIENCES*

500 600 KO
SCIENCE AND TECHNOLOGY.* (Text in Korean and English; summaries in English) 1955. irreg. exchange basis. Korea University, College of Science and Engineering, 1 Anam-Dong, Seoul 132, S. Korea.
Formerly: Goryo Daehakgyo Nonmunjip Science.

500 UN
SCIENCE AND TECHNOLOGY EDUCATION NEWSLETTER. (Supplement to: Bulletin of the Regional Office for Science and Technology for Africa) (Text in English) no. 9, 1978. Unesco, Regional Office for Science and Technology for Africa, Box 30592, Nairobi, Kenya.

500 UK ISSN 0300-3361
SCIENCE CHELSEA. 1965. irreg., vol. 8, 1979. £0.50($1.50) Chelsea College, Students Union, Manresa Road, London SW3 6LX, England. Ed. P. Ansell. adv. bk. rev. bibl. charts. illus. index. circ. 1,000.

500 JA
SCIENCE COUNCIL OF JAPAN. ANNUAL REPORT. (Text in English) 1950. a. exchange basis. Science Council of Japan - Nihon Gakujutsu Kaigi, 7-22-34 Roppongi, Minato-ku, Tokyo 106, Japan.

507.11 UK
SCIENCE EDUCATION IN THE REGION. 1965. biennial. 70p. London and Home Counties Regional Advisory Council for Technological Education, Tavistock House South, Tavistock Square, London WC1H 9LR, England. Ed. D. T. M. Bennett. circ. 1,500.

SCIENCE EDUCATION IN ZAMBIA. see *EDUCATION*

509 BE
SCIENCE ET TECHNOLOGIE ANNUAIRE/ WETENSCHAP EN TECHNOLOGIE JAARBOEK. 1970. a. Services de Programmation de la Politique Scientifique, Rue de la Science, 8, 1040 Brussels, Belgique.

500 US
SCIENCE FOR THE MODERN MIND. irreg. price varies. Macmillan Publishing Co., Inc., 866 Third Ave., New York, NY 10022.

500 US
SCIENCE MUSEUM OF MINNESOTA. MONOGRAPH. 1972. irreg. Science Museum of Minnesota, 30 E. 10th St., St. Paul, MN 55101. Ed. Bruce R. Erickson.

500 US ISSN 0161-4452
SCIENCE MUSEUM OF MINNESOTA. SCIENTIFIC PUBLICATIONS, NEW SERIES. 1966. irreg. $0.55. Science Museum of Minnesota, 30 E. 10th St., St. Paul, MN 55101. Ed. Bruce R. Erickson. Key Title: Scientific Publications of the Science Museum of Minnesota.
Supersedes: Science Museum of Minnesota. Scientific Bulletin; Formerly: Science Museum of Minnesota. Scientific Publications (ISSN 0080-5521)

500 AT
SCIENCE MUSEUM OF VICTORIA. MONOGRAPHS. 1977. irreg. price varies. Science Museum of Victoria, 304-328 Swanston St., Melbourne, Vic. 3000, Australia.

371.3 500 JM
SCIENCE NOTES AND NEWS. irreg. Association of Science Teachers of Jamaica, c/o Honorary Secretary, Olive Baxter, 46 Paddington Terrace, Kingston 6, Jamaica.
Study and teaching

500 FR ISSN 0080-7540
SCIENCE NOUVELLE.* irreg., 1970, no. 8. price varies. Editions R. Laffont, 6 Place Saint-Sulpice, Paris 6e, France.
Before 1970: Jeune Science.

500 UN ISSN 0080-7591
SCIENCE POLICY STUDIES AND DOCUMENTS. (Text in English or French) 1965. irreg.; no. 35, 1974. price varies. Unesco, 7-9 Place de Fontenoy, 75700 Paris, France (Dist. in U.S. by: Unipub, 345 Park Ave. S., New York NY 10010)

505 US
SCIENCE STUDENT EXPLORES. 1975. irreg. $7.97 per issue. Richards Rosen Press, 29 E. 21 St., New York, NY 10010. Ed. Ruth C. Rosen.
Grades 9-12

500 AT
SCIENCE TEACHERS ASSOCIATION OF QUEENSLAND. NEWSLETTER. 1961. irreg. Aus.$0.20 each issue. Science Teachers Association of Queensland, c/o J. Sinclair, 17 Indooroopilly Rd., Jaringa, Qld. 4068, Australia.

SCIENCE YEAR; World Book Science Annual. see *ENCYCLOPEDIAS AND GENERAL ALMANACS*

500 FR ISSN 0080-763X
SCIENCES. (1953-68, appeared in Revue Generale des Sciences Pures et Appliquees and Association Francaise pour l'Avancement des Sciences. Bulletin) 1936. irreg. 15 F.($20) Association Francaise pour l'Avancement des Sciences, 250 rue Saint-Jacques, Paris 5e, France.

SCIENCES: COMPREHENSIVE WORKS

500 600 JA
SCIENTIFIC AND TECHNICAL INFORMATION IN FOREIGN COUNTRIES/KAIGAIKI KAGAKU GIJUTSU JOHO SHIRYO. (Text in Japanese) irreg. Science and Technology Agency, Planning Bureau - Kagaku Gijutsu-cho Keikaku-kyoku, 2-2-1 Kasumigaseki, Chiyoda-ku, Tokyo 100, Japan.

500 600 SA ISSN 0080-7702
SCIENTIFIC AND TECHNICAL PERIODICALS PUBLISHED IN SOUTH AFRICA/WETENSKAPLIKE EN TEGNIESE TYDSKRIFTE IN SUID-AFRIKA UITGEGEE. a. R.1.50($1.50) Council for Scientific and Industrial Research, Publishing Division, Box 395, Pretoria 0001, South Africa. circ. 1,500.

500 600 SA ISSN 0080-7710
SCIENTIFIC AND TECHNICAL SOCIETIES IN SOUTH AFRICA/WETENSKAPLIKE EN TEGNIESE VERENIGINGS IN SUID-AFRIKA. a. R.2.50($3) Council for Scientific and Industrial Research, Publishing Division, Box 395, Pretoria 0001, South Africa. circ. 500.

500 600 CN ISSN 0586-7746
SCIENTIFIC AND TECHNICAL SOCIETIES OF CANADA/SOCIETES SCIENTIFIQUES ET TECHNIQUES DU CANADA. 1968. biennial. 5. National Research Council of Canada, Canada Institute for Scientific and Technical Information (CISTI), Ottawa, Ont. K1A 0S2, Canada.

505 HK ISSN 0586-5751
SCIENTIFIC DIRECTORY OF HONG KONG. 1968. quadrennial; latest 1978. price varies. Government Information Services, Beaconsfield House, Queen's Rd., Central, Victoria, Hong Kong, Hong Kong.

500 600 CN
SCIENTIFIC POLICY, RESEARCH AND DEVELOPMENT IN CANADA/POLITIQUE DES SCIENCES, LA RECHERCHES ET LE DEVELOPPEMENT AU CANADA. 1968. biennial. Can.$5. National Research Council of Canada, Canada Institute for Scientific and Technical Information (CISTI), Ottawa, Ont. K1A 0S2, Canada.

500 600 SA ISSN 0080-7761
SCIENTIFIC RESEARCH ORGANIZATIONS IN SOUTH AFRICA/WETENSKAPLIKE NAVORSINGSORGANISASIES IN SUID-AFRIKA. a. R.4($4.50) Council for Scientific and Industrial Research, Publishing Division, Box 395, Pretoria 0001, South Africa. circ. 500.

500 600 US ISSN 0085-5995
SCIENTIFIC, TECHNICAL AND RELATED SOCIETIES OF THE UNITED STATES. 9th edt. 1971. irreg. $14.25. National Academy of Sciences, 2101 Constitution Ave., Washington, DC 20418.

500 US ISSN 0080-777X
SCIENTISTS FORUM. 1969. irreg. $1 per issue. Chapman Grant, Ed. & Pub., 1114 Idaho St., Escondido, CA 92027. circ. 1,000.
  Formerly: Debunker.

500 UK ISSN 0080-8075
SCOTTISH JOURNAL OF SCIENCE. 1965. irreg. (approx. 1 pt. per yr) £2 per part. ‡ Scots Secretariat Pamphlets Organisation, Jess Cottage, Carlops, Penicuik, Midlothian EH26 9NF, Scotland. Ed. Archie Lamont. circ. 1,000.

501 100 US ISSN 0080-8970
SERIES IN THE PHILOSOPHY OF SCIENCE. 1962. irreg. price varies. ‡ University of Pittsburgh Press, 127 N. Bellefield Ave., Pittsburgh, PA 15260. Ed. Robert G. Colodny.

500.9 UK ISSN 0080-9241
SHERBORN FUND FACSIMILES. (Text mainly in English; occasionally in other European languages) 1959. irreg., 1973, no. 4. price varies. Society for the Bibliography of Natural History, c/o British Museum (Natural History), Cromwell Rd., London SW7 5BD, England.

500 US
SHEVCHENKO SCIENTIFIC SOCIETY. PROCEEDINGS OF THE SECTION OF MATHEMATICS AND PHYSICS. (Text in English and Ukrainian) 1964. vol. 6. irreg. $2 per copy. ‡ Shevchenko Scientific Society, 302 W. 13th St., New York, NY 10014. circ. 500.
  Supersedes in part its: Proceedings of the Section of Mathematics, Natural Science and Medicine (ISSN 0470-5017)

500 JA
SHIMANE UNIVERSITY. FACULTY OF SCIENCE. MEMOIRS. (Text in English and Japanese) 1966. a. Shimane University, Faculty of Science, 1060 Nishikawatsu-cho, Matsue-shi, Shimane-ken, Japan. Ed.Bd. circ. 600.

SHIVAJI UNIVERSITY, KOLHAPUR, INDIA. JOURNAL. HUMANITIES AND SCIENCES. see *HUMANITIES: COMPREHENSIVE WORKS*

505 JA ISSN 0583-0923
SHIZUOKA UNIVERSITY. FACULTY OF SCIENCE. REPORTS/SHIZUOKA DAIGAKU RIGAKUBU KENKYU HOKOKU. (Text in European languages) 1965. irreg. exchange basis. Shizuoka University, Faculty of Science - Shizuoka Daigaku Rigakubu, 836 Oya, Shizuoka-shi 422, Japan. Ed.Bd. circ. 400.

506 US ISSN 0080-9578
SIGMA ZETAN. 1927. a. free to members. Sigma Zeta, c/o George W. Welker, Ed., Ball State University, Muncie, IN 47306. circ. 1,200.

500.9 331.11 SI
SINGAPORE. MINISTRY OF SCIENCE AND TECHNOLOGY. NATIONAL SURVEY OF SCIENTIFIC MANPOWER. (Text in English) 1974. a. Ministry of Science and Technology, Singapore, Singapore.

500 SI
SINGAPORE. SCIENCE COUNCIL. ANNUAL REPORTS. 1972. a. Science Council, Singapore, Singapore. charts. illus. stat.

500 US ISSN 0081-0339
SMITHSONIAN OPPORTUNITIES FOR RESEARCH AND STUDY IN HISTORY ART SCIENCE. Title varies: Smithsonian Research Opportunities. 1964. irreg. free. ‡ Smithsonian Institution, Washington, DC 20560. index.
  Formerly: Smithsonian Institution Opportunities for Research and Advanced Study.

500 AG
SOCIEDAD CIENTIFICA ARGENTINA. CICLO DE CONFERENCIAS. irreg. Sociedad Cientifica Argentina, Comision de Cursos y Conferencias, Av. Santa Fe 1145, Buenos Aires, Argentina. illus.

509 MX
SOCIEDAD MEXICANA DE HISTORIA DE LA CIENCIA Y DE LA TECNOLOGIA. ANALES. 1969. irreg. $8. Sociedad Mexicana de Historia de la Ciencia y de la Tecnologia, Av. Dr. Vertiz 724, Mexico 12, D.F., Mexico. illus.

500 IT ISSN 0391-609X
SOCIETA E LA SCIENZA. 1977. irreg., no. 3, 1979. price varies. Liguori Editore s.r.l., Via Mezzocannone 19, 80134 Naples, Italy. Ed. Felice Ippolito.

500.9 FR
SOCIETE DES SCIENCES PHYSIQUES ET NATURELLES DE BORDEAUX. MEMOIRES. 1854. irreg., latest 1975/76. price varies. Bibliotheque Interuniversitaire de Bordeaux, Section des Sciences, Ancien Chemin Bernos, 33-Talence, France.

500.1 SZ ISSN 0037-9611
SOCIETE VAUDOISE DES SCIENCES NATURELLES. MEMOIRES. 1920. irreg. price varies. Societe Vaudoise des Sciences Naturelles, Palais de Rumine, 1005 Lausanne, Switzerland. adv. bibl. charts. illus. maps. index. Indexed: Biol.Abstr. Chem.Abstr.

500 US
SOCIETY FOR GENERAL SYSTEMS RESEARCH. ANNUAL MEETING PROCEEDINGS. a. $15 to individuals; institutions $20. Society for General Systems Research, Systems Science Institute, University of Louisville, Box 1055, Louisville, KY 40201.

500 US
SOCIETY FOR THE HISTORY OF DISCOVERIES. ANNUAL REPORT. 1961. a. membership. Society for the History of Discoveries, 5404 Thunder Hill Road, Columbia, MD 21043.

301 500 NE
SOCIOLOGY OF THE SCIENCES. (Text in English) 1977. irreg. price varies. D. Reidel Publishing Co., Box 17, 3300 AA Dordrecht, Netherlands (And Lincoln Building, 160 Old Derby St., Hingham, MA 02043) Ed. R. D. Whitley.

SOMERSET ARCHAEOLOGY AND NATURAL HISTORY. see *ARCHAEOLOGY*

SOOCHOW JOURNAL OF MATHEMATICAL & NATURAL SCIENCES. see *MATHEMATICS*

509 II
SOURCE MATERIALS ON THE HISTORY OF SCIENCE IN INDIA. irreg. price varies. Indian National Science Academy, Bahadur Zafar Marg, New Delhi 110002, India.

500 600 SA ISSN 0081-2455
SOUTH AFRICAN JOURNAL OF ANTARCTIC RESEARCH. 1971. a. R.5 per yr. Council for Scientific and Industrial Research, Co-Operative Scientific Programmes Group, Box 395, Pretoria 0001, South Africa. Ed. P.R. Condy. circ. 500.

500 US
SOUTH DAKOTA ACADEMY OF SCIENCE. PROCEEDINGS. 1916. a. $7. ‡ South Dakota Academy of Science, University of South Dakota, Dept. of Biology, Vermillion, SD 57069. Ed. Carroll Hanten. charts. illus. circ. 350(controlled) Indexed: Biol.Abstr.

500 CE ISSN 0081-3745
SPOLIA ZEYLANICA/BULLETIN OF THE NATIONAL MUSEUMS OF SRI LANKA. (Text in English) 1904. a. price varies. Department of National Museums, Box 854, Sir Marcus Fernando Mawatha, Colombo 7, Sri Lanka.

500 US
SPRINGER SERIES IN SOLID STATE SCIENCES. 1978. irreg., vol. 25, 1981. price varies. Springer-Verlag, 175 Fifth Ave., New York, NY 10010 (Also Berlin, Heidelberg, Vienna) Ed.Bd. (reprint service avail. fr9m ISI)

500 US ISSN 0081-3877
SPRINGER TRACTS IN NATURAL PHILOSOPHY. 1964. irreg., 1977, no. 29. price varies. Springer-Verlag, 175 Fifth Ave., New York, NY 10010 (also Berlin, Heidelberg, Vienna) Ed. B. D. Coleman. circ. 2,000. (reprint service avail. from ISI) Indexed: Math.R.
  Continues: Ergebnisse der Angewandten Mathematik.

500 CE
SRI LANKA ASSOCIATION FOR THE ADVANCEMENT OF SCIENCE. PROCEEDINGS. (Text in English) a. Sri Lanka Association for the Advancement of Science, 181/50 Bauddhaloka Mawatha, Colombo 7, Sri Lanka.

500 YU ISSN 0081-4024
SRPSKA AKADEMIJA NAUKA I UMETNOSTI. ODELJENJE PRIRODNO-MATEMATICKIH NAUKA. POSEBNA IZDANJA. (Text in Serbo-Croatian; summaries in French, English, German or Russian) 1950. irreg., 1972, no. 39. price varies. Srpska Akademija Nauka i Umetnosti, Knez Mihailova 35, 11001 Belgrade, Yugoslavia (Dist. by: Prosveta, Terazije 16, Belgrade, Yugoslavia) Ed. Jovan Belic. circ. 500. Indexed: Biol.Abstr. Ref.Zh.

060 500 YU
SRPSKA AKADEMIJA NAUKA I UMETNOSTI. POVREMENA IZDANJA. irreg. Srpska Akademija Nauka i Umetnosti, Knez Mihailova 35, 11001 Belgrade, Yugoslavia.

SCIENCES: COMPREHENSIVE WORKS

060 500 YU ISSN 0561-7383
SRPSKA AKADEMIJA NAUKA I UMETNOSTI. PREDAVANJA. 1961. irreg. Srpska Akademija Nauka i Umetnosti, Knez Mihailova 35, 11001 Belgrade, Yugoslavia.

SRPSKA AKADEMIJA NAUKA I UMETNOSTI SPOMENICA. see *HUMANITIES: COMPREHENSIVE WORKS*

500 600 GW
STIFTERVERBAND FUER DIE DEUTSCHE WISSENSCHAFT. TAETIGKEITSBERICHT. 1950. a. membership. ‡ Stifterverband fuer die Deutsche Wissenschaft, Brucker Holt 56, 4300 Essen, W. Germany (B.R.D.) circ. 10,000.
Supersedes: Stifterverband fuer die Deutsche Wissenschaft. Jahrbuch (ISSN 0081-5551)

500.9 BE
STUDIA ALGOLIGICA LOVANIENSIA. 1974. irreg. price varies. E. Story-Scientia, Prudens van Duyseplein 8, B-9000 Ghent, Belgium.

500 PL ISSN 0081-6590
STUDIA I MATERIALY Z DZIEJOW NAUKI POLSKIEJ. SERIA C. HISTORIA NAUK MATEMATYCZNYCH, FIZYKO-CHEMICZNYCH I GEOLOGICZNO-GEOGRAFICZNYCH. (Text in Polish; summaries in Russian and French) 1957. irreg., 1972, vol. 16. price varies. (Polska Akademia Nauk, Zaklad Historii Nauki i Techniki) Panstwowe Wydawnictwo Naukowe, Ul. Miodowa 10, Warsaw, Poland. Ed. W. Voise. bibl. illus.

500 PL ISSN 0081-6612
STUDIA I MATERIALY Z DZIEJOW NAUKI POLSKIEJ. SERIA E. ZAGADNIENIA OGOLNE. (Text in Polish; summaries in English, Russian and French) 1967. irreg., 1970, no. 4. price varies. (Polska Akademia Nauk, Zaklad Historii Nauki i Techniki) Panstwowe Wydawnictwo Naukowe, Ul. Miodowa 10, Warsaw, Poland (Dist. by Ars Polona-Ruch, Krakowskie Przedmiescie 7, Warsaw, Poland) Ed. W. Voise. index.

500 GW ISSN 0081-7376
STUDIEN ZUR WISSENSCHAFTSTHEORIE IM NEUNZEHNTEN JAHRHUNDERT. 1968. irreg., vol. 13, 1978. price varies. Verlag Anton Hain GmbH, Adelheidstr. 2, Postfach 1220, 6240 Koenigstein, W. Germany (B. R. D.)

500 GE ISSN 0081-7384
STUDIENBUECHEREI. 1970. irreg. price varies. VEB Deutscher Verlag der Wissenschaften, Postfach 1216, 108 Berlin, E. Germany (D.D.R.)

501 US ISSN 0081-8577
STUDIES IN THE FOUNDATIONS, METHODOLOGY AND PHILOSOPHY OF SCIENCE. 1967. irreg., 1971, no. 4. price varies. Springer-Verlag, 175 Fifth Ave., New York, NY 10010 (also Berlin, Heidelberg, Vienna) Ed. M. Bunge. (reprint service avail. from ISI)

500 608.7 US ISSN 0081-8615
STUDIES IN THE HISTORY OF DISCOVERIES. 1971. irreg., latest 1976. price varies. (Society for the History of Discoveries) University of Chicago Press, 5801 S. Ellis Ave., Chicago, IL 60637. Ed. David Woodward. (reprint service avail. from UMI,ISI)

509 NE
STUDIES IN THE HISTORY OF MODERN SCIENCE. (Text in English) 1977. irreg. price varies. D. Reidel Publishing Co., Box 17, 3300 AA Dordrecht, Netherlands (And Lincoln Building, 160 Old Derby St., Hingham, MA 02043) Eds. Robert S. Cohen, Erwin N. Hiebert, Everett Mendelsohn.

501 160 US
STUDIES IN THE LOGIC OF SCIENCE. 1971. irreg. price varies. University of California Press, 2223 Fulton St., Berkeley, CA 94720.

500 US
STUDIES IN THE NATURAL SCIENCES. 1973. irreg. price varies. (University of Miami, Center for Theoretical Studies) Plenum Press, 233 Spring St., New York, NY 10013. Ed.Bd.

500 SW ISSN 0081-8704
STUDIES IN THE THEORY OF SCIENCE. (Text in English) 1969. irreg. price varies. (Goeteborgs Universitet) Akademifoerlaget (Subsidiary of: Esselte Studium AB) Box 3075, S-400 10 Goeteborg, Sweden. Ed. Haakan Toernebohm.

354 SJ
SUDAN. NATIONAL COUNCIL FOR RESEARCH. SCIENCE POLICY AND ANNUAL REPORT. (Text in English) a, latest 1975/76. exchange basis. National Council for Research, Box 2404, Khartoum, Sudan.

SUDAN RESEARCH INFORMATION BULLETIN. see *HUMANITIES: COMPREHENSIVE WORKS*

SUDHOFFS ARCHIV. BEIHEFTE. see *MEDICAL SCIENCES*

SURVEY OF THE ACTIVITIES OF SCIENTIFIC UNIONS; SPECIAL AND SCIENTIFIC COMMITTEES OF I C S U IN THE FIELD OF INFORMATION. see *LIBRARY AND INFORMATION SCIENCES*

500 600 PL ISSN 0082-1241
SZCZECINSKIE TOWARZYSTWO NAUKOWE. SPRAWOZDANIA. 1960. irreg. price varies. Szczecinskie Towarzystwo Naukowe, Rycerska 3, 70-537 Szczecin, Poland.

500 PL ISSN 0137-5326
SZKICE LEGNICKIE. irreg., 1976, vol. 9. 45 Zl. (Legnickie Towarzystwo Przyjaciol Nauk) Ossolineum, Publishing House of the Polish Academy of Sciences, Rynek 9, Wroclaw, Poland (Dist. by: Ars Polona-Ruch, Krakowskie Przedmiescie 7, Warsaw, Poland)

TALLINNSKII POLITEKHNICHESKII INSTITUT. TRUDY. see *TECHNOLOGY: COMPREHENSIVE WORKS*

500.9 NZ ISSN 0496-8026
TANE. 1950. a. NZ.$2 for institutions. Auckland University Field Club, c/o Botany Department, University of Auckland, Private Bag, Auckland, New Zealand. illus.

500.9 US
TEBIWA MISCELLANEOUS PAPERS. 1958. irreg. $1 per no. Idaho Museum of Natural History, Idaho State University, Pocatello, ID 83209. Ed. Lucille B. Harten. abstr. 10-yr. cum.index in vol. 11. circ. 400. (also avail. in microform from UMI; reprint service avail. from UMI)
Formerly (until vol. 18): Tebiwa (ISSN 0040-0823)
Natural history

600 US
TECHNOCRACY. INFORMATION BRIEFS. irreg. Technocracy, Inc., Continental Headquarters, Savannah, OH 44874.

509 RM
TIBISCUS. SERIA STIINTELE NATURII. (Text in Romanian; summaries in German) a. Muzeul Banatului, Piata Huniade Nr.1, Timisoara, Romania.

TOPIC; a journal of the liberal arts. see *HUMANITIES: COMPREHENSIVE WORKS*

500.9 UK ISSN 0082-5344
TORQUAY NATURAL HISTORY SOCIETY. TRANSACTIONS AND PROCEEDINGS. 1909. a. 75p. Torquay Natural History Society, The Museum, Babbacombe Road, Torquay T21 1HG, England. Ed. Mrs. L. M. Gallant.

500 PL ISSN 0082-5522
TOWARZYSTWO NAUKOWE W TORUNIU. ROCZNIKI. (Text in Polish; summaries in German) a. price varies. Panstwowe Wydawnictwo Naukowe, Miodowa 10, Warsaw, Poland (Dist. by: Ars Polona-Ruch, Krakowskie Przedmiescie 7, Warsaw, Poland) Ed. Artur Hutnikiewicz.

500.9 SA ISSN 0041-1752
TRANSVAAL MUSEUM. ANNALS/TRANSVAAL MUSEUM ANNALE. (Text in Afrikaans, English, French and German) 1908. irreg. price varies. Transvaal Museum, Box 413, Pretoria, South Africa. Ed. Dr. Vari. illus. index. circ. 300(controlled)
Indexed: Biol.Abstr. Zoo.Rec.

500 CR ISSN 0069-2107
TROPICAL SCIENCE CENTER, COSTA RICA. OCCASIONAL PAPER. 1963. irreg.; no. 15, 1979. price varies. Tropical Science Center, Calle 1, No. 442, Apdo. 2959, San Jose, Costa Rica.

501 HU ISSN 0082-6707
TUDOMANYSZERVEZESI FUZETEK. 1965. irreg. price varies. (Magyar Tudomanyos Akademia) Akademiai Kiado, Publishing House of the Hungarian Academy of Sciences, P.O. Box 24, H-1363 Budapest, Hungary.

509 609 HU ISSN 0082-6715
TUDOMANYTORTENETI TANULMANYOK. 1961. irreg. price varies. (Magyar Tudomanyos Akademia) Akademiai Kiado, Publishing House of the Hungarian Academy of Sciences, P.O. Box 24, H-1363 Budapest, Hungary.

500 FI ISSN 0082-7002
TURUN YLIOPISTO. JULKAISUJA. SARJA A. I. ASTRONOMICA-CHEMICA-PHYSICA-MATHEMATICA. (Latin title: Annales Universitatis Turkuensis) (Text in English, German, French, Finnish) 1957. irreg. price varies. Turun Yliopisto - University of Turku, SF-20500 Turku 50, Finland.

TURUN YLIOPISTO. JULKAISUJA. SARJA C. SCRIPTA LINGUA FENNICA EDITA. see *HUMANITIES: COMPREHENSIVE WORKS*

500.9 GW ISSN 0068-0885
UEBERSEE-MUSEUM, BREMEN. VEROEFFENTLICHUNGEN. REIHE A: NATURWISSENSCHAFTEN. 1949. irreg. price varies. Uebersee-Museum, Bremen, Bahnhofsplatz 13, 2800 Bremen, W. Germany (B.R.D.)

500 US
UKRAINIAN STUDIES. (Text in Ukrainian, English) irreg. membership. Shevchenko Scientific Society, 302 W. 13th St., New York, NY 10014.

U.S. NATIONAL SCIENCE FOUNDATION. GUIDE TO PROGRAMS. see *EDUCATION — School Organization And Administration*

500 507.2 US ISSN 0083-2332
U. S. NATIONAL SCIENCE FOUNDATION. ANNUAL REPORT. 1951. a. price varies. U. S. National Science Foundation, 1800 G St., N.W., Washington, DC 20550 (Orders to: Supt. Doc., Washington, DC 20402)

500 US
U.S. NATIONAL SCIENCE FOUNDATION. FEDERAL FUNDS FOR RESEARCH, DEVELOPMENT, AND OTHER SCIENTIFIC ACTIVITIES. (Subseries of U.S. National Science Foundation. Surveys of Science Resource Series) a. U. S. National Science Foundation, 1800 G St., N.W., Washington, DC 20550 (Orders to: Supt. Doc., Washington, DC 20402)
Formerly: U.S. National Science Foundation. Federal Funds for Science (ISSN 0083-2359)

500 US ISSN 0083-2375
U. S. NATIONAL SCIENCE FOUNDATION. N S F FACTBOOK. 1971. irreg., 2nd ed. 1975. $44.50. Marquis Academic Media, 200 E. Ohio St., Chicago, IL 60611. index.

500 US ISSN 0080-2026
U. S. NATIONAL SCIENCE FOUNDATION. REVIEWS OF DATA ON SCIENCE RESOURCES. 1964. irreg. price varies. U. S. National Science Foundation, 1800 G St., N.W., Washington, DC 20550 (Orders to: Supt. Doc., Washington, DC 20402)

500 600 US ISSN 0083-2405
U. S. NATIONAL SCIENCE FOUNDATION. SURVEYS OF SCIENCE RESOURCES SERIES. irreg. price varies. U. S. National Science Foundation, 1800 G St., N.W., Washington, DC 20550 (Orders to: Supt. Doc., Washington, DC 20402)

500 IS
UNITED STATES - ISRAEL BINATIONAL SCIENCE FOUNDATION. ANNUAL REPORT. (Text in English) 1974. a. United States - Israel Binational Science Foundation, Jerusalem, Israel.

SCIENCES: COMPREHENSIVE WORKS

500   IS   ISSN 0333-5526
UNITED STATES-ISRAEL BINATIONAL SCIENCE FOUNDATION. PROJECT-REPORT ABSTRACTS. (Text in English) 1980. every 2-3 years. United States-Israel Binational Science Foundation, Jerusalem, Israel. Eds. Simson Carlebach, Edward L. Tepper.

500   FR   ISSN 0083-3673
UNIVERS HISTORIQUE. 1970. irreg. price varies. Editions du Seuil, 27 rue Jacob, 75261 Paris Cedex 06, France. Eds. Jacques Julliard & Michel Winock.

500   SP   ISSN 0075-7721
UNIVERSIDAD DE LA LAGUNA. FACULTAD DE CIENCIAS. ANALES. a (latest no. 9) 150 ptas. Universidad de la Laguna, Secretariado de Publicaciones, Laguna, Canary Islands, Spain.

UNIVERSIDAD DE LA REPUBLICA. FACULTAD DE HUMANIDADES Y CIENCIAS. PUBLICACIONES. see *HUMANITIES: COMPREHENSIVE WORKS*

500   PY
UNIVERSIDAD NACIONAL DE ASUNCION. INSTITUTO DE CIENCIAS. MEMORIA. irreg. Universidad Nacional de Asuncion, Asuncion, Paraguay.

500   PO   ISSN 0066-8079
UNIVERSIDADE DE LISBOA. FACULDADE DE CIENCIAS. INSTITUTO BOTANICO. ARTIGO DE DIVULGACAO. irreg. price varies. Universidade de Lisboa, Faculdade de Ciencias, Instituto Botanico, Lisbon 2, Portugal.

500   BL
UNIVERSIDADE FEDERAL DO RIO GRANDE DO SUL. INSTITUTO DE BIOCIENCIAS. BOLETIM. (Text in Portuguese; summaries occasionally in English) 1954. irreg.; nos. 35 & 36, 1978. price varies. ‡ Universidade Federal do Rio Grande do Sul, Instituto Central de Biociencias, Av. Luiz Englert s/n, 90000 Porto Alegre, Brazil. Ed. Bd. index. Indexed: Biol.Abstr. Chem.Abstr.
Former titles: Universidade Federal do Rio Grande do Sul. Instituto Central de Biociencias. Boletim & Universidade do Rio Grande do Sul. Instituto de Ciencias Naturais. Boletim (ISSN 0079-4058)

100   CS   ISSN 0068-2705
UNIVERSITA J. E. PURKYNE. FILOSOFICKA FAKULTA. SBORNIK PRACI. (Comprised of annual series A through I) (Text and summaries in Czech, English, French, German, Italian, Russian, Spanish) 1952. irreg., approx. a. exchange basis. Universita J. E. Purkyne, Filosoficka Fakulta, A. Novaka 1, 602 00 Brno, Czechoslovakia. bk. rev. abstr. bibl. illus. maps. circ. 600. Indexed: Bull.Signal.

001.3 500   GW   ISSN 0512-1523
UNIVERSITAET FRANKFURT. WISSENSCHAFTLICHE GESELLSCHAFT. SITZUNGSBERICHTE. 1962. irreg., vol. 18, 1981. price varies. (Wissenschaftliche Gesellschaft) Franz Steiner Verlag GmbH, Friedrichstr. 24, Postfach 5529, 6200 Wiesbaden, W. Germany (B.R.D.)

500   AU
UNIVERSITAET SALZBURG. DISSERTATIONEN. 1970. irreg., no. 9, 1978. price varies. (Universitaet Salzburg) Verband der Wissenschaftlichen Gesellschaften Oesterreichs, Lindengasse 37, A-1070 Vienna, Austria.

500   AU
UNIVERSITAET WIEN. DISSERTATIONEN. 1967. irreg., no. 140, 1978. price varies. Verband der Wissenschaftlichen Gesellschaften Oesterreichs, Lindengasse 37, A-1070 Vienna, Austria.

500   RM
UNIVERSITATEA BUCURESTI. ANALELE. STIINTELE NATURII. (Text in English, French, or Romanian) a. $10. Universitatea Bucuresti, Bd. 6h. Gheorghi-Dej Nr. 64, Bucharest, Romania.

500   FR   ISSN 0078-9887
UNIVERSITE DE PARIS. FACULTE DES LETTRES ET SCIENCES HUMAINES. PUBLICATIONS. SERIE ACTA. 1970. irreg. price varies. Presses Universitaires de France, 108 Bd. Saint Germaine, 75279 Paris Cedex 6, France (Service des Periodiques, 12 rue Jean de Beauvais, 75005 Paris)

505   CM   ISSN 0566-201X
UNIVERSITE DE YAOUNDE. FACULTE DES SCIENCES. ANNALES. 1968. irreg. free. Universite de Yaounde, Faculte des Sciences, Box 337, Yaounde, Cameroon (Dist. by: Service Central des Bibliotheques, Services des Publications, B. P. 1312, Yaounde, Cameroon) illus.
Continues: Universite Federale du Cameroun. Faculte des Sciences. Annales.

UNIVERSITY OF CALIFORNIA, LOS ANGELES. SCHOOL OF ENGINEERING AND APPLIED SCIENCE. RESEARCH DEVELOPMENT, AND PUBLIC SERVICE ACTIVITIES. see *TECHNOLOGY: COMPREHENSIVE WORKS*

500.9   US   ISSN 0075-5028
UNIVERSITY OF KANSAS. MUSEUM OF NATURAL HISTORY. MISCELLANEOUS PUBLICATIONS. 1946. irreg; latest no. 64, 1976. price varies. ‡ University of Kansas, Museum of Natural History, Lawrence, KS 66045. Ed. Richard Johnston. circ. 1,000. (reprint service avail. from UMI) Key Title: Miscellaneous Publications - University of Kansas, Museum of Natural History.

500.9   US   ISSN 0085-2465
UNIVERSITY OF KANSAS. MUSEUM OF NATURAL HISTORY. MONOGRAPHS. 1970. irreg.; latest no. 5, 1976. price varies. ‡ University of Kansas, Museum of Natural History, Lawrence, KS 66044. Ed. Richard Johnston. circ. 1,000. (reprint service avail. from UMI)
Natural history

500.9   US   ISSN 0091-7958
UNIVERSITY OF KANSAS. MUSEUM OF NATURAL HISTORY. OCCASIONAL PAPERS. 1971. irreg.; latest no. 66, 1977. ‡ University of Kansas, Museum of Natural History, Lawrence, KS 66044. Ed. Richard Johnston. circ. 1,500. (reprint service avail. from UMI)

500.9   US   ISSN 0075-5036
UNIVERSITY OF KANSAS. MUSEUM OF NATURAL HISTORY. PUBLICATIONS. 1946. irreg. University of Kansas, Museum of Natural History, Lawrence, KS 66045. (reprint service avail. from UMI)

500   US   ISSN 0022-8850
UNIVERSITY OF KANSAS SCIENCE BULLETIN. 1902. irreg., (approx. 5/yr.) $20 per vol. ‡ University of Kansas, Library Exchange & Gift Section, Lawrence, KS 66044. circ. 900. Indexed: Biol.Abstr. Chem.Abstr. Zoo.Rec.

500   KU
UNIVERSITY OF KUWAIT. JOURNAL(SCIENCE) (Text in English; summaries in Arabic) 1974. a. free. University of Kuwait, Faculty of Science, P.O. Box 5969, Kuwait. Ed. Riad Halwagy. circ. 1,000. Indexed: Biol.Abstr. Chem.Abstr. Excerp.Med. Math.R. Sci.Abstr.
Abstr.Health.Eff.Environ.Pollut. Anal.Abstr. Appl.Ecol.Abstr. Aqua.Sci. & Fish Abstr. Chem.Titles. I.M.M.Abstr. INIS Atomind. Microbiol.Abstr. Plant Breed.Abstr. Rev.Appl.Entomol. Rev.Plant.Path.

500   NR   ISSN 0075-7713
UNIVERSITY OF LAGOS. SCIENTIFIC MONOGRAPH SERIES. 1971. irreg. price varies. University of Lagos, Yaba, Lagos, Nigeria.

500   US   ISSN 0543-940X
UNIVERSITY OF MICHIGAN. GREAT LAKES RESEARCH DIVISION. SPECIAL REPORT. 1953. irreg., no. 51, 1974. free to scientists. University of Michigan, Great Lakes Research Division, Ann Arbor, MI 48105. (some back issues avail.)

069 500   US
UNIVERSITY OF NEBRASKA STATE MUSEUM. BULLETIN. 1956. irreg. free. University of Nebraska State Museum, Morrill Hall 212, Lincoln, NE 68508. Ed. Harvey L. Gunderson. abstr. bibl. charts. illus. circ. 5,000. (also avail. in microform from UMI)

500   US   ISSN 0077-796X
UNIVERSITY OF NEVADA. DESERT RESEARCH INSTITUTE. TECHNICAL REPORT. 1966. irreg. price varies. University of Nevada, Desert Research Institute, Social Sciences Center, Box 60220, Reno, NV 89506. Ed. Don D. Fowler. circ. 700-800. Indexed: Abstr.Anthropol.

500.9   US   ISSN 0078-6047
UNIVERSITY OF OREGON. MUSEUM OF NATURAL HISTORY. BULLETIN. 1965. irreg., no. 23, 1978. price varies. ‡ University of Oregon, Museum of Natural History, Eugene, OR 97403. circ. 1,000. Key Title: Bulletin - Museum of Natural History, University of Oregon.

500   SU
UNIVERSITY OF RIYADH. FACULTY OF SCIENCE. BULLETIN. (Text in English; summaries in Arabic) a. University of Riyadh, Faculty of Science, Riyadh, Saudi Arabia. charts. illus.

500   CN   ISSN 0080-665X
UNIVERSITY OF SASKATCHEWAN. INSTITUTE FOR NORTHERN STUDIES. ANNUAL REPORT. 1960. a. free. Institute for Northern Studies, University of Saskatchewan, Saskatoon, Sask. S7N 0W0, Canada. Ed. Dr. R. M. Bone. index. circ. 400.

500   GH   ISSN 0075-7225
UNIVERSITY OF SCIENCE AND TECHNOLOGY. JOURNAL. 1955. irreg., approx. a. University of Science and Technology, Kumasi, Ghana. Ed. A. B. K. Dadzle. bk. rev. circ. 500.
Nos. 1-6 issued as: Kumasitech.

UNIVERSITY OF WESTERN ONTARIO SERIES IN PHILOSOPHY OF SCIENCE. see *PHILOSOPHY*

001.3 500   US   ISSN 0084-3199
UNIVERSITY OF WYOMING PUBLICATIONS. 1922. irreg. price varies. ‡ University of Wyoming Library, Box 3334, Univ. Sta., Laramie, WY 82071. circ. 550.

500   YU   ISSN 0350-140X
UNIVERZITET U NOVOM SADU. PRIRODNO - MATEMATICKI FAKULTET. ZBORNIK RADOVA; review of research-faculty of sciences. (Text) 1971. irreg., no. 8, 1978. 160($4) Univerzitet u Novom Sadu, Prirodno-Matematicki Fakultet, Ilije Djuricica 4, 21001 Novi Sad, Yugoslavia. Ed. Bogoljub Stankovic. circ. 1,000. Indexed: Ref.Zhvr.

500   PL   ISSN 0076-0366
UNIWERSYTET LODZKI. ZESZYTY NAUKOWE. SERIA 2: NAUKI MATEMATYCZNO-PRZYRODNICZE. 1955. irreg. price varies. Uniwersytet Lodzki, Narutowicza 65, Lodz, Poland (Dist. by Ars Polona-Ruch, Krakowskie Przedmiescie 7, Warsaw, Poland) Ed. Wanda Leyko. circ. 380.

500   II   ISSN 0083-5013
UTTAR PRADESH, INDIA. SCIENTIFIC RESEARCH COMMITTEE MONOGRAPH SERIES.* (Text in English) irreg. price varies. Scientific Research Committee, Uttar Pradesh, Chhattar Manzil Palace, Lucknow, Uttar Pradesh, India.

VACUUM TECHNOLOGY DIRECTORY & BUYERS GUIDE. see *TECHNOLOGY: COMPREHENSIVE WORKS*

500 600   GW   ISSN 0083-5080
VADEMECUM DEUTSCHER LEHR- UND FORSCHUNGSSTAETTEN. 1954. irreg. DM.130. (Stifterverband fuer die Deutsche Wissenschaft) Gemeinnuetzige Verwaltungsgesellschaft fuer Wissenschaftspflege mbH, Brucker Holt 56, 4300 Essen, W. Germany (B.R.D.) adv.

500   US   ISSN 0083-5846
VERSTAENDLICHE WISSENSCHAFT. (Issues not numbered consecutively) 1952. irreg., vol. 115, 1980. price varies. Springer-Verlag, 175 Fifth Ave., New York, NY 10010 (also Berlin, Heidelberg, Vienna) (reprint service avail. from ISI)

507   US
WADSWORTH GUIDES TO SCIENCE TEACHING. irreg. Wadsworth Publishing Co., 10 Davis Dr., Belmont, CA 94002.

507   US   ISSN 0043-0323
WARD'S BULLETIN. 1962. irreg. free to teachers. Ward's Natural Science Establishment, Box 1712, Rochester, NY 14603. Ed. Bea Redfield. bk. rev. illus. circ. 100,000. Indexed: Biol.Abstr.
Study and teaching

500 620 JA
WASEDA UNIVERSITY. SCHOOL OF SCIENCE AND ENGINEERING. MEMOIRS/WASEDA DAIGAKU RIKOGAKUBU KIYO. (Text in English) 1922. a. Waseda University, School of Science and Engineering - Waseda Daigaku Rikogakubu, 4-170 Nishiokubo, Shinjuku-ku, Tokyo 160, Japan.

500 JA
WASEDA UNIVERSITY. SCIENCE AND ENGINEERING RESEARCH LABORATORY. REPORT. (Text in English) 1973. irreg. Waseda University, Science and Engineering Research Laboratory - Waseda Daigaku Rikogaku Kenkyusho, 17 Kikui-cho, Shinjuku-ku, Tokyo 162, Japan.

500 600 IS ISSN 0083-7849
WEIZMANN INSTITUTE OF SCIENCE, REHOVOT, ISRAEL. SCIENTIFIC ACTIVITIES. (Text in English) 1953. a. Weizmann Institute of Science, Rehovot, Israel. circ. 3,000.

500 ISSN 0083-7989
WENNER GREN CENTER INTERNATIONAL SYMPOSIUM SERIES. 1962. irreg., vol. 31, 1979. price varies. Pergamon Press Inc., Maxwell House, Fairview Park, Elmsford, NY 10523.

500 AT
WESTERN AUSTRALIAN NATURALIST SCIENTIFIC JOURNAL. 1950. 3/yr. Aus.$10. Western Australian Naturalists' Club, Naturalists' Hall, 53-65 Merriwa St., Nedlands, W. Australia 6009, Australia. Ed. D. L. Serventy. adv. circ. 350.
Formerly: Western Australian Naturalists' Club, Perth. Handbook (ISSN 0083-8748)

WHO'S WHO IN INDIAN SCIENCE. see *BIOGRAPHY*

500.2 UK ISSN 0309-3468
WILTSHIRE NATURAL HISTORY MAGAZINE. 1853. a. membership. Wiltshire Archaeological and Natural History Society, 41 Long St., Devizes, Wilts. SN10 1NS, England.
Supersedes in part (as of 1975): Wiltshire Archaeological and Natural History Magazine (ISSN 0084-0335)

500 US ISSN 0084-0505
WISCONSIN ACADEMY OF SCIENCES, ARTS AND LETTERS, TRANSACTIONS. 1870. a. $15 incl. Review and Triforium. Wisconsin Academy of Sciences, Arts and Letters, 1922 University Avenue, Madison, WI 53705. Ed. Dr. Forest Stearns. bk. rev. circ. 1,550.

500 YU ISSN 0350-0012
WISSENSCHAFTLICHE MITTEILUNGEN DES BOSNISCH-HERZEGOWINISCHEN LANDESMUSEUMS. NATURWISSENSCHAFT. (Text in German) Band 5, 1975. irreg. Zemaljski Muzej Bosne i Hercegovine, Vojvode Putnika 7, Sarajevo, Yugoslavia. Ed. Zeljka Bjelcic.

500 US
WORLD INSTITUTE CREATIVE FINDINGS. a. price varies. Gordon and Breach Science Publishers, One Park Ave., New York, NY 10016. Ed. Julius Stulman, Ervin Laszlo.

500 US
WORLD NATURALIST SERIES. irreg., latest 1973. W. W. Norton & Company, Inc., 500 Fifth Ave., New York, NY 10036.

500 600 US
WORLD OF THE FUTURE SERIES. irreg. M. Evans and Co., Inc., c/o J. B. Lippincott Co., Box 7, Philadelphia, PA 19105.

500 PL ISSN 0084-3024
WROCLAWSKIE TOWARZYSTWO NAUKOWE. PRACE. SERIA B. NAUKI SCISLE. (Text in Polish; summaries in English, French, and German) 1947. irreg., no. 202, 1979. price varies. Ossolineum, Publishing House of the Polish Academy of Sciences, Rynek 9, Wroclaw, Poland. Ed. Bronislaw Knaster.

500 PL ISSN 0371-4756
WROCLAWSKIE TOWARZYSTWO NAUKOWE. SPRAWOZDANIA. SERIA A. irreg., vol. 32, 1979. 30 Zl. Ossolineum, Publishing House of the Polish Academy of Sciences, Rynek 9, Wroclaw, Poland (Dist. by: Ars Polona-Ruch, Krakowskie Przedmiescie 7, Warsaw, Poland) Ed A. Galos.

500 US ISSN 0084-3113
WYKEHAM SCIENCE SERIES. 1970. irreg., no. 56, 1979. Crane, Russak & Company, Inc., 3 E. 44th St., New York, NY 10017.

500 US
YALE SERIES IN THE SCIENCES. 1970. irreg., latest 1972. Yale University Press, 92A Yale Sta., New Haven, CT 06520.

500 610 US ISSN 0084-3512
YALE STUDIES IN THE HISTORY OF SCIENCE AND MEDICINE. 1965. irreg; no. 11, 1976. price varies. Yale University Press, 92A Yale Sta., New Haven, CT 06520.
History

500 US ISSN 0096-3291
YEARBOOK OF SCIENCE AND THE FUTURE. 1969. a. $14.95. Encyclopaedia Britannica, Inc., 425 N. Michigan Ave, Chicago, IL 60611. Ed. James Ertel.
Formerly: Britannica Yearbook of Science and the Future (ISSN 0068-1199)

500 JA ISSN 0085-8366
YOKOHAMA NATIONAL UNIVERSITY. SCIENCE REPORTS. SECTION I: MATHEMATICS, PHYSICS, CHEMISTRY/ YOKOHAMA KOKURITSU DAIGAKU RIKA KIYO, DAI-1-RUI, SUGAKU, BUTSURIGAKU, KAGAKU. (Text in European languages) 1952. a. exchange basis only. Yokohama National University, Faculty of Education - Yokohama Kokuritsu Daigaku Kyoikugakubu, Tokiwadai 156, Hodogaya-ku, Yokohama 240, Japan.

500 ZA ISSN 0084-4950
ZAMBIA. NATIONAL COUNCIL FOR SCIENTIFIC RESEARCH. ANNUAL REPORT. 1968. a., latest 1978. National Council for Scientific Research, Box CH 158, Chelston, Lusaka, Zambia.

500 YU ISSN 0581-7528
ZEMALJSKI MUZEJ BOSNE I HERCEGOVINE. GLASNIK. PRIRODNE NAUKE. (Summaries in English, French or German) 1969 N.S. a. Zemaljski Muzej Bosne i Hercegovine, Vojevode Putnika 7, Sarajevo, Yugoslavia. Ed. Zeljka Bjelic. illus.
Formerly: Glasnik Zemaljskog Muzeja u Sarajevu.

500 PL ISSN 0084-5701
ZRODLA DO DZIEJOW NAUKI I TECHNIKI. 1957. irreg. price varies. (Polska Akademia Nauk, Zaklad Historii Nauki i Techniki) Ossolineum, Publishing House of the Polish Academy of Sciences, Rynek 9, 50-106 Wroclaw, Poland (Dist. by Ars Polona-Ruch, Krakowskie Przedmiescie 7, Warsaw, Poland) Ed. Bogdan Suchodolski.

SCIENCES: COMPREHENSIVE WORKS — Abstracting, Bibliographies, Statistics

500 016 FR
ASSOCIATION FRANCAISE POUR LA DIFFUSION DU LIVRE SCIENTIFIQUE, TECHNIQUE ET MEDICAL (BULLETINS COLLECTIFS) (First semester issues cover scientific and technical subjects; second semester issues cover medical subjects) 1978. irreg. free. Sodexport - Grem, 117 Bd Saint Germain, 75006 Paris, France. adv. circ. 10,000.

013 US ISSN 0084-7712
BATTELLE MEMORIAL INSTITUTE. PUBLISHED PAPERS AND ARTICLES. 1970. a. free. Battelle Memorial Institute, 505 King Avenue, Columbus, OH 43201. circ. 10,000. (processed)

500 016 BE
BELGIUM. FONDS NATIONAL DE LA RECHERCHE SCIENTIFIQUE. LISTE BIBLIOGRAPHIQUE DES TRAVAUX. BIBLIOGRAFISCHE LIJST VAN DE WERKEN. (Text in English, Flemish or French) triennial. Fonds National de la Recherche Scientifique, Rue d'Egmont 5, 1050 Brussels, Belgium. bibl. (back issues avail)

500 015 SZ ISSN 0067-6829
BIBLIOGRAPHIA SCIENTIAE NATURALIS HELVETICA. 1927. a. price varies. ‡ Bibliotheque Nationale Suisse, Hallwylstrasse 15, 3003 Berne, Switzerland. Ed. Rudolf Tank. circ. 700.

500 016 II
BIBLIOGRAPHY OF DOCTORAL DISSERTATIONS; NATURAL AND APPLIED SCIENCES. (Text in English) a. Rs.90. Association of Indian Universities, Rouse Avenue, New Delhi 110002, India.

503 603 016 UN ISSN 0067-7205
BIBLIOGRAPHY OF INTERLINGUAL SCIENTIFIC AND TECHNICAL DICTIONARIES. (Text in English, French and Spanish) 1951. irreg., 1969, 5th ed. Unesco, 7-9 Place de Fontenoy, 75700 Paris, France (Dist. in U.S. by: Unipub, 345 Park Ave. S., New York, NY 10010)

500 016 JA
DIRECTORY OF JAPANESE SCIENTIFIC PERIODICALS. (Text in English and Japanese) irreg., latest 1979. 6300 Yen. National Diet Library - Kokuritsu Kokkai Toshokan, 1-10-1 Nagata-cho, Chiyoda-ku, Tokyo 100, Japan.
8901 current periodicals in science and technology published in Japan

016 PK
DIRECTORY OF SCIENTIFIC PERIODICALS OF PAKISTAN. irreg. Rs.2($1) Pakistan Scientific and Technological Information Centre, House No. 6, Street No. 22, Sector F-7/2, Box 1217, Islamabad, Pakistan. Dir. A. R. Mohajir. circ. 500. (also avail. in microfilm)

500 016 II
DIRECTORY OF SCIENTIFIC RESEARCH IN INDIAN UNIVERSITIES. a. Rs.35. (University Grants Commission) Indian National Scientific Documentation Centre, Hillside Rd., New Delhi 110012, India. (Co-sponsor: Council of Scientific and Industrial Research)

311 FI ISSN 0355-2233
FINLAND. TILASTOKESKUS. TUTKIMUSTOIMINTA/FINLAND. STATISTIKCENTRALEN. FORSKNINGSVERKSAMHETEN/FINLAND. CENTRAL STATISTICAL OFFICE. RESEARCH ACTIVITY. (Section XXXVIII of Official Statistics of Finland) (Text in Finnish, Swedish and English) 1974. a. Fmk.12. Tilastokeskus, Annankatu 44, SF-00100 Helsinki 10, Finland (Subscr. to: Government Printing Centre, Box 516, SF-00100 Helsinki 10, Finland)

GUIDE TO AMERICAN SCIENTIFIC AND TECHNICAL DIRECTORIES. see *TECHNOLOGY: COMPREHENSIVE WORKS — Abstracting, Bibliographies, Statistics*

500 HU
HUNGARY. KOZPONTI STATISZTIKAI HIVATAL. TUDOMANYOS KUTATAS/ SCIENTIFIC RESEARCH. a. Statisztikai Kiado Vallalat, Kazas U. 10-12, P.O.B. 99, 1033 Budapest 3, Hungary.

500 016 II
INDIAN SCIENCE INDEX. (Text in English) 1975. a. Rs.50($10) Indian Documentation Service, Nai Subzi Mandi, Gurgaon 122001, Haryana, India. Ed. Satya Prakash.

500 010 AO ISSN 0074-008X
INSTITUTO DE INVESTIGACAO CIENTIFICA DE ANGOLA. BIBLIOGRAFICAS TEMATICAS. 1969. irreg., 1973, no. 19. free to qualified personnel. Instituto de Investigacao Cientifica de Angola, Departamento de Documentacao e Informacao, P.O. Box 3244, Luanda, Angola. Indexed: Trop.Abstr.

500 016 AT
JAMES COOK UNIVERSITY OF NORTH QUEENSLAND. RESEARCH AND PUBLICATIONS REPORT. (0312-9012) a. free. James Cook University of North Queensland, Townsville 4811, North Queensland, Australia.

500.9 016 SZ
KEY WORD INDEX OF WILDLIFE RESEARCH. (Text in English and German) 1974. a. $20. Swiss Wildlife Information Service, University of Zurich, Birchstrasse 15, CH-8050 Zurich, Switzerland. Ed. Rolf Auderegg. circ. 700.

500 US ISSN 0090-5232
L C SCIENCE TRACER BULLET. 1976? irreg. free.
U.S. Library of Congress, Science and Technology
Division, Washington, DC 20540.

500 015 TH ISSN 0125-4537
LIST OF SCIENTIFIC AND TECHNICAL
LITERATURE RELATING TO THAILAND.
(Text in English) 1964. irreg. $2 per no. (Thai
National Documentation Centre) Thailand Institute
of Scientific and Technological Research, 196
Phahonyothin Road, Bangkhen, Bangkok 9,
Thailand. circ. 1,000.

500 600 II
NATIONAL COMMITTEE ON SCIENCE AND
TECHNOLOGY. RESEARCH AND
DEVELOPMENT STATISTICS. a. Rs.15. National
Committee on Science and Technology, New Delhi
110029, India. charts. stat.

016 500 PL
POLITECHNIKA WROCLAWSKA. BIBLIOTEKA
GLOWNA I OSRODEK INFORMACJI
NAUKOWO-TECHNICZNEJ. PRACE
NAUKOWE. PRACE BIBLIOGRAFICZNE. 1975.
irreg., no. 7, 1979. price varies. Politechnika
Wroclawska, Wybrzeze Wyspianskiego 27, 50-370
Wroclaw, Poland (Dist. by: Ars Polona-Ruch,
Krakowskie Przedmiescie 7, Warsaw, Poland) Ed.
Marian Kloza. circ. 500.

500 016 US ISSN 0080-0619
REGIONAL SCIENCE RESEARCH INSTITUTE,
PHILADELPHIA. BIBLIOGRAPHY SERIES.
1961. irreg. price varies. Regional Science Research
Institute, 256 N. Pleasant St., Wentworth Bldg.,
Amherst, MA 01002. Ed. Benjamin H. Stevens.
(reprint service avail. from UMI)

500 016 RH
RHODESIA RESEARCH INDEX; register of current
research in Rhodesia. 1971. a. exchange basis.
Scientific Liaison Office, Box 8310, Causeway,
Zimbabwe (Orders to: Government Printer, Box
8062, Causeway, Zimbabwe) (Co-Sponsor:
University of Zimbabwe) index. circ. 500
(controlled) (processed)

500 600 016 US ISSN 0000-054X
SCIENTIFIC AND TECHNICAL BOOKS AND
SERIALS IN PRINT. 1972. a. $59. R.R. Bowker
Company, 1180 Ave. of the Americas, New York,
NY 10036 (Orders to P.O. Box 1807, Ann Arbor,
Mich. 48106)
  Formerly (until 1977): Scientific and Technical
Books in Print (ISSN 0000-0248)

500 016 TH ISSN 0125-4529
SCIENTIFIC SERIALS IN THAI LIBRARIES. (Text
in English) 1968. a. $36. Thailand Institute of
Scientific and Technological Research,
196phahonyothin Rd., Bang Khen, Bangkok 9,
Thailand.

500 011 TU
TURKISH DISSERTATION INDEX. (Text in
English) 1977. a. exchange basis. Turkish Scientific
and Technical Documentation Centre - Turkiye
Bilimsel ve Teknik Dokumantasyon, Ataturk Bulvari
221, Kavaklidere, Ankara, Turkey. abstr. circ.
2,500.

500 016 CN ISSN 0082-7657
UNION LIST OF SCIENTIFIC SERIALS IN
CANADIAN LIBRARIES/CATALOGUE
COLLECTIF DES PUBLICATIONS
SCIENTIFIQUES DANS LES BIBLIOTHEQUES
CANADIENNES. 1957. biennial; 8th. 1979.
Can.$95. National Research Council of Canada,
Canada Institute for Scientific and Technical
Information (CISTI), Ottawa, Ont. K1A OS2,
Canada. circ. 700. (also avail. in microfiche)

500 ZA
ZAMBIA. NATIONAL COUNCIL FOR
SCIENTIFIC RESEARCH. N C S R
BIBLIOGRAPHY. Short title: N C S R
Bibliography. 1976. irreg., latest 1979. K.1.50.
National Council for Scientific Research, Box CH
158, Chelston, Lusaka, Zambia.

500 016 ZA
ZAMBIA SCIENCE ABSTRACTS. 1977. a. National
Council for Scientific Research, Box CH 158,
Chelston, Lusaka, Zambia. Ed. W. C. Mushipi.

SHIPS AND SHIPPING

see Transportation—Ships and Shipping

SHOES AND BOOTS

see also Leather and Fur Industries

685.31 FR ISSN 0066-2526
ANNUAIRE DE LA CHAUSSURE ET DES CUIRS.
1905. a. 130 F. Editions Louis Johanet, 68 rue
Boursault, Paris 17, France.

685.31 658.8 US ISSN 0069-2387
CHAIN SHOE STORES AND LEASED SHOE
DEPARTMENT OPERATORS. 1962. a. $2 (free
with subscr. to Leather and Shoes) Rumpf
Publishing Division (Subsidiary of: Nickerson &
Collins Co.) 1800 Oakton St., Des Plaines, IL
60018. Ed. Elmer J. Rumpf. index.

CLOTHING AND FOOTWEAR INSTITUTE YEAR
BOOK AND MEMBERSHIP REGISTER. see
CLOTHING TRADE

685 FR ISSN 0071-4291
FEDERATION NATIONALE DE L'INDUSTRIE
DE LA CHAUSSURE DE FRANCE.
ANNUAIRE. 1952/53. irreg. 70 F. per no.
Federation Nationale de l'Industrie de la Chaussure
de France, 30 Ave. George V., 75008 Paris, France.
adv.

338 US ISSN 0095-1048
FOOTWEAR MANUAL. 1975. a. $125 to non-
members;$30 to members. American Footwear
Industries Association, Suite 900, 1611 N. Kent St.,
Arlington, VA 22209. stat.
  Continues: Facts & Figures on Footwear (ISSN
0362-3890)

338.4 US ISSN 0429-0208
FOOTWEAR NEWS FACT BOOK. 1954. irreg. free.
Footwear News, 7 E. 12th St., New York, NY
10003. illus.

685.31 CN
FOOTWEAR SHOEMAKING DIRECTORY. a.
Southam Communications Ltd., 1450 Don Mills
Rd., Don Mills, Ont. M3B 2X7, Canada. adv.
  Formerly: Canadian Shoemaking Directory &
Buyers' Guide.

LEATHER & FOOTWEARS/KAWA TO
HAKIMONO. see *LEATHER AND FUR
INDUSTRIES*

684.3 UK ISSN 0140-5578
SHOE RETAILERS MANUAL. 1977. biennial. £12.
New Century Publishing Co. Ltd., 84-88 Great
Eastern St., London EC2A 3ED, England. adv.

684.3 UK ISSN 0080-9349
SHOE TRADES DIRECTORY. (Headings and index
in English, French, German) 1948. N.S. 1976.
biennial. £17.50. New Century Publishing Co. Ltd.,
84-88 Great Eastern Street, London EC2A 3ED,
England. adv.

685.31 SA
SHOES AND LEATHER TRADES DIRECTORY
OF SOUTHERN AFRICA. 1977. a. R.20.
Thomson Publications S.A. (Pty) Ltd., Box 8308,
Johannesburg 2000, South Africa. Ed. Heinz
Engelhardt.

SHOES AND BOOTS — Abstracting, Bibliographies, Statistics

310 685 UK ISSN 0308-9398
FOOTWEAR INDUSTRY STATISTICAL REVIEW.
a. £8. British Footwear Manufacturers Federation,
72 Dean St., London W1V 5HB, England.

SMALL BUSINESS

see Business and Economics—Small
Business

SOCIAL SCIENCES: COMPREHENSIVE WORKS

300 AT ISSN 0156-160X
A N S O L BIBLIOGRAPHY SERIES. (Australian
National Social Sciences Library) 1978. irreg. price
varies. National Library of Australia, Sales and
Subscriptions Unit, Canberra, A.C.T. 2600,
Australia.

300 FI
AABO AKADEMI. STATSVETENSKAPLIGA
FAKULTETEN. MEDDELANDEN. (Text in
English, French and Swedish) 1956. irreg. free.
Aabo Akademi, Statsvetenskapliga - Swedish
University of Aabo, Faculty of Social Sciences,
Domkyrkotorget 3, 20500 Aabo 50, Finland. Ed.
Lauri Karvonen. circ. 150.
  Formed by the merger (from Jan 1979) of: Aabo
Akademi. Statsvetenskapliga Fakulteten.
Meddelanden. Serie A (ISSN 0355-4031) & Aabo
Akademi. Statsvetenskapliga Fakulteten.
Meddelanden. Serie B (ISSN 0355-4465)

ACADEMIA DE CIENCIAS POLITICAS Y
SOCIALES. BOLETIN. see *POLITICAL
SCIENCE*

300 AT
ACADEMY OF THE SOCIAL SCIENCES IN
AUSTRALIA. ANNUAL REPORT. a. membership.
Academy of the Social Sciences in Australia, 2Nd
Floor, National Library Bldg., Parkes, A.C.T. 2600,
Australia.

300 610 US
ADVANCES IN MEDICAL SOCIAL SCIENCE:
HEALTH AND ILLNESS AS VIEWED BY
ANTHROPOLOGY, GEOGRAPHY, HISTORY,
PSYCHOLOGY AND SOCIOLOGY. 1979? irreg.
Gordon and Breach Science Publishers, One Park
Ave., New York, NY 10016. Ed.Julio L. Ruffini.

AFRICA IN THE MODERN WORLD. see
HISTORY — History Of Africa

300 GE
AKADEMIE DER WISSENSCHAFTEN DER DDR.
ABHANDLUNGEN. ABTEILUNG
MATHEMATIK, NATURWISSENSCHAFTEN,
TECHNIK. 1975. irreg. price varies. Akademie-
Verlag, Leipziger Str. 3-4, 108 Berlin, E. Germany
(D.D.R.)

300 YU ISSN 0350-0039
AKADEMIJA NAUKA I UMJETNOSTI BOSNE I
HERCEGOVINE. ODELJENJE DRUSTVENIH
NAUKA. RADOVI. vol. 17, 1974. Akademija
Nauka i Umjetnosti Bosne i Hercegovine, Odeljenje
Drustvenih Nauka, Obala Vojvode Stepe 42,
Sarajevo, Yugoslavia. Hamdija Cemerlic.

300 572 CN
ALTERNATE ROUTES; a critical review. no.3,1979.
a. Can.$2.75. c/o Department of Anthropology,
Carleton University, Ottawa, Ont. K1S 5B6,
Canada. Ed.Bd.

980 300 BL ISSN 0002-709X
AMERICA LATINA. (Text in English, French,
Portuguese and Spanish) 1962. irreg. free. Centro
Latino-Americano de Pesquisas em Ciencias Sociais,
Caixa Postal 9012-ZC 02, 20000 Rio de Janeiro RJ,
Brazil. adv. bk. rev. charts. illus. index. circ. 1,300.
Indexed: Bull.Signal. Sociol.Abstr.

300 US ISSN 0065-6917
AMERICAN ACADEMY OF POLITICAL AND
SOCIAL SCIENCE. MONOGRAPHS. 1962. irreg.,
no. 17, 1973. $4 per copy. American Academy of
Political and Social Sciences, 3937 Chestnut St.,
Philadelphia, PA 19104. Ed. Richard D. Lambert.
circ. 15,500. (also avail. in microfiche; microfilm)

SOCIAL SCIENCES: COMPREHENSIVE WORKS

300 FR ISSN 0066-2607
ANNUAIRE DE L'AFRIQUE DU NORD. 1962. a. price varies. Centre National de la Recherche Scientifique, 15 Quai Anatole-France, 75700 Paris, France.

300 FR ISSN 0397-8249
ANNUAIRE DE L'URSS ET DES PAYS SOCIALISTES EUROPEENS. 1965. every 18 months. price varies. (Centre de Recherches sur l'URSS et les Pays de l'Est) Librairie Istra, 15 rue des Juifs, 67001 Strasbourg Cedex, France.
Formerly: Annuaire de l'U. R. S. S. (ISSN 0066-2704)

300 986.1 CK ISSN 0066-5045
ANUARIO COLOMBIANO DE HISTORIA SOCIAL Y DE LA CULTURA. 1963. irreg. exchange basis. Universidad Nacional de Colombia, Facultad de Ciencias Humanas, Apartado Aereo 14490, Ciudad Universitaria, Departamento de Historia, Bogota, D.E., Colombia. Ed. Jaime Jaramillo Uribe. circ. 5,000.

300 SP ISSN 0570-4324
ANUARIO IBEROAMERICANO; hechos y documentos. 1962. a. 600 plus.($8.50) Centro Iberoamericano de Cooperacion, Departamento de Documentacion Iberoamericana, Avda. Reyes Catolicas 3, Ciudad Universitaria, Madrid 3, Spain. (back issues avail.)

339.47 AU
ARBEITSGEMEINSCHAFT FUER LEBENSNIVEAUVERGLEICHE. SCHRIFTENREIHE. Variant title: Was Heisst Gut Leben? (Text in German; summaries in English) 1972. irreg. free. Arbeitsgemeinschaft fuer Lebensniveauvergleiche, Postfach 149, A-1131 Vienna, Austria. Ed. Lore Scheer. bibl. charts. circ. 2,000.

300 909 GW ISSN 0066-5827
ARBEITSHEFTE ZUR GEMEINSCHAFTSKUNDE. 1963. irreg. DM.4.80. Wochenschau-Verlag, Adolf-Damschke-Str. 105, 6231 Schwalbach, W. Germany (B.R.D.) Ed. Kurt Debus.

ARCHIWUM HISTORII FILOZOFII I MYSLI SPOLECZNEJ. see PHILOSOPHY

300 RH ISSN 0066-7781
ARNOLDIA RHODESIA. 1964. irreg. price varies. National Museums and Monuments Administration, P.O. Box 8540, Causeway, Salisbury, Zimbabwe. index. circ. 300.

ASPECTS OF GREEK AND ROMAN LIFE. see HISTORY

300 US
ASPEN CHRONICLE. 1972. a. $4. ‡ Aspen Institute for Humanistic Studies, 717 Fifth Ave., New York, NY 10022. charts. illus. circ. 9,000.
Former titles, until no. 10, 1977: Aspen Institute Chronicle; Until no. 8, 1975: Aspen Institute Quarterly.

300 VE
ATLANTIDA. 1974. irreg. Universidad Simon Bolivar, Division de Sociales y Humanidades, Valle de Sartenejas, Caracas, Venezuela.

BAR-ILAN: ANNUAL OF BAR-ILAN UNIVERSITY. see RELIGIONS AND THEOLOGY — Judaic

BARRON'S GUIDE TO GRADUATE SCHOOLS; the social sciences and psychology. see EDUCATION — Guides To Schools And Colleges

300 SZ ISSN 0067-4532
BASLER WIRTSCHAFTSWISSENSCHAFTLICHE VORTRAEGE. (Text in German, French, English) 1969. irreg. price varies. (Universitaet Basel, Wirtschaftswissenschaftliche Institut) Schulthess Polygraphischer Verlag AG, Zwingliplatz 2, 8001 Zurich, Switzerland.
Lectures presented at the University of Basel

300 GE
BEITRAEGE ZUR GESCHICHTE THUERINGENS.* 1968. irreg. Museen der Stadt Erfurt, Erfurt, E. Germany (D.D.R.) illus.

300 PY
BIBLIOTECA CLASICOS COLORADOS. 1975. irreg. Instituto Colorado de Cultura, Asuncion, Paraguay.

500 001.3 FI ISSN 0067-8481
BIDRAG TILL KAENNEDOM AV FINLANDS NATUR OCH FOLK. (Text in Finnish and Swedish) 1858. irreg. price varies. Societas Scientiarum Fennica, Snellmansgatan 9-11, SF-00170 Helsinki 17, Finland. Ed. Sven Erik Aastrom. circ. 700.

300 TU
BOGAZICI UNIVERSITY JOURNAL: MANAGEMENT, ECONOMIC AND SOCIAL SCIENCES/BOGAZICI UNIVERSITESI DERGISI: EY ONETICILIK, EKONOMI, VE SOSYAL BILIMLER. (Text in English or Turkish) 1973. a. $3. Bogazici Universitesi, Box 2, Istanbul, Turkey. bibl. stat.
Formerly: Bogazici University Journal: Social Sciences.

300 UK
BRAZIL, LAND OF THE PRESENT. no. 3, 1977. irreg. free. European Brazilian Bank Ltd., Bucklersbury House, Walbrook, London EC4N 8HP, England. Ed. J. J. A. Mirao. circ. 3,000.

300 US
BROOKINGS PAMPHLET SERIES. 1954? irreg. $10. Brookings Institution, 1775 Massachusetts Ave., N.W., Washington, DC 20036.
Former titles: Brookings Institution. Reprint (ISSN 0068-2810); Brookings Research Report Series (ISSN 0068-2829)

300 900 US ISSN 0068-2861
BROWN AND HALEY LECTURE SERIES. 1961. irreg., latest issue 1975. price varies. Rutgers University Press, 30 College Ave., New Brunswick, NJ 08903.

BULLETIN ECONOMIQUE ET SOCIAL DU MAROC. see BUSINESS AND ECONOMICS

BURT FRANKLIN AMERICAN CLASSICS IN HISTORY AND SOCIAL SCIENCES. see HISTORY — History Of North And South America

BURT FRANKLIN ESSAYS IN HISTORY, ECONOMICS, AND SOCIAL SCIENCES. see HISTORY

300 FR ISSN 0068-4953
CAHIERS BRETONS/AR GWYR. 1958-61, 1970 N.S. irreg. price varies. 29 rue des Meuliers, 77260 la Ferte-Sous-Jouarre, France.

300 CN ISSN 0068-5097
CAHIERS DE SCIENCES SOCIALES. 1963. a. price varies. University of Ottawa Press, 65 Hastey Ave., Ottawa, Ont. K1N 6N5, Canada. Ed. W. Badour. index.

300 UA
CAIRO PAPERS IN SOCIAL SCIENCES. 5/yr. £E5($12) to individuals; $15 (£E 7.50) to institutions. American University in Cairo, Social Research Center, 113 Sharia Kasr el Aini, Cairo, Egypt. Ed. Ali E. Hillal Dessouki, Mark C. Kennedy, Asaad Nadim.

300 978 US ISSN 0068-5615
CALIFORNIA HANDBOOK. 1969. irreg., 4th edt. 1981. $20. California Institute of Public Affairs, Box 10, Claremont, CA 91711. Eds. Thaddeus C. Trzyna and William Shank. index. circ. 2,500.

CAMBRIDGE COMMONWEALTH SERIES. see HISTORY

300 US ISSN 0149-6948
CASE ANALYSIS IN SOCIAL SCIENCE N SOCIAL THERAPY. 1977. irreg. price varies. Progresiv Publishr, 401 E. 32nd St., Rm. 1002, Chicago, IL 60616. Ed. Kenneth H. Ives. bk. rev. charts. stat. circ. 100. (back issues avail.) Indexed: Psychol.Abstr. Sociol.Abstr.

300 CN ISSN 0069-1844
CENTRE D'ETUDES ET DE DOCUMENTATION EUROPEENNES. CAHIERS. ANNALS. (Text in English and French) 1968. irreg., no. 4, 1979. $3. Universite de Montreal, Centre d'Etudes et de Documentation Europeennes, 3150rue Jean-Brilliant, C.P. 6128, Succursale A, Montreal, Que. H3C 3J7, Canada.

300 MC ISSN 0577-1730
CENTRE INTERNATIONAL D'ETUDE DES PROBLEMS HUMAINS. BULLETINS. irreg. price varies. Union Europeenne d'Editions, 17 rue de Millo, Monte Carlo, Monaco.

300 CV
CENTRO DE ESTUDOS DE CABO VERDE. REVISTA: SERIE DE CIENCIAS HUMANAS. Short title: Serie de Ciencias Humanas. (At head of title, 1973- : Junta de Investigacoes do Ultramar) (Summaries in English) 1973. irreg. Centro de Estudos de Cabo Verde, Praia, Sao Tiago, Cape Verde Islands. bibl. stat.

300 UY
CENTRO DE INFORMACIONES Y ESTUDIOS DEL URUGUAY. CUADERNOS. 1976. irreg. Centro de Informaciones y Estudios de Uruguay, Canelones 2047, Casilla de Correo 10587, Montevideo, Uruguay.

300 CS ISSN 0069-2298
CESKOSLOVENSKA AKADEMIE VED. ROZPRAVY. SV: RADA SPOLECENSKYCH VED. 1891. irreg., vol. 85, 1975. price varies. Academia, Publishing House of the Czechoslovak Academy of Sciences, Vodickova 40, 112 29 Prague 1, Czechoslovakia. circ. 1,000.

CHARLES E. MERRILL MONOGRAPH SERIES IN THE HUMANITIES AND SOCIAL SCIENCES. see HUMANITIES: COMPREHENSIVE WORKS

300 KO
CHIN-TAN SOCIETY. CHIN-TAN HAK-PO. (Summaries in English) 1940. a. Chin-Tan Society, c/o National Museum of Korea, Seoul, S. Korea. Ed. Yi Pyeng - do. bibl.

300 SX
CIMBEBASIA. SERIES B: CULTURAL HISTORY. (Text in English; summaries in German or French) 1962. irreg., vol.3, no.1, 1979. price varies. State Museum, Box 1203, Windhoek, South West Africa. charts. illus. circ. 1,000. Indexed: Biol.Abstr.

300 NE ISSN 0069-4290
CIVILISATIONS ET SOCIETES. 1965. irreg., no. 63, 1979. price varies. (Ecole Pratique des Hautes Etudes, Centre de Recherches Historiques, FR) Mouton Publishers, Noordeinde 41, 2514 GC The Hague, Netherlands (U.S. address: Mouton Publishers, c/o Walter de Gruyter, Inc., 200 Saw Mill River Rd., Hawthorne, NY 10532)

CIVILIZATION AND SOCIETY: STUDIES IN SOCIAL, ECONOMIC AND CULTURAL HISTORY. see HISTORY

300 AG
COLECCION DOCUMENTOS. 1974. irreg. Editorial Axis, Rosario, Argentina. illus.

300 CL
COLECCION FE E HISTORIA. 1977. irreg. Instituto Latinoamericano de Doctrinas y Estudios Sociales, Departamento de Publicaciones, Almirante Barroso 6, Casilla 1446 Correo 21, Santiago, Chile.

300 BE
COLLECTION "ARGUMENTS ET DOCUMENTS". 1973. irreg. Editions de l'Universite de Bruxelles, Parc Leopold, B-1040 Brussels, Belgium.

COLLEGE OF DAIRYING. JOURNAL; CULTURAL AND SOCIAL SCIENCES/ RAKUNO GAKUEN DAIGAKU KIYO, JINBUN SHAKAIKAGAKU HEN. see AGRICULTURE — Dairying And Dairy Products

COLOQUIO DE ESTUDOS LUSO BRASILEIROS. ANAIS. see LINGUISTICS

SOCIAL SCIENCES: COMPREHENSIVE WORKS

300   FI   ISSN 0355-256X
COMMENTATIONES SCIENTIARUM
SOCIALIUM. 1972. irreg. price varies. Societas
Scientiarum Fennica, Snellmansgatan 9-11, SF-
000170 Helsinki 17, Finland. Ed. Gunnar Fougstedt.
circ. 900.

300   EI   ISSN 0531-3724
COMMISSION OF THE EUROPEAN
COMMUNITIES. EXPOSE SUR L'EVOLUTION
SOCIALE DANS LA COMMUNAUTE.
(Published with its Rapport General sur l'Activite
des Communautes) (Editions also in German, Italian
and Dutch) 1968. a. 120 Fr. Office for Official
Publications of the European Communities, C.P.
1003, Luxembourg 1, Luxembourg (Dist. in U.S. by
European Communities Information Service, 2100
M St., N.W., Suite 707, Washington D.C. 20037)

300   FR
COMMUNAUTES MEDITERRANEENNES.
CAHIER. irreg., no. 3, 1976. Centre National de la
Recherche Scientifique, 15 Quai Anatole France,
75700 Paris, Italy.

300   US   ISSN 0147-4642
COMMUNICATION YEARBOOK. 1977. a. $29.95.
International Communication Association, Balcones
Research Center, 10,100 Burnet Rd., Austin, TX
78758. Ed. Dan Nimmo.

300 900   US   ISSN 0069-7907
COMPARATIVE STUDIES IN SOCIETY AND
HISTORY.* 1961. irreg. price varies. Columbia
University Press, 136 S. Broadway, Irvington-on-
Hudson, NY 10533.

300   CK
CONGRESO INTERNACIONAL DE VIVIENDA
POPULAR. no. 3, 1974. Col.$90. (Servicio Latino-
Americano y Asiatico de Vivienda Popular) Centro
de Investigacion y Accion Social, Carrera 5, No. 11-
53, Aptdo. Aereo 25916, Bogota, Colombia.

300 360   US
CONTEMPORARY EVALUATION RESEARCH.
1979. irreg. Sage Publications, Inc., 275 S. Beverly
Dr., Beverly Hills, CA 90212 (And Sage
Publications, Ltd., 28 Banner St., London EC1Y
8QE, England) Eds. Howard Freeman, Richard A.
Berk.

300   BL
CONTRIBUICOES EM CIENCIAS SOCIAIS. irreg.
Editora Campus Ltda (Subsidiary of: Elsevier
North-Holland, Inc) Rua Japeri 35, 20000 Rio de
Janeiro RJ, Brazil.

300 001.3   NE
CONTRIBUTIONS TO ASIAN STUDIES. 1971.
irreg., vol. 16, 1981. price varies. E. J. Brill, Oude
Rijn 33a-35, Leiden, Netherlands. Ed. K. Ishwaran.
(back issues avail)

300   TZ
COUNCIL FOR THE SOCIAL SCIENCES IN
EAST AFRICA. SOCIAL SCIENCE
CONFERENCE. PROCEEDINGS. a.
EAs.200($29) Council for the Social Sciences in
East Africa, Social Science Conference, University
of Dar-es-Salaam, Faculty of Arts and Social
Science, Box 35091, Dar-es-Salaam, Tanzania.
charts. stat.

300   PE
CRITICA ANDINA. 1978. irreg. $12 (to individuals;
$18 to institutions) Instituto de Estudios Sociales,
Director de Publicaciones, Casilla Postal 790,
Cusco, Peru. Dir. Marco Villasante. adv. bk. rev.
circ. 2,000.

300   PE
CUADERNOS DE SOCIEDAD Y POLITICA. 1976.
irreg. Cuadernos de Sociedad y Cultura, Apartado
11154, Correo Santa Beatriz, Lima, Peru.

CURRENT RESEARCH IN BRITISH STUDIES BY
AMERICAN AND CANADIAN SCHOLARS. see
HUMANITIES: COMPREHENSIVE WORKS

DATA BOOK OF SOCIAL STUDIES MATERIALS
AND RESOURCES. see *EDUCATION —
Teaching Methods And Curriculum*

300 900 400   II   ISSN 0045-9801
DECCAN COLLEGE. POSTGRADUATE &
RESEARCH INSTITUTE. BULLETIN. (Text in
English) a. q. $30. Deccan College, Postgraduate &
Research Institute, Poona 411006, India. bk. rev.
(back issues avail.)

300   US
DEVELOPING NATIONS MONOGRAPH SERIES
ONE. series 2, no. 2, 1974. irreg., no. 7 in prep.
Wake Forest University, Overseas Research Center,
Box 7805, Winston Salem, NC 27109.

DEVELOPMENT; a selected annotated bibliography.
see *BIBLIOGRAPHIES*

300   TH
DIRECTORY OF RESEARCH INSTITUTIONS IN
THAILAND. (Text in English) irreg. National
Research Council, Social Science Research Division,
Bangkok, Thailand.

300   II
DIRECTORY OF SOCIAL SCIENCE RESEARCH
INSTITUTIONS IN INDIA. (Subseries of the
Council's Research Information Series) (Text in
English) 1971. irreg. free. ‡ Indian Council of Social
Science Research, 35 Ferozshah Rd., New Delhi
110001, India. circ. 100.

300   KE   ISSN 0424-0928
EAST AFRICAN STUDIES. 1953. irreg. (Makerere
University, Makerere Institute of Social Research,
UG) East African Publishing House, Box 30571,
Lusaka Close, off Lusaka Rd., Nairobi, Kenya.
charts.

330   EI
ECONOMIC AND SOCIAL COMMITTEE OF THE
EUROPEAN COMMUNITIES. ANNUAIRE.
1960. irreg. free. Economic and Social Committee
of the European Communities, Service Presse et
Information, 2 rue Ravenstein, 1000 Brussels,
Belgium. circ. controlled.

300   SP
EDICIONES PENINSULA. SERIE
UNIVERSITARIA. HISTORIA, CIENCIA,
SOCIEDAD. no. 129, 1976. irreg. Ediciones
Peninsula, Provenza 278, Barcelona 8, Spain.

ENCYCLOPAEDIA AFRICANA. INFORMATION
REPORT. see *HISTORY*

ESSAYS ON THE ECONOMY AND SOCIETY OF
THE SUDAN. see *BUSINESS AND
ECONOMICS — Economic Situation And
Conditions*

305.8   CN   ISSN 0226-1928
ETHNOCULTURAL DIRECTORY OF ONTARIO.
(Text in English and French) 1977. irreg. Ministry
of Culture and Recreation, Multicultural
Development Branch, 77 Bloor St. W., Toronto,
Ont. M7A 2R9, Canada.

300   NE   ISSN 0071-271X
EUROPEAN COORDINATION CENTRE FOR
RESEARCH AND DOCUMENTATION IN
SOCIAL SCIENCES. PUBLICATIONS. 1971.
irreg. price varies. Mouton Publishers, Noordeinde
41, 2514 GC The Hague, Netherlands (U.S. addr:
Mouton Publishers, c/o Walter de Gruyter, Inc.,
200 Saw Mill River Road, Hawthorne, NY 10532)

300   US   ISSN 0364-7390
EVALUATION STUDIES REVIEW ANNUAL.
1976. a. $32.50. Sage Publications, Inc., 275 S.
Beverly Dr., Beverly Hills, CA 90212 (And Sage
Publications, Ltd., 28 Banner St., London EC1Y
8QE, England) Ed.Bd. (back issues avail.)

300 301   UK
EXPLORATIONS IN URBAN ANALYSIS. 1978.
irreg. price varies. Edward Arnold (Publishers) Ltd.,
41 Bedford Square, London WC1B 3DQ, England.

300   AT
FLINDERS UNIVERSITY OF SOUTH
AUSTRALIA. SCHOOL OF SOCIAL SCIENCES.
OCCASIONAL MONOGRAPH. 1973. irreg.
Flinders University of South Australia, School of
Social Sciences, Bedford Park, S.A. 5042, Australia.

FLORIDA STATE UNIVERSITY. CENTER FOR
YUGOSLAV-AMERICAN STUDIES,
RESEARCH, AND EXCHANGES.
PROCEEDINGS AND REPORTS OF
SEMINARS AND RESEARCH. see *HISTORY —
History Of Europe*

301 945   IT   ISSN 0544-1374
FONDAZIONE GIANGIACOMO FELTRINELLI.
ANNALI. 1958. a. price varies. Fondazione
Giangiacomo Feltrinelli, Via Romagnosi 3, 20121
Milan, Italy. bk. rev.

300   GW
GESELLSCHAFT, RECHT, WIRTSCHAFT. 1978.
irreg., vol. 5, 1980. price varies. Bibliographisches
Institut AG, Dudenstr. 6, Postfach 311, 6800
Mannheim 1, W. Germany (B.R.D.) Ed. Bd.

300   GW
GESELLSCHAFTSPOLITISCHE
BILDUNGSMATERIALIEN. 1976. irreg.
DM.10.80 per no. (Stiftung Gesellschaft und
Unternehmen) Deutscher Instituts-Verlag GmbH,
Gustav-Heinemann-Ufer 84-88, Postfach 510670,
5000 Cologne 51, W. Germany (B.R.D.) Ed. W.
Eberle, H. H. Wenkebach.

301   SW   ISSN 0072-5099
GOETEBORGS UNIVERSITET. SOCIOLOGISKA
INSTITUTIONEN. FORSKNINGS-RAPPORT.
(Text in Swedish; summaries in English) 1964. irreg.
price varies. Goeteborgs Universitet, Sociologiska
Institutionen, Karl Johansgatan 27, S-414 59
Goeteborg, Sweden.

331.2   UK
GREAT BRITAIN. GOVERNMENT ACTUARY.
OCCUPATIONAL PENSION BOARD. ANNUAL
REPORT. irreg. price varies. H.M.S.O., P.O. Box
569, London SE1 9NH, England.

300   UK
GREAT BRITAIN. SOCIAL SCIENCE RESEARCH
COUNCIL. BURSARY SCHEME. 1969. a. free.
Social Science Research Council, Postgraduate
Awards Division, 1 Temple Ave., London EC4Y
0BD, England. circ. 2,000.

300   UK   ISSN 0081-0444
GREAT BRITAIN. SOCIAL SCIENCE RESEARCH
COUNCIL. REPORT. 1966/67. a. Social Science
Research Council, 1 Temple Ave., London EC4Y
0BD, England.

300   UK   ISSN 0583-6948
GREAT BRITAIN. SOCIAL SCIENCE RESEARCH
COUNCIL. RESEARCH SUPPORTED BY THE
SOCIAL SCIENCE RESEARCH COUNCIL.
1967. a. £4. Social Science Research Council, 1
Temple Ave., London EC4Y 0BD, England. index.
circ. 1,500.

300   UK
GREAT BRITAIN. SOCIAL SCIENCE RESEARCH
COUNCIL. STUDENTSHIP HANDBOOK. 1966.
a. free. Social Science Research Council,
Postgraduate Awards Division, 1 Temple Ave.,
London EC4Y 0BD, England.

300 980   US
HANDBOOK OF LATIN AMERICAN STUDIES.
SOCIAL SCIENCES. biennial. price varies.
University Presses of Florida, 15 N.W. 15th St.,
Gainesville, FL 32603.

HARVARD PAPERBACKS. see *HUMANITIES:
COMPREHENSIVE WORKS*

300   IS
HEBREW UNIVERSITY OF JERUSALEM.
AUTHORITY FOR RESEARCH AND
DEVELOPMENT. CURRENT RESEARCH. (Vol.
1: Research; Vol. 2: Publications) (Text in English)
1964/65. a. Hebrew University of Jerusalem,
Jerusalem, Israel. Ed. R. Cohen. author index. circ.
controlled.
Formed by the merger of: Hebrew University of
Jerusalem. Authority for Research and
Development. Research Report: Humanities, Social
Sciences, Law, Education, Social Work, Library
(ISSN 0075-3645) & Hebrew University of
Jerusalem. Authority for Research and
Development. Research Report. Science and
Agriculture (ISSN 0075-3653) & Hebrew University
of Jerusalem. Authority for Research Report.
Medicine, Pharmacy, Dental Medicine (ISSN 0075-
3637)

SOCIAL SCIENCES: COMPREHENSIVE WORKS

HIROSHIMA UNIVERSITY. FACULTY OF GENERAL EDUCATION. MEMOIRS: STUDIES IN HUMANITIES AND SOCIAL SCIENCES. see *HUMANITIES: COMPREHENSIVE WORKS*

300 JA ISSN 0073-280X
HITOTSUBASHI JOURNAL OF SOCIAL STUDIES. 1960. s-a. 1500 Yen. Hitotsubashi University, Hitotsubashi Academy, 2-1 Naka, Kunitachi, Tokyo 186, Japan. Ed. S. Honda. circ. 940.

300 001.3 SA
HUMAN SCIENCES RESEARCH COUNCIL. ANNUAL REPORT. (Text in Afrikaans and English) 1969/70. a. free. ‡ Human Sciences Research Council, Private Bag X41, Pretoria 0001, South Africa. circ. 1,400.

300 001.3 SA
HUMAN SCIENCES RESEARCH COUNCIL. GENERAL INFORMATION. (Text in English) 1970. irreg. free. ‡ Human Sciences Research Council, Private Bag X41, Pretoria 0001, South Africa.

300 US
I S E R OCCASIONAL PAPERS. 1970. irreg., no. 14, 1978. $2 per no. University of Alaska, Institute of Social and Economic Research, 707 A St., Suite 206, Anchorage, AK 99501. Ed. Ronald Crowe. bibl.
 Formerly: I S E G R Occasional Papers.

300 NR
IBADAN SOCIAL SCIENCES SERIES. irreg., no. 7, 1976. Ibadan University Press, University of Ibadan, Ibadan, Nigeria.

300 US ISSN 0073-5183
ILLINOIS STUDIES IN THE SOCIAL SCIENCES. 1912. irreg. University of Illinois Press, 54 E. Gregory, Box 5081, Station A, Champaign, IL 61820. Ed. Bd. (reprint service avail. from UMI)

INDEX TO INTERNATIONAL PUBLIC OPINION. see *POLITICAL SCIENCE — International Relations*

300 II ISSN 0073-6694
INDIAN STATISTICAL INSTITUTE. ECONOMETRIC AND SOCIAL SCIENCES SERIES. RESEARCH MONOGRAPHS.* irreg. Statistical Publishing Society, 204/1 Barrackpore Trunk Rd., Calcutta 700035, India. Eds. P. C. Mahalanobis, C. R. Rao.

INSTITUT DES HAUTES ETUDES DE L'AMERIQUE LATINE. CENTRE D'ETUDES POLITIQUES, ECONOMIQUES ET SOCIALES. PUBLICATIONS MULTIGRAPHIEES. see *HISTORY — History Of North And South America*

300 BL
INSTITUTO JOAQUIM NABUCO DE PESQUISAS SOCIAIS. SERIE MONOGRAFIAS. 1975. irreg. $2.50 per no. Instituto Joaquim Nabuco de Pesquisas Sociais, Av. 17 de Agosto 2187, Recife, Brazil.

300 RM
INSTITUTUL PEDAGOGIC ORADEA. LUCRARI STIINTIFICE: SERIA STIINTE SOCIALE. (Continues in part its Lucrari Stiintifice: Seria Istorie, Stiinte Sociale, Pedagogie (1971-1972), its Lucrari Stiintifice: Seria A and Seria B (1969-1970), and its Lucrari Stiintifice (1967-68).) (Text in Rumanian, occasionally in English or French; summaries in Rumanian, French, English or German) 1973. a. Institutul Pedagogic Oradea, Calea Armatei Roseii Nr. 5, Oradea, Romania.

INTER-AMERICAN ECONOMIC AND SOCIAL COUNCIL. FINAL REPORT OF THE ANNUAL MEETING AT THE MINISTERIAL LEVEL. see *HISTORY — History Of North And South America*

301 NO ISSN 0522-4497
INTERNATIONAL PEACE RESEARCH INSTITUTE. BASIC SOCIAL SCIENCE MONOGRAPHS. 1967. irreg. International Peace Research Institute, Raadhusgt. 4, Oslo 1, Norway.

300 NE ISSN 0074-8404
INTERNATIONAL SOCIAL SCIENCE COUNCIL. PUBLICATIONS. irreg. price varies. Mouton Publishers, Noordeinde 41, 2514 GC The Hague, Netherlands (U.S. addr.: Mouton Publishers, c/o Walter de Gruyter, Inc. 200 Saw Mill River Road, Hawthorne, NY 10532)

INTERNATIONAL STUDIES IN SOCIOLOGY AND SOCIAL ANTHROPOLOGY. see *SOCIOLOGY*

300 320 UK ISSN 0074-9621
INTERNATIONAL YEAR BOOK AND STATESMEN'S WHO'S WHO. 1953. a. £50. Kelly's Directories, Ltd., Windsor Court, East Grinstead House, East Grinstead, West Sussex RH19 1XB, England. adv. index. circ. 3,750.

300 UK
INTERNATIONAL YEARBOOK OF ORGANIZATION STUDIES. 1980. a. Routledge & Kegan Paul Ltd., Broadway House, Newtown Rd., Henley-on-Thames, Oxon RG9 1EN, England (U.S. orders to: Routledge Journals, 9 Park St., Boston, MA 02108) Ed. David Dunkerley.

300 US ISSN 0362-8736
INTER-UNIVERSITY CONSORTIUM FOR POLITICAL AND SOCIAL RESEARCH. GUIDE TO RESOURCES AND SERVICES. 1963. a. free. Inter-University Consortium for Political and Social Research, Box 1248, Ann Arbor, MI 48106.

IRISH ECONOMIC AND SOCIAL HISTORY. see *HISTORY — History Of Europe*

300 IT ISSN 0391-321X
ISTITUZIONI CULTURALI. 1977. irreg., no. 5, 1979. Liguori Editore s.r.l., Via Mezzocannone 19, 80134 Naples, Italy. Ed. Guiliano Manacorda. circ. 2,000.

300 330 IS
JEWISH AGENCY FOR ISRAEL. OFFICE FOR ECONOMIC AND SOCIAL RESEARCH. ANNUAL. (Editions in Hebrew, English, French, Spanish) 1969. a. free. Jewish Agency for Israel, Office for Economic and Social Research, Box 92, Jerusalem, Israel. Ed. L. Berger.

300 US
JOURNAL OF INDO-EUROPEAN STUDIES MONOGRAPH SERIES. irreg., latest no. 2. Institute for the Study of Man, Inc., 1629 K St., N.W., Suite 520, Washington, DC 20006.

300 JA
JOURNAL OF INTERCULTURAL STUDIES. 1974. a. 2500 Yen($10) Kansai University of Foreign Studies, Intercultural Research Institute, 333 Ogura, Hirakata City, Osaka 573, Japan. Ed. Haruo Kozu. adv. bk. rev. charts. illus.

300 MW ISSN 0302-3060
JOURNAL OF SOCIAL SCIENCE. 1972. a, latest 1976. $7. Chancellor College, Box 280, Zomba, Malawi. Ed. Bd. bk. rev. circ. 500. (back issues avail.)

300 TH
JOURNAL OF SOCIAL SCIENCE REVIEW. 1976. irreg. $4. (Social Science Association of Thailand) Social Science Press, Box 5-84, Bangkok, Thailand. Ed. Likhit Dhiravegin.

300 JA
JOURNAL OF SOCIAL SCIENCES. (Text in English) no. 16, 1978. a. International Christian University - Kokusai Kiristokyo Daigaku, 3-10-2 Osawa, Mitaka, Tokyo 181, Japan. bk. rev.

300 BG
JOURNAL OF SOCIAL STUDIES. 1978. q. Tk.20($5) per. no. Center for Social Studies, c/o Department of Political Science, University of Dacca, Rm. No. 1107, Arts Bldg., Dacca 2, Bangladesh. Ed. B. K. Jahangin. adv. bk. rev. circ. 500.

900 US ISSN 0193-6131
JUNIOR EAGLE. 1979. irreg. $7.75. World Eagle, Inc., 64 Washburn Ave., Wellesley, MA 02181. Ed. Duncan L. Gibson.
 Study and teaching

300 II ISSN 0075-5176
KARNATAK UNIVERSITY, DHARWAD, INDIA. JOURNAL. SOCIAL SCIENCES. (Text in English) 1965. a. Rs.8($4) Karnatak University, C. S. Kanavi, Director, Prasaranga, Dharwad 580003, Karnataka, India. Ed. K. Chandrasekharaiah. circ. 500.

300 PL
KATOLICKI UNIWERSYTET LUBELSKI. WYDZIAL NAUK SPOLECZNYCH. ROZPRAWY. (Text in Polish; summaries in English or French) 1947. irreg. price varies. Katolicki Uniwersytet Lubelski, Towarzystwo Naukowe, Chopina 29, 20-023 Lublin, Poland. index. circ. 1,025.

KOBE UNIVERSITY OF MERCANTILE MARINE. REVIEW. PART 1. STUDIES IN HUMANITIES AND SOCIAL SCIENCE. see *HUMANITIES: COMPREHENSIVE WORKS*

KULTUR UND GESELLSCHAFT; Neue historische Forschungen. see *HISTORY*

KYUSHU INSTITUTE OF TECHNOLOGY. BULLETIN: HUMANITIES, SOCIAL SCIENCES/KYUSHU KOGYO DAIGAKU KENKYU HOKOKU, JINBUN-SHAKAI-KAGAKU. see *HUMANITIES: COMPREHENSIVE WORKS*

LAW AND PSYCHOLOGY REVIEW. see *LAW*

966.6 300 US
LIBERIAN STUDIES MONOGRAPH SERIES. 1972. irreg., no. 5, 1976. price varies. University of Delaware, Department of Anthropology, Newark, DE 19711. charts. illus.

966.6 300 US
LIBERIAN STUDIES RESEARCH WORKING PAPERS. 1971. irreg., no. 5, 1976. price varies. University of Delaware, Department of Anthropology, Newark, DE 19711. bibl.

LIBRARY OF LAW AND CONTEMPORARY PROBLEMS. see *LAW*

300 UK ISSN 0078-9224
LONDON SCHOOL OF ECONOMICS PAPERS IN SOVIET AND EAST EUROPEAN LAW, ECONOMICS AND POLITICS. 1964. irreg., 1967, no. 2. price varies. ‡ (London School of Economics and Political Science) Athlone Press, 90-91 Great Russell St., London WC1B 3PY, England (Dist. in U.S. by: Humanities Press Inc., 171 First Ave., Atlantic Highlands, NJ 07716) Ed. Prof. L. B. Schapiro.

309.1 US
LOUISIANA STATE OF THE STATE. 1970. irreg. State Planning Office, Box 44426, Capitol Sta., Baton Rouge, LA 70804. illus.

300 PP ISSN 0085-2902
LUKSAVE. 1970. irreg., latest issue Oct. 1976. K.1.50. Institute of Applied Social & Economic Research, Box 5854, Boroko, Papua New Guinea. Ed. R. J. May. circ. 2,000.

300 MY
M C D S OCCASIONAL PAPER SERIES. (Text in English) 1974. irreg., latest no. 5. M.$3.50. Malaysian Centre for Development Studies, Prime Minister's Department, Government Offices, Block K 11 & K 12, Jalan Duta, Kuala Lumpur, Malaysia. Ed. Engku M. Anuar.

300 CN ISSN 0076-1893
MCGILL UNIVERSITY, MONTREAL. CENTRE FOR DEVELOPING-AREA STUDIES. ANNUAL REPORT. 1967-68. a. free. McGill University, Centre for Developing-Area Studies, 815sherbrooke St. W., Montreal, Que. H3A 2K6, Canada.

300 CN ISSN 0702-8431
MCGILL UNIVERSITY, MONTREAL. CENTRE FOR DEVELOPING-AREA STUDIES. OCCASIONAL MONOGRAPH SERIES. 1969. irreg., no. 13, 1978. price varies. McGill University, Centre for Developing-Area Studies, 815 Sherbrooke St.W., Montreal, Que. H3A 2K6, Canada. Ed. Rosalind Boyd. circ. 1,000-1,500.
 Formerly: McGill University, Montreal. Centre for Developing-Area Studies. Occasional Paper Series (ISSN 0076-1907)

300 CN ISSN 0384-059X
MCGILL UNIVERSITY, MONTREAL. CENTRE FOR DEVELOPING-AREA STUDIES. WORKING PAPERS. 1975. irreg., no. 26, 1979. Can.$1. McGill University, Centre for Developing-Area Studies, 815 Sherbrooke St. W., Montreal, Que. H3A 2K6, Canada. Ed. Rosalind E. Boyd. circ. 200.

309 US
MAN-ENVIRONMENT SYSTEM IN THE LATE TWENTIETH CENTURY. irreg. Wadsworth Publishing Co., 10 Davis Dr., Belmont, CA 94002.

MAN IN SOUTHEAST ASIA. see *ANTHROPOLOGY*

300 GW
MANNHEIMER SOZIALWISSENSCHAFTLICHE STUDIEN. 1970. irreg., vol. 17, 1980. price varies. Verlag Anton Hain GmbH, Adelheidstr. 2, Postfach 1220, 6240 Koenigstein, W. Germany (B.R.D.) Ed. Bd.

300 CE
MARGA INSTITUTE. PROGRESS REPORT. (Text in English) 1973. irreg., no. 3, 1979. Marga Institute (Sri Lanka Centre for Development Studies), Box 601, 61 Issipathana Mawatha, Colombo 5, Sri Lanka. circ. 2,000.

300 NE ISSN 0076-6828
METHODS AND MODELS IN THE SOCIAL SCIENCES. 1971. irreg. price varies. Mouton Publishers, Noordeinde 41, 2514 GC The Hague, Netherlands (U.S. addr.: Mouton Publishers, c/o Walter de Gruyter, Inc., 200 Saw Mill River Road, Hawthorne, NY 10532)

300 US
MIDDLE STATES COUNCIL FOR THE SOCIAL STUDIES. JOURNAL. 1978. a. (occasionally 2/yr.) $5. Middle States Council for the Social Studies, c/o David Pierfy, Rider College, Box 6400, Lawrenceville, NJ 08648. Eds. Victor Shapiro, David Pierfy. bk. rev. circ. 500. (back issues avail.) Supersedes (1903-1978): Middle States Council for the Social Studies. Proceedings.

300 SP
MISION CIENTIFICA ESPANOLA EN HISPANOAMERICA. MEMORIAS. vol. 3, 1976. irreg. Direccion General de Relaciones Culturales, Madrid, Spain.

300 US ISSN 0077-0752
MONOGRAPHS AND TEXTS IN THE BEHAVIORAL SCIENCES.* irreg., 1971, no. 2. price varies. Gordon and Breach Science Publishers, 1 Park Avenue, New York, NY 10016.

MUSEE ROYAL DE L'AFRIQUE CENTRALE. ANNALES. SERIE IN 8. SCIENCES HUMAINES/KONINKLIJK MUSEUM VOOR MIDDEN-AFRIKA. ANNALEN. REEKS IN 8. MENSELIJKE WETENSCHAPPEN. see *HUMANITIES: COMPREHENSIVE WORKS*

NATIONAL INSTITUTE OF ECONOMIC AND SOCIAL RESEARCH, LONDON. ECONOMIC AND SOCIAL STUDIES. see *BUSINESS AND ECONOMICS*

300 UK ISSN 0077-491X
NATIONAL INSTITUTE OF ECONOMIC AND SOCIAL RESEARCH. ANNUAL REPORT. 1941. a. free. National Institute of Economic and Social Research, 2 Dean Trench St., Smith Sq., London SW1P 3HE, England. circ. 2,000.

300 RH
NATIONAL MUSEUMS AND MONUMENTS ADMINISTRATION. OCCASIONAL PAPERS. SERIES A: HUMAN SCIENCES. 1957. irreg. price varies. National Museums and Monuments Administration, P.O. Box 8540, Causeway, Salisbury, Zimbabwe. index. circ. 130.
Formerly: National Museums and Monuments of Rhodesia. Occasional Papers. Series A: Human Sciences. (ISSN 0304-5307); Supersedes in part: National Museums and Monuments of Rhodesia. Occasional Papers (ISSN 0027-9730)

300 US ISSN 0077-5274
NATIONAL OPINION RESEARCH CENTER. REPORT. 1941. irreg., no. 129, 1980. ‡ National Opinion Research Center, 6030 South Ellis, Chicago, IL 60637. Ed. Susan Campbell.

300 CH ISSN 0077-5835
NATIONAL TAIWAN UNIVERSITY. COLLEGE OF LAW. JOURNAL OF SOCIAL SCIENCE. (Text in Chinese or English) 1950. irreg. National Taiwan University, College of Law, Taipei, Taiwan, Republic of China.

300 US
NEW WORLDS NEWSLETTER. 1973. irreg? $10. Committee for the Future, Inc., 2325 Porter St. N.W., Washington, DC 20008. Ed. Ann Elizabeth Robinson. circ. 6,000.

300 330 NR ISSN 0078-074X
NIGERIAN INSTITUTE OF SOCIAL AND ECONOMIC RESEARCH. ANNUAL REPORT. 1954. a. free. Nigerian Institute of Social and Economic Research, Private Mail Bag 5, University of Ibadan, Ibadan, Nigeria.
Formerly: West African Institute of Social and Economic Research. Annual Report.

OCCASIONAL PAPERS IN ECONOMIC AND SOCIAL HISTORY. see *BUSINESS AND ECONOMICS — Economic Systems And Theories, Economic History*

300 AU
OESTERREICHISCHE AKADEMIE DER WISSENSCHAFTEN. KOMMISSION FUER SOZIAL-UND WIRTSCHAFTWISSENSCHAFTEN. VEROEFFENTLICHUNGEN. (Subseries of its Philosophisch-Historische Klasse. Sitzungsberichte) 1973. irreg., no. 9, 1976. price varies. Verlag der Oesterreichischen Akademie der Wissenschaften, Dr. Ignaz Seipel-Platz 2, 1010 Vienna, Austria. circ. 1,500.

300 US
OXFORD READINGS IN SOCIAL STUDIES. irreg. price varies. Oxford University Press, 200 Madison Ave., New York, NY 10016 (And Ely House, 37 Dover St., London W1X 4AH, England)

P S I: BROADSHEET SERIES AND MAJOR REPORTS. (Policy Studies Institute) see *POLITICAL SCIENCE*

P S I DISCUSSION PAPERS. (Policy Studies Institute) see *POLITICAL SCIENCE*

300 US ISSN 0079-1776
PHOENIX; journal of cultural and social thought. (Text in Ukranian and English) 1950. irreg. $1.75. Ukrainian Student Organization of Michnowsky, T.U.S.M., Box 113, Riverton, NJ 08077. Ed. Mykola Krawczuk. circ. 1,000.

300 PL ISSN 0574-9077
POLITECHNIKA CZESTOCHOWSKA. ZESZYTY NAUKOWE. NAUKI SPOLECZNO-EKONOMICZNE. (Text in Polish; summaries in English and Russian) 1964. irreg. Politechnika Czestochowska, Ul. Deglera 31, 42-200 Czestochowa, Poland (Dist. by: Ars Polona-Ruch, Krakowskie Przedmiescie 7, Warsaw, Poland) Ed. Mieczyslaw Stanczyk.

300 330 PL
POLITECHNIKA LODZKA. ZESZYTY NAUKOWE. NAUKI SPOLECZNO-EKONOMICZNE. (Text in Polish; summaries in English and Russian) 1974. irreg. price varies. Politechnika Lodzka, Ul. Zwirki 36, 90-924 Lodz, Poland (Dist. by: Ars Polona-Ruch, Krakowskie Przedmiescie 7, Warsaw, Poland) Ed. Leon Polanowski. circ. 383.

300 PL ISSN 0072-4718
POLITECHNIKA SLASKA. ZESZYTY NAUKOWE. NAUKI SPOLECZNE. (Text in Polish; summaries in English, and Russian) 1964. irreg. price varies. Politechnika Slaska, W. Pstrowskiego 7, 44-100 Gliwice, Poland (Dist by: Ars Polona, Krakowskie Przedmiescie 7, 00-068 Warsaw, Poland) Ed. Jerzy Broda.

300 PL ISSN 0324-9506
POLITECHNIKA WROCLAWSKA. INSTYTUT NAUK SPOLECZNYCH. PRACE NAUKOWE. MONOGRAFIE. (Text in Polish; summaries in English and Russian) 1971. irreg., no. 12, 1979. price varies. Politechnika Wroclawska, Wybrzeze Wyspianskiego 27, 50-370 Wroclaw, Poland (Dist. by: Ars Polona-Ruch, Krakowskie Przedmiescie 7, Warsaw, Poland) Ed. Marian Kloza.

300 PL ISSN 0324-9514
POLITECHNIKA WROCLAWSKA. INSTYTUT NAUK SPOLECZNYCH. PRACE NAUKOWE. STUDIA I MATERIALY. (Text in Polish; summaries in English and Russian) 1969. irreg., no. 10, 1979. price varies. Politechnika Wroclawska, Wybrzeze Wyspainskiego 27, 50-370 Wroclaw, Poland (Dist. by: Ars Polona-Ruch, Krakowskie Przedmiescie 7, Warsaw, Poland) Ed. Marian Kloza.

POLSKA AKADEMIA NAUK. ODDZIAL W KRAKOWIE. KOMISJA NAUKOWYCH. SPRAWOZDANIA Z POSIEDZEN. see *SCIENCES: COMPREHENSIVE WORKS*

300 PE
PONTIFICIA UNIVERSIDAD CATOLICA. REVISTA. N.S. 1977. irreg. Pontificia Universidad Catolica, Ave. Bolivar s/n, Pueblo Libre, Apartado 1761, Lima 21, Peru. Ed. Gerardo Alarco.

300 PE
PONTIFICIA UNIVERSIDAD CATOLICA DEL PERU. DEPARTAMENTO DE CIENCIAS SOCIALES. SERIE: EDICIONES PREVIAS. no. 5, 1975. irreg. Pontificia Universidad Catolica del Peru, Departamento de Ciencias Sociales, Fundo Pando s/n, Lima, Peru.

300 VC ISSN 0080-3960
PONTIFICIA UNIVERSITA GREGORIANA. ISTITUTO DI SCIENZE SOCIALI STUDIA SOCIALIA. (Multi-Language Text) 1955. irreg. price varies. Pontificia Universita Gregoriana, School of Social Sciences, Piazza della Pilotta 4, 00187 Rome, Italy. Ed. Theodor Mulder, S.J.

300 PL ISSN 0079-4716
POZNANSKIE TOWARZYSTWO PRZYJACIOL NAUK. KOMISJA NAUK SPOLECZNYCH. PRACE. (Text in Polish; summaries in English, French, German, Russian) 1922. irreg. price varies. Poznanskie Towarzystwo Przyjaciol Nauk, Mielzynskiego 27/29, 61-725 Poznan, Poland (Dist. by Ars Polona-Ruch, Krakowskie Przedmiescie 7, Warsaw, Poland)

300 US
PROBLEMS OF AMERICAN SOCIETY. irreg. price varies. Simon and Schuster, Inc., 630 Fifth Ave., New York, NY 10020 (Orders from: 1 W. 39th St., New York, N.Y. 10018)

300 UR ISSN 0079-5763
PROBLEMS OF THE CONTEMPORARY WORLD/PROBLEMES DU MONDE CONTEMPORAIN/PROBLEMAS DEL MUNDO CONTEMPORANEO. (Text in English, French, Spanish) 1969. irreg. available on exchange. Akademii Nauk S.S.S.R., Leninskii prospekt, 14, Moscow V-71, U. S. S. R. Ed. I. Grigulevich, D. Sc. circ. 500-1,000.

300 FR ISSN 0079-7448
PSYCHOTHEQUE. 1969. irreg. 19.95 F. Editions Jean Pierre Delarge, 10, rue Mayet, Paris 6e, France.

300 US
PUBLIC POLICY STUDIES IN THE SOUTH; a selected research guide. 1975. a. $5. Southern Center for Studies in Public Policy, Clark College, Atlanta, GA 30314.

PUBLICACOES CULTURAIS DA COMPANHIA. see *SCIENCES: COMPREHENSIVE WORKS*

300 US
QUANTITATIVE APPLICATIONS IN THE SOCIAL SCIENCES. (Subseries of: Sage University Papers) 1976. irreg. $3 per no. Sage Publications, Inc., 275 S. Beverly Dr., Beverly Hills, CA 90212 (And Sage Publications, Ltd., 28 Banner St., London EC1Y 8QE, England) Ed. Eric M. Uslaner. (back issues avail.)

300 US
READERS IN SOCIAL PROBLEMS. irreg. price varies. Harper and Row Publishers, Inc., 10 East 53rd St., New York, NY 10022.

300 II
RECENT TRENDS IN SOCIAL SCIENCES. 1975. irreg. Rs.20($4) Anu Prakashan, Shivaji Rd., Meerut 25001, India. Ed. Dr. Ram Nath Sharma. adv. bk. rev.

300 FR ISSN 0557-6989
RECHERCHES ANGLAISES ET AMERICAINES.
a. (Association Strasbourgeoise des Periodiques de Sciences Humaines) Universite de Strasbourg II, 22 rue Descartes, 67000 Strasbourg, France. Eds. S. Vauthier & A. Bleikasten.

RECHERCHES D'HISTOIRE ET DE SCIENCES SOCIALES/STUDIES IN HISTORY AND SOCIAL SCIENCES. see *HISTORY*

REFERENCE DATA ON SOCIOECONOMIC ISSUES OF HEALTH. see *MEDICAL SCIENCES*

331 CN ISSN 0708-1065
REGISTER OF ON-GOING LABOUR RESEARCH. (Supplement to: Labour, Capital and Society) 1978. a. free. McGill University, Centre for Developing Area Studies, 815 Sherbrooke St. W., Montreal, Que. H3A 2K6, Canada. Ed. Rosalind E. Boyd.

300 100 SZ
RENCONTRES INTERNATIONALES DE GENEVE. 1947. biennial. 36 Fr. Editions de la Baconniere S.A., Box 185, CH-2017 Boudry, Switzerland.

300 UN ISSN 0080-1348
REPORTS AND PAPERS IN THE SOCIAL SCIENCES. (Editions in English and French) 1955. irreg.; no. 30, 1974. price varies. Unesco, 7-9 Place de Fontenoy, 75700 Paris, France (Dist. in U.S. by: Unipub, 345 Park Ave. S., New York NY 10010)

RESEARCH JOURNAL: HUMANITIES AND SOCIAL SCIENCES. see *HUMANITIES: COMPREHENSIVE WORKS*

REVIEW JOURNAL OF PHILOSOPHY AND SOCIAL SCIENCE. see *PHILOSOPHY*

300 EC
REVISTA CIENCIAS SOCIALES. 1977. irreg. Universidad Central del Ecuador, Escuela de Sociologia y Ciencias Politicas, Apdo. 2349, Quito, Ecuador. Ed. Bd.

300 FR ISSN 0336-1578
REVUE DES SCIENCES SOCIALES DE LA FRANCE DE L'EST. 1971? a. price varies. Universite de Strasbourg II, 22 rue Descartes, 67084 Strasbourg, France. Ed. Freddy Raphael.

ROCKEFELLER FOUNDATION. WORKING PAPERS. see *AGRICULTURE — Agricultural Economics*

300 PL
ROCZNIKI NAUK SPOLECZNYCH. (Text in Polish; Summaries in English) 1949. a. price varies. Katolicki Uniwersytet Lubelski, Towarzystwo Naukowe, Chopina 29, 20-023 Lublin, Poland. circ. 820.

300 CE
ROYAL ASIATIC SOCIETY, CEYLON BRANCH. JOURNAL. 1958. a. Royal Asiatic Society, Ceylon Branch, Thurstan Rd., Colombo 3, Sri Lanka. bk. rev. bibl, illus.

RUSSIAN SERIES ON SOCIAL HISTORY. see *HISTORY — History Of Asia*

300.7 UK
S S R C STUDENTSHIP HANDBOOK; postgraduate studentships in the social sciences. 1970. a. free. Social Science Research Council, 1 Temple Ave., London EC4Y 0BD, England.
Formerly: Social Science Research Council (Gt. Brit.) Postgraduate Studentships in the Social Sciences.

300 SX
S.W.A. SCIENTIFIC SOCIETY. JOURNAL. Title varies: South West Africa Scientific Society Journal. (Text in English, Afrikaans or German) 1926. a. membership. S.W.A. Scientific Society, Box 67, Windhoek, South West Africa. illus.

300 US
SAGE CONTEMPORARY SOCIAL SCIENCE ANTHOLOGIES. 1978. irreg. $4.95. Sage Publications, Inc., 275 S. Beverly Dr., Beverly Hills, CA 90212 (And Sage Publications, Ltd., 28 Banner St., London EC1Y 8QE, England) (back issues avail.)

300 US
SAGE CONTEMPORARY SOCIAL SCIENCE ISSUES. 1974. irreg., 47 vols., 1978. $4.50. Sage Publications, Inc., 275 S. Beverly Dr., Beverly Hills, CA 90212 (And Sage Publications, Ltd., 28 Banner St., London EC1Y 8QE, England) (back issues avail.)

301 US
SAGE LIBRARY OF SOCIAL RESEARCH. 1973. irreg.(14-24/yr.) Sage Publications, Inc., 275 S. Beverly Dr., Beverly Hills, CA 90212 (And Sage Publications, Ltd., 28 Banner St., London EC1Y 8QE, England)

SCRIPTA HIEROSOLYMITANA. see *HUMANITIES: COMPREHENSIVE WORKS*

SERIES ON CONTEMPORARY JAVANESE LIFE. see *FOLKLORE*

300 JA
SHIMANE UNIVERSITY. FACULTY OF LAW AND LITERATURE. MEMOIRS. (Text in Japanese and English) 1973. a. Shimane University, Faculty of Law and Literature, 1060 Nishikawatsu-cho, Matsue-shi, Shimane-ken, Japan. Ed.Bd. circ. 400.

SOCIAAL-GEOGRAFISCHE STUDIEN. see *ANTHROPOLOGY*

300 900 NE ISSN 0081-0401
SOCIAAL-HISTORISCHE STUDIEN. (Text in Dutch; summaries in English or French) 1959. irreg., no. 6, 1973. price varies. (International Institute for Social History) Van Gorcum, Box 43, Assen, Netherlands.

300 IT
SOCIAL AND HUMAN FORECASTING DOCUMENTATION. (Text in English) a. (Institute for Futures Research and Education) Edizioni Previsionali, Via G. Paisiello 4, Rome, Italy.

301 CN ISSN 0316-313X
SOCIAL DEVELOPMENT. French edition: Developpement Social (ISSN 0316-3148) (Editions in English and French) 1972. irreg. (approx 4-5/yr.) membership. ‡ Canadian Council on Social Development, 55 Parkdale Avenue, Box 3505, Station C, Ottawa K1Y 4G1, Ont., Canada. Ed. Bozica Costigliola. circ. 6,000.

300 JA ISSN 0559-698X
SOCIAL DEVELOPMENT RESEARCH INSTITUTE. ORGANIZATION AND ACTIVITIES. (Text in English) irreg. Social Development Research Institute - Shakai Hosho Kenkyusho, 3-3-4 Kasumigaseki, Chiyoda-ku, Tokyo 100, Japan.

300 CN
SOCIAL SCIENCE FEDERATION OF CANADA. ANNUAL REPORT. a. free. Social Science Federation of Canada, 151 Slater St., Ottawa K1P 5H3, Canada. circ. 500.
Formerly: Social Science Research Council of Canada. Report (ISSN 0081-0452)

309.1 KO
SOCIAL SCIENCE JOURNAL. (Text in English) 1973. a. Korean National Commission for UNESCO, Box Central 64, Seoul, S. Korea. (Co-sponsor: Korean Social Science Research Council) bibl. stat.

300 US
SOCIAL SCIENCE REPORTS. 1950. irreg. price varies. Spartacus Press, Box 71, South Dartmouth, MA 02748.

300 CN ISSN 0081-0460
SOCIAL SCIENCE STUDIES. 1966. irreg. price varies. (University of Ottawa) University of Ottawa Press, 65 Hastey Ave., Ottawa, Ont. K1N 6N5, Canada.

330 II
SOCIAL SCIENCES RESEARCH SERIES. (Text in English) 1975. irreg. price varies. Indian Institute of Geography, 120/A Nehru Nagar East, Secunderabad 500026, Andhra Pradesh, India. Ed. B. N. Chaturuedi. circ. 1,000.
Supersedes: Health and Welfare of Andhra Pradesh Series (ISSN 0083-7776)

300 NR ISSN 0081-0487
SOCIAL SCIENTIST.* 1965. a. University of Ife, Economics Society, Ile-Ife, Nigeria.

300 301 UK
SOCIAL STRUCTURE AND SOCIAL CHANGE. 1977. irreg. price varies. Edward Arnold (Publishers) Ltd., 41 Bedford Square, London WC1B 3DQ, England.

300 US
SOCIAL STUDIES STUDENT INVESTIGATES. 1976. irreg. $7.97 per issue. Richards Rosen Press, 29 E. 21 St., New York, NY 10010. Ed. Ruth C. Rosen.
Grades 9-12

300 FR ISSN 0081-0894
SOCIETE DES OCEANISTES. PUBLICATIONS. 1951. irreg. price varies. Societe des Oceanistes, Musee de l'Homme, 75116 Paris, France. bk. rev. circ. 500.

SOCIOMEDICAL SCIENCES SERIES. see *MEDICAL SCIENCES*

300 320 CH
SOOCHOW JOURNAL OF SOCIAL & POLITICAL SCIENCES. 1977. irreg. $7 per no. Soochow University, Wai Shuang Hsi, Shih Lin, Taipei, Taiwan, Republic of China.

SOZIAL- UND WIRTSCHAFTSHISTORISCHE STUDIEN. see *BUSINESS AND ECONOMICS — Economic Systems And Theories, Economic History*

SOZIALWISSENSCHAFTLICHES JAHRBUCH FUER POLITIK. see *POLITICAL SCIENCE*

300 SZ
SOZIOOEKONOMISCHE FORSCHUNGEN. 1974. irreg., no. 10, 1978. price varies. Paul Haupt AG, Falkenplatz 14, CH-3001 Berne, Switzerland.

300 YU ISSN 0081-394X
SRPSKA AKADEMIJA NAUKA I UMETNOSTI. ODELJENJE DRUSTVENIH NAUKA. GLAS. (Text in Serbo-Croatian; summaries in French, English, German or Russian) 1951, N.S. irreg. price varies. Srpska Akademija Nauka i Umetnosti, Knez Mihailova 35, 11001 Belgrade, Yugoslavia (Dist. by: Prosveta, Terazije 16, Belgrade, Yugoslavia) Ed. Branislav Kojic. circ. 600. Indexed: Hist.Abstr.

300 YU ISSN 0081-3982
SRPSKA AKADEMIJA NAUKA I UMETNOSTI. ODELJENJE DRUSTVENIH NAUKA. POSEBNA IZDANJA. (Text in Serbo-Croatian; summaries in French, English, German or Russian) 1949, N.S. irreg. price varies. Srpska Akademija Nauka i Umetnosti, Knez Mihailova 35, 11001 Belgrade, Yugoslavia (Dist. by: Prosveta, Terazije 16, Belgrade, Yugoslavia) circ. 1,200. Indexed: Hist.Abstr.

300 913 720 YU ISSN 0081-4059
SRPSKA AKADEMIJA NAUKA I UMETNOSTI. ODELJENJE DRUSTVENIH NAUKA. SPOMENIK. (Text in Serbo-Croatian; summaries in French, English, German or Russian) 1950, N.S. irreg. price varies. Srpska Akademija Nauka i Umetnosti, Knez Mihailova 35, 11001 Belgrade, Yugoslavia (Dist. by: Prosveta, Terazije 16, Belgrade, Yugoslavia) circ. 1,200.

SRPSKA AKADEMIJA NAUKA I UMETNOSTI SPOMENICA. see *HUMANITIES: COMPREHENSIVE WORKS*

300 943.8 PL ISSN 0081-6574
STUDIA I MATERIALY Z DZIEJOW NAUKI POLSKIEJ. SERIA A. HISTORIA NAUK SPOLECZNYCH. (Text in Polish; summaries in English and French) 1957. irreg. price varies. (Polska Akademia Nauk, Zaklad Historii Nauki i Techniki) Panstwowe Wydawnictwo Naukowe, Ul. Miodowa 10, Warsaw, Poland. Ed. W. Voise.

STUDIES IN EAST AFRICAN SOCIETY AND HISTORY. see *HISTORY — History Of Africa*

STUDIES IN EUROPEAN POLITICS. see *POLITICAL SCIENCE*

STUDIES IN ORIENTAL CULTURE. see *HISTORY — History Of Asia*

STUDIES IN SOCIAL EXPERIMENTATION. see *SOCIOLOGY*

300 NE
STUDIES IN SOCIAL HISTORY. (Text in English) 1976. irreg. price varies. (International Institute for Social History) Martinus Nijhoff, Box 566, 2501 CN The Hague, Netherlands.

300 US
STUDIES IN THE HISTORY OF SCIENCE. vol.5, 1979. irreg. Burt Franklin & Co., Inc., 235 E. 44th St., New York, NY 10017. Ed. L. Pearce Williams.

300 NE ISSN 0081-8674
STUDIES IN THE SOCIAL SCIENCES. 1966. irreg. price varies. Mouton Publishers, Noordeinde 41, 2514 GC The Hague, Netherlands (U.S. addr: Mouton Publishers, c/o Walter de Gruyter, Inc., 200 Saw Mill River Road, Hawthorne, NY 10532)

300 SJ
SUDAN. ECONOMIC AND SOCIAL RESEARCH COUNCIL. BULLETIN. irreg. Economic and Social Research Council, Box 1166, Khartoum, Sudan.

300 SJ
SUDAN ECONOMIC AND SOCIAL RESEARCH COUNCIL. OCCASIONAL PAPER. irreg., no. 7, 1976. Economic and Social Research Council, 1Box 1166, Khartoum, Sudan. bibl.

300 SJ
SUDAN. ECONOMIC AND SOCIAL RESEARCH COUNCIL. RESEARCH REPORT. irreg.,no. 3, 1978. Economic and Social Research Council, Box 1166, Khartoum, Sudan.

SUDAN RESEARCH INFORMATION BULLETIN. see *HUMANITIES: COMPREHENSIVE WORKS*

SYNTHESE LIBRARY; monographs on epistemology, logic. methodology, philosophy of science and of knowledge, and the mathematical methods of social and behavioral sciences. see *PHILOSOPHY*

960 US
SYRACUSE UNIVERSITY. MAXWELL SCHOOL OF CITIZENSHIP AND PUBLIC AFFAIRS. FOREIGN AND COMPARATIVE STUDIES: AFRICAN SERIES. 1971. irreg., vol. 26, 1977. price varies. ‡ Syracuse University, Maxwell School of Citizenship and Public Affairs, 119 College Place, Syracuse, NY 13210. circ. 250. (processed)
Formerly (until vol. 25, 1976): Syracuse University. Program of East African Studies. Eastern African Studies.

300 PL ISSN 0082-1284
SZCZECINSKIE TOWARZYSTWO NAUKOWE. WYDZIAL NAUK SPOLECZNYCH. PRACE. (Text in Polish; summaries in English, German or Russian) 1959. irreg. price varies. Panstwowe Wydawnictwo Naukowe, Ul. Miodowa 10, Warsaw, Poland.

300 PL ISSN 0082-1292
SZCZECINSKIE TOWARZYSTWO NAUKOWE. WYDZIAL NAUK SPOLECZNYCH. WYDAWNICTWA. (Text in Polish; summaries in English or Russian) irreg. price varies. Panstwowe Wydawnictwo Naukowe, Miodowa 10, Warsaw, Poland (Dist. by Ars Polona-Ruch, Krakowskie Przedmiescie 7, Warsaw, Poland)

300 SZ ISSN 0080-7427
T.M. (Tatsachen und Meinungen) 1968. irreg., no. 41, 1978. price varies. Schweizerisches Ost-Institut - Swiss Eastern Institute, Jubilaeumsstr. 41, CH-3000 Berne 6, Switzerland.

300 HU ISSN 0082-1748
TARSADALOMTUDOMANYI KISMONOGRAFIAK. 1961. irreg. price varies. (Magyar Tudomanyos Akademia) Akademiai Kiado, Publishing House of the Hungarian Academy of Sciences, P.O. Box 24, H-1363 Budapest, Hungary.

300 NE
THEORY AND DECISION LIBRARY; an international series in the philosophy and methodology of the social and behavioral sciences. (Text in English) 1973. irreg. price varies. D. Reidel Publishing Co., P.O. Box 17, 3300 AA Dordrecht, Netherlands (And Lincoln Building, 160 Old Derby St., Hingham, MA 02043) Eds. Gerald Eberlein, Werner Leinfellner.

300 NO ISSN 0040-716X
TIDSSKRIFT FOR SAMFUNNSFORSKNING/ NORWEGIAN JOURNAL OF SOCIAL RESEARCH. (Text in Scandinavian languages; summaries in English) 1960. irreg. (6-8/yr.) Kr.140($28) Universitetsforlaget, Kolstadgt. 1, Box 2959-Toeyen, Oslo 6, Norway (Box 258, Irvington-on-Hudson, NY 10533) Ed. Dag Gjestland. adv. bk. rev. bibl. charts. stat. index. circ. 1,550. Indexed: SSCI.

TOPIC; a journal of the liberal arts. see *HUMANITIES: COMPREHENSIVE WORKS*

300 GW
TRANSFINES. 1977. irreg., no.15, 1979. price varies. Verlag Anton Hain GmbH, Adelhardstr. 2, Postfach 1220, 6240 Koenigstein, W. Germany (B.R.D.) Ed. Bd.
Formerly: Internationes.

300 SZ ISSN 0082-6022
TRAVAUX DE DROIT, D'ECONOMIQUE DE SOCIOLOGIE ET DE SCIENCES POLITIQUES. (Text in French, English) 1963. irreg. price varies. Librarie Droz, 11 rue Massot, 1211 Geneva, Switzerland. Ed. G. Busino. circ. 1,000.

300 GW
TUDUV-STUDIEN. REIHE SOZIALWISSENSCHAFTEN. 1976. irreg. price varies. Tuduv-Verlagsgesellschaft, Gabelsbergerstr. 15, 8000 Munich 2, W. Germany (B.R.D.)

300 UN
UNITED NATIONS RESEARCH INSTITUTE FOR SOCIAL DEVELOPMENT. RESEARCH NOTES. (Text in English) 1968. irreg.; latest issue 1974. United Nations Research Institute for Social Development, Palais des Nations, CH-1211 Geneva 10, Switzerland. Ed. Bd. bibl. charts. stat.

300 PE
UNIVERSIDAD DEL PACIFICO. CENTRO DE INVESTIGACION. SERIE: ENSAYOS. 1973. irreg; no. 12, sept. 1975. Universidad del Pacifico, Centro de Investigacion, Lima, Peru.

300 PE
UNIVERSIDAD DEL PACIFICO. DEPARTAMENTO DE CIENCIAS SOCIALES Y POLITICAS. SERIE: DEPARTAMENTOS ACADEMICOS. no. 3, 1975. irreg. Universidad del Pacifico, Departamento de Ciencias Sociais y Politicas, Lima, Peru.

300 CK
UNIVERSIDAD NACIONAL DE COLOMBIA. DIRECCION DE DIVULGACION CULTURAL. REVISTA. 1968. irreg. exchange basis. Universidad Nacional de Colombia, Direccion de Divulgacion Cultural, Apartado Aereo 14490, Bogota, D.E., Colombia. circ. 5,000.

300 CL
UNIVERSIDAD TECNICA DEL ESTADO. REVISTA. 1970. irreg. $4. Universidad Tecnica del Estado, Avda. Ecuador 3469, Correo 2, Santiago, Chile. illus.

500 BL
UNIVERSIDADE DO AMAZONAS. CENTRO DE PESQUISAS SOCIO-ECONOMICAS. BOLETIM TECNICO INFORMATIVO.* irreg. Universidade do Amazonas, Centro de Pesquisas Socio-Economicas, Divisao de Documentacao, Rua S. Bolivar 245, Caixa Postal 378, Manaus, Amazonas, Brazil.

300 100 BL ISSN 0041-8870
UNIVERSIDADE FEDERAL DO CEARA. DEPARTAMENTO DE CIENCIAS SOCIAIS E FILOSOFIA. DOCUMENTOS. (Text in English & Portuguese; summaries in English) 1967. irreg.; vol. 8, no. 2, 1977. Cr.$5.($6.) (Universidade Federal do Ceara, Departamento de Ciencias Sociais e Filosofia) Imprensa Universitaria do Ceara, 2762 Avda. da Universidade, C.P. 1257, Fortaleza BR Ceara, Brazil. Ed. Paulo Elpidio De Menezes Neto. adv. circ. 2,000.

300 BL
UNIVERSIDADE FEDERAL DO RIO GRANDE DO SUL. INSTITUTO DE FILOSOFIA E CIENCIAS HUMANAS. REVISTA. 1973. irreg. exchange basis. Universidade Federal do Rio Grande do Sul, Instituto de Filosofia e Ciencias Humanas, Porto Alegre, Rio Grande do Sul, Brazil. illus.

301.3 FR ISSN 0065-4949
UNIVERSITE D'AIX-MARSEILLE I. CENTRE D'ETUDES DES SOCIETES MEDITERRANEENNES. CAHIERS. 1966. a. Universite d'Aix-Marseille I (Universite de Provence), Centre d'Etudes des Societes Mediterraneenes, Service des Publications, 13621 Aix en Provence, France.

300 HT
UNIVERSITE D'ETAT. FACULTE D'ETHNOLOGIE. CENTRE DE RECHERCHES EN SCIENCES HUMAINES ET SOCIALES. REVUE. no. 26, 1975. irreg. Universite de l'Etat, Faculte d'Ethnologie, Centre de Recherches en Sciences Humaines et Sociales, Place des Heros de l'Independance, Port-au-Prince, Haiti.

UNIVERSITE DE DAKAR. FACULTE DES LETTRES ET SCIENCES HUMAINES. ANNALES. see *LITERATURE*

300 SZ ISSN 0075-8191
UNIVERSITE DE LAUSANNE. ECOLE DES SCIENCES SOCIALES ET POLITIQUES. PUBLICATIONS. 1970. irreg., no. 9, 1972. price varies. Librarie Droz, 11, rue Massot, 1211 Geneva 12, Switzerland. circ. 1,000.

300 400 FR ISSN 0078-9895
UNIVERSITE DE PARIS. FACULTE DES LETTRES ET SCIENCES HUMAINES. PUBLICATIONS. SERIE RECHERCHES. 1961. irreg. price varies. Presses Universitaires de France, 108 Bd. Saint Germaine, 75279 Paris Cedex 6, France (Service des Periodiques, 12 rue Jean de Beauvais, 75005 Paris)

300 FR ISSN 0563-9727
UNIVERSITE DES SCIENCES SOCIALES DE TOULOUSE. ANNALES. 1953. a. 25 F. Universite de Toulouse I (Sciences Sociales), Place Anatole France, 31070 Toulouse, France.

300 SA
UNIVERSITEIT VAN PRETORIA. PUBLIKASIES. NUWE REEKS. (Text in Afrikaans and English) irreg. R.1. University of Pretoria, Director of Public Relations, Hillcrest, Pretoria, South Africa.

300 US
UNIVERSITY OF CHICAGO. DIVISION OF THE SOCIAL SCIENCES. REPORTS. 1976. irreg. University of Chicago, Division of Social Sciences, Chicago, IL 60637. illus. circ. 16,000.

300 SA
UNIVERSITY OF DURBAN-WESTVILLE. INSTITUTE FOR SOCIAL AND ECONOMIC RESEARCH. ANNUAL REPORT. a. University of Durban-Westville, Institute for Social and Economic Research, Private Bag X54001, Durban 4000, South Africa.

300 900 US ISSN 0071-6197
UNIVERSITY OF FLORIDA MONOGRAPHS. SOCIAL SCIENCES. 1959. irreg. price varies. University Presses of Florida, 15 N.W. 15 St, Gainesville, FL 32603.

300 330 UK ISSN 0072-4629
UNIVERSITY OF GLASGOW. SOCIAL AND ECONOMIC RESEARCH STUDIES. 1966. irreg. price varies. ‡ Martin Robertson & Co. Ltd., 17 Quick Place, London N1 8HL, England. Ed. D. Martin.

300 330 UK ISSN 0072-4610
UNIVERSITY OF GLASGOW. SOCIAL AND ECONOMIC STUDIES. OCCASIONAL PAPERS. 1964. irreg. price varies. Oliver & Boyd, Croythorn House, 23 Ravelston Terrace, Edinburgh EH 4 3TJ, Scotland.

UNIVERSITY OF HONG KONG. CENTRE OF ASIAN STUDIES. OCCASIONAL PAPERS AND MONOGRAPHS. see *ORIENTAL STUDIES*

300 UK ISSN 0308-6119
UNIVERSITY OF LONDON. CONTEMPORARY CHINA INSTITUTE. RESEARCH NOTES AND STUDIES. 1976. irreg. price varies. University of London, School of Oriental and African Studies, Malet St., London WC1E 7HP, England.

325.3 UK ISSN 0076-0781
UNIVERSITY OF LONDON. INSTITUTE OF COMMONWEALTH STUDIES. ANNUAL REPORT. 1949/50. a. free. University of London, Institute of Commonwealth Studies, 27 Russell Sq., London WC1B 5DS, England.

300 UK ISSN 0076-0773
UNIVERSITY OF LONDON. INSTITUTE OF COMMONWEALTH STUDIES. COLLECTED SEMINAR PAPERS. 1967. irreg., no. 25, 1980. price varies. University of London, Institute of Commonwealth Studies, 27 Russell Sq., London WC1B 5DS, England. circ. 400.

325.3 UK ISSN 0076-0765
UNIVERSITY OF LONDON. INSTITUTE OF COMMONWEALTH STUDIES. COMMONWEALTH PAPERS. 1954. irreg., no. 21, 1978. price varies. Athlone Press, 90-91 Great Russell St., London WC1B 3PY, England.

300 330 AT ISSN 0076-6291
UNIVERSITY OF MELBOURNE. INSTITUTE OF APPLIED ECONOMIC AND SOCIAL RESEARCH. TECHNICAL PAPERS. 1968. irreg. price varies. University of Melbourne, Institute of Applied Economic and Social Research, Parkville, Victoria 3052, Australia.

300.7 KE
UNIVERSITY OF NAIROBI. INSTITUTE FOR DEVELOPMENT STUDIES. RESEARCH AND PUBLICATIONS. 1969. a. free. University of Nairobi, Institute for Development Studies, P.O. Box 30197, Nairobi, Kenya. circ. 2,000 (approx.)

300 SA ISSN 0070-7759
UNIVERSITY OF NATAL. INSTITUTE FOR SOCIAL RESEARCH. ANNUAL REPORT. 1958-59. a. free. University of Natal, Institute for Social Research, Durban, South Africa. Ed. L. Schlemmer. circ. 150(approx.)

300 US
UNIVERSITY OF NORTH CAROLINA, CHAPEL HILL. INSTITUTE FOR RESEARCH IN SOCIAL SCIENCE. TECHNICAL PAPERS. 1977. irreg., no. 6, 1981. I R S S Publications, Manning Hall 026A, Chapel Hill, NC 27514. Ed. Mary Ellen Marsden.

300 US
UNIVERSITY OF NORTH CAROLINA, CHAPEL HILL. INSTITUTE FOR RESEARCH IN SOCIAL SCIENCE. WORKING PAPERS IN METHODOLOGY. 1967. irreg., no. 10, 1978. I R S S Publications, Manning Hall 026A, Chapel Hill, NC 27514. Ed. Mary Ellen Marsden.

UNIVERSITY OF READING. GRADUATE SCHOOL OF CONTEMPORARY EUROPEAN STUDIES. OCCASIONAL PUBLICATION. see HISTORY — History Of Europe

UNIVERSITY OF SIND. RESEARCH JOURNAL. ARTS SERIES: HUMANITIES AND SOCIAL SCIENCES. see ART

300 BB
UNIVERSITY OF THE WEST INDIES. INSTITUTE OF SOCIAL AND ECONOMIC RESEARCH. OCCASIONAL PAPER. 1979. irreg. price varies. University of the West Indies, Institute of Social and Economic Research (Eastern Caribbean), Cave Hill, Barbados, W. Indies.

300 TR
UNIVERSITY OF THE WEST INDIES, TRINIDAD. INSTITUTE OF SOCIAL & ECONOMIC RESEARCH. OCCASIONAL PAPERS: GENERAL SERIES. 1977. irreg. price varies. University of the West Indies, Institute of Social & Economic Research, St. Augustine, Trinidad, West Indies. Eds. Jack Harewood, Marianne Remesar. charts. stat. circ. 220. (back issues avail.)

300 JA ISSN 0563-8054
UNIVERSITY OF TOKYO. INSTITUTE OF SOCIAL SCIENCE. ANNALS. (Text in English) 1953. a. free to research and educational institutions. ‡ University of Tokyo, Institute of Social Science, 7-3-1 Hongo, Bunkyo-ku, Tokyo 113, Japan. circ. 200.
Formerly: Social Science Abstracts.

300 UK ISSN 0307-0042
UNIVERSITY OF WALES. BOARD OF CELTIC STUDIES. SOCIAL SCIENCE MONOGRAPHS. 1975. irreg. price varies. (Board of Celtic Studies) University of Wales Press, 6 Gwennyth St., Cathays, Cardiff CF2 4YD, Wales. Ed. Harold Carter. (reprint service avail. from UMI)

301.4 US
UNIVERSITY OF WISCONSIN. INSTITUTE FOR RESEARCH ON POVERTY. BIBLIOGRAPHY SERIES. 1969? irreg., latest 1975. single copies free. University of Wisconsin-Madison, Institute for Research on Poverty, 1410 Social Science Bldg., 1180 Observatory Dr., Madison, WI 53706.

301.4 US
UNIVERSITY OF WISCONSIN. INSTITUTE FOR RESEARCH ON POVERTY. DISCUSSION PAPER SERIES. 1967. irreg., no. 348, 1976. single copies free. University of Wisconsin-Madison, Institute for Research on Poverty, 1410 Social Science Bldg., 1180 Observatory Dr., Madison, WI 53706.

301.4 US
UNIVERSITY OF WISCONSIN. INSTITUTE FOR RESEARCH ON POVERTY. MONOGRAPH SERIES. irreg. price varies. (University of Wisconsin-Madison, Institute for Research on Poverty) Academic Press, Inc., 111 Fifth Ave., New York, NY 10003.

301.4 US
UNIVERSITY OF WISCONSIN. INSTITUTE FOR RESEARCH ON POVERTY. SPECIAL REPORT SERIES. 1966? irreg., latest 1972. University of Wisconsin-Madison, Institute for Research on Poverty, 1410 Social Science Bldg., 1180 Observatory Dr., Madison, WI 53706.

301.45 US ISSN 0084-0769
UNIVERSITY OF WISCONSIN, MADISON. INSTITUTE FOR RESEARCH ON POVERTY. REPRINT SERIES. 1966. irreg., 1971, no. 61. free. University of Wisconsin-Madison, Institute for Research on Poverty, Social Sciences Building, 1180 Observatory Drive, Madison, WI 53706.

300 AT ISSN 0313-9921
UNIVERSITY OF WOLLONGONG. RESEARCH BULLETIN. no. 3, 1977. irreg. University of Wollongong, P.O. Box 1144, Wollongong, N.S.W. 2500, Australia.

300 ZA ISSN 0084-5108
UNIVERSITY OF ZAMBIA. INSTITUTE FOR AFRICAN STUDIES. COMMUNICATION. 1966. a. $5. University of Zambia, Institute for African Studies, Box 900, Lusaka, Zambia (Dist. by: Humanities Press, Inc., 171 First Ave., Atlantic Highlands, NJ 07016) Ed.Bd. circ. 750.

300 PL
UNIWERSYTET SLASKI W KATOWICACH. PRACE Z NAUK SPOLECZNYCH. 1975. irreg., 1976, no. 3. 32 Zl. Uniwersytet Slaski w Katowicach, Ul. Bankowa 14, 40-007 Katowice, Poland. Ed. Janusza Kolczynskiego.

URBAN HISTORY YEARBOOK. see HISTORY — History Of Europe

330 300 GW ISSN 0341-0846
VIERTELJAHRSCHRIFT FUER SOZIAL-UND WIRTSCHAFTSGESCHICHTE. BEIHEFTE. irreg., vol. 71, 1981. price varies. Franz Steiner Verlag GmbH, Friedrichstr. 24, Postfach 5529, 6200 Wiesbaden, W. Germany (B.R.D.)

VIETNAMESE STUDIES. see HISTORY — History Of Asia

300 060 FR ISSN 0083-6672
VISITI IZ SARSELIU. (Text in Ukrainian) 1963. irreg., no. 16, 1974. $2. Societe Scientifique Sevcenko, 29, rue des Bauves, 95200 Sarcelles, France. circ. 1,000.

300 GW
WERKSTATTPAPIERE; zur Analyse und Planung gesellschaftlicher Veraenderungen. 1972. irreg., no. 9, 1978. price varies. Verlag Anton Hain GmbH, Adelheidstr. 2, Postfach 1220, 6240 Koenigstein, W. Germany (B.R.D.) Ed. Helmut Klages.

300 US ISSN 0081-8682
WEST GEORGIA COLLEGE STUDIES IN THE SOCIAL SCIENCES. 1962. a. $3. West Georgia College, Division of Social Sciences, Carrollton, GA 30117. Ed. John C. Upchurch. adv. bk. rev. bibl. circ. 500.

300 US
WESTERN SOCIAL SCIENCE ASSOCIATION MONOGRAPH SERIES. irreg. Western Social Science Association, Social Science Bldg., Colorado State University, Fort Collins, CO 80523. bibl.

300 US ISSN 0512-4859
WILLIAM D. CARMICHAEL JR. LECTURE SERIES. irreg. North Carolina State University, Raleigh, NC 27607 (Order from: Box 5067, Raleigh, N. C. 27607)

300 US ISSN 0084-3326
YALE FASTBACKS. 1970. irreg., no.22,1980. price varies. Yale University Press, 92A Yale Sta., New Haven, CT 06520.

950 US ISSN 0513-4501
YALE SOUTHEAST ASIA STUDIES. MONOGRAPH SERIES. 1961. irreg., no. 20, 1976. Yale University, Southeast Asia Studies, 77 Prospect St., New Haven, CT 06520 (Dist. by: Cellar Book Shop, 18090 Wyoming, Detroit, MI 48221)

300 US ISSN 0084-4209
YIVO ANNUAL OF JEWISH SOCIAL SCIENCE. 1946. irreg; vol. 16, 1976. $15. Yivo Institute for Jewish Research, 1048 Fifth Ave., New York, NY 10028. Ed. David Roskies. index. circ. 1,500. Indexed: Hist.Abstr. Amer.Hist.&Life.

300 US ISSN 0084-4217
YIVO BLETER/YIVO PAGES. (Text in Yiddish; summaries in English) 1931. irreg; vol. 45, 1975. $10. Yivo Institute for Jewish Research, 1048 Fifth Ave., New York, NY 10028. Ed. Joshua A. Fishman. bk. rev. circ. 1,500. Indexed: Hist.Abstr. Amer.Hist.&Life.

100 300 JA ISSN 0513-5621
YOKOHAMA NATIONAL UNIVERSITY. HUMANITIES. SECTION 1: PHILOSOPHY AND SOCIAL SCIENCES/YOKOHAMA KOKURITSU DAIGAKU JIMBUN KIYO DAI-1-RUI, TETSUGAKU, SHAKAI KAGAKU. (Text in Japanese; summaries in English) 1953. a. Yokohama National University, Department of Sociology, 41 Shimizugaoka, Minami-ku, Yokohama 232, Japan.

SOCIAL SCIENCES: COMPREHENSIVE WORKS — Abstracting, Bibliographies, Statistics

300 016 US ISSN 0093-9188
ALTERNATIVES IN PRINT; an international catalog of books, pamphlets, periodicals and audiovisual materials. 1971. biennial. $39.95. (American Library Association, Social Responsibilities Round Table, Task Force on Alternatives in Print) Neal-Schuman Publishers, Inc., 64 University Place, New York, NY 10003 (Published outside North America by: Mansell Publishing Ltd., 3 Bloomsbury Place, London WC14 2QA, England) Ed.Bd.

016 300 II ISSN 0066-8478
ASIAN SOCIAL SCIENCE BIBLIOGRAPHY WITH ANNOTATIONS AND ABSTRACTS. (Text in English) 1952. a. Rs.85. (Institute of Economic Growth, Delhi) Vikas Publishing House Pvt. Ltd., Vikas House, 20/4 Industrial Area, Sahibabad, Distt. Ghaziabad U.P., India (Dist. by: UBS Publishers' Distributors Ltd., 5 Ansari Rd., New Delhi 110002, India) Ed. N. K. Goil.
Formerly: Southern Asia Social Science Bibliography.

300 314 BE ISSN 0067-5563
BELGIUM. INSTITUT NATIONAL DE
STATISTIQUE. STATISTIQUES SOCIALES.
(Text in Dutch and French) 1970. irreg. (1-4/yr.)
200 Fr. Institut National de Statistique, 44 rue de
Louvain, 1000 Brussels, Belgium.

300 016
BIBLIOGRAPHIE COURANTE D'ARTICLES DE
PERIODIQUES POSTERIEURS A 1944 SUR LES
PROBLEMES POLITIQUES, ECONOMIQUES
ET SOCIAUX/INDEX TO POST-1944
PERIODICAL ARTICLES ON POLITICAL,
ECONOMIC AND SOCIAL PROBLEMS. 1968.
a. (Fondation Nationale des Sciences Politiques,
FR) G.K. Hall & Co., 70 Lincoln St., Boston, MA
02111.

300 016 SZ ISSN 0067-6977
BIBLIOGRAPHIE DER SOZIALETHIK. 1956.
biennial. 80 Fr. Union de Fribourg, Institut
International des Sciences Sociales et Politiques,
Kleinschoenberg 10, CH-1700 Fribourg,
Switzerland. Eds. Arthur Utz, Brigitta von Galen,
Peter Paul Mueller. bk. rev. circ. 2,000.

300 US
BOOK REVIEW INDEX TO SOCIAL SCIENCE
PERIODICALS. a. $45. Pierian Press, 5000
Washtenaw Ave., Ann Arbor, MI 48104.

016 300 US
CLIO BIBLIOGRAPHY SERIES. 1972. irreg., no.
8,1981. price varies. American Bibliographical
Center-Clio Press, 2040 Alameda Padre Serra, Box
4397, Santa Barbara, CA 93103. Ed. Eric H.
Boehm.

D D R-PUBLIKATIONEN ZUR
IMPERIALISMUSFORSCHUNG,
AUSWAHLBIBLIOGRAPHIE. see *POLITICAL
SCIENCE — Abstracting, Bibliographies, Statistics*

011 II
I C S S R UNION CATALOGUE OF SOCIAL
SCIENCE PERIODICALS/SERIALS. (Text in
English) 1973. irreg. Rs.1530($460) (Indian Council
of Social Science Research) Social Science
Documentation Centre, 35 Ferozshah Rd., New
Delhi 110001, India. Ed. S. P. Agrawal. bibl. index.
circ. 1,000.

300 016 II
INDEX TO INDIAN PERIODICAL LITERATURE.
1963. a. Rs.100($30) Indian Documentation Service,
Nai Subzi Mandi, Gurgaon 122001, Haryana, India.
Ed. Satya Prakash.

300 011 TH ISSN 0125-5827
INDEX TO THAI PERIODICAL LITERATURE.
(Text in Thai) 1964. a. price varies. National
Institute of Development Administration, Library
and Information Center, Klongjan, Bangkapi,
Bangkok 24, Thailand. index. circ. 500.

016.3091 II
INDIA. MINISTRY OF EDUCATION AND
SOCIAL WELFARE. DEPARTMENT OF
SOCIAL WELFARE. DOCUMENTATION
SERVICE BULLETIN. 1968. a. free. ‡ Ministry of
Education and Social Welfare, Department of Social
Welfare, Shastri Bhavan, New Delhi 110001, India.
circ. controlled.

300 016 CK
INDICE DE ARTICULOS DE PUBLICACIONES
PERIODICAS EN EL AREA DE CIENCIAS
SOCIALES Y HUMANIDADES. 1975. irreg.
Instituto Colombiano para el Fomento de la
Educacion Superior, Division de Documentacion y
Fomento Bibliotecario, Bogota, Colombia.

300 016 UK ISSN 0076-051X
LONDON BIBLIOGRAPHY OF THE SOCIAL
SCIENCES. 1931. irreg. price varies. (British
Library of Political and Economic Science) Mansell
Publishing, 3 Bloomsbury Place, London WC1A
2QA, England (Dist. in U.S. by: Mansell, 22 S.
Broadway, Salem, NH 03079)
Subject catalog of the Library

300 NE ISSN 0077-6726
NETHERLANDS. CENTRAAL BUREAU VOOR
DE STATISTIEK. BIBLIOGRAFIE VAN
REGIONALE ONDERZOEKINGEN OP
SOCIAALWETENSCHAPPELIJK TERREIN.
BIBLIOGRAPHY OF REGIONAL STUDIES IN
THE SOCIAL SCIENCES. (Text in Dutch and
English) 1945. a., 1978 latest supplement. fl.14.45.
Centraal Bureau voor de Statistiek, Prinses
Beatrixlaan 428, Voorburg, Netherlands (Orders to:
Staatsuitgeverij, Christoffel Plantijnstraat, The
Hague, Netherlands)

300 016 US
NEW PAGES GUIDE TO ALTERNATIVE
PERIODICALS. 1980. a. $2.50. New Pages Press,
4426 S. Belsay Rd., Grand Blanc, MI 48439. Ed.Bd.
adv. illus.

300 016 II
PERIODICAL LITERATURE ON SOCIAL
SCIENCES AND AREA STUDIES. (Part 1:
Theoretical Studies; Part 2: Area Studies) (Text in
English) 1973. a. Jawaharlal Nehru University,
Library, New Mahrauli Rd., New Delhi 110057,
India.

016 300 KE
SOME CURRENT RESEARCH IN EAST AFRICA.
1964. irreg. East African Staff College, Box 30005,
Nairobi, Kenya.

960 US
SYRACUSE UNIVERSITY. FOREIGN AND
COMPARATIVE STUDIES. AFRICAN SERIES.
1977. irreg., no. 35, 1980. price varies. Syracuse
University, Foreign and Comparative Studies, 119
College Place, Syracuse, NY 13210.

972 US
SYRACUSE UNIVERSITY. FOREIGN AND
COMPARATIVE STUDIES. LATIN AMERICAN
SERIES. 1980. irreg., no. 2, 1981. price varies.
Syracuse University, Foreign and Comparative
Studies, 119 College Place, Syracuse, NY 13210.

950 US
SYRACUSE UNIVERSITY. FOREIGN AND
COMPARATIVE STUDIES. SOUTH ASIAN
SERIES. 1976. irreg., no. 6, 1980. price varies.
Syracuse University, Foreign and Comparative
Studies, 119 College Place, Syracuse, NY 13210.

950 US
SYRACUSE UNIVERSITY. FOREIGN AND
COMPARATIVE STUDIES. SOUTH ASIAN
SPECIAL PUBLICATIONS. 1976. irreg., no. 2,
1978. price varies. Syracuse University, Foreign and
Comparative Studies, 119 College Place, Syracuse,
NY 13210.

016 US ISSN 0565-0828
U.S. BUREAU OF THE CENSUS. CENSUS
BUREAU METHODOLOGICAL RESEARCH.
irreg. U.S. Bureau of the Census, Washington, DC
20233 (Orders to: Supt. of Documents, Washington,
DC 20402) Key Title: Census Bureau
Methodological Research.
Annotated list of papers and reports

300 015 JM
UNIVERSITY OF THE WEST INDIES. INSTITUTE
OF SOCIAL AND ECONOMIC RESEARCH.
OCCASIONAL BIBLIOGRAPHY SERIES. 1974.
irreg. University of the West Indies, Institute of
Social and Economic Research, Mona 7, Kingston,
Jamaica.

300 UN ISSN 0084-1870
WORLD LIST OF SOCIAL SCIENCE
PERIODICALS. (Text in English and French) irreg.
$12. Unesco, 7-9 Place de Fontenoy, 75700 Paris,
France (Dist. in U.S. by: Unipub, 345 Park Ave. S.,
New York NY 10010)

SOCIAL SERVICES AND WELFARE

*see also Blind; Deaf; Drug Abuse and
Alcoholism; Public Health and Safety*

353.9 US ISSN 0094-1174
ALASKA. DIVISION OF FAMILY AND
CHILDREN SERVICES. ANNUAL REPORT. a.
Division of Family and Children Services, Juneau,
AK 99801. illus. stat. Key Title: Annual Report -
Division of Family and Children Services (Juneau)

362.8 US ISSN 0362-6849
ALASKA NATIVE MEDICAL CENTER. ANNUAL
REPORT. a. Alaska Native Medical Center, Box 7-
741, Anchorage, AK 99510. illus. Key Title: Annual
Report - Alaska Native Medical Center.

360 US
ALBANY BULLETIN ON HEALTH AND
WELFARE LEGISLATION. 1927. w. during
legislative session. $50. State Communities Aid
Association, 105 E. 22nd St., New York, NY
10010. Ed. Beekman H. Pool.

360 614 CN ISSN 0381-4327
ALBERTA. DEPARTMENT OF SOCIAL
SERVICES AND COMMUNITY HEALTH.
ANNUAL REPORT. 1972. a. free. Department of
Social Services and Community Health, Seventh St.
Plaza, 11th Floor, 10030 107th St., Edmonton, Alta.
T5J 3E4, Canada. circ. 300.
Formerly: Alberta. Department of Health and
Social Development. Annual Report (ISSN 0084-
6163)

ALBERTA. HEALTH AND SOCIAL SERVICES
DISCIPLINES COMMITTEE. ANNUAL
REPORT. see *PUBLIC HEALTH AND SAFETY*

362.41 US ISSN 0065-7395
AMERICAN ASSOCIATION OF WORKERS FOR
THE BLIND. PROCEEDINGS. biennial. $4 to
non-members. American Association of Workers for
the Blind, Inc., 637 Investment Bldg., 1511 K St.
N.W., Washington, DC 20005. Ed. Teresa M.
DeFerrari.

362.41 US ISSN 0065-8359
AMERICAN FOUNDATION FOR THE BLIND.
ANNUAL REPORT. 1923. a. free. ‡ American
Foundation for the Blind, Inc., 15 W. 16 St, New
York, NY 10011. (also avail. in microfiche; reprint
service avail. from UMI)

361.7 US ISSN 0071-9617
AMERICAN FRIENDS SERVICE COMMITTEE.
ANNUAL REPORT. 1917. a. free to contributors.
‡ American Friends Service Committee, 1501
Cherry St., Philadelphia, PA 19102.

361 US
AMERICAN HUMANE ASSOCIATION.
NATIONAL SYMPOSIUM ON CHILD ABUSE.
INTERDISCIPLINARY PAPERS. no. 4, 1974.
irreg., 5th latest. $2. American Humane Association,
Children's Division, 5351 S. Roslyn St., Englewood,
CO 80111.

361.7 US
AMERICAN HUMANE ASSOCIATION ANNUAL
REPORT. 1952. a., 1974. ‡ American Humane
Association, 5351 S. Roslyn, Englewood, CO
80110. Ed. Warren Northwood. circ. 15,000.
Formerly: American Humane Association.
National Humane Report (ISSN 0065-8596)

361.6 US ISSN 0163-8300
AMERICAN PUBLIC WELFARE ASSOCIATION.
W-MEMO. 1975. 35/yr. $50. American Public
Welfare Association, 1125 15th St. N.W.,
Washington, DC 20005. (looseleaf format)

361 US
AMERICAN RED CROSS. ANNUAL REPORT.
1901. a. free. ‡ American Red Cross, 17th and D
Sts., N.W., Washington, DC 20006. circ. 30,000.
Formerly: American National Red Cross. Annual
Report (ISSN 0080-0384)

360 368.4 US ISSN 0191-118X
ANALYSIS OF WORKERS' COMPENSATION
LAWS. a. Chamber of Commerce of the U.S., 1615
H St., N.W., Washington, DC 20062.
Formerly: Analysis of Workmen's Compensation
Laws (ISSN 0577-5183)

ANNUAIRE H L M. (Habitations a Loyer Modere)
see *HOUSING AND URBAN PLANNING*

SOCIAL SERVICES AND WELFARE

309.1   US   ISSN 0094-9183
ANNUAL EDITIONS: READINGS IN SOCIAL PROBLEMS. Short title: Readings in Social Problems. a. $5.75. Dushkin Publishing Group, Guilford, CT 06437. illus.

361.3   AG
APUNTES DE TRABAJO SOCIAL. 1975. irreg. Editorial Ecro, Lavalle 2327, Buenos Aires, Argentina.

353.9 610   US
ARKANSAS. DIVISION OF REHABILITATION SERVICES. ANNUAL REPORT. 1940. a. Division of Rehabilitation Services, Box 3781, Little Rock, AR 72203. illus. stat. circ. 1,000.
Rehabilitation

368.4   AT
AUSTRALIAN SUPERANNUATION AND EMPLOYEE BENEFITS GUIDE. 1972. irreg.(approx. 10/yr) Aus.$220. C C H Australia Ltd., P.O. Box 230, North Ryde, N.S.W. 2113, Australia.
Formerly: Australian Superannuation and Employee Benefits Planning in Action (ISSN 0310-1347)

362.7   AU
AUSTRIA. STATISTISCHES ZENTRALAMT. JUGENDWOHLFAHRTSPFLEGE. vol. 327, 1972. a. S.65. Kommissionsverlag der Oesterreichischen Staatsdruckerei, Rennweg 12a, A-1037 Vienna, Austria.

371.3 360   IO
BALAI PENDIDIKAN VDAN LATIHAN TENAGH SOCIAL. LAPORAN. a. Balai Pendidikan dan Latihan Tenaga Sosial, Jl. Laksamana Laut R.E. Martadinata 112, Badung, Indonesia.
Study and teaching

613.62 360   BE
BELGIUM. MINISTERE DE LA SANTE PUBLIQUE ET DE LA FAMILLE. CENTRUM VOOR BEVOLKINGS- EN GEZINSSTUDIEN. TECHNISCH RAPPORT. (Text in Flemish) no. 6, 1975. irreg. Ministere de la Sante Publique et de la Famille, Cite Adinistrative de l'Etat, Quartier Vesale, B-1010 Brussels, Belgium. charts. stat.

360 614   BE
BELGIUM. MINISTERE DE LA SANTE PUBLIQUE ET DE LA FAMILLE. RAPPORT ANNUEL. 1954. a. Ministere de la Sante Publique et de la Famille, Cite Administrative de l'Etat, Bibliotheque, Quartier Vesale, 1010 Brussels, Belgium. charts. stat.

360   BL
BEMFAM. vol. 10, 1976. irreg. Sociedade Civil de Bem-Estar Familiar No Brasil, Rua das Laranjeiras 308, Rio de Janeiro, Brazil. Ed. Walter Rodrigues.

360   GW   ISSN 0067-9178
BLICK HINTER DIE FASSADE; Aspekte moderner Sozialarbeit. 1961. a. DM.90. Kodex-Verlag GmbH, Eugenstr. 16, 7000 Stuttgart 1, W. Germany (B.R.D.)

362.41   US   ISSN 0067-9186
BLINDNESS. 1964. a. $6 (free to members) American Association of Workers for the Blind, Inc., 1511 K St., Washington, DC 20005. Ed. George G. Mallinson.

361.6   BL
BRASILIA. FUNDACAO DO SERVICO SOCIAL DO DISTRITO FEDERAL. RELATORIO ANUAL DAS ATIVIDADES. a. Fundacao do Servico Social do Distrito Federal, Brasilia, Brazil.

360   BL
BRAZIL. SERVICO SOCIAL DO COMERCIO. ADMINISTRACAO REGIONAL DO ESTADO DE SAO PAULO. RELATORIA ANNUAL. 1958. a. free. ‡ Servico Social do Comercio, Administracao Regional do Estado de Sao Paulo, Rua Dr. Vila Nova, 228, Sao Paulo, Brazil. illus. circ. 2,000.

361   UK
BRITISH ASSOCIATION OF SOCIAL WORKERS. ANNUAL REPORT. 1970. a, no. 6, 1976. 50p. British Association of Social Workers, 16 Kent St., Birmingham B5 6RD, England. adv. bk. rev. bibl. tr.lit. circ. 14,000.

362.7   US   ISSN 0362-7063
CALIFORNIA. DEPARTMENT OF EDUCATION. OFFICE OF PROGRAM EVALUATION AND RESEARCH. INNOVATIVE PROGRAMS FOR CHILD CARE: EVALUATION REPORT. irreg. Department of Education, Office of Program Evaluation and Research, 721 Capitol Mall, Sacramento, CA 95814. illus. stat. Key Title: Innovative Programs for Child Care, Evaluation Report.

360   US
CAMPAIGNER. 1958. a. United Way for the Greater New Orleans Area, 211 Camp St., New Orleans, LA 70130. Ed. Margaret S. Cox. circ. 12,000.
Formerly: Torchlighter.

CANADA. DEPARTMENT OF NATIONAL HEALTH AND WELFARE. ANNUAL REPORT. see *PUBLIC HEALTH AND SAFETY*

360   CN
CANADIAN CONFERENCE ON SOCIAL DEVELOPMENT. PROCEEDINGS/COMPTE RENDU. (Text in English and French) 1938. biennial. price varies. ‡ Canadian Council on Social Development, 55 Parkdale Ave., Box 3505, Sta. C, Ottawa, Ont. K1Y 4G1, Canada.
Formerly: Canadian Conference on Social Welfare. Proceedings/Compte Rendu (ISSN 0068-8509)

300   CN   ISSN 0068-8584
CANADIAN COUNCIL ON SOCIAL DEVELOPMENT. ANNUAL REPORT/ RAPPORT ANNUEL. (Text in English and French) 1920. a. membership. Canadian Council on Social Development, 55 Parkdale Ave., Box 3505, Station C, Ottawa, Ont. K1Y 4G1, Canada. Ed. Bozica Costigliola. circ. 6,000.

CANADIAN NATIONAL INSTITUTE FOR THE BLIND. NATIONAL ANNUAL REPORT. see *BLIND*

362.4 616.8   CN   ISSN 0068-9424
CANADIAN PARAPLEGIC ASSOCIATION. ANNUAL REPORT. 1946. a. ‡ Canadian Paraplegic Association, 520 Sutherland Drive, Toronto, Ont. M4G 3V9, Canada.

CANADIAN PERSPECTIVE. see *BUSINESS AND ECONOMICS — Labor And Industrial Relations*

361.5   CN   ISSN 0068-9572
CANADIAN RED CROSS SOCIETY. ANNUAL REPORT. (Text in English and French) 1914. a. free. ‡ Canadian Red Cross Society, National Headquarters, 95 Wellesley St. E., Toronto, Ont M4Y 1H6, Canada. circ. 6,000.

CARITAS INTERNATIONALIS. INTERNATIONAL YEARBOOKS. see *RELIGIONS AND THEOLOGY*

CARITAS INTERNATIONALIS. REPORTS OF GENERAL ASSEMBLIES. see *RELIGIONS AND THEOLOGY*

361   GW   ISSN 0069-0570
CARITAS; JAHRBUCH DES DEUTSCHEN CARITASVERBANDES. 1968. a. DM.12.80($4) Deutscher Caritasverband, Karlstr. 40, 7800 Freiburg, W. Germany (B.R.D.)

360   AG
CENTRO LATINOAMERICANO DE TRABAJO SOCIAL. SERIE CELATS. 1976. irreg. Editorial Ecro, Lavalle 2327, Buenos Aires, Argentina.

360   UK   ISSN 0590-9783
CHARITIES DIGEST. 1882. a. £5.50. Family Welfare Association, 501-505 Kingsland Rd., London E8 4AU, England. Ed.Bd. adv. circ. 6,000. Classified digest of U.K. charities

574 530   US   ISSN 0069-2735
CHARLES F. KETTERING FOUNDATION. ANNUAL REPORT. 1961. a. free. Charles F. Kettering Foundation, 5335 Far Hills Ave., Dayton, OH 45429. Ed. Weir M. McBride. circ. 17,000.

362.7   US
CHILD WELFARE LEAGUE OF AMERICA. DIRECTORY OF MEMBER AGENCIES AND ASSOCIATE AGENCIES LISTING. (In 2 vols.) a. $10. Child Welfare League of America, Inc., 67 Irving Pl., New York, NY 10003. (reprint service avail. from UMI)
Formerly: Child Welfare League of America. Directory of Member Agencies and Associates (ISSN 0529-1674)

COLLEGES AND UNIVERSITIES WITH ACCREDITED UNDERGRADUATE SOCIAL WORK PROGRAMS. see *EDUCATION — Higher Education*

362.8 614   US   ISSN 0588-4543
COLORADO. STATE DEPARTMENT OF PUBLIC HEALTH. ANNUAL PROGRESS REPORT. STATE MIGRANT PLAN FOR PUBLIC HEALTH SERVICES. a. Department of Public Health, Denver, CO 80203. illus. stat. Key Title: Annual Progress Report. State Migrant Plan for Public Health Services.

309.2   UK   ISSN 0307-6067
COMMUNITY WORK. 1974. irreg. price varies. Routledge & Kegan Paul Ltd., Broadway House, Newtown Rd., Henley-on-Thames, Oxon. RG9 1EN, England (U.S. orders to: Routledge Journals, 9 Park St., Boston, MA 02108)

362   US   ISSN 0363-5600
COMPREHENSIVE ANNUAL SERVICES PROGRAM PLAN FOR THE STATE OF CALIFORNIA. 1976. a. Governor's Office, Sacramento, CA 95814. illus.

CONSUMERS AFFAIRS COUNCIL OF TASMANIA. ANNUAL REPORT. see *CONSUMER EDUCATION AND PROTECTION*

CONTEMPORARY EVALUATION RESEARCH. see *SOCIAL SCIENCES: COMPREHENSIVE WORKS*

360 327   FR
COUNCIL OF EUROPE. COMMITTEE OF INDEPENDENT EXPERTS ON THE EUROPEAN SOCIAL CHARTER. CONCLUSIONS. (Text in English; French edition also available) 1970. biennial. price varies. Council of Europe, Publications Section, 67006 Strasbourg, France (Dist. in U. S. by Manhattan Publishing Co., 225 Lafayette St., New York, N. Y. 10012)

360   BL
CRITICA SOCIAL. 1974. irreg. Universidade Catolica de Minas Gerais, Escola de Servico Social, Av. Dom Jose Gaspar 500, Belo Horizonte 30000, Minas Gerais, Brazil.

360   SP
CUADERNOS DE TRABAJO SOCIAL. 1973. irreg.; 1979, no. 4. price varies. (Universidad de Navarra, Escuela de Asistentes Sociales) Ediciones Universidad de Navarra, S.A., Plaza de los Sauces, 1 y 2, Baranain, Pamplona, Spain.

361   CY   ISSN 0070-2404
CYPRUS. DEPARTMENT OF SOCIAL WELFARE SERVICES. ANNUAL REPORT. (Text in Greek; summary in English available) 1952. a. free. Department of Social Welfare Services, c/o Director, Nicosia, Cyprus.

D.P.I. YELLOW PAGES. (Department of Public Institutions) see *PUBLIC ADMINISTRATION*

DELAWARE. DEPARTMENT OF HEALTH AND SOCIAL SERVICE. ANNUAL REPORT. see *PUBLIC HEALTH AND SAFETY*

353.9   US   ISSN 0090-3051
DELAWARE. DIVISION OF SOCIAL SERVICES. ANNUAL REPORT. 1970. a. free. Department of Health and Social Services, Division of Social Services, P.O. Box 309, Wilmington, DE 19899. Key Title: Annual Report of the Division of Social Services of the Department of Health and Social Services.
Report year ends June 30

SOCIAL SERVICES AND WELFARE

361 DK ISSN 0081-0584
DENMARK. SOCIALFORSKNINGSINSTITUTTET. BERETNING OM SOCIALFORSKNINGSINSTITUTTES VIRKSOMHED. Cover title: Denmark. Socialforskningsinstituttet. Socialforskningsinstituttets Virksomhed. 1960. a. price varies. Socialforskningsinstituttet - Danish National Institute of Social Research, Borgergade 28, DK-1300 Copenhagen K, Denmark.

301 DK
DENMARK. SOCIALFORSKNINGSINSTITUTTET. MEDDELELSE. 1972. irreg., no. 27, 1980. price varies. Socialforskningsinstituttet - Danish National Institute of Social Research, Borgergade 28, DK-1300 Copenhagen K, Denmark.

301 DK
DENMARK. SOCIALFORSKNINGSINSTITUTTET. PJECE. 1973. irreg., no. 8, 1978. price varies. Socialforskningsinstituttet - Danish National Institute of Social Research, 28 Borgergade, DK-1300 Copenhagen K, Denmark.

301 DK
DENMARK. SOCIALFORSKNINGSINSTITUTTET. PUBLIKATION. (Text in Danish; summaries in English) 1960. irreg., no. 94, 1979. price varies. Socialforskningsinstituttet - Danish National Institute of Social Research, Borgergade 28, DK-1300 Copenhagen K, Denmark.

301 DK
DENMARK. SOCIALFORSKNINGSINSTITUTTET. SMAATRYK. 1973. irreg., no. 10, 1977. Socialforskningsinstituttet - Danish National Institute of Social Research, Borgergade 28, DK-1300 Copenhagen K, Denmark.

301 DK
DENMARK. SOCIALFORSKNINGSINSTITUTTET. STUDIE. (Text in Danish; some with summaries in English) 1962. irreg., no. 38, 1979. price varies. Socialforskningsinstituttet - Danish National Institute of Social Research, Borgergade 28, DK-1300 Copenhagen K, Denmark.

360 DK
DENMARK. SOCIALFORSKNINGSINSTITUTTET. UNGDOMSFORLOEBSUNDERSOEGELSEN. RAPPORT. irreg. Socialforskningsinstituttet, Ungdomsforloebsundersoegelsen - Danish National Institute of Social Research, Borgergade 28, DK-1300 Copenhagen, Denmark.

301.3 361 US ISSN 0092-5470
DEVELOPMENTS IN HUMAN SERVICES SERIES. 1973. irreg., vol. 2, 1974. Human Sciences Press, 72 Fifth Ave., New York, NY 10011. Eds. H. Schulberg, F. Baker, S. Roen. index. (reprint service avail. from ISI,UMI)

360 UK
DICTIONARY OF SOCIAL SERVICES. 1971. irreg. £5 (hardcover);£2.95(paperback) National Council for Voluntary Organisations, 26 Bedford Square, London WC1B 3HU, England. Ed. Joan Clegg.

360 CN ISSN 0706-7860
DIRECTION (REGINA) 1978. irreg. Department of Social Services, 1920 Broad St., Regina, Sask. S4P 3V6, Canada. illus.

361.73 CK
DIRECTORIO NACIONAL DE INSTITUCIONES PRIVADAS FILANTROPICAS Y DE DESARROLLO SOCIAL. 1974. irreg. Accion en Colombia, Carrera 6 No. 69-A-23, Bogota, Colombia.

361.7 US ISSN 0091-1003
DIRECTORY. DIOCESAN AGENCIES OF CATHOLIC CHARITIES. UNITED STATES, PUERTO RICO AND CANADA. a. $3.50. National Conference of Catholic Charities, 1346 Connecticut Ave., N. W., Washington, DC 20036.

362 CN ISSN 0084-9871
DIRECTORY OF CANADIAN WELFARE SERVICES/REPERTOIRE DES SERVICES SOCIAUX CANADIENS. (Text in English and French) 1950. biennial (quarterly update) Can.$6.50. ‡ Canadian Council on Social Development, 55 Parkdale, Box 3505, Sta. C, Ottawa K1Y 1G1, Canada. circ. 1,500.

362 UK ISSN 0070-5268
DIRECTORY OF CHURCH OF ENGLAND SOCIAL SERVICES. biennial. Church of England, Board for Social Responsibility, Church House, Deans Yard, London, SW1P 3NZ, England.
Formerly: Directory of Church of England Moral and Social Welfare Work.

361 US ISSN 0070-5306
DIRECTORY OF COMMUNITY SERVICES IN MARYLAND. 1885. biennial. price varies. Health and Welfare Council of Central Maryland, Inc., 901 Court Square Bldg., 200 E. Lexington St., Baltimore, MD 21202. Ed. Beverly Rubenstein. index. circ. 6,000.

361.6 CN ISSN 0319-258X
DIRECTORY OF COMMUNITY SERVICES OF GREATER MONTREAL; welfare-health-recreation. (Text in English and French) 1956. biennial. Can.$10. Information and Referral Centre of Greater Montreal, 1800 Dorchester Blvd. W., Montreal H3H 2H2, Canada. circ. 4,000.
Formerly: Directory of Health, Welfare and Recreation Services of Greater Montreal (ISSN 0070-5640)

360 UK ISSN 0070-5624
DIRECTORY OF GRANT-MAKING TRUSTS. 1968. irreg. £25. Charities Aid Foundation, 48 Pembury Rd., Tonbridge TN9 2JD, Kent, England. Ed. J. D. Livingston Booth. circ. 2,000.

361.7 US ISSN 0161-2638
DIRECTORY OF JEWISH FEDERATIONS, WELFARE FUNDS AND COMMUNITY COUNCILS. 1936. a. $5. ‡ Council of Jewish Federations, 575 Lexington Ave., New York, NY 10022. index. circ. 1,000(approx.)
Formerly: Jewish Federations, Welfare Funds and Community Councils Directory (ISSN 0075-3734) List of Jewish federations, welfare funds and community councils in the U. S. and Canada

360 614 US ISSN 0419-2818
DIRECTORY OF JEWISH HEALTH AND WELFARE AGENCIES. 1952. irreg. price varies. Council of Jewish Federations, 575 Lexington Ave., New York, NY 10022.

362.8 US ISSN 0362-7179
DIRECTORY OF SERVICES FOR MIGRANT FAMILIES/DIRECTORIO DE SERVICIOS PARA FAMILIAS MIGRANTES. (Text in English and Spanish) 1975. irreg. Office of Education, Migrant Education Section, Springfield, IL 62777.

361 AT
DIRECTORY OF SOCIAL AGENCIES IN THE A.C.T. 1960. irreg. Aus.$1.50. Council of Social Service of the A.C.T., P.O. Box 195, Civic Square, A.C.T. 2608, Australia. Ed. Jean Moran.

360 614 US ISSN 0085-0012
DIRECTORY OF SOCIAL AND HEALTH AGENCIES OF NEW YORK CITY. 1883. biennial. $24. (Community Council of Greater New York, Inc.) Columbia University Press, 136 S. Broadway, Irvington-on-Hudson, NY 10533. Eds. Rowena McDade, William James Smith. circ. 7,000.

360 US ISSN 0082-2744
EAST TENNESSEE STATE UNIVERSITY. RESEARCH DEVELOPMENT COMMITTEE. PUBLICATIONS. (Former name of issuing body: Research Advisory Council) 1965. irreg., unnumbered. price varies. East Tennessee State University, Research Development Committee, Box 19450-A, Johnson City, TN 37601.

360 FR ISSN 0068-4902
ECONOMIES ET SOCIETES. SERIE P. RELATIONS ECONOMIQUES INTERNATIONALES. 1944. irreg. 42 F. Institut de Sciences Mathematiques et Economiques Appliquees, Paris, Institut Henri Poincare, 11 rue Pierre et Marie Curie, 75005 Paris, France. Dir. Jean Weiller. circ. 1,600.

360 370 UK
EDUCATION SOCIAL WORKER. 1946. a. free to qualified personnel; others £1.50. National Association of Social Workers in Education, 37 Papworth Gardens, London N7 8QP, England. Ed. Pat Ivan. adv. bk. rev. circ. 1,900.
Formerly: Education Welfare Officer (ISSN 0013-1598)

361 US ISSN 0071-0237
ENCYCLOPEDIA OF SOCIAL WORK. 1929. irreg., approx. every 6 yrs., no. 17, 1977. $42. National Association of Social Workers, Publications Department, 1425 H St. N.W., No. 600, Washington, DC 20005. Ed. John B. Turner. (reprint service avail. from UMI) Indexed: Abstr.Soc.Work.
Formerly: Social Work Year Book.

361 US ISSN 0090-4449
EVALUATION AND CHANGE. (At head of title: a Forum for Human Service Decision-Makers) 1972. irreg. price varies. Minneapolis Medical Research Foundation, Inc., 501 Park Avenue South, Minneapolis, MN 55415. (Co-sponsors: National Institute of Mental Health, Program Evaluation Resource Center) Ed. Laurence Kivens. bk. rev. illus. circ. 30,000. (back issues avail.) Indexed: Psychol.Abstr.
Formerly: Evaluation.

360 NE
FACT SHEET ON THE NETHERLANDS. (Text in English) irreg. Ministerie van Cultuur, Recreatie en Maatschappelijk Werk, Steenvoordelaan 370, Rijswijk (Z.H.), Netherlands.

FEDERATION FRANCAISE HANDISPORT. INFORMATIONS. see *SPORTS AND GAMES*

360 FI ISSN 0071-5336
FINLAND. SOSIAALI- JA TERVEYSMINISTERIO. SOSIAALISIA ERIKOISTUTKIMUKSIA/ FINLAND. MINISTRY OF SOCIAL AFFAIRS AND HEALTH. SPECIAL SOCIAL STUDIES. (Section XXXII of Official Statistics of Finland) (Text in Finnish and Swedish; summary in English) 1921. irreg. (4-6/yr.), no. 70, 1981. price varies. Sosiaali- ja Terveysministerio - Ministry of Social Affairs and Health, Snellmaninkatu 4-6, Box 267, SF-00170 Helsinki 17, Finland (Subscr. to: Government Printing Centre, Box 516, SF-00100 Helsinki 10, Finland) circ. 500.

360 FI ISSN 0071-5328
FINLAND. SOSIAALIHALLITUS. SOSIAALIHUOLTOTILASTON VUOSIKIRJA/ FINALND. NATIONAL BOARD OF SOCIAL WELFARE. YEARBOOK OF SOCIAL WELFARE STATISTICS/FINLAND. SOCIALSTYRELSEN. SOCIALVAARDSSTATISTISK AARSBOK. (Section XXI B of Official Statistics of Finland) (Text in Finnish and Swedish; summaries in English) 1959. a. Fmk.25. Sosiaalihallitus, Siltasaarenkatu 18 C, Helsinki, Finland. Ed. Kyllikki Korpi.

353.9 US ISSN 0094-6435
FLORIDA. DIVISION OF CORRECTIONS. FINANCIAL REPORT. a. Division of Corrections, Raiford, FL 32083. stat. Key Title: Financial Report of the Division of Corrections to the Department of Health and Rehabilitative Services.

360 GW ISSN 0071-7835
FORTBILDUNG UND PRAXIS. (Supplement to: Wege zur Sozialversicherung) 1949. irreg. price varies. Asgard-Verlag Dr. Werner Hippe KG, Einsteinstr. 10, Postfach 3080, 5205 St. Augustin 3, W. Germany (B.R.D.)

360 US ISSN 0190-3357
FOUNDATION CENTER. ANNUAL REPORT. 1956. a. free. Foundation Center, 888 7th Ave., New York, NY 10106.
Formerly: Foundation Center. Report (ISSN 0548-7269)

360 US
FOUNDATION CENTER NATIONAL DATA BOOK. 1975. a. $45. Foundation Center, 888 Seventh Ave., New York, NY 10106.

360 US
FOUNDATION GRANTS TO INDIVIDUALS. 1977. biennial. $15. Foundation Center, 888 Seventh Ave., New York, NY 10106.

352 BL
FUNDACAO DE ASSISTENCIA AOS MUNICIPIOS DO ESTADO DO PARANA. BOLETIM DOS MUNICIPIOS. 1972. irreg. free. Fundacao de Assistencia aos Municipios, Rua Voluntarios da Patria 547, Curitiba, Parana, Brazil.

SOCIAL SERVICES AND WELFARE

361.73   US
GIVING U.S.A. ANNUAL REPORT; a compilation of facts and trends on American philanthropy for the year. 1956. a. $10. ‡ American Association of Fund-Raising Counsel, Inc., 500 Fifth Ave., New York, NY 10036. Ed. Fred Schnaue. circ. 18,000.

GREAT BRITAIN. DEPARTMENT OF HEALTH AND SOCIAL SECURITY. HEALTH BUILDING NOTES. see *HOSPITALS*

GREAT BRITAIN. DEPARTMENT OF HEALTH AND SOCIAL SECURITY. HEALTH EQUIPMENT NOTES. see *HOSPITALS*

GREAT BRITAIN. DEPARTMENT OF HEALTH AND SOCIAL SECURITY. HOSPITAL IN-PATIENT INQUIRY. see *PUBLIC HEALTH AND SAFETY*

GREAT BRITAIN. DEPARTMENT OF HEALTH AND SOCIAL SECURITY. STATISTICAL AND RESEARCH REPORT SERIES. see *HOSPITALS*

368.4   UK
GREAT BRITAIN. DEPARTMENT OF HEALTH AND SOCIAL SECURITY. SOCIAL SECURITY STATISTICS. 1973. a. price varies. H.M.S.O., P.O. Box 569, London SE1 9NH, England. illus. stat.

362   UK   ISSN 0072-8756
GUIDE TO THE SOCIAL SERVICES. 1882. a. £5.50. ‡ Family Welfare Association, 501-505 Kingsland Rd., London E8 4AU, England. circ. 12,500

361.7   US
HARRY FRANK GUGGENHEIM FOUNDATION. REPORT. 1974. irreg. Harry Frank Guggenheim Foundation, 120 Broadway, New York, NY 10005.

362.6   US   ISSN 0090-2233
HAWAII. COMMISSION ON AGING. REPORT OF ACHIEVEMENTS OF PROGRAMS FOR THE AGING. (Report year ends June 30) 1970/71. biennial. Commission on Aging, 1149 Bethel St., Room 307, Honolulu, HI 96813. Key Title: Report of Achievements of Programs for the Aging.

362.7   US   ISSN 0362-6296
HAWAII DEPARTMENT OF HEALTH. MENTAL HEALTH SERVICES FOR CHILDREN AND YOUTH; children's MH services branch. a. Department of Health, Mental Health Division, Box 3378, Honolulu, HI 96801. stat. Key Title: Mental Health Services for Children and Youth.

362.2   US
HAWAII DEPARTMENT OF HEALTH. MENTAL HEALTH STATISTICAL SECTION. PSYCHIATRIC OUTPATIENT, INPATIENT AND COMMUNITY PROGRAMS. 1962. a. free. Department of Health, Mental Health Division, P.O. Box 3378, Honolulu, HI 96801.
     Formerly: Hawaii. Department of Health. Mental Health Statistical Section Psychiatric Outpatient Program (ISSN 0073-1048)

HAWAII. DEPARTMENT OF HEALTH. WAIMANO TRAINING SCHOOL AND HOSPITAL DIVISION (REPORT) see *HOSPITALS*

362 618.92   US
HAWAII. FAMILY HEALTH SERVICES DIVISION. CRIPPLED CHILDREN SERVICES BRANCH. REPORT. a. free. Department of Health, Family Health Services Division, Box 3378, Honolulu, HI 96801.
     Formerly: Hawaii. Children's Health Services Division. Crippled Children Branch Report (ISSN 0073-1013)

360   US
HEALTH, UNITED STATES. a. U. S. National Center for Health Statistics, Scientific and Technical Information Branch, 3700 East-West Highway, Hyattsville, MD 20782. (Co-sponsor: U.S. National Center for Health Services Research)

360   US
HOME CARE SERVICES IN NEW YORK STATE. Variant title: Directory of Home Care Services in New York. 1979. a. Office of Health Systems Management, Tower Bldg., Gov. Nelson A. Rockefeller Empire State Plaza, Albany, NY 12237.

361.6   HO
HONDURAS. SECRETARIA DE TRABAJO Y PREVISION SOCIAL. BOLETIN DE ESTADISTICAS LABORALES. a. Secretaria de Trabajo y Prevision Social, Tegucigalpa, Honduras.

365.6   US   ISSN 0094-0763
HUBER LAW SURVEY. irreg. Division of Corrections, Office of Information Management, Box 7925, Madison, WI 53707. stat.

360   PR   ISSN 0441-4144
HUMANIDAD. 1967. a. $2. Universidad de Puerto Rico, Escuela Graduada de Trabajo Social, Rio Piedras, PR 00931. Ed. Carmen F.Q. Rodriquez. bibl. cum. index: vols. 1-8, 1967-1974. circ. 2,000.

361   US   ISSN 0098-8278
I A S S W DIRECTORY; MEMBER SCHOOLS AND ASSOCIATIONS. irreg. International Association of Schools of Social Work, 345 E. 46th St., New York, NY 10017. Key Title: I A S S W Directory.
     Continues: International Association of Schools of Social Work. Directory of Members and Constitution.

362   US   ISSN 0361-3534
ILLINOIS. DEPARTMENT OF MENTAL HEALTH AND DEVELOPMENTAL DISABILIITIES. ANNUAL REPORT. 1917. a.(biennial until 1970) free. ‡ Department of Mental Health and Developmental Disabilities, 401 S. Spring St., Springfield, IL 62706. circ. 2,000.
     Formerly: Illinois. Department of Mental Health. Annual Report (ISSN 0073-4772)

362   US   ISSN 0091-6099
ILLINOIS. DEPARTMENT OF PUBLIC AID. ANNUAL REPORT. 1972. a. Department of Public Aid, 316 So. Second St., Springfield, IL 62762. Ed. Lois E. Rakov. circ. 10,000. Key Title: Annual Report - Illinois. Department of Public Aid.

IN A NUTSHELL. see *MEDICAL SCIENCES — Psychiatry And Neurology*

362.7   II
INDIAN COUNCIL FOR CHILD WELFARE. ANNUAL REPORT. (Text in English) a. Indian Council for Child Welfare, 4 Deen Dayal Upadhyaya Marg, New Delhi 110002, India.

INDIAN JOURNAL OF PSYCHIATRIC SOCIAL WORK. see *MEDICAL SCIENCES — Psychiatry And Neurology*

961   SG
INSTITUT FONDAMENTAL D'AFRIQUE NOIRE. RAPPORT ANNUEL. a. Institut Fondamental d'Afrique Noire, B.P. 206, Dakar, Senegal.

362.7   UY
INSTITUTO INTERAMERICANO DEL NINO. PUBLICACIONES SOBRE SERVICIO SOCIAL. irreg. Instituto Interamericano del Nino, Avda. 8 de Octubre no. 2904, Montevideo, Uruguay.

362.7   UY
INTERAMERICAN CHILDREN'S INSTITUTE. REPORT OF THE GENERAL DIRECTOR. a. Instituto Interamericano del Nino, Avda. 8 de Octubre no. 2904, Montevideo, Uruguay. illus.

361.77   SZ
INTERNATIONAL COMMITTEE OF THE RED CROSS. ANNUAL REPORT/RAPPORT D'ACTIVITE/INFORME DE ACTIVIDAD/ TAETIGKEITSBERICHT. (Text in English, French, German, and Spanish) a. 12 Fr. International Committee of the Red Cross, 17 Avenue de la Paix, 1211 Geneva, Switzerland.
     Red Cross

361   US   ISSN 0074-2961
INTERNATIONAL CONFERENCE OF SOCIAL WORK. CONFERENCE PROCEEDINGS. biennial, 18th San Juan, P.R., 1976. (International Council on Social Welfare) Columbia University Press, 136 S. Broadway, Irvington-on-Hudson, NY 10533.

360   US   ISSN 0074-3305
INTERNATIONAL CONFERENCE ON SOCIAL WELFARE. PROCEEDINGS. biennial, 1972, 16th, The Hague. International Conference on Social Welfare, 345 E. 46 St., New York, NY 10017.

360   SZ   ISSN 0074-4395
INTERNATIONAL COUNCIL OF VOLUNTARY AGENCIES. DOCUMENTS SERIES. (Text in English, French or Spanish) 1964. irreg. 5 Fr.($2.95) per no. International Council of Voluntary Agencies - Conseil International des Agences Benevoles, 17 Ave. de la Paix, 1202 Geneva, Switzerland.

360   SZ   ISSN 0074-4409
INTERNATIONAL COUNCIL OF VOLUNTARY AGENCIES. GENERAL CONFERENCE. RECORD OF PROCEEDINGS. (Issued in Council's Documents Series) 1962. irreg. International Council of Voluntary Agencies, 17 Ave. de la Paix, 1202 Geneva, Switzerland. Ed. Cyril Ritchie. adv. circ. 1,000.

360   FR   ISSN 0074-4425
INTERNATIONAL COUNCIL ON SOCIAL WELFARE. EUROPEAN SYMPOSIUM. PROCEEDINGS. (Edts. in French and English) 1959. biennial, 9th, 1977, Vienna. 25 F.($5) International Council on Social Welfare, Regional Office for Europe, Middle East and Mediterranean Area - Conseil International de l'Action Sociale, 9 rue Chardin, 75016 Paris, France.

INTERNATIONAL DIRECTORY OF PRISONERS' AID AGENCIES. see *CRIMINOLOGY AND LAW ENFORCEMENT*

361   US   ISSN 0538-9461
INTERNATIONAL RESCUE COMMITTEE ANNUAL REPORT. a. free. International Rescue Committee, 386 Park Avenue South, New York, NY 10016.

360   US   ISSN 0148-6802
INVEST YOURSELF. 1944. a. $2. ‡ Commission on Voluntary Service & Action, 475 Riverside Drive, New York, NY 10027 (Subscr. to: Invest Yourself Circulation Office, Peltoma Rd., Haddonfield, NJ 08033) Ed. Charles Hull Jacobs. circ. 10,000.

362   IS   ISSN 0075-1014
ISRAEL. CENTRAL BUREAU OF STATISTICS. DIAGNOSTIC STATISTICS OF HOSPITALIZED PATIENTS. (Subseries of its Special Series) (Text in Hebrew and English) 1950. a. price varies. Central Bureau of Statistics, Box 13015, Jerusalem, Israel.

ISRAEL SOCIETY FOR REHABILITATION OF THE DISABLED. ANNUAL. see *EDUCATION — Special Education And Rehabilitation*

362.7   JM
JAMAICA CHILDREN'S SERVICE SOCIETY. ANNUAL REPORT. a. Jamaica Children's Service Society, 79 Duke St., Kingston, Jamaica.

361   JA
JAPANESE REPORT TO THE INTERNATIONAL COUNCIL ON SOCIAL WELFARE. 1954. a. free. International Council on Social Welfare, Japanese National Committee, 3-3-4 Kasumigaseki, Chiyoda-ku, Tokyo, Japan.
     Formerly: International Conference of Social Work. Japanese National Committee. Progress Report (ISSN 0538-6039)

361   US   ISSN 0075-3742
JEWISH SOCIAL SERVICE YEARBOOK.* a. $6. Council of Jewish Federations, 575 Lexington Ave., New York, NY 10022. Ed. Alvin Chenkin.
     Analysis of service and financial statistics

360 296   US   ISSN 0021-6712
JEWISH SOCIAL WORK FORUM. 1964. a. $2. Yeshiva University, Wurzweiler School of Social Work, Alumni Association, 55 Fifth Ave., New York, NY 10003. Ed. Norman Linzer. adv. bk. rev. charts. circ. 950.

360 364.7   CN   ISSN 0225-4115
JUSTICE-DIRECTORY OF SERVICES/JUSTICE-REPERTOIRE DES SERVICES. (Text in English and French) a. Can.$15. Canadian Association for the Prevention of Crime, 55 Parkdale Ave., Ottawa, Ont. K1Y 1E5, Canada. Ed. R. Jubinville. circ. 800.
     Formerly: Directory of Correctional Services in Canada /Repertoire des Services de Correction du Canada (ISSN 0070-5381)

SOCIAL SERVICES AND WELFARE

362.7 US
KENTUCKY. DEPARTMENT OF HUMAN RESOURCES. ANNUAL REPORT. a. Department for Human Resources, Frankfort, KY 40601.
Incorporating: Kentucky. Department of Child Welfare. Annual Report.

360 KE ISSN 0075-594X
KENYA. PUBLIC SERVICE COMMISSION. ANNUAL REPORT. a. Government Printing and Stationery Department, Box 30128, Nairobi, Kenya.

KOSTEN EN FINANCIERING VAN DE GEZONDHEIDZORG IN NEDERLAND/COST OF HEALTH CARE IN THE NETHERLANDS. see PUBLIC HEALTH AND SAFETY

362 SZ ISSN 0075-708X
KRANKENHAUS-PROBLEME DER GEGENWART. 1967. irreg. price varies. Verlag Hans Huber, Laenggassstr. 76 und Marktgasse 9, CH-3000 Berne 9, Switzerland (Dist. by Williams & Wilkins Company, 428 E. Preston St., Baltimore, MD 21202) Eds. E. Haefliger, V. Elsasser.

361 US ISSN 0075-711X
KRESGE FOUNDATION. ANNUAL REPORT. 1924. a. free. Kresge Foundation, Standard Federal Savings Bldg., 2401 W. Big Beaver Rd., Box 3151, Troy, MI 48084. circ. 4,000(controlled)

361 SZ
LEAGUE OF RED CROSS SOCIETIES. BIENNIAL REPORT. (Editions in Arabic, English and French) biennial. free. League of Red Cross Societies, 17 Chemin des Crets, Petit-Saconnex, Box 276, 1211 Geneva 19, Switzerland.
Formerly: League of Red Cross Societies. Annual Report.

354 LB
LIBERIA. GENERAL SERVICES AGENCY. ANNUAL REPORT. a. General Services Agency, Box 9027, Monrovia, Liberia. stat.

354 LB
LIBERIA. MINISTRY OF LABOUR, YOUTH & SPORTS. ANNUAL REPORT. (Text in English) a. Ministry of Labour, Youth & Sports, Monrovia, Liberia. stat.

361 CN ISSN 0700-4982
LONDON COMMUNITY SERVICES DIRECTORY. 1975. a. Can.$10 (plus Can.$4 for cover) Information London, 294 Dundas St., London, Ont. N6B 1T6, Canada. circ. 600.

361.6 US ISSN 0362-8868
LOUISIANA. HEALTH AND HUMAN RESOURCES ADMINISTRATION COMPREHENSIVE ANNUAL SERVICES PROGRAM PLAN FOR SOCIAL SERVICES UNDER TITLE 20. a. Health and Human Resources Administration, Baton Rouge, LA 70804. illus. stat. Key Title: Comprehensive Annual Services Program Plan for Social Services Under Title 20.

354 CN
MANITOBA. SOCIAL SERVICES ADVISORY COMMITTEE. ANNUAL REPORT. a. free. Welfare Advisory Committee, 202-323 Portage Ave., Winnipeg, Man. R3B 2C1, Canada. Ed. Norma P. Dietz. circ. 5,000.
Formerly: Manitoba. Welfare Advisory Committee. Annual Report.

353.9 US ISSN 0095-4020
MASSACHUSETTS. DEPARTMENT OF PUBLIC WELFARE. STATE ADVISORY BOARD. ANNUAL REPORT. 1968. a. free. Department of Public Welfare, State Advisory Board, 600 Washington St., Boston, MA 02111. Ed. Raymond I. Stockwell, Jr. circ. 5,000. Key Title: Annual Report - Commonwealth of Massachusetts, Department of Public Welfare, State Advisory Board.

368.4 MF ISSN 0076-5538
MAURITIUS. MINISTRY OF SOCIAL SECURITY. ANNUAL REPORT. 1962. a, latest 1974. Rs.4. Ministry of Social Security, Port Louis, Mauritius (Orders to: Government Printing Office, Elizabeth II Ave., Port Louis, Mauritius)

360 610 US ISSN 0098-3616
MEDICAID RECIPIENT CHARACTERISTICS AND UNITS OF SELECTED MEDICAL SERVICES. (NCSS Report B-4 Supplement) a. U. S. National Center for Social Statistics, U.S. Dept. of Health, Education, and Welfare, 330 Independence Ave., S. W., Washington, DC 20201.

368.4 610 US ISSN 0091-8164
MEDICAID STATISTICS. (NCSS Report B-5) a. National Center for Social Statistics, Department of Health, Education and Welfare, 330 Independence Ave., S.W., Washington, DC 20201. stat. Key Title: Medicaid (Washington)

362 US ISSN 0076-6453
MENTAL HEALTH STATISTICS FOR ILLINOIS. 1930. a. free. ‡ Department of Mental Health and Developmental Disabilities, 401 S. Spring St., Springfield, IL 62706. circ. 1,100.
Formerly: Illinois. Department of Mental Health. Administrator's Data Manual.

353.9 US
MISSOURI. DIVISION OF YOUTH SERVICES. ANNUAL REPORT. 1955. a. free. Department of Social Services, Division of Youth Services, 402 Dix Rd., Box 447, Jefferson City, MO 65101. illus. stat. circ. 600.
Formerly: Missouri. State Division of Youth Services. Annual Report (ISSN 0098-0110)

362.1 US
MODERN NURSING HOME DIRECTORY OF NURSING HOMES IN THE UNITED STATES, U.S. POSSESSIONS AND CANADA. Title varies: Directory of Nursing Homes in the United States, U.S. Possessions and Canada. irreg. McGraw-Hill Book Co., 1221 Ave. of the Americas, New York, NY 10020 (Subscr. to: 230 W. Monroe St., Chicago, IL 60606)

353.9 US ISSN 0091-0996
MONTANA. DEPARTMENT OF SOCIAL AND REHABILITATION SERVICES. ANNUAL REPORT. (Section of: Governor's Annual Report) 1971/72. a. free. Department of Social and Rehabilitation Services, Box 4210, Helena, MT 59601. circ. 200. Key Title: Annual Report of the Department of Social and Rehabilitation Services to the Governor of Montana.
Continues: Montana. State Department of Public Welfare. Report.

362.4 UK
NATIONAL ASSOCIATION FOR DEAF/BLIND AND RUBELLA HANDICAPPED. NEWSLETTER. 1956. irreg. (approx. 3/yr.) 50p. National Association for Deaf-Blind and Rubella Handicapped, 164 Cromwell Lane, Coventry, Warwick CV4 8AP, England. Ed. Mrs. S. Brown. bibl. circ. 450 (controlled) (processed)
Formerly: National Association for Deaf/Blind and Rubella Children. Newsletter.

360 UK
NATIONAL ASSOCIATION OF ALMSHOUSES. YEARBOOK AND STATEMENT OF ACCOUNTS. a. 30p. per no. National Association of Almshouses, Wokingham, Berkshire RG11 5RU, England. Ed. Bd. stat.

301.45 361 US ISSN 0077-3352
NATIONAL ASSOCIATION OF JEWISH CENTER WORKERS. CONFERENCE PAPERS. 1962. a. $7.50. National Association of Jewish Center Workers, 15 E. 26 St, New York, NY 10010. Ed. Louis Kraft.

360 US
NATIONAL ASSOCIATION OF SOCIAL WORKERS. DIRECTORY OF AGENCIES: U.S. VOLUNTARY, INTERNATIONAL, VOLUNTARY INTERGOVERNMENTAL. 1973. irreg., 4th edt., 1980. $5.50. National Association of Social Workers, Publications Department, 1425 H St. N.W., No. 600, Washington, DC 20005. (reprint service avail. from UMI)

361.6 US
NATIONAL CONFERENCE OF STATE SOCIAL SECURITY ADMINISTRATORS. PROCEEDINGS. 1952. a. National Conference of State Social Security Administrators, P.O. Box 2543, Madison, WI 53701. circ. controlled.

360 UK
NATIONAL COUNCIL FOR VOLUNTARY ORGANIZATIONS. ANNUAL REPORT. a. 50p. National Council for Voluntary Organisations, 26 Bedford Sq, London WC1B 3HU, England. circ. 6,000.
Formerly: National Council of Social Service. Annual Report (ISSN 0077-409X)

360 UK ISSN 0077-4774
NATIONAL INSTITUTE SOCIAL SERVICES LIBRARY. 1964. irreg., no. 30, 1976. price varies. (National Institute for Social Work) George Allen & Unwin (Publishers) Ltd., 40 Museum St., London W.C.1, England.
Formerly: National Institute for Social Work Training Series.

361 US ISSN 0077-507X
NATIONAL JEWISH WELFARE BOARD. YEARBOOK. 1950-51. a. $4. National Jewish Welfare Board, 15 E. 26 St, New York, NY 10010. Ed. Morton Altman.

360 US
NATIONAL PRO-LIFE JOURNAL. 1976. irreg. Pro-Life Publications, Box 172, Fairfax, VA 22030. Ed. Audree Ryberg.

362.7 UK ISSN 0077-5754
NATIONAL SOCIETY FOR PREVENTION OF CRUELTY TO CHILDREN. ANNUAL REPORT. 1885. a. ‡ National Society for the Prevention of Cruelty to Children, 1 Riding House St., London, W1P 8AA, England. circ. 60,000.

NEPAL FAMILY PLANNING AND MATERNAL CHILD HEALTH BOARD. ANNUAL REPORT. see BIRTH CONTROL

NETHERLANDS. CENTRAAL BUREAU VOOR DE STATISTIEK. DIAGNOSESTATISTIEK BEDRIJFSVERENIGINGEN (OMSLAGLEDEN). SOCIAL INSURANCE SICKNESS STATISTICS. see INSURANCE

360 336 NE ISSN 0077-7072
NETHERLANDS. CENTRAAL BUREAU VOOR DE STATISTIEK. STATISTIEK VAN DE ALGEMENE BIJSTAND. STATISTICS OF PUBLIC ASSISTANCE. (Text in Dutch and English) 1965. a. fl.10.25. Centraal Bureau voor de Statistiek, Prinses Beatrixlaan 428, Voorburg, Netherlands (Orders to: Staatsuitgeverij, Christoffel Plantijnstraat, The Hague, Netherlands)

362 NE ISSN 0077-7099
NETHERLANDS. CENTRAAL BUREAU VOOR DE STATISTIEK. STATISTIEK VAN DE BEJAARDENOORDEN. HOMES FOR THE AGED. (Text in Dutch and English) 1950. a. fl.15.50. Centraal Bureau voor de Statistiek, Prinses Beatrixlaan 428, Voorburg, Netherlands (Orders to: Staatsuitgeverij, Christoffel Plantijnstraat, The Hague, Netherlands)

362.2 US ISSN 0098-6399
NEW JERSEY. DEPARTMENT OF HUMAN SERVICES. COMMUNITY MENTAL HEALTH PROJECTS SUMMARY STATISTICS. 1976. a. free. Department of Human Services, Division of Mental Health and Hospitals, Box 1237, Trenton, NJ 08625. Ed. Catherine Zelinski. circ. 250. Key Title: Community Mental Health Projects Summary Statistics.

353.9 US ISSN 0090-077X
NEW JERSEY. DEVELOPMENTAL DISABILITIES COUNCIL. ANNUAL REPORT. 1971. a. free. ‡ Developmental Disabilities Council, 108-110 N. Broad St., Box 1237, Trenton, NJ 08625. Ed. Virginia Morgan. circ. 2,000.
Supersedes: New Jersey Mental Retardation Planning Board. Annual Report.

NEW MEXICO. VETERANS' SERVICE COMMISSION. REPORT. see MILITARY

362.974 US ISSN 0090-4716
NEW YORK (STATE) DEPARTMENT OF SOCIAL SERVICES. BUREAU OF DATA MANAGEMENT AND ANALYSIS. PROGRAM ANALYSIS REPORT. 1954. irreg., no. 60, 1978. free. ‡ Department of Social Services, 40 N. Pearl St., Albany, NY 12243.
Formerly: New York (State) Department of Social Services. Bureau of Research. Program Analysis Report.

362.974   US   ISSN 0162-6302
NEW YORK(STATE) DEPARTMENT OF SOCIAL SERVICES. BUREAU OF DATA MANAGEMENT AND ANALYSIS. PROGRAM BRIEF. 1961. irreg. free. ‡ Department of Social Services, 40 N. Pearl St., Albany, NY 12243. Ed. Herbert Altrasso. illus. circ. 600-3,000.
  Formerly: New York (State) Department of Social Services. Bureau of Research. Program Brief. (ISSN 0361-6436)

360   NZ
NEW ZEALAND. DEPARTMENT OF SOCIAL WELFARE. REPORT. 1972. a. prices varies. Government Printing Office, Private Bag, Wellington, New Zealand. stat.

361   NZ   ISSN 0080-0392
NEW ZEALAND RED CROSS SOCIETY. REPORT. 1931. a. free. New Zealand Red Cross Society Inc., P.O. Box 12-140, Wellington North, New Zealand.

361   CN   ISSN 0078-0294
NEWFOUNDLAND. DEPARTMENT OF SOCIAL SERVICES. ANNUAL REPORT. 1950-51. a. free. Department of Social Services, St. John's, Newfoundland, Canada.

360   AU
NIEDEROESTERREICHISCHE SOZIALHILFE UND JUGENDWOHLFAHRTSPFLEGE. 1974. a. free. Amt der Niederoesterreichischen Landesregierung, Herrengasse 11-13, A-1014 Vienna, Austria. Ed. Herwig Schoen.

362.4   NR   ISSN 0078-0804
NIGERIAN NATIONAL ADVISORY COUNCIL FOR THE BLIND. ANNUAL REPORT. 1961-62. a. Nigerian National Advisory Council for the Blind, c/o Federal Ministry of Information, Lagos, Nigeria.

361.6   US   ISSN 0095-4942
NORTH CAROLINA. DEPARTMENT OF HUMAN RESOURCES. ANNUAL PLAN OF WORK. a. $10.75. Department of Human Resources, 325 N. Salisbury St., Raleigh, NC 27611. Key Title: Annual Plan of Work - Department of Human Resources.

361 362   US   ISSN 0095-6333
NORTH DAKOTA. SOCIAL SERVICE BOARD. AREA SOCIAL SERVICE CENTERS. (Subseries of: North Dakota. Social Service Board. Report) a. Social Service Board, Bismarck, ND 58501. stat. Key Title: Area Social Service Centers.

361   US   ISSN 0095-6325
NORTH DAKOTA. SOCIAL SERVICE BOARD. REPORT. irreg. Social Service Board, Bismarck, ND 58501. stat. Key Title: Report - Social Service Board of North Dakota.
  Continues: North Dakota. Public Welfare Board. Report.

353.9   US   ISSN 0094-6508
OHIO. DEPARTMENT OF MENTAL HEALTH AND MENTAL RETARDATION. ANNUAL FINANCIAL AND STATISTICAL REPORT. a. Department of Mental Health and Mental Retardation, Columbus, OH 43215.

361   US   ISSN 0078-4133
OHIO STATE UNIVERSITY. DISASTER RESEARCH CENTER. REPORT SERIES. 1968. irreg. Ohio State University, Disaster Research Center, 154 N. Oval Mall, 128 Derby Hall, Columbus, OH 43210.

360   US
OKLAHOMA. DEPARTMENT OF INSTITUTIONS, SOCIAL AND REHABILITATIVE SERVICES. ANNUAL REPORT. a. free. Public Welfare Commission, Department of Institutions, Social and Rehabilitative Services, P.O. Box 25352, Oklahoma City, OK 73125. Ed. L.E. Rader. charts, stat.
  Formerly: Oklahoma. Department of Public Welfare. Annual Report (ISSN 0078-4362)

360   US
OKLAHOMA. DEPARTMENT OF INSTITUTIONS, SOCIAL AND REHABILITATIVE SERVICES. CHART BOOK. a. Department of Institutions, Social and Rehabilitative Services, Box 25352, Oklahoma City, OK 73125. charts.

OLD AGE: A REGISTER OF SOCIAL RESEARCH. see *GERONTOLOGY AND GERIATRICS*

362.4   CN   ISSN 0700-3730
ONTARIO. ADVISORY COUNCIL ON THE PHYSICALLY HANDICAPPED. ANNUAL REPORT. 1976. a. Advisory Council on the Physically Handicapped, 801 Bay St., 3rd Floor, Toronto, Ont. M5S 1Z1, Canada. illus.

362   CN
ONTARIO. MINISTRY OF COMMUNITY AND SOCIAL SERVICES. SOCIAL ASSISTANCE REVIEW BOARD. ANNUAL REPORT OF THE CHAIRMAN. (Report Year Ends Mar. 31) a. Can.$1. Ministry of Community and Social Services, Toronto, Ont., Canada. illus.

OREGON. OFFICE OF COMMUNITY HEALTH SERVICES. LOCAL HEALTH SERVICES ANNUAL SUMMARY. see *PUBLIC HEALTH AND SAFETY*

360   DR
ORGANIZACIONES VOLUNTARIAS DE ACCION SOCIAL. CATALOGO. a. Fundacion Dominicana de Desarrollo, Apdo. Postal 857, Santo Domingo Z.P.1, Dominican Republic.

360   SP
ORIENTACION FAMILIAR. 1975. irreg.; 1979, no. 2. price varies. Ediciones Universidad de Navarra S.A., Plaza de los Sauces 1 y 2, Baranain, Pamplona, Spain.
  Family counseling

362.6   US
PENNSYLVANIA. ADMINISTRATION ON AGING. STATE PLAN ON AGING. a. Administration on Aging, Health & Welfare Bldg., Harrisburg, PA 17120.

361.6   US   ISSN 0098-8510
PENNSYLVANIA. DEPARTMENT OF PUBLIC WELFARE. PUBLIC WELFARE ANNUAL STATISTICS. 1972. a. Department of Public Welfare, Harrisburg, PA 17120. illus. Key Title: Public Welfare Annual Statistics.
  Continues: Pennsylvania. Department of Public Welfare. Public Welfare Report (ISSN 0479-8775)

361.6   US
PENNSYLVANIA. DEVELOPMENTAL DISABILITIES PLANNING COUNCIL. PENNSYLVANIA STATE PLAN. a. Developmental Disabilities Planning Council, Health & Welfare Bldg., Harrisburg, PA 17120.

362   US
PEOPLE. BIENNIAL REPORT. biennial. free. Department of Public Welfare, Centennial Bldg., St. Paul, MN 55155. bk. rev. circ. 9,000.
  Formerly: Minnesota Medical Assistance Biennial Report (ISSN 0085-347X)

360   US   ISSN 0079-1040
PERSPECTIVES IN SOCIAL WORK. 1966. irreg. ‡ Adelphi University School of Social Research, Garden City, NY 11530.

360   US
POLICY STUDIES IN EMPLOYMENT AND WELFARE. 1969. irreg., no. 29, 1977. price varies. Johns Hopkins University Press, Baltimore, MD 21218.

POLLING. see *MEDICAL SCIENCES*

301.44   US   ISSN 0091-0724
POVERTY IN SOUTH DAKOTA. a. ‡ Economic Opportunity Office, Capitol Building, 120 E. Capitol, Pierre, SD 57501. Ed. George J. Mauer. illus. stat.
  Formerly (until 1975): Annual Causes & Conditions of Poverty in South Dakota (ISSN 0091-0724)

360   US   ISSN 0163-8297
PUBLIC WELFARE DIRECTORY. 1939. a. $35. American Public Welfare Association, 1125 15th St. N.W., Washington, DC 20005. Ed. Amy Weinstein. circ. 5,000.

362   US   ISSN 0362-742X
PUBLIC WELFARE IN CALIFORNIA. a. Health and Welfare Agency, Department of Benefit Payments, 744 P St., Mail Sta. 12-81, Sacramento, CA 95814. illus.

362   UK   ISSN 0260-9584
QUAKER PEACE AND SERVICE. ANNUAL REPORT. 1927. a. free. Quaker Peace and Service, Friends House, Euston Road, London NW1 2BJ, England. Ed. Harvey Gillman. illus.
  Formerly: Friends Service Council. Annual Report (ISSN 0071-9609)

RALPH H. BLANCHARD MEMORIAL ENDOWMENT SERIES. see *INSURANCE*

361   US   ISSN 0091-2859
REGIONAL INSTITUTE OF SOCIAL WELFARE RESEARCH. ANNUAL REPORT. 1968-1969. a. free. 468 N. Milledge Ave., Box 152, Athens, GA 30603. Key Title: Annual Report - Regional Institute of Social Welfare Research.

360   NE
REGIONAL PLANNING. 1971. irreg., vol. 9, 1978. price varies. (United Nations Research Institute for Social Development, UN) Mouton Publishers, Noordeinde 41, 2514 GC The Hague, Netherlands (U.S. addr: Mouton Publishers, c/o Walter de Gruyter, Inc., 200 Saw Mill River Road, Hawthorne, NY 10532) bibl.

REPERTOIRE ADMINISTRATIF. see *POLITICAL SCIENCE*

360   PR   ISSN 0034-8937
REVISTA DE SERVICIO SOCIAL. 1940. irreg. Facultad de la Escuela de Trabajo Social, Apdo. 6679, Santurce, PR 00914. adv. bk. rev. bibl. charts. illus. index. circ. 1,000.

REVUE DU TRAVAIL. see *BUSINESS AND ECONOMICS — Labor And Industrial Relations*

360   BL   ISSN 0301-8156
RIO GRANDE DO SUL, BRAZIL. FUNDACAO DE ECONOMIA E ESTATISTICA. INDICADORES SOCIAIS. a. Cr.$45. Fundacao de Economia e Estatistica, Rua Siqueira Campos 1044, 4 Andar, Box 2355, 90000 Porto Alegre, Brazil. Ed. Edi Madalena Fracasso. (also avail. in microform)

362.1   US   ISSN 0091-3472
ROBERT WOOD JOHNSON FOUNDATION. ANNUAL REPORT. 1971. a. Robert Wood Johnson Foundation, Forrestal Center, Box 2316, Princeton, NJ 08540. Ed. Frank Kard. illus. circ. 20,000. Key Title: Annual Report-Robert Wood Johnson Foundation.

361.7   US   ISSN 0080-3391
ROCKEFELLER FOUNDATION. ANNUAL REPORT. 1914. a. free. Rockefeller Foundation, 1133 Ave. of the Americas, New York, NY 10036. index.

179.3   UK
ROYAL HUMANE SOCIETY. ANNUAL REPORT. 1774. a. free. ‡ Royal Humane Society, Watergate House, York Bldgs, Adelphi, London WC2N 6LE, England. circ. 800.

360   US   ISSN 0557-8183
RURAL ADVANCE. 1966. irreg. free. ‡ Rural Advancement Fund of the National Sharecroppers Fund, 2128 Commonwealth Ave., Charlotte, CA 28205. Ed. Bd. circ. 30,000.

361.8   US
ST. PAUL URBAN LEAGUE ANNUAL REPORT. 1924. a. free. St. Paul Urban League, 401 Selby Ave., St. Paul, MN 55102. Ed. L. G. Lambert. circ. 3,000. (tabloid format)

362.7   CN
SASKATCHEWAN. DEPARTMENT OF SOCIAL SERVICES. CHILD CARE STATISTICS. 1974. a. Department of Social Services, Regina, Sask., Canada.

360   CN   ISSN 0708-3882
SASKATCHEWAN. DEPARTMENT OF SOCIAL STATISTICS. ANNUAL REPORT. a. Department of Social Statistics, Regina, Sask., Canada. illus.

SCHOOLS OF SOCIAL WORK WITH ACCREDITED MASTER'S DEGREE PROGRAMS. see EDUCATION — Higher Education

301.3 GW ISSN 0080-7133
SCHRIFTENREIHE FUER LAENDLICHE SOZIALFRAGEN. 1951. irreg., no. 85, 1981. price varies. Agrarsoziale Gesellschaft e.V., Kurze Geismarstr. 23/25, 3400 Goettingen, W. Germany (B.R.D.) index.

360 SZ ISSN 0080-7419
SCHWEIZERISCHES SOZIALARCHIV. a. Schweizerisches Sozialarchiv, Neumarkt 28, 8001 Zurich, Switzerland.

SERIES IN CLINICAL AND COMMUNITY PSYCHOLOGY. see PSYCHOLOGY

361 CN ISSN 0317-4670
SERVICES FOR PEOPLE. 1945. a. free. Department of Human Resources, Parliament Buildings, Victoria, British Columbia, Canada.
Formerly: British Columbia. Department of Human Resources. Annual Report (ISSN 0068-1466)

360 JA
SHAKAI FUKUSHI NO DOKO. 1957. a. 320 Yen. National Council of Social Welfare - Zenkoku Shakai Fukushi Kyogikai, 3-3-4 Kasumigaseki, Chiyoda-ku, Tokyo, Japan. Ed. Yoshiyuki Kobayashi. circ. 3,000.

360 SI
SINGAPORE JOURNAL OF SOCIAL WORK. a. membership. Singapore Association of Social Workers, c/o Department of Social Work, University of Singapore, Singapore 10, Singapore.

SOCIAL SECURITY HANDBOOK. see INSURANCE

360 US
SOCIAL SERVICE DELIVERY SYSTEMS; an international annual. 1975. a. $18.50 cloth; $8.95 paper. Sage Publications, Inc., 275 S. Beverly Dr., Beverly Hills, CA 90212 (And Sage Publications, Ltd., 28 Banner St., London EC1Y 8QE, England) Eds. Daniel Thorsz, Joseph L. Vigilante. (back issues avail.)

362 US ISSN 0094-1220
SOCIAL SERVICES IN NORTH DAKOTA; annual report. 1973. a. Social Service Board, Bismarck, ND 58501.

361.6 CN ISSN 0317-4336
SOCIAL SERVICES IN NOVA SCOTIA. 1973. a. Department of Social Services, Halifax, Nova Scotia, Canada. illus. stat.
Continues: Welfare Services in Nova Scotia.

360 JA
SOCIAL WELFARE SERVICES IN JAPAN. 1960. a. 1000 Yen. International Council on Social Welfare, Japanese National Committee, 3-3-4 Kasumigaseki, Chiyoda-ku, Tokyo, Japan.

360 US ISSN 0081-055X
SOCIAL WORK AND SOCIAL ISSUES. 1969. irreg., 1977, no. 5. Columbia University Press, 136 South Broadway, Irvington-On-Hudson, NY 10533.

362.6 US
SOURCEBOOK ON AGING. 1977. irreg., 2nd edt. 1979. $39.50. Marquis Academic Media (Subsidiary of: Marquis Who's Who, Inc.) 200 E. Ohio St., Chicago, IL 60611.

SOUTH AFRICAN MEDICAL AND DENTAL COUNCIL. REGISTER OF SUPPLEMENTARY HEALTH SERVICE PROFESSIONS. see MEDICAL SCIENCES

SOUTH CAROLINA STATE PLAN FOR FRANCHISING, CONSTRUCTION AND MODERNIZATION OF HOSPITAL AND RELATED MEDICAL FACILITIES. see HOSPITALS

362.8 US ISSN 0094-372X
SOUTH DAKOTA INDIAN RECIPIENTS OF SOCIAL WELFARE. a. free. Department of Social Services, Program Analysis and Evaluation, State Office Bldg., Illinois St., Pierre, SD 57501. charts. stat.

360 SZ ISSN 0081-3249
SOZIALE SICHERHEIT; Beitraege zu ihrer Erforschung in Vergangenheit, Gegenwart und Zukunft. 1969. irreg., 1969, no. 2. price varies. Paul Haupt AG, Falkenplatz 14, 3001 Berne, Switzerland.

361 US ISSN 0585-1149
STATE COMMUNITIES AID ASSOCIATION ANNUAL REPORT. 1967. a. State Communities Aid Association, 105 E. 22nd St., New York, NY 10010. illus.
Formerly: State Charities Aid Association Annual Report.

361 US ISSN 0091-7192
STATISTICS ON SOCIAL WORK EDUCATION IN THE UNITED STATES. 1952. a. $4.50. ‡ Council on Social Work Education, 111 Eighth Ave., New York, NY 10011. circ. 1,400.
Formerly: Statistics on Social Work Education (ISSN 0081-5217)

360 NE ISSN 0039-1395
STICHTING STEDELIJKE RAAD VOOR MAATSCHAPPELIJK WELZIJN. INFORMATIE-BULLETIN. 1966. irreg. free. Stichting Stedelijke Raad voor Maatschappelijk Welzijn, Oude Boteringestraat 65, Groningen, Netherlands. Ed.Bd. bk. rev. bibl. circ. 1,500. (tabloid format)

STUDIECENTRUM VOOR JEUGDMISDADIGHEID. PUBLIKATIE/CENTRE D'ETUDE DE LA DELINQUANCE JUVENILE. PUBLICATION. see CRIMINOLOGY AND LAW ENFORCEMENT

363 378 GW
STUDIENSTIFTUNG. JAHRESBERICHT. a. free. Studienstiftung des Deutschen Volkes, Koblenzer Str. 77, 5300 Bonn 1, W. Germany (B.R.D.) illus. stat.

360 UK
STUDIES IN SOCIAL POLICY AND WELFARE. no. 6, 1978. irreg. £8. Heinemann Educational Books Ltd., 48 Charles St., London W1X 8AH, England. bibl.

SUMMARY INFORMATION ON MASTER OF SOCIAL WORK PROGRAMS. see EDUCATION — Higher Education

360 SW ISSN 0346-6019
SWEDEN. SOCIALSTYRELSEN. FOERFATTNINGSSAMLING: SOCIAL. 1976. irreg. (approx. 122/yr.) Kr.90. Socialstyrelsen - National Board of Health and Welfare, 106 30 Stockholm, Sweden. index. (looseleaf format)
Supersedes in part (1883-1976): Sweden. Medicinalvaesendet. Foerfattningssamling (ISSN 0346-5837)

360 SW
SWEDEN. SOCIALSTYRELSEN. REDOVISER. 1974, no. 36. irreg. (5-8/yr) price varies. (National Board of Health and Welfare) Liber Foerlag, Fack, S-162 89 Vaellingby, Sweden. charts. circ. 2,000.

360 US
TAFT CORPORATE FOUNDATION DIRECTORY. 1977. a. $125. Taft Corporation, 1000 Vermont Ave., N.W., Washington, DC 20005. Ed. Tara McCallum. index.

360 II
TATA INSTITUTE OF SOCIAL SCIENCES. CASE RECORDS. irreg. price varies. Tata Institute of Social Sciences, Sion-Trombay Rd., Deonar, Bombay 400008, India.

362 US ISSN 0082-3058
TEXAS. GOVERNOR'S COMMITTEE ON AGING. BIENNIAL REPORT. biennial. Governor's Committee on Aging, Box 12786, Capitol Station, Austin, TX 78711.

TRUE TO LIFE. see BIRTH CONTROL

360 US
TRUSTEES OF WEALTH; a biographical directory of private foundation and corporate foundation officers. 1975. a. $90. Taft Corporation, 1000 Vermont Ave. N.W., Washington, DC 20005. Ed. James Hickey. index. (back issues avail.)

360 US ISSN 0082-8556
U S O ANNUAL REPORT. a. free. ‡ United Service Organizations, Inc., 1146 19th St. N.W., Washington, DC 20036. Ed. Alan Krauath. circ. 15,000.

360 UN
UNITED NATIONS RESEARCH INSTITUTE FOR SOCIAL DEVELOPMENT. REPORT. 1963? irreg. (numbered within the year) unpriced. United Nations Research Institute for Social Development, Reference Centre, Palais des Nations, CH-1211 Geneva 10, Switzerland.

361.6 US ISSN 0190-373X
U.S. COMMUNITY SERVICES ADMINISTRATION. ANNUAL REPORT OF COMMUNITY SERVICES ADMINISTRATION. 1976. a. U.S. Community Services Administration, Washington, DC 20506. Key Title: Annual Report of Community Services Administration.
Formerly: U.S. Office of Economic Opportunity. Annual Report.

353.007 US ISSN 0091-6242
U.S. GENERAL SERVICES ADMINISTRATION. MANAGEMENT REPORT. a. U. S. General Services Administration, General Services Bldg., Eighteenth & F Sts., N.W., Washington, DC 20405. stat. Key Title: Management Report - General Services Administration.

360 US
U. S. NATIONAL CENTER FOR HEALTH STATISTICS. STANDARDIZED MICRO-DATA TAPE TRANSCRIPTS. a. U.S. National Center for Health Statistics, Scientific and Technical Information Branch, 3700 East-West Highway, Hyattsville, MD 20782.

362 US ISSN 0360-487X
U.S. SOCIAL AND REHABILITATION SERVICE. ANNUAL REPORT OF WELFARE PROGRAMS. a. U.S. Social and Rehabilitation Service, 330 C St., S.W., Washington, DC 20201. stat. Key Title: Annual Report of Welfare Programs.

362 US ISSN 0361-2643
U.S. SOCIAL AND REHABILITATION SERVICE. OFFICE OF MANAGEMENT. QUALITY CONTROL, STATES' CORRECTIVE ACTION ACTIVITIES. irreg. U.S. Social and Rehabilitation Service, 330 Independence Ave., S.W., Washington, DC 20201. Key Title: Quality Control: States' Corrective Action Activities.

360 US ISSN 0566-0327
U.S. SOCIAL SECURITY ADMINISTRATION. RESEARCH AND STATISTICS NOTES. irreg (1-2/mo) U.S. Department of Health, Education, and Welfare, U.S. Social Security Administration, Office of Research and Statistics, 6401 Security Blvd., Baltimore, MD 21235. stat. circ. 4,863.

360 US ISSN 0566-0335
U.S. SOCIAL SECURITY ADMINISTRATION. RESEARCH REPORT. no. 44, 1973. irreg. price varies per no. U.S. Social Security Administration, Office of Research and Statistics, 6401 Security Blvd., Baltimore, MD 21235. circ. 4,863 (controlled)

361 US
UNITED WAY OF AMERICA. INTERNATIONAL DIRECTORY. a. United Way of America, 801 N. Fairfax, Alexandria, VA 22313.
Former titles: United Way of America. Directory (ISSN 0083-3665); Directory of United Funds and Community Health and Welfare Councils (ISSN 0070-6523)

362 CN
UNITED WAY OF CANADA. DIRECTORY OF MEMBERS. (Text in French and English) 1963. irreg. Can.$3. ‡ United Way of Canada, 55 Parkdale, Box 3505, Sta. C, Ottawa K1Y 4G1, Canada. index. cum. index. (processed)
Formerly: Directory of Canadian Community Funds and Councils (ISSN 0084-9863)

300 330 AT ISSN 0076-6283
UNIVERSITY OF MELBOURNE. INSTITUTE OF APPLIED ECONOMIC AND SOCIAL RESEARCH. MONOGRAPHS. 1968. irreg. price varies. University of Melbourne, Institute of Applied Economic and Social Research, Parkville, Victoria 3052, Australia.

361.6 VE
VENEZUELA. MINISTERIO DE SANIDAD Y ASISTENCIA SOCIAL. MEMORIA Y CUENTA. 1936. a. Ministerio de Sanidad y Asistencia Social, Centro Simon Bolivar, Edificio sur, Caracas, Venezuela.

368 AU
VERBAND DER VERSICHERUNGSUNTERNEHMUNGEN OESTERREICHS. GESCHAEFTSBERICHT. 1956. a. free. Verband der Versicherungsunternehmungen Oesterreichs, Schwarzenbergplatz 7, A-1030 Vienna, Austria. circ. 750.
Formerly: Verband der Versicherungsunternehmungen Oesterreichs. Bericht ueber das Geschaeftsjahr (ISSN 0083-5501)

360 UK ISSN 0083-601X
VICTORIA LEAGUE FOR COMMONWEALTH FRIENDSHIP. ANNUAL REPORT. 1901. a. membership. ‡ Victoria League, 18 Northumberland Ave., London WC2N 5BJ, England.

VISTAS FOR VOLUNTEERS. see *HOSPITALS*

360 UK ISSN 0083-6907
VOLUNTARY SOCIAL SERVICES. 1928. a. £2.95. National Council for Voluntary Organisations, Bedford Square Press, 26 Bedford Sq., London WC1B 3HU, England.

361.7 US
WASHINGTON (STATE). ATTORNEY GENERAL'S OFFICE. CHARITABLE TRUST DIRECTORY. irreg. Attorney General's Office, Olympia, WA 98504.
Formerly: Washington (State). Attorney General's Office. Directory of Charitable Organizations and Trusts Registered with the Office of Attorney General (ISSN 0093-6693)

331.1 US ISSN 0091-4312
WASHINGTON (STATE). HUMAN RESOURCES AGENCIES. ANNUAL REPORT. 1970. biennial. State Office of Financial Management, Forecasting and Support Division, House Office Bldg., Olympia, WA 98504 (Dist. by: State Library, Olympia WA 98504) stat. Key Title: Annual Report. Human Resources Agencies (Olympia)

362 US ISSN 0083-8438
WEST VIRGINIA. COMMISSION ON AGING. ANNUAL PROGRESS REPORT. 1961. a. controlled free circ. Commission on Aging, State Capitol, Charleston, WV 25305. Ed. John Giles.

354 AT
WESTERN AUSTRALIA. DEPARTMENT FOR COMMUNITY WELFARE. ANNUAL REPORT. 1973. a. Department for Community Welfare, 81 St. Georges Terrace, Perth, W.A. 6000, Australia. stat.

360 US ISSN 0083-906X
WESTMINSTER SERIES. 1961. irreg., 1968, vol. 8. price varies. Pergamon Press, Inc., Maxwell House, Fairview Park, Elmsford, NY 10523. Ed. Farndale.

WHEELCHAIR TRAVELER. see *TRAVEL AND TOURISM*

361.7 UK
WILL TO CHARITY: THE CHARITIES' STORY BOOK. no. 4, 1974. a. £1.80. Seaforth Advertising, 8 Lennox Gardens, London SW1X 0DG, England. adv. illus.

360 US ISSN 0272-0493
WISE GIVING BULLETIN; a reporting and advisory service for contributors. 1944. irreg. single copies free. ‡ National Information Bureau, Inc., 419 Park Ave. South, New York, NY 10016. Ed. M. C. Van de Workeen.

360 US ISSN 0163-4313
WOODALL'S FLORIDA & SOUTHERN STATES RETIREMENT & RESORT COMMUNITIES DIRECTORY. 1976. a. $5.95. Woodall Publishing Co., 500 Bedford Pl., Highland Park, IL 60035. adv. circ. 50,000.
Former titles: Woodall's Retirement and Resort Communites Directory; Woodall's Mobile Home Park Directory (ISSN 0094-1891); Woodall's Mobile-Modular Living (ISSN 0084-1102); Incorporating: Woodall's Directory of Mobile Home Communities (ISSN 0093-7274)

WORKSHOP FOR CHILD CARE STAFF OF FLORIDA'S CHILD CARING FACILITIES. REPORT. see *CHILDREN AND YOUTH — About*

362 IT ISSN 0084-1625
WORLD CONGRESS OF THE DEAF. LECTURES AND PAPERS.* 1951. quadrennial, 1971, 6th, Paris. World Federation of the Deaf, c/o C. Magarotto, Secretary, Via Gregorio VII N. 120, 00165 Rome, Italy.

369.4 CN ISSN 0052-2678
WORLD COUNCIL OF YOUNG MENS SERVICE CLUBS. MINUTES OF THE GENERAL MEETING. 1962. a. ‡ World Council of Young Men's Service Clubs, Box K1N, Cambridge, Ont. N3H 5C6, Canada. (processed)

362 FR ISSN 0084-2044
WORLD MOVEMENT OF MOTHERS. REPORTS OF MEETINGS.* irreg., 1971, 9th, Strasbourg. World Movement of Mothers, c/o I. Mancaux, President, 9 rue Chardin, 75016 Paris.

301.4 FR
WORLD UNION FOR THE SAFEGUARD OF YOUTH. CONFERENCE PROCEEDINGS. (Edts. in English, French) 1960. triennial, 1972, 5th, Paris. World Union for the Safeguard of Youth, 28 Place Saint-Georges, 75442 Paris Cedex 9, France.
Formerly: World Union of Organizations for the Safeguard of Youth (ISSN 0084-2400)

353.9 614 US ISSN 0098-6984
WYOMING. DEPARTMENT OF HEALTH AND SOCIAL SERVICES. ANNUAL REPORT. a. Department of Health and Social Services, 317 Hathaway Bldg., Cheyenne, WY 82001. Key Title: Annual Report of the Health and Social Services.

267.3 US ISSN 0084-4292
Y M C A YEARBOOK AND OFFICIAL ROSTER. 1877. a. $30. ‡ National Council of Y M C As, 291 Broadway, New York, NY 10007. Ed. Stanley Haidl. circ. 2,000.

362.7 US
YOUTH-SERVING ORGANIZATIONS DIRECTORY. 1978. irreg., 2nd edt., 1980. $24. Gale Research Company, Book Tower, Detroit, MI 48226.

360 309.1 ZA ISSN 0084-4608
ZAMBIA. DEPARTMENT OF COMMUNITY DEVELOPMENT. REPORT. 1964. a (approx.), latest 1975. 10 n. Government Printer, P.O. Box 136, Lusaka, Zambia.

360 ZA ISSN 0084-4667
ZAMBIA. DEPARTMENT OF SOCIAL WELFARE. REPORT. 1964. a. Government Printer, P.O. Box 136, Lusaka, Zambia.

360 ZA ISSN 0081-0533
ZAMBIA. DEPARTMENT OF SOCIAL WELFARE. SOCIAL WELFARE RESEARCH MONOGRAPHS.* a. price varies. Government Printer, P.O. Box 136, Lusaka, Zambia.

360 ZA ISSN 0084-5035
ZAMBIA. PUBLIC SERVICE COMMISSION. REPORT. 1964. a. 10 n. Government Printer, P.O. Box 136, Lusaka, Zambia.

SOCIAL SERVICES AND WELFARE — Abstracting, Bibliographies, Statistics

309.1 016 US ISSN 0066-1104
AMERICAN UNIVERSITIES FIELD STAFF. LIST OF PUBLICATIONS. 1952. a. free. American Universities Field Staff, Inc., Box 150, Hanover, NH 03755. Ed. Manon L. Spitzer.

361 362 AT
AUSTRALIA. BUREAU OF STATISTICS. NEW SOUTH WALES OFFICE. HEALTH AND WELFARE SERVICES. 1972. a. Australian Bureau of Statistics., N. S. W. Office, St. Andrews House, Sydney Square, George St., Sydney, N. S. W. 2000, Australia. stat.

361 314 AU
AUSTRIA. STATISTISCHES ZENTRALAMT. OEFFENTLICHE FUERSORGE. vol. 360, 1974. a. S.55. Kommissionsverlag der Oesterreichischen Staatsdruckerei, Rennweg 12a, 1037 Vienna, Austria. circ. 400.

300 016 BL ISSN 0067-6608
BIBLIOGRAFIA BRASILEIRA DE CIENCIAS SOCIAIS. 1954. a. Cr.$300($15) Instituto Brasileiro de Informacao em Ciencia e Tecnologia, Rio de Janeiro, Brazil. bk. rev. circ. 300.
Supersedes: Bibliografia Economico-Social.

332 US
BIBLIOGRAPHY OF CORPORATE SOCIAL RESPONSIBILITY. 1971. a. $2 per no. Bank of America, Box 37000, San Francisco, CA 94137. circ. 5,000.
Formerly: Bibliography, Corporate Responsibility for Social Problems (ISSN 0361-6916)

CANADA. DEPARTMENT OF NATIONAL HEALTH AND WELFARE. LIBRARY. ACQUISITIONS. see *PUBLIC HEALTH AND SAFETY — Abstracting, Bibliographies, Statistics*

CANADA. STATISTICS CANADA. LIST OF CANADIAN HOSPITALS AND SPECIAL CARE FACILITIES/LISTE DES HOPITAUX CANADIENS ET DES ETABLISSEMENTS DE SOINS SPECIAUX. see *HOSPITALS — Abstracting, Bibliographies, Statistics*

360 UK ISSN 0144-610X
CHARTERED INSTITUTE OF PUBLIC FINANCE AND ACCOUNTANCY. PERSONAL SOCIAL SERVICES ESTIMATE STATISTICS. 1974. a. £10. Chartered Institute of Public Finance and Accountancy, 1 Buckingham Place, London SW1E 6HS, England. (back issues avail.)

310 360 UK ISSN 0309-653X
CHARTERED INSTITUTE OF PUBLIC FINANCE AND ACCOUNTANCY. PERSONAL SOCIAL SERVICES STATISTICS. ACTUALS. 1949-50. a. £10. Chartered Institute of Public Finance and Accountancy, 1 Buckingham Place, London SWE 6HS, England. stat. (back issues avail.)
Formerly: Chartered Institute of Public Finance and Accountancy. Local Health & Social Services Statistics (ISSN 0307-0506)

361.6 318 DR
DOMINICAN REPUBLIC. SECRETARIA DE SANIDAD Y ASISTENCIA PUBLICA. CUADROS ESTADISTICOS. irreg. Secretaria de Sanidad y Asistencia Publica, Ciudad Trujillo, Dominican Republic.

362 US ISSN 0093-6715
FLORIDA. DIVISION OF FAMILY SERVICES. ANNUAL STATISTICAL REPORT. a. Division of Family Services, Box 2050, Jacksonville, FL 32203. Key Title: Annual Statistical Report - Division of Family Services.

010 060 US ISSN 0071-8092
FOUNDATION DIRECTORY. 1960. biennial. $41.50. ‡ Foundation Center, 888 7th Ave., New York, NY 10106. Ed. Marianna O. Lewis. charts, stat. index. circ. 20,000. Indexed: ERIC.
Supersedes: American Foundations and Their Fields.

362.8 FR
FRANCE. CAISSE NATIONALE DES ALLOCATIONS FAMILIALES. ACTION SOCIALE. a. Caisse Nationale des Allocations Familiales, 23 rue Daviel, 75634 Paris Cedex 13, France. charts. stat.

362.5 FR
FRANCE. CAISSE NATIONALE DES ALLOCATIONS FAMILIALES. PRESTATIONS FAMILIALES. RESULTATS GENERAUX: RECETTES, DEPENSES, BENEFICIAIRES. a. Caisse Nationale des Allocations Familiales, 23 rue Daviel, 75634 Paris Cedex 13, France. charts. stat.

362 314   GW   ISSN 0072-3754
GERMANY (FEDERAL REPUBLIC, 1949-)
STATISTISCHES BUNDESAMT. FACHSERIE
13, REIHE 2,3: SOZIALHILFE;
KRIEGSOPFERFUERSORGE. a. price varies. W.
Kohlhammer-Verlag GmbH, Abt.
Veroeffentlichungen des Statistischen Bundesamtes,
Philipp-Reis-Str. 3, Postfach 421120, 6500 Mainz
42, W. Germany (B.R.D.)

362 314   GW   ISSN 0072-3762
GERMANY (FEDERAL REPUBLIC, 1949-)
STATISTISCHES BUNDESAMT. FACHSERIE
13, REIHE 6: OEFFENTLICHE JUGENDHILFE.
a. DM.9.50. W. Kohlhammer-Verlag GmbH, Abt.
Veroeffentlichungen des Statistischen Bundesamtes,
Philipp-Reis-Str. 3, Postfach 421120, 6500 Mainz
42, W. Germany (B.R.D.)

360   GR
GREECE. NATIONAL STATISTICAL SERVICE.
SOCIAL WELFARE AND HEALTH
STATISTICS. (Text in English and Greek) 1967. a.,
latest 1976. $1.50. National Statistical Service,
Publications and Information Division, 14-16
Lycourgou St., Athens 112, Greece.

361   US   ISSN 0093-7835
MICHIGAN. DEPARTMENT OF SOCIAL
SERVICES. PROGRAM STATISTICS. (Report
year Ends June 30) irreg. Department of Social
Services, 300 S. Capitol Ave., Lansing, MI 48926.
Key Title: Program Statistics - Michigan
Department of Social Services.

361   US   ISSN 0093-6774
MICHIGAN. DEPARTMENT OF SOCIAL
SERVICES. PUBLIC ASSISTANCE STATISTICS.
(Report year ends June 30) irreg. Department of
Social Services, Bureau of Quality Control and
Statistical Analysis, Lansing, MI 48933. Key Title:
Public Assistance Statistics (Lansing)

361.6   US   ISSN 0095-1633
NORTH DAKOTA. SOCIAL SERVICE BOARD.
STATISTICS. a. free. Social Service Board,
Bismarck, ND 58501. Key Title: Statistics - Social
Service Board, North Dakota.

360 315   CH
SOCIAL AFFAIRS STATISTICS OF TAIWAN/
CHUNG-HUA MIN KUO TAI-WAN SHENG
SHE HUI SHIH YEH TUNG CHI. (Text in
English and Chinese) a. Department of Social
Affairs, Nan-Tou Hsien, Taiwan, Republic of China.
stat.

362.1 310   US   ISSN 0148-8325
SOUTH DAKOTA. DEPARTMENT OF SOCIAL
SERVICES. ANNUAL MEDICAL REPORT. a.
Department of Social Services, Program Analysis
and Evaluation, State Office Bldg., Illinois St.,
Pierre, SD 57501. stat. Key Title: Annual Medical
Report (Pierre)

360 310   US   ISSN 0099-2305
SOUTH DAKOTA. STATE DEPARTMENT OF
PUBLIC WELFARE. RESEARCH AND
STATISTICS ANNUAL REPORT. a. State
Department of Public Welfare, Division of Research
and Statistics, Office Bldg. No. One, Pierre, SD
57501. stat. Key Title: Research and Statistics
Annual Report.

360 314   SW   ISSN 0082-0326
SWEDEN. STATISTISKA CENTRALBYRAAN.
STATISTISKA MEDDELANDEN. SUBGROUP S
(SOCIAL WELFARE STATISTICS) (Text in
Swedish; table heads and summaries in English)
1963 N.S. irreg. Kr.40. Liber Foerlag, Fack, S-162
89 Vaellingby, Sweden. circ. 1,300.

362.6 312   US   ISSN 0190-3896
U.S. ADMINISTRATION ON AGING. ELDERLY
POPULATION: ESTIMATES BY COUNTY. a.
U.S. Administration on Aging, Washington, DC
20201.

360 016   US
U.S. DEPARTMENT OF HEALTH, EDUCATION
AND WELFARE. CATALOG OF
PUBLICATIONS. irreg., latest 1975, next 1978.
free. U.S. Department of Health, Education and
Welfare, 330 Independence Ave. S.W., Washington,
DC 20201.

362.5   US   ISSN 0360-4594
U.S. FOOD AND NUTRITION SERVICE. FOOD
AND NUTRITION PROGRAMS. a. U.S.
Department of Agriculture, Food and Nutrition
Service, Dept. of Agriculture, 14th St. and
Independece Ave, S.W., Washington, DC 20250.
Key Title: Food and Nutrition Programs.

SOCIOLOGY

see also Folklore; Social Sciences:
Comprehensive Works; Social Services
and Welfare

614   FR   ISSN 0515-2925
ACTA MEDICA ET SOCIOLOGICA. 1962. irreg.,
1972, 6th, Varna. International Medical Association
for the Study of Living Conditions and Health, c/o
J. de Castro, 165, Av Charles de Gaulle, 92200
Neuilly-sur-Seine, France.

301   IT   ISSN 0065-1656
ACTA SCIENTIARUM SOCIALIUM. (Text in
English, French, German, Italian, Rumanian,
Spanish) 1959. irreg. price varies. Societa
Accademica Romena, Foro Traiano 1a, 00187
Rome, Italy.

301   MX
ACTA SOCIOLOGICA. SERIE PROMOCION
SOCIAL.* 1969. a. Universidad Nacional
Autonoma de Mexico, Facultad de Ciencias
Politicas y Sociales, Centro de Estudios del
Desarrollo, Ciudad Universitaria, Villa Obregon,
Mexico 20, D.F., Mexico. Ed. Ricardo Pozas
Arciniega. bibl. illus.

301.15   US   ISSN 0065-2601
ADVANCES IN EXPERIMENTAL SOCIAL
PSYCHOLOGY. 1964. irreg., vol. 12, 1979. price
varies. Academic Press, Inc., 111 Fifth Ave., New
York, NY 10003. Ed. Leonard Berkowitz. index.
(also avail. in microfiche)

ADVANCES IN FAMILY INTERVENTION
ASSESSMENT AND THEORY. see
PSYCHOLOGY

ADVANCES IN THE STUDY OF
COMMUNICATION AND AFFECT. see
PSYCHOLOGY

301   BE
AGGLOMERATION BRUXELLOISE; approche
geographique et sociologigue. 1971. irreg., vol. 3,
1974. (Universite Libre de Bruxelles, Institut de
Sociologie) Editions de l'Universite de Bruxelles,
Parc Leopold, B-1040 Brussels, Belgium.

AGORA (RAVENNA) see PHILOSOPHY

301.4   GW   ISSN 0170-7671
AGRARSOZIALE GESELLCHAFT. KLEINE
REIHE. 1970. irreg., no. 23, 1980. price varies.
Agrarsoziale Gesellschaft e.V., Kurze Geismarstr.
23/25, 3400 Goettingen, W. Germany(B.R.D.)

301.4 338.1   GW   ISSN 0065-437X
AGRARSOZIALE GESELLSCHAFT.
GESCHAEFTS- UND ARBEITSBERICHT. 1950/
51. a. free. Agrarsoziale Gesellschaft e.V., Kurze
Geismarstr. 23/25, 3400 Goettingen, W. Germany
(B.R.D.)
   Until 1968: Agrarsoziale Gesellschaft.
Arbeitsbericht.

301.4   GW   ISSN 0344-5712
AGRARSOZIALE GESELLSCHAFT.
MATERIALSAMMLUNG. 1953. irreg., no. 152,
1980. price varies. Agrarsoziale Gesellschaft e.V.,
Kurze Geismarstr. 23/25, 3400 Goettingen, W.
Germany(B.R.D.)

301.15   GW
ALLENSBACHER JAHRBUCH DER
DEMOSKOPIE. 1947/55. irreg. price varies.
(Institut fuer Demoskopie, Allensbach) Verlag fuer
Demoskopie, 7753 Allensbach, W. Germany (B. R.
D.) Eds. E. Noelle, E. P. Neumann. adv. bk. rev.
circ. 3,000.
   Former title: Jahrbuch der Oeffentlichen Meinung
(ISSN 0075-2347)

301   PE   ISSN 0065-6763
AMERICA - PROBLEMA. 1971. irreg.; no. 8, 1973.
price varies. ‡ (Instituto de Estudios Peruanos) I E
P Ediciones, Horacio Urteaga 694 (Campo de
Marte), Lima 11, Peru.

301.35   US   ISSN 0065-7999
AMERICAN COUNTRY LIFE ASSOCIATION.
PROCEEDINGS OF THE ANNUAL
CONFERENCE. (Each vol. has a distinctive title)
1919. a. $2. American Country Life Association,
Inc., 2118 S. Summit Ave., Sioux Falls, SD 57105.
circ. 500(approx.)

301   US   ISSN 0065-8197
AMERICAN ETHNOLOGICAL SOCIETY.
MONOGRAPHS. 1940. irreg., vol. 55, 1973. price
varies. (American Ethnological Society) West
Publishing Co., Box 3526, St. Paul, MN 55165
(Vols. before 1972 dist. by: University of
Washington Press, Seattle, WA 98105)

301.45   US
AMERICAN JEWISH COMMITTEE. INSTITUTE
OF HUMAN RELATIONS. PAPERBACK
SERIES. 1962. irreg., 1974. price varies. American
Jewish Committee, Institute of Human Relations,
165 E. 56th St., New York, NY 10022. Ed. Sonya
F. Kaufer.
   Formerly: American Jewish Committee. Institute
of Human Relations. Pamphlet Series. (ISSN 0065-
8928)

AMERICAN LECTURES IN SOCIAL AND
REHABILITATION PSYCHOLOGY. see
PSYCHOLOGY

301   US
AMERICAN SOCIOLOGICAL ASSOCIATION.
PROCEEDINGS OF ANNUAL MEETING. a. $2.
American Sociological Association, 1722 N St.,
N.W., Washington, DC 20036.

301   SP   ISSN 0066-1473
ANALES DE MORAL SOCIAL Y ECONOMICA.
1962. irreg. 125 ptas. Centro de Estudios Sociales
de la Santa Cruz del Valle de los Caidos, Madrid,
Spain (Distr. by: Aguilar, S.A. de Publicaciones,
Juan Bravo 38, Madrid 6, Spain)

301   PL
ANALIZY I PROBY TECHNIK BADAWCZYCH W
SOCJOLOGII. (Text in Polish; summaries in
English and Russian) irreg., 1975, vol.5. $12.50.
(Polska Akademia Nauk, Instytut Filozofii i
Socjologii) Ossolineum, Publishing House of the
Polish Academy of Sciences, Rynek 9, Wroclaw,
Poland (Dist. by: Ars Polona-Ruch, Krakowskie
Przedmiescie 7, Warsaw, Poland) Eds. Z.
Gostkowski, J. Lutynski.

ANCIENT GREEK CITIES REPORT. see
HOUSING AND URBAN PLANNING

301 330   FR
ANNALES D'ECONOMIE ET DE SOCIOLOGIE
RURALES. (Text in French; Summaries in English)
1972. irreg, 2-3 per year. Institut National de la
Recherche Agronomique, Departement d'Economie
et de Sociologie Rurales, 4 rue de Lasteyrie, 75016
Paris, France (Orders to: Service des Publications,
I.N.R.A., Route de Saint-Cyr, 78 Versailles, France)
charts. stat.
   Continues: Recherches d'Economie et de
Sociologie Rurales.

ANNALES UNIVERSITATIS MARIAE CURIE-
SKLODOWSKA. SECTIO I. PHILOSOPHIA-
SOCIOLOGIA. see PHILOSOPHY

301   IT   ISSN 0066-2275
ANNALI DI SOCIOLOGIA. 1964. a. Centro di Studi
Sociologici, Via Vincenzo Monti 11, 20123 Milan,
Italy. Ed. Oddone C. Poli. adv. bk. rev. Indexed:
Sociol.Abstr.

301   US   ISSN 0363-647X
ANNALS OF PHENOMENOLOGICAL
SOCIOLOGY. 1976. irreg. $7. University of
Oklahoma, Center for the Study of Phenomenology,
Dale Hall Tower, Dayton, OK 73019. Ed. D.
Lawrence Wieder. (back issues avail.) Indexed:
Curr.Cont.

301 FR ISSN 0066-2399
ANNEE SOCIOLOGIQUE. 1896. a. 160 F. Presses Universitaires de France, 108 Bd. Saint Germaine, 75279 Paris Cedex 6, France (Service des Periodiques, 12 rue Jean de Beauvais, 75005 Paris)

ANNUAL EDITIONS: READINGS IN HUMAN SEXUALITY. see *BIOLOGY*

301.42 US ISSN 0095-6155
ANNUAL EDITIONS: READINGS IN MARRIAGE AND FAMILY. Short title: Readings in Marriage and Family. a. $5.75. Dushkin Publishing Group, Sluice Dock, Guilford, CT 06437. illus.

301 US ISSN 0090-4236
ANNUAL EDITIONS: READINGS IN SOCIOLOGY. 1973. a. price varies. Dushkin Publishing Group, Sluice Dock, Guilford, CT 06437. illus.

301.18 US ISSN 0094-601X
ANNUAL HANDBOOK FOR GROUP FACILITATORS. a. $14.50 paperbound; $36.50 looseleaf. University Associates Publishers, 8517 Production Ave., San Diego, CA 92121. illus. (reprint service avail. from UMI)

301 US ISSN 0360-0572
ANNUAL REVIEW OF SOCIOLOGY. 1975. a. $20. Annual Reviews Inc., 4139 El Camino Way, Palo Alto, CA 94306. Ed. Alex Inkeles. bibl. cum.index. (back issues avail.; reprint service avail. from iSI)

ANUARIO DE SOCIOLOGIA Y PSICOLOGIA JURIDICAS. see *LAW*

309.1 US ISSN 0503-5422
APPALACHIAN REGIONAL COMMISSION. ANNUAL REPORT. 1965. a. free. U.S. Appalachian Regional Commission, 1666 Connecticut Ave. N.W., Washington, DC 20235. Ed. Elise F. Kendrick. circ. 6,000. (back issues available) Indexed: P.A.I.S.

301.2 PL ISSN 0066-6858
ARCHIWUM ETNOGRAFICZNE. 1951. irreg. price varies. Polskie Towarzystwo Ludoznawcze, Ul. Szewska 36, 50-139 Wroclaw, Poland (Dist. by Ars Polona-Ruch, Krakowskie Przedmiescie 7, Warsaw, Poland) index. circ. 1,000.

301 AT ISSN 0314-1705
AUSTRALIA. BUREAU OF STATISTICS. TASMANIAN OFFICE. EDUCATION. 1973. a. free. Australian Bureau of Statistics, Tasmanian Office, Box 66A, G.P.O., Hobart, Tasmania 7001, Australia. circ. 420.
 Supersedes: Australia. Bureau of Statistics. Tasmanian Office. Social (ISSN 0067-1061)

309 AT
AUSTRALIAN FRONTIER NEWSLETTER. 1964. irreg. membership. Australian Frontier, 422 Brunswick St., Fitzroy 3065, Australia. Ed. Pamela McLure. bk. rev. circ. 1,000.

301 AT
AUSTRALIAN NATIONAL UNIVERSITY. CANBERRA. DEPARTMENT OF DEMOGRAPHY. FAMILY AND FERTILITY CHANGE. no. 2, 1977. irreg. price varies. Australian National University, Department of Demography, Canberra, A.C.T. 2600, Australia.

301.2 015 BG
BANGLADESH DIRECTORY. (Text in English) a. Tk.125($10) Times Publications, 42-43, Purana Paltan, Dacca 2, Bangladesh.

301.4 BG ISSN 0070-8178
BANGLADESH RESEARCH AND EVALUATION CENTRE. REPORT.* (Text in English) a. Bangladesh Research and Evaluation Centre, 16 B, Rd. No 7, Dhanmondi, Bangladesh.

BEIRAT FUER WIRTSCHAFTS UND SOZIALFRAGEN. see *BUSINESS AND ECONOMICS*

301 GW
BEITRAEGE ZUR MITTELSTANDSFORSCHUNG. 1974. irreg., no. 75, 1981. price varies. (Institut fuer Mittelstandsforschung) Verlag Otto Schwartz und Co., Annastr. 7, 3400 Goettingen, W. Germany (B.R.D.) Eds. M. Ernst Kamp, F. Klein-Blenkers.

BEITRAEGE ZUR PSYCHOLOGIE UND SOZIOLOGIE DES KRANKEN MENSCHEN. see *PSYCHOLOGY*

301 US ISSN 0067-5830
BERKELEY JOURNAL OF SOCIOLOGY; critical review. 1955. a. $7. University of California, 410 Barrows Hall, Berkeley, CA 94720. Ed.Bd. adv. bk. rev. circ. 4,000. (back issues avail.) Indexed: Sociol.Abstr.
 Formerly (vols. 1-4, 1955-58): Berkeley Publications in Society and Institutions.

301 SZ ISSN 0067-6136
BERNER BEITRAEGE ZUR SOZIOLOGIE. 1959. irreg., vol. 18, 1977. price varies. (Universitaet Bern, Institut fuer Soziologie und Sozio-Oekonomische Entwicklungsfragen) Paul Haupt AG, Falkenplatz 14, CH-3001 Berne, Switzerland.

301.2 PL ISSN 0067-7655
BIBLIOTEKA ETNOGRAFII POLSKIEJ. (Text in Polish or English; summaries in English, French or German) 1958. a. price varies. (Polska Akademia Nauk, Instytut Historii Kultury Materialnej) Ossolineum, Publishing House of the Polish Academy of Sciences, Rynek 9, 50-106 Wroclaw, Poland (Dist. by Ars Polona-Ruch, Krakowskie Przedmiescie 7, Warsaw, Poland) Ed. Maria Frankowska.

301 CN ISSN 0703-1440
BIG COUNTRY CARIBOO MAGAZINE. a. Can.$5($6) Little Shepherd Publications Ltd., Box 4400, Quesnell, B.C. V2J 3J4, Canada. Ed. Heldor Schafer. adv. bk. rev. illus. circ. 3,000.

BIHAR RESEARCH SOCIETY. JOURNAL. see *HISTORY — History Of The Near East*

300 UY ISSN 0006-6508
BOLETIN URUGUAYO DE SOCIOLOGIA. 1961. 3/yr. $6. Juncal 1395, Casilla de Correo 1122, Montevideo, Uruguay. Dir. Mario Bon Espasandin.

301 GW ISSN 0068-0044
BONNER BEITRAEGE ZUR SOZIOLOGIE. 1964. irreg., no. 16, 1976. price varies. (Rheinische Friedrich-Wilhelms-Universitaet, Institut fuer Soziologie) Ferdinand Enke Verlag, Herdweg 63, 7000 Stuttgart 1, W. Germany (B.R.D.) Ed. G. Eisermann.

BRITISH POLITICAL SOCIOLOGY YEARBOOK. see *POLITICAL SCIENCE*

301 US
C U B COMMUNICATOR. m. $10. Concerned United Birthparents, Inc., Box 573, Milford, MA 01757.

301.35 301.364 BL
CADERNOS DE ESTUDOS RURAIS E URBANOS. 1968. a. Centro de Estudos Rurais e Urbanos, Cidade Unversitaria, Caixa Postal 8105, Sao Paulo, Brazil. Ed. Maria Isaura Pereira de Queiroz. bk. rev. bibl. circ. 350.

309 BL
CADERNOS DE LAZER. 1977. irreg. Editora Brasiliense, Rua Barao de Itapetininga 93, Sao Paulo, Brazil.

301 BE
CAHIERS D'ETUDE DE SOCIOLOGIE CULTURELLE. 1971. irreg., 1974, no. 3. (Universite Libre de Bruxelles, Institut de Sociologie) Editions de l'Universite de Bruxelles, Parc Leopold, B-1040 Brussels, Belgium.

368.4 FR
CAISSES CENTRALES DE MUTUALITE SOCIALE AGRICOLE. STATISTIQUES. (First part: Resultats d'Ensemble; second part: Resultats Detailles) 1969. a. 75 F. Union des Caisses Centrales de la Mutualite Agricole, 8 rue d'Astorg, 75380 Paris Cedex 8, France. stat.

301 UK ISSN 0068-6727
CAMBRIDGE PAPERS IN SOCIOLOGY. 1970. irreg., no. 5, 1975. $24.95 for latest vol. Cambridge University Press, Box 110, Cambridge CB2 3RL, England (and 32 E. 57 St., New York NY 10022) Eds. R. M. Blackburn, J. H. Goldthorpe. index.

301 UK ISSN 0068-6808
CAMBRIDGE STUDIES IN SOCIOLOGY. 1968. irreg., no. 10, 1978. $38.50 (cloth); $11.95(paper) for latest vol. Cambridge University Press, Box 110, Cambridge CB2 3RL, England (and 32 E. 57 St., New York, NY 10022) Eds. R. M. Blackburn, J. H. Goldthorpe. index.

CASE ANALYSIS IN SOCIAL SCIENCE N SOCIAL THERAPY. see *SOCIAL SCIENCES: COMPREHENSIVE WORKS*

309 II ISSN 0069-1631
CENTRAL INSTITUTE OF RESEARCH AND TRAINING IN PUBLIC COOPERATION, NEW DELHI. PUBLICATIONS. irreg., 1967, no. 4. Central Institute of Research and Training in Public Cooperation, New Delhi, India (Dist. by: International Publications Service, 114 E. 32nd St., New York, NY 10016)

301 FR ISSN 0071-8289
CENTRE D'ETUDES SOCIOLOGIQUES. TRAVAUX ET DOCUMENTS. 1969. irreg. price varies. Centre National de la Recherche Scientifique, Centre d'Etudes Sociologiques, Societe des Amis, 82 rue Cardinet, Paris (17e), France.

301.45 SA
CENTRE FOR INTERGROUP STUDIES. ANNUAL REPORT. Variant title: Abe Bailey Institute of Inter-Racial Studies. Annual Report. (Text in English & Afrikaans) 1968. a. free. Abe Bailey Institute of Inter-Racial Studies, Rondebosch, South Africa. Ed. Professor H.W. van der Merwe. bibl. circ. 2,200 (controlled)

301 US
CITY AND SOCIETY. 1977. irreg., vol. 3, 1978. price varies. Sage Publications, Inc., 275 S. Beverly Dr., Beverly Hills, CA 90212 (And Sage Publications, Ltd., 28 Banner St., London EC1Y 8QE, England) Ed. Gerald Suttles. (back issues avail.)

301 SP
COLECCION FUNDACION FOESSA. SERIE ESTUDIOS. 1969. irreg. (Fundacion Fomento de Estudios Sociales y Sociologia Aplicada) Euramerica, S.A., Mateo Inurria, 15, Madrid-16, Spain. bibl. charts.

301 BE ISSN 0069-5335
COLLECTION DE SOCIOLOGIE GENERALE ET DE PHILOSOPHIE SOCIALE. 1954. irreg. price varies. (Universite Libre de Bruxelles, Institut de Sociologie) Editions de l'Universite de Bruxelles, Parc Leopold, 1040 Brussels, Belgium.

301.364 US
COLUMBIA UNIVERSITY. CENTER FOR ADVANCED RESEARCH IN URBAN AND ENVIRONMENTAL AFFAIRS. WORKING PAPERS. 1976. irreg. Columbia University, Center for Advanced Research in Urban and Environmental Affairs, New York, NY 10027 (Dist. by J. Rietman, 167 Spring St., New York, NY 10012) illus.

COMMUNITY PSYCHOLOGY SERIES. see *PSYCHOLOGY*

301 US ISSN 0164-1247
COMPARATIVE STUDIES IN SOCIOLOGY. 1978. a. $17.25 to individuals; institutions $34.50. J A I Press, Box 1678, 165 W. Putnam Ave., Greenwich, CT 06830. Ed. Richard A. Tomasson.

301.3 US ISSN 0069-9055
CONNECTICUT URBAN RESEARCH REPORT. 1963. irreg., no. 26, 1979. price varies. University of Connecticut, Institute of Urban Research, Storrs, CT 06268.

301 IT ISSN 0391-1926
CONTRIBUTI DI SOCIOLOGIA. (Numbers not published consecutively) 1974. irreg., no. 63, 1980. price varies. Liguori Editore s.r.l., Via Mezzocannone 19, 80134 Naples, Italy. Ed. Franco Ferrarotti.

301 IT ISSN 0391-3171
CONTRIBUTI DI SOCIOLOGIA. READINGS. 1978. irreg., no. 4, 1979. price varies. Liguori Editore s.r.l., Via Mezzocannone 19, 80134 Naples, Italy. Ed. Franco Ferrarotti.

301.4 US ISSN 0147-1023
CONTRIBUTIONS IN FAMILY STUDIES. 1977. irreg. price varies. Greenwood Press, 88 Post Rd. W., Westport, CT 06881. Ed. Carol V. R. George.

301.4 US ISSN 0147-1031
CONTRIBUTIONS IN INTERCULTURAL AND COMPARATIVE STUDIES. 1976. irreg. $15.95 price varies. Greenwood Press, 88 Post Rd. W., Westport, CT 06881. Ed. Ann M. Pescatello.

301 US ISSN 0084-9278
CONTRIBUTIONS IN SOCIOLOGY. 1970. irreg. price varies. Greenwood Press, 88 Post Rd. W., Westport, CT 06881. Ed. Don Martindale.

301 II ISSN 0069-9659
CONTRIBUTIONS TO INDIAN SOCIOLOGY. n. S. 1957. a. Rs.40($10) (Institute of Economic Growth, Delhi, Asian Research Centre) Vikas Publishing House Pvt. Ltd., Vikas House, 20/4 Industrial Area, Sahibabad, Distt. Ghaziabad U.P., India (Dist. by: UBS Publishers' Distributors Ltd., 5 Ansari Rd., New Delhi 110002, India) T. N. Madan.

301.5 410 NE
CONTRIBUTIONS TO THE SOCIOLOGY OF LANGUAGE. 1972. irreg. price varies. Mouton Publishers, Noordeinde 41, 2514 GC The Hague, Netherlands (U.S. addr: Mouton Publishers, c/o Walter de Gruyter, Inc., 200 Saw Mill River Road, Hawthorne, NY 10532) Ed. Joshua A. Fishma.

CUADERNOS C I P C A (SERIE POPULAR) (Centro de Investigacion y Promocion del Campesinado) see *EDUCATION — Adult Education*

301 SP ISSN 0302-7724
CUADERNOS DE REALIDADES SOCIALES. no. 4, May 1974. irreg. 400 ptas.($11) Instituto de Sociologia Aplicada, Claudio Coello 141, Madrid, Spain. bk. rev. bibl. circ. 1,000.

251 AG ISSN 0070-1734
CUADERNOS DE SOCIOLOGIA.* 1961. irreg. price varies. Universidad Nacional de la Plata, Facultad de Humanidades y Ciencias de la Educacion, Calle 7 no. 776, La Plata, Argentina.

CURRENT PRACTICE IN FAMILY CENTERED COMMUNITY NURSING; a sociocultural framework. see *MEDICAL SCIENCES — Nurses And Nursing*

361 US ISSN 0164-1875
D R C BOOK & MONOGRAPH SERIES. 1968. irreg. Ohio State University, Disaster Research Center, 154 N. Oval Mall, 128 Derby Hall, Columbus, OH 43210.
Formerly: Ohio State University. Disaster Research Center. D R C - T R (ISSN 0078-4109)

361 US ISSN 0164-1867
D R C HISTORICAL AND COMPARATIVE DISASTERS SERIES. 1977. irreg. Ohio State University, Disaster Research Center, 128 Derby Hall, 154 Oval Mall, Columbus, OH 43210.

301.2 UR
DAGESTANSKII ETNOGRAFICHESKII SBORNIK. 1974. irreg. 1.49 Rub. Akademiya Nauk S.S.S.R., Dagestanskii Filial, Institut Istorii, Yazyka i Literatury, Ul. Gadzhieva, 45, Makhachkala, Daghestan, U.S.S.R. illus.

DENMARK. SOCIALFORSKNINGSINSTITUTTET. MEDDELELSE. see *SOCIAL SERVICES AND WELFARE*

DENMARK. SOCIALFORSKNINGSINSTITUTTET. PJECE. see *SOCIAL SERVICES AND WELFARE*

DENMARK. SOCIALFORSKNINGSINSTITUTTET. PUBLIKATION. see *SOCIAL SERVICES AND WELFARE*

DENMARK. SOCIALFORSKNINGSINSTITUTTET. SMAATRYK. see *SOCIAL SERVICES AND WELFARE*

DENMARK. SOCIALFORSKNINGSINSTITUTTET. STUDIE. see *SOCIAL SERVICES AND WELFARE*

309 MX ISSN 0011-9199
DESARROLLO; estudios sobre estructuracion social. 1965. irreg. Instituto Mexicano de Estudios Sociales, A. C. Londres 40, Mexico 6, D. F., Mexico. bibl.

DEVELOPMENTS IN HUMAN SERVICES SERIES. see *SOCIAL SERVICES AND WELFARE*

301 II
DIBRUGARH UNIVERSITY. CENTRE FOR SOCIOLOGICAL STUDY OF THE FRONTIER REGION. NORTH EASTERN RESEARCH BULLETIN. 1970. a. Rs.5. Dibrugarh University, Centre for Sociological Study of Frontier Region, Dept. of Sociology, Rajabheta, Dibrugarh, Assam, India. Ed. S.M. Dubey. bk. rev. bibl. circ. 500.

DIRECTORY OF UNPUBLISHED EXPERIMENTAL MENTAL MEASURES. see *PSYCHOLOGY*

301.4 BO
DOCUMENTOS INSTITUCIONALES OFICIALES. 1972. irreg. price varies. Centro de Investigaciones Sociales, Casilla 6931 - Correo Central, La Paz, Bolivia.

301 CN
DOSSIERS BEAUX-JEUX. 1976. irreg. Editions Bellarmin, 8100 Bd. Saint-Laurent, Montreal, Que. H2P 2L9, Canada. bibl.

301.2 US
DUBLIN SEMINAR FOR NEW ENGLAND FOLKLIFE. ANNUAL PROCEEDINGS. 1977. a. $7. Boston University Scholarly Publications, 25 Buick St., Boston, MA 02215. Ed. Peter Banes. adv. bibl. charts. illus. index. circ. 2,000. (back issues avail.)

EASTERN EUROPE REPORT: POLITICAL, SOCIOLOGICAL AND MILITARY AFFAIRS. see *POLITICAL SCIENCE*

301 UK
EDINBURGH STUDIES IN SOCIOLOGY. irreg (approx. 2 vols per year) price varies. Macmillan Press Ltd., 4 Little Essex St., London WC2R 3LF, England. Ed. Bd.

ENGINEERING AND SOCIETY SERIES. see *ENGINEERING*

301 NE
ERASMUS UNIVERSITEIT, ROTTERDAM. CENTRUM VOOR MAATSCHAPPIJGESCHIEDENIS. MEDEDELINGEN/INFORMATION BULLETIN. 1978. irreg., no. 7, 1979. Erasmus Universiteit, Rotterdam, Centrum voor Maatschappijgeschiedenis, Postbus 1738, Rotterdam, Netherlands.

309 BO
ESTUDIOS DE POBLACION Y DESARROLLO. 1974. irreg. price varies. Centro de Investigaciones Sociales, Casilla 6931 - Correo Central, La Paz, Bolivia.

301 BO
ESTUDIOS DE RECURSOS HUMANOS. 1978. irreg. Centro de Investigaciones Sociales, Casilla 6931, La Paz, Bolivia.

301.4 BO
ESTUDIOS DE SOCIOLOGIA FAMILIAR. 1975. irreg. Centro de Investigaciones Sociales, Casilla 6931 - Correo Central, La Paz, Bolivia.

301.364 BO
ESTUDIOS URBANOS. 1973. irreg. price varies. Centro de Investigaciones Sociales, Casilla 6931 - Correo Central, La Paz, Bolivia.

301 960 SG
ETUDES SENEGALAISES. 1949. irreg. Institut Fondamental d'Afrique Noire, Centre de Saint-Louis de Senegal, Universite de Dakar, B.P. 206, Dakar, Senegal. illus.

301 FR ISSN 0531-2663
EUROPEAN ASPECTS, SOCIAL STUDIES SERIES; a collection of studies relating to European integration. 1959. irreg. Council of Europe, Publications Section, 67000 Strasbourg, France (Dist. in U. S. by Manhattan Publishing Co., 225 Lafayette St., New York, N. Y. 10012)

EUROPEAN YEARBOOK IN LAW AND SOCIOLOGY. see *LAW*

EXPLORATIONS IN URBAN ANALYSIS. see *SOCIAL SCIENCES: COMPREHENSIVE WORKS*

301 BL
FACULDADE DE FILOSOFIA, CIENCIAS E LETRAS DE ARARAQUARA. CADEIRA DE SOCIOLOGIA E FUNDAMENTOS SOCIOLOGICOS DA EDUCAO. BOLETIM. 1965. irreg. Faculdade de Filosofia, Ciencias e Letras de Araraquara, Cadeira de Sociologia e Fundamentos Sociologicos da Educao, Praca Santos Dumont, C.P. 174, Araraquara, S.P., Brazil.

301.364 US ISSN 0160-9815
FOCUS: URBAN SOCIETY; an annual editions reader. 1978. a. Dushkin Publishing Group, Sluice Dock, Guilford, CT 06437.

301 FR ISSN 0080-116X
FRANCE. DELEGATION GENERALE A LA RECHERCHE SCIENTIFIQUE ET TECHNIQUE. REPERTOIRE NATIONAL DES CHERCHEURS: SCIENCES SOCIALES ET HUMAINES. TOME 1: ETHNOLOGIE, LINGUISTIQUE, PSYCHOLOGIE, PSYCHOLOGIE SOCIALE, SOCIOLOGIE. 1968. irreg. price varies. Documentation Francaise, 29-31 Quai Voltaire, 75340 Paris 07, France.

FREIE UNIVERSITAET BERLIN. OSTEUROPA-INSTITUT. PHILOSOPHISCHE UND SOZIOLOGISCHE VEROEFFENTLICHUNGEN. see *PHILOSOPHY*

301 330 BL
FUNDACAO CENTRO DE PESQUISAS ECONOMICAS E SOCIAIS DO PIAUI. RELATORIO DE ATIVIDADES. Cover title: Fundacao Centro de Pesquisas Economicas e Sociais do Piaui. Atividades C E P R O. irreg. Fundacao Centro de Pesquisas Economicas e Sociais do Piaui, Av. Miguel Rosa 3190/S, Caixa Postal 429, 6400 Teresina-Piaui, Brazil.

301 AG
FUNDACION BARILOCHE. DESARROLLOS SINERGICOS. PUBLICACIONES. irreg. Fundacion Bariloche, Desarrollos Sinergicos, Casilla de Correo 138, 8400 San Carlos de Bariloche - Rio Negro, Argentina.
Former titles: Fundacion Bariloche. Departamento de Sociologia. Publicaciones & Fundacion Bariloche. Departamento de Sociologia. Documentos de Trabajo (ISSN 0071-9838)

301.4 US
GENERAL MILLS AMERICAN FAMILY REPORT. no. 2, 1976. biennial. General Mills, Inc., 9200 Wayzata Blvd., Box 1113, Minneapolis, MN 55440.

301 US
GEORGE WASHINGTON UNIVERSITY. SOCIAL RESEARCH GROUP. ANNUAL REPORT. vol. 5, 1975. a. George Washington University, Social Research Group, Washington, DC 20052.

301 GH ISSN 0435-9380
GHANA JOURNAL OF SOCIOLOGY. 1965. s-a. $5. Ghana Sociological Association, c/o Department of Sociology, University of Ghana, Legon, Ghana.

301 SW ISSN 0072-5102
GOETEBORGS UNIVERSITET. SOCIOLOGISKA INSTITUTIONEN. MONOGRAFIER. (Text in Swedish; summaries in English) 1968. irreg., 1970, no. 3. Kr.25. Goeteborgs Universitet, Sociologiska Institutionen, Karl Johansgatan 27, S-414 59 Goeteborg, Sweden.

301 GW ISSN 0072-4874
GOETTINGER ABHANDLUNGEN ZUR SOZIOLOGIE. 1957. irreg., vol. 25, 1977. price varies. Ferdinand Enke Verlag, Herdweg 63, 7000 Stuttgart 1, W. Germany (B.R.D.) Eds. H. Plessner, H. P. Bahrdt.

GOLDEN BLADE. see *PHILOSOPHY*

301 PL ISSN 0072-5013
GORNOSLASKIE STUDIA SOCJOLOGICZNE. 1963. irreg. Slaski Instytut Naukowy, Ul. Francuska 12, Katowice, Poland (Dist. by Ars Polona-Ruch, Krakowskie Przedmiescie 7, Warsaw, Poland)

301   UK   ISSN 0072-5765
GREAT BRITAIN. CENTRAL STATISTICAL OFFICE. SOCIAL TRENDS. 1970. a. £16.50. Central Statistical Office, Great George St., London SW1P 3AQ, England (Avail. from: Open University Educational Enterprises Ltd., 12 Cofferidge Close, Stony Stratford, Milton Keynes MK11 1BY, England) charts. stat.

GREAT BRITAIN. DEPARTMENT OF THE ENVIRONMENT. REPORT ON RESEARCH AND DEVELOPMENT. see *ENVIRONMENTAL STUDIES*

301.3   UK   ISSN 0072-7008
GREAT BRITAIN. NATURAL ENVIRONMENT RESEARCH COUNCIL. REPORT. 1965-66. a. £4. Natural Environment Research Council, Alhambra House, 27-33 Charing Cross Rd., London WC2H 0AX, England (Avail. from H.M.S.O., c/o Liaison Officer, Atlantic House, Holborn Viaduct, London EC1P 1BN, England)

301   US   ISSN 0091-7052
GUIDE TO GRADUATE DEPARTMENTS OF SOCIOLOGY. a. $10. American Sociological Association, 1722 N. St. N.W., Washington, DC 20036.

HARD CHEESE; a journal of education. see *EDUCATION*

301   GW   ISSN 0073-1676
HEIDELBERGER SOCIOLOGICA. 1962. irreg. price varies. (Universitaet Heidelberg, Institut fuer Soziologie und Ethnologie) Verlag J.C.B. Mohr (Paul Siebeck), Wilhelmstr. 18, Postfach 2040, 7400 Tuebingen, W. Germany (B.R.D.) Ed. W. E. Muehlmann.

301   US   ISSN 0073-1986
HERITAGE OF SOCIOLOGY. 1964. irreg., latest 1978. price varies. University of Chicago Press, 5801 S. Ellis Ave., Chicago, IL 60637. Ed. Morris Janowitz. (reprint service avail. from UMI,ISI)

HISTORICA CARPATICA. see *POLITICAL SCIENCE*

301   FR   ISSN 0563-9743
HOMO. (Text in French; summaries in English) 1953. a. 17 F. Universite de Toulouse II (le Mirail), 109 bis, rue Vauquelin, 31081 Toulouse Cedex, France.

HONG KONG SOCIAL AND ECONOMIC TRENDS. see *BUSINESS AND ECONOMICS — Economic Situation And Conditions*

HOUSING. see *HOUSING AND URBAN PLANNING*

301.1   US   ISSN 0163-5182
HUMAN FACTORS SOCIETY ANNUAL MEETING. PROCEEDINGS. 1956? a. $20. Human Factors Society, Box 1369, Santa Monica, CA 90406.
    Formerly: Human Factors Society. Proceedings of the Annual Meeting (ISSN 0363-9797)

301   US   ISSN 0073-8646
I C R STUDIES. 1966. irreg., 1968, no. 3. price varies. ‡ Institute for Cross-Cultural Research, 4000 Albermarle St. N.W., Washington, DC 20016. Ed. T. L. Stoddard. circ. 6,000.

I D S RESEARCH REPORT. (Institute of Development Studies) see *BUSINESS AND ECONOMICS — International Development And Assistance*

301.2 991.4   PH   ISSN 0073-9537
I P C MONOGRAPHS. (Text in English) irreg., latest no. 2. price varies. Ateneo de Manila University, Institute of Philippine Culture, Box 154, Manila, Philippines. Ed. Alfonso De Guzman II.

301.2 991.4   PH   ISSN 0073-9545
I P C PAPERS. (Text in English) irreg., latest no. 12. price varies. Ateneo de Manila University, Institute of Philippine Culture, Box 154, Manila, Philippines. Ed. Alfonso De Guzman II.

309   PH
I P C POVERTY RESEARCH SERIES. irreg., no. 4, 1976. Ateneo de Manila University, Institute of Philippine Culture, Box 154, Manila, Philippines.

301   US
I S H I OCCASIONAL PAPERS IN SOCIAL CHANGE. 1976. irreg., no. 3, 1979. price varies. Institute for the Study of Human Issues, Inc., 3401 Science Ctr., Philadelphia, PA 19104. Ed. J. M. Jutkowitz. circ. 300-2,000.

301.15 340   SZ   ISSN 0344-1849
INSTITUT FUER KONFLIKTFORSCHUNG. SCHRIFTENREIHE. (Text in German) 1977. biennial. 22 Fr.($13.25) (1981 price) S. Karger AG, Allschwilerstrasse 10, P.O. Box, CH-4009 Basel, Switzerland. Ed. W. de Boor. circ. 1,000. (reprint service avail. from ISI) Indexed: Curr.Cont.

INSTITUT ZA KRIMINOLOSKA I SOCIOLOSKA ISTRAZIVANJA. ZBORNIK. see *CRIMINOLOGY AND LAW ENFORCEMENT*

301.45   UK
INSTITUTE OF RACE RELATIONS. ANNUAL REPORT. 1974/75. a. Institute of Race Relations, 247 Pentonville Rd., London N1 9NG, England.

INSTITUTE ON PLURALISM AND GROUP IDENTITY. WORKING PAPER SERIES. see *ETHNIC INTERESTS*

301.35   PE
INSTITUTO DE ESTUDIOS ANDINOS. CUADERNOS. 1978. irreg. Instituto de Estudios Andinos, Apartado 289, Huancayo, Peru. illus.

309   PE
INSTITUTO DE ESTUDIOS PERUANOS. COLECCION MINIMA. 1973. irreg. price varies. I E P Ediciones, Horacio Urteaga 694 (Campo de Marte), Lima 11, Peru.

309   PE
INSTITUTO DE ESTUDIOS PERUANOS. ESTUDIOS DE LA SOCIEDAD RURAL. 1969. irreg. price varies. I E P Ediciones, Horacio Urteaga 694 (Campo de Marte), Lima 11, Peru.

301   BL
INSTITUTO DE PLANEJAMENTO ECONOMICO E SOCIAL. RELATORIOS DE PESQUISA. 1971. irreg. price varies. Instituto de Planejamento Economico e Social, Rua Melvin Jones 5, Z C-00 Centro, Rio de Janeiro, Brazil.

301   BL
INSTITUTO JOAQUIM NABUCO DE PESQUISAS SOCIAIS. SERIE CURSOS E CONFERENCIAS. 1974. irreg. Instituto Joaquim Nabuco de Pesquisas Sociais, Av. 17 de Agosto 2187, Recife, Brazil.

301   BL
INSTITUTO JOAQUIM NABUCO DE PESQUISAS SOCIAIS. SERIE ESTUDOS E PESQUISAS. 1974. irreg. Instituto Joaquim Nabuco de Pesquisas Sociais, Av. 17 de Agosto 2187, Recife, Brazil.

301   AG   ISSN 0074-0357
INSTITUTO TORCUATO DI TELLA. CENTRO DE INVESTIGACIONES SOCIALES. DOCUMENTOS DE TRABAJO. 1965. irreg., 1973, no. 87. price varies. Instituto Torcuato di Tella, Conde 1717, Buenos Aires, Argentina. circ. 200.

362.7   FR   ISSN 0538-5490
INTERNATIONAL CHILDREN'S CENTRE. PARIS. REPORT OF THE DIRECTOR-GENERAL TO THE EXECUTIVE BOARD. irreg. International Children's Centre, Chateau de Longchamp, Bois de Boulogne, 75016 Paris, France.

616.8 362   FR   ISSN 0534-8021
INTERNATIONAL CHILDREN'S CENTRE. PARIS. TRAVAUX ET DOCUMENTS. 1950. irreg. International Children's Centre, Chateau de Longchamp, Bois de Boulogne, 75016 Paris, France.

320   FR
INTERNATIONAL COLLOQUY ABOUT THE EUROPEAN CONVENTION ON HUMAN RIGHTS. PROCEEDINGS. 1960. quintennial; 4th, 1975. Council of Europe, Directorate of Human Rights, 67006 Strasbourg, France (Dist. in U.S. by Manhattan Publishing Co., 225 Lafayette St., New York, N.Y. 10012)

INTERNATIONAL CONFERENCE OF SOCIOLOGY OF RELIGION. see *RELIGIONS AND THEOLOGY*

309   NE
INTERNATIONAL INSTITUTE FOR SOCIAL HISTORY. ANNUAL REPORT. 1936. a. free. International Institute for Social History, Box 19313, 1000 GH Amsterdam, Netherlands. circ. 1,000.

301   NE   ISSN 0074-8684
INTERNATIONAL STUDIES IN SOCIOLOGY AND SOCIAL ANTHROPOLOGY. 1963. irreg., vol. 30, 1981. price varies. E. J. Brill, Oude Rijn 33a-35, Leiden, Netherlands. Ed. K. Ishwaran.

INTERNATIONALES JAHRBUCH FUER RELIGIONSSOZIOLOGIE. see *RELIGIONS AND THEOLOGY*

301   MY
INTISARI; research journal of wider Malaysia. 1971. irreg. M.32. Malaysian Sociological Research Institute, Box 2112, Kuala Lumpur, Malaysia. Ed. Ahmad Bin Ibrahim. adv. bk. rev. bibl. circ. 3,000-4,000.

301   IS   ISSN 0075-1227
ISRAEL INSTITUTE OF APPLIED SOCIAL RESEARCH. RESEARCH REPORT. (Text in English) 1963-64. biennial. $12. ‡ Israel Institute of Applied Social Research, 19 Washington St., Box 7150, Jerusalem, Israel. Ed. Haya Gratch. circ. 3,000.

261   GW   ISSN 0075-2584
JAHRBUCH FUER CHRISTLICHE SOZIALWISSENSCHAFTEN. Title varies: Jahrbuch des Instituts fuer Christliche Sozialwissenschaften. 1960. a. DM.48. (Universitaet Muenster, Institut fuer Christliche Sozialwissenschaften) Verlag Regensberg, Daimlerweg 58, Postfach 6748/6749, 4400 Muenster, W. Germany (B.R.D.)

301 572   MY
JERNAL ANTROPOLOJI DAN SOSIOLOJI. (Text in English and Malay) 1972. a. M.$3. National University of Malaysia, Persatuan Kajimanusia Dan Kajimasharakat - Universiti Kebangsaan Malaysia, Bangi, Kajang, Selangor, Malaysia. bibl.

301.3   IS
JERUSALEM URBAN STUDIES. (Text in English) 1970. irreg. $2. Hebrew University of Jerusalem, Institute of Urban & Regional Studies, Jerusalem, Israel. Eds. Arieh Shahar, Erik Cohen. charts. circ. 1,000.

301   US   ISSN 0075-3866
JOHNS HOPKINS SERIES IN INTEGRATION AND COMMUNITY BUILDING IN EASTERN EUROPE. 1968. irreg. price varies. Johns Hopkins University Press, Baltimore, MD 21218. Ed. Jan F. Triska.

301   NR
KANO STUDIES; journal of Saharan and Sudanic research. 1973. a. (Abdullahi Bayero College) Oxford University Press (Nigerian Branch), P.M.B. 5095, Oxford House, Iddo Gate, Ibadan, Nigeria. Ed. John E. Lavers. adv. bk. rev.

334   IS
THE KIBBUTZ; interdisciplinary research review. (Text in Hebrew and English) a. price varies. Federation of Kibbutz Movements, Box 303, Tel Aviv 61-000, Israel. Ed. Shimon Shur.

301   KO
KOREAN JOURNAL OF SOCIOLOGY. a. 2000 Won($4.50) Korean Sociological Association, c/o Seoul National University, San 56-1 Sinrim-Dong, Kwanak-Ku 151, Seoul, S. Korea.

301   AT
LA TROBE SOCIOLOGY PAPERS. 1973. irreg. La Trobe University, Department of Sociology, School of Social Sciences, Bundoora, Vic. 3083, Australia.

LEGON FAMILY RESEARCH PAPERS. see *ANTHROPOLOGY*

301   US
LEO M. FRANKLIN MEMORIAL LECTURES IN HUMAN RELATIONS. 1951. a. Wayne State University Press, 5959 Woodward Ave., Detroit, MI 48202. (back issues avail)

SOCIOLOGY

301.2   PL   ISSN 0076-1435
LUD. (Text in Polish; summaries in English and German) 1895. a. 50 Zl. Polskie Towarzystwo Ludoznawcze, Ul. Szewska 36, 50-139 Wroclaw, Poland (Dist. by Ars Polona-Ruch, Krakowskie Przedmiescie 7, Warsaw, Poland) Ed. Jozef Burszta. bk. rev. index. circ. 800.

301   US
MAIN CURRENTS IN INDIAN SOCIOLOGY. 1976. irreg., latest, vol. 3. price varies. Carolina Academic Press, 2206 Chapel Hill Rd., Box 8791, Forest Hills Station, Durham, NC 27707. Ed. Giri Raj Gupta.

301   RH
MAMBO OCCASIONAL PAPERS. SOCIO-ECONOMIC SERIES. no. 4, 1975. irreg. Mambo Press, Box 779, Gwelo, Zimbabwe.

MAN AND SOCIETY/MANUSIA DAN MASYARAKAT. see *ANTHROPOLOGY*

MAN-ENVIRONMENT SYSTEMS/FOCUS SERIES. see *ENVIRONMENTAL STUDIES*

301 330   AU   ISSN 0506-9122
MATERIALIEN ZUR SOZIAL- UND WIRTSCHAFTSPOLITIK. 1963. irreg. price varies. (Institut fuer Angewandte Sozial- und Wirtschaftsforschung) Jupiter Verlag GmbH, Robertgasse 2, A-1020 Vienna, Austria.

301.45   UK   ISSN 0305-6252
MINORITY RIGHTS GROUP. REPORTS. 1970. irreg. (5/yr.) £3.50($7) Minority Rights Group, 36 Craven St., London WC2N 5NG, England. Ed. Ben Whitaker. bibl. illus. stat. circ. 1,500.

301   BO
MONOGRAFIAS DE POBLACION Y DESARROLLO. 1974. irreg. price varies. Centro de Investigaciones Sociales, Casilla 6931 - Correo Central, La Paz, Bolivia.

301   BO
MONOGRAFIAS DE RECURSOS HUMANOS. 1978. irreg. Centro de Investigaciones Sociales, Casilla 6931 - Correo Central, La Paz, Bolivia.

301.4   BO
MONOGRAFIAS DE SOCIOLOGIA FAMILIAR. 1974. irreg. price varies. Centro de Investigaciones Sociales, Casilla 6931 - Correo Central, La Paz, Bolivia.

301   US   ISSN 0077-3212
N A A C P ANNUAL REPORT. 1910. a. $1. National Association for the Advancement of Colored People, 1790 Broadway, New York, NY 10019. circ. 5,000. (also avail. in microform from BLH)

309.1   US   ISSN 0077-5266
NATIONAL OPINION RESEARCH CENTER. NEWSLETTER. 1967. irreg., no. 9, 1974. free. ‡ National Opinion Research Center, 6030 S. Ellis, Chicago, IL 60637. Ed. Susan Campbell. circ. 800.

301   CH   ISSN 0077-5851
NATIONAL TAIWAN UNIVERSITY JOURNAL OF SOCIOLOGY/TAI-WAN TA HSUEH SHE HUI HSUEH K'AN. (Text in Chinese and English) 1963. a. $2.50. ‡ National Taiwan University, Department of Sociology, 21 Hsu-Chow Road, Taipei, Taiwan 100, Republic of China. Ed. Albert R. O'Hara. bk. rev. circ. 300.

301.451   US   ISSN 0077-6483
NEGRO IN THE CONGRESSIONAL RECORD. irreg., 1971, vol. 10. $22.50. Humanities Press, Inc., Atlantic Highlands, NJ 07716. Eds. Peter M. Bergman, Jean McCarroll.

572 301.2   HU
NEPI KULTURA-NEPI TARSADALOM. (Text in Hungarian; summaries in German) 1968. irreg. (Magyar Tudomanyos Akademia, Neprajzi Kutato Csoport) Akademiai Kiado, Publishing House of the Hungarian Academy of Sciences, P.O. Box 24, H-1363 Budapest, Hungary. abstr. bibl. illus.

NEW BABYLON: STUDIES IN THE SOCIAL SCIENCES. see *PSYCHOLOGY*

NORWAY. STATISTISK SENTRALBYRAA. ARTIKLER/ARTICLES. see *BUSINESS AND ECONOMICS — Economic Systems And Theories, Economic History*

314 330.9   NO   ISSN 0085-4344
NORWAY. STATISTISK SENTRALBYRAA. SAMFUNNSOEKONOMISKE STUDIER/ SOCIAL ECONOMIC STUDIES. (Text in Norwegian; summaries in English) 1954. irreg. price varies. Statistisk Sentralbyraa, Box 8131 Dep., Oslo 1, Norway. circ. 2,000.

301 572   CN
P. E. I. COMMUNITY STUDIES. (Prince Edward Island) a. price varies. University of Prince Edward Island, Department of Sociology and Anthropology, Charlottetown, P.E.I. C1A 4P3, Canada. Ed. Satadal Das Gupta. circ. controlled.

301   PK   ISSN 0083-8306
PAKISTAN. DIRECTORATE OF RURAL WORKS PROGRAMME. EVALUATION REPORT.* (Text in English) 1963-64. a. Directorate of Rural Works Programme, Lahore, Pakistan.

301   IS
PAPERS IN SOCIOLOGY. 1972. a. $3. Hebrew University of Jerusalem, Department of Sociology, Givat Ram Campus, Jerusalem, Israel (Subscr. to: Jerusalem Academic Press, Box 2390, Jerusalem, Israel) abstr. (back issues avail.)

301   US   ISSN 0079-0192
PATTERNS OF AMERICAN PREJUDICE SERIES.* irreg., 1969, no. 4. Harper & Row Publishers, Inc., 10 E. 53rd St., New York, NY 10022.

309   RH
PEOPLE AND PROJECTS. 1971. irreg.,no. 15, 1979. Ministry of Education, Branch of Community Development Training, Private Bag 7724, Causeway, Salisbury, Zimbabwe. circ. 30,000.

301   PE   ISSN 0079-1075
PERU - PROBLEMA. 1971. irreg.; no. 17, 1978. price varies. (Instituto de Estudios Peruanos) I E P Ediciones, Horacio Urteaga 694 (Campo de Marte), Lima 11, Peru. Ed. Jose Matos Mar. bk. rev.
Social problems in contemporary Peru

301   PL
POLISH SOCIOLOGICAL BULLETIN. (Text in English) a. 75. (Polskie Towarzystwo Socjologiczne) Ossolineum, Publishing House of the Polish Academy of Sciences, Rynek 9, Wroclaw, Poland (Dist. by: Ars Polona-Ruch, Krakowskie Przedmiescie 7, Warsaw, Poland) Ed. J. Szacki.
Formerly: Polish Sociology.

POLITICAL POWER AND SOCIAL THEORY; a research annual. see *POLITICAL SCIENCE*

301   PL   ISSN 0079-3442
POLSKA AKADEMIA NAUK. ODDZIAL W KRAKOWIE. KOMISJA SOCJOLOGICZNA. PRACE. (Text in Polish; summaries in English, French, Russian) 1963. irreg., no. 44, 1979. price varies. Ossolineum, Publishing House of the Polish Academy of Sciences, Rynek 9, 50-106 Wroclaw, Poland (Dist. by Ars Polona-Ruch, Krakowskie Przedmiescie 7, Warsaw, Poland)

301   PL   ISSN 0079-3620
POLSKA 2000. 1970. irreg., 3-4 per year. price varies. (Polska Akademia Nauk, Komitet Badan i Prognoz "Polska 2000") Ossolineum, Publishing House of the Polish Academy of Sciences, Rynek 9, Wroclaw, Poland (Dist. by Ars Polona-Ruch, Krakowskie Przedmiescie 7, Warsaw, Poland) Ed. Antoni Rajkiewicz. circ. 2,000.

301   PO   ISSN 0079-4163
PORTUGAL. INSTITUTO NACIONAL DE ESTATISTICA. ESTATISTICAS DAS ORGANIZACOES SINDICAIS. a. Instituto Nacional de Estatistica, Av. Antonio Jose de Almeida, Lisbon 1, Portugal (Orders to: Imprensa Nacional, Casa da Moeda, Direccao Comercial, rua D. Francisco Manuel de Melo 5, Lisbon 1, Portugal)

301   PO
PORTUGAL. INSTITUTO NACIONAL DE ESTATISTICA. INDICADORES ECONOMICS-SOCIAIS/SOCIAL-ECONOMIC INDICATORS. (Supplements accompany some numbers) (Text in English and Portuguese) 1973. Esc.78. Instituto Nacional de Estatistica, Av. Antonio Jose de Almeida, 1, Lisbon, Portugal (Orders to: Imprensa Nacional, Casa da Moeda, Direccao Comercial, rua D. Francisco Manuel de Melo 5, Lisbon 1, Portugal)

301 650   US
PROBLEMS IN A BUSINESS SOCIETY. irreg. price varies. Wadsworth Publishing Co., 10 Davis Drive, Belmont, CA 94002.

301   NE   ISSN 0079-7804
PUBLICATIONS ON SOCIAL HISTORY. 1970. irreg., no. 8, 1974. price varies. (International Institute for Social History) Van Gorcum, Industrieweg 38, Assen, Netherlands (Dist. by ISBS, P.O. Box 4347, Portland, OR 97208)

301   IT
QUALITA DELLA VITA. 1978. irreg., no. 5, 1979. price varies. Edizioni Studium-Vita Nova, Via Crescenzio 63, 00193 Rome, Italy.

301   US   ISSN 0080-0023
RECENT SOCIOLOGY. 1969. irreg., latest, vol. 5. $2.95 pap. Macmillan Inc., 866 Third Ave., New York, NY 10022. Ed. Hans Peter Dreitzel.

301   US
RECONSTRUCTION OF SOCIETY SERIES. irreg. price varies. Oxford University Press, 200 Madison Ave., New York, NJ 07410 (And Ely House, 37 Dover St., London W1X 4AH, England) Eds. Robert Lana, Ralph Rosnow.

RELIGIONE E SOCIETA. see *RELIGIONS AND THEOLOGY*

RESEARCH IN LAW, DEVIANCE AND SOCIAL CONTROL. see *LAW*

369   US
RESEARCH IN RACE AND ETHNIC RELATIONS. a. $16.25 to individuals; institutions $32.50. J A I Press, Box 1678, 165 W. Putnam Ave., Greenwich, CT 06830. adv. bk. rev.
Race relations

301.24   US   ISSN 0163-786X
RESEARCH IN SOCIAL MOVEMENTS, CONFLICTS AND CHANGE. 1978. a. $17.25 to individuals; institutions $34.50. J A I Press, Box 1678, 165 W. Putnam Ave., Greenwich, CT 06830. Ed. Louis Kriesberg.

301.07   US   ISSN 0196-1152
RESEARCH IN SOCIAL PROBLEMS AND PUBLIC POLICY; a research annual. 1979. a. J A I Press, Box 1285, 165 W. Putnam Ave., Greenwich, CT 06830.

301   US   ISSN 0272-2801
RESEARCH IN THE INTERWEAVE OF SOCIAL ROLES: WOMEN AND MEN; a research annual. 1980. a. J A I Press, Box 1678, 165 W. Putnam Ave., Greenwich, CT 06830. Ed. Helen Z. Lopata.

301   AG
REVISTA DE PROBLEMAS ARGENTINOS Y AMERICANOS. 1942. a. Universidad Nacional de la Plata, Calle 7 No. 776, La Plata, Argentina.

301   CK
REVISTA DE SOCIOLOGIA. vol. 9, 1977. a. Universidad Pontificia Bolivariana, Facultad de Sociologia, Avda. la Playa 40-88, Apartado Aereo 1178, Medellin, Colombia. bibl. charts. stat.

301   RM   ISSN 0080-2646
REVUE ROUMAINE DES SCIENCES SOCIALES. SERIE DE SOCIOLOGIE. 1956. a. $8. (Academia de Stiinte Sociale si Politice) Editura Academiei Republicii Socialiste Romania, Calea Victoriei 125, Bucharest, Romania (Subscr. to: ILEXIM, Str. 13 Decembrie Nr. 3, P.O. Box 136-137, Bucharest, Romania) Ed. Constantin Ionescu. bk. rev.

RIJKSUNIVERSITEIT TE LEIDEN. INSTITUUT VOOR CULTURELE ANTROPOLOGIE EN SOCIOLOGIE DER NIET-WESTERSE VOLKEN. PUBLICATIE. see *ANTHROPOLOGY*

301.2 IT ISSN 0085-5731
RIVISTA DI ETNOGRAFIA.* 1946. a. L.5000. Via Alfrado Rocco No. 98, Naples, Italy. Ed. Giovanni Tucci.

301 PL ISSN 0080-3731
ROCZNIKI SOCJOLOGII WSI. STUDIA I MATERIALY. (Text in Polish; summaries in English and Russian) 1962. a. 60 Zl. (Polska Akademia Nauk, Instytut Filozofii i Socjologii) Ossolineum, Publishing House of the Polish Academy of Sciences, Rynek 9, Wroclaw, Poland (Dist. by Ars Polona-Ruch, Krakowskie Przedmiescie 7, Warsaw, Poland) Ed. B. Galeski. bk. rev. circ. 500.

301 UK ISSN 0307-1391
S S R C SURVEY ARCHIVE BULLETIN. no. 6, 1977. irreg. University of Essex, SSRC Survey Archive, Colchester CO4 3SQ, England. Ed. Marcia Taylor.

SAGE ANNUAL REVIEW OF SOCIAL AND EDUCATIONAL CHANGE. see *EDUCATION*

301 US
SAGE ANNUAL REVIEWS OF STUDIES IN DEVIANCE. 1977. a. $18.50 for hardcover; softcover $8.95. Sage Publications, Inc., 275 S. Beverly Drive, Beverly Hills, CA 90212 (And Sage Publications, Ltd., 28 Banner St., London EC1Y 8QE, England) Eds. Edward Sagarin, Charles Winick. (back issues avail.)

301 US
SAGE STUDIES IN INTERNATIONAL SOCIOLOGY. 1976. irreg. $7.50 for softcover; hardcover $15. (International Sociological Association) Sage Publications, Inc., 275 S. Beverly Dr., Beverly Hills, CA 90212 (And Sage Publications, Ltd., 28 Banner St., London EC1Y 8QE, England) bibl, charts, stat. (back issues avail.)

SAMISKE SAMLINGER. see *ANTHROPOLOGY*

301 GW
SCHRIFTEN ZUR MITTELSTANDSFORSCHUNG. 1962. irreg. price varies. (Institut fuer Mittelstandsforschung) Verlag Otto Schwartz und Co., Annastr. 7, 3400 Goettingen, W. Germany (B.R.D.) Eds. M. Ernst Kamp, F. Klein-Blenkers.

SCIENCE AND SOCIETY SERIES. see *SCIENCES: COMPREHENSIVE WORKS*

301 NE
SERIE WELSTANDSTOEZICHT. 1978. irreg. price varies. Vereniging van Nederlandse Gemeenten, Box 30435, 2500 GK The Hague, Netherlands.

SLOVANSKE STUDIE. see *HISTORY — History Of Europe*

301 330 NE ISSN 0560-3641
SOCIAAL-ECONOMISCHE RAAD. VERSLAG. a. Sociaal-Economische Raad, Bezuidenhoutseweg 60, The Hague, Netherlands.

301 US
SOCIAL CHANGE. 1973. a. $24. Gordon and Breach Science Publishers, One Park Ave., New York, NY 10016.

301 US
SOCIAL IMPACT ASSESSMENT SERIES. 1978. irreg. Westview Press, 5500 Central Ave., Boulder, CO 80301. Ed. Charles P. Wolf.

301 US ISSN 0363-3195
SOCIAL INDICATORS NEWSLETTER. 1973. irreg. free. Social Science Research Council, 1755 Massachusetts Ave. N.W., Washington, DC 20036. Ed. Nancy Carmichael. bk. rev. circ. 3,000.

301.2 KE
SOCIAL PERSPECTIVES. irreg. Central Bureau of Statistics, Social Statistics Section, Ministry of Finance and Planning, Box 30266, Nairobi, Kenya (Orders to: Government Printing and Stationery Office, Box 30128, Nairobi, Kenya) charts. stat.

301.15 SZ
SOCIAL STRATEGIES; monographs on sociology and social policy/monographien zur Soziologie und Gesellschaftspolitik. (Text in English, French, and German) 1974. irreg., no. 2, 1976. Social Strategies Publishers Co-Operative Society, c/o Soziologisches Seminar, Universitaet Basel, Gartenstrasse 112, CH-4052 Basel, Switzerland. Ed. Paul Trappe.

SOCIAL STRUCTURE AND SOCIAL CHANGE. see *SOCIAL SCIENCES: COMPREHENSIVE WORKS*

301 UY ISSN 0081-0649
SOCIEDAD URUGUAYA.* irreg. Editorial Arca, Colonia 1263, Montevideo, Uruguay.

SOCIO-ECONOMIC REVIEW OF PUNJAB. see *BUSINESS AND ECONOMICS — Economic Situation And Conditions*

301 IT
SOCIOLOGIA. no. 4, 1975. irreg. Societa Editrice Napoletana s.r.l., Corso Umberto I 34, 80138 Naples, Italy. Ed. Aurelio Paolinelli.

301 BL ISSN 0081-1742
SOCIOLOGIA II. (Subseries Of: Sao Paulo, Brazil (City) Universidade. Faculdade de Filosofia, Ciencias e Letras. Boletim) 1958. irreg. Universidade de Sao Paulo, Faculdade de Filosofia, Letras e Ciencias Humanas, Cidade Universitaria, "Armando de Salles Oliveira", Caixa Postal 8105, Sao Paulo, Brazil.

301 UG
SOCIOLOGICAL JOURNAL. (Text in English) 1971. a. Makerere University, Sociological Society, Box 7062, Kampala, Uganda. Ed. J.W.G. Karuri. bibl. charts. illus.

301.01 US ISSN 0081-1750
SOCIOLOGICAL METHODOLOGY. 1969. a. price varies. (American Sociological Association) Jossey-Bass Inc., Publishers, 433 California St., San Francisco, CA 94104. (also avail. in microform from UMI; back issues avail.; reprint service avail. from UMI)

301 DK
SOCIOLOGICAL MICROJOURNAL. (Text in English, French and German) 1967. a. Kr.35. Koebenhavns Universitet, Sociologisk Institut, 22 Linnegade, 1361 Copenhagen K, Denmark. Ed. K. Svalastoga. (back issues avail.)

301 572 US ISSN 0149-4872
SOCIOLOGICAL OBSERVATIONS. 1977. irreg., vol. 5, 1978. price varies. Sage Publications, Inc., 275 S. Beverly Dr., Beverly Hills, CA 90212 (And Sage Publications, Ltd., 28 Banner St., London EC1Y 8QE, England) Ed. John M. Johnson. (back issues avail.)

301 UK ISSN 0081-1769
SOCIOLOGICAL REVIEW. MONOGRAPH. 1958. irreg., no. 28, 1980. price varies. University of Keele, Keele, Staffordshire ST5 5BG, England. Eds. Prof. R. Frankenberg, Prof. W. M. Williams. Indexed: SSCI.

301 FR
SOCIOLOGIE PERMANENTE. 1978. irreg. Editions du Seuil, 27 rue Jacob, 75261 Paris Cedex 6, France. Dir. Alain Touraine.

301 BE
SOCIOLOGISCHE VERKENNINGEN. no. 2, 1972. irreg., no. 9, 1977. Leuven University Press, Krankenstraat 3, B-3000 Louvain, Belgium.

301 NR ISSN 0081-1807
SOCIOLOGIST.* 1968. a. University of Ibadan, Sociological Society, Ibadan, Nigeria.

SOCIOLOGY OF THE SCIENCES. see *SCIENCES: COMPREHENSIVE WORKS*

301 UR
SOTSIOLOGIYA KUL'TURY. 1974. a. 1.40 Rub. (Nauchno-Issledovatel'skii Institut Kul'tury, Otdel' Sotsiologicheskikh Issledovanii) Izdatel'stvo Sovetskaya Rossiya, Proezd Sapunova 13/15, Moscow K-12, U.S.S.R.
Formerly: Nauchno-Issledovatel'skii Institut Kul'tury. Trudy.

301.4 SA
SOUTH AFRICAN INSTITUTE OF RACE RELATIONS. (PUBLICATION) RR. 1962. irreg. price varies. South African Institute of Race Relations, Box 97, Johannesburg, South Africa. charts. stat.

301 SI
SOUTH-EAST ASIAN JOURNAL OF SOCIAL SCIENCES. 1968. s-a. (National University of Singapore, Department of Sociology) Chopmen Enterprises, 428 & 429 Katong Shopping Centre, Singapore 1543, Singapore. (Co-sponsor: Institute of Southeast Asian Studies) illus.
Formerly: South-East Asian Journal of Sociology.

301 GW ISSN 0340-7217
SOZIALE FORSCHUNG UND PRAXIS. 1947. irreg. price varies. (Universitaet Muenster, Sozialforschungsstelle) Verlag J.C.B. Mohr (Paul Siebeck), Wilhelmstr. 18, Postfach 2040, 7400 Tuebingen, W. Germany (B.R.D.)

301 AU
SOZIALFORSCHUNG. BEITRAEGE. 1969. irreg. price varies. Universitaet Linz, Abteilung fuer Wirtschaftssoziologie und Stadtforschung, A-4045 Linz/Donau, Austria. Ed. Friedrich Furstenberg. bk. rev. bibl. circ. 400.

300 GW ISSN 0340-8248
SOZIALFORSCHUNG UND GESELLSCHAFTSPOLITIK. 1972. irreg., no. 3, 1974. price varies. Ferdinand Enke Verlag, Herdweg 63, 7000 Stuttgart 1, W. Germany (B.R.D.) Eds. Chr. v. Ferber, W. Schulenberg, W. Strzelewicz.

301 GW ISSN 0340-9201
SOZIALISATION UND KOMMUNIKATION. 1974. irreg., no. 9, 1980. price varies. (Universitaet Erlangen-Nuernberg) Ferdinand Enke Verlag, Herdweg 63, 7000 Stuttgart 1, W. Germany (B.R.D.)

301 GW ISSN 0081-3265
SOZIOLOGISCHE GEGENWARTSFRAGEN. NEUE FOLGE. 1957. irreg., no. 43, 1977. price varies. Ferdinand Enke Verlag, Herdweg 63, 7000 Stuttgart 1, W. Germany (B.R.D.) Eds. L. Neundoerfer, H. Schelsky, F. H. Tenbruck.

SPAIN. INSTITUTO NACONAL DE INVESTIGACIONES AGRARIAS. ANALES. SERIE: ECONOMIA Y SOCIOLOGICA AGRARIAS. see *AGRICULTURE — Agricultural Economics*

301 333.7 AT
SPEAK. 1969. a. Aus.$0.10. c/o Audrey Windram, Ed., Conrad St., Longwood, S. A. 5153, Australia.

301 EI ISSN 0081-4989
STATISTICAL OFFICE OF THE EUROPEAN COMMUNITIES. STATISTIQUES SOCIALES. ANNUAIRE. (Text in French, German, Italian, Dutch, or French and German) a. 1500 Fr.($36.20) B.P. 1907, Luxembourg, Luxembourg (Dist. in the U.S. by: European Community Information Service, 2100 M St., NW, Suite 707, Washington, DC 20037)

309 IT
STRATIFICAZIONE E CLASSI SOCIALI IN ITALIA. QUADERNI DI RICERCA. 1976. irreg. (Fondazione Giovanni Agnelli) Editoriale Valentino, Via G. Giancosa 38, 10125 Turin, Italy.

STUDIEN ZUR LITERATUR- UND SOZIALGESCHICHTE SPANIENS UND LATEINAMERIKAS. see *LITERATURE*

301 US ISSN 0081-8291
STUDIES IN NEAR EASTERN CIVILIZATION. 1969, no. 2. irreg., latest no. 6. New York University Press, Washington Square, New York, NY 10003.

301 US
STUDIES IN SOCIAL DISCONTINUITY. irreg. price varies. Academic Press, Inc., 111 Fifth Ave., New York, NY 10003. Eds. C. Tilly, E. Shorter.

STUDIES IN SOCIAL ECONOMICS. see *BUSINESS AND ECONOMICS*

SOCIOLOGY

300 301 US
STUDIES IN SOCIAL EXPERIMENTATION. 1975. irreg., no. 4, 1975. price varies. Brookings Institution, 1775 Massachusetts Ave. N.W., Washington, DC 20036.

301 NE ISSN 0081-8518
STUDIES IN SOCIAL LIFE. 1953. irreg. price varies. Martinus Nijhoff, Box 566, 2501 CN The Hague, Netherlands. Ed. G. Beyer. Indexed: SSCI.

301 US ISSN 0148-656X
STUDIES IN SOCIAL THEORY. 1971. irreg. $1 per no. Institute for Humane Studies, 1177 University Drive, Menlo Park, CA 94025. bibl. circ. 5,000. (back issues avail.)

301 AT ISSN 0156-4420
STUDIES IN SOCIETY. 1978. irreg. price varies. George Allen & Unwin Australia Pty. Ltd., 8 Napier St, N. Sydney 2060, Australia. Ed. Colin Bell. bibl.

301 II
STUDIES IN SOCIOLOGY. Variant title: Rajasthan University Studies in Sociology. (Text in English and Hindi) vol. 4, 1973. a. Rs.1 per copy. University of Rajasthan, Gandhi Nagar, Jaipur 302004, India. Ed. T. K. N. Unnithan.

301 II
STUDIES IN SOCIOLOGY AND SOCIAL ANTHROPOLOGY. (Text in English) 1978. irreg. price varies. Hindustan Publishing Corp., 6-U.B. Jawahar Nagar, Delhi 110007, India. Ed. M. N. Srinivas.

301.1 US ISSN 0163-2396
STUDIES IN SYMBOLIC INTERACTION. 1978. a. $18.75 to individuals; institutions $37.50. J A I Press, Box 1678, 165 W. Putnam Ave., Greenwich, CT 06830. Ed. Norman K. Denzin. illus. Indexed: Ss.

309 960 ZA
STUDIES IN ZAMBIAN SOCIETY. irreg., no. 3, 1978. price varies. University of Zambia, School of Humanities and Social Sciences, Committee on Student Publications, Box 2379, Lusaka, Zambia. Ed. L. M. van den Berg.

301 NE ISSN 0081-8771
STUDIES OF DEVELOPING COUNTRIES. (Text mainly in English) 1963. irreg., no. 25, 1979. price varies. Van Gorcum, P.O. Box 43, Assen, Netherlands (Dist. by: Humanities Press, Inc., 171 First Ave., Atlantic Highlands, NJ 07716)
  Formerly: Non-European Societies.

STUDIES OF URBAN SOCIETY. see HOUSING AND URBAN PLANNING

301 HU ISSN 0082-1322
SZOCIOLOGIAI TANULMANYOK. 1966. irreg. price varies. (Magyar Tudomanyos Akademia) Akademiai Kiado, Publishing House of the Hungarian Academy of Sciences, P.O. Box 24, H-1363 Budapest, Hungary.

315 IS
TEL AVIV-YAFO. CENTER FOR ECONOMIC AND SOCIAL RESEARCH. YEARBOOK. (Text in Hebrew and English) no. 14, 1974. a. Center for Economic and Social Research, Tel Aviv, Israel. illus.
  Former titles: Tel Aviv-Yafo. Department of Research and Statistics. Yearbook; Tel Aviv Yearbook.

301 SP
TESTIGOS DE ESPANA. no. 9, 1974. irreg. 75 ptas. Plaza y Janes S.A., 21-33 Virgen de Guadeloupe, Esplugas de Llobregat, Spain.

301.451 TU ISSN 0082-6898
TURKISH REVIEW OF ETHNOGRAPHY/TURK ETNOGRAFYA DERGISI. 1956. a. price varies. General Directorate of Antiquities and Museums, Ankara, Turkey.
  Formerly: Turk Tarih-Arkeologya ve Etnografya Dergisi.

U N H C R REPORT. (United Nations High Commissioner for Refugees) see POLITICAL SCIENCE — International Relations

U S S R REPORT: BIOMEDICAL AND BEHAVIORAL SCIENCES. see MEDICAL SCIENCES

U S S R REPORT: POLITICAL AND SOCIOLOGICAL AFFAIRS. see POLITICAL SCIENCE

301 GW ISSN 0170-2416
UEBERSEE-MUSEUM, BREMEN. VEROEFFENTLICHUNGEN. REIHE E: HUMAN-OEKOLOGIE. 1978. irreg. price varies. Uebersee-Museum, Bremen, Bahnhofsplatz 13, 2800 Bremen, W. Germany(B.R.D.)

301 PR
UNIVERSIDAD DE PUERTO RICO. CENTRO DE INVESTIGACIONES SOCIALES. INFORME ANUAL. (Text in Spanish) 1974/75. a. free. Universidad de Puerto Rico, Centro de Investigaciones Sociales, Rio Piedras, PR 00931. Ed. Wenceslao Serro Deliz. bk. rev. bibl. circ. 1,000.

301 SZ
UNIVERSITAET ZUERICH. SOZIOLOGISCHES INSTITUT. BULLETIN. (Formerly co-sponsored by Fundacion Bariloche, Departamento de Sociologia) (Text in English and German; summaries in English) 1966. irreg., no. 36, 1979. 8 Fr. per no. ‡ Universitaet Zuerich, Soziologisches Institut, Zeltweg 63, 8032 Zurich, Switzerland. Ed. Peter Heintz. circ. 150.
  Formerly: Fundacion Bariloche. Boletin (ISSN 0071-982X)

572 301 FR
UNIVERSITE DE BORDEAUX II. CENTRE D'ETUDES ET DE RECHERCHES ETHNOLOGIQUES. CAHIERS. 1972. a. Universite de Bordeaux II, Centre d'Etudes et de Recherches Ethnologiques, 3 Place de la Victoire, 33000 Bordeaux, France.
  Ethnological, sociological, economic and psychological studies concerning overseas civilizations

301 BE ISSN 0066-2380
UNIVERSITE LIBRE DE BRUXELLES. INSTITUT DE SOCIOLOGIE. ANNEE SOCIALE. 1960. a. Editions de l'Universite de Bruxelles, 1 Parc Leopold, 1040 Brussels, Belgium.

301 BE ISSN 0068-2985
UNIVERSITE LIBRE DE BRUXELLES. INSTITUT DE SOCIOLOGIE. CAHIERS. 1951. irreg. price varies. Editions de l'Universite de Bruxelles, Parc Leopold, 1040 Brussels, Belgium.

UNIVERSITE NATIONALE DE COTE D'IVOIRE. ANNALES. SERIE F: ETHNOSOCIOLOGIE. see ANTHROPOLOGY

330 US
UNIVERSITY OF ALASKA. INSTITUTE OF SOCIAL AND ECONOMIC RESEARCH. RESEARCH SUMMARY. 1970. irreg., no. 8, 1981. free. University of Alaska, Institute of Social and Economic Research, 707 A St., Suite 206, Anchorage, Ak 99501. Ed. Ronald Crowe. bk. rev. charts. stat. circ. 1,900. (also avail. in microfiche; back issues avail.)

UNIVERSITY OF ALBERTA. DEPARTMENT OF RURAL ECONOMY. BULLETIN. see AGRICULTURE — Agricultural Economics

301 312 CN ISSN 0317-3119
UNIVERSITY OF ALBERTA. DEPARTMENT OF SOCIOLOGY. POPULATION RESEARCH LABORATORY. ALBERTA SERIES REPORT. 1973. irreg. University of Alberta, Department of Sociology, Population Research Laboratory, Tory Building, University of Alberta, Edmonton, Alberta, Canada.

301 NZ
UNIVERSITY OF AUCKLAND. DEPARTMENT OF SOCIOLOGY. PAPERS IN COMPARATIVE SOCIOLOGY. 1974. irreg., no. 7, 1977. price varies. University of Auckland, Department of Sociology, Private Bag, Auckland, New Zealand.

UNIVERSITY OF BIRMINGHAM. CENTRE FOR URBAN AND REGIONAL STUDIES. OCCASIONAL PAPERS. see HOUSING AND URBAN PLANNING

UNIVERSITY OF BIRMINGHAM. CENTRE FOR URBAN AND REGIONAL STUDIES. WORKING PAPER. see HOUSING AND URBAN PLANNING

301.15 US ISSN 0068-6085
UNIVERSITY OF CALIFORNIA, BERKELEY. INSTITUTE OF HUMAN DEVELOPMENT. ANNUAL REPORT.* a. University of California, Berkeley, Institute of Human Development, 1203 Tolman Hall, Berkeley, CA 94720.

UNIVERSITY OF CANTERBURY. DEPARTMENT OF PSYCHOLOGY AND SOCIOLOGY. RESEARCH PROJECTS. see PSYCHOLOGY

301 GH
UNIVERSITY OF GHANA. DEPARTMENT OF SOCIOLOGY. CURRENT RESEARCH REPORT SERIES. no. 2, 1972. irreg. University of Ghana, Department of Sociology, Legon, Ghana.

UNIVERSITY OF LAGOS. HUMAN RESOURCES RESEARCH UNIT. MONOGRAPH. see POPULATION STUDIES

301 330 JM
UNIVERSITY OF THE WEST INDIES. INSTITUTE OF SOCIAL AND ECONOMIC RESEARCH. WORKING PAPERS. no. 7, 1975. irreg. University of the West Indies, Institute of Social and Economic Research, Mona, Kingston 7, Jamaica.

URBAN ENVIRONMENT. see ARCHITECTURE

301 US
URBAN LIFE IN AMERICA. irreg. price varies. Oxford University Press, 200 Madison Ave., New York, NY 10016 (And Ely House, 37 Dover St., London W1X 4AH, England) Ed. Richard C. Wade.

301.364 US
URBAN OBSERVATORY OF SAN DIEGO. SPECIAL REPORT. 1975. irreg. $3.75. 202 C St., San Diego, CA 92101. Ed. Walter A. Lilly. bibl. charts. stat.

301.4 US ISSN 0083-5226
VANDERBILT SOCIOLOGY CONFERENCE. PROCEEDINGS. 1969. irreg. $10. ‡ Vanderbilt University Press, Box 1813, Sta. B, Nashville, TN 37235. Ed. Mayer N. Zald.

VIEWPOINT; minority outlook on current issues. see POLITICAL SCIENCE — Civil Rights

301.1 150 US
VOLUNTARY ACTION RESEARCH SERIES. (Includes separate monographs and annual volumes of Voluntary Action Research) 1972. a. Center for a Voluntary Society, 2936 Albermarle St., N.W., Washington, DC 20008.

WADSWORTH SERIES IN ANALYTIC ETHNOGRAPHY. see ANTHROPOLOGY

301 US
WADSWORTH SERIES IN SOCIOLOGY. irreg. Wadsworth Publishing Co., 10 Davis Dr., Belmont, CA 94002.

301 US
WILEY SERIES IN URBAN RESEARCH. 1971. irreg., unnumbered, latest, 1979. price varies. John Wiley & Sons, Inc., 605 Third Ave., New York, NY 10016. Ed. T.N. Clark.

WISSENSCHAFTLICHE PAPERBACKS; Sozial- und Wirtschaftsgeschichte. see BUSINESS AND ECONOMICS — Economic Systems And Theories, Economic History

301 178 SA ISSN 0084-2540
WORLD'S WOMAN'S CHRISTIAN TEMPERANCE UNION. CONVENTION REPORT. 1891. triennial. $4. World's Woman's Christian Temperance Union, 397 Voortrekker Rd., Parow East 7500, South Africa. Ed. Mrs. B. Hermanson. bk. rev. index. circ. 600.

WORLDWATCH PAPERS. see ENVIRONMENTAL STUDIES

YEARBOOK OF WORLD PROBLEMS AND HUMAN POTENTIAL. see POLITICAL SCIENCE — International Relations

SOCIOLOGY — Abstracting, Bibliographies, Statistics

301.42 AT
AUSTRALIA. BUREAU OF STATISTICS. DIVORCES. a. free. Australian Bureau of Statistics, P.O. Box 10, Belconnen, A.C.T. 2616, Australia. illus. circ. 1,500.

301 330 318 VE
INDICADORES SOCIOECONOMICOS Y DE COYUNTURA. no. 2, 1975. irreg. Direccion General de Estadistica y Censos Nacionales, Caracas, Venezuela.

301 016.3 UK ISSN 0085-2066
INTERNATIONAL BIBLIOGRAPHY OF THE SOCIAL SCIENCES. SOCIOLOGY. irreg., vol. 29, 1979. £32.50. Tavistock Publications Ltd., 11 New Fetter La., London EC4P 4EE, England (Dist. in U.S. by: Methuen Inc., 733 Third Ave., New York, N.Y. 10017)
 Title page also reads: International Bibliography of Sociology.

301.4 016 US ISSN 0094-7814
INVENTORY OF MARRIAGE AND FAMILY LITERATURE. 1974. a. price varies. Sage Publications, Inc., 275 S. Beverly Dr., Beverly Hills, CA 90212.
 Formerly: International Bibliography of Research in Marriage and the Family.

301.4 322.4 016 US
JOURNALS OF DISSENT AND SOCIAL CHANGE; a bibliography of titles in the California State University, Sacramento, library. 1969. irreg.; 4th ed., 1975; supplement 1978. free. ‡ California State University, Sacramento, Library, 2000 Jedsmith Dr., Sacramento, CA 95819. Ed. John Liberty. circ. controlled. (processed)

NEW PERIODICALS INDEX. see *LITERARY AND POLITICAL REVIEWS — Abstracting, Bibliographies, Statistics*

SOUND

see *Physics—Sound*

SOUND RECORDING AND REPRODUCTION

see also *Music*

789.9 US ISSN 0092-3486
ANNUAL INDEX TO POPULAR MUSIC RECORD REVIEWS. a. Scarecrow Press, Inc., Box 656, 52 Library St., Metuchen, NJ 08840. bibl.

621.389 US ISSN 0146-4701
AUDIO CRITIC. 1977. irreg. Audio Critic, Box 392, Bronxville, NY 10708. Ed. Peter Aczel.

621.389 AG
AUDIO UNIVERSAL. m. $25. Editorial Fotografia Universal, Muniz 1327/49, Buenos Aires, Argentina.

534 AT ISSN 0310-8902
AUSTRALIAN HI-FI ANNUAL. 1971. a. Australian Hi-Fi Publications Pty. Ltd., P.O. Box 341, Mona Vale, N.S.W. 2103, Australia. Eds. Ralphe Neill; Gary Cutler.

338.4 780 US
BILLBOARD TAPE/AUDIO/VIDEO SOURCEBOOK. a. $10. Billboard Directories, 2160 Patterson Street, Cincinnati, OH 45214. illus. circ. 45,000. (also avail. in microfilm)
 Formerly: Billboard International Tape Directory (ISSN 0090-645X)

253 US ISSN 0192-334X
DISCOGRAPHIES. irreg. price varies. Greenwood Press, 3 Post Rd. W., Westport, CT 06881.

621.389 AG
GUIA DE AUDIO. a. $2.50. Editorial Fotografia Universal, Muniz 1327/49, Buenos Aires, Argentina.

621.389 789.91 UK
HI FI NEWS & RECORD REVIEW ANNUAL. 1966. a. £1.05. Link House Publications, Ltd., Link House, Dingwall Ave., Croydon CR9 2TA, England. Ed. John Crabbe. adv.
 Formerly: Audio Annual (ISSN 0067-0545)

621.389 GW
HI-FI REPORT; Text-Handbuch der Zeitschrift Fonoforum. a. DM.19.80. Bielefelder Verlagsanstalt KG, Niederwall 53, Postfach 1140, 4800 Bielefeld, W. Germany (B.R.D.)

789.9 UK
HI-FI TEST ANNUAL. 1969. a. £1.50. Haymarket Publishing Ltd., 38-42 Hampton Rd., Teddington, Middx. TW11 0JE, England. Ed. Jonathan Kettle.
 Formerly: Hi-Fi Sound Annual (ISSN 0073-2044)

789.9 UK ISSN 0073-2060
HI-FI YEAR BOOK. 1964. a. £3.95. I P C Electrical-Electronic Press Ltd., Dorset House, Stamford Street, London SE1 9LU, England. adv. circ. 25,000.

621.3 US ISSN 0147-7676
HIGH FIDELITY'S BUYING GUIDE TO SPEAKER SYSTEMS. 1976. a. $1.95. A B C Leisure Magazines, Inc., 825 Seventh Ave., New York, NY 10019. Ed. William Tynan. adv. illus. circ. 95,900.

621.389 US ISSN 0161-4371
HIGH FIDELITY'S BUYING GUIDE TO TAPE SYSTEMS. 1972. a. $2.50 (single issue) A B C Leisure Magazines, Inc., 825 Seventh Ave., New York, NY 10019. Ed. William Tynan. adv. illus. circ. 95,000.
 Formerly: Buyer's Guide to the World of Tape (ISSN 0090-9033)

621.3 US ISSN 0090-3981
HIGH FIDELITY'S TEST REPORTS. 1973. a. $3.95 (single issue) A B C Leisure Magazines, Inc., 825 Seventh Ave., New York, NY 10019. Ed. William Tynan. adv. illus. circ. 96,900.

016.789 II ISSN 0302-6744
INDIAN RECORDS. (Text in English) irreg. Gramophone Company of India, Calcutta, India. bibl.

780 US
INTERNATIONAL RECORDING EQUIPMENT AND STUDIO DIRECTORY. 1968. a. $15. Billboard Directories, 2160 Patterson St., Cincinnati, OH 45214 (And 9000 Sunset Blvd., Los Angeles, CA 90069) circ. 45,000. (also avail. in microfilm from KTO)
 Former titles: International Recording Studio and Equipment Directory; International Directory of Recording Studios (ISSN 0067-8627)

MODERN RECORDING'S BUYER'S GUIDE. see *MUSIC*

PAUL'S RECORD MAGAZINE. see *MUSIC*

789.91 621.389 UK
RECORDING IN GREAT BRITAIN. a. membership. Association of Professional Recording Studios, 23 Chestnut Ave, Chorleywood, Herts. WD3 4HA, England.

621.389 BL
SOM; selecoes de Revista de Som. 1975. a. Cr.$300($5) Antenna Edicoes Tecnicas Ltda., Av. Marechal Floriano 143, 20080 Rio de Janeiro, Brazil. Gilberto Affonso Penna. adv.

621.387 AT
STEREO BUYER'S GUIDE. AMPLIFIERS. 1971. a. Australian Hi-Fi Publications Pty. Ltd., Box 341, Mona Vale, N.S.W. 2103, Australia. Ed. Ralphe Neill.

621.389 AT
STEREO BUYER'S GUIDE. CASSETTES. 1971. a. Australian Hi-Fi Publications Pty. Ltd., Box 341, Mona Vale, N.S.W. 2103, Australia. Ed. Ralphe Neill.

621.389 AT
STEREO BUYER'S GUIDE. DIRECTORY. 1971. a. Australian Hi-Fi Publications Pty. Ltd., Box 341, Mona Vale, N.S.W. 2103, Australia. Ed. Ralphe Neill.

621.389 AT
STEREO BUYER'S GUIDE. FM RADIO. 1971. a. Australian Hi-Fi Publications Pty. Ltd., Box 341, Mona Vale, N.S.W. 2103, Australia. Ed. Ralphe Neill.

621.389 AT
STEREO BUYER'S GUIDE. MANUAL. 1971. a. Australian Hi-Fi Publications Pty. Ltd., Box 341, Mona Vale, N.S.W. 2103, Australia. Ed. Ralphe Neill.

621.389 AT
STEREO BUYER'S GUIDE. SPEAKERS. 1971. a. Australian Hi-Fi Publications Pty. Ltd., Box 341, Mona Vale, N.S.W. 2103, Australia. Ed. Ralphe Neill.

621.389 AT
STEREO BUYER'S GUIDE. TURNTABLES. 1971. a. Australian Hi-Fi Publications Pty. Ltd., Box 341, Mona Vale, N.S.W. 2103, Australia. Ed. Ralphe Neill.

338.4 US ISSN 0090-6786
STEREO DIRECTORY & BUYING GUIDE. 1957. a. $1.95. Ziff-Davis Publishing Co., 1 Park Ave., New York, NY 10016. Ed. Arthur P. Salsberg. adv. circ. 160,000.
 Formerly: Stereo/Hi-Fi Directory (ISSN 0081-5470)

681.6 621.3 US
STEREO REVIEW'S TAPE RECORDING & BUYING GUIDE. 1965. a. $2.50. Ziff-Davis Publishing Co., One Park Ave, New York, NY 10016. Ed Arthur P. Salsberg. adv. circ. 130,000.
 Former titles: Tape Recording and Buying Guide (ISSN 0093-996X); Tape Recorder Annual.

SOUND RECORDING AND REPRODUCTION — Abstracting, Bibliographies, Statistics

620 011 US
AUDIO-CASSETTE DIRECTORY. 1972. biennial. $12. Cassette Information Services, Box 9559, Glendale, CA 91206. Ed. Gerald McKee. bk. rev.
 Formerly: Directory of Spoken-Voice Audio-Cassettes.

SPECIAL EDUCATION AND REHABILITATION

see *Education—Special Education and Rehabilitation*

SPORTS AND GAMES

see also *Sports and Games—Ball Games; Sports and Games—Bicycles and Motorcycles; Sports and Games—Boats and Boating; Sports and Games—Horses and Horsemanship; Sports and Games—Outdoor Life*

785.06 US ISSN 0361-221X
A A U BATON TWIRLING RULES AND REGULATIONS. Cover title: A A U Official Handbook: Baton Twirling. irreg. $3.50. Amateur Athletic Union of the United States, 3400 W. 86th St., Indianapolis, IN 46268. illus. Key Title: Baton Twirling Rules and Regulations.

796.4 US ISSN 0361-4654
A A U JUNIOR OLYMPIC HANDBOOK. a. Amateur Athletic Union of the United States, 3400 W. 86th St., Indianapolis, IN 46268. illus.

SPORTS AND GAMES

796.83   US
A A U OFFICIAL BOXING RULES AND GUIDE. quadrennial. $3. Amateur Athletic Union of the United States, 3400 W. 86 St., Indianapolis, IN 46268.

796.42   US   ISSN 0361-347X
A A U OFFICIAL TRACK AND FIELD HANDBOOK, RULES AND RECORDS. biennial. $3.50. Amateur Athletic Union of the United States, 3400 W. 86 St., Indianapolis, IN 46268.

796.41   US
A A U OFFICIAL WEIGHTLIFTING RULES AND GUIDE. a. $3.50. Amateur Athletic Union of the United States, 3400 W. 86 St., Indianapolis, IN 46268.

796   SW
AARETS BANDY. a. Kr.299. Stroembergs Idrottsboecker, Vittangigatan 27, Vaellingby, Stockholm, Sweden.

796   SW   ISSN 0567-4573
AARETS IDROTT. a. Kr.314. Stroembergs Idrottsboecker, Vittangigatan 27, Vaellingby, Stockholm, Sweden.

796.9   SW
AARETS ISHOCKEY. a. Kr.299. (Svenska Ishockeyfoerbundet) Stroembergs Idrottsboecker, Vittangigatan 27, Vaellingby, Stockholm, Sweden. illus.

796   FR   ISSN 0065-0579
ACADEMIE DES SPORTS, PARIS. ANNUAIRE. 1965. irreg. Academie des Sports, Paris, 34 rue de Penthievre, 75008 Paris, France.

790   CS
ALBUM SLAVNYCH SPORTOVCOV. irreg, vol. 4, 1976. price varies. Sport, Publishing House of the Central Committee of the Slovak Physical Culture Organization, Fucikova 14, 893 44 Bratislava, Czechoslovakia. illus.

796   UK   ISSN 0065-6690
AMATEUR ATHLETIC ASSOCIATION. HANDBOOK. 1925. a. £1. Amateur Athletic Association, 70 Brompton Rd., London SW3 1EE, England. Ed. B. Willis. adv. circ. 4,500.

797.2   US
AMATEUR ATHLETIC UNION OF THE UNITED STATES. ATHLETIC LIBRARY. OFFICIAL RULES FOR COMPETITIVE SWIMMING. Cover title: A A U Official Rules: Swimming. a. $3.50. Amateur Athletic Union of the United States, 3400 W. 86th St., Indianapolis, IN 46268. stat.

796   US   ISSN 0091-3405
AMATEUR ATHLETIC UNION OF THE UNITED STATES. OFFICIAL HANDBOOK OF THE A A U CODE. Cover title: A A U Code. a. $4. Amateur Athletic Union of the United States, 3400 W. 86th St., Indianapolis, IN 46268. illus. Key Title: Official Handbook of the A.A.U. Code.

797.2   US   ISSN 0093-5786
AMATEUR ATHLETIC UNION OF THE UNITED STATES. OFFICIAL RULES FOR WATER POLO. a. $3.50. Amateur Athletic Union of the United States, 3400 West 86th Street, Indianapolis, IN 46268. illus. Key Title: Official Rules for Water Polo.

796   US   ISSN 0516-8635
AMATEUR HOCKEY ASSOCIATION OF THE UNITED STATES. OFFICIAL GUIDE. a. $2.50. Amateur Hockey Association of the United States, c/o Hal Trumble, Exec.Dir., 2985 Broadmoor Valley Rd., Colorado Springs, CO 80906.

796   US
AMATEUR HOCKEY ASSOCIATION OF THE UNITED STATES. RULE BOOK. biennial. $2. Amateur Hockey Association of the United States, c/o Hal Trumble, Exec Dir., 2985 Broadmoor Valley Rd., Colorado Springs, CO 80906.

796.962   US   ISSN 0516-866X
AMATEUR SKATING UNION OF THE UNITED STATES. OFFICAL HANDBOOK. 1930. biennial. $2.50. ‡ Amateur Skating Union of the United States, 4423 W. Deming Place, Chicago, IL 60639. Ed. Milan Novak. circ. 1,500. (looseleaf format)

796   US   ISSN 0569-1796
AMATEUR WRESTLING NEWS. vol. 24, 1978. irreg. $10. Amateur Wrestling News, Box 80387, 1109 NW 36, Oklahoma City, OK 73146. Ed. John Hoke. adv.

790.1   FR
ANNEE SPORTIVE U.S.M.T. a. membership. Union Sportive Metropolitaine des Transports, 159 Bd de la Villette, Paris 10, France. adv.

796   FR   ISSN 0067-012X
ATHLETISME FRANCAIS. 1962. a. 15 F. Federation Francaise d'Athletisme, 10 rue Faubourg Poissonniere, 75480 Paris Cedex 10, France.

796   US   ISSN 0067-2408
AUTO RACING GUIDE. 1970. a. $1.50. Snibbe Publications, Inc., 523 Lakeview Rd., Clearwater, FL 33516. Ed. Don O'Reilly. circ. 100,000.

796.345   UK   ISSN 0067-2882
BADMINTON ASSOCIATION OF ENGLAND. OFFICIAL HANDBOOK. 1900. a. 50p. ‡ Badminton Association of England, 44/45 Palace Road, Bromley, Kent BR1 3JU, England. Ed. J.B.H. Bisseker. adv. index. circ. 5,500.

796.345   IE
BADMINTON IRELAND. 1977. a. (Badminton Union of Ireland) Sean Graham, 22 Moore St., Dublin 1, Ireland. illus.
Formerly: Irish Badminton Handbook.
Badminton

790.1   GW   ISSN 0341-7492
BEIHEFT ZU LEISTLINGSSPORT. (Text in English and French) 1975. irreg. DM.18. Verlag Bartels und Wernitz, Reinickendorfer Str. 113, Postfach 65 03 80, 1000 Berlin 65, W. Germany (B.R.D.) Ed. Stephan Starischka. adv. bibl. illus. stat. tr.lit. index. (back issues avail.)

796.082   US   ISSN 0067-6292
BEST SPORTS STORIES. 1944. a. $9.95. ‡ E. P. Dutton & Co., Inc., 201 Park Ave. S., New York, NY 10003. Eds. Irving T. Marsh & Edward Ehre.

371.7   US
BLUE BOOK OF COLLEGE ATHLETICS. 1901. a. $7. Rohrich Corp., Fidelity Bldg., Rm. 1017, 1904 E. 6th St., Cleveland, OH 44114. Ed. Floyd M. Robinson. circ. 6,000.

371.7   US   ISSN 0520-2973
BLUE BOOK OF JUNIOR COLLEGE ATHLETICS. 1958. a. $6. Rohrich Corp., Fidelity Bldg., Rm. 1017, 1940 E. 6th St., Cleveland, OH 44114. Ed. Floyd M. Robinson. circ. 2,000.

796.9   US   ISSN 0361-6398
BOSTON BRUINS OFFICIAL YEARBOOK. a. $2.50. R A Productions, Inc., Box 9100, Boston, MA 02114. illus.

790   US
BOSTON MARATHON. 1979. a. $2. Marathon Publications, Inc., 7 Water St., Boston, MA 02109. Ed. Peter Morrissey. adv. circ. 116,800.

796.83   US
BOXING GUIDE.* 1974. irreg. $0.60 per no. Salart House Inc., P.O. Box 642, Scottsdale, AZ 85252. Ed. Tommy Kay. adv. illus.

796.41   US
BOYS GYMNASTICS RULES. a. $2.25. National Federation of State High School Associations, Federation Place, Box 98, Elgin, IL 60120.

795.414   US
BRIDGE BIDDING GUIDE. 1968. a. $1.50. Snibbe Publications, Inc., 523 Lakeview Rd., Clearwater, FL 33516. Ed. Charles Mallon.

796   UK   ISSN 0068-1326
BRITISH ATHLETICS. 1964. a. £1.50. British Amateur Athletic Board, 70 Brompton Rd., London SW3 1PE, England.

796   UK   ISSN 0068-1938
BRITISH CYCLING FEDERATION. HANDBOOK. 1959. a. 50p. British Cycling Federation, 70 Brompton Rd, London SW3 1EN, England.
Formerly: British Cycling Federation. Racing Handbook.

796   GW
BUNDESINSTITUT FUER SPORTWISSENSCHAFT. BERICHTE UND ASPEKTE. biennial. Bundesinstitut fuer Sportwissenschaft, Hertzstrasse 1, 5023 Loevenich (Bez. Koeln), W. Germany (B.R.D.) illus.

796.5   UK   ISSN 0068-5267
CAIRNGORM CLUB JOURNAL. 1889. biennial, no. 98, 1980. £1. Cairngorm Club, c/o Secretary R. C. Shirreffs, 18 Bon-Accord Square, Aberdeen AB9 1YE, Scotland. Ed. D. Hawksworth. adv. index. circ. 420.

795.414   CN   ISSN 0707-9524
CANADIAN BRIDGE DIGEST. irreg. membership. Canadian Bridge Federation, 2692 Bendale Place, North Vancouver, B.C. V7H 1G9, Canada.
Formerly: Bridge Digest (ISSN 0317-9281)
Bridge

380.1 790.1   CN   ISSN 0316-7771
CANADIAN SPORTING GOODS & PLAYTHINGS. DIRECTORY. 1949. a. Can.$20($30) Lloyd Publications of Canada, Box 262, West Hill, Ont. M1E 4R5, Canada. Ed. J. Lloyd. adv. index. circ. 8,000.

CHARTERED INSTITUTE OF PUBLIC FINANCE AND ACCOUNTANCY. EDUCATION STATISTICS. UNIT COSTS. see *EDUCATION — Abstracting, Bibliographies, Statistics*

794.1   SZ
CHESS EXPRESS/SCHACH EXPRESS; international chess magazine. (Text in English and German) 1968. irreg (2/yr.) 33 Fr.($15) Michael Kuehnle, Ed. & Pub., Honggerstr. 80, CH-8037 Zurich, Switzerland. bk. rev. charts. illus.

796   US   ISSN 0084-8891
COLORADO SKI AND WINTER RECREATION STATISTICS. 1968. a. $20. University of Colorado, Graduate School of Business Administration, Boulder, CO 80309. Ed. Charles R. Goeldner. circ. 200.

382   BL
CONFEDERACAO BRASILEIRA DE DESPORTOS. RELATORIO. irreg. Confederacao Brasileira de Desportos, Rua da Alfandega, 70, Rio de Janeiro, Brazil. illus.

CORD SPORTFACTS GUNS GUIDE. see *HOBBIES*

796   GW   ISSN 0075-2401
DEUTSCHER TURNER-BUND. JAHRBUCH DER TURNKUNST. 1906. a. DM.12. Pohl Druckerei und Verlagsanstalt, Herzog-Ernst-Ring 1, Postfach 103, 3100 Celle, W. Germany (B.R.D.)

796 613.7   CN   ISSN 0708-6113
DIRECTORY OF SPORTS, RECREATION AND PHYSICAL EDUCATION. 1978. a. Sport Ontario, 559 Jarvis St., Toronto, Ont. M4Y 2J1, Canada.

796   GW   ISSN 0173-0843
DOKUMENTE ZUM HOCHSCHULSPORT. 1976. irreg., vol.6, 1979. price varies. (Freie Universitaet Berlin, Zentraleinrichtung Hochschulsport) Verlag Ingrid Czwalina, Reesenbuettler Redder 75, 2070 Ahrensburg, W. Germany (B.R.D.)

796.75   FR   ISSN 0071-4186
F. F. M. ANNUAIRE OFFICIEL. a. price varies. Federation Francaise de Motocyclisme, 36 rue d'Hauteville, 75010 Paris, France. adv.

798.8   SP   ISSN 0071-4119
FEDERACION ESPANOLA GALGUERA. ANUARIO Y MEMORIA DEPORTIVA. Cover title: Memoria Deportiva. 1939. a. Federacion Espanola Galguera, Barquillo 19, Madrid 4, Spain.

798   FR   ISSN 0071-4232
FEDERATION FRANCAISE DES SPORTS EQUESTRES. ANNUAIRE OFFICIEL.* irreg., 1967, 7th ed. 7 F. Federation Francaise des Sports Equestres, 164 Fg. Saint-Honore, 75008 Paris, France.

SPORTS AND GAMES

796 360   FR
FEDERATION FRANCAISE HANDISPORT. INFORMATIONS. 1976. irreg. 20 F. Federation Francaise Handisport, 1 Av. Pierre-Grenier, 92100 Boulogne, France. adv. circ. 5,000.
     Formerly: Federation Francaise de Sports pour Handicaps Physiques. Informations (ISSN 0395-7594)

799.3   CN   ISSN 0226-773X
FEDERATION OF CANADIAN ARCHERS. RULES BOOK. French edition: Federation Canadienne des Archers. Livret des Reglements (ISSN 0706-3180) (Editions in English and French) 1978. irreg. Can.$1. Federation of Canadian Archers, 333 River Rd., Vanier, Ont. K1L 8B9, Canada.

796.86   US
FENCING RULES FOR COMPETITIONS. irreg. price varies. Amateur Fencers League of America, 601 Curtis St., Albany, CA 94706.

799.1   SW
FISKE. a. Fritidsfiskarna, Box 14114, 104-41 Stockholm 14, Sweden. illus.
     Fishing

796   FR   ISSN 0071-9102
FRANCE-SPORTS. (Text in French; summaries in German, Italian, English, Spanish) 1954. biennial. 96 F. Creations, Editions et Productions Publicitaires, 1, Place d'Estienne d'Orves, 75009 Paris, France. Ed. Georges Prieux. adv. circ. 8,500.
     Directory of sport, camping, fishing and hunting articles

796.41   US
GIRLS GYMNASTICS MANUAL. biennial. $2.25. National Federation of State High School Associations, Federation Place, Box 98, Elgin, IL 60120.

796.41   US   ISSN 0270-2029
GIRLS GYMNASTICS RULES. a. $2.25. National Federation of State High School Associations, Federation Place, Box 98, Elgin, IL 60120.

796   US   ISSN 0072-4955
GOLF GUIDE. 1963. a. $1.50. Snibbe Publications, Inc., 523 Lakeview Rd., Clearwater, FL 33516. Ed. Joseph Gambatese.

796.352   SP
GOLFINFORMACION. Cover title: Golf Informacion. irreg. Ediciones Informativas y Deportivas, Avda. del Generalisimo, 60, Madrid, Spain. illus.

GUIDA DELLO SCIATORE. see *TRAVEL AND TOURISM*

796   AU   ISSN 0072-9698
HANDBALL UND FAUSTBALL IN OESTERREICH. irreg. Oesterreichischer Handball- und Faustball-Bund, Hauslabgasse 24, A-1050 Vienna, Austria. Ed. Friedrich Duschka.

796   UK   ISSN 0073-0416
HARPERS GUIDE TO SPORTS TRADE. 1948. a. £10.50. Harper Trade Journals Ltd., Harling House, 47-51 Great Suffolk St., London SE1 0BS, England. Ed. S. Blake. adv. circ. 3,600.

796   UK   ISSN 0073-3164
HOMING WORLD STUD BOOK. 1938. a. £1.85. Royal Pigeon Racing Association, 26 High St., Welshpool, Powys SY21 7JP, Wales. Ed. Ernest B. Harbourne.
     Deals with racing pigeons

796   SZ
I S U CONSTITUTION. (Text in English) biennial. 6 Fr. International Skating Union, Postfach, 7270 Davos-Platz, Switzerland.

796   SZ
I S U REGULATIONS. (Text in English) biennial; latest issue 1977. 12 Fr. International Skating Union, Postfach, 7270 Davos-Platz, Switzerland.

371.7   RM
INSTITUTUL PEDAGOGIC ORADEA. LUCRARI STIINTIFICE SERIA EDUCATIE FIZICA SI SPORT. (Continues in part its Lucrari Stiintifice : Seria Educatie Fizica, Biologie, Stiinte Medicale (1971-72), its Lucrari Stiintifice: Seria A and Seria B (1969-70), and its Lucrari Stiintifice (1967-68)) (Text in Rumanian, occasionally in English or French; summaries in Rumanian, English or German) 1967. a. Institutul Pedagogic Oradea, Calea Armatei Rosii Nr. 5, Oradea, Romania.

796   UK   ISSN 0074-137X
INTERNATIONAL ARCHERY FEDERATION. BULLETIN OFFICIEL. (Text in English and French) biennial; no. 26, 1974. price varies. International Archery Federation, 46 The Balk, Walton, Wakefield, England. Ed. Mrs. I. K. Frith. adv.

796 371   JA   ISSN 0074-1728
INTERNATIONAL ASSOCIATION OF PHYSICAL EDUCATION AND SPORTS FOR GIRLS AND WOMEN. PROCEEDINGS OF THE INTERNATIONAL CONGRESS. irreg., 1969, 6th, Tokyo. Japan Association of Physical Education for Women and Girls, 6-102 O.M.Y.C., 3-1 Jinen-cho Yoyogi, Shibuya-ku, Tokyo, Japan. circ. limited circ.
     Proceedings published in host country

796.345   UK
INTERNATIONAL BADMINTON FEDERATION. ANNUAL STATUTE BOOK. 1935. a. £1.50. International Badminton Federation, 24 Winchcombe House, Winchcombe St., Cheltenham, Glos., England. index.
     Formerly: International Badminton Federation. Annual Handbook (ISSN 0074-1981)

INTERNATIONAL MILITARY SPORTS COUNCIL. TECHNICAL BROCHURE/ CONSEIL INTERNATIONAL DU SPORT MILITAIRE. BROCHURE TECHNIQUE. see *MILITARY*

796   GR   ISSN 0074-7181
INTERNATIONAL OLYMPIC ACADEMY. REPORT OF THE SESSIONS. (Since 1968 issued in separate Greek, English and French vols) 1961. a; 13th, Olympia, Greece, 1973. $5 for non-qualified personnel. Hellenic Olympic Committee, 4 Kapsali St., Athens 138, Greece. cum.index: 1961-69. circ. 9,000.

796   FR   ISSN 0074-7645
INTERNATIONAL REFERENCE ANNUAL FOR BUILDING AND EQUIPMENT OF SPORTS, TOURISM, RECREATION INSTALLATIONS. 1970. a. price varies. Techno-Loisirs, 3 rue Sivel, Paris 14, France. adv. circ. 10,000.

790.1   US
INTERNATIONAL SERIES ON SPORTS SCIENCES. 1974. irreg. price varies. University Park Press, Chamber of Commerce Bldg., Baltimore, MD 21202. Eds. R. C. Nelson, C. A. Morehouse.

796   SZ   ISSN 0539-0168
INTERNATIONAL SKATING UNION. BESTIMMUNGEN UEBER DAS EISTANZEN. biennial. 12 Fr. International Skating Union, Postfach, 7270 Davos-Platz, Switzerland.

796   SZ   ISSN 0535-2479
INTERNATIONAL SKATING UNION. MINUTES OF CONGRESS. (Text in English) biennial, latest 1977, Paris. 8 Fr. International Skating Union, Postfach, 7270 Davos-Platz, Switzerland.

796   UK   ISSN 0539-0370
INTERNATIONAL SPORTING PRESS ASSOCIATION. BULLETIN. N.S.* irreg.; 1967, no. 15. International Sporting Press Association, c/o Bobby Naidoo, Tudor House, the Heath, Weybridge, Surrey, England.

796   GW
JAHRBUCH DER LEICHTATHLETIK. a. (Deutsches Leichtathletik-Verband) Verlag Bartels und Wernitz KG, Reinickendorfer Str. 113, 1000 Berlin 65, W. Germany (B.R.D) Ed. H. Vogel. circ. 5,000.

796   US   ISSN 0094-8705
JOURNAL OF PHILOSOPHY OF SPORT. 1974. a. $8. Philosophic Society for the Study of Sport, Box 5076, Champaign, IL 61820. Ed. Klaus V. Meier. bk. rev. circ. 235.

790.1 100   US   ISSN 0094-8705
JOURNAL OF THE PHILOSOPHY OF SPORT. 1974. a. $10. (Philosophic Society for the Study of Sport) Human Kinetics Publishers, Box 5076, Champaign, IL 61820. Ed. Klaus Meier. circ. 500.

796   FI   ISSN 0075-4684
KALASTUSPAIKKAOPAS. 1966. irreg.(approx. biennial) Fmk.20. Kalatalouden Keskusliitto - Federation of Finnish Fisheries Associations (Centralfoerbundet foer Fiskerihushaallning, Koydenpunojankatu 7 B 23, 00180 Helsinki 18, Finland. Ed. Bd. adv. index. circ. 4,000.

796   MY   ISSN 0085-2481
KARATE INTERNATIONAL ANNUAL. (Text in English and Chinese) 1971. a. M.$3.50($1.50) ‡ (Karate Association of Malaysia) Karate Budokan International Inc., 44 Pudu Road, Kuala Lumpur, Malaysia. Ed. Chew Choo Soot. adv. bk. rev. charts. illus. circ. 20,000.

796   HU
MAGYAR TESTNEVELESI FOISKOLA. TUDOMANYOS KOZLEMENYEK. (Summaries in French, German and Russian) 1954. irreg. 20 Ft. Magyar Testnevelesi Foiskola, Alkotas u.44, Budapest 12, Hungary. illus.

354   CN   ISSN 0703-0827
MANITOBA. LOTTERIES COMMISSION. ANNUAL REPORT. (Report year ends Mar. 31) 1971/72. a. Lotteries Commission, 415-155 Carlton St., Winnipeg, Man. RC3 3H8, Canada. illus. stat.

790.1   CK
MERIDIANO DEPORTIVO. 1975. irreg. c/o Efrain Tobon, Apdo. Aereo 8275, Medellin, Colombia.

790.1   CN   ISSN 0702-858X
MONDE DES LOISIRS. 1973. a. Can.$5. Confederation des Loisirs du Quebec, 1415 Jarry St. E., Montreal, Que. H2E 2Z7, Canada. circ. 1,500.

796   FR   ISSN 0077-1570
MOTOCYCLO CATALOGUE; guide technique du cycle et du motocycle. 1951. a. 79.15 F. Editions S.O.S.P., 59-61 Avenue de la Grande Armee, 75782 Paris Cedex 16, France. Ed. C. L. Lavaud. index.

790.1   CN
MOTONEIGISTE CANADIEN. (Text in French) 1975. a. C R V Publishing Co. Ltd., Suite 221, 3414 Park Ave., Montreal, Que. H2X 2H5, Canada. adv. illus.

MOTOR CYCLE DIARY. see *TRANSPORTATION — Automobiles*

796.7   US   ISSN 0090-2144
MOTOR RACING YEAR. (Vols for 1972-called also No. 3) 1971. a. price varies. W. W. Norton & Company, Inc., 500 Fifth Ave., New York, NY 10036. Ed. Anthony Pritchard. illus.

MOTORCYCLE BUYER'S GUIDE. see *TRANSPORTATION — Automobiles*

797.2   US   ISSN 0361-719X
N A G W S GUIDE. AQUATICS; tips and techniques for teachers and coaches. 1977. biennial. American Alliance for Health, Physical Education, Recreation and Dance, National Association for Girls and Women in Sport, 1900 Association Dr., Reston, VA 22091. illus. circ. 2,000.
     Formerly: Aquatics Guide (ISSN 0401-636X)

798 799
N A G W S GUIDE. ARCHERY-FENCING. 1938. a. $3.95. American Alliance for Health, Physical Education, Recreation, and Dance, National Association for Girls and Women in Sport, 1900 Association Dr., Reston, VA 22091. circ. 4,000. Indexed: ERIC.
     Former titles: Archery-Golf Guide; A A H P E R Archery-Riding Guide (ISSN 0065-700X)

790.1   US
N A G W S GUIDE. BADMINTON-SQUASH-RACQUETBALL. 1946. biennial. American Alliance for Health, Physical Education, Recreation and Dance, National Association for Girls and Women in Sport, 1900 Association Dr., Reston, VA 22091. circ. 13,000.

N A G W S GUIDE. BOWLING-GOLF. (National Association for Girls and Women in Sport) see *SPORTS AND GAMES — Ball Games*

SPORTS AND GAMES

797.21 US
N A G W S GUIDE. COMPETITIVE SWIMMING AND DIVING. 1949. a. American Alliance for Health, Physical Education, Recreation and Dance, National Association for Girls and Women in Sport, 1900 Association Dr., Reston, VA 22091. circ. 6,000.

796.41 US ISSN 0363-9282
N A G W S GUIDE. GYMNASTICS. 1963/65. biennial. American Alliance for Health, Physical Education, Recreation and Dance, National Association for Girls & Women in Sport, 1900 Association Dr., Reston, VA 22091. circ. 5,000. Indexed: ERIC.
Formerly: Gymnastics Guide.

797.21 US ISSN 0163-4267
N A G W S GUIDE. SYNCHRONIZED SWIMMING. 1949/51. a. American Alliance for Health, Physical Education, Recreation, and Dance, National Association for Girls and Women in Sport, 1900 Association Dr., Reston, VA 22091. circ. 1,000. Indexed: ERIC.

796.31 US
N A G W S GUIDE. TEAM HANDBALL, ORIENTEERING. 1976. biennial. American Alliance for Health, Physical Education, Recreation and Dance, National Association for Girls and Women in Sport, 1900 Association Dr., Reston, VA 22091. circ. 1,500.
Formerly (until 1981): N A G W S Guide. Team Handball, Racquetball, Orienteering (ISSN 0145-9767)

796 US ISSN 0077-3336
N A I A HANDBOOK. 1959. a. $6. National Association of Intercollegiate Athletics, 1221 Baltimore St., Kansas City, MO 64105. Ed. Harry Fritz.

796 US ISSN 0077-3344
N A I A OFFICIAL RECORD BOOK. 1958. a. $7.50. National Association of Intercollegiate Athletics, 1221 Baltimore, Kansas City, MO 64105. Ed. Charles Eppler. index. circ. 2,500.

790.1 US
N C A A DIRECTORY. 1976. a. $2. National Collegiate Athletic Association, Box 1906, U. S. Highway 50 and Nall Ave., Shawnee Mission, KS 66222. circ. 2,500.

797 US
N C A A GYMNASTICS RULES. 1967. a. $3. (National Collegiate Athletic Association) N C A A Publishing Service, Box 1906, Shawnee Mission, KS 66222.

790.1 US
N C A A TELEVISION COMMITTEE REPORT. 1952. a. $1.50. National Collegiate Athletic Association, Box 1906, U.S. Highway 50 and Nall Ave., Shawnee Mission, KS 66222. circ. 2,500.

796 CN ISSN 0079-5569
N.H.L. PRO HOCKEY. 1969. a. Can.$4.95. ‡ Paper Jacks Ltd., 330 Steelcase Rd., Markham, Ont. L3R 2M1, Canada. Ed. James Proudfoot. index. circ. 20,000.

796 US ISSN 0077-3794
NATIONAL COLLEGIATE ATHLETIC ASSOCIATION. ANNUAL REPORTS. 1966. a. $3. National Collegiate Athletic Association, U.S. Highway 50 and Nall Ave., Box 1906, Shawnee Mission, KS 66222. circ. 2,500.

796 US ISSN 0077-3808
NATIONAL COLLEGIATE ATHLETIC ASSOCIATION. CONVENTION PROCEEDINGS. 1906; 1967 as independent title. a. $3. National Collegiate Athletic Association, U.S. Highway 50 and Nall Ave., Box 1906, Shawnee Mission, KS 66222. circ. 2,500.

796 US ISSN 0077-3816
NATIONAL COLLEGIATE ATHLETIC ASSOCIATION. MANUAL. Cover title: N C A A Manual. 1906; 1966 as independent title. a. $3. National Collegiate Athletic Association, U.S. Highway 50 and Nall Ave., Box 1906, Shawnee Mission, KS 66222. circ. 7,500.

796.06 US ISSN 0094-4459
NATIONAL COLLEGIATE ATHLETIC ASSOCIATION. PROCEEDINGS OF THE SPECIAL CONVENTION. 1973. irreg. National Collegiate Athletic Association, Box 1906, Shawnee Mission, KS 66222. Key Title: Proceedings of the Special Convention of the National Collegiate Athletic Association.

796 US ISSN 0077-3824
NATIONAL COLLEGIATE CHAMPIONSHIPS. 1954. a. $3. National Collegiate Athletic Association, U.S. Highway 50 and Nall Ave., Box 1906, Shawnee Mission, KS 66222. circ. 2,700.
Formerly: National Collegiate Championships Record Book (ISSN 0148-9798)

796 US ISSN 0547-616X
NATIONAL DIRECTORY OF COLLEGE ATHLETICS (MEN'S EDITION) 1968. a. $12. (National Association of Collegiate Directors of Athletics) Ray Franks Publishing Ranch, P.O. Box 7068, Amarillo, TX 79109.

796 US ISSN 0092-5489
NATIONAL DIRECTORY OF COLLEGE ATHLETICS (WOMEN) 1973. a. $8. R Franks Publishing Ranch, Box 7068, Amarillo, TX 79109. Ed. Ray Franks. illus.
Formerly: National Directory of Women's Athletics (ISSN 0092-5489)

796.9 CN
NATIONAL HOCKEY LEAGUE. OFFICIAL RULE BOOK. 1931. a. Can.$1. National Hockey League, 920 Sun Life Bldg., Montreal, Canada. Ed. Brian O'Neill. illus.

790.1 US
NATIONAL RECREATIONAL, SPORTING AND HOBBY ORGANIZATIONS OF THE UNITED STATES. 1980. a. $25. Columbia Books, Inc., Suite 1336, 777 14th St. N.W., Washington, DC 20005. Eds. Craig Colgate Jr., Laurie Evans.

796.72 US
NATIONAL SPEEDWAY DIRECTORY. 1975. irreg., approx. biennial, latest 1980. $4.95. Dray Publishing Co., Box 188, Marne, MI 49435. Eds. Allan E. Brown, Ross Ferguson. adv. stat.
Formerly: Midwest Auto Racing Guide.

353.978 US ISSN 0091-942X
NEBRASKA. OFFICE OF ATHLETIC COMMISSIONER. REPORT. a. Office of Athletic Commissioner, Lincoln, NE 68509.

790.1 SZ
NEUE COLUMBUS; das grosse Jahrbuch von Spiel und Sport von Erfindungen, Entdeckungen und Abenteuern aus aller Welt. a. 26.50 Fr. Hallwag AG, Nordring 4, CH-3001 Berne, Switzerland. illus.

796.962 US
NEW YORK RANGERS YEARBOOK; official guide and records. a. $2 per copy. New York Rangers Hockey Club, Madison Square Garden, 4 Pennsylvania Plaza, New York, NY 10001. Ed. John Halligan. illus. stat.
Formerly: New York Rangers Blue Book.

790 NZ
NEW ZEALAND. COUNCIL FOR RECREATION AND SPORT. REPORT. 1974. a. NZ.$0.05. Council for Recreation and Sport, P.O. Box 5122, Wellington, New Zealand.

796 970 980 US
NORTH AMERICAN SOCIETY FOR SPORT HISTORY. PROCEEDINGS. a. membership. North American Society for Sport History, c/o Ronald A. Smith, 101 White Bldg., Penn State University, University Park, PA 16802. circ. 1,000.

796 US
NORTHERN CALIFORNIA GOLF ASSOCIATION. BLUE BOOK. 1961. a. $4 to non-members. Northern California Golf Association, Box 1157, Pebble Beach, CA 93953. Ed. Ronald R. Read. adv.

790 CN
NOVA SCOTIA. DEPARTMENT OF RECREATION. ANNUAL REPORT. 1974. a. Department of Recreation, 5151 George St., P.O. Box 864, Halifax, N.S. B3J 2V2, Canada. illus.

797.2 US
OFFICIAL A A U DIVING RULES. Running title: Diving Rules. a. $3.50. Amateur Athletic Union of the United States, 3400 W. 86th St., Indianapolis, IN 46268. illus.

796.8 US
OFFICIAL A A U JUDO RULES. biennial. $3.50. Amateur Athletic Union of the United States., 3400 W. 86th St., Indianapolis, IN 46268. illus.

797.2 US
OFFICIAL A A U SYNCHRONIZED SWIMMING HANDBOOK. Running title: Synchronized Swimming Rules. a. $3.50. Amateur Athletic Union of the United States, 3400 W. 86th St., Indianapolis, IN 46268. illus.

796.4 US ISSN 0361-2899
OFFICIAL A A U TRAMPOLINE AND TUMBLING HANDBOOK. Cover title: A A U Official Handbook: Trampoline & Tumbling. irreg. $5. Amateur Athletic Union of the United States, 3400 W. 86th St., Indianapolis, IN 46268. illus.

796.8 US
OFFICIAL A A U WRESTLING HANDBOOK. a. $3.50. Amateur Athletic Union of the United States, 3400 W. 86th St., Indianapolis, IN 46268. illus.

796.35 US ISSN 0362-3270
OFFICIAL FIELD HOCKEY RULES FOR SCHOOL GIRLS. irreg. United States Field Hockey Association, USFHA National Office, 4415 Buffalo Rd., North Chili, NY 14514.

796 US
OFFICIAL NATIONAL COLLEGIATE ATHLETIC ASSOCIATION ICE HOCKEY GUIDE. 1926. a. $3. (National Collegiate Athletic Association) N C A A Publishing Service, Box 1906, Shawnee Mission, KS 66222. circ. 10,000.

797.21 US
OFFICIAL NATIONAL COLLEGIATE ATHLETIC ASSOCIATION SWIMMING GUIDE. 1925. a. $3. (National Collegiate Athletic Association) N C A A Publishing Service, Box 1906, Shawnee Mission, KS 66222. circ. 8,200.

790.1 US
OFFICIAL NATIONAL COLLEGIATE ATHLETIC ASSOCIATION WATER POLO RULES. 1970. a. $1.50. (National Collegiate Athletic Association) N C A A Publishing Service, Box 1906, Shawnee Mission, KS 66222.

790.1 US
OFFICIAL NATIONAL COLLEGIATE ATHLETIC ASSOCIATION WRESTLING GUIDE. 1927. a. $3. (National Collegiate Athletic Association) N C A A Publishing Service, Box 1906, Shawnee Mission, KS 66222. circ. 10,000.

790.1 US
OFFICIAL RULES OF SPORTS AND GAMES. 1949. biennial. $25. Sportshelf, P.O. Box 634, New Rochelle, NY 10802. charts. illus.

790.1 UK
OLEANDER GAMES AND PASTIMES SERIES. a. Oleander Press, 17 Stansgate Ave., Cambridge CB2 2QZ, England (U.S. address: 210 Fifth Ave., New York, NY 10010)

796 CN
ONTARIO RINGETTE ASSOCIATION. OFFICIAL RULES. (Text in English and French) 1965. a. Can.$2. Ontario Ringette Association, 160 Vanderhoof Ave., Toronto, Ont. M4G 4B8, Canada. Ed. Wes Clark. circ. 5,000.

798 FR ISSN 0078-7035
OU MONTER A CHEVAL. 1964. a. 24 F. price varies. ‡ Guides Equestres, 38 rue Parmentier, 92200 Neuilly-sur-Seine, France. Dir. Agnes Lamoureux. adv. circ. 8,000.

796.962 US ISSN 0271-2636
PETERSEN'S PRO HOCKEY. 1980. a. $2.50. Petersen Publishing Co., 8490 Sunset Blvd., Los Angeles, CA 90069.

796 US ISSN 0079-550X
PRO AND AMATEUR HOCKEY GUIDE. 1967. a. $7.50. Sporting News Publishing Co., 1212 N. Lindbergh Blvd, St Louis, MO 63166.
Formerly: Pro Senior Hockey Guide.

SPORTS AND GAMES

796　　　　US　ISSN 0079-5577
PRO HOCKEY GUIDE. 1970. a. $1.50. Snibbe Publications, Inc., 523 Lakeview Rd., Clearwater, FL 33516. Ed. Jack Clary. circ. 1,000,0000.

794.1　　　　IT
QUADERNI DI SCACCHI: I GRANDI GIOCATORI. 1975. irreg. L.2500. Mursia Editore, Via Tadino 29, Milan, Italy. illus.

796　　　　UK　ISSN 0081-377X
RACEFORM UP-TO-DATE FORM BOOK ANNUAL. 1899. a. £8.75. Sporting Chronicle Publications Ltd., Thomson House, Withy Grove, Manchester M60 4BJ, England. Ed. K. Hussey. adv. circ. 10,000.

796　　　　UK　ISSN 0079-9424
RACING AND FOOTBALL OUTLOOK: RACING ANNUAL. 1909. a. £1. Webster's Publications Ltd., Onslow House, 60-66 Saffron Hill, London EC1N 8AY, England. circ. 40,000.
　　Formerly: Racing and Football Racing Annual.

790.1　658　　UK　ISSN 0144-624X
RECREATION MANAGEMENT HANDBOOK. 1975. biennial. £14.75. E. & F. N. Spon Ltd., 11 New Fetter Lane, London EC4P 4EE, England. circ. 2,500.
　　Formerly: Recreation Management Yearbook (ISSN 0306-3062)

796　　　　FR　ISSN 0080-1135
REPERTOIRE GENERAL DES CLUBS SPORTIFS DE FRANCE.* 1962. irreg. Editions du Forum, 13 rue Giacierre, Paris 13e, France.

796　　　　UK　ISSN 0080-4282
ROYAL CALEDONIAN CURLING CLUB. ANNUAL. 1838. a. £1.50. Royal Caledonian Curling Club, 2 Coates Crescent, Edinburgh EH3 7AN, Scotland. Ed. Robin W. Welsh. adv. circ. 4,600.

796　　　　UK　ISSN 0080-4819
RUFF'S GUIDE TO THE TURF AND THE SPORTING LIFE ANNUAL. 1842. a. £20. Mirror Group Newspapers Ltd., Sporting Life, 9 New Fetter Lane, London EC4A 1AR, England. Ed. Ken Oliver. adv.

794.1　　　　YU　ISSN 0045-6586
SAHOVSKI INFORMATOR/CHESS INFORMANT/SAHMATNYJ INFORMATOR. 1959. irreg. $16.50. (World Chess Federation - FIDE) Centar za Unapredjivanje Saha, 7 Jula 30, Box 739, Belgrade, Yugoslavia. Ed. Aleksandar Matarovic. circ. 22,000.
　　Chess

796　　　　FR
SKI FRANCAIS. m(Oct.-Feb.); every 3 months for rest of year. 14 F. Federation Francaise de Ski, 34, rue Eugene Flachat, 75017 Paris, France.

796　　　　US　ISSN 0080-9918
SKIER'S GUIDE. 1969. a. $1.50. Snibbe Publications, Inc., 523 Lakeview Rd., Clearwater, FL 33516. Ed. Jan McWilliams. circ. 300,000.

SOARING IN THE A.C.T. (Australian Capital Territory) see *AERONAUTICS AND SPACE FLIGHT*

790.1　　　　UK　ISSN 0560-6152
SOCIETY OF ARCHER-ANTIQUARIES. JOURNAL. 1958. a. membership. ‡ Society of Archer-Antiquaries, c/o D. Elmy, 61, Lambert Road, Bridlington, Yorkshire, England. Ed. E.G. Heath. bk. rev. charts. illus. circ. controlled.

790.1　　　　BE
SPORT INTERNATIONAL YEARBOOK. a. 150 Fr.($5) International Military Sports Council - Conseil International du Sport Militaire, Ave. des Abeilles 2, B-1050 Brussels, Belgium. Ed. J. Coumetou.

793　　　　NE　ISSN 0077-6777
SPORTACCOMMODATIE IN NEDERLAND/ SPORTS: PUBLIC ACCOMMODATION. (Text in Dutch and English) 1959. irreg. price varies. Centraal Bureau voor de Statistiek, Prinses Beatrixlaan 428, Voorburg, Netherlands (Orders to: Staatsuitgeverij, Christoffel Plantijnstraat, The Hague, Netherlands)

798　　　　UK　ISSN 0081-3761
SPORTING CHRONICLE "HORSES IN TRAINING". 1891. a. £6.50. Sporting Chronicle Publications Ltd., Thomson House, Withy Grove, Manchester, M60 4BJ, England. Ed. K. Hussey. adv. circ. 14,000.

790.1　　　　US
SPORTS AND RECREATIONAL PROGRAMS OF THE NATION'S UNIVERSITIES AND COLLEGES. 1958. every 5 years. National Collegiate Athletic Association, Box 1906, U.S. Highway 50 and Nall Ave., Shawnee Mission, KS 66222. circ. 3,000.

790.1　　　　US　ISSN 0198-6597
SPORTS COLLECTORS DIRECTORY. 1979. a. Urban Publications, 4928 N. 85th St., Milwaukee, WI 53225.

790.1　658.8　　US
SPORTS MANAGEMENT REVIEW. 1977. q. $85. Pacific Select Corp., 101 Lansdale Ave., San Francisco, CA 94127. Ed. Matt Levine. circ. 750. (looseleaf format)

790.1　338　　US
SPORTSGUIDE FOR INDIVIDUAL SPORTS; the master reference for individual sports marketing. 1980. a. $40. Sportsguide, Inc., 211 E. 43rd St., Suite 901, New York, NY 10017. Ed. Richard A. Lipsey. circ. 2,500.

790.1　338　　US　ISSN 0198-8190
SPORTSGUIDE FOR TEAM SPORTS; the master reference for team sports marketing. 1980. a. $40. Sportsguide, Inc., 211 E. 43rd St., Suite 901, New York, NY 10017. Ed. Richard A. Lipsey. circ. 2,500.

790.1　　　　NE
SPORTWETENSCHAPPELIJKE ONDERZOEKINGEN. 1978. irreg. price varies. Uitgeverij de Vriesborch, Jacobijnestraat 5, Haarlem, Netherlands. illus. circ. 1,500.

796　　　　GW　ISSN 0342-457X
SPORTWISSENSCHAFT UND SPORTPRAXIS. 1970. irreg., vol.34, 1979. price varies. Verlag Ingrid Czwalina, Reesenbuettler Redder 75, 2070 Ahrensburg, W. Germany (B. R. D.) Ed. Clemens Czwalina.
　　Formerly: Schriftenreihe fuer Sportwissenschaft und Sportpraxis (ISSN 0080-7141)

796　　　　GW　ISSN 0340-0956
SPORTWISSENSCHAFTLICHE DISSERTATIONEN. 1975. irreg., vol.14, 1979. price varies. Verlag Ingrid Czwalina, Reesenbuettler Redder 75, 2070 Ahrensburg, W. Germany (B. R. D.) Eds. Clemens Czwalina, Eike Jost.

STUDIES IN SPORT, PHYSICAL EDUCATION AND HEALTH. see *PHYSICAL FITNESS AND HYGIENE*

SUMMER BREEZES. see *CHILDREN AND YOUTH — For*

797　　　　US　ISSN 0081-9611
SURFBOARD BUILDERS' YEARBOOK. (Text in English, French and Spanish) 1963. a. $6. Transmedia, 9811 Edgelake Rd., La Mesa, CA 92041. Ed. Stephen M. Shaw. adv. circ. 10,000.

797.21　　　　US　ISSN 0163-2884
SWIMMING AND DIVING RULES. a. $1.75. National Federation of State High School Associations, Federation Place, Box 98, Elgin, IL 60120.
　　Formerly: Swimming & Diving Case Book (ISSN 0145-3831); Supersedes: Swimming Rules.

797.2　　　　US　ISSN 0082-0466
SWIMMING POOL WEEKLY/AGE - DATA AND REFERENCE ANNUAL. 1932. a. $10. Hoffman Publications, Inc., 3000 N.E. 30th Place, P.O. Box 11299, Fort Lauderdale, FL 33306. Ed. Henry Kinney. (reprint service avail. from UMI)

790　　　　KO
TAEHAN CHEYKHOE. CHEYUK CHONGSO. 1973. irreg. Korea Amateur Sports Association, 19 Mugyodong, Seoul, S. Korea. Ed.Bd. illus.

688.76　　　　FR
TECHNO-LOISIRS; guide international annuel de la construction et de l'Equipment pour le sport et les loisirs. (Text in various European languages and Esperanto) 1971. biennial. 50 F.($10) Editions Techno-Loisirs, 3 rue Sivel, 75014 Paris, France. Ed. Georges Caille. adv. bk. rev. play rev. bibl. illus. patents. stat. tr.lit. index. circ. 10,000. (also avail. in magnetic tape)

798　　　　US　ISSN 0083-3509
TROTTING AND PACING GUIDE; official handbook of harness racing. 1947. a. $2. United States Trotting Association, 750 Michigan Ave, Columbus, OH 43215. Ed. Philip Pikelny. index. circ. 5,000.

796.42　　　　US
UNITED STATES CROSS-COUNTRY COACHES ASSOCIATION. ANNUAL BUSINESS MEETING. MINUTES. a. free. United States Cross-Country Coaches Association, c/o Ken O'Brien, Sec., Boyden Gym, University of Massachusetts, Amherst, MA 01003.
　　Supersedes: United States Cross-Country Coaches Association. Proceedings; Which was formerly: United States Cross-Country and Distance Running Coaches Association. Proceedings (ISSN 0082-9706)

796.353　　　　US　ISSN 0083-3118
UNITED STATES POLO ASSOCIATION. YEARBOOK. 1890. a. $15. United States Polo Association, 1301 W. 22 St., Oak Brook, IL 60521. Ed. Ruthe Larson.

796.93　　　　US　ISSN 0083-3258
UNITED STATES SKI ASSOCIATION. DIRECTORY. a. $5. United States Ski Association, 1726 Champa St., Suite 300, Denver, CO 80202.

301.5　　　　AT
VICTORIA, AUSTRALIA. DEPARTMENT OF YOUTH, SPORT AND RECREATION. REPORT. a. free. 570 Bourke St., Melbourne 3000, Australia. stat. circ. 2,000.

639　　　　US　ISSN 0095-3253
WASHINGTON (STATE) GAME DEPARTMENT. APPLIED RESEARCH SECTION. BULLETIN. 1974. irreg. Game Department, 600 N. Capitol Way, Olympia, WA 98501. Key Title: Bulletin - Washington Game Department, Enviromental Management Division, Applied Research Section.

790.1　　　　UK
WELSH AMATEUR SWIMMING ASSOCIATION. HANDBOOK. irreg. 60p. Welsh Amateur Swimming Association, Honorary General Secretary, 45 Devon Place, Newport Mon., Wales. (looseleaf format)

796　　　　UK　ISSN 0084-0386
WINTER SPORTS IN SCOTLAND. 1970. a. free. Scottish Tourist Board, 23 Ravelston Terrace, Edinburgh EH4 3EU, Scotland.

794.6　　　　US　ISSN 0361-3976
WOMEN'S INTERNATIONAL BOWLING CONGRESS. PLAYING RULES. a. Women's International Bowling Congress, Inc., 5301 S. 76th St., Greendale, WI 53129. illus. Key Title: Playing Rules.

790.1　　　　UK
WOMEN'S SQUASH RACKETS ASSOCIATION. HANDBOOK. 1934. a. £1. ‡ Women's Squash Rackets Association, 345 Upper Richmond Rd. W., Sheen, London SW14 8QN, England. adv. circ. 3,500.

796.9　　　　US　ISSN 0095-7240
WORLD ALMANAC GUIDE TO PRO HOCKEY. irreg. $1.95. Bantam Books, Inc., 666 Fifth Ave., New York, NY 10019. illus.

794.1　　　　CS
WORLD STUDENT CHESS TEAM CHAMPIONSHIP. RESULTS. irreg., 20th, 1974, Teesside. price varies. (International Chess Federation) International Union of Students, 17th November St., 110 01 Prague 1, Czechoslovakia. charts. illus.

790.1 US
WRESTLING OFFICIALS MANUAL. a. $1.10.
National Federation of State High School
Associations, Federation Place, Box 98, Elgin, IL
60120.

790.1 US
WRESTLING RULES. a. $1.35. National Federation
of State High School Associations, Federation Place,
Box 98, Elgin, IL 60120.

YEAR BOOK OF SPORTS MEDICINE. see
MEDICAL SCIENCES

796 ZA ISSN 0084-506X
ZAMBIA. SPORTS DIRECTORATE. REPORT.
1968. a, latest 1973. 35 n. Government Printer, P.O.
Box 136, Lusaka, Zambia.

SPORTS AND GAMES — Abstracting, Bibliographies, Statistics

016.7966 US ISSN 0193-8584
BICYCLE RESOURCE GUIDE. 1974. a. $5. c/o
David J. Luebbers, Ed., 78 S. Jackson, Denver, CO
80209. bk. rev. bibl.
Formerly: Bicycle Bibliography (ISSN 0098-1230)

796.95 310 US ISSN 0163-7207
BOATING REGISTRATION STATISTICS. a.
National Association of Engine and Boat
Manufacturers, Box 5555, Grand Central Sta., New
York, NY 10017. stat.

338.4 CN ISSN 0575-979X
CANADA. STATISTICS CANADA. SPORTING
GOODS AND TOY INDUSTRIES/
FABRICATION D'ARTICLES DE SPORT ET DE
JOUETS. (Catalogue 47-204) (Text in English &
French) 1925. a. Can.$4.50($5.40) Statistics Canada,
Publications Distribution, Ottawa, Ont. K1A 0V7,
Canada. (also avail. in microform from MML)

790.1 UK ISSN 0142-1484
CHARTERED INSTITUTE OF PUBLIC FINANCE
AND ACCOUNTANCY. CHARGES FOR
LEISURE SERVICES. 1978. a. £5. Chartered
Institute of Public Finance and Accountancy, 1
Buckingham Place, London SW1E 6HS, England.
(back issues avail.)

790.1 UK ISSN 0141-187X
CHARTERED INSTITUTE OF PUBLIC FINANCE
AND ACCOUNTANCY. LEISURE ESTIMATE
STATISTICS. 1976. a. £10. Chartered Institute of
Public Finance and Accountancy, 1 Buckingham
Place, London SW1E 6HS, England. (back issues
avail.)

790 314 NE
NETHERLANDS. CENTRAAL BUREAU VOOR
DE STATISTIEK. STATISTIEK VAN DE
INKOMSTEN EN UITGAVEN DER OVERHEID
VOOR CULTUUR EN RECREATIE.
STATISTICS OF GOVERNMENT
EXPENDITURE ON CULTURE AND
RECREATION. (Text in Dutch and English) 1964.
a. fl.23.25. Centraal Bureau voor de Statistiek,
Prinses Beatrixlaan 428, Voorburg, Netherlands
(Orders to: Staatsuitgeverij, Christoffel
Plantijnstraat, The Hague, Netherlands)
Formerly: Netherlands.Centraal Bureau voor de
Statistiek. Statistiek van de Uitgaven der Overheid
voor Cultuur en Recreatie (ISSN 0077-7196)

796.95 US ISSN 0565-1530
U.S. COAST GUARD BOATING STATISTICS.
1960. a. free. ‡ U.S. Coast Guard, Commandant G-
BD-2, 400 Seventh St. S.W., Washington, DC
20591. Ed. A.L. Hakes. stat. circ. 15,000. (back
issues avail. to 1966)

799 310 US
U.S. FISH AND WILDLIFE SERVICE. NATIONAL
SURVEY OF HUNTING, FISHING AND
WILDLIFE-ASSOCIATED RECREATION. 1955.
irreg., 5th, 1977. U.S. Fish and Wildlife Service,
Washington, DC 20240. charts. illus. stat.

SPORTS AND GAMES — Ball Games

796 SW ISSN 0567-4565
AARETS FOTBOLL. a. Kr.314. Stroembergs
Idrottsboecker, Vittangigatan 27, Vaellingby,
Stockholm, Sweden.

796.332 US
ALL SOUTH CAROLINA FOOTBALL ANNUAL.
1956. a. $1.50. Southeastern Press, Inc., P.O. Box 3,
Columbia, SC 29202. Ed. Sidney L. Wise. adv.

796.3 SZ
ALMANACCO CALCISTICO SVIZZERO. (Text in
Italian) 1950. a. 10 Fr. Armando Libotte, Ed. &
Pub., Casella Postale, 6904 Lugano, Switzerland.
adv. stat. circ. 2,000.

796.357 US ISSN 0065-6739
AMATEUR SOFTBALL ASSOCIATION OF
AMERICA. OFFICIAL GUIDE AND RULE
BOOK. 1934. a. $2.25. Amateur Softball
Association of America, 2801 N.E. 50th St.,
Oklahoma City, OK 73111.

796.33 FR
ANNEE DU FOOTBALL. 1973. a. price varies.
Editions Calmann-Levy, 3, rue Auber, 75009 Paris,
France. Ed. Jacques Thibert. illus.

796.33 FR
ANNEE DU RUGBY. 1973. a. price varies. Editions
Calmann-Levy, 3 rue Auber, 75009 Paris, France.
Ed. Christian Montaignac. illus.

796.342 IT
ANNUARIO ILLUSTRATO DEL TENNIS. 1979. a.
L.5000($15.50) D M K Editrice s.r.l., Via Vitruvio
43, 20124 Milan, Italy (Subscr. to: via Boscovich
14, 20124 Milan, Italy) adv. illus. circ. 70,000.
Tennis

796 AT ISSN 0084-7291
AUSTRALIAN CRICKET YEARBOOK. 1970. a.
Aus.$3.50. Modern Magazines (Holdings) Ltd.,
Ryrie House, 15 Boundary St., Rushcutter's Bay,
N.S.W. 2011, Australia.

796 GW
BADMINTON. 1970. a. DM.6.90. (Deutscher
Badminton Verband) Oskar Klokow, Verlag und
Versandbuchhandlung, Kalandstr. 19, 2400 Luebeck,
W. Germany (B.R.D.) Ed. Oskar Klokow. stat.

796.3570 US ISSN 0067-4257
BASEBALL ANNUAL.* a. Whitestone Publications,
Fawcett Bldg, Greenwich, CT 06832. Ed. John
Devaney.

796.357 US
BASEBALL CASE BOOK. a. $1.45. National
Federation of State High School Associations,
Federation Place, Box 98, Elgin, IL 60120.

796.3 US ISSN 0067-4273
BASEBALL GUIDE. 1965. a. $1.50. Snibbe
Publications, Inc., 523 Lakeview Rd., Clearwater,
FL 33516. Ed. Jack Clary. circ. 1,000,000.

796.357 US
BASEBALL RULES. a. $1.10. National Federation of
State High School Associations, Federation Place,
Box 98, Elgin, IL 60120.

796.357 US
BASEBALL UMPIRES MANUAL. a. $1.10. National
Federation of State High School Associations,
Federation Place, Box 98, Elgin, IL 60120.

796.32 US ISSN 0525-4663
BASKETBALL CASE BOOK. a. $1.45. National
Federation of State High School Associations,
Federation Place, P.O. Box 98, Elgin, IL 60120. Ed.
Bruce B. Durbin. adv. illus. circ. 300,000.

796.3 US
BASKETBALL GUIDE. 1971. a. $1.50. Snibbe
Publications, Inc., 523 Lakeview Rd., Clearwater,
FL 33516. Ed. Jack Clary. circ. 600,000.
Formerly: Pro Basketball Guide (ISSN 0079-
5518)

796.323 US
BASKETBALL HANDBOOK. biennial. $1.10.
National Federation of State High School
Associations, Federation Place, Box 98, Elgin, IL
60120.

796.323 US
BASKETBALL OFFICIALS MANUAL. biennial.
$1.10. National Federation of State High School
Associations, Federation Place, Box 98, Elgin, IL
60120.

796.323 US
BASKETBALL RULES. a. $1.10. National Federation
of State High School Associations, Federation Place,
Box 98, Elgin, IL 60120.

796.323 US
BASKETBALL RULES - SIMPLIFIED AND
ILLUSTRATED. a. $1.75. National Federation of
State High School Associations, Federation Place,
Box 98, Elgin, IL 60120.

796.323 US
BASKETBALL STATISTICIANS' MANUAL. a.
$1.95. National Collegiate Athletic Association, Box
1906, U.S. Highway 50 and Nall Ave., Shawnee
Mission, KS 66222. stat.

796.357 US
BATTER PERFORMANCE HANDBOOK. 1980. a.
$3.50. Research Analysis Publications, Box 49213,
Los Angeles, CA 90049. Ed. Ronald H. Lewis. adv.
charts. stat.
Baseball

796.332 US
BIG EIGHT; a sport folio of America's super football
conference. 1972. a. $4.95. RAD Communications,
Box 20688, Oklahoma City, OK 73102 (Subscr. to:
Football Enterprises, Box 1775, Norman, OK
73070) Ed. Raymond H. Keitz. adv. charts. illus.
stat. circ. 85,000. (also avail. in microfilm;
microfiche; magnetic tape; Braille; talking book;
record; back issues avail.)

796.332 US
BLUE CHIPS; national recruiting magazine of
collegiate athletics. 1979. a. $4. RAD
Communications, Box 20688, Oklahoma City, OK
73102 (Subscr. to: Football Enterprises, Box 1775
Norman, OK 73070) Ed. Raymond H. Keitz. adv.
charts. illus. stat. circ. 30,000. (back issues avail.)

796.357 US
BOOK ON THE WORLD SERIES. 1969. a. $2.25. ‡
Baseball-for-Fans Publications, Box 49213, Los
Angeles, CA 90049. Ed. Ronald H. Lewis. adv.
charts. stat. circ. 3,000.

794.6 658.8 US ISSN 0068-0559
BOWLING AND BILLIARD BUYERS GUIDE.*
Title varies: Bowling Buyers Guide. 1961. a. $5.
National Bowlers Journal, Inc., 875 N. Michigan
Ave., Suite 3734, Chicago, IL 60611. Ed. Ernest H.
Ahlborn.

796 US ISSN 0068-0567
BOWLING GUIDE. 1969. a. $1.50. Snibbe
Publications, Inc., 523 Lakeview Rd., Clearwater,
FL 33516. Ed. Patrick J. McDonough. circ. 50,000.

796.357 CN ISSN 0226-577X
CANADIAN AMATEUR SOFTBALL
ASSOCIATION. FACTS & FIGURES. (Text in
English and French) 1975. a. free contr. circ.
Canadian Amateur Softball Association, 333 River
Rd., Vanier, Ont. K1L 8B9, Canada.

796.352 CN ISSN 0316-8131
CANADIAN AND PROVINCIAN GOLF
RECORDS. 1972. a. Royal Canadian Golf
Association, 696 Yonge St., Toronto, Ont. M4Y
2A7, Canada.
Formerly: Royal Canadian Golf Association.
National Tournament Records (ISSN 0316-8212)
Golf

796.352 CN ISSN 0084-8565
CANADIAN LADIES' GOLF ASSOCIATION.
YEAR BOOK. (Text in English & French) 1947. a.
Can.$1. Canadian Ladies' Golf Association, 333
River Road, Ottawa, Ontario, KIL 8B9, Canada.
Ed. L. John Whamond. adv. bk. rev. illus. stat.
index. circ. 10,000.

SPORTS AND GAMES — BALL GAMES

796.325   CN
CANADIAN VOLLEYBALL ANNUAL AND RULE BOOK. a. Can.$2. (Canadian Volleyball Association) Canadian Volleyball Publications, 333 River Rd., Vanier, Ont. K1L 8B9, Canada. circ. 10,000.

796.33   US   ISSN 0361-2988
COMPLETE HANDBOOK OF PRO FOOTBALL. (Subseries of: Signet Books) 1975. a. $2.50. New American Library (New York), 1633 Broadway, New York, NY 10019. Ed. Zander Hollander. illus.

796.334   US   ISSN 0363-6046
COMPLETE HANDBOOK OF SOCCER. 1976. a. $2.50. New American Library, Box 999, Bergenfield, NJ 07621. Ed. Zander Hollander. illus.

913   PK
CRICKET ANNUAL. (Text in English) a. Rs.5. Board of Control for Cricket in Pakistan, Rawalpindi, Pakistan.

796.358   AT   ISSN 0310-9356
CRICKET QUADRANT. 1973. irreg. Aus.$0.40 per no. Australian Cricket Society, A. C. T. Branch, 91 Gouger Street, Torrens, A. C. T. 2607, Australia. Ed. Julian Oakley.

796.342   US
CURTIS CASEWIT'S GUIDE TO TENNIS RESORTS. 1978. irreg. $2.50. Pilot Books, 347 Fifth Ave., New York, NY 10016.
Tennis

796.332   US
DALLAS COWBOYS OUTLOOK. 1967. a. $2.50. Sports Communications, Inc., P.O. Box 95, Waco, TX 76703. Ed. Dave Campbell. adv. circ. 55,622.

796.3   UK
EVENING TIMES WEE RED BOOK; the football annual. 1930? a. 14p. George Outram & Co. Ltd., 70 Mitchell Street, Glasgow G1 3LZ, Scotland. circ. 70,000.

796   FR   ISSN 0071-4267
FEDERATION INTERNATIONALE DE RUGBY AMATEUR. ANNUAIRE. 1965. a. International Amateur Rugby Federation, 7 Cite d'Antin, 75009 Paris, France.

796.332   UK   ISSN 0071-724X
FOOTBALL ASSOCIATION YEAR BOOK. 1949. a. £1.20. William Clowes (Publishers) Ltd., 31 Newgate, Beccles, Suffolk NR34 9QB, England. adv.

796.332   US   ISSN 0163-6200
FOOTBALL CASE BOOK. a. $1.45. National Federation of State High School Associations, Federation Place, Box 98, Elgin, IL 60120.

796.334   UK
FOOTBALL CHAMPIONS. a. £1.50. Purnell Books, Berkshire House, Queen St., Maidenhead, Berks. SL6 1NF, England.
Soccer

796.332   US   ISSN 0069-5548
FOOTBALL GUIDE. 1963. a. $1.50. Snibbe Publications, Inc., 523 Lakeview Rd., Clearwater, FL 33516. Ed. Jack Clary. circ. 1,000,000.
Formerly: College and Pro Football Guide.

796.332   US
FOOTBALL HANDBOOK. a. $1.10. National Federation of State High School Associations, Federation Place, Box 98, Elgin, IL 60120.

796.332   US
FOOTBALL OFFICIALS HANDBOOK. a. $1.10. National Federation of State High School Associations, Federation Place, Box 98, Elgin, IL 60120

796.332   US   ISSN 0071-7258
FOOTBALL REGISTER. 1966. a. $9. Sporting News Publishing Co., 1212 N. Lindbergh Blvd., St. Louis, MO 63166 (Orders to: Box 56, St. Louis, MO 63166) Ed. Howard M. Balzer.

796.332   US
FOOTBALL ROUNDUP. no. 12, 1971. a. $1.25. ‡ Lopez Publications, Inc., 21 West 26th St., New York, NY 10010. Ed. Herbert M. Furlow. adv. charts. illus. stat. circ. 185,000.
Football

796.332   US
FOOTBALL RULES. a. $1.10. National Federation of State High School Associations, Federation Place, Box 98, Elgin, IL 60120.

796.332   US
FOOTBALL RULES - SIMPLIFIED AND ILLUSTRATED. a. $2.25. National Federation of State High School Associations, Federation Place, Box 98, Elgin, IL 60120.

796.332   US
FOOTBALL STATISTICIAN'S MANUAL. a. $1.95. National Collegiate Athletic Association, Box 1906, U.S. Highway 50 and Nall Ave., Shawnee Mission, KS 66222. stat.

658   US   ISSN 0436-1474
GOLF COURSE SUPERINTENDENTS ASSOCIATION OF AMERICA. MEMBERSHIP DIRECTORY. Spine title: G C S A A Membership Directory. a. $25 to non-members. Golf Course Superintendents Association of America, 1617 St. Andrews Drive, Lawrence, KS 66044. Ed. Larry Goldsmith. circ. 5,000. Key Title: Membership Directory of the Golf Course Superintendents Association of America.

796.352   US   ISSN 0072-4947
GOLF COURSE SUPERINTENDENTS ASSOCIATION OF AMERICA. PROCEEDINGS OF THE INTERNATIONAL CONFERENCE AND SHOW. a. $10 ($3 to members) Golf Course Superintendents Association of America, 1617 St. Andrews Drive, Lawrence, Kansas. Ed. Larry Goldsmith. circ. 4,500.

796.352   FR
GOLF EN FRANCE; guide des terrains de golf francais. 1969. a. 22 F. Editions Person, 344 rue de Penthievre, 75008 Paris, France.
Golf

796   UK   ISSN 0072-4963
GOLF RULES ILLUSTRATED. 1969. quadrennial. £3.75. Munro-Barr Publications Ltd., 256 West George St., Glasgow G2 4QP, Scotland. Ed. A. J. Barr.

796   US   ISSN 0072-4971
GOLFER'S DIGEST. irreg. $7.95. ‡ D B I Books, Inc., One Northfield Plaza, Northfield, IL 60093. Ed. Earl Puckett.

796   UK   ISSN 0072-498X
GOLFER'S HANDBOOK. 1900. a. £12.50($30) Munro-Barr Publications Ltd., 256 West George St., Glasgow G2 4QP, Scotland. Ed. Percy Huggins. adv.

796.352   UK
GOLFING YEAR. a. £1.50. English Golf Union, c/o the Secretary, 12a Denmark St., Wokingham RG11 2BE, Berkshire, England. bk. rev. circ. 2,500.

796.3   UK   ISSN 0085-1566
HOCKEY ASSOCIATION. OFFICIAL HANDBOOK. 1900. a. £1. Hockey Association, 70 Brompton Rd., London SW3 1HB, England. index. cum. index. circ. 1,100.

796   920   US   ISSN 0090-2292
HOCKEY REGISTER. 1972. a. $9. Sporting News Publishing Co., 1212 N. Lindbergh Blvd., St. Louis, MO 63166. Eds. Larry Wigge, Frank Polnaszek. illus. stat.

796.397   US
HOW TO SCORE. 1945. irreg. $1. Sporting News Publishing Co., P.O. Box 56, St. Louis, MO 63166. Ed. Larry Wigge. bk. rev. charts. circ. 5,000.
Baseball scoring rules and forms

796   US
INSIDERS BASEBALL FACT BOOK. 1976. a. $13. Research Analysis Publications, Box 49213, Los Angeles, CA 90049. charts. stat.
Baseball

793   GW   ISSN 0534-6622
INTERNATIONAL AMATEUR BASKETBALL FEDERATION. OFFICIAL REPORT OF THE WORLD CONGRESS. irreg., 1976, 20th, Montreal. International Amateur Basketball Federation, Rugendas Str. 19, Munich/Solln., W. Germany (B.R.D.)

796.332   UK   ISSN 0074-610X
INTERNATIONAL FOOTBALL BOOK. 1959. a. £3.50. Souvenir Press Ltd., 95 Mortimer St., London WC1B 3PA, England. Ed. Eric G. Batty. circ. 5,000.

796.357   US
INTERNATIONAL SOFTBALL CONGRESS(YEAR) OFFICIAL YEARBOOK AND GUIDE. 1953. a. $1.50. International Softball Congress, 2523 W. 14th St., Greeley, CO 80631.

796.357   US   ISSN 0075-6385
KNOTTY PROBLEMS OF BASEBALL. 1950. irreg. $4. Sporting News Publishing Co., P.O. Box 56, St. Louis, MO 63166. Ed. Larry Wigge.

796.357   US   ISSN 0076-2849
MAJOR LEAGUE BASEBALL. 1965. a. $1.50. (Cord Communications Corp.) Simon & Schuster, Inc., 630 Fifth Ave., New York, NY 10020.

796.334   UK   ISSN 0308-8405
MANCHESTER UNITED FOOTBALL BOOK. 1966. a. £2.75. Stanley Paul & Co. Ltd., 3 Fitzroy Square, London W1P 6JD, England. Ed. David Meek. adv. bk. rev. illus. circ. 10,000.

796.32   US   ISSN 0362-3254
N A G W S GUIDE. BASKETBALL; official rules and interpretations. 1901. a. $3.75. American Alliance for Health, Physical Education, Recreation and Dance, National Association for Girls and Women in Sport, 1900 Association Dr., Reston, VA 22091. illus. circ. 23,000.
Formerly: Basketball Guide, with Official Rules and Standards (ISSN 0065-7018)

796   US
N A G W S GUIDE. BASKETBALL, VOLLEYBALL; tips and techniques for teachers and coaches. 1977. biennial. price varies. American Alliance for Health, Physical Education, Recreation and Dance, National Association for Girls and Women in Sport, Division for Girls and Women's Sports, Reston, VA 22091. charts. illus. circ. 3,000. Indexed: ERIC.

794.6   **796.86**   US
N A G W S GUIDE. BOWLING-GOLF. 1954/56. biennial. American Alliance for Health, Physical Education, Recreation, and Dance, National Association for Girls and Women in Sport, 1900 Association Dr., Reston, VA 22091. charts. illus. circ. 3,000. Indexed: ERIC.
Formerly: Bowling-Fencing Guide (ISSN 0099-0051)

796.355   US
N A G W S GUIDE. FIELD HOCKEY. 1950/52. biennial. price varies. American Alliance for Health, Physical Education, Recreation, and Dance, National Association for Girls and Women in Sport, 1900 Association Dr., Reston, VA 22091. circ. 15,000. Indexed: ERIC.
Supersedes in part: Field Hockey-Lacrosse Guide (ISSN 0065-7026)

796.334   US
N A G W S GUIDE. FLAG FOOTBALL, SPEEDBALL, SPEED-A-WAY. 1927. biennial. price varies. American Alliance for Health, Physical Education, Recreation, and Dance, National Association for Girls and Women in Sport, 1900 Association Dr., Reston, VA 22091. circ. 9,000. Indexed: ERIC.
Former titles: Soccer-Speedball-Flag Football Guide; Soccer-Speedball Guide (ISSN 0065-7034)

796   US
N A G W S GUIDE. LACROSSE. 1939. biennial. American Alliance for Health, Physical Education, Recreation and Dance, National Association for Girls and Women in Sport, 1900 Association Dr., Reston, VA 22091. circ. 15,000.

796.33   US   ISSN 0163-4747
N A G W S GUIDE. SOCCER. 1927. a. $2. American Alliance for Health, Physical Education, Recreation, and Dance, National Association for Girls and Women in Sport, 1900 Association Dr., Reston, VA 22091. illus. circ. 9,000.

SPORTS AND GAMES — BALL GAMES

796.4 US ISSN 0363-2504
N A G W S GUIDE. SOFTBALL. 1938. biennial. American Alliance for Health, Physical Education, Recreation, and Dance, National Association for Girls and Women in Sport, 1900 Association Dr., Reston, VA 22091. circ. 23,000. Indexed: ERIC.

796.342 US
N A G W S GUIDE. TENNIS. 1938. biennial. price varies. American Alliance for Health, Physical Education, Recreation, and Dance, National Association for Girls and Women in Sport, 1900 Association Dr., Reston, VA 22091. circ. 13,000. Indexed: ERIC.
Supersedes in part: Tennis-Badminton-Squash Guide (ISSN 0065-7042); Tennis-Badminton Guide.

796.325 US
N A G W S GUIDE. VOLLEYBALL. 1938. biennial. price varies. American Alliance for Health, Physical Education, Recreation, and Dance, National Association for Girls and Women in Sport, 1900 Association Dr., Reston, VA 22091. circ. 17,000. Indexed: ERIC.
Formerly: Volleyball Guide (ISSN 0065-7050)

796.357 US
N B C OFFICIAL YEARBOOK. 1935. a. $2.75. National Baseball Congress, Box 1420, Wichita, KS 67201. Ed. K. F. Harris. adv. circ. 10,000.
Formerly (until 1975): National Baseball Congress. Official Baseball Annual (ISSN 0077-3549)

796 US
N C A A BASEBALL ANNUAL GUIDE. 1980. a. National Collegiate Athletic Association, Publishing Department, Box 1906, Shawnee Mission, KS 66222.
Formerly: Official National Collegiate Athletic Association Baseball Guide (ISSN 0466-1478)

796.323 US
N C A A BASKETBALL RECORDS. 1975. a. $3. (National Collegiate Athletic Association) N C A A Publishing Service, Box 1906, Shawnee Mission, KS 66222. circ. 2,000.
Formerly (until 1979): Official National Collegiate Athletic Association Basketball Scores.

796.32 US
N C A A BASKETBALL RULES AND INTERPRETATIONS. 1967. a. $3. (National Collegiate Athletic Association) N C A A Publishing Service, Box 1906, Shawnee Mission, KS 66222. Ed. Lavonne Anderson. illus. circ. 25,000.
Former titles: Official National Collegiate Athletic Association Basketball Rules and Interpretations (ISSN 0163-2817); Official National Collegiate Athletic Association Basketball Rules (ISSN 0094-5234)

796.33 US
N.C.A.A. FOOTBALL RECORDS. 1969. a. $3. (National Collegiate Athletic Association) N C A A Publishing Service, Box 1906, U.S. Highway 50 and Nall Ave., Shawnee Mission, KS 66222. illus. stat. circ. 4,000.
Formerly: College Football Modern Record Book (ISSN 0092-881X)

796.32 US
N C A A ILLUSTRATED BASKETBALL RULES. a. $3. (National Collegiate Athletic Association) N C A A Publishing Service, Box 1906, Shawnee Mission, KS 66222.

796 US
N C A A LACROSSE GUIDE. a. $3. (National Collegiate Athletic Association) N C A A Publishing Service, Box 1906, Shawnee Mission, KS 66222.

796.332 US ISSN 0077-4588
NATIONAL FOOTBALL LEAGUE. RECORD MANUAL. 1947. a. $1.95. National Football League, 410 Park Ave., New York, NY 10022.
Statistics and records for teams and individual players

796.9 CN ISSN 0316-8174
NATIONAL HOCKEY LEAGUE. GUIDE. 1947. a. Can.$5. National Hockey League, 920 Sun Life Building, Montreal, Quebec, Canada. Ed. Ron Andrews.

796.323 US
NATIONAL WHEELCHAIR BASKETBALL ASSOCIATION. DIRECTORY. a. membership only. National Wheelchair Basketball Association, 110 Seaton Bldg., University of Kentucky, Lexington, KY 40506.

796.332 US
NEW YORK JETS OFFICIAL YEARBOOK. 1971. a. $2 per copy. (New York Jets Football Club Inc.) Football Publications Inc., 4100 Palisade Ave., Union City, NJ 07087. Ed. Frank Ramos. charts. illus. stat. circ. 60,000.

796.323 US
NEW YORK KNICKS YEARBOOK; official guide and record book. a. $1.50 per copy. New York Knickerbockers Basketball Club, 4 Pennsylvania Plaza, New York, NY 10001. Eds. Frank Blauschild, James Wergeles. charts. illus. stat.

796.357 US
OFFICIAL AMERICAN AND NATIONAL LEAGUE BASEBALL SCHEDULES AND RECORDS. a. $1.50. Sporting News Publishing Co., Box 56, St. Louis, MO 63166.

796.357 US ISSN 0162-5411
OFFICIAL BASEBALL DOPE BOOK. 1942. a. $7.50. Sporting News Publishing Co., 1212 N. Lindbergh Blvd., Box 56, St. Louis, MO 63166. Ed. Bd.
Formerly: Baseball Dope Book (ISSN 0067-4265)

796.357 US ISSN 0078-3838
OFFICIAL BASEBALL GUIDE. 1942. a. $7.50. Sporting News Publishing Co., 1212 N. Lindbergh Blvd., St. Louis, MO 63166.

796.357 US ISSN 0078-4605
OFFICIAL BASEBALL RECORD BOOK. Variant title: Sporting News Official Baseball Record Book. 1949. a. $7.50. Sporting News Publishing Co., 1212 N. Lindbergh Blvd., St. Louis, MO 63166. Ed. Craig Carter. (processed)
Formerly: One for the Book.

796.357 US ISSN 0162-542X
OFFICIAL BASEBALL REGISTER. 1940. a. $9. Sporting News Publishing Co., 1212 N. Lindbergh Blvd., St. Louis, MO 63166. Ed. Howard Balzer. cum.index (1940-73)
Formerly: Baseball Register (ISSN 0067-4281)

796.357 US ISSN 0078-3846
OFFICIAL BASEBALL RULES. 1950. a. $1.50. Sporting News Publishing Co., 1212 N. Lindbergh Blvd., St. Louis, MO 63166.

796.332 US
OFFICIAL N F L AND COLLEGIATE FOOTBALL SCHEDULES AND RECORDS. a. $1.50. Sporting News Publishing Co., Box 56, St. Louis, MO 63166.

796.3 US ISSN 0078-3862
OFFICIAL NATIONAL BASKETBALL ASSOCIATION GUIDE. 1958. a. $7.50. Sporting News Publishing Co., 1212 N. Lindbergh Blvd., St. Louis, MO 63166. Ed. Matt Winick.

796.357 US
OFFICIAL NATIONAL COLLEGIATE ATHLETIC ASSOCIATION BASEBALL GUIDE. 1958. a. $3. (National Collegiate Athletic Association) N C A A Publishing Service, Box 1906, Shawnee Mission, KS 66222. circ. 8,600.

796.323 US
OFFICIAL NATIONAL COLLEGIATE ATHLETIC ASSOCIATION BASKETBALL GUIDE. 1923. a. $3. (National Collegiate Athletic Association) N C A A Publishing Service, Box 1906, Shawnee Mission, KS 66222. circ. 12,000.

796.332 US
OFFICIAL NATIONAL COLLEGIATE ATHLETIC ASSOCIATION FOOTBALL GUIDE. 1889. a. $3. (National Collegiate Athletic Association) N C A A Publishing Service, Box 1906, Shawnee Mission, KS 66222. circ. 13,000.

796.33 US ISSN 0094-5226
OFFICIAL NATIONAL COLLEGIATE ATHLETIC ASSOCIATION FOOTBALL RULES & INTERPRETATIONS. Cover title: N C A A Official Football Rules & Interpretations. 1961. a. $3. (National Collegiate Athletic Association) N C A A Publishing Service, Box 1906, Shawnee Mission, KS 66222. Ed. David Nelson. circ. 24,000.

796.334 US
OFFICIAL NATIONAL COLLEGIATE ATHLETIC ASSOCIATION SOCCER GUIDE. 1927. a. $6. (National Collegiate Athletic Association) N C A A Publishing Service, Box 1906, Shawnee Mission, KS 66222. Ed. Donald Y. Yonker. circ. 11,700.

796.323 US
OFFICIAL READ-EASY BASKETBALL RULES. 1973. a. $1.50. (National Collegiate Athletic Association) N C A A Publishing Service, Box 1906, Shawnee Mission, KS 66222. Ed. Arnie Burdick. illus. circ. 5,200.

796.332 US
OFFICIAL READ-EASY FOOTBALL RULES. 1976. a. $1.50. (National Collegiate Athletic Association) N C A A Publishing Service, Box 1906, Shawnee Mission, KS 66222. Ed. Arnie Burdick. illus. circ. 4,200.

796.357 US ISSN 0078-3900
OFFICIAL WORLD SERIES RECORDS. 1953. a. $5. Sporting News Publishing Co., P.O. Box 56, St. Louis, MO 63166. Ed. Craig Carter. index.
World Series Records from 1903

796.358 PK
PAKISTAN BOOK OF CRICKET. (Text in English) 1976. a. Rs.10. Q. Ahmed, Pub., 3rd Floor, Spencers Bldg., I.I. Chundrigar Rd., G.P.O. Box 3721, Karachi, Pakistan. charts. illus.
Cricket

792.323 US ISSN 0192-2238
PETERSEN'S PRO BASKETBALL. 1977. a. $2.50. Petersen Publishing Co., 8490 Sunset Blvd., Los Angeles, CA 90069. Ed. Al Hall. circ. 85,000.
Basketball

796.357 US
PITCHER PERFORMANCE HANDBOOK. 1965. a. $3.50. ‡ Research Analysis Publications, Box 49213, Los Angeles, CA 90049. Ed. Ronald H. Lewis. adv. charts. stat. circ. 10,000.
Baseball

796.358 UK ISSN 0079-2314
PLAYFAIR CRICKET ANNUAL. a. £1. Queen Anne Press Ltd., Paulton House, 8 Shepherdess Walk, London N.1., England. Ed. Gordon Ross.

796.3 UK ISSN 0079-2322
PLAYFAIR FOOTBALL ANNUAL. 1948. a. £1.25. Queen Anne Press Ltd., Paulton House, 8 Shepherdess Walk, London N.1., England. Eds. L. Francis, P. Dunk.

796.357 US
PONY BASEBALL. BLUE BOOK. 1959. triennial. $1. ‡ Pony Baseball, Inc., Box 225, Washington, PA 15301. Ed. Roy Gillespie. circ. 3,000.
Formerly: Boys Baseball. Blue Book (ISSN 0068-0575)

796.352 US
PRIVATE COUNTRY CLUB GUEST POLICY DIRECTORY. 1979. a. $10. Pazdur Publishing Co., 2171 Campus Dr., Irvine, CA 92715. Ed. Edward F. Pazdur. adv. circ. 350,000.
Supersedes (1976-1979): Golf & Country Club Guest Policy Directory.

796.3305 US ISSN 0079-5526
PRO FOOTBALL. 1960. a. Petersen Publishing Co., 8490 Sunset Blvd., Los Angeles, CA 90069.
Formerly: Petersen's Pro Football Annual (ISSN 0079-1156)

796.332 US ISSN 0079-5534
PRO FOOTBALL. 1965. a. $1.75. (Cord Communications Corp.) Simon & Schuster, Inc., 630 Fifth Ave., New York, NY 10020.

796.334 US
PRO SOCCER GUIDE. 1976. a. $1.50. Snibbe Publications, Inc., 523 Lakeview Rd., Clearwater, FL 33516. Ed. Jim Henderson. circ. 250,000.

SPORTS AND GAMES — BICYCLES AND MOTORCYCLES

RACING AND FOOTBALL OUTLOOK: RACING ANNUAL. see *SPORTS AND GAMES*

796.3   UK   ISSN 0080-4088
ROTHMANS FOOTBALL YEARBOOK. 1970. a. £5.95 (paperback); £7.95(hardcover) (Rothmans of Pall Mall Ltd.) Queen Anne Press Ltd., Paulton House, 8 Shepherdess Walk, London N.1., England. Eds. Leslie Vernon, Jack Rollin. adv. circ. 71,000.

796.3   UK   ISSN 0080-4827
RUGBY FOOTBALL LEAGUE OFFICIAL GUIDE. a. Rugby Football League, 180 Chapeltown Road, Leeds LS7 4HT, England.

796.3   UK   ISSN 0080-7842
SCOTLAND-HOME OF GOLF. 1961. a. 65p. Scottish Tourist Board, 23 Ravelston Terrace, Edinburgh EH4 3EU, Scotland. circ. 15,000.

796.334   US   ISSN 0163-4763
SOCCER RULES. a. $1.10. National Federation of State High School Associations, Federation Place, Box 98, Elgin, IL 60120.

796.3   UK   ISSN 0081-038X
SOCCER YEAR BOOK FOR NORTHERN IRELAND. 1966. a. £1. Howard Publications, 112 Lisburn Rd., Belfast, Northern Ireland. Ed. Malcolm Brodie.

796.332   US   ISSN 0081-3788
SPORTING NEWS' NATIONAL FOOTBALL GUIDE. Cover title: National Football Guide. 1970. a. $7.50. Sporting News Publishing Co., 1212 N. Lindbergh Blvd., St. Louis, MO 63166. Ed.Bd. *Football*

796.3   US
SPORTS ALL STARS BASEBALL. 1953. a. $1.25. Maco Publishing Co., Inc., 380 Madison Ave., New York, NY 10017. Ed. Vito Stellino. adv. illus. circ. 150,000.

796.332   US
SPORTS QUARTERLY-FOOTBALL PROS. 1962. a. $1.25 newsstand sales only. Lopez Publications, Inc., 21 West 26th St., New York, NY 10010. Ed. Herbert M. Furlow. adv. circ. 250,000.

796   UK   ISSN 0081-3885
SQUASH RACKETS ASSOCIATION. HANDBOOK. 1930. a. £3.75. Squash Rackets Association, 70 Brompton Rd., London SW3 1DX, England. Ed. Ian Wright. adv. circ. 6,000.

796.257   US   ISSN 0161-2018
STREET & SMITH'S OFFICIAL YEARBOOK: BASEBALL. 1941. a. $1.95 not avail. by subscription. Conde Nast Publications Inc., 350 Madison Ave., New York, NY 10017. Ed. Gerard Kavanagh. adv.
   Formerly: Street and Smith's Baseball Yearbook (ISSN 0491-1520)

796.32   US   ISSN 0149-7103
STREET & SMITH'S OFFICIAL YEARBOOK: BASKETBALL. a. $1.95. Conde Nast Publications Inc., 350 Madison Ave., New York, NY 10017. Ed. Jim O'Brien. adv. illus.
   Formerly: Street and Smith's College & pro Official Basketball Yearbook (ISSN 0092-511X)

796.33   US   ISSN 0091-9977
STREET AND SMITH'S OFFICIAL YEARBOOK: COLLEGE FOOTBALL. a. $1.95. Conde Nast Publications Inc., 350 Madison Ave., New York, NY 10017. Ed. Gerard Kavanagh. adv. illus.

796.33   US   ISSN 0092-3214
STREET AND SMITH'S OFFICIAL YEARBOOK: PRO FOOTBALL. a. $1.95. Conde Nast Publications Inc., 350 Madison Ave., New York, NY 10017. Ed. Gerard Kavanagh. adv. illus. (reprint service avail. from UMI) Key Title: Street and Smith's Official Yearbook. Pro Football.

796.3   US   ISSN 0082-2833
TENNIS GUIDE. 1969. a. $1.50. Snibbe Publications, Inc., 523 Lakeview Rd., Clearwater, FL 33516. Ed. Neil Amdur. circ. 800,000.

796   SZ   ISSN 0570-2070
UNION OF EUROPEAN FOOTBALL ASSOCIATIONS. HANDBOOK OF U E F A. (Text in English, French and German) 1959. irreg. 95 Fr. for base vol., Fr. 30 for updates (3 yrs.) Union of European Football Associations - Union des Associations Europeennes de Football, 33 Jupiter Strasse, Case Postale 16, 3000 Berne 15, Switzerland.

796.342   US   ISSN 0083-1557
UNITED STATES LAWN TENNIS ASSOCIATION. YEARBOOK. 1937. a. $6. Harold O. Zimman, Inc., 156 Broad St., Lynn, MA 01901. adv. circ. 15,000.

796.343   US   ISSN 0083-3398
UNITED STATES SQUASH RAQUETS ASSOCIATION. OFFICIAL YEAR BOOK. 1925. a. $6. United States Squash Racquets Association, 211 Ford Rd., Bala-Cynwyd, PA 19004. adv. index. circ. 4,000.

796.325   US   ISSN 0083-3592
UNITED STATES VOLLEYBALL ASSOCIATION. OFFICIAL VOLLEYBALL GUIDE AND RULE BOOK. 1920. a. $3.50. ‡ United States Volleyball Association, Sales Office, 1750 E. Boulder St., Colorado Springs, CO 80909. Marvin D. Veronee. adv. index. circ. 17,000. (also avail. in microfiche)

796.325   US
VOLLEYBALL RULES. a. $1.10. National Federation of State High School Associations, Federation Place, Box 98, Elgin, IL 60120.

796   GW   ISSN 0083-9213
WHERE TO GOLF IN EUROPE. 1961. a. DM.18. John Jahr Verlag KG, Burchardstr. 14, 2000 Hamburg 1, W. Germany (B.R.D.)

WHO'S WHO IN BASEBALL. see *BIOGRAPHY*

796.33   US   ISSN 0091-6935
WHO'S WHO IN NATIONAL HIGH SCHOOL FOOTBALL. Variant title: Who's Who in National Athletics - High School Football. 1972-73. a. $14.95. National Josep Publishing Co., P.O. Box 1495, Pueblo, CO 81002. Ed. Frank Giannetto. illus. circ. 5,000.

796.342   US
WORLD OF TENNIS; a BP and commercial union yearbook. 5th, 1973. a. Simon & Schuster, Inc., 630 Fifth Ave., New York, NY 10020.

SPORTS AND GAMES — Bicycles And Motorcycles

796.6   FR
ANNEE DU CYCLISME. 1979. a. price varies. Editions Calmann-Levy, 3 rue Auber, 75009 Paris, France. illus.

BOTTIN AUTO-CYCLE-MOTO. see *TRANSPORTATION — Automobiles*

629.227 796.7   US
CHILTON'S MOTORCYCLE REPAIR MANUAL. 1974. irreg . price varies. Chilton Book Co., Automotive Editorial Department, Chilton Way, Radnor, PA 19089.

629.22   US   ISSN 0590-4641
CYCLE GUIDE ROAD TEST ANNUAL. a. $1.25. Quinn Publications, Inc. (Compton), Box 6040, Compton, CA 90224. illus.

796   US
CYCLE WORLD ROAD TEST ANNUAL. 1971. a. $2. C B S Consumer Publishing-West, 1499 Monrovia Ave., Newport Beach, CA 92663. Ed. Robert Atkinson. adv. charts. illus. tr.lit.

796   SZ   ISSN 0071-4283
FEDERATION INTERNATIONALE MOTOCYCLISTE. ANNUAIRE. (Including International Motorcycle Sporting Calendar) (Text in English and French) 1912. a. 3 Fr. International Motorcycle Federation, 19 Chemin William-Barbey, 1292 Chamesy-Geneva, Switzerland.

388.347   UK
GLASS'S MOTOR CYCLE CHECK BOOK. a. £2. Glass's Guide Service Ltd., Elgin House, St. George's Ave., Weybridge, Surrey KT13 0BX, England. adv.

796   AT   ISSN 0310-3137
JAGUAR JOURNAL OF AUSTRALIA. 1973. irreg. Aus.$0.50. Jaguar Clubs of Australia, 49 Tristania St., Doveton, Vic. 3177, Australia. Ed. H. G. Schendzielorz.

796   JA   ISSN 0446-6667
JAPAN'S BICYCLE GUIDE. (Text in English) 1951. a. exchange basis. Japan Bicycle Industry Association, 1-9-3 Akasaka, Tokyo 107, Japan. adv. stat.

796   UK   ISSN 0306-4867
MOTOR CYCLE AND CYCLE TRADER YEAR BOOK. 1970. a. £3. Wheatland Journals Ltd., 177 Hagden Lane, Watford WD1 8LW, England. Ed. Harold Briercliff. circ. 5,000.

380.1   US   ISSN 0091-3774
MOTORCYCLE BLUE BOOK. Variant title: Hap Jones Motorcycle and Scooter Blue Book. 1952. s-a. $6. H. Jones, Ed. & Pub., Box 3063, San Francisco, CA 94119.

629.227   NE
NETHERLANDS. CENTRAAL BUREAU VOOR DE STATISTIEK. PRODUKTIESTATISTIEKEN: RIJWIEL- EN MOTORRIJWIELINDUSTRIE. (Text in Dutch; summaries in English) a. fl.11.25. Centraal Bureau voor de Statistiek, Prinses Beatrixlaan 428, Voorburg, Netherlands (Orders to: Staatsuitgeverij, Christoffel Plantijnstraat, The Hague, Netherlands)

796   AT
PETER WEBSTER'S INTERNATIONAL SPEEDWAY REVIEW. 1977. a. Aus.$2.50. Leisure Boating and Speedway Magazines Pty. Ltd., Box 319, Avalon Beach, NSW 2107, Australia. Ed. Bd.
   Supersedes: Australian Speedway Yearbook (ISSN 0310-8368)

V K G JAHRBUCH. (Verband der Kraftfahrzeugteile- und Zweiradgrosshaendler e.V.) see *TRANSPORTATION — Automobiles*

SPORTS AND GAMES — Boats And Boating

797.1   US   ISSN 0065-9797
AMERICAN POWER BOAT ASSOCIATION. A P B A RULE BOOK. (In 5 vols: Parts 1-4 Racing Rules: Part 5 Racing Records, Commissions, Membership Directory) 1903. a. $3 ea. part to non-members. American Power Boat Association, 17640 E. Nine Mile Rd., E. Detroit, MI 48021. index.

796.95   FR
ANNEE BATEAUX. English edition: World of Yachting. 1977. a. Editions De Messine, 21 rue Pergolese, 75016 Paris, France. Eds. Gerald Asaria, Frank Page. illus. index. circ. 8,000. (back issues avail.)

797   FR
ANNUAIRE NAUTISME. 1963. a. 50 F.($10) Editions de Chabassol, 30 rue de Gramont, 75002 Paris, France. Ed. B. Laloup. adv.

797.1   IT
ANNUARIO DELLA NAUTICA. a. Nautica Editrice, Via Tevere 44, 00198 Rome, Italy. adv. illus.

797.1   US   ISSN 0067-9402
B I A CERTIFICATION HANDBOOK. 1956. a. $5. Boating Industry Association, 401 North Michigan, Chicago, IL 60611. index.
   Formerly: Boating Industry Associations Engineering Manual of Recommended Practices.

797   FR   ISSN 0067-8260
BIBLIOTHEQUE DE LA MER. 1970. irreg. price varies. Tchou Editeur, 6 rue du Mail, Paris 2e, France.

BLAKES HOLIDAYS AFLOAT. see *TRAVEL AND TOURISM*

SPORTS AND GAMES — HORSES AND HORSEMANSHIP

381.45   US   ISSN 0520-2949
BLUE BOOK, OFFICIAL INBOARD/OUTDRIVE BOAT TRADE-IN GUIDE. (Each ed. covers an 8 or 9 year period) a. $6.95. Intertec Publishing Corp., Abos Marine Publications Division, 9221 Quivira Rd., Overland Park, Kansas City, KS 66212. (reprint service avail. from UMI)

797.1   UK   ISSN 0306-3593
BOAT EQUIPMENT BUYERS' GUIDE. 1969. a. 4($5) Weald of Kent Publications(Tonbridge) Ltd., 47 High St., Tonbridge, Kent, England. Ed. L. V. Strong. adv.
    Former titles: Boatbuilders' & Chandlers' Directory of Suppliers (ISSN 0306-3593); Chandler and Boatbuilder Trade Directory (ISSN 0069-2662)

797   UK   ISSN 0067-933X
BOAT WORLD. 1964. a. £7. Haymarket Publishing Ltd., 38-42 Hampton Rd., Teddington, Middx. TW11 0JE, England. Ed. Colin Pringle. adv. bk. rev. circ. 10,000.

797.1   US   ISSN 0067-9399
BOATING GUIDE. 1972. a. $1.50. Snibbe Publications, Inc., 523 Lakeview Rd., Clearwater, FL 33516. Ed. Wilmer Kleinstuber. circ. 200,000.

796.9   380.1   US
BOATING INDUSTRY MARINE BUYERS GUIDE. a; vol. 35, no. 13. $5 per copy. ‡ Whitney Communications Corporation, Magazine Division, 150 E. 58th St., New York, NY 10022 (Subscr. to: Boating Industry, 270 St. Paul St., Denver, CO 80206) Ed. Charles A. Jones. adv. circ. controlled.

797   UK   ISSN 0309-1252
BRISTOW'S BOOK OF YACHTS. 1963. a. £3.95. Weald of Kent Publications (Tonbridge) Ltd., 47 High St., Tonbridge, Kent, England.
    Formed by the merger of: Bristow's Book of Motor Cruisers & Bristow's Book of Sailing Cruisers.

797.123   UK   ISSN 0068-2446
BRITISH ROWING ALMANACK. 1861. a. £2.25 to non-members. ‡ Amateur Rowing Association, 6 Lower Mall, London W6 9DJ, England. Ed. Bd. bk. rev. index.

797   UK   ISSN 0068-290X
BROWN'S NAUTICAL ALMANAC. 1858. a. £12.60. Brown, Son and Ferguson Ltd., 52 Darnley Street, Glasgow G41 2SG, Scotland. Eds. T. Nigel Brown, Capt. C. H. Cotter. adv. circ. 20,000.

797   FR   ISSN 0071-4194
FEDERATION FRANCAISE DE NATATION. ANNUAIRE. 1921. a. 55 F. Federation Francaise de Natation, 148 Av. Gambetta, 75020 Paris, France.

623.8   FI   ISSN 0356-7753
FINNISH BOATBUILDING INDUSTRY. (Text in: English, German, French) 1971. irreg. free. Suomen Vene- ja Moottoriyhdistys - Finnish Boat and Motor Association, Mariankatu 26 B 19, 00170 Helsinki 17, Finland.

797   FR   ISSN 0074-9648
INTERNATIONAL YEARBOOK OF THE UNDERWATER WORLD/ANNUAIRE INTERNATIONAL DU MONDE SOUS-MARIN. 1967-68. biennial. price varies. World Underwater Federation, 34 rue du Colisee, Paris 8e, France.

797   GW   ISSN 0075-627X
KLASINGS BOOTSMARKT INTERNATIONAL; YACHTEN UND BOOTE ZUBEHOER, AUSRUESTUNG, MOTOREN. 1968. a. DM.18. Verlag Delius, Klasing und Co., Siekerwall 21, Postfach 4809, 4800 Bielefeld, W. Germany (B.R.D.) Ed. Kai Krueger. adv. circ. 15,000.

797   UK   ISSN 0075-8272
LAZY MAN'S GUIDE TO HOLIDAYS AFLOAT. 1966. a. 50p. Boat Enquiries Ltd., 43 Botley Rd., Oxford OX2 0PT, England. adv. bk. rev. circ. 120,000.

797.14   US   ISSN 0076-0455
LOG OF THE STAR CLASS; official rule book. 1922. a. $3. ‡ International Star Class Yacht Racing Association, c/o C. Stanley Ogilvy, 943 Greacen Pt. Rd., Mamaroneck, NY 10543 (And 1545 Waukegan Rd., Glenview, IL 60025) Ed. Stanley Ogilvy. adv. circ. 3,200.

797   AT
MIRROR CLASS ASSOCIATION OF AUSTRALIA. YEARBOOK. 1969/70. a. Mirror Class Association of Australia, 29 Haines St., Hawthorn, Vic. 3122, Australia.

796.95   US   ISSN 0148-8740
MOTORBOAT & EQUIPMENT DIRECTORY. 1975. a. $2.95. Motorboat, Inc., 38 Commercial Wharf, Boston, MA 02110. (Affiliate: United Marine Publishing, Inc.) Ed. John R.W. Pear. adv. illus. circ. 92,000.

797.14   US   ISSN 0163-285X
NORTH AMERICAN YACHT REGISTER. 1903. a. $40. (Lloyd's Register of Shipping) Livingston Marine Services, Inc., 17 Battery Pl., New York, NY 10004. circ. 3,000.
    Supersedes (as of 1977): Lloyd's Register of American Yachts (ISSN 0076-0226)

797.1   US   ISSN 0029-8034
OCEAN LIVING. 1967. irreg. $1. Box 17463, Los Angeles, CA 90017. Eds. James Parkerson & Kerry Thornley. adv. bk. rev. illus. circ. 1,000. (processed)
    Formerly: Ocean Freedom.

797.1   SZ
OEFFENTLICHE SCHIFFAHRT AUF DEN SCHWEIZER SEEN. 1976. irreg. Birkhaeuser Verlag, Elisabethstr. 19, CH-4010 Basel, Switzerland.

797.1   US   ISSN 0193-3515
PACIFIC BOATING ALMANAC. NORTHERN CALIFORNIA & NEVADA. a. $6.95. Western Marine Enterprises, Inc., Box Q, Ventura, CA 93002. illus.
    Formerly: Sea Boating Almanac. Northern California and Nevada (ISSN 0363-7700)

797.9   US   ISSN 0148-1177
PACIFIC BOATING ALMANAC. PACIFIC NORTHWEST & ALASKA. a. $6.95. Western Marine Enterprises, Inc., Box Q, Ventura, CA 93002. illus.
    Formerly: Sea Boating Almanac. Pacific Northwest and Alaska (ISSN 0363-7999)

797.1   US   ISSN 0193-3507
PACIFIC BOATING ALMANAC. SOUTHERN CALIFORNIA, ARIZONA, BAJA. a. $6.95. Western Marine Enterprises, Inc., Box Q, Ventura, CA 93002. illus.
    Formerly: Sea Boating Almanac. Southern California, Arizona, Baja (ISSN 0363-6712)

796.95   UK   ISSN 0485-5175
ROVING COMMISSIONS; anthology of cruising logs. 1960. a. £3.90. R C C Press, William Blake House, Marshall St., London W 1, England. Ed. Boyd Campbell.

797.124   US
SAILBOAT & SAILBOAT EQUIPMENT DIRECTORY. 1967. a. $3.95. United Marine Publishing, Inc., Bernard A. Goldhirsh, 38 Commercial Wharf, Boston, MA 02110. adv. bk. rev. illus. circ. 95,000.
    Formerly (1967-1970): Sailboat Directory (ISSN 0581-3115)

623.82   UK   ISSN 0143-1153
SELL'S MARINE MARKET. a. £4. Sell's Publications Ltd., Sell's House, 39 East St., Epsom, Surrey KT17 1BQ, England.

797.1   UK
SOLENT YEARBOOK; solent cruising & racing association year book. 1910. a. £1.20. (Solent Cruising & Racing Association) Isle of Wight County Press Ltd., 29 High Street, Newport, Isle of Wight PO30 1ST, England. adv. charts. circ. 3,000.

796.9   US
WATERWAY GUIDE; the yachtsman's Bible. (Separate Northern, Southern, and Mid-Atlantic Editions) 1947. a. $4.95 per edition. ‡ Boating Industry Magazine, P.O. Box 1486, Annapolis, MD 21404. Ed. Cynthia Taylor. charts. illus.

797.1   BE   ISSN 0084-3237
YACHTING BELGE; revue annuelle et illustree des sports nautiques. 1962. a. 225 Fr. Editions EREL, 16 St. Sebastiaanstraat, 8400 Oostende, Belgium. Ed. Robert Lanoye. adv. bk. rev. circ. 10,000.

797.1   US   ISSN 0094-8136
YACHTING YEAR BOOK OF NORTHERN CALIFORNIA. a. $5. Pacific Inter-Club Yacht Association of Northern California, Publication Office, 68 Post St., R. 417, San Francisco, CA 94104. illus.

797.1   US
YACHTING'S BOAT BUYERS GUIDE. 1959. a. $2.95. Yachting Publishing Corporation, 50 W. 44 St., New York, NY 10036. Ed. Martha M. Lostrom. adv. index.
    Formerly: Boat Owners Buyers Guide (ISSN 0067-9321)

797.14   US   ISSN 0084-3261
YACHTSMAN'S GUIDE TO THE CARIBBEAN. 1964. irreg. latest issue 1975. $6.75. Seaport Publishing Co., c/o Ed. Clifford M. Montague, 843 Delray Ave., Grand Rapids, MI 49506. index.

797.14   US   ISSN 0084-327X
YACHTSMAN'S GUIDE TO THE GREAT LAKES. 1957. a. $4.75. Seaport Publishing Co., c/o Ed. Clifford M. Montague, 843 Delray Ave. S.E., Grand Rapids, MI 49506. index.

796.95   US   ISSN 0162-7635
YACHTSMAN'S GUIDE TO THE GREATER ANTILLES. a. $6.95. Tropic Isle Publishers, Box 340866, Coral Gables, FL 33134.

SPORTS AND GAMES — Horses And Horsemanship

798.2   NE
ALBUM VAN DRAF- EN RENSPORT. a. fl.25. N. V. Publico, Postbus 16043, 2500 BA The Hague, Netherlands. adv.

798   US
APPALOOSA HORSE; STUD BOOK AND REGISTRY. irreg., v. 15, 1973. price varies. Appaloosa Horse Club Inc., Box 8403, Moscow, ID 83843.

798   UK
ARAB HORSE STUD BOOK. 1919. a. price varies. Arab Horse Society, Sackville Lodge, Lye Green, Crowborough, Sussex TN6 1UU, England. circ. 1,000. (tabloid format)

798.4   AT   ISSN 0084-7402
AUSTRALIAN HORSE RACING ANNUAL.* 1969. a. $7 ea. Playfair Publishing Group, Box 52, Northbridge, N.S.W. 2063, Australia.

791.8   US
BRAND BOOK. 1972? biennial. $25. Westerners, San Diego Corral, Box 7174, San Diego, CA 92107.

636.1   CN   ISSN 0382-5795
CANADIAN HACKNEY STUD BOOK. 1905. irreg. Canadian Hackney Horse Society, c/o Canadian National Live Stock Records, Ottawa, Ont., Canada. illus.

796   UK   ISSN 0419-3806
DIRECTORY OF THE TURF. 1961. triennial. £11. Pacemaker Publications, 170 Kings Rd., London SW3 4UN, England. Ed. Peter Towers-Clark. adv. circ. 2,750.

798.4   IT
EUROPEAN RACING MANUAL. (Text in English, Italian) 1973. a. L.15000($20) Derby Societa Editrice, Corso di Porta Nuova 46, 20121 Milan, Italy.

798   BE
FASTES HIPPIQUES BELGES; revue annuelle illustree du sport equestre sur le galop, trot, jumping, elevage, dressage, tourisme equestre. 1957. a. 225 Fr. Editions EREL, 16, St. Sebastiaanstraat, 8400 Oostende, Belgium. Ed. R. Lanoye. adv. bk. rev. circ. 10,000.

636.1   SP   ISSN 0085-1337
GUIA DE LOS CABALLOS VERIFICADAS EN ESPANA. 1875. a. 1000 ptas. Sociedad de Fomento de la Cria Caballar de Espana, 6, Fernanflor, Madrid, Spain. circ. 2,000.

SPORTS AND GAMES — OUTDOOR LIFE

636.1   UK
HACKNEY HORSE SOCIETY YEAR BOOK. a. £3. Hackney Horse Society, British Equestrian Centre, Kenilworth, Warwickshire CV8 2LR, England.

636.1   UK
HACKNEY STUD BOOK. triennial. £6. Hackney Horse Society, British Equestrian Centre, Kenilworth, Warwickshire CV8 2LR, England.

798.2   US
HORSE ACTION. 1979. a. $2.95. Rich Publishing, Inc., Box 555, Temecula, CA 92390. adv. circ. 100,000.

791.8   US
HORSE & RIDER ALL-WESTERN YEARBOOK. 1973. a. $2.95. ‡ Rich Publishing, Inc., Box 555, Temecula, CA 92390. Ed. Ray Rich. adv. bk. rev. illus. circ. 47,000.

636.1   US   ISSN 0162-8127
HORSE CARE. 1979. a. $2.95. Rich Publishing, Inc., 41919 Moreno, Temecula, CA 92390. adv.

636.1   US
HORSE INDUSTRY DIRECTORY. 1972. a. $4. American Horse Council, Inc., 1700 K St N.W. No. 300, Washington, DC 20006. Ed. Georgine Winslett.

798.4   US
HORSE RACING GUIDE. 1973. a. $1.50. Snibbe Publications, Inc., 523 Lakeview Rd., Clearwater, FL 33516. Ed. Horace Wade.

636.1   US
HORSE WOMEN. 1978. a. Rich Publishing, Inc., Box 555, 41919 Moreno, Temecula, CA 92390. Ed. Marla Maeder. adv.

354   CN   ISSN 0317-7262
MANITOBA. HORSE RACING COMMISSION. ANNUAL REPORT. a. free. Horse Racing Commission, Winnipeg, Man., Canada. stat.

798   US
NATIONAL CUTTING HORSE ASSOCIATION. RULE BOOK. 1963. a. National Cutting Horse Association, P.O. Box 12155, Fort Worth, TX 76116. Ed. Zack T. Wood, Jr. circ. 4,000.

798   UK   ISSN 0079-9408
RACEHORSES. 1948. a. £22. Portway Press Ltd., Timeform House, Northgate, Halifax, Yorkshire HX1 1XE, England. Ed. J. D. Newton. adv. circ. 8,000.

798.2   UK   ISSN 0305-5892
REGISTER OF THOROUGHBRED STALLIONS. biennial. £25($61) Turf Newspapers Ltd., 55 Curzon St., London, W1Y 7PF, England.

798   AT
SOUTH AUSTRALIAN RACEHORSE. 1964. irreg. Bloodhorse Breeder's Association of Australia, South Australian Division, Box 1695, G.P.O. Adelaide, SA 5001, Australia. Ed. P. Duncan.

636.1   UK
STALLION REVIEW. 1912. a. £8. Thoroughbred Publishers Ltd., 26 Charing Cross Road, London WC2H 0DJ, England. adv. illus. circ. 6,000. (processed)

798   AT   ISSN 0311-8215
STUD AND STABLE. 1971. irreg. Aus.$0.10. Percival Publishing Co. Pty. Ltd., 862 Elizabeth St., Waterloo, NSW 2017, Australia.
     Formerly: Australasian Stud and Stable (ISSN 0310-6403)

798.2   US
TACK 'N TOGS BOOK; directory for retailers of supplies for horse and rider. 1971. a. $10. ‡ Miller Publishing Co., 2501 Wayzata Blvd., Box 67, Minneapolis, MN 55440. Ed. Douglas Dahl. adv. charts. stat. tr.lit. circ. 16,000 (controlled) (reprint service avail. from UMI)

798   US   ISSN 0082-4240
THOROUGHBRED RACING ASSOCIATIONS. DIRECTORY AND RECORD BOOK. 1955. a. free; limited distribution. ‡ Thoroughbred Racing Associations, 300 Marcus Ave., Suite 2W4, Lake Success, NY 11040. Ed. John I. Day. circ. 3,000.

798   AU   ISSN 0082-5646
TRABRENNEN. irreg. S.9. Zeitungsunternehmen "Sport", GmbH, Frankenberggasse 11/6, A-1040 Vienna, Austria. Ed. Kurt Kollross.

798   US
U S T A SIRES AND DAMS; the register. 1948. a. $30. United States Trotting Association, 750 Michigan Ave, Columbus, OH 43215. Ed. Walter Adamkosky. index. circ. 8,000.
     Formerly: Sires and Dams (ISSN 0083-3495)

798   US   ISSN 0083-3517
U S T A YEAR BOOK. 1939. a. $5. United States Trotting Association, 750 Michigan Ave, Columbus, OH 43215. Ed. Walter Adamkosky. index. circ. 8,000.

798   UK
WELSH PONY AND COB SOCIETY JOURNAL. 1962. a. membership. Welsh Pony and Cob Society, c/o T. E. Roberts, 6 Chalybeate St., Aberystwyth, Dyfed, Wales. Ed. Mrs. G. J. Mountain. adv. circ. 6,000.

SPORTS AND GAMES — Outdoor Life

796.52   US   ISSN 0065-082X
ACCIDENTS IN NORTH AMERICAN MOUNTAINEERING. 1948. a. $3. American Alpine Club, 113 E. 90 St., New York, NY 10028. Ed. John E. Williamson. circ. 8,000. (reprint service avail. from UMI)

796.5 910   GW
ADAC-CAMPINGFUEHRER. BAND 1: SUEDEUROPA. 1951. a. DM.16.80. ADAC Verlag GmbH, Baumgartnerstr. 53, 8 Munich 70, Postfach 70 01 26, West Germany (B.R.D.) Ed. H. Nitschke. adv. circ. 175,000.
     Supersedes in part: Internationaler Campingfuehrer (ISSN 0074-9753)

796.5 910   GW
ADAC-CAMPINGFUEHRER. BAND 2: DEUTSCHLAND, MITTEL- UND NORDEUROPA. 1952. a. DM.16.80. ADAC Verlag GmbH, Baumgartnerstr. 53, 8 Munich 70, Postfach 70 01 26, West Germany (B.R.D.) adv. circ. 60,000.

799.3   US   ISSN 0065-4213
AGE OF FIREARMS. irreg. $4.95. ‡ D B I Books, Inc., One Northfield Plaza, Northfield, IL 60093. Ed. Robert Held.

799.1   IT
AGEVOLAZIONI E VANTAGGI PER I PESCATORI FEDERATI. a. Federazione Italiana Pesca Sportiva, Viale Tiziano 70, Rome, Italy. Ed. Claudio Blasi. adv. circ. 800,000.
     Fishing

ALAN ROGERS' SELECTED SITES FOR CARAVANNING AND CAMPING IN EUROPE. see *TRAVEL AND TOURISM*

354.9   US   ISSN 0362-6962
ALASKA. DIVISION OF GAME. ANNUAL REPORT OF SURVEY-INVENTORY ACTIVITIES. a. Department of Fish and Game, Game Division, Juneau, AK 99801. illus. Key Title: Annual Report of Survey-Inventory Activities.

799   CN   ISSN 0318-4943
ALBERTA FISHING GUIDE. 1972. a. Can.$1.50. (Railton Publications Ltd.) George Mitchell, Ed. & Pub., 10519-128a Ave., Edmonton, Alta. T5E 0K2, Canada. adv. illus. circ. 15,000.

796.7   US
ALL ABOUT SNOWMOBILES. a. Argus Publishers Corp., Box 49659, Los Angeles, CA 90049.

796.5   IT
ALMANACCO ROULOTTE. 1977. a. Edigamma s.r.l., Piazza dei Sanniti 9, 00185 Rome, Italy. Ed. Tommaso Valentinetti.

796.5   GW   ISSN 0065-6534
ALPENVEREINS-JAHRBUCH. 1869. a. DM.16. Deutscher Alpenverein, Praterinsel 5, 8000 Munich 22, W. Germany (B.R.D.) (Co-sponsor: Oesterreichischer Alpenverein) index.

799.31   US   ISSN 0065-6747
AMATEUR TRAPSHOOTING ASSOCIATION. OFFICIAL TRAPSHOOTING RULES. a. free. Amateur Trapshooting Association, Vendalia, OH 45377. index.

796.52   US   ISSN 0065-6925
AMERICAN ALPINE JOURNAL. 1929. a. $12.50. American Alpine Club, 113 E. 90 St., New York, NY 10028. Ed. H. Adams Carter. bk. rev. index. circ. 5,000. (also avail. in microform from UMI; reprint service avail. from UMI)

796   US
ASSOCIATION OF INDEPENDENT CAMPS. BUYERS GUIDE AND CAMP DIRECTORY. 1959. a. $5. (Association of Independent Camps) Camp Consulting Services, Ltd., 14 Wesley Court, Huntington, NY 11743. Ed. Joanna W. Howe. adv. circ. 3,000.
     Formerly: Association of Private Camps. Buyers Guide and Camp Directory (ISSN 0519-1505)

796.5   FR   ISSN 0066-989X
ASSURANCES GENERALES DE FRANCE. INFORMATIONS.* 1970. irreg. price varies. Assurances Generales de France, 87 rue de Richelieu, Paris 2e, France.

799   CN   ISSN 0004-7384
AU GRAND AIR. 1961. irreg. Rod & Gun Publishing Corp. Ltd., 1219 Hotel de Ville, Montreal, Que., Canada. illus.

796   AT
AUSTRALIAN LADIES GOLF UNION. OFFICIAL YEARBOOK. 1932. a. Aus.$1. Australian Ladies Golf Union, Mrs. K. D. Brown, Honorary Secretary, 22 McKay Road, Rowville, Vic. 3178, Australia.

796.93   AT   ISSN 0084-7593
AUSTRALIAN SKI YEARBOOK. 1928. a. Aus.$2.50 ea. (Victorian Ski Association) Australian Ski Federation, 32 George St., Avalon Beach, N.S.W. 2107, Australia. Ed. Wendy J. Cross. adv. bk. rev. circ. 10,000.

799.1   US
B A S S FISHING GUIDE. 1974. a. $1.50. Bass Anglers Sportsman Society, Box 3044, Montgomery, AL 36117. Ed. Bob Cobb. circ. 100,000.

799.1   US
B A S S MASTER FISHING ANNUAL. 1973. a. $1.50. Bass Anglers Sportsman Society, Box 3044, Montgomery, AL 36117. Ed. Bob Cobb. circ. 371,000.

799.1   CN   ISSN 0709-7778
B. C. FRESH WATER FISHING GUIDE. 1958. a. Can.$2.95. Lee Straight Publications, 1375 W. 57th Ave, Vancouver, B.C. V6P 1S7, Canada. adv. illus. circ. 25,000.

799   CN   ISSN 0709-776X
B. C. SEA ANGLING GUIDE. 1973. a. Can.$2.95. Lee Straight Publications, 1375 W. 57th Ave., Vancouver, B.C. V6P 1S7, Canada. adv. illus. circ. 20,000.
     Formerly: B. C. Salt Water Salmon Guide.

799.2   UK   ISSN 0067-2947
BAILY'S HUNTING DIRECTORY. 1897. a. £7.75. J. A. Allen Ltd., 1 Lower Grosvenor Place, Buckingham Palace Road, London, SW1W OEL, England. adv.

799   US
BAKER DEER HUNTING ANNUAL. a. $1.95. Aqua-Field Publications, Inc., 728 Beaver Dam Rd., Point Pleasant, NJ 08742.

799.1   US   ISSN 0363-5538
BOB ZWIRZ' FISHING ANNUAL. a. $2.50. Charger Productions, Inc., 34249 Camino Capistrano, Capistrano Beach, CA 92624. illus.

381.45   US   ISSN 0362-6180
BUYERS' GUIDE FOR THE MASS ENTERTAINMENT INDUSTRY. a. $10. Billboard Publications, Inc., Amusement Business Division, Box 24970, Nashville, TN 37202 (Or 2160 Patterson St., Cincinnati, OH 45214) illus.
     Formerly: Amusement Equipment Buyers Guide; Incorporating: Facility Manager's Buyer's Guide & A B's Guide to Souvenirs and Novelties.

SPORTS AND GAMES — OUTDOOR LIFE

796   CN   ISSN 0382-8255
C O F NEWSLETTER. 1968. irreg. Canadian Orienteering Federation, 1B, 445 Gallard Blvd., Dorval, Que., Canada. illus. Key Title: COF Newsletter.
     Continues: Orienteering (ISSN 0380-9773)
     Orienteering

CALIFORNIA-NEVADA CAMPBOOK. see *TRAVEL AND TOURISM*

796.5   670   US
CAMP DIRECTORS PURCHASING GUIDE. 1964. a. $3. Klevens Publications, Inc., 7600 Ave. V, Littlerock, CA 93543. Ed. John Keller. adv. bk. rev. film rev, play rev. circ. 14,684(controlled) (back issues avail.)

796.5   IT
CAMPEGGIARE IN EUROPA. 1973. biennial. L.3500. Federazione Italiana del Campeggio e del Caravanning, Casella Postale 649, 50100 Florence, Italy.

796.5   IT
CAMPEGGIO ANNUARIO - TUTTOCAMPING. 1957. biennial. L.5000. Editoriale Aria Aperta, Via Durini 27, 20122 Milan, Italy. Ed. Guelfo La Manna. adv. circ. 7,000.
     Camping

796.54   US   ISSN 0068-6913
CAMPER'S DIGEST. 1970. irreg., 3rd edt., 1980. $7.95. ‡ D B I Books, Inc., One Northfield Plaza, Northfield, IL 60093. Eds. Erwin Bauer, Peggy Bauer.

CAMPER'S GUIDE TO AREA CAMPGROUNDS. see *TRAVEL AND TOURISM*

796.5   UK
CAMPING AND CARAVANNING IN BRITAIN. a. £2.75 to non-members. Automobile Association, Fanum House, Basingstoke, Hants RG21 2EA, England. adv.
     Formerly: Camping and Caravanning U. K.

CAMPING, CARAVANNING AND SPORTS EQUIPMENT TRADES DIRECTORY. see *BUSINESS AND ECONOMICS — Trade And Industrial Directories*

796.54   UK
CAMPING CLUB HANDBOOK AND SITES LIST. Camping Sites Yearbook. biennial. membership. Camping Club of Great Britain and Ireland Ltd., 11 Lower Grosvenor Place, London SW1W 0EY, England.
     Formerly: Camping Club of Great Britain and Ireland. Year Book with List of Camp Sites (ISSN 0068-6956)

796.5   IT
CAMPING-GUIDA. 1952. a. L.3500. Editoriale Aria Aperta, Via Durini 27, 20122 Milan, Italy. adv. circ. 10,000.
     Camping

CAMPING GUIDE. see *TRAVEL AND TOURISM*

796.54   US   ISSN 0068-6964
CAMPING GUIDE. 1972. a. $1.50. Snibbe Publications, Inc., 523 Lakeview Rd., Clearwater, FL 33516. Ed. James Winchester. circ. 200,000.

914.81   796.5   NO
CAMPINGBOKEN. 1966. a. Kr.15. Inter-Press A-S, P.O. Box 175, 1321 Stabekk, Norway. Ed. H. Moeller. adv. circ. 10,000.

796.5   910.202   IT
CAMPITUR: CAMPING, CARAVANING, VILLAGGI TURISTICI. 1973. a. L.4000. C P M Editrice s.a.s., Via Carducci 21, 20123 Milan, Italy. Ed. Ernesto Cavallini. adv. circ. 30,000.
     Camping

796.52   CN   ISSN 0068-8207
CANADIAN ALPINE JOURNAL. 1907. a. Can.$7. Alpine Club of Canada, P.O. Box 1026, Banff, Alberta T0L 0C0, Canada. Ed. Moira Irvine. bk. rev. index; cum.index (1907-1966) circ. 4,000.

796.5   AT
CARAVAN CAMPING DIRECTORY. a. membership. National Roads and Motorists Association, 151 Clarence T., Sydney, N.S.W. 2000, Australia.

799.2   IT   ISSN 0576-8888
CATALOGO BOLAFFI DEL CACCIATORE E DELLE ARMI. 1966. irreg.; no. 7, 1978. L.8000. Giulio Bolaffi Editore s.p.a., Via Cavour 17F, 10123 Turin, Italy. Ed. Umberto Allemandi. adv. illus. circ. 8,000.
     Hunting

796   917.1   CN
CATALOGUE OF CANADIAN RECREATION AND LEISURE RESEARCH. 1973. every 2-3 years. Can.$5. Ontario Research Council on Leisure, 77 Bloor St. W., 8th Floor, Toronto, Ont. M7A 2R9, Canada. circ. 5,000.

796   US
COLEMAN OUTDOOR ANNUAL. a. $1.95. Aqua-Field Publications, Inc., 728 Beaver Dam Rd., Point Pleasant, NJ 08742. Ed. Steve Ferber.
     Formerly: Coleman Camping Annual.

799.2   US   ISSN 0364-071X
COLT AMERICAN HANDGUNNING ANNUAL. 1975. a. $1.75. Aqua-Field Publications, 728 Beaver Dam Rd., Point Pleasant, NJ 08742. Ed. Steven Ferber. circ. 125,000.

333.78   UK
COMMONS, OPEN SPACES AND FOOTPATHS PRESERVATION SOCIETY. ANNUAL REPORT. a. Commons Open Spaces and Footpaths Preservation Society, 25A Bell St., Henley-on-Thames, Oxon RG9 2BA, England.

790   US   ISSN 0069-8903
CONGRESS FOR RECREATION AND PARKS. PROCEEDINGS. a. $8.35. National Recreation and Park Association, 1601 North Kent St., Arlington, VA 22209 (Order Tapes from: Leisure Sights and Sounds, Inc., Box 562, Columbia, MO 65201) Ed. Sidney G. Lutzin. index. (1969-1972 paperbound; since 1973 on cassettes)

711   UK
CONGRESS IN PARK AND RECREATION ADMINISTRATION. REPORTS. triennial. International Federation of Park and Recreation Administration, c/o Kenneth L. Morgan, Sec.Gen., The Grotto, Lower Basildon, Reading, Berkshire RG8 9NE, England.
     Formerly: World Congress in Public Park Administration. Reports (ISSN 0510-8225)

333.7   US   ISSN 0092-5764
CONNECTICUT WALK BOOK. 1937. irreg. $5.50. Connecticut Forest and Park Association, 1010 Main St., Box 389, East Hartford, CT 06108. illus.

796.54   UK   ISSN 0069-9527
CONTINENTAL CAMPING & CARAVAN SITES. 1964. a. £1. Link House Publications Ltd., Link House, Dingwall Ave., Croydon CR9 2TA, England. Ed. Heather Salter.

799.2   US   ISSN 0092-8216
CORD SPORTFACTS: HUNTING. irreg. Cord Communications Corp., 25 W. 43rd St., New York, NY 10022. illus.

796.93   US
CURTIS CASEWIT'S GUIDE TO SKI AREAS AND RESORTS. 1978. irreg. $2.50. Pilot Books, 347 Fifth Ave., New York, NY 10016.
     Skiing

D C C-CARAVAN MODELLFUEHRER. (Deutscher Camping Club e.V.) see *TRANSPORTATION — Automobiles*

D C C-CARAVANFUEHRER. (Deutscher Camping Club e.V.) see *TRAVEL AND TOURISM*

D C C-TOURISTIK SERVICE. (Deutscher Camping Club e.V.) see *TRAVEL AND TOURISM*

796.9   UK   ISSN 0309-5134
DAILY MAIL SKIER'S HOLIDAY GUIDE. a. £3. Ski Specialists, 4 Douro Place, London W85PH, England. illus.

799.1   US   ISSN 0145-613X
DAIWA FISHING ANNUAL. 1975. a. $1.75. Aqua-Field Publications, 728 Beaver Dam Rd., Point Pleasant, New York, NJ 08742. Ed. Steven Ferber.
     Formerly: Daiwa Sportfishing Annual.

799   US   ISSN 0146-6143
DIXIE GUN WORKS MUZZLELOADERS' ANNUAL. a. $1.95. Aqua-Field Publications, Inc., 728 Beaver Dam Rd, Point Pleasant, NJ 08742.

796.93   UK   ISSN 0070-718X
DOWNHILL ONLY JOURNAL. 1936. a. free to members. Downhill Only Club, c/o Ed. & Pub. D.N. Freund, Bannwald, Ballinger, Great Missenden, Bucks, England. adv. bk. rev. index. circ. 1,700.

EASTERN CANADA CAMPBOOK. see *TRAVEL AND TOURISM*

796.93   330   US   ISSN 0147-4243
ECONOMIC ANALYSIS OF NORTH AMERICAN SKI AREAS. a. $25. University of Colorado, Graduate School of Business Administration, Business Research Division, Boulder, CO 80309.
     Skiing

796.5   GW   ISSN 0071-2272
EUROPA CAMPING UND CARAVANING. INTERNATIONALER FUEHRER. (Text in English, French, and German) 1959. a. DM.14.80. Drei Brunnen Verlag, Postfach 1124, 7000 Stuttgart 1, W. Germany (B.R.D.) Ed. Heinz Dieter Schmoll.

797   SP
FEDERACION ESPANOLA DE NATACION. ANUARIO. 1950. a. 525 ptas.($8) Federacion Espanola de Natacion, Conde Penalver 61, Madrid-6, Spain.

799.17   US   ISSN 0163-5468
FIELD & STREAM BASS FISHING ANNUAL. C B S Publications, Consumer Publishing Group, 1515 Broadway, New York, NY 10036.

799   US
FIELD AND STREAM DEER HUNTING ANNUAL. 1978. a. newsstand sales only. C B S Publications, 1515 Broadway, New York, NY 10036. Ed. Glenn Sapir. circ. 250,000.

799.1   US   ISSN 0362-6385
FIELD & STREAM FISHING ANNUAL. $1.50. C B S Publications, Consumer Publishing Group, 1515 Broadway, New York, NY 10036. illus.

799.2   US   ISSN 0361-3011
FIELD & STREAM HUNTING ANNUAL. Short title: Hunting Annual. 1978. a. $1.50. C B S Publications, Consumer Publishing Group, 1515 Broadway, New York, NY 10036. illus.

799.1   US   ISSN 0430-6090
FISHERMEN'S DIGEST. irreg. $7.95. D B I Books, Inc., One Northfield Plaza, Northfield, IL 60093. Ed. Erwin A. Bauer. adv.

799.12   UK
FISHING WATERS; where to fish in England, Scotland and Wales. a. 90p. Link House Publications Ltd., Link House, Dingwall Ave., Croydon, CR9 2TA, England. Ed. Heather Salter.
     Formerly: Anglers' Annual (ISSN 0066-1783)

796.5   GW   ISSN 0071-7711
FORSCHUNGSSTELLE FUER JAGDKUNDE UND WILDSCHADENVERHUETUNG. SCHRIFTENREIHE. 1960. irreg., no. 8, 1978. price varies. Verlag Paul Parey (Hamburg), Spitalerstr. 12, 2000 Hamburg 1, W. Germany (B.R.D) Ed. Bd. bibl.illus. index. (reprint service avail. from ISI)

FRANCE-SPORTS. see *SPORTS AND GAMES*

799.1   US   ISSN 0071-5611
FRESH WATER FISHING GUIDE. 1970. a. $1.50. Snibbe Publications, Inc., 523 Lakeview Rd., Clearwater, FL 33516. Ed. Henry Shakespeare. circ. 200,000.

799   US
FRESHWATER FISHERMAN. a. $1.50. Aqua-Field Publications, Inc., 728 Beaver Dam Rd., Point Pleasant, NJ 08742. Ed. Steve Ferber.
     Formerly: Ferber's Freshwater Fisherman.

796.93   AU
FUER DIE SICHERHEIT IM BERGLAND. 1972. a. S.150. Oesterreichisches Kuratorium fuer Alpine Sicherheit, Prinz Eugen Str. 12, A-1040 Vienna, Austria. Ed. Eduard Rabofsky. circ. 3,000.

GOLDEN LIST OF BEACHES; believed to be free from sewage pollution. see ENVIRONMENTAL STUDIES

GOOD CAMPS GUIDE. see TRAVEL AND TOURISM

641.9477 US
GREAT LAKES CAMPBOOK. a. membership. American Automobile Association, 8111 Gatehouse Rd., Falls Church, VA 22047. illus.
Formerly (until 1980): Great Lakes Camping. R V and tent sites in Illinois, Indiana, Michigan, Ohio, Wisconsin

796 914.5 IT ISSN 0072-792X
GUIDA CAMPING D'ITALIA. 1958. a. L.4000. Federazione Italiana del Campeggio e del Caravanning, Casella Postale 649, 0100 Florence, Italy. adv.

796 CN ISSN 0705-8314
GUIDE DU CAMPING. 1976. a. Can.$1 per no. Association des Terrains de Camping et Caravaning du Quebec, 8775 Bd. Lacordaire, Ville St. Leonard, Que. H1R 2A9, Canada. illus.
Formerly: Guide Camping (ISSN 0383-2368)

796.5 FR
GUIDE OFFICIEL CAMPING-CARAVANING. a. (Federation Francaise de Camping et de Caravaning) Ediregie, 3 Cite d'Hauteville, B.P. 156, 75463 Paris Cedex 10, France. adv. circ. 135,000.

GUIDE TO CARAVAN AND CAMPING HOLIDAYS. see TRAVEL AND TOURISM

GUIDE TO SKIING IN MINNESOTA. see TRAVEL AND TOURISM

799.3 US ISSN 0072-9043
GUN DIGEST. a. $10.95. ‡ D B I Books, Inc., One Northfield Plaza, Northfield, IL 60093. Ed. Ken Warner.

799.2 US
GUN WORLD ANNUAL. 1973. a. $2.95. Gallant Publishing Co. Inc., 34249 Camino Capistrano, Capistrano Beach, CA 92624. illus.
Formerly: Gun World Hunting Guide (ISSN 0362-4749)

799.3 US ISSN 0072-906X
GUNS AND AMMO ANNUAL. a. $5.95. Petersen Publishing Co., Book Sales Division, 6725 Sunset Blvd., Los Angeles, CA 90028. Ed. Garry James.

799.3 US ISSN 0072-9078
GUNS ILLUSTRATED. 1969. a. $8.95. ‡ D B I Books, Inc., One Northfield Plaza, Northfield, IL 60093.

799.3 US ISSN 0073-0211
HANDLOADER'S DIGEST. irreg. $8.95. ‡ D B I Books, Inc., One Northfield Plaza, Northfield, IL 60093. Ed. John T. Amber.

919.4 796.74 AT ISSN 0085-1477
HERALD CARAVANNING GUIDE. 1931. a. Aus.$1 ea. Herald Travel Bureau, Newspaper House, 247 Collins St., Melbourne, Vic. 3000, Australia. Ed. D. H. Day.

796 AT
HEYBOB. 1959. a. price varies. University of Queensland, Bushwalking Club, St. Lucia, Qld. 4067, Australia. Ed. Robert Rankin.

796.552 II
HIMALAYAN JOURNAL. (Text in English) 1929. a. Rs.70. (Himalayan Club) Oxford University Press, Oxford House, Apollo Bunder, Box 31, Bombay 400001, India. Ed. Soli S. Mehta. adv. bk. rev. charts. illus. index. circ. 1,500. (tabloid format)

799.3 US ISSN 0073-3121
HOME GUNSMITHING DIGEST. 1970. irreg. $7.95. ‡ D B I Books, Inc., One Northfield Plaza, Northfield, IL 60093. Ed. Robert A. Steindler.

HOSTELING HOLIDAYS. see TRAVEL AND TOURISM

796.5 GW ISSN 0074-7122
INTERNATIONAL NATURIST GUIDE/ INTERNATIONALER FKK-REISEFUEHRER/ GUIDE NATURISTE INTERNATIONALE. a. DM.6.80. (International Naturist Federation) Richard Danehl's Verlag, Postfach 500344, 2000 Hamburg 50, W. Germany (B.R.D.) adv.

797 AT
IT. 1968. irreg. Aus.$0.10 per no. Canberra Bushwalking Club, Box 160, Canberra City, A.C.T. 2601, Australia.

796.5 CN
LEISUREWHEELS CAMPGROUND DIRECTORY. 1971. a. Can.$2.75. Tall Taylor Publishing Ltd., Box 40, Irricana, Alta. T0M 1B0, Canada. adv. circ. 10,000.

799.2 891.87 641.5 CS ISSN 0541-8836
MAGAZIN POLOVNIKA. a. 20 Kcs. Priroda, Krizkova 7, 894 17 Bratislava, Czechoslovakia. illus.

796 AT
MELBOURNE WALKER. 1929. a. Aus.$0.60 per no. Melbourne Amateur Walking and Touring Club, G.P.O. Box 2446v, Melbourne, Vic. 3001, Australia. Ed. Alan David Budge.

MIDEASTERN CAMPBOOK. see TRAVEL AND TOURISM

799.1 UK
MODERN INSHORE FISHING. 1974. irreg. 75p. R. D. Leakey, Ed. & Pub., Sutcliffe House, Settle, Yorkshire, England. bk. rev. circ. 16,000.

796.522 US ISSN 0027-2620
MOUNTAINEER; to explore, study, preserve and enjoy the natural beauty of Northwest America. 1907. m. plus special issues. $6. Mountaineers, Inc., 719 Pike St., Seattle, WA 98101. Ed. Verna Ness. adv. bk. rev. circ. 8,500.
Mountaineering

796.42 US ISSN 0362-9481
N A G W S GUIDE. TRACK AND FIELD. Short title: Track and Field Guide. 1937. a. American Alliance for Health, Physical Education, Recreation, and Dance, National Association for Girls and Women in Sport, 1900 Association Dr., Reston, VA 22091. circ. 15,000. Indexed: ERIC.

796.9 US ISSN 0148-1150
N A G W S RULES. SKIING. 1976. biennial. American Alliance for Health, Physical Education, Recreation and Dance, National Association for Girls and Women in Sport, 1900 Association Dr., Reston, VA 22091. circ. 1,500.

NATIONAL OUTDOOR LIVING DIRECTORY. see CONSERVATION

799.31 US ISSN 0077-5738
NATIONAL SKEET SHOOTING ASSOCIATION. RECORDS ANNUAL. 1947. a. $5. National Skeet Shooting Association, Box 28188, San Antonio, TX 78228. Ed. Milo Mims. adv. index. circ. 19,000.

354 NE
NETHERLANDS. MINISTERIE VAN CULTUUR, RECREATIE EN MAATSCHAPPELIJK WERK. OPENLUCHTRECREATIE. (Summaries in English and French) irreg. Ministerie van Cultuur, Recreatie en Maatschappelijk Werk, Steenvoordelaan 370, Rijswijk (Z.H.), Netherlands. illus.

799.1 US ISSN 0092-1734
NEW FISHING. 1953. a. $1.25. Maco Publishing Co. Inc., 380 Madison Ave., New York, NY 10017. Ed. John Brett. adv. circ. 140,000.

796.5 US ISSN 0077-8354
NEW HAMPSHIRE CAMPING GUIDE. 1969. a. free. ‡ (New Hampshire Campground Owners Association) Profiles Publishing Co., 2 Steam Mill Court, Box 1108, Concord, NH 03301. (Co-sponsor: New Hampshire Office of Vacation Travel) adv. circ. 200,000. (reprint service avail. from UMI)

NORSK FISKARALMANAKK. see FISH AND FISHERIES

NORTH CENTRAL CAMPBOOK. see TRAVEL AND TOURISM

917.4 US
NORTHEASTERN CAMPBOOK; including location maps. Cover title: R V and Tent Sites in Connecticut, Maine, Massachusetts, New Hampshire, New York, Rhode Island, Vermont. a. American Automobile Association, 8111 Gatehouse Rd., Falls Church, VA 22047. illus.
Former titles (until 1980): Northeastern Camping; Northeastern Camping and Trailering.

NORTHWESTERN CAMPBOOK; including location maps. see TRAVEL AND TOURISM

796 AU ISSN 0029-8840
OESTERREICHISCHER ALPENVEREIN. AKADEMISCHE SEKTION GRAZ. MITTEILUNGEN.* 1892. a. membership. Oesterreichischer Alpenverein, Akademische Sektion Graz, Rechbauerstr. 12, A-8010 Graz, Austria. Ed. J. Schurz. adv. bk. rev. illus. circ. 1,000.
Mountaineering

796.93 US
OFFICIAL NATIONAL COLLEGIATE ATHLETIC ASSOCIATION SKIING RULES. 1963. a. $1.50. (National Collegiate Athletic Association) N C A A Publishing Service, Box 1906, Shawnee Mission, KS 66222. circ. 1,000.

796.42 US
OFFICIAL NATIONAL COLLEGIATE ATHLETIC ASSOCIATION TRACK AND FIELD GUIDE. 1922. a. $3. (National Collegiate Athletic Association) N C A A Publishing Service, Box 1906, Shawnee Mission, KS 66222. circ. 10,000.

799.06 CN ISSN 0700-9909
OUTDOOR CREST. 1975. irreg. Toronto Anglers' and Hunters' Association, 61 Edgehill Rd., Islington, Ont. M9A 4N1, Canada. Ed. Peter Edwards. illus. circ. 1,200.
Formerly: Outdoor Crest Newsletter (ISSN 0700-9895)

799.1 US
OUTDOOR LIFE'S GUIDE TO FISHING THE MIDWEST. 1977. a. $1.95. Times Mirror Magazines, Inc., 380 Madison Ave., New York, NY 10017. Ed. John Culler. adv. illus. circ. 150,000. (reprint service avail. from UMI)

799.1 US
OUTDOOR LIFE'S GUIDE TO FISHING THE SOUTH. 1979. a. Times Mirror Magazines, Inc., 380 Madison Ave., New York, NY 10017. circ. 150,000. (reprint service avail. from UMI)

796.54 US
PARENTS' GUIDE TO ACCREDITED CAMPS. MIDWEST EDITION. 1952. a. $2.95 or with subscr. to Camping Magazine. ‡ American Camping Association, Bradford Woods, Martinsville, IN 46151. Ed. Glenn T. Job. index. circ. 5,000.
Supersedes in part: Directory of Accredited Camps for Boys and Girls (ISSN 0070-5047)

796.54 US
PARENTS' GUIDE TO ACCREDITED CAMPS. NORTHEAST EDITION. a. $2.95 or with subscr. to Camping Magazine. American Camping Association, Bradford Woods, Martinsville, IN 46151.
Supersedes in part: Directory of Accredited Camps for Boys and Girls (ISSN 0070-5047)

796.54 US
PARENTS' GUIDE TO ACCREDITED CAMPS. SOUTH EDITION. a. $2.95 or with subscr. to Camping Magazine. American Camping Association, Bradford Woods, Martinsville, IN 46151.
Supersedes in part: Directory of Accredited Camps for Boys and Girls (ISSN 0070-5047)

796.54 US
PARENTS' GUIDE TO ACCREDITED CAMPS. WEST EDITION. a. $2.95 or with subscr. to Camping Magazine. American Camping Association, Bradford Woods, Martinsville, IN 46151.
Supersedes in part: Directory of Accredited Camps for Boys and Girls (ISSN 0070-5047)

910.2 UK
PRACTICAL CAMPER'S SITES GUIDE. 1966. a.
£1. Haymarket Publishing Ltd., 38-42 Hampton
Rd., Teddington, Middx. TW11 0JE, England.
  Formerly: Camping Sites in Britain and France
(ISSN 0068-6980)

PRIRODNJACKI MUZEJ U BEOGRADU.
GLASNIK. SERIJA C: SUMARSTVO I LOV. see
FORESTS AND FORESTRY

796.5 US
PRIVATE CAMPGROUNDS & RV PARKS
BUYING GUIDE. 1971. a. $3. ‡ Campground
Marketing Associates, P.O. Box 121, Palos Verdes
Ests., CA 90274. Ed. Virginia J. Merrimer. adv.
stat. tr.lit. index. circ. 15,000(controlled)

796.54 US ISSN 0079-9610
RAND MCNALLY CAMPGROUND AND
TRAILER PARK GUIDE. a. Rand McNally & Co.,
P.O. Box 7600, Chicago, IL 60680.
  Formerly: Rand McNally Guidebook to
Campgrounds & Rand McNally Travel Trailer
Guide (ISSN 0079-9645)

796.5 US ISSN 0079-9629
RAND MCNALLY NATIONAL PARK GUIDE. a.
Rand McNally & Co., P.O. Box 7600, Chicago, IL
60680. Ed. Michael Frome.

790 US
RECREATION AND OUTDOOR LIFE
DIRECTORY. 1979. irreg. Gale Research
Company, Book Tower, Detroit, MI 48226. Ed.
Paul Wasserman.

799 US
REMINGTON HUNTING & SHOOTING GUIDE.
a. $1.95. Aqua-Field Publications, Inc., 728 Beaver
Dam Rd., Point Pleasant, NJ 08742.

ST. LAWRENCE UNIVERSITY. CONFERENCE
ON THE ADIRONDACK PARK
(PROCEEDINGS) see *CONSERVATION*

917.1 CN ISSN 0380-8343
SCOPE /WHEELERS CANADIAN
CAMPGROUND GUIDE. 1975. irreg. Merton
Publications Ltd., London, Ont., Canada. illus.
  Former titles: Scope/Woodall's Canadian
Campgrounds Directory (ISSN 0380-8335); Scope:
Recreational Vehicle & Camping News (ISSN 0048-
9743)

799 US
SCOTCH GAME CALL HUNTING ANNUAL. a.
$1.95. Aqua-Field Publications, Inc., 728 Beaver
Dam Rd., Point Pleasant, NJ 08742. Ed. Steve
Ferber.

SCOTLAND FOR FISHING. see *TRAVEL AND
TOURISM*

SCOTLAND FOR SEA ANGLING. see *TRAVEL
AND TOURISM*

796.522 UK ISSN 0080-813X
SCOTTISH MOUNTAINEERING CLUB.
JOURNAL. 1890. a. £1.30. (Scottish
Mountaineering Club) Scottish Mountaineering
Trust, 12 Newington Rd., Edinburgh, 9, Scotland.
Ed. W.D. Brooker. adv. bk. rev.

796.93 US
SKI MAGAZINE'S GUIDE TO CROSS COUNTRY
SKIING. 1974. a. $1.95. Times Mirror Magazines,
Inc., 380 Madison Ave., New York, NY 10017. Ed.
Michael Brady. adv. circ. 120,000. (reprint service
avail. from UMI)

796.93 US
SKI X-C. 1978. a. $2.50. Ziff-Davis Publishing Co.,
One Park Ave., New York, NY 10006. Ed. Harry
N. Roberts. circ. 150,000.
  Skiing

796.93 US
SKIERS' ALMANAC. 1960. a. $3. College Tower
Publications, 939 W. College St., Los Angeles, CA
90012. Ed. Russ Tiffany. adv. bk. rev. circ. 103,000.
  Skiing

796.95 CN
SNOWMOBILE SPORTS ANNUAL. 1974. a. Leisure
Sports Publications, 1255 Yonge St., Toronto, Ont.
M4T 1W6, Canada. Ed. Reg Fife. adv. illus.

SOUTH CENTRAL CAMPBOOK. see *TRAVEL
AND TOURISM*

799 US
SOUTHEASTERN ASSOCIATION OF FISH AND
WILDLIFE AGENCIES. PROCEEDINGS. 1947.
a. $8. Southeastern Association of Fish and Wildlife
Agencies, c/o Gary T. Myers, Sec.-Treas., Box
40747, Nashville, TN 37204. cum.index: vols. 1-15
(1947-61) (back issues avail.)
  Formerly: Southeastern Association of Game and
Fish Commissioners. Proceedings of the Annual
Conference (ISSN 0081-2943)

SOUTHEASTERN CAMPBOOK. see *TRAVEL
AND TOURISM*

799 US ISSN 0081-2986
SOUTHERN ANGLER'S AND HUNTER'S GUIDE.
1961. a. $2.50. Don J. Fuelsch, Ed. & Pub., P.O.
Box 2188, Hot Springs, AR 71901. adv. bk. rev.

SOUTHWESTERN CAMPBOOK. see *TRAVEL
AND TOURISM*

799.1 917.1 CN
SPORTFISHING. 1975. biennial. free. Canadian
Government Office of Tourism, Publications
Section, 150 Kent St., Ottawa K1A 0H6, Canada.
Ed. James Palmer.

799.1 US
SPORTS AFIELD FISHING ANNUAL. 1938. a.
$1.25. Hearst Magazines, Sports Afield, 250 W.
55th St., New York, NY 10019. Ed. Lamar
Underwood.

799.2 US ISSN 0490-5326
SPORTS AFIELD GUN ANNUAL. 1953. a. $1.25.
Hearst Magazines, Sports Afield, 250 W. 55th St.,
New York, NY 10019. Ed. Lamar Underwood.

796.5 US ISSN 0190-1249
SPORTS AFIELD OUTDOOR ALMANAC. 1973.
irreg. $1. Hearst Magazines, Sports Afield, 250 W.
55th St., New York, NY 10019. Ed. Ted Kesting.
illus.
  Formerly: Sports Afield Almanac (ISSN 0092-
7082)

796.5 US
SUSQUEHANNOCK HIKER. 1971. a. $2.
Susquenhannock Trail Club, c/o Elizabeth K. Ahn,
Sec., R.D. 6, No. 1, Ulysses, PA 16948. Ed. Robert
H. Knowles. illus. circ. 400.

797 AT
TASMANIAN TRAMP. 1933. biennial. price varies.
Hobart Walking Club, G.P.O. Box 753h, Hobart,
Tas. 7001, Australia. Ed.Bd. adv. circ. 1,000.

796.5 US ISSN 0049-3481
TETON. 1969. a. $1.50. Teton Magazine, Box 1903,
Jackson's Hole, WY 83001. Ed. Gene Downer. adv.
bk. rev. illus. circ. 30,000.

917.13 796.5 CN ISSN 0380-6197
THUNDER BAY CAMPING GUIDE. 1972. irreg.
Guide Publishing, Box 3074, Station P, Thunder
Bay, Ont. P7B 5E8, Canada. illus.

796.42 US
TRACK AND FIELD RULES AND RECORDS. a.
$1.75. National Federation of State High School
Associations, Federation Place, Box 98, Elgin, IL
60120.

796 US
TRAIL BLAZER'S ALMANAC. 1934. a. $0.50 per
no. Trail Blazer's Publishing Co., 206 W. Fourth St.,
Kewanee, IL 61443. Ed. W. Harry Harper. adv.
circ. 1,100,000c.

917 US
TRAILER LIFE'S RECREATIONAL VEHICLE
CAMPGROUND AND SERVICES DIRECTORY.
Running title: R V Campground & Services Guide.
1971. a. $9.95. Trailer Life Publishing Co., Inc.,
29901 Agoura Rd., Agoura, CA 91301. adv. illus.
circ. 375,000.
  Formerly: Good Sam Club's Recreational Vehicle
Owners Directory (ISSN 0090-3256); Trailer Life's
Recreational Vehicle Campground and Services
Guide (ISSN 0093-4283)

333.7 US
U.S. BUREAU OF OUTDOOR RECREATION.
RECREATION GRANTS-IN-AID MANUAL.
irreg. $9.75. U.S. Bureau of Outdoor Recreation,
U.S. Dept. of the Interior, Washington, DC 20240
(Orders to: Supt. of Documents, Washington. DC
20402) (looseleaf format)

U.S. FISH AND WILDLIFE SERVICE. NATIONAL
SURVEY OF HUNTING, FISHING AND
WILDLIFE-ASSOCIATED RECREATION. see
*SPORTS AND GAMES — Abstracting,
Bibliographies, Statistics*

799.1 US ISSN 0362-0700
U. S. FISH AND WILDLIFE SERVICE. SPORT
FISHERY AND WILDLIFE RESEARCH. 1958. a.
U.S. Fish and Wildlife Service, Washingto, DC
20240 (Orders to: Supt. Doc., Washington, DC
20402) illus. Key Title: Sport Fishery and Wildlife
Research.
  Formerly: U. S. Fish and Wildlife Service.
Progress in Sport Fishery Research (ISSN 0079-
6794)

719.32 333.7 US
U.S. NATIONAL PARK SERVICE. RESEARCH
REPORTS BY SERVICE PERSONNEL. 5-10
reports per year. U.S. National Park Service,
Interior Bldg., Washington, DC 20240 (Order from
NTIS, Springfield, VA 22161)

790.1 US
VIRGINIA OUTDOORS PLAN. 1965. quinquennial.
$5. Commission of Outdoor Recreation, Old Federal
Reserve Bldg., Franklin St./8th, Richmond, VA
23219. Ed. John W. Mitchell. illus. tr.lit. (back
issues avail.)
  Formerly (1965 report): Virginia's Common
Wealth.

796 AT
WALK. 1949. a. Aus.$1. Melbourne Bushwalkers,
G.P.O. Box 1751q, Melbourne, Vic. 3001, Australia.

WHEELERS RECREATIONAL VEHICLE RESORT
AND CAMPGROUND GUIDE: EASTERNER
EDITION. see *TRAVEL AND TOURISM*

WHEELERS RECREATIONAL VEHICLE RESORT
AND CAMPGROUND GUIDE: WESTERNER
EDITION. see *TRAVEL AND TOURISM*

796.93 US ISSN 0163-9684
WHITE BOOK OF SKI AREAS. U.S. AND
CANADA. 1976. a. $6.95. Inter-Ski Services, Inc.,
Box 3635, Georgetown Station, Washington, DC
20007. Eds. John R. Urciolo, Robert G. Enzel.
  Formerly: White Book of U.S. Ski Areas (ISSN
0145-6075)

917.59 US ISSN 0162-7384
WOODALL'S CAMPGROUND DIRECTORY.
ARIZONA EDITION. a. $1.95. Woodall Publishing
Co., 500 Hyacinth Pl., Highland Park, IL 60035.

917.59 US ISSN 0163-5328
WOODALL'S CAMPGROUND DIRECTORY.
ARKANSAS/MISSOURI EDITION. a. $1.95.
Woodall Publishing Co., 500 Hyacinth Pl, Highland
Park, IL 60035.

917.59 US ISSN 0162-7392
WOODALL'S CAMPGROUND DIRECTORY.
CALIFORNIA EDITION. a. $1.95. Woodall
Publishing Co., 500 Hyacinth Pl., Highland Park, IL
60035.

917.59 US ISSN 0163-5344
WOODALL'S CAMPGROUND DIRECTORY.
COLORADO EDITION. a. $1.95. Woodall
Publishing Co., 500 Hyacinth Pl., Highland Park, IL
60035.

917.59 US
WOODALL'S CAMPGROUND DIRECTORY.
DELAWARE/MARYLAND/VIRGINIA/
DISTRICT OF COLUMBIA EDITION. a. $1.95.
Woodall Publishing Co., 500 Hyacinth Pl., Highland
Park, IL 60035.

917.59 US ISSN 0162-7406
WOODALL'S CAMPGROUND DIRECTORY.
EASTERN EDITION. a. $5.95. Woodall Publishing
Co., 500 Hyacinth Pl., Highland Park, IL 60035.
  Supersedes in part: Woodall's Campground
Directory (ISSN 0362-3823)

917.59 US ISSN 0090-5151
WOODALL'S CAMPGROUND DIRECTORY.
FLORIDA CAMPGROUNDS EDITION. 1973. a.
$1.95. Woodall Publishing Co., 500 Hyacinth Place,
Highland Park, IL 60035. adv. illus.

917.59 US ISSN 0163-2493
WOODALL'S CAMPGROUND DIRECTORY.
IDAHO/OREGON/WASHINGTON EDITION. a.
$1.95. Woodall Publishing Co., 500 Hyacinth Pl.,
Highland Park, IL 60035.

917.59 US ISSN 0163-2485
WOODALL'S CAMPGROUND DIRECTORY.
ILLINOIS/INDIANA EDITION. a. $1.95.
Woodall Publishing Co., 500 Hyacinth Pl., Highland
Park, IL 60035.

917.59 US ISSN 0163-5336
WOODALL'S CAMPGROUND DIRECTORY.
KENTUCKY/TENNESSEE EDITION. a. $1.95.
Woodall Publishing Co., 500 Hyacinth Pl., Highland
Park, IL 60035.

917.59 US ISSN 0163-0121
WOODALL'S CAMPGROUND DIRECTORY.
MICHIGAN EDITION. a. $1.95. Woodall
Publishing Co., 500 Hyacinth Pl., Highland Park, IL
60035.

917.59 US ISSN 0163-0083
WOODALL'S CAMPGROUND DIRECTORY.
NEW ENGLAND STATES EDITION. a. $1.95.
Woodall Publishing Co., 500 Hyacinth Pl., Highland
Park, IL 60035.

917.59 US ISSN 0163-0113
WOODALL'S CAMPGROUND DIRECTORY.
NEW JERSEY/NEW YORK EDITION. a. $1.95.
Woodall Publishing Co., 500 Hyacinth Pl., Highland
Park, IL 60035.

917.59 US ISSN 0146-1362
WOODALL'S CAMPGROUND DIRECTORY.
NORTH AMERICAN/CANADIAN EDITION. a.
$8.95. Woodall Publishing Co., 500 Hyacinth Pl.,
Highland Park, IL 60035.
  Formerly: Woodall's Campground Directory.
North American Edition; Which superseded in part:
Woodall's Campground Directory (ISSN 0362-3823);
Which was formerly titled: Woodall's Trailering
Parks and Campgrounds (ISSN 0084-1110)

917.59 US ISSN 0163-5352
WOODALL'S CAMPGROUND DIRECTORY.
NORTH CAROLINA/SOUTH CAROLINA
EDITION. a. $1.95. Woodall Publishing Co., 500
Hyacinth Pl., Highland Park, IL 60035.

917.59 US ISSN 0163-1950
WOODALL'S CAMPGROUND DIRECTORY.
OHIO/PENNSYLVANIA EDITIONS. a. $1.95.
Woodall Publishing Co., 500 Hyacinth Pl., Highland
Park, IL 60035.

917.59 US ISSN 0163-240X
WOODALL'S CAMPGROUND DIRECTORY.
ONTARIO EDITION. a. $1.95. Woodall Publishing
Co., 500 Hyacinth Pl., Highland Park, IL 60035.

917.59 US ISSN 0162-7376
WOODALL'S CAMPGROUND DIRECTORY.
TEXAS EDITION. a. $1.95. Woodall Publishing
Co., 500 Hyacinth Pl., Highland Park, IL 60035.

917.59 US ISSN 0162-7414
WOODALL'S CAMPGROUND DIRECTORY.
WESTERN EDITION. a. $5.95. Woodall
Publishing Co., 500 Hyacinth Pl., Highland Park, IL
60035.
  Supersedes in part: Woodall's Campground
Directory (ISSN 0362-3823)

917.59 US ISSN 0163-0105
WOODALL'S CAMPGROUND DIRECTORY.
WISCONSIN EDITION. a. $1.95. Woodall
Publishing Co., 500 Hyacinth Pl., Highland Park, IL
60035.

WORLD RECORD GAME FISHES. see *FISH AND FISHERIES*

STATISTICS

see also specific subjects

318 MX
AGENDA ESTADISTICA. a. Secretaria de
Programacion y Presupuesto, Articulo 123 No. 88,
Mexico 1, D.F., Mexico (Orders to: Direccion
General de Estudios del Territorio Nacional,
Balderas 71, Col. Centro, Mexico 1, D.F., Mexico)

AGRICULTURAL STATISTICS OF GREECE. see
AGRICULTURE — Abstracting, Bibliographies, Statistics

312 US ISSN 0095-3431
ALABAMA'S VITAL EVENTS. 1971. a. $4.50.
Division of Vital Statistics, Montgomery, AL 36104.
Ed. Robert L. Shiller. illus. circ. 450. (also avail. in
microfiche)

317.123 CN ISSN 0317-3925
ALBERTA STATISTICAL REVIEW. a. Bureau of
Statistics, Park Square, 21st Floor, 10001 Bellamy
Hill, Edmonton, Alta. T5J 3B6, Canada. illus.

AMERICAN RADIO. see *COMMUNICATIONS — Abstracting, Bibliographies, Statistics*

310 US ISSN 0149-9963
AMERICAN STATISTICAL ASSOCIATION.
STATISTICAL COMPUTING SECTION.
PROCEEDINGS (OF THE ANNUAL
MEETING) 1976. a. American Statistical
Association, 806 15th St. N.W., Washington, DC
20005. stat.

311 US
AMERICAN STATISTICAL ASSOCIATION.
SURVEY RESEARCH SECTION.
PROCEEDINGS. 1978. a. American Statistical
Association, 806 15th St. N.W., Washington, DC
20005.
  Formerly: American Statistical Association.
Statistical Section. Proceedings.

016 US ISSN 0091-1658
AMERICAN STATISTICS INDEX.
(A comprehensive guide and index to the statistical
publications of the U.S. Government) 1973. m. with
q. and a. cumulations. price varies. ‡ Congressional
Information Service, 4520 East-West Hwy.,
Washington, DC 20014.

316 AO ISSN 0066-5193
ANGOLA. DIRECCAO DOS SERVICOS DE
ESTATISTICA. ANUARIO ESTATISTICO. 1933.
a. Esc.100. Direccao dos Servicos de Estatistica,
C.P. 1215, Luanda, Angola. circ. 1,000.

316 AO
ANGOLA. DIRECCAO DOS SERVICOS DE
ESTATISTICA. INFORMACOES
ESTATISTICAS. 1970. a. free. ‡ Direccao dos
Servicos de Estatistica, Ministerio do Planeamento e
Coordenacao Economica, C. P. 1215, Luanda,
Angola. stat. circ. 7,000.

ANNUAIRE DES STATISTIQUES DU
COMMERCE EXTERIEUR DU TOGO. see
BUSINESS AND ECONOMICS — Abstracting, Bibliographies, Statistics

317 CN ISSN 0066-3018
ANNUAIRE DU QUEBEC. 1914. a. (Bureau of
Statistics) Editeur Officiel du Quebec, 1283 Bd.
Charest Ouest, Quebec G1N 2C9, Canada. index.
circ. 6,000.

316.6 DM
ANNUAIRE STATISTIQUE DE BENIN. a, latest
1975. 2000 Fr.CFA. Institut National de la
Statistique et de l'Analyse Economique, B.P. 323,
Cotonou, Benin.
  Formerly: Annuaire Statistique du Dahomey.

314 BE ISSN 0066-3646
ANNUAIRE STATISTIQUE DE LA BELGIQUE.
(Text in Dutch and French) 1870. a. 720 Fr. Institut
National de Statistique, 44 rue de Louvain, 1000
Brussels, Belgium.
  Formerly (until 1960): Annuaire Statistique de la
Belgique et du Congo Belge.

314 FR ISSN 0066-3654
ANNUAIRE STATISTIQUE DE LA FRANCE.
1876. a. 180 F. Institut National de la Statistique et
des Etudes Economiques, 18, Bd A. Pinard, F
75675 Paris 14, France. circ. 3,500.

316 TI ISSN 0066-3689
ANNUAIRE STATISTIQUE DE LA TUNISIE. a,
latest 1974/75. Institut National de la Statistique,
27 rue de Liban, Tunis, Tunisia.

310 330 FR ISSN 0071-8793
ANNUAIRE STATISTIQUE DES TERRITOIRES
D'OUTRE MER. 1962. irreg. 25 F. Institut
National de la Statistique et des Etudes
Economiques, 18, Bd A. Pinard, F 75675 Paris 14,
France.

316 MR ISSN 0066-3719
ANNUAIRE STATISTIQUE DU MAROC. a. DH.45.
Direction de la Statistique, B.P. 178, Rabat,
Morocco.

316.6 TG
ANNUAIRE STATISTIQUE DU TOGO. 1966. a,
latest 1975-76(pub. 1978) 4000 Fr.CFA. Direction
de la Statistique, Boite Postale 118, Lome, Togo.
illus. stat.

ANNUAL BULLETIN OF ELECTRIC ENERGY
STATISTICS FOR EUROPE. see *ELECTRICITY
AND ELECTRICAL ENGINEERING —
Abstracting, Bibliographies, Statistics*

310 MY ISSN 0080-6439
ANNUAL STATISTICAL BULLETIN SARAWAK.
Variant title: Sarawak. Department of Statistics.
Annual Statistical Bulletin. Variant title: Sarawak
Annual Bulletin of Statistics. (Text in English) 1964.
a. M.$5. ‡ Department of Statistics, Federal
Complex, Jalan Simpang Tiga, Kuching, Sarawak,
Malaysia.

314 IT ISSN 0066-4545
ANNUARIO STATISTICO ITALIANO. a. L.6000.
Istituto Centrale di Statistica, Via C. Balbo, 16,
00100 Rome, Italy. circ. 4,500.

ANNUARIUM STATISTICUM ECCLESIAE/
STATISTIQUE DE L'EGLISE/STATISTICAL
YEARBOOK OF THE CHURCH. see
*RELIGIONS AND THEOLOGY — Abstracting,
Bibliographies, Statistics*

317 CU ISSN 0574-6132
ANUARIO ESTADISTICO DE CUBA. English
edition: Statistical Yearbook Compendium of the
Republic of Cuba. 1952. a. free. Comite Estatal de
Estadisticas, Direccion de Informacion y Relaciones
Internacionales, Centro de Informacion Cientifico-
Tecnico, Av. Tercera no. 4410, Municipio de Playa,
Havana, Cuba. circ. 1,000.
  Formerly (until 1971): Boletin Estadistico de
Cuba.

314 SP ISSN 0066-5177
ANUARIO ESTADISTICO DE ESPANA. (In two
editions: Edicion Extensa and Edicion Manual)
1912. a. Instituto Nacional de Estadistica, Avda.
Generalisimo 91, Madrid 16, Spain.

318 PY
ANUARIO ESTADISTICO DEL PARAGUAY.
1886. a. exchange basis. Direccion General de
Estadistica y Censos, Humaita 463, Asuncion,
Paraguay (Subscr. to: Casilla de Correo 1118,
Asuncion, Paraguay) Ed. Jose Diaz de Bedoya. circ.
1,500.

318 BL
ANUARIO ESTADISTICO DO BRASIL. 1916. a.
$50 price varies. ‡ Fundacao Instituto Brasileiro de
Geografia e Estatistica, Diretoria de Divulgacao,
Centro de Servicos Graficos, Av. Brasil 15671, ZC-
91 Rio de Janeiro RJ, Brazil. bk. rev. (back issues
avail)

310 BL
ANUARIO ESTADISTICO DO ESTADO DO RIO
DE JANEIRO. 1971. a. free. Fundacao Instituto de
Desenvolvimento Economico e Social, Rio de
Janeiro, Brazil. stat.
  Continues: Anuario Estatistico da Guanabara.

310 GW ISSN 0066-5673
ARBEITEN ZUR ANGEWANDTEN STATISTIK.
1967. irreg., vol. 22, 1980. price varies. Physica-
Verlag Rudolf Liebing GmbH und Co., Werner-von-
Siemens-Str. 5, Postfach 5840, 8700 Wuerzburg 1,
W. Germany (B.R.D.) Eds. K.-A. Schaeffer, P.
Schoenfeld, W. Wetzel.
  Formerly: Berlin. Freie Universitaet. Institut fuer
Statistik und Versicherungsmathematik. Berichte
(ISSN 0067-5865)

STATISTICS

314 GW ISSN 0072-162X
DAS ARBEITSGEBIET DER BUNDESSTATISTIK. (Editions in German, English, French) irreg. DM.23. (Statistisches Bundesamt) W. Kohlhammer-Verlag GmbH, Abt. Veroeffentlichungen des Statistischen Bundesamtes, Philipp-Reis-Str. 3, Postfach 421120, 6500 Mainz 42, W. Germany (B.R.D.)

318 AG
ARGENTINA. CENTRAL DE ESTADISTICAS NACIONALES. INFORME. 1976. irreg. $110. Central de Estadisticas Nacionales, Av. De Mayo 953, 1084 Buenos Aires, Argentina. Ed. Carlos A. Canto Yoy. circ. 500.

318 AG
ARGENTINA. COMISION NACIONAL DE VALORES. INFORMACION ESTADISTICA. irreg. Comision Nacional de Valores, 215 Hippolito Yrigoyen, Buenos Aires, Argentina.

318 AG
ARGENTINA. INSTITUTO NACIONAL DE ESTADISTICA Y CENSOS. ANUARIO ESTADISTICO. 1973. a. Instituto Nacional de Estadistica y Censos, Hipolito Yrigoyen 250, Buenos Aires, Argentina.

310 AG ISSN 0066-7196
ARGENTINA. INSTITUTO NACIONAL DE ESTADISTICA Y CENSOS. INFORME SERIE E: EDIFICACION. irreg. Instituto Nacional de Estadistica y Censos, Hipolito Yrigoyen 250, Buenos Aires, Argentina.

ARIZONA STATISTICAL REVIEW. see *BUSINESS AND ECONOMICS — Abstracting, Bibliographies, Statistics*

319 AT ISSN 0067-1754
AUSTRALIA. BUREAU OF STATISTICS. AUSTRALIAN CAPITAL TERRITORY. STATISTICAL SUMMARY. 1963. a. free. Australian Bureau of Statistics, P.O. Box 10, Belconnen, A.C.T. 2616, Australia. circ. 563.

AUSTRALIA. BUREAU OF STATISTICS. CENSUS OF TOURIST ACCOMODATION ESTABLISHMENTS: AUSTRALIA AND AUSTRALIAN CAPITAL TERRITORY. see *TRAVEL AND TOURISM — Abstracting, Bibliographies, Statistics*

338.4 AT
AUSTRALIA. BUREAU OF STATISTICS. MANUFACTURING COMMODITIES: PRINCIPAL ARTICLES PRODUCED. 1968-69. a. free. Australian Bureau of Statistics, P.O. Box 10, Belconnen, A.C.T. 2616, Australia. circ. 1,550.

338.4 AT
AUSTRALIA. BUREAU OF STATISTICS. MANUFACTURING COMMODITIES: PRINCIPAL MATERIALS USED. 1968-69. irreg., latest 1974-75. free. Australian Bureau of Statistics, P.O. Box 10, Belconnen, A.C.T. 2616, Australia. circ. 2,500.

338.4 AT
AUSTRALIA. BUREAU OF STATISTICS. MANUFACTURING ESTABLISHMENTS: SUMMARY OF OPERATIONS BY INDUSTRY CLASS. a. free. Australian Bureau of Statistics, Box 10, Belconnen, A.C.T. 2616, Australia. circ. 2,100.

319 AT ISSN 0067-0855
AUSTRALIA. BUREAU OF STATISTICS. NORTHERN TERRITORY STATISTICAL SUMMARY. 1960. a. Aus.$1.65. Australian Bureau of Statistics, P.O. Box 10, Belconnen, A.C.T. 2616, Australia. circ. 1,171.

319 AT
AUSTRALIA. BUREAU OF STATISTICS. POCKET YEAR BOOK OF AUSTRALIA. 1913. a. Aus.$1. Australian Bureau of Statistics, P.O. Box 10, Belconnen, A.C.T. 2616, Australia. circ. 1,825.
Formerly: Australia. Bureau of Statistics. Pocket Compendium of Australian Statistics (ISSN 0079-239X)

319.4 AT
AUSTRALIA. BUREAU OF STATISTICS. PUBLIC AUTHORITY FINANCE. PUBLIC AUTHORITY ESTIMATES. 1974. a. free. Australian Bureau of Statistics, P.O. Box 10, Belconnen, A.C.T. 2616, Australia. stat. circ. 2,000.

AUSTRALIA. BUREAU OF STATISTICS. PUBLIC AUTHORITY FINANCE. STATE AND LOCAL AUTHORITIES. see *BUSINESS AND ECONOMICS — Public Finance, Taxation*

312 AT
AUSTRALIA. BUREAU OF STATISTICS. QUEENSLAND OFFICE. AREA AND ESTIMATED POPULATION IN EACH QUEENSLAND LOCAL AUTHORITY AREA. a. free. Australian Bureau of Statistics, Queensland Office, 345 Ann St., Brisbane, Queensland 4000, Australia. stat. circ. 1,500. (processed)

319 AT ISSN 0067-091X
AUSTRALIA. BUREAU OF STATISTICS. SOUTH AUSTRALIAN OFFICE. DIVISIONAL STATISTICS. 1970. irreg. free. Australian Bureau of Statistics, South Australian Office, Box 2272, Adelaide, S.A. 5001, Australia.

319 AT ISSN 0085-493X
AUSTRALIA. BUREAU OF STATISTICS. TASMANIAN OFFICE. POCKET YEAR BOOK OF TASMANIA. 1913. a. Aus.$0.60. Australian Bureau of Statistics, Tasmanian Office, G.P.O. Box 66A, Hobart, Tas. 7001, Australia. circ. 3,300.

AUSTRALIA. BUREAU OF STATISTICS. VICTORIAN OFFICE. MANUFACTURING ESTABLISHMENTS: DETAIL OF OPERATIONS. see *BUSINESS AND ECONOMICS — Abstracting, Bibliographies, Statistics*

AUSTRALIA. BUREAU OF STATISTICS. VICTORIAN OFFICE. MANUFACTURING ESTABLISHMENTS: USAGE OF ELECTRICITY AND FUELS. see *ENERGY — Abstracting, Bibliographies, Statistics*

AUSTRALIA. BUREAU OF STATISTICS. VICTORIAN OFFICE. MINERAL PRODUCTION - VICTORIA. see *MINES AND MINING INDUSTRY — Abstracting, Bibliographies, Statistics*

994 319 AT ISSN 0067-1207
AUSTRALIA. BUREAU OF STATISTICS. VICTORIAN OFFICE. VICTORIAN POCKET YEARBOOK. 1956. a. Aus.$1. Australian Bureau of Statistics, Victorian Office, Box 2796Y, G.P.O. Melbourne, Victoria 3001, Australia. adv. bk. rev. index. circ. 3,400.

994 319 AT ISSN 0067-1223
AUSTRALIA. BUREAU OF STATISTICS. VICTORIAN OFFICE. VICTORIAN YEARBOOK. 1873. a. Aus.$10. Australian Bureau of Statistics, Victorian Office, Box 2796Y, G.P.O. Melbourne, Victoria 3001, Australia. Ed. H. L. Speagle. adv. bk. rev. bibl. index; cum.index: 1961-72. circ. 4,500.

AUSTRALIA. BUREAU OF STATISTICS. WESTERN AUSTRALIAN OFFICE. CATTLE AND PIGS: WESTERN AUSTRALIA. see *AGRICULTURE — Abstracting, Bibliographies, Statistics*

338.1 AT ISSN 0312-844X
AUSTRALIA. BUREAU OF STATISTICS. WESTERN AUSTRALIAN OFFICE. SHEEP, LAMBING AND WOOL CLIP. 1967/68. a. free. Australian Bureau of Statistics, Western Australian Office, 1-3 St. George's Tce., Perth, W.A. 6000, Australia. Ed. E. Binns. circ. 600. (processed)

319 AT
AUSTRALIA. BUREAU OF STATISTICS. YEAR BOOK AUSTRALIA. 1907. a. Aus.$10. Australian Bureau of Statistics, P.O. Box 10, Belconnen, A.C.T. 2616, Australia. circ. 11,948.
Former titles: Official Year Book of Australia (ISSN 0312-4746); Official Year Book of the Commonwealth of Australia (ISSN 0078-3927)

AUSTRALIAN ENERGY STATISTICS. see *ENERGY — Abstracting, Bibliographies, Statistics*

AUSTRIA. STATISTISCHES ZENTRALAMT. INDUSTRIE STATISTIK. see *BUSINESS AND ECONOMICS — Abstracting, Bibliographies, Statistics*

310 AU
AUSTRIA. STATISTISCHES ZENTRALAMT. MIKROZENSUS; JAHRESERGEBNISSE. (Subseries of its Beitraege zur Oesterreichischen Statistik) 1969. a. S.80. Kommissionsverlag der Oesterreichischen Staatsdruckerei, Rennweg 12A, 1037 Vienna, Austria. stat. circ. 500.

318 BF
BAHAMAS. DEPARTMENT OF STATISTICS. STATISTICAL ABSTRACT. 1969. a. $6. Department of Statistics, P.O. Box N 3904, Nassau, Bahamas.

318 BL
BAHIA. DEPARTAMENTO DE GEOGRAFIA E ESTATISTICA. PROVOADOS DO ESTADO DA BAHIA. 1947. Centro de Planejamento, Av. Luis Viana Filho, s/n-Paralela, Salvador, Brazil.

318 BL
BAHIA, BRAZIL (STATE). CENTRO DE PLANEJAMENTO. ANUARIO ESTATISTICO. 1972. a. Centro de Planejamento, Caixa Postal 321, 40000 Salvador, Bahia, Brazil.

312 BB
BARBADOS. REGISTRATION OFFICE. REPORT ON VITAL STATISTICS & REGISTRATIONS. a; latest edt. 1975. free. Registration Office, Bridgetown, Barbados, W. Indies. stat. circ. 100.

312 SZ
BASLER STATISTIK. 1976. irreg., no. 3, 1979. price varies. Statistisches Amt des Kantons Basel-Stadt, Clarastrasse 38, Postfach, CH-4021 Basel, Switzerland.

314 AU ISSN 0067-2319
BEITRAEGE ZUR OESTERREICHISCHEN STATISTIK. 1953. irreg. price varies. ‡ Oesterreichisches Statistisches Zentralamt, Nene Hofburg, Heldenplatz, 1014 Vienna, Austria.

314.93 BE
BELGIUM. INSTITUT NATIONAL DE STATISTIQUE. ANNUAIRE DE STATISTIQUES REGIONALES. 1976. a. 290 Fr. Institut National de Statistique, 44 rue de Louvain, 1000 Brussels, Belgium. charts. stat.

314 BE ISSN 0067-5431
BELGIUM. INSTITUT NATIONAL DE STATISTIQUE. ANNUAIRE STATISTIQUE DE POCHE. (Text in Dutch and French) 1965. a. 100 Fr. Institut National de Statistique, 44 rue de Louvain, 1000 Brussels, Belgium.

314 BE
BELGIUM. INSTITUT NATIONAL DE STATISTIQUE. COMMUNIQUE HEBDOMADAIRE. (Text in Dutch and French) w. 520 Fr. Institut National de Statistique, 44 rue de Louvain, 1000 Brussels, Belgium.

310 BE
BELGIUM. INSTITUT NATIONAL DE STATISTIQUE. ETUDES STATISTIQUES. irreg., nos. 58-61, 1980. 120 Fr. per no. Institut National de Statistique, 44 rue de Louvain, 1000 Brussels, Belgium.

BELGIUM. INSTITUT NATIONAL DE STATISTIQUE. STATISTIQUE DE LA NAVIGATION DU RHIN. see *TRANSPORTATION — Abstracting, Bibliographies, Statistics*

BELGIUM. INSTITUT NATIONAL DE STATISTIQUE. STATISTIQUE DE LA NAVIGATION INTERIEURE. see *TRANSPORTATION — Abstracting, Bibliographies, Statistics*

BELGIUM. INSTITUT NATIONAL DE STATISTIQUE. STATISTIQUE DES ACCIDENTS DE LA CIRCULATION SUR LA VOIE PUBLIQUE. see *PUBLIC HEALTH AND SAFETY — Abstracting, Bibliographies, Statistics*

STATISTICS

BELGIUM. INSTITUT NATIONAL DE STATISTIQUE. STATISTIQUE DES VEHICULES A MOTEUR NEUFS MIS EN CIRCULATION. see *TRANSPORTATION — Abstracting, Bibliographies, Statistics*

BELGIUM. INSTITUT NATIONAL DE STATISTIQUE. STATISTIQUE DU TOURISME ET DE L'HOTELLERIE. see *TRAVEL AND TOURISM — Abstracting, Bibliographies, Statistics*

BELGIUM. INSTITUT NATIONAL DE STATISTIQUE. STATISTIQUES DE LA CONSTRUCTION ET DU LOGEMENT. see *BUILDING AND CONSTRUCTION — Abstracting, Bibliographies, Statistics*

BELGIUM. INSTITUT NATIONAL DE STATISTIQUE. STATISTIQUES DEMOGRAPHIQUES. see *POPULATION STUDIES — Abstracting, Bibliographies, Statistcs*

BELGIUM. MINISTERE DE L'EDUCATION NATIONALE ET DE LA CULTURE FRANCAISE. ANNUAIRE STATISTIQUE DE L'ENSEIGNEMENT. see *EDUCATION — Abstracting, Bibliographies, Statistics*

314   BE
BELGIUM BASIC STATISTICS. French edition: Belgique Statistiques de Base. Dutch edition: Belgie Basis-Statistieken. German edition: Belgien Statistische Grundzahlen. Spanish edition: Belgica Estadisticas de Base. 1966. a. 100 Fr. Institut Belge d'Information et de Documentation - Belgian Information and Documentation Institute, Rue Montoyer 3, B-1040 Brussels, Belgium. circ. 30,000.

BIBLIOGRAPHIE SUISSE DE STATISTIQUE ET D'ECONOMIE POLITIQUE. see *BUSINESS AND ECONOMICS*

BIBLIOGRAPHY OF ECONOMIC AND STATISTICAL PUBLICATIONS ON TANZANIA. see *BUSINESS AND ECONOMICS — Abstracting, Bibliographies, Statistics*

BILDUNG IM ZAHLENSPIEGEL. see *EDUCATION — Abstracting, Bibliographies, Statistics*

BLUE BOOK OF FOOD STORE OPERATORS & WHOLESALERS. see *FOOD AND FOOD INDUSTRIES — Abstracting, Bibliographies, Statistics*

BOLIVIA. INSTITUTO NACIONAL DE ESTADISTICA. ANUARIO DE COMERCIO EXTERIOR. see *BUSINESS AND ECONOMICS — International Commerce*

BOLIVIA. INSTITUTO NACIONAL DE ESTADISTICA. ANUARIO DE ESTADISTICAS INDUSTRIALES. see *BUSINESS AND ECONOMICS — Production Of Goods And Services*

BOLIVIA. INSTITUTO NACIONAL DE ESTADISTICA. ESTADISTICAS REGIONALES DEPARTAMENTALES. see *PUBLIC ADMINISTRATION*

316.8   BS
BOTSWANA. CENTRAL STATISTICS OFFICE. STATISTICAL BULLETIN. q. R.1. Central Statistics Office, Ministry of Finance and Development Planning, Gaborone, Botswana (Orders to: Government Printer, Box 87, Gaborone, Botswana) illus.
    Formerly: Botswana. Central Statistical Office. Statistical Newsletter.

BRAZIL. COMISSAO DE FINANCIAMENTO DA PRODUCAO. ANUARIO ESTATISTICO. see *BUSINESS AND ECONOMICS — Abstracting, Bibliographies, Statistics*

BRAZIL. FUNDACAO INSTITUTO BRASILEIRO DE GEOGRAFIA E ESTATISTICA. DEPARTAMENTO DE ESTATISTICAS INDUSTRIAIS, COMERCIAIS E DE SERVICOS. EMPRESAS DE TRANSPORTE RODOVIARIO. see *TRANSPORTATION — Automobiles*

318   BL
BRAZIL. INSTITUTO BRASILEIRO DE GEOGRAFIA E ESTATISTICA. VEICULOS LICENCIADOS. 1967. a. $5 per no. Fundacao Instituto Brasileiro de Geografia e Estatistica, Av. Franklin Roosevelt, 146-a, 20000 Rio de Janerio, GB, Brazil.

310   BL
BRAZIL. SERVICO SOCIAL DO COMERCIO. ANUARIO ESTATISTICO. 1962. a. free. Servico Social do Comercio, Assessoria de Divulgacao e Promocao Institucional, Rua Voluntarios da Patria 169, 22270 Rio de Janeiro, Brazil. stat.

BRITISH LABOUR STATISTICS. YEAR BOOK. see *BUSINESS AND ECONOMICS — Abstracting, Bibliographies, Statistics*

319   VB
BRITISH VIRGIN ISLANDS. STATISTICS OFFICE. BALANCE OF PAYMENTS. irreg. Statistics Office, Finance Department, Road Town, Tortola, British Virgin Islands.

319   VB
BRITISH VIRGIN ISLANDS. STATISTICS OFFICE. NATIONAL INCOME AND EXPENDITURE. irreg. $3.50. Statistics Office, Finance Department, Road Town, Tortola, British Virgin Islands.

947   314   HU   ISSN 0521-4882
BUDAPEST STATISZTIKAI EVKONYVE. a. 155 Ft. (Kozponti Statisztikai Hivatal) Statisztikai Kiado Vallalat, Kaszas U.10-12, P.O.B.99, 1300 Budapest 3, Hungary.

947   314   HU   ISSN 0438-2242
BUDAPEST STATISZTIKAI ZSEBKONYVE. a. 30 Ft. (Kozponti Statisztikai Hivatal) Statisztikai Kiado Vallalat, Kaszas U.10-12, P.O.B.99, 1300 Budapest 3, Hungary.

316   316   BD
BURUNDI. DEPARTEMENT DES ETUDES ET STATISTIQUES. BULLETIN ANNUAIRE. a. 1100 Fr.CFA. Departement des Etudes et Statistiques, B.P. 156, Bujumbura, Burundi.

311   US
C I N D A S. ANNUAL REPORT. 1967. a. Center for Information and Numerical Data Analysis and Synthesis, c/o Y. S. Touloukian, Dir., Purdue University, 2595 Yeager Rd., West Lafayette, IN 47906.

319   TR
C.S.O. STATISTICAL BULLETINS. 1972. irreg. free. Central Statistical Office, Textel Building, 1, Edward Street, Port of Spain, Trinidad (or Govt. Printery, 2 Victoria Ave., Port of Spain, Trinidad)

312   US
CALIFORNIA COUNTY FACT BOOK. 1960. a. $10.60. County Supervisors Association of California, Suite 201, 11th & L Building, Sacramento, CA 95814. charts. stat. circ. 1,000.

316.7   CM
CAMEROON. DIRECTION DE LA STATISTIQUE ET DE LA COMPTABILITE NATIONALE. NOTE ACTUELLE DE STATISTIQUE. 1974. a. 7500 Fr.CFA. Direction de la Statistique et de la Comptabilite Nationale - Department of Statistics and National Accounts, Boite Postale 660, Yaounde, Cameroon. stat.

316   CM
CAMEROON. PROVINCIAL STATISTICAL SERVICE OF THE SOUTH WEST. ANNUAL STATISTICAL REPORT, SOUTH WEST PROVINCE. a. Service Provincial de la Statistique du Sud-Ouest, Box 93, Buea, Cameroon.

CANADA. STATISTICS CANADA. AGGREGATE PRODUCTIVITY MEASURES/MESURES GLOBALES DE PRODUCTIVITE. see *BUSINESS AND ECONOMICS — Abstracting, Bibliographies, Statistics*

CANADA. STATISTICS CANADA. AIR PASSENGER ORIGIN AND DESTINATION. CANADA-UNITED STATES REPORT/ ORIGINE ET DESTINATION DES PASSAGERS AERIENS. RAPPORT SUR LE TRAFIC CANADA-ETAT UNIS. see *TRANSPORTATION — Abstracting, Bibliographies, Statistics*

354.71   CN   ISSN 0703-2633
CANADA. STATISTICS CANADA. ANNUAL REPORT/RAPPORT ANNUEL. (Catalogue 11-201) (Text in English and French) 1919. a. free. Statistics Canada, Publications Distribution, Ottawa, Ont. K1A 0V7, Canada. (also avail. in microform from MML)

CANADA. STATISTICS CANADA. AVIATION STATISTICS CENTRE. SERVICE BULLETIN/ BULLETIN DE SERVICE DU CENTRE DES STATISTIQUES DE L'AVIATION. see *TRANSPORTATION — Abstracting, Bibliographies, Statistics*

CANADA. STATISTICS CANADA. BOATBUILDING AND REPAIR/ CONSTRUCTION ET REPARATION D'EMBARCATIONS. see *TRANSPORTATION — Abstracting, Bibliographies, Statistics*

CANADA. STATISTICS CANADA. BREWERIES/ BRASSERIES. see *FOOD AND FOOD INDUSTRIES — Abstracting, Bibliographies, Statistics*

CANADA. STATISTICS CANADA. BUILDING PERMITS. ANNUAL SUMMARY/PERMIS DE BATIR. see *BUILDING AND CONSTRUCTION — Abstracting, Bibliographies, Statistics*

CANADA. STATISTICS CANADA. CABLE TELEVISION/TELEDISTRIBUTION. see *COMMUNICATIONS — Abstracting, Bibliographies, Statistics*

317   CN   ISSN 0705-5765
CANADA. STATISTICS CANADA. CANADIAN STATISTICAL REVIEW. ANNUAL SUPPLEMENT TO SECTION 1/REVUE STATISTIQUE DU CANADA. SUPPLEMENT ANNUEL DE LA SECTION 1. (Catalog 11-206) (Text and summaries in English and French) 1961. a. £6($7.20) Statistics Canada, Publications Distribution, Ottawa. Ont. K1A 0V7, Canada. (also avail. in microform from MML)

CANADA. STATISTICS CANADA. CANE AND BEET SUGAR PROCESSORS/TRAITEMENT DU SUCRE DE CANNE ET DE BETTERAVES. see *FOOD AND FOOD INDUSTRIES — Abstracting, Bibliographies, Statistics*

CANADA. STATISTICS CANADA. CANVAS PRODUCTS AND COTTON AND JUTE BAG INDUSTRIES/INDUSTRIE DES ARTICLES EN GROSSE TOILE ET DES SACS DE COTON ET DE JUTE. see *TEXTILE INDUSTRIES AND FABRICS — Abstracting, Bibliographies, Statistics*

CANADA. STATISTICS CANADA. CARPET, MAT AND RUG INDUSTRY/INDUSTRIE DES TAPIS, DES CARPETTES ET DE LA MOQUETTE. see *TEXTILE INDUSTRIES AND FABRICS — Abstracting, Bibliographies, Statistics*

CANADA. STATISTICS CANADA. CAUSES OF DEATH, PROVINCES BY SEX AND CANADA BY SEX AND AGE/CAUSES DE DECES, PAR PROVINCES SELON LE SEXE ET LE CANADA SELON LE SEXE ET L'AGE. see *POPULATION STUDIES — Abstracting, Bibliographies, Statistcs*

CANADA. STATISTICS CANADA. COAL MINES/ MINES DE CHARBON. see *MINES AND MINING INDUSTRY — Abstracting, Bibliographies, Statistics*

CANADA. STATISTICS CANADA. COFFIN AND CASKET INDUSTRY/INDUSTRIE DES CERCUEILS. see *FUNERALS — Abstracting, Bibliographies, Statistics*

CANADA. STATISTICS CANADA. COMMUNICATIONS EQUIPMENT MANUFACTURERS/FABRICANTS D'EQUIPEMENT DE TELECOMMUNICATION. see *COMMUNICATIONS — Abstracting, Bibliographies, Statistics*

CANADA. STATISTICS CANADA. CONCRETE PRODUCTS MANUFACTURERS/FABRICANTS DE PRODUITS EN BETON. see *BUILDING AND CONSTRUCTION — Abstracting, Bibliographies, Statistics*

CANADA. STATISTICS CANADA. CONSOLIDATED GOVERNMENT FINANCE/ FINANCES PUBLIQUES CONSOLIDEES. see *BUSINESS AND ECONOMICS — Abstracting, Bibliographies, Statistics*

CANADA. STATISTICS CANADA. CORDAGE AND TWINE INDUSTRY /CORDERIE ET FICELLERIE (FABRICATION) see *TEXTILE INDUSTRIES AND FABRICS — Abstracting, Bibliographies, Statistics*

CANADA. STATISTICS CANADA. CORRUGATED BOX MANUFACTURERS/ FABRICANTS DE BOITES EN CARTON ONDULE. see *PAPER AND PULP — Abstracting, Bibliographies, Statistics*

CANADA. STATISTICS CANADA. COTTON YARN AND CLOTH MILLS/FILATURE ET TISSAGE DU COTON. see *TEXTILE INDUSTRIES AND FABRICS — Abstracting, Bibliographies, Statistics*

CANADA. STATISTICS CANADA. CRUDE PETROLEUM AND NATURAL GAS INDUSTRY/INDUSTRIE DU PETROLE BRUT ET DU GAZ NATUREL. see *PETROLEUM AND GAS — Abstracting, Bibliographies, Statistics*

CANADA. STATISTICS CANADA. DIRECT SELLING IN CANADA/VENTE DIRECTE AU CANADA. see *BUSINESS AND ECONOMICS — Abstracting, Bibliographies, Statistics*

CANADA. STATISTICS CANADA. DISTILLERIES. see *BEVERAGES — Abstracting, Bibliographies, Statistics*

CANADA. STATISTICS CANADA. ELECTRIC LAMP AND SHADE MANUFACTURERS/ INDUSTRIE DES LAMPES ELECTRIQUES ET DES ABAT-JOUR. see *ELECTRICITY AND ELECTRICAL ENGINEERING — Abstracting, Bibliographies, Statistics*

CANADA. STATISTICS CANADA. ELECTRIC POWER STATISTICS VOLUME 1: ANNUAL ELECTRIC POWER SURVEY OF CAPABILITY AND LOAD/STATISTIQUE DE L'ENERGIE ELECTRIQUE. VOLUME 1: ENQUETE ANNUELLE SUR LA PUISSANCE MAXIMALE ET SUR LA CHARGE DES RESEAUX. see *ELECTRICITY AND ELECTRICAL ENGINEERING — Abstracting, Bibliographies, Statistics*

CANADA. STATISTICS CANADA. ELECTRICAL CONTRACTING INDUSTRY/ ENTREPRENEURS D'INSTALLATIONS ELECTRIQUES. see *ELECTRICITY AND ELECTRICAL ENGINEERING — Abstracting, Bibliographies, Statistics*

CANADA. STATISTICS CANADA. ELEMENTARY-SECONDARY SCHOOL ENROLMENT/EFFECTIFS DES ECOLES PRIMAIRES ET SECONDAIRES. see *EDUCATION — Abstracting, Bibliographies, Statistics*

CANADA. STATISTICS CANADA. EMPLOYMENT, EARNINGS AND HOURS. SEASONALLY-ADJUSTED SERIES/EMPLOI, REMUNERATIONS ET HEURES; SERIES DESAISONNALISEES. see *BUSINESS AND ECONOMICS — Abstracting, Bibliographies, Statistics*

CANADA. STATISTICS CANADA. ENROLLMENT IN COMMUNITY COLLEGES/ EFFECTIFS DES COLLEGES COMMUNAUTAIRES. see *EDUCATION — Abstracting, Bibliographies, Statistics*

CANADA. STATISTICS CANADA. ESTIMATES OF POPULATION FOR CANADA AND THE PROVINCES/ESTIMATIONS DE LA POPULATION DU CANADA ET DES PROVINCES. see *POPULATION STUDIES — Abstracting, Bibliographies, Statistcs*

CANADA. STATISTICS CANADA. ESTIMATION OF POPULATION BY MARITAL STATUS, AGE AND SEX, CANADA AND PROVINCES/ ESTIMATIONS DE LA POPULATION SUIVANT L'ETAT MATRIMONIAL, L'AGE ET LE SEXE, CANADA ET PROVINCES. see *POPULATION STUDIES — Abstracting, Bibliographies, Statistcs*

CANADA. STATISTICS CANADA. EXPORTS- MERCHANDISE TRADE/EXPORTATIONS- COMMERCE DE MERCHANDISES. see *BUSINESS AND ECONOMICS — Abstracting, Bibliographies, Statistics*

CANADA. STATISTICS CANADA. FAMILY INCOMES(CENSUS FAMILIES) /REVENUS DES FAMILLE (FAMILLES DE RECENSEMENT) see *BUSINESS AND ECONOMICS — Abstracting, Bibliographies, Statistics*

CANADA. STATISTICS CANADA. FARM NET INCOME/REVENU NET AGRICOLE. see *AGRICULTURE — Abstracting, Bibliographies, Statistics*

CANADA. STATISTICS CANADA. FEDERAL GOVERNMENT EMPLOYMENT IN METROPOLITAN AREAS/EMPLOI DANS L'ADMINISTRATION FEDERALE REGIONS METROPOLITAINES. see *PUBLIC ADMINISTRATION — Abstracting, Bibliographies, Statistics*

CANADA. STATISTICS CANADA. FEDERAL GOVERNMENT FINANCE/FINANCES PUBLIQUES FEDERALES. see *BUSINESS AND ECONOMICS — Abstracting, Bibliographies, Statistics*

CANADA. STATISTICS CANADA. FELT AND FIBRE PROCESSING MILLS/INDUSTRIE DU FEUTRE ET DU TRAITEMENT DES FIBRES. see *TEXTILE INDUSTRIES AND FABRICS — Abstracting, Bibliographies, Statistics*

CANADA. STATISTICS CANADA. FINANCIAL STATISTICS OF EDUCATION/STATISTIQUES FINANCIERES DE L'EDUCATION. see *EDUCATION — Abstracting, Bibliographies, Statistics*

CANADA. STATISTICS CANADA. FISH PRODUCTS INDUSTRY/INDUSTRIE DE LA TRANSFORMATION DU POISSON. see *FISH AND FISHERIES — Abstracting, Bibliographies, Statistics*

CANADA. STATISTICS CANADA. FLOUR AND BREAKFAST CEREAL PRODUCTS INDUSTRY/MEUNERIE ET FABRICATION DE CEREALES DE TABLE. see *FOOD AND FOOD INDUSTRIES — Abstracting, Bibliographies, Statistics*

CANADA. STATISTICS CANADA. FOR-HIRE TRUCKING SURVEY/ENQUETE SUR LE TRANSPORT ROUTIER DE MARCHANDISES POUR COMPTE D'AUTRUI. see *TRANSPORTATION — Abstracting, Bibliographies, Statistics*

CANADA. STATISTICS CANADA. FOUNDATION GARMENT INDUSTRY/ INDUSTRIE DES CORSETS ET SOUTIENS- GORGE. see *CLOTHING TRADE — Abstracting, Bibliographies, Statistics*

CANADA. STATISTICS CANADA. FRUIT AND VEGETABLE PROCESSING INDUSTRIES/ PREPARATION DE FRUITS ET DE LEGUMES. see *FOOD AND FOOD INDUSTRIES — Abstracting, Bibliographies, Statistics*

CANADA. STATISTICS CANADA. FRUIT AND VEGETABLE PRODUCTION/PRODUCTION DE FRUITS ET DE LEGUMES. see *AGRICULTURE — Abstracting, Bibliographies, Statistics*

CANADA. STATISTICS CANADA. GAS UTILITIES (TRANSPORT AND DISTRIBUTION SYSTEMS) /SERVICES DE GAZ (RESEAUX DE TRANSPORT ET DE DISTRIBUTION) see *PETROLEUM AND GAS — Abstracting, Bibliographies, Statistics*

CANADA. STATISTICS CANADA. GENERAL REVIEW OF THE MINERAL INDUSTRIES/ REVUE GENERALE SUR LES INDUSTRIES MINERALES; mines, quarries and oil wells/mines, carrieres et puits de petrole. see *MINES AND MINING INDUSTRY — Abstracting, Bibliographies, Statistics*

CANADA. STATISTICS CANADA. GLASS AND GLASS PRODUCTS MANUFACTURERS/ FABRICANTS DE VERRE ET D'ARTICLES EN VERRE. see *CERAMICS, GLASS AND POTTERY — Abstracting, Bibliographies, Statistics*

CANADA. STATISTICS CANADA. HIGHWAY, ROAD, STREET AND BRIDGE CONTRACTING INDUSTRY/ ENTREPRENEURS DE GRANDE ROUTE, CHEMIN, RUE ET PONT. see *ENGINEERING — Abstracting, Bibliographies, Statistics*

CANADA. STATISTICS CANADA. HISTORICAL LABOUR FORCE STATISTICS, ACTUAL DATA, SEASONAL FACTORS, SEASONALLY ADJUSTED DATA/STATISTIQUES CHRONOLOGIQUES SUR LA POPULATION ACTIVE, CHIFFRES REELS, FACTEURS SAISONNIERS ET DONNEES DESAISONNALISEES. see *BUSINESS AND ECONOMICS — Abstracting, Bibliographies, Statistics*

CANADA. STATISTICS CANADA. HOMICIDE STATISTICS/STATISTIQUE DE L'HOMICIDE. see *CRIMINOLOGY AND LAW ENFORCEMENT — Abstracting, Bibliographies, Statistics*

CANADA. STATISTICS CANADA. HOSPITAL STATISTICS: PRELIMINARY ANNUAL REPORT/STATISTIQUE HOSPITALIERE: RAPPORT ANNUEL PRELIMINAIRE. see *HOSPITALS — Abstracting, Bibliographies, Statistics*

CANADA. STATISTICS CANADA. HOUSEHOLD FACILITIES AND EQUIPMENT/ L'EQUIPMENT MENAGER. see *HOME ECONOMICS — Abstracting, Bibliographies, Statistics*

CANADA. STATISTICS CANADA. HOUSEHOLD FURNITURE MANUFACTURERS/INDUSTRIE DES MEUBLES DE MAISON. see *INTERIOR DESIGN AND DECORATION — Abstracting, Bibliographies, Statistics*

CANADA. STATISTICS CANADA. IMPORTS- MERCHANDISE TRADE/IMPORTATIONS- COMMERCE DE MARCHANDISES. see *BUSINESS AND ECONOMICS — Abstracting, Bibliographies, Statistics*

CANADA. STATISTICS CANADA. INDEX OF FARM PRODUCTION/INDICE DE LA PRODUCTION AGRICOLE. see *AGRICULTURE — Abstracting, Bibliographies, Statistics*

CANADA. STATISTICS CANADA. INVESTMENT STATISTISTICS SERVICE BULLETIN/ BULLETIN DE SERVICE SUR LA STATISTIQUE DES INVESTISSEMENTS. see *BUSINESS AND ECONOMICS — Abstracting, Bibliographies, Statistics*

CANADA. STATISTICS CANADA. IRON AND STEEL MILLS/SIDERURGIE. see *METALLURGY — Abstracting, Bibliographies, Statistics*

CANADA. STATISTICS CANADA. KNITTING MILLS/BONNETERIE. see *CLOTHING TRADE — Abstracting, Bibliographies, Statistics*

CANADA. STATISTICS CANADA. LABOUR COSTS IN CANADA: EDUCATION, LIBRARIES AND MUSEUMS/COUTS DE LA MAIN D'OEUVRE AU CANADA. ENSEIGNEMENT, BIBLIOTHEQUES ET MUSEES. see *BUSINESS AND ECONOMICS — Abstracting, Bibliographies, Statistics*

CANADA. STATISTICS CANADA. LABOUR COSTS IN CANADA: FINANCE, INSURANCE AND REAL ESTATE/COUTS DE LA MAIN-D'OEUVRE AU CANADA: FINANCES, ASSURANCES, ET IMMEUBLE. see *BUSINESS AND ECONOMICS* — *Abstracting, Bibliographies, Statistics*

CANADA. STATISTICS CANADA. LIST OF CANADIAN HOSPITALS AND SPECIAL CARE FACILITIES/LISTE DES HOPITAUX CANADIENS ET DES ETABLISSEMENTS DE SOINS SPECIAUX. see *HOSPITALS* — *Abstracting, Bibliographies, Statistics*

CANADA. STATISTICS CANADA. LIVESTOCK AND ANIMAL PRODUCTS STATISTICS/STATISTIQUE DU BETAIL ET DES PRODUITS ANIMAUX. see *AGRICULTURE* — *Abstracting, Bibliographies, Statistics*

CANADA. STATISTICS CANADA. LOCAL GOVERNMENT FINANCE: REVENUE AND EXPENDITURE, ASSETS AND LIABILITIES, ACTUAL/FINANCES PUBLIQUES LOCALES: REVENUS ET DEPENSES, ACTIF ET PASSIF, CHIFFRES REELS. see *PUBLIC ADMINISTRATION* — *Abstracting, Bibliographies, Statistics*

CANADA. STATISTICS CANADA. MANUFACTURERS OF ELECTRIC WIRE AND CABLE/FABRICANTS DE FILS ET DE CABLES ELECTRIQUES. see *ELECTRICITY AND ELECTRICAL ENGINEERING*

CANADA. STATISTICS CANADA. MANUFACTURERS OF INDUSTRIAL CHEMICALS/FABRICANTS DE PRODUITS CHIMIQUES INDUSTRIELS. see *ENGINEERING* — *Abstracting, Bibliographies, Statistics*

CANADA. STATISTICS CANADA. MANUFACTURERS OF SOAP AND CLEANING COMPOUNDS/FABRICANTS DE SAVON ET DE PRODUITS DE NETTOYAGE. see *CLEANING AND DYEING* — *Abstracting, Bibliographies, Statistics*

CANADA. STATISTICS CANADA. MECHANICAL CONTRACTING INDUSTRY/LES ENTREPRENEURS D'INSTALLATIONS MECANIQUES. see *ENGINEERING* — *Abstracting, Bibliographies, Statistics*

CANADA. STATISTICS CANADA. MEN'S CLOTHING INDUSTRIES/INDUSTRIE DES VETEMENTS POUR HOMMES. see *CLOTHING TRADE* — *Abstracting, Bibliographies, Statistics*

CANADA. STATISTICS CANADA. MISCELLANEOUS MANUFACTURING INDUSTRIES/INDUSTRIES MANUFACTURIERES DIVERSES. see *BUSINESS AND ECONOMICS* — *Abstracting, Bibliographies, Statistics*

CANADA. STATISTICS CANADA. MISCELLANEOUS LEATHER PRODUCTS MANUFACTURERS/FABRICANTS D'ARTICLES DIVERS EN CUIR. see *LEATHER AND FUR INDUSTRIES* — *Abstracting, Bibliographies, Statistics*

CANADA STATISTICS CANADA. MISCELLANEOUS CLOTHING INDUSTRIES/INDUSTRIES DIVERSES DE L'HABILLEMENT. see *CLOTHING TRADE* — *Abstracting, Bibliographies, Statistics*

CANADA. STATISTICS CANADA. MISCELLANEOUS NON-METALLIC MINERAL PRODUCTS INDUSTRIES/INDUSTRIES DES PRODUITS MINERAUX NON-METALLIQUES DIVERS. see *MINES AND MINING INDUSTRY* — *Abstracting, Bibliographies, Statistics*

CANADA. STATISTICS CANADA. MISCELLANEOUS FOOD PROCESSORS/TRAITMENT DES PRODUITS ALIMENTAIRES DIVERS. see *FOOD AND FOOD INDUSTRIES* — *Abstracting, Bibliographies, Statistics*

CANADA. STATISTICS CANADA. MOTION PICTURE THEATRES AND FILM DISTRIBUTORS/CINEMAS ET DISTRIBUTEURS DE FILMS. see *MOTION PICTURES* — *Abstracting, Bibliographies, Statistics*

CANADA. STATISTICS CANADA. NON-RESIDENTIAL GENERAL BUILDING CONTRACTING INDUSTRY/INDUSTRIE DES ENTREPRISES GENERALES EN CONSTRUCTION NON DOMICILIAIRE. see *BUILDING AND CONSTRUCTION* — *Abstracting, Bibliographies, Statistics*

CANADA. STATISTICS CANADA. OFFICE FURNITURE MANUFACTURERS/INDUSTRIE DES MEUBLES DE BUREAU. see *INTERIOR DESIGN AND DECORATION* — *Abstracting, Bibliographies, Statistics*

CANADA. STATISTICS CANADA. ORNAMENTAL AND ARCHITECTURAL METAL INDUSTRY/INDUSTRIE DES PRODUITS METALLIQUES D'ARCHITECTURE ET D'ORNEMENT. see *METALLURGY* — *Abstracting, Bibliographies, Statistics*

CANADA. STATISTICS CANADA. PASSENGER BUS AND URBAN TRANSIT STATISTICS/STATISTIQUE DU TRANSPORT DES VOYAGEURS PAR AUTOBUS ET DU TRANSPORT URBAIN. see *TRANSPORTATION* — *Abstracting, Bibliographies, Statistics*

CANADA. STATISTICS CANADA. PETROLEUM REFINERIES/RAFFINERIES DE PETROLE. see *PETROLEUM AND GAS* — *Abstracting, Bibliographies, Statistics*

CANADA. STATISTICS CANADA. PRIVATE AND PUBLIC INVESTMENT IN CANADA, MID-YEAR REVIEW/INVESTISSEMENTS PRIVES ET PUBLICS AU CANADA. REVUE DE LA MI-ANNEE. see *BUSINESS AND ECONOMICS* — *Abstracting, Bibliographies, Statistics*

CANADA. STATISTICS CANADA. PRIVATE AND PUBLIC INVESTMENT IN CANADA. OUTLOOK/INVESTISSEMENTS PRIVES ET PUBLICS AU CANADA. PERSPECTIVES. see *BUSINESS AND ECONOMICS* — *Abstracting, Bibliographies, Statistics*

CANADA. STATISTICS CANADA. PRODUCTION AND VALUE OF MAPLE PRODUCTS/PRODUCTION ET VALEUR DES PRODUITS DE L'ERABLE. see *AGRICULTURE* — *Abstracting, Bibliographies, Statistics*

CANADA. STATISTICS CANADA. PRODUCTION OF POULTRY AND EGGS/PRODUCTION DE VOLAILLE ET OEUFS. see *AGRICULTURE* — *Abstracting, Bibliographies, Statistics*

CANADA. STATISTICS CANADA. PRODUCTS SHIPPED BY CANADIAN MANUFACTURERS/PRODUITS LIVRES PAR LES FABRICANTS CANADIENS. see *BUSINESS AND ECONOMICS* — *Abstracting, Bibliographies, Statistics*

CANADA. STATISTICS CANADA. PROVINCIAL GOVERNMENT ENTERPRISE FINANCE/FINANCES DES ENTREPRISES PUBLIQUES PROVINCIALES. see *BUSINESS AND ECONOMICS* — *Abstracting, Bibliographies, Statistics*

CANADA. STATISTICS CANADA. PROVINCIAL GOVERNMENT FINANCE, ASSETS, LIABILITIES, SOURCES AND USES OF FUNDS/FINANCES PUBLIQUES PROVINCIALES, ACTIF, PASSIF, SOURCES ET UTILISATIONS DES FONDS. see *BUSINESS AND ECONOMICS* — *Abstracting, Bibliographies, Statistics*

CANADA. STATISTICS CANADA. PROVINCIAL GOVERNMENT FINANCE, REVENUE AND EXPENDITURE (ESTIMATES) /FINANCES PUBLIQUES PROVINCIALES, REVENUS ET DEFENSES (PREVISIONS) see *BUSINESS AND ECONOMICS* — *Abstracting, Bibliographies, Statistics*

CANADA. STATISTICS CANADA. PULP AND PAPER MILLS/USINES DE PATES ET PAPIERS. see *FORESTS AND FORESTRY* — *Abstracting, Bibliographies, Statistics*

CANADA. STATISTICS CANADA. RADIO AND TELEVISION BROADCASTING/RADIODIFFUSION ET TELEVISION. see *COMMUNICATIONS* — *Abstracting, Bibliographies, Statistics*

CANADA. STATISTICS CANADA. RAILWAY FREIGHT TRAFFIC/TRAFIC MARCHANDISES FERROVIAIRE. see *TRANSPORTATION* — *Abstracting, Bibliographies, Statistics*

CANADA. STATISTICS CANADA. REPORT ON FUR FARMS/RAPPORT SUR LES FERMES A FOURRURE. see *LEATHER AND FUR INDUSTRIES* — *Abstracting, Bibliographies, Statistics*

CANADA. STATISTICS CANADA. RETAIL CHAIN STORES/MAGASINS DE DETAIL A SUCCURSALES. see *BUSINESS AND ECONOMICS* — *Abstracting, Bibliographies, Statistics*

CANADA. STATISTICS CANADA. ROAD MOTOR VEHICLES-FUEL SALES/VEHICULES AUTOMOBILES-VENTES DE CARBURANTS. see *TRANSPORTATION* — *Abstracting, Bibliographies, Statistics*

CANADA. STATISTICS CANADA. ROAD MOTOR VEHICLES-REGISTRATIONS/VEHICULES AUTOMOBILES-IMMATRICULATIONS. see *TRANSPORTATION* — *Abstracting, Bibliographies, Statistics*

CANADA. STATISTICS CANADA. SALARIES AND QUALIFICATIONS OF TEACHERS IN PUBLIC, ELEMENTARY AND SECONDARY SCHOOLS/TRAITEMENTS ET QUALIFICATIONS DES ENSEIGNANTS DES ECOLES PUBLIQUES, PRIMAIRES ET SECONDAIRES. see *EDUCATION* — *Abstracting, Bibliographies, Statistics*

CANADA. STATISTICS CANADA. SAWMILLS AND PLANING MILLS AND SHINGLE MILLS/SCIERIES ET ATELIERS DE RABOTAGE ET USINES DE BARDEAUX. see *FORESTS AND FORESTRY* — *Abstracting, Bibliographies, Statistics*

CANADA. STATISTICS CANADA. SCIENTIFIC AND PROFESSIONAL EQUIPMENT INDUSTRIES/FABRICATION DE MATERIEL SCIENTIFIQUE ET PROFESSIONNEL. see *INSTRUMENTS* — *Abstracting, Bibliographies, Statistics*

CANADA. STATISTICS CANADA. SHIPBUILDING AND REPAIR/CONSTRUCTION ET REPARATION DE NAVIRES. see *TRANSPORTATION* — *Abstracting, Bibliographies, Statistics*

CANADA. STATISTICS CANADA. SHORN WOOL PRODUCTION/PRODUCTION DE LAINE TONDUE. see *AGRICULTURE* — *Abstracting, Bibliographies, Statistics*

CANADA. STATISTICS CANADA. SLAUGHTERING AND MEAT PROCESSORS/ABATTAGE ET CONDITIONNEMENT DE LA VIANDE. see *FOOD AND FOOD INDUSTRIES* — *Abstracting, Bibliographies, Statistics*

CANADA. STATISTICS CANADA. SPORTING GOODS AND TOY INDUSTRIES/FABRICATION D'ARTICLES DE SPORT ET DE JOUETS. see *SPORTS AND GAMES* — *Abstracting, Bibliographies, Statistics*

CANADA. STATISTICS CANADA. SURGICAL PROCEDURES AND TREATMENTS/INTERVENTIONS CHIRURGICALES ET TRAITEMENTS. see *MEDICAL SCIENCES* — *Abstracting, Bibliographies, Statistics*

CANADA. STATISTICS CANADA. SURVEY OF CANADIAN NURSERY TRADES INDUSTRY/ ENQUETE SUR L'INDUSTRIE DES PEPINIERES CANADIENNES. see GARDENING AND HORTICULTURE — Abstracting, Bibliographies, Statistics

CANADA. STATISTICS CANADA. SURVEY OF PRODUCTION/RELEVE DE LA PRODUCTION. see BUSINESS AND ECONOMICS — Abstracting, Bibliographies, Statistics

CANADA. STATISTICS CANADA. TELECOMMUNICATIONS STATISTICS/ STATISTIQUE DES TELECOMMUNICATIONS. see COMMUNICATIONS — Abstracting, Bibliographies, Statistics

CANADA. STATISTICS CANADA. THERAPEUTIC ABORTIONS/AVORTEMENTS THERAPEUTIQUES. see BIRTH CONTROL — Abstracting, Bibliographies, Statistics

CANADA. STATISTICS CANADA. TOBACCO PRODUCTS INDUSTRIES/INDUSTRIE DU TABAC. see TOBACCO — Abstracting, Bibliographies, Statistics

CANADA. STATISTICS CANADA. TRANSPORTATION AND COMMUNICATIONS DIVISION. COMMUNICATIONS SERVICE BULLETIN/ COMMUNICATIONS-BULLETIN DE SERVICE. see COMMUNICATIONS — Abstracting, Bibliographies, Statistics

CANADA. STATISTICS CANADA. TRUSTEED PENSION PLANS-FINANCIAL STATISTICS/ REGIMES DE PENSIONS EN FIDUCIE STATISTIQUE FINANCIERE. see BUSINESS AND ECONOMICS — Abstracting, Bibliographies, Statistics

CANADA. STATISTICS CANADA. VEGETABLE OIL MILLS/MOULINS A HUILE VEGETALE. see FOOD AND FOOD INDUSTRIES — Abstracting, Bibliographies, Statistics

CANADA. STATISTICS CANADA. VENDING MACHINE OPERATORS/EXPLOITANTS DE DISTRIBUTEURS AUTOMATIQUES. see BUSINESS AND ECONOMICS — Abstracting, Bibliographies, Statistics

CANADA. STATISTICS CANADA. WATER TRANSPORTATION/TRANSPORT PAR EAU. see TRANSPORTATION — Abstracting, Bibliographies, Statistics

CANADA. STATISTICS CANADA. WOMEN'S AND CHILDREN'S CLOTHING INDUSTRIES/ INDUSTRIES DES VETEMENTS POUR DAMES ET POUR ENFANTS. see CLOTHING TRADE — Abstracting, Bibliographies, Statistics

CANADA. STATISTICS CANADA. WOODEN BOX FACTORIES/FABRIQUES DE BOITES EN BOIS. see PACKAGING — Abstracting, Bibliographies, Statistics

CANADA. STATISTICS CANADA. WOOL PRODUCTION AND SUPPLY/PRODUCTION ET STOCKS DE LAINE. see TEXTILE INDUSTRIES AND FABRICS — Abstracting, Bibliographies, Statistics

CANADA. STATISTICS CANADA. WOOL YARN AND CLOTH MILLS/FILATURE ET TISSAGE DE LA LAINE. see TEXTILE INDUSTRIES AND FABRICS — Abstracting, Bibliographies, Statistics

CANADA'S INTERNATIONAL INVESTMENT POSITION/BILAN CANADIEN DES INVESTISSEMENTS INTERNATIONAUX. see BUSINESS AND ECONOMICS — Abstracting, Bibliographies, Statistics

CANADA'S MINERAL PRODUCTION, PRELIMINARY ESTIMATE/PRODUCTION MINERALE DU CANADA, CALCUL PRELIMINAIRE. see MINES AND MINING INDUSTRY — Abstracting, Bibliographies, Statistics

310 338.9 JA
CATALOGUE OF STATISTICAL MATERIALS OF DEVELOPING COUNTRIES. (Text in English & Japanese) biennial. 1500 Yen. Institute of Developing Economies - Ajia Keizai Kenkyusho, 42 Ichigaya-Hommuracho, Shinjuku-ku, Tokyo 162, Japan.

317 CU
CENSO DE POBLACION Y VIVIENDAS. (Issued from 1972 as a number of Anuario Estadistico de Cuba) a. free. Comite Estatal de Estadisticas, Direccion de Informacion y Relaciones Internacionales, Centro de Informacion Cientifico-Tecnico, Av.Tercera no.4410, Municipio de Playa, Havana, Cuba.

CENSUS OF PRIVATE NON-PROFIT MAKING INSTITUTIONS IN FIJI. A REPORT. see BUSINESS AND ECONOMICS — Abstracting, Bibliographies, Statistics

CHARTERED INSTITUTE OF PUBLIC FINANCE AND ACCOUNTANCY. CHARGES FOR LEISURE SERVICES. see SPORTS AND GAMES — Abstracting, Bibliographies, Statistics

CHARTERED INSTITUTE OF PUBLIC FINANCE AND ACCOUNTANCY. CREMATORIA STATISTICS. ACTUALS. see PUBLIC HEALTH AND SAFETY

CHARTERED INSTITUTE OF PUBLIC FINANCE AND ACCOUNTANCY. EDUCATION ESTIMATES STATISTICS. see EDUCATION — Abstracting, Bibliographies, Statistics

CHARTERED INSTITUTE OF PUBLIC FINANCE AND ACCOUNTANCY. EDUCATION STATISTICS. ACTUALS. see EDUCATION — Abstracting, Bibliographies, Statistics

CHARTERED INSTITUTE OF PUBLIC FINANCE AND ACCOUNTANCY. FINANCIAL GENERAL & RATING STATISTICS. see BUSINESS AND ECONOMICS — Abstracting, Bibliographies, Statistics

CHARTERED INSTITUTE OF PUBLIC FINANCE AND ACCOUNTANCY. FIRE SERVICE STATISTICS. ACTUALS. see FIRE PREVENTION — Abstracting, Bibliographies, Statistics

CHARTERED INSTITUTE OF PUBLIC FINANCE AND ACCOUNTANCY. FIRE SERVICE STATISTICS. ESTIMATES. see FIRE PREVENTION — Abstracting, Bibliographies, Statistics

CHARTERED INSTITUTE OF PUBLIC FINANCE AND ACCOUNTANCY. HOMELESSNESS STATISTICS. see HOUSING AND URBAN PLANNING — Abstracting, Bibliographies, Statistics

CHARTERED INSTITUTE OF PUBLIC FINANCE AND ACCOUNTANCY. HOUSING ESTIMATE STATISTICS. see HOUSING AND URBAN PLANNING

CHARTERED INSTITUTE OF PUBLIC FINANCE AND ACCOUNTANCY. HOUSING MAINTENANCE & MANAGEMENT. ACTUALS STATISTICS. see HOUSING AND URBAN PLANNING

CHARTERED INSTITUTE OF PUBLIC FINANCE AND ACCOUNTANCY. HOUSING REVENUE ACCOUNTS. ACTUALS STATISTICS. see HOUSING AND URBAN PLANNING — Abstracting, Bibliographies, Statistics

CHARTERED INSTITUTE OF PUBLIC FINANCE AND ACCOUNTANCY. HOUSING RENTS. STATISTICS. see HOUSING AND URBAN PLANNING — Abstracting, Bibliographies, Statistics

CHARTERED INSTITUTE OF PUBLIC FINANCE AND ACCOUNTANCY. LEISURE ESTIMATE STATISTICS. see SPORTS AND GAMES — Abstracting, Bibliographies, Statistics

CHARTERED INSTITUTE OF PUBLIC FINANCE AND ACCOUNTANCY. LOCAL AUTHORITY AIRPORTS. ACCOUNTS AND STATISTICS. see TRANSPORTATION — Abstracting, Bibliographies, Statistics

CHARTERED INSTITUTE OF PUBLIC FINANCE AND ACCOUNTANCY. PERSONAL SOCIAL SERVICES ESTIMATE STATISTICS. see SOCIAL SERVICES AND WELFARE — Abstracting, Bibliographies, Statistics

CHARTERED INSTITUTE OF PUBLIC FINANCE AND ACCOUNTANCY. PERSONAL SOCIAL SERVICES STATISTICS. ACTUALS. see SOCIAL SERVICES AND WELFARE — Abstracting, Bibliographies, Statistics

CHARTERED INSTITUTE OF PUBLIC FINANCE AND ACCOUNTANCY. PLANNING AND DEVELOPMENT STATISTICS. ACTUALS. see PUBLIC ADMINISTRATION — Abstracting, Bibliographies, Statistics

CHARTERED INSTITUTE OF PUBLIC FINANCE AND ACCOUNTANCY. POLICE STATISTICS. ACTUALS. see CRIMINOLOGY AND LAW ENFORCEMENT — Abstracting, Bibliographies, Statistics

CHARTERED INSTITUTE OF PUBLIC FINANCE AND ACCOUNTANCY. POLICE STATISTICS. ESTIMATES. see CRIMINOLOGY AND LAW ENFORCEMENT — Abstracting, Bibliographies, Statistics

CHARTERED INSTITUTE OF PUBLIC FINANCE AND ACCOUNTANCY. PUBLIC LIBRARY STATISTICS. ACTUALS. see LIBRARY AND INFORMATION SCIENCES — Abstracting, Bibliographies, Statistics

CHARTERED INSTITUTE OF PUBLIC FINANCE AND ACCOUNTANCY. PUBLIC LIBRARY STATISTICS. ESTIMATES. see LIBRARY AND INFORMATION SCIENCES — Abstracting, Bibliographies, Statistics

CHARTERED INSTITUTE OF PUBLIC FINANCE AND ACCOUNTANCY. RATE COLLECTION STATISTICS. ACTUALS. see BUSINESS AND ECONOMICS — Abstracting, Bibliographies, Statistics

CHARTERED INSTITUTE OF PUBLIC FINANCE AND ACCOUNTANCY. WASTE COLLECTION STATISTICS. ACTUALS. see PUBLIC ADMINISTRATION — Abstracting, Bibliographies, Statistics

CHARTERED INSTITUTE OF PUBLIC FINANCE AND ACCOUNTANCY. WATER AND SEWAGE TREATMENT AND DISPOSAL STATISTICS. ACTUALS. see PUBLIC HEALTH AND SAFETY — Abstracting, Bibliographies, Statistics

CHARTERED INSTITUTE OF PUBLIC FINANCE AND ACCOUNTANCY. WATER SERVICES CHARGES STATISTICS. see WATER RESOURCES — Abstracting, Bibliographies, Statistics

318 CL
CHILE. INSTITUTO NACIONAL DE ESTADISTICAS. ANUARIO ESTADISTICO. a. Instituto Nacional de Estadisticas, Biblioteca, Casilla 7597-Correo 3, Santiago, Chile.

318 CL
CHILE. INSTITUTO NACIONAL DE ESTADISTICAS. COMPENDIO ESTADISTICO. 1971. biennial. Instituto Nacional de Estadisticas, Casilla 7597-Correo 3, Santiago, Chile. stat.

318 CL
CHILE. INSTITUTO NACIONAL DE ESTADISTICAS. SUB-DEPARTAMENTO CONSTRUCCION. BOLETIN DE EDIFICACION. irreg. Instituto Nacional de Estadisticas, Departamento de Estadisticas Economicas, Vicuna Mackenna 115, Casilla 677, Correo 22, Bogota, Colombia.
Formerly: Chile. Instituto Nacional de Estadisticas. Boletin de Edificacion.

STATISTICS

310 US ISSN 0190-602X
CHINA FACTS & FIGURES ANNUAL. 1978. a. $32.50 (vol. 1); $33.50 (vol. 2) Academic International Press, Box 555, Gulf Breeze, FL 32561. Ed. John L. Scherer. (back issues avail)

339 318 CR
CIFRAS DE CUENTAS NACIONALES. 1968. a. free. Banco Central de Costa Rica, Avda.Central, Calles 2 y 4, San Jose, Costa Rica (And: Apdo. 10058,San Jose, Costa Rica) charts. stat. circ. 300.

318 CK
COLOMBIA. DEPARTAMENTO ADMINISTRATIVO NACIONAL DE ESTADISTICA. ANUARIO DE JUSTICIA. Departamento Administrativo Nacional de Estadistica, Banco Nacional de Datos, Centro Administrativo Nacional, Avda. Eldorado, Bogota, Colombia.
Formerly: Colombia. Departamento Administrativo Nacional de Estadistica. Anuario General de Estadistica - Justicia.

318 CK
COLOMBIA. DEPARTAMENTO ADMINISTRATIVO NACIONAL DE ESTADISTICA. ANUARIO GENERAL DE ESTADISTICA - TRANSPORTES Y COMUNICACIONES. Departamento Administrativo Nacional de Estadistica, Banco Nacional de Datos, Centro Administrativo Nacional, Avda. Eldorado, Bogota, Colombia.

318 CK
COLOMBIA. DEPARTAMENTO ADMINISTRATIVO NACIONAL DE ESTADISTICA. ESTADISTICAS HISTORICAS. irreg. Departamento Administrativo Nacional de Estadistica, Apartado Aereo 80043, Avda. Eldovado, Bogota, Colombia.

519 AT ISSN 0069-7524
COMMONWEALTH SCIENTIFIC AND INDUSTRIAL RESEARCH ORGANIZATION. DIVISION OF MATHEMATICAL STATISTICS. TECHNICAL PAPER. 1954. irreg. Aus.$0.80 per issue. C. S. I. R. O., Division of Mathematical Statistics, 314 Albert St., E. Melbourne 3002, Victoria, Australia.

318 BL
COMPANHIA PARANAENSE DE ENERGIA. INFORME ESTATISTICO ANUAL. 1971. a. free. Companhia Paranaense de Energia, Assessoria de Planejamento, Rua Cel. Dulcidio, 800 Curitiba, 80000 Parana, Brazil. stat. (back issues avail)

317 GT ISSN 0588-912X
COMPENDIO ESTADISTICO CENTROAMERICANO. 1957. a. $8. General Treaty on Central American Economic Integration, Permanent Secretariat, 4A Avenida 10-25, Zona 14, Guatemala City, Guatemala.

314 IT ISSN 0069-7958
COMPENDIO STATISTICO ITALIANO. a. L.2500. Istituto Centrale di Statistica, Via Cesare Balbo 16, 00100 Rome, Italy. circ. 12,000.
Formerly: Compendio Statistico (ISSN 0390-640X)

314 GR ISSN 0069-8245
CONCISE STATISTICAL YEARBOOK OF GREECE. (Text in English and Greek) 1954. a., latest 1978. $3.50. National Statistical Service, Publications and Information Division, 14-16 Lycourgou St., Athens 112, Greece.

CONSTRUCTION IN CANADA/CONSTRUCTION AU CANADA. see *BUILDING AND CONSTRUCTION* — *Abstracting, Bibliographies, Statistics*

CONTROL AND SALE OF ALCOHOLIC BEVERAGES IN CANADA/CONTROLE ET LA VENTE DES BOISSONS ALCOOLIQUES AU CANADA/CONTROLE ET LA VENTES DES BOISSONS ALCOOLIQUES AU CANADA. see *BEVERAGES* — *Abstracting, Bibliographies, Statistics*

310 CR ISSN 0589-8544
COSTA RICA. DIRECCION GENERAL DE ESTADISTICA Y CENSOS. INVENTARIO DE LAS ESTADISTICAS NACIONALES. 1964. irreg., latest 1970. free on exchange. Direccion General de Estadistica y Censos, San Jose, Costa Rica.

CURRENT INDEX TO STATISTICS; applications-methods-theory. see *ABSTRACTING AND INDEXING SERVICES*

331.11 CN ISSN 0382-1102
CURRENT LABOUR FORCE STATISTICS FOR NOVA SCOTIA. 1966. a. free. Department of Labour and Manpower, Research Division, Box 697, Halifax, N.S. B3J 2T8, Canada. stat.

CYPRUS. DEPARTMENT OF STATISTICS AND RESEARCH. ANNUAL REPORT OF VACANCIES. see *BUSINESS AND ECONOMICS* — *Abstracting, Bibliographies, Statistics*

CYPRUS. DEPARTMENT OF STATISTICS AND RESEARCH. ANNUAL REPORT ON UNEMPLOYMENT. see *BUSINESS AND ECONOMICS* — *Abstracting, Bibliographies, Statistics*

CYPRUS. DEPARTMENT OF STATISTICS AND RESEARCH. CRIMINAL STATISTICS. see *CRIMINOLOGY AND LAW ENFORCEMENT* — *Abstracting, Bibliographies, Statistics*

CYPRUS. DEPARTMENT OF STATISTICS AND RESEARCH. MANPOWER SURVEY. see *BUSINESS AND ECONOMICS* — *Abstracting, Bibliographies, Statistics*

312 CY ISSN 0590-4862
CYPRUS. DEPARTMENT OF STATISTICS AND RESEARCH. STATISTICAL ABSTRACT. 1955. a. Mils.1250. Department of Statistics and Research, Ministry of Finance, Nicosia, Cyprus.

314 CY
CYPRUS. DEPARTMENT OF STATISTICS AND RESEARCH. STATISTICAL POCKET BOOK. 1978. a. free. Department of Statistics and Research, Ministry of Finance, Nicosia, Cyprus.

314.37 947 CS ISSN 0070-248X
CZECHOSLOVAKIA. FEDERALNI STATISTICKY URAD. STATISTICKA ROCENKA. (Text in Czech; summaries in English and Russian) 1957. approx. a $20 per no. Statni Nakladatelstvi Technicke Literary, Spalena 51, 113 02 Prague 1, Czechoslovakia. circ. 13,300.

314 DK ISSN 0070-3567
DENMARK. DANMARKS STATISTIK. STATISTISK AARBOG/STATISTICAL YEARBOOK. (Text in Danish; notes in English) 1896. a. Kr.39.15. Danmarks Statistik, Sejroegade 11, 2100 Copenhagen OE, Denmark. cum.index: 1769-1972.

314 DK ISSN 0039-0658
DENMARK. DANMARKS STATISTIK. STATISTISK TABELVAERK/STATISTICAL TABLES. 1835. irreg. price varies. Danmarks Statistik, Sejroegade 11, 2100 Copenhagen OE, Denmark.

314 DK ISSN 0070-3583
DENMARK. DANMARKS STATISTIK. STATISTISK TIARS-OVERSIGT. 1961. a. Kr.12.80. Danmarks Statistik, Sejroegade 11, 2100 Copenhagen OE, Denmark.

310 DK ISSN 0039-0674
DENMARK. DANMARKS STATISTIK. STATISTISKE EFTERRETNINGER. 1908. irreg. Kr.100. Danmarks Statistik, Sejroegade 11, 2100 Copenhagen OE, Denmark. stat.

310 DK
DENMARK. DANMARKS STATISTIK. STATISTISKE MEDDELELSER. 1852. irreg. price varies. Danmarks Statistik, Sejroegade 11, 2100 Copenhagen OE, Denmark.

314 DK ISSN 0039-0682
DENMARK. DANMARKS STATISTIK. STATISTISKE UNDERSOGELSER. 1958. irreg. price varies. Danmarks Statistik, Sejroegade 11, 2100 Copenhagen OE, Denmark.

310 US ISSN 0163-3384
DEVELOPMENTS IN STATISTICS. 1978. irreg. Academic Press, Inc., 111 Fifth Ave., New York, NY 10003. Ed. P. R. Krishnaiah.

310 US
DIRECTORY OF STATISTICIANS. 1961. triennial. American Statistical Association, 806 15 St., N.W., Washington, DC 20005.
Formerly: Statisticians and Others in Allied Professions (ISSN 0081-508X)

314 GW
DUESSELDORF IN ZAHLEN. 1902. a. DM.12. Amt fuer Statistik und Wahlen, Postfach 1120, 4000 Duesseldorf 1, W. Germany (B.R.D.) stat. circ. 550. (looseleaf format)

EDUCATION IN CANADA/EDUCATION AU CANADA. see *EDUCATION* — *Abstracting, Bibliographies, Statistics*

EDUCATION STATISTICS, NEW YORK STATE; prepared especially for members of the Legislature. see *EDUCATION* — *Abstracting, Bibliographies, Statistics*

315.6 UA
EGYPT. CENTRAL AGENCY FOR PUBLIC MOBILISATION AND STATISTICS. STATISTICAL YEARBOOK. (Text in Arabic and English) 1961. a. £E6($8) Central Agency for Public Mobilisation and Statistics, Box 2086, Nasr City, Cairo, Egypt.
Formerly: Statistical Handbook of Egypt.

318 ES ISSN 0080-5661
EL SALVADOR. DIRECCION GENERAL DE ESTADISTICA Y CENSOS. ANUARIO ESTADISTICO. a. free or exchange basis. Direccion General de Estadistica y Censos, San Salvador, El Salvador.

318 ES ISSN 0581-4111
EL SALVADOR. MINISTERIO DE PLANIFICACION Y COORDINACION DEL DESARROLLO ECONOMICO Y SOCIAL. INDICADORES ECONOMICOS Y SOCIALES. 1962. a. Ministerio de Planificacion y Coordinacion del Desarrollo Economico y Social, Seccion de Investigaciones Estadisticas, Casa Presidential, San Salvador, El Salvador. Ed.Bd. stat.

318 ES
EL SALVADOR EN CIFRAS. biennial. free or exchange basis. Direccion General de Estadistica y Censos, Calle Arce 953, San Salvador, El Salvador.

338 PR
ESTABLECIMIENTOS MANUFACTURERAS EN PUERTO RICO. a. free. Department of Labor, Bureau of Labor Statistics, 414 Barbosa Ave., Hato Rey, PR 00917. index. circ. 775.

310 PN
ESTADISTICA PANAMENA. SITUACION DEMOGRAFICA. SECCION 221. ESTADISTICAS VITALES. 1957. a. Bol.$.30. Direccion de Estadistica y Censo, Contraloria General, Apartado 5213, Panama. circ. 1,700.

318 PN ISSN 0378-2581
ESTADISTICA PANAMENA. SITUACION ECONOMICA. SECCION 312. PRODUCCION PECUARIA. 1954. a. Bol.$.30. Direccion de Estadistica y Censo, Contraloria General, Apartado 5213, Panama 5, Panama. circ. 1,500.

318 PN ISSN 0378-2573
ESTADISTICA PANAMENA. SITUACION ECONOMICA. SECCION 312. SUPERFICIE SEMBRADA Y COSECHA DE CAFE, TABACO Y CANA DE AZUCAR. 1954. a. Bol.$.30. Direccion de Estadistica y Censo, Contraloria General, Apartado 5213, Panama 5, Panama. circ. 1,500.

318   PN   ISSN 0553-0660
ESTADISTICA PANAMENA. SITUACION
ECONOMICA. SECCION 331-COMERCIO.
COMERCIO EXTERIOR. (Includes: annual and
preliminary reports) 1958. a. Bol.$2.50
annual report. Direccion de Estadistica y
Censo, Contraloria General, Apdo. 5213, Panama 5,
Panama. charts. stat. circ. 1,000.

318   PN   ISSN 0378-6730
ESTADISTICA PANAMENA. SITUACION
ECONOMICA. SECCION 343-344. HACIENDA
PUBLICA Y FINANZAS. 1958. a. Bol.$40.
Direccion de Estadistica y Censo, Contraloria
General, Apartado 5213, Panama 5, Panama. circ.
1,500.

318   PN   ISSN 0378-2530
ESTADISTICA PANAMENA. SITUACION
ECONOMICA. SECCION 351. PRECIOS
PAGADOS POR EL PRODUCTOR
AGROPECUARIO. 1973. a. Bol.$.30. Direccion de
Estadistica y Censo, Contraloria General, Apartado
5213, Panama 5, Panama. circ. 1,500.

318   PN   ISSN 0378-4991
ESTADISTICA PANAMENA. SITUACION
ECONOMICA. SECCION 352. HOJA DE
BALANCE DE ALIMENTOS. 1960. a. Bol.$.30.
Direccion de Estadistica y Censo, Contraloria
General, Apartado 5213, Panama 5, Panama. circ.
900.

318   PN   ISSN 0378-259X
ESTADISTICA PANAMENA. SITUACION
POLITICA, ADMINISTRATIVA Y JUSTICIA.
SECCION 631. JUSTICIA. 1967. a. Bol.$30.
Direccion de Estadistica y Censo, Contraloria
General, Apartado 5213, Panama 5, Panama. circ.
900.

318   PN   ISSN 0378-262X
ESTADISTICA PANAMENA. SITUACION
SOCIAL. SECCION 431. ASISTENCIA SOCIAL.
1957. a. Bol.$.30. Direccion de Estadistica y Censo,
Contraloria General, Apartado 5213, Panama 5,
Panama. circ. 1,100.

318   PN   ISSN 0378-6765
ESTADISTICA PANAMENA. SITUACION
SOCIAL. SECCION 451. ACCIDENTES DE
TRANSITO. 1958. a. Bol.$.30. Direccion de
Estadistica y Censo, Contraloria General, Apartado
5213, Panama 5, Panama. circ. 900.

318   VE
ESTADISTICA VENEZOLANA. irreg. Direccion
General de Estadistica y Censos Nacionales,
Caracas, Venezuela.

318   GT
ESTADISTICAS DE VEHICULOS EN
CIRCULACION EN GUATEMALA. 1972. irreg.
free. Direccion General de Estadistica, Ministerio
de Economia, 8A Calle no. 9-55, Zona 1,
Guatemala, Guatemala.

EXPORT STATISTICS OF AFGHANISTAN/
IHSA'IYAH-I AMUAL-I SADIRATI-I
AFGHANISTAN. see BUSINESS AND
ECONOMICS — Abstracting, Bibliographies,
Statistics

EXTERNAL TRADE STATISTICS OF GAMBIA.
see BUSINESS AND ECONOMICS —
Abstracting, Bibliographies, Statistics

315.4   II
FACTS ABOUT HARYANA. 1967. irreg. Director of
Public Relations, Chandigarh, India. stat. circ.
3,000.

FARM BUSINESS STATISTICS FOR SOUTH EAST
ENGLAND. see AGRICULTURE — Abstracting,
Bibliographies, Statistics

FERTILISER ASSOCIATION OF INDIA.
FERTILISER STATISTICS. see
AGRICULTURE — Abstracting, Bibliographies,
Statistics

310   FJ   ISSN 0071-4828
FIJI. BUREAU OF STATISTICS. ANNUAL
STATISTICAL ABSTRACT. 1969. a. $1.50. Bureau
of Statistics, Box 2221, Suva, Fiji. circ. 500.

310   FJ
FIJI. BUREAU OF STATISTICS. STATISTICAL
NEWS. no. 14, 1979. irreg. Bureau of Statistics, Box
2221, Suva, Fiji.

311   FI   ISSN 0355-2063
FINLAND. TILASTOKESKUS. KASIKIRJOJA/
FINLAND. STATISTIKCENTRALEN.
HANDBOECKER/FINLAND. CENTRAL
STATISTICAL OFFICE. HANDBOOKS. (Text in
Finnish and sometimes in Swedish and English)
1971. irreg. price varies. Tilastokeskus, Annankatu
44, SF-00100 Helsinki 10, Finland (Subscr. to:
Government Printing Centre, Box 516, SF-00100
Helsinki 10, Finland)

311   FI   ISSN 0355-208X
FINLAND. TILASTOKESKUS. TILASTOLLISIA
TIEDONANTOJA/FINLAND.
STATISTIKCENTRALEN. STATISTISKA
MEDDELANDEN/FINLAND. CENTRAL
STATISTICAL OFFICE. STATISTICAL
SURVEYS. (Text in Finnish and Swedish; some
summaries in English) 1906. irreg. price varies.
Tilastokeskus, Annankatu 44, SF-00100 Helsinki 10,
Finland (Subscr. to: Government Printing Centre,
Box 516, SF-00100 Helsinki 10, Finland)

381   US
FLORIDA. DEPARTMENT OF COMMERCE.
ANNUAL REPORT. 1969. a. free. ‡ Department
of Commerce, Secretary of Commerce, 107 West
Gaines St., Tallahassee, FL 32304. stat. circ.
controlled. (processed)

318   US   ISSN 0071-6022
FLORIDA STATISTICAL ABSTRACT. 1967. a.
$9.75 pap. University of Florida, College of Business
Administration, Bureau of Economic and Business
Research, Gainesville, FL 32611. Ed. Ralph B.
Thompson. circ. 2,200.

301   GW   ISSN 0373-7632
FLORISTISCH-SOZIOLOGISCHE
ARBEITSGEMEINSCHAFT. MITTEILUNGEN.
1928. irreg. price varies. ‡ Floristisch-Soziologische
Arbeitsgemeinschaft, Untere Karspuele 2, 3400
Goettingen, W. Germany (B.R.D.) Eds. H.
Dierschke, H. Haeupler, R. Tuexen. bk. rev.

310   US
FOUNDATION 500. a. $34.50. (Foundation Research
Service) Douglas M. Lawson Associates, 39 E. 51st
St., 3rd Fl., New York, NY 10022. Ed. David M.
Lawson.

314   FR
FRANCE. INSTITUT NATIONAL DE LA
STATISTIQUE ET DES ETUDES
ECONOMIQUES. COLLECTIONS. SERIE R,
REGIONS. 1969. irreg. 80 F. for 4 nos. Institut
National de la Statistique et des Etudes
Economiques, c/o Observatoire Economique de
Paris, Tour Gamma A, 195 rue de Bercy, 75582
Paris Cedex 12, France.

314   GW   ISSN 0071-9218
FRANKFURT AM MAIN. STATISTISCHES AMT
UND WAHLAMT. STATISTISCHES
JAHRBUCH. 1951. a. DM.16. Statistisches Amt
und Wahlamt, Kurt Schumacherstr. 41, 6000
Frankfurt 1, W. Germany (B.R.D.) circ. 1,300.

FROZEN FISHERY PRODUCTS. ANNUAL
SUMMARY. see FISH AND FISHERIES —
Abstracting, Bibliographies, Statistics

GAMBIA. CENTRAL STATISTICS
DEPARTMENT. EDUCATION STATISTICS. see
EDUCATION — Abstracting, Bibliographies,
Statistics

GAMBIA. CENTRAL STATISTICS
DEPARTMENT. TOURIST STATISTICS. see
TRAVEL AND TOURISM — Abstracting,
Bibliographies, Statistics

312   US   ISSN 0362-3904
GEORGIA. STATE DATA CENTER. CITY
POPULATION ESTIMATES. irreg. State Data
Center, 270 Washington St., S.W., Atlanta, GA
30334. Key Title: City Population Estimates.

317   US   ISSN 0085-1043
GEORGIA STATISTICAL ABSTRACT. 1951.
biennial. $14. University of Georgia, College of
Business Administration, Division of Research,
Athens, GA 30602. Ed. Lorena Akioka. circ. 1,200.

GERMANY (FEDERAL REPUBLIC, 1949-)
BUNDESANSTALT FUER ARBEIT.
BERUFSBERATUNG. ERGEBNISSE DER
BERUFSBERATUNGSSTATISTIK. see BUSINESS
AND ECONOMICS — Abstracting, Bibliographies,
Statistics

GERMANY (FEDERAL REPUBLIC, 1949-)
STATISTISCHES BUNDESAMT.
AUSGEWAEHLTE ZAHLEN FUER DIE
BAUWIRTSCHAFT. see BUILDING AND
CONSTRUCTION — Abstracting, Bibliographies,
Statistics

GERMANY (FEDERAL REPUBLIC, 1949-)
STATISTISCHES BUNDESAMT.
AUSSENHANDEL. REIHE 7:
SONDERBEITRAEGE. see BUSINESS AND
ECONOMICS — Abstracting, Bibliographies,
Statistics

GERMANY (FEDERAL REPUBLIC, 1949-)
STATISTISCHES BUNDESAMT. FACHSERIE
AUSLANDSSTATISTIK, REIHE 2:
PRODUZIERENDE GEWERBE IM AUSLAND.
see BUSINESS AND ECONOMICS —
Abstracting, Bibliographies, Statistics

GERMANY (FEDERAL REPUBLIC, 1949-)
STATISTISCHES BUNDESAMT. FACHSERIE
AUSLANDSSTATISTIK, REIHE 4: LOEHNE
UND GEHAELTER IM AUSLAND. see
BUSINESS AND ECONOMICS — Abstracting,
Bibliographies, Statistics

GERMANY (FEDERAL REPUBLIC, 1949-)
STATISTISCHES BUNDESAMT. FACHSERIE
AUSLANDSSTATISTIK, REIHE 5: PREISE UND
PREISINDIZES IM AUSLAND. see BUSINESS
AND ECONOMICS — Abstracting, Bibliographies,
Statistics

GERMANY (FEDERAL REPUBLIC, 1949-)
STATISTISCHES BUNDESAMT. FACHSERIE 1,
REIHE 1: GEBIET UND BEVOELKERUNG. see
POPULATION STUDIES — Abstracting,
Bibliographies, Statistcs

GERMANY (FEDERAL REPUBLIC, 1949-)
STATISTISCHES BUNDESAMT. FACHSERIE 2,
4: ZAHLUNGSSCHWIERIGKEITEN. see
BUSINESS AND ECONOMICS — Abstracting,
Bibliographies, Statistics

GERMANY (FEDERAL REPUBLIC, 1949-)
STATISTISCHES BUNDESAMT. FACHSERIE 3,
REIHE 2: BETRIEBS-, ARBEITS- UND
EINKOMMENSVERHAELTNISSE. see
AGRICULTURE — Abstracting, Bibliographies,
Statistics

GERMANY (FEDERAL REPUBLIC, 1949-)
STATISTISCHES BUNDESAMT. FACHSERIE 4,
REIHE 3.1: PRODUKTION IM
PRODUZIERENDEN GEWERBE. see BUSINESS
AND ECONOMICS — Abstracting, Bibliographies,
Statistics

GERMANY (FEDERAL REPUBLIC, 1949-)
STATISTISCHES BUNDESAMT. FACHSERIE 5,
REIHE 1: BAUTAETIGKEIT. see BUILDING
AND CONSTRUCTION — Abstracting,
Bibliographies, Statistics

GERMANY (FEDERAL REPUBLIC, 1949-)
STATISTISCHES BUNDESAMT. FACHSERIE 5,
REIHE 2: BEWILLIGUNGEN IM SOZIALEN
WOHNUNGSBAU. see BUILDING AND
CONSTRUCTION — Abstracting, Bibliographies,
Statistics

GERMANY (FEDERAL REPUBLIC, 1949-)
STATISTISCHES BUNDESAMT. FACHSERIE 6,
REIHE 3: EINZELHANDEL. see BUSINESS
AND ECONOMICS — Abstracting, Bibliographies,
Statistics

GERMANY (FEDERAL REPUBLIC, 1949-)
STATISTISCHES BUNDESAMT. FACHSERIE 6,
REIHE 5: WAHRENVERKEHR MIT BERLIN
(WEST) see BUSINESS AND ECONOMICS —
Abstracting, Bibliographies, Statistics

GERMANY (FEDERAL REPUBLIC, 1949-) STATISTISCHES BUNDESAMT. FACHSERIE 6, REIHE 6: WAHRENVERKEHR MIT DER DEUTSCHEN DEMOKRATISCHEN REPUBLIK UND BERLIN (OST) see *BUSINESS AND ECONOMICS — Abstracting, Bibliographies, Statistics*

GERMANY (FEDERAL REPUBLIC, 1949-) STATISTISCHES BUNDESAMT. FACHSERIE 7, REIHE 1: ZUSAMMENFASSENDE UEBERSICHTEN FUER DEN AUSSENHANDEL. see *BUSINESS AND ECONOMICS — Abstracting, Bibliographies, Statistics*

GERMANY (FEDERAL REPUBLIC, 1949-) STATISTISCHES BUNDESAMT. FACHSERIE 7, REIHE 2: AUSSENHANDEL NACH WAREN UND LAENDERN (SPEZIALHANDEL) see *BUSINESS AND ECONOMICS — Abstracting, Bibliographies, Statistics*

GERMANY (FEDERAL REPUBLIC, 1949-) STATISTISCHES BUNDESAMT. FACHSERIE 7, REIHE 3: AUSSENHANDEL NACH LAENDERN UND WARENGRUPPEN (SPEZIALHANDEL) see *BUSINESS AND ECONOMICS — Abstracting, Bibliographies, Statistics*

GERMANY (FEDERAL REPUBLIC, 1949-) STATISTISCHES BUNDESAMT. FACHSERIE 8, REIHE 2: EISENBAHNVERKEHR. see *TRANSPORTATION — Abstracting, Bibliographies, Statistics*

GERMANY (FEDERAL REPUBLIC, 1949-) STATISTISCHES BUNDESAMT. FACHSERIE 8, REIHE 3.3: STRASSENVERKEHRSUNFAELLE. see *TRANSPORTATION — Abstracting, Bibliographies, Statistics*

GERMANY (FEDERAL REPUBLIC, 1949-) STATISTISCHES BUNDESAMT. FACHSERIE 8, REIHE 4: BINNESCHIFFAHRT. see *TRANSPORTATION — Abstracting, Bibliographies, Statistics*

GERMANY (FEDERAL REPUBLIC, 1949-) STATISTISCHES BUNDESAMT. FACHSERIE 8, REIHE 5: SEESCHIFFAHRT. see *TRANSPORTATION — Abstracting, Bibliographies, Statistics*

GERMANY (FEDERAL REPUBLIC, 1949-) STATISTISCHES BUNDESAMT. FACHSERIE 8, REIHE 6: LUFTVERKEHR. see *TRANSPORTATION — Abstracting, Bibliographies, Statistics*

GERMANY (FEDERAL REPUBLIC, 1949-) STATISTISCHES BUNDESAMT. FACHSERIE 9, REIHE 2: AKTIENMAERKTE. see *BUSINESS AND ECONOMICS — Abstracting, Bibliographies, Statistics*

GERMANY (FEDERAL REPUBLIC, 1949-) STATISTISCHES BUNDESAMT. FACHSERIE 10. RECHTSPFLEGE. see *LAW — Abstracting, Bibliographies, Statistics*

GERMANY (FEDERAL REPUBLIC, 1949-) STATISTISCHES BUNDESAMT. FACHSERIE 11: BILDUNG UND KULTUR. see *EDUCATION — Abstracting, Bibliographies, Statistics*

GERMANY (FEDERAL REPUBLIC, 1949-) STATISTISCHES BUNDESAMT. FACHSERIE 12, REIHE 1: AUSGEWAEHLTE ZAHLEN FUER DAS GESUNDHEITSWESEN. see *PUBLIC HEALTH AND SAFETY — Abstracting, Bibliographies, Statistics*

GERMANY (FEDERAL REPUBLIC, 1949-) STATISTISCHES BUNDESAMT. FACHSERIE 16, REIHE 3: ARBEITERVERDIENSTE IM HANDWERK. see *BUSINESS AND ECONOMICS — Abstracting, Bibliographies, Statistics*

GERMANY (FEDERAL REPUBLIC, 1949-) STATISTISCHES BUNDESAMT. FACHSERIE 17, REIHE 1: PREISE UND PREISINDIZES FUER DIE LAND- UND FORSTWIRTSCHAFT. see *AGRICULTURE — Abstracting, Bibliographies, Statistics*

GERMANY (FEDERAL REPUBLIC, 1949-) STATISTISCHES BUNDESAMT. FACHSERIE 17, REIHE 2: PREISE UND PREISINDIZES FUER GEWERBLICHE PRODUKTE. ERZEUGERPREISE. see *BUSINESS AND ECONOMICS — Abstracting, Bibliographies, Statistics*

GERMANY (FEDERAL REPUBLIC, 1949-) STATISTISCHES BUNDESAMT. FACHSERIE 17, REIHE 3: INDEX DER GRUNDSTOFFRPREISE. see *BUSINESS AND ECONOMICS — Abstracting, Bibliographies, Statistics*

GERMANY (FEDERAL REPUBLIC, 1949-) STATISTISCHES BUNDESAMT. FACHSERIE 17, REIHE 4: MESSZAHLEN FUER BAULEISTUNGSPREISE UND PREISINDIZES FUER BAUWERKE. see *BUSINESS AND ECONOMICS — Abstracting, Bibliographies, Statistics*

GERMANY (FEDERAL REPUBLIC, 1949-) STATISTISCHES BUNDESAMT. FACHSERIE 17, REIHE 8: PREISE UND PREISINDIZES FUER DEN EIN- UND AUSFUHR. see *BUSINESS AND ECONOMICS — Abstracting, Bibliographies, Statistics*

GERMANY (FEDERAL REPUBLIC, 1949-) STATISTISCHES BUNDESAMT. FACHSERIE 17, REIHE 9: PREISE FUER VERKEHRSLEISTUNGEN. see *TRANSPORTATION — Abstracting, Bibliographies, Statistics*

GERMANY (FEDERAL REPUBLIC, 1949-) STATISTISCHES BUNDESAMT. FACHSERIE 17, REIHE 10: INTERNATIONALER VERGLEICH DER PREISE FUER DIE LEBENSERHALTUNG. see *BUSINESS AND ECONOMICS — Abstracting, Bibliographies, Statistics*

GERMANY (FEDERAL REPUBLIC, 1949-) STATISTISCHES BUNDESAMT. WARENVERZEICHNIS FUER DIE AUSSENHANDELSSTATISTIK. see *BUSINESS AND ECONOMICS — Abstracting, Bibliographies, Statistics*

318 GW
GERMANY (FEDERAL REPUBLIC, 1949-) STATISTISCHES BUNDESAMT. LAENDERBERICHTE. (Subseries of its Allgemeine Statistik des Auslandes; avail. for approx. 30 countries) irreg. price varies. W. Kohlhammer-Verlag GmbH, Abt. Veroeffentlichungen des Statistischen Bundesamtes, Philipp-Reis-Str. 3, Postfach 421120, 6500 Mainz 42, W. Germany (B.R.D.)

315 GW
GERMANY (FEDERAL REPUBLIC, 1949-) STATISTISCHES BUNDESAMT. LAENDERKURZBERICHTE. (Subseries of its Allgemeine Statistik des Auslandes; reports on over 100 countries available) 4/mo. DM.4.80 each. W. Kohlhammer-Verlag GmbH, Abt. Veroeffentlichungen des Statistischen Bundesamtes, Philipp-Reis-Str. 3, Postfach 421120, 6500 Mainz 42, W. Germany (B.R.D.)

310 GW ISSN 0072-4114
GERMANY (FEDERAL REPUBLIC, 1949-) STATISTISCHES BUNDESAMT. ZAHLENKOMPASS/STATISTICAL COMPASS/ BOUSSOLE DES CHIFFRES/COMPAS DE CIFRAS. (Editions in English, French, German and Spanish) a. DM.2. W. Kohlhammer-Verlag GmbH, Abt. Veroeffentlichungen des Statistischen Bundesamtes, Philipp-Reis-Str. 3, Postfach 421120, 6500 Mainz 42, W. Germany (B.R.D.)

GHANA. CENTRAL BUREAU OF STATISTICS. ECONOMIC SURVEY. see *BUSINESS AND ECONOMICS — Abstracting, Bibliographies, Statistics*

316 MF
GLANURES. (Text in English and French) a. free. Ministry of Information and Broadcasting, Government Centre, 6th Fl., Port Louis, Mauritius. circ. 5,000.

310 SW ISSN 0072-5110
GOETEBORGS UNIVERSITET. STATISTISKA INSTITUTIONEN. SKRIFTSERIE. PUBLICATIONS. (Text in Swedish or English) 1954. irreg., no. 16, 1974. price varies. Fack, S-104 05 Stockholm, Sweden.

314 UK ISSN 0072-5730
GREAT BRITAIN. CENTRAL STATISTICAL OFFICE. ANNUAL ABSTRACT OF STATISTICS. 1948. a. £8.50. Central Statistical Office, Great George St., London SW1P 3AQ, England (Avail. from: Open University Educational Enterprises Ltd., 12 Cofferidge Close, Stony Stratford, Milton Keynes MK11 1BY England)

314 UK ISSN 0261-1791
GREAT BRITAIN. CENTRAL STATISTICAL OFFICE. GUIDE TO OFFICIAL STATISTICS. 1976. biennial. £18.50. Central Statistical Office, Great George St., London SW1P 3AQ, England (Avail. from: Open University Educational Enterprises Ltd., 12 Cofferidge Close, Stony Stratford, Milton Keynes MK11 1BY, England)

314 UK ISSN 0261-1783
GREAT BRITAIN. CENTRAL STATISTICAL OFFICE. REGIONAL TRENDS. 1965. a. £11.95. Central Statistical Office, Great George St., London SW1P 3AQ, England (Avail. from: Open University Educational Enterprises Ltd., 12 Cofferidge Close, Stony Stratford, Milton Keynes MK11 1BY England) charts. stat.
Former titles: Great Britain. Central Statistical Office. Regional Statistics (ISSN 0308-146X); Great Britain. Central Statistical Office Abstracts of Regional Statistics (ISSN 0072-5749)

311 UK ISSN 0072-5757
GREAT BRITAIN. CENTRAL STATISTICAL OFFICE. RESEARCH SERIES. 1968. irreg. price varies. Central Statistical Office, Great George St., London SW1P 3AQ, England (Avail. from: Open University Educational Enterprises Ltd., 12 Cofferidge Close, Stony Stratford, Milton Keynes MK11 1BY, England)

311 UK ISSN 0081-8313
GREAT BRITAIN. CENTRAL STATISTICAL OFFICE. STUDIES IN OFFICIAL STATISTICS. irreg. price varies. Central Statistical Office, Great George St., London SW1P 3AQ, England (Avail. from: Open University Educational Enterprises Ltd., 12 Cofferidge Close, Stony Stratford, Milton Keynes MK11 1BY, England)

GREECE. NATIONAL STATISTICAL SERVICE. ANNUAL STATISTICAL SURVEY OF MINES, QUARRIES AND SALTERNS. see *MINES AND MINING INDUSTRY — Abstracting, Bibliographies, Statistics*

GREECE. NATIONAL STATISTICAL SERVICE. EDUCATION STATISTICS. see *EDUCATION — Abstracting, Bibliographies, Statistics*

GREECE. NATIONAL STATISTICAL SERVICE. EMPLOYMENT SURVEY CONDUCTED IN URBAN AND SEMI-URBAN AREAS. see *BUSINESS AND ECONOMICS — Abstracting, Bibliographies, Statistics*

GREECE. NATIONAL STATISTICAL SERVICE. RESULTS OF SEA FISHERY SURVEY BY MOTOR VESSELS. see *FISH AND FISHERIES — Abstracting, Bibliographies, Statistics*

GREECE. NATIONAL STATISTICAL SERVICE. SHIPPING STATISTICS. see *TRANSPORTATION — Abstracting, Bibliographies, Statistics*

GREECE. NATIONAL STATISTICAL SERVICE. SOCIAL WELFARE AND HEALTH STATISTICS. see *SOCIAL SERVICES AND WELFARE — Abstracting, Bibliographies, Statistics*

GREECE. NATIONAL STATISTICAL SERVICE. STATISTICS ON CIVIL, CRIMINAL AND REFORMATORY JUSTICE. see *CRIMINOLOGY AND LAW ENFORCEMENT — Abstracting, Bibliographies, Statistics*

STATISTICS

GREECE. NATIONAL STATISTICAL SERVICE. STATISTICS ON THE DECLARED INCOME OF LEGAL ENTITIES AND ITS TAXATION. see *BUSINESS AND ECONOMICS — Abstracting, Bibliographies, Statistics*

GREECE. NATIONAL STATISTICAL SERVICE. STATISTICS ON THE DECLARED INCOME OF PHYSICAL PERSONS AND ITS TAXATION. see *BUSINESS AND ECONOMICS — Abstracting, Bibliographies, Statistics*

GREECE. NATIONAL STATISTICAL SERVICE. TRANSPORT AND COMMUNICATION STATISTICS. see *TRANSPORTATION — Abstracting, Bibliographies, Statistics*

312   GU   ISSN 0085-1310
GUAM STATISTICAL ANNUAL REPORT. 1959. a. free. ‡ Department of Public Health and Social Services, Office of Vital Statistics, Box 2816, Agana, Guam. circ. controlled.

318   GT
GUATEMALA. DIRECCION GENERAL DE ESTADISTICA. ANUARIO ESTADISTICO. 1970. a. free. ‡ Direccion General de Estadistica, Ministerio de Economia, 8A Calle no. 9-55, Zona 1, Guatemala, Guatemala. charts. illus.

317.281   GT   ISSN 0017-5048
GUATEMALA. DIRECCION GENERAL DE ESTADISTICA. BOLETIN ESTADISTICO. 1967. a. free. ‡ Direccion General de Estadistica, Ministerio de Economia, 8A Calle no. 9-55, Zona 1, Guatemala, Guatemala. charts. mkt. circ. 2,500.

318   GT
GUATEMALA. DIRECCION GENERAL DE ESTADISTICA. DEPARTAMENTO DE ESTUDIOS ESPECIALES Y ESTADISTICAS CONTINUAS. PRODUCCION, VENTA Y OTROS INGRESOS DE LA ENCUESTA ANUAL DE LA INDUSTRIA MANUFACTURERA FABRIL. Variant title: Encuesta Industrial. a. Direccion General de Estadistica, Departamento de Estudios Especiales y Estadisticas Continuas, Guatemala, Guatemala.

317.29   HT   ISSN 0017-6788
HAITI. INSTITUT HAITIEN DE STATISTIQUE. BULLETIN TRIMESTRIEL DE STATISTIQUE. 1951. irreg; no. 104, 1976. free. Institut Haitien de Statistique, Departement des Finances et des Affaires Economique, Cite de l'Exposition, Blvd. Harry Truman, Port-au-Prince, Haiti. Dir. Jacques Vilgrain. charts. mkt. stat. circ. 500.

315   II   ISSN 0072-9728
HANDBOOK OF BASIC STATISTICS OF MAHARASHTRA STATE. (Editions in English and Marathi) 1960. a. Rs.1.30 for English edt.; Rs. 2.45 for Marathi edt. Directorate of Economics and Statistics, D.D. Bldg, Old Custom House, Bombay 400023, India. Ed. S. M. Vidwans.

HANDBUCH DER OESTERREICHISCHEN SOZIALVERSICHERUNG. see *INSURANCE — Abstracting, Bibliographies, Statistics*

317   US   ISSN 0073-2664
HISTORICAL STATISTICS OF THE UNITED STATES. 1949. irreg. special bicentennial edition, issued 1976, 6.00. U. S. Bureau of the Census, Dept. of Commerce, Washington, DC 20233 (Orders to: Supt. of Documents, Washington, DC 20402)

318   HO
HONDURAS EN CIFRAS. 1971. irreg. free. Banco Central de Honduras, Departamento de Estudios Economicos, Tegucigalpa, Honduras.

315   HK
HONG KONG. ANNUAL DIGEST OF STATISTICS. (Text in English) 1978. irreg. HK.$60. Census and Statistics Department, Kai Tak Commercial Bldg., 317 Des Voeux Rd., Central, Hong Kong, Hong Kong (Subscr. to: Government Information Service, Beaconsfield House, Queen's Rd., Central, Victoria, Hong Kong) charts. stat.

HONG KONG. ESTIMATES OF GROSS DOMESTIC PRODUCT. see *BUSINESS AND ECONOMICS — Abstracting, Bibliographies, Statistics*

362   US   ISSN 0090-6662
HOSPITAL STATISTICS; DATA FROM AMERICAN HOSPITAL ASSOCIATION ANNUAL SURVEY. 1946. a. $18.75 to non-members; members $15. American Hospital Association, 840 N. Lake Shore Dr., Chicago, IL 60611. Ed. Tamara Schiller. charts. stat. index. circ. 12,000. Key Title: Hospital Statistics.
Supersedes (since 1976): Survey of Hospital Charges (ISSN 0360-9316)

314   HU
HUNGARY. KOZPONTI STATISZTIKAI HIVATAL. TORTENETI STATISZTIKAI TANULMANYOK. 1975. irreg. Statisztikai Kiado Vallalat, Kaszas U.10-12, P.O.B.99, 1300 Budapest 3, Hungary.
Supersedes its: Torteneti Statisztikai Evkonyv.

947 314   HU   ISSN 0303-5344
HUNGARY. KOZPONTI STATISZTIKAI HIVATAL. TERULETI STATISZTIKAI EVKONYV. a. 112 Ft. Statisztikai Kiado Vallalat, Kaszas U.10-12., P.O.B.99, 1300 Budapest 3, Hungary.

312   US   ISSN 0362-9279
IDAHO. DEPARTMENT OF HEALTH AND WELFARE. ANNUAL SUMMARY OF VITAL STATISTICS. Cover title: Vital Statistics, Idaho. a. Department of Health and Welfare, Bureau of Research and Statistics, Boise, ID 83702. Key Title: Annual Summary of Vital Statistics (Boise)

317   US   ISSN 0073-456X
IDAHO STATISTICAL ABSTRACT. 1966. irreg.(approx. every 5 years) price varies. University of Idaho, Center for Business Development and Research, Moscow, ID 83843. Ed. Shaikh M. Ghazanfar. index. circ. 750. (back issues avail.)

IMPORTS STATISTICS OF AFGHANISTAN/IHSA'IYAH-I AMUAL-I VARIDATI-I AFGHANISTAN. see *BUSINESS AND ECONOMICS — Abstracting, Bibliographies, Statistics*

315   II   ISSN 0073-6163
INDIA. CENTRAL STATISTICAL ORGANIZATION. SAMPLE SURVEYS OF CURRENT INTEREST IN INDIA; REPORT. (Text in English) 1949-50. biennial. Rs.41.50($14.94) Central Statistical Organization, Sardar Patel Bhavan, Parliament St., New Delhi 110001, India. adv. circ. 400.

315   II   ISSN 0073-6155
INDIA. CENTRAL STATISTICAL ORGANIZATION. STATISTICAL ABSTRACT. (Text in English) 1950. a. Rs.163($58.68) Central Statistical Organization, Sardar Patel Bhavan, Sansad Marg, New Delhi 110001, India.

INDIAN PETROLEUM AND PETROCHEMICALS STATISTICS. see *PETROLEUM AND GAS — Abstracting, Bibliographies, Statistics*

310   II   ISSN 0073-6686
INDIAN STATISTICAL INSTITUTE. ANNUAL REPORT. 1932-1933. a. ‡ 203 Barrackpore Trunk Rd., Calcutta 700035, India. circ. 2,000.

310   II
INDIAN STATISTICAL INSTITUTE. LECTURE NOTES. 1961. irreg. price varies. Macmillan Company of India Ltd., c/o Indian Statistical Institute, 203 Barrackpore Trunk Rd., Calcutta 700035, India. (also avail. in microfilm)
Formerly: Indian Statistical Institute. Research and Training School. Publications.

310 519   II   ISSN 0073-6716
INDIAN STATISTICAL INSTITUTE. STATISTICS AND PROBABILITY SERIES. RESEARCH MONOGRAPHS.* irreg. Statistical Publishing Society, 204/1 Barrackpore Trunk Rd., Calcutta 700035, India. Eds. P. C. Mahalanobis, C. R. Rao.

310   II   ISSN 0073-6724
INDIAN STATISTICAL SERIES.* irreg, 1970, nos. 24, 25. price varies. Indian Statistical Institute, 203 Barrackpore Trunk Rd., Calcutta 700035, India.

INDICE DO BRASIL/BRAZILIAN INDEX YEARBOOK. see *BUSINESS AND ECONOMICS — Economic Situation And Conditions*

INDONESIA STATISTICS. see *BUSINESS AND ECONOMICS — Abstracting, Bibliographies, Statistics*

INDONESIA TOURIST STATISTICS. see *TRAVEL AND TOURISM — Abstracting, Bibliographies, Statistics*

311   US   ISSN 0538-3579
INTER-AMERICAN STATISTICAL INSTITUTE. COMMITTEE ON IMPROVEMENT OF NATIONAL STATISTICS. REPORT. (Editions in English, Spanish) 1951. irreg.; 12th, Lima, Peru, 1975 (pub. 1977) $4. Inter-American Statistical Institute, 1725 I St. N.W., Washington, DC 20006. circ. 1,500.

INTERNATIONAL COTTON INDUSTRY STATISTICS. see *TEXTILE INDUSTRIES AND FABRICS — Abstracting, Bibliographies, Statistics*

INTERNATIONAL MONETARY FUND. GOVERNMENT FINANCE STATISTICS YEARBOOK. see *BUSINESS AND ECONOMICS — Abstracting, Bibliographies, Statistics*

310   NE   ISSN 0074-8609
INTERNATIONAL STATISTICAL INSTITUTE. BULLETIN. PROCEEDINGS OF THE BIENNIAL SESSIONS. (Text in English, French, German, Italian, Spanish) 1895. biennial, 42nd, 1979, Manila. price varies. International Statistical Institute, Prinses Beatrixlaan 428, Box 950, 2270 AZ Voorburg, Netherlands. Indexed: Math.R.Stat.Theor.Meth.Abstr.
Edited by local organizing committees in the respective host countries of the session

310   NE
INTERNATIONAL STATISTICAL INSTITUTE. PROCEEDINGS OF SPECIALIZED MEETINGS. irreg. price varies. International Statistical Institute, Prinses Beatrixlaan 428, Box 950, 2270 AZ Voorburg, Netherlands.

INTERNATIONAL TEXTILE MACHINERY SHIPMENT STATISTICS. see *TEXTILE INDUSTRIES AND FABRICS — Abstracting, Bibliographies, Statistics*

IRAN YEARBOOK; a complete directory and encyclopedia of facts, data and statistics on Iran. see *HISTORY — History Of The Near East*

315   IQ
IRAQ. CENTRAL STATISTICAL ORGANIZATION. ANNUAL ABSTRACT OF STATISTICS. (Text in Arabic and English) a. ID.2($6) Central Statistical Organization, Publication and Public Relations Department, Baghdad, Iraq. stat. circ. 2,000.

319   IQ
IRAQ. CENTRAL STATISTICAL ORGANIZATION. STATISTICAL POCKET BOOK. a. ID.250. Central Statistical Organization, Baghdad, Iraq. stat.

314   IE   ISSN 0075-062X
IRELAND (EIRE) CENTRAL STATISTICS OFFICE. TUARASCAIL AR STAIDREAMH BEATHA. REPORT ON VITAL STATISTICS. 1864. a. 70p. Central Statistics Office, Earlsfort Terrace, Dublin 2, Ireland. circ. 800.

315.69   IS   ISSN 0081-4679
ISRAEL. CENTRAL BUREAU OF STATISTICS. STATISTICAL ABSTRACT OF ISRAEL/SHENATON STATISTI LE-YISRAEL. (Text in English and Hebrew) 1949-50. irreg., latest issue, no. 30, 1979. $20. Central Bureau of Statistics, Box 13015, Jerusalem, Israel.

310   IS   ISSN 0075-1111
ISRAEL. CENTRAL BUREAU OF STATISTICS. VITAL STATISTICS. (Subseries of its Special Series) (Text in Hebrew and English) 1965/66(publ. 1969) irreg., latest issue, no. 609, 1977. I£110. Central Bureau of Statistics, Box 13015, Jerusalem, Israel.

ITALY. ISTITUTO CENTRALE DI STATISTICA. ANNUARIO DI STATISTICHE INDUSTRIALI. see *BUSINESS AND ECONOMICS — Abstracting, Bibliographies, Statistics*

ITALY. ISTITUTO CENTRALE DI STATISTICA. ANNUARIO STATISTICO DEL COMMERCIO INTERNO. see *BUSINESS AND ECONOMICS — Abstracting, Bibliographies, Statistics*

ITALY. ISTITUTO CENTRALE DI STATISTICA. ANNUARIO STATISTICO DELLA NAVIGAZIONE MARITTIMA. see *TRANSPORTATION — Abstracting, Bibliographies, Statistics*

314 IT ISSN 0390-6434
ITALY. ISTITUTO CENTRALE DI STATISTICA. BOLLETINO MENSILE DI STATISTICA. irreg. price varies. Istituto Centrale di Statistica, Via Cesare Balbo 16, 00100 Rome, Italy.

ITALY. ISTITUTO CENTRALE DI STATISTICA. STATISTICA ANNUALE DEL COMMERCIO CON L'ESTERO. TOMO I. see *BUSINESS AND ECONOMICS — Abstracting, Bibliographies, Statistics*

ITALY. ISTITUTO CENTRALE DI STATISTICA. STATISTICA ANNUALE DEL COMMERCIO CON L'ESTERO. TOMO II. see *BUSINESS AND ECONOMICS — Abstracting, Bibliographies, Statistics*

314 NE
JAARBOEK EINDHOVEN. 1967. a. free. Gemeentebestuur, Stadhuis, Eindhoven, Netherlands. stat. illus. index.

JAMAICA. DEPARTMENT OF STATISTICS. ABSTRACT OF BUILDING AND CONSTRUCTION STATISTICS. see *BUILDING AND CONSTRUCTION*

317 JM
JAMAICA. DEPARTMENT OF STATISTICS. DEMOGRAPHIC STATISTICS. 1971. a; latest issue, 1973. $1. Department of Statistics, 9 Swallowfield Road, Kingston 5, Jamaica. stat. (back issues avail)

332 JM ISSN 0026-9638
JAMAICA. DEPARTMENT OF STATISTICS. MONETARY STATISTICS REPORT. 1957. a. Jam.$1. Department of Statistics, 9 Swallowfield Rd., Kingston 5, Jamaica. (processed)

318 JM
JAMAICA. DEPARTMENT OF STATISTICS. NATIONAL INCOME AND PRODUCT. (In Two Parts: Preliminary Report and Detailed Tables) 1975. a. Department of Statistics, 9 Swallowfield Road, Kingston 5, Jamaica.

319 JM
JAMAICA. DEPARTMENT OF STATISTICS. POCKETBOOK OF STATISTICS. 1978. irreg. Department of Statistics, 9 Swallowfield Rd., Kingston 5, Jamaica.

317 JM
JAMAICA. DEPARTMENT OF STATISTICS. STATISTICAL ABSTRACT. 1972. a. (published 9 months after year to which it relates) Jam.$3. Department of Statistics, 9 Swallowfield Rd, Kingston 5, Jamaica.
Formerly: Jamaica. Department of Statistics. Annual Abstract of Statistics (ISSN 0075-2983)

310 JA ISSN 0075-3173
JAPAN. BUREAU OF STATISTICS. ANNUAL REPORT ON FAMILY INCOME AND EXPENDITURES. a. 3600 Yen. Bureau of Statistics - Japan. Tokeikyoku, Office of the Prime Minister, 95 Wakamatsu-cho, Shinjuku-ku, Tokyo 162, Japan (Subscr. to Government Publications Service Center, 1-2-1 Kasumigaseki, Chiyoda-ku, Tokyo 100, Japan) circ. 600.

JAPAN. BUREAU OF STATISTICS. EMPLOYMENT STATUS SURVEY/JAPAN. SORIFU. TOKEIKYOKU. SHUGYOKOZO KIHON CHOSA. see *BUSINESS AND ECONOMICS — Abstracting, Bibliographies, Statistics*

312 JA ISSN 0075-3270
JAPAN. MINISTRY OF HEALTH AND WELFARE. STATISTICS AND INFORMATION DEPARTMENT. VITAL STATISTICS. Alternate title: Vital Statistics Japan. 1899. a. (in 2 vols.) 16200 Yen. Ministry of Health and Welfare, Statistics and Information Department, 42 Honmura-cho, Ichigaya, Shinjuku-ku, Tokyo 162, Japan (Order from: Health & Welfare Statistics Association, c/o Mezon Azabu, 5-13-14, Roppongi, Minato-ku, Tokyo, Japan)

315 JA ISSN 0075-3335
JAPAN STATISTICAL YEARBOOK. (Text in English and Japanese) 1949. a. 6800 Yen. Bureau of Statistics - Japan. Tokeikyoku, Office of the Prime Minister, 95 Wakamatsu-cho, Shinjuku-ku, Tokyo 162, Japan (Subscribe to: Government Publications Service Center, 1-2-1 Kasumigaseki, Chiyoda-Ku, Tokyo 100, Japan) circ. 650.

315 JO ISSN 0075-4013
JORDAN. DEPARTMENT OF STATISTICS. ANNUAL STATISTICAL YEARBOOK. (Text in Arabic and English) 1950. a. $15 incl. its External Trade Statistics. Department of Statistics, Amman, Jordan.

312.2 JO
JORDAN. DEPARTMENT OF STATISTICS. MORBIDITY STATISTICS. (Text in Arabic and English) 1969. a. $5. Department of Statistics, Amman, Jordan.

312 JO
JORDAN. DEPARTMENT OF STATISTICS. MULTI-PURPOSE HOUSEHOLD SURVEY. (Text in Arabic and English) 1972. a. $5. Department of Statistics, Amman, Jordan.

JYVASKYLA STUDIES IN COMPUTER SCIENCE, ECONOMICS AND STATISTICS. see *COMPUTER TECHNOLOGY AND APPLICATIONS*

316 NR
KADUNA STATE STATISTICAL YEARBOOK. 1975. a. Ministry of Economic Planning and Rural Development, Economic Planning Division, P.M. Bag 2032, Kaduna, Nigeria.
Continues: North Central State Statistical Yearbook.

316.69 NR
KANO STATE STATISTICAL YEAR BOOK. Economic Planning Division, Kano, Nigeria. stat.
Continues: Northern Nigeria. Ministry of Economic Planning. Statistical Year Book.

KENTUCKY. DEPARTMENT FOR HUMAN RESOURCES. SELECTED VITAL STATISTICS AND PLANNING DATA. see *PUBLIC HEALTH AND SAFETY — Abstracting, Bibliographies, Statistics*

316 KE ISSN 0300-2373
KENYA. CENTRAL BUREAU OF STATISTICS. AGRICULTURAL CENSUS (LARGE FARM AREAS) price varies. Central Bureau of Statistics, Ministry of Finance and Planning, Box 30266, Nairobi, Kenya (Orders to: Government Printing and Stationery Office, Box 30128, Nairobi, Kenya)

316 KE
KENYA. CENTRAL BUREAU OF STATISTICS. EMPLOYMENT AND EARNINGS IN THE MODERN SECTOR. a, latest 1972/73. price varies. Central Bureau of Statistics, Ministry of Finance and Planning, Box 30266, Nairobi, Kenya (Orders to: Government Printing and Stationery Office, Box 30128, Nairobi, Kenya)

310 DK
KOBENHAVNS STATISTISKE AARBOG; for Koebenhavn, Frederiksberg og Gentofte samt Hovedstadsregionen. (Text in Danish and English) 1923. a. Kr.30. Statistiske Kontor - Copenhagen Statistical Office, Nyropsgade 7, 1640 Copenhagen V, Denmark (Subscr. to: Danske Boghandleres Kommissionsanstalt, Siljangade 6-8, 2300 Copenhagen S, Denmark) Ed. Sigurd Haunso. circ. 3,000.

315 KO
KOREA(REPUBLIC). POPULATION & HOUSING CENSUS REPORT. 1960. quinquennial. 2003 Won. Bureau of Statistics, Economic Planning Board, 90 Gyeongun-Dong, Jongro-Gu, Seoul, S. Korea. Ed. Heung-Koo Kang. circ. 1,500.

315.367 KU
KUWAIT. CENTRAL STATISTICAL OFFICE. ANNUAL STATISTICAL ABSTRACT. (Text in Arabic and English) 1965. a. Central Statistical Office, Box 15, Kuwait. circ. 450.
Supersedes: Kuwait. Central Statistical Office. Monthly Statistical Bulletin (ISSN 0023-5768)

LABOUR FORCE SITUATION IN INDONESIA: PRELIMINARY FIGURES/KEADAAN ANGKATAN KERJA DI INDONESIA: ANGKA SEMENTARA. see *BUSINESS AND ECONOMICS — Abstracting, Bibliographies, Statistics*

315 LE ISSN 0075-8388
LEBANON. DIRECTION CENTRALE DE LA STATISTIQUE. RECUEIL DE STATISTIQUES LIBANAISES.* (Text in Arabic and French) 1963. a. free. Direction Centrale de la Statistique, Ministere du Plan, Beirut, Lebanon.

310 US
LECTURE NOTES IN STATISTICS. 1980. irreg., vol. 8, 1981. price varies. Springer-Verlag, 175 Fifth Ave., New York, NY 10010 (Also Berlin, Heidelberg, Vienna) Ed.Bd. (reprint service avail. from ISI)

315 LY ISSN 0075-9287
LIBYA. CENSUS AND STATISTICAL OFFICE. STATISTICAL ABSTRACT. (Text in Arabic and English) 1958. a. free. Census and Statistical Department, Ministry of Planning, Tripoli, Libya.

314.21 UK ISSN 0308-0900
LONDON FACTS AND FIGURES. (Subseries of: Greater London Council. Publication) 1972. irreg. free. Greater London Council, County Hall, London SE1 7PB, England.

314 LU ISSN 0076-1575
LUXEMBOURG. SERVICE CENTRAL DE LA STATISTIQUE ET DES ETUDES ECONOMIQUES. ANNUAIRE STATISTIQUE. 1955. a. 800 Fr. Service Central de la Statistique et des Etudes Economiques, B.P. 304, Luxembourg, Luxembourg.
Before 1962: Luxembourg. Office de la Statistique Generale. Annuaire Statistique.

312 LU
LUXEMBOURG. SERVICE CENTRAL DE LA STATISTIQUE ET DES ETUDES ECONOMIQUES. ANNUAIRE STATISTIQUE RETROSPECTIF. (Subseries of its Annuaire Statistique) 1960. every 10 yrs.; latest 1973. 800 Fr. Service Central de la Statistique et des Etudes Economiques, B.P. 304, Luxembourg, Luxembourg.

310 LU ISSN 0076-1591
LUXEMBOURG. SERVICE CENTRAL DE LA STATISTIQUE ET DES ETUDES ECONOMIQUES. COLLECTION D ET M: DEFINITIONS ET METHODES. 1966. irreg., no. 6, 1979. 100 Fr. per no. Service Central de la Statistique et des Etudes Economiques, B.P. 304, Luxembourg, Luxembourg.

338 MG
MALAGASY REPUBLIC. INSTITUT NATIONAL DE LA STATISTIQUE ET DE LA RECHERCHE ECONOMIQUE. RECENSEMENT INDUSTRIEL. 1969. a. or biennial. FMG.810. Institut National de la Statistique et de la Recherche Economique, Ministere des Finances et du Plan, B.P. 485, Antananarivo, Malagasy Republic.

310 MW ISSN 0076-3276
MALAWI. NATIONAL STATISTICAL OFFICE. HOUSEHOLD INCOME AND EXPENDITURE SURVEY. 1968. irreg. K.8.50($9.50) ‡ National Statistical Office, P.O. Box 333, Zomba, Malawi.

310 MW ISSN 0076-3284
MALAWI. NATIONAL STATISTICAL OFFICE. NATIONAL ACCOUNTS REPORT. 1967. a. K.3.50($3.90) ‡ National Statistical Office, P.O. Box 333, Zomba, Malawi.

316 MW
MALAWI STATISTICAL YEARBOOK. 1965. a. (after 1972) K.6.50. ‡ National Statistical Office, P.O. Box 333, Zomba, Malawi.
Supersedes: Malawi. National Statistical Office. Compendium of Statistics (ISSN 0076-3268)

315.95 MY ISSN 0542-3570
MALAYSIA. DEPARTMENT OF STATISTICS. ANNUAL BULLETIN OF STATISTICS. (Text in English) 1964. a, latest 1977. M.$3. Department of Statistics - Jabatan Perangkaan, Jalan Young, Kuala Lumpur 10-01, Malaysia.

MALAYSIA. DEPARTMENT OF STATISTICS. VITAL STATISTICS: PENINSULAR MALAYSIA. see *POPULATION STUDIES — Abstracting, Bibliographies, Statistcs*

314 MM ISSN 0081-4733
MALTA. CENTRAL OFFICE OF STATISTICS. ANNUAL ABSTRACT OF STATISTICS. a. £0.50($1.16) Central Office of Statistics, Auberge de Castille, Valletta, Malta (Subscr. to: Department of Information, Auberge de Castille, Valletta, Malta)

MANUFACTURING INDUSTRIES OF CANADA: SUB-PROVINCIAL AREAS/INDUSTRIES MANUFACTURIERES DU CANADA: NIVEAU INFRAPROVINCIAL. see *BUSINESS AND ECONOMICS — Abstracting, Bibliographies, Statistics*

MARKET RESEARCH HANDBOOK. see *BUSINESS AND ECONOMICS — Abstracting, Bibliographies, Statistics*

310 IT ISSN 0026-1424
METRON; rivista internazionale di statistica. (Text in several languages) 1920. irreg. $10. Universita degli Studi di Roma, Facolta di Scienze Statistiche Demografiche Ed Attuariali, Istituto di Statistica e Ricerca Sociale "C.Gini", Citta Universitaria, 00100 Rome, Italy. adv. bk. rev. abstr. charts. stat. index. cum.ind. irregularly. Indexed: Biol.Abstr.

MEXICO. DIRECCION GENERAL DE ESTADISTICA. ESTADISTICA INDUSTRIAL ANUAL. see *BUSINESS AND ECONOMICS — Abstracting, Bibliographies, Statistics*

317 US ISSN 0076-8308
MICHIGAN STATISTICAL ABSTRACT. 1955. a. $11.50. Michigan State University, Graduate School of Business Administration, Division of Research, Berkey Hall, East Lansing, MI 48824. Ed. David I. Verway.

318 BL
MINAS GERAIS, BRAZIL. DEPARTAMENTO DE ESTRADAS DE RODAGEM. SERVICO DE TRANSITO. ESTATISTICA DE TRAFEGO. 1969. a. free. Departamento de Estradas de Rodagem, Servico de Transito, Av. Andradas, 1120, 30000 Belo Horizonte, Brazil. stat. circ. 1,000.

319 VB
MONTSERRAT. STATISTICAL OFFICE. STATISTICAL DIGEST. no. 2, 1975. a. Statistical Office, Plymouth, Montserrat.

319 MR
MOROCCO. DIRECTION DE LA STATISTIQUE. STATISTIQUES RETROSPECTIVES. a. DH.16. Direction de la Statistique, B.P. 178, Rabat, Morocco.

312.2 NZ ISSN 0548-9911
MORTALITY AND DEMOGRAPHIC DATA. a. price varies. National Health Statistics Centre, P.O. Box 6314 Te Aro, Wellington 1, New Zealand. circ. controlled.

371.82 US ISSN 0097-9325
NEBRASKA STATISTICAL HANDBOOK. biennial. $4. Department of Economic Development, Division of Research, Box 94666, State Capitol, Lincoln, NE 68509.

634.9 NE
NEDERLANDSE BOSSTATISTIEK. 1952. irreg., latest 1971 (covers 1964-68) fl.9. Centraal Bureau voor de Statistiek, Prinses Beatrixlaan 428, Voorburg, Netherlands (Orders to: Staatsuitgeverij, Christoffel Plantijnstraat, The Hague, Netherlands) circ. 650.

315.49 NP
NEPAL. CENTRAL BUREAU OF STATISTICS. STATISTICAL POCKET BOOK. (Text in English) 1974. irreg. Rs.3.50. Central Bureau of Statistics, Kathmandu, Nepal. illus. circ. 2,000.

NETHERLANDS. CENTRAAL BUREAU VOOR DE STATISTIEK. PER LEERLING BESCHIKBAAR GESTELDE BEDRAGEN VOOR HET LAGER ONDERWIJS. AMOUNTS PER PUPIL PROVIDED FOR PRIMARY EDUCATION. see *EDUCATION — Abstracting, Bibliographies, Statistics*

314 NE
NETHERLANDS. CENTRAAL BUREAU VOOR DE STATISTIEK. REGIONAAL STATISTISCH ZAKBOEK. a. Centraal Bureau voor de Statistiek, Prinses Beatrixlaan 428, Voorburg, Netherlands (Orders to: Staatsuitgeverij, Christoffel Plantijnstraat, The Hague, Netherlands)

310 NE ISSN 0077-7064
NETHERLANDS. CENTRAAL BUREAU VOOR DE STATISTIEK. STATISTICAL STUDIES. 1953. irreg. price varies. Centraal Bureau voor de Statistiek, Prinses Beatrixlaan 428, Voorburg, Netherlands (Orders to: Staatsuitgeverij, Christoffel Plantijnstraat, The Hague, Netherlands)

NETHERLANDS. CENTRAAL BUREAU VOOR DE STATISTIEK. STATISTIEK VAN DE INVESTERINGEN IN VASTE ACTIVA IN DE NIJVERHEID. STATISTICS ON FIXED CAPITAL FORMATION IN INDUSTRY. see *BUSINESS AND ECONOMICS — Abstracting, Bibliographies, Statistics*

310 NE ISSN 0077-6947
NETHERLANDS. CENTRAAL BUREAU VOOR DE STATISTIEK. STATISTISCH BULLETIN. irreg. fl.45.50. Centraal Bureau voor de Statistiek, Voorburg, Netherlands, Netherlands (Orders to: Staatsuitgeverij, Christoffel Plantijnstraat, The Hague, Netherlands) circ. 3,500.

310 NE ISSN 0077-7463
NETHERLANDS. CENTRAAL BUREAU VOOR DE STATISTIEK. STATISTISCH ZAKBOEK. POCKET YEARBOOK. (Text in Dutch and English) 1944-46. a. fl.16. Centraal Bureau voor de Statistiek, Prinses Beatrixlaan 428, Voorburg, Netherlands (Orders to: Staatsuitgeverij, Christoffel Plantijnstraat, The Hague, Netherlands)

NETHERLANDS. CENTRAAL BUREAU VOOR DE STATISTIEK. STATISTISCHE ONDERZOEKINGEN. see *BUSINESS AND ECONOMICS — Abstracting, Bibliographies, Statistics*

314 NE
NETHERLANDS. CENTRALE COMMISSIE VOOR DE STATISTIEK. JAARVERSLAG. a. Centrale Commissie voor de Statistiek, The Hague, Netherlands.

317 NA ISSN 0077-6661
NETHERLANDS ANTILLES. BUREAU VOOR DE STATISTIEK. STATISTISCH JAARBOEK.* a. fl.6. Bureau voor de Statistiek, Fort Amsterdam, Netherlands Antilles.

312 US ISSN 0095-5523
NEW HAMPSHIRE VITAL STATISTICS. a. (with q. supplements) Bureau of Vital Records and Health Statistics, Concord, NH 03301.

338.4 NN
NEW HEBRIDES. BUREAU OF STATISTICS. BUSINESS LICENSES. PATENTS DELIVEREES. (Text and summaries in English and French) 1971. a. free. Bureau of Statistics, Port Vila, New Hebrides. stat. circ. 250. (processed)

387 NN
NEW HEBRIDES. BUREAU OF STATISTICS. OVERSEAS SHIPPING AND AIRCRAFT STATISTICS/STATISTIQUES DE NAVIGATION MARITIME ET AERIENNE INTERNATIONALES. (Text and Summaries in English and French) 1971. a. free. Bureau of Statistics, Port Vila, New Hebrides. stat. circ. 250. (processed)

317 US ISSN 0077-8575
NEW MEXICO STATISTICAL ABSTRACT. 1970. biennial. University of New Mexico, Bureau of Business and Economic Research, Albuquerque, NM 87131.

317 US ISSN 0077-9334
NEW YORK (STATE) DIVISION OF THE BUDGET. NEW YORK STATE STATISTICAL YEARBOOK. 1967. biennial. $5. Division of the Budget, State Capitol, Albany, NY 12224. index. circ. 6,000.

319 NZ ISSN 0077-9652
NEW ZEALAND. DEPARTMENT OF STATISTICS. ANNUAL REPORT OF THE GOVERNMENT STATISTICIAN. 1955. a. NZ.$0.65. Department of Statistics, Private Bag, Wellington, New Zealand (Subscr. to: Government Printing Office, Publications, Private Bag, Wellington, New Zealand)

NEW ZEALAND. DEPARTMENT OF STATISTICS. PART B: WAGES AND LABOUR. see *BUSINESS AND ECONOMICS — Labor And Industrial Relations*

310 NZ
NEW ZEALAND. DEPARTMENT OF STATISTICS. POPULATION CENSUS: INTERNAL MIGRATION. 1971. quinquennial. NZ.$3. Department of Statistics, Private Bag, Wellington, New Zealand.

NEW ZEALAND. DEPARTMENT OF STATISTICS. POPULATION CENSUS. LOCATION AND INCREASE OF POPULATION. PART A: POPULATION SIZE AND DISTRIBUTION. see *POPULATION STUDIES — Abstracting, Bibliographies, Statistcs*

NEW ZEALAND. DEPARTMENT OF STATISTICS. POPULATION CENSUS. LOCATION AND INCREASE OF POPULATION. PART B: POPULATION DENSITY. see *POPULATION STUDIES — Abstracting, Bibliographies, Statistcs*

319 NZ ISSN 0110-4586
NEW ZEALAND. DEPARTMENT OF STATISTICS. VITAL STATISTICS. a. NZ.$2.50. Department of Statistics, Private Bag, Wellington, New Zealand (Subscr. to: Government Printing Office, Publications, Private Bag, Wellington, New Zealand)

NEW ZEALAND. MINISTRY OF ENERGY. MINES DIVISION. ANNUAL RETURNS OF PRODUCTION FROM QUARRIES AND MINERAL PRODUCTION STATISTICS. see *MINES AND MINING INDUSTRY — Abstracting, Bibliographies, Statistics*

316 NR ISSN 0078-0626
NIGERIA. FEDERAL OFFICE OF STATISTICS. ANNUAL ABSTRACT OF STATISTICS. (Text in English) a. 12s. 6d. Federal Office of Statistics, Lagos, Nigeria.

314 SW ISSN 0078-1088
NORDISK STATISTISK AARSBOK/YEARBOOK OF NORDIC STATISTICS. (Subseries of: Nordisk Utredningsserie) (Text in Swedish and English) 1962. a. Nordiska Raadet - Nordic Council, Box 19506, S-104 32 Stockholm, Sweden. Ed. Harry de Sharengrad.

314 DK ISSN 0332-6527
NORDISK STATISTISK SKRIFTSERIE/ STATISTICAL REPORTS OF THE NORDIC COUNTRIES. (Text in Scandinavian languages; editions occasionally in English) 1954. irreg., no. 36, 1979. price varies. Nordisk Statistisk Sekretariat - Nordic Statistical Secretariat, Postbok 2550, DK-2100 Copenhagen OE, Denmark. circ. 1,000-4,500.

NORTH DAKOTA. JUDICIAL COUNCIL. ANNUAL REPORT. see *LAW*

NORWAY. STATISTISK SENTRALBYRAA. ALKOHOL OG ANDRE RUSMIDLER/ ALCOHOL AND DRUGS. see *DRUG ABUSE AND ALCOHOLISM — Abstracting, Bibliographies, Statistics*

844   STATISTICS

NORWAY. STATISTISK SENTRALBYRAA. ARBEIDSMARKEDSTATISTIKK/LABOUR MARKET STATISTICS. see *BUSINESS AND ECONOMICS — Abstracting, Bibliographies, Statistics*

NORWAY. STATISTISK SENTRALBYRAA. ELECTRISITESSTATISTIKK/ELECTRICITY STATISTICS. see *ENERGY — Abstracting, Bibliographies, Statistics*

NORWAY. STATISTISK SENTRALBYRAA. FAMILIE STATISTIKK/FAMILY STATISTICS. see *POPULATION STUDIES — Abstracting, Bibliographies, Statistcs*

NORWAY. STATISTISK SENTRALBYRAA. FOLKEMENGDEN ETTER ALDER OG EKTESKAPELIG STATUS/POPULATION BY AGE AND MARITAL STATUS. see *POPULATION STUDIES — Abstracting, Bibliographies, Statistcs*

NORWAY. STATISTISK SENTRALBYRAA. FORRETNINGS- OG SPAREBANKER/ COMMERCIAL AND SAVINGS BANKS. see *BUSINESS AND ECONOMICS — Abstracting, Bibliographies, Statistics*

NORWAY. STATISTISK SENTRALBYRAA. FRAMSKRIVING AV FOLKEMENGDEN: REGIONALE TALL/POPULATION PROJECTIONS: REGIONAL FIGURES. see *POPULATION STUDIES — Abstracting, Bibliographies, Statistcs*

NORWAY. STATISTISK SENTRALBYRAA. HELSEPERSONELLSTATISTIKK. see *MEDICAL SCIENCES — Abstracting, Bibliographies, Statistics*

NORWAY. STATISTISK SENTRALBYRAA. HELSESTATISTIKK/HEALTH STATISTICS. see *PUBLIC HEALTH AND SAFETY — Abstracting, Bibliographies, Statistics*

NORWAY. STATISTISK SENTRALBYRAA. INDUSTRISTATISTIKK/INDUSTRIAL STATISTICS. see *BUSINESS AND ECONOMICS — Abstracting, Bibliographies, Statistcs*

NORWAY. STATISTISK SENTRALBYRAA. JORDBRUKSSTATISTIKK/AGRICULTURAL STATISTICS. see *AGRICULTURE — Abstracting, Bibliographies, Statistics*

NORWAY. STATISTISK SENTRALBYRAA. KOMMUNE OG FYLKESTINGS VALGET/ MUNICIPAL AND COUNTY ELECTIONS. see *PUBLIC ADMINISTRATION — Abstracting, Bibliographies, Statistics*

NORWAY. STATISTISK SENTRALBYRAA. KREDITTMARKED STATISTIKK/CREDIT MARKET STATISTICS. see *BUSINESS AND ECONOMICS — Abstracting, Bibliographies, Statistics*

NORWAY. STATISTISK SENTRALBYRAA. KRIMINALSTATISTIKK/CRIMINAL STATISTICS: PRISONERS. see *CRIMINOLOGY AND LAW ENFORCEMENT — Abstracting, Bibliographies, Statistics*

NORWAY. STATISTISK SENTRALBYRAA. LOENNSSTATISTIKK/WAGE STATISTICS. see *BUSINESS AND ECONOMICS — Abstracting, Bibliographies, Statistics*

NORWAY. STATISTISK SENTRALBYRAA. NASJONALREGNSKAPL NATIONAL ACCOUNTS. see *BUSINESS AND ECONOMICS — Abstracting, Bibliographies, Statistics*

NORWAY. STATISTISK SENTRALBYRAA. OEKONOMISK UTSYN/ECONOMIC SURVEY. see *BUSINESS AND ECONOMICS — Abstracting, Bibliographies, Statistics*

NORWAY. STATISTISK SENTRALBYRAA. REISELIVSTATISKK/STATISTICS ON TRAVEL. see *TRAVEL AND TOURISM — Abstracting, Bibliographies, Statistics*

NORWAY. STATISTISK SENTRALBYRAA. SAMFERDSELSSTATISTIKK/TRANSPORT AND COMMUNICATION STATISTICS. see *TRANSPORTATION — Abstracting, Bibliographies, Statistics*

NORWAY. STATISTISK SENTRALBYRAA. SIVILRETTSSTATISTIKK/CIVIL JUDICIAL STATISTICS. see *CRIMINOLOGY AND LAW ENFORCEMENT — Abstracting, Bibliographies, Statistics*

NORWAY. STATISTISK SENTRALBYRAA. SKUGSTATSTIKK/FORESTRY STATISTICS. see *FORESTS AND FORESTRY — Abstracting, Bibliographies, Statistics*

314   NO   ISSN 0078-1932
NORWAY. STATISTISK SENTRALBYRAA. STATISTISK AARBOK/STATISTICAL YEARBOOK. (Subseries of its Norges Offisielle Statistikk) (Text in Norwegian and English) 1880. a. Kr.25. Statistisk Sentralbyraa, Box 8131 Dep., Oslo 1, Norway. circ. 25,000.

NORWAY. STATISTISK SENTRALBYRAA. STORTINGSVALG/PARLIAMENTARY ELECTIONS. see *PUBLIC ADMINISTRATION — Abstracting, Bibliographies, Statistics*

NORWAY. STATISTISK SENTRALBYRAA. UTDANNINGSSTATISTIKK: EDUCATIONAL STATISTICS. see *EDUCATION — Abstracting, Bibliographies, Statistics*

NORWAY. STATISTISK SENTRALBYRAA. UTENRIKSHANDEL/EXTERNAL TRADE. see *BUSINESS AND ECONOMICS — Abstracting, Bibliographies, Statistics*

NORWAY. STATISTISK SENTRALBYRAA. VAREHANDELSSTATISTIKK/WHOLESALE AND RETAIL TRADE STATISTICS. see *BUSINESS AND ECONOMICS — Abstracting, Bibliographies, Statistics*

319   AT   ISSN 0085-4441
OFFICIAL YEAR BOOK OF NEW SOUTH WALES. 1906. a. Aus.$9. Australian Bureau of Statistics, N.S.W. Office, St. Andrews House, Sydney Square, George St., Sydney, N.S.W. 2000, Australia.

665 338.2   AT   ISSN 0472-7584
OIL AND AUSTRALIA; the figures behind the facts. 1958. a. free. Australian Institute of Petroleum Ltd., 227 Collins St., Melbourne, Vic. 3000, Australia. Ed. G. Warden. stat.

317   CN
ONTARIO STATISTICS. 1964. a. price varies. Ministry of Treasury, Economics and Intergovernmental Affairs, Ontario Statistical Centre, Toronto M7A 1Z1, Ont., Canada. Ed. Shashi N. Sharma. circ. 6,000.
    Formerly: Ontario Statistical Review (ISSN 0078-5113)

312   US
OREGON PUBLIC HEALTH STATISTICS REPORT. Cover title: Oregon State Health Division, Vital Statistics Annual Report. 1960. a. $3. ‡ State Health Division, c/o State Office, 1400 S.W. Fifth Ave., Portland, OR 97201. stat. circ. 600.

ORGANIZATION FOR ECONOMIC COOPERATION AND DEVELOPMENT. INTER-REGIONAL DRY CARGO MOVEMENTS/MOUVEMENTS INTERREGIONAUX DE CARGAISONS SECHES. see *BUSINESS AND ECONOMICS — Abstracting, Bibliographies, Statistics*

315   PK   ISSN 0078-799X
PAKISTAN. STATISTICS DIVISION. KEY TO OFFICIAL STATISTICS.* (Text in English) 1962. irreg. Statistics Division, 63 Muslim Abab, Karachi 5, Pakistan (Order from: Manager of Publications, Government of Pakistan, 2nd Floor, Ahmad Chamber, Tariq Rd., P.E.C.H.S., Karachi 29, Pakistan)

315   PK   ISSN 0078-8007
PAKISTAN. STATISTICS DIVISION. N S S SERIES. (No. 1 also called National Sample Survey) 1960. irreg. Statistics Division, 63 Muslim Abab, Karachi 5, Pakistan (Order from: Manager of Publications, Government of Pakistan, 2nd Floor, Ahmad Chamber, Tariq Rd., P.E.C.H.S., Karachi 29, Pakistan)

315   PK
PAKISTAN. STATISTICS DIVISION. STATISTICAL YEARBOOK. (Text in English) 1952. a. Statistics Division, 63 Muslim Abab, Karachi 5, Pakistan (Order from: Manager of Publications, Government of Pakistan, 2nd Floor, Ahmad Chamber, Tariq Rd., P.E.C.H.S., Karachi 29, Pakistan)
    Supersedes: Pakistan. Statistical Division. Statistical Yearbook & Pakistan. Central Statistical Office. Statistical Yearbook (ISSN 0078-8023)

PAKISTAN INSTITUTE OF DEVELOPMENT ECONOMICS. STATISTICAL PAPERS. see *BUSINESS AND ECONOMICS — Abstracting, Bibliographies, Statistics*

315   PK   ISSN 0078-8473
PAKISTAN STATISTICAL ASSOCIATION. PROCEEDINGS. (Text in English) a. Rs.2. Pakistan Statistical Association, Institute of Statistics, University of the Punjab, Lahore, Pakistan.

318   PN   ISSN 0078-8996
PANAMA EN CIFRAS. 1953. a. Bl.0.35. Direccion de Estadistica y Censo, Contraloria General, Apartado 5213, Panama 5, Panama. circ. 1,000.

310   PP
PAPUA NEW GUINEA. BUREAU OF STATISTICS. HOUSEHOLD EXPENDITURE SURVEY. PRELIMINARY BULLETIN. (Text in English) 1975. irreg. Bureau of Statistics, P.O. Wards Strip, Papua New Guinea. Ed. J. J. Shadlow. charts. circ. 385.

319.5   PP
PAPUA NEW GUINEA. BUREAU OF STATISTICS. SUMMARY OF STATISTICS. (Text in English) 1970/71. a. Bureau of Statistics, P.O. Wards Strip, Papua New Guinea. illus. circ. 1,093.

PAPUA NEW GUINEA. BUREAU OF STATISTICS. WORKERS' COMPENSATION CLAIMS. see *INSURANCE — Abstracting, Bibliographies, Statistics*

338.4   US   ISSN 0556-3593
PENNSYLVANIA. DEPARTMENT OF COMMERCE. BUREAU OF STATISTICS. STATISTICS BY INDUSTRY AND SIZE OF ESTABLISHMENT. (Subseries of Pennsylvania Industrial Census Series) 1957. a. free. Department of Commerce, Bureau of Statistics, Research and Planning, 630B Health & Welfare Bldg., Harrisburg, PA 17120. Ed. W. Ronald Kresge. illus. stat. circ. 1,000. Key Title: Statistics by Industry and Size of Establishment (Harrisburg)

338.4   US   ISSN 0476-1103
PENNSYLVANIA STATISTICAL ABSTRACT. 1958. a. $5. Department of Commerce, Bureau of Statistics, Research and Planning, 630B Health & Welfare Bldg., Harrisburg, PA 17120 (Orders to: Bureau of Management Services, State Book Store, Box 1365, Harrisburg, PA 17125) stat.

PENSION PLANS IN CANADA/REGIMES DE PENSIONS AU CANADA. see *INSURANCE — Abstracting, Bibliographies, Statistics*

315   PH
PHILIPPINES. NATIONAL CENSUS AND STATISTICS OFFICE. SPECIAL REPORT. 1970. irreg., no. 5, 1975. National Census and Statistics Office, Ramon Magsaysay Blvd., Box 779, Manila, Philippines.

315   PH   ISSN 0554-0186
PHILIPPINES. NATIONAL CENSUS AND STATISTICS OFFICE. VITAL STATISTICAL REPORT. a, latest 1974. P.18($6) National Census and Statistics Office, Ramon Magsaysay Blvd., Box 779, Manila, Philippines.

319 AT ISSN 0079-2446
POCKET YEAR BOOK OF SOUTH AUSTRALIA. 1917. a. free. Australian Bureau of Statistics, South Australian Office, Box 2272 G.P.O., Adelaide, S.A. 5001, Australia.

319 AT ISSN 0085-4921
POCKET YEARBOOK OF NEW SOUTH WALES. 1913. a. Aus.$1 ea. Australian Bureau of Statistics, N.S.W. Office, St. Andrews House, Sydney Square, George St., Sydney, N.S.W. 2000, Australia.

314 PL ISSN 0079-2586
POLAND. GLOWNY URZAD STATYSTYCZNY. ATLAS STATYSTYCZNY. STATISTICAL ATLAS.* irreg. Glowny Urzad Statystyczny, Al. Niepodleglosci 208, 00-925 Warsaw, Poland.

314 PL ISSN 0079-2608
POLAND. GLOWNY URZAD STATYSTYCZNY. MALY ROCZNIK STATYSTYCZNY. CONCISE STATISTICAL YEARBOOK. (Editions in Polish, Russian, English, French and German) 1958. a. 30 Zl. Glowny Urzad Statystyczny, Al. Niepodleglosci 208, 00-925 Warsaw, Poland.

314.38 PL
POLAND. GLOWNY URZAD STATYSTYCZNY. MALY ROCZNIK STATYSTYKI MIEDZYNARODOWEJ. (Subseries of its: Seria Statystyka Miedzynarodowa) 1972. irreg. 125 Zl. Glowny Urzad Statystyczny, Departament Wydawaictw, Al. Niepodleglosci 208, Warsaw, Poland. illus. stat.

314 PL ISSN 0079-2756
POLAND. GLOWNY URZAD STATYSTYCZNY. ROCZNIK STATYSTYCZNY POWIATOW. STATISTICAL YEARBOOK OF COUNTIES. (Subseries of its: Statystyka Polski) 1970. a. 40 Zl. Glowny Urzad Statystyczny, Al. Niepodleglosci 208, 00-925 Warsaw, Poland.

314 PL ISSN 0079-2780
POLAND. GLOWNY URZAD STATYSTYCZNY. ROCZNIK STATYSTYCZNY. STATISTICAL YEARBOOK. (Text in Polish; summaries in English and Russian) 1921. a. Glowny Urzad Statystyczny, Al. Niepodleglosci 208, 00-925 Warsaw, Poland.

310 PL ISSN 0079-273X
POLAND. GLOWNY URZAD STATYSTYCZNY. ROCZNIK STATYSTYKI MIEDZYNARODOWEJ. YEARBOOK OF INTERNATIONAL STATISTICS.* irreg. Glowny Urzad Statystyczny, Al. Niepodleglosci 208, 00-925 Warsaw, Poland.

311 PL ISSN 0079-2845
POLAND. GLOWNY URZAD STATYSTYCZNY. STUDIA I PRACE STATYSTYCZNE. (Text in Polish; summaries in English and Russian) 1966. irreg. Glowny Urzad Statystyczny, Al. Niepodleglosci 208, 00-925 Warsaw, Poland.

310 PL ISSN 0079-2829
POLAND. GLOWNY URZAD STATYSTYCZNY,. ZESZYTY METODYCZNE. 1966. irreg., no. 33, 1979. price varies. Glowny Urzad Statystyczny, Al. Niepodleglosci 208, 00-925 Warsaw, Poland (Dist. by Ars Polona-Ruch, Ul. Krakowskie Przedmiescie 7, Warsaw, Poland)

POPULATION GROWTH IN SEYCHELLES. see POPULATION STUDIES — Abstracting, Bibliographies, Statistcs

POPULATION GROWTH OF IRAN. see POPULATION STUDIES

PORTUGAL. INSTITUTO NACIONAL DE ESTATISTICA. SERVICOS CENTRAIS. ESTATISTICAS DAS SOCIEDADES: CONTINENTE E ILHAS ADJACENTES. see BUSINESS AND ECONOMICS — Production Of Goods And Services

PORTUGAL. INSTITUTO NACIONAL DE ESTATISTICA. SERVICOS CENTRAIS. ESTATISTICAS DOS TRANSPORTES E COMMUNICACOES: CONTINENTE, ACORES E MADEIRA. see TRANSPORTATION

314 PO ISSN 0079-4112
PORTUGAL. INSTITUTO NACIONAL DE ESTATISTICA. ANUARIO ESTATISTICO. 1875. a. $150. Instituto Nacional de Estatistica, Av. Antonio Jose de Almeida, Lisbon 1, Portugal (Orders to: Imprensa Nacional, Casa da Moeda, Direccao Comercial, rua D. Francisco Manuel de Melo 5, Lisbon 1, Portugal)

314 PO
PORTUGAL. INSTITUTO NACIONAL DE ESTATISTICA. SERIE ESTATISTICAS REGIONAIS. 1970. irreg. Esc.70 per issue. Instituto Nacional de Estatistica, Av. Antonio Jose de Almeida, Lisbon, Portugal (Orders to: Imprensa Nacional, Casa da Moeda, Direccao Comercial, rua D. Francisco Manuel de Melo 5, Lisbon 1, Portugal) stat. circ. controlled.

314 PO
PORTUGAL (YEAR) (Editions in English and Portuguese) 1969. irreg. Esc.20. Instituto Nacional de Estatistica, Av. Antonio Jose de Almeida, 1078 Lisbon Codex, Portugal. stat. circ. 10,000 (Portuguese edt.); 1,500 (English edt.)
Formerly (until 1977): Portugal. Instituto Nacional de Estatistica. Servicos Centrais. Sinopse de Dados Estatisticos: Continente e Ilhas Adjacentes.

POULTRY MARKET STATISTICS. see AGRICULTURE — Abstracting, Bibliographies, Statistics

318 VE
PRODUCCION AGRICOLA - PERIODO DE VERANO. 1965. irreg.; latest issue 1976. free. Ministerio de Agricultura y Cria, Direccion de Planificacion y Estadistica, Division de Estadistica, Torre Norte-Piso 11, Centro Simon Bolivar, Caracas, Venezuela.

312 PR ISSN 0555-6511
PUERTO RICO. DIVISION OF DEMOGRAPHIC REGISTRY AND VITAL STATISTICS. ANNUAL VITAL STATISTICS REPORT.* (Text in Spanish and English) a. Division of Demographic Registry and Vital Statistics, San Juan, PR 00901.

QATAR YEARBOOK. see HISTORY — History Of The Near East

317 CN
QUEBEC (PROVINCE) BUREAU OF STATISTICS STATISTIQUES. 1962. q. Can.$15. Editeur Officiel du Quebec, 1283 Bd. Charest ouest, Quebec G1N 2C9, Canada. index. circ. 1,850.
Formerly (until Apr. 1981): Revue Statistique du Quebec (ISSN 0039-0550)

319 AT ISSN 0085-5316
QUEENSLAND POCKET YEARBOOK. 1950. a. Aus.$1.10. Australian Bureau of Statistics, Queensland Office, 345 Ann St., Brisbane, Qld. 4000, Australia. index. circ. 4,850.

319 AT ISSN 0085-5359
QUEENSLAND YEARBOOK. 1937. a. Aus.$6 per no. Australian Bureau of Statistics, Queensland Office, 345 Ann St., Brisbane, Qld. 4000, Australia. index. circ. 3,000.

318 BL
R S EM NUMEROS. 1976. a. Fundacao de Economia e Estatistica, Rua Siqueira Campos 1044, 9000 Porto Alegre, Brazil.

310 II ISSN 0079-9564
RAJASTHAN, INDIA. DIRECTORATE OF ECONOMICS AND STATISTICS. BASIC STATISTICS. (Text in English and Hindi) 1956. a. Rs.3. Directorate of Economics and Statistics, Krishi Bhawan, Jaipur, Rajasthan, India.

REGIONAL BREAKDOWN OF WORLD TRAVEL STATISTICS. see TRAVEL AND TOURISM

REPORT ON PASSENGER ROAD TRANSPORT IN ZAMBIA. see TRANSPORTATION — Abstracting, Bibliographies, Statistics

310 UK ISSN 0143-103X
RETURN OF OUTSTANDING DEBT. 1946. a. £10. Chartered Institute of Public Finance and Accountancy, 1 Buckingham Place, London SW1E 6HS, England. bk. England. stat. (back issues avail.)
Analysis of local authority debt in England and Wales and Scotland

370 US
RHODE ISLAND. DEPARTMENT OF EDUCATION. STATISTICAL TABLE. 1932. a. free. Department of Education, Office of Statistical Services, Roger Williams Bldg., Providence, RI 02908. Ed. Donley R. Taft. stat. circ. controlled. (tabloid format)

314 IT ISSN 0035-7960
ROMA E PROVINCIA ATTRAVERSO LA STATISTICA; dati mensili e annuali. 1956. a. L.800. per no. Camera di Commercio Industria Artigianato e Agricoltura di Roma, Via De'Burro 147, 00186 Rome, Italy. Ed. Dr. Leonida Attili. bk. rev. charts. stat. index. cum.index. circ. controlled.

315 MY ISSN 0080-5203
SABAH. DEPARTMENT OF STATISTICS. ANNUAL BULLETIN OF STATISTICS/SABAH. JABATAN PERANGKAAN. SIARAN PERANGKAAN TAHUNAN. 1964. a, latest 1977. M.$6. Department of Statistics, P.O. Box 500, Kota Kinabalu, Sabah, Malaysia. circ. 465.

310 US
ST. LOUIS STATISTICAL ABSTRACT. 1971. a. $25. University of Missouri-St. Louis, Library, c/o Dana C. Rooks, 8001 Natural Bridge Rd., St. Louis, MO 63121. index. circ. 150.

311 II ISSN 0581-4790
SAMVADADHVAM. (Text in English, Bengali, Hindi) 1956. irreg. ‡ Indian Statistical Institute, 203 Barrackpore Trunk Rd., Calcutta 700035, India. Ed. Bd. bk. rev. bibl, charts. illus. stat. circ. 2,500 (controlled)

SANITARY SERVICES IN TENNESSEE. see PUBLIC HEALTH AND SAFETY — Abstracting, Bibliographies, Statistics

318 AG
SANTIAGO DEL ESTERO. DIRECCION GENERAL DE INVESTIGACIONES ESTADISTICA Y CENSOS. ESTADISTICAS SOCIALES. a. free. Direccion General de Investigaciones Estadistica y Censos, Palacio de los Tribunales, Santiago del Estero, Argentina. Dir. Jose Humberto Alegre. stat.

319 MY ISSN 0080-6447
SARAWAK VITAL STATISTICS. (Text in English) 1966. a, latest 1976. M.$2. ‡ Department of Statistics, Federal Complex, Jalan Simpang Tiga, Kuching, Sarawak, Malaysia.

319 SU
SAUDI ARABIA. CENTRAL DEPARTMENT OF STATISTICS. STATISTICAL YEARBOOK. a. sR.30. Central Department of Statistics, Box 3735, Riyadh, Saudi Arabia.

SAUDI ARABIA. MINISTRY OF EDUCATION. EDUCATIONAL STATISTICS. see EDUCATION — Abstracting, Bibliographies, Statistics

SCHWEIZERISCHE BIBLIOGRAPHIE FUER STATISTIK UND VOLKSWIRTSCHAFT/ BIBLIOGRAPHIE SUISSE DE STATISTIQUE ET D'ECONOMIE POLITIQUE. see BIBLIOGRAPHIES

SCOTLAND. REGISTRAR GENERAL. ANNUAL REPORT. see POPULATION STUDIES — Abstracting, Bibliographies, Statistcs

314 UK
SCOTTISH ABSTRACT OF STATISTICS. 1971. a. £1.45. Scottish Office, Dover House, Whitehall, London SW1A 2AU, England (Avail. from H.M.S.O., c/o Liaison Officer, Atlantic House, Holborn Viaduct, London EC1P 1BN, England) circ. 350.
Superseded in 1971: Digest of Scottish Statistics.

316 SE
SEYCHELLES. PRESIDENT'S OFFICE. STATISTICS DIVISION. CENSUS. irreg. Rs.80. President's Office, Statistics Division, Box 206, Mahe, Seychelles (Subscr. to: Government Printer, Box 205, Union Vale, Mahe, Seychelles)

316 SE
SEYCHELLES. PRESIDENT'S OFFICE. STATISTICS DIVISION. STATISTICAL ABSTRACT. a. Rs.60. President's Office, Statistics Division, Box 206, Mahe, Seychelles (Subscr. to: Government Printer, Box 205, Union Vale, Mahe, Seychelles)

SEYCHELLES. PRESIDENT'S OFFICE. STATISTICS DIVISION. TOURISM AND MIGRATION REPORT. see *TRAVEL AND TOURISM — Abstracting, Bibliographies, Statistics*

310 SL ISSN 0080-9535
SIERRA LEONE IN FIGURES. a. free. Bank of Sierra Leone, P.O. Box 30, Freetown, Sierra Leone.

318 BL
SINOPSE ESTATISTICA DO BRASIL. (Summarizes data from Statistical Yearbook-Anuario Estatistico do Brasil) (Text in Portuguese or English) 1971. biennial. Cr.$80($25) Fundacao Instituto Brasileiro de Geografia e Estatistica, Diretoria de Divulgacao, Centro de Servicos Graficos, Av. Brasil 15671, Lucas ZC-91, Rio de Janeiro RJ, Brazil. charts. illus. circ. 5,000. (back issues avail)

312 NZ
SOCIAL TRENDS IN NEW ZEALAND. 1977. irreg. NZ.$4.50. Department of Statistics, Private Bag, Wellington, New Zealand.

316 SO
SOMALIA IN FIGURES. triennial. Central Statistical Department, State Planning Commission, Mogadishu, Somalia.

SOUTH AFRICA. DEPARTMENT OF AGRICULTURAL ECONOMICS AND MARKETING. DIVISION OF AGRICULTURAL MARKETING RESEARCH. ABSTRACT OF AGRICULTURAL STATISTICS. see *AGRICULTURE — Abstracting, Bibliographies, Statistics*

310 SA
SOUTH AFRICA. DEPARTMENT OF STATISTICS. ANNUAL REPORT OF THE STATISTICS ADVISORY COUNCIL AND OF THE SECRETARY OF STATISTICS. a. R.5.60. Department of Statistics, Private Bag X44, Pretoria 0001, South Africa. stat.

SOUTH AFRICA. DEPARTMENT OF STATISTICS. BUILDING PLANS PASSED AND BUILDINGS COMPLETED. see *BUILDING AND CONSTRUCTION — Abstracting, Bibliographies, Statistics*

531.6 310 SA ISSN 0301-8105
SOUTH AFRICA. DEPARTMENT OF STATISTICS. CENSUS OF ELECTRICITY, GAS AND STEAM. (Report No. 15-01) 1963. a., latest 1977. R.2.40. Department of Statistics, Private Bag X44, Pretoria 0001, South Africa (Orders to: Government Printer, Bosman St., Private Bag X85, Pretoria 0001,South Africa)

SOUTH AFRICA. DEPARTMENT OF STATISTICS. CENSUS OF MANUFACTURING. see *TECHNOLOGY: COMPREHENSIVE WORKS — Abstracting, Bibliographies, Statistics*

SOUTH AFRICA. DEPARTMENT OF STATISTICS. EDUCATION: COLOUREDS AND ASIANS. see *EDUCATION — Abstracting, Bibliographies, Statistics*

SOUTH AFRICA. DEPARTMENT OF STATISTICS. EDUCATION: WHITES. see *EDUCATION — Abstracting, Bibliographies, Statistics*

SOUTH AFRICA. DEPARTMENT OF STATISTICS. LABOUR STATISTICS: WAGE RATES, EARNINGS AND AVERAGE HOURS WORKED IN THE PRINTING AND NEWSPAPER INDUSTRY, ENGINEERING INDUSTRY, BUILDING INDUSTRY AND COMMERCE. see *BUSINESS AND ECONOMICS — Abstracting, Bibliographies, Statistics*

SOUTH AFRICA. DEPARTMENT OF STATISTICS. LOCAL GOVERNMENT STATISTICS. see *PUBLIC ADMINISTRATION — Abstracting, Bibliographies, Statistics*

SOUTH AFRICA. DEPARTMENT OF STATISTICS. MINING: FINANCIAL STATISTICS. see *MINES AND MINING INDUSTRY — Abstracting, Bibliographies, Statistics*

SOUTH AFRICA. DEPARTMENT OF STATISTICS. REPORT ON AGRICULTURAL AND PASTORAL PRODUCTION. see *AGRICULTURE — Abstracting, Bibliographies, Statistics*

SOUTH AFRICA. DEPARTMENT OF STATISTICS. REPORT ON BIRTHS: WHITE, COLOURED AND ASIANS. see *POPULATION STUDIES — Abstracting, Bibliographies, Statistcs*

SOUTH AFRICA. DEPARTMENT OF STATISTICS. REPORT ON MARRIAGES AND DIVORCES: SOUTH AFRICA. see *POPULATION STUDIES — Abstracting, Bibliographies, Statistcs*

SOUTH AFRICA. DEPARTMENT OF STATISTICS. REPORT ON PRICES. see *BUSINESS AND ECONOMICS — Abstracting, Bibliographies, Statistics*

SOUTH AFRICA. DEPARTMENT OF STATISTICS. ROAD TRAFFIC ACCIDENTS. see *TRANSPORTATION — Abstracting, Bibliographies, Statistics*

SOUTH AFRICA. DEPARTMENT OF STATISTICS. STATISTICS OF ADMINISTRATION BOARDS. see *PUBLIC ADMINISTRATION — Abstracting, Bibliographies, Statistics*

SOUTH AFRICA. DEPARTMENT OF STATISTICS. STATISTICS OF HOUSES AND DOMESTIC SERVANTS AND OF FLATS. see *HOUSING AND URBAN PLANNING — Abstracting, Bibliographies, Statistics*

SOUTH AFRICA. DEPARTMENT OF STATISTICS. STATISTICS OF MOTOR AND OTHER VEHICLES. see *TRANSPORTATION — Abstracting, Bibliographies, Statistics*

SOUTH AFRICA. DEPARTMENT OF STATISTICS. STATISTICS OF NEW VEHICLES REGISTERED. see *TRANSPORTATION — Abstracting, Bibliographies, Statistics*

SOUTH AFRICA. DEPARTMENT OF STATISTICS. SURVEY OF THE ACCOUNTS OF COMPANIES IN SECONDARY AND TERTIARY INDUSTRIES. see *BUSINESS AND ECONOMICS — Abstracting, Bibliographies, Statistics*

SOUTH AFRICA. DEPARTMENT OF STATISTICS. SURVEY OF THE ACCOUNTS OF MINING COMPANIES. see *MINES AND MINING INDUSTRY — Abstracting, Bibliographies, Statistics*

SOUTH AFRICA. DEPARTMENT OF STATISTICS. TOURISM AND MIGRATION. see *POPULATION STUDIES — Abstracting, Bibliographies, Statistcs*

SOUTH AFRICA. DEPARTMENT OF STATISTICS. TRANSFERS OF RURAL IMMOVABLE PROPERTY. see *REAL ESTATE — Abstracting, Bibliographies, Statistics*

SOUTH AFRICA; OFFICIAL YEARBOOK OF THE REPUBLIC OF SOUTH AFRICA. see *HISTORY — Abstracting, Bibliographies, Statistics*

316 SA ISSN 0081-2544
SOUTH AFRICAN STATISTICS. (Text in English and Afrikaans) 1968. biennial. R.7.50. Department of Statistics, Private Bag X44, Pretoria 0001, South Africa (Orders to: Government Printer, Bosman St., Private Bag X85, Pretoria 0001,South Africa)
Until 1966: South Africa. Department of Statistics. Statistical Year Book.

319 AT ISSN 0085-6428
SOUTH AUSTRALIAN YEARBOOK. 1966. a. Aus.$6. Australian Bureau of Statistics, South Australian Office, Box 2272, Adelaide, S.A. 5001, Australia.

317.57 US
SOUTH CAROLINA STATISTICAL ABSTRACT. 1972. a. $4.50. Budget and Control Board, Division of Research and Statistical Services, 1028 Sumter St., Suite 201, Columbia, SC 29201. Ed. Barry Strumpf. stat.

SOUTH DAKOTA. DEPARTMENT OF SOCIAL SERVICES. ANNUAL MEDICAL REPORT. see *SOCIAL SERVICES AND WELFARE — Abstracting, Bibliographies, Statistics*

SOUTH DAKOTA. STATE DEPARTMENT OF PUBLIC WELFARE. RESEARCH AND STATISTICS ANNUAL REPORT. see *SOCIAL SERVICES AND WELFARE — Abstracting, Bibliographies, Statistics*

312 US ISSN 0095-4802
SOUTH DAKOTA VITAL STATISTICS ANNUAL REPORT. a. Department of Health, Pierre, SD 57501.

310 NL
SOUTH PACIFIC COMMISSION. STATISTICAL BULLETIN. (Text in English or French) 1973. irreg., no. 15, 1978. free. South Pacific Commission, B.P. D5, Noumea, Cedex, New Caledonia.

317 US
SOUTHEASTERN HISTORICAL STATISTICS. Variant title: Historical Southeastern Statistics. 1961. a. free. ‡ Federal Reserve Bank of Atlanta, Box 1731, Atlanta, GA 30301. circ. 790.
Formerly (until 1978): Statistics on the Developing South (ISSN 0085-672X)

SOVIET ARMED FORCES REVIEW ANNUAL. see *MILITARY*

314 SP
SPAIN. INSTITUTO NACIONAL DE ESTADISTICA. INDICE DEL COSTE DE LA VIDA. 1971. a. Instituto Nacional de Estadistica, Avda. Generalisimo 91, Madrid 18, Spain.

310 US
SPRINGER SERIES IN STATISTICS. 1979. irreg. price varies. Springer-Verlag, 175 Fifth Ave., New York, NY 10010 (Also Berlin, Heidelberg, Vienna) Ed.Bd. (reprint service avail. from ISI)

315 CE
SRI LANKA YEARBOOK. (Text in English, Sinhala and Tamil) 1948. a. price varies. Department of Census and Statistics, Box 563, Colombo 7, Sri Lanka (Order from: Superintendent, Government Publications Bureau, Colombo, Sri Lanka) circ. 1,800.
Continues: Ceylon Yearbook.

312 968 SA ISSN 0585-1289
STATE OF SOUTH AFRICA; economic, financial and statistical yearbook for the Republic of South Africa. 1957. a. $30. Da Gama Publishers (Pty.) Ltd., 311 Locarno House, 20 Loveday St., Box 61464, Marshalltown 2107, South Africa (Dist. in U.S. by: W. S. Heinman, Imported Books, 400 E. 72nd St., New York, NY 10021) Ed. D. de Freitas. adv. circ. 10,000.

315 BG ISSN 0081-4628
STATISTICAL ABSTRACT FOR BANGLADESH.* (Text in English) a. Bureau of Statistics, Secretariat, Dacca 2, Bangladesh.

314 IC ISSN 0081-4652
STATISTICAL ABSTRACT OF ICELAND. 1930. irreg., latest 1974. ‡ Hagstofa Islands - Statistical Bureau of Iceland, Reykjavik, Iceland. Ed. Kl. Tryggvason.

314 IE ISSN 0081-4660
STATISTICAL ABSTRACT OF IRELAND. 1931. a. £2.10. Central Statistics Office, Earlsfort Terrace, Dublin 4, Ireland. circ. 2,000.

315 II ISSN 0081-4709
STATISTICAL ABSTRACT OF MAHARASHTRA STATE. (Text in English) a. Rs.1.30. Directorate of Economics and Statistics, D.D. Bldg., Old Custom House, Bombay 400023, India.

310 II ISSN 0081-4717
STATISTICAL ABSTRACT OF RAJASTHAN. (Text in English) 1958. a. Rs.10. Directorate of Economics and Statistics, Krishi Bhawan, Jaipur, Rajasthan, India.

315 CE ISSN 0081-4636
STATISTICAL ABSTRACT OF SRI LANKA. (Text in English, Sinhala and Tamil) 1949. a. price varies. Department of Census and Statistics, Box 563, Colombo 7, Sri Lanka (Order from: Superintendent, Government Publications Bureau, Colombo, Sri Lanka) index.

319 CJ
STATISTICAL ABSTRACT OF THE GOVERNMENT OF THE CAYMAN ISLANDS. 1975. irreg; 2nd, 1979. Department of Finance & Development, Grand Cayman Island, Cayman Islands, B.W.I. Dir. Thomas C. Jefferson.

317.3 US ISSN 0081-4741
STATISTICAL ABSTRACT OF THE UNITED STATES. 1878. a. price varies. U.S. Bureau of the Census, Dept. of Commerce, Washington, DC 20233 (Orders to: Supt. of Documents, Washington, DC 20402) (also avail. in microform from UMI)

311 IE ISSN 0081-4776
STATISTICAL AND SOCIAL INQUIRY SOCIETY OF IRELAND. JOURNAL. 1864. a. £2. Statistical and Social Inquiry Society of Ireland, c/o Economic and Social Research Institute, 4 Burlington Road, Dublin 4, Ireland. Ed. Robert O'Connor. cum.index: 1847-1947. circ. 700.

315 JA ISSN 0081-4792
STATISTICAL HANDBOOK OF JAPAN. (Text in English) 1958. a. 700 Yen. Bureau of Statistics - Japan. Tokeikyoku, Office of the Prime Minister, 95 Wakamatsu-cho, Shinjuku-ku, Tokyo 162, Japan (Subscribe to: Governement Publications Service Center, 1-2-1 Kasumigaseki, Chiyoda-Ku, Tokyo 100, Japan) circ. 700(approx.)

315 KO ISSN 0081-4806
STATISTICAL HANDBOOK OF KOREA/ TONGGYE SUCHUP. (Text in English) 1962. a. 860 Won. Bureau of Statistics, Economic Planning Board, Gyeongun-Dong, Jongro-Gu, Seoul, S. Korea. Ed. Heung-Koo Kang. circ. 2,000.

319 MY ISSN 0081-4814
STATISTICAL HANDBOOK OF SARAWAK. Variant title: Sarawak Statistical Handbook. (Text in English) 1966. a. M.$2. Department of Statistics, Federal Complex, Jalan Simpang Tiga, Kuching, Sarawak, Malaysia.

315 II
STATISTICAL HANDBOOK OF TAMIL NADU. (Text in English) 1969. a. Rs.6. Director of Statistics, Madras 600006, India (Subscr. to: Government Publication Depot, 166 Anna Rd., Madras 600002, India)

315 TH ISSN 0081-4822
STATISTICAL HANDBOOK OF THAILAND. (Text in English) 1965. irreg. $1.75. National Statistical Office, Lan Luang Rd., Bangkok, Thailand. circ. 1,000.

316.67 GH
STATISTICAL HANDBOOK OF THE REPUBLIC OF GHANA. a. NC.1.70. Information Services Department, Box 745, Accra, Ghana.

310 AF
STATISTICAL INFORMATION OF AFGHANISTAN/MA'LUMAT-I IHSA'IVI-I AFGHANISTAN. (Text in Persian or Pushto) no. 3, 1975/1976. Central Statistical Office, Nader Shah Minah, Block No. 4, Box 2002, Kabul, Afghanistan. stat.

310 JA ISSN 0561-922X
STATISTICAL NOTES OF JAPAN. (Text in English) 1953. irreg. Director of Statistical Standards, Administrative Management Agency, 3-1-1 Kasumigaseki, Chiyoda-ku, Tokyo, Japan.

315 II ISSN 0081-5012
STATISTICAL POCKET BOOK: INDIA. (Text in English) 1956. a. Rs.163($10.80) Central Statistical Organization, Sardar Patel Bhavan, Sansad Marg, New Delhi 110001, India.
Formerly: Statistical Pocket Book of the Indian Union.

315.8 AF
STATISTICAL POCKET-BOOK OF AFGHANISTAN. 1972. irreg. Department of Statistics, Kabul, Afghanistan. illus.

314 HU
STATISTICAL POCKET BOOK OF HUNGARY/ MAGYAR STATISZTIKAI ZSEBKONYV. (Edition in English, German, Hungarian, Russian) a. 40 Ft. (Kozponti Statisztikai Hivatal) Statisztikai Kiado Vallalat, Kaszas U.10-12., P.O.B.99, 1300 Budapest 3, Hungary.

315 PK ISSN 0081-5004
STATISTICAL POCKET-BOOK OF PAKISTAN. (Text in English) a. price varies. Statistics Division, 63 Muslim Abab, Karachi 5, Pakistan.

315 CE
STATISTICAL POCKET BOOK OF THE DEMOCRATIC SOCIALIST REPUBLIC OF SRI LANKA. (Text in English, Sinhala & Tamil) 1967. a. price varies. Department of Census and Statistics, Box 563, Colombo 7, Sri Lanka (Order from: Superintendent, Government Publications Bureau, Colombo, Sri Lanka) (back issues avail.)
Former titles: Statistical Pocket Book of Sri Lanka; Which continues: Statistical Pocket Book of Ceylon (ISSN 0585-1777)

319 TU
STATISTICAL POCKET BOOK OF TURKEY/ TURKIYE ISTATISTIK CEP YILLIGI. (Subseries of its Yayin) biennial. State Institute of Statistics - Devlet Istatistik Enstitusu, Necatibey Caddesi 114, Ankara, Turkey.

315.98 IO ISSN 0537-3808
STATISTICAL POCKETBOOK OF INDONESIA/ BUKU SAKU STATISTIK INDONESIA. (Subseries of its Statistik Tahunan) (Text in English and Indonesian) 1957. a. Central Bureau of Statistics - Biro Pusat Statistik, Jalan Dr. Sutomo 8, Box 3, Jakarta, Indonesia.
Continues: Statistik Indonesia.

317 US
STATISTICAL PROFILE OF IOWA. a. free. Iowa Development Commission, 250 Jewett Bldg., Des Moines, IA 50309. index.

310 US ISSN 0081-5020
STATISTICAL RESEARCH MONOGRAPHS. 1961. irreg., vol. 4, 1974. price varies. University of Chicago Press, 5801 S. Ellis Ave., Chicago, IL 60637. (Co-Sponsors: Institute of Mathematical Statistics; University of Chicago) (reprint service avail. from UMI,ISI)

353.9 US
STATISTICAL REVIEW OF GOVERNMENT IN UTAH. a. $5.50. Utah Foundation, 308 Continental Bank Bldg., Salt Lake City, UT 84101.

300.8 UN
STATISTICAL YEARBOOK FOR ASIA AND THE PACIFIC/ANNUAIRE STATISTIQUE POUR L'ASIE ET LE PACIFIQUE. (Text in English and French) 1968. a. United Nations Economic and Social Commission for Asia and the Pacific, United Nations Bldg., Rajadamnern Ave., Bangkok 2, Thailand (Dist. by United Nations Publications, Room LX-2300, New York, NY 10017; or Distribution and Sales Section, Palais des Nations, CH-1211 Geneva 10, Switzerland)
Formerly: Statistical Yearbook for Asia and the Far East (ISSN 0085-6711)

315 BG ISSN 0302-2374
STATISTICAL YEARBOOK OF BANGLADESH. (Text in English) 1964. a. $15. Bureau of Statistics, Secretariat, Dacca 2, Bangladesh. Ed. A. K. M. Ghulam Rabbani.
Formerly: Statistical Digest of Bangladesh.

314 GR ISSN 0081-5071
STATISTICAL YEARBOOK OF GREECE. (Text in English and Greek) a., latest 1978. $10. National Statistical Service, Publications and Information Division, 14-16 Lycourgou St., Athens 112, Greece.

319 IR
STATISTICAL YEARBOOK OF IRAN. (Editions in English and Farsi) 1966. a. (Farsi edt.) biennial (English edt.) Statistical Centre, Iran Novin Ave, Teheran, Iran. charts. illus. stat.

317.292 JM
STATISTICAL YEARBOOK OF JAMAICA. 1973. a. Jam.$1. Department of Statistics, 9 Swallowfield Rd, Kingston 5, Jamaica. illus.

STATISTICAL YEARBOOK OF THE REPUBLIC OF CHINA. see BUSINESS AND ECONOMICS — Abstracting, Bibliographies, Statistics

314 GE ISSN 0433-6844
STATISTISCHES TASCHENBUCH DER DDR. (Editions in Arabic, English, French, German, Russian, Spanish) a. M.6. (Staatliche Zentralverwaltung fuer Statistik) Staatsverlag der DDR, Otto-Grotewohl-Str. 17, 108 Berlin, E. Germany(D.D.R.)

314 BU
STATISTICHESKI GODISHNIK NA NARODNA REPUBLIKA BULGARIA. 1909. a. 7.28 lv. (Ministerstvo na Informatsiiata i Suobshteniiata) Izdatelstvo Nauka i Izkustvo, 6, Rouski Blvd., Sofia, Bulgaria. stat. circ. 2,000.

314 BU
STATISTICHESKI SPRAVOCHNIK. 1959. a. 0.90 lv. Ministerstvo na Informatsiiata i Suobshteniiata, 18, Ul. Graf Ignatiev, Sofia, Bulgaria. (Co-sponsor: Tsentralno Statistichesko Upravlenie) stat. circ. 5,500.

STATISTICS - ASIA & AUSTRALASIA: SOURCES FOR MARKET RESEARCH. see BIBLIOGRAPHIES

STATISTICS OF PRIVATELY OWNED ELECTRIC UTILITIES IN THE UNITED STATES. see ENERGY — Abstracting, Bibliographies, Statistics

310 016 US ISSN 0585-198X
STATISTICS SOURCES; a subject guide to data on industrial, business, social, educational, financial and other topics for the U.S. and selected foreign countries. irreg., 6th edt., 1980. $64. Gale Research Company, Book Tower, Detroit, MI 48226. Ed. Paul Wasserman.

STATISTIQUE CRIMINELLE DE LA BELGIQUE. see CRIMINOLOGY AND LAW ENFORCEMENT — Abstracting, Bibliographies, Statistics

STATISTIQUES DU COMMERCE EXTERIEUR DE MADAGASCAR. see BUSINESS AND ECONOMICS — Abstracting, Bibliographies, Statistics

STATISTISCHE STUDIEN. see BUSINESS AND ECONOMICS

314 AU ISSN 0081-5314
STATISTISCHES HANDBUCH FUER DIE REPUBLIK OESTERREICH. 1882. a. S.350. ‡ (Oesterreichisches Statistisches Zentralamt) Oesterreichische Staatsdruckerei, Vienna, Austria. adv. circ. 2,700.

314 GW ISSN 0081-5322
STATISTISCHES JAHRBUCH BERLIN. 1945. a. DM.50. (Statistisches Landesamt) Kulturbuch-Verlag GmbH, Passauer Str. 4, 1000 Berlin 30, W. Germany (B.R.D.)
Supersedes: Berlin in Zahlen.

314 GE
STATISTISCHES JAHRBUCH DER DDR. 1956. a. M.50. (Staatliche Zentralverwaltung fuer Statistik) Staatsverlag der DDR, Otto-Grotewohl-Str. 17, 108 Berlin, E. Germany (D.D.R.) stat.

314 SZ ISSN 0081-5330
STATISTISCHES JAHRBUCH DER SCHWEIZ/ ANNUAIRE STATISTIQUE DE LA SUISSE. 1891. a. price varies. (Statistisches Amt.) Birkhaeuser Verlag, Elisabethenstr. 19, CH-4010 Basel, Switzerland.

STATISTICS

314   GW
STATISTISCHES JAHRBUCH DER STADT AUGSBURG. irreg. Amt fuer Statistik und Stadtforschung, Von-Cobres-Str. 1, 8900 Augsburg 22, W. Germany (B.R.D.)

314   GW   ISSN 0081-5357
STATISTISCHES JAHRBUCH FUER DIE BUNDESREPUBLIK DEUTSCHLAND. 1952. a. DM.83. (Statistisches Bundesamt) W. Kohlhammer-Verlag GmbH, Abt. Veroeffentlichungen des Statistischen Bundesamtes, Philipp-Reis-Str. 3, Postfach 421120, 6500 Mainz 42, W. Germany (B.R.D.)

310   GW   ISSN 0077-2062
STATISTISCHES JAHRBUCH MUENCHEN. (Text and summaries in German and English) 1969. a. DM.25. Amt fuer Statistik und Datenanalyse, Tal 30, 8000 Munich 2, W. Germany (B.R.D.)

310   SW   ISSN 0081-5381
STATISTISK AARSBOK FOER SVERIGE. 1914. a. Kr.45. (Statistiska Centralbyraan) Liber Foerlag, Fack, S-162 89 Vaellingby, Sweden. circ. 12,300.

314   HU   ISSN 0073-4039
STATISZTIKAI EVKONYV/STATISTICAL YEARBOOK. (Text in Hungarian; since 1964 separate bilingual edition in English and Russian) 1871. a. 220 Ft. (Kozponti Statisztikai Hivatal) Statisztikai Kiado Vallalat, Kaszas U.10-12, P.O.B.99, 1300 Budapest 3, Hungary.

314   GW   ISSN 0072-3967
STUDIES ON STATISTICS. (Text in English) 1957. irreg. price varies. (Statistisches Bundesamt) W. Kohlhammer-Verlag GmbH, Abt. Veroeffentlichungen des Statistischen Bundesamtes, Philipp-Reis-Str. 3, Postfach 421120, 6500 Mainz 42, W. Germany (B.R.D.)

310   SJ
SUDAN. DEPARTMENT OF STATISTICS. STATISTICAL YEARBOOK. (Text in English) 1973. a. Department of Statistics, Box 700, Khartoum, Sudan.

314   FI   ISSN 0081-5063
SUOMEN TILASTOLLINEN VUOSIKIRJA/STATISTISK AARSBOK FOER FINLAND/STATISTICAL YEARBOOK OF FINLAND. (Text in English, Finnish and Swedish) 1879. a. Fmk.60. Tilastokeskus, Annankatu 44, SF-00100 Helsinki 10, Finland (Subscr. to: Government Printing Centre, Box 516, SF-00100 Helsinki 10, Finland) circ. 5,000.

318   SR
SURINAM. ALGEMEEN BUREAU VOOR DE STATISTIEK. NATIONALE REKENINGEN. (Subseries of: Suriname in Cijfers) irreg. Algemeen Bureau voor de Statistiek, Paramaribo, Surinam.

314   GW
SURVEY OF GERMAN FEDERAL STATISTICS/APERCU DE LA STATISTIQUE FEDERALE ALLEMANDE. (Editions in English and French) 1957. irreg. DM.10. (Statistisches Bundesamt) W. Kohlhammer-Verlag GmbH, Abt. Veroeffentlichungen des Statistischen Bundesamtes, Philipp-Reis-Str. 3, Postfach 421120, 6500 Mainz 42, W. Germany (B.R.D.)
    Formerly (1957-1970): Germany (Federal Republic, 1949-) Statisches Bundesamt Arbeiten (ISSN 0072-1611)

316   SQ   ISSN 0586-1357
SWAZILAND. CENTRAL STATISTICAL OFFICE. ANNUAL STATISTICAL BULLETIN. 1966. a, latest 1977. Central Statistical Office, P.O. Box 456, Mbabane, Swaziland. illus. circ. 800.

316   SQ
SWAZILAND. CENTRAL STATISTICAL OFFICE. ANNUAL SURVEY OF SWAZI NATION LAND. 1972/73. a, latest 1977/78. Central Statistical Office, P.O. Box 456, Mbabane, Swaziland. stat. circ. 500.

SWAZILAND. CENTRAL STATISTICAL OFFICE. COMMERCIAL TIMBER PLANTATION AND WOOD PRODUCTS STATISTICS. see *FORESTS AND FORESTRY — Abstracting, Bibliographies, Statistics*

SWEDEN. LUFTFARTSVERKET. AARSBOK. see *TRANSPORTATION — Abstracting, Bibliographies, Statistics*

309   SW
SWEDEN. STATISTISKA CENTRALBYRAAN. LEVNADSFOERHAALLANDEN AARSBOK/LIVING CONDITIONS YEARBOOK. (Subseries of: Sweden. Statistiska Centralbyraan. Sveriges Officiella Statistik) (Text in English and Swedish) 1975. a. Liber Foerlag, Fack, S-162 89 Vaellingby, Sweden. illus.

314   SW   ISSN 0082-0229
SWEDEN. STATISTISKA CENTRALBYRAAN. MEDDELANDEN I SAMORDNINGSFRAAGOR. 1966. irreg. (Statistiska Centralbyraan) Liber Foerlag, Fack, S-162 89 Vaellingby, Sweden.

SWEDEN. STATISTISKA CENTRALBYRAAN. STATISTISKA MEDDELANDEN. SUBGROUP BO (HOUSING AND CONSTRUCTION) see *BUILDING AND CONSTRUCTION — Abstracting, Bibliographies, Statistics*

314   SW   ISSN 0082-0350
SWEDEN. STATISTISKA CENTRALBYRAAN. URVAL SKRIFTSERIES/SELECTION SERIES. (Text in Swedish; summaries in English) 1969. irreg., 1970, no. 3. price varies. Liber Foerlag, Fack, S-162 89 Vaellingby, Sweden. circ. 500-1,000.

SWITZERLAND. DIRECTORATE GENERAL OF CUSTOMS. ANNUAL REPORT. see *BUSINESS AND ECONOMICS — Abstracting, Bibliographies, Statistics*

312.5   SZ
SWITZERLAND. STATISTISCHES AMT. HEIRATEN, LEBENDGEBORENE UND GESTORBENE IN DEN GEMEINDEN/MARIAGES, NAISSANCES ET DECES DANS LES COMMUNES. (Subseries of its Statistische Quellenwerke der Schweiz) 1971. irreg. 12 Fr. Statistisches Amt., Hallwylstr. 15, 3003 Berne, Switzerland. stat. circ. 750.

SWITZERLAND. STATISTISCHES AMT. SCHUELERSTATISTIK/STATISTIQUE DES ELEVES. see *EDUCATION — Abstracting, Bibliographies, Statistics*

SWITZERLAND: DIRECTORATE GENERAL OF CUSTOMS. ANNUAL STATISTICS. see *BUSINESS AND ECONOMICS — Abstracting, Bibliographies, Statistics*

315   SY   ISSN 0081-4725
SYRIA. CENTRAL BUREAU OF STATISTICS. STATISTICAL ABSTRACT. (Text in Arabic and English) 1948. a. $35. ‡ Central Bureau of Statistics, Damascus, Syria.

310   II   ISSN 0082-1578
TAMIL NADU. DEPARTMENT OF STATISTICS. ANNUAL STATISTICAL ABSTRACT. (Text in English) 1954-55. a. Rs.11. Director of Statistics, Madras 600006, India (Subscription to: Government Publication Depot, 166 Anna Road, Madras 600002, India)

312.8   TZ
TANZANIA. BUREAU OF STATISTICS. MIGRATION STATISTICS. 1968. irreg., latest 1970(pub. in 1972) Bureau of Statistics, Box 796, Dar es Salaam, Tanzania (Orders to: Government Publications Agency, Box 1801, Dar es Salaam, Tanzania)

TANZANIA. BUREAU OF STATISTICS. SURVEY OF INDUSTRIAL PRODUCTION. see *BUSINESS AND ECONOMICS — Abstracting, Bibliographies, Statistics*

TAX BURDEN ON TOBACCO. see *TOBACCO — Abstracting, Bibliographies, Statistics*

315   IS
TEL AVIV-YAFO. CENTER FOR ECONOMIC AND SOCIAL RESEARCH. RESEARCH AND SURVEYS SERIES/TEL-AVIV-YAFO. AAMERKAS LE-MECHKAR KALKALI VE-HEVRATI. MEHKARIM VE-SEKARIM. (Text in Hebrew and English) 1963, no. 12. irreg. I£20. Center for Economic and Social Research, Tel Aviv, Israel. Ed. H. Har-Paz. circ. 600.
    Formerly: Tel Aviv-Yafo. Research and Statistical Department. Special Surveys (ISSN 0082-2639)

317   US   ISSN 0082-2760
TENNESSEE STATISTICAL ABSTRACT. 1969. triennial. $15. University of Tennessee, Center for Business and Economic Research, Knoxville, TN 37916.

TEXAS BLUE BOOK OF LIFE INSURANCE STATISTICS. see *INSURANCE*

315   TH
THAILAND. NATIONAL STATISTICAL OFFICE. RESEARCH PAPER. 1975. irreg. National Statistical Office, Lan Luang Rd., Bangkok, Thailand.

THAILAND. NATIONAL STATISTICAL OFFICE. STATISTICAL BIBLIOGRAPHY. see *BIBLIOGRAPHIES*

TOURISM AND MIGRATION STATISTICS. see *TRAVEL AND TOURISM — Abstracting, Bibliographies, Statistics*

TRAVEL BETWEEN CANADA AND OTHER COUNTRIES/VOYAGES ENTRE LE CANADA ET LES AUTRES PAYS. see *TRAVEL AND TOURISM — Abstracting, Bibliographies, Statistics*

310   US
TREASURY ALASKA. Represents: Alaska. Department of Revenue. Treasury Division. Annual Financial Report. a. Department of Revenue, Treasury Division, Pouch SB, Juneau, AK 99811.

311   TR   ISSN 0082-6502
TRINIDAD AND TOBAGO. CENTRAL STATISTICAL OFFICE. ANNUAL STATISTICAL DIGEST. 1951. a; latest issue 1974-75. T.T.$3. Central Statistical Office, Textel Building, 1, Edward Street, Port of Spain, Trinidad (Subscr. to the Government Printer, 2 Victoria Ave., Port of Spain, Trinidad)

TRINIDAD AND TOBAGO. CENTRAL STATISTICAL OFFICE. BUSINESS SURVEYS. see *BUSINESS AND ECONOMICS — Economic Situation And Conditions*

317   TR
TRINIDAD AND TOBAGO. CENTRAL STATISTICAL OFFICE. POCKET DIGEST. 1973. a. Central Statistical Office, Textel Bldg., 1 Edward St., Port of Spain, Trinadad and Tobago (Orders to: Government Printing Office, 2 Victoria Ave., Port of Spain, Trinidad)

312   TR   ISSN 0082-6553
TRINIDAD AND TOBAGO. CENTRAL STATISTICAL OFFICE. POPULATION AND VITAL STATISTICS; REPORT. 1953. a. T.T.$2. Central Statistical Office, Textel Building, 1, Edward Street, Port of Spain, Trinidad (Subscr. to: Government Printery, 2 Victoria Ave., Port of Spain, Trinidad)

310   TR
TRINIDAD AND TOBAGO. CENTRAL STATISTICAL OFFICE. STAFF PAPERS. 1967. irreg. free. Central Statistical Office, Textel Building, 1, Edward Street, Port of Spain, Trinidad (or Govt. Printery, 2 Victoria Ave., Port of Spain, Trinidad)

310   TR   ISSN 0082-6561
TRINIDAD AND TOBAGO TODAY. 1966. irreg. T.T.$1. Central Statistical Office, Textel Building, 1, Edward Street, Port of Spain, Trinidad (Subscr. to: Government Printery, 2 Victoria Ave., Port of Spain, Trinidad)

TUNISIA. INSTITUT NATIONAL DE LA STATISTIQUE. RECENSEMENT DES ACTIVITES INDUSTRIELLES. see *BUSINESS AND ECONOMICS — Abstracting, Bibliographies, Statistics*

315 TU ISSN 0082-691X
TURKIYE ISTATISTIK YILLIGI/STATISTICAL YEARBOOK OF TURKEY. (Subseries of its Yayin) 1962. biennial. exchange basis. State Institute of Statistics, Necatibey Caddesi 114, Ankara, Turkey.

310 US
U.S.S.R. FACTS & FIGURES ANNUAL. 1977. a. $35 (vol. 1); $51 (vol. 2); $38.50 (vol. 3) Academic International Press, Box 555, Gulf Breeze, FL 32561. Ed. John L. Scherer. (back issues avail.)

310 060 UN ISSN 0082-7533
UNESCO STATISTICAL REPORTS AND STUDIES. (Editions in English and French) 1955. irreg. 1972, no. 18. price varies. Unesco, 7-9 Place de Fontenoy, 75700 Paris, France (Dist. in U.S. by: Unipub, 345 Park Ave. S., New York NY 10010)

310 UN ISSN 0082-7541
UNESCO STATISTICAL YEARBOOK. (Text in English and French) 1952. a. price varies. Unesco, 7-9 Place de Fontenoy, 75700 Paris, France (Dist. in U.S. by: Unipub, 345 Park Ave. S., New York NY 10010)

310 UN ISSN 0082-8459
UNITED NATIONS. STATISTICAL YEARBOOK. (Text in English and French) 1949. a. price varies. (United Nations Statistical Office) United Nations Publications, Room LX-2300, New York, NY 10017 (Or Distribution and Sales Section, Palais des Nations, CH-1211 Geneva 10, Switzerland)

U.S. ADMINISTRATION ON AGING. ELDERLY POPULATION: ESTIMATES BY COUNTY. see *SOCIAL SERVICES AND WELFARE — Abstracting, Bibliographies, Statistics*

317 US ISSN 0082-9455
U. S. BUREAU OF THE CENSUS. COUNTY AND CITY DATA BOOK. 1944. irreg. price varies. U.S. Bureau of the Census, Dept. of Commerce, Washington, DC 20233 (Orders to: Supt. of Documents, Washington, DC 20402)

311 US ISSN 0082-9536
U. S. BUREAU OF THE CENSUS. TECHNICAL NOTES. 1954. irreg. price varies. U. S. Bureau of the Census, Office of Asst. Director for Statistical Information, Washington, DC 20233.

310 US ISSN 0082-9544
U. S. BUREAU OF THE CENSUS. TECHNICAL PAPER. 1953. irreg., no. 43, 1978. price varies. U.S. Bureau of the Census, Dept. of Commerce, Washington, DC 20233 (Orders to: Supt. of Documents, Washington, DC 20402) Key Title: Technical Paper - U.S. Department of Commerce, Social and Economics Statistics Administration, Bureau of the Census.

310 US ISSN 0082-9552
U. S. BUREAU OF THE CENSUS. WORKING PAPERS. 1954. irreg. U.S. Bureau of the Census, Dept. of Commerce, Washington, DC 20233.

U.S. DEPARTMENT OF HOUSING AND URBAN DEVELOPMENT. STATISTICAL YEARBOOK. see *HOUSING AND URBAN PLANNING — Abstracting, Bibliographies, Statistics*

310 US
U.S. DEPARTMENT OF TRANSPORTATION. NATIONAL TRANSPORTATION STATISTICS. ANNUAL; a supplement to the summary of national transportation statistics. a. U. S. Department of Transportation, Statistical Information Reporting Branch, Office of the Assistant Secretary for Policy, Plans, and International Affairs, Washington, DC 20590 (Orders to Supt. of Documents, Washington, DC 20402) illus.
 Formed by the 1977 merger of: U.S. Department of Transportation. Energy Statistics & U.S. Department of Transportation. Summary of National Transportation Statistics (ISSN 0360-8980)

U.S. FISH AND WILDLIFE SERVICE. NATIONAL SURVEY OF HUNTING, FISHING AND WILDLIFE-ASSOCIATED RECREATION. see *SPORTS AND GAMES — Abstracting, Bibliographies, Statistics*

618.8 US
U.S. NATIONAL INSTITUTE OF MENTAL HEALTH. REPORT SERIES ON MENTAL HEALTH STATISTICS. SERIES D: CONFERENCE OR COMMITTEE REPORTS, AND ANALYTICAL REVIEWS OF LITERATURE. 1970. U.S. National Institute of Mental Health, Division of Biometry and Epidemiology, Survey and Reports Branch, 5600 Fishers Lane, Rockville, MD 20857. circ. 3,000-4,000. (also avail. in microfiche)

UNIVERSIDADE FEDERAL DE RIO DE JANEIRO. INSTITUTO DE MATEMATICA. MEMORIAS DE MATEMATICA. see *MATHEMATICS*

312.5 US
UTAH MARRIAGE AND DIVORCE ANNUAL REPORT. a. $5. Department of Social Services, Bureau of Health Statistics, 150 West North Temple, Suite 158, Box 2500, Salt Lake City, UT 84110.

VENEZUELA. MINISTERIO DE ENERGIA Y MINAS. APENDICE ESTADISTICO. see *ENERGY — Abstracting, Bibliographies, Statistics*

317.43 US ISSN 0092-5144
VERMONT FACTS AND FIGURES. irreg, latest 1975. Department of Budget & Management, Pavilion Office Building, Montpelier, VT 05602. stat.

312 US
VITAL STATISTICS OF IOWA. 1888. a. Department of Health, Statistical Services, Des Moines, IA 50319. stat. circ. 400.
 Supersedes (1970-1974): Iowa Detailed Report of Vital Statistics (ISSN 0362-9473)

310 CN
VITAL STATISTICS OF THE PROVINCE OF BRITISH COLUMBIA. 1944. a. Division of Vital Statistics, Department of Health, Victoria, B.C., Canada.

310 UR
VOPROSY STATISTIKI. (Subseries of: Latviiskii Gosudartstvennyi Universitet. Zinatniskie Raksti) irreg. 0.90 Rub. Latviiskii Gosudarstvennyi Universitet, Kafedra Statistiki i Planirovaniya Narodnogo Khozyaistva S.S.S.R., Bulvar Raynisa 19, Riga, U. S. S. R.

WASHINGTON (STATE). DEPARTMENT OF NATURAL RESOURCES. ANNUAL FIRE STATISTICS. see *FORESTS AND FORESTRY — Abstracting, Bibliographies, Statistics*

315.4 II ISSN 0511-5493
WEST BENGAL. BUREAU OF APPLIED ECONOMICS AND STATISTICS. STATISTICAL HANDBOOK. (Issuing body varies) (Text in English) 1960. a. price varies. Bureau of Applied Economics and Statistics, 1 Kiron Sankar Roy Rd., Calcutta 700001, India. stat.

365 US
WISCONSIN. DIVISION OF CORRECTIONS. OFFICE OF INFORMATION MANAGEMENT. ADMISSIONS TO JUVENILE INSTITUTIONS. (Subseries of its Statistical Bulletin) 1972. a. Division of Corrections, Office of Information Management, Box 7925, Madison, WI 53707. stat. (processed)
 Formerly: Wisconsin. Division of Corrections. Office of Information Management. Admissions to Juvenile Institutions.

310 US
WISCONSIN STATISTICAL ABSTRACT. irreg., latest, 1979. $9.50. Department of Administration, Document Sales and Distribution, 202 Thornton Ave., Madison, WI 53702.

WORLD MINERAL STATISTICS; world production, exports and imports. see *MINES AND MINING INDUSTRY — Abstracting, Bibliographies, Statistics*

379 US ISSN 0093-5530
WYOMING. DIVISION OF PLANNING, EVALUATION AND INFORMATION SERVICES. STATISTICAL REPORT SERIES. 1973. a. free. Division of Planning, Evaluation and Information Services, Cheyenne, WY 82001. stat. Key Title: Statistical Report Series (Cheyenne)

315.6 YE
YEMEN. CENTRAL STATISTICAL OFFICE. STATISTICAL YEARBOOK. (Text in Arabic and English) 1971. a. 20 rials. Central Statistical Office, Sana'a, Yemen. illus.

ZAMBIA. CENTRAL STATISTICAL OFFICE. AGRICULTURAL AND PASTORAL PRODUCTION (COMMERCIAL FARMS) see *AGRICULTURE — Abstracting, Bibliographies, Statistics*

ZAMBIA. CENTRAL STATISTICAL OFFICE. AGRICULTURAL AND PASTORAL PRODUCTION (NON-COMMERCIAL) see *AGRICULTURE — Abstracting, Bibliographies, Statistics*

ZAMBIA. CENTRAL STATISTICAL OFFICE. QUARTERLY AGRICULTURAL STATISTICAL BULLETIN. see *AGRICULTURE — Abstracting, Bibliographies, Statistics*

316 ZA ISSN 0084-4551
ZAMBIA. CENTRAL STATISTICAL OFFICE. STATISTICAL YEAR BOOK. 1967. a,latest 1971. K.3. Central Statistical Office, P.O. Box 1908, Lusaka, Zambia.

316 ZA ISSN 0084-456X
ZAMBIA. CENTRAL STATISTICAL OFFICE. VITAL STATISTICS. Variant title: Zambia. Central Statistical Office. Registered Births, Marriages and Deaths (Vital Statistics) 1965. a, latest 1975. K.0.20. Central Statistical Office, P.O. Box 1908, Lusaka, Zambia.

ZIMBABWE. CENTRAL STATISTICAL OFFICE. CENSUS OF PRODUCTION. see *BUSINESS AND ECONOMICS — Production Of Goods And Services*

ZIMBABWE. CENTRAL STATISTICAL OFFICE. INCOME TAX STATISTICS; analysis of assessments and loss statements. see *BUSINESS AND ECONOMICS — Abstracting, Bibliographies, Statistics*

SURGERY

see *Medical Sciences—Surgery*

TAXATION

see *Business and Economics—Public Finance, Taxation*

TEACHING METHODS AND CURRICULUM

see *Education—Teaching Methods and Curriculum*

TECHNOLOGY: COMPREHENSIVE WORKS

ACTA BOREALIA A. SCIENTIA. see *EARTH SCIENCES*

668.3 UK ISSN 0305-3199
ADHESIVES DIRECTORY. (Text in English, French, German and Italian) 1966. a. £3. Wheatland Journals Ltd., Penn House, Penn Place, Rickmansworth, Herts WD3 1SN, England. adv. charts. circ. 2,000.

ADVANCES IN ENVIRONMENTAL SCIENCE AND ENGINEERING. see *ENVIRONMENTAL STUDIES*

TECHNOLOGY: COMPREHENSIVE WORKS

600   US
ADVANCES IN MANUFACTURING SYSTEMS, RESEARCH AND DEVELOPMENT. 1971. irreg. price varies. Pergamon Press, Inc., Maxwell House, Fairview Park, Elmsford, NY 10523. Ed. J. Peklenik.

600   DK
AKADEMIET FOR DE VIDENSKABER. HANDBOG. Abbreviated title: A T V-H. irreg. Kr.40. Akademiet for de Tekniske Videnskaber, Lundtoftevej 266, 2800 Lyngby, Denmark.

600   CN   ISSN 0080-1526
ALBERTA RESEARCH COUNCIL. ANNUAL REPORT. 1919. a. free. Alberta Research Council, Publications Department, 11315 87th Ave., Edmonton, Alta. T6G 2C2, Canada.

ALBERTA RESEARCH COUNCIL. ATMOSPHERIC SCIENCES REPORTS. see SCIENCES: COMPREHENSIVE WORKS

ALBERTA RESEARCH COUNCIL. MEMOIRS. see SCIENCES: COMPREHENSIVE WORKS

600   CN
ALBERTA RESEARCH COUNCIL. REPORTS. 1919. irreg. price varies. Alberta Research Council, 11315-87th Ave., Edmonton, Alberta T6G 2C2, Canada.
    Formerly: Research Council of Alberta. Report (ISSN 0080-1607)

600   378   II   ISSN 0065-6623
ALTECH. 1950. a. on exchange basis. (Perarignar Anna University of Technology) Alagappa Chettiar College of Technology, Chepauk, Triplicane P.O., Madras 600005, Tamil Nadu, India. Ed. G. S. Laddha. circ. 1,000.

AMERICAN COUNCIL OF INDEPENDENT LABORATORIES. DIRECTORY. see SCIENCES: COMPREHENSIVE WORKS

600   US   ISSN 0065-8618
AMERICAN INDUSTRIAL ARTS ASSOCIATION. ADDRESSES AND PROCEEDINGS OF THE ANNUAL CONVENTION. (Each vol. has distinctive title) 1964. a. $525 paper. American Industrial Arts Association, Inc., N E A Headquarters Bldg., 1201 16th St. N.W., Washington, DC 20036. Ed. Esther Goldring.

600   US
AMERICAN INDUSTRIAL ARTS ASSOCIATION. FOCUS SERIES. 1971. irreg. price varies. American Industrial Arts Association, Inc., 1201 16th St. N.W., Washington, DC 20036. Ed. Colleen P. Stamm.

600   US   ISSN 0517-2306
AMERICAN INDUSTRIAL ARTS ASSOCIATION. MONOGRAPH SERIES. 1965. irreg. price varies. American Industrial Arts Association, Inc., N E A Headquarters Bldg., 1201 16th St., N.W., Washington, DC 20036.

621   US   ISSN 0163-5573
AMERICAN INSTITUTE OF INDUSTRIAL ENGINEERS. PROCEEDINGS OF THE SPRING ANNUAL CONFERENCE. 1950. a. $44 to non-members; members $22. American Institute of Industrial Engineers, Inc., 25 Technology Park/Atlanta, Norcross, GA 30092. charts. (reprint service avail. from UMI)

AMERICAN PETROLEUM INSTITUTE. COMMITTEE ON MEDICINE AND ENVIRONMENTAL HEALTH. MEDICAL RESEARCH REPORTS. see PUBLIC HEALTH AND SAFETY

600   US   ISSN 0097-2126
AMERICAN POWER CONFERENCE. PROCEEDINGS. 1952. a. price varies. American Power Conference, Illinois Institute of Technology, Chicago, IL 60616. Ed. Bette Haigh. index, cum.index (1938-1963) circ. 4,200-4,400.

350   600   US
AMERICAN PUBLIC WORKS ASSOCIATION. DIRECTORY. a. price varies. American Public Works Association, 1313 E. 60th St, Chicago, IL 60637.

ANTICIPATION; Christian social thought in a future perspective. see RELIGIONS AND THEOLOGY

600   AG   ISSN 0325-6278
ARGENTINA. INSTITUTO NACIONAL DE TECNOLOGIA INDUSTRIA. BOLETIN TECNICO. 1966. irreg. free. Instituto Nacional de Tecnologia Industrial, Leandro N. Alem 1067, Casilla de Correo 1359, 1001 Buenos Aires, Argentina. Ed. Bd. charts. circ. 500.

ASIA MONOGRAPH SERIES. see SCIENCES: COMPREHENSIVE WORKS

600   TH   ISSN 0572-4198
ASIAN INSTITUTE OF TECHNOLOGY. RESEARCH SUMMARY. 1962. a. Asian Institute of Technology, c/o Academic Secretary, P.O. Box 2754, Bangkok, Thailand.

600   FR   ISSN 0066-9288
ASSOCIATION FRANCAISE D'EXPERTS DE LA COOPERATION TECHNIQUE INTERNATIONALE. ANNUAIRE. 1965. a. $2. Association Francaise d'Experts de la Cooperation Technique Internationale, 150 Champs Elysees, 75008 Paris, France.

607   CN   ISSN 0707-3291
B C I T: THE CAREER CAMPUS. 1975. a. British Columbia Institute of Technology, 3700 Willingdon Ave., Burnaby, B.C., Canada. illus.
    Formerly: British Columbia Institute of Technology. Annual Report (ISSN 0381-260X)

B I A S JOURNAL. (Bristol Industrial Archaeological Society) see ENGINEERING

600   510   US
BALSKRISHNAN-NEUSTADT SERIES. irreg. price varies. Holt, Rinehart and Winston, Inc., 383 Madison Ave., New York, NY 10017.

BOMBAY TECHNOLOGIST. see CHEMISTRY

BRAZIL. CONSELHO NACIONAL DE DESENVOLVIMENTO CIENTIFICO E TECNOLOGICO. BOLETIM. see SCIENCES: COMPREHENSIVE WORKS

600   PL   ISSN 0068-4597
BYDGOSKIE TOWARZYSTWO NAUKOWE. WYDZIAL NAUK TECHNICZNYCH. PRACE. SERIA Z: (PRACE ZBIOROWE) 1966. irreg. price varies. Bydgoskie Towarzystwo Naukowe, Jezuicka 4, Bydgoszcz, Poland (Dist. by Ars Polona-Ruch, Krakowskie Przedmiescie 7, Warsaw, Poland)

C L A I M REPORT TO THE BRITISH LIBRARY AND DEVELOPMENT DEPARTMENT. (Centre for Library and Information Management) see SCIENCES: COMPREHENSIVE WORKS

C R I C RAPPORT DE RECHERCHE. (Centre National de Recherches Scientifiques et Techniques pour l'Industrie Cimentiere) see SCIENCES: COMPREHENSIVE WORKS

C S I R ANNUAL REPORT. (Council for Scientific and Industrial Research) see SCIENCES: COMPREHENSIVE WORKS

C. S. I. R. O. DIRECTORY. see SCIENCES: COMPREHENSIVE WORKS

C. S. I. R. O. FILM CATALOGUE. see SCIENCES: COMPREHENSIVE WORKS

C S I R ORGANIZATION AND ACTIVITIES. (Council for Scientific and Industrial Research) see SCIENCES: COMPREHENSIVE WORKS

CANADA. MINISTRY OF STATE FOR SCIENCE AND TECHNOLOGY. ANNUAL REPORT/RAPPORT ANNUEL. see SCIENCES: COMPREHENSIVE WORKS

CANADA. MINISTRY OF STATE FOR SCIENCE AND TECHNOLOGY. FEDERAL SCIENCE PROGRAMS. see SCIENCES: COMPREHENSIVE WORKS

600   500   BE   ISSN 0069-1968
CENTRE NATIONAL DE DOCUMENTATION SCIENTIFIQUE ET TECHNIQUE. RAPPORT D'ACTIVITE. 1964. a. contr. free circ. ‡ Centre National de Documentation Scientifique et Technique - National Center for Scientific and Technical Documentation, 4, Bd. de l'Empereur, B-1000 Brussels, Belgium. Dir. A. Cockx. index. circ. 2,500. Indexed: Bull.Signal.

600   CS   ISSN 0069-2301
CESKOSLOVENSKA AKADEMIE VED. ROZPRAVY. TV: RADA TECHNICKYCH VED. 1891. irreg., vol. 85, 1975. price varies. Academia, Publishing House of the Czechoslovak Academy of Sciences, Vodickova 40, 112 29 Prague 1, Czechoslovakia. circ. 1,000.

CHUO UNIVERSITY. FACULTY OF SCIENCE AND ENGINEERING. BULLETIN/CHUO DAIGAKU RIKOGAKUBU KIYO. see SCIENCES: COMPREHENSIVE WORKS

CODATA BULLETIN. (Committee on Data for Science and Technology) see SCIENCES: COMPREHENSIVE WORKS

600   SP
COLECCION TECNOLOGIA Y SOCIEDAD. 1978. irreg. price varies. Editorial Gustavo Gili, S.A., Rosellon 87-89, Barcelona 29, Spain.

600   CL
COMITE DE INVESTIGACIONES TECNOLOGICAS DE CHILE. biennial. Comite de Investigaciones Tecnologicas de Chile, Avda. Santa Maria 6500, Casilla 667, Santiago, Chile. illus.

600   AT   ISSN 0069-7184
COMMONWEALTH SCIENTIFIC AND INDUSTRIAL RESEARCH ORGANIZATION. ANNUAL REPORT. 1948. a. Aus.$2. C. S. I. R. O., 314 Albert St., E. Melbourne 3002, Victoria, Australia.

CONTRIBUTIONS TO THE HISTORY OF SCIENCE AND TECHNOLOGY IN BALTICS/IZ ISTORII ESTESTVOZNANIYA I TEKHNIKI PRIBALTIKI. see SCIENCES: COMPREHENSIVE WORKS

DAEDALUS. see MUSEUMS AND ART GALLERIES

600   US   ISSN 0164-2871
DESIGN NEWS. FLUID POWER. a. Cahners Publishing Co. (Chicago), Division of Reed Holdings, Inc., 5 S. Wabash Ave., Chicago, IL 60603 (Subscr. address: 270 St.Paul St., Denver, CO 80206)
    Formerly: Design News Annual. Fluid Power Edition.

600   US   ISSN 0164-2839
DESIGN NEWS. MATERIALS. a. Cahners Publishing Co. (Chicago), Division of Reed Holdings, Inc., 5 S. Wabash Ave., Chicago, IL 60603 (Subscr. address: 270 St. Paul St., Denver, CO 80206)
    Formerly: Design News Annual. Materials Edition.

DIRECTORY OF COMPUTERIZED INFORMATION IN SCIENCE AND TECHNOLOGY. see SCIENCES: COMPREHENSIVE WORKS

DIRECTORY OF SCIENTIFIC AND TECHNICAL ASSOCIATIONS IN ISRAEL. see SCIENCES: COMPREHENSIVE WORKS

DIRECTORY OF THE SCIENTISTS, TECHNOLOGISTS, AND ENGINEERS OF THE P C S I R. (Pakistan Council of Scientific and Industrial Research) see SCIENCES: COMPREHENSIVE WORKS

620   FR
ECOLE NATIONALE SUPERIEURE DE TECHNIQUES AVANCEES CENTRE D'EDITION ET DE DOCUMENTATION. RAPPORT D'ACTIVITE SUR LES RECHERCHES. irreg. Ecole Nationale Superieure de Techniques Avancees, Centre d'Edition et de Documentation, 32, Boulevard Victor, 75015 Paris, France.

ENERGY TECHNOLOGY REVIEW. see ENERGY

ENVIRONMENTAL SCIENCE AND TECHNOLOGY: A WILEY-INTERSCIENCE SERIES OF TEXTS AND MONOGRAPHS. see ENVIRONMENTAL STUDIES

TECHNOLOGY: COMPREHENSIVE WORKS

600   UK
EUROPEAN ELECTRO-OPTICS MARKETS AND TECHNOLOGY CONFERENCE. PROCEEDINGS. a, 2nd. 1974, Montreux, Switzerland. Mack Brooks Exhibitions, Ltd., 62-64 Victoria St., St. Albans, Herts. AL1 3XT, England. illus.

EXPERIENTIA. SUPPLEMENTUM. see *SCIENCES: COMPREHENSIVE WORKS*

600   US
FACHBERICHTE MESSEN-STEUERN-REGELN. 1977. irreg., vol. 5, 1980. price varies. Springer-Verlag, 175 Fifth Ave., New York, NY 10010 (Also Berlin, Heidelberg, Vienna) (reprint service avail. from ISI)

600 500   UK   ISSN 0071-4097
FAWLEY FOUNDATION LECTURES. 1954. a. 40p. University of Southampton, Highfield, Southampton SO9 5NH, England.

600   US   ISSN 0161-5319
FRONTIERS OF POWER TECHNOLOGY CONFERENCE. PROCEEDINGS. 6th, 1973. irreg. price varies. Oklahoma State University, College of Engineering, Engineering Extension, Stillwater, OK 74074.

600   GW   ISSN 0071-9749
FUEHRER DURCH DIE TECHNISCHE LITERATUR; Katalog technischer Werke fuer Studium und Praxis. 1900. a. DM.14.50. Fr. Weidemann's Buchhandlung (H.Witt), Georgstr. 11, Postfach 6406, 3000 Hannover, W. Germany (B.R.D.) Eds. K. Deichmann, H. Knigge. adv. circ. 25,000.

600   JA
FUKUI UNIVERSITY. FACULTY OF EDUCATION. MEMOIRS. SERIES 5: APPLIED SCIENCE AND TECHNOLOGY. (Text in Japanese; summmaries in English & Japanese) 1964. a. Fukui University, Faculty of Education, 9-1, 3-chome, Bunkyo, Fukui 910, Japan.

600   US
G A T F TECHNICAL SERVICES REPORT. 1967. irreg. $0.60 to members; $3.75 to non-members. ‡ Graphic Arts Technical Foundation, 4615 Forbes Ave., Pittsburgh, PA 15213. circ. controlled.

GERMANY (FEDERAL REPUBLIC,1949-) BUNDESMINISTERIUM FUER FORSCHUNG UND TECHNOLOGIE. BMFT FOERDERUNGSKATALOG. see *SCIENCES: COMPREHENSIVE WORKS*

GOVERNMENTAL RESEARCH ASSOCIATION DIRECTORY; directory of organizations and individuals professionally engaged in governmental research and related activities. see *SCIENCES: COMPREHENSIVE WORKS*

GREAT BRITAIN. SCIENCE RESEARCH COUNCIL. REPORT. see *SCIENCES: COMPREHENSIVE WORKS*

670   FR
GUIDE-ANNUAIRE OFFICIEL DE L'ARTISANAT ET DES METIERS. a. (Chambre de Metiers Departementale) Union Francaise d'Annuaires Professionnels, 13 Avenue Vladimir Komarov, B.P. 36, 78190 Trappes, France.

670   FR
GUIDE DE L'ARTISAN; chambres de metiers de France. a. (Chambre de Metiers Departementale) Union Francaise d'Annuaires Professionnels, 13 Avenue Vladimir Komarov, B.P. 36, 78190 Trappes, France.

GUIDE TO SCIENCE AND TECHNOLOGY IN EASTERN EUROPE. see *SCIENCES: COMPREHENSIVE WORKS*

GUIDE TO SCIENCE AND TECHNOLOGY IN THE ASIA/PACIFIC AREA. see *SCIENCES: COMPREHENSIVE WORKS*

GUMMA UNIVERSITY. FACULTY OF EDUCATION. ANNUAL REPORT: ART AND TECHNOLOGY SERIES. see *ART*

600   JA
HAKODATE TECHNICAL COLLEGE. RESEARCH REPORTS/HAKODATE KOGYO KOTO SENMON GAKKO KIYO. (Text in Japanese: summaries in English) 1967. a. Hakodate Technical College - Hakodate Kogyo Koto Senmon Gakko, 226 Tokura-cho, 2 Hakodate 042, Japan. illus.

600   US   ISSN 0440-3452
HARVARD MONOGRAPHS IN APPLIED SCIENCE. 1950. irreg. price varies. Harvard University Press, 79 Garden St., Cambridge, MA 02138.

HEIDELBERGER ARBEITSBUECHER. see *SCIENCES: COMPREHENSIVE WORKS*

HEIDELBERGER JAHRBUECHER. see *SCIENCES: COMPREHENSIVE WORKS*

HEIDELBERGER TASCHENBUECHER. see *SCIENCES: COMPREHENSIVE WORKS*

600   UK   ISSN 0307-5451
HISTORY OF TECHNOLOGY. 1976. a. price varies. Mansell Publishing, 3 Bloomsbury Pl., London WC1A 2QA, England (Dist. in U.S. by: Mansell, Merrimack Book Service, 99 Main St., Salem NH 03079) Eds. Rupert Hall, Norman Smith. Indexed: Hist.Abstr. Amer.Hist. & Life.

600   UK
HISTORY OF TECHNOLOGY SERIES. 1979. irreg. $49.50. Peter Peregrinus Ltd., Box 26, Hitchin, Herts SG5 1SA, England.

670   HK
HONG KONG INDUSTRIAL PRODUCTS DIRECTORY/HSIANG-KANG KUNG YEH CHIH PIN NIEN CHIEN. (Text in Chinese and English) 1974. irreg. HK.$50.00. Hsiang-Kang Kung i Chih Pin Chang Fa Chan Hsieh Hui., Handicrafts Manufacturers Development Association, P.O. Box: K-880, Chiu-Lung, Kowloon, Hong Kong. illus.

745.2   AU   ISSN 0018-7224
HUMAN INDUSTRIAL DESIGN. (Text in German) 1968. irreg. Verlag Dr. Herta Ranner, Zeismannsbrunngasse 1, A-1070 Vienna, Austria. Ed. H. Ranner. adv. bk. rev.

600   US
I F U. (Text in German) vol. 51, 1980. irreg. (Universitaet Stuttgart, Institut fuer Umformtechnik, GW) Springer-Verlag, 175 Fifth Ave., New York, NY 10010 (Also Berlin, Heidelberg, Vienna) Ed. K. Lange. (reprint service avail. from ISI)

620   IE
I I R S OCCASIONAL REPORT SERIES. 1975. irreg. Institute for Industrial Research and Standards, Ballymun Rd., Dublin 9, Ireland. bibl. charts.

INDIA. COMMITTEE ON SCIENCE AND TECHNOLOGY. ANNUAL REPORT. see *SCIENCES: COMPREHENSIVE WORKS*

354.54   II
INDIA. DEPARTMENT OF SCIENCE AND TECHNOLOGY. REPORT. (Text in English) 1971/72. a. free. ‡ Department of Science and Technology, Technology Bhavan, New Mehrauli Rd., New Delhi 110029, India.

600   II   ISSN 0073-6503
INDIAN INSTITUTE OF TECHNOLOGY, BOMBAY. SERIES.* (Text in English) 1968. irreg., 1971, no. 3. price varies. Indian Institute of Technology, Bombay, Powai, Bombay, India.

600   II   ISSN 0073-6511
INDIAN INSTITUTE OF TECHNOLOGY, MADRAS. ANNUAL REPORT. (Text in English) 1960. a. Rs.6.15. Indian Institute of Technology, Madras, The Registrar, Madras 36, India. circ. 500.

007   US   ISSN 0073-7623
INDUSTRIAL RESEARCH LABORATORIES OF THE U. S. irreg., 16th edt. 1979. $82.50. (Jaques Cattell Press) R. R. Bowker Company, 1180 Ave. of the Americas, New York, NY 10036 (Orders to P.O. Box 1807, Ann Arbor, Mich. 48106) (reprint service avail. from UMI)

600   NE   ISSN 0073-7739
INDUSTRIE ET ARTISANAT. 1965. irreg., 1968, no. 5. price varies. (Ecole Pratique des Hautes Etudes, Centre de Recherches Historiques, FR) Mouton Publishers, Noordeinde 41, 2514 GC The Hague, Netherlands (U.S. address: Mouton Publishers, c/o Walter de Gruyter, Inc., 200 Saw Mill River Rd., Hawthorne, NY 10532)

INSTITUT FUER DEN WISSENSCHAFTLICHEN FILM. PUBLIKATIONEN ZU WISSENSCHAFTLICHEN FILMEN. SEKTION TECHNISCHE WISSENSCHAFTEN, NATURWISSENSCHAFTEN. see *MOTION PICTURES*

620.1   US
INTERNATIONAL CONFERENCE ON PRESSURE VESSEL TECHNOLOGY. PAPERS. 1969. irreg., 3rd, 1977. price varies. American Society of Mechanical Engineers, Pressure Vessel Division, 345 E. 47th St., New York, NY 10017. bibl. illus. (also avail. in microfilm; microfiche)

600   NE   ISSN 0074-8951
INTERNATIONAL T N O CONFERENCE. (PROCEEDINGS) 1968. a. free. ‡ Netherlands Central Organization for Applied Scientific Research TNO, Information Department, P.O. Box 297, 2501 BD The Hague, Netherlands. Ed. A. Verbraeck. circ. 1,500.

607   JA   ISSN 0441-0734
JAPAN. GOVERNMENT INDUSTRIAL DEVELOPMENT LABORATORY, HOKKAIDO. REPORTS/HOKKAIDO KOGYO KAIHATSU SHIKENJO HOKOKU. 1966. irreg. Government Industrial Development Laboratory, Hokkaido - Hokkaido Kogyo Kaihatsu Shikenjo, 41-2 Higashi-tsukisamu, Toyohira-ku, Sapporo 061-01, Hokkaido, Japan.

Study and teaching

600   JA
JAPAN. GOVERNMENT INDUSTRIAL DEVELOPMENT LABORATORY, HOKKAIDO. TECHNICAL DATA/HOKKAIDO KOGYO KAIHATSU SHIKENJO GIJUTSU. 1961. irreg. Government Industrial Development Laboratory, Hokkaido - Hokkaido Kogyo Kaihatsu Shikenjo, 41-2 Higashi-tsukisamu, Toyohira-ku, Sapporo 06101, Hokkaido, Japan. charts.

JIWAJI UNIVERSITY. JOURNAL: SCIENCE, TECHNOLOGY & MEDICINE. see *SCIENCES: COMPREHENSIVE WORKS*

600   US
JOHNS HOPKINS STUDIES IN THE HISTORY OF TECHNOLOGY. 1967. irreg. price varies. Johns Hopkins University Press, Baltimore, MD 21218.

600 614   US   ISSN 0162-833X
JOURNAL OF THE NEW ALCHEMISTS. 1974. a. $25. (New Alchemy Institute) Stephen Greene Press, Box 1000, Brattleboro, VT 05301. Ed. Nancy Jack Todd. bk. rev. charts. illus. stat. circ. 5,000.

620   JA   ISSN 0453-2198
KANSAI UNIVERSITY TECHNOLOGY REPORTS/KANSAI DAIGAKU KOGAKU KENKYU HOKOKU. (Text in English) 1959. a. exchange basis. Kansai University, Faculty of Engineering - Kansai Daigaku Kogakubu, 3-3-35 Yamate-cho, Suita 564, Osaka, Japan.

600   US
KENTUCKY MANUFACTURING DEVELOPMENTS. a. Department of Commerce, Capitol Plaza Tower, Frankfort, KY 40601. Formerly (1966-1970): Manufacturing Developments in Kentucky.

KENYA NATIONAL ACADEMY FOR ADVANCEMENT OF ARTS AND SCIENCES. NEWSLETTER. see *SCIENCES: COMPREHENSIVE WORKS*

KORUNK TUDOMANYA. see *SCIENCES: COMPREHENSIVE WORKS*

745.2   NO
KUNSTINDUSTRIMUSEET I OSLO. AARBOK. (Summaries in English, German, French) 1893. irreg. Kr.50. Kunstindustrimuseet i Oslo, St. Olavs Gate, Oslo 1, Norway. Ed. Lauritz Opstad. bibl. illus.

TECHNOLOGY: COMPREHENSIVE WORKS

600   KO
KWAHAK KISUL YORAM/HANDBOOK OF SCIENCE AND TECHNOLOGY. 1970. a. Ministry of Science and Technology, Seoul, S. Korea. circ. 1,500.

KYOTO TECHNICAL UNIVERSITY. FACULTY OF INDUSTRIAL ARTS. MEMOIRS: SCIENCE AND TECHNOLOGY/KYOTO KOGEI SEN'I DAIGAKU KOGEIGAKUBU KIYO RIKO-HEN. see *SCIENCES: COMPREHENSIVE WORKS*

600   US   ISSN 0075-7926
LANDOLT-BOERNSTEIN, ZAHLENWERTE UND FUNKTIONEN AUS NATURWISSENSCHAFTEN UND TECHNIK. NEUE SERIE. GROUP 4: MACROSCOPIC AND TECHNICAL PROPERTIES OF MATTER. 1974. irreg., vol. 4, 1980. Springer-Verlag, 175 Fifth Ave., New York, NY 10010 (also Berlin, Heidelberg, Vienna) Ed. K. H. Hellwege. (reprint service avail. from ISI)

600   UK
LASER. 1966. irreg. £0.30 per no. ‡ 26 Selwood Rd., Addiscombe, Croydon CR0 7JR, Surrey, England. Ed. Bd. adv. bk. rev. bibl. charts. illus. circ. 100.

LEADING EDGE. see *SCIENCES: COMPREHENSIVE WORKS*

600   PL   ISSN 0076-0439
LODZKIE TOWARZYSTWO NAUKOWE. WYDZIAL V. NAUK TECHNICZNYCH. PRACE. 1963. irreg. price varies. Panstwowe Wydawnictwo Naukowe, Ul. Miodowa 10, Warsaw, Poland.

MCGRAW-HILL YEARBOOK OF SCIENCE AND TECHNOLOGY. see *SCIENCES: COMPREHENSIVE WORKS*

607   FR   ISSN 0071-9005
MEMOIRES O.R.S.T.O.M. 1961. irreg. price varies. Office de la Recherche Scientifique et Technique Outre-Mer, 70-74 Route d'Aulnay, 93140 Bondy, France.

METODICKY ZPRAVODAJ CS. SOUSTAVY VEDECKYCH, TECHNICKYCH A EKONOMICKYCH INFORMACI. see *LIBRARY AND INFORMATION SCIENCES*

600   JA
METROPOLITAN COLLEGE OF TECHNOLOGY, TOKYO. MEMOIRS/TOKYO-TORITSU KOKA TANKI DAIGAKU KENKYU HOKOKU. (Text in Japanese or English) 1973. a. Metropolitan Technical College - Tokyo-toritsu Koka Tanki Daigaku Gakujutsu Kenkyu Un'Eikai, 6-6 Asahigaoka Hino, Tokyo 191, Japan.

MIRRORED SPECTRUM; a collection of reports for the non-scientist and non-engineer about achievements in Canadian science and technology. see *SCIENCES: COMPREHENSIVE WORKS*

670   JA   ISSN 0540-469X
MITSUBISHI TECHNICAL BULLETIN. (Text mainly in English) 1962. irreg. Mitsubishi Heavy Industries Ltd., Technical Administration Dept., 2-5-1 Marunouchi, Chiyoda-ku, Tokyo 100, Japan. circ. 10,000.

600 020   HU   ISSN 0324-7341
MODSZERTANI KIADVANYOK/METHODS OF INFORMATION AND DOCUMENTATION. (Text in Hungarian; summaries in English, German, Russian) 1966. irreg., no. 44, 1976. price varies. Orszagos Muszaki Konyvtar es Dokumentacios Kozpont - Hungarian Central Technical Library and Documentation Centre, Reviczky utca 6, Box 12, 1428 Budapest, Hungary.

MONOGRAFIE Z DZIEJOW NAUKI I TECHNIKI. see *SCIENCES: COMPREHENSIVE WORKS*

600 330   HU   ISSN 0133-5707
MUSZAKI ES GAZDASAGI FEJLODES FO IRANYAI/MAIN TRENDS OF TECHNICAL AND ECONOMIC DEVELOPMENT. 1967. irreg., no. 15, 1976. price varies. Orszagos Muszaki Konyvtar es Dokumentacios Kozpont - Hungarian Central Technical Library and Documentation Centre, Reviczky u. 6, Box 12, 1428 Budapest, Hungary.

600   NE
N A T O ADVANCED STUDY INSTITUTE SERIES E: APPLIED SCIENCE. (Text in English) 1974. irreg. price varies. (North Atlantic Treaty Organization) Sijthoff & Noordhoff International Publishers b.v., Box 4, 2400 MA Alphen aan den Rijn, Netherlands (U.S. address: 20010 Century Blvd., Germantown, MD 20767)

NARODNI TECHNICKE MUZEUM. CATALOGUES OF COLLECTIONS. see *MUSEUMS AND ART GALLERIES*

600   CS   ISSN 0035-9378
NARODNI TECHNICKE MUZEUM. ROZPRAVY. (Text in Czech; summaries in English and German) 1962. 5-6/yr (approx) free. Narodni Technicke Muzeum, Kostelni 42, 170 78 Prague 7, Czechoslovakia. bibl.

600   CN   ISSN 0077-5584
NATIONAL RESEARCH COUNCIL, CANADA. PUBLICATIONS. 1953. irreg. price varies. National Research Council of Canada, Ottawa, Ont. K1A 0R6, Canada. circ. 1,000.

600   CN   ISSN 0077-5606
NATIONAL RESEARCH COUNCIL, CANADA. TECHNICAL TRANSLATION. 1947. irreg. price varies. National Research Council of Canada, Ottawa K1A 0R6, Ontario, Canada. circ. 100.

600   NZ   ISSN 0077-9601
NEW ZEALAND. DEPARTMENT OF SCIENTIFIC AND INDUSTRIAL RESEARCH. ANNUAL REPORT. 1927. a. price varies. Department of Scientific and Industrial Research, Box 9741, Wellington, New Zealand.

600   NZ   ISSN 0077-961X
NEW ZEALAND. DEPARTMENT OF SCIENTIFIC AND INDUSTRIAL RESEARCH. BULLETIN. 1927. irreg. price varies. Department of Scientific and Industrial Research, Box 9741, Wellington, New Zealand. index occasionally.

600   NZ   ISSN 0077-9636
NEW ZEALAND. DEPARTMENT OF SCIENTIFIC AND INDUSTRIAL RESEARCH. INFORMATION SERIES. 1948. irreg. price varies. Department of Scientific and Industrial Research, Box 9741, Wellington, New Zealand.

607   NZ   ISSN 0078-0162
NEW ZEALAND. NATIONAL RESEARCH ADVISORY COUNCIL. REPORT. 1965. a. price varies. Government Printing Office, Wellington, New Zealand.

607   NZ   ISSN 0078-0154
NEW ZEALAND. NATIONAL RESEARCH ADVISORY COUNCIL. SENIOR AND POST DOCTORAL RESEARCH FELLOWSHIP AWARDS FOR RESEARCH IN NEW ZEALAND GOVERNMENT DEPARTMENTS. 1968. a. free. National Research Advisory Council, P.O. Box 12240, Wellington, New Zealand. circ. 2,000.

NEWCOMEN SOCIETY FOR THE STUDY OF THE HISTORY OF ENGINEERING AND TECHNOLOGY. TRANSACTIONS. see *ENGINEERING*

NORGES TEKNISK-NATURVITENSKAPELIGE FORSKNINGSRAAD. AARSBERETNING. see *SCIENCES: COMPREHENSIVE WORKS*

600   CN
NOVA SCOTIA RESEARCH FOUNDATION CORPORATION. ANNUAL REPORT. a. Nova Scotia Research Foundation Corporation, 100 Fenwick St., Box 790, Dartmouth, N.S. B2Y 3Z7, Canada. Ed.Bd.

600   FR   ISSN 0071-9021
OFFICE DE LA RECHERCHE SCIENTIFIQUE ET TECHNIQUE OUTRE-MER. INITIATIONS DOCUMENTATIONS TECHNIQUES. 1962. irreg. price varies. Office de la Recherche Scientifique et Technique Outre-Mer, 70-74 Route d'Aulnay, 93140 Bondy, France.

OFFICE DE LA RECHERCHE SCIENTIFIQUE ET TECHNIQUE OUTRE-MER. RAPPORT D'ACTIVITE. see *SCIENCES: COMPREHENSIVE WORKS*

600   BL
OPEMA EM RITMO DE BRASIL JOVEM. 1968. irreg. free. (Ministerio dos Transportes, Operacao Maua) Assessoria de Relacoes Publicas, Editora, Promocoes e Publicidade Ltda., Av. Beira Mar 406, Grupo 906, Rio de Janeiro, Brazil. adv. illus. stat. circ. 60,000.

ORGANIZATION OF AFRICAN UNITY. SCIENTIFIC TECHNICAL AND RESEARCH COMMISSION. PUBLICATION. see *SCIENCES: COMPREHENSIVE WORKS*

ORGANIZATION OF AMERICAN STATES. REGIONAL SCIENTIFIC AND TECHNOLOGICAL PROGRAM. NEWSLETTER. see *SCIENCES: COMPREHENSIVE WORKS*

607   JA
OSAKA UNIVERSITY. INSTITUTE OF SCIENTIFIC AND INDUSTRIAL RESEARCH. MEMOIRS/OSAKA DAIGAKU SANGYO KAGAKU KENKYUSHO KIYO. (Text in European languages) 1941. a. exchange basis. Osaka University, Institute of Scientific and Industrial Research - Osaka Daigaku Sangyo Kagaku Kenkyusho, Yamadakami, Suita, Osaka 565, Japan. circ. 750.

600   US   ISSN 0078-6799
OSRAM-GESELLSCHAFT. TECHNISCH-WISSENSCHAFTLICHE ABHANDLUNGEN. 1953. irreg., no. 11, 1973. price varies. Springer-Verlag, 175 Fifth Ave., New York, NY 10010 (also Berlin, Heidelberg, Vienna) (reprint service avail. from ISI)

600   PK
P A S T I C TRANSLATIONS. 1957. irreg. free. Pakistan Scientific and Technological Information Centre, House No. 6, Street No. 22, Sector F-7/2, Box No. 1217, Islamabad, Pakistan. index issued separately. circ. 500. (also avail. in microfilm)
Formerly: P A N S D O C Translations (ISSN 0078-8368)

PAKISTAN COUNCIL OF SCIENTIFIC AND INDUSTRIAL RESEARCH. REPORT. see *SCIENCES: COMPREHENSIVE WORKS*

PERIODICALS THAT PROGRESSIVE SCIENTISTS SHOULD KNOW ABOUT. see *BIBLIOGRAPHIES*

PERIODICOS BRASILEIROS DE CIENCIAS E TECNOLOGIA. see *BIBLIOGRAPHIES*

PRAJNAN. see *SCIENCES: COMPREHENSIVE WORKS*

607   US
PROBABLE LEVELS OF R & D EXPENDITURES: FORECAST AND ANALYSIS. 1960? a. free. ‡ Battelle Memorial Institute, Columbus Laboratories, 505 King Avenue, Columbus, OH 43201. Ed. Dr. W. Halder Fisher. charts. stat. circ. controlled.

621.3   US   ISSN 0361-4689
R & D REVIEW (SCHENECTADY) irreg. General Electric Co., Research and Development Center, Schenectady, NY 12301. illus.

RAND REPORT SERIES. see *SCIENCES: COMPREHENSIVE WORKS*

REPORT TO S C A R ON SOUTH AFRICAN ANTARCTIC RESEARCH ACTIVITIES. (Scientific Committee for Antarctic Research) see *SCIENCES: COMPREHENSIVE WORKS*

RESEARCH IN PHILOSOPHY AND TECHNOLOGY. see *PHILOSOPHY*

RESEARCHER'S GUIDE TO WASHINGTON. see *SCIENCES: COMPREHENSIVE WORKS*

667.2   UK
REVIEW OF PROGRESS IN COLORATION AND RELATED TOPICS. 1970. a. Society of Dyers and Colourists, Box 244, Perkin House, Bradford, Yorkshire BD1 2JB, England. Ed. V. Simborowski. circ. 2,000.

RHEINISCH-WESTFAELISCHE AKADEMIE DER WISSENSCHAFTEN. VEROEFFENTLICHUNGEN. see *SCIENCES: COMPREHENSIVE WORKS*

TECHNOLOGY: COMPREHENSIVE WORKS

600   SW
S T U INVESTIGATION. irreg. Styrelsen foer Teknisk Utveckling, Information Section - National Swedish Board for Technical Development, Stockholm, Sweden. (Co-sponsor: Swedish State Power Board)

SAMBALPUR UNIVERSITY JOURNAL: SCIENCE AND TECHNOLOGY. see *SCIENCES: COMPREHENSIVE WORKS*

SASKATCHEWAN RESEARCH COUNCIL. ANNUAL REPORT. see *SCIENCES: COMPREHENSIVE WORKS*

SCIENCE AND ENGINEERING POLICY SERIES. see *SCIENCES: COMPREHENSIVE WORKS*

SCIENCE AND TECHNOLOGY. see *SCIENCES: COMPREHENSIVE WORKS*

SCIENCE ET TECHNOLOGIE ANNUAIRE/ WETENSCHAP EN TECHNOLOGIE JAARBOEK. see *SCIENCES: COMPREHENSIVE WORKS*

SCIENTIFIC AND TECHNICAL INFORMATION IN FOREIGN COUNTRIES/KAIGAKI KAGAKU GIJUTSU JOHO SHIRYO. see *SCIENCES: COMPREHENSIVE WORKS*

SCIENTIFIC AND TECHNICAL PERIODICALS PUBLISHED IN SOUTH AFRICA/ WETENSKAPLIKE EN TEGNIESE TYDSKRIFTE IN SUID-AFRIKA UITGEGEE. see *SCIENCES: COMPREHENSIVE WORKS*

SCIENTIFIC AND TECHNICAL SOCIETIES IN SOUTH AFRICA/WETENSKAPLIKE EN TEGNIESE VERENIGINGS IN SUID-AFRIKA. see *SCIENCES: COMPREHENSIVE WORKS*

SCIENTIFIC AND TECHNICAL SOCIETIES OF CANADA/SOCIETES SCIENTIFIQUES ET TECHNIQUES DU CANADA. see *SCIENCES: COMPREHENSIVE WORKS*

SCIENTIFIC POLICY, RESEARCH AND DEVELOPMENT IN CANADA/POLITIQUE DES SCIENCES, LA RECHERCHES ET LE DEVELOPPEMENT AU CANADA. see *SCIENCES: COMPREHENSIVE WORKS*

SCIENTIFIC RESEARCH ORGANIZATIONS IN SOUTH AFRICA/WETENSKAPLIKE NAVORSINGSORGANISASIES IN SUID-AFRIKA. see *SCIENCES: COMPREHENSIVE WORKS*

SCIENTIFIC, TECHNICAL AND RELATED SOCIETIES OF THE UNITED STATES. see *SCIENCES: COMPREHENSIVE WORKS*

600   607   US   ISSN 0080-830X
SCRIPPS CLINIC AND RESEARCH FOUNDATION. ANNUAL REPORT. 1924. a. free. Scripps Clinic and Research Foundation, 10666 N. Torrey Pines Rd., La Jolla, CA 92037. Ed. James O. Boylan. circ. 5,000.

600   GW
SIEMENS-NEWS. (Text in English) q. Siemens Aktiengesellschaft, Postfach 3240, 8520 Erlangen, W. Germany (B.R.D.) Ed. Willi Meier. circ. 10,000.

600   US   ISSN 0081-1491
SOCIETY FOR THE HISTORY OF TECHNOLOGY. MONOGRAPH SERIES. 1962. irreg., latest issue no. 8. Society for the History of Technology, c/o Carroll W. Pursell, Sec., Department of History, University of California, Santa Barbara, CA 93106.

SOUTH AFRICAN JOURNAL OF ANTARCTIC RESEARCH. see *SCIENCES: COMPREHENSIVE WORKS*

600   NE   ISSN 0077-7056
SPEUR- EN ONTWIKKELINGSWERK IN NEDERLAND/RESEARCH AND DEVELOPMENT ACTIVITIES IN THE NETHERLANDS. (Text in Dutch and English) 1959. irreg. fl.14.45. Centraal Bureau voor de Statistiek, Prinses Beatrixlaan 428, Voorburg, Netherlands (Orders to: Staatsuitgeverij, Christoffel Plantijnstraat, The Hague, Netherlands)

600   US
SPINOFF. a. U.S. National Aeronautics and Space Administration, Office of Space and Terrestrial Applications, Box 8756, Baltimore-Washington International Airport, MD 21240 (Orders to: Supt. of Documents, Washington, DC 20402) illus.

600   YU   ISSN 0081-3974
SRPSKA AKADEMIJA NAUKA I UMETNOSTI. ODELJENJE TEHNICKIH NAUKA. GLAS. (Text in Serbo-Croatian; summaries in French, English, German or Russian) 1949, N.S. irreg. price varies. Srpska Akademija Nauka i Umetnosti, Knez Mihailova 35, 11001 Belgrade, Yugoslavia (Dist. by: Prosveta, Terazije 16, Belgrade, Yugoslavia) Ed. Miroslav Nenadovic. circ. 500.

600   YU   ISSN 0081-4040
SRPSKA AKADEMIJA NAUKA I UMETNOSTI. ODELJENJE TEHNICKIH NAUKA. POSEBNA IZDANJA. (Text in Serbo-Croatian; summaries in French, English, German or Russian) 1950. irreg. price varies. Srpska Akademija Nauka i Umetnosti, Knez Mihailova 35, 11001 Belgrade, Yugoslavia (Dist. by: Prosveta, Terazije 16, Belgrade, Yugoslavia) circ. 600. Indexed: Ref.Zh.

600   PL   ISSN 0081-6604
STUDIA I MATERIALY Z DZIEJOW NAUKI POLSKIEJ. SERIA D. HISTORIA TECHNIKI I NAUK TECHNICZNYCH. (Text in Polish; summaries in English and French) 1958. irreg. price varies. (Polska Akademia Nauk, Zaklad Historii Nauki i Techniki) Panstwowe Wydawnictwo Naukowe, Ul. Miodowa 10, Warsaw, Poland. Ed. Waldemar Voise.

STUDIA I MATERIALY Z DZIEJOW NAUKI POLSKIEJ. SERIA E. ZAGADNIENIA OGOLNE. see *SCIENCES: COMPREHENSIVE WORKS*

STUDIES IN THE HISTORY OF DISCOVERIES. see *SCIENCES: COMPREHENSIVE WORKS*

620   SW
SWEDEN. STATENS JAERNVAEGARS CENTRALFOERVALTNING. GEOTEKNIK OCH INGENJOERGEOLOGI. MEDDELANDEN. (Text in Swedish; summaries in English) irreg., no. 38, 1979. Statens Jaernvaegars Centralfoervaltning - State Railways Central Administration, Geotechnical Department, S-105 50 Stockholm, Sweden.
    Formerly: Sweden. Statens Jaernvaegars Centralfoervaltning. Geotekniska Kontoret. Meddelanden.

600   500   UR
TALLINSKII POLITEKHNICHESKII INSTITUT. TRUDY. (Text in Russian; summaries in English and German) 1937. irreg., no. 375, 1975. price varies. Polutehniline Instituut, Ehitajate Tee 5, Tallinn, U.S.S.R. Ed. F. Vikhmann. circ. 350.

600   UK   ISSN 0082-2329
TECHNICAL SERVICE DATA (AUTOMOTIVE) 1935. a. £4.80. Palgrave Publishing Co. Ltd., 25 Windsor Street, Chertsey, Surrey, England. circ. 16,000.

600   GW   ISSN 0082-2361
TECHNIKGESCHICHTE IN EINZELDARSTELLUNGEN. 1967. irreg. price varies. (Verein Deutscher Ingenieure) V D I-Verlag GmbH, Graf Recke Str. 84, Postfach 1139, 4000 Duesseldorf 1, W. Germany (B.R.D.) circ. 200.

600   IS
TECHNION-ISRAEL INSTITUTE OF TECHNOLOGY. PRESIDENT'S REPORT. (Text in English) a. free to qualified personnel. Technion-Israel Institute of Technology, Haifa, Israel.
    Formerly: Israel Institute of Technology. President's Report and Reports of Other Officers (ISSN 0072-9329)

600   FR   ISSN 0082-2469
TECHNIQUES D'AUJOURD'HUI. 1970. irreg. price varies. Larousse, 17 rue du Montparnasse, 75280 Paris Cedex 06, France.

605   JA
TECHNIQUES INDUSTRIELLES DU JAPON. (Text in French) 1959. a. 2,000 Yen. Societe-Franco-Japonaise des Techniques Industrielles - Nichifutsu Kogyo Gijutsukai, 2-3 Kanda Surugadai, Chiyoda-ku, Tokyo 101, Japan.

600   GW   ISSN 0084-3091
TECHNISCHE AKADEMIE WUPPERTAL. BERICHTE. 1969. irreg. price varies. Vulkan-Verlag Dr. W. Classen, Hollestr. 1G, Postfach 103962, 4300 Essen, W. Germany (B.R.D.) adv. circ. 2,000.

658.5   745.2   GW   ISSN 0341-5570
TECHNO-TIP. 1970. m. DM.105. Vogel-Verlag KG, Max-Planck-Str. 7, 8700 Wuerzburg 1, W. Germany (B.R.D.) Ed.H. Groessl. adv. circ. 14,000(controlled)

600   GT
TECHNOLOGICAL MONOGRAPHS. (Text in Spanish; summaries in English) 1977. a. $15. Instituto Centro Americano de Investigacion y Tecnologia Industrial, Avda. la Reforma 4-47, Zona 10, Apdo. Postal 1552, Guatemala, Guatemala. charts.

TEKNISKA NOMENKLATURCENTRALEN PUBLIKATIONER. see *LINGUISTICS*

600   MY
TEKNOLOGI. (Text in English and Malay) 1977. irreg.? Technological University of Malaysia, Faculty of Electrical Engineering - Universiti Teknologi Malaysia, Fakulti Kejuruteraan Letrik, Jalan Gurney, Kuala Lumpur 15-02, Malaysia.

600   330   HU   ISSN 0133-3267
TEMADOKUMENTACIOS KIADVANYOK/ THEMATICAL REVIEWS. 1959. irreg. price varies. Orszagos Muszaki Konyvtar es Dokumentacios Kozpont - Hungarian Central Technical Library and Documentation Centre, Reviczky u. 6, Box 12, 1428 Budapest, Hungary.

605   JA   ISSN 0495-8020
TOKYO INSTITUTE OF TECHNOLOGY. BULLETIN. (Text in English) 1950. irreg. exchange basis. Tokyo Institute of Technology, 12-1, 2-chome, Okayama, Meguro-ku, Tokyo 152, Japan. abstr.

605   JA   ISSN 0495-8055
TOKYO INSTITUTE OF TECHNOLOGY. RESEARCH LABORATORY OF RESOURCES UTILIZATION. REPORT/SHIGEN KAGAKU KENKYUSHO. (Text in English) a. Tokyo Institute of Technology, Research Laboratory of Resources Utilization - Tokyo Kogyo Daigaku. Shigen Kagaku Kenkyusho, 2-2-1 Okayama, Meguro-ku, Tokyo 145, Japan.

600   JA   ISSN 0082-4747
TOKYO METROPOLITAN UNIVERSITY. FACULTY OF TECHNOLOGY. MEMOIRS/ TOKYO-TORITSU DAIGAKU KOGAKUBU HOKOKU. (Text in English) 1951. a. free. Tokyo Metropolitan University, Faculty of Technology - Tokyo-toritsu Daigaku Kogakubu, 2-1-1 Fukazawa, Setagaya-ku, Tokyo 158, Japan. Ed. Yoichi Higashi.

TREATISE ON MATERIALS SCIENCE & TECHNOLOGY. see *ENGINEERING — Engineering Mechanics And Materials*

600   UK
TREVITHICK SOCIETY. OCCASIONAL PUBLICATION. 1974. irreg. Trevithick Society, c/o Holman's Museum, Camborne, Cornwall, England.

TUDOMANYTORTENETI TANULMANYOK. see *SCIENCES: COMPREHENSIVE WORKS*

607   US
U.S. FEDERAL AVIATION ADMINISTRATION. SYSTEMS RESEARCH AND DEVELOPMENT. REPORT FAA-RD. 1958. irreg. price varies; announcements of new titles in FAA NEWS. U.S. Federal Aviation Administration, Systems Research and Development Service, 800 Independence Ave. S.W., Washington, DC 20591 (Order from: National Technical Information Service, 5285 Port Royal Rd., Springfield, VA 22151)

U.S. NATIONAL AERONAUTICS AND SPACE ADMINISTRATION. RESEARCH AND TECHNOLOGY OPERATING PLAN (RTOP) SUMMARY. see *AERONAUTICS AND SPACE FLIGHT*

338 600   US   ISSN 0083-2383
U.S. NATIONAL SCIENCE FOUNDATION. RESEARCH AND DEVELOPMENT IN INDUSTRY. (Subseries of U.S. National Science Foundation. Surveys of Science Resource Series) a. U. S. National Science Foundation, 1800 G St., N.W., Washington, DC 20550 (Orders to: Supt. Doc., Washington, DC 20402)

600   SP
UNIVERSIDAD POLITECNICA DE BARCELONA. PUBLICACION. no. 2, 1974. a. 750 ptas. Universidad Politecnica de Barcelona, Avda. Gregorio Maranon s/n, Barcelona 14, Spain.

600 378   CK
UNIVERSIDAD TECNOLOGICA DEL CHOCO. REVISTA. 1976. irreg. Universidad Tecnologica del Choco, Difusion Cultural, Carrera 2 no. 25-22, Quibdo, Choco, Colombia. Ed. Giorgio M. Manzini.

600 500   US   ISSN 0084-831X
UNIVERSITY OF CALIFORNIA, LOS ANGELES. SCHOOL OF ENGINEERING AND APPLIED SCIENCE. RESEARCH DEVELOPMENT, AND PUBLIC SERVICE ACTIVITIES. 1947. irreg., latest issue, 1973. University of California, Los Angeles, School of Engineering & Applied Science, 405 Hilgard Ave, Los Angeles, CA 90024. circ. 1,500.

600   II
UNIVERSITY OF RAJASTHAN. STUDIES IN ENGINEERING AND TECHNOLOGY. 1967. irreg. University of Rajasthan, Gandhi Nagar, Jaipur 302004, India.

UNIVERSITY OF SCIENCE AND TECHNOLOGY. JOURNAL. see *SCIENCES: COMPREHENSIVE WORKS*

600   PL
UNIWERSYTET SLASKI W KATOWICACH. WYDZIAL TECHNIKI. PRACE. irreg., 1975, vol. 5. price varies. Uniwersytet Slaski w Katowicach, Ul. Bankowa 14, 40-007 Katowice, Poland.

600   FI   ISSN 0357-9387
V T T SYMPOSIUM. (Text in official language of symposium) 1981. irreg. price varies. Valtion Teknillinen Tutkimuskeskus - Technical Research Centre of Finland, Vuorimiehentie 5, 02150 Espoo 15, Finland.

670   US
VACUUM TECHNOLOGY DIRECTORY & BUYERS GUIDE. 1966. a. free. Technical Publishing Co., 1301 S. Grove Ave., Barrington, IL 60010. Ed. C.J. Mosbacher. adv. circ. 32,000(controlled) Indexed: Chem. Abstr. Eng.Ind.

VADEMECUM DEUTSCHER LEHR- UND FORSCHUNGSSTAETTEN. see *SCIENCES: COMPREHENSIVE WORKS*

VALTION TEKNILLINEN TUTKIMUSKESKUS. TEKNILLINEN INFORMAATIOPALVELULAITOS. TIEDONANTO/TECHNICAL RESEARCH CENTRE OF FINLAND. TECHNICAL INFORMATION SERVICE. REPORT. see *LIBRARY AND INFORMATION SCIENCES*

WEIZMANN INSTITUTE OF SCIENCE, REHOVOT, ISRAEL. SCIENTIFIC ACTIVITIES. see *SCIENCES: COMPREHENSIVE WORKS*

WHERE AMERICA'S LARGE FOUNDATIONS MAKE THEIR GRANTS; who gets them and how much each receives. see *HUMANITIES: COMPREHENSIVE WORKS*

WHO'S WHO IN INDIAN ENGINEERING AND INDUSTRY. see *BIOGRAPHY*

600 010   US
WIRE TECHNOLOGY BUYER'S GUIDE. 1975. a. $20. Wire Technology, Inc., 137 E. 36th St., New York, NY 10016. Ed. Edmund D. Sickels. circ. 5,000.

WORLD OF THE FUTURE SERIES. see *SCIENCES: COMPREHENSIVE WORKS*

600   US   ISSN 0084-3121
WYKEHAM TECHNOLOGICAL SERIES. (Issues not numbered consecutively) 1970. irreg., no. 5, 1975. Crane, Russak & Company, Inc., 3 E. 44th St., New York, NY 10017.

605   JA
YAMAGUCHI UNIVERSITY. FACULTY OF ENGINEERING. TECHNOLOGY REPORTS. (Text in English) 1972. a. exchange basis. Yamaguchi University, Faculty of Engineering - Yamagachi Daigaku Kogakubu, Tokiwadai, Ube-shi 755, Japan.

ZRODLA DO DZIEJOW NAUKI I TECHNIKI. see *SCIENCES: COMPREHENSIVE WORKS*

TECHNOLOGY: COMPREHENSIVE WORKS — Abstracting, Bibliographies, Statistics

600 318   AG
ARGENTINA. INSTITUTO DE ASUNTOS TECNICOS. ESTADISTICAS. 1974. irreg. Instituto de Asuntos Tecnicos, Direccion de Estadistica, Palacio Municipal, Cordoba, Argentina. charts.

ASSOCIATION FRANCAISE POUR LA DIFFUSION DU LIVRE SCIENTIFIQUE, TECHNIQUE ET MEDICAL (BULLETINS COLLECTIFS) see *SCIENCES: COMPREHENSIVE WORKS — Abstracting, Bibliographies, Statistics*

BIBLIOGRAPHY OF INTERLINGUAL SCIENTIFIC AND TECHNICAL DICTIONARIES. see *SCIENCES: COMPREHENSIVE WORKS — Abstracting, Bibliographies, Statistics*

600 016   CS
DEJINY VYROBNICH SIL. irreg. price varies. Narodni Technicke Muzeum, Kostelni 42, 170 78 Prague 7, Czechoslovakia.

600 500 016   US   ISSN 0094-4505
GUIDE TO AMERICAN SCIENTIFIC AND TECHNICAL DIRECTORIES. 1972. triennial. $29.50. Todd Publications, Box 535, Rye, NY 10580. Ed. Barry T. Klein.

600 016   II
INDIAN INSTITUTE OF TECHNOLOGY, MADRAS. M.S., PH.D. DISSERTATION ABSTRACTS. (Text in English) a. Indian Institute of Technology, Madras, The Registrar, Madras 36, India.
  Supersedes: Indian Institute of Technology, Madras. Ph.D. Dissertation Abstracts.

016 600   PK
LISTS OF P A S T I C BIBLIOGRAPHIES. (Text in English) 1957. a. free. Pakistan Scientific and Technological Information Centre, House No. 6, Street No. 22, Sector F-7/2, Box 1217, Islamabad, Pakistan. Ed. Mumtaz Begum. circ. 500. (also avail. in microfilm)
  Formerly: Lists of P A N S Doc Bibliographies (ISSN 0078-835X)

600 016   CS
NARODNI TECHNICKE MUZEUM. BIBLIOGRAFIE. PRAMENY. (Text in Czech and German) 1970. irreg. price varies. Narodni Technicke Muzeum, Kostelni 42, 170 78 Prague 7, Czechoslovakia.

NATIONAL COMMITTEE ON SCIENCE AND TECHNOLOGY. RESEARCH AND DEVELOPMENT STATISTICS. see *SCIENCES: COMPREHENSIVE WORKS — Abstracting, Bibliographies, Statistics*

SCIENTIFIC AND TECHNICAL BOOKS AND SERIALS IN PRINT. see *SCIENCES: COMPREHENSIVE WORKS — Abstracting, Bibliographies, Statistics*

SCIENTIFIC SERIALS IN THAI LIBRARIES. see *SCIENCES: COMPREHENSIVE WORKS — Abstracting, Bibliographies, Statistics*

679 310   SA
SOUTH AFRICA. DEPARTMENT OF STATISTICS. CENSUS OF MANUFACTURING. (Report No. 10-21) biennial, latest 1972. price varies. Department of Statistics, Private Bag X44, Pretoria 0001, South Africa (Orders to: Government Printer, Bosman St., Private Bag X85, Pretoria 0001,South Africa)

016.05 600   UK
TECHNICAL AND SPECIALISED PERIODICALS PUBLISHED IN BRITAIN. Running title: Catalogue of Technical and Specialised Periodicals - a Selected List. a. Central Office of Information, Hercules Rd., London SE1 7DU, England (Dist. in U.S. by: British Publications, Inc., 11-03 46th Ave., Long Island City, New York, NY 11101)

600   US
THESES AND DISSERTATIONS ACCEPTED IN PARTIAL FULFILLMENT OF THE REQUIREMENTS FOR DEGREES GRANTED BY THE MICHIGAN TECHNOLOGICAL UNIVERSITY. (Subseries of Its: Library Publication) 1965. irreg., latest issue 1976. free. ‡ Michigan Technological University, Library, Houghton, MI 49931.

TELEPHONE AND TELEGRAPH

see *Communications—Telephone and Telegraph*

TEXTILE INDUSTRIES AND FABRICS

see also *Cleaning and Dyeing; Clothing Trade*

667 338.4   II   ISSN 0075-4005
AHMEDABAD TEXTILE INDUSTRY'S RESEARCH ASSOCIATION. JOINT TECHNOLOGICAL CONFERENCES. PROCEEDINGS. (Text in English) 1960. a. $7. Ahmedabad Textile Industry's Research Association, Polytechnic P.O., Ahmedabad 380015, India. circ. 1,000. Indexed: Text.Tech.Dig. World Text.Abstr.

677   II   ISSN 0065-4779
AHMEDABAD TEXTILE INDUSTRY'S RESEARCH ASSOCIATION. PROCEEDINGS OF THE MANAGEMENT CONFERENCE. (Text in English) 1956. a. $5. Ahmedabad Textile Industry's Research Association, Polytechnic P.O., Ahmedabad 380015, India. circ. 1,000.

677   SP
ALGODON HACE SUS CUENTAS. (Text in Spanish; summaries in English) 1956. biennial. 750 ptas. Servicio Comercial de la Industria Textil Algodonera, Ave. Jose Antonio, 670, Barcelona-10, Spain. stat. circ. 500.

677   II
ALL INDIA HANDLOOM EXPORTERS GUIDE. irreg. $10 per no. c/o S. Narayanan, 11-B Ramachandra Iyer St., Madras 600017, India.

ALL PAKISTAN TEXTILE MILLS ASSOCIATION. ANNUAL REPORT. see *BUSINESS AND ECONOMICS — Production Of Goods And Services*

677   US   ISSN 0065-7069
AMERICAN ASSOCIATION FOR TEXTILE TECHNOLOGY. TECHNICAL REVIEW AND REGISTER. (June issue of Modern Textiles) 1950. a. $1. American Association for Textile Technology, 1040 Ave. of the Americas, New York, NY 10018. Ed. F.A. McNeirney. adv. circ. 14,500. (also avail. in microform from UMI)

TEXTILE INDUSTRIES AND FABRICS

677.028   US
AMERICAN ASSOCIATION OF TEXTILE CHEMISTS AND COLORISTS. BUYER'S GUIDE. (Special issue of: Textile Chemist and Colorist) 1923. a. $40 to non-members; members $20. American Association of Textile Chemists and Colorists, P.O. Box 12215, Research Triangle Park, NC 27709. Ed. Jack Kissiah. adv. circ. 11,500. (reprint service avail. from UMI) Indexed: Chem.Abstr. Eng.Ind. Text.Tech.Dig. World Text.Abstr.
    Formerly: American Association of Textile Chemists and Colorists. Products Buyer's Guide (ISSN 0065-7352)

677.028   US
AMERICAN ASSOCIATION OF TEXTILE CHEMISTS AND COLORISTS. NATIONAL TECHNICAL CONFERENCE. BOOK OF PAPERS. 1974. a. $40 to non-members; members $20. American Association of Textile Chemists and Colorists, Box 12215, Research Triangle Park, NC 27709. (reprint service avail. from UMI)

677   US   ISSN 0065-8588
AMERICAN HOME ECONOMICS ASSOCIATION. TEXTILES AND CLOTHING SECTION. TEXTILE HANDBOOK. 1960. irreg., 5th edt., 1974. $6. ‡ American Home Economics Association, 2010 Massachusetts Ave. N.W., Washington, DC 20036.

677   FR   ISSN 0066-3697
ANNUAIRE STATISTIQUE DE L'INDUSTRIE FRANCAISE DU JUTE. 1953. a. Syndicat General de l'Industrie du Jute, 33 rue de Miromesnil, 75008 Paris, France.

ANNUAL BOOK OF A S T M STANDARDS. PART 32. TEXTILES--YARN, FABRICS, AND GENERAL TEST METHODS. see ENGINEERING — Engineering Mechanics And Materials

ANNUAL BOOK OF A S T M STANDARDS. PART 33. TEXTILES--FIBERS, ZIPPERS; HIGH MODULUS FIBERS. see ENGINEERING — Engineering Mechanics And Materials

677   US   ISSN 0094-9884
ANNUAL TEXTILE INDUSTRY TECHNICAL CONFERENCE. (PUBLICATION) a., formerly biennial. Institute of Electrical and Electronics Engineers, Inc., 445 Hoes Lane, Piscataway, NJ 08854.
    Formerly: Textile Industry Technical Conference. Record (ISSN 0082-3651)

677   IT
ANNUARIO DELL'INDUSTRIA ITALIANA DELLA MAGLIERIA E DELLA CALZETTERIA. (Text in Italian, French, German, English, Spanish) 1970. a. L.30000. (Italian Association of Knitwear Producers) Gesto s.r.l., Via Cesare Battisti 21, 20122 Milan, Italy. adv. circ. 15,000.

APPAREL BUYERS GUIDE YEAR BOOK. see BUSINESS AND ECONOMICS — Trade And Industrial Directories

646   US
APPAREL PLANT WAGES SURVEY. a. $25 to non-members; members $18. American Apparel Manufacturers Association, Suite 800, 1611 No. Kent St., Arlington, VA 22209.
    Supersedes in part: Apparel Plant Wages and Personnel Policies (ISSN 0084-6678)

677.2   SP   ISSN 0571-3609
ASOCIACION DE INVESTIGACION TEXTIL ALGODONERA. COLECCION DE MANUALES TECNICOS. irreg. Asociacion de Investigacion Textil Algodonera, Avda. Jose Antonio, 670, Barcelona, Spain. illus.
    Cotton

677.2   SP
ASOCIACION DE INVESTIGACION TEXTIL ALGODONERA. ESTUDIOS Y DOCUMENTOS. no. 2, 1976. irreg. Asociacion de Investigacion Textil Algodonera, Av. Jose Antonio 670, Barcelona, Spain.
    Cotton

677.3 636.3 319.4   AT
AUSTRALIA. BUREAU OF STATISTICS. TASMANIAN OFFICE. WOOL PRODUCTION AND DISPOSAL. a. Australian Bureau of Statistics, Tasmanian Office, Box 66A, Hobart, Tasmania 7001, Australia. circ. 550.
    Formerly: Australia. Bureau of Statistics. Tasmanian Office. Wool Production Statistics (ISSN 0571-9844)

746   SZ   ISSN 0067-849X
BIENNALE INTERNATIONALE DE LA TAPISSERIE. (Text in French and English) 1962. biennial. 15 Fr. International Centre of Ancient and Modern Tapestry - Centre International de la Tapisserie Ancienne et Moderne, 4 Av. Villamont, 1005 Lausanne, Switzerland. (Co-sponsor: Musee des Beaux-Arts, Lausanne) adv.

677   II   ISSN 0084-8859
C.T.T.S. ANNUAL. (Text and summaries in English) 1949. a. College of Textile Technology, Serampore, Students Union, Serampore, West Bengal, India. Ed. S.C. Ukil.

677.028   CN   ISSN 0068-9858
CANADIAN TEXTILE DIRECTORY. 1924. a. Can.$20($30) Lloyd Publications of Canada, Box 262, West Hill, Ont. M1E 4R5, Canada. Ed. J. Lloyd. adv. index. circ. 7,500.

677   US
CARPET AND RUG INSTITUTE. DIRECTORY. 1950. a. $10. Carpet and Rug Institute, Box 2048, Dalton, GA 30720. Ed. Richard N. Hopper.
    Formerly: Carpet and Rug Institute. Directory and Report (ISSN 0069-0740)

677   UK   ISSN 0069-0767
CARPET ANNUAL. 1931. a. £15. Haymarket Publishing Ltd., 38-42 Hampton Rd., Teddington, Middx. TW11 0JE, England.

667   UK
CARPET DYER INTERNATIONAL. 1978. a. £1.50($3.50) Textile Business Press Ltd., 91 Kirkgate, Bradford, West Yorkshire BD1 1TB, England. Ed. R.A.C. Mathews. circ. 5,000.

677   US   ISSN 0095-6457
CARPET SPECIFIER'S HANDBOOK. 1974. irreg., 3rd edt., 1979. $10. Carpet and Rug Institute, Box 2048, Dalton, GA 30720. illus.

677   US
CLARK'S DIRECTORY OF SOUTHERN TEXTILE MILLS. a. $10.50. Clark Publishing Co., Box 88, Greenville, SC 29602.

677.3   AT
COMMONWEALTH SCIENTIFIC AND INDUSTRIAL RESEARCH ORGANIZATION. CSIRO TEXTILE NEWS. 1954. a. free. C. S. I. R. O., Division of Textile Industry, Box 21, Belmont, Vic. 3216, Australia.
    Formerly: Commonwealth Scientific and Industrial Research Organization. Wool Research Laboratories. CSIRO Wool Textile News.
    Wool

677 530   AT
COMMONWEALTH SCIENTIFIC AND INDUSTRIAL RESEARCH ORGANIZATION. DIVISION OF TEXTILE PHYSICS. ANNUAL REPORT. 1970-71. a. Aus.$2. C. S. I. R. O., Division of Textile Physics, 338 Blaxland Rd., Ryde, N.S.W. 2112, Australia.

677.21   US   ISSN 0070-0673
COTTON INTERNATIONAL. 1914. a. $6. Meister Publishing Co., 37841 Euclid Ave., Wiloughby, OH 44094. Ed. Seton Ross. circ. 25,000.
    Formerly: Cotton Trade Journal International.

677   US   ISSN 0084-9502
CURTAIN, DRAPERY AND BEDSPREAD NATIONAL BUYERS GUIDE. 1954. a. $5. Columbia Communications, Inc., 370 Lexington Ave., New York, NY 10017. Ed. Rochelle Goldstein. adv. bk. rev. circ. 15,000 (controlled)

677   US   ISSN 0070-2943
DAVISON'S KNIT GOODS TRADE. 1891. a. $35. Davison Publishing Co., Box 477, Ridgewood, NJ 07451. Ed. Norman L. Vought.

677   US   ISSN 0363-5252
DAVISON'S SALESMAN'S BOOK. 1910. a. $20. Davison Publishing Co., P.O. Box 477, Ridgewood, NJ 07451. Ed. Norman L. Vought.
    Formerly: Davison's Textile Directory for Executives and Salesmen (ISSN 0070-2978)

677   US   ISSN 0070-2951
DAVISON'S TEXTILE BLUE BOOK. 1866. a. $50. Davison Publishing Co., P.O. Box 477, Ridgewood, NJ 07451. Ed. Norman L. Vought.

677   US
DAVISON'S TEXTILE BUYER'S GUIDE. 1934. a. $25. Davison Publishing Co., P.O. Box 477, Ridgewood, NJ 07451. Ed. Norman L. Vought.
    Formerly (until 1978): Davison's Textile Catalog and Buyer's Guide (ISSN 0070-296X)

DESIGN FROM SCANDINAVIA; a Scandinavian production in furniture, textiles, illumination, arts and crafts and industrial design. see INTERIOR DESIGN AND DECORATION — Furniture And House Furnishings

677.3   GW
DEUTSCHES WOLLFORSCHUNGSINSTITUT. VORTRAEGE. 1953. irreg. DM.10. Deutsches Wollforschungsinstitut, Technische Hochschule Aachen, Veltmanplatz 8, 5100 Aachen, W. Germany (B.R.D.)
    Wool

380.1   II
DIRECTORY OF WOOL, HOSIERY & FABRICS. (Text in English) 1950. a. Rs.30. Commerce Publications Limited, Manek Mahal, 90 Veer Nariman Rd., Churchgate, Bombay 400020, India. Ed. Vadilal Dagli.
    Formerly: India & Pakistan Wool, Hosiery & Fabrics.

E N I ANNUAL REPORT. (Ente Nazionale Idrocarburi) see ENERGY

677   SZ   ISSN 0084-5760
EIDGENOESSISCHE TECHNISCHE HOCHSCHULE ZUERICH. MITTEILUNGEN. TEXTILMASCHINENBAU UND TEXTILINDUSTRIE. (Text in German and English) 1943. irreg., 1967, no. 9. (Swiss Federal Institute of Technology) Buchdruckerei und Verlag Leemann AG, Arbenzstr. 20, 8034 Zurich, Switzerland.

677   US   ISSN 0080-6811
EMBROIDERY DIRECTORY. 1947. a. $5. Schiffli Lace and Embroidery Manufacturers Association, 512 23 St., Union City, NJ 07087. Ed. I. Leonard Seiler. adv. circ. 2,000.
    Former titles: Schiffli Digest and Directory; Schiffli Directory.

677 687   US
FAIRCHILD'S TEXTILE & APPAREL FINANCIAL DIRECTORY. 1974. a. $45. Fairchild Books, 7 East 12th St., New York, NY 10003. Ed. Robin Feldman. circ. 1,500.

677   US   ISSN 0071-4682
FIBER SCIENCE SERIES. 1970. irreg., vol. 8, 1979. price varies. Marcel Dekker, Inc., 270 Madison Ave., New York, NY 10016. Ed. L. Rebenfeld.

338.4   II
HANDBOOK OF THE INDIAN COTTON TEXTILE INDUSTRY. (Text in English) a. Rs.15. Cotton Textiles Export Promotion Council., Engineering Centre 9, 4 Mathew Rd., Bombay, India.

677
HISTORIC TEXTILES OF INDIA. (Text in English) 1972. irreg., vol. 2, 1973. Rs.200. Calico Museum of Textiles, Calico Mills Premises, Outside Jamalpur Gate, Ahmedabad, India. Ed. John Irwin.

677   US
I N D A ASSOCIATION OF THE NONWOVEN FABRICS INDUSTRY. TECHNICAL SYMPOSIUM PAPERS. (Former name of issuing body: International Nonwovens and Disposables Association) 1972? a. $70 to non-members; members $35. I N D A Association of the Nonwoven Fabrics Industry, 1700 Broadway, 25th Fl., New York, NY 10019.

677 SZ
I T M F DIRECTORY. biennial. free. ‡ International Textile Manufacturers Federation, Am Schanzengraben 29, Postfach, 8039 Zurich, Switzerland. Ed. Herwig M. Strolz.
  Formerly: I F C A T I Directory (ISSN 0445-0698)

677 UK ISSN 0073-604X
INDEX TO TEXTILE AUXILIARIES. 1967. biennial. £4.50. Textile Business Press Ltd., 91 Kirkgate, Bradford, West Yorkshire BD1 1TB, England (U.S. address: 205 E. 42nd St., New York, NY 10017)
  Published for the International Dyer

677.39 638 II
INDIAN JOURNAL OF SERICULTURE. (Text in English) 1962. a. Rs.7.50. Central Silk Board, Meghdoot, 95-B Marine Drive, Bombay 400002, India.
  Science and technology of silk industry

677.13 676.14 II ISSN 0073-6562
INDIAN JUTE MILLS ASSOCIATION. ANNUAL SUMMARY OF JUTE AND GUNNY STATISTICS. (Annual supplement to "Monthly Summary") (Text in English) 1955. a. Rs.25 per copy. Indian Jute Mills Association, Royal Exchange, 6 Netaji Subhas Rd., Calcutta 1, India. circ. 400.

677 676 II ISSN 0073-6570
INDIAN JUTE MILLS ASSOCIATION. LOOM AND SPINDLE STATISTICS. 1941. biennial. Rs.5. Indian Jute Mills Association, Royal Exchange, 6 Netaji Subhas Rd., Calcutta 1, India. circ. 500.

677 II
INDIAN TEXTILE ANNUAL & DIRECTORY. (Text in English) 1965. a. $10. Eastland Publications (Private) Ltd., 44 Chittaranjan Ave., Calcutta 12, India. Ed. J.R. Dutta. adv. bk. rev. charts. illus. pat. circ. 5,000.

667 338.4 US ISSN 0095-683X
INTERNATIONAL DIRECTORY OF THE NONWOVEN FABRICS INDUSTRY. 1970. biennial. $25 to non-members; members $15. I N D A Association of the Nonwoven Fabrics Industry, 1700 Broadway, 25th Fl., New York, NY 10019. Ed. Janet Rosen.
  Formerly: Directory for the Nonwoven Fabrics and Disposable Soft Goods Industries (ISSN 0070-5020)

667 677 SZ ISSN 0074-5898
INTERNATIONAL FEDERATION OF ASSOCIATIONS OF TEXTILE CHEMISTS AND COLORISTS. REPORTS OF CONGRESS. irreg., 11th, 1978, Italy. International Federation of Associations of Textile Chemists and Colorists, Box 93, CH-4133 Pratteln, Switzerland.

677 FR ISSN 0074-7602
INTERNATIONAL RAYON AND SYNTHETIC FIBRES COMMITTEE. TECHNICAL CONFERENCE. REPORTS. irreg. International Rayon and Synthetic Fibres Committee, 29, rue de Courcelles, 75008 Paris, France.

677 FR ISSN 0074-7610
INTERNATIONAL RAYON AND SYNTHETIC FIBRES COMMITTEE. WORLD CONGRESS. REPORT. irreg., 1971, 3rd, Munich. International Rayon and Synthetic Fibres Committee, 29 rue de Courcelles, 75008 Paris, France.
  Publisher and format of reports vary

677 UK ISSN 0074-9087
INTERNATIONAL TEXTILE MACHINERY. 1967. a. £2.50. Textile Business Press Ltd., 91 Kirkgate, Bradford, West Yorkshire BD1 1TB, England. Ed. Eugene P. Dempsey.
  Supersedes: Textile Recorder Annual and Machinery Review.

677 SZ
INTERNATIONAL TEXTILE MANUFACTURING. a. 20 Fr. International Textile Manufacturers Federation, Am Schanzengraben 29, Postfach 8039 Zurich, Switzerland. Ed. Herwig M. Strolz, Peter N. Scott.
  Formerly: Cotton and Allied Textile Industries (ISSN 0574-2315)

677 US
INTERNATIONAL TEXTILE REVIEW. 1979. a. $97. McGraw-Hill Publications Co. (Washington), 457 National Press Bldg., Washington, DC 20045. Ed. Paula York.

677 UR
KALININSKII NAUCHNO-ISSLEDOVATEL'SKII INSTITUT TEKSTIL'NOI PROMYSHLENNOSTI. NAUCHNO-ISSLEDOVATEL'SKIE TRUDY. 1971. irreg. 0.67 Rub. Kalininskii Nauchno-Issledovatel'skii Institut Tekstilnoi Promyshlennosti, Kalinin, U.S.S.R. illus.

677 338.4 US ISSN 0085-2562
KNITTING TIMES YEARBOOK. a. $10. National Knitwear and Sportswear Association, 51 Madison Ave., New York, NY 10010.

338.4 JA
MAN-MADE FIBERS OF JAPAN. (Text in English) biennial. $40. Japan Chemical Fibres Association, No. 3 Nihonbashi-Muromachi 3-chome, Chuo-ku, Tokyo 103, Japan. (Co-sponsor: Japan Silk and Synthetic Textiles Exporters' Association) illus.

677.02 CN ISSN 0381-551X
MANUAL OF THE TEXTILE INDUSTRY OF CANADA. 1928. a. Can.$10. Canadian Textile Journal Publishing Co., Ltd., 4920 de Maisonneuve Blvd. W., Suite 307, Montreal, Que. H3Z 1N1, Canada. Ed. W.A.B. Davidson.

677 US
MILL REPORT. 1976. irreg. Platt Saco Lowell, Drawer 2327, Greenville, SC 29602. charts. illus.

NATIONAL COTTONSEED PRODUCTS ASSOCIATION. TRADING RULES. see ENGINEERING — Chemical Engineering

NECKWEAR INDUSTRY DIRECTORY. see CLOTHING TRADE

PAKISTAN CENTRAL COTTON COMMITTEE. AGRICULTURAL SURVEY REPORT. see AGRICULTURE — Crop Production And Soil

PAKISTAN CENTRAL COTTON COMMITTEE. TECHNOLOGICAL BULLETIN. SERIES A. see AGRICULTURE — Crop Production And Soil

PAKISTAN CENTRAL COTTON COMMITTEE. TECHNOLOGICAL BULLETIN. SERIES B. see AGRICULTURE — Crop Production And Soil

677 UK
PLATT SACO LOWELL BULLETIN. 1928. a. contr.free circ. Box 55, Accrington BB5 0RN, Lancashire, England. Ed. D. J. Lloyd. adv. charts. illus. pat. tr.mk. index. circ. 5,397.
  Formerly: Saco-Lowell Bulletin (ISSN 0036-2182)
  House organ

677 US
PLATT SACO LOWELL REPLACEMENT PARTS NEWS. vol. 17, 1976. irreg. free to customers. Platt Saco Lowell, Replacement Parts Center, Box 327, Greenville, SC 29602. Ed. L. H. Irby. illus. circ. 3,000. (tabloid format)

677 PL ISSN 0076-0331
POLITECHNIKA LODZKA. ZESZYTY NAUKOWE. WLOKIENNICTWO. (Text in Polish; summaries in English and Russian) 1954. irreg. price varies. Politechnika Lodzka, Ul. Zwirki 36, 90-924 Lodz, Poland (Dist. by: Ars Polona-Ruch, Krakowskie Przedmiescie 7, Warsaw, Poland) Ed. Witold Zurek. circ. 383. Indexed: Chem.Abstr. World Text.Abstr. Text. Tech. Dig.

677.2 IT
RAPPORTO SULLA INDUSTRIA COTONIERA ITALIANA. (Supplement to: Industria Cotoniera) a. free. Associazione Cotoniera Italiana, 1 via Borgonuova 11, Milan, Italy.

677 FR ISSN 0080-102X
REPERTOIRE DES PRODUCTIONS DE L'INDUSTRIE COTONNIERE FRANCAISE. 1958. irreg. price varies; 70F for 1976-77 edition. (Syndicat General de l'Industrie Cotonniere Francaise et Textiles Allies) S P E I, 3 Av. Ruysdael, 75367 Paris Cedex 08, France.

677 CN ISSN 0704-7940
REPERTOIRE DES PRODUITS FABRIQUES AU QUEBEC. (Text in French) 1978. a. Centre de Recherche Industrielle de Quebec, Box 9038, 333 rue Franquet, Sainte-Foy, Que. G1V 4C7, Canada.

677.3 SA ISSN 0081-2560
S A W T R I TECHNICAL REPORT. 1952. irreg. $3. South African Wool and Textile Research Institute, Box 1124, Port Elizabeth 6000, South Africa. Ed. P. de W. Olivier. circ. 250. Indexed: World Text.Abstr.
  Wool

SHINSHU UNIVERSITY. FACULTY OF TEXTILE SCIENCE AND TECHNOLOGY. JOURNAL. SERIES A: BIOLOGY. see BIOLOGY

SHINSHU UNIVERSITY. FACULTY OF TEXTILE SCIENCE AND TECHNOLOGY. JOURNAL. SERIES C: CHEMISTRY. see ENGINEERING — Chemical Engineering

SHINSHU UNIVERSITY. FACULTY OF TEXTILE SCIENCE AND TECHNOLOGY. JOURNAL. SERIES D: ARTS. see ART

677 UK ISSN 0306-5154
SHIRLEY INSTITUTE PUBLICATIONS. S: SERIES. 1972. irreg. price varies. Shirley Institute, Manchester M20 8RX, England.

677.3 SA ISSN 0560-9941
SOUTH AFRICAN WOOL AND TEXTILE RESEARCH INSTITUTE. ANNUAL REPORT. (Text in Afrikaans and English) 1954. a. free. South African Wool and Textile Research Institute, Box 1124, Port Elizabeth 6000, South Africa. Ed. P. de W. Olivier. bibl. charts. illus. circ. 1,200.
  Wool

338.1 NZ
STATISTICAL ANALYSIS OF NEW ZEALAND WOOL PRODUCTION AND DISPOSAL. 1973. a. free. New Zealand Wool Marketing Corporation, 18 Brandon St., Wellington, New Zealand. stat.

677 SZ
STRUCTURE OF THE COTTON AND ALLIED TEXTILE INDUSTRIES. 1964. every 4 yrs. 20 Fr. International Textile Manufacturers Federation, Am Schanzengraben 29, Postfach 8039 Zurich, Switzerland. Ed. Peter N. Scott. charts. stat.

677.028 US
SYMPOSIUM ON TEXTILE FLAMMABILITY. PROCEEDINGS. 1973. a. price varies. LeBlanc Research Corporation, 5454 Post Rd., East Greenwich, RI 02818. Ed. R. Bruce LeBlanc. Indexed: Chem.Abstr.

677 FR ISSN 0082-1047
SYNDICAT GENERAL DE L'INDUSTRIE COTONNIERE FRANCAISE. ANNUAIRE. 1970. a. free. (Syndicat General de l'Industrie Cotonniere Francaise et Textiles Allies) Service de Presse Edition Information, 3 Av. Ruysdael, 75367 Paris Cedex 08, France. adv.

677 GW
TASCHENBUCH DER TEXTILEN RAUMAUSSTATTUNG. a. DM.29.80. Fachverlag Schiele und Schoen GmbH, Markgrafenstr. 11, 1000 Berlin 61, W. Germany (B.R.D.) Ed. Wilhelm Artz.

677 GW ISSN 0082-1837
TASCHENBUCH DES TEXTILEINZELHANDELS. 1962. a. Deutscher Fachverlag GmbH, Schumannstr. 27, Postfach 2625, 6000 Frankfurt 1, W. Germany (B.R.D.)

677 GW ISSN 0082-1896
TASCHENBUCH FUER DIE TEXTIL-INDUSTRIE. 1951. a. DM.32. Fachverlag Schiele und Schoen GmbH, Markgrafenstr. 11, 1000 Berlin 61, W. Germany (B.R.D.) Eds. M. Malthes, W. Lang. adv. circ. 5,000.

677.3 NZ
TECHNICAL PAPERS ON NEW ZEALAND WOOL. 1969. irreg. price varies. Wool Research Organization of New Zealand, Private Bag, Christchurch, New Zealand. Ed. L. F. Story. bibl. stat. circ. 150. Indexed: Chem.Abstr. World Text.Abstr.

677   FI
TEKSTIILITEOLLISUUDEN VUOSIKIRJA/ TEKSTILINDUSTRINS AARSBOK/TEXTILE INDUSTRY YEARBOOK. (Text in Finnish and Swedish; summaries in English) a. Tekstiiliteollisuuden Tyonantajaliitto, Aleksis Kivenkatu 10, 33210 Tampere 21, Finland. (Co-sponsor: Tekstiiliteollisuusyhdistys Tekstiilivaltuuskunta)

677   US
TEXSCOPE. EUROPEAN TEXTILE DISTRIBUTION. irreg. Werner Management Consultants, Inc., 111 W. 40th St., New York, NY 10018. charts. illus. stat.

677   US
TEXSCOPE: EUROPEAN OVERVIEW. irreg. Werner Management Consultants, Inc., 111 W. 40th St., New York, NY 10018. charts. illus. stat.

677   US
TEXSCOPE: OPEN END SPINNING. irreg., latest issue 1974. Werner Management Consultants, Inc., 111 W. 40th St., New York, NY 10018. charts. illus. stat.

677   US
TEXSCOPE: TEXTILE TECHNOLOGICAL INVESTMENT CLIMATE. irreg. Werner Management Consultants, Inc., 111 W. 40th St., New York, NY 10018. charts. illus. stat.

338.4   US   ISSN 0092-3540
TEXSCOPE; U S A TEXTILE INDUSTRY OVERVIEW. 1974. irreg., latest issue 1975. Werner Management Consultants, Inc., 111 W. 40th St., New York, NY 10018. stat. circ. (controlled) Key Title: Texscope (New York)

677   GW   ISSN 0082-3627
TEXTIL-INDUSTRIE UND IHRE HELFER. 1957. a. DM.38. Industrieschau-Verlagsgesellschaft, Berliner Allee 8, 6100 Darmstadt, W. Germany (B.R.D.)

677   338   SA
TEXTILE BUYER'S GUIDE AND DIRECTORY OF SOUTHERN AFRICA. 1965. biennial. R.20. Thomson Publications S.A. (Pty) Ltd., Box 8308, Johannesburg 2000, South Africa. Ed. Heinz Engelhardt. adv.

677   SZ
TEXTILE COUNTRY REPORTER. 1979. irreg. 20 Fr. International Textile Manufacturers Federation, Am Schanzengraben 29, Postfach, 8039 Zurich, Switzerland. Eds. Peter N. Scott, Herwig M. Strolz.
Supersedes in part: I F C A T I Newsletter.

677   UK   ISSN 0040-4969
TEXTILE HISTORY. 1968. a. £5($13) Pasold Research Fund Ltd., 23 St. James's Square, Bath, Avon BA1 2TT, England. Ed. K. G. Porting. adv. bk. rev. bibl. charts. illus. stat.

677   US
TEXTILE INDUSTRIES BUYERS GUIDE. (Special issue of Textile Industries) 1954. a. $5. W.R.C. Smith Publishing Co., 1760 Peachtree Road, N.W., Atlanta, GA 30357. Ed. Diane D. Burrell. adv. circ. controlled.

338.47   FR   ISSN 0474-6023
TEXTILE INDUSTRY IN O E C D COUNTRIES. 1953. irreg. $6. Organization for Economic Cooperation and Development, 2 rue Andre Pascal, 75775 Paris 16, France (U. S. orders to: O.E.C.D. Publications and Information Center, 1750 Pennsylvania Ave., N. W., Washington, D. C. 20006) (also avail. in microfiche)

677   UK
TEXTILE INSTITUTE. ANNUAL CONFERENCE. a. Textile Institute, 10 Blackfriars St., Manchester M3 5DR, England. Ed. P.W. Harrison. bibl. charts. illus. stat. Indexed: World Text.Abstr.

677   UK
TEXTILE INSTITUTE. ANNUAL REPORT. 1976. a. Textile Institute, 10 Blackfriars St., Manchester M3 5DR, England.

677   JA   ISSN 0082-366X
TEXTILE JAPAN/TEKISUTAIRU JAPAN. (Text in English) 1957. a. $12. Nihon Sen'i Shinbun Co., Ltd., 3-9 Hongo, Nihonbashi, Chuo-ku, Tokyo 103, Japan. Ed. Bd.

677   US   ISSN 0083-7407
TEXTILE MUSEUM JOURNAL. 1962. a. $6. Textile Museum, 2320 S. St. N.W., Washington, DC 20008. Ed. Petronel Lukens.
Supersedes: Workshop Notes Washington, D.C. Textile Museum.

677   US   ISSN 0495-369X
TEXTILE WORLD BUYER'S GUIDE/FACT FILE; McGraw-Hill's international textile magazine. (Special issue of Textile World) 1868. a. $6. McGraw-Hill Publications Co., 1221 Ave. of Americas, New York, NY 10020 (Subscr. to: 1175 Peachtree St. N.E., Atlanta, GA 30361) Ed. Laurence A. Christiansen, Jr. adv. circ. controlled. (also avail. in microfilm from UMI)

746   US
THREADS IN ACTION MONOGRAPH. irreg. H T H Publishers, 1607-A E. Edinger, Santa Ana, CA 92705.

677   UK   ISSN 0082-674X
TUFTING YEAR BOOK. 1966. a. £2.50. Textile Business Press, Ltd., 91 Kirkgate, Bradford, West Yorkshire BD1 1TN, England. Ed. D. T. Ward.
Supersedes: Skinner's Record Tufting Yearbook.

677   FI   ISSN 0355-3639
VALTION TEKNILLINEN TUTKIMUSKESKUS. TEKSTIILILABORATORIO. TIEDONANTO/ TECHNICAL RESEARCH CENTRE OF FINLAND. TEXTILE LABORATORY. REPORT. (Text mainly in Finnish, some in English or Swedish) 1972. irreg. price varies. Valtion Teknillinen Tutkimuskeskus - Technical Research Centre of Finland, Vuorimiehentie 5, 02150 Espoo 15, Finland.

677   AT
WOOL NEWS. 1954. irreg. free. Australian Wool Corporation, Public Relations Officer, Box 4867, Melbourne, Vic. 3000, Australia.
Formerly: Wool News Digest.

677.3   AT   ISSN 0084-1218
WOOL REVIEW. 1938. a. free. ‡ National Council of Wool Selling Brokers of Australia, Pastoral Exchange, 4 O'Connell St., Sydney, N.S.W., Australia.

677.3   US   ISSN 0084-1234
WOOLKNIT ANNUAL. Variant title: KnitOrations. 1939. a. $5. Woolknit Associates, Inc., 501 Madison Ave., New York, NY 10022. Ed. Mildred Faulk. adv. circ. 5,000.
Wool

677   BG   ISSN 0084-411X
YEARBOOK ON JUTE.* (Text in English) 1967/68. a. Asian Trade Publications, SWA (20) Gulshan Model Town, Dacca 12, Bangladesh.

TEXTILE INDUSTRIES AND FABRICS — Abstracting, Bibliographies, Statistics

677   AT   ISSN 0311-9882
AUSTRALIAN WOOL SALE STATISTICS. STATISTICAL ANALYSIS. PART A & B. (Issued in Two Parts) 1972. a. free. ‡ Australian Wool Corporation, Box 4867, Melbourne, Vic. 3001, Australia. Ed. R. S. Macdonald. circ. 700.
Former titles: Australian Wool (ISSN 0067-222X); Australian Wool Corporation. Statistical Analysis (ISSN 0084-764X)

677   CN   ISSN 0700-0278
CANADA. STATISTICS CANADA. CANVAS PRODUCTS AND COTTON AND JUTE BAG INDUSTRIES/INDUSTRIE DES ARTICLES EN GROSSE TOILE ET DES SACS DE COTON ET DE JUTE. (Catalogue 34-202) (Text in English and French) 1932. a. Can.$4.50($5.40) Statistics Canada, Publications Distribution, Ottawa, Ont. K1A 0V7, Canada. (also avail. in microform from MML)

677   CN   ISSN 0527-4893
CANADA. STATISTICS CANADA. CARPET, MAT AND RUG INDUSTRY/INDUSTRIE DES TAPIS, DES CARPETTES ET DE LA MOQUETTE. (Catalogue 34-221) (Text in English and French) 1960. a. Can.$4.50($5.40) Statistics Canada, Publications Distribution, Ottawa, Ont. K1A 0V7, Canada. (also avail. in microform from MML)

677.7   CN   ISSN 0527-4990
CANADA. STATISTICS CANADA. CORDAGE AND TWINE INDUSTRY /CORDERIE ET FICELLERIE (FABRICATION) (Catalogue 34-203) (Text in English and French) 1919-1920. a. Can.$4.50($5.40) Statistics Canada, Publications Distribution, Ottawa, Ont. K1A 0V7, Canada. (also avail. in microform from MML)

338.4   CN   ISSN 0527-5016
CANADA. STATISTICS CANADA. COTTON YARN AND CLOTH MILLS/FILATURE ET TISSAGE DU COTON. (Catalogue 34-205) (Text in English & French) 1918. a. Can.$4.50($5.40) Statistics Canada, Publications Distribution, Ottawa, Ont. K1A 0V7, Canada. (also avail. in microform from MML)

338.4   CN   ISSN 0700-0731
CANADA. STATISTICS CANADA. FELT AND FIBRE PROCESSING MILLS/INDUSTRIE DU FEUTRE ET DU TRAITEMENT DES FIBRES. (Catalogue 34-219) (Text in English & French) 1960. a. Can.$4.50($5.40) Statistics Canada, Publications Distribution, Ottawa, Ont. K1A 0V7, Canada. (also avail. in microform from MML)

338.4   CN   ISSN 0300-0265
CANADA. STATISTICS CANADA. WOOL PRODUCTION AND SUPPLY/PRODUCTION ET STOCKS DE LAINE. (Catalogue 23-205) (Text in English & French) 1939. a. Can.$3($3.60) Statistics Canada, Publications Distribution, Ottawa, Ont. K1A 0V7, Canada. (also avail. in microform from MML)

338.4   CN   ISSN 0300-1202
CANADA. STATISTICS CANADA. WOOL YARN AND CLOTH MILLS/FILATURE ET TISSAGE DE LA LAINE. (Catalogue 34-209) (Text in English & French) 1918. a. Can.$4.50($5.40) Statistics Canada, Publications Distribution, Ottawa, Ont. K1A 0V7, Canada. (also avail. in microform from MML)

677.2   314   IT   ISSN 0423-7269
EUROPEAN COTTON INDUSTRY STATISTICS. 1958. a. Associazione Cotoniera Italiana, Via Borgonuovo 11, 20121 Milan, Italy.

338.4   677   II
INDIAN COTTON TEXTILE INDUSTRY; ANNUAL STATISTICAL BULLETIN. (Text in English) 1968. a. Southern India Millowners' Association, Coimbatore, India. circ. 500.

677.2   SZ   ISSN 0538-6829
INTERNATIONAL COTTON INDUSTRY STATISTICS. 1958. a. 20 Fr. ‡ International Textile Manufacturers Federation, Am Schanzengraben 29, Postfach, 8039 Zurich, Switzerland. Ed. Peter N. Scott. charts. stat.
Cotton

677   FR   ISSN 0074-7599
INTERNATIONAL RAYON AND SYNTHETIC FIBRES COMMITTEE. STATISTICAL YEARBOOK. 1965. a. free. ‡ International Rayon and Synthetic Fibres Committee, 29 rue de Courcelles, 75008 Paris, France. circ. 3,500.

677.2   SZ
INTERNATIONAL TEXTILE MACHINERY SHIPMENT STATISTICS. 1975. a. 20 Fr. International Textile Manufacturers Federation, Am Schanzengraben 29, Postfach, 8039 Zurich, Switzerland. Ed. Peter N. Scott. charts. stat.
Formerly: International Cotton Industry Statistics. Supplement.

677   338.1   JA   ISSN 0447-5321
JAPAN COTTON STATISTICS AND RELATED DATA. 1953. a. $12. Japan Cotton Traders' Association - Nihon Menka Kyokai, Box Osaka Central 951, 1-8-2 Utsubu-Honmachi, Nishiku, Osaka, Japan.

677.39 II
SILK IN INDIA. biennial. Central Silk Board, 95-B Marine Drive, Bombay 400002, India. stat.

THEATER

see also Dance

792 SA
ALBANY SERIES OF PLAYS. irreg. latest no. 4, 1972. fl.30.50($15.25) per no. (Rhodes University, Speech and Drama Department) A. A. Balkema Ltd., P.O. Box 3117, Cape Town 8000, South Africa (And Box 1675, Rotterdam, Netherlands; in the U.S. and Canada, 99 Main St., Salem, NH 03079)

791 PL ISSN 0065-6526
ALMANACH SCENY POLSKIEJ. 1959/60. a. 75 Zl. (Polska Akademia Nauk, Instytut Sztuki) Wydawnictwa Artystyczne i Filmowe, Ul. Pulawska 61, Warsaw, Poland (Dist. by Ars Polona-Ruch, Krakowskie Przedmiescie 7, Warsaw, Poland) Ed. Kazimierz Andrzej Wysinski. circ. 1,500.

792 US
ALPHA PSI OMEGA: PLAYBILL. 1927. a. free contr. circ. Alpha Psi Omega National Theatre Honcrary, Eastern Illinois University, Charleston, IL 61920. Ed. Dr. D.P Garner. bk. rev. play rev. illus. stat. circ. 8,000-10,000.

792 US
AMERICAN THEATRE ANNUAL. 1976. a. $20. Gale Research Company, Book Tower, Detroit, MI 48226. Ed. Catharine R. Hughes. play rev. illus.
Incorporating: New York Theatre Annual (ISSN 0162-7333)

792 US ISSN 0065-8138
AMERICAN THEATRE ASSOCIATION. ANNUAL DIRECTORY OF MEMBERS. 1949. a. $7. American Theatre Association, 1000 Vermont Ave., N.W., Washington, DC 20005. Ed. Susan Holland. adv. circ. 6,000.
Formerly: American Educational Theatre Association. Annual Directory of Members.

ANGLICA GERMANICA: SERIES 2. see *LINGUISTICS*

792 FR ISSN 0066-3026
ANNUAIRE DU SPECTACLE. (Comprised of Four Volumes) 1956, 11th edt. a. 60 F. per volume; complete collection 220 F. Editions Raoult, 17 Faubourg Montmartre, 75009 Paris, France.

792 BL
ANNUARIO DO TEATRO BRASILEIRO. a. Ministerio da Educacao e Cultura, Servico Nacional de Teatro, Rio de Janeiro, Brazil. illus.

792 IT ISSN 0066-6661
ARCHIVIO DEL TEATRO ITALIANO. 1968. irreg; latest issue, 1976. price varies. Edizioni Il Polifilo, Via Borgonuovo 2, 20121 Milan, Italy. Ed. Giovanni Macchia.

792 UK ISSN 0143-8131
ARTISTES AND THEIR AGENTS. a. £2. John Offord (Publications) Ltd., Box 64, Eastbourne, East Sussex BN21 3LW, England.

792 950 US ISSN 0161-4908
ASIAN THEATRE REPORTS. a. University of Hawaii, Asian Theatre Organization, 1770 East-West Rd., Honolulu, HI 96822.

ASOCIACION ARGENTINA DE ACTORES. MEMORIA Y BALANCE. see *LABOR UNIONS*

792 AT
AUSTRALIAN VARIETY DIRECTORY. (Directory of variety and cabaret acts) a. Aus.$15. Showcast Publications Pty. Ltd, Box 141, Spit Junction, N. S. W. 2088, Australia.
Formerly: Variety Directory.

792.02 BG
BAHUBACANA. (Text in Bengali) 1978. irreg. Tk.3. Bahubacana Natyagosshthi, 11/2 Jaynag Rd., Bakshi Bazar, Dacca 1, Bangladesh. play rev.

792 GW ISSN 0067-6047
BERLIN, THEATER UND DRAMA. 1931. irreg. price varies. Colloquium Verlag, Unter den Eichen 93, 1000 Berlin 45, W. Germany (B.R.D.) circ. 1,000.

BERNARD SHAW SOCIETY JOURNAL. see *LITERATURE*

792 US
BEST PLAYS OF ... (YEAR) 1920. a. $17.95. Dodd, Mead & Co., Inc, 79 Madison Avenue, New York, NY 10013. Ed. Otis L. Guernsey, Jr. play rev. illus. tr.lit. (back issues avail)

792 US ISSN 0360-2788
BIBLIOGRAPHIC GUIDE TO THEATRE ARTS. a. G.K. Hall and Co., 70 Lincoln St., Boston, MA 02111.

792 US
BIOGRAPHICAL ENCYCLOPEDIA AND WHO'S WHO OF THE AMERICAN THEATRE. 1966. irreg. $82.50. James H. Heineman, Inc, 475 Park Ave., New York, NY 10022. Ed. Walter Rigdon.

792 380 UK ISSN 0142-5218
BRITISH ALTERNATIVE THEATRE DIRECTORY. 1979. a. £5. John Offord (Publications) Ltd., Box 64, Eastbourne, East Sussex BN21 3LW, England. Ed. Catherine Itzin.

792 380 UK ISSN 0306-4107
BRITISH THEATRE DIRECTORY. 1972. a. £7.75. John Offord (Publications) Ltd., Box 64, Eastbourne, East Sussex BN21 3LW, England. Ed. John Offord. adv.

792 US
CAHIERS CESAIRIENS. (Text in English and French) 1974. a. $6. Pennsylvania State University, Department of French, c/o Thomas A. Hale, University Park, PA 16802. Eds. Thomas A. Hale, Lilyan Kesteloot. bibl.
Amie Cesaire, poet, dramatist, political leader

CANADA COUNCIL. TOURING OFFICE. BULLETIN. see *ART*

CANADA COUNCIL ANNUAL REPORT AND SUPPLEMENT. see *ART*

792 CN ISSN 0380-9455
CANADA ON STAGE: CANADIAN THEATRE REVIEW YEARBOOK. 1974. a. Can.$19.95. Canadian Theatre Review Publications, 222 Admin Studies, York University, Downsview, Ont. M3J 1P3, Canada. Ed. Don Rubin. illus. index.

792 CN
CANADA'S LOST PLAYS; the developing mosaic. 1977. a. Can.$14.95 hardcover; Can.$8.95 softcover. Canadian Theatre Review, 4700 Keele St., Downsview, Ont. M3J 1P3, Canada. Ed. Anton Wagner. (back issues avail.)
Out of print plays from the formative period of 1917-1953

792 CN ISSN 0317-9044
CANADIAN DRAMA/ART DRAMATIQUE CANADIEN. (Text in English and French) vol. 2, 1976. s-a. Can.$6. University of Waterloo, Department of English, Waterloo, Ont. N2L 3G1, Canada. Ed. Rota Lister. adv. bk. rev. play rev, bibl, illus.

CANADIAN PLAY SERIES. see *LITERATURE*

792 CN ISSN 0705-5064
CANADIAN THEATRE CHECKLIST. a. Can.$2.75. Canadian Theatre Review Publications, York University, Downsview, Ont. M3J 1P3, Canada. Eds. Don Rubin, Mimi Mekler.

792 CN ISSN 0316-1323
CANADIAN THEATRE REVIEW YEARBOOK. 1974. a. Can.$10 to individuals; Can. $15 to libraries. Canadian Theatre Review Publications, York University, Downsview, Ont. M3J 1P3, Canada. Ed. Don Rubin. adv. bk. rev. illus. index. circ. 10,000.

658 791 US ISSN 0090-2985
CARNIVAL & CIRCUS BOOKING GUIDE. 1972. a. $3.50. Billboard Publications Inc., Amusement Business Division, Box 24970, Nashville, TN 37202. Ed. Paul Curran. adv. abstr. stat. circ. 14,800. (also avail. in microfilm)

790.2 US ISSN 0090-2993
CAVALCADE AND DIRECTORY OF ACTS & ATTRACTIONS. Variant title: Amusement Business's Cavalcade of Acts & Attractions. 1973. a. $18. Billboard Publications, Inc., Amusement Business Division, Box 24970, Nashville, TN 37202. illus.

792 US ISSN 0069-1372
CELEBRITY SERVICE INTERNATIONAL CONTACT BOOK; trade directory / entertainment industry. every 18 months. $8. Celebrity Service, Inc., 171 W. 57 St., New York, NY 10019. Ed. Barbara McGurn. adv.

792 US
CHICAGO RESOURCE DIRECTORY FOR THE PERFORMING ARTS. 1977. biennial. $6.95. Chicago Alliance for the Performing Arts, 176 W. Adams, Suite 2010, Chicago, IL 60603. Ed. Dorothy Keyser. index. circ. 1,000.

CINEMA AND SOCIETY. see *MOTION PICTURES*

792 BL
COLECAO TEATRO. no. 2, 1974. irreg. Universidade Federal do Rio Grande do Sul, Porto Alegre, Brazil. bibl.

792 IT
COLLANA DEL TEATRO DI ROMA. 1977. irreg. Officina Edizioni, Passeggiata di Ripetta 25, 00186 Rome, Italy.

792 780.65 AT
CONTACTS & FACILITIES; in the entertainment industry. 1963. a. Aus.$12. Showcast Publications Pty. Ltd, Box 141, Spit Junction, N. S. W. 2088, Australia.

792 US ISSN 0163-3821
CONTRIBUTIONS IN DRAMA AND THEATRE STUDIES. irreg. price varies. Greenwood Press, 8 Post Rd. W., Westport, CT 06881. Ed. Joseph Donohue.

800 UK
CORNISH PLAY SERIES. no. 4, 1973. irreg. 60p. Lodeneck Press, 14 Market St., Padstow, Cornwall, England.

792 US
COURSE GUIDE IN THE THEATRE ARTS AT THE SECONDARY SCHOOL LEVEL. no. 2, 1968. irreg., latest edt. 1975. $7.50. (Secondary School Theatre Conference) American Theatre Association, 1000 Vermont Ave., N.W., Washington, DC 20005. adv.
Formerly: Course Guide for High School Theatre (ISSN 0070-136X)

792 920 CN ISSN 0315-3290
CREATIVE CANADA. 1971. irreg. (University of Victoria, McPherson Library) University of Toronto Press, Front Campus, Toronto, Ont. M5S 1A6, Canada.

792 UK ISSN 0011-0892
CREATIVE DRAMA. 1949. a. £1.80($6) for 2 years. (Educational Drama Association) Stacey Publications, 1 Hawthorndene Rd., Hayes, Bromley, Kent, England. Ed. M. Cameron. adv. bk. rev. illus. cum.index at end of vol. (6 yrs). circ. 3,000.

792 GW ISSN 0070-4431
DEUTSCHES BUEHNEN-JAHRBUCH; Theatergeschichtliches Jahr- und Adressbuch. 1889. a. DM.43.20. (Genossenschaft Deutscher Buehnenangehoeriger) Buehnenschriften-Vertriebs-Gesellschaft, Feldbrunnenstr. 74, 2000 Hamburg 13, W. Germany (B.R.D.) adv.

791.53 GW ISSN 0070-4490
DEUTSCHES INSTITUT FUER PUPPENSPIEL. FORSCHUNG UND LEHRE. 1964. irreg. price varies. Deutsches Institut fuer Puppenspiel, Bergstr. 115, 4630 Bochum, W. Germany (B.R.D.) Ed. Fritz Wortelmann.

792 US ISSN 0070-5063
DIRECTORY OF AMERICAN COLLEGE THEATRE. 1967. irreg., latest edt. 1976. $7. American Theatre Association, 1000 Vermont Ave., N.W., Washington, DC 20005. Ed. Allen S. White. adv. index.

842 792 FR
DOCUMENTATION THEATRALE; fiches analytiques. 1974. a. 10 F. per copy. Universite de Paris X (Paris-Nanterre), Centre d'Etudes Theatrales, 200, Avenue de la Republique, 92001 Nanterre Cedex, France (Orders to: Librairie de Coupe-Papier, 19 rue de l'Odeon, 75006 Paris, France) (Co-sponsor: Centre de Recherches Historiques de l'Ecole des Hautes Etudes en Sciences Sociales) Eds. Jacqueline Jomaron, Bernard Faivre. bk. rev. abstr. bibl. film rev. play rev. index.

792 UK ISSN 0141-1179
DRAMAU'R BYD. (Text in Welsh) 1969. irreg. price varies. (Welsh Arts Council) University of Wales Press, 6 Gwennyth St., Cathays, Cardiff CF2 4YD, Wales. Ed.Gwyn Thomas. (reprint service avail. from UMI)

EDWARDIAN STUDIES. see *LITERATURE*

792.0942 US ISSN 0071-0032
ELIZABETHAN THEATRE. 1968. irreg.; 5th edt., 1975. price varies. Archon Books, (Subsidiary of: Shoe String Press, Inc.) 995 Sherman Ave., Hamden, CT 06514. adv.
Represents: International Conference on Elizabethan Theatre, University of Waterloo. Proceedings.

792 US ISSN 0361-2767
EMPIRICAL RESEARCH IN THEATRE. 1971-1975; reestablished 1980. a. Bowling Green State University, Center for Communications Research, 322 South Hall, Bowling Green, OH 43403. (Co-Sponsor: Speech Communication Association, Theatre Division) Ed. Briant Hamor Lee. bk. rev. circ. 500. (also avail. in microfiche) Indexed: Sociol.Abstr.

ENCORE. see *LITERATURE*

ENJOYING THE ARTS. see *DANCE*

792 780 US
ESSAYS ON ASIAN THEATER, MUSIC AND DANCE. vol. 3, 1974. irreg. price varies. Asia Society, 112 E. 64th St., New York, NY 10021.

ETUDES CINEMATOGRAPHIQUES. see *MOTION PICTURES*

800 IT
EVENTO TEATRALE. SEZIONE: AUTORI ITALIANI DEL NOVECENTO. 1976. irreg. Edizioni Abete, Corso Vittori Emanuele 39, 00186 Rome, Italy.

792 US
EXPERIMENT THEATRE; "one minute" poetic drama. irreg. $4.50. Experiment Press, 6565 N.E. Windermere Rd., Seattle, WA 98105. Ed. Carol Ely Harper.

792 CN
FACILITIES DIRECTORY/REPERTOIRE DES SALLES DE SPECTACLE. (In four volumes) (Text in English and French) 1980. annual updates. Can.$100. Canada Council, Touring Office, Box 1047, Ottawa, Ont. K1P 5V8, Canada. illus.

792 FR ISSN 0072-8063
GUIDE DU SHOW-BUSINESS; GUIDE PROFESSIONNEL DU SPECTACLE. 1963. a. 150 F. Societe d'Editions Radio-Phono, 11 rue Jean Bologne, 75016 Paris, France. Dir. Sabine Gay.

800 CN
HALLOWEEN; an occasional theatrical letter. no. 2, 1976. irreg. University of Western Ontario, Department of English, London, Ontario, Canada. Ed. James Reaney.

790 301.45 US
HAMBONE. 1974. a. Committee of Black Performing Arts, Harmong House, Stanford Univ., Stanford, CA 94305. Ed. Nate Mackey. illus.

800 792 UK ISSN 0260-7964
IRISH DRAMA SELECTIONS. 1981. irreg. price varies. Colin Smythe Ltd., Gerrards Cross, Buckinghamshire SL9 7AE, England (Dist. in U. S. by: Humanities Press Inc., 171 First Ave., Atlantic Highlands, N. J. 07716) Eds. Ann Saddlemyer, Joseph Ronsley.

792 IT ISSN 0075-1480
ISTITUTO DI STUDI PIRANDELLIANI E SUL TEATRO CONTEMPORANEO. 1967. irreg. Casa Editrice Felice le Monnier, Via Scipione Ammirato 100, C.P. 455, 50136 Florence, Italy.

792 IT
ISTITUZIONI CULTURALI PIEMONTESI. PUBBLICAZIONI. 1976. irreg. (Istituzioni Culturali Piemontesi) Cassa di Risparmio di Torino, Via XX Settembre 31, Turin, Italy.

792 BE
J E B THEATRE. irreg. (2-3/yr.) Direction Generale de la Jeunesse et des Loisirs, Galerie Ravenstein 78, 1000 Brussels, Belgium.

820 AU
JACOBEAN DRAMA STUDIES. (Text in English) 1972. irreg., no. 71, 1977. S.245. Universitaet Salzburg, Institut fuer Englische Sprache, Akademiestr. 24, A-5020 Salzburg, Austria. Ed. James Hogg. circ. 300.

LEEDS MEDIEVAL STUDIES. see *LITERATURE*

792 US
LONDON STAGE INFORMATION BANK. NEWSLETTER. 1971. irreg., approx. a. free. London Stage Project, Lawrence University, Box 599, Appleton, WI 54911. Ed. Ben Ross Schneider, Jr. circ. 800.
History of the London stage

791.53 GW ISSN 0076-6216
MEISTER DES PUPPENSPIELS. (Text generally in German; occasionally in Dutch, English and other languages) 1959. irreg. price varies. Deutsches Institut fuer Puppenspiel, Bergstr. 115, 4630 Bochum, W. Germany (B.R.D.) Ed. Fritz Wortelmann.

MINNESOTA DRAMA EDITIONS. see *LITERATURE*

MISSOURI SPEECH JOURNAL. see *COMMUNICATIONS*

MONOGRAPHS ON MUSIC, DANCE AND THEATER IN ASIA. see *DANCE*

792 384.55 NE
NEDERLANDS THEATER- EN TELEVISIE JAARBOEK. (Text in English and Dutch) 1950. a. price varies. Stichting Doneto, Vandelstraat 90, Amsterdam, Netherlands.

792 NE ISSN 0077-6688
NETHERLANDS. CENTRAAL BUREAU VOOR DE STATISTIEK. BEZOEK AAN VERMAKELIJKHEIDSINSTELLINGEN. ATTENDANCE AT PUBLIC ENTERTAINMENTS. (Text in Dutch and English) 1940-41. a. fl.6. Centraal Bureau voor de Statistiek, Prinses Beatrixlaan 428, Voorburg, Netherlands (Orders to: Staatsuitgeverij, Christoffel Plantijnstraat, The Hague, Netherlands)

792 NE
NETHERLANDS. CENTRAAL BUREAU VOOR DE STATISTIEK. MUZIEK EN THEATER. fl.22.68. Centraal Bureau voor de Statistiek, Prinses Beatrixlaan 428, Voorburg, Netherlands (Orders to: Staatsuitgeverij, Christoffel Plantijnstraat, The Hague, Netherlands)
Formerly: Netherlands. Centraal Bureau voor de Statistiek. Statistiek van het Gesubsidieerde Toneel.

792.02 800 II
NIVADAKA EKANKIKA. (Text in Marathi) 1977. a. Rs.18. Suparna Prakashan, 26 Parvati, Pune 411009, India.

792 US ISSN 0361-6606
O.O.B.A. GUIDEBOOK OF THEATRES. 1975. irreg. Off Off Broadway Alliance, 162 W. 56 St., New York, NY 10019. illus.

792 US
ON-STAGE STUDIES. Variant title: On-Stage Studies. 1976. a. $3. (Colorado Shakespeare Festival) University of Colorado, Department of Theatre and Dance, Boulder, CO 80309. Ed. Albert H. Nadeau. circ. 500.
Formerly: Colorado Shakespeare Festival Annual (ISSN 0198-831X)

800 792 UK ISSN 0141-1152
OXFORD THEATRE TEXTS. vol. 4, 1974. irreg. price varies. Colin Smythe Ltd., Gerrads Cross, Buckinghamshire SL9 7AE, England (Dist. in U.S. by: Humanities Press, 171 First Ave., Atlantic Highlands, N.J. 07716) illus.

792 016 US ISSN 0360-3814
PERFORMING ARTS RESOURCES. 1974. a. membership. Theatre Library Association, c/o Performing Arts Research Center, 111 Amsterdam at 65th St., New York, NY 10023. Eds. Ginnine Cocuzza, Barbara Naomi Cohen. circ. 700.

792 AT
PERFORMING ARTS YEAR BOOK OF AUSTRALIA. 1977. a. Aus.$25. Showcast Publications Pty. Ltd, Box 141, Spit Junction, N. S. W. 2088, Australia. illus.

822 UK ISSN 0554-3045
PLAYS. A CLASSIFIED GUIDE TO PLAY SELECTION. 1951. a. £1.60($5.50) Stacey Publications, 1 Hawthorndene Road, Hayes, Bromley, Kent, England. Ed. Roy Stacey. adv. bibl.

800 UK
PLAYS OF THE YEAR. 1949. irreg., no. 47, 1979. Elek Books Ltd., 54-58 Caledonian Rd, London N1 9RN, England.

792 809 US ISSN 0486-3739
RENAISSANCE DRAMA. a. Northwestern University Press, 1735 Benson Ave., Evanston, IL 60201. Ed. Leonard Barkan.

792 US ISSN 0098-647X
RESEARCH OPPORTUNITIES IN RENAISSANCE DRAMA. 1956. a. free. Modern Language Association of America, Conference on Research Opportunities in Renaissance Drama, c/o David M. Bergeron, Ed., Department of English, University of Kansas, Lawrence, KS 66045. adv. bk. rev. play rev. bibl. illus. circ. 1,700.

792 NE
SCENARIUM; Nederlandse reeks voor theaterwetenschap. 1977. a. fl.15. (Academische Raad, Sectie Theaterwetenschap) Walburg Pers, Zaadmarkt 842, Zutphen, Netherlands. (Co-sponsor: Toneelmuseum te Amsterdam) Eds. E. Alexander, W. Hogendoorn. circ. 1,250.

729 GW ISSN 0342-4553
SCHAUSPIELFUEHRER; der Inhalt der wichtigsten Theaterstuecke aus aller Welt. 1953. triennial. DM.90 per vol. (Universitaet Wien, Institut fuer Theaterwissenschaft, AU) Anton Hiersemann Verlag, Rosenberger. 113, Postfach 723, 7000 Stuttgart 1, W. Germany (B.R.D.) Ed. Margret Dietrich.

792 SZ
SCHWEIZERISCHE GESELLSCHAFT FUER THEATERKULTUR. JAHRBUECHER. 1928. a. price varies. Schweizerische Gesellschaft fuer Theaterkultur - Swiss Association for Theatre Research, c/o Lydia Benz-Burger, Richard Wagner-Strasse 19, 8002 Zurich, Switzerland.

792 SZ
SCHWEIZERISCHE GESELLSCHAFT FUER THEATERKULTUR. SCHRIFTEN. 1928. irreg., no. 15, 1978. Schweizerische Gesellschaft fuer Theaterkultur - Swiss Association for Theatre Research, c/o Lydia Benz-Burger, Richard-Wagner-Strasse 19, 8002 Zurich, Switzerland.

SHOWCALL. see *MUSIC*

792 AT
SHOWCAST DIRECTORY. (Directory of actors and actresses) 1963. a. Aus.$30. Showcast Publications Pty. Ltd., Box 141, Spit Junction, N.S.W. 2088, Australia.
Formerly: Showcast General Directory.

SO AND SO MAGAZINE. see *LITERATURE — Poetry*

THEATER — ABSTRACTING, BIBLIOGRAPHIES, STATISTICS

792 CN
SPONSORS' HANDBOOK FOR TOURING ATTRACTIONS. (Editions in English and French) 1975. irreg. Can.$5. Canada Council, Touring Office, Box 1047, Ottawa, Ont. K1P 5V8, Canada.

792 ZA
STAGE. (Text in English) 1956. irreg. price varies. Lusaka Theatre Club (Co-Op) Ltd., Box 615, Lusaka, Zambia. adv. bk. rev. play rev. circ. 300(controlled)

792 791.43 IE
STAGECAST-IRISH STAGE AND SCREEN DIRECTORY. 1962. biennial. £3.80. Stagecast Publications, 15 Eaton Square, Monkstown, Dublin County, Ireland. Ed. Derek Young. adv. illus. stat. (back issues avail.)

792 CN ISSN 0085-6770
STRATFORD FESTIVAL; souvenir book. 1953. a. Can.$3.50. ‡ Stratford Shakespearean Festival Foundation of Canada, Box 520, Stratford, Ont. N5A 6V2, Canada. Ed. Anne Selby.

792 CN ISSN 0085-6789
STRATFORD FESTIVAL STORY. 1954. a. free. Stratford Shakespearean Festival Foundation of Canada, Box 520, Stratford, Ont. N5A 6V2, Canada. Ed. Compiled By Publicity Department, Stratford Festival. illus. circ. controlled.

792 US ISSN 0081-6051
STUBS (METRO N.Y.); the seating plan guide for Western theatres, music halls, sports stadia. 1967. irreg. $2 postpd. (Stubs Publications) Meyer Schattner, Box 62, Pound Ridge, NY 10576. circ. 10,000.

792 PL
STUDIA I MATERIALY DO DZIEJOW TEATRU POLSKIEGO. 1957. irreg., vol.11, 1979. price varies. (Polska Akademia Nauk, Instytut Sztuki) Ossolineum, Publishing House of the Polish Academy of Sciences, Rynek 9, Wroclaw, Poland (Dist. by Ars Polona-Ruch, Krakowskie Przedmiescie 7, Warsaw, Poland)
Formerly: Studia i Materialy z Dziejow Teatru Polskiego (ISSN 0081-6647)

792 RM ISSN 0039-3991
STUDII SI CERCETARI DE ISTORIA ARTEI. SERIA TEATRU-MUZICA-CINEMATOGRAFIE. (Summaries in English, French, German and Russian) 1954. a. 25 lei($10) (Academia de Stiinte Sociale si Politice) Editura Academiei Republicii Socialiste Romania, Calea Victoriei 125, Bucharest, Romania (Subscr. to: ILEXIM, Str. 13 Decembrie Nr. 3, P.O. Box 136-137, Bucharest, Romania) bk. rev. illus. index.
History

792 US ISSN 0081-9387
SUMMER THEATRE DIRECTORY. 1968. a. $3.50. American Theatre Association, 1000 Vermont Ave., N.W., DC 20005. Ed. Kevin Hoggard. adv.

792 SZ
SZENE SCHWEIZ/SCENE SUISSE/SCENA SVIZZERA. 1973. a. 19 Fr. Schweizerische Gesellschaft fuer Theaterkultur - Swiss Association for Theatre Research, c/o Lydia Benz-Burger, Richard-Wagner-Strasse 19, 8002 Zurich, Switzerland.

792 US
T C G NATIONAL WORKING CONFERENCE. PROCEEDINGS. 1976. irreg. Theatre Communications Group, 355 Lexington Ave., New York, NY 10017. Ed. Peter Zeisler.

791 SA ISSN 0085-7416
T R U K-P A C T. (Transvaalse Raad vir die Uitvoerende Kunste-Performing Arts Council Transvaal) (Text in English & Afrikaans) 1968. irreg. free. ‡ Performing Arts Council Transvaal, Box 566, Pretoria 0001, South Africa. Ed. Ulrich G. Stark. circ. 13,000.

792 IT
TEATRO ITALIANO. 1975. a. Casa Editrice Einaudi, Via Biancamano 1, Turin 10129, Italy.

792 001.6 US
THEATER COMPUTER USERS GROUP NOTES. Short title: T C U G Notes. 1978. irreg. membership. Theater Sources, Inc., 104 N. St. Mary, Dallas, TX 75214. Ed. Mike Firth. adv. bk. rev. circ. 75. (back issues avail.)

792 NE
THEATER KLANKEN BEELD. 1970. irreg. Herengracht 168, Amsterdam, Netherlands.

THEATRE ANGELS. see *BUSINESS AND ECONOMICS — Investments*

792 US ISSN 0082-3821
THEATRE ANNUAL. 1942. a. $5. c/o Wallace Sterline, Ed., Department of Theatre Arts and Dance, College of Fine Arts and Applied Arts, University of Akron, Akron, OH 44325.

792 CN ISSN 0703-5640
THEATRE CANADA. SPECIAL BULLETIN. (Text in English and French) 1973. irreg. Theatre Canada, 45 Rideau St., Ottawa, Ont. K1N 5W8, Canada.

842 FR
THEATRE D'AUJOURD'HUI. 1976. irreg. price varies. Editons Klincksieck, 11 rue de Lille, Paris 7e, France.

792 UK
THEATRE DIRECTORY. 1964. biennial. £1.50($5) Stacey Publications, 1 Hawthorndene Rd., Hayes, Bromley, Kent, England. Ed. Roy Stacey. adv. circ. 2,000.

792 FR ISSN 0082-383X
THEATRE OUVERT. 1970. irreg. price varies. Editions Stock, 6 rue Casimir-Delavigne, Paris 6e, France.

792 US
THEATRE PERSPECTIVES. 1980. irreg. American Theatre Association, University-College Theatre Association, 1000 Vermont Ave., N.W., Washington, DC 20005. Ed. Anthony Graham-White.

792 US ISSN 0361-7947
THEATRE PROFILES; an informational handbook of nonprofit professional theatres in the United States. 1973. biennial. $12.95. Theatre Communications Group, 355 Lexington Ave., New York, NY 10017. illus.

792 US ISSN 0082-3848
THEATRE STUDENT SERIES. 1968. irreg. price varies. ‡ Richards Rosen Press, 29 East 21st. St., New York, NY 10010. Ed. Ruth C. Rosen. index from 1968.

792.02 US
THEATRE STUDIES. 1955. a. $2 to individuals; institutions $3. ‡ Ohio State University, Department of Theatre, 1089 Drake Union, 1849 Cannon Drive, Columbus, OH 43210. Ed. Bd. bk. rev. bibl. illus. cum.index vols. 1-20 in vol. 20 (1973-74) circ. 1,200. (also avail. in microfilm; back issues avail.) Indexed: G.Perf.Arts. T.D.S.I.

792.0973 US ISSN 0082-3856
THEATRE WORLD. a. $14.95. Crown Publishers, Inc., One Park Ave., New York, NY 10016.

792 CN
TOUR ORGANIZERS' HANDBOOK/GUIDE DU DIRECTEUR DE TOURNEES DE SPECTACLES. (Text in English and French) 1977. irreg., latest May, 1981. Can.$10. Canada Council, Touring Office, Box 1047, Ottawa, Ont. K1P 5V8, Canada.

790.2 CN
TOURING ARTISTS DIRECTORY. (Text in English and French) 1975. biennial. free. Canada Council, Touring Office, P.O. Box 1047, Ottawa, Ont. K1P 5V8, Canada. index.
Formerly: Touring Directory of the Performing Arts in Canada (ISSN 0317-5960)

790.2 CN ISSN 0317-5979
TOURNEES DE SPECTACLES. 1975. a. Can.$5($7) Conseil des Arts du Canada, Office des Tournees, Ottawa, Ont., Canada.

792 SP
UNIVERSIDAD DE MURCIA. CATEDRA DE TEATRO. CUADERNOS. 1978. irreg. Ediciones 23-27, Andres Baquero 7, Murcia, Spain.

792.07 TZ
UNIVERSITY OF DAR ES SALAAM. THEATRE ARTS DEPARTMENT. ANNUAL REPORT. a. University of Dar es Salaam, Theatre Arts Department, Box 35091, Dar es Salaam, Tanzania.

792 UR ISSN 0507-3952
VOPROSY TEATRA; sbornik statei i materialov. 1965. a. 1.45 Rub. Vserossiiskoe Teatral'noe Obshchestvo, Ul. Gorkogo, 16, Moscow, U. S. S. R. (Co-sponsor: Institut Istorii Iskusstv) bibl. illus.

WHO DOES WHAT: A GUIDE TO NATIONAL ASSOCIATIONS, SERVICE ORGANIZATIONS AND UNIONS OPERATING IN MOST AREAS OF THE ARTS. see *ART*

WHO'S WHERE; who's where in show business. see *COMMUNICATIONS — Radio And Television*

WHO'S WHO: A GUIDE TO FEDERAL AND PROVINCIAL DEPARTMENTS AND AGENCIES, THEIR FUNDING PROGRAMS, AND THE PEOPLE WHO HEAD THEM. see *ART*

WHO'S WHO IN THE THEATRE. see *BIOGRAPHY*

792 AU
WIENER FORSCHUNGEN ZUR THEATER UND MEDIENWISSENSCHAFT. 1972. irreg. price varies. (Universitaet Wien, Institut fuer Theaterwissenschaft) Wilhelm Braumueller, Universitaets-Verlagsbuchhandlung GmbH, Servitengasse 5, A-1092 Vienna, Austria. Ed. Margaret Dietrich. index. circ. 1,000.
Formerly: Vienna. Universitaet. Institut fuer Theaterwissenschaft. Wissenschaftliche Reihe (ISSN 0083-6176)

792 AU ISSN 0072-4262
WIENER GESELLSCHAFT FUER THEATERFORSCHUNG. JAHRBUCH. 1944. a. price varies. Wiener Gesellschaft fuer Theaterforschung, Batthyanystiege, Hofburg, A-1010 Vienna, Austria. Ed. Franz Hadamowsky.

792 AU
WIENER GESELLSCHAFT FUER THEATERFORSCHUNG. JAHRBUCH. 1954. irreg., no. 22, 1978. price varies. Verband der Wissenschaftlichen Gesellschaften Oesterreichs, Lindengasse 37, A-1070 Vienna, Austria. Ed. Franz Hadamovsky.

YEARBOOK OF CULTURAL & ARTISTIC ACTIVITIES/MUNYEYUNGAM. see *ART*

THEATER — Abstracting, Bibliographies, Statistics

792 016 UK
B T I BIBLIOGRAPHIC SERIES. no. 4, 1975. irreg. membership. British Theatre Institute, 30 Clareville St., London SW7 5AW, England.

792 016 CN ISSN 0707-5456
DIRECTORY OF CANADIAN PLAYS AND PLAYWRIGHTS. 1977. irreg. free contr. circ. Playwright's Co-Op, 8 York St., 6th Floor, Toronto, Ont. M5J 1R2, Canada. illus.

TOBACCO

679.7 FR
ANNALES DU TABAC. 1963. a. free to qualified personnel. Service d'Exploitation Industrielle des Tabacs et Allumettes, 53 Quai d'Orsay, 75340 Paris, France. Ed. Jean Waterlot. bibl.

633.71 II
CENTRAL TOBACCO RESEARCH INSTITUTE AND ITS REGIONAL RESEARCH STATIONS. ANNUAL REPORT. (Text in English) 1967. a. exchange basis. Central Tobacco Research Institute, Rajahmundry 533104, India. Ed. Bd. charts. stat. circ. 150.
Absorbed: Central Tobacco Research Institute. Annual Report; Tobacco Research Station, Hunsur, Report; Wrapper & Hookah Tobacco Research Station Report.

679.7 US ISSN 0077-3468
COORDINATOR. 1942. a. $75 to non-members. National Association of Tobacco Distributors, Inc., 58 E. 79 St., New York, NY 10021. Ed. W. B. Bennett.

COUNCIL FOR TOBACCO RESEARCH--U.S.A. REPORT. see *DRUG ABUSE AND ALCOHOLISM*

679.7 FR
FEDERATION DES DEBITANTS DE TABAC DE L'ILE-DE-FRANCE. ANNUAIRE OFFICIEL. 1952. a. 180 F.($20) Pym Editeur, 27 rue Hermel, 75018 Paris, France. adv. bk. rev. annual index.

679.7 BL
INSTITUTO BAHIANO DO FUMO. BOLETIM INFORMATIVO: COMERCIO EXTERIOR - ESPORTACAO DE FUMO EM FOLHAS. irreg. Instituto Bahiano do Fumo, Rua de Belgica, 2, Edificio Roosevelt, Salvador-Bahia, Brazil.

331.88 SZ ISSN 0579-8302
INTERNATIONAL UNION OF FOOD AND ALLIED WORKERS' ASSOCIATIONS. TOBACCO WORKERS' TRADE GROUP BOARD. MEETING. irreg. International Union of Food and Allied Workers' Associations - Union Internationale des Travailleurs de l'Alimentation et des Branches Connexes, Secretariat, Rampe du Pont-Rouge 8, CH-1213 Petit-Lancy/Geneva, Switzerland.

679.7 658.8 MF
MAURITIUS. TOBACCO BOARD. ANNUAL REPORT. 1932. a. Tobacco Board, Plaine Lauzun, Mauritius. circ. 325. Indexed: Tob.Abstr.

679.7 NE
MONOGRAFIEEN OVER KLEIPIJPEN. vol. 8, 1976. irreg. fl.2.50. ICON, Raadhuisstr. 2, 4797 AX Willemstad, Netherlands. Ed. Niels Augustin. circ. 500. (back issues avail.)

633.71 NR
NIGERIAN TOBACCO COMPANY. ANNUAL REPORT AND ACCOUNTS. 1964. a. free. Nigerian Tobacco Company, Western House, 8/10 Broad St., Lagos, Nigeria.
Formerly: Nigerian Tobacco Company. Report (ISSN 0078-0820)

679.7 UK ISSN 0081-0355
SMOKER'S HANDBOOK; of recommended retail prices. 1882. a. $5. International Trade Publications Ltd., Queensway House, 2 Queensway, Redhill, Surrey RH1 1QS, England. Ed. Freda Troughton. adv.

338.1 SA
SOUTH AFRICA. TOBACCO BOARD. ANNUAL REPORT/JAARVERSLAG. 1939/40. a. $0.95. Tobacco Board, P.O. Box 934, Pretoria, South Africa. stat. circ. 1,000.
Continues: South Africa. Tobacco Industry Control Board. Report.

679.7 US ISSN 0082-4593
TOBACCO ASSOCIATES. ANNUAL REPORT. 1948. a. free. Tobacco Associates, Inc., 1306 Annapolis Dr., Suite 102, Raleigh, NC 27605. cum.index: 1948-1972. circ. 13,500.

679.7 US
TOBACCO MERCHANTS ASSOCIATION OF THE UNITED STATES. NATIONAL BULLETIN. 1924. irreg. membership. Tobacco Merchants Association of the United States, Statler Hilton, Seventh Ave. & 33rd St., New York, NY 10001. Ed. Marvin K. Bloom. circ. controlled. (looseleaf format)

338.1 II
TOBACCO NEWS. (Text in English) 1951. m. Tobacco Board, Box 451, Lakshmipuram, Guntur 522007, India.
Formerly: Indian Tobacco (ISSN 0445-8192)

633.71 US
TOBACCO REPRINT SERIES. 1954. irreg. free to qualified personnel. Tobacco Literature Service, North Carolina State University, 2314 D.H. Hill Library, Raleigh, NC 27650. Ed. Carmen M. Marin. charts. illus. circ. 150(controlled) (tabloid format)

679.7 US ISSN 0082-4623
TOBACCO SCIENCE YEARBOOK. 1958. a. $15. Lockwood Trade Journal Co., Inc., 551 Fifth Ave., New York, NY 10017. index. (reprint service avail. from UMI)

679.7 UK ISSN 0082-4631
TOBACCO TRADE YEAR BOOK AND DIARY. a. $5. International Trade Publications Ltd., Queensway House, 2 Queensway, Redhill, Surrey RH1 1QS, England. Ed. Freda Troughton. adv.

U. S. BUREAU OF ALCOHOL, TOBACCO AND FIREARMS. ANNUAL REPORT. see *LAW*

658.8 679.7 US ISSN 0083-3479
UNITED STATES TOBACCO JOURNAL SUPPLIER DIRECTORY. 1963. a. $25 free to subscribers; non-subscribers $10. B M T Publications, Inc., 254 W. 31st St., New York, NY 10001. Ed. I. Babson. adv. index. circ. 8,000.

679.7 US ISSN 0084-2273
WORLD TOBACCO DIRECTORY. 1938. a. $60. International Trade Publications Ltd., Queensway House, Redhill, Surrey RH1 1QS, England. Ed. Michael F. Barford. adv.

679.7 RH ISSN 0080-2875
ZIMBABWE-RHODESIA. TOBACCO RESEARCH BOARD. ANNUAL REPORT AND ACCOUNTS. 1954/55. a. free. ‡ Tobacco Research Board, P.O. Box 1909, Salisbury, Zimbabwe. circ. 660.

TOBACCO — Abstracting, Bibliographies, Statistics

338.4 CN ISSN 0300-0249
CANADA. STATISTICS CANADA. TOBACCO PRODUCTS INDUSTRIES/INDUSTRIE DU TABAC. (Catalogue 32-225) (Text in English & French) 1918. a. Can.$4.50($5.40) Statistics Canada, Publications Distribution, Ottawa, Ont. K1A 0V7, Canada. (also avail. in microform from MML)

658.8 336 310 US ISSN 0563-6191
TAX BURDEN ON TOBACCO. 1966. a. Tobacco Tax Council, 5407 Patterson Ave., Richmond, VA 23226. stat.

633.71 679.7 317 US
U.S. AGRICULTURAL MARKETING SERVICE. ANNUAL REPORT ON TOBACCO STATISTICS. (Subseries of U.S.D.A. Statistical Bulletin) a. U.S. Agricultural Marketing Service, Washington, DC 20250 (Orders to: Supt. Doc., Washington, DC 20402) stat. (tabloid format)

TRADE AND INDUSTRIAL DIRECTORIES

see *Business and Economics — Trade and Industrial Directories*

TRANSPORTATION

see also *Transportation — Air Transport; Transportation — Automobiles; Transportation — Railroads; Transportation — Roads and Traffic; Transportation — Ships and Shipping; Transportation — Trucks and Trucking*

380.5 CN ISSN 0318-4757
ALBERTA. DEPARTMENT OF TRANSPORTATION. ANNUAL REPORT. a. Department of Transportation, 320 Legislative Bldg., Edmonton, Alta. T5K 2B6, Canada.

388.322 US
AMERICAN BUS ASSOCIATION. REPORT. 1927. a. American Bus Association, 1025 Connecticut Ave., Washington, DC 20036. stat.
Incorporating (as of 1977): Bus Facts.

380.5 FR ISSN 0066-3549
ANNUAIRE NATIONAL DES TRANSPORTS. 1948. a. Editions Louis Johanet, 68 rue Boursault, 75017 Paris, France. adv.

380.5 UN ISSN 0066-3859
ANNUAL BULLETIN OF TRANSPORT STATISTICS FOR EUROPE. (Text in English, French and Russian) 1950. a.; latest 1974. price varies. United Nations Economic Commission for Europe, Palais des Nations, 1200 Geneva 10, Switzerland (Or United Nations Publications, Room LX-2300, New York, NY 10017)

380.5 SP
ANO DEL TRANSPORTE. 1976. a. 1000 ptas. Edisport S.L., Isaac Peral 12, Madrid, Spain. illus.

380.5 BL
ANUARIO BRASILEIRO DE TRANSPORTES. 1974. a. $10. Publicacoes Informativas Ltda., Rua Caetes 139, 05016 Sao Paulo, Brazil. Ed. J.C. Salles Neto. adv. circ. 15,000.

380.52 BL
ANUARIO ESTATISTICO DOS TRANSPORTES. 1970. a. free. Empresa Brasileira de Planejamento de Transportes, G E I P O T, San Quadro 3 LoteA, 70,040 Brasilia, DF, Brazil. circ. 1,000.

380.1 US
ARABIAN TRANSPORT DIRECTORY. irreg., latest 1980. $75. Inter-Crescent Publishing Co., Inc., Box 8481, Dallas, TX 75205.

AUSTRALIA. BUREAU OF STATISTICS. RAIL, BUS, AND AIR TRANSPORT. see *TRANSPORTATION — Railroads*

380.5 CN
B.C. MOTOR TRANSPORT DIRECTORY. 1977. a. British Columbia Motor Transport Association, 4090 Graveley St., Burnaby, B.C. V5C 3T6, Canada. adv.

B I C-CODE. see *PACKAGING*

380.5 US
BATTERY COUNCIL INTERNATIONAL. CONVENTION MINUTES. a. $25. ‡ Battery Council International, 111 E. Wacker Dr., Chicago, IL 60601. abstr. charts. illus. stat. circ. 750.

338.3 US ISSN 0363-3764
BUS RIDE: BUS INDUSTRY DIRECTORY. Spine title: Bus Industry Directory. 1972. biennial. $12.50. Friendship Publications, Inc., Box 1472, Spokane, WA 99210. Ed. William A. Luke. abstr. circ. 2,000.

380.5 CN ISSN 0068-9912
CANADA. TRANSPORT COMMISSION. ANNUAL REPORT. (Text in English and French) a. free. Transport Commission, 275 Slater St., Ottawa, Ont. K1A 0N9, Canada (Subscr. to: Supply and Services Canada, Publications Division, Ottawa, Ont. K1A 0S9, Canada)

386 CN ISSN 0068-9467
CANADIAN PORTS AND SEAWAYS DIRECTORY. 1934. a. Can.$22. Southam Communications Ltd., 1450 Don Mills Rd., Don Mills, Ont. M3B 2X7, Canada. Ed. Doug Seip. index. circ. 3,000.

388.4 CN ISSN 0316-7933
CANADIAN URBAN TRANSIT ASSOCIATION. PROCEEDINGS. 1973. a. Canadian Urban Transit Association, 1138 Bathurst St., Toronto, Ont. M5R 3H2, Canada.
Formerly: Canadian Transit Association. Proceedings (ISSN 0316-7941)

TRANSPORTATION

711.7 II ISSN 0069-1690
CENTRAL ROAD RESEARCH INSTITUTE, NEW DELHI. ROAD RESEARCH PAPER. (Text in English) 1956. irreg., 1969, no. 108. free. Central Road Research Institute, P.O. Central Road Research Institute, New Delhi 110020, India. (Affiliate: Council of Scientific and Industrial Research) circ. controlled. Indexed: Chem.Abstr. Eng.Ind.

380.5 UK ISSN 0306-9559
CHARTERED INSTITUTE OF TRANSPORT. HANDBOOK. a. Chartered Institute of Transport, 80 Portland Place, London W1N 4DP, England.

380.5 US
CHICAGO AREA TRANSPORTATION STUDY. ANNUAL REPORT. a. Chicago Area Transportation Study, 300 W. Adams St., Chicago, IL 60606. charts. illus.

385 EI ISSN 0069-679X
COMMISSION OF THE EUROPEAN COMMUNITIES. STUDIES: TRANSPORT SERIES.* (Text in Dutch, English, French, German, Italian) 1966. irreg. 200 Fr. Office for Official Publications of the European Communities, C.P. 1003, Luxembourg, Luxembourg (Dist. in U.S. by: European Community Information Service, 2100 M St., NW, Suite 707, Washington, DC 20037)

353.9 US ISSN 0362-9503
CONNECTICUT. AUDITORS OF PUBLIC ACCOUNTS. REPORT ON DEPARTMENT OF TRANSPORTATION, BUREAU OF RAIL AND MOTOR CARRIER SERVICES. triennial. Auditors of Public Accounts, Hartford, CT 06115. illus. Key Title: Report on Department of Transportation, Bureau of Rail and Motor Carrier Services.

388 US ISSN 0069-9039
CONNECTICUT MASTER TRANSPORTATION PLAN. 1971. a. Department of Transportation, Bureau of Staff Services, c/o Director of Planning, Bureau of Planning & Research, 24 Wolcott Hill Rd., Wethersfield, CT 06109. circ. 2,000.
  Incorporating (as of 1973): Connecticut Highway Needs Report.

380.52 380.1 GW
CONTAINER CONTACTS. 1971. a. DM.16. K.O. Storck und Co. Verlag und Druckerei GmbH, Stahltwiete 7, 2000 Hamburg 50, W. Germany (B.R.D.) Ed. H. Meder.

658.7 UK
CONTAINERISATION INTERNATIONAL YEARBOOK. a. £28. National Magazine Co. Ltd., 72 Broadwick St., London W1V 2BP, England.

CONTAINERIZATION AND MATERIAL HANDLING ANNUAL. see *PACKAGING*

CONTAINERS. see *PACKAGING*

387 388 FR
COURRIER DU TRANSPORTEUR; publicite directe specialisee pour le transport. 1975. irreg. 250 F. Editions Gozlan, 94, rue Saint-Lazare, 75009 Paris, France. circ. 16,000.
  Formerly: Transporanonces.

380.5 CY
CYPRUS. DEPARTMENT OF STATISTICS AND RESEARCH. ROAD MOTOR TRANSPORT SAMPLE SURVEY. a. Mils.250. Department of Statistics and Research, Ministry of Finance, Nicosia, Cyprus.

380.5 GW ISSN 0070-4210
DEUTSCHE KRAFTFAHRTFORSCHUNG UND STRASSENVERKEHRSTECHNIK. 1938. irreg. (Verein Deutscher Ingenieure) V D I-Verlag GmbH, Graf Recke Str. 84, Postfach 1139, 4000 Duesseldorf 1, W. Germany (B.R.D.) circ. 500.

380.5 GW
DEUTSCHE VERKEHRSWISSENSCHAFTLICHE GESELLSCHAFT. SCHRIFTENREIHE. REIHE A. DOKUMENTATION. vol. 12, 1974. irreg. DM.21. Deutsche Verkehrswissenschaftliche Gesellschaft, Apostelnstr. 11, 5000 Cologne 1, W. Germany (B.R.D.) Ed. K. Thielen.

380.5 NE
DEVELOPMENTS IN TRANSPORT STUDIES. 1980. irreg. price varies. Martinus Nijhoff, Box 442, The Hague, Netherlands.

380.5 US
DWIGHT'S SPECIAL TRUCK EQUIPMENT MANUAL. 1963. a. Dwight Publishing Company, 4782 N. Cumberland Blvd., Milwaukee, WI 53211. Ed. Roth D. Row. circ. 4,500.

380.5 001.5 PN ISSN 0378-7389
ESTADISTICA PANAMENA. SITUACION ECONOMICA. SECCIONES 333 Y 334. TRANSPORTES Y COMUNICACIONES. 1958. a. Bl..30. Direccion de Estadistica y Censo, Contraloria General, Apartado 5213, Panama 5, Panama. circ. 1,100.

380.5 SZ ISSN 0071-3120
EUROPEAN PASSENGER TIMETABLE CONFERENCE MINUTES. (Text in French and German) 1923. a. membership. Chemins de Fer Federaux Suisses - Swiss Federal Railways, Hochschulstr. 6, CH-3030 Berne, Switzerland. circ. 550 (controlled)

353.9 US ISSN 0095-2060
FLORIDA. DEPARTMENT OF TRANSPORTATION. ANNUAL REPORT. 1915. a. free. Department of Transportation, Burns Bldg., Tallahassee, FL 32301. illus. stat. circ. 1,000. Key Title: Annual Report - State of Florida, Department of Transportation.

388.3 US ISSN 0092-0177
FLORIDA. DIVISION OF MOTOR VEHICLES. TAGS AND REVENUE. 1928. a. free. Department of Highway Safety and Motor Vehicles, Division of Motor Vehicles, Neil Kirkman Building, Tallahassee, FL 32304. circ. 1,000.

385.1 GW ISSN 0341-0951
FORSCHUNG STADTVERKEHR. (Text in English and German) 1968. irreg., no. 27, 1980. price varies. (Bundesministerium fuer Verkehr) Kirschbaum Verlag, Siegfriedstr. 28, Postfach 210209, 5300 Bonn 2, W. Germany (B.R.D.) Ed. Bd. abstr. circ. 3,000.

388 UK ISSN 0071-9471
FREIGHT INDUSTRY YEARBOOK; classified reference and guide for transport vehicle manufacturers, operators and users. 1950. a. £8.95. Transport and Distribution Press, 118 Ewell Rd., Surbiton, Surrey, England. Ed. E. M. G. Gibbins. adv. circ. 2,000.
  Formerly: Good Vehicle Year Book.

385.1 GH ISSN 0072-4408
GHANA. RAILWAY AND PORTS ADMINISTRATION. REPORT. 1912. a. NC.6. Railway and Ports Administration, P.O. Box 251, Takoradi, Ghana.

388 UK
GLASS'S COMMERCIAL VEHICLE CHECK BOOK. a. £2.50. Glass's Guide Service Ltd., Elgin House, St. George's Ave., Weybridge, Surrey KT13 0BX, England. adv.

380.5 GW ISSN 0073-019X
HANDBUCH OEFFENTLICHER VERKEHRSBETRIEBE. 1952. biennial. price varies. (Verband Oeffentlicher Verkehrsbetriebe) Erich Schmidt Verlag (Bielefeld), Viktoriastr. 44A, Postfach 7330, 4800 Bielefeld 1, W. Germany (B.R.D.) adv.

658.7 US
HANDLING & SHIPPING. PRESIDENTIAL ISSUE. (Vols for 1970-72 compiled by the editors of Handling & Shipping) a. $8 (single issue) Penton-IPC, 614 Superior Ave., W., Cleveland, OH 44113. Ed. Henry Becker. adv. illus. (reprint service avail. from UMI)

I T F PANORAMA. (International Transport Worker's Federation) see *LABOR UNIONS*

353.9 US ISSN 0095-5019
ILLINOIS. DEPARTMENT OF TRANSPORTATION. ANNUAL REPORT. 1972. a. Department of Transportation, Springfield, IL 62706. Key Title: Annual Report - Illinois Department of Transportation.

380.5 SW
INGENIOERSVETENSKAPSAKADEMIEN. TRANSPORTFORSKNINGSKOMMISSION. RAPPORTER. 1976. irreg. (5-10/yr) price varies. Ingenioersvetenskapsakademien, Transportforskningskommission - Royal Swedish Academy of Engineering Sciences, Grev Turegatan 12 A, 114 46 Stockholm, Sweden.

388 PL
INSTYTUT TRANSPORTU SAMOCHODOWEGO. ZESZYTY NAUKOWE. (Text in Polish; summaries in English and Russian) 1962. irreg., (approx 4-6 per year) Instytut Transportu Samochodowego, Stalingradzka 40, Warsaw, Poland. bk. rev. illus. stat. pat. circ. controlled.

385.1 BE ISSN 0378-1968
INTERNATIONAL STATISTICAL HANDBOOK OF URBAN PUBLIC TRANSPORT/RECUEIL INTERNATIONAL DE STATISTIQUES DES TRANSPORTS PUBLICS URBAINS/ INTERNATIONALES STATISTIK-HANDBUCH FUER DEN OEFFENTLICHEN STADTVERKEHR. 1964. irreg. 3300 Fr.($110) International Union of Public Transport, 19, Ave. de l'Uruguay, B-1050 Brussels, Belgium.
  Supersedes: International Union of Public Transport. Transports Publics dans les Principales Villes du Monde (ISSN 0539-113X)

INTERNATIONAL SYMPOSIUM ON THE AERODYNAMICS AND VENTILATION OF VEHICLE TUNNELS. PROCEEDINGS. see *ENGINEERING — Civil Engineering*

380.1 US ISSN 0094-7466
INTERNATIONAL SYMPOSIUM ON TRANSPORT AND HANDLING OF MINERALS. MINERALS TRANSPORTATION; PROCEEDINGS. 1971. irreg. price varies. Miller Freeman Publications, Inc., 500 Howard St., San Francisco, CA 94105. bibl. illus. Key Title: Minerals Transportation.

INTERNATIONAL TRANSPORT WORKERS' FEDERATION REPORT ON ACTIVITIES. see *LABOR UNIONS*

386 BE ISSN 0074-9311
INTERNATIONAL UNION FOR INLAND NAVIGATION. ANNUAL REPORT. (Editions in English, French, and German) 1953. a. free. International Union for Inland Navigation - Union Internationale de la Navigation Fluviale, 19 rue de la Presse, 1000 Brussels, Belgium.

380.5 BE
INTERNATIONAL UNION OF PUBLIC TRANSPORT. PROCEEDINGS OF THE INTERNATIONAL CONGRESS. biennial. price varies. International Union of Public Transport, 19, Ave. de l'Uruguay, 1050 Brussels, Belgium.
  Formerly: International Union of Public Transport. Reports and Proceedings of the International Congress (ISSN 0074-9494)

380.5 BE ISSN 0378-1976
INTERNATIONAL UNION OF PUBLIC TRANSPORT. TECHNICAL REPORTS OF THE CONGRESSES. French edition: Union Internationale des Transports Publics. Rapports Techniques des Congres Internationaux. German edition: Internationaler Verband fuer Oeffentliches Verkehrswesen. Technische Berichte zu den Internationalen Kongressen. (Editions in English, French, and German) 1885. biennial. price varies. International Union of Public Transport, 19, Avenue de l'Uruguay, B-1050 Brussels, Belgium. adv. circ. 18,000.

380.5 PK ISSN 0075-5109
KARACHI PORT TRUST. YEAR BOOK OF INFORMATION, PORT OF KARACHI, PAKISTAN. (Text in English) 1961. a. Rs.20. Karachi Port Trust, I.A. Quiraishi, Karachi, Pakistan.

629.2 DK
L D V BOGEN. 1960. a. Landsforeningen Danske Vognmaend, Jens Kofodsgade 1, 1268 Copenhagen K, Denmark. cum.index (1960-1980 in no. 21)

380.5 US ISSN 0149-4007
LAND USE AND TRANSPORTATION. 1977. a. free. National Research Council, Transportation Research Board, 2101 Constitution Ave. N.W., Washington, DC 20418. Ed. Steven Bloomfield. circ. 5,500.

LIBERIA. MINISTRY OF COMMERCE, INDUSTRY AND TRANSPORTATION. ANNUAL REPORT. see *BUSINESS AND ECONOMICS — Production Of Goods And Services*

388.322 UK ISSN 0076-0013
LITTLE RED BOOK, CLASSIFIED TO ALL PUBLIC TRANSPORT FLEET OWNERS AND OPERATORS AND VEHICLE MANUFACTURERS. 1899. a. price varies. Ian Allan Ltd., Terminal House, Shepperton, Middlesex TW17 8AS, England. Ed. John Parke. adv. circ. 2,250.
Formerly: Passenger Transport Year Book.

380.5 US
M A P A ANNUAL TRANSPORTATION REPORT. 1974. a. free. Omaha-Council Bluffs Metropolitan Area Planning Agency, 7000 W. Center Rd., Suite 200, Omaha, NE 68106. circ. 400.

353.9 US ISSN 0094-5048
MAINE. DEPARTMENT OF TRANSPORTATION. ANNUAL REPORT. 1973. a. Department of Transportation, Augusta, ME 04330. illus. stat. Key Title: Annual Report - Maine Department of Transportation.

380.5 MF ISSN 0076-5554
MAURITIUS. MINISTRY OF WORKS AND INTERNAL COMMUNICATIONS. REPORT. a, latest 1976. price varies. Government Printing Office, Elizabeth II Ave., Port Louis, Mauritius.

380.5 US
MODERN TIRE DEALER PRODUCTS CATALOG. 1972. a. included in subscr. to Modern Tire Dealer. ‡ Bill Communications Inc., 633 Third Ave., New York, NY 10017. Ed. Stephen LaFerre. adv. circ. 34,000(controlled) (reprint service avail. from UMI)

380.5 NZ
MOTOR INDUSTRY YEAR BOOK. 1947. a. New Zealand Motor Trade Federation, Box 390, Wellington, New Zealand. Ed. H. Snijders.

381.41 US ISSN 0094-2790
MOVEMENT OF CALIFORNIA FRUITS AND VEGETABLES BY RAIL, TRUCK, AND AIR. a. free. Federal-State Market News Service, 1220 N St., Sacramento, CA 95814. stat.

380.5 US
N F T A ANNUAL REPORT. 1967. a. free. Niagara Frontier Transportation Authority, 181 Ellicott St., Buffalo, NY 14203. Ed. John C.Seal. circ. 500.

380.5 US
N F T A PORT OF BUFFALO HANDBOOK. 1967. biennial. free. Niagara Frontier Transportation Authority, 181 Ellicott St., Buffalo, NY 14203. Ed. John C. Seal. adv.

NATIONAL INSTITUTE FOR TRANSPORT AND ROAD RESEARCH. ANNUAL REPORT/ NASIONALE INSTITUUT VIR VERVOER- EN PADNAVORSING. JAARVERSLAG. see *ENGINEERING — Civil Engineering*

380.5 US ISSN 0148-849X
NATIONAL RESEARCH COUNCIL. TRANSPORTATION RESEARCH BOARD. BIBLIOGRAPHY. no. 57, 1976. irreg. price varies. National Research Council, Transportation Research Board, 2101 Constitution Ave., Washington, DC 20418. bibl.

380.5 US ISSN 0361-1981
NATIONAL RESEARCH COUNCIL. TRANSPORTATION RESEARCH BOARD. RECORD. 1963. irreg., no. 175, 1976. price varies. National Research Council, Transportation Research Board, 2101 Constitution Ave., Washington, DC 20418.

387 623.89 AT ISSN 0077-6262
NAVIGATION. 1959. a. $1.50. Australian Institute of Navigation, Box 2250 G.P.O, Sydney, N.S.W, Australia. Ed. S. Cohen. adv. bk. rev. circ. 600.

388 387 NE ISSN 0077-7358
NETHERLANDS. CENTRAAL BUREAU VOOR DE STATISTIEK. STATISTIEK VAN HET PERSONENVERVOER. STATISTICS OF PASSENGER TRANSPORT. (Text in Dutch and English) 1943. a. fl.12.35. Centraal Bureau voor de Statistiek, Prinses Beatrixlaan 428, Voorburg, Netherlands (Orders to: Staatsuitgeverij, Christoffel Plantijnstraat, The Hague, Netherlands)

380.5 US
NEW JERSEY. DEPARTMENT OF TRANSPORTATION. ANNUAL REPORT. 1894. a. free. Department of Transportation, 1035 Parkway Ave., Box 101, Trenton, NJ 08625.
Former titles, 1975-1977: New Jersey. Department of Transportation. Highlight of Activities; 1970-1974: New Jersey. Department of Transportation. Report of Operations (ISSN 0085-395X); Until 1970: New Jersey. Department of Transportation. Annual Report.

380 NZ ISSN 0110-3458
NEW ZEALAND. DEPARTMENT OF STATISTICS. TRANSPORT STATISTICS. a. NZ.$2.50. Department of Statistics, Private Bag, Wellington, New Zealand (Subscr. to: Government Printing Office, Publications, Private Bag, Wellington, New Zealand)

380.5 NZ ISSN 0085-4123
NEW ZEALAND. MINISTRY OF TRANSPORT. ANNUAL REPORT. 1969. a. price varies. Government Printing Office, Private Bag, Wellington, New Zealand.

354.931 NZ
NEW ZEALAND. URBAN PUBLIC PASSENGER TRANSPORT COUNCIL. REPORT. a. NZ.$0.10. New Zealand Urban Public Passenger Transport Council, Wellington, New Zealand. stat.

312.44 US ISSN 0092-9913
OREGON. MOTOR VEHICLES DIVISION. OREGON MOTORCYCLE ACCIDENTS. 1970. a. free. Department of Transportation, Motor Vehicles Division, Salem, OR 97310. stat. circ. 300. Key Title: Oregon Motorcycle Accidents.

380.5 II ISSN 0079-2381
POCKET BOOK OF TRANSPORT STATISTICS OF INDIA. 1968. a; latest edition in print 1972-73. $12.96. Ministry of Shipping and Transport, Transport Research Division, I D A Bldg, Jamnagar House, Shahjahan Rd., New Delhi 110011, India (Orders to: Controller of Publications, Civil Lines, Delhi 110006, India)
Formerly: India Transport Statistics.

387 US ISSN 0085-5030
PORT OF NEW ORLEANS ANNUAL DIRECTORY. 1969. a. free. Port of New Orleans, 2 Canal St., Box 60046, New Orleans, LA 70160. Ed. Nat Chesnut. adv. bk. rev. charts. illus. stat. circ. 18,000 (controlled)

380.5 301.16 314 PO
PORTUGAL. INSTITUTO NACIONAL DE ESTATISTICA. SERVICOS CENTRAIS. ESTATISTICAS DOS TRANSPORTES E COMMUNICACOES: CONTINENTE, ACORES E MADEIRA. (Text in French, Portuguese) irreg. Instituto Nacional de Estatistica, Servicos Centrais, Avda. Antonio Jose de Almeida 1, Lisbon, Portugal.

380.5 JA
PROBLEMS OF TRANSPORTATION IN JAPAN. (Text in English) 1975. irreg. Institute of Transportation Economics - Un'Yu Chosakyoku, 2-5-6 Izumicho Kokubunji, Tokyo, Japan.

380.5 FR ISSN 0079-6972
PROMOTRANS.* 1970. irreg. price varies. Association pour la Promotion Sociale et la Formation Professionelle dans les Transports Routiers, 124 Av. de la Republique, Paris 11e, France.

353.9 US
PUBLIC TRANSPORTATION IN OREGON. 1969. a. free. Department of Transportation, Public Transit Division, 129 Transportation Bldg., Salem, OR 97310. Ed. Jalaine Madura. illus. circ. 500.
Formerly: Oregon. Mass Transit Division. Annual Report (ISSN 0090-3906)

387 623.8 UK ISSN 0080-0422
REED'S NAUTICAL ALMANAC. (In two editions: European & American) 1931. a. £6.95 for each edt. Thomas Reed Industrial Press, 36/37 Cock Lane, London EC1A 9BY, England. Ed. O. M. Watts. index.

380.5 US ISSN 0516-9445
REFERENCE BOOK OF HIGHWAY PERSONNEL. a. $2.50. American Association of State Highway and Transportation Officials, 444 N. Capitol St. N.W., Suite 225, Washington, DC 20001.

384 380.52 UK
ROUTES; directory of International Freighting Services. 1973. a. £3. Maclean-Hunter Ltd., 30 Old Burlington St., London W1X 2 AE, England. Ed. Stephen Taylor. adv. bk. rev. circ. 3,000.

380.5 US ISSN 0362-2800
SAN FRANCISCO BAY AREA RAPID TRANSIT DISTRICT. ANNUAL REPORT. 1958. a. San Francisco Bay Area Rapid Transit District, 800 Madison St., Oakland, CA 94607. Ed. Michael Healy. illus. circ. 5,000. Key Title: Annual Report - San Francisco Bay Area Rapid Transit District.

380.1 CN ISSN 0707-9184
SNOWMOBILE ACCIDENTS, MANITOBA. 1972. a. contr. free circ. Department of Highways, Safety Division, Box 15, Bldg. 15, 139 Tuxedo Blvd., Winnipeg, Man. R3N 0H6, Canada.

380.5 US ISSN 0362-2843
SOUTHERN CALIFORNIA RAPID TRANSIT DISTRICT. ANNUAL REPORT. 1964. a. Southern California Rapid Transit District, 425 S. Main, Los Angeles, CA 90013. illus. circ. 5,000. Key Title: Annual Report - Southern California Rapid Transit District.

380.5 EI ISSN 0081-4962
STATISTICAL OFFICE OF THE EUROPEAN COMMUNITIES. STATISTIQUES DES TRANSPORTS. ANNUAIRE. (Text in French, German, Italian, Dutch) a. B.P. 1907, Luxembourg, Luxembourg (Dist. in the U.S. by: European Community Information Service, 2100 M St., NW, Suite 707, Washington, DC 20037)

380.5 UK
STEAM & ORGAN YEAR BOOK & PRESERVED TRANSPORT GUIDE. 1976. a. 60p. Traction Engine Enterprises, 216 Coventry Rd., Hinckley, Leicestershire LE1O 0NG, England. Ed. C. L. Deith.

380.5 CN ISSN 0706-7658
TRANSIT FACT BOOK & MEMBERSHIP DIRECTORY. 1969. a. membership. ‡ Canadian Urban Transit Association, 234 Eglinton Ave. E., Suite 301, Toronto, Ont. M4P 1K5, Canada. Ed. R.A. Harvey. adv. circ. 500.
Formerly (until 1977): Transit Fact Book (ISSN 0082-5913)

380 UN ISSN 0041-1396
TRANSPORT & COMMUNICATIONS BULLETIN FOR ASIA & THE FAR EAST. 1950. irreg., no. 52, 1978. price varies. United Nations Economic and Social Commission for Asia and the Pacific, United Nations Bldg., Rajadamnern Ave., Bangkok 2, Thailand (Dist. by: United Nations Publications, Room LX-2300, New York, NY 10017; or Distribution and Sales Section, Palais des Nations, CH-1211 Geneva 10, Switzerland) bk. rev. charts. illus. stat. Indexed: P.A.I.S.

380.5 II
TRANSPORT INDUSTRY AND TRADE ANNUAL. 1963. a. $10. Praveen Corp., Sayajigani, Baroda 390005, India. Ed. C. M. Pandit. circ. 2,500.
Formerly: Transport Industry and Trade Journal (ISSN 0041-1477)

388 UK ISSN 0306-9435
TRANSPORT MANAGER'S HANDBOOK. 1970. a. £11.95. ‡ Kogan Page Ltd., 120 Pentonville Rd., London N1 9JN, England. Ed. David Lowe. adv. charts. illus.

380.5 PL ISSN 0137-4435
TRANSPORT MUSEUMS. (Yearbook of the International Association of Transport Museums) (Text in English) irreg., vol. 4, 1979. (Centralne Muzeum Morskie, Gdansk) Ossolineum, Publishing House of the Polish Academy of Sciences, Rynek 9, Wroclaw, Poland (Subscr. to: International Association of Transport Museums, Zeughaus Str. 1-5, Cologne, W. Germany (B.R.D.)) (Co-sponsor: International Association of Transport Museums)

380 AT
TRANSPORT SERVICES DIRECTORY. 1968. a. Trade Directories, P.O. Box 94, Morningside, Qld 4170, Australia.

380.5 UK
TRANSPORT STUDIES GROUP. ANNUAL SEMINAR ON RURAL PUBLIC TRANSPORT. PAPERS AND PROCEEDINGS. 1972. a. £6. Transport Studies Group, Polytechnic of Central London, 35 Marylebone Rd., London NW1 5LS, England. Ed. Peter R. White. circ. 150.

331.88 MY
TRANSPORT WORKERS UNION. TRIENNIAL REPORT. (Text in English) triennial. Transport Workers Union, Transport Workers House, 21 Jalan Barat, Petaling Jaya, Malaysia.

380.5 US ISSN 0164-1689
TRANSPORTATION LAW SEMINAR. PAPERS AND PROCEEDINGS. 1971. a. Association of Interstate Commerce Commission Practitioners, 1112 ICC Bldg., Washington, DC 20423.

380.5 CN
TRANSPORTATION R & D IN CANADA. 1963. biennial. Can.$6($6) Roads and Transportation Association of Canada, 1765 St. Laurent Bd., Ottawa, Ont. K1G 3V4, Canada. Ed. C. A. Davies. index. circ. 800. (processed)
    Former titles: Transportation Research in Canada (ISSN 0381-8284); Road Research in Canada.

380.5 US ISSN 0091-2468
TRANSPORTATION RESEARCH FORUM. PROCEEDINGS: ANNUAL MEETING. 1962. a. $25. (Transportation Research Forum) Richard B. Cross Co., 103 S. Howard St., Box 405, Oxford, IN 47971 (Dist. by Grant C. Vietsch, 181 East Lake Shore Drive, Chicago Ill., 60611) illus. stat. Key Title: Proceedings. Annual Meeting - Transportation Research Forum.

TRANSPORTATION STATISTICS IN THE UNITED STATES. see BUSINESS AND ECONOMICS — Domestic Commerce

380.5 US ISSN 0447-9181
TRANSPORTATION TELEPHONE TICKLER. (Published in a national edition in 3 vols. and 10 regional editions) 1950. a. $40 per set. Journal of Commerce, 110 Wall St., New York, NY 10005 (Subscr. addr.: Journal of Commerce, 445 Marshall St., Phillipsburg, NJ 08865) adv. index. circ. 60,000.

621.8 658.7 GW ISSN 0082-5964
TRANSPORTIEREN UMSCHLAGEN LAGERN. 1967. irreg. DM.36. Hestra-Verlag, Postfach 4244, 6100 Darmstadt 1, W. Germany (B.R.D.) adv. bk. rev.

TRUCK & BUS TESTS & SPECS. see TRANSPORTATION — Trucks And Trucking

380.5 US ISSN 0082-9404
U. S. BUREAU OF THE CENSUS. CENSUS OF TRANSPORTATION. 1963. quinquennial. price varies. U.S. Bureau of the Census, Dept. of Commerce, Washington, DC 20233 (Orders to: Supt. of Documents, Washington, DC 20402)

U.S. DEPARTMENT OF TRANSPORTATION. NATIONAL TRANSPORTATION STATISTICS. ANNUAL; a supplement to the summary of national transportation statistics. see STATISTICS

353.85 US ISSN 0092-3117
U. S. DEPARTMENT OF TRANSPORTATION. FISCAL YEAR BUDGET IN BRIEF.* a. U. S. Department of Transportation, Office of Budget, 400 Seventh St., S.W., Washington, DC 20590. Key Title: Budget in Brief - Department of Transportation (Washington)

380.5 US ISSN 0099-2267
U.S. DEPARTMENT OF TRANSPORTATION. OFFICE OF UNIVERSITY RESEARCH. AWARDS TO ACADEMIC INSTITUTIONS BY THE DEPARTMENT OF TRANSPORTATION. a. U.S. Department of Transportation, Office of University Research, 400 7th St., S.W., Washington, DC 20590. Key Title: Awards to Academic Institutions by the Department of Transportation.

388.3 US
U. S. FEDERAL HIGHWAY ADMINISTRATION. HIGHWAY AND URBAN MASS TRANSPORTATION. 1972. irreg (2-3/yr) price varies. U.S. Federal Highway Administration, Washington, DC 20590. Ed. Elizabeth Samson. charts. illus.

UNIVERSITY OF BIRMINGHAM. DEPARTMENT OF TRANSPORTATION AND ENVIRONMENTAL PLANNING. RESEARCH JOURNAL. see ENVIRONMENTAL STUDIES

625.7 016 US ISSN 0068-6115
UNIVERSITY OF CALIFORNIA, BERKELEY. INSTITUTE OF TRANSPORTATION STUDIES. LIBRARY REFERENCES. 1955. irreg., no. 78, 1978. free. University of California, Berkeley, Institute of Transportation Studies Library, 412 McLaughlin Hall, Berkeley, CA 94720. Ed. Beverly Hickok.

385.1 CN
UNIVERSITY OF MANITOBA. CENTER FOR TRANSPORTATION STUDIES. ANNUAL REPORT. 1969. a. free. University of Manitoba, Center for Transportation Studies, Rm. 515, University Centre, Winnipeg, Manitoba R3T 2N2, Canada.

385.1 CN ISSN 0076-3977
UNIVERSITY OF MANITOBA. CENTER FOR TRANSPORTATION STUDIES. OCCASIONAL PAPER. 1968. irreg. University of Manitoba, Center for Transportation Studies, Rm. 515, University Centre, Winnipeg, Man. R3T 2N2, Canada.

385 CN ISSN 0316-7984
UNIVERSITY OF MANITOBA. CENTER FOR TRANSPORTATION STUDIES. RESEARCH REPORT. 1967. irreg. price varies. University of Manitoba, Center for Transportation Studies, Rm. 515, University Centre, Winnipeg, Man. R3T 2N2, Canada.

380.5 CN ISSN 0076-3993
UNIVERSITY OF MANITOBA. CENTER FOR TRANSPORTATION STUDIES. SEMINAR SERIES ON TRANSPORTATION. PROCEEDINGS. 1967. a. Can.$3. University of Manitoba, Center for Transportation Studies, Rm. 515, University Centre, Winnipeg, Man. R3T 2N2, Canada.
    Incorporating: Colloquim Series on Transportation. Proceedings (ISSN 0069-584X)

380.5 CN ISSN 0318-1251
UNIVERSITY OF TORONTO-YORK UNIVERSITY. JOINT PROGRAM IN TRANSPORTATION. ANNUAL REPORT. a. University of Toronto-York University Joint Program in Transportation, 42 St. George St., Toronto, Ont. M5S 2E4, Canada.

380.5 PL
UNIWERSYTET GDANSKI. WYDZIAL EKONOMIKI TRANSPORTU. ZESZYTY NAUKOWE. EKONOMIKA TRANSPORTU LADOWEGO. (Text in Polish; summaries in English and Russian) 1971. irreg. price varies. Uniwersytet Gdanski, Ul. Czerwonej Armii 110, 81-824 Sopot, Poland. circ. 300.

380.5 UR
VSESOYUZNYI NAUCHNO-ISSELDOVATEL'SKII INSTITUT TRANSPORTNOGO STROITEL'STVA. TRUDY. vol. 106, 1977. irreg. 0.83 Rub. per no. Izdatel'stvo Transport, Basmannyi Tupik, 6a, Moscow B-175, U.S.S.R. Ed.Bd. circ. 1,000.

343 US ISSN 0095-6082
WASHINGTON (STATE) LEGISLATURE. TRANSPORTATION COMMITTEE. REPORT. irreg. Legislature, Transportation Committee, Olympia, WA 98501. Key Title: Report of the Legislative Transportation Committee.

353.9 US ISSN 0091-4967
WASHINGTON (STATE). TRANSPORTATION AGENCIES. ANNUAL REPORT. 1971. a. State Office of Financial Management, Forecasting and Support Division, House Office Bldg., Olympia, WA 98504 (Dist. by: State Library, Olympia WA 98504) Key Title: Annual Report. Transportation Agencies. State of Washington.

381 AT ISSN 0083-8691
WESTERN AUSTRALIA. OFFICE OF DIRECTOR GENERAL OF TRANSPORT. ANNUAL REPORT. 1968. a. contr.free circ. ‡ Director General of Transport, 68 St. George's Terrace, Perth, Australia. Ed. J. E. Knox. circ. 800.

354 AT
WESTERN AUSTRALIA. TRANSPORT COMMISSION. ANNUAL REPORT OF THE COMMISSIONER OF TRANSPORT. 1934. a. Transport Commission, 136-138 Stirling Highway, Nedlands, W.A. 6009, Australia. circ. 200.

380.5 NE
WORLD CONFERENCE ON TRANSPORT RESEARCH. PROCEEDINGS. irreg., 3rd, 1977, Rotterdam. $76.50. Martinus Nijhoff, Box 442, The Hague, Netherlands (Dist. in the U.S. and Canada by: Kluwer Boston, Inc., 160 Old Derby St., Hingham, MA 02043)

TRANSPORTATION — Abstracting, Bibliographies, Statistics

388.3 US ISSN 0360-9154
ALASKA ACCIDENT STATISTICS. a. Department of Public Safety, Planning and Research, Pouch N, Juneau, AK 99801. illus.

338 AO
ANGOLA. DIRECCAO DOS SERVICOS DE ESTATISTICA. ESTATISTICA DOS VEICULOS MOTORISADOS. 1967. a. ‡ Direccao dos Servicos de Estatistica, Ministerio do Planeamento e Coordenacao Economica, C.P. 1215, Luanda, Angola. circ. 750.

315.2 JA
ANNUAL STATISTICS OF ACTUAL PRODUCTION OF RAILWAY CARS/TETSUDO SHARYOTO SEISAN DOTAI TOKEI NENPO. (Text in Japanese) 1954. a. Ministry of Transport, Data Processing Division - Un'Yu-sho Daijin Kanbo. Joho Kanri-bu, Minister's Secretariat, 2-1-3 Kasumigaseki, Chiyoda-ku, Tokyo 100, Japan.

387 318 AG
ARGENTINA. INSTITUTO NACIONAL DE ESTADISTICA Y CENSOS. NAVEGACION COMMERCIAL ARGENTINA. 1961. a. Instituto Nacional de Estadistica y Censos, Hipolito Yrigoyen 250, Buenos Aires, Argentina. charts. stat.

AUSTRALIA. BUREAU OF STATISTICS. NEW SOUTH WALES OFFICE. TRANSPORT AND COMMUNICATION. see BUSINESS AND ECONOMICS — Abstracting, Bibliographies, Statistics

387 382 319 AT
AUSTRALIA. BUREAU OF STATISTICS. OVERSEAS AND COASTAL SHIPPING. 1974. a. free. Australian Bureau of Statistics, Box 10, Belconnen, A.C.T. 2616, Australia. circ. 700.
    Formerly: Australia. Bureau of Statistics. Overseas Shipping Cargo.

AUSTRALIA. BUREAU OF STATISTICS. TASMANIAN OFFICE. TRADE AND SHIPPING. see BUSINESS AND ECONOMICS — Abstracting, Bibliographies, Statistics

388 II ISSN 0067-6462
BASIC ROAD STATISTICS OF INDIA. Hindi edition: Mool Sarak Ankrey. 1948. a; latest editions in print: 1974-75(English edt.) 1970-71(Hindi edt.) Rs.79.40 for Hindi edt.; $3.78 for English edt. Ministry of Shipping and Transport, Transport Research Division, I D A Bldg., Jamnagar House, Shahjahan Rd, New Delhi 110011, India (Orders to: Controller of Publications, Civil Lines, Delhi 110006, India)

386　　　　　　　　BE　ISSN 0067-5520
BELGIUM. INSTITUT NATIONAL DE STATISTIQUE. STATISTIQUE DE LA NAVIGATION DU RHIN. (Text in Dutch and French) 1949. a. 70 Fr. per no. Institut National de Statistique, 44 rue de Louvain, 1000 Brussels, Belgium.

386　　　　　　　　BE　ISSN 0067-5539
BELGIUM. INSTITUT NATIONAL DE STATISTIQUE. STATISTIQUE DE LA NAVIGATION INTERIEURE. (Text in Dutch and French) 1971. a. 45 Fr. Institut National de Statistique, 44 rue de Louvain, 1000 Brussels, Belgium.

338.4　　　　　　　BE　ISSN 0067-5555
BELGIUM. INSTITUT NATIONAL DE STATISTIQUE. STATISTIQUE DES VEHICULES A MOTEUR NEUFS MIS EN CIRCULATION. (Text in Dutch and French) 1955. a. 208 Fr. Institut National de Statistique, 44 rue de Louvain, B-1000 Brussels, Belgium.

380.5　　　　　　　AU　ISSN 0067-6306
BESTANDS-STATISTIK DER KRAFTFAHRZEUGE IN OESTERREICH. 1956. a. S.460. ‡ (Oesterreichisches Statistisches Zentralamt) Verlag Neue Technik Ges. m.b.H., Walfischgasse 15, A-1010 Vienna, Austria. adv. circ. 650.

016　947　387　　　US
BIBLIOGRAPHY OF PERIODICAL ARTICLES ON MARITIME AND NAVAL HISTORY. a., latest 1972. $3.50. Marine Historical Associations, Inc., c/o Mystic Seaport Museum Stores, Inc., Mystic, CT 06355.

388.31　310　　　　BL
BRAZIL. SUPERINTENDENCIA DO DESENVOLVIMENTO DO NORDESTE. DEPARTAMENTO DE SERVICOS BASICOS DA SUDENE. ESTATISTICA DE TRAFEGO NO NORDESTE. (In 3 vols: I-Maranhao, Piaui, Ceara, Rio Grande do Norte; II-Sergipe, Bahia; III-Paraiba, Pernambuco, Alagoas) 1972. a. Superintendencia do Desenvolvimento do Nordeste, Departamento de Servicos Basicos da Sudene, Av. Prof. Moraes Rego, Edf. da Sudene, Cidade Universitaria, Brazil. stat. index. circ. controlled.

623.82　016　　　　UK
BRITISH SHIP RESEARCH ASSOCIATION. B. S. R. A. BIBLIOGRAPHIES. 1963. irreg. £5($12) per no. British Ship Research Association, Wallsend Research Station, Wallsend, Tyne and Wear NE28 6UY, England. bibl.

387.7　　　　　　　CN　ISSN 0705-4343
CANADA. STATISTICS CANADA. AIR PASSENGER ORIGIN AND DESTINATION. CANADA-UNITED STATES REPORT/ ORIGINE ET DESTINATION DES PASSAGERS AERIENS. RAPPORT SUR LE TRAFIC CANADA-ETAT UNIS. (Catalogue 51-205) (Text in English and French) 1968. a. Can.$25($30) Statistics Canada, Publications Distribution, Ottawa, Ont. K1A 0V7, Canada. (also avail. in microform from MML)

387.7　　　　　　　CN　ISSN 0068-7057
CANADA. STATISTICS CANADA. AVIATION STATISTICS CENTRE. SERVICE BULLETIN/ BULLETIN DE SERVICE DU CENTRE DES STATISTIQUES DE L'AVIATION. (Catalog 51-004) (Text in English and French) 1968. irreg (service bulletin) Can.$15($18) Statistics Canada, Publications Distribution, Ottawa, Ont, K1A 0V7, Canada. (also avail. in microform from MML)

623.82　　　　　　CN　ISSN 0527-4834
CANADA. STATISTICS CANADA. BOATBUILDING AND REPAIR/ CONSTRUCTION ET REPARATION D'EMBARCATIONS. (Catalogue 42-205) (Text in English and French) 1920. a. Can.$4.50($5.40) Statistics Canada, Publications Distribution, Ottawa, Ont. K1A 0V7, Canada. (also avail. in microform from MML)

388　　　　　　　　CN　ISSN 0382-0939
CANADA. STATISTICS CANADA. FOR-HIRE TRUCKING SURVEY/ENQUETE SUR LE TRANSPORT ROUTIER DE MARCHANDISES POUR COMPTE D'AUTRUI. (Catalogue 53-224) (Text in English & French) 1970. a. Can.$6($7.20) Statistics Canada, Publications Distribution, Ottawa, Ont. K1A 0V7, Canada. (also avail. in microform from MML)

388　　　　　　　　CN　ISSN 0383-5766
CANADA. STATISTICS CANADA. PASSENGER BUS AND URBAN TRANSIT STATISTICS/ STATISTIQUE DU TRANSPORT DES VOYAGEURS PAR AUTOBUS ET DU TRANSPORT URBAIN. (Catalogue 53-215) (Text in English and French) 1956. a. Can.$6($7.20) Statistics Canada, Publications Distribution, Ottawa, Ont. K1A 0V7, Canada. (also avail. in microform from MML)

385　　　　　　　　CN　ISSN 0317-3445
CANADA. STATISTICS CANADA. RAILWAY FREIGHT TRAFFIC/TRAFIC MARCHANDISES FERROVIAIRE. (Catalogue 52-205) (Text in English and French) 1921. a. Can.$10($12) Statistics Canada, Publications Distribution, Ottawa, Ont. K1A 0V7, Canada. (also avail. in microform from MML)

388.3　　　　　　　CN　ISSN 0703-654X
CANADA. STATISTICS CANADA. ROAD MOTOR VEHICLES-FUEL SALES/VEHICULES AUTOMOBILES-VENTES DE CARBURANTS. (Catalogue 53-218) (Text in English & French) 1960. a. Can.$4.50($5.40) Statistics Canada, Publications Distribution, Ottawa, Ont. K1A 0V7, Canada. (also avail. in microform from MML)
　Formerly: Canada. Statistics Canada. Motor Vehicle. Part 2. Motive Fuel Sales/Vehicules a Moteur. Partie 2. Ventes des Carburants (ISSN 0527-5830)

388.3　　　　　　　CN　ISSN 0706-067X
CANADA. STATISTICS CANADA. ROAD MOTOR VEHICLES-REGISTRATIONS/ VEHICULES AUTOMOBILES-IMMATRICULATIONS. (Catalogue 53-219) (Text in English & French) 1960. a. Can.$4.50($5.40) Statistics Canada, Publications Distribution, Ottawa, Ont. K1A 0V7, Canada. (also avail. in microform from MML)

623.82　　　　　　CN　ISSN 0527-6144
CANADA. STATISTICS CANADA. SHIPBUILDING AND REPAIR/ CONSTRUCTION ET REPARATION DE NAVIRES. (Catalogue 42-206) (Text in English & French) 1937. a. Can.$4.50($5.40) Statistics Canada, Publications Distribution, Ottawa, Ont. K1A 0V7, Canada. (also avail. in microform from MML)

387　　　　　　　　CN　ISSN 0380-0342
CANADA. STATISTICS CANADA. WATER TRANSPORTATION/TRANSPORT PAR EAU. (Catalogue 54-205) (Text in English and French) 1946. a. Can.$7($8.40) Statistics Canada, Publications Distribution, Ottawa, Ont. K1A 0V7, Canada. (also avail. in microform from MML)

387　　　　　　　　UK　ISSN 0008-7572
CASUALTY RETURN STATISTICAL SUMMARY. 1890. a (plus quarterly reports) £5. Lloyd's Register of Shipping, 71 Fenchurch St., London EC3M 4BS, England. Ed. J. P. Cashman.
　Formerly: Merchant Ships Totally Lost, Broken up Etc.

387.7　310　　　　UK　ISSN 0143-540X
CHARTERED INSTITUTE OF PUBLIC FINANCE AND ACCOUNTANCY. LOCAL AUTHORITY AIRPORTS. ACCOUNTS AND STATISTICS. 1979. a. £5. Chartered Institute of Public Finance and Accountancy, 1 Buckingham Place, London SW1E 6HS, England. (back issues avail.)

385.1　016　　　　US　ISSN 0069-9314
CONTAINERIZATION: A BIBLIOGRAPHY. 1967. a. $3. Northwestern University, Transportation Center, Leverone Hall, 2001 Sheridan Rd., Evanston, IL 60201. Ed. Dorothy V. Ramm.
　Formerly: Bibliography on Economics of Containerization.

388.1　312.4　　　CY　ISSN 0574-8399
CYPRUS. DEPARTMENT OF STATISTICS AND RESEARCH. MOTOR VEHICLES AND ROAD ACCIDENTS. 1960. a. Mils.250. Department of Statistics and Research, Ministry of Finance, Nicosia, Cyprus.

387　314　　　　　DK　ISSN 0070-3486
DANMARKS SKIBE OG SKIBSFART/DANISH SHIPS AND SHIPPING. (Subseries of its Statistiske Meddelelser) 1921. a. Kr.11.13. Danmarks Statistik, Sejroegade 11, 2100 Copenhagen OE, Denmark.

380.5　016　　　　US　ISSN 0070-6809
DOCTORAL DISSERTATIONS ON TRANSPORTATION. 1969. irreg. $3 for latest supplement. Northwestern University, Transportation Center, 2001 Sheridan Rd., Evanston, IL 60201.

385.1　　　　　　　FI　ISSN 0430-5272
FINLAND. TILASTOKESKUS. LIIKENNETILASTOLLINEN VUOSIKIRJA/ FINLAND. STATISTIKCENTRALEN. SAMFAERDSELSTATISTISKAARSBOK/ FINLAND. CENTRAL STATISTICAL OFFICE. YEARBOOK OF TRANSPORT STATISTICS. (Section XXXVI of Official Statistics of Finland) (Text in Finnish, Swedish and English) 1959. a. Fmk.28. Tilastokeskus, Annankatu 44, SF-00100 Helsinki 10, Finland (Subscr. to: Government Printing Centre, Box 516, SF-00100 Helsinki 10, Finland)

380.5　　　　　　　FR
FRANCE. DEPARTEMENT DES STATISTIQUES DE TRANSPORT. ANNUAIRE STATISTIQUE DES TRANSPORTS. a. Departement des Statistiques de Transport, Ministere des Transports, 55-57 rue Brillat-Savarin, 75658 Paris Cedex 13, France. circ. 1,000.

380.5　　　　　　　FR
FRANCE. DEPARTEMENT DES STATISTIQUES DE TRANSPORT. MEMENTO DE STATISTIQUES DES TRANSPORTS. a. Departement des Statistiques de Transport, Ministere des Transports, 55-57 rue-Brillat-Savarin, 75658 Paris Cedex 13, France.

388　314　　　　　GW　ISSN 0072-405X
GERMANY (FEDERAL REPUBLIC, 1949-) STATISTISCHES BUNDESAMT. FACHSERIE 8, REIHE 3: STRASSENVERKEHR. irreg. price varies. W. Kohlhammer-Verlag GmbH, Abt. Veroeffentlichungen des Statistischen Bundesamtes, Philipp-Reis-Str. 3, Postfach 421120, 6500 Mainz 42, W. Germany (B.R.D.)

614　312　　　　　GW　ISSN 0072-4068
GERMANY (FEDERAL REPUBLIC, 1949-) STATISTISCHES BUNDESAMT. FACHSERIE 8, REIHE 3.3: STRASSENVERKEHRSUNFAELLE. m and a. DM.44.40. W. Kohlhammer-Verlag GmbH, Abt. Veroeffentlichungen des Statistischen Bundesamtes, Philipp-Reis-Str. 3, Postfach 421120, 6500 Mainz 42, W. Germany (B.R.D.)

387.74 310	UK	ISSN 0306-3577
GREAT BRITAIN. CIVIL AVIATION AUTHORITY. C A A MONTHLY STATISTICS. 1973. a. £36. Civil Aviation Authority, C A A House, 45-59 Kingsway, London, England.
Formerly: Business Monitor Civil Aviation Series.

388.1	UK	ISSN 0072-6893
GREAT BRITAIN. DEPARTMENT OF TRANSPORT. HIGHWAY STATISTICS. 1963. a. price varies. Department of Transport, 2 Marsham St., London SW1P 3EB, England (Avail. from H.M.S.O., c/o Liaison Officer, Atlantic House, Holborn Viaduct, London EC1P 1BN, England)

387	GR	ISSN 0072-7423
GREECE. NATIONAL STATISTICAL SERVICE. SHIPPING STATISTICS. 1967. a., latest 1976. $2.50. National Statistical Service, Publications and Information Div., 14-16 Lycourgou St., Athens 112, Greece.

301.6 380.5	GR
GREECE. NATIONAL STATISTICAL SERVICE. TRANSPORT AND COMMUNICATION STATISTICS. (Text in Greek) 1967. a., latest 1976. $2.50. National Statistical Service, Publications and Information Division, 14-16 Lycourgou St., Athens 112, Greece.

380.5 016	US	ISSN 0533-5485
GUIDE TO TRAFFIC SAFETY LITERATURE. 1955. a. $5. 444 N. Michigan Ave., Chicago, IL 60611.

385	II
INDIAN RAILWAYS YEARBOOK. (Text in English) 1973/74. a. Railway Board, Directorate of Statistics and Economics, Joint Director, Public Relations, New Delhi 110001, India.

387 629.1 016	UN	ISSN 0074-249X
INTERNATIONAL CIVIL AVIATION ORGANIZATION. INDEXES TO I C A O PUBLICATIONS. ANNUAL CUMULATION. (Text in English) a; latest edition 1974. price varies. International Civil Aviation Organization - Organisation de l'Aviation Civile Internationale, P.O. Box 400, Succursale: Place de l'Aviation Internationale, 1000 Sherbrooke Street West, Montreal, Quebec H3A 2R2, Canada.

385	FR
INTERNATIONAL UNION OF RAILWAYS. TALBLEAUX ET GRAPHIQUES. (Text in French; tables of contents in English, French and German) 1963. irreg. International Union of Railways, 14 rue Jean Rey, 75015 Paris, France. charts.

380.3 310	IS
ISRAEL. CENTRAL BUREAU OF STATISTICS. ROAD ACCIDENTS WITH CASUALTIES. (Text in English and Hebrew) 1950. irreg., latest issue, no. 627, 1978. price varies. Central Bureau of Statistics, P.O.B. 13015, Jerusalem, Israel.

387 314	IT	ISSN 0075-1898
ITALY. ISTITUTO CENTRALE DI STATISTICA. ANNUARIO STATISTICO DELLA NAVIGAZIONE MARITTIMA. a. L.10000. Istituto Centrale di Statistica, Via Cesare Balbo 16, 00100 Rome, Italy.

659.1	US
MEDIA GUIDE INTERNATIONAL. AIRLINE INFLIGHT/TRAVEL MAGAZINES EDITION. 1976. a. $25. Directories International, 1718 Sherman Ave., Evanston, IL 60201. Ed. Marilyn Justman.
Formerly: Media Guide International. Airline Inflight Magazines Edition.

380.5 016	BE	ISSN 0378-195X
METRO: A BIBLIOGRAPHY. 1964. biennial. 1800 Fr.($45) International Union of Public Transport, 19, Avenue de l'Uruguay, 1050 Brussels, Belgium. (back issues avail.)

388.34 310	JA	ISSN 0463-6635
MOTOR VEHICLE STATISTICS OF JAPAN. (Text in English) a. Japan Automobile Manufacturers Association - Nihon Jidosha Kogyokai, Ote-machi Bldg., 1-6-1 Ote-machi, Chiyoda-ku, Tokyo 100, Japan. illus. stat.

387	JA	ISSN 0469-4783
NAGOYA PORT STATISTICS ANNUAL/NAGOYAKO TOKEI NENPO. (Text in Japanese) 1958. a. Nagoya Port Authority - Nagoyako Kanri Kumiai, 1-8-21 Irifune, Minato-ku, Nagoya 455, Japan. stat.

388.1	NE	ISSN 0077-7234
NETHERLANDS. CENTRAAL BUREAU VOOR DE STATISTIEK. STATISTIEK VAN DE VERKEERSONGEVALLEN OP DE OPENBARE WEG. STATISTICS OF ROAD-TRAFFIC ACCIDENTS. (Text in Dutch and English) 1947-48. a. fl.20.25. Centraal Bureau voor de Statistiek, Prinses Beatrixlaan 428, Voorburg, Netherlands (Orders to: Staatsuitgeverij, Christoffel Plantijnstraat, The Hague, Netherlands)

380.5	NO
NORWAY. STATISTISK SENTRALBYRAA. SAMFERDSELSSTATISTIKK/TRANSPORT AND COMMUNICATION STATISTICS. (Subseries of its Norges Offisielle Statistikk) (Text in Norwegian and English) 1958. a. Kr.20. Statistisk Sentralbyraa - Central Bureau of Statistics, Box 8131-Dep., Oslo 1, Norway.

388 310	PP
PAPUA NEW GUINEA. BUREAU OF STATISTICS. STATISTICAL BULLETIN: REGISTERED MOTOR VEHICLES. (Text in English) 1962. a. Bureau of Statistics, P.O. Wards Strips, Papua New Guinea. circ. 484.

314 387	PL	ISSN 0079-2667
POLAND. GLOWNY URZAD STATYSTYCZNY. ROCZNIK STATYSTYCZNY GOSPODARKI MORSKIEJ. YEARBOOK OF SEA ECONOMY STATISTICS. (Subseries of its: Statystyka Polski) 1969. irreg. 65 Zl. Glowny Urzad Statystyczny, Al. Niepodleglosci 208, 00-925 Warsaw, Poland. stat. illus. charts. circ. 1,040.

380.5 314	PL	ISSN 0079-2802
POLAND. GLOWNY URZAD STATYSTYCZNY. ROCZNIK STATYSTYCZNY TRANSPORTU. YEARBOOK OF TRANSPORT STATISTICS. (Subseries of its: Statystyka Polski) 1967. irreg. 77 Zl. Glowny Urzad Statystyczny, Al. Niepodleglosci 208, 00-925 Warsaw, Poland.

387 317	PL	ISSN 0079-2837
POLAND. GLOWNY URZAD STATYSTYCZNY. STATYSTYKA ZEGLUCI SRODLADOWEJ I DROG WODNYCH SRODLADOWYCH.* (Subseries of Its Seria Statystyka Polski Materialy Statystyczne) a. 15 Zl. Glowny Urzad Statystyczny, Al. Niepodleglosci 208, 00-925 Warsaw, Poland.

310 385	US
RAILWAY STATISTICAL MANUAL. irreg. price varies. Association of American Railroads, American Railroads Bldg., 1920 L St., N.W., Washington, DC 20036.

388.1	ZA
REPORT ON PASSENGER ROAD TRANSPORT IN ZAMBIA. 1968. a, latest 1974. K.40. Central Statistical Office, P.O. Box 1908, Lusaka, Zambia.

312.44	SA	ISSN 0584-195X
SOUTH AFRICA. DEPARTMENT OF STATISTICS. ROAD TRAFFIC ACCIDENTS. (Report No. 12-01) a., latest 1977. R.5. Department of Statistics, Private Bag X44, Pretoria 0001, South Africa (Orders to: Government Printer, Bosman St., Private Bag X85, Pretoria 0001,South Africa)

388.3 310	SA
SOUTH AFRICA. DEPARTMENT OF STATISTICS. STATISTICS OF MOTOR AND OTHER VEHICLES. (Report No. 12-03) 1972. a., latest 1977. R.5. Department of Statistics, Private Bag X44, Pretoria 0001, South Africa (Orders to: Government Printer, Bosman St., Private Bag X85, Pretoria 0001,South Africa)

388	SA
SOUTH AFRICA. DEPARTMENT OF STATISTICS. STATISTICS OF NEW VEHICLES REGISTERED. (Report No. 12-02) a., latest covers 1978. R.5. Department of Statistics, Private Bag X44, Pretoria 0001, South Africa (Orders to: Government Printer, Bosman St., Private Bag X85, Pretoria 0001,South Africa)
Formerly: South Africa. Department of Statistics. Statistics of New Vehicles Licensed.

614.86	SP	ISSN 0085-655X
SPAIN. DIRECCION GENERAL DE TRAFICO. ANUARIO ESTADISTICO DE ACCIDENTES. BOLETIN INFORMATIVO. 1962. a. 600 ptas. Direccion General de Trafico, Gabinete de Estudios, Calle J. Valcarcel 28, Madrid 27, Spain. circ. 1,500.

614.86	SP	ISSN 0085-6568
SPAIN. DIRECCION GENERAL DE TRAFICO. ANUARIO ESTADISTICO GENERAL. 1960. a. 650 ptas. Direccion General de Trafico, Gabinete de Estudios, Calle J. Valcarcel 28, Madrid 27, Spain. circ. 2,500.

388.1	UN	ISSN 0081-5160
STATISTICS OF ROAD TRAFFIC ACCIDENTS IN EUROPE. 1956. a; latest 1978. price varies. United Nations Economic Commission for Europe, Palais des Nations, 1200 Geneva 10, Switzerland (Or United Nations Publications, Room LX-2300, New York, NY 10017)

387.7	SW	ISSN 0348-2251
SWEDEN. LUFTFARTSVERKET. AARSBOK. 1976. a. Kr.20. Luftfartsverket - National Civil Aviation Administration, S-601 79 Norrkoeping, Sweden. stat.

380	SW	ISSN 0082-0334
SWEDEN. STATISTISKA CENTRALBYRAAN. STATISTISKA MEDDELANDEN. SUBGROUP T (TRANSPORT AND OTHER FORMS OF COMMUNICATION) (Text in Swedish; table heads and summaries in English) 1963 N.S. irreg. Kr.130. Liber Foerlag, Fack, S-162 89 Vaellingby, Sweden. circ. 1,000.

314.94 338.4	SZ
SWITZERLAND. STATISTISCHES AMT. EINGEFUEHRTE MOTORFAHRZEUGE/VEHICULES A MOTEUR IMPORTES. (Subseries of Statistische Quellenwerke der Schweiz) (Text in French and German) irreg. Statistisches Amt., Publikationsdienst, Hallwylstrasse 15, CH-3003 Berne, Switzerland.
Continues in part: Switzerland. Statistisches Amt. Eingefuehrte Motorfahrzeuge; in Verkehr Gesetzte Neue Motorfahrzeuge.

388	SZ
SWITZERLAND. STATISTISCHES AMT. IN VERKEHR GESETZTE NEUE MOTORFAHRZEUGE/VEHICULES A MOTEUR NEUFS MIS EN CIRCULATION. (Subseries of Statistische Quellenwerke der Schweiz) (Text in French and German) irreg. Statistisches Amt., Publikationsdienst, Hallwylstrasse 15, CH-3003 Berne, Switzerland.
Continues in part: Switzerland. Statistisches Amt. Eingefuehrte Motorfahrzeuge: In Verkehr Gesetzte Neue Motorfahrzeuge.

380.5 315	CH
TAIWAN ANNUAL STATISTICAL REPORT OF TRANSPORTATION/TAI-WAN SHENG CHIAO TUNG TUNG CHI NIEN PAO. (Text in Chinese and English) a. Taiwan Sheng Cheng Fu Chiao Tung Chu, Nan-Tou Hsien, Taiwan, Republic of China. stat.

380.5 016   US   ISSN 0083-0380
U. S. DEPARTMENT OF TRANSPORTATION. BIBLIOGRAPHIC LISTS. 1969. irreg. U. S. Department of Transportation, Library Services Division, 400 Seventh St. N.W., Washington, DC 20590 (Order from: National Technical Information Service, 5285 Port Royal Rd., Springfield, VA 22151)

016   US
U.S. NATIONAL HIGHWAY TRAFFIC SAFETY ADMINISTRATION.TECHNICAL REPORTS; a bibliography. a. U.S. National Highway Traffic Safety Administration, 400 Seventh St., S.W., Washington, DC 20590.

623.89 310   UY
URUGUAY. CENTRO DE NAVEGACION TRANSATLANTICA. ESTADISTICA. irreg. Centro de Navegacion Transatlantica, Montevideo, Uruguay.

388.1   US   ISSN 0509-7967
WASHINGTON STATE TRAFFIC ACCIDENT FACTS. a. free. State Patrol, Olympia, WA 98504. circ. 5,000.

386   US
WATERBORNE COMMERCE OF THE PORT OF BOSTON. 1970. a. free. Massachusetts Port Authority, 99 High St., Boston, MA 02110. circ. controlled. (looseleaf format)

380.5   SZ   ISSN 0302-7902
WORLD TRANSPORT DATA/STATISTIQUES MONDIALES DE TRANSPORT. (Text in English and French) 1973. triennial. 70 Fr. International Road Transport Union, 1 rue de Varembe, B.P. 44, CH-1211 Geneva 20, Switzerland. (back issues avail.)

384 314   YU   ISSN 0513-0794
YUGOSLAVIA. SAVEZNI ZAVOD ZA STATISTIKU. SAOBRACAJ I VEZE. (Subseries of its Statisticki Bilten) (Edition also in English) 100 din.($5.56) Savezni Zavod za Statistiku, Uzun Mirkova 1, Belgrade, Yugoslavia. illus. circ. 1,100.

TRANSPORTATION — Air Transport

387.7   US   ISSN 0271-065X
A O P A'S AIRPORTS U.S.A. 1962. a. $10. Aircraft Owners and Pilots Association, Box 5800, Washington, DC 20014. Ed. Janice Knestout Colvin. circ. 100,000.
Formerly: Aircraft Owners and Pilots Association. A O P A Airport Directory (ISSN 0065-4906)

387.7   UK   ISSN 0065-0838
ACCIDENTS TO AIRCRAFT ON THE BRITISH REGISTER. 1949. price varies. Civil Aviation Authority, C A A House, 45-59 Kingsway, London WC2B 6TE, England.

387.7   FR   ISSN 0065-3721
AEROPORT DE PARIS. RAPPORT DU CONSEIL D'ADMINISTRATION. (Editions in English and French) a. free. Aeroport de Paris - Paris Airport Authority, Service Documentation et Statistiques, Orly Sud 103, 94396 Orly Aerogare Cedex, France.

387.7   FR   ISSN 0078-947X
AEROPORT DE PARIS. SERVICE STATISTIQUE. STATISTIQUE DE TRAFIC. 1951. price and frequency determined on service basis. Aeroport de Paris - Paris Airport Authority, Service Documentation et Statistiques, Orly Sud 103, 94396 Orly Aerogare Cedex, France.

387.7   NZ   ISSN 0065-4817
AIR NEW ZEALAND. ANNUAL REPORT. 1965. a. Air New Zealand Ltd, Private Bag, Auckland 1, New Zealand (U. S. Address: Suite 1000, 510 W. 6th St., Los Angeles, CA 90014) circ. 6,000.

387.7   US
AIR TRANSPORT. 1937. a. Air Transport Association of America, 1709 New York Ave., N.W., Washington, DC 20006. circ. 5,000(controlled)

AIR TRANSPORT (LONDON) see AERONAUTICS AND SPACE FLIGHT

387.7   UK
AIR TRANSPORT AND TRAVEL INDUSTRY TRAINING BOARD. REPORT AND STATEMENT OF ACCOUNTS. 1967. a. 60p. ‡ Air Transport and Travel Industry Training Board, Staines House, 158-162 High Street, Staines, Middlesex TW18 4AS, England. stat. circ. controlled.

387.7   CN   ISSN 0065-485X
AIR TRANSPORT ASSOCIATION OF CANADA. ANNUAL REPORT. a. Air Transport Association of Canada, 747 Metropolitan Life Bldg., 99 Bank St., Ottawa, Ont. K1P 6B9, Canada.

387.7   CN
AIR TRANSPORTATION ANNUAL. 1975? a. Shipping Register Publications, Ltd. (Subsidiary of: Anchor Press) Suite 504, 1434 St. Catherine St. W., Montreal, Que. H3G 1R4, Canada. Ed. O. J. Silva. adv. circ. 5,000.

387.7   US
AIR TRAVEL ANSWERS. 1979. a. $2.95. Aerofacts, Box 11347, McCarren International Airport, Las Vegas, NV 89111. Ed. Mike Minear. circ. 2,000.

387.7   RH
AIR ZIMBABWE ANNUAL REPORT. 1968. a. free. Air Zimbabwe Corporation, P.O. Box AP. 1, Salisbury Airport, Salisbury, Zimbabwe. circ. 2,000.
Formerly: Air Rhodesia Annual Report.

AIRLINE GUIDE TO STEWARDESS & STEWARDS CAREER. see OCCUPATIONS AND CAREERS

387.7   US   ISSN 0095-4683
AIRLINE HANDBOOK. 1972. a. $10. AeroTravel Research Publications, Box 3694, Cramston, RI 02910. Ed. Paul K. Martin. illus.

AIRMAN'S INFORMATION MANUAL (FALLBROOK) see AERONAUTICS AND SPACE FLIGHT

387.72   US   ISSN 0065-4930
AIRWAY PIONEER; YEARBOOK OF THE SOCIETY OF AIRWAY PIONEERS. a. available to members only. Society of Airway Pioneers, P.O. Box 17020, San Diego, CA 92117.

387.7 347   AG   ISSN 0066-7188
ARGENTINA. INSTITUTO NACIONAL DE DERECHO AERONAUTICO Y ESPACIAL. 1947, no. 2. irreg; latest issue, 1974. free. Instituto Nacional de Derecho Aeronautico y Espacial, Edificio Condor, Comodoro Pedro Zanni 250, Buenos Aires, Argentina.

341.46   US
AVIATION CASES IN THE COURTS. irreg., approx. 2/yr. $75. Hawkins Publishing Co., Inc., 933 N. Kenmore St., Suite 220, Arlington, VA 22201. Ed. Carl R. Eyler, R.C. Morefield.

387.7   US
AVIATION TELEPHONE DIRECTORY: PACIFIC AND WESTERN STATES. (Published in 5 regional editions) 1946. a. $9.95. E. A. Brennan & Co., Inc., 9355 Chapman Ave., Garden Grove, CA 92641. adv. circ. 3,000.
Formerly (until 1979): Pacific Coast Aviation Directory.

387.7   US   ISSN 0069-1437
CENSUS OF U.S. CIVIL AIRCRAFT. 1965. a. U.S. Federal Aviation Administration., Office of Management Systems, Department of Transportation, Washington, DC 20591 (Orders to: NTIS, Springfield, VA 22161)

387.7   SZ
CIVIL JET TRANSPORT. AVIONIC EQUIPMENT. a. updates (to base vol.) Interavia S.A., 86 Ave. Louis Cassai, Case Postale 162, CH-1216 Cointrin/Geneva, Switzerland.

387   AT
CONTACT. 1958. irreg. 3. (Air Force Association, Victoria Division) Air Force Club of Victoria, Air Forces Memorial Centre, 6 Ste. Helens Court, Vermont, Vic. 3133, Australia. Ed. W. Bakker.

CURRENT AVIATION STATISTICS. see AERONAUTICS AND SPACE FLIGHT

387.7   US   ISSN 0094-5390
DIRECTORY OF OKLAHOMA AIRPORTS. biennial. Aeronautics Commission, 424 United Founders Tower Bldg., Oklahoma City, OK 73112. illus.
Continues: Oklahoma Airport Directory.

387   SP   ISSN 0421-4986
ESTADISTICAS DE LA AVIACION CIVIL EN ESPANA. a. Ministerio del Aire, Subsecretaria de Aviacion Civil, Princessa 88, Madrid, Spain.

387.7   UN   ISSN 0071-2558
EUROPEAN CIVIL AVIATION CONFERENCE (REPORT OF SESSION) (Issued as a subseries of Air Transport. Series D: Reports) (Editions in English, French and Spanish) 1955. triennial since 1961 with intermediate sessions; 8th triennial, Strasbourg, 1973; 6th intermediate, Paris, 1974. price varies. International Civil Aviation Organization - Organisation de l'Aviation Civile Internationale, P.O. Box 400, Succursale: Place de l'Aviation Internationale, 1000 Sherbrooke Street West, Montreal, Quebec H3A 2R2, Canada.

387.7   UK   ISSN 0068-1229
GREAT BRITAIN. BRITISH AIRPORTS AUTHORITY. ANNUAL REPORT AND ACCOUNTS. a. £2. British Airports Authority, 2 Buckingham Gate, London S.W.1, England (Avail. from H.M.S.O., c/o Liaison Officer, Atlantic House, Holborn Viaduct, London EC1P 1BN, England) illus.

387.7   UK
GREAT BRITAIN. CIVIL AVIATION AUTHORITY. GENERAL AVIATION SAFETY INFORMATION. irreg. £4. Civil Aviation Authority, CAA House, 45-59 Kingsway, London WC2B 6TE, England.

387.7   UK
GREAT BRITAIN. CIVIL AVIATION AUTHORITY. AIR TRANSPORT USERS COMMITTEE ANNUAL REPORT. a. price varies. Civil Aviation Authority, CAA House, 45-59 Kingsway, London WC2B 6TE, England.

387.7   UK   ISSN 0072-5641
GREAT BRITAIN. CIVIL AVIATION AUTHORITY. CIVIL AVIATION PUBLICATIONS. 1946. irreg. price varies. Civil Aviation Authority, C A A House, 45-59 Kingsway, London WC2B 6TE, England.

387.71   UK   ISSN 0306-3569
GREAT BRITAIN. CIVIL AVIATION AUTHORITY. ANNUAL REPORT AND ACCOUNTS. 1949. a. price varies. Civil Aviation Authority, C A A House, 45-59 Kingsway, London WC2B 6TE, England.
Formerly: Great Britain. Air Transport Licensing Board. Report (ISSN 0072-5617)

387.7   UK
GREAT BRITAIN. CIVIL AVIATION AUTHORITY. ANNUAL STATISTICS. 1973. a. price varies. Civil Aviation Authority, CAA House, 45-59 Kingsway, London WC2B 6TE, England.

387.7   UK
GREAT BRITAIN. CIVIL AVIATION AUTHORITY. INTERNATIONAL REGISTER OF CIVIL AIRCRAFT. a(plus monthly supplements) £75. Civil Aviation Authority, CAA House, 45-59 Kingsway, London WCB 6TE, England.

386.736   FR
GUIDE PRATIQUE DES AEROPORTS ET DE L'AVIATION COMMERCIALE. 1975. a. 40 F. 30 rue de Trevise, 75009 Paris, France.

TRANSPORTATION — AIR TRANSPORT

387.72 US ISSN 0147-4030
HOW TO FLY FOR LESS; consumer's guide to low cost air charters and other travel bargains. 1976. a. $5. Travel Information Bureau, Box 105, Kings Park, NY 11754. Ed. Jens Jurgen. charts. circ. 20,000. (back issues avail.)
Formerly: Charter Flight Directory.

387 CN ISSN 0376-642X
I A T A REVIEW. (Text in English) 1966. irreg. International Air Transport Association., Box 550, International Aviation Square, 1000 Sherbrooke St., Montreal, Que. H3A 2R4, Canada. circ. controlled.
Formerly: I A T A News Review (ISSN 0085-199X)

387 UN ISSN 0074-2481
I C A O CIRCULARS. (Editions in English, French, Spanish; some also issued in Russian) 1951, no. 18. irreg. price varies. International Civil Aviation Organization - Organisation de l'Aviation Civile Internationale, P.O. Box 400, Succursale: Place de l'Aviation Internationale, 1000 Sherbrooke Street West, Montreal, Quebec H3A 2R2, Canada.

387.7 CN
INTERNATIONAL AIR TRANSPORT ASSOCIATION. ANNUAL REPORT. (Text in English, French and Spanish) 1945. a. Can.$10. International Air Transport Association, Box 550, International Aviation Square, 1000 Sherbrooke St. W., Montreal, Que. H3A 2R4, Canada.
Continues: Air Transport Association. Annual General Meeting Reports and Proceedings; Which was formerly: International Air Transport Association. Bulletin (ISSN 0074-1329)

387 UN ISSN 0074-221X
INTERNATIONAL CIVIL AVIATION ASSOCIATION. AERONAUTICAL AGREEMENTS AND ARRANGEMENTS. ANNUAL SUPPLEMENT. (Text in English) 1965. a. $1. International Civil Aviation Organization - Organisation de l'Aviation Civile Internationale, P.O. Box 400, Succursale: Place de l'Aviation Internationale, 1000 Sherbrooke Street West, Montreal, Quebec H3A 2R2, Canada.

387.7 UN ISSN 0074-2287
INTERNATIONAL CIVIL AVIATION ORGANIZATION. AIR NAVIGATION PLAN. AFRICA-INDIAN OCEAN REGION. (Editions in English, French and Spanish) 1954. irreg; 18th, 1974. price varies. International Civil Aviation Organization - Organisation Civile Internationale, P.O. Box 400, Succursale: Place de l'Aviation Internationale, 1000 Sherbrooke Street West, Montreal, Quebec H3A 2R2, Canada.

387.7 UN
INTERNATIONAL CIVIL AVIATION ORGANIZATION. AIR NAVIGATION PLAN. CARIBBEAN REGION. (Editions in English, French and Spanish) 1956. irreg; 7th, 1974. $10.50. International Civil Aviation Organization - Organisation de l'Aviation Civile Internationale, P.O. Box 400, Succursale: Place de l'Aviation Internationale, 1000 Sherbrooke Street West, Montreal, Quebec H3A 2R2, Canada.
Third meeting: International Civil Aviation Organization. Air Navigation Plan. Caribbean and South American Regions. (ISSN 0074-2295)

387.7 UN ISSN 0074-2309
INTERNATIONAL CIVIL AVIATION ORGANIZATION. AIR NAVIGATION PLAN. EUROPEAN REGION. (Editions in English, French and Spanish) 1957. irreg; 9th, 1975. price varies. International Civil Aviation Organization - Organisation de l'Aviation Civile Internationale, P.O. Box 400, Succursale: Place de l'Aviation Internationale, 1000 Sherbrooke Street West, Montreal, Quebec H3A 2R2, Canada.

387.7 UN ISSN 0074-2317
INTERNATIONAL CIVIL AVIATION ORGANIZATION. AIR NAVIGATION PLAN. MIDDLE EAST AND SOUTH EAST ASIA REGIONS. (Supersedes its Middle East Region & its South East Asia Region) (Edts. in English, French, Spanish) irreg; 9th, 1975. price varies. International Civil Aviation Organization - Organisation de l'Aviation Civile Internationale, P.O. Box 400, Succursale: Place de l'Aviation Internationale, 1000 Sherbrooke Street West, Montreal, Quebec H3A 2R2, Canada.

387.7 UN ISSN 0074-2325
INTERNATIONAL CIVIL AVIATION ORGANIZATION. AIR NAVIGATION PLAN. NORTH ATLANTIC, NORTH AMERICAN AND PACIFIC REGIONS. (Supersedes its North Atlantic Region and its Pacific Region) (Edts. in English, French, Spanish) irreg; 8th, 1975. price varies. International Civil Aviation Organization - Organisation de l'Aviation Internationale, P.O. Box 400, Succursale: Place de l'Aviation Internationale, 1000 Sherbrooke Street West, Montreal, Quebec H3A 2R2, Canada.

387.7 UN ISSN 0074-2368
INTERNATIONAL CIVIL AVIATION ORGANIZATION. ASSEMBLY. REPORT AND MINUTES OF THE LEGAL COMMISSION. (Editions in English, French, Russian, Spanish) irreg; 21st, Montreal, 1974. price varies. International Civil Aviation Organization - Organisation de l'Aviation Civile Internationale, P.O. Box 400, Succursale: Place de l' Aviation Internationale, 1000 Sherbrooke Street West, Montreal, Quebec H3A 2R2, Canada.

387.7 UN ISSN 0074-2376
INTERNATIONAL CIVIL AVIATION ORGANIZATION. ASSEMBLY. REPORT OF THE ECONOMIC COMMISSION. irreg.; 18th, 1971. price varies. International Civil Aviation Organization - Organisation de l'Aviation Civile Internationale, P.O. Box 400, Succursale: Place de l'Aviation Internationale, 1000 Sherbrooke Street West, Montreal, Quebec H3A 2R2, Canada.

387.7 UN ISSN 0074-235X
INTERNATIONAL CIVIL AVIATION ORGANIZATION. ASSEMBLY. RESOLUTIONS. (Editions in English, French, Russian, Spanish) 1965, 15th. irreg; 21st, Montreal, 1974. price varies. International Civil Aviation Organization - Organisation de l'Aviation Civile Internationale, P.O. Box 400, Succursale: Place de l'Aviation Internationale, 1000 Sherbrooke Street West, Montreal, Quebec H3A 2R2, Canada.

387 UN
INTERNATIONAL CIVIL AVIATION ORGANIZATION. COUNCIL. ANNUAL REPORT. (Editions in English, French, Russian, Spanish) a; latest, 1974. price varies. International Civil Aviation Organization - Organisation de l'Aviation Civile Internationale, P.O. Box 400, Succursale: Place de l'Aviation Internationale, 1000 Sherbrooke Street West, Montreal, Quebec H3A 2R2, Canada.

387 UN ISSN 0074-2422
INTERNATIONAL CIVIL AVIATION ORGANIZATION. DIGESTS OF STATISTICS. SERIES AT. AIRPORT TRAFFIC. (Classification of its Digest of Statistics, issued from 1947. Digest and Series numbering maintained separately) (Editions in English, French, Russian, Spanish) 1960. a; no. 14, 1973. price varies. International Civil Aviation Organization - Organisation de l'Aviation Civile Internationale, P.O. Box 400, Succursale: Place de l'Aviation Internationale, 1000 Sherbrooke Street West, Montreal, Quebec H3A 2R2, Canada.
Monthly and yearly statistics for airports open to international traffic

387 UN ISSN 0074-2430
INTERNATIONAL CIVIL AVIATION ORGANIZATION. DIGESTS OF STATISTICS. SERIES F. FINANCIAL DATA. (Classification of its Digest of Statistics, issued from 1947. Digest and Series numbering maintained separately) (Edts. in English, French, Spanish, Russian) 1959, no. 13. a; latest issue, no. 28, 1974. price varies. International Civil Aviation Organization - Organisation de l'Aviation Civile Internationale, P.O. Box 400, Succursale: Place de l'Aviation Internationale, 1000 Sherbrooke Street West, Montreal, Quebec H3A 2R2, Canada.

387 UN ISSN 0074-2449
INTERNATIONAL CIVIL AVIATION ORGANIZATION. DIGESTS OF STATISTICS. SERIES FP. FLEET, PERSONNEL. (Classification of its Digest of Statistics, issued from 1947. Digest and Series numbering maintained separately) (Editions in English, French, Spanish, Russian) 1959, no. 13. a; latest issue, no. 27, 1973. price varies. International Civil Aviation Organization - Organisation de l'Aviation Civile Internationale, P.O. Box 400, Succursale: Place de l'Aviation Internationale, 1000 Sherbrooke Street West, Montreal, Quebec H3A 2R2, Canada.

387 UN ISSN 0074-2457
INTERNATIONAL CIVIL AVIATION ORGANIZATION. DIGESTS OF STATISTICS. SERIES R. CIVIL AIRCRAFT ON REGISTER. (Classification of its Digest of Statistics, issued from 1947. Digest and Series numbering maintained separately) (Edts. in English, French, Spanish, Russian) 1961. a; no. 13, 1974. price varies. International Civil Aviation Organization - Organisation de l'Aviation Internationale, P.O. Box 400, Succursale: Place de l'Aviation Internationale, 1000 Sherbrooke Street West, Montreal, Quebec H3A 2R2, Canada.

387 UN ISSN 0074-2465
INTERNATIONAL CIVIL AVIATION ORGANIZATION. DIGESTS OF STATISTICS. SERIES T. TRAFFIC. (Classification of its Digest of Statistics, issued from 1947. Digest and Series numbering maintained separately) (Edts. in English, French, Spanish, Russian) 1960, no. 18. a, no. 33, 1974. price varies. International Civil Aviation Organization - Organisation de l'Aviation Civile Internationale, P.O. Box 400, Succursale: Place de l'Aviation Internationale, 1000 Sherbrooke Street West, Montreal, Quebec H3A 2R2, Canada.
Monthly and yearly traffic statistics for scheduled airlines, information also provided by country

387.7 UN ISSN 0074-2503
INTERNATIONAL CIVIL AVIATION ORGANIZATION. LEGAL COMMITTEE. MINUTES AND DOCUMENTS (OF SESSIONS) (Editions in English, French and Spanish) irreg.; 21st, Montreal, 1974. price varies. International Civil Aviation Organization - Organisation de l'Aviation Civile Internationale, P.O. Box 400, Succursale: Place de l'Aviation Internationale, 1000 Sherbrooke Street West, Montreal, Quebec H3A 2R2, Canada.

658 US ISSN 0538-7442
INTERNATIONAL FEDERATION OF OPERATIONAL RESEARCH SOCIETIES. AIRLINE GROUP (A G I F O R S) PROCEEDINGS. 1961. a. $40. International Federation of Operational Research Societies, Airline Group, c/o Dr. Leonard G. Klinger, Ed., 10700 S. W. 134 Terrace, Miami, FL 33176. circ. 300. (processed; back issues avail.)

341.46 AG
JORNADAS NACIONALES DE DERECHO AERONAUTICO Y ESPACIAL. TRABAJOS. irreg. Universidad Nacional de Cordoba, Instituto de Derecho Aeronautico y Espacial, Ciudad Universitaria, Cordoba, Argentina.

387.7 US
LIST OF UNITED STATES AIR CARRIERS. irreg. free. U.S. Civil Aeronautics Board, 1825 Connecticut Avenue, N.W., Washington, DC 20428.

387.7 MW ISSN 0076-3055
MALAWI. DEPARTMENT OF CIVIL AVIATION. ANNUAL REPORT. a, latest 1968. K.0.30. Government Printer, P.O. Box 37, Zomba, Malawi.

387.7 CN
MIRABEL AIRPORT DIRECTORY. 1975. a. Anchor Press, 1434 St. Catherine St. W., Montreal, Canada.

387.7   KE   ISSN 0077-2666
NAIROBI AIRPORT. ANNUAL REPORT.* 1958. a. Director of Aerodromes, P.O. Box 19001, Nairobi, Kenya.

387.7   US
NATIONAL TRANSPORTATION SAFETY BOARD SERVICE. 1972. irreg. (approx. 8-10/yr.) $155. Hawkins Publishing Co., Inc., Suite 220, 933 No. Kenmore St., Arlington, VA 22201. Ed.Carl R. Eyler. circ. 66. (looseleaf format)

387.7   NE   ISSN 0077-7137
NETHERLANDS. CENTRAAL BUREAU VOOR DE STATISTIEK. STATISTIEK VAN DE LUCHTVAART. CIVIL AVIATION STATISTICS. (Text in Dutch and English) 1949. a. fl.14.45. Centraal Bureau voor de Statistiek, Prinses Beatrixlaan 428, Voorburg, Netherlands (Orders to: Staatsuitgeverij, Christoffel Plantijnstraat, The Hague, Netherlands)

387.7   US   ISSN 0091-6978
NEW JERSEY AIRPORT DIRECTORY. 1968. irreg., latest 1981. ‡ Department of Transportation, 1035 Parkway Ave., Trenton, NJ 08625. illus.

PACIFIC AVIATION YEARBOOK. see AERONAUTICS AND SPACE FLIGHT

387.7   US
PENNSYLVANIA. BUREAU OF AVIATION. AVIATION NEWSLETTER. irreg. free. Bureau of Aviation, Capital City Airport, New Cumberland, PA 17070.

307.71   US
PORT AUTHORITY OF NEW YORK & NEW JERSEY. AVIATION DEPARTMENT. AIRPORT STATISTICS. a. Port Authority of New York & New Jersey, Aviation Department, Aviation Economics Division, 65 N One World Trade Center, New York, NY 10048. stat.

387.7   AT
QANTAS AIRWAYS. REPORT.* (Subseries of: Australia. Parliament. Parliamentary Papers) a. Aus.$0.65 per no. Australian Government Publishing Service, Box 84, Canberra, A.C.T. 2600, Australia. illus.

387.7   FR   ISSN 0080-066X
REGISTRE AERONAUTIQUE INTERNATIONAL. 1966. a (with m. suppl.) 630 F. Bureau Veritas, Service Aeronautique, 31 rue Henri Rochefort, B.P. 170, 75821 Paris Cedex 17, France.

387.7   UN   ISSN 0085-5596
REVIEW OF ECONOMIC SITUATION OF AIR TRANSPORT. (Issued in ICAO Circular Series) (Editions in English, French and Spanish; 1974 edition also in Russian) 1965. triennial since 1965. $1.75. International Civil Aviation Organization - Organisation de l'Aviation Civile Internationale, P.O. Box 400, Succursale: Place de l'Aviation Internationale, 1000 Sherbrooke Street West, Montreal, Quebec H3A 2R2, Canada.

387.7   SZ
SCHWEIZERISCHE ZIVILLUFTFAHRT/ AVIATION CIVILE SUISSE. a. Bundesamt fuer Zivilluftfahrt - Federal Office for Civil Aviation (Office Federal de l'Aviation Civile), Inselgasse, CH-3003 Berne, Switzerland.
Supersedes (from 1975): Schweizerische Luftverkehrsstatistik/Statistique du Trafic Aerien Suisse.

387.7   CN   ISSN 0081-4571
STATE OF THE AIR TRANSPORT INDUSTRY. (Director General'S report to the Annual General Meeting of the International Air Transport Association) (Text in English, French and Spanish) 1945. a. free; limited distribution. ‡ International Air Transport Association, Box 550, International Aviation Square, 1000 Sherbrooke St. W., Montreal, Que. H3A 2R4, Canada. circ. controlled.

387.7   US   ISSN 0082-9609
U. S. CIVIL AERONAUTICS BOARD. AIRCRAFT OPERATING COST AND PERFORMANCE REPORT. 1965. a. price varies. U.S. Civil Aeronautics Board, Washington, DC 20428 (Orders to: Supt. Doc., Washington, DC 20402)

387.7   US
U.S. FEDERAL AVIATION ADMINISTRATION. NATIONAL AVIATION SYSTEM: CHALLENGES OF THE DECADE AHEAD. 1969. irreg., latest issues, 1976. $2. U. S. Federal Aviation Administration, 800 Independence Ave., S.W., Washington, DC 20590 (Orders to: Supt. of Documents, Washington, DC 20402) illus. circ. 3,000.
Formerly: Federal Aviation Administration. National Aviation System Policy Summary (ISSN 0092-4555)

387.74   US
U.S. NATIONAL TRANSPORTATION SAFETY BOARD. AIRCRAFT ACCIDENT REPORTS. (Formerly issued by Department of Transportation) irreg. $35 (brief format $40) U.S. National Transportation Safety Board, Washington, DC 20590 (Orders to: National Technical Information Service, 5825 Port Royal Rd., Springfield, VA 22151)

387.7   FR
WESTERN EUROPEAN AIRPORT ASSOCIATION. STATISTIQUES DE TRAFIC. (Text in English and French) irreg. 90 F. Western European Airport Association, 291, Bd. Raspail, 75014 Paris, France. (Co-Sponsor: International Civil Airport Association)

387.7   SZ   ISSN 0084-1366
WORLD AIR TRANSPORT STATISTICS. 1956. a, latest 1978. $25. International Air Transport Association, Industry Research Division, 26 Chemin de Joinville, Box 160, 1216 Cointrin-Geneva, Switzerland. (back issues avail.)

387.7   US   ISSN 0084-1374
WORLD AIRLINE RECORD. 1948. irreg., 7th edt. 1972, with q. supplements. $43.50. Roadcap Aviation Publications, 1030 S. Green Bay Rd., Lake Forest, IL 60045. Ed. Roy R. Roadcap.

387.736   UK
WORLD AIRPORTS CONFERENCE. PROCEEDINGS. irreg., 5th, 1976. (Institution of Civil Engineers) Thomas Telford Ltd., Publications Division, 26-34 Old St., London EC1V 9AD, England.

TRANSPORTATION — Automobiles

629.2   GW
ADAC-SCHRIFTENREIHE. JUGENDVERKEHRSERZIEHUNG. 1963. irreg. Allgemeiner Deutscher Automobil-Club e.V., Abteilong Verkehrserziehung und -Aufklaerung, Baumgartnerstr. 53, 8000 Munich 70, W. Germany (B.R.D.)

629.2   US   ISSN 0065-2555
ADVANCES IN ENGINEERING. irreg. price varies. Society of Automotive Engineers, 400 Commonwealth Dr., Warrendale, PA 15096.

AMERICAN ASSOCIATION FOR AUTOMOTIVE MEDICINE. PROCEEDINGS. see MEDICAL SCIENCES

343   US   ISSN 0093-4062
AMERICAN AUTOMOBILE ASSOCIATION. DIGEST OF MOTOR LAWS. (Vols. for 1965-73 Compiled by its Legal Dept) a. $4. American Automobile Association, 8111 Gatehouse Road, Falls Church, VA 22047. Ed. Melitta Hartung. circ. 75,000. Key Title: Digest of Motor Laws.

629.1 629.2   FR
ANCIENS ELEVES DE L'ECOLE TECHNIQUE D'AERONAUTIQUE ET DE CONSTRUCTION AUTOMOBILE. ANNUAIRE. a. Association des Anciens Eleves de l'Ecole Technique d'Aeronautique et de Construction Automobile, 1 rue Bouterie, 75005 Paris, France.

388.3   FR
ANNEE AUTOMOBILE. (Editions in English, French & German) 1953. a. 75 rue Voltaire, 92532 Levallois-Perret Cedex, France. Eds. Ami Guichard, Jean P. Thibault. adv. circ. 15,000 English edt.; 20,000 French edt.; 10,000 German edt.

629.2   FR
ANNUAIRE NATIONAL AUTOMOBILE. 1946. a. 145 F. Editions Gozlan, 94 rue Saint-Lazare, 75442 Paris 9, France.
Formerly: Annuaire General Automobile (ISSN 0066-314X)

629.286   BL
ANUARIO DA INDUSTRIA BRASILEIRA DE AUTOPECAS/YEARBOOK OF THE BRAZILIAN INDUSTRY OF AUTOMOTIVE PARTS. (Text in English, Portuguese) 1977. a. (Sindicato Nacional da Industria de Componentes para Veiculos Automotores) G. & C. Gomes, Av. Paulista 807, Sao Paulo, Brazil. illus.

388 629.286   UK   ISSN 0260-664X
AUSTIN HEALEY YEAR BOOK. 1978. a. Magpie Publishing Co., Holmerise, Seven Hills Rd., Cobham, Surrey, England. illus.

629.2   SA
AUTO DATA DIGEST. 1974. a. R.17.50. Mead & McGrouther (Pty) Ltd., Box 741, Johannesburg, South Africa. Ed.Bd.

629.2   GW
AUTO-KATALOG. 1957. a. DM.7.50. Vereinigte Motor-Verlage GmbH und Co. KG, Leuschnerstr. 1, Postfach 1042, 7000 Stuttgart 1, W. Germany (B. R. D.) Ed. Klaus Freund. adv. abstr. index. circ. 265,000.
Formerly: Auto-Modelle.

629.2   SZ   ISSN 0067-2416
AUTO-UNIVERSUM.* 1958. a. $12.50. International Automobile Parade, 10 Pfadackerstr., CH-8957 Spreitenbach, Switzerland (Dist. by International Publications Service, 114 E. 32nd St., New York, N.Y. 10016)
Before 1971: Automobile World.

629.2   FR   ISSN 0067-2424
AUTOCATALOGUE; guide technique de mecanique automobile. (Text in English, French, German, Italian, Spanish) 1913. a. 95.25 F. Editions S.O.S.P., 59-61 Avenue de la Grande Annee, 75782 Paris Cedex 16, France. Ed. C.L. Lavaud. index.

629.2 621.38   US   ISSN 0587-5919
AUTOMOBILE ELECTRONIC EQUIPMENT. 1970/71. irreg. price varies. Pergamon Press, Inc., Maxwell House, Fairview Park, Elmsford, NY 10523.

629.2   II   ISSN 0067-2548
AUTOMOBILE NEWS ANNUAL. (Text in English) 1947. a. Rs.15. Gidwaney's Publishing Co., 401 Arun Chambers, Tardeo Rd., Bombay 400034, India. Ed. Kishu Gidwaney.

629.2   SZ   ISSN 0084-7674
AUTOMOBILE YEAR/ANNEE AUTOMOBILE/ AUTO-JAHR. (Editions in English, French, German, Greek and Spanish) 1953. a. 59 Fr. Edita S.A., 3 rue de la Vigie, CH-1000 Lausanne 9, Switzerland. Ed. Douglas Armstrong. adv. circ. 45,000.

629   US
AUTOMOTIVE ENCYCLOPEDIA. 1981. biennial. Goodheart-Willcox Co., Inc., 123 West Taft Drive, South Holland, IL 60473. Eds. William K. Toboldt, Larry Johnson. index.

380.5   II
AUTOMOTIVE INDUSTRY OF INDIA - FACTS & FIGURES. (Text in English) 1966. a. Rs.25. All-India Automobile and Ancillary Industries Association, 80 Dr. Annie Besant Rd., Worli, Bombay 400018, India. Ed. S. Panikar. circ. 1,000.
Formerly: Automotive and Ancillary Industry.

629.2   US
AUTOMOTIVE NEWS MARKET DATA BOOK. 1933. a. $12.50. Crain Automotive Group Inc. (Subsidiary of: Crain Communications, Inc.) 965 E. Jefferson Ave., Detroit, MI 48207.
Formerly: Automotive News Almanac (ISSN 0067-2580)

629.286   CN   ISSN 0068-9629
AUTOMOTIVE SERVICE DATA BOOK. 1935. a. Can.$7($9) Maclean-Hunter Ltd., 481 University Ave., Toronto, Ont. M5W 1A7, Canada. Ed.E. Belitsky. adv.

TRANSPORTATION — AUTOMOBILES

629.286   MX
AUTOMOTRIZ. 1968. a. 125($80) Editorial Innovacion, Espana 396, Mexico 13, D.F., Mexico. Ed. Cesar Macazaga. adv.

629.2   US   ISSN 0067-4338
BASIC AUTO REPAIR MANUAL. 1968. irreg., latest edt. no. 8. $5.95. Petersen Publishing Co., Book Sales Division, 6725 Sunset Blvd., Los Angeles, CA 90028. Ed. Spence Murray.

629.2   US   ISSN 0067-4362
BASIC BODYWORK AND PAINTING. 1969. irreg., latest edt. no. 4. $3.95. Petersen Publishing Co., Book Sales Division, 6725 Sunset Blvd., Los Angeles, CA 90028. Ed. Miles Schofield.

629.2   US   ISSN 0067-4370
BASIC CAMS, VALVES AND EXHAUST SYSTEMS. 1968. irreg., latest edt. no. 4. $3.95. Petersen Publishing Co., Book Sales Division, 6725 Sunset Blvd., Los Angeles, CA 90028. Ed. Miles Schofield.

629.2   US   ISSN 0067-4389
BASIC CARBURETION AND FUEL SYSTEMS. 1968. irreg., no. 6, 1977. $4.95. Petersen Publishing Co., 8490 Sunset Blvd., Los Angeles, CA 90069.

629.2   US   ISSN 0067-4397
BASIC CHASSIS, SUSPENSION AND BRAKES. 1969. irreg., latest edt. no. 4. $3.95. Petersen Publishing Co., Book Sales Division, 6725 Sunset Blvd., Los Angeles, CA 90028. Ed. Miles Schofield.

629.2   US   ISSN 0067-4400
BASIC CLUTCHES AND TRANSMISSIONS. 1968. irreg., latest edt. no. 4. $3.95. Petersen Publishing Co., Book Sales Division, 6725 Sunset Blvd., Los Angeles, CA 90028. Ed. Miles Schofield.

629.2   US   ISSN 0067-4427
BASIC IGNITION AND ELECTRICAL SYSTEMS. 1969. irreg., latest edt. no. 5. $3.95. Petersen Publishing Co., Book Sales Division, 6725 Sunset Blvd., Los Angeles, CA 90028. Ed. Bd.

388.3   DK
BILISMEN I DANMARK. 1967. a. free. Automobil-Importoerernes Sammenslutning, Ryvangs Alle 68, 2900 Hellerup, Denmark. Ed. Erik Ebsen Petersen.

388.3   CN   ISSN 0316-4896
BLACK BOOK VEHICLE IDENTIFICATION GUIDE. (Text in English and French) 1973. a. Can.$4.95. Wm. Ward Publishing Co. Ltd., 85 Ellesmere Rd., Suite 201, Scarborough, Ont. M1R 4B8, Canada. circ. 13,000.

796 380.1   FR
BOTTIN AUTO-CYCLE-MOTO. 1894. a. $37. Societe Didot Bottin, 28 rue du Docteur Finlay, 75738 Paris Cedex 15, France.
Formerly: Bottin de l'Auto et du Cycle.

318   BL
BRAZIL. FUNDACAO INSTITUTO BRASILEIRO DE GEOGRAFIA E ESTATISTICA. DEPARTAMENTO DE ESTATISTICAS INDUSTRIAIS, COMERCIAIS E DE SERVICOS. EMPRESAS DE TRANSPORTE RODOVIARIO. irreg. $10. Fundacao Instituto Brasileiro de Geografia e Estatistica, Departamento de Estatisticas Industriais, Comerciais e de Servicos, Av. Brazil 15671, ZC-91 Rio de Janeiro, Brazil.

388.3   CN   ISSN 0707-5014
BRITISH COLUMBIA MOTOR TRANSPORT DIRECTORY. 1978. a. Can.$7.50. Automotive Transport Association of British Columbia, 4090 Graveley St., Burnaby, B.C. V5C 3T6, Canada.

629.222   UK
BUYERS' GUIDE TO THE MOTOR INDUSTRY OF GREAT BRITAIN. a. £5 to non-members. Society of Motor Manufacturers and Traders Ltd., Forbes House, Halkin St., London SW1X 7DS, England.

CANADIAN AUTOMOTIVE AFTERMARKET DIRECTORY/MARKETING GUIDE. see BUSINESS AND ECONOMICS — Trade And Industrial Directories

629.2   US
CAR AND DRIVER BUYERS GUIDE. 1957. a. $1.75. Ziff-Davis Publishing Co., 1 Park Ave., New York, NY 10016. Ed. William Jeanes. adv. circ. 155,000.
Formerly: Car and Driver Yearbook (ISSN 0069-0260)

388 658.8   US
CAR PRICES. 1965. a. $1.95 per no. People's Publishing Co., Inc., 1440 W. Walnut St., Compton, CA 90220. Ed. Ray Krupa. adv. stat. circ. 100,000.
Formerly: American Car Prices.

CARAVAN FACTFINDER. see TRAVEL AND TOURISM

629.286   IT
CATALOGO MOTORISTICO. (Text in English, French, German, Italian) 1962. a. L.5000. Azienda Cataloghi Italiani, Piazzale Lugano 9, 20158 Milan, Italy. Ed. Lucio Torella. adv. circ. 35,000(controlled)

629.2   FR   ISSN 0069-1097
CATALOGUE DES CATALOGUES AUTOMOBILE. a. 72 F. 1 Avenue Felix-Faure, Paris 15, France.

388.3   BE
CATALOGUE GENERAL DE L'INDUSTRIE ET DU COMMERCE AUTOMOBILE DE BELGIQUE. (Text in Dutch, English, French and German) 1950. a. Chambre Syndicale du Commerce Automobile de Belgique, Bd. de la Woluwe 46, 1200 Brussels, Belgium. adv.

388.3 918.904   UY
CENTUR. 1977. a. free. Centro Automovilista del Uruguay, Artigas 1773, Montevideo, Uruguay. Ed.Ever Cabrera Tornielli. adv. circ. 10,000.

CHAMBRE SYNDICALE NATIONALE DES ELECTRICIENS ET SPECIALISTES DE L'AUTOMOBILE. ANNUAIRE. see ELECTRICITY AND ELECTRICAL ENGINEERING

629.28   US   ISSN 0069-3634
CHILTON'S AUTO REPAIR MANUAL; American cars from 1975 to 1981. 1968. a. price varies. Chilton Book Co., Automotive Editorial Department, Chilton Way, Radnor, PA 19089.

629.2   US
CHILTON'S IMPORT AUTOMOTIVE REPAIR MANUAL. 1971. irreg., 5th edt., 1979, covers 1973-79. price varies. Chilton Book Co., Automotive Editorial Department, Chilton Way, Radnor, PA 19089. Ed. Bd.
Former titles: Chilton's Import Car Repair Manual (ISSN 0084-8743); Chilton's Foreign Car Repair Manual.

629.28   US   ISSN 0363-2393
CHILTON'S MOTOR-AGE PROFESSIONAL AUTOMOTIVE SERVICE MANUAL. 1976. a. Chilton Book Co., Chilton Way, Radnor, PA 19089. illus.
Formerly: Chilton's Automotive Service Manual.

338.4   US   ISSN 0361-9397
CHILTON'S MOTOR-AGE PROFESSIONAL LABOR GUIDE AND PARTS MANUAL. 1976. irreg. Chilton Co. Inc., Chilton Way, Radnor, PA 19089. illus.
Formerly: Chilton's Motor Age Labor Guide and Parts Manual.

629.224   US
CHILTON'S TRUCK AND VAN REPAIR MANUAL; gasoline and diesel engines. (The 1974 edt. covers 1965-1974) 1971. irreg., latest edt., 1980, covers 1973-80. price varies. Chilton Book Co., Automotive Editorial Department, Chilton Way, Radnor, PA 19089.
Formerly: Chilton's Truck Repair Manual (ISSN 0045-6721)

629.2   US   ISSN 0069-8008
COMPLETE VOLKSWAGEN BOOK. 1969. irreg., latest edt. no. 4. $3.95. Petersen Publishing Co., Book Sales Division, 6725 Sunset Blvd., Los Angeles, CA 90028.

629.22   CN   ISSN 0708-3963
CONSUMER BULLETIN/BULLETIN AUX CONSOMMATEURS. 1972. irreg. Can.$15. Automobile Protection Association - Association pour la Protection Automobile, 292 ouest, Bd. St. Joseph, Montreal, Que. H2V 2N7, Canada. circ. 12,000.

CONTINENTAL MOTORING HOLIDAYS. see TRAVEL AND TOURISM

629.2 621.38   US
CONVERGENCE: INTERNATIONAL COLLOQUIUM ON AUTOMOTIVE ELECTRONIC TECHNOLOGY. PROCEEDINGS. biennial. $25. Society of Automotive Engineers, 400 Commonwealth Dr., Warrendale, PA 15096. (Co-sponsor: Institute of Electrical and Electronics Engineers;)

629.22   US
CORVETTE, SPORTSCAR OF AMERICA. 1976. a. $34.50. Michael Bruce Associates, P.O. Box 396, Powell, OH 43065. Ed. Michael B. Antonick. illus. circ. 5,000.
Formerly(until vol. 3): Corvette, the Sensuous American (ISSN 0362-3777)

659.1   US   ISSN 0070-2277
CYCLE BUYERS GUIDE. 1968. a. $2.50 (free to subscribers of Cycle) Ziff-Davis Publishing Co., One Park Ave., New York, NY 10016. Ed. Cook Neilson. adv. circ. 140,000.

796.5   GW
D C C-CARAVAN MODELLFUEHRER. a. (Deutscher Camping Club e.V.) D C C-Wirtschaftsdienst und Verlag GmbH, Postfach 400428, 8000 Munich 40, W. Germany (B.R.D.) adv. circ. 15,000.
Camping

629.2   UK
DAILY MAIL MOTOR SHOW REVIEW. a. Associated Newspapers Group Ltd., Carmelite House, Carmelite St., London EC4Y 0JA, England. illus.

343 388   US
DRIVERS LICENSE GUIDE; U. A. & Canadian edition. 1966. a. $8.45. Drivers License Guide Company, 1492 Oddstad Drive, Redwood City, CA 94063. Ed. Keith Doerge. circ. 30,000.

629.2   US
EDMUND'S AUTO-PEDIA. 1973. a. $2.50. Edmund Publications Corp., 515 Hempstead Tpke., West Hempstead, NY 11552. charts. illus. circ. 200,000.

629.2   US
EDMUND'S CAR PRICES. 1970. a. $2.50. Edmund Publications Corp., 515 Hempstead Tpke., West Hempstead, NY 11552. charts. illus. circ. 200,000.

629.2   US
EDMUND'S VAN, PICKUP, OFF ROAD VEHICLES. 1978. a. $2.50. Edmund Publications Corp., 515 Hemstead Tpke, Hempstead, NY 11552.

629.2   US   ISSN 0489-5606
ENGINEERING KNOW-HOW IN ENGINE DESIGN. 1953. a. Society of Automotive Engineers, 400 Commonwealth Dr., Warrendale, PA 15096. illus.

ESTADO DE SAO PAULO; AMALISE E ACOMPANHEMENTO DO MERCADO DE ENERGIA ELECTRICA DOS AUTOPRODUCTORES. see ELECTRICITY AND ELECTRICAL ENGINEERING

388.3   BE
ETUDE DU MARCHE AUTOMOBILE BELGE.* (Editions in Dutch and French) a. Chambre Syndicale du Commerce Automobile de Belgique, Bd. de la Woluwe 46, 1200 Brussels, Belgium.

338.3   FR
ETUDES ET DOCUMENTATION DE LA R.T.A. (Revue Technique Automobile) irreg. Editions pour l'Automobile et l'Industrie, 20-22 rue de la Saussiere, 92100 Boulogne-Billancourt, France. charts. illus.

TRANSPORTATION — AUTOMOBILES

338.3   FR
FICHES TECHNIQUES R.T.A. (Revue Technique Automobile) 1978. irreg. prices varies. Editions Techniques pour l'Automobile et l'Industrie, 20-22 rue de la Saussiere, 92100 Boulogne-Billancourt, France. charts. illus. (looseleaf format)

338.3   FR
FICHES TECHNIQUES R.T.C. (Revue Technique Carrosserie) irreg. price varies. Editions Techniques pour l'Automobile et l'Industrie, 20-22 rue de la Saussiere, 92100 Boulogne-Billancourt, France. charts. illus. (looseleaf format)

338.3   FR
FICHES TECHNIQUES R.T.D. (Revue Technique Diesel) irreg. price varies. Editions Techniques pour l'Automobile et l'Industrie, 20-22 rue de la Saussiere, 92100 Boulogne-Billancourt, France.

629.2   US   ISSN 0071-5670
FIX YOUR CHEVROLET. 1954. irreg. $6. ‡ Goodheart-Willcox Co., Inc., 123 W. Taft Dr., South Holland, IL 60473. Ed. Bill Toboldt. index.

629.2   US   ISSN 0071-5689
FIX YOUR FORD. 1954. irreg. $6. ‡ Goodheart-Willcox Co., Inc., 123 W. Taft Dr., South Holland, IL 60473. Ed. Bill Toboldt. index.

629.2   US   ISSN 0071-5697
FIX YOUR VOLKSWAGEN. 1960. a. $6. ‡ Goodheart-Willcox Co., Inc., 123 West Taft Dr., South Holland, IL 60473. Ed. Larry Johnson. index.

GENERAL MOTORS PUBLIC INTEREST REPORT. see BUSINESS AND ECONOMICS — *Production Of Goods And Services*

388   629.2   US
GENERAL MOTORS SYMPOSIA SERIES. 1971. irreg. price varies. Plenum Press, 233 Spring St., New York, NY 10013.

629.2   GW   ISSN 0072-145X
GERMAN MOTOR TRIBUNE. 1951. a. DM.17. (Export-Service Dupke) Broenner Verlag Breidenstein GmbH, Stuttgarter Str. 18-24, 6000 Frankfurt, W. Germany (B.R.D.) Ed. Werner Siebeneicher. adv. circ. 10,000.
    Export directory

388   UK
GLASS'S CAR CHECK BOOK. a. £3.50. Glass's Guide Service Ltd., Elgin House, St. George's Ave., Weybridge, Surrey KT13 0BX, England. adv.

629.2   US
GOLD BOOK. s-a. $14. Quentin Craft, Ed. & Pub., 910 Tony Lama St., El Paso, TX 79915.

GUESTHOUSES, FARMHOUSES AND INNS IN BRITAIN. see *TRAVEL AND TOURISM*

916.9   MG
GUIDE ROUTIER ET TOURISTIQUE: MADAGASCAR, REUNION, MAURICE, COMORES ET SEYCHELLES. a. Automobile Club de Madagascar, Service du Guide Routier, B.P. 571, Antananarivo, Malagasy Republic. illus.

629.2   GW   ISSN 0073-0157
HANDBUCH FUER BERUFSKRAFTFAHRER.* irreg. price varies. Krueger-Verlag, Westenhellweg 9, Postfach 227, 4600 Dortmund 1, W. Germany (B.R.D.)

614.86   388   JA   ISSN 0386-1112
I A T S S RESEARCH. 1977. a. $5. International Association of Traffic and Safety Sciences, 6-20, 2-chome, Yaesu, Chuo-Ku, Tokyo 104, Japan. Ed.Bd. circ. 1,000.

629.2   US   ISSN 0098-3551
I E E E VEHICULAR TECHNOLOGY CONFERENCE. RECORD. irreg., latest 1976. Institute of Electrical and Electronics Engineers, Inc., 445 Hoes Lane, Piscataway, NJ 08854. illus. Key Title: Record - Vehicular Technology Conference.

629.2   IT   ISSN 0073-7291
INDUSTRIA ITALIANA DEL CICLO E DEL MOTOCICLO. ANNUARIO. (Text in English, French, German, Italian, Spanish) 1960. a. free. Associazione Nazionale Ciclo, Motociclo e Accessori, Via M. Macchi 32, Milan, Italy. adv. index. circ. 12,000.

629.2   FR   ISSN 0073-7747
INDUSTRIE FRANCAISE DES MOTEURS A COMBUSTION INTERNE; repertoire alphabetique des constructeurs. 1953. biennial. 30 F. Syndicat des Constructeurs de Moteurs a Combustion Interne, 10 Av. Hoche, 75382 Paris, France.

629.286   US
INTERNATIONAL CONFERENCE ON VEHICLE STRUCTURAL MECHANICS. PROCEEDINGS. 1975. biennial. Society of Automotive Engineers, 400 Commonwealth Dr., Warrendale, PA 15096.

629.276   US
INTERNATIONAL CONGRESS OF AUTOMOTIVE SAFETY. PROCEEDINGS. irreg., 2nd, 1973. price varies. International Congress on Automotive Safety, 3512 Graysby Ave., San Pedro, CA 90732.

629.2   UR
KONSTRUKTORSKO-TEKHNOLOGICHESKII INSTITUT AVTOMATIZATSII AVTOMOBILSTROENIYA. SBORNIK TRUDOV. irreg. price varies. Konstruktorsko-Tekhnologicheskii Institut Avtomatizatsii Avtomobilstroeniya, Chelyabinsk, U.S.S.R. illus.

629.2   GW   ISSN 0341-468X
KRAFTFAHRT-BUNDESAMT. STATISTISCHE MITTEILUNGEN. 1954. a. DM.72. Kirschbaum Verlag, Siegfriedstr. 28, Postfach 210209, 5300 Bonn 2, W. Germany (B.R.D.) charts. stat. circ. 400.

629.22   US
M G INTERNATIONAL. 1973. a. $12.95. c/o R. L. Knudson, Ed., Box 2332, Springfield, MA 01101. illus.
    Former titles (in 1975): M G World (ISSN 0098-2741); 1973-1974: Classic M G Yearbook.

338.476   US   ISSN 0146-9932
M V M A MOTOR VEHICLE FACTS AND FIGURES. 1976. a. single copies free. ‡ Motor Vehicle Manufacturers Association of the U.S. Inc., 300 New Center Bldg., Detroit, MI 48202. Key Title: Motor Vehicle Facts & Figures.
    Formed by the merger of: Automobile Facts and Figures (ISSN 0067-253X) & Motor Truck Facts (ISSN 0077-1643)

338.3   FR
MOTEURS DIESEL. irreg. (no. 5, 1979) Editions Techniques pour l'Automobile et l'Industrie, 20-22 rue de la Saussiere, 92100 Boulogne-Billancourt, France. charts. illus.

629.2   US
MOTOR AUTO REPAIR MANUAL. 1938. a. $16.95. Hearst Magazines, Book Division, 250 West 55th Street, New York, NY 10019. index.
    Formerly: Motor's Auto Repair Manual (ISSN 0098-1745)
    Mechanical repair procedures for American-made cars

629.2   UK   ISSN 0077-1589
MOTOR CYCLE DIARY. 1928. a. 51p-83p. I P C Business Press Ltd., 40 Bowling Green Lane, London E. C. 1, England. Ed. E. Liggins. circ. 7,000.

629.28   US   ISSN 0094-1514
MOTOR HANDBOOK. a. Hearst Books, Motor Books Department, 224 W.57th St., New York, NY 10019. illus.
    Continues: Motor's Handbook.

629.222   UK   ISSN 0077-1597
MOTOR INDUSTRY OF GREAT BRITAIN. 1926. a. £22. Society of Motor Manufacturers and Traders Ltd., Forbes House, Halkin St., London, SW1X 7DS, England. circ. 1,000.

338.476   JA
MOTOR INDUSTRY OF JAPAN. (Text in English) 1972. a. free. Toyota Motor Sales Co. Ltd., No. 3-18, 2-chome, Kudan-Minami, Chiyoda-ku, Tokyo 102, Japan. charts. illus. stat. circ. 7,000.

MOTOR MANUAL. see *TRANSPORTATION — Trucks And Trucking*

629.2   US   ISSN 0077-1716
MOTOR PARTS AND TIME GUIDE. 1910. a. $26. Hearst Books, Motor Books Department, 224 W.57th St., New York, NY 10019. Ed. David Lewis. circ. 50,000.
    Formerly: Motor's Flat Rate and Parts Manual.

388.3   SW   ISSN 0077-1619
MOTOR TRAFFIC IN SWEDEN. Swedish edition: Bilismen i Sverige. 1948. a. Kr.35. (Sveriges Bilindustri- och Bilgrossistfoerening - Association of Swedish Automobile Maufacturers and Wholesalers) AB Bilstatistik, Box 5514, S-114 85 Stockholm, Sweden.

629.28   US   ISSN 0098-3624
MOTOR TRUCK REPAIR MANUAL. a. $21.95. Hearst Books, Motor Book Department, 250 W. 55th St., New York, NY 10019. Ed. Louis C. Forier.
    Formerly: Motor Truck & Diesel Repair Manual (ISSN 0077-1724)

629.286   JA
MOTOR VEHICLE ENGINEERING SPECIFICATIONS-JAPAN. (Text in Japanese) a. 9000 Yen. Society of Automotive Engineers of Japan, Inc., 10-2,Goban-cho, Chiyoda-ku, Tokyo 102, Japan.

796.75   US   ISSN 0077-1678
MOTORCYCLE BUYER'S GUIDE. 1970. a. $2.95. Petersen Publishing Co., 8490 Sunset Blvd., Los Angeles, CA 90069.

388.5   US   ISSN 0091-5793
MOTORCYCLE FACTS. a. free. National Safety Council, Statistics Division, 444 N. Michigan Ave., Chicago, IL 60611. illus. stat.

388.3   US
N A F A ANNUAL REFERENCE BOOK. 1960. a. $5. National Association of Fleet Administrators, Inc., 295 Madison Ave., New York, NY 10017. Ed. Robert Berke. adv. stat. circ. 2,500.
    Formerly: N A F A Conference Brochure & Reference Book (ISSN 0550-8843)

629.222   UK
NATIONAL MOTOR MUSEUM PICTORIAL GUIDE. 1959. a. 50p. (National Motor Museum Trust) Montagu Ventures Ltd., Beaulieu, Hampshire, England. Ed. Michael Sedgewick. adv. illus. stat. circ. 60,000.

629.28   US
NATIONAL SERVICE DATA; DOMESTIC. a. $24.95. Mitchell Manuals, Inc., Box 80427, San Diego, CA 92138. illus.

629   NN
NEW HEBRIDES. BUREAU OF STATISTICS. NEW MOTOR VEHICLE REGISTRATIONS AND MOTOR VEHICLES ON THE REGISTER/ NOUVELLES IMMATRICULATIONS ET VEHICULES AUTOMOBILES IMMATRICULES. (Text in English, French) 1972. a. free. Bureau of Statistics, Port Vila, New Hebrides. stat.

629.2   US   ISSN 0475-1876
OLD CAR VALUE GUIDE. Variant title: Old Car Value Guide Annual. vol. 5, 1976. a. $7.95. Quentin Craft, Ed. & Pub., 910 Tony Lama St., El Paso, TX 79915. illus.

338.3   CN
ONTARIO. MINISTRY OF TRANSPORTATION AND COMMUNICATIONS. MOTOR VEHICLE ACCIDENT FACTS. 1957. a. free. Ministry of Transportation and Communications, 1201 Wilson Ave., Downsview, Ont. M3M 1J8, Canada. illus. stat.
    Continues: Ontario. Ministry of Transportation and Communications. Highway Traffic Collisions.

388.3   629.2   CN
OPPORTUNITIES UNLIMITED. biennial. free. Automotive Industries Association of Canada, 1306 Wellington St., Ottawa, Ont. K1Y 3B2, Canada. circ. 40,000.

388   MR
PARC AUTOMOBILE DU MAROC. (Text in French) a. DH.15. Direction de la Statistique, Box 178, Rabat, Morocco.

TRANSPORTATION — RAILROADS

388   US   ISSN 0485-3695
ROLLS-ROYCE OWNERS' CLUB, DIRECTORY AND REGISTER.* 1951. biennial. membership. Rolls-Royce Owners' Club Inc., c/o Adrian A. West, Box 725, Morrisville, VT 05661. circ. 5,000(controlled) (tabloid format)

629.28   US   ISSN 0362-8205
S A E HANDBOOK. 1905. a. $65. Society of Automotive Engineers, 400 Commonwealth Dr., Warrendale, PA 15096.

388   US
S A E TECHNICAL PAPERS. irreg. $1.95 to non-members. Society of Automotive Engineers, 400 Commonwealth Dr., Warrendale, PA 15096. index; cum.index: 1965-1978. (also avail. in microfiche; back issues avail.)

629.28   US   ISSN 0096-736X
S A E TRANSACTIONS. a. price varies. Society of Automotive Engineers, 400 Commonwealth Dr., Warrendale, PA 15096. index. (also avail. in microfiche)

338.476   FR
S D A I; syndicat de la distribution pour l'automobile et l'industrie. 1966. a. (Syndicat National de la Distribution pour l'Automobile et l'Industrie) Centre d'Editions Publicitaires Perrin, 100 Bd. de Sebastopol, 75003 Paris, France. adv.

388   SI
SINGAPORE MOTORING GUIDE. 1980. a. S.$4. Times Directories Private Ltd., 530 Cuppage Centre, 55 Cuppage Rd., Singapore 0922, Singapore. circ. 12,000.

SOCIEDAD ESPANOLA DE AUTOMOVILES DE TURISMO. MEMORIA Y BALANCE. see *TRAVEL AND TOURISM*

629.286   JA
SOCIETY OF AUTOMOTIVE ENGINEERS OF JAPAN. TRANSACTIONS. (Text in Japanese; summaries in English) biennial. 5000 Yen. Society of Automotive Engineers of Japan, Inc, 10-2, Goban-cho, Chiyoda-ku, Tokyo 102, Japan.

629.28   US   ISSN 0585-086X
STAPP CAR CRASH CONFERENCE PROCEEDINGS. 10th, 1967. a. Society of Automotive Engineers, 400 Commonwealth Dr., Warrendale, PA 15096.

388.3   629.2   IT   ISSN 0039-4254
STYLE AUTO; architettura della carrozzeria. (Text in Italian or English) 1964. a. L.5000($10) softbound; L.8000 ($13) hardbound. Style Auto Editrice, Corso Adriatico 26, 10129 Turin, Italy. Ed. Mario Dinarich. adv. illus.

388   SZ
SWITZERLAND. STATISTISCHES AMT. STRASSENVERKEHRSUNFAELLE/ACCIDENTS DE LA CIRCULATION ROUTIERE EN SUISSE. (Subseries of Statistische Quellenwerke der Schweiz) (Text in German and French) 1963. a. 11 Fr. Statistisches Amt., Hallwylstrasse 15, CH-3003 Berne, Switzerland. stat.

629.2   GW
TASCHENFACHBUCH DER KRAFTFAHRZEUGBETRIEBE. 1953. a. DM.13.50. Krafthand-Verlag Walter Schulz, St.-Anna-Str. 26, 8939 Bad Woerishofen, W. Germany (B.R.D.) Ed. Walter Schulz

338   629.2   GW   ISSN 0083-548X
TATSACHEN UND ZAHLEN AUS DER KRAFTVERKEHRSWIRTSCHAFT. 1927. a. price varies. Verband der Automobilindustrie, Westendstr. 61, Postfach 174249, 6000 Frankfurt 17, W. Germany (B.R.D.) (back issues avail.)

917.4   US
TOURBOOK: CONNECTICUT, MASSACHUSETTS, RHODE ISLAND. Cover title: Connecticut, Massachusetts, Rhode Island Tourbook. a. membership. American Automobile Association, 8111 Gatehouse Rd., Falls Church, VA 22047. illus.
   Supersedes in part: Northeastern Tour Book (ISSN 0468-6853)

917.4   US
TOURBOOK: MAINE, NEW HAMPSHIRE, VERMONT. Cover title: Maine, New Hampshire, Vermont Tour Book. a. membership. American Automobile Association, 8111 Gatehouse Rd., Falls Church, VA 22047.
   Supersedes in part: Northeastern Tour Book (ISSN 0468-6853)

338.3   JA
TOYOTA IN BRIEF. a. Toyota Motor Sales Co. Ltd. - Toyota Jidosha Hanbai K.K., Public Relations Department, 2-3-18 Kudan Minami, Chiyoda-ku, Tokyo 102, Japan. charts. stat.
   Press information

629.283   US   ISSN 0091-6056
U. S. FEDERAL HIGHWAY ADMINISTRATION. MOTOR VEHICLE REGISTRATIONS BY STANDARD METROPOLITAN STATISTICAL AREAS. irreg. U. S. Federal Highway Administration, 400 Seventh St., S.W., Washington, DC 20590. stat. Key Title: Motor Vehicle Registrations by Standard Metropolitan Statistical Areas.

629.2   GW
V K G JAHRBUCH; Mitgliederverzeichnis. 1969. a. DM.9. Verband der Kraftfahrzeugteile- und Zweiradgrosshaendler e.V., Oberstr. 36-42, 4030 Ratingen, W. Germany (B.R.D.) Ed. Hans H. Eichler. adv. bk. rev. bibl. charts. stat. circ. 1,200.

629.2   380.1   GW
V K G JAHRBUCH. 1969. a. Verband der Kraftfahrzeugteile- und Zweiradgrosshaendler e.V., Postfach 1680, Oberstr. 36-42, 4030 Ratingen, W. Germany (B.R.D.) adv.

388.1   DK   ISSN 0083-5358
VEJTRANSPORTEN I TAL OG TEKST. (Text in Danish; notes in English) 1959. a. Kr.71. Automobil-Importoerernes Sammenslutning, Ryvangs Alle 68, 2900 Hellerup, Denmark. Ed. Erik Ebsen Petersen. index; cum.index every 7 years.

629.2   338   GW
VERBAND DER AUTOMOBILINDUSTRIE. JAHRESBERICHT. a. price varies. Verband der Automobilindustrie, Westendstr. 61, Postfach 174249, 6000 Frankfurt 17, W. Germany (B.R.D.)
   Formerly: Verband der Automobilindustrie. Taetigkeitsbericht (ISSN 0083-5471)

629.386   SZ
VEREINIGUNG SCHWEIZERISCHER STRASSENFACHMAENNER. VERSUCHSBERICHT. vol. 5, 1974. irreg. Vereingung Schweizerischer Strassenfachmaenner, Seefeldstr 9, 8008 Zurich, Switzerland. charts. stat.

629.222   US   ISSN 0363-4639
VINTAGE AUTO ALMANAC. 1977. a. $7.95. Hemmings Motor News, Box 256, Bennington, VT 05201 (Subscr. address: Box 945, Bennington, VT 05201) Ed. David Brownell. illus. circ. 16,000.

629.2   US   ISSN 0083-7229
WARD'S AUTOMOTIVE YEARBOOK. 1938. a. $50. Ward's Communications, Inc., 28 W. Adams, Detroit, MI 48226. Ed. Harry A. Stark. adv. bk. rev. charts. illus. stat. index. circ. 5,000.

338.476   US
WARD'S WHO'S WHO AMONG U.S. MOTOR VEHICLE MANUFACTURERS. 1977. irreg. $29.75. Ward's Communications, Inc., 28 W. Adams St., Detroit, MI 48226. Eds. David C. Smith, Patricia J. Williams. adv. bk. rev. charts. illus. stat. index. circ. 5,000.

388.3   GW
WAS KOSTET DER GESCHAEFTSWAGEN? vol. 11, 1977. a. DM.14.80. ADAC Verlag GmbH, Baumgartnerstr. 53, 8000 Munich 70, W. Germany (B.R.D.) circ. 7,000.
   Formerly(until vol. 15, 1979/80): Was Kostet Mein Auto?

629.2   US   ISSN 0092-3583
WASHINGTON (STATE). DEPARTMENT OF MOTOR VEHICLES. RESEARCH AND TECHNOLOGY. RESEARCH REPORT. 1965. irreg., no. 042, 1977. $2. ‡ Department of Motor Vehicles, Research & Technology, Olympia, WA 98504. Ed. Dr. Carl L. Klingberg. circ. 100. Key Title: Research Report - Department of Motor Vehicles Research and Technology Division (Olympia)

388.4   US
WORLD AUTOMOTIVE MARKET. 1931. a. $10. Automobile International, 386 Park Ave. South, New York, NY 10016. Ed. Bernard Zinober. circ. 3,500.

338.476   US   ISSN 0084-1463
WORLD CARS. 1962. a. $29.75. (Automobile Club d'Italia, IT) Herald Books, Box 17E, Pelham, NY 10803.

629.2   US   ISSN 0085-8307
WORLD MOTOR VEHICLE DATA. a. $25. Motor Vehicle Manufacturers Association of the U.S., Inc., 300 New Center Bldg., Detroit, MI 48202.

629.222   338.4   US
WORLD TRENDS IN PASSENGER-CAR PRODUCTION AND ENGINES. 1964. irreg., 1967, 2nd ed. free; limited distribution. ‡ Ethyl Corporation, Research Laboratories, 1600 W. Eight Mile Rd., Ferndale, MI 48220. Ed. Burr J. French.
   Formerly: Free-World Trends in Passenger-Car Production and Engines (ISSN 0071-9331)

TRANSPORTATION — Railroads

625.1   US
AMERICAN RAILWAY ENGINEERING ASSOCIATION. PROCEEDINGS. a. $25. American Railway Engineering Association, 59 E. van Buren St., Chicago, IL 60604.

625.1   GW   ISSN 0341-0463
ARCHIV FUER EISENBAHNTECHNIK. 1952. a. price varies. Hestra-Verlag, Holzhofallee 33, Postfach 4244, 6100 Darmstadt 1, W. Germany (B.R.D.) adv.

625
ASSOCIATION OF AMERICAN RAILROADS. DATA SYSTEMS DIVISION. PAPERS. a. price varies. Association of American Railroads, American Railroads Bldg., 1920 L St., N.W., Washington, DC 20036.

385   388.322   AT
AUSTRALIA. BUREAU OF STATISTICS. RAIL, BUS, AND AIR TRANSPORT. (Text in English) 1972. a. free. Australian Bureau of Statistics, P.O. Box 10, Belconnen, A.C.T. 2616, Australia. circ. 1,800.

385.1   UK   ISSN 0068-242X
BRITISH RAILWAYS BOARD. REPORT AND STATEMENT OF ACCOUNTS. 1963. a. price varies. British Railways Board, Euston Square, Box 100, London NW1 2DZ, England (Also avail from: H.M.S.O., c/o Liaison Officer, Atlantic House, London EC1P 1BW, England)

385.1   CM
CAMEROON REGIE NATIONALE DES CHEMINS DE FER. COMPTE RENDU DE GESTION. a. Regie Nationale des Chemins de Fer, Douala, Cameroon.

385   CM
CAMEROON. REGIE NATIONALE DES CHEMINS DE FER. STATISTIQUES. irreg. Regie Nationale des Chemins de Fer, Douala, Cameroon. illus.

385   CN
CANADA. STATISTICS CANADA. RAILWAY TRANSPORT/TRANSPORT FERROVIAIRE. (Issued in 6 Parts, Catalogue 52-207 through 52-212) (Text in English and French) 1919. a. each part price separately. Statistics Canada, Publications Distribution, Ottawa, Ont. K1A 0V7, Canada. (also avail. in microform from MML)

TRANSPORTATION — RAILROADS

385 708   CN   ISSN 0384-6903
CANADIAN DIRECTORY OF RAILWAY MUSEUMS AND DISPLAYS. a. Can.$2.95. Lancelot Press, Windsor, Ont., Canada. Ed. David Stephens. adv. illus.

625.2   US
CAR AND LOCOMOTIVE CYCLOPEDIA. 1879. quadrennial. $60. Simmons-Boardman Publishing Corporation, 350 Broadway, New York, NY 10013. Ed. K. Ellsworth. adv. bibl. charts. illus. circ. 6,500.

625   US   ISSN 0069-1623
CENTRAL ELECTRIC RAILFANS' ASSOCIATION. BULLETIN. 1938. irreg., no. 117, 1978. membership. Central Electric Railfans' Association, Box 503, Chicago, IL 60690. Ed. Bd. circ. 2,000.

625 385   PL
CENTRALNY OSRODEK BADAN I ROZWOJU TECHNIKI KOLEJNICTWA. PRACE COBIRTK. (Text in Polish; summaries in English, French, German, Russian) 1959. irreg (approx 4-5/yr) price varies. Wydawnictwa Komunikacji i Lacznosci, Kazimierzowska 52, Warsaw, Poland. Ed. Bd. circ. 1,400 (controlled)

385.1   US   ISSN 0069-6048
COLORADO RAIL ANNUAL. 1963. a.(none published 1975) price varies. ‡ (Colorado Railroad Historical Foundation, Inc.) Colorado Railroad Museum, Box 10, Golden, CO 80401. Ed. Cornelius W. Hauck. adv. bk. rev. index. circ. 3,000-6,000.

625.1   GW   ISSN 0072-1549
D B REPORT. 1965. a. price varies. (Deutsche Bundesbahn) Hestra-Verlag, Holzhofallee 33, Postfach 4244, 6100 Darmstadt 1, W. Germany (B.R.D.) adv.

385   UK   ISSN 0309-1465
DEVELOPING RAILWAYS. 1966. a. £1.40. I P C Transport Press Ltd., Division of IPC Business Press, Dorset House, Stamford Street, London S.E.1, England. (reprint service avail. from UMI)
    Former titles: International Railway Progress (ISSN 0074-7572); Overseas Railways.

621.2   US   ISSN 0070-4830
DIESEL LOCOMOTIVE QUESTION & ANSWER MANUAL. 1950. irreg. $5. Railway Fuel and Operating Officers Association, 10335 S. Hale, Chicago, IL 60643.
    Formerly: Diesel Electric Locomotive Examination Book.

385   SZ
EISENBAHNGESCHICHTE DER VEREINIGTEN STAATEN VON AMERIKA. 1977. irreg. Birkhaeuser Verlag, Elisabethenstr. 19, CH-4010 Basel, Switzerland.

625.1   GW   ISSN 0071-0075
ELSNERS TASCHENBUCH DER EISENBAHNTECHNIK. a. DM.29.80. Tetzlaff Verlag GmbH, Havelstr. 9, 6100 Darmstadt 1, W. Germany (B.R.D.) circ. 6,000.

EURAIL GUIDE; how to travel Europe and all the world by train. see *TRAVEL AND TOURISM*

385.1   SZ   ISSN 0071-2264
EUROPEAN COMPANY FOR THE FINANCING OF RAILWAY ROLLING STOCK. ANNUAL REPORT. Short title: EURFIMA Annual Report. (Text in French; summaries in English) 1957. a. free. European Company for the Financing of Railway Rolling Stock, Rittergasse 20, CH-4001 Basel 1, Switzerland.

385   FI   ISSN 0506-3876
FINNISH STATE RAILWAYS. (Text in English) 1965. a. ‡ Valtionrautatiet - Finnish State Railways, P.O. Box 488, SF-00101 Helsinki, Finland. illus. circ. 4,000.

625.1 385   UK   ISSN 0073-9839
INSTITUTION OF RAILWAY SIGNAL ENGINEERS. PROCEEDINGS. 1912. a. £4. Institution of Railway Signal Engineers, 21 Avalon Rd, Earley Reading Berks, England. Ed. L. G. Mackean. adv. circ. 1,500.

385   FR   ISSN 0074-7580
INTERNATIONAL RAILWAY STATISTICS. STATISTICS OF INDIVIDUAL RAILWAYS. irreg. 40 F. International Union of Railways, 14-16, rue Jean Rey, 75015 Paris, France.

625.1   GW   ISSN 0075-2479
JAHRBUCH DES EISENBAHNWESENS. 1950. a. price varies. (Deutsche Bundesbahn) Hestra-Verlag, Holzhofallee 33, Postfach 4244, 6100 Darmstadt 1, W. Germany (B.R.D.) adv.

385   GW   ISSN 0075-2576
JAHRBUCH FUER BUNDESBAHNBEAMTE. 1968. a. DM.51.50. Walhalla- und Praetoria-Verlag Georg Zwichenpflug, Dolomitenstr. 1, Postfach 301, 8400 Regensburg 1, W. Germany (B.R.D.)

385.1   UK   ISSN 0075-3033
JANE'S FREIGHT CONTAINERS. a. £37.50. Jane's Publishing Co., Paulton House, 8 Shepherdess Walk, London N.1., England. Ed. Patrick Finlay.

385.1 625.1   UK   ISSN 0075-3084
JANE'S WORLD RAILWAYS. a. £37.50. Jane's Publishing Co., Paulton House, 8 Shepherdess Walk, London N.1., England. Ed. Paul Goldsack.

385   JA   ISSN 0546-093X
JAPANESE NATIONAL RAILWAYS. FACTS AND FIGURES. a. free. Japanese National Railways - Nihon Kokuyu Tetsudo, International Dept., 1-6-5 Marunouchi, Chiyoda-ku, Tokyo 100, Japan. illus. stat.

625.1   US
JOINT RAILROAD CONFERENCE. CONFERENCE RECORD. a. $8. Institute of Electrical and Electronics Engineers, Inc, 445 Hoes Lane, Piscataway, NJ 08854.
    Supersedes: Joint Railroad Technical Conference. Preprint (ISSN 0075-3998)

625.26   US   ISSN 0076-0285
LOCOMOTIVE MAINTENANCE OFFICERS ASSOCIATION. ANNUAL PROCEEDINGS.* 1940. a. $6., or $10. for both convention report and the annual proceedings. Locomotive Maintenance Officers Association, 3144 Brereton Ct., Huntington, WV 25705. index.

625.26   US   ISSN 0076-0293
LOCOMOTIVE MAINTENANCE OFFICERS ASSOCIATION. PRECONVENTION REPORT;* full text of all seven technical committee reports on diesel locomotive and M.U. train maintenance. a. $10 for both preconvention report and the annual proceedings. Locomotive Maintenance Officers Association, 3144 Brereton Ct., Huntington, WV 25705. Ed. C.M. Lipcomb. index.

385   MW   ISSN 0076-3330
MALAWI RAILWAYS. ANNUAL REPORTS AND ACCOUNTS. Title varies: Malawi Railways. Directors' Reports and Accounts. 1932. a. free. Malawi Railways, Ltd., P.O. Box 5144, Limbe, Malawi. circ. 500.

MODEL RAILWAY CONSTRUCTOR ANNUAL. see *HOBBIES*

621.2   US
MODERN LOCOMOTIVE HANDBOOK. 1950. irreg. $6. Railway Fuel and Operating Officers Association, 10335 S. Hale, Chicago, IL 60643.

385   US   ISSN 0077-3387
NATIONAL ASSOCIATION OF REGULATORY UTILITY COMMISSIONERS. PROCEEDINGS. a. $25. National Association of Regulatory Utility Commissioners, 1102 Interstate Commerce Commission Bldg., Box 684, Washington, DC 20044.
    Formerly: National Association of Railroad and Utilities Commissioners. Proceedings.

385   NZ
NEW ZEALAND. RAILWAYS DEPARTMENT. ANNUAL REPORT. a. Railways Department, Wellington, New Zealand. illus. stat.

385   SW
NORDENS JAERNVAEGAR. (Text in English and Swedish) 1966. a. Kr.40($9) Frank Stenvalls Foerlag, Malmgatan 3, S-211 32 Malmoe, Sweden. Ed. Frank Stenvall. illus. circ. 200. (back issues avail.)

385.1   PK
PAKISTAN RAILWAYS. YEARBOOK OF INFORMATION. (Text in English) a. Pakistan Railways, Moghalpura, Pakistan.
    Continues: Pakistan Western Railway. Yearbook of Information (ISSN 0078-8511)

385   US
PASSENGER TRAIN ANNUAL. 1975. a. $7.95. (Passenger Train Journal Publishing Co.) P.T.J. Publishing, Inc., Box 397, Park Forest, IL 60466. bk. rev. bibl.

625.1   US
RAIL TRANSPORTATION PROCEEDINGS. 1970. a. $30. American Society of Mechanical Engineers, Rail Transportation Division, United Engineering Center, 345 E. 47th St., New York, NY 10017. (also avail. in microfiche; microfilm)

385.26   US
RAILROAD STATION HISTORICAL SOCIETY. RAILROAD STATION MONOGRAPH. 1970. irreg; 1973, no. 4. price varies. J-B Publishing Co., 430 Ivy Ave., Crete, NE 68333. Ed. Bd. bibl. illus. circ. 500.

657 385   US
RAILWAY ACCOUNTING RULES. irreg. price varies. Association of American Railroads, American Railroads Bldg., 1920 L. St., N.W., Washington, DC 20036.

385   UK   ISSN 0079-9513
RAILWAY DIRECTORY AND YEARBOOK. a. £13. I P C Transport Press Ltd., Division of IPC Business Press, Dorset House, Stamford St., London SE1 9LU, England. (reprint service avail. from UMI)

385   US   ISSN 0079-9521
RAILWAY FUEL AND OPERATING OFFICERS ASSOCIATION. PROCEEDINGS. a. $12. Railway Fuel and Operating Officers Association, 10335 S. Hale, Chicago, IL 60643.

385   US
RAILWAY LINE CLEARANCES. a. $17. National Railway Publication Co., 424 W. 33rd St., New York, NY 10001.

385   US   ISSN 0094-2278
RAILWAY PASSENGER CAR ANNUAL. 1974. a. $7.50. R P C Publications, Box 296, Godfrey, IL 62035. Ed. W. David Randall. circ. 1,500.

625.1   GW   ISSN 0079-9548
RAILWAY TECHNICAL REVIEW. (Text in English) 1952. a. price varies. Hestra-Verlag, Holzhofallee 33, Postfach 4244, 6100 Darmstadt 1, W. Germany (B.R.D.) adv.

385   UK   ISSN 0082-5891
RAILWAY WORLD ANNUAL. 1947. a. price varies. Ian Allan Ltd., Terminal House, Shepperton, Middlesex TW17 8AS, England. Ed. Michael Harris. circ. 12,500.
    Formerly: Trains Annual & Trains Illustrated Annual.

385   II   ISSN 0080-1933
REVIEW OF ACCIDENTS ON INDIAN GOVERNMENT RAILWAYS. (Text in English) 1957-58. a. Railway Board, Directorate of Safety, Joint Director, Public Relations, New Delhi 110001, India.

625.1   US   ISSN 0080-3316
ROADMASTERS AND MAINTENANCE OF WAY ASSOCIATION OF AMERICA. PROCEEDINGS. 1883. a. free to members and advertisers. Richard B. Cross Co., 103 S. Howard St., Box 405, Oxford, IN 47971. Ed. Richard B. Cross. circ. 2,000.

385.1   SZ   ISSN 0080-6048
SANKT GALLER BEITRAEGE ZUM FREMDENVERKEHR UND ZUR VERKEHRSWIRTSCHAFT: REIHE VERKEHRSWIRTSCHAFT. 1970. irreg. price varies. (Hochschule St. Gallen fuer Wirtschafts- und Sozialwissenschaften, Institut fuer Fremdenverkehr und Verkehrswirtschaft) Paul Haupt AG, Falkenplatz 14, 3001 Berne, Switzerland.

385.314   BL
SISTEMA FERROVIARIO R F F S A. irreg. Rede Ferroviaria Federal, S.A., Departamento Geral de Estadistica, Rio de Janeiro, Brazil. illus.

385   BE   ISSN 0081-119X
SOCIETE NATIONALE DES CHEMINS DE FER BELGES. RAPPORT ANNUEL. 1926/27. a. ‡ Nationale Maatschappij der Belgische Spoorwegen, 85 rue de France, B-1070 Brussels, Belgium. circ. controlled.

385   US   ISSN 0362-8213
SOUND APPROACH TO THE RAILROAD MARKET. a. Railway Equipment and Publication Co., 424 W. 33rd St., New York, NY 10001. illus.

385.1   US   ISSN 0081-542X
STEAM PASSENGER SERVICE DIRECTORY. 1966. a. $3. ‡ Empire State Railway Museum, P.O. Box 666, Middletown, NY 10940. Ed. Marvin H. Cohen. circ. 15,000.

385   SW   ISSN 0081-9964
SVERIGES JAERNVAEGAR/RAILWAYS OF SWEDEN. (Subseries of Sveriges Officiella Statistik: Transport- och Kommunikationsvaesen) 1953. a. Kr.42. Statens Jaernvaegars Centralfoervaltning - State Railways Central Administration, S-105 50 Stockholm, Sweden. circ. 1,000.
    Supersedes: Allmaen Jaernvaegsstatistik; Statens Jaernvaegar.

625.1   001.53   JA
SYMPOSIUM ON THE USE OF CYBERNETICS ON THE RAILWAY. (Text in Japanese; summaries available separately in English) 1964. a. Japan Railway Cybernetics Association - Nihon Tetsudo Saibanetikkusu Kyogikai, 2-5-18 Otemachi, Tokyo 100, Japan.
    Cybernetics

385   CH
TAIWAN RAILWAY. (Text in Chinese and English) 1963. irreg. Taiwan Railway Administration, Taipei, Taiwan, Republic of China. Ed. J. Fan. illus. circ. 2,000.

625.1   AU
TECHNISCHE UNIVERSITAET WIEN. INSTITUT FUER EISENBAHNWESEN, SPEZIALBAHNEN UND VERKEHRSWIRTSCHAFT. ARBEITEN. 1971. biennial. ‡ Technische Universitaet Wien, Institut fuer Eisenbahnwesen, Spezialbahnen und Verkehrswirtschaft, Karlsplatz 13, A-1040 Vienna, Austria. Edwin Engel.

385.1   FR   ISSN 0579-8256
THROUGH EUROPE BY TRAIN. 1951. irreg. free. International Union of Railways, 14 rue Jean Rey, 75015 Paris, France.

385.1   NO
TRANSPORTOEKONOMISK INSTITUTT. AARSBERETNING. 1965. a. free. Transportoekonomisk Institutt - Institute of Transport Economics, Grenseveien 86, Oslo 6, Norway. Ed. Tore Thjoemoee.
    Formerly: Norges Teknisk-Naturvitenskapelige Forskningsraad. Transportoekonomisk Institutt. Aarsberetning (ISSN 0078-124X)

385   US   ISSN 0163-4674
U.S. FEDERAL RAILROAD ADMINISTRATION. OFFICE OF SAFETY. ACCIDENT/INCIDENT BULLETIN. no. 144, 1975. a. U.S. Federal Railroad Administration, Office of Safety, Washington, DC 20590. Key Title: Accident/Incident Bulletin.
    Formerly: U.S. Federal Railroad Administration. Office of Safety. Accident Bulletin (ISSN 0092-1645)

625.1   UR
VSESOYUZNYI NAUCHNO-ISSLEDOVATEL'SKII INSTITUT VAGONOSTROENIYA. TRUDY. irreg. 1.10 Rub. Vsesoyuznyi Nauchno-issledovatel'skii Institut Vagonostroeniya, Moscow, U. S. S. R. illus.

380.3   CS
VYZKUMNY USTAV SPOJU. SBORNIK PRACI. (Text in Czech; summaries in English, French, German, Russian) 1974. 2-3/yr. 10 Kcs. per no. Nakladatelstvi Dopravy a Spoju, Hybernska 5, 115 78 Prague 1, Czechoslovakia (Subscr. to: Artia, Ve Smeckach 30, 111 27 Prague 1) Ed. Miroslav Joachim. charts illus.

385   CN   ISSN 0085-8188
WESTERN CANADIAN STEAM LOCOMOTIVE DIRECTORY. 1969. biennial. $1. Richard L. Coulton, Ed. & Pub., Bentley, Alberta, T0C 0J0, Canada. circ. 100.

385   US   ISSN 0084-3997
YEARBOOK OF RAILROAD FACTS. 1965. a. free. ‡ Association of American Railroads, Economics and Finance Department, 1920 L. St., N.W., Washington, DC 20036. circ. 40,000(approx.)

TRANSPORTATION — Roads And Traffic

see also Engineering — Civil Engineering

624   US   ISSN 0360-6996
A R T B A OFFICIALS AND ENGINEERS DIRECTORY, TRANSPORTATION AGENCY PERSONNEL. a. price varies. American Road and Transportation Builders Association, A R T B a Bldg., 525 School St., S.W., Washington, DC 20024.

388   CR   ISSN 0525-8693
ACCIDENTES DE TRANSITO EN COSTA RICA. 1952. irreg., latest 1977. exchange basis. Direccion General de Estadistica y Censos, Apartado 10163, San Jose, Costa Rica. stat.

625.7   CN   ISSN 0065-5988
ALBERTA RESEARCH COUNCIL. HIGHWAY RESEARCH. 1962. irreg. price varies. Alberta Research Council, 11315 87th Ave., Edmonton, Alberta T6G 2C2, Canada.

388.312   US
AMERICAN ASSOCIATION OF STATE HIGHWAY AND TRANSPORTATION OFFICIALS. PROCEEDINGS. a. $10. American Association of State Highway and Transportation Officials, 444 N. Capitol St. N.W., Suite 225, Washington, DC 20001.

AMERICAN ASSOCIATION OF STATE HIGHWAY AND TRANSPORTATION OFFICIALS. SUB-COMMITTEE ON COMPUTER TECHNOLOGY. PROCEEDINGS. NATIONAL CONFERENCE. see *COMPUTER TECHNOLOGY AND APPLICATIONS*

388.1   US
ASSOCIATION OF HIGHWAY OFFICIALS OF THE NORTH ATLANTIC STATES. PROCEEDINGS. a. price varies. Association of Highway Officials of the North Atlantic States, 1035 Parkway Ave., Trenton, NJ 08618.

388   AT   ISSN 0067-1185
AUSTRALIA. BUREAU OF STATISTICS. VICTORIAN OFFICE. ROAD TRAFFIC ACCIDENTS INVOLVING CASUALTIES. 1952. q. and a. free. Australian Bureau of Statistics, Victorian Office, Box 2796Y, G.P.O. Melbourne, Victoria 3001, Australia.

388   625.7   AT   ISSN 0572-1431
AUSTRALIAN ROAD RESEARCH BOARD. PROCEEDINGS. 1962. biennial. Australian Road Research Board, 156 (Bag 4), Nunawading, Vic. 3131, Australia.

BICYCLE RESOURCE GUIDE. see *SPORTS AND GAMES — Abstracting, Bibliographies, Statistics*

388   BO
BOLIVIA. SERVICIO NACIONAL DE CAMINOS. INFORME ANUAL.* 1956. a. Servicio Nacional de Caminos, Av. 20 de Octubre No.311, Casilla No. 1485, La Paz, Bolivia. circ. controlled.

388   BL
BRASILIA. DEPARTAMENTO DE ESTRADOS DE RODAGEM DO DISTRITO FEDERAL. DIRETORIA GERAL. RELATORIA ANUAL. a. Departamento de Estrados de Rodagem do Distrito Federal, Diretoria Geral, Secretaria de Viacao e Obras, Brasilia, Brazil.

388.1   FR
CAISSE NATIONALE DES AUTOROUTES. RAPPORT ANNUEL. a. Caisse Nationale des Autoroutes, 56 rue de Lille, 75007 Paris, France. illus.

625.7   US   ISSN 0068-5887
CALIFORNIA TRANSPORTATION AND PUBLIC WORKS CONFERENCE. PROCEEDINGS. 1949. a. price varies. University of California, Berkeley, Institute of Transportation Studies, 108 McLaughlin Hall, Berkeley, CA 94720. Ed. Wolfgang S. Homburger. index.cum.index: vols. 1-10.
    Formerly: California Street and Highway Conference. Proceedings.

388.314   CN   ISSN 0702-8733
CANADIAN HIGHWAY CARRIERS GUIDE. 1972. a. Can.$22. Southam Communications Ltd., 450 Don Mills Rd., Don Mills, Ont. M3B 2X7, Canada. Ed. Douglas Seip. adv.

388   UN
CENSUS OF MOTOR TRAFFIC ON MAIN INTERNATIONAL TRAFFIC ARTERIES. (Text in English and French) a. United Nations Economic Commission for Europe, Palais des Nations, 1200 Geneva 10, Switzerland (Or United Nations Publications, Room LX-2300, New York, NY 10017)
    Formerly: Census of Traffic on Main International Traffic Arteries (ISSN 0566-7631)

388.312   US   ISSN 0069-6013
COLORADO. DEPARTMENT OF HIGHWAYS. TRAFFIC VOLUME STUDY. Cover title: Colorado Traffic Volume Study. 1952. biennial. $5. Department of Highways, 4201 East Arkansas, Denver, CO 80222.

388.312   US   ISSN 0413-7647
COLORADO'S ANNUAL HIGHWAY REPORT. a. Department of Highways, 4201 E. Arkansas Ave., Denver, CO 80222.

388.1   II
COMMERCE YEARBOOK OF ROAD TRANSPORT. (Text in English) a. Rs.35. Commerce Publications Limited, Manek Mahal, 90 Veer Nariman Rd., Churchgate, Bombay 400020, India.

625.7   US
CONSTRUCTION DIRECTORY; a directory and catalog of highway and heavy construction in New England. 1948. a. $3. Construction Industries of Massachusetts, Inc., 20 Kilby St, Boston, MA 02109. Ed. Herbert Resnick.
    Formerly: New England Road Builders Association. N E R B A Annual Directory (ISSN 0077-8281)

388.1   CR
COSTA RICA. MINISTERIO DE OBRAS PUBLICAS Y TRANSPORTES. MEMORIAS. irreg. Ministerio de Obras Publicas y Transportes, San Jose, Costa Rica.
    Continues: Costa Rica. Ministerio de Transportes. Memoria (ISSN 0589-8617)

388   US   ISSN 0070-329X
DELAWARE. DEPARTMENT OF HIGHWAYS AND TRANSPORTATION. TRAFFIC SUMMARY. 1957. a. $5. Department of Transportation, P. O. Box 778, Dover, DE 19901. Ed. John J. Kirwan. circ. 300-500.

388.1   US   ISSN 0147-6939
FATAL ACCIDENT REPORTING SYSTEM; ANNUAL REPORT. 1975. a. U.S. National Highway Traffic Safety Administration, National Center for Statistics and Analysis, Washington, DC 20590 (Orders to: Supt. of Documents, Washington, DC 20402) circ. 4,000. (also avail. in microfiche)

338.31   GW   ISSN 0171-1547
FORSCHUNG STADTVERKEHR: SONDERREIHE/URBAN TRANSPORT RESEARCH: SPECIAL SERIES. (Text in English and German) 1973. irreg., no. 8, 1979. price varies. (Bundesministerium fuer Verkehr) Kirschbaum Verlag, Siegfriedstr. 28, Postfach 210209, 5300 Bonn 2, W. Germany (B.R.D.) circ. 3,000.

388   GW
GERMANY (FEDERAL REPUBLIC), BUNDESMINISTERIUM FUER VERKEHR. STRASSENBAUBERICHT. irreg. Bundesministerium fuer Verkehr, 5300 Bonn, W. Germany (B.R.D.) illus.

TRANSPORTATION — ROADS AND TRAFFIC

388.1 UK
GREAT BRITAIN. DEPARTMENT OF TRANSPORT. ROADS IN ENGLAND. (Issued in the series of Reports and papers of the House of Commons. Report Year Ends Mar. 31) a. price varies. Department of Transport, 2 Marsham St., London SW1P 3EB, England (Avail. from H.M.S.O., c/o Liaison Officer, Atlantic House, Holborn Viaduct, London EC1P 1BN, England) illus.

HIGHWAY RESEARCH RECORD; general report on road research work done in India during (year).
see *ENGINEERING — Civil Engineering*

388.1 II
I R C SPECIAL PUBLICATION. no. 13, 1973. irreg. Rs.15. Indian Roads Congress, Jamnagar House, Shahjahan Rd., New Delhi 110011, India. bibl. charts.

388 II ISSN 0376-4788
INDIAN ROADS CONGRESS. HIGHWAY RESEARCH BOARD BULLETIN. (Text in English) s-a. Rs.5 per. no. Indian Roads Congress, Jamnagar House, Shahjahan Rd., New Delhi 110011, India. Ed. P. C. Bhasin. circ. 5,000.
Supersedes (1975): Indian Roads Congress. Road Research Bulletin (ISSN 0073-6643)

388.1 625.7 FR ISSN 0074-7815
INTERNATIONAL ROAD CONGRESSES. PROCEEDINGS. (Editions Available in English and French) quadrennial since 1964; 1975, 15th, Mexico. Permanent International Association of Road Congresses, 43 Ave. du President Wilson, 75116 Paris, France.
Roads and streets

625.7 JA ISSN 0075-3319
JAPAN ROAD ASSOCIATION. ANNUAL REPORT OF ROADS. (Text in English; summaries in French) 1961. a. free. Japan Road Association - Nihon Doro Kyokai, Shoyukaikan, 3-3-3 Kasumigaseki, Chiyoda-ku, Tokyo 100, Japan.

388.1 AU ISSN 0075-7306
KURATORIUM FUER VERKEHRSSICHERHEIT. KLEINE FACHBUCHREIHE. (Text in German; summaries in English and French) 1959. irreg., no. 15, 1979. price varies. ‡ Kuratorium fuer Verkehrssicherheit, Oelzeltgasse 3, A-1030 Vienna, Austria. Ed. K. J. Hoefner. cum. index: 1959-1971. Indexed: Psychol.Abstr. Hwy.Res.Abstr. Psychopharmacol.Abstr.

388.3 US ISSN 0094-6265
MARYLAND. STATE HIGHWAY ADMINISTRATION. TRAFFIC TRENDS. irreg. free. State Highway Administration, Box 717, 300 W. Preston St., Baltimore, MD 21203. stat. Key Title: Traffic Trends.

388 US
MISSOURI. DIVISION OF HIGHWAY SAFETY. HIGHWAY SAFETY PLAN. 1971. a. ‡ Division of Highway Safety, 2634 Industrial Drive, Jefferson City, MO 65101. Ed. R.N. Echols. circ. controlled.
Former titles: Missouri's Annual Highway Safety Program; Missouri Annual Highway Safety Work Program (ISSN 0091-1097)

388.1 AT
NATIONAL ASSOCIATION OF AUSTRALIAN STATE ROAD AUTHORITIES. GUIDE TO THE ACTIVITIES, PUBLICATIONS AND STANDARDS OF N A A S R A. a. free. National Association of Australian State Road Authorities, Box J 141, Brickfield Hill, Sydney, N.S.W. 2000, Australia.
Formerly: National Association of Australian State Road Authorities. Guide to the Publications and Policies of N A A S R A.

625.7 388.31 US ISSN 0077-5614
NATIONAL COOPERATIVE HIGHWAY RESEARCH PROGRAM REPORTS. 1964. irreg. price varies. National Research Council, Transportation Research Board, 2101 Constitution Ave., Washington, DC 20418. circ. 2,500-4,000.
Roads and streets

625.7 US ISSN 0547-5570
NATIONAL COOPERATIVE HIGHWAY RESEARCH PROGRAM SYNTHESIS OF HIGHWAY PRACTICE. 1969. irreg. price varies. National Research Council, Transportation Research Board, 2101 Constitution Ave. N.W., Washington, DC 20418.

388.1 SA
NATIONAL INSTITUTE FOR TRANSPORT AND ROAD RESEARCH. BULLETINS. Alternative title: C S I R Research Reports. (Text in Afrikaans and English) 1956. irreg., no. 17, 1980. National Institute for Transport and Road Research - Nasionale Instituut vir Vervoer- en Padnavorsing, Box 395, Pretoria 0001, South Africa.

388.1 SA
NATIONAL INSTITUTE FOR TRANSPORT AND ROAD RESEARCH. P A D SERIES. Alternate title: C S I R Special Reports. irreg., PAD 42, 1979. National Institute for Transport and Road Research - Nasionale Instituut vir Vervoer- en Padnavorsing, Box 395, Pretoria 0001, South Africa.

625 SA
NATIONAL INSTITUTE FOR TRANSPORT AND ROAD RESEARCH. TECHNICAL METHODS FOR HIGHWAYS/NASIONALE INSTITUUT VIR VERVOER- EN PADNAVORSING. TEGNIESE METODES VIR HOOTWEE. 1978. irreg., TMH 4, 1978. price varies. National Institute for Transport and Road Research, Box 395, Pretoria 0001, South Africa.

388.312 SA
NATIONAL INSTITUTE FOR TRANSPORT AND ROAD RESEARCH. TECHNICAL RECOMMENDATIONS FOR HIGHWAYS/ NASIONALE INSTITUUT VIR VERVOER- EN PADNAVORSING. TEGNIESE RIGLYNE VIR HOOFWEE. 1970. irreg. National Institute for Transport and Road Research, Box 395, Pretoria 0001, South Africa.

388.1 SA
NATIONAL INSTITUTE FOR TRANSPORT AND ROAD RESEARCH. TECHNICAL REPORT/ NASIONALE INSTITUUT VIR VERVOER- EN PADNAVORSING. TEGNIESE VERSLAG. irreg. National Institute for Transport and Road Research, Box 395, Pretoria 0001, South Africa.

625 001.642 SA
NATIONAL INSTITUTE FOR TRANSPORT AND ROAD RESEARCH. USER MANUALS FOR COMPUTER PROGRAMS/NASIONALE INSTITUUT VIR VERVOER- EN PADNAVORSING. GEBRUIKERSHANDBOEKE VIR REKENAARPROGRAMME. 1976. irreg., P 6, 1980. National Institute for Transport and Road Research, Computer Information Centre for Transportation, Box 395, Pretoria 0001, South Africa.

388.1 US
NEBRASKA. DEPARTMENT OF ROADS. HIGHWAY STATISTICS: STATE AND LOCAL ROAD AND STREET DATA FOR (YEAR) a. Department of Roads, Highway Statistical Unit, Lincoln, NE 68508. illus.
Formerly: Nebraska Highway Statistics: State and Local Construction Mileage (ISSN 0099-0442)

388 US ISSN 0091-844X
NEBRASKA. DEPARTMENT OF ROADS. TRAFFIC ANALYSIS UNIT. CONTINUOUS TRAFFIC COUNT DATA AND TRAFFIC CHARACTERISTICS ON NEBRASKA STREETS AND HIGHWAYS. 1968. a. Department of Roads, Planning Division, P.O. Box 94759, Lincoln, NE 68509. circ. controlled.

388.1 NE ISSN 0077-748X
NETHERLANDS. CENTRAAL BUREAU VOOR DE STATISTIEK. TOEPASSING DER WEGENVERKEERSWET. STATISTICS OF THE APPLICATION OF THE ROAD TRAFFIC ACT. (Text in Dutch and English) 1951-52. irreg. fl.6. Centraal Bureau voor de Statistiek, Prinses Beatrixlaan 428, Voorburg, Netherlands (Orders to: Staatsuitgeverij, Christoffel Plantijnstraat, The Hague, Netherlands)

388 US
NEVADA. DEPARTMENT OF TRANSPORTATION. PLANNING DIVISION. STATUS OF ROAD SYSTEMS. 1960. a. free. ‡ Department of Transportation, 1263 S. Stewart St., Carson City, NV 89712. cum.index: (1960-70) circ. 100.
Formerly: Nevada. Department of Highways. Planning Survey Division. Status of Road Systems (ISSN 0077-7870)

388.1 NZ ISSN 0549-0030
NEW ZEALAND. ROAD RESEARCH UNIT. BULLETIN. 1965. irreg. NZ.$2. Road Research Unit, Wellington, New Zealand. bk. rev. charts. illus. circ. 800.

338.3 US
NORTH CAROLINA. DEPARTMENT OF TRANSPORTATION. OFFICE OF HIGHWAY SAFETY. SUMMARY OF ACTIVITIES. a. free. Department of Transportation, Office of Highway Safety, Raleigh, NC 27600. illus. stat.
Formerly: North Carolina Governor's Highway Safety Program. Summary of Activities (ISSN 0361-2295)

388 614 US
NORTH DAKOTA'S HIGHWAY SAFETY WORK PROGRAM. 1967. a. free to qualified personnel. ‡ Highway Department, Traffic Safety Programs Division, Capitol Grounds, Bismarck, ND 58505. circ. controlled. (looseleaf format)

388.1 US
OKLAHOMA. DEPARTMENT OF TRANSPORTATION. SUFFICIENCY RATING REPORT AND NEEDS STUDY: OKLAHOMA STATE TRANSPORTATION. 1966. biennial. free. Department of Transportation, Planning Division, 200 N.E. 21st., Oklahoma City, OK 73105. illus. circ. 200.
Formerly: Oklahoma. Department of Highways. Sufficiency Rating Report and Needs Study: Oklahoma State Highways (ISSN 0094-6230)

388.31 US
OKLAHOMA TURNPIKE AUTHORITY. ANNUAL REPORT TO THE GOVERNOR. 1954. a. free. Turnpike Authority, 3500 North Eastern, P.O. Box 11357, Oklahoma City, OK 73111. charts. stat. circ. 1,000 (approx.)

388 US
OREGON TRUCK ACCIDENTS. a. free. ‡ Department of Transportation, Motor Vehicles Division, Salem, OR 97310. circ. 250.

388.1 II
ORISSA STATE ROAD TRANSPORTATION CORPORATION. ANNUAL ADMINISTRATION REPORT. (Text in English) 1974-75. a. State Road Transportation Corporation, Cuttack 753001, India. stat.

388.1 US ISSN 0092-8941
PUERTO RICO HIGHWAY IMPROVEMENT PROGRAM. 1963. a. Wilbur Smith and Associates, 4500 Jackson Boulevard, Columbia, SC 29202. illus.

625.7 US ISSN 0079-8142
PURDUE UNIVERSITY. ROAD SCHOOL. PROCEEDINGS OF ANNUAL ROAD SCHOOL. (Subseries of: Engineering Bulletin. Engineering Extension Series) 1924. a. single copy free. Purdue University, School of Civil Engineering, West Lafayette, IN 47907. Ed. D. G. Shurig. circ. 2,500.

385.1 388 UK ISSN 0307-6822
ROAD ACCIDENTS IN GREAT BRITAIN. (Joint publication with Scottish Development Department and the Welsh Office) 1969. a. price varies. Department of the Environment, 2 Marsham St., London SW1P 3EB, England (Avail. from H.M.S.O., c/o Liaison Officer, Atlantic House, Holborn Viaduct, London EC1P 1BN, England)

388 625.7 UK ISSN 0080-3294
ROAD NOTES. irreg. price varies. Transport and Road Research Laboratory, Old Wokingham Rd., Crowthorne, Berks. RG7 6AU, England (Avail. from H.M.S.O., Atlantic House, Holborn Viaduct, London EC1P 1BN, England)

614.8 SA ISSN 0035-7391
ROBOT. (Text in Afrikaans & English) 1962. irreg. free. ‡ National Road Safety Council, Rondalia Building, Visagie St., Private Bag X147, Pretoria, South Africa. Ed. T. Botha. bk. rev. illus. stat. circ. 50,000

388.3 CN
SASKATCHEWAN. GOVERNMENT INSURANCE OFFICE. PROVINCE OF SASKATCHEWAN MOTOR VEHICLE TRAFFIC ACCIDENTS. ANNUAL REPORT. a. Government Insurance Office, Regina, Saskatchewan, Canada.

614.8 US ISSN 0361-3461
SOUTH DAKOTA HIGHWAY SAFETY WORK PROGRAM. irreg. $2.03. Division of Highway Safety, Pierre, SD 57501.

614.8 US
STATE OF MICHIGAN'S ANNUAL HIGHWAY SAFETY PLAN. 1968. a. free. Office of Highway Safety Planning, 7150 Harris Dr., Lansing, MI 48913. illus, stat. circ. 50.
Formerly (until 1978): Michigan. Office of Highway Safety Planning. Annual Highway Safety Work Plan. (ISSN 0094-1069)

338.1 SW ISSN 0347-6030
SWEDEN. STATENS VAEG- OCH TRAFIKINSTITUT. RAPPORT. (Text in Swedish and English; summaries in English) 1971. irreg. (10-15/yr.) free. Statens Vaeg- och Trafikinstitut, Fack, S-581 01 Linkoeping, Sweden. circ. 300-500. (processed)

354.485 SW ISSN 0347-6057
SWEDEN. STATENS VAEG- OCH TRAFIKINSTITUT. VERKSAMHETSBERAETTELSE. English edition: Sweden. National Road and Traffic Research Institute. Annual Report. a. Statens Vaeg- och Trafikinstitut, Fack, 581 01 Linkoeping, Sweden.

388.314 333.77 DK
TECHNICAL UNIVERSITY OF DENMARK. INSTITUTE OF ROADS, TRANSPORT AND TOWN PLANNING. REPORT. irreg., no. 19, 1978. Polytekniske Laereanstalt, Danmarks Tekniske Hoejskole, Instituttet for Vejbygning, Trafikteknik og Byplanlaegning, Bygning 115, DK-2800 Lyngby, Denmark.

353.9 US ISSN 0095-1994
TENNESSEE. DEPARTMENT OF SAFETY. ANNUAL REPORT. a. free to qualified personnel. Department of Safety, Andrew Jackson State Office Bldg., Nashville, TN 37219. Key Title: Annual Report - Department of Safety.

388.31 AU ISSN 0300-1997
TIROLER VERKEHRSWIRTSCHAFTLICHE ZAHLEN. 1972. a. S.100($5) ‡ Institut fuer Verkehr und Tourismus, Wilhelm-Greil-Str. 14, A-6010 Innsbruck, Austria. Eds. Dr. Helmut Lamprecht, Klaus Wergles. stat. circ. 300.

388 US ISSN 0082-5859
TRAFFIC LAWS COMMENTARY. 1963. irreg., latest 1976. price varies. National Committee on Uniform Traffic Laws and Ordinances, 1776 Massachusetts Avenue, N.W., Washington, DC 20036 (Orders to: Supt. of Documents, U.S. Government Printing Office, Washington, DC 20402)

388.1 US
TRAFFIC SAFETY; a report on activities under the Highway Safety Act of 1966. 1966. a. U.S. National Highway Traffic Safety Administration, 400 Seventh St. N.W., Washington, DC 20590. (Prepared with: U.S. Federal Highway Administration)

388.1 SA ISSN 0379-4792
TRANSPORT AND ROAD DIGEST/VERVOER-EN PADOORSIGTE. 1977. irreg., no. 20, 1980. National Institute for Transport and Road Research - Nasionale Instituut vir Vervoer- en Padnavorsing Suid-Afrika, Box 395, Pretoria 0001, South Africa. Ed. B. M. Davies. circ. 3,000.

388 625.7 UK
TRANSPORT AND ROAD RESEARCH. 1955. a. price varies. Transport and Road Research Laboratory, Old Wokingham Rd., Crowthorne, Berks. RG7 6AU, England (Avail. from H.M.S.O., Atlantic House, Holborn Viaduct, London EC1P 1BN, England)
Formerly: Road Research (ISSN 0080-3308)

388.1 UK
TRANSPORT STATISTICS GREAT BRITAIN. (Joint publication with the Scottish Development Department and Welsh Office) 1976. a. price varies. ‡ Department of Transport, 2 Marsham St., London SW1P 3EB, England (Avail. from H.M.S.O., c/o Liaison Officer, Atlantic House, Holborn Viaduct, London EC1P 1BN, England) circ. 2,000.
Incorporating: Great Britain. Department of the Environment. Highway Statistics & Passenger Transport in Great Britain (ISSN 0079-0133)

625.7 388 US ISSN 0360-859X
TRANSPORTATION RESEARCH BOARD SPECIAL REPORT. 1952. irreg. price varies. National Research Council, Transportation Research Board, 2101 Constitution Ave, Washington, DC 20418. circ. 2,500-4,000.
Until no. 144, 1974: Highway Research Board Special Publication (ISSN 0077-5622)

625.7 388 US ISSN 0361-1981
TRANSPORTATION RESEARCH RECORD. 1963. irreg. price varies. National Research Council, Transportation Research Board, 2101 Constitution Ave. N. W., Washington, DC 20418. circ. 2,500-4,000. Indexed: Ocean.Abstr. Pollut.Abstr.
Formerly until 1974: Highway Research Record (ISSN 0073-2206)

388 CN ISSN 0581-8079
TRAVEL ON SASKATCHEWAN HIGHWAYS. a. free. Department of Highways and Transportation, Planning Branch, 1855 Victoria Ave., Regina, Sask. S4P 3V5, Canada.

385.1 US ISSN 0082-6359
TRI-STATE TRANSPORTATION COMMISSION. PUBLIC TRANSPORT SERVICES TO NON C/B/D EMPLOYMENT CONCENTRATIONS; PROGRESS REPORT. 1967. irreg. ‡ Tri-State Transportation Commission, One World Trade Center, New York, NY 10048. circ. 30,000.

388.3 US ISSN 0098-3209
U. S. DEPARTMENT OF TRANSPORTATION. ANNUAL REPORT ON HIGHWAY SAFETY IMPROVEMENT PROGRAMS. 1974. a. U. S. Department of Transportation, 400 Seventh St. N.W., Washington, DC 20590 (Order from: Supt. of Documents, Washington DC 20402) stat. Key Title: Annual Report on Highway Safety Improvement Programs.

625.7 US ISSN 0361-4204
U.S. FEDERAL HIGHWAY ADMINISTRATION. FEDERALLY COORDINATED PROGRAM OF HIGHWAY RESEARCH AND DEVELOPMENT. 1975. a. U.S. Federal Highway Administration, Dept. of Transportation, Washington, DC 20591 (Orders to: Supt. Doc., Washingto, D.C. 20402) illus. Key Title: Federally Coordinated Program of Highway Research and Development.
Continues: U.S. Federal Highway Administration. Research and Development Program.

388.3 US
U.S. FEDERAL HIGHWAY ADMINISTRATION. HIGHWAY STATISTICS. 1945. a. $5-10. U.S. Federal Highway Administration, Highway Statistics Division, Washington, DC 20590 (Orders to: Supt. of Documents, U.S. Government Printing Office, Washington, DC 20402) Ed. A. French.

388.3 US ISSN 0361-5332
UTAH. DEPARTMENT OF TRANSPORTATION. HIGHWAY SAFETY PROGRAM, ANNUAL REPORT. 1975. a. Department of Transportation, Salt Lake City, UT 84100. stat. Key Title: Highway Safety Program, Annual Report.

388 310 GW ISSN 0083-5021
V W Z. (Verkehrswirtschaftliche Zahlen) 1954. a. free. Bundesverband des Deutschen Gueterfernverkehrs e.V., Haus des Strassenverkehrs, Postfach 930 260, D-6000 Frankfurt-93, W. Germany (B.R.D.) Ed. P. Kaumanns. circ. 6,000.

388.31 AU ISSN 0042-4048
VERKEHRSPSYCHOLOGISCHER INFORMATIONSDIENST. 1962. irreg. (2-3/yr.) free. Kuratorium fuer Verkehrssicherheit, Verkehrspsychologisches Institut, Oelzeltgasse 3, A-1031 Vienna, Austria. Ed. K. Hoefner. circ. 2,500.

388.1 625.7 US
VIRGINIA HIGHWAY AND TRANSPORTATION CONFERENCE. PROCEEDINGS. 1947. a. Department of Highways and Transportation, 1401 E. Broad St., Richmond, VA 23219. (Co-sponsor: Virginia Military Institute) cum.index: 1947-69(except 1968) circ. 750.
Formerly: Virginia Highway Conference. Procceedings (ISSN 0083-6370)

388 AT ISSN 0310-6330
WESTERN AUSTRALIA. MAIN ROADS DEPARTMENT. TECHNICAL REPORT. 1973. irreg. Main Roads Department, Waterloo Crescent, East Perth, W.A. 6000, Australia.

388 US ISSN 0084-0572
WISCONSIN. DEPARTMENT OF TRANSPORTATION. DIVISION OF PLANNING AND BUDGET. HIGHWAY MILEAGE DATA. (Former name of issuing body: Division of Planning) 1946. a. $5. Department of Transportation, Division of Planning, Box 7913, 4802 Sheboygan Ave., Madison, WI 53702. circ. 200.

388 US ISSN 0084-0580
WISCONSIN. DEPARTMENT OF TRANSPORTATION. DIVISION OF PLANNING. HIGHWAY TRAFFIC. Short title: Wisconsin Highway Traffic. 1968. a. $8. Department of Transportation, Transportation Network Statistics Section, 4802 Sheboygan Ave., Box 7913, Madison, WI 53707. circ. 300.
Formerly: Wisconsin. Division of Highways. System Planning Section. Highway Traffic in Wisconsin Cities (ISSN 0512-0624)

388.3 US ISSN 0098-5082
WISCONSIN. DIVISION OF HIGHWAY SAFETY COORDINATION. HIGHWAY SAFETY REPORT TO THE LEGISLATURE. a. Division of Highway Safety Coordination, Office of the Governor, Room 1121 - State Office Building, 1 W. Wilson St., Madison, WI 53702. Key Title: Highway Safety Report to the Legislature.

WISCONSIN ACCIDENT FACTS. see *PUBLIC HEALTH AND SAFETY*

388 US
WISCONSIN TRAFFIC DATA - AUTOMATIC TRAFFIC RECORDER; monthly average daily traffic. Short title: Wisconsin Traffic Data - A T R. 1970. a. $13.95. Department of Transportation, Transportation Network Statistics Section, 4802 Sheboygan Ave., Box 7913, Madison, WI 53707. circ. 125.
Former titles: Wisconsin. Department of Transportation. Automatic Traffic Recorder Data; Wisconsin. Department of Transportaion. Traffic Planning Section. Automatic Recorder Station Traffic Data (ISSN 0091-6080)

353.9 US ISSN 0098-5058
WYOMING. GOVERNOR'S OFFICE OF HIGHWAY SAFETY. ANNUAL REPORT. a. free. Governor's Office of Highway Safety, Cheyenne, WY 82001. Key Title: Annual Report of the Wyoming Governor's Office of Highway Safety.

TRANSPORTATION — Ships And Shipping

387 BE
ACADEMIE DE MARINE. COMMUNICATIONS/MARINE ACADEMIE. MEDEDELINGEN. (Text in Dutch and French; summaries in English and French) 1936/37. irreg. (approx. a) 630 Fr. Uitgeverij de Sikkel N.V., Nijverheidsstraat 8, 2150 Malle, Belgium. Ed. Walter Debrock. bibl. illus.

387 IT
AGENDA NAUTICA. a. Istituto Idrografico della Marina, Piazza Osservatorio, 16126 Genova, Italy.

TRANSPORTATION — SHIPS AND SHIPPING

387 US
AMERICAN BUREAU OF SHIPPING. RECORD. 1869. a. with m. supplements. $235. American Bureau of Shipping, 65 Broadway, New York, NY 10006.

387.1 US ISSN 0091-5491
AMERICAN MARINE REGISTER. a. with q. supplements. $100. Box 5468, North Little Rock, AR 72119. illus.

387 US ISSN 0065-9207
AMERICAN MARITIME LIBRARY. 1970. irreg. (Mystic Seaport, Inc.) Wesleyan University Press, 55 High St., Middletown, CT 06457.

387.5 US
AMERICAN MERCHANT MARINE CONFERENCE. PROCEEDINGS. 1935. a. $6.25. ‡ Propeller Club of the United States, 1730 M St., N.W., Suite 413, Washington, DC 20036. Ed. Jasper S. Baker. circ. 2,500 (controlled)

385.77 US
ANALYSIS OF WORLD TANK SHIP FLEET. 1942. a. $10. Sun Oil Company, Economics and Industry Affairs, 240 Radnor-Chester Road, St. Davids, PA 19087. circ. 1,000.

623.82 US ISSN 0097-8442
ANCIENT INTERFACE. Represents: A I A A Symposium on the Aero/Hydronautics of Sailing. Proceedings. (Subseries of: American Institute of Aeronautics and Astronautics, Los Angeles Section. Monographs) 1970. a. Western Periodicals Co., 13000 Raymer St., North Hollywood, CA 91605. illus.

387 FR ISSN 0066-2550
ANNUAIRE DE LA MARINE MARCHANDE. 1904. a. 115 F. Comite Central des Armateurs de France, 73 Bld. Haussmann, 75008 Paris, France. adv. circ. 650.

387 FR ISSN 0180-9962
ANNUAIRE DES MAREES POUR L'AN, TOME 2. PORTS D'OUTRE MER. 1958. a. price varies. Service Hydrographique et Oceanographique de la Marine, 3 Ave. Octave Greard, 75200 Paris Naval, France (Subscr. address: E.P.S.H.O.M., B.P. 426, 29275 Brest Cedex, France)

ANNUAIRE MARITIME. see *LAW*

623.82 JA ISSN 0448-3294
ANNUAL STATISTICS OF MARITIME SAFETY. (Text in Japanese) 1950. a. Maritime Safety Agency - Kaijo Hoancho, 2-1-3 Kasumigaseki, Chiyoda-ku, Tokyo 100, Japan. stat.

623.89 AT
ANNUAL SUMMARY OF AUSTRALIAN NOTICES TO MARINERS. a. free. Department of the Navy, Hydrographic Service, Sydney, Australia. illus. index.
Navigation

387 620 UK
ANNUAL SUMMARY OF MERCHANT SHIPS LAUNCHED/COMPLETED IN THE WORLD. 1892. a (plus quarterly reports) £5. Lloyd's Register of Shipping, 71 Fenchurch St., London EC3M 4BS, England. Ed. J. P. Cashman.
Formerly: Annual Summary of Merchant Ships Launched in the World (ISSN 0066-4391)

386 BL
ANUARIO DE PORTOS E NAVIOS. a. Cr.$350. Revista Tecnica e Informativa Ltda, Rua Leandro Martins 10, Caixa Postal 2791, Rio de Janeiro, Brazil. Ed. Brasilio Accioly. adv. charts. stat.

387 UK
ARAB MARITIME DATA. 1978. a. £32.50($65) Benn Publications Ltd., 25 New Street Square, London EC4A 3JA, England. Ed. John D. Hewitt. charts. stat. tr.lit. index.

387 623.8 629.1 FR ISSN 0066-9814
ASSOCIATION TECHNIQUE MARITIME ET AERONAUTIQUE, PARIS. BULLETIN. (Text in French; Summaries in English and French) 1890. a. 310 F. to non-members. Association Technique Maritime et Aeronautique, 47, rue de Monceau, 75008 Paris, France. index. (back issues available) Indexed: Appl.Mech.Rev.

623.8 387 AT
AUSTRALIAN SHIPPING AND SHIPBUILDING. 1947. a. price varies. Australian Government Publishing Service, P.O. Box 84, Canberra, A.C.T. 2600, Australia.

387.5 BG
BANGLADESH SHIPPING DIRECTORY. (Text in English) a. Tk.46. Bangladesh Ocean Publications, Box 316, 1314/A Bangabandhu Rd., Chittagong, Bangladesh. illus.

387 SP
BARCELONA PORT; guia de servicios del puerto de Barcelona. 1978. a. 400 ptas.($10) Publicaciones Men - Car, Paseo de Colon 24, Barcelona, Spain. Eds. Juan y Manuel Cardona. adv. circ. 10,000.
Formerly: Port(Year)

387 II
BASIC PORT STATISTICS OF INDIA. 1970. a., latest edition in print 1976/1977. $27.54. Ministry of Shipping and Transport, Transport Research Division, I D A Bldg., Jamnagar House, Shahjahan Rd., New Delhi 110011, India (Orders to: Controller of Publications, Civil Lines, Delhi 110006, India)
Former titles: Port Transport Statistics of India; India Ports and Shipping Statistics.

387 BE
BELGIUM. ADMINISTRATION DE LA MARINE ET DE LA NAVIGATION INTERIEURE. RAPPORT ANNUEL SUR L'EVOLUTION DE LA FLOTTE DE PECHE. a. Administration de la Marine et de la Navigation Interieure, 30 rue Belliard, 1040 Brussels, Belgium.
Continues: Belgium. Administration de la Marine. Rapport Annuel sur l'Evolution de la Flotte de Peche.

623.89 PL ISSN 0067-7728
BIBLIOTEKA NAWIGATORA. 1972. irreg. 25 Zl. Wyzsza Szkola Morska w Gdyni - Merchant Marine Academy, Czerwonych Kosynierow 83, 81-225 Gdynia, Poland (Dist. by Ars Polona-Ruch, Krakowskie Przedmiescie 7, Warsaw, Poland) bk. rev. circ. 500.

387 UK ISSN 0142-2553
BRITISH SHIPPING REVIEW. a. General Council of British Shipping, 30-32 St. Mary Axe, London EC3A 8ET, England.

387 UK ISSN 0068-2659
BRITISH TRANSPORT DOCKS BOARD. ANNUAL REPORT AND ACCOUNTS. 1963. a. free. British Transport Docks Board, Melbury House, Melbury Terrace, London N.W.1., England.

386 UK ISSN 0068-2683
BRITISH WATERWAYS BOARD. ANNUAL REPORT AND ACCOUNTS. 1963. a. price varies. British Waterways Board, Melbury House, Melbury Terrace, London NW1 6JX, England (Avail. from: H.M.S.O., c/o Liaison Officer, Atlantic House, London EC1P 1BW, England)

387.5 FR
BULLETIN OFFICIEL DE LA MARINE MARCHANDE. Imprimerie Nationale, Service des Ventes, 59128 Flers en Escrebieux, France.

BULLINGER'S POSTAL AND SHIPPERS GUIDE FOR THE UNITED STATES AND CANADA. see *COMMUNICATIONS — Postal Affairs*

387 BE
C M I YEAR BOOK. a. International Maritime Committee - Comite Maritime International, c/o Henry Voet-Genicot, Borzestraat 17, B-2000 Antwerp, Belgium.
Supersedes in part (since 1978): International Maritime Committee. Documentation (ISSN 0538-8643)

380.5 CN
CANADA. NATIONAL HARBOURS BOARD. PORT DIRECTORY. (Text in English and French) a. free. National Harbours Board, Ottawa, Ont. K1A 0N6, Canada.
Formerly: Canada. National Harbours Board. Annual Report (ISSN 0068-7928)

CANADIAN PORTS AND SEAWAYS DIRECTORY. see *TRANSPORTATION*

387 CN ISSN 0708-0727
CANADIAN SHIPPING PROJECT NEWSLETTER. 1976. a. free contr. circ. Memorial University of Newfoundland, Maritime History Group, St. John's, Nfld. A1C 5S7, Canada.

CANALS BOOK. see *TRAVEL AND TOURISM*

387 AG
CENTRO DE NAVEGACION TRANSATLANTICA. C.N.T. HANDBOOK. RIVER PLATE HANDBOOK FOR SHIPOWNERS AND AGENTS. Cover title: Centro de Navegacion Transatlantica. C.N.T. Year Book; Ship Owners' and Agents' Handbook, River Plate Ports. (Text in English) 1972. biennial. $30. ‡ Centro de Navegacion Transatlantica, 25 de Mayo 489, Buenos Aires, Argentina. Ed. Victor L. M. Fricker. adv. circ. 2,000.
Continues a similar publication issued 1933-1966 as: MAR Year Book.

387 CE
CEYLON SHIPPING CORPORATION. ANNUAL REPORT & STATEMENT OF ACCOUNTS. (Text in English) a. Ceylon Shipping Corporation, Box 1718, Colombo, Sri Lanka.

387 US
CHARTERING ANNUAL. 1953. a. $40. Maritime Research, Inc., 11 Broadway, New York, NY 10004. adv.

387 BG
CHITTAGONG PORT AUTHORITY. YEARBOOK. (Text in English) a. Chittagong Port Authority, Box 2013, Chittagong, Bangladesh.
Formerly: Chittagong Port Trust. Yearbook of Information (ISSN 0069-3723)

387 US
COAST MARINE AND TRANSPORTATION DIRECTORY. a. $12. Pacific Shipper, Inc., 1050 Sansome St., San Francisco, CA 94111.

387.5 FR ISSN 0069-5815
COLLOQUES INTERNATIONAUX D'HISTOIRE MARITIME. TRAVAUX.* 1957. irreg., 1967, 9th. price varies. Ecole Pratique des Hautes Etudes, 45-47 rue des Ecoles, Paris 5e, France.

387.5 UK
COMECON MERCHANT SHIPS ANNUAL. 1977. a. £6.95. Kenneth Mason Publications Ltd., 13-14 Homewell, Havant, Hants. PO9 1EF, England. Ed. Lord Greenway.

387 II
COMMERCE YEARBOOK OF PORTS, SHIPPING AND SHIPBUILDING. (Text in English) 1974. a. Rs.30. Commerce Publications Limited, Manek Mahal, 90 Veer Nariman Rd., Churchgate, Bombay 400020, India. Ed. Vadilal Dagli. illus. stat.
Continues: Commerce Yearbook of Shipping and Shipbuilding.

387.2 AT ISSN 0084-909X
COMPANY OF MASTER MARINERS OF AUSTRALIA. JOURNAL. 1936". a. Aus.$2($0.50) ea. Company of Master Mariners of Australia, Box 46, Williamstown, Vic. 3016, Australia.

623.82 FR
CONSTRUCTION NAUTIQUE FRANCAISE/ FRENCH BOATING EXPORT. (Text in English, French, Spanish) 1976. a. 35 F. Interval Editions, 3 rue Fortia, 13001 Marseille, France. illus.

354.44 623.8 FR
CONSTRUCTION NAVALE; rapport du conseil d'administration, assemblee generale ordinaire. irreg. free. Chambre Syndicale des Constructeurs de Navires et de Machines Marines, 47, rue de Monceau, 75008 Paris, France.

387.5 CY ISSN 0070-2439
CYPRUS. DEPARTMENT OF STATISTICS AND RESEARCH. SHIPPING STATISTICS. 1954. a. Mils.250($250) Department of Statistics and Research, Ministry of Finance, Nicosia, Cyprus.
Supersedes in part: Cyprus. Department of Statistics and Research. Shipping and Aviation Statistics; Which was formerly: Cyprus. Department of Statistics and Research. Statistics of Imports, Exports and Shipping.

TRANSPORTATION — SHIPS AND SHIPPING

387   BL
DADOS ESTATISTICOS DA MOVIMENTACAO DE CARGA E PASSAGEIROS. Cover title: Dados Estatisticos da Navegacao. a. Empresa de Navegacao de Amazonia, S.A., Setor de Processamento de Dados Estatisticos, Av. Presidente Vargas 41, Belem, Para, Brazil. stat.

387   GW   ISSN 0070-4148
DIE DEUTSCHE HANDELSFLOTTE. 1954. irreg. DM.385. Seehafen-Verlag Erik Blumenfeld, Celsiusweg 15, Postfach 1347, 2000 Hamburg 50, W. Germany (B.R.D.) adv.

387   GW   ISSN 0070-4377
DEUTSCHER KUESTEN-ALMANACH; ein Nachschlagewerk fuer die Berufs- und Sportschiffahrt in Nord- und Ostsee und auf den deutschen Seeschiffahrts-strassen. a. DM.29.80. Kroegers Buch- und Verlagsdruckerei, Blankeneser Bahnhofstr. 17, Postf. 550270, 2000 Hamburg 55, W. Germany (B.R.D.)
    Formerly: Deutscher Fischerei-Almanach.

623.82   GW
DEUTSCHER SCHIFFBAU. 1962. a. free. Verband der Deutschen Schiffbauindustrie e.V., An der Alster 1, 2000 Hamburg 1, W. Germany (B.R.D.)
Shipbuilding

387   UK   ISSN 0070-6310
DIRECTORY OF SHIPOWNERS, SHIPBUILDERS AND MARINE ENGINEERS. 1902. a. £6.50($15.25) incl. postage) I P C Industrial Press Ltd., 33-39 Bowling Green Lane, London EC1R ONE, England. Ed. John Pratt. index.

387.1   AT
DOG WATCH. 1943. a. Aus.$3. ‡ Shiplovers Society of Victoria, G.P.O. Box 1169K, Melbourne, Victoria, 3001, Australia. Eds. S.A.E. Strom, T. E. Goldfinch. adv. bk. rev. circ. 2,500.
    Formerly: Annual Dog Watch (ISSN 0066-3921)

387   US
DOMESTIC WATERBORNE TRADE OF THE UNITED STATES. a. U.S. Maritime Administration, GAO Bldg., 14th & E Sts., N.W., Washington, DC 20230 (Orders to: Supt. of Documents, Washington, DC 20402)
    Continues: Domestic Oceanborne and Great Lakes Commerce of the United States (ISSN 0070-7058)

387   BL
EMPRESA DE NAVEGACAO DA AMAZONIA. ESTATISTICA DA NAVEGACAO. a. Empresa de Navegacao da Amazonia, Av. Presidente Vargas 41, Belem, Para, Brazil. Dir. Eugenio Marques Frazao. charts.

387   347.75   GW
ENTSCHEIDUNGEN DES BUNDESOBERSEEAMTES UND DER SEEAMTER DER BUNDESREPUBLIK DEUTSCHLAND. 1975. m. DM.144. K.O. Storck und Co. Verlag und Druckerei GmbH, Stahltwiete 7, 2000 Hamburg 50, W. Germany (B.R.D.) Ed. H. Meder.

387   NO
EUROPEAN RIG- AND SUPPLY SHIP OWNERS. (Text in English) a. Kr.50($10) Selvig Publishing A-S, Box 9070 Vaterland, Oslo 1, Norway.

387   SW   ISSN 0015-5268
F I V MEDDELANDEN. 1931. irreg. (approx. 2-3/yr.) membership. Foereningen foer Inre Vattenvaegar, c/o Olle Renck, Ed., Pyrolavaegen 38, 181 60 Lidingoe, Sweden. illus. stat. cum.index: 1928-1965. circ. 400.

387   UK
FAIRPLAY WORLD SHIPPING YEAR BOOK. a. £18. Fairplay Publications Ltd., 52-54 Southwark St., London S.E.1., England.

387   NO
FEARNLEYS REVIEW. a. free. Fearnleys, Box 1158 - Sentrum, Oslo 1, Norway. charts. stat.
    Formerly: Fearnly & Egers Chartering Co. Review.

347.75   387   US
FEDERAL MARITIME COMMISSION SERVICE. 1970. irreg., 10-12/yr. $170. Hawkins Publishing Co., Inc., 933 North Kenmore St., Suite 220, Arlington, VA 22201. Eds. Carl R. Eyler, R.C. Morefield. (looseleaf format)

387   UK
FINANCIAL TIMES WORLD SHIPPING YEARBOOK. a. £14($42) Financial Times, Bracken House, 10 Cannon St., London EC4P 4BY, England.

FORD'S DECK PLAN GUIDE. see *TRAVEL AND TOURISM*

387   GW
FRACHT-SCHIFFAHRTS-KONFERENZEN. 1954. a. DM.32. K.O. Storck und Co. Verlag und Druckerei GmbH, Stahltwiete 7, 2000 Hamburg 50, W. Germany(B.R.D.) Ed. H. Meder.

387   FR
FRANCE. COMMISSION CENTRALE POUR LA NAVIGATION DU RHIN. RAPPORT ANNUEL. (Issued in 2 Vols.) 1835. a. 17 F. vol. 1; 40F vol. 2. ‡ Commision Centrale pour la Navigation du Rhin, Palais du Rhin, Strasbourg, France. charts. stat.

387.164   380.1   GW
GEFAHRGUT KONTAKTE/DANGEROUS CARGO CONTACTS. 1976. a. DM.16. K.O. Storck und Co. Verlag und Druckerei GmbH, Stahltwiete 7, 2000 Hamburg 50, W. Germany (B.R.D.) Ed. H. Meder.

387   UK
GENERAL COUNCIL OF BRITISH SHIPPING. ANNUAL REPORT. a. General Council of British Shipping, 30-32 St. Mary Axe, London EC3A 8ET, England.

387.5   UK   ISSN 0072-6591
GREAT BRITAIN. MERCANTILE NAVY LIST. a, with monthly supplements. H.M.S.O., P.O.B. 569, London SE1 9NH, England.

387   CN
GREAT LAKES NAVIGATION. 1917. a. Can.$5. Anchor Press, 1434 St. Catherine St. W., Montreal, Que. H3G 1R4, Canada. Ed. O. J. Silva. adv.

386   US   ISSN 0072-7318
GREAT LAKES RED BOOK. 1903. a. $4.50. Fourth Seacoast Publishing Co. Inc., Box 145, St. Clair Shores, MI 48080. Ed. Amelia G. Sasso. adv. index. circ. 6,000.

386   US   ISSN 0072-7490
GREENWOOD'S GUIDE TO GREAT LAKES SHIPPING. 1958. a. $35 (approx.) Freshwater Press, Inc, 258, The Arcade, Cleveland, OH 44114. Ed. John O. Greenwood. adv. circ. 3,700.

387   JA
GUIDE TO THE PORT OF YOKOHAMA. (Includes Map) a. (Text in English) irreg. free. Port and Harbor Bureau, Industry and Trade Center Bldg., Yamashita-cho, Nakaku, Yokohama, Japan.

387   GW
HAMBURG THE QUICK PORT; also Bremen and Weserports. (Text in English) 1958. a. DM.12. K.O. Storck und Co. Verlag und Druckerei GmbH, Stahltwiete 7, 2000 Hamburg 50, W. Germany (B.R.D.) Ed. H. Meder.

948   DK   ISSN 0085-1418
HANDELS- OG SOEFARTSMUSEET PAA KRONBORG. AARBOG. (Text in Danish; summaries in English or German) 1942. a. membership. Handels- og Soefartsmuseet paa Kronborg, DK-3000 Helsingoer, Denmark. Eds. Henning Henningsen, Hanne Poulsen. adv. illus. cum.index 5. circ. 2,500.

387.5   IO
INDONESIAN SHIPPING DIRECTORY. (Text in English) 1975. biennial. Rps.8000. Marindo Press, Jalan Kramat Raya 146, Jakarta, Indonesia. Ed. Danito Darwas. adv. illus. circ. 2,000.

387.1   FR   ISSN 0073-7720
INDUSTRIE DE LA MANUTENTION DANS LES PORTS FRANCAIS. 1964. a. Union Nationale des Industries de la Manutention dans les Ports Francais, 76 Av. Marceau, Paris 8e, France.

386   US
INLAND RIVER GUIDE. 1972. a. $25. ‡ Waterways Journal, Inc., 319 N. Fourth St., 666 Security Bldg., St. Louis, MO 63102. Ed. Dan Owen. adv. circ. 2,500. (looseleaf format)

386   US
INLAND RIVER RECORD. 1945. a. $20. ‡ Waterways Journal, Inc., 319 N. Fourth St., 666 Security Bldg., St. Louis, MO 63102. Ed. Dan Owen. adv. circ. 1,800.

INTERNATIONAL CARGO HANDLING COORDINATION ASSOCIATION. RAPPORTS DES COMITES NATIONAUX. see *BUSINESS AND ECONOMICS — International Commerce*

385   FR
INTERNATIONAL COMMISSION OF MARITIME HISTORY. COLLOQUES. ACTES. 1957. irreg. Service d'Edition et de Vente des Publications de l'Education Nationale, 13 rue du Four, 75006 Paris, France.

623.89   FR   ISSN 0538-6128
INTERNATIONAL CONFERENCE ON LIGHTHOUSES AND OTHER AIDS TO NAVIGATION. (REPORTS) (Includes: "Discussion Reports" which are in French and English) 1929. quinquennial. 200 (Swiss francs) International Association of Lighthouse Authorities - Association Internationale de Signalisation Maritime, 43 Avenue du President Wilson, Paris 16, France.
Navigation

387   BE
INTERNATIONAL HARBOUR CONGRESS. PROCEEDINGS/INTERNATIONAAL HAVENKONGRES. VERSLAGBOEK/ CONGRES PORTUAIRE INTERNATIONAL. COMPTE-RENDU/INTERNATIONALE HAFENTAGUNG. BERICHTE. irreg., 7th, 1979. Koninklijke Vlaamse Ingenieursvereniging, Jan van Rijswijcklaan 58, B-2000 Antwerp, Belgium.

623.89   BE
INTERNATIONAL NAVIGATION CONGRESS. PAPERS: INLAND NAVIGATION. (Text in English and French; summaries in English and French) quadrennial, 24th, 1977, Leningrad. 2250 Fr. Permanent International Association of Navigation Congresses, 155 rue de la Loi, 1040 Brussels, Belgium.

623.89   BE
INTERNATIONAL NAVIGATION CONGRESS. PAPERS: OCEAN NAVIGATION. (Text in English and French; summaries in English and French) quadrennial, 24th, 1977, Leningrad. 2250 Fr. Permanent International Association of Navigation Congresses, 155 rue de la Loi, 1040 Brussels, Belgium.

380.5   623.89   BE
INTERNATIONAL NAVIGATION CONGRESS. PROCEEDINGS. (Text in English) quadrennial, 24th, 1977, Leningrad. Permanent International Association of Navigation Congresses, 155, rue de la Loi, 1040 Brussels, Belgium. circ. 4,000.

387   UK
INTERNATIONAL OFFSHORE CRAFT CONFERENCE. PROCEEDINGS. irreg; 2nd 1977. $50. Thomas Reed Industrial Press, Saracen's Head Bldg., 36-37 Cock Lane, London EC1A 9BY, England. Ed. Kenneth D. Troup.

623.8   UK   ISSN 0074-8358
INTERNATIONAL SHIPPING AND SHIPBUILDING DIRECTORY. 1966. a. £35 for 2 vols. Benn Publications Ltd., 25 New Street Square, London EC4A 3JA, England. Ed. Richard Daykin. adv. circ. 2,162.

ITALY. ISTITUTO CENTRALE DI STATISTICA. ANNUARIO STATISTICO DELLA NAVIGAZIONE MARITTIMA. see *TRANSPORTATION — Abstracting, Bibliographies, Statistics*

387   US   ISSN 0160-2241
JACKSONVILLE PORT HANDBOOK. 1974. a. $5 (or with subscr. to Jacksonville Seafarer) Howard Publications, Inc., 33 S. Hogan St., Suite 4-F, Box 4728, Jacksonville, FL 32201. Ed. Hayes H. Howard. adv. circ. 5,000. (also avail. in microform from UMI)

TRANSPORTATION — SHIPS AND SHIPPING

JANE'S FIGHTING SHIPS. see *MILITARY*

387   UK   ISSN 0075-305X
JANE'S SURFACE SKIMMERS. a. £25. Jane's Publishing Co., Paulton House, 8 Shepherdess Walk, London N.1., England. Ed. Roy McLeavy.

623.8   JA
JAPAN. SHIP RESEARCH INSTITUTE. PAPERS/ SENPAKU GIJUTSU KENKYUSHO OBUN HOKOKU. (Text in European languages) 1951. irreg. Ship Research Institute - Un'Yu-sho Senpaku Gijutsu Kenkyusho, Ministry of Transport, 6-38-1 Shinkawa, Mitaka-shi, Tokyo 181, Japan.

387   JA
JAPAN PORT INFORMATION. (Text in English) 1969. biennial. 7500 Yen($46) (Ships Agency Committee of Japan - Japan Inbestazusha) Japan Press Ltd, 2-12-8 Kita Aoyama, Minato-ku, Tokyo 107, Japan. Ed. Yoshio Wada.

387   GW   ISSN 0075-6474
KOEHLERS FLOTTENKALENDER. JAHRBUCH FUER SCHIFFAHRT UND HAEFEN. 1901. a. DM.14.80. Koehlers Verlagsgesellschaft mbH, Steintorwall 17, Postfach 371, 4900 Herford, W. Germany (B.R.D.) Ed. Hans Georg Prager. adv. bk. rev. abstr. charts. illus. stat. circ. 20,000.

386   US   ISSN 0075-7748
LAKE CARRIERS' ASSOCIATION. ANNUAL REPORT. 1885. a. not for sale. Lake Carriers' Association, 1411 Superior Ave. N.W., Cleveland, OH 44113. Ed. John A. Packard. index. circ. 600.

LAZY WAY TO BOOK YOUR CAR FERRIES. see *TRAVEL AND TOURISM*

387   UK   ISSN 0260-7387
LIST OF SHIPOWNERS. 1980. a. Lloyd's Register of Shipping, 71 Fenchurch St., London EC3M 4BS, England.

387.2   BE
LISTE OFFICIELLE DES NAVIRES DE MER BELGES ET DE LA FLOTTE DE LA FORCE NAVALE. irreg. Administration de la Marine et de la Navigation Interieure, 30 rue Belliard, 1040 Brussels, Belgium. illus.

387   UK   ISSN 0076-020X
LLOYD'S MARITIME ATLAS, INCLUDING A COMPREHENSIVE LIST OF PORTS AND SHIPPING PLACES OF THE WORLD. 1951. biennial. £9. Lloyd'S of London Press Ltd., Sheepen Place, Colchester, Essex CO3 3LP, England. circ. 7,000.

387   UK
LLOYD'S NAUTICAL YEARBOOK & CALENDAR. 1898. a. £8. Lloyd's of London Press Ltd., Sheepen Place, Colchester, Essex CO3 3LP, England. Ed. P. R. Fisher. adv. circ. 10,000.
Formerly: Lloyd's Calendar & Nautical Book (ISSN 0076-0196)

387   UK   ISSN 0076-0234
LLOYD'S REGISTER OF SHIPPING. STATISTICAL TABLES. 1885. a. £3. Lloyd'S Register of Shipping, 71 Fenchurch St, London EC3M 4BS, England. Ed. J. P. Cashman.

387   UK
LLOYD'S REGISTER OF SHIPS. a (with monthly supplements) £8. Lloyd's Register of Shipping, 71 Finchurch St., London EC3M 4BS, England.

387   UK
LONDON SHIPPING CONTACTS. (Text in English) 1978. a. Rystom and Storck Publications Ltd., Downham Market, Norfolk PE38 9BX, Great Britain (Subscr. to: Storck Shipping Publications, 15 Half Moon Street, London W.1, Great Britain) Ed. Stuart Pearce.

387   SW   ISSN 0024-6328
LONGITUDE;* a magazine of the Seven Seas. a. Kr.24.50. J. E. Carlstedt Foerlag AB, Maester Samuelsgatan 1, 111 44 Stockholm, Sweden. charts. illus.

623.82 331.88   CN   ISSN 0383-7769
MAIN DECK. 1943. irreg. Shipyard General Workers' Federation of British Columbia, 1219 Nanaimo St., Vancouver, B.C., Canada. illus.

387   GW   ISSN 0542-6758
MARE BALTICUM. (Text in English, German, Polish, and Scandinavian languages) 1965. irreg. DM.20. Ostseegesellschaft e.V., Johnsallee 18, 2000 Hamburg 13, W. Germany (B.R.D.) Ed. Hans Georg Prager. adv. bk. rev. bibl. charts. illus. index. (back issues avail.)

387   AT
MARINE BOARD OF HOBART. ANNUAL REPORT. a. Marine Board of Hobart, Franklin Wharf, Tasmania 7000, Australia.

387   US   ISSN 0076-4450
MARINE CATALOG. 1943. a. $15. Simmons-Boardman Publishing Corporation, 508 Birch St., Bristol, CT 06010. Ed. Robert Ware. adv. circ. 7,500.

387   US
MARINE CATALOG BUYERS GUIDE. 1942. a. $15. Simmons Boardman Publishing Corporation, 508 Birch St., Bristol, CT 06010. Ed. Robert Ware. adv.

623.87 387   US   ISSN 0076-4469
MARINE ENGINEERING/LOG ANNUAL MARITIME REVIEW AND YEARBOOK ISSUE. 1942. a. $2. Simmons-Boardman Publishing Corporation, 508 Birch St., Bristol, CT 06010. Ed. Robert Ware. adv. circ. 20,714. (also avail. in microform from UMI)

387   CN
MARINE EQUIPMENT DIRECTORY. 1917. a. Can.$10. Anchor Press, 1434 St. Catherine St. W., Suite 504, Montreal, Que. H3G 1R4, Canada. Ed. O. J. Silva. adv.

387   FR   ISSN 0076-4485
MARINE MARCHANDE. (Special series of: Journal de la Marine Marchande) 1948. a. 180 F. Journal de la Marine Marchande, S. A., 190 Bd. Haussmann, 75008 Paris, France. Ed. M. Christian Moreux. index.

623.8   JA
MARINE STANDARDIZATION IN JAPAN. (Text in Japanese) a. 1,500 Yen. Japan Marine Standards Association, Sumitomo Toranomon Bldg., 7 Shiba Kotohira-cho, Minato-ku, Tokyo 105, Japan.
Formerly: Marine Standardization.

623.8   US
MARINE TECHNOLOGY SOCIETY. ANNUAL CONFERENCE PROCEEDINGS. Short title: Oceans (Year) 1974, no. 9. a. Marine Technology Society, 1730 M St. N.W., Washington, DC 20036. (Co-sponsor: Institute of Electrical and Electronics Engineers Conference on Engineering in the Ocean Environment) bibl. charts.

MARINER'S CATALOG. see *EARTH SCIENCES — Oceanography*

387   UK   ISSN 0307-8590
MARITIME MONOGRAPHS AND REPORTS. 1970. irreg. price varies. National Maritime Museum, Romney Rd., Greenwich SE10 9NF, England (U.S. subscr. to: Mystic Seaport Museum Stores, Mystic, CT 06355) bibl. illus.

387   US   ISSN 0076-650X
MERCHANT VESSELS OF THE UNITED STATES. a. U.S. Coast Guard, Dept. of Transportation, 400 7th Street, S.W., Washington, DC 20590 (Orders to: Supt. of Documents, Washington, DC 20402)

387   UK
MONEY AND SHIPS. 1971. a. £50. Seatrade Publications Ltd., Fairfax House, Colchester CO1 1RJ, England.

387   CN
MONTREAL PORT GUIDE & DIRECTORY. 1970. a. Anchor Press, 1434 St. Catherine St. W., Montreal, Canada.

387   US   ISSN 0077-2615
MYSTIC SEAPORT MANUSCRIPTS INVENTORY. 1964. irreg., 1966, no. 5. free; selective distribution. ‡ Mystic Seaport, Inc., G.W. Blunt White Library, Mystic, CT 06355.

387   UK   ISSN 0077-5185
NATIONAL MARITIME BOARD. (GREAT BRITAIN) YEAR BOOK. 1922. a. 50p. National Maritime Board, 17-18 Bury St., London EC3A 5AH, England.

NATIONAL MARITIME MUSEUM. OCCASIONAL LECTURE SERIES. see *MUSEUMS AND ART GALLERIES*

387.5   PK
NATIONAL SHIPPING CORPORATION. REPORT AND ACCOUNTS. (Text in English) a. National Shipping Corporation, N S C Bldg., Moulvi Tamizuddin Khan Rd., Karachi, Pakistan.

387   US   ISSN 0028-0380
NATIONAL WATERWAYS CONFERENCE NEWSLETTER. 1964. irreg. (5-6/yr.) $15. ‡ National Waterways Conference, Inc., 1130 17th St., N.W., Washington, DC 20036. Ed. Claude C. Duncan. bk. rev. charts. illus. circ. 2,400. (processed)

387   FR   ISSN 0077-6270
NAVIS; annuaire de la marine marchande, de la construction navale et des ports. 1942. a. 270 F. Rene Moreux et Cie, 190, Boulevard Haussmann, 75008 Paris, France. Ed. Christian Moreux. index.

386 314   NE   ISSN 0077-7102
NETHERLANDS. CENTRAAL BUREAU VOOR DE STATISTIEK. STATISTIEK VAN DE INTERNATIONALE BINNENVAART. STATISTICS OF THE INTERNATIONAL INLAND SHIPPING. (Text in Dutch and English) 1948. a. fl.19.65. Centraal Bureau voor de Statistiek, Prinses Beatrixlaan 428, Voorburg, Netherlands (Orders to: Staatsuitgeverij, Christoffel Plantijnstraat, The Hague, Netherlands)

387.5   NE   ISSN 0077-7129
NETHERLANDS. CENTRAAL BUREAU VOOR DE STATISTIEK. STATISTIEK VAN DE KOOPVAARDIJVLOOT. STATISTICS OF THE MERCHANT MARINE. (Text in Dutch and English) 1949. irreg. fl.7.85. Centraal Bureau voor de Statistiek, Prinses Beatrixlaan 428, Voorburg, Netherlands (Orders to: Staatsuitgeverij, Christoffel Plantijnstraat, The Hague, Netherlands)

387   NE   ISSN 0077-7250
NETHERLANDS. CENTRAAL BUREAU VOOR DE STATISTIEK. STATISTIEK VAN DE ZEEVAART. STATISTICS OF SEABORNE SHIPPING. (Text in Dutch and English) 1948. a. fl.20.25. Centraal Bureau voor de Statistiek, Prinses Beatrixlaan 428, Voorburg, Netherlands (Orders to: Staatsuitgeverij, Christoffel Plantijnstraat, The Hague, Netherlands)

386   NE   ISSN 0077-7269
NETHERLANDS. CENTRAAL BUREAU VOOR DE STATISTIEK. STATISTIEK VAN HET BINNENLANDS GOEDERENVERVOER. STATISTICS OF INTERNAL GOODS TRANSPORT IN THE NETHERLANDS. (Text in Dutch and English) 1948-49. a. fl.14.45. Centraal Bureau voor de Statistiek, Prinses Beatrixlaan 428, Voorburg, Netherlands (Orders to: Staatsuitgeverij, Christoffel Plantijnstraat, The Hague, Netherlands)

387   NE   ISSN 0077-7552
NETHERLANDS. COMMISSIE ZEEHAVENOVERLEG. JAARVERSLAG. 1970. a. free. Commissie Zeehavenoverleg, Koningskade 4, The Hague, Netherlands.
Dutch seaport advisory board annual report

387   NZ   ISSN 0545-7866
NEW ZEALAND SHIPPING DIRECTORY. 1962. a. $2.25. Mercantile Gazette of New Zealand Ltd., Box 20-034, Christchurch 5, New Zealand. Ed. E. R. Edmonds. adv. illus.

387.5   JA
NIHON SHOSEN SEMPUKU TOKEI. 1972. a. free. Japanese Shipowners' Association, Research Division - Nihon Senshu Kyokai, c/o Kaiun Bldg., 2-6-4 Hirakawacho, Chiyoda-ku, Tokyo 102, Japan. circ. 2,800.

387   NO   ISSN 0549-7000
NORSKE VERITAS CLASSIFICATION AND REGISTRY OF SHIPPING. PUBLICATION. (Text in English) 1957. irreg., no. 108,1979. free. Norske Veritas, Box 300, 1322 Hoevik, Norway.

TRANSPORTATION — SHIPS AND SHIPPING

623.82   FR   ISSN 0078-2157
NOUVEAUTES TECHNIQUES MARITIMES.
(Special series of: Journal de la Marine Marchande)
a. 160 F. Journal de la Marine Marchande, S. A.,
190 Boulevard Haussmann, 75008 Paris, France. Ed.
M. Christian Moreux. index.
Shipbuilding

386.8   US   ISSN 0093-1799
OFFICIAL PORT OF DETROIT WORLD
HANDBOOK. 1973. a. $4.50. Fourth Seacoast
Publishing Co. Inc., Box 145, St. Clair Shores, MI
48080. Ed. Roger J. Buysse. adv. illus. circ. 10,000.

387.1   US   ISSN 0094-8454
OFFICIAL SOUTHERN CALIFORNIA PORTS
MARITIME DIRECTORY AND GUIDE. 1974. a.
$10. Civic-Data Corp., 404 S. Bixel St., Los
Angeles, CA 90017. illus.

387   FR   ISSN 0474-5884
ORGANIZATION FOR ECONOMIC
COOPERATION AND DEVELOPMENT.
MARITIME TRANSPORT COMMITTEE.
MARITIME TRANSPORT. 1954. a. $8.50.
Organization for Economic Cooperation and
Development, 2 rue Andre Pascal, 75775 Paris 26,
France (U. S. orders to: O.E.C.D. Publications and
Information Center, 1750 Pennsylvania Ave., N.
W., Washington, D. C. 20006) (also avail. in
microfiche)

387.5   NO
PLATOU REPORT. a. free. R. S. Platou A-S, Box
1357, Vika, Oslo 1, Norway. illus.

623.8   PL   ISSN 0416-7287
POLITECHNIKA GDANSKA. ZESZYTY
NAUKOWE. BUDOWNICTWO OKRETOWE.
(Text in Polish; summaries in English and Russian)
1957. irreg. price varies. Politechnika Gdanska,
Majakowskiego 11/12, 81-952 Gdansk 6, Poland
(Dist. by: Osrodek Rozpowszechniania Wydawnictw
Naukowych Pan, Palac Kultury i Nauki, 00-901
Warsaw, Poland)

387   II
POOMPUHAR SHIPPING CORPORATION.
ANNUAL REPORT. (Text in English) 1975. a.
Poompuhar Shipping Corporation Ltd., Kuralagam,
Madras 600001, India.

627.2   JA
PORT AND HARBOUR TECHNICAL RESEARCH
INSTITUTE. GUIDE/KOWAN GIJUTSU
KENKYUSHO. GUIDE. irreg. exchange basis. Port
and Harbour Technical Research Institute - Un'Yu-
sho Kowan Gijutsu Kenkyusho, 3-1-1 Nagase,
Yokosuka 239, Kanagawa, Japan. illus.

387   JM
PORT EUSTAMANTE HANDBOOK. 1972. a. free.
Shipping Association of Jamaica, Confederation Life
Building, 5-7 King Street, P.O. Box 40, Kingston 15,
Jamaica. (Co-sponsor: Port Authority of Jamaica)
Ed. T. A. Gambrill. circ. 1,700.
Formerly(until 1977): Port of Kingston
Handbook.

387   US   ISSN 0079-3981
PORT OF BALTIMORE HANDBOOK. 1946.
biennial since 1957. free. ‡ Maryland Port
Administration, World Trade Center Baltimore,
Baltimore, MD 21202. Ed. Donald Klein. circ.
12,000.

387   UK
PORT OF BRISTOL. HANDBOOK. 1886. a. free to
qualified personnel. Port of Bristol Authority, St.
Andrews Rd., Avonmouth, Bristol BS11 9DQ,
England. Ed. Rodney Stone. adv. circ. 4,000.

387   JA
PORT OF OSAKA/OSAKAKO. (Text in Japanese
and English) a. free. Port and Harbour Bureau -
Osaka-shi Kowan-Kyoku, 2-8-24 Chikko, Minato-
ku, Osaka 552, Japan. stat.

387   GR
PORT OF PIRAEUS AUTHORITY. ANNUAL
REPORT. a. Port of Piraeus Authority, Akti
Miaouli II, Merarchias Corner, Piraeus, Greece.

387   GR
PORT OF PIRAEUS AUTHORITY. STATISTICAL
REPORT. (Text in English and Greek) 1913. m.
Port of Piraeus Authority, Akti Miaouli II,
Merarchias Corner, Piraeus, Greece. adv. circ.
4,000.
Supersedes: Port of Piraeus Authority. Statistical
Bulletin (ISSN 0079-399X)

387.1   JA
PORT OF TOKYO. 1951. a. free. Port and Harbor
Bureau, 3-8 Marunouchi, Chiyoda-ku, Tokyo, Japan.
illus.

315.2   JA
PORT OF YOKOHAMA. ANNUAL REPORT. (Text
in Japanese and English) a. free. Port and Harbor
Bureau, Industry and Trade Center Bldg.,
2Yamashita-cho, Nakaku, Yokohama, Japan. stat.

387.1   CN
PORTS ANNUAL. 1972. a. Anchor Press, 1434, St.
Catherine St. W., Montreal, Quebec Province,
Canada. illus.

387   AT
PORTS OF NEW SOUTH WALES JOURNAL.
1976. irreg. Maritime Services Board, Public
Relations Section, G.P.O. Box 32, Sydney, N.S.W.
2001, Australia. adv. illus.

387   SA
PORTS OF SOUTH AFRICA. a. R.9. Industrial
Publishing Co. (Pty) Ltd., Box 4886, Johannesburg
2000, South Africa. adv.

387 382   UK   ISSN 0079-4066
PORTS OF THE WORLD. 1896. a. £31. Benn
Publications Ltd., 25 New Street Square, London
EC4A 3JA, England. Ed. A. R. Daykin. adv. index.
circ. 2,566.

387   CN
QUEBEC PORT GUIDE & DIRECTORY. a.
Shipping Register Publications Ltd. (Subsidiary of:
Anchor Press) Suite 504, 1434 St. Catherine St. W.,
Montreal, Que.H3G 1R4, Canada. Ed. O.J. Silva.
adv.

387   FR
REGISTRE MARITIME. 1929. a (with m. suppl.) 450
F. Bureau Veritas, Service Maritime, 31 rue Henri
Rochefort, 75821 Paris Cedex 17, France.
Supersedes in part: Registre International de
Classification de Navires et d'Aeronefs (ISSN 0080-
0678)

387.2   UN   ISSN 0085-560X
REVIEW OF MARITIME TRANSPORT. (Editions
in English, French, Spanish) 1969. a; latest issue,
1977. price varies; standing order basis. United
Nations Conference on Trade and Development,
Distribution and Sales Section, Palais des Nations,
CH-1211 Geneva 10, Switzerland (Or United
Nations Publications, Rm. A-3315, New York, N.Y.
10017)

623.81   UK   ISSN 0373-529X
ROYAL INSTITUTION OF NAVAL ARCHITECTS.
SUPPLEMENTARY PAPERS. a. £15($38) Royal
Institution of Naval Architects, 10 Upper Belgrave
St., London SW1X 8BQ, England. illus.
Naval architecture

623.81   UK   ISSN 0035-8967
ROYAL INSTITUTION OF NAVAL ARCHITECTS.
TRANSACTIONS. 1860. a. £25 to non-members.
Royal Institution of Naval Architects, 10 Upper
Belgrave St., London SW1X 8BQ, England. Ed. P.
W. Ayling. circ. 6,400. Indexed: Br.Tech.Ind.
Naval architecture

359.97   US   ISSN 0163-2833
S A R STATISTICS. (Search and Rescue) a. U.S.
Coast Guard, 400 Seventh St. S.W., Washington,
DC 20591.

387   MY   ISSN 0080-522X
SABAH. MARINE DEPARTMENT. ANNUAL
REPORT. (Text in English) 1961. a, latest 1976.
M.$2. Marine Department, Labuan, Sabah,
Malaysia.

387   UK
ST. JAMES PRESS CAR FERRY GUIDE. 1979. a.
St. James Press Publications Ltd., 5-11 Worship St.,
London EC2A 2AY, England.

387   US
SAVANNAH PORT HANDBOOK. 1981. a. $5.
Howard Publications, Inc., 33 S. Hogan St., Suite 4-
F, Box 4728, Jacksonville, FL 32201. Ed. Hayes H.
Howard. adv. circ. 9,500.

387.2   GW
SCHIFF UND ZEIT. 1973. irreg., vol. 6, 1977.
DM.16.80. (Deutsche Gesellschaft fuer Schiffahrts-
und Marinegeschichte e. V.) Koehlers
Verlagsgesellschaft mbH, Steintorwall 17, Postfach
371, 4900 Herford, W. Germany (B.R.D.) Ed.
Jochen Brennecke. illus.

SCHIFFBAU-NORMUNG. see *METROLOGY AND
STANDARDIZATION*

623.82   US   ISSN 0080-6803
SCHIFFBAUTECHNISCHE GESELLSCHAFT.
JAHRBUCH. a. price varies. (GW) Springer-
Verlag, 175 Fifth Ave, New York, NY 10010 (also
Berlin Heidelberg, Vienna) (reprint service avail.
from ISI)
Shipbuilding

387 382   CN   ISSN 0080-8423
SEAPORTS AND THE SHIPPING WORLD.
ANNUAL ISSUE. 1957. a. not for sale. Gallery
Publications Ltd., 4634 St. Catherine St. W.,
Montreal, Que H3Z 2W6, Canada. Ed. Brian
Gallery. adv. circ. 1,300.
Directory of those involved in shipping/marine
industry in Canada

382   UK   ISSN 0141-4151
SEATRADE GUIDE TO ARAB SHIPPING. 1978. a.
included with subscription to Seatrade. Seatrade
Publications Ltd., Fairfax House, Colchester CO1
IRJ, England. Ed. Gary Gimson. adv.

387   UK   ISSN 0141-4585
SEATRADE GUIDE TO EEC SHIPPING. 1978. a.
£18 included with subscr. to Seatrade. Seatrade
Publications Ltd., Fairfax House, Colchester CO1
IRJ, England.

387   UK   ISSN 0142-5064
SEATRADE GUIDE TO LATIN AMERICAN
SHIPPING. 1979. a. £15 (combined subscription
with Seatrade £18) Seatrade Publications Ltd.,
Fairfax House, Colchester, Essex CO1 1RJ,
England.

387   UK   ISSN 0142-5056
SEATRADE U.S. YEARBOOK. 1979. a. £15
(combined subscription with Seatrade £18) Seatrade
Publications Ltd., Fairfax House, Colchester, Essex
CO1 1RJ, England. Ed. P. Goldman. adv.

SEFUNIM. see *ARCHAEOLOGY*

387.7   MM   ISSN 0080-9268
SHIPPING AND AVIATION STATISTICS OF THE
MALTESE ISLANDS. a. £0.25. Central Office of
Statistics, Auberge de Castille, Valletta, Malta
(Subscr. to: Department of Information, Auberge de
Castille, Valletta, Malta)

387.5   GW
SHIPPING STATISTICS YEARBOOK. 1973.
biennial. price varies. Institut fuer
Seeverkehrswirtschaft Bremen - Institute of Shipping
Economics, Werderstr. 73, D-2800 Bremen 1, W.
Germany (B.R.D.) stat. (back issues avail.)

387   NO
SKANDINAVISKE SKIPSREDERIER/YEARBOOK
OF SCANDINAVIAN SHIPOWNERS. (Text in
English) a. Kr.90. Per Selvig A-S, Kongensgt. 6,
Oslo 1, Norway.

387   NO
SKIPSFARTENS INNKJOEPSBOK. a. Instituttet for
Merkantil Informasjon A-S, N. Kirkebyvei 11, 1350
Lommedalen, Norway. adv. circ. 5,000.

387 380.1   GW
SOCIALIST SHIPPING CONTACTS. 1979. a.
DM.16. K.O. Storck und Co. Verlag und Druckerei
GmbH, Stahltwiete 7, 2000 Hamburg 50, W.
Germany(B.R.D.) Ed. H. Meder.

TRANSPORTATION — TRUCKS AND TRUCKING

623.8 US ISSN 0081-1661
SOCIETY OF NAVAL ARCHITECTS AND MARINE ENGINEERS. TRANSACTIONS. 1893. a. $35. Society of Naval Architects and Marine Engineers, One World Trade Center, Suite 1369, New York, NY 10048. index. circ. 5,000. Indexed: Ocean.Abstr. Pollut.Abstr.

387 AG
SOUTH AMERICAN PORTS HANDBOOK. (Text in English) 1974. biennial. $55. Agencia Maritima Internacional S.A., Av. Julio Roca 710, 1067 Buenos Aires, Argentina. Ed. Frank V. H. Wylie. illus. circ. 1,500.
Formerly (until 1976): Owners, Masters, Brokers and Agents Handbook on S. American Caribbean and Pacific Ports in Venezuela, Colombia, Panama, Ecuador, Peru, Bolivia and Chile.

387.1 US ISSN 0160-2233
SOUTH FLORIDA PORTS HANDBOOK. 1976. a. $5. Howard Publications, Inc., 33 S. Hogan St. Suite 4-F, Box 4728, Jacksonville, FL 32201. Ed. Hayes H. Howard. adv. circ. 10,000.

387.5 UK
SOVIET MERCHANT SHIPS. 1969. a. £6.95. Kenneth Mason Publications Ltd., Homewell, Havant Hants, PO9 1EF, England. Ed. Lord Greenway.

387 US ISSN 0081-4768
STATISTICAL ANALYSIS OF WORLD'S MERCHANT FLEETS SHOWING AGE, SIZE, SPEED AND DRAFT BY FREQUENCY GROUPINGS. 1956. a. since 1975; previously biennial. U.S. Maritime Administration, Office of Trade and Statistics, GAO Bldg., 14th & E Sts., N.W., Washington, DC 20230 (Orders to: Supt. of Documents, Washington, DC 20402)

386 NE ISSN 0077-7161
STATISTIEK VAN DE SCHEEPVAARTBEWEGING IN NEDERLAND/ CENSUS OF INLAND SHIPPING IN THE NETHERLANDS AT LOCKS AND BRIDGES. (Text in Dutch and English) 1946. a. fl.11.85. Centraal Bureau voor de Statistiek, Prinses Beatrixlaan 428, Voorburg, Netherlands (Orders to: Staatsuitgeverij, Christoffel Plantijnstraat, The Hague, Netherlands)

387 GW ISSN 0073-0203
STATISTIK DES HAMBURGISCHEN STAATES; Handel und Schiffahrt des Hafens Hamburg. 1845. a. DM.20. ‡ Statistisches Landesamt, Steckelhoern 12, 2000 Hamburg 11, W. Germany (B.R.D.)

387.164 GW
STOWAGE AND SEGREGATION TO I M D G CODE. 1973. a. DM.32. K. O. Storck und Co. Verlag und Druckerei GmbH, Stahltwiete 7, 2000 Hamburg 50, W. Germany(B.R.D.) Ed. H. Meder.

STUBBS DIRECTORY; professional and commercial products and services. see BUSINESS AND ECONOMICS — Trade And Industrial Directories

SVEUCILISTE U ZAGREBU. FAKULTET STROJARSTVA I BRODOGRADNJE. ZBORNIK RADOVA. see ENGINEERING — Mechanical Engineering

387 GW
TAEGLICHER HAFENBERICHT. JAHRESAUSGABE. a. DM.25. Seehafen-Verlag Erik Blumenfeld, Celsiusweg 8, Postfach 1347, 2000 Hamburg 50, W. Germany(B.R.D.) charts.stat.

387 US
TAMPA PORT HANDBOOK. 1978. a. $5. Howard Publications, Inc., 33 S. Hogan St., Suite 4-F, Box 4728, Jacksonville, FL 32201. Ed. Hayes H. Howard. adv. circ. 5,500.

TOWARDS A SHIPPING POLICY FOR THE EEC. see BUSINESS AND ECONOMICS — International Commerce

387.5 JA
TOYAMA MERCANTILE MARINE COLLEGE. JOURNAL/TOYAMA SHOSEN KOTO SENMON GAKKO KENKYU SHUROKU. (Text in Japanese; some articles in English) 1968. a. Toyama Mercantile Marine College - Toyama Shosen Koto Senmon Gakko, 1-2 Ebie Neriai, Shinminato, Toyama 933-02, Japan. Ed. Henshu Iinkai. illus. circ. 140.

387 US ISSN 0082-5867
TRAFFIC REPORT OF THE ST. LAWRENCE SEAWAY. U.S. Saint Lawrence Seaway Development Corporation, 800 Independence Ave. S.W., Washington, DC 20591.

387.5 FR
TRANSPORT MARITIME: ETUDES ET STATISTIQUES. 1956. a. 30 F. Comite Central des Armateurs de France, 73 bld. Haussmann, 75008 Paris, France. circ. 4,500.
Formerly: Marine Marchand: Etudes et Statistiques (ISSN 0069-6439)

387.1 TI
TUNISIA. OFFICE DES PORTS NATIONAUX. BULLETIN ANNUEL DES STATISTIQUES. Cover title: Tunisia. Office des Ports Nationaux. Trafic Maritime. a. Office des Ports Nationaux, Tunis, Tunisia.

387.1 US ISSN 0083-0305
U.S. ARMY. CORPS OF ENGINEERS. PORT SERIES. 1921. irreg. U.S. Army, Corps of Engineers., Washington, DC 20310 (Orders to: Supt. Doc., Washington, DC 20402)

287 US ISSN 0083-0755
U. S. FEDERAL MARITIME COMMISSION. ANNUAL REPORT. 1962. a. free. U.S. Federal Maritime Commission., 1110 L St. N. W., Washington, DC 20573.

387 US ISSN 0083-1670
U. S. MARITIME ADMINISTRATION. ANNUAL REPORT. 1950. a. U.S. Maritime Administration, GAO Bldg., 14th Sts., N.W., Washington, DC 20230 (Orders to: Supt. of Documents, Washington, DC 20402)

387 623.8 US ISSN 0083-1697
U. S. MARITIME ADMINISTRATION. TECHNICAL REPORT INDEX, MARITIME ADMINISTRATION RESEARCH AND DEVELOPMENT. 1967. a. U.S. Maritime Administration, GAO Bldg., 14th & E Sts., N.W., Washington, DC 20230 (Orders to: Supt. of Documents, Washington, DC 20402)

387 US ISSN 0083-3207
U. S. SAINT LAWRENCE SEAWAY DEVELOPMENT CORPORATION. ANNUAL REPORT. 1954/55. a. U.S. Saint Lawrence Seaway Development Corporation, 800 Independence Ave. S.W., Washington, DC 20591.

387 PL
UNIWERSYTET GDANSKI. WYDZIAL EKONOMIKI TRANSPORTU. ZESZYTY NAUKOWE. EKONOMIKA TRANSPORTU MORSKIEGO. (Text in Polish; summaries in English and Russian) 1971. irreg. price varies. Uniwersytet Gdanski, Ul. Czerwonej Armii 110, 81-824 Sopot, Poland. circ. 300.

386 333.91 SP
VALENCIA PORT; guia del servicios del puerto de Valencia. 1978. a. 400 ptas. Publicaciones Men-Car, Paseo de Colon 24, Barcelona 2, Spain. Eds. Juan and Manuel Cardona. adv. circ. 10,000.

VIRGINIA PORT AUTHORITY. BOARD OF COMMISSIONERS. ANNUAL REPORT. see BUSINESS AND ECONOMICS — International Commerce

VIRGINIA PORT AUTHORITY. FOREIGN TRADE ANNUAL REPORT: THE PORTS OF VIRGINIA. see BUSINESS AND ECONOMICS — International Commerce

387 II
WATER TRANSPORT STATISTICS OF INDIA. 1969. a. $11.70. Ministry of Shipping and Transport, Transport Research Division, I D A Bldg., Jamnagar House, Shahjahan Rd., New Delhi 11001, India (Orders to: Controller of Publications, Civil Lines, Delhi 110006, India)
Formerly: India (Republic) Ministry of Shipping and Transport. Statistics of Water Transport Industries (ISSN 0081-5144)

387 US ISSN 0083-7725
WATERBORNE COMMERCE OF THE UNITED STATES. a. (in 5 separate parts) price varies. U.S. Army Corps of Engineers, Waterborne Commerce Statistics Center, Box 61280, New Orleans, LA 70161.

387.5 AT
WESTERN AUSTRALIAN COASTAL SHIPPING COMMISSION. ANNUAL REPORT. a. contr.circ. Coastal Shipping Commission, P.O. Box 394, Fremantle, Australia. stat.

387 NO
WHERE TO BUILD-WHERE TO REPAIR. (Text in English) a. Kr.65. Per Selvig A-S, Kongensgt. 6, Oslo 6, Norway.

387 380.1 GW
WIE ERREICHE ICH WEN? 1958. a. DM.16. K.O. Storck und Co. Verlag und Druckerei GmbH, Stahltwiete 7, 2000 Hamburg 50, W. Germany(B.R.D.) Ed. H. Meder.

387 NO
WORLD BULK TRADES. a. free. Fearnleys, Box 1158 - Sentrum, Oslo 1, Norway. charts. stat.

387.164 US ISSN 0162-0088
WORLD WIDE SHIPPING GUIDE. 1976. a. $35. World Wide Shipping Guide, Inc., 77 Moehring Dr., Blauvelt, NY 10913. adv. circ. 12,500.

TRANSPORTATION — Trucks And Trucking

388.324 UK ISSN 0308-9304
A B C FREIGHT GUIDE. a. A B C Travel Guides Ltd., World Timetable Centre, Dunstable, Bedfordshire LU6 3EB, England. adv. circ. 3,500.
Formerly: A B C Goods Transport Guide (ISSN 0001-0421)

388 CN ISSN 0084-6171
ALBERTA MOTOR TRANSPORT DIRECTORY. 1947. a. Can.$13. ‡ Alberta Trucking Association, P. O. Box 5520, Station A, 5112 3 St. S.E., Calgary, Alberta T2H 1X9, Canada. adv. bk. rev. circ. 3,000.
Formerly: Alberta Shippers Guide.

388.3 US ISSN 0065-7271
AMERICAN ASSOCIATION OF MOTOR VEHICLE ADMINISTRATORS. ANNUAL CONFERENCE. PROCEEDINGS. 1957. a. American Association of Motor Vehicle Administrators, 1201 Connecticut Ave., N.W., Suite 910, Washington, DC 20036. Ed. Robert S. Brown, Jr. circ. 2,500.

388.324 US ISSN 0146-0781
AMERICAN MOTOR CARRIER DIRECTORY: ILLINOIS-MISSOURI EDITION. a. $38. Guide Services, Inc., 6291 Barfield Rd. N.E., Box 720455, Atlanta, GA 30328.

338.324 US ISSN 0146-0803
AMERICAN MOTOR CARRIER DIRECTORY: MIDDLE ATLANTIC EDITION. a. $38. Guide Services, Inc., 6291 Barfield Rd. N.E., Box 720455, Atlanta, GA 30328.
Formerly: American Motor Carrier Directory: New York-New Jersey Edition.

388.324 US ISSN 0146-0811
AMERICAN MOTOR CARRIER DIRECTORY: NEW ENGLAND EDITION. a. $38. Guide Services, Inc., 6291 Barfield Rd. N.E., Box 720455, Atlanta, GA 30328.

388.324 US
AMERICAN MOTOR CARRIER DIRECTORY: NORTH AMERICAN EDITION. s-a. $92.50. Guide Services, Inc., Box 720455, 6291 Barfield Rd. N.E., Atlanta, GA 30328.
Formerly: American Motor Carrier Directory: National Edition (ISSN 0569-6356)

388.324 US ISSN 0146-079X
AMERICAN MOTOR CARRIER DIRECTORY: SOUTHEASTERN EDITION. a. $38. Guide Services, Inc., 6291 Barfield Rd. N.E., Box 720455, Atlanta, GA 30328.

388.324 US ISSN 0569-6364
AMERICAN MOTOR CARRIER DIRECTORY: SPECIALIZED SERVICES EDITION. a. $38. Guide Services, Inc., Box 720455, 6291 Barfield Rd. N.E., Atlanta, GA 30328.

388.4 US
AMERICAN TRUCKING TRENDS. a. American Trucking Associations, Inc., 1616 P St. N.W., Washington, DC 20036.
Former titles: American Trucking Trends. Statistical Report; American Trucking Associations Report (ISSN 0066-0892)

388.322 UK ISSN 0068-4376
BUSES ANNUAL. a. price varies. Ian Allan Ltd., Terminal House, Shepperton, Middlesex TW17 8AS, England. Ed. Gavin Booth. circ. 10,500.

388.3 CN ISSN 0068-9734
CANADIAN SPECIAL TRUCK EQUIPMENT MANUAL; directory of truck equipment. 1959. a. Can.$5. Maclean-Hunter, Ltd, 481 University Ave, Toronto, Ont. M5W 1A7, Canada. Ed. Rolf Lockwood. index.

388.324 CN
CANADIAN TRUCK MARKETING. a. Can.$25. Wadham Publications Ltd., 109 Vanderhoof Ave, Toronto, Ont. M4G 2J2, Canada. Ed. Barry M. Holmes. circ. 7,720.

388.3 US
F & O S. EXECUTIVE AND OWNERSHIP REPORT. (Financial and Operating Statistics) a. $100 cr with subscr. to 2 other F & O S publications. American Trucking Associations, Inc., 1616 P St. N.W., Washington, DC 20036.

388.324 US
FINANCIAL ANALYSIS OF THE FOR-HIRE TANK TRUCK INDUSTRY. 1973. a. National Tank Truck Carriers, Inc., 1616 P St., N.W., Washington, DC 20036.

388.3 US ISSN 0099-2445
FINANCIAL ANALYSIS OF THE MOTOR CARRIER INDUSTRY. a. American Trucking Associations, Inc., 1616 P St., N.W., Washington, DC 20036. illus. stat.

388.324 UK
HAULAGE MANUAL. 1970. a. £3. Road Haulage Association, 22 Upper Woburn Place, London WC1H OES, England. Ed. John Ockenden. adv. stat. index. circ. 18,000.

629.2 SZ ISSN 0073-4292
I N U F A: INTERNATIONALER NUTZFAHRZEUG-KATALOG/ INTERNATIONAL CATALOGUE FOR COMMERCIAL VEHICLES. 1958. a. 24 Fr. Vogt-Schild AG, Dornacherstr. 39, 4501 Solothurn 1, Switzerland. adv. bk. rev. circ. 6,500.

388.3 IS ISSN 0075-1057
ISRAEL. CENTRAL BUREAU OF STATISTICS. MOTOR VEHICLES. (Subseries of its Special Series) (Text in Hebrew; summaries in English) irreg., latest issue, no. 633, 1978. I£90. Central Bureau of Statistics, Box 13015, Jerusalem, Israel.

388.324 US
MOTOR CARRIER STATISTICAL SUMMARY. q. American Trucking Associations, Inc., 1616 P St. N.W., Washington, DC 20036.
Formed by the merger of: Intercity Truck Tonnage (ISSN 0534-607X) & Truck Beat.

388.3 UK ISSN 0077-1600
MOTOR MANUAL.* irreg. L.1.25. Hamlyn Group, 42 The Centre, Feltham, Middlesex, England.

MOTORCYCLE BUYER'S GUIDE. see TRANSPORTATION — Automobiles

MOTORING IN MALAYA. see TRAVEL AND TOURISM

388.324 US ISSN 0077-586X
NATIONAL TANK TRUCK CARRIER DIRECTORY. 1954. a. $9.50. National Tank Truck Carriers, Inc., 1616 P St. N.W., Washington, DC 20036. Ed. Melinda Duncan. adv. circ. 2,500.

388.3 NE
NETHERLANDS. CENTRAAL BUREAU VOOR DE STATISTIEK. STATISTIEK DER MOTORVOERTUIGEN. STATISTICS OF MOTOR VEHICLES. (Text in Dutch and English) 1966. a. fl.10.75. Centraal Bureau voor de Statistiek, Prinses Beatrixlaan 428, Voorburg, Netherlands (Orders to: Staatsuitgeverij, Christoffel Plantijnstraat, The Hague, Netherlands)
Formerly: Netherlands. Centraal Bureau voor de Statistiek. Statistiek der Motorrijtuigen (ISSN 0077-698X)

381 US ISSN 0093-1195
OFFICIAL MOTOR HOME TRADE-IN GUIDE. a. $6.95. Intertec Publishing Corp., Technical Publications Division, 9221 Quivira Rd., Overland Park, KS 66212. (reprint service avail. from UMI)

381.45 US ISSN 0094-1131
OFFICIAL TRUCK CAMPER TRADE-IN GUIDE. a. $6.95. (Techincal Publications Division) Intertec Publishing Corp., 9221 Quivira Rd., Overland Park, KS 66212. stat. (reprint service avail. from UMI)

388.324 US
ROADWISE. 1949. a. $2.50. (Montana Motor Carriers Association, Inc.) Motor Carrier Service Inc., 1727 11th Ave., Helena, MT 59601. Ed. B. G. Havdahl. adv. circ. 3,500.

385.1 US
ST. PAUL, MINNESOTA. TWIN CITIES AREA METROPOLITAN TRANSIT COMMISSION. ANNUAL REPORT. 1969. a. free. Twin Cities Area Metropolitan Transit Commission, 801 American Center Bldg., St. Paul, MN 55101 (Dist. by Natl. Technical Information Service, Springfield, Va. 22151) Ed. Roger L. Downey. circ. 7,000.
Formerly: St. Paul, Minnesota. Metropolitan Transit Commission. Annual Report (ISSN 0082-710X)

388.324 CN ISSN 0707-0365
SASKATCHEWAN MOTOR TRANSPORT GUIDE. 1973. a. Saskatchewan Trucking Association, 1335 Wallace St., Regina, Sask. S4N 3Z5, Canada. Ed. Tom Durbin. adv. circ. 2,000.

388.3 SA
TRANSPORT MANAGER'S HANDBOOK; incorporating Commercial Transport Equipment Index. 1967. a. R.45. (Federation of Road Transport Associations) Thomson Publications S.A. (Pty) Ltd., P.O. Box 8308, Johannesburg 2000, South Africa. Ed. Heinz Engelhardt. adv. circ. 3,014.
Formerly: Commercial Transport Handbook and Buyer's Guide for S.A. (ISSN 0069-6676)

388.3 US ISSN 0082-6499
TRINC'S BLUE BOOK OF THE TRUCKING INDUSTRY. 1945. a. $145. Trinc Transportation Consultants, (Subsidiary of: Dun & Bradstreet, Inc.) 475 L'Enfant Plaza S.W., Suite 4200, Box 23091, Washington, DC 20024. Ed. C. E. Graver.

388.324 AT
TRUCK & BUS TESTS & SPECS. 1979. a. Aus.$6.50. Shennen Publishing & Publicity Co., 64 Kippax St., Surry Hills, N.S.W. 2010, Australia. Ed. F. Shennen. illus.

338.324 US ISSN 0190-3101
TRUCK & VAN BUYER'S GUIDE. a. $1.95. Petersen Publishing Co., 8490 Sunset Blvd., Los Angeles, CA 90069.

388.3 US ISSN 0362-5737
TRUCK BROKER DIRECTORY. a. J. J. Keller & Associates, Inc., 145 W. Wisconsin Ave., Neenah, WI 54956. adv.

388.324 CN ISSN 0564-3392
TRUCK DATA BOOK. vol. 34, 1981. a. Can.$17. Sanford Evans Publishing Ltd., 1077 St. James St., Box 6900, Winnipeg, Man. R3Q 3B1, Canada. Ed. C.B. Wagner.

388.324 US ISSN 0517-5666
TRUCK TAXES BY STATES. 1950. a. American Trucking Associations, Inc., 1616 P St. N.W., Washington, DC 20036.

388.3 US
WAREHOUSING/DISTRIBUTION DIRECTORY. 1963. a. $38. ‡ (Local and Short Haul Carriers Conference) Guide Services, Inc., 6291 Barfield Rd. N.E., Box 720455, Atlanta, GA 30328. Ed. W. M. Hite. circ. 12,000.
Former titles: National Distribution Directory of Local Cartage-Short Haul Carriers Warehousing (ISSN 0364-9539); National Distribution Directory (ISSN 0077-4219)

TRAVEL AND TOURISM

914.2 UK
A A/G B ROAD ATLAS. (Automobile Association - Great Britain) 1973. a. £8.95 to non-members. (Automobile Association) Geographia Ltd., 93 St. Peter's St., St. Albans, Herts. AL1 3EH, England.

910.2 916.76 KE
A A GUIDE TO MOTORING IN KENYA. 1966. a. EAs.42($6.50) (Automobile Association of East Africa) Nairobi News Publishers Ltd., P.O. Box 30339, Nairobi, Kenya. Ed. H. J. Reuter. adv. bk. rev. circ. 7,000.
Supersedes: Official Touring Guide to East Africa (ISSN 0078-3897)

917.3 US ISSN 0090-8614
A L A SIGHTS TO SEE BOOK. 1973. a. membership. ‡ Automobile Legal Association, Auto & Travel Club, 888 Worcester St., Wellesley, MA 02181. illus. circ. 30,000.
Formerly: Automobile Legal Association. A L A Green Book.

910.1 647.94 US
A Y H HANDBOOK. 1939. a. $1.25. American Youth Hostels, Inc., National Campus, Delaplane, VA 22025. Ed. Sam Shayon. adv. circ. 80,000.
Formerly: American Youth Hostels Guide and Handbook (ISSN 0066-1201)

914.2 UK
ACTIVITY HOLIDAYS IN BRITAIN. 1974. a. 60p. Farm Holiday Guides Ltd., 18 High St., Paisley PA1 2BX, Scotland.

ADAC-CAMPINGFUEHRER. BAND 1: SUEDEUROPA. see SPORTS AND GAMES — Outdoor Life

ADAC-CAMPINGFUEHRER. BAND 2: DEUTSCHLAND, MITTEL- UND NORDEUROPA. see SPORTS AND GAMES — Outdoor Life

910 US
ADVENTURE TRAVEL (NEW YORK) 1972. biennial. $7.95. Adventure Guides, Inc., 36 E. 57 St., New York, NY 10022. Ed. Pat Dickerman.
Formerly (until 1976): Adventure Trip Guide (ISSN 0084-5965)

916 915 HK
AFRICAN, MEDITERRANEAN AND ORIENTAL TRAVEL; handbook of international travel and tourism. 1963. a. $25. Travintal Ltd., Box 1237, G.P.O., Hong Kong, Hong Kong. Ed. Nina Casimaty. adv. bk. rev. bibl. charts. illus. index. circ. 10,000.
Former titles: African and Oriental Holiday (ISSN 0084-5981); African Middle and Far East Holiday

AGENT'S HOTEL GAZETTEER: AMERICA. see HOTELS AND RESTAURANTS

AGENT'S HOTEL GAZETTEER: RESORTS. see HOTELS AND RESTAURANTS

AIR TRAVEL ANSWERS. see TRANSPORTATION — Air Transport

910.09 US ISSN 0065-4868
AIR TRAVEL BARGAINS. 1965. a. $2.95. Air Travel Bargains Worldwide Guidebook, Box 897, Coconut Grove, Miami, FL 33133 (Dist. by Simon & Schuster) Ed. Jim Woodman. adv. circ. 50,000.

TRAVEL AND TOURISM

796.54   UK   ISSN 0065-5686
ALAN ROGERS' SELECTED SITES FOR CARAVANNING AND CAMPING IN EUROPE. 1968. a. £1.45. Deneway Guides and Travel Ltd., P.O. Box 286, Rottingdean, Brighton, BN2 8AY, England. adv. circ. 25,000.

917.98   US
ALASKA ALMANAC: FACTS ABOUT ALASKA. 1976. a. $3.95. Alaska Northwest Publishing Co., Box 4-EEE, Anchorage, AK 99509 (Circ. office: 130 Second Ave. South, Edmonds, WA 98020) illus.
   Formerly: Facts About Alaska (ISSN 0361-7823)

910.2   917   US   ISSN 0065-5848
ALASKA TRAVEL GUIDE. 1960. a. $4.95. Box 21038, Salt Lake City, UT 84121. Ed. Larry Lake. adv. bk. rev. circ. 52,000.

917.3   CN   ISSN 0707-3151
ALGOMA OUTDOORS. 1977. a. free contr. circ. Algoma Kinniwabi Travel Association, 553 Queen St. E., Sault Ste. Marie, Ont. P6A 2A3, Canada. illus.

917.9   US
ALL ABOUT ARIZONA, THE HEALTHFUL STATE. biennial. $4.95. Harian Publications, One Vernon Ave., Floral Park, NY 11001. Ed. Thomas B. Lesure.

910.2   II   ISSN 0065-6291
ALL INDIA GOVERNMENT TRAVELLERS BUNGALOWS ANNUAL RECORDER.* (Text in English) 1967. triennial. price varies. Hardy & Ally, 8-44 Regal Bldg., Box 184, New Delhi 1, India. Ed. K. N. Malhotra.

910.09   917   US   ISSN 0533-0653
ALL OF MEXICO AT LOW COST. biennial. $3.45. Harian Publications, One Vernon Ave., Floral Park, NY 11001. Ed. Norman D. Ford. charts.

910.09   GW
ALPENPAESSE ALPENSTRASSEN; ADAC-Reisefuehrer. 1969. irreg. DM.19380. (Allgemeiner Deutscher Automobil-Club e.V.) ADAC Verlag GmbH, Baumgartnerstr. 53, 8 Munich 70, Postfach 70 01 26, W. Germany (B.R.D.) adv. circ. 15,000.

917   US   ISSN 0569-1966
AMERICA BY CAR. 1958. biennial. $4.95. Harian Publications, One Vernon Ave., Floral Park, NY 11001. Ed. Norman D. Ford.

917.3   US   ISSN 0363-535X
AMERICAN EXECUTIVE TRAVEL COMPANION. Cover title: Guide to Traveling on Business in 50 States. 1976. a. Guides to Multinational Business, Inc., Box 92, Boston, MA 02138.

910.2   US   ISSN 0066-0884
AMERICAN TRAIL SERIES. irreg. Arthur H. Clark Co., 1264 S. Central Ave., Glendale, CA 91204.

915.1   CH
ANNUAL REPORT ON TOURISM STATISTICS, REPUBLIC OF CHINA. (Text in Chinese and English) 1972. a. Taipei Tourism Bureau, Box 1490, Taipei, Taiwan, Republic of China. illus.

914.504   IT
ANNUARIO GENERALE DELLE IMPRESE DI VIAGGIO E TURISMO. 1970. a. L.8000. Pubbliturist, Via Natale Battaglia 27, 20127 Milan, Italy. adv. circ. 10,000.

915   916   HK
ARAB COUNTRIES; handbook for the businessman and traveller. 1975. a. $10. Travintal Ltd., Box 1237, G.P.O., Hong Kong, Hong Kong. Ed. Nina Casimaty. adv. bk. rev. bibl. charts. illus. index. circ. 10,000.

910   YU
ARENATURIST. 1972. a. free. Arenaturist, Pula, Yugoslavia. Ed. Marijan Fistrovic.

910.202   HK
ASIA TRAVEL TRADE DIRECTORY. 1977. a. HK.$30. Interasia Publications, 200 Lockhart Rd., 13th Floor, Hong Kong, Hong Kong. adv. illus.

AUSTRALIAN-AMERICAN NEWS N.S.W. ANNUAL EDITION. see POLITICAL SCIENCE — International Relations

919.4   AT
AUSTRALIAN TOURIST COMMISSION. ANNUAL REPORT. 1968. a. Australian Tourist Commission, 414 St. Kilda Rd, Melbourne, Vic. 3004, Australia. illus. stat. (back issues avail.)

910   FI   ISSN 0355-2896
AUTOLLA ULKOMAILLE. 1965. a. Fmk.18. Autoliitto r.y. - Automobile and Touring Club of Finland, Kansakoulukatu 10, 00100 Helsinki 10, Finland. Ed. Reijo Kaukinen. circ. 7,000.
   Formerly: Kansainvalinen Automatkailu (ISSN 0075-4900)

910.09   UK
B A H R E P INTERNATIONAL HOTEL DIRECTORY. (British Association of Hotel Representatives) St. James Press Publications Ltd., 5-11 Worship St., London EC2A 2AY, England.

910.09   GW
DIE BADEPLAETZE IN DAENEMARK. triennial. DM.16.80. ADAC Verlag GmbH, 8 Munich 70, Baumgartnerstr. 53, Postfach 700086, W. Germany (B.R.D.)

910.09   GW
DIE BADEPLAETZE IN JUGOSLAWIEN. triennial. DM.16.80. ADAC Verlag GmbH, 8 Munich 70, Baumgartnerstr. 53, Postfach 700086, W. Germany (B.R.D.)

917.2   US   ISSN 0067-2955
BAJA CALIFORNIA TRAVEL SERIES. 1965. irreg., approx. 2/yr., vol. 39, 1977. $20 (approx.)per vol. ‡ Dawson's Book Shop, 535 N. Larchmont Blvd, Los Angeles, CA 90004. Eds. Edwin Carpenter, Glen Dawson. index in some volumes.cum.index planned. circ. 350.

919.7   BB
BARBADOS. PARKS AND BEACHES COMMISSION. ANNUAL REPORT. a. Parks and Beaches Commission, P.O. Box 111, Trident House, Bridgetown, Barbados.

919.704   BB
BARBADOS TOURIST BOARD. ANNUAL REPORT. no. 14, 1972. a. $3. Barbados Tourist Board, Bridgewater, Barbados, W. Indies. charts. illus.

914   US   ISSN 0146-8707
BAXTER'S EURAILPASS TRAVEL GUIDE. 1971. a. $5.95. Rail-Europe, Box 3255, Alexandria, VA 22302. Ed. Dr. Robert Baxter.

917   US
BAXTER'S U.S.A. BUS TRAVEL GUIDE. 1973. a. $5.95. Rail-Europe, Box 3255, Alexandria, VA 22302. Ed. Dr. Robert Baxter.

917   US
BAXTER'S U.S.A. TRAIN TRAVEL GUIDE. 1973. a. $5.95. Rail-Europe, Box 3255, Alexandria, VA 22302. Ed. Dr. Robert Baxter.

910.3   UK
BED AND BREAKFAST IN BRITAIN. 1955. a. 95p. ‡ Herald Advisory Services, 23A Brighton Rd, South Croydon, Surrey, CR2 6UE, England. Ed. Crispin Williams.
   Formed by the merger of: Bed and Breakfast in South and Southwest England (ISSN 0067-4761) & Bed and Breakfast in Wales, Northern England and Scotland (ISSN 0067-477X)

914.2   UK
BED & BREAKFAST STOPS. 1975. a. 60p. Farm Holiday Guides Ltd., 18 High St., Paisley PA1 2BX, Scotland.

910.4   UK   ISSN 0084-7755
BED, BREAKFAST AND EVENING MEAL. 1963. a. 60p. Starfish Books Ltd., Starfish House, Brook Farm Rd., Cobham, Surrey KT11 3AY, England. Ed. J.L. Harding. circ. 35,000.

910.2   UK   ISSN 0067-5342
BELFAST AND NORTHERN IRELAND DIRECTORY. 1852. a. £17.50. Century Services, Ltd., 51-59 Donegall St., Belfast BT1 2GB, N. Ireland. adv. circ. 3,000.

910 330   SZ   ISSN 0067-6152
BERNER STUDIEN ZUM FREMDENVERKEHR. 1966. irreg. price varies. (Universitaet Bern, Forschungsinstitut fuer Fremdenverkehr) Verlag Peter Lang AG, Muenzgraben 2, Postfach, CH-3000 Berne 7, Switzerland. Ed. J. Krippendorf.

796.95   914.2   UK
BLAKES HOLIDAYS AFLOAT. 1974. a. free. Blakes (Norfolk Broads Holidays) Ltd., Wroxham, Norwich NR12 8DH, England.
   Formed by merger of: Blakes International Holidays Afloat & Norfolk Broads Holidays Afloat (ISSN 0078-1142)

917.04   CN
BLUEWATER CIRCLE DRIVES. a. free. J. D. Thomson Tourist Promotions Ltd., R. R. No. 5 Dresden, Ontario N0P 1MD, Canada. adv. illus.

917.04   CN
BLUEWATER VACATION GUIDE; Lake Huron and Georgian Bay. 1969. a. free. J. D. Thomson Tourist Promotions Ltd., RR No. 5 Dresden, Ontario N0P 1MD, Canada. Ed. N.E. Thomson. adv. illus. circ. 27,000(controlled)

910.2   UK
BRITAIN WELCOMES COACHES. 1978. a. free to qualified personnel. Lewis Publications Ltd., 31 Castle St., Kingston upon Thames, Surrey KT1 1ST, England. Ed. David Jacobson. adv. circ. 15,000.

910.2   UK   ISSN 0068-2667
BRITISH TOURIST AUTHORITY. ANNUAL REPORT. 1969. a. £0.60. British Tourist Authority, 64-65 St. James St., London S.W.1, England. circ. 8,500.
   Formerly: British Travel and Holidays Association. Annual Report.

914.2   UK   ISSN 0068-2616
BRITISH TOURIST AUTHORITY. DIGEST OF TOURIST STATISTICS. 1969. irreg. £4. British Tourist Authority, 64-65 St. James' St., London SW1A 1NF, England.

910.2   UK   ISSN 0068-273X
BROADS BOOK. 1966. a. £1.15. Link House Publications Ltd, Link House, Dingwall Ave, Croydon, CR9 2TA, England. Ed. Heather Salter.

BUSINESSMAN'S DIRECTORY OF R.O.C. see BUSINESS AND ECONOMICS — Trade And Industrial Directories

914   FR   ISSN 0068-5151
CAHIERS DU TOURISME. (Issued in 5 parts: A-France; C-Recherche Fondamentale et Appliquee: Methodologie; D-Statistiques; E-Divers) 1963. irreg., no. 130,1980. price varies. Universite d'Aix-Marseille III (Universite de Droit, d'Economie et des Sciences.), Centre des Hautes Etudes Touristiques, 18 rue de l'Opera, 13100 Aix-en-Provence, France. circ. 300.

918.104   BL
CALENDARIO CULTURAL DO BRASIL. 1976. a. Conselho Federal de Cultura, Rio de Janeiro, Brazil. illus.

917   796.5   US
CALIFORNIA-NEVADA CAMPBOOK. Cover title: R V & Tent Sites in California, Nevada. a. membership. American Automobile Association, 8111 Gatehouse Rd., Falls Church, VA 22047.
   Formerly (until 1980): California-Nevada Camping.

796.5   917   US   ISSN 0094-0054
CAMPER'S GUIDE TO AREA CAMPGROUNDS. 1965. irreg; latest 1973. $3.95. c/o Marilee B. Pearsall, Timber Ridge Dr., Box 68-A, Coal Valley, IL 61240. illus. circ. 15,000.

910.2   914   FR   ISSN 0076-7735
CAMPING, CARAVANING IN FRANCE. Also known as: Michelin Annual Camping Guide for France. (Text in English, French, German and Dutch) a. $6.95. Michelin, Services de Tourisme, 75341 Paris Cedex 7, F 75341 Paris 7e, France (U.S. subscr. address: Michelin Guides and Maps, Box 5022, New Hyde Park, NY 11042)

917   796.5   US
CAMPING GUIDE. a. free. Department of Economic Development, 480 Cedar St., St. Paul, MN 55101. circ. 75,000.

CAMPINGBOKEN. see *SPORTS AND GAMES — Outdoor Life*

CAMPITUR: CAMPING, CARAVANING, VILLAGGI TURISTICI. see *SPORTS AND GAMES — Outdoor Life*

914.2　　　　UK　ISSN 0069-0066
CANALS BOOK. 1966. a. £1.15. Link House Publications Ltd, Link House, Dingwall Ave, Croydon, CR9 2TA, England. Ed. Heather Salter.

910.2　　　　UK　ISSN 0069-0317
CARAVAN & CHALET SITES GUIDE. a. £1. Haymarket Publishing Ltd., 38-42 Hampton Rd., Teddington, Middx. TW11 0JE, England.
　　Formerly: Caravan Sites in Britain and Ireland.

914.2　388.3　　UK
CARAVAN FACTFINDER. 1972. a. 85p. Link House Publications Ltd., Link House, Dingwall Ave., Croydon CR9 2TA, England. Ed. A. W. Bradford.
　　Incorporating: Caravan Yearbook (ISSN 0069-0333)

910.2　　　　AT　ISSN 0069-0295
CARAVAN MANUAL AND TOURIST PARK GUIDE.* 1948. a. $1.25. Age Publications, 250 Spencer St, Melbourne, 3000, Victoria, Australia.
　　Formerly: Caravan and Touring Manual.

910.2　914　　UK
CARAVAN SITES. 1955. a. 90p. Link House Publications Ltd., Link House, Dingwall Ave., Croydon CR9 2DY, England. Ed. Heather Salter.
　　Formerly: Caravan Sites and Mobile Home Parks (ISSN 0069-0309)
　　Guide to officially recognised caravan sites in Great Britain and Ireland

CARIBBEAN FREE TRADE ASSOCIATION. DIRECTORY. see *BUSINESS AND ECONOMICS — Trade And Industrial Directories*

917.2　　　　BB
CARIBBEAN TOURISM RESEARCH CENTRE. NEWSLETTER. Short title: C T R C Newsletter. 1977. irreg. Caribbean Tourism Research Centre, Mervue, Marine Gardens, Christ Church, Barbados, West Indies.

919.704　　　BB
CARIBBEAN TOURISM STATISTICS. 1977. irreg. Caribbean Tourism Research Centre, Mervue, Marine Gardens, Christ Church, Barbados, West Indies.

972　917　　CN　ISSN 0705-2731
CARIBBEAN YEAR BOOK. 1929. a. $36. Caribook Ltd., 1255 Yonge St., Toronto, Ont. M4T 1W6, Canada. Ed. Colin Rickards. adv. circ. 5,000.
　　Formerly (until vol. 48, 1977/78): West Indies and Caribbean Year Book (ISSN 0083-8233)

CATALOGUE OF CANADIAN RECREATION AND LEISURE RESEARCH. see *SPORTS AND GAMES — Outdoor Life*

918　　　　CJ
CAYMAN ISLANDS HOLIDAY GUIDE. 1972. s-a. $2. (Department of Tourism) Northwester Company Ltd., P.O. Box 243, George Town, Grand Cayman, British West Indies. Ed. Jim Graves. circ. 100,000.

CENTUR. see *TRANSPORTATION — Automobiles*

910.2　914　　UK　ISSN 0069-3456
CHILDREN WELCOME; happy Family Holiday Guide. 1956. a. 95p. ‡ Herald Advisory Services, 23A Brighton Rd., South Croydon, Surrey, CR2 6UE, England. Ed. Peter Stanley Williams. index.

CIRCLES OF FRIENDS: 200 NEW WAYS TO MAKE FRIENDS IN WASHINGTON DC. see *CLUBS*

910.4　　　　US
CITYGUIDE-THE SAN FRANCISCO BAY AREA AND NORTHERN CALIFORNIA. 1978. a. $4.95. Danella Publications, Box C, Sausalito, CA 94966. Ed. Bella Levin. adv. (back issues avail.)

910.2　914　　UK　ISSN 0069-4886
COACH TOURS IN BRITAIN & IRELAND. 1924. a. free. Galleon World Travel Ltd., Galleon House, King St., Maidstone, Kent ME14 1EG, England (Dist. in U.S. by: Fourways Travel Ltd., 950 Third Ave., New York, NY 10022) index.

910.2　　　　UK
COACHES & PARTIES WELCOME. 1977. a. free to qualified personnel. Lewis Publications Ltd., 31 Castle St., Kingston upon Thames, Surrey KT1 1ST, England. Ed. David Jacobson. adv. circ. 25,000.

910.202　　　CK
COLOMBIA. CORPORACION NACIONAL DE TURISMO. BOLETIN DE INVESTIGACIONES E INFORMACIONTURISTICA. 1970. irreg.; latest issue, 1974. free. Corporacion Nacional de Turismo, Apartado Aereo 8400, Bogota, Colombia. illus. circ. 2,500.

910　796.5　　UK
COME CRUISING. 1975. a. 50p. Boat Enquiries Ltd., 43 Botley Rd., Oxford 0X2 0PT, England.

CONFERENCES MEETINGS & EXHIBITIONS WELCOME. see *MEETINGS AND CONGRESSES*

917　　　　US
CONNECTICUT WEST. 1970. a. $0.60. Foothills Trader, Central Ave., New Hartford, CT 06057. Ed. Lillian J. Ludlam. adv. bibl. circ. 20,000.

CONTINENTAL CAMPING & CARAVAN SITES. see *SPORTS AND GAMES — Outdoor Life*

914.7　388　　UK
CONTINENTAL MOTORING HOLIDAYS. 1972. a. 50. Contemporary Press Ltd., 21A Alma Square, London NW8 9QA, England. Ed. Brian Hedges.

796　　　　US　ISSN 0147-3867
COUNTRY VACATIONS U.S.A. biennial. $5.95. Farm and Ranch Vacations, Inc., 36 E. 57 St., New York, NY 10022. Ed. Pat Dickerman.
　　Former titles: Farm, Ranch and Country Vacations; Farm, Ranch and Countryside Guide; Farm and Ranch Vacation Guide (ISSN 0085-0438)

910.4　382　　CY
CYPRUS. TOURISM ORGANISATION. ANNUAL REPORT. a. Tourism Organisation, Nicosia, Cyprus. charts. stat.

910.2　　　　GW　ISSN 0078-3943
D C C-CAMPING FUEHRER EUROPA. 1950. a. DM.9.80. (Deutscher Camping-Club e.V.) D C C-Wirtschaftsdienst und Verlag GmbH, Postfach 400428, 8000 Munich 40, W. Germany (B.R.D.) adv. circ. 45,000.

796.5　　　　GW
D C C-CARAVANFUEHRER. a. (Deutscher Camping Club e.V.) D C C-Wirtschaftsdienst und Verlag GmbH, Mandlstr. 28, 8000 Munich 40, W. Germany (B.R.D.) circ. 15,000.
　　Camping

796.5　　　　GW
D C C-TOURISTIK SERVICE. a. (Deutscher Camping Club e.V.) D C C-Wirtschaftsdienst und Verlag GmbH, Postfach 400428, 8000 Munich 40, W. Germany (B.R.D.) adv.
　　Camping

910　　　　AT
DAWSONS GUIDE TO AUSTRALIAN & WORLDWIDE HOTELS. a. Dawson Publications Pty. Ltd., Tramore House, Killarney Heights, Sydney, N.S.W. 2087, Australia. adv.

914.404　　　FR
DICTIONNAIRE DES COMMUNES (MICHELIN) irreg. $25.50. Michelin, Service de Tourisme, 46 Av de Breteuil, 75341 Paris Cedex 7, France (U. S. subscr. address: Michelin Guides and Maps, Box 5022, New Hyde Park, Ny 11042)

910.2　　　　FR　ISSN 0070-6515
DIRECTORY OF TRAVEL AGENCIES. 1950. a. membership. ‡ International Hotel Association, 89 Faubourg Saint-Honore, 75008 Paris, France. circ. 7,000.

DOMOVA POKLADNICA. see *LITERATURE*

914.2　　　　UK
EAST ANGLIA GUIDE. 1973. a. 60p. East Anglia Tourist Board, 14 Museum St., Ipswich, England. Ed. Mrs. K. Mason. circ. 35,000.

915　　　　JA　ISSN 0424-0944
EAST ASIA TRAVEL ASSOCIATION. PROCEEDINGS OF THE GENERAL MEETING.* 1967. irreg. East Asia Travel Association, c/o Japan National Tourist Organization, 2-13 Yurakucho, Tokyo, Japan.

916.7　　　　HK
EASTERN AFRICA; handbook of international travel and tourism. 1970. a. $8.75. Travintal Ltd., Box 1237, G.P.O., Hong Kong, Hong Kong. Ed. Nina Casimaty. adv. bk. rev. bibl. charts. illus. index. circ. 10,000.

917　796.5　　US　ISSN 0363-2091
EASTERN CANADA CAMPBOOK. Cover title: R V and Tent Sites in New Brunswick, Newfoundland, Nova Scotia, Ontario, Prince Edward Island, Quebec. a. membership. American Automobile Association, 8111 Gatehouse Rd., Falls Church, VA 22047.
　　Formerly (until 1980): Eastern Canada Camping.

910.2　338.4　　SP　ISSN 0070-864X
ECONOMIC REVIEW OF WORLD TOURISM. (Editions in: English, French) biennial. $24. World Tourism Organization, Avenida del Generalisimo, 59, Madrid-16, Spain.

918.1　　　　BL
EMPRESA BRASILEIRA DE TURISMO. ANUARIO ESTATISTICO. 1970. a (with supplement) price varies. Empresa Brasileira de Turismo, Praca Maua 7, Rio de Janeiro 20081, Brazil (Subscr. to: rua Ribeiro 272, 22040 Rio de Janeiro, Brazil) stat.

918.104　　　BL
EMPRESA BRASILEIRA DE TURISMO. CALENDARIO TURISTICO. English edition: Empresa Brasileira de Turismo. Tourist Calendar. French edition: Empresa Brasileira de Turismo. Calendrier Touristique. a. Empresa Brasileira de Turismo, Praca Maua 7, Rio de Janeiro 20000, Brazil.

914.2　　　　UK
ENGLAND'S BEST HOLIDAYS. 1974. a. 60p. Farm Holiday Guides Ltd., 18 High St., Paisley PA1 2BX, Scotland.

914.2　　　　UK
ENJOY SCOTLAND. 1972. a. Scottish Tourist Board, 23 Ravelston Terrace, Edinburgh EH4 3EU, Scotland. charts. illus. circ. 1,250,000.
　　Formerly: Scotland: a World of a Difference.

914　385　　US　ISSN 0085-0330
EURAIL GUIDE; how to travel Europe and all the world by train. 1971. a. $9.95. Eurail Guide Annual, 27540 Pacific Coast Highway, Malibu, CA 90265. Eds. Marvin L. Saltzman, Kathryn S. Muileman.

EUROPA CAMPING UND CARAVANING. INTERNATIONALER FUEHRER. see *SPORTS AND GAMES — Outdoor Life*

910.202　　　IT
EUROPA FACILE. 1971. irreg., latest edt. 1979. L.3600 to non-members. Touring Club Italiano, Corso Italia 10, 20122 Milan, Italy. adv. illus. circ. 50,000.
　　Continues: Touring Club Italiano. Servizio Informazioni Turistiche. Fascicoli di Documentazione per i Viaggi in Europa.

910　　　　GW
EUROPAEISCHER FERNWANDERWEG. 1975. irreg., latest no. 6. DM.12.80. J. Fink-Kuemmerly und Frey Verlag GmbH, Gebelsbergstr. 41, 7000 Stuttgart 1, W. Germany (B.R.D.)

910.09　　　US　ISSN 0429-9639
FABULOUS MEXICO; where everything costs less. biennial. $2.50 per issue. Harian Publications, One Vernon Ave., Floral Park, NY 11001.

919　　　　FK
FALKLAND ISLANDS JOURNAL. (Text in English) 1967. a. 60p. ‡ Ross House, Stanley, Falkland Islands, South Atlantic. Ed.Bd. illus. circ. 400.

910.2   UK   ISSN 0071-3740
FAMILY HOLIDAY GUIDE. 1953. a. 75p. ‡ Lewis Publications Ltd., 31 Castle St., Kingston Upon Thames, Surrey KT1 1ST, England. Ed. David Jacobson. adv. circ. 75,000.

914.2   IE
FARM HOLIDAYS IN IRELAND. 1970. a. $3. Libra House Ltd., Box 1127, Dublin 8, Ireland. Ed. Cathal Tyrrell. circ. 53,650.

647.94   US   ISSN 0197-9477
FASTFACTS U.S.A. HOTEL MOTEL LOCATOR. 1979. irreg. $25. Denhamwood, Inc., 4069 Hayvenhurst Ave., Encino, CA 91436.

917   US
FESTIVALS SOURCEBOOK; a reference guide to fairs, festivals and celebrations in agriculture, antiques, the arts, theatre and drama, arts and crafts, community, dance, ethnic events, film, folk, food and drink, history, Indians, marine, music, seasons and wildlife. 1977. irreg. $50. Gale Research Company, Book Tower, Detroit, MI 48226. Ed. Paul Wasserman.

910.2   US
FIELDING'S CARIBBEAN. 1968. a. $10.95. Fielding Publications, 105 Madison Ave., New York, NY 10016. (Affiliate: William Morrow and Company, Inc.) index.
  Former titles: Fielding's Caribbean, Including Cuba; (until 1979): Fielding's Guide to the Caribbean Plus the Bahamas (ISSN 0071-4755)

910.2   US   ISSN 0192-5326
FIELDING'S EUROPE. 1948. a. $10.95. Fielding Publications, 105 Madison Ave., New York, NY 10016. (Affiliate: William Morrow and Company, Inc.) Auth. Temple Fielding. index.
  Formerly: Fielding's Travel Guide to Europe.

647   US   ISSN 0191-0329
FIELDING'S FAVORITES: HOTELS & INNS, EUROPE. 1972. a. $4.95. Fielding Publications, 105 Madison Ave., New York, NY 10016. (Affiliate: William Morrow and Company, Inc.)
  Formerly: Fielding's Selected Favorites: Hotels and Inns, Europe (ISSN 0092-9506)

910.2   US   ISSN 0095-6406
FIELDING'S LOW-COST EUROPE. 1967. a. $5.95. Fielding Publications, 105 Madison Ave., New York, NY 10016. (Affiliate: William Morrow and Company, Inc.) Auth. Nancy & Temple Fielding.
  Formerly: Fielding's Super Economy Europe (ISSN 0071-4798)

910.2   US   ISSN 0071-478X
FIELDING'S SELECTIVE SHOPPING GUIDE TO EUROPE. 1957. a. $4.95. Fielding Publications, 105 Madison Ave., New York, NY 10016. (Affiliate: William Morrow and Company, Inc.) Auth. Nancy And Temple Fielding. index.

FINANCIAL TIMES WORLD HOTEL DIRECTORY. see *HOTELS AND RESTAURANTS*

919.04   US   ISSN 0191-2321
FODOR'S AUSTRALIA, NEW ZEALAND AND THE SOUTH PACIFIC. a. $13.95. David McKay Co., 2 Park Ave., New York, NY 10016. Ed. Robert C. Fisher. illus.

910.2   US   ISSN 0071-6340
FODOR'S AUSTRIA. 1951. a. $11.95. David McKay Co., 2 Park Ave., New York, NY 10016. Eds. Eugene Fodor, Robert Fisher.

910.2   US   ISSN 0071-6359
FODOR'S BELGIUM AND LUXEMBOURG. 1951. biennial. $10.95. David McKay Co., 2 Park Ave., New York, NY 10016. Eds. Eugene Fodor, Robert Fisher.

914.4   US
FODOR'S BUDGET FRANCE. 1980. $4.95. David McKay Co., 2 Park Ave., New York, NY 10016.

910   US   ISSN 0270-787X
FODOR'S BUDGET ITALY. irreg. $4.95. David McKay Co., 2 Park Ave., New York, NY 10016. Ed. Richard Moore.

917.9   US   ISSN 0192-9925
FODOR'S CALIFORNIA. irreg., 2nd edt. 1980. $9.95. David McKay Co., 2 Park Ave., New York, NY 10016.

910.2   US   ISSN 0098-2547
FODOR'S CARIBBEAN, BAHAMAS AND BERMUDA. 1962. a. $9.95. David McKay Co., 2 Park Ave., New York, NY 10016. Eds. Eugene Fodor, Robert Fisher.
  Formerly: Fodor's Guide to the Caribbean, Bahamas, and Bermuda (ISSN 0071-6561)

910   US   ISSN 0270-8183
FODOR'S CENTRAL AMERICA. a. $13.95. David McKay Co., 2 Park Ave., New York, NY 10016. Ed. Robert C. Fisher.

910.09   US   ISSN 0160-3914
FODOR'S CRUISES EVERYWHERE. 1977. a. $9.95. David McKay Co., 2 Park Ave., New York, NY 10016. Eds. Eugene Fodor, Robert Fisher. illus.

910.2   US   ISSN 0071-6367
FODOR'S CZECHOSLOVAKIA. 1970. irreg. $12.95. David McKay Co., 2 Park Ave., New York, NY 10016. Eds. Eugene Fodor, Robert Fisher.

916   US   ISSN 0147-8176
FODOR'S EGYPT. 1977. a. $9.95. David McKay Co., 2 Park Ave., New York, NY 10016. Eds. Eugene Fodor, Robert Fisher. illus.

914   US
FODOR'S EUROPE TALKING. 1975. irreg. $7.95. David McKay Co., 2 Park Ave., New York, NY 10016. Ed. Eugene Fodor. illus.

917   US   ISSN 0192-3730
FODOR'S FAR WEST. 1975. biennial. $4.95. David McKay Co., 2 Park Ave., New York, NY 10016. Eds. Eugene Fodor, Robert Fisher. illus.

917.5   US
FODOR'S FLORIDA. irreg., 2nd edt. 1980. $9.95. David McKay Co., 2 Park Ave., New York, NY 10017.

910.2   US   ISSN 0071-6383
FODOR'S FRANCE. 1951. a. $9.95. David McKay Co., 2 Park Ave., New York, NY 10016. Eds. Eugene Fodor, Robert Fisher.

910.2   US   ISSN 0192-0952
FODOR'S GERMANY: WEST AND EAST. 1951. a. $10.95. David McKay Co., 2 Park Ave., New York, NY 10016. Eds. Eugene Fodor, Robert Fisher.
  Formerly: Fodor's Germany (ISSN 0071-6391)

910.2   US   ISSN 0071-6405
FODOR'S GREAT BRITAIN. 1951. a. $11.95. David McKay Co., 2 Park Ave., New York, NY 10016. Eds. Eugene Fodor, Robert Fisher.

910.2   US   ISSN 0071-6413
FODOR'S GREECE. 1951. a. $9.95. David McKay Co., 2 Park Ave., New York, NY 10016. Eds. Eugene Fodor, Robert Fisher.

910.2   US   ISSN 0071-6375
FODOR'S GUIDE TO EUROPE. 1959. a. $9.95. David McKay Co., 2 Park Ave., New York, NY 10016. Eds. Eugene Fodor, Robert Fisher.

910.2   US   ISSN 0071-6421
FODOR'S HAWAII. 1961. a. $9.95. David McKay Co., 2 Park Ave., New York, NY 10016. Eds. Eugene Fodor, Robert Fisher.

910.2   US   ISSN 0071-643X
FODOR'S HOLLAND. 1951. biennial. $11.95. David McKay Co., 2 Park Ave., New York, NY 10016.

910.2   US
FODOR'S INDIA & NEPAL. 1963. biennial. $14.95. David McKay Co., 2 Park Ave., New York, NY 10016.
  Formerly: Fodor's India (ISSN 0071-6456)

910.2   US   ISSN 0071-6464
FODOR'S IRELAND. 1968. a. $9.95. David McKay Co., 2 Park Ave., New York, NY 10016.

910.2   US   ISSN 0071-6588
FODOR'S ISRAEL. 1967. a. $9.95. David McKay Co., 2 Park Ave., New York, NY 10016.

910.2   US   ISSN 0071-6472
FODOR'S ITALY. 1951. a. $12.95. David McKay Co., 2 Park Ave., New York, NY 10016.

910.2   US   ISSN 0098-1613
FODOR'S JAPAN AND KOREA. 1962. a. $13.95. David McKay Co., 2 Park Ave., New York, NY 10016.
  Supersedes in part: Fodor's Japan and East Asia (ISSN 0071-6480)

910.2   US   ISSN 0071-6596
FODOR'S LONDON. 1971. a. $5.95. David McKay Co., 2 Park Ave., New York, NY 10016.

910.2   US   ISSN 0071-6499
FODOR'S MEXICO. 1972. a. $10.95. David McKay Co., 2 Park Ave., New York, NY 10016.

917   US   ISSN 0192-5571
FODOR'S MIDWEST. 1975. irreg. $7.95. David McKay Co., 2 Park Ave., New York, NY 10016. illus.

917   US   ISSN 0192-3412
FODOR'S NEW ENGLAND. 1975. biennial. $7.95. David McKay Co., 2 Park Ave., New York, NY 10016. illus.

917   US
FODOR'S NEW YORK. 1975. irreg. $7.95. David McKay Co., 2 Park Ave., New York, NY 10016. illus.
  Formerly: Fodor's New York & New Jersey.

914.4   US   ISSN 0149-1288
FODOR'S PARIS. 1973. biennial. $5.95. David McKay Co., 2 Park Ave., New York, NY 10016.

910.2   US   ISSN 0071-6510
FODOR'S PORTUGAL. 1951. a. $10.95. David McKay Co., 2 Park Ave., New York, NY 10016.

910.2   US   ISSN 0071-6529
FODOR'S SCANDINAVIA. 1951. a. $13.95. David McKay Co., 2 Park Ave., New York, NY 10016.

917   US   ISSN 0147-8680
FODOR'S SOUTH. 1975. biennial. $9.95. David McKay Co., 2 Park Ave., New York, NY 10016. illus.

910.2   US   ISSN 0071-6537
FODOR'S SOUTH AMERICA. 1966. a. $10.95. David McKay Co., 2 Park Ave., New York, NY 10016.

910.2   US   ISSN 0160-8991
FODOR'S SOUTHEAST ASIA. 1975. biennial. $13.95. David McKay Co., 2 Park Ave., New York, NY 10016.
  Supersedes in part: Fodor's Japan and East Asia (ISSN 0071-6480)

917   US   ISSN 0147-8656
FODOR'S SOUTHWEST. 1975. biennial. $7.95. David McKay Co., 2 Park Ave., New York, NY 10016. illus.

914.7   US   ISSN 0095-1358
FODOR'S SOVIET UNION. 1975. biennial. $13.95. David McKay Co., 2 Park Ave., New York, NY 10016. Eds. E. Fodor, R. C. Fisher. illus.

910.2   US   ISSN 0071-6545
FODOR'S SPAIN. 1955. a. $10.95. David McKay Co., 2 Park Ave., New York, NY 10016. Eds. Eugene Fodor, Robert Fisher.

910.2   US   ISSN 0071-6553
FODOR'S SWITZERLAND. 1951. a. $11.95. David McKay Co., 2 Park Ave., New York, NY 10016.

910.2   US   ISSN 0071-6618
FODOR'S TURKEY. 1969. a. $11.95. David McKay Co., 2 Park Ave., New York, NY 10016.

917   US   ISSN 0147-8745
FODOR'S U.S.A. 1976. a. $10.95. David McKay Co., 2 Park Ave., New York, NY 10016. illus.

910.2   US   ISSN 0071-657X
FODOR'S YUGOSLAVIA. 1951. a. $11.95. David McKay Co., 2 Park Ave., New York, NY 10016.

TRAVEL AND TOURISM

387.2 US ISSN 0096-1353
FORD'S DECK PLAN GUIDE. Short title: Deck Plan Guide. 1974. base vol. plus annual updates. $40. Ford's Travel Guides, Box 505, 22151 Clarendon St., Woodland Hills, CA 91365. illus.

910.2 FR ISSN 0071-8734
FRANCE EN POCHE. TOTAL GUIDE.* 1970. a. Editions Vrille-Copalic, 32 Boulevard Flandrin, Paris 16e, France.

917 UK
FREIGHTHOPPERS' MANUAL FOR NORTH AMERICA. 1981. irreg. £1.95. Travelaid Publishing, Box 369, London NW3 4ER, England.

910 AU ISSN 0071-948X
FREMDENVERKEHR IN OESTERREICH. (Subseries of: Beitraege zur Oesterreichischen Statistik) 1956/57. a. S.420. ‡ (Oesterreichisches Statistisches Zentralamt) Carl Ueberreuter, Alserstr. 24, Postfach 60, A-1095 Vienna, Austria. circ. 600.

914 UK
FRENCH FARM AND VILLAGE HOLIDAY GUIDE. (Text in English and French) a. $4.95. Duo Publishing Ltd., 1 Hermes St, London N1, England. Ed. J. H. McCartney. illus. circ. 50,000.

790 US
FUNPARKS DIRECTORY. Variant title: Amusement Business's Funparks Directory. 1961. a. $18. Billboard Publications, Inc., Amusement Business Division, Box 24970, Nashville, TN 37202. Ed. Steve Rogers. adv. circ. 5,200. (also avail. in microfilm)
Formerly: Funspots Directory (ISSN 0071-9951)
Annual market report and directory of amusement parks, tourist attractions and zoos in North America

910.2 UK ISSN 0071-996X
FURNISHED HOLIDAY HOMES & CARAVANS. 1958. a. 95p. ‡ Herald Advisory Services, 23A Brighton Rd., South Croydon, Surrey, CR2 6UE, England. Ed. Crispin Williams. index.

918.304 CL ISSN 0431-1930
GEOCHILE. 1951. irreg. (Sociedad Geografica de Chile) Lord Cochrane S.A., Providencia 711, Santiago, Chile. illus.

917 US ISSN 0533-8387
GEORGIA WELCOME CENTER. RESEARCH REPORT. 1968. irreg. free. (Department of Community Development) University of Georgia, College of Business Administration, Athens, GA 30601. Ed. Polly W. Hein. stat.

914.104 UK
GLIMPSE OF LONDON WITH AMERICAN EXPRESS. 1965. a. free. (American Express International, US) Warner Publicity Ltd., 11 Old Bond St., London W.1, England. Ed. Michael Cope. circ. 50,000.

914.2 UK
GOFF'S GUIDE TO CATER YOURSELF HOLIDAYS. 1977. a. 50p. London and Continental Publishing Ltd., 42-43 Gerrard St., London W1V 7LP, England. Ed. Robert Redman.

796.5 UK ISSN 0142-5978
GOOD CAMPS GUIDE. 1976. a. £1. Deneway Guides and Travel Ltd., Box 286, Rottingdean, Brighton, Sussex BN2 8AY, England. Ed. Alan Rogers. adv. circ. 30,000.

914.95 GR ISSN 0432-6105
GREECE. (Text in English) 1950. a. National Tourist Organisation of Greece, General Direction of Promotion, Odos Amerikis 2, Athens, Greece. illus.

916 332.6 HK
GREECE AS LINK BETWEEN ARAB COUNTRIES AND THE WEST; handbook for the businessman and investor. 1979. a. $4.20. Travintal Ltd., Box 1237, G.P.O., Hong Kong, Hong Kong. Nina Casimaty. adv. bk. rev. bibl. charts. illus. index. circ. 10,000.

914.2 388 UK
GUESTHOUSES, FARMHOUSES AND INNS IN BRITAIN. a. £2.75 to non-members. Automobile Association, Fanum House, Basingstoke, Hants RG21 2EA, England. adv.
Formerly: Automobile Association. Budget Guide.

647 SP
GUIA DE HOTELES: ESPANA. (Includes some material in English, French, German, Italian, Portuguese and Swedish) a. 350 ptas. Direccion General de Empresas y Actividades Turisticas, Madrid-16, Spain. illus.
Continues: Hoteles de Spana; Guia Oficial Abreviada.

918.204 AG
GUIA DE TURISMO. 1977. a. Ediciones Cicerone, Peru 327, Buenos Aires, Argentina. Ed. Alberto Gorlier.

910.202 SP
GUIA DE VALENCIA: TURISTICA, URBANA, COMERCIAL. 1960. a. 225 ptas. Ediciones Gaisa, Gran via Marques de Turia 64, Valencia 5, Spain. Ed. S. L. Gaisa. illus. circ. 3,000.

917.204 HO
GUIA OFICIAL DE CENTRO-AMERICA. 1922. irreg. Apartado 494, Tegucigalpa, Honduras.

910.202 AG
GUIA PEUSER DE TURISMO ARGENTINA Y SUDAMERICANA.* irreg. Peuser S.A., San Martin 200, Buenos Aires, Argentina. illus.
Continues: Turismo, Guia Peuser (ISSN 0533-4675)

918.104 AG
GUIA TURISTICA DE ROSARIO Y SANTE FE. vol. 13, 1975. irreg. Talleres Graficos Amalevi, Calle Mendoza 1851, Rosario, Santa Fe, Argentina. Ed. Rafael Vinas Paris. adv. illus.

910.202 AG
GUIA TURISTICA Y DE CALLES DE LA CIUDAD DE MAR DEL PLATA. Cover title: Guia Filcar Mar del Plata. irreg. Arg.$10. Filcar, Saavedra 138, Buenos Aires, Argentina. illus.

918.704 VE
GUIA TURISTICA Y HOTELES DE VENEZUELA Y EL CARIBE. (Text in English & Spanish) 1971. a. $6. Guiturven, Av. Francisco de Miranda, Edificio Banco Caracas, Torre Norte, Apdo. 51881, Chacao, Caracas, Venezuela. Ed. Felix Contreras Berdial. adv. charts. illus. circ. 25,000.

796 IT
GUIDA DELLO SCIATORE. a; 1969/70 no. 12. (Federazione Italiana Sport Invernali) Milano Sole Editore, Via Denti 2, 20133 Milan, Italy. adv.

914.504 IT ISSN 0487-3750
GUIDA SARDEGNA D'OGGI. Title varies: Sardegna d'Oggi; Guida Practica. 1955. irreg., 7th, 1976. L.4800. Poliedrica Editrice, Plaza Bologna 1 bis, Rome, Italy. charts. illus.

642.5 901.202 FR
GUIDE DES RELAIS ROUTIERS. (Editions in English and Dutch) 1934. a. 30 F. 6 rue de l'Isly, 75008 Paris, France. Ed. Bertrand de Saulieu. adv. charts. circ. 70,000; english edt. 20,000; belgian edt. 5,000; dutch edt. 5,000.

642.5 910.202 FR
GUIDE KLEBER FRANCE. (Text in French, summaries in English) 1961. a. 49.80 F. R.C.P. Edition, 6 Villa Emile Bergerat, 92200 Neuilly sur Seine, France (Dist. by: French European Publications, 610 Fifth Ave., New York, NY 10020) Ed. Jean Didier. adv. charts.

914.2 UK
GUIDE TO BRITAIN'S BEST HOLIDAYS. 1968. a. 70p. Farm Holiday Guides Ltd., 18 High St., Paisley PA1 2BX, Scotland.

910 US
GUIDE TO CANADA. 1972. a. Rand McNally & Co., 8225 N. Central Pk., Skokie, IL 60076 (Orders to: Box 7600, Chicago, IL 60680) Ed. Len Hilts.
Formerly: Explore Canada (ISSN 0085-0373)

796.5 UK
GUIDE TO CARAVAN AND CAMPING HOLIDAYS. 1975. a. 60p. Farm Holiday Guides Ltd., 18 High St., Paisley PA1 2BX, Scotland.

917 796.93 US
GUIDE TO SKIING IN MINNESOTA. a. free. Department of Economic Development, 480 Cedar St., St. Paul, MN 55101. circ. 10,000.
Incorporating: Guide to Downhill Skiing in Minnesota & Guide to Cross Country Skiing in Minnesota.

959 TH
GUIDE TO THAILAND. (Text in English) 1969. a. $2. Temple Publicity Services, 4Th Floor, British Airways Building, 133/19 Gaysorn Road, P.O. Box 316, Bangkok, Thailand. circ. 5,000.

910.2 AT ISSN 0072-9809
HANDBOOK OF FIJI. 1962. irreg., 4th ed., 1980. Aus.$11.95. Pacific Publications (Australia) Pty. Ltd., G.P.O. Box 3408, Sydney, N.S.W. 2001, Australia. Ed. Stuart Inder.

910.2 II ISSN 0073-0378
HARDY'S ENCYCLOPAEDIA GUIDE TO AGRA, JAIPUR, DELHI, VARANASI.* (Text in English) 1970. a. price varies. Hardy & Ally, 8-44 Regal Bldg., Box 184, New Delhi 1, India. Ed. K. N. Malhotra.

919 US ISSN 0197-8527
HAWAII ON 25 DOLLARS A DAY. a. $4.95. Frommer-Pasmantier Publishing Corp., 205 E. 42nd St., New York, NY 10017.
Formerly: Hawaii on 20 Dollars a Day.

919.69 US ISSN 0066-412X
HAWAII VISTORS BUREAU. ANNUAL RESEARCH REPORT. 1953. a. $15 to non-members. Hawaii Visitors Bureau, Research Committee, 2270 Kalakaua Ave., Honolulu, HI 96815. Ed. Evelyn K. Richardson. circ. 3,000.

HERALD CARAVANNING GUIDE. see *SPORTS AND GAMES* — *Outdoor Life*

910.2 UK
HOLIDAY CAMPS AND CENTRES DIRECTORY. 1947. a. 50p. Stone and Cox (Publications) Ltd., 44 Fleet Street, London EC4Y 1BS, England.
Formerly: Holiday Camps Directory and Magazine (ISSN 0073-2966)

914 UK ISSN 0073-3024
HOLIDAYS IN BRITAIN. 1924. a. free. Galleon World Travel Ltd., Galleon House, King St., Maidstone, Kent ME14 1EG, England (Dist. in U.S. by: Fourways Travel Ltd., 950 Third Ave., New York, NY 10022) index.

914.2 UK
HOLIDAYS IN THE SUN, DEVON, CORNWALL, SOMERSET AND DORSET. 1965. a. 55p. Starfish Books Ltd., Starfish House, Brook Farm Road, Cobham, Surrey KT11 3AY, England.
Formerly: Devon and Cornwall Holidays in the Sun (ISSN 0070-461X)

914.2 UK
HOLIDAYS IN WALES. 1974. a. 60p. Farm Holiday Guides Ltd., 18 High St., Paisley PA1 2BX, Scotland.

HOLY PLACES OF PALESTINE. see *RELIGIONS AND THEOLOGY*

915 HK
HONG KONG STREETS AND PLACES. (Text in English and Chinese) no. 2, 1978. a. Government Land Surveyor, Lands and Survey Dept., Murray Bldg., Garden Rd., Hong Kong, Hong Kong.

917 780 UK
HONKY TONKIN': A TRAVEL GUIDE TO AMERICAN MUSIC. 1980. biennial. £2.95. Travelaid Publishing, Box 369, London NW3 4ER, England.

910.2 UK ISSN 0073-3431
HOSEASONS HOLIDAYS BOATS AND BUNGALOWS HIRE. 1946. a. free. Hoseasons, Sunway House, Oulton Broad, Lowestoft, Suffolk NR32 3LT, England.

647.94 US
HOSTELING HOLIDAYS. 1956. a. free. American Youth Hostels, Inc., Metropolitan New York Council, 132 Spring St., New York, NY 10012. circ. 50,000.

HOTELFUEHRER DEUTSCHLAND. see *HOTELS AND RESTAURANTS*

914 647 UK
I A T A TRAVEL AGENTS DIRECTORY OF EUROPE. (Text in English and French) 1980. biennial. £20. Morgan-Grampian Book Publishing Co., 30 Calderwood St., Woolwich, London SE18 6QH England. Ed. Jane Doyle. adv. circ. 1,500.

338.4 US
I C T A DIRECTORY. a. Institute of Certified Travel Agents, 148 Linden St., Box 56, Wellesley, MA 02181.
Formerly: I C T A Roster (ISSN 0094-3517)

917.04 US
I LOVE NEW YORK: THE FINGER LAKES TRAVEL GUIDE. 1951. a. $0.75. Finger Lakes Association, Inc., 309 Lake Street, Penn Yan, NY 14527. Ed. Conrad T. Tunney. adv. circ. 55,000.
Formerly: Finger Lakes Travel Guide.

910.09 US
IMPACT OF TRAVEL ON STATE ECONOMIES. 1976. a. $20. U S Travel Data Center, 1899 L St., N.W., Washington, DC 20036.

915.4 II
INDIA AT A GLANCE.* a. Rs.15. Commercial Publications Bureau, Post Box No. 3005, New Delhi, India.

910 915 AT
INDONESIA DO-IT-YOURSELF. 1976. a. $6. Palmii 49 Park St., South Yarra, Vic., Australia. illus.

917.204 CR
INSTITUTO COSTARRICENSE DE TURISMO.. MEMORIA ANUAL. a. Instituto Costarricense de Turismo, San Jose, Costa Rica. illus.

910.2 BE ISSN 0074-5979
INTERNATIONAL FEDERATION OF JOURNALISTS AND TRAVEL WRITERS. OFFICIAL LIST/REPERTOIRE OFFICIEL. (Text in English, French) 1965. irreg., 1975, latest issue. International Federation of Journalists and Travel Writers, c/o J. P. Delfeld, Pres., 32 rue de l'Automne, 1050 Brussels, Belgium.

910.2 SZ ISSN 0074-9133
INTERNATIONAL TOURING ALLIANCE. MINUTES OF THE GENERAL ASSEMBLY. (Text in English and French) 1898. a. free. International Touring Alliance, 2 Quai Gustave Ador, Geneva, Switzerland.

917 US
INTERNATIONAL TRAVEL GUIDE TO FLORIDA. (Text in English, French, German, Portuguese and Japanese) 1969. a. Hal Herman, Box 2226, Hollywood, FL 33020. Ed. Bernard Block. index. circ. 250,000 (controlled)

915.69 IS ISSN 0075-1405
ISRAEL TOURIST STATISTICS/HA-TAYARUT BE-YISRAEL. (Subseries of the Bureau's Special Series) (Text in Hebrew and English) irreg., latest issue, no. 623, 1978. I£140. Central Bureau of Statistics, Box 13015, Jerusalem, Israel.

910.2 GW ISSN 0075-2150
JAEGER'S INTERTRAVEL; world guide to travel agencies, tour operators, countries, towns and hotels. (Text in English) 1959. a. DM.84. Jaeger-Verlag GmbH, Holzhofallee 38a, Postfach 110320, 6100 Darmstadt, W. Germany (B.R.D.) adv.

382 GW ISSN 0075-2649
JAHRBUCH FUER FREMDENVERKEHR. 1950. a. DM.25. Deutsches Wirtschaftswissenschaftliches Institut fuer Fremdenverkehr, Hermann-Sack-Str. 2, Postfach 264, 8000 Munich 33, W. Germany (B.R.D.) circ. 500 (approx.)

917 UK ISSN 0447-3280
JAMAICA ANNUAL.* 1973. a. Arawak Press Ltd., 53 Cadogan Gardens, London SW3 2TH, England. adv. charts. illus.

910.2 UK ISSN 0075-3750
JEWISH TRAVEL GUIDE. 1950. a. $8.95. Jewish Chronicle Publications, 25 Furnival St., London EC4A 1JT, England. Ed. S. Lightman. adv. index. circ. 10,000.
World guide for Jewish travellers

915 JO
JORDAN. MINISTRY OF TOURISM AND ANTIQUITIES. TOURISM ANNUAL REPORT. (Text in Arabic) a. Ministry of Tourism & Antiquities, Box 224, Amman, Jordan. circ. 700.

915.6 JO
JORDAN. MINISTRY OF TOURISM AND ANTIQUITIES. TOURIST ARRIVALS IN NUMBERS. Variant title: Jordan. Ministry of Tourism and Antiquities. Travel Statistics. (Text in English) a. Ministry of Tourism & Antiquities, Box 224, Amman, Jordan. circ. 1,000.

916.891 RH
JUMBO GUIDE TO RHODESIA. $3. Wilrey Publications, P.O. Box 3430, Salisbury, Zimbabwe. illus.

KARNATAKA. DEPARTMENT OF TOURISM. ANNUAL REPORT. see *PUBLIC ADMINISTRATION*

914.304 GW
KAUPERTS DEUTSCHLAND STAEDTE-, HOTEL- UND REISEFUEHRER. a. DM.25. Adressbuch-Gesellschaft Berlin mbH, Friedrichstr. 210, 1000 Berlin 61, W. Germany (B.R.D.)

338.4 KE
KENYA. CENTRAL BUREAU OF STATISTICS. MIGRATION AND TOURISM STATISTICS. 1971. irreg., latest 1973 (covers 1968-71) Central Bureau of Statistics, Box 30266, Nairobi, Kenya (Orders to: Government Printing and Stationery Office, Box 30128, Nairobi, Kenya)

KULTURNOPOLITICKY KALENDAR. see *MEETINGS AND CONGRESSES*

914.04 UK
LAKELAND RAMBLER. 1933. a. 60p. Lakescene Publications, 12 Lonsdale St., Carlisle, Cumbria, England. Ed. Roland Taylor. adv. bk. rev. illus. circ. 5,000. (tabloid format)

910.2 US
LATIN AMERICAN TRAVEL GUIDE & PAN AMERICAN HIGHWAY GUIDE (MEXICO-CENTRAL-SOUTH AMERICA) 1966. irreg., approx. biennial, latest 1980. $9.95. Compsco Publishing Co., 663 Fifth Ave., New York, NY 10022. Ed. Ernst A. Jahn. adv. bk. rev. circ. 125,000.
Former titles: Latin American Travel Guide; Latin American Travel and Pan American Highway Guide (ISSN 0075-8159)

914 387 UK
LAZY WAY TO BOOK YOUR CAR FERRIES. 1970. a. £0.25. Car Ferry Enquiries Ltd., 9A Spur Rd., Isleworth, Middlesex, England. Ed. Roger Frankland. tr.lit. circ. 25,000.

917.104 CN
LEISURE STUDY CANADA/LOISIRES AU CANADA. (Text in English & French) irreg. (Department of the Secretary of State, Arts and Culture Branch) Comstat Consulting Services, Ltd., 100 Sparks St., Suite 403, Ottawa, Ont. K1P 5B7, Canada.

917.4 US
LEISUREGUIDE - BOSTON. 1978. a. Leisureguides,Inc., 11501 N.W. Second Ave., Miami, FL 33168. adv. circ. 3,050,000.

917 US
LEISUREGUIDE - CHICAGO. 1971. a. Leisureguides, Inc., 11501 N.W. Second Ave., Miami, FL 33168. adv. circ. 4,850,000.

917 US
LEISUREGUIDE - GRAND STRAND (MYRTLE BEACH, S.C.) 1977. a. Leisureguides, Inc., 11501 N.W. Second Ave., Miami, FL 33168. adv. circ. 3,100,000.

917 US
LEISUREGUIDE - HOUSTON. 1978. a. Leisureguides, Inc., 11501 N.W. Second Ave., Miami, FL 33168. adv. circ. 3,000,000.

917 US
LEISUREGUIDE - LOUISVILLE. 1979. a. Leisureguides, Inc., 11501 N.W. Second Ave., Miami, FL 33168. adv. circ. 1,700,000.

917.5 US
LEISUREGUIDE - ORLANDO. 1980. a. Leisureguides, Inc., 11501 N.W. Second Ave., Miami, FL 33168. adv. circ. 3,100,000.

917.2 US
LEISUREGUIDE - PUERTO RICO. 1980. a. Leisureguides, Inc, 11501 N.W. Second Ave., Miami, FL 33168. adv. circ. 3,300,000.

917 US
LEISUREGUIDE - TAMPA BAY. 1979. a. Leisureguides, Inc., 11501 N.W. Second Ave., Miami, FL 33168. circ. 2,500,000.

917 US
LEISUREGUIDE - THE FLORIDA GOLD COAST. 1974. a. Leisureguides, Inc., 11501 N.W. Second Ave., Miami, FL 33168. adv. circ. 5,950,000.

917.04 US ISSN 0192-2920
LET'S GO: THE BUDGET GUIDE TO ITALY. 1981. a. $5.50. (Harvard Student Agencies) E. P. Dutton & Co., Inc., 201 Park Ave. S., New York, NY 10003. Ed. Jeremy Metz.

910.2 914 US ISSN 0075-8868
LET'S GO: THE STUDENT GUIDE TO EUROPE. 1960. a. $4.95. E. P. Dutton & Co., Inc., 201 Park Ave. S., New York, NY 10003. adv. circ. 60,000.

917.04 US ISSN 0090-788X
LET'S GO: THE STUDENT GUIDE TO THE UNITED STATES AND CANADA. 1973. irreg. $3.95. ‡ E. P. Dutton & Co., Inc., 201 Park Ave. S., New York, NY 10032. illus.

354 LB
LIBERIA. MINISTRY OF INFORMATION, CULTURAL AFFAIRS & TOURISM. ANNUAL REPORT TO THE SESSION OF THE LEGISLATURE. (Text in English) a. Ministry of Information, Cultural Affairs and Tourism, Monrovia, Liberia.

910.2 960 UK
LIBYA PAST AND PRESENT SERIES. 1970. irreg., (approx. 2 per year) 1970, vol. 3. price varies. Oleander Press, 17 Stansgate Ave., Cambridge CB2 2QZ, Eng (U.S. address: 210 Fifth Ave., New York, N.Y. 10010) Eds. Wayne Schlepp and Philip Ward.
Formerly: Libyan Travel Series (ISSN 0075-9309)

LIVING IN MALAWI. see *BUSINESS AND ECONOMICS — Economic Situation And Conditions*

LONDON RED GUIDE. see *GEOGRAPHY*

914.2 UK
LONDON: YOUR SIGHTSEEING GUIDE. a. 80p.($3.60) British Tourist Authority, 4 Bromwells Rd., London SW4 0BJ, England.

916 MW
MALAWI TOURISM REPORT. 1970. a. K.1.50($1.70) ‡ National Statistical Office, Box 333, Zomba, Malawi. stat. (processed)
Formerly: Malawi. National Statistical Office. Tourist Report (ISSN 0085-302X)

MALTA YEARBOOK. see *POLITICAL SCIENCE*

917.104 CN
MANITOBA VACATION GUIDE, CANADA. 1972. a. Department of Tourism and Cultural Affairs, 200 Vaughan St., Winnipeg, Man. R3C 1T5, Canada. Ed. Victor Pasta. illus.
Formerly: Manitoba Vacation Handbook.

916.1 NO
MED BIL I EUROPA. 1951. a. membership. Norges Automobil-Forbund, Storgaten 2, Postboks 494, Oslo 1, Norway.

914.404 FR
MICHELIN GREEN GUIDE SERIES: ALPES. 1978. irreg. $6.95. Michelin, Services de Tourisme, 46 Av. de Breteuil, 75341 Paris 7, France (U.S. subscr. address: Michelin Guides and Maps, Box 5022, New Hyde Park, NY 11040)

TRAVEL AND TOURISM

914.36 FR
MICHELIN GREEN GUIDE SERIES: AUSTRIA. (Editions in English, French & German) irreg. $6.95 per no. Michelin, Services de Tourisme, 46 Avenue de Breteuil, F 75341 Paris 7, France (U.S. subscr. adddress: Michelin Guides and Maps, Box 5022, New Hyde Park, NY 11042)

914.404 FR
MICHELIN GREEN GUIDE SERIES: AUVERGNE. 1977. irreg. $6.95. Michelin, Services de Tourisme, 46 Av. de Breteuil, 75341 Paris 7, France (U.S. subscr. address: Michelin Guides and Maps, Box 5022, New Hyde Park, NY 11040)

914.404 FR
MICHELIN GREEN GUIDE SERIES: BELGIQUE. (Text in French) irreg. $6.95 per no. Michelin, Service de Tourism, 6 Av de Breteuil, 75341 Paris Cedex 7, France (U. S. subscr. address: Michelin Guides and Maps, Box 5022, New Hyde Park, NY 11042)

914.404 FR
MICHELIN GREEN GUIDE SERIES: BELGIUM-LUXEMBURG. (Text in Dutch) irreg. $6.95. Michelin, Service de Tourisme, 46 Ave de Breteuil, 75346 Paris Cedex 7, France (U.S. subscr. address: Michelin Guides and Maps, Box 5022, New Hyde Park, NY 11042)

914.404 FR
MICHELIN GREEN GUIDE SERIES: BOURGOGNE. irreg. $6.95. Michelin, Service de Tourisme, 46 Av. de Breteuil, 75341 Paris 7, France (U.S. subscr. address: Michelin Guides and Maps, P.O. Box 5022, New Hyde Park, NY 11040)

914.4 FR
MICHELIN GREEN GUIDE SERIES: BRITTANY. (Editions in English & French) irreg. $6.95 per no. Michelin, Services de Tourisme, 46 Avenue de Breteuil, F 75341 Paris 7, France (U.S. subscr. address: Michelin Guides and Maps, P.O. Box 5022, New Hyde Park, NY 11042)

914.404 FR
MICHELIN GREEN GUIDE SERIES: CAUSSES CEVENNES. irreg. Michelin, Service de Tourisme, 46 Av de Breteuil, 75341 Paris 7, France (U.S. subscr. address: Michelin Guides and Maps, Box 5022, New Hyde Park, NY 11040)

914.4 FR
MICHELIN GREEN GUIDE SERIES: CHATEAUX OF THE LOIRE. (Editions in English, French & German) irreg. $6.95 per no. Michelin, Services de Tourisme, 46 Avenue de Breteuil, F 75341 Paris 7, France (U.S. subscr. address: Michelin Guides and Maps, Box 5022, New Hyde Park, NY 11042)

914.404 FR
MICHELIN GREEN GUIDE SERIES: CORSE. irreg. $6.95. Michelin, Service de Tourisme, 46 Av. de Breteuil, 75341 Paris 7, France (U.S. subscr. address: Michelin Guides and Maps, Box 5022, New Hyde Park, NY 11040)

914.404 FR
MICHELIN GREEN GUIDE SERIES: COTE ATLANTIQUE. irreg. Michelin, Service de Tourisme, 46 Av de Breteuil, 75341 Paris 7, France (U.S. subscr. address: Michelin Guides and Maps, Box 5022, New Hyde Park, NY 11042)

914.4 FR
MICHELIN GREEN GUIDE SERIES: DORDOGNE. English edition: Michelin Green Guide Series: Perigord. (Text in English) irreg. $6.95. Michelin, Services de Tourism, 46 Ave de Breteuil, 75341 Paris Cedex 7, France (U.S. subscr. address: Michelin Guides and Maps, Box 5022, New Hyde Park, NY 11042)

914.404 FR
MICHELIN GREEN GUIDE SERIES: ENVIRONS DE PARIS. irreg. $6.95. Michelin, Service de Tourisme, 46 Av de Breteuil, 75341 Paris 7, France (U.S. subscr. address: Michelin Guides and Maps, Box 5022, New Hyde Park, NY 11040)

914.4 FR
MICHELIN GREEN GUIDE SERIES: FRENCH RIVIERA. (Editions in English and French) irreg. $6.95 per no. Michelin, Services de Tourisme, 46 Avenue de Breteuil, F 75341 Paris 7, France (U.S. Subscr. address: Michelin Guides and Maps, Box 5022, New Hyde Park, NY 11042)

914.3 FR
MICHELIN GREEN GUIDE SERIES: GERMANY. (Editions in English, French and German) irreg. $6.95 per no. Michelin, Services de Tourisme, 46 Avenue de Breteuil, F 75341 Paris 7, France (U.S. subscr. address: Michelin Guides and Maps, Box 5022, New Hyde Park, NY 11042)

914.5 FR
MICHELIN GREEN GUIDE SERIES: ITALY. (Editions in English, French, German & Italian) irreg. $6.95 per no. Michelin, Services de Tourisme, 46 Avenue de Breteuil, F 75341 Paris 7, France (U.S. subscr. address: Michelin Guides and Maps, Box 5022, New Hyde Park, NY 11042)

914.404 FR
MICHELIN GREEN GUIDE SERIES: JURA. irreg. $6.95. Michelin, 46 Av de Breteuil, 75341 Paris 7, France (U.S. subscr. address: Michelin Guides and Maps, Box 5022, New Hyde Park, NY 11040)

914.2 FR
MICHELIN GREEN GUIDE SERIES: LONDRES. (Text in French; English edition available) irreg. $6.95 per no. Michelin, Services de Tourisme, 46 Avenue de Breteuil, F 75341 Paris 7, France (U.S. subscr. address: Michelin Guides and Maps, Box 5022, New Hyde Park, NY 11042)

916.4 FR
MICHELIN GREEN GUIDE SERIES: MAROC. (Text in French) irreg. $6.95 per no. Michelin, Services de Tourisme, 46 Avenue de Breteuil, F 75341 Paris 7, France (U.S. subscr. address: Michelin Guides and Maps, Box 5022, New Hyde Park, NY 11042)

917.4 FR
MICHELIN GREEN GUIDE SERIES: NEW YORK (CITY) (Text in English and French) irreg. $6.95 per no. Michelin, Services de Tourisme, 46 Avenue de Breteuil, F 75341 Paris 7, France (U.S. subscr. address: Michelin Guides and Maps, Box 5022, New Hyde Park, NY 11042)

914.404 FR
MICHELIN GREEN GUIDE SERIES: NORD DE LA FRANCE. irreg. $6.95. Michelin, Service de Tourisme, 46 Av de Breteuil, 75341 Paris 7, France (U.S. subscr. address: Michelin Guides and Maps, Box 5022, New Hyde Park, NY 11040)

914.4 FR
MICHELIN GREEN GUIDE SERIES: NORMANDY. (Editions in English & French) irreg. $6.95 per no. Michelin, Services de Tourisme, 46 Avenue de Breteuil, F 75341 Paris 7, France (U.S. subscr. address: Michelin Guides and Maps, Box 5022, New Hyde Park, NY 11042)

914.4 FR
MICHELIN GREEN GUIDE SERIES: PARIS. (Editions in English, French & German) irreg. $6.95 per no. Michelin, Services de Tourisme, 46 Avenue de Breteuil, F 75341 Paris 7, France (U.S. subscr. address: Michelin Guides and Maps, Box 5022, New Hyde Park, NY 11042)

914.904 FR
MICHELIN GREEN GUIDE SERIES: PAYS BAS. irreg. $6.95. Michelin, Service de Tourisme, 46 Av de Breteuil, 75341 Paris 7, France (U.S. subscr. address: Michelin Guides and Maps, Box 5022, New Hyde Park, NY 11040)

914.69 FR
MICHELIN GREEN GUIDE SERIES: PORTUGAL. (Editions in English & French) irreg. $6.95 per no. Michelin, Services de Tourisme, 46 Avenue de Breteuil, F 75341 Paris 7, France (U.S. subscr. address: Michelin Guides and Maps, Box 5022, New Hyde Park, NY 11042)

914.404 FR
MICHELIN GREEN GUIDE SERIES: PROVENCE. (Editions in English and French) 1980. irreg. $6.95. Michelin, Service de Tourisme, 46 Av. de Breteuil, 75341 Paris 7, France (U.S. subscr. address: Michelin Guides and Maps, Box 5022, New Hyde Park, NY 11040)

914.404 FR
MICHELIN GREEN GUIDE SERIES: PYRENEES. irreg. $6.95. Michelin, Service de Tourisme, 46 Av. de Breteuil, 75341 Paris 7, France (U.S. subscr. address: Michelin Guides and Maps, Box 5022, New Hyde Park, NY 11040)

914.404 FR
MICHELIN GREEN GUIDE SERIES: ROME. (Text in French) irreg. $6.95. Michelin, Service de Tourisme, 46 Ave de Breteuil, 75341 Paris Cedex 7, France (U.S. subscr. address: Michelin Guides and Maps, Box 5022, New Hyde Park, NY 11042)

914.6 FR
MICHELIN GREEN GUIDE SERIES: SPAIN. (Editions in English, French, German & Spanish) irreg. $6.95 per no. Michelin, Services de Tourisme, 46 Avenue de Breteuil, F 75341 Paris 7, France (U.S. subscr. address: Michelin Guides and Maps, Box 5022, New Hyde Park, NY 11042)

914.94 FR
MICHELIN GREEN GUIDE SERIES: SWITZERLAND. (Editions in English, French & German) irreg. $6.95 per no. Michelin, Services de Tourisme, 46 Avenue de Breteuil, F 75341 Paris 7, France (U.S. subscr. address: Michelin Guides and Maps, Box 5022, New Hyde Park, NY 11042)

914.404 FR
MICHELIN GREEN GUIDE SERIES: VALLEE DU RHONE. irreg. $6.95. Michelin, Service de Tourisme, 46 Av. de Breteuil, 75341 Paris 7, France (U.S. subscr. address: Michelin Guides and Maps, Box 5022, New Hyde Park, NY 11040)

914.404 FR
MICHELIN GREEN GUIDE SERIES: VOSGES. (Editions in French and German) irreg. $6.95. Michelin, Service de Tourisme, 46 Av de Breteuil, 75341 Paris 7, France (U.S. subscr. address: Michelin Guides and Maps, Box 5022, New Hyde Park, NY 11040)

910.2 914 FR ISSN 0076-7743
MICHELIN RED GUIDE SERIES: BENELUX. (Text in Dutch, English, French and German) a. $10.95. Michelin, Services de Tourisme, 75341 Paris 7, 75341 Paris 7e, France (U.S. subscr. address: Box 5022, New Hyde Park, NY 11042)

910.2 914 FR ISSN 0076-7778
MICHELIN RED GUIDE SERIES: FRANCE. (Text in English, French, German and Italian) a. $12.95. Michelin, Services de Tourisme, 75341 Paris 7, 75341 Paris 7e. France, France (U.S. subscr. address: Box 5022, New Hyde Park, NY 11042)

910.2 914 FR ISSN 0076-7751
MICHELIN RED GUIDE SERIES: GERMANY. (Text in English, French, German and Italian) a. $12.95. Michelin, Services de Tourisme, 75341 Paris 7, 75341 Paris 7e, France (U.S. subscr. address: Box 5022, New Hyde Park, NY 11042)

914.204 FR
MICHELIN RED GUIDE SERIES: GREAT BRITAIN AND IRELAND. (Text in English, French, German and Italian) a. $11.95. Michelin, Services de Tourisme, 46 Avenue de Breteuil, 75341 Paris 7, France (U.S. subscr. address: Michelin Guides and Maps, Box 5022, New Hyde Park, NY 11042) illus.

914.21 FR
MICHELIN RED GUIDE SERIES: GREATER LONDON. (Text in English, French, German & Italian) a. $2.95. Michelin, Services de Tourisme, 46 Avenue de Breteuil, 75341 Paris 7, France (U.S. subscr. address: Michelin Guides and Maps, Box 5022, New Hyde Park, N.Y. 11042) illus.

914 FR ISSN 0076-7786
MICHELIN RED GUIDE SERIES: ITALY. (Text in English, French, German and Italian) a. $11.95. Michelin, Services de Tourisme, 75341 Paris 7, 75341 Paris 7e, France (U.S. subscr. address: Box 5022, New Hyde Park, NY 11042)

910.2 914 FR ISSN 0076-7794
MICHELIN RED GUIDE SERIES: PARIS. (Notes: in two editions: (1) Multilingual (Dutch, French, German & English) and (2) English) a. $2.95. Michelin, Services de Tourisme, 75341 Paris 7, 75341 Paris 7e, France (U.S. subscr. address: Box 5022, New Hyde Park, NY 11042)

910.2 914 FR ISSN 0076-776X
MICHELIN RED GUIDE SERIES: SPAIN & PORTUGAL. (Text in English, French, German, Italian, Portuguese and Spanish) a. $9.95. Michelin, Services de Tourisme, 75341 Paris 7, 75341 Paris 7e, France (U.S. subscr. address: Box 5022, New Hyde Park, NY 11042)

TRAVEL AND TOURISM   889

914.6   UK
MICHELIN SPAIN. 1974. irreg. £3. Michelin Tyre Co.Ltd., Tourist Service, 81 Fulham Rd., London SW3 6RD, England. illus.

917   796.5   US
MIDEASTERN CAMPBOOK. Cover title: R V and Tent Sites in Delaware, District of Columbia, Maryland, New Jersey, Pennsylvania, Virginia, West Virginia. a. membership. American Automobile Association, 8111 Gatehouse Rd., Falls Church, VA 22047.
    Formerly (until 1980): Mideastern Camping.

910   US   ISSN 0361-1361
MILEPOST: ALL-THE-NORTH TRAVEL GUIDE; all-the-north-travel-guide. 1948. a. $7.95. Alaska Northwest Publishing Co., Box 4-EEE, Anchorage, AK 99509 (Circ. Office: 130 Second Ave. S., Edmonds, WA 98020) Ed. Robert A. Henning. adv. charts. illus. stat. circ. 60,000.

917   UK
MONEYWISE GUIDE TO NORTH AMERICA. 1962. a. £3.50. Travelaid Publishing, Box 369, London NW3 4ER, England. Eds. Michael von Haag, Anna Crew.

910.09   US
MOTORCOACH TOUR MART. 1978. a. $12.50. Grace J. Talmage & Associates, 2600 Martin Rd., Willow Grove, PA 19090. Ed. Grace J. Talmage. circ. 18,000.

910.2   MY   ISSN 0077-1694
MOTORING IN MALAYA.* Variant title: A a M Handbook. 1932. every 18 mos. $3. free to members. (Automobile Association of Malaya) Technical Publications Malaya, 10 Clove Hall Rd., Penang, Malaysia. Ed. Mrs. K. S. Lim.

MOVING TO OTTAWA/HULL. see *REAL ESTATE*

MOVING TO SASKATCHEWAN. see *REAL ESTATE*

MOVING TO TORONTO & AREA. see *REAL ESTATE*

MOVING TO VANCOUVER & B.C. see *REAL ESTATE*

MULTINATIONAL EXECUTIVE TRAVEL COMPANION. see *BUSINESS AND ECONOMICS — International Commerce*

910.202   US
NATIONAL DIRECTORY OF FREE TOURIST ATTRACTIONS. 1976. irreg. $2.95. Pilot Books, 347 Fifth Ave., New York, NY 10016. Ed. Raymond Carlson.

910.09   US
NATIONAL DIRECTORY OF FREE VACATION & TRAVEL INFORMATION. 1977. irreg. $2.95. Pilot Books, 347 Fifth Ave., New York, NY 10016. Ed. Raymond Carlson.

910.202   US
NATIONAL DIRECTORY OF LOW-COST TOURIST ATTRACTIONS. 1979. biennial. $3.50. Pilot Books, 347 Fifth Ave., New York, NY 10016. Ed. Raymond Carlson.

910.202   US
NATIONAL DIRECTORY OF THEME PARKS AND AMUSEMENT AREAS. 1978. irreg. $2.95. Pilot Books, 347 Fifth Ave., New York, NY 10016. Ed. Raymond Carlson.

910.09   US
NATIONAL TRAVEL EXPENDITURE STUDY: SUMMARY REPORT. 1975. a. $27. U S Travel Data Center, 1899 L. St., N.W., Washington, DC 20036.

910 310   NE   ISSN 0077-7447
NETHERLANDS. CENTRAAL BUREAU VOOR DE STATISTIEK. STATISTIEK VREEMDELINGENVERKEER. TOURISM STATISTICS. (Text in Dutch and English) 1952. a. fl.17.55. Centraal Bureau de Statistiek, Prinses Beatrixlaan 428, Voorburg, Netherlands (Orders to: Staatsuitgeverij, Christoffel Plantijnstraat, The Hague, Netherlands)

910.2   NE
NETHERLANDS. CENTRAAL BUREAU VOOR DE STATISTIEK. VAKANTIEONDERZOEK. (Text in Dutch and English) 1954. irreg. price varies. Centraal Bureau voor de Statistiek, Prinses Beatrixlaan 428, Voorburg, Netherlands (Orders to: Staatsuitgeverij, Christoffel Plantijnstraat, The Hague, Netherlands)
    Formerly: Vakantiebesteding van de Nederlandse Bevolking (ISSN 0077-7501)

917.1   CN   ISSN 0703-6566
NEW BRUNSWICK. DEPARTMENT OF TOURISM. ANNUAL REPORT. (Text in English and French) 1972. a. Department of Tourism, 796 Queen St., Fredericton, N.B., Canada. illus.

910.2 917.4   US   ISSN 0077-8222
NEW ENGLAND GUIDE; guide to travel and history. 1958. a. $2.25. Profiles Publishing Co., 2 Steam Mill Court, Box 1108, Concord, NH 03301. Ed. Susan S. Rahmlow. adv. index. circ. 200,000. (reprint service avail. from UMI)

910.2 915.2   JA   ISSN 0077-8591
NEW OFFICIAL GUIDE: JAPAN. (Text in English) 1952. irreg. 5000 Yen($15.) (Japan National Tourist Organization - Nihon Boeki Shuppansha) Japan Travel Bureau, Inc., 2-1 Yotsuya, Shinjuku-ku, Tokyo 160, Japan. index.
    Formerly: Japan: the Official Guide.

917.53   US   ISSN 0097-8213
NEW SETTLER'S GUIDE FOR WASHINGTON, D.C. AND COMMUNITIES IN NEARBY MARYLAND AND VIRGINIA. a. $2.95. R. B. Minogue, 8824 Tuckerman Lane, Potomac, MD 20854. illus.

919.31   NZ   ISSN 0110-0831
NEW ZEALAND ANNUAL. 1901. a. NZ.$3. Wilson and Horton Ltd., 149 Queen St., Auckland, New Zealand. illus. circ. 35,000.

919.3   NZ
NEW ZEALAND VISITOR STATISTICS. 1973. a. free. Department of Tourist and Publicity, Box 95, Wellington, New Zealand. adv.

916.69   NR
NIGERIA TOURIST GUIDE/GUIDE DU TOURISME NIGERIEN. Variant title: National Tourist Guide of Nigeria. 1969. irreg. Nigerian Tourist Board, 44 Norman Williams St., P.O. Box 2944, Lagos, Nigeria. illus.

910.09   US
NOMAD. 1967. irreg. Other Scenes, c/o John Wilcock, Ed., Box 4137, Grand Central Sta., New York, NY 10017. circ. 1,000. (reprint service avail. from UMI)

910.2   UK   ISSN 0078-1150
NORFOLK HOLIDAY HANDBOOK. 1960. a. 75p. Hoseasons, Sunway House, Oulton Broad, Lowestoft, Suffolk NR32 3LT, England.
    Formerly: Norfolk Holiday Hints Handbook.

917.5   US   ISSN 0546-3432
NORMAN FORD'S FLORIDA. biennial. $4.95 per no. Harian Publications, One Vernon Ave., Floral Park, NY 11001. Ed. Norman D. Ford. charts. illus.

917 796.5   US
NORTH CENTRAL CAMPBOOK. Cover title: R V and Tent Sites in Iowa, Minnesota, Nebraska, North Dakota, South Dakota. a. membership. American Automobile Association, 8111 Gatehouse Rd., Falls Church, VA 22047.
    Formerly (until 1980): North Central Camping.

917.8   US
NORTHWESTERN CAMPBOOK; including location maps. Cover title: R V and Tent Sites in Idaho, Montana, Oregon, Washington, Wyoming. a. membership. American Automobile Association, 8111 Gatehouse Rd., Falls Church, VA 22047. illus.
    Former titles (until 1980): Northwestern Camping; Northwestern Camping and Trailering.

917.04   US
NUDIST PARK GUIDE. 1966. a. $5.95. American Sunbathing Association, 810 N. Mills Ave, Orlando, FL 32803. Ed. Roland Senecal. adv. circ. 10,000.

914.2   UK
OLIVER'S GUIDE TO THE CITY OF LONDON. 1970. a. £2. Oliver's Guides, 37 Amwell St., London EC1, England. Ed. Victoria Burgess. circ. 2,000. (back issues avail.)

950.04   US   ISSN 0162-5950
ON-YOUR-OWN GUIDE TO ASIA. a. $3.95. Volunteers in Asia, Inc., Box 4543, Stanford, CA 94305. (Co-sponsor: Charles E. Tuttle Company)

382   FR
ORGANIZATION FOR ECONOMIC COOPERATION AND DEVELOPMENT. TOURISM COMMITTEE. TOURISM POLICY AND INTERNATIONAL TOURISM IN O E C D MEMBER COUNTRIES. a. $14.50. Organization for Economic Cooperation and Development, 2, rue Andre-Pascal, 75775 Paris 16e, France (U.S. orders to: O.E.C.D. Publications and Information Center, 1750 Pennsylvania Ave. N.W., Washington, D.C. 20006) (also avail. in microfiche; back issues available)
    Continues: International Tourism Policy in OECD Member Countries.

917.11   CN   ISSN 0707-803X
OUTWEST MAGAZINE. 1975. irreg. Western Canada Advertising, Burnaby, B.C., Canada. illus.

914   UK   ISSN 0030-7378
OVER THE HILLS. 1920. a. membership(nonmembers 20p per no.) ‡ Holiday Fellowship Ltd, 142 Great North Way, London NW4 1EG, England. Ed. M. J. Carter. adv. bk. rev. circ. 50,000.

OWEN'S COMMERCE AND TRAVEL AND INTERNATIONAL REGISTER. see *BUSINESS AND ECONOMICS — International Commerce*

PACIFIC BOATING ALMANAC. NORTHERN CALIFORNIA & NEVADA. see *SPORTS AND GAMES — Boats And Boating*

PACIFIC BOATING ALMANAC. PACIFIC NORTHWEST & ALASKA. see *SPORTS AND GAMES — Boats And Boating*

PACIFIC BOATING ALMANAC. SOUTHERN CALIFORNIA, ARIZONA, BAJA. see *SPORTS AND GAMES — Boats And Boating*

919   US
PACIFIC DESTINATIONS HANDBOOK. 1977. a. $75 (free to members) Pacific Area Travel Association, 274 Brannan St., San Francisco, CA 94107. a. illus. circ. 4,000.
    Formerly: Pacific Area Destination Handbook (ISSN 0363-4817)

915   AT   ISSN 0311-0826
PACIFIC TRAVEL DIRECTORY. 1973. a. Aus.$7.50. c/o Pacific Airlines News, Box 1, Surfers Paradise, Qld. 4217, Australia. Ed. A. H. McRobbie.

910.2   UK   ISSN 0078-7833
PAINTING HOLIDAYS. 1924. a. free. Galleon World Travel Ltd., Galleon House, King St., Maidstone, Kent ME14 1EG, England (Dist. in U.S. by: Fourways Travel Ltd., 950 Third Ave., New York, NY 10022)

915.47   PK   ISSN 0552-8968
PAKISTAN HOTEL GUIDE. (Text in English) 1957. a. Rs.15($3) Maulai Enterprise, J-6/2 al-Naseer, Federal B Area, Block No. 1, Off Sir Shah Sulaiman Rd., Karachi 19, Pakistan. Ed. Syed Wali Ahmad Maulai. adv. charts. stat. circ. 5,000. (back issues avail.)

910.202   PK
PAKISTAN HOTELS & TOURISM. 1975. a. Rs.5. Bhatti Publications, 103/B Gulberg, Lahore, Pakistan. Ed. Mukhtar Bhatti. adv.

910.4   US   ISSN 0553-0601
PAN AM'S WORLD GUIDE; encyclopedia of travel. a., latest issue 23rd ed. $6.95. Pan American World Airways, Pan Am Bldg., New York, NY 10017. adv. charts. illus. circ. 50,000.

910.2　　　　　　AT
PAPUA NEW GUINEA HANDBOOK. 1954. a. Aus.$11.95. Pacific Publications (Australia) Pty. Ltd., P.O. Box 3408, G.P.O., Sydney, N.S.W. 2001, Australia. Ed. John Carter. adv. index.
Formerly: Handbook of Papua and New Guinea (ISSN 0072-9868)

914.504　　　　　　IT
PASSEGGIATE NEL LAZIO. 1977. irreg. (Regione Lazio, Assessorato al Turismo) Bulzoni Editore, Via dei Liburni, 00185 Rome, Italy.

910.2　914　　　UK　ISSN 0079-130X
PETS WELCOME. 1961. a. 95p. ‡ Herald Advisory Services, 23A Brighton Rd., South Croydon, Surrey CR2 6UE. Ed. Peter Stanley Williams.

299　910　　　　　US
PILGRIM'S GUIDE TO PLANET EARTH. 1974. irreg. $8.95. Spiritual Community Publications, Box 1080, San Rafael, CA 94902. Ed. Parmatma Singh Khalsa. circ. 17,500.

917.04　　　　　　US
PORTLAND AND THE PACIFIC NORTHWEST. 1975. a. $5.50. Fox Publishing Co., 320 S. W. Stark, Suite 519, Portland, OR 97204. Ed. Susan Monti. adv. circ. 12,000.

914.69　　　　　　PO
PORTUGAL. INSTITUTO NACIONAL DE ESTATISTICA. ESTATISTICAS DO TURISMO. a. Esc.120. Instituto Nacional de Estatistica, Av. Antonio Jose de Almeida, Lisbon, Portugal (Orders to: Imprensa Nacional, Casa da Moeda, Direccao Comercial, rua D. Francisco Manuel de Melo 5, Lisbon 1, Portugal)

354.717　　　　　　CN
PRINCE EDWARD ISLAND. DEPARTMENT OF TOURISM, PARKS AND CONSERVATION. ANNUAL REPORT. a. free. Department of Tourism, Parks and Conservation, Box 2000, Charlottetown, P.E.I. C1A 7N8, Canada. stat. circ. 200.
Formerly: Prince Edward Island. Department of the Environment and Tourism. Annual Report.

QUADERNI DE "LA TERRA SANTA". see RELIGIONS AND THEOLOGY

353.9　　　　CN　ISSN 0481-2786
QUEBEC (PROVINCE) DEPARTMENT OF TOURISM, FISH AND GAME. ANNUAL REPORT. a. free. Quebec (Province) Department of Tourism, Fish and Game, Quebec, P.Q., Canada.

917.1　　　　CN　ISSN 0702-6943
QUEBEC AT A GLANCE. vol. 9, 1978. a. free contr. circ. Department of Intergovernmental Affairs, 1225 Place Georges V, Quebec G1R 4Z7, Canada. Ed. Myles O'Farrell. bk. rev. illus. circ. 12,000.

910.2　　　　US　ISSN 0079-9637
RAND MCNALLY DISCOVER HISTORIC AMERICA. 1971. a. Rand McNally & Co., P.O. Box 7600, Chicago, IL 60680.
Formerly: Rand McNally Vacation Guide.

910.2　914　　　　UK
RECOMMENDED COUNTRY HOTELS OF BRITAIN. 1973. a. £1.50. Herald Advisory Services, 23a Brighton Rd., South Croydon, Surrey CR2 6UE, England. Ed. Peter Stanley Williams.

910.2　914　　　UK　ISSN 0080-0252
RECOMMENDED WAYSIDE INNS OF BRITAIN. 1962. a. £1.50. ‡ Herald Advisory Services, 23A Brighton Rd., South Croydon, Surrey CR2 6UE, England. Ed. Peter Stanley Williams.

314　910.202　　　　SP
REGIONAL BREAKDOWN OF WORLD TRAVEL STATISTICS. (Editions in English, French, Spanish) a. $20. World Tourism Organization, Avda. del Generalisimo 59, Madrid 16, Spain.

910.2　　　　　　GW
REISEN IN DEUTSCHLAND; DEUTSCHES HANDBUCH FUER FREMDENVERKEHR. Volume 1 (ISSN 0171-5240); Volume 2 (ISSN 0171-5224); Volume 3. 1925. a. (3 volumes) DM.15 per vol. Jaeger-Verlag GmbH, Holzhofallee 38a, Postfach 110320, 6100 Darmstadt, W. Germany (B.R.D.) adv.

910.09　　　　TZ　ISSN 0564-836X
REPORT ON TOURISM STATISTICS IN TANZANIA. (Formerly issued by its Central Statistical Bureau) 1968. irreg. Bureau of Statistics, Box 796, Dar es Salaam, Tanzania (Orders to: Government Publications Agency, Box 1801, Dar es Salaam, Tanzania)

910.09　　　　　　US
RETIREMENT PARADISES OF THE WORLD. biennial. $4.95. Harian Publications, One Vernon Ave, Floral Park, NY 11001. Ed. Norman D. Ford. illus.
Supersedes: Bargain Paradises of the World (ISSN 0408-568X)

910.2　　　　　　UK
SCHOOLS AND COLLEGES WELCOME. 1978. a. free to qualified personnel. Lewis Publications Ltd., 31 Castle St., Kingston upon Thames, Surrey KT1 1ST, England. Ed. David Jacobson. adv. circ. 20,000.

914.1　　　　　　UK
SCOTLAND: CAMPING AND CARAVAN SITES; camping and caravan sites. 1960. a. 70p. Scottish Tourist Board, 23 Ravelston Terrace, Edinburgh EH4 3EU, Scotland. adv. circ. 60,000.
Former titles: Scotland for Touring Caravans; Scotland for Caravan Holidays.

910.2　799.1　　　UK　ISSN 0080-7834
SCOTLAND FOR FISHING. a. 65p. Scottish Tourist Board, 23 Ravelston Terrace, Edinburgh EH4 3EU, Scotland. circ. 20,000.

914.2　　　　　　UK
SCOTLAND FOR HILLWALKING. 1971. irreg. 80p. Scottish Tourist Board, 23 Ravelston Terrace, Edinburgh EH4 3EU, Scotland. Ed. Donald J. Bennet. illus. (back issues avail.)

910.2　799.1　　　　UK
SCOTLAND FOR SEA ANGLING. a. 60p. Scottish Tourist Board, 23 Ravelston Terrace, Edinburgh EH4 3EU, Scotland.

914.1　　　　　　UK
SCOTLAND FOR THE MOTORIST. 1977. irreg. 60p. Scottish Tourist Board, 23 Ravelston Terrace, Edinburgh EH4 3EU, Scotland.

SCOTLAND-HOME OF GOLF. see SPORTS AND GAMES — Ball Games

914.1　　　　　　UK
SCOTLAND: IN FAMOUS FOOTSTEPS. 1976. irreg. 30p. Scottish Tourist Board, 23 Ravelston Terrace, Edinburgh EH4 3EU, Scotland.

914.2　　　　　　UK
SCOTLAND: SELF CATERING ACCOMMODATION. 1971. a. 75p. Scottish Tourist Board, 23 Ravelston Terrace, Edinburgh EH4 3EU, Scotland. charts. circ. 5,000.

914.2　　　　　　UK
SCOTLAND: TRAVEL TRADE GUIDE. 1969. a. Scottish Tourist Board, 23 Ravelston Terrace, Edinburgh EH4 3EU, Scotland.

914.1　　　　　　UK
SCOTLAND: WHERE TO STAY, BED AND BREAKFAST. a. 75p. Scottish Tourist Board, 23 Ravelston Terrace, Edinburgh EH4 3EU, Scotland.
Formerly: Where to Stay in Scotland. Bed & Breakfast; Supersedes in part: Where to Stay in Scotland (ISSN 0083-9221)

914.1　　　　　　UK
SCOTLAND: WHERE TO STAY, HOTELS AND GUEST HOUSES. 1947. a. 75p. Scottish Tourist Board, 23 Ravelston Terrace, Edinburgh EH4 3EU, Scotland. circ. 65,000.
Formerly: Where to Stay in Scotland. Hotels & Guest Houses; Supersedes in part: Where to Stay in Scotland (ISSN 0083-9221)

910.2　　　　　　UK
SCOTLAND: 1001 THINGS TO SEE. 1970. irreg. 90p. Scottish Tourist Board, 23 Ravelston Terrace, Edinburgh EH4 3EU, Scotland.
Former titles: Scotland: 600 Things to See; Scottish Castles and Historic Houses (ISSN 0080-7931); Scotlands Castles.

914.2　　　　　　UK
SCOTLAND'S BEST HOLIDAYS. 1974. a. 60p. Farm Holiday Guides Ltd., 18 High St., Paisley PA1 2BX, Scotland.

919.4　　　　　　AT
SEE AUSTRALIA. 1977. a (in four parts) Aus.$12($15) Research Publications Pty. Ltd., 418 Canterbury Rd., Surrey Hills, Vic. 3127, Australia. Ed. Helen Greenwood. circ. 2,000.

917.29　　　　　　PR
SELECTED STATISTICS OF THE TOURISM INDUSTRY IN PUERTO RICO. a;latest issue, 1977-78. free. ‡ Tourism Company of Puerto Rico, Office of Statistics and Economic Studies, G.P.O. Box B N, San Juan, PR 00936. Ed. Bolivar Roman. charts. stat. circ. 1,250. (processed)

914.2　　　　　　UK
SELF-CATERING AND FURNISHED HOLIDAYS. 1968. a. 70p. Farm Holiday Guides Ltd., 18 High St., Paisley PA1 2BX, Scotland.
Formerly: Furnished Holidays in Britain.

910.2　　　　UK　ISSN 0080-8679
SELF CATERING HOLIDAYS. 1958. a. 75p. Starfish Books Ltd., Starfish House, Brook Farm Road, Cobham, Surrey KT11 3AY, England.

914.2　　　　　　UK
SELF CATERING IN BRITAIN. a. £2.75 to non-members. Automobile Association, Fanum House, Basingstoke, Hants RG21 2EA, England. Ed. Joan Fensome.
Formerly: Guide to Holiday Houses, Cottages and Chalets.

910.2　　　　FR　ISSN 0080-8768
SEMAINIER BEAUX PAYS DE FRANCE.* 1970. a. price varies. Editions B. Arthaud, 6 rue de Mezieres, Grenoble, France.
Formerly: Semainier de Paris.

916.8　　　　　　SA
SHELL TOURIST GUIDE TO SOUTH AFRICA. a. R.4.40. Chris van Rensburg Publications (Pty) Ltd., Box 25272, Marshalltown 2107, South Africa. adv.

915.95　　　　　　SI
SINGAPORE TOURIST PROMOTION BOARD. ANNUAL STATISTICAL REPORT ON VISITOR ARRIVALS. 1969. a. S.$15. ‡ Singapore Tourist Promotion Board, Tudor Court, Tanglin Road, Singapore 1024, Singapore. charts. stat. circ. 1,500. (tabloid format)

914.6　388.3　　　　SP
SOCIEDAD ESPANOLA DE AUTOMOVILES DE TURISMO. MEMORIA Y BALANCE. a. Sociedad Espanola de Automoviles de Turismo, S.A., Avda. Generalisimo 146, Madrid 16, Spain. charts. stat.

910.2　　　　US　ISSN 0081-2579
SOUTH AMERICAN HANDBOOK. a. Rand McNally & Co., P.O. Box 7600, Chicago, IL 60680.

917　796.5　　　　US
SOUTH CENTRAL CAMPBOOK. Cover title: R V and Tent Sites in Arkansas, Kansas, Missouri, Oklahoma, Texas. a. membership. American Automobile Association, 8111 Gatehouse Rd., Falls Church, VA 22047.
Formerly (until 1980): South Central Camping (ISSN 0364-7161)

917　796.5　　　　US
SOUTHEASTERN CAMPBOOK. Cover title: R V and Tent Sites in Alabama, Florida, Georgia, Kentucky, Louisiana, Mississippi, North Carolina, South Carolina, Tennessee. a. membership. American Automobile Association, 8111 Gatehouse Rd., Falls Church, VA 22047.
Formerly (until 1980): Southeastern Camping.

916.8　916.9　　　　SA
SOUTHERN AFRICA AND THE INDIAN OCEAN ISLANDS TRAVEL TRADE DIRECTORY. 1974. a. $15. Da Gama Publishers (Pty) Ltd., 311 Locarno House, 20 Loveday St., Box 61464, Marshalltown 2107, South Africa. Ed. Daphne de Freitas. adv. circ. 10,000.

338.47   SA
SOUTHERN AFRICAN AND INDIAN OCEAN ISLANDS TRAVEL INDUSTRY'S YEARBOOK, DIRECTORY AND WHO'S WHO. Short title: Southern Africa's Travel Industry. 1976. a. R.10. World Freight & Markets (Pty) Ltd., Box 6202, Johannesburg, South Africa.

917   796.5   US
SOUTHWESTERN CAMPBOOK. Cover title: R V and Tent Sites in Arizona, Colorado, New Mexico, Utah. a. membership. American Automobile Association, 8111 Gatehouse Rd., Falls Church, VA 22047.
    Formerly (until 1980): Southwestern Camping.

910   SP
SPAIN. MINISTERIO DE COMERCIO Y TURISMO. ESTADISTICAS DE TURISMO. a. free. Ministerio de Comercio y Turismo, Alcala 44, Madrid 14, Spain.
    Formerly: Spain. Ministerio de Informacion y Turismo. Estadisticas de Turismo (ISSN 0081-346X)

SPIRITUAL COMMUNITY GUIDE; the new consciousness source book. see *RELIGIONS AND THEOLOGY — Other Denominations And Sects*

SPORTFISHING. see *SPORTS AND GAMES — Outdoor Life*

910.2   UK   ISSN 0081-4385
STARFISH BOOK OF FARM AND COUNTRY HOLIDAYS. 1969. a. 55p. Starfish Books Ltd., P. and J. Harding, Starfish House, Brook Farm Road, Cobham, Surrey KT11 3AY, Surrey, England.

917.41   US   ISSN 0097-1189
STATE O'MAINE FACTS. 12th ed., 1977. a. $1.95. Courier-Gazette, Inc., 1 Park Drive, Rockland, ME 04841. Ed. Chester C. Nash. illus.
    Continues: Maine Facts.

914.2   UK
STATELY HOMES, MUSEUMS, CASTLES AND GARDENS. a. £1.95 to non-members. Automobile Association, Fanum House, Basingstoke, Hants RG21 2EA, England. adv.
    Formerly: Britain's Heritage.

915.1   HK
STATISTICAL REVIEW OF TOURISM IN HONG KONG. (Text in English) 1974. a. HK.$20($4) Hong Kong Tourist Association, Box 2597, Hong Kong, Hong Kong.
    Supersedes: Hong Kong Tourist Association. Digest of Annual Statistics.

STATISTICS ON TOURISM AND HOTEL INDUSTRY IN FIJI. see *HOTELS AND RESTAURANTS*

910   GW
STRAND EUROPA. 1974. irreg. DM.16.80. ADAC Verlag GmbH, Baumgartnerstr. 53, 8000 Munich 70, W. Germany (B.R.D.) adv. circ. 10,000.

910.09   US   ISSN 0191-3468
SUNSET WESTERN TRAVEL ADVENTURES. 1979. a. $2.95 per no. Lane Publishing Co., 80 Willow Rd., Menlo Park, CA 94025.

910.09   US
SURVEY OF STATE TRAVEL OFFICES. 1973. a. $20. U S Travel Data Center, 899 L. St., N.W., Washington, DC 20036.

338.7   II
TAMIL NADU TOURISM DEVELOPMENT CORPORATION. ANNUAL REPORT. (Text in English) a. Tamil Nadu Tourism Development Corporation, Shivalaya Bldg., 16 Commander-in-Chief Rd., Madras 600008, India.

910   HK
TANZANIA; handbook of international travel and tourism. 1979. a. $3.95. Travintal Ltd., Box 1237, G.P.O., Hong Kong, Hong Kong. Ed. Nina Casimaty. adv. bk. rev. bibl. charts. illus. index. circ. 10,000.

914.2   UK
TASTE OF SCOTLAND. 1972. irreg. Scottish Tourist Board, 23 Ravelston Terrace, Edinburgh EH4 3EU, Scotland. illus.

914.3   GW
TECHNISCHE SEHENSWUERDIGKEITEN IN DEUTSCHLAND. BAND 1: SCHLESWIG-HOLSTEIN, NIEDERSACHSEN, HAMBURG, BREMEN; ADAC-Reisefuehrer. 1976. irreg., vol. 2, 1978. DM.16.80. ADAC Verlag GmbH, Baumgartnerstr. 53, 8000 Munich 70, W. Germany (B.R.D.)

914.3   GW
TECHNISCHE SEHENSWUERDIGKEITEN IN DEUTSCHLAND. BAND 2: NORDRHEIN-WESTFALEN; ADAC reisefuehrer. 1976. irreg. DM.16.80. ADAC Verlag GmbH, Baumgartnerstr. 53, 8000 Munich 70, W. Germany (B.R.D.)

914.3   GW
TECHNISCHE SEHENSWUERDIGKEITEN IN DEUTSCHLAND. BAND 3: HESSEN, RHEINLAND-PFALZ, SAARLAND, BADEN-WUERTTEMBERG; ADAC-Reisefuehrer. 1976. irreg. DM.16.80. ADAC Verlag GmbH, Baumgartnerstr. 53, 8000 Munich 70, W. Germany (B.R.D.)

914.3   GW
TECHNISCHE SEHENSWUERDIGKEITEN IN DEUTSCHLAND. BAND 4: BAYERN, BERLIN; ADAC-Reisefuehrer. 1976. irreg. DM.16.80 per no. ADAC Verlag GmbH, Baumgartnerstr. 53, 8000 Munich 70, W. Germany (B.R.D.)

910.202   US
TEMPORARY MILITARY LODGING AROUND THE WORLD. 1971. irreg., 3rd edt. 1977. $3.95. Military Marketing Services, Inc., Box 4010, Arlington, VA 22204.

914   IT   ISSN 0040-3652
TERAMO; le notizie del turismo. (Text in English, French, German and Italian) 1959. irreg. free. Ente Provinciale per Il Turismo di Teramo, Teramo, Italy. Dir. Giammario Sgattoni. bk. rev. charts. illus. tr.lit. circ. 20,000(annually)

910.2   914   UK   ISSN 0082-3805
THAMES BOOK. 1966. a. £1.15. Link House Publications Ltd., Link House, Dingwall Ave., Croydon CR9 2TA, England. Ed. Heather Salter.

917.404   US
THIS IS RHODE ISLAND. 1964. biennial. free. ‡ Department of Economic Development, One Weybosset Hill, Providence, RI 02903.

910.2   919   US
THRUM'S ALL ABOUT HAWAII. 1970, 91st edition. a. $3.50. S B Printers, Inc., P.O. Box 100, Honolulu, HI 96810. Ed. Arlene King Duncan. adv. circ. 25,000.
    Former titles: Almanac of the Pacific (ISSN 0065-6461) & All About Hawaii.

910.2   917   US   ISSN 0082-4267
THRUWAY-INTERSTATE HIGHWAY GUIDE; travel directory for New York State, including Vermont, New Jersey and Ontario. 1954. a. $1. Richard M. McGrath, Dover Rd., Barneveld, NY 13304. Ed. Delores W. McGrath. index.

THUNDER BAY CAMPING GUIDE. see *SPORTS AND GAMES — Outdoor Life*

917.6   US   ISSN 0361-4948
TOURBOOK: ALABAMA, LOUISIANA, MISSISSIPPI. Cover title: Alabama, Louisiana, Mississippi TourBook. a. membership. American Automobile Association, 8111 Gatehouse Rd., Falls Church, VA 22047. illus.

917.89   US   ISSN 0362-3599
TOURBOOK: ARIZONA, NEW MEXICO. Variant title: Arizona, New Mexico Tour Book. a. membership. American Automobile Association, 8111 Gatehouse Rd., Falls Church, VA 22047. illus.

917.6   US
TOURBOOK: ARKANSAS, KANSAS, MISSOURI, OKLAHOMA. Cover title: Arkansas, Kansas, Missouri, Oklahoma TourBook. a. membership. American Automobile Association, 8111 Gatehouse Rd., Falls Church, VA 22047.

917.15   US   ISSN 0363-1788
TOURBOOK: ATLANTIC PROVINCES AND QUEBEC. Cover title: Atlantic Provinces and Quebec; New Brunswick Newfoundland, Nova Scotia, Prince Edward Island, Quebec TourBook. a. membership. American Automobile Association, 8111 Gatehouse Rd., Falls Church, VA 22047. (Co-sponsor: Canadian Automobile Association) illus.

917.9   US
TOURBOOK: CALIFORNIA, NEVADA. Cover title: California, Nevada TourBook. a. membership. American Automobile Association, 8111 Gatehouse Rd., Falls Church, VA 22047.

917.8   US   ISSN 0362-9821
TOURBOOK: COLORADO, UTAH. Cover title: Colorado, Utah TourBook. a. membership. American Automobile Association, 8111 Gatehouse Rd., Falls Church, VA 22047.

917.59   US   ISSN 0516-9674
TOURBOOK: FLORIDA. 1965. a. membership. American Automobile Association, 8111 Gatehouse Rd., Falls Church, VA 22047. illus. Key Title: Florida Tour Book.

917.5   US   ISSN 0361-4956
TOURBOOK: GEORGIA, NORTH CAROLINA, SOUTH CAROLINA. Cover title: Georgia, North Carolina, South Carolina TourBook. a. membership. American Automobile Association, 8111 Gatehouse Rd., Falls Church, VA 22047. illus.

917   US
TOURBOOK: HAWAII. Cover title: Hawaii TourBook. a. membership. American Automobile Association, 8111 Gatehouse Rd., Falls Church, VA 22047.

917.9   US   ISSN 0363-2695
TOURBOOK: IDAHO, MONTANA, WYOMING. Cover title: Idaho, Montana, Wyoming TourBook. a. membership. American Automobile Association, 8111 Gatehouse Rd., Falls Church, VA 22047. illus.
    Supersedes in part: Northwestern Tour Book (ISSN 0094-078X); Continues: Northwestern States.

917   US
TOURBOOK: ILLINOIS, INDIANA, OHIO. Cover title: Illinois, Indiana, Ohio, TourBook. a. membership. American Automobile Association, 8111 Gatehouse Rd., Falls Church, VA 22047.

917.68   US   ISSN 0361-4964
TOURBOOK: KENTUCKY, TENNESSEE. Cover title: Kentucky, Tennessee TourBook. a. membership. American Automobile Association, 8111 Gatehouse Rd., Falls Church, VA 22047. illus.

917   US
TOURBOOK: MICHIGAN, WISCONSIN. Cover title: Michigan, Wisconsin TourBook. a. membership. American Automobile Association, 8111 Gatehouse Rd., Falls Church, VA 22047.

917   US   ISSN 0364-0086
TOURBOOK: MID-ATLANTIC. Cover title: Mid-Atlantic-Delaware, District of Columbia, Maryland, Virginia, West Virginia TourBook. a. membership. American Automobile Association, 8111 Gatehouse Rd., Falls Church, VA 22047.

917   US
TOURBOOK: NEW JERSEY, PENNSYLVANIA. Cover title: New Jersey, Pennsylvania TourBook. a. membership. American Automobile Association, 8111 Gatehouse Rd., Falls Church, VA 22047.

917   US
TOURBOOK: NEW YORK. Cover title: New York TourBook. a. membership. American Automobile Association, 8111 Gatehouse Rd., Falls Church, VA 22047.

917   US
TOURBOOK: NORTH CENTRAL. Cover title: North Central-Iowa, Minnesota, Nebraska, North Dakota, South Dakota TourBook. a. membership. American Automobile Association, 8111 Gatehouse Rd., Falls Church, VA 22047.

917   US
TOURBOOK: ONTARIO. Cover title: Ontario TourBook. a. membership. American Automobile Association, 8111 Gatehouse Rd., Falls Church, VA 22047.

TRAVEL AND TOURISM

917 US
TOURBOOK: TEXAS. Cover title: Texas TourBook. a. membership. American Automobile Association, 8111 Gatehouse Rd., Falls Church, VA 22047.

917.12 US ISSN 0362-3602
TOURBOOK: WESTERN CANADA AND ALASKA. Cover title: Western Canada and Alaska; Alberta, British Columbia, Manitoba, Saskatchewan, Northwest Territories, Yukon Territory and Alaska TourBook. a. American Automobile Association, 8111 Gatehouse Rd., Falls Church, VA 22047. illus.

914.2 UK
TOURING GUIDE TO ENGLAND. 1974. a. £10.95 to non-members. Automobile Association, Fanum House, Basingstoke, Hants RG21 2EA, England.

914.1 UK
TOURING GUIDE TO IRELAND. 1975. a. £9.95 to non-members. Automobile Association, Fanum House, Basingstoke, Hants RG21 2EA, England.

914.1 UK
TOURING GUIDE TO SCOTLAND. 1975. a. £9.95 to non-members. Automobile Association, Fanum House, Basingstoke, Hants RG21 2EA, England.

914.2 UK
TOURING GUIDE TO WALES. 1975. a. £9.95 to non-members. Automobile Association, Fanum House, Basingstoke, Hants RG21 2EA, England.

910.2 UK ISSN 0144-8099
TOURISM; statements of marketing intent. a. British Tourist Authority, 64 St. James St., London SW1A 1NF, England.

338.4 UN
TOURISM IN AFRICA. ANNUAL BULLETIN. 1972. a. free. United Nations Economic Commission for Africa - Commission Economique pour l'Afrique, Box 3001, Addis Ababa, Ethiopia (Dist. by: United Nations Publications, Room LX-2300, New York, NY 10017; or Distribution and Sales Section, Palais des Nations, CH-1211 Geneva 10, Switzerland) circ. 400.

338.4 US
TOURISM IN ARKANSAS; ACTIVITY REPORT. 1972. irreg., latest 1977. Department of Parks and Tourism, Tourism Division, 149 State Capitol, Little Rock, AR 72201. illus.

914.95 GR ISSN 0082-545X
TOURISM IN GREECE. (Text in English) 1961. a. $10. Hellenews Ltd., 39 Amaroussiou-Halandriou Rd., Amaroussion, Athens, Greece. Ed. D. G. Kalofolias. adv. circ. 28,000.

338.4 VB
TOURISM IN THE BRITISH VIRGIN ISLANDS. 1973. a. $3. Statistics Office, Finance Department, Road Town, Tortola, British Virgin Islands. stat.

910.2 CN
TOURISM INDUSTRY ASSOCIATION OF CANADA. CONVENTION REPORT. 1946. a. Travel Industry Association of Canada, Suite 1016, 130 Albert St, Ottawa, Ontario K1P 5G4, Canada. adv. circ. 2,000.
Former titles: Travel Industry Association of Canada. Convention Report (ISSN 0082-612X); Canadian Tourist Association. Proceedings.

915 JO
TOURISM RESEARCH BULLETIN/NASHRAT AL-ABHATH ASSYIAHIYAH. (Text in Arabic) 1971. a. Ministry of Tourism & Antiquities, Box 224, Amman, Jordan. circ. 500.

917.104 CN
TOURIST GUIDE/TOURISTIQUE. (Text in French & English) a. Can.$2.50. Editeur Limite-Ltd., 300 Arran Ave., St. Lambert, Que. J4R 1K5, Canada. Ed. Lucien Fontaine. adv. circ. 50,000.

380.058 ET ISSN 0564-0490
TRADE DIRECTORY AND GUIDE BOOK TO ETHIOPIA. 1954. a. Eth.$10($4.80) Ethiopian Chamber of Commerce, Box 517, Addis Ababa, Ethiopia. (reprint service avail. from ISI)

TRAILER LIFE'S RECREATIONAL VEHICLE CAMPGROUND AND SERVICES DIRECTORY.
see SPORTS AND GAMES — Outdoor Life

910 SP ISSN 0082-6103
TRAVEL ABROAD: FRONTIER FORMALITIES. (Editions in: English, French) 1955. a. $54. World Tourism Organization, Avenida del Generalisimo, 59, Madrid-16, Spain.

917.123 CN
TRAVEL ALBERTA-ANNUAL REVIEW. 1973. a. Travel Alberta, Suite 320, the Boardwalk, 10310-102 Ave., Edmonton, Alta., Canada. illus.

910.09 US
TRAVEL DATA LOCATOR INDEX; a reference guide to current data on travel and recreation. irreg. $12. U S Travel Data Center, 1899 L St., N.W., Washington, DC 20036.

919.3 NZ
TRAVEL EXECUTIVES OF NEW ZEALAND. 1968. a. NZ.$2. Mercantile Gazette of New Zealand Ltd., Box 20-034, Christchurch 5, New Zealand. Ed. E.R. Edmonds. adv.

910 SA
TRAVEL GUIDE, S.A. a. R.1.90. Promco (Pty) Ltd., 601 Pier House, Heerengracht, Cape Town, South Africa. Ed. L.D. Solomon. adv.

914.1 US
TRAVEL GUIDE TO EUROPE. triennial. $5. American Automobile Association, 8111 Gatchouse Rd., Falls Church, VA 22047. illus.
Formed by the merger of: British Isles and Ireland Travel Guide (ISSN 0095-1579) & Central Europe and Scandinavia Travel Guide (ISSN 0094-3657) & Eastern Europe Travel Guide (ISSN 0094-8632) & Southern Europe Travel Guide (ISSN 0094-3614)

910.09 US
TRAVEL IN AMERICA. irreg. $20. U S Travel Data Center, 1899 L St., N.W., Washington, DC 20036.

914.95 GR
TRAVEL IN GREECE. (Text in Greek) 1970. a. Dr.80($4) Hellenews Ltd., 39 Amaroussiou-Halandriou Rd., Amaroussion, Athens, Greece. Ed. D. G. Kalofolias.

910.2 US ISSN 0082-6146
TRAVEL INDUSTRY PERSONNEL DIRECTORY. 1951. a. $12. American Traveler, Inc., 2 W. 46 St., New York, NY 10036. Ed. Bette Sweeney. adv. index. circ. 7,000.

910.09 US
TRAVEL MARKET YEARBOOK (1980); the yearbook of travel facts, figures and trends. 1965. a. $48. Ziff Davis Publishing Co., Public Transportation and Travel Division, One Park Ave., New York, NY 10036. Ed. Penny Neubert. adv. charts. stat. index. circ. 6,000.
Former titles (until 1980): Travel Marketing; Travel Market Yearbook (ISSN 0564-1632)

910.09 US
TRAVEL OUTLOOK FORUM. PROCEEDINGS. a. $30. U S Travel Data Center, 1899 L St., N.W., Washington, DC 20036. (Co-sponsor: Travel Research Association)

914.2 UK ISSN 0082-7932
TRAVEL TRADE DIRECTORY, U K AND IRELAND. 1958. a. £12.50. Morgan-Grampian (Publishers) Ltd., Morgan-Grampian House, Calderwood St., London SE18 6QH, England. Ed. Jane Doyle. adv. circ. 5,800.

910 AT
TRAVEL TRADE YEARBOOK. 1965. s-a. I P C Business Press (Australia) Pty. Ltd., 3-13 Queen St., Chippendale, N.S.W. 2008, Australia. Ed. Kaye Tanner. circ. 2,850.

910 US
TRAVEL TRENDS IN THE UNITED STATES AND CANADA. 1960. irreg., latest edt., 1978. $25. University of Colorado, Graduate School of Business Administration, Boulder, CO 80309. Ed. Charles R. Goelder. circ. 1,100.
Formerly: Travel Trends in the United States and Canadian Provinces (ISSN 0082-6200)

910.202 US
TRAVEL WEEKLY'S WORLD TRAVEL DIRECTORY; official guide to the worldwide travel industry. 1970. a. $45. Ziff-Davis Publishing Co., Public Transportation and Travel Division, One Park Ave., New York, NY 10016. adv. tr. lit. circ. 7,500.
Formerly: World Travel Directory.

910.2 UK ISSN 0082-6219
TRAVEL WORLD YEAR BOOK AND DIARY. 1955. a. £3. Blandford Business Press, Pembroke House, Wellesley Rd., Croydon CR9 2BX, England. index.

916.2 UK
TRAVELAID GUIDE TO EGYPT. 1981. biennial. £5.95. Travelaid Publishing, Box 369, London NW3 4ER, England.

914.9 UK
TRAVELAID GUIDE TO GREECE. 1978. biennial. £3.75. Travelaid Publishing, Box 369, London NW3 4ER, England.

910.202 642.57 US
TRAVELER'S DIRECTORY OF FAST-FOOD RESTAURANTS. 1979. irreg. $3.50. Pilot Books, 347 Fifth Ave., New York, NY 10016. Ed. Kathleen Gruber.

917.204 MX
TRAVELERS GUIDE TO MEXICO. (Text in English) 1969. a. Mex.$60 per no. Chris A. Luhnow, Ed. & Pub., Paseo de la Reforma 380-3, Mexico 6, D.F., Mexico. adv. circ. 191,564.

916 UK ISSN 0140-1300
TRAVELLER'S GUIDE TO AFRICA. 1978. a. £7.45($14.95) International Communications Ltd., 63 Long Acre, London WC2E 9JH, England. Ed. Gill Garb. bk. rev. illus. stat. circ. 5,000. (also avail. in microfilm; back issues avail.)

915.6 UK ISSN 0140-1319
TRAVELLER'S GUIDE TO THE MIDDLE EAST. 1977. a. £7.45($14.95) International Communications Ltd., 63 Long Acre, London WC2E 9JH, England. Ed. Gill Garb. illus. stat. circ. 5,000. (also avail. in microfilm; back issues avail.)

917 US
TRAVELOG. 1960. a. $2. ‡ Travelog Publications, Box 11156, Fort Worth, TX 76109. Ed. Daniel Carlos Miller. adv. illus. circ. 125,000.

910 310 TR ISSN 0082-6537
TRINIDAD AND TOBAGO. CENTRAL STATISTICAL OFFICE. INTERNATIONAL TRAVEL REPORT. 1955. a; latest issue 1975. T.T.$1. Central Statistical Office, Textel Building, 1, Edward Street, Port of Spain, Trinidad (Subscr. to: Government Printery, 2 Victoria Ave., Port of Spain, Trinidad)

910.2 GW
DER TROTTER; d z g info. 1975. irreg. (4-6/yr.) DM.30 membership. Deutsche Zentrale fuer Globetrotter, c/o Ludmilla Tueting, Ed., Mittenwalder Str. 7, D-1000 Berlin 61, W. Germany (B.R.D.) bk. rev. abstr. charts. illus. stat. index. circ. 1,200. (back issues avail.)
Formerly: Globetrotter.

719.32 US ISSN 0083-2316
U. S. NATIONAL PARK SERVICE. HISTORICAL HANDBOOK SERIES. 1950. irreg. U. S. National Park Service, Interior Bldg., Washington, DC 20240 (Orders to: Supt. Doc., Washington, DC 20402)

719.32 US ISSN 0083-2324
U. S. NATIONAL PARK SERVICE. SOURCE BOOKS SERIES. 1942. irreg. U. S. National Park Service, Interior Bldg., Washington, DC 20240.

914 FR
UNIVERSITE D'AIX-MARSEILLE III. CENTRE DES HAUTES ETUDES TOURISTIQUES. COLLECTION "ESSAIS". 1976. irreg. no. 101,1981. price varies. Universite d'Aix-Marseille III(Universite de Droit, d'Economie et des Sciences), Centre des Hautes Etudes Touristiques, 18, rue de l'Opera, 13100 Aix-en-Provence, France.

914 FR ISSN 0065-4965
UNIVERSITE D'AIX-MARSEILLE III. CENTRE DES HAUTES ETUDES TOURISTIQUES. ETUDES ET MEMOIRES. 1963. irreg. no. 99, 1981. price varies. Universite d'Aix-Marseille III (Universite de Droit, d'Economie et des Sciences), Centre des Hautes Etudes Touristiques, 18 rue de l'Opera, 13100 Aix-en-Provence, France.

914.3 GW ISSN 0083-5250
VARTA FUEHRER DURCH DEUTSCHLAND, WESTLICHER TEIL UND BERLIN; ausgewaehlte Hotels und Restaurants. 1957. a. price varies. Redaktion VARTA-Fuehrer, Seedammweg 55, Postfach 2307, 6380 Bad Homburg, W. Germany (B.R.D.) circ. 100,000.

910.2 UK ISSN 0260-910X
VISIT CALIFORNIA WITH FYFE ROBERTSON. 1981. a. £1.95. Lewis Publications Ltd., 31 Castle St., Kingston-upon-Thames, Surrey KT1 1ST, England. Ed. David Jacobson. adv. circ. 30,000.

914.1 UK
WALKS AND TRAILS IN SCOTLAND. 1977. irreg. 60p. Scottish Tourist Board, 23 Ravelston Terrace, Edinburgh EH4 3EU, Scotland.

WASHINGTON (STATE) NATURAL RESOURCES AND RECREATION AGENCIES. ANNUAL REPORT. see CONSERVATION

910.2 UK ISSN 0260-9061
WEEKENDER. 1981. a. 85p. Lewis Publications Ltd., 31 Castle St., Kingston-upon-Thames, Surrey KT1 1ST, England. Ed. David Jacobson. adv. circ. 50,000.

914 DK ISSN 0085-8048
WELCOME TO FINLAND. (Text in English, French and German) 1962. a. Kr.35. Anders Nyborg A-S, Internationalt Forlag, Rungstedvej 13, 2970 Hoersholm, Denmark.

914.1 UK ISSN 0260-4426
WEST OF SCOTLAND VISITOR; a complete tourist guide to the West of Scotland. 1979. a. £0.20. Scotsman Publications, 20 North Bridge, Edinburgh EH1 1YT, Scotland. illus.

917.12 US
WESTERN CANADA ALASKA CAMPBOOK. Cover title: R V and Tent Sites in Alberta, British Columbia, Manitoba, Northwest Territories, Saskatchewan, Yukon Territory and Alaska. a. membership. American Automobile Association, 8111 Gatehouse Rd., Falls Church, VA 22047.

914.204 UK
WHAT'S ON NORTH WEST. a. free. Intercity Publications (N.W.) Ltd., 128 Northenden Rd., Sale, Cheshire, England. adv. illus. circ. 100,000.

917.04 US
WHEELCHAIR TRAVELER. 1963. biennial. $7.95. Annand Enterprises, Ball Hill Rd., Milford, NH 03055. Ed. Douglass R. Annand. adv. circ. 6,000.

796 US
WHEELERS RECREATIONAL VEHICLE RESORT AND CAMPGROUND GUIDE: EASTERNER EDITION. (Issued in regional editions) 1972. a. $4.95. Print Media Services, Ltd., 1521 Jarvis Ave., Elk Grove Village, IL 60007. Ed. Lois Edtrom. adv. circ. 100,000.
Supersedes: Wheelers Recreational Vehicle Resort and Campground Guide - Northeasterner Edition & Wheelers Recreational Vehicle Resort and Campground Guide - Southeasterner Edition; Which was formerly titled: Wheelers Trailer Resort and Campground Guide (ISSN 0090-600X)

917 US ISSN 0362-9759
WHEELERS RECREATIONAL VEHICLE RESORT AND CAMPGROUND GUIDE: NORTH AMERICAN EDITION. a. $6.95. Print Media Services, Ltd., 1521 Jarvis Ave., Elk Grove Village, IL 60007. Ed. Lois V. Edstrom.

796 US
WHEELERS RECREATIONAL VEHICLE RESORT AND CAMPGROUND GUIDE: WESTERNER EDITION. a. $3.95. Print Media Services Ltd., 1521 Jarvis Ave., Elk Grove Village, IL 60007. Ed. Lois V. Edstrom. adv. illus.

WHERE TO EAT & ENTERTAIN-SINGAPORE. see HOTELS AND RESTAURANTS

WHERE TO EAT IN CANADA. see HOTELS AND RESTAURANTS

910 709 US
WORLD CULTURAL GUIDES. irreg. Holt Rinehart and Winston, Inc., General Book Division, 383 Madison Ave., New York, NY 10017.

910 SP
WORLD TOURISM ORGANIZATION. COLLECTION OF TECHNICAL BULLETINS. (Editions in: English, French & Spanish) 18/yr. $35. World Tourism Organization, Avda. del Generalisimo 59, Madrid 16, Spain.
Until 1976 issued as: International Union of Official Travel Organizations. Technical Bulletin (ISSN 0579-692X)

TRAVEL AND TOURISM —
Abstracting, Bibliographies, Statistics

910 319.4 AT
AUSTRALIA. BUREAU OF STATISTICS. CENSUS OF TOURIST ACCOMODATION ESTABLISHMENTS: AUSTRALIA AND AUSTRALIAN CAPITAL TERRITORY. 1973. irreg., latest 1973-74. free. Australian Bureau of Statistics, Box 10, Belconnen, A.C.T. 2616, Australia. stat. circ. 2,000.

319 BB
BARBADOS. STATISTICAL SERVICE. DIGEST OF TOURISM STATISTICS. m. Statistical Service, National Insurance Building, Fairchild St., Bridgetown, Barbados, W. Indies.

910.2 BE ISSN 0067-5547
BELGIUM. INSTITUT NATIONAL DE STATISTIQUE. STATISTIQUE DU TOURISME ET DE L'HOTELLERIE. (Text in Dutch and French) a. 35 Fr. Institut National de Statistique, 44 rue de Louvain, 1000 Brussels, Belgium.

916.8 316 BS
BOTSWANA. CENTRAL STATISTICS OFFICE. TOURIST STATISTICS. 1974. a., latest 1978. R.1. Central Statistics Office, Ministry of Finance and Development Planning, Gaborone, Botswana (Orders to: Government Printer, Box 87, Gaborone, Botswana) charts, stat.

301.32 312 CY
CYPRUS. DEPARTMENT OF STATISTICS AND RESEARCH. TOURISM, MIGRATION AND TRAVEL STATISTICS. (Text in English and Greek) 1973. a. Mils.750. Department of Statistics and Research, Ministry of Finance, Nicosia, Cyprus.

312.8 910 GM
GAMBIA. CENTRAL STATISTICS DEPARTMENT. TOURIST STATISTICS. (Formerly issued by Central Statistics Division) a., latest 1978/1979. d.11. Central Statistics Department, Wellington St., Banjul, Gambia.

910 314 GW ISSN 0072-1999
GERMANY (FEDERAL REPUBLIC, 1949-) STATISTISCHES BUNDESAMT. FACHSERIE 6, REIHE 7: REISEVERKEHR. irreg. price varies. W. Kohlhammer-Verlag GmbH, Abt. Veroeffentlichungen des Statistischen Bundesamtes, Philipp-Reis-Str. 3, Postfach 421120, 6500 Mainz 42, W. Germany (B. R. D.)

338.4 IO
INDONESIA TOURIST STATISTICS. 1975. a. Directorate General of Tourism - Direktorat Jenderal Pariwisata, Jalan Kramat Raya, Box 409, Jakarta, Indonesia.

910 310 IS
ISRAEL. CENTRAL BUREAU OF STATISTICS. TRAVELING HABITS SURVEY. (Text in English and Hebrew) 1972. irreg. price varies. Central Bureau of Statistics, P.O.B. 13015, Jerusalem, Israel.

332.1 314 NO
NORWAY. STATISTISK SENTRALBYRAA. REISELIVSTATISKK/STATISTICS ON TRAVEL. (Subseries of its Norges Offisielle Statistikk) (Text in Norwegian and English) 1977. a. Kr.15. Statistisk Sentralbyraa, Box 8131 Dep., Oslo 1, Norway. stat. circ. 1,200.

910 314 PL
POLAND. GLOWNY URZAD STATYSTYCZNY. TURYSTYKA. (Subseries of: Statystyka Polski) 1969. a. 10 Zl. Glowny Urzad Statystyczny, Al. Niepodleglosci 208, 00-925 Warsaw, Poland.

960 316 SE
SEYCHELLES. PRESIDENT'S OFFICE. STATISTICS DIVISION. TOURISM AND MIGRATION REPORT. a. Rs.15. President's Office, Statistics Division, Box 206, Mahe, Seychelles (Subscr. to: Government Printer, Box 205, Union Vale, Mahe, Seychelles.)

SOUTH AFRICA. DEPARTMENT OF STATISTICS. TOURISM AND MIGRATION. see POPULATION STUDIES — Abstracting, Bibliographies, Statistcs

319 FJ
TOURISM AND MIGRATION STATISTICS. irreg., latest 1978. $1. Bureau of Statistics, Box 2221, Suva, Fiji.

910 016 SP
TOURISM COMPENDIUM. (Editions in: English, French & Spanish) 1959. a. $24. World Tourism Organization, Avenida del Generalisimo, 59, Madrid-16, Spain.
Formerly: Tourist Bibliography (ISSN 0082-5468)

338.4 CN ISSN 0317-6738
TRAVEL BETWEEN CANADA AND OTHER COUNTRIES/VOYAGES ENTRE LE CANADA ET LES AUTRES PAYS. (Catalogue 66-201) (Text in English and French) 1920. a. Can.$7($8.40) Statistics Canada, Publications Distribution, Ottawa, Ont. K1A 0V7, Canada. (also avail. in microform from MML)

910 314 BU
TURIZUM/TURISM. (Text in Bulgarian and English) 1967. irreg. 0.74 lv. per issue. Ministerstvo na Informatsiiata i Suobshteniiata, 18, Ul. Graf Ignatiev, Sofia, Bulgaria. (Co-sponsor: Tsentralno Statistichesko Upravlenie) stat. circ. 690.

910.2 SP
WORLD TRAVEL STATISTICS/STATISTIQUES DU TOURISME MONDIAL/ESTADISTICAS DEL TURISMO MUNDIAL. (Text in English, French & Spanish) 1953. a. 188 ptas. World Tourism Organization, Avenida del Generalisimo, 59, Madrid-16, Spain. (looseleaf format)
Formerly: International Travel Statistics (ISSN 0074-9184)

910.09 YU
YUGOSLAVIA. SAVEZNI ZAVOD ZA STATISTIKU. TURIZAM. (Subseries of its Statisticki Bilten) a. 30 din.($1.67) Savezni Zavod za Statistiku, Uzun Mirkova 1, Belgrade, Yugoslavia. stat.

UROLOGY AND NEPHROLOGY

see Medical Sciences — Urology and Nephrology

VETERINARY SCIENCE

636.089 IE ISSN 0066-9768
A. V. S. JOURNAL.* 1961. a. Association of Veterinary Students of Great Britain and Ireland, Veterinary College of Ireland, Ballsbridge, Dublin, 4, Ireland.

636.089 DK ISSN 0065-1699
ACTA VETERINARIA SCANDINAVICA. SUPPLEMENTUM. (Text in English, German or French; summaries in English, German and a Scandinavian language) 1961. irreg. Kr.410 incl. main vols. (Societatum Veteranariarum Scandanivacarum) Danske Dyrlaegeforening, Alhambravej 15, DK-1826 Copenhagen V, Denmark. Indexed: Ind.Med.

ADELAIDE. INSTITUTE OF MEDICAL AND VETERINARY SCIENCE. ANNUAL REPORT OF THE COUNCIL. see MEDICAL SCIENCES

VETERINARY SCIENCE

636.089   US   ISSN 0065-3519
ADVANCES IN VETERINARY SCIENCE AND COMPARATIVE MEDICINE. 1953. irreg., vol. 23, 1979. price varies. Academic Press Inc., 111 Fifth Ave, New York, NY 10003. Eds. C.A. Brandly, E.L. Jungherr. index. (also avail. in microfiche) Indexed: Ind.Med.
Continues: Advances in Veterinary Science.

636.089   US
AMERICAN ANIMAL HOSPITAL ASSOCIATION. ANNUAL MEETING SCIENTIFIC PROCEEDINGS. a. $25 for non-members; members $20. American Animal Hospital Association, 3612 E. Jefferson Blvd., Box 6429, South Bend, IN 46660.

636.089   US   ISSN 0065-7182
AMERICAN ASSOCIATION OF EQUINE PRACTITIONERS. PROCEEDINGS OF THE ANNUAL CONVENTION. 1956, 2nd convention. a. $15. American Association of Equine Practitioners, Route 5, 14 Hillcrest Circle, Golden, CO 80401. Ed. Frank Milne. circ. 2,500. (also avail. in microfilm from UMI; back issues avail.)

636.089   US   ISSN 0098-3543
AMERICAN ASSOCIATION OF VETERINARY LABORATORY DIAGNOSTICIANS. PROCEEDINGS OF ANNUAL MEETING. 19th, 1976. a. $15. American Association of Veterinary Laboratory Diagnosticians, c/o M. W. Vorhies, Sec. Treas, Department of Veterinary Science, South Dakota State University, Brookings, SD 57007. bibl. illus. circ. 580. Key Title: Proceedings of Annual Meeting - American Association of Veterinary Laboratory Diagnosticians.

636   US   ISSN 0569-7832
AMERICAN SOCIETY OF ANIMAL SCIENCE. WESTERN SECTION PROCEEDINGS. 1950? a. $6. American Society of Animal Science, Western Section, 309 W. Clark St., Champaign, IL 61820. circ. 600.

636.089   US   ISSN 0066-1147
AMERICAN VETERINARY MEDICAL ASSOCIATION. DIRECTORY. a. $30. ‡ American Veterinary Medical Association, 930 N. Meacham Rd., Schaumburg, IL 60196. Ed. A.V. Tennyson. adv. circ. 32,000. (also avail. in microfilm)

636.089   SP
ANALES DE LA UNIVERSIDAD HISPALENSE. SERIE: VETERINARIA. irreg. price varies. Universidad de Sevilla, San Fernando 4, Seville, Spain. charts, illus.

636.089   UK   ISSN 0142-6591
ANIMAL HEALTH TRUST. ANNUAL REPORT. 1963. a. £1. Animal Health Trust, Lanwades Hall, Kennet, Newmarket, Suffolk CB8 7PN, England (and 122 E. 55th St., New York, N.Y. 10022) Ed.Bd. adv. bk. rev. charts. illus. index. circ. 3,500. Indexed: Biol.Abstr.
Formerly: Animal Health (ISSN 0003-3502)

636.089   UN   ISSN 0066-1872
ANIMAL HEALTH YEARBOOK. (Text in English, French and Spanish) 1957. a. price varies. Food and Agriculture Organization of the United Nations, Distribution and Sales Section, Via delle Terme di Caracalla, 00100 Rome, Italy (Dist. in U.S. by: Unipub, 345 Park Ave. S., New York, NY 10010)

636   AT
ANIMAL QUARANTINE. 1972. irreg. free. Department of Health, Box 100, Woden, A. C. T. 2606, Australia. circ. 4,000.

639.089   PL   ISSN 0301-7737
ANNALES UNIVERSITATIS MARIAE CURIE-SKLODOWSKA. SECTIO DD. MEDICINA VETERINARIA. (Text in Polish or English; summaries in English, French, German, Russian) 1949. a. Uniwersytet Marii Curie-Sklodowskiej, Plac Marii Curie-Sklodowskiej 5, 20-031 Lublin, Poland. Ed. G. Staskiewicz. Indexed: Landwirt.Zentralbl. Vet.Bull.

636.089   BL
ANUARIO BRASILEIRO DE MEDICINA VETERINARIA. a. Publicacoes Informativas Ltda., Rua Caete 139, 05016 Sao Paulo, Brazil. Ed. J.C. Salles Neto. adv. circ. 10,000.

636.089   FR   ISSN 0007-9944
CAHIERS DE MEDECINE VETERINAIRE. 1928. irreg. Rhone-Poulenc-Specia, 26 Av. de l'Observatoire, Paris (14e), France. bk. rev. bibl. charts. illus.

636.089   CN   ISSN 0068-7316
CANADA. AGRICULTURE CANADA. HEALTH OF ANIMALS BRANCH. BOVINE TUBERCULOSIS AND BRUCELLOSIS. irreg. free. Agriculture Canada, Health of Animals Branch, Ottawa, Canada.

636   UK   ISSN 0069-6927
COMMONWEALTH BUREAU OF ANIMAL HEALTH. REVIEW SERIES. 1952. irreg. price varies. (Commonwealth Bureau of Animal Health) Commonwealth Agricultural Bureaux, Farnham House, Farnham Royal, Slough SL2 3BN, England. (also avail. in microfiche; back issues avail.)

636.089   AT   ISSN 0069-7273
COMMONWEALTH SCIENTIFIC AND INDUSTRIAL RESEARCH ORGANIZATION. DIVISION OF ANIMAL HEALTH. ANNUAL REPORT. 1966-67. a. free. C. S. I. R. O., Division of Animal Health, Private Bag No. 1, Parkville 3052, Victoria, Australia. circ. 1,000. Indexed: Ind.Vet. Vet.Bull.

COMPARATIVE ANIMAL NUTRITION. see BIOLOGY — Zoology

636.089   CU
CUBA. CENTRO DE INFORMACION Y DOCUMENTACION AGROPECUARIO. BOLETIN DE RESENAS. SERIE: VETERINARIA. 1974. irreg. $5. Centro de Informacion y Documentacion Agropecuario, Calle 11 no. 1057, Gaveta Postal 4149, Havana 4, Cuba.

636.089   CY
CYPRUS. CHIEF VETERINARY OFFICER. ANNUAL REPORT. (Text in English) a. Chief Veterinary Officer, Nicosia, Cyprus.

636.089   UK   ISSN 0260-0498
EUROVET BULLETIN. 1978. irreg. £1.50 to non-members. Eurovet, c/o C.B. Alers Hankey, Secy., British Veterinary Association, 7 Mansfield St., London W1AM 0AT, England.

636.089   GW   ISSN 0301-2794
FORTSCHRITTE DER VETERINAERMEDIZIN/ ADVANCES IN VETERINARY MEDICINE. (Supplement to: Zentralblatt fuer Veterinaermedizin, Series A, Series B, and Series C which is under the title: Anatomia, Histologia, Embryologia) 1958. irreg. price varies. Verlag Paul Parey (Berlin), Lindenstr. 44-47, 1000 Berlin 61, W. Germany (B.R.D.) bibl. illus. index. Indexed: Biol.Abstr.

636.089   FR
FRANCE. CENTRE NATIONAL DE RECHERCHE ZOOTECHNIQUE. DEPARTEMENT DE GENETIQUE ANIMALE. BULLETIN TECHNIQUE. 1968. irreg. Centre Nationale de Recherche Zoologique, Departement de Genetique Animale, Station de Genetique Quantitative et Appliquee, Bibliotheque, 78350 Jouy en Josas, France. circ. 500. Indexed: Anim.Breed.Abstr.
Formerly: France. Centre National de Recherche Zoologique. Departement de Genetique Animale. Bulletin Technique.

636.089   IT
GUIDA DI VETERINARIA E ZOOTECNIA; Italian directory of veterinary drugs, feed additives and manufacturers. (Text in Italian) 1966. irreg., 3rd edt., 1979. $35. Organizzazione Editoriale Medico-Farmaceutica, Via Edolo 42, Box 10434, 20125 Milan, Italy. Ed. Silvia Marini.

INDIAN POULTRY INDUSTRY YEARBOOK. see AGRICULTURE — Poultry And Livestock

636.089   II   ISSN 0304-7067
INDIAN VETERINARY RESEARCH INSTITUTE. ANNUAL REPORT. (Text in English) 1947/48. a. exchange basis. Indian Veterinary Research Institute, Mukteswar-Kumaon, Izatnagar, Uttar Pradesh, India.
Continues: Muktesar, India. Imperial Veterinary Research Institute. Report.

636   CN   ISSN 0581-3263
INFORMATION VETERINAIRE. vol. 19, 1977. irreg. free. Universite de Montreal, Faculte de Medecine Veterinaire, C.P. 5000, St. Hyacinthe, Que. J2S 7C6, Canada. Ed. Dr. Louis Phillippe Phaneuf. Indexed: Ind.Vet.

636.089   IR
INSTITUTE RAZI. ARCHIVES. (Text and summaries in English and French) 1940. a. free. Razi Institute, Boite Postale 656, Teheran, Iran. Eds. H. Mirshamsy, M. Ardehali.
Formerly: Institut d'Hessarek. Archives.

INSTITUTUL AGRONOMIC "ION IONESCU DE LA BRAD" LUCRARI STIINTIFICE II ZOOTEHNIE - MEDICINA VETERINARA. see AGRICULTURE — Poultry And Livestock

636.089   UK   ISSN 0074-4026
INTERNATIONAL CONGRESS ON ANIMAL REPRODUCTION AND ARTIFICIAL INSEMINATION. PROCEEDINGS. 1948. quadrennial., 7th, 1972, Munich; 8th, 1976, Krakow. $60. International Standing Committee on Physiology and Pathology of Animal Reproduction, c/o Prof. J. A. Laing, Royal Veterinary College, Hawkshead House, Hawkshead Lane, N. Mymms, Hatfield, Herts., England. Ed. M. Tischner. circ. 2,000.

636.089   GW   ISSN 0074-6975
INTERNATIONAL MEETING ON CATTLE DISEASES. REPORTS. (Each report published in the host country) (Text in English, French, German) biennial, 10th, Mexico, 1978. World Association for Buiatrics, Boigneville-91920, France, Bischofsholer Damm 15 (Rinderklinik), 3000 Hannover, W. Germany (B.R.D.)

636.7   US
INTERNATIONAL SYMPOSIUM ON CANINE HEARTWORM DISEASE. PROCEEDINGS. 1969. irreg., 2d, Jacksonville, 1971. $12. ‡ University of Florida, Institute of Food and Agricultural Sciences, Department of Veterinary Science, Gainesville, FL 32611. Ed. Richard E. Bradley. bibl. illus.

636.089   AU   ISSN 0075-2606
JAHRBUCH FUER DEN OESTERREICHISCHEN TIERARZT. 1950. a. S.208. Alois Goeschl und Co., Trummelhofgasse 12, A-1190 Vienna, Austria. Ed. Hiltraud Lechner.

636   JA   ISSN 0453-0535
JAPAN. NATIONAL INSTITUTE OF ANIMAL HEALTH. ANNUAL REPORT/NORIN-SHO KACHIKU EISEI SHIKENJO NENPO. (Text in Japanese) 1960. a. contr. circ. National Institute of Animal Health - Norin-sho Kachiku Eisei Shikenjo, Extension and Information Service, 1500 Josuihon-cho, Kodaira, Tokyo 187, Japan.

636   US   ISSN 0075-4129
JOURNAL OF ANIMAL SCIENCE. SUPPLEMENT. irreg., latest issue 1974. $8. American Society of Animal Science, 309 W. Clark St., Champaign, IL 61820. Ed. R.A. Merkel. Indexed: Ind.Med.

636.089 630   DK   ISSN 0368-7171
KONGELIGE VETERINAER- OG LANDBOHOEJSKOLE. AARSKRIFT. (Text mainly in English) 1917. a. Kr.45. Kongelige Veterinaer- og Landbohoejskole - Royal Veterinary and Agricultural University, Bulowsvej 13, DK-1870 Copenhagen V, Denmark. Ed. H. E. Jensen. circ. (controlled) Indexed: Biol.Abstr. Curr.Cont.

636.089   MW   ISSN 0076-3365
MALAWI. DEPARTMENT OF VETERINARY SERVICES AND ANIMAL INDUSTRY. ANNUAL REPORT. a, latest 1973. K.1.50. Government Printer, P.O. Box 37, Zomba, Malawi.

636.089   MY   ISSN 0460-8518
MALAYSIAN VETERINARY JOURNAL. (Text in English) 1955. a. M.$4. Malaysian Veterinary Association, c/o Central Animal Facility, Faculty of Medicine, University of Malaya, Kuala Lumpur, Malaysia. Ed. T. Mahendranathan. adv. bk. rev. charts. illus. circ. 350.

636.089　　　　US　ISSN 0076-6542
MERCK VETERINARY MANUAL; A
HANDBOOK OF DIAGNOSIS AND THERAPY
FOR THE VETERINARIAN. 1955. irreg., 5th edt.,
1979. $16.50. Merck and Co., Inc, Rahway, NJ
07065. Ed. Otto H. Siegmund, D.V.M.

636.089　　　　AT　ISSN 0085-4026
NEW SOUTH WALES VETERINARY
PROCEEDINGS. 1965. a. price varies. Australian
Veterinary Association, N.S.W. Division, 76
Parramatta Rd., Camperdown, N.S.W. 2050,
Australia. adv. circ. 1,000.

636.089　　　　NO　ISSN 0078-6713
NORGES VETERINAERHOEGSKOLE.
AARSBERETNING/VETERINARY COLLEGE
OF NORWAY. ANNUAL REPORT. 1937. a. free.
Norges Veterinaerhoegskole, Postboks 8146, Oslo-
Dep, Oslo 1, Norway.

636.089　　　　PL　ISSN 0079-3647
POLSKIE ARCHIWUM WETERYNARYJNE. (Text
in Polish and English; summaries in English, Polish
and Russian) 1951. irreg., 1972, vol. 15, fasc. 4.
price varies. (Polska Akademia Nauk, Komitet Nauk
Weterynaryjnych) Panstwowe Wydawnictwo
Naukowe, Miodowa 10, Warsaw, Poland (Dist by
Ars Polona-Ruch, Krakowskie Przedmiescie 7,
Warsaw, Poland) Ed. Edmund Prost. bibl, charts,
illus. Indexed: Biol.Abstr. Chem.Abstr. Ind.Med.

636.089　　　　US　ISSN 0146-6429
SOCIETY OF VECTOR ECOLOGISTS. BULLETIN.
1974. a. $15 to institutions. Society of Vector
Ecologists, Inc., Educational Foundation, 3827 W.
Chapman Ave., Orange, CA 92668. Ed. Minoo B.
Madon. circ. 250. Indexed: Chem.Abstr. Key Title:
Bulletin of the Society of Vector Ecologists.

636.089　　　　US
U.S. DEPARTMENT OF AGRICULTURE.
ANIMAL AND PLANT HEALTH INSPECTION
SERVICE. REPORTED ARTHROPOD-BORNE
ENCEPHALITIDES IN HORSES AND OTHER
EQUIDAE. 1966. a. free. ‡ U.S. Animal and Plant
Health Inspection Service, Federal Building,
Hyattsville, MD 20782. illus. stat. Indexed:
Bibl.Agri.

636.089　　　　US　ISSN 0082-8750
UNITED STATES ANIMAL HEALTH
ASSOCIATION. PROCEEDINGS OF THE
ANNUAL MEETING. 1969, no. 73. a. $12.50.
United States Animal Health Association, 6924
Lakeside Ave., Suite 205, Richmond, VA 23228.
circ. 1,000. (back issues avail.) Indexed: Ind.Med.
Continues: United States Livestock Sanitary
Association. Proceedings.

636.089　　　　GT
UNIVERSIDAD DE SAN CARLOS DE
GUATEMALA. FACULTAD DE MEDICINA
VETERINARIA Y ZOOTECNIA REVISTA. (Text
in Spanish; summaries in Spanish and English)
1962. irreg. exchange basis. Universidad de San
Carlos de Guatemala, Facultad de Medicina
Veterinaria y Zootecnia, Ciudad Universitaria, Zona
12, Guatemala.

636　　　　CN　ISSN 0383-8455
UNIVERSITE DE MONTREAL. ECOLE DE
MEDECINE VETERINAIRE. ANNUAIRE. 1968.
a. Universite de Montreal, Ecole de Medecine
Veterinaire, C.P. 6128, Montreal, Que., Canada.
Formerly: Ecole de Medecine Veterinaire, Saint-
Hyacinthe, Quebec. Annuaire (ISSN 0383-8447)

636　　　　US　ISSN 0076-9711
UNIVERSITY OF MISSOURI, COLUMBIA.
VETERINARY MEDICAL DIAGNOSTIC
LABORATORY. ANNUAL REPORT. 1967. a.
University of Missouri-Columbia, Veterinary
Medical Diagnostic Labrary, Columbia, MO 65201.
Ed. L. G. Morehouse. circ. 800.

636.089　　　　VE
VETERINARIA TROPICAL. (Text in Spanish;
summaries in English & Spanish) irreg. available on
exchange. Instituto de Investigaciones Veterinarias,
Apdo. Postal 70, Maracay 300, Venezuela. Ed.Bd.
bibl. charts. illus.
Formerly (until 1976): Instituto de
Investigaciones Veterinarias. Boletin.

636　　　　NZ
VETERINARY SURGEONS IN NEW ZEALAND;
registered under the Veterinary Surgeons Act 1956
& persons entitled to use the title or description of
veterinary practitioner. 1957. a. price varies.
Government Printing Office, Mulgrave St,
Thorndon, Wellington, New Zealand. circ. 1,000.

636.089　　　　AT
VICTORIAN VETERINARY PROCEEDINGS.
1950. a. Aus.$4.50. Australian Veterinary
Association, Victorian Division, 272 Brunswick Rd.,
Brunswick, Vic. 3056, Australia. Ed. Dr. Ivan Caple.
adv. circ. 1,000. Indexed: Ind. Vet.

636.089　　　　GR　ISSN 0084-1404
WORLD ASSOCIATION FOR THE
ADVANCEMENT OF VETERINARY
PARASITOLOGY. PROCEEDINGS OF
CONFERENCE. (Publisher varies) 1963. biennial,
8th, 1977, Sydney. $15. ‡ World Association for the
Advancement of Veterinary Parasitology, c/o C.A.
Himonas, Sec.-Treas., Department of Applied
Helminthology & Entomology, School of Veterinary
Medicine, Aristotelian University, Thessalonika,
Greece. Ed. Bd.

WORLD DIRECTORY OF VETERINARY
SCHOOLS. see *EDUCATION — Guides To
Schools And Colleges*

636.089　　　　SZ　ISSN 0084-2435
WORLD VETERINARY ASSOCIATION.
CATALOGUE OF VETERINARY FILMS AND
FILMS OF VETERINARY INTEREST. (Text in
English; synopeses in English, French or German)
1966. irreg., latest edition 1975. 40 Fr. World
Veterinary Association, 70, Rte. du Pont Butin,
1213 Petit-Lancy/GE, Switzerland. circ. 400.

636.089　　　　SZ　ISSN 0084-2443
WORLD VETERINARY CONGRESS.
PROCEEDINGS. quadrennial, 21st, 1979, Moscow,
U.S.S.R. $30. World Veterinary Congress, c/o
World Veterinary Association, 70 Route du Pont
Butin, 1213 Petit-Lancy/GE, Switzerland (Published
by the organizing committee of each congress; for
21st Congress, inquire: USSR National Organizing
Committee, Bld. B1, Room 404, Orlikov Per. 1/11,
Moscow, USSR)

VETERINARY SCIENCE —
Abstracting, Bibliographies, Statistics

636.089 016　　　　US
ACCUMULATIVE VETERINARY INDEX. 1960. s-
a., cumulated annually and every 5 yrs. $17.50.
Index Inc., Box 35, Arvada, CO 80001. Ed. Dr. V.
D. Stauffer.
Formerly: Veterinary Index.

WATER RESOURCES

see also *Environmental Studies*

333.7 628　　　　US
ADVANCED WATER CONFERENCE.
PROCEEDINGS. irreg, 3rd, 1971. price varies.
Oklahoma State University, College of Engineering,
Engineering and Industrial Extension, Stillwater,
OK 74074.

333.9　　　　CN　ISSN 0580-535X
AGASSIZ CENTER FOR WATER STUDIES.
RESEARCH REPORT. irreg. Agassiz Center for
Water Studies, Winnipeg, Man., Canada. bibl.

627　　　　US　ISSN 0066-0612
AMERICAN SOCIETY OF CIVIL ENGINEERS.
URBAN WATER RESOURCES RESEARCH
PROGRAM. TECHNICAL MEMORANDUM.
1968. irreg. price varies. American Society of Civil
Engineers, 345 E. 47th St., New York, NY 10017
(Subscr. to: NTIS, Port Royal Rd., Springfield, VA
22161)

333.91　　　　US　ISSN 0066-1171
AMERICAN WATER RESOURCES
CONFERENCES. ANNUAL PROCEEDINGS.
1965. a. $15. American Water Resources
Association, St. Anthony Falls Hydraulic
Laboratory, Mississippi River at Third Ave., S. E.,
Minneapolis, MN 55414.

628　　　　US　ISSN 0360-814X
AMERICAN WATER WORKS ASSOCIATION.
PROCEEDINGS, A W W A ANNUAL
CONFERENCE. a. American Water Works
Association, 6666 W. Quincy Ave., Denver, CO
80235. illus. (reprint service avail. from UMI, BLH)
Key Title: Proceedings, A W W A Annual
Conference.

627　　　　BL
ANAIS HIDROGRAFICOS. 1933. a. free. Ministerio
da Marinha, Diretoria de Hidrografia e Navegacao,
Rio de Janeiro, Brazil. charts. illus. stat. circ.
controlled.

333.91　　　　US　ISSN 0161-4924
ANNUAL NEW MEXICO WATER
CONFERENCE. PROCEEDINGS. 1956. a. New
Mexico Water Resources Research Institute, Box
3167, New Mexico State University, Las Cruces,
NM 88003. circ. 500.

333.91　　　　US
ANNUAL REPORT ON GROUND WATER IN
ARIZONA. (Subseries of: Arizona Water
Commission Bulletin) a. free. Department of Water
Resources, 99 E. Virginia, Phoenix, AZ 85004.
charts. illus. stat.

331.91　　　　FI　ISSN 0356-7133
AQUA FENNICA. (Text in English; summaries in
Finnish) 1971. a. Fmk.50. Vesiyhdistys r.y. - Water
Association, P.O. Box 721, 00101 Helsinki 10,
Finland. Ed. Pertti Sevna. adv. charts. illus. circ.
350. (back issues avail)

333.91　　　　US　ISSN 0360-7461
ARIZONA. WATER COMMISSION. BULLETIN.
irreg. Department of Water Resources, Suite 800,
Phoenix, AZ 85004.
Formerly: Arizona. State Land Department.
Water Resources Report (ISSN 0403-0699)

333.91　　　　US　ISSN 0571-0278
ARKANSAS. GEOLOGICAL COMMISSION.
WATER RESOURCES CIRCULARS. 1955. irreg.,
no. 12, 1975. price varies. Geological Commission,
Vardell Parham Geology Center, 3815 West
Roosevelt Rd., Little Rock, AR 72204. (back issues
avail.)

333.9　　　　US　ISSN 0067-043X
AUBURN UNIVERSITY. WATER RESOURCES
RESEARCH INSTITUTE. ANNUAL REPORT.
1965. a. free. ‡ Auburn University, Water Resources
Research Institute, 202 Hargis Hall, Auburn, AL
36849. Ed. Lesley P. Cooper. circ. 600.

628　　　　MW　ISSN 0084-7925
BLANTYRE WATER BOARD. ANNUAL REPORT
AND STATEMENT OF ACCOUNTS. 1967. a. ‡
Blantyre Water Board, Box 30369, Chichiri,
Blantyre 3, Malawi. stat. circ. 500.

627　　　　BL
BRAZIL. MINISTERIO DO INTERIOR.
RELATORIO SINTETICO, ANDAMENTO DO
PROGRAMA DE IRRIGACAO DO NORDESTE.
irreg. Ministerio do Interior, Brasilia, Brazil. illus.

333.9　　　　CN　ISSN 0068-1873
BRITISH COLUMBIA. DEPARTMENT OF
LANDS, FORESTS AND WATER RESOURCES.
WATER RESOURCES SERVICE. REPORT. 1964.
a. free. Department of Lands, Forests and Water
Resources, Water Resources Service, Victoria, B.C.,
Canada.

333.91　　　　CN
BRITISH COLUMBIA WATER AND WASTE
ASSOCIATION. PROCEEDINGS OF THE
ANNUAL CONFERENCE. a. free. Fisheries and
Environment Canada, Fontaine Bldg, 200 Sacre-
Coeur Blvd., Hull, Que. K1A 0H3, Canada. charts.
illus.

333.9　　　　　US　　ISSN 0084-8263
CALIFORNIA. DEPARTMENT OF WATER
RESOURCES. BULLETIN. a. price varies.
Department of Water Resources, P.O. Box 388,
Sacramento, CA 95802. circ. controlled.

333.9　　　　　US　　ISSN 0092-9158
CALIFORNIA. DEPARTMENT OF WATER
RESOURCES. INVENTORY OF WASTE
WATER PRODUCTION AND WASTE WATER
RECLAMATION PRACTICES IN
CALIFORNIA. (Subseries of its Bulletin) a. price
varies. Department of Water Resources, P.O. Box
388, Sacramento, CA 95802.

363.6　　　　　US
CALIFORNIA. STATE WATER RESOURCES
CONTROL BOARD. PROGRAM GUIDE. a.
State Water Resources Control Board, Box 100,
Sacramento, CA 95801. illus.
　　Former titles: California. State Water Resources
Control Board. Annual Program Guide; California.
State Water Resources Control Board. Annual State
Strategy (ISSN 0361-4506)

333.91　　　　US　　ISSN 0090-5968
CALIFORNIA STATE WATER PROJECT.
(Subseries of California. Dept. of Water Resources.
Bulletin) 1963. a. price varies. ‡ Department of
Water Resources, P.O. Box 388, Sacramento, CA
95802. illus. stat. circ. controlled. (back issues
available)

354　　　　　　CN　　ISSN 0704-3139
CANADA. HYDROGRAPHIC SERVICE.
ANNUAL REPORT. a. free. Fisheries and
Environment Canada, Information Service
Directorate, Fontaine Bldg, 200 Sacre-Coeur Blvd,
Hull, Que. K1A 0H3, Canada. illus.

333.91 016　　　NE
CATALOGUS VAN NEDERLANDSE
ZEEKAARTEN EN ANDERE
HYDROGRAFISCHE PUBLIKATIES/CATALOG
OF CHARTS AND OTHER HYDROGRAPHIC
PUBLICATIONS. (Text in Dutch and English)
1874. a. fl.12. Ministerie van Defensie, c/o
Hydrographer of the Royal Netherlands Navy, Box
90704, 2509 LS The Hague, Netherlands.
　　Formerly: Netherlands. Departement van Marine.
Catalogus van Nederlandse Zeekaarten en
Boekwerken.

628　　　　　　SW　　ISSN 0009-1111
CHALMERS TEKNISKA HOGSKOLA.
INSTITUTIONEN FOER
VATTENFOERSOERJNINGS OCH
AVLOPPSTEKNIK. PUBLIKATIONSSERIE B;
Current reports on research in water supply and
sewage disposal. (Text in Swedish; summaries in
English) 1962. irreg. Kr.90. Chalmers Tekniska
Hoegskola, Institutionen Foer Vattenfoersoerjnings
och Avloppsteknik, S-412 96 Goeteborg 5, Sweden.
charts. illus.

333.91　　　　US　　ISSN 0069-4657
CLEMSON UNIVERSITY. WATER RESOURCES
RESEARCH INSTITUTE. REPORT. 1967. irreg.,
no. 67, 1977. free; limited distribution. Clemson
University, Water Resources Research Institute,
Clemson, SC 29631.

333.91　　　　US　　ISSN 0092-2684
COLORADO WATER RESOURCES CIRCULARS.
1948. irreg., latest issue no. 36. $1-3. Division of
Water Resources, Water Conservation Board, 823
State Centennial Bldg., 1313 Sherman St., Denver,
CO 80203. (Co-sponsor: U.S. Geological Survey)
illus.
　　Continues: Colorado. Water Conservation Board.
Ground Water Series. Circular (ISSN 0160-0974)

333.9　　　　　US　　ISSN 0360-6864
COLUMBIA RIVER WATER MANAGEMENT
REPORT. 1971. a. free. U.S. Army Corps of
Engineers, Columbia River Water Management
Group, Box 2870, Portland, OR 97208. illus.

COMISION DE INTEGRACION ELECTRICA
REGIONAL. RECURSOS ENERGETICOS DE
LOS PAISES DE LA C I E R. see *PETROLEUM
AND GAS*

333.9　　　　　US　　ISSN 0363-8170
COORDINATION DIRECTORY OF STATE AND
FEDERAL AGENCY WATER AND LAND
RESOURCES OFFICIALS. a. Missouri River Basin
Commission, Suite 403, 10050 Regency Circle,
Omaha, NE 68114.
　　Formerly: Directory of Federal and State
Officials Engaged in Water Resource Development.

333.91　　　　US
CURRENTS. 1973. irreg. free. Oregon State
University, Sea Grant College Program, Sea Grant
Communications, AdS A418, Corvallis, OR 97331.
bk. rev. bibl. circ. 4,000. (back issues avail)

333.91　　　　US　　ISSN 0045-9844
DELAWARE BASIN BULLETIN. 1959. irreg.
membership or free upon request. ‡ Water
Resources Association of the Delaware River Basin,
Box 867, Davis Rd., Valley Forge, PA 19481. Ed.
Paul M. Felton. charts. illus.

333.91　　　　US
DELAWARE RIVER BASIN WATER RESOURCES
CONFERENCE. PROCEEDINGS. 1962. a.
membership. Water Resources Association of the
Delaware River Basin, Box 867, Davis Rd., Valley
Forge, PA 19481.

551.4　627　　　GW　　ISSN 0340-5176
DEUTSCHES GEWAESSERKUNDLICHES
JAHRBUCH. DONAUGEBIET. 1898. a. avail. on
exchange. Bayer Landesamt fuer Wasserwirtschaft,
Lazarettstr. 67, 8000 Munich 19, W. Germany
(B.R.D.) charts. stat. circ. 500.

551.4　627　　　GW　　ISSN 0340-5184
DEUTSCHES GEWAESSERKUNDLICHES
JAHRBUCH. KUESTENGEBIET DER NORT-
UND OSTSEE. 1941. a. DM.40. Landesamt fuer
Wasserhaushalt und Kuesten, Saarbrueckenstr. 38,
2300 Kiel 1, W. Germany (B.R.D.) Ed. Mr. Benn.
stat. index;cum. index. circ. controlled.

551　627　　　　GW
DEUTSCHES GEWAESSERKUNDLICHES
JAHRBUCH. RHEINGEBIET: ABSCHNITT
MAIN. 1898. a. avail. on exchange. Bayer
Landesamt fuer Wasserwirtschaft, Lazarettstr. 67,
8000 Munich 19, W. Germany (B.R.D.) charts.
stat. circ. 500.

628　　　　　　GW　　ISSN 0012-0030
DOKUMENTATIONSZENTRALE WASSER
SCHRIFTENREIHE. 1963. irreg. price varies.
(Fraunhofer-Gesellschaft) Erich Schmidt Verlag
(Bielefeld), Viktoriastr. 44A, 4800 Bielefeld 1, W.
Germany B.R.D. adv. bk. rev. bibl. circ. 750.
　　Formerly: Deutscher Arbeitskreis Wasser.
Schriftenreihe.

627　620　　　　US
DREDGING SEMINAR. PROCEEDINGS. vol. 5,
1973. irreg. Texas A & M University, Center for
Dredging Studies, College Station, TX 77843.
charts.

627　　　　　　US
ENGINEERING COMMITTEE ON OCEANIC
RESOURCES. PROCEEDINGS OF THE
GENERAL ASSEMBLY. irreg., 2nd, 1975, Tokyo.
Engineering Committee on Oceanic Resources,
2101 Constitution Ave. N.W., Washington, DC
20418.

627　　　　　　UN
FAO IRRIGATION AND DRAINAGE PAPERS.
irreg.; 1972, no. 12. price varies. Food and
Agriculture Organization of the United Nations,
Distribution and Sales Section, Via delle Terme di
Caracalla, I-00100 Rome, Italy (Dist. in U.S. by:
Unipub, 345 Park Ave. S., New York, NY 10010)

627　　　　　　FI　　ISSN 0355-0982
FINLAND. VESTIENTUTKIMUSLAITOS.
JULKASUJA/FINLAND. WATER RESEARCH
INSTITUTE. PUBLICATIONS. (Text in Finnish;
summaries in English) 1972. irreg. price varies.
Valtion Painatuskeskus - Government Printing
Centre, Annankatu 44, 00100 Helsinki 10, Finland.
illus.

333.91　　　　FR　　ISSN 0071-853X
FRANCE. DELEGATION GENERALE A LA
RECHERCHE SCIENTIFIQUE ET TECHNIQUE.
RECHERCHE DANS LE DOMAINE DE L'EAU:
REPERTOIRE DES LABORATOIRES. 1964.
irreg. 14 F. Documentation Francaise, 29-31 Quai
Voltaire, 75340 Paris 07, France.

333.91　　　　US　　ISSN 0149-2462
GEORGIA. WATER RESOURCES SURVEY.
HYDROLOGIC REPORT. 1974. irreg. price varies.
‡ Department of Natural Resources, Geologic and
Water Resources Division, 19 Hunter St., Rm. 400,
Atlanta, GA 30334. Ed. L. P. Stafford.

333.7　333.7　　GW
GERMANY (FEDERAL REPUBLIC, 1949-).
BUNDESANSTALT FUER
GEWAESSERKUNDE. JAHRESBERICHT. 1949-
1962;1974. a. Bundesanstalt fuer Gewaesserkunde,
Kaiserin-Augusta-Anlagen 15, 5400 Koblenz, W.
Germany (B.R.D.) illus.

333.9　　　　　UK　　ISSN 0072-7245
GREAT BRITAIN. WATER RESOURCES BOARD.
PUBLICATION. 1966(o.p.) irreg. Water Resources
Board, Reading Bridge House, Reading, Berks,
England (Avail. from H.M.S.O., Atlantic House,
Holborn Viaduct, London EC1P 1BN, England)

333.9　　　　　UK　　ISSN 0072-7253
GREAT BRITAIN. WATER RESOURCES BOARD.
REPORT. 1963-64. a. price varies. Water Resources
Board, Reading Bridge House, Reading, Berks,
England (Avail. from H.M.S.O., c/o Liaison Officer,
Atlantic House, Holborn Viaduct, London EC1P
1BN, England)

333.9　　　　　US
GREAT LAKES BASIN COMMISSION. ANNUAL
REPORT. 1968. a. free. Great Lakes Basin
Commission, Box 999, 3475 Plymouth Rd., Ann
Arbor, MI 48106.

977　016　　　　US　　ISSN 0072-7326
GREAT LAKES RESEARCH CHECKLIST. 1959. s-
a. free. ‡ Great Lakes Commission, 2200 Bonisteel
Blvd., Ann Arbor, MI 48109. Ed. A. G. Ballert.
circ. 650. (also avail. in microfilm from UMI;
reprint service avail. from UMI)

551.4　　　　　CN
INDEX DE REFERENCES: INVENTAIRE DES
STATIONS HYDROMETRIQUES. 1968. irreg.
Can.$2. Ministere des Richesses Naturelles, 1620
Bd. de l'Entente, Quebec G1S 4N6, Canada. illus.
circ. 400.

333.91　　　　RM
INSTITUTUL DE STUDII, CERCETARI SI
PROIECTARI PENTRU GOSPODARIREA
APELOR. STUDII DE ECONOMIA APELOR.
(Summaries in English, French and Russian.) 1972.
irreg. Institutul de Studii, Cercetari si Proiectari
Pentru Gospodarirea Apelor, Splaiul Independentei 294,
Bucharest, Romania. illus.

333.9　　　　　PL　　ISSN 0074-0586
INSTYTUT GOSPODARKI WODNEJ. PRACE.*
(Text in Polish; summaries in English and Russian)
1961. irreg., 1971, no. 4, vol. 6. $8 per volume.
Wydawnictwa Komunikacji i Lacznosci, Ul.
Kazimierzowska 52, Warsaw, Poland (Dist. by Ars
Polona-Ruch, Krakowskie Przedmiescie 7, Warsaw,
Poland)

631.6　　　　　II　　ISSN 0538-5768
INTERNATIONAL COMMISSION ON
IRRIGATION AND DRAINAGE. REPORT.
(Text in English) 1951. a. International Commission
on Irrigation and Drainage - Commission
Internationale des Irrigations et du Drainage, 48
Nyaya Marg, Chanakyapuri, New Delhi 110021,
India. circ. 2,000(controlled)

333.91　　　　IT
INTERNATIONAL CONFERENCE ON WATER
LAW AND ADMINISTRATION.
BACKGROUND PAPER. (Text in various
European languages) no. 2, 1976. irreg. $40.
International Association for Water Law, Via
Montevideo 5, 00197 Rome, Italy. circ. 400.

627　　　　　　UK
INTERNATIONAL SYMPOSIUM ON WAVE AND
TIDAL ENERGY. PROCEEDINGS. 1978. irreg.
price varies. British Hydromechanics Research
Association, Cranfield, Bedford MK43 0AJ,
England (Dist. in U.S. by: Air Science Co., Box
143, Corning, N. Y. 14830) Eds. H. S. Stephens, C.
A. Stapleton.

INTERNATIONAL WATER CONFERENCE.
PROCEEDINGS. see ENGINEERING —
Hydraulic Engineering

628.1　　　UK　ISSN 0074-9583
INTERNATIONAL WATER SUPPLY CONGRESS.
PROCEEDINGS. (Text in English and French)
1949. biennial, 12th, 1978, Kyoto. price varies.
International Water Supply Association, 1, Queen
Anne's Gate, London SW1H 9BT, England. circ.
3,000.

333.91　　　US　ISSN 0535-4676
INTERSTATE COMMISSION ON THE POTOMAC
RIVER BASIN. PROCEEDINGS. a. Interstate
Commission on the Potomac River Basin, 1055
First St., Rockville, MD 20850.

627　　　　　　PK
IRRIGATION RESEARCH INSTITUTE, LAHORE.
REPORT. 1973. irreg. Irrigation Research Institute,
The Mall, Lahore, Pakistan.

333.91　614.7　US
JOURNAL OF FRESHWATER. 1977. a.
membership. Freshwater Biological Research
Foundation, 2500 Shadywood Rd., Box 90, Navarre,
MN 55392. illus. circ. controlled.

JOURNAL OF SOIL AND WATER
CONSERVATION IN INDIA. see
CONSERVATION

333.91　　　US　ISSN 0160-2659
KANSAS WATER RESOURCES RESEARCH
INSTITUTE. ANNUAL REPORT. 1964. a. Kansas
Water Resources Research Institute, 146D Waters
Hall, Manhattan, KS 66502.

628　551.4　US
LOUISIANA WATER RESOURCES RESEARCH
INSTITUTE. ANNUAL REPORT. 1965/66. a.
Louisiana Water Resources Research Institute,
Louisiana State University, 146 Engineering
Drawing Building, Baton Rouge, LA 70803. circ.
controlled.

MAJI REVIEW. see ENERGY

354　　　　CN　ISSN 0318-3912
MANITOBA. WATER SERVICES BOARD.
ANNUAL REPORT. 1973. a. Water Services
Board, 1445 Pembina Highway, Winnipeg, Man.
R3T 2C4, Canada.

333.91　　　US　ISSN 0076-4817
MARYLAND. GEOLOGICAL SURVEY. WATER
RESOURCES BASIC DATA REPORT. 1966.
irreg., no. 11, 1980. price varies. Geological Survey,
Merryman Hall, Johns Hopkins University,
Baltimore, MD 21218.

MEXICO. SECRETARIA DE AGRICULTURA Y
RECURSOS HIDRAULICOS. INFORME
ESTADISTICOS. see AGRICULTURE —
Agricultural Economics

628　　　　　　US
MICHIGAN STATE UNIVERSITY. INSTITUTE OF
WATER RESEARCH. ANNUAL REPORT. 1966.
a. free. ‡ Michigan State University, Institute of
Water Research, 334 Natural Resources Bldg., East
Lansing, MI 48824. Ed. Mrs. Mayanne Richardson.
illus. circ. 100 - 200. (processed; reprint service
avail. from UMI)

628　　　　US　ISSN 0580-9746
MICHIGAN STATE UNIVERSITY. INSTITUTE OF
WATER RESEARCH. TECHNICAL REPORT.
1968. irreg., latest no. 47. price varies. Michigan
State University, Institute of Water Research, 334
Natural Resources Bldg., East Lansing, MI 48824
(Order from: National Technical Information
Service, 5285 Port Royal Rd., Springfield, VA
22151) (back issues avail.; reprint service avail. from
UMI)

333.9　　　US　ISSN 0076-9533
MISSISSIPPI WATER RESOURCES
CONFERENCE. PROCEEDINGS. 1966. a.
Mississippi State University, Water Resources
Research Institute, Mississippi State, MS 39762. Ed.
Elizabeth Hawkins.

333.91　551.4　US　ISSN 0076-9614
MISSOURI. DIVISION OF GEOLOGICAL
SURVEY AND WATER RESOURCES. WATER
RESOURCES REPORT. 1956. irreg., no. 30, 1974.
price varies. Department of Natural Resources,
Division of Geology and Land Survey, Box 250,
Rolla, MO 65401. Ed. Barbara Harris. circ. 1,000-
2,000.

333.9　　　US　ISSN 0092-7945
MISSOURI RIVER BASIN COMMISSION.
ANNUAL REPORT. 1972/73. a. Missouri River
Basin Commission, Suite 403, 10050 Regency
Circle, Omaha, NE 68114. illus. Key Title: Annual
Report - Missouri River Basin Commission.

333.9　　　US　ISSN 0077-1201
MONTANA. WATER RESOURCES BOARD.
INVENTORY SERIES. 1968. irreg., no. 16, 1970.
$1.50. Department of Natural Resources and
Conservation, 32 S. Ewing St., Helena, MT 59601.

628　　　　　　US
MONTANA UNIVERSITY JOINT WATER
RESOURCES RESEARCH CENTER. ANNUAL
REPORT. a. Montana University Joint Water
Resources Research Center, Montana State
University, Bozeman, MT 59717. abstr.

333.91　　　SA
N I W R INFORMATION SHEET. irreg. free.
National Institute for Water Research, Box 395,
Pretoria 0001, South Africa.

627　　　　　　JA
NAGOYA UNIVERSITY. WATER RESEARCH
INSTITUTE. ANNUAL REPORT/SUIKEN
KAGAKU KENKYUJO NENPO. (Text in
Japanese) 1974. a. Nagoya University, Water
Research Institute - Nagoya Daigaku Suishitsu
Kagaku Kenkyu Shisetsu, Furo-cho, Chikusa-ku,
Nagoya 464, Japan. illus.

333.91　　　　　US
NATIONAL CONFERENCE ON COMPLETE
WATER USE. PROCEEDINGS. vol. 3, 1976. a.
American Institute of Chemical Engineers, 345 E.
47th St., New York, NY 10017. (Co-sponsor: U.S.
Environmental Protection Agency) charts.

NATIONAL WATERWAYS CONFERENCE
NEWSLETTER. see TRANSPORTATION —
Ships And Shipping

333.9　　　US　ISSN 0092-6442
NEBRASKA. NATURAL RESOURCES
COMMISSION. STATE WATER PLAN
PUBLICATION (LINCOLN) irreg. Natural
Resources Commission, Box 94725, Statehouse
Station, Lincoln, NE 68509. illus.

333.9　　　US　ISSN 0077-6394
NEBRASKA WATER RESOURCES RESEARCH
INSTITUTE, UNIVERSITY OF NEBRASKA.
ANNUAL REPORT OF ACTIVITIES. a. free.
Nebraska Water Resources Research Institute,
University of Nebraska, Lincoln, NE 68503.

NEW ZEALAND AGRICULTURAL
ENGINEERING INSTITUTE. ANNUAL
REPORT. see AGRICULTURE — Crop
Production And Soil

333.9　　　US　ISSN 0078-1525
NORTH CAROLINA STATE UNIVERSITY.
WATER RESOURCES RESEARCH INSITUTE.
REPORT. 1966. irreg., no. 102, 1974. $4. ‡ North
Carolina State University, Water Resources
Research Institute, 124 Riddick Building, Raleigh,
NC 27607. Ed. F. E. McJunkin. circ. 300-1,000.
Indexed: Sel.Water Res.Abstr.

333.9　　　US　ISSN 0092-2528
OKLAHOMA WATER RESOURCES RESEARCH
INSTITUTE. ANNUAL REPORT. 1966. a.
Oklahoma Water Resources Research Institute,
1203 Whitehurst Hall, Stillwater, OK 74074. illus.
circ. 200. Key Title: Annual Report of the
Oklahoma Water Resources Research Institute.

333.9　　　CN　ISSN 0078-5156
ONTARIO. MINISTRY OF THE ENVIRONMENT.
GROUND WATER BULLETIN. 1961. irreg. free.
Ministry of the Environment, Water Resources
Branch, 135 St. Clair Ave. W., Toronto, Ont. M4V
1P5, Canada.

333.91　　　US　ISSN 0078-5849
OREGON STATE UNIVERSITY. WATER
RESOURCES RESEARCH INSTITUTE. WATER
RESEARCH SUMMARY. 1966. biennial. contr.
free circ. Oregon State University, Water Resources
Research Institute, Corvallis, OR 97330. Ed.
William H. Buckley.

POLIMERY V MELIORATSII I VODNOM
KHOZYAISTVE. see ENGINEERING —
Hydraulic Engineering

333.91　　　　　US
POTOMAC ISSUES. a. free. Interstate Commission
on the Potomac River Basin, 1055 First St.,
Rockville, MD 20850.

333.91　　　　　US
POTOMAC REPORT. 1945. irreg. ‡ Interstate
Commission on the Potomac River Basin, 1055
First St., Rockville, MD 20850. Ed. Kevin C.
Flynn. circ. 10,000.
　Formerly: Annual Potomac Report.

333.91　　　　　US
POTOMAC RIVER BASIN WATER QUALITY
REPORTS. a. Interstate Commission on the
Potomac River Basin, 1055 First St., Rockville, MD
20850.
　Formerly: Potomac River Water Quality Network
(ISSN 0539-2047)

354.712　　　　CN
PRAIRIE PROVINCES WATER BOARD ANNUAL
REPORT. (First report covers period Oct. 30, 1969-
Mar. 31, 1972) 1972. a. free. ‡ Prairie Provinces
Water Board, Rm. 306, Motherwell Bldg., 1901
Victoria Ave., Regina, Sask. S4P 3R4, Canada. circ.
300.

333.7　　　　　UR
PROBLEMY POLES'YA. 1972. irreg. 2.61 Rub.
Akademiya Navuk Belarusskai S.S.R., Leninskii
prospekt 68, Minsk, U.S.S.R. bibl. illus.

333.9　　　US　ISSN 0079-6956
PROJECT SKYWATER. ANNUAL REPORT. 1967.
a. U.S. Water and Power Resources Service,
Engineering and Research Center, Box 25007,
Denver Federal Center, Denver, CO 80225.

333.91　016　US　ISSN 0079-7766
PUBLICATIONS IN WATER RESEARCH AT
OREGON STATE UNIVERSITY. a. Oregon State
University, Water Resources Research Institute,
Corvallis, OR 97330. Ed. William H. Buckley. circ.
controlled.

333.91　　　UN　ISSN 0080-0589
REGIONAL CONFERENCE ON WATER
RESOURCES DEVELOPMENT IN ASIA AND
THE FAR EAST. PROCEEDINGS. (Subseries of
Water Resources Series) irreg., 10th, Manila, 19772
(pub. 1973) price varies. United Nations Economic
and Social Commission for Asia and the Pacific,
United Nations Bldg., Rajadamnern Ave., Bangkok
2, Thailand (Dist. by: United Nations Publications,
Room LX-2300, New York, NY 10017; or
Distribution and Sales Section, Palais des Nations,
CH-1211 Geneva 10, Switzerland)

551.5　　　　　TI
RESOURCES EN EAU DE TUNISIE. (Text in
French) irreg. Division des Resources en Eau,
Tunis, Tunisia. illus.

333.91　　　　　II
RIVER BEHAVIOUR AND CONTROL. (Text in
English) vol. 9, 1976. a. River Research Institute,
11-a Free School St., Calcutta 700016, India.

620　　　　PL　ISSN 0035-9394
ROZPRAWY HYDROTECHNICZNE. (Text in
Polish; summaries in English and Russian) 1956.
irreg., 1976, no. 36. price varies. (Polska Akademia
Nauk, Instytut Budownictwa Wodnego) Panstwowe
Wydawnictwo Naukowe, Miodowa 10, Warsaw,
Poland (Dist. by: Ars Polona - Ruch, Krakowskie
Przedmiescie 7, Warsaw, Poland) Indexed:
Chem.Abstr.

WATER RESOURCES

354.7   CN   ISSN 0586-5522
SASKATCHEWAN. WATER SUPPLY BOARD. ANNUAL REPORT. 1966. a. Water Supply Board, 2345 Broad St., Regina, Sask. S4P 1Y1, Canada.

628.167   US
SEAWATER AND DESALTING. 1980. irreg. price varies. Springer-Verlag, 175 Fifth Ave., New York, NY 10010 (Also Berlin, Heidelberg, Vienna) (reprint service avail. from ISI)
Desalination

333.91   SA
SOUTH AFRICA. WATER RESEARCH COMMISSION. ANNUAL REPORT. 1971. a. free. Water Research Commission - Waternavorsingskommissie, Box 824, Pretoria 0001, South Africa. illus. circ. 700.

627   RM
STUDII DE IRIGATII SI DESECARI. (Text in Romanian; summaries in English and French) a. Academia de Stiinte Agricole si Silvice, Institutul de Cercetari Pentru Imbunatatiri Funciare, B-dul Marasti, 61, Bucharest, Romania (Subscr. to: ILEXIM, Str. 13 Decembrie Nr. 3, P.O. Box 136-137, Bucharest, Romania)

553   US   ISSN 0093-0539
SUMMARY OF GROUND WATER DATA FOR TENNESSEE. irreg. free. Division of Water Resources, 6213 Charlotte Ave., Nashville, TN 37209. illus.

333.9   UK   ISSN 0081-959X
SURFACE WATER YEAR BOOK OF GREAT BRITAIN. 1961. a. price varies. Water Resources Board, Reading Bridge House, Reading, Berks, England (Avail. from H.M.S.O., c/o Liaison Officer, Atlantic House, Holborn Viaduct, London EC1P 1BN, England)

333.9   US   ISSN 0094-6427
SUSQUEHANNA RIVER BASIN COMMISSION. ANNUAL REPORT. 1972. a. free. Susquehanna River Basin Commission, 1721 N. Front St., Harrisburg, PA 17102. illus. Key Title: Annual Report - Susquehanna River Basin Commission.

333.91 627   US
SUSQUEHANNA RIVER BASIN COMMISSION. PUBLICATION. no. 50, 1977. irreg. Susquehanna River Basin Commission, 5012 Lenker St., Mechanicsburg, PA 17055.

333.9   US   ISSN 0082-1012
SYMPOSIUM ON WATER RESOURCES RESEARCH. PROCEEDINGS. 1965. a. $5. Ohio State University, Water Resources Center, 1791 Neil Ave., Columbus, OH 43210.

333.91   GW   ISSN 0073-0319
TECHNISCHE UNIVERSITAET HANNOVER. INSTITUT FUER SIEDLUNGSWASSERWIRTSCHAFT. VEROEFFENTLICHUNGEN. 1957. irreg., no. 44, 1977. price varies. Technische Universitaet Hannover, Institut fuer Siedlungswasserwirtschaft, Welfengarten 1, 3000 Hannover, W. Germany (B.R.D.)

333.9   US
TENNESSEE. DIVISION OF WATER QUALITY CONTROL. ANNUAL REPORT. (Report year ends June 30) 1972. a. free. ‡ Division of Water Quality Control, 621 Cordell Hull Bldg., Nashville, TN 37219. Ed. S. Jones. circ. 250.

627 333.91   US
TEXAS. DEPARTMENT OF WATER RESOURCES. REPORT. 1950. irreg. free. Department of Water Resources, P.O. Box 13087, Capitol Station, Austin, TX 78711. Indexed: Sel.Water Res.Abstr.
Former titles (1965-1977): Texas. Water Development Board. Report (ISSN 0082-3562); (until 1965): Texas. Water Commission. Bulletin.

333.9   US
TEXAS WATER RESOURCES INSTITUTE. TECHNICAL REPORT. irreg. Texas A & M University, College Station, TX 77843. illus.

333.9   US
U.S. BUREAU OF RECLAMATION. MID-PACIFIC REGION. REPORT. 1974. a. free. U.S. Water and Power Resources Service, Mid-Pacific Regional Office, 2800 Cottage Way, Sacramento, CA 95825.
Supersedes: Central Valley Project (California) Annual Report (ISSN 0084-8662)

333.9   US   ISSN 0361-2651
U.S. DEPARTMENT OF THE ARMY. PROJECTS RECOMMENDED FOR DEAUTHORIZATION, ANNUAL REPORT. 1975. a. U.S. Department of the Army, Washington, DC 20310 (Orders to: National Technical Information Service, 5285 Port Royal Rd., Springfield, VA 22151) Key Title: Projects Recommended for Deauthorization, Annual Report.

614.7   US
U.S. ENVIRONMENTAL PROTECTION AGENCY. WATER PLANNING DIVISION. WATER QUALITY STRATEGY PAPER. 1973. a. free. U.S. Environmental Protection Agency, Water Planning Division, WH-554, Waterside Mall, East Tower, Room 815, 401 M St., S.W., Washington, DC 20460. circ. 7,500.

333.91   US
U. S. OFFICE OF WATER RESEARCH AND TECHNOLOGY. ANNUAL REPORT; cooperative water research and training. 1965. a. (approx.) free. U. S. Office of Water Research and Technology, Washington, DC 20240. circ. 2,000 (controlled) (some back issues avail.)
Formerly: U. S. Office of Water Resources Research. Annual Report (ISSN 0565-9442)

U.S. WATER AND POWER RESOURCES SERVICE. ANNUAL REPORT. see
CONSERVATION

U.S. WATER AND POWER RESOURCES SERVICE. ENGINEERING MONOGRAPH. see
ENGINEERING — Hydraulic Engineering

333.91   US
U.S. WATER AND POWER RESOURCES SERVICE. ENGINEERING AND RESEARCH CENTER. RESEARCH REPORTS. 1963. irreg., no. 28, 1977. price varies. U.S. Water and Power Resources Service, Engineering and Research Center, Box 25007, Denver Federal Center, Denver, CO 80225. (back issues avail.)
Formerly: U.S. Bureau of Reclamation. Engineering and Research Center. Research Reports (ISSN 0501-7467)

333.91   US   ISSN 0065-5953
UNIVERSITY OF ALASKA. INSTITUTE OF WATER RESOURCES. ANNUAL REPORT. 1975. a. free. University of Alaska, Institute of Water Resources, Fairbanks, AK 99701. Ed. Alan C. Paulson. circ. 1,500. (also avail. in microfiche)

333.91   CN
UNIVERSITY OF ALBERTA. WATER RESOURCES CENTRE. PUBLICATION. no. 2, 1973. irreg. University of Alberta, Water Resources Centre, Edmonton, Alberta, Canada. Ed. Rolf Kellerhals.

333.91   US   ISSN 0068-6298
UNIVERSITY OF CALIFORNIA, DAVIS. WATER RESOURCES CENTER. ANNUAL REPORT. 1964. a. free. University of California, Davis, Water Resources Center, Davis, CA 95616. Ed. J. Herbert Snyder. circ. 1,200. Indexed: Sel.Water Res.Abstr.

333.91   US   ISSN 0068-6301
UNIVERSITY OF CALIFORNIA, DAVIS. WATER RESOURCES CENTER. CONTRIBUTIONS. 1957. irreg (5-7 nos. per yr.) free. ‡ University of California, Davis, Water Resources Center, Davis, CA 95616. circ. 600. Indexed: Sel.Water Res.Abstr.

333.9   US   ISSN 0069-9063
UNIVERSITY OF CONNECTICUT. INSTITUTE OF WATER RESOURCES. REPORT SERIES. 1966. irreg., no. 29, 1978. free; some numbers priced. ‡ University of Connecticut, Institute of Water Resources, Storrs, CT 06268. Dir. Victor E. Scottron.

333.7   US
UNIVERSITY OF CONNECTICUT. INSTITUTE OF WATER RESOURCES. WETLANDS CONFERENCE. PROCEEDINGS. (Subseries of its Report) 1973. irreg., 3rd, 1976. University of Connecticut, Institute of Water Resources, Box U-37, Storrs, CT 06268. charts. illus. (also avail. in microfiche from NTI) Indexed: Sel.Water Res.Abstr.

333.9 628   US
UNIVERSITY OF DELAWARE. WATER RESOURCES CENTER. ANNUAL REPORT. 1965. a. free. University of Delaware, Water Resources Center, 42 E. Delaware Ave., Newark, DE 19711. Ed. Robert D. Varrin. circ. 125.

333.9 628   US   ISSN 0073-1293
UNIVERSITY OF HAWAII. WATER RESOURCES RESEARCH CENTER. COLLECTED REPRINTS. 1969. biennial. free. ‡ University of Hawaii, Water Resources Research Center, 2540 Dole St., Honolulu, HI 96822. Ed. Faith N. Fujimura. circ. 600. (also avail. in microfiche from NTI)

333.9 628   US   ISSN 0073-1307
UNIVERSITY OF HAWAII. WATER RESOURCES RESEARCH CENTER. TECHNICAL REPORT. 1967. irreg., no. 122, 1979. free. ‡ University of Hawaii, Water Resources Research Center, 2540 Dole St., Honolulu, HI 96822. Ed. Faith N. Fujimura. circ. 300. (also avail. in microfiche from NTI)

333.91   US
UNIVERSITY OF HAWAII. WATER RESOURCES RESEARCH CENTER. WORKSHOP SERIES. 1976. irreg. University of Hawaii, Water Resources Research Center, 2540 Dole St., Honolulu, HI 96822.

333.9 627   US   ISSN 0073-4616
UNIVERSITY OF IDAHO. WATER RESOURCES RESEARCH INSTITUTE. ANNUAL REPORT. 1965. a. free. University of Idaho, Water Resources Research Institute, Moscow, ID 83843. Ed. John S. Gladwell. circ. 300-500.

333.91   US   ISSN 0073-5434
UNIVERSITY OF ILLINOIS AT URBANA-CHAMPAIGN. WATER RESOURCES CENTER. ANNUAL REPORT. 1965. a. free. ‡ University of Illinois at Urbana-Champaign, Water Resources Center, Urbana, IL 61801. Ed. Glenn E. Stout. (also avail. in microform from NTI)

333.91   US   ISSN 0073-5442
UNIVERSITY OF ILLINOIS AT URBANA-CHAMPAIGN. WATER RESOURCES CENTER. RESEARCH REPORT. 1966. irreg., no. 128, 1977. free. ‡ University of Illinois at Urbana-Champaign, Water Resources Center, Urbana, IL 61801. Ed. Glenn E. Stout. (also avail. in microform from NTI)

627 333.9   AT   ISSN 0077-8818
UNIVERSITY OF NEW SOUTH WALES. WATER RESEARCH LABORATORY, MANLY VALE. LABORATORY RESEARCH REPORTS. 1959. irreg., no. 156, 1980. price varies. University of New South Wales, Water Research Laboratory, King St., Manly Vale, N.S.W. 2093, Australia. Indexed: Sel.Water Res.Abstr.

333.9 628   US
UNIVERSITY OF RHODE ISLAND. WATER RESOURCES CENTER. ANNUAL REPORT. 1965. a. ‡ University of Rhode Island, Water Resources Center, Kingston, RI 02881. Ed. A. Ralph Thompson. circ. 800.

333.91   US
UNIVERSITY OF WYOMING. WATER RESOURCES RESEARCH INSTITUTE. MISCELLANEOUS PUBLICATIONS. 1966. irreg., no. 77, 1980. University of Wyoming, Water Resources Research Institute, Box 3067, University Station, Laramie, WY 82071. (back issues avail.)

333.9   US   ISSN 0084-3210
UNIVERSITY OF WYOMING. WATER RESOURCES RESEARCH INSTITUTE. WATER RESOURCES SERIES. 1966. irreg., no. 75, 1979. free. University of Wyoming, Water Resources Research Institute, Box 3067, University Sta., Laramie, WY 82070. Indexed: Sel.Water Res.Abstr.

354.66   UV
UPPER VOLTA. DIRECTION DE
L'HYDRAULIQUE ET DE L'EQUIPEMENT
RURAL. SERVICE I.R.H. RAPPORT
D'ACTIVITES. irreg. Direction de l'Hydraulique et
de l'Equipement Rural, Service I.R.H., Ministere du
Plan, du Developpement Rural, de l'Environnement
et du Tourisme, Ouagadougou, Upper Volta.

VALENCIA PORT; guia del servicios del puerto de
Valencia. see TRANSPORTATION — Ships And
Shipping

VANDERBILT UNIVERSITY. DEPARTMENT OF
ENVIRONMENTAL AND WATER
RESOURCES ENGINEERING. TECHNICAL
REPORTS. see ENVIRONMENTAL STUDIES

353.9   US   ISSN 0095-1978
VIRGINIA. STATE WATER CONTROL BOARD.
ANNUAL REPORT. 1973. a. free. State Water
Control Board, 2111 N. Hamilton St., P.O. Box
11143, Richmond, VA 23230. illus. Key Title:
Annual Report of the Virginia State Water Control
Board.

353.9   US
VIRGINIA. STATE WATER CONTROL BOARD.
BASIC DATA BULLETIN. 1930. irreg., no. 44,
1975. State Water Control Board, 2111 N.
Hamilton St., Box 11143, Richmond, VA 23230.

353.9   US
VIRGINIA. STATE WATER CONTROL BOARD.
INFORMATION BULLETIN. no. 527, 1977. irreg.
State Water Control Board, 2111 N. Hamilton St.,
Box 11143, Richmond, VA 23230.

353.9   US
VIRGINIA. STATE WATER CONTROL BOARD.
PLANNING BULLETIN. no. 304, 1976. irreg.
State Water Control Board, 2111 N. Hamilton St.,
Box 11143, Richmond, VA 23230.

333.91   US
VIRGINIA. WATER RESOURCES RESEARCH
CENTER. BULLETIN. irreg., latest no. 112. free
within Virginia; out-of-state $4 per no. Water
Resources Research Center, Virginia Polytechnic
Institute and State University, 617 N. Main St.,
Blacksburg, VA 42060. abstr. bibl. illus. (also avail.
in microfilm from UMI; back issues avail.)

614   333.7   HU
VIZGAZDALKODAS ES KORNYEZETVEDELEM.
irreg. price varies. Orszagos Vizugyi Foigazgatosag,
Kazinczy u. 37B, Budapest 7, Hungary. illus.

628.1   HU
VIZMINOSEGI ES VIZTECHNOLOGIAI
KUTATASI EREDMENYEK/RESEARCH IN
WATER QUALITY AND WATER
TECHNOLOGY. (Text and summaries in English
or Hungarian (1958/68, Hungarian only)) 1969.
irreg. Vizgazdalkodasi Tudomanyos Kutato
Kozpont., Kvassay J.ut 1, 1095 Budapest 9,
Hungary.

627   BU
VODNI PROBLEMI. 1975. irreg. 1 lv. per issue.
(Bulgarska Akademiia na Naukite, Institut po Vodni
Problemi) Publishing House of the Bulgarian
Academy of Sciences, Ul. Akad. G. Bonchev, 1113
Sofia, Bulgaria. circ. 800.
 Supersedes: Bulgarska Akademiia na Naukite.
Institut po Vodni Problemi. Izvestiia.

608   540   US   ISSN 0083-6915
VOM WASSER; ein Fachbuch fuer Wasserchemie und
Wasserreinigungstechnik. biennial. price varies.
(Gesellschaft Deutscher Chemiker, Fachgruppe
Wasserchemie, GW) Verlag Chemie International,
Inc., Plaza Center, Ste. E, 1020 N.W. 6th St.,
Deerfield Beach, FL 33441 (And Pappelallee 3,
Postfach 1260, 6940 Weinheim, W. Germany
(B.R.D.)) adv. (reprint service avail. from ISI)

333.91   US
WASHINGTON (STATE). DEPARTMENT OF
ECOLOGY. WATER SUPPLY BULLETINS.
1921. irreg., no. 35, 1970. price varies. Department
of Ecology, Olympia, WA 98504. (back issues
avail.)

333.9   US   ISSN 0083-7598
WASHINGTON (STATE) WATER RESEARCH
CENTER, PULLMAN. REPORT. 1967. irreg.,
latest issue no. 16. free. ‡ Water Research Center,
Washington State University, Pullman, WA 99163.
Indexed: Sel.Water Res.Abstr.

628.1   333.7   GW   ISSN 0511-3520
WASSER-KALENDER; Jahrbuch fuer das gesamte
Wasserfach. 1966. a. price varies. Erich Schmidt
Verlag (Berlin), Genthiner Str. 30g, 1000 Berlin 30,
W. Germany (B.R.D.) Ed. H. Huebner. charts. stat.
circ. 3,000.

333.7   628.1   GW   ISSN 0512-5030
WASSER UND ABWASSER IN FORSCHUNG
UND PRAXIS. (Text in German; summaries in
English and French) 1969. irreg., vol. 15, 1977.
price varies. Erich Schmidt Verlag(Bielefeld),
Viktoriastr. 44A, 4800 Bielefeld, W. Germany
(B.R.D.)

333.7   340   628.1   GW   ISSN 0508-1254
WASSERRECHT UND WASSERWIRTSCHAFT.
1960. irreg., vol. 18, 1978. price varies. Erich
Schmidt Verlag (Berlin), Genthiner Str. 30g, 1000
Berlin 30, W. Germany (B.R.D.) bibl. charts. illus.
stat.

627   US   ISSN 0083-7636
WATER. (Subseries of A I Ch E Symposium Series)
irreg., latest 1975. $15. American Institute of
Chemical Engineers, 345 E. 47 St., New York, NY
10017. Ed. S. Fourdrinier.

628.1   CN   ISSN 0318-0468
WATER & POLLUTION CONTROL. DIRECTORY
AND HANDBOOK. (Title varies slightly) 1962. a.
Can.$25. Southam Communications Ltd., 1450 Don
Mills Road, Don Mills, Ontario M3B 2X7, Canada.
Ed. Tom Davey. adv. bk. rev. illus. circ. 8,238.
 Formerly: Water & Pollution Control Directory
(ISSN 0511-3555)

338.7   II
WATER AND POWER DEVELOPMENT
CONSULTANCY SERVICES. ANNUAL
REPORT AND STATEMENT OF ACCOUNTS.
(Report year ends Mar. 31) (Text in English) a.
Water and Power Development Consultancy
Services (India) Ltd., Kailash, 26 K. G. Marg, New
Delhi 110001, India.

333.91   US
WATER DEVELOPMENT SUPPLY AND
MANAGEMENT. 1978. irreg., vol. 14, 1980. price
varies. Pergamon Press, Inc., Maxwell House,
Fairview Park, Elmsford, NY 10523 (And
Headington Hill Hall, Oxford OX3 0BW, England)

363.6   JA
WATER JAPAN/SUIDO SANGYO SHIMBUN;
Japan's waterworks yearbook. (Text in English) a.
free. Japan Water Works Association, Osaka Godo
Bldg., 1-5 Doyama-cho, Kita-ku, Osaka, Japan. Ed.
Hiroshi Ishimaru. adv. illus.

333.91   CN   ISSN 0383-5472
WATER QUALITY DATA FOR ONTARIO
STREAMS & LAKES. a. free. Ministry of the
Environment, Water Resources Branch, 135 St.
Clair Ave. W., Toronto, Ont. M4Y 1P5, Canada.

628   681.2   US
WATER QUALITY INSTRUMENTATION. 1972.
irreg. Instrument Society of America, 400 Stanwix
St., Pittsburgh, PA 15222.

628.1   AT   ISSN 0085-8021
WATER RESEARCH FOUNDATION OF
AUSTRALIA. REPORTS. 1959. irreg. Water
Research Foundation of Australia Ltd., Box 47,
Kingsford, N.S.W. 2032, Australia. Indexed:
Aus.Sci.Ind.
 Incorporating: Water Research Foundation of
Australia. Bulletin (ISSN 0085-8013)

333.91   US
WATER RESOURCES ASSOCIATION OF THE
DELAWARE RIVER BASIN. ALERTING
BULLETIN. irreg. no. 136, Nov. 1977.
membership. Water Resources Association of the
Delaware River Basin, Box 867, Davis Rd., Valley
Forge, PA 19481.

553.7   PR
WATER RESOURCES DATA FOR PUERTO RICO.
1968. irreg., latest 1974. free. U. S. Geological
Survey, Water Resources Div., District Chief, Box
34168, Fort Buchanan, PR 00934. (Co-Sponsor:
Puerto Rico Aqueduct and Sewer Authority) charts.
stat. circ. 300-500. Indexed: Sel.Water Res. Abstr.

333.91   UN   ISSN 0082-8130
WATER RESOURCES DEVELOPMENT SERIES.
1951. irreg., no. 47, 1976. price varies. United
Nations Economic and Social Commission for Asia
and the Pacific, The United Nations Building,
Rajamnern Ave., Bangkok 2, Thailand, NY 10017
(Dist. by: United Nations Publications, Room LX-
2300, New York, NY 10017; or Distribution and
Sales Section, Palais des Nations, CH-1211 Geneva
10, Switzerland)

333.91   620   US
WATER RESOURCES MONOGRAPHS. 1971.
irreg., no. 5, 1980. American Geophysical Union,
2000 Florida Ave. N.W., Washington, DC 20009.
(reprint service avail. from ISI)

333.9   US
WATER RESOURCES REPORT SERIES. irreg. $3.
Texas Tech University, Lubbock, TX 79409 (Orders
to:, Box 4630)
 Formerly: Civil Engineering Report Series (ISSN
0095-1692)

551.4   333.9   US   ISSN 0095-1250
WATER RESOURCES RESEARCH IN VIRGINIA,
ANNUAL REPORT. 1970. a. free (free to Virginia
residents) Water Resources Research Center,
Virginia Polytechnic Institute and State University,
617 N. Main St., Blacksburg, VA 24060. Dir.
William R. Walker. (reprint service avail. from
UMI)

551.4   333.9   US   ISSN 0518-6374
WATER RESOURCES SUMMARY. 1962. irreg.;
latest issue, 1973. price varies. ‡ Geological
Commission, Vardell Parham Geology Center, 3815
W. Roosevelt Rd, Little Rock, AR 72204. illus.

333.9   US   ISSN 0095-4659
WEST VIRGINIA. DEPARTMENT OF NATURAL
RESOURCES. ANNUAL REPORT ON THE
COMPREHENSIVE WATER RESOURCES
PLAN. a. Department of Natural Resources, State
Capitol, Charleston, WV 25305. Key Title: Annual
Report on the Comprehensive Water Resources
Plan.

333.91   US
WESTERN WASHINGTON STATE COLLEGE.
AQUATIC STUDIES PROGRAM. TECHNICAL
REPORT SERIES. 1964. irreg., no. 26, 1978. free.
Western Washington University, Aquatic Studies
Program, Bellingham, WA 98225. charts. illus.
stat.
 Formerly: Western Washington State College.
Institute for Freshwater Studies. Technical Report
Series.

333.91   CN   ISSN 0315-3010
WESTWATER; notes on water research in western
Canada. 1972. irreg. free. University of British
Columbia, Westwater Research Centre, Vancouver,
B.C. V6T 1W5, Canada. Ed. A.H.J. Dorcey. bk. rev.
illus. circ. 1,600.

333.91   UK
WHO'S WHO IN THE WATER INDUSTRY. 1975.
a. £8. (National Water Council) Wheatland Journals
Ltd., Penn House, Penn Place, Rickmansworth,
Herts WD3 1SN, England. Ed. R. Clarke. adv. circ.
4,500.

627   333.91   AU
WIENER MITTEILUNGEN: WASSER,
ABWASSER, GEWAESSER. 1968. irreg. price
varies. Technische Universitaet Wien, Institut fuer
Wasserversorgung, Abwasserreinigung und
Gewaesserschutz, A-1040 Vienna, Austria. circ. 300-
400.

333.91   627   ZA   ISSN 0084-4705
ZAMBIA. DEPARTMENT OF WATER AFFAIRS.
REPORT. 1964. a. 30 n. Government Printer, P.O.
Box 136, Lusaka, Zambia.

WATER RESOURCES — Abstracting, Bibliographies, Statistics

627 016   II   ISSN 0523-302X
BIBLIOGRAPHY ON IRRIGATION, DRAINAGE, RIVER TRAINING AND FLOOD CONTROL/ BIBLIOGRAPHIE RELATIVE AUX IRRIGATIONS, AU DRAINAGE, A LA REGULARISATION DES COURS D'EAU ET LA MATRISE DES CRUES. (Text in English and French) 1954-56. a. $2.50 per copy. International Commission on Irrigation and Drainage - Commission Internationale des Irrigations et du Drainage, 48 Nyaya Marg, Chanakyapuri, New Delhi 110021, India. bk. rev. circ. 2,200. (back issues avail.)

333.91 310   UK   ISSN 0141-7835
CHARTERED INSTITUTE OF PUBLIC FINANCE AND ACCOUNTANCY. WATER SERVICES CHARGES STATISTICS. 1978. a. £3. Chartered Institute of Public Finance and Accountancy, 1 Buckingham Place, London SW1E 6HS, England. (back issues avail.)

GERMANY(FEDERAL REPUBLIC, 1949-). BUNDESANSTALT FUER GEWAESSERKUNDE. HYDROLOGISCHE BIBLIOGRAPHIE. see *EARTH SCIENCES — Abstracting, Bibliographies, Statistics*

GERMANY (FEDERAL REPUBLIC, 1949-) STATISTISCHES BUNDESAMT FACHSERIE 19, REIHE 2: WASSERVERSORGUNG UND ABWASSERBESEITIGUNG. see *ENERGY — Abstracting, Bibliographies, Statistics*

NEW ZEALAND AGRICULTURAL ENGINEERING INSTITUTE. CURRENT PUBLICATIONS. see *AGRICULTURE — Abstracting, Bibliographies, Statistics*

338.4   US   ISSN 0094-4335
STATISTICS FOR WATER UTILITIES INCLUDING WATER AUTHORITIES IN PENNSYLVANIA. a. free. Department of Commerce, Bureau of Statistics, Research and Planning, 630B Health & Welfare Bldg., Harrisburg, PA 17120.

WELDING

see *Metallurgy — Welding*

WOMEN'S INTERESTS

301.412   US
A M A: WOMEN IN AFRICAN AND AMERICAN WORLDS. 1975. irreg. $21. African Bibliographic Center, P.O. Box 13096, Washington, DC 20009. Ed. Linda Fink Matthews. bk. rev. circ. 500.

396   PK
ALL PAKISTAN WOMEN'S ASSOCIATION. TRIENNIAL CONFERENCE REPORT. (Text in English) triennial. All Pakistan Women's Association, Information and Research Bureau, 67-B Garden Rd., Karachi 3, Pakistan.

051   US
BETTER HOMES AND GARDENS BRIDES BOOK. 1980. a. $2. Meredith Corporation, 1716 Locust St., Des Moines, IA 50336. adv. circ. 600,000.

301.412   PO
CADERNOS CONDICAO FEMININA. 1975. irreg. price varies. Comissao da Condicao Feminina, Ave. Elias Garcia 12, 1093 Lisbon Codex, Portugal. circ. 1,300.

301.412   CN   ISSN 0705-6028
CANADA. ADVISORY COUNCIL ON THE STATUS OF WOMEN. ANNUAL REPORT. 1976. a. Advisory Council on the Status of Women, 63 Sparks St., Box 1541, Station B, Ottawa, Ont. K1P 5R5, Canada.

301.42   US   ISSN 0147-104X
CONTRIBUTIONS IN WOMEN'S STUDIES. 1978. irreg. Greenwood Press, 88 Post Rd. W., Westport, CT 06881.

301.412   BO
ESTUDIOS DE PROMOCION FEMENINA. 1978. irreg. Centro de Investigaciones Sociales, Casilla 6931 - Correo Central, La Paz, Bolivia.

301   US
FEMALE STUDIES. irreg., no. 10, 1975. $5. Feminist Press, Box 334, Old Westbury, NY 11568. bibl.

301.412   US   ISSN 0145-8299
FEMINIST PRESS. NEWS/NOTES. 1970. irreg. free. Feminist Press, Box 334, Westbury, NY 11568. Ed. Bd. bibl. circ. 35,000.

FEMMES EN LITTERATURE. see *LITERATURE*

640   GW
FRAU MIT HERZ. 1948. w. DM.1.30 per no. Sonnenverlag GmbH, Bismarckstr. 4, Postfach 720, 7570 Baden-Baden, W. Germany (B.R.D.) Ed. P. Kulig. adv. circ. 405,399.

301.412   SZ
LA FRONDE. (Text in French) irreg. M L F, Case Postale 3268, CH-1000 Lausanne, Switzerland. (newspaper)

354   GH
GHANA. NATIONAL COUNCIL ON WOMEN AND DEVELOPMENT. ANNUAL REPORT. 1976. a. National Council on Women and Development, Box M.53, Accra, Ghana. circ. 3,000.

346.969   US   ISSN 0092-9190
HAWAII. STATE COMMISSION ON THE STATUS OF WOMEN. ANNUAL REPORT.* 1972. a. State Commission on the Status of Women, Kamamalu Building, Room 510, 250 South King St., Honolulu, HI 96813. illus. Key Title: Annual Report - State of Hawaii. State Commission on the Status of Women.

052   SI
HER WORLD ANNUAL. 1976. a. S.$6 per no. Times Periodicals Private Ltd., 422 Thomson Rd., Singapore 1129, Singapore. circ. 25,000.

301.41   US   ISSN 0091-8121
HONOLULU. MAYOR'S COMMITTEE ON THE STATUS OF WOMEN. ANNUAL REPORT. 1972. a. free. Mayor's Committee on the Status of Women, Honolulu, HI 96813.

301.412   US
IMAGE OF WOMAN. irreg. price varies. Abner Schram Enterprises, Ltd., 36 Park St., Montclair, NJ 07042.

301.412   US
INDEX/DIRECTORY OF WOMEN'S MEDIA. a. $8. Women's Institute for Freedom of the Press, 3306 Ross Place, N.W., Washington, DC 20008. Ed. Martha Leslie Allen.

301.412   IO
INDONESIAN WOMEN'S CONGRESS. BULLETIN/KONGRES WANITA INDONESIA. BERITA. (Text in Indonesian) irreg. Indonesian Women's Congress, Jl. H.O.S. Cokroaminoto 67, Jakarta, Indonesia.

640   GW
INGRID. 1977. m. DM.2 per no. Sonnenverlag GmbH, Bismarckstr. 4, Postfach 720, 7570 Baden-Baden, W. Germany (B.R.D.) Ed.H. Eilers. adv.

989.2   PY
INSTITUTO FEMENINO DE INVESTIGACIONES HISTORICAS. ANUARIO. 1971. irreg. Instituto Femenino de Investigaciones Historicas, Asuncion, Paraguay.

396   US   ISSN 0538-2912
INTER-AMERICAN COMMISSION OF WOMEN. NEWS BULLETIN. Spanish edition: Inter-American Commission of Women. Noticiero (ISSN 0538-2920) 1953. irreg., latest no. 33. (Inter-American Commission of Women (C I M)) Organization of American States, General Secretariat of the Organization of American States, Department of Publications, Washington, DC 20006.

396   US   ISSN 0538-2920
INTER-AMERICAN COMMISSION OF WOMEN. NOTICIERO. English edition: Inter-American Commission of Women. News Bulletin (ISSN 0538-2912) 1951. irreg., latest no. 33. (Inter-American Commission of Women (C I M)) Organization of American States, General Secretariat of the Organization of American States, Washington, DC 20006.

301.412   SW
KVINNEBULLETIN. irreg. Grupp 8, Odengatan 102, Stockholm, Sweden.

301.412   US
LADY-UNIQUE-INCLINATION-OF-THE-NIGHT. 1976. a. $3. Sowing Circle Press, Box 803, New Brunswick, NJ 08903. Ed. Kay F. Turner. adv. bk. rev. bibl. illus. circ. 1,500. (back issues avail.) Indexed: Alt.Press Ind.

LAW & WOMEN SERIES. see *LAW*

920 301.412   FR
MEMOIRE DES FEMMES. 1978. irreg. price varies. Editions Syros, 1 rue de Varenne, 75006 Paris, France.

301.412   US
MICHIGAN OCCASIONAL PAPERS IN WOMEN'S STUDIES. 1978. irreg. $1-3. University of Michigan, Women's Studies Program, 1058 LSA Building, Ann Arbor, MI 48109. adv. circ. 400. Indexed: Wom.Stud.Abstr.
   Supersedes (1974-1978): University of Michigan Papers in Women's Studies.

301.412 618   US
MONTHLY EXTRACT. 1972. irreg. $5.50 for 6 nos. New Moon Communications, Box 3488, Ridgeway Station, Stamford, CT 06905. Ed. Bd. circ. 1,500. (also avail. in microform from BLH)

301.412   SW   ISSN 0027-1101
MORGONBRIS. 1904. irreg. (8-10/yr.) Kr.20. Sveriges Socialdemokratiska Kvinnofoerbund, Box 1317, 111 83 Stockholm, Sweden. Ed. Eva Swedenmark. charts. illus.
   Women's liberation movement

301.412   US   ISSN 0047-830X
MOVING OUT; feminist literary & arts journal. 1971. a. $3.50. 4866 Third, Rm. 207, Wayne State University, Detroit, MI 48202. Eds. Margaret Kaminski, Gloria Dyc. adv. bk. rev. illus. circ. 2,500. (also avail. in microform from BLH; back issues avail) Indexed: Wom.Stud.Abstr.
   Women's liberation movement

376   US
NATIONAL ADVISORY COUNCIL ON WOMEN'S EDUCATIONAL PROGRAMS. ANNUAL REPORT. 1975. a. U.S. National Advisory Council on Women's Educational Programs, 1832 M St., N.W., Washington, DC 20036.

301.412   US   ISSN 0029-0815
NO MORE FUN AND GAMES; a journal of female liberation. 1968. irreg. c/o Cell 16, 14A Eliot St., Cambridge, MA 01238. Ed. Dana Densmore.

301.412   CN
ONTARIO. STATUS OF WOMEN COUNCIL. ANNUAL REPORT. 1974. a. Ontario Status of Women Council, Toronto, Canada. illus.

OPEN DOOR INTERNATIONAL FOR THE EMANCIPATION OF THE WOMAN WORKER. REPORT OF CONGRESS. see *BUSINESS AND ECONOMICS — Labor And Industrial Relations*

301.412   CN   ISSN 0319-1001
PEDESTAL. 1974. irreg. Can.$3($3.50) 6854 Iverness, Vancouver, B.C. V5X 4G2, Canada. illus.
   Formerly: Women Can (ISSN 0319-0994)

PERFORMING WOMAN; a national directory of professional women musicians. see *MUSIC*

301.412   PO
PORTUGAL. COMISSAO DA CONDICAO FEMININA. COLECCAO INFORMAR AS MULHERES. 1979. irreg. Comissao da Condicao Feminina, Avda. Elias Garcia 12, 1093 Lisbon Codex, Portugal.

301.412 800   US   ISSN 0364-7609
PRIMAVERA. 1975. irreg. $3.90 per issue. University of Chicago, Ida Noyes Hall, 1212 E. 59th St., Chicago, IL 60637. Ed.Bd. adv. circ. 1,000.

PROFESSIONAL WOMEN AND MINORITIES; a manpower data resource service. see OCCUPATIONS AND CAREERS

917.306 323.4   US
RAZON MESTIZA. a. $1974. Concilio Mujeres, c/o D-Q University, Box 409, Davis, CA 95616. Ed. Dorinda Moreno. adv. bk. rev. circ. 2,000. Chicana interests

RED MENACE; a libertarian socialist newsletter. see POLITICAL SCIENCE

ROOM; a woman's literary journal. see LITERATURE — Poetry

ROSTER OF WOMEN IN POLITICAL SCIENCE. see POLITICAL SCIENCE

S H A R E; a directory of feminist library workers. (Sisters Have Resources Everywhere) see LIBRARY AND INFORMATION SCIENCES

301.412   CN   ISSN 0380-8297
SASKATCHEWAN. ADVISORY COUNCIL ON THE STATUS OF WOMEN. PUBLICATION. 1974. irreg. Advisory Council on the Status of Women, 214-230 22nd St. E., Saskatoon, Sask. S7K 0E9, Canada.

301.412   UK   ISSN 0140-5810
SCOTTISH WOMEN'S LIBERATION JOURNAL. 1977. irreg. £1.50 for 4 nos. Scottish Women's Liberation Journal Collective, c/o 23 Marchmont Crescent, Endinburgh, Scotland. Ed.Bd. bk. rev.

301.412   US
SHAMELESS HUSSY REVIEW. 1969. a. $1.25. Shameless Hussy Press, Box 3092, Berkeley, CA 94703. circ. 1,000. (processed; also avail. in microfilm from BLH)
Formerly (1969-1971): Remember Our Fires.

301.412 296   IS
TODAA. 1976. 2/yr. I£5. Israel Feminist Movement, Jerusalem Branch, P.O.B. 9258, Jerusalem, Israel.

301.412   AT   ISSN 0310-9496
W. E. L. (VICTORIA) PAPERS. 1974 N.S. 1977. irreg. Aus.$2 to non-members. Women's Electoral Lobby (Victoria), 420 Canterbury Rd., Surrey Hills, Vic. 3127, Australia.

301   CN
WAGES FOR HOUSEWORK. CAMPAIGN BULLETIN. 1976. 2-3/yr. Can.$3. Toronto Wages for Housework Committee, Box 38, Ste E, Toronto, Ont. M6H 4E1, Canada. bk. rev. circ. 10,000. (tabloid format)

301.412   US
WHO'S WHO AND WHERE IN WOMEN'S STUDIES. 1975. irreg. $12.50 cloth, $6 paper. Feminist Press, Box 334, Old Westbury, NY 11568.

WINDHAVEN; feminist fantasy & science fiction. see LITERATURE

331.4   II
WOMEN IN A DEVELOPING ECONOMY. 1975. irreg. Allied Publishers Private Ltd., 15 Graham Rd., Ballard Estate, Bombay 400038, India.

WOMEN IN CONTEXT: DEVELOPMENT AND STRESSES. see MEDICAL SCIENCES

WOMEN IN THE WORKING WORLD. see BUSINESS AND ECONOMICS — Labor And Industrial Relations

WOMEN - POEMS. see LITERATURE — Poetry

WOMEN TALKING, WOMEN LISTENING. see LITERATURE — Poetry

301.412   US
WOMEN'S COLLECTION NEWSLETTER. 1974. irreg. free. Northwestern University, Library, Special Collections Department, Evanston, IL 60201. Ed. Sarah Sherman. abstr. bibl. circ. 1,250.

346.013   US
WOMEN'S NEWSLETTER. irreg. $5. National Lawyers Guild (Washington), National Committee on Women's Oppression, c/o Nan Hunter, Holmes, Hunter, Polikoff & Bodley, P.C., 1319 F St., Washington, DC 20004.

301.41   US   ISSN 0092-6639
WOMEN'S ORGANIZATIONS & LEADERS DIRECTORY. 1973. a. $54. Today Publications and News Service, Inc., National Press Building, Washington, DC 20004. Ed. Myra E. Barrer.

301.412   UK
WOMEN'S ORGANIZATIONS IN GREAT BRITAIN. 1974. irreg (every 2 or 3 years) 40p.($1) National Council for Voluntary Organisations, 26 Bedford Square, London WC1B 3HV, England.

920.72   UK
WORLD WHO'S WHO OF WOMEN. 1973. every 18 mos. price varies. Melrose Press Ltd., 17-21 Churchgate St., Soham, Ely, Cambridgeshire CB7 5DS, England (U.S. subscr. to: International Biographical Centre, c/o Biblio Distribution Centre, 81 Adams Drive, Totowa, NJ 07512) Ed. Dr. Ernest Kay. illus.

920 376   UK
WORLD WHO'S WHO OF WOMEN IN EDUCATION. 1978. irreg. price varies. Melrose Press Ltd., 17-21 Churchgate St., Soham, Ely, Cambridgeshire CB7 5DS, England (U.S. subscr. to: International Biographical Centre, c/o Biblio Distribution Centre, 81 Adams Drive, Totowa, NJ 07512)

800   US
XANTHIPPE; feminist literary magazine. vol. 3, 1976. a. $0.75. California State University, San Jose, Women's Center, 177 S. 10th St., San Jose, CA 95192. adv. bibl.

301.412   US
YEARBOOK IN WOMEN'S POLICY STUDIES. 1976. a. $18.50 for hardcover; softcover $8.95. Sage Publications,Inc., 275 S. Beverly Dr., Beverly Hills, CA 90212 (And Sage Publications Ltd., 28 Banner St., London C1Y 8QE, England) Eds. Jane Roberts Chapman, Margaret Gates. (back issues avail.)

13TH MOON; a feminist literary magazine. see LITERATURE

WOMEN'S INTERESTS — Abstracting, Bibliographies, Statistics

301.412 016   GW   ISSN 0344-1415
DIE FRAUENFRAGE IN DEUTSCHLAND. BIBLIOGRAPHIE. 1951. a. DM.25. (Deutscher Akademikerinnenbund) K. G. Saur Verlag KG, Peossenbacherstr. 2, 8000 Munich 71, W. Germany (B.R.D.)

ZOOLOGY

see Biology—Zoology

Cessations

323   US
A IS A LIBERTARIAN DIRECTORY; access to ideas. 1971-1972. irreg (approx 1/yr) Mega, 9730 Hyne Road, Brighton, MI 48116.

610.73   US   ISSN 0065-9495
A N A CLINICAL SESSIONS. 1966-19?? biennial (alternates with ANA Clinical Conferences) American Nurses Association, 2420 Pershing Rd., Kansas City, MO 64108.

363   US
A S P C A YELLOW PAGES. discontinued. irreg. American Society for the Prevention of Cruelty to Animals, 441 E. 92nd St., New York, NY 10028.

621.38   AT   ISSN 0001-2920
A W A TECHNICAL REVIEW. 1935-1977 (vol. 16, no. 2) irreg. Amalgamated Wireless (Australasia) Ltd., 47 York St., Sydney, N.S.W. 2000, Australia.

333.91 627 551.4   AT   ISSN 0311-7979
A W R C ACTIVITIES. 1976-197? a. Australian Water Resources Council, Box 5, Canberra, A.C.T. 2600, Australia

960   BE   ISSN 0567-6592
ACADEMIE ROYALE DES SCIENCES D'OUTRE MER. REVUE BIBLIOGRAPHIQUE/ KONINKLIJKE ACADEMIE VOOR OVERZEESE WETENSCHAPPEN. BIBLIOGRAFISCH OVERZICHT. 1965-197? a. Academie Royale des Sciences d'Outre-Mer, Rue Defacqz 1, 1050 Brussels, Belgium.

658.4   IT
ACCADEMIA NAZIONALE DI RAGIONERA PAPERS ON BUSINESS ADMINISTRATION. 1974 (only one vol. published) irreg. Casa Editrice Dott. A. Giuffre, Via Statuto 2, Milan 20121, Italy.

540   DK   ISSN 0065-1133
ACTA CHEMICA SCANDINAVICA. SUPPLEMENTUM. 1963-197? irreg. (reprint service avail. from ISI) Munksgaard, 35 Noerre Soegade, DK-1370 Copenhagen K, Denmark.

378.1   US   ISSN 0362-5923
ACTIVITY PROGRAMMERS SOURCEBOOK. discontinued. a. (National Entertainment Conference) Billboard Publications, Inc., Amusement Business Division, Box 24970, Nashville, TN 37202.

270   US   ISSN 0065-2067
ADVANCE OF CHRISTIANITY THROUGH THE CENTURIES. discontinued. irreg. Wm. B. Eerdmans Publishing Co., 255 Jefferson Ave., S.E., Grand Rapids, MI 49502.

616.97   US   ISSN 0163-1578
ADVANCES IN ASTHMA & ALLERGY. 1974-1978; suspended. irreg. Fisons Corp., Two Preston Ct., Bedford, MA 01730.

610.28   US   ISSN 0065-2261
ADVANCES IN BIOMEDICAL ENGINEERING AND MEDICAL PHYSICS. 1967-197? irreg. John Wiley & Sons, Inc., 605 Third Ave., New York, NY 10016.

629.132   US   ISSN 0065-4841
AIR SAFETY FORUM. discontinued after 1973. a. Air Line Pilots Association International (AFL-CIO), Engineering and Air Safety Division, 1625 Massachusetts Avenue, N.W., Washington, DC 20036.

410   US   ISSN 0084-6112
ALABAMA LINGUISTIC AND PHILOLOGICAL SERIES. 1964-197? irreg. University of Alabama Press, Box 2877, University, AL 35486.

920   US
ALABAMA'S DISTINGUISHED. 1974 (issued only once) biennial. Reese Publishers, Box 614, Albertville, AL 35950.

636   US
ALASKA. DEPARTMENT OF FISH AND GAME. GAME DIVISION. INTERIOR MOOSE AND MOOSE DISEASE STUDIES. series completed. irreg. Department of Fish and Game, Game Division, Subport Bldg., Juneau, AK 99801.
    Formerly: Alaska. Department of Fish and Game. Game Division. Interior Moose Studies.

614   US
ALASKA. DEPARTMENT OF HEALTH AND SOCIAL SERVICES. QUARTERLY. 1938-19??; discontinued. irreg. (approx. 4/yr.) (back issues avail.) Department of Health and Social Services, Pouch H-01, Juneau, AK 99811.
    Former titles: Alaska's Health and Social Services; Alaska's Health and Welfare (ISSN 0002-4597)

799.1   US   ISSN 0361-3984
ALASKA FISHING GUIDE; by the editors of Alaska magazine. 1974-197? a. Alaska Northwest Publishing Co., Box 4-EEE, Anchorage, AK 99509

799.2   US   ISSN 0095-5760
ALASKA HUNTING GUIDE; by the editors of Alaska magazine. 1974-197? a. Alaska Northwest Publishing Co., Box 4-EEE, Anchorage, AK 99509

362   US   ISSN 0065-583X
ALASKA STATE PLAN FOR THE CONSTRUCTION OF HOSPITALS AND MEDICAL FACILITIES. 1950-19??; discontinued. a. Department of Health and Social Services, Pouch H, Juneau, AK 99811.

616.97   DK
ALLERGY. SUPPLEMENTUM. 1950-197? irreg. (reprint service avail. from ISI) Munksgaard, 35 Noerre Soegade, DK-1370 Copenhagen K, Denmark.
    Formerly: Acta Allergologica. Supplementum (ISSN 0065-096X)

620   US   ISSN 0002-6123
ALLIS-CHALMERS ENGINEERING REVIEW. 1936-1976 (vol. 41, no. 1). irreg. (also avail. in microform from UMI) Allis-Chalmers Corp., Box 512, Milwaukee, WI 53201.

940   GW
ALT-HILDESHEIM; Zeitschrift fuer Stadt und Stift Hildesheim. 1919-197? a. (Stadtarchiv Hildesheim) Verlag August Lax, 3200 Hildesheim, W. Germany (B.R.D.)

796.3   US   ISSN 0090-4414
AMATEUR ATHLETIC UNION OF THE UNITED STATES. OFFICIAL A A U BASKETBALL HANDBOOK. 1918-19??; discontinued. biennial. Amateur Athletic Union of the United States, 3400 W. 86 St., Indianapolis, IN 46268.

635   UK
AMATEUR GARDENING GUIDE; an amateur gardening publication. 1912-197? a. I P C Magazines Ltd., Tower House, Southampton St., London, WC2E 9QF, England.
    Supersedes: Percy Thrower's Guide to Modern Gardening (ISSN 0065-6712)

317   US   ISSN 0065-6771
AMERICA EN CIFRAS. (10 Booklets and Supplement) 1960-1977 (9th edt.) irreg. (Inter-American Statistical Institute) Organization of American States, General Secretariat, Department of Publications, 17th & Constitution Ave. N.W., Washington, DC 20006.

333 339   US   ISSN 0065-6984
AMERICAN ASSOCIATION FOR CONSERVATION INFORMATION. YEARBOOK. 1954-1976. a. American Association for Conservation Information, c/o Jay Kaffka, Arkansas Game & Fish Commission, Little Rock, Cheyenne, AR 72201.

378 US ISSN 0065-7239
AMERICAN ASSOCIATION OF COMMUNITY AND JUNIOR COLLEGES. GOVERNMENTAL AFFAIRS SPECIAL. ceased Sep. 1979. irreg. American Association of Community and Junior Colleges, One Dupont Circle N.W., Washington, DC 20036.

296 US
AMERICAN FEDERATION OF JEWS FROM CENTRAL EUROPE. PROCEEDINGS. 1965-197?: discontinued. a(not issued in 1977) American Federation of Jews from Central Europe, Inc., 570 Seventh Ave., New York, NY 10018.

617.7 US
AMERICAN SOCIETY OF OCULARISTS. SELECTED PAPERS AND DISCUSSIONS FROM THE ANNUAL MEETING. discontinued. a. Thieme-Stratton, Inc., 381 Park Ave. S., New York, NY 10016.

327 BE ISSN 0066-2135
ANNALES D'ETUDES INTERNATIONALES/ ANNALS OF INTERNATIONAL STUDIES. 1770-1979. a. (Universite de Geneve, Institut Universitaire de Hautes Etudes Internationales Alumni Association, SZ) Etablissements Emile Bruylant, 67 rue de la Regence, 1000 Brussels, Belgium.

610 FR
ANNEE DU MEDECIN. 1976-1979. a. (Hopital Broussais - Paris) Flammarion Medecine - Sciences, 20 rue de Vaugirard, 75006 Paris, France

331 US
ANNUAL LABOR-MANAGEMENT CONFERENCE ON COLLECTIVE BARGAINING AND LABOR LAW. 1971-1976. a. (Institute of Industrial and Labor Relations, College of Business and Public Administration) University of Arizona College of Business and Public Administration, Division of Economic and Business Research, Institute of Industrial and Labor Relations, Tucson, AZ 85721.

342 UK ISSN 0570-2658
ANNUAL SURVEY OF COMMONWEALTH LAW. 1965-197? a. Oxford University Press, Press Rd., Neasden, London NW10 ODD, England.

780 CL ISSN 0066-4928
ANTOLOGIA DEL FOLKLORE MUSICAL CHILENO. ceased 1970, vol. 5. irreg. Universidad de Chile, Instituto de Investigaciones Musicales, Av. Bernardo O'Higgins 1058, Casilla 10-D, Santiago, Chile.

387 SP
ANUARIO DE LA INDUSTRIA NAUTICA ESPANOLA. 1977-197? a. Yate y Motonautica, Diputacion 304, Barcelona 9, Spain.

861 AG
ANUARIO DE POETAS CONTEMPORANEOS. 1976-1979. a. Club de Poetas, Casilla de Correo 5685/CC, 1000 Buenos Aires, Argentina.

370 US ISSN 0570-4200
ANUARIO DEL DESARROLLO DE LA EDUCACION, LA CIENCIA Y LA CULTURA EN AMERICA LATINA. 1964-19?? a. Organization of American States, Dept. of Publications, Department of Publications, Washington, DC 20006.

320.9 IS
ARAB VIEW. 1970-197? irreg. Ministry for Foreign Affairs, Research Division, Jerusalem, Israel.

617.7 SZ ISSN 0066-5851
ARBEITSMEDIZINISCHE FRAGEN IN DER OPHTHALMOLOGIE/PROBLEMS OF INDUSTRIAL MEDICINE IN OPHTHALMOLOGY. 1969-197? irreg. (reprint service avail. from ISI) S. Karger AG, Allschwilerstrasse 10, P.O. Box, CH-4009 Basel, Switzerland.

690 SA ISSN 0084-6708
ARCHITECTS, BUILDERS, AND CONTRACTORS BLUE-BOOK. 1952-1980? a. Communications Group, Business Press Division, White-Ray House, 51 Wale St., Box 335, Cape Town 8000, South Africa.

617.585 US ISSN 0092-7651
ARCHIVES OF PODIATRIC MEDICINE AND FOOT SURGERY. 1973-1979(vol. 5) irreg. Futura Publishing Co., 295 Main St., Box 333, Mount Kisco, NY 10549.

913 PE
ARCHIVO GENERAL DE LA NACION. REVISTA. 1972-1978, no.4-5. a. Peru. Instituto Nacional de Cultura, Jr. Manuel Cuadros s/n, Palacio de Justica, Aptdo. 3124, Lima, Peru.

489 FI ISSN 0066-6998
ARCTOS; ACTA PHILOLOGICA FENNICA. SUPPLEMENTUM. 1968-19?? irreg. Klassillis-Filologinen Yhdistys, Hallituskatu 11-13, Helsinki 17, Finland.

980 US
ARIZONA LATIN AMERICAN CONFERENCE PAPERS. 1973-1977. a. (back issues avail.) Arizona State University, Center for Latin American Studies, Tempe, AZ 85281.

951 US ISSN 0084-6805
ASIA IN THE MODERN WORLD SERIES. 1961-19?? irreg. (back issues avail.) St. John's University Press, Grand Central and Utopia Parkways, Jamaica, NY 11439.

181 US ISSN 0084-6813
ASIAN INSTITUTE TRANSLATIONS. 1961-197? irreg. St. John's University Press, Grand Central and Utopia Parkways, Jamaica, NY 11439.

181 US ISSN 0066-8443
ASIAN PHILOSOPHICAL STUDIES. 1962-197? irreg. St. Johns University Press, Grand Central & Utopia Parkway, Jamaica, NY 14439.

630 CR ISSN 0074-0756
ASOCIACION INTERAMERICANA DE BIBLIOTECARIOS Y DOCUMENTALISTAS AGRICOLAS. BOLETIN TECNICO. 1966-1979. irreg,; no. 17, 1978. Asociacion Interamericana de Bibliotecarios y Documentalistas Agricolas, Apdo. No. 74, Turrialba, Costa Rica.

378.15 US ISSN 0066-9563
ASSOCIATION OF GRADUATE SCHOOLS IN ASSOCIATION OF AMERICAN UNIVERSITIES. JOURNAL OF PROCEEDINGS AND ADDRESSES. 1949-19?? a. Princeton University, Graduate School, Princeton, NJ 08540.

676 FR
ASSOCIATION TECHNIQUE DE L'INDUSTRIE PAPETIERE. CIRCULAIRE. ceased. irreg. Association Technique de l'Industrie Papetiere, 154 Boulevard Haussman, Paris 8, France.

676 FR
ASSOCIATION TECHNIQUE DE L'INDUSTRIE PAPETIERE. QUELQUES NOUVELLES. ceased. irreg. Association Technique de l'Industrie Papetiere, 154 Boulevard Haussman, Paris 8, France.

971 016 CN ISSN 0571-7817
ATLANTIC PROVINCES CHECKLIST. 1957-1965 (vol.9) a. Atlantic Provinces Library Association, c/o School of Library Service, Dalhousie University, Halifax, N.S. B3H 4H8, Canada.

330 FR ISSN 0067-026X
ATLAS D'ATTRACTION URBAINE. 1966-19?? irreg. (Ecole Pratique des Hautes Etudes, Centre d'Etudes des Techniques Economiques Modernes) Centrale des Revues, Dunod, B. P. 119, 93104 Montreuil Cedex, France.

621.389 US
AUDIO DIGEST. 1976-197? a. Davis Publications, Inc., 380 Lexington Ave., New York, NY 10017.

332.6 319 AT
AUSTRALIA. BUREAU OF STATISTICS. OVERSEAS INVESTMENTS: OVERSEAS BORROWINGS BY COMPANIES IN AUSTRALIA. 1971-1976. irreg. (approx. 1/yr.) (processed) Australian Bureau of Statistics, P.O. Box 10, Belconnen, A.C.T. 2616, Australia.

360 319.4 AT
AUSTRALIA. BUREAU OF STATISTICS. PUBLIC AUTHORITY FINANCE. STATE GOVERNMENTS: SOCIAL SERVICES. 1971-1974. a. Australian Bureau of Statistics, P.O. Box 10, Belconnen, A.C.T. 2616, Australia.

331 319 AT
AUSTRALIA. BUREAU OF STATISTICS. VICTORIAN OFFICE. INDUSTRIAL ACCIDENTS AND WORKERS COMPENSATION. 1957-1979. a. Australian Bureau of Statistics, Victorian Office, Box 2796Y, G.P.O. Melbourne, Victoria 3001, Australia. Formerly: Australia. Bureau of Statistics. Victorian Office Industrial Accidents and Workers Compensation. Statistics (ISSN 0067-1134)

090 AT ISSN 0310-9879
AUSTRALIAN AND PACIFIC BOOK PRICES CURRENT. 1973-197?. a. (back issues avail.) O.P. Books Pty. Ltd., 31 Adolphus St., Balmain, N.S.W. 2041, Australia.

025 US
AUTOMATION EFFORTS AT THE COLUMBIA UNIVERSITY LIBRARIES. PROGRESS REPORT. 1968/69-197? irreg. (back issues avail) Columbia University Libraries, Systems Office, 535 W. 114 St., New York, NY 10027.

299 US
AVTOKEFALNAIA AMERIKANSKAIA PRAVOSLAVNAIA TSERKOV. EZHEGODNIK PRAVOSLAVNOI TSERKVI V AMERIKE. 1975-1979. a. Orthodox Church in America, Box 675, Syosset, NY 11791.

382.17 CL ISSN 0067-3013
BALANZA DE PAGOS DE CHILE. ceased in 1975. a. Banco Central de Chile, Departamento de Informaciones Economicas y Estadisticas, Casilla 967, Santiago, Chile.

630 639.2 BB
BARBADOS. MINISTRY OF AGRICULTURE AND FISHERIES. BULLETIN. ceased. irreg. Ministry of Agriculture and Fisheries, Bridgetown, Barbados, W. Indies.

690 GW ISSN 0067-4575
BAU UND BAUSTOFF HANDBUCH. 1966-197? a. Gert Wohlfarth GmbH Verlag Fachtechnik und Mercator-Verlag, Koehnenstr. 5-11, 4100 Duisburg 1, W. Germany (B.R.D.)

020 GW ISSN 0522-6201
BEITRAEGE ZUM BUECHEREIWESEN. REIHE B: QUELLEN UND TEXTE. 1967-1978(vol. 6); series completed. irreg. Verlag Otto Harrassowitz, Taunusstr. 6, Postfach 2929, 6200 Wiesbaden, W. Germany (B.R.D.)

016 US
BESTERMAN WORLD BIBLIOGRAPHIES. discontinued. irreg. Rowman and Littlefield, 81 Adams Drive, Totowa, NJ 07512.

800 SZ ISSN 0067-6330
BESTSELLERS DU MONDE ENTIER. 1969-197? irreg. Edito-Service S.A., Ch. de Roches 9, Case Postale 307, 1211 Geneva 6, Switzerland.

526.8 FR ISSN 0067-6934
BIBLIOGRAPHIE CARTOGRAPHIQUE INTERNATIONALE. 1946-1975. a. Centre National de la Recherche Scientifique, Laboratoire Intergeo, 191, rue Saint-Jacques, 75005 Paris, France

913 GE ISSN 0067-6950
BIBLIOGRAPHIE DER CHEMISCH-ARCHAEOLOGISCHEN LITERATUR. (Supplement to "Alt-Thueringen") 1967-197? irreg. Museum fuer Ur- und Fruehgeschichte Thueringens, Amalienstr., 53 Weimar, E. Germany (D.D.R.)

830 016 GW
BIBLIOGRAPHISCHES HANDBUCH DER DEUTSCHEN LITTERATURWISSENSCHAFT 1945-1969. 1973-1979 (vol.3) irreg. Vittorio Klostermann, Frauenlobstr. 22, Postfach 900601, D-6000 Frankfurt 90, W. Germany (B.R.D.)

945 IT
BIBLIOTECA DI STORIA LOMBARDA
MODERNA E CONTEMPORANEA. STUDI E
RICERCHE. ceased. irreg., no. 4, 1976. SugarCo
s.r.l., Viale Tunisia 41, Milan, Italy.

800 SZ ISSN 0067-8457
BIBLIOTHEQUE RENCONTRE DES LETTRES
ANCIENNES ET MODERNES. 1970-197? irreg.
Edito-Service S.A., Ch. de Roches 9, Case Postale
307, 1211 Geneva 6.

010 US ISSN 0360-2516
BILLBOARD INDEX. ceased. irreg. University
Microfilms International, Indexing Services, 300 N.
Zeeb Rd., Ann Arbor, MI 48106.

686.2 UK ISSN 0306-4077
BINDERY DATA INDEX. 1975-197? a. Benn
Publications Ltd., 25 New Street Square, London
EC4A 3JA, England

574.192 US ISSN 0067-8686
BIOCHEMICAL PREPARATIONS. 1949-197? irreg.
John Wiley & Sons, Inc., 605 Third Ave., New
York, NY 10016.

630 016 CR
BOLETIN PARA BIBLIOTECAS AGRICOLAS.
1964-19?? q. Instituto Interamericano de Ciencias
Agricolas de la O E A, Centro Interamericano de
Documentacion e Informacion Agricola, Apartado
74, Turrialba, Costa Rica.

332.64 AG
BOLSA DE COMERCIO DE ROSARIO. BOLETIN
INFORMATIVO. ceased. s-m. Bolsa de Comercio
de Rosario, Centro de Documentacion para
Exportaciones, Rosario, Santa Fe, Argentina.

350 GW ISSN 0340-6377
BONNER ORIENTALISTISCHE STUDIEN. 1954-
1975 (vol. 30); series completed. irreg. Verlag Otto
Harrassowitz, Taunusstr. 6, Postfach 2929, 6200
Wiesbaden, W. Germany (B.R.D.)

070.5 US
BOOKHUNTER'S GUIDE TO THE NORTHEAST.
1977-1979. biennial. Ephemera and Books, Box
19681, San Diego, CA 92119.

808.1 US ISSN 0067-6276
BORESTONE MOUNTAIN POETRY AWARDS.
1948-19?? a. Pacific Books, Publishers, P. O. Box
558, Palo Alto, CA 94302.

784 CN ISSN 0382-5604
BOUSCUEIL; bulletin d'information de l'Alliance
Chorale Canadienne. 1971-1978 (no. 17, Mar.)
irreg. Alliance Chorale Canadienne, 1052 Avenue
Laurien Ouest, Montreal, Que. H2V 2K8, Canada.

778.5 BL
BRASIL CINEMA. ceased. irreg. Empresa Brasileira
de Filmes, Av. 13 de Maio no. 41, Rio de Janeiro,
Brazil.
  Formerly: Catalogo de Filmes Brasileiros (ISSN
0576-8942)

631.0913 BL
BRAZIL. INSTITUTO BRASILEIRO DE
DESENVOLVIMENTO FLORESTAL. PROJETO
DE DESENVOLVIMENTO E PESQUISA
FLORESTAL. COMUNICACAO TECNICA.
1976-1977 (no. 19) irreg. Instituto Brasileiro de
Desenvolvimento Florestal, Brasilia, Brazil.

631.0913 BL
BRAZIL. INSTITUTO BRASILEIRO DE
DESENVOLVIMENTO FLORESTAL.PROJETO
DE DESENVOLVIMENTO E PESQUISA
FLORESTAL. SERIE DIVULGACAO. 1976-1978
(no. 15) irreg. Instituto Brasileiro de
Desenvolvimento Florestal, Brasilia, Brazil.

332 US ISSN 0073-9065
C F A MONOGRAPH SERIES. 1967-19?? irreg.
Institute of Chartered Financial Analysts, P.O. Box
3668, Charlottesville, VA 22903.

574.192 US
C R C HANDBOOK OF BIOCHEMISTRY AND
MOLECULAR BIOLOGY; selected data for
molecular biology. 1968-197? irreg. C R C Press,
Inc., 2000 N.W. 24th St., Boca Raton,
FL 33431.
  Formerly: Handbook of Biochemistry (ISSN
0072-9736)

677 626.3 AT ISSN 0310-8163
C. S. I. R. O. SHEEP AND WOOL RESEARCH.
discontinued. a. C. S. I. R. O., 314 Albert St., East
Melbourne, Vic. 3002, Australia.

551.34 CN ISSN 0068-7723
CANADA. ATMOSPHERIC ENVIRONMENT
SERVICE. ICE OBSERVATIONS: CANADIAN
ARCTIC. 1964-1970. irreg. Atmospheric
Environment Service, 4905 Dufferin St.,
Downsview, Ont. M3H 5T4, Canada

551.34 CN ISSN 0068-7731
CANADA. ATMOSPHERIC ENVIRONMENT
SERVICE. ICE OBSERVATIONS: CANADIAN
INLAND WATERWAYS. 1964-1970. a.
Atmospheric Environment Service, 4905 Dufferin
St, Downsview M3H 5T4, Ont., Canada.

551.34 CN ISSN 0068-774X
CANADA. ATMOSPHERIC ENVIRONMENT
SERVICE. ICE OBSERVATIONS: EASTERN
CANADIAN SEABOARD. 1964-1970. irreg.
Atmospheric Environment Service, 4905 Dufferin
St., Downsview, Ont. M3H 5T4, Canada.

572 CN ISSN 0068-8002
CANADA. NATIONAL MUSEUMS, OTTAWA.
PUBLICATIONS IN ETHNOLOGY/CANADA.
MUSEES NATIONAUX. PUBLICATIONS
D'ETHNOLOGIE. 1970-1975. irreg. (back issues
avail.) (National Museum of Man) National
Museums of Canada, Ottawa, Ont. K1A OM8,
Canada.

398 CN
CANADA. NATIONAL MUSEUMS, OTTAWA.
PUBLICATIONS IN FOLK CULTURE/
CANADA, MUSEES NATIONAUX.
PUBLICATIONS DE CULTURE
TRADITIONNELLE. 1971-1973. irreg. (back issues
avail.) (National Museum of Man) National
Museums of Canada, Ottawa, Ont. K1A 0M8,
Canada.

900 CN ISSN 0068-8010
CANADA. NATIONAL MUSEUMS, OTTAWA.
PUBLICATIONS IN HISTORY/CANADA.
MUSEES NATIONAUX. PUBLICATIONS
D'HISTOIRE. 1970-1974. irreg. (back issues avail.)
(National Museum of Man) National Museums of
Canada, Ottawa, Ont. K1A OM8, Canada.

338.4 CN
CANADA. STATISTICS CANADA. CANNED
AND FROZEN PROCESSED FOODS/
ALIMENTS, CONDITIONNES EN BOITES ET
CONGELES. (Catalog 32-212) discontinued. a.
Statistics Canada, User Advisory Services, Ottawa
K1A 0T6, Canada.

374.9 CN ISSN 0700-1444
CANADA. STATISTICS CANADA. CONTINUING
EDUCATION: ELEMENTARY-SECONDARY/
EDUCATION PERMANENTE: NIVEAU
ELEMENTAIRE-SECONDAIRE. (Catalog 81-224)
1969-197? a. Statistics Canada, User Services,
Ottawa, Ont. K1A 0T6, Canada.
  Formerly: Canada. Statistics Canada. Continuing
Education. Part 1: Elementary-Secondary
Institutions/Education Permanente. Partie 1:
Etablissements de l'Elementaire-Secondaire.

374.9 CN ISSN 0700-141X
CANADA. STATISTICS CANADA. CONTINUING
EDUCATION: UNIVERSITIES/EDUCATION
PERMANENTE: UNIVERSITES. (Catalog 81-225)
1970/71-197? a. Statistics Canada, User Services,
Ottawa, Ont. K1A 0T6, Canada.
  Formerly: Canada. Statistics Canada. Continuing
Education. Part 2: Post-Secondary Level/Education
Permanente. Partie 2: Niveau Postsecondaire.

310 622 CN ISSN 0318-8841
CANADA. STATISTICS CANADA. CONTRACT
DRILLING FOR PETROLEUM AND OTHER
CONTRACT DRILLING/FORAGE DE PUITS
DE PETROLE A FORFAIT ET AUTRE
FORAGE A FORFAIT. (Catalogue 26-207) 1938-
197? a. Statistics Canada, User Services, Ottawa
Ont. K1A OT6, Canada.

637 CN ISSN 0068-7111
CANADA. STATISTICS CANADA. DAIRY
STATISTICS/STATISTIQUE LAITIERE. (Catalog
23-201) 1933-197? a. Statistics Canada, User
Services, Ottawa, Ont. K1A 0T6, Canada.

378 CN ISSN 0382-411X
CANADA. STATISTICS CANADA.
EDUCATIONAL STAFF IN COMMUNITY
COLLEGES/PERSONNEL D'ENSEIGNEMENT
DES COLLEGES COMMUNAUTAIRES. (Catalog
81-227) 1970-197? a. Statistics Canada, User
Services, Ottawa, Ont. K1A 0T6, Canada.
  Formerly: Canada. Statistics Canada. Statistical
Profiles of Educational Staff in Community
Colleges/Profiles Statistiques sur le Personnel
d'Enseignement des Colleges Communautaires
(ISSN 0382-4128)

338.4 CN ISSN 0575-8440
CANADA. STATISTICS CANADA. ESTIMATES
OF PRODUCTION AND DISAPPEARANCE OF
MEATS/ESTIMATION DE LA PRODUCTION
ET DE LA DISPARITION DES VIANDES.
(Catalogue 32-220) 1922-197? a. Statistics Canada,
User Services, Ottawa, Ont. K1A 0T6, Canada.

338.1 317 CN ISSN 0703-4857
CANADA. STATISTICS CANADA. FARM
INCOME AND PRICES SECTION. FARM
CASH RECEIPTS/RECETTES MONETAIRES
AGRICOLES. (Catalog 21-201) 1945-197? a.
Statistics Canada, User Services, Ottawa, Ont. K1A
0T6, Canada.

338.2 CN ISSN 0319-4957
CANADA. STATISTICS CANADA. FELDSPAR
AND QUARTZ MINES/MINES DE
FELDSPATH ET DE QUARTZ. (Catalogue 26-
208) 1927-197? a. Statistics Canada, User Services,
Ottawa, Ont. K1A 0T6, Canada.

338.2 CN ISSN 0380-4968
CANADA. STATISTICS CANADA. GOLD
QUARTZ AND COPPER-GOLD-SILVER
MINES/MINES DE QUARTZ AURIFERE ET
MINES DE CUIVRE-OR-ARGENT. (Catalogue
26-209) 1958-197? a. Statistics Canada, User
Services, Ottawa, Ont. K1A 0T6, Canada.
  Formerly: Canada. Statistics Canada. Placer Gold
Mines, Gold Quartz Mines and Copper-Gold-Silver
Mines/Placers d'Or Mines de Quartz Aurifere et
Mines de Cuivre-Or-Argent (ISSN 0068-7138)

610.73 331.2 CN ISSN 0576-016X
CANADA. STATISTICS CANADA. HEALTH
MANPOWER SECTION. ANNUAL SALARIES
OF HOSPITAL NURSING PERSONNEL/
TRAITEMENTS ANNUELS DU PERSONNEL
INFIRMIER DES HOPITAUX. (Catalogue 83-401)
1972-197? biennial. Statistics Canada, User Services,
Ottawa, Ont. K1A 0T6, Canada.

338.4 CN ISSN 0384-3300
CANADA. STATISTICS CANADA. LEATHER
GLOVE FACTORIES/FABRIQUES DE GANTS
EN CUIR. (Catalogue 33-204) 1924-197? a.
Statistics Canada, User Services, Ottawa, Ont. K1A
0T6, Canada.

338.2 CN ISSN 0382-4020
CANADA. STATISTICS CANADA.
MANUFACTURING INDUSTRIES DIVISION.
POTASH MINES/MINES DE POTASSE. (Catalog
26-222) 1974-197? a. Statistics Canada, User
Services, Ottawa, Ont. K1A 0T6, Canada.

338 317 CN ISSN 0076-4248
CANADA. STATISTICS CANADA.
MANUFACTURING INDUSTRIES OF
CANADA: TYPE OF ORGANIZATION AND
SIZE OF ESTABLISHMENT/INDUSTRIES
MANUFACTURIERES DU CANADA: FORME
D'ORGANISATION ET TAILLE DES
ETABLISSEMENTS. (Catalog 31-210) 1946-197?
a. Statistics Canada, User Services, Ottawa Ont.
K1A 0T6, Canada.
  Formerly: Manufacturing Industries of Canada.

338.2 CN ISSN 0575-9048
CANADA. STATISTICS CANADA.
MISCELLANEOUS METAL MINES/MINES
METALLIQUES DIVERSES. (Catalog 26-219)
1927-197? a. Statistics Canada, User Services,
Ottawa, Ont. K1A 0T6, Canada.

338.2 CN ISSN 0380-6952
CANADA. STATISTICS CANADA.
MISCELLANEOUS NON-METAL MINES/
MINES NON METALLIQUES DIVERSES.
(Catalog 26-220) 1927-197? a. Statistics Canada,
User Services, Ottawa, Ont. K1A 0T6, Canada.

CESSATIONS

363.2   CN   ISSN 0575-9331
CANADA. STATISTICS CANADA. POLICE ADMINISTRATION STATISTICS/ STATISTIQUE DE L'ADMINISTRATION POLICIERE. (Catalog 85-204) 1960-197? a. Statistics Canada, User Advisory Services, Ottawa, Ont. K1a 0T6, Canada.

381   CN   ISSN 0704-5387
CANADA. STATISTICS CANADA. PUBLIC WAREHOUSING/ENTREPOSAGE PUBLIC. (Catalogue 63-212) 1944-197? a. Statistics Canada, User Services, Ottawa, Ont. K1A 0T6, Canada.
    Formerly(until 1977): Canada. Statistics Canada. Warehousing-General Merchandise and Refrigerated Goods/Entreposage-Entrepots de Merchandises et Installations Frigorifiques.

388   CN   ISSN 0706-3105
CANADA. STATISTICS CANADA. ROAD AND STREET LENGTH AND FINANCING/VOIES PUBLIQUES, LONGUEUR ET FINANCEMENT. (Catalogue 53-201) 1928-197? a. Statistics Canada, User Services, Ottawa K1A 0T6, Ont., Canada.
    Formerly: Canada. Statistics Canada. Road and Street Mileage and Expenditure/Voies Publiques: Longueur et Depenses (ISSN 0410-5869)

387   CN   ISSN 0318-8914
CANADA. STATISTICS CANADA. SHIPPING REPORT. PART 1: INTERNATIONAL SEABORNE SHIPPING (BY COUNTRY) / TRANSPORT MARITIME. PARTIE 1: TRANSPORT MARITIME INTERNATIONAL (PAR PAYS) (Catalogue 54-202) 1938-197? a. Statistics Canada, User Services, Ottawa, Ont. K1A 0T6, Canada.

387   CN   ISSN 0318-8930
CANADA. STATISTICS CANADA. SHIPPING REPORT. PART 3: COASTWISE SHIPPING/ TRANSPORT MARITIME. PARTIE 3: NAVIGATION NATIONALE. (Catalogue 54-204) 1938-197? a. Statistics Canada, User Services, Ottawa, Ont. K1A 0T6, Canada.

387   CN   ISSN 0575-9757
CANADA. STATISTICS CANADA. SHIPPING REPORT. PART 4: ORIGIN AND DESTINATION FOR SELECTED PORTS/ TRANSPORT MARITIME. PARTIE 4: ORIGINE ET DESTINATION POUR CERTAINS PORTS. (Catalogue 54-206) 1962-197? a. Statistics Canada, User Services, Ottawa, Ont. K1A 0T6, Canada.

387   CN   ISSN 0318-8949
CANADA. STATISTICS CANADA. SHIPPING REPORT. PART 5: ORIGIN AND DESTINATION FOR SELECTED COMMODITIES/TRANSPORT MARITIME. PARTIE 5: ORIGINE ET DESTINATION DE CERTAINES MARCHANDISES. (Catalogue 54-207) 1961-197? a. Statistics Canada, User Services, Ottawa, Ont. K1A 0T6, Canada.

338.2   CN   ISSN 0703-7406
CANADA. STATISTICS CANADA. SILVER-COBALT MINES AND SILVER-LEAD-ZINC MINES/MINES D'ARGENT-COBALT ET MINES D'ARGENT-PLOMB-ZINC. (Catalog 26-216) 1927-197? a. Statistics Canada, User Services, Ottawa K1A 0T6, Canada.

364   CN   ISSN 0319-8227
CANADA. STATISTICS CANADA. STATISTICS OF CRIMINAL AND OTHER OFFENCES/ STATISTIQUE DE LA CRIMINALITE. (Catalogue 85-201) 1876-197? a. Statistics Canada, User Services, Ottawa, Ont. K1A 0T6, Canada.

338.2   CN   ISSN 0575-9846
CANADA. STATISTICS CANADA. STONE QUARRIES/CARRIERES. (Catalog 26-217) 1926-197? a. Statistics Canada, User Services, Ottawa, Ont. K1A 0T6, Canada.

338.4   CN
CANADA. STATISTICS CANADA. TRAVEL, TOURISM AND OUTDOOR RECREATION - A STATISTICAL DIGEST/VOYAGES, TOURISME ET LOISIRS DE PLEIN AIR-RESUME STATISTIQUE. (Catalog 66-202) 1972-197? a. Statistics Canada, User Services, Ottawa, Ont. K1A 0T6, Canada.

614 312   CN
CANADA. STATISTICS CANADA. TUBERCULOSIS STATISTICS. VOLUME 1: TUBERCULOSIS MORBIDITY AND MORALITY/LA STATISTIQUE DE LA TUBERCULOSE, VOLUME I: MORBIDITE ET MORTALITE. (Catalog 83-206) 1937-197? a. Statistics Canada, User Services, Ottawa, Ont. K1A 0T6, Canada.

614 312   CN   ISSN 0381-8845
CANADA. STATISTICS CANADA. TUBERCULOSIS STATISTICS. VOLUME 2: INSTITUTIONAL FACILITIES, SERVICES AND FINANCES/LA STATISTIQUE DE LA TUBERCULOSE, VOLUME 2: INSTALLATIONS, SERVICES ET FINANCE DES ETABLISSEMENTS. (Catalog 83-207) 1954-197? a. Statistics Canada, User Services, Ont. K1A 0T6, Canada.

378   CN   ISSN 0700-2181
CANADA. STATISTICS CANADA. UNIVERSITY FINANCIAL STATISTICS/UNIVERSITES STATISTIQUES FINANCIERES. (Catalogue 81-212) 1964-197? a. Statistics Canada, User Services, Ottawa, Ont. K1A 0T6, Canada.
    Formerly(until 1977): Canadian Universities: Income and Expenditure/Universities Canadiennes: Recettes et Depenses.

330 971 317   CN   ISSN 0705-5331
CANADA: OFFICIAL HANDBOOK OF PRESENT CONDITIONS AND RECENT PROGRESS/ CANADA: REVUE OFFICIELLE DE LA SITUATION ACTUELLE ET DES PROGRES RECENTS. (Catalogue 11-203 or 11-203f) 1930-197? a. Statistics Canada, User Services, Ottawa, Ont. K1A 0T6, Canada.

971 317   CN   ISSN 0068-8142
CANADA YEARBOOK. (Catalog 11-202) 1867-197? a. Statistics Canada, User Services, Ottawa, Ont. K1A 0T6, Canada.

791   CN   ISSN 0068-872X
CANADIAN FILMOGRAPHY SERIES. 1965. ceased with no. 11. irreg. Canadian Film Archives, 1762 Carling, Ottawa, Ont. K2A 2H7, Canada.

629.2   US   ISSN 0147-7684
CAR CARE HANDBOOK. 1977-197? a. (Popular Science Publishing Co.) Times Mirror Magazines, Inc., 380 Madison Ave., New York, NY 10017.

948.5 355   SW   ISSN 0069-0597
CARL X GUSTAF-STUDIER. 1965-1979 (no. 8) irreg. Kungliga Militaerhoegskolan, Militaerhistoriska Avdelningen - Royal Armed Forces Staff College, 100 45 Stockholm 90, Sweden.

624.1833   FR
CENTRE D'ETUDES ET DE RECHERCHES DE L'INDUSTRIE DES LIANTS HYDRAULIQUES, PARIS. RAPPORT D'ACTIVITE. ceased. Centre d'Etudes et de Recherches de l'Industrie des Liants Hydrauliques, 23, rue de Cronstadt, Paris 75015, France.

350   FR   ISSN 0069-1852
CENTRE D'ETUDES PRATIQUES D'INFORMATIQUE ET D'AUTOMATIQUE. COLLECTION. 1971-197? irreg. Centrale des Revues, Dunod, B. P. 119, 93104 Montreuil Cedex, France.

800   SZ   ISSN 0069-2840
CHEFS-D'OEUVRE DE LA SCIENCE-FICTION. 1970-197? irreg. Edito-Service S.A., Ch. de Roches 9, Case Postale 307, 1211 Geneva 6, Switzerland.

630.24 668.8   US
CHEMAGRO COURIER. 1962-1977. irreg. Mobay Chemical Corporation, Chemagro Agricultural Division, P.O. Box 4913, Hawthorn Rd., Kansas City, MO 64120

352   US
CITIZENS CONFERENCE ON STATE LEGISLATURES. INFORMATION BULLETIN. 1972-197?; discontinued. irreg. Legis 50-Center for Legislative Improvement, 7503 Maron, Greenwood Plaza, Englewood, CO 80110.

352   US   ISSN 0578-3364
CITIZENS CONFERENCE ON STATE LEGISLATURES. RESEARCH MEMORANDUM. 1970, no. 3. Legis 50-Center for Legislative Improvement, 7503 Maron, Greenwood Plaza, Englewood, CO 80110.

910.2   US   ISSN 0069-4401
CLARK GUIDEBOOKS. 1956-1976 (3 vols.) irreg. Arthur H. Clark Co., 1264 S. Central Ave., Glendale, CA 91204.

370   US   ISSN 0069-4495
CLASSICS IN EDUCATION. 1975-197? irreg. Teachers College Press, Teachers College, Columbia University, 1234 Amsterdam Ave., New York, NY 10027.

616.8 618   US   ISSN 0069-4797
CLINICAL APPROACHES TO THE PROBLEMS OF CHILDHOOD: THE LANGLEY PORTER CHILD PSYCHIATRY SERIES. 1965-1971 (vol. 5) irreg. Science & Behavior Books, Inc., Box 11457, Palo Alto, CA 94306.

616.994   US   ISSN 0069-4800
CLINICAL CONFERENCE ON CANCER. PAPERS. discontinued. a. (University of Texas, M.D. Anderson Hospital and Tumor Institute) Year Book Medical Publishers, Inc., 35 E. Wacker Dr., Chicago, IL 60601.

332.6   SP
COLEGIO DE AGENTES DE CAMBIO Y BOLSA DE BARCELONA. SERVICIO DE ESTUDIOS E INFORMACION. EVOLUCION DE CAPITAL Y RENTA EN LA INVERSION EN ACCIONES. 1973-1979. a. Colegio de Agentes de Cambio y Bolsa de Barcelona, Servicio de Estudios e Informacion, Paseo Isabel II s/n, Barcelona, Spain.

378.0025   US   ISSN 0588-2990
COLLEGES CLASSIFIED; a guide for counselors, parents and students. ceased in 1975. irreg. Chronicle Guidance Publications, Inc., Aurora St., Moravia, NY 13118.

539   NE   ISSN 0533-3180
COLLOQUES A M P E R E. discontinued. irreg., vol. 18, 1975. (Group for the Study of Atoms and Molecules from Radio-Electric Research) North Holland Publishing Co., P.O. Box 211, 1000 AE Amsterdam, Netherlands.

551.31   IT   ISSN 0084-8948
COMITATO GLACIOLOGICO ITALIANO. BOLLETTINO. 1914-1977. a. Comitato Glaciologico Italiano, Via Academia delle Scienze N. 5, I-10123 Turin, Italy.

338   US   ISSN 0084-8964
COMMITTEE FOR ECONOMIC DEVELOPMENT. SUPPLEMENTARY PAPER. 1959-197? irreg. Committee for Economic Development, 477 Madison Ave., New York, NY 10022.

338.9   AT   ISSN 0591-0129
COMMITTEE FOR ECONOMIC DEVELOPMENT OF AUSTRALIA. C E D A OCCASIONAL PAPERS. 1969-1978 (Jan.) irreg. Committee for Economic Development of Australia, 186 Exhibition St., Melbourne, Vic 3000, Australia.

338.9   AT
COMMITTEE FOR ECONOMIC DEVELOPMENT OF AUSTRALIA. C E D A SUPPLEMENTARY PAPERS. 1967-1979 (Mar.) irreg (5-6/yr) Committee for Economic Development of Australia, 186 Exhibition St., Melbourne, Vic 3000, Australia.

634.9   AT
COMMONWEALTH SCIENTIFIC AND INDUSTRIAL RESEARCH ORGANIZATION. DIVISION OF FOREST RESEARCH. BULLETINS. 1932-1975 (no.47) irreg. C. S. I. R. O., Division of Forest Research, Banks St., Yarralumla, A.C.T. 2600, Australia.
    Formerly: Australia. Forestry and Timber Bureau. Bulletins (ISSN 0067-1452)

634.9   AT
COMMONWEALTH SCIENTIFIC AND
INDUSTRIAL RESEARCH ORGANIZATION.
DIVISION OF FOREST RESEARCH.
LEAFLETS. 1932-1976 (no.127). irreg. C. S. I. R.
O., Division of Forest Research, Banks St.,
Yarralumla, A.C.T. 2600, Australia.
    Formerly: Australia. Forestry and Timber Bureau.
Leaflets (ISSN 0067-1479)

631.7   AT   ISSN 0069-7443
COMMONWEALTH SCIENTIFIC AND
INDUSTRIAL RESEARCH ORGANIZATION.
DIVISION OF IRRIGATION RESEARCH.
REPORT. 1962/63 (suspended). a. C.S.I.R.O.,
Division of Irrigation Research, Private Bag, Griffith
N.S.W. 2680, Australia.

301   US
COMMUNITY DEVELOPMENT ABSTRACTS.
1964-1970 (vol. 2) Sociological Abstracts, Inc., Box
22206, San Diego, CA 92122.

610   US   ISSN 0160-6980
CONTINUING EDUCATION FOR HEALTH
CARE PROVIDERS. 1974-1977(vol. 2) irreg.
Futura Publishing Co., 295 Main Street, Box 333,
Mount Kisco, NY 10549.
    Formerly: Continuing Education in Nursing
Home Administration (ISSN 0094-6192)

327   US   ISSN 0045-849X
COOPERATOR. 1968?-19??; suspended. a. (also avail.
in microfilm from UMM) International Cooperation
Council, Inc., 8570 Wilshire Blvd., Beverly Hills,
CA 90211.
    Supersedes: Challenge (ISSN 0009-0980)

185   US
CORPUS COMMENTARIORUM IN
ARISTOTELEM. VERSIO ANGLICA.
discontinued. irreg. Mediaeval Academy of
America, 1430 Massachusetts Ave., Cambridge, MA
02138.

185   US
CORPUS COMMENTARIORUM IN
ARISTOTOLEM. VERSIO ARABICA.
discontinued. irreg. Mediaeval Academy of
America, 1430 Massachusetts Ave., Cambridge, MA
02138.

185   US
CORPUS COMMENTARIORUM IN
ARISTOTOLEM. VERSIO HEBRAICA.
discontinued. irreg. Mediaeval Academy of
America, 1430 Massachusetts Ave., Cambridge, MA
02138.

185   US
CORPUS COMMENTARIORUM IN
ARISTOTOLEM. VERSIO LATINA. discontinued.
irreg. Mediaeval Academy of America, 1430
Massachusetts Ave., Cambridge, MA 02138.

364 016   CN   ISSN 0070-0509
CORRECTIONAL LITERATURE PUBLISHED IN
CANADA/OUVRAGES DE CRIMINOLOGIE
PUBLIES AU CANADA. 1964-197? irreg.
Canadian Association for the Prevention of Crime,
55 Parkdale Ave., Ottawa, Ontario K1Y 1E5,
Canada.

668.55   US   ISSN 0070-0533
COSMETIC FORMULARY. (Title varies: Cosmetic
and Pharmaceutical Catalog and Formulary) 1965-19??
biennial. Allured Publishing Corp., Box 318,
Wheaton, IL 60187.

913 016   US   ISSN 0070-072X
COUNCIL FOR OLD WORLD ARCHAEOLOGY:
C O W A SURVEYS AND BIBLIOGRAPHIES.
AREA 1: BRITISH ISLE. 1958-19?? irreg., planned
to become triennial. Council for Old World
Archaeology, Boston University, 232 Bay State Rd.,
Boston, MA 02215.

913 016   US   ISSN 0070-0738
COUNCIL FOR OLD WORLD ARCHAEOLOGY:
C O W A SURVEYS AND BIBLIOGRAPHIES.
AREA 2: SCANDINAVIA. 1959-19?? irreg.,
planned to become triennial. Council for Old World
Archaeology, Boston University, 232 Bay State Rd.,
Boston, MA 02215.

913 016   US   ISSN 0070-0746
COUNCIL FOR OLD WORLD ARCHAEOLOGY:
C O W A SURVEYS AND BIBLIOGRAPHIES.
AREA 3: WESTERN EUROPE: PART 1. 1959-
19?? irreg., planned to become triennial. Council for
Old World Archaeology, Boston University, 232
Bay State Rd., Boston, MA 02215.

913 016   US   ISSN 0070-0754
COUNCIL FOR OLD WORLD ARCHAEOLOGY:
C O W A SURVEYS AND BIBLIOGRAPHIES.
AREA 3: WESTERN EUROPE: PART 2. 1959-
19?? irreg., planned to become triennial. Council for
Old World Archaeology, Boston University, 232
Bay State Rd., Boston, MA 02215.

913 016   US   ISSN 0070-0762
COUNCIL FOR OLD WORLD ARCHAEOLOGY:
C O W A SURVEYS AND BIBLIOGRAPHIES.
AREA 4: WESTERN MEDITERRANEAN. 1959-
19?? irreg., planned to become triennial. Council for
Old World Archaeology, Boston University, 232
Bay State Rd., Boston, MA 02215.

913 016   US   ISSN 0070-0797
COUNCIL FOR OLD WORLD ARCHAEOLOGY:
C O W A SURVEYS AND BIBLIOGRAPHIES.
AREA 7: EASTERN MEDITERRANEAN. 1957-
19?? irreg., planned to become triennial. Council for
Old World Archaeology, Boston University, 232
Bay State Rd., Boston, MA 02215.

913 016   US   ISSN 0070-0800
COUNCIL FOR OLD WORLD ARCHAEOLOGY:
C O W A SURVEYS AND BIBLIOGRAPHIES.
AREA 8: EUROPEAN RUSSIA. 1958-19?? irreg.,
planned to become triennial. Council for Old World
Archaeology, Boston University, 232 Bay State Rd.,
Boston, MA 02215.

913 016   US   ISSN 0070-0819
COUNCIL FOR OLD WORLD ARCHAEOLOGY:
C O W A SURVEYS AND BIBLIOGRAPHIES.
AREA 9: NORTHEAST AFRICA. 1959-19??
irreg., planned to become triennial. Council for Old
World Archaeology, Boston University, 232 Bay
State Rd., Boston, MA 02215.

913 016   US   ISSN 0070-0827
COUNCIL FOR OLD WORLD ARCHAEOLOGY:
C O W A SURVEYS AND BIBLIOGRAPHIES.
AREA 10. NORTHWEST AFRICA. 1957-19??
irreg., planned to become triennial. Council for Old
World Archaeology, Boston University, 232 Bay
State Rd., Boston, MA 02215.

913 016   US   ISSN 0070-0835
COUNCIL FOR OLD WORLD ARCHAEOLOGY:
C O W A SURVEYS AND BIBLIOGRAPHIES.
AREA 11. WEST AFRICA. 1958-19?? irreg.,
planned to become triennial. Council for Old World
Archaeology, Boston University, 232 Bay State Rd.,
Boston, MA 02215.

913 016   US   ISSN 0070-0843
COUNCIL FOR OLD WORLD ARCHAEOLOGY:
C O W A SURVEYS AND BIBLIOGRAPHIES.
AREA 12. EQUATORIAL AFRICA. 1959-19??
irreg., planned to become triennial. Council for Old
World Archaeology, Boston University, 232 Bay
State Rd., Boston, MA 02215.

913 016   US   ISSN 0070-0851
COUNCIL FOR OLD WORLD ARCHAEOLOGY:
C O W A SURVEYS AND BIBLIOGRAPHIES.
AREA 13. SOUTH AFRICA. 1959-19?? irreg.,
planned to become triennial. Council for Old World
Archaeology, Boston University, 232 Bay State Rd.,
Boston, MA 02215.

913 016   US   ISSN 0070-086X
COUNCIL FOR OLD WORLD ARCHAEOLOGY:
C O W A SURVEYS AND BIBLIOGRAPHIES.
AREA 14. EAST AFRICA. 1959-19?? irreg.,
planned to become triennial. Council for Old World
Archaeology, Boston University, 232 Bay State Rd.,
Boston, MA 02215.

913 016   US   ISSN 0070-0878
COUNCIL FOR OLD WORLD ARCHAEOLOGY:
C O W A SURVEYS AND BIBLIOGRAPHIES.
AREA 15. WESTERN ASIA. 1959-19?? irreg.,
planned to become triennial. Council for Old World
Archaeology, Boston University, 232 Bay State Rd.,
Boston, MA 02215.

913 016   US   ISSN 0070-0886
COUNCIL FOR OLD WORLD ARCHAEOLOGY:
C O W A SURVEYS AND BIBLIOGRAPHIES.
AREA 16. SOUTHERN ASIA. 1959-19?? irreg.,
planned to become triennial. Council for Old World
Archaeology, Boston University, 232 Bay State Rd.,
Boston, MA 02215.

913 016   US   ISSN 0070-0894
COUNCIL FOR OLD WORLD ARCHAEOLOGY:
C O W A SURVEYS AND BIBLIOGRAPHIES.
AREA 17. FAR EAST. 1959-19?? irreg., planned to
become triennial. Council for Old World
Archaeology, Boston University, 232 Bay State Rd.,
Boston, MA 02215.

913 016   US   ISSN 0070-0916
COUNCIL FOR OLD WORLD ARCHAEOLOGY:
C O W A SURVEYS AND BIBLIOGRAPHIES.
AREA 18. NORTHERN ASIA. 1957-19?? irreg.,
planned to become triennial. Council for Old World
Archaeology, Boston University, 232 Bay State Rd.,
Boston, MA 02215.

913 016   US   ISSN 0070-0924
COUNCIL FOR OLD WORLD ARCHAEOLOGY:
C O W A SURVEYS AND BIBLIOGRAPHIES.
AREA 19. SOUTHEAST ASIA. 1959-19?? irreg.,
planned to become triennial. Council for Old World
Archaeology, Boston University, 232 Bay State Rd.,
Boston, MA 02215.

913 016   US   ISSN 0070-0932
COUNCIL FOR OLD WORLD ARCHAEOLOGY:
C O W A SURVEYS AND BIBLIOGRAPHIES.
AREA 20. INDONESIA. 1957-19?? irreg., planned
to become triennial. Council for Old World
Archaeology, Boston University, 232 Bay State Rd.,
Boston, MA 02215.

913 016   US   ISSN 0070-0940
COUNCIL FOR OLD WORLD ARCHAEOLOGY:
C O W A SURVEYS AND BIBLIOGRAPHIES.
AREA 21. PACIFIC ISLANDS. 1958-19?? irreg.,
planned to become triennial. Council for Old World
Archaeology, Boston University, 232 Bay State Rd.,
Boston, MA 02215.

913 016   US   ISSN 0070-0959
COUNCIL FOR OLD WORLD ARCHAEOLOGY:
C O W A SURVEYS AND BIBLIOGRAPHIES.
AREA 22. AUSTRALIA. 1959-19?? irreg., planned
to become triennial. Council for Old World
Archaeology, Boston University, 232 Bay State Rd.,
Boston, MA 02215.

787   US   ISSN 0092-8887
CREATIVE GUITAR INTERNATIONAL. 1973-
1979 (Oct.). irreg. Mockingbird Press, Box 7,
Alpine, TX 79830.

548.1 548.8   US   ISSN 0070-167X
CRYSTAL STRUCTURES. 1963-1971 (vol. 6, pt. 2)
irreg., John Wiley & Sons, Inc.,
605 Third Ave., New York, NY 10016.

810   US
CULTURAL ACTIVIST. discontinued. irreg.
(processed) c/o Broms, 219 W. 81st St., New York,
NY 10024.

630   CY
CYPRUS. AGRICULTURAL RESEARCH
INSTITUTE. PROGRESS REPORT. 1966-1974
(no. 22) irreg. Agricultural Research Institute,
Nicosia, Cyprus.

616.845   SZ   ISSN 0070-2889
DATA PROCESSING IN MEDICINE/
DATENVERARBEITUNG IN DER MEDIZIN.
1968-197? irreg. (aprox. 1/yr.) (reprint service avail.
from ISI) S. Karger AG, Allschwilerstrasse 10, P.O.
Box, CH-4009 Basel, Switzerland.

268   US   ISSN 0070-3222
DEEMS LECTURESHIP. 1966-1970. irreg. New
York University Press, Washington Sq, New York,
NY 10003.

069.950   US
DESERT SPEAKS; the story of the Arizona-Sonora
Desert Museum. 1972-1979. irreg. Arizona-Sonora
Desert Museum, Inc., Rt. 9, Box 900, Tucson, AZ
85704.

576 GW ISSN 0084-9758
DEUTSCHE GESELLSCHAFT FUER HYGIENE UND MIKROBIOLOGIE. BERICHTE UEBER TAGUNGEN. 1906-19??; ceased after no. 35. biennial. Gustav Fischer Verlag, Wollgrasweg 49, Postfach 720193, 7000 Stuttgart 70, W. Germany (B.R.D.)

572 970.1 US ISSN 0095-2907
DICKSON MOUNDS MUSEUM ANTHROPOLOGICAL STUDIES. 1971-1980. irreg. Illinois State Museum, Springfield, IL 62706.

617.6 US ISSN 0085-0004
DIRECTORY OF REGISTERED DENTISTS AND REGISTERED DENTAL HYGIENISTS IN CONNECTICUT. 1961-19?? a. Department of Health Services, 79 Elm St., Hartford, CT 06115.

338.4 ZA
DIRECTORY OF ZAMBIAN INDUSTRY. discontinued. biennial. Zambia Industrial and Mining Corp. Ltd., Zimco Information and Publicity Unit, Box 30090, Lusaka, Zambia.

629.22 US ISSN 0090-8185
DIRT BIKE BUYER'S GUIDE. discontinued. Hi-Torque Publications, Inc., 16200 Ventura Boulevard, Encino, CA 91436.

780 070.5 AU
DOBLINGER'S NEWS LETTER. 1973-1976. a. Musikverlag Ludwig Doblinger, Dorotheergasse 10, A-1011 Vienna, Austria

781.98 AU ISSN 0070-6795
DOBLINGERS VERLAGSNACHRICHTEN. 1968-1978. a. Musikverlag Ludwig Doblinger, Postfach 882, Dorothergasse 10, A-1010 Vienna, Austria

665.5 BL
DOCUMENTO ABRIL. 1975-197? irreg. Editora Abril Ltda, Avda. Otaviano Alves de Lima 800, Caixa Postal 2372, Sao Paulo, Brazil.

020 FR ISSN 0070-6817
DOCUMENTOLOGIE. 1970-19?? irreg. Centrale des Revues Dunod Gauthier-Villars, B. P. 119, 93104 Montreuil Cedex, France.

330 FR ISSN 0070-6957
DOCUMENTS ET RECHERCHES SUR L'ECONOMIE DES PAYS BYZANTINS, ISLAMIQUES ET SLAVES ET LEURS RELATIONS COMMERCIALES AU MOYEN AGE. 1958-19?? irreg. (Ecole Pratique des Hautes Etudes, FR) Editions Mouton et Cie, 7 rue Dupuytren, 75005 Paris, France.

381 US ISSN 0364-586X
DOWNTOWN MALL ANNUAL & URBAN DESIGN REPORT. 1975-1978. a. Alexander Reports Corp., Downtown Research and Development Center, 270 Madison Ave., Suite 1505, New York, NY 10016.
Formerly (until 1977): Downtown Malls (ISSN 0098-7557)

301 US ISSN 0145-1715
DOWNTOWN PLANNING & DEVELOPMENT ANNUAL. 1977-1978. a. Alexander Reports Corp., Downtown Research & Development Center, 270 Madison Ave., Suite 1505, New York, NY 10016.

614 US
DRUG ABUSE COUNCIL. HANDBOOK. ceased Dec. 1980. irreg. Drug Abuse Council, Inc., 1828 L St. N.W., Washington, DC 20036.

614 US ISSN 0091-2662
DRUG ABUSE COUNCIL. PUBLIC POLICY. ceased Dec. 1980. 2-3/yr. Drug Abuse Council, Inc., 1828 L St. N.W., Washington, DC 20036.

614 US
DRUG ABUSE COUNCIL. SPECIAL STUDIES. ceased Dec. 1980. irreg. Drug Abuse Council, Inc., 1828 L St. N.W., Washington, DC 20036.

614.7 US
E I S ANNUAL REVIEW. (Environmental Impact Statement) published only once, 1978? a. Information Resources Press, 1700 N. Moore St., Ste. 700, Arlington, VA 22209.

070.5 US ISSN 0070-9107
EDITORIAL OFFICES IN THE WEST. 1969-197? biennial. Simon Public Relations, Inc., 11661 San Vicente Blvd., Los Angeles, CA 90049.

370 UN
EDUCATIONAL RESEARCH AND PRACTICE. 1971-197? irreg. Unesco Institute for Education - Unesco Institut fuer Paedagogik, Feldbrunnenstr. 70, 2000 Hamburg 13, W. Germany (B.R.D.)

621.3 US ISSN 0095-084X
ELECTRICAL INSTALLATION & REPAIR PROJECTS. discontinued. a. Davis Publications, Inc., 380 Lexington Ave., New York, NY 10017.
Formerly: Electrical Guide.

621.38 DK
ELEKTRONIK NYT BUYERS GUIDE. 1972-197? a. Thomson Communications (Scandinavia) A-S, Hestemoellestraede 6, DK-1464 Copenhagen K, Denmark.

510 FR ISSN 0070-9999
ELEMENTS DE MATHEMATIQUE. (Subseries of Actualites Scientifiques et Industrielles) ceased. irreg. Editions Hermann, 293 rue Lecourbe, 75015 Paris, France.

614.7 US
ENVIRONMENTAL LEADERS FORUM. PROCEEDINGS. 1973-197?; ceased. irreg. New York State College of Agriculture and Life Sciences, Cornell University, Mailing Room, Research Park, Ithaca, NY 14853.

332.6 NZ
EQUITY INVESTMENT. discontinued. a. Berl Publications Ltd., Box 10010, Wellington, New Zealand.

016 US
ETHNIC PRESS IN THE UNITED STATES; lists of foreign language, nationality and ethnic newspapers and periodicals in the U. S. 1924-1974. irreg. American Council for Nationalities Service, 20 W. 40th St., New York, NY 10018.

330 FR ISSN 0071-2043
ETUDES EUROPEENNES. 1963-19?? irreg. (Ecole Pratique des Hautes Etudes, Division des Aires Culturelles, FR) Editions Mouton et Cie, 7 rue Dupuytren, 75005 Paris, France.

341.24 US ISSN 0095-7607
EUROPEAN PARLIAMENT DIGEST. 1973-197? irreg. Rowman and Littlefield, 81 Adams Dr., Totowa, NJ 07512.

614 US
EUTHANASIA CONFERENCE. EXCERPTS FROM PAPERS AND DISCUSSIONS. 1968-1978: 10 yr. compilation, 1980. a. Concern for Dying, 250 W. 57th St., New York, NY 10019.

338 PE
EXPORTACIONES MINERAS DEL PERU. irreg. Banco Minero del Peru, Division de Planeamiento, Lima, Peru.

613.2 UN ISSN 0071-6979
F A O ATOMIC ENERGY SERIES. 1959-19?? irreg., 1966, no. 6. Food and Agriculture Organization of the United Nations, Distribution and Sales Section, Via delle Terme di Caracalla, 00100 Rome, Italy

641 UN ISSN 0425-5089
F A O NUTRITION MEETING FOR EUROPE. REPORT. (Subseries of Food and Agriculture Organization of the United Nations. F A O Nutrition Meetings Report Series) 1958-19?? Food and Agriculture Organization of the United Nations, Distribution and Sales Section, Via delle Terme di Caracalla, I-00100 Rome, Italy.

641 UN ISSN 0532-0305
F A O NUTRITION SPECIAL REPORTS. 1962-19?? Food and Agriculture Organization of the United Nations, Distribution and Sales Section, Via delle Terme di Caracalla, I-00100 Rome, Italy.

338.1 UN ISSN 0428-9625
F A O PAPERS ON DEMAND ANALYSIS. 1959-19?? Food and Agriculture Organization of the United Nations, Distribution and Sale Section, Via delle Terme di Caracalla, I-00100 Rome, Italy.

375 636 UN ISSN 0429-9388
F A O/W H O EXPERT PANEL ON VETERINARY EDUCATION. REPORT OF THE MEETING. 1962-19?? Food and Agriculture Organization of the United Nations, Distribution and Sales Section, Via delle Terme di Caragalla, I-00100 Rome, Italy.

010 NE ISSN 0074-5820
F I D ANNUAL REPORT. 1970-19?? a. International Federation for Documentation, Box 30115, 2500 GC The Hague, Netherlands.
Until 1972: International Federation for Documentation. Secretary General. Report.

029 NE
F I D/E T OCCASIONAL PAPERS. discontinued. irreg., no. 2, 1975. International Federation for Documentation, Committee on Education and Training, Hofweg 7, 2511 AA The Hague, Netherlands.

658 US ISSN 0163-5514
FEDERAL CONTROLS. 1978-1981. irreg. (looseleaf format) Bureau of National Affairs, Inc., 1231 25th St., N.W., Washington, DC 20037.

330.9 US
FEDERAL RESERVE BANK OF MINNEAPOLIS. ANNUAL STATISTICAL REVIEW. ceased. a. Federal Reserve Bank of Minneapolis, Research Department, 250 Marquette Ave., Minneapolis, MN 55480.

331.88 BE ISSN 0430-2419
FEDERATION INTERNATIONALE DES SYNDICATS CHRETIENS D'OUVRIERS AGRICOLES. TRAVAILLEUR DE LA TERRE. ceased. irreg. Federation Internationale des Syndicats Chretiens d'Ouvriers Agricoles, 27 rue de l'Association, Brussels, Belgium.

791 US ISSN 0085-0535
FILM AND TV FESTIVAL DIRECTORY. 1970-197?; discontinued. Backstage Publications, Inc., 165 West 46th St., New Yor, NY 10036.

789.91 621.389 NE
FONOWEEK; platen/tapes/apparatuur. 1975-1979? w. Uitgeversmaatschappij C. Misset B.V., Box 4, Doetinchem, Netherlands.

800 GW ISSN 0077-1953
FONTES ET COMMENTATIONES. 1960-19?? irreg. (Universitaet Muenster, Institut fuer Epigraphik) Aschendorffsche Verlagsbuchhandlung, Soester Str 13, 4400 Muenster, W. Germany (B.R.D.)

636 UN ISSN 0428-9552
FOOD AND AGRICULTURE ORGANIZATION OF THE UNITED NATIONS. ANIMAL HEALTH BRANCH. ANIMAL HEALTH MONOGRAPH. 1960-19?? Food and Agriculture Organization of the United Nations, Distribution and Sales Section, Via delle Terme di Caracalla, I-00100 Rome, Italy.

338.1 UN ISSN 0071-6952
FOOD AND AGRICULTURE ORGANIZATION OF THE UNITED NATIONS. COMMODITY REFERENCE SERIES. 1961-19?? irreg., 1970, vol. 28. Food and Agriculture Organization of the United Nations, Distribution and Sales Section, Via delle Terme di Caracalla, 00100 Rome, Italy

639.2 UN
FOOD AND AGRICULTURE ORGANIZATION OF THE UNITED NATIONS. FISHERY COMMITTEE FOR THE EASTERN CENTRAL ATLANTIC. REPORT OF THE SESSION. ceased. irreg. Food and Agriculture Organization of the United Nations, Distribution and Sales Section, Via delle Terme di Caracalla, I-00100 Rome, Italy.

338.1 UN ISSN 0532-0690
FOOD AND AGRICULTURE ORGANIZATION OF THE UNITED NATIONS. FORESTRY AND FOREST PRODUCTS DIVISION. WORLD FOREST PRODUCTS STATISTICS. 1955-19?? irreg. Food and Agriculture Organization of the United Nations, Distribution and Sales Section, Via delle Terme di Caracalla, I-00100 Rome, Italy.

634.9 UN ISSN 0428-9374
FOOD AND AGRICULTURE ORGANIZATION OF THE UNITED NATIONS. FORESTRY OCCASIONAL PAPER. 1955-19?? irreg. Food and Agriculture Organization of the United Nations, Distribution and Sales Section, Via delle Terme di Caracalla, I-00100 Rome, Italy.

630 UN ISSN 0428-9390
FOOD AND AGRICULTURE ORGANIZATION OF THE UNITED NATIONS. INDEX OF AGRICULTURAL INSTITUTIONS IN EUROPE. ceased. Food and Agriculture Organization of the United Nations, Distribution and Sales Section, Via delle Terme di Caracalla, I-00100 Rome, Italy.

636 UN ISSN 0532-0348
FOOD AND AGRICULTURE ORGANIZATION OF THE UNITED NATIONS. INTERAMERICAN MEETING ON ANIMAL PRODUCTION AND HEALTH. REPORT. (Subseries of Food and Agriculture Organization of the United Nations. Animal Production and Health Division. Meeting Report) ceased. Food and Agriculture Organization of the United Nations, Distribution and Sales Section, Via delle Terme di Caracalla, I-00100 Rome, Italy.

338.1 UN
FOOD AND AGRICULTURE ORGANIZATION OF THE UNITED NATIONS.REVIEW OF FAO FIELD PROGRAMMES. 1973-197? irreg. Food and Agriculture Organization of the United Nations, Distribution and Sales Section, Via delle Terme di Caracalla, 00100 Rome, Italy.

332.4 US ISSN 0363-5430
FOREIGN EXCHANGE RATES AND RESTRICTIONS. 1972-197? a. Ernst & Whinney, 1300 Union Commerce Bldg., Cleveland, OH 44115.

951.24 CH ISSN 0304-1204
FREE CHINA TODAY. 1963-1974 (vol.3) a. Epoch Publicity Agency, 8 Nanking East Rd., P.O. Box 1642, Taipei, Taiwan, Republic of China.
Formerly: Free China (ISSN 0071-9315)

361 UN
FREEDOM FROM HUNGER CAMPAIGN/ ACTION FOR DEVELOPMENT. 1965-19?? irreg. Food and Agriculture Organization of the United Nations, Distribution and Sales Section, Via delle Terme di Caracalla, 00100 Rome, Italy.
Formerly: Freedom from Hunger Campaign/Ideas and Action Bulletin (ISSN 0046-502X) & Freedom from Hunger Campaign/Campaign Development Bulletin.

910 GW ISSN 0071-9439
FREIBURGER GEOGRAPHISCHE ARBEITEN. 1961-1972?; suspended. irreg. (Deutsche Forschungsgemeinschaft) Hans Ferdinand Schulz Verlag, Friedrichring 13, 7800 Freiburg, W. Germany (B.R.D.)

574 NE ISSN 0071-965X
FRONTIERS OF BIOLOGY. 1967-1979 (vol. 48). irreg. Elsevier North-Holland Biomedical Press, P.O. Box 211, 1000 AE Amsterdam, Netherlands.

330 US ISSN 0362-6911
FRONTIERS OF ECONOMICS. discontinued. irreg. University Publications, Box 47, Blacksburg, VA 24060.

370 BL
FUNDACAO CARLOS CHAGAS. DEPARTAMENTO DE PESQUISAS EDUCACIONAIS. PROFISSOES. 1969-19?? irreg. Fundacao Carlos Chagas, Departamento de Pesquisas Educacionais, Av. Francisco Morato 1565, 05513 Sao Paulo, SP, Brazil.

370 BL
FUNDACAO CARLOS CHAGAS. DEPARTAMENTO DE PESQUISAS EDUCACIONAIS. SIMPOSIOS. 1970-197? irreg. Fundacao Carlos Chagas, Departamento de Pesquisas Educacionais, Av. Francisco Morato 1565, 05513 Sa Paulo,SP, Brazil.

310 GM
GAMBIA. CENTRAL STATISTICS DEPARTMENT. STATISTICAL WORKING PAPER. (Formerly issued by Central Statistics Division) discontinued. irreg. Central Statistics Department, Wellington St., Banjul, Gambia.

665.7 US ISSN 0065-8391
GAS UTILITY AND PIPELINE INDUSTRY PROJECTIONS. 1966-19??; discontinued. irreg. American Gas Association, Statistics Directorate, 1515 Wilson Blvd., Arlington, VA 22209.

616.3 SZ ISSN 0071-7843
GASTROENTEROLOGISCHE FORTBILDUNGSKURSE FUER DIE PRAXIS. 1969-197? irreg. (reprint service avail. from ISI) S. Karger AG, Allschwilerstrasse 10, P.O. Box, CH-4009 Basel, Switzerland.
Formerly: Fortbildungskurse fuer Praktische Gastroenterologie.

016 330 US
GEORGIA STATE UNIVERSITY. COLLEGE OF BUSINESS ADMINISTRATION. REPORT OF PUBLICATIONS AND RESEARCH. 1973-1978. a. (reprint service avail. from UMI and ISI) Georgia State University, College of Business Administration, Business Publishing Division, University Plaza, Atlanta, GA 30303.
Supersedes: Georgia State University. School of Business Administration. Report of Publications by the Faculty.

368 GW
GERMANY (FEDERAL REPUBLIC, 1949-). BUNDESVERSICHERUNGSAMT. TAETIGKEITSBERICHT. 1975-197? irreg. Bundesversicherungsamt, Reichpietschufer 72-76, 1000 Berlin 30, W. Germany (B.R.D.)

332.1 314 GW ISSN 0072-2014
GERMANY (FEDERAL REPUBLIC, 1949-) STATISTISCHES BUNDESAMT. FACHSERIE 9, REIHE 1: BODEN- UND KOMMUNALKREDITINSTITUTE. ceased 1979. a; supplements monthly numbers. W. Kohlhammer-Verlag GmbH, Abt. Veroeffentlichungen des Statistischen Bundesamtes, Philipp-Reis-Str. 3, Postfach 421120, 6500 Mainz 42, W. Germany (B.R.D.)

614 AT ISSN 0085-1124
GOOD HEALTH. 1932-1977(no. 140) irreg. Department of Public Health, 158 Rundle St., Adelaide, S.A. 5000, Australia.

353 US ISSN 0072-5145
GOVERNMENT CONTRACTS GUIDE. 1967-197? irreg. Commerce Clearing House, Inc, 4025 W. Peterson Ave, Chicago, IL 60646.

685.31 AT
GRAPHIC PICTORIAL SHOE AND LEATHER INDUSTRY; buyers guide for footwear, leather & allied industry. 1928-197? a. Lawrence Publishing Co. Pty. Ltd., Box 1813, Sydney, N.S.W. 2001, Australia.

331 UK ISSN 0072-5943
GREAT BRITAIN. DEPARTMENT OF EMPLOYMENT. TRAINING INFORMATION PAPERS. ceased. irreg. Department of Employment, 8 St. James's Square, London SW1Y 4JB, England.

554 UK ISSN 0366-4198
GREAT BRITAIN. INSTITUTE OF GEOLOGICAL SCIENCES. BULLETIN OF THE GEOLOGICAL SURVEY OF GREAT BRITAIN. 1939-1979(no. 70) irreg. Institute of Geological Sciences, Exhibition Rd., London SW7 2DE, England

622 551 UK
GREAT BRITAIN.INSTITUTE OF GEOLOGICAL SCIENCES. MINERAL MONOGRAPHS. 1952-197? irreg. Institute of Geological Sciences, Exhibition Rd., London SW7 2DE, England

300 UK
GREAT BRITAIN. SOCIAL SCIENCE RESEARCH COUNCIL. FELLOWSHIPS. 1969-197? irreg. Social Science Research Council, Postgraduate Awards Division, 1 Temple Ave., London EC4Y 0BD, England.

333.91 US ISSN 0533-196X
GREAT LAKES COMMISSION. REPORT TO THE STATES. ceased 1976. biennial. Great Lakes Commission, 2200 Bonisteel Blvd., Ann Arbor, MI 48109.

658 FR
GUIDE DE L'ORGANISATION DE L'INFORMATIQUE ET DE LA FORMATION. 1964-1975. a. Editions Olivier Lesourd, 252 rue du Faubourg Saint-Honore, 75008 Paris, France.
Former titles: Guide de l'Organisation et de la Modernisation des Industries et Collectives (ISSN 0066-3204); Guide de l'Organisation, des Techniques de Direction et de la Modernisation des Entreprises.

891.8 FR ISSN 0072-8071
GUIDE DU SLAVISTE. 1969-1973. irreg. Institut d'Etudes Slaves, 9 rue Michelet, F - 75006 Paris, France.

621.48 SZ ISSN 0072-8136
GUIDE INTERNATIONAL DES MACHINES, APPAREILS, OUTILS. 1932-197? a. Hugo Buchser S.A., 4 Tour de l'Ile, CH-1211 Geneva 11, Switzerland.

658.8 US ISSN 0072-8314
GUIDE TO CONSUMER MARKETS. (Subseries of: Conference Board. Report) 1960-1978. a. Conference Board, Inc., 845 Third Ave., New York, NY 10022.
Formerly: Graphic Guide to Consumer Markets (ISSN 0072-551X)

374 US ISSN 0363-0927
GUIDE TO EXTERNAL AND CONTINUING EDUCATION. ceased in 1978. a. Chronicle Guidance Publications, Inc., Moravia, NY 13118.

378.0025 US ISSN 0145-8035
GUIDE TO GRADUATE AND PROFESSIONAL STUDY. 1970-1979. a. Chronicle Guidance Publications, Inc., Moravia, NY 13118.

500 600 US ISSN 0072-8934
GUIDES TO INFORMATION SOURCES IN SCIENCE AND TECHNOLOGY. 1963-19?? irreg. John Wiley & Sons, Inc., 605 Third Ave, New York, NY 10016.

551.9 US ISSN 0072-9817
HANDBOOK OF GEOCHEMISTRY. 1969-1978(complete) irreg. Springer-Verlag, 175 Fifth Ave., New York, NY 10010

378.3 US
HANDBOOK ON U.S. STUDY FOR FOREIGN NATIONALS. 1955-197? irreg. Institute of International Education, 809 United Nations Plaza, New York, NY 10017.
Formerly: Handbook on International Study: for Foreign Nationals (ISSN 0440-193X); Supersedes in part: Handbook on International Study (ISSN 0072-9965)

530 US ISSN 0085-140X
HANDBUCH DER PHYSIK/ENCYCLOPEDIA OF PHYSICS. 1955 (series complete in 54 vols. irreg. (reprint service avail. from ISI) Springer Verlag, 175 Fifth Ave., New York, NY 10010

301.15 US ISSN 0085-1442
HARRIS SURVEY YEARBOOK OF PUBLIC OPINION; a compendium of current American attitudes. 1970-1973. irreg (approx. a.) Louis Harris and Associates, Inc., 630 Fifth Ave., New York, NY 10020.

368 US
HEALTH INSURANCE ASSOCIATION OF AMERICA. CONSUMER AND PROFESSIONAL RELATIONS DIVISION. EXTENT OF GROWTH--PRIVATE HEALTH INSURANCE COVERAGE IN THE UNITED STATES. 1945-19??; discontinued. a. Health Insurance Association of America, Consumer and Professional Relations Division, 919 Third Ave., New York, NY 10022.
Formerly: Extent of Voluntary Health Insurance in the United States.

910.2 UK ISSN 0073-2958
HOLIDAY BOOK. 1946-197? a. Purnell & Sons Ltd., Paulton House, Shepherdess Walk, London N. 1., England.

001.3 US ISSN 0073-3148
HOME UNIVERSITY LIBRARY. discontinued. irreg. Oxford University Press, 200 Madison Ave., New York, NY 10016

626.2　　　　US　　ISSN 0073-3482
HOT ROD YEARBOOK. 1962-19?? a. (also avail. in microform from UMI) Petersen Publishing Co., 8490 Sunset Blvd., Los Angeles, CA 90069.
　　Formerly: Hot Rod Magazine Yearbook.

621.3　　　　UK
I E E REVIEWS. (Special issue of I E E Proceedings) 1970-1979(Dec.). a. (also avail. in microfiche) Institution of Electrical Engineers, Box 26, Hitchin, Herts. SG5 1SA, England.

016.792　　　　US　　ISSN 0095-2087
I M P DIRECTORY. 1975-1979. irreg. International Mimes & Pantomimists, Rte. 3, The Valley Studio, Spring Green, WI 53588.

622 517　　　　US　　ISSN 0073-4462
IDAHO BUREAU OF MINES AND GEOLOGY. PAMPHLET. 1921-1977 (no. 167) irreg. Bureau of Mines and Geology, Department of Lands, Moscow, ID 83843.

629.2　　　　US　　ISSN 0073-5582
IMPORT CAR BUYER'S GUIDE. 1971-197? a. Petersen Publishing Co., 8490 Sunset Blvd., Los Angeles, CA 90069.

574.072 016　　　　US　　ISSN 0090-0753
INDEX OF TISSUE CULTURE; a guide to literature in the field. 1966-19?? a. Tissue Culture Association, Inc., One Bank St., Suite 210, Gaithersburg, MD 20760.
　　Formerly: Current Tissue Culture Literature (ISSN 0011-3948)

016.050　　　　US　　ISSN 0073-5949
INDEX TO LITTLE MAGAZINES. 1948-19?? biennial. Swallow Press, Inc., 811 W. Junior Terr., Chicago, IL 60613.

610　　　　US
INDIANA STATE MEDICAL ASSOCIATION. JOURNAL: ROSTER AND YEARBOOK ISSUE. 1908-19?? a. (also avail. in microfiche from UMI) Indiana State Medical Association, 3935 N. Meridan St., Indianapolis, IN 46208.

614.7　　　　UK　　ISSN 0306-8285
INDUSTRIAL POLLUTION CONTROL YEARBOOK. 1974-197? a. Fuel & Metallurgical Journals Ltd., Queensway House, 2 Queensway, Redhill, Surrey RH1 1QS, England.

323.4　　　　US
INEQUALITY IN EDUCATION. 1969-1978(Sep.). irreg. (also avail. in microform from UMI) Center for Law and Education, Inc., Gutman Library, 6 Appian Way, Cambridge, MA 02138.

600　　　　GW
INFORMATION HEUTE. ceased. irreg. Otto Maier Verlag, Marktstr. 22, 7980 Ravensburg, W. Germany (B.R.D.).

796.357　　　　US
INSIDERS BASEBALL COMPENDIUM. discontinued. a. Baseball-for-Fans Publications, 11860 Kiowa Ave., Box 49213, Los Angeles, CA 90049.

891.8　　　　FR　　ISSN 0078-9968
INSTITUT D'ETUDES SLAVES, PARIS. ANNUAIRE. 1964-1973. a. Institut d'Etudes Slaves, 9 rue Michelet, F-75006 Paris, France.

630 338.1　　　　CR
INSTITUTO INTERAMERICANO DE CIENCIAS AGRICOLA DE LA OEA. HEMISPHERIC AND HUMANISTIC PROJECTION: I I C A REPORT. 1972-1978. irreg. Instituto Interamericano de Ciencias Agricolas de la O E A, Secretariado, Apdo 55, Coronado, Prov. San Jose, Costa Rica.

530　　　　NE
INSTITUUT VOOR KERNPHYSISCH ONDERZOEK. PROGRESS REPORT. discontinued. irreg. a. Instituut voor Kernphysisch Onderzoek - Institute for Nuclear Physics Research, Box 4395, 1009 AJ Amsterdam, Netherlands.

500 620　　　　US
INTERCOLLEGE RESEARCH. 1968-1979 (Jun.) biennial. Pennsylvania State University, Vice President for Research and Graduate Studies, 207 Old Main Building, University Park, PA 16802.

020　　　　NZ
INTERFACE N.Z. suspended with no. 5, Nov. 1978. irreg. (processed) National Library of New Zealand, General Services Division, Private Bag, Wellington, New Zealand.

341 539 016　　　　UN　　ISSN 0538-4893
INTERNATIONAL ATOMIC ENERGY AGENCY. LAW LIBRARY. BOOKS AND ARTICLES IN THE I A E A LAW LIBRARY. LIST. 1968-19?? irreg. International Atomic Energy Agency - Agence Internationale de l'Energie Atomique, Kaertner Ring 11, Box 590, A-1011 Vienna, Austria

301.4　　　　UK　　ISSN 0074-3259
INTERNATIONAL CONFERENCE ON PLANNED PARENTHOOD. PROCEEDINGS. 1967/68-19?? irreg., 1967, 8th, Santiago. International Planned Parenthood Federation, 18-20, Lower Regent St., London SW1Y 4PW, England.

551.46　　　　US　　ISSN 0092-0002
INTERNATIONAL DECADE OF OCEAN EXPLORATION. PROGRESS REPORT. 1973-1981(July) a. (also avail. in microfiche) U.S. Environmental Data and Information Service, U.S. National Oceanic and Atmospheric Administration, Rockville, MD 20852.

029　　　　HU
INTERNATIONAL FEDERATION FOR DOCUMENTATION. COMMITTEE FOR DEVELOPING COUNTRIES. OCCASIONAL PUBLICATIONS. 1974-1975. irreg. Hungarian Central Technical Library and Documentation Centre - Technoinform, Reviczky u. 6, 1428 Budapest, P.O.B. 12, Hungary.

301.4 613　　　　UK　　ISSN 0074-7386
INTERNATIONAL PLANNED PARENTHOOD FEDERATION. PROCEEDINGS OF THE CONFERENCE OF THE EUROPE AND NEAR EAST REGION. discontinued. irreg. International Planned Parenthood Federation, 18-20 Lower Regent St., London SW1Y 4PW, England.

312　　　　UK　　ISSN 0074-7394
INTERNATIONAL PLANNED PARENTHOOD FEDERATION. WORKING PAPERS. (Nos. 3 & 4 out of Print) 1967-197? irreg; latest issue, no. 5. International Planned Parenthood Federation, 18-20 Lower Regent St., London SW1Y 4PW, England.

382　　　　US
INTERNATIONAL REFERENCE HANDBOOK OF MARKETING, MANAGEMENT AND ADVERTISING ORGANIZATIONS. 1972-1977? irreg., 5th edt., 1977. World Trade Academy Press, Inc., 50 E. 42nd St., New York, NY 10017.
　　Formerly: International Reference Handbook of Services, Organizations, Diplomatic Representation, Marketing and Advertising Channels (ISSN 0074-7653)

531 540　　　　US　　ISSN 0074-7785
INTERNATIONAL REVIEWS IN AEROSOL PHYSICS AND CHEMISTRY. 1971-197? (ceased with vol. 3) q. (also avail. in microform from MIM,UMI) Pergamon Press, Inc., Maxwell House, Fairview Park, Elmsford, NY 10523

540 660　　　　US　　ISSN 0074-9508
INTERNATIONAL UNION OF PURE AND APPLIED CHEMISTRY. COMPTES RENDUS OF IUPAC CONFERENCE. 1920-197? biennial since 1947; 1975, 25th, Jerusalem. Pergamon Press, Inc., Maxwell House, Fairview Park, Elmsford, NY 10523

658 382 338　　　　GW
DIE INTERNATIONALE UNTERNEHMUNG. discontinued. irreg. Verlag Anton Hain GmbH, Muehlgasse 3, Postfach 180, 6554 Meisenheim, W. Germany (B.R.D.).

378.1　　　　US　　ISSN 0075-0174
INVENTORY OF PROGRAMS IN MARYLAND'S PRIVATE AND PUBLIC UNIVERSITIES AND COLLEGES. discontinued. a. Council for Higher Education, 2100 Guilford Ave., Baltimore, MD 21218.

630 636.089　　　　CL　　ISSN 0539-239X
INVESTIGACION Y PROGRESO AGRICOLA. 1967-1977(vol. 9) irreg. Instituto de Investigaciones Agropecuarias, Casilla 5427, Santiago, Chile.

368　　　　IT　　ISSN 0075-1537
ISTITUTO NAZIONALE PER L'ASSICURAZIONE CONTRO LE MALATTIE, ROME. BILANCIO CONSUNTIVO. ceased in Jan. 1980. a. Istituto Nazionale per l'Assicurazione Contro le Malattie, Via C. Colombo 210, Rome, Italy.

591　　　　SA　　ISSN 0075-207X
J. L. B. SMITH INSTITUTE OF ICHTHYOLOGY. OCCASIONAL PAPER. (Continues numbering of publication issued under former name of body, Dept. of Ichthyology, Rhodes University) 1964-197?; suspended. irreg. Rhodes University, J. L. B. Smith Institute of Ichthyology, Grahamstown 6140, South Africa.

781.57 016　　　　US
JAZZ PUBLICITY II; newly revised and expanded bibliography of names and addresses of hundreds of international jazz critics and magazines. 1970-1974. irreg. (back issues avail.) Reese Markewich, Ed. & Pub., Bacon Hill, Pleasantville, NY 10570.

338.9 301　　　　CN　　ISSN 0541-623X
KEITH CALLARD LECTURE SERIES. 1965-197? irreg. (McGill University, Centre for Developing - Area Studies) McGill-Queen's University Press, 1020 Pine Ave. W., Montreal, Que. H3A 1A2, Canada.

547　　　　US　　ISSN 0075-6067
KINETICS AND MECHANISMS OF POLYMERIZATION. 1967-1972. irreg., 1972, vol. 3. Marcel Dekker, Inc., 270 Madison Ave., New York, NY 10016.

301　　　　GW
KOELNER BEITRAEGE ZUR SOZIALEN FORSCHUNG UND ANGEWANDTEN SOZIOLOGIE. 1966-197? irreg. Verlag Anton Hain GmbH, Muehlgasse 3, Postfach 180, 6554 Meisenheim, W. Germany (B.R.D.)

540　　　　NE
KONINKLIJKE NEDERLANDSE CHEMISCHE VERENIGING. CHEMISCH JAARBOEK. 1899-197? a. Koninklijke Nederlandse Chemische Vereniging, Burnierstraat 1, The Hague, Netherlands.

616.9　　　　GE　　ISSN 0067-5113
KREBSFORSCHUNG. BEITRAEGE. 1953-197? irreg., vol. 14, 1974. Verlag Theodor Steinkopff, Loschwitzer Str. 32, 8053 Dresden, E. Germany (D.D.R.)

301　　　　GW
KULTURELLER WANDEL. 1974-197? irreg. Verlag Anton Hain GmbH, Muehlgasse 3, Postfach 180, 6554 Meisenehim, W. Germany (B.R.D.)

025　　　　US　　ISSN 0065-9088
L T P PUBLICATIONS. ceased 1975 (no. 19) irreg., latest, no. 19, 1975. American Library Association, Library Technology Program, 50 E. Huron St., Chicago, IL 60611.

347.599　　　　PH
LAW PRACTICE FOR THE SENIOR LAWYER. (Subseries of Law Institute Series) 1968-1971. irreg. University of the Philippines, Law Center, Diliman, Quezon City, Philippines.

336　　　　FR　　ISSN 0075-8906
LA LETTRE. 1970-197? irreg. Syndicat du Personnel d'Encadrement de l'Edition et de la Librairie, 64 rue Taitbout, 75009 Paris, France.

020　　　　SA　　ISSN 0024-2101
LIBRA. 1969. a. since 1972. University of Port Elizabeth, Library, Private Bag X6058, Port Elizabeth 6000, South Africa.

026　　　　UK　　ISSN 0075-9058
LIBRARY ASSOCIATION. REFERENCE, SPECIAL AND INFORMATION SECTION. NORTH WESTERN GROUP. OCCASIONAL PAPERS. 1958-19?? irreg. Library Association, North Western Group, London, Ridgmount Street, London, W.C.1, England.

020　　　　UK
LIBRARY ASSOCIATION. STUDENTS HANDBOOK. ceased. a. Library Association, 7 Ridgmount St., London WC1E 7AE, England.

410 AT
LINGUISTIC COMMUNICATIONS. 1970-1976. irreg. Monash University, Clayton, Vic. 3168, Australia.

595.7 FR
LISTE D'IDENTIFICATION DES ENTOMOPHAGES. 1956-19??(vol.5) irreg. (International Organization for Biological Control) Librairie le Francois, 91 Bd. Saint-Germain, Paris (6e), France.

900 FR ISSN 0076-0129
LIVRE ET SOCIETES. 1958-19?? irreg. (Ecole Pratique des Hautes Etudes, Division des Aires Culturelles, FR) Editions Mouton et Cie, 7 rue Dupuytren, 75005 Paris, France.

338.9 CN ISSN 0076-1915
MCGILL UNIVERSITY, MONTREAL. CENTRE FOR DEVELOPING-AREA STUDIES. REPRINT SERIES. discontinued in 1980. irreg. McGill University, Centre for Developing-Area Studies, 815 Sherbrooke St. W., Montreal, Que H3A 2K6, Canada.

100 US
MACMILLAN NEW STUDIES IN ETHICS SERIES. discontinued. irreg. Saint Martins Press, 175 Fifth Avenue, New York, NY 10010.

330 FR ISSN 0076-4205
MANUELS PRATIQUES D'ECONOMIE. 1970-197? irreg. Centrale des Revues, Dunod, B. P. 119, 93104 Montreuil Cedex, France.

301.2 SZ
MARXIST ANTHROPOLOGY. discontinued. irreg. Elsevier Sequoia S.A., Box 851, 1001 Lausanne 1, Switzerland.

020 US ISSN 0076-4728
MARY C. RICHARDSON LECTURE. (Cumulative Volumes Included in the Geneseo Studies in Library Science Series) 1958-19?? a. State University of New York, College at Geneseo, School of Library and Information Science, Geneseo, NY 14454.

378.1 US ISSN 0361-140X
MARYLAND. COUNCIL FOR HIGHER EDUCATION. ANNUAL REPORT AND RECOMMENDATIONS. 1968-197? (discontinued). irreg. Council for Higher Education, 2100 Guilford Ave., Baltimore, MD 21218.
Formerly: Maryland. Council for Higher Education. Annual Report (ISSN 0076-4736)

620.11 GW
MATERIALKUNDLICH-TECHNISCHE REIHE. 1976-197? irreg. Gebrueder Borntraeger Verlagsbuchhandlung, Johannesstr. 3A, 7000 Stuttgart 1, W. Germany (B. R. D.).

547 540 US ISSN 0076-5791
MECHANISMS OF MOLECULAR MIGRATIONS. 1968-197? irreg. John Wiley & Sons, Inc., 605 Third Ave, New York, NY 10016.

250 180 US
MEDIEVAL AND RENAISSANCE STUDIES. 1968-1974 (no.7) irreg. St. John's University, Hill Monastic Manuscript Library, Collegeville, MN 56321.

551 US ISSN 0076-6836
METHODS AND TECHNIQUES IN GEOPHYSICS. 1960-19?? irreg. John Wiley & Sons, Inc., 605 Third Ave, New York, NY 10016.

370.196 US ISSN 0047-7141
MICHIGAN STATE UNIVERSITY. CENTER FOR INTERNATIONAL PROGRAMS. INTERNATIONAL REPORT. 1971-197?; discontinued. a. Michigan State University, Center for International Programs, East Lansing, MI 48823.

370 US ISSN 0093-870X
MINNESOTA. DEPARTMENT OF EDUCATION. BIENNIAL REPORT. discontinued. biennial. Department of Education, St. Paul, MN 55101.

557 US ISSN 0076-9169
MINNESOTA. GEOLOGICAL SURVEY. BULLETIN. 1889-1968 (no. 45) irreg. Geological Survey, University of Minnesota, 1633 Eustis St., St. Paul, MN 55108.

614.8 US ISSN 0093-2558
MINNESOTA ALCOHOL PROGRAMS FOR HIGHWAY SAFETY; an overview with statistics. 1972-1978. irreg. Department of Public Safety, 207 Transportation Bldg., St. Paul, MN 55155.

792 US
MISE-EN-SCENE. 1976; published only once. irreg. c/o Louis Gianetti, 4080 Crawford Hall, Case Western Reserve University, Cleveland, OH 44106.

670 US
MISSISSIPPI MANUFACTURING ATLAS. discontinued. irreg. Mississippi Research and Development Center, 3825 Ridgewood Rd., Jackson, MS 39205.

616.97 US
MODERN CONCEPTS OF ALLERGY. 1969-1977. 3-4/yr. (back issues avail) Warren H. Green, 8356 Olive Blvd., St. Louis, MO 63132.

616.1 US
MODERN CONCEPTS OF CARDIOLOGY. 1968-1977. 3-4/yr. (back issues avail) Warren H. Green, 8356 Olive Blvd., St. Louis, MO 63132.

616.5 US
MODERN CONCEPTS OF DERMATOLOGY. 1972-1977. 3-4/yr. (back issues avail) Warren H. Green, 8356 Olive Blvd., St. Louis, MO 63132.

610 US
MODERN CONCEPTS OF EDUCATION. 1968-1977. 3-4/yr. (back issues avail) Warren H. Green, 8356 Olive Blvd., St. Louis, MO 63132.

613.62 US
MODERN CONCEPTS OF INDUSTRIAL MEDICINE. 1968-1977. 3-4/yr. (back issues avail) Warren H. Green, 8356 Olive Blvd., St. Louis, MO 63132.

610 US ISSN 0544-6511
MODERN CONCEPTS OF MEDICAL VIROLOGY, ONCOLOGY AND CYTOLOGY. 1969-1977. irreg. Warren H. Green, 8356 Olive Blvd., St. Louis, MO 63132.

616.8 US
MODERN CONCEPTS OF NEUROLOGY. 1967-1977. 3-4/yr. (back issues avail) Warren H. Green, 8356 Olive Blvd., St. Louis, MO 63132.

617.3 US
MODERN CONCEPTS OF ORTHOPEDIC SURGERY. 1967-1977. 3-4/yr. (back issues avail) Warren H. Green, 8356 Olive Blvd., St. Louis, MO 63132.

616.07 US
MODERN CONCEPTS OF PATHOLOGY. 1968-1977. 3-4/yr. (back issues avail) Warren H. Green, 8356 Olive Blvd., St. Louis, MO 63132.

610 US
MODERN CONCEPTS OF PHILOSOPHY. 1967-1977. 3-4/yr. (back issues avail) Warren H. Green, 8356 Olive Blvd., St. Louis, MO 63132.

616.2 US
MODERN CONCEPTS OF PULMONARY DISEASE. 1968-1977. 3-4/yr. (back issues avail) Warren H. Green, 8356 Olive Blvd., St. Louis, MO 63132.

615.842 US
MODERN CONCEPTS OF RADIOLOGY, NUCLEAR MEDICINE AND ULTRASOUND. 1967-1977. 3-4/yr. (back issues avail) Warren H. Green, 8356 Olive Blvd., St. Louis, MO 63132.

617 US
MODERN CONCEPTS OF SURGERY. 1971-1977. 3-4/yr. (back issues avail) Warren H. Green, 8356 Olive Blvd., St. Louis, MO 63132.

100 US ISSN 0085-3542
MONOGRAPHS IN MODERN CONCEPTS OF PHILOSOPHY. 1970-1977. irreg. Warren H. Green, 8356 Olive Blvd., St. Louis, MO 63132.

157.6 615.1 SZ ISSN 0301-3057
MONOGRAPHS ON DRUGS. discontinued. irreg. (reprint service avail. from ISI) S. Karger AG, Allschwilerstrasse 10, P.O. Box, CH-4009 Basel, Switzerland.

379.1 US ISSN 0090-6743
MONTANA. DEPARTMENT OF PUBLIC INSTRUCTION. DESCRIPTIVE REPORT OF PROGRAM ACTIVITIES FOR VOCATIONAL EDUCATION. (Report Year Ends June 30) discontinued. a. Department of Public Instruction, Helena, MO 59601.

333.9 US
MONTANA. WATER RESOURCES DIVISION PROGRESS REPORT OF THE MONTANA STATE WATER PLAN. discontinued. biennial. Water Resources Division, Sam W. Mitchell Bldg., Helena, MT 59601.

581 US ISSN 0027-1187
MORRIS ARBORETUM BULLETIN. 1935-1975 (vol. 26) a. (also avail. in microform from UMI) Morris Arboretum, Univ. of Pennsylvania, 9414 Meadowbrook Ave., Philadelphia, PA 19118.

796.7 US ISSN 0091-8822
MOTOR SPORT YEARBOOK. discontinued 1974. a. Collier Books, 866 Third Avenue, New York, NY 10022.

500 600 FR ISSN 0077-1775
MOYENS DE LA RECHERCHE SCIENTIFIQUE ET TECHNIQUE EN HAUTE-NORMANDIE. 1969-19?? a. Chambre Regionale de Commerce et d'Industrie de Haute-Normandie, Palais des Consuls, Quai de la Bourse, Rouen, France.

783 CN ISSN 0384-5133
MUSIQUE LITURGIQUE. ceased. irreg. Abbaye Benedictine de Mont-Laurier, Mont Laurier, Que., Canada.

309.2 NO
N I B R OCCASIONAL PAPER. ceased Dec. 1979. irreg. Norsk Institutt for By- og Regionforskning - Norwegian Institute of Urban and Regional Research, Nycoveien 1, Box 15 Grefsen, Oslo 4, Norway.

534 AT ISSN 0311-8983
NATIONAL ACOUSTIC LABORATORIES, SYDNEY. ANNUAL REPORT. 1962/62-1976/77 (temporarily suspended) a. National Acoustic Laboratories, 5 Hickson Rd., Millers Point, N.S.W., Australia.
Formerly: Commonwealth Acoustic Laboratories, Sydney. Annual Report (ISSN 0069-6870)

668.4 US
NATIONAL CELLULAR PLASTICS CONFERENCE. PROCEEDINGS. ceased in 1976. irreg. 17th, 1974, Washington DC. Technomic Publishing Co., Inc., 265 Post Rd. W., Westport, CT 06880.

301.4 US ISSN 0077-4162
NATIONAL COUNCIL ON FAMILY RELATIONS. ANNUAL MEETING PROCEEDINGS. 1966-197? a. (processed) National Council on Family Relations, 1219 University Ave., S.E., Minneapolis, MN 55414.

029.5 US ISSN 0077-524X
NATIONAL OBSERVER INDEX. 1969-197? a. (also avail. in microfilm) Dow Jones & Co., Inc., P.O. Box 300, Princeton, NJ 08540.

330 910.03 US
NATIONAL SYMPOSIUM ON THE STATE OF THE BLACK ECONOMY. SELECTED PROCEEDINGS. ceased in 1979. irreg. University of Michigan, Graduate School of Business Administration, Division of Research, Ann Arbor, MI 48109.

665.7 UK
NATURAL GAS MANUAL. 1972-197? triennial. Scientific Surveys Ltd., 4 Burkes Parade, Beaconsfield, Bucks, England.

505 US ISSN 0085-3860
NATURE/SCIENCE ANNUAL. 1970-1978. a. Time-Life Books, Inc. (Subsidiary of: Time, Inc.) 777 Duke Street, Alexandria, VA 22314.

500.9 AU ISSN 0083-6141
NATURHISTORISCHES MUSEUM IN WIEN. FLUGBLATT. 1957-19?? irreg. Naturhistorisches Museum in Wien, Burgring 7, A-1014 Vienna, Austria.

363.2   US   ISSN 0091-9195
NEBRASKA. COMMISSION ON LAW
ENFORCEMENT AND CRIMINAL JUSTICE.
CRIMINAL JUSTICE ACTION PLAN.
discontinued. irreg. Commission on Law
Enforcement and Criminal Justice, Box 94946,
Lincoln, NE 68509.

364   US   ISSN 0091-9128
NEBRASKA. COMMISSION ON LAW
ENFORCEMENT AND CRIMINAL JUSTICE.
CRIMINAL JUSTICE COMPREHENSIVE PLAN.
1969-197?; discontinued. irreg. Commission on Law
Enforcement and Criminal Justice, Box 94946,
Lincoln, NE 68509.

016   NE
NEDERLANDS BIBLIOTHEEK EN LEKTUUR
CENTRUM. INDEX. 1977-19?? 10/yr. De
Horstink, Box 400, 3800 AK Amersfoort,
Netherlands.

370   AT   ISSN 0077-8230
NEW ENGLAND PAPERS ON EDUCATION.
1966-197? irreg. University of New England,
Faculty of Education, Armidale, N.S.W. 2351,
Australia.

331.7   US
NEW MEXICO. EMPLOYMENT SERVICES
DEPARTMENT. ANNUAL RURAL
MANPOWER SERVICE REPORT. ceased. a.
Employment Services Department, 401 Broadway
N.E., P.O. Box 1928, Albuquerque, NM 87103.
    Formerly: New Mexico. Employment Security
Commission. Annual Rural Manpower Service
Report (ISSN 0077-8559)

378   AT   ISSN 0310-0103
NEW SOUTH WALES. HIGHER EDUCATION
BOARD. HIGHER EDUCATION HANDBOOK.
1973-1980. a. Higher Education Board, 13th Floor,
189 Kent St., Sydney, NSW 2000, Australia.

639   AT   ISSN 0077-8788
NEW SOUTH WALES. STATE FISHERIES.
RESEARCH BULLETIN. 1938-1976(no. 14) irreg.
State Fisheries, Chief Secretary's Dept., Sydney,
N.S.W., Australia.

010   US
NEW YORK INDEX. ceased. irreg. University
Microfilms International, Indexing Services, 300 N.
Zeeb Rd., Ann Arbor, MI 48106.

338 319   NZ   ISSN 0077-9865
NEW ZEALAND. DEPARTMENT OF
STATISTICS. INDUSTRIAL PRODUCTION.
ceased in 1973/74. a. Department of Statistics,
Private Bag, Wellington, New Zealand

639   NZ   ISSN 0078-0111
NEW ZEALAND. MARINE DEPARTMENT.
ANNUAL REPORT ON FISHERIES. 1928-1975.
a. Marine Department, P.O. Box 10142, Wellington,
New Zealand.

330 319   NZ
NEW ZEALAND ECONOMIC STATISTICS. ceased
in 1977. irreg. Bank of New Zealand, P. O. Box
2392, Wellington, New Zealand.

655 658   US
NEWSPAPER REQUIREMENTS. 1950-19?? irreg.,
1973, 19th ed. (Electrographic Corp.) Reilly-Lake
Shore Graphics, 812 W. Van Buren St., Chicago, IL
60607.
    Formerly (until 1975): Reilly-Lake Shore
Graphics. R O P Color Requirements Report (ISSN
0080-0783)

367   NE   ISSN 0028-9582
NEWSSEEKER. 1960-1979. a. (processed) World
Amateur Press Association, Box 7, 1170 AA
Badhoevedorp, Netherlands.

536.56   NE
NORTH-HOLLAND SERIES IN LOW
TEMPERATURE PHYSICS. 1968-19?? irreg., vol.
3, 1974. North-Holland Publishing Co., Box 211,
1000 AE Amsterdam, Netherlands.

639   NO   ISSN 0078-1843
NORWAY. FISKERIDIREKTORATET. SKRIFTER.
SERIE FISKERI. 1942-1971 (vol. 5, no. 3) irreg.
Fiskeridirektoratet - Directorate of Fisheries, Box
1870-72. N-5011 Bergen-Nordnes, Norway.

614 616   CN   ISSN 0078-2319
NOVA SCOTIA. DEPARTMENT OF
BACTERIOLOGY. ANNUAL REPORT. ceased. a.
Department of Public Health, Halifax, N.S., Canada.

614 616.07   CN   ISSN 0078-2351
NOVA SCOTIA. DEPARTMENT OF
PATHOLOGY. ANNUAL REPORT. ceased. a.
Department of Public Health, Department of
Pathology, Halifax, N.S., Canada.

600   CN   ISSN 0078-2483
NOVA SCOTIA RESEARCH FOUNDATION.
BULLETIN. 1963-1972. irreg. Nova Scotia
Research Foundation, Box 790, Dartmouth, N.S.
B2Y 3Z7, Canada.

610.73   US   ISSN 0078-2831
NURSING EDUCATION MONOGRAPHS. 1962-
19?? irreg. Teachers College Press, 1234 Amsterdam
Ave., New York, NY 10027.

331.88   GH
O A T U U INFORMATION TIPS. 1976-197? (no
longer in print) irreg. Organization of African Trade
Union Unity, Box M 386, Accra, Ghana.

340   US   ISSN 0078-3161
OCEANA DOCKET CLASSICS. 1957-1966. irreg.
Oceana Publications Inc., Dobbs Ferry, NY 10522.

663   FR   ISSN 0078-3412
OENOLOGIE PRATIQUE. 1970-197? irreg. Centrale
des Revues, B. P. 119, 93104 Montreuil Cedex,
France.

796.323   US
OFFICIAL N B A AND COLLEGE BASKETBALL
SCHEDULES. discontinued. a. Sporting News
Publishing Co., Box 56, St. Louis, MO 63166.

686.2   UK   ISSN 0308-4485
OFFSET DATA INDEX. 1971-197? a. Benn
Publications Ltd., 25 New Street Square, London
EC4A 3JA, England.

550   UK   ISSN 0078-3692
OFFSHORE EUROPE. 1968-197? biennial. Scientific
Surveys Ltd., 4 Burkes Parade, Beaconsfield, Bucks
HP9 1NS, England.

658   US   ISSN 0078-4087
OHIO STATE UNIVERSITY. COLLEGE OF
ADMINISTRATIVE SCIENCE. MONOGRAPH.
1967-19?? (temporarily suspended) irreg. Ohio State
University, College of Administrative Science,
Hagerty Hall, 1775 College Rd., Columbus, OH
43210.

649   US
ONE PARENT FAMILY; a magazine for single
parents. 1976 (only 1 vol. published) irreg. Single
Parent Resource Center, 3896 24th St., San
Francisco, CA 94114.

658   NE
ORGANISATIONS, PEOPLE, SOCIETY/O P S.
1967-197? irreg. Van Gorcum, Box 43, Assen,
Netherlands.
    Formerly: Technology and Democratic Society
(ISSN 0082-2604)

808.8   US
OSAWATOMIE. discontinued 197? irreg. John Brown
Book Club, Box 14422, San Francisco, CA 94114.

797.1   US   ISSN 0094-8101
OUTBOARD BOATING HANDBOOK. ceased. a.
Times Mirror Magazines, Inc., 380 Madison Ave.,
New York, NY 10017.

312   US   ISSN 0146-7646
P R B REPORT. 1966-1978 (Nov.) irreg. Population
Reference Bureau, Inc., 1337 Conn. Ave., N.W.,
Washington, DC 20036.
    Supersedes: P R B Selection (ISSN 0085-5014) &
Population Profile (ISSN 0085-5006)

370   US
P R E P. REPORTS. (Putting Research into
Educational Practice) ceased with no. 40, 1973.
irreg. (looseleaf format) U.S. National Institute of
Education, 1200 19th St. N.W., Washington, DC
20208.

327   US
PACEM IN TERRIS. 1965-19?? irreg. Center for the
Study of Democratic Institutions, 2056 Eucalyptus
Hill Rd., Santa Barbara, CA 93108.

300   US   ISSN 0553-0407
PAN AMERICAN UNION. DEPARTMENT OF
SOCIAL AFFAIRS. STUDIES AND
MONOGRAPHS. 1961-1970. irreg. Organization of
American States, Department of Publications,
Washington, DC 20006.

331   PP   ISSN 0085-4719
PAPUA NEW GUINEA. DEPARTMENT OF
LABOUR. INDUSTRIAL REVIEW. 1963-1972.
irreg. Department of Labour, Konedobu, Papua New
Guinea.

370   SW
PEDAGOGISKA MONOGRAFIER UMEAA. 1970-
1978 (no. 20) irreg. Umeaa Universitet, Pedagogiska
Institutionen, S-901 87 Umeaa, Sweden.

618.9   US   ISSN 0097-5257
PEDIATRIC NEPHROLOGY. 1974-197? irreg.
Thieme-Stratton, Inc., 381 Park Ave. South, New
York, NY 10016.

800   US   ISSN 0553-4917
PENGUIN MODERN POETS. 1962-19?? irreg.
Penguin Books, Inc., 625 Madison Ave., New York,
NY 10022.

630   US
PENNSYLVANIA STATE UNIVERSITY.
RESEARCH IN THE COLLEGE OF
AGRICULTURE. 1969-1979 (Oct.) biennial.
Pennsylvania State University, Vice President for
Research and Graduate Studies, 207 Old Main
Building, University Park, PA 16802.

550   US
PENNSYLVANIA STATE UNIVERSITY.
RESEARCH IN THE COLLEGE OF EARTH
AND MINERAL SCIENCES. 1967-1977 (Mar.)
biennial. Pennsylvania State University, Vice
President for Research and Graduate Studies, 207
Old Main Building, University Park, PA 16802.

620   US
PENNSYLVANIA STATE UNIVERSITY.
RESEARCH IN THE COLLEGE OF
ENGINEERING. 1969-1979 (Apr.) biennial.
Pennsylvania State University, Vice President for
Research and Graduate Studies, 207 Old Main
Building, University Park, PA 16802.

613   US
PENNSYLVANIA STATE UNIVERSITY.
RESEARCH IN THE COLLEGE OF HEALTH,
PHYSICAL EDUCATION, AND RECREATION.
1968-1976 (Feb.) biennial. Pennsylvania State
University, Vice President for Research and
Graduate Studies, 207 Old Main Bldg., University
Park, PA 16802.
    Supersedes(1974-1978): Pennsylvania State
University. Research in the College of Science.

612   US
PENNSYLVANIA STATE UNIVERSITY.
RESEARCH IN THE COLLEGE OF HUMAN
DEVELOPMENT. 1968-1977 (Aug.) biennial.
Pennsylvania State University, Vice President for
Research and Graduate Studies, 207 Old Main
Bldg., University Park, PA 16802.

610   US
PENNSYLVANIA STATE UNIVERSITY.
RESEARCH IN THE COLLEGE OF MEDICINE.
1967-1976 (Jun.) biennial. Pennsylvania State
University, Vice President for Research and
Graduate Studies, 207 Old Main Building,
University Park, PA 16802.

001.3   US
PENNSYLVANIA STATE UNIVERSITY.
RESEARCH IN THE COLLEGE OF THE
LIBERAL ARTS. 1970-1978 (Jan.) biennial.
Pennsylvania State University, Vice President for
Research and Graduate Studies, 207 Old Main
Building, University Park, PA 16802.

370   BL
PESQUISAS EDUCACIONAIS. 1969-19?? irreg.
Fundacao Carlos Chagas, Departamento de
Pesquisas Educacionais, Biblioteca, Av. Francisco
Morato 1565, 05513 Sao Paulo SP, Brazil.

629.222   US
PETERSEN'S MINI-CARS. 1978-197? a. Petersen Publishing Co., 6725 Sunset Blvd., Los Angeles, CA 90028.

052   UK   ISSN 0031-8337
PHOENIX; a poetry magazine. 1967-1975 (no. 13) irreg. (back issues avail) (North West Arts Association) Harry Chambers, Ed. & Pub., Treovis Farm Cottage, Upton Cross, Liskeard, Cornwall PL14 5BQ, England.

617.3   US
PODIATRIC MEDICINE AND SURGERY; a monograph series. 1973-1979(vol. 10) irreg. Futura Publishing Co, 295 Main Street, Box 333, Mount Kisco, NY 10549.

811   US   ISSN 0032-2199
POETRY VENTURE. (Supplements) 1968-1974 (vol. 6, no. 2) s-a; delayed, 1974 publ. 1977. (also avail. in microfiche) Valkyrie Press, Inc., 2135 First Ave. S., St. Petersburg, FL 33712.

371.2   US
POLICY ANALYSIS AND EDUCATION SERIES. discontinued. irreg. Teachers College Press, Teachers College, Columbia University, 1234 Amsterdam Ave., New York, NY 10027.

917.406   323.4   FR
POLSKA W EUROPIE; Pologne en Europe. Discontinued. irreg. (tabloid format) Union des Federalistes Polonais, 20 rue Legendre, 75017 Paris, France.

270   US   ISSN 0079-3833
POPES THROUGH HISTORY. 1961-1968(no. 3) irreg., 1968, vol. 3. Paulist Press, 545 Island Rd., Ramsey, NJ 07446.

016   301.3   US   ISSN 0091-2263
POPULATION AND THE POPULATION EXPLOSION: A BIBLIOGRAPHY. 1970-1976 (pub. 1979). a. Whitston Publishing Co., Inc., Box 958, Troy, NY 12181.

615   610   US   ISSN 0094-9264
PRINCIPLES AND TECHNIQUES OF HUMAN RESEARCH AND THERAPEUTICS. 1974-1977(vol. 15) irreg. Futura Publishing Co., 295 Main St., Box 333, Mount Kisco, NY 10549.

655   US   ISSN 0079-533X
PRINTING MAGAZINE PURCHASING GUIDE. 1938-19?? a. Walden-Mott Corporation, 466 Kinderkamack Rd., Oradell, NJ 07649.

700   US
PRODUCT DIRECTORY; a guide to art materials and equipment. 1966-197?; discontinued. a. American Artist Reprints, (Subsidiary of: Billboard Publications, Inc.) 1515 Broadway, New York, NY 10036.
    Formerly: American Artist Product Directory.

616.8   614   US
PROGRESS IN COMMUNITY MENTAL HEALTH. ceased with vol. 3, 1975. irreg. Brunner-Mazel, Inc., 19 Union Sq. W., New York, NY 10003.

539.7   523.01   NE   ISSN 0079-6247
PROGRESS IN ELEMENTARY PARTICLE AND COSMIC RAY PHYSICS. 1954-19?? irreg. North Holland Publishing Co., P.O. Box 211, 1000 AE Amsterdam, Netherlands.

300   510   NE
PROGRESS IN MATHEMATICAL SOCIAL SCIENCES. 1973-19?? irreg. Elsevier Scientific Publishing Co., Box 211, 1000 AE Amsterdam, Netherlands

615.7   US
PROGRESS IN PSYCHIATRIC DRUG TREATMENT. 1975-1976. irreg. Brunner-Mazel, Inc., 19 Union Sq. W., New York, NY 10003.

620   NE   ISSN 0555-4276
PROGRESS IN SOLID MECHANICS. 1961-19?? irreg., 1963, vol. 4. North-Holland Publishing Co., Box 211, 1000 AE Amsterdam, Netherlands.

338   BL
PROJETO. 1972-197? a. Editora Abril Ltda., Av. Otaviano Alves de Lima, 800, Sao Paulo, Brazil.

350   IS   ISSN 0079-7499
PUBLIC ADMINISTRATION IN ISRAEL AND ABROAD. 1960-1979. a. Israel Institute of Public Administration, P.O. Box 1077, Jerusalem, Israel.

020   CN   ISSN 0317-4921
PUBLIC LIBRARIES IN CANADA/BIBLIOTHEQUES PUBLIQUES DU CANADA. (Catalogue 81-205) 1958-197? a. Statistics Canada, User Services, Ottawa, Ont. K1A 0T6, Canada.
    Formerly: Canada. Statistics Canada. Survey of Libraries. Part 1: Public Libraries/Releve des Bibliotheques. Partie 1: Bibliotheques Publiques.

371.3   IT   ISSN 0079-9726
RASSEGNA INTERNAZIONALE DEL FILM SCIENTIFICO - DIDATTICO. (International Festival of Scientific and Educational Film) 1956-1975 (ceased with vol.18). biennial. Universita degli Studi di Padova, Centro per la Cinematografia Scientifica, 35100 Padua, Italy.

152   BE   ISSN 0080-0058
RECHERCHES DE PSYCHOLOGIE EXPERIMENTALE ET COMPAREE. 1968-1973 (no. 5) irreg. (Universite Catholique de Louvain, Faculte de Psychologie et des Sciences de l'Educations) Vander Publishing, 148 Mechelsestraat, B-3000 Louvain, Belgium.

650   338   AT   ISSN 0085-5456
REGISTER OF COMPANIES IN NEW SOUTH WALES. 1969-197? a. Universal Business Directories Pty. Ltd., 64 Talavera Rd., North Ryde, N.S.W. 2113, Australia.
    Formerly: Register of Manufacturing Industries in New South Wales.

741   NE   ISSN 0486-3887
RENEWAL OF TOWN AND VILLAGE. 1965-19?? irreg. International Union of Local Authorities, Wassenaarseweg 45, 2596 CG The Hague, Netherlands.

791.43   500   GW   ISSN 0034-5202
RESEARCH FILM/FILM DE RECHERCHE/FORSCHUNGSFILM. 1952-197? irreg. Institut fuer den Wissenschaftlichen Film, Nonnenstieg 72, 3400 Goettingen, W. Germany (B.R.D.)

551.5   PO
RESUMO METEOROLOGICO. ceased. irreg. Instituto Nacional de Meteorologia e Geofisica, Servios Centrais, Rua Saraiva de Carvalho 2, Lisbon, Portugal.

341   327   GW   ISSN 0080-4800
RUESTUNGSBESCHRAENKUNG UND SICHERHEIT. 1960-19?? irreg. (Deutsche Gesellschaft fuer Auswaertige Politik e.V.) Alfred Metzner Verlag GmbH, Zeppelinallee 43, Postfach 970148, 6000 Frankfurt 97, W. Germany (B.R.D.)

370   US   ISSN 0036-1941
S T A EDUCATOR. 1969-1974 (ceased in Apr. with vol. 4, no. 3) irreg. Stockton Teachers Association, Box 8465, Stockton, CA 95204.
    Formerly: S T A Digest.

282   016   US   ISSN 0080-5483
ST. LOUIS UNIVERSITY. PIUS XII LIBRARY. PUBLICATIONS. 1970-197? irreg. St. Louis University, Pius XII Memorial Library, 3655 W. Pine Blvd., St. Louis, MO 63108.

810   820   AU   ISSN 0080-5718
SALZBURGER STUDIEN ZUR ANGLISTIK UND AMERIKANISTIK. 1971-19?? irreg. Wilhelm Braumueller, Universitaets-Verlagsbuchhandlung GmbH, Servitengasse 5, 1092 Vienna, Austria.

001.3   GW   ISSN 0080-5815
SAMMLUNG DIALOG. 1965-19?? irreg. Nymphenburger Verlagshandlung, Romanstr. 16, 8000 Munich 19, W. Germany (B.R.D.)

027   949.4   SZ
SCHWEIZERISCHES BUNDESARCHIV. STUDIEN UND QUELLEN/ETUDES ET SOURCES/STUDI E FONTI. 1975-1978; suspended. a. Schweizerisches Bundesarchiv, Archivstrasse 24, CH-3003 Berne, Switzerland.

370   FR   ISSN 0080-7648
SCIENCES DE L'EDUCATION. 1970-197? irreg. Centrale des Revues, B. P. 119, 93104 Montreuil Cedex, France.

500   IC
SCIENTIA ISLANDICA/SCIENCE IN ICELAND. 1940-1970(no.2). irreg. Visindafelag Islendinga - Societas Scientiarum Islandica (Icelandic Scientific Society), Haskolabokasafn, 101 Reyjkavik, Iceland.

362   UK   ISSN 0080-7885
SCOTLAND. SCOTTISH HOME AND HEALTH DEPARTMENT. HOSPITAL DESIGN IN USE. discontinued in 1969. irreg. H.M.S.O., P.O. Box 569, London SE1 9NH, England.

362   UK   ISSN 0307-9597
SCOTTISH SOCIAL WORK STATISTICS. 1971-1975. a. H.M.S.O., P.O. Box 569, London SE1 9NH, England.

910   US   ISSN 0361-137X
SELECTED ALASKA HUNTING & FISHING TALES. 1970-197? irreg., vol. 4, 1976. Alaska Northwest Publishing Co., Box 4-EEE, Anchorage, AK 99509

020   US   ISSN 0361-9966
SEMINAR ON THE ACQUISITION OF LATIN AMERICAN LIBRARY MATERIALS. RESOLUTIONS AND LISTS OF COMMITEES. ceased with no. 23, 1978. irreg. University of Massachusetts, Seminar on the Acquisition of Latin American Library Materials, Amherst, MA 01002.

027   US
SEMINAR ON THE ACQUISITION OF LATIN AMERICAN LIBRARY MATERIALS. RESOLUTIONS AND LIST OF COMMITTEES. ceased with 1978/79 publication. a. Seminar on the Acquisition of Latin American Library Materials, c/o Benson Latin American Collection, University of Texas at Austin, Austin, TX 78712.

918.1   BL
SEMINARIO DE ESTUDOS BRASILEIROS. ANAIS. (Subseries of its Publicacoes) 1971-197? irreg. Universidade de Sao Paulo, Instituto de Estudos Brasileiros, C.P. 11.154, C.O. 8191, Sao Paulo, Brazil.

635.9   US
SHOWTIME. 1978-1979(vol. 2) a. Intertec Publishing Corp., Box 12901, Overland Park, KS 66212.

301.412   UK
SHREW. 1969-197? irreg. Women's Liberation Workshop, 42 Earlham St., London W. C. 2., England.

616.15   016   US
SICKLE CELL HEMOGLOBINOPATHIES: A COMPREHENSIVE BIBLIOGRAPHY. ceased with 1973/75 edition. irreg. (back issues avail) Whitston Publishing Co., Inc., Box 958, Troy, NY 12181.

500   BE   ISSN 0085-6282
SOCIETE ROYALE DES SCIENCES DE LIEGE. MEMOIRES IN 8. suspended since 1977. a. Societe Royale des Sciences de Liege, 15 Ave. des Tilleuls, 4000 Liege, Belgium.
    Contains: Colloques Internationaux D'Astrophysique de Liege. Comptes Rendus.

615.842   JM
SOCIETY OF RADIOGRAPHERS. NEWSLETTER. ceased. a. Society of Radiographers, Jamaica Ltd., c/o University Hospital of the West Indies, Mona, St. Andrew, Jamaica.

664.1   SW   ISSN 0038-0466
SOCKER HANDLINGAR; communications from the Swedish Sugar Corporation. 1951-1978 (vol. 29, no. 2) irreg. Svenska Sockerfabriks AB, Box 17050, S-200 10 Malmoe 17, Sweden.

530   US
SOLAR ENERGY HANDBOOK. 1977-197? a. Times Mirror Magazines, Inc., 380 Madison Ave., New York, NY 10017.

621.47   536   AT   ISSN 0584-0651
SOLAR ENERGY PROGRESS IN AUSTRALIA AND NEW ZEALAND. 1962-197? a. International Solar Energy Society, Australian and New Zealand Section, Box 26, Highett, Vic. 3190, Australia.

CESSATIONS

618.97   US   ISSN 0071-6111
SOUTHERN CONFERENCE ON
GERONTOLOGY REPORT. (Subseries of: Florida University, Gainesville. Center for Gerontology Studies and Programs) 1951-19?? a. University Presses of Florida, 15 N.W. 15th St., Gainesville, FL 32603.

973   US   ISSN 0081-3036
SOUTHERN HISTORICAL PUBLICATIONS. 1965-1976 (no. 20) irreg. University of Alabama Press, Box 2877, University, AL 35486.

554.1 549   GE   ISSN 0070-7228
STAATLICHES MUSEUM FUER MINERALOGIE UND GEOLOGIE, DRESDEN. ABHANDLUNGEN. 1954-19?? a. Verlag Theodor Steinkopff, Loschwitzer Str. 32, 8053 Dresden, E. Germany (D.D.R.)
     Formerly (until 1965): Staatliches Museum fuer Mineralogie und Geologie, Dresden. Jahrbuch.

347.9   US   ISSN 0081-4482
STATE COURT SYSTEMS. 1950-1978. irreg. Council of State Governments, Box 11910, Iron Works Pike, Lexington, KY 40578.

378   US   ISSN 0098-4132
STATE DIRECTORY OF HIGHER EDUCATION INSTITUTIONS AND AGENCIES IN MARYLAND. 1973-197?; discontinued. a. Council for Higher Education, 93 Main St., Annapolis, MD 21401.

310   US   ISSN 0081-475X
STATISTICAL ABSTRACT OF VIRGINIA. 1966-19??; suspended. irreg. Thomas Jefferson Center for Political Economy, University of Virginia, Rouss Hall, Charlottesville, VA 22901.

318   US   ISSN 0585-1432
STATISTICAL COMPENDIUM OF THE AMERICAS. 1969-1971. irreg. Organization of American States, Dept. of Publications, Department of Publications, Washington, DC 20006.

370 310   UK   ISSN 0081-4784
STATISTICAL GUIDES IN EDUCATIONAL RESEARCH. 1966-197? irreg. Manchester University Press, Oxford Rd., Manchester M13 9PL, England.

020 310   GW   ISSN 0081-5241
STATISTIK DER KOMMUNALEN OEFFENTLICHEN BIBLIOTHEKEN DER BUNDESREPUBLIK. 1961-197? a. Deutscher Bibliotheksverband e. V., Arbeitsstelle fuer das Bibliothekswesen, Fehrbelliner Platz 3, 1000 Berlin 31, W. Germany (B.R.D.)
     Formerly: Statistik der Oeffentlichen Buechereien der Bundesrepublik.

610.73   US
STEWART NURSING CONFERENCE SERIES. discontinued. irreg. Teachers College Press, Teachers College, Columbia University, 1234 Amsterdam Ave., New York, NY 10027.

266   NO   ISSN 0585-3273
STUDIA MISSIONALIA UPSALIENSIA. 1956-197? irreg. Lunde Forlag og Bokhandel A-S, Box 540, C. Sundtsgt. 2, Bergen, Norway.

100   SZ   ISSN 0081-6825
STUDIA PHILOSOPHICA. 1941-1977(no. 37) a. (Societe Suisse de Philosophie) Verlag fuer Recht und Gesellschaft AG, Bundesstr. 15, CH-4054 Basel, Switzerland.

669 622   PL   ISSN 0081-704X
STUDIA Z DZIEJOW GORNICTWA I HUTNICTWA. (Subseries of: Polska Akademia Nauk. Instytut Historii Kultury Materialnej. Studia i Materialy) 1957-1970. irreg. (Polska Akademia Nauk, Instytut Historii Kultury Materialnej) Ossolineum, Publishing House of the Polish Academy of Sciences, Rynek 9, 50-106 Wroclaw, Poland

100   US
STUDIES IN CONTEMPORARY PHILOSOPHY. ceased 1974. irreg., vol. 2, 1973. New York University Press, Washington Sq, New York, NY 10003.

332   NE
STUDIES IN FINANCIAL ECONOMICS. 1975-19?? irreg. North-Holland Publishing Co., Box 211, 1000 AE Amsterdam, Netherlands.

300   US
STUDIES OF NATIONALITIES IN THE USSR. discontinued after one book, 1978. irreg. (Stanford University, Hoover Institution on War, Revolution and Peace) Hoover Institution Press, Stanford, CA 94305.

370   NE
STUDIES ON EDUCATION. 1973-19?? irreg. Elsevier Scientific Publishing Co., Box 211, 1000 AE Amsterdam, Netherlands

341.57   NE
STUDIES OVER INTERNATIONAAL ECONOMISCH RECHT. 1977-1980. irreg. (T.M.C. Asser Institute) Tjeenk Willink-Noorduijn B.V., Industrieweg 1, Box 48, Culemborg, Netherlands.

551.46   US
SUMMARY OF MARINE ACTIVITIES OF THE COASTAL PLAINS REGION. discontinued. a. Coastal Plains Center for Marine Development Services, 1518 Harbour Dr., Wilmington, NC 28401.

541.3   US   ISSN 0081-9573
SURFACE AND COLLOID SCIENCE. 1969-1976 (vol. 9) irreg. John Wiley & Sons, Inc., 605 Third Ave., New York, NY 10016.

610   US   ISSN 0091-1747
SYNDROME IDENTIFICATION. 1973-19?? irreg. (looseleaf format) National Foundation-March of Dimes, 1275 Mamaroneck Ave., White Plains, NY 10605.

547.596   US   ISSN 0082-1152
SYNTHETIC PROCEDURES IN NUCLEIC ACID CHEMISTRY. 1968-197? irreg. John Wiley & Sons, Inc., 605 Third Ave, New York, NY 10016.

027.7747   US   ISSN 0094-5900
SYRACUSE UNIVERSITY. LIBRARIES. ANNUAL REPORT. ceased in 1973. a. Syracuse University, Libraries, Bird Library, Rm. 100, Syracuse, NY 13210.

960 015   US   ISSN 0586-3414
SYRACUSE UNIVERSITY. PROGRAM OF EAST AFRICAN STUDIES. EAST AFRICAN BIBLIOGRAPHIC SERIES. 1965-1969 (no. 3) irreg. Syracuse University, Program of East African Studies, 119 College Pl., Syracuse, NY 13210.

960 015   US   ISSN 0586-3422
SYRACUSE UNIVERSITY. PROGRAM OF EAST AFRICAN STUDIES. OCCASIONAL BIBLIOGRAPHIES. discontinued with no. 27, 1975. irreg. Syracuse University, Program of East African Studies, 119 College Pl., Syracuse, NY 13210.

960 015   US   ISSN 0586-3430
SYRACUSE UNIVERSITY. PROGRAM OF EAST AFRICAN STUDIES. OCCASIONAL PAPERS. discontinued. irreg. Syracuse University, Program of East African Studies, 119 College Pl., Syracuse, NY 13210.

960 015   US
SYRACUSE UNIVERSITY. PROGRAM OF EAST AFRICAN STUDIES. SPECIAL PUBLICATIONS. 1966-1975 (no. 7) irreg. Syracuse University, Program of East African Studies, 119 College Pl., Syracuse, NY 13210.

791.45   US   ISSN 0082-1381
T V "FREE" FILM SOURCE BOOK. 1949-1975. a. Broadcast Information Bureau, Inc., 30 E. 42nd St., New York, NY 10017.

791.4   US   ISSN 0363-9487
T V SEASON. discontinued with 1977-78 edt. a. Oryx Press, 2214 N. Central at Encanto, Suite 103, Phoenix, AZ 85004.

629.13   US
TECH NOTES. 1961-1977 (no.99) irreg. Singer Company, Kearfott Division, 1150 McBride Ave., Little Falls, NJ 07424.

690   FI   ISSN 0355-337X
TECHNICAL RESEARCH CENTRE OF FINLAND. PUBLICATION. BUILDING TECHNOLOGY AND COMMUNITY DEVELOPMENT. 1972-1981. irreg. Valtion Teknillinen Tutkimuskeskus - Technical Research Centre of Finland, Vuorimiehentie 5, 02150 Espoo 15, Finland.

620   FI   ISSN 0355-3396
TECHNICAL RESEARCH CENTRE OF FINLAND. PUBLICATION. ELECTRICAL AND NUCLEAR TECHNOLOGY. 1973-1981. irreg. Valtion Teknillinen Tutkimuskeskus - Technical Research Centre of Finland, Vuorimiehentie 5, 02150 Espoo 15, Finland.

600   FI   ISSN 0355-3388
TECHNICAL RESEARCH CENTRE OF FINLAND. PUBLICATION. MATERIALS AND PROCESSING TECHNOLOGY. 1972-1981. irreg. Valtion Teknillinen Tutkimuskeskus - Technical Research Centre of Finland, Vuorimiehentie 5, 02150 Espoo 15, Finland.

600   FI
TECHNICAL RESEARCH CENTRE OF FINLAND. TIEDONANTO. 1972-1981. irreg. Valtion Teknillinen Tutkimuskeskus - Technical Research Centre of Finland, Vuorimiehentie 5, 02150 Espoo 15, Finland.

330   FR   ISSN 0082-2485
TECHNIQUES ECONOMIQUES MODERNES. ESPACE ECONOMIQUE. 1963-19?? irreg. (Ecole Pratique des Hautes Etudes, Centre d'Etudes des Techniques Economiques Modernes) Centrale des Revues, Dunod, B. P. 119, 93104 Montreuil Cedex, France.

330   FR   ISSN 0082-2493
TECHNIQUES ECONOMIQUES MODERNES. HISTOIRE ET PENSEE ECONOMIQUE. 1964-19?? irreg. (Ecole Pratique des Hautes Etudes, Centre d'Etudes des Techniques Economiques Modernes) Centrale des Revues, Dunod, B. P. 119, 93104 Montreuil Cedex, France.

330   FR   ISSN 0082-2507
TECHNIQUES ECONOMIQUES MODERNES. PRODUCTION ET MARCHES. 1964-19?? irreg. (Ecole Pratique des Hautes Etudes, Centre d'Etudes des Techniques Economiques Modernes) Centrale des Revues, Dunod, B. P. 119, 93104 Montreuil Cedex, France.

362.8   US   ISSN 0091-8385
TECHNIQUES OF MARRIAGE AND FAMILY COUNSELING. (Represents papers presented at the Institutes annual workshops) 1972-197?; discontinued. a. American Institute of Family Relations, 5287 Sunset Blvd., Los Angeles, CA 90027.

669   US   ISSN 0082-2558
TECHNIQUES OF METALS RESEARCH. 1968-197? irreg. John Wiley & Sons, Inc., 605 Third Ave., New York, NY 10016.

660.2   GE   ISSN 0082-2566
TECHNISCHE FORTSCHRITTSBERICHTE; landtechnische Zeitschrift der DDR. 1923-197. irreg., vol. 63, 1974. Verlag Theodor Steinkopff, Loschwitzer Str. 32, 8053 Dresden, E. Germany (D.D.R.)

620   DK
TEKNISK NYT BUYERS GUIDE. 1962-197? a. Thomson Communications (Scandinavia) A-S, Hestemoellestraede 6, DK-1464 Copenhagen K, Denmark.

620   US   ISSN 0071-0369
TENNESSEE VALLEY AUTHORITY. ENGINEERING LABORATORY. RESEARCH IN THE FIELDS OF CIVIL ENGINEERING, MECHANICAL ENGINEERING, INSTRUMENTATION. 1965-1972. biennial. Tennessee Valley Authority, Engineering Laboratory, Knoxville, TN 37902.

796.3 910   US   ISSN 0082-2825
TENNIS FOR TRAVELERS. 1966-197? irreg. (back issues avail) Richards Industries, Inc., Affiliate of Richards Industries, Inc., 407 Blade St., Cincinnati, OH 45216.

610 EC ISSN 0040-3679
TERAPIA. 1945-1977, vol. 62, no. 444. irreg.
Laboratorios "Life", Apdo. 458, Quito, Ecuador.

344.764 US ISSN 0091-0848
TEXAS. WATER QUALITY BOARD. AGENCY
PUBLICATION. ceased in 1977. irreg. Water
Quality Board, Box 13246, Capitol Station, Austin,
TX 78711.

614.772 US ISSN 0082-3570
TEXAS. WATER QUALITY BOARD. BIENNIAL
REPORT. (Report year ends August 31) ceased in
1977. biennial. Water Quality Board, P.O. Box
13246 Capitol Station, Austin, TX 78711.

677 AT
TEXTILE COUNCIL OF AUSTRALIA. TEXTILE
INFORMATION SERVICE. 1963-1977 (Nov.)
irreg. Textile Council of Australia, Accountants
House, 5th Floor, 124 Exhibition St., Melbourne,
Vic. 3000, Australia.

028 GW
THEMEN DER ZEIT. ceased. irreg. Otto Maier
Verlag, Marktstr. 22, 7980 Ravensburg, W.
Germany (B.R.D.)

370 US
THEORY AND RESEARCH IN TEACHING
SERIES. discontinued. irreg. Teachers College
Press, Teachers College, Columbia University, 1234
Amsterdam Ave., New York, NY 10027.

320 US ISSN 0082-4178
THOMAS JEFFERSON CENTER FOR POLITICAL
ECONOMY. RESEARCH MONOGRAPHS. 1959-
19?? irreg. Thomas Jefferson Center for Political
Economy, University of Virginia, Rouss Hall,
Charlottesville, VA 22901.

016 US
TIO SAM Y USTED. (discontinued) biennial. Cruzada
Spanish Publications, Box 650909, Miami, FL 33165.

679.7 UK ISSN 0082-4607
TOBACCO RESEARCH COUNCIL. RESEARCH
PAPERS. discontinued. irreg. Tobacco Research
Council, Glen House, Stag Place, London S.W.1,
England.

679.7 UK ISSN 0082-4615
TOBACCO RESEARCH COUNCIL. REVIEW OF
ACTIVITIES. (Supersedes Report of the Council
issued under its former name: Tobacco
Manufacturers' Standing Committee) discontinued.
irreg. Tobacco Research Council, Glen House, Stag
Place, London S.W.1, England.

694 DK
TRAE NYT BUYERS GUIDE. discontinued. a.
Thomson Communications (Scandinavia) A-S,
Hestemoellestraede 6, DK-1464 Copenhagen K,
Denmark.

910.2 US ISSN 0072-8772
TRAVEL ROUTES AROUND THE WORLD:
GUIDE TO TRAVELING AROUND THE
WORLD BY PASSENGER-CARRYING
FREIGHTERS. 1935-197? a. Harian Publications,
One Vernon Ave., Floral Park, NY 11001.

179.3 US
TRAVELING WITH YOUR PET. 1969-197? biennial.
American Society for the Prevention of Cruelty to
Animals, c/o Public Relations Dept., 441 E. 92nd
St., New York, NY 10028.

667.6 US ISSN 0082-6278
TREATISE ON COATINGS. 1966-1972(vol. 7)
irreg. Marcel Dekker, Inc., 270 Madison Ave.,
New York, NY 10016.

810 US
TRUCK. 1970-1979 (ceased with no.21) irreg. Truck
Press, c/o David Wilk, Ed., Box 4544, Industrial
Station, St. Paul, MN 55104.

320.9 CN ISSN 0706-9820
UNICAN. 1978-1979 (April) irreg. Council for
Canadian Unity, 2055 Peel St., Suite 1000,
Montreal, Que. H3A 1V4, Canada.

338.9 US ISSN 0082-8637
U. S. AGENCY FOR INTERNATIONAL
DEVELOPMENT. PROPOSED FOREIGN AID
PROGRAM, SUMMARY PRESENTATION TO
CONGRESS. 1963-19?? a. U.S. Agency for
International Development, Dept. of State,
Washington, DC 20523

382 US ISSN 0093-9692
U.S. DEPARTMENT OF COMMERCE. EFFECTS
OF POLLUTION ABATEMENT ON
INTERNATIONAL TRADE. 1953-1979 (Sep.) a.
U.S. Department of Commerce, Fourteenth St.
Between Constitution Ave. and E. St. N.W.,
Washington, DC 20203

309.2 US
U.S. DEPARTMENT OF HOUSING AND URBAN
DEVELOPMENT. COMMUNITY
DEVELOPMENT EVALUATION SERIES. 1971-
1973 (ceased in May with no. 15) irreg. U. S.
Department of Housing and Urban Development,
451 Seventh St. SW, Washington, DC 20410.

352.7 016 US ISSN 0364-0930
U.S. DEPARTMENT OF HOUSING AND URBAN
DEVELOPMENT. OFFICE OF
INTERNATIONAL AFFAIRS. FOREIGN
PUBLICATIONS ACCESSIONS LIST. ceased with
no. 46, Mar. 1978. irreg. U. S. Department of
Housing and Urban Development, Division of
Information Sciences, Documentation & Publications
Branch, Washington, DC 20410.

320 US ISSN 0084-2257
U.S. DEPARTMENT OF STATE. WORLD
STRENGTH OF THE COMMUNIST PARTY
ORGANIZATIONS. ANNUAL REPORT; report
by the President to Congress. (Subseries of its
International Organization and Conference Series;
also issued in House Documents Series) 1948-1974.
a. U.S. Department of State, Bureau of Intelligence
and Research, 2201 C St. N.W., Washington, DC
20250

333.74 339.49 US ISSN 0069-9101
U.S. DEPARTMENT OF THE INTERIOR.
CONSERVATION BULLETINS. ceased with no.
42, 1962. irreg. U.S. Department of the Interior,
Washington, DC 20240

339.49 US ISSN 0069-9152
U.S. DEPARTMENT OF THE INTERIOR.
CONSERVATION YEARBOOK. 1965-1969(no. 5)
irreg. U.S. Department of the Interior, Washington,
DC 20240
  Includes: U.S. Department of the Interior. Annual
Report (ISSN 0083-0321)

353.3 658.3 US ISSN 0093-3716
U. S. DEPARTMENT OF THE INTERIOR.
OFFICE OF PERSONNEL MANAGEMENT.
ANNUAL MANPOWER PERSONNEL
STATISTICS. 1964-1973(no. 8) a. U. S.
Department of the Interior, Washington, DC 20240.

614.8 US ISSN 0083-0364
U. S. DEPARTMENT OF THE INTERIOR.
SAFETY CONFERENCE GUIDES. ceased with
no. 30 B, 1961. irreg. U.S. Department of the
Interior., Washington, DC 20240.

551.5 US ISSN 0083-0631
U. S. FEDERAL COUNCIL FOR SCIENCE AND
TECHNOLOGY. INTERDEPARTMENTAL
COMMITTEE FOR ATMOSPHERIC SCIENCES.
I C A S REPORTS. 1960-1977 (Sep.) a. U.S.
National Science Foundation, 1800 G. St.,
Washington, DC 20550

634.9 US ISSN 0083-2987
U.S. FOREST SERVICE. PACIFIC NORTHWEST
FOREST AND RANGE EXPERIMENT
STATION. ANNUAL REPORT. 1936-1971. a.
U.S. Forest Service, Pacific Northwest Forest and
Range Experiment Station, 809 N.E. Sixth Ave.,
Portland, OR 97232.

018 US ISSN 0148-5644
U.S. LIBRARY OF CONGRESS. ACCESSIONS
LIST: AFGHANISTAN. 1978-1980. a. U.S. Library
of Congress, Overseas Operations Division,

629.13 US ISSN 0068-5682
U.S. NATIONAL AERONAUTICS AND SPACE
ADMINISTRATION. JET PROPULSION
LABORATORY. TECHNICAL
MEMORANDUM. 1960-19?? irreg. (also avail. in
microfiche) U.S. National Aeronautics and Space
Administration, Jet Propulsion Laboratory,
California Institute of Technology, CA 91109

363.6 US ISSN 0094-7857
U.S. NATIONAL SCIENCE FOUNDATION.
DIVISION OF ENVIRONMENTAL SYSTEMS
AND RESOURCES. SUMMARY OF AWARDS.
ceased Jul. 1978. a. National Science Foundation,
1800 G St. N.W., Washington, DC 20550

353.5 US ISSN 0361-4530
U.S. SOLICITOR FOR THE DEPARTMENT OF
THE INTERIOR. SOLICITOR'S REVIEW. 1971-
1973(Jul.) irreg. U.S. Department of the Interior, C
St. Between 18th and 19th Sts., N.W., Washington,
DC 20240.

380 BL
UNIVERSIDADE FEDERAL DO PARANA.
MUSEU DE ARQUEOLOGIA E ARTES
POPULARES. CADERNOS DE ARTES E
TRADICOES POPULARES. 1973-1975, vol. II, no.
2. irreg. Universidade Federal do Parana, Museu de
Arqueologia e Artes Populares, Rua 15 de
Novembro, No. 567, 83200 Paranagua, Parana,
Brazil.

300 261 GW ISSN 0077-1945
UNIVERSITAET MUENSTER. INSTITUT FUER
CHRISTLICHE SOZIALWISSENSCHAFTEN.
SCHRIFTEN. 1955-19?? irreg. Aschendorffsche
Verlagsbuchhandlung, Soester Str. 13, Postfach
1124, 4400 Muenster, W. Germany (B. R. D.)

510 FR ISSN 0078-9909
UNIVERSITE DE PARIS VI (PIERRE ET MARIE
CURIE). INSTITUT HENRI POINCARE.
SEMINAIRE CHOQUET. INITIATION A
L'ANALYSE. (Sub-series of: Mathematica
Seminosa) 1962-1978. a., in 1-2 fascicules.
Universite de Paris VI (Pierre et Marie Curie),
Institut Henri Poincare, Secretariat Mathematique,
P.O. Box 93-05, Paris 5e, France.

510 FR ISSN 0079-0036
UNIVERSITE DE PARIS VI (PIERRE ET MARIE
CURIE). INSTITUT HENRI POINCARE.
SEMINAIRE LIONS. (Subseries of Mathematica
Seminosa) 1968-69. irreg. Universite de Paris VI
(Pierre et Marie Curie), Institut Henri Poincare,
Secretariat Mathematique, 11 rue Pierre et Marie
Curie, Paris 5e, France.

020 CN ISSN 0318-7179
UNIVERSITY AND COLLEGE LIBRARIES IN
CANADA/BIBLIOTHEQUES DES
UNIVERSITES ET DES COLLEGES DU
CANADA. (Catalogue 81-206) 1958-197? a.
Statistics Canada, User Services, Ottawa, Ont. K1A
0T6, Canada.
  Formerly(until 1972): Canada. Statistics Canada.
Survey of Libraries. Part 2: Academic Libraries/
Releve des Bibliotheques. Partie 2: Bibliotheques
Scolaires.

535 US ISSN 0066-7609
UNIVERSITY OF ARIZONA. OPTICAL
SCIENCES CENTER. NEWSLETTER. 1967-19??
irreg.(approx. 3-5 issues per year) University of
Arizona, Optical Sciences Center, Tucson, AZ
85721.

535 US ISSN 0066-7617
UNIVERSITY OF ARIZONA. OPTICAL
SCIENCES CENTER. TECHNICAL REPORT.
1965-19?? irreg. University of Arizona, Optical
Sciences Center, Tucson, AZ 85721.

980 US ISSN 0092-2242
UNIVERSITY OF CALIFORNIA, LOS ANGELES.
LATIN AMERICAN CENTER. LATIN
AMERICAN ACTIVITIES AND RESOURCES.
1964-19?? a. (processed) University of California,
Los Angeles, Latin American Center, 405 Hilgard
Avenue, Los Angeles, CA 90024.

340 UK ISSN 0075-7691
UNIVERSITY OF LAGOS. LAW SERIES.
discontinued. irreg. Evans Brothers Ltd., Montague
House, Russell Sq., London W.C.1, England.

381 US ISSN 0093-4623
UNIVERSITY OF MICHIGAN. GRADUATE SCHOOL OF BUSINESS ADMINISTRATION. PROCEEDINGS OF THE ANNUAL BUSINESS CONFERENCE. 1969-1979. a. University of Michigan, Graduate School of Business Administration, Ann Arbor, MI 48104.

919.4 AT ISSN 0066-7730
UNIVERSITY OF NEW ENGLAND. EXPLORATION SOCIETY. REPORT. 1960-197? irreg. University of New England, Exploration Society, Armidale, N.S.W., Australia.

505 SI ISSN 0083-405X
UNIVERSITY OF SINGAPORE SCIENCE JOURNAL. 1962-197? irreg. (Lee Foundation) University of Singapore Science Society, Union House, Bukit Timah Rd., Singapore 10, Singapore.

352 US ISSN 0082-3406
UNIVERSITY OF TEXAS, AUSTIN. COUNTY AUDITORS' INSTITUTE. PROCEEDINGS. 1959-1976 (18th) a. University of Texas at Austin, Lyncon B. Johnson School of Public Affairs, Austin, TX 78712.

336.2 US ISSN 0082-3430
UNIVERSITY OF TEXAS, AUSTIN. INSTITUTE FOR TAX ASSESSORS. PROCEEDINGS. 1959-1977 (18th) a. University of Texas at Austin, Lyncon B. Johnson School of Public Affairs, Drawer Y, Austin, TX 78712.

639 US ISSN 0083-7539
UNIVERSITY OF WASHINGTON. DEPARTMENT OF OCEANOGRAPHY. FISHERY REPORT. 1956-19?? irreg. University of Washington, Dept. of Oceanography, Seattle, WA 98105.

551.46 US ISSN 0083-7547
UNIVERSITY OF WASHINGTON. DEPARTMENT OF OCEANOGRAPHY. SPECIAL REPORT. 1962-19?? irreg. University of Washington, Dept. of Oceanography, Seattle, WA 98105.

614.7 301.31 CN
UNIVERSITY OF WATERLOO. FACULTY OF ENVIRONMENTAL STUDIES. OCCASIONAL PAPER. 1972-197? irreg. University of Waterloo, Faculty of Environmental Studies, Waterloo, Ont. N2L 3G1, Canada.
Formerly: University of Waterloo. Division of Environmental Studies. Occasional Paper (ISSN 0317-8633).

338.1 AT ISSN 0083-8705
UNIVERSITY OF WESTERN AUSTRALIA. INSTITUTE OF AGRICULTURE. RESEARCH REPORT: AGRICULTURAL ECONOMICS. 1961-197? irreg. University of Western Australia Press, Nedlands, Western Australia, Australia

617.6 US
UPDATE IN CLINICAL DENTISTRY. 1978-1979. a. American Dental Association, 211 E. Chicago Ave.. Chicago, IL 60611.

617.6 US
UPDATE IN ENDODONTICS. 1979 (discontinued). a. American Dental Association, 211 E. Chicago Ave.. Chicago, IL 60611.

617.6 US
UPDATE IN ORAL SURGERY. 1977-1979; discontinued. a. American Dental Association, 211 E. Chicago Ave., Chicago, IL 60611.
Formerly (1971-1975): Advances in Oral Surgery (ISSN 0065-3039)

617.643 US
UPDATE IN ORTHODONTICS. 1977-1979; discontinued. a. American Dental Association, 211 E. Chicago Ave., Chicago, IL 60611.
Formerly (1970-1975): Advances in Orthodontics (ISSN 0065-3063)

617.632 US
UPDATE IN PERIODONTICS. 1977-1979; discontinued. a. American Dental Association, 211 E. Chicago Ave., Chicago, IL 60611.
Formerly (1970-1975): Advances in Periodontics (ISSN 0065-3128)

617.6 US
UPDATE IN PREVENTIVE DENTISTRY. 1979 (discontinued). a. American Dental Association, 211 E. Chicago Ave., Chicago, IL 60611.

439.5 SW ISSN 0083-4661
UPPSALA UNIVERSITET. INSTITUTIONEN FOER NORDISKA SPRAAK. SKRIFTER. 1953-1967 (no.15); dissertations now published in Studia Philologiae Scandinavicae Upsaliensia. irreg. Uppsala Universitet, Institutionen foer Nordiska Spraak, Box 513, S-751-25 Uppsala, Sweden.

333 US ISSN 0083-470X
URBAN LAND INSTITUTE. RESEARCH REPORT. 1959-197? irreg. (also avail. in microfilm) Urban Land Institute, 1200 18th St. N.W., Washington, DC 20036.

339.4 US ISSN 0083-4718
URBAN LAND INSTITUTE. TECHNICAL BULLETIN. 1945-197? irreg. (also avail. in looseleaf format) Urban Land Institute, 1200 18th St.N.W., Washington, DC 20036.

628 DK
VARME OG SANITETS NYT BUYERS GUIDE. discontinued. a. Thomson Communications (Scandinavia) A-S, Hestemoellestraede 6, DK-1464 Copenhagen K, Denmark.

616.95 016 US ISSN 0090-8479
VENEREAL DISEASE BIBLIOGRAPHY. (Supplement to: Venereal Disease Bibliography 1966-1970) 1972-1975. a. Whitson Publishing Co. Inc., Box 958, Troy, NY 12181.

090.75 BE
VEREENIGING DER ANTWERPSCHE BIBLIOPHIELEN. PUBLICATIONS. 1877-1961 (3rd series, no. 4) irreg. Vereeniging der Antwerpsche Bibliophielen, Museum Plantin-Moretus, Vrijdamarkt 22, B-2000 Antwerp, Belgium.

800 UK ISSN 0083-582X
VERSE SPEAKING ANTHOLOGY. discontinued. every 3 or 4 yrs. Poetry Society Inc., 21 Earls Court Square, London S.W.5, England.

200 US ISSN 0083-6281
VINCENTIAN STUDIES. 1968-19?? irreg. St. John's University Press, Jamaica, NY 11439.

630 US ISSN 0362-6490
VIRGINIA. AGRICULTURAL OPPORTUNITIES DEVELOPMENT PROGRAM. ANNUAL REPORT. discontinued. a. Department of Agriculture and Commerce, Box 1165, Richmond, VA 23209.

371.3 UK ISSN 0083-6680
VISUAL EDUCATION YEARBOOK. ceased in 1979. a. National Committee for Audio-Visual Aids in Education, 254 Belsize Rd., London NW6 4BY, England.

320 GE ISSN 0083-6982
WAERMELEHRE UND WAERMEWIRTSCHAFT IN EINZELDARSTELLUNGEN. 1926-197? irreg., vol. 22, 1974. Verlag Theodor Steinkopff, Loschwitzer Str. 32, 8053 Dresden, E. Germany (D.D.R.)

350 US
WASHINGTON REPORT ON FEDERAL LEGISLATION FOR CHILDREN. ceased, 1980. q? Child Welfare League of America, 1346 Connecticut Ave. N.W., Washington, DC 20036.
Formerly: Washington Report on Legislation for Children and What You Can do About It (ISSN 0508-0924)

917 557 US ISSN 0083-8489
WEST VIRGINIA GEOLOGICAL SURVEY. ARCHAEOLOGICAL SERIES. 1965-19?? irreg. Geological and Economic Survey, Morgantown, WV 26505.

557 US ISSN 0083-8500
WEST VIRGINIA GEOLOGICAL SURVEY. BULLETIN. 1901-19?? irreg. Geological and Economic Survey, Morgantown, WV 26505.

557 US ISSN 0083-8519
WEST VIRGINIA GEOLOGICAL SURVEY. CIRCULARS. 1965-19?? irreg. Geological and Economic Survey, Morgantown, WV 26505.

557 US ISSN 0083-8527
WEST VIRGINIA GEOLOGICAL SURVEY. GEOLOGICAL PUBLICATIONS. VOLUMES. 1899-19?? irreg. Geological and Economic Survey, Morgantown, WV 26506.

380.1 AT
WESTERN AUSTRALIA. SEED BOARD. CHAIRMAN'S REPORT. 1971-197? irreg. Western Australia Seed Board, Perth, Australia.

947 GW ISSN 0580-1540
WESTFAELISCHE WILHELMS-UNIVERSITAET MUENSTER. SLAVISCH-BALTISCHES SEMINAR. 1958-197? irreg. Verlag Anton Hain GmbH, Muehlgasse 3, Postfach 180, 6554 Meisenheim, W. Germany (B.R.D.)

100 US
WISDOM OF TIBET SERIES. discontinued. irreg. Harper and Row Publishers, Inc., 10 E. 53 St., New York, NY 10022.

200 US ISSN 0084-117X
WOODSTOCK PAPERS: OCCASIONAL ESSAYS FOR THEOLOGY. ceased with no. 8, 1967. irreg. Paulist Press, 545 Island Rd., Ramsey, NJ 07446.

616.8 AU ISSN 0084-2206
WORLD PSYCHIATRIC ASSOCIATION. BULLETIN. 1969-197? biennial. World Psychiatric Association, c/o Prof. P. Berner, Psychiatrische Universitaetsklinik, Lazarettgasse 14, A-1097 Vienna, Austria.

590 BL ISSN 0084-5582
ZOOLOGIA. (Subseries of Sao Paulo, Brazil (City) Universidade. Faculdade de Filosofia, Ciencias e Letras. Boletim) 1937-1973 (vol. 30) irreg., 1965, no. 25. Universidade de Sao Paulo, Faculdade de Filosofia, Letras e Ciencias Humanas, Cidade Universitaria, "Armando de Salles Oliveira", C.P. 8191, Sao Paulo, Brazil.

Index to Publications of International Organizations

Titles listed with page numbers refer to entries included in the Classified List of this Directory. Titles listed without page numbers refer to entries in the 20th edition of *Ulrich's International Periodicals Directory*. The index is divided into four sections: publications of international organizations, of international congresses, of the European Communities, and of the United Nations.

INTERNATIONAL ORGANIZATIONS

A D B Quarterly Review (Asian Development Bank)

A G A R D Bulletin (Advisory Group for Aerospace Research and Development)

A I C A R C Bulletin

A. I. J. P. Yearbook (International Association of Philatelic Journalists) 478

A I L A Bulletin (Association Internationale de Linguistique Appliquee)

A I L/Doc (Association of International Libraries) 525

A I O S P Bulletin (International Association for Educational and Vocational Guidance)

A L A M A R Informativo (Asociacion Latinoamericana de Armadores)

A.P.D.S.A. Journal (Asian Pacific Dental Student Association) 608

A P O Annual Report (Asian Productivity Organization) 220

A S A I H L. Seminar Reports (Association of Southeast Asian Institutions of Higher Learning) 333

A S P A C Newsletter of Cultural and Social Affairs (Asian and Pacific Council)

A S P A C Seminar on Audio-Visual Education. Proceedings (Asian and Pacific Council) 441

Academie Internationale d'Histoire des Sciences. Collection des Travaux 778

Acta Chirurgiae Maxillo-Facialis 624

Acta Colloquii Didacticii Classici 540

Acta Geneticae Medicae et Gemellologiae

Acta Haematologica

Acta Musicologica

Acta Radiologica. Series 1: Diagnosis

Acta Radiologica. Series 2: Oncology, Radiation Therapy, Physics and Biology

Adelphi Papers

Advances in Myocardiology 606

African Bulletin

African Development Bank. Report by the Board of Directors/Banque Africaine de Developpement. Rapport du Conseil d'Administration 199

African Journal of Plant Protection/Revue Africaine de la Protection des Vegetaux

African News Sheet 497

African Tax Systems

Afro Asian Economic Review

Afro-Asian Publications 439

ALGOL Bulletin 270

Aluminum Smelters 641

America Cooperativa

America Latina 795

Americas

Amnesty International Report 719

Anales Galdosianos 559

Anciens Pay et Assemblees d'Etats 708

Andrologia

Animalia

Annales de l'Economie Publique, Sociale et Cooperative/Annals of Public and Cooperative Economy

Annales des Falsifications et de l'Expertise Chimique

Annals of Glaciology 291

Annotated Bibliography of Literature on Cooperative Movements in South-East Asia

Annuaire des Arachnologistes Mondiaux 127

Annual Report on Results of Treatment in Gynecological Cancer 604

Annual Reports on Competition Policy in O E C D Member Countries 220

Anthos

Antropologia Social 47

Anuario Estadistico Centroamericano de Comercio Exterior 151

Anuario Interamericano de Derechos Humanos/Inter-American Yearbook on Human Rights 522

Apiacta

Applied Neurophysiology

Arab Bulletin

Archiv fuer Rechts- und Sozialphilosophie/Archives de Philosophie du Droit et de Philosophie Sociale/Archives for Philosophy of Law and Social Philosophy

Archiv fuer Rechts- und Sozialphilosophie. Beihefte. Neue Folge 687

Archiv fuer Religionspsychologie 763

Asia/Pacific Consumer

Asia-Pacific Scouting

Asian and Pacific Council. Cultural and Social Centre. Annual Report 442

Asian and Pacific Council. Food and Fertilizer Technology Center. Extension /Technical Bulletin

Asian Bulletin

Asian Institute of Technology. Research Summary 850

Asian Labour

Asian News Sheet

Asian Pacific Quarterly of Cultural and Social Affairs (Asian and Pacific Council)

Asian Peoples' Anti-Communist League. Charts About Chinese Communists on the Mainland 442

Asian Peoples' Anti-Communist League. China. Pamphlet 708

Asian Productivity Organization. A P O News

Asian Productivity Organization. Review of Activities of National Productivity 220

Asociacion

Asociacion Interamericana de Bibliotecarios y Documentalistas Agricolas. Boletin Especial 12

Asociacion Interamericana de Bibliotecarios y Documentalistas Agricolas. Boletin Informativo.

Asociacion Latinoamericana de Libre Comercio. Estadisticas de Comercio Exterior--Serie A-Exportaciones 193

Asociacion Latinoamericana de Libre Comercio. Estadisticas de Comercio Exterior-Serie B-Importaciones 193

Asociacion Latinoamericana de Libre Comercio. Estadisticas de Comercio Exterior - Serie C - Importaciones Zonales 193

Asociacion Latinoamericana de Libre Comercio. Lista Consolidada de Concesiones 193

Asociacion Latinoamericana de Libre Comercio. Lista Nacional de Argentina 193

Asociacion Latinoamericana de Libre Comercio. Lista Nacional de Brasil 193

Asociacion Latinoamericana de Libre Comercio. Lista Nacional de Chile 193

Asociacion Latinoamericana de Libre Comercio. Lista Nacional de Colombia 193

Asociacion Latinoamericana de Libre Comercio. Lista Nacional de Ecuador 193

Asociacion Latinoamericana de Libre Comercio. Lista Nacional de Mexico 193

Asociacion Latinoamericana de Libre Comercio. Lista Nacional de Paraguay 193

Asociacion Latinoamericana de Libre Comercio. Lista Nacional de Peru 193

Asociacion Latinoamericana de Libre Comercio. Serie Instrumentos 193

Association Euratom-Ital. Annual Report 13

Association Internationale d'Etudes du Sud-Est Europeen. Bulletin

Association Internationale d'Etudes Patristiques. Bulletin d'Information et de Liaison

Association Internationale du Droit Commercial et du Droit Affaires. Groupe Francais. Travaux 522

Association Internationale pour l'Histoire du Verre. Bulletin 244

Association of Commonwealth Universities. Annual Report of the Council Together with the Accounts of the Association 334

Association of Institutes for European Studies. Annuaire 449

Association of Institutes for European Studies. Year-Book 449

Association of Southeast Asian Institutions of Higher Learning. Newsletter 334

Astin Bulletin 497

Atlantic Mail 522

Atomic Physics 702

Audiology

Auto-Universum 869

Automatic Data Processing Information Bulletin 270

Automatica

B E N E L U X Economic Union. Conseil Central de l'Economie. Rapport du Secretaraire sur l'Activite du Conseil 220

B I C-Code 672

Babel

Bank for International Settlements. Annual Report 169

Bank for International Settlements. Monetary and Economic Department. International Commodity Position. General Survey 169

Batiment International/Building Research and Practice

Bears-Their Biology and Management 127

Benelux Publikatieblad/Bulletin Benelux 740

Benelux Tijdschrift/Revue Benelux

Biblia Revuo

Bibliographia I U L A

Bibliographie de la Philosophie/Bibliography of Philosophy

Bibliographie Internationale de l'Humanisme et de la Renaissance 756

Bibliography on Irrigation, Drainage, River Training and Flood Control/Bibliographie Relative aux Irrigations, au Drainage, a la Regularisation des Cours d'Eau et la Matrise des Crues 900

Biochemical Education

Biotelemetry and Patient Monitoring

Boreas

Brahmavidya 669

Bronches-Broncho-Pneumologie

Building and Wood

Bulletin d'Archeologie Sud-Est Europeenne. 59

Bulletin de Philosophie Medievale 687

Bulletin du Bibliophile

Bulletin for International Fiscal Documentation

Bulletin G C I D (International Commission on Irrigation and Drainage, Greek National Committee)

Bulletin Geodesique

Bulletin of Information on Current Research on Human Sciences Concerning Africa/Bulletin d'Information sur les Recherches dans les Sciences Humaines Concernant l'Afrique

Bulletin of Peace Proposals

Bulletin Volcanologique 303

Bureau International de l'Heure. Rapport Annuel 81

Bureau International des Societes Gerant les Droits d'Enregistrement et de Reproduction Mecanique. Bulletin 733

C B Bulletin/Bulletin O C (International Commission on Rules for the Approval of Electrical Equipment, Certification Body)

C C I A Background Information (World Council of Churches, Commission on International Affairs)

C E R N Annual Report (European Organization for Nuclear Research) 695

C E R N Courier (European Organization for Nuclear Research)

C E R N-H E R A Reports (European Organization for Nuclear Research) 695

C E R N Reports (European Organization for Nuclear Research) 696

C E R N School of Computing. Proceedings (European Organization for Nuclear Research) 696

C E R N School of Physics. Proceedings (European Organization for Nuclear Research) 696

C.I.A. Revue (Confederation Internationale des Accordeonistes) 658

C I B Directory of Building Research Information and Development Organizations (International Council for Building Research, Studies and Documentation) 135

C.I.C.A.E. Bulletin d'Information (Confederation Internationale des Cinemas d'Art et d'Essai) 649

C I M M Y T Today (Centro Internacional de Mejoramiento de Maiz y Trigo) 42

C I N D A 700

C I N T E R F O R. Estudios y Monografias (Centro Interamericano de Investigacion y Documentacion Sobre Formacion Profesional) 315

C I N T E R F O R - Documentacion (Centro Interamericano de Investigacion y Documentacion Sobre Formacion Profesional)

C I R A Bulletin (Centre International de Recherches sur l'Anarchisme)

C. I. R. P. Annals

C M I News Letter (International Maritime Committee)

C M I Year Book 877

Cahiers de Droit Fiscal International

Cahiers Ligures de Prehistoire et d'Archeologie 59

Carre Bleu

Catalogo de Publicaciones Latinoamericanas Sobre Formacion Profesional 668

Catalogus Musicus 658

Catalogus Translationem et Commentatorium 578

Centre International d'Etude des Problems Humains. Bulletins 796

Centre International de Documentation Arachnologiques. Liste des Travaux Arachnologiques 110

Centre International de Documentation Economique et Sociale Africaine. Monographies Documentaires 439

Centre International de Documentation et Sociale Africaine. Enquetes Bibliographiques 439

Centre International de Liaison des Ecoles de Cinema et de Television. Bulletin d'Informations 267

Centro de Estudios Monetarios Latinoamericanos. Ensayos 171

Centro Interamericano de Investigacion y Documentacion Sobre Formacion Profesional. Boletin

Centro Interamericano de Investigacion y Documentacion Sobre Formacion Profesional. Cuadro Comparativo y Fichas Descriptivas

Centro Interamericano de Investigacion y Documentacion Sobre Formacion Profesional. Informes 329

Centro Interamericano de Investigacion y Documentacion Sobre Formacion Profesional. Serie Bibliografica 315

Centro Latino Americano de Pesquisas em Ciencias Sociais. Boletim Bibliografia

Centro Latinoamericano de Demografia. Boletin Demografico

Centro Latinoamericano de Economia Humana. Publicaciones

Chemistry International

Chemoreception Abstracts

INDEX TO PUBLICATIONS OF INTERNATIONAL ORGANIZATIONS 919

Children in the Tropics

Child's Brain

Ch'indaba

Christian Democratic Study and Documentation Center. Cahiers d'Etudes 709

Christian Democratic World Union. Information Bulletin 709

Christian Peace Conference

Chronicle of Parliamentary Elections and Developments 709

Chronobiologia

Church Alert

Church and the Jewish People

Ciencia Interamericana

Circulation Auditing Around the World 167

Cites Unies

Civilisations

CODATA Bulletin (Committee on Data for Science and Technology) 781

Colecciones Basicas C I N T E R F O R (Centro Interamericano de Investigacion y Documentacion Sobre Formacion Profesional) 329

Collection of Documents for the Study of International Non-Governmental Relations 522

Colombo Plan Bureau. Technical Cooperation under the Colombo Plan. Report 199

Colombo Plan for Co-operative Economic and Social Development in Asia and the Pacific. Consultative Committee. Report 199

Comision Espanola de Cooperacion Con la UNESCO. Revista de Informacion

Comissao de Integracao Eletrica Regional. Informe do Coordenador Tecnico 352

Comite Euro-International du Beton. Bulletin d'Information 135

Comite International de Dachau. Bulletin 451

Comite International des Poids et Mesures. Comite Consultatif d'Electricite. (Rapport et Annexes) 636

Comite International des Poids et Mesures. Comite Consultatif de Photometrie et Radiometrie.(Rapport et Annexes) 636

Comite International des Poids et Mesures. Comite Consultatif de Thermometrie. Rapports et Annexes 636

Comite International des Poids et Mesures. Comite Consultatif des Unites (Rapport et Annexes) 636

Comite International des Poids et Mesures. Comite Consultatif pour la Definition de la Seconde. (Rapport et Annexes) 636

Comite International des Poids et Mesures. Comite Consultatif pour la Definition du Metre (Rapport et Annexes) 636

Comite International des Poids et Mesures. Comite Consultatif pour les Etalons des Mesure des Rayonnements Ionisants (Rapport et Annexes) 636

Commission for the Geological Map of the World. Bulletin 288

Commonwealth Agricultural Bureaux. List of Research Workers 14

Commonwealth Bureau of Agricultural Economics. Annotated Bibliographies. Series B: Agricultural Policy and Rural Development in Africa 24

Commonwealth Bureau of Animal Breeding and Genetics. Technical Communications 44

Commonwealth Bureau of Animal Health. Review Series 894

Commonwealth Bureau of Horticulture and Plantation Crops. Horticultural Review 415

Commonwealth Bureau of Horticulture and Plantation Crops. Research Review 415

Commonwealth Bureau of Horticulture and Plantation Crops. Technical Communications 415

Commonwealth Bureau of Nutrition. Annotated Bibliographies 666

Commonwealth Bureau of Nutrition. Technical Communications 665

Commonwealth Bureau of Pastures and Field Crops. Bulletin 34

Commonwealth Bureau of Soils. Technical Communications 34

Commonwealth Forestry Bureau. Technical Communication 408

Commonwealth Forestry Bureau Annotated Bibliographies 412

Commonwealth Geological Liaison Office. Liaison Report 292

Commonwealth Geological Liaison Office. Newsletter

Commonwealth Geological Liaison Office. Special Publication 292

Commonwealth Institute of Biological Control. Technical Communications 102

Commonwealth Mycological Institute. Phytopathological Papers 114

Commonwealth Universities Yearbook 335

Communication Arts International

Communist Program 709

Compendio Estadistico Centroamericano 838

Compendium of University Entrance Requirements for First Degree Courses in the United Kingdom 335

Composers of the Americas/Compositores de America 658

Concern

Confederacion Latinoamericana de Asociaciones Cristianas de Jovenes. Carta 764

Conscience et Liberte

Consejo Superior Universitario Centroamericano. Actas de la Reunion Ordinaria 335

Consejo Superior Universitario Centroamericano. Publicaciones 335

Consequence

Consumer Review

Consumers Directory 279

Controller

Convenios Centroamericanos de Integration Economica. 199

Convergence

Convergence: International Colloquium on Automotive Electronic Technology. Proceedings 870

Cooperative Press in South-East Asia 504

Cooperative Trade Directory for Southeast Asia 180

Corporate Taxation in Latin America

COSPAR Technique Manual (Committee on Space Research) 7

COSPAR Transactions (Committee on Space Research) 7

Cotton. Part 1: Monthly Review of the World Situation

Cotton. Part 2: World Statistics

Council of Europe. Concise Handbook 522

Council of Europe. Council for Cultural Cooperation. Annual Report 720

Council of Europe. Directorate of Legal Affairs. Information Bulletin on Legislative Activities

Council of Europe. Documentation Centre for Education in Europe. Newsletter/Faits Nouveaux

Council of Europe. Documentation Section and Library. Bibliographical Bulletin. Series: Legal Affairs.

Council of Europe. Documentation Section and Library. Bibliographical Bulletin. Series: Political and Economic Affairs.

Council of Europe. Documentation Section and Library. Bibliographical Bulletin. Series: Social Affairs

Council of Europe. European Treaty Series 522

Council of Europe. Exchange of Information Between the Member States on Their Legislative Activity and Regulations (New Series) 522

Council of Europe. Parliamentary Assembly. Documents; Working Papers/Documents de Seance 522

Council of Europe. Parliamentary Assembly. Orders of the Day, Minutes of Proceedings/Ordres du Jour, Proces Verbaux 522

Council of Europe. Parliamentary Assembly. Texts Adopted by the Assembly/Textes Adoptes Par l'Assemblee 522

Council of Europe. Standing Committee on the European Convention on Establishment (Individuals). Periodical Report. 718

Council of Europe Film Weeks 649

Council of Europe Forum

Courrier du Secretariat International de l'Enseignement Universitaire des Sciences Pedagogiques

Crocodiles 128

Cybernetic Medicine

Cytologia/Kitorogia

D E

D E - Bulletin (Democratization of Education)

Democratic Journalist

Desarrollo del Tropico Americano

Desert Locust Control Organization for Eastern Africa. Annual Report 34

Design Abstracts International

Deutschland - Frankreich

Diamond World Review

Directory of Travel Agencies 884

Directory of Water Pollution Research Laboratories 385

Documentation Bulletin for South-East Asia

Don Universel du Sang

Drug and Alcohol Dependence

E A A A Newsletter (European Association of Advertising Agencies) 5

E B U Monographs, Legal and Administrative Series (European Broadcasting Union) 267

E B U Review. Geneva Edition (Programmes, Adminstration, Law) (European Broadcasting Union)

E B U Seminars for Producers and Directors of Educational Television for Schools and Adults (European Broadcasting Union) 267

E B U Workshops for Producers and Directors of Television Programmes for Children and Young People (European Broadcasting Union) 267

E C A R B I C A Journal (International Council on Archives, East and Central African Regional Branch)

E F I L Documentation (European Federation for Intercultural Learning) 342

E F I L Newsletter (European Federation for Intercultural Learning)

E F T A Bulletin (European Free Trade Association)

E F T A Trade (European Free Trade Association) 195

E S A Bulletin (European Space Agency)

E U M E N Action (Entr'aide Universitaire Mondiale) 336

Earthquake Engineering and Structural Dynamics

East African Freshwater Fisheries Research Organization. Annual Report 396

East Asia Travel Association. Proceedings of the General Meeting 884

Echo

Economic Review of World Tourism 884

Economie Familiale/Home Economics

Ecumenical Review

Education in Europe. Section 1: Higher Education and Research 336

Education in Europe. Section 2: General and Technical Education 317

Education in Europe. Section 3: Out-Of-School Education 317

Education in Europe. Section 4 (General) 317

Educational Statistics Yearbook 317

Electrochimica Acta

Electroencephalography and Clinical Neurophysiology

Elektrizitaetsverwertung/Electrique/Electrical Service

Enfant en Milieu Tropical

Engineering Industries in O E C D Member Countries: New Basic Statistics 222

Entomologische Zeitschrift

Environmental Policy and Law

Environmental Policy and Law Papers 385

Enzyme

Epilepsia

Episodes

Ergebnisse der Limnologie 307

Estadistica

Etudes de Cas de Conflits Internationaux 721

EUDISED R & D Bulletin (Documentation Centre for Education in Europe)

Eurocontrol 8

Europastimme

European and Mediterranean Plant Protection Organization. E P P O Bulletin/Bulletin O E P P 35

European and Mediterranean Plant Protection Organization. Publications. Series B: Plant Health Newsletter 35

European Aspects, Law Series 511

European Aspects, Social Studies Series 813

European Association for Animal Production. Publications 44

European Association for Animal Production. Symposia on Energy Metabolism 44

European Association of Exploration Geophysicists. Constitution and By-Laws, Membership List. 304

European Co-Operation 523

European Commission of Human Rights. Annual Review/Compte Rendu Annual 511

European Commission of Human Rights. Decisions and Reports

European Committee on Crime Problems. Bulletin on Legislative Activities 281

European Congress on Molecular Spectroscopy. Proceedings 249

European Coordination Centre for Research and Documentation in Social Sciences. Publications 797

European Council of Jewish Community Services. Exchange

European Court of Human Rights. Publications. Series A: Judgments and Decisions/Cour Europeenne des Droits de l'Homme. Publications. Serie a: Arrets et Decisions 718

European Curriculum Studies 348

European Demographic Information Bulletin

European Economic Review

European Federation of Finance House Associations. Annual Report 172

European Federation of Finance House Associations. Newsletter

European Free Trade Association. Annual Report 195

European Information Centre for Nature Conservation. Newsletter. Nature

European Journal of Biochemistry

European Journal of Political Research

European League for Economic Cooperation. Publications 199

European League for Economic Cooperation. Report of the Secretary General on the Activities of E. L. E. C. 199

European Organisation for Civil Aviation Electronics. General Assembly. Annual Report 8

European Organization for Nuclear Research. Liste des Publications Scientifiques/List of Scientific Publications 700

European Research

European Southern Observatory. Annual Report 82

European Taxation

European Yearbook 90

Exchange of Information on Research in European Law/Echange d'Informations sur les Recherches en Droit Europeen 521

Expression

Extensions and Corrections to the U D C 529

Eyelights

F. D. I. Newsletter

F.I.D./C.R. Report Series (International Federation for Documentation) 530

F I D Directory (International Federation for Documentation) 530

F I D News Bulletin (International Federation for Documentation)

F I D/R I Meetings Reports (International Federation for Documentation, Committee on Research on the Theoretical Basis of Information) 530

F I D/R I Series on Problems of Information Science (International Federation for Documentation, Committee on Research on the Theoretical Basis of Information) 530

F. I. E. J. Bulletin (Federation Internationale des Editeurs de Journaux et Publications)

F I F A News (International Federation of Association Football)

F I S Bulletin (International Ski Federation)

F I T Newsletter/F I T Nouvelles (International Federation of Translators)

Faith and Order Papers 765

Family Planning in Five Continents 131

Federacion Panamericana de Associaciones de Facultades de Medicina. Boletin

Federation Internationale de Gymnastique. Bulletin

Federation Internationale de Rugby Amateur. Annuaire 824

Federation Internationale des Professeurs de Francais. Bulletin

Federation Internationale Motocycliste. Annuaire 826

Fernschach

Flashes from the Trade Unions

Fluoride

Folia Linguistica 544

Folia Phoniatrica

Fontes Artis Musicae

Food Consumption in the O. E. C. D. Countries/ Consommation de Denrees Alimentaires dans les Pays de l'O.C.D.E. 404

Food Irradiation Information/Informations sur l'Irradiation des Denrees

Forum

Fred och Frihet/Pax et Libertas

Free Labour World

Friends of I B B Y Newsletter (International Board on Books for Young People)

Futuribles

Futurology

General Treaty for Central American Economic Integration. Permanent Secretariat. Carta Informativa

General Treaty for Central American Economic Integration. Permanent Secretariat. Newsletter 200

Geodex Retrieval System for Geotechnical Abstracts

Geodynamics International 304

Geographical Distribution of Financial Flows to Less Developed Countries. (Disbursements) 200

Geothermics

Giornale Storico della Lunigiana e del Territorio Lucense

Guide-Annuaire de l'Equipement Agricole 32

Guide to European Taxation. Taxation of Companies in Europe

Guides to European Taxation: Taxation of Patent Royalties, Dividends, Interest in Europe

Guitarra

Hague Conference on Private International Law. Actes et Documents 523

Handbook on the U.S.-German Tax Convention 229

Hebrew Christian

Histopathology

Human Rights Bulletin

Hydrological Sciences Bulletin/Bulletin des Sciences Hydrologiques

I A A E E Monographs (International Association for the Advancement of Ethnology and Eugenics) 50

I A A E E Reprint (International Association for the Advancement of Ethnology and Eugenics) 50

I A B C News (International Association of Business Communicators)

I A G A News (International Association of Geomagnetism and Aeronomy) 304

I A G Communications (Applied Information Processing Group)

I. A. J. R. C. Journal (International Association of Jazz Record Collectors)

I A L News (International Association of Laryngectomees)

I A S L Newsletter (International Association of School Librarianship)

I A T A Review (International Air Transport Association.) 868

I B A Review (International Bauxite Association)

I B I Newsletter (Intergovernmental Bureau for Informatics)

I C A Regional Bulletin

I C A S A L S Newsletter (International Center for Arid and Semi-Arid Land Studies)

I. C. C. Information (International Chamber of Commerce)

I C E L References (International Council on Environmental Law) 390

I C E M Review (International Council for Educational Media)

I C E S Oceanographic Data Lists and Inventories 310

I C F T U Economic & Social Bulletin (International Confederation of Free Trade Unions)

I C I A Information Bulletin (International Center of Information on Antibiotics) 686

I C I D Bulletin (International Commission on Irrigation and Drainage.)

I C L A S Bulletin (International Council for Laboratory Animal Science)

I C M A Newsletter (International City Management Association)

I C M C Newsletter (International Catholic Migration Commission)

I C O M News/Nouvelles de l'I.C.O.M. (International Council of Museums)

I C P A Quarterly Bulletin (International Commission for the Prevention of Alcoholism)

I C V A News (International Council of Voluntary Agencies)

I E C Bulletin (International Electrotechnical Commission)

I E C Catalogue of Publications (International Electrotechnical Commission) 360

I E E E International Conference on Acoustics, Speech and Signal Processing. Conference Record (Institute of Electrical and Electronics Engineers, Inc.) 354

I E E E International Symposium on Electrical Insulation. Conference Record (Institute of Electrical and Electronics Engineers, Inc.) 354

I E S A Information

I F A P News/F I P A Nouvelles (International Federation of Agricultural Producers)

I F H P News Sheet (International Federation for Housing and Planning)

I F I P Information Bulletin (International Federation for Information Processing) 530

I F L A Directory (International Federation of Library Associations and Institutions) 531

I F L A Journal (International Federation of Library Associations and Institutions)

I F L A Publications (International Federation of Library Associations and Institutions) 531

I. F. L. Nieuws (International Friendship League)

I. F. T. Journal (International Foundation for Telemetering)

I G F-Journal (International Graphical Federation)

I I A S A Annual Report (International Institute for Applied Systems Analysis) 272

I L P E S Cuadernos. Serie 1: Apuntes de Clase (Instituto Latinamericano de Planificacion Economica y Social)

I M A C S News (International Association for Mathematics and Computers in Simulation)

I M F News (International Metalworkers Federation)

I M F Studies (International Metalworkers Federation) 628

I M P H O S Congress Proceedings/World Phosphate Rock Institute. Proceedings (Institut Mondial du Phosphate) 373

I M U Canberra Circular (International Mathematical Union) 585

I M Z Bulletin (International Music Centre)

I P I Report (International Press Institute)

I P P F Co-Operative Information Service (International Planned Parenthood Federation)

I P P F News (International Planned Parenthood Federation)

I P R A Studies in Peace Research (International Peace Research Association) 721

I P S F News Bulletin (International Pharmaceutical Students Federation)

I. P. T. C. Newsletter (International Press Telecommunications Council) 269

I R R I Annual Report (International Rice Research Institute) 42

I S C U Newsletter (International Council of Scientific Unions)

I S M E Yearbook (International Society for Music Education) 659

I S O Bulletin (International Organization for Standardization)

I S O International Standards (International Organization for Standardization) 637

I S O Memento (International Organization for Standardization) 637

I S T A News Bulletin (International Seed Testing Association)

I S U Constitution (International Skating Union) 820

I S U Regulations (International Skating Union) 820

I T A Bulletin (Institut du Transport Aerien)

I T C Information Booklets 422

I T C Journal

I T C - Publications. Series A (Photogrammetry) (International Training Centre for Aerial Survey) 422

I T M F Directory (International Textile Manufacturers Federation) 856

I T T Elektrisches Nachrichtenwesen (International Telephone and Telegraph Corporation)

I T U Review

I U B S Newsmagazine (International Union of Biological Sciences)

I U C N Annual Report (International Union for Conservation of Nature and Natural Resources) 276

I U C N Bulletin (International Union for Conservation of Nature and Natural Resources)

I. U. G. G. Chronicle (International Union of Geodesy and Geophysics)

I U L A (Publication) (International Union of Local Authorities) 742

I U L A Newsletter/I U L A Nouvelles/I U L A Nachrichten (International Union of Local Authorities)

I U P I W Views (International Union of Petroleum & Industrial Workers)

I U S S P Papers 727

I U S Sport Bulletin/Bulletin Sportif de l' U. I. E./ Boletin Deportivo de la U. I. E. (International Union of Students)

I W G I A Documents (International Work Group for Indigenous Affairs) 50

I W G I A Newsletter (International Work Group for Indigenous Affairs) 50

Ibero-American Bureau of Education. Information and Publications Department Series V: Technical Seminars and Meetings 318

ICE (International Glaciological Society)

Ichthyologica

Indicadores Economicos Centroamericanos

Individual Psychology News Letter

Inform Quarterly Newsletter

Informaciones F I D/C L A (International Federation for Documentation, Comision Latinoamericana)

Informaciones Sindicales Continentales

Information Bulletin for Catholic Rural Organizations

Information, Computer and Communications Policy 200

Informations Universitaires et Professionnelles Internationales

Infoterm Series (International Information Centre for Terminology, Vienna) 545

Ingenieria Sanitaria

INDEX TO PUBLICATIONS OF INTERNATIONAL ORGANIZATIONS

Inspel

Institut International du Froid. Bulletin/International Institute of Refrigeration. Bulletin

Institut Panafricain pour le Developpement. Annuaire des Anciens Etudiants

Institut Panafricain pour le Developpement. Travaux Manuscrits 28

Instituto Indigenista Interamericano Serie de Ediciones Especiales 50

Instituto Interamericano de Ciencios Agricolas de la O E A. Documentos Oficiales 16

Instituto Interamericano del Nino. Boletin

Instituto Interamericano del Nino. Publicaciones Sobre Servicio Social 806

Instituto Panamericano de Geografia e Historia. Boletin Aereo

Inter-African Phyto-Sanitary Commission. Publication 36

Inter-American Bar Association. Letter to Members 513

Inter-American Center of Tax Administrators. Informativo/Newsletter

Inter-American Centre for Agricultural Documentation and Information. Documentacion e Informacion Agricola 25

Interamerican Children's Institute. Report of the General Director 806

Inter-American Commission of Women. News Bulletin 900

Inter-American Commission of Women. Noticiero 900

Inter-American Council for Education, Science, and Culture. Final Report 318

Inter-American Council of Commerce and Production. Uruguayan Section. Publicaciones 200

Interamerican Defense College. Library Bulletin/Colegio Interamericano de Defensa. Boletin de la Biblioteca

Inter-American Development Bank. Annual Report 174

Inter-American Development Bank. Institute for Latin American Integration. Annual Report 200

Inter-American Economic and Social Council. Final Report of the Annual Meeting at the Ministerial Level 469

Inter-American Institute of Agricultural Sciences. Informe Anual 16

Inter-American Institute of Agricultural Sciences. Technical Advisory Council. Junta Directiva. Reunion Anual. Resoluciones y Documentos 16

Inter-American Nuclear Energy Commission. Final Report 703

Inter-American Press Association. Committee on Freedom of the Press. Report 711

Inter-American Press Association. Minutes of the Annual Meeting 505

Inter-American Review of Bibliography/Revista Interamericana de Bibliografia

Inter-American Statistical Institute. Committee on Improvement of National Statistics. Report 841

Inter-American Tropical Tuna Commission. Bulletin/Comision Interamericana del Atun Tropical. Boletin 398

Inter-American Tropical Tuna Commission. Data Report 397

Inter-American Tropical Tuna Commission. Informe Anual. Annual Report 398

Interdependence

Intergovernmental Committee for European Migration. Review of Achievements 727

InterMedia

International Abstracts in Operations Research

International Advertising Association. United Kingdom Chapter. Concise Guide to International Markets 5

International Air Transport Association. Annual Report 868

International Alban Berg Society. Newsletter 660

International Animated Film Association. Bulletin 650

International Archery Federation. Bulletin Officiel 820

International Arthurian Society. Bibliographical Bulletin 578

International Association for Bridge and Structural Engineering. Reports of the Working Commissions 375

International Association for Byzantine Studies. Bulletin d'Information et de Coordination 455

International Association for Cross-Cultural Psychology. Newsletter

International Association for Mass Communication Research. Letter from the President 264

International Association for Plant Tissue Culture. Newsletter

International Association for Shell and Spatial Structures. Bulletin 375

International Association for the Exchange of Students for Technical Experience. Annual Report 342

International Association of Agricultural Librarians and Documentalists. Quarterly Bulletin

International Association of Dentistry for Children. Journal

International Association of Engineering Geology. Bulletin

International Association of French Studies. Cahiers 565

International Association of Geodesy. Central Bureau for Satellite Geodesy. Bibliography 428

International Association of Geodesy. Central Bureau for Satellite Geodesy. Information Bulletin 423

International Association of Geodesy. Commission Permanente des Marees Terrestres. Marees Terrestres Bulletin d'Information 423

International Association of Hydrogeologists. Memoires 308

International Association of Labour History Institutions. Bibliographische Information

International Association of Law Libraries. Directory 531

International Association of Liberal Religious Women. Newsletter 765

International Association of Lighthouse Authorities. I.A.L.A. Bulletin/Association Internationale de Signalisation Maritime. Bulletin de l'A I S M

International Association of Philatelic Journalists. Bulletin 478

International Association of Theoretical and Applied Limnology. Communications 308

International Association of University Professors & Lecturers. Communication 337

International Association of Volcanology and Chemistry of the Earth's Interior. Newsletter 305

International Astronomical Union. Transactions and Highlights 82

International Atlantic Salmon Foundation. Newsletter.

International Baccalaureate Office. Annual Bulletin 319

International Badminton Federation. Annual Statute Book 820

International Bibliography of Selected Police Literature 285

International Bibliography of the Forensic Sciences 602

International Biennial Exhibition of Prints in Tokyo 75

International Brain Research Organization Monograph Series 619

International Bureau of Fiscal Documentation. Annual Report 230

International Bureau of Fiscal Documentation. Publication 230

International Cargo Handling Coordination Association. Rapports des Comites Nationaux 196

International Cataloguing

International Center of Tropical Agriculture. Annual Report 16

International Center of Tropical Agriculture. Information Bulletin 16

International Center of Tropical Agriculture. Reference Bulletins 16

International Center of Tropical Agriculture. Technical Bulletin 16

International Centre for Settlement of Investment Disputes. Annual Report 203

International Centre of Insect Physiology and Ecology. Annual Report 122

International Chamber of Commerce. Handbook 179

International Chamber of Commerce. United States Council. Report 179

International Child Welfare Review

International Children's Center. Courrier

International Children's Centre. Paris. Report of the Director-General to the Executive Board 814

International Children's Centre. Paris. Travaux et Documents 814

International Christian Broadcasters Bulletin

International Civil Defence

International Classification

International College of Dentists. European Section. Newsletter 609

International Commission for Uniform Methods of Sugar Analysis. Report of the Proceedings of the Session 405

International Commission of Jurists. Review

International Commission on Irrigation and Drainage. Congress Reports 381

International Commission on Irrigation and Drainage. Report 896

International Commission on Large Dams. Bulletin 375

International Commission on Radiological Protection. Report 622

International Committee for Historical Science. Bulletin d'Information 433

International Committee of the Red Cross. Annual Report/Rapport d'Activite/Informe de Actividad/Taetigkeitsbericht 806

International Committee on Urgent Anthropological and Ethnological Research. Bulletin 50

International Confederation of Free Trade Unions. Features 506

International Confederation of Free Trade Unions. World Congress Reports 506

International Confederation of Societies of Authors and Composers 677

International Conference on Plutonium and Other Actinides. Proceedings 251

International Conference on Water Law and Administration. Background Paper. 896

International Congress of University Adult Education. Journal

International Congress Science Series 626

International Consumer

International Cooperative Alliance. Cooperative Series 181

International Copper Information Bulletin

International Cotton Advisory Committee. Country Statements Presented in Connection with the Plenary Meetings 36

International Cotton Industry Statistics 857

International Cotton-System Fibre Consumption Statistics

International Council for Bird Preservation. British Section. Report 125

International Council for the Exploration of the Sea. Annales Biologiques 104

International Council for the Exploration of the Sea. Bulletin Statistique 310

International Council for the Exploration of the Sea. Cooperative Research Reports 311

International Council for the Exploration of the Sea. Journal du Conseil 311

International Council of Scientific Unions. Year Book 784

International Council of Voluntary Agencies. Documents Series 806

International Council of Women. Newsletter/Conseil International des Femmes. Newsletter

International Council on Archives. Microfilm Committee. Bulletin 531

International Customs Journal/Bulletin International des Douanes 230

International Dairy Federation. Annual Bulletin/ Federation Internationale de Laiterie. Bulletin Annuel 41

International Dairy Federation. Annual Memento/ Federation Internationale de Laiterie. Memento Annuel 41

International Dairy Federation. Catalogue of I D F Publications. Catalogue des Publications de la F I L 25

International Dairy Federation. International Standard/Federation Internationale de Laiterie. Norme Internationale 41

International Dental Federation. News Letter/ Federation Dentaire Internationale. News Letter

International Dental Journal

International Development Review/Revista del Desarrollo Internacional/Revue du Developpment Internacional

International Directory of Antiquarian Booksellers/ Repertoire International de la Librairie Ancienne 759

International Directory of Prisoners' Aid Agencies 281

International Egg Commission. Market Review Situation & Outlook Report

International Egg Commission. Six-Monthly Statistical Bulletin

International Electrotechnical Commission. Annuaire/ International Electrotechnical Commission. Handbook 355

International Electrotechnical Commission. Report on Activities 355

International Federation for Documentation. P-Notes 531

International Federation for Housing and Planning. Directory 485

International Federation of Commerical Clerical and Technical Employees. Newsletter

International Federation of Journalists and Travel Writers. Official List/Repertoire Officiel 887

International Federation of Secondary Education Teachers. International Bulletin/Federation Internationale des Professeurs de l'Enseignement Secondaire Officiel, Bulletin International/ Internationale Vereinigung der Lehrer an Offentlichen Hoheren Schulen. Internationale Zeitschrift

International Fiscal Association. Yearbook 523

International Fiscal Harmonization Series 230

International Folk Music Council. Yearbook 660

International Forum of Light Music in Radio 267

International Graphical Federation. Report of Activities 507

International Gravimetric Bureau. Bulletin d'Information 305

International Group for Scientific Research in Stomatology. Bulletin

International Handbook of Universities and Other Institutions of Higher Education 337

International Hotel Guide 482

International Humanism

International Hydrographic Bulletin

International Hydrographic Organization. Yearbook 311

International Hydrographic Review

International Institute for Land Reclamation and Improvement. Annual Report 36

International Institute for Land Reclamation and Improvement. Bibliography 25

International Institute for Land Reclamation and Improvement. Bulletin 36

International Institute for Land Reclamation and Improvement. Publication 36

International Institute of Seismology and Earthquake Engineering. Bulletin 305

International Institute of Seismology and Earthquake Engineering. Earthquake Report 305

International Institute of Seismology and Earthquake Engineering. Lecture Note 305

International Institute of Seismology and Earthquake Engineering. Progress Report 305

International Institute of Seismology and Earthquake Engineering. Report of Individual Study by Participants to I I S E E 305

International Institute of Seismology and Earthquake Engineering. Year Book 305

International Institute on the Prevention and Treatment of Alcoholism. Selected Papers 287

International Journal of Biometeorology

International Journal of Cancer

International Journal of Dermatology

International Journal of Early Childhood

International Journal of Government Auditing/Revue Internationale de la Verification des Comptes Publics/Revista Internacional de Entidades Fiscalizadoras Superiores

International Journal of Group Tensions

International Journal of Gynaecology and Obstetrics

International Journal of Health Education

International Journal of Law Libraries.

International Journal of Leprosy and Other Mycobacterial Diseases

International Journal of Oral Surgery

International Journal of Physical Education/ Internationale Zeitschrift fuer Sportpaedagogik

International Journal of Psycho-Analysis

International Journal of Sport Psychology

International Journal of Systematic Bacteriology

International League for Human Rights. Annual Report 718

International Linguistic Association. Monograph 545

International Linguistic Association. Special Publications 545

International Maize and Wheat Improvement Center. Research Bulletin 42

International Man-Made Fibre Production Statistics

International Medical Directory 596

International Military Sports Council. Technical Brochure/Conseil International du Sport Militaire. Brochure Technique 639

International Music Council. German Committee. Referate Informationen

International Naturist Guide/Internationaler FKK- Reisefuehrer/Guide Naturiste Internationale 830

International News Items

International North Pacific Fisheries Commission. Annual Report 398

International North Pacific Fisheries Commission. Bulletin 398

International Nursing Review

International Oil Scouts Association. Official Publication

International Organization

International Organization of Consumers Unions. Proceedings 280

International Orthopaedics

International Pacific Halibut Commission (U.S. and Canada). Annual Report 398

International Pacific Halibut Commission (U.S. and Canada). Scientific Reports 398

International Pacific Salmon Fisheries Commission. Annual Report 398

International Pacific Salmon Fisheries Commission. Bulletin 398

International Pacific Salmon Fisheries Commission. Progress Report 398

924 INDEX TO PUBLICATIONS OF INTERNATIONAL ORGANIZATIONS

International Pathology

International Peace Research Institute. Basic Social Science Monographs 798

International Peace Research Newsletter

International Peat Society. Bulletin/Internationale Moor- und Torf-Gesellschaft. Mitteilungen 37

International Plant Protection Center. Infoletter

International Polar Motion Service. Annual Report/ Kokusai Kyoku-Undo Kansoku Jigyo Nenpo 82

International Polar Motion Service. Monthly Notes/ Kokusai Kyoku-Undo Kansoku Jigyo Geppo

International Police Association. Meeting of the International Executive Council 282

International Police Association. Travel Scholarships 282

International Political Science Abstracts/ Documentation Politique Internationale

International Population Conference. Proceedings 727

International Press Institute. Survey 505

International Prisoners Aid Association. Newsletter

International Psychologist

International Railway Statistics. Statistics of Individual Railways 873

International Rayon and Synthetic Fibres Committee. Statistical Yearbook 857

International Reading Association. Annual Report 319

International Record

International Reformed Bulletin

International Rehabilitation Review

International Rescue Committee Annual Report 806

International Review for Business Education/Revue Internationale pour l'Enseignement Commercial/ Internationale Zeitschrift fuer Kaufmaennisches Bildungswesen/Rivista Internazionale per la Cultura Commerciale/Revista Internacional la Ensenanza Comercial

International Review of Administrative Sciences

International Review of Mission

International Review of the Red Cross

International Rubber Digest

International Secretariat of Entertainment Trade Unions. Newsletter 507

International Seismological Centre. Bulletin

International Silk Association. Monthly Newsletter

International Skating Union. Bestimmungen ueber das Eistanzen 820

International Social Science Council. Publications 798

International Social Security Association. Etudes et Recherches/Studies and Research 499

International Social Security Review

International Social Work

International Society of Criminology. Bulletin 282

International Society of Plant Morphologists. Yearbook 116

International Society of Soil Science. Bulletin

International Solid Waste and Public Cleansing Association. Information Bulletin

International Specialty Conference on Cold-Formed Steel Structures. (Proceedings) 628

International Sporting Press Association. Bulletin. N.S. 820

International Statistical Handbook of Urban Public Transport/Recueil International de Statistiques des Transports Publics Urbains/Internationales Statistik-Handbuch fuer den Oeffentlichen Stadtverkehr 862

International Statistical Review/Revue International de Statistique

International Studies Notes

International Sugar Organization. Annual Report 37

International Sugar Organization Statistical Bulletin

International Surgery

International Symposium on Canine Heartworm Disease. Proceedings 894

International Textile, Garment and Leather Workers' Federation. World Digest

International Textile Machinery Shipment Statistics 857

International Textile Manufacturing 856

International Theatre

International Tin Research Council. Annual Report 628

International Trade Union Committee of Solidarity with the Workers and People of Chile. Bulletin 722

International Trade Union News

International Transplutonium Element Symposium. Proceedings 251

International Union against Cancer. Manual/Union Internationale Contre le Cancer. Manuele 605

International Union for Inland Navigation. Annual Report 862

International Union for Vacuum Science, Technique and Applications. News Bulletin

International Union of Alpine Associations. Bulletin/ Union Internationale des Associations d'Alpinisme. Bulletin

International Union of Crystallography. Structure Reports 251

International Union of Food and Allied Workers' Associations. News Bulletin

International Union of Geodesy and Geophysics. Monograph 423

International Union of Geodesy and Geophysics. Proceedings of the General Assembly 423

International Union of Physiological Sciences. Newsletter 126

International Union of Public Transport. Technical Reports of the Congresses 862

International Union of Tenants. International Information

International Whaling Commission. Report 398

International Wheat Council. Annual Report 16

International Wheat Council. Market Report

International Wheat Council. Record of Operations of Member Countries 16

International Wheat Council. Secretariat Papers 16

International Women's News 722

International Yearbook of the Underwater World/ Annuaire International du Monde Sous-Marin 827

Internationale Berg- und Seilbahn-Rundschau/ International Aerial Tramway Review

Internationale Gesellschaft fuer Geschichte der Pharmazie. Veroeffentlichungen. Neue Folge 685

Internationale Gesellschaft fuer Urheberrecht. Yearbook 677

Internationale Stiftung Mozarteum. Mitteilungen

Internationale Vereinigung zur Foerderung des Studiums der Hegelschen Philosophie. Veroeffentlichung 689

Internationales Institut fuer den Frieden. Cultural Anniversaries Series 491

Internationales Jahrbuch fuer Kartographie 423

Inter-Parliamentary Bulletin

Inter-Parliamentary Union. Series: "Reports and Documents" 711

Interpressgrafik

Interrescue Information

Intervirology

Inventaria Archaeologica Belgique 61

Inventaria Archaeologica Ceskoslovensko 61

Inventaria Archaeologica Denmark 61

Inventaria Archaeologica Deutschland 61

Inventaria Archaeologica Espana 62

Inventaria Archaeologica France 62

Inventaria Archaeologica Great Britain 62

Inventaria Archaeologica Italia 62

Inventaria Archaeologica Jugoslavija 62

Inventaria Archaeologica Norway 62

Inventaria Archaeologica Oesterreich 62

Inventaria Archaeologica Pologne 62

Inventaria Archaeologica Ungarn 62

Jahrbuch fuer Liturgik und Hymnologie 766

Jazzforschung/Jazz Research 660

Journal de Genetique Humaine

Journal of Cardiovascular Surgery

Journal of Glaciology

Journal of Hydraulic Research

Journal of Maxillofacial Surgery

Journal of Northwest Atlantic Fishery Science

Journal of Organizational Communication

Journal of Police Science and Administration

Journal of Reading

Journal of Rural Cooperation

Journal of Structural Learning

Journal of Terramechanics

Journal of Traffic Medicine

Journalists' Affairs

Jugend und Buch

Justice et Service

Kidma

Kidney International

Klassische Homoeopathie

La Zona Norte. Informa 17

Labor Press and Information

Labor Professional Action

INDEX TO PUBLICATIONS OF INTERNATIONAL ORGANIZATIONS

Labor-Transport

Latin American Bulletin

Lead and Zinc Statistics

League of Red Cross Societies. Biennial Report 807

Leben und Umwelt

Lethaia

Library, Documentation and Archives Serials 539

Ligue Internationale Contre la Concurrence Deloyale. Annuaire

Ligue Internationale Contre la Concurrence Deloyale. Communication

LINKletter

Literacy Discussion

Local Finance

Log of the Star Class 827

Lotus

Lymphology

M.I.I. Series (Muslim Intellectuals' International) 769

Market Frontier News

Materiaux & Constructions/Materials & Structures

Ma'yanot 392

Medailles

Medecine d'Afrique Noire

Medical & Biological Engineering & Computing

Memento de l'O.I.V. (Office International de la Vigne et du Vin) 86

Metallography

Metro: a Bibliography 866

Metrologia

Microtables Imports-Exports of O E C D Countries 197

Microwave Power Symposium. Proceedings 356

Migration Bulletin

Migration News

Migration Today 728

Military Balance 639

Ministerial Formation

Monthly Letter on Evangelism

Monumentum

Muslim World

N A F O Statistical Bulletin 399

N A T O Handbook (North Atlantic Treaty Organization) 722

N A T O Nyt (North Atlantic Treaty Organization)

N A T O Review (North Atlantic Treaty Organization)

Nature and Environment Series 277

Naturopa

Neuroendocrinology

New Perspectives

News from O E C D

News Service

NEWSIDIC

Nonviolence et Societe

Nordisk Statistisk Aarsbok/Yearbook of Nordic Statistics 843

Nordisk Statistisk Skriftserie/Statistical Reports of the Nordic Countries 843

Nordisk Statutsamling 516

Noticias de Galapagos

Nuclear Law Bulletin

Numen

O A S. General Secretariat. Annual Report (Organization of American States) 470

O E C D Economic Outlook (Organization for Economic Cooperation & Development)

O E C D Financial Statistics/Statistiques Financieres de l'OCDE (Organization for Economic Cooperation and Development) 162

O E C D Halden Reactor Project (Organization for Economic Cooperation and Development) 704

O E C D Observer

O I E C Bulletin (Catholic International Education Office)

O I R T Information (International Radio and Television Organization)

O.I.V. Bulletin (Office International de la Vigne et du Vin)

Olympic Review

One World

Onoma

Orbis

Orbis Geographicus 425

Organ Building Periodical/Zeitschrift fuer Orgelbau (International Society of Organbuilders) 662

Organisation Internationale pour l'Etude des Langues Anciennes Par Ordinateur. Revue/International Organization for Ancient Languages Analysis by Computer. Review

Organization for Economic Cooperation and Development. Activities of O E C D: Report by the Secretary General 200

Organization for Economic Cooperation and Development. Catalogue of Publications 93

Organization for Economic Cooperation and Development. Cement Industry. Industrie du Ciment 138

Organization for Economic Cooperation and Development. Council. Code de la Liberation des Mouvements de Capitaux. Code of Liberalisation of Capital Movements 175

Organization for Economic Cooperation and Development. Development Assistance Committee. Report by the Chairman on the Annual Review 200

Organization for Economic Cooperation and Development. Development Cooperation 200

Organization for Economic Cooperation and Development. Development Centre. Employment Series 210

Organization for Economic Cooperation and Development. Economic Surveys: Austria 188

Organization for Economic Cooperation and Development. Economic Surveys: Australia 188

Organization for Economic Cooperation and Development. Economic Surveys: Belgium-Luxembourg Economic Union 188

Organization for Economic Cooperation and Development. Economic Surveys: Canada 188

Organization for Economic Cooperation and Development. Economic Surveys: Denmark 188

Organization for Economic Cooperation and Development. Economic Surveys: France 188

Organization for Economic Cooperation and Development. Economic Surveys: Germany 188

Organization for Economic Cooperation and Development. Economic Surveys: Greece 188

Organization for Economic Cooperation and Development. Economic Surveys: Iceland 188

Organization for Economic Cooperation and Development. Economic Surveys: Ireland 188

Organization for Economic Cooperation and Development. Economic Surveys: Italy 188

Organization for Economic Cooperation and Development. Economic Surveys: Japan 188

Organization for Economic Cooperation and Development. Economic Surveys: Netherlands. 188

Organization for Economic Cooperation and Development. Economic Surveys: Norway 188

Organization for Economic Cooperation and Development. Economic Surveys: Portugal 188

Organization for Economic Cooperation and Development. Economic Surveys: Spain 188

Organization for Economic Cooperation and Development. Economic Surveys: Sweden 188

Organization for Economic Cooperation and Development. Economic Surveys. Switzerland 188

Organization for Economic Cooperation and Development. Economic Surveys: Turkey 189

Organization for Economic Cooperation and Development. Economic Surveys: United Kingdom 189

Organization for Economic Cooperation and Development. Economic Surveys: United States 189

Organization for Economic Cooperation and Development. Economic Surveys: Socialist Federal Republic of Yugoslavia 189

Organization for Economic Cooperation and Development. Electricity Supply Industry. l'Industrie de l'Electricite 357

Organization for Economic Cooperation and Development. Employment of Special Groups 210

Organization for Economic Cooperation and Development. Energy Statistics 364

Organization for Economic Cooperation and Development. Guide to Legislation on Restrictive Business Practices. Supplements 197

Organization for Economic Cooperation and Development. Historical Statistics. Statistiques Retrospectives 162

Organization for Economic Cooperation and Development. Industrial Production. Production Industrielle 224

Organization for Economic Cooperation and Development. Industrial Statistics. Statistiques Industrielles 162

Organization for Economic Cooperation and Development. Inter-Regional Dry Cargo Movements/Mouvements Interregionaux de Cargaisons Seches 162

Organization for Economic Cooperation and Development. Labour Force Statistics (Yearbook) / Statistiques de la Population Active 162

Organization for Economic Cooperation and Development. Labour Statistics/Statistiques de la Population Active

Organization for Economic Cooperation and Development. Liaison Bulletin Between Development Research and Training Institutes 200

Organization for Economic Cooperation and Development. Liaison Bulletin Between Research and Training Institutes 224

Organization for Economic Cooperation and Development. Library. Catalogue of Periodicals/ Catalogue des Periodiques 93

Organization for Economic Cooperation and Development. Library. Ouvrages et Periodiques Nouveaux Catalogues a la Bibliotheque/New Books and Periodicals Catalogued at the Library

Organization for Economic Cooperation and Development. Library. Special Annotated Bibliography; Automation. Bibliographie Speciale Analytique 274

Organization for Economic Cooperation and Development. Main Economic Indicators/ Principaux Indicateurs Economiques (Organization for Economic Cooperation and Development)

Organization for Economic Cooperation and Development. Maritime Transport Committee. Maritime Transport 880

Organization for Economic Cooperation and Development. Nuclear Energy Agency. Activity Report 704

Organization for Economic Cooperation and Development. Oil Statistics/Statistiques Petrolieres 682

Organization for Economic Cooperation and Development. Revenue Statistics of OECD Member Countries 162

Organization for Economic Cooperation and Development. Reviews of Manpower and Social Policies 210

Organization for Economic Cooperation and Development. Social Affairs Division. Developing Job Opportunities 667

Organization for Economic Cooperation and Development. Social Affairs Division. Employment of Special Groups 210

Organization for Economic Cooperation and Development. Special Committee for Iron and Steel. Iron and Steel Industry 629

Organization for Economic Cooperation and Development. Special Committee for Oil. Oil Statistics. Supply and Disposal 680

Organization for Economic Cooperation and Development. Statistics of Foreign Trade. Series A: Monthly Bulletin/Statistiques du Commerce Exterieur. Serie A: Bulletin Mensuel (Organization for Economic Cooperation and Development)

Organization for Economic Cooperation and Development. Statistics of Foreign Trade. Series B: Tables by Reporting Countries /Statistiques du Commerce Exterieur. Serie B: Tableaux Par Pays Declarants

Organization for Economic Cooperation and Development. Statistics of Foreign Trade. Series C: Tables by Commodities. Imports and Exports/ Statistiques du Commerce Exterieur. Serie C: Tableaux Par Produits 162

Organization for Economic Cooperation and Development. Survey of Electric Power Equipment. Enquete sur l'Equipment Electrique 382

Organization for Economic Cooperation and Development. Tourism Committee. Tourism Policy and International Tourism in O E C D Member Countries 889

Organization of African Unity. Health, Sanitation and Nutrition Commission. Proceedings and Report 753

Organization of African Unity. Inter- African Bureau for Soils. Bibliographie 25

Organization of African Unity. Scientific Technical and Research Commission. Publication 788

Organization of American States. Department of Cultural Affairs. Estudios Bibliotecarios 534

Organization of American States. Department of Cultural Affairs Manuales del Bibliotecario 534

Organization of American States. Department of Scientific Affairs. Newsletter.

Organization of American States. Department of Scientific Affairs. Report of Activities 788

Organization of American States. Department of Scientific Affairs. Serie de Biologia: Monografias 106

Organization of American States. Department of Scientific Affairs. Serie de Fisica: Monografias 697

Organization of American States. Department of Scientific Affairs. Serie de Matematica: Monografias 588

Organization of American States. Department of Scientific Affairs. Serie de Quimica: Monografias 247

Organization of American States. General Assembly. Actas y Documentos 723

Organization of American States. Official Records. Indice y Lista General 471

Organization of the Petroleum Exporting Countries. Annual Review and Record 681

Organization of the Petroleum Exporting Countries. Annual Statistical Bulletin 681

Out of School Scientific and Technical Education 788

P A D F News (Pan American Development Foundation)

P A /Planning and Administration

P C R Information (World Council of Churches, Programme to Combat Racism) 766

P. T. T. I. Studies (Postal Telegraph and Telephone International)

Pan American Associations in the United States; A Directory with Supplementary Lists of Other Associations. Inter-American and General 523

Pan American Development Foundation. Annual Report 201

Pan American Institute of Geography and History. Commission on Geophysics. Boletin 306

Pan American Institute of Geography and History. Commission on History. Bibliografias 471

Pan American Institute of Geography and History. Commission on History. Guias 471

Pan American Institute of Geography and History. Commission on History. Historiografias Americanas 471

Pan American Institute of Geography and History. Commission on History. Historiadores de America 471

Pan American Institute of Geography and History. Commission on History. Monumentos Historicos y Arqueologicos 471

Pan American Medical Women's Alliance. Newsletter 598

Panorama

Panorama Democrate Chretien 713

Panorama Democrate Chretien/Panorama Democrata Cristiano/Christlich Demokratisches Panorama

Paraplegia

Participation 713

Pax et Libertas

Peace and the Sciences

Peace Courier

Pedofauna 38

People

Periodic Bulletin of the International Office of Cocoa and Chocolate and the International Sugar Confectionary Manufacturers' Association

Permanent International Altaistic Conference (PIAC). Newsletter 671

Phonetica

Phosphorus in Agriculture/Phosphore et Agriculture

Photogrammetria

Phycologia

Phytomorphology

Planetarian

Planning & Administration

Polar Bears 130

Police Chief 283

Police Labor Review

Potash Review

Programa Comunista

Progress in Water Technology

Psychotherapy and Psychosomatics

Publications on Social History 815

Pulp and Paper Industry in the O E C D Member Countries and Finland/Industrie des Pates et Papiers dans les Pays Membres de l'OCDE et la Finlande 675

Pulp and Paper/Pates et Papiers

Quality

Quarterly Bulletin on Solar Activity

R & D Projects in Documentation and Librarianship

Radio - Television

Rail International

Reading Research Quarterly

Reading Teacher

Reformation Review

Reformed World

Rejuvenation

Repertorium Plantarum Succulentarum 117

Research in Reproduction

Research into Disease 599

Research on Transport Economics/Recherche en Matiere d'Economie des Transports

Resumenes Analiticos C I N T E R F O R (Centro Interamericano de Investigacion y Documentacion sobre Formacion Profesional)

Review of Contemporary Law

Review of Fisheries in OECD Member Countries 399

Review of Income and Wealth

Review of International Cooperation/Revue de la Cooperation Internationale/Revista de la Cooperacion Internacional

Review of Population Reviews

Review of Public and Co-Operative Economy in Israel. 181

Review of the World Wheat Situation 19

INDEX TO PUBLICATIONS OF INTERNATIONAL ORGANIZATIONS

Revista FELABAN (Federacion Latinoamericana de Bancos)

Revista Geofisica

Revista Geografica

Revista Interamericana de Planificacion

Revista Internacional de Vivienda Rural/International Rural Housing Journal 487

Revista Latinoamericana de Quimica

Revista Rotaria

Revue Africaine et Malgache de Psychologie

Revue de Bio-Mathematique/Biomathematics

Revue de Coree

Revue des Parlementaires de Langue Francaise

Revue Internationale de Police Criminelle

Revue Internationale des Industries Agricoles. Bulletin Analytique

Rivista di Studi Liguri

Rotarian

Rubber Statistical Bulletin

S T P Notes (Inter-Union Commission of Solar Terrestrial Physics) 83

Sabouraudia

Scandinavian Journal of History

Science Film

Scientia Horticulturae

Scientific World

Sedimentology

Seed Science and Technology

Selected Documents of the International Petroleum Industry 681

Selected Monographs on Taxation 232

Selection of International Railway Documentation/ Abrege de Documentation Ferroviaire Internationale/Auszuege aus der Internationalen Eisenbahn-Dokumentation/Resumen de Documentacion Ferroviaria Internacional

Sennacieca Revuo 723

Sharing

Shooting Sport/Tir Sportif/Tiro Deportivo/Schiess-Sport

Societe Internationale de Psycho-Prophylaxie Obstetricale. Bulletin Officiel

Solnechnaya Radiatsiya i Radiatsionnyi Balans (Mirovaya Set)/Solar Radiation and Radiation Balance Data (the World Network)

Sols Africains/African Soils

Sources of Contemporary Jewish Thought/Mekevot 557

South Pacific Commission. Annual Report 723

South Pacific Commission. Handbook 715

South Pacific Commission. Information Circular 715

South Pacific Commission. Information Document 715

South Pacific Commission. Technical Paper 715

Southeast Asian Archives 445

South-East Asian Spectrum

Speleological Abstracts/Bulletin Bibliographique Speleologique

Statistical Theory and Method Abstracts

Strategic Survey 723

Structure of the Cotton and Allied Textile Industries 856

Studi Genuensi 65

Studies in Conservation

Studies in Export Promotion 198

Studies in Social History 801

Studies on Tax Administration Series 232

Studies on Taxation and Economic Development 232

Supplementary Service to European Taxation

Survey

Survey of the Activities of Scientific Unions; Special and Scientific Committees of I C S U in the Field of Information 536

T. U. I. A. F. P. W. Information

Taraxacum

Tax News Service

Taxon

Teachers of the World

Terra et Aqua

Texas Yearbook 681

Textile Industry in O E C D Countries 857

Theatre en Pologne/Theatre in Poland

Theosophist

Thrombosis and Haemostasis

Through Europe by Train 874

Tidal Gravity Corrections

Torah Education

Tourism Compendium 893

Trade Unions International of Workers in Commerce. Bulletin

Trade Unions International of Workers in Commerce. News

Translation News 553

Transnational Associations/Associations Transnationales

Transport Museums 864

Transport Workers of the World

Travel Abroad: Frontier Formalities 892

Travel Research Journal

Tropical Ecology

Tuberculosis "T"

Typographical Journal

U I A Information (Union Internationale des Architectes)

U.I.A.M.S. Bulletin Trimestriel (International Union for Moral and Social Action)

U.I.A.M.S. Informations (International Union for Moral and Social Action)

U I C C Bulletin (International Union Against Cancer)

U I S Bulletin (Union Internationale de Speleologie)

U I T B B Information (Trade Unions International of Workers of the Building, Wood and Building Materials Industries)

U I T P Biblio-Index (International Union of Public Transport)

U I T P Revue (International Union of Public Transport)

U R S I Information Bulletin (International Union of Radio Science)

Union Douaniere et Economique de l'Afrique Centrale. Bulletin des Statistiques Generales

Union Internationale de Protection de l'Enfance. Bibliotheque. Liste

Union Mondiale des Organisations Syndicales sur Bases Economique et Sociale Liberales. Conferences: Rapport 507

Union of European Football Associations. Handbook of U E F A 826

Verband

Visual Merchandising

Voix du Silence/Voice of Silence

Volunteer

Vox Sanguinis

Vsemirnoe Profsoyuznoe Dvizhenie

W C O T P Annual Report (World Confederation of Organizations of the Teaching Profession) 345

W C O T P Theme Study (World Confederation of Organizations of the Teaching Profession) 325

W F D Y News (World Federation of Democratic Youth)

W I Z O Review (Women's International Zionist Organization)

W R I Newsletter

Water Research

Welding in the World/Soudage dans le Monde

Wereldverbond van Bouwvakarbeiders- en Houtbewerkersorganisaties. Bulletin

White Ribbon Bulletin

Whole World Handbook: a Student Guide to Work, Study and Travel Abroad 343

Widening Horizons

Word and Deed 771

Work Accomplished by the Inter- American Juridicical Committee During Its Meeting 521

World Advertising Expenditures (International Advertising Association.) 6

World Aeronautical Records 11

World Agriculture/Agriculture dans le Monde

World Air Transport Statistics 869

World Alliance of Y M C A's Directory 262

World Aluminum Abstracts

World Association for Christian Communication. Journal

World Bibliography of Social Security/Bibliographie Universelle de Securite Sociale

World Council of Churches. Office of Education. Education Newsletter

World Directory of Mathematicians 591

World Fertility Survey. Basic Documentation 731

World Highways

World Hockey

World Journal of Surgery

World List of Family Planning Agencies 133

World List of Universities, Other Institutions of Higher Education and University Organizations 333

World Medical Association. General Assembly. Proceedings 601

World Methodist Historical Society. News Bulletin.

World Mining Congress. Report 647

World Scout Bureau. Biennial Report 257

World Scouting/Scoutisme Mondial

World Scouting Newsletter/Bulletin du Scoutisme Mondial

World Student Chess Team Championship. Results 822

World Student Christian Federation. Dossier 768

World Student News/Etudiants du Monde

World Tourism Organization. Collection of Technical Bulletins 893

World Trade Union Movement

World Transindex

World Transport Data/Statistiques Mondiales de Transport 867

World Travel/Tourisme Mondial

World Travel Statistics/Statistiques du Tourisme Mondial/Estadisticas del Turismo Mundial 893

World Union for the Safeguard of Youth. Bulletin

World University Service. Annual Report 343

World University Service. Programme of Action 343

World Veterinary Association. Catalogue of Veterinary Films and Films of Veterinary Interest 895

World Veterinary Association. News Items

World Veterinary Association. News Letter

World Wheat Statistics 26

World Youth/Jeunesse du Monde/Juventud del Mundo

World Zionist Organziation Press Service

Y M C A World Communique

Y M C A's of the World 262

Yearbook of Human Rights 719

Yearbook of International Congress Proceedings 725

Yearbook of International Organizations 725

Yearbook of World Problems and Human Potential 725

Young Cinema and Theatre/Jeune Cinema et Theatre

Young Cinema International

Zahlestafeln der Physikalisch-Chemischen Untersuchungen des Rheins sowie der Mosel/Tableaux Numeriques des Analyses Physico-Chimiques des Eaux du Rhin Ainsi Que de la Moselle. 390

Zeitschrift fuer Fremdenverkehr/Revue de Tourisme/Tourist Review

Zhenshchiny Mira

Zionist Literature

Zshurnalist 506

INTERNATIONAL CONGRESS PROCEEDINGS

Acoustical Imaging: Recent Advances in Visualization and Characterization 706

Acta Concilium Ophthalmologicum 615

Acta Endocrinologica Congress. Advance Abstracts 611

Acta Endocrinologica Panamericana 611

Acta Medica et Sociologica 811

Acts IMEKO 636

Actualites Protozoologiques 119

Advances in Water Pollution Research 383

Afro-Asian Peoples' Conference. Proceedings 439

Afro-Asian Peoples' Solidarity Organization. Council. Documents of the Session 439

Allergologicum; Transactions of the Collegium Internationale 603

American Constitutional and Legal History 466

Annual International Congress Calendar 626

Asian Conference on Occupational Health. Proceedings 495

Asian Pacific Congress of Cardiology. Symposia 606

Assembly of Western European Union. Proceedings

Astronautical Research 7

Baptist World Alliance. Congress Reports 771

Biometeorology; Proceedings 101

Bronches-Broncho-Pneumologie

Brown Boveri Symposia. Proceedings 352

Canadian Society for Immunology. International Symposium. Proceedings 603

Caritas Internationalis. International Yearbooks 764

Caritas Internationalis. Reports of General Assemblies 764

Carnegie-Rochester Conference Series on Public Policy

Carotenoids Other Than Vitamin A 110

Chemistry of Natural Products 252

Clinical Neurosurgery; Proceedings 619

Colloques Internationaux d'Histoire Maritime. Travaux 877

Colloquium on the Law of Outer Space. Proceedings 7

Commonwealth Entomological Conference. Report 120

Commonwealth Press Union. Record of Quadrennial Conference 504

Commonwealth Space-Flight Symposium. Proceedings 7

Comparative Education Society in Europe. Proceedings of the General Meeting 315

Confederation Europeene pour la Therapie Physique. Congress Reports 594

Conference on United Nations Procedures. Report 720

Congres International d'Histoire des Sciences. Actes 781

Congreso Regional Sobre Documentacao. Anais 528

Congress in Park and Recreation Administration. Programme 626

Congress in Park and Recreation Administration. Reports 829

Congress International Medical de Pays de Langue Francaise de l'Hemisphere Americain. Rapports et Communications 594

Congress of International Congress Organizers and Technicians. Proceeding 626

Coordination Chemistry 246

Council for the Social Sciences in East Africa. Social Science Conference. Proceedings 797

Criminology, Criminal Law, Penology 281

Developments in Biological Standardization 603

Drug-Induced Diseases 594

E A P R Abstracts of Conference Papers (European Association for Potato Research) 34

Electra

Elizabethan Theatre 859

Etudes Historiques 432

Eucarpia 114

European Association for Animal Production. Symposia on Energy Metabolism 44

European Association for Personnel Management. Congress Reports 220

European Brewery Convention. Proceedings of the International Congress 86

European Civil Aviation Conference (Report of Session) 867

European Conference of Local and Regional Authorities. Documents 741

European Conference of Local and Regional Authorities. Official Reports of Debates 741

European Conference of Local and Regional Authorities. Texts Adopted 741

European Conference on Microcirculation. Proceedings 607

European Congress of Anaesthesiology. Proceedings 604

European Congress of Cardiology. Abstracts of Papers 607

European Congress of Cardiology. (Proceedings) 607

European Congress of Perinatal Medicine. Proceedings 615

European Congress on Electron Microscopy 124

European Congress on Molecular Spectroscopy. Proceedings 249

European Federation of Finance House Associations. Conference Proceedings 172

European Grassland Federation. Proceedings of the General Meeting 35

European League for Economic Cooperation. Reports of the International Congress 199

European Ophthalmological Society. Congress. Abstracts 616

European Organization for Quality Control. Conference Proceedings 637

European Passenger Timetable Conference Minutes 862

European Purchasing Conference. (Proceedings) 218

European Society of Toxicity. Proceedings 684

INDEX TO PUBLICATIONS OF INTERNATIONAL ORGANIZATIONS 929

European Symposium on Chemical Reaction Engineering. Proceedings 372

European Symposium on Concrete Pavements. Reports 375

Experimental Mechanics; Proceedings 379

Federation of European Biochemical Societies. (Proceedings of Meeting) 111

Food and Agriculture Organization of the United Nations Conference. Report 15

Fracht-Schiffahrts-Konferenzen 878

Hybrid Microelectronics Symposium. (Papers) 354

I C H P E R Congress Proceedings (International Council on Health, Physical Education and Recreation) 596

I E E E International Conference on Communications. Conference Record 264

I E E E International Symposium on Circuits and Systems. Proceedings 354

I F A C Symposium on Multivariable Technical Control Systems. Proceedings (International Federation of Automatic Control) 382

I F L A Annual (International Federation of Library Associations and Institutions) 531

I N S E R M Symposia

I T C-U N E S C O International Seminar. Proceedings (International Institute for Aerial Survey and Earth Sciences) 386

Immunopathology 603

Instrumentation in the Pulp and Paper Industry 675

Inter-American Commission of Women. Special Assembly. Final Act/Comision Interamericana de Mujeres. Asamblea Extraordinaria. Acta Final 718

Inter-American Conference on Indian Life. Acta/ Congresos Indigenistas Interamericanos. Acta 50

Inter-American Development Bank. Board of Governors. Proceedings of the Meeting 174

Intergovernmental Council for Automatic Data Processing. Proceedings of Conference 272

Inter-Guiana Geological Conference. Proceedings 295

International Academy of Legal Medicine and of Social Medicine. (Congress Reports) 613

International Academy of Oral Pathology. Proceedings 609

International Actuarial Congress. Transactions 499

International Aeronautic Federation. Annual Information Bulletin 8

International African Seminar. Studies Presented and Discussed 440

International Amateur Basketball Federation. Official Report of the World Congress 824

International Anatomical Congress. Proceedings 596

International Arthurian Society. Report of Congress/ Societe Internationale Arthurienne. Rapports du Congres 565

International Association for Bridge and Structural Engineering. Final Report (of Congress) 375

International Association for Bridge and Structural Engineering. Preliminary Report (of Congress) 375

International Association for Cereal Chemistry. Working and Discussion Meetings Reports 405

International Association for Classical Archaeology. Proceedings of Congress 61

International Association for Cross-Cultural Psychology. International Conference. Selected Papers 736

International Association for Hydraulic Research. Congress Proceedings 381

International Association for Scientific Study of Mental Deficiency. Proceedings of International Congress 619

International Association of Applied Psychology. Proceedings of Congress 736

International Association of Chain Stores. Report of Plenary Session 218

International Association of Democratic Lawyers. Congress Report 513

International Association of Logopedics and Phoniatrics. Reports of Congress 619

International Association of Meteorology and Atmospheric Physics. Report of Proceedings of General Assembly

International Association of Milk Control Agencies. Proceedings of Annual Meetings 41

International Association of Museums of Arms and Military History. Congress Reports 653

International Association of Philatelic Journalists. Minutes of Annual Congresses 479

International Association of Physical Education and Sports for Girls and Women. Proceedings of the International Congress 820

International Association of Plant Breeders for the Protection of Plant Varieties. Congress Reports 115

International Association of Seed Crushers. Proceedings of the Annual Congress 16

International Association of State Lotteries. (Reports of Congress) 230

International Association of Thalassotherapy. Congress Reports 596

International Association of Workers for Maladjusted Children. Congress Reports 345

International Astronomical Union. General Assembly. Proceedings 82

International Astronomical Union. Proceedings of Symposia 82

International Beekeeping Congress. Reports 16

International Biodeterioration Symposium. Proceedings. Biodeterioration of Materials 123

International Biometeorological Congress. Summaries and Reports Presented to the Congress 104

International Biophysics Congress. Abstracts 110

International Botanical Congress. Abstracts of Papers 115

International Botanical Congress. Proceedings 115

International Catecholamine Symposium. Proceedings 252

International Centre of Fertilizers. World Congress. Acts 36

International Ceramic Congress. Proceedings 244

International Clay Conference. Proceedings 244

International Clean Air Congress. Proceedings 386

International College of Psychosomatic Medicine. Proceedings of the Congress 620

International Colloquium on Plant Analysis and Fertilizer Problems. Proceedings 36

International Colloquium on Rapid Mixing and Sampling Techniques Applicable to the Study of Biochemical Reactions. Proceedings 111

International Commission of Agricultural Engineering. Reports of Congress 36

International Commission of Sugar Technology. Proceedings of the General Assembly 405

International Commission on Illumination. Proceedings 355

International Commission on Irrigation and Drainage. Congress Reports 381

International Commission on Large Dams. Transactions 375

International Commission on Trichinellosis. Proceedings 608

International Committee for Standardization in Hematology. Symposia 613

International Committee of Onomastic Sciences. Congress Proceedings 545

International Comparative Literature Association. Proceedings of the Congress 566

International Confederation for Agricultural Credit. Assembly and Congress Reports 28

International Confederation of Free Trade Unions. World Congress Reports 506

International Conference in Particle Technology. Proceedings 703

International Conference of Agricultural Economists. Proceedings 28

International Conference of Building Officials. Accumulative Supplements to the Codes 136

International Conference of Building Officials. Analysis of Revisions to the Uniform Building Code 136

International Conference of Building Officials. Building Department Administration 136

International Conference of Building Officials. Dwelling Construction Under the Uniform Building Code 136

International Conference of Building Officials. One and Two Family Dwelling Code 136

International Conference of Building Officials. Plan Review Manual 136

International Conference of Building Officials. Uniform Code for the Abatement of Dangerous Buildings 137

International Conference of Building Officials. Uniform Fire Code 137

International Conference of Building Officials. Uniform Housing Code 137

International Conference of Building Officials. Uniform Mechanical Code 137

International Conference of Social Work. Conference Proceedings 806

International Conference of Sociology of Religion 765

International Conference on Acoustics. Reports 706

International Conference on Calorimetry and Thermodynamics. Proceedings 700

International Conference on Cloud Physics. Proceedings 633

International Conference on Computer Communications.(Proceedings) 272

International Conference on Computing Fixed Points with Applications. Proceedings 586

International Conference on Conduction and Breakdown in Dielectric Liquids. Proceedings

International Conference on Congenital Malformations. Proceedings 596

International Conference on Cybernetics and Society. Proceedings 272

International Conference on Education. Final Report/ Conference International de l'Education. Rapport Final 319

International Conference on Endodontics. Transactions 610

International Conference on Experimental Meson Spectroscopy. Proceedings 705

International Conference on Fluid Sealing. Proceedings 382

International Conference on Global Impacts of Applied Microbiology. Proceedings 123

International Conference on Health and Health Education. Proceedings 694

International Conference on High Energy Physics and Nuclear Structure. Proceedings 703

International Conference on Intra-Uterine Contraception. Proceedings 615

International Conference on Ion Implantation in Semiconductors. Proceedings 355

International Conference on Large High Voltage Electric Systems. Proceedings 355

International Conference on Lead. Proceedings 628

International Conference on Lighthouses and Other Aids to Navigation. (Reports) 878

International Conference on Liquefied Natural Gas. Papers 679

International Conference on Oral Biology. Proceedings 610

International Conference on Phenomena in Ionized Gases. Proceedings 697

International Conference on Physics of Semiconductors. Proceedings 355

International Conference on Piagetian Theory and the Helping Professions. Proceedings 319

International Conference on Plutonium and Other Actinides. Proceedings 251

International Conference on Pressure Vessel Technology. Papers 851

International Conference on Production Disease in Farm Animals. Proceedings 45

International Conference on Shielding Around High Energy Accelerators. Papers 703

International Conference on Social Welfare. Proceedings 806

International Conference on Soil Mechanics and Foundation Engineering. Proceedings 375

International Conference on Structural Mechanics in Reactor Technology. Proceedings

International Conference on the Environmental Impact of Aerospace Operations in the High Atmosphere. (Proceedings) 386

International Conference on the Physics of Electronic and Atomic Collisions. Papers 703

International Conference on the Theory and Applications of Differential Games. Proceedings 355

International Conference on Thermoelectric Energy Conversion. Proceedings 355

International Conference on Vehicle Structural Mechanics. Proceedings 871

International Conference on Water Pollution Research. Proceedings 387

International Congress for Byzantine Studies. Acts/Congres International des Etudes Byzantines. Actes 433

International Congress for Child Psychiatry. Proceedings 620

International Congress for Cybernetics. Proceedings. Actes 272

International Congress for Logic, Methodology and Philosophy of Science. Proceedings 784

International Congress for Papyrology. Proceedings 61

International Congress for Stereology. Proceedings 379

International Congress for the Study of Pre-Columbian Cultures of the Lesser Antilles. Proceedings 50

International Congress of Acarology. Proceedings 128

International Congress of Accountants. Proceedings 167

International Congress of Allergology. Abstracts of Reports of Discussion and of Communications 603

International Congress of Allergology. Proceedings 603

International Congress of Angiology. Proceedings 607

International Congress of Anthropological and Ethnological Sciences. Proceedings 50

International Congress of Archives. Proceedings 531

International Congress of Automatic Control. Proceedings 272

International Congress of Automotive Safety. Proceedings 871

International Congress of Biochemistry. Proceedings 111

International Congress of Cell Biology. Summaries of Reports and Communications 119

International Congress of Chemotherapy. Proceedings 684

International Congress of Cybernetic Medicine. Proceedings 596

International Congress of Electroencephalography and Clinical Neurophysiology (Proceedings) 620

International Congress of Endocrinology. Proceedings 611

International Congress of Entomology 121

International Congress of Food Science and Technology. Proceedings 405

International Congress of Graphoanalysts. Proceedings 736

International Congress of Hematology. Proceedings 613

International Congress of Histochemistry and Cytochemistry. Proceedings 111

International Congress of Home Economics. Report 479

International Congress of Human Genetics. Abstracts 122

International Congress of Life Assurance Medicine. Proceedings 499

International Congress of Linguists. Proceedings 545

International Congress of Microbiology. Proceedings 123

International Congress of Nephrology. Proceedings 625

International Congress of Neurological Sciences. Abstracts and Descriptions of Contributions of the Scientific Program 620

International Congress of Neurological Surgery. Abstracts of Papers 620

International Congress of Occupational Therapy. Proceedings 596

International Congress of Parasitology. Proceedings 128

International Congress of Pharmaceutical Sciences. Proceedings

International Congress of Physical Medicine. Abstracts of Papers Presented 596

International Congress of Plastic and Reconstructive Surgery. Transactions 624

International Congress of Primatology. Proceedings 50

International Congress of Psychology. Proceedings 736

International Congress of Psychopathological Art. Program. Programme 676

International Congress of Psychosomatic Medicine in Obstetrics and Gynaecology. Proceedings 615

International Congress of Psychosurgery. Proceeding 620

International Congress of Psychotherapy. Proceedings/Verhandlungen/Comptes Rendus 620

International Congress of Pure and Applied Chemistry. (Lectures) 246

International Congress of Radiation Research. Proceedings 703

International Congress of Radiology. (Reports) 622

International Congress of Sugarcane Technologists. Proceedings 405

International Congress of Verdi Studies. Proceedings. 660

International Congress of Zoology. Proceedings 129

International Congress on Alcoholism and Drug Dependence. Proceedings 287

International Congress on Animal Reproduction and Artificial Insemination. Proceedings 894

International Congress on Canned Foods. Report 405

International Congress on Canned Foods. Texts of Papers Presented and Resolutions/Congres International de la Conserve. Textes des Communications 405

International Congress on Catalysis. Proceedings 255

International Congress on Clinical Chemistry. Abstracts 111

International Congress on Clinical Chemistry. Papers 111

International Congress on Clinical Chemistry. Proceedings 111

International Congress on Combustion Engines. Proceedings 382

International Congress on Hormonal Steroids. Abstracts of Papers Presented 611

International Congress on Hygiene and Preventive Medicine. Proceedings 694

International Congress on Medical Librarianship. Proceedings 531

International Congress on Metallic Corrosion. (Proceedings) 628

International Congress on Muscle Diseases. Abstracts 596

International Congress on Occupational Health. Proceedings 495

International Congress on the History of Art. Proceedings 75

International Congress Series 626

International Congresses on Tropical Medicine and Malaria. (Proceedings) 608

International Convocation on Immunology. Papers 603

International Cooperative Alliance. Congress Report 181

International Cotton Advisory Committee. Country Statements Presented in Connection with the Plenary Meetings 36

International Council for Bird Preservation. Proceedings of Conferences 125

International Council for Building Research, Studies and Documentation. Congress Reports 137

International Council for Laboratory Animal Science. Proceedings of the Symposium 596

International Council for Scientific Management. Proceedings of World Congress 215

International Council for the Exploration of the Sea. Rapports et Proces-Verbaux des Reunions 311

International Council of Homehelp Services. Reports of Congress 479

International Council of Voluntary Agencies. General Conference. Record of Proceedings 806

International Council on Archives. East and Central Africa Regional Branch. General Conference Proceedings 531

International Council on Social Welfare. European Symposium. Proceedings 806

International Data Processing Conference. Proceedings 272

International Diabetes Federation. Proceedings of Congress 611

International Economic Association. Proceedings of the Conferences and Congresses 145

International Electron Devices Meeting. Abstracts 355

International Falcon Movement. Conference Reports 258

International Federation for Documentation. Proceedings of Congress 531

International Federation for Medical Psychotherapy. Congress Reports 620

International Federation for Modern Languages and Literature. Congress Reports 545

International Federation of Agricultural Producers. General Conference Proceedings 16

International Federation of Asian and Western Pacific Contractors' Associations. Proceedings of the Annual Convention 137

International Federation of Associations of Textile Chemists and Colorists. Reports of Congress 856

International Federation of Catholic Universities. General Assembly. (Report) 337

International Federation of Fruit Juice Producers. Proceedings. Berichte. Rapports 405

International Federation of Fruit Juice Producers. Proceedings of Congress. Compte-Rendu du Congres 86

International Federation of Medical Students' Associations. Reports of General Assembly 596

International Federation of Operational Research Societies. Airline Group (A G I F O R S) Proceedings 868

International Federation of Plantation, Agricultural and Allied Workers. Report of the Secretariat to the I F P A A W World Congress 29

International Federation of Prestressing. Congress Proceedings 379

International Gas Union. Proceedings of Conferences 680

International Geographical Union. Report of Congress 423

International Grassland Congress. Proceedings 36

International Harbour Congress. Proceedings/ Internationaal Havenkongres. Verslagboek/Congres Portuaire International. Compte-Rendu/ Internationale Hafentagung. Berichte 878

International Hop Growers Convention. Report of Congress 42

International Horticultural Congress. Proceedings 415

International Humanist and Ethical Union. Proceedings of the Congress 689

International Hydrographic Conference. Reports of Proceedings 311

International I U P A C Congress of Pesticide Chemistry. Proceedings 36

International Institute for Sugar Beet Research. Reports of the Winter Congress 37

International Institute of Administrative Sciences. Reports of the International Congress 743

International Institute of Differing Civilizations. (Session Papers) 721

International Institute of Ibero-American Literature. Congress Proceedings. Memoria 566

International Institute of Philosophy. Actes 689

International Institute of Public Finance. Papers and Proceedings 230

International Institute of Refrigeration. Proceedings of Commission Meetings 430

International Institute on the Prevention and Treatment of Drug Dependence. Selected Papers 287

International Joint Conference on Artificial Intelligence. Advance Papers of the Conference 272

International Journal of Psycho-Analysis

International Law Association. Reports of Conferences 523

International League of Societies for the Mentally Handicapped. World Congress Proceedings. 736

International Leprosy Congress. Transactions 608

International Literary and Artistic Association. Proceedings and Reports of Congress 491

International Machine Tool Design and Research Conference. Proceedings 583

International Medical Congress. Year Book 596

International Meeting of Animal Nutrition Experts. Proceedings 45

International Meeting on Cattle Diseases. Reports 894

International Metalworkers' Congress. Reports 628

International Mineralogical Association. Proceedings of Meetings 644

International Narcotic Conference. Report: Proceedings of Annual Conference 287

International Navigation Congress. Proceedings 878

International Olive Growers Federation. Congress Reports 37

International Olympic Academy. Report of the Sessions 820

International Organization for Cooperation in Health Care. General Assembly. Report 596

International Organization for the Study of the Old Testament. Proceedings of the International Congress 765

International Organization of Citrus Virologists. Proceedings of the Conference 415

International P. E. N. Congress. Report 566

International Peace Research Association. Proceedings of the Conference 722

International Philatelic Federation. General Assembly. Proces-Verbal 479

International Photobiological Congress. Proceedings 111

International Playground Association. Conference Report 258

International Political Science Association. World Congress 711

International Population Conference. Proceedings 727

International Potash Institute. Colloquium. Compte Rendu 37

International Potash Institute. Congress Report 37

International Powder Metallurgy Conference. Proceedings-Modern Developments in Powder Metallurgy 628

International Pressure Die Casting Conferences. Proceedings 583

International Publishers Association. Proceedings of Congress 759

International Quantum Electronics Conference. Digest of Technical Papers 356

International Rayon and Synthetic Fibres Committee. Technical Conference. Reports 856

International Rayon and Synthetic Fibres Committee. World Congress. Report 856

International Real Estate Federation. Reports of Congress 761

International Road Congresses. Proceedings 875

International Rubber Study Group. Summary of Proceedings of the Group Meetings and Assemblies 777

International School of Physics "Enrico Fermi." Proceedings 697

International School of Physics "Ettore Majorana," Erice, Italy. Proceedings 703

International Seaweed Symposium. Proceedings 116

International Sedimentological Congress. Guidebook 295

International Seminar on Reproductive Physiology and Sexual Endocrinology. Proceedings 126

International Skating Union. Minutes of Congress 820

International Social Security Association. Technical Reports of Assemblies 499

International Society for Performing Arts. Libraries and Museums. Congress Proceedings 75

International Society for Research on the Moors. Report of Congress 423

International Society for Rock Mechanics. Congress. Proceedings 376

International Society for Terrain-Vehicle Systems. Proceedings of International Conference 376

International Society of Blood Transfusion. Proceedings of the Congress 607

International Society of Geographical Pathology. Proceedings of the Conference 596

International Society of Internal Medicine. Congress Proceedings 596

International Society of Orthopaedic Surgery and Traumatology. Proceedings of Congresses 616

International Society of Urology. Reports of Congress 625

International Statistical Institute. Bulletin. Proceedings of the Biennial Sessions 841

INDEX TO PUBLICATIONS OF INTERNATIONAL ORGANIZATIONS

International Superphosphate and Compound Manufacturers Association Limited. Technical Meeting. Proceedings 37

International Symposia on Comparative Law. Proceedings/Colloques Internationaux de Droit Compare. Travaux 513

International Symposium on Adsorption-Desorption Phenomena. Proceedings 255

International Symposium on Aerobiology. Proceedings 752

International Symposium on Animal and Plant Toxins. Proceedings 111

International Symposium on Atherosclerosis. Proceedings 607

International Symposium on Brain-Endocrine Interaction. Proceedings 611

International Symposium on Canine Heartworm Disease. Proceedings 894

International Symposium on Comparative Endocrinology. Proceedings 611

International Symposium on Crop Protection. Proceedings 37

International Symposium on Fault-Tolerant Computing. Proceedings 272

International Symposium on Growth Hormone. Abstracts 126

International Symposium on Molecular Biology. Proceedings 119

International Symposium on Nitrite in Meat Products. Proceedings 405

International Symposium on Nitrogen Fixation. Proceedings 246

International Symposium on Nonlinear Acoustics. Abstracts of Papers 706

International Symposium on Pharmacological Treatment in Burns. Proceedings 616

International Symposium on Plastic and Reconstructive Surgery of the Face and Neck. Proceedings 624

International Symposium on Regional Development. Papers and Proceedings 485

International Symposium on Residual Gases in Electron Tubes. Proceedings 356

International Symposium on Subscriber Loop and Services. Proceedings 356

International Symposium on Surface Physics. Solid-Vacuum Interface. Proceedings

International Symposium on the Continuous Cultivation of Microorganisms. Proceedings 123

International Symposium on Transport and Handling of Minerals. Minerals Transportation; Proceedings 862

International T N O Conference. (Proceedings) 851

International Television Symposium and Technical Exhibit, Montreux. (Papers) 267

International Thermal Spraying Conference. Preprint of Papers 631

International Thyroid Conference. Proceedings 611

International Touring Alliance. Minutes of the General Assembly 887

International Trade Conference of Workers of the Building, Wood and Building Materials Industries. (Brochure) 137

International Trade Union Conference for Action Against Apartheid. Resolution 718

International Transplutonium Element Symposium. Proceedings 251

International Union against Cancer. Proceedings of Congress 605

International Union against Tuberculosis. Conference Proceedings 623

International Union for Conservation of Nature and Natural Resources. Proceedings and Papers of the Technical Meeting 276

International Union for Conservation of Nature and Natural Resources. Proceedings of the General Assembly 276

International Union for Quaternary Research. Congress Proceedings 295

International Union of Biological Sciences. General Assemblies. Proceedings 104

International Union of Building Societies and Savings Associations. Congress Proceedings 174

International Union of Crystallography. Abstracts of the Triennial Congress 251

International Union of Food and Allied Workers' Associations. Meeting of the Executive Committee. I. Documents of the Secretariat. II. Summary Report 507

International Union of Food and Allied Workers' Associations. Tobacco Workers' Trade Group Board. Meeting 861

International Union of Forest Research Organizations. Congress Proceedings/Rapports du Congres/Kongressberichte 409

International Union of Local Authorities. Reports of Congress 749

International Union of Physiological Sciences. Proceedings of Congress 126

International Union of Prehistoric and Protohistoric Sciences. Proceedings of Congress 50

International Union of Producers and Distributors of Electrical Energy. (Congress Proceedings) 356

International Union of Public Transport. Proceedings of the International Congress 862

International Union of Radio Science. Proceedings of General Assemblies 267

International Union of School and University Health and Medicine. Congress Reports 319

International Union of Students. Congress Resolutions 337

International Water Conference. Proceedings 381

International Water Supply Congress. Proceedings 897

Internationaler Kongress fuer Reprographie und Information. Fachreferate und Plenarvortraege 693

Inter-Parliamentary Union. Conference Proceedings/Union Interparlementaire. Comptes Rendus des Conferences 722

Istituto Internazionale di Studi Liguri. Collezione di Monografie Preistoriche Ed Archeologiche 62

Kongresa Libro 546

Latin American Food Production Conference Summary Report 405

Latin Language Mathematicians Group. Actes et Travaux du Congres 586

Los Alamos Symposium on Mathematics in the Natural Sciences. Proceedings 586

Lutheran World Federation. Proceedings of the Assembly 772

Macromolecular Chemistry 253

Marine Biology; Proceedings of the Interdisciplinary Conference 105

Mathematics and Computers in Simulation

Meeting of International Organizations for the Joint Study of Programs and Activities in the Field of Agriculture in Europe. Report 18

Miles International Symposium 119

Molecular Biology; Proceedings of the International Conference 119

Mushroom Science 116

N A F O Annual Report 398

National/International Sculpture Conference. Proceedings 77

North Atlantic Treaty Organization. Expert Panel on Air Pollution Modeling. Proceedings 388

North Pacific Fur Seal Commission. Proceedings of the Annual Meeting 130

Open Door International for the Emancipation of the Woman Worker. Report of Congress 210

Organization of American States. Permanent Council. Decisions Taken at Meetings (Cumulated Edition) 471

Pacific Chemical Engineering Congress. Proceedings 373

Pacific Science Association. Congress and Inter-Congress Proceedings 788

Parapsychology Foundation. Proceedings of International Conferences 676

Pax Romana 775

Perugia Quadrennial International Conferences on Cancer. Proceedings 606

Photochemistry 255

Power Systems Computation Conference. P S C C Proceedings 369

Progress in Land Reform 19

Regional Conference on Water Resources Development in Asia and the Far East. Proceedings 897

Reinforced Plastics Congress 707

Report of the General Assembly of the Members of the International Office of Cocoa and Chocolate and the International Sugar Confectionary Manufacturers' Association 407

Rubber Research Institute of Malaysia. Planters Conference Proceedings 777

S D C E International Die Casting Congress. Transactions (Society of Die Casting Engineers, Inc.) 583

Scandinavian Corrosion Congress. Proceedings 629

Social Welfare Services in Japan 809

Society for International Development. World Conference Proceedings 201

South Pacific Commission. Report of S P C Technical Meetings 715

Spores 118

State of the Air Transport Industry 869

Study of Time 84

Symposium (International) on Combustion 256

Symposium Anaesthesiologiae Internationale. Berichte 604

Trade Unions International of Chemical, Oil and Allied Workers. International Trade Conference. Documents 507

Transplantation Today 625

U I C C Technical Report Series (International Union Against Cancer) 606

U N I T A R Conference Reports (United Nations Institute for Training and Research) 524

U S A-Japan Computer Conference. Proceedings 274

Unesco. Records of the General Conference. Proceedings 724

Unesco. Records of the General Conference. Resolutions 724

Union Academique Internationale. Compte Rendu de la Session Annuelle du Comite 493

Union Mondiale des Organisations Syndicales sur Bases Economique et Sociale Liberales. Conferences: Rapport 507

Union of European Pedopsychiatrists. Proceedings 621

United Nations of the Next Decade Conference. Report 724

Wenner Gren Center International Symposium Series 794

Western Hemisphere Nutrition Congress. Proceedings 666

World Airports Conference. Proceedings 869

World Association for Educational Research. Congress Reports 325

World Association for the Advancement of Veterinary Parasitology. Proceedings of Conference 895

World Association of Girl Guides and Girl Scouts. Report of Conference 257

World Confederation for Physical Therapy. Proceedings of the Congress 601

World Conference on Animal Production. Proceedings 46

World Conference on Transport Research. Proceedings 864

World Congress of Anaesthesiologists. Proceedings 604

World Congress of Psychiatry. Proceedings 621

World Congress of the Deaf. Lectures and Papers 810

World Congress of the Deaf. Proceedings. 286

World Congress on Fertility and Sterility. Proceedings 109

World Congress on the Prevention of Occupational Accidents and Diseases. Proceedings 496

World Council of Churches. General Assembly. Assembly-Reports 768

World Council of Churches. Minutes and Reports of the Central Committee Meeting 768

World Council of Young Mens Service Clubs. Minutes of the General Meeting 810

World Crafts Council. General Assembly. Proceedings of the Biennial Meeting 80

World Energy Conference. Plenary Conferences. Transactions 364

World Federation for Mental Health. Proceedings of Annual Meetings 739

World Jersey Cattle Bureau. Conference Reports 46

World Medical Association. General Assembly. Proceedings 601

World Movement of Mothers. Reports of Meetings 810

World Muslim Conference. Proceedings 770

World O R T Union. Congress Report (Organization for Rehabilitation Through Training) 325

World Union for the Safeguard of Youth. Conference Proceedings 810

INDEX TO PUBLICATIONS OF INTERNATIONAL ORGANIZATIONS 933

World Veterinary Congress. Proceedings 895

World Zionist Organization. General Council. Addresses, Debates, Resolutions 771

World Zionist Organization. Zionist Congress. Kongres Ha-Tsiyoni. Hahlatot 717

World's Poultry Science Association. Report of the Proceedings of International Congress 46

World'S Woman's Christian Temperance Union. Convention Report 817

EUROPEAN COMMUNITIES

Bibliographie de Jurisprudence Europeenne Concernant les Decisions Judiciares Relatives aux Traites Institutant les Communautes Europeennes 521

Bulletin of the European Communities

Bulletin of the European Communities. Supplement 184

Bureau Euristop. Cahiers d'Information 702

Bureau Euristop. Informations Technico-Economiques. 702

Central Nucleaire Ardennes 702

Centrale Elletronucleare Latina. Relazione Annuale 702

Centrale Nucleare Garigliano. Relazione Annuale 702

Commission of the European Communities. Annual Reports on the Progress of Research Work Promoted by the ECSC 751

Commission of the European Communities. Cahiers de Reconversion Industrielle 221

Commission of the European Communities. Centre for Information and Documentation. Annual Report: Program Biology-Health Protection 102

Commission of the European Communities. Collection d'Economie du Travail 221

Commission of the European Communities. Collection d'Economie et Politique Regionale 143

Commission of the European Communities. Collection d'Hygiene et de Medecine du Travail 495

Commission of the European Communities. Collection du Droit du Travail 206

Commission of the European Communities. Collection Objectifs Generaux Acier 643

Commission of the European Communities. Collection Physiologie et Psychologie du Travail 206

Commission of the European Communities. Community Law 522

Commission of the European Communities. Conjoncture Energetique dans la Communaute 362

Commission of the European Communities. Directorate of Taxation. Inventory of Taxes 227

Commission of the European Communities. Directory 522

Commission of the European Communities. Documentation Bulletin.

Commission of the European Communities. Dublin Office. Community Report

Commission of the European Communities. Etudes: Serie Aide au Developpement 199

Commission of the European Communities. Etudes: Serie Concurrence- Rapprochement des Legislations 221

Commission of the European Communities. Etudes: Serie Energie 362

Commission of the European Communities. Etudes: Serie Industrie 221

Commission of the European Communities. Etudes: Serie Informations Internes sur l'Agriculture 27

Commission of the European Communities. Etudes: Serie Politique Sociale 709

Commission of the European Communities. Expose Annuel sur les Activities d'Orientation Professionnelle dans la Communaute 335

Commission of the European Communities. Expose Annuel sur les Activities des Services de Main-d'Ouvre des Etats Membres de la Communaute 206

Commission of the European Communities. Expose sur l'Evolution Sociale dans la Communaute 797

Commission of the European Communities. Financial Report 227

Commission of the European Communities. Investments in the Community Coalmining and Iron and Steel Industries. Report on the Survey 643

Commission of the European Communities. Marches Agricoles: Serie "Prix". Produits Animaux 27

Commission of the European Communities. Marches Agricoles: Serie "Prix". Produits Vegetaux 27

Commission of the European Communities. Recueils de Recherches Charbon 642

Commission of the European Communities. Report on Competition Policy/Rapport sur la Politique de Concurrence 221

Commission of the European Communities. Studies: Agricultural Series 27

Commission of the European Communities. Studies: Economic and Financial Series 143

Commission of the European Communities. Studies: Transport Series 862

Commission of the European Communities. Terminology Office. Terminology Bulletin/Bulletin de Terminologie 542

Comunita Europee

Court of Justice of the European Communities. Recueil de la Jurisprudence 522

Debates of the European Parliament 523

Developments in the European Communities. Report

Documentation Europeenne - Serie Agricole 14

Documentation Europeenne - Serie Syndicale et Ouvriere 207

E E/Epargne Europe

E U R O N O R M 637

Economic and Social Committee of the European Communities. Annuaire 797

Economic and Social Committee of the European Communities. Bulletin d'Information

Etudes Universitaires sur l'Integration Europeenne/ University Studies on European Integration 721

Euro Abstracts Section I. Euratom and EEC Research

European Atomic Energy Community. Contamination Radioactive des Denrees Alimentaires dans les Pays de la Communaute 751

European Atomic Energy Community. Resultats des Mesures de la Radioactivite Ambiante dans les Pays de la Communaute: Air-Retombee-Eaux 751

European Coal and Steel Community. Consultative Committee. Handbook 199

European Coal and Steel Community. Consultative Committee. Yearbook 199

European Community

European Court of Human Rights. Publications. Series B: Pleadings, Oral Arguments and Documents/Cour Europeenne des Droits de l'Homme. Publications. Serie B: Memoires, Plaidoiries et Documents 718

European Economic Community Savings Bank Group. Report 172

European Economy

European Investment Bank. Annual Report 172

European Parliament. Bulletin

European Parliament. Documents de Seance 523

European Parliament. Informations 523

European Social Fund. Annual Report on the Activities of the New European Social Fund 345

Eurostat. Agriculture. Monthly Statistics. Eggs

Fontes et Aciers/Ghise ed Acciai/Roheisen und Stahlerzeugnisse/Ruwijer en Stallprodukten 643

General Commission on Safety and Health in the Iron and Steel Industry. Report 495

General Report on the Activities of the European Communities 186

Information Service of the European Communities. Newsletter on the Common Agricultural Policy 28

Information Service of the European Communities. Trade Union News 506

Joint Meeting of the Members of the Consultative Assembly of the Council of Europe and of the Members of the European Parliamentary Assembly. Official Report of Debates 722

Joint Nuclear Research Center, Ispra, Italy. Annual Report 703

Kernenergiecentrale van 50 MWE; Doodeward. Jaarverslag 368

Kernkraft Lingen. Jahresbericht 703

Kernkraft Zentrale, Gundremmingen. Jahresberichte 703

Kernkraftwerk Obrigheim. Jahresbericht 704

Mines Safety and Health Commission. Report/Organe Permanent pour la Securite dans les Mines e Houille. Rapport 644

Niveaux de Contamination Radioactive du Milieu Ambiant et de la Chaine Alimentaire 753

Official Journal of the European Communities. C Series: Information and Notices

Official Journal of the European Communities. L Series: Legislation

Publications Juridiques Concernant l'Integration Europeenne; Bibliographie Juridique. Supplement 521

Statistical Office of the European Communities. Associes Statistique du Commerce Exterieur. Annuaire 164

Statistical Office of the European Communities. Aussenhandel: Analitische Ubersichten. Foreign Trade: Analytical Tables 164

Statistical Office of the European Communities. Balances of Payments Yearbook 232

Statistical Office of the European Communities. Basic Statistics 164

Statistical Office of the European Communities. Commerce Exterieur: Nomenclature des Pays 198

Statistical Office of the European Communities. Commerce Exterieur: Products C E C A 164

Statistical Office of the European Communities. Energy Statistics. Yearbook 364

Statistical Office of the European Communities. Foreign Trade: Monthly Statistics

Statistical Office of the European Communities. Foreign Trade: Standard Country Classification 164

Statistical Office of the European Communities. General Statistical Bulletin

Statistical Office of the European Communities. Industrial Statistics

Statistical Office of the European Communities. Iron & Steel

Statistical Office of the European Communities. Monthly Bulletin of General Statistics

Statistical Office of the European Communities. National Accounts. Yearbook 164

Statistical Office of the European Communities. Overseas Associates. Annuaire Statistiques des Etats Africains et Malgache 164

Statistical Office of the European Communities. Quarterly Bulletin of Energy Statistics

Statistical Office of the European Communities. Recettes Fiscales. Annuaire 164

Statistical Office of the European Communities. Siderurgie Annuaire 630

Statistical Office of the European Communities. Social Statistics

Statistical Office of the European Communities. Statistical Studies and Surveys

Statistical Office of the European Communities. Statistique Agricole 20

Statistical Office of the European Communities. Statistiques des Transports. Annuaire 863

Statistical Office of the European Communities. Statistiques Industrielles Annuaire 164

Statistical Office of the European Communities. Statistiques Sociales. Annuaire 816

Statistical Office of the European Communities. Yearbook Regional Statistics 164

Studies on the Radioactive Contamination of the Sea. Annual Report 754

Vocational Training

30 Jours d'Europe

UNITED NATIONS

A D I Quarterly News Letter

A F R O Technical Papers (Regional Office for Africa) 750

Adult Education Information Notes

African Target/Objectifs Africains

African Trade/Commerce Africain

Agricultural Economics Bulletin for Africa 26

Agrindex

Aircraft Accident Digest 7

Animal Health Yearbook 894

Annotated Accessions List of Studies and Reports in the Field of Science Statistics 87

Annual Bulletin of Coal Statistics for Europe 641

Annual Bulletin of Electric Energy Statistics for Europe 359

Annual Bulletin of Gas Statistics for Europe/Bulletin Annuel du Statistiques de Gaz pour l'Europe 678

Annual Bulletin of General Energy Statistics for Europe 364

Annual Bulletin of Transport Statistics for Europe 861

Annual Fertilizer Review 33

Annual Summary of Information on Natural Disasters 303

Anuario Hidrologico del Istmo Centroamericano 307

Arid Zone Research 288

Art 71

Asian Bibliography

Asian Industrial Development News

Asian Population Programme News 725

Asian Population Studies Series 725

Atencion Medica

Atomic Energy Review/Revue d'Energie Atomique

Awareness List/Bulletin Signaletique (U N)

Basic Facts about the United Nations 719

Bibliographical Services Throughout the World 88

Bibliographie, Documentation, Terminologie

Bibliography of Interlingual Scientific and Technical Dictionaries 794

Bibliography on Human Reproduction, Family Planning, and Population Dynamics 133

Book Promotion News

Bulletin of Labour Statistics

Bulletin on Narcotics

C E P A L Review

C I N D A 700

C I S Abstracts (Centre International d'Informations de Securite et d'Hygiene du Travail)

Carnets de l'Enfance/Assignment Children

Catalogue of Reproductions of Paintings Prior to 1860 73

Catalogue of Reproductions of Paintings, 1860-1973 73

Census of Motor Traffic on Main International Traffic Arteries 874

Centro Latinoamericano de Administracion Medica. Traducciones 593

Centro Latinoamericano de Demografia. Publicaciones P I S P A L (Programa de Investigaciones Sociales Sobre Problemas de Poblacion Relevantes para Politicas de Poblacion en America Latina) 726

Centro Latinoamericano de Demografia. Textos de Divulgacion 726

Centro Pan-Americano de Febre Aftosa. Boletin

Ceres

Codex Committee on Pesticide Residues. Report of the Meeting 751

Commodity Trade Statistics

Composition of the W M O

Connaissance de l'Orient. Collection Unesco d'Oeuvres Representatives 562

Connect

INDEX TO PUBLICATIONS OF INTERNATIONAL ORGANIZATIONS 935

Cooperative Educational Abstracting Service

Copyright

Copyright Bulletin

Copyright Laws and Treaties of the World. Supplements 676

Cultures

Delegations to the United Nations 720

Demographic Yearbook 727

Dengue Newsletter for the Americas

Development Education Exchange

Development Forum

Diogenes/Revue Diogene

Direction of Trade Statistics

Disarmament

Documentation, Libraries and Archives: Bibliographies and Reference Works 539

Documentation, Libraries and Archives: Studies and Research 529

Droit d'Auteur

E S C A P Country Monograph Series 727

Earth Sciences Series 288

Ecology and Conservation Series 103

Economic and Social Survey of Asia and the Pacific 185

Economic Bulletin for Africa

Economic Bulletin for Asia and the Pacific

Economic Bulletin for Europe

Economic Survey of Europe 185

Economic Survey of Latin America 185

Educacion Medica y Salud

Education in Asia and Oceania: Reviews, Reports and Notes 317

Educational Building Digest

Educational Studies and Documents 317

Enfants du Monde

Engineering Laboratories Series 367

Estimated World Requirements of Narcotic Drugs 684

Estimated World Requirements of Narcotic Drugs, Supplement 684

European Civil Aviation Conference (Report of Session) 867

Everyman's United Nations 721

Experiments and Innovations in Education

F A O African Regional Meeting on Animal Production and Health. Report of the Meeting. 44

F A O Agricultural Development Papers 14

F A O Agricultural Studies 14

F A O Commodity Review and Outlook 28

F A O Documentation-Current Bibliography (Food and Agriculture Organization of the United Nations)

F A O Fisheries Circulars 396

F A O Fisheries Reports 396

F A O Fisheries Studies 396

F A O Fisheries Technical Paper 396

F A O Food Additive Control Series 404

F A O Forestry and Forest Products Studies 408

F A O Forestry Development Papers 408

F A O Legislative Series 14

F A O Library List of Recent Accessions 24

F A O Manuals in Fisheries Science 396

F A O Nutrition Meetings Report Series 666

F A O Nutritional Study 666

F A O Plant Protection Bulletin

F A O Regional Conference for Africa 14

F A O Regional Conference for Asia and the Far East. Report 14

F A O Regional Conference for Europe. Report of the Conference 14

F A O Regional Conference for Latin America. Report 14

F A O Regional Conference for the Near East. Report 14

F A O Terminology Bulletin 15

Facts About the World Bank

FAO Irrigation and Drainage Papers (Food and Agriculture Organization of the United Nations) 896

Farm Management Notes for Asia and the Far East 28

Fertilizer Industry Series 35

Finance and Development

Food and Agricultural Legislation

Food and Agriculture Organization of the United Nations. Agricultural Planning Studies 28

Food and Agriculture Organization of the United Nations. Asia and the Far East Commission on Agricultural Statistics. Periodic Report 24

Food and Agriculture Organization of the United Nations. Basic Texts 15

Food and Agriculture Organization of the United Nations. Committee for Inland Fisheries of Africa. CIFA Reports 397

Food and Agriculture Organization of the United Nations. Committee for Inland Fisheries of Africa. CIFA Technical Papers 397

Food and Agriculture Organization of the United Nations. Commodity Policy Studies 28

Food and Agriculture Organization of the United Nations. European Inland and Fisheries Advisory Commission. E I F A C Newsletter 397

Food and Agriculture Organization of the United Nations. Forest Tree Seed Directory 408

Food and Agriculture Organization of the United Nations. National Grain Policies 42

Food and Agriculture Organization of the United Nations. Plant Protection Committee for Southeast Asia and Pacific Region. Information Letter 35

Food and Agriculture Organization of the United Nations. Plant Protection Committee for Southeast Asia and Pacific Region. Quarterly Newsletter

Food and Agriculture Organization of the United Nations. Plant Protection Committee for Southeast Asia and Pacific Region. Technical Document 35

Food and Agriculture Organization of the United Nations. Production Yearbook 28

Food and Agriculture Organization of the United Nations. Soils Bulletins 35

Food and Agriculture Organization of the United Nations. Trade Yearbook 28

Food and Agriculture Organization of the United Nations. World Soil Resources Reports 35

Food and Agriculture Organization of the United Nations Conference. Report 15

Food and Nutrition

Food and Nutrition Bulletin

Food Industry Studies 404

Foreign Trade Statistics of Africa. Series A: Direction of Trade 156

Foreign Trade Statistics of Africa. Series B: Trade by Commodity 156

Forestry Newsletter of the Asia-Pacific Region 409

Freedom from Hunger Campaign. Basic Studies 404

Freedom from Hunger Campaign. F F H C Report 28

Fundamentals of Educational Planning 342

Fundamentals of Educational Planning. Lecture-Discussion Series 342

G A T T Studies in International Trade (General Agreement on Tariffs and Trade) 196

General Agreement on Tariffs and Trade. Basic Instruments and Selected Documents Series. Supplement 196

General Agreement on Tariffs and Trade. G A T T Activities in (Year) 196

General Agreement on Tariffs and Trade. International Trade 196

General Catalogue of Unesco and Unesco-Sponsored Publications 717

General Fisheries Council for the Mediterranean. Proceedings and Technical Papers. Debats et Documents Techniques 397

General Fisheries Council for the Mediterranean. Reports of the Sessions 397

General Fisheries Council for the Mediterranean. Studies and Reviews 397

Gilberto Amado Memorial Lecture 523

Global Atmospheric Research Programme. G A R P Special Reports 633

Global Atmospheric Research Programme. Publication Series 633

Glossary of Health Care Terminology 595

Guide to National Bibliographical Information Centres 530

Habitat News

Half-Yearly Bulletin of Electric Energy Statistics for Europe

Health Physics Research Abstracts 756

Human Rights Bulletin

I A E A Library Film Catalog (International Atomic Energy Agency) 700

I A R C Monographs on the Evaluation of the Carcinogenic Risk of Chemicals to Humans (International Agency for Research on Cancer) 605

I A R C Scientific Publications (International Agency for Research on Cancer) 605

I C A O Bulletin (International Civil Aviation Organization)

I C A O Circulars (International Civil Aviation Organization) 868

I L O Information (International Labour Office)

I L O Publications (International Labour Office)

I M C O News
(Inter-Governmental Maritime Consultative Organization)

I M F Survey (International Monetary Fund)

I. M. S. Newsletter (International Marine Science)

I N I S Atomindex (International Nuclear Information System)

I N I S Newsletter

I N I S Reference Series 531

Ideas and Action Bulletin

Impact of Science on Society

Index Translationum 531

Indian Ocean Fishery Commission. Report of the Session 397

Indo-Pacific Fisheries Council. Regional Studies 397

Industrial Development Abstracts

Industrial Planning and Programming Series 200

Industrial Property

Industrial Property, Statistics/Propriete Industrielle, Statistiques

Innovation

Instituto de Nutricion de Centro America y Panama. Informe Anual 666

Intergovernmental Oceanographic Commission. Technical Series 310

International Atomic Energy Agency. Annual Report 703

International Atomic Energy Agency. Bulletin

International Atomic Energy Agency. Legal Series 513

International Atomic Energy Agency. Panel Proceedings Series 703

International Atomic Energy Agency. Power Reactors in Member States 703

International Atomic Energy Agency. Proceedings Series 703

International Atomic Energy Agency. Safety Series 752

International Atomic Energy Agency. Technical Directories 703

International Atomic Energy Agency. Technical Report Series 703

International Book Year Newsletter

International Catalogue of Occupational Safety and Health Films 496

International Centre for Theoretical Physics. Annual Report 696

International Centre for Theoretical Physics. Monthly Bulletin

International Civil Aviation Association. Aeronautical Agreements and Arrangements. Annual Supplement 868

International Civil Aviation Organization. Air Navigation Plan. Africa-Indian Ocean Region 868

International Civil Aviation Organization. Air Navigation Plan. Caribbean Region 868

International Civil Aviation Organization. Air Navigation Plan. European Region 868

International Civil Aviation Organization. Air Navigation Plan. Middle East and South East Asia Regions 868

International Civil Aviation Organization. Air Navigation Plan. North Atlantic, North American and Pacific Regions 868

International Civil Aviation Organization. Airworthiness Committee. Report of Meeting 8

International Civil Aviation Organization. All-Weather Operations Panel. Report of Meeting 8

International Civil Aviation Organization. Assembly. Report and Minutes of the Legal Commission 868

International Civil Aviation Organization. Assembly. Report of the Economic Commission 868

International Civil Aviation Organization. Assembly. Report of the Technical Commission 8

International Civil Aviation Organization. Assembly. Resolutions 868

International Civil Aviation Organization. Automated Data Interchange Systems Panel. Report of Meeting 8

International Civil Aviation Organization. Council. Annual Report 868

International Civil Aviation Organization. Digests of Statistics. Series AT. Airport Traffic 868

International Civil Aviation Organization. Digests of Statistics. Series F. Financial Data 868

International Civil Aviation Organization. Digests of Statistics. Series FP. Fleet, Personnel 868

International Civil Aviation Organization. Digests of Statistics. Series R. Civil Aircraft on Register 868

International Civil Aviation Organization. Digests of Statistics. Series T. Traffic 868

International Civil Aviation Organization. Digests of Statistics. Series TF. Traffic Flow 868

International Civil Aviation Organization. Indexes to I C A O Publications. Annual Cumulation 866

International Civil Aviation Organization. Legal Committee. Minutes and Documents (of Sessions) 868

International Civil Aviation Organization. Library Information: Recent Accessions and Selected Articles

International Civil Aviation Organization. Obstacle Clearance Panel. Report of Meeting 8

International Civil Aviation Organization. (Panel On) Application of Space Techniques Relating to Aviation. Report of Meeting 8

International Civil Aviation Organization. Report of the Air Navigation Conference 8

International Civil Aviation Organization. Sonic Boom Panel. Report of the Meeting 9

International Civil Aviation Organization. Technical Panel on Supersonic Transport. Report of Meeting 9

International Civil Aviation Organization. Visual Aids Panel. Report of Meeting 9

International Conference on Education. Final Report/ Conference International de l'Education. Rapport Final 319

International Copyright Information Centre. Information Bulletin 677

International Council for Philosophy and Humanistic Studies. Bulletin 689

International Court of Justice. Yearbook 523

International Designs Bulletin

International Digest of Health Legislation

International Directory of Occupational Safety and Health Services and Institutions 495

International Finance Corporation. Report 174

International Financial Statistics

International Histological Classification of Tumours 605

International Indian Ocean Expedition. Collected Reprints 311

International Institute for Educational Planning. Occasional Papers 342

International Institute for Labour Studies. International Educational Materials Exchange. List of Available Materials 159

International Institute for Labour Studies. Public Lecture Series 208

International Institute for Labour Studies. Publications 208

International Institute for Labour Studies. Research Series 208

International Labour Conference. Reports to the Conference and Record of Proceedings 208

International Labour Documentation

International Labour Office. Legislative Series

International Labour Office. Minutes of the Governing Body

International Labour Office. Official Bulletin. Series A

International Labour Office. Special Report of the Director-General on the Application of the Declaration Concerning the Policy of Apartheid of the Republic of South Africa 718

International Labour Review

International Monetary Fund. Annual Report of the Executive Board 174

International Monetary Fund. Annual Report on Exchange Arrangements and Exchange Restrictions 174

International Monetary Fund. Balance of Payments Yearbook 213

International Monetary Fund. Pamphlet Series 174

International Monetary Fund. Selected Decisions of the International Monetary Fund and Selected Documents 174

International Monetary Fund. Staff Papers

International Monetary Fund. Summary Proceedings of the Annual Meeting of the Board of Governors 174

International Narcotics Control Board. Comparative Statement of Estimates and Statistics on Narcotic Drugs Furnished by Governments in Accordance with the International Treaties 287

International Oceanographic Tables 311

International Poplar Commission. Session Reports 409

International Review of Criminal Policy 282

International Rice Commission. Newsletter

International Social Development Review

International Social Science Journal

International Studies in Education 319

International Telecommunication Union. Central Library. List of Recent Acquisitions/Union Internationale des Telecommunications. Bibliotheque Centrale. Liste de Acquisitions Recentes/Union Internacional de Telecomunicaciones. Biblioteca Central. Lista de Adquisiciones Recientes f

International Telecommunication Union. Central Library. Liste des Periodiques. List of Periodicals. Lista de Revistas 266

International Telecommunication Union. Central Library. Listes des Publications Annuelles. List of Annuals. Lista de Publicaciones Anuales 266

INDEX TO PUBLICATIONS OF INTERNATIONAL ORGANIZATIONS

International Telecommunication Union. List of Telegraph Offices Open for International Service 269

International Telecommunication Union. Operational Bulletin

International Telecommunication Union. Report on the Activities 269

International Trade Forum

International Understanding at School

Investment Africa

Joint F A O/W H O Codex Alimentarius Commission. Report of the Session 752

Joint F A O/W H O Expert Committee on Food Additives Report 405

Joint F A O/W H O Expert Committee on Nutrition. Report 666

Journal of Development Planning 200

Labor Education

Labour and Society

Land Reform, Land Settlement and Cooperatives/ Reforme Agraire, Colonisation et Cooperatives Agricoles/Reforma Agraria, Colonizacion y Cooperativas

List of Cables Forming the World Submarine Network 269

List of Destination Indicators and Telex Identification Codes 269

List of International Telephone Routes 269

Locust Newsletter

Marques Internationales

Meeting of International Organizations for the Joint Study of Programs and Activities in the Field of Agriculture in Europe. Report. 18

Meeting on Soil Correlation for North America. (Report) 37

Meeting on Soil Survey Correlation and Interpretation for Latin America. Report 37

Meetings on Atomic Energy

Mekong Bulletin

Monographs on Education 320

Monographs on Oceanographic Methodology 311

Monthly Bulletin of Statistics (FAO)

Museum

Museums and Monuments Series 654

N A T I S-News 533

Natural Resources Research 289

Nature and Resources

New Aquisitions in the U N E C A Library

New Trends in Biology Teaching 105

New Trends in Chemistry Teaching 247

New Trends in Integrated Science Teaching 350

New Trends in Mathematics Teaching 587

New Trends in Physics Teaching 697

Notas Sobre la Economia y el Desarrollo de America Latina

Nuclear Fusion/Fusion Nucleaire

Objective: Justice

Occupational Safety and Health Series 496

Oficina Sanitaria Panamericana. Boletin

Operational Hydrology Reports 308

Palestine Refugees Today

Pan American Health

Pan American Health Organization. Bulletin

Periodicals of Asia and Oceania

Permanent Missions to the United Nations/Missions Permanentes Aupres des Nations Unies a Geneve et Orga Principaux des Nations Unies

Perspectivas

Perspectives

Pharmacopoeia Internationalis/International Pharmacopoeia 685

Plant Genetic Resources Newsletter 278

Population Education in Asia Newsletter 321

Population Newsletter

Population Studies 729

Progress in Land Reform 19

Propriete Industrielle

Prospects

Prostaglandins in Fertility Control 106

Public Administration and Finance Newsletter 745

Public Health Papers 754

Quarterly Bulletin of Statistics for Asia and the Pacific

Quarterly Bulletin of Steel Statistics for Europe/ Bulletin Trimestriel de Statistiques de l'Acier pour l'Europe

Quarterly Statistical Bulletin for Africa

Race Question in Modern Science 53

Radiation Dosimetry Data; Catalogue 622

Regional Conference on Water Resources Development in Asia and the Far East. Proceedings 897

Regional Planning 808

Report on the World Health Situation 754

Reports and Papers in the Social Sciences 800

Reports and Papers on Mass Communications 265

Reports on Marine Science Affairs 312

Resolutions of the General Assembly of the United Nations 723

Review of Economic Situation of Air Transport 869

Review of Maritime Transport 880

Revue Internationale des Sciences Sociales

Sample Surveys in the ESCAP Region 163

Science Policy Studies and Documents 790

Selected List of Catalogues for Short Films and Filmstrips 651

Social and Labour Bulletin

Social Development Newsletter

Social Science Journal 800

State of Food and Agriculture 20

Statistical Indicators for Asia and the Pacific

Statistical Yearbook for Asia and the Pacific/Annuaire Statistique pour l'Asie et le Pacifique 847

Statistical Yearbook for Latin America/Anuario Estadistico de America Latina

Statistics of Road Traffic Accidents in Europe 866

Statistics of World Trade in Steel 630

Studies and Documents on Cultural Policies 493

Studies and Reports in Hydrology Series 308

Studies in Compulsory Education 323

Studies on Selected Development Problems in Various Countries in the Middle East 201

Study Abroad/Etudes a l'Etranger/Estudios en el Extranjero 343

Table of International Telex Relations and Traffic 269

Teachers' Associations. Associations d'Enseignants. Asociaciones de Personal Docente 345

Technical Papers in Hydrology Series 308

Telecommunication Journal

Tourism in Africa. Annual Bulletin 892

Training for Agriculture and Rural Development 330

Transport & Communications Bulletin for Asia & the Far East 863

Tungsten Statistics

U I E Monographs (Unesco Institute for Education) 323

U N C T A D Guide to Publications (United Nations Conference on Trade and Development) 165

U N D E X (United Nations Documents Index)

U N H C R (United Nations High Commissioner for Refugees)

U N H C R Report (United Nations High Commissioner for Refugees) 723

U N I D O Documents Checklist (United Nations Industrial Development Organization)

U N I D O Newsletter (United Nations Industrial Development Organization)

U N I S I S T Boletin de Informacion

U N I S I S T Newsletter (Unesco Programme of International Cooperation in Scientific and Technological Information)

U N I S I S T Newsletter. Russian Edition (Unesco Programme of International Cooperation in Scientific and Technological Information)

U N I T A R Conference Reports (United Nations Institute for Training and Research) 524

U N I T A R News (United Nations Institute for Training and Research) 211

U N I T A R-P S Series (Peaceful Settlement) (United Nations Institute for Training and Research) 723

U N I T A R Regional Studies (United Nations Institute for Training and Research) 724

U N Monthly Chronicle

Unasylva

Unesco. Centro de Documentacion Cultural, Havana. Informaciones Trimestriales

Unesco. Oficina Regional de Educacion para America Latina y le Caribe. Boletin de Educacion

Unesco. Records of the General Conference. Proceedings 724

Unesco. Records of the General Conference. Resolutions 724

Unesco. Regional Office for Culture and Book Development in Asia. Newsletter

Unesco. Regional Office for Education in Asia and Oceania. Bulletin 323

Unesco. Regional Office for Science and Technology for Africa

Unesco. Regional Office for Science and Technology for Latin American and the Caribbean. Boletin

Unesco. Report of the Director-General on the Activities of the Organization 724

Unesco. Scientific Maps and Atlases and Other Related Publications 95

Unesco Asian Fiction Series 575

Unesco Chronicle

Unesco Courier

Unesco Earthquake Study Missions 306

Unesco Features

Unesco Handbook of International Exchanges 343

Unesco Journal of Information Science, Librarianship and Archives Administration

Unesco List of Documents and Publications

Unesco Source Books on Curricula and Methods 351

Unesco Statistical Reports and Studies 849

Unesco Statistical Yearbook 849

Unesco Technical Papers in Marine Science 312

Unicef Information Bulletin

Unicef News

Union Postale

Union Postale Universelle 266

Union Postale Universelle. Statistique des Services Postaux 266

U. N. Annual Bulletin of Housing and Building Statistics for Europe 139

United Nations. Commission on International Trade Law. Report on the Work of Its Session 524

United Nations. Commission on International Trade Law. Yearbook 524

United Nations. Current Bibliographical Information

United Nations. Disarmament Commission. Official Records 640

United Nations. Division of Narcotic Drugs. Information Letter

United Nations. Economic and Social Council. Index to Proceedings 724

United Nations. Economic and Social Council. Official Records 724

United Nations. General Assembly. Index to Proceedings 724

United Nations. International Law Commission. Yearbook 524

United Nations. International Narcotics Control Board. Statistics on Narcotic Drugs Furnished by Governments in Accordance with the International Treaties and Maximum Levels of Opium Stocks 754

United Nations. Multilateral Treaties in Respect of Which the Secretary-General Performs Depositary Functions 524

United Nations. Permanent Central Narcotics (Opium) Board. Report of the International Narcotics Control Board on Its Work 754

United Nations. Population and Vital Statistics Report

United Nations. Regional Centre for Demographic Training and Research in Latin America. Serie A/ Centro Latinoamericano de Demografia. Serie A: Informes sobre Investigaciones Realizadas 729

United Nations. Regional Centre for Demographic Training and Research in Latin America. Serie C/ Centro Latinoamericano de Demografia. Serie C: Informes sobre Investigaciones Realizadas Por los Alumnos del Centro 730

United Nations. Regional Centre for Demographic Training and Research in Latin America. Serie D 730

United Nations. Regional Centre for Demographic Training and Research in Latin America. Serie I/ Centro Latinoamericano de Demografia. Serie I: Recopilacion de Trabajos Sobres Paises 730

United Nations. Security Council. Index to Proceedings 724

United Nations. Security Council. Official Records 724

United Nations. Statistical Yearbook 849

United Nations. Trade and Development Board. Official Records 201

United Nations. Trade and Development Board. Official Records. Supplements 724

United Nations. Trusteeship Council. Index to Proceedings 724

United Nations. Trusteeship Council. Official Records 724

United Nations. Trusteeship Council. Official Records. Supplements 724

United Nations. Yearbook 724

United Nations and What You Should Know about It 724

United Nations Congress on the Prevention of Crime and the Treatment of Offenders. Report 284

United Nations Economic and Social Commission for Asia and the Pacific. Development Programming Techniques Series 201

United Nations Economic and Social Commission for Asia and the Pacific. Mineral Resources Development Series 647

United Nations Economic and Social Commission for Asia and the Pacific. Regional Economic Cooperation Series 201

United Nations Economic and Social Commission for Asia and the Pacific. Social Development Division. Social Work Training and Teaching Materials Newsletter

United Nations Economic and Social Commission for Asia and the Pacific. Statistical Newsletter

United Nations Economic Commission for Western Asia. Population Bulletin

United Nations Industrial Development Organization. Guides to Information Sources 165

United Nations Institute for Training and Research. Report of the Executive Director 724

United Nations Juridical Yearbook 524

United Nations Legislative Series 524

United Nations Library. Geneva. Monthly List of Books Catalogued in the Library of the United Nations/Nations Unies. Bibliotheque Geneva. Liste Mensuelle d'Ouvrages Catalognes a la Bibliotheque des Nations Unies

United Nations Library. Monthly List of Selected Articles/Nations Unies. Bibliotheque. List Mensuelle d'Articles Selectionnes

United Nations Regional Cartographic Conference for Asia and the Far East. Proceedings of the Conference and Technical Papers 426

United Nations Research Institute for Social Development. Report 809

United Nations Research Institute for Social Development. Research Notes 801

United Nations Social Defense Research Institute. Publication 724

United Nations Statistical Office. Monthly Bulletin of Statistcs

Uniterra

Vaccination Certificate Requirements for International Travel/Certificats de Vaccination Exiges dans les Voyages Internationaux 755

Vienna International Centre. Library. Library Acquisitions

Volunteer Service Bulletin

W H O Chronicle (World Health Organization)

W H O Technical Report Series (World Health Organization) 601

W M O Bulletin (World Meteorological Organization)

Waste Management Research Abstracts 757

Water Resources Development Series 899

Weekly Epidemiological Record

World Animal Review

World Bank. Economic Development Institute. E D I Seminar Papers 202

World Bank Atlas 202

World Bank Staff Occasional Papers 202

World Cartography 428

World Cultural Heritage 656

World Directory of Dental Schools 332

World Directory of Medical Schools/Repertoire Mondial des Ecoles de Medecine 332

World Directory of Post-Basic and Post-Graduate Schools of Nursing 332

World Directory of Schools of Pharmacy 332

World Directory of Schools of Public Health 332

World Directory of Social Science Institutions

World Directory of Veterinary Schools 332

World Economic Survey 191

World Energy Supplies 364

World Food Problems 406

World Food Programme News

World Grain Trade Statistics 43

World Health

World Health Organization. Bulletin

World Health Organization. Monograph Series 755

World Health Organization. Regional Office for Africa. Report of the Regional Committee. 755

World Health Organization. Regional Office for Africa. Report of the Regional Director 755

World Health Organization. Regional Office for the Eastern Mediterranean. Biennial Report of the Regional Director 755

World Health Organization. Regional Office for the Western Pacific. Annual Report of the Regional Director to the Regional Committee for the Western Pacific 756

World Health Organization. Regional Office for the Western Pacific. Report on the Regional Seminar on the Role of the Hospital in the Public Health Programme 481

World Health Organization. Work of W H O 756

World Health Organization. World Health Assembly and the Executive Board. Handbook of Resolutions and Decisions. 756

World Health Statistics Annual 757

World Health Statistics Quarterly

World List of Social Science Periodicals 803

World Meteorological Congress. Abridged Report with Resolutions 635

World Meteorological Congress. Proceedings 635

World Meteorological Organization. Annual Reports 635

World Meteorological Organization. Basic Documents and Official Reports 635

World Meteorological Organization. Executive Committee Reports: Abridged Reports with Resolutions 636

World Meteorological Organization. Report on Marine Science Affairs 313

World Meteorological Organization. Reports of Sessions of Regional Associations 636

World Meteorological Organization. Reports of Sessions of Technical Commissions 636

World Meteorological Organization. Special Environmental Reports 390

World Meteorological Organization. Technical Notes 636

World Meteorological Organization. Weather Reporting. Volume A: Observing Stations

World Trade Annual 198

World Trade Annual Supplement 198

World Weather Watch Planning Reports 636

Yearbook of Common Carrier Telecommunication Statistics/Annuaire Statistique des Telecommunications du Secteur Public 265

Yearbook of Fishery Statistics 400

Yearbook of Forest Products 413

Yearbook of International Trade Statistics 166

Year Book of Labour Statistics. 166

Yearbook of National Accounts Statistics 166

Yearbook on Human Rights 719

Your United Nations 436

ISSN Index

Titles in the Bowker Serials Bibliography data base *(Ulrich's, Irregular Serials and Annuals,* and *Ulrich's Quarterly)* with ISSN are listed in this index. For title change, a reference is given to the ISSN of the new title. If a title has changed and a new ISSN has not been assigned (or has not been entered in the Bowker serial record), a reference to the new title will be given. Duplicate listing of ISSN, with references to new titles and/or new ISSN, indicates that the serial has split. Ceased titles (published in the Cessations sections of *Ulrich's, Irregular Serials,* and *Ulrich's Quarterly)* are identified by the symbol †.

0000-0019	Publishers Weekly
0000-0043	Irregular Serials and Annuals
0000-0051	Previews†
0000-0078	L J/S L J Hot Line
0000-0094	Bowker Serials Bibliography Supplement see 0000-0507
0000-0140	Subject Collections
0000-0159	Subject Guide to Books in Print
0000-0167	Subject Guide to Children's Books in Print
0000-0175	Ulrich's International Periodicals Directory
0000-0183	Whitaker's Five-Year Cumulative Book List *changed to* Whitaker's Three-Year Cumulative Book List
0000-0191	Who's Who in American Art
0000-0205	Who's Who in American Politics
0000-0213	Willing's Press Guide
0000-0221	Internationales Bibliotheks-Handbuch
0000-0248	Scientific and Technical Books in Print see 0000-054X
0000-0256	Who's Who in der Politik
0000-0264	Subject Guide to Forthcoming Books
0000-0280	Book/Guide: Mystery, Detective and Suspense Stories†
0000-0302	Mystery & Detection Annual.
0000-0329	I B I D
0000-0345	Canadian Serials Directory/Repertorie des Publications Seriees Canadiennes
0000-037X	Educational Media Yearbook
0000-0388	International Index to Film Periodicals
0000-0434	Magazine Industry Market Place
0000-0450	Information Industry Market Place
0000-0507	Ulrich's Quarterly
0000-0515	Books in Series in the United States
0000-0523	Sources of Serials
0000-054X	Scientific and Technical Books and Serials in Print
0000-0574	Medical Books and Serials in Print
0000-0612	Religious Books and Serials in Print
0000-0620	Publishers and Distributors of the United States see 0000-0671
0000-0671	Publishers, Distributors and Wholesalers of the United States
0001-0006	Mississippi News and Views†
0001-0022	A A A M Quarterly *changed to* A A A M Quarterly Journal
0001-0049	A A C E Bulletin see 0161-6315
0001-0057	A A C S B Bulletin†
0001-0065	A A C T E Publication Service
0001-009X	A A L C Reporter
0001-0111	A A M A Apparel Management Letter†
0001-012X	A A M A Newsletter†
0001-0154	A A M V A Bulletin
0001-0162	A. A. P. M. Quarterly Bulletin see 0094-2405
0001-0170	A A P S News Letter
0001-0189	A A Q
0001-0197	A. A. R. N. Newsletter
0001-0200	A A R P News Bulletin
0001-0235	Advertising Techniques
0001-0251	A A T S E E L Newsletter
0001-026X	A A U P Bulletin see 0190-2946
0001-0278	A A U W Journal see 0161-5661
0001-0286	A A U W New York Division. Newsletter *changed to* A A U W New Yorker
0001-0308	A A Z P A Newsletter
0001-0316	A et U†
0001-0332	A. B. B. Noticias
0001-0340	A B Bookman's Weekly
0001-0367	A B C - Nieuwsmagazine†
0001-0375	Die A B C-Zeitung
0001-0391	A B C Air Cargo Guide and Directory see 0141-6529
0001-0405	A B C der Schuhfabrikation see 0036-7052
0001-0413	A B C Film Review *changed to* Film Review
0001-0421	A B C Goods Transport Guide see 0308-9304
0001-043X	B & C News see 0163-447X
0001-0456	A B C Pol Sci
0001-0464	A B C Radio Guide
0001-0472	A B C Rail Guide
0001-0480	A B C Shipping Guide
0001-0502	A. B. D
0001-0510	A B L C Journal see 0306-1264
0001-0529	A B M A C Bulletin *changed to* Taiwan Medical and Social Review
0001-0545	A B N Correspondence
0001-0553	A B P - Association Belge des Paralyses. Bulletin
0001-0561	A B P I News
0001-0588	A C A News†
0001-0596	A C B Management
0001-060X	A.C.C.A. Canberra Comment see 0045-561X
0001-0618	A. C. C. E. Reporter
0001-0626	A C C E S S *changed to* A C C E L
0001-0634	Chemical Abstracts Service Source Index
0001-0650	A C E
0001-0669	A C E C Review
0001-0677	A C E N News†
0001-0693	A C E Research†
0001-0707	A C H A News
0001-0715	A. C. I. Informazioni
0001-0723	A C I L Bulletin†
0001-0731	A C
0001-0766	A C M C Bulletin†
0001-0774	A C M Newsletter see 0317-5006
0001-0782	Association for Computing Machinery. Communications
0001-0790	A C O S News
0001-0812	A C P A Newsletter *changed to* P I R I Newsletter
0001-0847	A. D. A. Forecast see 0095-8301
0001-0855	A D A News
0001-0863	A D A Newsletter *changed to* A D A Leadership Bulletin
0001-0871	A D A World
0001-088X	A D C Newsletter
0001-0898	A D E Bulletin
0001-091X	Al-Adib
0001-0928	A D K Nuusbrief *changed to* S A D K Nuusbrief
0001-0936	A D L Bulletin
0001-0944	A D M
0001-0979	A D T V - Nachrichten
0001-0987	A D V-Informationsdienst
0001-0995	A D W - Umschau†
0001-1002	A E A-M Newsletter/Journal
0001-1010	A E B U
0001-1029	A E C L Review
0001-1037	A E D S Journal
0001-1045	A E D S Monitor
0001-1053	A E G - Schakels
0001-1061	A E G - Telefunken al Dia
0001-107X	A E G - Telefunken Progress
0001-1088	A E Rho Monitor *changed to* Playback
0001-1096	A E Ue
0001-110X	A U E W E S Journal
0001-1118	A E U Reports
0001-1126	A F A Informationen
0001-1134	A F E R
0001-1150	A F L - C I O Library Acquisition List
0001-1169	American Federationist see 0149-2489
0001-1177	A F L-C I O Free Trade Union News
0001-1185	A F L-C I O News
0001-1193	A F R A Boletin Informativo
0001-1207	A. F. R E
0001-1223	A F S Cast Metals Research Journal see 0008-7467
0001-1231	A. F. Universite *changed to* Action Francaise Etudiante
0001-124X	A F V-G2
0001-1274	A G A
0001-1282	A G A News†
0001-1290	Agasvets†
0001-1304	A. G. Bush Library Abstracts†
0001-1320	A G E C O - Documentation Siderurgique
0001-1339	A G I E S
0001-1355	A G R A News
0001-1371	A G V A News *changed to* A G V A Newsletter
0001-138X	A. H. A. Newsletter
0001-1398	A. H. A. Review
0001-1401	Aussenhandelsdienst der Industrie- und Handelskammern und Wirtschaftsverbaende
0001-1428	A H I L Quarterly *changed to* H R L S D Journal
0001-1436	A. H. R. C. Chronicle
0001-1444	A I A A Bulletin see 0004-6213
0001-1452	A I A A Journal
0001-1460	A I A A Student Journal
0001-1479	A I A Journal

0001-1487 A I A Memo
0001-1495 Asociacion Interamericana de Bibliotecarios y Documentalistas Agricolas. Boletin Informativo.
0001-1509 Political Africa†
0001-1509 All India Congress Committee. Political and Economic Review†
0001-1517 A I C C News
0001-1541 A I Ch E Journal
0001-155X American Industrial Development Council. A I D C Journal *see* 0279-6430
0001-1568 A. I. Digest *changed to* Advanced Animal Breeder
0001-1576 A I F L D Report
0001-1584 A. I. L. A.
0001-1606 A I L Newsletter
0001-1622 A I M S Newsletter
0001-1630 A I O E Labour News
0001-1649 A I P Educational Newsletter†
0001-1657 A. I. P. Information & Publication Newsletter†
0001-1665 A I P Newsletter *see* 0164-5420
0001-1673 A I Z
0001-1681 A J R Information
0001-169X A K†
0001-1703 A L A F O. Revista
0001-1746 A L A Washington Newsletter
0001-1754 A. L. B. A. Bowls
0001-1762 A L E C Report
0001-1770 A L S A C News
0001-1789 A Lampada
0001-1800 Atualidades Medicas†
0001-1819 A. M. A. *changed to* Report
0001-1827 A M A Audio News Journal†
0001-1835 A M A International Health Bulletin†
0001-1843 American Medical News
0001-1851 A M A X Journal
0001-186X A M B A C. Noticiero
0001-1878 A M C H A M Newsletter
0001-1894 A M C of A Newsletter
0001-1908 A M D I Bollettino
0001-1932 A M News - Southern Africa
0001-1940 Ampujainlehti
0001-1967 A M S Management Bulletin *see* 0090-3825
0001-1975 A M T D A Journal *see* 0308-9274
0001-1983 A M Z
0001-1991 A.N.A. Club Bulletin *see* 0029-6090
0001-2025 A.N.F.I.A. Notiziario di Informazioni
0001-2033 A.N.F.I.A. Notiziario Statistico
0001-2041 A N N Y
0001-205X American Newspaper Publishers Association, Research Institute. R.I. Bulletins. *changed to* Presstime
0001-2068 A N U Historical Journal
0001-2076 A N Z Bank Quarterly Survey†
0001-2084 A O P A Pilot
0001-2092 A O R N Journal
0001-2114 A P A Monitor
0001-2122 A. P. A. V. E. Revue
0001-2130 A P C A Abstracts†
0001-2173 A P D F Newsletter
0001-2181 A P E C
0001-2203 A P L A Bulletin
0001-2211 A P L Technical Digest *changed to* Johns Hopkins A P L Technical Digest
0001-2246 A P R A Journal
0001-2252 A P W A Newsletter
0001-2270 A P W A Reporter
0001-2289 A R A Log
0001-2297 A R E R S
0001-2300 A R G R Journal
0001-2319 A R M P News†
0001-2327 A R S H A Bulletin
0001-2335 A. R. S. Hai Sird
0001-2343 Archiv fuer Rechts- und Sozialphilosophie
0001-2351 A S A E Transactions
0001-2378 A S A Newsletter†
0001-2386 A. S. B. Bulletin
0001-2394 A. S. B. E. Letter
0001-2408 A S B S D Bulletin
0001-2416 A S C A Newsletter
0001-2424 A S C A P Today
0001-2432 A S C E Publications Abstracts
0001-2440 A S E A Bulletin
0001-2459 A S E A Journal
0001-2475 A S H A
0001-2483 A S H P Newsletter
0001-2491 A S H R A E Journal
0001-2505 A S H R A E Transactions
0001-2521 Aslib Book List
0001-253X Aslib Proceedings
0001-2548 A S L P Bulletin
0001-2556 A S M. Bibliography Series
0001-2580 A S P A C Newsletter of Cultural and Social Affairs
0001-2599 A S P A C Quarterly of Cultural and Social Affairs *changed to* Asian Pacific Quarterly of Cultural and Social Affairs
0001-2602 A S P B A E Journal†
0001-2610 Planning
0001-2629 A S R C T Newsletter†
0001-2637 A S T A Travel News
0001-2645 A S T E Bulletin *see* 0360-5930
0001-2653 A S T M S Journal
0001-2661 A. T. A. Associazione Tecnica dell'Automobile
0001-267X A T A News
0001-2688 Auto Touring
0001-2696 Acta Technica Belgica. Revue A T B: Metallurgie
0001-2718 A T E Newsletter
0001-2726 A T F Monthly Report *changed to* A T F Annual Report
0001-2734 A. T. G. Bulletin
0001-2750 A T O - A C E Newsletter†
0001-2769 A T P A S Bulletin *see* 0308-6895
0001-2777 A T R
0001-2785 A T Z
0001-2807 A U P E L F. Revue
0001-2815 Tissue Antigens
0001-2823 A. U. T. Bulletin
0001-2831 A-V
0001-2858 A V A Magazine
0001-2866 A V A Member-Gram
0001-2874 A V C Bulletin
0001-2890 A V Communication Review *see* 0148-5806
0001-2904 A V S News
0001-2912 A Votre Sante†
0001-2920 A W A Technical Review†
0001-2939 A W I N Newsletter
0001-2947 A W R Bulletin
0001-2955 Hosteler†
0001-2971 A A H E College and University Bulletin *see* 0162-7910
0001-298X Aakerifoeretagaren-Transportoeren *see* 0348-0356
0001-3013 Aannemer *changed to* Bouwbedrijf
0001-3048 Aaron Burr Association. Chronicle
0001-3056 Arrow (Kenosha)
0001-3064 Aavesh
0001-3072 Abacus
0001-3099 Abacus
0001-3102 Abbia
0001-3110 Abbigliamento Italiano *changed to* Abbigliamento
0001-3129 Abeille & Erable
0001-3137 Abeille de France *changed to* Abeille de France et l'Apiculteur
0001-3145 Abeilles et Fleurs
0001-3153 Abel
0001-3161 Aberdeen-Angus Journal *see* 0194-9543
0001-317X Aberdeen-Angus Review
0001-3188 Aberdeen Chamber of Commerce Journal
0001-3196 University of Aberdeen. African Studies Group. Bulletin
0001-320X University of Aberdeen Review
0001-3218 Abitare
0001-3234 Abolition News
0001-3242 About the House
0001-3269 Abracadabra
0001-3285 Abrasive Methods *changed to* Abrasive Engineering Society. Magazine
0001-3307 Abraxas†
0001-3331 Abridged Index Medicus
0001-334X Abridged Readers' Guide to Periodical Literature
0001-3358 Abril†
0001-3374 Absatzwirtschaft
0001-3382 Abside
0001-3390 Abstract Review
0001-3404 Abstracts and Book Title Index Card Service (ABTICS)
0001-3412 Abstracts for Social Workers *see* 0148-0847
0001-3420 Abstracts for the Advancement of Industrial Utilization of Cereal Grains†
0001-3439 Abstracts from Current Scientific and Technical Literature
0001-3447 Abstracts from Technical and Patent Publications
0001-3455 Abstracts in Anthropology
0001-3463 Abstracts of Bulgarian Scientific Literature. Agriculture and Forestry. Veterinary Medicine.
0001-3471 Abstracts of Bulgarian Scientific Literature. Biology and Biochemistry
0001-348X Abstracts of Bulgarian Scientific Literature. Economics and Law
0001-3498 Abstracts of Bulgarian Scientific Literature. Geology and Geography
0001-3501 Bulletin d'Analyses de la Litterature Scientifique Bulgare. Linguistique et Litterature
0001-351X Abstracts of Bulgarian Scientific Literature. Mathematics, Physics, Astronomy, Geophysics, Geodesy
0001-3528 Abstracts of Bulgarian Scientific Literature. Philosophy, Psychology and Pedagogics *changed to* Abstracts of Bulgarian Scientific Literature. Philosophy, Sociology, Science of Sciences, Psychology and Pedagogics
0001-3536 Abstracts of Bulgarian Scientific Medical Literature
0001-3552 Abstracts of Efficiency Studies in the Hospital Service *changed to* Great Britain. Department of Health and Social Security. Notes on Good Practices
0001-3560 Abstracts of English Studies
0001-3579 Abstracts of Entomology
0001-3587 Abstracts of Folklore Studies†
0001-3595 Abstracts of Hospital Management Studies *see* 0194-4908
0001-3609 Abstracts of Instructional Materials in Vocational and Technical Education *changed to* Resources in Vocational Education
0001-3617 Abstracts of Mycology
0001-3625 Abstracts of North American Geology†
0001-3633 Abstracts of Photographic Science & Engineering Literature†
0001-3641 Abstracts of Research and Related Materials in Vocational and Technical Education *changed to* Resources in Vocational Education
0001-365X Abstracts of Romanian Scientific and Technical Literature
0001-3668 Abstracts of the Current Literature on TB and Other Respiratory Diseases
0001-3676 Abstracts of Uppsala Dissertations in Science
0001-3684 Excerpta Criminologica *see* 0166-6231
0001-3692 Abstracts on Hygiene *see* 0260-5511
0001-3706 Abwassertechnik *see* 0342-4022
0001-3714 Revista de Microbiologia
0001-3722 Abyss
0001-3730 Acacia Clarion
0001-3749 Academe *see* 0190-2946
0001-3757 Academia Argentina de Letras. Boletin
0001-3765 Academia Brasileira de Ciencias. Anais
0001-3773 Academia Colombiana. Boletin
0001-3781 Academia das Ciencias de Lisboa. Boletim
0001-3803 Academia Medico Quirurgica Espanola. Anales†
0001-3811 Academia Militar de Chorrillos. Revista
0001-382X Academia Nacional de la Historia. Boletin
0001-3838 Academia Nacional de Medicina. Boletim
0001-3846 Academia Paulista de Letras. Revista
0001-3854 Academia Peruana de Cirugia Revista
0001-3862 Academia Portena del Lunfardo. Boletin
0001-3889 Academia Republicii Socialiste Romania. Buletin de Informare Stiintifica. Geologie, Geografie†
0001-3897 Lingvistica-Filologie†
0001-3900 Academia Republicii Socialiste Romania. Buletin de Informare Stiintifica. Seria Matematica Astronomie†
0001-3919 Teoria si Istoria Literaturii si Artei; Buletin de Informare Stiintifica†
0001-3927 Academia Sinica. Institute of Chemistry. Bulletin
0001-3935 Academia Sinica. Institute of Ethnology. Bulletin
0001-3943 Academia Sinica.Institute of Zoology.Bulletin
0001-3951 Academic Achievement
0001-396X Academic Therapy
0001-3978 Academie Bulgare des Sciences. Comptes Rendus
0001-3986 Academie d'Agriculture de France./ Comptes Rendus des Seances
0001-3994 Academie d'Architecture
0001-4001 Chirurgie
0001-401X Academie de Droit International de la Haye. Recueil des Cours
0001-4044 Academie des Sciences d'Outre-Mer, Paris. Comptes Rendus des Seances
0001-4060 Academie Internationale du Tourisme. Revue
0001-4079 Academie Nationale de Medecine. Bulletin
0001-4087 Academie Polonaise des Sciences. Bulletin. Serie des Sciences Biologiques
0001-4095 Academie Polonaise des Sciences. Bulletin. Serie des Sciences Chimiques
0001-4109 Academie Polonaise des Sciences. Bulletin. Serie des Sciences de la Terre
0001-4117 Academie Polonaise des Sciences. Bulletin. Serie des Sciences Mathematiques, Astronomiques et Physiques
0001-4125 Academie Polonaise des Sciences. Bulletin. Serie des Sciences Techniques
0001-4133 Academie Royale des Sciences, des Lettres et des Beaux-Arts de Belgique. Classe des Lettres et Sciences Morales et Politiques. Bulletin
0001-4141 Academie Royale des Sciences des Lettres et des Beaux-Arts de Belgique. Classe des Sciences. Bulletin
0001-415X Academie Royale des Sciences, des Lettres et des Beaux Arts de Belgique. Commission Royale d'Histoire. Bulletin
0001-4168 Academie Royale de Medecine de Belgique. Bulletin *changed to* Academie Royale de Medecine de Belgique. Bulletin et Memoires
0001-4176 Academie Royale des Sciences d'Outre-Mer. Bulletin des Seances
0001-4192 Academie Veterinaire de France. Bulletin
0001-4214 Revue Roumaine de Biochimie
0001-4230 Academus;
0001-4249 Academy Bookman
0001-4265 Academy of General Dentistry. Journal *see* 0363-6771
0001-4273 Academy of Management. Journal
0001-4281 Academy of Medicine of Cleveland. Bulletin *changed to* Cleveland Physician
0001-4303 Academy of Medicine of Toledo and Lucas County. Bulletin
0001-4311 Academy of Medicine, Toronto. Bulletin
0001-4338 Academy of Sciences of the U S S R. Izvestiya. Atmospheric and Oceanic Physics
0001-4346 Mathematical Notes
0001-4354 Academy of Sciences of the U S S R. Izvestiya. Physics of the Solid Earth

0001-4362 Population Biocharacterist *changed to* Health Evaluation Review
0001-4370 Academy of Sciences of the U S S R. Oceanology
0001-4389 Pharmacology and Therapeutics in Dentistry
0001-4397 Acadiana Profile
0001-4400 Acao
0001-4419 Accademia delle Scienze di Torino. Atti. Part I. Classe di Scienze Fisiche, Matematiche e Naturali
0001-4427 Accademia Medica Lombarda. Atti
0001-4435 Accademia Nazionale dei Lincei. Classe di Scienze Fisiche Matematiche e Naturali. Rendiconti
0001-4443 Accademia Nazionale di Agricoltura. Annali†
0001-4451 Accademie e Biblioteche d'Italia
0001-446X Accelerator
0001-4478 Accelerator
0001-4486 Accent†
0001-4508 Accent on Living
0001-4516 Accent on Youth
0001-4559 Acciaio
0001-4567 Acciaio Inossidabile
0001-4575 Accident Analysis & Prevention
0001-4583 Accidents Claims Journal
0001-4591 Accidents, How They Are Caused and How to Prevent Them†
0001-4605 Accion
0001-4613 Accion Conjunta
0001-4648 Accordion Horizons†
0001-4656 Accordion Times
0001-4664 Accountancy
0001-4672 Accountancy Age
0001-4680 Accountancy, Business & Insurance Review
0001-4699 Accountancy Ireland
0001-4702 Accountant Journal *changed to* Institute of Chartered Accountants of Sri Lanka. Journal
0001-4710 Accountant
0001-4729 Accountant
0001-4737 Accountants Digest
0001-4745 Accountants' Journal
0001-4753 Accountants' Journal
0001-4761 Accountant's Magazine
0001-477X Accountants Market Place *changed to* C P A's Market Place
0001-4788 Accounting and Business Research
0001-4796 Accounting & Data Processing Abstracts
0001-4818 Accounting Forum
0001-4826 Accounting Review
0001-4834 Accounting Trends†
0001-4842 Accounts of Chemical Research
0001-4850 Acero y Energia
0001-4869 Achaab
0001-4877 Achats et Entretien du Materiel Industriel *changed to* Achats et Entretien-Equipement Industriel
0001-4893 Acheteurs
0001-4907 Achievement
0001-4923 Acier
0001-4931 Acier dans le Monde
0001-494X Acme
0001-4958 Aconcagua Iberoamerica-Europa†
0001-4966 Acoustical Society of America. Journal
0001-4974 Acoustics Abstracts
0001-4982 Inquinamento
0001-5008 Acquisitions Nouvelles en Pathologie Cardio-Vasculaire
0001-5040 Acropole†
0001-5059 Across from City Hall
0001-5067 Acrow Review
0001-5075 Act
0001-5083 Act
0001-5105 Academiae Aboensis, Series B: Mathematics, Science, Engineering
0001-5113 Acta Adriatica
0001-5121 Acta Agriculturae Scandinavica
0001-513X Acta Agronomica
0001-5148 Acta Allergologica *see* 0105-4538
0001-5156 Acta Anaesthesiologica *see* 0374-4965
0001-5164 Acta Anaesthesiologica Belgica
0001-5172 Acta Anaesthesiologica Scandinavica
0001-5180 Acta Anatomica
0001-5199 Acta Apostolicae Sedis. Commentarium Officiale
0001-5202 Acta Arachnologica
0001-5210 Acta Archaeologica
0001-5229 Acta Archaeologica Carpathica
0001-5237 Acta Astronomica
0001-5253 Acta Biochimica et Biophysica
0001-5261 Acta Biochimica Iranica†
0001-527X Acta Biochimica Polonica†
0001-5288 Acta Biologica
0001-5296 Acta Biologica Cracoviensia. Botanica
0001-530X Acta Biologica Cracoviensia. Zoologia
0001-5318 Acta Biologica et Medica Germanica
0001-5326 Acta Biologica Venezuelica
0001-5334 Acta Biologicae Experimentalis Sinica†
0001-5342 Acta Biotheoretica
0001-5350 Acta Botanica
0001-5369 Acta Botanica Fennica
0001-5377 Acta Cancerologica
0001-5385 Acta Cardiologica
0001-5393 Acta Chemica Scandinavica *see* 0302-4377
0001-5393 Acta Chemica Scandinavica *see* 0302-4369
0001-5407 Acta Chimica
0001-5415 Acta Chirurgiae Orthopaedicae et Traumatologiae Cechoslovaca
0001-5423 Acta Chirurgiae Plasticae
0001-5431 Acta Chirurgica
0001-544X Acta Chirurgica Austriaca
0001-5458 Acta Chirurgica Belgica
0001-5466 Acta Chirurgica Italica
0001-5474 Acta Chirurgica Iugoslavica
0001-5482 Acta Chirurgica Scandinavica
0001-5490 Acta Cientifica†
0001-5504 Acta Cientifica Venezolana
0001-5520 Acta Crystallographica *see* 0567-7394
0001-5547 Acta Cytologica
0001-5555 Acta Dermato-Venereologica
0001-5563 Acta Diabetologica Latina
0001-5571 Acta Diurna†
0001-558X Acta Electronica
0001-5598 Acta Endocrinologica
0001-5601 Acta Entomologica Bohemoslovaca
0001-561X Acta Entomologica Fennica
0001-5628 Acta Ethnographica
0001-5636 Acta Forestalia Fennica
0001-5644 Acta Gastro-Enterologica Belgica
0001-5652 Human Heredity
0001-5660 Acta Geneticae Medicae et Gemellologiae
0001-5679 Acta Geodaetica, Geophysica et Montanistica
0001-5687 Acta Geographica
0001-5695 Acta Geologica
0001-5709 Acta Geologica Polonica
0001-5717 Acta Geologica Sinica
0001-5725 Acta Geophysica Polonica
0001-5733 Acta Geophysica Sinica
0001-5741 Acta Gerontologica
0001-575X Acta Gerontologica et Geriatrica Belgica *changed to* Rejuvenation
0001-5768 Acta Gerontologica Japonica *changed to* Yokufukai Geriatric Journal
0001-5776 Acta Ginecologica
0001-5792 Acta Haematologica
0001-5806 Acta Haematologica Japonica
0001-5814 Acta Haematologica Polonica
0001-5822 Acta Hepato- Splenologica *changed to* Hepato-Gastroenterology
0001-5830 Acta Historiae Artium
0001-5849 Acta Historica
0001-5857 Acta Historica Leopoldina
0001-5865 Acta Historica Medicinae, Stomatologiae, Pharmaciae, Veterinae
0001-5881 Acta Homoeopathica *see* 0301-1402
0001-589X Acta Iberica Radiologica-Cancerologica
0001-5903 Acta Informatica
0001-592X Acta Juridica
0001-5938 Acta Leprologica
0001-5946 Acta Linguistica
0001-5954 Acta Mathematica
0001-5962 Acta Mathematica
0001-5970 Acta Mechanica
0001-5989 Acta Medica
0001-5997 Acta Medica
0001-6004 Acta Medica Auxologica
0001-6012 Acta Medica Costarricense
0001-6020 Acta Medica de Tenerife
0001-6039 Acta Medica Italica di Medicina Tropicale e Subtropicale e di Gastroenterologia
0001-6055 Acta Medica Nagasakiensia
0001-6071 Acta Medica Philippina
0001-608X Acta Medica Polona
0001-6098 Acta Medica Romana
0001-6101 Acta Medica Scandinavica
0001-611X Acta Medica Universitatis Kagoshimaensis
0001-6136 Acta Medica Veterinaria
0001-6152 Acta Medicinae Okayama. *see* 0386-300X
0001-6160 Acta Metallurgica
0001-6179 Acta Meteorologica Sinica
0001-6187 Acta Microbiologica
0001-6195 Acta Microbiologica Polonica
0001-6209 Acta Microbiologica Sinica
0001-6217 Acta Morphologica
0001-6225 Acta Morphologica Neerlando-Scandinavica
0001-6233 Acta Mozartiana
0001-6241 Acta Musicologica
0001-625X Acta Mycologica
0001-6268 Acta Neurochirurgica
0001-6276 Acta Neurologica
0001-6284 Acta Neurologica et Psychiatrica Belgica *see* 0300-9009
0001-6284 Acta Neurologica et Psychiatrica Belgica *see* 0300-8967
0001-6306 Acta Neurologica Latinamericana
0001-6314 Acta Neurologica Scandinavica
0001-6322 Acta Neuropathologica
0001-6330 Acta Obsterica et Gynaecologica Japonica†
0001-6349 Acta Obstetricia et Gynecologica Scandinavica
0001-6357 Acta Odontologica Scandinavica
0001-6365 Acta Odontologica Venezolana
0001-6373 Acta Oeconomica
0001-6381 Acta Oncologica†
0001-6381 Acta Oncologica
0001-639X Acta Ophthalmologica
0001-6403 Acta Ophthalmologica Iugoslavica
0001-6411 Acta Ordinis Fratrum Minorum
0001-642X Acta Ordinis Sancti Augustini
0001-6438 Acta Orientalia
0001-6446 Acta Orientalia
0001-6454 Acta Ornithologica
0001-6462 Acta Orthopaedica Belgica
0001-6470 Acta Orthopaedica Scandinavica
0001-6489 Acta Oto-Laryngologica
0001-6497 Acta Oto-Rhino-Laryngologica Belgica
0001-6500 Acta Oto-Rino-Laringologica Ibero-Americana
0001-6519 Acta Otorrinolaringologica Espanola
0001-6527 Acta Paediatrica
0001-6535 Acta Paediatrica Belgica
0001-6543 Acta Paediatrica Japonica
0001-6551 Acta Paediatrica Latina
0001-656X Acta Paediatrica Scandinavica
0001-6578 Acta Paediatrica Sinica
0001-6586 Acta Paedopsychiatrica
0001-6594 Acta Palaeobotanica
0001-6616 Acta Palaeontologica Sinica
0001-6624 Acta Pathologica et Microbiologica Scandinavia *see* 0365-4184
0001-6632 Acta Pathologica Japonica
0001-6640 Acta Pediatrica Espanola
0001-6659 Acta Pharmaceutica Hungarica
0001-6667 Acta Pharmaceutica Jugoslavica
0001-6675 Acta Pharmaceutica Suecica
0001-6683 Acta Pharmacologica et Toxicologica
0001-6691 Acta Philologica Scandinavica
0001-6705 Acta Physica
0001-6713 Acta Physica Austriaca
0001-6721 Acta Universitatis Szegediensis de Attila Jozsef Nominatae. Acta Physica et Chemica
0001-673X Acta Physica Polonica
0001-6748 Acta Physioligica et Pharmacologia Neerlandica†
0001-6756 Acta Physiologica
0001-6764 Acta Physiologica Latino Americana
0001-6772 Acta Physiologica Scandinavica
0001-6780 Acta Phytopathologica
0001-6799 Acta Phytotaxonomica et Geobotanica
0001-6810 Acta Politica
0001-6829 Acta Poloniae Historica
0001-6837 Acta Poloniae Pharmaceutica†
0001-6845 Acta Polytechnica Scandinavica. Electrical Engineering Series
0001-6853 Acta Polytechnica Scandinavica. Chemistry Including Metallurgy Series
0001-6861 Acta Polytechnica Scandinavica. Mathematics and Computing Machinery Series *see* 0355-2713
0001-687X Acta Polytechnica Scandinavica. Mechanical Engineering Series
0001-6888 Acta Polytechnica Scandinavica. Physics Including Nucleonics Series *see* 0355-2721
0001-6896 Acta Psiquiatrica y Psicologica de America Latina
0001-690X Acta Psychiatrica Scandinavica
0001-6918 Acta Psychologica
0001-6934 Acta Rheumatologica Scandinavica *see* 0300-9742
0001-6942 Acta Sagittariana
0001-6950 Acta Scholae Medicinalis Universitatis in Kioto†
0001-6969 Acta Scientiarum Mathematicarum
0001-6977 Acta Societatis Botanicorum Poloniae
0001-6985 Acta Societatis Medicorum Upsaliensis *see* 0300-9734
0001-6993 Acta Sociologica
0001-7000 Acta Stomatologica Belgica
0001-7019 Acta Stomatologica Croatica
0001-7035 Acta Technica
0001-7043 Ceskoslovenska Akademie Ved. Acta Technica
0001-7051 Acta Theriologica
0001-706X Acta Tropica
0001-7078 Acta Tuberculosea et Pneumologica Belgica *changed to* European Journal of Respiratory Diseases
0001-7108 Current Literature of Blood†
0001-7124 Acta Universitatis Carolinae: Biologica
0001-7132 Acta Universitatis Carolinae: Geologica
0001-7140 Acta Universitatis Carolinae: Mathematica et Physica
0001-7159 Acta Universitatis Lundensis Sectio: Medica, Mathematica, Scientiae Rerum Naturalium†
0001-7167 Acta Universitatis Palackianae, Facultatis Medicae
0001-7175 Acta Universitatis Szegediensis de Attila Jozsef Nominatae. Acta Bibliothecaria
0001-7183 Acta Urologica Belgica
0001-7191 Acta Urologica Japonica
0001-7205 Acta Veterinaria
0001-7213 Acta Veterinaria
0001-7221 Acta Veterinaria Japonica
0001-723X Acta Virologica
0001-7248 Acta Vitaminologica *see* 0300-8924
0001-7264 Acta Zoologica
0001-7272 Acta Zoologica
0001-7280 Acta Zoologica et Pathologica Antverpiensia
0001-7299 Acta Zoologica Fennica
0001-7302 Acta Zoologica Sinica
0001-7310 Actas Dermo-Sifiliograficas
0001-7329 Actas Luso Espanolas de Neurologia y Psiquiatria *see* 0300-5062
0001-7345 Actes Pontificaux†
0001-7353 Actinides and Lanthanides Reviews†
0001-737X Action (Louisville)
0001-7388 Action (New York)†
0001-7396 Action (Albany)
0001-740X Action†
0001-7418 Action Automobile et Touristique
0001-7426 Action et Pensee†
0001-7442 Action Line (Baltimore)
0001-7450 Action Municipale
0001-7469 Action Nationale
0001-7477 Action Poetique
0001-7485 Action-Reaction *see* 0360-1897

ISSN	Title
0001-7507	Action Sociale
0001-7523	Action Veterinaire
0001-754X	Active Handicapped†
0001-7558	Active Service
0001-7566	Actividade Economica de Angola
0001-7574	C E E D. Actividades†
0001-7582	Actividades Petroleras
0001-7590	Activist†
0001-7604	Activitas Nervosa Superior
0001-7612	Activities of the Communist World Organizations†
0001-7620	ACTivity
0001-7639	Actual
0001-7647	Actual Specifying Engineer see 0164-5242
0001-7655	Actualidad Economica
0001-7671	Actualidad Pediatrica†
0001-768X	Actualidades de Japon
0001-7701	General Relativity and Gravitation
0001-771X	Actualite Economique
0001-7728	Actualite Juridique: Edition Droit Administratif
0001-7736	Actualite Juridique: Edition Propriete Immobiliere see 0001-7728
0001-7744	Actualite Missionnaire†
0001-7752	Actualite Pedagogique a l'Etranger†
0001-7760	Actualite Publicitaire
0001-7779	Actualite Terminologique
0001-7787	Actualites Cereales changed to Actualites Agricoles
0001-7795	Actualites et Culture Veterinaires†
0001-7809	Actualites Marines†
0001-7817	Actualites Odonto-Stomatologiques
0001-7825	Actuary
0001-7833	Actuel†
0001-7841	Actuele Onderwerpen-Reeks
0001-785X	Aktuelle Chirurgie
0001-7868	Aktuelle Urologie
0001-7884	Acustica
0001-7892	Ad
0001-7906	AD-Cards†
0001-7914	Ad Change
0001-7922	Ad Club News
0001-7930	Ad Fontes
0001-7949	Ad Lib
0001-7957	Ad Libs†
0001-7965	Ad Marginem
0001-7973	Ad Rem†
0001-7981	Behavioral Science in Progress†
0001-799X	Adalbert-Stifter-Institut des Landes Oberoesterreich. Vierteljahresschrift
0001-8007	Adam
0001-8015	Adam International Review
0001-8023	Adam Magazine†
0001-804X	Adansonia
0001-8066	Adcrafter
0001-8074	Addiction and Drug Abuse Report see 0160-967X
0001-8082	Addictions†
0001-8090	Adding Life to Years†
0001-8112	A D E G - Kaufmann
0001-8120	A D E G - Kurier
0001-8139	Adelaar
0001-8147	Adelaide Church Guardian
0001-8163	University of Adelaide. Graduates Union. Monthly Newsletter and Gazette
0001-8171	Adem
0001-818X	Adept Quarterly
0001-8198	Adhaesion
0001-8201	Adhesion Society of Japan. Journal
0001-821X	Adhesives Age
0001-8228	Adhuna Sahitya
0001-8236	Adirondac
0001-8244	Behavior Genetics
0001-8252	Adirondack Life
0001-8260	Adler
0001-8279	Der Adler
0001-8295	Admap
0001-8309	Administracion y Desarrollo
0001-8317	Administratieve Arbeid†
0001-8325	Administration
0001-8333	Quarterly Journal of Administration
0001-835X	Administrative Digest
0001-8368	Administrative Law Review
0001-8376	Administrative Management
0001-8384	Administrative Officer changed to Management Service Alert & The Administrative Officer
0001-8392	Administrative Science Quarterly
0001-8406	Administrative Science Review
0001-8422	Administrator's Digest
0001-8430	Administrators Notebook
0001-8449	Adolescence
0001-8473	Adult & Continuing Education Today
0001-8481	Adult Education
0001-849X	Adult Education
0001-8503	Adult Education in Finland
0001-8511	Adult Education in Nova Scotia
0001-852X	Adult Education in the Public Schools†
0001-8546	Adult Jewish Education†
0001-8554	Adult Leadership changed to Lifelong Learning: the Adult Years
0001-8562	Advance (Chicago)
0001-8570	Advance (St. Louis)†
0001-8570	Advance (St. Louis) see 0360-7119
0001-8589	Advance (Springfield)
0001-8597	Advance (New York) changed to Labor Unity
0001-8600	Advance Abstracts of Contributions on Fisheries and Aquatic Sciences in India†
0001-8619	Advance Australia
0001-8627	Advanced Battery Technology
0001-8635	Advanced Documentation List†
0001-8651	Advanced Publications†
0001-8678	Advances in Applied Probability
0001-8686	Advances in Colloid and Interface Science
0001-8694	Advances in Education
0001-8708	Advances in Mathematics
0001-8716	Advances in Molecular Relaxation Processes see 0378-4487
0001-8724	Advances in Neurological Sciences
0001-8732	Advances in Physics
0001-8740	Adveniat
0001-8759	Advent Christian Missions
0001-8767	Adventbode changed to Advent
0001-8775	Adventure†
0001-8783	Adventure†
0001-8791	Journal of Vocational Behavior
0001-8805	Adventure Road
0001-8813	Adventure Time†
0001-8821	Adventurer
0001-883X	Adventures in Western New York History
0001-8848	Excerpta Medica. Section 38: Adverse Reactions Titles
0001-8856	Advertentieblad
0001-8864	Advertisement Parade
0001-8880	Adweek†
0001-8899	Advertising Age
0001-8902	Advertising & Marketing for Manufacturers†
0001-8910	Advertising & Marketing News changed to National Business Review
0001-8929	Newspaper News changed to Advertising News
0001-8961	Advertising Quarterly changed to Advertising Magazine
0001-8988	Advertlink
0001-8996	Advocate (San Mateo)
0001-9003	Advocate (New York)
0001-9011	Adyar
0001-902X	Brahmavidya
0001-9038	Aegir
0001-9046	Aegyptus
0001-9054	Aequationes Mathematicae
0001-9062	Aerial
0001-9070	Aerial Applicator
0001-9089	Sardegna-Agricoltura (Varese)
0001-9097	Aero
0001-9100	Aero
0001-9127	Aeroespacio
0001-9127	Aerospacio
0001-9135	Aero Field
0001-9151	Aero Graphic
0001-916X	Aero Mundial
0001-9178	Aero Philatelist Annals†
0001-9186	Aero-Revue
0001-9194	Aerograph Research Notes†
0001-9216	Aerological Data of Japan
0001-9224	Aerologische Berichte
0001-9232	Aero Modeller
0001-9240	Aeronautical Journal
0001-9259	Aeronautical Quarterly
0001-9267	Aeronautical Society of India. Journal
0001-9275	Aeronautique et l'Astronautique
0001-9283	Aeroporika Nea Kai Pathetike changed to Aeroporika Nea
0001-9291	Aerosol Age
0001-9313	Aerosol Report
0001-9321	Aerospace
0001-933X	Aerospace
0001-9364	Aerospace Historian
0001-9372	Aerospace International
0001-9380	Aerospace Maintenance Safety see 0364-7145
0001-9402	Aerospace Medicine see 0095-6562
0001-9410	Aerospace Medicine and Biology; a Continuing Bibliography
0001-9429	Aerospace Safety see 0279-9308
0001-9445	Flieger-Revue
0001-9453	Aerotecnica changed to Aerotecnica, Missili e Spazio
0001-9461	Aerovoz
0001-947X	Aerzteblatt Baden-Wuerttemberg
0001-9488	Aerzteblatt Rheinland-Pfalz
0001-9496	Aerztliche Forschung†
0001-950X	Aerztliche Fortbildung†
0001-9518	Aerztliche Jugendkunde
0001-9526	Das Aerztliche Laboratorium
0001-9534	Aerztliche Praxis
0001-9542	Aerztliche Tonbandzeitung
0001-9550	Aesceala
0001-9569	Aesculape†
0001-9585	Aetna-Izer
0001-9593	Aevum
0001-9607	Affaersekonomi changed to Affaersekonomi Management
0001-9615	Affaires
0001-9623	Affairs of State†
0001-9658	Affaersvaerlden-Finanstidningen changed to Affaersvaerlden
0001-9666	Affiches d'Alsace et de Lorraine-Moniteur des Soumissions et des Ventes de Bois de l'Est
0001-9674	Affirmation
0001-9682	Afghanistan
0001-9690	Aficion Espanola
0001-9704	Afinidad
0001-9712	Afrasian Markets changed to Export Gazette
0001-9720	Africa see 0020-5877
0001-9739	Africa
0001-9747	Africa
0001-9755	Africa
0001-9763	Africa†
0001-978X	Africa Diary
0001-9798	Africa Digest see 0306-8412
0001-981X	Africa Institute. Bulletin changed to Africa Institute Bulletin
0001-9828	Africa Quarterly
0001-9836	Africa Report
0001-9844	Africa Research Bulletin. Series A: Political, Social and Cultural
0001-9852	Africa Research Bulletin. Series B: Economic, Financial and Technical
0001-9860	Africa Samachar
0001-9879	Africa-Tervuren
0001-9887	Africa Today
0001-9909	African Affairs
0001-9925	African Aquarist†
0001-9933	African Arts
0001-9941	African Books Newsletter
0001-995X	African Bookshelf changed to Diplomatic Bookshelf & Review
0001-9968	African Challenge changed to Today's Challenge
0001-9976	African Communist
0001-9984	African Development see 0140-833X
0001-9992	African Historical Studies see 0361-7882
0002-001X	African Insurance Record
0002-0028	African Journal of Medical Sciences see 0309-3913
0002-0036	African Journal of Tropical Hydrobiology and Fisheries
0002-0044	African Labour News
0002-0052	African Law Digest
0002-0079	African M I M S see 0140-4415
0002-0087	African Notes
0002-0095	African Opinion
0002-0109	Behind the News
0002-0117	African Review
0002-0133	African Recorder
0002-015X	African Scientist†
0002-015X	African Scientist changed to African Scientist and Technologist
0002-0168	African Social Research
0002-0184	African Studies
0002-0192	African Studies Association of the United Kingdom. Bulletin see 0305-862X
0002-0206	African Studies Review
0002-0214	African Studies Newsletter
0002-0222	African Succulent Plant Society. Bulletin†
0002-0230	African Target
0002-0249	African Trader
0002-0265	African Violet Magazine
0002-0273	African Wildlife
0002-029X	Africana Bulletin
0002-0303	Africana Library Journal see 0095-1080
0002-0311	Africana Marburgensia
0002-032X	Africana Notes and News
0002-0338	Africasia changed to Afrique-Asie
0002-0346	Afrika†
0002-0397	Afrika Spectrum
0002-0419	Afrika Studiecentrum. Documentatieblad
0002-0427	Afrika und Uebersee
0002-0443	Journal of Nursing Administration
0002-046X	Afrique & Culture
0002-0478	Afrique Contemporaine
0002-0486	Afrique et l'Asie changed to Afrique et l'Asie Modernes
0002-0508	Afrique Litteraire et Artistique
0002-0516	Afrique Medicale
0002-0524	Afrique Mon Pays
0002-0532	Afrique Nouvelle†
0002-0540	Afrique Service
0002-0575	Afrique Urbaine†
0002-0575	Afro-American Studies see 0308-6860
0002-0591	Afro-Asia
0002-0605	Afro-Asian and World Affairs
0002-0613	Afro Asian Economic Review
0002-0621	Afro-Asian Journalist
0002-063X	Afro-Asian Labour Bulletin see 0031-5443
0002-0648	Afro-Asia Peoples changed to Solidarity
0002-0664	Lotus
0002-0672	Afrox News
0002-0699	After Beat†
0002-0702	After Dark
0002-0710	Agrarische Rundschau
0002-0729	Age and Ageing
0002-0737	Age de la Science†
0002-0745	Age of Achievement
0002-0753	Age of Tomorrow
0002-0761	Agence d'Informations Europeennes. Bulletin
0002-077X	Revue Parlementaire
0002-0788	Agency Items changed to Agency News Items
0002-0796	Agenda
0002-080X	Agenor
0002-0826	Agent Commercial
0002-083X	Agente
0002-0869	Agenzia di Viaggi
0002-0877	Agenzia Economica Finanziaria
0002-0893	Agenzia Nazionale Informazioni Turistiche
0002-0907	Aggiornamenti Clinicoterapeutici changed to Gazzetta Medica Italiana-Aggiornamenti Clinicoterapeutici
0002-0915	Aggiornamenti di Terapia Oftalmologica
0002-0923	Aggiornamenti in Ematologia
0002-0931	Aggiornamenti in Ostetricia e Ginecologia see 0026-4784
0002-094X	Aggiornamenti Sociali

ISSN	Title
0002-0958	Aggiornamento Pediatrico
0002-0966	Aging
0002-0974	Aging & Human Development see 0091-4150
0002-0982	Aging in the News†
0002-0990	Agmazine
0002-1008	Krankenpflege
0002-1016	Agora
0002-1024	Agra Europe
0002-1032	Agra University Journal of Research (Science).
0002-1040	Agradoot
0002-1059	Agraringenieur see 0341-2520
0002-1067	Agrarirodalmi Szemle
0002-1075	Landbouw-Economisch Instituut. Agrarisch Weekoverzicht
0002-1105	Agrartorteneti Szemle
0002-1113	Magyar Tudomanyos Akademia. Agrartudomanyok Osztalya. Kozlemenyek changed to Agrartudomanyi Kozlemenyek
0002-1121	Agrarwirtschaft
0002-113X	Agrekon
0002-1148	Agressologie
0002-1164	Agri Finance
0002-1172	Agri Hortique Genetica
0002-1180	Agri Marketing
0002-1199	Agri-Pick-Up
0002-1202	Agricoltore
0002-1210	Agricoltore Ferrarese
0002-1229	Agricoltore Trevisano
0002-1237	Agricoltura
0002-1245	Agricoltura Aretina
0002-1253	Agricoltura Bergamasca†
0002-1261	Agricoltura delle Venezie
0002-127X	Agricoltura d'Italia
0002-1288	Agricoltura Nostra
0002-1296	Agricoltura Romagnola
0002-130X	Agriculteur du Sud-Est
0002-1318	Agricultor
0002-1334	Agricultura
0002-1342	Agricultura al Dia
0002-1350	Agricultura de las Americas
0002-1369	Agricultural and Biological Chemistry Journal
0002-1377	Agricultural & Veterinary Chemicals and Agricultural Engineering
0002-1393	South Africa. Department of Agricultural Technical Services. Agricultural Bulletins
0002-1407	Agricultural Chemical Society of Japan. Journal
0002-1415	Agricultural Co-Operative Bulletin
0002-1423	U.S. Department of Agriculture. Economics, Statistics, and Cooperatives Service. Agricultural Economics Research
0002-1431	Agricultural Economist
0002-144X	Agricultural Education
0002-1458	Agricultural Engineering
0002-1466	U.S. Department of Agriculture. Economics, Statistics, and Cooperatives Service. Agricultural Finance Review
0002-1474	Agricultural Gazette of New South Wales
0002-1482	Agricultural History
0002-1490	Agricultural History Review
0002-1504	A I C Review see 0044-684X
0002-1512	Agricultural Letter
0002-1520	Agricultural Literature of Czechoslovakia
0002-1547	Agricultural Machinery Journal
0002-1555	Agricultural Marketing†
0002-1571	Agricultural Marketing
0002-1598	Agricultural Meteorology Fertilizer Progress
0002-1601	U.S. Crop Reporting Board. Agricultural Prices
0002-161X	Agricultural Research
0002-1628	Agricultural Research Journal of Kerala
0002-1660	U.S. Department of Agriculture. Economics, Statistics, and Cooperatives Service. Agricultural Situation
0002-1679	Agricultural Situation in India
0002-1687	Agriculture
0002-1695	Agriculture†
0002-1709	Agriculture
0002-1717	Agriculture Abroad
0002-1725	Agriculture and Agro-Industries Journal
0002-1733	Agriculture Checklist
0002-1741	Agriculture Decisions
0002-175X	Agriculture in Northern Ireland
0002-1776	Agriculture Pakistan
0002-1784	Agrisul
0002-1792	Agro-Industrialist†
0002-1806	Agro-Meteorological Bulletin changed to Israel. Meteorological Service. Monthly Agroclimatic Data
0002-1814	Agro-Service
0002-1822	Agroborealis
0002-1830	Agrochemia
0002-1849	Agrochemia
0002-1857	Agrochimica
0002-1865	Agrohemija
0002-1873	Agrokemia es Talajtan
0002-1881	Agrokhimiya
0002-189X	Agrometeorolosko Porocilo
0002-1903	Agronomia
0002-1911	Agronomia Lusitana
0002-192X	Agronomia Tropical
0002-1938	Agronomics†
0002-1946	Agronomie Tropicale
0002-1954	Agronomski Glasnik
0002-1962	Agronomy Journal
0002-1970	Agros
0002-1989	Agrotehnicar
0002-1997	Agrotis
0002-2004	Agua†
0002-2012	Agway Cooperator
0002-2039	Ahijuna
0002-2047	Ahora
0002-2055	Ahorro
0002-2063	Aid Newsletter changed to A M S A Newsletter
0002-208X	Aidai-Echoes
0002-2098	Aika see 0355-0303
0002-2101	Aikakan Himiakan Amsagir
0002-211X	Aikya†
0002-2136	Ain Agricole
0002-2144	Ain Shams Medical Journal
0002-2152	Air Actualites
0002-2160	Air Almanac
0002-2179	Air and Space Age†
0002-2187	Air and Water News†
0002-2195	Air B P†
0002-2209	Air Cadet News
0002-2225	Air Carrier Financial Statistics
0002-2241	Air Classics
0002-225X	Air Comprime
0002-2268	Air Conditioning & Refrigeration in India
0002-2276	Air Conditioning, Heating and Refrigeration News
0002-2284	Building Systems Design changed to Energy Engineering
0002-2306	Air-Cushion Vehicles†
0002-2314	Air Europa
0002-2330	Air Force Accounting and Finance Technical Digest changed to Accounting and Finance Tech Digest
0002-2349	Air Force and Space Digest changed to Air Force Magazine
0002-2357	Air Force Civil Engineer see 0362-188X
0002-2365	Air Force Comptroller
0002-2373	Air Force Driver changed to Driver
0002-2381	Air Force Policy Letter for Commanders
0002-2403	Air Force Times
0002-2411	Air Line Employee
0002-242X	Air Line Pilot
0002-2454	Air Navigation Radio Aids
0002-2462	Air Pictorial
0002-2470	Air Pollution Control Association. Journal
0002-2489	Air Pollution Notes changed to Solid Waste Management
0002-2497	Air Pollution Titles
0002-2527	U D S Air Quality Control Digest changed to Air Quality Control Digest
0002-2535	Air Reservist Magazine
0002-2543	Air Transport World
0002-2551	Air Transportation see 0148-7469
0002-256X	Air Transport Magazine see 0005-2132
0002-2578	Air Travel changed to TravelScene
0002-2586	Air University Library Index to Military Periodicals
0002-2594	Air University Review
0002-2608	Air/Water Pollution Report
0002-2616	Air Weather Service Observer
0002-2624	Airadio News
0002-2640	Airconditioning and Refrigeration Business
0002-2659	Aircraft
0002-2667	Aircraft Engineering
0002-2675	Aircraft Illustrated
0002-2683	Aircraft Industry Record
0002-2691	A. O. P. A. Magazine
0002-2705	Airfix
0002-2713	Airframe changed to British Aerospace News
0002-2721	Airline Fleet Record
0002-273X	Airline Management and Marketing†
0002-2748	Airline Newsletter
0002-2756	Airman
0002-2764	Airman's Information Manual. Part 1: Basic Flight Manual and ATC Procedures
0002-2772	Airman's Information Manual. Part 2: Airport Directory†
0002-2802	Airport Forum
0002-2810	Airport News changed to Western Aviation-Airport News
0002-2829	Airport Services Management
0002-2837	Airport Times
0002-2853	Airports International
0002-2861	Airway Pioneer
0002-287X	Airways see 0032-0617
0002-2888	Airways International†
0002-2896	Airways Magazine changed to Airways Inflight
0002-2926	Aiton Review†
0002-2942	Asian Economies
0002-2950	Ajour changed to Ajour-Industri-Teknikk
0002-2969	Biologicheskii Zhurnal Armenii
0002-2977	Akademie der Wissenschaften und der Literatur. Geistes- und Sozialwissenschaftliche Klasse. Abhandlungen
0002-2985	Akademie der Wissenschaften und der Literatur, Mainz. Klasse der Literatur. Abhandlungen
0002-2993	Akademie der Wissenschaften und der Literatur, Mainz. Mathematisch-Naturwissenschaftliche Klasse. Abhandlungen
0002-3000	Akademische Monatsblaetter
0002-3019	Akademischer Dienst
0002-3027	Akademiya Meditsinskikh Nauk S. S. S. R. Vestnik
0002-3035	Akademiya Nauk Armyanskoi S. S. R. Izvestiya. Seriya Fizika
0002-3043	Akademiya Nauk Armyanskoi S. S. R. Izvestiya. Seriya Matematika
0002-3051	Akademiya Nauk Armyanskoi S. S. R. Izvestiya. Seriya Mekhanika
0002-306X	Akademiya Nauk Armyanskoi S. S. R. Izvestiya. Seriya Tekhnicheskikh Nauk
0002-3078	Akademiya Nauk Azerbaidzhanskoi S. S. R. Doklady
0002-3086	Akademiya Nauk Azerbaidzhanskoi S. S. R. Izvestiya. Seriya Biologicheskikh Nauk
0002-3094	Akademiya Nauk Azerbaidzhanskoi S. S. R. Izvestiya. Seriya Ekonomicheskikh Nauk
0002-3108	Akademiya Nauk Azerbaidzhanskoi S. S. R. Izvestiya. Seriya Fiziko-Tekhnicheskikh i Matematicheskikh Nauk
0002-3116	Akademiya Nauk Azerbaidzhanskoi S. S. R. Izvestiya. Seriya Istoriya, Filosofiya i Pravo
0002-3124	Akademiya Nauk Azerbaidzhanskoi S. S. R. Izvestiya. Seriya Nauki o Zemle
0002-3132	Akademiya Nauk Azerbaidzhanskoi S.S.R. Izvestiya. Seriya Yazykoznanie, Literatura i Iskusstva
0002-3140	Akademiya Nauk Estonskoi S.S.R. Izvestiya. Fizika. Matematika
0002-3159	Akademiya Nauk Estonskoi S. S. R. Izvestiya. Obshchestvennye Nauki
0002-3167	Akademiya Nauk Gruzinskoi S. S. R. Soobshcheniya
0002-3175	Akademiya Nauk Kazakhskoi S. S. R. Izvestiya. Seriya Geologicheskaya
0002-3183	Akademiya Nauk Kazakhskoi S. S. R. Seriya Biologicheskaya
0002-3191	Akademiya Nauk Kazakhskoi S. S. R. Izvestiya. Seriya Fiziko-Matematicheskaya
0002-3205	Akademiya Nauk Kazakhskoi S. S. R. Izvestiya. Seriya Khimicheskaya
0002-3213	Akademiya Nauk Kazakhskoi S. S. R. Vestnik
0002-3221	Akademiya Nauk Kirgizskoi S. S. R. Izvestiya
0002-323X	Akademiya Nauk Latviiskoi S. S. R. Izvestiya. Seriya Fizicheskikh i Tekhnicheskikh Nauk
0002-3248	Akademiya Nauk Latviiskoi S. S. R. Izvestiya. Seriya Khimicheskaya
0002-3264	Akademiya Nauk S. S. S. R. Doklady
0002-3299	Akademiya Nauk S. S. S. R. Institut Geologii Rudnykh Mestorozhdenii, Petrografii, Mineralogii i Geokhimii. Trudy
0002-3310	Akademiya Nauk S. S. S. R. Izvestiya. Energetika i Transport
0002-3329	Akademiya Nauk S. S. S. R. Izvestiya. Seriya Biologicheskaya
0002-3337	Akademiya Nauk S. S. S. R. Izvestiya. Seriya Fizika Zemli
0002-3345	Akademiya Nauk S. S. S. R. Izvestiya. Seriya Geologicheskaya
0002-3353	Akademiya Nauk S. S. S. R. Izvestiya. Seriya Khimicheskaya
0002-3361	Akademiya Nauk S. S. S. R. Izvestiya. Seriya Matematicheskaya
0002-337X	Akademiya Nauk S. S. S. R. Izvestiya. Seriya Neorganicheskie Materialy
0002-3388	Akademiya Nauk S. S. S. R. Izvestiya. Tekhnicheskaya Kibernetika
0002-3418	Akademiya Nauk S. S. S. R. Sibirskoe Otdelenie Izvestiya. Seriya Biologicheskikh i Meditsinskikh Nauk
0002-3426	Akademiya Nauk S. S. S. R. Sibirskoe Otdelenie. Izvestiya Seriya Khimicheskikh Nauk
0002-3434	Akademiya Nauk S. S. S. R. Sibirskoe Otdelenie. Izvestiya. Seriya Tekhnicheskikh Nauk
0002-3442	Akademiya Nauk S. S. S. R. Vestnik
0002-3450	Akademiya Nauk S. S. S. R. Institut Okeanologii. Trudy
0002-3469	Akademiya Nauk Tadzhikskoi S. S. R. Doklady
0002-3477	Akademiya Nauk Tadzhikskoi S. S. R. Izvestiya. Otdelenie Biologicheskikh Nauk
0002-3485	Akademiya Nauk Tadzhikskoi S. S. R. Izvestiya. Otdelenie Fiziko-Matematicheskikh i Geologo-Khimicheskikh Nauk
0002-3493	Akademiya Nauk Turkmenskoi S. S. R. Izvestiya. Seriya Biologicheskikh Nauk
0002-3507	Akademiya Nauk Turkmenskoi S. S. R. Izvestiya. Seriya Fiziko-Tekhnicheskikh, Khimicheskikh i Geologicheskikh Nauk
0002-3515	Akademiya Nauk S. S. S. R. Izvestiya. Seriya Fizika Atmosfery i Okeana
0002-3523	Akademiya Nauk Ukrainskoi S. S. R. Dopovidi. Seriya Geologiya, Geofizyka, Khimiya ta Biologiya
0002-3531	Akademiya Nauk Ukrains'koi Rsr. Dopovidi. Seria a Fiziko-Matematichni ta Tekhnichni Nauki
0002-354X	Akademiya Navuk Belarusskai S. S. R. Doklady
0002-3558	Akademiya Navuk Belarusskai S.S.R. Vesti. Serryya Biyalagichnykh Navuk

ISSN INDEX

ISSN	Title
0002-3566	Akademiya Navuk Belarusskai S. S. R. Vestsi. Seryya Fizika- Tekhnichnykh Navuk
0002-3574	Akademiya Navuk Belarusskai S. S. R. Vestsi. Seryya Fizika- Matematychnykh Navuk
0002-3582	Akademiya Navuk Belarusskai S. S. R. Vestsi. Seryya Gramadskikh Navuk
0002-3590	Akademiya Navuk Belarusskai S. S. R. Vestsi. Seryya Khimichnykh Navuk
0002-36C4	Akademiya Navuk Belarusskai S. S. R. Vestsi. Seryya Sel'skagaspadarchykh Navuk
0002-3612	Akaroa Mail
0002-3620	Akashi
0002-3639	Akhand Anand
0002-3655	Akher Saa
0002-368X	Akita Journal of Rural Medicine
0002-3701	Akron Dental Society. Bulletin
0002-371X	Akron Law Review
0002-3728	Akros
0002-3744	Aktie
0002-3752	Die Aktiengesellschaft
0002-3760	Aktion†
0002-3787	Aktualne Problemy Informacji i Dokumentacji
0002-3809	Aktuelle Freie Praxis†
0002-3825	Aktuelle Kulturpolitik†
0002-3833	Aktuelle Probleme der Buergerlichen Philosophie *changed to* Referateblatt Philosophie. Reihe E. Aktuelle Probleme und Kritik der Buergerlichen Philosophie
0002-3841	Aktuelle Sammlung†
0002-385X	Aktuelle Steuer-Informationen *changed to* Steuer-Telex
0002-3884	Aktuellt Politik och Samhaelle *see* 0345-0635
0002-3892	Akuntansi & Administrasi
0002-3906	Akusherstvo i Ginekologiya
0002-3914	Akusticheskii Zhurnal
0002-3922	Akvariet
0002-3930	Akvarium a Terarium
0002-3949	Akwesasne Notes
0002-3957	Akzente
0002-3965	Al-Ousbou' al-Arabi
0002-3973	Al-Abhath
0002-3931	Al-Ahad
0002-399X	Al-Dirasat al-Islamiyah
0002-4015	Al-Ma'arif
0002-4023	Al-Machriq†
0002-4031	Arab Academy of Damascus. Journal
0002-4058	Al-Maskukat
0002-4066	Ai Nostri Amici
0002-4074	Al-Ta'awun
0002-4082	Al-Turath Al-Sha'bi
0002-4090	A L A
0002-4112	Alabama Academy of Science. Journal
0002-4120	Alabama Architect†
0002-4139	Alabama Association of Secondary School Principals. Bulletin
0002-4147	Alabama Baptist Historian
0002-4155	Alabama Builder
0002-4163	Alabama Business
0002-4171	Alabama Conservation
0002-418X	Alabama Contractor
0002-4198	Alabama Dental Association. Journal
0002-4201X	Alabama Food Merchants Journal
0002-4228	Alabama Forest Products *changed to* Alabama Forests
0002-4236	Alabama Historical Quarterly
0002-4252	Alabama Journal of Medical Sciences
0002-4260	Alabama Junior College Librarian *changed to* Alabama Junior College Library Association Newsletter
0002-4279	Alabama Law Review
0002-4287	Alabama Lawyer
0002-4295	Alabama Librarian
0002-4309	Alabama Municipal Journal
0002-4325	Alabama Purchasor
0002-4333	Alabama Retail Trade *see* 0002-4163
0002-4341	Alabama Review
0002-435X	Alabama School Journal
0002-4368	Alabama Social Welfare
0002-4384	Alabama Trucker
0002-4392	Alam Attijarat
0002-4406	Alambre
0002-4414	Alameda-Contra Costa Medical Association. Bulletin
0002-4422	Alamo
0002-4430	Alan Watts Journal†
0002-4457	Alaska Beverage Analyst
0002-4465	Alaska Conservation Review
0002-4473	Alaska Construction and Oil Report *changed to* Alaska Construction and Oil
0002-4481	Alaska Economic Trends
0002-449X	Alaska Industry
0002-4503	Alaska Journal†
0002-4511	Alaska Land Lines *changed to* Alaska's Resources
0002-452X	Alaska Law Journal *see* 0093-1039
0002-4546	Alaska Nurse
0002-4554	A M U Press Alaskana Series (Alaska Methodist University) *changed to* A P U Press Alaskana Series
0002-4562	Alaska
0002-4570	Sourdough
0002-4597	Alaska's Health and Welfare *changed to* Alaska. Department of Health and Social Services. Quarterly
0002-4600	Alata Internazionale
0002-4619	Alauda
0002-4627	Alba
0002-4643	Albania Oggi
0002-4651	Albania Report
0002-466X	Albany County Agriculture News *changed to* Extension News-Albany/ Rensselaer/Saratoga/Washington Counties
0002-4678	Albany Law Review
0002-4686	Albany Regional Medical Program. Report†
0002-4708	Albert Einstein Medical Center. Journal†
0002-4716	Alberta Amateur *see* 0049-5778
0002-4724	Alberta Business Trends *see* 0317-3925
0002-4740	Alberta Calls
0002-4759	Alberta Conservative†
0002-4767	Alberta Farm Economist†
0002-4775	Alberta Gazette
0002-4783	Alberta Historical Review *see* 0316-1552
0002-4805	Alberta Journal of Educational Research
0002-4821	Alberta Law Review
0002-483X	Library Association of Alberta. Bulletin†
0002-4848	Alberta Medical Bulletin†
0002-4856	Alberta Motorist
0002-4872	Alberta Oil and Gas Industry. Monthly Statistics *see* 0706-1447
0002-4902	Alberta Transport Reporter
0002-4910	Albertina Studien†
0002-4929	Albrecht-Thaer-Archiv *changed to* Archiv fuer Acker- und Pflanzenbau und Bodenkunde
0002-4937	Album
0002-4953	Albuquerque Archaeological Society Newsletter
0002-4961	Albus
0002-497X	Alcalde
0002-4988	Alcan Magazine†
0002-4996	Alcan News
0002-5003	Alcan Review *changed to* Aluminum Review
0002-5011	Alchimist†
0002-502X	Alcoholism
0002-5038	Alcoholism Review
0002-5054	Alcool ou Sante
0002-5062	Alcor
0002-5089	Aldebaran Review
0002-5097	Alderley and Wilmslow and Knutsford Advertiser
0002-5100	Aldrichimica Acta
0002-5119	Aldus
0002-5127	Aleh
0002-5135	Alemanha Internacional†
0002-5151	Alergia
0002-5178	Alerta†
0002-5186	Alerte Atomique
0002-5208	Alexanor
0002-5216	Alfa
0002-5224	Alfred Hitchcock's Mystery Magazine
0002-5232	Algebra and Logic
0002-5240	Algebra Universalis
0002-5267	Algemeen Maconniek Tijdschrift
0002-5275	Algemeen Nederlands Tijdschrift voor Wijsbegeerte
0002-5283	Algemeen Politieblad van het Koninkrijk der Nederlanden
0002-5291	Algeria. Institut Pedagogique National. Bureau de Documentation et d'Information Scolaires Universitaires et Professionnelles. Informations et Documents†
0002-5305	Algeria. Sous-Direction des Statistiques. Bulletin de Statistiques Generales *changed to* Algeria. Direction des Statistiques et de la Comptabilite Nationale. Bulletin Trimestriel de Statistiques
0002-5313	Algerien en Europe
0002-5321	Universite d'Alger. Publications Scientifiques. Serie A: Mathematiques
0002-533X	Universite d'Alger. Publications Scientifiques. Serie B: Sciences Physiques
0002-5348	Algo
0002-5364	Algol *see* 0195-9379
0002-5380	Ali Nuove
0002-5399	Alieia
0002-5402	Alimenta
0002-5410	Alimentation au Quebec
0002-5429	Alimentazione Animale *see* 0390-0487
0002-5445	Aliupseeri *see* 0355-726X
0002-5453	Alive†
0002-5461	Alive (St. Louis)
0002-547X	Alive(Harrisonburg)
0002-5488	Alkahest†
0002-5496	Alkohol-Industrie
0002-550X	Alkoholdebatt
0002-5518	Alkoholfraagen *see* 0345-0732
0002-5526	Alkoholikysymys
0002-5534	All-Africa Church Music Association. Journal†
0002-5542	All-Church Press Newspapers
0002-5550	All Clear†
0002-5569	All England Law Reports
0002-5577	All Hands†
0002-5585	All-India Anglo-Indian Association. Review
0002-5593	All India Reporter
0002-5623	All the World
0002-5631	Alla Bottega
0002-564X	Allam- es Jogtudomany
0002-5658	Allattani Kozlemenyek
0002-5666	Alle den Volcke
0002-5674	Alle Hens
0002-5682	Alle Kvinner†
0002-5690	Allegheny County Pharmacist
0002-5704	Allegro
0002-5712	Allemagnes d'Aujourd'hui
0002-5720	Allemagne Internationale†
0002-5739	Allen Memorial Art Museum. Bulletin
0002-5747	Allergia
0002-5755	Allergie und Immunologie
0002-5771	Allers
0002-578X	Allers
0002-5798	Allgemeine Bau-Zeitung
0002-5801	Allgemeine Bauzeitung
0002-581X	Allgemeine Deutsche Gesellen-Zeitung†
0002-5836	Allgemeine Deutsche Lehrerzeitung *see* 0342-0671
0002-5844	Allgemeine Fleischer Zeitung
0002-5852	Allgemeine Forst- und Jagdzeitung
0002-5860	Allgemeine Forstzeitschrift
0002-5879	Allgemeine Forstzeitung
0002-5887	Allgemeine Homoeopathische Zeitung
0002-5895	Allgemeine Hotel-und Gaststaetten-Zeitung
0002-5909	Allgemeine Missionsnachrichten *see* 0341-082X
0002-5917	A P R
0002-5925	Allgemeine Schweizerische Militaerzeitschrift
0002-5933	Allgemeine Sparkasse in Linz. Kurz Notiert
0002-5941	Allgemeine Unabhaengige Juedische Wochenzeitung *see* 0340-272X
0002-5968	Allgemeine Vermessungs-Nachrichten
0002-5984	Nachrichten der Fachorganisationen *changed to* Bindereport
0002-5992	Allgemeiner Muehlen-Markt
0002-600X	Allgemeiner Samen- und Pflanzen Anzeiger
0002-6018	Allgemeines Statistisches Archiv
0002-6034	Alliance
0002-6050	Alliance Israelite Universelle en France. Cahiers
0002-6069	Alliance Journal†
0002-6093	Alliance Review
0002-6107	Allied Industrial Worker
0002-6123	Allis-Chalmers Engineering Review†
0002-614X	Alloy Digest
0002-6158	Allpress
0002-6166	Allround-Collector Address-List
0002-6174	Allsvensk Samling *changed to* Sverigekontakt
0002-6182	Allt i Hemmet
0002-6190	Allt om Hobby
0002-6204	Allt Om Mat
0002-6212	Alluminio
0002-6239	Alma *changed to* Paz e Alegria
0002-6247	Alma Mater†
0002-6271	Almanaque Aeronautico†
0002-628X	Almas
0002-6298	Der Almbauer
0002-6301	Aloe
0002-631X	Aloft
0002-6328	Along the Boardwalk†
0002-6336	Alpen
0002-6344	Alpengarten
0002-6352	Alpenlaendische Bienenzeitung
0002-6379	Alpha
0002-6387	Kappan
0002-6395	Alpha-Mathematische Schuelerzeitschrift
0002-6409	Alpha News Digest *changed to* Alpha News
0002-6425	Alphabet†
0002-6433	Alphabet
0002-6441	Alphabetic Subject Index to Petroleum Abstracts
0002-645X	Alphian *changed to* Alphian
0002-6468	Alpi Venete
0002-6476	Alpine Garden Society. Quarterly Bulletin
0002-6484	Alpinismus
0002-6492	Alpino
0002-6506	Alt for Damerne
0002-6514	Alt-Katholische Kirchenzeitung
0002-6522	Alt-Katholische Kirchenzeitung
0002-6530	Microform Review
0002-6549	Alta Direccion
0002-6557	Alta Frequenza
0002-6565	Alte und Moderne Kunst
0002-6573	Das Altenheim
0002-6611	Alternative
0002-662X	Alternative Press Index
0002-6638	Alternatives: Perspectives on Society and Environment *changed to* Alternatives
0002-6646	Das Altertum
0002-6662	Altra Italia
0002-6670	Der Altsprachliche Unterricht
0002-6689	Aluminium
0002-6697	World Aluminum Abstracts
0002-6700	Johns Hopkins Hospital School of Nursing. Alumni Magazine
0002-6778	Amaru†
0002-6786	Amaterska Scena
0002-6794	Amatersky Film
0002-6808	Amateur Athlete *changed to* A A U News and Amateur Athlete
0002-6816	Amateur Baseball News
0002-6832	Amateur Gardening
0002-6840	Amateur Photographer
0002-6859	Amateur Radio
0002-6867	Amateur Stage
0002-6875	Amateurtuinder
0002-6883	Amateur Winemaker
0002-6905	Ambassade van de U. S. S. R. in Nederland. Informatie-Bulletin†
0002-6913	Ambassador†

ISSN INDEX 947

0002-6921 Ambassador of Peace *changed to* Young Companion
0002-693X Amber-Hi-Lites
0002-6948 Ambiance de Paris
0002-6956 Ambience†
0002-6964 Ambienti†
0002-6972 Ambit
0002-6980 Ambix
0002-6999 Ambt en Plicht
0002-7006 Ambulatory Pediatric Association. Newsletter
0002-7014 Ameghiniana
0002-7022 Amentia
0002-7030 America
0002-7049 America
0002-7057 Cooperative America *changed to* America Cooperativa
0002-7065 America: History and Life. Part A: Article Abstracts and Citation
0002-7081 America Indigena
0002-709X America Latina
0002-7103 Woman Physician *see* 0091-7427
0002-712X American Academy of Arts and Sciences. Bulletin
0002-7138 American Academy of Child Psychiatry. Journal
0002-7146 American Academy of Gold Foil Operators. Journal *changed to* Operative Dentistry
0002-7154 American Academy of Ophthalmology and Otolaryngology. Transactions *see* 0161-6420
0002-7162 American Academy of Political and Social Science. Annals
0002-7170 Council on the Study of Religion. Bulletin
0002-7189 American Academy of Religion. Journal
0002-7197 Independent Agent
0002-7200 American Agent and Broker
0002-7219 American Agriculturist and Rural New Yorker
0002-7227 American Aircraft Modeler†
0002-7235 Alumni Register *changed to* Illinois State University Alumni News
0002-7251 American Animal Hospital Association Bulletin *see* 0587-2871
0002-726X American Annals of the Deaf
0002-7286 American Anthropological Association. Newsletter *see* 0098-1605
0002-7294 American Anthropologist
0002-7316 American Antiquity
0002-7324 American Archives of Rehabilitation Therapy
0002-7359 American Art Journal
0002-7367 American Artisan†
0002-7375 American Artist
0002-7405 American Association for the Advancement of Slavic Studies. Newsletter
0002-7413 American Association of Colleges for Teacher Education. Bulletin
0002-7421 American Association of Dental Examiners. Board Bulletin
0002-743X American Association of Fund-Raising Counsel. Bulletin *see* 0436-0257
0002-7448 American Association of Nurse Anesthetists. Journal *see* 0094-6354
0002-7464 American Association of Petroleum Geologists. Bulletin *see* 0149-1423
0002-7472 American Association of State Libraries. President's Newsletter *see* 0044-9660
0002-7480 American Association of Teacher Educators in Agriculture. Journal
0002-7499 American Association of Teachers of Esperanto Quarterly Bulletin
0002-7502 American Association of Workers for the Blind. Dictionary Catalogue†
0002-7510 American Association of Workers for the Blind. News and Views
0002-7529 American Astrology
0002-7537 American Astronomical Society. Bulletin
0002-7545 American Automatic Merchandiser
0002-7561 American Banker
0002-757X American Baptist
0002-7596 American Bar Association Journal
0002-760X American Bar News†
0002-7618 American Bard†
0002-7626 American Bee Journal
0002-7634 American Beef Producer†
0002-7642 American Behavioral Scientist
0002-7650 American Benedictine Review
0002-7669 American Bibliography of Agricultural Economics†
0002-7677 American Bicyclist & Motorcyclist
0002-7685 American Biology Teacher
0002-7707 American Book Publishing Record
0002-7715 American Breeds Magazine†
0002-7723 American Brewer
0002-7731 American Building Supplies
0002-7766 American Business Law Journal
0002-7774 Report on Alcohol *see* 0161-1267
0002-7782 American Cage-Bird Magazine
0002-7790 American Catholic Historical Society of Philadelphia. Records
0002-7804 American Cemetery
0002-7812 American Ceramic Society Bulletin
0002-7820 American Ceramic Society Journal
0002-7839 American Chamber of Commerce Executives. Journal†
0002-7847 American Chamber of Commerce in Japan. Journal
0002-7863 American Chemical Society. Journal
0002-788X American Choral Foundation. Research Memorandum Series
0002-7898 American Choral Review
0002-7901 American Christmas Tree Growers' Journal *see* 0569-3845
0002-791X American Church News *see* 0149-4244
0002-7928 American Cinematographer
0002-7936 American City *see* 0149-337X
0002-7944 American College Health Association. Journal
0002-7952 A C H Action
0002-7960 American College of Chest Physicians Bulletin *see* 0149-6719
0002-7979 American College of Dentists. Journal
0002-7987 American College of Foot Orthopedists Newsletter
0002-8002 American College of Nurse-Midwives. Bulletin *see* 0091-2182
0002-8010 American College of Physicians. Bulletin *see* 0161-7478
0002-8029 American College of Preventive Medicine Newsletter
0002-8037 American College of Radiology Bulletin
0002-8045 American College of Surgeons. Bulletin
0002-8053 American Comparative Literature Association Newsletter *changed to* Heliconian
0002-8061 American Concrete Institute. Journal
0002-807X American Cooner
0002-8088 American Corrective Therapy Journal
0002-810X American Craftmen's Council Outlook *changed to* A C C Outlook
0002-8118 American Criminal Law Quarterly *changed to* American Criminal Law Review
0002-8126 American Criminologist
0002-8134 American Crosby Clipper *changed to* American Clipper
0002-8142 American Dachshund
0002-8150 American Dahlia Society. Bulletin
0002-8169 American Dairy Review
0002-8177 American Dental Association. Journal
0002-8193 American Dialect Society Newsletter
0002-8207 American Dialect Society. Publications
0002-8215 American Dialog
0002-8223 American Dietetic Association. Journal
0002-8231 American Society for Information Science. Journal
0002-824X American Druggist
0002-8258 American Drycleaner
0002-8266 American Dyestuff Reporter
0002-8274 American Ecclesiastical Review†
0002-8282 American Economic Review
0002-8290 American Economist
0002-8304 American Education
0002-8312 American Educational Research Journal
0002-8320 American Entomological Society. Transactions
0002-8339 American Esperanto Magazine†
0002-8347 American Stock Exchange Stock Reports
0002-8371 American Fabrics *see* 0091-0864
0002-838X American Family Physician
0002-8398 American Farm Bureau Federations Official News Letter *see* 0197-5617
0002-8401 American Farm Youth†
0002-8436 American Fencing
0002-8444 American Fern Journal
0002-8452 American Field
0002-8460 American Film Institute. Education Membership Newsletter†
0002-8487 American Fisheries Society. Transactions
0002-8525 American Flint
0002-8533 American Forensic Association. Journal
0002-8541 American Forests
0002-855X American Foundation for the Blind Newsletter
0002-8568 American Fruit Grower
0002-8576 American Funeral Director
0002-8584 American Gas Association Monthly
0002-8592 American Genealogist
0002-8606 American Geophysical Union. Transactions *see* 0096-3941
0002-8614 American Geriatrics Society. Journal
0002-8622 American-German Review†
0002-8630 American Girl (Braille Edition)
0002-8630 American Girl (Inkprint Edition)
0002-8649 American Glass Review
0002-8657 American Gold News
0002-8665 American Grocer
0002-8681 American Hampshire Herdsman
0002-869X American Harp Journal
0002-8703 American Heart Journal
0002-8711 American Helicopter Society. Journal
0002-872X American Hereford Journal
0002-8738 American Heritage
0002-8746 American Highways *see* 0147-4820
0002-8754 American Histadrut Cultural Exchange Institute. Bulletin†
0002-8762 American Historical Review
0002-8770 American History Illustrated
0002-8789 American Home†
0002-8797 American Horologist and Jeweler *see* 0279-6198
0002-8800 American Horticultural Magazine *see* 0096-4417
0002-8819 American Horticultural Society News and Views *see* 0096-4417
0002-8835 American Hungarian Review†
0002-8843 American Idea†
0002-886X American Import/Export Bulletin
0002-8886 American Indian Law Newsletter
0002-8908 American Industry
0002-8916 American Inkmaker
0002-8940 Report on Food Markets
0002-8959 American Institute of Food Distribution. Weekly Digest
0002-8975 American Institute of Hypnosis. Journal
0002-8983 American Institute of Landscape Architects. Journal†
0002-8991 American Institute of Planners. Journal *see* 0194-4363
0002-9017 American International Travel
0002-9033 American-Israel Economic Horizons
0002-9041 American Jewelry Manufacturer
0002-905X American Jewish Archives
0002-9068 American Jewish Historical Quarterly *see* 0164-0178
0002-9076 American Jewish Times-Outlook
0002-9084 American Jewish World
0002-9092 American Journal of Agricultural Economics
0002-9106 American Journal of Anatomy
0002-9122 American Journal of Botany
0002-9130 American Journal of Building Design *changed to* Western Building Design
0002-9149 American Journal of Cardiology
0002-9157 American Journal of Clinical Hypnosis
0002-9165 American Journal of Clinical Nutrition
0002-9173 American Journal of Clinical Pathology
0002-919X American Journal of Comparative Law
0002-9203 American Journal of Correction *see* 0190-2563
0002-9211 American Journal of Digestive Diseases *see* 0163-2116
0002-922X American Journal of Diseases of Children
0002-9246 American Journal of Economics and Sociology
0002-9254 American Journal of Enology and Viticulture
0002-9262 American Journal of Epidemiology
0002-9270 American Journal of Gastroenterology
0002-9289 American Journal of Hospital Pharmacy
0002-9297 American Journal of Human Genetics
0002-9300 American Journal of International Law
0002-9319 American Journal of Legal History
0002-9327 American Journal of Mathematics
0002-9343 American Journal of Medicine
0002-936X American Journal of Nursing
0002-9378 American Journal of Obstetrics and Gynecology
0002-9386 American Journal of Occupational Therapy *see* 0161-326X
0002-9394 American Journal of Ophthalmology
0002-9416 American Journal of Orthodontics
0002-9432 American Journal of Orthopsychiatry
0002-9440 American Journal of Pathology
0002-9459 American Journal of Pharmaceutical Education
0002-9467 American Journal of Pharmacy and the Sciences Supporting Health *see* 0163-464X
0002-9475 American Journal of Philology
0002-9483 American Journal of Physical Anthropology
0002-9491 American Journal of Physical Medicine
0002-9505 American Journal of Physics
0002-9513 American Journal of Physiology
0002-9521 American Journal of Proctology *see* 0162-6566
0002-953X American Journal of Psychiatry
0002-9548 American Journal of Psychoanalysis
0002-9556 American Journal of Psychology
0002-9564 American Journal of Psychotherapy
0002-9572 American Journal of Public Health and the Nation's Health *see* 0090-0036
0002-9580 American Journal of Roentgenology, Radium Therapy and Nuclear Medicine *see* 0361-803X
0002-9599 American Journal of Science
0002-9602 American Journal of Sociology
0002-9610 American Journal of Surgery
0002-9629 American Journal of the Medical Sciences
0002-9637 American Journal of Tropical Medicine and Hygiene
0002-9645 American Journal of Veterinary Research
0002-9653 Dimensions in American Judaism†
0002-9661 American Judoman
0002-9688 American Labor†
0002-970X American Landrace
0002-9718 American Laundry Digest
0002-9726 American Leather Chemists Association. Journal
0002-9734 American Legion Magazine
0002-9742 American Legion Press Association News-Letter
0002-9750 American Legislator†
0002-9769 American Libraries
0002-9777 American Library Association. Adult Services Division Newsletter†
0002-9785 American Library Association. Library Education Division. Newsletter†
0002-9793 American Library Directory Updating Service
0002-9815 American Literary Accents†
0002-9823 American Literary Realism: 1870-1910
0002-9831 American Literature
0002-9858 American Machinist
0002-9866 American Marine Engineer
0002-9874 American Maritime Cases
0002-9882 American Maritime Officer
0002-9890 American Mathematical Monthly
0002-9904 American Mathematical Society. Bulletin
0002-9912 American Mathematical Society. New Publications *see* 0361-4794
0002-9920 American Mathematical Society. Notices

0002-9939	American Mathematical Society. Proceedings
0002-9947	American Mathematical Society. Transactions
0002-9955	American Medical Association. Journal *see* 0098-7484
0002-9963	American Medical Technologists. Journal
0002-9971	American Medical Writers Association. Bulletin *see* 0090-046X
0002-9998	American Metal Market
0003-0007	American Meteorological Society. Bulletin
0003-0023	American Microscopical Society. Transactions
0003-0031	American Midland Naturalist
0003-004X	American Mineralogist
0003-0066	American Motor Carrier
0003-0074	A M A News *changed to* American Motorcyclist
0003-0082	American Museum Novitates
0003-0090	American Museum of Natural History. Bulletin
0003-0104	American Music Center. Newsletter
0003-0112	American Music Teacher
0003-0139	American Musicological Society. Journal
0003-0147	American Naturalist
0003-0155	American Neptune
0003-0163	American Newspaper Boy
0003-0171	American Notes & Queries
0003-018X	American Nuclear Society Transactions
0003-0198	American Nurseryman
0003-0201	American Observer *see* 0037-2242
0003-021X	American Oil Chemists' Society. Journal
0003-0228	American Fiddlers News
0003-0228	American Old Time Fiddlers News *see* 0003-0228
0003-0236	American Opinion
0003-0244	American Optometric Association. Journal
0003-0252	American Orchid Society Bulletin
0003-0279	American Oriental Society. Journal
0003-0287	American Osteopathic Association. Journal
0003-0295	American Oxonian
0003-0309	American Paint and Wallpaper Dealer *changed to* American Paint and Wallcoverings Dealer
0003-0317	American Paint Journal *see* 0098-5430
0003-0325	American Painting Contractor
0003-0341	American Paper Institute. Monthly Statistical Summary
0003-0376	American Pen†
0003-0392	American Perfumer and Cosmetics *see* 0361-4387
0003-0406	Abstracts of Air and Water Conservation Literature†
0003-0422	Abstracts of Refining Literature *changed to* A P I Abstracts/Literature
0003-0430	American Petroleum Institute. Abstracts of Refining Patents *changed to* A P I Abstracts/Patents
0003-0457	American Petroleum Institute. Division of Statistics & Economics. Weekly Statistical Bulletin
0003-0465	American Pharmaceutical Association. Journal *see* 0160-3450
0003-0473	American Philatelist
0003-0481	American Philosophical Quarterly
0003-049X	American Philosophical Society. Proceedings
0003-0503	American Physical Society. Bulletin
0003-0511	American Pigeon Journal
0003-052X	American Place Theatre. News†
0003-0538	American Podiatry Association. Journal
0003-0546	American Poet
0003-0554	American Political Science Review
0003-0562	American Polygraph Association. Journal *changed to* Polygraph
0003-0570	American Portuguese Cultural Society. Journal *see* 0098-4981
0003-0589	American Potato Journal
0003-0619	American Primrose, Primula, and Auricula Society, Quarterly
0003-0619	American Primrose Society. Quarterly *see* 0003-0619
0003-0627	Pharmacy Times
0003-0635	American Protestant Hospital Association. Bulletin
0003-0651	American Psychoanalytic Association. Journal
0003-066X	American Psychologist
0003-0678	American Quarterly
0003-0686	American Racing Pigeon News
0003-0694	American Railway Engineering Association. Bulletin
0003-0708	American Rationalist
0003-0716	American Record Guide
0003-0724	American Recorder
0003-0732	American Red Cross Youth Journal†
0003-0740	American Red Cross Youth News *changed to* Young Horizons
0003-0775	American Report†
0003-0805	American Review of Respiratory Disease
0003-0813	American Review of World Health
0003-0821	American Rhododendron Society. Quarterly Bulletin
0003-083X	American Rifleman
0003-0848	American Risk and Insurance Association. Commission on Insurance Terminology. Bulletin†
0003-0856	American Road Builder *see* 0149-4511
0003-0864	American Rock Garden Society Bulletin
0003-0872	American Rodding†
0003-0880	American Roofer and Building Improvement Contractor
0003-0899	American Rose Magazine
0003-0902	American Salesman
0003-0910	American Scandinavian Review *see* 0098-857X
0003-0929	American Scene *changed to* Gilcrease Magazine of American History and Art
0003-0937	American Scholar
0003-0945	American School & University
0003-0953	American School Board Journal
0003-0961	American School News†
0003-097X	American Schools of Oriental Research. Bulletin
0003-0988	American Scientific Affiliation. Journal
0003-0996	American Scientist
0003-1003	American Secondary Education
0003-1011	American Security Council Washington Report
0003-102X	American Sephardi
0003-1038	American Shoemaking
0003-1046	American Small Stock Farmer†
0003-1054	American Society for Geriatric Dentistry. Journal
0003-1062	American Society for Horticultural Science. Journal
0003-1070	American Society for Psychical Research. Journal
0003-1089	American Society for the Study of Orthodontics. Journal†
0003-1097	American Society Legion of Honor Magazine
0003-1100	American Society of Civil Engineers. Engineering Mechanics Division. Newsletter†
0003-1119	American Society of Civil Engineers. Proceedings
0003-1135	American Society of Civil Engineers. Structural Division. Newsletter†
0003-1143	American Society of Civil Engineers. Surveying & Mapping Division. Newsletter†
0003-1151	American Society of Civil Engineers. Waterways & Harbors Division. Newsletter†
0003-116X	American Society of Farm Managers and Rural Appraisers. Journal
0003-1178	American Society of Newspaper Editors. Bulletin
0003-1194	American Society of Psychosomatic Dentistry and Medicine. Journal
0003-1208	American Society of Safety Engineers. Journal *see* 0099-0027
0003-1216	American Society of Sugar Beet Technologists. Journal
0003-1224	American Sociological Review
0003-1232	American Sociologist
0003-1240	American Soft Drink Journal†
0003-1275	Soybean Profits†
0003-1283	American Speech
0003-1291	American Statistical Association. Journal
0003-1305	American Statistician
0003-1313	American String Teacher
0003-1321	American Studies International
0003-1348	American Surgeon
0003-1356	American Surgical Dealer†
0003-1372	American Symphony Orchestra League. Newsletter *see* 0271-2687
0003-1380	American Teacher
0003-1399	American Theological Library Association. Newsletter
0003-1402	American Theosophist
0003-1410	American Transcendental Quarterly
0003-1429	American Translator†
0003-1437	American Trial Lawyers Association Newsletter *see* 0364-8125
0003-1445	American Turf Monthly
0003-1453	American University Law Review
0003-1461	American Vegetable Grower
0003-147X	American Vegetarian-Hygienist†
0003-1488	American Veterinary Medical Association. Journal
0003-1496	American Vocational Journal *see* 0164-9175
0003-150X	American Water Works Association. Journal
0003-1518	American Way
0003-1534	American West
0003-1550	American Zionist
0003-1569	American Zoologist
0003-1585	America's First Zoo *see* 0003-3537
0003-1593	America's Future
0003-1607	America's Textile Reporter†
0003-1615	The Americas
0003-1623	Amerikanischer Wirtschaftsbrief
0003-1631	Amerikas Latvietis
0003-1666	Amersfoortse Stemmen†
0003-1674	A M E X *changed to* A M E X Canada
0003-1682	Amgueddfa†
0003-1690	Amherst Alumni News *changed to* Amherst
0003-1704	Ami du Peuple
0003-1712	Amica *changed to* A M I C A Bulletin
0003-1720	Amicizia
0003-1739	Amicizia Ebraico-Cristiana di Firenze. Bollettino
0003-1747	Amico dell'Arte Cristiana
0003-1755	Amiga
0003-1763	Aminco Laboratory News†
0003-1771	Amis-Coop
0003-178X	Amis de Han Ryner. Cahiers
0003-1798	Amis de la Radiesthesie
0003-1801	Amis de l'I.B.A.N.A.(Publication) *changed to* Ecole Nationale Superieure de Biologie Appliquee a la Nutrition et a l'Alimentation. Cahiers
0003-181X	Amis de Milosz
0003-1828	Amis de Napoleon 3rd. Bulletin Interne
0003-1844	Amis des Roses
0003-1852	Amis du Chateau de Pau. Bulletin
0003-1860	Amis du Film & de la Television
0003-1879	Amistad†
0003-1887	S O S Amitie France. Bulletin National
0003-1895	Amities Catholiques Francaises
0003-1909	Amities Spirituelles. Bulletin
0003-1917	Amministrazione Socialista
0003-1933	Amnesty Action
0003-1941	Amnesty International Monthly *see* 0308-6887
0003-195X	Among Friends
0003-1968	Among Ourselves
0003-1976	Among the Deep Sea Fishers
0003-1984	Amor Artis Bulletin†
0003-1992	Amperland
0003-200X	Amphora
0003-2018	Ampleforth Journal
0003-2026	Ampo
0003-2034	Amposta
0003-2042	Ampul
0003-2050	Amro Beursnieuws
0003-2069	Amsterdam in de Markt†
0003-2077	Amsterdam-Rotterdam Bank. Economic Quarterly Review†
0003-2093	Amtlich Nicht Notierte Wertpapiere - Geregelter Freiverkehr an der Wiener Boerse
0003-2107	Amtliche Veterinaernachrichten
0003-2115	Amtlicher Anzeiger
0003-2131	Amtliches Kreisblatt fuer den Kreis Herzogtum Lauenburg
0003-214X	Berlin Wertpapierboerse. Amtliches Kursblatt
0003-2158	Wertpapierboerse in Stuttgart. Amtliches Kursblatt
0003-2166	Wiener Warenboerse. Amtliches Kursblatt. Holz und Kolonialwaren.
0003-2174	Wiener Warenboerse. Amtliches Kursblatt. Rohhaeute und Felle, Leder Treibriemen und Technische Lederartikel
0003-2190	Amtliches Schulblatt fuer den Regierungsbezirk Duesseldorf
0003-2204	Amtliches Schulblatt fuer die Volks-, Real- und Berufsschulen fuer den Bezirksregierung Trier
0003-2220	Amtsblatt der Oesterreichischen Justizverwaltung
0003-2239	Amtsblatt der Stadt Kapfenberg
0003-2247	Wels, Stadt. Amtsblatt
0003-2255	Wiener Neustadt. Amtsblatt der Stadt *changed to* Wiener Neustadt. Amtsblatt der Statutarstadt
0003-2263	Germany (Federal Republic, 1949-) Bundesminister fuer das Post- und Fernmeldewesen. Amtsblatt
0003-2271	Amtsblatt fuer das Land Vorarlberg
0003-228X	Amtsblatt fuer den Regierungsbezirk Aurich†
0003-2328	Amtsblatt fuer die Erzdioezese Bamberg
0003-2336	Der Amtsvormund
0003-2344	Amusement Business
0003-2360	An Lef Kernewek
0003-2387	Al-Nashra *changed to* Al-Arabiyya
0003-2409	Anaesthesia
0003-2417	Der Anaesthesist
0003-2425	Anais Azevedos†
0003-2433	Anais Brasileiros de Dermatologia
0003-2441	Anais de Farmacia e Quimica de Sao Paulo
0003-245X	Anais Paulistas de Medicina e Cirurgia
0003-2468	Analecta Bollandiana
0003-2476	Analecta Cisterciensia
0003-2484	Anales Cientificos
0003-2492	Anales de Bromatologia
0003-2506	Anales de Mecanica y Electricidad
0003-2514	Anales de Medicina *see* 0517-6832
0003-2514	Anales de Medicina *see* 0517-6824
0003-2530	Anales del Instituto Corachan
0003-2549	Anales del Servicio de Psiquiatria
0003-2557	Anales Espanoles de Odontoestomatologia†
0003-2565	Beogradski Univerzitet. Pravni Fakultet. Anali
0003-2573	Analise Social
0003-2581	Analisis-Confirmado
0003-259X	Analisis de Actualidades Societicas†
0003-2603	Analog Science Fact-Science Fiction *see* 0161-2328
0003-262X	Analyse et Prevision *changed to* Futuribles
0003-2638	Analysis
0003-2646	Analysis of Current Developments in the Soviet Union†
0003-2654	Analyst
0003-2662	Analyst
0003-2670	Analytica Chimica Acta
0003-2689	Analytical Abstracts
0003-2697	Analytical Biochemistry
0003-2700	Analytical Chemistry
0003-2719	Analytical Letters
0003-2727	Anaqueles†
0003-2751	Anarchy†
0003-276X	Anatomical Record
0003-2778	Anatomical Society of India. Journal
0003-2786	Anatomischer Anzeiger

0003-2794 Anbar Management Services Abstracts *see* 0001-4796
0003-2808 Anbar Management Services Bibliography *see* 0261-0108
0003-2816 Anbar Management Services Joint Index *see* 0261-0094
0003-2824 Anblick
0003-2832 Anchor *changed to* Golden Gate Aquarist
0003-2840 Anchor
0003-2867 Ancilla
0003-2883 Ancora†
0003-2891 Andar per Ceramiche
0003-2905 Andean Air Mail and Peruvian Times†
0003-2913 Andelsbladet
0003-2921 Esotera
0003-293X Anderson College News
0003-2948 Andes
0003-2956 Andhra Agricultural Journal
0003-2964 Andhra Pradesh Productivity Council Journal
0003-2972 Andover Newton Quarterly
0003-2980 Andrews University Seminary Studies
0003-2999 Anesthesia and Analgesia
0003-3006 Anesthesia Progress
0003-3014 Anesthesie, Analgesie, Reanimation
0003-3022 Anesthesiology
0003-3030 Ange Gardien
0003-3049 Angeiologie
0003-3057 Angel Hair†
0003-3073 Angheliaforos *changed to* Anichti Orizontes-Angheliaforos
0003-3081 Angelicum
0003-3103 Angels
0003-312X Die Angestelltenversicherung
0003-3138 Angewandte Kosmetik *see* 0342-2968
0003-3146 Angewandte Makromolekulare Chemie
0003-3154 Angewandte Ornithologie
0003-3162 Angewandte Parasitologie
0003-3170 Angiologia
0003-3189 Angiologica *see* 0303-6847
0003-3197 Angiology
0003-3219 Angle Orthodontist
0003-3227 Angler Tierzucht *changed to* Angler Rinderzucht
0003-3235 Anglers' Digest
0003-3243 Angler's Mail
0003-3251 Anglia
0003-326X Anglica
0003-3278 Anglican Digest
0003-3286 Anglican Theological Review
0003-3294 Angling
0003-3308 Angling Times
0003-3316 Anglo American Trade News *changed to* Atlantic
0003-3324 Anglo-Continental Dental Society. Journal
0003-3332 Anglo-German Medical Review†
0003-3340 Anglo-German Review
0003-3359 Anglo-Israel Trade Journal
0003-3367 Anglo-Jewish Art and History†
0003-3375 Anglo-Norwegian Trade Journal
0003-3383 Anglo-Spanish Quarterly Review
0003-3391 Anglo Swiss Times†
0003-3405 Anglo-Welsh Review
0003-3413 Angola. Direccao dos Servicos de Estatistica. Boletim Mensal
0003-343X Instituto de Investigacao Cientifica de Angola. Relatorios e Communicacoes
0003-3448 Laboratorio de Engenharia de Angola. Boletim Informativo†
0003-3456 Angola. Direccao Provincial dos Servicos de Geologia e Minas. Boletim
0003-3464 Angora Goat & Mohair Journal
0003-3472 Animal Behaviour
0003-3480 Animal Blood Groups and Biochemical Genetics
0003-3499 Animal Breeding Abstracts
0003-3502 Animal Health *see* 0142-6591
0003-3510 Animal Health Age†
0003-3537 Animal Kingdom
0003-3545 Animal Life†
0003-3553 Animal Nutrition & Health
0003-3561 Animal Production
0003-357X Animal Protection *changed to* A S P C A Bulletin
0003-3588 Animal Science Journal of Pakistan *changed to* Bangladesh Journal of Animal Science
0003-3596 Animal Welfare Institute. Information Report
0003-360X Animaldom
0003-3618 Animals *changed to* Wildlife
0003-3626 Animals' Champion and the Way to Health
0003-3634 Animals: Defender & Anti-Vivisection News
0003-3642 Animals Magazine *changed to* Animal Forum
0003-3650 Animaux de Laboratoire. Revue Bibliographique
0003-3669 Animo
0003-3685 Ankara Universitesi. Veteriner Fakultesi. Dergisi
0003-3693 Ankertros
0003-3707 Ankh†
0003-3715 Anleggsmaskinen
0003-3723 Ann Arbor Argus†
0003-3731 Ann Arbor Review†
0003-374X Anna
0003-3758 Annabel
0003-3766 Annabella
0003-3774 Annabelle
0003-3790 Annals of Science
0003-3804 Annalen der Physik
0003-3839 Annales Agronomiques
0003-3847 Annales Botanici Fennici
0003-3855 Annales Chirurgiae et Gynaecologiae Fenniae *see* 0355-9521
0003-3863 Annales Collegii Medici Antverpiensis
0003-3871 Annales d'Anatomie Pathologique *changed to* Annales de Pathologie
0003-388X Annales de Biologie Animale, Biochemie, Biophysique *see* 0181-1916
0003-3898 Annales de Biologie Clinique
0003-3901 Annales de Bourgogne
0003-391X Annales de Bretagne et des Pays de l'Ouest(Anjou, Maine, Touraine)
0003-3928 Annales de Cardiologie et d'Angeiologie
0003-3936 Annales de Chimie *changed to* Annales de Chimie: Science des Materiaux
0003-3944 Annales de Chirurgie
0003-3952 Annales de Chirurgie Infantile *see* 0180-5738
0003-3960 Annales de Chirurgie Plastique
0003-3979 Societe Francaise de Dermatologie et de Syphiligraphie. Bulletin *see* 0151-9638
0003-3987 Anales de Edafologia y Agrobiologia
0003-3995 Annales de Genetique
0003-4002 Annales de Genetique et de Selection Animale
0003-4010 Annales de Geographie
0003-4029 Annales de Geophysique
0003-4037 Annales de la Nutrition et de l'Alimentation
0003-4045 Annales de la Propagation de la Foi *changed to* Solidaires
0003-4053 Annales de l'Amelioration des Plantes
0003-4061 Annales de l'Anesthesiologie Francaise
0003-407X Annales de l'Economie Collective *changed to* Annales de l'Economie Publique, Sociale et Cooperative
0003-4088 Annales de Limnologie
0003-4096 Annales de Medecine et de Pharmacie de Reims *see* 0301-4444
0003-410X Annales de Medecine Interne
0003-4118 Annales de Medecine Veterinaire
0003-4126 Annales de Medecine des Accidents et du Trafic Traumatologie
0003-4134 Annales de Normandie
0003-4142 Annales de Paleontologie
0003-4150 Annales de Parasitologie Humaine et Comparee
0003-4169 Annales de Physique
0003-4177 Annales de Phytopathologie
0003-4185 Annales de Radiologie
0003-4193 Annales de Recherches Veterinaires
0003-4215 Annales de Speleologie†
0003-4223 Annales de Technologie Agricole
0003-4231 Annales de Zoologie- Ecologie Animale†
0003-424X Annales de Zootechnie
0003-4266 Annales d'Endocrinologie
0003-4274 Annales des Falsifications et de l'Expertise Chimique
0003-4274 Annales des Falsifications de l'Expertise Chimique et Toxicologique
0003-4282 Annales des Mines
0003-4290 Annales des Mines de Belgique
0003-4312 Annales des Sciences Forestieres
0003-4320 Annales des Sciences Naturelles. Botanique et Biologie Vegetale
0003-4339 Annales des Sciences Naturelles. Zoologie et Biologie Animale
0003-4347 Annales des Telecommunications
0003-4355 Annales d'Histochimie *see* 0145-5680
0003-4363 Annales d'Hygiene de Langue Francaise *changed to* Medecine et Nutrition
0003-4371 Annales d'Oculistique *see* 0181-5512
0003-438X Annales d'Oto-Laryngologie et de Chirurgie Cervico Faciale
0003-4398 Annales du Midi
0003-4401 Annales d'Urologie
0003-441X Annales-Economies, Societes, Civilisations
0003-4428 Annales Entomologici Fennici
0003-4436 Annales Historiques de la Revolution Francaise
0003-4444 Annales Homeopathiques Francaises
0003-4452 Annales Internationales de Criminologie
0003-4460 Annales Medicales de Nancy
0003-4479 Annales Medicinae Experimentalis et Biologiae Fenniae *see* 0302-2137
0003-4487 Annales Medico-Psychologiques
0003-4495 Annales Paediatrici Japonici
0003-4509 Annales Pharmaceutiques Francaises
0003-4517 Annales Scientifiques Textiles Belges†
0003-4525 Annales Textiles†
0003-4533 Annales Universitatis Saraviensis. Reihe: Medizin
0003-4541 Annales Zoologici
0003-455X Annales Zoologici Fennici
0003-4568 Annali della Carita
0003-4576 Annali della Facolta di Agraria
0003-4584 Italy. Ministero della Pubblica Istruzione. Annali della Pubblica Istruzione
0003-4592 Annali di Chimica
0003-4606 Annali di Freniatria e Scienze Affini
0003-4614 Annali di Idrologia†
0003-4622 Annali di Matematica
0003-4630 Annali di Medicina Navale
0003-4649 Annali di Microbiologia Ed Enzimologia
0003-4657 Annali di Ostetricia e Ginecologia (1879-1971) *see* 0300-0087
0003-4665 Annali di Ottamologia e Clinica Oculista
0003-4673 Annali di Radiologia Diagnostica
0003-4681 Annali di Stomatologia
0003-469X Annali Italiani di Chirurgia
0003-4703 Annali Italiani di Dermatologia Clinica e Sperimentale
0003-4711 Annali Italiani di Pediatria†
0003-472X Annali Sclavo
0003-4738 Annals of Allergy
0003-4746 Annals of Applied Biology
0003-4754 Annals of Botany
0003-4762 Annals of Clinical Research
0003-4789 Annals of General Practice *see* 0300-8495
0003-4797 Annals of Good St. Anne
0003-4800 Annals of Human Genetics
0003-4819 Annals of Internal Medicine
0003-4827 Annals of Iowa
0003-4835 Annals of Library Science and Documentation
0003-4843 Annals of Mathematical Logic
0003-4851 Annals of Mathematic Statistics *changed to* Annals of Probability
0003-4851 Annals of Mathematical Statistics *see* 0090-5364
0003-486X Annals of Mathematics
0003-4878 Annals of Occupational Hygiene
0003-4886 Annals of Ophthalmology
0003-4894 Annals of Otology, Rhinology and Laryngology
0003-4908 Rheumatology and Physical Medicine *see* 0300-3396
0003-4916 Annals of Physics
0003-4932 Annals of Surgery
0003-4940 Annals of the Holy Childhood *changed to* It's Our World
0003-4967 Annals of the Rheumatic Diseases
0003-4975 Annals of Thoracic Surgery
0003-4983 Annals of Tropical Medicine and Parasitology
0003-4991 Annals of Wyoming
0003-5009 Annals of Zoology
0003-5017 L'Annee Biologique
0003-5033 Annee Psychologique
0003-505X Annonces de l'Industrie†
0003-5076 Annotated Bibliography of Economic Geology†
0003-5084 Annotated Bibliography of Literature Produced by the Cooperative Movements in South-East Asia *changed to* Annotated Bibliography of Literature on Cooperative Movements in South-East Asia
0003-5092 Annotationes Zoologica Japonenses
0003-5106 Announced Reprints†
0003-5114 Conference Board. Announcements of Mergers and Acquisitions
0003-5149 Annuario di Diritto Comparato e di Studi Legislativi
0003-5157 Annuarium Historiae Conciliorum
0003-5165 Annunciatore Poligrafico
0003-5181 Another Mother for Peace
0003-519X Die Anregung
0003-5203 Annrinya
0003-5211 Anritsu Technical Bulletin
0003-5238 Der Anschnitt†
0003-5246 "Ansearchin" News
0003-5254 Ansgarsledaren
0003-5262 Ansgarsposten
0003-5270 Anstoesse
0003-5300 Answer†
0003-5319 Antaeus
0003-5327 Antarctic
0003-5335 Antarctic Journal of the United States
0003-5351 Antarktiese Bulletin
0003-536X Antena
0003-5378 Antenna
0003-5386 Antenna
0003-5394 Antenne Medicale
0003-5408 Antenni†
0003-5424 Anthos
0003-5459 Anthropologica
0003-5467 Royal Anthropological Institute of Great Britain and Ireland. Library. Anthropological Index *changed to* Anthropological Index to Current Periodicals in the Library of the Museum of Mankind
0003-5475 Anthropological Journal of Canada
0003-5483 Anthropological Linguistics
0003-5491 Anthropological Quarterly
0003-5505 Anthropological Society of Nippon. Journal
0003-5513 Anthropological Survey of India. Bulletin
0003-5521 L'Anthropologie
0003-553X Anthropologie
0003-5548 Anthropologischer Anzeiger
0003-5556 Anthropologist
0003-5564 Anthropology U C L A
0003-5572 Anthropos
0003-5580 Anti-Apartheid News
0003-5599 Anti-Corrosion Methods and Materials
0003-5602 A R Staatkunde
0003-5610 Anti-Vivisectionist *changed to* Animal Welfare
0003-5629 Antibiotica
0003-5637 Antibiotiki
0003-5645 Antichita Viva
0003-5653 Antiek
0003-5661 Antigonish Review
0003-567X Antik Tanulmanyok
0003-5688 Antike Kunst
0003-5696 Antike und Abendland
0003-5718 Antilliaanse Nieuwsbrief

0003-5734 Antincendio e Protezione Industriale *changed to* Antincendio e Protezione Civile
0003-5742 Antioch College Reports *changed to* Antioch Report
0003-5769 Antioch Review
0003-5785 Antiquarian Horology and the Proceedings of the Antiquarian Horological Society
0003-5793 Antiquariat†
0003-5815 Antiquaries Journal
0003-5823 Antique Airplane Association News
0003-5831 Antique Automobile
0003-584X Antique Collecting
0003-5858 Antique Collector
0003-5866 Antique Dealer and Collectors' Guide
0003-5874 Antique Finder *see* 0003-584X
0003-5882 Antique Monthly
0003-5890 Antique Motor News and Atlantic Auto Advertiser *changed to* Antique Motor News
0003-5904 Antique Outboarder
0003-5912 Antique Trader *see* 0161-8342
0003-5939 Antiques *see* 0161-9284
0003-5947 Antiques Dealer
0003-5963 Antiques Journal
0003-598X Antiquity
0003-5998 Antiseptic
0003-6021 Antitrust & Trade Regulation Report
0003-603X Antitrust Bulletin
0003-6048 Antitrust Law and Economics Review
0003-6056 Antitrust Law Journal
0003-6064 Antonianum
0003-6072 Antonie van Leeuwenhoek Journal of Microbiology and Serology *changed to* Antonie van Leeuwenhoek Journal of Microbiology
0003-6099 Antriebstechnik
0003-6102 Antropologia e Historia de Guatemala (IDAEH)
0003-6110 Antropologica
0003-6129 Antropolognytt *changed to* Antropologiska Studier
0003-6137 Antropos
0003-6145 Antroposofia
0003-6161 Antur
0003-617X Antwerp Bee-Argus
0003-6188 Antwerps Havennieuws†
0003-620X Anukta
0003-6218 Anuvad
0003-6226 Anvil
0003-6234 Das Anwaltbuero†
0003-6242 Anyagmozgatas-Csomagolas
0003-6277 Anzeiger des Oesterreichischen Buchhandels
0003-6285 Anzeiger des Reiches der Gerechtigkeit
0003-6293 Anzeiger fuer die Altertumswissenschaft
0003-6307 Anzeiger fuer Schaedlingskunde und Pflanzenschutz *see* 0340-7330
0003-6315 Anzeiger Solothurn-Lebern
0003-6323 Aomori-ken Nogyo Kisho Junpo
0003-6331 Agriculture in Aomori
0003-634X Apalachee Diary
0003-6358 Apartment Construction News *see* 0146-0919
0003-6366 Apartment Ideas *changed to* Metropolitan Home
0003-6374 Apartment Owners News
0003-6390 Apeiron
0003-6412 Apercu Technique-Technisch Overzicht (A T O)
0003-6420 Aperture
0003-6439 Apex
0003-6455 Apiacta
0003-6471 Apicultor†
0003-648X Apicultural Abstracts
0003-6498 Apka Swasthya
0003-6501 Aplikace Matematiky
0003-6528 Apollo
0003-6536 Apollo
0003-6552 Aposento Alto
0003-6560 Apothecary
0003-6579 Apothekersblad
0003-6587 Appalachia Journal
0003-6595 Appalachia
0003-6609 Appalachia Medicine†
0003-6617 Appalachian Lookout†
0003-6625 Appalachian Outlook
0003-6633 Appalachian South
0003-6641 Appalachian Trailway News
0003-665X Appaloosa News
0003-6668 Apparecchi Elettrodomestici Nella Casa Moderna
0003-6676 Apparecchiature Idrauliche e Pneumatiche *see* 0374-3225
0003-6684 Apparel Executive†
0003-6749 Appel de Saint Vincent de Paul†
0003-6757 Appita
0003-6765 Apple†
0003-6773 Appliance Engineer *see* 0003-6781
0003-6781 Appliance
0003-679X Appliance Manufacturer
0003-6803 Appliance Service News
0003-6811 Applicable Analysis
0003-682X Applied Acoustics
0003-6838 Applied Biochemistry and Microbiology
0003-6846 Applied Economics
0003-6854 Applied Electrical Phenomena†
0003-6862 Applied Entomology and Zoology
0003-6870 Applied Ergonomics
0003-6889 Applied Graphics†
0003-6900 Applied Mechanics Reviews
0003-6919 Applied Microbiology *see* 0099-2240
0003-6935 Applied Optics
0003-6943 Applied Photography†
0003-6951 Applied Physics Letters
0003-696X Applied Plastics†
0003-6978 Journal of Applied Pneumatics
0003-6986 Applied Science and Technology Index
0003-6994 Applied Scientific Research
0003-701X Applied Solar Energy
0003-7028 Applied Spectroscopy
0003-7052 Appraisal
0003-7060 Appraisal Digest
0003-7079 Appraisal Institute Digest
0003-7087 Appraisal Journal
0003-7095 Appraiser
0003-7109 Apprenticeship News
0003-7117 Approach
0003-7125 Approach Magazine†
0003-7133 Approaches; a Periodical of Poems by Kentuckians *changed to* Kentucky Poetry Review
0003-7176 Apres - Demain
0003-7206 Aqua
0003-7214 Aqua
0003-7222 Aqua Vite
0003-7230 New Aquarian Agent *changed to* Astrology-the New Aquarian Agent
0003-7257 Aquarien Magazin
0003-7265 Die Aquarien-und Terrarien-Zeitschrift
0003-7273 Aquarist and Pondkeeper
0003-729X Aquarium
0003-7303 Aquarius
0003-7311 Aquatic Biology Abstracts *see* 0140-5373
0003-7338 Aqueduct News *see* 0092-0622
0003-7354 Aquin
0003-7362 Aquinas
0003-7397 Arab Film and Television Center News
0003-7400 Arab Journal†
0003-7419 Arab News and Views†
0003-7435 Arab Oil Review
0003-7443 Arab Petroleum
0003-7451 A R R
0003-746X Arab Veterinary Medical Association. Journal
0003-7478 Arab World†
0003-7486 Arabian Horse News†
0003-7494 Arabian Horse World
0003-7508 Arabica
0003-7524 Arable Farmer *see* 0300-2829
0003-7540 Araksha
0003-7559 Araldo di S. Antonio
0003-7567 Aramco World
0003-7583 Ararat
0003-7591 Arbeidskundig Tijdschrift *changed to* Bedrijfsvoering
0003-7605 Arbeit
0003-7613 Die Arbeit
0003-7621 Arbeit, Beruf, und Arbeitslosenhilfe *changed to* Arbeit und Beruf
0003-763X Arbeit und Leistung *see* 0340-2444
0003-7648 Arbeit und Recht
0003-7656 Arbeit und Wirtschaft
0003-7664 Arbeits- und Sozialrecht
0003-7710 Arbeitsgemeinschaft fuer Jugendpflege und Jugendfuersorge. Mitteilungen *changed to* Forum Jugendhilfe
0003-7729 Arbeitsgemeinschaft Oesterreichischer Entomologen. Zeitschrift
0003-7737 Saarlaendische Arbeitnehmer *changed to* Arbeitnehmer
0003-7745 Arbeitskreis Holz *changed to* A K Holz
0003-7753 Arbeitsmedizin, Sozialmedizin, Arbeitshygiene *see* 0300-581X
0003-7761 Arbeitsrecht in Stichworten
0003-777X Arbeitsrecht und Arbeitslosenversicherung
0003-7796 Arbeitstechnische Merkhefte der Waldarbeit
0003-780X Die Arbeitsvorbereitung
0003-7818 Arbejdsgiveren
0003-7826 Arbejdslederen
0003-7834 Arbetsmiljoe
0003-7842 Arbetsledaren
0003-7850 Arbetsmarknaden
0003-7869 Arbiter
0003-7877 Arbitration
0003-7885 Arbitration in the Schools
0003-7893 Arbitration Journal
0003-7907 Arbitro
0003-7915 Arbol de Fuego: Poesia
0003-7931 Arboricultural Association Journal *see* 0307-1375
0003-794X Arboriculture Fruitiere
0003-7958 Arborist's News *changed to* Journal of Arboriculture
0003-7966 Arbos†
0003-7974 L'Arc
0003-7982 Arcadia
0003-7990 Arcadie
0003-8008 Archaeologia Austriaca
0003-8032 Archaeologiai Ertesito
0003-8059 Archaeological Society of Central New York. Bulletin†
0003-8067 Archaeological Society of Delaware. Bulletin
0003-8075 Archaeological Society of Japan. Journal
0003-8091 A S A Newsletter *changed to* A S A Journal
0003-8105 Archaeologischer Anzeiger
0003-8121 Archaeology and Physical Anthropology in Oceania
0003-813X Archaeometry
0003-8148 Archeia tes Pharmakeutikes (Athens)
0003-8156 Archeocivilisation†
0003-8164 Archeologia†
0003-8172 Archeologia Classica†
0003-8172 Archeologia Classica
0003-8180 Archeologia Polski
0003-8199 Archeological Newsletter†
0003-8210 Archeologie
0003-8229 Archeologie Vivante
0003-8237 Archer†
0003-8237 Archer
0003-827X Archery World
0003-8288 Archibald Newsletter†
0003-8296 Archidiocesi di Monreale. Bollettino Ecclesiastico
0003-8369 Archimede
0003-8377 Archimedes
0003-8385 Archimedes
0003-8393 Architect
0003-8407 Architect & Builder
0003-8415 Architect
0003-8423 Architect & Contractor
0003-8431 Architect & Surveyor *see* 0308-4930
0003-844X Architect Consulting Engineer-Product Bulletin Directory *changed to* Product Bulletin Directory.
0003-8458 Architekonike Kai Dikosmese†
0003-8466 Architects' Journal
0003-8490 Architecture Culture
0003-8504 Architectural Design
0003-8512 Architectural Design, Cost and Data *changed to* Design, Cost & Data
0003-8520 Architectural Digest
0003-8547 Architectural Glass & Aluminium†
0003-8555 Architectural Institute of Japan. Transactions
0003-858X Architectural Record
0003-8598 Architectural Record Newsletter†
0003-8601 Architectural Research and Teaching *changed to* Journal of Architectural Research
0003-861X Architectural Review
0003-8628 Architectural Science Review
0003-8644 Arkhitektura
0003-8652 Architecture and Building Industry
0003-8679 Architecture Canada†
0003-8695 Architecture d'Aujourd'hui (Paris, 1929)
0003-8709 Architecture East Midlands
0003-8717 Architecture Francaise *changed to* Architecture d'Aujourd'hui (Paris, 1940)
0003-8725 Architecture in Australia *changed to* Architecture Australia
0003-8733 Architecture New Jersey
0003-875X Der Architekt
0003-8768 Der Architekt und der Bauingenieur
0003-8784 Architektur und Kultiviertes Wohnen *changed to* Architektur und Wohnen
0003-8792 Architektur und Wohnform *see* 0173-8046
0003-8806 Architektur Wettbewerbe *see* 0341-2784
0003-8814 Architektura
0003-8830 Architettura
0003-8849 Archiv
0003-8857 Archiv
0003-8865 Archiv der Gegenwart
0003-8873 Archiv der Internationalen Stefan Zweig-Gesellschaft
0003-8881 Julius Klaus- Stiftung. Archiv *see* 0300-984X
0003-889X Archiv der Mathematik
0003-8903 Archiv der Pharmazie
0003-8911 Archiv des Oeffentlichen Rechts
0003-892X Archiv des Voelkerrechts
0003-8938 Archiv for Pharmaci og Chemi
0003-8946 Archiv fuer Begriffsgeschichte
0003-8962 Archiv fuer das Eisenhuettenwesen
0003-8970 Archiv fuer das Studium der neueren Sprachen und Literaturen
0003-8989 Archiv fuer deutsche Postgeschichte
0003-8997 Archiv fuer die Civilistische Praxis
0003-9012 Archiv fuer die Gesamte Virusforschung *see* 0304-8608
0003-9020 Archiv fuer Druck und Papier†
0003-9039 Archiv fuer Elektrotechnik
0003-9047 Archiv fuer Energiewirtschaft
0003-9055 Archiv fuer Experimentelle Veterinaermedizin
0003-9063 Archiv fuer Fischereiwissenschaft
0003-908X Archiv fuer Gartenbau
0003-9098 Archiv fuer Gefluegelkunde
0003-9101 Archiv fuer Geschichte der Philosophie
0003-911X Archiv fuer Geschwulstforschung
0003-9128 Archiv fuer Gynaekologie *see* 0170-9925
0003-9136 Archiv fuer Hydrobiologie
0003-9152 Archiv fuer Japanische Chirurgie
0003-9160 Archiv fuer Katholisches Kirchenrecht
0003-9179 Archiv fuer Kinderheilkunde *see* 0300-8630
0003-9187 Archiv fuer Dermatologische Forschung *see* 0340-3696
0003-9195 Archiv fuer klinische und experimentelle Ohren-, Nasen- und Kehlkopfheilkunde *see* 0302-9530
0003-9209 Archiv fuer Kommunalwissenschaften
0003-9217 Basic Research in Cardiology
0003-9225 Archiv fuer Kriminologie
0003-9233 Archiv fuer Kulturgeschichte
0003-925X Archiv fuer Lebensmittelhygiene, Insbesondere fuer Fleisch-, Fisch- und Milchhygiene *changed to* Archiv fuer Lebensmittel Hygiene, Fleisch-, Fisch- und Milchhygiene

ISSN INDEX 951

0003-9268 Archiv fuer Mathematische Logik und Grundlagenforschung
0003-9276 Archiv fuer Mikrobiologie *see* 0302-8933
0003-9284 Archiv fuer Molluskenkunde
0003-9292 Archiv fuer Musikwissenschaft
0003-9306 Archiv fuer Naturschutz und Landschaftsforschung
0003-9314 Archiv fuer Oeffentliche und Freigemeinnuetzige Unternehmen
0003-9322 Oesterreichische Akademie der Wissenschaften. Archiv fuer Oesterreichische Geschichte
0003-9330 Archiv fuer Orthopaedische und Unfallchirurgie *see* 0344-8444
0003-9357 Zeitschrift fuer Physiotherapie
0003-9365 Archiv fuer Protistenkunde
0003-9373 Archiv fuer Psychiatrie und Nervenkrankheiten
0003-9381 Archiv fuer Reformationsgeschichte
0003-9403 Archiv fuer Sippenforschung
0003-9411 Archiv fuer Technisches Messen - A T M *see* 0171-8096
0003-942X Archiv fuer Tierernaehrung
0003-9438 Archiv fuer Tierzucht
0003-9446 Archiv fuer Toxikologie *see* 0340-5761
0003-9462 Archiv fuer Vaterlaendische Geschichte und Topographie
0003-9470 Archiv Ostdeutscher Familienforscher
0003-9489 Archiva Veterinaria†
0003-9497 Archivalische Zeitschrift
0003-9500 Der Archivar
0003-9519 Archive for History of Exact Sciences
0003-9527 Archive for Rational Mechanics and Analysis
0003-9535 Archives
0003-9543 Archives Advocate†
0003-956X Archives Belges de Dermatologie et de Syphiligraphie *see* 0301-8636
0003-9578 Archives Belges de Medecine Sociale, Hygiene, Medecine du Travail et Medecine Legale
0003-9586 Archives d'Anatomie, d'Histologie et d'Embryologie
0003-9594 Archives d'Anatomie Microscopique et de Morphologie Experimentale
0003-9608 Archives d'Anatomie Pathologique *changed to* Archives d'Anatomie et de Cytologie Pathologiques
0003-9616 Archives de Biochimie et Cosmetologie†
0003-9632 Archives de Philosophie
0003-9640 Archives de Psychologie
0003-9659 Archives de Sociologie des Religions *changed to* Archives de Sciences Sociales des Religions
0003-9667 Archives de Zoologie Experimentale et Generale
0003-9675 Archives des Lettres Modernes
0003-9683 Archives des Maladies du Coeur et des Vaisseaux
0003-9691 Archives des Maladies Professionnelles de Medecine du Travail et de Securite Sociale
0003-9705 Archives des Sciences
0003-9721 Revue Diplomatique *changed to* Archives Diplomatiques et Consulaires
0003-973X Archives d'Ophtalmologie *see* 0181-5512
0003-9748 Archives et Bibliotheques de Belgique
0003-9756 European Journal of Sociology
0003-9764 Archives Francaises de Pediatrie
0003-9772 Archives Francaises des Maladies de l'Appareil Digestif *see* 0399-8320
0003-9780 Archives Internationales de Pharmacodynamie et de Therapie
0003-9802 Archives Internationales de Sociologie de la Cooperation et du Developpement
0003-9810 Archives Internationales d'Histoire des Sciences
0003-9829 Archives Italiennes de Biologie
0003-9837 Archives Juives
0003-9845 Archives Mediterraneennes de Medecine
0003-9853 Archives of American Art. Journal
0003-9861 Archives of Biochemistry and Biophysics
0003-987X Archives of Dermatology
0003-9888 Archives of Diseases in Childhood
0003-9896 Archives of Environmental Health
0003-990X Archives of General Psychiatry
0003-9918 Archives of Hygiene
0003-9926 Archives of Internal Medicine
0003-9934 Archives of Medical Hydrology
0003-9942 Archives of Neurology
0003-9950 Archives of Ophthalmology
0003-9969 Archives of Oral Biology
0003-9977 Archives of Otolaryngology
0003-9985 Archives of Pathology *see* 0363-0153
0003-9993 Archives of Physical Medicine and Rehabilitation
0004-0002 Archives of Sexual Behavior
0004-0010 Archives of Surgery
0004-0029 Archives of Traditional Music. Trimester Report†
0004-0037 Archives Roumaines de Pathologie Experimentale et de Microbiologie
0004-0053 Archivio Botanico e Biogeografico Italiano
0004-0061 Archivio de Vecchi
0004-007X Archivio di Chirurgia Toracica e Cardiovascolare†
0004-0088 Archivio di Filosofia
0004-0096 Archivio di Fisiologia
0004-010X Archivio di Medicina Interna
0004-0118 Archivio di Ortopedia *changed to* Archivio di Ortopedia e Reumatologia
0004-0126 Archivio di Ostetricia e Ginecologia
0004-0134 Archivio di Ottalmologia *see* 0300-0109
0004-0142 Archivio di Patologia e Clinica Medica†
0004-0150 Archivio di Psicologia, Neurologia e Psichiatria
0004-0169 Archivio di Scienze Biologiche
0004-0177 Archivo di Studi Urbani e Regionali
0004-0185 Archivio Monaldi per la Tisiologia e le Malattie dell'Apparato Respiratorio
0004-0193 Archivio E.Maragliano di Patologia e Clinica
0004-0207 Archivio Glottologico Italiano
0004-0215 Archivio Italiano delle Malattie dell'Apparato Digerente†
0004-0223 Archivio Italiano di Anatomia e di Embriologia
0004-0231 Archivio Italiano di Anatomia e Istologia Patologica†
0004-024X Archivio Italiano di Chirurgia†
0004-0258 Archivio Italiano di Otologia, Rinologia e Laringologia *see* 0301-3693
0004-0266 Archivio Italiano di Patologia e Clinica dei Tumori
0004-0274 Archivio Italiano di Pediatria e Puericoltura†
0004-0320 Archivio Stomatologico
0004-0339 Archivio Storico Italiano
0004-0347 Archivio Storico Lodigiano
0004-0355 Archivio Storico per la Calabria e la Lucania
0004-0363 Archivio Storico per la Sicilia Orientale
0004-0371 Archivio Storico Ticinese
0004-038X Archivmitteilungen
0004-0398 Archivni Casopis
0004-0401 Archivo de Ciencias Biologicas y Naturales, Teoricas y Aplicadas
0004-041X Archivio di Medicina Mutualistica†
0004-0428 Archivo Espanol de Arte
0004-0444 Archivo Historico de Miraflores. Boletin
0004-0452 Archivo Ibero-Americano
0004-0460 Archivio Italiano di Dermatologia, Venereologia e Sessuologia *changed to* Archivo Italiano di Urologia e Nefrologia
0004-0479 Archivio Veterinario Italiano
0004-0495 Archivos Argentinos de Reumatologia†
0004-0509 Archivos Argentinos de Tisiologia y Neumonologia
0004-0517 Archivos Argentinos Enfermedades del Aparato Digestivo
0004-0525 Archivos Bolivianos de Medicina
0004-0533 Archivos de Biologia y Medicina Experimentales
0004-0541 Archivos de Criminologia, Neuro-Psiquiatria y Disciplinas Conexas
0004-055X Archivos de Historia Potosina
0004-0568 Archivos de Medicina Experimental
0004-0576 Archivos de Neurobiologia
0004-0584 Archivos de Pediatria del Uruguay
0004-0592 Archivos de Zootecnia
0004-0606 Archivos Dominicanos de Pediatria
0004-0614 Archivos Espanoles de Urologia
0004-0622 Archivos Latinoamericanos de Nutricion
0004-0630 Archivos Leoneses
0004-0657 Archivum Chirurgicum Neerlandicum *changed to* Netherlands Journal of Surgery
0004-0665 Archivum Franciscanum Historicum
0004-0673 Archivum Heraldicum
0004-0681 Archivum Histologicum Japonicum
0004-069X Archivum Immunologiae et Therapiae Experimentalis†
0004-0703 Archivum Linguisticum
0004-0711 Archiwista
0004-072X Archiwum Automatyki i Telemechaniki
0004-0738 Archiwum Budowy Maszyn†
0004-0754 Archiwum Gornictwa
0004-0762 Archiwum Historii Medycyny
0004-0770 Archiwum Hutnictwa
0004-0789 Archiwum Hydrotechniki
0004-0797 Archiwum Inzynierii Ladowej
0004-0800 Archiwum Mechaniki Stosowanej *changed to* Archives of Mechanics
0004-0819 Arcispedale S. Anna di Ferrara†
0004-0835 Arcoscenico
0004-0843 Arctic
0004-0851 Arctic and Alpine Research
0004-086X Arctic Circular†
0004-0878 Arctic Development Digest *see* 0704-4836
0004-0894 Area
0004-0908 Area Development Magazine
0004-0916 U.S. Department of Labor. Employment and Training Administration. Area Trends in Employment and Unemployment
0004-0924 Areatopics *changed to* Norweb News
0004-0932 Arena
0004-0967 Arepo†
0004-0975 Arethusa
0004-0983 Argentina
0004-0991 Argentina Automotriz
0004-1009 Argentina. Biblioteca del Congreso. Boletin
0004-1017 Argentina. Direccion Nacional de Estadistica y Censos. Boletin de Estadistica *see* 0325-1969
0004-1017 Argentina. Direccion Nacional de Estadistica y Censos. Boletin de Estatistica *see* 0325-1950
0004-1025 Argentina. Direccion Nacional de Asistencia Nacional. DAS
0004-1033 Pergamino, Argentine Republic. Estacion Experimental Agropecuario. Boletin de Divulgacion†
0004-105X Argentina Grafica
0004-1068 Argentina. Ministerio de Trabajo y Prevision. Boletin de Biblioteca *see* 0403-0133
0004-1076 Argentina. Servicio de Hidrografia Naval. Boletin
0004-1084 Argentine Science Fiction Review
0004-1106 Argentinos Lietuviu Balsas
0004-1114 Argosy
0004-1130 Argot†
0004-1149 Argument for Frihet och Raett
0004-1157 Das Argument
0004-1165 Argus
0004-1173 Argus
0004-1181 Argus
0004-119X Argus des Collectivites
0004-1203 Argus des Pharmaciens
0004-1211 Argus-Journal
0004-122X Argus Menager *see* 0019-9354
0004-1238 Arhitektura-Urbanizam *see* 0350-3666
0004-1246 Arhiv Bioloskih Nauka†
0004-1262 Arhiv za Poljoprivredne Nauke
0004-1270 Arhiv za Pravne i Drustvene Nauke
0004-1289 Arhiv za Zastitu Majke i Djeteta
0004-1297 Arhivski Pregled
0004-1300 Aria Compressa
0004-1319 Arid Lands Research Newsletter†
0004-1327 Ariel
0004-1335 Ariel
0004-1343 Ariel
0004-1351 Arion†
0004-136X Arithmetic Teacher
0004-1378 Arizona Academy of Science Journal *changed to* Arizona-Nevada Academy of Science Journal
0004-1386 Arizona Advocate
0004-1394 Arizona Alumnus
0004-1408 Arizona and the West
0004-1424 Arizona Bar Journal
0004-1440 Arizona Business Bulletin *see* 0093-0717
0004-1459 Arizona Dental Journal†
0004-1467 Arizona Economic Indicators
0004-1475 Arizona Education News *changed to* Alert (Phoenix)
0004-1483 Arizona English Bulletin
0004-1491 Arizona Farmer-Ranchman
0004-1505 Arizona Grocer
0004-1521 Arizona Highways
0004-153X Arizona Law Review
0004-1548 Arizona Librarian†
0004-1556 Arizona Medicine
0004-1564 Arizona Mobile Citizen
0004-1572 Arizona Modern Business and Industry *see* 0193-7480
0004-1580 Arizona-New Mexico Contractor & Engineer *see* 0193-7472
0004-1599 Arizona Nurse
0004-1602 Arizona Pharmacist *changed to* New Arizona Pharmacist
0004-1610 Arizona Quarterly
0004-1629 Arizona Review
0004-1637 Arizona Roadrunner
0004-1653 Arizona Teacher *see* 0194-8849
0004-167X Ark
0004-1688 Ark *changed to* Ark (1978)
0004-1696 Ark-Light Newsletter *see* 0094-0488
0004-1718 Arkansas Archeologist
0004-1726 Arkansas Banker
0004-1742 Arkansas Business and Economic Review
0004-1750 Arkansas Cattle Business
0004-1769 Arkansas Dental Journal
0004-1777 Arkansas Department of Education Newsmagazine
0004-1785 Arkansas Farm Research
0004-1807 Arkansas Game & Fish
0004-1815 Arkansas Grocer
0004-1823 Arkansas Historical Quarterly
0004-1831 Arkansas Law Review
0004-184X Arkansas Libraries
0004-1858 Arkansas Medical Society. Journal
0004-1866 Arkansas Municipalities *changed to* City & Town
0004-1874 Arkansas Oil and Gas Statistical Bulletin
0004-1882 Arka-Tech
0004-1890 Arkansas Valley Journal
0004-1904 Arkham Collector†
0004-1912 Arkheologiia
0004-1920 Arkhimedes
0004-1939 Arkhitektura S S S R
0004-1947 Arkhiv Anatomii, Gistologii i Embriologii
0004-1955 Arkhiv Patologii
0004-1963 Arhiv za Farmaciju
0004-1971 Arkitekt
0004-198X Arkitekten
0004-1998 Arkitektnytt
0004-1998 Arkitektnytt *issued with* 0332-6578
0004-2005 A T
0004-2013 Arkitektur *changed to* Arkitektur DK
0004-2021 Swedish Review of Architecture
0004-203X Arkiv
0004-2048 Arkiv for Astronomi†
0004-2056 Chemica Scripta
0004-2064 Arkiv for Geofysik†
0004-2080 Arkiv foer Matematik
0004-2099 Arkiv for Mineralogi och Geologi†
0004-2102 Arkiv for Sjoerett

ISSN	Title
0004-2110	Arkiv for Zoologi see 0300-3256
0004-2129	Arkkitehti
0004-2145	Arma
0004-2153	Armament Data Sheets
0004-217X	Armchair Detective
0004-2188	Armed Forces Comptroller
0004-220X	Armed Forces Journal see 0196-3597
0004-2218	Armed Forces Medical Journal, India changed to Medical Journal Armed Forces, India
0004-2226	Armed Forces Writer & Journalist changed to National Association of Government Communicators. News
0004-2234	Armee changed to Armees d'Aujourd'hui
0004-2242	Armee et Defense
0004-2269	Armee-Motor
0004-2277	Armee-Rundschau
0004-2285	Armeiski Pregled
0004-2293	Armenia Today
0004-2307	Armenian-American Outlook changed to A.M.A.A. News
0004-2315	Armenian Church
0004-2323	Armenian Digest
0004-2331	Armenian Guardian†
0004-234X	Armenian Mirror - Spectator
0004-2358	Armenian Reporter
0004-2366	Armenian Review
0004-2374	Armenian Weekly
0004-2382	Armenian Welfare Association of New York News
0004-2404	Armenytt
0004-2412	Armieri
0004-2420	Armor
0004-2447	Arms Control and National Security†
0004-2455	Army
0004-2463	Army, Air Force & Naval Air Statistical Record
0004-2471	United States Army Aviation Digest
0004-248X	Army Aviation
0004-2498	Army Digest see 0093-8440
0004-251X	Army Journal see 0314-1039
0004-2528	Army Logistician
0004-2536	Army Museum Newsletter
0004-2544	Army Orders†
0004-2552	Army Quarterly and Defence Journal
0004-2560	Army Research and Development changed to Army R D and A
0004-2579	Army Reserve Magazine
0004-2595	Army Times
0004-2609	Army Vehicle and Military Aircraft Data Sheets
0004-2617	Arnold Air Letter
0004-2625	Arnold Arboretum. Journal
0004-2633	Arnoldia
0004-265X	Ars Sutoria
0004-2668	Arquipelago changed to Voz di Povo
0004-2676	Arquitecto Peruano
0004-2706	Arquitectura
0004-2714	Arquivo de Patologia
0004-2722	Arquivo do Distrito de Aveiro
0004-2730	Arquivos Brasileiros de Endocrinologia e Metabologia
0004-2749	Arquivos Brasileiros de Oftalmologia
0004-2757	Arquivos Brasileiros de Psicologia Aplicada changed to Arquivos Brasileiros de Psicologia
0004-2765	Arquivos Brasileiros de Tuberculose e Doencas do Torax
0004-2773	Arquivos Catarinenses de Medicina
0004-2781	Arquivos de Angola
0004-279X	Arquivos de Biologia†
0004-2803	Arquivos de Gastroenterologia
0004-2811	Arquivos de Higiene e Saude Publica†
0004-282X	Arquivos de Neuro-Psiquiatria
0004-2838	Universidade Federal de Minas Gerais. Curso de Odontologia. Arquivos do Centro de Estudos
0004-2846	Arredare la Casa
0004-2854	Arredorama
0004-2870	Ars Aequi
0004-2889	Ars Buddhica
0004-2897	Ars Medici
0004-2919	Ars Organi
0004-2927	Ars Pharmaceutica
0004-296X	Art Alliance Bulletin
0004-2978	Art & Antiques Weekly
0004-2986	Art and Archaeology Newsletter
0004-2994	Art and Archaeology Technical Abstracts
0004-301X	Art and Australia
0004-3028	Art & Craft in Education changed to Art & Craft
0004-3044	Art and Life
0004-3052	Art and Man
0004-3060	Indianapolis Museum of Art. Bulletin changed to Indianapolis Museum of Art. News Letter
0004-3079	Art Bulletin
0004-3087	Art Chretien
0004-3095	Art d'Eglise
0004-3109	Art Direction
0004-3117	Art du Sol et des Murs changed to Art du Sol-Officiel des Revetements
0004-3125	Art Education
0004-3133	Art Enfantin
0004-315X	Art et Curiosite
0004-3168	Art et Decoration
0004-3184	Art Gallery
0004-3206	Art Gallery of South Australia. Bulletin†
0004-3214	Art in America
0004-3222	Art Index
0004-3230	Art International
0004-3249	Art Journal
0004-3265	Art Material Trade News
0004-3273	Art News
0004-329X	Art of the Americas. Bulletin†
0004-3303	Art Quarterly†
0004-3303	Art Quarterly
0004-3354	Arta
0004-3389	De Arte
0004-3397	Qui Arte Contemporanea
0004-3400	Arte Cristiana
0004-3419	Arte e Poesia
0004-3443	Arte Lombarda
0004-3451	Arterama
0004-346X	Arte Tipografico
0004-3478	Arteregalo
0004-3486	Artes
0004-3494	Artes Graficas see 0164-1905
0004-3508	Artes Graficas en Mexico
0004-3516	Artes Hispanicas†
0004-3524	Artes/Letras
0004-3532	Artforum
0004-3540	Artha
0004-3559	Artha Vijnana
0004-3567	Artha-Vikas
0004-3575	Arthaniti
0004-3583	Arthritis and Rheumatic Diseases Abstracts†
0004-3591	Arthritis and Rheumatism
0004-3605	Arthur D. Little.Industrial Bulletin changed to Arthur D. Little Inc. Bulletin
0004-3613	Arthur Young Journal
0004-363X	Arti e Mercature
0004-3648	Artibus Asiae
0004-3664	Articles on Neoplasia changed to Current Articles on Neoplasia
0004-3672	Articoli Casalinghi
0004-3680	Artifact
0004-3702	Artificial Intelligence
0004-3710	Artificial Kidney Bibliography see 0363-2369
0004-3729	Artificial Limbs†
0004-3737	Artigiano Modenese
0004-3745	Artigliere
0004-3753	Artigos Selecionados
0004-377X	Artikkelindeks Foer Bygg†
0004-3788	Artilleri-Tidskrift
0004-3796	Artillerie, Armee & Technik
0004-380X	Artillerie Rundschau†
0004-3818	Artilleriiskii Zhurnal
0004-3826	Artillery Journal
0004-3834	Artis
0004-3842	Artis
0004-3869	Artisan Staff Association Magazine changed to A S A Magazine
0004-3885	Artist
0004-3893	Artist Junior see 0004-3052
0004-3907	Artistes et Varietes
0004-3931	Arts and Activities
0004-394X	Arts and Sciences
0004-3958	Arts Asiatiques
0004-3966	Arts en Auto
0004-3974	Arts en Sociale Verzekering
0004-3982	Arts et Industries
0004-3990	Arts et Manufactures
0004-4008	Arts et Metiers
0004-4024	Arts in Society†
0004-4032	Arts in Virginia
0004-4059	Arts Magazine (New York)
0004-4067	Arts Management
0004-4083	Arts of Asia
0004-4091	Arts Review
0004-4113	Artscanada
0004-4121	Artweek
0004-413X	Arunodayam
0004-4148	Arx†
0004-4156	Aryan Path
0004-4164	Aryana
0004-4172	Arzneimittel-Forschung
0004-4180	Arzt in Niederoesterreich
0004-4202	As We Are†
0004-4210	Asahi Glass Company. Research Laboratory. Reports
0004-4229	Asbarez
0004-4237	Asbestos
0004-4245	Asbestos Worker
0004-4253	Asbury Seminarian
0004-427X	Ascent†
0004-4288	Aschehougs Leksikonservice†
0004-4296	Asecolda†
0004-430X	Aseguradores
0004-4318	Asfalt
0004-4326	Ashanti Times†
0004-4334	Ashford Advertiser
0004-4342	Achkhar
0004-4350	Ashland Dealer†
0004-4377	Ashtree Echo
0004-4385	Asi†
0004-4407	Asia (Bulletin)†
0004-4423	Asia Bulletin†
0004-4431	Asia Calling†
0004-444X	Asia Christian Colleges Association. Bulletin†
0004-4458	Asia Foundation Program Quarterly†
0004-4466	Asia Letter
0004-4474	Asia Magazine
0004-4482	Asia Major†
0004-4490	Asia Notebook changed to Japan Publications Guide
0004-4504	Asia Scene see 0300-4341
0004-4520	Asian Almanac
0004-4547	Asian Books Newsletter
0004-4555	Asian Economic Review
0004-458X	Asian Industry changed to Asian Business
0004-4598	Asian Institute of Technology. Newsletter changed to A I T Review
0004-4601	Asian Labour
0004-461X	Asian Medical Journal
0004-4628	Asian Outlook
0004-4636	Asian Printer†
0004-4644	Asian Recorder
0004-4652	Asian Review and Arts and Letters see 0038-2841
0004-4660	Asian Student†
0004-4679	Asian Studies
0004-4687	Asian Survey
0004-4695	Asiatic Research Bulletin†
0004-4709	Asiatic Society, Bombay. Journal
0004-4717	Asiatische Studien
0004-4725	Asie Nouvelle
0004-4741	Asociacion Argentina Criadores de Cerdos. Revista
0004-4768	Asociacion Bioquimica Argentina. Revista
0004-4776	Asociacion Colombiana de Facultades de Medicina. Cronica†
0004-4784	Asociacion Costarricense de Bibliotecarios. Boletin
0004-4792	Asociacion Cultural Humboldt. Boletin
0004-4806	Asociacion de Ex-Alumnos de la Escuela Nacional de Bibliotecarios. Boletin
0004-4814	Asociacion Franco-Mexicana de Ingenieros y Tecnicos. Boletin
0004-4822	Asociacion Geologica Argentina. Revista
0004-4830	Asociacion Medica Argentina. Revista
0004-4849	Asociacion Medica de Puerto Rico. Boletin
0004-4857	Asociacion Mexicana de Facultades y Escuelas de Medicina. Boletin
0004-4865	Asociacion Nacional de Industriales. Revista Trimestral changed to Asociación Nacional de Industriales. Revista Bimestral
0004-4873	Asociacion Numismatica Argentina. Revista
0004-4881	Asociacion Odontologica Argentina. Revista
0004-489X	Asociacion para Evitar la Ceguera en Mexico. Archivos
0004-4911	Aspect†
0004-4946	Aspetti Letterari
0004-4954	Asphalt†
0004-4962	Aspire
0004-4970	Asprenas
0004-4989	Assam Information
0004-4997	Assam Review and Tea News
0004-5004	Assay see 0147-6629
0004-5012	Assayad
0004-5020	Assegai
0004-5063	Assembly Engineering
0004-5071	Assessors Journal
0004-508X	Assessors News Letter/A N L changed to Assessment Digest
0004-5098	Assicurazione
0004-511X	Assicurazioni
0004-5128	Carnets de l'Enfance
0004-5136	Assignments in Management
0004-5144	Education Sanitaire et Nurtritionnelle d'Afrique Centrale
0004-5152	Assistant Librarian
0004-5187	Associacao Bahiana de Bibliotecarios. Informa
0004-5195	Associacao Brasileira de Pesquisas sobre Plantas Aromaticas e Oleos Essenciais. Boletim
0004-5209	Associacao Comercial de Lourenco Marques. Boletim†
0004-5217	Associacao Comercial do Amazonas. Boletim
0004-5225	Associacao Medica Brasileira. Boletim
0004-5233	Associacao Medica Brasileira. Jornal
0004-5241	Associacao Medica Brasileira. Revista
0004-525X	Associacao Medica de Minas Gerais. Revista
0004-5268	Associacao Medica do Rio Grande do Sul. Revista changed to Revista A M R I G S
0004-5276	Associacao Paulista de Cirurgioes Dentistas. Revista
0004-5292	Association and Society Manager
0004-5306	Association Canadienne d'Education. Bulletin
0004-5314	Association Canadienne des Bibliothecaires de Langue Francaise. Bulletin see 0315-2340
0004-5322	Association de Geographes Francais. Bulletin
0004-5349	Association des Anciens Eleves des Ecoles Techniques Superieures de Geneve. Bulletin Technique changed to Association des Anciens Eleves de l'Ecole d'Ingenieurs de Geneve. Bulletin Technique
0004-5365	Association des Bibliothecaires Francais. Bulletin d'Informations
0004-5381	Association des Instituteurs Reunis du Grand - Duche de Luxembourg. Bulletin changed to Ecole et Vie
0004-539X	Association des Medecins de Langue Francaise du Canada. Bulletin
0004-5403	Association for Asian Studies. Newsletter
0004-5411	Association for Computing Machinery. Journal
0004-542X	Association for Psychoanalytic Medicine. Bulletin

0004-5438 Association for Recorded Sound Collections Journal
0004-5446 Association for the Advancement of Medical Instrumentation. Journal (JAAMI) *see* 0090-6689
0004-5454 Association for the Study of Perception. Journal
0004-5462 Revue Technique des Industries du Cuir
0004-5497 Association Francaise pour l'Etude du Cancer. Bulletin *see* 0007-4551
0004-5500 Association Francaise pour l'Etude du Quaternaire. Bulletin
0004-5519 Association Generale des Medecins de France.Bulletin
0004-5527 Association Guillaume Bude. Bulletin
0004-5535 Art
0004-5543 Association Internationale des Numismates Professionels. Bulletin-Circular
0004-5551 Association Internationale d'Etudes du Sud-Est Europeen. Bulletin
0004-556X Association Internationale Permanente des Congres de la Route. Bulletin
0004-5586 Feuillets de l'ANAS *changed to* Revue Francaise de Service Social
0004-5608 Association of American Geographers. Annals
0004-5616 Association of American Medical Colleges. Bulletin†
0004-5624 Association of Broadcasting Staff Bulletin *see* 0306-7602
0004-5632 Annals of Clinical Biochemistry
0004-5640 Association of College and University Concert Managers. Bulletin *changed to* Association of College, University and Community Arts Administrators. Bulletin
0004-5659 Association of College Unions-International. Bulletin
0004-5667 Association of College Unions International. Union Wire
0004-5675 Association of Collegiate Schools of Planning. Bulletin
0004-5683 Association of Economic Geographers. Annals
0004-5691 Association of Engineering Geologists. Bulletin
0004-5713 Association of Engineers, Kerala State. Journal
0004-5721 Association of Food and Drug Officials of the United States. Quarterly Bulletin *see* 0195-4865
0004-573X Association of Marshall Scholars and Alumni. Newsletter *changed to* Marshall News
0004-5748 Association of Nova Scotia Land Surveyors *see* 0380-9242
0004-5756 Association of Official Analytical Chemists. Journal
0004-5764 Association of Official Seed Analysts. News Letter
0004-5772 Association of Physicians of India. Journal
0004-5780 Association of Public Analysts. Journal
0004-5799 Association of Public Passenger Transport Operators. Journal†
0004-5810 Association of Teachers of Japanese. Journal-Newsletter *changed to* Association of Teachers of Japanese. Journal
0004-5837 Association of the Bar of the City of New York. Record
0004-5845 Association of University Evening Colleges. Newsletter
0004-5853 Association of Urban Universities Newsletter
0004-5861 Association pour le Developpement International de l'Observatoire de Nice. Bulletin d'Information *changed to* Association pour le Developpement International de l'Observatoire de Nice. Bulletin
0004-587X Association Suisse des Electriciens. Bulletin
0004-5888 Association Technique de l'Industrie Papetiere. Feuillets Bibliographiques. *changed to* Centre Technique du Papier. Feuillets Bibliographiques
0004-5896 Association Technique de l'Industrie Papetiere. Revue
0004-590X Associazione degli Africanisti Italiani. Bollettino
0004-5918 Notiziario
0004-5934 Associazione Italiana Biblioteche. Bollettino d'Informazioni
0004-5950 Associazione Italiana Industriali Tintori Stampatori e Finitori Tessili. Notiziario
0004-5969 Associazione Italiana per l'Assistenza Agli Spastici. Notiziaro *changed to* Associazione Italiana Assistenza Spastici. Notiziaro
0004-5977 Associazione Italiana Veterinari per Piccoli Animali.Bollettino
0004-5985 Associazione Nazionale Ex Internati. Bollettino Ufficiale
0004-5993 Associazione Nazionale Mutilati e Invalidi di Guerra. Sezione di Roma. Notiziario
0004-6000 Associazione Romana di Entomologia. Bollettino
0004-6019 Assurance Francaise
0004-6027 Assurances
0004-6035 Assurances Banques Transports†
0004-6043 Assureur Conseil
0004-6051 Assyrian Star
0004-606X Aste Giudiziarie
0004-6078 Asti Informazioni Economiche
0004-6086 Astma- og Allergi-Nytt
0004-6094 Astra
0004-6108 Astra
0004-6116 Astrado
0004-6124 Astral Projection†
0004-6132 Astrolabio
0004-6140 Astrological Magazine
0004-6167 Astrologische Gids
0004-6175 Astrologischer Auskunftsbogen
0004-6183 Astrology
0004-6191 Astrology Guide
0004-6205 Astronautica Acta. *see* 0094-5765
0004-6213 Astronautics & Aeronautics
0004-623X Astronautyka
0004-6248 Bulletin of the Astronomical Institutes of Czechoslovakia
0004-6256 Astronomical Journal
0004-6264 Astronomical Society of Japan. Publications
0004-6272 Astronomical Society of the Pacific. Leaflet†
0004-6280 Astronomical Society of the Pacific. Publications
0004-6299 Astronomicheskii Zhurnal
0004-6302 Astronomie
0004-6310 Astronomie in der Schule
0004-6337 Astronomische Nachrichten
0004-6345 Astronomisk Tidsskrift
0004-6361 Astronomy and Astrophysics
0004-637X Astrophysical Journal
0004-6388 Astrophysical Letters
0004-6396 Astrophysics
0004-640X Astrophysics and Space Science
0004-6434 At Cooper Union
0004-6450 At Home with the South African Permanent†
0004-6469 New Packaging
0004-6477 Atem *see* 0341-3403
0004-6485 Atemschutz-Informationen†
0004-6493 Atene e Roma
0004-6507 Atenea *changed to* Nueva Atenea
0004-6523 Pre-Medico
0004-6531 Ateneo Parmense. Acta Bio-Medica
0004-654X Ateneo Parmense. Acta Naturalia
0004-6558 Ateneo Veneto
0004-6574 Athenaeum
0004-6590 Athenee
0004-6604 Athens Annals of Archaeology
0004-6612 Athens Chamber of Commerce and Industry. Monthly Bulletin
0004-6620 Institut Pasteur Hellenique. Archives
0004-6647 Athletic Director
0004-6655 Athletic Journal
0004-6663 Athletics Arena *changed to* Athletics Arena International
0004-6671 Athletics Weekly
0004-668X Atletiekwereld
0004-6698 Athletik
0004-6701 Atlanta
0004-671X Atlanta Economic Review *see* 0163-531X
0004-6736 Atlante
0004-6744 Atlantic Advocate
0004-6752 Atlantic Baptist
0004-6760 Atlantic Community Quarterly
0004-6787 Atlantic Mirror†
0004-6795 Atlantic Monthly
0004-6809 Atlantic Naturalist†
0004-6817 Atlantic Observer-Knickbocker International†
0004-6825 Atlantic Provinces Inter-University Committee on the Sciences. Newsletter
0004-6833 Atlantic Psychologist†
0004-6841 Atlantic Report
0004-6868 Atlantic Truck Transport Review
0004-6914 Marine/Atlantische Welt†
0004-6922 Atlas *changed to* Atlas-Air France
0004-6930 Atlas *see* 0161-6528
0004-6965 Atmanirvrithi
0004-6973 Atmosphere *see* 0705-5900
0004-6981 Atmospheric Environment
0004-699X Air Pollution Abstracts†
0004-7007 Atoka
0004-7015 Atom
0004-7023 Atom
0004-7031 Atom-Informationen
0004-7058 Atom News
0004-7066 Atom und Strom
0004-7074 Atomic Absorption and Flame Emission Spectroscopy Abstracts *see* 0309-1813
0004-7082 Atomic Data *see* 0092-640X
0004-7090 Atomic Energy in Australia
0004-7104 Atomic Energy Law Journal
0004-7112 Atomic Energy Review
0004-7120 Atomic Energy Society of Japan. Journal
0004-7139 I N I S Atomindex
0004-7147 Atomkernenergie *see* 0171-5747
0004-7155 ATOMKI Kozlemenyek
0004-7163 Atomnaya Energiya
0004-7171 Atomo e Industria
0004-718X Atomo Petrolio Elettricita
0004-7198 Kerntechnik *see* 0171-5747
0004-7201 Izotoptechnika
0004-721X Atomwirtschaft *see* 0365-8414
0004-7228 Atoomenergie en Haar Toepassingen *changed to* Energie-Spectrum
0004-7244 Att Bo
0004-7252 Attentie Met Oog en Oor *changed to* Attentie
0004-7279 Atterraggio Forzato
0004-7287 Societa degli Ingegneri e degli Architetti in Torino. Atti e Rassegna Tecnica
0004-7309 Attualita di Laboratorio
0004-7317 Attualita di Ostetricia e Ginecologia
0004-7325 Attualita Mediche
0004-7333 Attualita Mondiali *changed to* Informozioni e Attualita Mondiali
0004-7341 Atuagagdliutit
0004-7368 Actualides Pernambucanas
0004-7376 Au Fil du Rail
0004-7384 Au Grand Air
0004-7392 Auberge de la Jeunesse
0004-7414 Auburn Pharmacist
0004-7422 Auckland City Art Gallery Quarterly†
0004-7430 Auckland Rugby League. League News
0004-7449 Auckland Star
0004-7465 Auctioneer
0004-7473 Audecibel
0004-7481 Audenshaw Papers
0004-749X Audience†
0004-7503 Audience†
0004-7546 Audio Amateur
0004-7554 Audio Engineering Society. Journal
0004-7570 Audio Visual Journal
0004-7589 Audio-Visual Language Journal
0004-7597 Educational Media International
0004-7600 Audiovizualis Kozlemenyek
0004-7619 Audiotecnica
0004-7627 Audiovisivi
0004-7635 Audiovisual Instruction *see* 0196-6979
0004-7651 Auditor
0004-7686 American Birds
0004-7694 Audubon Magazine
0004-7708 Auerbach Computer Characteristics Digest *see* 0361-2783
0004-7716 Auerbach Computer Notebook International†
0004-7724 Auerbach Data Communications Reports
0004-7732 Auerbach Data Handling Reports†
0004-7740 Auerbach Graphic Processing Reports†
0004-7759 Auerbach Minicomputer Reports *changed to* Auerbach General Purpose Minicomputer Reports
0004-7775 Auerbach Software Reports *changed to* Auerbach Applications Software Reports
0004-7775 Auerbach Software Reports *changed to* Auerbach Systems Software Reports
0004-7783 Auerbach Standard E D P Reports
0004-7791 Auerbach Time Sharing Reports
0004-7805 Aufbau
0004-7813 Aufbau
0004-7821 Aufbau
0004-783X Aufbereitungs-Technik
0004-7848 Aufbruch
0004-7864 Der Aufstieg
0004-7872 Auftrag
0004-7880 Auftrag
0004-7899 Ran
0004-7902 Der Augenarzt
0004-7910 Augenoptik
0004-7929 Der Augenoptiker
0004-7937 Der Augenspiegel
0004-7945 Augsburg Echo
0004-7953 Augsburg in Zahlen
0004-7961 Augsburger Kulturnachrichten
0004-797X Augusta Magazine
0004-7988 Augustan
0004-7996 Augustana College Bulletin
0004-8003 Augustiniana
0004-8011 Augustinianum
0004-802X Augustinus
0004-8038 Auk
0004-8046 Aum *changed to* Aum: the Message of Sri Chinmoy
0004-8054 Aural News
0004-8062 Aurea Parma
0004-8070 Auricle
0004-8089 Aurora
0004-8097 Ausbau *changed to* Technik Heute
0004-8100 Der Ausbilder
0004-8119 Ausblick
0004-8127 Ausgrabungen und Funde
0004-8135 Auslandsreisen
0004-8143 Ausonia
0004-816X Austria. Statistisches Zentralamt. Aussenhandel Oesterreichs
0004-8178 Aussenhandelsdienst
0004-8186 Der Aussenhandelskaufmann
0004-8194 Aussenpolitik
0004-8208 Aussenpolitische Korrespondenz
0004-8216 Aussenwirtschaft
0004-8232 Aussenwirtschaftsdienst des Betriebs-Berater *see* 0340-7926
0004-8240 Aussprache†
0004-8259 Aussteuer Bett und Couch *changed to* Haustex
0004-8267 Austin Dental News *changed to* Tenth Times
0004-8275 Austral News *changed to* Australian Trading News
0004-8283 Australian Citrus News
0004-8291 Australian and New Zealand Journal of Medicine
0004-8305 Australasian Baker & Millers' Journal *see* 0311-1385
0004-8313 Australasian Beekeeper
0004-8321 Australasian Catholic Record
0004-833X Australasian Corrosion Engineering
0004-8356 Australasian Grocer *see* 0156-0352
0004-8364 Australasian Institute of Mining and Metallurgy. Proceedings

0004-8372 Australasian Insurance and Banking Record *changed to* Insurance Record of Australia & New Zealand
0004-8380 Australasian Journal of Dermatology
0004-8399 Australasian Journal of Pharmacy *changed to* Australian Journal of Pharmacy
0004-8402 Australasian Journal of Philosophy
0004-8437 Australasian Post
0004-8453 Australasian Printer
0004-8461 Australasian Radiology
0004-847X Australasian Soft Drink Journal *changed to* Beverage Review
0004-8488 Australasian Sportsgoods and Toy Retailer
0004-8496 Australasian Stamp Collector
0004-850X A N Z Bank Business Indicators
0004-8526 Australia. Bureau of Statistics. Western Australian Office. Building Operations
0004-8534 Australia. Commonwealth Bureau of Census and Statistics. Western Australian Office. Building Permits and Approvals *changed to* Australia. Bureau of Statistics. Western Australian Office. Building Approvals
0004-8542 Australia. Bureau of Statistics. Western Australian Office. Monthly Statistical Summary *changed to* Australia. Bureau of Statistics. Western Australian Office. Monthly Summary of Statistics
0004-8577 Australia. Bureau of Statistics. Quarterly Estimates of National Income and Expenditure
0004-8585 Australia. Bureau of Statistics. Western Australian Office. Quarterly Statistical Abstract†
0004-8607 Australia International†
0004-8615 Australia Newsletter
0004-8623 Australian Academic and Research Libraries
0004-8631 Australian Accountant
0004-8658 Australian and New Zealand Journal of Criminology
0004-8666 Australian and New Zealand Journal of Obstetrics and Gynecology
0004-8674 Australian & New Zealand Journal of Psychiatry
0004-8682 Australian and New Zealand Journal of Surgery
0004-8690 Australian & New Zealand Journal of Sociology
0004-8704 Australian Antique Collector
0004-8712 V A C C Journal
0004-8720 Australian Automotive Engineering and Equipment *changed to* Automotive Engineer
0004-8739 Australian Baptist
0004-8747 Australian Bird Bander *see* 0155-0438
0004-8755 Australian Book Review
0004-8763 Australian Bookseller and Publisher
0004-8771 Australian Bride Magazine
0004-878X Australian Builder
0004-8798 Australian Building Science and Technology
0004-8801 Australian Business Communications†
0004-881X Australian Ceramic Society. Journal
0004-8828 Australian Chemical Engineering
0004-8836 Australian Chemical Processing & Engineering *changed to* P A C E
0004-8844 Australian Children Limited *see* 0313-6620
0004-8852 Australian Christian
0004-8887 Australian Coin Review
0004-8895 Australian College of Dental Surgeons. Annals. *changed to* Royal Australasian College of Dental Surgeons. Annals
0004-8909 Australian College of Speech Therapists. Journal *changed to* Australian Journal of Human Communication Disorders
0004-8917 Australian Computer Journal
0004-8941 Australian Credit Manager *changed to* Credit Review
0004-895X Australian Cricket *changed to* Australian Cricket Newspaper
0004-8992 Australian Economic History Review
0004-900X Australian Economic Papers
0004-9018 Australian Economic Review
0004-9026 Australian Education Index
0004-9034 Australian Electrical World *changed to* Australian Electrical World (1980)
0004-9042 Australian Electronics Engineering
0004-9050 Australian Entomological Society. Journal
0004-9069 Australian External Territories†
0004-9077 Australian Family Safety
0004-9085 Australian Fashion News *see* 0312-0325
0004-9093 Australian Economic News†
0004-9107 Australian Fish Trades Review
0004-9115 Australian Fisheries
0004-9123 Australian Flying
0004-9131 Australian Food Manufacturer and Distributor†
0004-914X Australian Forest Research
0004-9158 Australian Forestry
0004-9166 Australian Gas Journal
0004-9174 Australian Gemmologist
0004-9182 Australian Geographer
0004-9190 Australian Geographical Studies
0004-9204 Australian Gliding
0004-9212 Australian Golf *changed to* Australian Golf (1978)
0004-9239 Australian Grapegrower *changed to* Australian Grapegrower & Winemaker
0004-9263 Australian Harness Sport
0004-928X Australian Home Beautiful
0004-9298 Australian Home Journal
0004-9301 Australian Hot Rodding Review†
0004-931X Australian House and Garden
0004-9328 Australian Humanist†
0004-9344 A.I.A.S. Newsletter
0004-9352 Australian Institute of Metals. Journal *see* 0160-7952
0004-9360 Australian Jewish Historical Society. Journal and Proceedings
0004-9379 Australian Jewish News
0004-9387 Australian Journal of Adult Education
0004-9395 Australian Journal of Agricultural Economics
0004-9409 Australian Journal of Agricultural Research
0004-9417 Australian Journal of Biological Sciences
0004-9425 Australian Journal of Chemistry
0004-9433 Australian Journal of Dairy Technology
0004-9441 Australian Journal of Education
0004-945X Australian Journal of Experimental Biology and Medical Science
0004-9468 Australian Journal of French Studies
0004-9484 Australian Journal of Music Education
0004-9492 Australian Journal of Physical Education *see* 0312-827X
0004-9506 Australian Journal of Physics
0004-9514 Australian Journal of Physiotherapy
0004-9522 Australian Journal of Politics and History
0004-9530 Australian Journal of Psychology
0004-9549 Search
0004-9557 Australian Journal of Social Issues
0004-9565 Australian Journal of Social Work *see* 0312-407X
0004-9573 Australian Journal of Soil Research
0004-9581 Australian Journal of Statistics
0004-959X Australian Journal of Zoology
0004-9611 Australian Law Journal
0004-962X Australian Leather Journal, Boot and Shoe Recorder
0004-9638 Australian Left Review
0004-9646 Australian Legal Monthly Digest
0004-9654 Australian Liberal
0004-9662 Communion
0004-9689 Australian Library News†
0004-9697 Australian Literary Studies
0004-9700 Australian Lithographer *changed to* Australian Lithographer, Printer, and Packager
0004-9719 Australian Machinery and Production Engineering
0004-9727 Australian Mathematical Society. Bulletin
0004-9735 Australian Mathematical Society. Journal *changed to* Australian Mathematical Society. Journal. Series A
0004-9743 Australian Meteorological Magazine
0004-9751 Australian Mineral Industry. Quarterly Review
0004-976X Australian Mining
0004-9808 Australian Municipal Journal
0004-9816 Australian National Bibliography
0004-9832 Australian National University News
0004-9840 Australian Natural History
0004-9867 Australian Newsagent and Stationer
0004-9875 Australian Numismatic Journal
0004-9883 Australian Numismatic Society. Report
0004-9891 Australian Official Journal of Patents, Trade Marks, and Designs
0004-9905 Australian Outdoors
0004-9913 Australian Outlook
0004-9921 Australian Packaging
0004-993X Australian Paediatric Journal
0004-9956 Australian Parks *see* 0311-8223
0004-9964 Australian Photography
0004-9972 Australian Physicist
0004-9980 Australian Pistol Shooters' Bulletin
0005-0008 Australian Plants
0005-0016 Australian Plastics and Rubber Journal†
0005-0024 Australian Police Journal
0005-0059 Australian Presbyterian Life
0005-0067 Australian Psychologist
0005-0075 Australian Public Affairs Information Service
0005-0083 Australian Purchasing
0005-0091 Australian Quarterly
0005-0105 Australian Railway Historical Society. Bulletin
0005-0113 Australian Rationalist
0005-0148 Australian Refrigeration, Air Conditioning and Heating
0005-0164 Australian Road Research
0005-0180 Australian Safety News
0005-0199 Australian School Librarian
0005-0229 Australian Science Index
0005-0237 Australian Seacraft
0005-0245 Australian Shooters Journal
0005-0253 Australian Skindivers
0005-0261 Australian Society of Accountants. Bulletin
0005-0296 Australian Stamp Monthly
0005-030X Australian Student†
0005-0318 Australian Sugar Journal
0005-0326 Australian Surveyor
0005-0334 Australian Teacher of the Deaf
0005-0342 Australian Temperance Advocate *changed to* Temperance Advocate
0005-0350 Australian Thoroughbreds
0005-0369 Australian Timber Journal and Building Products Merchandiser *changed to* Australian Forest Industries Journal
0005-0377 Australian Tradition†
0005-0385 Australian Transport
0005-0393 Australian Traveller†
0005-0407 Australian Trotting Register
0005-0415 Australian University†
0005-0431 Australian Welding Journal
0005-044X Australian Wine, Brewing & Spirit Review†
0005-0458 Australian Women's Weekly
0005-0474 Australia's Neighbors *changed to* Dyason House Papers
0005-0482 Australijas Latvietis
0005-0490 Austria Export
0005-0504 I F E F, Austria Sekcio. Bulteno
0005-0512 Austria-Philatelist
0005-0520 Austrian Information
0005-0539 Austro-Motor
0005-0555 Austroflug
0005-0563 Austropack
0005-0571 Auszuege aus den Gebrauchsmustern
0005-058X Auszuege aus den Patentanmeldungen *changed to* Auszuege aus den Auslegeschriften
0005-0598 Auszuege aus Presseartikeln
0005-0601 Aut Aut
0005-0628 Author
0005-0652 Authority in Crisis†
0005-0660 Authorship
0005-0695 Autospark
0005-0709 Auto Age
0005-0717 Auto and Flat Glass Journal
0005-0725 Auto Club News Pictorial
0005-0733 Auto Dealers' Digest
0005-0768 Auto-Journal
0005-0776 Auto Laundry News
0005-0792 Auto-Motor
0005-0822 Auto Racing†
0005-0830 Autorevue
0005-0857 Auto-Technik
0005-0865 Auto Trim News
0005-0873 Autovisie
0005-0881 Auto-Volt
0005-089X Auto-Writing *changed to* I I S T Bulletins
0005-0903 Autoaccessorio
0005-0911 Autobody and the Reconditioned Car
0005-092X Autocar
0005-0938 Autocar et Cargo Routier†
0005-0946 Autoclub
0005-0954 Autoclub
0005-0962 Autoclub & Via *changed to* Via!
0005-0989 Autohaus
0005-0997 Autokampioen
0005-1004 Autolinea†
0005-1012 Automat
0005-1020 Automated Education Letter†
0005-1039 Automaten-Markt
0005-1047 Automatic Control *see* 0146-4116
0005-1055 Automatic Documentation and Mathematical Linguistics
0005-1071 Automatic Machining
0005-108X Automatic Welding
0005-1098 Automatica
0005-1101 Automatica si Electronica *changed to* Electrotehnica, Electronica si Automatica. Automatica si Electronica
0005-1128 Automatie
0005-1136 Automatik *see* 0026-0339
0005-1152 Automation
0005-1160 Automation *see* 0146-1737
0005-1179 Automation and Remote Control
0005-1187 Automation Council News
0005-1225 Automation Journal of Japan *changed to* A M J Newsletter
0005-1233 Automatisch-Verkaufen†
0005-1241 Automatisme *changed to* Nouvel Automatisme
0005-125X Automatizace
0005-1268 Automatizacija Poslovanja
0005-1284 Automazione e Strumentazione
0005-1292 Automatic Monitoring & Measuring
0005-1306 Automobil-Industrie
0005-1314 Revue Automobile
0005-1330 Automobile
0005-1349 Automobile
0005-1357 Automobile Abstracts *see* 0309-0817
0005-1373 Automobile Club di Milano. Notiziario Economico
0005-139X Automobile in Southern Africa *see* 0304-8721
0005-1403 Automobile India
0005-1411 Automobile Law Reports Insurance Decisions
0005-142X Automobile News
0005-1438 Automobile Quarterly
0005-1454 Automobilismo e Automobilismo Industriale
0005-1462 Automobilist *changed to* Away
0005-1470 Automotive Age (1978)
0005-1489 Automotive Chain Store
0005-1497 Automotive Cooling Journal
0005-1500 Automotive Design Engineering *see* 0307-6490
0005-1519 Automotive Fleet
0005-1527 Automotive Industries *changed to* Chilton's Automotive Industries
0005-1543 Automotive Market Report and Auto Week
0005-1551 Automotive News
0005-156X Automotive News of the Pacific Northwest

ISSN INDEX

ISSN	Title
0005-1578	Automotive Retailer
0005-1586	Automotive Service
0005-1594	Automobile International
0005-1608	Automotor
0005-1616	Automovil de Venezuela
0005-1659	Autoparade†
0005-1683	Autorama
0005-1691	Auto Revista
0005-1713	Autorevue
0005-173X	Autosport
0005-1748	Autosprint
0005-1756	Autostrade
0005-1772	Autotoerist
0005-1780	Autotransportes "Tres Estrellas de Oro"
0005-1799	Autoveteranen
0005-1802	Autoweek
0005-1810	Autowelt†
0005-1829	Autoworld
0005-1845	Auvergne Litteraire†
0005-1853	Auxiliaire des Fabricants de Cartonnages, Transformateurs de Papier, Industries et Arts Graphiques *changed to* Cartonnages et Complexes
0005-1861	Volunteer Leader
0005-1888	Avalanche†
0005-1896	Avances en Alimentacion y Mejora Animal
0005-190X	Avant-Garde†
0005-1918	Avant Garde
0005-1926	Avant Gardener
0005-1934	A M
0005-1942	A. D. Correspondence
0005-1950	Avedik
0005-1969	Avenirs
0005-1977	Aventure Sous-Marine
0005-1985	Avenue
0005-1993	Aves
0005-2027	Avia
0005-2035	Avia
0005-2043	Avia Aeroespacial
0005-206X	Aviacao e Astronautica *changed to* Aviacao em Revista
0005-2078	Aviacion
0005-2086	Avian Diseases
0005-2094	Aviasport
0005-2108	Aviation et Astronautique *changed to* La Conquete de l'Air-Aviastro
0005-2116	National Aeronautics†
0005-2124	Aviation Historical Society of New Zealand. Journal
0005-2132	Aviation Magazine International
0005-2140	Aviation Mechanics Bulletin
0005-2159	Aviation Reports
0005-2167	Aviation Studies International. Official Price List
0005-2175	Aviation Week & Space Technology
0005-2183	Aviatsiya i Kosmonavtika
0005-2205	Aviazione di Linea Difesa e Spazio *changed to* Aviazione
0005-2213	Avicoltura *changed to* Rivista di Avicoltura
0005-2221	Aviculteur Quebecois
0005-223X	Avicultura
0005-2248	Avicultura Brasileira
0005-2264	Avio-Nieuws *see* 0017-6818
0005-2272	Avion
0005-2280	Avis-Kronik-Index *see* 0106-147X
0005-2299	Labour and National Insurance
0005-2302	Avtomaticheskaya Svarka
0005-2310	Avtomatika i Telemekhanika
0005-2329	Avtomatika, Telemekhanika i Svyaz
0005-2337	Avtomobil'naya Promyshlennost'
0005-2345	Avtomobil'nyi Transport
0005-2353	Avtomobil'nye Dorogi
0005-2361	Avvenire Agricolo (Parma)
0005-237X	Awake
0005-2388	Awakener
0005-2426	Axial
0005-2442	Ayrshire Cattle Society's Journal
0005-2450	Ayrshire Digest
0005-2469	Ayu
0005-2477	Ayurved Vikas
0005-2485	Ayurveda-Bharati
0005-2493	Ayurveda Doot
0005-2515	Azad Mazdur
0005-2523	Azerbaidzhan Tibb Zhurnaly
0005-2531	Azerbaidzhanskii Khimicheskii Zhurnal
0005-254X	Azimut
0005-2558	Azione
0005-2566	Azione Cooperativa
0005-2574	Aziya i Afrika Segodnya
0005-2590	Aztec Engineer†
0005-2604	Aztlan *changed to* Aztlan-International Journal of Chicano Studies Research
0005-2612	B A C I E Journal
0005-2639	B A G-Nachrichten
0005-2647	B A R C News
0005-2655	B A S F Review†
0005-2671	B A S R A Journal
0005-268X	B & T
0005-2698	B-U Nachrichten
0005-2701	B & Z†
0005-2728	B B A-Bioenergetics
0005-2736	B B A-Biomembranes
0005-2744	B B A-Enzymology
0005-2760	B B A-Lipids & Lipid Metabolism
0005-2779	B. B. A. Nieuws†
0005-2787	B B A-Nucleic Acids and Protein Synthesis
0005-2795	B B A-Protein Structure
0005-2809	B B B Tribune
0005-2817	British Broadcasting Corporation. B B C Engineering
0005-2825	B B C-Nachrichten
0005-2833	Bokrevy
0005-2868	B C I R A Abstracts of Foundry Literature *see* 0141-2930
0005-2876	B C L A Reporter
0005-2884	B. C. Motorist *changed to* Westworld
0005-2892	B. C. Power Engineer
0005-2906	B. C. Professional Engineer
0005-2930	B. C. Sports & Recreation Magazine†
0005-2949	B. C. Studies
0005-2957	B. C. Teacher
0005-2965	British Columbia Teachers' Federation. Newsletter
0005-2981	B D K-Mitteilungen†
0005-299X	B D V-Dienst Niedersachsen†
0005-3015	B. E. A. Bulletin
0005-3023	B E A Magazine *changed to* Topline
0005-3031	B E F A-Mitteilungen
0005-304X	B E M A Bulletin
0005-3066	B. H. P. Review
0005-3074	B. H. P. Technical Bulletin
0005-3082	B I B-Liner
0005-3090	B I C C Bulletin†
0005-3112	B I I L
0005-3120	Bibliotheque de Travail Junior
0005-3147	B I N O P Bulletin *changed to* Orientation Scolaire et Professionnelle
0005-3155	B I O S
0005-3163	B. I. R. E
0005-318X	B I T S
0005-3198	B L M
0005-3201	B M/E
0005-3228	B N A Policy & Practice Series
0005-3252	B.O.A.C. Review *changed to* British Airways News
0005-3279	B R A Review
0005-3287	Betriebssicherheit - B S
0005-3295	B S C S Newsletter†
0005-3295	B S C S Newsletter *see* 0162-3613
0005-3309	B. S. I. News
0005-3317	B. S. I. Quarterly *changed to* Building Societies Institute. Journal
0005-3325	B S P Magazine
0005-3333	B S R
0005-3341	B S S R Quarterly Newsletter *changed to* B S S R Newsletter
0005-335X	Bibliotheque de Travail
0005-3368	B T A/Buerotechnik und Automation *changed to* Buerotechnik Automation und Organisation
0005-3376	B T E-Werbedienst *changed to* B T E Marketing-Berater
0005-3392	B T O News
0005-3414	Bibliotheque de Travail 2d Degre
0005-3430	B V A Bulletin
0005-3457	B V N. Boletin Informativo
0005-3465	B Z
0005-3473	B Z B
0005-3503	Babel
0005-3538	Babson Alumni Bulletin *changed to* Babson Bulletin
0005-3546	Babson's Washington Service *changed to* Babson's Washington Service
0005-3554	Baby & Junior
0005-3562	Baby & Tiener†
0005-3570	Baby Care
0005-3589	Baby Talk *changed to* Baby Talk Magazine
0005-3597	Bacchus Journal
0005-3600	Bach
0005-3635	Back Stage
0005-3643	Back to Godhead
0005-366X	Backstretch
0005-3678	Bacteriological Reviews *see* 0146-0749
0005-3686	Bad und Kueche†
0005-3708	Bad Homburger Veranstaltungsspiegel Kurzeitung
0005-3724	Baden-Wuerttembergisches Verwaltungsblat *see* 0340-3505
0005-3740	Badger Farm Bureau News
0005-3759	Badger History
0005-3767	Badger Legionnaire
0005-3775	Badger Sportsman
0005-3783	Badia Greca di Grottaferrata. Bollettino
0005-3791	Badminton
0005-3805	Badminton Gazette
0005-3821	Archaeographie
0005-383X	Baecker und Konditor
0005-3848	Baender, Bleche, Rohre
0005-3856	Baessler Archiv
0005-3864	Det Baesta ur Reader's Digest (Swedish Edition)
0005-3872	Baeuerlicher Ratgeber†
0005-3880	Bagdala
0005-3899	Baghdad Chamber of Commerce. Weekly Bulletin
0005-3902	Baghdad Observer
0005-3910	Bagin
0005-3929	Bagolah
0005-3937	Bagvertising Weekly
0005-3945	Baha'i-Briefe†
0005-3953	Bahamas
0005-3961	Bahamas Weekly and Nassau Tourist News *changed to* Nassau and Paradise Island.Tourist News
0005-397X	Bahamian Review
0005-3988	Bahana
0005-3996	Hadshot Hahistadrut
0005-4003	Baileya
0005-4011	Bajan & South Caribbean
0005-402X	Bakelite Review†
0005-4054	Baker, Confectioner, Caterer *see* 0005-4100
0005-4062	Baker-Konditor
0005-4070	Baker Street Journal
0005-4089	Bakers Digest
0005-4097	Bakers Journal
0005-4100	Bakers Review
0005-4119	Bakers Weekly *see* 0005-4127
0005-4127	Bakery Production and Marketing
0005-4135	New Student Baker *changed to* Student Baker
0005-4143	Baking Research Association. Abstracts *see* 0300-421X
0005-4151	Baking Industries Journal
0005-416X	Baking Industry
0005-4178	Bakkersvakblad *changed to* Bakker
0005-4186	Baksteen
0005-4194	Bal Bharati
0005-4208	Bal Sandesh
0005-4216	Balance
0005-4224	Balance of Payments Reports
0005-4232	Balance Sheet
0005-4240	Banque Populaire Suisse. Balance Sheet Prospectus
0005-4259	Balans
0005-4267	Balcony Square
0005-4275	Balde Branco
0005-4283	Bulgarski Ezik
0005-4291	Baljivan
0005-4313	Balkan Studies
0005-433X	Ball State University Forum
0005-4348	Ballet-Who *see* 0705-8063
0005-4356	E M U Faculty-Staff News. Library Supplement *changed to* Eastern Michigan University Faculty-Staff News. Center of Educational Resources Supplement
0005-4364	Ballon Kurier
0005-4380	Ballroom Dancing Times
0005-4399	Ballsout
0005-4402	Balneologia Polska
0005-4410	Balon
0005-447X	Baltimore Bulletin of Education†
0005-4488	Baltimore City Public Schools Staff Newsletter and Community Newsletter *changed to* Baltimore City Public Schools Staff Newsletter
0005-4496	Baltimore Engineer
0005-450X	Baltimore Jewish Times
0005-4518	Baltimore Museum of Art Record†
0005-4526	Baltische Briefe
0005-4534	Baltische Hefte
0005-4542	Bama'arakha
0005-4550	Chambre de Commerce et d'Industrie du Mali. Circulaire Mensuelle d'Information *changed to* Chambre de Commerce et d'Industrie du Mali. Bulletin Trimestriel
0005-4569	Bamat Hatzarkhan†
0005-4577	Israel. Ministry of Agriculture. Department of Fisheries. Bamidgeh
0005-4585	Banas
0005-4593	Banca d'Italia. Bollettino
0005-4607	Banca Nazionale del Lavoro. Quarterly Review
0005-4615	Banca y Comercio
0005-4623	Bancaria
0005-4631	Bancni Vestnik
0005-464X	Banco Central de Chile. Boletin Mensual
0005-4658	Banco Central de Costa Rica. Revista†
0005-4666	Banco Central de Honduras. Revista Trimestral†
0005-4674	Banco Central de la Republica Argentina. Boletin Estadistico
0005-4682	Banco Central de la Republica Dominicana. Boletin Mensual
0005-4690	Banco Central de Nicaragua. Boletin Trimestral *changed to* Banco Central de Nicaragua. Boletin Anual
0005-4704	Banco Central de Reserva de El Salvador. Revista Mensual
0005-4712	Banco Central de Reserva del Peru. Boletin
0005-4720	Banco Central de Venezuela. Revista
0005-4739	Banco Central del Ecuador. Boletin
0005-4747	Banco Central del Uruguay. Boletin Estadistico Mensual
0005-4755	Banco Central del Uruguay. Seleccion de Temas Economicos
0005-4763	Banco Central do Brasil. Boletim
0005-478X	Banco de Angola. Boletim Trimestral†
0005-4798	Banco de Espana. Boletin Estadistico
0005-4801	Banco de Fomento Nacional. Boletim de Informacao†
0005-481X	Banco de Guatemala. Boletin Estadistico
0005-4828	Banco de la Republica. Revista
0005-4844	Economia y Finanzas
0005-4852	Banco de Vizcaya. Noticiario Economico
0005-4860	Banco di Sicilia. Informazioni Sulla Congiuntura
0005-4879	Banco do Brasil. Boletim
0005-4887	Banco Nacional Ultramarino. Boletim Trimestral†
0005-4909	Band
0005-4917	Band†
0005-4925	Band- und Flechtindustrie
0005-4933	Band Journal
0005-4968	Bandwagon
0005-4976	Baner Ac Amserau Cymru *changed to* Y Faner
0005-4984	Bangkok Bank. Monthly Review
0005-4992	Banif's Investment Bulletin
0005-500X	Banijya Barta
0005-5018	Bank- en Effectenbedrijf
0005-5026	Bank and Quotation Record
0005-5034	Bank-Betrieb *changed to* Die Bank
0005-5042	Bank Board Letter

ISSN	Title
0005-5050	Bank Equipment News see 0146-0900
0005-5069	Bank Installment Lending Newsletter
0005-5077	Bank Karamchari
0005-5085	Der Bankkaufmann
0005-5093	Bank Markazi Iran Bulletin
0005-5115	Bank Negara Malaysia. Quarterly Economic Bulletin changed to Bank Negara Malaysia. Bulletin Ekonomi Suku Tahunan/Quarterly Economic Bulletin
0005-5123	Bank News
0005-5131	Bank Notes
0005-514X	Bank of Canada Statistical Summary see 0045-1460
0005-5158	Bank of Canada Weekly Financial Statistics
0005-5166	Bank of England Quarterly Bulletin
0005-5174	Bank of Finland. Monthly Bulletin
0005-5182	Bank of Ghana. Quarterly Economic Bulletin
0005-5190	Bank of Greece. Monthly Statistical Bulletin
0005-5204	Bank of Hawaii Monthly Review
0005-5212	Bank of India. Bulletin
0005-5220	Bank of Israel. Bulletin changed to Bank of Israel. Economic Review
0005-5239	Bank of Jamaica. Bulletin
0005-5247	Bank of Japan. Economic Statistics Monthly
0005-5263	Bank of Korea. Monthly Statistical Review changed to Bank of Korea. Monthly Economic Statistics
0005-5271	Bank of Libya. Economic Research Division. Economic Bulletin
0005-528X	Bank of London & South America. Revista Mensual†
0005-5298	Bank of London and South America Review
0005-5301	Bank of Mauritius. Quarterly Review
0005-531X	Bank of Montreal Business Review
0005-5328	Bank of Nova Scotia. Monthly Review
0005-5336	Bank of Sudan. Economic and Financial Bulletin changed to Bank of Sudan. Economic and Financial Statistics Review
0005-5344	Bank of Taiwan Quarterly
0005-5352	Bank of Thailand. Monthly Bulletin changed to Bank of Thailand. Quarterly Bulletin
0005-5360	Bank of Tokyo Semiannual Report changed to Bank of Tokyo Annual Report
0005-5379	Bank of Tokyo Weekly Review changed to Tokyo Financial Review
0005-5387	Bank One
0005-5395	Banker
0005-5409	Banker & Tradesman
0005-5417	Bankers Digest changed to Special Office Brief
0005-5425	Bankers Digest
0005-5433	Banker's Letter of the Law
0005-5441	Bankers' Magazine
0005-545X	Bankers Magazine
0005-5468	Bankers' Magazine of Australasia
0005-5484	Banketbakkerij
0005-5492	Banking changed to A B A Banking Journal
0005-5506	Banking Law Journal
0005-5514	Banking News changed to Maryland Banking Quarterly
0005-5522	Bankinsurance News
0005-5530	Bankruptcy Law Reports
0005-5549	Bankvaerlden
0005-5557	Banner
0005-5565	Banneret
0005-5573	Bano
0005-5581	Banque
0005-559X	Banque Centrale des Etats de l'Afrique de l'Ouest. Notes d'Information et Statistiques
0005-5603	Banque de Port-Said. Revue Economique Trimestrielle
0005-5611	Banque Nationale de Belgique. Bulletin
0005-562X	Banque Nationale de Paris. Revue†
0005-5662	Bantu Education Journal
0005-5670	Banyaszati es Kohaszati Lapok - Kohaszat
0005-5689	Baptist Bulletin
0005-5697	Baptist Challenge
0005-5700	Baptist Herald
0005-5719	Baptist History and Heritage
0005-5727	Baptist Leader
0005-5735	Indiana Baptist Observer
0005-5743	Baptist Program
0005-5751	Baptist Progress
0005-576X	Baptist Quarterly
0005-5778	Baptist Record
0005-5786	Baptist Times
0005-5794	Baptist Witness
0005-5808	Baptist World
0005-5816	N A B E News†
0005-5824	Bar Examiner
0005-5840	Bar-Server†
0005-5859	Barat Review†
0005-5859	Barat Review
0005-5867	Baraza
0005-5883	Barba
0005-5891	Barbados Museum and Historical Society. Journal
0005-5913	Barclays Trade Review see 0250-2402
0005-5921	Barco Pesquero†
0005-593X	Observer
0005-5948	Bardic Echoes
0005-5956	Barid Hollanda
0005-5972	Barke†
0005-5980	Barmer Ersatzkasse changed to Die Barmer
0005-5999	Barmherzigkeit
0005-6006	Barn i Hem-Skola-Samhaelle
0005-6014	Barnard Bulletin
0005-6049	Baromfiipar changed to Baromfitenyesztes es Feldolgozas
0005-6073	Barron's
0005-609X	Baseball Digest
0005-6103	Basic Journal Abstracts†
0005-6111	Basilicata
0005-6138	Basis
0005-6146	Basis
0005-6154	Basketbal
0005-6162	Basketball
0005-6170	Basketball Weekly
0005-6189	Basler Predigten
0005-6197	Basse Normandie Automobile
0005-6200	Basta Ya
0005-6219	Basteria
0005-6227	Bat Research News
0005-6235	Bateaux
0005-6243	Bates Student
0005-626X	Baths Service changed to Baths Service and Recreation Management
0005-6278	Batiment
0005-6294	Batir changed to Batiment-Batir
0005-6308	Baatnytt
0005-6324	Baton Rouge
0005-6332	Battaglia Letteraria
0005-6340	Battaglie Postelegrafoniche
0005-6359	Battery Man
0005-6367	Batting the Breeze
0005-6375	Battleacts†
0005-6383	Bau†
0005-6391	Bau; Fachzeitschrift fuer Bautechnik, Baupraxis, und Baumaschinen
0005-6413	Bau changed to Wuerttembergische Bau-Berufsgenossenschaft. Mitteilungen
0005-6421	Bau & Bauindustrie†
0005-643X	Bau und Baustoff
0005-6448	Der Baustoffmarkt
0005-6456	Bauindustrie
0005-6464	Bau- und Moebelschreiner
0005-6472	Bauamt und Gemeindebau see 0005-6847
0005-6480	Baubeschlag Magazin mit Praktikus changed to Baubeschlag Magazin
0005-6499	Bingo
0005-6510	Bauen und Fertighaus
0005-6529	Bauen und Wohnen
0005-6545	Bauen mit Holz
0005-6553	Bauen und Siedeln
0005-6561	Der Bauer
0005-657X	Bauern und Gaertner†
0005-6618	Das Baugeruest
0005-6626	Baugeschaeft und Bauunternehmer
0005-6634	Baugewerbe
0005-6642	Bauinformation changed to Bauinformation Wissenschaft und Technik
0005-6650	Bauingenieur
0005-6677	Baum Bugle
0005-6685	Baumaschine Baugeraet Baustoff changed to Baumaschine - Baugeraet - Baustelle
0005-6693	Baumaschine und Bautechnik
0005-6707	Baumaschinen und Baugeraette Revue†
0005-6715	Baumaschinen- und Baugeraete-Handel
0005-6723	B D Baumaschinendienst
0005-674X	Baumeister
0005-6758	Bauplanung - Bautechnik
0005-6766	Baupraxis
0005-6782	Bausparkasse der Rheinprovinz†
0005-6790	Baustein
0005-6804	Baustoff- und Baubedarfs-Grosshandel
0005-6839	Bauunternehmer changed to Bau; Fachzeitschrift fuer Betriebsfuehrung und Kalkulation
0005-6847	Die Bauverwaltung
0005-6855	Bauwelt
0005-6863	Bauwirtschaft (B W)
0005-6871	Bauzeitung
0005-688X	Das Bauzentrum
0005-6928	New England Architect changed to Architecture: New England
0005-6936	Bay State F L Bulletin changed to Massachusetts Foreign Language Bulletin
0005-6944	Bay State Librarian
0005-6952	Bayavaya Uskalos
0005-6960	Bayer-Berichte
0005-6987	Bayer-Mitteilungen fuer die Gummi-Industrie
0005-6995	Bayerische Akademie der Wissenschaften. Mathematisch-Naturwissenschaftliche Klasse. Abhandlungen
0005-7002	Bayerische Beamtenzeitung†
0005-7029	Bayerische Boerse in Muenchen. Amtliches Kursblatt
0005-7045	Bayerische Gemeindezeitung
0005-7053	Bayerische Kleingaertner†
0005-7061	Das Bayerische Kraftfahrzeughandwerk
0005-7088	Der Metzgermeister
0005-7096	Bayerische Standesamt changed to Das Standesamt
0005-710X	Bayerische Akademie der Wissenschaften. Philosophisch-Historische Klasse
0005-7118	Bayerischer Landesverein fuer Familienkunde. Blaetter
0005-7126	Bayerisches Aerzteblatt
0005-7142	Bayerisches Justizministerialblatt
0005-7150	Bayerisches Landwirtschaftliches Jahrbuch
0005-7169	Bayerisches Landwirtschaftliches Wochenblatt
0005-7177	Bayerisches Sonntagsblatt fuer die Katholische Familie
0005-7185	Bayerisches Staatsministerium des Innern. Ministerialamtsblatt der bayerischen inneren Verwaltung
0005-7193	Bayerisches Staatsministerium fuer Arbeit und Soziale Fuersorge Amtsblatt. see 0340-1790
0005-7207	Bayerisches Staatsministerium fuer Unterricht und Kultus. Amtsblatt
0005-7215	Bayern in Zahlen
0005-7223	Bayern Nachrichten†
0005-7231	Bayernturner
0005-724X	Baylor Business Studies
0005-7258	Baylor Dental Journal
0005-7266	Baylor Geological Studies Bulletin
0005-7274	Baylor Law Review
0005-7282	Bayreuther Gemeindeblatt
0005-7312	Bazuin
0005-7320	Beacon
0005-7339	Beacon
0005-7347	Beacon
0005-7363	Beaconette
0005-7371	Be'ad Ve- Neged
0005-738X	Beaken
0005-7398	Beam
0005-7401	Beamte im Lande Bremen
0005-741X	Der Beamte in Rheinland-Pfalz
0005-7428	Bearing Engineer†
0005-7436	Beato Angelo
0005-7460	Beautiful British Columbia
0005-7495	Beauty Tips†
0005-7509	Beaux-Arts
0005-7517	Beaver
0005-7525	Beaver
0005-7533	Bebidas
0005-755X	Beckman Report
0005-7568	Bedding
0005-7576	Bedford Stuyvesant Youth in Action Monthly Newsletter
0005-7584	Bedford Transport†
0005-7592	Bedfordshire Magazine
0005-7606	Bedriftsoekonomen
0005-7614	Bedrijf en Techniek
0005-7622	Maandblad voor Bedrijfsadministratie en Organisatie
0005-7630	Bedrijfsjournalist†
0005-7649	Bedrijfspluimveehouder changed to Pluimveehouderij
0005-7657	Bedrijfsvervoer changed to Vervoer en Transporttechniek
0005-7665	Bedside Nurse changed to Journal of Nursing Care
0005-7673	Bedsitter
0005-7681	Det Bedste fra Reader's Digest (Danish Edition)
0005-769X	Beduin
0005-7703	Bee Craft
0005-7711	Bee-Hive changed to United Technologies Bee-Hive
0005-772X	Bee World
0005-7738	Beef
0005-7754	Beekeeping
0005-7770	Beer Wholesaler
0005-7789	Beet
0005-7797	F B U-Befael
0005-7800	Begegnung
0005-7819	Begegnung mit Polen
0005-7843	Behavioural Sciences and Community Development changed to Behavioural Sciences and Rural Development
0005-786X	Behavioral Research in Highway Safety†
0005-7878	Behavior Research Methods and Instrumentation
0005-7886	Behavior Science Notes see 0094-3673
0005-7894	Behavior Therapy
0005-7916	Journal of Behavior Therapy and Experimental Psychiatry
0005-7924	Behavior Today
0005-7932	Behavioral Neuropsychiatry
0005-7940	Behavioral Science
0005-7959	Behaviour
0005-7967	Behaviour Research and Therapy
0005-7983	Behind the Headlines
0005-7991	Das Behinderte Kind
0005-8009	Bei Uns
0005-8017	Beihefte Zum Geologischen Jahrbuch see 0341-6429
0005-8017	Beihefte Zum Geologischen Jahrbuch see 0341-6410
0005-8017	Beihefte Zum Geologischen Jahrbuch see 0341-6399
0005-8017	Beihefte Zum Geologischen Jahrbuch see 0341-6402
0005-8025	Beitraege aus der Plasmaphysik
0005-8041	Beitraege zur Biologie der Pflanzen
0005-805X	Beitraege zur Entomologie
0005-8068	Beitraege zur Geschichte der Arbeiterbewegung
0005-8076	Beitraege zur Geschichte der deutschen Sprache und Literatur
0005-8084	Beitraege zur Linguistik und Informationsverarbeitung
0005-8092	Literaturkunde. Beitraege
0005-8106	Musikwissenschaft. Beitraege
0005-8114	Beitraege zur Namenforschung
0005-8122	Beitraege zur Naturkundlichen Forschung in Suedwestdeutschland

ISSN INDEX

ISSN	Title
0005-8149	Beitraege zur Orthopaedie und Traumatologie
0005-8157	Beitraege zur Paedagogischen Arbeit
0005-8165	Beitraege zur Pathologie *see* 0344-0338
0005-8173	Beitraege zur Physik der Atmosphaere
0005-8181	Romanische Philologie. Beitraege
0005-819X	Beitraege zur Tabakforschung *see* 0173-783X
0005-8203	Beitraege zur Tropischen und Subtropischen Landwirtschaft und Tropen Veterinaermedizin *see* 0301-567X
0005-8211	Beitraege zur Vogelkunde
0005-822X	Bejaarden *changed to* Senior
0005-8238	B E K - Bruecke *changed to* Barmer Bruecke
0005-8246	Germany (Democratic Republic). Amt fuer Erfindungs- und Patentwesen. Bekanntmachungen
0005-8254	Bekhan Wa Bedan
0005-8262	Beklaednadsfolket
0005-8270	Bekleidung und Maschenware
0005-8289	Bekleidung und Waesche
0005-8297	Beku Nyusu
0005-8319	Belarus'
0005-8327	Belaruskaja Carkva
0005-8335	Maandblad Belasting Beschouwingen
0005-8343	Beleggers-Belangen *changed to* Financieel Economisch Weekblad Beleggers Belangen
0005-8351	Belfagor
0005-8378	Belgian Chamber of Commerce in Great Britain Journal *changed to* Business Contact
0005-8386	Het Beste Uit Reader's Digest (Belgian-Flemish Edition)
0005-8394	Belgian Trade Review *changed to* Belgian American Trade Review
0005-8408	Belgicatom
0005-8424	Belgique Laitiere/Belgisch Zuivelbedrijf *changed to* Lait et Nous
0005-8440	Tijdschrift voor Geneeskunde
0005-8459	Belgische Duivensport
0005-8467	Belgische Fruitrevue
0005-8483	Belgische Tuinbouw
0005-8491	Belgium: Economic and Technical Information
0005-8521	Belgium. Ministere des Affaires Economiques. Bibliotheque Centrale (Fonds Quetelet). Accroissements
0005-853X	Belgium. Ministere des Finances. Administration des Contributions. Bulletin des Contributions/Bulletin der Belastingen
0005-8556	Bell Journal of Economics and Management Science *see* 0361-915X
0005-8564	Bell Laboratories Record
0005-8572	Bell Ringer
0005-8580	Bell System Technical Journal
0005-8602	Bella
0005-8610	Bellamy - Nieuws
0005-8629	Belleza y Moda
0005-8645	Bellona
0005-8661	Beloit Poetry Journal
0005-867X	Belora
0005-8688	Beltone Institute for Hearing Research. Translations
0005-8696	Benavides
0005-8726	Benedictines
0005-8734	Benediktijns Tijdschrift
0005-8742	Benediktusbote
0005-8750	U.S. Unemployment Insurance Service. Benefit Series Service, Unemployment Insurance
0005-8769	Benelux Economische en Statistisch Kwartaalbericht/Bulletin Trimestriel Benelux Economique et Statistique *changed to* Benelux Tijdschrift
0005-8777	Benelux Publikatieblad
0005-8785	Benfica
0005-8793	Bengal Medical Journal
0005-8807	Bengal: Past and Present
0005-8815	Bengali Literature
0005-8823	Benn's Hardware Price List
0005-884X	Bent of Tau Beta Pi
0005-8858	Benzin & Olie Bladet
0005-8866	Beratende Ingenieure
0005-8874	Berea Alumnus
0005-8890	Berean Searchlight
0005-8904	Denmark. Forsoegslaboratoriet. Beretning *changed to* Denmark. Statens Husdyrbrugsudvalg. Beretning
0005-8912	B H M. Berg- und Huettenmaennische Monatshefte
0005-8920	Bergbauwissenschaften und Verfahrenstechnik†
0005-8939	Winter-Bergkamerad†
0005-8939	Winter-Bergkamerad *see* 0340-1294
0005-8947	Bergmann-Echo
0005-8955	Bergomun
0005-8963	Der Bergsteiger
0005-8971	Bergverks-Nytt
0005-898X	Bergvriend
0005-8998	Bericht over Rassenkeuze *changed to* Rassenbericht
0005-9013	Berichte Biochemie und Biologie†
0005-9021	Bunsengesellschaft fuer Physikalische Chemie. Berichte
0005-9048	Berichte Physiologie, Physiologische Chemie und Pharmakologie†
0005-9056	Berichte ueber Die Allgemeine und Spezielle Pathologie
0005-9064	Berichte ueber Die Gesamte Gynaekologie und Geburtshilfe Sowie Deren Grenzgebiete
0005-9072	Berichte ueber Die Gesamte Biologie Abt. A: Berichte ueber Die Wissenschaftliche Biologie *see* 0005-9013
0005-9080	Berichte ueber Landwirtschaft
0005-9099	Berichte zur deutschen Landeskunde
0005-9102	Berichte zur Raumforschung und Raumplanung
0005-9110	Berichten van de Afdeling Volkskredietwezen
0005-9129	Berita Bibliografi *changed to* Berita Idayu Bibliografi
0005-9137	Berita L.I.P.I.
0005-9145	Berita Selulosa
0005-9153	Berita Shell
0005-9161	Berkeley Barb†
0005-9188	Berkeley Tribe†
0005-9196	Berkshire News
0005-920X	Berkshire Review
0005-9218	Berliet-Informations
0005-9226	Berlin
0005-9242	Berlin-Flugplan
0005-9250	Berlin Programm
0005-9269	Der Berliner Baer
0005-9277	Berliner Bank. Wirtschaftsbericht
0005-9285	Betten-Magazin
0005-9293	Berliner Leben†
0005-9315	Berliner Liberale Zeitung
0005-9323	Berliner Sozialversicherungs beamte und angestellte†
0005-9331	Berliner Statistik
0005-934X	Berliner Studentenzeitung
0005-9358	Berliner Turnzeitung
0005-9366	Berliner und Muenchener Tieraerztliche Wochenschrift
0005-9374	Sozialistische Politik
0005-9382	Bermudian
0005-9390	Sint Bernardus
0005-9404	Berner Briefmarken-Zeitung
0005-9412	Berner Wochen Bulletin
0005-9420	Berner Zeitschrift fuer Geschichte und Heimatkunde
0005-9439	Bernice P. Bishop Museum Bulletin
0005-9455	Bertelsmann Briefe
0005-9471	Beruf und Gesinnung
0005-948X	Berufliche Bildung *changed to* Gewerkschaftliche Bildungspolitik
0005-9498	Berufs-Dermatosen *see* 0343-2432
0005-9501	Berufsberatung und Berufsbildung
0005-951X	Die Berufsbildende Schule
0005-9528	Berufsbildende Schule Oesterreichs†
0005-9536	Berufsbildung
0005-9544	Die Berufsgenossenschaft
0005-9560	Berufstaetige Frau Oesterreichs
0005-9579	Besco News†
0005-9587	Besier's Hauswirtschaftliche†
0005-9595	Besser Verpacken *changed to* O V Z-Mitteilungen
0005-9609	Besseres Obst
0005-9617	Best in Documents†
0005-9625	Best Sellers
0005-9633	Best Sermons
0005-9641	Best Songs†
0005-965X	Best Wishes
0005-9668	Das Beste aus Reader's Digest (German Edition)
0005-9676	Beste aus Reader's Digest (Swiss-German Edition)
0005-9684	Det Beste fra Reader's Digest (Norwegian Edition)
0005-9692	Het Beste uit Reader's Digest (Dutch Edition)
0005-9706	Best's Review. Life/Health Insurance Edition
0005-9714	Best's Review. Property-Liability Insurance Edition *see* 0161-7745
0005-9722	Best's Weekly Digest *changed to* Best's Insurance Management Reports: Life-Health Edition
0005-9730	Bestsellers *see* 0164-9876
0005-9749	Bet Ha-Talmud
0005-9757	Beta Phi Mu Newsletter
0005-9765	Betail
0005-9773	Betar Jagat
0005-9781	Betelgeuse†
0005-979X	Beth Mikra
0005-9803	Bethany Guide†
0005-9811	Bethany Nazarene College Today†
0005-982X	Bethel College Bulletin
0005-9838	Bethlehem Express
0005-9846	Beton
0005-9854	Beton Arme
0005-9889	Beton i Zhelezobeton
0005-9897	Beton-Landbau
0005-9900	Beton- und Stahlbetonbau
0005-9919	Betoniuote
0005-9927	Betonstein-Zeitung *see* 0373-4331
0005-9935	Der Betrieb
0005-9943	Betrieb und Absatz
0005-9951	Betriebliche Altersversorgung
0005-996X	Betriebsausruestung
0005-9986	Betriebswirtschafts-Magazin
0006-0003	Buerotext *changed to* Sysdata und Buerotechnik
0006-0011	Betriebswirtschaftliche Blaetter fuer die Praxis der Sparkassen und Girozentralen *changed to* Betriebswirtschaftliche Blaetter fuer die Praxis der Sparkassen und Landesbanken/Girozentralen
0006-002X	Betriebswirtschaftliche Forschung und Praxis
0006-0038	Better America
0006-0046	Better Breeding
0006-0054	Better Broadcasts News
0006-0062	Better Business†
0006-0070	Better Camping†
0006-0089	Better Crops with Plant Food
0006-0100	Better Driving†
0006-0119	Better Editing†
0006-0127	Better Education
0006-0151	Better Homes and Gardens
0006-016X	Better Investing
0006-0178	Better Letters
0006-0186	Better Management
0006-0194	Better Radio and Television
0006-0208	Better Roads
0006-0216	Better Supervision†
0006-0224	Better Times
0006-0232	Better Tomorrows†
0006-0240	Better Transit Bulletin *see* 0029-4039
0006-0291	Between Ourselves *changed to* Horizons
0006-0305	Between the Lines *see* 0145-160X
0006-0313	Beursbengel
0006-033X	Bevar
0006-0356	Beverage Bulletin. Southern California
0006-0364	Beverage Industry News
0006-0372	Beverage Media
0006-0399	Beverages
0006-0410	Beverly Review
0006-0429	Bewusster Leben
0006-0453	Bezpecnost a Hygiena Prace
0006-0461	Bhagirath
0006-047X	Bharat Medical Journal†
0006-0488	Bharat Sevak
0006-0496	Bharatha Darshan
0006-050X	Bharati Te Videshi Sahita
0006-0518	Bhavan's Journal
0006-0526	Bhopal Regional College of Education. Journal†
0006-0534	Bhubaneswar Review
0006-0542	Bhushan's World Trade Enquiries
0006-0569	Biafra Time
0006-0577	Bianco e Nero
0006-0585	Bibbia e Oriente
0006-0593	Bibel heute
0006-0607	Bibel-Journalen
0006-0615	Bibel und Gemeinde
0006-0623	Bibel und Kirche
0006-064X	Bibel und Liturgie
0006-0658	Bibeltrogna Vaenner Missionstidning
0006-0674	Bible Advocate and Herald of the Coming Kingdom *changed to* Bible Advocate
0006-0690	Bible Collector
0006-0704	Bible et Son Message
0006-0712	Bible et Terre Sainte *changed to* Monde de la Bible
0006-0720	Bible et Vie Chretienne†
0006-0739	Bible Friend
0006-0747	Bible in New York *changed to* BibleWorld
0006-0755	Bible Society News *changed to* Word in Action: the Bible in the World
0006-0763	Bible Lands
0006-0771	Bible Readers' Union Bulletin *changed to* Dor le-Dor
0006-078X	Bible Searchers
0006-0798	Bible Searchers: Teacher
0006-0801	American Bible Society Record
0006-081X	Bible Standard and Herald of Christ's Kingdom
0006-0828	Bible-Time
0006-0836	Bible Today
0006-0844	Bible Translator *changed to* Practical Papers for the Bible Translator
0006-0844	Bible Translator *changed to* Technical Papers for the Bible Translator
0006-0860	Biblia
0006-0879	Biblia Revuo
0006-0887	Biblica
0006-0895	Biblical Archeologist
0006-0909	Biblical Missions
0006-0917	Biblical Theology
0006-0925	Biblical Viewpoint
0006-0941	Bibliofilia
0006-0968	Bibliografia Argentina de Artes y Letras†
0006-0976	Bibliografia Brasileira Mensal†
0006-0992	Bibliografia Classificada
0006-100X	Bibliografia Economica de Mexico
0006-1018	Bibliografia Elettrotecnica
0006-1026	Bibliografia Historica de Espana e Hispanoamerica
0006-1034	Bibliografia Internazionale di Scienze ed Arti
0006-1042	Bibliografia Italiana di Idraulica
0006-1050	Bibliografia Medica Internacional†
0006-1069	Bibliografia Mexicana
0006-1077	Bibliografia Nazionale Italiana
0006-1085	Bibliografia Venezolana
0006-1093	Bibliografia Zawartosci Czasopism
0006-1107	Statni Knihovna C S R. Bibliograficky Casopis†
0006-1115	Bibliograficky Katalog C S S R: Clanky v Ceskych Casopisech
0006-1123	Spolecenske Vedy. Rada 2: Bibliografie Ekonomicke Literatury *see* 0139-5203
0006-114X	Bibliografija Jugoslavije
0006-1158	Bibliografija Jugoslovenske Periodike

0006-1166 Bibliografija Prispelih Knjiga Clanaka Iz Strucnih Casopisa i Drugih Dokumenata
0006-1174 Bibliograma
0006-1182 Bibliographia I U L A-I F H P *changed to* Bibliographia I U L A
0006-1190 Bibliographia Africana
0006-1204 Bibliographia Anastatica *see* 0303-4550
0006-1212 Bibliographia Asiatica
0006-1220 Bibliographia Asiatica *changed to* Asien-Bibliographie
0006-1239 Bibliographia Geodaetica
0006-1247 Bibliographia Neuroendocrinologica
0006-1255 Bibliographic Index
0006-1271 Bibliographical Bulletin for Welding and Allied Processes†
0006-128X Bibliographical Society of America. Papers
0006-1298 Bibliographie Africaine
0006-1301 Bibliographie Agricole Courante Roumaine†
0006-131X Bibliographie Americaniste
0006-1328 Centre Technique du Cuir. Bibliographie Analytique et Signaletique
0006-1336 Bibliographie de Belgique
0006-1344 Bibliographie de la France
0006-1352 Bibliographie de la Philosophie
0006-1360 Bibliographie der Deutschen Bibliographien *see* 0301-4614
0006-1387 Bibliographie der Pflanzenschutzliteratur
0006-1409 Bibliographie der Uebersetzungen deutschsprachiger Werke
0006-1417 Bibliographie der Wirtschaftspresse
0006-1433 Bibliographie, Documentation, Terminologie
0006-1441 Bibliographie du Quebec
0006-145X Bibliographie Fremdsprachiger Werke ueber Deutschland und Persoenlichkeiten des Deutschen Sprachgebietes *changed to* Fremdsprachige Germanica
0006-1468 Bibliographie Staat und Recht der Deutschen Demokratischen Republik (Vierteljahresbibliographie)†
0006-1476 World Bibliography of Social Security
0006-1484 Bibliographies of Atomic Energy Literature†
0006-1506 Bibliographische Berichte
0006-1522 Bibliography and Index of Geology Exclusive of North America *see* 0098-2784
0006-1530 Bibliography of Agriculture
0006-1557 Bibliography of Indian Fisheries
0006-1565 Bibliography of Reproduction
0006-1573 Bibliography of Systematic Mycology
0006-1581 Shu Mo Chi Kan. Bibliography Quarterly
0006-159X Biblion†
0006-1603 Bibliophilie *see* 0399-9742
0006-1611 Biblioteca
0006-152X Biblioteca Americana de Autores. Boletin†
0006-1546 Biblioteca de Menendez Pelayo. Boletin
0006-1554 Biblioteca della Liberta
0006-1562 Biblioteca do Sejur. Boletim
0006-1570 Tribunal Justica Estado da Guanabara. Biblioteca. Boletim
0006-1697 Biblioteca "Jose Artigas". Boletin
0006-1700 Biblioteca Labronica Notiziario
0006-1719 Universidad Nacional Autonoma de Mexico. Instituto de Investigaciones Bibliograficas. Boletin
0006-1727 Biblioteca Nacional Jose Marti. Revista
0006-1751 Biblioteca y Hemeroteca de Servicios Electricos del Gran Buenos Aires. Boletin Bibliografico *changed to* Servicios Electricos del Gran Buenos Aires S.A. Boletin Bibliografico
0006-176X Bibliotecas
0006-1778 Biblioteconomia
0006-1786 Bibliotek for Laeger
0006-1794 Bibliotekar
0006-1808 Bibliotekar'
0006-1816 Bibliotekar
0006-1824 Bibliotek 70
0006-1832 Bibliotekarstvo
0006-1840 Biblioteket Presenterar Nya Boecker
0006-1859 Biblioteki Z. N. E. P.A.N. Biuletyn Informacyjny
0006-1867 Biblioteksbladet
0006-1913 Bibliotheca Orientalis
0006-1921 Bibliotheca Sacra
0006-193X Bibliotheck
0006-1948 Technische Hogeschool te Delft. Bibliotheek. Aanwinsten
0006-1956 Bibliotheekgids
0006-1964 Der Bibliothekar
0006-1972 Bibliotheksdienst
0006-1980 Bibliotheque de l'Ecole des Chartes
0006-1999 Bibliotheque d'Humanisme et Renaissance
0006-2006 Bulletin des Bibliotheques de France
0006-2014 Biblische Zeitschrift
0006-2022 Biblos
0006-2030 Biblos
0006-2057 Bichitra†
0006-2073 Bicycling
0006-2081 Biddend Nazareth
0006-209X Bielarus
0006-2103 Bielefelder Katalog *changed to* Bielefelder Katalog - Klassik
0006-2111 Bien-Etre Social Canadien *changed to* Digeste Social
0006-212X Die Biene
0006-2138 Bienen
0006-2146 Bienenvater
0006-2154 Bienenwelt
0006-2189 Big Farmer Entrepreneur
0006-2189 Big Farmer *see* 0006-2189
0006-2219 Bihar Industries
0006-2227 Bij de Haard
0006-2235 Bijbellessen voor de Kinderen
0006-2243 Bijbellessen voor de Sabbatschool
0006-2251 Industriele Eigendom. Bijblad
0006-226X Bijblijven
0006-2278 Bijdragen
0006-2286 Bijdragen tot de Geschiedenis
0006-2294 Bijdragen tot de Taal-, Land- en Volkenkunde
0006-2308 Bijeen
0006-2316 Bijou
0006-2324 Biken Journal
0006-2340 Bilanz
0006-2359 Bilanz- und Buchhaltungs-Praxis
0006-2367 Bilbransjen/Bilteknisk Fagblad
0006-2375 Bild der Wissenschaft
0006-2383 Bild und Ton
0006-2391 Bildende Kunst
0006-2405 Bildermaerchen†
0006-2413 Bildlexikon der Nutzhoelzer
0006-2421 Bildmessung und Luftbildwesen
0006-243X Bildnerische Erziehung†
0006-2448 Bildor
0006-2456 Bildung und Erziehung
0006-2464 Bilen og Baden *changed to* Bilen, Motor og Sport
0006-2502 Bill of Rights Newsletter *see* 0160-7731
0006-2510 Billboard
0006-2529 Bille-Anzeigen-Rundschau
0006-2537 Billed Bladet
0006-2545 Billiards & Snooker†
0006-2553 Billiken
0006-2561 Savez Sindikata Jugoslavije. Centralni Vec. Bilten
0006-257X Bilten Dokumentacije. Biljna Proizvodnja
0006-2588 Bilten Dokumentacije. Elektrotehnika
0006-2596 Bilten Dokumentacije. Goriva i Maziva
0006-260X Bilten Dokumentacije. Gradevinarstvo i Arhitektura
0006-2618 Bilten Dokumentacije. Hemija i Hemijska Industrija
0006-2626 Bilten Dokumentacije. Industrija Tekstila i Papira
0006-2634 Bilten Dokumentacije. Masinska Tehnologija i Radne Masine
0006-2642 Bilten Dokumentacije. Metalurgija
0006-2650 Bilten Dokumentacije. Pogonske Masine i Masinski Delovi
0006-2669 Bilten Dokumentacije. Prehrambena Industrija
0006-2677 Bilten Dokumentacije. Rudarstvo i Geologija
0006-2685 Bilten Dokumentacije. Saobracaj
0006-2693 Bilten Dokumentacije. Silikatna Industrija
0006-2707 Bilten Dokumentacije. Stocna Proizvodnja i Veterinarstvo
0006-2715 Bilten Dokumentacije. Sumarstvo i Drvna Industrija
0006-2731 Bilten Pravne Sluzbe J N A
0006-2766 Bim
0006-2774 Iranian Journal of Plant Pathology
0006-2790 Bimestre†
0006-2804 Binario
0006-2812 Binden en Bouwen
0006-2847 Binnenschiffahrts-Nachrichten
0006-2855 Bio-Medical Insight
0006-2863 Bio-Dynamics
0006-2871 Bio-Graphic Quarterly†
0006-2898 Biomedical Engineering *see* 0309-1902
0006-2901 Bioastronautics Report†
0006-291X Biochemical and Biophysical Research Communications
0006-2928 Biochemical Genetics
0006-2936 Biochemical Journal *see* 0306-3275
0006-2936 Biochemical Journal *see* 0306-3283
0006-2944 Biochemical Medicine
0006-2952 Biochemical Pharmacology
0006-2960 Biochemistry
0006-2979 Biochemistry
0006-3002 Biochimica et Biophysica Acta
0006-3029 Biofizika
0006-3037 Biogenic Amines and Transmitters in the Nervous System
0006-3045 Biograf-Bladet
0006-3053 Biography Index
0006-3061 Bioinorganic Chemistry *changed to* Journal of Inorganic Biochemistry
0006-307X Biokhimiya
0006-3088 Biologia
0006-3096 Biologia
0006-310X Biologia Culturale†
0006-3118 Biologia Gabonica
0006-3126 Biology of the Neonate
0006-3134 Biologia Plantarum
0006-3142 Biologiai Kozlemenyek/Biological Publications *changed to* Biologia
0006-3150 Biologica Latina†
0006-3169 Biological Abstracts
0006-3177 Biological and Agricultural Index
0006-3185 Biological Bulletin
0006-3193 Biological Bulletin†
0006-3207 Biological Conservation
0006-3223 Biological Psychiatry
0006-3231 Cambridge Philosophical Society. Biological Reviews
0006-324X Biological Society of Washington. Proceedings
0006-3258 Biologie et Gastro-Enterologie *see* 0399-8320
0006-3266 Biologie Medicale
0006-3274 Der Biologieunterricht
0006-3282 Biologische Abhandlungen
0006-3290 Biologische Rundschau
0006-3304 Biologisches Zentralblatt
0006-3320 Kongelige Danske Videnskabernes Selskab. Biologiske Skrifter
0006-3339 Biologist
0006-3347 Biologist
0006-3355 Biology and Human Affairs
0006-3363 Biology of Reproduction
0006-338X Biomedical Electronics
0006-3398 Biomedical Engineering
0006-341X Biometrics
0006-3428 Biometrie Humaine *see* 0183-5688
0006-3436 Biometrie-Praximetrie
0006-3444 Biometrika
0006-3452 Biometrische Zeitschrift
0006-3479 Bionomic Briefs†
0006-3487 Bionomica
0006-3495 Biophysical Journal
0006-3509 Biophysics
0006-3517 Biophysik *see* 0301-634X
0006-3525 Biopolymers
0006-3533 Bioquimica Clinica *changed to* Acta Bioquimica Clinica Latinoamericana
0006-3541 BioResearch Index *changed to* Biological Abstracts/R R M(Reports, Reviews, Meetings)
0006-355X Biorheology
0006-3568 BioScience
0006-3576 Biosophia
0006-3584 Biota
0006-3592 Biotechnology and Bioengineering
0006-3606 Biotropica
0006-3614 Birbal
0006-3630 Bird-Banding *changed to* Journal of Field Ornithology
0006-3649 Bird Life
0006-3657 Bird Study
0006-3665 Birds
0006-3673 Birds and Country
0006-3681 Birlik
0006-369X Birmingham
0006-3703 Birmingham ABC & Midland Counties Railway Time Tables†
0006-3711 Birmingham Bar Association. Bulletin
0006-3746 University of Birmingham Chemical Engineer†
0006-3754 Birmingham World
0006-3762 Birney Arrow†
0006-3770 Birra e Malto
0006-3797 Biscuits, Biscottes, Panification Industrielle, Produits Dietetiques, Chocolat, Confiserie *changed to* Revue des Industries de la Biscuiterie, Biscotterie, Chocolaterie, Confiserie
0006-3800 In the Field of Building†
0006-3819 Bisdomblad
0006-3827 Bismoi
0006-3835 Bit
0006-3843 Bit
0006-3878 Bitaon Heyl Ha'avir
0006-3886 Bitidningen
0006-3894 Bits and Pieces†
0006-3894 Bits & Pieces
0006-3908 Bitterroot
0006-3916 Bitumen
0006-3924 Bitumen, Teere, Asphalte, Peche und verwandte Stoffe†
0006-3924 Bitumen, Teere, Asphalte, Peche *changed to* Strassen- und Tiefbau Vereinigt mit Strasse-Bruecke-Tunnel, Bitumen-Teere-Asphalts-Peche
0006-3932 Bitzaron: the Hebrew Monthly of America *changed to* Bitzaron: a Quarterly of Hebrew Letters
0006-3940 Biuletyn Biblioteki Jagiellonskiej
0006-3967 Biuletyn Historii Sztuki
0006-3975 Biuletyn Informacyjny†
0006-3983 Biblioteka Narodowa. Biuletyn Informacyjny
0006-3991 Polska Akademia Nauk. Instytut Krajow Socjalistycznych. Biuletyn Informacyjny
0006-4017 Biuletyn Numizmatyczny
0006-4025 Poland. Glowny Urzad Statystyczny. Biuletyn Statystyczny
0006-4033 Zydowski Instytut Historyczny w Polsce. Biuletyn
0006-4041 Byulleten' Eksperimental'noi Biologii i Meditsiny
0006-4068 Bjelovarski List
0006-4076 Blaa Stjaernan
0006-4084 Black Academy Review†
0006-4106 Black Belt Magazine
0006-4114 Black Business Digest†
0006-4122 Black Careers
0006-4149 Black Diamond
0006-4165 Black Enterprise
0006-4173 Black Hills Anemone *changed to* Black Hills State TODAY
0006-4203 Black News
0006-4246 Black Scholar
0006-4254 Black Student†
0006-4262 Black Swamp Review†
0006-4289 Black Times: Voices of the National Community†
0006-4297 Black Vanguard
0006-4300 Black Voice

0006-4319 Black World†
0006-4327 Blackboard Bulletin
0006-4335 Blackcountryman
0006-4351 Blackpool Hotel & Guest House Association Ltd. Journal
0006-4378 Blaetter der freien Volksbuehne Berlin
0006-4386 Blaetter fuer Agrarrecht†
0006-4394 Blaetter fuer den Deutschlehrer
0006-4416 Blaetter fuer deutsche und internationale Politik
0006-4424 Blaetter fuer Fraenkische Familienkunde
0006-4440 Blaetter fuer Grundstuecks-, Bau- und Wohnungsrecht
0006-4459 Blaetter fuer Heimatkunde
0006-4475 Blaetter fuer Steuerrecht, Sozial Versicherung und Arbeitsrecht
0006-4483 Blaetter fuer Volksliteratur
0006-4491 Blaetter fuer Zuercherische Rechtsprechung
0006-4505 Blagovest
0006-4513 Blagues
0006-4521 Blaisdell Papers
0006-453X Blake Newsletter *changed to* Blake
0006-453X Blake Newsletter *see* 0160-628X
0006-4548 Blake Studies
0006-4556 Blaaklint *see* 0345-1593
0006-4564 B T N†
0006-4572 Blanco y Negro
0006-4580 B. L. A. S. A. Newsletter *changed to* African Library Association of S.A. Newsletter
0006-4610 Blaue, Alpwirtschaftliche Monatsblaetter
0006-4629 Blaue Kreuz
0006-4637 Der Blaue Peter
0006-4645 A en D
0006-4653 Blauwe Kruis
0006-4661 Blauwe Wimpel
0006-467X Bleb *changed to* Ark
0006-4688 Blech - Rohre - Profile
0006-4696 Blessings of Liberty
0006-4718 Blick und Bild
0006-4734 Blick ins Fleischer-Fachgeschaeft
0006-4750 Blick vom Hochhaus
0006-4769 Blickpunkt
0006-4777 Blijde Boodschap
0006-4785 Blijdorp Geluiden
0006-4793 Blikkenslager- Roer-og Sanitets Mesteren *see* 0106-8881
0006-4815 Blind Citizen
0006-4823 Blind Welfare
0006-4831 Blindas Tidskrift†
0006-4858 Zeitschrift fuer das Blinden- und Sehbehindertenbildungswesen
0006-4866 Blindenwelt *changed to* Die Blindenselbsthilfe
0006-4874 Blindmaker *see* 0305-733X
0006-4882 Blitz
0006-4890 Bloc
0006-4904 Der Block
0006-4912 Blodau'r Ffair
0006-4920 Bloemenvriend
0006-4939 Bloemfontein Nuusbrief
0006-4947 Bloemheuwel-Nuus
0006-4955 Blomster
0006-4963 Blomster-Branschen
0006-4971 Blood; the Journal of Hematology *changed to* Blood
0006-498X Blood Group News†
0006-4998 Blood-Horse
0006-5005 Blood Therapy Journal
0006-5013 Bloodlines Journal *changed to* Bloodlines
0006-5021 Blue Anchor
0006-503X Blue and Gold Triangle of Lamba Kappa Sigma
0006-5048 Blue and White†
0006-5056 Bluebook†
0006-5064 Blue Cloud Quarterly†
0006-5099 Blue Jay
0006-5102 Blue Triangle†
0006-5137 Bluegrass Unlimited
0006-5153 Blues Unlimited
0006-5161 Blues World
0006-517X Bluestocking†
0006-5188 Bluestone†
0006-5196 Blumea
0006-5218 Blumenau em Cadernos
0006-5226 Blumenfreundin Blumenpost
0006-5242 Blut
0006-5250 Blutalkohol
0006-5269 Blyttia
0006-5277 B'nai B'rith Messenger
0006-5307 Scripts†
0006-5323 Trade and Industry *changed to* British Business
0006-5331 Board of Trade Newsletter *see* 0164-7059
0006-534X Board Manufacture Practice *see* 0306-4123
0006-5358 Boardman
0006-5366 Boat & Motor Dealer
0006-5374 Boating
0006-5404 Boating Industry
0006-5412 Bobbin
0006-5420 Scientific Pest Control†
0006-5439 Bode van het Heil in Christus
0006-5455 Boden und Gesundheit
0006-5463 Boden, Wand, Decke
0006-5471 Die Bodenkultur
0006-548X Bodensee Hefte
0006-5498 Bodine Motorgram
0006-5501 Body
0006-5528 National Defense Medical Journal
0006-5544 Boek der Boeken *changed to* Schrift
0006-5560 Boekenband
0006-5579 Boekengids
0006-5587 Boekverkoper
0006-5595 Boer *changed to* Boer en de Tuinder
0006-5609 Boer en Tuinder
0006-5617 Boerderij
0006-5625 Boerenleenbank *changed to* Rabobank
0006-5633 Boern & Unge
0006-5641 Boersenblatt fuer den Deutschen Buchhandel
0006-565X Boersenblatt fuer den Deutschen Buchhandel. Frankfurter Ausgabe
0006-5692 Bogens Verden
0006-5706 Bogormen
0006-5714 Bogoslovlje
0006-5722 Bogoslovni Vestnik
0006-5730 Bogtrykkerbladet
0006-5749 Bogvennen
0006-5765 B B R
0006-5773 Boi
0006-5781 Bois
0006-579X Bois et Forets des Tropiques
0006-5803 Boissons de France "Saines et Legeres"
0006-5811 Bok og Bibliotek
0006-582X Bokbladet
0006-5846 Bokvaennen
0006-5854 Boletim Cultural da Guine Portuguesa
0006-5862 B I G
0006-5870 Boletim da Pesca
0006-5897 Boletim de Bibliografia Portuguesa
0006-5900 Boletim de Custos
0006-5919 Boletim de Desenvolvimento de Pessoal†
0006-5927 Boletim de Estudos de Pesca
0006-5935 Boletim de Minas
0006-5943 Boletim de Psicologia
0006-5951 Boletim do Leite
0006-596X Boletim do Porto de Lisboa
0006-5978 Portos e Caminhos de Ferro de Mocambique *changed to* Mozambique. Direccao Nacional dos Portos e Caminhos de Ferro. Revista Trimestral.
0006-5994 Boletim Geoelectrico
0006-6001 Mozambique. Servico Meteorologico. Boletim Geomagnetico Preliminar
0006-601X Boletim-Geral do Ultramar†
0006-6044 Mozambique. Servico Meteorologico. Boletim Meteorologico para a Agricultura
0006-6052 Boletim Meteorologico para a Agricultura†
0006-6060 Boletim Mineiro de Geografia
0006-6079 Boletim Paulista de Geografia
0006-6087 B R
0006-6095 Mozambique. Servico Meteorologico. Boletim Seismique
0006-6109 Boletim Sismico
0006-6117 Boletim Tecnico da Petrobras
0006-6125 Boletin Agropecuario del Alto Valle
0006-6133 Boletin Bibliografice de Revista "Signos"†
0006-6141 Boletin Bibliografico Boliviano
0006-6168 Boletin Bibliografico Mexicano
0006-6176 Boletin Chileno de Parasitologia
0006-6184 Boletin Cultural y Bibliografico†
0006-6192 Escuela Interamericana de Bibliotecologia. Boletin de Adquisiciones†
0006-6206 Boletin de Arte
0006-6249 Boletin de Estudios Economicos
0006-6257 Boletin de Estudios Oaxaquenos
0006-6265 Boletin de Filologia Espanola
0006-6273 Boletin de Formacion Cooperativa
0006-6281 Boletin de Geologia
0006-629X Boletin de Higiene y Epidemiologia *changed to* Revista Cubana de Higiene y Epidemiologia
0006-6303 Boletin de Historia y Antiguedades
0006-6311 Boletin de Informacion Dental
0006-632X Boletin de Informacion Educativa
0006-6338 Boletin de la Propiedad Industrial
0006-6346 Argentina. Ministerio de Trabajo y Seguridad Social. Boletin de Legislacion
0006-6354 Boletin de Noticias†
0006-6362 Boletin del Deposito Legal de Obras Impresas *see* 0525-3675
0006-6389 Boletin Informativo
0006-6397 Boletin Informativo Sobre Estudios Latinoamericanos en Europa *see* 0301-6676
0006-6419 Boletin Juridico Militar
0006-6435 Boletin Mensual Climatologico
0006-6451 Boletin Meteorologico de El Salvador†
0006-646X Boletin Naval
0006-6486 Boletin Produccion Animal†
0006-6494 Boletin Radiofonico T.V.
0006-6508 Boletin Uruguayo de Sociologia
0006-6508 Boletin Uruguayo de Sociologia
0006-6524 Bolignyt
0006-6532 Bolivarian Review†
0006-6540 Bolivia
0006-6559 Bolivia - Land of Promise†
0006-6567 Bollettino delle Malattie dell'Orrecchio, della Gola, del Naso
0006-6575 Bollettino di Pesca *changed to* Bollettino di Pesca, Piscicoltura e Idrobiologia
0006-6583 Bollettino di Studi Latini
0006-6591 Bollettino Storico Piacentino
0006-6605 I S L Bollettino Bibliografico†
0006-6613 Bollettino Bibliografico Internazionale per l'Apostolato delle Edizioni
0006-6621 Bollettino Bibliografico per le Scienze Morali e Sociale
0006-663X Bollettino Ceciliano
0006-6648 Bollettino Chimico Farmaceutico
0006-6656 D O X A. Bollettino
0006-6664 Bollettino dei Brevetti per Invenzioni, Modelli e Marchi
0006-6680 Bollettino delle Accessioni di Periodici e Libri
0006-6699 Studio di Restauro Strini. Bollettino
0006-6702 Italy. Azienda Autonoma delle Ferrovie dello Stato. Bollettino di Documentazione
0006-6710 Bollettino di Geodesia e Scienze Affini
0006-6729 Bollettino di Geofisica, Teorica ed Applicata
0006-6745 Bollettino di Libri Antichi e Moderni di Varia Cultura Esauriti e Rari
0006-6753 Italy. Laboratorio di Idrobiologia. Bollettino di Pesca Piscicoltura e Idrobiologia
0006-6761 Bollettino di Psicologia Applicata
0006-677X Bollettino d'Oculistica
0006-6788 Bollettino Ecclesiastico *changed to* Arcidiocesi di Reggio Calabria. Rivista Pastorale
0006-6796 Bollettino Economico
0006-680X Bollettino Emerografico di Economia Internazionale
0006-6826 Bollettino-Metallografico e di Odonto-Stoma-Tologia
0006-6834 Dati Meteorologico della Puglia e Luciania *changed to* Osservazioni di Meteorologia Agraria della Puglia e Basilicata
0006-6842 Italy. Consiglio dell'Ordine dei Medici di Torino. Bollettino Ordine dei Medici†
0006-6850 Bollettino Quindicinale dell'Emigrazione†
0006-6869 Bollettino Storico della Svizzera Italiana
0006-6877 Bollettino Tecnico Geloso
0006-6885 Bollettino Termomeccanica
0006-6893 Bollettino Tributario d'Informazioni
0006-6907 Bollettino Vincenziano
0006-6915 Bolsa de Valores de Mexico. Weekly Bulletin
0006-6923 Bolsa de Comercio de Buenos Aires. Boletin *changed to* Bolsa
0006-6931 Bolsa de Comercio de Rosario. Revista
0006-694X Bolsa de Valores do Rio de Janeiro. Boletim de Documentacao†
0006-6958 Bolwerk
0006-6966 Yelmo
0006-6974 Bombay Market
0006-6982 Bombay Natural History Society. Journal
0006-6990 Bon Appetit
0006-7016 Bona
0006-7024 Bona Espero
0006-7040 Bond and Money Market Review†
0006-7059 Bond Line
0006-7067 Standard & Poor's Bond Outlook *see* 0091-8415
0006-7075 Bondholder's Register
0006-7091 Bondsspaarbanken
0006-7113 Bonifatiusblatt
0006-7156 Bonner Meteorologische Abhandlungen
0006-7164 Bonner Zahlen†
0006-7172 Bonner Zoologische Beitraege
0006-7180 Bonsai Bulletin
0006-7199 Bonytt *see* 0029-6783
0006-7229 Book Collecting World
0006-7237 Book Collector
0006-7245 Book Exchange
0006-7253 Book-Keepers Journal *see* 0143-9359
0006-7261 Book Market†
0006-727X Book News†
0006-7288 Book News *changed to* Tartan Book Sales Catalog
0006-7296 Book News Letter
0006-730X Book-Of-The-Month Club News
0006-7318 Book Production Industry *see* 0273-8724
0006-7326 Book Review Digest
0006-7334 Rucksack
0006-7342 Book Reviews of the Month
0006-7350 Book Shopper Newsletter†
0006-7369 Book World
0006-7377 Bookbird
0006-7385 Booklist
0006-7393 Bookmark
0006-7407 Bookmark
0006-7415 Bookmark†
0006-7423 Books
0006-7431 Books Abroad *changed to* World Literature Today
0006-7458 Books and Libraries at the University of Kansas
0006-7474 Books at Iowa
0006-7482 Books for Your Children
0006-7490 Books from Finland
0006-7504 Books from Hungary *see* 0324-3451
0006-7512 Books in Polish or Relating to Poland
0006-7520 Books of the Southwest
0006-7539 Bookseller
0006-7547 Bookseller
0006-7555 Bookseller Pustak Vikreta Baroda
0006-7563 Bookstore Journal
0006-7571 Boom-Pers Combinatie
0006-758X Boor
0006-7598 Boosey and Hawkes. Newsletter
0006-7601 Boost
0006-761X Boot- und Schiffbau†

0006-7636 Boote
0006-7644 Bootswirtschaft
0006-7652 Bor- es Cipotechnika
0006-7660 Bordeaux Chirurgical†
0006-7679 Borden Review of Nutrition Research†
0006-7695 Borderline Magazine†
0006-7709 Bore Da
0006-7717 Boreal *changed to* Boreal International
0006-7725 Borec
0006-7741 Borgazdasag
0006-775X Borghese
0006-7768 Borgyogyaszati es Venerologiai Szemle
0006-7784 Boris Kidric Institute of Nuclear Sciences. Bulletin
0006-7792 Boern og Boeger
0006-7806 Borneo Research Bulletin
0006-7822 Boron in Glass
0006-7849 Borsa dei Noli
0006-7857 Borsa Marmi
0006-7865 Borussen-Echo
0006-7873 Disaster Prevention
0006-789X Bosch Technische Berichte
0006-7903 Bose Institute. Transactions
0006-792X Boss
0006-7938 Children's Hospital Medical Center, Boston. News *changed to* Children's World
0006-7946 Boston City Record
0006-7954 Boston College Industrial and Commercial Law Review *see* 0161-6587
0006-7989 Boston
0006-7997 Boston Museum Bulletin *changed to* M F A Bulletin
0006-8004 Boston Public Schools Review
0006-8020 Boston Symphony Orchestra Program Book-Notes *changed to* Boston Symphony Orchestra Program
0006-8039 Boston University Journal†
0006-8047 Boston University Law Review
0006-8055 Botanica Marina
0006-8063 Academia Sinica. Botanical Bulletin
0006-8071 Botanical Gazette
0006-808X Botanical Magazine *changed to* Botanical Magazine, Tokyo
0006-8098 Botanical Museum Leaflets
0006-8101 Botanical Review
0006-811X Botanical Society of Bengal. Bulletin
0006-8128 Botanical Survey of India. Bulletin
0006-8136 Botanicheskii Zhurnal
0006-8144 Botanikai Kozlemenyek
0006-8152 Botanische Jahrbuecher fuer Systematik, Pflanzengeschichte und Pflanzengeographie
0006-8160 Botanische Tuinen en Het Belmonte Arboretum der Landbouwhogeschool Te Wageningen Mededelingen†
0006-8179 Botanische Staatssammlung Muenchen. Mitteilungen
0006-8187 Botanisk Tidsskrift
0006-8195 Botaniska Notiser
0006-8209 Bote
0006-8217 Bote aus der Apotheke†
0006-8225 Bote fuer Tirol
0006-8233 Both Sides Now
0006-8241 Bothalia
0006-825X Boticario
0006-8276 Botschafter des Kommenden Koenigs
0006-8284 Boucherie Francaise
0006-8292 Boulanger-Patissier *see* 0224-5027
0006-8306 Boumi Temple News
0006-8314 Boundary-Layer Meteorology
0006-8330 Bouwbelangen
0006-8349 Bouwen aan de Nieuwe Aarde
0006-8357 Plan
0006-8365 Bouwliteratuur Documentatie
0006-8373 Bouwmachines
0006-8381 Bouwondernemer
0006-8403 Bow and Arrow
0006-8411 Bowlers Journal and Billiard Revue *see* 0164-9183
0006-842X Bowling Magazine
0006-8438 Bowling Notizie
0006-8446 Bowling Proprietor
0006-8454 Bowls in N.S.W
0006-8470 Box y Lucha
0006-8489 Boxboard Containers
0006-8497 Boxe Ring
0006-8519 Boxing News
0006-8527 Boxoffice
0006-8535 Boxwood Bulletin
0006-8543 Boyce Thompson Institute for Plant Research, Inc. Contributions†
0006-8551 Boys and Girls†
0006-856X Boys Baseball Bulletin *changed to* Pony Baseball Newsletter
0006-8578 Boys Brigade Gazette
0006-8586 Boys Club Bulletin
0006-8594 Boys Clubs of America. Journal *see* 0272-6513
0006-8608 Boys' Life (Inkprint Edition)
0006-8616 Brabant
0006-8624 Brabantia
0006-8632 Brabantse Leeuw
0006-8640 Bracara Augusta
0006-8667 Brackety - Ack
0006-8675 Bradfield College Chronicle
0006-8705 Bragantia
0006-8721 Brahmavadin
0006-873X Braille Book Review (Inkprint Edition)
0006-8748 Braille Cardinal
0006-8756 Braille Chess Magazine
0006-8764 Braille Digest
0006-8772 Braille Forum
0006-8780 Braille Journal of Physiotherapy
0006-8799 Braille Mainichi *changed to* Braille Mainichi Weekly
0006-8810 Braille Mirror
0006-8829 Braille Monitor (Inkprint Edition)
0006-8837 Braille Musical Magazine
0006-8845 New Braille Musician *see* 0364-7501
0006-8853 Braille News Summary
0006-887X Braille Radio Times
0006-8888 Braille Rainbow
0006-8896 Braille Science Journal
0006-890X Braille Sporting Record
0006-8918 Braille Star Theosophist
0006-8926 Braille Sunday School Quarterly†
0006-8942 Braille Variety News†
0006-8950 Brain
0006-8969 Brain and Nerve
0006-8977 Brain, Behavior and Evolution
0006-8985 Brain News
0006-8993 Brain Research
0006-9000 Brainstorms
0006-9019 Brake and Front End Service *changed to* Brake and Front End
0006-9027 Brand *changed to* Brand en Brandweer
0006-9035 Brand Aus
0006-9043 Brandeis University Bulletin
0006-9051 Brandfoersvar
0006-906X Die Brandhilfe
0006-9078 Branding Iron
0006-9086 Brandon's Shipper & Forwarder
0006-9108 Brandverhuetung und Brandbekaempfung *see* 0343-3560
0006-9116 Brandwacht
0006-9124 Brandweer†
0006-9132 Brangus Journal
0006-9140 Branicevo
0006-9159 Die Branntweinwirtschaft
0006-9191 Brasil Jovem
0006-9205 Brasil-Medico
0006-9248 Bratislavske Lekarske Listy
0006-9256 Bratrsky Vestnik
0006-9264 Bratstvo
0006-9272 Bratstvo
0006-9280 Brauereibesitzer und Braumeister *changed to* Brauerei Journal
0006-9299 Braunkohle Waerme und Energie *see* 0341-1060
0006-9310 Brautechnik Aktuell
0006-9329 Brauwelt
0006-9337 Brauwissenschaft
0006-9361 Brazil. Biblioteca da Camara dos Deputados. Boletim *changed to* Brazil. Camara dos Deputados. Documentacao e Informacao
0006-937X Brazil. Conselho Nacional de Economia. Revista
0006-9388 Brazil. Departamento de Agricultura. Boletim†
0006-9418 Faculdade de Farmacia e Odontologia de Ribeirao Preto. Boletim *changed to* Faculdade de Farmacia e Odontologia de Ribeirao Preto- Revista
0006-9434 Brazil. Ministerio da Fazenda. Nucleo Regional de Administracao. Boletin Informativo *changed to* Brazil. Ministerio a Fazenda. Boletim Informativo a Secao de Documentacao
0006-9442 Brazil. Ministerio da Saude. Departamento Nacional de Endemias Rurais. Divisao de Cooperacao e Divulgacao. Boletim Bibliografico†
0006-9469 Pernambuco. Secretaria do Saneamento, Habitacao e Obras. Boletin Tecnico
0006-9477 Brazila Esperantisto
0006-9485 Brazilian Bulletin†
0006-9493 Brazilian Business†
0006-9507 Brazilian News Briefs
0006-9515 Bread of Life
0006-9523 Break-In
0006-954X Brecon and Radnor Farmer
0006-9558 Uit in West-Brabant
0006-9566 Bref Rhone Alpes
0006-9574 Bremer Missionsschiff
0006-9582 Bremer Schulblatt
0006-9604 Brennpunkt
0006-9612 B W K
0006-9620 Brennstoff-Chemie†
0006-9620 Brennstoffchemie *see* 0014-0058
0006-9639 Bres-Planete *changed to* Bres'
0006-9647 Bretagne Reelle
0006-9655 Brethren Journal
0006-9663 Brethren Life and Thought
0006-9671 Breton News *changed to* Carn
0006-968X Breve, Il Gruppo, la Cultura, l'Idee
0006-9698 Breviora
0006-9701 Brewers Bulletin
0006-971X Brewers Digest
0006-9728 Brewers' Guardian
0006-9736 Brewer
0006-9752 Brewing Trade Review *changed to* Brewing Review
0006-9760 Brick and Clay Record
0006-9779 Brickbats & Bouquets
0006-9787 Brides & Setting Up Home
0006-9795 Bride's Magazine *see* 0161-1992
0006-9809 Bridge of Eta Kappa Nu
0006-9817 Bridge†
0006-9825 Bridge
0006-9833 Bridge
0006-9841 Bridge Bulletin
0006-985X Bridge d'Italia
0006-9868 Bridge Magazine
0006-9876 Bridge World
0006-9884 Bridgeport Hospital News
0006-9892 Bridgeport News
0006-9906 Bridge Tidningen
0006-9914 Bridgeur
0006-9922 Brief *changed to* American Council for Judaism. Issues
0006-9949 Brief aus Wahlwies
0006-9965 Brief of the School of Law
0006-9973 Briefe an den Chef
0006-9981 Briefe an den Mitarbeiter
0006-999X Briefe an den Mitmenschen
0007-0009 Briefe fuer junge Steuerfachleute
0007-0017 Briefed†
0007-0025 Briefing Papers
0007-0041 Briefmarken-Spiegel
0007-0068 Briefs
0007-0076 Brieven Aan de Chef†
0007-0084 Brigade Leader
0007-0106 Brigham Young University Studies
0007-0130 Brighton Historical Society. Newsletter *changed to* Brighton Newsletter
0007-0149 Brighton Park Life
0007-0157 Brightonian
0007-0173 Brio
0007-0181 Bristol Building and Design Centre. Newsletter *changed to* Bristol Newsletter
0007-019X Bristol Medico-Chirurgical Journal
0007-0203 Britannia
0007-0211 Brith
0007-022X British Agents Review *changed to* British Commercial Agents Review
0007-0238 British Amateur Journalist
0007-0262 British Antarctic Survey. Bulletin
0007-0270 British Archaeological Abstracts
0007-0289 British Archer
0007-0297 British Astronomical Association. Journal
0007-0300 British Baker
0007-0319 British Bandsman
0007-0327 British Bee Journal
0007-0335 British Birds
0007-0343 British Book News
0007-0351 British Boot and Shoe Institution. Journal *see* 0142-0534
0007-036X British Bulletin of Publications on Latin America, the West Indies, Portugal and Spain *changed to* British Bulletin of Publications on Latin America, the Caribbean, Portugal and Spain
0007-0378 British Bulletin of Spectroscopy *see* 0307-0026
0007-0394 British Ceramic Society. Publications
0007-0408 British Chamber of Commerce in Brazil. Information Circular
0007-0416 British Chamber of Commerce of Turkey. Trade Journal
0007-0432 British Chemist†
0007-0440 British Chess Magazine
0007-0459 British Citizen
0007-0467 British Clothing Manufacturer
0007-0475 B C U R A Monthly Bulletin†
0007-0483 British Columbia Catholic
0007-0513 British Columbia Government News†
0007-0521 British Columbia Hospital News *changed to* B C H A News
0007-053X British Columbia Library Quarterly†
0007-0548 British Columbia Lumberman
0007-0556 British Columbia Medical Journal
0007-0564 British Columbia Music Educator
0007-0572 British Columbia Orchardist†
0007-0580 British Columbia School Trustee†
0007-0599 British Corrosion Journal
0007-0602 British Deaf News
0007-0610 British Dental Journal
0007-0629 British Dental Surgery Assistant
0007-0637 British Education Index
0007-0653 British Endodontic Society Journal *see* 0143-2885
0007-0661 British Engineer†
0007-067X British Esperantist
0007-0688 British Farmer and Stockbreeder
0007-0696 British Federation of Master Printers. Members Circular *see* 0307-7195
0007-070X British Food Journal
0007-0718 British Foundryman
0007-0726 British Friesian Journal
0007-0734 British Goat Society. Monthly Journal
0007-0742 British Golf Greenkeeper *changed to* Golf Greenkeeping & Course Maintenance
0007-0750 British Grassland Society. Journal *see* 0142-5242
0007-0769 British Heart Journal
0007-0777 British Homing World
0007-0785 British Homoeopathic Journal
0007-0807 British Hotelier and Restaurateur
0007-0815 British Humanities Index
0007-0823 British Industry and Engineering
0007-084X British Interplanetary Society Journal
0007-0858 British Italian Trade Review
0007-0866 British Jeweller & Watch Buyer
0007-0874 British Journal for the History of Science
0007-0882 British Journal for the Philosophy of Science
0007-0890 British Journal of Addiction
0007-0904 British Journal of Aesthetics
0007-0912 British Journal of Anaesthesia
0007-0920 British Journal of Cancer
0007-0939 British Journal of Chiropody
0007-0947 British Journal of Clinical Practice
0007-0955 British Journal of Criminology
0007-0963 British Journal of Dermatology

0007-0971 British Journal of Diseases of the Chest
0007-098X British Journal of Disorders of Communication
0007-0998 British Journal of Educational Psychology
0007-1005 British Journal of Educational Studies
0007-1013 British Journal of Educational Technology
0007-1021 British Journal of Experimental Pathology
0007-1048 British Journal of Haematology
0007-1056 British Journal of Herpetology
0007-1064 British Journal of Hospital Medicine
0007-1072 British Journal of Industrial Medicine
0007-1080 British Journal of Industrial Relations
0007-1099 British Journal of Marketing *see* 0309-0566
0007-1102 British Journal of Mathematical and Statistical Psychology
0007-1110 British Journal of Medical Education *see* 0308-0110
0007-1129 British Journal of Medical Psychology
0007-1137 British Journal of Non-Destructive Testing
0007-1145 British Journal of Nutrition
0007-1161 British Journal of Ophthalmology
0007-117X British Journal of Oral Surgery
0007-1188 British Journal of Pharmacology
0007-1196 British Journal of Photography
0007-120X British Journal of Physical Education
0007-1218 British Journal of Physiological Optics
0007-1226 British Journal of Plastic Surgery
0007-1234 British Journal of Political Science
0007-1242 British Journal of Preventive and Social Medicine *changed to* Journal of Epidemiology & Community Medicine
0007-1250 British Journal of Psychiatry
0007-1269 British Journal of Psychology
0007-1285 British Journal of Radiology
0007-1293 British Journal of Social and Clinical Psychology *see* 0144-6665
0007-1293 British Journal of Social and Clinical Psychology *see* 0144-6657
0007-1307 British Journal of Social Psychiatry†
0007-1315 British Journal of Sociology
0007-1323 British Journal of Surgery
0007-1331 British Journal of Urology
0007-134X British Journal of Venereal Diseases
0007-1358 British Kinematography, Sound & Television *see* 0305-6996
0007-1366 British Lawn Tennis *see* 0306-7920
0007-1366 British Lawn Tennis *changed to* Tennis
0007-1374 British Legion Journal *see* 0308-4949
0007-1390 British Master Patternmaker *changed to* British Pattern & Mould Maker
0007-1404 British Medical Abstracts†
0007-1412 British Medical Book List *see* 0140-2722
0007-1420 British Medical Bulletin
0007-1439 British Medical Index *see* 0140-2722
0007-1447 British Medical Journal
0007-1455 British Medical Register of Holiday Accommodation†
0007-1463 British Mouthpiece
0007-1471 British Museum (Natural History) Bulletin. Geology
0007-148X British Museum (Natural History) Bulletin. Mineralogy *see* 0007-1471
0007-1498 British Museum (Natural History) Bulletin. Zoology
0007-1501 British Museum (Natural History). Bulletin. Entomology
0007-151X British Museum Quarterly†
0007-1528 British Mycological Society. Bulletin
0007-1536 British Mycological Society. Transactions
0007-1544 British National Bibliography
0007-1552 British National Film Catalogue
0007-1587 British Nuclear Energy Society. Journal *see* 0140-4067
0007-1595 British Ornithologists' Club. Bulletin
0007-1609 British Patents Abstracts
0007-1617 British Phycological Journal
0007-1625 British Plastics *see* 0306-3534
0007-1633 British Polio Fellowship. Bulletin
0007-1641 British Polymer Journal†
0007-165X British-Portuguese Chamber of Commerce. Monthly Bulletin *changed to* British-Portuguese Chamber of Commerce. Monthly Magazine
0007-1668 British Poultry Science
0007-1676 British Practice in International Law
0007-1684 British Printer
0007-1692 British Psychological Society. Bulletin
0007-1706 British Racehorse *see* 0260-7468
0007-1714 British Railways Board. Monthly Review of Technical Literature
0007-1722 British Record†
0007-1749 N L L Announcement Bulletin *changed to* British Reports, Translations and Theses
0007-1757 British Road Federation. Bulletin†
0007-1765 British Ship Research Association. Journal
0007-1773 British Society for Phenomenology. Journal
0007-1781 British Society of Commerce. Review
0007-179X British Society of Dowsers. Journal
0007-1803 British-Soviet Friendship
0007-1811 British Stationer *changed to* C T N
0007-1838 British Steelmaker
0007-1846 British Studies Monitor
0007-1854 British Sugar Beet Review
0007-1862 British Tax Guide
0007-1870 British Tax Review
0007-1889 British Technology Index *see* 0260-6593
0007-1897 British Toys *see* 0308-6712
0007-1900 British Travel News
0007-1927 British Vegetarian *see* 0260-3233
0007-1935 British Veterinary Journal
0007-1951 British Weekly and Christian World *changed to* British Weekly and Christian Record
0007-196X Brittonia
0007-1986 Public Health
0007-1994 Broadcast Engineering
0007-2001 Broadcast Journal†
0007-201X Broadcasters Bulletin
0007-2028 Broadcasting
0007-2044 Broadsheet
0007-2052 China Policy Study Group. Broadsheet
0007-2109 Broadside and the Free Press†
0007-2133 Broadway
0007-215X Brodogradnja
0007-2168 Broed *see* 0345-181X
0007-2176 Broiler Industry
0007-2184 Bromeliad Society Bulletin *see* 0090-8738
0007-2192 Bromides in Agriculture
0007-2214 Bron†
0007-2222 Bronches *changed to* Bronches-Broncho-Pneumologie
0007-2249 Bronx County Historical Society. Journal
0007-2257 Bronx County Medical Society. Bulletin *changed to* Bronx Medicine
0007-2265 Bronx Real Estate and Building News
0007-2273 Bronxboro
0007-229X Brookings Bulletin
0007-2303 Brookings Papers on Economic Activity
0007-232X Brooklyn Barrister
0007-2346 Brooklyn Heights Press and Cobble Hill News
0007-2354 Brooklyn Insurance Brokers Association. Bulletin *changed to* Messenger Reporter
0007-2362 Brooklyn Law Review
0007-2370 Brooklyn Longshoreman
0007-2397 Brooklyn Public Library Bulletin
0007-2400 Broom and Broom Corn News
0007-2419 Brot und Gebaeck *changed to* Getreide, Mehl und Brot
0007-2427 Broteria: Ciencias Naturais
0007-2435 Brotherhood
0007-2443 Brotherhood of Maintenance of Way Employes. Journal *see* 0146-0625
0007-2451 Brothers Newsletter
0007-246X Die Brotindustrie
0007-2478 Brown Alumni Monthly
0007-2486 Brown Boveri Review
0007-2494 Brown Gold
0007-2516 Brown Swiss Bulletin
0007-2524 Brownie
0007-2532 Browning Newsletter *see* 0095-4489
0007-2540 Browning Sentinel
0007-2559 Browser†
0007-2567 Brud Ar Yez Hag Ar Vro *changed to* Brud Nevez
0007-2583 Bruecke
0007-2605 Bruecke†
0007-2613 Die Bruecke
0007-2621 Bruel & Kjaer Technical Review
0007-2648 Brug
0007-2656 Brug†
0007-2664 Bruehl
0007-2672 Brulot
0007-2680 Burns Beitraege fuer Klinische Chirurgie *see* 0023-8236
0007-2699 Brunswickan
0007-2702 Brushes *see* 0305-7321
0007-2710 Brushware
0007-2729 B. B. B. Agenda†
0007-2737 Brygmesteren
0007-2745 Bryologist
0007-2753 B't
0007-2761 Buch der Zeit
0007-277X Buch und Bildung
0007-2788 Druck und Verarbeitung
0007-2796 Buchhaendler Heute
0007-280X Landesmuseum fuer Kaernten. Buchreihe.
0007-2818 Buck Investment Letter†
0007-2826 Buckeye Beverage Journal *changed to* Ohio Beverage Journal
0007-2834 Buckeye Farm News
0007-2842 ADAC Motorwelt
0007-2869 Bucknell Review
0007-2885 Budapest
0007-2893 Budapester Rundschau
0007-2907 Budavox Telecommunication Review
0007-2974 Budivel'ni Materialy i Konstruktsii
0007-2982 Budo-Sport
0007-2990 Budownictwo Okretowe
0007-3008 Budownictwo Wiejskie *changed to* Budownictwo Rolnicze
0007-3016 Buecherkommentare
0007-3032 Buechergilde
0007-3040 Buecherschau
0007-3059 Buecherschiff
0007-3067 Der Buechsenmacher
0007-3075 Die Buehne
0007-3083 Die Buehnengenossenschaft
0007-3091 Buehnentechnische Rundschau
0007-3113 Buenos Aires Musical
0007-3121 Der Buerger im Staat
0007-3148 Bueromarkt
0007-3156 Bueromaschinen-Mechaniker *see* 0340-2185
0007-3164 Buerotechnische Praxis†
0007-3172 Buerotechnische Sammlung
0007-3199 Buffalo Magazine *see* 0149-5070
0007-3229 Build
0007-3245 Builder†
0007-3261 Builder (Columbus)
0007-327X Builder/Architect *see* 0193-7472
0007-3288 Builders' Merchants' Journal *changed to* Builders and Home Improvement Merchants Journal
0007-3296 Builders Report Pacific *changed to* Building Industry Digest
0007-330X Builders' Weekly Guide†
0007-3318 Building
0007-3326 Building Abstracts Service C I B
0007-3334 Building Alaska†
0007-3342 Building & Construction
0007-3350 Building & Contract Journal
0007-3369 S. A. Building Products News
0007-3377 Building & Heating Product Guide
0007-3385 Building and Management *see* 0319-7018
0007-3393 Building & Realty Record
0007-3407 Building Design & Construction
0007-3415 Building Construction in Texas†
0007-3423 Building Design
0007-344X Building Equipment & Materials for South Africa
0007-3458 Building Equipment News *changed to* Building Equipment and Materials
0007-3490 Building Operating Management
0007-3504 Building Materials†
0007-3512 Building Materials & Equipment
0007-3520 Building Materials Merchandiser *see* 0194-1321
0007-3555 Building Permit Activity in Florida
0007-3563 Building Permit Values
0007-3571 Building Practice
0007-358X Building Products News
0007-3598 Building Progress†
0007-3601 Building Research†
0007-361X Building Research News
0007-3628 Building Science *see* 0360-1323
0007-3636 Building Science Abstracts†
0007-3644 Building Services Contractor
0007-3652 Building Societies' Gazette
0007-3679 Building Stone News
0007-3687 Building Supply Dealer
0007-3695 Building Supply News
0007-3709 Building Technology and Management
0007-3717 Building Tradesman
0007-3725 Buildings
0007-3733 Asian Regional Institute for School Building Research. Newsletter
0007-3741 Buitenlandse Boek
0007-375X Nieuwsbrief†
0007-3768 Buitenspoor
0007-3776 Bukhgalterskii Uchet
0007-3784 Buletin de Informare in Bibliologie
0007-3792 Buletin de Informare Pedagogica *changed to* Probleme de Pedagogie Contemporana
0007-3806 Buletin de Informare Stiintifica Biologie†
0007-3822 Buletin de Informare Stiintifica. Fizica†
0007-3830 Istorie-Arheologie†
0007-3849 Buletin de Informare Stiintifica. Matematica, Mecanica, Astronomie†
0007-3857 Psihologie; Buletin de Informare Stiintifica†
0007-3865 Sociologie; Buletin de Informare Stiintifica†
0007-3873 Stiinte Economice; Buletin de Informare Stiintifica†
0007-3881 Stiinte Juridice; Buletin de Informare Stiintifica†
0007-389X Vyzkumny Ustav Rybarsky a Hydrobiologicky. Bulletin
0007-3903 Bulgaria Today
0007-3911 Bulgarian Films
0007-3938 Bulgarsko Geologichesko Druzhestvo. Spisanie
0007-3946 Bulgarian Review
0007-3954 Bulgarian Trade Unions
0007-3970 Bulgarska Akademiia na Naukite. Institut po Fiziologiia na Rasteniiata "Metodii Popov." Izvestiia *changed to* Fiziologiia na Rasteniiata
0007-3989 Bulgarska Akademiia na Naukite. Spisanie
0007-3997 Bulgarski Knigopis. Seriia 1: Knigi, Notni, Graficheski i Kartografski
0007-4004 Bulgarski Voin
0007-4012 Bulgarsko Foto
0007-4020 Otkrytiya, Izobreteniya, Promyshlennye Obraztsy, Tovarnye Znaki
0007-4039 Bulletin
0007-4047 Bulletin; Belgium's News Weekly in English
0007-4063 Centre de Documentation Siderurgique. Bulletin Analytique
0007-4071 Bulletin Analytique de Documentation Politique, Economique et Sociale Contemporaine
0007-408X Bulletin Analytique de Linguistique Francaise
0007-4098 Bulletin Analytique d'Entomologie Medicale et Veterinaire

0007-4101 Bulletin Analytique Petrolier
0007-411X Bulletin Annote des Lois et Decrets
0007-4128 Bulletin Baudelairien
0007-4136 Bulletin Belge de Metrologie
0007-4144 Bulletin Bi-Mensuel des Tirages
0007-4152 Bulletin Bibliographique de Documentation Technique des Charbonnages de France *changed to* Bulletin Bibliographique de Documentation Technique du Groupement des Industries Extractives
0007-4160 Bulletin Bibliographique International du Machinisme Agricole
0007-4187 Bulletin Biologique de la France et de la Belgique
0007-4209 Bulletin Critique du Livre Francais
0007-4217 Bulletin de Correspondance Hellenique
0007-4225 Belgium. Ministere des Communications. Bulletin de Documentation†
0007-4233 Laboratoire de Recherches et de Controle du Caoutchouc. Bulletin de Documentation Bibliographique *changed to* L R C C Bulletin Bibliographique
0007-4241 Bulletin de Documentation Ceramique *changed to* CERINDEX: Bulletin de Documentation Ceramique
0007-4268 Bulletin de Documentation Pratiques des Impots Directs et des Taxes sur le Chiffre d'Affaires *changed to* Bulletin de Documentation Pratique des Impots Directs et des Droits d'Enregistrement
0007-4276 Bulletin de Documentation Pratique des Taxes sur le Chiffre d'Affaires *changed to* Bulletin de Documentation Pratique des Taxes sur le Chiffre d'Affaires et des Contributions Indirectes
0007-4284 Bulletin de Geophysique
0007-4292 Bulletin de la Librairie Ancienne et Moderne†
0007-4306 Belgium. Administration Penitentiaire. Bulletin
0007-4314 A. I. M. Bulletin
0007-4322 Bulletin de Litterature Ecclesiastique
0007-4330 Bulletin de l'Oeuvre Apostolique
0007-4349 Bulletin de l'Oeuvre d'Orient
0007-4357 Bulletin de Madagascar†
0007-4365 Bulletin de Medecine Legale et de Toxicologie Medicale *changed to* Journal de Medecine Legale
0007-4373 A U P E L F. Bulletin de Nouvelles Breves *see* 0226-7454
0007-439X Bulletin de Physiopathologie Respiratoire *see* 0271-9983
0007-4411 Bulletin de Psychologie Scolaire et d'Orientation
0007-442X Bulletin de Theologie Ancienne et Medievale
0007-4438 Institut de Science Financiere et d'Assurances. Bulletin des Actuaires Diplomes
0007-4462 Data from the Greek Economic Life *see* 0041-0543
0007-4489 Bulletin des Lettres
0007-4497 Bulletin des Sciences Mathematiques
0007-4500 Bulletin des Soies et Soieries *changed to* Textilyon: Bulletin des Soies et Soieries
0007-4519 Bulletin des Transports
0007-4535 Bulletin d'Information des Centrales Electriques†
0007-4543 France. Commissariat a l'Energie Atomique. Bulletin d'Informations Scientifiques et Techniques.†
0007-4551 Bulletin du Cancer
0007-456X Connaissance et Formation Par le Levre et l'Audiovisuel *changed to* Livres de France
0007-4578 Bulletin Economique du Cambresis
0007-4586 Bulletin Economique et Social du Maroc
0007-4594 E G U Bulletin
0007-4616 Bulletin Folklorique de l'Ile de France *changed to* Traditions de l'Ile de France
0007-4624 Bulletin for International Fiscal Documentation
0007-4632 Bulletin Geodesique
0007-4640 Bulletin Hispanique
0007-4659 Bulletin Historique et Scientifique de l'Auvergne
0007-4667 Bulletin Hygiene du Travail†
0007-4675 Bulletin Immobilier
0007-4683 Japanese Communist Party. Central Committee. Bulletin: Information for Abroad
0007-4691 Bulletin Mathematique
0007-4705 Bulletin Medical Franco-Japonais
0007-4713 France. Institut National de la Statistique et des Etudes Economiques. Bulletin Mensuel de Statistique
0007-473X Bulletin Monumental
0007-4748 O. et M. Bulletin *changed to* Service Central d'Organisation et Methodes. Revue
0007-4756 Bulletin of Applied Linguistics†
0007-4764 American Journal of Art Therapy
0007-4780 Bulletin of Bibliography and Magazine Notes *changed to* Bulletin of Bibliography
0007-4799 Bulletin of Business Research†
0007-4802 Bulletin of Canadian Petroleum Geology
0007-4810 Bulletin of Concerned Asian Scholars
0007-4837 Bulletin of Dental Education
0007-4845 Bulletin of Endemic Diseases
0007-4853 Bulletin of Entomological Research
0007-4861 Bulletin of Environmental Contamination and Toxicology
0007-4888 Bulletin of Experimental Biology and Medicine
0007-4896 Bulletin of Grain Technology
0007-490X Bulletin of Hispanic Studies
0007-4918 Bulletin of Indonesian Economic Studies
0007-4926 Bulletin of Information on Current Research on Human Sciences Concerning Africa
0007-4942 Volunteer Service Bulletin
0007-4950 Bulletin of Labour Statistics
0007-4969 Bulletin of Legal Developments
0007-4977 Bulletin of Marine Science
0007-4985 Bulletin of Mathematical Biophysics *see* 0092-8240
0007-4993 Bulletin of Mathematical Statistics
0007-5000 Bulletin of Mechanical Engineering Education†
0007-5019 Bulletin of Paedagogical Research
0007-5027 Laboratory Medicine
0007-5035 Bulletin of Peace Proposals
0007-5043 Bulletin of Physical Education
0007-5051 Bulletin of Polish Medical Science and History†
0007-506X Bulletin of Prosthetics Research
0007-5094 Science and Public Affairs Bulletin of the Atomic Scientists *see* 0096-3402
0007-5116 Bulletin of the European Communities
0007-5124 Experimental Animals
0007-5132 Bulletin of the History of Dentistry
0007-5140 Bulletin of the History of Medicine
0007-5159 Bulletin of Tibetology
0007-5167 Bulletin of Zoological Nomenclature
0007-5175 Bulletin Officiel Annote de Tous les Ministeres *changed to* Documentation Communale
0007-5183 Bulletin Officiel de la Propriete Industrielle *see* 0223-4092
0007-5191 Sport en Roumanie
0007-523X Bulletin on Narcotics
0007-5248 Bulletin on Rheumatic Diseases
0007-5256 Bulletin Ornithologique
0007-5264 Bulletin Quotidien d'Afrique
0007-5272 Bulletin Quotidien d'Informations Textiles
0007-5280 Belgium. Institut Royal Meteorologique. Bulletin Quotidien du Temps
0007-5302 Bulletin Signaletique des Telecommunications
0007-5310 Bulletin Signaletique. Part 101: Information Scientifique et Technique *see* 0301-0309
0007-5329 Mathematiques Appliques-Informatique-Automatique *changed to* Bulletin Signaletique. Part 110: Informatique-Automatique-Recherche Operationnelle-Gestion-Economie
0007-5337 Bulletin Signaletique. Part 120: Astronomie - Physique Spatiale - Geophysique
0007-5345 Bulletin Signaletique. Part 130: Physique *see* 0397-7757
0007-5353 Bulletin Signaletique. Part 140: Electricite-Electronique *changed to* Bulletin Signaletique. Part 140: Eldoc-Electrotechnique
0007-5353 Bulletin Signaletique. Part 140: Electricite-Electronique *changed to* Bulletin Signaletique. Part 145: Eldoc-Electronique
0007-537X Bulletin Signaletique. Part 160: Structure de la Matiere I *see* 0301-3332
0007-537X Bulletin Signaletique. Part 160: Structure de la Matiere 1 *see* 0301-3359
0007-5388 Bulletin Signaletique. Part 161. Structure de la Matiere II *see* 0304-1298
0007-5396 Bulletin Signaletique. Part 170: Chimie
0007-5442 Bulletin Signaletique. Part 330: Sciences Pharmacologiques - Toxicologie
0007-5450 Bulletin Signaletique. Part 340: Microbiologie-Virologie-Immunologie
0007-5469 Bulletin Signaletique. Part 350. Pathologie Generale et Experimentale *see* 0301-133X
0007-5477 Bulletin Signaletique. Part 351: Revue Bibliographique Cancer
0007-5485 Bulletin Signaletique. Part 360. Biologie et Physiologie Animale *see* 0181-0006
0007-5493 Bulletin Signaletique. Part 361. Endocrinologie et Reproduction *see* 0180-9989
0007-5507 Bulletin Signaletique. Part 362: Diabete - Maladies Metaboliques *changed to* Bulletin Signaletique. Part 362: Diabete. Obesite. Maladies Metaboliques
0007-5515 Bulletin Signaletique. Part 370. Biologie et Physiologie Vegetales *changed to* Bulletin Signaletique. Part 370: Biologie et Physiologie Vegetales. Sylviculture
0007-5523 Bulletin Signaletique. Part 380: Agronomie-Zootechnie-Phytopathologie-Industries Alimentaires *see* 0181-0030
0007-5531 Bulletin Signaletique. Part 390: Psychologie - Psychopathologie - Psychiatrie
0007-554X Bulletin Signaletique. Part 519: Philosophie
0007-5558 Bulletin Signaletique. Part 520: Sciences de l'Education
0007-5566 Bulletin Signaletique. Part 521: Sociologie - Ethnologie
0007-5574 Bulletin Signaletique. Part 522: Histoire des Sciences et des Techniques
0007-5582 Bulletin Signaletique. Part 523: Histoire et Science de la Litterature
0007-5590 Bulletin Signaletique. Part 524: Sciences du Langage
0007-5612 Bulletin Signaletique. Part 526: Art et Archeologie
0007-5620 Bulletin Signaletique. Part 527: Sciences Religieuse *see* 0180-9296
0007-5639 Bulletin Signaletique. Part 528: Science Administrative *see* 0150-8695
0007-5647 Bulletin Signaletique. Part 730: Combustibles - Energie
0007-5655 Bulletin Signaletique. Part 740: Metaux - Metallurgie
0007-5663 Bulletin Signaletique. Part 761: Microscopie Electronique-Diffraction Electronique
0007-5671 Bulletin Signaletique. Part 780: Polymeres *see* 0397-7730
0007-568X Bulletin Signaletique. Part 880: Genie Chimique - Industries Chimique et Parachimique
0007-5698 Bulletin Signaletique. Part 885: Eau et Assainissement-Pollution Atmospherique *see* 0301-3499
0007-5701 Bulletin Signaletique. Part 890: Industries Mecaniques-Genie Civil-Transports-Techniques Aerospatiales *see* 0223-4246
0007-571X Bulletin Signaletique. Part 900. Bulletin des Traductions *see* 0378-6803
0007-5728 Bulletin Synoptique de Documentation Thermique *see* 0337-4092
0007-5736 Bulletin Technique
0007-5744 Bulletin Technique de la Suisse Romande
0007-5752 Bureau Veritas. Bulletin Technique
0007-5779 Bulletins of American Paleontology
0007-5787 Bullettino delle Scienze Mediche
0007-5795 Bullettino Storico Empolese
0007-5809 Bullettino Storico Pistoiese
0007-5817 Bumazhnaya Promyshlennost'
0007-5833 Bund der Deutschen Katholischen Jugend. Informationsdienst
0007-5841 Bund der Oeffentlich Bestellten Vermessungsingenieure e.V. Mitteilungsblatt *changed to* B D V I - Forum
0007-585X Germany (Federal Republic, 1949-) Bundesanstalt fuer Arbeit. Amtliche Nachrichten
0007-5868 Bundesversorgungsblatt *changed to* Bundesarbeitsblatt
0007-5876 Die Bundesbahn
0007-5884 Bundesbaublatt
0007-5892 Bundesforschungsanstalt fuer Forst- und Holzwirtschaft in Reinbeck. Mitteilungen
0007-5914 Bundesgesundheitsblatt
0007-5922 Austria. Hoehere Bundeslehr- und Versuchanstalt fuer Wein- und Obstbau. Mitteilungen
0007-5930 Die Bundesverwaltung
0007-5949 Die Bundeswehr
0007-5965 Das Bunte Blatt
0007-5973 Bunte Blumenwelt
0007-5981 Bunte Oesterreich *changed to* Bunte
0007-599X Bunte Tierwelt
0007-6007 Bur
0007-6015 Burbujas
0007-6023 Burda Bunte Bild Rezepte†
0007-6031 Burda Moden
0007-604X Bureau
0007-6074 Bureaux de France
0007-6090 France. Bureau de Recherches Geologiques et Minieres. Bulletin. Section 2. Geologie Appliquee *changed to* France. Bureau de Recherches Geologiques et Minieres. Bulletin. Section 2: Geologie des Gites Mineraux
0007-6104 France. Bureau de Recherches Geologiques et Minieres. Bulletin. Section 1: Geologie de la France
0007-6112 France. Bureau de Recherches Geologiques et Minieres. Bulletin. Section 4: Geologie Generale
0007-6120 France. Bureau de Recherches Geologiques et Minieres. Bulletin. Section III: Hydrogeologie *see* 0300-936X
0007-6155 Philippines. Bureau of Agricultural Economics. Bureau of Agricultural Economics Reporter†
0007-6163 Bureau of Government Research Bulletin†
0007-6171 University of Rhode Island. Bureau of Government Research. Newsletter
0007-618X U. S. Bureau of the Census. Bureau of the Census Catalog
0007-6201 Burgen und Schloesser
0007-621X Burgenlaendische Forschungen
0007-6228 Burgenlaendische Gemeinschaft
0007-6236 Burgenlaendische Heimatblaetter
0007-6244 Burgenlaendische Landwirtschaftskammer. Mitteilungsblatt
0007-6252 Burgenlaendisches Leben

0007-6260 Buried History
0007-6279 Burlington County Times Advertiser
0007-6287 Burlington Magazine
0007-6295 Burma Medical Journal
0007-6309 Burning Bush
0007-6325 B T O/Buerotechnik und Organization *changed to* Buerotechnik Automation und Organisation
0007-6333 Burroughs Bulletin
0007-6341 Burroughs Clearing House
0007-635X Bus and Truck Transport
0007-6376 Busara†
0007-6376 Busara
0007-6392 Buses
0007-6406 Business Abroad†
0007-6414 Business Administration *see* 0140-8453
0007-6422 Business Advertising†
0007-6430 Business Analyst
0007-6449 Business and Administration *changed to* Institute of Administration and Commerce of South Africa. Journal
0007-6457 Business and Economic Dimensions
0007-6465 Business and Economic Review
0007-6473 Business and Finance†
0007-6473 Business and Finance
0007-6481 Business and Financial Indicators†
0007-6503 Business and Society
0007-6511 Business and Society†
0007-652X Business and Technology Sources†
0007-6562 Business Comments†
0007-6570 Business and Commercial Aviation
0007-6589 Business Conditions *changed to* Economic Perspectives
0007-6597 Business Conditions Digest
0007-6600 Business Conditions in Argentina†
0007-6627 Business Credit and Hire Purchase Journal
0007-6635 Business Day
0007-6651 Business Digest
0007-6678 Business Education Forum
0007-6686 Business Education Journal
0007-6694 Business Education World
0007-6708 Business Equipment Digest
0007-6716 Business Equipment Guide
0007-6732 Business Systems & Equipment
0007-6740 Business Facts and Figures
0007-6767 Business Forms Reporter
0007-6775 Business Graphics†
0007-6783 Business Herald
0007-6791 Business History
0007-6805 Business History Review
0007-6813 Business Horizons
0007-6821 Business in Brief
0007-683X Business in Nebraska
0007-6856 Business Inquiry†
0007-6864 Business Insurance
0007-6872 Business International
0007-6880 Business Latin America
0007-6899 Business Lawyer
0007-6902 Business Literature
0007-6929 Industrial Management *changed to* Industrial Management & Data Systems
0007-6937 Business Management†
0007-6945 Business Memo from Belgium
0007-6953 Business Opportunities Digest
0007-6961 Business Periodicals Index
0007-6988 Business Products *changed to* Special Report to Office Products Industry
0007-6996 Business Quarterly
0007-7011 Federal Reserve Bank of Philadelphia Business Review
0007-702X Federal Reserve Bank of Dallas. Business Review *see* 0149-5364
0007-7038 Business Review and Economic News from Israel
0007-7046 Business Screen *see* 0005-3635
0007-7062 Business Service Checklist†
0007-7070 Business South Africa *changed to* Business S A
0007-7097 Business Systems & Equipment
0007-7100 Business Today
0007-7119 Business Travel *changed to* Business Travel World
0007-7127 Business Trends in New York State
0007-7135 Business Week
0007-7151 Businessman
0007-716X Businessman & the Law
0007-7178 Businessmen's Expectations
0007-7194 Buskap og Avdraatt
0007-7216 Bustan†
0007-7224 Bustleton-Somerton News Gleaner *changed to* Bustleton News
0007-7232 Busy Bees' News
0007-7240 Butane Propane
0007-7259 Butane-Propane News
0007-7267 Butcher Workman†
0007-7275 Butter-Fat
0007-7283 Butterfield Express
0007-7291 Butterfly
0007-7305 Butterick Home Catalog *changed to* Butterick Sewing World
0007-7313 Butterley Foundry News†
0007-7321 Butterworths Consolidated Legislation Service of South Africa. Monthly Bulletin
0007-7356 Buvar
0007-7364 Buxom Belle Courier
0007-7380 Buyers' Guide
0007-7402 Buyers Purchasing Digest
0007-7429 Byarozka
0007-7437 Byelorussian-American Union. Bulletin†
0007-7445 Bygd
0007-7453 Bokvaennen *see* 0345-7982
0007-7461 Bygg *see* 0332-5326
0007-747X Bygge Fagene
0007-7488 Bygge Nyt
0007-7496 Byggehaandvaerket
0007-750X Byggeindustrien
0007-7518 Byggekunst
0007-7542 Bygglitteratur†
0007-7550 Byggmaestaren
0007-7569 Byggnadsarbetaren
0007-7577 Byggnadsindustrin
0007-7585 Byggnadsingenjoren- Team
0007-7593 Byggnadskonst
0007-7607 Byggnadstidningen
0007-7615 Byggnadsvaerlden
0007-7631 Byminner
0007-764X Hospital Equipment
0007-7658 Byplan
0007-7666 U. S. S. R. Gosudarstvennyi Komitet Soveta Ministrov po Voprosam Truda i Zarabotnoi Platy. Byulleten
0007-7674 Byulleten' Inostrannoi Kommercheskoi Informatsii
0007-7682 Moskovskoe Obshchestvo Ispytatelei Prirody. Geologicheskii Otdel. Byulleten'
0007-7690 Byulleten' Stroitel'noi Tekhniki
0007-7704 Byzantinische Zeitschrift
0007-7712 Byzantinoslavica
0007-7720 Canadian Review of American Studies
0007-7739 C A E News
0007-7763 C A H P E R Journal
0007-7771 C. A. H. S. Journal
0007-778X Cal
0007-7798 C A L F News
0007-7801 C A M
0007-7836 C A R D A N. Fiches Analytiques†
0007-7844 Council for the Advancement of Small Colleges. Newsletter†
0007-7852 C. A. S. I. Transactions†
0007-7860 C A T C A Journal
0007-7887 C. A. U. T. Bulletin
0007-7895 C. A. U. T. Newsletter *see* 0007-7887
0007-7909 C & T
0007-7925 Select†
0007-7933 C B E Bulletin *changed to* Basic Education
0007-7941 C B M News
0007-795X C B Magazine
0007-7968 C. B. R. I. Abstracts
0007-7976 C C A R Journal *see* 0149-712X
0007-7984 C C B Outlook (Inkprint Edition)
0007-7992 Accounting Articles
0007-800X C C I T U Labour Bulletin†
0007-8018 C D A Newsletter *see* 0703-5764
0007-8026 C D I U P A. Bulletin Bibliographique *see* 0223-9159
0007-8034 C E A Forum
0007-8042 C E A - C T A News
0007-8050 C E A Advisor
0007-8069 C E A Critic
0007-8077 O E C D. Isotope Generator Information Centre *changed to* O E C D. Newsletter on Isotopic Generators and Batteries
0007-8093 C E A P Bulletin†
0007-8123 C E C Newsletter *changed to* Last Word
0007-8131 C E C Update
0007-814X C E D A G Informativo†
0007-8158 C E D A M Notiziario Bibliografico
0007-8166 C. E. D. Contact†
0007-8174 C. E. D. Dokumentoj†
0007-8204 English Education
0007-8212 C E F News *changed to* C-E-F Trailblazer
0007-8220 C E F P Journal
0007-8247 C E N
0007-8255 C E N
0007-8263 C E N P H A. Boletim
0007-8271 C E N S I S Quindicinale di Note e Commenti
0007-828X C E N T O Newsletter†
0007-8301 C. E. R. I. L. H. Bulletin Analytique
0007-8328 C E R N Reports
0007-8336 C E S I N News
0007-8344 C F Letter *see* 0091-536X
0007-8352 C G D Betriebstraete-Mitteilungen
0007-8360 C G Information *changed to* C G-Kurier
0007-8387 C I A S Centro de Investigacion y Accion *see* 0325-1306
0007-8395 Ciba Journal *changed to* CIBA-Geigy Journal
0007-8409 Ciba Technical Notes *see* 0142-4904
0007-8417 C.I.C.I.A.M.S. News/Nouvelles/Nachrichten
0007-8433 C I L Oval†
0007-8441 C I M M Y T Annual Report on Maize and Wheat Improvement *see* 0304-5439
0007-8441 C I M M Y T Annual Report on Maize and Wheat Improvement *see* 0304-548X
0007-845X C I M Notes *changed to* Cleveland Institute of Music (Newsletter)
0007-8484 C I R F Abstracts *changed to* T & D Abstracts
0007-8506 C. I. R. P. Annals
0007-8514 C I S Index
0007-8530 C. K. of A. Journal
0007-8549 C L A Journal
0007-8557 C L A Newsletter
0007-8565 Cumann Leabharlannaithe Scoile. C L S Bulletin
0007-8573 C L U Journal
0007-8581 C. M. A. A. Newsletter†
0007-8603 C M A S Bulletin d'Information
0007-8611 C. M. B. Newsletter
0007-862X C M D†
0007-8646 C. M. J. Quarterly *changed to* Shalom
0007-8654 C M M
0007-8670 C M R†
0007-8689 C. M. S. News *see* 0311-0737
0007-8700 C. N. A. P. T. Bulletin†
0007-8727 C. N. E. E. M. A. Bulletin d'Information
0007-8735 C. N. E. E. M. A. Etudes
0007-8743 C. N. E. E. M. A. Nouvelles
0007-8751 C. N. E. N. Notiziario
0007-8794 C O N E S C A L
0007-8808 C O P H Bulletin
0007-8816 C O P N I P List†
0007-8824 C O P P E Boletim Informativo *changed to* C O P P E Noticiario
0007-8832 C O S M E P Newsletter *changed to* C O S M E P Newsletter (1981)
0007-8859 C O T A L
0007-8867 C P A†
0007-8875 C. P. C. Monthly Report†
0007-8883 C P C U News
0007-8891 C P E C Taxpayers News
0007-8905 C P H Commentator
0007-8921 C P S Reporter
0007-893X C Q
0007-8948 C Q Elettronica
0007-8956 C Q Guide to Current American Government
0007-8964 C Q Ham Radio
0007-8972 Foodservice & Hospitality
0007-8980 C R C Critical Reviews in Analytical Chemistry
0007-8999 C R C Critical Reviews in Environmental Control
0007-9006 C R C Critical Reviews in Food Technology *see* 0099-0248
0007-9014 C R C Critical Reviews in Radiological Sciences and Nuclear Medicine *see* 0147-6750
0007-9030 C R D A News *see* 0147-8222
0007-9030 Illinois Drug Process *see* 0147-8222
0007-9049 C R E Information
0007-9057 C R V Newsletter†
0007-9065 C S A Quarterly Review†
0007-9073 C S C. Newsletter
0007-9081 C.S.E.R. Selezione *see* 0391-3457
0007-9103 C. S. I. R. O. Wildlife Research *see* 0310-7833
0007-9111 C S I R Library Information & Accessions†
0007-912X C S I R O Abstracts *see* 0311-5836
0007-9138 C S I R O Food Preservation Quarterly *see* 0310-9070
0007-9154 C S I R Recorder†
0007-9162 C S I R Research Review *changed to* C S I R Publications
0007-9197 C S U Collegian *changed to* Fort Collins Journal
0007-9200 C T A Action *changed to* C T A/N E A Action
0007-9219 C T V D: Cinema-TV-Digest
0007-9227 C W A News
0007-9235 Ca-A Cancer Journal for Clinicians
0007-9243 Ca Va
0007-926X Cabellian†
0007-9278 Cabinet Maker and Retail Furnisher
0007-9286 Cable *changed to* World Spotlight
0007-9294 Cablecasting-Cable TV Engineering†
0007-9308 Cables & Transmission *changed to* Commutation et Transmission
0007-9316 Cabore
0007-9332 Cacaos, Cafes, Sucres
0007-9340 Cacau Atualidades†
0007-9359 Cacciatore Siciliano
0007-9367 Cactus and Succulent Journal
0007-9375 Cactus and Succulent Journal of Great Britain
0007-9383 Cactus Comments
0007-9391 Cad†
0007-9405 Cadenza
0007-9421 Cadernos de Biblioteconomia, Arquivistica e Documentacao
0007-943X Cadernos de Jornalismo e Comunicacao
0007-9456 Cadet Journal and Gazette
0007-9472 Cadres and Profession *changed to* Cadres C F D T
0007-9480 Caducee
0007-9499 Caementum
0007-9502 Caesaraugusta
0007-9510 Cafe, Cacao, The
0007-9537 Cafe Solo
0007-9545 Cafeteria Motel Bladet *changed to* Cafeteria Bladet
0007-9553 Caffe
0007-9561 Cage & Aviary Birds
0007-957X Civilisation Libertaire
0007-9596 Cahiers Astrologiques
0007-960X Cahiers Bibliques Trimestriels *changed to* Cahiers Evangile
0007-9618 Cahiers Bourbonnais et du Centre
0007-9626 Cahiers Bruxellois
0007-9650 Cahiers d'Action Litteraire
0007-9669 Cahiers de l'Actualite Religieuse et Sociale
0007-9677 Cahiers d'Agriculture Pratique des Pays Chauds *see* 0395-9481
0007-9685 Cahiers d'Anesthesiologie
0007-9693 Cahiers d'Archeologie et d'Histoire du Berry

0007-9715 Cahiers de Bibliographie Therapeutique Francaise. Edition Medicale
0007-9723 Cahiers de Biologie Marine
0007-9731 Cahiers de Civilisation Medievale
0007-974X Cahiers de Droit
0007-9758 Cahiers de Droit Europeen
0007-9766 Cahiers de Geographie du Quebec
0007-9774 Cahiers de Josephologie
0007-9782 Cahiers de Kinesitherapie
0007-9790 Cahiers de la Ceramique, du Verre et des Arts du Feu
0007-9804 Association Belge de Documentation. Cahiers de la Documentation/Bladen voor de Documentatie
0007-9812 Cahiers de la Methode Naturelle *changed to* Cahiers de la Methode Naturelle en Medecine
0007-9820 Cahiers de la Puericultrice
0007-9839 Cahiers de la Reconciliation
0007-9847 Cahiers de la Renaissance Vaudoise
0007-9855 Cahiers de l'Afrique Occidentale et de l'Afrique Equatoriale
0007-9863 Cahiers de l'Enfance Inadaptee
0007-9898 Cahiers de l'Iroise
0007-9901 Cahiers de l'Optique de Contact
0007-991X Cahiers de l'Oronte
0007-9936 Cahiers de Medecine Interprofessionnelle
0007-9944 Cahiers de Medecine Veterinaire
0007-9952 France. Institut National de Recherche et de Securite pour la Prevention des Accidents du Travail et des Maladies Professionnelles. Cahiers de Notes Documentaires
0007-9960 Cahiers de Nutrition et de Dietetique
0007-9979 Cahiers de Reeducation & de Readaptation Fonctionnelles
0007-9987 Cahiers de Sociologie Economique
0007-9995 Cahiers de Sociologie et de Demographie Medicales
0008-0004 Cahiers de Topologie et Geometrie Differentielle†
0008-0012 Cahiers de Tunisie
0008-0020 Cahiers des Ameriques Latines. Serie - Sciences de l'Homme *changed to* Cahiers des Ameriques Latines
0008-0039 Cahiers des Naturalistes
0008-0047 Cahiers des Religions Africaines
0008-0055 Cahiers d'Etudes Africaines
0008-0063 Cahiers d'Etudes Cathares
0008-008X Cahiers d'Histoire
0008-0098 Cercle Ernest Renan. Cahiers
0008-0101 Cahiers du Chemin†
0008-011X Cahiers du Cinema
0008-0128 Club de la Grammaire. Cahiers
0008-0136 Cahiers du Communisme
0008-0152 Cahiers du Monde Hispanique et Luso-Bresilien (Caravelle)
0008-0160 Cahiers du Monde Russe et Sovietique
0008-0179 Cahiers du Nursing *see* 0703-9484
0008-0195 Cahiers Economiques de Bruxelles
0008-0209 Cahiers Economiques et Sociaux
0008-0217 Cahiers Francais
0008-0241 Cahiers Geologiques
0008-025X Cahiers Haut-Marnais
0008-0268 Cahiers Integres de Medecine†
0008-0276 Cahiers Internationaux de Sociologie
0008-0284 Cahiers Internationaux de Symbolisme
0008-0292 Cahiers J E B *changed to* J E B
0008-0292 Cahiers J E B *changed to* J E B Special
0008-0292 Cahiers J E B Cahiers *changed to* J E B-Points
0008-0306 Cahiers Jean Tousseul†
0008-0314 Cahiers Laennec†
0008-0322 Cahiers Libres de Leon Emery
0008-0330 Cahiers Lyonnais d'Histoire de la Medecine†
0008-0365 Cahiers Naturalistes
0008-0373 Cahiers Numismatiques
0008-0381 Cahiers O.R.S.T.O.M. Serie Hydrologie
0008-039X Cahiers O.R.S.T.O.M. Serie Oceanographie†
0008-0403 Cahiers O.R.S.T.O.M. Serie Sciences Humaines
0008-0411 Cahiers Oceanographiques†
0008-042X Cahiers Pedagogiques
0008-0438 Cahiers Pierre Loti
0008-0446 Cahiers pour l'Analyse†
0008-0454 Cahiers Raciniens
0008-0462 Cahiers Rationalistes
0008-0497 Cahiers Vilfredo Pareto
0008-0519 Caiet de Documentare Cinematografica
0008-0527 Caiet Pentru Literatura si Istoriografie
0008-0535 Cake and Cockhorse
0008-0543 Cal-Tax News
0008-056X Calabria Nobilissima
0008-0578 Calavo Newsletter *changed to* Calavo Newsletter
0008-0586 Calcified Tissue Abstracts
0008-0594 Calcified Tissue Research *see* 0171-967X
0008-0616 Calcoin News
0008-0624 Calcolo
0008-0632 Calculi
0008-0659 Calcutta Mathematical Society. Bulletin
0008-0667 Calcutta Medical Journal
0008-0675 Calcutta Municipal Gazette
0008-0683 Calcutta Statistical Association. Bulletin
0008-0691 University of Calcutta. Department of English. Bulletin
0008-0705 University of Calcutta.University College of Medicine. Bulletin
0008-0713 Caledon Venster
0008-0721 Calendar
0008-073X Calendar of Coming Meetings of Interest to Historians†
0008-0756 Calendar of Events in the New Pennsylvania *changed to* Pennsylvania Quarterly Calendar of Events
0008-0764 Calendar of Forthcoming Scientific and Technological Meetings to Be Held in Israel
0008-0772 Calendar of Sports Events†
0008-0802 California A F L - C I O News
0008-0829 California Academy of Sciences. Academy Newsletter
0008-0837 California Agency Bulletin *changed to* California Independent Agent
0008-0845 California Agriculture
0008-0853 California Agriculture Department Biennial Report†
0008-0861 California Air Environment
0008-0896 California Apparel News
0008-090X California-Arizona Cotton
0008-0918 California Bowling News
0008-0926 California Business
0008-0934 California C P A Quarterly
0008-0942 California Cattleman
0008-0950 California Courier
0008-0969 California Covenanter *changed to* Pacific Southwest Covenanter
0008-0977 California Dental Association. Journal
0008-0985 California Dental Association. Newsletter†
0008-1000 California. Division of Mines and Geology. Bulletin
0008-1019 California Elementary Administrator†
0008-1027 California Engineer
0008-1051 California Farmer
0008-106X Western Financial Journal
0008-1078 California Fish and Game
0008-1086 California Food Mart News *changed to* Grocers' Spotlight West
0008-1094 California Forestry and Forest Products
0008-1108 California Future Farmer†
0008-1116 California Garden
0008-1124 California Grange News
0008-1140 California Highway Patrolman
0008-1167 California Historical Society. Notes *see* 0095-6465
0008-1175 California Historical Quarterly *see* 0162-2897
0008-1191 California Industrial Relations Reports
0008-1205 California Journal
0008-1213 California Journal of Educational Research *changed to* Educational Research Quarterly
0008-1221 California Law Review
0008-123X California Librarian†
0008-1248 California Livestock News *changed to* California Sheepman's Quarterly
0008-1256 California Management Review
0008-1264 California Medicine *see* 0093-0415
0008-1272 California Men's and Women's Stylist *changed to* Mens Apparel News
0008-1280 California Mental Health Research Digest†
0008-1299 California Mining Journal
0008-1302 California Monthly
0008-1310 California Nurse
0008-1329 Pacific Oil World
0008-1337 California Optometrist Association. Journal *changed to* California Optometry
0008-1345 Nord Nytt
0008-1353 California Palace of the Legion of Honor. Bulletin†
0008-1361 California Pelican
0008-1388 California Pharmacy *changed to* California Pharmacist
0008-140X California Probation, Parole and Correctional Association. Journal *changed to* Crime and Corrections
0008-1418 California Professor
0008-1426 California Public Survey†
0008-1434 California Publisher
0008-1442 California Rancher *changed to* California Grower & Rancher
0008-1450 California Real Estate Magazine
0008-1477 California Safety News†
0008-1485 California Savings and Loan Journal
0008-1493 California School Administrator†
0008-1515 California School Employee
0008-154X California Shavian
0008-1558 California Southern Baptist
0008-1566 California State Employee
0008-1574 California State Publications
0008-1582 California Tech
0008-1604 California Vector Views
0008-1612 California Veterinarian
0008-1639 California Western Law Review
0008-1647 Western Tide *changed to* U S I U International News
0008-1655 California Wineletter
0008-1663 California Woman
0008-1671 California Youth Authority Quarterly
0008-1698 Call (New York)
0008-1701 Call Board
0008-1728 Call
0008-1736 Call Number†
0008-1744 Call Number
0008-1760 Calore
0008-1779 Calvary Review
0008-1787 Calvijn
0008-1795 Calvin Theological Journal
0008-1833 Camag Bibliography Service
0008-1841 Camara Argentina de Productos Quimicos. Boletin Informativo
0008-185X Camara de Comercio de Bogota. Boletin
0008-1868 Comerciante
0008-1876 Camara de Comercio de la Guaira. Boletin Estadistico.
0008-1884 Camara de Comercio de Lima. Boletin Semanal
0008-1892 Comercio y Produccion
0008-1906 Camara de Comercio Luso-Americana. Boletim
0008-1914 Camara de Comercio Uruguayo-Britanica. Revista
0008-1922 Camara Nacional de Comercio de Managua. Boletin *changed to* Camara de Comercio de Nicaragua. Boletin Comercial
0008-1930 Camara Oficial de Comercio, Industria y Navegacion de Barcelona. Boletin
0008-1949 Camera Textil de Mexico. Revista Tecnica *changed to* Revista Tecnica Textil-Vestido
0008-1973 Cambridge Law Journal
0008-1981 Cambridge Philosophical Society. Proceedings. Mathematical and Physical Sciences *see* 0305-0041
0008-199X Cambridge Quarterly
0008-2007 Cambridge Review
0008-2023 Cambridgeshire, Huntingdon & Peterborough Life
0008-2031 Camden County Record
0008-204X Camellia Journal
0008-2058 Cameo Newsletter *changed to* New York State Office for the Aging. Newsletter
0008-2066 Camera
0008-2074 Camera
0008-2082 CamerArt
0008-2090 Camera Canada
0008-2104 Camera Club Journal
0008-2112 Camara de Industria y Comercio Argentino-Alemana. Boletin
0008-2120 Camera di Commercio di Milano *changed to* Realta Economica
0008-2139 Camera di Commercio Industria Artigianato e Agricoltura. Dati e Notizie†
0008-2147 Camera di Commercio, Industria, Artigianato e Agricoltura di Belluno. Rassegna Economica
0008-2155 Camera Mainichi
0008-2163 Camera Nu *changed to* Camera Palet
0008-2171 Camera Thirty-Five
0008-218X Cameral†
0008-2198 Chambre de Commerce, d'Industrie et des Mines du Cameroun.Bulletin d'Information
0008-221X Camillusbode
0008-2236 Caminos
0008-2244 Caminos del Aire
0008-2252 Camion
0008-2260 Cammino
0008-2279 Cammino Economico
0008-2295 Camp Management†
0008-2309 Campaign
0008-2325 Campeggio Italiano
0008-2341 Campesino
0008-235X Campesino
0008-2376 Camping Magazine
0008-2384 Camping & Caravaning
0008-2406 C S E News
0008-2414 Camping-Caravanning-Revue
0008-2430 Camping Industry
0008-2449 Camping Journal *changed to* Caravan Camping-Journal
0008-2465 Campo
0008-2473 El Campo
0008-2481 Campus (Lennoxville)
0008-249X Campus Call†
0008-2503 Campus Crier
0008-2511 Campus Estrien
0008-252X Campus Leader
0008-2538 Campus Life
0008-2554 Canada Agriculture
0008-2562 Canada Armenian Press *changed to* Canada Armenian Press. Newsletter
0008-2570 Canada. Statistics Canada. Air Carrier Operations in Canada/Operations des Transporteurs Aeriens au Canada
0008-2589 Canada. Bureau of Statistics. Credit Statistics. *see* 0380-0741
0008-2597 Canada. Bureau of Statistics. Industry Division. Air Conditioning and Equipment *changed to* Canada. Statistics Canada. Air Conditioning & Refrigeration Equipment
0008-2600 Canada. Statistics Canada. Biscuits and Confectionery/Biscuits et Confiserie†
0008-2619 Canada. Statistics Canada. Production of Canada's Leading Minerals/Production es Principaux Mineraux du Canada†
0008-2627 Canada. Statistics Canada. Restaurant Statistics/Statistique des Restaurants
0008-2635 Canada Courier
0008-2643 Canada. Department of Fisheries and Forestry. Bi-Monthly Research Notes *see* 0228-9989
0008-2651 Canada. Statistics Canada. Consumption, Production and Inventories of Rubber/Consommation, Production et Stocks de Caoutchouc
0008-266X Canada. Statistics Canada. Service Bulletin. Energy Statistics†

0008-2686 Canada. Fisheries Research Board. Journal *see* 0706-652X
0008-2694 Canada Income Tax Guide
0008-2708 Canada Labour Service
0008-2732 Canada Poultryman
0008-2740 Canada Tax Cases
0008-2759 Canada Tax Service
0008-2775 Canadan Uutiset
0008-2791 Canada's Mental Health
0008-2805 Canadian
0008-2813 Canadian Administrator
0008-2821 Canadian Aeronautics and Space Journal
0008-2821 Canadian Journal of Remote Sensing
0008-283X Canadian Affairs†
0008-283X Canadian Affairs†
0008-2848 Canadian Aircraft Operator
0008-2856 Canadian Anaesthetists' Society. Journal
0008-2864 Canadian Arabian News
0008-2872 Canadian Architect
0008-2880 Canadian Armed Forces Review *changed to* Government and Military Business
0008-2899 C A H P E R Journal
0008-2902 Canadian Association of Radiologists. Journal
0008-2937 Canadian Author & Bookman
0008-2945 Canadian Automotive Trade
0008-2953 Canadian Aviation
0008-2961 Canadian Ayrshire Review
0008-297X Canadian Banker *see* 0315-6230
0008-2988 Canadian Baptist
0008-3003 Canadian Bar Review
0008-3011 Canadian Beverage Review
0008-3038 Broadcaster
0008-3046 Canadian Botanical Association. Bulletin
0008-3054 Canadian Boy†
0008-3070 Canadian Building
0008-3089 Canadian Building Abstracts
0008-3097 Canadian Building Digest
0008-3127 Canadian Cartographer
0008-3143 Cattlemen
0008-3151 Canadian Certified Accountant *see* 0318-742X
0008-316X Canadian Chartered Accountant *see* 0317-6878
0008-3178 Canadian Chemical Education†
0008-3186 Canadian Chemical Processing
0008-3194 Canadian Chiropractic Association. Journal
0008-3208 Canadian Church Historical Society Journal
0008-3216 Canadian Churchman
0008-3224 Canadian Cleaner & Launderer
0008-3232 Canadian Clothing Journal
0008-3240 Canadian Co-Operative Digest†
0008-3267 Canadian Consulting Engineer
0008-3275 Canadian Consumer
0008-3283 Canadian Controls & Instrumentation *see* 0705-3193
0008-3291 Canadian Copper
0008-3305 Canadian Council for International Co-Operation. Bulletin†
0008-3313 Canadian Council of Professional Engineers. News Brief/Communique†
0008-3321 Canadian Council of Resource Ministers. References†
0008-3348 Canadian Criminal Cases
0008-3356 Canadian Current Law
0008-3364 Canadian Datasystems
0008-3372 Canadian Dental Association. Journal
0008-3380 Canadian Dental Hygienist
0008-3399 Canadian Dietetic Association. Journal
0008-3402 Canadian Dimension
0008-3429 Canadian Doctor
0008-3437 Canadian Documentation Centre, Fitness and Sport. Bulletin†
0008-3445 Canadian Education Association. Newsletter
0008-3453 Canadian Education Index
0008-3461 Canadian Electronics Engineering
0008-347X Canadian Entomologist
0008-3488 Canadian Estate and Gift Tax Reports *changed to* Canadian Estate Planning and Administration Reports
0008-350X Canadian Family Physician
0008-3518 Canadian Farm Economics
0008-3526 Canadian Farm Equipment Dealer†
0008-3534 Canadian Federation of Music Teachers' Associations. News Bulletin *see* 0319-6356
0008-3542 Canadian Feed & Grain Journal†
0008-3550 Canadian Field-Naturalist
0008-3577 Canadian Flight
0008-3585 Canadian Florist, Greenhouse and Nursery
0008-3631 Canadian Forum
0008-364X Canadian Funeral Service *see* 0319-3225
0008-3658 Canadian Geographer
0008-3674 Canadian Geotechnical Journal
0008-3682 Canadian Golf Review†
0008-3690 Canadian Government Publications Monthly Catalogue *see* 0709-0412
0008-3704 Canadian Grocer
0008-3712 Canadian Guide
0008-3720 Canadian Hairdresser
0008-3739 Canadian Hereford Digest
0008-3747 Canadian High News *changed to* Teen Generation
0008-3755 Canadian Historical Review
0008-3763 Canadian Home Economics Journal
0008-3771 Canadian Home Leaguer
0008-378X Canadian Horse
0008-3798 Canadian Hospital *see* 0317-7645
0008-3801 Canadian Hotel & Restaurant
0008-381X Canadian Imperial Bank of Commerce. Commercial Letter *changed to* Canadian Imperial Bank of Commerce. Spectrum
0008-3828 Canadian Independent Adjuster
0008-3836 Canadian Industrial Equipment News
0008-3844 Canadian Information Processing Society. Quarterly Bulletin *see* 0315-5986
0008-3860 Canadian Institute of Food Technology Journal/Institut Canadien de Technologie Alimentaire. *see* 0315-5463
0008-3879 Canadian Insurance
0008-3887 Canadian Interiors
0008-3895 Canadian Jaycee
0008-3909 Canadian Jersey Breeder
0008-3917 Canadian Jeweller
0008-3925 Canadian Jewish Chronicle Review *see* 0008-3941
0008-3941 Canadian Jewish News
0008-395X Canadian Jewish Weekly†
0008-3968 Canadian Journal of African Studies
0008-3984 Canadian Journal of Animal Science
0008-3992 Arms Collecting
0008-3992 Canadian Journal of Arms Collecting *see* 0008-3992
0008-4018 Canadian Journal of Biochemistry
0008-4026 Canadian Journal of Botany
0008-4034 Canadian Journal of Chemical Engineering
0008-4042 Canadian Journal of Chemistry
0008-4050 Canadian Journal of Comparative Medicine
0008-4069 Canadian Journal of Corrections *see* 0704-9722
0008-4077 Canadian Journal of Earth Sciences
0008-4085 Canadian Journal of Economics
0008-4093 Canadian Journal of Genetics and Cytology
0008-4107 Canadian Journal of History
0008-4115 Canadian Journal of History of Sport and Physical Education
0008-4123 Canadian Journal of Hospital Pharmacy
0008-4131 Canadian Journal of Linguistics
0008-4158 Canadian Journal of Medical Technology
0008-4166 Canadian Journal of Microbiology
0008-4174 Canadian Journal of Occupational Therapy
0008-4182 Canadian Journal of Ophthalmology
0008-4190 Canadian Journal of Pharmaceutical Sciences
0008-4204 Canadian Journal of Physics
0008-4212 Canadian Journal of Physiology and Pharmacology
0008-4220 Canadian Journal of Plant Science
0008-4239 Canadian Journal of Political Science
0008-4247 Canadian Journal of Psychiatric Nursing
0008-4255 Canadian Journal of Psychology
0008-4263 Canadian Journal of Public Health
0008-4271 Canadian Journal of Soil Science
0008-428X Canadian Journal of Surgery
0008-4298 Studies in Religion
0008-4301 Canadian Journal of Zoology
0008-4328 Canadian Labor Law Reports
0008-4336 Canadian Labour
0008-4344 Canadian Lacombe Breeders Association. Newsletter
0008-4352 Canadian Library Journal
0008-4360 Canadian Literature†
0008-4387 Canadian Marketer†
0008-4409 Canadian Medical Association Journal
0008-4417 Canadian Mennonite†
0008-4425 Canadian Messenger of the Sacred Heart
0008-4433 Canadian Metallurgical Quarterly†
0008-4433 Canadian Metallurgical Quarterly
0008-4441 Canadian Metalworking/Machine Production†
0008-445X Canadian Military Engineer
0008-4468 Canadian Military Journal
0008-4476 Canadian Mineralogist
0008-4492 Canadian Mining Journal
0008-4506 Canadian Modern Language Review
0008-4522 Canadian Motorcycling *changed to* Cycle C M A
0008-4530 Canadian Motorist
0008-4549 Canadian Music Educator
0008-4557 Canadian Commission for UNESCO. Bulletin
0008-4565 Canadian News Facts
0008-4573 Canadian Numismatic Journal†
0008-4581 Canadian Nurse
0008-459X Canadian Nurseryman *see* 0315-4874
0008-4611 Canadian Occupational Safety
0008-462X Canadian Office Products and Stationery
0008-4638 Canadian Journal of Operational Research and Information Processing *see* 0315-5986
0008-4654 Canadian Packaging
0008-4662 Canadian Paint and Finishing†
0008-4670 Patent Office Record (Canada)
0008-4689 Canadian Patent Reporter
0008-4697 Peace Research
0008-4719 Canadian Periodical Index
0008-4735 Canadian Petroleum
0008-4743 Canadian Pharmaceutical Journal
0008-4751 Canadian Physiotherapy Association Journal/Association Canadienne de Physiotherapie Revue *see* 0300-0508
0008-476X Canadian Plant Disease Survey
0008-4778 Canadian Plastics
0008-4786 Canadian Podiatrist
0008-4794 Canadian Postmaster
0008-4808 Canadian Poultry Review†
0008-4816 Canadian Printer and Publisher
0008-4824 Canadian Psychiatric Association Journal *see* 0706-7437
0008-4840 Canadian Public Administration
0008-4859 Canadian Publishers Directory
0008-4867 Canadian Pulp and Paper Industry
0008-4875 Canadian Rail
0008-4883 Canadian Railway Club. Official Proceedings *changed to* Canadian Railway Club. Newsletter
0008-4891 Canadian Reader
0008-4905 Canadian Realtor *changed to* Canadian Real Estate
0008-4913 Canadian Register *see* 0383-1620
0008-493X Canadian Research & Development *see* 0319-1974
0008-4948 Canadian Review of Sociology and Anthropology
0008-4956 Canadian Rockhound
0008-4972 Canadian Sailor
0008-4980 Canadian Shipping and Marine Engineering†
0008-4999 Canadian Slavic Studies/Revue Canadienne d'Etudes Slaves *see* 0090-8290
0008-5006 Canadian Slavonic Papers
0008-5022 Canadian Society of Exploration Geophysicists. Journal
0008-5030 Canadian Society of Forensic Science Journal
0008-5049 Canadian Sociology and Anthropology Association. Bulletin†
0008-5057 Canadian Spectroscopy *see* 0045-5105
0008-509X Canadian Statistical Review/Revue Statistique du Canada
0008-5103 Canadian Surveyor
0008-5111 Canadian Tax Journal
0008-512X Canadian Tax Papers
0008-5138 Canadian Tax Reports
0008-5146 Canadian Teacher
0008-5154 Canadian Technical Information News *changed to* Canadian Technical and Scientific Information News Journal
0008-5162 Canadian Telephone and Cable Television Journal *see* 0318-0069
0008-5170 Canadian Textile Journal
0008-5189 Canadian Tobacco Grower
0008-5197 Canadian Tourism†
0008-5200 Canadian Transportation and Distribution Management
0008-5219 Canadian Travel Courier
0008-5235 Canadian Tuberculosis and Respiratory Disease Association. Bulletin *changed to* Canadian Lung Association. Bulletin
0008-5243 Canadian U F O Report
0008-5251 Canadian Underwriter
0008-5278 Canadian Vending
0008-5286 Canadian Veterinary Journal
0008-5294 Canadian Weather Review
0008-5308 Canadian Weekly Law Sheet
0008-5316 Canadian Weekly Publisher *see* 0380-8025
0008-5324 Canadian Welder & Fabricator
0008-5332 Canadian Welfare *see* 0704-5263
0008-5340 Western Canadian Journal of Anthropology
0008-5367 Canadian Wings *see* 0701-1369
0008-5383 Canadian Zionist
0008-5391 Canadiana
0008-5405 Canard Enchaine
0008-5413 Canberra Consumer
0008-5421 Canberra Post
0008-543X Cancer
0008-5448 Cancer Bulletin
0008-5456 Cancer Chemotherapy Abstracts *changed to* Cancer Therapy Abstracts
0008-5464 Cancer News
0008-5472 Cancer Research
0008-5480 Cancro
0008-5502 Candle *see* 0308-9703
0008-5510 Candle (Overland Park)
0008-5537 Baked Snack Industry *changed to* Candy & Snack Industry
0008-5545 Candy Marketer
0008-5553 Cane Growers Quarterly Bulletin
0008-557X Canner Packer *see* 0192-7132
0008-5588 Canning and Packing *see* 0040-795X
0008-560X Canning Trade *changed to* Food Production/Management
0008-5618 Cannocchiale
0008-5626 Canoe-Camper
0008-5642 Canoeing in Britain *see* 0308-7565
0008-5650 Canon Law Abstracts
0008-5677 Canteras y Explotaciones
0008-5685 Canterbury Chamber of Commerce. Economic Bulletin
0008-5693 Canterbury Diocesan Notes
0008-5715 Cantiere *see* 0029-6325
0008-5723 Canto dell'Assemblea†
0008-5731 Canto Gregoriano
0008-5758 Canyon Cinemanews *changed to* Cinemanews
0008-5774 Capaha Arrow
0008-5782 Cape Cod Illustrated†
0008-5790 Cape Librarian
0008-5804 Cape of Good Hope. Department of Nature Conservation. Newsletter *changed to* Cape of Good Hope. Department of Nature Conservation and Museum Services. Annual Report
0008-5812 Cape Rock Journal *see* 0146-2199

ISSN	Title
0008-5820	Cape Town Photographic Society Syllabus
0008-5839	Capital
0008-5847	Capital
0008-5855	Capital Changes Reports
0008-5871	Capital en Accion *changed to* San Juan en Accion
0008-588X	Capital Goods Review
0008-591X	Capitolium†
0008-5936	Capper's Weekly
0008-5944	Capricho
0008-5952	C C C O News Notes
0008-5960	Capsule News†
0008-5979	Captions†
0008-5987	Car
0008-6002	Car and Driver
0008-6010	Car Craft
0008-6029	Car-del Scribe
0008-6037	Car Mechanics
0008-6053	Car Rental & Leasing Insider Newsletter
0008-607X	Car Wash Review *changed to* American Carwash Review
0008-6088	Cara
0008-6096	Carabinier de Lausanne
0008-610X	Carabiniere
0008-6118	Caracola
0008-6126	Caractere TPG
0008-6134	Caracteres
0008-6142	Caravan
0008-6150	Caravan
0008-6169	Caravan Bladet
0008-6177	Caravaning
0008-6185	Caravaning
0008-6193	Caravanner
0008-6207	Caravel†
0008-6215	Carbohydrate Research
0008-6223	Carbon
0008-6231	Carbon Black Abstracts†
0008-624X	Carcanet *see* 0308-2636
0008-6258	Carcinogenesis Abstracts
0008-6266	Commonwealth Forestry Bureau. Card Title Service
0008-6274	Cardamom News *changed to* Cardamom
0008-6290	Cardinal Poetry Quarterly†
0008-6312	Cardiology
0008-6320	Cardiologia nel Mondo
0008-6339	Cardiologia Pratica
0008-6347	Cardiology Digest *see* 0148-5199
0008-6355	Cardiovascular Nursing
0008-6363	Cardiovascular Research
0008-6371	Cardiovascular Research Center Bulletin
0008-638X	Care†
0008-641X	Cargill Crop Bulletin
0008-6436	Caribbean Challenge
0008-6444	Caribbean Conservation Association. Newsletter *changed to* Caribbean Conservation News.
0008-6460	Caribbean Journal of Science and Mathematics
0008-6495	Caribbean Quarterly
0008-6509	Caribbean Report†
0008-6517	Caribbean Research Institute. Quarterly Report†
0008-6525	Caribbean Review
0008-6533	Caribbean Studies
0008-655X	Caridade
0008-6568	Caries Research
0008-6576	Carillon
0008-6592	Carinski Pregled
0008-6606	Carinthia 1
0008-6614	Caritas
0008-6622	Caritas-Korrespondenz
0008-6630	Carleton *see* 0315-1859
0008-6649	Carleton Miscellany†
0008-6657	Laboratoire Carlsberg. Comptes Rendus des Travaux *see* 0105-1938
0008-6665	Carmel
0008-6673	Carmelus
0008-6681	Carnegie Magazine
0008-669X	Carnets de Zoologie
0008-6711	Carnivore Genetics Newsletter
0008-672X	Carolina Christian
0008-6738	Carolina Cooperator *see* 0195-3346
0008-6746	Carolina Country
0008-6762	Carolina Genealogist
0008-6770	Carolina Golfer
0008-6789	Carolina Highways
0008-6797	Carolina Quarterly
0008-6800	Carolina Sportsman
0008-6819	Carolinian†
0008-6835	Carovana†
0008-6843	Carpenter
0008-6851	Carpet Review *see* 0308-4507
0008-6878	Carre Bleu
0008-6886	Carrefour
0008-6894	Carrell
0008-6908	Carreteras
0008-6916	Carriage Journal
0008-6924	Carrier Reports
0008-6932	Carroll Business Bulletin
0008-6940	Carrosserie
0008-6959	Carrozziere Italiano
0008-6975	Cars & Parts
0008-6983	Carta Cultural de Venezuela
0008-7009	Cartactual
0008-7017	Carte Blanche
0008-7025	Carte Segrete
0008-7033	Carthusian
0008-7041	Cartographic Journal
0008-705X	Cartonnagebedrijf
0008-7068	Cartoonist Profiles
0008-7076	Cartophilic Notes & News
0008-7092	Carwash Journal
0008-7114	Caryologia
0008-7122	Casa
0008-7149	Casa de la Cultura Ecuatoriana. Revista
0008-7157	Casa de las Americas
0008-7165	Casa do Douro Boletim†
0008-7173	Casa Vogue
0008-7181	Casabella
0008-719X	Casana
0008-7203	Casas y Jardines
0008-7211	Cascade Caver
0008-722X	Cascades†
0008-7238	Case and Comment
0008-7246	Case & Counsel
0008-7254	Case Western Reserve Journal of International Law
0008-7262	Case Western Reserve Law Review
0008-7289	Cash Box
0008-7297	Cash Crop Farming
0008-7300	Cashew Bulletin
0008-7319	Cashier
0008-7327	C & S
0008-7335	Casopis Lekaru Ceskych
0008-7343	Narodni Muzeum. Casopis: Oddil Historicky
0008-7351	Narodni Muzeum. Casopis: Oddil Prirodovedny
0008-736X	Casopis pro Mezinarodni Pravo
0008-7378	Casopis pro Mineralogii a Geologii
0008-7394	Casopis pro Pestovani Matematiky
0008-7408	Cassa di Risparmio delle Provincie Lombarde Quarterly
0008-7416	Cassa di Soccorso e Malattia per i Dipendenti dell'Azienda Trasporti Municipali di Milano. Bollettino d'Informazione
0008-7424	Cassazione Penale
0008-7440	Cassella-Riedel Archiv
0008-7467	International Cast Metals Journal
0008-7475	Castanea
0008-7483	Casteel
0008-7491	Castello
0008-7505	Castillos de Espana
0008-7513	Casting Engineering
0008-7521	Castings
0008-753X	Castoro
0008-7548	Burmah International
0008-7556	Castrum Peregrini
0008-7564	Casual Living and Summer and Casual Furniture *changed to* Casual Living
0008-7572	Casualty Return Statistical Summary
0008-7580	Casualty Simulation
0008-7599	Cat
0008-7602	Cat Fancy
0008-7610	Catalogo Nacional del Envase, Embalaje y Artes Graficas Aplicadas
0008-7629	Catalogue & Index
0008-7645	Catalysis Reviews *see* 0360-2451
0008-7661	Catalyst (Peterborough)
0008-767X	Catalyst (Philadelphia)
0008-7688	Catalyst for Environmental Quality *changed to* Catalyst for Environment/Energy
0008-7696	Catch
0008-770X	Catch Society of America. Journal†
0008-7726	Catechist
0008-7734	Catechistes *changed to* Temps et Paroles
0008-7742	Catechistes d'Aujourd'hui *changed to* Points de Repere
0008-7750	Universidad de Granada. Catedra Francisco Suarez. Anales
0008-7777	Caterer & Hotelkeeper
0008-7807	Catering Executive†
0008-7815	Catering Industry Employee
0008-7823	Catering Quarterly†
0008-7831	Catering Times
0008-784X	Caterpillar†
0008-7866	Cathcart Chronicle
0008-7874	Cathedral Age
0008-7882	Cathode Press†
0008-7890	Catholic Action News
0008-7904	Catholic Advance
0008-7912	Catholic Biblical Quarterly
0008-7920	Catholic Book Review *changed to* Canadian Book, Film and Record Review
0008-7939	Religious Book Review
0008-7947	Catholic Business Education Review†
0008-7971	Catholic Chronicle
0008-7998	Catholic Digest
0008-8005	Catholic Documentation†
0008-8013	Catholic Education Today†
0008-8021	Catholic Film Newsletter *see* 0362-0875
0008-8048	Catholic Forester
0008-8064	Catholic Gazette
0008-8072	Catholic Herald
0008-8080	Catholic Historical Review
0008-8099	Catholic Hospital *changed to* C. H. A. C. Review
0008-8102	Medical Service
0008-8110	Catholic Institutional Management†
0008-8129	Catholic Journalist
0008-8137	Catholic Lawyer
0008-8145	Catholic Leader
0008-8161	Catholic Library Association. Northern Illinois Unit. Newsletter
0008-817X	Catholic Library Association. Northern Ohio Unit. Newsletter
0008-8188	Parish & Lending Library News *changed to* Parish and Community Libraries News
0008-820X	Catholic Library World
0008-8218	Catholic Life
0008-8226	Catholic Medical Quarterly
0008-8234	Catholic Messenger
0008-8242	Catholic Mind
0008-8250	Catholic News†
0008-8269	Catholic Nurse†
0008-8277	Catholic Peace Fellowship Bulletin
0008-8285	Catholic Periodical and Literature Index
0008-8293	Catholic Pictorial
0008-8307	Catholic Press Directory
0008-8315	Catholic Review (Baltimore)
0008-8323	Catholic Review (New York)
0008-8331	Catholic Rural Life
0008-834X	Catholic School Editor†
0008-8366	Catholic Standard
0008-8374	Catholic Traveler
0008-8390	Catholic University Law Review
0008-8404	Catholic Virginian
0008-8412	Catholic Voice
0008-8420	Catholic Weekly
0008-8439	Catholic Weekly
0008-8447	Catholic Witness
0008-8455	Catholic Woman's Journal
0008-8463	Catholic Worker
0008-8471	Catholic Workman
0008-848X	Catholic World *changed to* New Catholic World
0008-8498	Catholica†
0008-8501	Catholica
0008-851X	Catholica Unio
0008-8528	Catolicismo
0008-8536	Catonsville Roadrunner
0008-8544	Cats Magazine
0008-8552	Cattleman
0008-8579	Caustic
0008-8609	Cavalier Daily
0008-8625	Caves and Karst
0008-8641	Caxtonian†
0008-865X	Cayuga County Farm and Home News
0008-8668	Cebu y Derivados
0008-8676	Cecidologia Indica
0008-8684	Cedars-Sinai Medical Center Compass
0008-8692	Ceiba
0008-8706	Celebriamo
0008-8714	Celestial Mechanics
0008-8722	Celik
0008-8730	Cell & Tissue Kinetics
0008-8749	Cellular Immunology
0008-8757	Cellule
0008-8765	Cellulosa e Carta
0008-8773	Celtic News *changed to* Carn
0008-8781	Celuloide
0008-8803	Cement
0008-8811	Cement
0008-882X	Cement
0008-8838	Cement & Concrete†
0008-8846	Cement and Concrete Research
0008-8854	Cement Technology *see* 0308-8855
0008-8862	Cement, Lime and Gravel *see* 0305-9421
0008-8870	Cement og Beton *see* 0029-1307
0008-8889	Cement Special
0008-8897	Cement, Wapno, Gips
0008-8900	Cemento-Hormigon
0008-8927	Cemento Portland
0008-8935	Cenacolo
0008-8943	Cenhadwr†
0008-8951	Cenicafe
0008-896X	Cenobio
0008-8978	Centaur†
0008-8986	Centauros
0008-8994	Centaurus
0008-9001	Centenary College Conglomerate
0008-901X	Centennial Review *see* 0162-0177
0008-9036	Center for Children's Books. Bulletin
0008-9044	Center for Chinese Research Materials. Newsletter
0008-9052	University of Michigan. Center for Coordination of Ancient and Modern Studies. Newsletter†
0008-9079	Center for Law Enforcement Research Information†
0008-9087	Center for Research Libraries. Newsletter *see* 0275-4924
0008-9095	Center for Soviet and East-European Studies in the Performing Arts. Bulletin
0008-9117	Center Forum†
0008-9125	Center for the Study of Democratic Institutions. Center Magazine
0008-9133	Center for Teaching About Peace and War. Newsletter
0008-9141	Cento
0008-915X	Centri Meccanografici Ed Elettronici *changed to* Management e Informatica
0008-9168	Centraal Orgaan voor de Handel in Aardappelen, Groenten en Fruit†
0008-9176	Central African Journal of Medicine
0008-9184	Central African Zionist Digest
0008-9192	Central Asiatic Journal
0008-9206	Central Bank News†
0008-9214	Central Bank News Digest *changed to* C. B. Review
0008-9222	Central Bank of Ceylon. Bulletin
0008-9230	Central Bank of Cyprus. Bulletin
0008-9249	Central Bank of Egypt. Economic Review
0008-9257	Central Bank of Iraq. Quarterly Bulletin
0008-9265	Central Bank of Jordan. Quarterly Bulletin *changed to* Central Bank of Jordan. Monthly Statistical Bulletin
0008-9273	Central Bank of Malta. Quarterly Review
0008-9281	Central Bank of Nigeria. Economic and Financial Review

0008-929X Central Bank of Nigeria. Monthly Report
0008-9303 Philippine Financial Statistics
0008-9311 Central Bible Quarterly†
0008-9346 Central Constructor†
0008-9362 Central Europe Journal†
0008-9389 Central European History
0008-9397 Central Glass and Ceramic Research Institute. Bulletin
0008-9400 Central Ideas†
0008-9419 Central Illinois Historical Messenger *changed to* Historical Messenger
0008-9427 Central Inland Fisheries Research Institute. Bulletin
0008-9443 Central Japan Journal of Orthopaedic & Traumatic Surgery
0008-9451 Central Michigan Life
0008-946X Central New York Academy of Medicine. Bulletin
0008-9478 Central New York Regional Medical Program. Bulletin†
0008-9486 Central New Yorker
0008-9494 Central News†
0008-9508 Central Opera Service Bulletin
0008-9524 Central Pennsylvania Labor News
0008-9559 Central States Archaeological Journal
0008-9575 Central States Speech Journal
0008-9583 Centralblatt fuer das Gesamte Forstwesen
0008-9591 Centralny Osrodek Informacji Budownictwa. Biuletyn-Informacja *changed to* Biuletyn Informacyjny o Budownictwie
0008-9605 Centre Catholique des Intellectuels Francais. Recherches et Debats
0008-9613 Centre d'Amitie Internationale. Revue d'Art-Tourisme-Culture
0008-9621 Centre de Conjoncture Africaine et Malgache. Bulletin d'Information *changed to* C C A M Information
0008-963X Centre de Documentation Siderurgique. Circulaire d'Informations *see* 0035-1563
0008-9648 Centre de Formation des Journalistes. Feuillets
0008-9664 Centre de Recherche et d'Information Socio-Politiques. Etudes Africaines†
0008-9672 Societe Nationale des Petroles d'Aquitaine. Centre de Recherches de Pau. Bulletin *see* 0396-2687
0008-9680 Centre de Recherches et d'Etudes Oceanographiques. Travaux
0008-9699 Universite Libre de Bruxelles. Centre d'Etude des Pays de l'Est. Revue du Centre d'Etude des Pays de l'Est et du Centre National pour l'Etude des Etats de l'Est *changed to* Universite Libre de Bruxelles. Centre d'Etude des Pays de l'Est. Revue des Pays de l'Est
0008-9702 Centre d'Etude des Matieres Plastiques. Bulletin de Documentation
0008-9710 Shikshak
0008-9737 Universite Libre de Bruxelles. Centre d'Etudes de Recherche Operationnelle. Cahiers
0008-9761 Centre d'Etudes Socialistes. Cahiers†
0008-9788 Centre d'Information Civique, Paris. Etudes
0008-980X Centre International d'Etude des Textiles Anciens. Bulletin de Liaison
0008-9818 Centre International d'Etudes Romanes. Bulletin *changed to* Centre International d'Etudes Romanes. Revue Trimestrielle
0008-9826 Centre Medical†
0008-9842 Federation Protestante de France. Centre d'Etudes et de Documentation. Bulletin *changed to* Centre Protestant d'Etudes et de Documentation. Bulletin
0008-9850 Centre Scientifique et Technique du Batiment. Cahiers
0008-9869 Centre Technique du Bois. Bulletin Bibliographique
0008-9877 Centre Technique du Bois. Bulletin d'Informations Techniques
0008-9885 Centre Technique du Bois. Cahiers
0008-9907 Centro America Odontologica
0008-9915 Instituto de Investigacao Cientifica de Mocambique. Centro de Documentacao Cientifica. Boletim†
0008-9931 Portugal. Ministerio do Ultramar. Centro de Documentacao Tecnico-Economica. Boletim Bibliografico
0008-9958 Centro de Estudios Monetarios Latinoamericanos. Boletin Mensual *changed to* Centro de Estudios Monetarios Latinoamericanos. Boletin Bimensual
0008-9966 Centro de Estudios. Sociales del Valle de los Caidos. Boletin *changed to* Revista de Estudios Sociales
0008-9990 Centro de Historia del Estado Falcon. Boletin
0009-000X Regno-Documenti
0009-0026 Centro di Documentazione Sul Movimento dei Disciplinati. Quaderni
0009-0034 Centro Interamericano de Vivienda y Planeamiento. Lista de Nuevas Adquisiciones†
0009-0042 Centro Interamericano de Vivienda y Planeaminento. Suplemento Informativo *changed to* S I N D U. Noticiero
0009-0050 Centro Latino Americano de Fisica Noticia
0009-0069 Centro Latino-Americano de Pesquisas Em Ciencias Sociais. Bibliografia†
0009-0069 Centro Latino Americano de Pesquisas em Ciencias Sociais. Boletim Bibliografia
0009-0085 Centro Nacional de Informacion de Ciencias Medicas. Revista de Resumenes. Cuaderno 2. Cirugia†
0009-0093 Centro Nacional de Informacion de Ciencias Medicas. Revista de Resumenes. Cuaderno 4. Higiene, Epidemiologia, Medios de Diagnostico y Otros†
0009-0107 Centro Nacional de Informacion de Ciencias Medicas. Revista de Resumenes. Cuaderno 1. Medicina†
0009-0115 Centro Nacional de Informacion de Ciencias Medicas. Revista de Resumenes. Cuaderno 3. Pediatria†
0009-0123 Centro Naval. Boletin
0009-0131 Centro Pan-Americano de Febre Aftosa. Boletin
0009-014X Centro Regional de Pesquisas Educacionais Jaoa Pinheiro. Boletim Informativo
0009-0158 Century
0009-0166 Century†
0009-0174 Ceol
0009-0190 Ceramic Arts & Crafts
0009-0204 Ceramic Awareness Bulletin†
0009-0212 Ceramic Forum†
0009-0220 Ceramic Industry
0009-0247 Ceramic Scope
0009-0255 Ceramic Society of Japan. Journal
0009-0263 Ceramic Trade News & Catalog File *changed to* Ceramic Teaching Projects and Trade News
0009-0271 Ceramica Informazione
0009-028X Ceramic Italian nell'Edilizia *changed to* Ceramica per l'Edilizia International
0009-0301 Ceramics *see* 0305-7623
0009-031X Ceramics Japan
0009-0328 Ceramics Monthly
0009-0336 Ceramique Moderne
0009-0344 Cercle d'Etudes Numismatiques. Bulletin
0009-0352 Cereal Chemistry
0009-0360 Cereal Science Today *see* 0146-6283
0009-0379 Ceres
0009-0387 Cerkev v Sedanjem Svetu
0009-0395 Cernakov Odkaz *changed to* Slobodne Slovensko
0009-0409 Certificated Engineer
0009-0417 Certified Accountants Journal *see* 0306-2406
0009-0425 Certified General Accountant *see* 0318-742X
0009-0433 Certified Milk†
0009-0441 Cerveny Kvet
0009-045X Cervi's Rocky Mountain Journal *changed to* Rocky Mountain Journal
0009-0468 Ceska Literatura
0009-0476 Ceska Mykologie
0009-0484 Ceske Listy†
0009-0492 Ceskoslovenska Akademie Ved. Vestnik
0009-0506 Ceskoslovenska Armada
0009-0514 Ceskoslovenska Dermatologie
0009-0522 Ceskoslovenska Epidemiologie, Mikrobiologie, Imunologie
0009-0530 Ceskoslovenska Farmacie
0009-0549 Ceskoslovenska Fotografie
0009-0557 Ceskoslovenska Fysiologie
0009-0565 Ceskoslovenska Gastroenterologie a Vyziva
0009-0573 Ceskoslovenska Hygiena
0009-0581 Ceskoslovenska Neurologie *see* 0301-0597
0009-059X Ceskoslovenska Oftalmologie
0009-0603 Ceskoslovenska Otolaryngologie
0009-0611 Ceskoslovenska Patologie
0009-062X Ceskoslovenska Psychologie
0009-0638 Ceskoslovenska Rusistika
0009-0646 Ceskoslovenska Spolecnost Mikrobiologicka. Bulletin
0009-0654 Ceskoslovenska Stomatologie
0009-0670 Rybarstvi
0009-0689 Ceskoslovenske Zdravotnictvi
0009-0697 Ceskoslovensky Architekt
0009-0700 Ceskoslovensky Casopis pro Fysiku
0009-0719 Ceskoslovensky Hornik a Energetik
0009-0727 Ceskoslovensky Kolorista
0009-0735 Ceskoslovensky Rozhlas a Televize
0009-0743 Ceskoslovensky Sach
0009-0751 Ceskoslovensky Vojak
0009-0778 Cesky Bratr
0009-0786 Cesky Jazyk a Literatura
0009-0794 Cesky Lid
0009-0808 Ceux des F F A
0009-0816 Ceylon Coconut Planter's Review
0009-0824 Ceylon Coconut Quarterly
0009-0832 Sri Lanka Journal of Historical and Social Studies
0009-0840 Ceylon Journal of the Humanities *changed to* Sri Lanka Journal of the Humanities
0009-0859 Ceylon Labour Gazette *changed to* Sri Lanka Labour Gazette
0009-0867 Sri Lanka Library Review
0009-0875 Ceylon Medical Journal
0009-0883 Ceylon National Bibliography *changed to* Sri Lanka National Bibliography
0009-0891 Ceylon Veterinary Journal
0009-0905 Avicultura Industrial
0009-0913 Chacra *changed to* Campo Moderno y Chacra
0009-0921 Chain Merchandiser
0009-093X Chain Saw Age
0009-0948 Chain Saw Industry & Power Equipment Dealer
0009-0964 Chalk Talk
0009-0972 Chalkmarks†
0009-0980 Challenge *see* 0045-849X
0009-0999 Challenge (London, 1961)
0009-1006 Challenge (London)
0009-1014 Challenge (Sandbach)
0009-1049 Challenge (New York)
0009-1057 Challenge†
0009-1065 New Stationer
0009-1073 Challenge (Richmond)
0009-1103 Chalmers†
0009-1111 Chalmers Tekniska Hogskola. Institutionen Foer Vattenfoersoerjnings och Avloppsteknik. Publikationsserie B
0009-112X Chalmers Tekniska Hoegskola. Institutionen foer Skeppshydromekanik. Rapport
0009-1138 Dublin Chamber of Commerce Journal *changed to* Trade-Links Journal
0009-1146 Chamber of Commerce of the U.S. Newsletter
0009-1154 Chamber of Commerce of the U.S. Association Letter
0009-1162 Chamberof Mines Journal *changed to* Mining and Engineering
0009-1189 Chambre de Commerce et d'Industrie de Meurthe et Moselle. Bulletin Mensuel *changed to* Commerce et Industrie
0009-1197 Chambre de Commerce de Bruxelles. Bulletin Officiel *changed to* Entreprendre
0009-1200 Chambre de Commerce et d'Industrie de Marseille. Cahiers de Documentation†
0009-1219 Chambre de Commerce et d'Industrie de Paris. Bulletin Mensuel
0009-1227 Chambre de Commerce et d'Industrie de Rouen. Bulletin Economique
0009-1235 Chambre de Commerce Francaise du Japon. Bulletin†
0009-126X Chambre Syndicale des Mines de Fer de France. Bulletin Technique
0009-1286 Chaminade College Newsletter *changed to* Chaminade University Newsletter
0009-1308 Champignon
0009-1316 Champignoncultuur
0009-1324 Champion†
0009-1332 Champak
0009-1359 Chandrabhaga
0009-1367 Change *see* 0335-1971
0009-1383 Change
0009-1391 Changes (New York)
0009-1413 Changing Education†
0009-1421 Changing Schools†
0009-143X Changing Times
0009-1456 Channel *see* 0025-4142
0009-1464 Channel (New Paltz)
0009-1480 Gambit†
0009-1499 Channel Viewer *changed to* Channel TV Times
0009-1502 Channels (Omaha)
0009-1510 Channels (New York)
0009-1529 Channels of Blessing
0009-1537 Chanoyu Quarterly
0009-1537 Chanoyu *see* 0009-1537
0009-1553 Chantecoq†
0009-1561 Chanticleer
0009-1588 Chantiers
0009-1596 Chantiers Cooperatifs
0009-160X Les Chantiers du Cardinal
0009-1618 Chantiers Pedagogiques
0009-1626 Children's Book Review†
0009-1634 Chapeaux et Coiffures de France *see* 0047-8512
0009-1642 Chaplain *see* 0149-4236
0009-1650 Chappaqua Speculator†
0009-1669 Character Potential
0009-1685 Charbonnages de France. Publications Techniques
0009-1707 Charing Cross Hospital Gazette *changed to* Charing Cross Medical Gazette
0009-1715 Charisma *changed to* Ark
0009-1723 Charity and Children
0009-1731 Charivari†
0009-174X Charlatan: Interdisciplinary Journal†
0009-1766 Charles C. Adams Center for Ecological Studies. Occasional Papers
0009-1774 Charles S. Peirce Society. Transactions
0009-1790 Charlotte-Mecklenburg School Report†
0009-1804 Charm
0009-1812 Charm†
0009-1820 Charmant†
0009-1839 Charme†
0009-1847 Charolais Banner
0009-1863 Chart-Of-The-Week
0009-1871 Chartcraft Weekly Service
0009-188X Chartered Accountant
0009-1898 Chartered Accountant in Australia
0009-1901 Chartered Engineer†
0009-191X Chartered Mechanical Engineer
0009-1928 Chartered Secretary
0009-1936 Chartered Surveyor
0009-1944 Chartotheca Translationum Alphabetica
0009-1952 Chase
0009-1960 Chasovoi
0009-1987 Chat
0009-1995 Chatelaine
0009-2002 Chaucer Review

ISSN INDEX

ISSN	Title
0009-2010	Chaud-Froid-Plomberie
0009-2029	Chauffage - Ventilation - Conditionnement
0009-2037	Chauffage-Plomberie
0009-2053	Chaussure et la Mode see 0025-3898
0009-2061	Chavhata Weekly
0009-2088	Joint Council on Economic Education. Checklist
0009-2096	Checklist of Congressional Hearings see 0195-3761
0009-2126	Cheering Words
0009-2142	Cheese Reporter
0009-2185	Chelsea
0009-2207	Chemexcil Export Bulletin
0009-2223	Chemia Analityczna
0009-2231	Chemia Stosowana. Seria A: Zagadnienia Technologii Chemicznej changed to Chemia Stosowana
0009-224X	Chemia Stosowana. Seria B. Zagadnienia Inzynierii i Apartury Chemicznej changed to Inzynieria Chemiczna
0009-2258	Chemical Abstracts
0009-2266	Chemical Abstracts - Applied Chemistry Sections see 0090-8363
0009-2274	Chemical Abstracts - Macromolecular Sections
0009-2282	Chemical Abstracts - Organic Chemistry Sections
0009-2290	Chemical Abstracts - Physical and Analytical Chemistry Sections
0009-2304	Chemical Abstracts - Biochemistry Sections
0009-2312	Chemical Age
0009-2320	Chemical Age of India
0009-2347	Chemical and Engineering News
0009-2355	Chemical and Petroleum Engineering
0009-2363	Chemical & Pharmaceutical Bulletin
0009-2371	Chemical and Process Engineering see 0370-1859
0009-238X	Chemical-Biological Activities(CBAC)
0009-2398	Chemical Bond
0009-2401	Chemical Bulletin
0009-241X	Chemical Communications see 0022-4936
0009-2436	Chemical Economy and Engineering Review
0009-2452	Chemical Engineer and Transactions of the Institution of Chemical Engineers changed to Chemical Engineer
0009-2460	Chemical Engineering
0009-2479	Chemical Engineering Education
0009-2495	Chemical Engineering Progress
0009-2509	Chemical Engineering Science
0009-2517	Chemical Engineering World
0009-2525	Chemical Equipment
0009-2533	Chemical Era
0009-2541	Chemical Geology
0009-255X	Chemical Highlights
0009-2576	Chemical Industry News
0009-2584	Chemical Industry Report†
0009-2592	Chemical Instrumentation see 0190-4094
0009-2606	Chemical Market Abstracts see 0161-8032
0009-2614	Chemical Physics Letters
0009-2622	Chemical Processing see 0305-439X
0009-2630	Chemical Processing
0009-2649	Chemical Processing & Engineering see 0302-7678
0009-2657	Chemical Purchasing
0009-2665	Chemical Reviews
0009-2673	Chemical Society of Japan. Bulletin
0009-2681	Chemical Society, London. Quarterly Reviews see 0306-0012
0009-269X	Chemical Substructure Index
0009-2703	Chemtech
0009-2703	Chemical Technology see 0009-2703
0009-2711	Chemical Titles
0009-272X	Chemical Week
0009-2738	Chemicals & Allied Products Export News
0009-2746	Chemicals-International
0009-2754	Chemicals, Quarterly Industry Report†
0009-2770	Chemicke Listy
0009-2789	Chemicky Prumysl
0009-2797	Chemico-Biological Interactions
0009-2800	Chemie-Anlagen und Verfahren
0009-2819	Chemie der Erde
0009-2827	Chemie en Techniek†
0009-2835	Chemie fuer Labor und Betrieb
0009-2843	Chemie in der Schule
0009-2851	Chemie in Unserer Zeit
0009-286X	Chemie-Ingenieur-Technik
0009-2886	Chemik
0009-2894	Chemiker-Zeitung
0009-2908	Chemin
0009-2916	Cheminot
0009-2924	Chemins de Fer
0009-2932	Chemisch Weekblad changed to Chemisch Magazine
0009-2932	Chemisch Weekblad changed to Chemisch Weekblad/Chemische Courant
0009-2940	Chemische Berichte
0009-2959	Chemische Industrie
0009-2967	Chemische Industrie International
0009-2975	Chemischer Informationsdienst
0009-2983	Chemische Rundschau
0009-2991	Chemie Kunststoffe Aktuell. Mitteilungen.
0009-3017	Chemisier l'Elegance Masculine changed to Elegance Masculine-Mylord
0009-3025	Chemist
0009-3033	Chemist and Druggist
0009-3041	Chemist & Drugstore News
0009-305X	Chemistry see 0190-597X
0009-3068	Chemistry and Industry
0009-3076	Chemistry and Industry in New Zealand
0009-3084	Chemistry and Physics of Lipids
0009-3092	Chemistry and Technology of Fuels and Oils
0009-3106	Chemistry in Britain†
0009-3114	Chemistry in Canada
0009-3122	Chemistry of Heterocyclic Compounds
0009-3130	Chemistry of Natural Compounds
0009-3149	Chemists Review†
0009-3157	Chemotherapy
0009-3165	Chemotherapy
0009-3173	Chempress
0009-3203	Cherie Moda
0009-322X	Cherokee Nation News changed to Cherokee Advocate
0009-3238	Cherry Circle
0009-3254	Chesapeake and Ohio Historical Newsletter
0009-3262	Chesapeake Science see 0160-8347
0009-3297	Cheshire Smile
0009-3300	Chesopiean
0009-3319	Chess
0009-3335	Chess Digest†
0009-3343	Chess in Australia
0009-3351	Chess Life & Review
0009-336X	Chess 'n Checkers' changed to Pool Checker Masters
0009-3378	Kyoto University. Chest Disease Research Institute. Bulletin
0009-3386	Chester White Journal
0009-3394	Chestnut Hill Local
0009-3408	Chetwynd Reporter changed to Chetwynd Echo
0009-3424	Chez Nous
0009-3432	Chhandita
0009-3440	Chiang Mai Medical Bulletin
0009-3459	Chiba Medical Society. Journal
0009-3467	Monthly Report of Meteorology, Chiba Prefecture
0009-3483	Chic
0009-3491	Chicago Academy of Sciences. Bulletin
0009-3513	Chicago Bowler
0009-3521	Chicago Daily Hide and Tallow Bulletin
0009-353X	Chicago Dental Society Fortnightly Review see 0091-1666
0009-3548	Chicago Fire Fighter
0009-3556	Chicago Genealogist
0009-3564	Chicago Herpetological Society. Bulletin
0009-3572	Chicago Illini
0009-3580	Chicago Journalism Review†
0009-3599	Chicago-Kent Law Review changed to Chicago-Kent Law Review
0009-3602	Chicago Magazine†
0009-3610	Chicago Maroon
0009-3629	Chicago Medical School Quarterly†
0009-3637	Chicago Medicine
0009-3645	Chicago P N Y X
0009-3653	Chicago Police Star†
0009-3661	Chicago Psychoanalytic Literature Index
0009-367X	Chicago Purchasor
0009-3696	Chicago Review
0009-3718	Chicago Studies
0009-3734	University of Chicago. Pritzker School of Medicine. Alumni Association. Bulletin
0009-3769	Chicagoland's Real Estate Advertiser
0009-3777	Chicano Community Newspaper changed to Chicano
0009-3785	Chichester News
0009-3793	Chicory
0009-3807	Chief
0009-3831	Education of Earth Science
0009-384X	Chiiki Fukushi
0009-3858	Chikitsak Samaj
0009-3866	Storage Battery
0009-3874	Animal Husbandry
0009-3882	Child and Family
0009-3890	Child and Man
0009-3904	Child Care†
0009-3920	Child Development
0009-3939	Child Development Abstracts and Bibliography
0009-3947	Child Education
0009-3963	Child Health Investigation†
0009-3971	Child Life
0009-398X	Child Psychiatry and Human Development
0009-3998	Child Psychiatry Quarterly
0009-4005	Child Study Journal
0009-4013	Child Wear†
0009-4021	Child Welfare
0009-403X	Childbirth Education†
0009-4048	Childbirth without Pain Education Association. Newsletter
0009-4056	Childhood Education
0009-4064	Children see 0361-4336
0009-4072	Mental Retardation News
0009-4080	Children's Digest
0009-4099	Children's Digest see 0272-7145
0009-4102	Friend
0009-4110	Children's Hospital Notes
0009-4129	Childrens Hospital of the District of Columbia. Clinical Proceedings see 0092-7813
0009-4137	Children's House Magazine changed to Children's House/Children's World
0009-4153	Children's Own
0009-4161	Children's Playmate
0009-417X	Children's Styles
0009-4196	Children's Theatre Review
0009-420X	Children's World
0009-4218	Child's Guardian
0009-4226	Chile - Economic Notes†
0009-4234	Chile-Economic Background Information†
0009-4242	Chile. Ejercito. Anexo Historico. Memorial
0009-4277	Chiltern Life†
0009-4285	Chimes
0009-4293	Chimia
0009-4315	Chimica e l'Industria
0009-4323	Chimie Actualites
0009-4331	Chimie Analytique see 0365-4877
0009-4366	Chimie et Technique
0009-4374	Chimica Therapeutica
0009-4382	China Glass & Tableware
0009-4404	China News Analysis
0009-4412	China Notes
0009-4420	China Pictorial
0009-4439	China Quarterly
0009-4447	China Reconstructs
0009-4455	China Report
0009-4471	China Today†
0009-448X	China Trade Report
0009-4501	Chinatown News
0009-451X	Chinchilla-Zucht†
0009-4528	Chinese Bulletin changed to Chinese-Canadian Bulletin
0009-4536	Chinese Chemical Society. Journal
0009-4544	Chinese Culture
0009-4552	Chinese Economic Studies
0009-4560	Chinese Education
0009-4579	Chinese Journal of Administration
0009-4587	Chinese Journal of Microbiology changed to Chinese Journal of Microbiology and Immunology
0009-4595	Chinese Language Teachers Association. Journal
0009-4609	Chinese Law and Government
0009-4617	Chinese Literature
0009-4625	Chinese Sociology and Anthropology
0009-4633	Chinese Studies in History
0009-4641	Chinese Voice
0009-465X	Ch'ing Documents
0009-4668	Ching Feng
0009-4684	Chirimo
0009-4692	Chirogram†
0009-4706	Chiropodist
0009-4714	Chiropody Review
0009-4722	Der Chirurg
0009-4749	Chirurgia degli Organi di Movimento
0009-4757	Chirurgia e Patologia Sperimentale
0009-4765	Chirurgia Gastroenterologica (Italian Edition)
0009-4773	Chirurgia Italiana
0009-4781	Chirurgia Maxillofacialis and Plastica
0009-479X	Chirurgia Narzadow Ruchu i Ortopedia Polska
0009-4811	Chirurgia Triveneta
0009-482X	Chirurgia Veterinaria†
0009-4838	Chirurgien-Dentiste de France
0009-4846	Chirurgische Praxis
0009-4854	Monthly Review of Geology
0009-4862	Chitalishte
0009-4870	Chitrali
0009-4889	Chitty's Law Journal
0009-4897	Map
0009-4900	Map's Companion
0009-4919	Chlodnictwo
0009-4935	Choc-Talk
0009-4943	Chocolaterie, Confiserie de France changed to Revue des Industries de la Biscuiterie, Biscotterie, Chocolaterie, Confiserie
0009-4951	Chogin Research changed to L T C B Research
0009-496X	Choice
0009-4978	Choice
0009-4986	Choice†
0009-4994	Choisir
0009-501X	Choppers Magazine changed to Choppers & Big Bike Magazine
0009-5028	Choral Journal
0009-5036	Der Chordirigent
0009-5044	Chorleiter†
0009-5052	Christ et France-sur le Roc
0009-5060	Der Christ im Zwanzigsten Jahrhundert
0009-5087	Christ und Buch
0009-5109	Christ und Welt changed to Deutsche Zeitung Christ und Welt
0009-5117	Christadelphian
0009-5133	Christelijk-Historisch Tijdschrift
0009-5141	Christelijk Oosten
0009-515X	Onze Vacatures
0009-5176	Christelijke Muziekbode
0009-5184	Die Christengemeinschaft
0009-5192	Christenlehre
0009-5206	Christian†
0009-5206	Christian see 0092-8372
0009-5214	Christian Adventurer
0009-5222	Christian Advocate changed to Today's Ministry
0009-5230	Christian Anti-Communism Crusade. Newsletter
0009-5249	Christian Attitudes on Jews and Judaism see 0144-2902
0009-5265	Christian Beacon
0009-5273	Christian Bookseller
0009-5281	Christian Century
0009-5303	Christian Communications
0009-5311	Christian Cynosure
0009-5338	Christian Endeavor World
0009-5346	Christian Family†

ISSN INDEX

ISSN	Title
0009-5354	Christian Herald (Chappaqua)
0009-5362	Christian Heritage†
0009-5370	Christian Home
0009-5389	Christian Home & School
0009-5397	Christian Institutes of Islamic Studies Bulletin *changed to* Christian Institutes of Islamic Studies Bulletin. (1978)
0009-5400	Christian Labor Herald
0009-5419	Christian Leader
0009-5427	Christian Life
0009-5435	Christian Living
0009-5443	Christian Medical Association of India. Journal
0009-5451	Christian Medical College Alumni Journal
0009-546X	Christian Medical Society Journal
0009-5478	Christian Messenger
0009-5486	Christian Minister
0009-5494	Christian Monthly
0009-5508	Today's Christian Mother *changed to* Today's Christian Parent
0009-5516	Christian News
0009-5524	Christian News Bulletin†
0009-5532	Christian News from Israel
0009-5540	Christian Nurse
0009-5559	Christian Order
0009-5567	Christian Peace Conference
0009-5575	Christian Record
0009-5583	Christian Record Talking Magazine
0009-5591	Christian Recorder†
0009-5605	Christian Rural Fellowship. Bulletin
0009-5613	Christian Science Journal
0009-563X	Christian Science Sentinel
0009-5648	Christian Socialist
0009-5656	Christian Standard
0009-5664	Christian Statesman
0009-5672	Christian Teacher
0009-5680	Vanguard
0009-5699	Christian Voice
0009-5702	Christian Woman
0009-5710	Christiane
0009-5729	Christianisme au Vingtieme Siecle
0009-5745	Christianity and Crisis
0009-5753	Christianity Today
0009-5761	Christlich-Paedagogische Blaetter
0009-577X	Die Christliche Frau
0009-5796	Christliche Innerlichkeit
0009-580X	Christoffel-Blindenmission. Bericht
0009-5818	Christophorus
0009-5826	Youth Alive *see* 0190-6569
0009-5834	Christus
0009-5850	Die Christus-Post
0009-5869	Christus en Israel†
0009-5877	Christus Rex *changed to* Social Studies
0009-5885	Christusruf†
0009-5893	Chromatographia
0009-5907	Chromatographic Reviews *see* 0021-9673
0009-5915	Chromosoma
0009-5931	Chronica
0009-594X	Chronica
0009-5958	Chronicle†
0009-5974	Chronicle†
0009-5990	Chronicle of the Horse
0009-6008	Chronicle of U.S. Classic Postal Issues
0009-6024	Chronicles of Oklahoma
0009-6040	Chronique de l'IRSAC
0009-6059	Chronique de Politique Etrangere *changed to* Studia Diplomatica
0009-6067	Chronique d'Egypte
0009-6075	Chronique des Mines et de la Recherche Miniere *changed to* France. Bureau de Recherches Geologiques et Minieres. Bulletin. Section 2: Geologie des Gites Mineraux
0009-6083	Transport Echo
0009-6121	Chronique Sociale de France†
0009-6148	Chroniques de l'Art Vivant†
0009-6172	Chronmy Przyrode Ojczysta
0009-6180	Chronos
0009-6199	Chrysalist
0009-6202	Chubu Institute of Technology. Memoirs
0009-6210	Chuck Wagon
0009-6229	Chugoku Agricultural Research *changed to* Kinki Chugoku Agricultural Research
0009-6237	Chugoku Electric Power Co. Technical Laboratory Report
0009-6245	Chulpan Moonwha
0009-6253	Chung-Ang Herald
0009-6261	Chung Chi Bulletin
0009-6296	Chuo Law Review
0009-630X	Church Advocate
0009-6318	Church and Community†
0009-6326	Church and People *changed to* Together
0009-6334	Church & State
0009-6342	Church and Synagogue Libraries
0009-6350	Church Army Review
0009-6369	Church Bulletin
0009-6385	Church Growth Bulletin *see* 0273-7183
0009-6393	Church Herald
0009-6407	Church History
0009-6415	Church Labor Letter
0009-6423	Media: Library Services Journal
0009-6431	Church Management: The Clergy Journal
	Church Music *see* 0305-4438
0009-644X	Church Musician
0009-6466	Church Musician
0009-6474	Church News
0009-6482	Church Observer
0009-6490	Church of England Historical Society (Diocese of Sydney). Journal
0009-6504	Church of God Missions
0009-6512	Church of Ireland Gazette
0009-6520	Church of Light Quarterly
0009-6539	Church Panorama†
0009-6547	Church Quarterly†
0009-6555	Church Renewal†
0009-6563	Church Scene
0009-6571	Church Teacher *see* 0307-5982
0009-658X	Church Times
0009-6598	Church Woman
0009-6601	Church World
0009-661X	Churchman
0009-6628	Churchman
0009-6636	Churchman's Magazine
0009-6652	Casting and Forging *changed to* Casting, Forging & Heat Treatments
0009-6679	Cibles
0009-6687	Ciceroniana
0009-6709	Ciel et Terre
0009-6717	Ciencia Aeronautica
0009-6725	Ciencia e Cultura
0009-6733	Ciencia e Investigacion
0009-675X	Ciencia Interamericana
0009-6768	Ciencia y Naturaleza
0009-6776	Ciencias
0009-6784	Ciencias Administrativas
0009-6792	Ciencias Neurologicas
0009-6806	Ciencias Sociales
0009-6814	Cigar Makers' Official Journal†
0009-6822	Cigarette Card News and Trade Card Chronicle
0009-6830	Cimaise
0009-6849	Cimarron Review
0009-6865	Cimone
0009-6873	Cincinnati Journal of Medicine *see* 0163-0075
0009-6881	Cincinnati Law Review
0009-689X	Cincinnati
0009-6903	Cincinnati Purchasor
0009-6911	Cinderella Philatelist
0009-692X	Cine al Dia
0009-6946	Cine Cubano
0009-6954	Cine News
0009-6970	Cine Technicians' Association of South India. Journal *changed to* C.T.A. Journal
0009-7004	Cineaste
0009-7012	Cineclube do Porto. Boletim Circular *see* 0704-061X
0009-7020	Cinecronache
0009-7039	Cineforum
0009-7047	Cinema
0009-7063	Cinema†
0009-7071	Cinema Canada†
0009-7101	Cinema/Canada (Montreal)
0009-708X	Cinema de Amadores
0009-7101	Cinema Journal
0009-711X	Cinema Nuovo
0009-7128	Cinema Pratique
0009-7144	Cinema Rangam†
0009-7152	Cinema e Societa
0009-7160	Cinemasud
0009-7179	Cinematografia in Presa†
0009-7187	Cinematografia Ita
0009-7195	Cines d'Orient†
0009-7209	Cinesiologie
0009-7225	Cinque Foil
0009-7241	Circolo Letterario†
0009-725X	Circolo Matematico di Palermo. Rendiconti
0009-7268	Circolo Speleologico Romano. Notiziario
0009-7284	Circuit Magazine†
0009-7292	Circuit News
0009-7306	Circuits Manufacturing
0009-7314	Colegio Oficial de Farmaceutico. Circular Farmaceutica
0009-7322	Circulation
0009-7330	Circulation Research
0009-7349	Circulo
0009-7357	Circulo Odontologico de Rosario. Revista
0009-7365	Circus *changed to* Circus (1979)
0009-7373	Cirque dans l'Univers
0009-7381	Cirugia del Uruguay
0009-739X	Cirugia Espanola
0009-7403	Cirugia Plastica Uruguaya
0009-7411	Cirugia y Cirujanos
0009-7438	Citatel
0009-7446	Citation
0009-7489	Cahiers de Cite Libre†
0009-7489	Cahiers de Cite Libre
0009-7497	Citeaux
0009-7500	Cites et Villes†
0009-7527	Cithara
0009-7535	Cities and Villages
0009-7543	Citizen
0009-756X	Citizen's Business
0009-7578	Citrograph
0009-7586	Citrus and Vegetable Magazine
0009-7594	Citrus Industry Magazine
0009-7608	Citrus World
0009-7616	Citta di Milano†
0009-7624	Patavium
0009-7632	Citta di Vita
0009-7640	Citta e Societa
0009-7667	Cittadino Canadese
0009-7675	City†
0009-7683	City Almanac
0009-7691	City Art Museum of Saint Louis. Bulletin *changed to* St. Louis Art Museum. Bulletin
0009-7705	City Beautiful
0009-7713	City Business Courier
0009-7721	City Club Comments *changed to* City Club Gadfly
0009-7748	City Press†
0009-7756	Ciudad de Dios
0009-7764	Civic Administration *see* 0315-1972
0009-7772	Civic Affairs
0009-7799	Civic Leader†
0009-7802	Civiele Verdediging *changed to* Noodzaak
0009-7810	Civil Air Patrol News
0009-7845	Civil Engineer in South Africa
0009-7853	Civil Engineering (New York) *see* 0360-0556
0009-7861	Civil Engineering and Public Works Review *see* 0305-6473
0009-787X	Civil Engineering, Construction & Public Works Journal†
0009-7888	Civil Engineering Contractor
0009-7918	Civil Liberties Bulletin†
0009-7926	Civil Liberties in New York *changed to* N. Y. Civil Liberties
0009-7934	Civil Liberties Reporter
0009-7942	Rights, Opportunities, Action Reporter†
0009-7950	Civil Rights Court Digest
0009-7969	Civil Rights Digest *changed to* Perspectives: A Civil Rights Quarterly
0009-7985	Civil Service Journal†
0009-8000	Civil Service Leader
0009-8019	Civil Service News Releases *changed to* Civil Service News
0009-8027	Civil Service Opinion *changed to* Opinion
0009-8035	Civil Service Review
0009-8051	Civil Service Sports Quarterly†
0009-806X	Civil Transport Data Sheets
0009-8078	Civil War History
0009-8086	Civil War Round Table Digest
0009-8094	Civil War Times Illustrated
0009-8108	Civil War Token Society. Journal
0009-8132	Civilingenjoersfoerbundets Tidskrift *see* 0348-6087
0009-8140	Civilisations
0009-8159	Civilt Foersvar
0009-8167	Civilta Cattolica
0009-8175	Civilta' della Strada†
0009-8191	Civitas
0009-8205	Cizi Jazyky ve Skole
0009-8213	Clan McLaren Society, U S A. Quarterly
0009-8221	Clare Market Review†
0009-823X	Claridad
0009-8256	Clarin Economico
0009-8264	Clark County School Letter *changed to* Educator
0009-8272	Clark Now
0009-8280	C L A S S: Reading†
0009-8299	Classe e Stato†
0009-8310	Classic Car
0009-8329	Classic Film Collector *see* 0275-8423
0009-8337	Classical Bulletin
0009-8345	Classical Folia
0009-8353	Classical Journal
0009-8361	Classical Outlook
0009-837X	Classical Philology
0009-8388	Classical Quarterly
0009-840X	Classical Review
0009-8418	Classical World
0009-8426	Classici del Giallo
0009-8434	Classification Management
0009-8450	Classified Abstract Archive of the Alcohol Literature†
0009-8477	Classified Documentation List of Current Scientific Literature. Monthly Bulletin *changed to* C S M C R I Documentation List Monthly Bulletin
0009-8485	Classroom Interaction Newsletter *changed to* Journal of Classroom Interaction
0009-8507	Claudia
0009-8515	Claudia
0009-8523	Clausthaler Geologische Abhandlungen
0009-8531	Claverite
0009-854X	Clavier
0009-8558	Clay Minerals
0009-8566	Canadian Clay & Ceramics
0009-8574	Clay Science
0009-8582	Claycraft *see* 0306-1841
0009-8590	Claymore
0009-8604	Clays and Clay Minerals
0009-8620	Clean Water Report
0009-8639	Manual of Maintenance *changed to* Maintenance Buyers Guide
0009-8647	Clean Air
0009-8655	Clearing House
0009-8663	Clearinghouse Announcements in Science & Technology†
0009-8671	Clearinghouse on Self-Instructional Materials for Health Care Facilities. Bulletin†
0009-868X	Clearinghouse Review
0009-8698	Clearway
0009-8701	Cleft Palate Journal
0009-871X	Clemson University. College of Architecture. Semester Review
0009-8728	Cleo en la Moda
0009-8736	Clergy Review
0009-8744	Clerk *changed to* A P E X
0009-8752	Clessidra
0009-8787	Cleveland Clinic Quarterly
0009-8809	Cleveland Engineering
0009-8817	Cleveland Food Dealer
0009-8825	Cleveland Jewish News
0009-8833	Cleveland Medical Library. Bulletin
0009-8841	Cleveland Museum of Art. Bulletin

0009-885X Cleveland Public Library Staff Association. News and Views
0009-8876 Cleveland State Law Review
0009-8884 Business Bulletin†
0009-8892 Clevelander
0009-8906 Clic Fotografiamo
0009-8914 Clima Commerce International
0009-8930 Climate Control
0009-8957 Climatological Data for Jakarta Observatory
0009-8965 Climb
0009-8973 Climber and Rambler
0009-8981 Clinica Chimica Acta
0009-899X Clinica de Endocrinologia y Metabolismo. Boletin†
0009-9007 Clinica Europea
0009-9015 Clinica Geral†
0009-9023 Clinica Ortopedica†
0009-9031 Clinica Ostetrica e Ginecologica *see* 0304-0313
0009-9031 Ostetrica e Ginecologia Clinica
0009-904X Clinica Otorinolaringoiatrica *changed to* Nuova, Clinica Otorinolaringoiatrica
0009-9058 Clinica Pediatrica
0009-9066 Clinica Psichiatrica
0009-9074 Clinica Terapeutica
0009-9082 Clinica Veterinaria
0009-9090 Clinical Allergy
0009-9104 Clinical and Experimental Immunology
0009-9112 Clinical Anesthesia†
0009-9120 Clinical Biochemistry
0009-9139 Quarterly Literature Reports. Clinical Biochemistry†
0009-9147 Clinical Chemistry
0009-9155 Clinical Electroencephalography
0009-9163 Clinical Genetics
0009-918X Clinical Neurology
0009-9201 Clinical Obstetrics and Gynecology: a Quarterly Periodical
0009-921X Clinical Orthopaedics and Related Research
0009-9228 Clinical Pediatrics
0009-9236 Clinical Pharmacology and Therapeutics
0009-9244 Clinical Psychologist
0009-9252 Clinical Radiology *changed to* Japanese Journal of Clinical Radiology
0009-9260 Clinical Radiology
0009-9279 Clinical Research
0009-9295 Clinical Symposia
0009-9309 Clinical Toxicology
0009-9325 Clinical Trials Journal
0009-9333 Clinicas Obstetricas y Ginecologicas
0009-9341 Clinician
0009-935X Clinique
0009-9368 La Clinque, Ophtalmologique
0009-9376 Clio
0009-9384 Clio: Devoted to Commercials
0009-9414 Clipsheet†
0009-9422 Clique
0009-9430 Clock Tower
0009-9449 C M A Close-Up
0009-9465 Clothes *see* 0161-973X
0009-9473 Clothesline *changed to* National Clothesline
0009-9503 Club
0009-9511 Club Alpino Italiano. Rivista Mensile *changed to* Club Alpino Italiano. Rivista
0009-952X Club and Institute Journal
0009-9538 Club Committee & Northern Free Trade News
0009-9546 Club du Griffon d'Arret a Poil Dur Korthal. Bulletin
0009-9562 Club Folk†
0009-9570 Club Francais de la Medaille
0009-9589 Club Management
0009-9597 Club Managers Journal *changed to* Secretaries and Managers Journal of Australia
0009-9600 Fussball Club Pforzheim. Club-Nachrichten
0009-9627 Club Operations†
0009-9635 Club Secretary
0009-9651 Clube Filatelico de Portugal. Boletim
0009-966X Clube Militar Naval. Anais
0009-9678 Salcofoon
0009-9716 C M I Descriptions of Pathogenic Fungi and Bacteria
0009-9724 Co-Ed
0009-9740 Co-Op Highlights
0009-9759 Co-Op Maandblad†
0009-9767 Co-Op Report†
0009-9805 Cooperative Information Bulletin *changed to* Cooperative Perspective
0009-9813 Co-Operative Management & Marketing *see* 0307-8604
0009-9821 Co-Operative News
0009-9848 Co-Operative Review
0009-9856 Co-Operatives Quarterly
0009-9864 Co-Partnership *changed to* Industrial Participation
0009-9872 Coach and Athlete *changed to* Coach and Athlete Magazine
0009-9880 Coaching Clinic
0009-9899 Coaching Journal and Bus Review
0009-9902 Coagulation *see* 0301-0147
0009-9910 Coal Age
0009-9929 Coal and Steel†
0009-9945 Coal Miner†
0009-9961 Coal Mining & Processing
0009-997X Coal News
0009-9988 Coal Research†
0009-9996 Canada. Statistics Canada. Coarse Grains Review/Revue des Cereales Secondaire†
0010-0005 Coast
0010-0013 Shoe-the Coast Shoe Reporter
0010-003X Coat of Arms
0010-0056 Cobbers†
0010-0064 Cobouw
0010-0072 Sonntagsblatt - Coburger Heimatglocken
0010-0099 Cockpit *changed to* Vliegtuigparade
0010-0102 Cockpit
0010-0110 Cockpit
0010-0137 Cocoa Statistics†
0010-0145 Coconut Bulletin *changed to* Indian Coconut Journal
0010-0161 Cocuk Sagligi ve Hastaliklari Dergisi
0010-017X Coda
0010-0188 Codes Larcier
0010-0196 Codex
0010-020X Codicillus
0010-0226 Coeur
0010-0234 Coeur et Medecine Interne
0010-0250 Coffee Mazdoor Sahakari
0010-0277 Cognition
0010-0285 Cognitive Psychology
0010-0293 Cogwheel
0010-0307 Cohesion†
0010-0331 Coiffure
0010-034X Coiffure de Paris
0010-0358 Coiffure et Beaute†
0010-0366 Coimbra Medica†
0010-0374 Coin Dealer
0010-0390 Coin Monthly *changed to* Coin Monthly(1980)
0010-0404 Coin-Op *see* 0092-2811
0010-0412 Coin Prices
0010-0420 Coin Slot *see* 0043-9304
0010-0439 Coin, Stamp, Antique News *see* 0702-3162
0010-0439 Canadian Stamp News
0010-0447 Coin World
0010-0455 Coinage
0010-0471 Coins
0010-0501 Coke and Chemistry U. S. S. R.†
0010-0501 Coke and Chemistry U.S.S.R.
0010-0528 Coke Research Report *see* 0305-9545
0010-0536 Coke Review *see* 0305-8131
0010-0544 Colada
0010-0552 Colby Library Quarterly
0010-0560 Colegio de Abogados de la Ciudad de Buenos Aires. Boletin Informativo
0010-0579 Colegio de Abogados de Puerto Rico. Revista
0010-0587 Colegio de Abogados. Revista
0010-0595 Colegio de Bibliotecarios Colombianos.(Revista)†
0010-0609 Colegio de Ingenieros Arquitectos y Agrimensores de Puerto Rico. Revista
0010-0617 Colegio de Ingenieros de Caminos, Canales y Puertos. Boletin de Informacion
0010-0633 Colegio de Profesores de Venezuela. Seccional No. 1. Boletin. Informativo
0010-0641 Colegio Medico de El Salvador. Archivas
0010-065X Coleopterists' Bulletin
0010-0676 Colfeian
0010-0684 Colgate *changed to* Colgate Scene
0010-0692 Collage†
0010-0722 Collana di Monografie Turistiche†
0010-0730 Collectanea Botanica
0010-0749 Collectanea Franciscana
0010-0757 Collectanea Mathematica
0010-0765 Collection of Czechoslovak Chemical Communications
0010-0773 Collections - Femme Chic
0010-0781 Collections Baur. Bulletin
0010-079X Collective Bargaining Negotiations & Contracts
0010-0803 Collective Bargaining Review
0010-0811 Collectivites-Express
0010-082X Collector
0010-0838 Collectors Club Philatelist
0010-0846 Collectors News
0010-0854 Collector's World†
0010-0862 College *changed to* St. John's Review
0010-0870 College and Research Libraries
0010-0889 College and University
0010-0900 College and University Business *see* 0194-2263
0010-0919 College and University Business Officer *see* 0147-877X
0010-0935 College and University Personnel Association. Journal
0010-0943 College and University Safety Newsletter
0010-0951 College Board Review
0010-096X College Composition and Communication
0010-0986 College Echoes†
0010-0994 College English
0010-1001 Education et Societe†
0010-101X College Law Bulletin†
0010-1028 College Library Notes†
0010-1044 College of Dental Surgeons of the Province of Quebec. Information *changed to* Order of Dentists of Quebec. Information
0010-1052 University of North Dakota. College of Education. Record *see* 0360-5027
0010-1060 College of Emporia Compass†
0010-1087 College of Physicians of Philadelphia. Transactions & Studies
0010-1095 College of Physicians, Surgeons and Gynecologists of South Africa. Transactions *changed to* College of Medicine of South Africa. Transactions
0010-1117 College Press Review
0010-1125 College Press Service
0010-1133 Journal of College Radio
0010-115X College Store Journal
0010-1168 College Student Personnel Abstracts
0010-1176 College Student Personnel Institute. Newsletter†
0010-1184 College Student Survey *see* 0146-3934
0010-1192 College Voice
0010-1206 Collegian
0010-1214 Collegiate Journalist†
0010-1222 Collegiate News and Views
0010-1249 Collegio
0010-1265 Collezionista-Italia Filatelica
0010-1281 Colliery Guardian
0010-129X Collins Signal Magazine†
0010-1303 Colloid Journal of the U S S R
0010-1311 Colloquium†
0010-132X Colloqui Cremonese
0010-1338 Colloquia Germanica
0010-1346 Colloquium†
0010-1354 Colloquium Mathematicum
0010-1370 Colombia. Departamento Administrativo Nacional de Estadistica. Boletin Mensual de Estadistica
0010-1389 Colombia. Ministerio de Defensa. Boletin
0010-1397 Colombia Today
0010-1400 Universidad Nacional de Colombia. Facultad de Medicina. Revista
0010-1419 Colombo Plan Newsletter
0010-1427 Colombophilie Belge
0010-1435 Colonial Courier
0010-1443 C N L
0010-1451 Coloquio/Artes
0010-146X Color Engineering†
0010-1478 Color Engineering†
0010-1494 Colorado and Rocky Mountain Motor Carrier *changed to* Highland Highways
0010-1516 Colorado Beverage Analyst
0010-1524 Colorado Business Review
0010-1532 Colorado C P A Report†
0010-1540 Colorado Councillor
0010-1567 Colorado Editor
0010-1583 Colorado Engineer
0010-1605 Colorado F.P.†
0010-163X Colorado Journal of Pharmacy
0010-1648 Colorado Magazine *changed to* Colorado Heritage
0010-1656 Colorado Manpower Review
0010-1664 Colorado Municipalities
0010-1672 Colorado Music Educator
0010-1680 Colorado Nurse
0010-1699 Colorado Outdoors
0010-1702 Colorado Prospector
0010-1710 Colorado Quarterly
0010-1729 Colorado Rancher and Farmer
0010-1737 Colorado School Journal
0010-1745 Colorado School of Mines. Mineral Industries Bulletin *see* 0192-6179
0010-1753 Colorado School of Mines Quarterly
0010-1761 Colorado State Library Newsletter
0010-1788 Colores y Pinturas
0010-1796 Colorado-Rocky Mountain West†
0010-180X Colour Material
0010-1818 Colour Review
0010-1826 Colourage
0010-1834 Cols-Bleus
0010-1842 Colstonian
0010-1850 Coltivatore e Giornale Vinicolo Italiano
0010-1869 Columbia
0010-1877 Columbia Basin Farmer
0010-1885 Columbia College Pre-Med†
0010-1893 Columbia Daily Spectator
0010-1907 Columbia Forum†
0010-1915 Columbia Jester
0010-1923 Columbia Journal of Law and Social Problems
0010-1931 Columbia Journal of Transnational Law
0010-194X Columbia Journalism Review
0010-1958 Columbia Law Review
0010-1966 Columbia Library Columns
0010-1982 Columbia Review
0010-1990 C. S. P. A. A. Bulletin
0010-2008 Columbia Survey of Human Rights Law *see* 0090-7944
0010-2016 Columbia University. Ancient Near Eastern Society. Journal
0010-2024 Columbian
0010-2032 Squires *changed to* Squires Newsletter
0010-2059 Columbus Business Forum†
0010-2075 Column *changed to* Scan
0010-2083 Columni
0010-2091 Columns
0010-2105 Comarca de Suzano
0010-2113 Combat†
0010-2121 Combat
0010-213X Combat Crew
0010-2148 Combattente della Liberta
0010-2156 Toesj/Combo
0010-2164 International Laboratory
0010-2172 Combustion†
0010-2180 Combustion and Flame
0010-2202 Combustion Science & Technology
0010-2237 Comentarios Bibliograficos Americanos
0010-2245 Comercio
0010-2253 Comercio
0010-227X Comercio & Mercados
0010-2288 Comercio Colombo Americano

ISSN	Title
0010-2296	Comercio Ecuatoriano
0010-2326	Comercio Hispano Britanico
0010-2334	Comercio Portugues *changed to* Comercio, Industria, Servicos
0010-2342	Comercio y Produccion
0010-2350	Comercio y Produccion
0010-2369	Comhar
0010-2377	Coming up *changed to* Perspective (Berkeley)
0010-2385	Comino
0010-2407	Comissao de Desenvolvimento Economico do Estado do Amazonas. Boletim Informativo
0010-2415	Comite Belge d'Histoire des Sciences. Notes Bibliographiques
0010-2423	Economic and Social Committee of the European Communities. Bulletin d'Information
0010-2431	Olympic Review
0010-244X	Comites de Prevention du Batiment et des Travaux Publics. Cahiers
0010-2458	Officiel des Comites d'Entreprise et Services Sociaux
0010-2482	Commanders Digest *see* 0270-9015
0010-2504	Commando *changed to* Paratus
0010-2512	Commandos *changed to* Junior Life
0010-2520	Comme les Autres
0010-2539	Comment†
0010-2547	Comment (London)
0010-2555	Comment
0010-2571	Commentarii Mathematici Helvetici
0010-2598	Commentarium pro Religiosis et Missionariis
0010-2601	Commentary
0010-2628	Commentationes Mathematicae Universitatis Carolinae
0010-2644	Commentator†
0010-2652	Commentator
0010-2660	Comments on Argentine Trade
0010-2679	Comments on Astrophysics and Space Physics *see* 0146-2970
0010-2687	Comments on Atomic and Molecular Physics
0010-2695	Comments on Earth Sciences: Geophysics *changed to* Comments on Geochemistry and Cosmochemistry
0010-2709	Comments on Nuclear & Particle Physics
0010-2725	Commerce
0010-2733	Commerce International
0010-2741	Commerce
0010-275X	Commerce
0010-2768	Commerce
0010-2776	Commerce†
0010-2784	Commerce & Industry†
0010-2806	Commerce des Combustibles†
0010-2814	Commerce du Levant
0010-2822	Commerce Education *changed to* Journal of Commerce Education
0010-2830	Commerce Franco-Suisse
0010-2849	Commerce in France
0010-2873	Commerce Moderne Urbanisme et Commerce *see* 0396-714X
0010-2881	Australia. Perth Chamber of Commerce. Commerce News†
0010-2911	Commercial Bulletin
0010-292X	Commercial Car Journal
0010-2938	Commercial Courier
0010-2946	Decor and Contract Furnishing
0010-2954	Commercial Expansion Reporter *see* 0036-3456
0010-2962	Commercial Financing *see* 0160-5178
0010-2997	Australian Commercial Fishing & Marketing
0010-3004	Commercial Grower†
0010-3004	Commercial Grower *see* 0308-3268
0010-3012	Commercial Herald
0010-3039	Commercial Journal
0010-3047	Commercial Kitchen and Dining Room *see* 0190-8553
0010-3055	Commercial Law Journal
0010-3063	Commercial Motor
0010-308X	Commercial Opinion *changed to* Commerce
0010-3098	Commercial Record
0010-3101	Oregon Feed, Seed and Suppliers Association. Commercial Review
0010-311X	Commercial Teacher
0010-3136	Commercial Vehicles†
0010-3144	Commercial West
0010-3160	Commercium
0010-3179	Commission
0010-3209	Commission on Accreditation of Service Experiences. Newsletter *changed to* American Council on Education. Office on Educational Credit and Credentials. Newsletter
0010-3225	Commodity Chart Service
0010-3233	Commodity Trade Statistics
0010-3241	Commodity Yearbook Statistical Abstract Service
0010-3276	Common Life
0010-3292	Common Market Law Review
0010-3314	Commonplace Book
0010-3322	Commons, Open Spaces and Footpaths Preservation Society, Journal
0010-3330	Commonweal
0010-3349	Commonwealth
0010-3357	Commonwealth
0010-3365	Commonwealth
0010-3373	Commonwealth Education Liaison Committee Newsletter†
0010-3403	Commonwealth Jeweller and Watchmaker *changed to* Jeweller, Watchmaker and Giftware
0010-3411	Commonwealth
0010-3438	Commonwealth Secretariat Rice Bulletin†
0010-3446	Communaute Autogestion†
0010-3454	Communaute Chretienne
0010-3497	Communicatio Socialis
0010-3500	Communication Arts International
0010-3519	Communication Arts
0010-3527	Communication Disorders†
0010-3543	Communication Reports
0010-3551	Communicationes de Historia Artis Medicinae
0010-356X	Communications
0010-3586	Communications Business *changed to* Communications and Cable TV Business
0010-3608	Communications in Behavioral Biology *changed to* Behavioral and Neural Biology
0010-3616	Communications in Mathematical Physics
0010-3624	Communications in Soil Science and Plant Analysis
0010-3632	Communications News
0010-3640	Communications on Pure and Applied Mathematics
0010-3675	Communications *see* 0362-4277
0010-3683	Communicator†
0010-3691	Communidades†
0010-3705	Communio
0010-3713	Communio Viatorum
0010-3721	Comminique *changed to* Wood County Board of Education. This Week and Next
0010-3756	Communist Viewpoint
0010-3772	Community
0010-3780	Community Comments *changed to* Community Service Newsletter
0010-3802	Community Development Journal
0010-3829	Community Development Society. Journal
0010-3837	Community Health†
0010-3845	Community Health *changed to* Post Rock
0010-3853	Community Mental Health Journal
0010-3861	Community Mental Health Services. Newsletter *changed to* Access (Tallahassee)
0010-3888	Community School and Its Administration†
0010-3896	Community Schools Gazette *changed to* Community Homes Gazette
0010-3918	Community Teamwork†
0010-3926	Commutation et Electronique†
0010-3926	Commutation et Electronique *changed to* Commutation et Transmission
0010-3934	Compact
0010-3942	Compact†
0010-3950	Compagnie des Ecrivains Mediterraneens et des Amis des Lettres. Bulletin
0010-3969	Companheiros
0010-3985	Companion of St. Francis and St. Anthony
0010-3993	Companion†
0010-4019	Company Law Journal†
0010-4027	Company News and Notes
0010-4035	Comparative and General Pharmacology *see* 0306-3623
0010-4043	Comparative and International Education Society. Newsletter
0010-4051	Comparative and International Law Journal of Southern Africa
0010-4078	Comparative Drama
0010-4086	Comparative Education Review
0010-4108	Comparative Group Studies *see* 0090-5526
0010-4116	Comparative Law Review
0010-4124	Comparative Literature
0010-4132	Comparative Literature Studies
0010-4140	Comparative Political Studies
0010-4159	Comparative Politics
0010-4167	Comparative Romance Linguistics Newsletter
0010-4175	Comparative Studies in Society and History
0010-4191	Compass (Asbury Park) *changed to* Compass Quarterly
0010-4205	A I C S Compass
0010-4213	Compass
0010-4248	Compensation Review
0010-4299	Comple
0010-4310	Component Technology†
0010-4329	Comportamiento Humano
0010-4337	Composer
0010-4353	Composers, Authors and Artists of America
0010-4361	Composites
0010-437X	Compositio Mathematica
0010-4388	Compost Science *changed to* Bio Cycle
0010-4396	Compostelle *changed to* Compostelle, Cahiers du Centre d'Etudes Compostellanes
0010-440X	Comprehensive Psychiatry
0010-4418	Comprendre
0010-4426	Compressed Air
0010-4442	Computable
0010-4469	Computer Abstracts
0010-4477	Computer Age
0010-4485	Computer Aided Design
0010-4507	Computer and Information Systems *see* 0191-9776
0010-4523	Computer Applications Service†
0010-4531	Computer Bulletin†
0010-4531	Computer Bulletin
0010-454X	Computer Characteristics Review *see* 0093-416X
0010-4558	Computer Decisions
0010-4566	Computer Design
0010-4582	Computer Display Review
0010-4590	Computer Education
0010-4620	Computer Journal
0010-4647	Computer News *issued with* 0010-4469
0010-4655	Computer Physics Communications
0010-4663	Computer Praxis *see* 0013-5720
0010-468X	Computer Programs in Biomedicine
0010-4728	Computer Science Newsletter *see* 0315-4661
0010-4736	Computer Services†
0010-4760	Computer Survey
0010-4787	Computer Weekly
0010-4795	Computers and Automation *see* 0361-1442
0010-4809	Computers and Biomedical Research
0010-4817	Computers and the Humanities
0010-4825	Computers in Biology and Medicine
0010-4833	Computers in Medicine Abstracts†
0010-4841	Computerworld
0010-485X	Computing
0010-4868	Computing Newsletter for Schools of Business
0010-4884	Computing Reviews
0010-4892	Computing Surveys *see* 0360-0300
0010-4906	Computopia
0010-4914	Comte de Jette Bulletin
0010-4930	Comune Democratico
0010-4949	Comune di Bologna. Notiziario Settimanale *changed to* Bologna
0010-4957	Comune di Roma. Ufficio di Statistica e Censimento. Bollettino Statistico
0010-4965	Comune di Rome. Ufficio de Statistica e Censimento. Notiziario Statistico Memsile
0010-4973	Comuni d'Europa
0010-5023	Comunidad†
0010-504X	Comunita
0010-5058	Comunita Europee
0010-5066	Comunita Internazionale
0010-5074	Comunita Israelitica di Milano. Bollettino
0010-5082	Combustion, Explosion and Shock Waves
0010-5090	Con Edison Library Bulletin
0010-5120	Concept of Pakistan
0010-5147	Conceptos de Matematica
0010-5155	Conceptus
0010-5163	Concern *changed to* Concern Magazine/Newsfold
0010-5171	Concern†
0010-5198	Concerning Food & Nutrition†
0010-5201	Concerning Poetry
0010-5228	Conciliatore
0010-5244	Concord†
0010-5252	Concordia
0010-5260	Concordia Historical Institute Quarterly
0010-5287	Concordia Torch
0010-5309	Concours Medical
0010-5317	Concrete
0010-5325	Precast Concrete
0010-5333	Concrete Construction
0010-5341	Concrete Construction and Architecture
0010-535X	Concrete Industry Bulletin
0010-5368	Concrete Products
0010-5376	Concrete Quarterly
0010-5392	Conditional Reflex *see* 0093-2213
0010-5414	Condor†
0010-5422	Condor
0010-5457	Confectioner
0010-5465	Confectionery and Tobacco News *changed to* C T N
0010-5473	Confectionery Production
0010-549X	Confederacion de Camaras Nacionales de Comercio. Carta Semanal
0010-5503	Confederacion Sudamericana de Asociaciones Cristianas de Jovenes. Noticias *changed to* Asociacion
0010-5511	Confederate Historical Society. Journal†
0010-5546	Conference Board Record *changed to* Across the Board
0010-5554	Conference Board Statistical Bulletin
0010-5562	Conference of Local Environmental Health Administrators. Newsletter
0010-5589	Conferences du Cenacle
0010-5597	Conferences, Exhibitions and Executive Travel *changed to* Conferences and Exhibitions International
0010-5600	Conferencias
0010-5619	Confezione Italiana
0010-5627	Confit†
0010-5635	Confidencias†
0010-566X	Confidential Detective Cases†
0010-5678	Confinia Neurologia *see* 0302-2773
0010-5686	Confinia Psychiatrica†
0010-5694	Confins
0010-5708	Confort
0010-5716	Confrontation
0010-5732	Confronto†
0010-5732	Confronto
0010-5740	Congiuntura Estera
0010-5759	Congiuntura Italiana
0010-5767	Congo-Afrique *see* 0049-8513
0010-5775	Congo Disque
0010-5783	Congo Magazine *changed to* Zaire Ya Sika

972 ISSN INDEX

0010-5805 Congo. Centre National de la Statistique et des Etudes Economiques. Bulletin Mensuel de la Statistique
0010-5813 Congregation Cistercienne de Senaque et de la Pieuse Ligue Universelle pour les Ames de l'Abbaye de Lerins. (Publication) *changed to* Lerins
0010-5821 Congregational Library. Bulletin
0010-583X Congregational Monthly *see* 0306-7262
0010-5856 Congregationalist
0010-5872 American Jewish Congress. Congress Bi-Weekly *see* 0163-1365
0010-5880 Congress Bulletin†
0010-5899 Congressional Digest
0010-5902 Congressional Monitor
0010-5910 Congressional Quarterly Service. Weekly Report
0010-5929 Coniglicoltura
0010-5937 Conjunto
0010-5945 Conjuntura Economica
0010-5953 Connaissance de la Campagne†
0010-5961 Connaissance de la Mer†
0010-597X Connaissance de la Vigne et du Vin
0010-5938 Connaissance des Arts *changed to* Connaissance des Arts-Plaisir
0010-6003 Connaissance des Plastiques†
0010-602X Connaitre la Wallonie
0010-6038 Connchord
0010-6046 Connecticut Action†
0010-6054 Connecticut Antiquarian
0010-6070 Connecticut Bar Journal
0010-6089 Connecticut C P A
0010-6097 Connecticut Conference Missioner†
0010-6100 Connecticut Conservation Reporter
0010-6119 Connecticut Government
0010-6127 Connecticut Health Bulletin
0010-6135 Connecticut Industry *changed to* C B I A News
0010-6143 Connecticut. Labor Department. Bulletin
0010-6151 Connecticut Law Review
0010-616X Connecticut Libraries
0010-6178 Connecticut Medicine
0010-6208 Connecticut Purchaser *changed to* New England Purchaser/Connecticut Purchaser
0010-6216 Connecticut Review†
0010-6224 Connecticut School Library Association. Newsletter
0010-6232 Connecticut State Dental Association. Journal
0010-6240 Connecticut Teacher†
0010-6259 Connecticut Woodlands
0010-6267 Connection†
0010-6275 Connoisseur
0010-6283 Connoisseur's Guide†
0010-6291 Conocimiento de la Nueva Era
0010-6305 Conoscenza
0010-6313 Conparlist
0010-6348 Conquiste del Lavoro
0010-6356 Conradiana
0010-6364 Argentina. Consejo Nacional de Investigaciones Cientificas y Tecnicas. Informaciones
0010-6364 Revista de Sociologia
0010-6364 Universidad de Antioquia. Departamento de Antropologia. Boletin de Antropologia
0010-6410 Conselho Estadual de Educacao de Sao Paulo. Acta
0010-6429 Consensus *changed to* Momentum
0010-6445 Conservacionista†
0010-6453 Conservation Contractor
0010-6461 Conservation Education Association Newsletter
0010-647X Conservation News†
0010-6488 Conservation Report
0010-6496 Conservation Volunteer *changed to* Minnesota Volunteer
0010-650X Conservationist
0010-6518 Conservative and Unionist Central Office. Monthly News *changed to* Conservative and Unionist Central Office. Conservative News
0010-6542 Conservative Judaism
0010-6550 Conservatoire de Musique de Geneve. Bulletin
0010-6569 Consiglio di Stato
0010-6593 Consommation
0010-6607 Constabulary Gazette
0010-6615 Constellation
0010-6623 Constitutional and Parliamentary Information
0010-6631 Construcao Sao Paulo
0010-6658 Constructeur
0010-6674 Construction
0010-6690 Construction in Southern Africa
0010-6704 Construction
0010-6712 Construction Advisor
0010-6739 Construction Digest
0010-6747 Construction Electrique *changed to* Industries Electriques et Electroniques
0010-6755 Construction Equipment Distribution
0010-6763 Construction Equipment Magazine *see* 0192-3978
0010-6771 Construction Equipment Operation and Maintenance
0010-678X Construction Foreman's & Supervisor's Letter
0010-6798 Construction Francaise *see* 0335-2021
0010-6828 Construction Industries and Trade Journal *changed to* Construction Industries and Trade Annual
0010-6836 Construction Labor Report
0010-6844 Construction Methods and Equipment *see* 0270-1588
0010-6852 Construction Moderne
0010-6860 Construction News
0010-6879 Construction Plant Hire *changed to* Plant Hire
0010-6887 Construction Products
0010-6895 Construction Products & Technology†
0010-6917 Construction Review
0010-6925 Construction Specifier
0010-6941 Construction West
0010-695X Constructional Review
0010-6968 Constructioneer
0010-6976 Constructions Equipements pour les Loisirs
0010-6992 Constructive Action for Good Mental Health *changed to* Constructive Action for Good Health
0010-700X Constructive Triangle
0010-7018 Constructor
0010-7034 Construire
0010-7042 Consudel
0010-7050 Consulente Immobiliare
0010-7069 Consultant (Greenwich)
0010-7077 Consultant (Midland)
0010-7085 Consultant (Wake)
0010-7093 Consulting Engineer
0010-7107 Consulting Engineer (Barrington)
0010-7115 Consumers Affairs Bulletin *changed to* Co-Op Consumers
0010-7123 Consumer Bulletin *see* 0095-2222
0010-7131 Consumer Buying Prospects *changed to* Economic Prospects
0010-7158 Consumer Education Forum
0010-7174 Consumer Reports
0010-7182 Consumers Digest
0010-7190 Consumers Voice
0010-7212 Contabilidad Administracion *changed to* Contaduria. Administracion
0010-7220 Austria Contact
0010-7239 Contact
0010-7247 Contact(London, 1955) *see* 0309-4928
0010-7255 Contact (Bromley)
0010-7263 Contact†
0010-728X Contact Lens Medical Bulletin *see* 0360-1358
0010-7301 Contact Point
0010-731X Contactblad
0010-7328 O A A G. Bulletin†
0010-7336 Die Contactlinse
0010-7352 Container in Italia e nel Mondo *changed to* Eurotransports Illustrato-Container in Italia e nel Mondo
0010-7360 Container News
0010-7379 Containerisation International
0010-7387 Containers and Packaging†
0010-7395 Contamination Control *see* 0090-2519
0010-7409 Contamination Newsletter†
0010-7468 Contemporary Authors
0010-7476 Contemporary Education
0010-7484 Contemporary Literature
0010-7492 Contemporary Literature in Translation
0010-7514 Contemporary Physics
0010-7522 Contemporary Poland
0010-7530 Contemporary Psychoanalysis
0010-7549 Contemporary Psychology
0010-7557 Contemporary Religions in Japan *changed to* Japanese Journal of Religious Studies
0010-7565 Contemporary Review
0010-7573 Contemporary Writers in Christian Perspective†
0010-7581 Contenido
0010-759X Contents of Contemporary Mathematical Journals *see* 0361-4794
0010-7603 Contents Pages: Electronics and Electricity†
0010-7611 Contents Pages of Iranian Science and Social Science Journals†
0010-762X Contenuti
0010-7646 Jaybee
0010-7662 Contigo
0010-7697 Continental Bulletin
0010-7719 Continental Iron and Steel Trade Reports
0010-7727 Continental Magazine
0010-7735 Continental Paint and Resin News
0010-7743 Continentaler Stahlmarkt
0010-776X Continuing Education Report†
0010-7778 Continuous Learning†
0010-7794 Conto Dertien *changed to* Tussen Ons in
0010-7816 Contra Costa County School Bulletin
0010-7824 Contraception
0010-7832 Contract
0010-7840 Contract Bridge Bulletin
0010-7859 Contract Journal *changed to* Contract Journal(1979)
0010-7867 Contracting and Construction Engineer *changed to* Resources Industry-Quarry Mine & Construction Equipment
0010-7875 Contracting in the Carolinas
0010-7883 Contractor and Plant Manager†
0010-7891 Contractor
0010-793X Contrary Investor
0010-7948 Contrast
0010-7956 Contratista
0010-7964 Contrepoint
0010-7972 Instituto Ecuatoriano de Ciencias Naturales. Contribuciones
0010-7980 University of Wyoming
0010-7999 Contributions to Mineralogy and Petrology
0010-8014 Controcorrente
0010-8022 Control and Instrumentation
0010-8030 Control and Science Record†
0010-8049 Control Engineering
0010-8065 Control Systems
0010-8073 Controller
0010-8081 Controlli Numerici e Macchine *changed to* Controlli Numerici Macchine a C N Robot Industriali
0010-809X Controspazio
0010-8103 Controvento
0010-8111 Convegno Musicale
0010-812X Convegno
0010-8138 Convenience Store Journal†
0010-8146 Convergence
0010-8154 Convergence
0010-8170 Conversation et Traduction
0010-8189 Converter
0010-8197 Converting Industry *see* 0032-8707
0010-8200 Conveyancer and Property Lawyer
0010-8227 Convivium†
0010-8235 Convivium, Filosofia, Psicologia, Humanidades
0010-8243 Convorbiri Literare
0010-8251 Cook County Highway News†
0010-8286 Cooks Continental Timetable *see* 0144-7475
0010-8294 Cooks Staff Magazine *changed to* World of Thomas Cook
0010-8316 Cooperacion Libre
0010-8332 Cooperation
0010-8340 Cooperation *changed to* Cooperation-Distribution-Consommation
0010-8359 Cooperation Agricole
0010-8367 Cooperation and Conflict
0010-8375 Cooperation et Developpement *see* 0395-9481
0010-8383 Cooperation Technique *see* 0395-9481
0010-8391 Cooperative Accountant
0010-8413 Cooperative Builder
0010-843X Cooperative Education Association Newsletter
0010-8448 Cooperative Farmer
0010-8456 Cooperativismo & Nordeste†
0010-8464 Cooperator
0010-8472 Cooperator†
0010-8480 Cooperazione di Credito
0010-8499 Cooperazione e Societa
0010-8502 Cooperazione Educativa
0010-8510 Cooperazione Italiana
0010-8529 Coopercotia
0010-8537 Cooper's Hero-Hobby
0010-8545 Coordination Chemistry Reviews
0010-857X Copper†
0010-8596 Copper Abstracts *see* 0309-2216
0010-8626 Copyright
0010-8634 Copyright Bulletin
0010-8650 Cor et Vasa
0010-8669 Coranto
0010-8677 Corcoran Gallery of Art Bulletin†
0010-8685 Cord
0010-8707 Corduroy†
0010-8723 C O R E S T A
0010-8731 Cork Historical and Archaeological Society. Journal
0010-874X Cork Weekly Examiner & Weekly Herald *changed to* Irish Weekly Examiner
0010-8758 Cormoran†
0010-8766 Cormoran y Delfin
0010-8782 Cornell Countryman
0010-8790 Cornell Engineer
0010-8804 Cornell Hotel & Restaurant Administration Quarterly
0010-8812 Cornell International Law Journal
0010-8820 Cornell Journal of Social Relations
0010-8839 Cornell Law Forum
0010-8847 Cornell Law Review
0010-8855 Cornell Newsletter, Chemicals-Pesticides Program†
0010-8863 Cornell Plantations
0010-8871 Cornell Program in Oral History. Bulletin†
0010-888X Cornell International Agricultural Development Bulletin *changed to* Cornell International Agricultural Bulletin
0010-8898 Cornell University Medical College Alumni Quarterly
0010-8901 Cornell Veterinarian
0010-8936 Coronet†
0010-8944 Corpoandes *changed to* Corporacion de los Andes. Revista
0010-8952 Corporate Communications Report
0010-8987 Corporate Planning
0010-8995 Corporate Practice Commentator
0010-9029 Correction Sidelights†
0010-9045 Corrections Digest
0010-9053 Corrective Psychiatry and Journal of Social Therapy *see* 0093-1551
0010-9061 Correio Agro-Pecuario
0010-9088 Correio Serrano
0010-9096 Correo del Delta
0010-910X Correo del Sur
0010-9118 Correo Economico
0010-9142 Corridor *changed to* Wordworks
0010-9150 Corriere Nucleare†
0010-9169 Corriere dei Ciechi
0010-9177 Corriere dei Congressi†
0010-9185 Corriere dei Piccoli
0010-9193 Corriere dei Trasporti
0010-9207 Corriere del Farmacista
0010-9215 Corriere del Teatro
0010-9223 Corriere dell'Aviatore
0010-9231 Corriere di Caracas

ISSN	Title
0010-924X	Corriere d'Italia
0010-9258	Corriere Fitopatologico
0010-9274	Corriere Italiano
0010-9282	Corriere Sindacale†
0010-9290	Corriere Stenografico
0010-9304	Corrispondenza Socialista
0010-9312	Corrosion
0010-9320	Corrosion Abstracts†
0010-9339	Corrosion Abstracts
0010-9347	Corrosion Control Abstracts
0010-9355	Corrosion Engineering
0010-9371	Corrosion Prevention and Control
0010-938X	Corrosion Science
0010-941X	Body Fashions see 0360-3520
0010-9428	Corset, Bra & Lingerie Magazine changed to Intimate Fashion News
0010-9436	Corset de France
0010-9452	Cortex
0010-9525	Cosmic Research
0010-9533	Cosmoglotta
0010-9541	Cosmopolitan
0010-955X	Cosmopolitan Contact
0010-9568	Cosmorama Pictorial
0010-9576	Cosmos
0010-9592	Cost and Management
0010-9606	Cost Engineer
0010-9614	Cost Engineering†
0010-9622	Value Engineering Digest/Defense Contract Guide changed to Value Engineering and Management Digest/Defense Contract Guide
0010-9630	Camara de Comercio. Boletin Informativo changed to Comercio
0010-9649	Costruire Laterizi
0010-9657	Costruttori Romani
0010-9665	Costruzioni
0010-9673	Costruzioni Metalliche
0010-9681	Cote d'Azur Agricole et Horticole
0010-972X	Cote d'Azur Agricole et Horticole. Bulletin Bibliographique
0010-9746	Cotswold Life
0010-9789	Cotton and General Economic Review changed to Cotton Outlook
0010-9797	Cotton Digest
0010-9800	Cotton Gin and Oil Mill Press
0010-9835	Cotton's Progress†
0010-9843	Cottonwood see 0147-149X
0010-9851	Couleurs
0010-986X	Coulisse Diplomatique see 0015-3516
0010-9886	Council Fire
0010-9894	Council for Research in Music Education. Bulletin
0010-9916	Council for the Protection of Rural England. Quarterly Bulletin
0010-9924	Church Council of Greater Seattle. Occasional News changed to Source (Seattle)
0010-9932	Tanners' Council of America, Inc. Council News
0010-9940	Council of Associations of University Student Personnel Services. Journal†
0010-9959	Council of Planning Librarians. Exchange Bibliographies†
0010-9959	Council of Planning Librarians. Exchange Bibliography see 0193-970X
0010-9967	Council on Abandoned Military Posts. Periodical
0010-9975	American Council on Consumer Interests. Newsletter
0010-9983	Council of Library Technology. Newsletter changed to Council on Library/Media Technical Assistants. Newsletter
0010-9991	Councilor
0011-0000	Counseling Psychologist
0011-0019	Counselor
0011-0027	Counselor
0011-0035	Counselor Education and Supervision
0011-0043	Counselor's Information Service†
0011-0051	Count Dracula Society Quarterly changed to Castle Dracula
0011-0086	Country & Western Express
0011-0094	Country and Western Roundabout
0011-0108	Country & Western Spotlight
0011-0124	Country Churchman
0011-0132	Country Gentlemen's Magazine
0011-0140	Country Guide
0011-0159	Country Landowner
0011-0167	Country Life changed to National Country Life
0011-0175	Country Life†
0011-0183	Country Life in British Columbia
0011-0191	Country Living
0011-0205	Country Living
0011-0213	Country Quest
0011-023X	Country-Side
0011-0248	Country Song Roundup
0011-0256	Country Standard
0011-0264	Countryman
0011-0272	Countryman
0011-0280	Countryside see 0363-8723
0011-0299	Countrywide Sports†
0011-0302	Countrywoman
0011-0310	County Councils Gazette
0011-0353	County Progress
0011-037X	Courage†
0011-0396	Courier
0011-040X	Courier (New York)†
0011-0418	Courier (Syracuse)
0011-0426	Courier
0011-0434	Voedingsblad
0011-0442	Courrier Australien
0011-0450	Courrier Avicole
0011-0469	Courrier: Cahiers d'Etudes et d'Informations changed to Association des Eleves et Anciens Eleves de l'Ecole Nationale Superieure des Postes et Telecommunications. Cahiers d'Etudes et d'Information
0011-0477	Courrier de la Nature, Homme et l'Oiseau
0011-0485	Courrier de la Normalisation
0011-0493	Courrier de la Republique
0011-0507	Courrier des Echecs
0011-0515	Courrier des Messageries Maritimes changed to Compagnie Generale Maritime. Courrier
0011-0523	Courrier d'Information-Rearmement Moral changed to Tribune de Caux
0011-0531	Centre International d'Etudes Poetiques. Courrier
0011-0558	Courrier du Secretariat International de l'Enseignement Universitaire des Sciences Pedagogiques
0011-0566	Courrier du Verre changed to Architecture de Lumiere Courrier du Verre
0011-0574	Courrier Europeen
0011-0604	Courrier Industriel et Scientifique
0011-0620	Courrier Musical de France
0011-0639	Courrier Vauclusien
0011-0647	Court Review
0011-0655	Couture†
0011-0671	Covenant Companion
0011-0701	Cover Note†
0011-071X	Covered Bridge Topics
0011-0728	Covjek i Prostor
0011-0736	Coyote's Journal
0011-0744	Craft Horizon changed to American Craft
0011-0752	Craft, Model & Hobby Industry
0011-0779	Craftsman changed to Make It with Leather
0011-0787	Cranberries
0011-0795	Cranbrook Magazine†
0011-0809	Crane News†
0011-0825	Cranial Academy Newsletter
0011-0833	Crawdaddy; Magazine of Rock see 0163-9404
0011-0841	Crazy Horse
0011-085X	C R C Critical Reviews in Solid State Sciences changed to C R C Critical Reviews in Solid State & Materials Sciences
0011-0868	Creationist†
0011-0876	Creative Camera
0011-0884	Creative Crafts
0011-0892	Creative Drama
0011-0906	Creative Plastics†
0011-0930	Creative Writing
0011-0973	Credit and Financial Management
0011-0981	Credit and Financial Newsletter
0011-099X	Credit Communal de Belgique. Bulletin Trimestriel
0011-1007	Credit Executive
0011-1023	Credit Suisse. Bulletin
0011-1031	Credit Retailer
0011-1058	Credit Union Executive
0011-1066	Credit Union Magazine
0011-1074	Credit World
0011-1090	Credito Popolare
0011-1104	Creditreform
0011-1139	Creel†
0011-1147	Creem
0011-1155	Creighton Law Review
0011-1163	Cremationieuws
0011-1171	Crescendo
0011-118X	Crescendo International
0011-1198	Cresset
0011-1201	Creuset, la Voix des Cadres changed to Cadres et Maitrise
0011-121X	Cri du Monde†
0011-1228	Crianca e Escola changed to Escola Fundamental
0011-1236	Cricket
0011-1244	Cricket
0011-1252	Cricket Quarterly†
0011-1260	Cricketer changed to Cricketer International
0011-1287	Crime & Delinquency
0011-1295	Crime Control Digest
0011-1309	Crime Detective†
0011-1317	Criminal Law Bulletin
0011-1325	Criminal Law Journal
0011-1333	Criminal Law Quarterly
0011-1341	Criminal Law Reporter
0011-135X	Criminal Law Review
0011-1368	Criminalia†
0011-1376	Criminologist
0011-1384	Criminology
0011-1392	Cripple Care News
0011-1406	Crisi e Letteratura
0011-1422	Crisis (New York, 1910)
0011-1430	Crisis & Change
0011-1449	Cristallo
0011-1457	Cristianismo y Sociedad
0011-1465	Christ to the World
0011-1473	Criterio
0011-1481	Criterion†
0011-149X	Critic (Chicago)
0011-1503	Critica
0011-1511	Critica d'Arte
0011-152X	Critica Marxista
0011-1538	Critica Sociale†
0011-1546	Critica Sociologica
0011-1554	Critica Storica
0011-1562	Critical Quarterly
0011-1589	Criticism
0011-1597	Criticon
0011-1600	Critique
0011-1619	Critique: Studies in Modern Fiction
0011-1627	Croatia Press
0011-1643	Croatica Chemica Acta
0011-1651	Croce
0011-166X	Crochet†
0011-1686	Croissance des Jeunes Nations
0011-1694	Crol
0011-1708	Cromos
0011-1716	T.T.P.I. Trade Gazette
0011-1724	Cronaca Politica
0011-1732	Cronache Calabresi
0011-1740	Cronache d'Altri Tempi
0011-1759	Chronica Dermatologica
0011-1767	Cronache di Archeologia e di Storia dell'Arte
0011-1775	Cronache Economiche
0011-1783	Cronache Farmaceutiche
0011-1791	Cronica de Holanda
0011-1805	Cronica Medica†
0011-1813	Cronica Universitaria†
0011-183X	Crop Science
0011-1848	Crop Science Society of Japan. Proceedings changed to Japanese Journal of Crop Science
0011-1864	Crops & Soils
0011-1872	Crops in India
0011-1880	Croquet Gazette
0011-1899	Cross
0011-1910	Cross & Cockade Journal
0011-1910	Cross and Crown see 0162-6760
0011-1945	Cross Country News
0011-1953	Cross Currents
0011-1961	Cross of Languedoc
0011-197X	Cross Tie Bulletin see 0097-4536
0011-1988	Crossbow
0011-2011	Crossed Flags†
0011-202X	Crossroads†
0011-2038	Crossroads
0011-2054	Crossroads
0011-2070	Crow's Forest Products Digest†
0011-2089	Croydon Advertiser
0011-2100	Crucible
0011-2119	Crucible
0011-2127	Crusade
0011-2135	Crusade for Education
0011-2143	Crusade Messenger changed to Crusader
0011-2151	Crusader
0011-216X	Crustaceana
0011-2186	Crux
0011-2194	Cruzada Eucaristica
0011-2208	Cruzado
0011-2216	Cruzeiro
0011-2224	Cry California
0011-2232	Ceylon Journal of Medical Science
0011-2240	Cryobiology
0011-2259	Cryogenic Information Report
0011-2275	Cryogenics
0011-2283	Cryogenics and Industrial Gases†
0011-2291	Immortality Magazine†
0011-2305	Crystal Lattice Defects
0011-2313	C S A and the Consumer
0011-2321	Ctenar
0011-2348	Cuaderno Cultural
0011-2356	Cuadernos Americanos
0011-2364	Cuadernos de Arquitectura
0011-2372	Cuadernos de Botanica Canaria
0011-2380	Cuadernos de Critica
0011-2399	Cuadernos de Economia
0011-2445	Cuadernos de Literatura
0011-2453	Cuadernos de Orientacion Familiar
0011-2488	Cuadernos de Ruedo Iberico
0011-250X	Cuadernos Hispanoamericanos
0011-2526	Cuadernos Latinoamericanos de Economia Humana changed to Centro Latinoamericano de Economia Humana. Publicaciones
0011-2534	Cuadernos para el Dialogo†
0011-2550	Cuadernos Trimestrales de Poesia
0011-2569	Cuadernos Universitarios
0011-2577	Cuadernos Valencianos de Historia de la Medicina y de la Ciencia
0011-2585	Cuba - Foreign Trade†
0011-2593	Cuba Internacional
0011-2607	Cuba Noticias Economicas
0011-2615	Cuba. Oficina Nacional de Invenciones, Informacion Tecnica y Marcas. Boletin Oficial
0011-2623	Cuba Socialista†
0011-2631	Cuban Studies Newsletter/Boletin de Estudios Cubanos see 0361-4441
0011-264X	Cucciolo
0011-2658	Cue see 0028-7369
0011-2666	Cue of Theta Alpha Phi
0011-2674	Cuento
0011-2690	Cuir
0011-2704	Cuisine et Vins de France
0011-2720	Cukoripar
0011-2747	Cultivador Moderno
0011-2755	Cultura
0011-2763	Cultura Boliviana
0011-2771	Cultura e Scuola
0011-278X	Cultura Hispanica
0011-2798	Cultura nel Mondo
0011-2801	Cultura Popolare
0011-281X	Cultura Turcica
0011-2828	Cultural Affairs†
0011-2836	Cultural Comercial
0011-2852	Cultural Forum†

0011-2860 Cultural Hermeneutics *changed to* Philosophy and Criticism
0011-2879 Cultural News from Germany *changed to* Kulturbrief - A German Review
0011-2837 Cultural News from India
0011-2895 Cultural Research Institute. Bulletin
0011-2925 Culture Francaise
0011-2941 Groningen
0011-295X Cultures et Developpement
0011-2976 Cumberland Presbyterian
0011-2984 Cumbria
0011-300X Cumulative Book Index
0011-3018 Cumulative Index to Nursing Literature *see* 0146-5554
0011-3026 Cumulative Stock Profits
0011-3034 Cuoio Pelli Materie Concianti
0011-3050 Cupula†
0011-3069 Curator
0011-3093 Curlew
0011-3107 Curling *changed to* Svensk Curling
0011-3115 Curling Review
0011-3123 Current
0011-3131 Current
0011-3158 Current Abstracts of Chemistry & Index Chemicus
0011-3166 Current Abstracts of the Soviet Press *see* 0011-3425
0011-3174 University of Illinois at Urbana-Champaign. College of Agriculture. Current Affairs
0011-3182 Current Affairs Bulletin
0011-3190 Indo-Pacific Fisheries Council. Current Affairs Bulletin†
0011-3204 Current Anthropology
0011-3212 Current Archaeology
0011-3220 Cryogenic Data Center. Current Awareness Service *see* 0364-0868
0011-3239 Current Bibliography for Aquatic Sciences and Fisheries *see* 0140-5373
0011-3247 Current Bibliography of Epidemiology†
0011-3255 Current Bibliography on African Affairs
0011-3301 Current Bibliography on Science and Technology: Earth Science, Mining and Metallurgy
0011-3344 Current Biography
0011-3352 Current Books for Academic Libraries *see* 0360-473X
0011-3360 Current Compensation References
0011-3379 C C-A F V/Current Contents, Agricultural, Food and Veterinary Sciences *see* 0090-0508
0011-3387 C C-B S E/Current Contents, Behavioral, Social and Educational Sciences *see* 0092-6361
0011-3395 Current Contents/Engineering and Technology *see* 0095-7917
0011-3409 Current Contents/Life Sciences
0011-3417 Current Contents, Physical and Chemical Sciences *changed to* Current Contents/Physical, Chemical & Earth Sciences
0011-3425 Current Digest of the Soviet Press
0011-3433 Current Documents from the German Democratic Republic
0011-3468 Current Events (Fredericton)
0011-3484 Current Events
0011-3492 Current Events (Inkprint Edition)
0011-3506 Current Food Additives Legislation†
0011-3514 Current Geographical Publications
0011-3522 Current Hawaiiana
0011-3530 Current History
0011-3557 Current Index to Conference Papers†
0011-3565 Current Index to Journals in Education
0011-3573 Current Indian Statutes
0011-359X Current Journals in Baker Library. Part One - Author and Title†
0011-3603 Current Journals in Baker Library. Part Two - Subject†
0011-3611 Current Laboratory Practice†
0011-362X Current Law
0011-3638 Current Leather Literature
0011-3646 Current Legal Bibliography
0011-3654 Current Literature in Traffic and Transportation
0011-3662 Current Literature on Aging
0011-3689 Current Medical Abstracts for Practitioners†
0011-3700 Current Medical Practice
0011-3719 Current Medicine for Attorneys
0011-3727 Current Municipal Problems
0011-3735 Current Musicology
0011-3751 Current Notes on International Affairs *see* 0311-7995
0011-3778 Current Papers in Electrical & Electronics Engineering
0011-3786 Current Papers in Physics
0011-3794 Current Papers on Computers & Control
0011-3824 Current Podiatry
0011-3832 Current Practices
0011-3840 Current Problems in Surgery
0011-3867 Current Publications in Population/Family Planning†
0011-3867 Current Publications in Family Planning *see* 0039-3665
0011-3883 Current Scene
0011-3891 Current Science
0011-3905 Current Science (Inkprint Edition)
0011-3913 Current Slang†
0011-3921 Current Sociology
0011-3948 Current Tissue Culture Literature *see* 0090-0753
0011-3964 Current Topics in Radiation Research†
0011-3972 U.S. Bureau of Labor Statistics. Current Wage Developments
0011-3999 Current Work in the History of Medicine
0011-4006 Currents *changed to* ChemEcology
0011-4014 Currents in Modern Biology *see* 0303-2647
0011-4022 Curriculum†
0011-4049 Curriculum Theory Network *see* 0362-6784
0011-4057 Cursillo
0011-4065 Curtain, Drapery & Bedspread Magazine
0011-4081 Curved Horn Newspaper *changed to* Fordham University. Review
0011-409X Cushman Foundation for Foraminiferal Research. Contributions *see* 0096-1191
0011-4103 Custodian's Letter
0011-4111 Custom Applicator
0011-412X Custom Tailor
0011-4146 Customs Bulletin
0011-4154 Customs Imports and Exports Journal
0011-4162 Cutis
0011-4170 Cutler-Hammer Record
0011-4189 Cutting Tool Engineering
0011-4200 Cuvar Jadrana
0011-4219 Cybernetic Medicine
0011-4227 Cybernetica
0011-4235 Cybernetics
0011-4243 Cybernetics Abstracts
0011-426X Cycle†
0011-4278 Cycle Guide
0011-4286 Cycle World
0011-4294 Cycles
0011-4316 Cycling
0011-4324 Cycling & Motorcycling *changed to* Cycling & Motorcycling with the Scooter
0011-4332 Cycling News *changed to* South African Cyclist
0011-4359 Cyclo-Flame
0011-4367 Cyclotron Trading Services
0011-4375 Cygnet
0011-4383 Cykel- och Sporthandlaren
0011-4391 Cykel-och Mopednytt
0011-4413 Cyklistika
0011-4421 Cylchgrawn Llyfrgell Genedlaethol Cymru
0011-443X Cylinder Theory Reports
0011-4448 Cymru'r Plant
0011-4456 Cyprus Bulletin
0011-4464 Cyprus. Department of Statistics & Research. Quarterly Statistical Digest
0011-4472 Cyprus. Department of Statistics and Research. Imports and Exports Statistics
0011-4480 Cyprus. Ministry of Labour and Social Insurance. Quarterly Review *changed to* Cyprus. Ministry of Labour and Social Insurance. Labour Review
0011-4499 Cyrano de Paris
0011-4529 Cytobios
0011-4537 Cytogenetics *see* 0301-0171
0011-4553 Czasopismo Stomatologiczne
0011-4561 Czasopismo Techniczne
0011-457X Czechoslovak Engineering Sciences Abstracts†
0011-4588 Czechoslovak Film
0011-4596 Czechoslovak Film Press News *changed to* Film News
0011-460X Czechoslovak Foreign Trade
0011-4618 Czechoslovak Heavy Industry
0011-4626 Czechoslovak Journal of Physics. Section B *changed to* Czechoslovak Journal of Physics
0011-4634 Czechoslovak Life
0011-4642 Czechoslovak Mathematical Journal
0011-4650 Czechoslovak Motor Review
0011-4677 Czechoslovak Woman
0011-4685 Quattroruote Mare†
0011-4693 D/A *see* 0161-5785
0011-4707 D A C News
0011-4723 D A Review
0011-4731 D A S U P
0011-474X D A V Magazine
0011-4758 D B - Kundenbrief
0011-4766 D B-Deutsche Bauzeitung-Die Bauzeitung *changed to* Deutsche Bauzeitung-db
0011-4782 D B Z
0011-4812 D D R-Sport
0011-4820 D D R-Verkehr
0011-4839 D D Z†
0011-4871 D E S A L Reportaje†
0011-4898 D E W Technische Berichte *changed to* Thyssen Edelstahl Technische Berichte
0011-4901 D F V L R - Nachrichten
0011-491X D F Z
0011-4928 D G Z
0011-4936 D. H. Lawrence Review
0011-4952 D I N Mitteilungen
0011-4979 D. I. Y. Trade
0011-4987 D K-Mitteilungen
0011-4995 D L-Q T C *changed to* CQ DL
0011-5002 D L W Informationen zur Bau- und Einrichtungspraxis *changed to* D L W Nachrichten
0011-5010 D L Z
0011-5029 D M
0011-5037 D M A A Washington Newsletter *changed to* D M M A Government Affairs Report
0011-5045 D M G Newsletter†
0011-5053 D M I-Nachrichten *see* 0342-0957
0011-5061 Deadline Data on World Affairs
0011-507X D N Z International
0011-5088 D. O
0011-510X D P W V - Nachrichten
0011-5118 D R C Newsletter *changed to* D R C Africa News
0011-5126 D R P A Log *changed to* Delaware Valley Business Magazine
0011-5134 D R P Bulletin
0011-5142 D S F-Journal
0011-5150 D S H Abstracts
0011-5169 D S T Z-Deutsche Stenografenzeitung
0011-5177 D. V. B. A. Publicaciones Tecnicas
0011-5185 D W I - Berichte†
0011-5193 D W V-Mitteilungen
0011-5207 Da-a /U dela
0011-5223 Dacca University Studies. Part A: Humanities
0011-5231 Dachshund
0011-524X Dade County Teacher *changed to* U. T. D. Today
0011-5258 Dados
0011-5266 Daedalus (Cambridge)
0011-5282 DAF Trucks Magazine
0011-5290 Daffodil Journal
0011-5304 Dagspressen
0011-5320 Daheim Bei der W A G
0011-5339 Dahl, Dunn & Hargitt's Moving Average Commodity Service†
0011-5347 Large Dams
0011-5355 Daiichi Kogyo Seiyaku Review
0011-5371 Daily Athenaeum
0011-538X Daily Blessing
0011-5398 Daily Cardinal
0011-5401 Daily Construction Service
0011-541X Daily Gleaner-Farmers Weekly
0011-5428 Daily Gleaner-Food Supplement
0011-5444 Daily Kent Stater
0011-5452 Daily Law Journal Record *changed to* Journal Record
0011-5460 Daily News Record
0011-5495 Daily Telegraph Magazine *changed to* Telegraph Sunday Magazine
0011-5509 Daily Variety
0011-5517 South Africa. Weather Bureau. Daily Weather Bulletin/Daaglikse Weerbulletin
0011-5525 Daily Word
0011-5533 Daily World
0011-5541 Dainichi-Nippon Cables Review
0011-555X Dairy and Ice Cream Field *changed to* Dairy Field
0011-5568 Dairy Council Digest
0011-5576 Dairy Farmer
0011-5592 Dairy Goat Journal
0011-5606 Dairy Guide
0011-5614 Dairy Herd Management
0011-5622 Dairy Industries *see* 0308-8197
0011-5649 Dairy Industry News
0011-5657 Dairy Industry Newsletter
0011-5673 Dairy Record
0011-5681 Dairy Science Abstracts
0011-569X Dairy Shorthorn Journal *changed to* Shorthorn Journal
0011-5703 U.S. Department of Agriculture. Economics, Statistics and Cooperatives Service. Dairy Situation
0011-572X Dairyman
0011-5738 Dairynews
0011-5746 Milk Reporter *changed to* Milk Marketer
0011-5754 Dais
0011-5762 Dak Tar
0011-5770 Dakota Catholic Action
0011-5800 Dalesman
0011-5819 Dalhousie Gazette
0011-5827 Dalhousie Review
0011-5835 Dallas
0011-5843 Dallas Bible College News *changed to* Dallas Bible College Herald
0011-586X Dallas Medical Journal
0011-5894 Daltons Weekly
0011-5908 Damals
0011-5916 Damernas Vaerld
0011-5924 Textiel-Visie: Damesmodevakblad
0011-5940 Damn You
0011-5959 Damspel
0011-5975 Dan Smoot Report†
0011-5991 Dance Films Association and Dance Society Newsletter *changed to* Dance Films Association Newsletter
0011-6009 Dance
0011-6017 Dance News
0011-6025 Dance News and Recall
0011-6033 Dance Perspectives†
0011-605X Dancing Times
0011-6068 Dandy
0011-6076 Danfoss Journal
0011-6084 Danish Journal
0011-6092 Danish Medical Bulletin
0011-6106 Danmarks Amstraad
0011-6114 Danmarks Geologiske Undersoegelse
0011-6130 Danmarks Havfaskeri *see* 0011-6270
0011-6149 Danmarks Nationalbank. Monetary Review
0011-6157 Danmarksposten
0011-6165 Dansbalans *changed to* Nevo-Nieuws
0011-6173 Danses
0011-6181 Dansk Arbejde
0011-6203 Dansk Artilleri-Tidsskrift
0011-6211 Dansk Botanisk Arkiv
0011-622X Dansk Brandvaern *changed to* Brandvaern
0011-622X Brandfare og Brandvaernn *changed to* Brandvaern
0011-6238 Dansk Bridge

ISSN	Title
0011-6262	Dansk Familieblad
0011-6270	Dansk Fiskeritidende
0011-6297	Dansk Geologisk Forening. Bulletin
0011-6319	Dansk Institutions Tidsskrift
0011-6327	Dansk Jagt
0011-6335	Dansk-Kemi†
0011-6335	Dansk-Kemi
0011-6351	Nye Dansk Landbrug†
0011-636X	Dansk Mejeritidende†
0011-6378	Dansk Missionsblad
0011-6386	Dansk Musiktidsskrift†
0011-6394	Dansk Ornithologisk Forenings Tidsskrift
0011-6408	Dansk Paedagogisk Tidsskrift
0011-6424	Dansk Pelsdyravl
0011-6440	Dansk Radio Industri see 0033-9970
0011-6459	Dansk Reklame changed to Markedsfoering
0011-6475	Dansk Skovforenings Tidsskrift
0011-6491	Dansk Svejsetidende changed to Svejsetidende
0011-6505	Dansk Teknisk Tidsskrift
0011-6513	Dansk Tidsskrift for Farmaci†
0011-6513	Dansk Tidsskrift for Farmaci see 0302-248X
0011-6548	Dansk Vejtidsskrift
0011-6556	Danske Bogmarked
0011-6564	Danske Dyrlaegeforening. Medlemsblad changed to Dansk Veterinaertidsskrift
0011-6572	Danske Kommuner
0011-6629	Danske Vognmaend
0011-6637	Darbininkas
0011-6645	Daring Confessions
0011-6653	Daring Romance changed to My Personal Love Secrets
0011-667X	Dark Horse
0011-6688	Dark Shadows
0011-6696	Umma
0011-6718	Darpon
0011-6726	D'Ars
0011-6734	Darshana International
0011-6750	Dartmouth College Library Bulletin
0011-6769	Dartnell Office Adminstration Service
0011-6777	Dartnell Sales and Marketing Service
0011-6793	Darwiniana
0011-6823	Data Journal changed to Tass News and Journal
0011-6831	Data Management†
0011-684X	Data Processing
0011-6858	Data Processing Digest
0011-6874	Data Processing Magazine†
0011-6882	Data Processing Practitioner†
0011-6890	Data Processor
0011-6912	Data Systems
0011-6947	Data Trend see 0311-7731
0011-6963	Datamation
0011-6971	Dataweek†
0011-698X	Dateline Delhi
0011-7005	Datenjournal
0011-7013	Daughters of the American Revolution Magazine
0011-703X	Davar
0011-7048	Davka
0011-7064	Dawn†
0011-7080	Day by Day
0011-7099	Day to Remember
0011-7102	Daybreak
0011-7110	Israel. Ministry of Agriculture. Department of Fisheries. Dayig u-Midgeh be-Yisrael
0011-7129	Daytime T V
0011-7137	Dayton USA
0011-7145	Db, the Sound Engineering Magazine
0011-7153	D. C. Gazette
0011-7161	Echo (De Aar)
0011-7188	De Paul Law Review
0011-7196	Deadwood†
0011-720X	Deaf American
0011-7218	Dealerscope
0011-7234	Dean Sherman's Forest Industry Affairs Letter
0011-7250	Decalogue Journal
0011-7269	Deccan Geographer
0011-7285	Deciduous Fruit Grower
0011-7293	Decimal Currency and Metrication News†
0011-7307	Decision (Minneapolis)
0011-7315	Decision Sciences
0011-7323	Decisions of the Comptroller General of the United States
0011-7331	U. S. Department of the Interior. Decisions of the Department of the Interior
0011-734X	Deco Trefoil†
0011-7358	Decor
0011-7374	Decorating Contractor changed to Builder and Decorator
0011-7382	Decorating Craft Ideas Made Easy see 0192-3706
0011-7404	Decorating Retailer
0011-7412	Decorating Your First Home†
0011-7420	Decoration - Ameublement
0011-7447	Decuscope
0011-7455	Dedalo
0011-7471	Deep-Sea Research and Oceanographic Abstracts see 0198-0149
0011-7471	Deep-Sea Research see 0198-0149
0011-748X	Defence Science Journal
0011-7498	Defender (Wilmington)
0011-7501	Defender
0011-7528	Defenders of Wildlife News see 0162-6337
0011-7552	Defense de l'Occident
0011-7560	Defense des Distillateurs Ambulants et des Bouilleurs de Cru
0011-7579	Defense des Vegetaux
0011-7587	Defense Law Journal
0011-7595	Defense Management Journal
0011-7609	Defense Manager†
0011-7625	Defense Transportation Journal
0011-7633	Defensor-Chieftain
0011-7641	Defesa Nacional
0011-7668	Deficience Mentale
0011-7676	Definition†
0011-7684	Dein Freund†
0011-7692	Dein Reich Komme
0011-7706	Deirdre
0011-7714	Dekalb Literary Arts Journal
0011-7722	Delavska Enotnost
0011-7730	Delaware Archaeology†
0011-7749	Delaware Geological Survey Reports of Investigations
0011-7765	Delaware History
0011-7773	Delaware Library Association Bulletin
0011-7781	Delaware Medical Journal
0011-779X	Delaware Today
0011-7803	D V I Magazine changed to Delaware Valley Business Magazine
0011-782X	Delfts Bouwkundig Studenten Gezelschap Styles. Mededelingen
0011-7846	Delhi Law Times
0011-7854	Delhi Medical Journal
0011-7862	Deli News
0011-7870	Delinquency and Society†
0011-7889	Delirante
0011-7897	Deliverer
0011-7919	Delmarva Poultry & Farm
0011-7927	Delmarva Report
0011-7935	Delo
0011-7943	Delo in Varnost
0011-796X	Delphin
0011-7978	Delta
0011-7986	Delta
0011-7994	Delta
0011-801X	Delta see 0025-570X
0011-8028	Delta Epsilon Sigma Bulletin
0011-8036	Delta Farm Press
0011-8044	Delta Kappa Gamma Bulletin
0011-8052	Delta Pi Epsilon Journal
0011-8060	Paper Book
0011-8079	Deltawerken
0011-8087	Deltion Diikiseos Epichiriseon
0011-8095	Deltion Dimotikis Vivliothikis Hermoupoleos†
0011-8109	International Committee on Irrigation and Drainage. Greek National Committee. Bulletin changed to Bulletin G C I D
0011-8117	Greek Speleological Society. Deltion
0011-8133	National Foundation "King Paul." Deltion changed to Protovoulia
0011-8141	DeLuxe General Rewind†
0011-815X	Demag Kurier
0011-8168	Demain
0011-8176	Demama
0011-8184	D E Mly
0011-8192	Democrat†
0011-8206	Democratic German Report†
0011-8214	Democratic Journalist
0011-8222	Democratie Moderne
0011-8249	Demografia
0011-8257	Demografia y Economia
0011-8265	Demografie
0011-8281	Demography and Development Digest
0011-829X	Demokraat
0011-8303	Die Demokratische Gemeinde
0011-8311	Die Demokratische Schule
0011-832X	Demos
0011-8338	Demosta
0011-8346	Radio Waves and Examination
0011-8362	Den'gi i Kredit
0011-8370	Denken en Doen
0011-8389	Electric Furnace Steel
0011-8419	Denmark. Civilforsvarsstyrelsen. Orientation†
0011-8427	Denmark Quarterly Review
0011-8435	Radio, TV, HiFi & Electronics
0011-8451	Densei Technical Journal
0011-8478	Electrophotography
0011-8486	Dental Abstracts
0011-8516	Dental Association of South Africa. Journal
0011-8524	Dental Cadmos
0011-8532	Dental Clinics of North America
0011-8540	Dental Concepts
0011-8559	Dental-Dienst
0011-8567	Dental Digest see 0033-6572
0011-8575	Dental Echo
0011-8583	Dental Economics
0011-8591	Dental Guidance Council for Cerebral Palsy. Bulletin changed to Dental Guidance Council on the Handicapped. Journal
0011-8605	Dental Health†
0011-863X	Dental Industry News
0011-8656	Das Dental-Labor
0011-8664	Dental Laboratory News
0011-8672	Dental Laboratory Review
0011-8680	Dental Management
0011-8699	Dental Mirror
0011-8702	Dental Outlook
0011-8710	Dental Practice
0011-8729	Dental Practitioner and Dental Record see 0300-5712
0011-8737	Dental Products Report
0011-8745	National University of Iran. Dental School. Journal
0011-8761	Dental Student Newsletter
0011-877X	Dental Student changed to Dental Student/Dentalpractice
0011-8788	Dental Survey
0011-8796	Dental Technician
0011-8818	Dentists Marketplace
0011-8826	Denver Art Museum. Quarterly†
0011-8834	Denver Law Journal
0011-8850	Denver Public Library News see 0020-1405
0011-8869	Denver Quarterly
0011-8877	Osmania Medical College. Department of History of Medicine. Bulletin see 0304-9558
0011-8885	Department Store Employees Union. Local Twenty One Guide
0011-8893	Department Store Management changed to Department Store Economist
0011-8907	Department Store Suppliers changed to I.R.D.S.
0011-8915	Department Store Workers' Union. Local 1-S News
0011-8931	Depeche Commerciale et Agricole
0011-8958	Depeche Mode
0011-8966	Depositaire de France
0011-8974	Derby changed to Esquire & Derby
0011-8982	Derby Enterprise see 0144-6118
0011-8990	Derbyshire Life and Countryside
0011-9008	Derevoobrabatyvayushchaya Promyshlennost'
0011-9016	Dergi†
0011-9024	Dermato-Venerologie changed to Revista de Medicina Interna, Neurologie, Psihiatrie, Neurochirurgie, Dermato-Venerologie. Dermato-Venerologie
0011-9032	Dermatologia†
0011-9040	Dermatologia Ibero Latino-Americana†
0011-9040	Dermatologia Ibero Latino-Americano changed to Medicina Cutanea Ibero-Latino-Americana
0011-9059	International Journal of Dermatology
0011-9075	Dermatologica
0011-9083	Dermatologische Monatsschrift
0011-9091	Dermatology and Urology/Hifu to Hitsunyo changed to Nishi Nihon Journal of Dermatology
0011-9105	Dermatology Digest see 0160-7685
0011-9113	Derriere le Miroir
0011-9121	Belgian Patents Report changed to Belgian Patents Abstracts
0011-913X	Japanese Patents Report
0011-9148	Deryn
0011-9156	Des Moines. Public Library. Monthly Memo
0011-9164	Desalination changed to Membrane Science and Desalination
0011-9172	Desalination Abstracts
0011-9199	Desarrollo
0011-9202	Desarrollo Administrativo†
0011-9210	Descant
0011-9229	Desert Call
0011-9237	Desert
0011-9245	Design
0011-9261	Design
0011-927X	Design†
0011-9288	Design & Components in Engineering†
0011-9296	Design & Development†
0011-930X	Design and Environment changed to Urban Design Newsletter
0011-9318	Design Australia†
0011-9342	Design Engineering
0011-9350	Design Engineering
0011-9369	Design from Scandinavia
0011-9393	Design International changed to Design International. Issue B
0011-9393	Design International changed to Design International. Issue A
0011-9407	Design News
0011-9415	Design Quarterly
0011-9423	Designer
0011-9431	Designer
0011-944X	Designscape
0011-9474	Desmos
0011-9490	Dessa Mina Minsta
0011-9512	Dessinateurs et Techniciens changed to Dessin et Technique
0011-9520	Dessins et Modeles Internationaux changed to International Designs Bulletin
0011-9539	Dessous Elegants see 0010-9436
0011-9547	Destellos Evangelicos†
0011-9555	Destin changed to Destin International
0011-9563	Destino
0011-9571	Detail
0011-958X	Detergents and Specialities see 0090-8878
0011-9598	Detonator changed to Envoy
0011-9601	Detroit Dental Bulletin
0011-9636	Detroit Institute of Arts. Bulletin
0011-9644	Detroit Jewish News
0011-9652	Detroit Lawyer
0011-9660	Detroit and Suburban Lutheran
0011-9679	Detroit Schools changed to Call to Action
0011-9687	Detroit Society for Genealogical Research. Magazine
0011-9695	Detroit Teacher
0011-9709	Detroiter†
0011-9717	Detskaya Literatura
0011-9725	Dettaglio Tessile e dell'Abbigliamento†
0011-9741	Deutsch als Fremdsprache
0011-975X	Die Deutsche Buehne

0011-9734 Deutsche Agrartechnik *see* 0323-3308
0011-9822 Deutsche Akademie fuer Staedtebau und Landesplanung. Mitteilungen
0011-9830 Deutscher Altphilologen-Verband. Mitteilungsblatt
0011-9849 Der Deutsche Apotheker
0011-9857 Deutsche Apotheker Zeitung
0011-9865 Deutsche Architektur *changed to* Architektur der DDR
0011-9873 Der Deutsche Arzt
0011-9881 Deutsche Aussenpolitik
0011-989X Deutsche Automobil Revue
0011-9911 Deutsche Baumeister†
0011-992X Deutsche Baumschule
0011-9938 Der Deutsche Beamte
0011-9946 Deutsche Berufs- und Fachschule *see* 0340-904X
0011-9954 Deutsche Bibliographie. Das Deutsche Buch
0011-9989 Deutsche Buecherschau†
0012-0006 Deutsche Bundesbank. Monatsberichte
0012-0022 Deutsche Circus-Zeitung *changed to* Die Circuszeitung
0012-0030 Dokumentationszentrale Wasser Schriftenreihe
0012-0049 Deutsche Drogisten Zeitung
0012-0057 Deutsche Eisenbahntechnik *see* 0323-3553
0012-0073 Deutsche Entomologische Zeitschrift
0012-0081 Der Deutsche Fall Schirmjaeger
0012-0103 Sozialistische Finanzwirtschaft
0012-0111 Deutsche Fischerei-Zeitung *changed to* Zeitschrift fuer die Binnenfischerei der DDR
0012-012X Der Deutsche Forstmann
0012-0138 Deutsche Gaertnerboerse *changed to* G B und G W - Gaertner Boerse und Gartenwelt
0012-0162 Deutsche Gefluegelwirtschaft *see* 0340-3858
0012-0197 Deutsche Gesellschaft fuer Geologische Wissenschaften. Berichte. Reihe A: Geologie und Palaeontologie, Reihe B: Mineralogie und Lagerstaettenforschung†
0012-0200 Deutsche Gesellschaft fuer Versicherungsmathematik. Blaetter
0012-0219 Das Deutsche Gesundheitswesen
0012-0227 Deutsche Getraenke-Industrie
0012-0235 Deutsche Gewaesserkundliche Mitteilungen
0012-0251 Deutsche Handelskammer in Oesterreich (Bulletin)
0012-026X Deutsche Hebammen-Zeitschrift
0012-0278 Deutsche Hebe- und Foerdertechnik
0012-0286 Deutsche Hotel Zeitung *changed to* D G Deutsche Gaststaette/Deutsche Hotel-Zeitung Gastwirt und Hotelier
0012-0294 Der Deutsche Hugenott
0012-0308 Deutsche Hydrographische Zeitschrift
0012-0316 Deutsche Ingenieurschule *see* 0340-448X
0012-0324 Deutsche Jaeger-Zeitung *changed to* Jaeger
0012-0332 Deutsche Jugend
0012-0340 Deutsche Kameramann *see* 0343-5571
0012-0375 Deutsche Kunst und Denkmalpflege
0012-0391 Deutsche Landwirtschaft *see* 0023-3811
0012-0413 Deutsche Lebensmittel-Rundschau
0012-0421 Deutsche Lehrerzeitung
0012-043X Deutsche Literaturzeitung
0012-0448 Das Deutsche Malerblatt
0012-0464 Deutsche Mechaniker Zeitung†
0012-0472 Deutsche Medizinische Wochenschrift
0012-0480 Deutsche Milchwirtschaft
0012-0502 Deutsche Musikbibliographie
0012-0510 Deutsche National-Zeitung
0012-0529 Deutsche Nationalbibliographie. Reihe A: Neuerscheinungen des Buchhandels
0012-0537 Deutsche Nationalbibliographie. Reihe B: Neuerscheinungen Ausserhalb des Buchhandels
0012-0545 Deutsche Nationalbibliographie. Reihe C: Dissertationen und Habilitationsschriften
0012-0553 Der Deutsche Pelztierzuechter
0012-057X Deutsche Polizei
0012-0596 Deutsche Post
0012-060X Deutsche Rechtsprechung
0012-0618 Deutsche Rentenversicherung
0012-0626 Deutsche Rheologische Gesellschaft. Berichte *see* 0340-8388
0012-0634 Der Deutsche Rundfunk- Einzelhandel
0012-0650 Deutsche Schachblaetter
0012-0677 Deutsche Schaefereizeitung
0012-0685 Der Deutsche Schreiner
0012-0693 Die Deutsche Schrift
0012-0707 Deutsche Schuetzenzeitung
0012-0723 Das Deutsche Schuhmacherhandwerk
0012-0731 Die Deutsche Schule
0012-074X Deutsche Krankenpflege-Zeitschrift
0012-0758 Deutsche Seiler-Zeitung
0012-0766 Deutsche Sparkassenzeitung
0012-0774 Deutsche Steuer-Zeitung: Ausgabe A *changed to* Deutsche Steuer-Zeitung
0012-0782 Deutsche Steuer-Zeitung. Ausgabe B *changed to* Deutsche Steuer-Zeitung. Eildienst
0012-0790 Deutsche Stomatologie der D D R *see* 0302-4725
0012-0804 Der Deutsche Strassenverkehr
0012-0812 Deutsche Studien
0012-0820 Der Deutsche Tabakbau
0012-0839 Deutsche Textiltechnik *see* 0323-3804
0012-0847 Deutsche Tieraerztliche Wochenschrift *see* 0341-6593
0012-0855 Der Deutsche Tischlermeister
0012-0863 Deutsche Uhrmacher-Zeitschrift *see* 0017-1689
0012-0871 Deutsche Umschau
0012-0901 D V Z
0012-091X Deutsche Versicherungszeitschrift†
0012-0928 Deutsche Verwaltungspraxis
0012-0936 Deutsche Vierteljahrsschrift fuer Literaturwissenschaft und Geistesgeschichte
0012-0944 Neue Volkskunst
0012-0960 Allgemeine Deutsche Weinfachzeitung *changed to* Die Weinwirtschaft
0012-0979 Der Deutsche Weinbau
0012-0987 Deutsche Wissenschaftliche Kommission fuer Meeresforschung. Berichte *see* 0341-6836
0012-0995 Deutsche Wohnungswirtschaft
0012-1010 Zahn- Mund- und Kieferheilkunde
0012-1029 Deutsche Zahnaerztliche Zeitschrift
0012-1037 Zeitschrift fuer Neurologie *see* 0340-5354
0012-1045 Deutsche Zeitschrift fuer Philosophie
0012-1053 Deutsche Zeitschrift fuer Verdauungs- und Stoffwechselkrankheiten
0012-1061 Deutscher Germanisten-Verband. Mitteilungen
0012-107X Deutscher Aerokurier *changed to* Aerokurier
0012-1088 Deutscher Alpenverein
0012-1096 Deutscher Drucker
0012-110X Der Fass- und Weinkuefer
0012-1118 Deutscher Jaeger *see* 0340-7829
0012-1126 Deutscher Kantinen Anzeiger *changed to* Kantinen Anzeiger
0012-1134 Deutscher Lebensmittelgrosshandel
0012-1142 Deutscher Lebensmittelhandel
0012-1169 Deutscher Palaestina-Verein. Zeitschrift
0012-1177 Deutscher Studenten-Anzeiger
0012-1185 Deutscher Verein fuer Oeffentliche und Private Fuersorge. Nachrichtendienst
0012-1193 Deutsches Adelsblatt
0012-1207 Deutsches Aerzteblatt
0012-1215 Deutsches Architektenblatt
0012-1223 Deutsches Archiv fuer Erforschung des Mittelalters
0012-1231 D A R
0012-124X Deutsches Dachdecker-Handwerk *changed to* Das Dachdecker-Handwerk
0012-1258 Deutsches Elektrohandwerk *changed to* D E - der Elektromeister und Deutsches Elektrohandwerk
0012-1274 Deutsches Handwerksblatt
0012-1282 Deutsches Industrieinstitut Beitraege†
0012-1290 Deutsches Institut fuer Wirtschaftsforschung. Vierteljahrshefte zur Wirtschaftsforschung
0012-1304 Deutsches Institut fuer Wirtschaftsforschung. Wochenbericht
0012-1312 Jahrbuch fuer Volkskunde und Kulturgeschichte *changed to* Jahrbuch fuer Volkskunde und Kulturgeschichte. Neue Folge
0012-1320 Deutsches Medizinisches Journal†
0012-1339 Deutsches Museum. Abhandlungen und Berichte
0012-1347 Deutsches Steuerrecht
0012-1355 Deutsches Tieraerzteblatt
0012-1363 Deutsches Verwaltungsblatt
0012-1371 Deutsches Volksheimstaettenwerk. Informationsdienst
0012-138X Deutsches Waffen-Journal
0012-1398 Deutschkurse
0012-1401 Deutschland - Frankreich
0012-141X Deutschland-Magazin
0012-1428 Deutschland Archiv
0012-1444 Deutschland-Informationen†
0012-1452 Der Deutschland- Sammler
0012-1460 Deutschunterricht
0012-1479 Zielsprache Deutsch
0012-1487 Deutschunterricht in Suedafrika
0012-1509 Deux Mille
0012-1533 Developing Economies
0012-155X Development and Change
0012-1576 Development Digest
0012-1584 Development Forum
0012-1592 Development, Growth and Differentiation
0012-1606 Developmental Biology
0012-1622 Developmental Medicine and Child Neurology
0012-1630 Developmental Psychobiology
0012-1649 Developmental Psychology
0012-1657 Developpement et Civilisations
0012-1665 Devenir Historico
0012-1673 Devil's Advocate†
0012-1681 Devon and Cornwall Notes and Queries
0012-1703 Devon Life
0012-1711 Devotion au Saint-Esprit *see* 0396-969X
0012-172X Dewey Newsletter†
0012-1746 Dharma
0012-1754 Di Cyan and Brown Bulletin *changed to* Di Cyan Bulletin
0012-1762 Dia Medico
0012-1770 Diabete†
0012-1770 Diabete *see* 0338-1684
0012-1789 Diabete et Nutrition
0012-1797 Diabetes
0012-1800 Diabetes in the News
0012-1819 Diabetes Literature Index†
0012-1827 Diabetes Newsletter
0012-1851 Diabetiker *see* 0341-8812
0012-186X Diabetologia
0012-1878 Diafora
0012-1886 Diaghonios†
0012-1894 Diagnosi - Laboratorio e Clinica†
0012-1908 Internal Medicine News & Diagnosis News
0012-1916 Diagnostica†
0012-1924 Diagnostica
0012-1932 Diagnostyka Laboratoryjna
0012-1959 Diakonia
0012-1967 Diakonia
0012-1975 Diakonie im Rheinland
0012-1983 Diakonische Werk (das) *changed to* Diakonie Report
0012-1991 Dial
0012-2009 D A I R S and Systems for Instruction Newsletter
0012-2017 Dialectica
0012-2025 Dialetti d'Italia
0012-2033 Dialog
0012-2041 Dialog
0012-205X Dialoghi
0012-2068 Dialogi
0012-2084 Dialogo
0012-2092 Dialogo
0012-2106 Dialogos
0012-2114 Dialogos
0012-2122 Dialogos
0012-2130 Dialogue†
0012-2157 Dialogue: A Journal of Mormon Thought
0012-2165 Dialogue†
0012-2173 Dialogue
0012-2181 Dialogue
0012-219X Dialogue
0012-2203 Dialogue†
0012-2211 Dialogue (New York, 1962) Braille edition of 0012-222X
0012-222X Dialogue (New York, 1962)†
0012-2238 Dialogue (New York, 1966)†
0012-2246 Dialogue (Milwaukee)
0012-2262 Dialogue (Washington)
0012-2270 Dialogue Calcutta *changed to* Dialogue India
0012-2289 Dialogue on Campus
0012-2297 Dialoguer
0012-2300 Diamond News and South African Jeweller
0012-2319 Diamond Walnut News
0012-2327 Diana
0012-2335 Diana
0012-2343 Diana
0012-2351 Diana Armi
0012-236X Diane
0012-2378 Diapason
0012-2386 Diario Italiano†
0012-2416 Dibevo
0012-2432 Dickens Studies Newsletter
0012-2440 Dickensian
0012-2459 Dickinson Law Review
0012-2467 Dictionnaire Permanent de la Construction
0012-2475 Dictionnaire Permanent Droit des Affaires
0012-2483 Dictionnaire Permanent Entreprise Agricole
0012-2491 Dictionnaire Permanent Fiscal
0012-2505 Dictionnaire Permanent Rural *changed to* Dictionnaire Permanent Rural (Droit, Social, Agricole)
0012-2513 Dictionnaire Permanent Social
0012-253X Die Casting Engineer
0012-2548 Diecasting & Metal Moulding
0012-2556 Diemaking, Diecutting and Converting *see* 0163-9234
0012-2564 Dienen und Fuehren *changed to* Unterwegs
0012-2572 Dienender Glaube
0012-2580 Sonntagschulmitarbeiter
0012-2602 Diesel and Gas Turbine Progress *changed to* Diesel Progress North American
0012-2610 Diesel Equipment Superintendent
0012-2629 Diesel-Lehti
0012-2645 Dietsche Warande en Belfort
0012-2653 Difesa Sociale
0012-2661 Differential Equations
0012-267X Diffusion Data *see* 0377-6883
0012-2688 Difofu
0012-2696 Difusion Economica
0012-2718 Digest des Revues Techniques *changed to* Bulletin Bibliographique des Laboratoires Professionnels Francais et Belge
0012-2726 Australia. Bureau of Statistics. Digest of Current Economic Statistics
0012-2734 U.S. National Labor Relations Board. Digest of Decisions of the National Labor Relations Board *changed to* Classified Index of N.L.R.B. and Related Court Decisions
0012-2742 Digest of Investment Advices
0012-2750 Digest of Labour Cases
0012-2769 Digest of Neurology & Psychiatry
0012-2777 Digest of Opinions of the Attorney General
0012-2785 U.S. Library of Congress. Congressional Research Service Digest of Public Bills and Resolutions

ISSN INDEX

ISSN	Title
0012-2807	Journal for Special Educators of the Mentally Retarded *changed to* Journal for Special Educators
0012-2815	Digest of the Soviet Ukrainian Press†
0012-2823	Digestion
0012-2831	Digital Integrated Circuit D.A.T.A. Book†
0012-284X	Dikobraz
0012-2858	Diliman Review
0012-2866	Dimanche
0012-2874	Dime Novel Round-Up
0012-2882	Dimension
0012-2890	Dimension: Journal of Pastoral Concern†
0012-2904	Dimensioni
0012-2920	Dimossiotis
0012-2939	Dinamica Economica
0012-2947	Dinamica Rural
0012-2971	Dines Letter
0012-3005	Dinaman
0012-3013	Dinteria
0012-3021	Diocesan Digest
0012-303X	Diogene†
0012-3048	Diogenes
0012-3064	Dion
0012-3072	Diplomania *see* 0016-4364
0012-3080	Diplomatic Bookshelf *changed to* Diplomatic Bookshelf & Review
0012-3099	U.S. Department of State. Diplomatic List
0012-3110	Diplomatist
0012-3129	Diplomlandwirt *see* 0340-7810
0012-3137	Dippy Post†
0012-3145	Spain. Direccion General de Archivos y Bibliotecas. Boletin†
0012-3161	Power Electronics†
0012-317X	Energy Digest
0012-3188	Direct Marketing Magazine
0012-320X	Direction et Gestion des Entreprises
0012-3218	Direction for Youth Leaders†
0012-3226	Direction of Trade *changed to* Direction of Trade Statistics
0012-3234	Directions
0012-3242	Director
0012-3250	Director†
0012-3250	Director
0012-3277	Directory of Chemical Producers-U.S.A.
0012-3293	Directory of Published Proceedings. Series SEMT-Science, Engineering, Medicine and Technology
0012-3307	Directory of Published Proceedings. Series SSH-Social Sciences/Humanities
0012-3323	Direttore Commerciale
0012-3331	Direzione Aziendale
0012-334X	Dirigente Amministrativo
0012-3358	Dirigente Construtor
0012-3366	Dirigente Industrial
0012-3374	Dirigente Rural
0012-3382	Diritti della Scuola
0012-3390	Diritto Aereo
0012-3404	Diritto del Lavoro
0012-3412	Diritto delle Radiodiffusioni e delle Telecomunicazioni
0012-3420	Diritto di Autore
0012-3439	Diritto e Giurisprudenza
0012-3447	Diritto e Pratica Tributaria
0012-3455	Diritto Ecclesiastico
0012-3471	Diritto Internazionale†
0012-348X	Diritto Marittimo
0012-351X	Discipline and Grievances
0012-3528	Discobolo
0012-3536	Discographer
0012-3544	Discographical Forum
0012-3560	Discoteca Alta Fedelta *changed to* Discoteca Hi Fi
0012-3579	Discount Merchandiser
0012-3587	Discount Store News
0012-3625	Discovery (New Haven)
0012-3633	Discovery (Toledo)
0012-3641	Discovery (Northbrook)
0012-365X	Discrete Mathematics
0012-3668	Discretio
0012-3676	Discus
0012-3684	Discussion sur l'Alphabetisation *see* 0024-4503
0012-3692	Chest
0012-3706	Diseases of the Colon and Rectum
0012-3714	Diseases of the Nervous System *see* 0160-6689
0012-3722	Disk
0012-3730	Diskus
0012-3765	Dispatcher
0012-3773	Dispensing Optician
0012-3781	Display International†
0012-3803	Display World *see* 0094-4610
0012-3811	Disposables and Nonwovens
0012-382X	Disque-Ton†
0012-3846	Dissent (New York)
0012-3862	Dissertationes Mathematicae
0012-3870	Dissertationes Pharmaceuticae et Pharmacologicae *see* 0301-0244
0012-3900	Distributie en Zelfbediening,D6†
0012-3927	Distribution/Warehouse Cost Digest *changed to* Warehouse and Physical Distribution Productivity
0012-3935	Distribution d'Aujourd'Hui
0012-3951	Distribution Worldwide *see* 0195-7244
0012-396X	C M I Distribution Maps of Plant Diseases
0012-3978	Distribuzione Moderna
0012-3986	Distributive Worker
0012-3994	District Council Nine Newsletter
0012-401X	District Heating
0012-4028	District Mail
0012-4036	District Management†
0012-4044	District Nursing *see* 0301-0821
0012-4060	District of Columbia Dental Society. Journal
0012-4079	District of Columbia Nurses Association. Quarterly Review†
0012-4087	Distrofia Muscolare
0012-4109	D I T
0012-4125	Dithmarschen
0012-4133	Detail
0012-4141	Divadelni Noviny
0012-4168	Dive *changed to* Dive Business
0012-4206	Divine Life
0012-4214	Divine Word Messenger†
0012-4222	Divinitas
0012-4230	Divorce Chats
0012-4249	Israel. Knesset. Divrei Haknesset
0012-4257	Divus Thomas
0012-4265	Divya Vani
0012-4273	Dix-Septieme Siecle
0012-4281	Dixie Contractor
0012-4303	Dixon Line†
0012-4311	El Djezair
0012-432X	Djur-Expressen
0012-4338	Djur och Natur†
0012-4346	Djurskyddet
0012-4354	Dnipro
0012-4370	Do It Yourself
0012-4389	Do It yourself-Markt *changed to* Muster und Farbe
0012-4397	Do It Yourself Retailing
0012-4400	Doberman News†
0012-4419	Dock and Harbour Authority
0012-4427	Docket
0012-4435	Doctor
0012-4443	Doctor Communist†
0012-446X	Doctrine and Life
0012-4478	Document Reproductie
0012-4486	Documenta Ophthalmologica
0012-4494	Documentacion Administrativa
0012-4508	Documentaliste
0012-4516	Documentatie
0012-4524	Documentatie Verkeerseconomie en Aanverwante Onderwerpen
0012-4532	Documentatieblad *changed to* Justitiele Verkenningen
0012-4540	Netherlands. Ministerie van Onderwijs en Wetenschappen. Documentatieblad
0012-4559	Documentatio Geographica *see* 0341-2431
0012-4567	Nationale Maatschappij der Belgische Spoorwegen. Documentatie
0012-4575	Documentation - Europe Post
0012-4583	Documentation - Technique, Scientifique et Commerciale
0012-4591	International Cooperative Alliance. Regional Office and Education Centre for South-East Asia. Documentation Bulletin *changed to* Documentation Bulletin for South-East Asia
0012-4613	Documentation Catholique
0012-4621	Documentation Commerciale et Comptable
0012-463X	Documentation East-European Agricultural Literature†
0012-4648	Documentation Economique
0012-4656	Documentation Francaise Illustree†
0012-4680	Documentation Rapide du Chef d'Enterprise *see* 0395-451X
0012-4699	Documentation Sociale†
0012-4702	Electricite de France. Documentation Technique
0012-4710	Documentazione Sui Paesi dell'Est
0012-4729	Documenti di Architettura†
0012-4737	Documenti di Vita Comunale
0012-4745	Documenti Sul Comunismo
0012-4753	Documentos
0012-477X	Documents et Debats
0012-4788	Documents et Statistiques†
0012-480X	Dodge Construction News
0012-4826	Doelmatig Bedrijfsbeheer *changed to* D B-Tijdschrift voor Doelmatig Bedrijfsbeheer
0012-4834	Dog Fancy
0012-4850	Dog News *see* 0309-1031
0012-4877	Dog Review of Southern Africa†
0012-4885	Dog World
0012-4893	Dog World
0012-4907	Dogar's General Knowledge Digest
0012-4915	Dogs in Canada
0012-4931	Dohanyipar
0012-494X	Doklady - Earth Science Sections
0012-4958	Doklady Biochemistry
0012-4966	Doklady Biological Sciences
0012-4974	Doklady Biophysics
0012-4982	Doklady Botanical Sciences
0012-4990	Doklady Chemical Technology
0012-5008	Doklady Chemistry
0012-5016	Doklady Physical Chemistry
0012-5024	Dokumentacija za Gradevinarstvo i Arhitekturu
0012-5032	Dokumentacja Geograficzna
0012-5059	D F W Dokumentation-Information
0012-5067	Dokumentation der Deutschen Binnenschiffahrt
0012-5075	Dokumentation der Gesetze und Verordnungen Osteuropas
0012-5091	Dokumentation der Zeit†
0012-5105	Dokumentation fuer Bodenmechanik - Grundbau, Felsmechanik - Ingenieurgeologie
0012-5113	Dokumentation - Jugendfoschung,Jugendhe,Jugendpolitik *see* 0342-3964
0012-513X	Dokumentation Sozialmedizin, Oeffentlicher Gesundheitsdienst, Arbeitsmedizin
0012-5148	Dokumentation Strasse
0012-5156	Dokumentation Wasser
0012-5172	Dokumente
0012-5180	Documentation Study
0012-5229	Doll Talk
0012-5237	Dollar-Bonds & Euro-Bonds
0012-5253	Dolphin *changed to* Dewan Perintis
0012-5261	Dolphin Book Club News
0012-527X	Domei News†
0012-5288	Domenica
0012-5296	Domenica del Corriere
0012-530X	Domestic Equipment Trader
0012-5318	Domestic Heating *see* 0308-9614
0012-5326	Domestic Heating News *see* 0308-8561
0012-5342	Dominion Engineer
0012-5350	Dominion Law Reports
0012-5369	Domov
0012-5377	Domus
0012-5393	Don
0012-5407	Don Universel du Sang
0012-5415	Donauraum†
0012-5423	Der Donauschwabe
0012-544X	Dono
0012-5458	Dookola Swiata
0012-5474	Doorbraak
0012-5482	Doorkijk
0012-5490	Doors to Latin America†
0012-5504	Doortocht
0012-5512	Dopester†
0012-5520	Doprava
0012-5547	Dorf Aktuell *see* 0340-7837
0012-5555	Dorfschule†
0012-5563	Dornier-Post
0012-5571	Road
0012-5598	Dorset Farmer
0012-5601	Doshkil'ne Vykhovannya
0012-561X	Doshkol'noe Vospitanie
0012-5636	Dostignuca
0012-5652	Dotacion
0012-5660	Dotaito Nyusus Reta†
0012-5679	Dots and Taps
0012-5687	Dottore in Scienze Agrarie
0012-5695	Douai Magazine
0012-5709	Double Liaison
0012-5717	Douglas Library Notes†
0012-5725	Dow Diamond *changed to* Elements
0012-5768	Down Beat
0012-5776	Down East Magazine
0012-5784	Down Library Lane†
0012-5806	Downside Review
0012-5814	Downstate Reporter
0012-5822	Downtown Idea Exchange
0012-5849	Dr. Shelton's Hygienic Review
0012-5857	Draegerheft
0012-5865	Draft Horse Journal
0012-5873	Drag Racing†
0012-5881	Dragoco Report
0012-589X	Dragon
0012-5911	Draht
0012-592X	Draht-Welt
0012-5938	Drake Law Review
0012-5946	Drama
0012-5954	Drama and Theatre†
0012-5962	Drama Review
0012-5989	Dramatics
0012-6004	Dramatists Guild Quarterly
0012-6012	Dramma
0012-6020	Drapers Record
0012-6055	Drehpunkt
0012-6063	Die Drei
0012-6071	Dreihammer
0012-608X	Dreikoenigsbote
0012-6098	Dreiser Newsletter
0012-6101	Dresdner Monats-Blaetter
0012-611X	Dressmaking
0012-6128	Dressvertising Weekly
0012-6136	Drevarsky Vyskum
0012-6144	Drevo
0012-6152	Drew Gateway
0012-6160	Drexel Library Quarterly
0012-6179	Drexel Technical Journal
0012-6187	Drie Talen
0012-6209	Rijksuniversiteit te Groningen. Nedersaksisch Instituut. Driemaandelijkse Bladen
0012-6217	Drift
0012-6225	Drill Bit
0012-6233	Water Supply Management
0012-6241	Drilling-D C W
0012-625X	Drinks International
0012-6268	Der Dritte Weg
0012-6322	Drogerie-Journal
0012-6330	Drogist
0012-6349	Drogistenblad Vergulde Gaper *changed to* D W
0012-6357	Drogownictwo
0012-6365	Droit d'Auteur
0012-6373	Droit de Vivre
0012-639X	Droit et Economie
0012-6411	Droit et Liberte
0012-642X	Droit Maritime Francais
0012-6438	Droit Social
0012-6454	Drovers Journal
0012-6462	Druck - Print
0012-6470	Druck und Papier
0012-6489	Druckformenherstellung
0012-6497	Druckluft-Praxis
0012-6500	Der Druckspiegel
0012-6519	Druckwelt
0012-6527	Drug and Cosmetic Industry
0012-6535	1199 News

ISSN	Title
0012-6543	Drug and Therapeutics Bulletin
0012-6551	Drug Digest†
0012-656X	Drug Information Bulletin see 0092-8615
0012-6578	Drug Intelligence & Clinical Pharmacy
0012-6586	Drug Merchandising
0012-6608	Drug Research Reports: The Blue Sheet
0012-6616	Drug Topics
0012-6624	Drug Trade News see 0090-2454
0012-6624	Drug Trade News changed to Product Marketing
0012-6632	Drugarce
0012-6640	Druggist†
0012-6667	Drugs
0012-6675	Drugs and Drug Abuse Education changed to Washington Drug Review
0012-6683	Drugs Made in Germany
0012-6691	Drugs of Today changed to Medicamentos de Actualidad / Drugs of Today
0012-6713	Drukkerswereld changed to Repro en Druk
0012-6721	Drum
0012-673X	Drum
0012-6748	Drum Corps News
0012-6756	Druzhba Narodov
0012-6764	Druzina in Dom
0012-6772	Drvna Industrija
0012-6780	Dryad
0012-6799	Dryade
0012-6802	Drycleaners News
0012-6829	Drycleaning World changed to Laundry Cleaning World
0012-6837	Du
0012-6845	Du und die Welt changed to Medizin Heute
0012-6853	Dual Dictionary Coordinate Index to Petroleum Abstracts see 0162-329X
0012-6861	Dublin Historical Record
0012-687X	Dublin Magazine
0012-6896	Dublin University Law Review†
0012-690X	Dubrovacki Vjesnik
0012-6918	Dubuque Leader
0012-6934	Duca-Post
0012-6942	Duckett's Register†
0012-6950	Ducks Unlimited
0012-6977	Duepiu
0012-7019	Duesseldorfer Amtsblatt
0012-7027	Duesseldorfer Hefte
0012-7035	Duff's Turf Guide changed to Computaform
0012-7043	Duiker Krant
0012-7051	Duitse Kroniek
0012-706X	Duivengazet
0012-7078	Duke Divinity School Review
0012-7086	Duke Law Journal
0012-7094	Duke Mathematical Journal
0012-7108	Duke University Library Newsletter
0012-7116	Duluthian
0012-7124	Dundee Chamber of Commerce Journal see 0306-0241
0012-7132	Dune Buggies & Hot VWs
0012-7159	Dunlop Industrial Rubber News
0012-7167	Dunn & Hargitt's Commodity Service
0012-7175	Dun's Review
0012-7183	Duodecim
0012-7205	Duquesne Review†
0012-7213	Duquesne University Law Review see 0093-3058
0012-7221	Durban High School Old Boys' Club. Bulletin
0012-723X	Durban Museum Novitates
0012-7264	Durez Molder
0012-7280	Durham University Journal
0012-7299	Duroc News
0012-7302	Dust†
0012-7310	Dutch-Australian Weekly
0012-7337	D V M Newsmagazine
0012-7353	Dyna
0012-7361	Dyna
0012-7388	Dynamic Maturity see 0148-799X
0012-7396	Dynamic Supervision
0012-740X	Dynamische Psychiatrie
0012-7418	Dynamite / International
0012-7434	Dysk Olimpijski†
0012-7450	E A R O P H News and Notes
0012-7469	E A S A changed to Engineers' News
0012-7477	E A Z
0012-7485	E B B A News changed to North American Bird Bander
0012-7493	E B U Review. Part B: General and Legal changed to E B U Review. Geneva Edition (Programmes, Adminstration, Law)
0012-7507	E D C
0012-7515	E D N Magazine
0012-7515	E E E-Magazine of Circuit Design Engineering see 0012-7515
0012-7523	E D P Analyzer
0012-7531	E D P Daily†
0012-754X	E D P Industry Report and Market Review changed to E D P Industry Report
0012-7558	E D P Weekly
0012-7566	E D U C O M Bulletin
0012-7590	E E G-E M G
0012-7612	E E I Statistical Releases. Electric Output
0012-7639	E E O†
0012-7647	E. F. D. S. S. News see 0013-8231
0012-7655	E F T A Bulletin
0012-7671	E G
0012-768X	E. I. M. Mededelingen
0012-7701	E L F
0012-771X	E L N A Bulteno see 0030-5065
0012-7744	E.M.G. Handmade Gramophones. Monthly Letter
0012-7760	E M N I D-Informationen
0012-7779	E M O Bulletin
0012-7787	E M O National Digest see 0317-3518
0012-7795	E-M Synchronizer
0012-7809	E N A P I†
0012-7817	E N P A S
0012-7825	Eos
0012-7841	E P I C Bulletin†
0012-7876	E. R. A. Journal†
0012-7892	E R D A
0012-7922	E R I C News Plus†
0012-7957	E R T (Electronics-Radio-TV) see 0355-4503
0012-7965	E S/Espana Semanal changed to Espana Hoy
0012-7981	E S G - Nachrichten
0012-799X	E S R O / E L D O Bulletin changed to E S A Bulletin
0012-8007	E S S A World see 0014-0821
0012-8015	Essor Economique et Commercial
0012-8023	E T V Newsletter
0012-8031	Elektrotechnische Zeitschrift. Ausgabe B see 0170-1711
0012-804X	E U R I S I†
0012-8058	E und M
0012-8074	Elektronik-Zeitung
0012-8082	Eagle (Washington)
0012-8090	Eagle (Milwaukee)
0012-8104	Eagle and Boys' World
0012-8112	Eagle
0012-8139	Early American
0012-8147	Early American Industries Association. Chronicle
0012-8155	Early American Life
0012-8163	Early American Literature
0012-8171	Early Childhood Education
0012-8198	Earnshaw's Infants' & Children's Review see 0161-2786
0012-821X	Earth and Planetary Science Letters
0012-8228	Earth Science
0012-8236	Earth Science Bulletin
0012-8244	Earth Science Journal†
0012-8252	Earth Science Reviews
0012-8287	Earthquake Notes
0012-8295	East
0012-8309	East Africa Journal†
0012-8317	Journal of the East Africa Natural History Society and National Museum
0012-8325	East African Agricultural and Forestry Journal
0012-8333	East Africa Journal of Rural Development changed to Eastern Africa Journal of Rural Development
0012-8341	East African Management Journal†
0012-835X	East African Medical Journal
0012-8376	East and West
0012-8384	East and West Series
0012-8392	East Anglian Magazine
0012-8406	East Asia Millions
0012-8414	East Asian Cultural Studies
0012-8430	East Europe†
0012-8449	East European Quarterly
0012-8457	East European Trade
0012-8465	East London Papers†
0012-8473	Perspective
0012-8481	East Midland Geographer
0012-849X	East Pakistan. Bureau of Statistics. Monthly Bulletin of Statistics changed to Monthly Statistical Bulletin of Bangladesh
0012-8503	East Pakistan Bureau of Statistics. Weekly Information Service†
0012-852X	East Riding Archaeologist
0012-8538	East Side Chamber of Commerce Newsletter
0012-8546	East Sussex Farmer
0012-8570	East-West
0012-8589	East/West
0012-8597	East-West Center Magazine
0012-8627	East-West Digest
0012-8635	East-West Review†
0012-8643	Eastbournian
0012-8651	Easter Seal Bulletin changed to Easter Seal Communicator
0012-866X	Eastern Africa Economic Review
0012-8678	Eastern Africa Law Review
0012-8686	Eastern Anthropologist
0012-8708	Eastern Buddhist
0012-8724	Eastern Cape Naturalist
0012-8732	Eastern Churches News Letter
0012-8740	Eastern Churches Review changed to Sobornost
0012-8759	Eastern Dental Society Bulletin
0012-8767	Eastern Economist
0012-8775	Eastern European Economics
0012-8783	International Journal of Politics
0012-8791	Eastern Evening News
0012-8805	Eastern Fruit Grower†
0012-8813	Eastern Horizon
0012-8821	Eastern Journal of International Law
0012-883X	Eastern Kansas Register
0012-8848	Eastern Librarian†
0012-8848	Eastern Librarian
0012-8856	Eastern Metals Review changed to Engineering & Metals Review
0012-8864	Eastern News
0012-8872	Eastern Pharmacist
0012-8880	Eastern Railway Magazine
0012-8899	Eastern Massachusetts Regional Library System. Eastern Region News
0012-8902	Eastern Review Magazine see 0094-3649
0012-8945	Eastern Utilization Research and Development Division. Publications and Patents changed to Eastern Regional Research Center. Publications and Patents
0012-8953	Eastern Worker
0012-897X	Eastman Organic Chemical Bulletin
0012-8996	Eaton Livia†
0012-9003	Information Eaux
0012-9011	Ebony
0012-902X	Ecclesia†
0012-9038	Ecclesia
0012-9046	Ecclesia changed to Kiongozi
0012-9054	Ecclesiastica Xaveriana changed to Theologica Xaveriana
0012-9089	Echo†
0012-9097	Echo†
0012-9119	Echo
0012-9127	Echo(Bethal)
0012-9135	Echo
0012-9143	Echo
0012-916X	Economic Echo from Yugoslavia changed to Yugoslavia Echo
0012-9178	Echo Africain
0012-9224	Echo de la Liberte de l'Ouest
0012-9232	Echo de la Presse et de la Publicite
0012-9240	Echo de la Timbrologie
0012-9259	Echo de l'Imprimerie et des Arts Graphiques see 0012-9232
0012-9267	Echo des Depositaires des Libraires et des Marchands de Journaux
0012-9283	Echo des Recherches
0012-9305	Echo uit Afrika changed to Echo uit Afrika en Andere Werelddelen
0012-9321	Echoes
0012-933X	Echoes
0012-9348	Echos de la Medecine see 0336-8653
0012-9356	Echos du Monde Classique
0012-9372	Echo's voor de Textielkleinhandel†
0012-9380	Eclair
0012-9402	Eclogae Geologicae Helvetiae
0012-9410	Eco
0012-9429	Eco Contemporaneo
0012-9437	Eco-Cuoio delle Industrie e del Commercio del Cuoio e delle Calzature
0012-9445	Eco de Nayarit
0012-9453	Eco degli Oratori e dei Circoli Giovanili
0012-947X	Eco del Seguro
0012-9488	Eco della Riviera
0012-9496	Eco della Scuola Nuova
0012-9518	Eco dell'Educazione Ebraica
0012-9526	Eco dell'Industria Tessile
0012-9534	Eco d'Italia
0012-9542	Eco-Tessili
0012-9550	Ecole de Specialisation de l'Artillerie Anti-Aerienne. Bulletin d'Information
0012-9569	Ecole en Afrique†
0012-9577	Ecole et la Vie
0012-9585	Ecole Maternelle Francaise
0012-9593	Ecole Normale Superieure. Annales Scientifiques
0012-9607	Ecologia Agraria
0012-9615	Ecological Monographs
0012-9623	Ecological Society of America. Bulletin
0012-9631	Ecologist changed to Ecologist (1979)
0012-9658	Ecology
0012-9666	Ecology Today†
0012-9674	Econ Notes changed to Ohio Council on Economic Education. Newsletter
0012-9682	Econometrica
0012-9690	Economia†
0012-9704	Economia
0012-9712	Economia
0012-9720	Economia
0012-9747	Economia Aretina
0012-9763	Economia Dominicana
0012-9771	Economia e Credito
0012-978X	Economia e Lavoro
0012-9798	Economia e Storia
0012-9801	Economia Internacional
0012-981X	Economia Internazionale
0012-9828	Economia Internazionale delle Fonti di Energia†
0012-9836	Economia Montana
0012-9844	Economia Mundial
0012-9852	Economia Nuova per Un Mondo Nuovo
0012-9860	Economia Salvadorena
0012-9879	Economia Trentina
0012-9887	Economia y Administracion
0012-9895	Economia y Ciencias Sociales
0012-9917	Economic Abstracts changed to Key to Economic Science
0012-9925	Economic Activity
0012-9933	Economic and Business Bulletin see 0148-6195
0012-995X	Economic & Business Review
0012-9968	Economic and Financial Review†
0012-9976	Economic and Political Weekly
0012-9984	Economic and Social Review
0012-9992	East African Community. Economic and Statistical Review
0013-0001	Economic Botany
0013-001X	Economic Brief†
0013-0028	Commercial Bank of Greece. Economic Bulletin
0013-0044	Economic Bulletin of Ghana
0013-0079	Economic Development and Cultural Change
0013-0095	Economic Geography
0013-0109	Economic Geology see 0361-0128

0013-0125 Economic Indicators
0013-0133 Economic Journal
0013-0141 Economic Leaflets
0013-015X Economic News about Turkey†
0013-0168 Economic News Bulletin
0013-0176 Economic News of Bulgaria
0013-0184 Economic Notes
0013-0192 Economic Observer†
0013-0206 Economic Opportunity Report
0013-0222 Economic Planning
0013-0249 Economic Record
0013-0257 Economic Report from Germany†
0013-0265 Economic Reporter
0013-0273 Economic Review
0013-0281 Economic Review†
0013-029X Economic Review
0013-0303 Economic Review
0013-0311 Economic Review and Report *changed to* International Understanding
0013-032X Economic Review of the Arab World†
0013-0346 Economic Situation in the Community *changed to* European Economy
0013-0354 Economic Society of Australia and New Zealand. New South Wales and Victorian Branches. Economic Papers
0013-0362 Economic Studies
0013-0370 Goetabanken
0013-0389 Economic Times
0013-0397 Economic Topics Series
0013-0400 Economic Trends
0013-0419 Revista Economica
0013-0427 Economica
0013-0435 Economia de Cordoba
0013-0443 Economicos Tachydromos
0013-0451 Economics of Planning†
0013-0451 Economics of Planning
0013-0478 Economie
0013-0494 Economie Appliquee
0013-0508 Economie Electrique
0013-0516 Economie et Humanisme
0013-0524 Economie et Medecine Animales†
0013-0532 Economie in Limburg *changed to* G. O. M.-Economie in Limburg
0013-0540 Economie Libanaise et Arabe
0013-0559 Economie Rurale
0013-0575 Economisch en Sociaal Tijdschrift
0013-0583 Economisch-Statistische Berichten
0013-0613 Economist
0013-0621 Economist
0013-063X Economist
0013-0648 Economista
0013-0656 Economista
0013-0664 Arab Economist†
0013-0672 Economiste Egyptien
0013-0680 Ecos
0013-0699 Ecos de Portugal
0013-0702 Ecotass
0013-0710 Ecrits de Paris
0013-0761 Ecumenical Courier
0013-077X Czech Ecumenical News
0013-0788 National†
0013-0796 Ecumenical Review
0013-080X Ecumentist
0013-0818 Edda
0013-0826 Die Edelkatze
0013-0842 Edesipar
0013-0877 Edilizia alle Fiere
0013-0885 Edilizia Moderna†
0013-0893 Edinburgh Academy Chronicle
0013-0907 Edinburgh Dental Hospital Gazette
0013-0915 Edinburgh Mathematical Society. Proceedings
0013-0923 Edition†
0013-0931 Editor†
0013-094X Editor & Publisher-the Fourth Estate
0013-0958 Editorial Research Reports
0013-0966 Editorials on File
0013-0974 Editor's Notebook†
0013-0982 Edizioni Nostre *changed to* Pagine Aperte
0013-1008 Edmonton Public Library. News Notes. *see* 0319-2156
0013-1016 Edmundite
0013-1024 EdPress Newsletter *changed to* EdPress News
0013-1032 Edubusiness†
0013-1067 Educacion
0013-1075 Educacion
0013-1083 Educacion Dental
0013-1091 Educacion Medica y Salud
0013-1105 Educador Social
0013-1113 Educadores
0013-1121 Educate†
0013-113X Educateur
0013-1148 Educateur et Bulletin Corporatif
0013-1156 Education
0013-1164 Education
0013-1172 Education
0013-1180 Education
0013-1199 Education
0013-1202 Education *changed to* Education News
0013-1202 Education *changed to* Education Journal
0013-1210 Education Abstracts†
0013-1229 Education and Culture *changed to* Council of Europe Forum
0013-1237 Education & Training of the Mentally Retarded
0013-1245 Education and Urban Society
0013-1253 Education Canada
0013-1261 Education Daily
0013-127X Education Digest
0013-1288 Education Enfantine
0013-1296 Education Equipment
0013-130X Education Equipment and Services Review†
0013-1318 Education et Developpement
0013-1326 Education for Teaching *see* 0309-877X
0013-1334 Education Gazette
0013-1342 Education Gazette and Teachers' Aid
0013-1350 Education in Chemistry
0013-1369 French News *changed to* France Education
0013-1377 Education in Science
0013-1385 Education Index
0013-1407 Education Libraries Bulletin
0013-1415 Education Musicale
0013-1423 Education
0013-1431 Education News
0013-144X Education Newsletter *changed to* Education San Diego County
0013-1458 Education of the Visually Handicapped
0013-1474 Education Physique et Sport
0013-1482 Education Quarterly
0013-1490 Education Quebecoise†
0013-1504 Education Recaps†
0013-1512 Education Reporter
0013-1520 Education Summary
0013-1547 Education Today
0013-1555 Education-Training Market Report
0013-1563 Education Trends *changed to* Outlook in Education
0013-1571 Education U. S. A.
0013-158X Education Weekly†
0013-1598 Education Welfare Officer *changed to* Education Social Worker
0013-1601 Educational Administration Abstracts
0013-161X Educational Administration Quarterly
0013-1628 Educational Administration Reporter†
0013-1644 Educational and Psychological Measurement
0013-1652 Educational Books and Equipment†
0013-1660 Educational Broadcasting Review *see* 0093-8149
0013-1679 Educational Bulletin *changed to* D P I Dispatch
0013-1687 Educational Courier
0013-1725 Educational Forum
0013-1733 Educational Forum
0013-1741 Educational Freedom
0013-175X Educational Horizons
0013-1768 Educational India
0013-1792 Educational Magazine
0013-1806 Educational Marketer
0013-1814 Educational Media†
0013-1830 Transvaal. Education Department. Educational News Flashes
0013-1849 Educational Perspectives
0013-1857 Educational Philosophy and Theory
0013-1865 Educational Product Report *changed to* E P I E Report
0013-1873 Educational Record
0013-1881 Educational Research
0013-189X Educational Researcher
0013-1911 Educational Review
0013-192X Educational Review
0013-1946 Educational Studies
0013-1954 Educational Studies in Mathematics
0013-1962 Educational Technology
0013-1970 Educational Broadcasting International
0013-1989 Educational Theatre Journal *see* 0192-2882
0013-1997 Educational Theatre News
0013-2004 Educational Theory
0013-2012 Educator
0013-2020 Educator
0013-2047 South Dakota Education Association. Educators' Advocate
0013-2055 Educator's Dispatch†
0013-2071 Educazione Alla Sicurezza
0013-208X Educazione Musicale†
0013-2098 Educazione Sanitaria *changed to* Educazione Sanitaria e Medicina Preventiva
0013-2101 Eendracht *changed to* W I K
0013-211X Eendrachtbode†
0013-2128 Eerste Hulp†
0013-2136 Eesti Loodus
0013-2144 Akademiya Nauk Estonskoi S. S. R. Izvestiya. Biologiya
0013-2152 Eesti Post†
0013-2160 Efemerides Costarricenses†
0013-2179 Effektivt Forsvar†
0013-2187 Effektivt Landbrug
0013-2195 Effeta
0013-2209 Efficacy†
0013-2217 Effluent and Water Treatment Journal
0013-2225 Effort *changed to* Jeu de Dames
0013-2233 Efluvios†
0013-2241 Egerer Zeitung
0013-225X Egeszseg†
0013-2268 Egeszsegtudomany
0013-2276 Egeszsegugyi Gazdasagi Szemle
0013-2306 Egg Industry†
0013-2322 Eglise Canadienne
0013-2330 Eglise en Alsace
0013-2349 Eglise et Theologie
0013-2357 Eglise Qui Chante
0013-2365 Eglise Vivante†
0013-2373 Egretta
0013-2381 Egypt Travel Magazine
0013-239X Egypte Contemporaine
0013-2403 Egyptian Cotton Gazette
0013-2411 Egyptian Medical Association. Journal
0013-242X Egyptian Orthopaedic Journal
0013-2438 Egyptian Pharmaceutical Journal†
0013-2446 Egyptian Public Health Association Journal
0013-2454 Egyptian Surgical Society Quarterly Review
0013-2462 Ehe *changed to* Partner Beratung
0013-2470 Ehe und Familie
0013-2489 Rundbrief Ehemaliger Schueler und Freunde der Schulbrueder
0013-2497 Eichholzbrief
0013-2500 Eier-Wild-Gefluegel-Markt
0013-2519 Eigen Huis *changed to* Eigen Huis en Interieur
0013-2527 Eigene Garten - Eigene Haus *changed to* Das Eigene Haus
0013-2551 Eight O'Clock
0013-256X 1820
0013-2578 1860 Settler
0013-2586 Eighteenth-Century Studies
0013-2594 Eighteen Month Forecast of Japan's Economy *changed to* Quarterly Forecast of Japan's Economy by the S. A. Method
0013-2608 Eigse
0013-2624 Eimreidin
0013-2640 Eine Welt der Vereinten Nationen
0013-2659 Einheit
0013-2667 Einheit und Fortschritt†
0013-2683 Eire-Ireland
0013-2705 Eisbericht
0013-2713 Eisdiele & Milchbar†
0013-273X Journal of Hygienic Chemistry
0013-2756 Eisenbahn
0013-2764 Eisenbahn-Amateur
0013-2772 Eisenbahn-Landwirt
0013-2780 Eisenbahnpraxis
0013-2799 Eisenbahner
0013-2802 Eisenbahner. Ausgabe A & B *changed to* D B
0013-2810 Der Eisenbahningenieur
0013-2829 Eisenbahntechnik
0013-2837 Eisenbahn-technische Praxis
0013-2845 Eisenbahntechnische Rundschau
0013-2853 Eisenwaren-Boerse
0013-2861 Eisenwaren-Zeitung
0013-287X Eisma's Schildersblad
0013-2888 Either/Or†
0013-2896 Ejendomsmaegleren
0013-2918 Ejercito
0013-2926 Ekalabya
0013-2934 Ekistic Index
0013-2942 Ekistics
0013-2969 Wiadomosci Ekologiczne
0013-2977 Ekonomen
0013-2985 Ekonomia†
0013-2993 Ikonomicheska Misul
0013-3000 Ekonomicheskii Byulleten Niderlandov
0013-3019 Ekonomicheskie Nauki
0013-3027 Ekonomicko-Matematicky Obzor
0013-3035 Ekonomicky Casopis
0013-3051 Ekonomika i Zhizn'
0013-306X Ekonomika Poljoprivrede *changed to* Ekonomika Proizvodnje Hrane
0013-3078 Ekonomika Preduzeca *changed to* Ekonomika Udruzenog Rada
0013-3086 Ekonomika Radyanskoi Ukrainy
0013-3094 Ekonomika Sel'skogo Khozyaistva
0013-3108 Ekonomika Stavebnictva
0013-3116 Ekonomika Stroitel'stva
0013-3124 Ekonomika Zemedelstvi *changed to* Ekonomika Polnohospodarstva
0013-3132 Ekonomicheskaya Gazeta
0013-3167 Ekonomisk Revy
0013-3175 Ekonomiska Laeget†
0013-3183 Ekonomiska Samfundets Tidskrift
0013-3191 Ekonomist
0013-3205 Ekonomista
0013-3213 Ekonomska Analiza
0013-3221 Radna Jedinica *changed to* Organizacija Samoupravljanja OUR
0013-323X Ekonomska Misao
0013-3256 Ekonomska Revija
0013-3264 Ekonomski Anali
0013-3272 Ekonomski Glasnik
0013-3299 Ekran
0013-3302 Ekran
0013-3310 Zhurnal Eksperimental'noi i Klinicheskoi Meditsiny
0013-3329 Eksperimental'naya Khirurgiya i Anesteziologiya
0013-3345 Ekspress-Informatsiya. Aviastroenie
0013-3353 Ekspress-Informatsiya. Automobilestroenie
0013-3361 Ekspress-Informatsiya. Avtomobil'nyi Transport
0013-3388 Ekspress-Informatsiya. Detali Mashin
0013-3396 Ekspress-Informatsiya. Elektricheskie Mashiny i Apparaty
0013-340X Ekspress-Informatsiya. Elektricheskie Stantsii, Seti i Sistemy
0013-3418 Ekspress-Informatsiya. Elektronika
0013-3426 Ekspress-Informatsiya. Fotokinoapparatura. Nauchnaya i Prikladnaya Fotografiya
0013-3434 Ekspress-Informatsiya. Garazhi i Garazhnoe Oborudovanie
0013-3442 Ekspress-Informatsiya. Gidroenergetika
0013-3450 Ekspress-Informatsiya. Gornorudnaya Promyshlennost'
0013-3469 Ekspress-Informatsiya. Gorodskoi Transport
0013-3477 Ekspress-Informatsiya. Iskusstvennye Sooruzheniya na Avtomobil'nykh Dorogakh
0013-3485 Ekspress-Informatsiya. Ispytatel'nye Pribory i Stendy

980 ISSN INDEX

0013-3493 Ekspress-Informatsiya. Khimicheskaya Tekhnologiya Pererabotki Vysokopolimernykh Materialov
0013-3507 Ekspress-Informatsiya. Khimiya i Pererabotka Nefti i Gaza
0013-3515 Ekspress-Informatsiya. Khimia i Tekhnologiya Neorganicheskikh Veshchestv
0013-3523 Ekspress-Informatsiya. Kontrol'no-Izmeritel'naya Tekhnika
0013-3531 Ekspress-Informatsiya. Korrozia i Zashchita Metallov
0013-354X Ekspress-Informatsiya. Kozhevenno-Obuvnaya Promyshlennost' *changed to* Ekspress-Informatsiya. Kozhevennaya Promyshlennost'
0013-354X Ekspress-Informatsiya. Kozhevenno-Obuvnaya Promyshlennost' *changed to* Ekspress-Informatsiya. Obuvnaya Promyshlennost'
0013-3558 Ekspress-Informatsiya. Lokomotivostroenie Vagonostroenie
0013-3574 Ekspress-Informatsiya. Myasnaya i Molochnaya Promyshlennost'
0013-3582 Ekspress-Informatsiya. Nefte- i Gazodobyvayushchaya Promyshlennost'
0013-3590 Ekspress-Informatsiya. Obogashchenie Poleznykh Iskopaemykh
0013-3604 Ekspress-Informatsiya. Organizatsiya Perevozok, Avtomatica, Telemekhanica i Svyaz' na Zheleznykh Dorogakh
0013-3612 Ekspress-Informatsiya. Pishchevaya Promyshlennost'
0013-3620 Ekspress-Informatsiya. Pod'emno-Transportnoe Mashinostroenie
0013-3639 Ekspress-Informatsiya. Porshnevye i Gazoturbinnye Dvigateli
0013-3663 Ekspress-Informatsiya. Promyshlennyi Organicheskii Sintez
0013-3671 Ekspress-Informatsiya. Promyshlennyi Transport
0013-368X Ekspress-Informatsiya. Protsessy i Apparaty Khimicheskikh Proizvodstv
0013-3698 Ekspress-Informatsiya. Put' i Stroitel'stvo Zheleznykh Dorog
0013-3701 Ekspress-Informatsiya. Radiolokatsiya, Televidenie, Radiosvyaz'
0013-371X Ekspress-Informatziya. Radiotekhnika Sverkhvysokikh Chastot i Kvantovaya Radiotekhnika *changed to* Ekspress-Informatsiya. Radiotekhnika Sverkhvysokikh Chastot
0013-371X Ekspress-Informatziya. Radiotekhnika Sverkhvysokikh Chastot i Kvantovaya Radiotekhnika *changed to* Ekspress-Informatsiya. Kvantovaya Radiotekhnika
0013-3728 Ekspress-Informatsiya. Rezhushchie Instrumenty
0013-3736 Ekspress-Informatsiya. Rybnaya Promyshlennost'
0013-3744 Ekspress-Informatsiya. Sel'skokhozyaistvennye Mashiny i Orudiya. Mekhanizatsiya Sel'skokhozyaistvennykh Rabot
0013-3752 Ekspress-Informatsiya. Silikatnye Stroitel'nye Materialy
0013-3760 Ekspress-Informatsiya. Sinteticheskie Vysokopolimernye Materialy
0013-3779 Ekspress-Informatsiya. Sistemy Avtomaticheskogo Upravleniya
0013-3787 Ekspress-Informatsiya. Steklo, Keramika i Ogneupory
0013-3795 Ekspress-Informatsiya. Stroitel'stvo i Ekspluatatsiya Avtomobilnykh Dorog
0013-3809 Ekspress-Informatsiya. Sudostroenie
0013-3825 Ekspress-Informatsiya. Tara i Upakovka *changed to* Ekspress-Informatsiya. Tara i Upakovka. Konteinery
0013-3833 Ekspress-Informatsiya. Tekhnicheskaya Ekspluatatsiya Podvizhnogo Sostava i Tyaga Poezdov
0013-3841 Ekspress-Informatsiya. Tekhnicheskaya Kibernetika
0013-385X Ekspress-Informatsiya. Tekhnologiya i Oborudovanie Kuznechno-Shtampovochnogo Proizvodstva
0013-3868 Ekspress-Informatsiya. Tekhnologiya i Oborudovanie Liteinogo Proizvodstva
0013-3876 Ekspress-Informatsiya. Tekhnologiya i Oborudovanie Mekhanosborochnogo Proizvodstva
0013-3884 Ekspress-Informatsiya. Tekstil'naya Promyschlennost'
0013-3892 Ekspress-Informatsiya. Tedriya i Praktika Nauchnoi Informatsii
0013-3906 Ekspress-Informatsiya. Teploenergetika
0013-3914 Ekspress-Informatsiya. Traktorostroenie
0013-3922 Ekspress-Informatsiya. Transport i Khranenie Nefti i Gaza
0013-3930 Ekspress-Informatsiya. Tsellyulozno-Bumazhnaya Promyshlennost'
0013-3957 Ekspress-Informatsiya. Ugol'naya Promyshlennost'
0013-3965 Ekspress-Informatsiya. Vodnyi Transport
0013-3973 Ekspress-Informatsiya. Vozdushnyi Transport
0013-3981 Ekspress-Informatsiya. Vychislitel'naya Tekhnika
0013-399X El
0013-4007 El Branschen
0013-4023 El Paso Archaeology
0013-4031 El Paso Economic Review *see* 0162-1041
0013-404X El Salvador. Direccion General de Estadistica y Censos. Boletin Estadistico
0013-4066 Elan
0013-4082 Elders
0013-4090 E L D O - E S R O Scientific and Technical Review *changed to* E S A Journal
0013-4112 Electric Heat and Air Conditioning *see* 0190-1370
0013-4139 Electric Power Statistics (Washington)
0013-4147 Electric Railway Society. Journal
0013-4155 Electric Technology U. S. S. R.
0013-4163 Electric Traction
0013-4171 Electric Vehicles for Industry
0013-418X Electrical & Electronic Trader
0013-421X Electrical and Electronics Techician Engineer *see* 0306-8552
0013-4228 Electrical and Radio Trading
0013-4236 Electrical Apparatus Service-Volt/Age *see* 0190-1370
0013-4244 Electrical Business
0013-4252 Electrical Communication
0013-4260 Electrical Construction and Maintenance
0013-4279 Electrical Contractor
0013-4287 Electrical Contractor and Maintenance Supervisor
0013-4295 Electrical Contractor and Retailer *see* 0308-7174
0013-4309 Electrical Engineer
0013-4317 Electrical Equipment
0013-4333 Electrical Equipment News
0013-435X Electrical India
0013-4376 Electrical Power Engineer
0013-4384 Electrical Review
0013-4414 Electrical Times
0013-4430 Electrical Wholesaling
0013-4449 Electrical Workers' Journal *changed to* I B E W Journal
0013-4457 Electrical World
0013-4465 Electricidade
0013-4481 Electricite
0013-449X Electricite de France. Direction des Etudes et Recherches. Bulletin. Serie A: Nucleaire, Hydraulique, Thermique
0013-4503 Electricite de France. Direction des Etudes et Recherches. Bulletin. Serie B: Reseaux Electriques, Materiels Electriques
0013-4511 Electricite de France. Direction des Etudes et Recherches. Bulletin. Serie C: Mathematiques-Informatique
0013-452X Electricite pour Vous
0013-4538 Electricity and Electronics
0013-4546 Electricity in Building *see* 0362-1324
0013-4562 Electrified Industry†
0013-4562 Electrified Industry *see* 0194-4746
0013-4589 Electro Optics
0013-4597 Electrophysiological Technologists' Association. Proceedings and Journal *see* 0307-5095
0013-4600 Electro-Procurement *see* 0163-6197
0013-4619 Electro Radio Mercuur *changed to* Elektrotechnisch Vakblad E R M
0013-4627 Elektrotechniek
0013-4635 Electro-Technology†
0013-4643 Electro-Technology
0013-4651 Electrochemical Society. Journal
0013-466X Electrochemical Society of India. Journal
0013-4678 Electrochemical Society of Japan. Journal (Denki Kagaku) *changed to* Electrochemistry and Industrial Physical Chemistry
0013-4686 Electrochimica Acta
0013-4694 Electroencephalography and Clinical Neurophysiology
0013-4708 Electrolysis Digest
0013-4716 Electromechanical Design†
0013-4740 Electron
0013-4759 Electron *see* 0315-1182
0013-4767 Electron
0013-4775 Electroanalytical Abstracts
0013-4783 Electronic Age†
0013-4791 Electronic & Appliance Specialist†
0013-4805 S. E. R. T. Journal *see* 0141-061X
0013-4813 Electronic Application News
0013-4821 Electronic Applications Bulletin *changed to* Electronic Components and Applications
0013-483X Electronics Today *see* 0047-9624
0013-4848 Electronic Capabilities†
0013-4864 Electronic Components *see* 0307-2401
0013-4872 Electronic Design
0013-4880 Electronic Distributing and Marketing *see* 0191-9075
0013-4899 Electronic Engineer *changed to* E E Systems Engineering Today
0013-4902 Electronic Engineering
0013-4910 Electronic Equipment News
0013-4929 Electronic Instrument Digest†
0013-4937 Electronic News
0013-4945 Electronic Packaging and Production
0013-4953 Electronic Products Magazine
0013-4961 Electronic Progress
0013-497X Electronic Servicing
0013-4988 Electronic Technician *see* 0363-5821
0013-4996 Electronics Trends(Washington) *changed to* Electronic Market Trends
0013-5011 Electronic Trends: International†
0013-502X Electronica
0013-5046 Elternblatt†
0013-5054 Electronica y Fisica Aplicada†
0013-5062 Electronicien
0013-5070 Electronics
0013-5097 Electronics Abstracts Journal *see* 0361-3313
0013-5100 Electronics and Communications
0013-5119 Electronics and Communications Abstracts
0013-5127 Electronics and Power
0013-5135 Electronics Australia
0013-5143 Electronics Digest†
0013-516X Electronics for You
0013-5178 Electronics Illustrated *see* 0025-6587
0013-5186 Electronics and Instrumentation
0013-5194 Electronics Letters
0013-5208 Electronics Record†
0013-5216 Electronics Today *changed to* Electronics Today International
0013-5224 Electronics Weekly
0013-5232 Electronics World†
0013-5259 Electronique Industrielle *see* 0398-1851
0013-5267 Electronique Medicale†
0013-5305 Electroplating and Metal Finishing *see* 0309-3018
0013-5313 Electrotecnia Popular
0013-5321 Electrotehnica *changed to* Electrotehnica, Electronica si Automatica. Electrotehnica
0013-5348 Eleftherotypia
0013-5364 Eleganza
0013-5372 Elektricheskie Stantsii
0013-5380 Elektrichestvo
0013-5399 Elektrie
0013-5402 Elektrik Muhendisligi
0013-5410 Elektrikeren
0013-5437 Elektrische Bahnen
0013-5445 E M A - Elektrische Maschinen
0013-5453 I T T Elektrisches Nachrichtenwesen
0013-5461 Elektrizitaet
0013-547X Elektrizitaet†
0013-547X Elektrizitaet *see* 0340-7519
0013-5488 Elektrizitaetsverwertung
0013-5496 Elektrizitaetswirtschaft
0013-550X Elektro
0013-5518 Elektro-Anzeiger
0013-5542 E H - Elektro Handel
0013-5550 Elektro Nachrichten
0013-5569 Der Elektro-Praktiker
0013-5577 Elektromarkt
0013-5585 Biomedizinische Technik
0013-5607 Elektron *changed to* Elektron-International
0013-5615 Elektronaut
0013-5623 Elektronica en Telecommunicatie
0013-5631 Elektronik
0013-564X Elektronik-Teknik & Marknad *changed to* Elektroniknyheterna
0013-5658 Elektronik
0013-5666 Elektronik-Anzeiger *see* 0720-101X
0013-5674 Elektronik Journal
0013-5690 Elektronikk
0013-5704 Angewandte Informatik
0013-5712 Elektronische Informationsverarbeitung und Kybernetik
0013-5720 Elektronische Rechenanlagen mit Computer-Praxis
0013-5739 Elektronnaya Obrabotka Materialov
0013-5747 Elektronorm (1947-1977) *see* 0011-4952
0013-5755 Elektroprivreda
0013-5763 Elektropromishlenost i Priborostroene
0013-5771 Elektrosvyaz'
0013-578X Elektrotechnicky Casopis
0013-5798 Elektrotechnicky Obzor
0013-581X Elektrotechnik
0013-5828 Elektrotehnicar
0013-5844 Elektrotehnika
0013-5852 Elektrotehniski Vestnik
0013-5860 Elektrotekhnika
0013-5879 Elektroteknikeren
0013-5887 Elektrowirtschaft
0013-5895 Elektuur
0013-5909 Elelmezesi Ipar
0013-5917 Elelmiszertudomany†
0013-5917 Elelmiszertudomany *see* 0302-7368
0013-5925 Element und Fertigbau
0013-5933 Elementa
0013-5941 Elementary Counselor *see* 0036-6536
0013-595X Elementary Electronics *see* 0279-585X
0013-5968 Elementary English *see* 0360-9170
0013-5976 Elementary School Guidance & Counseling
0013-5984 Elementary School Journal
0013-5992 Elementary Teacher's Ideas and Materials Workshop
0013-600X Elemente
0013-6018 Elemente der Mathematik
0013-6026 Elements, Produits, Services
0013-6042 Elenco dei Quotidiani e Periodici Italiani†
0013-6050 Elenco Ufficiale dei Protesti Cambiari Levati Nella Provincia di Torino
0013-6069 Elepaio
0013-6077 Elet es Tudomany
0013-6085 Eletronica Popular
0013-6093 Elettrificazione
0013-6115 Elettrodomus†
0013-6123 Elettronica e Telecomunicazioni
0013-6131 Elettrotecnica
0013-6158 Elevator World
0013-6166 Eleventh District Dental Society. Bulletin
0013-6182 Elim Evangel

ISSN	Title
0013-6190	Elinstallatoeren
0013-6204	Eliot Sharp's Tax Exempt Newsletter *changed to* Eliot Sharp's Municipal Newsletter
0013-6212	Elisabethbode
0013-6220	Elisha Mitchell Scientific Society. Journal
0013-6247	Elizabeth†
0013-6255	Elizabethan†
0013-6263	Elks Magazine
0013-6271	Elektrotechnika
0013-6298	Elle
0013-6301	Ellery Queen's Anthology
0013-631X	Ellery Queen's Mystery Magazine. Braille Edition†
0013-6328	Ellery Queen's Mystery Magazine
0013-6336	Ellinika
0013-6352	Eloquenza
0013-6360	Eloquenza Siciliana
0013-6379	Elovilag†
0013-6379	Elovilag *see* 0007-7356
0013-6395	Elseviers Magazine
0013-6409	Elsevier Select
0013-6417	Elta
0013-6425	Elteknik *changed to* Elteknik Med Aktuell Elektronik
0013-6433	Schweizer Zeitschrift fuer die Junge Familie *changed to* Wir Eltern
0013-6441	Elternblatt
0013-645X	Der Elternbrief
0013-6468	Eltheto
0013-6484	Elvis Monthly
0013-6506	Emajl-Keramika-Staklo
0013-6514	Emanon
0013-6522	Emantalehti
0013-6530	Embalagem
0013-6549	Emballage
0013-6557	Emballage Digest
0013-6565	Emballage Moderne *changed to* Cartonnages & Emballages Modernes
0013-6573	Emballages
0013-6581	Emballering
0013-6603	Embotellador
0013-662X	Ementario da Legislacao do Petroleo
0013-6638	Ementario Forense
0013-6646	Emergency Health Services Newsletter
0013-6654	Emergency Medicine
0013-6662	Emerita
0013-6670	E S Q
0013-6697	Emigrato Italiano
0013-6700	Emigrazione
0013-6719	Emmanuel
0013-6727	Emory Magazine
0013-6735	Empire City Pharmacist
0013-6743	Forum (Syracuse)
0013-676X	Empire State Geogram
0013-6786	Empire State Iris Society Newsletter
0013-6794	Empire State Mason
0013-6808	Employee Benefit Plan Review
0013-6816	Employee Relations Bulletin
0013-6824	Employee Relations in Action
0013-6832	Employers' Review
0013-6840	U.S. Bureau of Labor Statistics. Employment and Earnings
0013-6859	Great Britain. Department of Employment. Gazette
0013-6867	Australia. Bureau of Statistics. Employment and Unemployment *changed to* Australia. Bureau of Statistics. Civilian Employees
0013-6875	Employment Relations Abstracts *changed to* Work Related Abstracts
0013-6883	Employment Review
0013-6891	Empoli
0013-6905	Empress Chinchilla Breeder
0013-6913	Emuna†
0013-6921	En Avant
0013-6956	En Haa†
0013-6964	En Marche
0013-6972	En Viaje†
0013-6980	Enact
0013-6999	Enamelling Newsletter†
0013-7006	Encephale
0013-7057	Encore: a Quarterly of Verse & Poetic Arts
0013-7065	Encounter†
0013-7073	Encounter
0013-7081	Encounter(Indianapolis)
0013-709X	Encounter Today
0013-7103	Encres Vives
0013-7111	Encuentro†
0013-712X	Encyclopaedia Africana. Information Report
0013-7138	Encyclopaedia Moderna
0013-7146	Encyclopedie Politique Arabe. Documents et Notes
0013-7154	End-Use Markets for Plastics
0013-7170	Endeavour
0013-7200	Endocrinologia Experimentalis
0013-7219	Endocrinologia Japonica
0013-7227	Endocrinology
0013-7235	Endocrinology Index
0013-7243	Endocrinologya y Terapeutica†
0013-7251	Endokrinologie
0013-726X	Endoscopy
0013-7278	Energetik
0013-7286	Energetika
0013-7294	Energetyka
0013-7308	Energia Elettrica
0013-7316	Energia es Atomtechnika
0013-7324	Energia Nuclear
0013-7332	Energia Nucleare
0013-7340	Energie†
0013-7359	Energie
0013-7405	Energieanwendung
0013-7421	Energietechnik
0013-743X	Energiewirtschaftliche Tagesfragen
0013-7448	Energija
0013-7456	Energomashinostroenie
0013-7464	Energy *changed to* Energy Dialogue
0013-7472	Energy and Character
0013-7480	Energy Conversion *see* 0196-8904
0013-7510	Energy Info
0013-7529	Energy International†
0013-7537	Energy Management Report *issued with* 0031-6466
0013-7545	Enfance
0013-7553	Enfant
0013-7561	Enfant en Milieu Tropical
0013-757X	Enfants du Monde
0013-7596	Enfys
0013-7618	Engage *see* 0164-5528
0013-7626	Japanese Society for Horticultural Science. Journal
0013-7634	New Information on Horticulture *changed to* New Information on Horticulture: Flowers
0013-7642	Engelhard Industries Technical Bulletin†
0013-7669	Engenharia†
0013-7707	Engenharia (Revista) *changed to* Engenharia na Industria
0013-7707	Engenharia *changed to* Engenharia Civil
0013-7723	Engenheiro Moderno†
0013-774X	Engine Data Sheets
0013-7758	Engineer
0013-7766	Engineer of Southern California
0013-7774	Engineering
0013-7782	Engineering
0013-7790	Engineering and Construction World *see* 0043-8375
0013-7804	Engineering and Contract Record
0013-7812	Engineering and Science
0013-7820	Engineering and Science Review
0013-7839	Engineering Bulletin†
0013-7855	Engineering Capacity Register *see* 0306-0179
0013-7871	Engineering: Cornell Quarterly
0013-788X	Engineering Cybernetics
0013-7898	Engineering Designer†
0013-7901	Engineering Digest
0013-791X	Engineering Economist
0013-7928	Facts from Gatorland†
0013-7936	Engineering Forum
0013-7944	Engineering Fracture Mechanics
0013-7952	Engineering Geology
0013-7960	Engineering Index *see* 0162-3036
0013-7979	Engineering Index Card-A-Lert†
0013-7987	Engineering Industries & Trade Journal
0013-8010	Engineering Journal
0013-8029	Engineering Journal
0013-8037	Engineering Manpower Bulletin†
0013-8045	Engineering Materials and Design
0013-8053	Engineering Production†
0013-8061	Engineering News
0013-8061	Engineering News
0013-807X	Engineering News-Record
0013-8088	Engineering Outlook at the University of Illinois at Urbana-Champaign *changed to* Engineering Outlook
0013-810X	Engineering Research News
0013-8118	Engineering Societies of New England. Journal *changed to* New England Engineering Journal
0013-8126	Engineering Technician in the News *changed to* Certified Engineering Technician
0013-8134	Engineering Times
0013-8142	Engineers and Engines Magazine
0013-8150	Engineers' Club of St. Louis. Journal
0013-8169	Engineers' Digest
0013-8177	Coast Guard Engineer's Digest
0013-8185	Englisch
0013-8193	Englische an Volkshochschulen *see* 0342-6173
0013-8215	English
0013-8223	English Churchman
0013-8231	English Dance and Song
0013-824X	English for Immigrants†
0013-8266	English Historical Review†
0013-8266	English Historical Review
0013-8274	English Journal
0013-8282	English Language Notes
0013-8290	English Language Teaching *see* 0307-8337
0013-8304	E L H
0013-8312	English Literary Renaissance
0013-8339	English Literature in Transition (1880-1920)
0013-8355	English Quarterly
0013-8363	English Record
0013-8371	English-Speaking Union News
0013-838X	English Studies
0013-8398	English Studies in Africa
0013-8401	English Westerners' Brand Book
0013-841X	English Westerners' Tally Sheet
0013-8436	Enigma
0013-8444	Engineers
0013-8452	Enjoy Houston
0013-8460	Vinyls and Polymers
0013-8487	Enlite†
0013-8495	Enoch Pratt Free Library. Staff Reporter
0013-8509	Enquiry
0013-8517	Enquiry
0013-8533	Ensanian Physicochemical Institute. Journal
0013-8541	Enjay Magazine *changed to* Exxon Chemicals Magazine
0013-855X	Ensayo
0013-8576	Techniques Industrielles
0013-8584	Enseignement Mathematique
0013-8592	Ensemble
0013-8606	Ensign
0013-8614	Ensino Secundario
0013-8622	Ente Provinciale per Il Turismo di Nuoro. Notiziario
0013-8630	Entente Africaine
0013-8657	Enterprise
0013-8665	Enterprise†
0013-8673	Enterprise
0013-8711	Entomologica Scandinavica
0013-872X	Entomological News
0013-8738	Entomological Review
0013-8746	Entomological Society of America. Annals
0013-8754	Entomological Society of America. Bulletin
0013-8762	Entomological Society of India. Bulletin of Entomology
0013-8770	Entomology *changed to* Insect
0013-8789	Entomological Society of Southern Africa. Journal
0013-8797	Entomological Society of Washington. Proceedings
0013-8800	Entomologie et Phytopathologie Appliquees
0013-8819	Entomologische Arbeiten aus dem Museum G. Frey, Tutzing-Bei Muenchen
0013-8827	Entomologische Berichten
0013-8835	Entomologische Blaetter fuer Biologie und Systematik der Kaefer
0013-8843	Entomologische Zeitschrift
0013-8851	Entomologiske Meddelelser
0013-886X	Entomologisk Tidskrift
0013-8886	Entomologiste
0013-8894	Entomologist's Gazette
0013-8908	Entomologist's Monthly Magazine
0013-8916	Entomologist's Record
0013-8924	Entomology Abstracts
0013-8932	Entomology Circular
0013-8940	South Africa. Department of Agricultural Technical Services. Entomology Memoirs
0013-8959	Entomophaga
0013-8967	Entomops
0013-8975	Entr'Acte
0013-8991	Entre/Nous *changed to* Hydro-Presse
0013-9009	Entre Nous Houston
0013-9017	Entrelineas
0013-9033	Entrepreneur en Plomberie-Chauffage *see* 0032-1591
0013-9041	Entrepreneur Menuisier
0013-905X	Entreprise
0013-9084	Entropie
0013-9092	Entscheidung
0013-9114	Entwicklung und Zusammenarbeit
0013-9130	Environnement
0013-9149	Environment†
0013-9157	Environment
0013-9165	Environment and Behavior
0013-9173	Environment & Planning *see* 0308-518X
0013-9181	Environment Information Access *see* 0093-3287
0013-919X	Environment Monthly†
0013-9203	Environment Report
0013-9211	Environment Reporter
0013-922X	Environmental Action
0013-9238	Environmental Control News for Southern Industry
0013-9254	Environmental Education *see* 0095-8964
0013-9262	Environmental Engineering *see* 0374-356X
0013-9270	Environmental Health
0013-9289	Environmental Health *changed to* Indian Journal of Environmental Health
0013-9319	Environmental Mutagen Society Newsletter *see* 0027-5107
0013-9327	Environmental Pollution *see* 0143-1471
0013-9327	Environmental Pollution *see* 0143-148X
0013-9343	Environmental Quarterly†
0013-9351	Environmental Research
0013-936X	Environmental Science & Technology
0013-9386	Environmental Spectrum
0013-9394	Envoi
0013-9408	Envoy
0013-9416	Enzymes in Medicine
0013-9424	Enzymologia *see* 0300-8177
0013-9432	Enzyme
0013-9440	EOS
0013-9475	Epatologia
0013-9491	Ephemerides Iuris Canonici
0013-9505	Ephemerides Liturgicae
0013-9513	Ephemerides Theologicae Lovanienses
0013-9521	Epicier
0013-953X	Epicure†
0013-9548	Epicurean
0013-9556	Epidemiological Review†
0013-9564	Epigraphia Indica
0013-9572	Epigraphica
0013-9580	Epilepsia
0013-9599	Excerpta Medica. Section 50: Epilepsy
0013-9610	Episcopal Recorder
0013-9629	Episcopalian
0013-9645	Epistemologie Sociologique†
0013-9653	Epistolodidaktika
0013-9661	Epites es Epitesuzettudomany
0013-967X	Epitesugyi Szemle

ISSN	Title
0013-9688	Genike Stratiotike Epitheoresis†
0013-9696	Greek Review of Social Research
0013-970X	Epitoanyag
0013-9718	Epoca
0013-9726	Epoca
0013-9734	Epos, a Quarterly of Poetry†
0013-9742	Epuletgepeszet
0013-9750	Equal Justice†
0013-9777	Equal Opportunity in Federal Government *changed to* Spotlight on Affirmative Employment Programs
0013-9815	Equals One
0013-9823	Equestrian Journal
0013-9831	Equestrian Trails
0013-984X	Equinews
0013-9874	Equipment Industriel†
0013-9882	Equipment Mechanique des Chantiers *changed to* Equipement Mecanique, Carrieres et Materiaux
0013-9890	Equity News
0013-9912	Er Ruft
0013-9920	Era
0013-9939	E R A
0013-9947	Eranos
0013-9963	Erbe und Auftrag
0013-998X	Erdbau
0013-9998	Die Erde
0014-0007	Erdkreis
0014-0015	Erdkunde
0014-0023	Der Erdkundeunterricht
0014-0031	Az Erdo
0014-004X	Erdoel-Erdgas Zeitschrift
0014-0058	Erdoel und Kohle, Erdgas, Petrochemie
0014-0066	Erdogazdasag es Faipar
0014-0082	Erfahrungsheilkunde
0014-0090	Erfahrungswissenschaftliche Blaetter (EWB)
0014-0104	Erfolgs- und Erwerbspost
0014-0112	Ergokratische Schule fuer Dauernden. Frieden (Publication) *changed to* Die Ergokratische Schule
0014-0120	Ergonomia
0014-0139	Ergonomics
0014-0147	Erhversoekonomisk Tidsskrift
0014-0155	Erhvervs-Bladet
0014-0163	Eric/Crier Newsletter†
0014-0171	Ericsson Review
0014-018X	Ericsson Technics†
0014-0198	Erkenntnistheorie, Philosophische Probleme der Methodologie und Logik *changed to* Referateblatt Philosophie. Reihe D. Erkenntnistheorie, Wissenschaftstheorie, Methodologie, Logik
0014-0201	Ermlandbriefe
0014-021X	Ernaehrungs-Umschau
0014-0228	Ernaehrungsdienst
0014-0236	Die Ernaehrungsindustrie
0014-0244	Ernaehrungswirtschaft
0014-0252	Eroeffnungen
0014-0260	ERREu
0014-0279	Die Ersatzkasse
0014-0309	Erwerbsobstbau
0014-0317	Dynamic
0014-0325	Erziehung und Unterricht
0014-0333	Erziehungskunst
0014-0341	Escalpelo
0014-0368	Escort†
0014-0376	Escribano
0014-0384	Escrow Newsletter†
0014-0392	Escudo
0014-0422	Universidad de Panama. Escuela de Bibliotecologia. Boletin
0014-0430	Argentina. Escuela Superior de Guerra. Revista *changed to* Argentina. Escuela de Defensa Nacional. Revista
0014-0449	Escursionismo
0014-0457	Escutcheon†
0014-049X	Espana Agraria *changed to* Espana Agricola
0014-0511	Espana Libre
0014-0546	Espanol en Australia
0014-0554	Espansione
0014-0562	Esparavel
0014-0570	Espectaculos†
0014-0589	Espectator
0014-0597	Espejo†
0014-0600	Esperanta Ligilo
0014-0619	Der Esperantist
0014-0635	Esperanto
0014-0643	Esperanto en Skotlando
0014-0651	Esperanto-Gazeto†
0014-066X	Esperanto-Lingvo Internacia
0014-0678	Esperienza
0014-0686	Esperienze Amministrative
0014-0694	Espero
0014-0708	Espiral†
0014-0716	Espiritu
0014-0724	Espoir
0014-0732	Espoir du Monde
0014-0740	Esportazione
0014-0759	Esprit
0014-0767	Esprit Createur
0014-0775	Esprit et Vie
0014-0783	Esprit Libre
0014-0791	Esquire *see* 0194-9535
0014-0805	Esquire's Good Grooming Guide†
0014-0813	Esquiu
0014-0821	N O A A
0014-083X	Essay and General Literature Index
0014-0848	Essay Proof Journal
0014-0856	Essays in Criticism
0014-0864	Essays in Economics
0014-0880	Essence
0014-0902	Essenze-Derivati Agrumari
0014-0910	Essex Countryside
0014-0937	Essex County Medical Society. Bulletin
0014-0945	Essex Farmers Journal
0014-0953	Essex Institute. Historical Collections
0014-097X	Esso Agricola
0014-0988	Esso Air World *changed to* Exxon Air World
0014-0996	Esso Aviation News Digest *changed to* Exxon Aviation News Digest
0014-1003	Esso Dealer
0014-1011	Esso Magazine
0014-102X	Esso News *changed to* Esso in Malaysia
0014-1038	Esso Rivista
0014-1046	Essobron
0014-1054	Essofoon
0014-1062	Essor du Comminges
0014-1089	Est
0014-1100	Est Sesia
0014-1127	Estacion Experimental. Dr. Mario Cassinoni. Facultad de Agronomia. Boletin Tecnico†
0014-1135	Estadistica
0014-1151	Spain. Instituto Nacional de Estadistica. Estadistica Espanola
0014-1178	Estado das Culturas e Previsao de Colheitas
0014-1186	Estafeta Literaria *changed to* Nueva Estafeta
0014-1194	Estano
0014-1208	Estanzuela - Investigacion Agricola†
0014-1216	Estate Planning
0014-1224	Estate Planning Checklists and Forms
0014-1240	Estates Gazette
0014-1259	Estates Times
0014-1267	Est et Ouest
0014-1275	Estetica Ambrosiana
0014-1283	Esteticka Vychova
0014-1291	Estetika
0014-1313	Estetyka†
0014-1321	Estheticienne
0014-133X	Estilo *see* 0325-0229
0014-1356	Estomatologia
0014-1364	Estomatologia e Cultura
0014-1372	Estonian Events *changed to* Baltic Events
0014-1380	Extra Twenty-Two Hundred South
0014-1399	Estrella
0014-1410	Estudios Americanos
0014-1429	Estudios Andinos
0014-1437	Estudios Biblicos
0014-1445	Estudios Centro Americanos
0014-1453	Estudios Clasicos
0014-1461	Estudios de Derecho
0014-147X	Estudios de Historia Moderna y Contemporanea de Mexico
0014-1496	Estudios Geograficos
0014-150X	Estudios Historicos Sobre San Sebastian. Boletin
0014-1518	Estudios Internacionales†
0014-1534	Estudios de Asia y Africa
0014-1542	Estudios Sindicales y Cooperativos†
0014-1550	Estudios Sobre el Communismo
0014-1577	Estudios Sobre la Union Sovietica†
0014-1585	Estudos Agronomicos
0014-1593	Estudos de Psicanalise
0014-1607	Estudos Leopoldenses
0014-1623	Estudos Politicos e Sociais
0014-1631	L'Etain et ses Usages
0014-164X	ETC
0014-1658	Eter-Aktuellt
0014-1666	Eterna Sabiduria - Spanish Braille for Theosophists†
0014-1682	Eternity
0014-1682	Evangelical Newsletter
0014-1690	Ethical Record
0014-1704	Ethics
0014-1712	Ethiopia in the World Press†
0014-1720	Ethiopia Observer†
0014-1739	Ethiopian Geographical Journal†
0014-1747	Ethiopian Library Association. Bulletin
0014-1755	Ethiopian Medical Journal
0014-178X	Ethnie Francaise
0014-1798	Ethnographia
0014-1801	Ethnohistory
0014-181X	Ethnologische Zeitschrift
0014-1828	Ethnology
0014-1836	Ethnomusicology
0014-1844	Ethnos
0014-1895	Etoile de la Foire
0014-1909	Etruscan
0014-1917	Etude Comparative Benelux sur les Salaires†
0014-1933	Economie et les Finances des Pays Arabes *see* 0013-0664
0014-1941	Etudes
0014-195X	Etudes Anglaises
0014-1968	Etudes Ardennaises *see* 0035-3272
0014-1976	Etudes Balkaniques
0014-1992	Etudes Cinematographiques
0014-200X	Etudes Classiques
0014-2018	Etudes Dahomeennes
0014-2026	Etudes de Lettres
0014-2034	Etudes Economiques†
0014-2042	Banque Francaise et Italienne. Etudes Economiques
0014-2069	Banque des Etats de l'Afrique Centrale. Etudes et Statistiques
0014-2077	Etudes Evangeliques†
0014-2085	Etudes Francaises
0014-2093	Etudes Franciscaines†
0014-2107	Etudes Freudiennes
0014-2115	Etudes Germaniques
0014-2123	Etudes Internationales
0014-2131	Etudes Internationales de Psycho-Sociologie Criminelle
0014-214X	Etudes Litteraires
0014-2158	Etudes Normandes
0014-2166	Etudes Philosophiques
0014-2182	Etudes Rurales
0014-2190	Etudes Slaves et Est-Europeennes *changed to* Cahiers Culturels
0014-2204	Etudes Sociales
0014-2212	Etudes Sociales et Syndicales
0014-2239	Etudes Theologiques et Religieuses
0014-2247	Etudes Tsiganes
0014-2255	World Student News
0014-2263	Etyka
0014-2271	Eucharist
0014-2298	Euhemer
0014-2301	E U M I G - Lupe
0014-2328	Euphorion
0014-2336	Euphytica
0014-2352	Euro Abstracts *changed to* Euro Abstracts Section I. Euratom and EEC Research
0014-2387	Euro Piano
0014-2409	EUROCOM Press Information†
0014-2425	Euromed
0014-2433	Euromoney
0014-2441	Euromonitor Review *see* 0308-3446
0014-2476	Europa-Archiv
0014-2484	Europa Chemie
0014-2492	Europa Ethnica
0014-2514	Europa Industrie Revue. Maschinenmarkt und Elektrotechnik *see* 0341-5783
0014-2522	Europa-Korrespondenz
0014-2530	Europa Libera
0014-2549	Europa Medica†
0014-2557	Europa Medica
0014-2565	Revista Clinica Espanola
0014-2573	Europa Medicophysica
0014-2581	Europa Nazione
0014-259X	Eurosport *see* 0340-739X
0014-2603	Europa Star
0014-2611	Europa-Union *changed to* Europaeische Zeitung Europa-Union
0014-262X	Europa-Verkehr†
0014-2638	Europaeer Diskutieren†
0014-2662	Europaeische Integration
0014-2670	Europaeische Mode nach Mass
0014-2697	Europaeische Technische Informationen *changed to* Lagern und Fordern
0014-2700	Europaeisches Immobilien Journal†
0014-2727	Europastimme
0014-2735	Welthandels Informationen/Europa Technik *changed to* World Trade Information
0014-2751	Europe
0014-276X	Europe & Oil†
0014-2794	Europe-Echecs
0014-2816	Europe France Outremer *changed to* Europe Outre-Mer
0014-2824	Europe Oil-Telegram
0014-2832	Europe Orientale†
0014-2840	Witchcraft *see* 0085-8250
0014-2859	European Board Markets†
0014-2867	European Business Review†
0014-2875	European Chemical News
0014-2883	European Civil Engineering
0014-2891	European Community
0014-2905	European Documentation - a Survey
0014-2921	European Economic Review
0014-293X	European Federation for the Protection of Waters. Information Bulletin†
0014-2948	European Grocery Letter
0014-2956	European Journal of Biochemistry
0014-2964	European Journal of Cancer
0014-2972	European Journal of Clinical Investigation
0014-2980	European Journal of Immunology
0014-2999	European Journal of Pharmacology
0014-3006	European Judaism
0014-3014	European Marketing Research Review *changed to* European Research
0014-3022	European Neurology
0014-3030	European Numismatics
0014-3057	European Polymer Journal
0014-3065	Potato Research
0014-3073	European Railways
0014-3081	European Review†
0014-309X	European Shipbuilding†
0014-309X	European Shipbuilding†
0014-3103	European Studies *changed to* Exploring Europe
0014-3111	European Studies Review
0014-312X	European Surgical Research
0014-3138	European Taxation
0014-3146	European Teacher
0014-3154	European Transport Law
0014-3162	European Trends
0014-3170	European University News
0014-3189	Europeo
0014-3197	Europese Documentatie†
0014-3219	Europublica Combinations Flugplan
0014-3235	Eurosud
0014-3243	Eurotec
0014-3251	Eurotransports Illustrato *changed to* Eurotransports Illustrato-Container in Italia e nel Mondo
0014-326X	Evangelische-Lutherische Kirche in Thueringen. Amtsblatt
0014-3278	Eva
0014-3286	Eva
0014-3294	Eva†
0014-3308	Eva Express

ISSN INDEX

ISSN	Title
0014-3316	Evaluation Engineering
0014-3324	Evangelical Baptist
0014-3332	Evangelical Beacon
0014-3340	Evangelical Friend
0014-3359	Evangelical Missions Quarterly
0014-3367	Evangelical Quarterly
0014-3375	Evangelical Truth
0014-3383	Evangelie en Maatschappij
0014-3391	Evangelisch-Lutherische Kirche in Bayern. Ausgabe Oberfranken. Sonntagsblatt
0014-3405	Evangelisch-Soziale Warte *changed to* S V A-Zeitung
0014-3413	Der Evangelische Erzieher
0014-3421	Evangelische Kinderpflege fuer Kindergarten, Hort, Heim und Familie *see* 0342-7145
0014-343X	Evangelische Kirche in Deutschland. Amtsblatt
0014-3472	Evangelische Missionszeitschrift *changed to* Zeitschrift fuer Mission
0014-3480	Der Evangelische Religionslehrer an Beruflichen Schulen
0014-3502	Evangelische Theologie
0014-3529	Evangelische Landeskirche in Wuerttemberg. Amtsblatt
0014-3553	Evangelischer Nachrichtendienst in der DDR
0014-3561	Evangelisches Gemeindeblatt Berlin†
0014-3588	Evangelisches Gemeindeblatt fuer Muencher *changed to* Muenchner Gemeindeblatt
0014-360X	Evangelisches Gemeindeblatt fuer Wuerttemberg
0014-3618	Evangelisches Schulblatt†
0014-3626	Evangelist
0014-3642	Evanjelicky Hlasnik
0014-3650	Evans-Novak Political Report
0014-3669	Evansville Public Library and Vanderburgh County Public Library. Staff News Bulletin *changed to* Evansville-Vanderburgh County Public Library. Staff News Bulletin
0014-3677	Evansville-Vanderburgh School Corporation. Public Schools Bulletin†
0014-3685	Eve†
0014-3693	Evelyn Waugh Newsletter
0014-3731	Event *changed to* Metropinion
0014-374X	Event
0014-3804	Everywoman's Daily Horoscope *changed to* Popular Astrology
0014-3812	Eve's Weekly
0014-3820	Evolution
0014-3839	Panelectronics
0014-3847	Evolution Medicale
0014-3855	Evolution Psychiatrique
0014-3863	Evoluzione Agricola
0014-3871	EWG-Warenhandel
0014-388X	Ex-C B I Roundup
0014-3901	Ex Libris†
0014-3928	Ex Ore Infantium
0014-3936	Ex-Serviceman
0014-3944	Ex-Umbra
0014-3952	Exakte Aesthetk†
0014-3960	Examen de la Situacion Economica de Mexico
0014-3979	Examiner
0014-4010	Exceptional Child Education Abstracts *see* 0160-4309
0014-4029	Exceptional Children
0014-4037	Excerpta Botanica. Sectio A: Taxonomica et Chorologica
0014-4045	Excerpta Botanica. Section B: Sociologica
0014-4053	Excerpta Medica. Section 1: Anatomy, Anthropology, Embryology & Histology
0014-4061	Excerpta Medica. Section 2: Physiology
0014-407X	Excerpta Medica. Section 3: Endocrinology
0014-4088	Excerpta Medica. Section 4: Microbiology-Bacteriology, Virology, Mycology and Parasitology *changed to* Excerpta Medica. Section 4: Microbiology-Bacteriology, Mycology and Parasitology
0014-4096	Excerpta Medica. Section 5: General Pathology and Pathological Anatomy
0014-410X	Excerpta Medica. Section 6: Internal Medicine
0014-4118	Excerpta Medica. Section 7: Pediatrics *changed to* Excerpta Medica. Section 7: Pediatrics and Pediatric Surgery
0014-4126	Excerpta Medica. Section 8: Neurology and Neurosurgery
0014-4134	Excerpta Medica. Section 9: Surgery
0014-4142	Excerpta Medica. Section 10: Obstetrics and Gynecology
0014-4150	Excerpta Medica. Section 11: Otorhinolaryngology
0014-4169	Excerpta Medica. Section 12: Ophthalmology
0014-4177	Excerpta Medica. Section 13: Dermatology and Venereology
0014-4185	Excerpta Medica. Section 14: Radiology
0014-4193	Excerpta Medica. Section 15: Chest Diseases, Thoracic Surgery and Tuberculosis
0014-4207	Excerpta Medica. Section 16: Cancer
0014-4215	Excerpta Medica. Section 17: Public Health, Social Medicine & Hygiene
0014-4223	Excerpta Medica. Section 18: Cardiovascular Diseases and Cardiovascular Surgery
0014-4231	Excerpta Medica. Section 19: Rehabilitation and Physical Medicine
0014-424X	Excerpta Medica. Section 20: Gerontology and Geriatrics
0014-4258	Excerpta Medica. Section 21: Developmental Biology and Teratology
0014-4266	Excerpta Medica. Section 22: Human Genetics
0014-4274	Excerpta Medica. Section 23: Nuclear Medicine
0014-4282	Excerpta Medica. Section 24: Anesthesiology
0014-4290	Excerpta Medica. Section 25: Hematology
0014-4304	Excerpta Medica. Section 26: Immunology, Serology and Transplantation
0014-4312	Excerpta Medica. Section 27: Biophysics, Bio-Engineering and Medical Instrumentation
0014-4320	Excerpta Medica. Section 28: Urology and Nephrology
0014-4339	Excerpta Medica. Section 29: Biochemistry *see* 0300-5372
0014-4355	Excerpta Medica. Section 31: Arthritis and Rheumatism
0014-4363	Excerpta Medica. Section 32: Psychiatry
0014-4371	Excerpta Medica. Section 33: Orthopedic Surgery
0014-438X	Excerpta Medica. Section 34: Plastic Surgery
0014-4398	Excerpta Medica. Section 35: Occupational Health and Industrial Medicine
0014-4436	Exchange†
0014-4444	Exchange
0014-4460	Exchange and Mart
0014-4487	Exchangite
0014-4509	Executive
0014-4525	Executive Fitness Newsletter
0014-4533	Executive Grocer†
0014-455X	Executive Housekeeper
0014-4568	Executive Life†
0014-4576	Executive Mens Arts Series *changed to* Executive Mens Advertising Service
0014-4584	Executive Reading
0014-4592	Executives Wealth Report†
0014-4622	Exeter University Gazette
0014-4665	Exhibition Bulletin
0014-4673	Exil et Liberte†
0014-4681	Existential Psychiatry†
0014-469X	Exlibris-Nyt
	Expanded Shale Concrete Facts *changed to* Expanded Shale Lightweight Concrete Facts
0014-4703	Expansion
0014-4711	Cahiers de l'Expansion Regionale *see* 0240-9925
0014-472X	Expecting
0014-4738	Expedition
0014-4754	Experientia
0014-4762	Experientiae
0014-4770	Experiment
0014-4797	Experimental Agriculture
0014-4800	Experimental & Molecular Pathology
0014-4819	Experimental Brain Research
0014-4827	Experimental Cell Research
0014-4835	Experimental Eye Research
0014-4851	Experimental Mechanics
0014-486X	Experimental Medicine and Microbiology†
0014-4878	Experimental Medicine and Surgery†
0014-4886	Experimental Neurology
0014-4894	Experimental Parasitology
0014-4908	Experimentelle Pathologie
0014-4916	Experimentation Animale†
0014-4924	Experimentelle Technik der Physik
0014-4932	Experiodica
0014-4940	Explicator
0014-4959	Exploration†
0014-4967	Explorations *see* 0360-6511
0014-4975	Explorations
0014-4983	Explorations in Economic History
0014-4991	Explore†
0014-5009	Explorer
0014-5017	Explorer
0014-5025	Explorers Journal
0014-5033	Exploring
0014-5041	Explosion Hunger-1975
0014-505X	Explosives & Pyrotechnics
0014-5068	Explosivstoffe
0014-5076	Exponent
0014-5084	Export
0014-5092	Export
0014-5106	Export Anzeiger†
0014-5114	Export-Berater
0014-5122	Export Courier
0014-5149	Export-Import News
0014-5165	Export Management†
0014-5173	Export Polygraph International
0014-5181	Export Shipping Manual
0014-519X	Export
0014-5203	Revista Mensal de Exportacao
0014-5211	Exportmarkten
0014-522X	Expositor Bautista
0014-5238	Expositor Biblico
0014-5246	Expository Times
0014-5254	Expovisie
0014-5262	Express†
0014-5270	Express
0014-5289	Express Documents
0014-5297	International Business Intelligence
0014-5327	Expression
0014-5343	Expression
0014-5351	Expression†
0014-536X	Expression One
0014-5378	Extebank Monthly Economic Report
0014-5386	Extemporale
0014-5394	Extensao em Minas Gerais
0014-5408	Extension Service Review *see* 0162-9875
0014-5416	Extensions†
0014-5424	Extensions and Corrections to the U D C
0014-5432	External Affairs *see* 0381-4874
0014-5440	New Zealand Foreign Affairs Review
0014-5459	External Studies Gazette
0014-5467	Stamp Digest
0014-5475	American Digest of Foreign Orthopaedic Literature†
0014-5483	EXtrapolation
0014-5491	Eye, Ear, Nose & Throat Monthly *see* 0145-5613
0014-5513	Eyeopener
0014-553X	F A A Aviation News *see* 0362-7942
0014-5548	F. A. B. I. Revue d'Information
0014-5556	F A C T A Newsletter
0014-5564	F. A. I. Abstract Service
0014-5580	F A O Documentation-Current Index *changed to* F A O Documentation-Current Bibliography
0014-5599	F A O Aquaculture Bulletin†
0014-5610	F A O Forestry and Forest Industries Bulletin for Latin America†
0014-5629	F A O Information *changed to* World Agriculture, Forestry and Fisheries
0014-5637	F A O Plant Protection Bulletin
0014-5645	FAPIG
0014-5661	F & S Index International
0014-567X	F & S Index of Corporations and Industries *changed to* Predicasts F & S Index United Startes
0014-5688	F B I Law Enforcement Bulletin
0014-570X	F C H News Briefs
0014-5718	F C I B Bulletin *changed to* F C I B International Bulletin
0014-5734	F C N L Washington Newsletter
0014-5742	F C X Patron†
0014-5750	F D A Papers *see* 0362-1332
0014-5769	F D G B-Rundschau
0014-5777	F. D. I. Newsletter
0014-5785	F E & Z N.
0014-5793	F E B S Letters
0014-5807	F E N
0014-5815	F F Communications
0014-5831	F F H Mitteilungen
0014-584X	Incorporates; F H D-Zeitung *changed to* Schweizer Soldat
0014-5866	Informaciones F I D/C L A
0014-5874	F I D News Bulletin
0014-5890	F I G A News
0014-5904	F I R A Bulletin
0014-5912	F. I. R. O. Quaderni
0014-5920	F L A C S
0014-5939	F L C Newsletter
0014-5955	F M G-Fachblatt
0014-5963	F M *changed to* Vox; Hebdomadaire Militaire
0014-5998	F. N. Orienterung
0014-6013	F O A Orienterar Om
0014-603X	F. O. I. Center Report
0014-6048	F. O. Licht's Europaeisches Zuckerjournal *changed to* F. O. Licht's International Sugar Report
0014-6056	F. O. Lichts's International Molasses Report
0014-6072	F. P. A. Journal *see* 0309-6866
0014-6080	F P C News (U.S. Federal Power Commission) *changed to* F E R C News
0014-6102	F R C C *changed to* F R C C Newsletter
0014-6110	F R E N *changed to* Florida Rural Electric News
0014-6137	F R I Monthly Portfolio
0014-6145	Der Sportjournalist
0014-6153	F u Pressedienst Wissenschaft†
0014-6161	F V I†
0014-6196	Fabian News
0014-620X	Fabric Forecast
0014-6226	Fabrieksorganisatie†
0014-6234	Fabriksarbetaren
0014-6242	Fabula
0014-6269	Face au Risque
0014-6277	Face-To-Face
0014-6285	Facettes
0014-6293	Fachberater
0014-6315	Fachberater fuer das Deutsche Kleingartenwesen
0014-634X	Fachblatt der Bundesinnung der Metallgiesser, Guertler, Graveure, Metalldrucker†
0014-6366	F F S B *changed to* Handels-Magazin F S B und Fachblatt fuer Selbstbedienung
0014-6374	Fachhefte fuer Chemigraphie, Lithographie und Tiefdruck
0014-6382	Fachpresse
0014-6404	Fachschule
0014-6412	Fachzeitschrift Papier, Buerobedarf, Schreibwaren *changed to* Fachzeitung fuer den Buerofachhandel ueber Papier, Buerobedarf, Schreibwaren
0014-6420	Facilities for Atmospheric Research *see* 0091-2026
0014-6447	Die Fackel
0014-6455	Fackfoereningsroerelsen *see* 0346-895X

ISSN	Title
0014-6463	Facklaeraren
0014-6471	Fackliga Vaerldsrorelsen
0014-648X	Universita degli Studi di Perugia. Facolta di Medicina e Chirurgia. Annali
0014-6501	F B; A Fact Book on Higher Education *changed to* Fact Book for Academic Administrators
0014-651X	Fact Finder
0014-6536	De Facto *changed to* Uni-Press Purchasing
0014-6544	Purchasing
0014-6552	Factory Equipment & Materials for Southern Africa
0014-6579	Factory Equipment News
0014-6595	Factory Mutual Record
0014-6609	Facts
0014-6617	Facts and Comparisons
0014-6633	Facts on Dental Health & Smoking†
0014-6641	Facts on File
0014-665X	Lisbon. Universidade. Faculdade de Ciencias. Revista. Serie 2. Seccao A. Ciencias Matematicas†
0014-6676	Revista de Farmacia e Bioquimica
0014-6684	Faculdade de Farmacia e Odontologia de Araraquara. Revista *changed to* Faculdade de Ciencias Farmaceuticas de Araraquara. Revista
0014-6714	Universidad de la Republica. Facultad de Arquitectura. Revista
0014-6722	Universidad Nacional de Cordoba. Facultad de Ciencias Medicas. Revista
0014-6730	Universidad de Zaragoza. Facultad de Medicina. Archivos
0014-6749	Universite de Toulouse II (le Mirail). Annales
0014-6781	Saint Augustine's College. Faculty Research Journal
0014-679X	Faenza
0014-6803	Fahr mit Uns
0014-6811	Fahr Betriebsleben
0014-682X	Fahrlehrer†
0014-6838	Fahrschule
0014-6846	Fahrt Frei
0014-6854	Der Fahrzeug- und Metall-Lackierer
0014-6862	Fahrzeug und Karosserie
0014-6870	Fahrzeughandel
0014-6889	Faims et Soifs des Hommes
0014-6897	Faipar
0014-6900	Fair
0014-6919	Fair Employment Report
0014-6927	Fair Lady
0014-6943	Fairchild Tropical Garden Bulletin
0014-6951	Faire Face
0014-696X	Fairfield County Economy
0014-6978	Fairfield County Press
0014-6986	Fairplay Shipping Journal *see* 0307-0220
0014-6994	Fait Public†
0014-7001	Faith and Form
0014-701X	Faith and Freedom
0014-7028	Faith and Thought
0014-7036	Faith and Unity†
0014-7044	Faith for Daily Living
0014-7052	Facts and Tendencies
0014-7079	Falcon†
0014-7095	Famiglia Cristiana
0014-7109	Familia†
0014-7117	Familia
0014-7125	Familia Crista
0014-7133	Familie Journalen
0014-7141	Familien
0014-715X	Familienblatt
0014-7168	Familienfreund†
0014-7176	Familienverband Avenarius. Familienzeitschrift
0014-7184	Famille Nouvelle
0014-7192	Family and School
0014-7206	Family Circle
0014-7214	Family Coordinator *changed to* Family Relations
0014-7230	Family Handyman
0014-7249	Family Health
0014-7257	Family Health Bulletin
0014-7265	Family History
0014-7273	Family Houseboating *see* 0093-6782
0014-7281	Family Law
0014-729X	Family Law Quarterly
0014-7303	Family Life
0014-7311	Family Perspective
0014-732X	Family Physician
0014-7338	Family Planning *see* 0309-1112
0014-7346	Family Planning News *changed to* Pathways in Population Planning
0014-7354	Family Planning Perspectives
0014-7362	Family Planning Quarterly†
0014-7370	Family Process
0014-7389	Family Puzzlers
0014-7397	Family Safety
0014-7427	Family Weekly
0014-7435	Famous Artists Magazine†
0014-7443	Famous Monsters of Filmland
0014-7451	Famous Photographers†
0014-7478	Fanfare†
0014-7486	Fangst og Fiske *changed to* Maritime News
0014-7494	Fant†
0014-7501	Fante di Quadri
0014-7532	Far East *see* 0048-251X
0014-7540	Far East Architect and Builder *changed to* Asian Building & Construction
0014-7559	Far East Engineer†
0014-7567	Far East Medical Journal *see* 0301-0376
0014-7575	Far East Reporter
0014-7583	Far East Trade and Development†
0014-7591	Far Eastern Economic Review
0014-7605	Far Eastern University Journal
0014-7613	F A R Horizons Newletter†
0014-763X	Far West Magazine
0014-7648	Far West News *changed to* Far West Ski News
0014-7656	Faraday
0014-7664	Faraday Society. Discussions *see* 0301-7249
0014-7672	Faraday Society. Transactions *see* 0300-9599
0014-7672	Faraday Society. Transactions *see* 0300-9238
0014-7680	Die Farbe
0014-7699	Farbe und Lack
0014-7702	Farbe und Raum
0014-7710	Farben-Chemiker†
0014-7710	Farben-Chemiker *see* 0015-038X
0014-7737	Farbenkreis, Oesterreichischen Malerzeitung
0014-7745	Fare Box
0014-777X	Jern og Farge *changed to* Jernvare Bygg Hobby
0014-7788	Farhang-e Iran Zamin
0014-7796	Farm
0014-7818	Big Farm Management
0014-7826	Farm and Dairy
0014-7834	Farm & Power Equipment
0014-7842	Farm and Ranch Bulletin
0014-7850	Farm Building Express
0014-7869	Farm Building News
0014-7877	Farm Buildings Digest
0014-7885	Farm Chemicals and Croplife *see* 0092-0053
0014-7893	Farm City Week Newsletter
0014-7907	Farm Credit Banks of Baltimore. News & Views†
0014-7923	Farm Economics
0014-7931	Farm Economist *changed to* Oxford Agrarian Studies
0014-7958	Farm Equipment
0014-7974	U.S. Department of Agriculture. Economic Research Service. Farm Income Situation *see* 0099-1066
0014-7982	Farm Index†
0014-7990	Farm Industry News
0014-8008	Farm Journal
0014-8016	Farm Labor
0014-8024	Farm Letter
0014-8032	Farm Light & Power
0014-8040	Farm Machine Design Engineering†
0014-8059	Farm Management
0014-8067	Farm Mechanisation
0014-8075	Farm Policy
0014-8091	Farm Quarterly†
0014-8105	Farm Safety Review
0014-8113	Farm Service News *changed to* N J D A Report
0014-8121	Farm Store Merchandising
0014-813X	Farm Supplier
0014-8148	Farm Technology *see* 0190-2423
0014-8156	Farm Tempo U. S. A
0014-8164	Farmaceuten†
0014-8172	Farmaceuticky Obzor
0014-8180	Farmaceutico
0014-8199	Farmaceutisk Tidende
0014-8202	Farmaceutski Glasnik
0014-8210	Farmacevtisk Revy
0014-8229	Farmacevtski Vestnik
0014-8237	Farmacia
0014-8245	Farmacia Nuova
0014-8253	Farmacia Sociale
0014-8261	Farmacja Polska
0014-827X	Farmaco
0014-8288	Farmacognosia
0014-8296	Terapeutica Razonada†
0014-8318	Farmakologiya i Toksikologiya
0014-8326	Farmakoterapi
0014-8334	Farmand
0014-8342	Farmatsevtychnyi Zhurnal
0014-8350	Farmer
0014-8369	Farmer & Parliament
0014-8377	Farmer-Labor Press
0014-8393	Farmers Club. Journal
0014-8415	Farmers' Friend
0014-8423	Farmers Guardian
0014-844X	Farmers Newsletter
0014-8458	Farmers Union Herald *changed to* Co-op Country News
0014-8466	Farmers Weekly
0014-8482	Farmers Weekly
0014-8504	Farming in Zambia
0014-8512	Foreign Acquisitions Newsletter
0014-8520	Farmis - Reptilen
0014-8539	Farmland *see* 0093-5832
0014-8547	Farmweek
0014-8555	Il Faro
0014-8563	Faro Dominical *changed to* Marchemos
0014-8571	Farogh-I-Urdu
0014-858X	Farol†
0014-8598	Faarskoetsel
0014-8601	Pharmacy
0014-8628	Faserforschung und Textiltechnik *changed to* Acta Polymerica
0014-8644	Fashion Accessories
0014-8660	Fashion Calendar
0014-8679	Fashion Forecast
0014-8695	Fashion Week†
0014-8709	Fashionweek *see* 0312-0325
0014-8725	Fast Food *see* 0097-8043
0014-8733	Fast Grunn
0014-8741	Fasteners†
0014-875X	Fastline Monthly†
0014-8776	Fate
0014-8784	Res Medicae
0014-8814	Fathers of the Church
0014-8822	Fathom (Norfolk)
0014-8830	Fatima Findings
0014-8849	Fatos & Fotos
0014-8865	U.S. Department of Agriculture. Economics, Statistics, and Cooperatives Service. Fats and Oils Situation
0014-8873	Fatti E Notizie
0014-8881	Fauna
0014-889X	S. W. A. N. S
0014-8903	Fauna och Flora
0014-892X	Faversham Papers
0014-8946	Feasta
0014-8962	Feddes Repertorium
0014-8970	Die Feder
0014-9004	Federal Accountant *changed to* Government Accountant's Journal
0014-9039	Federal Bar Journal
0014-9047	Federal Bar News
0014-9063	Federal Contracts Report
0014-9071	Federal Employee
0014-908X	Federal Fire Council News Letter†
0014-9128	Federal Probation
0014-9136	Washington Environmental Protection Report
0014-9144	Federal Reserve Bank of Atlanta. Monthly Review *changed to* Federal Reserve Bank of Atlanta. Economic Review
0014-9152	Federal Reserve Bank of Kansas City. Monthly Review *see* 0161-2387
0014-9160	Federal Reserve Bank of New York. Monthly Review *see* 0147-6580
0014-9179	Federal Reserve Bank of Richmond. Monthly Review *see* 0094-6893
0014-9187	Federal Reserve Bank of St. Louis. Review
0014-9195	Federal Reserve Bank of San Francisco. Monthly Review *see* 0363-0021
0014-9209	Federal Reserve Bulletin
0014-9225	Federal Statistics Users' Conference. Newsletter
0014-9233	Federal Times
0014-9241	Federalist *changed to* World Citizen/Federalist Letter
0014-9268	Federaliste Europeen
0014-9284	Federatie Contact *changed to* Contour
0014-9306	Federation of State Medical Boards of the United States. Federation Bulletin
0014-9314	Federation of Synagogues of South Africa. Federation Chronicle
0014-9322	International Dental Federation. News Letter
0014-9330	Federation des Entreprises de l'Industrie des Fabrications Metalliques, Mecaniques, Electriques et de la Transformation des Matieres Plastiques. Bulletin d'Information Mensuel *changed to* Federation des Entreprises de l'Industrie des Fabrications Metalliques, Mecaniques, Electriques et de la Transformation des Matieres Plastiques. Revue Mensuelle
0014-9349	Federation des Industries Belges. Bulletin *changed to* Federation des Entreprises de Belgique. Bulletin
0014-9357	Federation des Societes d'Histoire Naturelle de Franche-Comte. Bulletin *changed to* Societe d'Histoire Naturelle du Doubs. Bulletin
0014-9365	Federation Francaise des Societes de Sciences Naturelles. Revue *see* 0336-8300
0014-9373	Entreprise Europeenne
0014-939X	Federation Nationale de l'Industrie Laitiere. Bulletin d'Information
0014-9411	Federation News
0014-942X	Federation News
0014-9438	American Beekeeping Federation. News Letter
0014-9446	Federation of American Societies for Experimental Biology. Federation Proceedings
0014-9454	Federation of Canadian Archers. Official Bulletin *see* 0319-2571
0014-9470	Federation of Indian Chambers of Commerce and Industry. Fortnightly Review *changed to* Economic Trends
0014-9489	F. W. I. News
0014-9497	Federazione Italiana Medici Igienisti. Bolletino d'Informazioni Agli Iscritti
0014-9500	Federazione Medica
0014-9519	Federazione Nazionale Stampa Italiana. Bollettino†
0014-9527	Quaerendo
0014-9535	Feed Industry Review
0014-9543	Feed Bulletin
0014-9551	Feed/Grain Equipment Times *see* 0163-4119
0014-956X	Feed Management
0014-9578	U.S. Department of Agriculture. Economics, Statistics, and Cooperatives Service. Feed Situation
0014-9586	Feed Trade
0014-9594	Feedback *changed to* Feedback for Improving Vocational-Technical and Career Education
0014-9608	Feedback†

ISSN	Title
0014-9616	Feedlot *changed to* Feedlot Management
0014-9624	Feedstuffs
0014-9632	Feet†
0014-9659	Fegato
0014-9667	Chung Kung Yen Chiu
0014-9675	Fei-Ching Yueh-Pao
0014-9683	Feingeraetetechnik
0014-9691	Feinkost-Revue
0014-9705	Die Feinkostwirtschaft
0014-9713	Feinwerktechnik *see* 0340-1952
0014-9721	Feiten, Cijfers, Meningen *changed to* Voetganger
0014-973X	Feju
0014-9748	Feld und Wald
0014-9756	Feld Wald Wasser
0014-9764	Feldgrau†
0014-9772	Fel'dsher i Akusherka
0014-9780	Feldweibel
0014-9799	Feldwirtschaft
0014-9802	Feliciter
0014-9810	Fellowship
0014-9829	Fellowship for Freedom in Medicine. Bulletin *see* 0305-9324
0014-9837	Fellowship in Prayer
0014-9853	Femina
0014-9861	Femina
0014-987X	Femina and Woman's Life†
0014-9888	Feminidades†
0014-9896	Femme Chic†
0014-990X	Femme d'Aujourd'hui et Patrie Suisse-Actualites *changed to* Femme d'Aujourd'hui
0014-9918	Femme-Lines
0014-9926	Femme Pratique
0014-9934	Femmes au Village
0014-9942	Femmes Chefs d'Entreprise
0014-9950	Femmes d'Aujourd'hui
0014-9969	Fenarete-Letture d'Italia
0014-9977	Fence Industry
0014-9985	Fendt-Nachrichten†
0015-0002	Fenix
0015-0010	Fennia
0015-0029	Das Fenster
0015-0037	Ferguson-Florissant Schools
0015-0045	Actualite Agricole
0015-0053	Fermentatio *changed to* Cerevisia
0015-0061	Fermentation Research Institute. Report
0015-007X	Fermettes et Residences Secondaires *changed to* Combat Nature
0015-0096	Fernmelde Impulse†
0015-010X	Der Fernmelde-Ingenieur
0015-0118	Fernmelde Praxis
0015-0126	Fernmeldetechnik
0015-0134	Fernseh-Informationen
0015-0142	Fernseh- und Kino-Technik
0015-0150	Fernsehen und Bildung
0015-0177	Ferrocarriles *changed to* Ferrocarriles Mexicanos
0015-0185	Ferrocarriles y Tranvias
0015-0193	Ferroelectrics
0015-0207	Ferronales
0015-0215	Ferroviere
0015-0223	Ferskvandsfiskeribladet
0015-0231	Fertigteilbau und industrialisiertes Bauen *see* 0340-2967
0015-024X	Fertigungstechnik und Betrieb
0015-0258	Feed and Farm Supplies *changed to* Milling Feed and Fertiliser
0015-0266	Fertiliser News
0015-0282	Fertility and Sterility
0015-0290	Fertilizer Abstracts
0015-0304	Fertilizer International
0015-0312	Fertilizer Solutions
0015-0320	Der feste Grund
0015-0339	Feste Prophetische Wort†
0015-0347	Festina Lente
0015-0355	Festiniog Railway Magazine
0015-0363	Festival
0015-0371	Fetes et Saisons
0015-038X	Fette - Seifen - Anstrichmittel
0015-0398	Feu Vert
0015-0401	Feuerungstechnik - Gebaeudetechnik
0015-041X	Feuille Anarchiste
0015-0428	Feuille Officielle de la Protection Civile
0015-0444	Feuillets d'Electroradiologie *changed to* Feuillets de Radiologie
0015-0452	Feuillets du Praticien
0015-0479	Fiamma†
0015-0495	Fiat Lux
0015-0509	Fib-Aktuellt
0015-0517	Fibonacci Quarterly
0015-0525	Fibra
0015-0533	Fibre and Fabric†
0015-0541	Fibre Chemistry
0015-055X	Fibre e Colori *see* 0033-9067
0015-0568	Fibre Science and Technology
0015-0576	Fibula†
0015-0592	Fichero Bibliografico Hispanoamericano
0015-0606	Fichero Medico Terapeutico Purissimus
0015-0649	Fiddlehead
0015-0657	Field
0015-0673	Field & Stream
0015-069X	Field Crop Abstracts
0015-0703	Field Museum of Natural History Bulletin
0015-0711	Arkansas Archeological Society. Field Notes
0015-072X	Field Notes
0015-0746	Fieldiana: Botany
0015-0754	Fieldiana: Zoology
0015-0762	Fields *changed to* Christian Missions in Many Lands
0015-0770	Fields Within Fields...Within Fields†
0015-0797	Fiere e Mostre
0015-0800	Fifth Estate
0015-0819	Fifth Wheel
0015-0827	Fifty Millesimal
0015-0835	Figaro
0015-0843	Figaro Litteraire†
0015-0851	Figurino Moderno
0015-086X	Figyelo
0015-0878	Fiinta Romaneasca†
0015-0886	Fiji Agricultural Journal
0015-0894	Fiji. Bureau of Statistics. Current Economic Statistics
0015-0908	Fiji Farmer†
0015-0916	Fiji. Government Printing Department. Publications Bulltin
0015-0932	Fikrun Wa Fann
0015-0940	Filatelia Italiana
0015-0959	Filatelie
0015-0967	Filatelija
0015-0975	Filatelista
0015-0983	Filateli'ya S. S. S. R.
0015-0991	Filipino-American Herald
0015-1009	Filipino Teacher
0015-1017	Film *changed to* L B Levende Billeder
0015-1025	Film
0015-1033	Film
0015-1041	Film
0015-105X	Film *see* 0046-368X
0015-1068	Film a Doba
0015-1076	Film & Foto
0015-1084	Film en Televisie
0015-1106	Film and Television Technician
0015-1114	Film und Ton-Magazin
0015-1122	Film Artiste†
0015-1130	Film Bild Ton *changed to* A V-Praxis
0015-1149	Film-Echo/Filmwoche
0015-1157	Film Bulletin†
0015-1165	Film Bulletin
0015-1173	Film Canadiana: The Canadian Film Institute Yearbook of Canadian Cinema
0015-1181	Film Collectors Registry†
0015-119X	Film Comment
0015-1203	Critic
0015-1211	Film Culture
0015-1238	Film Fan Monthly†
0015-1262	Film Francais-Cinematographie Francais *see* 0397-8702
0015-1270	Film Heritage†
0015-1289	Film Index
0015-1297	Film Information†
0015-1300	Film Italiano†
0015-1319	Film Journal Advertiser†
0015-1327	Film Library Quarterly
0015-1335	Film-Lyd-Bildet†
0015-1343	Film News *see* 0195-1017
0015-1351	Film og Kino
0015-136X	Polish Film
0015-1378	Film/Pop-Telescoop *changed to* Pop-Telescoop
0015-1386	Film Quarterly
0015-1416	Film, Szinhaz, Muzsika
0015-1424	Fernseh und Film Technikum†
0015-1440	Film und Recht
0015-1459	Film User *see* 0305-2249
0015-1467	Film Weekly†
0015-1475	Film World
0015-1505	Filmclub Action-Mitteilungen
0015-1513	Filmcritica
0015-1521	Filme Cultura†
0015-1521	Film e Cultura *changed to* Filme Cultura
0015-153X	Filmfacts†
0015-1548	Filmfare
0015-1556	Filmjournalen
0015-1564	Filmkompas *changed to* 3 D Filmkompas
0015-1572	Filmkritik
0015-1580	Filmkultura
0015-1599	Filmkunst
0015-1602	Filmlist *see* 0037-4830
0015-1610	Filmmakers' Newsletter *see* 0194-4339
0015-1629	Filmograph
0015-1645	Filmovy Prehled
0015-1653	Filmowy Osrodek Badawczo - Rozwojowy "Techfilm". Przeglad Dokumentacyjny
0015-1661	Filmrutan
0015-1688	Films in Review
0015-1696	Filmschau
0015-1734	Filmspiegel
0015-1742	Filmtheater-Praxis *changed to* Filmtheater-Praxis - Werbung Heute
0015-1750	Filmo-Bibliografischer Jahresbericht
0015-1777	Filologia e Letteratura *changed to* Critica Letteraria
0015-1785	Filologiai Kozlony
0015-1807	Filoloski Pregled
0015-1815	Filomata
0015-1823	Filosofia
0015-1831	Filosoficky Casopis
0015-184X	Filosofska Misul
0015-1858	Filosofskie Nauki
0015-1866	Filozofija
0015-1874	Filson Club History Quarterly
0015-1882	Filtration & Separation
0015-1890	Filtration Engineering†
0015-1904	Findivert†
0015-1912	Finance†
0015-1920	Finance a Uver
0015-1939	Finance & Commerce *changed to* Finance & Society
0015-1955	Finance and Trade Review
0015-1963	Finance Facts
0015-1971	Finance Taxation & Company Law
0015-198X	Financial Analysts Journal
0015-1998	Financial Executive
0015-2005	Financial Express
0015-2013	Financial Mail
0015-2021	Financial Post
0015-203X	Great Britain. Central Statistical Office. Financial Statistics
0015-2056	Financial Times of Canada
0015-2064	Financial World
0015-2072	Financieel Overheidsbeheer
0015-2080	Financiele Flitsen
0015-2099	Financiele Koerier
0015-2102	Financiero
0015-2110	Financing Agriculture
0015-2129	Financing Foreign Operations
0015-2137	Finansi i Kredit
0015-2145	Finansije
0015-2153	Finanstidende
0015-2161	Finansy S.S.S.R.
0015-217X	Finante si Credit†
0015-2188	Finanz-Revue
0015-2196	Finanz-Rundschau
0015-220X	Finanz und Wirtschaft
0015-2218	Finanzarchiv
0015-2226	Finanzas al Dia
0015-2242	Finanziere
0015-2250	Finanzjournal mit Gebuehren-und Verkehrssteuerrundschau
0015-2269	Finanznachrichten
0015-2277	Finanzrechtliche Erkenntnisse des Verwaltungsgerichtshofes
0015-2285	Findings†
0015-2293	Fine
0015-2307	Fine Arts†
0015-2315	Finis Terrae†
0015-234X	Finish†
0015-2358	Finishers' Management
0015-2366	Finite String *changed to* American Journal of Computational Linguistics
0015-2374	Sueder-Elbe Wochenblatt fuer Sued Hamburg *changed to* Elbe Wochenblatt
0015-2390	Finland. Tilastokeskus. Tilastokatsauksia
0015-2412	Finnfacts
0015-2420	Finnische Handelsrundschau *changed to* Technik und Form aus Finnland
0015-2439	Finnish American Chamber of Commerce Newsletter *changed to* Finnish American Chamber of Commerce Newsletter Including Finnfacts Newsletter
0015-2447	Finnish Game Research
0015-2455	Finnish Paper and Timber†
0015-2463	Finnish Trade Review
0015-248X	Finsk Tidskrift
0015-2498	Finska Kemistsamfundet. Meddelanden *see* 0355-1628
0015-2501	Finska Laekaresaellskapet. Handlingar
0015-251X	Finskij Torgovyj Zurnal
0015-2528	Fiori di S. Antonio
0015-2536	Fiorisce Un Cenacolo
0015-2544	Fire
0015-2552	Fire Chief
0015-2560	Fire Command
0015-2579	Fire Control Notes *changed to* Fire Management Notes
0015-2587	Fire Engineering
0015-2595	Fire Fighting in Canada
0015-2609	Fire International
0015-2617	Fire Journal
0015-2625	Fire News
0015-2641	Fire Protection Review
0015-2668	Fire Service Information
0015-2684	Fire Technology
0015-2706	Firenze Agricola
0015-2714	Fireside Chats
0015-2722	Firing Line
0015-2730	Firmenkraftfahrer†
0015-2749	First *see* 0199-2066
0015-2757	First Hawaiian Bank. Economic Indicators
0015-2773	First National Bank of Chicago. Business and Economic Review†
0015-2781	First National Bank of Chicago. International Economic Review†
0015-279X	Citibank. Monthly Economic Letter
0015-2803	First to Final
0015-2811	Fiscaal Tijdschrift voor de Euromarkt *changed to* Intertax (Dutch Edition)
0015-282X	Fiscalite du Marche Commun *changed to* Intertax
0015-2838	Fisch und Fang
0015-2846	Fischer Edition News†
0015-2854	Das Fischerblatt
0015-2862	Fischers Tarif Nachrichten fuer Eisenbahn und Kraftwagen
0015-2897	Fish and Game Sportsman *see* 0709-1532
0015-2900	Fish Boat/Sea Food Merchandising
0015-2919	Fish Culturist
0015-2927	Fish Friers Review
0015-2943	Fish Trades Gazette *changed to* Fish Trader
0015-2951	Fisheries of Canada†
0015-2978	Fisherman†
0015-2986	Fisherman
0015-2994	Fishermen's News
0015-3001	Fishery Technology
0015-301X	Fishing and Hunting News
0015-3028	Fishing Gazette
0015-3036	Fishing News
0015-3044	Fishing News International

ISSN	Title
0015-3052	Tackle & Guns
0015-3060	Fishing Tackle Trade News
0015-3079	Fishing World
0015-3087	Fishpaste†
0015-3095	Fiskaren
0015-3109	Fiskehandleren
0015-3117	Norway. Fiskeridirektoratet. Skrifter. Serie Havundersoekelser
0015-3125	Fiskeritidskrift foer Finland
0015-3133	Fiskets Gang
0015-3141	Fitness and Health†
0015-3176	Five Associated University Libraries. Newsletter†
0015-3184	Five/Six see 0149-7820
0015-3206	Fizika
0015-3214	Fizika i Khimiya Obrabotki Materialov
0015-3222	Fizika i Tekhnika Poluprovodnikov
0015-3230	Fizika Metallov i Metallovedenie
0015-3249	Fizika Tverdogo Tela
0015-3257	Fizikai Szemle
0015-3265	Fiziko-Matematichesko Spisanie
0015-3273	Fiziko-tekhnicheskie Problemy Razrabotki Poleznykh Iskopremykh
0015-329X	Fiziologicheskii Zhurnal
0015-3303	Fiziologiya Rastenii
0015-3311	Fiziologichnyi Zhurnal
0015-332X	Fizkul'tura i Sport
0015-3338	Fjaederfae
0015-3346	Fjarmalatidindi
0015-3354	Fjoerfe
0015-3362	Flacara
0015-3370	Flag Bulletin
0015-3389	Flair
0015-3400	Flakten
0015-3419	Flama†
0015-3427	Flambeau
0015-3435	Flambeau
0015-346X	Flame Notes†
0015-3478	Flamingo†
0015-3486	Flammes Vives
0015-3494	Flash
0015-3508	Flash
0015-3516	Flash Actualite
0015-3524	Flash Art changed to Flash Art
0015-3532	Flavour Industry see 0143-8441
0015-3540	Fleanende Krie
0015-3567	Fleet Owner
0015-3575	Fleisch
0015-3583	Fleisch und Feinkost†
0015-3605	Fleischer Offerten-Dienst changed to Fleisch-Lebensmittel-Markt
0015-3613	Die Fleischerei
0015-363X	Die Fleischwirtschaft
0015-3648	Fleur de Lys
0015-3680	Der Flieger
0015-3699	Luftwaffe
0015-3702	Flight Comment
0015-3710	Flight International
0015-3737	Flight Safety Bulletin
0015-3753	Floor & Wall Covering News†
0015-3761	Floor Covering Weekly
0015-377X	Flooring & Carpet Specifier†
0015-3796	B P P
0015-380X	Flora
0015-3818	Flora og Fauna
0015-3826	Floresta
0015-3834	Floricoltura Pesciatina
0015-3842	Florida A A A Motorist
0015-3850	Florida Academy of Sciences. Quarterly Journal see 0098-4590
0015-3869	Florida Agriculture
0015-3877	Florida Alligator changed to Independent Florida Alligator
0015-3885	Florida Sportsman
0015-3893	Florida Anthropologist
0015-3907	Florida Architect†
0015-3915	Florida Bar Journal
0015-3923	Florida Builder
0015-3931	Florida Cancer News
0015-394X	Florida Catholic Newspaper
0015-3958	Florida Cattleman and Livestock Journal
0015-3974	Florida Conservation News
0015-3982	Florida Contractor and Builder changed to Florida Construction Industry
0015-3990	Florida Dental Journal
0015-4008	Florida Department of Agriculture. Division of Plant Industry. News Bulletin changed to Florida. Department of Agriculture and Consumer Service. Plant Industry News
0015-4016	Florida Education changed to Forum (Tallahassee)
0015-4024	Florida Educational Research and Development Council. Research Bulletin
0015-4032	Florida Engineering Society. Journal
0015-4040	Florida Entomologist
0015-4059	Florida Explorer
0015-4067	Florida Family Physician
0015-4075	Florida Field Report see 0015-4091
0015-4083	Florida Food & Grocery News
0015-4091	Florida Grower and Rancher
0015-4105	Florida Health Notes†
0015-4113	Florida Historical Quarterly
0015-4121	Florida Industrial Arts Quarterly Bulletin
0015-413X	Florida Journal of Commerce/Seafarer see 0160-225X
0015-4148	Florida Medical Association Journal
0015-4164	Florida Municipal Record
0015-4172	Florida Naturalist
0015-4180	Communique (Hollywood)
0015-4199	Florida Nurse
0015-4202	Florida Pharmaceutical Journal see 0161-746X
0015-4210	Florida Planning and Development see 0145-5885
0015-4237	Florida Prisoner Statistics†
0015-4245	Florida Purchaser
0015-4253	Florida Quarterly†
0015-4261	Florida Reading Quarterly
0015-427X	Florida Restaurant, Hotel & Motel Journal
0015-4288	Florida School Herald
0015-4296	Florida Schools
0015-430X	Florida State University. Institute for Social Research. Governmental Research Bulletin†
0015-4318	Florida Supplement
0015-4326	Florida Trend
0015-4334	Florida Truck News
0015-4369	Florida Wildlife
0015-4377	Florist
0015-4385	Florist
0015-4393	Florist
0015-4407	Florist & Nursery Exchange see 0037-0797
0015-4415	Florist Trade Magazine
0015-4423	Florists' Review
0015-4431	Flottans Maen
0015-444X	Flourish†
0015-4458	Flow Line
0015-4466	Flower and Feather
0015-4482	Home Garden see 0014-7230
0015-4490	Flower News
0015-4504	Flowering Plants of Africa
0015-4512	Flue Cured Tobacco Farmer
0015-4520	Mitteldeutscher Kurier
0015-4539	Fluessiges Obst
0015-4547	Flug Revue
0015-4555	Flughafen - Revue
0015-458X	Flug und Modell-Technik
0015-4598	Flugsport-Informationen
0015-461X	Fluid
0015-4628	Fluid Dynamics
0015-4636	Fluid Milk and Cream Report†
0015-4644	Fluid Power Abstracts
0015-4652	Fluid Power International see 0011-9350
0015-4660	Fluid Sealing Abstracts
0015-4687	Fluidics Quarterly
0015-4709	Fluorescence News†
0015-4717	Fluoridation Reporter†
0015-4725	Fluoride
0015-4733	Flur und Furche
0015-4741	Fly Fisherman
0015-475X	Flyghorisont
0015-4776	Flygposten
0015-4784	Flygrevyn
0015-4792	FlygvapenNytt
0015-4806	Flying
0015-4814	Flying A
0015-4822	Flying Angel
0015-4830	Flying Lady
0015-4849	Flying Models
0015-4857	Flying Physician
0015-4865	Aerospace Review†
0015-4873	Flying Saucer News
0015-489X	Flying Saucers changed to Search-Flying Saucers
0015-4911	Flyleaf†
0015-492X	Flyv
0015-4938	Canadian Journal of Radiography, Radiotherapy, Nucleography see 0319-4434
0015-4946	Focus
0015-4954	Focus†
0015-4970	Focus (Chicago)†
0015-4997	Focus
0015-5004	Focus (New York, 1950)
0015-5012	Bausch & Lomb Focus changed to Educational Focus
0015-5020	National Committee on the Education of Migrant Children. Focus†
0015-5039	Focus (New York, 1964)†
0015-5047	Focus (Columbus, 1967)
0015-5055	South Africa International
0015-5063	Focus on Public Affairs changed to Focus on Governmental Affairs
0015-508X	Focus/Midwest
0015-5098	Focus on Industry and Commerce
0015-511X	Focus on Exceptional Children
0015-5128	Focus on Film
0015-5136	Focus on Guidance see 0193-7375
0015-5152	Focus on Indiana Libraries
0015-5160	Focus on Jamaica
0015-5179	Focus on Saskatchewan Libraries
0015-5195	Focus: Social and Preventive Medicine
0015-5209	Foden News
0015-5217	Foer Biblisk Tro see 0345-1453
0015-5225	Foerbundet Svenska Finlandsfrivilliga. Tidning
0015-5233	Foerdermittel-Journal
0015-5241	Foerdern und Heben
0015-525X	Foerderungsdienst
0015-5268	F I V Meddelanden
0015-5276	Foeretagaren
0015-5284	Foersamlings- och Pastorsfoervaltning
0015-5292	Foerskolan
0015-5306	Foersvarstjaenstemannen
0015-5314	Fogorvosi Szemle
0015-5322	Fogra-Literaturdienst
0015-5330	Fogra-Mitteilungen
0015-5349	F O I Digest
0015-5357	Foi et Vie
0015-5365	Foi et Vie de l'Eglise au Diocese de Toulouse
0015-5373	Foil
0015-539X	Fold es Eg
0015-5403	Foldrajzi Ertesito
0015-5411	Foldrajzi Kozlemenyek
0015-542X	Foldtani Kozlony
0015-5438	Folger Library Newsletter
0015-5446	Folha Bancaria
0015-5454	Folha Medica
0015-5470	Folia Allergologica see 0303-8432
0015-5489	Folia Biochimica et Biologica Graeca
0015-5497	Folia Biologica
0015-5500	Folia Biologica
0015-5519	Folia Clinica et Biologica†
0015-5527	Folia Clinica Internacional†
0015-5543	Folia Forestalia
0015-5551	Folia Geobotanica et Phytotaxonomica
0015-556X	Folia Haematologica
0015-5578	Folia Hereditaria et Pathologica
0015-5586	Folia Histochemica et Cytochemica
0015-5594	Folia Humanistica
0015-5608	Folia Medica†
0015-5616	Folia Medica Cracoviensia
0015-5632	Folia Microbiologica
0015-5640	Folia Morphologica
0015-5659	Folia Morphologica†
0015-5667	Folia Ophthalmologica Japonica
0015-5675	Folia Orientalia
0015-5683	Folia Parasitologica
0015-5691	Folia Pharmacologica Japonica
0015-5705	Folia Phoniatrica
0015-5713	Folia Primatologica
0015-5721	Folia Psychiatrica et Neurologica Japonica
0015-573X	Folia Quaternaria
0015-5748	Folia Veterinaria
0015-5756	Folio (Birmingham)
0015-5764	Folio†
0015-5772	Folio
0015-5780	Folio (Waltham)
0015-5799	Folio Pharmaceutica
0015-5802	Folium Diocesanum Bauzanense-Brixinense
0015-5810	Folk og Fritid
0015-5829	Folk Style
0015-5837	Folkeskolen
0015-5845	Folkevirke
0015-5853	Folkforsvaret†
0015-5861	Folkets Vael changed to Folkets-Vael/DKSN-RIA Informerar
0015-587X	Folklore
0015-5888	Folklore
0015-5896	Folklore
0015-590X	Folklore Brabancon
0015-5918	Folklore de France
0015-5926	Folklore Forum
0015-5950	Folklore Society of Greater Washington Newsletter
0015-5969	Folklore Suisse
0015-6000	Follia di New York
0015-6019	Contrary Investor Follow-up Service
0015-6027	Fomento†
0015-6035	Fomento de la Produccion
0015-6043	Revista de Fomento Social
0015-606X	Fondazione Giorgio Ronchi. Atti
0015-6078	Fonderia
0015-6086	Fonderie Italiana
0015-6094	Fonderie-Fondeur d'Aujourd'hui
0015-6108	Fonderie Belge
0015-6116	Fondeur d'Aujour'mui see 0015-6094
0015-6124	Fondo Nacional de las Artes. Informativo†
0015-6132	Confederacion Espanola de Cajas de Ahorros. Fondo para la Investigacion Economica y Social. Boletin de Documentacion
0015-6140	Fono Forum
0015-6159	Platenwereld†
0015-6167	Foenstret
0015-6175	Fontane-Blaetter
0015-6183	Fontes Archaeologici Pragenses
0015-6191	Fontes Artis Musicae
0015-6205	Fonti Vive
0015-6213	Food Agriculture and Plantation Journal
0015-6221	Food and Agricultural Legislation
0015-6256	Food and Cookery Review
0015-6264	Food and Cosmetics Toxicology
0015-6272	Food and Drug Packaging
0015-6280	Food & Equipment Product News changed to Foodservice Product News
0015-6302	Hospitality-Food & Lodging see 0148-0766
0015-6310	Food & Nutrition News
0015-6329	Food and Nutrition Notes and Reviews
0015-6337	Food Chemical News
0015-6353	Food Distributors News
0015-6361	Food, Drug, Cosmetic Law Journal
0015-637X	Food Engineering
0015-6388	Food Executive
0015-6396	Food Farming and Agriculture
0015-640X	Food Fish Situation and Outlook see 0091-8105
0015-6418	Food from Poland
0015-6426	Food Hygienic Society of Japan. Journal
0015-6442	Food in Canada
0015-6450	Food Industries of South Africa
0015-6469	Food Ingredients & Equipment see 0149-5895
0015-6477	Food Manufacture
0015-6493	Food Merchants Advocate
0015-6507	Food Outlook
0015-6515	Food Plant Ideas
0015-6523	Food Processing
0015-6531	Food Processing Industry

ISSN	Title
0015-654X	Food Product Development *changed to* Food Development
0015-6558	Food Promotions
0015-6566	Food Research Institute Studies in Agricultural Economics, Trade, and Development *changed to* Food Research Institute Studies
0015-6574	Food Science and Technology Abstracts
0015-6582	Food-Scope†
0015-6604	Food Service Magazine *see* 0092-5845
0015-6639	Food Technology
0015-6647	Food Technology in Australia
0015-6655	Food Technology in New Zealand
0015-6663	Food Trade News
0015-6671	Food Trade Review
0015-668X	Food World *changed to* World Food Review
0015-6698	Foodpack
0015-6701	Foodpress
0015-6728	Foodsman
0015-6752	Football Clinic†
0015-6760	Football Digest
0015-6795	Football Record
0015-6809	Footplate
0015-6817	Footwear Fashions
0015-6825	Footwear Manufacturers Journal†
0015-6833	Footwear News
0015-6841	Footwear Weekly *see* 0306-3437
0015-685X	For Reference
0015-6868	For Teens Only†
0015-6884	For the Defense
0015-6892	For You from Czechoslovakia
0015-6906	Forage and Grassland Progress
0015-6914	Forbes
0015-6922	Forbes Magazine's Restaurant Guide†
0015-6930	Forbrukeren
0015-6949	Foerbundskontakt *changed to* Soedra-Kontakt
0015-6957	Forces
0015-6981	Ford Estate
0015-699X	Ford Foundation Letter
0015-7007	Ford-Nachrichten
0015-7015	Ford Times
0015-7023	Ford Truck Times
0015-7031	Ford Wereld†
0015-704X	Fordham Law Review
0015-7058	Ford's Freighter Travel Guide
0015-7066	Ford's International Cruise Guide
0015-7074	Forecast *changed to* Graffiti
0015-7082	Forecast Data Bank Cumulative Sheets
0015-7090	Forecast for Home Economics
0015-7104	Advance Weather Forecasts†
0015-7120	Foreign Affairs
0015-7139	Foreign Affairs Bulletin
0015-7155	Foreign Affairs Reports
0015-7163	Foreign Agriculture
0015-718X	Foreign Language Annals
0015-7198	Foreign Language Beacon
0015-7228	Foreign Policy
0015-7244	Foreign Projects Newsletter
0015-7260	Foreign Radio Amateur Callbook Magazine
0015-7279	Foreign Service Journal
0015-7287	U.S. Department of State. Foreign Service List†
0015-7309	Foreign Trade/Commerce Exterieur *see* 0068-7251
0015-7309	Pakistan. Statistics Division. Foreign Trade
0015-7317	Foreign Trade Bulletin
0015-7325	Foreign Trade Review
0015-7333	Foreman's Letter
0015-735X	Forensic
0015-7368	Forensic Science Society. Journal
0015-7384	Forest and Bird
0015-7392	Forest and Timber
0015-7406	Forest Farmer
0015-7414	Forest Fire Control Abstracts
0015-7422	Forest History *see* 0094-5080
0015-7430	Forest Industries
0015-7449	Forest Log
0015-7457	Forest Notes
0015-7473	Forest Products Journal
0015-7481	Forest Research Institute and Colleges, Dehra Dun. Quarterly News Letter
0015-749X	Forest Science
0015-7503	Foresta
0015-7511	Foresters Miscellany
0015-752X	Forestry
0015-7538	Forestry Abstracts
0015-7546	Forestry Chronicle
0015-7546	Forestry Chronicle *issued with* 0068-8991
0015-7562	Forestry Economics *changed to* Social Sciences in Forestry
0015-7570	Forestry Marketing Bulletin *changed to* Sawlog
0015-7589	Forests & People
0015-7597	Foret
0015-7619	Foeretagsekonomi Bokfoeraren-Revisorn
0015-7627	Forex Service
0015-7635	Forge
0015-766X	Form
0015-7678	Form
0015-7694	Form und Geist
0015-7708	Form und Technik *see* 0012-6470
0015-7716	Forma et Functio†
0015-7724	Formage des Materiaux *changed to* Travail des Metaux Par Deformation
0015-7732	Formage et Traitements des Metaux *see* 0024-9130
0015-7740	Format
0015-7759	Format
0015-7767	Formazione e Lavoro
0015-7775	Graveur Flexograf
0015-7783	Formosan Medical Association. Journal
0015-7791	Formosan Science
0015-7805	Forms of Business Agreements
0015-7813	Fornvaennen
0015-7821	Foro Internacional
0015-783X	Foro Italiano
0015-7848	Foro Napoletano
0015-7856	Foro Padano
0015-7864	Foro Penale
0015-7880	Foersaakringstidningen
0015-7899	Forschung im Ingenieurwesen
0015-7902	Forschungen zur Volks- und Landeskunde
0015-7910	Vierteljahresberichte - Probleme der Entwicklungslaender
0015-7929	Forsikringstidende
0015-7937	Forskning och Framsteg
0015-7945	Norges Almenvitenskapelige Forskiningsraad. Forskningsnytt
0015-7953	Institutet foer Metallforskning. Forskningsverksamheten
0015-7961	Der Forst- und Holzwirt
0015-797X	Forstliche Mitteilungen
0015-7988	Forstliche Umschau
0015-7996	Forstpflanzen-Forstsamen
0015-8003	Forstwissenschaftliches Centralblatt
0015-8011	Foersvarsmedicin†
0015-802X	Fort Beaufort Advocate
0015-8038	Fort Dodge Biochemic Review†
0015-8054	Fort Hare Papers
0015-8070	Fort Ticonderoga Museum. Bulletin
0015-8089	Fort Worth
0015-8097	Fort Worth Commercial Recorder
0015-8100	Forth Valley Chamber of Commerce Quarterly Bulletin *changed to* Central Scotland Chamber of Commerce Quarterly Bulletin
0015-8119	Forthcoming Books
0015-8127	Fortnightly Journal of Industry & Commerce
0015-8135	Fortpflanzung, Besamung und Aufzucht der Haustiere. Biologie, Pathologie und Hygiene†
0015-8151	Fortschritte auf dem Gebiete der Roentgenstrahlen und der Nuklearmedizin *see* 0340-1618
0015-816X	Fortschritte der Kieferorthopaedie
0015-8178	Fortschritte der Medizin
0015-8186	Fortschritte der Mineralogie
0015-8194	Fortschritte der Neurologie, Psychiatrie und Ihrer Grenzgebiete *changed to* Fortschritte der Neurologie - Psychiatrie
0015-8208	Fortschritte der Physik
0015-8216	Fortschrittliche Betriebs Fuehrung *changed to* Fortschrittliche Betriebsfuehrung und Industrial Engineering
0015-8224	Der Fortschrittliche Landwirt
0015-8240	Fortuna Italiana
0015-8259	Fortune
0015-8275	Fortune News
0015-8283	Forty Acres and a Mule†
0015-8291	Education Forum†
0015-8305	Forum (Washington, D.C.)
0015-8313	Forum
0015-8321	Forum†
0015-833X	Forum
0015-8356	Forum (Chicago, 1965)
0015-8364	Forum†
0015-8372	Forum†
0015-8380	Forum†
0015-8399	Forum (Scranton)
0015-8402	Forum
0015-8410	Forum (Houston)
0015-8445	Forum
0015-8453	Forum - Revista Invatamintului Superior
0015-847X	Forum Botanicum
0015-8488	Forum de la Force Terrestre
0015-8496	Forum der Letteren
0015-850X	Forum des Praktischen Arztes
0015-8518	Forum for Modern Language Studies
0015-8526	Forum for the Advancement of Toxicology in Colleges of Pharmacy. Newsletter *changed to* Forum for the Advancement of Toxicology
0015-8534	Forum Haus Ortlohn. Freundesbrief
0015-8542	Forum of Education
0015-8550	Forum on Public Affairs†
0015-8577	Forumeer
0015-8585	Foervaltningsraettslig Tidskrift
0015-8593	Forward *changed to* Media Spectrum
0015-8615	Forward *changed to* Civil Aviation in Pakistan: Half-Yearly Newsletter
0015-8623	Forward in Erie *changed to* Forward
0015-8631	Forward in Europe *changed to* Council of Europe Forum
0015-864X	Forward Markets Bulletin
0015-8658	Forward Trends *see* 0305-7526
0015-8666	Forza 7
0015-8682	Foto
0015-8690	Foto-Film-Ton
0015-8704	Foto-Kino Revija
0015-8712	Foto-Magazin
0015-8720	Foto Notiziario
0015-8755	Foto & Film Prisma†
0015-8798	Fotografernet
0015-8801	Fotografia *see* 0324-8453
0015-881X	Fotografia Universal
0015-8828	Fotografie
0015-8836	Fotografie
0015-8844	Fotohaendler *see* 0340-6644
0015-8852	Fotohandel
0015-8879	Fotokino-Magazin
0015-8895	Foton
0015-8909	Fotonyheterna
0015-8933	Foundation Facts
0015-8941	Foundation for Reformation Research. Bulletin of the Library *changed to* Sixteenth Century Bibliography
0015-895X	Foundation for Reformation Research. Newsletter *changed to* Center for Reformation Research. Newsletter
0015-8968	Foundation Law Review
0015-8976	Foundation News
0015-8984	Foundation Time
0015-8992	Foundations
0015-900X	Foundations of Language†
0015-900X	Foundations of Language *see* 0378-4177
0015-9018	Foundations of Physics
0015-9026	F.W.P. Journal *changed to* Founding, Welding, Production Engineering Journal
0015-9034	Foundry *see* 0360-8999
0015-9042	Foundry Trade Journal
0015-9050	Foundry Worker
0015-9069	Fountainhead
0015-9077	Four and Five
0015-9093	Peace and Freedom
0015-9107	Four Quarters
0015-9115	Four States Genealogist
0015-9123	Four Wheeler
0015-914X	Fourier
0015-9174	Fourrure et Peau en Poil
0015-9182	Foursquare World Advance
0015-9190	Fourth Estate
0015-9212	Fox-Report†
0015-9220	Foxfire
0015-9239	Foyers Mixtes
0015-9247	Fra Fysikkens Verden
0015-9255	Fra Haug og Heidni
0015-9271	Fracastoro
0015-928X	Fragen der Freiheit
0015-9298	Fragmenta Balcanica Musei Macedonici Scientiarum Naturalium
0015-9301	Fragmenta Faunistica
0015-931X	Fragmenta Floristica et Geobotanica
0015-9336	Fragments *changed to* Banque Populaire Suisse. Journal
0015-9344	Fragmentarium
0015-9352	Fraktemann
0015-9360	Saadd och Skoerd *see* 0021-7433
0015-9379	Franc-Rire
0015-9387	Francais au Nigeria
0015-9395	Francais dans le Monde
0015-9409	Francais Moderne
0015-9417	France/Loisirs†
0015-9425	France-Cuir†
0015-9433	France-Theatre
0015-9441	France a Table†
0015-9476	France-Algerie†
0015-9484	France Alimentaire
0015-9506	France Catholique *changed to* France Catholique-Ecclesia
0015-9530	France. Commissariat General au Tourisme. Bulletin Mensual de Statistique du Tourisme *changed to* France. Secretariat d'Etat au Tourisme. Statistiques du Tourisme
0015-9549	France Dimanche
0015-9557	Societe d'Edition de Periodiques Sportifs
0015-9565	France Graphique
0015-9573	France Horlogere
0015-959X	France Informations
0015-9603	France. Institut National de la Sante et de la Recherche Medicale. Bulletin *changed to* France. Institut National de la Sante et de la Recherche Medicale. Bulletin d'Information
0015-962X	France Medicale†
0015-9646	France. Ministere de l'Agriculture. Bulletin Technique d'Information (1945) *changed to* France. Ministere de l'Agriculture. Bulletin Technique d'Information
0015-9654	France. Ministere de l'Economie et des Finances. Statistiques et Etudes Financieres *changed to* France. Ministere de l'Economie et des Finances. Statistiques et Etudes Financieres. Finance Publique. Serie Bleue
0015-9670	France Mutualite
0015-9689	France Peche
0015-9697	France Pharmacie
0015-9700	France-Pologne, Peuples Amis
0015-9719	France. Ministere de la Defense Nationale. Bulletin d'Information Technique et Scientifique
0015-9727	France. Ministere de la Defense Nationale. Bulletin Officiel
0015-9735	France. Secretariat d'Etat a la Marine. Bulletin d'Information de la Marine Nationale
0015-9743	Problemes Politiques et Sociaux
0015-9751	France-U.S.A
0015-9786	Francis Bolen's Newsletter
0015-9794	Franciscaans Leven
0015-9808	Franciscan
0015-9816	Franciscan Herald
0015-9840	Franciscana
0015-9867	Franco-British Trade Review *changed to* Info
0015-9875	Franco Vida†
0015-9905	Frankenland

ISSN	Title
0015-9921	Frankford News Gleaner
0015-993X	Frankfurter Blaetter fuer Heimatvertriebene
0015-9964	Frankfurter Gastronomie
0015-9972	Frankfurter Handwerk†
0015-9980	Frankfurter Hausfrauen Zeitung†
0015-9999	Frankfurter Hefte
0016-0008	Frankfurter Lehrerblatt†
0016-0024	Frankfurter Wochenschau
0016-0032	Franklin Institute. Journal
0016-0040	Franklin Township Sentinel
0016-0059	Franse Boek *changed to* Rapports Franse Boek
0016-0067	Franziskanische Studien
0016-0075	Investment Survey of Warrants *changed to* F R A Warrant Service
0016-0083	Fraser's Circular
0016-0105	Fraternal Monitor
0016-0113	Fraternity Month†
0016-0121	Frau
0016-013X	Frau im Beruf
0016-0148	Frau im Leben
0016-0180	Frau und Mutter
0016-0202	Frau und Politik
0016-0210	Die Frau von Heute
0016-0229	Frauen der Ganzen Welt
0016-0237	Der Frauenarzt
0016-0245	Frauenkulter *changed to* Frau und Kultur
0016-0288	Fred och Frihet
0016-0296	Freddo
0016-030X	Free China Review
0016-0318	Free China Weekly
0016-0326	Free Church Chronicle
0016-0334	Free Church of Scotland. Monthly Record
0016-0342	Free Enterprise *changed to* American Patriot
0016-0350	Free Labour World
0016-0369	Free Lance
0016-0377	Free-Lance Report
0016-0393	Free News & Feature Service
0016-0415	Free Press
0016-0423	Boston Free Press†
0016-0431	Free Press Weekly Report on Farming *see* 0317-8552
0016-044X	Free Ranger Inter-Tribal News Service *changed to* Alternative Media Magazine
0016-0458	Free State Libraries
0015-0474	Free Trader†
0015-0504	Freedom
0016-0512	Freedom & Union†
0016-0520	Freedom at Issue
0016-0547	Freedom First
0016-0555	Freedom Magazine
0016-0571	Freedom of Vision
0016-061X	Freedomways
0016-0644	Freeland†
0016-0652	Freeman
0016-0660	Freemason
0016-0679	Freeport Memorial Library. News Bulletin†
0016-0687	Freethinker
0016-0695	Freezer Provisioning and Portion Control *see* 0192-2807
0016-0709	Freiburger Studentenzeitung
0016-0717	Freiburger Universitaetsblaetter
0016-0725	Freiburger Zeitschrift fuer Philosophie und Theologie
0016-075X	Freie Lehrerstimme
0016-0768	Freie Presse-Korrespondenz
0016-0776	Freie Religion
0016-0784	Die Freie Wohnungswirtschaft
0016-0792	F D P Informationsdienst
0016-0806	Freies Bayern
0016-0814	Freies Leben
0016-0830	Freigeistige Aktion *changed to* Der Humanist
0016-0849	Freight
0016-0857	Freight *changed to* Commercial Transport
0016-0857	Freight *changed to* Freight World
0016-0865	Freight & Container Transportation
0016-0873	Freight Management
0016-0881	Freight News *changed to* Freight News Weekly
0016-089X	Freighter Travel News
0016-0903	Freiheitlicher Oberoesterreichischer Landeslehrer Verein. Zeitschrift *changed to* Freiheitlicher Oberoesterreichischer Lehrerverein. Zeitschrift
0016-0911	Die Freiheitsglocke
0016-092X	Der Freiwillige
0016-0938	Freizeit-Mode *see* 0340-739X
0016-0946	Der Freizeitgaertner
0016-0954	Fremdenverkehr-Reiseland-Oesterreich *changed to* Reiseland Oesterreich
0016-0962	Fremdenverkehr *see* 0342-4774
0016-0970	Fremdsprachen
0016-0997	Fremonitor
0016-1004	Fremont Schools
0016-1012	Fremsyn
0016-1020	Fremtiden
0016-1039	French-American Commerce
0016-1047	French Canadian and Acadian Genealogical Review
0016-1071	French Historical Studies
0016-108X	French Notes & Queries†
0016-1098	French Patents Abstracts
0016-1101	French Railway Techniques
0016-111X	French Review
0016-1136	Frequenz
0016-1144	Freres d'Armes
0016-1152	Fresenius' Zeitschrift fuer Analytische Chemie
0016-1160	Fresno County Medical Society. Bulletin
0016-1187	Freundin
0016-1209	Freyr
0016-1217	Fri Koepenskap
0016-1225	Friar Magazine†
0016-1233	Friday Flash
0016-1268	Friend
0016-1276	Friend of Animals
0016-1284	Friend O'Wildlife
0016-1292	Friendly Companion
0016-1314	Friendly World†
0016-1322	Friends Journal
0016-1330	Friends of the San Bernardino County Library. News Letter
0016-1349	Friends of Youth Newsletter *changed to* Target
0016-1357	Friends' Quarterly
0016-1365	Friends World News
0016-1373	Fries Landbouwblad
0016-1381	Friesch Rundvee-Stamboek. Mededelingen *changed to* Friese Veefokkerij
0016-1403	Friesia
0016-1411	Frigotechnica *changed to* Frigotherma
0016-142X	Frihet
0016-1438	Frimaerkesamleren
0016-1446	Fripounet
0016-1454	Friseurhandwerk Friseurspiegel
0016-1470	Friseurwelt
0016-1489	Frisur *see* 0323-410X
0016-1500	Fritidsgaarden†
0016-1519	Fritt Kjoepmannskap
0016-1527	Fritzsche-D & O Library Bulletin
0016-1535	Friuli Medico
0016-1543	Foersvarsforskningsreferat
0016-156X	Der Froehliche Kreis
0016-1586	From Italy
0016-1594	From Italy Clothing *see* 0016-1586
0016-1608	From New York†
0016-1616	From Nine to Five
0016-1624	From the California State Librarian†
0016-1632	From the State Capitals. Agriculture and Food Products†
0016-1640	From the State Capitals. Airport Construction and Financing†
0016-1659	From the State Capitals. Civil Defense†
0016-1667	From the State Capitals. Federal Action Affecting the States†
0016-1675	From the State Capitals. Fire Administration†
0016-1683	From the State Capitals. Fish and Game Regulation†
0016-1691	From the State Capitals. General Bulletin†
0016-1705	From the State Capitals. Highway Financing and Construction†
0016-1713	From the State Capitals. Housing and Redevelopment†
0016-1721	From the State Capitals. Industrial Development†
0016-173X	From the State Capitals. Institutional Building†
0016-1748	From the State Capitals. Insurance Regulation†
0016-1756	From the State Capitals. Judicial Administration†
0016-1764	From the State Capitals. Juvenile Delinquency and Family Relations†
0016-1772	From the State Capitals. Labor Relations†
0016-1780	From the State Capitals. Liquor Control†
0016-1799	From the State Capitals. Merchandising†
0016-1802	From the State Capitals. Milk Control†
0016-1810	From the State Capitals. Motor Vehicle Regulation†
0016-1829	From the State Capitals. Off-Street Parking†
0016-1837	From the State Capitals. Parks and Recreation Trends†
0016-1845	From the State Capitals. Personnel Management†
0016-1853	From the State Capitals. Police Administration†
0016-1861	From the State Capitals. Public Assistance and Welfare Trends†
0016-187X	From the State Capitals. Public Health†
0016-1888	From the State Capitals. Public Utilities†
0016-1896	From the State Capitals. Racial Relations†
0016-190X	From the State Capitals. School Construction†
0016-1926	From the State Capitals. Sewage and Waste Disposal†
0016-1934	From the State Capitals. Small Loans, Sales Finance, Banking†
0016-1942	From the State Capitals. Taxes - Local Non-Property†
0016-1950	From the State Capitals. Tourist Business Promotion†
0016-1969	From the State Capitals. Unemployment Compensation†
0016-1977	From the State Capitals. Urban Transit and Bus Transportation†
0016-1985	From the State Capitals. Wage-Hour Regulation†
0016-1993	From the State Capitals. Water Supply†
0016-2000	From the State Capitals. Workmen's Compensation†
0016-2027	Front
0016-2043	Front Page Detective
0016-2078	Frontier†
0016-2086	Frontier†
0016-2094	Frontier
0016-2108	Frontier News
0016-2116	Frontier Nursing Service. Quarterly Bulletin
0016-2132	Frontiera
0016-2159	Frontiers
0016-2167	Frontiers of Plant Science
0016-2175	Frontlijn
0016-2183	Frontpage
0016-2191	Frozen Food Age
0016-2205	Frozen Foods
0016-2213	Confructa
0016-2221	Fruechte und Gemuese
0016-2248	Fruit Belge
0016-2256	Fruit Trades Journal
0016-2264	Fruit of the Vine
0016-2272	Fruit Varieties and Horticultural Digest *see* 0091-3642
0016-2280	Fruit World and Market Grower
0016-2299	Fruits
0016-2302	Fruitteelt
0016-2310	Frutticoltura
0016-2329	Ftiziologia *changed to* Revista de Igiena, Bacteriologie, Virusologie, Parazitologie, Pneumoftiziologie. Pneumoftiziologie
0016-2353	Fuehrungskraefte Foerdern†
0016-2361	Fuel
0016-237X	Ful-, Orr-, Gegegyogyaszat
0016-2388	Fuel Abstracts and Current Titles *see* 0140-6701
0016-240X	Fules
0016-2418	Fueloil and Oil Heat *see* 0148-9801
0016-2426	Fuer Alle
0016-2434	Fuer Arbeit und Besinnung
0016-2442	Fuer Heute
0016-2450	Fuer Sie
0016-2469	Fuerstenfelder Grenzlandecho
0016-2477	Fuerza Nueva
0016-2485	Revista de las Fuerzas Armadas
0016-2493	Fuji Bank Bulletin
0016-2507	Keio University. Fujihara Memorial Faculty of Engineering. Proceedings. *changed to* Keio Engineering Reports
0016-2515	Fujitsu
0016-2523	Fujitsu Scientific & Technical Journal
0016-2531	Red Double-Barred Cross
0016-254X	Fukuoka Acta Medica
0016-2558	Fukuoka District Meteorological Observatory. Unusual Meteorological Report
0016-2566	Fukuoka District Meteorological Observatory. Technical Times
0016-2574	Fukuoka Prefecture. Monthly Report of Meteorology
0016-2582	Fukushima Medical Journal
0016-2590	Fukushima Journal of Medical Science
0016-2604	Fulcrum
0016-2612	Fuldaer Geschichtsblaetter
0016-2620	Full Cry
0016-2639	Filmmuseum-Cinemateek *changed to* Filmmuseum-Cinemateek-Journaal
0016-2655	Fun for Middlers *changed to* Rainbow
0016-2663	Functional Analysis and Its Applications
0016-2671	Fund Guide Internationak *changed to* Portfolio and Fund Guide International
0016-268X	Fund Raising Management
0016-2698	Fundacion Jimenez Diaz. Boletin
0016-2701	Fundacion John Boulton. Boletin Historico
0016-271X	Fundacion Roux-Ocefa. Archivos
0016-2728	Fundament
0016-2736	Fundamenta Mathematicae
0016-2744	Fundamentalist
0016-2760	FundScope†
0016-2779	Die Fundstelle
0016-2787	Funeral Forum
0016-2809	Funeral Service Journal
0016-2817	Funk Fachhaendler
0016-2825	Funk-Technik
0016-2841	Funkschau
0016-285X	Funktsional'nyi Analiz i Ego Prilozheniya
0016-2876	Fuoco
0016-2884	Fur Age Weekly
0016-2892	Fur and Feather, Rabbits and Rabbit Keeping *changed to* Fur and Feather
0016-2906	Fur & Feathers
0016-2914	Fur Bulletin
0016-2922	Fur-Fish-Game
0016-2930	Fur Market Review *changed to* Fur Review
0016-2949	Fur Parade *changed to* Fur Parade International
0016-2957	Fur and Leather Review *changed to* Fur Review
0016-2965	Fur Taker
0016-2973	Fur Trade Journal of Canada *see* 0381-8535
0016-3007	Home Furnishing†
0016-3015	Furnishing World *see* 0007-9278
0016-304X	Furniture Design & Manufacturing
0016-3058	Furniture History
0016-3066	Furniture News *see* 0194-360X
0016-3074	Furniture South
0016-3082	Furniture Warehouseman *see* 0092-7449
0016-3090	Furniture Workers Press
0016-3104	Furniture World and Furniture Buyer and Decorator
0016-3112	Furrow
0016-3120	Furrow

ISSN INDEX

ISSN	Title
0016-3139	Fuersorger
0016-3155	Fusion
0016-3171	Fusion Facts†
0016-318X	Fusion Facts†
0016-321X	Fussball-Jugend
0016-3228	Der Fussballtrainer
0016-3236	Fussboden-Zeitung
0016-3244	Futur†
0016-3252	Futura
0016-3260	Future
0016-3287	Futures
0016-3295	Futures Market Service
0016-3317	Futurist
0016-3325	Futuro
0016-3341	Futurum†
0016-335X	4H-Journalen
0016-3376	Fyzika ve Skole *changed to* Matematika a Fyzika ve Skole
0016-3384	Fysioterapeuten
0016-3392	Fysisk Tidsskrift
0016-3406	G A
0016-3414	G A O Review
0016-3422	G A T F Newsletter†
0016-3449	G C A Newsletter *changed to* Voice for Girls
0016-3457	G D I Information
0016-3465	G D I Test Universal *see* 0016-3457
0016-3473	G D I Topics *changed to* Brennpunkte
0016-3481	G. D. R. Peace Council. Information
0016-349X	G D R Review
0016-3503	G. E. N
0016-3511	G F M-Mitteilungen zur Markt- und Absatzforschung†
0016-3511	G F M-Mitteilungen zur Markt- und Absatzforschung *changed to* Marktforschung
0016-3538	G I T
0016-3554	G L C A Newsletter†
0016-3562	G L V Mitteilungen
0016-3570	GmbH-Rundschau
0016-3597	G O†
0016-3600	G P *see* 0002-838X
0016-3619	G R A Reporter
0016-3627	G S N. Gesneriad Saintpaulia News
0016-3635	Grossmont Educator *changed to* G E A Educator
0016-3651	Wasser/Abwasser *changed to* Wasser/Abwasser-G W F
0016-366X	G W: George Washington University Magazine *changed to* G W Times
0016-3678	Gaangsport
0016-3694	Gabriel
0016-3708	Gabriele
0016-3716	Gaceta
0016-3724	Gaceta
0016-3759	Gaceta de la Universidad
0016-3767	Gaceta Economica
0016-3775	Gaceta Hipica
0016-3783	Gaceta Ilustrada
0016-3791	Honduras. Corte Suprema de Justicia. Gaceta Judicial
0016-3805	Gaceta Matematica
0016-3813	Gaceta Medica de Mexico
0016-3821	Gaceta Medica Espanola
0016-383X	Gaceta Militar y Naval
0016-3848	Gaceta Politecnica
0016-3856	Gaceta Pre Militar†
0016-3864	Gaceta Rural
0016-3880	Gacetilla Agricola de Holanda†
0016-3899	Gacetilla Austral
0016-3902	Garten- und Freizeitmarkt
0016-3910	Gaiato
0016-3929	Gairm
0016-3945	Musical Instruments News *changed to* Music Trade in Japan
0016-3953	Gakushuin Economic Papers
0016-397X	Gala *changed to* Gala International
0016-3988	Galamukani!
0016-3996	Galaxia
0016-4003	Galaxy
0016-4011	Galencia Acta
0016-402X	Galeon
0016-4038	Galerie *changed to* Arts-Magazine
0016-4046	Galerie Raymond Creuze. Bulletin
0016-4054	Galesburg Labor News
0016-4070	Gallagher Report
0016-4089	Gallaudet Today
0016-4097	Galleria
0016-4119	Gallia
0016-4127	Gallia Prehistoire
0016-4143	Der Galneukirchner Bote
0016-4151	El Gallo News
0016-416X	Gallo
0016-4178	Galloway News
0016-4186	Galloway Times†
0016-4194	Gallup Opinion Index
0016-4216	Galpakabita
0016-4224	Galvano *changed to* Galvano-Organo-Traitements de Surface
0016-4240	Galvanotecnica
0016-4259	Gam on Yachting
0016-4275	Gambit
0016-4283	Gambit
0016-4313	Gamecock
0016-4321	Gamekeeper and Countryside
0016-433X	Gamekeepers' Gazette *changed to* W A G B I Magazine
0016-4356	Gamesletter *see* 0016-4364
0016-4364	Gamesman
0016-4380	Gamma
0016-4402	Gan Vanof
0016-4437	Gandhi Marg (English Edition)†
0016-4453	Gangan
0016-4461	Ganganatha Jha Research Institute. Journal *changed to* Ganganatha Jha Kendriya Sanskrit Vidyapeetha. Journal
0016-447X	Ganigo
0016-4496	Ophthalmology
0016-4518	Ganmitram
0016-450X	GANN Journal
0016-4518	Ganterie-Vetements de Peau†
0016-4542	Garage & Officina
0016-4550	Garage, Tankstelle und Servicestation *changed to* Tankstelle und Garage
0016-4569	Garcia de Orta
0016-4577	Garden Club of America. Bulletin
0016-4585	Garden Journal†
0016-4585	Garden Journal *changed to* Garden
0016-4593	Garden News
0016-4607	Garden Path
0016-4615	Garden Stater
0016-4623	Garden Supplies Retailer
0016-4631	Garden Writers Bulletin
0016-464X	Gardener
0016-4682	Gardeners Chronicle/Horticultural Trade Journal
0016-4690	Gargoyle
0016-4712	Garment Worker
0016-4720	Garten und Landschaft
0016-4739	Gaertnerischer Fachhandel *see* 0016-3902
0016-4739	Das Gartenamt
0016-4747	Gartenbau
0016-4755	Gartenbau†
0016-4763	Der Gartenbauingenieur
0016-4771	Gartenbauwirtschaft mit Gartenbau Nachrichten *changed to* Gartenbauwirtschaft
0016-478X	Gartenbauwissenschaft
0016-4798	Gartenwelt *changed to* G B und G W - Gaertner Boerse und Gartenwelt
0016-4801	Gary Library Bulletin *changed to* Gary Graphique
0016-4828	Gas
0016-4836	Gas Magazine *see* 0161-4851
0016-4844	Gas Abstracts
0016-4852	Gas and Oil Power *see* 0308-4795
0016-4860	Gas & Sanitair Mercuur†
0016-4879	Gas Appliance Merchandising
0016-4887	Gas Chromatography Abstracts *see* 0301-388X
0016-4895	Gas Chromatography Literature-Abstracts & Index
0016-4909	Gas Erdgas†
0016-4909	Gas - Erdgas
0016-4925	Gas in Industry and Commerce *changed to* Natural Gas
0016-4933	Gas in Industry *see* 0194-2468
0016-495X	Gas Liquefatti - le Apparecchiature
0016-4968	Gas Processing/Canada *see* 0319-5759
0016-4976	Gas Scope
0016-4984	Gas Marketing *see* 0308-7026
0016-4992	Gas Showroom *see* 0308-7026
0016-500X	Gas Turbine Magazine *see* 0149-4147
0016-5018	Gas, Wasser, Waerme
0016-5026	Gas World
0016-5034	Gas-Beispiele†
0016-5042	Gasoline News
0016-5069	Monthly Gasoline Stand
0016-5077	Gastro-Enterologie Quotidienne
0016-5085	Gastroenterology
0016-5093	Gastroenterology Abstracts and Citations†
0016-5107	Gastrointestinal Endoscopy
0016-5115	Gastronomie *changed to* Plaisirs
0016-5123	Gastronomie-Rundschau
0016-5131	Gastronomie und Gastlichkeit *changed to* Tafelfreuden
0016-5158	Gastwirt
0016-5166	Gastwirt und Hotelier *changed to* D G Deutsche Gaststaette/Deutsche Hotel-Zeitung Gastwirt und Hotelier
0016-5182	Gasverwendung†
0016-5190	Gateway
0016-5204	Gateway
0016-5239	Gaudeamus
0016-5247	Gaudeamus
0016-5263	Gaveshana†
0016-5271	Gawein *changed to* Gedrag
0016-5298	Gay Scene
0016-5301	Gayana: Botanica
0016-531X	Gayana: Zoologica
0016-5328	Gaz d'Aujourd'Hui
0016-5352	Gaz, Woda i Technika Sanitarna
0016-5360	Gazdasag
0016-5379	Gazer
0016-5395	Gazeta Cukrownicza
0016-5409	Gazeta da Farmacia
0016-5425	Gazeta de Pinheiros
0016-5433	Gazeta Matematica. Serie A *changed to* Gazeta Matematica
0016-5441	Gazetta Matematica. Serie B *changed to* Gazeta Matematica
0016-545X	Gazeta Medica da Bahia†
0016-5468	Gazeta Mobil
0016-5484	Gazette†
0016-5492	Gazette
0016-5506	Gazette Apicole
0016-5514	Gazette de la Region du Nord
0016-5522	Association des Archivistes Francais. Gazette des Archives
0016-5530	Gazette des Beaux-Arts
0016-5530	Gazette des Beaux Arts
0016-5557	Gazette Medicale de France
0016-5565	Gazette Numismatique Suisse
0016-5573	Gazette Officielle du Tourisme
0016-5581	Gazovaya Promyshlennost'
0016-559X	Gazzetta Antiquaria
0016-5603	Gazzetta Chimica Italiana
0016-5611	Gazzetta Commerciale
0016-5638	Gazzetta delle Arti
0016-5646	Gazzetta Farmaceutica†
0016-5654	Gazzetta Filatelica
0016-5662	Gazzetta Internazionale di Medicina e Chirurgia
0016-5670	Gazzetta Medica Italiana *changed to* Gazzetta Medica Italiana-Aggiornamenti Clinicoterapeutici
0016-5697	Gazzetta Sanitaria
0016-5700	Rilancio
0016-5719	Gazzettino della Scuola
0016-5727	Gebaeudigereiniger-Handwerk *changed to* Rationell Reinigen
0016-5735	Gebetsapostolat und Seelsorge
0016-5743	Gebrauchsgraphik *see* 0302-9794
0016-5751	Geburtshilfe und Frauenheilkunde
0016-576X	Dienst am Wort - Gedanken zur Sonntagspredigt
0016-5778	Gedeeld Domein
0016-5786	Gedistilleerd, Wijn, Bier en Frisdranken†
0016-5794	Gefaehrdetenhilfe
0016-5808	Gefaehrliche Ladung
0016-5816	Die Gefiederte Welt
0016-5824	Gefluegel-Boerse
0016-5832	Geflugel und Kleinvieh *changed to* Schweizerische Gefluegelzeitung
0016-5840	Gegenbaurs Morphologisches Jahrbuch
0016-5859	Gegenwart
0016-5867	Gegenwart
0016-5875	Gegenwartskunde
0016-5883	Gehoert-Gelesen
0016-5913	Geisinger Medical Center. Bulletin
0016-5921	Geist und Leben
0016-593X	Surgery
0016-5956	Gekkan Kibbutz *changed to* Cooperative Life
0016-5964	Monthly Journal of Gasoline Service Stations
0016-5972	Petroleum Monthly
0016-5980	Pharmaceuticals Monthly
0016-5999	Gelatiere Italiano
0016-6006	Die Gelben Hefte
0016-6022	Geliotekhnika
0016-6030	Gem†
0016-6049	Gemeenteblad van Amsterdam
0016-6057	Gemeentefinancien *changed to* B & G
0016-6065	Gemeenteleven
0016-6073	Die Gemeinde
0016-609X	Gemeindebote
0016-6103	Gemeindebote *changed to* Kirche in Marburg
0016-6111	Gemeindebrief
0016-612X	Die Gemeindekasse
0016-6146	Gemeindekurier
0016-6154	Evangelische Pfarrgemeinde A.B. Wien-Favoriten-Christuskirche. Gemeindebrief
0016-6170	Gemeindeverwaltung in Rheinland - Pfalz
0016-6200	Gemeinsames Amtsblatt des Landes Baden-Wuerttemberg
0016-6219	Gemeinschaft der Wohnungseigentuemer - Informationen
0016-6227	Gemeinwirtschaft
0016-6235	Gemengde Branche(1948) *changed to* Gemengde Branche(1978)
0016-6243	Gemischtwarenhandel
0016-6251	Gems
0016-626X	Gems & Gemology
0016-6278	Gems and Minerals
0016-6286	Gemuese
0016-6308	Gemueseproduktion *changed to* Industriemaessige Gemueseproduktion Prosit
0016-6316	Genadeklanken
0016-6324	Contemporary Library Trends
0016-6332	Genealogical Helper
0016-6359	Genealogical Magazine of New Jersey
0016-6367	Genealogical Quarterly†
0016-6375	Genealogie
0016-6383	Genealogists' Magazine
0016-6405	Geneologist's Post *changed to* Pennsylvania Traveler-Post
0016-6421	Genealogy Club of America Magazine *see* 0098-7689
0016-643X	Geneeskunde†
0016-643X	Geneeskunde
0016-6448	Geneeskunde en Sport
0016-6464	Geneeskundige Gids†
0016-6472	Genen en Phaenen
0016-6480	General and Comparative Endocrinology
0016-6499	General and Municipal Workers' Union
0016-6502	General Aviation
0016-6510	General Aviation *changed to* General Aviation News: the Green Sheet
0016-6537	General Federation Clubwoman *changed to* G F W C Clubwoman
0016-6545	General Insurance Guide
0016-6553	General Linguistics
0016-657X	Strobotactics†
0016-660X	General Topology and Its Applications *see* 0166-8641
0016-6634	Genesee Valley Buyer *changed to* Purchasing Professional
0016-6642	Genesee Valley Chemunications
0016-6669	Genesis 2
0016-6677	Genetic Psychology Monographs
0016-6685	Genetica Agraria
0016-6693	Genetica Iberica
0016-6707	Genetica
0016-6715	Genetica Polonica

0016-6723 Genetical Research
0016-6731 Genetics
0016-674X Genetics Abstracts
0016-6758 Genetika
0016-6766 Genetika i Selektsiia
0016-6774 Geneve-Afrique†
0016-6812 Genie Civil
0016-6820 Genie Construction
0016-6839 Genie Medical
0016-6847 Genie Rural
0016-6855 Genii-the Conjurors' Magazine
0016-6863 Genio Rurale
0016-6871 Genitori
0016-6898 Genos
0016-6901 Genova
0016-691X Genova Statistica *changed to* Notiziario Statistico Mensile
0016-6928 Genre
0016-6936 Gens Nostra, "Ons Geslacht"
0016-6944 Gente
0016-6952 Gente
0016-6960 Gentes
0016-6979 Gentlemen's Quarterly
0016-6987 Genus
0016-6995 Geobios
0016-7002 Geochemical Journal
0016-7029 Geochemistry International
0016-7037 Geochimica et Cosmochimica Acta
0016-7053 Geocom Bulletin
0016-7061 Geoderma
0016-7088 Geodesy and Aerophotography *see* 0361-4433
0016-7096 Geodeticky a Kartograficky Obzor
0016-710X Geodetski List
0016-7118 Geodezia es Kartografia
0016-7126 Geodeziya i Kartografiya
0016-7134 Geodezja i Kartografia
0016-7142 Geoexploration
0016-7169 Geofisica Internacional
0016-7177 Geofizikai Kozlemenyek
0016-7185 Geoforum
0016-7193 Geograficky Casopis
0016-7207 Geografiya v Shkole
0016-7215 Geografisch Tijdschrift
0016-7223 Geografisk Tidsskrift
0016-7231 Geografiska Annaler *see* 0435-3676
0016-7231 Geografiska Annaler *see* 0435-3684
0016-724X Geografiska Notiser
0016-7266 Geografski Horizont
0016-7274 Geografski Obzornik
0016-7282 Geographia Polonica
0016-7290 Geographica
0016-7312 Geographica Helvetica
0016-7339 Geographical Abstracts B (Biogeography, Climatology & Cartography) *see* 0305-1900
0016-7363 Geographical Analysis
0016-7371 Geographical Association of Nigeria. Journal *see* 0029-0084
0016-738X Geographical Association of Tanzania Journal
0016-7398 Geographical Journal
0016-7401 Geographical Knowledge
0016-741X Geographical Magazine
0016-7428 Geographical Review
0016-7436 Geographical Review of Afghanistan
0016-7444 Geographical Review of Japan
0016-7452 Geographische Berichte
0016-7460 Geographische Rundschau
0016-7479 Geographische Zeitschrift
0016-7487 Geography
0016-7509 Geography Teacher
0016-7517 Geography Teacher
0016-7525 Geokhimiya
0016-7533 Geologia y Metalurgia
0016-7541 Geologic Notes
0016-755X Geologica Bavarica
0016-7568 Geological Magazine
0016-7576 Geological, Mining and Metallurgical Society of India. Bulletin
0016-7584 Geological, Mining and Metallurgical Society of India. Quarterly Journal
0016-7592 Geological Society of America. Abstracts with Programs
0016-7606 Geological Society of America. Bulletin
0016-7614 Geological Society of Australia. Journal
0016-7622 Geological Society of India. Journal
0016-7630 Geological Society of Japan. Journal
0016-7649 Geological Society. Journal
0016-7657 Geological Society of South Africa. Quarterly News Bulletin
0016-7665 Geological Survey of Japan. Bulletin
0016-7673 South Australia. Geological Survey. Bulletin
0016-7681 South Australia. Geological Survey. Report of Investigations
0016-769X Geologicheskii Zhurnal Armenii
0016-7703 Geologichnii Zhurnal
0016-772X Geologicky Pruzkum
0016-7738 Geologicky Zbornik
0016-7746 Geologie en Mijnbouw
0016-7762 Izvestiya Vysshikh Uchebnykh Zavedenii. Seriya Geologiya i Razvedka
0016-7789 Geologija
0016-7797 Geologische Blaetter fuer Nordost-Bayern und Angrenzende Gebiete
0016-7800 Geologische Bundesanstalt, Vienna. Jahrbuch
0016-7843 Geologische Gesellschaft, Vienna. Mitteilungen *changed to* Oesterreichische Geologische Gesellschaft. Mitteilungen
0016-7851 Geologisches Jahrbuch *see* 0341-6429
0016-7851 Geologisches Jahrbuch *see* 0341-6410
0016-7851 Geologisches Jahrbuch *see* 0341-6399
0016-7851 Geologisches Jahrbuch *see* 0341-6402
0016-786X Geologiska Foereningens i Stockholm Foerhandlinger
0016-7878 Geologists' Association. Proceedings
0016-7886 Geologiya i Geofizika
0016-7894 Geologiya Nefti i Gaza
0016-7908 Geologiya Rudnykh Mestorozhdenii
0016-7924 Geoloski Vjesnik
0016-7932 Geomagnetism and Aeronomy
0016-7940 Geomagnetizm i Aeronomiya
0016-7959 Geometra
0016-7967 Geometre
0016-7975 Geominas
0016-7983 Geophysical Abstracts†
0016-8009 Royal Astronomical Society Geophysical Journal
0016-8017 Japan. Meteorological Agency. Geophysical Magazine
0016-8025 Geophysical Prospecting
0016-8033 Geophysics
0016-8041 Leipzig. Universitaet. Geophysikalisches Institut. Veroeffentlichungen. Zweite Serie *changed to* Geophysik und Geologie
0016-8076 George Washington Law Review
0016-8084 Georgetown Dental Journal
0016-8092 Georgetown Law Journal
0016-8106 Georgetown Medical Bulletin
0016-8114 Georgia Journal of Science
0016-8122 Georgia Agricultural Research
0016-8130 Georgia Alumni Record
0016-8149 Georgia AnchorAge
0016-8157 Georgia Augusta
0016-8173 Georgia Business
0016-8181 Georgia C. P. A†
0016-819X Georgia Dental Association. Journal
0016-822X Georgia Engineer
0016-8238 Georgia Entomological Society. Journal
0016-8254 Georgia Farmer†
0016-8262 Georgia Future Farmer
0016-8270 Georgia Game and Fish *changed to* Outdoors in Georgia
0016-8289 Georgia Government Review *see* 0160-323X
0016-8297 Georgia Historical Quarterly
0016-8300 Georgia Law Review
0016-8319 Georgia Librarian
0016-8335 Georgia Nursing
0016-8351 Georgia Professional Engineer
0016-8378 Georgia Rehabilitation News†
0016-8386 Georgia Review
0016-8408 Georgia Social Science Journal
0016-8416 Georgia State Bar Journal
0016-8424 Georgia State University Signal
0016-8432 Georgia Straight
0016-8440 Georgia Tech Alumnus *changed to* Tech Topics
0016-8459 Georgia Tech Engineer *changed to* Exponent
0016-8467 Georgian
0016-8483 Geoscience Documentation
0016-8491 Geotechnical Abstracts
0016-8505 Geotechnique
0016-8521 Geotectonics
0016-853X Geotektonika
0016-8548 Geotektonische Forschungen
0016-8556 Geotimes
0016-8564 Geotitles Weekly
0016-8572 Gep
0016-8580 Gepgyartastechnologia
0016-8599 Geraniums around the World
0016-8610 Gereformeerd Theologisch Tijdschrift
0016-8629 Gereformeerde Kerken in Noord-Brabant en Limburg. Kerkblad
0016-8637 Gerencia
0016-8688 Geriatrics Digest†
0016-8696 Gerlands Beitraege zur Geophysik
0016-870X Gerling-Informationen fuer Geschaeftsfreunde†
0016-8718 German American Trade News *see* 0192-0103
0016-8726 German Constructions†
0016-8742 German Exporter *see* 0033-0876
0016-8769 German International
0016-8777 German Life and Letters
0016-8785 German Medical Monthly†
0016-8793 German News
0016-8807 German Patents Abstracts
0016-8823 German Postal Specialist
0016-884X Philosophy and History
0016-8858 German Tribune
0016-8866 Germana Esperanta Fervojista Asocio. Bulteno
0016-8882 Germanic Notes
0016-8890 Germanic Review
0016-8904 Germanisch-Romanische Monatsschrift
0016-8912 Germanistik
0016-8920 Germantown Courier
0016-8939 Crier
0016-8963 Germany Stamp News
0016-898X Gerontologia *see* 0304-324X
0016-8998 Gerontologia Clinica†
0016-8998 Gerontologia Clinica *see* 0304-324X
0016-9005 Gerontologie
0016-9013 Gerontologist
0016-9021 Geschaeftsmann und Christ
0016-903X Geschaeftsmappe fuer Gemeinden und Standesaemter†
0016-9048 Geschaeftsreisen *changed to* Verband
0016-9056 Geschichte in Wissenschaft und Unterricht
0016-9064 Geschichten aus dem Wienerwald *changed to* W Wintern
0016-9072 Geschichtsunterricht und Staatsburgerkunde
0016-9080 Gesellschaft fuer Natur- und Voelkerkunde Ostasiens. Nachrichten
0016-9099 Gesellschaft und Politik
0016-9102 Gesellschaftspolitische Kommentare
0016-9129 Gesetz- und Verordnungsblatt fuer Schleswig-Holstein
0016-9145 Gesher
0016-9153 Gesichertes Leben
0016-9161 Gesnerus
0016-920X Gesta
0016-9218 Gestions Hospitalieres
0016-9226 Gesund durch Sauna†
0016-9234 Gesund Leben
0016-9242 Gesunde Mensch†
0016-9250 Gesundes Leben
0016-9269 Gesundheit in Betrieb und Familie
0016-9277 Gesundheits-Ingenieur *see* 0172-8199
0016-9285 Gesundheitsnachrichten
0016-9293 Gesundheitspolitik†
0016-9307 Gesundheitspolitische Umschau
0016-9315 Gesundheitswesen und Desinfektion *see* 0340-997X
0016-9323 Getraenke-Industrie
0016-9331 Getraenkehandel
0016-934X Getroster Tag
0016-9366 Gettysburg Seminary Bulletin
0016-9374 Geuzen Penning†
0016-9390 Gewaltfreie Aktion
0016-9412 Gewerbliche Rundschau *changed to* Unternehmungsfuehrung im Gewerbe
0016-9420 Gewerblicher Rechtsschutz und Urheberrecht
0016-9439 Gewerkschafter im Handwerk
0016-9447 Gewerkschaftliche Monatshefte
0016-9455 Gewerkschaftliche Rundschau
0016-9463 Gewerkschafts Presse
0016-9471 Das Gewissen
0016-948X Geyer's Dealer Topics
0016-9498 Gezinsblad
0016-9501 Gezond Limburg
0016-951X Gezondheid en Ziekenfonds†
0016-9528 Gezondheidszorg†
0016-9536 Ghana Geographical Association. Bulletin
0016-9544 Ghana Journal of Science†
0016-9552 Ghana Library Journal
0016-9560 Ghana Medical Journal
0016-9579 Ghana News
0016-9587 Ghana Review
0016-9595 Ghana Teacher's Journal *changed to* Ghana Journal of Education
0016-9609 Ghana Today *changed to* New Ghana
0016-9617 Ghana Workers' Bulletin *changed to* T U C Newsletter
0016-9625 Gheoponica
0016-9633 Ghost Dance
0016-965X Giardino Fiorito
0016-9668 Gib Acht
0016-9676 Stamp Monthly
0016-9684 Gibson Report
0016-9706 Gidroliznaya i Lesokhimicheskaya Promyshlennost'
0016-9714 Gidrotekhnicheskoe Stroitel'stvo
0016-9722 Gidrotekhnika i Melioratsiya
0016-9730 Gids
0016-9757 Giervalk-Gerfaut
0016-9765 Giesserei
0016-9773 Giesserei-Erfahrungsaustausch
0016-9781 Giesserei-Praxis
0016-979X Giesserei Rundschau
0016-9803 Giessereitechnik
0016-982X Gieterij
0016-9846 Gift & Tableware Reporter *see* 0163-2175
0016-9854 Gift Buyer International
0016-9862 Gifted Child Quarterly *see* 0098-7565
0016-9870 Gifted Pupil
0016-9889 Gifts & Decorative Accessories
0016-9900 Gigiena i Sanitariya
0016-9919 Gigiena Truda i Professional'nye Zabolevaniya
0016-9935 Technology and Industries†
0016-9943 Gil Vicente†
0016-9951 Gilbert and Sullivan Journal
0016-9986 Gildenweg
0016-9994 Giligia†
0017-0003 Gimlaoth
0017-0011 Ginekologia Polska
0017-002X Jugoslavenska Ginekologija i Opstetricija
0017-0038 Ginger
0017-0046 Ginnasta
0017-0054 Giocattoli
0017-0062 Gioia
0017-0070 Giornale Botanico Italiano
0017-0089 Giornale Critico della Filosofia Italiana
0017-0097 Giornale degli Economisti e Annali di Economia
0017-0100 Giornale degli Uccelli
0017-0119 Giornale dei Distillatori
0017-0127 Giornale dei Genitori
0017-0135 Giornale degli Allevatori
0017-0143 Giornale del Bieticoltore
0017-0151 Commercio Turismo
0017-016X Giornale del Genio Civile
0017-0186 Giornale del Mezzogiorno
0017-0208 Giornale della Cogne
0017-0216 Giornale della Libreria
0017-0224 Giornale dell'Arteriosclerosi†
0017-0224 Giornale dell'Arteriosclerosi
0017-0232 Giornale dello Spettacolo

ISSN INDEX 991

ISSN	Title
0017-0240	Giornale dell'Officina
0017-0259	Giornale di Barga
0017-0267	Giornale di Batteriologia, Virologia e Immunologia ed Annali dell'Ospedale Maria Vittoria di Torino *see* 0301-1453
0017-0267	Giornale di Batteriologia, Virologia e Immunologia ed Annali dell'Ospedale Maria Vittoria di Torino *see* 0301-1445
0017-0275	Giornale di Clinica Medica
0017-0283	Giornale di Fisica
0017-0291	Giornale di Geologia
0017-0305	Giornale di Gerontologia
0017-0313	Giornale di Igiene e Medicina Preventiva
0017-0321	Giornale di Malattie Infettive e Parassitarie
0017-033X	Giornale di Mathematiche di Battaglini
0017-0364	Giornale di Medicina Militare
0017-0380	Giornale di Microbiologia
0017-0399	Giornale di Psichiatria e di Neuropatologia†
0017-0429	Giornale Economico
0017-0437	Giornale Italiano delle Malattie del Torace
0017-0445	Giornale Italiano di Chemioterapia
0017-0453	Giornale Italiano di Chirurgia
0017-0461	Giornale Italiano di Filologia
0017-047X	Giornale Italiano di Patologia e Scienze Affini
0017-0496	Giornale Storico della Letteratura Italiana
0017-050X	Giornale Storico della Lunigiana e del Territorio Lucense
0017-0518	Giornalismo Europeo
0017-0526	Giovane Critica
0017-0534	Giovane Montagna
0017-0542	Gioventu Evangelica
0017-0550	Girard Home News
0017-0569	Girl Crusader
0017-0577	Girl Scout Leader
0017-0593	Girls' Brigade Gazette
0017-0615	Gissing Newsletter
0017-0623	Giurisprudenza Italiana
0017-0631	Giustizia Civile
0017-064X	Giustizia Nuova
0017-0658	Giustizia Penale
0017-0682	Gjuteriet
0017-0690	Glaces et Verres†
0017-0704	Glacier Francais
0017-0712	Glaciological Notes *see* 0149-1776
0017-0720	Glad Tidings
0017-0739	Glad Tidings of Good Things
0017-0747	Glamour
0017-0755	Glarmestertidende
0017-0763	Glas-Email-Keramo-Technik†
0017-0771	Glas Istre
0017-078X	Glas och Porslin
0017-0798	Glas Omladine
0017-0801	Glas Podravine
0017-081X	Glas Podrinja
0017-0828	Glas Trebinja
0017-0852	Glasforum
0017-0860	Glasgow Chamber of Commerce. The Journal
0017-0879	Glasgow Herald Trade Review†
0017-0887	Glasgow Illustrated
0017-0895	Glasgow Mathematical Journal
0017-0917	Glasgow University Guardian
0017-0925	Glasnik
0017-0933	Glasnik Advokatske Komore Vojvodine
0017-0941	Glasnik Hemijskog Drustva
0017-095X	Glasnik Matematicki
0017-0976	Glasnik Poljoprivredne Proizvodnje, Prerade i Plasmana
0017-0984	Glass
0017-0992	Glass Age
0017-100X	Glass and Ceramics
0017-1018	Glass Digest
0017-1026	Glass Industry
0017-1042	Glass, Potteries and Ceramic Journal *changed to* Glass, Potteries and Ceramic Annual
0017-1050	Glass Technology
0017-1069	Glass Workers News
0017-1077	Glass Workshop
0017-1085	Glastechnische Berichte
0017-1093	Glasteknisk Tidskrift
0017-1107	Glaswelt/Deutsche Glaserzeitung
0017-1123	Glaube und Tat
0017-1131	Gleaner *changed to* Rutgers Gleaner
0017-114X	Gleanings in Bee Culture
0017-1166	Gledista
0017-1174	Glenbow†
0017-1182	Glenmary's Challenge
0017-1204	Globe and Laurel
0017-1212	Globe and Mail Report on Business
0017-1220	Globen
0017-1239	Glocke†
0017-1247	Glocke
0017-1263	Glos Nauczycielski
0017-1271	Glossa
0017-1298	Glotta
0017-131X	Gloucestershire Farmer
0017-1336	Giovani in Dialogo
0017-1344	Glowna Biblioteka Lekarska. Biuletyn
0017-1352	Gloxinian
0017-1360	Glucose Informatie†
0017-1379	Glueckauf
0017-1387	Glueckauf-Forschungshefte
0017-1395	Glueckliches Leben-der Stille Weg *changed to* Lebensschutz
0017-1409	Gnade und Herrlichkeit
0017-1417	Gnomon
0017-1425	Gnosis†
0017-1433	Go (Burlingame)
0017-1441	Go (Charlotte)
0017-1476	Go Greyhound
0017-1484	Goa Today
0017-1506	Gobbles
0017-1522	Goetheana Periodico Literario
0017-1549	Goettingische Gelehrte Anzeigen
0017-1557	Gold Bulletin
0017-1573	Gold und Silber
0017-1581	Golden Eye
0017-159X	Golden Magazine *see* 0009-3971
0017-162X	Golden West Purchasor
0017-1638	Di Goldene Keit
0017-1646	Der Goldene Pfennig
0017-1654	Die Sphinx
0017-1670	Goldmanns Mitteilungen fuer den Buchhandel
0017-1689	Goldscmiede Zeitung - European Jeweler und Deutsche Uhrmacherzeitschrift
0017-1697	Goldsmith-Nagan Bond and Money Market Letter
0017-1700	Goleuad
0017-1727	Golf
0017-176X	Golf Digest
0017-1794	Golf Journal
0017-1808	Golf
0017-1816	Golf Monthly
0017-1824	Golf Shop Operations
0017-1832	Golf Singapore Review
0017-1840	Golf Superintendent *see* 0192-3048
0017-1867	Golf/U.S.A†
0017-1883	Golf World
0017-1891	Golf World
0017-1905	Golfdom†
0017-1905	Golfdom *see* 0148-3706
0017-1913	Golfer
0017-1948	Golos Radzimy
0017-1956	Goltdammer's Archiv fuer Strafrecht
0017-1964	Gomitolo
0017-1972	Gong
0017-1999	Gong
0017-2014	Gonubie Gazette *changed to* Times of Gonubie
0017-2022	Good Counsel†
0017-2030	Good Earth
0017-2049	Good Farming†
0017-2073	Good Health *see* 0306-462X
0017-2081	Good Housekeeping
0017-209X	Good Housekeeping
0017-212X	Good News†
0017-2138	Good News *changed to* New York Good News
0017-2146	Good News
0017-2154	Good News Broadcaster
0017-2162	Good News Crusades *changed to* Mountain Movers
0017-2170	Good Packaging
0017-2189	Good Reading *changed to* Good Reading for Everyone
0017-2197	Good Times†
0017-2219	Goodyear Revue†
0017-2227	Gopher Historian *see* 0148-6659
0017-2235	Gopher Music Notes
0017-2243	Gordian
0017-2251	Christian Scholar's Review
0017-226X	Gornik
0017-2278	Gornyi Zhurnal
0017-2286	Gorskostopanska Nauka
0017-2294	Gorteria
0017-2308	Goshen College Bulletin
0017-2332	Gospel Carrier
0017-2340	Gospel Herald
0017-2359	Gospel Messenger
0017-2367	Gospel Standard
0017-2375	Gospel Tidings
0017-2383	Gospel Truth
0017-2391	Gospel Witness
0017-2405	Gospodarka Materialowa
0017-2413	Gospodarka Paliwami i Energia
0017-2421	Gospodarka Planowa
0017-243X	Gospodarka Rybna
0017-2448	Gospodarka Wodna
0017-2456	Gospodarstvo
0017-2480	Gottes Wort
0017-2499	Gottesdienst und Kirchenmusik
0017-2510	Gotteskinder *changed to* Regenbogen
0017-2529	Gouden Sleutels
0017-2537	Gouden Uren
0017-2545	Gould's Position
0017-2553	Gourmet
0017-257X	Government and Opposition
0017-2588	Government Business Worldwide *changed to* Defense & Economy World Report & Survey
0017-2596	Government Contractor
0017-260X	Government Employee Relations Report
0017-2618	Government Equipment Reports *changed to* Defense & Economy World Report & Survey
0017-2626	Government Executive
0017-2642	Government Product News
0017-2650	Government Purchasing Digest *see* 0017-2642
0017-2669	Government Standard
0017-2677	Governmental Research Newsletter *see* 0364-3921
0017-2693	Gown
0017-2707	Gownsman†
0017-2715	Goya
0017-2723	Gozdarski Vestnik
0017-2731	Kirjapainotaito-Graafikko
0017-2758	Gracas do Servo de Deus: Padre Cruz
0017-2774	Gradbeni Vestnik
0017-2782	Grade Teacher *changed to* Instructor and Teacher
0017-2804	Graduate Careers
0017-2812	Graduate Careers in Science and Technology†
0017-2839	Graduate Research in Education and Related Disciplines *changed to* Graduate Research in Urban Education and Related Disciplines
0017-2863	Graffitti†
0017-2871	Grafia *changed to* Druk en Papier
0017-288X	Grafia
0017-2898	Grafica
0017-291X	Grafico
0017-2928	Grafico
0017-2944	Grafiek
0017-2952	Grafische Literatuur Centrale
0017-2960	Grafiscope
0017-2979	Grafisk Faktorstidning
0017-2987	Grafisk Revy *see* 0017-288X
0017-2995	Grafiske Fag
0017-3002	Grafiskt Forum
0017-3029	Grain Age
0017-3045	Grain and Fire
0017-3053	Grain Bulletin†
0017-3061	Grain Market News and Feed Market News *see* 0364-099X
0017-3061	Grain Market News and Feed Market News *see* 0364-2046
0017-307X	Revue Technique Automobile
0017-3088	Gralswelt
0017-310X	Gramophone
0017-3118	Gran Pavese
0017-3126	Gran Tiramolla
0017-3134	Grana
0017-3142	Grande Hotel
0017-3150	Grande Ronde Review
0017-3185	Grani
0017-3207	Granite Cutters Journal
0017-3223	Granma
0017-324X	Granthagar
0017-3258	Grapevine†
0017-3266	Graphia
0017-3274	Graphic Antiquarian
0017-3282	Graphic Arts Abstracts
0017-3290	Graphic Arts Bulletin†
0017-3304	Graphic Arts Buyer
0017-3312	Graphic Arts Monthly and the Printing Industry
0017-3320	Graphic Arts Patent Abstracts†
0017-3339	Graphic Arts Product News†
0017-3347	Graphic Arts Progress *changed to* Graphic Arts Literature Abstracts
0017-3355	Graphic Arts Supplier News *see* 0198-9065
0017-3363	Graphic Arts Unionist *changed to* Union Tabloid
0017-341X	Graphic Trends†
0017-3436	Graphicus
0017-3444	Graphik Werbung und Formgebung *changed to* Graphik
0017-3452	Graphis
0017-3479	Graphische Revue Oesterreichs
0017-3487	Graphs and Notes on the Economic Situation in the Community *changed to* European Economy
0017-3495	Grasas y Aceites
0017-3517	Grass Roots Forum
0017-3525	Grasso Mededelingen *changed to* Grassortiment
0017-3541	Grassroots Editor
0017-3568	Gravure *see* 0163-9234
0017-3576	Gravure Technical Association Bulletin
0017-3584	Gray and Ductile Iron News *see* 0362-0425
0017-3592	Graybar Outlook
0017-3606	Grazhdanskaya Aviatsiya
0017-3630	Great Britain. Central Statistical Office. Statistical News
0017-3657	Great Britain Journal
0017-3665	Great Lakes News Letter
0017-3673	Great Plains Journal
0017-3681	Great Plains National Instructional Television Library Newsletter *changed to* G P Newsletter
0017-369X	Great Speckled Bird†
0017-3711	Greater Indianapolis *changed to* Indianapolis
0017-3754	Greater Milwaukee Dental Bulletin
0017-3762	Delaware Valley Business Fortnight†
0017-3770	Greater Pittsburgh†
0017-3789	Portland Commerce *changed to* Portland Magazine
0017-3797	Greater Rochester Commerce†
0017-3819	Grecia de Ayer, de Hoy y de Siempre
0017-3827	Grecourt Review
0017-3835	Greece and Rome
0017-3851	Greek Bibliography†
0017-386X	Greek Gazette
0017-3886	Greek Observer
0017-3894	Greek Orthodox Theological Review
0017-3916	Greek, Roman and Byzantine Studies
0017-3924	Green and White
0017-3932	Green Book
0017-3940	Green Cross†
0017-3967	Green Island
0017-3975	Green Pyne Leaf
0017-3983	Green Revolution
0017-3991	Green River Current
0017-4009	Green River Review
0017-4017	Green Tree†
0017-4041	Greenfield Review

ISSN INDEX

ISSN	Title
0017-4068	Greenleaf†
0017-4076	Green's Commodity Market Comments
0017-4084	Greensboro Review
0017-4092	Greensward
0017-4106	Greeting Card Magazine *changed to* Greetings
0017-4114	Gregorianum
0017-4122	Gregoriusblad†
0017-4149	Grenoble Universite. Faculte des Lettres et Sciences Humaines. Centre de Documentation et de Recherches Bibliographiques. Bulletin d'Information†
0017-4157	Greyhound
0017-4165	Greyhound Owner & Breeder
0017-4181	Grial
0017-419X	Gridley Wave
0017-4203	Griekenland Bulletin *changed to* Internationale Korrespondentie
0017-422X	Griffin Report of New England *changed to* Griffin Report of Food Marketing
0017-4254	Grille
0017-4289	Grit
0017-4297	Grit and Steel
0017-4300	Grito†
0017-4319	Grits and Grinds
0017-4327	Grits and Grinds (Swedish edition)†
0017-4335	Grive
0017-4343	Grlica
0017-4351	Grocer
0017-436X	Grocer Management/Western†
0017-4378	Grocers' and Storekeepers' Journal of Western Australia
0017-4394	Grocers' Spotlight
0017-4440	Grocery Review
0017-4459	Groei†
0017-4467	Groei *changed to* Management Facetten
0017-4483	Groene Amsterdammer
0017-4491	Groenten en Fruit
0017-4505	Grondboor en Hamer
0017-4521	Groninger Landbouwblad
0017-453X	Gronk
0017-4548	Gronkopings Veckoblad
0017-4556	Groenland
0017-4572	Groothandel in Levensmiddelen *changed to* Levensmiddelenmarkt
0017-4599	Gross Wartenberger Heimatblatt
0017-4602	Entschluss
0017-4610	Grosse Pointe Public Library. Newsletter
0017-4645	Grosswetterlagen Europas
0017-4653	Ground Engineering
0017-4661	Ground Water
0017-4688	Grounds Maintenance
0017-4696	Groundsman
0017-470X	Group Health and Welfare News *see* 0164-0542
0017-4718	Group Leader's Workshop
0017-4726	Group Practice *see* 0199-5103
0017-4734	Group Psychotherapy *changed to* Group Psychotherapy, Psychodrama & Sociometry
0017-4742	Group Research Report
0017-4750	Group Travel
0017-4769	Oregon Quality Newsletter *changed to* Oregon Development
0017-4777	Grower
0017-4785	Grower
0017-4793	Growth
0017-4807	Growth and Acquisition Guide†
0017-4815	Growth and Change
0017-4831	Growth Fund Guide
0017-484X	Growth Stock Digest†
0017-4858	Grubensicherheit *changed to* Arbeit und Sicherheit
0017-4866	Grudnaya Khirurgiya
0017-4874	Die Waage
0017-4904	Grundfoerbaettring†
0017-4912	Grundig Technische Informationen
0017-4920	Grundlagen der Landtechnik
0017-4939	Grundlagenstudien aus Kybernetik und Geisteswissenschaft
0017-4947	Gruppenpsychotherapie und Gruppendynamik
0017-4955	Gruzlica i Choroby Pluc *changed to* Pneumonologia Polska
0017-4971	Guaira†
0017-498X	Guajana
0017-4998	Guanabara Industrial†
0017-5005	Guardia Nacional
0017-5013	Guardian†
0017-5021	Guardian
0017-503X	Guards Magazine
0017-5048	Guatemala. Direccion General de Estadistica. Boletin Estadistico
0017-5056	Guatemala Indigena
0017-5064	Guatemala Pediatrica
0017-5110	Guernsey Breeders' Journal
0017-5137	Der Gueterverkehr
0017-5145	Guia Aeronautico
0017-5153	Guia Guarani
0017-5161	Guia para Maestros de Ninos†
0017-5188	Guida Allo Spettacolo
0017-520X	Guidance Exchange
0017-5218	Guidance Report†
0017-5226	Guide
0017-5234	Today's Guide
0017-5242	Guide *see* 0039-2022
0017-5250	Guide des Parents d'Eleves
0017-5269	Guide Post
0017-5285	Guide to Indian Periodical Literature
0017-5293	Guide to Microforms in Print *see* 0164-0747
0017-5307	Guide to Social Science and Religion in Periodical Literature
0017-5315	Guide to the American Left *changed to* Directory of the American Left
0017-5323	Guidepost
0017-5331	Guideposts
0017-534X	Guider
0017-5366	Guild Gardener. Newsletter†
0017-5374	Guild Gazette *changed to* Guild and City Gazette
0017-5382	Guild Guide *see* 0194-2174
0017-5390	Guild Practitioner
0017-5404	Guild Reporter
0017-5412	Guilde du Livre
0017-5439	Guilds of Weavers, Spinners and Dyers. Quarterly Journal *changed to* Weavers Journal
0017-5455	Guion
0017-5463	Guitar Player
0017-5471	Guitar Review
0017-548X	Guitare et Musique Chansons Poesie
0017-5498	Guitarra
0017-5501	Gujarat Labour Gazette
0017-551X	Gujarat Law Reporter
0017-5528	Gujarat Law Times
0017-5536	Gujarat Revenue Tribunal Law Reporter
0017-5544	Guldsmedebladet
0017-5560	Gulf Coast Lumberman and Building Distributor *see* 0192-4389
0017-5587	Gulf Review†
0017-5595	Gummi, Asbest, Kunststoffe
0017-5609	Gummibereifung
0017-5617	Gun Report
0017-5625	Gun Talk
0017-5633	Gun Week
0017-5641	Gun World
0017-565X	Gumma Journal of Medical Science *changed to* Gumma Reports on Medical Sciences
0017-5668	Gumma University. Faculty of Education. Science Reports
0017-5676	Guns
0017-5684	Guns & Ammo
0017-5692	Guns Review
0017-5706	Gurukul Kangri Vishwavidyalaya
0017-5714	Gurukula Prakashana†
0017-5730	Gustav-Adolf-Blatt
0017-5749	Gut
0017-5757	Gute Fahrt
0017-5765	Gute Nachrichten
0017-5773	Gute Reise
0017-5781	Die Gute Tat
0017-579X	Gute Reise
0017-5803	Die Gute Tat
0017-5811	Le Gutenberg
0017-582X	Guter Rat
0017-5838	Guthrie Clinic Bulletin *see* 0094-369X
0017-5846	Guy†
0017-5854	Guyana Business
0017-5862	Guyana Information Bulletin (1979)
0017-5870	Guy's Hospital Gazette
0017-5897	Gwyddonydd(y)
0017-5900	Gyermekgyogyaszat
0017-5919	Gymnasieingenjoeren *changed to* T L I-Ingenjoeren
0017-5927	Gymnasieskolen
0017-5935	Das Gymnasion†
0017-5943	Gymnasium
0017-5951	Gymnasium Helveticum
0017-596X	Gymnastikk og Turn
0017-5978	Gymnastikledaren
0017-5986	Gynecologic Investigation *see* 0378-7346
0017-5994	Der Gynaekologe
0017-6001	Gynaekologische Rundschau
0017-601X	Gynecologie et Obstetrique et Federation des Societes de Gynecologie et d'Obstetrique. Bulletin *see* 0368-2315
0017-6028	Gynecologie Pratique *see* 0301-2204
0017-6036	Gyogyszereszet
0017-6044	Gyogyszereszeti es Gyogyszerterapias Dokumentacios Szemle *changed to* Gyogyszerterapias Dokumentacios Szemle
0017-6052	Gyorstajekoztato a Magyar Konyvtartudomanyi Irodalomrol *see* 0133-736X
0017-6087	Gypsy Lore Society. Journal†
0017-6095	Gypsies for Christ
0017-6109	H A Bulletin†
0017-6117	H & S Reports
0017-6125	H & W†
0017-6141	H C I Journal *see* 0144-3704
0017-615X	H C R Bulletin *changed to* U N H C R
0017-6176	H E A News Flash†
0017-6192	H N O
0017-6206	H. P†
0017-6214	H R D News *see* 0098-1435
0017-6222	H R I S Abstracts
0017-6230	H S M A Bulletin and Idea Exchange *changed to* H S M A World
0017-6249	H S U Brand
0017-6257	H S V - Post
0017-6265	H T A Contact *changed to* H T A Today
0017-6273	H T A Horizon†
0017-629X	HTS'er†
0017-6303	H U D Challenge Magazine *changed to* Challenge (Washington)
0017-6311	H U D Newsletter
0017-632X	Haagse Jazz Club
0017-6346	Habinjan
0017-6354	Habinyan
0017-6362	Habit
0017-6370	Habitat
0017-6397	Habitat†
0017-6400	Habitation
0017-6419	Habitation
0017-6443	Habonneh†
0017-6451	Hacettepe Bulletin of Medicine-Surgery
0017-646X	Hahinukh
0017-6478	Hacia la Luz
0017-6486	Hacienda
0017-6508	Hadashot Me Hachaim Hadatiyim Be Israel
0017-6516	Hadassah Magazine
0017-6524	Hadoar
0017-6540	Hadtortenelmi Kozlemenyek
0017-6559	Haematologia
0017-6575	Haematologica Latina†
0017-6583	Haerterei-Technische Mitteilungen (HTM)
0017-6605	Encouragement
0017-6613	Kir-Ou-Kirk
0017-6621	Hahnemannian
0017-6656	Haiku *see* 0703-1831
0017-6664	Haiku Highlights *see* 0364-359X
0017-6680	Addis Ababa University. College of Technology. Library Bulletin
0017-6699	Hailer†
0017-6702	Hair & Beauty
0017-6710	Hair and Makeup Trends†
0017-6729	Hair Beauty Magazine†
0017-6737	Hair Magic†
0017-6761	Hairdressers' Journal
0017-677X	Hairenik
0017-6788	Haiti. Institut Haitien de Statistique. Bulletin Trimestriel de Statistique
0017-6796	Hakku
0017-680X	Halle aux Cuirs†
0017-6818	I D†
0017-6834	Halve Maen
0017-6842	Ham Radio *see* 0148-5989
0017-6850	Hamaapil
0017-6869	Hamburg Air
0017-6877	Hamburg in Zahlen
0017-6885	Hamburg Journal†
0017-6915	Hamburger Aerzteblatt
0017-6931	Hamburger Export-Woche
0017-694X	Hamburger Hafen-Nachrichten und Schiffsabfahrten *see* 0341-0862
0017-6966	Hamburger Lehrerzeitung
0017-6982	Hamburger Sport-Mitteilungen
0017-6990	Hamburger Vorschau
0017-7024	Hamdard Medical Digest *changed to* Hamdard Medicus
0017-7032	Hamdden†
0017-7040	Hamevaser
0017-7059	Hamifal
0017-7067	Hamilton Alumni Review
0017-7083	Hamizrah Hehadash
0017-7091	Hamlonai
0017-7113	Hampshire
0017-7121	Hampshire Farmer
0017-7148	Hand Vol Pluis
0017-7156	Handarbeit
0017-7164	Handasa W'adrikhalut
0017-7172	Handbags and Accessories *changed to* Fashion Accessories
0017-7180	Handbal
0017-7199	Handbook of Basic Economic Statistics
0017-7202	Handbuch des Bauherrn
0017-7210	Handbuch des Hausbesitzers†
0017-7229	Der Handel
0017-7237	Handel en Nywerheid†
0017-7245	Handel Zagraniczny
0017-7253	Handelingen der Staten-Generaal
0017-7261	Agentur
0017-7288	Handelsbelangen
0017-7296	Handelsblatt
0017-730X	Handelskammer Hamburg. Mitteilungen *changed to* Hamburger Wirtschaft
0017-7318	Handelslaget
0017-7326	Handelsnytt
0017-7334	Chambre de Commerce Neerlandaise pour la Belgique et le Luxembourg. Revue Commerciale
0017-7342	Denmark. Danmarks Statistik. Handelsstatistiske Meddelelser. Maanedsstatistik over Udenrigshandelen. Monthly Bulletin of Foreign Trade
0017-7350	Handelswoche
0017-7377	Handes Amsorya
0017-7385	Handling & Shipping *changed to* Handling & Shipping Management
0017-7393	Handloader
0017-7407	Handweaver and Craftsman†
0017-7415	Handwerken Ariadne *changed to* Ariadne
0017-7423	Handy Shipping Guide
0017-7431	Hanford Project News *changed to* Hanford News
0017-744X	Korea Development Bank. Monthly Economic Review
0017-7458	Hannibal Labor Press†
0017-7466	Hannoversche Land- und Forstwirtschaftliche Zeitung
0017-7474	Hannoversches Pferd
0017-7482	Hanover News
0017-7490	Hans Sachs *changed to* Schuh-Service-Magazin
0017-7504	Hansa
0017-7520	Animal Reproduction Techniques
0017-7539	Hanson's Latin America Letter
0017-7547	Japanese Journal of Criminal Psychology
0017-7555	Haolam Hazeh
0017-7563	Happening in New York†

0017-7571	Hapraklit	0017-887X	Health	0018-0157	Helsenytt
0017-758X	Harangue	0017-8896	Health and Physical Education Bulletin see 0707-3186	0018-0173	Helvetia Archaeologica changed to Archaeologie der Schweiz
0017-7636	Harbour and Shipping			0018-0181	Helvetica Chirurgica Acta
0017-7644	Hard Fibres†	0017-890X	Health and Strength	0018-019X	Helvetica Chimica Acta
0017-7652	Hardlines Wholesaling†	0017-8926	Ofakim	0018-0211	Helvetica Odontologica Acta see 0036-7702
0017-7660	Hardware Age	0017-8950	Health Education		
0017-7679	Hardware & Farm Equipment	0017-8969	Health Education Journal	0018-022X	Helvetica Paediatrica Acta
0017-7687	Hardware Consultant see 0361-5294	0017-8977	Health Foods Retailing	0018-0238	Helvetica Physica Acta
0017-7695	Hardware Merchandiser see 0017-7741	0017-8993	Health Information Digest†	0018-0246	Hem och Fritid
0017-7709	Hardware Merchandiser	0017-9019	Health Insurance Underwriter	0018-0254	Hem och Samhaelle
0017-7717	Hardware Merchandising	0017-9027	Health Insurance Viewpoints	0018-0262	Hembygden
0017-7725	Hardware Retailer see 0164-7695	0017-9035	Health Laboratory Science†	0018-0270	Hemecht
0017-7733	Hardware Review	0017-9043	Health News†	0018-0297	Hemerocallis Journal
0017-7741	Hardware Trade Journal	0017-9051	Health-Pac changed to Health-Pac Bulletin	0018-0300	Hemisphere
0017-7768	Harefuah			0018-0319	Hemispherica
0017-7776	Harian Press changed to Harian Creative Press	0017-906X	Health, Physical Education, and Recreation Microcard Bulletin see 0090-5119	0018-0327	Hemmets Journal
				0018-0335	Hemmets Vaen
0017-7792	Harlequin			0018-0343	Hemtraedgaarden
0017-7806	Harmonica Accordeon et Musique	0017-9078	Health Physics	0018-0351	Hemvaernet
0017-7830	Die Harmonika	0017-9086	Weekly Government Abstracts. Health Planning see 0199-9974	0018-036X	Hendrik Pierson Vereniging (Publication) changed to Hendrik Pierson Stichting (Publication)
0017-7849	Harmonizer				
0017-7857	Harness Horse	0017-9116	Health Services Journal		
0017-7865	Israel Pharmaceutical Journal	0017-9124	Health Services Research	0018-0386	Hennepin Reporter
0017-7873	Harper's Bazaar	0017-9132	Health Trends	0018-0394	Hennes†
0017-789X	Harper's†	0017-9140	Health Visitor	0018-0408	Henry E. Huntington Library and Art Gallery. Calendar of Exhibitions changed to Huntington Library, Art Gallery and Botanical Gardens. Calendar
0017-7903	Harpers Wine and Spirit Gazette	0017-9159	Healthways Magazine		
0017-7911	Harpoen	0017-9167	Healthy Living		
0017-792X	Harpsichord	0017-9175	Hear This		
0017-7938	Harris-Report†	0017-9183	Hearing		
0017-7946	Harrison Tape Catalog changed to Harrison Tape Guide	0017-9205	Hearing Dealer see 0092-4466	0018-0416	Henry Ford Hospital Medical Journal
		0017-9248	Heart Bulletin†	0018-0424	Henry George News
0017-7954	Harry S. Truman Library Institute Research Newsletter see 0363-1028	0017-9256	Heart of America Purchaser	0018-0432	Hep changed to Hip
		0017-9272	Heartbeat of St. Joseph's Hospital	0018-0440	Hephaistos
0017-7962	Hartford Agent	0017-9280	Hearth and Home†	0018-0467	Herald
0017-7970	Hartford Hospital Bulletin	0017-9299	Hearthstone†	0018-0475	Herald of Christian Science
0017-7989	Hartford Studies in Literature see 0196-2280	0017-9302	Hearts of Oak Journal	0018-0491	Herald of Health
		0017-9310	International Journal of Heat and Mass Transfer	0018-0505	Herald of Health
0017-7997	Wild Raspberry			0018-0521	Herald of Library Science
0017-8012	Harvard Business Review	0017-9329	Heat Engineering	0018-053X	Heraldo del Espiritismo see 0034-4478
0017-8020	Harvard Business School Bulletin	0017-9345	Heat Treating	0018-0548	Heraldo Mercantil Internacional
0017-8039	Harvard Civil Rights-Civil Liberties Law Review	0017-9353	Heating, Air Conditioning & Refrigeration	0018-0556	Heraldos del Rey changed to Conquistadores
0017-8047	Harvard Divinity Bulletin	0017-937X	Heating and Ventilating Engineer and Journal of Air Conditioning	0018-0572	Herb Grower Magazine
0017-8055	Harvard Educational Review			0018-0580	Herba Hungarica
0017-8063	Harvard International Law Journal	0017-9388	Heating and Ventilating News see 0017-9396	0018-0599	Herba Polonica
0017-808X	Harvard Journal on Legislation			0018-0602	Herbage Abstracts
0017-8098	Harvard Lampoon	0017-9396	H & V News	0018-0629	Hercules Chemist
0017-8101	Harvard Law Record	0017-9396	Heating and Ventilating Review	0018-0637	Hercynia
0017-811X	Harvard Law Review	0017-940X	Heating/Piping/Air Conditioning	0018-0645	Herder-Korrespondenz
0017-8128	Harvard Law School Bulletin	0017-9418	Heating, Plumbing, Air Conditioning	0018-0661	Hereditas
0017-8136	Harvard Library Bulletin	0017-9426	Heavy Construction News	0018-067X	Heredity
0017-8144	Harvard Project Physics. Newsletter†	0017-9434	Heavy Duty Trucking	0018-0688	Herefordshire Farmer
0017-8152	Harvard Public Health Alumni Bulletin	0017-9442	Hebezeuge und Foerdermittel	0018-070X	Black Music Review†
0017-8160	Harvard Theological Review	0017-9477	Hebrew Christian	0018-0718	Heritage of Vermilion County
0017-8179	Harvard Today†	0017-9485	Hechos y Dichos†	0018-0726	Heritage-Southwest Jewish Press
0017-8195	Harvest Farm Magazine	0017-9493	Hed Hahinukh	0018-0734	Herkenning
0017-8209	Harvest Years see 0163-2027	0017-9507	Hedeselskabets Tidsskrift	0018-0742	Hermanus News†
0017-8217	Harvester	0017-9515	Heemschut	0018-0750	Hermathena
0017-8225	Harvester	0017-9523	Heer en Mode†	0018-0777	Hermes
0017-8233	Haryana Cooperation	0017-9531	Heerbaan changed to Wereld en Zending	0018-0785	Hermes Exchange†
0017-8241	Haryana Health Journal			0018-0793	Herold
0017-825X	Haryana Journal of Education	0017-9566	Heghapoghagan Albom	0018-0807	Herold
0017-8268	Haryou-Act News†	0017-9590	Heights	0018-0815	Herold des Kostbaren Blutes
0017-8276	Harzburger Hefte see 0302-6671	0017-9604	Die Heilberufe	0018-0831	Herpetologica
0017-8284	Ha-Sifrut	0017-9612	Das Heilige Band	0018-084X	Herpetological Review
0017-8306	Hasler-Mitteilungen	0017-9620	Heiliger Dienst	0018-0858	Der Herr
0017-8314	Hassadeh	0017-9647	Heilpaedagogische Forschung	0018-0866	Husholdningslaereren (Vaeloese)
0017-8322	Hastings Law Journal	0017-9655	Vierteljahrsschrift fuer Heilpaedagogik und ihre Nachbargebiete	0018-0874	Herrenjournal
0017-8330	Hat Worker†			0018-0890	Hers
0017-8357	Hatchet	0017-9671	Heim und Anstalt	0018-0904	Hertfordshire Countryside Illustrated see 0306-672X
0017-8381	Hatvertising Weekly	0017-968X	Heim und Herd changed to Bauspar-Journal		
0017-839X	Hauenstein Verlag. Mitteilungsblatt changed to Ring-Post			0018-0912	Hertha
		0017-9698	Heima Er Bezt	0018-0920	Hervormd Arnhem
0017-8403	Haus und Grund	0017-9701	Die Heimat	0018-0939	Hervormd Nederland
0017-842X	Hausfrau	0017-9728	Heimat und Kirche†	0018-0947	Hervormd Wageningen
0017-8438	Haustechnische Rundschau	0017-9736	Heimat und Staat†	0018-0955	Hervormde Gemeente Musselkanaal. Kerkblad
0017-8454	Hauswirtschaft und Wissenschaft	0017-9752	Heimat-Zeitung Roemerstaedter Laendchen		
0017-8462	Hauswirtschaftsmeisterin changed to Rationelle Hauswirtschaft			0018-0971	Herzogia
		0017-9779	Heimatland	0018-098X	Hesperia
0017-8470	Der Hautarzt	0017-9787	Heimatland Lippe	0018-0998	Hesperide†
0017-8497	Havebladet	0017-9809	Das Heimatmuseum Alsergrund	0018-1005	Hesperis-Tamuda
0017-8500	Haven	0017-9817	Heimatschutz	0018-1013	Hesperus†
0017-8519	Havenloods	0017-9833	Heimatwerk	0018-103X	Hessische Blaetter fuer Volksbildung
0017-8527	Hawadess	0017-9841	Heimen	0018-1056	Hessische Erzieher†
0017-8535	Hawaii AFL-CIO News	0017-985X	Heimevernsbladet	0018-1064	Hessische Familienkunde
0017-8543	Hawaii Beverage Guide	0017-9868	Die Heimstatt	0018-1072	Hessische Gaertner
0017-8551	Hawaii Business and Industry changed to Hawaii Business	0017-9876	Heimtex	0018-1080	Hessische Gross- und Aussenhandel changed to Grosshandel-Aussenhandel
		0017-9884	Heirs		
0017-8578	Hawaii Guardsman changed to Pupukahi	0017-9906	H L H, Zeitschrift fuer Heizung, Lueftung, Klimatechnik, Haustechnik	0018-1099	Hessische Jugend
				0018-1102	Hessische Standesbeamte†
0017-8586	Hawaii Library Association Journal	0017-9914	Hejnal Mariacki	0018-1110	Hestesport
0017-8616	Hawaii Dental Association. Journal	0017-9922	Helan Medical Magazine	0018-1129	Het Torentje
0017-8624	Hawaiian Shell News	0017-9930	Helferbrief see 0173-7872	0018-1137	Heterofonia
0017-8632	Hawkeye United Methodist changed to Hawkeye	0017-9949	Die Helferin des Arztes	0018-1145	Heuristics
		0017-9957	Helgolaender Wissenschaftliche Meeresuntersuchungen see 0174-3597	0018-1153	Hewlett-Packard Journal
0017-8640	Hay Guetron			0018-1188	Hey Lady
0017-8667	Hayastanyaitz Yegeghetzy	0017-9965	Helicopter World†	0018-1196	Heythrop Journal
0017-8675	Hayahad Digest	0017-9973	Helictite	0018-120X	HiCall
0017-8683	Aiastani Kensabanakan Andes	0017-9981	Helikon	0018-1226	Hi-Fi News & Record Review
0017-8691	Hayatsiv	0017-999X	Helikon Vilagirodalmi Figyelo	0018-1242	Hi-Tension News
0017-8705	Areiniki Dzain	0018-0009	Helinium	0018-1269	Hiballer Miner changed to Hiballer Contractor Miner
0017-8713	Head, Heart, Hands & Health in Virginia	0018-0025	Hellenic-American Chamber of Commerce. Newsletter		
0017-8721	Head Start Newsletter			0018-1277	Hibernia changed to Hibernia Weekly
0017-8748	Headache	0018-0033	Hellenic Herald	0018-1285	Hidalguia
0017-8756	Headland changed to New Headland	0018-0041	Hellenic Review	0018-1293	Hide and Leather Bulletin
0017-8764	Headlight	0018-005X	Hellenic Shipping International	0018-1307	Hides and Skins Quarterly†
0017-8799	Heads Up†	0018-0068	Ellenike Kteniatrike	0018-1315	Hidro Mecanica en la Construccion Mexicana
0017-8810	Healdsburg Tribune-Enterprise and Scimitar	0018-0076	Hellenicos Erythros Stavros Neotitos		
		0018-0084	Hellenika	0018-1323	Hidrologiai Kozlony
0017-8829	Healing Hand	0018-0106	Hellenism	0018-1331	Hidrologija i Meteorologija†
0017-8837	Health	0018-0114	Helmantica	0018-134X	Hidrotehnica, Gospodarirea Apelor, Meteorologia changed to Hidrotehnica
0017-8845	Health see 0308-602X	0018-0130	Helminthological Society of Washington. Proceedings		
0017-8853	Health†				
0017-8861	Health	0018-0149	Helse		

ISSN	Title
0018-1353	Hidrotehnicka Bibliografija
0018-1382	HiFi Stereophonie
0018-1390	Skin Research
0018-1404	Clinical Dermatology
0018-1412	High Change & Unitholder†
0018-1420	High Country
0018-1439	High Energy Chemistry
0018-1447	High Energy Physics Index
0018-1455	High Fidelity
0018-1463	High Fidelity/Musical America
0018-1471	High Plains Journal
0018-148X	High Points
0018-1493	High School Journal
0018-1501	High Speed Ground Transportation Journal *see* 0197-6729
0018-151X	High Temperature Physics *changed to* High Temperature
0018-1535	High Temperature Science
0018-1544	High Temperatures - High Pressures
0018-1552	High Voltage Engineering Corporation Newsletter
0018-1560	Higher Education
0018-1579	Higher Education and National Affairs
0018-1587	Higher Education and Research in the Netherlands
0018-1595	Secondary Education *see* 0143-1749
0018-1609	Higher Education Review
0018-1617	Highland Hotelkeeper & Touristmaker
0018-1625	Highlights
0018-1641	Highlights at B P L *changed to* Bloomfield Public Library Highlights
0018-165X	Highlights for Children
0018-1663	Highlights of Agricultural Research
0018-1676	Highway
0018-1684	Highway
0018-1692	Highway Builder
0018-1706	Highway Common Carrier Newsletter
0018-1722	Highway Mail
0018-1730	Highway Research Abstracts *changed to* Transportation Research Abstracts
0018-1749	Highway Research News *see* 0095-2656
0018-1757	Highway Transport
0018-1765	Highway User *see* 0094-7393
0018-1773	Highways *see* 0142-6168
0018-1781	Highways. Current Literature *see* 0091-1410
0018-179X	Hika
0018-1803	Leather Technology
0018-1811	Leather Chemistry
0018-182X	Hikone Ronso
0018-1846	Hill and Dale News
0018-1854	Hillbilly†
0018-1862	Hillel Gate
0018-1870	St. Edwards University Students
0018-1889	Himachal Agricultural Newsletter
0018-1897	Himavanta
0018-1900	Himmat
0018-1919	Hind Mazdoor†
0018-1927	Hinduism
0018-1935	Hindustan Antibiotics Bulletin
0018-1943	Hindustan Chamber Review
0018-1951	Statistical Quality Control
0018-1978	Hinterland
0018-1986	Hints to Potato Growers
0018-2001	Hippokrates†
0018-201X	Hippologisk Tidsskrift
0018-2028	Hiradastechnika
0018-2036	Hiram Poetry Review
0018-2044	Hiroshima Medical Association. Journal
0018-2052	Hiroshima Journal of Medical Sciences
0018-2060	Hiroshima University. Faculty of Engineering. Bulletin
0018-2079	Hiroshima Mathematical Journal
0018-2087	Hiroshima Daigaku Igaku Zasshi
0018-2095	His
0018-2117	Hisairdec News
0018-2125	Hispalis Medica
0018-2133	Hispania
0018-2141	Hispania
0018-215X	Hispania Sacra
0018-2168	Hispanic American Historical Review
0018-2176	Hispanic Review
0018-2184	Hispano
0018-2192	Hispano Americano
0018-2206	Hispanofila
0018-2214	Histochemical Journal
0018-2222	Histochemie/Histochemistry/Histochimie *see* 0301-5564
0018-2230	Histoire de la Medecine†
0018-2257	Histoire Sociale
0018-2265	Historium *changed to* Historium en Su Nueva Dimension
0018-2273	Historama
0018-2281	Historia
0018-229X	Historia
0018-2311	Historia
0018-2338	Historia Mexicana
0018-2346	Historia Natural y pro Natura
0018-2354	Historia y Vida
0018-2362	Historiallinen Aikakauskirja
0018-2370	Historian
0018-2389	Historic Aviation†
0018-2397	Historic Kern
0018-2400	Historic Maury
0018-2419	Historic Preservation
0018-2427	Historica
0018-2435	Historical Abstracts *see* 0363-2725
0018-2443	Historical Aviation Album
0018-2451	Historical Firearms Society of South Africa. Journal
0018-246X	Historical Journal
0018-2478	Historical Journal of Japan
0018-2486	Historical Magazine of the Protestant Episcopal Church
0018-2494	Historical Methods Newsletter *see* 0161-5440
0018-2508	Historical New Hampshire
0018-2516	Historical Review
0018-2524	Historical Review of Berks County
0018-2532	Historical Society of Haddonfield. Bulletin
0018-2540	Historical Society of Nigeria. Journal
0018-2559	Historical Studies
0018-2567	Historical Wyoming†
0018-2575	Historicky Casopis
0018-2583	Historie a Vojenstvi
0018-2591	Historiographer
0018-2605	Das Historisch-Politische Buch
0018-2613	Historische Zeitschrift
0018-2621	Historisches Jahrbuch
0018-263X	Historisk Tidsskrift
0018-2648	History
0018-2656	History and Theory
0018-2664	History Book Club Review
0018-2680	History of Education Quarterly
0018-2699	History of Education Society Bulletin
0018-2702	History of Political Economy
0018-2710	History of Religions
0018-2737	History of the Twentieth Century†
0018-2745	History Teacher
0018-2753	History Today
0018-2761	Hit
0018-277X	Hitachi Review
0018-2788	Hitachi Zosen Technical Review
0018-2796	Hitotsubashi Journal of Commerce and Management
0018-280X	Hitotsubashi Journal of Economics
0018-2818	Hitotsubashi Review
0018-2842	Hjemmet
0018-2869	Hlas l'Udu
0018-2885	Hoard's Dairyman
0018-2893	Hobart Weldworld
0018-2907	Hobbies
0018-2923	Hobby
0018-2931	Hobby Bulletin *changed to* H B Model & Techniek
0018-294X	Bookworm
0018-2958	Hochfrequenztechnik und Elektroakustik†
0018-2974	Hochschulwesen
0018-2982	Hockey Circle
0018-2990	Hockey e Pattinaggio†
0018-3008	Hockey Field
0018-3016	Hockey News
0018-3032	Hockey Sport
0018-3040	Hodowla Roslin, Aklimatyzacja i Nasiennictwo
0018-3059	Hoechstrichterliche Finanzrechtsprechung
0018-3067	Hoeden & Boetiek†
0018-3075	Tidsskriftet den Hoegre Skolen *changed to* Skoleforum
0018-3083	Die Hoehere Schule†
0018-3091	Hoehle
0018-3105	Hoehlenpost
0018-3113	Hoer zu
0018-3121	Hoergeschaedigte Kinder
0018-3156	Hoesch *changed to* Estel
0018-3164	Hoffheimer Nachrichten†
0018-3172	Hofstra Chronicle *changed to* Chronicle
0018-3180	Hog Farm Management
0018-3199	Hog Guide
0018-3210	Hogar
0018-3229	Hogar Cristiano
0018-3245	Hohe Bruecke
0018-3253	Hohenzollerische Heimat
0018-327X	Hoiku No Tomo
0018-3288	Hoja de Informacion Economica
0018-3296	Hoja del Lunes de Lugo
0018-330X	Hoja del Lunes de Orense
0018-3326	Hoja Tisiologica
0018-3334	Hojskolebladet
0018-3342	Health Care
0018-3350	Health and Physical Education
0018-3369	Review of Tuberculosis for Public Health Nurse
0018-3377	Hokkaido Journal of Orthopedic & Traumatic Surgery
0018-3393	Hokkaido University of Education. Journal. Section 2 B. Biology, Geology and Agriculture
0018-3415	Hokkaido National Agricultural Experiment Station. Research Bulletin
0018-3431	Hokkaido Librarians Study Circle. Bulletin
0018-344X	Hokkaido University. Faculty of Agriculture. Journal
0018-3458	Hokkaido University. Faculty of Fisheries. Bulletin
0018-3466	Hokkaido University. Faculty of Fisheries. Memoirs
0018-3474	Hokkaido University. Faculty of Science. Journal. Series 4: Geology and Mineralogy
0018-3482	Hokkaido University. Faculty of Science. Journal. Series I: Mathematics *changed to* Hokkaido Mathematical Journal
0018-3490	Agriculture in Hokkaido
0018-3504	Hokkaido Central Fisheries Experiment Station. Monthly Report
0018-3512	Holectechniek†
0018-3520	Holiday *see* 0161-7184
0018-3539	Holiday Inn *changed to* Holiday Inn Companion
0018-3555	Holidays in Romania
0018-3563	Holland Herald
0018-3571	Holland Shipbuilding, Marine Engineering and Shipping Herald *changed to* Holland Shipbuilding
0018-358X	Holland Shipping and Trading *changed to* Holland's Export Magazine
0018-3598	Hollandia Varia†
0018-3601	Hollands Maandblad
0018-361X	Hollandse Huis†
0018-3628	Hollar
0018-3636	Hollingsworth Register
0018-3644	Hollins Critic
0018-3652	Hollins Symposium†
0018-3660	Hollywood Reporter
0018-3687	Holstein-Friesian Journal
0018-3695	Holstein-Friesian World *see* 0199-4239
0018-3709	Holsteiner Pferd *changed to* Pferde
0018-3717	Holt Investment Advisory
0018-3725	Holy Cross
0018-3733	Holy Cross Purple
0018-3741	Holy Name Monthly
0018-375X	Holz-Kunststoff
0018-3768	Holz als Roh- und Werkstoff
0018-3776	Holz im Handwerk
0018-3784	Holz-Kurier
0018-3792	Holz-Zentralblatt
0018-3806	Holzarbeiter-Zeitung
0018-3814	Holzbau
0018-3822	H O B-Die Holzbearbeitung
0018-3830	Holzforschung
0018-3849	Holzforschung und Holzverwertung
0018-3857	Holzindustrie
0018-3881	Holztechnologie
0018-3911	Home and Auto Retailer *see* 0162-8801
0018-392X	Home and Building
0018-3946	Home and Family
0018-3954	Home and Garden Supply Merchandiser *changed to* Garden Supply Retailer
0018-3962	Home and Health
0018-3970	Home Builder News
0018-3997	Home Business Digest *changed to* Mail Order Selling & Small Business World
0018-4004	Home Ec News
0018-4012	Home Echoes
0018-4020	Home Economics Research Abstracts
0018-4039	Home Finders Directory
0018-4047	Home Furnishings Daily *see* 0162-9158
0018-4055	Home Goods Retailing
0018-4063	Home Improvements *see* 0146-5996
0018-4071	Home Life
0018-408X	Home Missions
0018-411X	Home Office Report†
0018-4128	Home Rule†
0018-4160	Homefinder
0018-4187	Homemaker
0018-4195	Perspectives-In Long Term Care†
0018-4209	Homemakers's Magazine
0018-4217	Homemakers Guide
0018-4225	Homeopathie Francaise†
0018-4233	Homes and Gardens
0018-4241	Homes Overseas
0018-425X	Homesewing Trade News
0018-4268	Homiletic and Pastoral Review
0018-4276	Homiletische Monatshefte
0018-4284	Homin Ukrainy
0018-4292	Homine
0018-4314	Revue l'Homme Libre
0018-4322	Homme Nouveau
0018-4349	Hommes et Commerce-Horizons et Conjoncture *changed to* Hommes et Commerce
0018-4365	Hommes et Migrations
0018-4373	Hommes et Organisations d'Afrique Noire *changed to* Groupes et Societes d'Afrique Noire
0018-4381	Hommes et Techniques
0018-439X	Hommes et Terres du Nord
0018-4403	Hommes Libres
0018-4411	Hommes Volants
0018-442X	Homo
0018-4446	Homeopathic Sandesh
0018-4454	Homoeopathic Science Quarterly
0018-4462	Homoeopathic Vikas
0018-4489	Homoeopathisch Maandblad *changed to* Homeopathisch Tijdschrift
0018-4519	Art & Architecture
0018-4527	Hondenwereld
0018-4535	Honduras Pediatricia
0018-4551	Honey
0018-456X	Honeyguide
0018-4578	Hong Kong Economic Papers
0018-4586	Hong Kong Enterprise
0018-4594	Hong Kong Manager
0018-4616	Hong Kong Travel Bulletin
0018-4632	Honnold Library Record†
0018-4640	Honolulu Magazine *see* 0441-2044
0018-4659	Honolulu Weekly Snooper
0018-4675	Honourable Company of Master Mariners. Journal
0018-4683	Hoof Beats
0018-4691	Dimensie
0018-4705	Hoofdlijnen
0018-4721	Hoosharar
0018-473X	Hoosier Banker
0018-4748	Hoosier Farmer
0018-4756	Hoosier Genealogist
0018-4764	Hoosier Independent
0018-4772	Hoosier Legionnaire
0018-4780	Hoosier Outdoors
0018-4799	Hoosier Purchasor
0018-4810	Hoosier Schoolmaster

ISSN INDEX

ISSN	Title
0018-4829	Hooyce†
0018-4837	Hopeapeili†
0018-4845	Hopfen-Rundschau
0018-4861	Hopital a Paris
0018-487X	Hopitaux Civils et Militaires. Gazette
0018-4888	Hoppe-Seyler's Zeitschrift fuer Physiologische Chemie
0018-4896	Hoppenstedt-Monatskurstabellen *changed to* Hoppenstedt Kurstabellen - Kursanalysen
0018-4918	Horatio Alger Newsboy *see* 0028-9396
0018-4926	Horeca Ondernemer *changed to* Gastvrij
0018-4934	Hoerelsen
0018-4942	Die Horen
0018-4950	Horisont
0018-4977	Horizon (New York)
0018-4985	Horizons *changed to* Alberta Council on Aging News
0018-5000	Horizons in Leisure†
0018-5019	Horizons Unlimited
0018-5027	Horizontes
0018-5043	Hormone and Metabolic Research
0018-5051	Hormones *see* 0301-0163
0018-506X	Hormones and Behavior
0018-5078	Horn Book Magazine
0018-5086	Hornet
0018-5108	Horological Journal
0018-5116	Horoscope
0018-5124	Horoscope Quotidien Eclair
0018-5140	Horse and Hound
0018-5159	Horse & Rider
0018-5167	Horse and Show Inc†
0018-5205	Horsefeathers
0018-5213	Horseless Carriage Gazette
0018-5221	Horseman
0018-523X	Horseman and Fair World
0018-5256	Horsemen's Journal
0018-5264	Horsetrader
0018-5272	Horticultura†
0018-5272	Horticulture *see* 0106-0546
0018-5280	Horticultural Abstracts
0018-5299	Horticultural Research
0018-5302	Horticultural Society of New York. Bulletin†
0018-5329	Horticulture
0018-5337	Hortikultura
0018-5345	HortScience
0018-5361	Hose & Nozzle
0018-537X	Hosiery Abstracts
0018-5388	Hosiery and Textile Journal
0018-5396	Hosiery and Underwear
0018-540X	Hosiery Newsletter
0018-5418	Hosiery Report
0018-5442	Arquivos dos Hospitais e da Faculdade de Ciencias Medicas da Santa Casa de Sao Paulo
0018-5477	Hospital *see* 0308-0234
0018-5493	Hospital Abstract Service†
0018-5507	Hospital Abstracts
0018-5515	Hospital and Health Care *changed to* Australian Hospital
0018-5523	Hospital & Health Services Administration
0018-5523	Hospital Administration *see* 0018-5523
0018-5531	Hospital Administration
0018-554X	Hospital Administration in Canada *changed to* Health Care
0018-5558	Hospital Affairs in New York State†
0018-5566	Health Care Product News
0018-5574	Hospital Association of New York State. News
0018-5582	Hospital Building and Engineering *see* 0300-5720
0018-5590	Hospital Bureau Market News†
0018-5604	Asociacion Medica de los Ferrocarriles Nacionales de Mexico. Revista Medica
0018-5612	Hospital de Mataro. Anales†
0018-5620	Hospital Equipment & Supplies
0018-5639	Hospital Financial Management
0018-5647	Hospital for Joint Diseases. Bulletin
0018-5663	Hospital Forum
0018-568X	Hospital General
0018-5701	Hospital Highlights *changed to* Highlights
0018-571X	Hospital International†
0018-5728	Hospital Law Manual & Quarterly Service
0018-5736	Hospital Literature Index
0018-5779	Hospital Pharmacy *changed to* White Sheet
0018-5787	Hospital Pharmacy
0018-5795	Hospital Physician
0018-5809	Hospital Practice
0018-5817	Hospital Progress
0018-5825	Hospital Purchasing *see* 0300-5461
0018-5833	Hospital R. S. A
0018-5841	Hospital Supervision *see* 0363-020X
0018-585X	Hospital Supervisor's Bulletin
0018-5868	Hospital Topics
0018-5876	Hospital Tribune
0018-5884	Hospital Vargas. Archivos
0018-5906	Hospitales y Clinicas
0018-5914	Hospitalia
0018-5922	Hospitalier
0018-5930	Hospitalis
0018-5949	Hospitality
0018-5973	Hospitals
0018-5981	Hospitals' Association Journal†
0018-599X	Hospodar
0018-6007	Hot Car
0018-6023	Hot Rod Industry News†
0018-6031	Hot Rod
0018-6066	Hotel *changed to* Motel/Restaurant Voice
0018-6074	Hotel and Club Voice *changed to* Motel/Restaurant Voice
0018-6082	Hotel & Motel Management
0018-6104	Catering and Hotel Management
0018-6120	Hotel-Gasthof-Pension/H G P *changed to* Hotel 2000
0018-6139	Hotel Gazette of South Australia
0018-6171	Hotel Motel and Restaurant
0018-618X	Hotel/Motel Buyer's Directory†
0018-6201	Hotel & Restaurant
0018-621X	Hotel Restaurant
0018-6228	Hotel Review *changed to* Host
0018-6279	Hoteles de Colombia
0018-6287	Hotelier
0018-6309	Hotellerie Magazine
0018-6317	Hotelli- ja Ravintolalehti *changed to* Vitriini
0018-6333	Hotelnews
0018-6341	Practice in Prosthodontics
0018-6368	Houille Blanche
0018-6384	Hounds and Hunting
0018-6392	House & Bungalow
0018-6406	House & Garden
0018-6414	House and Home *see* 0161-0619
0018-6422	House Beautiful
0018-6430	House Beautiful's Building Manual
0018-6457	House Beautiful's Home Decorating
0018-6465	House Beautiful's Home Remodeling
0018-6473	House Buyer
0018-6481	House of Tang Family News
0018-649X	House Physician Reporter†
0018-6503	Housecraft
0018-652X	Housewares Promotions
0018-6554	Housing Affairs Letter
0018-6562	Housing and People†
0018-6570	Housing and Planning References
0018-6597	Housing and Renewal Index *see* 0094-2324
0018-6600	Housing and Urban Affairs Daily
0018-6619	Housing and Urban Development Trends
0018-6627	Housing Authority Journal
0018-6651	Housing Review
0018-666X	H D A World†
0018-6678	Houston
0018-6686	Houston Geological Society. Bulletin
0018-6694	Houston Law Review
0018-6708	Houston, Texas. Museum of Fine Arts Bulletin
0018-6732	Houtwereld
0018-6740	Houtz†
0018-6759	Hovercraft World
0018-6775	Hovering Craft and Hydrofoil *changed to* High-Speed Surface Craft
0018-6805	Howard Collector†
0018-6813	Howard Law Journal
0018-6856	Hoy Dia
0018-6899	Hromkla
0018-6902	Hrvatska Revija
0018-6910	Hrvatski Katolicki Glasnik
0018-6929	Hsien Tai Hsueh Yuan *changed to* Chieh-Hsueh Yu Wen-Hua
0018-6937	Hsin Ju Chia
0018-6945	Hsinhua Selected News Items *changed to* Hsinhua Weekly
0018-6953	Huaral
0018-6961	Hubbard School System Office of Curriculum and Instruction. Digest Newsletter *changed to* Insight(Hubbard)
0018-6988	Hudba a Zvuk†
0018-6996	Hudebni Rozhledy
0018-7003	Hudebni Veda
0018-702X	Hudson Review
0018-7054	Ovum
0018-7070	Huisarts en Wetenschap
0018-7089	Huisgenoot
0018-7097	Huismuziek
0018-7119	Huizer Kerkblad
0018-7127	Hule Mexicano y Plasticos
0018-7135	Human Side *changed to* Human Side of Supervision
0018-7143	Human Biology
0018-7151	Human Context†
0018-716X	Human Development
0018-7178	Human Ecology Forum
0018-7186	Human Events
0018-7194	Human Events
0018-7216	Human Geography
0018-7224	Human Industrial Design
0018-7232	Human Issue
0018-7240	Human Mosaic
0018-7259	Human Organization
0018-7267	Human Relations
0018-7275	Human Relations-Tips and Trends *see* 0097-8345
0018-7283	Human Relations News of Chicago
0018-7291	Human Relations Training News *changed to* Social Change
0018-7305	Human Voice *see* 0145-983X
0018-7321	Humana
0018-733X	Humane Society of the United States. News *changed to* Humane Society of the United States News (1977)
0018-7348	Humangenetik *see* 0340-6717
0018-7356	Humanidades
0018-7364	Humanisme
0018-7372	Humanisme et Entreprise
0018-7380	Humanist *see* 0306-512X
0018-7399	Humanist
0018-7402	Humanist in Canada
0018-7410	Humanist News *changed to* Humanist Newsletter
0018-7429	Humanist Outlook
0018-7437	Quest†
0018-7445	Humanitas
0018-7453	Humanitas†
0018-7461	Humanitas
0018-7488	Humanitas†
0018-7496	Humanitas *changed to* Studies in Formative Spirituality
0018-750X	Humanite Rouge
0018-7518	Humanities Scientifique *changed to* Documents et Recherches-Sciences
0018-7526	Humanities†
0018-7534	Humanities. Classes de Lettres. Sections Modernes *changed to* Documents et Recherches
0018-7542	Humanities Association Review
0018-7550	Humanities. Classes de Lettres. Section Classiques *changed to* Documents et Recherches
0018-7569	Humanities. Cycle d'Observation. Classes de 4 et 3 *changed to* Documents et Recherches
0018-7577	Humanities in the South
0018-7615	Humboldt
0018-7623	Humboldt (Portuguese Edition)
0018-7666	Humpty Dumpty's Magazine for Little Children *see* 0273-7590
0018-7682	Die Hundewelt
0018-7690	Hundsport
0018-7704	Hungara Vivo
0018-7712	Hungarian Agricultural Review
0018-7720	Hungarian Building Bulletin
0018-7739	Hungarian Exporter *changed to* New Hungarian Exporter
0018-7747	Hungarian Foreign Trade
0018-7755	Hungarian Heavy Industries *changed to* Hungarian Machinery
0018-7763	Hungarian Review
0018-7771	Hungarian Technical Abstracts
0018-778X	Hungarian Trade Union News
0018-7798	Hungarofilm Bulletin
0018-7801	Ipari es Epitoipari Statisztikai Ertesito
0018-781X	Statisztikai Havi Kozlemenyek
0018-7828	Teruleti Statisztika
0018-7852	Hunterdon Historical Newsletter
0018-7879	Hunting Dog
0018-7887	Hunting Group Review
0018-7895	Huntington Library Quarterly
0018-7909	Huon News
0018-7917	Huron Church News
0018-7925	Huron Road Hospital. Scientific Bulletin *changed to* Huron Road Hospital. Scientific Bulletin
0018-7933	Hurra Juventus
0018-795X	Hus og Hjem
0018-7968	Husbyggaren
0018-7976	Huset Vaart
0018-7984	Husfreyjan
0018-7992	Hushaallslaeraren
0018-800X	Husipar
0018-8018	Husmandshjemmet *changed to* Landbrugsmagasinet Husmandshjemmet
0018-8026	Husmodern
0018-8034	Husmorbladet
0018-8050	Hutmacher-, Modisten- und Schirrmacher-Zeitung
0018-8069	Hutnicke Listy
0018-8077	Hutnik
0018-8085	Hutoipar
0018-8093	Hvedekorn
0018-8107	Hvidvare-Nyt
0018-8115	Hydata†
0018-8131	Hydraulic Pneumatic Power *see* 0306-4069
0018-814X	Hydraulics and Pneumatics
0018-8158	Hydrobiologia
0018-8166	Hydrobiological Journal
0018-8182	Hydrocarbon News *see* 0031-6466
0018-8190	Hydrocarbon Processing
0018-8212	Hydrospace *changed to* Offshore Services & Technology
0018-8220	Hydrotechnical Construction
0018-8239	Hygien Forum†
0018-8247	Khigiena i Zdraveopazvane
0018-8263	Hygienist
0018-8271	Hymn
0018-8298	Hymylehti
0018-831X	Hyperbaric Medicine Newsletter *changed to* Pressure
0018-8336	Hyphen
0018-8344	Hypnosis Quarterly
0018-8352	Hypothese†
0018-8360	Hyresgaesten
0018-8387	I A G Journal *see* 0579-5486
0018-8395	T A M
0018-8409	I A P A News
0018-8425	Institute of Administrative Research. Research Bulletin *changed to* H M L I Research Bulletin
0018-8433	I A S A Newsletter
0018-8441	I A S L I C Bulletin
0018-845X	I A S L I C Newsletter
0018-8476	I A T U L Proceedings
0018-8484	I A U News *changed to* Polygraph-I A U News
0018-8492	International Association of University Professors & Lecturers. Communication
0018-8506	Bulletin d'Information de la Region Parisienne *see* 0396-9975
0018-8514	I and N Reporter
0018-8522	I B A Municipal Statistical Bulletin

ISSN	Title
0018-8530	I. B. A. News†
0018-8549	I B A Statistical Bulletin
0018-8557	I B B - Information†
0018-8565	I B B Bulletin *changed to* I B E Bulletin
0018-8573	I B B R I S *see* 0300-5801
0018-8581	I B E A S
0018-859X	I B E W - A F L -C I O. Local 1470 Journal
0018-8603	I. B. Flash-Edition Batiment†
0018-8611	I B I S
0018-862X	I B L A
0018-8638	I B M Iran News Bulletin†
0018-8646	I B M Journal of Research and Development
0018-8654	I B M Kwartaalschrift *changed to* I B M Monitor
0018-8662	I B M Nachrichten
0018-8670	I B M Systems Journal
0018-8689	I B M Technical Disclosure Bulletin
0018-8697	I B Nachrichten
0018-8700	I B P. Boletim *changed to* Petroleo e Petroquimica
0018-8735	I C A Information†
0018-8743	I C A Information Bulletin *changed to* I C A Regional Bulletin
0018-8751	I C A News†
0018-876X	I C A Newsletter
0018-8778	I C A O Bulletin
0018-8786	Icare
0018-8794	Instituto Colombiano Agropecuario. Revista I C A
0018-8808	I C A S A L S Newsletter
0018-8816	I C A T U Review
0018-8824	I C B
0018-8832	I C C News *changed to* I. C. C. Information
0018-8840	I C C Newsletter *changed to* I B I Newsletter
0018-8859	I C C Practitioners' Journal
0018-8867	I.C.C.W. News Bulletin
0018-8875	I C D Letterette
0018-8883	Institut Canadien d'Education des Adultes. Bulletin *changed to* I. C. E. A. Bulletin de Liaison
0018-8891	I. C. E. A. Cahiers
0018-8905	I C E M News *changed to* Migration Bulletin
0018-8913	I. C. F. Quarterly
0018-8921	I C F T U Economic & Social Bulletin
0018-8948	I C I A Information Bulletin
0018-8972	I C N Calling†
0018-8999	I C O M News
0018-9006	I C P A Quarterly Bulletin
0018-9014	I C P Quarterly *see* 0097-8396
0018-9022	I C R H Newsletter
0018-9030	I C S I D Information Bulletin *see* 0145-2118
0018-9049	I C S S R Newsletter
0018-9065	I C V A News
0018-9073	I D B Newsletter†
0018-9081	I D I A†
0018-9103	I D O R T
0018-9111	Probleme de Documentare si Informare
0018-912X	Discover the Bible
0018-9138	I E C Bulletin
0018-9146	I. E. E. - I. E. R. E. Proceedings - India
0018-9154	I E E E Almanack
0018-9162	Computer
0018-9189	I E E E Grid
0018-9197	I E E E Journal of Quantum Electronics
0018-9200	I E E E Journal of Solid State Circuits
0018-9219	I E E E Proceedings
0018-9235	I E E E Spectrum
0018-9243	I E E E Student Journal†
0018-9251	I E E E Transactions. Aerospace and Electronic Systems
0018-926X	I E E E Transactions. Antennas and Propagation
0018-9278	I E E E Transactions. Audio & Electroacoustics *see* 0096-3518
0018-9286	I E E E Transactions. Automatic Control
0018-9294	I E E E Transactions. Biomedical Engineering
0018-9308	I E E E Transactions. Broadcast & Television Receivers *see* 0098-3063
0018-9316	I E E E Transactions. Broadcasting
0018-9324	I E E E Transactions. Circuit Theory *see* 0098-4094
0018-9332	I E E E Transactions. Communication Technology *see* 0090-6778
0018-9340	I E E E Transactions. Computers
0018-9359	I E E E Transactions. Education
0018-9367	I E E E Transactions. Electrical Insulation
0018-9375	I E E E Transactions. Electromagnetic Compatibility
0018-9383	I E E E Transactions. Electron Devices
0018-9391	I E E E Transactions. Engineering Management
0018-9405	I E E E Transactions. Engineering Writing and Speech *see* 0361-1434
0018-9413	I E E E Transactions. Geoscience Electronics *see* 0196-2892
0018-9421	I E E E Transactions. Industrial Electronics and Control Instrumentation
0018-943X	I E E E Transactions. Industry and General Applications *see* 0093-9994
0018-9448	I E E E Transactions. Information Theory
0018-9456	I E E E Transactions. Instrumentation and Measurement
0018-9464	I E E E Transactions. Magnetics
0018-9472	I E E E Transactions. Systems, Man & Cybernetics
0018-9480	I E E E Transactions. Microwave Theory and Techniques
0018-9499	I E E E Transactions. Nuclear Science
0018-9502	I E E E Transactions. Parts, Materials and Packaging *see* 0148-6411
0018-9510	I E E E Transactions. Power Apparatus and Systems
0018-9529	I E E E Transactions. Reliability
0018-9537	I E E E Transactions. Sonics and Ultrasonics
0018-9545	I E E E Transactions. Vehicular Technology
0018-9553	I E E News *see* 0013-5127
0018-9561	I E E T E Bulletin
0018-957X	I. E. N. Pubblicazioni
0018-9596	I E Review
0018-9618	I. E. S. Lighting Review
0018-9626	I E S P E. Boletim
0018-9634	I F A N Bulletin. Serie A: Sciences Naturelles
0018-9642	I F A N Bulletin. Series B: Sciences Humaines
0018-9650	I F A P News
0018-9685	I F L A News *see* 0340-0352
0018-9693	I F L-Mitteilungen
0018-9707	I. F. L. Nieuws
0018-9715	I F M - S E I Bulletin
0018-9723	I. F. M. A. News
0018-9731	I F O Studien
0018-974X	I F O Schnelldienst
0018-9758	I. F. Stone's Weekly†
0018-9766	I G A Grocergram
0018-9774	I G C Monthly†
0018-9782	I G F-Journal
0018-9790	I G T - Nieuws
0018-9804	I G U Bulletin
0018-9812	I H B Review
0018-9820	I H Engineering Review
0018-9839	I H K Wuppertal. Wirtschaftliche Mitteilungen
0018-9847	I. H. V. E. Journal *see* 0142-3630
0018-9855	I I C
0018-9863	I I C A. Documentacao
0018-9871	I I E Report†
0018-988X	Status Report
0018-9898	I. I. R. B.†
0018-9901	I I T Tecnologia
0018-991X	I J A Report
0018-9936	I K Z
0018-9944	I L A Catalyst *changed to* Catalyst (Des Moines)
0018-9952	I L A Intercambio Latinoamericano†
0018-9960	I L A R News
0018-9979	I L A Reporter
0018-9995	I L P A Reporter
0019-0012	I M C Journal
0019-0020	I M M Abstracts
0019-0055	I. M. S. A. Signal Magazine
0019-0063	I M S Bulletin
0019-0071	I M Z Bulletin
0019-008X	Imboniselo
0019-0136	INFO
0019-0144	I N F O Journal
0019-0152	I N P A Advertising Newsletter
0019-0160	International Newspaper Promotion Association Advertising Copy Service Newsletter
0019-0179	Inpho
0019-0187	I N P S Boletim Informativo *changed to* Informe I N P S
0019-0195	I N P S. Mensario Estatistico
0019-0209	France. Institut National de la Statistique et des Etudes Economiques. Annales
0019-0217	Inspel
0019-0225	Argentina. Instituto Nacional de Tecnologia Industrial. Boletin I N T I. *see* 0325-934X
0019-0233	I. N. T. Informativo
0019-0241	Inqabayokulinda
0019-025X	I P A Forum†
0019-0268	I P A Review
0019-0276	I. P. A. S. E. Biblioteca Informa
0019-0292	I P E G. Boletim Informativo†
0019-0314	I P I Report
0019-0322	I. P. I. Rural News
0019-0330	I P M Digest
0019-0349	Instituut voor Plantenziektenkundig Onderzoek. Mededeling
0019-0357	I P P F Medical Bulletin
0019-0365	International Philosophical Quarterly
0019-039X	I P S F News Bulletin
0019-0403	I P S S Bulletin
0019-0411	I. P. V. D. F. Boletim Mensal†
0019-042X	I R A L
0019-0446	I R B Revista
0019-0454	I. R. Concepts†
0019-0462	I. R. I. Journal†
0019-0497	I R M P Impact†
0019-0500	I R R A Newsletter
0019-0535	Workers' Power†
0019-0543	I S A C S Bulletin
0019-0551	Instrumentation Index
0019-056X	I S A L Abstracts†
0019-0578	I S A Transactions
0019-0586	I S B A Journal
0019-0594	Iscor News
0019-0608	I S C P A Bulletin *changed to* Tickmark
0019-0616	I S C U S Bulletin *changed to* Amity
0019-0624	I S E A Communique
0019-0632	I S I Bulletin
0019-0640	Standard and Poor's I S L Daily Stock Price Index. American Stock Exchange. *changed to* Standard & Poor's Daily Stock Price Record. American Exchange
0019-0659	Standard and Poor's I S L Daily Stock Price Index. New York Stock Exchange *changed to* Standard & Poor's Daily Stock Price Record. New York Stock Exchange
0019-0691	I S S Letter *changed to* T A I S S A Letter
0019-0713	I S T A News Bulletin
0019-0748	I T A Bulletin
0019-0756	I T A Bulletin†
0019-0772	I T A-Engenharia†
0019-0780	I T A Studies
0019-0799	I T F Newsletter
0019-0810	I T L†
0019-0829	I T L Review of Applied Linguistics
0019-0837	I T Novine
0019-0845	I T R
0019-0853	I T U Review
0019-0861	I U E News
0019-087X	I U L A Newsletter
0019-0888	I U S Y Survey *changed to* I U S Y Bulletin
0019-0896	I V L Nytt
0019-0918	I V S
0019-0926	I Y F European Bulletin†
0019-0934	Iade
0019-0942	Iatrika Pepragmena
0019-0950	Iatriki
0019-0977	Ibarske Novosti
0019-0993	Ibero-Romania†
0019-1000	Ibid
0019-1019	Ibis
0019-1027	Icarus
0019-1035	Icarus
0019-1043	ICE
0019-1051	Ice Cap News
0019-106X	Ice Cream & Frozen Confectionery
0019-1078	Hagtidindi
0019-1108	Ichthyologica
0019-1140	Iconolatre
0019-1159	Idaho Agricultural Science†
0019-1167	Idaho Business and Economic Review†
0019-1175	Idaho Transportation Department. Highway Information
0019-1183	Idaho Education News *changed to* I E A Reporter (1976)
0019-1205	Idaho Law Review
0019-1213	Idaho Librarian
0019-1221	Idaho Pharmacist
0019-1248	Idaho Wildlife Review *changed to* Idaho Wildlife
0019-1256	Idaho Woodland Farmer†
0019-1264	Idaho Yesterdays
0019-1272	Idea†
0019-1280	Idea
0019-1299	Idea
0019-1310	Idea Source Guide
0019-1329	Idea Zoofila†
0019-1345	Ideal Companion
0019-1353	Ideal Education
0019-1361	Ideal Home
0019-137X	Ideals
0019-1388	Ideas
0019-140X	Ideas y Valores
0019-1426	Ideen des Exakten Wissens *see* 0340-0220
0019-1434	Idees pour Tous
0019-1442	Ideggyogyaszati Szemle
0019-1450	Identification News
0019-1485	Idiom†
0019-1507	Idisze Szriftn
0019-1523	Idrijski Razgledi
0019-1531	Iets
0019-154X	If†
0019-1558	Ifju Zenebarat
0019-1566	Spiegel der Wirtschaft *see* 0170-3617
0019-1574	Japana Medicina Revuo
0019-1582	Medicine and Gospel
0019-1590	Medical Science and Medical Care
0019-1604	Medicine and Biology
0019-1612	Studies on History of Medicine
0019-1620	Revista de Igiena, Bacteriologie, Virusologie, Parazitologie, Pneumoftiziologie. Igenia
0019-1639	Igiene e Sanita Pubblica
0019-1647	Igiene Mentale
0019-1655	Igiene Moderna
0019-1663	Igitur Revista Literaria
0019-1671	Iglesia Evangelica del Rio de la Plata. Revista Parroquial
0019-168X	Igloos
0019-1698	Ignis
0019-1701	Ihre Brigitte†
0019-171X	Ija Webonere
0019-1728	Ikai Jiho
0019-1736	Journal of Medical Instruments
0019-1744	Ikon
0019-1752	Ikon
0019-1779	Ilanga
0019-1795	Iliff Review
0019-1809	Illiana Genealogist
0019-1817	Illiana Research Report†
0019-1825	Illinet Output *changed to* Off-Line
0019-1833	Illinois Agricultural Economics
0019-1841	Illinois Alumni News
0019-185X	Illinois Banker
0019-1868	Illinois Baptist
0019-1876	Illinois Bar Journal

0019-1892 Illinois Beverage Journal
0019-1906 Illinois Braille Messenger (Inkprint Edition)
0019-1914 Illinois Building News
0019-1922 Illinois Business Review
0019-1930 Illinois Central Magazine *changed to* Illinois Central Gulf News
0019-1949 Illinois County and Township Official
0019-1957 Illinois Courts Bulletin
0019-1965 Illinois Dental Hygienists' Association. Bulletin
0019-1973 Illinois Dental Journal
0019-1981 Illinois Business and Economic Development *see* 0161-7885
0019-199X Illinois. Department of Public Health. Division of Disease Control. Weekly Report *changed to* Illinois. Department of Public Health. Division of Disease Control. Monthly Report
0019-2015 Illinois Engineer
0019-2023 Illinois English Bulletin
0019-2031 Illinois Geographical Society. Bulletin
0019-204X Illinois Health Messenger
0019-2058 Illinois History
0019-2074 Illinois Journal of Health, Physical Education and Recreation
0019-2082 Illinois Journal of Mathematics
0019-2090 Illinois Labor Bulletin†
0019-2104 Illinois Libraries
0019-2112 Illinois Master Plumber
0019-2120 Illinois Medical Journal
0019-2139 Illinois Municipal Review
0019-2147 Illinois Music Educator
0019-2155 Illinois Parks & Recreation
0019-2163 Illinois Pharmacist *see* 0147-8222
0019-2171 Illinois Police Association. Official Journal
0019-2201 Illinois Research
0019-221X Illinois School Board Journal
0019-2228 Illinois School Research *see* 0163-822X
0019-2236 Illinois Schools Journal
0019-2252 Illinois State Academy of Science. Transactions
0019-2260 Illinois State Chamber of Commerce. Current Report *changed to* Voice of Illinois Business
0019-2279 Illinois State Federation of Labor and Congress of Industrial Organizations. Weekly News Letter
0019-2287 Illinois State Historical Society. Journal
0019-2295 Illinois Quarterly
0019-2309 Illinois Truck News
0019-2317 Illinois Wildlife
0019-2325 Illovo Digest†
0019-2333 Illuminating Engineering *see* 0360-6325
0019-2333 Illuminating Engineering *see* 0099-4480
0019-2341 Illuminating Engineering Institute of Japan. Journal
0019-235X Illumination Annual *changed to* Divine Path
0019-2368 Illuminations *see* 0046-5410
0019-2376 Illuminator
0019-2384 Illumino-Tecnica
0019-2406 Illustrated Carpenter and Builder *see* 0306-3194
0019-2414 Illustrated Life Rhodesia *changed to* Illustrated Life & Talk
0019-2422 Illustrated London News
0019-2430 Illustrated Weekly of India
0019-2457 Illustration 63
0019-2465 Illustrator
0019-2473 Illustrazione Pubblicitaria
0019-2481 Illustre Protestant†
0019-249X Illustrerad Motor Sport
0019-2511 Illustrierte Rundschau der Gendarmerie
0019-252X Ilmailu
0019-2538 Ilocos Review
0019-2546 I L T A M Newsletter for Information Technology in Israel
0019-2554 Ilusao
0019-2562 Ilusion y Aventura†
0019-2570 Ilustrovana Politika
0019-2597 Im Lande der Bibel
0019-2635 Revue du Cinema
0019-2651 Image Technology†
0019-2678 Images
0019-2694 Imago†
0019-2708 Imballaggio
0019-2716 Imbongi
0019-2724 Imfama (Inkprint Edition)
0019-2732 Der Imkerfreund
0019-2740 Immagini /Forma *changed to* Immagini/Technika
0019-2759 Immanuel's Witness *see* 0308-5252
0019-2767 Immext†
0019-2775 Immigration Bar Bulletin
0019-2783 Immortality Newsletter *see* 0362-0085
0019-2791 Immunochemistry *see* 0161-5890
0019-2805 Immunology
0019-2813 Casting Digest
0019-2821 Impact (Wheaton)
0019-2848 Impact†
0019-2856 Impact (Columbia)
0019-2864 Impact-Africa
0019-2872 Impact of Science on Society
0019-2880 Impacto
0019-2899 Impacts
0019-2902 Imparcial
0019-2910 Imperial Oil Review *see* 0380-903X
0019-2929 Impermeabile Europeo†
0019-2945 Impianti Industriali†
0019-2953 Implement & Tractor
0019-2961 Import†
0019-297X Import Bulletin *changed to* Journal of Commerce Import Bulletin
0019-2988 Importer *changed to* Importer/ Electronics
0019-3003 Impresa Pubblica
0019-302X Imprimerie Nouvelle
0019-3038 Imprint
0019-3046 Imprint
0019-3054 Imprint
0019-3062 Imprint
0019-3089 Improving College and University Teaching
0019-3097 Impuls
0019-3100 In†
0019-3127 Animaland
0019-3135 In Brief†
0019-3143 In Britain
0019-3151 In de Rechte Straat
0019-316X In de Waagschaal
0019-3178 In- en Uitvoer Nieuws
0019-3186 In Famiglia
0019-3194 In Jewish Bookland *changed to* Jewish Books in Review
0019-3216 In Particular†
0019-3224 Printing Industry†
0019-3232 In-Plant Printer
0019-3240 In-Plant Reprographics†
0019-3259 In Review
0019-3267 In Step *changed to* Lutherans in Step
0019-3275 In the Beginning
0019-3283 In Touch
0019-3291 In Transit
0019-333X Monthly Newspaper Techniques *changed to* Newspaper Techniques
0019-3356 Incentive Marketing *see* 0305-2230
0019-3364 Incentive Marketing (New York)
0019-3399 Inchieste di Urbanistica e Architettura
0019-3402 Co-Incidences *changed to* Incidences (1979)
0019-3410 Incidenza
0019-3429 Income Opportunities
0019-3437 Income-Tax Journal
0019-3453 Income Tax Reports
0019-3461 Incomes Data Report
0019-347X Incontri Culturali
0019-3488 Incontri Meridionali
0019-3496 Incontro
0019-350X Incorporated British Institute of Certified Carpenters. Journal
0019-3518 Weekly Law Reports
0019-3526 Incorporated Law Society of Northern Ireland. Gazette
0019-3534 Incorporated Linguist
0019-3542 Incredible Idaho†
0019-3550 Incunable†
0019-3569 I N D A C
0019-3577 Indagationes Mathematicae *issued with* 0023-3358
0019-3585 Indeks
0019-3593 Indonesian Biological and Agricultural Index/Indeks Biologi Dan Pertanian di Indonesia *changed to* Index of Biology, Agriculture and Agro Economy
0019-3607 Index of Indonesian Learned Periodicals
0019-3631 Independent *changed to* Western Sunday Independent.
0019-3658 Independent Adjuster
0019-3666 Independent American
0019-3674 Independent Banker
0019-3682 Independent Coal Operator
0019-3720 Independent Formosa†
0019-3747 Independent School†
0019-3755 Independent School Bulletin *see* 0145-9635
0019-3763 Independent Shavian
0019-378X Index Analytique†
0019-3798 Index Bibliographique de Botanique Tropicale†
0019-3801 Index Bibliographique du Vide - Vacuum Index†
0019-3828 Index Chemicus Registry System
0019-3836 Index de la Litterature Nucleaire Francaise†
0019-3844 Index India
0019-3852 Index Indo-Asiaticus
0019-3860 Index: Industrial Extension for the Forest Products Industry†
0019-3879 Index Medicus
0019-3887 Index Medicus Danicus†
0019-3895 Index of Fungi
0019-3909 Index of Dermatology and Dermapathology *see* 0090-1245
0019-3917 Index of Mathematical Papers
0019-3925 Index of New Products
0019-3933 Index of Rheumatology
0019-3941 Index of Veterinary Specialities
0019-3968 Index to Australian Book Reviews
0019-3976 Index to Current E E G Literature *see* 0013-4694
0019-3984 Index to Current Malaysian, Singapore, and Brunei Periodicals†
0019-3992 Index to Dental Literature
0019-400X Index to Foreign Legal Periodicals
0019-4018 Index to Forthcoming Russian Books
0019-4026 Index to Indian Economic Journals
0019-4034 Index to Indian Legal Periodicals
0019-4042 Index to Indian Medical Periodicals
0019-4069 Index to Latin American Periodicals†
0019-4077 Index to Legal Periodicals
0019-4085 Index to Office Equipment & Supplies *see* 0305-635X
0019-4093 Index to Periodical Articles Related to Law
0019-4107 Index to Religious Periodical Literature *see* 0149-8428
0019-4115 Index to the Literature of Magnetism†
0019-4123 Index Veterinarius
0019-4131 Indexer
0019-414X India Book House News
0019-4158 India Calling
0019-4166 India Cultures Quarterly
0019-4174 India. Central Statistical Organization. Monthly Abstract of Statistics
0019-4182 India in Industries
0019-4204 India. Ministry of Finance. Finance Library. Weekly Bulletin
0019-4212 India News
0019-4220 India Quarterly
0019-4239 India Today and Tomorrow
0019-4247 Indian Academy of Applied Psychology. Journal
0019-4255 Indian Academy of Dentistry. Journal
0019-4263 Indian Academy of Medical Sciences. Annals *changed to* National Academy of Medical Sciences. Annals
0019-4271 Indian Academy of Philosophy. Journal
0019-428X Indian Academy of Sciences. Proceedings
0019-4298 Indian Administrative & Management Review *changed to* Indian Review of Management and Future
0019-4301 Indian Advocate
0019-4328 Indian Agricultural News Digest†
0019-4336 Indian Agriculturist
0019-4344 Journal of Indian and Buddhist Studies
0019-4352 Indian and Eastern Engineer
0019-4360 Indian & Eastern Pharmacy
0019-4379 Indian & Foreign Review
0019-4387 Indian Anthropological Society. Journal
0019-4395 Indian Antiquary
0019-4417 Indian Aviation
0019-4425 Indian Bee Journal
0019-4433 Indian Book Industry
0019-4441 Indian Book Review Supplement
0019-445X Indian Books
0019-4476 Indian Business Review†
0019-4484 Indian Cashew Journal
0019-4492 Indian Ceramics
0019-4506 Indian Chemical Engineer
0019-4514 Indian Chemical Journal
0019-4522 Indian Chemical Society. Journal
0019-4530 Indian Church History Review
0019-4549 Indian Coffee
0019-4557 Indian Communist†
0019-4565 Indian Concrete Journal
0019-4581 Indian Cooperative Review
0019-459X Indian Cotton Mills Federation. Journal
0019-4603 Indian Dairyman
0019-4611 Indian Dental Association, Journal
0019-462X Indian Drugs
0019-4638 Indian Drugs and Pharmaceuticals Industry
0019-4646 Indian Economic and Social History Review
0019-4654 Indian Economic Diary
0019-4662 Indian Economic Journal
0019-4670 Indian Economic Review
0019-4689 Indian Education
0019-4697 Indian Education Abstracts
0019-4700 Indian Educational Review
0019-4719 Indian Engineering Exporter
0019-4727 Indian-Eskimo Association of Canada Bulletin *see* 0073-6341
0019-4735 Indian Export Trade Journal
0019-4751 Indian Exporter Quarterly†
0019-476X Indian Factories Journal
0019-4778 Indian Farm Mechanization
0019-4786 Indian Farming
0019-4794 Indian Finance
0019-4808 Indian Food Packer
0019-4816 Indian Forester
0019-4824 Indian Geographical Journal
0019-4832 Indian Heart Journal
0019-4840 Indian Historian *changed to* Wassaja/ The Indian Historian
0019-4867 Indian Homoeopathic Gazette
0019-4875 Indian Horticulture
0019-4883 Indian Hotelier and Caterer
0019-4905 Indian Institute of Advanced Study, Simla. Bulletin *changed to* I I A S Newsletter
0019-4913 Indian Institute of Architects. Journal
0019-4921 Indian Institute of Bankers. Journal
0019-493X Indian Institute of Metals. Transactions
0019-4948 Indian Institute of Public Opinion. Quarterly Economic Report
0019-4956 Indian Institute of Road Transport. Monthly Bulletin
0019-4964 Indian Institute of Science. Journal
0019-4972 Indian Institute of World Culture. Transactions
0019-4980 I I T C Bulletin
0019-4999 Indian Investment Centre. Monthly Newsletter
0019-5006 Indian Journal of Adult Education
0019-5014 Indian Journal of Agricultural Economics
0019-5022 Indian Journal of Agricultural Science
0019-5030 Indian Journal of American Studies
0019-5049 Indian Journal of Anaesthesia
0019-5057 Indian Journal of Animal Health
0019-5065 Indian Journal of Applied Chemistry *see* 0019-4522
0019-5073 Indian Journal of Applied Psychology

0019-5081 Indian Journal of Biochemistry *see* 0301-1208
0019-509X Indian Journal of Cancer
0019-5103 Indian Journal of Chemistry *changed to* Indian Journal of Chemistry. Section A: Inorganic, Physical, Theoretical and Analytical Chemistry
0019-5111 Indian Journal of Chest Diseases *changed to* Indian Journal of Chest Diseases and Allied Sciences
0019-512X Indian Journal of Commerce
0019-5146 Indian Journal of Dairy Science
0019-5154 Indian Journal of Dermatology
0019-5162 Indian Journal of Dermatology and Venerology *changed to* Indian Journal of Dermatology, Venereology and Leprology
0019-5170 Indian Journal of Economics
0019-5189 Indian Journal of Experimental Biology
0019-5197 Indian Journal of Experimental Psychology†
0019-5200 Indian Journal of Genetics and Plant Breeding
0019-5219 Indian Journal of Gerontology
0019-5227 Indian Journal of Helminthology
0019-5235 Indian Journal of History of Science
0019-5243 Indian Journal of Homoeopathic Medicine
0019-5251 Indian Journal of Horticulture
0019-526X Indian Journal of Hospital Pharmacy
0019-5278 Indian Journal of Industrial Medicine
0019-5286 Indian Journal of Industrial Relations
0019-5294 Indian Journal of International Law
0019-5308 Indian Journal of Labour Economics
0019-5316 Indian Journal of Marketing
0019-5340 Indian Journal of Medical Research
0019-5359 Indian Journal of Medical Sciences
0019-5375 Indian Journal of Mental Retardation
0019-5383 Indian Journal of Meteorology and Geophysics *changed to* Mausam
0019-5391 Indian Journal of Occupational Health
0019-5413 Indian Journal of Orthopaedics
0019-5421 Indian Journal of Otolaryngology
0019-543X Indian Journal of Parapsychology *see* 0031-1782
0019-5448 Indian Journal of Pathology & Bacteriology *changed to* Indian Journal of Pathology & Microbiology
0019-5456 Indian Journal of Pediatrics
0019-5464 Indian Journal of Pharmaceutical Education
0019-5472 Indian Journal of Pharmacy *changed to* Indian Journal of Pharmaceutical Sciences
0019-5480 Indian Journal of Physics and Proceedings of the Indian Association for the Cultivation of Science
0019-5499 Indian Journal of Physiology and Pharmacology
0019-5502 Indian Journal of Plant Physiology
0019-5510 Indian Journal of Political Science
0019-5529 Indian Journal of Poultry Science
0019-5537 Indian Journal of Power and River Valley Development
0019-5545 Indian Journal of Psychiatry
0019-5553 Indian Journal of Psychology
0019-5561 Indian Journal of Public Administration
0019-557X Indian Journal of Public Health
0019-5588 Indian Journal of Pure and Applied Mathematics
0019-5596 Indian Journal of Pure & Applied Physics
0019-560X Indian Journal of Radiology
0019-5618 Indian Journal of Science and Industry *changed to* Indian Journal of Agricultural Research
0019-5618 Indian Journal of Science and Industry *changed to* Indian Journal of Animal Research
0019-5626 Indian Journal of Social Research
0019-5634 Indian Journal of Social Work
0019-5642 Indian Journal of Sociology
0019-5650 Indian Journal of Surgery
0019-5669 Indian Journal of Technology
0019-5677 Indian Journal of the History of Medicine
0019-5685 Indian Journal of Theology
0019-5693 Indian Journal of Theoretical Physics
0019-5707 Indian Journal of Tuberculosis
0019-5715 Indian Journal of Veterinary Science and Animal Husbandry *changed to* Indian Journal of Animal Sciences
0019-5723 Indian Labour Journal
0019-5731 Indian Law Institute. Journal
0019-574X Indian Leather
0019-5758 Indian Leather Technologists' Association. Journal
0019-5766 Indian Libertarian†
0019-5774 Indian Librarian
0019-5782 Indian Library Association. Bulletin
0019-5790 Indian Library Science Abstracts
0019-5804 Indian Literature
0019-5820 Indian Management Abstracts
0019-5839 Indian Mathematical Society. Journal
0019-5847 Indian Medical Association. Journal
0019-5855 Indian Medical Forum
0019-5863 Indian Medical Gazette
0019-5898 Indian Medical Record
0019-5901 Indian Merchants' Chamber. Journal
0019-591X Indian Military Academy Journal
0019-5928 Indian Mineralogist
0019-5936 Indian Minerals
0019-5944 Indian Mining & Engineering Journal
0019-5952 Indian Modeller
0019-5979 Indian Movie News *changed to* Indian Malay Movie News
0019-5987 Indian Museum Bulletin
0019-5995 Indian Music Journal
0019-6002 Indian National Bibliography
0019-6029 Indian News
0019-6037 Indian News Index†
0019-6045 Indian Oil and Soap Journal†
0019-6053 Indian P.E.N.
0019-6061 Indian Pediatrics
0019-607X Indian Perfumer
0019-6088 Indian Periodicals Record *changed to* Journal of Indexing & Reference Work
0019-6096 Indian Philosophy & Culture†
0019-610X Indian Plastics Review†
0019-6126 Indian Political Science Review
0019-6134 Indian Ports
0019-6142 Indian Poultry Gazette
0019-6150 Indian Poultry Review
0019-6169 Indian Practitioner
0019-6177 Indian Press Index
0019-6185 Indian Print & Paper
0019-6193 Indian Progress
0019-6207 Indian Promenade
0019-6223 Indian Publisher and Bookseller
0019-6231 Indian Pulp and Paper
0019-624X Indian Radio Amateur
0019-6258 Indian Railway Gazette
0019-6266 Indian Railway Technical Bulletin
0019-6274 Indian Railways
0019-6282 Indian Record
0019-6290 Indian Recorder & Digest†
0019-6304 Indian Review
0019-6312 Indian Rubber & Plastics Age
0019-6320 Indian Rubber Bulletin†
0019-6339 Indian Science Abstracts
0019-6347 Indian Seafoods
0019-6355 Indian Silk
0019-6363 Indian Society of Agricultural Statistics. Journal
0019-6371 Indian Society of Earthquake Technology. Bulletin
0019-638X Indian Society of Soil Science. Journal
0019-6398 International Journal of Contemporary Sociology
0019-6401 Indian Spices
0019-641X Indian Steel Age
0019-6428 Indian Sugar
0019-6436 Indian Textile Journal
0019-6444 Indian Trade Journal
0019-6452 Indian Truth
0019-6460 Indian Vegetarian Congress Quarterly
0019-6479 Indian Veterinary Journal
0019-6487 Indian Witness
0019-6495 Indian Writing Today†
0019-6509 Indiana
0019-6517 Indiana Alumni
0019-6525 Indiana Audubon Quarterly
0019-6533 Indiana Business and Industry
0019-6541 Indiana Business Review
0019-655X Indiana Covered Bridge Society. Newsletter
0019-6568 Indiana Dental Association. Journal
0019-6576 Indiana. Department of Public Welfare. Semi-Annual Statistical Series
0019-6584 Indiana English Journal *changed to* Indiana English
0019-6606 Indiana Family Planner *see* 0146-1117
0019-6614 Indiana Folklore
0019-6622 Indiana Freemason
0019-6630 Indiana Herald
0019-6649 Indiana History Bulletin
0019-6665 Indiana Law Journal
0019-6673 Indiana Magazine of History
0019-6681 Indiana Nurse†
0019-6711 Indiana Publisher
0019-672X Indiana Reading Quarterly
0019-6738 Indiana Slant
0019-6746 Indiana Social Studies Quarterly
0019-6754 Indiana State Board of Health Bulletin
0019-6762 Indiana State Library. Extension Division Bulletin
0019-6770 Indiana State Medical Association. Journal
0019-6789 Indiana Statesman
0019-6797 Indiana Teacher *see* 0300-6298
0019-6800 Indiana University Bookman
0019-6819 Indiana University. Folklore Institute. Journal *changed to* Folklore Institute. Journal
0019-6827 Indiana University. Graduate Library School Alumni Newsletter
0019-6835 Viewpoints *see* 0160-8398
0019-6851 India's Stamp Journal
0019-686X Indica
0019-6908 Indicateur Universel des P. T. T
0019-6916 Luxembourg. Service Central de la Statistique et des Etudes Economiques. Indicateurs Rapides
0019-6924 Indicator
0019-6932 Indicator
0019-6940 Indicator Digest
0019-6959 Indicatore Cartotecnico
0019-6967 Indicatore Grafico
0019-6975 Indice
0019-6991 Indice Cultural de Venezuela
0019-7009 Indice de Precios al Consumidor para San Salvador, Mejicanos y Villa Delgado *changed to* Indice de Precios al Consumidor
0019-7017 Indice de Precios al Consumidor para Familias Obreras en Puerto Rico
0019-7025 Indice de Precios al Consumidor
0019-7033 Indice Economico Colombiano
0019-7041 Indice General de Publicaciones Periodicas Latinoamericanas.Humanidades y Ciencias Sociales†
0019-705X Indice Medico Colombiano
0019-7068 Indice Medico Espanol
0019-7084 Indice Penale
0019-7114 Indiscret de Paris
0019-7122 Inditer
0019-7149 Individual Psychologist†
0019-7157 Individual Psychology News Letter
0019-7165 Individualist
0019-7181 Indo-African Trade Journal†
0019-719X Indo-Asia
0019-7203 Indo-Asian Culture *changed to* Indian Horizons
0019-7211 Indo-British Review
0019-7246 Indo-Iranian Journal
0019-7262 Indogermanische Forschungen
0019-7289 Indonesia (Ithaca)
0019-7297 Indonesia Letter
0019-7319 Indonesian Abstracts
0019-7351 Indonesian Planned Parenthood Association News†
0019-7378 Indus Digest†
0019-7394 Industria
0019-7408 Industria
0019-7424 Industria *changed to* Industrie Revu
0019-7432 Comercio e Industria
0019-7459 Industria Alimenticia
0019-7467 Industria Avicola
0019-7475 Industria Britanica†
0019-7483 Industria Conserve
0019-7491 Industria Cotoniera
0019-7521 Industria del Legno e del Mobile
0019-753X Industria del Mobile
0019-7548 Industria della Carta
0019-7556 Industria della Gomma
0019-7564 Industria della Vernice
0019-7602 Industria e Desenvolvimento
0019-7610 Industria Italiana dei Laterizi
0019-7629 Industria Italiana dei Plastici *changed to* Europlast
0019-7637 Industria Italiana del Cemento
0019-7645 Industria Italiana Elettrotecnica ed Elettronica
0019-7661 Industria Lombarda
0019-767X Industria Meridionale†
0019-7688 Industria Militar
0019-7696 Industria Mineraria
0019-770X Industria Portuguesa†
0019-7718 Industria & Produtividade
0019-7734 Industria Saccarifera Italiana
0019-7742 Industria Textil Sud Americana
0019-7750 Industria Textila *changed to* Industria Usoara-Textile, Tricotaje, Confectii Textile
0019-7769 Industria Toscana
0019-7777 Industria Turistica
0019-7785 Industria Usoara *changed to* Industria Usoara-Pielarie, Confectii de Piele, Prelucrarea Cauciucului si Maselor Plastice, Sticla, Ceramica Fina, Articole Casnice, Utilaje Pentru Industria Usoara
0019-7793 Industrial Accountant
0019-7807 Industrial Ad-Reply: Delaware Valley Edition
0019-7815 Industrial Advertising & Marketing *changed to* Advertising & Marketing
0019-7823 Industrial Aerodynamics Abstracts
0019-784X Industrial and Commercial Photographer
0019-7858 Industrial and Commercial Training
0019-7866 Industrial and Engineering Chemistry†
0019-7890 Industrial and Engineering Chemistry Product Research and Development *see* 0196-4321
0019-7912 Industrial and Labor Relations Forum
0019-7920 Industrial and Labor Relations Report
0019-7939 Industrial and Labor Relations Review
0019-7971 Industrial Archaeology
0019-7998 Industrial Art Methods *see* 0363-132X
0019-8013 Industrial Banker *see* 0097-8345
0019-8021 Industrial Bulletin
0019-8056 Industrial Canada†
0019-8064 Industrial Ceylon
0019-8099 Industrial Courier
0019-8102 Industrial Court Reporter
0019-8110 Industrial Design *see* 0192-3021
0019-8137 Industrial Development and Manufacturers Record
0019-8145 Industrial Diamond Review
0019-8153 Industrial Distribution
0019-8161 Industrial Distributor News
0019-817X Industrial Ecology†
0019-8188 Industrial Economist
0019-8196 Industrial Editor†
0019-820X Industrial Egypt
0019-8218 Industrial Engineer†
0019-8226 Engineering Management†
0019-8234 Iindustrial Engineering
0019-8242 Industrial Engineering and Management
0019-8277 Industrial Equipment News
0019-8285 Industrial Equipment News
0019-8307 Industrial Fabric Products Review
0019-8315 Industrial Finishing *see* 0309-3018
0019-8323 Industrial Finishing
0019-8358 Industrial Gerontology *see* 0161-2514
0019-8366 Industrial Health
0019-8382 Industrial Hygiene Digest
0019-8390 Industrial Hygiene Review†
0019-8404 Industrial Index
0019-8412 Industrial India

0019-8439 Industrial Japan *changed to* Dentsu's Japan Marketing/Advertising
0019-8447 Industrial Laboratory
0019-8455 Industrial Machinery News
0019-8463 Industrial Maintenance & Plant Operation
0019-8471 Industrial Management
0019-848X Sloan Management Review
0019-8498 Industrial Marketing
0019-8501 Industrial Marketing Management
0019-8528 Industrial Mathematics
0019-8536 Industrial Medicine and Surgery *see* 0362-4064
0019-8544 Industrial Minerals
0019-8552 Industrial Models & Patterns
0019-8579 Industrial Nottingham
0019-8587 Industrial Philippines
0019-8609 Industrial Photography and Commercial Camera *changed to* Industrial and Commercial Photography
0019-8617 Industrial Progress
0019-8625 Industrial Property
0019-8641 Industrial Purchasing Agent
0019-865X Industrial Purchasing News
0019-8668 Industrial Recovery
0019-8676 Industrial Relations
0019-8684 Industrial Relations *changed to* Personnel Today
0019-8692 Industrial Relations Journal
0019-8706 Industrial Relations Law Digest†
0019-8714 Industrial Relations News
0019-8722 Industrial Research *see* 0160-4074
0019-8757 Industrial Safety
0019-8765 Industrial Safety & Health Bulletin
0019-8773 Industrial Security *see* 0145-9406
0019-8781 Industrial Society
0019-879X Industrial Supervisor
0019-8803 Industrial Times
0019-8838 Industrial Tribunal Reports†
0019-8846 Industrial Tyneside *changed to* Industrial Tyne & Wear
0019-8854 Progress Wales
0019-8862 Industrial Water Engineering
0019-8870 Industrial Worker
0019-8889 Industrial World
0019-8897 Industrialisierung des Bauens†
0019-8897 Industrialisierung des Bauens *see* 0013-5925
0019-8927 Industrialization Forum
0019-8935 Industrials: Four Hundred & Twenty Five Canadian Weekly Stock Charts *see* 0383-2945
0019-8943 Industrias de la Alimentacion†
0019-896X Die Industrie
0019-8978 Industrie†
0019-8986 Industrie- und Handelskammer Frankfurt am Main.Mitteilungen
0019-8994 Ostschwaebische Wirtschaft *changed to* Wirtschaft in Ostwuerttemberg
0019-901X Industrie Alimentari
0019-9028 Industrie & Nachwuchs†
0019-9036 Industrie-Anzeiger
0019-9044 Industrie Ceramique
0019-9060 Industrie du Petrole en Europe-Gaz-Chimie *changed to* Industrie du Petrole - Gaz - Chimie
0019-9079 I E A - Industrie, Elektrik und Elecktronik
0019-9087 Industrie Francaise du Coton et des Fibres Alliees
0019-9095 Industrie Hoteliere de France et d'Outre Mer *changed to* Industrie Hoteliere
0019-9109 Industrie Lackierbetrieb
0019-9125 Producteur de Lait
0019-9141 Industrie-Post
0019-9168 Messe Industriespiegel
0019-9176 Industrie Textile
0019-9192 Industrie und Handel
0019-9206 Profit
0019-9214 Der Industrie- und Handelsvertreter
0019-9230 Industriel de Cote d'Ivoire
0019-9249 Industriele Eigendom
0019-9257 Industriell Teknik†
0019-9265 Industrielle Einkauf *changed to* Beschaffung Aktuell
0019-9281 Management-Zeitschrift
0019-929X Industriemagazin
0019-9303 Industriemeister Nachrichten
0019-932X Industries Atomiques *changed to* Industries Atomiques et Spatiales
0019-9354 Industries et Techniques
0019-9362 Industries et Travaux d'Outre-Mer
0019-9370 Industries Mecaniques
0019-9389 Industries Nautiques
0019-9397 Proclim *changed to* Promoclim A: Applications Thermiques et Aerauliques
0019-9397 Proclim *changed to* Promoclim B: Bulletin du Genie Climatique
0019-9419 Industrijska Istrazivanja
0019-9427 Industritjaenstemannen
0019-9435 Industry
0019-9443 Industry & Finance
0019-9451 Industry & Trade Review
0019-946X Industry of Free China
0019-9494 Industry Today†
0019-9508 Infancia e Juventude
0019-9516 Infant and Nursery School Equipment
0019-9524 Infanteria
0019-9532 Infantry
0019-9540 Infantry Journal
0019-9559 Infants to Teens Wear Buyers
0019-9567 Infection and Immunity
0019-9591 Infirmiere *see* 0301-0813
0019-9605 Infirmiere Canadienne
0019-9613 Infirmiere Francaise
0019-9656 Info
0019-9680 Infor-Austria†
0019-9702 Inform - Letter *changed to* Inform Quarterly Newsletter
0019-9710 Informa
0019-9729 Informacao Agricola
0019-9737 Informacao Semanal C A C E X
0019-9753 Informacio - Elektronika
0019-9761 Informacion Comercial Espanola. Boletin Semanal
0019-977X Informacion Comercial Espanola. Revista Mensual
0019-9788 Informacion Educativa *changed to* Argentina. Centro Nacional de Documentacion e Informacion Educativa. Informaciones y Documentos
0019-9796 Informacion Farmaceutica
0019-9818 Informaciones del Brasil†
0019-9826 Informatsiya o Bibliotechnom Dele i Bibliografii za Rubezhom
0019-9834 Informacja Ekspresowa
0019-9869 Informador
0019-9885 Informateur *changed to* Etudes Rwandaises; l'Informateur
0019-9893 Informateur de la Quinzaine
0019-9907 Informatie
0019-9915 Informatik
0019-9923 Informatika
0019-9931 Information about the Oil Industry/For the Oil Industry
0019-994X Information Agricole
0019-9958 Information and Control
0019-9966 Information and Records Management *see* 0095-4853
0019-9974 Information Bulletin for the Southern Hemisphere†
0019-9982 Information Bulletin on Isotopic Generators†
0019-9990 Information *see* 0345-5300
0020-000X Information de Sages-Femmes†
0020-0018 Information Dentaire
0020-0026 Information d'Histoire de l'Art†
0020-0034 Information Dietetique
0020-0042 Information Display†
0020-0050 Information Economique Africaine
0020-0085 Information from the Peace Movement of the German Democratic Republic
0020-0093 Information Geographique
0020-0107 Information Juive
0020-0123 Information Litteraire
0020-0131 Information Los Angeles *changed to* Key (Los Angeles)
0020-014X Information Medicale et Paramedicale
0020-0166 Tajekoztato a Kulfoldi Kozgazdasagi Irodalomrol. Series A
0020-0174 Information on Rehabilitering
0020-0190 Information Processing Letters
0020-0220 Information Retrieval & Library Automation Newsletter *changed to* Information Retrieval & Library Automation
0020-0239 Information Science Abstracts
0020-0247 Information Science in Canada†
0020-0255 Information Sciences
0020-0263 Information Scientist *see* 0165-5515
0020-0271 Information Storage and Retrieval *see* 0306-4573
0020-028X Hopital, Information Therapeutique†
0020-0298 Information Transports
0020-0301 Information ueber Aktuelle Probleme der Marxistisch-Leninistischen Philosophie in der UdSSR *changed to* Informationsbulletin. Aktuelle Probleme der Philosophie der UdSSR
0020-031X Informationsdienst fuer die Private Krankenversicherung *see* 0343-9321
0020-0328 Informationen aus dem Philosophischen Leben in der DDR *changed to* Informationsbulletin. aus dem Philosophischem Leben der DDR
0020-0336 Informationen aus Orthodontie und Kieferorthopaedie
0020-0344 Informationen fuer die Fischwirtschaft
0020-0352 Informationen fuer Die Frau
0020-0379 Informationen ueber die Fischwirtschaft des Auslandes
0020-0387 Informationen zur Kernforschung und Kerntechnik
0020-0395 Soziologische Forschung in der DDR. Informationen
0020-0409 Informations Aeronautiques *changed to* Informations Aeronautiques et Spatiales
0020-0417 Informations & Documents
0020-0425 Informations Bancaires et Financieres
0020-0433 Informations Canadiennes
0020-0441 Informations Catholiques Internationales
0020-045X Informations-Chimie
0020-0468 Informations du Caoutchouc *changed to* Informations du Caoutchouc et des Plastiques
0020-0476 Informations Etudes Outre-Mer†
0020-0484 Federation des Comites d'Alliance Ouvriere. Informations Ouvrieres
0020-0492 Informations Rapides de l'Administration Francaise
0020-0506 Statistiques des Enseignements
0020-0530 Informations Universitaires et Professionnelles Internationales
0020-0549 Informationsdienst des Deutschen Rates der Europaeischen Bewegung
0020-0581 Informationsdienstkartei (i D K) *changed to* Fachdokumentation Agrargeschichte
0020-0611 Informatique *see* 0337-6729
0020-062X Informatique & Gestion
0020-0638 Informativni Bilten Radnickog Sveucilista "Mosa Pijade"
0020-0654 Informativo Bamerindus
0020-0662 Informatology†
0020-0670 P. I. M. R. Informator Patentowy†
0020-0689 Informatore Agrario
0020-0697 Informatore Botanico Italiano
0020-0700 Informatore del Marmista
0020-0719 Informatore di Ortoflorofrutticoltura
0020-0727 Informatore Filatelico
0020-0735 Informatore Fitopatologico
0020-0743 Informatore Medico-Sociale
0020-076X Informatore Turistico
0020-0778 Informatore Zootecnico
0020-0786 Informazione Industriale
0020-0794 Informazione Mediterranea
0020-0816 Informazioni Sociali
0020-0832 Estacion Experimental Agropecuaria Pergamino. Informe Tecnico *see* 0325-1799
0020-0832 Pergamino. Estacion Experimental Agropecuaria. Informe Tecnico *see* 0325-1799
0020-0840 Informer
0020-0883 Informes de la Construccion
0020-0891 Infrared Physics
0020-0905 Ingegnere
0020-0913 Ingegnere Italiano†
0020-0921 Ingegnere Libero Professionista†
0020-093X Ingegneria Chimica
0020-0948 Ingegneria Civile
0020-0956 Ingegneria Ferroviaria
0020-0964 Ingegneria Meccanica
0020-0980 Ingegneria Sanitaria
0020-1014 Ingenieria Arquitectura Construccion
0020-1022 Ingenieria Civil
0020-1030 Ingenieria e Industria
0020-1049 Ingenieria Electrica y Mecanica
0020-1057 Ingenieria Hidraulica en Mexico *changed to* Recursos Hidraulicos
0020-1065 Ingeneria Internacional Construccion *see* 0043-8375
0020-1073 Ingenieria Naval
0020-1081 Ingenieria Quimica†
0020-109X Ingenieria y Arquitectura†
0020-1103 Ingenieria y Ciencia
0020-1111 Ingeniero Andino
0020-112X Ingeniero Westinghouse†
0020-1138 Ingenieur
0020-1154 Ingenieur-Archiv
0020-1162 Ingenieur Chimiste
0020-1170 Der Ingenieur der Deutschen Bundespost
0020-1197 Ingenieurs *changed to* Ingenieurs: Equipement Industriel/Industriele Uitrusting
0020-1200 Ingenieurs de l'Automobile
0020-1227 Ingenieurs et Techniciens†
0020-1227 Ingenieur et Technicien *changed to* Revue de l'Entreprise
0020-1235 Ingenieursblad
0020-1243 Ingenioer- og Bygningsvaesen *changed to* Ingenioeren
0020-126X Ingenioerens Ugeblad *changed to* Ingenioeren
0020-1278 Ingenjoersvetenskapsakademiens Meddelanden†
0020-1308 Inglewood Public Library Quarterly Report
0020-1324 Respiratory Care *changed to* Respiratory Care (1980)
0020-1332 Inherited
0020-1340 Iniziativa Europea *changed to* Sinistra Europea
0020-1359 Iniziativa Isontina
0020-1383 Injury
0020-1391 Injury Valuation Reports and Special Research Reports
0020-1405 Inkling
0020-1413 Inkoop *changed to* Bedrijfsvoering
0020-1421 Inkop†
0020-1448 Inlaendsk Tidningstaxa
0020-1456 Inland
0020-1464 Inland Africa
0020-1502 Inland Printer/American Lithographer *changed to* American Printer and Lithographer
0020-1510 Inland Register
0020-1537 Inland Seas
0020-1553 Inner Space†
0020-1561 Innere Kolonisation *see* 0341-1869
0020-157X Innes Review
0020-1588 Innisfail Canegrower
0020-1596 Inniu
0020-160X Innkjoep
0020-1618 Innominate
0020-1626 Du Pont Innovation†
0020-1642 Innsbrucker Theater- und Konzertspiegel
0020-1650 Inorganic & Nuclear Chemistry Letters
0020-1669 Inorganic Chemistry
0020-1685 Inorganic Materials
0020-1693 Inorganica Chimica Acta
0020-1707 Inpho Oesterreich
0020-1715 Input - Kentucky Quarterly†
0020-1723 Inquirer
0020-1731 Inquiry†
0020-174X Inquiry

0020-1758 Japan Printer
0020-1766 Printing World
0020-1774 Inscape
0020-1790 Insect Biochemistry
0020-1804 Insecta Matsumurana
0020-1812 Insectes Sociaux
0020-1820 Insectocutor News
0020-1839 Insektenboerse *see* 0013-8843
0020-1847 Inside Detective
0020-1855 Inside Education
0020-1863 Inside Kenya Today
0020-1871 Insieme
0020-1901 Insight†
0020-191X Insight: Notre Dame†
0020-1928 Insight (Grand Rapids)
0020-1936 Insight
0020-1944 Insight (Washington)
0020-1960 Insight & Opinion *changed to* Insight Publication
0020-1987 Insight
0020-2002 Insinoorilehti†
0020-2010 Insinooriuutiset
0020-2029 Insite
0020-2045 Netherlands. Inspectie voor het Brandweerwezen. Maandelijkse Mededelingen
0020-2053 Inspection News *changed to* Equifax News
0020-2061 Inspiration
0020-207X Installateur
0020-2088 Installateur Rhone-Alpes†
0020-2096 Installatie
0020-2118 Installatore Italiano
0020-2126 Installment Retailing *changed to* N A I C Reporter
0020-2134 Instantanes Criminologiques
0020-2142 Instantanes Medicaux
0020-2150 Instantanes Techniques†
0020-2177 Institut Archeologique du Luxembourg. Bulletins
0020-2185 Institut Belge du Petrole. Annales
0020-2207 Institut d'Amenagement et d'Urbanisme de la Region Parisienne. Cahiers *changed to* Institut d'Amenagement et d'Urbanisme de la Region d'Ile de France. Cahiers
0020-2215 Universite Libre de Bruxelles. Institut de Sociologie. Revue
0020-2223 Institut des Actuaires Francais. Bulletin Trimestriel
0020-2231 Institut Scientifique et Technique des Peches Maritimes. Revue des Travaux
0020-2266 Institut Economique et Social des Classes Moyennes. Bulletin d'Information
0020-2304 Institut fuer Orientforschung. Mitteilungen†
0020-2312 Institut fuer Raumordnung. Informationen†
0020-2312 Institut fuer Raumordung. Informationen *see* 0303-2493
0020-2339 Institut Henri Poincare. Annales. Section A: Physique Theorique
0020-2347 Institut Henri Poincare. Annales. Section B: Calcul des Probabilites et Statistiques
0020-2355 Institut International d'Administration Publique. Bulletin *changed to* Revue Francais d'Administration Publique
0020-2363 Institut Maurice Thorez. Cahiers *see* 0221-5047
0020-2371 Institut Napoleon. Revue
0020-238X Institut National de la Recherche Agronomique de Tunisie. Documents Techniques
0020-2398 France. Institut National de la Statistique et des Etudes Economiques. Departements et Territoires d'Outre Mer. Bulletin Bibliographique
0020-2401 Institut National des Appellations d'Origine des Vins et Eaux-de-Vie. Bulletin
0020-241X Institut National des Industries Extractives. Bulletin Technique "Mines et Carrieres"†
0020-2428 Institut National des Industries Extractives. Fiches de Documentation
0020-2436 Belgium. Institut National du Logement, Bulletin d'Information /Informatie Bulletin
0020-2444 Institut Pasteur. Annales *see* 0300-4910
0020-2444 Institut Pasteur. Annales *see* 0300-5410
0020-2452 Institut Pasteur. Bulletin
0020-2460 Institut Pasteur d'Algerie. Archives
0020-2479 Institut Pasteur de la Guyane Francaise. Archives
0020-2487 Institut Pasteur de Lyon. Revue
0020-2495 Institut Pasteur de Madagascar. Archives
0020-2509 Institut Pasteur de Tunis. Archives
0020-2517 Institut Royal Meteorologique de Belgique Contributions†
0020-2525 Belgium. Institut Royal Meteorologique. Observations Geophysiques
0020-2533 Belgium. Institut Royal Meteorologique. Observations Ionospheriques et du Rayonnement Cosmique
0020-2541 Belgium. Institut Royal Meteorologique. Observations Synoptiques
0020-255X Belgium. Institut Royal Meteorologique. Publications
0020-2568 Institut Technique du Batiment et des Travaux Publics. Annales
0020-2576 Institut Textile de France. Bulletin Scientifique
0020-2606 Institute for Defence Studies and Analyses. Journal
0020-2614 Pennsylvania State University. Institute for Research on Land and Water Resources. Newsletter
0020-2622 Institute for Social Research. Newsletter
0020-2630 Institute for the Study of Nonviolence Journal†
0020-2649 Institute for the Study of the U S S R. Bulletin†
0020-2665 Institute for Workers' Control. Bulletin *see* 0306-1892
0020-2673 Young Men's Institute. Institute Journal
0020-2681 Institute of Actuaries. Journal
0020-269X Institute of Actuaries Students' Society. Journal
0020-2703 University of Ghana. Institute of African Studies. Research Review
0020-2711 Institute of Animal Technicians. Journal
0020-272X Institute of Bankers in Ireland. Journal
0020-2738 Institute of Bankers. Journal
0020-2746 Motor Management
0020-2754 Institute of British Geographers. Transactions
0020-2762 Institute of Burial and Cremation Administration. Journal
0020-2770 Institute of Civil Defence. Journal
0020-2800 Institute of Consulting Engineers. Journal
0020-2827 Institute of Developing Economies. Library Bulletin
0020-2835 Institute of Development Studies Bulletin *see* 0308-5872
0020-2843 Institute of Early American History and Culture. News Letter
0020-2851 Institute of Economic Research. Journal
0020-286X Institute of Electrical Communication Engineers of Japan. Journal *changed to* Institute of Electronics and Communication Engineers of Japan. Journal
0020-2878 Railway Electric Rolling Stocks
0020-2886 Institute of Fuel. Journal *changed to* Institute of Energy. Journal
0020-2894 University of London. Institute of Historical Research, Bulletin
0020-2908 Landscape Design
0020-2916 Institute of Management Sciences Bulletin *see* 0092-2102
0020-2924 Institute of Marine Engineers. Transactions *see* 0309-3948
0020-2932 Institute of Mathematics and Its Application. Journal
0020-2940 Measurement and Control
0020-2959 Institute of Medical Laboratory Technology. Gazette *see* 0307-5656
0020-2967 Institute of Metal Finishing. Transactions
0020-2983 Institute of Mine Surveyors of South Africa. Journal
0020-3009 Institute of Navigation. Journal *changed to* Journal of Navigation
0020-3017 Institute of Outdoor Drama Newsletter
0020-3025 Institute of Pacific Research. Journal
0020-3033 Institute of Paper Chemistry. Abstract Bulletin
0020-3041 Institute of Paper Chemistry. Keyword Supplement *changed to* Institute of Paper Chemistry. Keyword Index to Abstract Bulletin
0020-3076 Petroleum Review
0020-3084 Institute of Physical and Chemical Research. Reports
0020-3092 Institute of Physical and Chemical Research. Scientific Papers
0020-3106 Institute of Public Health. Bulletin
0020-3114 Institute of Rail Transport. Journal
0020-3130 Institute of Science Technology. Bulletin
0020-3157 Institute of Statistical Mathematics. Annals
0020-3165 University of Dacca. Institute of Statistical Research and Training. Bulletin *changed to* Journal of Statistical Research
0020-3173 Institute of the Motor Industry. Journal *see* 0020-2746
0020-319X Institute of Weights and Measures Administration Monthly Review *see* 0302-3249
0020-3203 Institute of Wood Science. Journal
0020-322X Institutet Foer Maltdrycksforskning. Meddelande†
0020-3238 Institution of Agricultural Engineers. Journal and Proceedings *see* 0308-5732
0020-3246 Institution of Chemical Engineers. Diary
0020-3254 Institution of Chemists (India). Journal
0020-3270 Institution of Electrical Engineers. Proceedings *changed to* I E E Proceedings Part A: Covering Reviews, Physical Science, Measurement and Instrumentation, Management and Education
0020-3270 Institution of Electrical Engineers. Proceedings *see* 0143-7097
0020-3270 Institution of Electrical Engineers. Proceedings *changed to* I E E Proceedings Part I: Solid-State and Electron Devices
0020-3270 Institution of Electrical Engineers. Proceedings *see* 0143-7038
0020-3270 Institution of Electrical Engineers. Proceedings *changed to* I E E Proceedings Part C: Generation, Transmission and Distribution
0020-3270 Institution of Electrical Engineers. Proceedings *changed to* I E E Proceedings Part D: Control Theory and Applications
0020-3270 Institution of Electrical Engineers. Proceedings *changed to* I E E Proceedings Part E: Computers and Digital Techniques
0020-3270 Institution of Electrical Engineers. Proceedings *changed to* I E E Proceedings Part G: Electronic Circuits and Systems
0020-3270 Institution of Electrical Engineers. Proceedings *changed to* I E E Proceedings Part F: Communications, Radar and Signal Processing
0020-3289 Institution of Engineers and Shipbuilders in Scotland. Transactions
0020-3297 Institution of Engineers, Australia. Civil Engineering Transactions
0020-3300 Institution of Engineers, Australia. Electrical Engineering Transactions
0020-3319 Institution of Engineers, Australia. Journal *changed to* Engineers Australia
0020-3327 Institution of Engineers, Australia. Mechanical and Chemical Engineering Transactions *changed to* Institution of Engineers, Australia. Mechanical Engineering Transactions
0020-3327 Institution of Engineers, Australia. Mechanical and Chemical Engineering Transactions *changed to* Institution of Engineers, Australia. Chemical Engineering Transactions
0020-3335 Institution of Engineers-In-Charge. Transactions
0020-3343 Institution of Engineers (India). Bulletin
0020-3351 Institution of Engineers (India). Chemical Engineering Division. Journal
0020-336X Institution of Engineers (India). Civil Engineering Division. Journal
0020-3378 Institution of Engineers (India). Electronics and Telecommunication Engineering Division. Journal
0020-3386 Institution of Engineers (India). Electrical Engineering Division. Journal
0020-3394 Institution of Engineers (India). Mining and Metallurgy Division. Journal
0020-3408 Institution of Engineers (India). Mechanical Engineering Division. Journal
0020-3416 Institution of Engineers (India). Public Health Engineering Division. Journal *changed to* Institution of Engineers (India). Environmental Engineering Division. Journal
0020-3424 Institution of Fire Engineers Quarterly *changed to* Fire Engineers Journal
0020-3432 Institution of Gas Engineers. Journal *see* 0306-6444
0020-3459 Institution of Highway Engineers. Journal *see* 0306-6452
0020-3475 Institution of Marine Technologists. Journal
0020-3483 Institution of Mechanical Engineers. Proceedings
0020-3505 Institution of Municipal Engineers. Journal *changed to* Chartered Municipal Engineer
0020-3513 Institution of Public Health Engineers. Journal *see* 0300-5925
0020-3521 Institution of Radio and Electronics Engineers, Australia. Proceedings *see* 0314-4321
0020-3556 Institution of Water Engineers. Journal *see* 0309-1600
0020-3572 Institutional Distribution
0020-3580 Institutional Investor
0020-3599 Institutional Laundry *changed to* Laundry Cleaning World
0020-3602 Institutional Management *see* 0144-3704
0020-3610 Institutions/Volume Feeding Management *changed to* Institutions
0020-3629 Instituto Agronomico do Sul. Escola de Agronomia Eliseu Maciel. Arquivos de Entomologia. Serie A & Serie B
0020-3637 Instituto Americano de Estudios Vascos. Boletin
0020-3645 Instituto Barraquer. Anales
0020-3653 Instituto Biologico. Arquivos
0020-3661 Instituto Biologico da Bahia. Boletim
0020-367X Instituto Brasil-Estados Unidos. Boletim
0020-3688 Instituto Brasileiro de Bibliografia e Documentacao. Noticias†
0020-370X Instituto Caro y Cuervo. Noticias Culturales†
0020-3718 Instituto Cultural Peruano Norteamericano. Boletin
0020-3726 Instituto de Angola. Boletim
0020-3734 Instituto de Angola. Boletim Analitico
0020-3742 Instituto de Angola. Boletim Bibliografico
0020-3750 Universidad Nacional Mayor de San Marcos. Instituto de Biologia Andina. Archivos *changed to* Archivos de Biologia Andina

0020-3769 Instituto de Biologia Aplicada. Publicaciones†
0020-3777 Lisbon. Instituto de Biologia Maritima. Notas e Estudos *changed to* Notas e Estudos. Serie Recursos e Ambiente Aquaticos
0020-3785 Instituto de Cardiologia de Mexico. Archivos†
0020-3807 Instituto de Ciencias Sociales. Revista
0020-3815 Instituto de Cultura Puertorriquena. Revista
0020-3823 Instituto de Derecho Privado. Boletin
0020-3831 Academia de Ciencias de Cuba. Instituto de Documentacion e Information Cientifica y Tecnica. Boletin
0020-384X Instituto de Estudios Asturianos. Boletin
0020-3858 Estudios Medicos y Biologicos. Boletin
0020-3866 Instituto de Estudios Politicos. Boletin
0020-3874 Universidade de Sao Paulo. Instituto de Estudos Brasileiros. Revista
0020-3882 Instituto de Fomento Pesquero. Boletin Cientifico *changed to* Serie Investigacion Pesquera
0020-3890 Instituto de Geografia e Historia Militar do Brasil. Revista
0020-3912 Instituto de Investigacao Cientifica de Angola. Boletim
0020-3939 Instituto de Investigaciones Geologicas. Boletin
0020-3947 Anales de Antropologia
0020-3955 Instituto de Investigaciones Medica. Bulletin†
0020-3963 Instituto de Zoonosis e Investigacion Pecuaria Revista
0020-3971 I. M. M. E. Boletin
0020-398X Instituto de Pesquisas e Experimentacao Agropecuarias do Sul. Biblioteca. Boletim Bibliografico. *changed to* Rio Grande do Sul. Unidade Executiva de Pesquisa Agropecuaria Estadual. Boletim Bibliografico
0020-4005 Instituto de Prevision Social. Boletin
0020-4013 Instituto de Salubridad y Enfermedades Tropicales, Revista *see* 0034-8384
0020-4021 Instituto de Zoologia "Dr. Augusto Nobre". Publicacoes
0020-403X Istituto di Patologia del Libro "Alfonso Gallo." Bollettino *changed to* Istituto Centrale per la Patologia del Libro "Alfonso Gallo." Bollettino
0020-4048 Instituto Ingenieros Civiles de Espana. Boletim Informativo *changed to* Instituto de la Ingenieria de Espana. Hoja Informativa
0020-4056 Instituto Interamericano del Nino. Boletin
0020-4064 Instituto Italiano di Cultura. Bulletin†
0020-4102 Instituto Nacional de Antropologia e Historia. Boletin†
0020-4129 Instituto Nacional de Investigaciones Agronomicas. Anales†
0020-4137 Instituto Nacional de Investigaciones Agronomicas. Boletin†
0020-4145 Instituto Nacional de la Vivienda. Boletin Interior de Informacion†
0020-4153 Instituto Nacional de Pesca del Ecuador. Boletin Cientifico y Tecnico†
0020-4161 Argentina. Instituto Nacional de Tecnologia Agropecuaria. Departamento de Especializacion. Publicacion Didactica
0020-417X Universidad de Oriente. Instituto Oceanografico. Boletin
0020-4188 Instituto Panamericano de Geografia e Historia. Boletin Aereo
0020-4196 Instituts fuer Landeskunde. Neueingaenge der Bibliothek und Kartensammlung†
0020-4218 Instituto Historico e Geografico de Juiz de Fora
0020-4226 Institutul de Cercetari Piscicole. Buletinul *changed to* Institutul de Cercetari si Proiectari Alimentare. Sectia Cercetare Piscicola. Buletinul de Cercetari Piscicole
0020-4234 Institutul Geologie si Geofizica. Memoire
0020-4242 Institutul Politehnic "Gheorghe Gheorghiu-Dej." Buletin
0020-4269 Instructional Materials Intercom†
0020-4277 Instructional Science
0020-4285 Instructor *changed to* Instructor and Teacher
0020-4293 Instrument and Apparatus News
0020-4307 Instrument and Control Engineering†
0020-4323 Instrument Practice for Process Control and Automation†
0020-4331 Instrumentalist
0020-434X Instrumentatie†
0020-4358 Honeywell Instrumentatie Nieuws
0020-4366 Instrumentation†
0020-4382 Instrumentation Technology
0020-4390 Instrumentenbau-Zeitschrift
0020-4404 Instruments and Control Systems *see* 0164-0089
0020-4412 Instruments and Experimental Techniques
0020-4420 Instruments & Laboratoires†
0020-4455 Instytut Gospodarstwa Spolecznego. Biuletyn
0020-4463 Instytut Medycyny Morskiej w Gdansku. Biuletyn/Institute of Marine Medicine in Gdansk. Bulletin *changed to* Instytut Medycyny Morskiej i Tropikalnej w Gdyni. Bulletin
0020-4471 Instytut Metali Niezelaznych. Przeglad Dokumentacyjny
0020-448X Instytut Ochrony Roslin. Biuletyn
0020-4498 Instytut Urbanistyki i Architektury. Biuletyn†
0020-4501 Instytut Urbanistyki i Architektury. Przeglad Informacyjny†
0020-451X Instytut Lacznosci. Prace
0020-4528 Instytut Obrobki Skrawaniem. Zeszyty Naukowe
0020-4536 Insula
0020-4544 Insulation/Circuits
0020-4579 Insurance Adjuster
0020-4587 Insurance Advocate
0020-4595 Insurance Agent and Broker in Canada *see* 0008-3879
0020-4609 Insurance and Actuarial Society of Glasgow. Newsletter
0020-4617 Insurance Broker *see* 0384-5958
0020-4625 Insurance Broker-Age†
0020-4633 Insurance Brokers' Monthly *changed to* Brokers' Monthly & Insurance Adviser
0020-465X Insurance Counsel Journal
0020-4668 Insurance Economics Surveys
0020-4676 Insurance Exchange Magazine *changed to* Illinois Underwriter
0020-4684 Insurance Field
0020-4706 Insurance Index†
0020-4722 Insurance Law Journal†
0020-4730 Insurance Law Reports: Fire & Casualty
0020-4749 Insurance Law Reports: Life, Health & Accident *changed to* Insurance Law Reports: Life
0020-4757 Insurance Lines
0020-4765 Insurance Literature
0020-4773 Insurance Mail
0020-4781 Insurance News
0020-479X Insurance Record
0020-4803 Insurance Record
0020-4811 Insurance Review
0020-482X Insurance Salesman *changed to* Insurance Sales
0020-4846 Insuranceweek
0020-4854 Intanda News
0020-4862 Integrateducation
0020-4870 Integrated Management
0020-4889 Integrated Personnel Services Index†
0020-4900 Intelligence Digest
0020-4919 Intensive Agriculture
0020-4927 Inter
0020-4943 Inter-American Economic Affairs
0020-4978 Inter-American Music Bulletin†
0020-4986 Inter-American News†
0020-5001 Inter Auto Ecoles de France/Inter Auto Route
0020-5028 Inter/Ed†
0020-5036 Inter Electronique
0020-5044 Integre C.H.U†
0020-5052 Nordens Kristne Laeger Meddelelser *changed to* Inter Medicos
0020-5079 Inter-Parliamentary Bulletin
0020-5087 Inter-School & Inter-Varsity Christian Fellowship
0020-5095 Inter-State Milk Producers Review *see* 0195-5314
0020-5109 Andy Warhol's Interview *see* 0149-8932
0020-5117 Interaction
0020-5125 Interafrique Presse
0020-5133 Interamerican
0020-5141 Interamerican Scene
0020-515X Interauteurs
0020-5168 Interavia: World Review of Aviation-Astronautics-Avionics
0020-5176 Interavia Air Letter
0020-5192 Inter Cambio
0020-5206 Interceptor
0020-5214 Interceram
0020-5222 Interchange†
0020-5230 Interchange
0020-5249 Intercollegiate Review
0020-5265 Intercom
0020-5273 Intercom
0020-5281 Intercom *changed to* U M E A Replay
0020-529X Interconair Aviazione e Marina Internazionale
0020-5303 Intercontinental Press *see* 0162-5594
0020-532X Intercultural Education†
0020-5338 Interdiscipline
0020-5346 Intereconomics
0020-5362 Interesse
0020-5389 Interest and Dividends†
0020-5397 Interet Europeen: Europe et Regions
0020-5419 Interface (Bethesda)
0020-5427 Interface *changed to* S I G C U E Bulletin
0020-5451 Interfaith Observer
0020-5478 Interim†
0020-5494 Interior Design
0020-5508 Interior Design
0020-5516 Interiors *changed to* Interiors: for the Contract Design Professional
0020-5532 Interline Reporter
0020-5540 Interlingvistika Informa Servo
0020-5559 Interlink
0020-5567 Interlinks†
0020-5575 Interlit
0020-5583 Intermedia News and Feature Service
0020-5605 Intermediair
0020-5613 Intermediaire des Chercheurs et Curieux
0020-5621 Intermediaire des Genealogistes
0020-563X Intermediate Teacher
0020-5656 Intermountain Contractor
0020-5664 Intermountain Economic Review *see* 0195-8550
0020-5672 Intermountain Farmer *changed to* I F A Cooperator
0020-5680 Intermountain Food Retailer
0020-5702 Transport Management *changed to* Distributie en Transport Management
0020-5710 Internacia Esperanto-Muzeo en Wien. Informilo
0020-5737 Internal *changed to* New York University Report
0020-5745 Internal Auditor
0020-5761 Internal Revenue Bulletin
0020-577X Internasjonal Politikk
0020-5796 International Abstract†
0020-580X International Abstracts in Operations Research
0020-5818 International Abstracts of Biological Sciences
0020-5826 International Accountant†
0020-5834 International Advertiser†
0020-5842 International Aerospace Abstracts
0020-5850 International Affairs
0020-5869 International Affairs
0020-5877 International African Bibliography
0020-5885 International Alliance of Theatrical Stage Employees and Moving Picture Machine Operators of the United States and Canada. Official Bulletin
0020-5893 International and Comparative Law Quarterly
0020-5907 International Anesthesiology Clinics
0020-5915 International Archives of Allergy and Applied Immunology
0020-5923 International Archives of Occupational Health *see* 0340-0131
0020-5931 International Art Market
0020-594X International Association for Analog Computation. Proceedings *see* 0378-4754
0020-5958 International Association for Mathematical Geology. Journal
0020-5966 International Association of Agricultural Librarians and Documentalists. Quarterly Bulletin
0020-5974 I A E I News
0020-6008 International Association of Personnel in Employment Security. News
0020-6016 International Association of Pupil Personnel Workers. Journal
0020-6024 International Association of Scientific Hydrology. Bulletin *see* 0303-6936
0020-6032 International Association of Universities. Bulletin
0020-6059 International Associations *changed to* Transnational Associations
0020-6067 International Atomic Energy Agency. Bulletin
0020-6075 List of Bibliographies on Nuclear Energy†
0020-6091 Audiology
0020-6105 International Aviation Review†
0020-6113 International Bank Credit Analyst
0020-613X International Behavioural Scientist
0020-6148 International Beverage News
0020-6156 International Bibliography of Automatic Control†
0020-6164 International Biodeterioration Bulletin
0020-6172 International Boat Industry
0020-6180 International Bookbinder†
0020-6199 International Bottler and Packer
0020-6202 International Brahman Review†
0020-6229 International Broadcast Engineer
0020-6245 International Bulletin for the Printing and Allied Trades†
0020-6261 International Bureau of Education. Bulletin/Bureau International d'Education. Bulletin *see* 0303-3899
0020-627X International Business Contacts†
0020-6288 International Business Equipment
0020-6296 International Centre for Local Credit. Bulletin *changed to* Local Finance
0020-630X International Centre for Theoretical Physics. Monthly Bulletin
0020-6318 International Chemical Engineering
0020-6326 International Chemical Register
0020-6334 International Chemical Worker *see* 0162-637X
0020-6342 International Child Welfare Review
0020-6350 International Christian Broadcasters Bulletin
0020-6369 International Civil Defence
0020-6377 International Civil Engineering Monthly†
0020-6385 Commerce Today *changed to* Business America
0020-6393 International Commission of Jurists. Review
0020-6407 International Conciliation†
0020-6415 International Construction
0020-6423 International Construction Reporter
0020-6431 International Consumer
0020-644X International Cooperative Training Journal *see* 0090-9580
0020-6466 International Council for the Exploration of the Sea. Journal du Conseil
0020-6482 International Credit Bank. Quarterly Review†
0020-6490 International Currency Review

0020-6504 International Cycle Sport
0020-6512 International Defense Review
0020-6520 International DeMolay Cordon
0020-6539 International Dental Journal
0020-6555 International Development Review
0020-6563 International Digest of Health Legislation
0020-6571 International Drug Therapy Newsletter
0020-658X International Dyer, Textile Printer, Bleacher and Finisher
0020-6598 International Economic Review
0020-6601 International Educational and Cultural Exchange†
0020-661X International Egg Commission. Market Review Situation & Outlook Report
0020-6628 International Egg Commission. Six-Monthly Statistical Bulletin
0020-6644 International Electronics†
0020-6652 International Executive
0020-6660 International Federation for Housing and Planning Bulletin *changed to* I F H P News Sheet
0020-6687 International Federation of European Contractors of Building and Public Works Review *see* 0014-9373
0020-6695 International Federation of Gynaecology and Obstetrics. Journal *see* 0020-7292
0020-6709 International Federation of Pedestrians. International Bulletin *changed to* Voice of the Pedestrian
0020-6717 International Financial News Survey *see* 0047-083X
0020-6725 International Financial Statistics
0020-675X International Flying Farmer
0020-6768 International Folk Music Council. Bulletin
0020-6776 International Food Register
0020-6784 International Forum
0020-6806 International Friendship League. Newsletter
0020-6814 International Geology Review
0020-6830 International Grafik
0020-6857 International Guide to Indic Studies†
0020-6903 International Hotel Directory
0020-6911 International Hotel Review
0020-692X International Humanism
0020-6938 International Hydrographic Bulletin
0020-6946 International Hydrographic Review
0020-6970 Institut International du Froid. Bulletin
0020-6997 International Insurance Monitor
0020-7004 International Intertrade Index
0020-7020 International Journal
0020-7039 International Journal
0020-7047 International Journal for Philosophy of Religion
0020-7055 International Journal for Radiation Physics and Chemistry *see* 0146-5724
0020-7063 International Journal of Accounting Education and Research
0020-7071 International Journal of American Linguistics
0020-708X International Journal of Applied Radiation and Isotopes
0020-7098 International Journal of Arbitration
0020-711X International Journal of Biochemistry
0020-7128 International Journal of Biometeorology
0020-7136 International Journal of Cancer
0020-7144 International Journal of Clinical and Experimental Hypnosis
0020-7152 International Journal of Comparative Sociology
0020-7160 International Journal of Computer Mathematics
0020-7179 International Journal of Control
0020-7187 International Journal of Early Childhood
0020-7209 International Journal of Electrical Engineering Education
0020-7217 International Journal of Electronics
0020-7225 International Journal of Engineering Science
0020-7233 International Journal of Environmental Studies
0020-725X International Journal of Fertility
0020-7268 International Journal of Fracture Mechanics *changed to* International Journal of Fracture
0020-7276 International Journal of Game Theory
0020-7284 International Journal of Group Psychotherapy
0020-7292 International Journal of Gynaecology and Obstetrics
0020-7306 International Journal of Health Education
0020-7314 International Journal of Health Services
0020-7322 International Journal of Insect Morphology and Embryology
0020-7330 International Journal of Legal Research†
0020-7349 International Journal of Leprosy *see* 0148-916X
0020-7357 International Journal of Machine Tool Design and Research
0020-7365 International Journal of Magnetism†
0020-7373 International Journal of Man-Machine Studies
0020-7381 International Journal of Mass Spectrometry and Ion Physics
0020-739X International Journal of Mathematical Education in Science and Technology
0020-7403 International Journal of Mechanical Sciences
0020-7411 International Journal of Mental Health
0020-7438 International Journal of Middle East Studies
0020-7446 International Journal of Neurology
0020-7454 International Journal of Neuroscience
0020-7462 International Journal of Non-Linear Mechanics
0020-7470 International Journal of Nondestructive Testing *see* 0140-072X
0020-7489 International Journal of Nursing Studies
0020-7497 International Journal of Offender Therapy *see* 0306-624X
0020-7500 International Journal of Orthodontics
0020-7500 International Journal of Orthodontics *see* 0002-9416
0020-7519 International Journal for Parasitology
0020-7527 International Journal of Physical Distribution *changed to* International Journal of Physical Distribution & Materials Management
0020-7535 International Journal of Powder Metallurgy *see* 0361-3488
0020-7543 International Journal of Production Research
0020-7578 International Journal of Psycho-Analysis
0020-7594 Journal International de Psychologie
0020-7608 International Journal of Quantum Chemistry
0020-7616 International Journal of Radiation Biology
0020-7624 International Journal of Rock Mechanics and Mining Sciences *see* 0148-9062
0020-7632 International Journal of Slavic Linguistics and Poetics
0020-7640 International Journal of Social Psychiatry
0020-7659 International Journal of Sociology
0020-7667 International Journal of Sociology of the Family
0020-7675 International Journal of Sociometry and Sociatry *changed to* Handbook of International Sociometry.
0020-7683 International Journal of Solids and Structures
0020-7691 International Journal of Speleology†
0020-7705 International Journal of Symbology†
0020-7713 International Journal of Systematic Bacteriology
0020-7721 International Journal of Systems Science
0020-773X International Journal of the Addictions
0020-7748 International Journal of Theoretical Physics
0020-7756 International Labour Documentation
0020-7764 International Labour Office. Legislative Series
0020-7772 International Labour Office. Official Bulletin *see* 0378-5882
0020-7772 International Labour Office. Official Bulletin *see* 0378-5890
0020-7780 International Labour Review
0020-7799 International Language Reporter *changed to* Eco-Logos
0020-7810 International Lawyer
0020-7829 International Legal Materials
0020-7837 International Library Review
0020-7845 International Licensing
0020-7853 International Lighting Review
0020-7888 International Management
0020-7896 International Management Information Business Digest†
0020-7918 International Marine Science†
0020-7926 International Mathematical News
0020-7977 International Microform Journal of Legal Medicine
0020-7985 International Migration
0020-7993 International Migration Review
0020-8000 International Mining Equipment *see* 0010-1281
0020-8019 International Molders' and Allied Workers' Journal
0020-8027 International Monetary Fund. Staff Papers
0020-8051 International Musician
0020-806X International Narcotic Report *see* 0148-4648
0020-8086 International News Items
0020-8094 International News Letter *changed to* International Report
0020-8124 International Nursing Index
0020-8132 International Nursing Review
0020-8140 International Odd Fellow
0020-8159 International Operating Engineer
0020-8167 International Ophthalmology Clinics
0020-8183 International Organization
0020-8191 International Paper Board Industry
0020-8205 International Pathology
0020-8213 International Peace Research Newsletter
0020-823X International P. E. N. Bulletin of Selected Books
0020-8248 International Perfumer *see* 0305-0319
0020-8256 International Pest Control
0020-8264 International Pharmaceutical Abstracts
0020-8272 International Pharmacopsychiatry
0020-8280 International Photo Technik
0020-8299 International Photographer
0020-8302 International Piano Library Bulletin†
0020-8337 International Polar Motion Service. Monthly Notes
0020-8345 International Political Science Abstracts†
0020-8345 International Political Science Abstracts
0020-8353 Potters Herald
0020-8361 International Press Bulletin
0020-837X International Press Journal
0020-8388 International Printing Pressmen and Assistants Union of North America. News and Views *changed to* International Printing and Graphic Communications Union. News and Views
0020-8396 International Prisoners Aid Association. Newsletter
0020-840X International Problems
0020-8426 International Psychiatry Clinics†
0020-8434 International Public Relations Review *see* 0033-3700
0020-8442 Rail International
0020-8450 International Railway Journal
0020-8477 International Rehabilitation Review
0020-8485 International Relations†
0020-8493 International Reporter
0020-8507 International Reports
0020-8523 International Review of Administrative Sciences
0020-8566 International Review of Education
0020-8574 International Review of History and Political Science
0020-8582 International Review of Mission
0020-8590 International Review of Social History
0020-8604 International Review of the Red Cross
0020-8647 International Ropeway Review†
0020-8655 International Rubber Digest
0020-8663 International Seed Testing Association. Proceedings *changed to* Seed Science and Technology
0020-8671 International Seismological Centre. Bulletin
0020-8698 International Silk Association. Bulletin *changed to* International Silk Association. Monthly Newsletter
0020-8701 International Social Science Journal
0020-871X International Social Security Review
0020-8728 International Social Work
0020-8760 International Society of Soil Science. Bulletin
0020-8779 International Statistical Institute Review *see* 0306-7734
0020-8787 Stewardess and Flight Service *changed to* Passenger & In-Flight Service
0020-8795 International Stock Report *see* 0364-5711
0020-8809 International Student Newsletter *changed to* F.S.S.C. Newsletter
0020-8817 International Studies
0020-8833 International Studies Quarterly
0020-8841 International Sugar Journal
0020-885X International Sugar Organization Statistical Bulletin
0020-8868 International Surgery
0020-8876 International Swimmer
0020-8892 International Teamster
0020-8914 International Textiles
0020-8922 Interior
0020-8930 International Theatre
0020-8957 International Trade Forum
0020-8981 International Trade Review
0020-899X International Trade Union News
0020-9007 International Transport Workers' Journal†
0020-9015 International Travel *changed to* Travelweek
0020-9023 International Trotter and Pacer *changed to* Harness Horsemen International
0020-9058 I U C N Bulletin
0020-9066 International Union for Vacuum Science, Technique and Applications. News Bulletin
0020-9074 International Union of Food and Allied Workers' Associations. News Bulletin
0020-9090 International Whaling Statistics
0020-9104 Wheelspin News
0020-9112 International Wildlife
0020-9120 International Women's News
0020-9139 International Woodworker
0020-9147 Elektrowaerme International *see* 0340-3521
0020-9147 Elektrowaerme International *see* 0340-3513
0020-9155 International Zoo-News
0020-9163 Internationale - A. M. R.
0020-9171 Internationale Berg- und Seilbahn-Rundschau
0020-918X I B R
0020-9198 Internationale Bibliographie der Versicherungsliteratur†
0020-9201 Internationale Bibliographie der Zeitschriftenliteratur
0020-921X I B N
0020-9236 Internationale Elektronische Rundschau *changed to* Nachrichten-Elektronik
0020-9252 Internationale Kirchliche Zeitschrift
0020-9260 Internationale Luftwaffen Revue *changed to* Luftwaffen Revue
0020-9309 Internationale Revue der gesamten Hydrobiologie
0020-9317 Internationale Spectator
0020-9325 Internationale Stiftung Mozarteum. Mitteilungen
0020-9341 Internationale Transport-Zeitschrift
0020-935X Internationale Wirtschaft
0020-9368 Internationale Wirtschafts-Briefe
0020-9376 Internationale Zeitschrift fuer Angewandte Physiologie Einschliesslich Arbeitsphysiologie *see* 0301-5548
0020-9384 Gas Waerme International
0020-9392 Internationale Zeitschrift fuer Klinische Pharmakologie, Therapie und Toxikologie *see* 0340-0026

0020-9406 Internationale Zeitschrift fuer Vitamin-Forschung *see* 0300-9831
0020-9422 Internationaler Holzmarkt
0020-9430 Internationales Afrikaforum
0020-9449 Internationales Asienforum
0020-9457 Internationales Biographisches Archiv
0020-9465 Internationales Europaforum *see* 0049-7134
0020-9473 Internationales Freies Wort
0020-9481 Internationales Gewerbearchiv
0020-949X Internationales Handbuch
0020-9503 Internationales Recht und Diplomatie
0020-9511 Internationales Verkehrswesen
0020-952X Internationella Studier
0020-9538 Interni
0020-9546 Internist
0020-9554 Der Internist
0020-9562 Internist Observer†
0020-9570 Internistische Praxis
0020-9597 Interplanetary News
0020-9619 Interpressgrafik
0020-9635 Interpretation
0020-9643 Interpretation
0020-966X Buffalo and Erie County Public Library Bulletin
0020-9678 Interpreter
0020-9686 Interpreter Releases
0020-9694 Quarterly Report on Public Welfare in Arkansas†
0020-9708 Interracial Books for Children *see* 0146-5562
0020-9716 Interstages
0020-9724 Interstampa della Capitale†
0020-9732 Interstate Oil Compact Commission. Committee Bulletin
0020-9740 Interstellar Communication
0020-9759 Intervalo†
0020-9791 Intimate Apparel *see* 0360-3520
0020-9805 Intimate Confessions
0020-9813 Intimate Story
0020-983X Into Europe *changed to* New Europe
0020-9848 Intra-Science Chemistry Reports *see* 0276-8585
0020-9864 Intrepid
0020-9872 Inuttituut
0020-9880 Invalidensport *changed to* Behindertensport
0020-9902 Invention Intelligence
0020-9910 Inventiones mathematicae
0020-9929 Inverness Courier
0020-9937 Investicni Vystavba
0020-9953 Investigacion Pesquera
0020-9961 Investigaciones en Sociologia
0020-9988 Investigative Ophthalmology *see* 0146-0404
0020-9996 Investigative Radiology
0021-0005 Investigative Urology
0021-0013 Investigator
0021-0021 Investimenti e Prospettive
0021-003X Investing, Licensing & Trading Conditions Abroad
0021-0048 Investment Analyst
0021-0064 Investment & Marketing
0021-0072 Investment Bulletin
0021-0080 Investment Dealers' Digest
0021-0110 Investment Quality Trends
0021-0153 Investor
0021-0161 Investors Chronicle and Stock Exchange Gazette
0021-0226 Investors' Profit Guide
0021-0250 Inward Light
0021-0269 Inyala News
0021-0277 Inzinierske Stavby
0021-0293 Inzhenernyi Zhurnal *changed to* Inzhenerno- Fizicheskii Zhurnal
0021-0307 Inzicht
0021-0315 Inzynieria i Budownictwo
0021-0331 Io
0021-0358 Ionian
0021-0374 Ionospheric Data
0021-0382 Ionospheric Data in Japan
0021-0390 Ionospheric Predictions†
0021-0404 Ios
0021-0420 Iowa Adult Education Association. Newsletter *changed to* I A L L Eye-Opener
0021-0439 Iowa Architect
0021-0447 Iowa Association of School Librarians/ Library Lines *changed to* Iowa Media Message
0021-0455 Iowa Bird Life
0021-0463 Business and Industry
0021-0471 Iowa Conservationist
0021-048X Iowa Dental Bulletin
0021-0498 Iowa Dental Journal
0021-0501 Iowa Engineer
0021-051X Iowa Farm Bureau Spokesman
0021-0528 Iowa Food Dealer
0021-0536 Iowa Journal of Social Work *changed to* Social Development Issues
0021-0552 Iowa Law Review
0021-0560 Iowa Legionnaire
0021-0579 Iowa Library Quarterly†
0021-0587 Iowa Medical Society. Journal
0021-0609 Iowa Music Educator
0021-0617 Iowa P T A Bulletin
0021-0633 Iowa Police Journal
0021-065X Iowa Review
0021-0668 Iowa School Board Dialogue
0021-0676 Iowa Science Teachers Journal
0021-0684 Iowa State Journal of Science *see* 0092-6345
0021-0692 Iowa State University. Iowa Agriculture and Home Economics Experiment Station. Research Bulletin Series
0021-0706 Iowa Transit *changed to* Hawkeye Engineer
0021-0714 Iowa Veterinarian†
0021-0722 Iowan
0021-0730 Iowa's People†
0021-0749 Ipargazdasag
0021-0757 Ipari Energiagazdalkodas *changed to* Energiagazdalkodas
0021-0765 Ipirotiki Estia
0021-0773 Iqbal Review
0021-079X Iran Oil Journal
0021-0803 Iran Trade and Industry
0021-0846 Iranian Library Association Bulletin
0021-0854 Iranian Petroleum Institute. Bulletin
0021-0862 Iranian Studies
0021-0870 Iranica Antiqua
0021-0889 Iraq
0021-0897 Iraq Natural History Museum. Bulletin *changed to* Iraq Natural History Research Center and Museum. Bulletin
0021-0900 Iraq. Central Statistical Organization. Summary of Foreign Trade Statistics
0021-0919 Iraq. Statistics Bureau. Quarterly Bulletin of Foreign Trade Statistics†
0021-0927 Iraqi Medical Professions' Association. Journal
0021-0935 Ireland *changed to* Ireland Today
0021-0943 Ireland of the Welcomes
0021-0951 Ireland's Own
0021-096X Ireland's Press and Print
0021-0978 Irenikon
0021-0986 I R G-M I R Bulletin *changed to* Nonviolence et Societe
0021-1001 Iris
0021-101X Iris an Gharda *changed to* Garda Review
0021-1028 Irish Accountant and Secretary†
0021-1036 Irish Agricultural and Creamery Review
0021-1052 Irish Astronomical Journal
0021-1060 Irish Banking Review
0021-1079 Irish Bee-Keeper
0021-1087 Irish Builder and Engineer
0021-1095 Irish Catering Review
0021-1109 Irish Chemist and Druggist *changed to* Irish Pharmacy Journal
0021-1133 Irish Dental Association. Journal
0021-1141 Irish Electrical Industries Review
0021-115X Irish Engineers *see* 0332-1711
0021-1168 Irish Farmers' Journal
0021-1176 Irish Farming News
0021-1184 Irish Field
0021-1192 Irish Forestry
0021-1206 Irish Georgian Society. Quarterly Bulletin
0021-1214 Irish Historical Studies
0021-1222 Irish Independent
0021-1249 Irish Journal of Agricultural Economics and Rural Sociology
0021-1257 Irish Journal of Education
0021-1273 Irish Jurist
0021-1281 Irish Law Times and Solicitors' Journal
0021-129X Irish Medical Association. Journal *changed to* Irish Medical Journal
0021-1303 Irish Messenger of the Sacred Heart *changed to* Sacred Heart Messenger
0021-1311 Irish Naturalists' Journal
0021-132X Irish Numismatics
0021-1338 Irish Nurses' Journal *changed to* World of Irish Nursing
0021-1354 Irish Nursing News *changed to* Irish Nursing Newsletter
0021-1362 Irish Plumbing & Heating Engineer *changed to* Irish H & V News
0021-1370 Irish Statistical Bulletin
0021-1389 Irish Sword
0021-1397 Irish Tatler & Sketch
0021-1419 Irish Travel Trade News
0021-1427 Irish University Review
0021-1443 Irish World and Gaelic American
0021-1451 Irish Yachting and Motorboating *changed to* Ireland Afloat
0021-1478 Irodalomtortenet
0021-1486 Irodalomtorteneti Kozlemenyek
0021-1494 Irohin Yoruba
0021-1508 Iron Age
0021-1516 Iron Age Metalworking International *see* 0163-030X
0021-1524 Iron and Steel *see* 0308-9142
0021-1532 Statistical Office of the European Communities. Iron & Steel
0021-1559 Iron and Steel Engineer
0021-1575 Iron and Steel Institute of Japan. Journal
0021-1583 Iron and Steel Institute of Japan. Transactions
0021-1591 Iron and Steel Monthly Statistics *see* 0308-9770
0021-1605 Iron and Steel Translations *changed to* Ferrous and Non-Ferrous Science and Technology Lists-British Industrial and Scientific International Translations
0021-1613 Iron & Steel Journal of India
0021-1621 Iron Worker†
0021-163X Ironworker
0021-1648 Food Irradiation /Irradiation des Aliments (Issn 0021-1648) *see* 0301-049X
0021-1656 Irrigation Age
0021-1664 Irrigation and Power
0021-1672 Irrigation and Power Abstracts
0021-1680 Irrigazione
0021-1710 Iscani†
0021-1737 Isenkraemmerbladet *changed to* Forbrugsgoder
0021-1753 Isis
0021-1761 Iskra
0021-177X Iskusstvo
0021-1788 Iskusstvo Kino
0021-1796 Isla Literaria†
0021-180X Al-Islam
0021-1818 Der Islam
0021-1826 Islam and the Modern Age
0021-1834 Islamic Culture
0021-1842 Islamic Quarterly
0021-1850 Islamic Review†
0021-1869 Islander
0021-1885 Isolation et Revetements *see* 0244-2019
0021-1893 Isotope†
0021-1907 Isotope and Radiation Research
0021-1915 Isotopenpraxis
0021-1923 Isotopes and Radiation Technology†
0021-1931 Isotopics
0021-194X Israel
0021-1958 Israel Annals of Psychiatry and Related Disciplines
0021-1974 Israel Book World *changed to* Jerusalem Post Literary Supplement
0021-1982 Israel. Central Bureau of Statistics. Monthly Bulletin of Statistics
0021-1990 Israel. Central Bureau of Statistics. Foreign Trade Statistics Quarterly *changed to* Israel. Central Bureau of Statistics. Annual Foreign Trade Statistics
0021-2008 Israel. Central Bureau of Statistics. Monthly Price Statistics
0021-2016 Israel Diamonds
0021-2032 Israel Digest of Press and Events in Israel and the Middle East *changed to* Israel Digest
0021-2040 Israel Economist
0021-2059 Israel Exploration Journal
0021-2067 Israel Export and Trade Journal
0021-2075 Israel Financial Review
0021-2083 Israel Horizons
0021-2091 Israel Illustrated *see* 0007-7038
0021-2113 Israel Investors' Reporter *changed to* Israel Business
0021-213X Israel Journal of Botany
0021-2148 Israel Journal of Chemistry
0021-2164 Israel Journal of Earth Sciences
0021-2172 Israel Journal of Mathematics
0021-2180 Israel Journal of Medical Sciences
0021-2199 Israel Journal of Physiotherapy
0021-2202 Israel Journal of Technology
0021-2210 Israel Journal of Zoology
0021-2229 Israel Labour Party Bulletin†
0021-2237 Israel Law Review
0021-2245 Israel†
0021-2253 Israel Medical Association. Quarterly Review
0021-2261 Israel. Meteorological Service. Monthly Weather Report. Series B (Observational Data)
0021-227X Israel Museum News
0021-2288 Israel Numismatic Journal†
0021-230X Israel Seaman
0021-2318 I S L I C Bulletin
0021-2326 Israel. Ministry of Justice. Patent Office. Patents and Designs Journal
0021-2334 Die Gemeinde
0021-2342 Israelitisches Wochenblatt fuer die Schweiz
0021-2350 Israel's Oriental Problems *changed to* Challenge
0021-2369 Issue†
0021-2377 Issues & Studies
0021-2385 Issues in Criminology†
0021-2415 Istarski Mozaik
0021-2423 Istina
0021-2431 Istituto Carlo Forlanini. Annali†
0021-244X Istituto Centrale del Restauro. Bollettino†
0021-2458 Istituto di Architettura e Urbanistica. Rassegna
0021-2474 Istituto di Studi Romani. Rassegna d'Informazioni
0021-2482 Istituto Italiano degli Attuari. Giornale
0021-2490 Istituto Italiano di Cultura. Newsletter†
0021-2504 Istituto Lombardo Accademia di Scienze e Lettere. Rendiconti. A
0021-2512 Istituto Mobiliare Italiano. Quarterly Economic Review
0021-2520 Istituto Nazionale della Previdenza Sociale. Atti Ufficiali
0021-2539 I N A I L Notiziario Statistico
0021-2547 Istituto Sieroterapico Milanese. Bollettino
0021-2555 Istituto Storico e di Cultura dell'Arma del Genio. Bollettino
0021-2571 Istituto Superiore di Sanita. Annali
0021-258X Istituto Tecnico
0021-2598 Istituto Vaccinogeno e dei Consorzi Provinciali Antitubercolari. Rivista
0021-261X Istmo
0021-2636 Istoricheski Pregled
0021-2644 Istorijski Glasnik
0021-2652 Istorijski Zapisi
0021-2660 Istoriya S. S. S. R.
0021-2679 Istruzione Tecnica *see* 0535-899X
0021-2717 It Starts in the Classroom
0021-2725 It-Torca
0021-2733 Italdoc
0021-2741 Italia

0021-275X Italia Agricola
0021-2768 Italia che Scrive
0021-2776 Italia Forestale e Montana
0021-2792 Italia Medica
0021-2806 Italia Missionaria
0021-2822 Italia Nostra
0021-2830 Italia Numismatica
0021-2849 Italia Scacchistica
0021-2857 Italia Sul Mare
0021-2865 Italia Vinicola ed Agraria
0021-2873 Italian American Business
0021-2881 Italian Books and Periodicals
0021-289X Italian Business†
0021-2903 Italian Chamber of Commerce in Chicago. Bulletin
0021-2911 Italian Economic Survey
0021-292X Italian General Review of Dermatology
0021-2938 Italian Journal of Biochemistry
0021-2946 Italian Production
0021-2954 Italian Quarterly†
0021-2970 Italiana Stil Maglia
0021-2989 Italian Stock Market
0021-2997 Italian Trade Topics
0021-3004 Italian Trends
0021-3012 Italiani nel Mondo
0021-3020 Italica (New York)
0021-3063 Italy - Documents and Notes
0021-3071 Annali della Sanita Pubblica
0021-308X Italy and Nigeria
0021-3098 Italy Canada Trade
0021-3101 Italy. Centro per la Statistica Aziendale. Index
0021-3136 Italy. Istituto Centrale di Statistica. Bollettino Mensile di Statistica
0021-3144 Italy. Ministero dei Trasporti e dell' Aviazione Civile. Azienda Autonoma delle Ferrovie dello Stato. Bollettino Statistico Mensile
0021-3152 Italy. Ministero delle Poste e delle Telecomunicazioni. Comunicazioni Postali Con l'Estero. Bollettino Mensile
0021-3187 Itineraires
0021-3209 Itinerarium
0021-3217 It's Good Psychology
0021-3225 Jugoslavica Physiologica et Pharmacologica. Acta. Serija C
0021-3233 Yunost'
0021-3241 Iura
0021-325X Ius Canonicum
0021-3268 Iustitia
0021-3276 Ivy Leaf
0021-3284 Iwate Medical Association. Journal
0021-3306 Iyyun
0021-3314 Outdoor America
0021-3349 Izmeritel'naya Tekhnika
0021-3357 Izmir Chamber of Commerce Review
0021-3365 Izobretatel' i Ratsionalizator
0021-3381 Izraz
0021-339X Fountain
0021-3411 Izvestiya Vysshikh Uchebnykh Zavedenii. Seriya Fizika
0021-342X Timiryazevskaya Sel'skokhozyaistvennaya Akademiya. Izvestiya
0021-3438 Izvestiya Vysshikh Uchebnykh Zavedenii. Seriya Chernaya Metallurgiya
0021-3446 Izvestiya Vysshikh Uchebnykh Zavedenii. Seriya Matematika
0021-3454 Izvestiya Vysshikh Uchebnykh Zavedenii. Seriya Priborostroenie
0021-3462 Izvestiya Vysshikh Uchebnykh Zavedenii. Seriya Radiofizika
0021-3470 Izvestiya Vysshikh Uchebnykh Zavedenii. Seriya Radioelektronika
0021-3489 Izvestiya Vysshikh Uchebnykh Zavedenii. Seriya Tekhnologiya Legkoi Promyshlennosti
0021-3497 Izvestiya Vysshikh Uchebnykh Zavedenii. Seriya Tekhnologiya Tekstil'noi Promyshlennosti
0021-3500 J A F News Letter†
0021-3519 J A G Journal
0021-3527 J A G Bulletin *see* 0094-8381
0021-3551 Japan Agricultural Research Quarterly
0021-356X J. B. Speed Art Museum Bulletin
0021-3578 J C I World
0021-3594 B J E Bulletin *changed to* Up-to-Date with B J E
0021-3608 J E E
0021-3616 J E I
0021-3624 J E I
0021-3632 J E M F Newsletter *changed to* J E M F Quarterly
0021-3640 J E T P Letters
0021-3659 J E T S Journal†
0021-3667 Journal of General Education
0021-3675 Japanese Journal of Medical Electronics and Biological Engineering
0021-3705 J N F Illustrated
0021-3713 J N K V V News
0021-3721 J N K V V Research Journal
0021-3748 J O L A Technical Communications†
0021-3756 J O T (Journal fuer Oberflaechentechnik) *changed to* Oberflaeche und J O T
0021-3764 J. S. M. E. Bulletin
0021-3772 J T A Daily News Bulletin
0021-3780 J W B Circle
0021-3799 J. W. V. A. Bulletin
0021-3802 Formule 1
0021-3810 Jacetania
0021-3829 Jack and Jill (Inkprint Edition)
0021-3837 Jack London Newsletter
0021-3845 Jack-Pine Warbler
0021-3861 Jacksonville
0021-387X Jacobsen's Fats & Oils Bulletin
0021-3888 Jadeed Science
0021-3896 Jaegerblatt
0021-390X Jag
0021-3918 Jagawani
0021-3926 Jagd und Jaeger in Rheinland-Pfalz
0021-3942 Der Jagdgebrauchshund
0021-3950 Der Jagdspaniel
0021-3969 Jagriti
0021-3977 Jagt og Fiskeri
0021-3985 Jahrbuch der Absatz - und Verbrauchsforschung
0021-3993 Jahrbuch fuer Internationales Recht *changed to* German Yearbook of International Law
0021-4000 Jahrbuch fuer Psychologie, Psychotherapie, und Medizinische Anthropologie *see* 0300-869X
0021-4019 Jahrbuecher fuer Geschichte Osteuropas
0021-4027 Jahrbuecher fuer Nationaloekonomie und Statistik
0021-4035 Jain Jagran
0021-4043 Jain Journal
0021-4051 Jakt-Fiske-Friluftsliv
0021-406X Jaktmaker och Fiskevatten
0021-4078 Jalkine
0021-4086 Jamaica and West Indian Review
0021-4094 Jamaica Chamber of Commerce Journal
0021-4108 Jamaica. Department of Statistics. Rural Retail Price Index *see* 0302-9336
0021-4116 News Review
0021-4124 Jamaica Journal
0021-4132 Jamaica Public Health
0021-4140 Jamaican Nurse
0021-4159 Jamaican Weekly Gleaner
0021-4167 Missionland
0021-4183 James Joyce Quarterly
0021-4191 Jamia Educational Quarterly†
0021-4205 Jana Sangh Patrika
0021-4213 Janaman
0021-4221 Janata
0021-423X Jantantra
0021-4248 Janus†
0021-4256 Janus†
0021-4264 Janus
0021-4272 Janus & S C T H
0021-4280 Japan Academy. Proceedings *changed to* Japan Academy. Proceedings. Series A: Mathematical Sciences
0021-4280 Japan Academy. Proceedings *changed to* Japan Academy. Proceedings. Series B: Physical and Biological Sciences
0021-4299 Japan-America Society of Washington. Bulletin
0021-4302 Japan Architect
0021-4329 Japan Automotive News
0021-4345 Japan Camera Trade News
0021-4353 Japan Christian Activity News
0021-4361 Japan Christian Quarterly
0021-437X Japan Diabetic Society. Journal
0021-4388 Japan Economic Journal
0021-4396 Japan Foundrymen's Society. Journal
0021-440X Japan Harvest
0021-4418 Japan Illustrated†
0021-4426 Japan Institute of Metals. Bulletin
0021-4434 Japan Institute of Metals. Transactions
0021-4450 Japan Interpreter
0021-4469 Japan Labour Bulletin
0021-4477 Japan Lumber Journal
0021-4485 Japan. Maritime Safety Agency. Hydrographic Department. Hydrographic Bulletin
0021-4493 Japan Medical Association. Journal
0021-4507 Japan Medical Gazette
0021-4515 Japan Medical News
0021-4523 Japan Metal Bulletin
0021-4531 Japan Missionary Bulletin
0021-454X Japan Orthodontic Society. Journal
0021-4566 Japan Petroleum Weekly
0021-4574 Japan Plastics
0021-4582 Japan Plastics Age
0021-4590 Japan Quarterly
0021-4604 Japan Report
0021-4620 Japan Sea Regional Fisheries Research Laboratory. Bulletin
0021-4639 Japan Sewage Works Association. Journal
0021-4647 Japan Shipbuilding & Marine Engineering
0021-4655 Japan Socialist Review
0021-4663 Japan Society for Aeronautical and Space Sciences. Journal
0021-4671 Japan Society for Cancer Therapy. Journal
0021-468X Japan Society of Civil Engineers. Journal
0021-4701 Japan Society of London. Bulletin
0021-471X Japan Society of Mathematical Education. Journal
0021-4728 Japan Society of Mechanical Engineers. Journal
0021-4736 Japan Stock Journal
0021-4744 Japan Telecommunications Review
0021-4752 Japan Textile News *changed to* J T N
0021-4760 Japan Trade Bulletin *changed to* Focus Japan
0021-4779 Japan Welding News†
0021-4787 Japan Welding Society. Journal
0021-4795 Japan Wood Research Society. Journal
0021-4809 Japanese Archives of Internal Medicine
0021-4817 Japanese Association for Infectious Diseases. Journal
0021-4825 Japanese Association of Mineralogists, Petrologists and Economic Geologists. Journal
0021-4833 Economic Survey of Japan
0021-4841 Japanese Economic Studies
0021-485X Japanese Forestry Society. Journal
0021-4868 Japanese Heart Journal
0021-4876 Japan Institute of Metals. Journal
0021-4884 Japanese Journal of Allergology
0021-4906 Japanese Journal of Antibiotics
0021-4914 Japanese Journal of Applied Entomology and Zoology
0021-4922 Japanese Journal of Applied Physics
0021-4930 Japanese Journal of Bacteriology
0021-4949 Japanese Journal of Cancer Clinics
0021-4957 Japanese Journal of Child Psychiatry *changed to* Japanese Journal of Child & Adolescent Psychiatry
0021-4965 Japanese Journal of Clinical and Experimental Medicine
0021-4973 Japanese Journal of Clinical Dermatology
0021-4981 Japanese Journal of Clinical Electron Microscopy *changed to* Journal of Clinical Electron Microscopy
0021-499X Japanese Journal of Dermatology: Series A & B
0021-5007 Japanese Journal of Ecology
0021-5015 Japanese Journal of Educational Psychology
0021-5023 Japanese Journal of Ethnology
0021-5031 Japanese Journal of Experimental Medicine
0021-504X Japanese Journal of Genetics
0021-5066 Japanese Journal of Geophysics†
0021-5074 Japanese Journal of Human Genetics
0021-5082 Japanese Journal of Hygiene
0021-5090 Japanese Journal of Ichthyology
0021-5104 Japanese Journal of Limnology
0021-5112 Japanese Journal of Medical Science and Biology
0021-5120 Japanese Journal of Medicine
0021-5139 Japanese Journal of Microbiology *changed to* Microbiology and Immunology
0021-5147 Japanese Journal of Nutrition
0021-5155 Japanese Journal of Ophthalmology
0021-5163 Japanese Journal of Oral Surgery
0021-5171 Japanese Journal of Parasitology
0021-518X Japanese Journal of Pediatrics
0021-5198 Japanese Journal of Pharmacology
0021-5201 Japanese Weekly on Pharmacy and Chemistry
0021-521X Japanese Journal of Physiology
0021-5228 Japanese Journal of Plastic & Reconstructive Surgery
0021-5236 Japanese Journal of Psychology
0021-5244 Japanese Journal of Studies on Alcohol
0021-5252 Japanese Journal of Thoracic Surgery
0021-5260 Japanese Journal of Tropical Agriculture
0021-5279 Japanese Journal of Tuberculosis and Chest Diseases†
0021-5287 Japanese Journal of Urology
0021-5295 Japanese Journal of Veterinary Science
0021-5309 Japanese Journal of Zootechnical Science
0021-5325 Japanese Orthopaedic Association. Journal
0021-5333 Japanese Patents Abstracts *see* 0011-913X
0021-5341 Japanese Periodicals Index. Humanities and Social Science Section
0021-535X Japanese Poetry in English†
0021-5368 Japanese Psychological Research
0021-5376 Food and Nutrition
0021-5384 Japanese Society of Internal Medicine. Journal
0021-5392 Japanese Society of Scientific Fisheries. Bulletin
0021-5406 Japanese Society of Starch Science. Journal
0021-5414 Japanese Sociological Review
0021-5449 Jardin des Arts *changed to* Arts-Magazine
0021-5465 Jardin Ouvrier de France
0021-5481 Jardins de France
0021-5503 Jardin et Logis *changed to* Ami des Fleurs
0021-5511 Jarmuvek, Mezogazdasagi Gepek
0021-552X Jaernhandlaren
0021-5546 Jaernvaegteknik†
0021-5554 Jaune et la Rouge
0021-5562 Javeriana
0021-5570 Jax
0021-5597 Jazykovedny Casopis
0021-5600 Jazz
0021-5619 Jazz - Rhythm & Blues *changed to* Jazz
0021-5627 Jazz & Pop†
0021-5635 Jazz Forum
0021-5643 Jazz Hot
0021-5651 Jazz Journal *see* 0140-2285
0021-566X Jazz Magazine
0021-5678 Jazz Monthly†
0021-5686 Jazz Podium
0021-5694 Jazz Report
0021-5708 Musikrevue†
0021-5716 Jazz Times
0021-5724 Jazzfreund
0021-5740 Je Crois
0021-5759 Jeune Garde *see* 0701-8746
0021-5767 Jean's Journal of Poems *changed to* Jean's Journal
0021-5775 Jedinstvo

0021-5783 Jedleseet†
0021-5791 Jednota
0021-5805 Jednotna Skola
0021-5813 Jeevan Jauban
0021-5821 Jefferson Medical College Alumni Bulletin
0021-583X J. E. M.†
0021-5848 J E N-Bulteno (Junularo Esperantista de Nord-Ameriko *see* 0030-5065
0021-5856 Jenaer Jahrbuch†
0021-5864 Jenaer Rundschau
0021-5872 Jenga
0021-5880 Jeopardy
0021-5899 Jernindustri
0021-5902 Jernkontorets Annaler *changed to* Jernkontorets Annaler. Edition A
0021-5902 Jernkontorets Annaler *changed to* Jernkontorets Annaler. Edition B
0021-5929 Jersey
0021-5945 Jersey Concrete†
0021-5953 Jersey Journal
0021-5961 Jersey Publisher
0021-5988 Jesuit
0021-5996 Jet
0021-6003 Jet Cargo News
0021-602X Jetline Schedules
0021-6038 Jeugd
0021-6054 Jeugdboekengids
0021-6062 Jeugdnatuurwachter
0021-6070 J N
0021-6089 Jeune Afrique
0021-6100 Jeune Revolutionnaire
0021-6119 Jeune (S)†
0021-6127 Quebec Science
0021-6135 Jeunes
0021-6151 Jeunes Avocats
0021-616X Jeunes des Auberges
0021-6194 Jeunesse an Deux Mille
0021-6208 Jeunesse et Orgue
0021-6224 Jeunesses Numismatiques *changed to* Vie Numismatique
0021-6232 Revue Internationale des Jeux et Jouets
0021-6240 Jevrejski Pregled
0021-6259 Jewel of Africa
0021-6267 Jewelers' Circular-Keystone
0021-6275 Jeweller and Metalworker *see* 0307-580X
0021-6283 Jewelry Clip Review *changed to* Costume Jewelry Review
0021-6291 Jewelry Workers' Bulletin
0021-6305 Jewish Affairs
0021-6313 Jewish Affairs
0021-6321 Jewish Braille Review
0021-633X Jewish Chronicle
0021-6348 Jewish Civic Press
0021-6356 Jewish Collegiate Observer *changed to* Kol Yavneh
0021-6364 San Francisco Jewish Bulletin
0021-6372 Jewish Community Center Program Aids
0021-6380 Jewish Current Events
0021-6399 Jewish Currents
0021-6410 Jewish Digest
0021-6429 Jewish Education
0021-6437 Jewish Exponent
0021-6445 Jewish Floridian
0021-6453 Jewish Frontier
0021-6461 Jewish Gazette
0021-647X Jewish Herald
0021-6488 Jewish Herald-Voice
0021-6534 Jewish Journal of Sociology
0021-6542 Jewish Labor Movement. Bund Archives. Bulletin†
0021-6550 Jewish Ledger
0021-6569 Jewish Liberation Journal†
0021-6577 Jewish Life
0021-6585 Jewish Memorial Hospital Bulletin†
0021-6615 Jewish Observer
0021-6623 Jewish Observer and Middle East Review†
0021-6631 Jewish Parent†
0021-664X Jewish Peace Fellowship Newsletter *see* 0080-9160
0021-6658 Jewish Post and Opinion
0021-6666 Jewish Press (Omaha)
0021-6674 Jewish Press (Brooklyn)
0021-6682 Jewish Quarterly Review
0021-6690 Jewish Review *changed to* Religious Zionist Movement News Letter
0021-6704 Jewish Social Studies
0021-6712 Jewish Social Work Forum
0021-6739 Jewish Standard
0021-6747 Jewish Standard
0021-6755 Jewish Telegraph
0021-6763 J T A Weekly News Digest
0021-6771 Jewish Times
0021-678X Jewish Transcript
0021-6801 Jewish Vanguard
0021-681X Jewish Vegetarian
0021-6852 Jewish Week and American Examiner
0021-6860 Jewish Weekly News
0021-6879 Jewish Western Bulletin
0021-6887 Jewish Youth Monthly *changed to* Jewish Youth
0021-6895 Jews & the Jewish People
0021-6909 Jews in Eastern Europe†
0021-6917 Jez
0021-6925 Jezik
0021-6933 Jezik in Slovstvo
0021-6941 Jezyk Polski
0021-695X Jicarilla Chieftain
0021-6968 Jikeikai Medical Journal
0021-6976 Jiwan Dhara
0021-6984 Free World
0021-700X Jnanadhara
0021-7026 Job
0021-7042 Jobber and Warehouse Executive
0021-7050 Jobber News
0021-7069 Jobber Topics
0021-7077 Joblinglass†
0021-7093 Jobson's Investment Digest of Australia and New Zealand
0021-7115 Jockey Club
0021-7131 Joedisk Orientering
0021-714X Joel†
0021-7158 Joeygram *changed to* Calliope
0021-7166 Jogtudomanyi Kozlony
0021-7174 Johann Wilhelm Klein
0021-7182 Johannesburg Stock Exchange Monthly Bulletin
0021-7190 John Herling's Labor Letter
0021-7204 John Liner Letter
0021-7212 John Marshall Journal of Practice and Procedure *see* 0270-854X
0021-7220 John Milton Talking Book
0021-7239 John Rylands Library. Bulletin *see* 0301-102X
0021-7255 Johns Hopkins Magazine
0021-7263 Johns Hopkins Medical Journal
0021-7271 Johnson Drillers Journal
0021-728X Johnsonian News Letter
0021-7298 Information and Documentation
0021-7301 Desfile
0021-731X Joint Acquisitions List of Africana
0021-7328 Progress in Economic Education
0021-7336 National Defence College Gazette
0021-7344 Jok†
0021-7379 Jonge Handen *changed to* Warempel
0021-7387 Jonge Kampvechter
0021-7395 Jonge Kerk
0021-7417 Stakkato
0021-7433 Traktor Journalen
0021-7441 Jordbruksekonomiska Meddelanden
0021-745X Jordbrukskasseroerelsen *see* 0346-9670
0021-7476 Jorden Runt
0021-7484 Jordens Folk - Etnografisk Revy†
0021-7514 Jornal Brasileiro de Neurologia
0021-7522 Jornal de Estomatologia
0021-7557 Jornal de Pediatria
0021-7565 Jornal de Poesia
0021-7573 Jornal do Medico
0021-759X Josephinum Newsletter
0021-7603 Josephite Harvest
0021-7611 Joslin Diabetes Foundation. Newsletter
0021-762X Journal Asiatique
0021-7638 Journal Bandeirante†
0021-7654 Journal Belge de Rhumatologie et de Medecine Physique
0021-7662 Journal d'Agriculture Tropical et de Botanique Appliquee *changed to* Journal d'Agriculture Traditionelle et de Botanique Appliquee
0021-7670 Journal d'Analyse Mathematique
0021-7689 Journal de Chimie Physique et de Physicochimie Biologique
0021-7697 Journal de Chirurgie
0021-7719 Journal de Conchyliologie
0021-7735 Journal de France des Appellations d'Origine
0021-7743 Journal de Genetique Humaine
0021-7751 Journal de Kinesitherapie *see* 0302-427X
0021-776X Journal de la Construction de la Suisse Romande
0021-7778 Journal de la Corse Agricole
0021-7786 Journal de la Marine Marchande
0021-7794 Journal de la Paix - Pax Christi
0021-7808 Journal de l'Amateur d'Art
0021-7816 Journal de l'Equipement Electrique et Electronique
0021-7824 Journal de Mathematiques Pures et Appliquees
0021-7832 Journal de Mecanique
0021-7859 Journal de Medecine de Besancon†
0021-7867 Bordeaux Medical
0021-7875 Journal de Medecine de Caen
0021-7883 Journal de Medecine de Lyon
0021-7891 Journal de Medecine de Montpellier†
0021-7905 Journal de Medecine de Strasbourg†
0021-7913 Journal de Medecine et de Chirurgie Pratiques
0021-7921 Journal de Microscopie *see* 0399-0311
0021-7921 Journal de Microscopie *see* 0395-9279
0021-793X Journal de Pharmacologie
0021-7948 Journal de Physiologie
0021-7956 Journal de Psychologie Normale et Pathologique
0021-7964 Journal de Radiologie d'Electrologie et de Medecine Nucleaire *see* 0227-9363
0021-7972 Journal de Recherches Atmospheriques
0021-7980 Journal de Semiologie Medicale†
0021-7999 Journal Dentaire du Quebec
0021-8006 Journal Historique des Bernier
0021-8014 Journal des Combattants
0021-8022 Journal des Communautes
0021-8030 Journal des Communes
0021-8049 Journal des Finances
0021-8057 Journal des Horticulteurs et Maraichers. *changed to* Horticulteurs et Maraichers Romands
0021-8065 Journal des Ingenieurs
0021-8073 Journal des Instituteurs et des Institutrices
0021-8081 Journal des Medecins du Nord & de l'Est
0021-8111 Journal des Sciences Medicales de Lille
0021-812X Journal des Tribunaux
0021-8138 Journal d'Hotel
0021-8170 Journal du Droit International
0021-8189 Journal du Four Electrique et des Industries Electrochimiques
0021-8197 Journal du Textile
0021-8200 Journal d'Urologie et de Nephrologie *see* 0248-0018
0021-8219 Journal Europeen de Toxicologie *changed to* European Journal of Toxicology and Environmental Hygiene
0021-8227 Journal Export
0021-8235 Journal for Anthroposophy
0021-8243 Journal for Geography/Tydskrif vir Aardrykskunde *see* 0378-5327
0021-8251 Journal for Research in Mathematics Education
0021-8278 Journal for Technical and Vocational Education in South Africa
0021-8286 Journal for the History of Astronomy
0021-8294 Journal for the Scientific Study of Religion
0021-8308 Journal for the Theory of Social Behaviour
0021-8324 Journal Francais de Medecine et Chirurgie Thoraciques†
0021-8332 Journal Francais d'Oto-Rhino-Laryngologie et Chirurgie Maxillo-Faciale
0021-8340 Journal Francais Langenscheidt†
0021-8359 Journal fuer Hirnforschung
0021-8367 Journal fuer Marktforschung†
0021-8375 Journal fuer Ornithologie
0021-8383 Journal fuer praktische Chemie
0021-8405 Journal Mondial de Pharmacie†
0021-8413 Journal Musical Francais-Musica Disques†
0021-8421 Journal of Abdominal Surgery
0021-843X Journal of Abnormal Psychology
0021-8448 Journal of Accountancy
0021-8456 Journal of Accounting Research
0021-8464 Journal of Adhesion
0021-8480 Journal of Adventist Education
0021-8499 Journal of Advertising Research
0021-8502 Journal of Aerosol Science
0021-8510 Journal of Aesthetic Education
0021-8537 Journal of African History
0021-8553 Journal of African Law
0021-8561 Journal of Agricultural and Food Chemistry
0021-857X Journal of Agricultural Economics
0021-8588 Journal of Agricultural Meteorology
0021-8596 Journal of Agricultural Science
0021-860X Journal of Agriculture†
0021-8618 Journal of Agriculture of Western Australia
0021-8626 Journal of Agriculture-South Australia†
0021-8634 Journal of Agricultural Engineering Research
0021-8642 Journal of Air Law and Commerce
0021-8650 Journal of Air Traffic Control
0021-8669 Journal of Aircraft
0021-8677 Journal of Alcohol Education *see* 0090-1482
0021-8685 Bulletin of Alcoholism *see* 0309-1635
0021-8693 Journal of Algebra
0021-8707 Journal of Allergy *see* 0091-6749
0021-8715 Journal of American Folklore
0021-8723 Journal of American History
0021-8731 Journal of American Indian Education
0021-874X Journal of American Insurance
0021-8758 Journal of American Studies
0021-8758 British Association for American Studies. Newsletter *see* 0021-8758
0021-8766 Journal of Analytical Chemistry of the U S S R
0021-8774 Journal of Analytical Psychology
0021-8782 Journal of Anatomy
0021-8790 Journal of Animal Ecology
0021-8804 Journal of Animal Morphology and Physiology
0021-8812 Journal of Animal Science
0021-8820 Journal of Antibiotics
0021-8839 Journal of Apicultural Research
0021-8847 Journal of Applied Bacteriology
0021-8855 Journal of Applied Behavior Analysis
0021-8863 Journal of Applied Behavioral Science
0021-8871 Journal of Applied Chemistry *see* 0142-0356
0021-888X Journal of Applied Chemistry of the U S S R
0021-8898 Journal of Applied Crystallography
0021-8901 Journal of Applied Ecology
0021-891X Journal of Applied Electrochemistry
0021-8928 Journal of Applied Mathematics and Mechanics
0021-8936 Journal of Applied Mechanics
0021-8944 Journal of Applied Mechanics and Technical Physics
0021-8952 Journal of Applied Meteorology
0021-8960 Journal of Applied Nutrition
0021-8979 Journal of Applied Physics
0021-8987 Journal of Applied Physiology *see* 0161-7567
0021-8995 Journal of Applied Polymer Science
0021-9002 Journal of Applied Probability
0021-9010 Journal of Applied Psychology
0021-9029 Journal of Applied Social Psychology
0021-9037 Journal of Applied Spectroscopy
0021-9045 Journal of Approximation Theory
0021-9053 Journal of Arizona History
0021-9061 Journal of Arkansas Education *see* 0161-7753

0021-907X Journal of Art History
0021-9088 Journal of Art Studies
0021-9096 Journal of Asian and African Studies
0021-910X Journal of Asian History
0021-9118 Journal of Asian Studies
0021-9126 Journal of Asiatic Studies
0021-9134 Journal of Asthma Research
0021-9150 Atherosclerosis
0021-9169 Journal of Atmospheric and Terrestrial Physics
0021-9177 Journal of Auditory Research
0021-9185 Journal of Autism and Childhood Schizophrenia *see* 0162-3257
0021-9193 Journal of Bacteriology
0021-9207 Journal of Band Research
0021-9215 Journal of Bank Research
0021-9223 Journal of Basic Engineering†
0021-9223 Journal of Basic Engineering *see* 0098-2202
0021-9223 Journal of Basic Engineering *see* 0094-4289
0021-9231 Journal of Biblical Literature
0021-924X Journal of Biochemistry
0021-9258 Journal of Biological Chemistry
0021-9266 Journal of Biological Education
0021-9274 Journal of Biological Psychology-Worm Runner's Digest†
0021-9282 Journal of Biological Sciences
0021-9290 Journal of Biomechanics
0021-9304 Journal of Biomedical Materials Research
0021-9312 Journal of Biomedical Systems
0021-9339 Journal of Black Poetry *changed to* Kitabu Cha Jua
0021-9347 Journal of Black Studies
0021-9355 Journal of Bone and Joint Surgery: American Volume
0021-9363 Journal of Botany of the United Arab Republic *changed to* Egyptian Journal of Botany
0021-9371 Journal of British Studies
0021-938X Journal of Broadcasting
0021-9398 Journal of Business (Chicago)
0021-9401 Journal of Business (South Orange)
0021-941X Journal of Business Administration
0021-9428 Journal of Business & Social Studies
0021-9436 Journal of Business Communication
0021-9444 Journal of Business Education
0021-9460 Journal of Business Law
0021-9487 Journal of Canadian Petroleum Technology
0021-9495 Journal of Canadian Studies
0021-9509 Journal of Cardiovascular Surgery
0021-9517 Journal of Catalysis
0021-9525 Journal of Cell Biology
0021-9533 Journal of Cell Science
0021-9541 Journal of Cellular Physiology
0021-955X Journal of Cellular Plastics
0021-9568 Journal of Chemical and Engineering Data
0021-9576 Journal of Chemical Documentation *see* 0095-2338
0021-9584 Journal of Chemical Education
0021-9592 Journal of Chemical Engineering of Japan
0021-9606 Journal of Chemical Physics
0021-9614 Journal of Chemical Thermodynamics
0021-9622 Journal of Chemicals and Allied Industries
0021-9630 Journal of Child Psychology and Psychiatry and Allied Disciplines
0021-9649 Journal of Christian Camping
0021-9657 Journal of Christian Education
0021-9665 Journal of Chromatographic Science
0021-9673 Journal of Chromatography
0021-9681 Journal of Chronic Diseases
0021-969X Journal of Church and State
0021-9703 Journal of Church Music
0021-972X Journal of Clinical Endocrinology and Metabolism
0021-9738 Journal of Clinical Investigation
0021-9746 Journal of Clinical Pathology
0021-9754 Journal of Clinical Pharmacology and New Drugs *see* 0091-2700
0021-9762 Journal of Clinical Psychology
0021-9770 Journal of College Placement
0021-9789 Journal of College Student Personnel
0021-9797 Journal of Colloid and Interface Science
0021-9800 Journal of Combinatorial Theory *see* 0097-3165
0021-9800 Journal of Combinatorial Theory *see* 0095-8956
0021-9819 Journal of Commerce
0021-9827 Journal of Commerce
0021-9835 Journal of Commerce & Independent Review *changed to* Journal of Commerce-Review
0021-9843 Journal of Commerce & Industry *changed to* Journal of Commerce, Industry & Transportation
0021-9851 Journal of Commerce
0021-986X Journal of Commercial Bank Lending
0021-9878 Journal of Commodity Trading *see* 0092-7864
0021-9886 Journal of Common Market Studies
0021-9894 Journal of Commonwealth Literature
0021-9908 Journal of Commonwealth Political Studies *see* 0306-3631
0021-9916 Journal of Communication
0021-9924 Journal of Communication Disorders
0021-9932 Journal of Comparative Administration *see* 0095-3997
0021-9940 Journal of Comparative and Physiological Psychology
0021-9967 Journal of Comparative Neurology
0021-9975 Journal of Comparative Pathology
0021-9983 Journal of Composite Materials
0021-9991 Journal of Computational Physics
0022-0000 Journal of Computer and System Sciences
0022-0019 Journal of Conchology
0022-0027 Journal of Conflict Resolution
0022-0035 Journal of Connoisseurship and Art Technology†
0022-0043 Journal of Constitutional & Parliamentary Studies
0022-0051 Journal of Constitutional Law *see* 0377-0907
0022-006X Journal of Consulting and Clinical Psychology
0022-0078 Journal of Consumer Affairs
0022-0086 Journal of Consumer Credit Management
0022-0094 Journal of Contemporary History
0022-0116 Journal of Contemporary Psychotherapy
0022-0124 Journal of Continuing Education in Nursing
0022-0132 Journal of Cooperative Education
0022-0140 Journal of Extension
0022-0159 Journal of Correctional Education
0022-0167 Journal of Counseling Psychology
0022-0175 Journal of Creative Behavior
0022-0183 Journal of Criminal Law
0022-0191 Journal of Criminal Law
0022-0205 Journal of Criminal Law, Criminology and Police Science *see* 0091-4169
0022-0213 Journal of Critical Analysis
0022-0221 Journal of Cross Cultural Psychology
0022-023X Ophthalmic Surgery
0022-0248 Journal of Crystal Growth
0022-0256 Journal of Cuneiform Studies
0022-0264 Journal of Current Laser Abstracts
0022-0272 Journal of Curriculum Studies
0022-0280 Journal of Cybernetics *see* 0196-9722
0022-0299 Journal of Dairy Research
0022-0302 Journal of Dairy Science
0022-0310 Journal of Data Education
0022-0329 Data Management *see* 0148-5431
0022-0337 Journal of Dental Education
0022-0345 Journal of Dental Research
0022-0353 Journal of Dentistry for Children
0022-0361 Journal of Detergents and Collective Chemistry and Physics *changed to* Journal of Collective Chemistry and Physics
0022-037X Journal of Developing Areas
0022-0388 Journal of Development Studies
0022-0396 Journal of Differential Equations
0022-040X Journal of Differential Geometry
0022-0418 Journal of Documentation
0022-0426 Journal of Drug Issues
0022-0434 Journal of Dynamic Systems, Measurement and Control
0022-0442 Journal of Earth Sciences
0022-0450 Journal of East Asiatic Studies
0022-0469 Journal of Ecclesiastical History
0022-0477 Journal of Ecology
0022-0485 Journal of Economic Education
0022-0493 Journal of Economic Entomology
0022-0507 Journal of Economic History
0022-0515 Journal of Economic Literature
0022-0531 Journal of Economic Theory
0022-0558 Journal of Ecumenical Studies
0022-0566 Journal of Education
0022-0574 Journal of Education (Boston)
0022-0582 Sierra Leone Journal of Education
0022-0590 Journal of Education and Psychology
0022-0604 Journal of Education for Librarianship
0022-0612 Journal of Education for Social Work
0022-0620 Journal of Educational Administration and History
0022-0639 Journal of Educational Administration
0022-0655 Journal of Educational Measurement
0022-0663 Journal of Educational Psychology
0022-0671 Journal of Educational Research
0022-068X Journal of Educational Research and Extension
0022-0698 Journal of Educational Technology *see* 0007-1013
0022-0701 Journal of Educational Thought
0022-071X Journal of Elastoplastics. *see* 0095-2443
0022-0728 Journal of Electroanalytical Chemistry and Interfacial Electrochemistry
0022-0736 Journal of Electrocardiology
0022-0744 Journal of Electron Microscopy
0022-0752 Journal of Embryology and Experimental Morphology
0022-0787 Journal of Employment Counseling
0022-0795 Journal of Endocrinology
0022-0809 Engineering Education
0022-0817 Journal of Engineering for Industry
0022-0825 Journal of Engineering for Power
0022-0833 Journal of Engineering Mathematics
0022-0841 Journal of Engineering Physics
0022-0868 Journal of English and Germanic Philology *see* 0363-6941
0022-0884 Journal of English Teaching Techniques†
0022-0892 Journal of Environmental Health
0022-0906 Journal of Environmental Sciences
0022-0914 Journal of Ethiopian Law†
0022-0922 Journal of Ethiopian Studies†
0022-0930 Journal of Evolutionary Biochemistry and Physiology
0022-0949 Journal of Experimental Biology
0022-0957 Journal of Experimental Botany
0022-0965 Journal of Experimental Child Psychology
0022-0973 Journal of Experimental Education
0022-0981 Journal of Experimental Marine Biology and Ecology
0022-099X Journal of Experimental Medical Sciences†
0022-1007 Journal of Experimental Medicine
0022-1015 Journal of Experimental Psychology *see* 0096-1515
0022-1015 Journal of Experimental Psychology *see* 0097-7403
0022-1015 Journal of Experimental Psychology *see* 0096-3445
0022-1023 Journal of Experimental Research in Personality *see* 0092-6566
0022-1031 Journal of Experimental Social Psychology
0022-104X Journal of Experimental Zoology
0022-1066 Journal of Family Law
0022-1074 Journal of Family Welfare
0022-1082 Journal of Finance
0022-1090 Journal of Financial and Quantitative Analysis
0022-1104 Journal of Fire & Flammability
0022-1112 Journal of Fish Biology
0022-1120 Journal of Fluid Mechanics
0022-1139 Journal of Fluorine Chemistry
0022-1147 Journal of Food Science
0022-1155 Journal of Food Science and Technology
0022-1163 Journal of Food Technology
0022-1171 Journal of Forensic Medicine†
0022-1171 Journal of Forensic Medicine *see* 0379-0738
0022-1198 Journal of Forensic Sciences
0022-1201 Journal of Forestry
0022-121X Journal of Fuel and Heat Technology *see* 0367-1119
0022-1228 Journal of Fukien History
0022-1236 Journal of Functional Analysis
0022-1244 Journal of Gem Industry
0022-1252 Journal of Gemmology and Proceedings of the Gemmological Association of Great Britain
0022-1260 Journal of General and Applied Microbiology
0022-1279 Journal of General Chemistry of the U S S R
0022-1287 Journal of General Microbiology
0022-1295 Journal of General Physiology
0022-1309 Journal of General Psychology
0022-1317 Journal of General Virology
0022-1325 Journal of Genetic Psychology
0022-1341 Journal of Geography
0022-135X Journal of Geography
0022-1368 Journal of Geological Education
0022-1376 Journal of Geology
0022-1384 Journal of Geology of the United Arab Republic *changed to* Egyptian Journal of Geology
0022-1392 Journal of Geomagnetism and Geoelectricity
0022-1406 Journal of Geophysical Research *see* 0196-2256
0022-1414 Journal of Geriatric Psychiatry
0022-1422 Journal of Gerontology
0022-1430 Journal of Glaciology
0022-1449 Journal of Graphoanalysis
0022-1457 Journal of Health and Physical Education *changed to* Journal of Health, Physical Education and Recreation
0022-1465 Journal of Health and Social Behavior
0022-1473 Journal of Health, Physical Education, Recreation *changed to* Journal of Physical Education, Recreation and Dance
0022-1481 Journal of Heat Transfer
0022-149X Journal of Helminthology
0022-1511 Journal of Herpetology
0022-152X Journal of Heterocyclic Chemistry
0022-1538 Journal of High Temperature Science *see* 0018-1536
0022-1546 Journal of Higher Education
0022-1554 Journal of Histochemistry and Cytochemistry
0022-1562 Journal of Historical Research
0022-1570 Journal of Home Economics
0022-1589 Journal of Horticultural Science
0022-1597 Hospital and Community Psychiatry
0022-1600 Journal of Hospital Dental Practice
0022-1619 Journal of Hospital Pharmacy *see* 0025-7621
0022-1651 Journal of Human Relations†
0022-166X Journal of Human Resources
0022-1678 Journal of Humanistic Psychology
0022-1686 Journal of Hydraulic Research
0022-1694 Journal of Hydrology
0022-1708 Journal of Hydrology (N.Z.)
0022-1716 Journal of Hydronautics
0022-1724 Journal of Hygiene
0022-1732 Journal of Hygiene, Epidemiology, Microbiology and Immunology
0022-1759 Journal of Immunological Methods
0022-1767 Journal of Immunology
0022-1775 Journal of Indian History
0022-1791 Journal of Indian Philosophy
0022-1805 Journal of Individual Psychology
0022-1813 Man/Society/Technology
0022-1821 Journal of Industrial Economics
0022-183X Journal of Industrial Engineering
0022-1856 Journal of Industrial Relations
0022-1864 Journal of Industrial Teacher Education
0022-1872 Journal of Industry
0022-1880 Journal of Industry and Trade
0022-1899 Journal of Infectious Diseases

0022-1902 Journal of Inorganic and Nuclear Chemistry
0022-1910 Journal of Insect Physiology
0022-1929 Journal of Insurance
0022-1937 Journal of Interamerican Studies and World Affairs
0022-1945 Journal of Interdisciplinary Cycle Research
0022-1953 Journal of Interdisciplinary History
0022-1961 Journal of Internal Medicine *changed to* Internal Medicine
0022-197X Journal of International Affairs
0022-1988 Journal of International and Comparative Studies *see* 0091-2573
0022-1996 Journal of International Economics
0022-2003 Journal of International Law and Economics
0022-2011 Journal of Invertebrate Pathology
0022-202X Journal of Investigative Dermatology
0022-2038 Journal of Irreproducible Results
0022-2054 Journal of J. J. Group of Hospitals and Grant Medical College
0022-2062 Journal of Japanese Botany
0022-2070 Journal of Japanese Chemistry
0022-2089 Journal of Jewish Communal Service
0022-2097 Journal of Jewish Studies
0022-2100 Journal of Jinsen Medical Sciences
0022-2119 Journal of Karyopathology
0022-2135 Journal of Labelled Compounds *see* 0362-4803
0022-2143 Journal of Laboratory and Clinical Medicine
0022-2151 Journal of Laryngology and Otology
0022-216X Journal of Latin American Studies
0022-2186 Journal of Law and Economics
0022-2194 Journal of Learning Disabilities
0022-2208 Journal of Legal Education
0022-2216 Journal of Leisure Research
0022-2224 Visible Language
0022-2232 Journal of Librarianship
0022-2240 Journal of Library Automation
0022-2259 Journal of Library History, Philosophy and Comparative Librarianship
0022-2267 Journal of Linguistics
0022-2275 Journal of Lipid Research
0022-2283 Journal of Livestock and Agriculture *changed to* St. Joseph Journal of Livestock and Agriculture
0022-2291 Journal of Low Temperature Physics
0022-2305 Journal of Lubrication Technology
0022-2313 Journal of Luminescence
0022-2321 Journal of Macromolecular Science, Part D: Reviews in Polymer Processing and Technology *see* 0360-2559
0022-233X Journal of Macromolecular Science. Part A. Chemistry
0022-2348 Journal of Macromolecular Science. Part B. Physics
0022-2356 Journal of Macromolecular Science, Part C. Reviews in Macromolecular Chemistry
0022-2364 Journal of Magnetic Resonance
0022-2372 Journal of Mammalogy
0022-2380 Journal of Management Studies
0022-2399 Journal of Management Studies
0022-2402 Journal of Marine Research
0022-2410 Journal of Maritime Law and Commerce
0022-2429 Journal of Marketing
0022-2437 Journal of Marketing Research
0022-2445 Journal of Marriage and the Family
0022-2453 Journal of Materials. (J M L S A) *see* 0090-3973
0022-2461 Journal of Materials Science
0022-247X Journal of Mathematical Analysis and Applications
0022-2488 Journal of Mathematical Physics
0022-2496 Journal of Mathematical Psychology
0022-250X Journal of Mathematical Sociology
0022-2518 Indiana University Mathematics Journal
0022-2526 Studies in Applied Mathematics
0022-2542 Journal of Mechanical Engineering Science
0022-2550 Government Mechanical Laboratory of Japan. Journal
0022-2569 Journal of Mechanisms *see* 0094-114X
0022-2577 Journal of Medical Education
0022-2585 Journal of Medical Entomology
0022-2593 Journal of Medical Genetics
0022-2607 Medical Laboratory Technology *see* 0308-3616
0022-2615 Journal of Medical Microbiology
0022-2623 Journal of Medicinal Chemistry
0022-2631 Journal of Membrane Biology
0022-264X Journal of Mental Deficiency Research
0022-2658 Journal of Mental Health
0022-2666 Journal of Mental Subnormality *see* 0374-633X
0022-2704 Journal of Microbiology of the United Arab Republic *changed to* Egyptian Journal of Microbiology
0022-2712 Journal of Micrographics
0022-2720 Journal of Microscopy
0022-2739 Journal of Microwave Power
0022-2747 Journal of Milk and Food Technology *see* 0362-028X
0022-2755 Journal of Mines, Metals and Fuels
0022-2771 Journal of Mississippi History
0022-278X Journal of Modern African Studies
0022-2798 Journal of Modern Education
0022-2801 Journal of Modern History
0022-281X Journal of Modern Literature
0022-2828 Journal of Molecular and Cellular Cardiology
0022-2836 Journal of Molecular Biology
0022-2844 Journal of Molecular Evolution
0022-2852 Journal of Molecular Spectroscopy
0022-2860 Journal of Molecular Structure
0022-2879 Journal of Money, Credit & Banking
0022-2887 Journal of Morphology *see* 0362-2525
0022-2895 Journal of Motor Behavior
0022-2909 Journal of Music Theory
0022-2917 Journal of Music Therapy
0022-2925 Journal of Narrative Technique
0022-2933 Journal of Natural History
0022-2941 Journal of Natural Sciences and Mathematics
0022-295X Journal of Navy Civilian Manpower Management *see* 0364-0426
0022-2968 Journal of Near Eastern Studies
0022-2976 Journal of Necromantic Numismatics
0022-2984 Journal of Negro Education
0022-2992 Journal of Negro History
0022-300X Journal of Nematology
0022-3018 Journal of Nervous and Mental Disease
0022-3026 Journal of Neuro-Visceral Relations *see* 0300-9564
0022-3034 Journal of Neurobiology
0022-3042 Journal of Neurochemistry
0022-3050 Journal of Neurology, Neurosurgery and Psychiatry
0022-3069 Journal of Neuropathology and Experimental Neurology
0022-3077 Journal of Neurophysiology
0022-3085 Journal of Neurosurgery
0022-3093 Journal of Non-Crystalline Solids
0022-3107 Journal of Nuclear Energy *see* 0306-4549
0022-3115 Journal of Nuclear Materials
0022-3123 Journal of Nuclear Medicine *see* 0161-5505
0022-3131 Journal of Nuclear Science and Technology
0022-314X Journal of Number Theory
0022-3158 Journal of Nursing Education
0022-3166 Journal of Nutrition
0022-3174 Indian Journal of Nutrition and Dietetics
0022-3182 Journal of Nutrition Education
0022-3190 Journal of Obstetrics and Gynaecology of India
0022-3204 Journal of Obstetrics and Gynaecology of the British Commonwealth *see* 0306-5456
0022-3212 Journal of Occupational Medicine *see* 0096-1736
0022-3239 Journal of Optimization Theory and Applications
0022-3247 Journal of Oral Medicine
0022-3255 Journal of Oral Surgery
0022-3263 Journal of Organic Chemistry
0022-3271 Journal of Organic Chemistry of the U S S R
0022-328X Journal of Organometallic Chemistry
0022-3298 Journal of Orgonomy
0022-3301 Journal of Oriental Research
0022-331X Journal of Oriental Studies
0022-3336 Journal of Outdoor Education
0022-3344 Journal of Pacific History
0022-3352 J.P.T. Journal of Paint Technology *see* 0361-8773
0022-3360 Journal of Paleontology
0022-3379 Journal of Palynology
0022-3387 Journal of Parapsychology
0022-3395 Journal of Parasitology
0022-3409 Journal of Pastoral Care
0022-3417 Journal of Pathology
0022-3425 Journal of Peace *see* 0022-3433
0022-3433 Journal of Peace Research
0022-345X Journal of Pediatric Ophthalmology *changed to* Journal of Pediatric Ophthalmology and Strabismus
0022-3468 Journal of Pediatric Surgery
0022-3476 Journal of Pediatrics
0022-3484 Journal of Periodontal Research
0022-3492 Journal of Periodontology
0022-3506 Journal of Personality
0022-3514 Journal of Personality and Social Psychology
0022-3522 Journal of Petroleum Technology
0022-3530 Journal of Petrology
0022-3549 Journal of Pharmaceutical Sciences
0022-3557 Journal of Pharmaceutical Sciences of the United Arab Repubic *see* 0301-5068
0022-3565 Journal of Pharmacology and Experimental Therapeutics
0022-3573 Journal of Pharmacy and Pharmacology
0022-3581 Journal of Phi Rho Sigma
0022-359X Journal of Philippine Librarianship†
0022-3603 Journal of Philippine Statistics
0022-3611 Journal of Philosophical Logic
0022-362X Journal of Philosophy
0022-3638 Journal of Photographic Science
0022-3646 Journal of Phycology
0022-3654 Journal of Physical Chemistry
0022-3662 Journal of Physical Education
0022-3670 Journal of Physical Oceanography
0022-3689 Journal of Physics A-General *see* 0305-4470
0022-3697 Journal of Physics and Chemistry of Solids
0022-3700 Journal of Physics B: Atomic and Molecular Physics
0022-3719 Journal of Physics C: Solid State Physics
0022-3727 Journal of Physics D: Applied Physics
0022-3735 Journal of Physics E: Scientific Instruments
0022-3743 Journal of Physics of the Earth
0022-3751 Journal of Physiology
0022-376X Journal of Planning and Property Law *see* 0307-4870
0022-3778 Journal of Plasma Physics
0022-3786 D E Journal *see* 0147-6998
0022-3794 Journal of Podiatric Medicine
0022-3808 Journal of Political Economy
0022-3816 Journal of Politics
0022-3824 Journal of Polygraph Studies *changed to* Journal of Polygraph Science
0022-3840 Journal of Popular Culture
0022-3859 Journal of Postgraduate Medicine
0022-3867 Journal of Practical Nursing
0022-3883 Journal of Presbyterian History
0022-3891 Journal of Personality Assessment
0022-3905 Journal of Property Management
0022-3913 Journal of Prosthetic Dentistry
0022-3921 Journal of Protozoology
0022-393X Journal of Psychedelic Drugs *changed to* Journal of Psychoactive Drugs
0022-3948 Journal of Psychiatric Nursing *see* 0360-5973
0022-3956 Journal of Psychiatric Research
0022-3964 Journal of Psychoanalysis in Groups *see* 0093-4763
0022-3972 Journal of Psychological Researches
0022-3980 Journal of Psychology
0022-3999 Journal of Psychosomatic Research
0022-4006 Journal of Public Health Dentistry
0022-4014 Journal of Public Law *see* 0094-4076
0022-4030 Journal of Purchasing *see* 0094-8594
0022-4049 Journal of Pure and Applied Algebra
0022-4057 Journal of Pure and Applied Sciences
0022-4065 Journal of Quality Technology
0022-4073 Journal of Quantitative Spectroscopy and Radiative Transfer
0022-409X Journal of Range Management
0022-4103 Journal of Reading
0022-4111 Journal of Reading Behavior
0022-412X Journal of Recreational Mathematics
0022-4138 Journal of Refrigeration†
0022-4146 Journal of Regional Science
0022-4154 Journal of Rehabilitation
0022-4162 Journal of Rehabilitation in Asia
0022-4170 Journal of Rehabilitation of the Deaf
0022-4189 Journal of Religion
0022-4197 Journal of Religion and Health
0022-4200 Journal of Religion in Africa
0022-4219 Journal of Religious Education *see* 0276-0770
0022-4227 Journal of Religious History
0022-4235 Journal of Religious Thought
0022-4243 Journal of Reprints for Antitrust Law & Economics
0022-4251 Journal of Reproduction and Fertility
0022-426X Journal of Research and Development in Education
0022-4278 Journal of Research in Crime and Delinquency
0022-4286 Journal of Research in Indian Medicine
0022-4294 Journal of Research in Music Education
0022-4308 Journal of Research in Science Teaching
0022-4316 U. S. National Bureau of Standards. Journal of Research. Section C: Engineering and Instrumentation†
0022-4324 Journal of Research on the Lepidoptera
0022-4332 U. S. National Bureau of Standards. Journal of Research. Section A. Physics and Chemistry *see* 0160-1741
0022-4340 U. S. National Bureau of Standards. Journal of Research. Section B. Mathematical Sciences *see* 0160-1741
0022-4359 Journal of Retailing
0022-4367 Journal of Risk and Insurance
0022-4375 Journal of Safety Research†
0022-4383 Journal of San Diego History
0022-4391 Journal of School Health
0022-4405 Journal of School Psychology
0022-4413 Journal of Science and Engineering Research
0022-4421 Journal of Science and Technology *see* 0302-2587
0022-443X Journal of Science of Labour
0022-4456 Journal of Scientific and Industrial Research
0022-4464 Journal of Secondary Education *see* 0145-2061
0022-4472 Journal of Sedimentary Petrology
0022-4480 Journal of Semitic Studies
0022-4499 Journal of Sex Research
0022-4502 Journal of Ship Research
0022-4510 Journal of Small Animal Practice
0022-4529 Journal of Social History
0022-4537 Journal of Social Issues
0022-4545 Journal of Social Psychology
0022-4553 Journal of Societal Issues†
0022-4561 Journal of Soil and Water Conservation
0022-457X Journal of Soil and Water Conservation in India
0022-4588 Journal of Soil Science
0022-4596 Journal of Solid State Chemistry
0022-460X Journal of Sound and Vibration
0022-4618 Journal of South African Botany
0022-4634 Journal of Southeast Asian Studies
0022-4642 Journal of Southern History
0022-4650 Journal of Spacecraft and Rockets
0022-4669 Journal of Special Education
0022-4677 Journal of Speech and Hearing Disorders
0022-4685 Journal of Speech and Hearing Research
0022-4693 Journal of Spelean History
0022-4707 Journal of Sports Medicine and Physical Fitness
0022-4715 Journal of Statistical Physics

0022-4723 Journal of Steel Castings Research
0022-4731 Journal of Steroid Biochemistry
0022-474X Journal of Stored Products Research
0022-4758 Journal of Strain Analysis *see* 0309-3247
0022-4766 Journal of Structural Chemistry
0022-4774 Journal of Structural Learning
0022-4782 Journal of Submicroscopic Cytology
0022-4790 Journal of Surgical Oncology
0022-4804 Journal of Surgical Research
0022-4812 Journal of Symbolic Logic
0022-4820 Journal of Systems Engineering *see* 0308-9541
0022-4839 Journal of Systems Management
0022-4847 Journal of Taiwan Agricultural Research *changed to* Journal of Agricultural Research of China
0022-4855 Journal of Tamil Studies
0022-4863 Journal of Taxation
0022-4871 Journal of Teacher Education†
0022-4871 Journal of Teacher Education
0022-4898 Journal of Terramechanics
0022-4901 Journal of Texture Studies
0022-4928 Journal of the Atmospheric Sciences
0022-4936 Journal of the Chemical Society. Chemical Communications
0022-4944 Chemical Society, London. Journal. Section A: Inorganic, Physical and Theoretical Chemistry *see* 0300-9246
0022-4952 Chemical Society, London. Journal. Section C: Organic Chemistry *see* 0300-922X
0022-4979 Kranatak University. College of Education. Journal
0022-4987 Journal of the Dianetic Sciences *changed to* Dianetic Journal Notes
0022-4995 Journal of the Economic and Social History of the Orient
0022-5002 Journal of the Experimental Analysis of Behavior
0022-5010 Journal of the History of Biology
0022-5029 Journal of the History of Buddhism†
0022-5037 Journal of the History of Ideas
0022-5045 Journal of the History of Medicine and Allied Sciences
0022-5053 Journal of the History of Philosophy
0022-5061 Journal of the History of the Behavioral Sciences
0022-507X Journal of the Indian Medical Profession
0022-5088 Journal of the Less-Common Metals
0022-5096 Journal of the Mechanics and Physics of Solids
0022-510X Journal of the Neurological Sciences
0022-5118 Journal of the New African Literature and the Arts†
0022-5126 Journal of the Reading Specialist *changed to* Reading World
0022-5134 Journal of the Royal Artillery
0022-5142 Journal of the Science of Food and Agriculture
0022-5150 Denison University. Journal of the Scientific Laboratories
0022-5169 Journal of the West
0022-5177 Journal of the West Australian Nurses†
0022-5185 Journal of Theological Studies
0022-5193 Journal of Theoretical Biology
0022-5207 Journal of Therapy
0022-5215 Journal of Thermal Analysis
0022-5223 Journal of Thoracic and Cardiovascular Surgery
0022-5231 Journal of Thought
0022-524X Journal of Transpersonal Psychology
0022-5258 Journal of Transport Economics and Policy
0022-5266 Journal of Transport History
0022-5274 Journal of Transportation Medicine
0022-5282 Journal of Trauma
0022-5290 Journal of Tropical Geography *changed to* Singapore Journal of Tropical Geography
0022-5304 Journal of Tropical Medicine and Hygiene
0022-5320 Journal of Ultrastructure Research
0022-5339 Journal of Undergraduate Mathematics
0022-5347 Journal of Urology
0022-5355 Journal of Vacuum Science and Technology
0022-5363 Journal of Value Inquiry
0022-5371 Journal of Verbal Learning and Verbal Behavior
0022-538X Journal of Virology
0022-5398 Journal of Vitaminology *see* 0301-4800
0022-5401 Journal of West African Languages
0022-541X Journal of Wildlife Management
0022-5428 Columbia Journal of World Business
0022-5436 Journal of World History
0022-5444 Journal of World Trade Law
0022-5452 Journal of Yugoslav Foreign Trade
0022-5460 Journal of Zoology
0022-5495 Journal Pratique de Droit Fiscal et Financier *changed to* Journal de Droit Fiscal
0022-5509 Journalism†
0022-5517 Journalism Educator
0022-5525 Journalism Monographs
0022-5533 Journalism Quarterly *see* 0196-3031
0022-5541 Journalist
0022-555X Journalist
0022-5568 Zhurnalist
0022-5576 Der Journalist
0022-5584 Journalist
0022-5592 Journalisten
0022-5622 Journee des Fruits & Legumes
0022-5630 Journee du Batiment
0022-5649 Journee Vinicole
0022-5665 Journeyman Barber *changed to* Journeyman Barber and Beauty Culture
0022-5673 Journeyman Roofer and Waterproofer
0022-5681 Jours de France
0022-569X Joy†
0022-5703 Joy & Light
0022-5711 Jucunda Laudatio
0022-572X Judaica
0022-5738 Judaica Bohemiae
0022-5746 Judaica Book Guide†
0022-5754 Judaica Book News
0022-5762 Judaism
0022-5770 Judean
0022-5789 Judge
0022-5800 Judicature
0022-5819 Judo
0022-5827 Judo Echo *changed to* Budo Echo
0022-5835 Judo Illustrated
0022-5843 Judo Kokokan†
0022-5851 Judy
0022-5878 Jugend & Technik
0022-5886 Jugend Film Fernsehen *see* 0341-6860
0022-5894 Jugend in Arbeit *changed to* Jugend in Schule und Beruf
0022-5908 Jugend Kurier†
0022-5916 Jugend und Buch
0022-5924 Jugenddorf-Zeitung *changed to* Klinge
0022-5932 Jugendherberge
0022-5940 Jugendhilfe
0022-5959 Jugendpost
0022-5967 Jugendwacht
0022-5975 Jugendwohl
0022-6009 Jugi
0022-6017 Jugoslavenska Advokatura†
0022-6025 Jugoslavia Pervojisto
0022-6033 Jugoslavija
0022-6041 Yugoslavskie Profsoyuzy
0022-605X Jugoslawische Touristenzeitung
0022-6068 Jugoslovenska i Inostrana Dokumentacija Zastite na Radu
0022-6076 Jugoslovenska Revija za Kriminologiju i Krivicno Pravo
0022-6084 Jugoslovenska Revija za Medjunarodno Pravo
0022-6130 Jugoslovensko Vinogradarstvo i Vinarstvo
0022-6157 Juguetes y Juegos de Espana
0022-6165 Juillard†
0022-6173 Juilliard News Bulletin
0022-6181 Juke Box
0022-6203 Juncture - Where Ideas Meet†
0022-6211 June and School Friend *changed to* June and Pixie
0022-622X Junge Christliche Arbeitnehmer. Werkbrief *changed to* C A J Junge Christliche Arbeitnehmer
0022-6246 Das Junge Elektrohandwerk
0022-6262 Der Junge Florist
0022-6270 Junge Gaertner†
0022-6289 Junge Gemeinde
0022-6297 Junge Generation
0022-6300 Der Junge Kaufmann
0022-6319 Junge Kirche
0022-6335 Der Junge Metallhandwerwer
0022-6343 Junge Sammler
0022-6351 Jung Soldat; Kinderzeitschrift der Heilsarmee *changed to* D J S
0022-636X Junge Stimme†
0022-6378 Der Junge Textilverkaeufer
0022-6394 Junger Tischler†
0022-6416 Junge Wirtschaft
0022-6424 Jungfreiheitliche†
0022-6432 Junghandwerker im Kraftfahrzeug-Betrieb *see* 0341-5627
0022-6440 Eisenhardt-Post
0022-6467 Jungscharhelfer
0022-6475 Junior
0022-6483 Junior Age
0022-6491 Junior Astronomy News
0022-6505 Junior Bookshelf
0022-6521 Junior Church Paper†
0022-653X Junior College Journal *see* 0190-3160
0022-6548 Junior College Research Review *changed to* Junior College Resource Review
0022-6556 Junior Dental *changed to* Junior Dental e Bocca Nuda
0022-6564 Junior Education Equipment *changed to* Primary & Middle School Equipment
0022-6572 Junior Farmer and 4-H Enthusiast
0022-6599 Junior Hi Challenge *changed to* Junior High New Life Literature
0022-6602 Texas Historian
0022-6610 Institution of General Technician Engineers Journal *see* 0308-650X
0022-6629 Junior Keynotes
0022-6637 Junior League *changed to* Junior League Review
0022-6645 Jet Cadet *changed to* R-A-D-A-R
0022-6653 Junior Literature *changed to* Junior New Life Literature
0022-6661 Junior Members Round Table. News Notes *changed to* Footnotes
0022-667X Junior News
0022-6688 Junior Scholastic
0022-6696 Junior Statesman *changed to* Junior State Report
0022-670X Junior Student
0022-6718 Junior Trails
0022-6726 Quest (St. Louis)†
0022-6734 Junta Nacional da Cortica Boletim *changed to* Instituto dos Produtos Florestais- Cortica. Boletim
0022-6742 Junta Nacional da Marinha Mercante. Boletim *changed to* Portugal. Direccao Geral de Marinha do Comercio. Boletim
0022-6769 Juntendo Medical Journal
0022-6777 Juridica†
0022-6785 Juridical Review
0022-6793 Jurimetrics Journal
0022-6807 Juris
0022-6815 Jurisprudence Association. Journal
0022-6823 Jurisprudence Automobile
0022-6831 Jurisprudence du Port d'Anvers
0022-684X Jurisprudencia e Doutrina
0022-6858 Jurist
0022-6874 Juristen *changed to* Juristen og Oekonomen
0022-6882 Juristenzeitung
0022-6890 Juristische Analysen†
0022-6912 Juristische Blaetter
0022-6920 Juristische Rundschau
0022-6939 Juristische Schulung
0022-6947 J U S
0022-6955 Jus
0022-6963 Jus Gentium
0022-6971 Jussens Venner
0022-698X Just Between Office Girls *changed to* Office Guide for Working Women
0022-6998 P L A Newsletter *see* 0163-5506
0022-7013 Justice
0022-7048 Justice Weekly
0022-7056 Justicia
0022-7064 Justiz-Ministerial-Blatt fuer Hessen
0022-7099 Jute and Jute Fabrics- Pakistan *changed to* Jute and Jute Fabrics-Bangladesh
0022-7102 Jute and Synthetics Review†
0022-7137 Jutro Polski
0022-7145 Juvenile Braille Monthly†
0022-7153 Juvenile Court Judges Journal *see* 0161-7109
0022-7161 Juvenile Merchandising
0022-717X Juvenile Rechabite†
0022-7196 Juventud
0022-720X Juventud en Accion†
0022-7218 Juventud Panadera
0022-7226 Juzen Medical Society. Journal
0022-7234 Jyotish Kalp†
0022-7242 K. A. C. B. Auto Revue
0022-7250 K A G P Journal *see* 0090-5089
0022-7269 K A H P E R Journal
0022-7277 K & C
0022-7293 K B S-Rapporter
0022-7307 K E A. Publications *changed to* K E A. Research Publications
0022-7323 K F Z Werkstaette
0022-734X K L A Bulletin
0022-7358 K L A Bulletin
0022-7390 K M U Monthly Newsletter *changed to* K M U News Report
0022-7404 K-Rautaviesti *see* 0355-3086
0022-7412 K U L S A A Newsletter
0022-7439 K. V. P. News
0022-7447 K. W. F.-Nieuws
0022-7463 Kaarsvlam
0022-7471 Kachiku to Eiyo†
0022-748X Kadima
0022-7498 Kadmos
0022-7501 Kaelte *see* 0343-2246
0022-751X Kaelte-und Klima Rundschau *changed to* Temperatur Technik
0022-7528 Kaelte Klima-Praktiker *changed to* K I Klima, Kaelte, Heizung
0022-7552 Kaerntner Gemeindeblatt
0022-7560 Kaerntner Heimatleben
0022-7579 Kaerntner Landes-Zeitung
0022-7587 Kaerntner Museumsschriften
0022-7595 Kaerntner Naturschutzblaetter
0022-7609 Kaffee und Tee Markt
0022-7625 Science
0022-7633 Science and Technology Information Service
0022-765X Toyama Science and Technical Documents
0022-7668 Japan Association for Philosophy of Science. Journal
0022-7676 Chemical Engineering
0022-7684 Chemistry and Chemical Industry
0022-7692 Journal of History of Science
0022-7706 Monthly Report of Agricultural Meteorology, Kagoshima Prefecture
0022-7714 Kahertaja
0022-7722 Acta Anatomica Nipponica
0022-7757 Kairos
0022-7765 Kairos
0022-779X Kaiserswerther Mitteilungen
0022-7803 Shipping
0022-782X Kajian Ekonomi Malaysia
0022-7838 Kakao und Zucker
0022-7846 Kakteen und Andere Sukkulenten†
0022-7854 Japanese Journal of Nuclear Medicine
0022-7862 Kakyevole
0022-7870 Kalaikathir
0022-7889 Kalakeli
0022-7900 Kalbos Kultura
0022-7919 Kaleidoscope
0022-7927 Kaleidoscope†
0022-7935 Kalendarium†
0022-7943 Kali†
0022-796X Kalibreur
0022-7978 Kalimat Al-Mar'ah
0022-7994 Kalki
0022-8028 Kalyan

0022-8036 Kalyan Kalpataru†
0022-8052 Kamakoti Vani
0022-8060 Kameradengruss†
0022-8109 Kamera und Schule
0022-8117 Kamerad Tier
0022-8133 Kameralehti
0022-8141 University of Leiden. Kamerlingh Onnes Laboratory. Communications
0022-815X Japan T A P P I
0022-8168 Paper & Pulp Statistical Monthly
0022-8176 Kamm und Schere
0022-8184 Kammer-Nachrichten
0022-8192 Kammerspiele Muenchen *changed to* Muenchner Kammerspiele
0022-8206 Campana
0022-8214 Kampanje!
0022-8230 Kampf dem Krieg
0022-8249 Kampf dem Laerm *changed to* Zeitschrift fuer Laermbekaempfung
0022-8257 Kampftruppen
0022-8265 Kampioen
0022-8273 Kamratposten
0022-8281 Kanadai Magyarsag
0022-829X Kanaski Srbobran
0022-8311 Journal of Radiology and Physical Therapy†
0022-832X Kanazawa University. Faculty of Technology. Memoirs
0022-8338 Kanazawa University. Science Reports
0022-8346 Kandang Kerbau Hospital Bulletin *changed to* Singapore Journal of Obstetrics & Gynaecology
0022-8354 Kandelaar
0022-8362 Nursing
0022-8370 Japanese Journal of Nursing Research
0022-8397 Kanot-Nytt
0022-8400 Kansai Medical School. Journal *changed to* Kansai Medical University. Journal
0022-8419 Kansallis-Osake-Pankki. Economic Review
0022-8427 Kansantaloudellinen Aikakauskirja
0022-8435 Kansas!
0022-8443 Kansas Academy of Science. Transactions
0022-8451 Kansas Anthropological Association. Newsletter *changed to* Kansas Anthropological Association. Journal
0022-8478 Kansas Banker
0022-8486 Kansas Bar Association Journal
0022-8494 Kansas Beverage News
0022-8516 Kansas City Grocer
0022-8524 Kansas City Jewish Chronicle
0022-8532 Kansas Economic Development Report
0022-8540 Kansas Electric Farmer *see* 0091-9586
0022-8559 Kansas Engineer
0022-8567 Kansas Entomological Society. Journal
0022-8575 Kansas Farm Bureau News
0022-8591 Kansas Fish and Game
0022-8605 Kansas Food Dealers Bulletin
0022-8613 Kansas Government Journal
0022-8621 Kansas Historical Quarterly *see* 0149-9114
0022-863X Kansas Job Opportunities
0022-8648 Kansas Journal of Sociology *changed to* Mid-American Review of Sociology
0022-8664 Kansas Kernels
0022-8672 Kansas Law Enforcement Journal *changed to* Kansas Peace Officer
0022-8699 Kansas Medical Society. Journal
0022-8702 Kansas Music Review
0022-8710 Kansas Nurse
0022-8729 Kansas Ornithological Society. Bulletin
0022-8737 Kansas Publisher
0022-8745 Kansas Quarterly
0022-8753 Kansas Restaurant
0022-8761 Kansas School Board Journal
0022-877X Kansas School Naturalist
0022-8788 Kansas Speech and Hearing Association Journal
0022-8796 Kansas State Dental Association. Journal
0022-880X Kansas. State Department of Education. Special Education Section. Typical Report†
0022-8818 Kansas State Teachers College Alumni Association. Alumni News *changed to* Spotlight (Emporia)
0022-8826 Kansas Stockman
0022-8834 Kansas Teacher
0022-8842 Kansas Transporter
0022-8850 University of Kansas Science Bulletin
0022-8869 Kansas Water News
0022-8877 Kant-Studien
0022-8885 Kantinen
0022-8893 Kantoor en Efficiency
0022-8907 Kantoor-School-Huis
0022-8923 Kanu-Sport
0022-894X Kappa Delta Epsilon Current
0022-8958 Kappa Delta Pi Record
0022-8974 Karachi University Gazette
0022-8982 Karakter *changed to* Interaktie
0022-8990 Karamu
0022-9008 Karate and Oriental Arts
0022-9024 Karayollari Teknik Bulteni
0022-9032 Kardiologia Polska
0022-9040 Kardiologiya
0022-9059 Karlovacki Tjednik
0022-9075 Karma Album Review†
0022-9083 Karnatak Granthalaya
0022-9091 Karnatak Law Journal
0022-9113 Kartei der Praktischen Medizin
0022-913X Karting
0022-9148 Kartofel' i Ovoshchi
0022-9156 Der Kartoffelbau
0022-9164 Kartographische Nachrichten
0022-9172 Karty Dokumentacyjne
0022-9199 Karys
0022-9202 Fossils
0022-9210 Kashmir Affairs
0022-9229 Kasityo ja Teollisuus
0022-9237 Kasr-El-Aini Journal of Surgery
0022-9245 Kasseler Sonntagsblatt
0022-9253 Kastner & Oehler Firmen-Zeitung
0022-9261 Kasturi
0022-927X Kasvatus
0022-9288 Katallagete
0022-9296 Katedra
0022-930X Katera i Yakhty
0022-9318 Katha-Sahitya
0022-9326 Kathakali†
0022-9334 Katholieke Kleuterschool
0022-9342 Archief van de Kerken
0022-9350 Metamedica
0022-9369 Katholieke Gezondheidszorg *changed to* Maatschappelijke Gezondheidszorg
0022-9377 Katholische Frauenbewegung Oesterreichs. Fuehrungsblatt
0022-9385 Katholische Gedanke *see* 0340-8280
0022-9393 Katholische Hochschuljugend Oesterreichs-Blaetter
0022-9407 Katholischen Missionen *changed to* K M - Die Katholischen Missionen
0022-9415 Katilolehti
0022-9423 Katipo
0022-9431 Katolikus Szemle
0022-9458 Katsaus
0022-9466 Kauchuk i Rezina
0022-9474 Kaufhaus und Warenhaus
0022-9482 Kaunis Koti *see* 0355-2950
0022-9490 Kauppa ja Koti
0022-9504 Kaupparekisteri
0022-9520 Kautschuk und Gummi. Kunststoffe
0022-9539 Kaviamuthu
0022-9547 Kavita
0022-9555 Kayak
0022-9563 Kayhan-E-Bacheha
0022-9571 Kaytannon Maamies
0022-9601 Keel Ja Kirjandus
0022-961X Keen Teen
0022-9636 Keeping Posted
0022-9644 Keeping Posted with N C S Y
0022-9652 Keeping the Record Straight†
0022-9660 Keeping up with Elementary Education *changed to* Educating Children: Early and Middle Years
0022-9679 Keesing's Contemporary Archives
0022-9687 Kehilwenyane
0022-9695 Keidanren Review
0022-9709 Keio Economic Studies
0022-9717 Keio Journal of Medicine
0022-9725 Economic Science
0022-9733 Economic Review
0022-9741 Economic Review
0022-975X Journal of Political Economy
0022-9768 Journal of Economics
0022-9776 Tuberculosis
0022-9784 Kelderblom
0022-9792 Keltia
0022-9806 Keltner Commodity Letter
0022-9822 Kemian Teollisuus *see* 0355-1628
0022-9830 Kemija u Industriji
0022-9857 Kemio Internacia†
0022-9865 Kemisti
0022-9873 Kemixon Reporter
0022-9881 Kemphaan
0022-989X Kempo Nyusu
0022-9903 Kempton Park Parade†
0022-992X Kenko Hoken Shimbun
0022-9938 Public Health Education
0022-9946 Longer and Healthier Life
0022-9954 Kenkyuseika Yoshisyu *see* 0385-6437
0022-9962 Kennel Gazette
0022-9970 K en O
0022-9997 Monthly Report of Price and Wage in Construction Engineering
0023-0006 Kensington News *changed to* Far Northeast News
0023-0014 Kent Archaeological Review
0023-0022 Kent Farmer
0023-0030 Kent Life
0023-0049 Kent Messenger
0023-0057 Kentaur
0023-0065 Kentering†
0023-0073 Kentuckiana Purchasor
0023-0081 Kentucky Academy of Science. Transactions
0023-009X Kentucky Accountant *changed to* Bottom Line
0023-0103 Kentucky Ancestors
0023-0111 Kentucky Banker
0023-012X Kentucky Beverage Journal
0023-0146 Kentucky Civil War Round Table. Bulletin
0023-0162 Kentucky Dental Association. Journal
0023-0170 Kentucky Education News *see* 0164-3959
0023-0189 Kentucky Elementary School Principal
0023-0197 Kentucky English Bulletin
0023-0200 Kentucky Farm Bureau News
0023-0219 Kentucky Farmer
0023-0227 Kentucky Folklore Record
0023-0235 Kentucky Happy Hunting Ground
0023-0243 Kentucky Historical Society. Register
0023-0251 Kentucky Labor News
0023-026X Kentucky Law Journal
0023-0294 Kentucky Medical Association. Journal
0023-0316 Kentucky Nurses Association Newsletter
0023-0324 Kentucky Press
0023-0332 Kentucky Romance Quarterly
0023-0359 Kentucky School Journal†
0023-0367 Kentucky State Bar Journal *see* 0164-9345
0023-0421 Kenya Farmer†
0023-0421 Kenya Farmer
0023-0448 Kenya Police Review
0023-0464 Kenya Teacher Journal
0023-0472 Kenya Weekly News
0023-0480 Kep- es Hangtechnika
0023-0499 Kerala Commerce and Industry
0023-0510 Kerala Law Journal
0023-0529 Kerala Law Times
0023-0537 Kerala Sree
0023-0553 Keramik-Freunde der Schweiz. Mitteilungsblatt
0023-0561 Keramische Zeitschrift
0023-057X Kereskedelmi Szervezes†
0023-0588 Kerk en Wereld†
0023-0596 Kerkblad
0023-0618 Kerkbode van Gereformeerde Kerken in Noord en Zuid-Holland
0023-0626 Kerknieuws van de Hervormde Gemeente Schoonebeek†
0023-0634 Kern County Dental Society Newsletter
0023-0642 Kernenergie
0023-0650 Kerngetallen van Europese Effecten
0023-0669 Kerngetallen van Nederlandse Effecten
0023-0677 Kerteszet es Szoleszet *see* 0133-381X
0023-0685 Kerugma
0023-0693 Kerygma
0023-0707 Kerygma und Dogma
0023-0715 Keshet†
0023-0723 Kesho *changed to* Africa Ya Kesho
0023-0731 Keuken
0023-074X Kexue Tongbao
0023-0758 Key (Grand Rapids)†
0023-0766 Key (Philadelphia)
0023-0774 Key Figures to European Securities
0023-0782 Key Houston
0023-0790 U.S. Department of State. Key Officers in Foreign Service Posts
0023-0804 Key Reporter
0023-0812 Key Dallas *changed to* Key (Dallas)
0023-0820 Key: This Week in San Francisco and Northern California
0023-0839 Key to Christian Education
0023-0855 Key to the Dayton Scene *changed to* Key Dayton Scene
0023-0863 Key to Toronto
0023-0952 Keya-the Journal for You†
0023-0979 Keynotes *changed to* L. O. M. A. Resource
0023-0987 Keystone Folklore Quarterly *see* 0149-8444
0023-0995 Keystone Motorist
0023-1010 Khad Patrika
0023-1029 Khadi Gramodyog
0023-1037 Khadya Vigyan
0023-1045 Khao Kan-Faifa
0023-1053 Khao Setthakit Kan-Kaset
0023-1061 Khartoum†
0023-107X Khatoon Mashriq
0023-1088 Kheti
0023-1096 Khilauna
0023-110X Khimicheskaya Promyshlennost'
0023-1118 Khimicheskie Volokna
0023-1126 Khimicheskoe i Neftyanoe Mashinostroenie
0023-1134 Khimiko-farmatsevticheskii Zhurnal
0023-1142 Khimiya i Zhizn'
0023-1150 Khimiya Prirodnykh Soedinenii
0023-1169 Khimiya i Tekhnologiya Topliv i Masel
0023-1177 Khimiya Tverdogo Topliva
0023-1185 Khimiya v Sel'skom Khozyaistve
0023-1193 Khimiya Vysokikh Energii
0023-1207 Khirurgiya
0023-1215 Khlebopekarnaya i Konditerskaya Promyshlennost'
0023-1223 Khliborob Ukrainy
0023-1231 Khlopkovodstvo
0023-124X Kholodil'naya Tekhnika
0023-1258 Khudozhnik
0023-1274 Kibernetika
0023-1282 Kick to Corruption
0023-1290 Kicker-Sportmagazin
0023-1304 Kidney
0023-1312 Kids†
0023-1347 Kieler Milchwirtschaftliche Forschungsberichte
0023-1355 Kigyoho Kenkyu†
0023-1363 Kijk op het Noorden
0023-1371 Farming Mechanization
0023-138X Quarterly Information of Sugar Industry
0023-1398 Komuna
0023-1401 Kilpailunvapauslehti *see* 0356-5092
0023-141X Kim/Trefle *changed to* Kim
0023-1428 Kamya Muhendisligi
0023-1436 Kin
0023-1444 Kind en Zondag
0023-1452 Kindai Chugoku Kenkya Senta Iho†
0023-1479 Contemporary Architecture
0023-1487 Der Kinderarzt
0023-1495 Kinderaerztliche Praxis
0023-1509 Kinderdorfbote
0023-1517 Kindergartner
0023-1525 Textiel-Visie: Kindermodevakblad
0023-1533 Kinderzeitung
0023-1541 Kine Weekly†
0023-1568 Kinesis
0023-1576 Kinesitherapie Scientifique
0023-1584 Kinetics and Catalysis
0023-1606 Kingbird
0023-1614 Kingdom Digest

ISSN	Title
0023-1630	Libya. Census and Statistical Department. Monthly Cost of Living Index for Tripoli Town
0023-1649	Kingsman
0023-1657	Kinki University. Bulletin of Pharmacy
0023-1673	Kino
0023-1681	Kinomekhanik
0023-169X	Kinotechnik
0023-1703	Kinship
0023-1711	Kinyu Keizai
0023-172X	Kioskejer-Bladet
0023-1738	Kipling Journal
0023-1746	Kiplinger Agricultural Letter
0023-1754	Kiplinger Florida Letter
0023-1762	Kiplinger Tax Letter
0023-1770	Kiplinger Washington Letter
0023-1789	Kirche
0023-1797	Kirchenblatt fuer die Reformierte Schweiz:
0023-1800	Der Kirchenchor
0023-1819	Der Kirchenmusiker
0023-1827	Kirchliches Amtsblatt fuer das Bistum Essen
0023-1843	Kirjastolehti
0023-1851	Kiryat Sefer
0023-186X	Kirke og Kultur
0023-1878	Kiserletes Orvostudomany
0023-1886	Kiswahili
0023-1894	Kitab†
0023-1908	Kitikanto Medical Journal
0023-1916	Kitano Hospital Journal of Medicine
0023-1924	Kitazato Archives of Experimental Medicine
0023-1932	Kitchen Business
0023-1940	Kiva
0023-1967	Kiwanis Magazine
0023-1975	Kizito
0023-1983	Kjemi
0023-1991	Kjoleteknikk og Fryserinaering see 0048-9301
0023-2017	Klagenfurt
0023-2025	Klassekampen
0023-2033	Akroterion
0023-2041	Klei en Keramiek changed to Klei/Glas/Keramiek
0023-2068	Kleine Chorzeitung
0023-2076	Kleintier-Praxis
0023-2084	Kleio
0023-2106	Kleuterwerld changed to Wereld van het Jonge Kind
0023-2114	Kliatt Paperback Book Guide changed to Kliatt Young Adult Paperback Book Guide
0023-2130	Klinicheskaya Khirurgiya
0023-2149	Klinicheskaya Meditsina
0023-2157	Klinika Oczna
0023-2165	Klinische Monatsblaetter fuer Augenheilkunde und fuer Augenarztliche Fortbildung
0023-2173	Klinische Wochenschrift
0023-2181	Klok en Klepel
0023-219X	Klub changed to Klub i Khudozhestvennaya Samodeyatel'nost'
0023-2203	Klub Slowenischer Studenten in Wien. Information
0023-222X	Die Kluge Hausfrau
0023-2238	Kmecki Glas
0023-2246	Kneipp
0023-2254	Kneipp Blaetter
0023-2262	Knight†
0023-2270	Knight's Industrial Reports see 0309-0558
0023-2289	Knip
0023-2300	Knitting Times
0023-2335	Knitting Industry
0023-236X	Ekspress-Informatsiya. Knizhnaya Torgoulya
0023-2378	Knizhnoe Obozrenie
0023-2386	Knjigovoda
0023-2394	Knjigovodstvo
0023-2408	Knjizevnost
0023-2416	Knjizevne Novine
0023-2424	Knjiznica
0023-2432	Konditor-Zeitung
0023-2459	Know Canada
0023-2467	A P S S Know How (Associated Public School Systems) changed to H M L I Research Bulletin
0023-2483	Know Your World changed to Know Your World Extra
0023-2491	Knowledge Industry Report†
0023-2505	Kobber- og Blikkenslagermesteren
0023-2513	Kobe Journal of Medical Sciences
0023-2521	Kobe Plant Protection and Plant Quarantine Information
0023-2548	Kobieta i Zycie
0023-2556	Kobunshi Kagaku changed to Kobunshi Ronbunshu
0023-2564	Polymer Application
0023-2572	Kochniano Anees
0023-2599	Kodai Mathematical Seminar Reports changed to Kodai Mathematical Journal
0023-2602	Kodak Dealer News
0023-2610	Kodin Kuvalehti
0023-2629	Koebenhavns Havneblad
0023-2637	Koeling†
0023-2645	Koelner Monatszahlen
0023-2653	Koelner Zeitschrift fuer Soziologie und Sozialpsychologie
0023-2661	Koeltechniek
0023-267X	Koepel†
0023-2688	Koepmannen
0023-2696	Koerpererziehung†
0023-270X	Koers
0023-2718	Kyushu University. Faculty of Engineering. Technology Reports
0023-2726	N A L News
0023-2734	Kogyo Kagaku Zasshi see 0369-4577
0023-2742	Kohle und Heizoel
0023-2750	Koinonia†
0023-2777	Factory Management
0023-2785	Essences of Japan
0023-2807	Mind and Society
0023-2815	Koks i Khimiya
0023-2823	Koks, Smola, Gaz
0023-2831	Journal of Dental Health
0023-284X	Aircraft Engineering
0023-2858	Japan Air Self Defense Force. Aeromedical Laboratory. Reports
0023-2866	Journal of International Law and Diplomacy
0023-2912	Kolloidnyi Zhurnal
0023-2939	Kolorisztikai Ertesito
0023-2947	Kolpingblatt
0023-2963	Komal Patra
0023-298X	Komfort in Haus und Garten†
0023-3005	Die Kommenden
0023-3013	Kommentar
0023-303X	Kommentare zum Zeitgeschehen
0023-3048	Oesterreichische Akademie der Wissenschaften. Kommission fuer Musikforschung. Mitteilungen
0023-3056	Kommunal Litteraturtjaenst
0023-3064	Kommunal Skoltidning see 0347-5484
0023-3072	Kommunal Tidskrift see 0347-5484
0023-3080	Kommunikation†
0023-3099	Kommunist
0023-3102	Kommunist Belorussii
0023-3110	Kommunist Ukrainy
0023-3129	Kommunisti Tochikiston
0023-3161	Komunikasi
0023-317X	Komuna Esperanto-Gazeto
0023-3188	Komunikaty Mazursko-Warminskie
0023-3196	Komunist
0023-320X	Komunist
0023-3234	Konditorei und Cafe
0023-3250	Der Konditormeister
0023-3277	Konepajamies
0023-3285	Konevodstvo i Konnyi Sport
0023-3293	Konfeksjon†
0023-3307	Kongelige Danske Videnskabernes Selskab. Historisk-Filosofiske Skrifter
0023-3315	Kongelige Danske Videnskabernes Selskab. Oversigt over Selskabets Virksomhed
0023-3323	Kongelige Danske Videnskabernes Selskab. Matematisk-Fysiske Meddelelser
0023-3331	Kongelige Danske Videnskabernes Selskab. Matematisk-Fysiske Skrifter†
0023-334X	Agricultural Chemicals Monthly
0023-3358	Koninklijke Nederlandse Akademie van Wetenschappen. Series A: Mathematical Sciences. Proceedings
0023-3366	Koninklijke Nederlandse Adademie van Wetenschappen. Series B: Physical Sciences. Proceedings changed to Koninklijke Nederlandse Akademie van Wetenschappen. Series B: Palaeontology, Geology, Physics and Chemistry. Proceedings
0023-3374	Biological and Medical Sciences. Proceedings changed to Koninklijke Nederlandse Akademie van Wetenschappen Series C: Biological and Medical Sciences. Proceedings
0023-3390	Koninklijke Shell-Post changed to Shell-Post
0023-3404	Koninklijke Academie voor Nederlandse Taal- en Letterkunde. Verslagen en Mededelingen
0023-3412	Tractatenblad van het Koninkrijk der Nederlanden
0023-3420	Konjunktur und Krise†
0023-3439	Konjunktur von Morgen
0023-3447	Konjunkturberichte
0023-3455	Konjunkturdienst changed to Konjunktur
0023-3463	Konjunkturlaget
0023-3471	Konjunkturni Barometar
0023-348X	Konjunkturni Pregled
0023-3498	Konjunkturpolitik
0023-3501	Konkreet
0023-3544	Konkuriito Jaanaru see 0387-1061
0023-3552	Konkurs-, Treuhand- und Schiedsgerichtswesen
0023-3560	Konsertnytt
0023-3579	Konservatorium Nuus
0023-3587	Konservnaya i Ovoshchesushil'naya Promyshlennost'
0023-3595	Konsonanz
0023-3609	Konsthistorisk Tidskrift
0023-3625	Konstruktion im Maschinen-, Apparate- und Geraetebau changed to Konstruktion
0023-3633	Konstruktiver Ingenieurbau Berichte
0023-365X	Kontakt
0023-3668	Kontakt†
0023-3676	Kontakt Drei und Zwanzig
0023-3692	Kontakto
0023-3714	Kontor-Nyt
0023-3730	Kontorteknikk see 0332-8201
0023-3749	Kontraste Impuls
0023-3757	Kontur
0023-3765	Kontynenty
0023-3773	Konyvtari Figyelo
0023-3811	Kooperation
0023-382X	Kooperationen
0023-3838	K L F Tidskrift see 0024-015X
0023-3846	Kooperatoeren
0023-3862	Koepmannen
0023-3870	Koppeling
0023-3889	Korea Exchange Bank. Monthly Review
0023-3897	Korea Herald
0023-3900	Korea Journal
0023-3919	Korea Observer
0023-3927	Korea Research Society for Dental Materials. Journal
0023-3935	Korea Times
0023-3943	Korea Trade
0023-3951	Korea Week
0023-396X	Korean Business Journal
0023-3978	Korean Economic Journal
0023-3986	Korean Journal of International Law
0023-401X	Korean Journal of Public Health
0023-4028	Korean Medical Association. Journal
0023-4036	Korean Nature
0023-4044	Journal of Social Sciences and Humanities
0023-4052	Korean Scientific Abstracts
0023-4060	Koreana Quarterly
0023-4079	Koreansk Journal
0023-4087	Korneuburger Kulturnachrichten
0023-4095	Koroze a Ochrana Materialu
0023-4117	Korpsblad Rijkspolitie changed to Rijkspolitie Magazine
0023-4125	Korrespondens /Utbildningskontakt
0023-4133	Korrosion
0023-4141	Korrosion och Ytskydd changed to Modern Ytbehandling
0023-415X	Kortars
0023-4168	Kosmetik-Parfum-Drogen-Rundschau mit Aerosol-Aspect†
0023-4176	Kosmetikerinnen-Fachzeitung - Parfuemerie Journal changed to Kosmetik International
0023-4184	Kosmetische Monatsschrift†
0023-4192	Kosmicheskaya Biologiya i Meditsina changed to Kosmicheskaya Biologiya i Aviakosmicheskaya Meditsina
0023-4206	Kosmicheskie Issledovaniya
0023-4214	Kosmobiologie
0023-4222	Kosmorama
0023-4230	Kosmos
0023-4249	Kosmos. Series A. Biologia
0023-4257	Kosmos Tis Psychis
0023-4265	Kostenrechnungs-Praxis
0023-4281	Kotiliesi
0023-429X	Kountry Korral†
0023-4303	Kovave†
0023-4311	Kovoexport changed to Kovoexport-Investa
0023-432X	Kovove Materialy
0023-4338	Kozarstvi
0023-4346	Kozgazdasagi Szemle
0023-4354	Kozhevenno-Obuvnaya Promyshlennost'
0023-4362	Kozlekedestudomanyi Szemle
0023-4370	Kraaiennest†
0023-4389	Kracht van Omhoog
0023-4397	Kraftfahrzeug und Motorrad-Kurier changed to Kraftfahrzeug-Gewerbe Suedbaden
0023-4400	Der Kraftfahrzeugvermieter
0023-4419	K F T
0023-4427	Kraftfutter
0023-4435	Krafthand
0023-4443	Kraftverkehr
0023-4478	Krakowskie Studia Prawnicze
0023-4486	Krankendienst
0023-4494	Krankengymnastik
0023-4508	Krankenhaus-Umschau
0023-4516	Der Krankenhausarzt
0023-4524	Krankenversicherung
0023-4567	Kratylos
0023-4583	Kredietbank. Weekly Bulletin
0023-4591	Kredit und Kapital
0023-4605	Kresge Art Center Bulletin†
0023-4613	Krestanska Revue
0023-4621	Kridangan
0023-463X	Der Kriegsblinde
0023-4648	Kriegsgraeberfuersorge
0023-4656	Krikos
0023-4664	Krikos Ton Vathmoforon
0023-4672	Krila Armije
0023-4699	Kriminalistik
0023-4702	Kriminalistik und Forensische Wissenschaften
0023-4710	Krishak Samachar
0023-4729	Krishan
0023-4737	Krishanu
0023-4745	Krishnachura
0023-4753	Kristall und Technik
0023-4761	Kristallografiya
0023-477X	Kristaus Karaliaus Laivas
0023-4788	Kristet Samhaellsliv†
0023-4796	Kristliga Esperantofoerbundets Medlemsblad
0023-4818	Kritika
0023-4826	Kritike
0023-4834	Kritische Justiz
0023-4842	Kritischer Katholizismus†
0023-4850	Krmiva
0023-4869	Kroeber Anthropological Society. Papers
0023-4877	Krokodil
0023-4885	Krolikovodstvo i Zverovodstvo
0023-4893	Kroniek van Afrika changed to African Perspectives
0023-4907	Kroniek van het Ambacht/Klein- en Middenbedrijf
0023-4923	Kronika
0023-4931	Kroonkroniek

ISSN INDEX 1011

ISSN	Title
0023-494X	Kruidenier *changed to* Food-Magazine
0023-4958	Krul's Maandblad voor Stoom- en Chemische Wasserijen Ververijen en Wassalons
0023-4974	Kryl'ya Rodiny
0023-4982	Ktaadn
0023-4990	Kudzu†
0023-5008	Kuehn Archiv†
0023-5016	Kuerbiskern
0023-5032	Air Cleaning
0023-5040	Kukuruza
0023-5059	Kulde *see* 0048-9301
0023-5067	Kulfold Mezogazdasaga†
0023-5075	Kulfoldi Folyoiratok Tartalomjegyzeke†
0023-5083	Kulisy
0023-5113	Kultur
0023-5121	Kulturberichte aus Niederoesterreich
0023-513X	Kultur Un Lebn
0023-5148	Kultura
0023-5156	Kultura
0023-5164	Kultura
0023-5172	Kultura i Spoleczenstwo
0023-5180	Kul'tura i Zhyttya
0023-5199	Kul'tura i Zhizn'
0023-5202	Kultura Slova
0023-5210	Kulturberichte aus Tirol
0023-5229	Kulturgemeinschaft "der Kreis." Mitteilungen
0023-5237	Kulturgeografi†
0023-5245	Kulturgeografiske Skrifter
0023-5253	Kulturni Radnik
0023-5261	Kulturni Zivot
0023-5296	Kumamoto University. Faculty of Engineering. Technical Reports
0023-530X	Kumamoto University. Institute of Constitutional Medicine. Bulletin
0023-5318	Kumamoto Journal of Science. Series A: Mathematics, Physics and Chemistry *changed to* Kumamoto Journal of Science. Mathematics
0023-5326	Kumamoto Medical Journal
0023-5334	Kumamoto University. Faculty of Engineering. Memoirs
0023-5342	Kumar
0023-5350	Kungliga Skogs- och Lantbruksakademien. Tidskrift
0023-5369	Kungliga Krigsvetenskapsakademien. Handlingar och Tidskrift
0023-5377	Kungliga Svenska Vetenskapsademiens. Handlingar†
0023-5385	Kunnallistekniikka
0023-5393	Kunst des Orients
0023-5415	Kunst og Kultur†
0023-5423	Die Kunst und das Schoene Heim
0023-5431	Kunst und Kirche
0023-544X	Kunst und Literatur
0023-5458	Kunst und Stein
0023-5466	Kunst und Unterricht
0023-5474	Kunstchronik
0023-5490	Kunstgeschichtliche Anzeigen†
0023-5504	Der Kunsthandel
0023-5512	Kunstnachrichten
0023-5520	Kunststoffberater
0023-5539	Kunststoff Dokumentum
0023-5555	Kunststoff-Rundschau *see* 0023-5520
0023-5563	Kunststoffe
0023-5571	K I B *see* 0343-3129
0023-558X	Kunststoffe - Plasticos *changed to* Plasticos Universales
0023-5598	Kunststoffe-Plastics
0023-5601	Kunststofftechnik *see* 0023-5520
0023-561X	Das Kunstwerk
0023-5628	Kupfer-Mitteilungen *see* 0309-2216
0023-5636	Kurdish Facts†
0023-5652	Kursbuch
0023-5660	Kurukshetra
0023-5679	Kurume Medical Journal
0023-5687	Kurz und Buendig
0023-5695	Kurzauszuege aus dem Schrifttum fuer das Eisenbahnwesen *changed to* Information Eisenbahn
0023-5717	Kuspi
0023-5725	Kusunoki Noho
0023-5733	Kutlwano
0023-5741	Kuuloviesti
0023-575X	Kuwait al-Youm
0023-5768	Kuwait. Central Statistical Office. Monthly Statistical Bulletin *changed to* Kuwait. Central Statistical Office. Annual Statistical Abstract
0023-5776	Kuwait Medical Association. Journal
0023-5792	Al-Kuwaiti
0023-5806	Kuznechno-shtampovochnoe Proizvodstvo
0023-5814	Kvakera Esperantisto
0023-5822	Kvaellsstunden
0023-5830	Kvasny Prumysl
0023-5849	Kvety
0023-5857	Kvinner og Klaer
0023-5865	Kwartalnik Architektury i Urbanistyki
0023-5873	Kwartalnik Geologiczny
0023-5881	Kwartalnik Historii Kultury Materialnej
0023-589X	Kwartalnik Historii Nauki i Techniki
0023-5903	Kwartalnik Historyczny
0023-5911	Kwartalnik Neofilologiczny
0023-592X	Kwartalnik Opolski
0023-5938	Kwartalnik Pedagogiczny
0023-5946	Kybernetik *see* 0340-1200
0023-5954	Kybernetika
0023-5962	Kyklos
0023-5970	Kylteknisk Tidskrift *see* 0048-9301
0023-5989	Kymppi
0023-5997	Educational Review
0023-6004	Polar News
0023-6012	Kyoto Prefectural University of Medicine. Medical Society. Journal
0023-6020	Fire Prevention
0023-6039	Kyoto University. Bulletin of Stomatology
0023-6063	Kyoto University. Faculty of Engineering. Memoirs
0023-6071	Kyoto University. Institute for Chemical Research. Bulletin
0023-608X	Kyoto University. Journal of Mathematics
0023-6098	Kyoto University. Misaki Marine Biological Institute. Bulletin
0023-6101	Kyoto University of Education. Bulletin. Series B: Mathematics and Natural Science
0023-611X	Kypros
0023-6128	Kyrios†
0023-6144	Kyushu Neuro-Psychiatry
0023-6152	Kyushu University. Faculty of Agriculture. Journal
0023-6160	Kyushu University. Faculty of Engineering. Memoirs
0023-6179	Kyushu University. Faculty of Science. Memoirs. Series D: Geology
0023-6195	Kyushu University. Research Institute for Applied Mechanics. Reports
0023-6217	L. A. M. Y. A. Revista Mensual
0023-6225	L A R C Reports†
0023-6241	L & N *changed to* Family Lines
0023-625X	L B I News
0023-6268	L G A-Rundschau
0023-6276	L G M Mededelingen
0023-6284	L.I. Almanac *changed to* Long Island Almanac
0023-6292	L I D News Bulletin†
0023-6306	L K A B-Tidningen†
0023-6314	L K H H Accountant *see* 0147-2208
0023-6322	Laerarinnornas Missionsfoerening. Meddelande till L M F
0023-6330	L M S-Lingua
0023-6349	L O G A
0023-6357	L P A News
0023-6365	L S A Bulletin
0023-6373	L S C R R C Newsletter†
0023-6381	L S E Engineering Bulletin
0023-639X	L S E Magazine
0023-6403	L S U/Alumni News
0023-6411	L S U Engineering News
0023-642X	L V I Teknillingen Aikakaus-Lehti *changed to* L V I
0023-6438	Lebensmittel-Wissenschaft und Technologie
0023-6446	La-Yaaran
0023-6454	Lab World
0023-6462	Labeo
0023-6470	Labo-Pharma *see* 0458-5747
0023-6489	Labor
0023-6497	Labor
0023-6500	Labor Arbitration Awards
0023-6519	Labor Chronicle
0023-6527	Labor Developments Abroad†
0023-6535	Labor Education News *changed to* Workers Education Local 189. Newsletter
0023-6543	Labor Education Viewpoints†
0023-656X	Labor History
0023-6578	Labor in Print†
0023-6586	Labor Law Journal
0023-6594	Labor Leader
0023-6616	Labor Record
0023-6632	Labor Safety Newsletter *changed to* Labor Newsletter
0023-6640	Labor Today
0023-6667	Labor World
0023-6675	Laboratoire Central des Industries Electriques. Bulletin d'Information *changed to* L C I E-Informations
0023-6683	Laboratoires Squibb. Recueil de Nouvelles†
0023-6691	Laboratorio
0023-6705	Laboratorio de Engenharia de Mocambique. Boletim Tecnico de Informacoes *changed to* Laboratorio de Engenharia de Mocambique. Boletin Tecnico
0023-6713	Soul Illustrated *changed to* Soul
0023-6721	Laboratoriums-Praxis†
0023-6748	Laboratornoe Delo (po Voprosam Meditsiny)
0023-6764	Laboratory Animal Science
0023-6772	Laboratory Animals
0023-6780	L A C News Letter *see* 0308-9568
0023-6799	Laboratory Digest†
0023-6810	Laboratory Equipment
0023-6829	Laboratory Equipment Digest
0023-6837	Laboratory Investigation
0023-6853	Laboratory Practice
0023-6861	Laboratory Primate Newsletter
0023-687X	Laboratory Safety Newsletter *changed to* Campus Safety
0023-6888	Laborer
0023-6896	Labour and Employment Gazette
0023-690X	Labour Arbitration Cases
0023-6934	Labour Gazette
0023-6942	Labour History
0023-6950	Labour in Exile
0023-5969	Labour in Israel
0023-6977	Labour Law Journal
0023-6985	Labour Monthly
0023-6993	Labour Organiser
0023-7000	Labour Research
0023-7027	Labour Woman†
0023-7035	Labour World
0023-7043	Labris *changed to* Ko-Ko
0023-7051	Lacerta
0023-7078	Lackawanna Jurist
0023-7086	Lacrosse
0023-7094	Lada'at
0023-7108	Ladder†
0023-7116	Laeder och Skor *see* 0040-4845
0023-7124	Ladies' Home Journal (Inkprint Edition)
0023-7140	Ladue Public Schools Bulletin
0023-7159	Ladugaardsfoermannen
0023-7167	Lady
0023-7175	Lady *see* 0343-3366
0023-7183	Ladycom
0023-7191	Lady's Circle
0023-7205	Laekartidningen
0023-7213	Laeknabladid
0023-7256	Lagena
0023-7272	Lagos Weekend
0023-7280	Lagrimal Trifurca
0023-7299	Lahey Clinic Foundation Bulletin
0023-7302	Lait
0023-7310	Lajpat Bhawan Journal *changed to* Better Life
0023-7329	Lake Carriers' Association Bulletin
0023-7345	Lakeland Boating
0023-7353	Lakimies
0023-7361	Lakimiesuutiset
0023-737X	Lakokrasochnye Materialy i Ikh Primenenie
0023-7388	Lal-Baugh
0023-7396	Lalit Kala Contemporary
0023-740X	Lalita *changed to* Priya
0023-7418	Lamp
0023-7426	Lamp Journal *see* 0162-9077
0023-7442	Lampetten
0023-7450	Lana Moda
0023-7477	Lancaster County Historical Society. Journal
0023-7485	Lancaster Farming
0023-7493	Lance
0023-7515	Lanciana
0023-7523	Land
0023-7531	Land
0023-754X	Land
0023-7558	Der Land- und Forstwirtschaftliche Betrieb
0023-7574	Land & Liberty
0023-7582	Land en Water†
0023-7590	Land & Water Development *changed to* Land & Water
0023-7612	Land and Water Law Review
0023-7639	Land Economics
0023-7655	Land Pollution Reporter
0023-768X	Land Use Digest
0023-7698	Land van Valkenburg
0023-7701	Land Worker
0023-7728	Landarzt *see* 0341-9835
0023-7736	Landbode
0023-7744	Landbote
0023-7752	Landbouw en Plantenziekten†
0023-7760	Landbouwdocumentatie
0023-7779	Landbouwweekblad
0023-7787	Landbouwkundig Tijdschrift
0023-7795	Landbouwmechanisatie
0023-7817	Bedrijfsontwikkeling. Editie Akkerbouw *changed to* Bedrijfsontwikkeling
0023-7825	Landbouwwereldnieuws
0023-7833	Landbrukstidende
0023-7841	Koninklijk Instituut voor de Tropen. Afdeling Agrarisch Onderzoek. Landendocumentatie
0023-785X	Landers Film Reviews
0023-7868	Schleswig- Holstein Kultusminister. Nachrichtenblatt
0023-7876	Landesamtsblatt fuer das Burgenland
0023-7884	Landesgesetzblatt fuer das Land Salzburg
0023-7906	Landesmuseum fuer Naturkunde zu Muenster in Westfalen. Abhandlungen
0023-7922	Landesversicherungsanstalt Hessen. Nachrichten
0023-7930	Landfall
0023-7949	Landis und Gyr Mitteilungen
0023-7957	Landjugend
0023-7965	Landman
0023-7973	Landmaschinen-Handwerk-Handel
0023-7981	Landmaschinen-Markt *see* 0341-695X
0023-799X	Landowning in Scotland
0023-8007	Die Landpost
0023-8015	Landsbygdens Folk
0023-8023	Landscape
0023-8031	Landscape Architecture†
0023-804X	Landscape Industry
0023-8058	Landschaft und Stadt
0023-8066	Landskap *changed to* Landskab
0023-8074	Landstingens Tidskrift
0023-8082	Fachzeitschrift fuer Alle Bereiche der Agrartechnik *changed to* Landtechnik
0023-8104	Das Landvolk
0023-8112	Landwirt
0023-8120	V W D - Landwirtschaft und Ernaehrung
0023-8147	Landwirtschaftliche Forschung
0023-8163	Landwirtschaftliche Zeitschrift Rheinland
0023-8171	Landwirtschaftliches Jahrbuch der Schweiz
0023-818X	Landwirtschaftliches Zentralblatt. Abteilung 1: Landtechnik
0023-8198	Landwirtschaftliches Zentralblatt. Abteilung 2: Pflanzliche Produktion
0023-8201	Landwirtschaftliches Zentralblatt. Abteilung 3: Tierzucht, Tierernaehrung, Fischerei

ISSN	Title
0023-821X	Landwirtschaftliches Zentralblatt. Abteilung 4: Veterinaermedizin
0023-8228	Langage Total
0023-8236	Langenbecks Archiv fuer Chirurgie
0023-8244	Langenscheidt's English Monthly†
0023-8252	Langenscheidt's Sprach-Illustrierte
0023-8279	Language - Teaching Abstracts see 0306-6304
0023-8287	Language and Automation†
0023-8295	L L B A
0023-8309	Language and Speech
0023-8317	Language and Style
0023-8325	Language Association of Eastern Africa. Journal
0023-8333	Language Learning
0023-8341	Language Sciences†
0023-8368	Langue Francaise
0023-8376	Langues Modernes
0023-8384	Lansing Labor News
0023-8414	Lantern
0023-8422	Lantern
0023-8430	Lantmaestaren
0023-8457	Lapidary Journal
0023-8473	Laputa Gazette and Faculty News†
0023-8481	Lara Lamont
0023-849X	Laerartidningen
0023-8503	Lares
0023-8511	Larvae du Golden Gate
0023-852X	Laryngoscope
0023-8533	Las Polski
0023-8546	Las Vegas Voice
0023-8554	Laser changed to Laser und Elektro-Optik
0023-8589	Laser Focus see 0275-1399
0023-8597	Laser Journal†
0023-8600	Laser Report
0023-8627	Chinese Studies in Philosophy
0023-8635	Last Day Messenger
0023-8651	Last Post
0023-866X	Lastauto Omnibus
0023-8678	Lastbilen
0023-8686	Lastebilen
0023-8694	Lastechniek
0023-8716	Lather
0023-8740	Latin American Books Newsletter
0023-8759	Latin American Calendar†
0023-8767	Latin American Digest
0023-8791	Latin American Research Review
0023-8805	Latin American Studies Association Newsletter
0023-8813	Latin American Theatre Review
0023-8821	Latin Teaching
0023-883X	Latinitas
0023-8856	Latomus
0023-8864	Lattante
0023-8872	Laettbetong
0023-8880	Latte
0023-8899	Latvija
0023-8902	Latvija Amerika
0023-8910	Latvijas P S R Preses Hronika
0023-8929	Akademiya Nauk Latviiskoi S. S. R. Izvestiya
0023-8937	Laufende Mitteilungen Zum Stand der Politischen Bildung in der Bundesrepublik Deutschland†
0023-8961	Laundry and Cleaning
0023-897X	Laundry & Cleaning International
0023-8988	Laurel Messenger
0023-8996	Laurel of Phi Kappa Tau
0023-9003	Laurel Review†
0023-9003	Laurel Review see 0145-8388
0023-9011	Laurentian University Review
0023-902X	Laurentianum
0023-9038	Laval Administration
0023-9046	Laval Medical see 0301-1534
0023-9054	Laval Theologique et Philosophique
0023-9062	Lavender Band
0023-9070	Lavoro e Medicina†
0023-9089	Lavoro Italiano
0023-9097	Lavoro Neuropsichiatrico
0023-9119	Lavoro Sud†
0023-9135	Lavoura
0023-9143	Lavoura Arrozeira
0023-9151	Lavoura e Cooperativismo changed to Agricultura Brasileira
0023-916X	Law
0023-9178	Law and Computer Technology
0023-9186	Law and Contemporary Problems
0023-9208	Law and Policy in International Business
0023-9216	Law & Society Review
0023-9224	Law and the Social Order changed to Arizona State Law Journal
0023-9232	New South Wales Weekly Notes see 0312-1674
0023-9240	Law Books Published
0023-9267	Law Institute Journal
0023-9275	Law Librarian
0023-9283	Law Library Journal
0023-9291	Royal National Institute for the Blind. Law Notes. Extracts
0023-9305	Law Notes see 0094-5277
0023-933X	Law Quarterly Review
0023-9348	Law Reports
0023-9356	Buffalo Law Review
0023-9364	Law Society Gazette
0023-9372	Law Society Journal
0023-9380	Law Society's Gazette
0023-9399	Law Thesaurus
0023-9402	Lawn Care
0023-9429	Lawn Tennis changed to Tennissport
0023-9437	Lawyer
0023-9445	Lawyer of the Americas
0023-9461	Lawyers Marketplace
0023-947X	Lawyer's Medical Journal
0023-9488	Lawyers' Recreation
0023-9518	Laymen's Movement Review changed to Trends (Rye)
0023-9526	Lazio
0023-9534	Le Havre changed to Escale
0023-9542	Leabharlann
0023-9550	Lead
0023-9569	Lead Abstracts
0023-9577	Lead and Zinc Statistics
0023-9585	Leader
0023-9593	Leader†
0023-9607	Leaflet
0023-964X	Leaflet
0023-9666	Leaguer
0023-9674	Lealtad
0023-9682	Learn
0023-9690	Learning & Motivation
0023-9704	Learning for Living changed to British Journal of Religious Education
0023-9712	Learning Resources†
0023-9739	Leather
0023-9747	Leather and Shoes
0023-9755	L I R I Monthly Circular
0023-9763	Leather Manufacturer
0023-9771	Leather Science
0023-978X	Leather Titles Service†
0023-9798	Leathergoods
0023-9801	Leathergoods Buyer†
0023-981X	Leatherneck
0023-9828	Leathers
0023-9836	Leaves of Twin Oaks
0023-9852	Lebanese Medical Journal
0023-9860	Lebanon. Direction Centrale de la Statistique. Bulletin Statistique Mensuel
0023-9879	Lebe Dich Gesund
0023-9887	Leben see 0303-4283
0023-9895	Leben und Gesundheit
0023-9909	Lebende Sprachen
0023-9917	Lebendige Erde
0023-9925	Lebendige Familie changed to Praxis Bilden und Erziehen
0023-9933	Lebendige Schule†
0023-9941	Lebendiges Zeugnis
0023-995X	Lebenshilfe changed to Geistige Behinderung
0023-9968	Thema Null changed to Blaue Feder
0023-9976	Lebensmittel-Grosshandel/Susswaren-Zeitung changed to Food and Nonfood
0023-9984	Lebensmittelhandel
0023-9992	Lebensmittel Praxis
0024-001X	Lebensmittelhaendler see 0047-4282
0024-0028	Lebensmittelindustrie
0024-0036	Lebensmittelpost see 0047-4282
0024-0044	Lebensversicherungs-Medizin
0024-0052	Lebensweiser
0024-0060	Lebone la Kgalalelo Isibani Sobu Ngcwele changed to Lebone la Kgalalelo
0024-0079	Lecciones y Ensayos†
0024-0087	Lectura†
0024-0095	Lectura†
0024-0109	Lectura para Todos†
0024-0125	Lecture et Tradition
0024-015X	Ledarforum
0024-0168	Ledarskap och Loensamhet
0024-0176	Das Leder
0024-0184	Leder Echo
0024-0192	L S L
0024-0214	Lederwaren-Report
0024-0222	Ledger†
0024-0230	Lediga Platser
0024-0249	Leeds African Studies Bulletin
0024-0257	Leeds Arts Calendar
0024-0273	Leeds Journal
0024-0281	Leeds Philosophical and Literary Society. Proceedings. Literary and Historical Section
0024-029X	Communist News
0024-0303	Left
0024-032X	Lega Navale
0024-0338	Legal Aid Briefcase changed to N L A D A Briefcase
0024-0354	Legal Eagles News changed to Lawyer-Pilots Bar Association Journal
0024-0362	Legal Executive
0024-0370	Legal Record
0024-0389	Legerkoerier
0024-0400	Leggi
0024-0419	Leggi delle Comunita' Europee†
0024-0435	Legion
0024-0451	Legionair
0024-046X	New Jersey School Boards Association. Legislative Bulletin changed to New Jersey School Leader
0024-0478	Legislative Conference Reporter changed to P S C Clarion
0024-0486	Legislative Research Checklist changed to State Government Research Checklist
0024-0494	Legislative Roundup
0024-0508	Legislator
0024-0524	Legislazione Italiana
0024-0532	Legno changed to Mondolegno
0024-0540	Legon Observer†
0024-0567	Lehigh Valley Safety News
0024-0575	Ligstafel/Lehlasedi
0024-0591	Spark
0024-0605	Lehrer in Friseurklassen†
0024-0613	Leibesuebungen changed to T U S - Turnen und Sport
0024-0621	Leica-Fotografie
0024-063X	Leica Photography
0024-0648	Leicester & County Chamber of Commerce Journal
0024-0656	Leicestershire Farmer see 0306-0160
0024-0664	Leicestershire Historian
0024-0672	Rijksmuseum van Natuurlijke Historie. Zoologische Mededelingen
0024-0699	Leipuri
0024-0702	Leistung
0024-0710	Leisure Painter
0024-0729	Leisure Time
0024-0737	Der Leitende Angestellte
0024-0745	Lekarz Wojskowy
0024-0761	Lemouzi
0024-0788	Lenau-Forum
0024-0796	Lenguaje y Ciencias
0024-0818	Leningradskii Universitet. Vestnik. Seriya Ekonomika, Filosofiya i Pravo
0024-0826	Leningradskii Universitet. Vestnik. Seriya Fizika i Khimiya
0024-0834	Leningradskii Universitet. Vestnik. Seriya Geologiya i Geografiya
0024-0842	Leningradskii Universitet. Vestnik. Seriya Istoriya, Yazyk i Literatura
0024-0850	Leningradskii Universitet. Vestnik. Seriya Matematika, Mekhanika i Astronomiya
0024-0869	Leninyan Ugiov
0024-0877	Lenkurt Demodulator changed to G T E Lenkurt Demodulator
0024-0885	Lentaja†
0024-0893	Lente (Inkprint Edition)
0024-0907	Lenzinger Berichte
0024-0915	Leo Baeck Institut. Bulletin
0024-0923	Leodiensian
0024-094X	Leonardo: Art Science and Technology
0024-0958	Leone
0024-0966	Lepidopterist's Society. Journal
0024-0974	Lepidopterological Society of Japan. Transactions
0024-0982	Lepra Magazine changed to Lepra News
0024-0990	Podiatry Management Letter
0024-1008	Lepro see 0386-3980
0024-1016	Leprologia
0024-1024	Leprosy in India
0024-1040	Lerindustrien
0024-1059	Lernen und Leisten see 0340-6040
0024-1067	Les
0024-1075	Leserzeitschrift†
0024-1083	Lesestunde mit dem Grossen Freizeit-Programm
0024-1091	Leshonenu La'am
0024-1105	Lesnictvi
0024-1113	Lesnoe Khozyaistvo
0024-1121	Lesotho-Canada†
0024-1156	Letectvi a Kosmonautika
0024-1164	Lethaia
0024-1172	Letopis' Gazetnykh Statei
0024-1180	Letopis na Periodichna Pechat see 0300-1962
0024-1180	Letopis na Periodichna Pechat see 0300-1954
0024-1199	Letopis' Pechatnykh Proizvedenii Izobrazitel'nogo Iskusstva
0024-1202	Letopis' Zhurnal'nykh Statei
0024-1210	Letras
0024-1229	Letras de Ayer y de Hoy
0024-1245	Letras Potosinas
0024-1261	Let's Find Out
0024-1288	Let's Live
0024-1296	Letter to Libraries see 0194-2999
0024-130X	Letterato
0024-1318	Lettere al Nuovo Cimento
0024-1326	Lettere d'Affari
0024-1334	Lettere Italiane
0024-1350	Lettore di Provincia
0024-1369	Lettres
0024-1377	Lettres et Medecins†
0024-1385	Lettres et Poesie
0024-1393	Lettres Francaises†
0024-1407	Lettres Nouvelles†
0024-1415	Lettres Romanes
0024-1423	Lettrisme
0024-1431	Lettura Stenografica
0024-144X	Letture
0024-1458	Cineschedario - Letture Drammatiche
0024-1466	Leukemia Abstracts
0024-1482	Leuvense Bijdragen
0024-1490	Levant Morgenland
0024-1504	Levante
0024-1512	Leveltari Kozlemenyek
0024-1520	Levende Natuur
0024-1539	Levende Talen
0024-1555	H L changed to Levensmiddelenmarkt
0024-1563	Leviathan see 0360-1765
0024-1571	Levnedsmiddelbladet see 0105-6654
0024-158X	Legislacao Federal e Marginalia
0024-1598	Lex
0024-161X	Lexington Philharmonic Society Newsletter
0024-1628	Lexington Theological Quarterly
0024-1636	Ley
0024-1644	Ley
0024-1652	Rijksmuseum van Natuurlijke Historie. Zoologische Verhandelingen
0024-1660	Leyland Journal†
0024-1679	Leyte-Samar Studies
0024-1687	Liaison†
0024-1709	Federation Nationale des Anciens Combattants et Coalets des Transmissions. Liaison des Transmissions
0024-1717	Liaisons
0024-1725	Liaisons Sociales

ISSN INDEX

ISSN	Title
0024-1733	Al Liamm
0024-1741	Liaudies Balsas†
0024-175X	Libelle
0024-1784	Liberal
0024-1792	Liberal Catholic
0024-1806	Liberal Context†
0024-1814	Liberal Debatt see 0345-3685
0024-1822	Liberal Education
0024-1830	Liberal Opinion
0024-1849	Liberal Party Organisation. Liberal News
0024-1857	Liberal Ungdom
0024-1873	Liberation
0024-189X	Liberation†
0024-1903	Liberation News Service
0024-1911	Liberation News Service
0024-1962	Liberian Age
0024-1970	Liberian Law Journal
0024-1989	Liberian Studies Journal
0024-1997	Liberta
0024-2004	Libertarian
0024-2012	Libertarian Connection†
0024-2012	Libertarian Connection changed to Connection(Fairfax)
0024-2020	Liberte
0024-2047	Libertijn†
0024-2055	Liberty (Washington, 1906)
0024-2063	Liberty
0024-208X	Liberty see 0360-3342
0024-2098	Liberty Letter changed to Spotlight (Washington)
0024-2101	Libra†
0024-211X	Librachat
0024-2128	Librairie Ancienne et Moderne. Bulletin changed to Bulletin du Bibliophile
0024-2144	Libraries in International Development. Newsletter†
0024-2152	Librarium
0024-2160	Library
0024-2179	Library & Information Science Abstracts
0024-2187	Library Associate†
0024-2195	Library Association Record
0024-2209	Library Binder see 0090-8746
0024-2217	Library Bookseller
0024-2225	State University of New York. Upstate Medical Center. Library Bulletin†
0024-2233	Library Chronicle (Philadelphia)
0024-2241	Library Chronicle (Austin)
0024-225X	Library-College Journal see 0091-7281
0024-2276	Library Counselor†
0024-2284	Library for the Blind and Physically Handicapped. Newsletter†
0024-2292	Library Herald
0024-2306	Library History
0024-2330	Library Keynotes
0024-2349	Library Leaves
0024-2357	Library Lines
0024-2365	Contra Costa County Library Link
0024-2373	Library Literature
0024-239X	Library Materials on Africa see 0305-862X
0024-2411	Library Notes†
0024-242X	Washington University. School of Medicine Library. Library Notes
0024-2438	Library Notes
0024-2446	North Dakota Library Notes†
0024-2454	Library Occurrent
0024-2462	Library Opinion†
0024-2489	Library Periodicals Directory†
0024-2497	Library Progress†
0024-2500	Library Publicity Clippings
0024-2519	Library Quarterly
0024-2527	Library Resources & Technical Services
0024-2535	Library Review
0024-2543	Library Science with a Slant to Documentation
0024-2551	Library Service News
0024-2578	Library System†
0024-2586	Library Technology Reports
0024-2594	Library Trends
0024-2608	Library World
0024-2616	Library World see 0307-4803
0024-2632	L S A
0024-2640	Libreria
0024-2659	Libreria
0024-2667	Libri
0024-2683	Libri e Riviste d'Italia
0024-273X	Libro Espanol
0024-2756	Libros†
0024-2764	Licensed Beverage Journal
0024-2772	Licensed Bookmaker & Betting Office Proprietor
0024-2780	Licensed Retailer
0024-2802	Licensee
0024-2810	Lichamelijke Opvoeding
0024-2829	Lichenologist
0024-2845	Lichtbogen
0024-2853	Lichthoeve-Kinderwerk changed to Lichthoeve
0024-2861	Lichttechnik
0024-287X	Licitationen
0024-2888	Licke Novine
0024-2896	Lide a Zeme
0024-290X	Lied und Chor
0024-2926	Lien Entre Meres et Peres de Pretres
0024-2934	Lien Wallon
0024-2942	Liens
0024-2950	Lietuviu Dienos
0024-2969	Litovskii Fizicheskii Sbornik
0024-2969	Litovskii Fizicheskii Zbornik
0024-2977	Litovskii Matematicheskii Sbornik
0024-2977	Akademiya Nauk Litovskoi S.S.R. Litovskoii Matematicheskii Sbornik
0024-2985	Akademiya Nauk Litovskoi S. S. R. Trudy. Seriya A. Obshchestvennye Nauki
0024-2993	Akademiya Nauk Litovskoi S. S. R. Trudy. Seriya B. Khimiya, Tekhnika, Fizicheskaya Geografiya
0024-3000	Akademiya Nauk Litovskoi S. S. R. Trudy. Seriya C. Biologicheskie Nauki
0024-3019	Life†
0024-3019	Life (Chicago)
0024-3027	Life and Breath changed to Life & Lung
0024-3035	Life and Health
0024-3043	Life and Health
0024-306X	Life and Work
0024-3078	Life Association News
0024-3086	Life-Boat
0024-3094	Life Boy Link†
0024-3132	Life Insurance Planning
0024-3140	Life Insurance Selling
0024-3159	Life International†
0024-3167	Life Lines†
0024-3175	Life of Faith changed to Family
0024-3183	Life Office Management Association. Bulletin changed to L. O. M. A. Resource
0024-3191	Systems & Procedures Review changed to L. O. M. A. Resource
0024-3205	Life Sciences (1973)
0024-3221	Life Underwriters Association of the City of New York. Bulletin
0024-3264	Ligament
0024-3272	Ligdraer
0024-3299	Light and Life see 0162-1890
0024-3345	Light Metal Age
0024-3353	Light of New York†
0024-3361	Light of the Moon
0024-337X	Light Engineering†
0024-3388	Light Steam Power changed to Steam Power
0024-3396	Lightbearer
0024-340X	Lighter
0024-3418	Lighting Equipment News
0024-3434	Ligne de Communication†
0024-3442	Ligstraal/Umsebe/Umtha
0024-3450	Liguorian
0024-3469	Liiketaloudellinen Aikakauskirja
0024-3477	Lijecnicki Vjesnik†
0024-3485	Lillabulero†
0024-3493	Lille Chirurgical
0024-3507	Lille Medical
0024-3523	Limba Romana
0024-354X	Limen
0024-3558	Limi
0024-3566	Limiar
0024-3582	Limnological Society of Southern Africa. Newsletter see 0377-9688
0024-3590	Limnology and Oceanography
0024-3604	Limnos see 0037-0487
0024-3612	Limonadier de Paris
0024-3620	Limosa
0024-3639	Linacre Quarterly
0024-3647	Linage†
0024-3663	Lincoln Business†
0024-3671	Lincoln Herald
0024-368X	Lincoln Law Review
0024-3698	Lincoln Library Bulletin
0024-3701	Lincolnian
0024-371X	Lincolnshire Life
0024-3744	Linea Grafica
0024-3752	Linea Italiana
0024-3760	Linea Maschile e Femminile†
0024-3779	Linea Z
0024-3787	Lineamaglia
0024-3795	Linear Algebra and Its Applications
0024-3809	Linear Integrated Circuit D.A.T.A. Book
0024-3817	Lineastruttura
0024-3825	Linen Supply News see 0195-0118
0024-3833	Linens/Domestics & Bath Products
0024-3841	Lingua
0024-385X	Lingua e Stile
0024-3868	Lingua Nostra
0024-3876	Lingue del Mondo
0024-3892	Linguistic Inquiry
0024-3906	Linguistic Reporter
0024-3914	Linguistic Society of Japan. Journal
0024-3922	Linguistica
0024-3930	Linguistische Berichte
0024-3949	Linguistics
0024-3957	Linguistique
0024-3965	Lingvologia Revuo
0024-3973	Linieofficeren
0024-399X	Link†
0024-4007	Link
0024-4015	Link-Up
0024-4023	Linking Ring
0024-404X	Links
0024-4058	Linnaean News-Letter
0024-4066	Linnean Society. Biological Journal
0024-4074	Linnean Society. Botanical Journal
0024-4082	Linnean Society. Zoological Journal
0024-4104	Linn's Weekly Stamp News see 0161-6234
0024-4112	Linoticias†
0024-4139	Linzer Theaterzeitung
0024-4147	Linzer Woche
0024-4155	Legkaya Atletika
0024-4163	Lion
0024-4171	Lion en Espanol
0024-4198	Len i Konoplya
0024-4198	Lion
0024-4201	Lipids
0024-421X	Liquefied Petroleum Gas Report
0024-4228	Liquified Natural Gas†
0024-4236	Liquor Store Magazine
0024-4244	Lira
0024-4260	Lisbon. Instituto Gulbenkian de Cienca. Arquivo. Section A. Estudos Matematicos e Fisico-Matematicos†
0024-4279	Instituto Maternal, Lisbon. Revista Clinica see 0302-4326
0024-4309	List-O-Tapes
0024-4317	List of Accessions to the Science Museum Library
0024-4333	List of Selected Articles on I C A O and Civil Aviation changed to International Civil Aviation Organization. Library Information: Recent Accessions and Selected Articles
0024-4341	List of Technical Studies and Experimental Housing Projects†
0024-435X	Listen
0024-4384	Listen†
0024-4392	Listener
0024-4406	Listener in T V changed to Scene
0024-4414	Listening
0024-4430	Listino Ufficiale della Borsa Valori di Torino
0024-4449	Listy Cukrovarnicke
0024-4457	Listy Filologicke
0024-4465	Listy Sv. Frantiska
0024-449X	Liteinoe Proizvodstvo
0024-4503	Literacy Discussion
0024-4511	Literary Cavalcade
0024-452X	Literary Criterion
0024-4538	American Reference Books Annual
0024-4546	Literary Guild Newsletter†
0024-4554	Literary Half-Yearly
0024-4562	Literary Herald†
0024-4570	Literary Quarterly of the Yugoslav Pen-Centre†
0024-4589	Literary Review
0024-4597	Literary Sketches
0024-4600	Literary Studies
0024-4619	Literary Times
0024-4627	Der Literat
0024-4635	Literatur- Eildienst Roche changed to Hexagon Roche
0024-4643	Literatur in Wissenschaft und Unterricht
0024-4651	Literatur-Schnelldienst Kunststoffe und Kautschuk changed to Literatur-Schnelldienst Kunststoffe Kautschuk Fasern
0024-4678	Literatur Zum Bibliothekswesen†
0024-4686	Literatura i Mastatstva
0024-4694	Literatura Kajero
0024-4708	Literatura Ludowa
0024-4724	Literatura v Shkole
0024-4740	Literature and Ideology see 0702-7532
0024-4759	Literature and Psychology
0024-4767	Literature East & West
0024-4775	Literature, Music, Fine Arts
0024-4783	Literature on Economic Development and Planning - a Select Bibliography†
0024-4791	Literaturen Zbor
0024-4805	Rat fuer Formgebung. Literaturhinweise
0024-4813	Literaturna Misul
0024-4821	Literaturna Ukrayina
0024-483X	Literaturnaya Armeniya
0024-4848	Literaturnaya Gazeta
0024-4856	Literaturnaya Rossiya
0024-4864	Literaturnyi Azerbaidzhan
0024-4872	Literaturrundschau
0024-4902	Lithology and Mineral Resources
0024-4910	Lithopinion†
0024-4929	Lithoprinter
0024-4937	Lithos
0024-4945	Lithuanian Medical Bulletin
0024-4953	Litmus
0024-497X	Litologiya i Poleznye Iskopaemye
0024-4988	Litterair Paspoort†
0024-4996	Litterature de Jeunesse†
0024-5011	Little Bronzed Angel
0024-502X	Little Flower†
0024-5054	Little Review
0024-5062	Little Ship
0024-5070	Little Square Review†
0024-5089	Lituanus
0024-5100	Liturgisches Jahrbuch
0024-5119	Life and Worship see 0305-4438
0024-5127	Liv og Helse†
0024-5135	Livarski Vestnik
0024-5143	Live Lines
0024-5151	Liverpool Bulletin
0024-516X	U.S. Department of Agriculture. Economics, Statistics, and Cooperatives Service. Livestock and Meat Situation
0024-5178	Livestock Breeder Journal
0024-5208	Livestock Market Digest
0024-5224	Living
0024-5232	Living Blues
0024-5240	Living Church
0024-5259	Living Health Newsletter†
0024-5267	Living Judaism
0024-5275	Living Light
0024-5283	Living Museum
0024-5291	Living Tapes†
0024-5305	Living Wilderness
0024-5313	Livingston County Agricultural News
0024-5321	Livornocronaca
0024-533X	Livre et l'Estampe
0024-5348	Livres
0024-5364	Livros de Portugal changed to Livros de Portugal. Suplemento
0024-5372	Livrustkammaren
0024-5380	Livs
0024-5399	Livsmedelsteknik

ISSN	Title
0024-5402	Ljevarstvo
0024-5410	Ljusglimtar
0024-5437	Llais Llyfrau *changed to* Llais Llyfrau/Book News from Wales
0024-5445	Llan
0024-5461	Lloydia *see* 0163-3864
0024-547X	Lloyds Bank Review
0024-5488	Lloyd's Law Reports
0024-5496	Lloyd's Loading List
0024-550X	Lloyd's Log
0024-5518	Local Government Administration
0024-5526	Local Government Bulletin
0024-5534	Local Government Chronicle
0024-5542	Local Government Finance *see* 0305-9014
0024-5569	Local Government Journal of Western Australia
0024-5577	Munisipale en Openbare Dienste†
0024-5585	Local Historian
0024-5607	Local Preachers
0024-5615	Local Self-Government
0024-5623	All India Institute of Local Self Government. Quarterly Journal
0024-5631	Local Taxation†
0024-5658	Locating Gold *changed to* Locating Gold, Gems, & Minerals
0024-5666	Locations & Ventes
0024-5674	Locations Vacances
0024-5690	Locke Report
0024-5704	Lockheed Orion Service Digest
0024-5712	Lockheed Reports *changed to* Airborne A S W Log
0024-5720	Locksmith Ledger and Security Register *changed to* Locksmith Ledger
0024-5739	Loco-Revue
0024-5747	Locomotive Engineer
0024-5755	Lodging and Food-Service News
0024-5763	Lodigiano Sudmilano
0024-5771	Lodzki Numizmatyk
0024-5798	Log
0024-581X	Log Analyst
0024-5828	Log of Mystic Seaport
0024-5844	Logistics Review *see* 0047-4991
0024-5887	Logos
0024-5895	Lohos
0024-5917	Lok Rajya
0024-5925	Lok Udyog
0024-5941	Lokomotivtechnik†
0024-595X	Loktantra Samiksha
0024-5968	S D A Dentist
0024-5976	Lon og Virke *see* 0105-032X
0024-5984	London Archaeologist
0024-5992	Spokesman
0024-600X	London Calling
0024-6018	London Clinic Medical Journal†
0024-6026	London Corn Circular
0024-6034	London Diary of Social Events†
0024-6042	London Hilton Magazine
0024-6050	London Hospital Gazette†
0024-6069	London Information
0024-6077	London Letter†
0024-6085	London Magazine
0024-6093	London Mathematical Society. Bulletin
0024-6107	London Mathematical Society. Journal
0024-6115	London Mathematical Society. Proceedings
0024-6123	London Mystery Magazine *see* 0307-9112
0024-6131	London Philatelist
0024-614X	London Review
0024-6158	London Society. Journal
0024-6166	London Times Index†
0024-6174	London Town
0024-6182	London Weekly Advertiser
0024-6190	London Weekly Diary of Social Events
0024-62C4	London Welshman
0024-6220	Long Cane News Letter
0024-6247	Long Island Builder
0024-6255	Long Island Catholic
0024-6263	Long Island Courant†
0024-628X	Long Island Forum
0024-6258	Long Island University Magazine†
0024-63C1	Long Range Planning
0024-631X	Long Room
0024-6328	Longitude
0024-6336	Look†
0024-6344	Look and Learn†
0024-6352	Look & Listen
0024-6360	Look Around
0024-6379	Look at Finland
0024-6387	Look Fortnightly
0024-64C9	Looking Ahead *changed to* Looking Ahead and Projection Highlights
0024-6417	Looking Back
0024-6425	Lookout
0024-6433	Lookout
0024-6441	Looming
0024-645X	Loon
0024-6476	Looys
0024-6484	Lorain Labor Leader
0024-6492	Lore
0024-65C6	Lorian
0024-6514	Loris
0024-6522	Los Angeles
0024-6530	Los Angeles Bar Bulletin *see* 0162-2900
0024-6549	Los Angeles Citizen
0024-6557	Los Angeles County Museum of Art. Bulletin
0024-6565	Los Angeles County Regional Plannning Commission. Quarterly Bulletin *see* 0363-5775
0024-6573	Los Angeles Free Press
0024-6581	Image†
0024-659X	Los Angeles Neurological Societies. Bulletin
0024-6603	Eisenwaren Allgemeine
0024-6611	Loshen und Leben
0024-662X	Loteria
0024-6638	Lotta Contro la Tubercolosi *changed to* Lotta Contro la Tubercolosi e le Malattie Polmonari Sociali
0024-6646	Lotta Operaia
0024-6654	Lottery Gazette
0024-6662	Lottoroscopo
0024-6670	Lotus Bleu
0024-6689	Intergroup Relations Newsletter†
0024-6689	Intergroup Relations Newsletter†
0024-6697	Lou Pais
0024-6719	Loughborough University of Technology Gazette
0024-6727	Louis Braille
0024-6735	Louisiana Agriculture
0024-6743	Louisiana Baptist Builder
0024-6751	Louisiana Business Review
0024-6778	Louisiana Conservationist
0024-6786	Louisiana Dental Association. Journal
0024-6794	Louisiana Engineer
0024-6816	Louisiana History
0024-6832	Louisiana Insurer
0024-6840	Louisiana L P-Gas News
0024-6859	Louisiana Law Review
0024-6867	L L A Bulletin
0024-6875	Louisiana Methodist†
0024-6891	Louisiana-Revy
0024-6905	Louisiana Schools *see* 0162-2773
0024-6913	Louisiana Senior Citizen†
0024-6921	Louisiana State Medical Society. Journal
0024-693X	Louisiana Studies *changed to* Southern Studies: an Interdisciplinary Journal of the South
0024-6948	Louisville
0024-6956	Louvain Medical
0024-6964	Louvain Studies
0024-6980	Lov og Rett
0024-6999	Lovacki Vjesnik
0024-7014	Lovec
0024-7022	Lovejoy's Guidance Digest
0024-7030	Low Bidder
0024-7049	Low Cost Automation Review†
0024-7057	Lowell Observatory Bulletin
0024-7065	Lowry-Cocroft's Review of the Food Service Literature†
0024-7073	Loyola News
0024-709X	Liquefied Petroleum Gas
0024-7103	L P-Gas
0024-7111	Lraber Asarakakan Gitutyunneri
0024-7154	Lubrication Engineering
0024-7162	Lubrificazione Industriale e per Autoveicoli *changed to* Oleodinamica-Pneumatica-Lubrificazione
0024-7170	Lucas Engineering Review
0024-7189	Luce
0024-7197	Luce e Immagini
0024-7200	Luci Sulla Via†
0024-7219	Lucknow Librarian
0024-7235	Lucy Moda†
0024-7243	Lufkin Line
0024-7251	Luft- und Kaeltetechnik
0024-7286	Luister
0024-7294	Lumber Co-Operator
0024-7324	Lumen Vitae
0024-7332	Lumiere
0024-7340	Lumiere du Monde
0024-7359	Lumiere et Vie
0024-7367	Lumo
0024-7375	Luna Monthly *changed to* Luna
0024-7383	Luonnon Tutkija
0024-7391	Luscinia
0024-7413	Luso-Brazilian Review
0024-7421	Lustrum
0024-743X	Lutheran
0024-7448	Lutheran Education
0024-7456	Lutheran Forum
0024-7464	Lutheran Layman
0024-7472	Lutheran Libraries
0024-7480	Lutheran Messenger for the Blind
0024-7499	Lutheran Quarterly†
0024-7502	Lutheran Scholar *see* 0362-708X
0024-7510	Lutheran Sentinel
0024-7537	Lutheran Spokesman
0024-7545	Lutheran Standard
0024-7553	Lutheran Theological Journal
0024-7561	Lutheran Welfare in New Jersey *changed to* Lutheran Times in New Jersey
0024-757X	Lutheran Witness
0024-7588	Lutheran Witness-Reporter Edition†
0024-7596	Lutheran Women
0024-760X	Lutheran World†
0024-7618	Lutherische Monatshefte
0024-7626	Die Lutherkirche
0024-7634	Lutra
0024-7642	Lutte Contre le Cancer
0024-7650	Lutte Ouvriere
0024-7669	Lux
0024-7685	Lux Vera
0024-7693	Luz
0024-7707	Luz (Skokie)
0024-7715	Luz Apostolica†
0024-7723	Luz del Cosmos†
0024-7731	Luz Y Verdad†
0024-774X	Lyd & Tone†
0024-7758	Journal of Reproductive Medicine
0024-7766	Lymphology
0024-7774	Lynx
0024-7782	Lyon Chirurgical
0024-7790	Lyon Medical
0024-7804	Lyon Pharmaceutique
0024-7812	Lyons Music News *see* 0093-0164
0024-7820	Lyric
0024-7839	Lyric Opera News
0024-7847	Lyrica Germanica†
0024-7863	Lys Mykyta
0024-7871	Lyudyna i Svit
0024-788X	M A C Flyer
0024-7898	M. A. C. Gopher
0024-791X	M A S C A Newsletter *see* 0198-0106
0024-7944	M & B Laboratory Bulletin†
0024-7952	M B A†
0024-7960	M B A A Technical Quarterly
0024-7987	M C M Newsletter
0024-7995	M C-Nytt
0024-8002	M D en Espanol
0024-8010	Medical Newsmagazine *changed to* M D Magazine
0024-8029	M D Moebel Interior Design *changed to* M D
0024-8045	M D S
0024-807X	M D'S Wife *see* 0163-0512
0024-810X	M E D *changed to* Medical Electronics
0024-8118	M. E. N. Economic Weekly
0024-8134	M F C News
0024-8142	M F M-Moderne Fototechnik
0024-8150	M.G.A. Bulletin *changed to* Mushroom Journal
0024-8169	M G Conquest†
0024-8185	M.H.S. Miscellany
0024-8207	M I Contact *changed to* Marconi Instruments Contact
0024-8215	M L A International Bibliography of Books and Articles on the Modern Languages and Literatures
0024-8223	M L A Newsletter
0024-8231	M. L. B. Log
0024-824X	M'-le Magazine de Madame†
0024-8258	M. M. E. A. Music News *see* 0147-2550
0024-8266	Astronomical Society of Southern Africa. Monthly Notes
0024-8282	M O N Y News
0024-8320	M R A Information Service *changed to* New World News
0024-8339	M R und V/Metall-Reinigung und Vorbehandlung-Oberflaechen Technik *changed to* Oberflaechentechnik
0024-8347	M R I Quarterly
0024-8355	M Report
0024-8363	M S A Monthly Bulletin
0024-8398	M S H A
0024-841X	M S Keynotes *changed to* M S Messenger
0024-8428	M S O A Journal
0024-8444	M S S C Exchange
0024-8452	M S S P A Bugle†
0024-8460	M S U Business Topics
0024-8479	M S U Mathematics Letter
0024-8487	M T A News
0024-8495	Weekly Bulletin
0024-8509	M T M
0024-8517	M T T
0024-8525	M T Z
0024-8533	Meridiano Dodici
0024-8541	Maailma ja Me
0024-855X	Maal og Minne
0024-8568	Maalarilehti
0024-8592	Drenthe
0024-8606	Maandblad Suiker Unie
0024-8614	Maandblad tegen de Kwakzalverij
0024-8622	Maandblad voor Accountancy en Bedrijfshuishoudkunde
0024-8649	Maandblad voor de Varkensfokkerij *changed to* Maandblad voor de Varkensfokkerij en -Mesterij
0024-8657	Maandblad voor het Land- en Tuinbouwonderwijs
0024-8665	Nederduitse Gereformeerde Kerk van Natal Gemeente Vryheid. Maandbrief
0024-8673	Maandschrift Economie
0024-8681	Maandschrift voor Bijenteelt
0024-8703	Maandstatistiek Buitenlandse Handel†
0024-8711	Netherlands. Centraal Bureau voor de Statistiek. Maandstatistiek van Bevolking en Volksgezondheid
0024-872X	Netherlands. Centraal Bureau voor de Statistiek. Maandstatistiek van de Binnenlandse Handel *changed to* Netherlands. Centraal Bureau voor de Statistiek. Maandstatistiek van de Binnenlandse Handel en Dienstverlening
0024-8738	Netherlands. Centraal Bureau voor de Statistiek. Maandstatistiek van de Buitenlandse Handel per Goederensoort
0024-8746	Netherlands. Centraal Bureau voor de Statistiek. Maandstatistiek van de Buitenlandse Handel per Land
0024-8754	Netherlands. Centraal Bureau voor de Statistiek. Maandstatistiek van de Landbouw
0024-8762	Maandstatistiek van Het Financiewezen†
0024-8770	Netherlands. Centraal Bureau voor de Statistiek. Maandstatistiek Verkeer en Vervoer
0024-8789	Maanedsskrift for Praktisk Laegegering *changed to* Tidsskrift for Praktisk Laegegering
0024-8797	Maanmittausinsinoori *see* 0356-7869
0024-8819	Maarakennus ja Kuljetus

ISSN INDEX

ISSN	Title
0024-8827	Maatalous
0024-8835	Scientific Agricultural Society of Finland. Journal
0024-8843	Maatschappijbelangen
0024-8886	Macabre
0024-8894	Macaroni Journal
0024-8908	McCall's
0024-8924	McCall's Needlework & Crafts
0024-8940	McCall's Fabrics Plus†
0024-8959	Macchine
0024-8967	Macchine e Motori Agricoli
0024-8975	McCormick Quarterly†
0024-8991	McDonnell Douglas Spirit
0024-9009	Macedonian Tribune
0024-9017	Macelleria Italiana
0024-9025	McGill Dental Review
0024-9033	McGill Journal of Education
0024-9041	McGill Law Journal
0024-905X	McGill Medical Journal
0024-9068	McGill News
0024-9076	McGill University, Montreal. Industrial Relations Centre. Review
0024-9092	Machine and Machinery
0024-9106	Machine and Tool Blue Book
0024-9114	Machine Design
0024-9122	Machine Design & Control†
0024-9130	Machine Moderne
0024-9130	Machine Moderne see 0047-536X
0024-9149	Machine-Outil
0024-9157	Machine Shop and Engineering Manufacture†
0024-9165	Machine Tool Engineering†
0024-9173	Machine-Tool Review
0024-919X	Machinery and Production Engineering
0024-9203	Machinery Lloyd
0024-9211	Machinery Market and the Machinery and Engineering Materials Gazette
0024-922X	Machines and Tooling see 0144-6622
0024-9238	Machines Francaises†
0024-9246	Machinisme Agricole Tropical
0024-9262	Maclean's
0024-9270	McMaster University Library Research News
0024-9297	Macromolecules
0024-9300	Mad
0024-9319	Mad
0024-9327	Mad og Gaester†
0024-9335	Mada
0024-9343	Madam
0024-9351	Madam
0024-936X	Madame
0024-9378	Made in Europe changed to Made in Europe. General Merchandise
0024-9386	Made in Poland†
0024-9394	Mademoiselle
0024-9408	Mademoiselle Gymnast see 0162-9867
0024-9424	Madhumeh changed to Diabetic Association of India. Journal
0024-9432	Madhuri
0024-9459	Madhya Pradesh Law Journal
0024-9467	Madhya Pradesh Medical Journal†
0024-9475	Laboratory Enquiry Service
0024-9483	Madison Avenue
0024-9521	Indonesian Journal of Geography
0024-953X	Madjalah Manager†
0024-9548	Madjalah Persatuan Dokter Gigi Indonesia
0024-9556	Madjalah Pertanian
0024-9564	Madjalah Kedokteran Surabaja see 0303-7932
0024-9572	Madonna changed to Sacred Heart Messenger
0024-9580	Madonna di Barbana
0024-9599	Madonna di Castelmonte
0024-9602	Madras Agricultural Journal
0024-9610	Madras Labour Gazette. changed to Tamil Nadu Labour Journal
0024-9629	Spain. Consejo Superior de Investigaciones Cientificas. Instituto de Farmacologia Experimental. Archivos changed to Archivas de Farmacologia y Toxicologia
0024-9637	Madrono
0024-9645	Maelkeritidende changed to Danish Dairy Industry
0024-9653	Maelstrom†
0024-9661	Der Maerker
0024-967X	Maerkische Zeitung
0024-9688	Maerklin-Magazin
0024-9696	Maestro
0024-9718	Mafeking Mail and Botswana Guardian
0024-9726	Magadh University Journal
0024-9742	Magazin der Grosskuechen und Kantinen changed to Grosskuechen und GV
0024-9750	Magazin fuer Fortschrittliche Haustechnik und Wohnkultur†
0024-9769	Magazin fuer Haus und Wohnung
0024-9785	Magazin Vier und Zwanzig changed to Initiative
0024-9793	Media Industry Newsletter
0024-9807	Magazine Litteraire
0024-9815	Maclean see 0383-8714
0024-9823	Magazine of Bank Administration
0024-9831	Magazine of Concrete Research
0024-984X	Magazine of Fantasy and Science Fiction
0024-9858	Magazine of Wall Street
0024-9866	Magazyn Polski
0024-9874	Magazzini & Trasporti
0024-9890	Maghreb see 0336-6324
0024-9904	Magic Cauldron
0024-9912	Magische Welt
0024-9920	Magistrate
0024-9939	Magistrate
0024-9947	Maglie Calze Industria
0024-9955	Magna Graecia
0024-9963	Magneet-Revue
0024-998X	Magnetohydrodynamics
0024-9998	Kongresszentralblatt fuer die Gesamte Innere Medizin see 0301-584X
0025-0007	Magnificat
0025-0015	Magnitnaya Gidrodinamika
0025-0023	Magnus changed to Finish
0025-0031	Maguey†
0025-004X	Magyar Allatorvosok Lapja
0025-0058	Magyar Aluminium
0025-0066	Magyar Belorvosi Archivum
0025-0074	Magyar Epitoipar
0025-0082	Magyar Epitomuveszet
0025-0090	Magyar Filozofiai Szemle
0025-0104	Magyar Fizikai Folyoirat
0025-0112	Magyar Folyoiratok Repertoriuma see 0133-6894
0025-0120	Magyar Geofizika
0025-0139	Magyar Grafika
0025-0147	Magyar Jog†
0025-0147	Magyar Jog see 0034-6829
0025-0155	Magyar Kemiai Folyoirat
0025-0163	Magyar Kemikusok Lapja
0025-0171	Magyar Konyvszemle
0025-018X	Magyar Mezogazdasag
0025-0198	Magyar Mezogazdasagi Bibliografia
0025-021X	Magyar Noorvosok Lapja
0025-0228	Magyar Nyelv
0025-0236	Magyar Nyelvor
0025-0244	Magyar Onkologia
0025-0252	Magyar Orvosi Bibliografia
0025-0260	Magyar Pedagogia
0025-0279	Magyar Pszichologiai Szemle
0025-0287	Magyar Radiologia
0025-0295	Magyar Sebeszet
0025-0309	Magyar Textiltechnika
0025-0317	Magyar Traumatologia, Orthopedia es Helyreallito-Sebeszet
0025-0325	Magyar Tudomany
0025-0333	Magyar Tudomanyos Akademia. Biologiai Tudomanyok Osztalya. Kozlemenyek
0025-0341	Magyar Tudomanyos Akademia. Konyvtar. Kiadvanyok
0025-035X	Magyar Tudomanyos Akademie. Matematikai es Fizikai Tudomanyok Osztalya. Kozlemenyek changed to Alkalmazott Matematikai Lapok
0025-0368	Magyar Tudomanyos Akademia. Nyelv- es Irodalomtudomanyi Osztaly. Kozlemenyek
0025-0376	Magyar Tudomanyos Akademia. Filozofiai es Tortenettudomanyi Osztaly. Kozlemenyek
0025-0384	Magyar Zene
0025-0392	Maharashtra
0025-0406	Maha Bodhi
0025-0414	Mahajanmer Lagna
0025-0422	Maharaja Sayajirao University of Baroda. Journal
0025-0430	Maharashtra Co-Operative Quarterly
0025-0449	Maharashtra, India. Directorate of Industries. Industrial Bulletin†
0025-0465	Maharashtra Law Journal
0025-0473	Maharashtra Parichaya†
0025-0481	Maharashtra Quarterly Bulletin of Economics and Statistics
0025-049X	Mahenjodaro
0025-0503	Mahfil: a Quarterly of South Asian Literature see 0091-5637
0025-0511	Die Mahnung
0025-052X	Maehrisch-Schlesische Heimat†
0025-0538	Maia
0025-0546	Mail
0025-0562	Mail Trade
0025-0570	Main Currents in Modern Thought†
0025-0597	Main Roads
0025-0619	Maine Business Indicators
0025-0643	Maine Fish and Game Magazine see 0360-005X
0025-0651	Maine Law Review
0025-0678	Maine Life
0025-0686	Maine Manpower
0025-0694	Maine Medical Association. Journal
0025-0708	Maine Nature
0025-0716	Maine, New Hampshire, Vermont Beverage Journal
0025-0732	Maine on the Grow changed to Mark Maine News
0025-0759	Maine State Labor News changed to Maine Labor News
0025-0775	Maine Teacher
0025-0783	Maine Times
0025-0791	Maine Townsman
0025-0805	Maine Water Utilities Association. Journal
0025-0813	Mainichi Graphic
0025-083X	Mainliner
0025-0848	Mainly
0025-0856	Mainostaja see 0357-2862
0025-0864	Mainosuutiset
0025-0872	Maintenance changed to Maintenance Management
0025-0880	Maintenance
0025-0899	Maintenance Engineering†
0025-0902	Maintenance Engineering
0025-0910	Maintenance News†
0025-0929	Maintenance Supplies
0025-0937	Maison-Dieu
0025-0945	Maison et Jardin
0025-0953	Maison Francaise
0025-0996	Maitre Imprimeur
0025-1003	International Phonetic Association. Journal
0025-102X	Majallaht
0025-1038	Diwan al-Tadween al-Qanouni Majallat changed to Adala
0025-1046	Majallat Shi'r
0025-1089	Makedonski Jazik
0025-1119	Makerere Medical Journal
0025-1127	Matekon
0025-1135	Makina Muehendisleri Odasi Haftalik Haberler Gazetesi
0025-1151	Making Music†
0025-116X	Makromolekulare Chemie
0025-1178	Mala Ukrstenica
0025-1186	Malabar Herald†
0025-1208	Maladosts'
0025-1216	Malahat Review
0025-1224	Malamalama†
0025-1232	Maaleri
0025-1240	Malawi Mwezi Uno/Malawi This Month changed to Boma Lathu
0025-1267	Malawi Patent Journal and Trade Marks Journal
0025-1275	Malayan Forester see 0302-2935
0025-1283	Malayan Law Journal
0025-1291	Malayan Nature Journal
0025-1305	Malaysia†
0025-1313	Quarterly Bulletin of Statistics Relating to the Mining Industry of Malaysia
0025-1321	Malaysian Agricultural Journal
0025-133X	Malaysian Journal of Education†
0025-133X	Malaysian Journal of Education changed to South-East Asian Journal of Educational Studies
0025-1348	Malaysian Management Review
0025-1372	Malerzeitung Drei Schilde
0025-1380	Mallasjuomat see 0356-3014
0025-1399	Mallige
0025-1402	Malm changed to Graengeskontakten
0025-1410	Malmoe Museum. Aktuellt†
0025-1429	Studia Historyczne
0025-1437	Malta. Central Office of Statistics. Quarterly Digest of Statistics
0025-1445	Maltechnik-Restauro
0025-1453	Malyatko
0025-1461	Mammalia
0025-1496	Man
0025-150X	Man and His Music†
0025-1518	Man and Metal
0025-1526	Man and Society†
0025-1534	Man and World
0025-1542	Man-Environment-Communication Center Report†
0025-1550	Man-Environment Systems
0025-1569	Man in India
0025-1577	Man in New Guinea changed to Research in Melanesia
0025-1593	Man on Earth
0025-1615	Manab Mon
0025-1623	Manage
0025-1631	Management†
0025-164X	Management
0025-1658	Management
0025-1666	Management Abstracts see 0307-3580
0025-1674	Management Accountant
0025-1682	Management Accounting
0025-1690	Management Accounting
0025-1704	Management & Operations†
0025-1720	Management Consultant†
0025-1739	Management Controls changed to Management Focus
0025-1747	Management Decision
0025-1771	Management Ideas
0025-178X	Management in Nigeria
0025-1798	Management Index†
0025-1801	Management Industrial see 0374-4795
0025-181X	Management International Review
0025-1828	Management Japan
0025-1836	Management Horizons
0025-1844	Management News changed to Managers' Forum
0025-1860	Management Quarterly
0025-1887	Monthly Review of Management Research
0025-1895	Management Review
0025-1909	Management Science
0025-1925	Management Today
0025-1933	Management's Bibliographic Data†
0025-1941	Managerial Planning
0025-195X	Manager's Letter†
0025-1968	Manager's Magazine
0025-1976	Manas
0025-1984	Manas
0025-1992	Manchester Chamber of Commerce. Record
0025-200X	Manchester Guardian Weekly
0025-2018	Manchester Medical Gazette changed to Mediscope
0025-2026	Manchester Review†
0025-2034	Manchester School of Economic and Social Studies
0025-2042	Manchete
0025-2077	Manequim
0025-2085	Manhattan Almanac changed to Metropolitan Almanac
0025-2093	Manhattan College Engineer
0025-2123	Manhattan Review†
0025-214X	Manicomio Judiciario Heitor Carrilho. Arquivos
0025-2166	Manifold
0025-2174	Manion Forum†
0025-2182	Manitoba changed to Manitoba Business Review

ISSN INDEX

ISSN	Title
0025-2190	Manitoba Archaeological Newsletter *see* 0705-2669
0025-2204	Manitoba Association of School Librarians Newsletter *see* 0315-9124
0025-2239	Manitoba Co-Operator
0025-2247	Manitoba Dental Association. Bulletin
0025-2255	Manitoba Medical Review†
0025-2271	Manitoba Professional Engineer
0025-2298	Manitoban
0025-231X	Mankato State Daily Reporter *changed to* Mankato State Independent
0025-2328	Mankind
0025-2336	Mankind
0025-2344	Mankind Quarterly
0025-2352	Mannskapsavisa *changed to* Forsvarets Forum
0025-2360	Mannus *changed to* Volksleben
0025-2379	Manoir-Express *changed to* Manoir-Echo
0025-2387	Manovella
0025-2395	Manpower Magazine *changed to* Worklife Magazine
0025-2433	Manpower Trends *changed to* Maryland Labor Market Dimensions
0025-2441	ManRoot†
0025-245X	Man's Conquest†
0025-2468	Man's Illustrated†
0025-2476	Man's Magazine
0025-2484	Manse Mail†
0025-2492	Manteia
0025-2506	Mantova
0025-2514	Manuelle Medizin
0025-2522	Manufacturers Agent
0025-2530	Manufacturers' Monthly
0025-2549	Manufacturing & the Law
0025-2557	Manufacturing Chemist and Aerosol News
0025-2565	Manufacturing Clothier
0025-2573	Manufacturing Confectioner
0025-2581	Manufacturing Optics International
0025-259X	Manufaktur *see* 0332-5520
0025-2603	Manuscripta
0025-2611	Manuscripta Mathematica
0025-2638	Manuskripte
0025-2646	Manutencion y Almacenaje
0025-2654	Manutention-Stockage *see* 0397-3816
0025-2670	Many Smokes
0025-2689	Mapocho†
0025-2697	Die Mappe
0025-2700	Maquinas & Metais†
0025-2700	Maquinas e Metais
0025-2719	Maquinas y Equipos
0025-2727	Mar *changed to* Clube Naval Revista
0025-2735	Mar y Pesca
0025-2743	Marathon World
0025-2751	Marathwada University Journal
0025-2778	Marburger Umschau
0025-28C8	March of Education†
0025-2840	Marche Suisse des Machines
0025-2859	Marches Tropicaux et Mediterraneens
0025-2867	Marcolian
0025-2883	Marconi Review
0025-2891	Marechal
0025-2905	Maree de France
0025-2913	Marg
0025-2921	Margin
0025-293X	Marginales
0025-2948	Marginalien
0025-2956	Margriet
0025-2972	Maria
0025-2980	Mariages
0025-2999	Mariahilfer Pfarrbote
0025-3006	Marian†
0025-3014	Marianist
0025-3022	Mariannhill
0025-3030	Maricopa Urban Teachers Association Newsletter
0025-3049	Marie-Claire
0025-3057	Marie-France
0025-3065	Regard de Foi
0025-3073	Marien Report†
0025-309X	Marina Italiana
0025-3103	Marina Mercantile
0025-312X	Marine & Recreation News
0025-3138	Marine and Air Catering†
0025-3146	Marine Biological Association of India. Journal
0025-3154	Marine Biological Association of the United Kingdom. Journal
0025-3162	Marine Biology
0025-3170	Marine Corps Gazette
0025-3197	Marine Digest
0025-3200	Marine Engineer and Naval Architect *changed to* Shipbuilding & Marine Engineering International
0025-3219	Marine Engineering/Log
0025-3227	Marine Geology
0025-3235	Marine Geophysical Researches
0025-3243	Marine News
0025-3251	Marine Observer
0025-325X	Marine Pollution Bulletin
0025-3278	Marine Products *changed to* Marine Retailer
0025-3286	Marine Resources Digest/Marine Biology Digest†
0025-3294	Marine-Rundschau
0025-3308	Marine Science Contents Tables†
0025-3316	Marine Technology
0025-3324	Marine Technology Society Journal
0025-3340	Marineblad
0025-3359	Mariner's Mirror
0025-3357	Mariners Weather Log
0025-3375	Marinnytt
0025-3383	Marion
0025-3391	Maritime *see* 0161-9373
0025-3405	Maritime Co-Operator *see* 0703-5357
0025-3413	Maritime Command Trident
0025-3421	Maritime Exchange Bulletin *changed to* Maritime Association of the Port of New York. Newsletter
0025-343X	Maritime Farmer and Co-Operative Dairyman
0025-3448	Maritime Reporter and Engineering News
0025-3464	Maritime Worker
0025-3472	Maritimes
0025-3480	Marjolaine
0025-3499	Mark Twain Journal
0025-3502	Markedsfoering
0025-3510	Markedskommunikasjon†
0025-3529	Marker *changed to* Arch
0025-3537	Market
0025-3545	West Virginia. Department of Agriculture. Market Bulletin
0025-3553	Market Frontier News
0025-3561	Market Industries News
0025-357X	Market Place
0025-3588	Market Research *see* 0308-3047
0025-3596	Market Research Abstracts
0025-360X	Market Research Facts and Trends
0025-3618	Market Research Society. Journal
0025-3626	Marketer *see* 0093-5832
0025-3634	Marketing
0025-3642	Marketing
0025-3650	Marketing
0025-3669	Marketing & the Law *changed to* Marketing in Action
0025-3677	U.S. Department of Agriculture. Economic Research Service. Marketing and Transport Situation *see* 0099-1066
0025-3685	Marketing/Communications†
0025-3707	Marketing Image
0025-3715	Marketing Horizons
0025-3723	Marketing in Europe
0025-3731	Marketing in Hungary
0025-374X	Marketing Information Guide†
0025-3774	Marketing Journal
0025-3790	Marketing News
0025-3812	Marketing World†
0025-3820	Markham Review
0025-3847	Markkinointi-Myyntiniehet *see* 0357-2862
0025-3855	Marknaden
0025-3863	Markt
0025-3871	Marktwirtschaft†
0025-3871	Marktwirtschaft *see* 0302-6671
0025-388X	Maroc-Medical†
0025-3898	Maroquinerie-Voyage-Parapluie-Chaussure
0025-3901	Maroquinerie, Sellerie et Bagages de France
0025-391X	Marple's Business Roundup *changed to* Marple's Business Newsletter
0025-3928	Marquee
0025-3936	Marques Internationales
0025-3944	Marquetarian
0025-3952	Marquette Business Review†
0025-3960	Marquette Engineer
0025-3979	Marquette Journal
0025-3987	Marquette Law Review
0025-3995	Marquette Tribune
0025-4002	Marquette University Magazine *changed to* Marquette Today
0025-4010	Marriage *changed to* Marriage and Family Living
0025-4029	Mars in Cathedra
0025-4037	Mars-Magazine
0025-4053	Marseille Medical
0025-4061	Mart
0025-407X	Martinella di Milano
0025-4088	Chambre de Commerce et d'Industrie de la Martinique. Bulletin *see* 0396-2458
0025-4096	Maruee
0025-410X	Marx Memorial Library. Quarterly Bulletin
0025-4118	Marxism Today
0025-4134	Marxist Veekshanam
0025-4142	Maryland and Delaware Genealogist
0025-4150	Maryland Baptist
0025-4169	Maryland Bar Journal
0025-4177	Maryland C. P. A. Quarterly†
0025-4185	Maryland Conservationist
0025-4193	Maryland Crime Report *changed to* Maryland Crime Control Directory
0025-4207	Maryland-Delaware-D. C. Press News
0025-4215	Maryland Fruit Grower
0025-4223	Maryland Herpetological Society. Bulletin
0025-4231	Maryland Historian
0025-424X	Maryland Historical Magazine
0025-4258	Maryland History Notes *changed to* Maryland Historical Society. News and Notes
0025-4266	Maryland Horse
0025-4274	Maryland Law Review
0025-4282	Maryland
0025-4290	Maryland Municipal News *changed to* Municipal Maryland
0025-4304	Maryland Music Educator
0025-4312	Maryland P T A Bulletin
0025-4339	Maryland Pharmacist
0025-4347	Maryland State Dental Association. Journal
0025-4355	Maryland State Medical Journal
0025-4363	Maryland Teacher†
0025-4371	Maryland University School of Medicine Bulletin
0025-438X	Maryland Veterinarian†
0025-4398	Mas Chistes†
0025-441X	Masada
0025-4428	Masalah Bangunan
0025-4436	Die Maschine
0025-4444	Maschine und Werkzeug
0025-4452	Maschinen- und Stahlbauindustrie in Oesterreich *changed to* Maschinen und Stahlbau
0025-4460	Maschinenbau†
0025-4479	Maschinenbau und Fertigungstechnik der U d S S R
0025-4487	Maschinenbautechnik
0025-4495	Der Maschinenschaden
0025-4517	Maschinenwelt-Elektrotechnik
0025-4533	MascuLines
0025-4541	Mashinostroene
0025-455X	Mashinostroitel'
0025-4568	Mashinovedenie
0025-4576	Mashriq
0025-4584	Maske und Kothurn
0025-4606	Maskin
0025-4614	Maskinbefaelet
0025-4622	Maskinstationen *changed to* Maskinstationen og Landbrugslederen
0025-4630	Maslozhirovaya Promyshlennost'
0025-4649	Mason Clinic Bulletin
0025-4657	Masonic Tribune
0025-4673	Masonry
0025-4681	Masque
0025-469X	Masque
0025-4711	Mass Media Ministries. Bi-Weekly Newsletter *see* 0361-865X
0025-472X	Mass Spectrometry Bulletin
0025-4738	Massachusetts Bureau of Library Extension. Newsletter *changed to* Currents (Boston)
0025-4762	Massachusetts C P A Review
0025-4770	Massachusetts College of Pharmacy. Bulletin
0025-4789	Massachusetts Daily Collegian
0025-4797	Massachusetts Heritage†
0025-4819	Massachusetts Institute of Technology. Research Laboratory of Electronics. Quarterly Progress Report *changed to* Massachusetts Institute of Technology. Research Laboratory of Electronics. R L E Progress Report
0025-4827	Massachusetts Law Quarterly *see* 0163-1411
0025-4835	Massachusetts Physician *see* 0192-2963
0025-4851	Massachusetts Professional Engineer *changed to* New England Engineering Journal
0025-486X	Massachusetts Review
0025-4878	Massachusetts State Labor Council AFL-CIO Newsletter
0025-4894	Massachusetts Teacher
0025-4908	Massachusetts Trends in Employment and Unemployment *changed to* Massachusetts Trends, Labor Force, Employment, Unemployment
0025-4916	Massachusetts Wildlife
0025-4924	Massimario de Il Foro Italiano
0025-4932	Massimario della Giurisprudenza Italiana
0025-4940	Massimario di Giurisprudenza del Lavoro
0025-4959	Massis
0025-4975	Master Baker, Confectioner & Caterer
0025-4983	Master Builders' Journal
0025-4991	Master Carriers Journal *changed to* Freight Carriers
0025-5009	Master Detective
0025-5017	Master Drawings
0025-5025	Master Plumber and Heating Contractor†
0025-505X	Master Plumber of South Australia
0025-5068	Masterpainter *changed to* British Decorator
0025-5092	Masters Abstracts
0025-5106	Master's Thesis Abstracts Bulletin†
0025-5114	Masthead
0025-5122	Matemaattisten Aineiden Aikakauskirja
0025-5149	Matematicheskii Sbornik
0025-5157	Matematicki Vesnik
0025-5165	Mathematica Slovaca
0025-5173	Matematika v Shkole
0025-5181	Matematikai Lapok
0025-519X	Mater Ecclesiae
0025-522X	Materia Medica Nordmark
0025-5238	Materia Medica Polona
0025-5246	Materiaal, Metodiek, Mededelingen *changed to* M.3
0025-5254	Material Handling Engineering
0025-5262	Material und Organismen
0025-5270	Materiale Plastice
0025-5289	Materialehaandtering og Transport Nyt *see* 0106-1666
0025-5297	Materialpruefung
0025-5300	Materials Engineering
0025-5319	Materials Evaluation
0025-5327	Materials Handling and Management†
0025-5335	Materials Management & Distribution
0025-5343	Materials Handling News
0025-5351	Materials on Asia and Africa-Accession List and Review
0025-536X	Materials Protection *see* 0094-1492
0025-5378	Materials Reclamation Weekly
0025-5386	Materials Research and Standards/MIRS *see* 0090-1210
0025-5394	Materials Research Bulletin
0025-5408	Materials Science and Engineering
0025-5416	

0025-5432	Materiaux & Constructions	0025-6641	MedBooks†	0025-7753	Medicina Clinica
0025-5440	Materidouska	0025-665X	Medborgaren	0025-7761	Medicina Clinica e Sperimentale†
0025-5459	Materie Plastiche ed Elastomeri	0025-6668	Norske Myrselskap. Meddelelser see 0332-5229	0025-777X	Medicina Contemporanea†
0025-5467	Materiel d'Enterprise changed to Construction			0025-7788	Medicina Cutanea changed to Medicina Cutanea Ibero-Latino-Americana
0025-5475	Maternal and Child Care†	0025-6676	Meddelelser om Groenland changed to Greenland Geoscience		
0025-5491	Maternidade e Infancia			0025-7796	Medicina Danas
0025-5505	Mathematica	0025-6676	Meddelelser om Groenland changed to Greenland Biosciences	0025-7818	Medicina del Lavoro
0025-5513	Mathematica Japonica			0025-7826	Medicina Dello Sport
0025-5521	Mathematica Scandinavica	0025-6676	Meddelelser om Groenland changed to Greenland, Man and Society	0025-7834	Medicina e Morale
0025-553X	Mathematicae Notae			0025-7842	Medicina Espanola
0025-5548	Mathematical Algorithms†	0025-6692	Medecin du Quebec	0025-7850	Journal of Medicine changed to Journal of Medicine (Clinical, Experimental and Theoretical)
0025-5556	Mathematical Association of India. Bulletin	0025-6714	Etudes Medicales		
		0025-6722	Medecine du Sport		
0025-5564	Mathematical Biosciences	0025-6730	Medecine et Gastronomie†	0025-7869	Revista de Medicina Interna, Neurologie, Psihiatrie, Neuro-Chirurgie, Dermato-Venerologie. Medicina Interna
0025-5572	Mathematical Gazette	0025-6749	Medecine et Hygiene		
0025-5580	Mathematical Log	0025-6757	Medecine et Travail		
0025-5602	Mathematical Pie	0025-6773	Medecine Infantile		
0025-5610	Mathematical Programming	0025-6781	Medecine Interne		
0025-5629	Mathematical Reviews	0025-6811	Medecine Practicienne†	0025-7877	Medicina Nei Secoli
0025-5637	Mathematical Sciences Employment Register†	0025-682X	Medecine Tropicale	0025-7893	Medicina Psicosomatica
		0025-6838	Medecins de Groupe	0025-7907	Medicina Rural†
0025-5653	Mathematical Spectrum	0025-6854	Bedrijfsontwikkeling. Editie Tuinbouw changed to Bedrijfsontwikkeling	0025-7915	Medicina Sociale
0025-5661	Mathematical Systems Theory			0025-7923	Medicina Tedesca
0025-567X	Matematicheskie Zametki	0025-6862	Mededelingenblad Bedrijfsorganisatie	0025-7931	Respiration
0025-5688	Delta-K	0025-6870	Medhjalparen changed to E F S Paa Vaeg	0025-794X	Medicina Tropical changed to Revista Cubana de Medicina Tropical
0025-570X	Mathematics Magazine				
0025-5718	Mathematics of Computation	0025-6870	Medhjalparen changed to E F S Start	0025-7958	Medicina Tropical
0025-5726	Mathematics of the U S S R-Izvestija	0025-6897	Media & Methods	0025-7966	Medicinar
0025-5734	Mathematics of the U S S R - Sbornik	0025-6900	Marketing & Media Decisions	0025-7974	Medicine
0025-5742	Mathematics Student	0025-6919	Media-Informatiedienst	0025-7982	Medicine and Medicaments Courier
0025-5750	Mathematics Student Journal changed to Mathematics Student	0025-6927	Medianite	0025-7990	Medicine and Science in Sports see 0195-9131
		0025-6943	Medical Abstract Service†		
0025-5769	Mathematics Teacher	0025-696X	Medical & Biological Engineering see 0140-0118	0025-8008	Medicine & Surgery
0025-5785	Mathematics Teaching			0025-8016	Medicine Europeene
0025-5793	Mathematika	0025-6978	Medical and Biological Illustration see 0140-511X	0025-8032	Medicine Today†
0025-5807	Der Mathematikunterricht			0025-8040	Medicinsk Forum
0025-5831	Mathematische Annalen	0025-6986	Medical Annals of the District of Columbia†	0025-8067	Medicinska Revija
0025-584X	Mathematische Nachrichten			0025-8091	Medicinski Glasnik
0025-5858	Universitaet Hamburg. Mathematisches Seminar. Abhandlungen	0025-7001	Medical Aspects of Human Sexuality†	0025-8105	Medicinski Pregled
		0025-701X	Medical Association for Prevention of War. Proceedings	0025-8113	Medicinski Radnik
0025-5866	Der Mathematische und Naturwissenschaftliche Unterricht			0025-8121	Medicinski Razgledi
		0025-7028	Medical Association of Georgia. Journal	0025-813X	Medico†
0025-5874	Mathematische Zeitschrift	0025-7036	Medical Association of Thailand. Journal	0025-8148	Medico d'Italia
0025-5904	Mathitiki Estia	0025-7044	Medical Association of the State of Alabama. Journal	0025-8164	Medico-Legal Bulletin
0025-5912	Mati			0025-8172	Medico-Legal Journal
0025-5920	Matica	0025-7052	Science Book Finder	0025-8180	Medico Moderno†
0025-5939	Letopis Matice Srpske	0025-7060	Medical Book News	0025-8202	Medicos†
0025-5947	Matieland	0025-7079	Medical Care	0025-8210	Medicus†
0025-5955	Matilda Ziegler Magazine for the Blind	0025-7087	Medical Care Review	0025-8229	Medjimurje
0025-5963	Matkailumaailma	0025-7095	Medical Centre Journal	0025-8237	Medion†
0025-598X	Matrix	0025-7109	Medical Checklist	0025-8245	Medisch Contact
0025-5998	Matrix and Tensor Quarterly	0025-7117	Medical Chronicle	0025-8253	Mediscope
0025-6005	Matter	0025-7125	Medical Clinics of North America	0025-8261	Options Mediterraneennes†
0025-6021	Mature Years	0025-7133	Medical College and Hospital, Calcutta. Bulletin	0025-827X	Mediterranean Diplomatic Observer
0025-603X	Mature Years-New Directions†			0025-8296	Mediterranee
0025-6048	Mauricien Medical	0025-7141	Medical College of Virginia Quarterly	0025-830X	Meditsinskii Zhurnal Uzbekistana
0025-6056	Mauritius. Central Statistical Office. Bi-Annual Digest of Statistics	0025-715X	Medical Counterpoint	0025-8318	Meditsinskaya Gazeta
		0025-7168	Medical Digest	0025-8326	Meditsinskaya Parazitologiya i Parazitarnye Bolezni
0025-6064	Mauritius Times	0025-7176	Medical Digest see 0149-0273		
0025-6072	Mausolee	0025-7184	Medical Digest	0025-8334	Meditsinskaya Radiologiya
0025-6099	Mavoschool changed to Nieuw Zicht	0025-7192	Medical Ecology and Clinical Research†	0025-8342	Meditsinskaya Sestra
0025-6102	Max-Planck-Gesellschaft zur Foerderung der Wissenschaften Mitteilungen changed to Max-Planck-Gesellschaft zur Foerderung der Wissenschaften Berichte und Mitteilungen	0025-7206	Medical Economics	0025-8350	Medium
		0025-7222	Medical Electronics & Communications Abstracts	0025-8377	Saskatchewan Association of Media Specialists. Medium changed to Medium
		0025-7230	Medical Electronics News changed to Medical Electronics and Equipment News		
				0025-8393	Medizin in Bild und Ton†
0025-6129	May Day Pictorial News	0025-7257	Medical Group Management	0025-8407	Medizin und Ernaehrung†
0025-6137	May Trends	0025-7265	Medical Group News	0025-8415	Medizin und Sport
0025-6153	Maydica	0025-7273	Medical History	0025-8423	Medizinal-Markt Acta Medicotechnica
0025-6161	Mayfair	0025-729X	Medical Journal of Australia	0025-8431	Medizinhistorisches Journal
0025-617X	Mayfair News changed to Mayfair-Northeast News	0025-7303	Medical Journal of Malaya see 0300-5283	0025-844X	Medizinische Bild†
				0025-8458	Medizinische Klinik
0025-6188	Mayibuye	0025-732X	Medical Letter on Drugs and Therapeutics	0025-8466	Das Medizinische Laboratorium
0025-6196	Mayo Clinic Proceedings			0025-8474	Medizinische Monatsschrift see 0342-9601
0025-6218	Mazputnins	0025-7338	Medical Library Association. Bulletin		
0025-6234	Mbioni	0025-7346	National Library of Medicine Current Catalog Proofsheets	0025-8482	Medizinische Neuerscheinungen
0025-6242	Mvelaphanda			0025-8490	Der Medizinische Sachverstaendige
0025-6269	Me	0025-7354	Medical Marketing & Media	0025-8504	Medizinische Technik see 0344-9416
0025-6277	Me Naiset	0025-7389	Medical Missionary changed to Medical Mission Sisters News	0025-8512	Die Medizinische Welt
0025-6285	Meander			0025-8539	Nordisk Numismatisk Union. Medlemsblad
0025-6293	Meanjin Quarterly changed to Meanjin	0025-7397	Medical-Moral Newsletter		
0025-6307	Measurement and Evaluation in Guidance	0025-7400	Medical Officer see 0300-8347	0025-8547	Foerfattaren
		0025-7435	Medical Post	0025-8555	Medjunarodni Problemi
0025-6315	National Council on Measurement in Education. Measurement News	0025-7451	Medical Quarterly see 0046-9130	0025-8571	Medusa
		0025-746X	Medical Radiography and Photography	0025-8601	Medycyna Doswiadczalna i Mikrobiologia
0025-6323	Measurements and Data see 0148-0057	0025-7478	Medical Record		
0025-6331	Measuring for Medicine & the Life Sciences†	0025-7486	Medical Record News	0025-861X	Medycyna Komunikacyjna
		0025-7494	Medical Research Bulletin	0025-8628	Medycyna Weterynaryjna
0025-634X	Meat†	0025-7508	Medical Research Engineering	0025-8636	Medycyna Wiejska
0025-6358	Meat Board Reports	0025-7532	Medical Society of the County of Kings and Academy of Medicine of Brooklyn. Bulletin changed to K C M S Bulletin	0025-8644	M T
0025-6374	Meat Industry			0025-8652	Meetings and Conventions
0025-6390	Meat Processing changed to Meat Processing International			0025-8679	Megamot
				0025-8687	Megaphone (Canton)
0025-6412	Meat Trades Journal	0025-7540	Medical Socioeconomic Research Sources†	0025-8695	Megaphone (Dallas)
0025-6447	M A G see 0531-755X			0025-8709	Megaphone (Georgetown)
0025-6455	Meccanica	0025-7559	Medical Staff in Action†	0025-8717	Meglio
0025-6463	Meccano Magazine†	0025-7567	Medical-Surgical Review†	0025-8725	Meharri-Dent
0025-6471	Mech	0025-7583	Medical Times	0025-8733	Nagoya University. Cosmic-Ray Research Laboratory. Proceedings
0025-6501	Mechanical Engineering	0025-7605	Medical Tribune see 0279-9340		
0025-651X	Mechanical Engineering News	0025-7613	Medical University of South Carolina. Medical University News changed to Medical University of South Carolina. Medical University Review	0025-8741	Meidensha Review changed to Meiden Review
0025-6528	Mechanical Handling see 0025-5351				
0025-6536	Mechanical Sciences Abstracts changed to Mechanical Sciences			0025-875X	Meie Post
				0025-8768	Meie Tee
0025-6544	Mechanics of Solids	0025-7621	Medical World	0025-8776	Meieriposten
0025-6552	Mechanik	0025-7648	Medicamenta†	0025-8784	Meiklejohn Civil Liberties Library. Acquisitions changed to What's Happening to the Law
0025-6560	Mechanisch Transport en Opslag changed to Bedrijfstransport	0025-7656	Medicamentos de Actualidad changed to Medicamentos de Actualidad/Drugs of Today		
0025-6579	South African Materials Handling News			0025-8792	Mein Eigenheim
0025-6587	Mechanix Illustrated	0025-7664	Medicamundi	0025-8814	Mein Standpunkt
0025-6595	Mechanizacia	0025-7672	Medicare Report	0025-8822	Angewandte Sozialforschung. Journal
0025-6609	Mecman-Technique	0025-7680	Medicina	0025-8830	M E J
0025-6625	Medailles	0025-7699	Medicina	0025-8857	Mekeel's Stamp News
0025-6633	Medal Collector	0025-7729	Medicina	0025-8865	Mekhanika Polimerov

ISSN INDEX   1017

ISSN	Title
0025-8873	Mekhanizatsiya i Avtomatizatsiya Proizvodstva
0025-8881	Mekhanizatsiya i Elektrifikatsiya Sotsialisticheskogo Sel'skogo Khozyaistva
0025-889X	Mekhanizatsiya Sil'skogo Gospodarstva
0025-8903	Mekhanizatsiya Stroitel'stva
0025-8911	Melanges de Science Religieuse
0025-892X	Melanges Malraux Miscellany
0025-8938	Melbourne University Law Review
0025-8954	Mele
0025-8970	Melk en Zuivel *changed to* Zuivelkoerier
0025-8989	Melliand Textilberichte International *see* 0341-0781
0025-8997	Melodie
0025-9004	Melodie und Rhythmus
0025-9012	Melody Maker
0025-9020	Melos *see* 0170-8791
0025-9039	Melyepitestudomanyi Szemle
0025-9047	Memeler Dampfboot
0025-9055	Memento General Tequi Quincaillerie
0025-9063	Memisa Nieuws
0025-9071	Memo
0025-908X	Memo from Belgium
0025-9101	Memo Key *changed to* Office Skills for the Business Studies Teacher
0025-911X	Center for Research on Learning and Teaching. Memo to the Faculty
0025-9128	Revue de Metallurgie. Memoires Scientifiques
0025-9136	Defense Academy. Memoirs
0025-9144	Memon Alam
0025-9152	Mexico. Direccion de Estadistica y Estudios Economicos. Memorandum Tecnico
0025-9160	Memorial de l'Artillerie Francaise
0025-9179	Memorial des Percepteurs et Receveurs des Communes
0025-9195	Memoires C.E.R.E.S.
0025-9209	Memphis State Business Review *changed to* Mid-South Quarterly Business Review
0025-9225	Menadzer u Privredi *changed to* Privreda i Rukovodjenje
0025-9233	Menckeniana
0025-9241	Mendel Newsletter
0025-925X	Mendeleev Chemistry Journal
0025-9268	Mendocino County Historical Society. Newsletter
0025-9284	Menninger Clinic. Bulletin
0025-9292	Menninger Perspective
0025-9314	Mennonitische Rundschau
0025-9322	Mennonite†
0025-9330	Mennonite
0025-9349	Mennonite Brethren Herald
0025-9357	Mennonite Historical Bulletin
0025-9365	Mennonite Life
0025-9373	Mennonite Quarterly Review
0025-9381	Mennonite Historical Society *see* 0148-4036
0025-939X	Menorah
0025-9411	Men's and Boys' Wear Buyers
0025-942X	Men's Art Service
0025-9438	Men's Clip Review *changed to* Menswear Advertising
0025-9446	Mens en Boek *changed to* Bibliotheek en Samenleving
0025-9454	Mens en Maatschappij
0025-9462	Mens en Melodie
0025-9470	Mens en Onderneming *changed to* Mens en Organisatie
0025-9489	Humanist
0025-9497	Men's Fashions
0025-9500	Men's Hairstylist and Barber's Journal
0025-9519	Men's Wear
0025-9527	Men's Wear
0025-9535	Men's Wear of Canada
0025-9543	Mensa Bulletin
0025-956X	Mensaje
0025-9586	Mensajero Forestal
0025-9608	Mensch und Welt†
0025-9616	Das Menschenrecht
0025-9632	Mental Health†
0025-9640	Mental Health Court Digest
0025-9667	Mental Health in Australia
0025-9675	Mental Health Scope
0025-9683	M H†
0025-9691	Mental Retardation Abstracts *see* 0191-1600
0025-9748	Mercado da Borracha no Brasil. Boletin Mensual
0025-9756	Mercado de Valores
0025-9764	Mercados de Grasas y Acietes†
0025-9780	Corriere Mercantile Politico d'Informazioni
0025-9799	Mercantile Gazette of New Zealand
0025-9810	Mercantile Law Reporter†
0025-9829	Mercato Metalsiderurgico
0025-9837	Mercator *see* 0533-070X
0025-9845	Mercer Actuarial Bulletin
0025-9853	Mercer Cluster
0025-987X	Mercer Law Review
0025-9888	Merchandising Week *see* 0362-3920
0025-990X	Mercian Geologist
0025-9918	Merck Sharp & Dohme Review
0025-9926	Mercur
0025-9934	Mercure
0025-9950	Mercurius
0025-9969	Mercury
0025-9977	Mercy Profile
0025-9985	Finland. Merentutkimuslaitos. Julkaisu *see* 0357-1076
0025-9993	Meres es Automatika
0026-0002	Meresugyi Kozlemenyek
0026-0010	Mergers & Acquisitions
0026-0029	Merian
0026-0045	Merino Breeders' Journal
0026-0061	Merkt
0026-007X	Merkenblad B E N E L U X
0026-0088	Merkonomi
0026-0096	Merkur
0026-010X	Merkur Magazin fuer Volksgesundheit
0026-0118	Merkuriusz Polski-Zycie Akademickie†
0026-0126	Merleg
0026-0142	Merova Technika *changed to* Ceskoslovenska Standardizace
0026-0150	Merrill-Palmer Quarterly of Behavior and Development
0026-0169	Merrimac *changed to* M T I Reporter
0026-0185	Mesias
0026-0193	Mesures Regulation Automatisme
0026-0215	Message de l'Immaculee†
0026-0223	Message de Verite†
0026-0231	Message
0026-024X	Messager
0026-0258	Messager de la Haute Savoie
0026-0266	Messager de l'Exarchat du Patriarche Russe en Europe Occidentale
0026-0274	Messager Evangelique
0026-0290	Messages du Secours Catholique
0026-0304	Messaggero dei Ragazzi
0026-0312	Messaggero di S. Antonio
0026-0339	Messen und Pruefen
0026-0347	Messen-Steuern-Regeln
0026-0355	Messenger
0026-0363	Messenger
0026-0371	Messenger
0026-0401	Messidor
0026-0428	Messtechnische Briefe fuer Elektrisches Messen Mechanischer Groessen
0026-0436	Mester†
0026-0452	Meta
0026-0460	Metaal & Kunststof
0026-0479	Metaal en Techniek
0026-0487	Metaalbewerking
0026-0509	Metabolismo
0026-0517	Metal
0026-0525	Metal Building Review
0026-0533	Metal Bulletin
0026-0541	Metal Construction & British Welding Journal *see* 0307-7896
0026-055X	Metal Fabricating News
0026-0568	Metal Fabricator
0026-0576	Metal Finishing
0026-0584	Metal Finishing Abstracts
0026-0606	Metal Finishing Plants and Processes
0026-0614	Meidensha Review *changed to* Kinzoku Hyomen Gijutsu
0026-0622	Metal Forming *changed to* Metallurgia: the Journal of Metals Technology, Metal Forming and Thermal Processing
0026-0630	U D S Metal Joining Digest *changed to* Metal Joining Digest
0026-0649	Metal Polisher, Buffer and Plater†
0026-0657	Metal Powder Report
0026-0665	Metal Progress
0026-0673	Metal Science and Heat Treatment
0026-0681	Metal Science Journal *see* 0306-3453
0026-069X	Metal Stamping
0026-0703	Metal Trades Department. Bulletin†
0026-072X	Metal Worker
0026-0738	Metalektro Visie
0026-0746	Metall
0026-0754	Metallarbetaren
0026-0762	Metalle
0026-0770	Metallgesellschaft Aktiengesellschaft. Review of the Activities
0026-0789	Metallhandwerk & Metalltechnik *changed to* Metall-Handwerk und Technik
0026-0797	Metalloberflaeche
0026-0800	Metallography
0026-0819	Metallovedenie i Termicheskaya Obrabotka Metallov
0026-0827	Metallurg
0026-0835	Metallurgia *changed to* Metallurgia: the Journal of Metals Technology, Metal Forming and Thermal Processing
0026-0843	Metallurgia Italiana
0026-0851	C R M Metallurgical Reports
0026-086X	Metallurgical Transactions *see* 0360-2133
0026-0878	Metallurgie *changed to* Entreprises Rhone Alpes
0026-0894	Metallurgist
0026-0908	Metallverarbeitung
0026-0924	Metals Abstracts
0026-0932	Metals Abstracts Index
0026-0940	Metals and Materials
0026-0959	Metals and Minerals Review
0026-0967	Metals Engineering Quarterly†
0026-0967	Metals Engineering Quarterly *see* 0026-0665
0026-0975	Metals Week
0026-0983	Metalurgia
0026-0991	Metalurgia y Electricidad
0026-1009	Metalworking Digest
0026-1017	Metalworking Economics†
0026-1025	Metalworking News
0026-1033	Metalworking Production
0026-105X	Metanoia†
0026-1068	Metaphilosophy
0026-1076	Metapsichica
0026-1084	Metaux
0026-1092	Meteor
0026-1114	Meteoritics
0026-1122	Israel. Meteorological Service. Meteorologia Be-Israel
0026-1130	Meteorological and Geoastrophysical Abstracts
0026-1149	Meteorological Magazine
0026-1165	Meteorological Society of Japan. Journal
0026-1173	Meteorologicke Zpravy
0026-1181	Meteorologie
0026-119X	Meteorologiya i Gidrologiya
0026-1203	Meteorologische Abhandlungen
0026-1211	Meteorologische Rundschau
0026-1238	Methodist History
0026-1246	Methodist Homes Quarterly *changed to* Horizon
0026-1254	Methodist Message *changed to* Pelita Methodist
0026-1262	Methodist Recorder
0026-1270	Methods of Information in Medicine
0026-1289	Metiers Graphiques
0026-1297	Metlfax
0026-1300	Zemedelska Informatika
0026-1319	Metodiky pro Zavadeni Vysledku Vyzkumu do Praxe
0026-1327	Metra†
0026-1335	Metrika
0026-1343	Metro
0026-136X	Intelligence Report *changed to* Metro Denver
0026-1378	Metro Memo†
0026-1386	Metroeconomica
0026-1394	Metrologia
0026-1408	Metrology and Inspection
0026-1416	Metron†
0026-1424	Metron
0026-1467	Metropolitan *changed to* Metro (Redondo Beach)
0026-1475	Metropolitan†
0026-1483	Metropolitan Area Digest†
0026-1491	Metropolitan Computer News†
0026-1505	Metropolitan Council of the Twin Cities Area. Newsletter†
0026-1513	Metropolitan Life Insurance Company. Statistical Bulletin
0026-1521	Metropolitan Museum of Art. Bulletin
0026-153X	Metropolitan Nashville Board of Education. News and Views
0026-1556	Metropolitan Pensioner
0026-1564	Metropolitan Restaurant News
0026-1580	Metropolitan Star
0026-1599	Metropolitan Washington Board of Trade News
0026-1602	Metsa Ja Puu
0026-1610	Communicationes Instituti Forestalis Fenniae
0026-1629	Metsastys ja Kalastus
0026-1637	Metterdaad†
0026-1645	Metzger und Wurster
0026-1653	Meubles et Decors *changed to* Decors
0026-1688	Mevo
0026-1696	Mexican-American Review
0026-170X	Mexican Life†
0026-1726	Mexico Agricola
0026-1734	Mexico. Archivo General de la Nacion. Boletin
0026-1750	Universidad Nacional Autonoma de Mexico. Revista
0026-1769	Mexico. Direccion General de Estadistica. Revista de Estadistica
0026-1777	Instituto Politecnico Nacional. Escuela National de Ciencias Biologicas. Revista Anales
0026-1785	Mexico Farmaceutico
0026-1793	Mexico Heroico
0026-1807	Mexico Industrial
0026-1815	Mexico Mercantil
0026-184X	Mexico Today
0026-1858	Mexletter
0026-1866	Meyers Modeblatt
0026-1882	Mezhdunarodnyi Sel'skokhozyaistvennyi Zhurnal
0026-1890	Mezogazdasagi Technika
0026-1904	Mezogazdasagi Vilagirodalom
0026-1912	Eurosud - Il Mezzogiorno e le Comunita' Europee
0026-1939	Mi Mladi
0026-1947	Miami Business Review†
0026-1955	Miami Valley Dairyman†
0026-1971	Mias†
0026-198X	Michel-Rundschau
0026-1998	Michigan A F L - C I O News
0026-2005	Michigan Academician
0026-2013	Michigan Association of Secondary School Principals' Bulletin
0026-2021	Michigan Beverage News
0026-203X	Michigan Botanist
0026-2048	Michigan Business Education Association. News Bulletin
0026-2056	Michigan Business Review *changed to* University of Michigan Business Review
0026-2072	Michigan Christian Advocate
0026-2080	Michigan College Personnel Association Journal
0026-2102	Michigan Dental Association. Journal
0026-2110	Michigan Documents
0026-2129	Teacher's Voice
0026-2137	Michigan Engineer
0026-2145	Michigan Entomologist *see* 0090-0222
0026-2161	Michigan Farm News
0026-2188	Michigan Heritage *changed to* Family Trails
0026-2196	Michigan History
0026-220X	Michigan Hospitals

0026-2218 Michigan in Books
0026-2226 Michigan Journal of Secondary Education *changed to* Secondary Education Today
0026-2234 Michigan Law Review
0026-2242 Michigan Librarian
0026-2250 Michigan Magazine Index
0026-2277 Michigan Manufacturer and Financial Record
0026-2285 Michigan Mathematical Journal
0026-2293 Michigan Medicine
0026-2315 Michigan Milk Messenger
0026-2323 Michigan Motor Carrier-Folks *changed to* Michigan Trucking Today
0026-2331 Michigan Municipal Review
0026-234X Michigan Music Educator
0026-2358 Michigan Natural Resources
0026-2366 Michigan Nurse
0026-2374 Michigan Osteopathic Journal
0026-2382 Michigan Out-Of-Doors
0026-2412 Michigan Purchasing Management
0026-2420 Michigan Quarterly Review
0026-2439 Michigan School Board Journal
0026-2447 Michigan State Bar Journal *changed to* Michigan Bar Journal
0026-2455 Michigan State Economic Record
0026-2463 Michigan State University Alumni Magazine
0026-2471 Michigan Technic
0026-248X Michigan Tradesman *see* 0193-0257
0026-2501 Michigan's Health
0026-251X Michigan's Occupational Health
0026-2528 Mic Mac News
0026-2536 Micro-Library Bulletin
0026-2544 Micro News Bulletin *see* 0149-9300
0026-2560 Micro Tips
0026-2579 Microbial Genetics Bulletin
0026-2595 Microbiologia Espanola
0026-2609 Bacteriologia, Virusologia, Parazitologia, Epidemiologia *see* 0301-7338
0026-2617 Microbiology
0026-2633 Microbios
0026-265X Microchemical Journal
0026-2668 Microcosm†
0026-2676 Microcritica
0026-2684 Microdoc
0026-2692 Microelectronics Journal
0026-2706 Microelectronics Abstracts†
0026-2714 Microelectronics and Reliability
0026-2722 Microelectronics Digest†
0026-2730 Microfacts Advertising Reference File†
0026-2749 Micrographics Newsletter
0026-2765 Micrographics News & Views†
0026-2781 Micronesian Reporter
0026-279X Micronesica
0026-2803 Micropaleontology
0026-2811 Journal of Microphotography *changed to* Journal of Micrographics
0026-2838 Microscopy
0026-2846 Microstructures†
0026-2854 Microtecnic
0026-2862 Microvascular Research
0026-2870 University of Utah. Microwave Device and Physical Electronics Laboratory Quarterly Report
0026-2889 Microwave Energy Applications Newsletter
0026-2897 Microwave Journal
0026-2900 Microwave Tube D.A.T.A. Book
0026-2927 Mid-America
0026-2935 Mid-America Insurance
0026-2943 Mid-Atlantic Apothecary *see* 0003-6560
0026-296X Mid-Continent Banker
0026-2986 Mid-Continent Mortician†
0026-3001 Mid East†
0026-3028 Mid-Monmouth Panorama
0026-3036 Mid-Towner†
0026-3044 Mid-West Contractor
0026-3052 Mid-West Truckman
0026-3060 Mid-Western Banker
0026-3079 American Studies
0026-3095 Middle East Business Digest *changed to* Africa Middle East Business Digest
0026-3117 Middle East Express
0026-3133 Middle East Information Series *see* 0097-9791
0026-3141 Middle East Journal
0026-315X Middle East Monitor†
0026-315X Middle East Monitor
0026-3176 Middle East Perspective
0026-3184 Middle East Studies Association Bulletin
0026-3192 Middle East Trade
0026-3206 Middle Eastern Studies
0026-3214 Middle Way
0026-3222 Middlesex Hospital Journal
0026-3230 MidEast Report
0026-3249 Midland
0026-3257 Midland Bank Review
0026-3273 Midland Industrialist
0026-3281 Midland Medical Review
0026-3311 Midlands Industry and Commerce
0026-332X Midstream
0026-3338 Midwest Automotive News
0026-3346 Midwest Chaparral
0026-3354 Midwest Eighty-Eight Manufacturing
0026-3362 Midwest Electrical News†
0026-3370 Midwest Engineer
0026-3397 Midwest Journal of Political Science *see* 0092-5853
0026-3400 Midwest Landscaping *see* 0194-7257
0026-3419 Midwest Modern Language Association Bulletin
0026-3427 Midwest Motor Transport News
0026-3435 Midwest Motorist
0026-3443 Midwest Museums Conference, American Association of Museums. Quarterly
0026-3451 Midwest Quarterly
0026-346X Midwest Review of Public Administration
0026-3478 Midwestern Dentist
0026-3486 Midwestern Druggist†
0026-3494 Midwestern Nigeria Gazette *changed to* Bendel State Gazette
0026-3516 Midwife and Health Visitor *see* 0306-9699
0026-3524 Midwives Chronicle
0026-3532 Mie Medical Journal
0026-3540 Miedzynarodowe Czasopismo Rolnicze
0026-3559 Maize News
0026-3567 Miesiecznik Literacki
0026-3575 Migrant
0026-3583 Migration News
0026-3591 Migrations
0026-3605 Mijn Stokpaardje
0026-3613 Mijnwerker†
0026-3621 Mike Shayne Mystery Magazine
0026-363X Mikhtav Lehaver
0026-3648 Mikologiya i Fitopatologiya
0026-3664 Mikrobiologichnyi Zhurnal
0026-3672 Mikrochimica Acta
0026-3680 Mikrokosmos
0026-3702 Mikroskopie
0026-3710 Mil
0026-3729 Camera di Commercio Industria Artigianato e Agricoltura di Milano. Notiziario Commerciale
0026-3737 Milap Weekly
0026-3745 Milbank Memorial Fund Quarterly *see* 0160-1997
0026-3753 Milch-Praxis *changed to* Die Milchpraxis und Rindermast
0026-3761 Milch-Fettwaren-Eier-Handel
0026-377X Milchsuppe
0026-3788 Milchwissenschaft
0026-380X Milestones
0026-3826 Militaergeschichtliche Mitteilungen
0026-3842 Militaerpsykologiske Meddelelser
0026-3850 Militaert Tidsskrift
0026-3869 Militaire Spectator
0026-3877 Militant
0026-3885 Militant
0026-3893 Militant Truth
0026-3907 Militaer-Kuechenchef
0026-3915 Militaria†
0026-3923 Militaerwesen†
0026-3931 Military Affairs
0026-394X Military Aircraft & Missile Data Sheets
0026-3958 Military Chaplain
0026-3974 Military Digest
0026-3982 Military Engineer
0026-3990 Military Government Journal and Newsletter *see* 0045-7035
0026-4008 Military Historical Society. Bulletin
0026-4016 Military History Journal
0026-4032 Military Journalist *changed to* Military Media Review
0026-4040 Military Law Review
0026-4067 Military Market
0026-4075 Military Medicine
0026-4083 Military Modelling
0026-4105 Military Police Journal†
0026-4121 Military Record of Atomic C B R Happenings
0026-413X Military Research Letter
0026-4148 Military Review
0026-4156 Militia Christi
0026-4164 Miljoespegeln
0026-4172 Milk Industry
0026-4180 Milk Producer
0026-4199 Milk Producer
0026-4210 Milk Vendor
0026-4229 Milking Shorthorn Journal *see* 0145-8264
0026-4253 Mill News Letter
0026-427X Millinery and Boutique
0026-4296 Milling *changed to* Milling Feed and Fertiliser
0026-430X Mills Stream
0026-4318 Milton College Blue and Gold
0026-4326 Milton Quarterly
0026-4342 Milwaukee Commerce
0026-4350 Milwaukee Courier
0026-4377 Milwaukee Reader
0026-4385 Mimos
0026-4407 North and South
0026-4415 Minaret *changed to* Minaret Monthly International
0026-4423 Mind
0026-4431 Mynd
0026-4458 Mind over Matter†
0026-4474 Mindszenty Report
0026-4490 Mine Medical Officers' Association of South Africa. Proceedings
0026-4504 Mine Ventilation Society of South Africa. Journal
0026-4512 Mined-Land Conservation†
0026-4520 Mineracao Metalurgia
0026-4539 Earth and Mineral Sciences
0026-4547 Mineral Industries Newsletter
0026-4555 California Geology
0026-4563 Mineral Research and Exploration Institute of Turkey. Bulletin
0026-4571 Mineral Wealth
0026-458X Minerales
0026-4598 Mineralium Deposita
0026-4601 Mineralogical Abstracts
0026-461X Mineralogical Magazine
0026-4628 Mineralogical Record
0026-4652 Minerals Research Laboratory Bulletin *changed to* Minerals Research Laboratory Newsletter
0026-4660 Minerals Science and Engineering
0026-4679 Mineria
0026-4695 Minerva
0026-4709 Minerva Aerospaziale
0026-4717 Minerva Anestesiologica
0026-4725 Minerva Cardioangiologica
0026-4733 Minerva Chirurgica *changed to* Minerva Chirurgica-Chirurgia
0026-4741 Minerva Dermatologica *changed to* Giornale Italiano di Dermatologia e Venereologia
0026-475X Minerva Dietologica *changed to* Minerva Dietologica e Gastroenterologica
0026-4768 Minerva Fisiconucleare
0026-4776 Minerva Gastroenterologica *changed to* Minerva Dietologica e Gastroenterologica
0026-4784 Minerva Ginecologica
0026-4792 Minerva Idroclimatologica *see* 0391-1624
0026-4806 Minerva Medica
0026-4814 Minerva Medica Giuliana
0026-4822 Minerva Medica Siciliana
0026-4830 Minerva Medicobibliografica
0026-4849 Minerva Medicolegale
0026-4857 Minerva Mediconucleare *changed to* Journal of Nuclear Medicine and Allied Sciences
0026-4865 Minerva Medicopsicologica
0026-4873 Minerva Nefrologica
0026-4881 Minerva Neurochirurgica *changed to* Journal of Neurological Sciences
0026-489X Minerva Nipiologica *changed to* Rivista di Pediatria Preventiva e Sociale-Nipiologia
0026-4903 Minerva Oftalmologica
0026-4911 Minerva Ortopedica
0026-492X Minerva Ospedaliera. la Settimana degli Ospedali. le Medico Ospedaliero
0026-4938 Minerva Otorinolaringologica
0026-4946 Minerva Pediatrica
0026-4954 Minerva Pneumologica
0026-4962 Minerva Radiologica *see* 0033-8362
0026-4970 Minerva Stomatologica
0026-4989 Minerva Urologica
0026-4997 Minervas Kvartalsskrift†
0026-5012 Mines and Factories Journal†
0026-5020 Mines and Minerals†
0026-5039 Mines & Oils; Four Hundred & Fifty Canadian Weekly Stock Charts *see* 0383-2953
0026-5047 Mines et Metallurgie
0026-5055 Mines
0026-5063 Mineur d'Auvergne
0026-5071 Mineurs de France
0026-508X Mingay's Electrical Supplies Guide
0026-5098 Mingay's News *changed to* Mingay's Retailer & Merchandiser
0026-5101 Mingay's Price Service
0026-5128 Miniature Book News
0026-5152 Mining and Minerals Engineering *see* 0369-1632
0026-5160 Mining Congress Journal
0026-5179 Mining Engineer
0026-5187 Mining Engineering
0026-5195 Mining Equipment News
0026-5209 Mining Geology
0026-5217 Mining Industry & Trade Journal *changed to* Mining Industry & Trade Annual
0026-5225 Mining Journal
0026-5233 Mining Magazine
0026-5241 Mining Record
0026-525X Mineral Resources Review
0026-5268 Chamber of Mines of South Africa. Mining Survey
0026-5284 Belgium. Ministere de l'Education Nationale et de la Culture Francaise. Bulletin d'Information *changed to* Belgium. Ministere de l'Education Nationale et de la Culture Francaise. Revue
0026-5292 Cuba. Ministerio del Commercio Exterior. Revista
0026-5306 Ministerium
0026-5314 Ministry
0026-5322 Trinidad and Togabo. Ministry of Petroleum and Mines. Monthly Bulletin *changed to* Trinidad and Tobago. Ministry of Energy and Energy-Based Industries. Monthly Bulletin
0026-5330 Ministry Theological Review†
0026-5357 Minkus Stamp Journal *changed to* Minkus Stamp & Coin Journal
0026-5365 Minneapolis District Dental Journal
0026-5381 Minnesota A. A. A. Motorist
0026-539X Minnesota Academy of Science. Journal
0026-5411 Minnesota Chemist
0026-542X Minnesota Department of Agriculture. Agronomy Services Newsletter†
0026-5438 Minnesota. Department of Education. Public Library Newsletter
0026-5446 Minnesota Education News *changed to* M E Advocate
0026-5454 Minnesota Education Report *changed to* Education Update
0026-5462 Minnesota Engineer†

1020 ISSN INDEX

0026-5489 Minnesota Food Guide
0026-5497 Minnesota History
0026-5500 Minnesota Horticulturist
0026-5519 Minnesota I R C News
0026-5527 Minnesota Journal of Education†
0026-5535 Minnesota Law Review
0026-5543 Minnesota Legal Register
0026-5551 Minnesota Libraries
0026-556X Minnesota Medicine
0026-5578 Minnesota Municipalities *changed to* Minnesota Cities
0026-5586 Minnesota Nursing Accent
0026-5594 Minnesota Optometrist
0026-5616 Minnesota Pharmacist
0026-5624 Minnesota Police Journal
0026-5632 Minnesota Press
0026-5659 Minnesota Reading Quarterly†
0026-5667 Minnesota Review
0026-5675 Minnesota Science
0026-5683 Minnesota Sheriff
0026-5691 Minnesota Technolog
0026-5705 Minnesota Welfare *changed to* People (St. Paul)
0026-5713 Minority Report
0026-5721 Minus One
0026-573X Minute
0026-5748 Minuzzolo *changed to* L. G. Argomenti
0026-5756 Mio Bebe
0026-5764 Mio Lavora†
0026-5772 M I P E L
0026-5780 Mira
0026-5799 Miracle Library
0026-5802 Miraculous Medal
0026-5810 Miroir du Centre
0026-5829 Mirovaya Ekonomika i Mezhdunarodnye Otnosheniya
0026-5837 Mirror
0026-5845 Mirror
0026-5853 Hospital Equipment Service
0026-587X Miscellanea Francescana
0026-5888 Miscellanea Storica della Valdelsa
0026-5896 Miscellany
0026-590X Miscellany
0026-5918 Miss Chatelaine *changed to* Flare
0026-5934 Bakkerswereld
0026-5942 Bouwwereld
0026-5950 Horeca
0026-5977 Missi
0026-5985 Hier en Elders
0026-5993 Missile/Ordnance Letter
0026-6000 Espace†
0026-6019 Missili e Spazio *changed to* Aerotecnica, Missili e Spazio
0026-6027 Mission *see* 0199-4433
0026-6035 Mission de l'Eglise
0026-6043 Missionary Aviation *changed to* Mission Aviation
0026-6051 Missionary News Service
0026-606X Missionary Research Library. Occasional Bulletin *changed to* International Bulletin of Missionary Research
0026-6078 Missionary Review†
0026-6086 Missionhurst
0026-6094 Mondo e Missione
0026-6108 Missioni Domenicane
0026-6116 Missions-Etrangeres
0026-6124 Missions. Messages
0026-6132 Missionsbaneret
0026-6159 Mississippi Banker
0026-6167 Mississippi Business Review
0026-6175 Mississippi E P A News
0026-6205 Mississippi Farm Bureau News
0026-6213 Mississippi Farm Report†
0026-6221 Mississippi Farm.Research *see* 0091-4460
0026-6248 Mississippi Folklore Register
0026-6256 Mississippi Game and Fish
0026-6264 Mississippi Grocers' Guide
0026-6272 Mississippi Language Crusader
0026-6280 Mississippi Law Journal
0026-6299 Mississippi Legion-Aire
0026-6302 Mississippi Library News *changed to* Mississippi Libraries
0026-6310 Mississippi Magic†
0026-6329 Mississippi Methodist Advocate *changed to* Mississippi United Methodist Advocate
0026-6337 Mississippi Municipalities
0026-6353 Mississippi Notes *changed to* Mississippi Music Educator
0026-637X Mississippi Quarterly
0026-6388 Mississippi R N
0026-6396 Mississippi State Medical Association. Journal
0026-640X Mississippi State University. Forest Products Utilization Laboratory. Research Report
0026-6418 Mississippi Valley Journal of Business and Economics *changed to* Review of Business and Economic Research
0026-6426 Mississippi Valley Lumberman *see* 0092-0681
0026-6434 Mississippi Valley Stockman-Farmer *see* 0192-7140
0026-6442 Mississippi's Business
0026-6477 Missouri Architect
0026-6485 Missouri Bar. Journal
0026-6493 Missouri Botanical Garden. Annals
0026-6507 Missouri Botanical Garden Bulletin
0026-6515 Missouri Conservationist
0026-6523 Missouri Dental Association. Journal *see* 0273-3463
0026-6531 Missouri Disaster Planning and Operations Newsletter *see* 0364-0337
0026-6558 Missouri Engineer
0026-6566 Missouri Family Doctor
0026-6574 Missouri Farm Bureau News
0026-6582 Missouri Historical Review
0026-6590 Missouri Historical Society. Bulletin†
0026-6604 Missouri Law Review
0026-6612 Missouri L P-Gas Talks *changed to* M L P G A News
0026-6620 Missouri Medicine
0026-6647 Missouri Municipal Review
0026-6655 Missouri Nurse
0026-6663 Missouri Pharmacist
0026-6671 Missouri Press News
0026-6698 Missouri School Board
0026-6701 Missouri School Music
0026-671X Missouri Speleology
0026-6728 Missouri Teamster
0026-6736 Missouri Valley Adult Education Association. Journal
0026-6744 Missouri Valley Adult Education Association. Newsletter
0026-6760 Mita Journal of Economics
0026-6779 Die Mitarbeit
0026-6787 Mithila Institute of Post Graduate Studies and Research in Sanskrit Learning. Bulletin
0026-6809 M E R I's Monthly Circular. Survey of Economic Conditions in Japan
0026-6817 Mitsubishi Heavy Industries Technical Review
0026-6825 Mitsui Technical Review
0026-6833 Mitteilungen aus Baltischem Leben
0026-6841 Mitteilungen aus der Gebiete der Lebensmetteluntersuchung und Hygiene
0026-6868 Mitteilungen aus der Rheinischen Rinderzucht
0026-6876 Mitteilungen aus Statistik und Verwaltung der Stadt Wien
0026-6884 Mitteilungen der Deutschen Patentanwaelte
0026-6892 Industrie- und Handelskammer Reutlingen. Mitteilungen
0026-6906 Wiener Urania. Mitteilungen
0026-6922 Oberoesterreichisches Volksbildungswerk. Mitteilungen
0026-6930 Mitteilungen fuer den Aussenhandel†
0026-6949 Mitteilungen ueber Textilindustrie *changed to* Mittex: Mitteilungen ueber Textilindustrie
0026-6957 Dokumentation fuer Umweltschutz und Landespflege
0026-6965 Mitteilungsblatt der Genossenschaftlichen Frauenorganisation†
0026-6973 Mitteilungsblatt fuer Dolmetscher und Uebersetzer
0026-6981 Mizan: U S S R-China-Africa-Asia†
0026-699X Mizrachi Weg†
0026-7007 Mizrachi Woman
0026-7023 Mlad Borec
0026-7031 Mladost
0026-704X Mljekarstvo
0026-7058 Mlynsko-Pekarensky Prumysl a Technika Skladovani Obili
0026-7066 Mnemonic
0026-7074 Mnemosyne
0026-7090 Moebelvaerlden *see* 0345-7737
0026-7104 Mobila
0026-7112 Mobile
0026-7120 Mobile and Recreational Housing Merchandiser *see* 0191-9768
0026-7139 Mobile Home *see* 0306-5839
0026-7147 Mobile Home Park Management *changed to* Mobile Home Park Management & Developer
0026-7163 Mobile Home Reporter & Recreation Vehicle News *changed to* Manufactured Housing Reporter
0026-7171 Mobile Homes & Recreational Vehicles in Canada *changed to* Canadian Recreational Vehicle Industry
0026-7198 Mobile Living
0026-7201 Mobile Living in Canada *changed to* Mobile Living in Canada-Manufactured Homes/Canada
0026-7228 Mobilia
0026-7244 Moccasin
0026-7252 Moda dei Bimbi
0026-7279 Mode
0026-7309 Model Car Science†
0026-7317 Model Cars *see* 0036-5432
0026-7325 Model Engineer
0026-7333 Model Maker and Model Boats *changed to* Model Boats
0026-7341 Model Railroader
0026-735X Model Railway Constructor
0026-7368 Model Railways
0026-7384 Modelbouwer
0026-7392 Modele Magazine
0026-7406 Modele Reduit d'Avion
0026-7414 Modele Reduit de Bateau
0026-7422 Modelleisenbahner
0026-7430 Modena *changed to* Modena Economica
0026-7449 Moderat Debatt
0026-7457 Modern Age
0026-7465 Modern & Classical Language Bulletin *see* 0318-5176
0026-7473 Modern Applications News for Design and Manufacturing
0026-7481 Modern Asia
0026-749X Modern Asian Studies
0026-7503 Modern Austrian Literature
0026-7511 Modern Beauty Shop *changed to* Modern Salon
0026-752X Modern Boating
0026-7538 Modern Brewery Age
0026-7546 Modern Bride
0026-7554 Modern Caravan *changed to* Caravanning Monthly
0026-7562 Modern Casting
0026-7570 Modern Ceylon Studies
0026-7597 Modern Churchman
0026-7600 Modern Concepts of Cardiovascular Disease
0026-7619 Modern Concrete
0026-7635 Modern Converter†
0026-7651 Modern Dairy
0026-766X Modern Dance and Dancer†
0026-7678 Modern Data *changed to* Minimicro News
0026-7686 Modern Datateknik†
0026-7694 Modern Drama
0026-7708 Modern English *see* 0306-9346
0026-7716 Modern Farming
0026-7724 Modern Fiction Studies
0026-7732 Modern Fishing
0026-7759 Modern Franchising†
0026-7775 Modern Geology
0026-7791 Modern Government *see* 0360-7941
0026-7805 Modern Grocer
0026-7813 Modern Gymnast *see* 0162-9867
0026-7821 Modern Haiku
0026-783X Modern Hospital *see* 0160-7480
0026-7848 Modern Images
0026-7856 Modern International Drama
0026-7864 Modern Jeweler *see* 0193-208X
0026-7872 Modern Kantoor†
0026-7899 Modern Knitting Management
0026-7902 Modern Language Journal
0026-7910 M L N
0026-7929 Modern Language Quarterly
0026-7937 Modern Language Review
0026-7945 Modern Languages
0026-7953 Modern Law and Society
0026-7961 Modern Law Review
0026-7988 Modern Living
0026-8003 Modern Machine Shop
0026-8011 Modern Man†
0026-802X Modern Manufacturing *changed to* Factory
0026-802X Modern Manufacturing *changed to* Factory Management
0026-8038 Modern Materials Handling
0026-8046 Modern Maturity
0026-8054 Modern Media
0026-8089 Modern Medicine of Australia *see* 0312-875X
0026-8097 Modern Medicine of Canada
0026-8119 Modern Medicine of New Zealand
0026-8127 Modern Metals
0026-8135 Modern Milk Hauler
0026-8143 Modern Motor
0026-816X Modern Needlecraft
0026-8178 Modern Nursing Home *see* 0160-7480
0026-8194 Drug News
0026-8208 Modern Office Procedures
0026-8216 Modern Ondernemerschap *changed to* Ondernemers-Visie
0026-8224 Modern Packaging†
0026-8232 Modern Philology
0026-8240 Modern Photography
0026-8259 Modern Plant Operation and Maintenance†
0026-8267 Modern Plastering
0026-8275 Modern Plastics
0026-8283 Modern Plastics International
0026-8291 Modern Poetry in Translation
0026-8305 Modern Poetry Studies
0026-8313 Modern Power & Engineering
0026-833X Modern Purchasing
0026-8348 Modern Railroads *changed to* Modern Railroads/Rail Transit
0026-8356 Modern Railways
0026-8364 Refrigeration and Air Conditioning
0026-8380 Modern Review
0026-8399 Modern Romances
0026-8402 Modern Schoolman
0026-8410 Modern Schools†
0026-8429 Modern Screen†
0026-8437 Modern Society†
0026-8445 Modern Steel Construction
0026-8453 Modern Stores and Offices†
0026-8461 Modern Sunbathing Quarterly†
0026-847X Modern Design/Modern Textil†
0026-8488 Modern Textiles Magazine
0026-8496 Modern Tire Dealer
0026-850X Modern Tramway and Light Railway Review *see* 0144-1655
0026-8526 Modern Treatment†
0026-8534 Modern Utopian *changed to* Communities; a Journal of Cooperative Living
0026-8542 Modern Veterinary Practice
0026-8550 Modern Vocational Trends†
0026-8577 Moderna Spraak
0026-8585 Moderna Transporter†
0026-8593 Moderne Frau *see* 0031-630X
0026-8607 Das Moderne Heim
0026-8615 Holz- und Kunststoffverarbeitung
0026-8623 Moderne Jordflytning *changed to* Anlaegsteknik
0026-864X Die Moderne Kueche
0026-8666 Moderne Sprachen
0026-8674 Moderne Welt†

ISSN INDEX 1021

ISSN	Title
0026-8682	Moderner Markt
0026-8704	Modernes Hotel
0026-8712	Modernes Wohnen
0026-8720	Moderni Rizeni
0026-8739	Modes & Travaux
0026-8747	Modes de Paris
0026-8755	Modetelegramm
0026-8771	Modische Linie (Ausgabe B)
0026-878X	Modische Maschen
0026-8828	Modus Operandi
0026-8836	Moebel und Raum†
0026-8844	Moebel und Wohnraum
0026-8852	Moellen
0026-8860	Mofussil
0026-8887	Moissons de l'Esprit†
0026-8895	Moj Pas
0026-8917	Wood Industry
0026-8925	Molecular and General Genetics
0026-8933	Molecular Biology
0026-8941	Molecular Crystals and Liquid Crystals *see* 0140-6566
0026-895X	Molecular Pharmacology
0026-8968	Molecular Photochemistry
0026-8976	Molecular Physics
0026-8984	Molekulyarnaya Biologiya
0026-8992	Molennieuws
0026-900X	Molineria y Panaderia
0026-9018	Molini d'Italia
0026-9026	Molochnaya Promyshlennost'
0026-9034	Molochnoe i Myasnoe Skotovodstvo
0026-9042	Moloda Ukrayina
0026-9050	Molodaya Gvardiya
0026-9077	Molodoi Kommunist
0026-9093	Molula-Qhooa
0026-9107	Molybdaen-Dienst†
0026-9115	Molykote†
0026-9131	Momento
0026-914X	National Catholic Educational Association. Momentum
0026-9166	Mon Jardin et Ma Maison
0026-9174	Mon Journal Confidences *changed to* Confidences
0026-9190	Monastic Studies†
0026-9204	Monat†
0026-9212	Interkantonale Kontrollstelle fuer Heilmittel. Monatsbericht
0026-9220	Oesterreichische Landwirtschaft. Monatsberichte
0026-9239	Monatsblaetter fuer Freiheitliche Wirtschaftspolitik
0026-9247	Monatshefte fuer Chemie
0026-9255	Monatshefte fuer Mathematik
0026-9263	Monatshefte fuer Veterinaermedizin
0026-9271	Monatshefte fuer Deutschen Unterricht
0026-928X	Monatskurse fuer Die Aerztliche Fortbildung
0026-9298	Monatsschrift fuer Kinderheilkunde
0026-9301	Monatsschrift fuer Kriminologie und Strafrechtsreform
0026-931X	Monatsschrift fuer Lungenkrankheiten und Tuberkulosebekaempfung†
0026-9328	Monatsschrift fuer Ohrenheilkunde und Laryngo-Rhinologie†
0026-9328	Monatsschrift fuer Ohrenheilkunde und Laryngo-Rhinologie *changed to* Laryngologie, Rhinologie, Otologie Vereinigt mit Monatsschrift fuer Ohrenheilkunde
0026-9336	Monatsschrift fuer Unfallheilkunde, Versicherungs- , Versorgungs- und Verkehrsmedizin *see* 0341-5694
0026-9344	Formerly (Until Vol. 7, 1977); Mondo Lingvo Problemo *see* 0165-2672
0026-9352	Monday Morning†
0026-9360	Monde
0026-9379	Monde de l'Electricite
0026-9387	Monde des Philatelistes
0026-9395	Monde Diplomatique
0026-9417	Monde Gitan
0026-9425	Monde Juif
0026-9433	Monde Libertaire
0026-9441	Travaux Souterrains†
0026-9468	Mondo†
0026-9484	Mondo Agricolo
0026-9492	Mondo Aperto
0026-9506	Mondo Bancario
0026-9522	Mondo Economico
0026-9530	Mondo Finanziario†
0026-9557	Mondo Occidentale *changed to* Americana
0026-9565	Mondo Odontostomatologico
0026-959X	Moneda y Credito
0026-9611	Moneta e Credito
0026-9638	Jamaica. Department of Statistics. Monetary Statistics Report
0026-9646	Moneysworth
0026-9654	Mongolia Society Bulletin *changed to* Mongolian Studies
0026-9662	Monist
0026-9670	Moniteur Africain du Commerce et de l'Industrie *changed to* Moniteur Africain
0026-9689	Moniteur des Pharmacies et des Laboratoires
0026-9697	Moniteur des Travaux Agricoles et des Battages *see* 0027-2272
0026-9700	Moniteur des Travaux Publics et du Batiment
0026-9719	M.O.C.I.
0026-9727	Moniteur du Regne de la Justice
0026-9735	Moniteur Professionel de l'Electricite
0026-9743	Monitor
0026-9751	Monitor *see* 0198-7208
0026-976X	Monitor Ecclesiasticus
0026-9778	Monitore Ostetrico-Ginecologico di Endocrinologia e del Metabolismo
0026-9786	Monitore Zoologico Italiano
0026-9794	Monkey
0026-9808	Monmouth Educator
0026-9816	Monmouthshire Farmer
0026-9832	Monographien zur Geschichte des Mittelalters
0026-9840	Monroe News Leader
0026-9859	Monsanto Magazine†
0026-9875	Montan-Berichte *see* 0005-8912
0026-9883	Montan-Rundschau *see* 0005-8912
0026-9891	Montana
0026-9905	Montana Agriculture
0026-9913	Montana Beverage News
0026-9921	Montana Business Quarterly
0026-993X	Montana Education *changed to* M.E.A. Today
0026-9964	Montana Law Forum
0026-9972	Montana Law Review
0026-9980	Montana League of Cities & Towns. Newsletter
0026-9999	Montana Legionnaire
0027-0008	Montana Masonic News
0027-0016	Montana Outdoors†
0027-0024	Montana Wool Grower
0027-0032	Montaneros de Aragon
0027-0040	Montazhnye i Spetsial'nye Raboty v Stroitel'stve
0027-0059	Montclair, N.J. Art Museum. Bulletin
0027-0067	Montclair Public Schools†
0027-0075	Montclair Schools
0027-0105	Montes
0027-0113	Museo Nacional de Historia Natural. Communicaciones Zoologicas
0027-0121	Museo Nacional de Historia Natural. Communicaciones Botanicas
0027-013X	Universidad de la Republica. Facultad de Ingenieria y Agrimensura. Boletin
0027-0148	Montfort
0027-0156	Montgomery-Bucks Dental Society. Bulletin
0027-0172	Month
0027-0180	New Zealand. Department of Statistics. Monthly Abstract of Statistics
0027-0199	Monthly Bank Clearings
0027-0202	Monthly Bibliography of Medical Reviews†
0027-0210	Monthly Bulletin of African Materials†
0027-0229	Monthly Bulletin of Agricultural Economics and Statistics (FAO) *changed to* Monthly Bulletin of Statistics (FAO)
0027-0237	Egypt. Central Agency for Public Mobilisation and Statistics. Monthly Bulletin of Foreign Trade
0027-0245	Iraq. Central Statistical Organization. Monthly Bulletin of Foreign Trade Statistics *changed to* Iraq. Central Statistical Organization. Quarterly Bulletin of Foreign Trade Statistics
0027-0253	Monthly Bulletin of Ionospheric Characteristics Recorded at Johannesburg and Capetown *changed to* Monthly Bulletin of Ionospheric Characteristics Recorded at Johannesburg and Hermanus
0027-0261	Indian Bureau of Mines. Bulletin of Mineral Statistics and Information
0027-027X	Monthly Business Failures
0027-0288	U. S. Library of Congress. Monthly Checklist of State Publications
0027-0296	Monthly Climatic Data for the World
0027-030X	Monthly Commentary on Indian Economic Conditions
0027-0334	Pakistan Central Cotton Committee. Monthly Cotton Review
0027-0342	Ontario. Ministry of Agriculture and Food. Monthly Crop and Live Stock Report
0027-0377	Zambia. Central Statistical Office. Monthly Digest of Statistics
0027-0385	Monthly Digest of Tax Articles
0027-0407	Monthly Film Bulletin
0027-0415	Monthly Frequency Tables of Visibility, Cloud & Wind
0027-0431	M I M S
0027-044X	U. S. Bureau of Labor Statistics. Monthly Labor Review
0027-0458	Monthly Listings of Neuro-Psychiatric Literature†
0027-0482	Monthly Radiation Summary
0027-0490	Monthly Radiation Values for Bergen, Norway
0027-0504	Monthly Railway Statistics
0027-0512	International Canada
0027-0520	Monthly Review
0027-0539	Australia. Bureau of Statistics. Monthly Review of Business Statistics *changed to* Australia. Bureau of Statistics. Monthly Summary of Statistics
0027-0547	Monthly Statistics of Foreign Trade of India
0027-0555	Monthly Statistics of Japan
0027-0563	Monthly Statistics of Korea
0027-0571	Monthly Summary of Australian Conditions *see* 0314-755X
0027-058X	Monthly Summary of Business Conditions in Southern California
0027-0598	Monthly Summary of Jute and Gunny Statistics
0027-0601	Pakistan Jute Association. Monthly Summary of Jute Goods Statistics *changed to* Quarterly Summary of Jute Goods Statistics
0027-061X	Monthly Technical Review
0027-0628	Monthly Trade Bulletin *changed to* Jamaica. Department of Statistics. External Trade Summary Tables
0027-0636	Great Britain. Meteorological Office. Monthly Weather Report
0027-0644	Monthly Weather Review
0027-0660	Monti e Boschi *see* 0390-6736
0027-0695	Ecole Publique *changed to* Trans-Parent
0027-0709	Montreal General Hospital News
0027-0725	Montreal. Museum of Fine Arts. Quarterly Review†
0027-0733	Monument in Cantos and Essays
0027-0741	Monumenta Nipponica
0027-075X	Monumental News-Review *see* 0160-7243
0027-0768	Monuments Historiques de la France
0027-0776	Monumentum
0027-0806	Moody Monthly
0027-0814	Moody's Bank & Finance Manual
0027-0830	Moody's Handbook of Common Stocks
0027-0849	Moody's Industrials
0027-0857	Moody's Municipals and Governments
0027-0865	Moody's O T C Industrials
0027-0873	Moody's Public Utilities
0027-0881	Moody's Stock Survey†
0027-089X	Moody's Transportation
0027-0903	Moon *see* 0165-0807
0027-0911	Moon Magazine
0027-092X	Moonshine Can
0027-0954	Moose
0027-0962	Moottoriviesti *see* 0041-4468
0027-0970	Moottori *see* 0356-4827
0027-0989	Mopac News
0027-1004	Morality in Media Newsletter
0027-1012	North American Moravian
0027-1020	Moravian Music Foundation. News Bulletin *see* 0147-7013
0027-1047	Morehouse College Bulletin
0027-1055	Moreland News and Views
0027-1071	Morgagni
0027-1098	Morgan Horse
0027-1101	Morgonbris
0027-111X	Mormon Americana
0027-1136	Mornaricki Glasnik
0027-1144	Morning Rays†
0027-1160	Morocco Tourism
0027-1179	Morokami
0027-1187	Morris Arboretum Bulletin†
0027-1195	Morsingboen
0027-1209	Morsko Ribarstvo
0027-1217	Morskoi Flot
0027-1241	Mortgage Banker *changed to* Mortgage Banking
0027-125X	Morton Arboretum Quarterly
0027-1268	Mortuary Management
0027-1276	Mosaic
0027-1284	Mosaic
0027-1306	Moscow News
0027-1314	Moscow University Chemistry Bulletin
0027-1322	Moscow University Mathematics Bulletin
0027-1330	Moscow University Mechanics Bulletin
0027-1349	Moscow University Physics Bulletin
0027-1357	Moskovskii Universitet. Vestnik. Seriya 12: Pravo
0027-1365	Moskovskii Universitet. Vestnik. Seriya Ekonomika, Filosofiya *changed to* Moskovskii Universitet. Vestnik. Seriya 7: Ekonomika
0027-1365	Moskovskii Universitet. Vestnik. Seriya Ekonomika, Filosofiya *changed to* Moskovskii Universitet. Vestnik. Seriya 8: Filosofiya
0027-1381	Moskovskii Universitet. Vestnik. Seriya 5: Geografiya
0027-139X	Moskovskii Universitet. Vestnik. Seriya Istoricheskie Nauki *changed to* Moskovskii Universitet. Vestnik. Seriya 9: Istoriya
0027-1403	Moskovskoe Obshchestvo Ispytatelei Prirody. Biologicheskii Otdel. Byulleten'
0027-1411	Moskva
0027-142X	Mosquito News
0027-1438	Most
0027-1446	Mosul University. College of Medicine. Annals
0027-1454	Mosupa - Tsela
0027-1470	Mot-Bau
0027-1500	Mother
0027-1535	Mother Earth News
0027-1543	Mother India
0027-1551	Mothers' Manual
0027-156X	Mothers-to Be/American Baby *see* 0044-7544
0027-1594	Motion Picture Daily†
0027-1616	Motion Picture Herald *see* 0146-5023
0027-1624	Motion Picture Magazine
0027-1632	Motion Pictures Technical Bulletin
0027-1667	Motive†
0027-1675	Moto†
0027-1683	Moto Revija
0027-1691	Motociclismo
0027-1713	Motor
0027-173X	Motor
0027-1721	Motor
0027-1748	Motor
0027-1772	Motor Age

ISSN	Title
0027-1780	Motor Boat and Yachting
0027-1799	Motor Boating & Sailing
0027-1802	Motor Business
0027-1829	Motor Caravan & Camping *changed to* Motorcaravan & Motorhome Monthly
0027-1837	Motor Cycle
0027-1845	Motor Cycle and Cycle Trader
0027-1853	Motor Cycle News
0027-187X	Motor Cyclist Illustrated
0027-1888	Motor-Dienst und Erdoel-Nachrichten *changed to* Motor und Erdoel
0027-190X	Motor in Canada
0027-1926	Motor Italia
0027-1934	Motor News *changed to* Michigan Living-A A A Motor News
0027-1950	Motor Reise Revue
0027-1977	Motor Service
0027-1985	Motor Service
0027-2000	Motor Ship
0027-2019	Motor Sport
0027-2027	Motor Trade Executive
0027-2035	Motor Trade Journal
0027-2043	Motor Trader
0027-2051	Motor Trader and Fleet Operator
0027-206X	Motor Transport
0027-2078	Motor Transportation Hi-Lights
0027-2086	Motor Travel
0027-2094	Motor Trend
0027-2108	Motor Truck
0027-2116	Motor Truck News *changed to* Iowa Trucking Lifeliner
0027-2124	Motor West
0027-2140	Motorbranschen
0027-2159	Motorbranschens Registeringsstatistik *see* 0027-2140
0027-2167	Enthusiast
0027-2175	Revs Motorcycle News (Revs)
0027-2205	Motorcyclist
0027-2213	Motorfoereren
0027-2221	Motorhome Life *see* 0164-503X
0027-223X	Motorindia
0027-2248	Motoring
0027-2256	Motoring Life
0027-2264	Motoring News
0027-2272	Motorisation Agricole
0027-2299	Motorist
0027-2302	Motorists Guide to New & Used Car Prices
0027-2310	Motorland
0027-2337	Motorliv
0027-2345	Motorman
0027-2361	Motorpraxis†
0027-237X	Das Motorrad
0027-2396	Motrix
0027-2485	Mount Allison Record
0027-2493	Mount Holyoke Alumnae Quarterly
0027-25C7	Mount Sinai Journal of Medicine
0027-2515	Mount to the Stars
0027-2523	Mount Washington Observatory News Bulletin
0027-2531	Thoroughbred Mid-America
0027-254X	Mountain Geologist
0027-2558	Mountain Life and Work
0027-2566	Mountain†
0027-2574	Mountain Path
0027-2582	Mountain-Plains Library Quarterly *see* 0145-6180
0027-2590	Mountain States Banker
0027-2612	Mountain Visitor
0027-2620	Mountaineer
0027-2639	Mousaion
0027-2647	Tele-Moustique
0027-2663	Mouvement
0027-2671	Mouvement Social
0027-2701	Movie Maker
0027-271X	Movie Mirror
0027-2736	Movie News
0027-2779	Movie World†
0027-2787	Movieland and TV Time *changed to* Teen Bag
0027-2809	Movimento di Liberazione in Italia *changed to* Italia Contemporanea
0027-2817	Movimento Operaio e Socialista
0027-2833	Movoznavstvo
0027-2841	Moyen Age
0027-2858	Mozaiek Katholiek Verbond voor Kinderbescherming. Maandblad†
0027-2892	Moznayim
0027-2906	M.S. for Medical Secretaries†
0027-2914	Muanyag es Gumi
0027-2930	El Mueble
0027-2949	Die Muehle und Mischfuttertechnik
0027-2957	Muell und Abfall
0027-2965	Mueller Clipper
0027-2973	Muenchener Medizinische Wochenschrift
0027-2981	Muenchner Woche
0027-299X	Das Muenster
0027-3007	Muenzen und Medaillen
0027-3015	Muszaki Egyetemi Konyvtaros
0027-3023	Muszaki Lapszemle. Anyagmozgatas, Csomagolas
0027-3031	Muhammad Speaks *see* 0161-8644
0027-304X	Muhendis ve Makina
0027-3090	Mukomol'no-elevatornaya i Kombikormovaya Promyshlennost'
0027-3104	Mukta
0027-3120	Mulino
0027-3139	Mullard Technical Communications *changed to* Electronic Components and Applications
0027-3147	Multi†
0027-3155	Multihull International
0027-3163	Multihull Sailing
0027-3171	Multivariate Behavioral Research
0027-318X	Munca Sanitara *changed to* Viata Medicala-Cadre Medii
0027-3198	Zahnaerztlicher Anzeiger
0027-321X	Office International de Bibliographie. Communications Mundaneum
0027-3228	Mundartfreunde Oesterreichs. Mitteilungen
0027-3244	Mundo Cristao†
0027-3252	Mundo Cristiano
0027-3287	Mundo Economico
0027-3295	Mundo Electrico
0027-3309	Mundo Hispanico†
0027-3317	Mundo Hospitalario†
0027-3325	Mundo Maderero
0027-335X	Mundo Social†
0027-3384	Mundus
0027-3392	Mundus
0027-3600	Mundus Artium
0027-3414	Munibe
0027-3422	Municipal Administration & Engineering
0027-3430	Municipal and Public Services Journal
0027-3449	Municipal Attorney
0027-3457	Municipal Engineering
0027-3465	Municipal Engineers Journal
0027-349X	Municipal Journal *see* 0027-3430
0027-3503	Municipal Law Court Decisions
0027-352X	Municipal League of Seattle and King County. Municipal News
0027-3538	Municipal Ordinance Review
0027-3546	Municipal Recreation Pools, Rink & Parks *changed to* Pool Industry Canada
0027-3554	New York Municipal Reference & Research Center Notes†
0027-3562	Municipal Review
0027-3570	Municipal South†
0027-3589	Municipal World
0027-3597	Municipality
0027-3600	Munka
0027-3619	Munkavedelem
0027-3627	Munson-Williams-Proctor Institute. Bulletin
0027-3635	Muotisorja *see* 0355-192X
0027-3643	Muoviviesti *see* 0355-7839
0027-3651	Murermesteren
0027-366X	Murimi†
0027-3678	Murmesteren
0027-3686	Murray Hill News
0027-3716	Murrelet
0027-3724	Musart†
0027-3724	Musart *see* 0363-6569
0027-3740	Muscular Dystrophy Journal
0027-3759	Muscular Dystrophy News *changed to* M D A News
0027-3767	Musee Carnavalet. Bulletin
0027-3775	Musee du Soir†
0027-3783	Musee Ingres. Bulletin
0027-3791	Musee National de Varsovie. Bulletin
0027-3805	Musee Neuchatelois
0027-3813	Museen in Koeln. Bulletin
0027-3821	Musees de Geneve
0027-383X	Musees et Collections Publiques de France
0027-3848	Musees et Monuments Lyonnais. Bulletin
0027-3856	Musees Royaux des Beaux-Arts de Belgique. Bulletin
0027-3872	Musei e Gallerie d'Italia
0027-3880	Museo Argentino de Ciencias Naturales "Bernardino Rivadavia" e Instituto Nacional de Investigaciones de la Ciencias Naturales. Revista y Communicaciones
0027-3899	Museo de Ciencias Naturales. Boletin
0027-3902	Museo de Historia Natural de San Rafael. Revista Cientifica de Investigaciones *changed to* Museo de Historia Natural de San Rafael. Revista
0027-3910	Museo Nacional de Historia Natural. Boletin
0027-3945	Museo Nacional de Historia Natural. Noticiario Mensual
0027-3953	Museo Nazionale del Cinema. Notiziario
0027-3961	Museo Trentino del Risorgimento e della Lotta per la Liberta. Bollettino
0027-397X	Museologist
0027-3988	Museu Bocage. Arquivos
0027-3996	Museum
0027-4003	Museum
0027-4011	Museum *see* 0098-3373
0027-402X	Museum Alliance Quarterly *changed to* Terra
0027-4038	Museum Boymans-van Beuningen. Bulletin†
0027-4038	Museum Boymans-van Beuningen. Bulletin†
0027-4046	Museum Graphic†
0027-4054	Museum Helveticum
0027-4062	New Brunswick Museum. Museum Memo†
0027-4062	New Brunswick Museum. Memo *see* 0703-0606
0027-4070	Museum National d'Histoire Naturelle, Paris. Bulletin
0027-4089	Museum News
0027-4097	Museum Notes
0027-4100	Harvard University. Museum of Comparative Zoology. Bulletin
0027-4127	Museum of Modern Art. Members Newsletter†
0027-4135	Museum of the Fur Trade Quarterly
0027-4143	Museumjournaal
0027-4151	Museums Association Monthly Bulletin *see* 0307-2525
0027-416X	Museums Journal
0027-4178	Museumskunde†
0027-4186	Museumsnytt
0027-4194	Courrier Roumain
0027-4208	Music *see* 0164-3150
0027-4216	Music & Artists†
0027-4224	Music and Letters
0027-4240	Music Article Guide
0027-4259	Music at Georgia†
0027-4275	Music Box
0027-4283	Music Cataloging Bulletin
0027-4291	Music City News
0027-4305	Music Clubs Magazine
0027-4313	Music Director *see* 0046-4155
0027-4321	Music Educators Journal
0027-433X	Music in Education†
0027-4348	Music Index
0027-4364	Music Journal
0027-4372	Music Leader
0027-4380	Notes (Ann Arbor)
0027-4399	Music Maker
0027-4402	Music Ministry†
0027-4410	Music News from Prague
0027-4437	Music Now
0027-4445	Music Review
0027-4461	Music Teacher
0027-447X	Music Tempo
0027-4488	Music Trades
0027-4496	Music World†
0027-450X	Musica
0027-4518	Musica
0027-4526	Musica e Dischi
0027-4534	Musica Iberoamericana
0027-4542	Musica Jazz
0027-4569	Musicae Sacrae Ministerium
0027-4577	Musical Box Society. Bulletin *changed to* Musical Box Society International. Bulletin
0027-4585	Musical Denmark
0027-4615	Musical Merchandise Review
0027-4623	Musical Opinion
0027-4631	Musical Quarterly
0027-464X	Musical Salvationist
0027-4658	Musical Show
0027-4666	Musical Times
0027-4674	Musicalbrande
0027-4682	Musicasia†
0027-4690	Impulse
0027-4704	Musik in der Schule
0027-4712	Musik-Informationen
0027-4720	Musik och Ljudteknik
0027-4747	Musik und Bildung
0027-4755	Musik und Gesellschaft
0027-4763	Musik und Gottesdienst
0027-4771	Musik und Kirche
0027-478X	Musikern
0027-4798	Musikerziehung
0027-4801	Die Musikforschung
0027-481X	Musikhandel
0027-4828	Das Musikinstrument
0027-4836	Musiklivet-Vaar Saang
0027-4844	Musikrevy
0027-4879	Muslim Africa
0027-4887	Muslim Digest
0027-4895	Muslim Review
0027-4909	Muslim World
0027-4917	Mustang Review†
0027-4925	Muster
0027-4933	Muszaki-Gazdasagi Tajekoztato
0027-4941	Muszaki Lapszemle. Uzemszervezes, Iparagazdasag
0027-495X	Muszaki Lapszemle. Banyaszat
0027-4968	Muszaki Lapszemle. Elektrotechnika, Hiradastechnika *changed to* Muszaki Lapszemle. Elektrotechnika
0027-4976	Muszaki Lapszemle. Elelmiszeripar
0027-4984	Muszaki Lapszemle. Energia
0027-4992	Muszaki Lapszemle. Faipar, Papir-es Nyomdaipar
0027-500X	Muszaki Lapszemle. Fizika, Meres- es Muszertechnika, Automatika
0027-5018	Muszaki Lapszemle. Gepeszet
0027-5026	Muszaki Lapszemle. Kemia Vegyipar
0027-5034	Muszaki Lapszemle. Kohaszat, Onteszet
0027-5042	Muszaki Lapszemle. Kozlekedes
0027-5050	Muszaki Lapszemle. Melyepites, Vizepites
0027-5069	Muszaki Lapszemle. Textilipar, Bor- es Borfeldolgozoipar
0027-5085	Muszaki Tudomany
0027-5093	Mut
0027-5107	Mutation Research
0027-5115	Mutech Chemical Engineering Journal†
0027-5123	Mutisia
0027-514X	Muttersprache
0027-5158	Mutual Benefit Estate and Tax Letter
0027-5182	Mutual Funds Guide
0027-5190	Mutual Beneficial Association of Rail Transportation Employees. Mutual Magazine
0027-5212	Mutualiste de Touraine
0027-5239	Mutualite
0027-5247	Muveszettorteneti Ertesito
0027-5255	Muzejni a Vlastivedna Prace
0027-5263	Muzeum
0027-5271	Muzicka Omladina
0027-528X	Muziek Expres
0027-5298	Muziek Mercuur
0027-5301	Muziekhandel
0027-531X	Muzika
0027-5336	Muzsika
0027-5344	Muzyka

ISSN INDEX

ISSN	Title
0027-5352	Muzykal'naya Zhizn'
0027-5360	Muzzle Blasts
0027-5379	My Baby†
0027-5387	My Devotions
0027-5409	My Home and Family
0027-5417	My i Svit
0027-5425	My Career
0027-5433	My Magazine of India
0027-545X	My Story
0027-5468	My Volk
0027-5484	My Weekly Reader (Summer Editions) *changed to* Bubblegum Gazette
0027-5484	My Weekly Reader (Summer Editions) *see* Jellybean Jamboree
0027-5484	My Weekly Reader (Summer Editions) *changed to* Peppermint Press
0027-5492	Myasnaya Industriya S.S.S.R.
0027-5506	Myastenia Gravis Foundation. Newsletter
0027-5514	Mycologia
0027-5522	Mycological Papers
0027-5530	Mycopathologia et Mycologia - Applicata *see* 0301-486X
0027-5549	Mycophile
0027-5557	Mykosen
0027-5565	Mylpaal
0027-5573	Mysindia†
0027-5581	Mysl Polska
0027-559X	Mysore Commerce
0027-5603	Mysore Economic Review
0027-5611	Mysore Industrial Diary†
0027-562X	Mysore Labour Journal *changed to* Karnataka Labour Journal
0027-5638	Mysterium
0027-5662	N A A F I News
0027-5670	A. D. A. S. Quarterly Review
0027-5689	N. A. B. A. Review
0027-5697	N A B E T News
0027-5700	N A B P Quarterly *changed to* N A B P Newsletter
0027-5719	N A C†
0027-5727	N A C C Attack *see* 0571-8597
0027-5735	N A C D L Journal *see* 0360-5361
0027-5743	N A C O News and Views *changed to* County News
0027-576X	N A C W P I Journal
0027-5778	Cars and Trucks *changed to* Automotive Executive
0027-5786	N.A.D.A. Auto Auction True Values Guide *changed to* N.A.D.A. Dealers Wholesale Auto Auction Report
0027-5824	N A F S A Newsletter
0027-5832	N A H B Journal *changed to* NA H B Builder
0027-5840	N A H B Washington Scope *changed to* NA H B Builder
0027-5859	N A I I News Memo
0027-5867	N A I I Press Samplings
0027-5883	N A I S Report†
0027-5891	Two Wheeler Dealer
0027-5905	N A L L D Journal
0027-5913	N A M M Music Retailer News
0027-5921	N A M Reports *see* 0191-5215
0027-593X	N A N T I S News
0027-5948	N A O T Notes *changed to* Organ Teacher
0027-5956	Air Pollution Abstracts†
0027-5964	N A P I A Bulletin
0027-5980	N A R G U S Bulletin†
0027-5999	N A S C A R Newsletter
0027-6006	N. A. S. C. Quarterly
0027-6014	N A S P A Journal
0027-6022	N A S W News
0027-6030	N A T E S A Scope
0027-6049	N A T News
0027-6057	N A T O Letter *changed to* N A T O Review
0027-609X	N A V A News
0027-6103	N A W G A Management and Controller's Bulletin
0027-6111	N & M†
0027-612X	N B C News *see* 0380-8599
0027-6138	N B O Abstracts
0027-6146	N.B.O.B. Orgaan *changed to* Unie van Beveiligings- en Bewakingspersoneel. Orgaan
0027-6154	N. B. O. Building Information Bulletin†
0027-6162	N B R I Information Sheet
0027-6170	N C A A News
0027-6189	N C A E News Bulletin
0027-6197	N C A R B Bulletin
0027-6219	N C A Today
0027-6227	N C A W E News
0027-6235	N C C D News†
0027-6243	N C C-Interface
0027-6251	N C C P A Newsletter
0027-6278	N. C. D. C. Bulletin
0027-6308	N C E Today *changed to* Nexus
0027-6316	N C I Newsletter†
0027-6332	N C M A Newsletter *changed to* Contract Management
0027-6340	N C S A W Report *changed to* Society for Animal Rights Report
0027-6359	N C Scene
0027-6367	N. C. W. News
0027-6383	Prosecutor
0027-6405	N E A Reporter
0027-6413	N E A Research Bulletin†
0027-6421	N E C News
0027-643X	N E D A Journal/Electronic Merchandising
0027-6464	N E R B A *changed to* C I M Construction Journal
0027-6499	N F A Reports†
0027-6502	N F I Bulletin *changed to* Hardware Today
0027-6510	N F Legal Legislative Reporter News Bulletin *see* 0458-9599
0027-6529	N. G. Z.
0027-6537	N. H. Conservation Commission News
0027-6545	N H D S Newsletter
0027-6553	N H K Technical Journal
0027-6561	N H K Technical Report
0027-657X	N H K Laboratories Note
0027-6588	N H S A A
0027-6596	N H S C News
0027-660X	N. H. School Boards Association Newsletter
0027-6618	N I A *changed to* Tijdschrift voor Marketing
0027-6634	N I E Journal *changed to* Journal of Indian Education
0027-6642	N I F Weekly
0027-6669	N I M Abstracts†
0027-6685	N I N
0027-6731	N I T Newsletter *see* 0193-578X
0027-6766	N K B
0027-6774	N K B Research Monthly *see* 0385-2350
0027-6782	N L G I Spokesman
0027-6790	N L L Review *see* 0140-2773
0027-6804	N L N News†
0027-6839	N M L Technical Journal
0027-6855	N M U Pilot
0027-6863	N O D A Bulletin
0027-6871	N O M D A Spokesman
0027-6898	N P L Technical Bulletin
0027-6901	N P N Bulletin
0027-691X	N R A Newsletter
0027-6928	N R C D Bulletin *see* 0306-2880
0027-6944	N H F A Reports *see* 0149-2276
0027-6952	N R I Journal†
0027-6979	N R T A Journal
0027-6987	N R T A News Bulletin
0027-7002	National Society for Programmed Instruction. Journal *changed to* Performance & Instruction
0027-7010	N S S News
0027-7029	New South Wales Contract Reporter
0027-7037	N T A Journal
0027-7045	N T D R A Dealer News
0027-7053	N T L Institute News and Reports†
0027-707X	N T Z Nachrichtentechnische Zeitschrift
0027-7088	N U B E News *changed to* B I F U Report
0027-7096	N U E A Spectator *see* 0162-4024
0027-710X	Centrale Suiker Maatschappij. Voorlichtingsblad *changed to* C S M Informatie
0027-7126	Nya Argus
0027-7134	N. Y. L. A. Bulletin
0027-7142	N Y L I C Review
0027-7150	N Y P M A Bulletin
0027-7169	N Y S S A Bulletin *see* 0095-2273
0027-7177	N. Z. Baptist
0027-7185	N. Z. Electrical Industry
0027-7193	N. Z. H. Maandblad†
0027-7207	New Zealand Institute of Architects Journal
0027-7215	N Z L A Newsletter *see* 0110-4373
0027-724X	New Zealand Shipping Gazette
0027-7266	N Z T C A Journal
0027-7274	N. Z. Truth
0027-7282	N. Z. Valuer
0027-7304	Na Pua Okika o Hawaii Nei/Orchids of Hawaii *see* 0099-8745
0027-7312	Na Stroikakh Rossii
0027-7320	Na Vijven
0027-7339	Naaimachine-Nieuws
0027-7347	Naamloos Nieuws *changed to* Milacroniek
0027-7355	Naar Morgen
0027-7363	Nach der Arbeit
0027-7371	Nachal'naya Shkola
0027-738X	Nachrichten aus Chemie und Technik *see* 0341-5163
0027-7398	Nachrichten aus der Aerztlichen Mission
0027-7401	Oesterreichisches Chemiefaser-Institut. Nachrichten
0027-741X	Nachrichten fuer Aussenhandel
0027-7428	Nachrichten fuer Die Zivile Luftfahrt, Deutsche Demokratische Republik
0027-7436	Nachrichten fuer Dokumentation
0027-7444	Nachrichten fuer Seefahrer
0027-7452	Nachrichtenblatt der Bayerischen Entomologen
0027-7460	Deutsche Gesellschaft fuer Geschichte der Medizin, Naturwissenschaft und Technik. Nachrichtenblatt
0027-7479	Nachrichtenblatt des Deutschen Pflanzenschutzdienstes
0027-7487	Nachrichtenblatt fuer die Buersten- und Pinselindustrie
0027-7495	Nachrichtentechnik *changed to* Nachrichtentechnik-Elektronik
0027-7509	Nacion
0027-7525	Nadel Faden Fingerhut†
0027-7533	Naeringsrevyen
0027-7541	Nafta
0027-755X	Nafta
0027-7568	Nagaoka Technical College. Research Reports
0027-7576	Nagarjun
0027-7584	Nagarlok
0027-7592	Nagoya Port Statistics Monthly
0027-7606	Nagoya City University. Medical Association. Journal
0027-7614	Japan. Government Industrial Research Institute, Nagoya. Technical News
0027-7622	Nagoya Journal of Medical Science
0027-7630	Nagoya Mathematical Journal
0027-7649	Nagoya Medical Journal
0027-7657	Nagoya University. Faculty of Engineering. Memoirs
0027-7681	Naho
0027-769X	Die Nahrung
0027-7703	Nahrungsmittel
0027-7711	Nailaer Zeitung†
0027-772X	Lead and Zinc
0027-7738	Names
0027-7746	Namib Times
0027-7754	Namibia
0027-7762	Namrugram†
0027-7770	Nanak Prakash Patrika
0027-7797	Nanyang University. Bulletin *changed to* Chronicle. Nanyang University. Newsletter
0027-7800	Napa-Solano Dental Society. District Six. Newsletter *changed to* Oracle
0027-7819	Napjaink
0027-7827	Napoleon
0027-7835	Napoli Nobilissima
0027-7843	Napred
0027-7851	Narciso
0027-786X	Narcotics Control Digest
0027-7886	Narod†
0027-7894	Narod Polski
0027-7908	Narodna Armija
0027-7924	Narodna Tvorchist' ta Etnografiya
0027-7932	Narodne Novine
0027-7940	Narodne Noviny
0027-7959	Narodni Borac
0027-7975	Narodni List
0027-7983	Narodni Sumar
0027-8009	Narodni Vybory
0027-8017	Narodno Stvaralastvo - Folklor
0027-8025	Narodno Zdravlje
0027-8033	Narodnoe Obrazovanie
0027-8041	Narody Azii i Afriki
0027-805X	Narragansett Naturalist†
0027-8068	Nas Chov
0027-8076	Revija
0027-8084	Nas Jezik
0027-8092	Nas Put/Our Way *see* 0702-3855
0027-8106	Nas Svijet
0027-8114	Nas Vesnik†
0027-8122	Nasa Rec
0027-8149	Nasa Stampa
0027-8157	Nasa Strucna Skola
0027-8165	Nasa Zakonitost
0027-819X	Nase Planine
0027-8203	Nase Rec
0027-8211	Nase Vojsko
0027-8238	Nash Sovremennik
0027-8246	Nash Swit
0027-8254	Nashe Slovo
0027-8262	Nasi Dani
0027-8270	Nasi Zbori
0027-8319	Nasza Droga
0027-8327	Panorama Polska
0027-8335	Natal University News†
0027-8343	Natal Wildlife
0027-8351	Nataller *changed to* Tempo
0027-8378	Nation
0027-8394	Nation
0027-8408	Nation Europa
0027-8416	National Association of College Admissions Counselors. Newsletter
0027-8424	National Academy of Sciences. Proceedings
0027-8432	National Academy of Sciences. National Academy of Engineering. National Research Council. Institute of Medicine. News Report
0027-8459	National Adoptalk *changed to* Adoptalk
0027-8467	N A C News
0027-8505	National Agricultural Library Catalog
0027-8513	National Alliance
0027-8521	National Amateur
0027-853X	National AMMVET
0027-8548	National and Grindlays Review *changed to* Grindlays Bank Review
0027-8556	National Antiques Review†
0027-8572	National Assembly Library Review
0027-8580	National Assembly Review
0027-8602	National Association of Colleges and Teachers of Agriculture. Journal *see* 0149-4910
0027-8610	National Association of Educational Broadcasters Newsletter *changed to* Current (Washington)
0027-8629	National Association of Private Psychiatric Hospitals. Journal
0027-8637	National Association of Private Psychiatric Hospitals. News Letter
0027-8645	National Association of Regulatory Utility Commissioners. Bulletin
0027-8653	National Association of Secondary School Principals. Bulletin *see* 0192-6365
0027-8661	National Association of Soil and Water Conservation Districts. Tuesday Letter *see* 0047-8733
0027-867X	National Association of Summer Sessions. Newsletter *changed to* North American Association of Summer Sessions. Newsletter
0027-8688	National Association of Watch and Clock Collectors. Bulletin

0027-870X National Association of Women Deans and Counselors. Journal *see* 0094-3460
0027-8718 National Athletic Trainers Association. Journal *see* 0160-8320
0027-8742 National Bank of Egypt. Economic Bulletin
0027-8750 National Bank of Ethiopia. Quarterly Bulletin
0027-8769 National Beauty School Journal
0027-8777 National Bibliography of Botswana
0027-8785 National Board Examiner
0027-8793 National Bowlers Journal and Billiard Revue *see* 0164-9183
0027-8807 National Builder
0027-8815 National Buildings Organisation. Journal
0027-8823 U. S. National Bureau of Standards. Technical News Buletin *see* 0093-0458
0027-8831 National Business Woman
0027-8858 National Cactus & Succulent Journal
0027-8866 Cancer Care and the National Cancer Foundation. Report About the Services Your Contributions Support
0027-8874 U. S. National Cancer Institute. Journal
0027-8882 National Candy Wholesaler *see* 0162-5136
0027-8890 National Capital Pharmacist
0027-8912 National Catholic Guidance Conference Journal *see* 0160-7960
0027-8920 National Catholic Register
0027-8939 National Catholic Reporter
0027-8947 China, Republic. National Central Library. Bulletin
0027-8955 National Chamber of Trade Journal *changed to* Distributor
0027-8963 National Chinchilla Breeders of Canada. Bulletin
0027-8971 National Christian News
0027-898X National Chronicle
0027-9013 National Civic Review
0027-9021 National Coffee Association News Letter *changed to* National Coffee Association of U.S.A., Inc. Newsletter
0027-9048 American Bankruptcy Law Journal
0027-9064 National Contract Management Journal *changed to* National Contract Management Journal(1980)
0027-9072 National Council for Homemaker Service. News *changed to* National HomeCaring Council. News
0027-9080 National Cremation *changed to* Cremationist of North America
0027-9099 National Custodian *changed to* Cleaning Management
0027-9102 National Decency Reporter
0027-9110 National Defence Academy. Journal†
0027-9129 N. D. A. Quarterly
0027-9145 National Diary
0027-9153 Japan. National Diet Library. Monthly Bulletin
0027-9161 Japan. National Diet Library. Newsletter
0027-917X N. D. T. I. Review
0027-9188 National Education
0027-9196 National Educational Secretary
0027-920X National Elementary Principal *changed to* Principal (Arlington)
0027-9218 National Engineer
0027-9226 National Farmers Union Washington Newsletter
0027-9234 National Federation of Housing Societies. Quarterly Bulletin *changed to* Voluntary Housing
0027-9242 National Federation of Science Abstracting and Indexing Services. Federation Newsletter *see* 0090-0893
0027-9250 National Fisherman
0027-9269 National Fluoridation News
0027-9277 U.S. Department of Agriculture. Economic Research Service. National Food Situation *see* 0161-4274
0027-9285 National 4-H News
0027-9293 National Franchise Reports†
0027-9315 National Future Farmer
0027-9323 National Gallery of Canada. Bulletin *changed to* National Gallery of Canada. Annual Bulletin
0027-9331 National Gardener
0027-934X National Genealogical Society Quarterly
0027-9358 National Geographic
0027-9374 National Geographical Journal of India
0027-9382 National Geophysical Research Institute. Bulletin *changed to* Geophysical Research Bulletin
0027-9390 National Glass Budget
0027-9404 National Guardian *changed to* Scottish Licensed Trade Guardian
0027-9412 National Guardsman *see* 0163-3945
0027-9420 National Health Federation. Bulletin
0027-9439 National Hearing Aid Journal *see* 0091-2166
0027-9447 National Hog Farmer
0027-9455 National Horseman
0027-9471 National Humane Newsletter *changed to* Animal Protection News
0027-948X National Humane Review *changed to* Animal Protection News
0027-9498 National Humane Shoptalk *changed to* Animal Protection News
0027-9501 National Institute Economic Review
0027-951X Japan. National Institute of Animal Health Quarterly
0027-9528 National Institute of Sciences of India. Bulletin *changed to* Indian National Science Academy. Bulletin
0027-9544 National Jeweler
0027-9552 National Jewish Monthly
0027-9560 National Journal *see* 0360-4217
0027-9609 National Leaders Magazine
0027-9617 National League Journal of Insured Savings Associations *see* 0095-781X
0027-9625 National Legal Magazine *see* 0041-2538
0027-9633 National Library News
0027-9641 National Library of Medicine Current Catalog
0027-965X National Library of Medicine News
0027-9668 National Live Stock Producer†
0027-9676 National Medical and Dental Association. Bulletin
0027-9684 National Medical Association. Journal
0027-9692 National Medical Journal *changed to* National Integrated Medical Association Journal
0027-9706 National Merchandiser†
0027-9714 National Messenger
0027-9722 National Model Railroad Association. Bulletin
0027-9730 National Museums and Monuments of Rhodesia. Occasional Papers *changed to* National Museums and Monuments Administration. Occasional Papers. Series B: Natural Sciences
0027-9730 National Museums and Monuments of Rhodesia. Occasional Papers *changed to* National Museums and Monuments Administration. Occasional Papers. Series A: Human Sciences
0027-9749 National Music Council Bulletin
0027-9765 National News†
0027-9773 National News Letter
0027-9781 National News of the Blind
0027-9803 National Observer†
0027-9811 National Oceanographic Data Center. Newsletter†
0027-9838 National P T A Bulletin†
0027-9846 National Palace Museum Bulletin
0027-9854 National Palace Museum Newsletter
0027-9862 National Parking Association. Newsletter *changed to* Parking World
0027-9870 National Parks & Conservation Magazine
0027-9889 National Petroleum News
0027-9897 National Pharmaceutical Association. Journal
0027-9900 National Pilots Association News Bulletin *changed to* National Pilots Association News
0027-9927 National Press Club Record
0027-9935 National Press Photographer *changed to* News Photographer
0027-9943 National Program Letter
0027-9951 National Prospector's Gazette & Treasure Hunter's News
0027-996X National Provisioner
0027-9978 National Public Accountant
0027-9994 National Real Estate Investor
0028-0003 National Renaissance Bulletin
0028-0011 National Research Council of Thailand. Journal
0028-002X National Retailer *changed to* R M A Report
0028-0038 National Review
0028-0046 National Review Bulletin
0028-0054 National Review of Criminal Sciences
0028-0062 National Review of Social Sciences
0028-0089 National Rural Letter Carrier
0028-0097 National Safety
0028-0100 National Safety News
0028-0119 National Science Museum. Bulletin *see* 0385-2431
0028-0119 National Science Museum. Bulletin. *see* 0385-244X
0028-0119 National Science Museum. Bulletin *see* 0385-2423
0028-0127 National Sculpture Review
0028-0135 National Service to Regional Councils. Special Reports *see* 0196-4003
0028-0143 National Service to Regional Councils. Newsletter *changed to* National Association of Regional Councils. Regional Focus
0028-0151 National Service to Regional Councils. Regional Review†
0028-016X National Sheriff
0028-0186 National Society for Medical Research. Bulletin
0028-0194 Society of Professors of Education. Quarterly Review *changed to* Society of Professors of Education
0028-0208 National Speed Sport News
0028-0216 N S S Bulletin
0028-0259 Greece. National Statistical Service. Monthly Statistical Bulletin of Public Finance *changed to* Greece. National Statistical Service. Statistical Bulletin of Public Finance
0028-0267 National Stock Dog
0028-0275 National Taiwan University. College of Medicine. Memoirs
0028-0283 National Tax Journal
0028-0291 National Technical Report
0028-0305 National Timber Industry *changed to* Western Timber Industry
0028-0313 National Tuberculosis and Respiratory Disease Association Bulletin *see* 0092-5659
0028-0321 National U. Weekly
0028-033X National Underwriter. Life & Health Insurance Edition
0028-0348 National Union Catalog
0028-0356 National Union of the Footwear, Leather and Allied Trades Monthly Journal and Report *changed to* National Union of the Footwear, Leather and Allied Trades Journal and Report
0028-0372 National Voter
0028-0380 National Waterways Conference Newsletter
0028-0399 National Westminster Bank Review
0028-0402 National Wildlife
0028-0410 National Wool Grower
0028-0429 National Writers Club. Bulletin for Professional Members *changed to* Professional Freelance Writers Directory
0028-0437 Der Nationale Demokrat
0028-0453 Nationaloekonomisk Tidsskrift
0028-047X Nation's Business
0028-0488 Nation's Cities *changed to* Nation's Cities Weekly
0028-0496 Nation's Health
0028-050X Nations Nouvelles
0028-0518 Nation's Restaurant News
0028-0526 Nation's Schools *see* 0194-2263
0028-0534 Native Nevadan
0028-0542 Native Voice
0028-0550 Natturufraedingurinn
0028-0577 Natur, Kultur und Jagd *see* 0340-4277
0028-0585 Natur og Museum
0028-0593 Natur und Heimat
0028-0607 Natur und Land
0028-0615 Natur und Landschaft
0028-0623 Natur-und Nationalparke†
0028-0631 Natura
0028-064X Natura
0028-0666 Natura Mosana
0028-0674 Natura
0028-0682 Natural and Applied Science Bulletin
0028-0704 Natural Health World
0028-0712 Natural History
0028-0720 Natural History Society of Northumberland Durham and Newcastle Upon Tyne. Transactions *see* 0144-221X
0028-0739 Natural Resources Journal
0028-0747 Natural Resources Lawyer
0028-0755 Natural Rubber News
0028-0763 Natural Science in Schools
0028-0771 Naturalist
0028-0798 Naturaliste Canadien
0028-0801 Naturalistes Belges
0028-081X Der Naturarzt
0028-0828 Naturbrunnen *changed to* Der Mineralbrunnen
0028-0836 Nature
0028-0844 Nature and Resources and Man and Biosphere Programme. Bulletin *changed to* Nature and Resources
0028-0852 Nature Conservancy News
0028-0860 Nature Study
0028-0887 Naturen
0028-0895 Naturens Verden
0028-0909 Nature's Path
0028-0917 Naturforschende Gesellschaft zu Freiburg. Berichte
0028-0925 Naturfreund
0028-0933 Naturgemaesser Land- und Gartenbau
0028-0941 Naturheilpraxis
0028-095X Naturhistorisches Museum in Wien. Monatsprogramm
0028-0968 Naturisme
0028-0976 Naturist und Welt
0028-0992 Naturkunde in Westfalen *changed to* Natur- und Landschaftskunde in Westfalen
0028-100X Naturopath
0028-1018 Naturschutz- und Naturparke
0028-1026 Naturstein
0028-1034 Die Naturstein- Industrie
0028-1042 Die Naturwissenschaften
0028-1050 Naturwissenschaftliche Rundschau
0028-1077 Natuur en Landschap *changed to* Natuur en Milieu
0028-1085 Natuur en Museum
0028-1093 Natuur en Techniek
0028-1115 Natya
0028-1123 Nauchen Zhivot
0028-1131 Nauchno-tekhnicheskaya Informatsiya
0028-1212 Filologicheskie Nauki
0028-1220 Nauncni Skupovi u SFRJ i u Inostranstvu *see* 0350-011X
0028-1239 Nauka i Religiya
0028-1247 Nauka i Suspil'stvo
0028-1255 Nauka i Tekhnika
0028-1263 Nauka i Zhizn'
0028-1271 Nauka Polska
0028-128X N A U N L U
0028-1298 Naunyn-Schmiedeberg's Archives of Pharmacology
0028-1301 Natur und Museum
0028-131X Nautakarja
0028-1336 Nautical Magazine
0028-1344 Nautilus
0028-1352 Nautilus
0028-1379 Nautisk Tidskrift
0028-1409 Naval Affairs

ISSN	Title
0028-1417	Naval Aviation News
0028-1425	Naval Engineers Journal
0028-1441	Naval Research Logistics Quarterly
0028-145X	Naval Research Reviews†
0028-1468	Naval Stores Review and Terpene Chemicals *changed to* Naval Stores Review
0028-1484	Naval War College Review
0028-1492	Navalkatha
0028-1506	Navbharat Times
0028-1514	Navetex
0028-1522	Navigation (Washington)
0028-1530	Navigation
0028-1549	Revue de la Navigation Fluviale Europeenne, Ports et Industries
0028-1565	Navigatoer *changed to* Nyt Navigatoer-Navigatoer Nyt
0028-1581	Navioneer
0028-159X	Navires Ports & Chantiers
0028-1603	Navis
0028-1611	Navitecnia
0028-162X	Navnirman
0028-1646	Navy *changed to* Navy International
0028-1654	Navy Chaplains Bulletin
0028-1662	Navy News
0028-1670	Navy News
0028-1689	Navy: the Magazine of Sea Power *changed to* Sea Power
0028-1697	Navy Times
0028-1700	Nazareth
0028-1727	Nea Agrotiki Epitheorisis
0028-1735	Nea Hestia
0028-1743	Middle East Council of Churches. News Bulletin†
0028-1751	Near East Foundation News
0028-176X	Near East Report
0028-1778	Near North News
0028-1786	Nebelspalter
0028-1794	Nebraska Alumnus
0028-1808	Nebraska Beverage Analyst
0028-1816	Nebraska Bird Review
0028-1824	Nebraska College of Agriculture Quarterly *changed to* Farm, Ranch and Home Quarterly
0028-1832	Nebraska Dental Association. Journal
0028-1840	Nebraska Education News *changed to* Nebraska Ed News
0028-1859	Nebraska History
0028-1867	Nebraska Journal of Economics and Business *see* 0160-6557
0028-1875	Nebraska Legionnaire
0028-1883	Nebraska Library Association Quarterly
0028-1891	Nebraska Mortar and Pestle
0028-1913	Nebraska Newspaper
0028-1921	Nebraska Nurse
0028-193X	Nebraska on the March†
0028-1948	Nebraska Retailer
0028-1964	Nebraskaland
0028-1972	Nedelet†
0028-1980	Nedeljne Novine
0028-1999	Nedeljne Novosti
0028-2006	Nederduitse Gereformeerde Teologiese Tydskrif
0028-2014	Nederland-Israel
0028-2022	Nederland-USSR Instituut. Maandberichten
0028-2030	Nederlands Archief voor Kerkgeschiedenis
0028-2049	Nederlands Archievenblad
0028-2057	Nederlands Bosbouw Tijdschrift
0028-2073	Nederlands Korfbalblad
0028-2081	Nederlandsch Maandblad voor Philatelie
0028-209X	Netherlands Milk and Dairy Journal
0028-2103	Nederlands Militair Geneeskundig Tijdschrift
0028-2111	Nederlands Tandartsenblad
0028-212X	Nederlands Theologisch Tijdschrift
0028-2138	Netherlands International Law Review
0028-2146	Nederlands Tijdschrift *changed to* NOT U-Mededelingen
0028-2154	Nederlands Tijdschrift voor Criminology *changed to* Tijdschrift voor Criminologie
0028-2170	Nederlands Tijdschrift voor Medische Studenten†
0028-2189	Nederlands Tijdschrift voor Natuurkunde *changed to* Nederlands Tijdschrift voor Natuurkunde A en B
0028-2197	Nederlands Tijdschrift voor Psychiatrie *changed to* Tijdschrift voor Psychiatrie
0028-2200	Nederlands Tijdschrift voor Tandheelkunde
0028-2219	Nederlands Transport
0028-2227	Nederlands Weekblad voor de Groothandel in Levensmiddelen†
0028-2243	European Journal of Obstetrics and Gynecology *see* 0301-2115
0028-2251	Nederlandsch-Turksche Vereeniging. Berichten†
0028-226X	Nederlandsche Leeuw
0028-2278	Nederlandse Gedachten
0028-2294	Nederlandse Onderneming *changed to* Onderneming
0028-2308	Nederlandse Sport Federatie. Technisch Bulletin *changed to* Nederlandse Sport Federatie. Technische Mededelingen
0028-2324	Nederlandse Vereniging van Huisvrouwen Afdeling Amsterdam. Maandbericht†
0028-2332	Nederlandse Vereniging van Vrouwen met Academische Opleiding. Mededelingen
0028-2340	Nederlandse Vereniging voor Zeegeschiedenis. Mededelingen
0028-2359	Needle's Eye
0028-2375	Neent†
0028-2383	Neerlandia
0028-2391	Neerlands Postduiven Orgaan
0028-2405	Neerlands Volksleven
0028-2413	Nef
0028-2421	Neftekhimiya
0028-243X	Neftyanik
0028-2448	Neftyanoe Khozyaistvo
0028-2456	Negocios y Bancos
0028-2464	Negotiation Research Digest†
0028-2472	Negotiations News *changed to* New Jersey School Leader
0028-2480	Negro American Literature Forum *see* 0148-6179
0028-2502	Negro Braille Magazine
0028-2510	Negro Heritage *changed to* Black Heritage
0028-2529	Negro History Bulletin
0028-2537	Negro Traveler & Conventioneer
0028-2545	Niege et Glace *changed to* Ski-Flash Magazine
0028-2553	Neill Letter of Contrary Opinion *changed to* Fraser Opinion Letter
0028-2561	Neirofiziologiya
0028-2588	Neman
0028-2596	Nematologica
0028-260X	Nemuno Krastas
0028-2626	Nemzetor
0028-2642	Neo Aftokinito
0028-2677	Neophilologus
0028-2685	Neoplasma
0028-2693	Neos Kosmos
0028-2707	Nepal Gazette Translation Service *changed to* Nepal Recorder
0028-2715	Nepal Medical Association. Journal
0028-2723	Nepal Press Digest
0028-2731	Nepal Press Report
0028-274X	Nepal Rastra Bank. Quarterly Economic Bulletin
0028-2758	Nepal Review Monthly†
0028-2766	Nephron
0028-2774	Neprajzi Kozlemenyek
0028-2782	Neptune Nautisme
0028-2790	Neptunus
0028-2804	Der Nervenarzt
0028-2812	Nestor
0028-2820	Net
0028-2847	Netherhall News†
0028-2855	Netherlands-American Trade
0028-2871	Amsterdam. Bureau van Statistiek. Maandbericht
0028-2898	Netherlands. Centraal Bureau voor de Statistiek. Maandschrift
0028-2901	Netherlands Economic Bulletin for the Foreign Press *changed to* Holland Info
0028-291X	Statistisch Kwartaaloverzicht Hilversum
0028-2928	Netherlands Journal of Agricultural Science
0028-2944	Netherlands Journal of Plant Pathology
0028-2960	Netherlands Journal of Zoology
0028-2979	Netherlands. Ministerie van Cultuur, Recreatie en Maatschappelijk Werk. Centrale Afdeling Internationale Betrekkingen. Informatie Bulletin
0028-2987	Netherlands. Ministerie van Onderwijs en Wetenschappen. Pedagogische Bibliografie
0028-2995	Netherlands Patents Report
0028-3002	Netherlands. Rijksmuseum. Bulletin
0028-3029	Netsu Kanri *see* 0302-1289
0028-3037	Network
0028-3045	Networks
0028-3053	Neue Technik und Wirtschaft†
0028-307X	Der Angestellte
0028-3088	Neue Betriebswirtschaft†
0028-3096	Neue Blaetter des Theaters in der Josefstadt
0028-310X	Neue Blaetter fuer Taubstummenbildung *see* 0342-4898
0028-3118	Das Neue Buch
0028-3126	Die Neue Buecherei
0028-3134	Der Neue Bund
0028-3142	Neue Deutsche Hefte
0028-3150	Neue deutsche Literatur
0028-3169	Das Neue Erlangen
0028-3177	Die Neue Gesellschaft
0028-3193	Das Neue Handwerk
0028-3207	Neue Huette
0028-3223	Neue Illustrierte Wochenschau
0028-3231	Neue Justiz
0028-324X	Der Neue Kaufmann
0028-3258	Neue Kommentare
0028-3274	Der Neue Mahnruf
0028-3282	Neue Museumskunde
0028-3290	Neue Musikzeitung
0028-3304	Die Neue Ordnung in Kirche, Staat, Gesellschaft, Kultur
0028-3312	Neue Physik
0028-3320	Neue Politische Literatur
0028-3339	Neue Produkte
0028-3347	Neue Rundschau
0028-3355	Neue Sammlung
0028-3363	Neue Stafette
0028-3371	Neue Stenographische Praxis
0028-338X	Neue Steuerpraxis
0028-3398	Neue Technik
0028-3401	Neue Technik im Buero
0028-341X	Neue Uhrmacher-Zeitung *changed to* Schmuck und Uhren
0028-3444	Neue Wege
0028-3452	Neue Werbung
0028-3460	Neue Wirtschafts-Briefe
0028-3479	Zeitschrift fuer Parapsychologie und Grenzgebiete der Psychologie
0028-3495	Neue Zeitschrift fuer Missionswissenschaft
0028-3509	Neue Zeitschrift fuer Musik†
0028-3509	Neue Zeitung fuer Musik *see* 0170-8791
0028-3517	Neue Zeitschrift fuer Systematische Theologie und Religionsphilosophie
0028-3525	Neue Zeitschrift fuer Wehrrecht
0028-3533	Neuen Buecher†
0028-355X	DNV
0028-3568	Zions Freund
0028-3576	Die Neueren Sprachen
0028-3584	Der Neuerer
0028-3592	Neues Beginnen *changed to* Theorie und Praxis der Sozialen Arbeit
0028-3606	Neues Bei Uns *changed to* STEWEAG-Rundschau
0028-3614	Neues Dorf
0028-3622	Neues Forum
0028-3630	Neues Jahrbuch fuer Geologie und Palaeontologie, Monatshefte
0028-3649	Neues Jahrbuch fuer Mineralogie. Monatshefte
0028-3657	Neues Leben
0028-3665	Neues Leben
0028-3673	Neues Optikerjournal
0028-3681	Neues Polizeiarchiv
0028-3711	Neuheiten und Erfinderdienst *changed to* Erfinder und Neuheitendienst
0028-3754	Neuphilologische Mitteilungen
0028-3770	Neuro-Chirurgie
0028-3797	Neuropaediatrie *see* 0174-304X
0028-3800	Neurobiologia
0028-3819	Neurochirurgia
0028-3827	Neuroendocrine Control Mechanism
0028-3835	Neuroendocrinology
0028-3843	Neurologia i Neurochirurgia Polska
0028-386X	Revista de Medicina Interna, Neurologie, Psihiatrie, Neuro-Chirurgie, Dermato-Venerologie. Neurologie, Psihiatrie, Neuro-Chirurgie
0028-3886	Neurology India
0028-3894	Neuropatologia Polska
0028-3908	Neuropharmacology
0028-3916	Neuropsichiatria
0028-3924	Neuropsichiatria Infantile
0028-3932	Neuropsychologia
0028-3940	Neuroradiology
0028-3959	Neuroscience Translations *see* 0097-0549
0028-3967	Neurosciences Research Program Bulletin
0028-3975	Neurospora Newsletter
0028-3983	Neusprachliche Mitteilungen aus Wissenschaft und Praxis
0028-4009	Neva
0028-4017	Nevada Business Review *changed to* Nevada Review of Business and Economics
0028-4033	Nevada Education Journal
0028-4041	Nevada Highway News†
0028-405X	Nevada Highways and Parks *changed to* Nevada
0028-4068	Nevada Libraries *changed to* Highroller
0028-4076	Nevada Notes
0028-4084	Nevada Outdoors and Wildlife Review†
0028-4092	Nevada State Bar Journal *see* 0092-6086
0028-4106	Nevada State Library. Official Nevada Publications
0028-4114	Neve International
0028-4122	Nevesport Illustrato
0028-4130	New†
0028-4149	New Magazine†
0028-4165	New African†
0028-4173	Witches Newsletter *see* 0049-7754
0028-419X	New America
0028-4203	New America & Canadian Poetry†
0028-4211	New American Review *changed to* American Review
0028-4238	New Associations and Projects
0028-4246	New Atlantis†
0028-4254	New Aurora
0028-4270	New Beacon (Inkprint Edition)
0028-4289	New Blackfriars
0028-4297	New Book Review†
0028-4300	New Books
0028-4319	New Books in Business and Economics *changed to* Harvard University. Graduate School of Business Administration. Baker Library. Recent Additions to Baker Library
0028-4327	New Books on Family Planning
0028-4335	New Books on World Affairs *changed to* Council Spotlight Book Notes
0028-4351	New Brunswick Economic Statistics
0028-436X	New Building *changed to* New Building Projects
0028-4378	New Business Incorporations
0028-4386	New Canadian
0028-4408	New Captain George's Whizzbang†
0028-4416	New Christian
0028-4424	New Church Messenger
0028-4459	New Coin
0028-4467	New Collage Magazine
0028-4475	New Commonwealth *see* 0305-750X
0028-4491	New Construction
0028-4505	New Cornwall†
0028-4513	New Dawn†

0028-4521 New Dawn *changed to* Dawn
0028-453X New Day
0028-4548 New Day†
0028-4556 New Day *changed to* New Century
0028-4564 Ontario New Democrat
0028-4572 New Democrat†
0028-4599 New Dimensions†
0028-4602 New Dimensions in Education *see* 0317-0349
0028-4629 New Directions
0028-4637 New Driver†
0028-4645 New Edinburgh Review
0028-4653 New England Advertising Week
0028-4661 New England Apparel Retailer *changed to* New England Fashion Retailer
0028-4688 New England Bride
0028-470X New England Construction
0028-4718 New England Dairyman *changed to* Yankeemilk News
0028-4726 New England Economic Review
0028-4734 New England Electrical News†
0028-4742 New England Furniture News
0028-4750 New-England Galaxy†
0028-4769 New England Grocery Merchandiser
0028-4785 New England Historical and Genealogical Register
0028-4793 New England Journal of Medicine
0028-4807 New England Journal of Optometry
0028-4815 New England Journeys
0028-4823 New England Law Review
0028-4831 New England Letter *changed to* New England Report
0028-484X New England Printer and Publisher
0028-484X New England Printer and Lithographer *see* 0028-484X
0028-4858 New England Purchaser *changed to* New England Purchaser/Connecticut Purchaser
0028-4866 New England Quarterly: An Historical Review of New England Life and Letters
0028-4874 New England Railroad Club. Official Proceedings
0028-4882 New England Reading Association. Journal
0028-4890 New England Real Estate Journal
0028-4912 New England Social Studies Bulletin
0028-4920 New England Square Dance Caller
0028-4939 New England Water Works Association. Journal
0028-4947 New Englander *changed to* New England Business
0028-4955 New Entomologist
0028-4963 New Equipment Digest
0028-4971 New Equipment News
0028-498X New Equipment News
0028-4998 New Era
0028-5013 New Era†
0028-5021 New Era
0028-5048 New Era
0028-5056 New Era Laundry & Cleaning Lines
0028-5064 New Ethicals *see* 0311-905X
0028-5072 New Factory Report†
0028-5080 New Forerunner†
0028-5099 New Future *changed to* News and Views: for Young Workers
0028-5102 New Generation
0028-5110 New Geographical Literature and Maps†
0028-5129 New Germany Reports†
0028-5137 New Guard
0028-5145 New Guinea and Australia, the Pacific and South-East Asia†
0028-5153 New Guinea Bulletin†
0028-5161 New Guinea Periodical Index
0028-517X New Guinea Psychologist†
0028-5188 New Guinea Research Bulletin†
0028-5196 New Hampshire Alumnus
0028-520X New Hampshire Audubon News *changed to* New Hampshire Audubon
0028-5234 New Hampshire Educator
0028-5242 New Hampshire Highways
0028-5250 New Hampshire Horizons†
0028-5269 N H L A Newsletter
0028-5277 New Hampshire Motor Transport†
0028-5285 New Hampshire Natural Resources
0028-5293 New Hampshire Polyglot
0028-5307 New Hampshire Profiles
0028-5315 New Hampshire Quarter Notes
0028-5331 New Haven I N F O
0028-5374 New Horizons
0028-5382 New Horizons in Education
0028-5390 New Hungarian Quarterly
0028-5404 New Idea
0028-5412 New Illustrator *changed to* Light on the Word for Adult Teachers
0028-5420 New in Dentistry†
0028-5439 New Individualist Review†
0028-5455 New Jersey Academy of Science. Bulletin
0028-5463 New Jersey Academy of Science. Newsletter
0028-5498 New Jersey Air, Water and Waste Management Times *changed to* New Jersey Outdoors
0028-5501 New Jersey Association of Certified Dental Laboratories, Inc. Bulletin
0028-5528 N J A O P S Journal
0028-5536 New Jersey Banker
0028-5544 New Jersey Bell
0028-5552 New Jersey Beverage Journal
0028-5560 New Jersey Business
0028-5579 New Jersey Business Woman
0028-5587 New Jersey Club Woman and Even'tide
0028-5595 New Jersey Correction News
0028-5609 New Jersey Council News
0028-5617 New Jersey County Government†
0028-5633 New Jersey Days†
0028-565X New Jersey Dental Laboratory Industry. Bulletin
0028-5668 New Jersey Division of Veterans Services Information Bulletin. *changed to* New Jersey Bureau of Veterans Services Information Bulletin
0028-5676 New Jersey Economic Review†
0028-5684 New Jersey Education *see* 0199-4557
0028-5706 New Jersey Equine Industry News
0028-5714 New Jersey Federation of Planning Officials. Federation Planner
0028-5722 New Jersey Federation of Planning Officials. Federation Planning Information Reports
0028-5730 New Jersey Genesis Quarterly
0028-5757 New Jersey History
0028-5765 New Jersey Journal of Optometry
0028-5773 New Jersey Journal of Pharmacy
0028-5781 New Jersey Labor Herald
0028-579X New Jersey Landings
0028-5803 New Jersey Law Journal
0028-5811 New Jersey Libraries
0028-582X New Jersey Messenger
0028-5838 New Jersey Motor Truck Association. Bulletin
0028-5846 New Jersey Municipalities
0028-5854 New Jersey Music and Arts†
0028-5862 New Jersey Nature News *changed to* New Jersey Audubon
0028-5870 N J S N A Newsletter *changed to* New Jersey Nurse
0028-5897 New Jersey Parent Teacher
0028-5900 New Jersey Professional Engineer
0028-5919 New Jersey Realtor
0028-5927 N. J. S. D. C. Research Bulletin
0028-5935 New Jersey Speech and Hearing Association. Journal
0028-5951 New Jersey State Bar Journal
0028-5994 New Jersey's Finest
0028-6001 New Journal
0028-601X New Journal of Statistics and Operational Research
0028-6044 New Leader
0028-6052 Money Management and Unitholder
0028-6060 New Left Review
0028-6079 New Life
0028-6087 New Literary History
0028-6095 New Literature on Automation
0028-6109 New Magazine
0028-6125 New Messenger (Braille Edition)†
0028-6141 New Mexico Beverage Journal
0028-6168 New Mexico Business†
0028-6184 New Mexico Extension News†
0028-6192 New Mexico Farm & Ranch
0028-6206 New Mexico Historical Review
0028-6214 New Mexico Law Review
0028-6222 New Mexico Libraries†
0028-6230 New Mexico Lobo
0028-6249 New Mexico Magazine
0028-6257 New Mexico Municipal League. Municipal Reporter
0028-6265 New Mexico Musician
0028-6273 New Mexico Nurse
0028-6281 New Mexico Professional Engineer
0028-629X New Mexico Review and Legislative Journal
0028-6303 New Mexico School Review
0028-632X New Mexico Tax Bulletin
0028-6338 New Mexico Wildlife
0028-6354 New Morality
0028-6362 New Musical Express
0028-6370 New Nation†
0028-6389 New Norfolk *changed to* Tidewater Virginian
0028-6397 New Orleans Port Record
0028-6400 New Orleans Review
0028-6419 New Outlook
0028-6427 New Outlook
0028-6435 New Outlook for the Blind *see* 0145-482X
0028-6443 New Philosophy
0028-6451 New Physician
0028-6478 New Poetry *changed to* Brouhaha
0028-6486 New Polish Publications
0028-6494 New Politics†
0028-6524 New Product Newsletter *changed to* International New Product Newsletter
0028-6532 New Race
0028-6540 New Rambler
0028-6559 New Records
0028-6567 New Reference Books at U C L A†
0028-6575 New Renaissance
0028-6583 New Republic
0028-6591 New Research Centers
0028-6605 New Review *changed to* New Review of East-European History (1981)
0028-6605 New Review *see* 0381-9140
0028-6613 New Scholar
0028-6621 New Scholasticism
0028-663X New School Bulletin†
0028-6656 New Schools Exchange Newsletter†
0028-6664 New Scientist
0028-6672 New Scotian *changed to* Maritimer
0028-6680 New Serial Titles
0028-6699 New Serial Titles-Classed Subject Arrangement
0028-6702 New Ships *see* 0172-9314
0028-6729 New Society
0028-6745 New South *see* 0093-9293
0028-6761 New South Wales Government Publications. Monthly List
0028-677X New South Wales Industrial Gazette
0028-6788 New South Wales Library Bulletin†
0028-6796 New South Wales Official Publications Received in the Library of New South Wales
0028-680X Australia. Bureau of Statistics. New South Wales Office. Monthly Summary of Statistics
0028-6818 New South Wales. Soil Conservation Service Journal
0028-6826 New South Wales Statistical Bulletin†
0028-6834 New Spotlight
0028-6842 New Statesman
0028-6869 New Technical Books
0028-6877 New Testament Abstracts
0028-6885 New Testament Studies
0028-6907 New Trail
0028-6966 New Window†
0028-6974 New Woman
0028-6990 New World
0028-7008 New World
0028-7016 New World *see* 0149-970X
0028-7032 New World
0028-7067 New World Review
0028-7075 New Worlds
0028-7091 New York Academy of Medicine. Bulletin
0028-7105 New York Academy of Medicine. News Notes
0028-7113 New York Academy of Sciences. Transactions†
0028-7113 New York Academy of Sciences. Transactions
0028-7121 New York Amsterdam News
0028-713X New York Auto Repairs
0028-7164 New York Construction News
0028-7180 New York Column†
0028-7199 New York Entomological Society. Journal
0028-7210 New York Fish and Game Journal
0028-7229 New York Folklore Quarterly *see* 0361-204X
0028-7237 New York Genealogical and Biographical Record
0028-7245 New York Generator
0028-7253 New-York Historical Society Quarterly
0028-727X New York Holstein Friesian News
0028-7288 New York Convention & Visitors Bureau. Quarterly Calendar of Events
0028-7296 New York Journal of Dentistry
0028-730X New York L P N
0028-7318 New York Law Forum *see* 0145-448X
0028-7342 New York Letter Carriers' Outlook
0028-7350 New York Library Club Bulletin
0028-7369 New York Magazine
0028-7385 New York Motorist
0028-7431 New York Podiatrist
0028-7466 New York Public Library. Bulletin *see* 0160-0168
0028-7474 New York Purchasing Review *see* 0192-7973
0028-7482 New York Quarterly
0028-7490 New York Retailer†
0028-7504 New York Review of Books
0028-7512 New York State Archeological Association. Bulletin *changed to* New York State Archeological Association. Bulletin and Journal
0028-7539 New York State Banker
0028-7547 New York State Bar Journal
0028-7555 New York State Bulletin *changed to* New York State Register
0028-7563 New York State Conference of Mayors and Other Municipal Officials. Legal Bulletin
0028-7571 New York State Dental Journal
0028-758X New York State Dental Society of Anesthesiology. Bulletin *changed to* New York State Dental Society of Anesthesiology. Newsletter
0028-7598 New York State Education†
0028-761X New York State Housing and Community Renewal Reporter†
0028-7628 New York State Journal of Medicine
0028-7636 New York State Law Digest
0028-7644 New York State Nurses Association. Journal
0028-7652 New York State Nurses Association. Report
0028-7679 New York State Planning News
0028-7687 New York State Psychologist
0028-7709 New York State School Boards Association Journal
0028-775X New York State Speech Association. Reports
0028-7768 New York State Statistical Reporter†
0028-7776 New York State Taxpayer *changed to* C P E S Taxpayer
0028-7784 New York Theatre Critics' Reviews
0028-7806 New York Times Book Review
0028-7814 New York Times Large Type Weekly
0028-7830 New York Times School Weekly
0028-7849 New York Times Student Weekly†
0028-7857 New York University. Center for International Studies. Policy Papers†
0028-7865 New York University Journal of Dentistry†
0028-7873 New York University Journal of International Law and Politics
0028-7881 New York University Law Review
0028-789X New York University Medical Center News
0028-7903 New York University Medical Quarterly

0028-7911 New York University Post-Graduate Medical School. Inter-Clinic Information Bulletin
0028-792X New Yorker
0028-7938 New York's Food and Life Sciences Quarterly
0028-7946 New Yugoslav Law *see* 0350-2252
0028-7962 New Zealand Archaeological Association. Newsletter
0028-7989 New Zealand Camellia Bulletin
0028-7997 New Zealand Christian Pacifist *changed to* C P S Bulletin
0028-8004 New Zealand Coal
0028-8012 New Zealand Commerce
0028-8020 New Zealand Company Director and Sharemarket Survey *changed to* New Zealand Company Director & Executive
0028-8039 New Zealand Countrywoman
0028-8047 New Zealand Dental Journal
0028-8063 New Zealand Electrical Journal *see* 0110-1668
0028-8071 New Zealand Electrician
0028-808X New Zealand Engineering
0028-8098 New Zealand Farmer
0028-8101 New Zealand Financial Times
0028-811X New Zealand. Forest Service. Forest Research Institute. Research Leaflet†
0028-8128 New Zealand Furnishing and Appliance World†
0028-8136 New Zealand Gardener
0028-8144 New Zealand Geographer
0028-8160 New Zealand Hardware Journal
0028-8179 New Zealand Holiday†
0028-8187 New Zealand Home Journal†
0028-8195 New Zealand Horological Journal
0028-8209 New Zealand Horse & Pony
0028-8217 New Zealand Hospital
0028-8225 New Zealand Institute of Chemistry. Journal *changed to* Chemistry in New Zealand
0028-8233 New Zealand Journal of Agricultural Research
0028-825X New Zealand Journal of Botany
0028-8268 New Zealand Journal of Dairy Technology *see* 0300-1342
0028-8276 New Zealand Journal of Educational Studies
0028-8284 New Zealand Journal of Forestry
0028-8292 New Zealand Journal of Geography
0028-8306 New Zealand Journal of Geology and Geophysics
0028-8314 New Zealand Journal of Health, Physical Education and Recreation
0028-8322 New Zealand Journal of History
0028-8330 New Zealand Journal of Marine and Freshwater Research
0028-8349 New Zealand Journal of Medical Laboratory Technology
0028-8357 New Zealand Journal of Public Administration *changed to* Public Sector
0028-8365 New Zealand Journal of Science
0028-8373 New Zealand Law Journal
0028-8381 New Zealand Libraries
0028-8403 New Zealand Local Government
0028-8411 New Zealand Manufacturer†
0028-842X New Zealand Marine Sciences Newsletter
0028-8438 New Zealand Meat Producer†
0028-8446 New Zealand Medical Journal
0028-8454 New Zealand Medical Record†
0028-8470 New Zealand Model Railway Journal
0028-8489 New Zealand Monthly Review
0028-8497 New Zealand National Bibliography
0028-8500 New Zealand News U.K.
0028-8519 New Zealand Newsletter *changed to* Letter from New Zealand
0028-8527 New Zealand Numismatic Journal
0028-8535 New Zealand Nursing Journal
0028-8543 New Zealand Outdoor
0028-856X New Zealand Patent Office Journal
0028-8594 New Zealand Plumbing Review
0028-8608 New Zealand Potter
0028-8616 New Zealand Poultry World
0028-8624 New Zealand Railway Observer
0028-8632 New Zealand Rationalist and Humanist
0028-8640 New Zealand Export Review†
0028-8659 New Zealand School Journal
0028-8667 New Zealand Science Review
0028-8675 Service Station News *changed to* Motor Trade News
0028-8683 New Zealand Slavonic Journal
0028-8705 New Zealand Society of Periodontology. Bulletin *changed to* New Zealand Society of Periodontology. Journal
0028-8713 New Zealand Speech Therapists Journal
0028-8721 New Zealand Stamp Monthly
0028-873X New Zealand Stock Market Review†
0028-8748 New Zealand Tablet
0028-8756 New Zealand Tenders Gazette
0028-8799 New Zealand Trotting Calendar
0028-8802 New Zealand Wildlife
0028-8829 New Zealand Woman's Weekly
0028-8837 Newark *changed to* Metro-Newark!
0028-8845 Newark Beth Israel Medical Center. Journal†
0028-8853 Newark Churchman *changed to* Voice(Newark)
0028-887X Newcastle Medical Journal†
0028-8888 Newfoundland Gazette
0028-8918 Newport History
0028-8926 Newport Newstory†
0028-8942 News About Z-39 *see* 0163-626X
0028-8969 News & Letters
0028-9000 News Digest - International
0028-9019 News Explorer
0028-9035 News for Farmer Cooperatives *see* 0364-0736
0028-9043 Habitat
0028-9051 News for You
0028-9094 News from Pondy
0028-9116 News from Romania
0028-9132 News from South Africa†
0028-9140 News from the Center†
0028-9159 News from the Gutter
0028-9167 News from the Home Front *changed to* National Asthma Center News
0028-9175 News from the Library†
0028-9183 News from the Vineyards†
0028-9191 News Front
0028-9205 News in Engineering
0028-9221 News 'n Views†
0028-923X News, Notes, and Quotes
0028-9256 Newark Museum. News Notes
0028-9264 News of New York
0028-9272 News of Norway
0028-9280 News of the World
0028-9299 News of the World's Children
0028-9302 News of the Yivo
0028-9310 News on Russian Medicine and Biochemistry
0028-9329 Scholastic News Pilot
0028-9337 News Review†
0028-9353 News Trade Weekly
0028-9361 News Trails
0028-937X News-View†
0028-9388 Newsagent†
0028-9396 Newsboy
0028-940X Bangkok Standard *changed to* Living in Thailand
0028-9418 Newsette
0028-9426 Newsletter for Birdwatchers
0028-9434 Newsletter for Research in Psychology *see* 0092-394X
0028-9442 Newsletter from behind the Iron Curtain
0028-9450 Newsletter of Computer Archaeology†
0028-9469 Newsletter on Comparative Studies of Communism†
0028-9485 Newsletter on Intellectual Freedom
0028-9493 Newsletter on Isotopic Generators and Batteries†
0028-9507 Newsletter on Newsletters
0028-9523 Newsletter on the State of the Culture†
0028-9531 Newsman
0028-954X Newspaper Collector's Gazette†
0028-9558 Newspaper Controller
0028-9566 Trabajador del Periodismo
0028-9574 Newsreel†
0028-9582 Newsseeker†
0028-9590 Newstime
0028-9604 Newsweek
0028-9620 Neydhartinger Moorpost
0028-9639 Nharireyomurindi
0028-9647 Nhluvuko
0028-9655 Nia Voceto *changed to* Kalejdoskopo
0028-9663 Niagara Frontier
0028-9698 Nice Historique
0028-9744 Niederoesterreichische Landes-Landwirtschaftskammer. Amtlicher Marktbericht
0028-9752 Niederrheinische Industrie- und Handelskammer Duisberg Wesel zu Duisberg. Wirtschaftliche Mitteilungen *changed to* NiederrheinKammer
0028-9760 Niedersaechsische Wirtschaft
0028-9779 Niedersaechsische Gemeinde
0028-9787 Niedersaechsischer Staatsanzeiger
0028-9795 Niedersaechsisches Aerzteblatt
0028-9809 Niekas†
0028-9817 Nieman Reports
0028-9825 Nieuw Archief voor Wiskunde
0028-9833 Nieuw Geluid
0028-9841 Nieuw Ruimzicht *changed to* Ruimzicht
0028-985X Nieuw Tijdschrift voor Wiskunde
0028-9868 Nieuw Vlaams Tijdschrift
0028-9876 Nieuw Wereld Nieuws
0028-9892 Nieuwe Linie
0028-9906 Nieuwe Literatuur over Oorlog en Vrede *changed to* Trans-Actie
0028-9922 Nieuwe Taalgids
0028-9930 Nieuwe West Indische Gids
0028-9949 Nieuws Uit Zuid-Afrika†
0028-9965 Nieuwsblad voor de Boekhandel
0028-999X Verantwoord Levensverkeer
0029-0009 Nigeria English Studies Association Journal
0029-0017 Nigeria. Federal Office of Statistics. Digest of Statistics
0029-0025 Nigeria Lawyers' Quarterly
0029-0041 Nigeria Trade Journal
0029-005X Nigerian Christian
0029-0076 Nigerian Field
0029-0084 Nigerian Geographical Journal
0029-0092 Nigerian Journal of Economics & Social Studies
0029-0106 Nigerian Journal of Islam
0029-0114 Nigerian Journal of Science
0029-0122 Nigerian Libraries
0029-0130 Nigerian Opinion†
0029-0157 Nigerian Schoolmaster
0029-0173 Nigrizia
0029-0181 Nihon Butsuri Gakkaishi *changed to* Physics
0029-019X Science Council of Japan. Monthly Report
0029-0211 Japan Gas Association. Journal
0029-022X Society of Rubber Industry. Journal
0029-0238 Japanese Journal of Smooth Muscle Research
0029-0254 Japanese Poultry Science
0029-0262 Japanese Economic Indicators
0029-0270 Japan Society of Mechanical Engineers. Transactions
0029-0289 Mycological Society of Japan. Transactions
0029-0297 Japanese Stomatological Society. Journal
0029-0300 Folia Endocrinologica Japonica
0029-0319 Nihon no Jidosha†
0029-0327 Japan Science and Technology
0029-0335 Journal of Japanese Scientists
0029-0343 Japanese Association of Physical Medicine, Balneology and Climatology. Journal
0029-0351 Japan Plastics Journal
0029-036X Japan Refrigeration and Air Conditioning News
0029-0378 Japan Institute of Labour. Journal
0029-0386 Acta Neonatologica Japonica
0029-0394 Journal of Food Science and Technology
0029-0408 Japanese Television
0029-0416 Horological Institute of Japan. Journal
0029-0424 Nihon University Journal of Medicine
0029-0432 Nihon University. School of Dentistry. Journal
0029-0440 Niigata Medical Journal
0029-0459 Nijhoff Information
0029-0467 Nijhoff's Index Op Nederlandse en Vlaamse Periodieken†
0029-0483 Japan Chemical Industry Association Monthly
0029-0491 Nikkei Business
0029-0505 Nikkyoso Kyoiku Shimbun
0029-0513 Nikon World
0029-0521 Nillmijmeringen†
0029-0556 Nineteen†
0029-0564 Nineteenth-Century Fiction
0029-0572 Human Medicine
0029-0580 Ninth District Conditions *changed to* Federal Reserve Bank of Minneapolis. Quarterly Review
0029-0602 Japanese Association of Groundwater Hydrology. Journal
0029-0610 Society of the Science of Soil and Manure of Japan. Journal
0029-0629 Japanese Journal of Fertility and Sterility
0029-0645 Japan Broncho-Esophagological Society. Journal
0029-0653 Japan Precious Metals and Watch News
0029-067X Musashino Electrical Communication Laboratory. Review of the Electrical Communication Laboratories
0029-0688 Niranjan
0029-0696 Nirmok
0029-070X Nisarg Ane Arogya
0029-0718 Nishi Nihon Kisho Geppo†
0029-0726 Nishi Nihon Journal of Urology
0029-0734 Nissan Diesel Review
0029-0742 Nissan Graphic
0029-0769 Niti†
0029-0769 NITI
0029-0777 Nitrogen
0029-0785 Poultry Researches
0029-0793 Annales de Physique Biologique & Medicale *changed to* Journal de Biophysique et Medecine Nucleaire
0029-0807 No Eyed Monster
0029-0815 No More Fun and Games
0029-0823 No More Hiroshimas†
0029-0831 Brain and Development
0029-084X No Walls Broadsheet†
0029-0858 Nobel Hefte
0029-0882 Agriculture and Better Farming
0029-0904 Nogyo No Kairyo†
0029-0912 Agriculture and Economy
0029-0920 Noi Donne
0029-0939 Noi Giovani
0029-0947 Noise & Vibration Bulletin
0029-0963 Nok Lapja
0029-0971 Agricultural Machinery News
0029-098X Nokigu Nyusu *changed to* Agricultural Machinery News
0029-1013 Canada. Statistics Canada. Non-Ferrous Scrap Metal†
0029-1021 Non-Destructive Testing *see* 0308-9126
0029-103X Non-Foods Merchandising
0029-1056 Non-Manual Worker in the Free Labour World *changed to* International Federation of Commerical Clerical and Technical Employees. Newsletter
0029-1080 Noncello
0029-1102 Nonferrous Report†
0029-1137 Noord-Amsterdammer
0029-1145 Noord-Brabant
0029-1161 Nor Or
0029-117X Norch *changed to* Doris
0029-1188 Nord e Sud
0029-1196 Nordfriesland
0029-120X Nord Economique
0029-1218 Nord-Ostsee-Kanal
0029-1226 Norden
0029-1234 Nordens Tidning†
0029-1242 Nordeste
0029-1269 Nordhaeuser Nachrichten
0029-1277 Nordic Hydrology
0029-1285 Nordisk Administrativt Tidsskrift
0029-1307 Nordisk Betong
0029-1315 Nordisk Domssamling
0029-1323 Nordisk Exlibris Tidsskrift

1028 ISSN INDEX

0029-1331 Nordisk Fagpresse *see* 0106-0120
0029-134X Nordisk Filateli
0029-1358 Nordisk Foersaekringstidskrift
0029-1374 Nordisk Hygienisk Tidskrift *see* 0355-3140
0029-1382 Nordisk Jaernbane Tidskrift
0029-1390 Nordisk Kriminalteknisk Tidsskrift
0029-1404 Nordisk Kvaekartidskrift *see* 0345-6005
0029-1412 Nordisk Matematisk Tidskrift *changed to* Normat: Nordisk Matematisk Tidskrift
0029-1420 Nordisk Medicin
0029-1439 Nordisk Mejeri-Tidsskrift *see* 0106-7265
0029-1447 Nordisk Missions Tidsskrift *changed to* Mission
0029-1455 Nordisk Psykiatrisk Tidsskrift†
0029-1463 Nordisk Psykologi
0029-1471 Nordisk Tidskrift foer Doevundervisningen *changed to* Nordisk Tidskrift foer Hoersel och Doevundervisning
0029-148X Nordisk Tidskrift Foer Bok- och Biblioteksvaesen
0029-1501 Nordisk Tidskrift for Vetenskap, Konst och Industri
0029-1544 Nordisk Tidsskrift for Special-Optikere *changed to* Nordisk Tidsskrift for Optikere
0029-1552 Nordisk Tidsskrift for Tale og Stemme†
0029-1579 Nordisk Veterinaermedicin
0029-1587 Nordiska Institutet Foer Faergforskning. Litteraturoversigt
0029-1595 Nordost-Archiv
0029-1609 Nordwestdeutsche Gesellschaft fuer Innere Medizin. Kongressbericht
0029-1617 Nordwestdeutsches Handwerk
0029-1633 Norfolk and Western
0029-1641 Norfolk Botanical Garden Society Bulletin
0029-165X Norfolk Fair
0029-1668 Norges Apotekerforenings Tidsskrift
0029-1676 Norges Bank. Economic Bulletin
0029-1684 Norges Bondeblad *changed to* Bondebladet
0029-1692 Norges Forsvar
0029-1706 Norges Industri
0029-1714 Universitetet i Trondheim. Norges Tekniske Hoegskole. Biblioteket. Meldinger og Boklister
0029-1722 Norges Utenrikshandel
0029-1730 Norges Vel†
0029-1757 Monthly Statistics on Agriculture, Forestry and Fisheries
0029-1773 Norin Tosho Shiryo Geppo
0029-1781 Normalizace *changed to* Ceskoslovenska Standardizace
0029-179X Normalizacja
0029-1803 Normandie Industrielle
0029-1811 Normandie Protestante *changed to* Nord-Normandie
0029-182X Norois
0029-1838 Norrlaendsk Tidskrift
0029-1846 Norseman
0029-1854 Norsk Artilleri-Tidsskrift
0029-1862 Norsk Bibliografisk Bibliotek
0029-1870 Norsk Bokfortegnelse Aarskatalog
0029-1889 Norske Bokhandlertidende *changed to* Bok og Samfunn
0029-1897 Norwegian Journal of Entomology†
0029-1900 Norsk Fagfoto
0029-1919 Norsk Faktortidende
0029-1927 Norsk Farmaceutisk Selskap. Meddelelser
0029-1935 Norsk Farmaceutisk Tidsskrift
0029-1943 Norsk Filosofisk Tidsskrift
0029-1951 Norsk Geografisk Tidsskrift
0029-196X Norsk Geologisk Tidsskrift
0029-1978 Norsk Grafisk Tidsskrift
0029-1986 Norsk Hagetidend
0029-1994 Norsk Idrett
0029-2001 Norske Laegeforening. Tidsskrift
0029-201X Norsk Luftmilitaert Tidsskrift
0029-2028 Norsk Militaert Tidsskrift
0029-2044 Norsk Musikerblad
0029-2052 Norsk Pedagogisk Tidskrift
0029-2060 Norsk Retstidende
0029-2079 Norsk Sjoemannsforbund. Medlemsblad
0029-2087 Norsk Skogbruk
0029-2095 Norsk Skogindustri
0029-2109 Norsk Skole
0029-2117 Norsk Skoleblad *issued with* 0042-2029
0029-2117 Norsk Skoleblad
0029-2125 Norsk Skomakertidende
0029-2133 Norsk Skotoey *changed to* SKO
0029-2141 Norsk Slektshistorisk Tidsskrift
0029-215X Norsk Styrmandsblad
0029-2168 Norsk Tekstiltidende
0029-2176 Norsk Teologisk Tidsskrift
0029-2184 Norsk Tidende for det Industrielle Rettsvern. Del III: Moenstre
0029-2192 Norsk Tidende for det Industrielle Rettsvern. Del II: Varemerker
0029-2206 Norsk Tidende for det Industrielle Rettsvern. Del I: Patenter
0029-2214 Norsk Tidsskrift for Misjon
0029-2222 Norsk Tidsskrift for Sjovesen
0029-2249 Norsk Tidsskrift om Alkoholspoersmaalet *changed to* Tidsskrift om Edruskapsspoersmaal
0029-2257 Norsk Ukeblad
0029-2265 Norsk V V S
0029-2273 Norsk Veterinaertidsskrift
0029-229X Norske Skogforsoksvesen. Meddelelser†
0029-2303 Norske Tannlaegeforenings Tidende
0029-2311 Norske Videnskaps-Akademi. Historisk-Filosofisk Klasse. Avhandlinger Two
0029-2338 Norske Videnskaps-Akademi. Matematisk-Naturvidenkapelig Klasse. Skrifter *changed to* Norske Videnskaps-Akademi. Naturvidenskapelig Klasse. Skrifter
0029-2354 Norte
0029-2362 North
0029-2397 North American Review
0029-2419 North Carolina Anvil
0029-2427 North Carolina Architect
0029-2435 North Carolina Christian Advocate
0029-2451 North Carolina Education
0029-246X North Carolina Folklore *changed to* North Carolina Folklore Journal
0029-2478 North Carolina Foreign Language Teacher *changed to* North Carolina Foreign Language Review
0029-2494 North Carolina Historical Review
0029-2508 North Carolina Journal of Speech *changed to* North Carolina Journal of Speech Communication
0029-2516 North Carolina Law Enforcement Journal
0029-2524 North Carolina Law Review
0029-2540 North Carolina Libraries
0029-2559 North Carolina Medical Journal
0029-2567 North Carolina Museum of Art. Bulletin
0029-2575 North Carolina Museum of Art. Calendar of Art Events
0029-2591 North Carolina Public Schools†
0029-2605 North Carolina Report†
0029-2613 North Carolina School Boards Association Bulletin
0029-263X North Carolina Veterinarian
0029-2648 North Central Association Quarterly
0029-2680 North Country Libraries†
0029-2699 North Country Reference & Research Resources Council. Newsletter
0029-2702 North Dakota Employment Trends†
0029-2710 North Dakota History
0029-2729 North Dakota Industrial News *changed to* North Dakota B I D D for Progress
0029-2737 North Dakota Journal of Education
0029-2745 North Dakota Law Review
0029-2753 North Dakota Music Educator
0029-2761 North Dakota Outdoors
0029-277X North Dakota Quarterly
0029-2788 North Dakota Rural Electric Magazine *changed to* North Dakota R E C Magazine
0029-280X North East Coast Institution of Engineers and Shipbuilders. Transactions
0029-2818 North East Group for the Study of Labour History Bulletin
0029-2842 North Jersey Business Review *changed to* Jersey Business Review
0029-2850 North Jersey Highlander
0029-2877 North Loop News
0029-2885 East Midlands Bibliography
0029-2907 North Texas Retailer *changed to* Retailer and Marketing News
0029-2923 North West Lancashire Chamber of Commerce Journal *changed to* Forum
0029-294X North Wind-Skagway's Newspaper†
0029-2958 North Woods Call
0029-2982 Northeast Business
0029-2990 Northeast Horseman
0029-3032 Northeastern News
0029-3067 Northern Circuit†
0029-3083 Northern Engineer
0029-3091 Northern Illinois University Business Report†
0029-3105 Northern Ireland Legal Quarterly
0029-3113 Northern Ireland Libraries *see* 0023-9542
0029-313X Northern Junket
0029-3148 Northern Lights
0029-3156 Northern Logger and Timber Processer
0029-3164 Northern Miner
0029-3172 Northern Minnesota Educator
0029-3180 Northern Minnesota Review†
0029-3199 Northern Neighbors
0029-3210 Northern Railway Newsletter
0029-3253 Northian
0029-3261 Northland
0029-327X Northliner Magazine
0029-3296 Northwest Anthropological Research Notes
0029-330X Northwest Architect *changed to* Architecture Minnesota
0029-3326 Northwest Association of Secondary and Higher Schools. Committee on Research and Service. Newsletter. *changed to* Northwest Association of Schools and Colleges, Committee on Research and Service. Newsletter
0029-3334 Northwest Community Hospital Medical Bulletin
0029-3350 Northwest Farm Equipment Journal
0029-3369 Northwest Folklore†
0029-3393 Northwest Motor
0029-3407 Northwest Ohio Quarterly
0029-3415 Northwest Passage
0029-3423 Northwest Review
0029-3431 Salmon-Trout Steelheader
0029-344X Northwest Science
0029-3458 Northwest Skier *changed to* Northwest Skier and Northwest Sports
0029-3466 Northwest Sportsman†
0029-3474 Northwest Technocrat
0029-3482 Northwestern Engineer
0029-3490 Northwestern Jeweler
0029-3504 Northwestern Lumber Dealer *see* 0092-0681
0029-3512 Northwestern Lutheran
0029-3520 Northwestern Management Reporter†
0029-3539 Northwestern Miller†
0029-3547 Unigard Mutuality†
0029-3555 Northwestern Ontario Timber Operators' Association. Log Book†
0029-3563 Northwestern Report†
0029-3571 Northwestern University Law Review
0029-358X Northwestern University Medical School Magazine *changed to* Northwestern University Medical Center Magazine
0029-3601 Norveg
0029-361X Norvega Esperantisto
0029-3628 Norway
0029-3636 Norway. Statistisk Sentralbyraa. Statistisk Maanedshefte /Monthly Bulletin of Statistics
0029-3644 Norwegian American Commerce
0029-3652 Norwegian Archaeological Review
0029-3660 Norwegian Commercial Banks Financial Review
0029-3679 Norwegian Fishing and Maritime News *changed to* Maritime News
0029-3709 Norwegian Shipping News
0029-3717 Nos Lettres *changed to* Nos Lettres. Informations
0029-3725 Nos Oiseaux
0029-3741 Theatre Amateur *see* 0398-0049
0029-375X Nosotros
0029-3768 Nostra Voce
0029-3776 Nostre Scuole
0029-3784 Nostri Cani
0029-3792 Nostri Ragazzi
0029-3806 Nostro Mondo†
0029-3814 Nostro Tempo
0029-3822 Nota Bene
0029-3857 Notaro
0029-3865 Centro Brasileiro de Pesquisas. Fisicas. Notas de Fisica†
0029-3873 C E N I D. Notas Informativas
0029-3881 Notas Sobre la Economia y el Desarrollo de America Latina
0029-389X Notatki Plockie
0029-3903 Note di Pastorale Giovanile
0029-392X Note Stiri de Cenaclu
0029-3946 Notes a Tempo
0029-3954 Notes Africaines
0029-3962 Notes and Abstracts of American and International Education
0029-3970 Notes and Queries
0029-3997 France. Commissariat a l'Energie Atomique. Notes d'Information
0029-4004 Notes et Etudes Documentaires
0029-4012 F E E Notes
0029-4020 Tarlton Law Library. Notes
0029-4039 Notes from Underground
0029-4047 Notes on Contemporary Literature
0029-4055 Notes on Current Politics *see* 0307-7039
0029-4063 Commercial Bank of Greece. Notes on Foreign Trade *changed to* Commercial Bank of Greece. Notes on Foreign Trade and Main Economic Data
0029-4071 Notes on Mississippi Writers
0029-408X Notes on Selected Acquisitions†
0029-4098 Notes on Tin
0029-4101 Notes on Water Pollution *see* 0307-6652
0029-411X Nothing Doing in London†
0029-4128 Noticia Geomorfologica
0029-4136 Noticiarie a Imprensa Falada e Escrita
0029-4144 Noticiario-Odontologia
0029-4152 Noticias
0029-4160 Fundacion Servicio para el Agricultor. Noticias Agricolas
0029-4187 Noticias de Suecia†
0029-4195 Noticias del Trabajo
0029-4225 Noticias Medicas
0029-425X Noticiero de la Fe
0029-4306 Notitiae
0029-4314 Notiziario Agricolo
0029-4322 Notiziario d'Arte
0029-4330 Notiziario di Aviazione Civile *changed to* Aviazione Civile
0029-4349 Notiziario della Lega Italiana per la Lotta Contro i Tumori e dei Centri Oncologici†
0029-4357 Notiziario di Aviazione†
0029-4365 Notiziario di Caccia e Pesca-Tiro a Volo
0029-4373 Notiziario Famiglie Numerose
0029-4381 I S T A T. Notiziario
0029-439X Notiziario Medico Farmaceutico
0029-4403 Notiziario Orto Frutticolo dei Prodotti Agricolo-Alimentari *changed to* Notiziario Ortofrutticolo e dei Prodotti Agricolo-Alimentari e Floricoli
0029-442X Notiziario Tecnico Worthington
0029-4438 Notizie Olivetti
0029-4446 Notizie per gli Industriali della Provincia di Siena *changed to* Informatore Industriale
0029-4454 Notizie Rapide *changed to* E D P Notizie
0029-4462 Notnaya Letopis'
0029-4470 Notornis

ISSN INDEX 1029

0029-4497	Notre Dame Alumnus *changed to* Notre Dame Magazine	0029-5671	Recherche	0029-702X	O E C D Foreign Trade Statistics. Series A *changed to* Organization for Economic Cooperation and Development. Statistics of Foreign Trade. Series A: Monthly Bulletin/ Statistiques du Commerce Exterieur. Serie A: Bulletin Mensuel
0029-4500	Notre Dame English Journal	0029-568X	Nucleus		
0029-4519	Notre Dame Journal of Education†	0029-5690	Nucleus		
0029-4527	Notre Dame Journal of Formal Logic	0029-5701	Nuestra Arquitectura		
0029-4535	Notre Dame Lawyer	0029-571X	Nuestra Historia		
0029-4543	Notre Dame Technical Review	0029-5728	Nuestra Industria. Revista Economica†		
0029-4551	Notre Formation *changed to* Objectif Formation	0029-5736	Nuestra Industria. Revista Tecnologia†	0029-7038	Organization for Economic Cooperation and Development. Liaison Bulletin Between Research and Training Institutes
		0029-5736	Revista Tecnologica		
0029-456X	Notre Temps	0029-5752	Nuestro Amigo		
0029-4578	Notres	0029-5760	Nuestro Anhelo		
0029-4586	Nottingham French Studies	0029-5787	Nuestro Holando	0029-7054	O E C D Observer
0029-4594	Notulae Entomologicae	0029-5795	Nuestro Tiempo	0029-7062	Organization for Economic Cooperation and Development. Provisional Oil Statistics/Statistiques Petrolieres Provisoires *changed to* Organization for Economic Cooperation and Development. Oil Statistics/Statistiques Petrolieres
0029-4608	Notulae Naturae	0029-5809	Nuestros Ninos		
0029-4616	Noturno†	0029-5825	Nueva Forma		
0029-4624	Nous	0029-585X	Nueva Pompeya		
0029-4632	Nous Deux Presente	0029-5868	Nueva Revista de Filologia Hispanica		
0029-4659	Nouveau Cinemonde†	0029-5884	Nuevo Ambiente *changed to* Habitat		
0029-4675	Nouveau Journal de Charpente-Menuiserie-Parquets	0029-5914	Nuklearna Energija		
		0029-5922	Nukleonika	0029-7070	O. E. C. T. A. Review *changed to* O. E. C. T. A. Reporter
0029-4705	Alliance Israelite Universelle en France. Oeuvre Scolaire. Nouveaux Cahiers	0029-5949	Numaga		
		0029-5973	Numen	0029-7089	O G B-Bildungsfunktionaer†
0029-4713	Le Nouvel Observateur	0029-5981	International Journal for Numerical Methods in Engineering	0029-7097	O I R T Information
0029-4721	Nouvelle Critique			0029-7119	O.I.V. Bulletin
0029-4748	Nouvelle Famille Educatrice	0029-599X	Numerische Mathematik	0029-7135	O L A Bulletin
0029-4756	Nouvelle France	0029-6007	Numero Economique du Vendredi	0029-7143	O L O G O S
0029-4764	Nouvelle Frontiere	0029-6015	Numisma	0029-7151	O L W
0029-4772	Nouvelle Hygiene	0029-6023	Numismatic Circular	0029-716X	O M I Farm News
0029-4780	Nouvelle Revue d'Optique *see* 0150-536X	0029-6031	Numismatic Literature	0029-7178	O. M. I. Missions†
		0029-604X	Numismatic News	0029-7194	O M V - Zeitschrift
0029-4799	Nouvelle Revue Franc-Comtoise	0029-6058	Numismatic Scrapbook Magazine†	0029-7208	O P Z-Dokumentation *changed to* O P W Z-Dokumentation
0029-4802	Nouvelle Revue Francaise	0029-6058	Numismatic Scrapbook *see* 0010-0447		
0029-4810	Nouvelle Revue Francaise d'Hematologie	0029-6066	Numismatic Society of India. Journal	0029-7216	O R M P Newsletter
		0029-6074	Numismaticke Listy	0029-7224	Cahiers O.R.S.T.O.M. Serie Entomologie Medicale et Parasitologie
0029-4837	Nouvelle Revue Pedagogique†	0029-6082	Numismatisches Nachrichtenblatt		
0029-4845	Nouvelle Revue Theologique	0029-6090	Numismatist	0029-7232	Cahiers O.R.S.T.O.M. Serie Geologie
0029-4861	Nouvelles Benelux Nieuws *changed to* Benelux Nouvelles/Nieuws	0029-6112	Nuntempa Bulgario†	0029-7240	Cahiers O.R.S.T.O.M. Serie Hydrobiologie *changed to* Revue d'Hydrobiologie Tropicale
		0029-6139	Nuorten Sarka		
0029-487X	Nouvelles de Chretiente	0029-6147	Nuova Antologia		
0029-4888	Nouvelles de l'Estampe	0029-6155	Nuova Corrente	0029-7259	Cahiers O.R.S.T.O.M. Serie Pedologie
0029-490X	Nouvelles Esthetiques	0029-6163	Nuova Critica	0029-7275	O S S T F. Bulletin *changed to* O S S T F. Forum
0029-4918	Nouvelles Etudes Marxistes	0029-6171	Nuova Economia		
0029-4926	Nouvelles Graphiques	0029-618X	Nuova Era	0029-7283	O S U Research Review†
0029-4934	Nouvelles Industrielles et Commerciales et de Midi-Pyrenees	0029-6198	Nuova Gazzetta di Calabria	0029-7291	O T C Chart Manual
		0029-6201	Nuova Rassegna	0029-7305	O. T. C. Market Chronicle *see* 0360-1773
0029-4950	Nouvelles Universitaires Europeennes	0029-621X	Nuova Rivista Internazionale		
0029-4969	Nova	0029-6228	Nuova Rivista Musicale Italiana	0029-7313	O T F Reporter *see* 0316-3903
0029-4977	Nova†	0029-6236	Nuova Rivista Storica	0029-7321	O. T. Kaner
0029-4985	Nova	0029-6244	Nuova Rivista Tributaria	0029-733X	O T O†
0029-4993	Nova	0029-6252	Nuova Tecnica Ospedaliera *changed to* Tecnica Ospedaliera	0029-7356	Oak Leaf
0029-5000	Nova Acta Regiae Societatis Scientiarum Upsaliensis			0029-7372	Oak Ridge Associated Universities. Newsletter
		0029-6260	Nuova Venezia		
0029-5019	Nova Ecclesia	0029-6279	Nuova Veterinaria†	0029-7380	Oakhamian
0029-5027	Nova et Vetera	0029-6287	Nuovi Annali di Igiene e Microbiologia	0029-7399	Aomori Prefecture. Monthly Report of Meteorology
0029-5035	Nova Hedwigia	0029-6295	Nuovi Argomenti		
0029-5051	Nova Proizvodnja	0029-6309	Nuovo Agora Omaggio	0029-7402	Die Oase
0029-506X	Nova Scotia *changed to* Nova Scotia Times	0029-6317	Nuovo Bollettino Bibliografico Sardo	0029-7410	Oasis
		0029-6325	Nuovo Cantiere	0029-7410	Expression *see* 0029-7410
0029-5078	Nova Scotia Export Quarterly†	0029-6333	Nuovo Chirone	0029-7429	Ob/Gyn Digest *see* 0148-5164
0029-5094	Nova Scotia Medical Bulletin	0029-635X	Nuovo Didaskaleion†	0029-7437	Ob. Gyn. News
0029-5108	Nova Scotia Teachers Union Newsletter *see* 0382-408X	0029-6368	Nuovo Diritto	0029-7461	Savez Geodetskih Inzenjera i Geometara Hrvatske. Obavijesti *changed to* Savez Geodetskih Inzenjera i Geometara Hrvatske. Geodet
		0029-6376	Nuovo Mezzogiorno		
0029-5116	Novas de Alegria	0029-6384	Nuovo Osservatore		
0029-5124	Novaya i Noveishaya Istoriya	0029-6406	Nursery Business		
0029-5132	Novel: A Forum on Fiction	0029-6414	Nursery Days	0029-747X	Obcan
0029-5140	Novena *see* 0308-0617	0029-6422	Nursery World	0029-7488	Oberflaeche *changed to* Oberflaeche und J O T
0029-5159	Novidades Fotoptica	0029-6430	Nurseryman and Garden Centre		
0029-5167	Novinar	0029-6457	Nursing†	0029-7496	Oberfraenkische Wirtschaft
0029-5175	Novinarstvo	0029-6465	Nursing Clinics of North America	0029-7518	Oberlin Alumni Magazine
0029-5191	Novinky Literatury: Prehled Informativni Literatury	0029-6473	Nursing Forum	0029-7526	Oberlin Review
		0029-649X	Nursing Homes	0029-7534	Oberoesterreichische F P O-Nachrichten fuer Freiheit und Recht
0029-5205	Novinky Literatury: Zdravotnictvi	0029-6503	Nursing Journal of India		
0029-5248	Noviny Vnitrniho Obchodu	0029-6511	Nursing Mirror	0029-7542	Oberoesterreichische Gemeindezeitung
0029-5264	Novitur†	0029-652X	Nursing News *changed to* Connecticut Nursing News	0029-7550	Oberoesterreichische Heimatblaetter
0029-5272	Novosti			0029-7569	Oberoesterreichisches Reise-Journal
0029-5280	Novoe Vremya	0029-6538	New Hampshire Nursing News	0029-7585	Obiter Dicta
0029-5302	Novy Orient	0029-6546	Nursing News	0029-7593	Objective: Justice
0029-5310	Novy Shliakh	0029-6554	Nursing Outlook	0029-7615	Objets et Mondes
0029-5329	Novyi Mir	0029-6562	Nursing Research	0029-7623	Obogashchenie Rud
0029-5337	Novyj Zhurnal	0029-6570	Nursing Standard	0029-764X	Andragogija
0029-5345	Now	0029-6589	Nursing Times	0029-7658	Obrero Ferroviario
0029-5353	Now *changed to* Focus on Montana Agriculture	0029-6597	Nutida Musik	0029-7666	Observateur des Assurances
		0029-6600	Nutrition *see* 0308-4329	0029-7674	Observation, Opinion, Orientation *changed to* Poumons
0029-5388	Nowe Drogi	0029-6619	Nutrition Abstracts and Reviews *see* 0309-1295		
0029-5396	Nowe Rolnictwo			0029-7682	Belgium. Institut Royal Meteorologique. Observations Climatologiques
0029-540X	Nowotwory	0029-6619	Nutrition Abstracts and Reviews *see* 0309-135X		
0029-5426	Ag-Chem Age			0029-7690	Belgium. Institut Royal Meteorologique. Observations d'Ozone
0029-5442	Nsanja Ya Olonda	0029-6627	Nutrition Information Bulletin *see* 0309-0531		
0029-5450	Nuclear Technology			0029-7704	Observatory
0029-5469	Nuclear Canada	0029-6635	Nutrition Reports International	0029-7712	Observer
0029-5477	Nuclear Data *see* 0092-640X	0029-6643	Nutrition Reviews	0029-7720	Observer†
0029-5477	Nuclear Data *see* 0090-3752	0029-6651	Nutrition Society, Proceedings	0029-7739	Observer
0029-5485	Nuclear Energy *changed to* Nuclear Engineer	0029-666X	Nutrition Today	0029-7747	Stern College for Women. Observer
		0029-6686	Nutzfahrzeug	0029-7763	Obshchestvennye Nauki v Uzbekistane
0029-5493	Nuclear Engineering and Design	0029-6694	Nuus Oor Afrika	0029-7771	Obst- und Weinbau *changed to* Obst - Wein - Garten
0029-5507	Nuclear Engineering International	0029-6708	Nuwe Protestant		
0029-5515	Nuclear Fusion	0029-6716	Nux	0029-7798	Obst und Garten
0029-5523	Nuclear India	0029-6724	Ny Boky No Loharanom-Pandrosoana†	0029-781X	Revista de Pediatrie, Obstetrica, Ginecologie. Obstetrica si Ginecologie
0029-5531	Nuclear Industry	0029-6732	NY Fremtid		
0029-554X	Nuclear Instruments and Methods	0029-6759	Ny Politik	0029-7828	Obstetrical and Gynecological Survey
0029-5558	Nuclear Magnetic Resonance Abstracts Service *changed to* Nuclear Magnetic Resonance Literature-Abstracts & Index	0029-6783	Nye Bonytt	0029-7836	Obstetricia y Ginecologia Latino Americana
		0029-6791	Nyelvtudomanyi Kozlemenyek		
		0029-6813	Nykytekstiili	0029-7844	Obstetrics and Gynecology
		0029-683X	Nyt for Hospitalslaboranter	0029-7852	Obzor
0029-5574	Nuclear News	0029-6848	Nyt Fra Historien	0029-7860	Obzornik
0029-5582	Nuclear Physics *changed to* Nuclear Physics, Section A	0029-6864	Norwegian Journal of Zoology†	0029-7879	Occident†
		0029-6872	O A C Newsletter *see* 0361-2678	0029-7887	Occult Gazette *changed to* Royal Cosmic Theology
0029-5582	Nuclear Physics *see* 0550-3213	0029-6880	O A G Pocket Flight Guide		
0029-5604	Nuclear Safety	0029-6902	O A S Chronicle†	0029-7909	Occupational Hazards
0029-5612	Nuclear Science Abstracts†	0029-6910	O & M	0029-7917	Occupational Health
0029-5620	Nuclear Science Information of Japan	0029-6953	Biologico	0029-7925	Occupational Health Newsletter *changed to* Environmental Health and Safety News
0029-5639	Nuclear Science and Engineering	0029-6961	O C L A E Revista		
0029-5647	Nuclear Science Journal				
0029-5655	Nuclear Standards News				

0029-7933 Occupational Health Nursing
0029-7941 Occupational Health Review†
0029-7968 U.S. Bureau of Labor Statistics. Occupational Outlook Quarterly
0029-7976 Occupational Psychology *see* 0305-8107
0029-7984 Occupational Safety and Health Abstracts *see* 0302-7651
0029-800X British Journal of Occupational Therapy
0029-8018 Ocean Engineering
0029-8026 Ocean Industry
0029-8034 Ocean Living
0029-8042 Ocean Oil Weekly Report
0029-8069 Ocean Science News
0029-8077 Oceania
0029-8085 Oceanic Citation Journal *see* 0093-6901
0029-8093 Oceanic Index *see* 0093-6901
0029-8115 Oceanic Linguistics
0029-8123 Oceanite
0029-8131 Oceanographical Society of Japan. Journal
0029-814X Oceanologia et Limnologia Sinica†
0029-8158 Oceanology†
0029-8174 Oceans
0029-8182 Oceanus
0029-8190 Ochanomizu Women's University. Natural Science Report
0029-8204 Ochrana Prirody *changed to* Pamatky a Priroda
0029-8220 Ochrona Pracy
0029-8239 Ochrona Roslin
0029-8247 Ochrona Zabytkow
0029-8263 Ocrotirea Naturii si a Mediului Inconjurator
0029-8271 Octagon
0029-828X Octobre
0029-8328 Oculus
0029-8336 Odbrana
0029-8344 Odbrana i Zastita
0029-8360 Der Odenwald
0029-8387 Odjek
0029-8395 Odontoiatria
0029-8409 Odontologia
0029-8417 Odontologia Chilena
0029-8425 Odontologia Uruguaya
0029-8433 Odontological Bulletin
0029-8441 Odontologisk Revy *changed to* Swedish Dental Journal
0029-845X Scandinavian Journal of Dental Research
0029-8468 Odontologiska Foreningens Tidskrift
0029-8476 Odontologiste des Hopitaux†
0029-8484 Odontology
0029-8492 Odontoprotesti
0029-8506 Odontostomatological Progress
0029-8514 Odrodzenie i Reformacja w Polsce
0029-8522 Odu
0029-8530 Odvjetnik
0029-8549 Oecologia
0029-8557 Oecologica Plantarum *see* 0243-7651
0029-8573 Das Oeffentliche Gesundheitswesen
0029-8581 Das Oeffentliche Haushaltswesen in Oesterreich
0029-859X Die Oeffentliche Verwaltung
0029-8603 Oeffentliche Wirtschaft *changed to* Oeffentliche Wirtschaft und Gemeinwirtschaft
0029-862X Oeil
0029-8638 Oekonomik Gartenbau†
0029-8646 Oekonomisk Kronik
0029-8654 Oekumenische Rundschau
0029-8662 Oel- und Gasfeuerung
0029-8689 Oel
0029-8697 Oelhydraulik und Pneumatik
0029-8700 Oil World
0029-8719 Oertliche Raumheizung†
0029-8727 Oes†
0029-8735 Oeste†
0029-8751 Oesterreich-Nederland
0029-876X Oesterreichische Krankenhaus Zeitung
0029-8778 Academia
0029-8786 Oesterreichische Aerztezeitung
0029-8832 Oesterreichische Akademie der Wissenschaften. Philosophisch-Historische Klasse. Sitzungsberichte
0029-8840 Oesterreichischer Alpenverein. Akademische Sektion Graz. Mitteilungen
0029-8859 Oesterreichische Apotheker-Zeitung
0029-8867 Oesterreichische Arbeitsgemeinschaft fuer Rehabilitation. Information
0029-8875 Der Oesterreichische Arzt
0029-8883 Oesterreichische Autorenzeitung
0029-8891 Oesterreichische Bauzeitung
0029-8905 Oesterreichische Bauernzeitung
0029-8913 Oesterreichische Bibliographie
0029-8921 Oesterreichische Blaetter fuer Gewerblichen Rechtsschutz und Urheberrecht
0029-8956 Brandverhuetung
0029-8964 Oesterreichische Buchbinder, Kartonage-, Etui-, Kassetten- und Papierwarenerzeuger
0029-8972 Oesterreichische Camping & Caravaning Revue *changed to* Oesterreichische Camping Revue
0029-8980 Oesterreichische Caritas Zeitschrift *changed to* Caritas
0029-8999 Oesterreichische Dachdecker- und Pflasterer-Zeitung *changed to* Dach und Wand Abdichtung
0029-9006 Oesterreichische Dentisten-Zeitschrift
0029-9030 Die Oesterreichische Feuerwehr
0029-9057 Der Oesterreichische Filmamateur
0029-9065 Der Oesterreichische Friseur
0029-9073 Strassengueterverkehr
0029-9081 Oesterreichische Fussbodenzeitung
0029-909X Oesterreichische Galerie. Mitteilungen
0029-9103 Oesterreichische Gastgewerbe-Zeitung
0029-9111 Oesterreichische Gefluegelwirtschaft
0029-912X Oesterreichische Gemeinde-Zeitung
0029-9138 Oesterreichische Geographische Gesellschaft. Mitteilungen
0029-9146 Oesterreichische Gesellschaft fuer Filmwissenschaft. Mitteilungen *changed to* Oesterreichische Gesellschaft fuer Filmwissenschaft, Kommunikations- und Medienforschung. Mitteilungen
0029-9154 Oesterreichische Gesellschaft fuer Holzforschung. Schrifttumskarteidienst
0029-9162 Oesterreichische Glaserzeitung
0029-9170 Das Oesterreichische Graphische Gewerbe
0029-9189 Oesterreichische Hausbesitz
0029-9200 Die Oesterreichische Hoehere Schule
0029-9219 Oesterreichische Ingenieur Zeitschrift *changed to* Oe I Z. Oesterreichische Ingenieur Zeitschrift
0029-9227 Der Oesterreichische Installateur
0029-9235 Oesterreichische Installateurzeitung
0029-9243 Der Oesterreichische Jungarbeiter
0029-9251 Oesterreichische Juristen-Zeitung
0029-926X Oesterreichische Kunststoff Zeitung *changed to* Oesterreichische Kunststoff-Zeitschrift
0029-9278 Laenderbank Boerseninformationen
0029-9286 Oesterreichische Leder- und Haeutewirtschaft
0029-9294 Oesterreichische Mechaniker *changed to* Mechanik
0029-9308 Oesterreichische Monatshefte
0029-9316 Oesterreichische Musikzeitschrift
0029-9324 Oesterreichische Naehmaschinen- und Fahrrad-Zeitung *changed to* Oesterreichische Naehmaschinen- und Zweirad-Zeitung
0029-9332 Oesterreichische Nationalbank.Mitteilungen des Direktoriums
0029-9340 Oesterreichische Notariats-Zeitung
0029-9359 Oesterreichische Numismatische Gesellschaft. Mitteilungen
0029-9367 C W F
0029-9375 Oesterreichische Osthefte
0029-9383 Oesterreichische Paedagogische Warte *changed to* K L O E Impulse
0029-9391 Oesterreichische Papier-Zeitung
0029-9405 Oesterreichische Raumausstatterzeitung
0029-9421 Oesterreichische Schachzeitung†
0029-943X Oesterreichische Schlosser-und Maschinenbauerzeitung†
0029-9448 Oesterreichische Schmiede-Zeitung†
0029-9456 Oesterreichische Schuhhaendler *changed to* Schuh-Revue
0029-9464 Oesterreichische Schuhmacher-Zeitung *changed to* Der Oesterreichische Schuhmarkt
0029-9499 Der Oesterreichische Spengler und Kupferschmied
0029-9502 Oesterreichische Foerster Zeitung
0029-9510 Oesterreichische Steuer und Wirtschaftskartei
0029-9529 Oesterreichische Steuer-Zeitung
0029-9537 Austria Tabakwerke A. G. Fachliche Mitteilungen†
0029-9545 Oesterreichische Textil-Mitteilungen
0029-9553 Oesterreichische Textil Zeitschrift *changed to* Mode und Material
0029-9561 Oesterreichische Trafikanten-Zeitung
0029-957X Der Oesterreichische Volkswirt
0029-9588 Oesterreichische Wasserwirtschaft
0029-9596 Oesterreichische Zahnaerzte-Zeitung
0029-960X Oesterreichische Zeitschrift fuer Aussenpolitik
0029-9618 Oe Z E
0029-9626 Oesterreichische Zeitschrift fuer Kunst und Denkmalpflege
0029-9634 Oesterreichische Zeitschrift fuer Oeffentliches Recht. Neue Folge *see* 0378-3073
0029-9642 Oesterreichische Zeitschrift fuer Stomatologie
0029-9650 Oesterreichische Zeitschrift fuer Vermessungswesen *changed to* Oesterreichische Zeitschrift fuer Vermessungswesen und Photogrammetrie
0029-9669 Oesterreichische Zeitschrift fuer Volkskunde
0029-9677 Oesterreichische Zimmermeister
0029-9685 Oesterreichische Zoll und Steuer Nachrichten
0029-9693 Oesterreichischen Arbeitsgemeinschaft fuer Ur- und Fruhgeschichte. Mitteilungen
0029-9707 Oesterreichisches Institut fuer Raumplanung. Mitteilungen
0029-9715 Oesterreichischer Alpenverein. Mitteilungen
0029-9723 Oesterreichischer Blindenverband. Mitteilungen
0029-9731 Oesterreichischer Brieftaubensport
0029-974X Kameradschaft der Wiener Panzer-Division. Mitteilungsblatt
0029-9758 Der Oesterreichische Kleingaertner
0029-9766 Oesterreichischer Kleintierzuechter
0029-9774 Oesterreichischer Luftfahrt Pressedienst
0029-9782 Oesterreichischer Markenanzeiger
0029-9790 Oesterreichischer Personenverkehr
0029-9812 Oesterreichischer Yachtsport
0029-9820 Oesterreichisches Archiv fuer Kirchenrecht
0029-9839 Oesterreichisches Bank-Archiv
0029-9847 Oesterreichisches Cafe Journal
0029-9855 Elektro & Radio *changed to* Elektro Journal
0029-9863 Oesterreichisches Forschungsinstitut fuer Wirtschaft und Politik. Berichte und Informationen
0029-988X Oesterreichisches Hotel-und Gastronomie-Journal
0029-9898 Oesterreichisches Institut fuer Wirtschaftsforschung. Monatsberichte
0029-9901 Oesterreichisches Jugendrotkreuz. Arbeitsblaetter
0029-991X Oesterreichisches Klerus Blatt
0029-9928 Oesterreichisches Kolpingblatt
0029-9936 Leben-Wirken *changed to* Mensch und Ziel
0029-9944 Oesterreichisches Patentblatt
0029-9952 Oesterreichisches Standesamt
0029-9960 Austria. Statistisches Zentralamt. Statistische Nachrichten
0029-9987 Oesterreichs Fischerei
0029-9995 Oesterreichs Paddelsport
0030-0004 Oesterreichs Presse, Werbung, Graphik
0030-0012 Oesterreichs Weidwerk
0030-0047 Of Consuming Interest
0030-0055 Of Sea and Shore
0030-0071 Off Our Backs
0030-0098 Offene Kreis†
0030-0101 Offene Tore
0030-011X Offene Tueren
0030-0128 Office
0030-0136 Office Administration *see* 0001-835X
0030-0144 Office Products *changed to* Office Products Dealer
0030-0179 Office Equipment & Methods
0030-0187 Office Equipment News
0030-0217 Management in Action *see* 0025-1747
0030-0233 Office Products Dealer†
0030-0241 Office Products News
0030-025X Office Supervisor's Bulletin
0030-0268 Officer
0030-0276 Official Airline Guide. North American Quick Reference Edition
0030-0284 Official Board Markets
0030-0292 Official Container Directory
0030-0306 Official Detective Stories
0030-0314 Official Gazette of Guyana
0030-0322 Official Guide of the Railways and Steam Navigation Lines of the United States, Puerto Rico, Canada, Mexico and Cuba, Airline Schedules *see* 0190-6704
0030-0330 Official Journal (Patents)
0030-0349 Official Journal of Industrial and Commercial Property
0030-0357 Official Motor Freight Guide
0030-0365 Official Oil in North Dakota *see* 0363-2512
0030-0373 Official Railway Equipment Register
0030-039X Officiel de la Couleur
0030-0403 Officiel de la Couture et de la Mode de Paris
0030-0411 Officiel de la Droguerie
0030-042X Officiel de la Librairie†
0030-0438 Officiel de la Photographie et du Cinema
0030-0446 Officiel de l'Ameublement; Ameublement Informations
0030-0454 Officiel de l'Automobile
0030-0462 Officiel des Plastiques et du Caoutchouc
0030-0500 Officiel des Spectacles
0030-0519 Officiel du Cycle, du Motocycle et de la Motoculture
0030-0551 Officier de Reserve *changed to* Ares
0030-0586 Offizieller Salzburger Wochenspiegel
0030-0594 Offsetpraxis
0030-0608 Offshore
0030-0624 Oficina Moderna
0030-0632 Oficina Sanitaria Panamericana. Boletin
0030-0667 Revista de Chirurgie, Oncologie, O.R.L., Radiologie, Stomatologie. Oftalmologie
0030-0675 Oftal'mologicheskii Zhurnal
0030-0683 Ofthalmologika Chronika
0030-0691 Ogam
0030-0705 Oggi
0030-0713 Oglas za Pomorce
0030-0721 Ogonek
0030-073X Ogoniok
0030-0756 Ogrodnictwo
0030-0764 Ohio Academy of Science News
0030-0772 Ohio AFL-CIO News and Views
0030-0780 Ohio Archivist *changed to* Society of Ohio Archivists Newsletter
0030-0799 Ohio Association of School Librarians' Bulletin *changed to* Ohio Media Spectrum
0030-0861 Ohio Contractor
0030-0888 Ohio Family Physician News
0030-090X Ohio Florists Association. Bulletin
0030-0918 Ohio Forestry Association. Bulletin
0030-0926 Ohio Grange
0030-0934 Ohio History
0030-0950 Ohio Journal of Science
0030-0977 Ohio Library Trustee
0030-0985 Ohio Motorist
0030-0993 Ohio Nurses Review
0030-1019 Ohio Parent Teacher *see* 0199-0918
0030-1027 Ohio Pharmacist

ISSN	Title
0030-1043	Ohio Report on Research and Development in Biology, Agriculture and Home Economics *changed to* Ohio Report on Research and Development in Agriculture, Home Economics, and Natural Resources
0030-1051	Ohio Researcher†
0030-1078	Ohio School Boards Journal
0030-1086	Ohio Schools
0030-1094	Ohio State Bar Association Report
0030-1116	Ohio State Lantern
0030-1124	Ohio State Medical Journal
0030-1132	Ohio State University. College of Medicine. Journal
0030-1140	Ohio State University. Institute of Polar Studies. Newsletter†
0030-1159	Ohio State University Libraries Notes†
0030-1167	Ohio State University Monthly
0030-1183	Ohio Tavern News
0030-1191	Ohio Trucking News *changed to* Ohio Truck Times
0030-1205	Ohio University Post *changed to* Post
0030-1213	Ohio Veterinarian *changed to* Ohio Veterinary Medical Association. Newsletter
0030-1221	Ohio Wesleyan Magazine
0030-123X	Ohio Woodlands/Conservation in Action
0030-1248	Ohioana Quarterly
0030-1256	Ohio's Health
0030-1264	Ohmio†
0030-1272	Ohnicek
0030-1299	Oikos
0030-1302	Oikoumenikon
0030-1310	Oil-Lifestream of Progress
0030-1329	Oil & Chemical Worker
0030-1337	Oil and Colour Chemists' Association. Journal
0030-1345	Oil & Gas Discoveries†
0030-1353	Oil, Gas & Petrochem Equipment
0030-1361	Oil and Gas Firing *see* 0307-1219
0030-1388	Oil and Gas Journal
0030-1396	Oil and Gas Tax Quarterly
0030-1418	Oil Caravan Weekly
0030-1426	Oil, Chemical and Atomic Workers International Union. Union News
0030-1442	Oil Mill Gazetter
0030-1450	Oil News
0030-1469	Oil, Paint and Drug Reporter *see* 0090-0907
0030-1485	Oil Technologists Association of India. Journal
0030-1507	Oils and Oilseeds Journal
0030-1515	Oilweek
0030-1523	Oise Agricole
0030-1531	Oiseau et la Revue Francaise d'Ornithologie
0030-154X	Okajima's Folia Anatomica Japonica Medical Association of Okayama. Journal
0030-1558	Mathematical Journal of Okayama University
0030-1566	Okeanologiya
0030-1574	Okhota i Okhotnich'e Khozyaistvo
0030-1582	Okhrana Truda i Sotsial'noe Strakhovanie
0030-1590	Okki
0030-1612	Oklahoma Union Farmer
0030-1620	Oklahoma
0030-1639	Oklahoma Banker
0030-1647	Oklahoma Bar Association. Journal *changed to* Oklahoma Bar Journal
0030-1655	Oklahoma Beverage News
0030-1663	Oklahoma Business Bulletin
0030-1671	Oklahoma C. P. A†
0030-168X	Oklahoma Cowman
0030-1698	Oklahoma Current Farm Economics
0030-1701	Oklahoma Daily
0030-171X	Oklahoma Gazette
0030-1728	Oklahoma Geology Notes
0030-1736	Oklahoma Labor Market
0030-1744	Oklahoma Law Review
0030-1752	Oklahoma Librarian
0030-1760	Oklahoma Mason
0030-1779	Oklahoma Nurse
0030-1787	Oklahoma Observer
0030-1795	Oklahoma Odd Fellow
0030-1809	Oklahoma Parent-Teacher
0030-1817	Oklahoma Reader
0030-1833	Oklahoma Retailer
0030-1841	Oklahoma State Dental Association. Journal *changed to* Oklahoma Dental Association Journal
0030-1868	Oklahoma State Medical Association. Journal
0030-1876	Oklahoma Teacher
0030-1884	Oklahoma Today
0030-1892	Oekonomi og Politik
0030-1906	Okonomisk Revy
0030-1914	Okonomisk Virksomhedsledelse *changed to* Lederskab og Loensomhed
0030-1922	Oktobar
0030-1949	Oktyabr'
0030-1957	Old Bottle Magazine
0030-1965	Old English Newsletter
0030-1973	Old Lady of Threadneedle Street
0030-199X	Old Man
0030-2007	Old Motor
0030-2023	Old-Time New England
0030-2031	Old Timers' Bulletin
0030-204X	Old West
0030-2058	Das Oldenburger Sportpferd
0030-2066	Oldenburgische Familienkunde
0030-2074	Oleagineux
0030-2082	
0030-2104	Oleodinamica-Pneumatica *changed to* Oleodinamica-Pneumatica-Lubrificazione
0030-2112	Olie *changed to* Shell-Venster
0030-2120	Incorporates Oljebladet *see* 0006-2367
0030-2139	Olomeinu
0030-2147	Oltre il Cielo
0030-2155	Oltremare†
0030-2163	Olympian
0030-2171	Olympic Training Film Profiles *changed to* Training Film Profiles
0030-218X	Oma
0030-2201	Omaha District Dental Society. Chronicle
0030-221X	Omaha Profile
0030-2228	Omega
0030-2236	Omen
0030-2244	Omin Kasin *see* 0355-1873
0030-2260	Omnia Medica et Therapeutica
0030-2279	Omnibus-Revue
0030-2287	Omnipraticien Francais
0030-2295	Omnis
0030-2317	Instytut Metali Niezelaznych. Biuletyn
0030-2325	On Course†
0030-2333	On Dit
0030-2341	On Target
0030-2368	On the Road
0030-2376	On the Sound†
0030-2384	On the Track†
0030-2392	On Watch
0030-2406	Oncologia si Radiologia *changed to* Revista de Chirurgie, Oncologie, O.R.L., Radiologie, Oftalmolgie, Stomatologie. Oncologie
0030-2406	Oncologia si Radiologia *see* 0481-6684
0030-2414	Oncology
0030-2422	Ondas
0030-2430	Onde Electrique
0030-2449	Onder Chevron Vlag *changed to* Chevron Motor
0030-2457	Onder de Vlam
0030-2465	Onderstepoort Journal of Veterinary Research
0030-2473	Onderwijs en Media†
0030-2481	Onderwijs en Opvoeding
0030-2503	One Church
0030-2511	One-Design and Offshore Yachtsman *changed to* Yacht Racing/Cruising
0030-252X	One in Christ
0030-2546	1001 Custom & Rod Ideas†
0030-2554	1001 Decorating Ideas
0030-2562	One/Two†
0030-2597	Musicologica
0030-2600	Art of Music
0030-2619	Onlooker
0030-2627	Onomastica†
0030-2635	Ons Beroepsonderwijs *changed to* Beroepsonderwijs
0030-2643	Ons Bou *changed to* Tagtig
0030-2651	Ons Erfdeel
0030-266X	Ons Fruitteeltblad *changed to* Boer en de Tuinder
0030-2678	Ons Geestelijk Leven
0030-2686	Ons Huis
0030-2694	Ons Jeug
0030-2708	Ons Jonge Platteland(OJP)
0030-2716	Ons Kompas†
0030-2724	Ons Leger
0030-2732	Ons Platteland
0030-2740	Ons Politeuma *changed to* Ons Burgerschap
0030-2759	Reisiesduif *changed to* Racing Pigeon
0030-2767	Ons Trekpaard†
0030-2775	Ons Vee
0030-2783	Ons Wapen
0030-2791	Ons Zeewezen *see* 0165-8182
0030-2805	Ons Ziekenhuis†
0030-2813	Japan Journal of Logopedics and Phoniatrics
0030-2821	Science of Hot Springs
0030-283X	Ontario Association of Children's Aid Societies. Journal
0030-2848	Ontario Churchman
0030-2856	Ontario College of Pharmacy. Bulletin†
0030-2864	Ontario Dental Association. Journal
0030-2872	Ontario. Ministry of Agriculture and Food. Monthly Dairy Report.
0030-2902	Ontario Education
0030-2910	Ontario Film Association. Bulletin *changed to* Newsletter Called Fred
0030-2929	Ontario Fish and Wildlife Review
0030-2937	Ontario Gazette
0030-2945	Families
0030-2953	Ontario History
0030-297X	Ontario Hydro News *changed to* Hydro News
0030-2988	Ontario Hydro Research Quarterly†
0030-2996	Ontario Library Review
0030-3011	Ontario Mathematics Gazette
0030-302X	Ontario Medical Review
0030-3038	Ontario Milk Producer
0030-3046	Ontario Naturalist *changed to* Seasons
0030-3054	Ontario Psychologist
0030-3062	Opal
0030-3070	Ontario Register
0030-3089	Ontario Reports
0030-3097	Ontario Securities Commission. Monthly Bulletin *changed to* O S C Bulletin
0030-3100	Ontario Securities Commission. Weekly Summary *changed to* O S C Bulletin
0030-3119	Ontario Showcase
0030-3127	Ontario Statute Citator
0030-3135	Ontladingen
0030-3143	Ontode *changed to* Banyaszati es Kohaszati Lapok - Ontode
0030-3151	Ontological Thought *changed to* Emissary
0030-316X	Ontwaak!
0030-3186	Onward-Voorwaarts *changed to* Volkstem
0030-3194	Onze Eigen Tuin
0030-3208	Onze Luchtmacht
0030-3224	Onze Vogels
0030-3232	Onze Wereld
0030-3259	Oomoto
0030-3267	Oorspronkelijk Christendom
0030-3275	Oost en West
0030-3283	Civis Mundi
0030-3291	Oostenrijkse Handelsdelegatie in Nederland *changed to* Oostenrijkse Economische Berichten
0030-3305	Op Cit
0030-3321	Op de Rails
0030-333X	Op Leeftijd *changed to* Leef Tijd
0030-3348	Opakowanie
0030-3356	Opbouw
0030-3372	Open
0030-3399	Open Deur
0030-3402	Open Deur
0030-3429	Open Forum
0030-3437	Open Road and the Professional Driver
0030-3445	Open Shelf†
0030-3453	Open Venster
0030-3461	Openbaar Vervoer
0030-347X	Openbare Bibliotheek *changed to* Bibliotheek en Samenleving
0030-3488	Openbare Uitgaven†
0030-3496	Public Work, Construction & Transport *changed to* Public Works
0030-350X	Openings†
0030-3518	Oper und Konzert
0030-3526	Opera
0030-3542	Opera
0030-3577	Opera/Canada
0030-3585	Opera Journal
0030-3593	European Intelligence
0030-3607	Opera News
0030-3615	Operation L A P L†
0030-3623	Operational Research Quarterly *see* 0160-5682
0030-3631	Operations Forestieres et de Scierie
0030-364X	Operations Research
0030-3658	Operations Research/Management Science
0030-3666	Operations Research Society of America. Bulletin *see* 0161-0295
0030-3690	Opernwelt
0030-3720	Ophthalmic Literature
0030-3739	Ophthalmic Optician
0030-3747	Ophthalmic Research
0030-3755	Ophthalmologica
0030-3763	Ophthalmologist
0030-3771	Opinie *see* 0167-093X
0030-3798	Opinion†
0030-3836	Klank en Weerklank
0030-3844	Oppervlaktetechnieken van Metalen
0030-3879	Opsaal
0030-3887	Opsearch
0030-3895	Opstina
0030-3909	Optica Acta
0030-3917	Optica Pura y Aplicada
0030-3925	Optical Journal and Review of Optometry *see* 0147-7633
0030-3941	Optical Society of America. Journal
0030-395X	Optical Spectra
0030-3976	Opticien Belge
0030-3984	Opticien-Lunetier
0030-3992	Optics and Laser Technology
0030-400X	Optics and Spectroscopy
0030-4018	Optics Communications
0030-4026	Optik
0030-4034	Optika i Spektroskopiya
0030-4042	Optiko-mekhanicheskaya Promyshlennost'
0030-4050	Optima
0030-4069	Optimist
0030-4077	Opto-Electronics *see* 0306-8919
0030-4085	Optometric Management
0030-4093	Optometric Weekly *changed to* Optometric Monthly
0030-4107	Optometric World
0030-4115	Optometrie
0030-4123	Optometrie
0030-4131	Opus†
0030-414X	Opuscula Medica
0030-4166	Or Hamizrach†
0030-4174	Ora et Labora
0030-4182	Orafo Orologiaio
0030-4190	Orafo Valenzano
0030-4204	Oral Health
0030-4212	Oral Research Abstracts†
0030-4220	Oral Surgery, Oral Medicine and Oral Pathology
0030-4239	Orang Peladang
0030-4255	Orange County Business
0030-4263	Orange County Genealogical Society. Quarterly *changed to* Orange County California Genealogical Society Quarterly
0030-4271	Orange County Farm News
0030-428X	Orange County Illustrated
0030-4298	Orange County Jewish Heritage
0030-431X	Orangeburg Historical and Genealogical Record
0030-4328	Oranje-Nassau Post†
0030-4336	Orante
0030-4344	Oratoire

ISSN	Title
0030-4352	Oratoriana
0030-4360	Organismo†
0030-4379	Orbis
0030-4387	Orbis (Philadelphia)
0030-4395	Orbis Geographicus
0030-4425	Orbis
0030-4433	Orbit
0030-445X	Orbita†
0030-4468	Das Orchester
0030-4476	Orchid Review
0030-4484	Orchideeen
0030-4492	Ord och Bild
0030-4506	Ordem dos Medicos. Boletim
0030-4514	Order of Scottish Clans Lion Rampant†
0030-4530	Ordine Nuovo *changed to* Linea
0030-4549	Ordinismo
0030-4565	Ordre National des Medecins. Bulletin
0030-4581	Ordu Dergisi
0030-459X	Ore
0030-4603	Oregon Agri-Record
0030-4611	Oregon Agriculture
0030-462X	Oregon Beverage Analyst
0030-4638	Oregon Business Review†
0030-4646	Oregon Churchman *changed to* Oregon Episcopal Churchman
0030-4654	Oregon Commercial Fisheries Newsletter *changed to* Oregon Commercial Fisheries
0030-4662	Oregon Daily Emerald
0030-4670	Oregon Dental Association. Journal
0030-4689	Oregon Education
0030-4697	Oregon Grange Bulletin
0030-470C	Oregon Health Bulletin
0030-4727	Oregon Historical Quarterly
0030-4735	Oregon Library News
0030-4743	Oregon Music Educator
0030-4751	Oregon Nurse
0030-476X	Oregon Optometrist *see* 0274-6549
0030-4778	Oregon Ornamental and Nursery Digest *changed to* Ornamentals Northwest Newsletter
0030-4794	Oregon Science Teacher
0030-4808	Oregon Sportsman and Conservationist
0030-4816	Oregon State Bar Bulletin
0030-4832	Oregon State University. Forest Research Laboratory. Index†
0030-4840	Oregon Teamster
0030-4859	Oregon Voter Digest
0030-4867	Orella
0030-4875	Orfeo
0030-4883	Organ
0030-4905	Organi di Trasmissione
0030-4913	Organic Gardening and Farming *see* 0163-3449
0030-4921	Organic Magnetic Resonance
0030-493X	Organic Mass Spectrometry
0030-4948	Organic Preparations and Procedures International
0030-4956	Organic Reactivity†
0030-4964	Organisation Gestion des Enterprises
0030-4972	Organisation Internationale pour l'Etude des Langues Anciennes Par Ordinateur. Revue
0030-5006	Organische Land -und Gartenkultur
0030-5014	Organisert†
0030-5022	Organizacija Kadrovska Politika *see* 0350-1531
0030-5049	Organizacion Mercantil *changed to* Noticia Comercial del Oriente
0030-5057	Organizacja - Metody - Technika
0030-5065	E L N A Newsletter
0030-5073	Organizational Behavior and Human Performance
0030-5081	Organizer†
0030-509X	Organizzazione Ferroviaria
0030-5111	Organometallic Chemistry Reviews. Section A: Subject Reviews *see* 0022-328X
0030-512X	Annual Surveys *see* 0022-328X
0030-5138	Organometallic Compounds
0030-5146	Organometallics in Chemical Synthesis†
0030-5154	Organon†
0030-5162	Organorama
0030-5170	Orgue
0030-5189	Oriens Antiquus
0030-5197	Oriens Extremus
0030-5227	Orient
0030-5243	South Pacific Travel Trade News *changed to* Thomsons Travel
0030-5251	Orientacion Docente
0030-526X	Orientacion Economica†
0030-5294	Oriental Art
0030-5308	Oriental Economist
0030-5316	Oriental Geographer
0030-5324	Oriental Insects
0030-5332	Oriental Institute. Journal
0030-5340	Oriental Rug
0030-5357	Oriental Society of Australia. Journal
0030-5375	Orientalia
0030-5383	Orientalia Christiana Periodica
0030-5391	Orientalistische Literaturzeitung
0030-5405	Orientamenti Pedagogici
0030-5413	Orientamenti Sociali
0030-543X	Orientation Professionnelle
0030-5464	Orientations
0030-5472	Oriente Europeo†
0030-5480	Oriente Moderno
0030-5499	Orientering *changed to* Ny Tid
0030-5502	Orientering
0030-5510	Orientierung
0030-5529	Origin Technical Journal
	The Original Art Report
0030-5537	University of Victoria. Department of Hispanic and Italian Studies. Original Works†
0030-5545	Original Works; Art, Poetry, Fiction†
0030-5553	Oriole
0030-557X	Orion
0030-5596	Orita
0030-560X	Orizont
0030-5618	Orizzonti Aperti
0030-5634	Orizzonti Professionali
0030-5642	Orkester Journalen
0030-5650	Orkestra
0030-5669	Orleans Parish Medical Society. Bulletin
0030-5677	Ormanci Gazetesi
0030-5685	Ornis Fennica
0030-5693	Ornis Scandinavica
0030-5707	Ornithologische Beobachter
0030-5715	Ornithologische Gesellschaft in Bayern. Anzeiger
0030-5723	Ornithologische Mitteilungen
0030-5731	Ornithologische Arbeitsgruppe Mitteilungen
0030-5758	Oro y Hora
0030-5774	Orphan's Messenger and Advocate of the Blind *changed to* St. Joseph's Messenger and Advocate of the Blind
0030-5790	Orpheus
0030-5804	Orphic Lute
0030-5812	Orta Dogu†
0030-5839	Orthodox Word
0030-5855	Orthopaedic Medicine Surgery *see* 0009-9325
0030-5863	Orthopaedics/Oxford
0030-5871	Orthopaedieschuhmachermeister *changed to* Orthopaedieschuhtechnik
0030-588X	Orthopaedische Praxis
0030-5898	Orthopedic Clinics of North America
0030-5901	Orthopedic Surgery
0030-591X	Orthopod
0030-5928	Orthotics and Prosthetics
0030-5936	Ortodoncia
0030-5944	Ortodontia
0030-5952	Ortodox Kyrkotidning
0030-5979	Ortopedici e Sanitari
0030-5987	Ortopediya, Travmatologiya i Protezirovaniye
0030-5995	Die Ortskrankenkasse
0030-6002	Orvosi Hetilap
0030-6010	Orvosi Konyvtaros
0030-6029	Orvosi Szemle†
0030-6037	Orvoskepzes
0030-6045	Orvostudomany
0030-6053	Oryx
0030-6061	Orzecznictwo Sadow Polskich i Komisji Arbitrazowych
0030-6088	Osaka District Meteorological Observatory. Monthly Report
0030-6096	Osaka City Medical Journal
0030-610X	Osaka Economic Papers *changed to* Osaka Daigaku Keizaigaku-Osaka Economic Papers
0030-6118	Osaka Medical College. Journal
0030-6126	Osaka Journal of Mathematics
0030-6134	Osaka Institute of Technology. Memoirs. Series B: Liberal Arts
0030-6142	Osaka Medical College. Bulletin
0030-6150	Osaka Odontological Society. Journal
0030-6169	Osaka University. Medical Journal
0030-6177	Osaka University. Faculty of Engineering. Technology Reports
0030-6185	Osgoode Hall Law Journal
0030-6193	Osiguranje i Privreda
0030-6207	Journal of the Oslo City Hospitals
0030-6223	Osnovaniya, Fundamenty i Mekhanika Gruntov
0030-6223	Osnovaniya, Fundamenty i Mekhanika Gruntov
0030-6231	Ospedale
0030-624X	Ospedale al Mare. Archivo.
0030-6258	Ospedali d'Italia
0030-6266	Ospedali d'Italia-Chirurgia
0030-6274	Ospedali Italiani-Pediatria
0030-6282	Polska Akademia Nauk. Osrodek Dokumentacji i Informacji Naukowej. Biuletyn *changed to* Zagadnienia Informacji Naukowej
0030-6290	Osservatore Legale
0030-6304	Osservatore Politico Letterario
0030-6320	Osservatore Tributario e Rassegna Tributaria
0030-6339	Ostdeutscher Literatur-Anzeiger†
0030-6355	Ostehandleren
0030-6363	Osten
0030-6371	Osteopathic Physician†
0030-638X	Osteroder Zeitung
0030-6398	Oesterreich-Polen, Austria-Polska
0030-6428	Osteuropa
0030-6436	Osteuropa-Naturwissenschaft und Technik†
0030-6444	Osteuropa-Recht
0030-6452	Osteuropaeische Rundschau†
0030-6460	Osteuropa-Wirtschaft
0030-6479	Ostfriesland
0030-6487	Ostkirchliche Studien
0030-6495	Ostkusten *see* 0347-4275
0030-6509	Osto ja Materiaalijohto *see* 0356-7931
0030-6517	Ostomy Quarterly
0030-6533	Osuuskauppalehti
0030-655X	Otazky Miru a Socialismu
0030-6568	Other Scenes
0030-6576	Other Voices†
0030-6584	Otia
0030-6592	Oto†
0030-6614	Oto-Laryngological Society of Australia. Journal
0030-6630	Oto-Rino-Laringologia Italiana†
0030-6649	Oto-Rino Laringologie
0030-6657	Otolaryngologia Polska
0030-6665	Otolaryngologic Clinics of North America
0030-6673	Audio-Digest Otorhinolaryngology
0030-6681	Otrok in Druzina
0030-669X	Otsuka Pharmaceutical Factory. Journal
0030-6703	Ottar
0030-6711	Otto Rank Association. Journal
0030-672X	Oud-Holland
0030-6738	Oud Utrecht
0030-6746	Oude Paden
0030-6754	Ouest Industriel, Maritime, Agricole et Commercial
0030-6762	Our Age†
0030-6770	Our American Heritage Committee News Bulletin
0030-6789	Our Animals
0030-6797	Our Boys
0030-6800	Our Children
0030-6819	Educating in Faith
0030-6835	Animals
0030-6843	Our Family
0030-6851	Our Fourfooted Friends
0030-686X	Our Generation
0030-6878	Our Lady of the Sacred Heart. A *changed to* Annals Magazine
0030-6886	Our Lady's Digest
0030-6894	Our Little Friend
0030-6916	Our Navy†
0030-6924	Our Northland Diocese
0030-6932	Our Paper
0030-6940	Our Public Lands
0030-6959	Our Special
0030-6967	Our Sunday Visitor
0030-6983	Our World
0030-6991	Ouranos-Giel-Insolite *see* 0472-2744
0030-7009	Out of Sight
0030-7025	Outdoor California
0030-7033	Outdoor Education
0030-705X	Outdoor Illinois *see* 0148-3390
0030-7068	Outdoor Indiana
0030-7076	Outdoor Life
0030-7084	Outdoor Lighting *changed to* Lighting Systems
0030-7092	Outdoor News Bulletin
0030-7106	Outdoor Oklahoma
0030-7122	Outdoor Power Products for Recreational and Garden Merchandising *see* 0381-5528
0030-7130	Outdoor Recreation Action†
0030-7157	Wonderful West Virginia
0030-7165	Outdoor World†
0030-7173	Outdoors Magazine *see* 0004-9905
0030-7181	Outdoors Unlimited
0030-719X	Outlook†
0030-7203	Outlook *see* 0306-7262
0030-7211	Outlook
0030-7238	Outlook
0030-7246	Standard & Poor's Outlook
0030-7254	Outlook
0030-7270	Outlook on Agriculture
0030-7289	Outpost
0030-7297	Outposts
0030-7300	Outreach *changed to* Intercom
0030-7319	Outrider
0030-7327	Outward Bound
0030-7335	Over Alle Grenser
0030-7343	Over the Bridge†
0030-7351	Standard and Poor's Over-The-Counter *changed to* Standard & Poor's Daily Stock Price Record. Over the Counter Exchange
0030-736X	Over-the-Counter Securities Review *changed to* O T C Review
0030-7378	Over the Hills
0030-7386	Overbrook Adviser
0030-7408	Overflow†
0030-7416	Overland
0030-7424	Overseas
0030-7432	Overseas Building Notes
0030-7440	Overseas Development†
0030-7440	Overseas Development
0030-7475	Uebersee-Post - Europa-Post
0030-7491	Overseas Review *see* 0307-7039
0030-7505	Trinidad and Tobago. Central Statistical Office. Overseas Trade. Monthly Report
0030-7513	Overseas Trading
0030-7521	Overseas Visitor to United Kingdom
0030-7548	Overtones†
0030-7556	Overview
0030-7564	Overview(Chicago)
0030-7572	Ovtsevodstvo
0030-7580	Owl of Minerva
0030-7602	Owlet
0030-7629	Ox Head
0030-7645	Oxford
0030-7653	Oxford Economic Papers
0030-7661	Oxford Medical School Gazette
0030-767X	Oxford University. Institute of Statistics. Bulletin *see* 0305-9049
0030-7688	Oxfordshire Farmer *changed to* Oxford Farmer
0030-7696	Oxidation and Combustion Reviews†
0030-770X	Oxidation of Metals
0030-7718	Afn Shvel
0030-7726	Hokkaido University. Research Institute of Applied Electricity. Bulletin
0030-7734	Kyushu University. Research Institute for Applied Mechanics. Bulletin

ISSN	Title
0030-7750	Ozarker
0030-7769	Ozarks Mountaineer
0030-7777	Ozone Data for the World
0030-7785	R. A. I.-Orgaan *changed to* R. A. I. Actueel
0030-7793	P A N S *see* 0143-6147
0030-7807	P. A. R. Analysis
0030-7815	P A R D Bulletin
0030-7823	P and I†
0030-7831	P & S Quarterly *changed to* P & S Journal
0030-784X	P B S Aktuell
0030-7858	P Ch C Journal of Educational Research
0030-7866	P C M - P C E†
0030-7874	P C M R Message†
0030-7904	P E D
0030-7912	Pegg/Professional Engineer, Geologist, Geophysicist
0030-7920	Panorama Economico Latinoamericano
0030-7947	P E P *changed to* P S I: Broadsheet Series and Major Reports
0030-7955	Mundo Policial
0030-7963	P F M
0030-798X	P H P
0030-7998	P I B Monthly *changed to* P I B Monthly Service-Leading National Advertisers Monthly Service
0030-8005	P I C I C News
0030-8013	P I E F Newsletter *changed to* Studies in Visual Communications
0030-803X	P I Q (Process Industries Quarterly)
0030-8048	P J G B *changed to* Philatelist and Philatelic Journal of Great Britain
0030-8056	P K
0030-8064	Port of London
0030-8080	P M.†
0030-8099	P M A Newsletter
0030-8102	P M E A News
0030-8110	Photomethods for Industry *see* 0146-0153
0030-8129	P M L A
0030-8137	Piano World and Music Trades Review *see* 0305-7178
0030-8145	P M Newsletter *see* 0141-1241
0030-8153	P. M. O. Notes
0030-817X	P N E U Journal *changed to* W E S Journal
0030-8196	P N P A Press
0030-820X	P P G Products
0030-8218	P P S T A Herald
0030-8226	P R Aids' Party Line
0030-8242	Profodcil Bulletin
0030-8250	P. R. S. Journal
0030-8269	P S
0030-8277	P S A Journal
0030-8285	P. S. for Private Secretaries
0030-8315	P. S.-Postscript to Education *changed to* Alumnews
0030-8323	P. S. Public Schools in Action
0030-834X	P T B Mitteilungen Forschen und Pruefen
0030-834X	P T B Mitteilungen *see* 0030-834X
0030-8366	P T T Bedrijf
0030-8374	P T T Informations
0030-8382	Telecommunicatie
0030-8390	P T T-Zbornik *changed to* P T T Novice
0030-8404	P U D O C Bulletin
0030-8412	P. U.-Kaner
0030-8420	P. U. R. Executive Information Service
0030-8439	P V
0030-8447	Paarl Post
0030-8455	Paarlse Padwyser *changed to* Strooidak
0030-8471	Pace†
0030-851X	Pacific Affairs
0030-8528	Pacific Bakers News
0030-8536	Pacific Banker and Business
0030-8544	Pacific Builder and Engineer
0030-8560	Pacific Business Magazine
0030-8579	Pacific Citizen
0030-8587	Pacfic Coast Nurseryman and Garden Supply Dealer *see* 0192-7159
0030-8617	Pacific Coast Society of Orthodontists. Bulletin
0030-8625	Pacific Community†
0030-8633	Pacific Community *changed to* Asia Pacific Community
0030-8641	Pacific Discovery
0030-865X	Pacific Factory
0030-8668	Pacific Fruit News
0030-8676	Pacific Historian
0030-8684	Pacific Historical Review
0030-8692	Pacific Hosteller
0030-8706	Pacific Hotel-Motel News†
0030-8714	Pacific Insects
0030-8722	Pacific Islands Monthly
0030-8730	Pacific Journal of Mathematics
0030-8757	Pacific Law Journal
0030-8765	P M L/Life *changed to* Soundings (Newport Beach)
0030-8781	Pacific Neighbors
0030-879X	Pacific News
0030-8803	Pacific Northwest Quarterly
0030-8811	Pacific Northwest Underwriter†
0030-882X	Pacific Northwesterner
0030-8838	Pacific Orchid Society of Hawaii. Bulletin *see* 0099-8745
0030-8846	Pacific Purchasor
0030-8854	Pacific Research and World Empire Telegrams *changed to* Pacific Research
0030-8870	Pacific Science
0030-8889	Pacific Science Association. Information Bulletin
0030-8897	Pacific Search *changed to* Search
0030-8900	Pacific Shipper
0030-8919	Pacific Sociological Review
0030-8943	Pacific Traffic
0030-8951	Pacific Travel News
0030-896X	Pacific Tribune
0030-8978	Pacific Viewpoint
0030-8986	Pacific Yachting
0030-8994	Pacifican
0030-9001	Pack *changed to* Pack-Distribution
0030-901X	Pack-o-Fun *see* 0146-6607
0030-9028	Package Development *see* 0274-4996
0030-9044	Package Engineering
0030-9060	Packaging
0030-9087	Packaging Abstracts *see* 0260-7409
0030-9095	Packaging Bulletin *see* 0091-0120
0030-9109	Packaging Design†
0030-9109	Packaging Design *see* 0032-8510
0030-9117	Packaging Digest
0030-9125	Packaging/India
0030-9133	Packaging News
0030-9141	Packaging Technology *changed to* Packaging Technology and Management
0030-9168	Packer
0030-9176	Packing and Shipping
0030-9184	Packung und Transport im Chemiebetrieb. *see* 0343-7183
0030-9192	Padova e la sua Provincia
0030-9206	Padova Economica
0030-9214	Padre Santo
0030-9222	Padres' Trail
0030-9230	Paedagogica Historica
0030-9257	Paedagogik Heute†
0030-9265	Paedagogik und Schule in Ost und West
0030-9273	Paedagogische Rundschau
0030-9281	Paedagogisches Institut der Stadt Wien. Mitteilungen
0030-929X	Paedagogisches Institute Salzburg. Mitteilungen *changed to* Paedagogische Mitteilungen
0030-9311	Paediatrica Indonesiana
0030-932X	Paediatrie und Grenzgebiete
0030-9338	Paediatrie und Paedologie
0030-9362	Paediatrische Praxis
0030-9362	Page
0030-9389	Pages
0030-9397	Pages†
0030-9400	Pagine di Storia della Medicina *see* 0025-7877
0030-9427	Pahlavi Medical Journal *changed to* Iranian Journal of Medical Sciences
0030-9435	Paideia
0030-9443	Paikallislehdisto
0030-9451	Pain
0030-946X	Paint and Resin Patents
0030-9478	Paint and Varnish Production *see* 0098-7786
0030-9508	Paint Manufacture *changed to* Paint and Resin
0030-9516	Paint Oil and Colour Journal *see* 0370-1158
0030-9524	Paint Technology *see* 0369-9420
0030-9532	Painter & Allied Trades Journal
0030-9540	Paintindia
0030-9567	Pais e Filhos
0030-9575	Pajara Pinta†
0030-9583	Pajtas
0030-9591	Pak Jamhuriat
0030-9605	Pak-Scout
0030-9613	Pakin
0030-9621	Pakistan Accountant
0030-963X	Pakistan Affairs
0030-9648	Pakistan Armed Forces Medical Journal
0030-9656	Pakistan Army Journal
0030-9664	Pakistan Book News†
0030-9672	Pakistan. Central Statistical Office. Statistical Bulletin *changed to* Pakistan. Statistics Division. Statistical Bulletin
0030-9680	Pakistan Chemist & Druggist†
0030-9699	Pakistan Cottons
0030-9702	Pakistan Council for National Integration. Review†
0030-9710	Pakistan Dental Review
0030-9729	Pakistan Development Review *see* 0304-095X
0030-9745	Pakistan Economist
0030-9753	Pakistan Engineer
0030-977X	Pakistan Exports
0030-9788	Pakistan Geographical Review
0030-9796	Pakistan Historical Society. Journal
0030-9818	Pakistan Journal of Forestry
0030-9826	Pakistan Journal of Geriatrics†
0030-9834	Pakistan Journal of Health
0030-9842	Pakistan Journal of Medical Research
0030-9850	Pakistan Journal of Pharmacy
0030-9869	Pakistan Journal of Psychology†
0030-9877	Pakistan Journal of Science
0030-9885	Pakistan Journal of Scientific and Industrial Research
0030-9893	Pakistan Journal of Soil Science *changed to* Bangladesh Journal of Soil Science
0030-9907	Pakistan Journal of Surgery, Gynaecology, and Obstetrics
0030-9915	Pakistan Journal of Veterinary Science *changed to* Bangladesh Veterinary Journal
0030-9923	Pakistan Journal of Zoology
0030-994X	Pakistan Labour Cases
0030-9958	All Pakistan Legal Decisions
0030-9966	Pakistan Library Bulletin
0030-9974	Pakistan Management Review
0030-9982	Pakistan Medical Association. Journal
0030-9990	Pakistan Medical Forum†
0031-0018	Pakistan Medical Review
0031-0026	Pakistan. Ministry of Information & Broadcasting. Progress of the Month†
0031-0042	Pakistan News Digest *changed to* Weekly Commentary and Pakistan News Digest
0031-0050	Pakistan Press Index†
0031-0069	Pakistan Quarterly†
0031-0077	Pakistan Review†
0031-0085	Pakistan Science Abstracts
0031-0093	Pakistan Stamps
0031-0107	Pakistan Studies†
0031-0115	Pakistan Tax Decisions
0031-0123	Pakistan Weather Review-Monthly Weather Report
0031-0131	Pakkaus
0031-014X	Palabra y el Hombre
0031-0158	El Palacio
0031-0166	Paladijn
0031-0174	Palaeobotanist
0031-0182	Palaeogeography, Palaeoclimatology, Palaeoecology
0031-0204	Palaeontological Society of Japan. Transactions and Proceedings
0031-0220	Palaeontologische Zeitschrift
0031-0247	Palaeovertebrata
0031-0255	Palaestra
0031-0263	Palaestra Latina†
0031-028X	Palatino
0031-0301	Paleontological Journal
0031-031X	Paleontologicheskii Zhurnal
0031-0328	Palestine Exploration Quarterly
0031-0336	Palestine Refugees Today
0031-0344	Palestra
0031-0352	Paletten
0031-0360	Palimpsest
0031-0379	Palladio
0031-0387	Pallas
0031-0395	Pallottis Werk
0031-0417	Palm Beach Life
0031-0425	Palm Springs Life
0031-0433	Palmer Writer†
0031-0441	Palmos Tou Geneous†
0031-045X	Palomino Horses
0031-0468	Palontorjunta
0031-0476	Palontorjuntateknikka
0031-0492	Palynological Bulletin *see* 0022-3379
0031-0506	Pamatky Archeologicke
0031-0514	Pamietnik Literacki
0031-0522	Pamietnik Teatralny
0031-0530	Pamir Monthly *changed to* Pamir Magazine
0031-0549	Pammatone
0031-0557	Pamphleteer Monthly
0031-0565	Pan-African Journal
0031-0573	Pan American Health Organization. Gazette *changed to* Pan American Health
0031-0581	Revista Geografica
0031-059X	Pan American Review
0031-0603	Pan-Pacific Entomologist
0031-0611	Pan Pipes of Sigma Alpha Iota
0031-0646	Panama Canal Review
0031-0662	Pancevac
0031-0697	Pandecte Neon Noman Kediataghmaton
0031-0735	Panel
0031-0743	Excerpta Medica. Section 49: Forensic Science
0031-076X	Panhandle
0031-0778	Panidealistische Umschau†
0031-0786	Panjab Past and Present
0031-0794	Panjab University Economist *changed to* Pakistan Economic and Social Review
0031-0808	Panminerva Medica
0031-0824	Panorama
0031-0840	Panorama *changed to* Colorado Women's College. Bulletin
0031-0859	Panorama
0031-0867	Panorama
0031-0875	Panorama
0031-0883	Panorama
0031-0891	Panorama Ballesterense *changed to* Reportero
0031-0913	Panorama Democrate Chretien
0031-093X	Panorama Economico†
0031-0948	Panorama Medical†
0031-0964	Panorama Polnocy
0031-0972	Panpere
0031-0980	Panstwo i Prawo
0031-0999	Pantheon
0031-1006	Panther *changed to* Advocate (Johnstown)
0031-1014	Pantograph
0031-1049	Papeis Avulsos de Zoologia
0031-1057	Papel
0031-1065	Papeles de Son Armadans
0031-1081	Paper Age
0031-109X	Printing Abstracts
0031-1103	Paper and Twine Journal
0031-1111	Paper Bulletin *see* 0142-5307
0031-112X	Paper Facts and Figures
0031-1138	Paper, Film and Foil Converter
0031-1146	Paper Maker†
0031-1154	Paper-Maker *see* 0306-8234
0031-1162	Paper Money
0031-1170	Paper Sales
0031-1189	Paper Technology *see* 0306-252X
0031-1197	Paper Trade Journal
0031-1200	Paper Trends
0031-1219	Paperbacks in Print
0031-1227	Paperboard Packaging

ISSN	Title
0031-1235	Paperbound Books in Print
0031-1243	Paperi ja Puu
0031-1251	Papers in Linguistics: International Journal of Human Communication
0031-126X	Papers in Meteorology and Geophysics
0031-1278	Papers in Psychology†
0031-1286	Papers of Woodrow Wilson
0031-1294	Papers on Language and Literature
0031-1308	Papeterie
0031-1316	Papeterist
0031-1324	Papetier de France
0031-1332	Papetier Libraire
0031-1340	Das Papier
0031-1359	Papier- und Buchgewerbe-Rundschau
0031-1367	Papier Carton et Cellulose
0031-1375	Papier und Druck
0031-1383	Papiergeschichte†
0031-1391	Papierhandels-Fachblatt
0031-1405	Der Papiermacher
0031-1413	Papierwereld
0031-1421	Papir a Celuloza
0031-143X	Papirhandleren
0031-1448	Papiripar
0031-1456	Pappershandlaren
0031-1464	Papua New Guinea Agricultural Journal
0031-1472	Papua and New Guinea Journal of Education
0031-1480	Papua New Guinea Medical Journal
0031-1510	Papua New Guinea Overseas Migration *changed to* Papua New Guinea International Migration
0031-1529	Papua New Guinea. Quarterly Retail Price Index *see* 0094-8616
0031-1537	Papua and New Guinea. Quarterly Summary of Statistics *changed to* Papua New Guinea. Abstract of Statistics
0031-1553	Parabas
0031-1561	Paraboles
0031-1588	Parachutist
0031-1596	Parade
0031-160X	Parade
0031-1618	Parade and Foto-Action
0031-1642	Parag
0031-1650	Paragone
0031-1669	Paragraphs
0031-1677	Paraguay. Direccion General de Estadistica y Censos. Boletin Estadistico
0031-1685	Paraguay Industrial y Comercial
0031-1693	Paraguay Today
0031-1715	Parallelo Trentotto
0031-1723	Parameters
0031-1731	Parametro
0031-174X	Parana em Paginas
0031-1758	Paraplegia
0031-1766	Paraplegia News
0031-1782	Parapsychology
0031-1790	Parapsychology Bulletin†
0031-1804	Parapsychology Review
0031-1812	Parasitica
0031-1820	Parasitology†
0031-1820	Parasitology
0031-1847	Parazitologiya
0031-1855	Pardon
0031-1863	Parent Educator†
0031-188X	Parents' Bulletin
0031-1898	Parents et Instituteurs†
0031-1901	Parents et Maitres
0031-191X	Parents' Magazine and Better Family Living *changed to* Parents' Magazine
0031-1928	Lexington School for the Deaf. Parents' Newsletter. *changed to* Sounds of Lexington
0031-1936	Parents Voice
0031-1952	Parfuemerie und Kosmetik
0031-1979	Parichiti
0031-2002	Paris District. Journal des Communes
0031-2010	Paris Gaz Relations *changed to* Gaz Relations
0031-2029	Paris Match
0031-2037	Paris Review
0031-2045	Paris-Sud
0031-2053	Pariser Kurier
0031-2061	Parish Councils Review *see* 0308-3594
0031-207X	Parish News†
0031-2088	Parishioner
0031-2096	Pariyal Kalyan
0031-210X	Park
0031-2118	Park Administration
0031-2126	Park East
0031-2134	Park Maintenance
0031-2142	Park News†
0031-2150	Grist
0031-2177	Parkdalian
0031-2193	Parking
0031-2207	Dierenpark Wassenaar Zoo. Parknieuws
0031-2215	Parks and Recreation
0031-2223	Parks and Recreation
0031-224X	Parks and Sports Grounds
0031-2282	Parliamentarian
0031-2290	Parliamentary Affairs
0031-2312	Parmamedica
0031-2320	Parnasso
0031-2347	Paroisse et Liturgie *changed to* Communautes et Liturgies
0031-2355	Parola del Passato
0031-2363	Parola del Popolo
0031-2371	Parola e Il Libro
0031-2398	Parole di Vita
0031-2428	Parrocchia
0031-2436	Parson and Parish
0031-2444	U.S. Agency for International Development. Participant Journal†
0031-2460	Particle Accelerators
0031-2479	Particles and Nuclei
0031-2487	Particulate Matter
0031-2509	Partiinaya Zhizn' Activist†
0031-2517	Activist†
0031-2525	Partisan Review
0031-2533	Partisans†
0031-255X	Partizanov Vesnik
0031-2568	Partners
0031-2576	Parts Line
0031-2584	Pas a Pas†
0031-2592	Paseo del Rio Showboat
0031-2606	Pashupalan†
0031-2606	Pashupalan *see* 0023-1088
0031-2614	Pasicrisie Belge
0031-2622	Pasidibala
0031-2630	Pasinomie
0031-2649	Pasque Petals
0031-2657	Pasquino
0031-2665	Passaic County Historical Society. Bulletin†
0031-2673	Passaic County Medical Society. Bulletin
0031-2681	Passauer Bistumsblatt
0031-269X	Passe-Partout
0031-2703	Passenger Pigeon
0031-2711	Passerelle
0031-272X	Passport
0031-2738	Password
0031-2746	Past and Present: a Journal of Historical Studies
0031-2754	Pastor Evangelico *changed to* Obrero Cristiano
0031-2762	Pastoral Life
0031-2789	Pastoral Psychology
0031-2800	Pastoralblaetter
0031-2819	Pastoralist and Grazier Newsletter
0031-2827	Wissenschaft und Praxis in Kirche und Gesellschaft *see* 0720-6259
0031-2835	Patent and Trademark Review
0031-286X	Patent Journal Including Trademarks and Models
0031-2878	Patent Licensing Gazette *changed to* World Technology
0031-2894	Patentblatt
0031-2908	Patentni Glasnik
0031-2916	Finland. Patentti- ja Rekisterihallitus. Patenttilehti/Patenttidning/Patent Gazette
0031-2932	Path of Truth
0031-2940	Pathfinder
0031-2959	Schweizerische Zeitschrift fuer Allgemeine Pathologie und Bakteriologie *see* 0304-3568
0031-2967	Pathologia Europaea†
0031-2975	Pathologia Veterinaria *see* 0300-9858
0031-2991	Patologicheskaya Fiziologiya i Eksperimental'naya Terapiya
0031-3009	Pathologie Biologie
0031-3017	Pathologist
0031-3025	Pathology
0031-3033	Pathways
0031-305X	Patient Care
0031-3068	Patisserie Francaise Illustree
0031-3076	Patissier de l'Ile-De-France
0031-3084	Patna Journal of Medicine
0031-3092	Patna University Journal
0031-3106	Patologia
0031-3114	Patologia Polska
0031-3122	Patranu
0031-3130	Patria Indipendente
0031-3149	Patrimonium
0031-3165	Patronat Francais
0031-3173	Patronato Genovese Pronatura "A. Anfossi." Notiziario†
0031-3181	Patrys
0031-3203	Pattern Recognition
0031-3211	Patterns *see* 0146-1397
0031-322X	Patterns of Prejudice
0031-3238	Patterson's California Beverage Gazetteer
0031-3246	Paukenslag
0031-3262	Paunch
0031-3270	Pauze
0031-3289	Pavliha
0031-3297	Pavo
0031-3300	Pax†
0031-3319	Pax Bulletin *see* 0306-7645
0031-3327	Pax et Libertas
0031-3335	Pax Regis
0031-3351	Pay Planning
0031-336X	Pay Planning Checklist and Forms
0031-3386	Pays Bas-Normand
0031-3394	Pays Lorrain
0031-3408	Paz e Terra†
0031-3416	Pcela
0031-3432	Peabody Journal of Education
0031-3440	Peabody Notes
0031-3459	Peabody Reflector
0031-3467	Peace
0031-3491	Peace and Freedom
0031-3513	Peace and the Sciences
0031-353X	Peace Monitor
0031-3548	Peace News
0031-3564	Peace Plans
0031-3572	Peace Press
0031-3580	Excerpta Medica. Section 48: Gastroenterology
0031-3599	Peace Research Abstracts Journal
0031-3602	Peacemaker
0031-3610	Peach-Times
0031-3629	Peak
0031-3637	Peak District Mines Historical Society. Bulletin
0031-3653	Peanut Farmer
0031-3661	Peanut Journal and Nut World
0031-367X	Peat Abstracts
0031-3696	Pebble
0031-370X	Peche au Canada†
0031-3718	Peche et les Poissons
0031-3726	Peche Maritime
0031-3734	Pecheur et Chasseur Suisses *changed to* Nature Information
0031-3742	Pecheurs d'Hommes
0031-3750	Pecsi Muszaki Szemle
0031-3777	Pedagogia e Vita
0031-3785	Pedagogiai Szemle
0031-3793	Pedagogic Reporter
0031-3807	Pedagogija
0031-3815	Pedagogika
0031-3823	Pedagogisch Forum *changed to* Pedagogisch Tijdschrift
0031-3831	Scandinavian Journal of Educational Research
0031-384X	Pedagoski Rad
0031-3858	Pedagoski Zivot
0031-3866	Pedale d'Oro
0031-3874	Arrive *changed to* Walk
0031-3882	Pediatria
0031-3890	Pediatria
0031-3904	Revista de Pediatrie, Obstetrica, Ginecologie. Pediatrie
0031-3912	Pediatria e Puericultura
0031-3920	Pediatria Moderna
0031-3939	Pediatria Polska
0031-3947	Pediatria Pratica
0031-3955	Pediatric Clinics of North America
0031-3963	Pediatric Conferences
0031-398X	Pediatric News
0031-3998	Pediatric Research
0031-4005	Pediatrics
0031-4013	Pediatrics Digest *changed to* Pediatrics Digest (1979)
0031-4021	Pediatre (Lyon)
0031-403X	Pediatriya
0031-4048	Pediatriya, Akusherstvo ta Ginekologiya
0031-4056	Pedobiologia
0031-4064	Pedologist
0031-4072	Pegasus *see* 0318-5753
0031-4080	Pegasus Journal
0031-4099	Peiling
0031-4110	Peking Informers
0031-4129	Peking Review
0031-4137	Pelagos
0031-4145	Pelerin du Vingtieme Siecle
0031-4153	Pelican
0031-417X	Pelita
0031-4188	Pellervo
0031-4226	Pembrokeshire Farmer
0031-4242	Pen Woman
0031-4250	Pendle Hill Pamphlets
0031-4269	Pendulum of Time and the Arts
0031-4285	Peninsula
0031-4293	Peninsula Living
0031-4307	Peninsula Poets
0031-4315	Penmen's News Letter
0031-4331	Penn Dental Journal
0031-434X	Pennsylvania Angler
0031-4358	Pennsylvania Archaeologist
0031-4366	Pennsylvania Board of Probation and Parole. Monthly Statistical Report
0031-4374	Pennsylvania Board of Probation and Parole. Quarterly Statistical Report *see* 0031-4366
0031-4382	Pennsylvania Business Survey
0031-4390	Pennsylvania C P A Spokesman
0031-4404	Pennsylvania Chiefs of Police Association Bulletin
0031-4412	Pennsylvania Contractor
0031-4420	Pennsylvania Dental Association. Newsletter†
0031-4439	Pennsylvania Dental Journal
0031-4455	Pennsylvania Education
0031-4463	Pennsylvania Farm Economics *see* 0014-7923
0031-4471	Pennsylvania Farmer
0031-448X	Pennsylvania Flower Growers. Bulletin
0031-4498	Pennsylvania Folklife
0031-4501	Pennsylvania Forests
0031-451X	Pennsylvania Game News
0031-4528	Pennsylvania History
0031-4536	Pennsylvania Holstein News
0031-4544	Pennsylvania Human Relations Report†
0031-4552	Pennsylvania Jewish Life
0031-4579	Pennsylvania Library Association. Bulletin
0031-4587	Pennsylvania Magazine of History and Biography
0031-4595	Pennsylvania Medicine
0031-4609	Pennsylvania Message
0031-4617	Pennsylvania Nurse
0031-4625	Pennsylvania Optometrist†
0031-4633	Pennsylvania Pharmacist
0031-4641	Pennsylvania Professional Engineer *changed to* Engineer
0031-465X	Pennsylvania Psychiatric Quarterly†
0031-4668	Pennsylvania School Boards Association. Bulletin *see* 0162-3559
0031-4676	Pennsylvania School Journal
0031-4684	Pennsylvania State Modern Language Association. Bulletin
0031-4692	Pennsylvania Traveler *changed to* Pennsylvania Traveler-Post
0031-4706	Pennsylvania Veterinarian†
0031-4722	Pennsylvanian
0031-4730	Pensador†
0031-4749	Pensamento
0031-4757	Pensamiento Politico†
0031-4765	Pensamiento y Accion

0031-4773 Pensee
0031-4781 Pensee Catholique
0031-479X La Pensee Francaise
0031-4803 Pensez Plastiques
0031-4811 Pensiero†
0031-482X Pensiero Mazziniano
0031-4838 Pensiero Nazionale
0031-4846 Pensiero Politico
0031-4854 Pensioen Bulletin
0031-4862 Pension & Welfare News *see* 0098-1753
0031-4870 Pentagon
0031-4889 Pentagramma
0031-4897 Pentecostal Evangel
0031-4900 International Pentecostal Holiness Advocate
0031-4919 Pentecostal Messenger
0031-4927 Pentecostal Testimony
0031-4935 Penthouse
0031-496X Penzugyi Szemle
0031-4978 People *changed to* Pix-People
0031-4986 People†
0031-4994 People†
0031-5001 People†
0031-501X People (Kansas City)
0031-5028 People's Action†
0031-5036 People's Korea
0031-5044 People's World
0031-5052 Peoria Labor News
0031-5087 Pepinieristes Horticulteurs Maraichers
0031-5117 Perception & Psychophysics
0031-5125 Perceptual and Motor Skills
0031-5133 Perceptual-Cognitive Development†
0031-5141 Perchtoldsdorfer Pfarrbote
0031-5168 Percussionist and Percussive Notes *changed to* Percussionist
0031-5168 Percussionist and Percussive Notes *changed to* Percussive Notes
0031-5176 Perets
0031-5184 Perfect Home
0031-5192 Perfekt Kindermode
0031-5206 Perfekt Mode
0031-5214 Performance (Washington) *see* 0148-5407
0031-5222 Performing Arts
0031-5230 Performing Arts in Canada
0031-5249 Performing Arts Review
0031-5257 Performing Right *see* 0309-0019
0031-529X Periodica de Re Morali Canonica Liturgica
0031-5303 Periodica Mathematica Hungarica
0031-5311 Periodica Polytechnica. Chemical Engineering
0031-532X Periodica Polytechnica. Electrical Engineering
0031-5338 Periodica Polytechnica. Mechanical Engineering
0031-5346 Periodica Polytechnica. Architecture
0031-5397 Periodontology Today
0031-5400 Peripherals Weekly *changed to* Peripherals Digest
0031-5427 Periscope
0031-5435 Perito Industriale
0031-5443 N. T. U. C. Perjuangan
0031-5451 Perkins School of Theology Journal
0031-546X Perlin et Pinpin
0031-5478 Permanences
0031-5486 Permanencia
0031-5508 Permanent International Altaistic Conference (PIAC). Newsletter
0031-5516 Permanent Way
0031-5524 Permanent Way Institution. Journal and Report of Proceedings
0031-5532 P S I†
0031-5540 Perpetual Motion Journal†
0031-5559 Perpustakaan†
0031-5567 Nederlandse Hervormde Kerk. Persbureau. Weekbulletin
0031-5575 Persklaar *changed to* Intercom
0031-5591 Personal Injury Valuation Handbooks
0031-5605 Personal
0031-5621 Personalist *changed to* Pacific Philosophical Quarterly
0031-563X Personality†
0031-5648 Personality *changed to* Family Radio & TV
0031-5656 Personeelbeleid
0031-5672 Der Personenverkehr
0031-5680 Personenvervoer
0031-5699 Personhistorisk Tidskrift
0031-5702 Personnel
0031-5729 Personnel Administrator
0031-5737 Personnel and Guidance Journal
0031-5745 Personnel Journal
0031-5753 Personnel Literature
0031-5761 Personnel Management
0031-577X Personnel Management Abstracts
0031-5788 International Personnel Management Association. Personnel News *changed to* I P M A News
0031-580X Personnel Policies Forum *see* 0361-7467
0031-5818 Australia. Department of Labour and National Service. Personnel Practice Bulletin *changed to* Work and People
0031-5826 Personnel Psychology
0031-5834 Personnel Quarterly *changed to* L. O. M. A. Resource
0031-5842 Persoon en Gemeenschap
0031-5850 Persoonia
0031-5869 Persoverzicht
0031-5885 Perspective (Augusta) *changed to* Update (Augusta)
0031-5893 Perpective (St. Louis)†
0031-5915 Perspective†
0031-5923 Perspective
0031-5931 Perspective†
0031-594X Peace Courier
0031-5958 Perspectives; Journal of General and Liberal Studies *see* 0148-1959
0031-5974 Federation Nationale des Clubs Perspectives et Realities *changed to* Perspectives et Realities
0031-5982 Perspectives in Biology and Medicine
0031-5990 Perspectives in Psychiatric Care
0031-6016 Perspectives of New Music
0031-6032 Perspectives Psychiatriques
0031-6059 Perspektywy
0031-6067 Peru. Biblioteca Nacional. Boletin
0031-6067 Peru. Biblioteca Nacional. Boletin
0031-6075 Pesca Italiana
0031-6083 Pesca y Marina
0031-6091 Pescare
0031-6105 Peshawar Times†
0031-6121 Pest Control
0031-613X Pesticide Science
0031-613X Parasite Immunology
0031-6148 Pesticides
0031-6156 Pesticides Monitoring Journal
0031-6164 Pesum Padam
0031-6180 P S M *changed to* Pets/Supplies/Marketing
0031-6202 Pet Product Marketing and Garden Supplies - the Pet Trade Journal
0031-6229 Petermanns Geographische Mitteilungen
0031-6237 Petfish Monthly *changed to* Petfish Practical Fishkeeping Monthly
0031-6245 Petfood Industry
0031-6253 Petit Journal du Brasseur
0031-6261 Petit Meunier
0031-627X Petit Moniteur des Assurances
0031-6296 Petnaest Dana
0031-630X Petra
0031-6318 Petri-Heil
0031-6326 Petro/Chem Engineer *see* 0031-6466
0031-6334 Petrobras†
0031-6342 PetroChemical News
0031-6350 Petrol si Gaze *changed to* Mine, Petrol si Gaze
0031-6369 Arab Oil & Gas
0031-6407 Petroleo Interamericano *see* 0093-7851
0031-6415 Petroleo y Mineria de Venezuela
0031-6423 Petroleum Abstracts
0031-6431 Modern Bulk Transporter
0031-644X Petroleum and TBA Marketer *see* 0362-7799
0031-6458 Petroleum Chemistry U.S.S.R.
0031-6466 Petroleum Engineer International
0031-6474 Fruit by Telegraph
0031-6482 Petroleum Mirror
0031-6490 Petroleum Outlook
0031-6504 Petroleum Press Service *see* 0306-395X
0031-6512 Petroleum Refining Developments†
0031-6520 Excerpta Medica. Section 47: Virology
0031-6539 Petroleum Taxation Report *changed to* Petroleum Taxation/Legislation Report
0031-6547 Petroleum Times *changed to* International Petroleum Times
0031-6555 Petroleum Today†
0031-6563 Petrolieri d'Italia
0031-6571 Petrolio
0031-658X Petronio
0031-6598 Petrotecnica
0031-6601 Petticoat
0031-661X Peuple
0031-6644 Pewter Collectors' Club of America. Bulletin
0031-6652 Pez y la Serpiente
0031-6660 Pfaelzer Bauer
0031-6679 Pfaelzer Heimat
0031-6687 Pfaelzer Saenger
0031-6695 Pfalz am Rhein
0031-6709 Pfarrbrief
0031-6725 Pfizer Spectrum†
0031-6733 Pflanzenarzt
0031-6741 Pflanzenernaehrung und Duengung†
0031-675X Pflanzenschutzberichte
0031-6768 Pfluegers Archiv
0031-6776 Pflugschar†
0031-6784 Die Pforte
0031-6792 Peradarstvo
0031-6806 Phaphama!
0031-6814 Phare
0031-6822 Pharetra
0031-6849 Pharma Times
0031-6857 Pharmaca
0031-6865 Pharmaceutica Acta Helvetiae
0031-6873 Pharmaceutical Journal
0031-6881 Pharmaceutical Journal
0031-689X Pharmaceutical Research Institute. Bulletin
0031-6903 Pharmaceutical Society of Japan. Journal
0031-6911 Pharmaceutisch Weekblad
0031-692X Pharmacien
0031-6938 Pharmacien de France
0031-6954 Pharmacien Rural
0031-6962 Pharmacists Quarterly
0031-6970 European Journal of Clinical Pharmacology
0031-6989 Pharmacological Research Communications
0031-6997 Pharmacological Reviews
0031-7004 Pharmacologist
0031-7012 Pharmacology
0031-7020 Rational Drug Therapy
0031-7039 Pharmacotoxicologia et Therapia Clinica†
0031-7039 Pharmacotoxicologia et Therapia *changed to* Pharmaco-Toxicologia Clinica
0031-7047 Pharmacy in History
0031-7063 Pharmacy News
0031-7071 Pharmacy Trade
0031-708X Pharmakeftikon Deltion
0031-7098 Pharmakopsychiatrie - Neuro-Psychopharmakologie *changed to* Pharmacopsychiatria
0031-7101 Pharmanews†
0031-711X Die Pharmazeutische Industrie
0031-7128 Pharmazeutische Rundschau
0031-7136 Pharmazeutische Zeitung
0031-7144 Die Pharmazie
0031-7152 Pharmindex
0031-7160 Pharos
0031-7179 Pharos
0031-7187 Phare†
0031-7209 Phi Delta Epsilon News & Scientific Journal
0031-7217 Phi Delta Kappan
0031-7233 Philadelphia
0031-725X Philadelphia College of Pharmacy and Science Bulletin
0031-7268 Philadelphia County Dental Society. Bulletin
0031-7276 Philadelphia Dental Laboratory Association Journal
0031-7306 Philadelphia Medicine
0031-7314 Philadelphia Museum of Art. Bulletin
0031-7322 Philadelphia Purchasor
0031-7349 South Africa. Philatelic Services. Philatelic Bulletin/Filateliebulletin *changed to* South Africa. Philatelic Services and Intersapa. Philatelic Bulletin/Filateliebulletin
0031-7357 Philatelic Magazine *see* 0261-3107
0031-7365 Philatelic Trader and Stationer *changed to* Philatelic Trader
0031-7373 Philatelist *changed to* Philatelist and Philatelic Journal of Great Britain
0031-7381 Philatelic Exporter
0031-739X Philately
0031-7403 Philately from Australia
0031-7438 Philippine Abstracts
0031-7446 Philippine Agricultural Situation
0031-7454 Philippine Agriculturist
0031-7462 Philippine Architecture & Building Journal
0031-7489 Philippine Business Index
0031-7497 Philippine Dental Association. Journal
0031-7500 Philippine Economic Journal
0031-7527 Philippine Educational Forum
0031-7535 Philippine Federation of Private Medical Pactitioners. Journal
0031-7543 Philippine Fishing Journal
0031-7551 Philippine Geographical Journal
0031-756X Philippine Geologist *changed to* Geological Society of the Philippines. Journal
0031-7578 Philippine Health Journal
0031-7608 Philippine Journal of Cancer
0031-7616 Philippine Journal of Child-Youth Development
0031-7624 Philippine Journal of Education
0031-7632 Philippine Journal of Leprosy
0031-7640 Philippine Journal of Nutrition
0031-7659 Philippine Journal of Ophthalmology
0031-7667 Philippine Journal of Pediatrics
0031-7675 Philippine Journal of Public Administration
0031-7683 Philippine Journal of Science
0031-7691 Philippine Journal of Surgical Specialties
0031-7705 Philippine Journal of Veterinary Medicine
0031-7713 Philippine Junior Red Cross Magazine
0031-7721 Philippine Law Journal
0031-7748 Philippine Medical Association. Journal
0031-7764 Philippine Progress†
0031-7780 Philippine Review of Business and Economics
0031-7799 Philippine Scientific Journal
0031-7802 Philippine Social Sciences and Humanities Review
0031-7810 Philippine Sociological Review
0031-7829 Philippine Statistician
0031-7837 Philippine Studies
0031-7845 Philippine Tax Journal
0031-7853 Philippine Women's University Administrative News
0031-787X Philippines Labor Relations Journal
0031-7888 Philippines Transportation
0031-7896 Philips Cronache *changed to* Cronache
0031-790X Philips Music Herald†
0031-7926 Philips Technical Review
0031-7934 P T R
0031-7942 Phillips Exeter Bulletin
0031-7969 Philobiblon
0031-7977 Philological Quarterly
0031-7985 Philologus
0031-7993 Philosopher's Index
0031-8000 Philosophia
0031-8019 Philosophia Mathematica
0031-8027 Philosophia Naturalis
0031-8035 Philosophia Reformata
0031-8043 Philosophical Association. Journal
0031-8051 Philosophical Books
0031-806X Philosophical Forum
0031-8078 Philosophical Journal†
0031-8086 Philosophical Magazine
0031-8094 Philosophical Quarterly
0031-8108 Philosophical Review
0031-8116 Philosophical Studies

ISSN	Title	ISSN	Title	ISSN	Title
0031-8124	Philosophische Probleme der Sozialistischen Bewusstseinsbildung und der Moral *changed to* Referateblatt Philosophie. Reiche C. Philosophische Probleme des Geistigen Lebens, Marxistisch-Leninistische Ethik	0031-9155	Physics in Medicine and Biology	0032-0234	Piraiki-Patraiki
		0031-9163	Physics Letters *changed to* Physics Letters. Section A: General, Atomic and Solid State Physics	0032-0242	Pirkka
				0032-0250	Pirquet Bulletin of Clinical Medicine *changed to* Virchow-Piquet Medical Society. Proceedings
		0031-9163	Physics Letters *changed to* Physics Letters. Section B: Nuclear, Elementary Particle and High-Energy Physics	0032-0269	Pirsch *see* 0340-7829
0031-8132	Philosophische Probleme der Naturwissenschaften *changed to* Referateblatt Philosophie. Reihe B. Philosophische Probleme der Wissenschaften			0032-0277	Piscator
				0032-0285	Piscines
				0032-0293	Pit & Quarry
		0031-9163	Physics Letters *see* 0370-1573	0032-0307	Pitman Journal *changed to* Memo International
		0031-9171	Physics of Fluids		
		0031-918X	Physics of Metals and Metallography	0032-0315	Pittsburgh Business Review
0031-8140	Philosophische Probleme des Sozialistischen Aufbaus und der Technischen Revolution *changed to* Referateblatt Philosophie. Reihe A. Dialektischer und Historischer Materialismus, Philosophische Probleme des Sozialismus	0031-9198	Physics of Sintering *see* 0350-820X	0032-0323	Pittsburgh Catholic
		0031-9201	Physics of the Earth and Planetary Interiors	0032-0331	Pittsburgh Legal Journal
				0032-034X	Pittsburgh Musician
		0031-921X	Physics Teacher	0032-0358	Pittsburgh Symphony Orchestra Program
		0031-9228	Physics Today	0032-0374	Catholic Guild News *changed to* Word for Word
		0031-9236	Physik der Kondensierten Materie/ Physique de la Matiere Condensee/ Physics of Condensed Matter *changed to* Zeitschrift fuer Physik. Section B: Condensed Matter		
				0032-0382	Pivot
0031-8159	Philosophische Rundschau			0032-0390	Pix *changed to* Pix-People
0031-8167	Philosophische Zeitspiegel			0032-0404	Pjichk
0031-8175	Philosophischer Literaturanzeiger	0031-9244	Physik in der Schule	0032-0412	Plain Rapper
0031-8183	Philosophisches Jahrbuch	0031-9252	Physik in Unserer Zeit	0032-0420	Plain Truth (Pasadena)
0031-8191	Philosophy	0031-9260	Physikalische Berichte *see* 0170-7434	0032-0439	Plain Truth
0031-8205	Philosophy and Phenomenological Research	0031-9279	Physikalische Blaetter	0032-0447	Plains Anthropologist
		0031-9287	Physikalische Medizin und Rehabilitation	0032-0455	Plainsong
0031-8213	Philosophy and Rhetoric			0032-0463	Plaintiff *changed to* Medicine Jug
0031-8221	Philosophy East and West	0031-9295	Der Physikunterricht	0032-0471	Boum
0031-823X	Philosophy Forum *see* 0260-4027	0031-9309	Physiologia Bohemoslovaca	0032-048X	Plaisir de France *changed to* Connaissance des Arts-Plaisir
0031-8248	Philosophy of Science	0031-9317	Physiologia Plantarum		
0031-8256	Philosophy Today	0031-9325	Physiological Chemistry and Physics	0032-048X	Plaisir de France *changed to* Connaissance des Arts - Plaisir de France
0031-8264	Philotelia	0031-9333	Physiological Reviews		
0031-8272	Philwomenian	0031-9341	Physiological Society of Japan. Journal		
0031-8280	Phlebologie *changed to* Societe Francaise de Phlebologie. Bulletin	0031-935X	Physiological Zoology	0032-0498	Plaisir de la Maison
		0031-9368	Physiologie Vegetale	0032-0501	Plaisirs de la Peche
0031-8299	Phoenix	0031-9376	Physiologist	0032-051X	Plaisirs Equestre
0031-8310	Phoenix	0031-9384	Physiology and Behavior	0032-0528	Plamuk
0031-8329	Phoenix	0031-9392	Physiotherapie	0032-0536	PLAN
0031-8337	Phoenix†	0031-9406	Physiotherapy	0032-0544	Plan *changed to* Plan Canada
0031-8353	Phoenix Jewish News	0031-9414	Physis	0032-0552	Plan
0031-837X	Phoenix Quarterly	0031-9422	Phytochemistry	0032-0560	Plan
0031-8388	Phonetica	0031-9430	Phytologia	0032-0579	Plan
0031-8396	Phoni Tou Evangeliou	0031-9449	Phytomorphology	0032-0587	Plan Ahead
0031-8426	Phosphorus and Potassium	0031-9457	Phyton	0032-0595	Plan and Print
0031-8434	Phosphorus in Agriculture	0031-9465	Phytopathologia Mediterranea†	0032-0609	Plan og Arbeid
0031-8442	Photo	0031-9473	Phytopathological Society of Japan. Annals	0032-0617	Plane & Pilot
0031-8450	Photo-Cine-Expert *changed to* Photo-Cine-Expert (1979)			0032-0633	Planetary & Space Science
		0031-9481	Phytopathologische Zeitschrift	0032-065X	Planned Parenthood Report†
0031-8469	Photo-Cine-Review *see* 0369-9641	0031-949X	Phytopathology	0032-0668	Planned Savings
0031-8477	Photo-Cinema, Film, Amateur-Son *see* 0398-9372	0031-9503	Phytopathology News	0032-0676	Planner
		0031-9511	Phytoprotection	0032-0684	Planning & Changing
0031-8485	Photo Dealer†	0031-952X	Pi Mu Epsilon Journal	0032-0692	Planning and Development in the Netherlands
0031-8515	Photographic Processor	0031-9538	Pianeta		
0031-8523	Photo Interpretation	0031-9546	Piano Guild Notes	0032-0706	Planning Comment†
0031-8531	Photo Marketing	0031-9554	Piano Quarterly	0032-0714	Planning Outlook
0031-854X	Photo News	0031-9562	Piano Technician's Journal	0032-0749	Planovane Hospodarstvi
0031-8566	Photo Screen	0031-9570	Pianura	0032-0757	Planovoe Khozyaistvo
0031-8574	Photo-Technik und - Wirtschaft†	0031-9589	Picchiarello	0032-0765	Planseeberichte fuer Pulvermetallurgie
0031-8582	Canadian Photography	0031-9600	Piccolo Missionario	0032-0773	Plant Administration and Engineering *see* 0315-9183
0031-8590	Photo Trade News	0031-9619	Picket Post		
0031-8604	Photo Trade of Japan	0031-9635	Pictorial†	0032-0781	Plant and Cell Physiology
0031-8639	Photo Typesetting	0031-9643	Pictorial Life *changed to* Gold Coast Pictorial	0032-079X	Plant and Soil
0031-8647	Photo Weekly			0032-0803	Plant Breeding Abstracts
0031-8655	Photochemistry and Photobiology	0031-9651	Pictorial News Review	0032-0811	Plant Disease Reporter *see* 0191-2917
0031-8663	Photogrammetria	0031-926X	Picturegoer†	0032-082X	Plant Engineering
0031-8671	Photogrammetric Engineering *see* 0099-1112	0031-9678	Pictures & Prints†	0032-0838	Plant Engineers†
		0031-9686	Pictures on Exhibit	0032-0846	Plant Life
0031-868X	Photogrammetric Record	0031-9694	Picturescope†	0032-0854	Plant Operating Management†
0031-8701	Photographic Abstracts	0031-9708	Pie	0032-0870	Plant Pathology Circular
0031-871X	Photographic Applications in Science, Technology and Medicine *see* 0360-7216	0031-9716	Pierian Spring†	0032-0889	Plant Physiology
		0031-9732	Pig Breeders Gazette	0032-0897	Plant Protection Abstracts
		0031-9740	Pig Farmer	0032-0919	Plant Science Bulletin
0031-8728	Photographic Business and Product News *changed to* Studio Photography	0031-9759	Pig Farming	0032-0935	Planta
		0031-9767	Pig International (American Edition) *see* 0148-2173	0032-0943	Planta Medica
0031-8736	Photographic Journal			0032-0951	Planter
0031-8744	Photographic Processing	0031-9775	Pig Progress†	0032-096X	Planters Bulletin
0031-8760	Photographic Science and Engineering	0031-9783	Pigeon News	0032-0978	Planters' Chronicle
0031-8779	Photographic Trade News	0031-9791	Piggin String	0032-0986	Planters Journal and Agriculturist
0031-8809	Photography	0031-9813	Pilgrim Society Notes	0032-0994	Plantes Medicinales et Phytotherapie
0031-8817	Photography and Travel *changed to* Creative Photography	0031-983X	Pin High†	0032-101X	Plants & Gardens
		0031-9856	Pine Cone	0032-1028	Plasma Physics
0031-8833	Photon	0031-9864	Rap†	0032-1036	Plasterer and Cement Mason
0031-8841	Photoplatemakers Bulletin	0031-9872	Pinellas Teacher *changed to* Action (Clearwater)	0032-1052	Plastic and Reconstructive Surgery
0031-885X	Photoplay			0032-1060	Plastic Industry Notes†
0031-8868	Phronesis	0031-9880	Pingrin	0032-1079	Plastic Laminating†
0031-8876	Phytiatrie-Phytopharmacie	0031-9899	Pinheiros Farmaceutico†	0032-1087	Plastic-Revue Edition Schweiz†
0031-8884	Phycologia	0031-9902	Pinkster Protestant	0032-1095	Plastica
0031-8892	Phykos	0031-9910	Pinpointer	0032-1109	Plasticke Hmoty a Kaucuk *changed to* Plasty a Kaucuk
0031-8906	Phylon	0031-9929	Pins and Needles		
0031-8922	Physica Fennica *see* 0031-8949	0031-9945	Pintores	0032-1117	Plasticonstruction *see* 0343-3129
0031-893X	Physica Norvegica†	0031-9953	Pinturas y Acabados Industriales	0032-1133	Plasticos em Revista
0031-893C	Physica Norvegica *see* 0031-8949	0031-9961	Rivista degli Infermieri	0032-1141	Plasticos y Resinas†
0031-8949	Physica Scripta	0031-997X	Pioneer	0032-115X	Plastics Abstracts
0031-8957	Physica Status Solidi (B). Basic Research	0031-9988	Pioneer†	0032-1168	Plastics and Rubber Weekly
		0032-0005	Pioneer America	0032-1176	Plastics Design & Processing
0031-8965	Physica Status Solidi (A). Applied Research	0032-0021	Pioneer Woman	0032-1192	Plastics in Engineering†
		0032-003X	Pioner	0032-1206	Plastics Industry News, Japan
0031-8973	Physical Education Newsletter	0032-0048	Pionerskaya Pravda	0032-1214	Plastics Industry Notes†
0031-8981	Physical Educator	0032-0099	Pionir-Kekec	0032-1222	Plastics, Paint and Rubber *changed to* Plastics and Rubber News
0031-899X	Physical Review *see* 0556-2791	0032-0102	Pioneriya		
0031-9007	Physical Review Letters	0032-0110	Pionyrske Noviny *changed to* Sedmicka Pionyru	0032-1249	Plastics, Rubber and Leather Industries Journal
0031-9015	Physical Society of Japan. Journal				
0031-9023	Physical Therapy	0032-0129	Pioppi Coltura e Arboricoltura da Legno *changed to* Arboricoltura da Legno	0032-1257	Plastics Technology
0031-9031	Physicians' Association of Madras. Journal			0032-1265	Plastics Trends
		0032-0145	Pipe Line Industry	0032-1273	Plastics World
0031-904X	Physicians' Basic Index†	0032-0153	Pipe Line News *see* 0148-4443	0032-129X	Plastiques Informations *see* 0032-1303
0031-9058	Physicians' Drug Manual	0032-0161	Pipe Smoker's Ephemeris	0032-1303	Plastiques Modernes et Elastomers
0031-9066	Physician's Management	0032-017X	Pipe World	0032-1311	Plastnytt
0031-9074	Physicians Market Place	0032-0196	Pipeline & Underground Utilities Construction	0032-132X	Plastvaerldent†
0031-9082	Physico-Chemical Biology			0032-1338	Plastverarbeiter
0031-9090	Physics and Chemistry of Glasses	0032-020X	Pipes and Pipelines International	0032-1346	Plateau
0031-9104	Physics and Chemistry of Liquids	0032-0218	Pippin	0032-1354	Plateau†
0031-9112	Physics Bulletin	0032-0226	P I R A Newspaper Information Service *changed to* P I R A Newsbrief	0032-1370	Platform
0031-9120	Physics Education			0032-1389	Platform
0031-9147	Physics in Canada				

ISSN INDEX

0032-1397	Plating see 0360-3164	0032-2733	Polimlje	0032-4019	Polyphonie see 0035-3736
0032-1400	Platinum Metals Review	0032-2741	Polio-France	0032-4027	Polysar Progress (1965) changed to Polysar Progress (1978)
0032-1419	Plattdeutsche Post	0032-2768	Poliplasti e Plastici Rinforzati changed to Poliplasti e Plastici Rinforzati (1978)	0032-4035	Polyscope Automatik und Elektronik
0032-1435	Plavi Vjesnik†			0032-4051	Polytechnic
0032-1451	Playback†	0032-2776	Polish Academy of Sciences. Review	0032-406X	Polytechnic Engineer
0032-146X	Playbill	0032-2784	Polish Affairs	0032-4078	Polytechnisch Tijdschrift: Bouwkunde, Wegen- en Waterbouw
0032-1478	Playboy	0032-2792	Polish American Journal	0032-4086	Polytechnisch Tijdschrift: Elektrotechniek/Elektronica
0032-1486	Players Magazine	0032-2806	Polish American Studies		
0032-1508	Playhour	0032-2814	Polish Building Abstracts	0032-4094	Polytechnisch Tijdschrift: Procestechniek
0032-1516	Playing Fields†	0032-2822	Polish Co-Operative Review	0032-4108	Polytechnisch Tijdschrift: Werktuigbouw
0032-1532	Playmen	0032-2849	Polish Economic Survey	0032-4116	Polytechnische Bildung und Erziehung
0032-1540	Plays	0032-2865	Polish Export-Import	0032-4124	Polyteknikeren
0032-1567	Playthings	0032-2873	Polish Facts and Figures†	0032-4132	Pomhaj Boh
0032-1583	Psychologie	0032-2881	Polish Foreign Trade	0032-4140	Pomiary-Automatyka-Kontrola
0032-1591	Plomberie-Chauffage et Climatisation	0032-289X	Polish Literature	0032-4159	Pomme de Terre Francaise
0032-1605	Plomjo	0032-2903	Polish Machinery News†	0032-4167	Pommern
0032-1613	Plow	0032-2911	Polish Maritime News	0032-4175	Pomologie Francaise†
0032-1621	Plug	0032-2938	Polish Medical Journal†	0032-4183	Pomona Today
0032-163X	Plumb Line	0032-2946	Polish Music	0032-4205	Pompebledden
0032-1656	Plumbing	0032-2954	Polish News	0032-4213	Ponny see 0346-4687
0032-1672	Plumbing Equipment News and Heating Engineer see 0308-373X	0032-2962	Polish Perspectives	0032-4221	Pont†
		0032-2989	Polish Scientific Periodicals-Contents†	0032-423X	Ponte
0032-1680	Wholesaler	0032-2997	Polish Sociological Bulletin	0032-4264	Pony Express
0032-1702	Plus†	0032-3004	Polish Technical and Economic Abstracts	0032-4272	Pool 'n Patio
0032-1729	Plutonium-Dokumentation changed to Plutonium-Dokumentation/ Transplutonium-Elemente			0032-4280	Pool News see 0194-5351
		0032-3012	Polish Technical Review	0032-4299	Poona Agricultural College Magazine
		0032-3020	Polish Weekly	0032-4302	Poor Richard's Almanack†
0032-1737	Plymouth Bulletin	0032-3039	Polish Western Affairs	0032-4310	Poor Richard's Report see 0516-9623
0032-1753	Plymouth Traveler†	0032-3055	Politecnica	0032-4329	Poor's Investment Advisory Survey changed to Standard & Poor's Investment Advisory Survey
0032-1761	Plyn	0032-3063	Politica del Diritto		
0032-177X	Plywood & Panel	0032-3101	Politica Internazionale (Florence)		
0032-1788	Plywood World changed to Wood World	0032-3128	Political Affairs	0032-4337	Pootaardappelhandel changed to Pootaardappelwereld
		0032-3152	Political Companion		
0032-1796	Pobeda	0032-3160	Memo from C O P E	0032-4345	Pop-Foto/Tuney Tunes changed to Popfoto
0032-180X	Pochvovedenie	0032-3179	Political Quarterly		
0032-1826	Pocket List of Railroad Officials	0032-3187	Political Science	0032-4353	Pope Speaks
0032-1869	Podnikova Organizace	0032-3195	Political Science Quarterly	0032-4361	El Popola Cinio
0032-1877	Poe Newsletter see 0090-5224	0032-3209	Political Scientist	0032-437X	Popolo del Friuli-Venezia Giulia
0032-1885	Poem	0032-3217	Political Studies	0032-4388	Popoyan
0032-1893	Poesia de Venezuela	0032-3225	Politicheskoe Samoobrazovanie	0032-4418	Populaer Filateli
0032-1907	Poesia en la Calle	0032-3233	Politicka Ekonomie	0032-4442	Populaer Radio og TV Teknik changed to Populaer Radio
0032-194X	Poet	0032-3241	Politicka Misao		
0032-1958	Poet and Critic	0032-325X	Politico	0032-4450	Popular Bridge
0032-1966	Poet Lore	0032-3268	Politics	0032-4469	Camping
0032-1974	Cahiers de Litterature et de Poesie: Poetes et Leurs Amis	0032-3276	Politics	0032-4477	Popular Ceramics
		0032-3284	Politics and Money	0032-4485	Popular Electronics
0032-1982	Poeti della Nuova Italia	0032-3292	Politics and Society	0032-4493	Popular Flying
0032-1990	Poeti Italiani Contemporanei†	0032-3306	Politics†	0032-4507	Popular Gardening†
0032-2016	Poetica	0032-3322	Politie-Dierenbescherming	0032-4515	Popular Government
0032-2024	Poetique	0032-3330	Politiek changed to Politiek Perspectief	0032-4523	Popular Hot Rodding
0032-2032	Poetry	0032-3349	Politiek en Cultuur	0032-4531	Popular Imported Cars changed to Small Cars /Magazine
0032-2040	Poetry & Audience	0032-3357	Politiidrett		
0032-2059	Poetry Australia	0032-3365	Politiikka	0032-454X	Popular Mechanics†
0032-2067	Poetry Bag	0032-3381	Politika-Ekspres	0032-4558	Popular Mechanics
0032-2075	Poetry India†	0032-339X	Politikin Zabavnik	0032-4574	Popular Motoring
0032-2083	Poetry Market	0032-342X	Politique Etrangere changed to Politique Etrangere de la France	0032-4582	Popular Photography
0032-2105	Poetry Nippon			0032-4590	Popular Photography's Woman†
0032-2113	Poetry Northwest	0032-3438	Politische Dokumentation†	0032-4604	Popular Plastics changed to Popular Plastics and Rubber
0032-2148	Poetry Prevue see 0148-9666	0032-3438	Politische Dokumentation		
0032-2156	Poetry Review	0032-3446	Die Politische Meinung	0032-4620	Popular Rotorcraft Flying
0032-2164	Poetry Singapore	0032-3462	Politische Studien	0032-4639	Popular Science and Technology
0032-2172	Poetry Society of America. Bulletin	0032-3489	Politisk Tidskrift	0032-4647	Popular Science
0032-2199	Poetry Venture†	0032-3497	Polity	0032-4655	Popular Talisman Bulletin
0032-2202	Poetry Wales	0032-3500	Polityka	0032-4663	Population
0032-2229	Serie Poeyana changed to Poeyana	0032-3519	Die Polizei	0032-468X	Population Bulletin
0032-2237	Poezja	0032-3527	Die Polizei im Lande Berlin	0032-4698	Population Chronicle†
0032-2245	Pogledi	0032-3535	Polizei Technik Verkehr	0032-4701	Population Index
0032-2253	Pogledi i Iskustva u Odgoju i Obrazovanju	0032-3543	Polizeimagazin	0032-471X	Population Review
		0032-3551	Polizeischau	0032-4728	Population Studies
0032-227X	Poids Lourd	0032-356X	Polizia Moderna	0032-4736	Incorporating - Population Statistics Hilversum see 0028-291X
0032-2288	Poilu Lorrain	0032-3578	Polja		
0032-230X	Point of View	0032-3594	Polka		
0032-2318	Point of View	0032-3608	Polled Hereford World	0032-4744	Por Alquimia
0032-2326	Point Three	0032-3616	Pollen et Spores	0032-4752	Poradnik Bibliotekarza
0032-2334	Point to Point Communication see 0305-3601	0032-3624	Pollution Abstracts	0032-4779	Polymer Friends for Rubber, Plastics and Fiber
		0032-3632	Pollution Atmospherique		
0032-2342	Pointer†	0032-3640	Pollution Engineering	0032-4787	Porodica i Dijete
0032-2369	Points et Contrepoints	0032-3659	Pollution Equipment News	0032-4795	Poroshkovaya Metallurgiya
0032-2377	Poirieria	0032-3667	Polo	0032-4809	Port
0032-2385	Poissonnier Belge	0032-3675	Pologne et les Affaires Occidentales	0032-4817	Port of Baltimore Bulletin
0032-2393	Pojistny Obzor	0032-3683	Polonia	0032-4825	Port of Houston
0032-2407	Pokret	0032-3713	Polska Bibliografia Analityczna Mechaniki	0032-4833	Port of Karachi†
0032-2415	Pokrof			0032-4841	Port of Norfolk News Letter†
0032-2423	Pokroky Matematiky, Fyziky a Astronomie	0032-3721	Polska Sztuka Ludowa	0032-485X	Port of Sydney see 0313-4075
		0032-373X	Polski Przeglad Chirurgiczny	0032-4868	Port of Toledo News
0032-2431	Pola Esperantisto	0032-3756	Polski Tygodnik Lekarski	0032-4876	Port of Yokohama. Monthly Statistics
0032-244X	Poland/American Edition	0032-3764	Polski Archiwum Hydrobiologii	0032-4884	Portals of Prayer
0032-2458	Poland and Germany (East & West)†	0032-3772	Polskie Archiwum Medycyny Wewnetrznej	0032-4892	Portcullis
0032-2466	Poland China World			0032-4906	Porter Library Bulletin changed to Kansas State College of Pittsburg. Library Bulletin
0032-2474	Polar Record	0032-3780	Polskie Pismo Entomologiczne		
0032-2482	Polar Times	0032-3799	Annales Societatis Mathematicae Polonae. Series 1: Commentationes Mathematicae		
0032-2490	Polarforschung			0032-4914	Portico
0032-2504	Pole et Tropiques			0032-4922	Presence Orthodoxe
0032-2520	Polet	0032-3802	Polskie Towarzystwo Jezykoznawcze. Biuletyn	0032-4930	Portland Physician
0032-2547	Poletarac			0032-4949	Porto di Livorno
0032-2555	Police	0032-3829	Polyclinic Journal†	0032-4957	Porto di Savona
0032-2563	Police†	0032-3837	Polygraph changed to Polygraph-I A U News	0032-4965	Porto di Venezia
0032-258X	Police Journal			0032-4973	Portos e Navios
0032-2598	Police Life	0032-3845	Der Polygraph	0032-4981	Portrait changed to University of Maryland Magazine
0032-2601	Police Times changed to Police Times and Police Command	0032-3861	Polymer		
		0032-3896	Polymer Journal	0032-499X	Portraits of Prominent U.S.S.R. Personalities†
0032-261X	Police World	0032-390X	Polymer Mechanics changed to Mechanics of Composite Materials		
0032-2628	Policia Portuguesa Revista Ilustrada†			0032-5007	International Freighting Weekly
0032-2636	Policlinico. Sezione Chirurgica	0032-3918	Polymer News	0032-5015	Ports O'Call
0032-2644	Policlinico. Sezione Pratica	0032-3926	Polymer Report. Japan†	0032-5023	Portsmouth Chamber of Commerce. Newsletter changed to Portsmouth Chamber of Commerce. Report
0032-2652	Policy	0032-3934	Polymer Preprints		
0032-2660	Policy, Fact and Comment changed to P R P Comment	0032-3942	Polymer Science & Technology Post		
		0032-3950	Polymer Science, U. S. S. R	0032-5031	Portugal-an Information Review
0032-2679	Policy Holder Insurance Journal	0032-3969	Polymerics†	0032-504X	Portugal. Direccao-Geral dos Servicos Florestais e Aquicolas. Gabinete de Estudos Economicos e Estatisticos. Cadernos†
0032-2687	Policy Sciences†	0032-3977	Quarterly Literature Reports. Polymers†		
0032-2695	Policy Sciences	0032-3985	Polymya		
0032-2709	Poligrafico Italiano	0032-3993	Polymus†		
0032-2717	Poligrafiya	0032-4000	Polynesian Society. Journal	0032-5066	Portugal Evangelico
0032-2725	Polimery				

ISSN	Title
0032-5082	Portugal. Instituto Nacional de Estatistica. Boletim Mensal
0032-5090	Laboratorio Nacional de Engenharia Civil. Boletim Mensal de Informacao
0032-5112	Portugal Ministerio da Economia. Comissao Reguladora do Comercio de Arroz. Informacao Bibliografica do Arroz†
0032-5120	Portugal Ministerio da Saude e Assistencia, Direccao-Geral da Assistencia. Informacao Social†
0032-5139	Portugal. Ministerio dos Negocios Estrangeiros. Boletim de Informacao Economica†
0032-5147	Portugaliae Acta Biologica
0032-5155	Portugaliae Mathematica
0032-5163	Portuguese Journal
0032-5171	Poruka Borca
0032-5198	Poseidon
0032-5201	Possev
0032-521X	Posh†
0032-5228	Positions Lutheriennes
0032-5236	Post
0032-5244	Post†
0032-5252	Post Magazine and Insurance Monitor
0032-5260	Post Mark†
0032-5279	Post Mortem
0032-5287	Post Office Electrical Engineers' Journal
0032-5295	Post Office Engineering Union Journal
0032-5309	Post Office Telecommunications Journal†
0032-5317	Postal and Telegraph Herald
0032-5325	Postal Bell
0032-5333	Postal Bulletin
0032-5341	Postal History Journal
0032-535X	Postal Journal
0032-5368	Postal Life
0032-5376	Postal Record
0032-5384	Postal Supervisor
0032-5392	Postal Worker
0032-5406	Poste e Telecomunicazioni
0032-5414	Postepy Astronomii
0032-5422	Postepy Biochemii
0032-5430	Postepy Fizyki
0032-5449	Postepy Higieny i Medycyny Doswiadczalnej
0032-5457	Postepy Nauk Rolniczych
0032-5473	Postgraduate Medical Journal
0032-5481	Postgraduate Medicine
0032-549X	Posthalter-Kurier
0032-5503	Postmaennens Tidning
0032-552X	Postmasters Gazette
0032-5546	Potash Review
0032-5554	Potato and Onion World†
0032-5562	Potato Chipper changed to Chipper/Snacker
0032-5570	Potato Councillor
0032-5589	Potato Grower News
0032-5600	Potencia
0032-5619	Potentials in Marketing
0032-5635	Potomac Appalachian Trail Club. Bulletin changed to Potomac Appalachian
0032-5643	Potomac View changed to Potomac View on Lung Health
0032-566X	Potravinar
0032-5678	Pottery Quarterly
0032-5686	Poty Cuntu
0032-5708	U.S. Department of Agriculture. Economics, Statistics, and Cooperatives Service. Poultry and Egg Situation
0032-5716	Poultry and Eggs Marketing
0032-5724	Poultry Digest
0032-5732	Poultry Farmer
0032-5740	Poultry Guide
0032-5767	Poultry International
0032-5775	Poultry Market Review
0032-5783	Poultry Press
0032-5791	Poultry Science
0032-5805	Poultry Tribune
0032-5813	Poultry World
0032-5821	Le Poumon & le Coeur
0032-583X	Pour la Vie
0032-5856	Poverty
0032-5864	Poverty & Human Resources Abstracts see 0099-2453
0032-5880	Povratak u Zivot
0032-5899	Powder Metallurgy
0032-5910	Powder Technology
0032-5929	Power
0032-5937	Power & Plant in Southern Africa
0032-5953	Power Engineer†
0032-5961	Power Engineering
0032-5996	Power Farming and Better Farming Digest see 0311-1911
0032-6003	Power for Living
0032-6011	Power for Today
0032-6038	Power Laundry & Cleaning News†
0032-6046	Power Life changed to Freeway
0032-6054	Power Management†
0032-6062	Power Record
0032-6070	Power Transmission Design
0032-6089	Powerboat
0032-6143	Poznaj Swiat
0032-6151	Poznaj Swoj Kraj
0032-616X	Pozoriste
0032-6178	Prabuddha Bharata
0032-6186	Praca i Zabezpieczenia Spoleczne
0032-6194	Praca Skolna
0032-6208	Prace a Mzda
0032-6216	Instytut Elektrotechniki. Prace
0032-6232	Instytut Naftowy. Prace
0032-6240	Instytut Technologii Drewna. Prace
0032-6259	Instytut Tele- i Radiotechniczny. Prace
0032-6267	Mineralogia Polonica
0032-6275	Muzeum Ziemi. Prace
0032-6283	Przemyslowy Instytut Telekomunikacji. Prace
0032-6291	Pracovni Lekarstvi
0032-6305	Practica Oto-Rhino-Laryngologica see 0301-1569
0032-6313	Practica Otologica Kyoto
0032-6321	Practical Accountant
0032-633X	Practical Anthropology see 0091-8296
0032-6348	Practical Boat Owner
0032-6356	Practical Camper
0032-6364	Practical Christianity
0032-6372	Practical Electronics
0032-6380	Scholastic Voice
0032-6399	Practical Gardening
0032-6410	Practical Knowledge
0032-6429	Practical Lawyer
0032-6437	Practical Motorist
0032-6445	Practical Photography
0032-6453	Practical Psychology
0032-647X	Television (London, 1934)
0032-6488	Practical Woodworking
0032-6518	Practitioner
0032-6534	Praehistorische Forschungen
0032-6542	Der Praeparator
0032-6550	Pragati
0032-6569	Prager Volkszeitung
0032-6577	Pragmatist in Art†
0032-6585	Prague Bulletin of Mathematical Linguistics
0032-6593	Praha - Moskva
0032-6607	Prairie Club Bulletin
0032-6615	Prairie Farmer
0032-6623	Prairie Gleaner
0032-6631	Prairie Lore
0032-664X	Prairie Messenger
0032-6674	Prairie School Review
0032-6682	Prairie Schooner
0032-6690	Prajnan
0032-6704	Praksa
0032-6720	Prakticke Zubni Lekarstvi
0032-6739	Prakticky Lekar
0032-6747	Prakticna Zena
0032-6755	Praktiker
0032-6763	Praktiko†
0032-6771	Praktische Forstwirt fuer die Schweiz changed to Schweizer Foerster
0032-678X	Praktische Metallographie
0032-6801	Der Praktische Schaedlingsbekaempfer
0032-681X	Der Praktische Tierarzt
0032-6828	Praline
0032-6836	Pram Retailer†
0032-6844	Pram & Nursery Trader
0032-6852	Pramo
0032-6860	Prapor
0032-6879	Prasna
0032-6887	Pratfall†
0032-6895	Materiaux et Techniques
0032-6909	Pratique du Soudage†
0032-6909	Pratique du Soudage see 0035-127X
0032-6917	Pratishruti
0032-6925	Prato - Storia e Arte
0032-6933	Pratt Cannon changed to Pratt Reports
0032-695X	Pravna Misla
0032-6968	Pravna Misul
0032-6984	Pravny Obzor
0032-6992	Pravoslavnaya Zhyzn
0032-700X	Pravoslavno Misao
0032-7018	Pravoslavnaya Rus'
0032-7034	Praxis der Kinderpsychologie und Kinderpsychiatrie
0032-7042	Praxis der Mathematik
0032-7050	Praxis der Naturwissenschaften. Biologie im Unterricht der Schulen
0032-7069	Praxis der Pneumologie see 0342-7498
0032-7077	Praxis der Psychotherapie see 0171-791X
0032-7085	Praxis des Neusprachlichen Unterrichts
0032-7107	Worship and Preaching
0032-7123	Precision†
0032-7131	Precision
0032-714X	Precision Metal
0032-7166	Predicasts changed to Predicasts Forecasts
0032-7174	Predicasts Electronic Trends changed to Electronics Trends(Cleveland)
0032-7182	Prediction
0032-7212	Der Prediger und Katechet
0032-7220	Predskolska Vychova
0032-7239	Preet Lari
0032-7247	Prefabbricare
0032-7255	Prefabbricazione
0032-7263	Preface
0032-7271	Pregled
0032-7298	Pregled Problema Mentalno Retardiranih Osoba
0032-731X	Pregled Zakonodavstva u Stranim Drzavama
0032-7328	Prehlad Lesnickej, Drevarskej, Celulozovej a Papiernickej Literatury
0032-7336	Prehled Lesnicke a Myslivecke Literatury
0032-7344	Novinky Literatury: Prehled Pedagogicke Literatury changed to Prehled Pedagogicke Literatury Dokumentacni Listkova Sluzba
0032-7352	Prehledy Leteckotechnicke Literatury
0032-7360	Prehledy Leteckotechnicke Literatury
0032-7379	Prehledy Potravinarske Literatury
0032-7387	Premier Plan†
0032-7409	Premio
0032-7425	Prenatal
0032-7433	Prensa Confidencial
0032-745X	Prensa Medica Argentina
0032-7468	Prensa Medica Mexicana
0032-7476	Prent 190
0032-7484	Preparative Biochemistry
0032-7506	Prepodavanie Istorii v Shkole
0032-7514	Prepravni a Tarifni Vestnik
0032-7522	Presbyterian Guardian
0032-7530	Presbyterian Herald
0032-7549	Presbyterian Journal
0032-7557	Presbyterian Life changed to United Presbyterian A.D.
0032-7565	Presbyterian Outlook
0032-7573	Presbyterian Record
0032-7581	Rush-Presbyterian-St. Luke's Medical Bulletin†
0032-759X	Presbyterian Survey
0032-7611	Prescribers' Journal
0032-762X	Presence
0032-7638	Presence Africaine
0032-7654	Presence des Lettres et des Arts Emergences
0032-7654	Presence des Letteres et des Arts see 0032-7654
0032-7662	Presence du Cinema
0032-7689	Presencia
0032-7697	Present
0032-7700	Present Truth and Herald of Christ's Epiphany
0032-7719	Presente†
0032-7727	Presenza Pastorale
0032-7735	Preservation News
0032-7751	President
0032-7778	Wisconsin Library Association. President's Newsletter changed to W L A Newsletter
0032-7786	Preslia
0032-7794	Germany (Federal Republic, 1949-) Presse- und Informationsamt. Bulletin
0032-7808	Press and Public Relations
0032-7816	Press Booklets
0032-7824	Press Woman
0032-7832	Presse Actualite
0032-7840	Presse der Sowjetunion
0032-7859	Belgium. Commissariat General au Tourisme. Bulletin
0032-7867	Presse Medicale see 0301-1518
0032-7875	Presse Thermale et Climatique
0032-7883	Pressens Tidning
0032-7891	Presseschau Ostwirtschaft
0032-7905	Pressespiegel Blicknach Drueben changed to Pressespiegel aus Zeitungen und Zeitschriften der DDR
0032-7913	Pressluft changed to Drucklufttechnik
0032-7921	Prestige de l'Hotellerie, de la Restauration et du Tourisme
0032-793X	Prestressed Concrete Institute. Journal
0032-7948	South Africa. Weather Bureau. Newsletter/Nuusbrief
0032-7956	Pretres Diocesains
0032-7964	Pretzel Baker†
0032-7972	Preussenland
0032-8006	Prevention
0032-8014	Prevention of Blindness News changed to Prevent Blindness News
0032-8022	Prevention Routiere
0032-8030	Prevention Routiere dans l'Entreprise
0032-8049	Previdencia Social†
0032-8057	Previdenza Agricola
0032-8065	Previdenza Sociale
0032-8081	Previdenza Sociale Nella Stampa Estera†
0032-809X	Previdenza Sociale nell'Artigianato
0032-8103	Preview
0032-8111	Preview†
0032-812X	Previsoes Ionosfericas M U F
0032-8138	Przeglad Bibliograficzny Pismiennictwa Ekonomicznego
0032-8146	Priapus
0032-8154	Pribory i Sistemy Upravleniya
0032-8162	Pribory i Teknika Eksperimenta
0032-8170	Price Waterhouse Review
0032-8197	Pride
0032-8200	Priest
0032-8219	Landbouw-Economisch Instituut. Prijsstatistiek
0032-8227	Prikazi in Studije
0032-8235	Prikladnaya Matematika i Mekhanika
0032-8243	Prikladnaya Mekhanika
0032-8251	Primalinea
0032-826X	Primary Bookshelf†
0032-8278	Primary Days
0032-8286	Primary Friend
0032-8308	Primary Producer changed to Dairyman's Digest and Primary Producer
0032-8316	Primary Treasure
0032-8324	Primate News
0032-8332	Primates
0032-8340	Primavera
0032-8359	Prime Areas
0032-8367	Primer Acto†
0032-8375	Primera Plana
0032-8383	Primicia
0032-8391	Princess Tina changed to Tina
0032-8405	Princeton Engineer
0032-843X	Princeton University. Art Museum. Record
0032-8448	Princeton University Cutaneous Research Project Reports
0032-8456	Princeton University Library Chronicle
0032-8472	Principe de Viana
0032-8480	Principes
0032-8499	Prinsejagt
0032-8502	Prinses†
0032-8510	Print
0032-8529	Print

0032-8537 Print Collector's Newsletter
0032-8553 Print Project Amerika†
0032-8561 Print Room†
0032-857X Printindia
0032-8588 Printing and Publishing
0032-8596 Printing Equipment and Materials *changed to* Printing Today
0032-860X Printing Impressions
0032-8626 Printing News
0032-8634 Printing Plates†
0032-8642 Printing Product Information Cards
0032-8650 Printing Management *see* 0032-860X
0032-8677 Printing Salesman's Herald
0032-8685 Printing Technology *see* 0308-4205
0032-8707 Printing Trades Journal†
0032-8715 Printing World
0032-8731 Priroda
0032-874X Priroda
0032-8758 Prirodovedne Prace Ustavu C S A V v Brne
0032-8766 Prirodni Vedy ve Skole
0032-8774 Prirucka Casopisu Zena a Moda *changed to* Prakticka Zena
0032-8790 Prism International
0032-8804 Prisma Lectuurvoorlichting / Book Reviews for Public Libraries
0032-8812 Prisma†
0032-8847 Prismet
0032-8855 Prison Journal
0032-8863 Prison Officers Magazine
0032-8871 Private Carrier
0032-888X Private Eye
0032-8898 Private Library
0032-8901 Private Pilot
0032-891X Private Practice
0032-8928 Private Practice News†
0032-8936 Private Printer & Private Press†
0032-8944 Private Wirtschaft†
0032-8960 Privreda
0032-8979 Privredna Izgradnja
0032-8995 Privredni Vjesnik
0032-9002 Privredno Pravni Prirucnik
0032-9010 Prizewinner
0032-9037 Pro Magazin
0032-9053 Pro Football Weekly
0032-9061 Pro
0032-907X Pro Medico
0032-9088 Pro Medico
0032-9096 Pro Metal†
0032-910X Pro Patria
0032-9126 Pro-Sports
0032-9134 Pro Tem
0032-9142 Pro Veritate
0032-9150 Proa
0032-9177 Probe (Santa Barbara)
0032-9185 Probe
0032-9193 Probe (Rockville Centre)
0032-9215 Probe (Memphis)
0032-9223 Problemas
0032-9231 Probleme Agricole†
0032-9258 Probleme des Friedens und des Sozialismus
0032-9266 Probleme Economice†
0032-9290 Problemes d'Outre-Mer†
0032-9304 Problemes Economiques
0032-9312 Problemes Sociaux Congolais *changed to* Problemes Sociaux Zairois
0032-9320 Problemes Sovietiques†
0032-9339 Problemi
0032-9347 Problemi della Pedagogia
0032-9355 Problemi della Sicurezza Sociale†
0032-9363 Problemi di Gestione
0032-9371 Problemi na Izkustvoto
0032-938X Problemi Spoljne Trgovine i Konjunkture
0032-9398 Problemist
0032-941X Problems of Communism
0032-9428 Problemy Osvoeniya Pustyn'
0032-9436 Problems of Economics
0032-9444 Problems of Forensic Medicine & Criminalistics†
0032-9452 Journal of Ichthyology
0032-9460 Problems of Information Transmission
0032-9479 Problems of the Peoples of the USSR†
0032-9487 Problemy
0032-9495 Problemy Alkoholizmu
0032-9509 Problemy Endokrinologii i Gormonoterapii *changed to* Problemy Endokrinologii
0032-9517 Problemy Inwestowania i Rozwoju
0032-9525 Problemy Transportu Samochodowego†
0032-9533 Problemy Tuberkuleza
0032-9541 Problemy Uczelni i Instytutow Medycznych
0032-955X Procedes et Equipements Electroniques†
0032-9568 Proceedings in Print
0032-9576 Journal of Technical Physics
0032-9592 Process Biochemistry
0032-9606 Process Engineering, Plant and Control *see* 0370-1859
0032-9614 Process Journal *changed to* S L A D E Journal
0032-9622 Proche-Orient Chretien
0032-9630 Proche-Orient Etudes Economiques
0032-9649 Proche Orient Etudes Juridiques
0032-9665 Prodotti di Marca
0032-9673 Prodotto Chimico e Aerosol Selezione
0032-9681 Produccion
0032-9703 Producers Guild of America. Journal
0032-9711 Producers' Price-Current
0032-972X Producers Review†
0032-9738 Product Design and Development
0032-9746 Product Design Engineering†
0032-9754 Product Engineering
0032-9762 Product Finishing
0032-9770 Product Licensing Index *changed to* P L I Know How
0032-9789 American Hotel and Motel Association. Product News. *changed to* American Hotel and Motel Association. Buyers Guide for Hotels & Motels.
0032-9797 European Plant Equipment News†
0032-9819 Production
0032-9827 Alberta Drilling Progress and Pipeline Receipts, Weekly Report
0032-9827 Weekly Production and Drilling Statistics *see* 0032-9827
0032-9843 Production and Inventory Management
0032-9878 Production Journal
0032-9908 Productividad
0032-9924 Productivity
0032-9932 Productivity Letter†
0032-9940 Products Finishing
0032-9967 Produktion
0032-9975 Produktivnost
0032-9983 Produrre
0032-9991 Produttivita
0033-0000 Produzione Animale
0033-0019 Proefstation voor de Groenten- en Fruitteelt onder Glas. Mededelingen
0033-0043 Professional Builder
0033-0051 Professional Engineer (Washington)
0033-0078 Professional Engineer
0033-0086 Professional Engineer in Nova Scotia *see* 0225-851X
0033-0094 Professional Fishermen's Association of Tasmania Magazine
0033-0108 Professional Flashes†
0033-0116 Professional Gardener *changed to* Grounds Management Forum
0033-0124 Professional Geographer
0033-0132 Professional Golfer *changed to* P G A Magazine
0033-0140 Professional Medical Assistant
0033-0159 Professional Nutritionist
0033-0167 Professional Photographer
0033-0175 Professional Psychology
0033-0183 Professional Public Service *changed to* Professional Institute of the Public Service of Canada. Journal
0033-0191 Professional Sanitation Management
0033-0205 Professioni Infermieristiche
0033-0213 Professions et Entreprises
0033-0221 Professor
0033-023X Profile†
0033-0248 Profile†
0033-0256 Profile *changed to* Harbinger (Detroit)
0033-0264 Profils Poetiques des Pays Latins
0033-0280 Profit Sharing
0033-0299 Profitable Hobby Merchandising *changed to* Profitable Craft Merchandising
0033-0337 Program
0033-0353 Norsk Rikskringkasting. Programbladet
0033-037X Programme Communiste
0033-0388 Johannesburg Film Society. Programme News
0033-0396 Programmed Learning & Educational Technology
0033-0418 Programmer
0033-0434 Progres
0033-0442 Progres Islamique†
0033-0450 Progres Medical
0033-0469 Progres Scientifique
0033-0477 Progresele Stiintei†
0033-0485 Progreso
0033-0507 Progresos de Patologia y Clinica†
0033-0515 Progresos de Pediatria y Puericultura†
0033-0523 Progresos de Terapeutica Clinica†
0033-054X Progress
0033-0566 Progress
0033-0574 Progress
0033-0582 Progress
0033-0590 Progress†
0033-0604 Progress against Cancer
0033-0612 Progress & Care
0033-0620 Progress in Cardiovascular Diseases
0033-0655 Progress in Organic Coatings
0033-0663 Progress of Education
0033-068X Progress of Theoretical Physics
0033-0698 Progres Social
0033-0701 Progressi in Patologia Cardiovascolare
0033-071X Progressi in Radiologia
0033-0728 Progressio
0033-0736 Progressive
0033-0744 Progressive Agriculture in Arizona
0033-0752 Progressive Architecture
0033-0760 Progressive Farmer
0033-0779 Progressive Fish-Culturist
0033-0787 Progressive Grocer
0033-0795 Progressive Labor *changed to* P L. Progressive Labor Magazine
0033-0809 Progressive Plastics†
0033-0817 Progressive Railroading
0033-0825 Progressive Teacher
0033-0833 Progressive Woman†
0033-085X Progressive World
0033-0868 Progresso Fotografico
0033-0876 Technic International
0033-0884 Projet
0033-0892 Project - Guidelines to Equal Opportunity *see* 0006-4122
0033-0906 Project Concern News *changed to* Concern News
0033-0914 Project
0033-0922 Project on Linguistics Analysis Reports†
0033-0957 Projekt
0033-0981 Proletaire
0033-099X Prolipsis Ton Atychimaton
0033-1007 Prologue (Medford)
0033-1023 National Arts Centre. Calendar of Events
0033-1031 Prologue (Washington)
0033-1058 Promeny
0033-1066 Promesses
0033-1082 Promethee
0033-1090 Promien
0033-1112 Promoting Church Music *see* 0307-6334
0033-1120 Promotion des Affaires
0033-1139 Promotor de Educacion Cristiana
0033-1147 Prompt
0033-1155 Promyshlennaya Energetika
0033-118X Promyshlennoe Stroitel'stvo
0033-1201 Pronab
0033-1228 Proof Sheet
0033-1236 Proofs
0033-1260 Propane / Canada
0033-1279 Propel
0033-1287 Properties
0033-1295 Property and Compensation Reports
0033-1309 Property Journal
0033-1317 Property Mail†
0033-1333 Prophetic News and Israel's Watchman *see* 0033-135X
0033-1341 Prophetic Newsletter
0033-135X Prophetic Witness
0033-1368 Prophylaxe†
0033-1368 Prophylaxe (Heidelberg) *see* 0340-7047
0033-1376 Propiedad Intelectual†
0033-1384 Propos en l'Air
0033-1392 Propos Utiles aux Medecins
0033-1414 Propria Cures (PC)
0033-1422 Proprieta Edilizia Lombarda
0033-1430 Propriete Industrielle Bulletin Documentaire
0033-1449 Propriete Industrielle Nucleaire†
0033-1465 Proscopos
0033-1481 Prospect
0033-1503 Prospectives *changed to* Futuribles
0033-1511 Prospectives
0033-152X Prospector
0033-1538 Prospects in Education *changed to* Prospects
0033-1546 University of Michigan Journal of Law Reform
0033-1562 Prospetti†
0033-1570 Nuove Prospettive
0033-1597 Prostor
0033-1600 Prostor in Cas†
0033-1619 Prosveta
0033-1627 Prosveten Glasnik
0033-1635 Prosvetni Rabotnik
0033-1643 Prosvetni Delavec
0033-1651 Prosvetni Pregled
0033-166X Prosvjeta
0033-1678 Prosvjetni List
0033-1686 Prosvjetni Rad
0033-1708 Protection
0033-1716 Protection
0033-1724 Protection Civile et Securite Industrielle *changed to* Securite Civile et Industrielle
0033-1732 Protection of Metals
0033-1759 Protestant en de Weg *changed to* Tenminste
0033-1767 Protestantesimo
0033-1783 Protetyka Stomatologiczna
0033-1791 Proteus
0033-1805 Proteus
0033-1821 Protistologica
0033-183X Protoplasma
0033-1848 Prove di Letteratura
0033-1856 Provence Historique
0033-1864 Providence Hospital of Southfield. Medical Bulletin†
0033-1872 Province de Liege-Tourisme
0033-1880 Province du Maine
0033-1902 Provincia di Forli in Cifre
0033-1910 Provincia di Padova in Cifre
0033-1929 Provincia Social
0033-1937 Provoker
0033-1945 Provost Parade
0033-1953 Proyecto Hidrometeorologico Centroamericano. Boletin Informativo†
0033-1988 Prumysl Potravin
0033-2003 Przeglad Antropologiczny
0033-2011 Przeglad Artystyczny *changed to* Sztuka
0033-202X Przeglad Biblioteczny
0033-2038 Przeglad Budowlany
0033-2046 Przeglad Dokumentacyjny Materialow Ogniotrwalych
0033-2054 Przeglad Dokumentacyjny Maszyn Rolniczych
0033-2062 Przeglad Dokumentacyjny Elektrotechniki
0033-2070 Przeglad Dokumentacyjny Polskiego i Zagranicznego Pismiennictwa Kolejowego
0033-2089 Elektronika
0033-2097 Przeglad Elektrotechniczny
0033-2100 Przeglad Epidemiologiczny
0033-2119 Przeglad Gastronomiczny
0033-2127 Przeglad Geodezyjny
0033-2135 Przeglad Geofizyczny
0033-2143 Przeglad Geograficzny
0033-2151 Przeglad Geologiczny
0033-216X Przeglad Gorniczy
0033-2178 Przeglad Historyczno-Oswiatowy†
0033-2186 Przeglad Historyczny
0033-2194 Przeglad Humanistyczny

0033-2208 Przeglad Kolejowy Drogowy *see* 0137-284X
0033-2216 Przeglad Kolejowy Elektrotechniczny *see* 0137-2858
0033-2224 Przeglad Kolejowy Mechaniczny *see* 0137-2963
0033-2232 Przeglad Komunikacyjny
0033-2240 Przeglad Lekarski
0033-2259 Przeglad Mechaniczny
0033-2275 Przeglad Odlewnictwa
0033-2283 Przeglad Orientalistyczny
0033-2291 Przeglad Papierniczy
0033-2313 Przeglad Piekarski i Cukierniczy
0033-2321 IB. Informacja Biezaca
0033-233X Bibliografia Analityczna Bibliotekoznawstwa i Informacji Naukowej
0033-2348 Przeglad Pismiennictwa Zagadnien Informacji
0033-2356 Przeglad Socjologiczny†
0033-2364 Przeglad Spawalnictwa
0033-2372 Przeglad Statystyczny
0033-2380 Przeglad Techniczny Tygodnik
0033-2399 Przeglad Telekomunikacyjny
0033-2402 Przeglad Ustawodawstwa i Czasopism Prawniczych Socjalistycznych Krajow Europy
0033-2410 Przeglad Wlokienniczy
0033-2429 Przeglad Wybranych Czasopism Prawniczych Krajow Zachodnich
0033-2437 Przeglad Zachodni
0033-2445 Przeglad Zachodnich Czasopism Ekonomicznych
0033-2453 Przeglad Zagranicznej Literatury Naukowej z Zakresu Genetyki i Hodowli Roslin
0033-2461 Przeglad Zbozowo-Mlynarski
0033-247X Przeglad Zoologiczny
0033-2488 Przekroj
0033-2496 Przemysl Chemiczny
0033-250X Przemysl Spozywczy
0033-2518 Przewodnik Bibliograficzny
0033-2526 Przeglad Dermatologiczny
0033-2534 Przyjaciolka
0033-2542 Psallite
0033-2550 Psalterium
0033-2569 Psi Chi Newsletter
0033-2577 Psihijatrijska Njega/Psychiatric Care *changed to* Vjesnik Medicinskih Sestara i Medicinskih Tehnicara Hrvatske
0033-2585 Psionic Medicine
0033-2615 Psyche
0033-2623 Psyche
0033-264X Psychiatria Clinica
0033-2658 Psychiatria et Neurologia Japonica:
0033-2666 Psychiatria, Neurologia, Neurochirurgia†
0033-2674 Psychiatria Polska
0033-2682 Psychiatric Communications†
0033-2690 Psychiatric Forum
0033-2704 Psychiatric News
0033-2712 O P. Psychiatric Opinion *see* 0163-2655
0033-2720 Psychiatric Quarterly†
0033-2720 Psychiatric Quarterly
0033-2739 Psychiatrie, Neurologie und Medizinische Psychologie
0033-2747 Psychiatry
0033-2755 Psychiatry and Medical Practice Bulletin†
0033-2771 Psychiatry Digest *changed to* Psychiatry Digest (1980)
0033-278X Psychiatry in Medicine *see* 0091-2174
0033-2798 Psychic *see* 0147-7625
0033-2801 Psychic News
0033-2828 Psychoanalytic Quarterly
0033-2836 Psychoanalytic Review
0033-2844 Physchogram
0033-2852 Psychologia
0033-2860 Psychologia Wychowawcza
0033-2879 Psychologica Belgica
0033-2887 Psychological Abstracts
0033-2895 Psychological Association of Trinidad and Tobago. Journal
0033-2909 Psychological Bulletin
0033-2917 Psychological Medicine
0033-2925 Psychological Perspectives
0033-2933 Psychological Record
0033-2941 Psychological Reports
0033-295X Psychological Review
0033-2968 Psychological Studies
0033-2976 Psychologie *see* 0036-7869
0033-2984 Psychologie Francaise
0033-2992 Psychologie und Praxis
0033-300X Psychologie v Ekonomicke Praxi
0033-3018 Psychologische Beitraege
0033-3034 Psychologische Menschenkenntnis
0033-3042 Psychologische Rundschau
0033-3085 Psychology in the Schools
0033-3093 Psychology Quarterly
0033-3107 Psychology Today
0033-3115 Psycholoog
0033-3123 Psychometrika
0033-3131 Psychonomic Science†
0033-314X Psychopathologie Africaine
0033-3158 Psychopharmacology
0033-3166 Psychopharmacology Abstracts
0033-3174 Psychosomatic Medicine
0033-3182 Psychosomatics
0033-3190 Psychotherapy and Psychosomatics
0033-3204 Psychotherapy: Theory, Research and Practice†
0033-3212 Psykisk Haelsa
0033-3239 Ptitsevodstvo
0033-3247 Pubblicista
0033-3255 Pubblicita e Vendita
0033-3263 Pubdisco News
0033-3271 Public Address Engineers Journal *changed to* Public Address
0033-328X Public Administration *changed to* Australian Journal of Public Administration
0033-3298 Public Administration
0033-3301 Public Administration†
0033-331X Public Administration Abstracts and Index of Articles *changed to* Documentation in Public Administration
0033-3328 Public Administration News and Views *see* 0149-8797
0033-3336 Public Administration Recruiter *see* 0149-8797
0033-3344 Public Administration Review
0033-3352 Public Administration Review
0033-3360 Public Administration Survey
0033-3387 Public Affairs Bulletin†
0033-3395 Public Affairs Comment
0033-3409 Public Affairs Information Service. Bulletin
0033-3417 Public Affairs Report
0033-3425 Public Aid in Illinois†
0033-3433 Public Cleansing *see* 0306-6509
0033-3441 Public Contract Law Journal
0033-345X Public Employee Press
0033-3468 Public Enterprise Recorder
0033-3476 Public Finance
0033-3484 Public Health†
0033-3492 Public Health†
0033-3506 Public Health
0033-3514 Public Health Court Digest
0033-3522 Public Health Laboratory
0033-3530 Public Health News†
0033-3549 HSMHA Health Reports *see* 0090-2918
0033-3557 Public Interest
0033-3565 Public Law
0033-3573 Public Library of Youngstown and Mahoning County. Staff Bulletin *changed to* Biblio-Files
0033-3581 Public Library Trustee
0033-3603 Public Lighting
0033-3611 Public Management
0033-362X Public Opinion Quarterly
0033-3638 Public Personnel Review *see* 0091-0260
0033-3646 Public Policy
0033-3654 Public Power
0033-3662 Public Relations *see* 0307-9252
0033-3670 Public Relations Journal
0033-3689 Public Relations Journal of India
0033-3697 Public Relations News
0033-3700 Public Relations Quarterly
0033-3719 Public Relations Reporter†
0033-3727 P R Revue
0033-3735 Public Roads
0033-3743 Public Safety Systems†
0033-3751 Public Schools of New York City. Staff Bulletin *changed to* Learning in New York
0033-376X Public Servant
0033-3778 Public Service Magazine
0033-3786 Public Service Review
0033-3794 Public Undertakings
0033-3808 Public Utilities Fortnightly
0033-3816 Public Welfare
0033-3840 Public Works
0033-3867 Publicaciones Cientificas Alter
0033-3875 Publication Management†
0033-3883 Publicationes Mathematicae
0033-3913 Media News Keys
0033-3921 Publicity Review
0033-3948 Publieke Werken *see* 0046-5577
0033-3956 Publik†
0033-3972 Publisher†
0033-3999 Publitransport
0033-4006 Publizistik
0033-4014 Pueblo†
0033-4030 Puerto Rico Libre†
0033-4049 Puerto Rico Living
0033-4073 Pneumonologie/Pneumonology *see* 0341-2040
0033-4081 Pulp and Paper
0033-409X Pulp & Paper International
0033-4103 Pulp & Paper Magazine of Canada *see* 0316-4004
0033-4111 Pulp Era†
0033-4138 Christian Ministry
0033-4146 Pulpit Digest *see* 0160-838X
0033-4154 Pulpwood Production and Timber Harvesting *see* 0160-6433
0033-4162 Pulse†
0033-4170 Pulse (Lafayette)†
0033-4197 Pulse (Tulsa)
0033-4200 Pulse Beat
0033-4219 Pulse of Public Continuing & Adult Education
0033-4227 Pulse of Youth
0033-4235 Pulso
0033-4251 Pult
0033-426X Pumps-Pompes-Pumpen
0033-4278 Punch
0033-4286 Pungolo del Sud
0033-4294 Pungolo Verde
0033-4308 Punjab Educational Journal†
0033-4316 Punjab Fruit Journal
0033-4324 Punjab Horticultural Journal
0033-4332 Punjab Law Reporter
0033-4340 Punjab Medical Journal
0033-4359 Haryana Veterinarian
0033-4367 Punto de Partida
0033-4375 Punto de Vista†
0033-4391 Punto Omega
0033-4405 Puppenspiel und Puppenspieler
0033-4421 Puppet Post†
0033-443X Puppetry Journal
0033-4448 Purchasing
0033-4456 Purchasing Bulletin *see* 0306-1922
0033-4472 Purchasing Journal *see* 0309-7242
0033-4480 Purchasing Week *see* 0093-1659
0033-4502 Purdue Alumnus
0033-4510 Purdue Engineer
0033-4529 Purdue Pharmacist
0033-4537 Purdue University. School of Electrical Engineering. Annual Research Summary
0033-4545 Pure and Applied Chemistry
0033-4553 Pure and Applied Geophysics
0033-4561 Pure-Bred Dogs, American Kennel Gazette
0033-4588 Pure Verite
0033-4596 Pure Water†
0033-4642 Purple Thumb†
0033-4669 Purpose†
0033-4677 Pursuit & Symposium†
0033-4685 Pursuit
0033-4693 Pustakalaya
0033-4707 Pustakalaya Sandesh
0033-4715 Put' i Putevoe Khozyaistvo
0033-474X Pyrenees
0033-4758 Pythagoras†
0033-4766 Pythagoras
0033-4774 Q B Beam
0033-4782 A F C I Q. Bulletin
0033-4790 Q I M P Quarterly
0033-4804 Q L†
0033-4812 Q S T
0033-4820 Q T C
0033-4839 Qadmoniot
0033-4863 Quaderni del Conoscitore di Stampe *changed to* Conoscitore di Stampe
0033-4898 Quaderni Dello Sport
0033-491X Quaderni di Clinica Ostetrica e Ginecologica
0033-4928 Quaderni di Criminologia Clinica *changed to* Rassegna Penitenziaria e Criminologica
0033-4936 Quaderni di Dibattito Politico
0033-4952 Quaderni di Sociologia
0033-4960 Quaderni Ibero-Americani
0033-4979 Quaderni Sclavo di Diagnostica Clinica e di Laboratorio
0033-4987 Quaderni Urbinati di Cultura Classica
0033-4995 Quadrangle†
0033-5002 Quadrant
0033-5010 Quadrant
0033-5029 Quadrante Sardo†
0033-5037 Quaestiones Entomologicae
0033-5045 Quaker Campus
0033-5053 Quaker History
0033-5061 Quaker Life
0033-507X Quaker Monthly
0033-5088 Quaker Religious Thought
0033-5096 Quaker Service Bulletin
0033-510X Quaker Service Bulletin†
0033-5118 Electrical Contractor
0033-5126 Qualitaet und Zuverlaessigkeit
0033-5134 Qualitas Plantarum et Materiae Vegetabiles *see* 0377-3205
0033-5142 Qualite. Revue Pratique de Controle Industriel
0033-5169 Quality
0033-5177 Quality and Quantity
0033-5207 Quality Control and Applied Statistics
0033-5231 Quality of Sheffield and South Yorkshire
0033-5231 Quality of Sheffield *see* 0033-5231
0033-524X Quality Progress
0033-5266 Quarry
0033-5274 Quarry Managers' Journal *see* 0305-9421
0033-5290 Quarterly Analysis of Failures
0033-5304 Quarterly Bibliography of Economics
0033-5312 Quarterly Blue Book on Joint Stock Companies in India
0033-5320 Canada. Statistics Canada. Quarterly Bulletin of Agricultural Statistics†
0033-5339 Building *changed to* Building Statistics
0033-5347 Quarterly Check -List of Ethnology & Sociology†
0033-5371 Quarterly Check-List of Economics & Political Science†
0033-5398 Quarterly Check-List of Literary History: English, French, German†
0033-5452 Quarterly Construction Statistics
0033-5479 Quarterly Dental Review *see* 0300-5712
0033-5487 Quarterly Digest of Urban and Regional Research†
0033-5495 Quarterly Economic Review
0033-5509 U. S. Federal Trade Commission. Quarterly Financial Report: United States Manufacturing Corporations *see* 0098-681X
0033-5517 Quarterly Inventory of Economic Research on New England†
0033-5525 Quarterly Journal of Crude Drug Research
0033-5533 Quarterly Journal of Economics
0033-555X Quarterly Journal of Experimental Psychology
0033-5568 Quarterly Journal of Forestry
0033-5576 Quarterly Journal of Indian Studies in Sciences†

ISSN INDEX 1041

ISSN	Title
0033-5584	Quarterly Journal of Indian Studies in Social Sciences *changed to* Asian Economic and Social Review
0033-5592	Quarterly Journal of Indian Studies in Technical Knowledge†
0033-5606	Quarterly Journal of Mathematics
0033-5614	Quarterly Journal of Mechanics and Applied Mathematics
0033-5622	Quarterly Journal of Medicine
0033-5630	Quarterly Journal of Speech
0033-5649	Quarterly Journal of Studies on Alcohol *see* 0096-882X
0033-5657	Quarterly Journal of Surgical Sciences
0033-5665	Quarterly Journal of Taiwan Land Credit
0033-5673	Psychiatria et Neurologia Japonica
0033-569X	Quarterly of Applied Mathematics
0033-5711	Quarterly Predictions of National Income and Expenditure
0033-572X	Quarterly Report to Investors in Puerto Rican Securities†
0033-5738	Quarterly Reports on Sulfur Chemistry
0033-5754	Quarterly Review of Agricultural Economics *see* 0156-7446
0033-5762	Quarterly Review of Australian Education. *changed to* Australian Education Review
0033-5770	Quarterly Review of Biology
0033-5789	Quarterly Review of Drilling Statistics
0033-5800	Quarterly Review of Historical Studies
0033-5819	Quarterly Review of Literature *changed to* Quarterly Review of Literature Contemporary Poetry Series
0033-5835	Quarterly Reviews of Biophysics
0033-5843	Australia. Bureau of Statistics. Quarterly Summary of Australian Statistics.†
0033-5851	Quarterly Summary of Business Statistics, New York State
0033-586X	Quartet *see* 0011-9210
0033-5878	Quatre Verites
0033-5894	Quaternary Research
0033-5908	Quatro Rodas
0033-5916	Quattroruote
0033-5924	Quattrosoldi†
0033-5940	Que Tal
0033-5967	Quebec Home & School News
0033-5975	Quebec Industriel
0033-5983	Quebec Official Gazette
0033-5991	Quebec/Travail
0033-6009	Queen *see* 0141-0547
0033-6017	Queen
0033-6025	Queen's Highway†
0033-6033	Queens Medical Magazine
0033-6041	Queen's Quarterly
0033-6068	Queensborough
0033-6076	Queensland Agricultural Journal
0033-6084	Queensland Country Life
0033-6092	Queensland Country Woman
0033-6106	Queensland Dairyfarmer
0033-6114	Queensland Electrical Contractor
0033-6122	Queensland Fruit and Vegetable News
0033-6130	Queensland Garden *changed to* Queensland Home & Garden
0033-6149	Queensland Government Mining Journal
0033-6157	Queensland Heritage†
0033-6165	Q. Industry†
0033-6173	Queensland Journal of Agricultural and Animal Sciences
0033-6181	Queensland Justice of the Peace and Reports *see* 0312-1658
0033-6203	Queensland Motor Industry *changed to* Q A C C Motor Trader
0033-6211	Queensland Nurses Journal†
0033-622X	Incorporates; Queensland Shopkeeper *see* 0034-6144
0033-6238	Queensland Teachers' Journal
0033-6246	Die Quelle
0033-6262	Querce
0033-6270	Query
0033-6289	Quest *changed to* New Quest
0033-6297	Quest (Champaign)
0033-6300	Little Magazine
0033-6319	Quest (Chardon)
0033-6327	Quest (Pullman)
0033-6335	Questa Sicilia
0033-6343	Question†
0033-6351	Questions Actuelles du Socialisme
0033-636X	Questions Internat
0033-6378	Questitalia
0033-6386	Quetta Times
0033-6416	Quick Frozen Foods International
0033-6432	Quid
0033-6440	Quiet Please *changed to* Noise News Digest
0033-6467	Quill†
0033-6475	Quill
0033-6483	Quill
0033-6491	Quill and Quire
0033-6505	Quill and Scroll
0033-6521	Quimica e Industria
0033-653X	Quimica Iberoamericana†
0033-6548	Quincailliers de France *changed to* Quincailliers de France-l'Argus Menager
0033-6556	Quincy College Bulletin
0033-6564	Quintessence
0033-6572	Quintessence International
0033-6599	Quintessenz Journal
0033-6610	Quis Custodiet *changed to* Law & Justice
0033-6637	Quo Vadis
0033-6645	Quoi de Neuf
0033-6661	Quondam
0033-667X	Quote Magazine
0033-6688	Quotes Ending†
0033-6696	R. A. C. S. Newsletter†
0033-670X	R A E C Gazette *changed to* Torch
0033-6718	R. A. E. News
0033-6726	R A K-Information *see* 0346-5764
0033-6734	R A News
0033-6742	R A P
0033-6750	R A P R A Abstracts
0033-6769	R A S
0033-6777	R A S Kennel Control Journal
0033-6785	R A U-Rapport
0033-6807	R & D Management
0033-6815	R. & L. News
0033-6831	R C A Review
0033-684X	R C M Magazine
0033-6858	R. C. M. P. Quarterly
0033-6866	R-C Modeler
0033-6874	Refa Nachrichten
0033-6882	R E L C Journal
0033-6890	Reticuloendothelial Society. Journal
0033-6904	R E S News Exchange
0033-6912	R I B A Library Bulletin *changed to* Architectural Periodicals Index
0033-6939	R I C S Abstracts and Reviews *changed to* R I C S Library Information Service Abstracts and Reviews
0033-6947	R I C S Technical Information Service. Weekly Briefing *changed to* R I C S Library Information Service.Weekly Briefing
0033-6955	R I L M Abstracts of Music Literature
0033-6963	R I O Newsletter
0033-6971	R J
0033-698X	R L A
0033-7021	R N
0033-703X	R O C
0033-7048	R O S C
0033-7056	R. P. A. Bulletin
0033-7064	R P M Weekly
0033-7072	R Q
0033-7099	R S A World
0033-7102	Railway Control Systems *see* 0033-8826
0033-7129	R S I
0033-7137	R.T.A. Journal *changed to* N.T.A. Journal
0033-7145	R T E Guide
0033-7153	R T N D A Communicator
0033-7161	R T T Y Journal
0033-7196	R W D S U Record
0033-720X	R X Sports and Travel
0033-7218	R Z-Illustrierte Romanzeitung
0033-7226	Raadgevend-Ingenieur†
0033-7234	Raam†
0033-7242	Rabbits in Canada
0033-7250	Rabels Zeitschrift fuer auslaendisches und internationales Privatrecht
0033-7269	Raccolto *see* 0040-3776
0033-7277	Race *see* 0306-3968
0033-7285	Race News
0033-7293	Race Relations†
0033-7315	Race Relations and Industry
0033-7323	Race Relations Bulletin *see* 0142-971X
0033-7331	Race Relations Law Survey†
0033-734X	Race Relations News
0033-7366	Racing & Football Outlook
0033-7374	Racing Car News
0033-7390	Racing Pigeon
0033-7404	Racing Pigeon Pictorial
0033-7412	Racing Report†
0033-7420	Racing Specialist
0033-7439	Racing Star Weekly
0033-7447	Racquette
0033-7455	Das Rad
0033-7463	Rad
0033-748X	Denmark. Statens Husholdningsraad. Raad og Resultater Med Tekniske Meddelelser
0033-7498	Rad und Schiene *changed to* Blickpunkt D B
0033-7501	Radar
0033-751X	Radar and Electronics *changed to* I. P. R. E. Review
0033-7528	Radcliffe Quarterly
0033-7536	Informacije Rade Koncar
0033-7544	Radford Review†
0033-7552	Radiaesthesie-Geopathie-Strahlenbiologie
0033-7560	Radiation Botany *see* 0098-8472
0033-7579	Radiation Effects
0033-7587	Radiation Research
0033-7617	Radical America
0033-7625	Radical Humanist
0033-7641	Radical Therapist†
0033-765X	Radio
0033-7668	Radio - Plans
0033-7676	Radio - Television
0033-7684	Radio Active *changed to* Scan
0033-7692	Radio Aids to Marine Navigation
0033-7706	Radio Amateur Callbook Magazine
0033-7714	Radio and Electrical Retailing
0033-7722	Radio and Electronic Engineer
0033-7730	Radio & Electronics
0033-7749	Radio & Television
0033-7757	Radio und Television *changed to* R T V
0033-7765	Radio & Television Weekly *see* 0194-5866
0033-7781	Radio Chassis Television
0033-779X	Radio Club of America. Proceedings
0033-7803	Radio Communication Techniques Electroniques et Audiovisuelles *see* 0397-6424
0033-782X	Radio Constructor *see* 0374-4361
0033-7838	Radio Control Models & Electronics
0033-7846	Radio, Electrical & Furniture Merchandiser†
0033-7854	Radio Electronica *changed to* R E-Radio Electronica
0033-7862	Radio-Electronics
0033-7870	Radioelectronics and Communications Systems
0033-7889	Radio Engineering and Electronic Physics
0033-7897	Radio Fernseh Phono Praxis
0033-7900	Radio Fernsehen Elektronik
0033-7919	Radio Industria *changed to* Radioindustria-Elettronica-Televisione
0033-7927	Radio Japan News
0033-7935	Radio Mentor Electronic†
0033-7943	Radio Mozambique†
0033-7951	Radio Nederland
0033-796X	Radio Portugal Listeners Magazine†
0033-7986	Radio Propagation Predictions for Southern Africa
0033-7994	Radio R E F
0033-8001	Radio Research Laboratories. Journal
0033-801X	Radio Research Laboratories. Review
0033-8028	Radio Revue TV-Electronique Industrielle
0033-8036	Radio Rivista
0033-8052	Radio Technica
0033-8060	Radio Times
0033-8079	Radio Times of India†
0033-8087	R T H†
0033-8095	Radio-TV-Electronic Service *changed to* R T E
0033-8109	Radio-TV Wereld *see* 0027-5298
0033-8133	Radio y Television
0033-8141	Radio y Television Practica
0033-815X	Radio Z S
0033-8168	Radio-Amater
0033-8176	Radiobiologia, Radioterapia e Fisica Medica *see* 0003-4673
0033-8184	Radiobiologia-Radioterapia
0033-8192	Radiobiologiya
0033-8206	Radiobiology†
0033-8214	Radiobote
0033-8222	Radiocarbon
0033-8230	Radiochimica Acta
0033-8249	Radiochimie†
0033-8257	Radiocorriere-TV
0033-8273	Radiographer
0033-8281	Radiography
0033-829X	Radioisotope Report *changed to* Radiation Report
0033-8303	Radioisotopes
0033-8311	Radiokhimiya
0033-832X	Der Radiologe
0033-8338	Radiologia
0033-8346	Radiologia Clinica et Biologica *see* 0378-9837
0033-8354	Radiologia Diagnostica
0033-8362	Radiologia Medica
0033-8389	Radiologic Clinics of North America
0033-8397	Radiologic Technology
0033-8400	Radiological Health Data and Reports. *see* 0091-6722
0033-8419	Radiology
0033-8427	Radiology/Today & Tomorrow†
0033-8443	Radiophysics and Quantum Electronics
0033-8451	Radioprotection
0033-846X	Radioschau *changed to* Elektronikschau
0033-8478	Radiotechnika
0033-8486	Radiotekhnika
0033-8494	Radiotekhnika i Elektronika
0033-8508	Radiotelegrafen
0033-8516	Radiovy Konstrukter *changed to* Amaterske Radio B
0033-8532	Radius
0033-8540	Radmarkt
0033-8559	Imunoloski Zavod. Radovi
0033-8567	Centar za Proucanje i Suzbijanje Alkoholizma i Drugih Ovisnosti. Radovi
0033-8575	Radovi Medicinskog Fakulteta u Zagrebu
0033-8583	Radovi Poljoprivrednog Fakulteta Univerziteta u Sarajevu
0033-8591	Raduga
0033-8605	Radyans'ka Osvita
0033-8613	Radyans'ke Literaturoznavstvo
0033-8621	Rag
0033-8648	Ragguaglio Librario
0033-8656	Ragione
0033-8672	Ragtimer
0033-8680	Rehabilitacia
0033-8699	Rahnema-Ye Ketab
0033-8702	Raiffeisenblatt fuer Niederoesterreich und Wien†
0033-8710	Raiffeisenbote
0033-8729	Spoor
0033-8737	R M F
0033-8745	Rail News
0033-8761	Railroad Magazine *see* 0163-7266
0033-877X	Railroad Model Craftsman
0033-8788	U.S. Railroad Retirement Board. Quarterly Review
0033-8796	Railroad Yardmaster
0033-880X	Railroading *changed to* Railroading Series
0033-8818	Railway Advocate
0033-8826	Railway Age
0033-8834	Railway and Canal Historical Society Journal
0033-8842	Railway and Locomotive Historical Society. Bulletin *see* 0090-7847
0033-8850	Railway Carmen's Journal

1042 ISSN INDEX

0033-8869 Railway Clerk/Interchange
0033-8885 S.A. Railway Engineering *changed to* Railways Southern Africa
0033-8893 Railway Forum†
0033-8907 Railway Gazette *see* 0373-5346
0033-8915 Railway Locomotives and Cars *see* 0033-8826
0033-8923 Railway Magazine
0033-8931 Railway Modeller
0033-894X Railway Research & Engineering News. Section A
0033-8958 Railway Research & Engineering News. Section B
0033-8966 Railway Research & Engineering News. Sections D,E,F and G
0033-8974 Railway Review *changed to* Transport Review
0033-8990 Railway Steel Topics†
0033-9008 Railway Technical Research Institute (J N R). Quarterly Reports
0033-9016 Railway Track and Structures
0033-9032 Railway World
0033-9040 Railways Institute Magazine
0033-9067 Textilia
0033-9075 Raison Presente
0033-9083 Rajasthan Board Journal of Education
0033-9105 Rajasthan Srama Patrika†
0033-9113 Rakam
0033-9121 Rakennuslehti
0033-913X Rakennustekniikka
0033-9148 Rallye Racing
0033-9156 Ramakrishna Mission Institute of Culture. Bulletin
0033-9164 Ramparts†
0033-9172 Ranch Romances†
0033-9180 Randolph-Macon Alumni Bulletin *changed to* Randolph-Macon College. Bulletin
0033-9199 Range
0033-9202 Rangefinder
0033-9229 Ranger Rick's Nature Magazine
0033-9237 Rangers Scout
0033-9245 Ransomer
0033-9261 Rapid Handler
0033-9296 Rapport†
0033-930X Racquet
0033-9318 Rasprostranenie Pechati
0033-9334 Rassegna Chimica
0033-9342 Rassegna Cinofila†
0033-9350 Camera di Commercio di la Spezia. Rassegna Commerciale *see* 0391-7983
0033-9377 Rassegna dei Lavori Pubblici
0033-9385 Rassegna Del Lavoro
0033-9407 Rassegna del Mercato
0033-9415 Rassegna dell' Arbitrato
0033-9423 Rassegna della Letteratura Italiana
0033-9431 Rassegna della Letteratura Odontoiatrica
0033-944X Rassegna della Letteratura Sui Cicli Economici
0033-9458 Rassegna della Stampa
0033-9466 Rassegna dell'Istruzione Secondaria
0033-9482 Rassegna di Cultura e Vita Scolastica
0033-9504 Rassegna di Diritto Cinematografico, Teatrale e della Radiotelevisione
0033-9512 Rassegna di Diritto Pubblico
0033-9539 Rassegna di Ipnosi e Medicina Psicosomatica
0033-9547 Rassegna di Legislazione Italiana Nei Rapporti Internazionali†
0033-9555 Rassegna di Medicina Sperimentale
0033-9571 Rassegna di Pedagogia
0033-958X Rassegna di Politica e di Storia
0033-9598 Rassegna di Scienze Filosofiche
0033-9601 Rassegna di Servizio Sociale
0033-961X Rassegna di Statistiche del Lavoro
0033-9628 Rassegna di Studi Penitenziari *changed to* Rassegna Penitenziaria e Criminologica
0033-9636 Rassegna di Studi Psichiatrici
0033-9644 Rassegna di Teologia
0033-9652 Rassegna Ed Archivio di Chirurgia
0033-9687 Rassegna Grafica
0033-9695 Rassegna Internazionale di Clinica e Terapia
0033-9709 Rassegna Internazionale di Meccanica *changed to* Rassegna di Meccanica
0033-9725 Rassegna Italiana di Linguistica Applicata
0033-9733 Rassegna Italiana di Ricerca Psichica
0033-975X Rassegna Lucchese
0033-9768 Rassegna Medica e Culturale†
0033-9776 Rassegna Medica Sarda
0033-9784 Rassegna Melodrammatica
0033-9792 Rassegna Mensile di Israel
0033-9806 Rassegna Musicale Curci
0033-9814 I S L E. Rassegna Parlamentare - Schedario Legislativo
0033-9822 Rassegna Petrolifera
0033-9830 Rassegna Quindicinale dell'Agricoltura *changed to* Ecomese
0033-9849 Rassegna Sindacale
0033-9857 Associazione Italiana per i Rapporti Culturali Con l'Unione Sovietica. Rassegna Sovietica
0033-9865 Rassegna Speleologica Italiana†
0033-9873 Rassegna Storica del Risorgimento
0033-9881 Rassegna Storica Toscana
0033-9903 Rassegna Tecnica Enel *changed to* Rassegna Tecnica di Problemi dell'Energia Elettrica
0033-9911 Rassegna Trimestrale di Odontoiatria
0033-992X Rassegna di Urologia e Nefrologia†
0033-9938 Raster†
0033-9946 Rastitel'nye Resursy
0033-9962 Rateko
0033-9970 Radiobranchen
0033-9970 Rateksa *see* 0033-9970
0033-9989 Der Ratgeber
0033-9997 Ratgeber fuer Kranke und Gesunde *changed to* Ratgeber aus der Apotheke
0034-0006 Ratio
0034-0014 Ratio *see* 0035-6816
0034-0030 Individualist
0034-0049 Rational Living
0034-0057 Rationalisierung
0034-0065 Rationalist
0034-0073 Rationelles Buero *see* 0340-3491
0034-0081 Formerly; Raumausstatter *changed to* Raum und Textil
0034-009X Raumausstattung Report†
0034-0103 Raumfahrtforschung *changed to* Zeitschrift fuer Flugwissenschaften - Weltraumforschung
0034-0111 Raumforschung und Raumordnung
0034-012X Rautakaupan Uutiset
0034-0138 Rave†
0034-0146 Raven
0034-0162 Ray Palmer's Forum†
0034-0170 Rayito
0034-0197 Rayons
0034-0200 Rays of Sunshine *see* 0039-5412
0034-0227 Razgledi
0034-0235 Razon y Fe
0034-0243 Razonoda Miliona
0034-026X Razvedka i Okhrana Nedr
0034-0286 Re: Arts and Letters *changed to* RE: Artes Liberales
0034-0294 Re: Search†
0034-0308 Reach
0034-0316 Reach Out†
0034-0324 Reaching Out *changed to* Feelings
0034-0332 Reactor Technology†
0034-0359 Read Magazine
0034-0367 Readaption *see* 0705-9094
0034-0375 Reader's Digest
0034-0383 Reader's Digest (Asian Edition)
0034-0391 Reader's Digest (Australian Edition)
0034-0405 Reader's Digest (British Edition)
0034-0413 Reader's Digest (Canadian-English Edition)
0034-0421 Reader's Digest (Indian Edition)
0034-043X Reader's Digest (Japanese Edition)
0034-0448 Reader's Digest (New Zealand Edition)
0034-0456 Reader's Digest (South African Edition)
0034-0464 Readers' Guide to Periodical Literature
0034-0472 Reading
0034-0502 Reading Horizons
0034-0510 Reading Improvement
0034-0537 Reading Newsreport†
0034-0545 Reading Quarterly†
0034-0553 Reading Research Quarterly
0034-0561 Reading Teacher
0034-057X Reaktorn
0034-0588 Real†
0034-0596 Real Academia de Ciencias Exactas, Fisicas y Naturales. Revista
0034-060X Real Academia de Cordoba de Ciencias, Bellas Letras y Nobles Artes. Boletin
0034-0618 Real Academia de Farmacia. Anales
0034-0626 Real Academia de la Historia. Boletin
0034-0634 Real Academia Nacional de Medicina. Anales
0034-0642 Real Confessions
0034-0669 Real Estate and Stock Journal
0034-0677 Real Estate Appraiser *see* 0271-258X
0034-0693 Real Estate Investment Planning Checklist and Forms
0034-0707 Real Estate Forum
0034-0715 Real Estate Insider Newsletter
0034-0723 Real Estate Investment Ideas
0034-0731 Real Estate Investment Planning
0034-074X Real Estate Journal
0034-0758 Real Estate Law Brief Case
0034-0766 Real Estate News (New York)
0034-0774 Real Estate Record and Builder's Guide
0034-0790 Real Estate Review
0034-0804 Real Estate Today
0034-0839 Real Life Confessions
0034-0847 Real Living
0034-0855 Real Property, Probate and Trust Journal
0034-0863 Real Sociedad Arqueologica. Boletin Arqueologico
0034-0871 Real Sociedad Espanola de Fisica y Quimica. Anales. Serie A: Fisica *changed to* Real Sociedad Espanola de Fisica y Quimica. Anales de Fisica
0034-088X Real Sociedad Espanola de Fisica y Quimica. Anales. Serie B: Quimica *changed to* Real Sociedad Espanola de Fisica y Quimica. Anales de Quimica
0034-0898 Real West
0034-091X Realist†
0034-0936 Realites Libyennes
0034-0960 Reality
0034-0979 Reality
0034-0987 Reality Magazine
0034-0995 Realta
0034-1029 Realta Sovietica
0034-1037 Realtor Headlines†
0034-1045 Realty and Building
0034-1053 Realty and Chain Store Renting Leads *changed to* Realty
0034-1061 Realty Review†
0034-107X Reaper
0034-1096 Reassurance *see* 0153-3614
0034-1118 Rebe und Wein
0034-1134 Reblooming Iris Reporter
0034-1142 Rec Naroda
0034-1169 C L R Recent Developments
0034-1185 Recent Publications on Governmental Problems
0034-1193 Recenti Progressi in Medicina
0034-1207 Recenzija
0034-1215 Rechabite
0034-1223 Recherche Aerospatiale
0034-1231 C A R D A N. Bulletin d'Information et de Liaison†
0034-124X Recherche Sociale
0034-1258 Recherches de Science Religieuse
0034-1266 Recherches de Theologie Ancienne et Medievale
0034-1274 Recherches Economiques de Louvain
0034-1282 Recherches Sociographiques
0034-1290 Rechnoi Transport
0034-1312 Recht der Jugend und des Bildungswesens
0034-1320 Recht der Schiffahrt
0034-1339 Recht im Amt
0034-1347 R W P
0034-1355 Rechtsarchiv der Wirtschaft *changed to* Recht der Wirtschaft
0034-1363 Rechtspflegerblatt
0034-1371 Rechtsprechung der Bau-Ausfuehrung *changed to* Rechtsprechung Zum Privaten Baurecht
0034-138X Rechtsprechung in Strafsachen
0034-1398 Rechtstheorie
0034-1401 Formerly; Rechtswissenschaftliche Dokumentation *changed to* Bibliographie Staat und Recht
0034-141X Reclamation Era *changed to* Era (Denver)
0034-1436 Reclamation Safety News *see* 0270-4447
0034-1452 Recommend: Florida
0034-1479 Reconciliation Quarterly
0034-1487 Reconstruction
0034-1495 Reconstructionist
0034-1509 Rencontre Orient Occident†
0034-1517 Record†
0034-1525 Lancashire Authors' Association. Record
0034-1541 Record
0034-155X Record Collector
0034-1568 Record Collector
0034-1576 Record Mirror
0034-1592 Record Research
0034-1606 Record Retailer *changed to* Music Week
0034-1614 Record Stockman
0034-1622 Record World
0034-1630 Recorded Sound
0034-1649 Recorder
0034-1657 Recorder†
0034-1665 Recorder and Music
0034-1673 Recording Engineer-Producer
0034-1703 Records and Statistics†
0034-1711 Records Management Journal†
0034-172X Records Management Quarterly *changed to* A R M A Records Management Quarterly
0034-1738 Records of Huntingdonshire
0034-1746 Records of the Month†
0034-1770 Recreation Management
0034-1827 Recruiting Trends
0034-1835 Recueil Dalloz-Sirey
0034-1843 Recueil de Medecine Veterinaire d'Alfort
0034-1851 Recueil des Brevets d'Invention
0034-186X Recueil des Travaux Chimiques des Pays-Bas
0034-1878 Recueil Juridique de l'Est Securite Sociale
0034-1886 Recueil Officiel des Marques de Fabrique et de Commerce†
0034-1894 Recueil Penant *see* 0336-1551
0034-1916 Recuperatie
0034-1924 Recuperation
0034-1932 Recusant History
0034-1940 Red and Black
0034-1959 Red and Green
0034-1967 Red Cedar Review
0034-1975 Red Clay Reader†
0034-1983 Red Cross Newsletter *changed to* Good Neighbor
0034-1991 Panorama
0034-2009 Red Hill Press *see* 0147-4936
0034-2017 Red Mole *see* 0142-6575
0034-2025 Red Notes
0034-2033 Red Poll News
0034-2041 Red Shield *changed to* Red Shield News
0034-2068 Red Star Weekly
0034-2076 Red Tape
0034-2092 Redaktions-Archiv
0034-2106 Redbook
0034-2114 Reddingwezen
0034-2122 Redeemer's Voice
0034-2130 Redlands Bulldog
0034-2165 Redstart
0034-2173 Redwood Empire Dental News
0034-2181 Redwood Rancher
0034-219X Reed's Aircraft & Equipment News†
0034-2203 Reed's Marine Equipment News *see* 0140-8046
0034-2211 Reeducation
0034-222X Reeducation Orthophonique
0034-2238 Reel
0034-2246 Referateblatt zur Raumordnung *see* 0341-2512

ISSN INDEX 1043

0034-2254 Referatekartei Korrosion-Korrosionsschutz†
0034-2262 Bibliographie Philosophie
0034-2289 Referativnyi Zhurnal. Avtomatika, Telemekhanika i Vychislitel'naya Tekhnika
0034-2297 Referativnyi Zhurnal. Avtomobil'nyi i Gorodskoi Transport
0034-2300 Referativnyi Zhurnal. Biologiya
0034-2319 Referativnyi Zhurnal. Ekonomika Promyshlennosti
0034-2327 Referativnyi Zhurnal. Elektrotekhnika i Energetika
0034-2335 Referativnyi Zhurnal. Farmakologiya. Khimioterapevticheskie Sredstva. Toksikologiya
0034-2343 Referativnyi Zhurnal. Fizika
0034-2351 Referativnyi Zhurnal. Geodeziya *changed to* Referativnyi Zhurnal. Geodeziya Aeros' Emka
0034-236X Referativnyi Zhurnal. Geofizika
0034-2378 Referativnyi Zhurnal. Geografiya
0034-2386 Referativnyi Zhurnal. Gornoe Delo
0034-2394 Gornye Mashiny *changed to* Referativnyi Zhurnal. Gornoe i Neftepromyslovye Mashinostroenie
0034-2408 Referativnyi Zhurnal. Issledovanie Kosmicheskogo Prostranstva
0034-2416 Referativnyi Zhurnal. Khimicheskoe i Kholodil'noe Mashinostroenie *changed to* Referativnyi Zhurnal. Khimicheskoe, Neftepererabatyvayschchee i Polimernoe Mashinostroenie
0034-2424 Referativnyi Zhurnal. Kotlostroenie
0034-2432 Referativnyi Zhurnal. Legkaya Promyshlennost'
0034-2440 Referativnyi Zhurnal. Lesovedenie i Lesovodstvo
0034-2459 Referativnyi Zhurnal. Mashinostroitel'nye Materialy, Konstruktsii i Raschet Detale; Mashin. Gidroprivod
0034-2467 Referativnyi Zhurnal. Matematika
0034-2475 Referativnyi Zhurnal. Meditsinskaya Geografiya
0034-2483 Referativnyi Zhurnal. Mekhanika
0034-2491 Referativnyi Zhurnal. Metallurgiya
0034-2505 Referativnyi Zhurnal. Metrologiya i Izmeritel'naya Tekhnika
0034-2513 Referativnyi Zhurnal. Nasosostroenie i Kompressorstroenie *changed to* Referativnyi Zhurnal. Nasosostroenie i Kompressorostroenie. Kholodil'noe Mashinostroenie
0034-2521 Referativnyi Zhurnal. Oborudovanie Pishchevoi Promyshlennosti
0034-253X Referativnyi Zhurnal. Organizatsiya Upravleniya Promyshlennostyu *changed to* Referativnyi Zhurnal. Organizatsiya Upravleniya
0034-2548 Referativnyi Zhurnal. Pochvovedenie i Agrokhimiya
0034-2556 Referativnyi Zhurnal. Promyshlennyi Transport
0034-2564 Referativnyi Zhurnal. Raketostroenie
0034-2572 Referativnyi Zhurnal. Svarka
0034-2580 Referativnyi Zhurnal. Tekhnologiya i Oborudovanie Tsellyulozno-vumazhnogo i Poligraficheskogo Proizvodstva
0034-2599 Referativnyi Zhurnal. Tekhnologiya Mashinostroeniya
0034-2602 Referativnyi Zhurnal. Traktory i Sel'skokhozyaistvennye Mashiny i Orudiya
0034-2610 Referativnyi Zhurnal. Truboprovodnyi Transport
0034-2629 Referativnyi Zhurnal. Turbostroyeniye
0034-2637 Referativnyi Zhurnal. Voprosy Tekhnicheskogo Progressa i Organizatsii Proizvodstva v Mashinostroenii
0034-2645 Referativnyi Zhurnal. Vzaimodeistvie Raznykh Vidov Transporta i Konteinernye Perevozki
0034-2653 Referativnyi Zhurnal. Yadernye Reaktory
0034-2661 Referativnyi Zhurnal. Zhivotnovodstvo i Veterinariya
0034-267X Referativnyi Zhurnal. Radiotekhnika
0034-2688 Referatovy Vyber z Anestesiologie a Resuscitace
0034-2696 Referatovy Vyber z Chirurgie
0034-270X Referatovy Vyber z Chorob Infekcnich
0034-2718 Referatovy Vyber z Dermatovenerologie
0034-2726 Referatovy Vyber z Endokrinologie
0034-2734 Referatovy Vyber z Fysiologie
0034-2742 Referatovy Vyber z Gastroenterologie
0034-2750 Referatovy Vyber z Gerontologie a Geriatrie
0034-2769 Referatovy Vyber z Kardiologie, Fysiologie a Patologie Obehoveho Ustroji
0034-2777 Referatovy Vyber z Lekarenstvi
0034-2785 Referatovy Vyber z Lekarskeho Tisku o Vychove a Doskolovani Zdravotnickych Pracovniku
0034-2793 Referatovy Vyber z Neurologie
0034-2807 Referatovy Vyber z Oftalmologie
0034-2815 Referatovy Vyber z Onkologie
0034-2823 Referatovy Vyber z Ortopedie, Traumatologie a Pribuznych Oboru
0034-2831 Referatovy Vyber z Otorhinolaryngologie a Foniatrie
0034-284X Referatovy Vyber z Patologicke Anatomie
0034-2858 Referatovy Vyber z Pediatrie
0034-2866 Referatovy Vyber z Porodnictvi a Gynekologie
0034-2874 Referatovy Vyber z Rentgenologie
0034-2882 Referatovy Vyber z Revmatologie
0034-2890 Referatovy Vyber z Pneumologie a Tuberkulosy
0034-2904 Referatovy Vyber ze Sportovni Mediciny
0034-2912 Japan. National Diet Library. Reference
0034-2939 Reflector
0034-2947 Reflector
0034-2955 Reflector
0034-2963 Reflector
0034-2971 Reflets et Perspectives de la Vie Economique
0034-298X Reflets Guildiens†
0034-3005 Reflexion *changed to* Revista Canadiense de Estudios Hispanicos
0034-3013 Kontakt und Reflexionen *changed to* Kontakt
0034-3021 Reformatio
0034-303X Reformation Review
0034-3048 Reformation Today
0034-3056 Reformed World
0034-3064 Reformed Review
0034-3072 Reformed Theological Review
0034-3102 Refractories
0034-3110 Refractories Journal
0034-3129 Refrigerated Transporter
0034-3137 Refrigeration
0034-3145 Refrigeration Service and Contracting
0034-3153 Refuah Veterinarith
0034-317X Regan Report on Hospital Law
0034-3188 Regan Report on Medical Law
0034-3196 Regan Report on Nursing Law
0034-320X Regards sur le Comite d'Etablissement d'Orly Sud
0034-3218 Regelrecht
0034-3250 Regensburger Bistumsblatt
0034-3269 Der Reggeboge
0034-3285 T V Panorama *changed to* Panorama/Ons Land
0034-3293 Regio Basiliensis
0034-3315 Region Six Sentinel
0034-3323 Regional Action
0034-3331 Regional and Urban Economics-Operational Methods *changed to* Regional Science & Urban Economics
0034-334X International Seismological Centre. Regional Catalogue of Earthquakes
0034-3358 Regional Cultural Institute. Journal
0034-3366 Regional Development Newsletter *see* 0310-5946
0034-3374 Regional Plan News *changed to* R P A News
0034-3382 Incorporating; Regional Review Quarterly *see* 0196-4003
0034-3390 Regional Spotlight
0034-3404 Regional Studies
0034-3412 Regione e Potere Locale
0034-3420 Region's Agenda
0034-3439 Regionwide†
0034-3471 Regmaker
0034-348X Regmi Research Series
0034-3498 Regno
0034-3501 Rehabilitation in South Africa
0034-351X Japanese Journal of Rehabilitation Medicine
0034-3528 Rehabilitation†
0034-3536 Die Rehabilitation
0034-3552 Rehabilitation Counseling Bulletin
0034-3579 Rehabilitation Literature
0034-3587 Rehabilitation Record *changed to* U.S. Health Care Financing Administration Record
0034-3609 Rehovot
0034-3617 Reinforced Plastics
0034-3625 Reiniger und Waescher
0034-3633 Reino
0034-3641 Reinsurance Reporter
0034-365X Reinwardtia
0034-3668 Deutsche Reisebuero-Zeitung
0034-3676 Reiseliv i Norge *changed to* Reiseliv
0034-3684 Reiss-Davis Clinic Bulletin†
0034-3692 Reiter Revue International
0034-3714 Refrigeration
0034-3722 Refrigeration and Air Conditioning Technology *changed to* Techniques of Refrigeration and Air Conditioning
0034-3749 Rekenschap
0034-3765 Relacoes Humanas†
0034-3773 Relais
0034-3781 Relations
0034-379X Relations Industrielles
0034-3803 Relations Latines
0034-3811 Relations Publiques Informations
0034-382X Relay Association Journal *changed to* Cablevision News
0034-3838 Relazioni†
0034-3846 Relazioni Internazionali
0034-3854 Etocomunicazione *changed to* Etocom (1980)
0034-3862 Relazioni Sociali†
0034-3897 Relics
0034-3935 Religioese Graphik
0034-3943 Religion and Church in the Communist Orbit†
0034-3951 Religion and Society
0034-396X Religion and Society *see* 0093-2582
0034-3978 R C D A-Religion in Communist Dominated Areas
0034-3986 Religion in Life *see* 0270-9287
0034-401X Religion Teacher's Journal
0034-4036 Religiose nell' Apostolato Diretto
0034-4044 Religious & Theological Abstracts
0034-4052 Religious and Theological Resources†
0034-4060 Religious Book Review Index
0034-4079 Religious Broadcasting
0034-4087 Religious Education
0034-4095 Religious Humanism
0034-4109 R N A Newsletter
0034-4117 Religious Periodicals Index†
0034-4125 Religious Studies
0034-4141 Reluire *changed to* Art et Metiers du Livre
0034-4168 Remag
0034-4176 Remainders' Book Italiano
0034-4184 Remanso
0034-4192 Remarques Africaines *changed to* Ramerques Arabo-Africaines
0034-4206 Remedes des Corps et des Ames *see* 0048-7228
0034-4214 Remedial Education
0034-4230 Reminder†
0034-4249 Remodeling Contractor
0034-4257 Remote Sensing of Environment
0034-4265 Removals and Storage
0034-4273 Rempart
0034-4281 Renaissance *changed to* New Reformation
0034-429X Renaissance and Reformation
0034-4311 Renaissance Deux-Mille *changed to* Tribune Gaulliste
0034-4338 Renaissance Quarterly
0034-4346 Renascence
0034-4354 Rencontres Sous le Signe de la Langue Francaise
0034-4362 Renderer *see* 0090-8932
0034-4370 Rendez-Vous
0034-4397 Rendez-Vous de la Mode
0034-4400 Rendezvous
0034-4419 Rendiconti
0034-4427 Rendiconti di Matematica
0034-4435 Renegotiation
0034-4451 Renfro Valley Bugle
0034-446X Renovacion
0034-4478 Renovacion
0034-4486 Renovatio
0034-4494 Renovation *see* 0041-5103
0034-4508 Rensselaer Engineer
0034-4516 Rent-All Magazine
0034-4524 Rental Equipment Register
0034-4532 Rental Laundry Management *changed to* Laundry Cleaning World
0034-4540 Rentner und Pensionist
0034-4567 Repertoire Bibliographique de la Philosophie
0034-4575 Repertoire des Voyages
0034-4583 Repertoire Permanent des Groupes Financiers et Industriels *changed to* Repertoire des Groupes d'Entreprise
0034-4591 Repertorio Analitico della Stampa Italiana. Quotidiani e Periodici
0034-4613 Repertorio Centroamericano†
0034-463X Repertorium Verpakte Geneesmiddelen Periodiek Overzicht voor Artsen *changed to* Repertorium Farmaceutische Specialites Periodiek Overzicht voor Artsen
0034-4648 Repertuar Khudozhestvennoi Samodeyatel'nosti
0034-4656 Varta Report
0034-4664 Report from Germany†
0034-4672 Report of Ionosphere and Space Research in Japan *changed to* Solar Terrestrial Environmental Research in Japan
0034-4680 Report on Education of the Disadvantaged
0034-4699 Report on Education Research
0034-4702 Report on Preschool Education
0034-4745 Reportage
0034-4753 Reporter
0034-4761 Reporter
0034-477X New Jersey Association for Health, Physical Education and Recreation Reporter
0034-4788 Reporter
0034-4796 Reporter for Conscience' Sake
0034-480X Reporter of Construction Equipment *see* 0149-5240
0034-4818 Reportero Industrial
0034-4826 I A B C Notebook†
0034-4834 Reporting on Governments
0034-4842 Union of Japanese Scientists and Engineers. Reports of Statistical Application Research
0034-4869 Reports on Higher Education *changed to* W I C H E Reports
0034-4877 Reports on Mathematical Physics†
0034-4877 Reports on Mathematical Physics
0034-4885 Reports on Progress in Physics
0034-4893 Representation
0034-4907 Representative Research in Social Psychology
0034-4915 Representor
0034-4923 Reprint Bulletin
0034-4931 Reprints from the Soviet Press
0034-4958 Reproduction
0034-4966 Reproduction Paper News Bulletin *changed to* Reproduction Bulletin
0034-4974 Reproductions Review *see* 0198-9065

0034-5016 China, Republic. National Central Library. Newsletter
0034-5024 South Africa. Department of Statistics. Bulletin of Statistics
0034-5040 Republica Argentina. Transporte Aereo. Noticiero
0034-5059 Republican†
0034-5067 Republican Battle Line *see* 0145-1677
0034-5075 Republican Journal
0034-5091 Res Gestae
0034-5105 Resale Weekly
0034-5113 Research†
0034-5121 Research and Farming
0034-513X Research and Industry
0034-5148 Research and Sponsored Programs at Notre Dame *changed to* Notre Dame Report
0034-5156 Research Association of Powder Technology, Japan. Journal. *see* 0386-6157
0034-5164 Research Communications in Chemical Pathology and Pharmacology
0034-5172 Alberta Research Council. Bulletins
0034-5180 Alberta Research Council. Information Series
0034-5199 Research/Development *see* 0160-4074
0034-5202 Research Film†
0034-5210 Research in African Literatures
0034-5229 Research in Education *see* 0098-0897
0034-5237 Research in Education
0034-5245 Research in Librarianship
0034-5253 Research in Reproduction
0034-5261 Research in the Life Sciences
0034-527X Research in the Teaching of English
0034-5288 Research in Veterinary Science
0034-5296 Research Index
0034-530X Hokkaido University. Research Institute for Catalysis. Journal
0034-5318 Research Institute for Mathematical Sciences. Publications
0034-5326 Research into Higher Education Abstracts
0034-5334 Research Management
0034-5342 Research News†
0034-5350 Research Papers in Physical Education
0034-5369 University of North Carolina. Institute for Research in Social Science. Research Reviews.†
0034-5377 American Alliance for Health, Physical Education and Recreation. Research Quarterly *changed to* Research Quarterly for Exercise and Sport
0034-5393 California University Center for Research and Development in Higher Education. Research Reporter
0034-5407 American Institute for Economic Research. Research Reports
0034-5415 Research Reports in Social Science†
0034-5423 Research Reports in the Social Sciences
0034-5431 Research Society of Pakistan. Journal
0034-5458 Researcher†
0034-5466 Researches on Population Ecology
0034-5474 Resena de Hispanoamerica†
0034-5490 Reservbefal
0034-5504 Reserve Bank of Australia. Statistical Bulletin
0034-5512 Reserve Bank of India. Bulletin
0034-5520 Reserve Bank of Malawi. Economic and Financial Review *see* 0376-5725
0034-5539 Reserve Bank of New Zealand. Bulletin
0034-5555 Resident and Staff Physician
0034-5571 Resin Review
0034-5598 Resistenza
0034-5636 Resort Management
0034-5652 Resource†
0034-5660 Resources for Youth Ministry
0034-5687 Respiration Physiology
0034-5695 Respond†
0034-5709 Response
0034-5725 Response
0034-575X Ressorgiment
0034-5792 Restaurante
0034-5806 Restaurator
0034-5814 Restauratoeren
0034-5822 Restoration & Eighteenth Century Theatre Research
0034-5830 Restoration Herald
0034-5857 Results of the Business Survey Carried out Among Heads of Enterprises in the Community
0034-5865 Resumen†
0034-5873 Abstracts of Military Bibliography
0034-5873 Resumenes Analiticos Sobre Defensa y Seguridad Nacional/Abstracts of Military Bibliography *see* 0034-5873
0034-5881 Resumenes de Articulos Cientificos y Tecnicos. Serie A: Quimica Industrial *changed to* Alerta Informativa. Serie A: Quimica Industrial
0034-589X Resumenes de Articulos Cientificos y Tecnicos. Serie B: Fisica Aplicada *changed to* Alerta Informativa. Serie B: Fisica Aplicada
0034-5903 Resumenes de Articulos Cientificos y Tecnicos. Serie C: Ciencia y Tecnica de los Metales *changed to* Alerta Informativa. Serie C: Ciencia y Tecnica de los Metales
0034-5911 Resumenes de Articulos Cientificos y Tecnicos. Serie D: Ingenieria y Tecnologia Varias *changed to* Alerta Informativa. Serie D: el Mundo Rural
0034-592X Resumenes de Articulos. Cientificos y Tecnicos. Serie E: Economia de la Empresa *see* 0210-7023
0034-5946 Mozambique. Servico Meteorologico. Resumos Meteorologicas para a Aeronautica
0034-5954 Resumos Meteorologicos para a Aeronautica
0034-5970 Resurgence
0034-5989 Retail Ad News†
0034-5997 Retail Advertising Week
0034-6012 Retail Business
0034-6020 Retail Chemist *see* 0009-3033
0034-6039 Retail Clerks Advocate†
0034-6047 Retail Control
0034-6055 Retail Food Price Bulletin *see* 0028-6168
0034-6063 Retail Jeweller
0034-6071 Retail Labor Report *see* 0148-7930
0034-608X Retail Lumberman
0034-6098 Retail Newsagent, Bookseller and Stationer *changed to* Retail Newsagent
0034-611X Retail Price Indices *see* 0302-9336
0034-6136 Retail World
0034-6144 Retailer of Queensland
0034-6152 Retarded
0034-6160 Retired Officer
0034-6179 Retirement Life
0034-6187 Rettens Gang
0034-6195 Rjettur
0034-6209 Reuma
0034-6217 Reuma Bulletin
0034-6233 Reumatologia
0034-6241 Reus Avicola y Agricola
0034-625X Revealing Confession
0034-6268 Revealing Romances
0034-6276 Reveil de Djibouti *changed to* Nation Djibouti
0034-6284 Reveil Missionnaire
0034-6292 Reveil Socialiste de Lannemezan
0034-6306 Reveille
0034-6314 Revetements Sols et Murs†
0034-6322 American Logistics Association Review
0034-6330 Review
0034-6349 Review: Worldwide Reinsurance
0034-6357 Review
0034-6373 Review and Expositor
0034-6381 Review and Herald *see* 0161-1119
0034-6403 Review of Agricultural Economics Malaysia
0034-6438 Review of Plant Pathology
0034-6446 Review of Black Political Economy
0034-6454 Review of Business
0034-6462 Alaska Review of Business and Economic Conditions *see* 0162-5403
0034-6489 Review of Communist Scientific and Political Publications (Soviet Union)†
0034-6497 Review of Czechoslovak Medicine
0034-6500 Turkiye Is Bankasi. Review of Economic Conditions
0034-6519 Bank Leumi Economic Review
0034-6527 Review of Economic Studies
0034-6535 Review of Economics and Statistics
0034-6543 Review of Educational Research
0034-6551 Review of English Studies
0034-656X Review of Existential Psychology and Psychiatry†
0034-6578 Review of Ghana Law
0034-6586 Review of Income and Wealth
0034-6594 Review of Indonesian and Malayan Affairs
0034-6608 Review of International Cooperation
0034-6616 Review of Marketing and Agricultural Economics
0034-6624 Review of Medical and Veterinary Mycology
0034-6632 Review of Metaphysics
0034-6640 Review of National Literatures
0034-6659 Nutrition and Food Science
0034-6667 Review of Palaeobotany and Palynology
0034-6675 Review of Physical Chemistry of Japan
0034-6683 Review of Physics in Technology *see* 0305-4624
0034-6691 Review of Polarography
0034-6705 Review of Politics
0034-6713 Review of Popular Astronomy†
0034-6721 Review of Religions
0034-6748 Review of Scientific Instruments
0034-6756 Standard & Poor's Review of Securities Regulation
0034-6764 Review of Social Economy
0034-6772 Review of Soviet Medical Sciences†
0034-6780 Review of Surgery *see* 0149-7944
0034-6799 Review of the Economic Conditions in Italy
0034-6802 Review of the News
0034-6810 Review of the River Plate
0034-6829 Magyar Jog es Kulfoldi Jogi Szemle
0034-6853 Reviews of Geophysics & Space Physics
0034-6861 Reviews of Modern Physics
0034-687X Reviews of Pure and Applied Chemistry†
0034-6888 Revija
0034-6896 Revija Skolstva i Prosvetna Dokumentacija
0034-690X Revija za Kriminalistiko in Kriminologijo
0034-6918 Revision og Regnskabsvaesen
0034-6926 Revista A P H
0034-6934 Revista Aerea Latinoamericana
0034-6942 Revista Aeronautica
0034-6950 Revista Aguas e Energia Eletrica de Sao Paulo†
0034-6969 Revista Alamar†
0034-6977 Revista Alentejana
0034-6985 Anales de Legislacion Argentina
0034-6993 Revista Argentina de Angiologia
0034-7019 Revista Argentina de Ciencia Politica
0034-7027 Revista Argentina de Psicologia
0034-7043 Revista Arhivelor
0034-706X Revista Bancaria Brasileira
0034-7078 Revista Biblica
0034-7086 Revista Bibliotecilor†
0034-7094 Revista Brasileira de Anestesiologia
0034-7108 Revista Brasileira de Biologia
0034-7116 Revista Brasileira de Cancerologia
0034-7124 Revista Brasileira de Cirurgia
0034-7140 Revista Brasileira de Economia
0034-7159 Revista Brasileira de Energia Eletrica†
0034-7167 Revista Brasileira de Enfermagem
0034-7175 Revista Brasileira de Estatistica
0034-7183 Revista Brasileira de Estudos Pedagogicos
0034-7191 Revista Brasileira de Estudos Politicos
0034-7205 Revista Brasileira de Filosofia
0034-7213 Revista Brasileira de Folclore
0034-723X Revista Brasileira de Geografia
0034-7256 Revista Brasileira de Malariologia e Doencas Tropicais
0034-7264 Revista Brasileira de Medicina
0034-7272 Revista Brasileira de Odontologia
0034-7280 Revista Brasileira de Oftalmologia
0034-7299 Revista Brasileira de Oto-Rino-Laringologia
0034-7302 Revista Brasileira de Patologia Clinica
0034-7310 Revista Brasileira de Pesquisas Medicas e Biologicas
0034-7329 Revista Brasileira de Politica Internacional
0034-7337 Revista Brasileira de Saude Mental
0034-7353 Revista Campinense de Cultura
0034-7361 C E C. Revista
0034-737X Ceres
0034-7388 Revista Chilena de Neuropsiquiatria
0034-7396 Revista Chilena de Pediatria†
0034-740X Revista Chilena de Entomologia
0034-7418 Revista Colombiana de Ciencias Quimico Farmaceuticas
0034-7426 Revista Colombiana de Matematicas
0034-7434 Revista Colombiana de Obstetricia y Ginecologia
0034-7442 Revista Colombiana de Pediatria y Puericultura
0034-7450 Revista Colombiana de Psiquiatria
0034-7477 Revista Conservadora del Pensiamento Centroamericano *changed to* Revista del Pensamiento Centroamericano
0034-7485 Revista Cubana de Ciencia Agricola
0034-7493 Revista Cubana de Cirugia
0034-7507 Revista Cubana de Estomatologia
0034-7515 Revista Cubana de Farmacia
0034-7523 Revista Cubana de Medicina
0034-7531 Revista Cubana de Pediatria
0034-754X Revista Cultului Mozaic
0034-7558 Bolsa de Valores de Sao Paulo. Revista
0034-7566 Revista da Construcao Civil
0034-7582 Revista da Madeira
0034-7590 Revista de Administracao de Empresas
0034-7604 Revista de Administracao Municipal
0034-7612 Revista de Administracao Publica
0034-7620 Revista de Administracion Publica
0034-7639 Revista de Administracion Publica
0034-7647 Revista de Aeronautica y Astronautica
0034-7655 Revista de Agricultura
0034-7671 Revista de Agricultura *changed to* Ciencias de las Agriculturas
0034-7698 Revista de Agroquimica y Tecnologia de Alimentos
0034-7701 Revista de Antropologia
0034-771X Revista de Archivos, Bibliotecas y Museos
0034-7728 Revista de Bellas Artes†
0034-7736 Revista de Biologia
0034-7744 Revista de Biologia Tropical
0034-7752 Revista de Chimie
0034-7779 Revista de Ciencias Economicas *see* 0325-0814
0034-7779 Revista de Ciencias Economicas *see* 0325-0830
0034-7787 Revista de Ciencias Juridicas†
0034-7817 Revista de Ciencias Sociales
0034-7825 Revista de Compendios de Articulos de Economia
0034-7833 Revista de Conservatorio
0034-7841 Revista de Criminalistica do Rio Grande do Sul
0034-785X Revista de Cultura Brasilena
0034-7868 Revista de Derecho
0034-7876 Revista de Derecho Comercial
0034-7884 Revista de Derecho Deportivo
0034-7892 Revista de Derecho Internacional y Ciencias Diplomaticas
0034-7906 Revista de Derecho, Jurisprudencia y Administracion
0034-7914 Revista de Derecho Penal y Criminologia†
0034-7922 Revista de Derecho Privado
0034-7930 Revista de Derecho Puertorriqueno
0034-7949 Revista de Derecho Y Ciencias Politicas
0034-7957 Revista de Derecho y Ciencias Sociales *changed to* Revista de Derecho
0034-7965 Revista de Derecho y Legislacion†
0034-7973 Revista de Diagnostico Biologico†
0034-7981 Revista de Dialectologia y Tradiciones Populares
0034-8007 Revista de Direito Administrativo
0034-8015 Revista de Direito Publico
0034-8023 Revista de Ciencia Politica

0034-804X Revista de Economia Latinoamericana
0034-8058 Revista de Economia Politica *changed to* Revista de Politica Economia
0034-8066 Revista de Economia y Estadistica
0034-8074 Revista de Educacion
0034-8082 Revista de Educacion
0034-8090 Revista de Enfermagem†
0034-8104 Revista de Engenharia do Estado da Guanabara
0034-8112 Revista de Engenharia Mackenzie
0034-8139 Revista de Entomologia de Mocambique†
0034-8147 Revista de Espiritualidad
0034-8155 Revista de Estudios Agro-Sociales
0034-8163 Revista de Estudios de la Vida Local
0034-8171 Revista de Estudios de Teatro *changed to* Instituto Nacional de Estudios de Teatro. Boletin
0034-818X Revista de Estudios Hispanicos
0034-8198 Revista de Etnografie si Folclor
0034-8201 Revista de Farmacia e Odontologia
0034-821X Revista de Ferreteria y Ramos Generales
0034-8228 Revista de Filosofia†
0034-8236 Revista de Filosofia
0034-8244 Revista de Filosofia†
0034-8252 Revista de Filosofia
0034-8260 Revista de Filozofie
0034-8279 Revista de Geofisica
0034-8287 Revista de Ginecologia e d'Obstetricia†
0034-8295 Revista de Guimaraes
0034-8309 Revista de Historia
0034-8317 Revista de Historia†
0034-8325 Revista de Historia de America
0034-8333 Revista de Ideas Esteticas†
0034-8341 Revista de Indias
0034-835X Revista de Informacao Legislativa
0034-8368 Revista de Intendencia
0034-8376 Revista de Investigacion Clinica†
0034-8384 Revista de Investigacion en Salud Publica†
0034-8392 Revista de Istorie si Teorie Literara
0034-8406 Revista de la Defensa Nacional†
0034-8414 Revista de la Fuerza Aerea
0034-8422 Revista de la Integracion†
0034-8422 Revista de la Integracion *changed to* Integracion Latinoamericana
0034-8430 Revista de la Sanidad de Policia *changed to* Peru. Fuerzas Policiales. Revista de la Sanidad
0034-8457 Revista de las Fuerzas Armadas
0034-8473 Revista de las Fuerzas Armadas
0034-8481 Revista de Legislacion Argentina
0034-8511 Revista de Marina
0034-852X Revista de Marina
0034-8538 Revista de Marina del Peru
0034-8546 Revista de Marinha
0034-8554 Revista de Medicina
0034-8562 Revista de Medicina Social y del Trabajo
0034-8570 Revista de Metalurgia
0034-8589 Revista de Neumologia y Cirugia de Torax
0034-8597 Revista de Neuro-Psiquiatria
0034-8600 Revista de Nutricion y Aterosclerosis
0034-8619 Revista de Obras Publicas
0034-8627 Revista de Obras Sanitarias de la Nacion
0034-8635 Revista de Occidente
0034-8643 Revista de Otorrinolaringologia
0034-8651 Revista de Pedagogia†
0034-866X Revista de Tecnologia Educativa
0034-8678 Revista de Pedagogie
0034-8686 Revista de Planeacion y Desarrollo
0034-8694 Revista de Planificacion†
0034-8708 Revista de Plasticos Modernos
0034-8716 Revista de Politica Internacional
0034-8724 Revista de Politica Social
0034-8732 Revista de Prevencion
0034-8740 Revista de Psicoanalisis
0034-8759 Revista de Psihologie
0034-8767 Revista de Psiquiatria Dinamica
0034-8775 Revista de Publicaciones Navales
0034-8783 Revista de Referate in Bibliologie
0034-8791 Filosofie-Logica; Revista de Referate, Recenzii si Sinteze†
0034-8805 Istorie- Etnografie Revista de Referate, Recenzii si Sinteze†
0034-8813 Lingvistica-Filologie; Revista de Referate, Recenzii si Sinzeze†
0034-8821 Psihologie; Revista de Referate Recenzii si Sinteze†
0034-883X Sociologie; Revista de Referate Recenzii si Sinteze†
0034-8848 Stiinte Economice; Revista de Referate, Recenzii si Sinteze†
0034-8856 Stiinte Juridice; Revista de Referate, Recenzii si Sinteze†
0034-8864 Teoria si Istoria Literaturii si Artei; Revista de Referate, Recenzii si Sinteze†
0034-8872 Revista de Resumenes†
0034-8880 Revista de Revistas
0034-8899 Revista de Sanidad e Higiene Publica
0034-8902 Revista de Santander
0034-8910 Revista de Saude Publica
0034-8937 Revista de Servicio Social
0034-8961 Revista de Telecomunicacion
0034-897X Revista de Trabajo
0034-8988 Revista de Trabajo
0034-8996 Revista de Urologia†
0034-9003 Costa Rica. Archivo Nacional. Revista
0034-9011 Revista del Cafe
0034-902X Circulo Odontologico del Sur. Revista†
0034-9046 Revista del Ejercito
0034-9054 Revista del Ejercito y Armada
0034-9070 Revista del Hogar
0034-9089 I D I E M. Revista
0034-9097 Revista del Mexico Agrario
0034-9100 Revista del Pacifico†
0034-9119 Revista del Suboficial
0034-9127 Czechoslovak Glass Review *changed to* Glass Review
0034-9135 Rivista dell' Informazione
0034-9143 Revista Dental de Chile
0034-916X Rivista di Ingegneria Agraria
0034-9178 Revista Diesel†
0034-9186 Diners
0034-9194 Revista Diplomatica e Internacional
0034-9208 Revista do Ar
0034-9216 Revista do Arquivo Municipal
0034-9224 Revista do Comercio de Cafe
0034-9240 Revista do Servico Publico
0034-9259 Revista dos Criadores
0034-9267 Revista dos Transportes
0034-9275 Revista dos Tribunais
0034-9283 Revista Economica
0034-9291 Revista Economica†
0034-9305 Revista Ecuatoriana de Educacion
0034-9313 Revista Ecuatoriana de Medicina y Ciencias Biologicas
0034-933X Sol
0034-9356 Revista Espanola de Anestesiologia y Reanimacion
0034-9372 Revista Espanola de Derecho Canonico
0034-9380 Revista Espanola de Derecho Internacional
0034-9399 Revista Espanola de Derecho Militar
0034-9402 Revista Espanola de Fisiologia
0034-9410 Revista Espanola de Gerontologia
0034-9429 Revista Espanola de la Opinion Publica
0034-9437 Revista Espanola de las Enfermedades del Aparato Digestivo
0034-9445 Revista Espanola de Obstetricia y Ginecologia
0034-9453 Revista Espanola de Oto-Neuro-Oftalmologia y Neurocirugia
0034-9461 Revista Espanola de Pedagogia
0034-947X Revista Espanola de Pediatria
0034-9488 Revista Espanola de Seguros
0034-9496 Revista Farmaceutica
0034-950X Revista Ferroviaria
0034-9518 Revista Financiera
0034-9526 Revista Finlay†
0034-9534 Revista Fiscal e de Legislacao de Fazenda†
0034-9542 Revista Gaucha de Odontologia
0034-9550 Revista Genealogica Latina
0034-9569 Revista General de Marina
0034-9577 Revista Geografica de Valparaiso
0034-9585 Revista Goiana de Medicina
0034-9593 Revista Hispanica Moderna
0034-9607 I M C Y C. Revista
0034-9615 Revista Iberica de Endocrinologia
0034-9623 Revista Iberica de Parasitologia
0034-9631 Revista Iberoamericana
0034-964X Revista Iberoamericana de Seguridad Social†
0034-9658 Revista Ibys
0034-9666 Revista Imposto Fiscal
0034-9690 Revista Interamericana de Psicologia
0034-9704 Revista Interamericana de Radiologia
0034-9712 Revista Internacional de Sociologia
0034-9720 Revista Internacional y Diplomatica
0034-9739 Revista Juridica
0034-9747 Revista Juridica de Buenos Aires†
0034-9771 Revista Latinoamericana de Microbiologia†
0034-9771 Revista Latinoamericana de Microbiologia
0034-978X Revista Latinoamericana de Psicologia
0034-9798 Revista Latinoamericana de Siderurgia *changed to* Siderurgia Latinoamericana
0034-9801 Revista Latinoamericana de Sociologia
0034-981X Revista Literaria Azor
0034-9828 Cenit
0034-9844 Manana
0034-9852 Revista Manizales
0034-9860 Revista Maritima Brasileira
0034-9887 Revista Medica de Chile
0034-9895 Revista Medica de Corrientes
0034-9909 Revista Medica de Costa Rica
0034-9917 Revista Medica de Valparaiso
0034-9925 Revista Medica del Hospital General de Mexico S.S.A.
0034-9933 Revista Medica del Paraguay
0034-9941 Revista Medica do Estado da Guanabara *see* 0100-0195
0034-995X Revista Medicala
0034-9976 Revista Mexicana de Ciencia Politica *changed to* Revista Mexicana de Ciencias Politicas y Sociales
0034-9984 Revista Mexicana de Cirugia, Ginecologia y Cancer
0035-0001 Revista Mexicana de Electricidad
0035-001X Revista Mexicana de Fisica
0035-0028 Revista Mexicana de Ingenieria y Arquitectura
0035-0044 Revista Mexicana de la Propiedad Industrial y Artistica
0035-0052 Revista Mexicana de Pediatria
0035-0079 Revista Mexicana de Psicologia†
0035-0087 Revista Mexicana de Sociologia
0035-0109 Revista Militar
0035-0117 Revista Militar
0035-0125 Revista Militar Brasileira
0035-0133 Revista Militar de Guatemala
0035-0141 Revista Militar del Peru
0035-015X Revista Militar y Naval
0035-0168 Revista Minelor *changed to* Mine, Petrol si Gaze
0035-0176 Revista Mineria, Geologia y Mineralogia
0035-0184 Revista Municipal†
0035-0192 Revista Musical Chilena
0035-0206 Revista Muzeelor *changed to* Revista Muzeelor si Monumentelor. Muzee
0035-0214 Revista Nacional da Pesca
0035-0222 Revista Nacional de Agricultura
0035-0257 Revista Odontologica *see* 0325-1071
0035-0265 Revista Odontologica de Concepcion
0035-0273 Revista Odontologica de Merida *changed to* Universidad de Los Andes. Facultad de Odontologia. Revista
0035-0281 Revista Odontologica de Puerto Rico
0035-029X Revista Padurilor *changed to* Revista Padurilor-Industria Lemnului, Celuloza si Hirtie. Industria Lemnului
0035-029X Revista Padurilor *changed to* Revista Padurilor - Industria Lemnului, Celuloza si Hirtie. Celuloza si Hirtie
0035-029X Revista Padurilor *changed to* Revista Padurilor-Industria Lemnului, Celuloza si Hirtie, Silvicultura si Exploatarea Padurilor
0035-0303 Revista para Parvulos y Principiantes
0035-0311 Revista para Uniones de Adultos *changed to* Accion
0035-032X Revista para Uniones de Intermedios *changed to* Ahora
0035-0338 Revista para Jovenes *changed to* Adelante
0035-0346 Revista para Uniones de Primarios
0035-0354 Revista Paraguaya de Sociologia
0035-0362 Revista Paulista de Medicina
0035-0370 Revista Peruana de Derecho Internacional
0035-0389 Revista Portuguesa de Ciencias Veterinarias
0035-0397 Revista Portuguesa de Estomatologia e Cirurgia Maxilo-Facial
0035-0400 Revista Portuguesa de Filosofia
0035-0419 Revista Portuguesa de Quimica
0035-0427 Revista Referativo de la Construccion *changed to* Servicio Referativo de la Construccion
0035-0435 Revista Romana de Drept
0035-0443 Revista Rotaria
0035-0451 Revista Signos de Valparaiso
0035-0478 Sur
0035-0486 Revista Tamaulipas
0035-0494 Revista Tecnica Iem
0035-0516 Revista Telegrafica Electronica
0035-0524 Revista Textil
0035-0532 Revista Transporturilor *changed to* Revista Transporturi Auto, Navale si Aeriene
0035-0559 Revista Uruguaya de Patologia Clinica *changed to* Revista Uruguaya de Patologia Clinica y Microbiologia
0035-0567 Rivista Veneta†
0035-0575 Revista Venezolana de Folklore†
0035-0583 Revista Venezolana de Sanidad y Asistencia Social
0035-0591 Revista Venezolana de Urologia
0035-0605 Revista do Livro†
0035-0621 Revolution Africaine
0035-0656 Revue "A" /Tijdschrift "A" *changed to* Journal "A"
0035-0672 Revue Administrative
0035-0699 Revue Algerienne des Sciences Juridiques, Politiques et Economiques *changed to* Revue Algerienne des Sciences Juridiques, Economiques et Politiques
0035-0702 Revue Algologique *see* 0181-1568
0035-0710 Revue Analytique d'Education Physique et de Sport†
0035-0729 Revue
0035-0737 Revue Archeologique
0035-0745 Revue Archeologique de l'Est et du Centre-Est
0035-0753 Revue Archeologique du Centre de la France
0035-077X Revue Belge d'Archeologie et d'Histoire de l'Art
0035-0788 Revue Belge de Droit International
0035-0796 Revue Belge de Geographie
0035-0818 Revue Belge de Philologie et d'Historie
0035-0826 Revue Belge de Psychologie et de Pedagogie
0035-0834 Revue Belge de Securite Sociale
0035-0869 Revue Belge d'Histoire Contemporaire
0035-0877 Revue Belge d'Histoire Militaire
0035-0885 Revue Belge d'Homoeopathie
0035-0893 Revue Benedictine
0035-0907 Revue Biblique
0035-0915 Revue Canadienne de Biologie
0035-0931 Revue Congolaise des Sciences Humaines†
0035-0958 Revue Critique de Droit International Prive
0035-0966 Revue Critique de Jurisprudence Belge
0035-0974 Revue d'Allemagne *changed to* Revue d'Allemagne et des Pays de Langue Allemande
0035-0990 Revue d'Ascetique et de Mystique *changed to* Revue d'Histoire de la Spiritualite
0035-1008 Revue d'Auvergne
0035-1016 Revue de Belles-Lettres
0035-1024 Revue de Bio-Mathematique
0035-1032 Revue de Chimie Minerale

0035-1040 Revue de Chirurgie Orthopedique et Reparatrice de l'Appareil Moteur
0035-1059 Revue de Comminges
0035-1067 Revue de Cytologie et de Biologie Vegetales *see* 0181-7582
0035-1075 Defense Nationale
0035-1083 Revue de Droit Intellectuel l'Ingenieur-Conseil
0035-1091 Revue de Droit International de Sciences Diplomatiques et Politiques
0035-1105 Revue de Droit International et de Droit Compare
0035-1113 Revue de Droit Social
0035-1121 Revue de Geographie Alpine
0035-113X Revue de Geographie de Lyon
0035-1148 Revue de Geographie de Montreal *see* 0705-7199
0035-1156 Revue de Geographie du Maroc
0035-1164 Revue de Geographie Physique et de Geologie Dynamique *see* 0241-1407
0035-1172 Revue de Kinesitherapie *see* 0302-427X
0035-1199 Revue de la Cooperation Scolaire†
0035-1210 Revue de la France Libre
0035-1237 Revue de la Police Nationale
0035-1245 Revue de la Presse Arabe
0035-1253 Revue de la Protection†
0035-1261 Revue de la Securite
0035-127X Revue de la Soudure
0035-1288 Revue de l'Agenais
0035-1296 Revue de l'Agriculture
0035-130X Revue de l'Alcoolisme
0035-1318 Revue de l'Aluminium
0035-1326 Revue de l'Art
0035-1334 Revue de Laryngologie-Otologie-Rhinologie
0035-1342 Revue de l'Avranchin et du Pays de Granville
0035-1350 Revue de l'Economie du Centre-Est
0035-1369 Revue de l'Economie Meridionale
0035-1377 Revue de l'Education Physique
0035-1385 Revue de l'Embouteillage et des Industries Connexes *changed to* Revue Conditionnement des Liquides-Embouteillage
0035-1393 Revue de l'Enseignement Philosophique
0035-1415 Revue de l'Est *changed to* Revue d'Etudes Comparatives Est-Ouest.
0035-1423 Revue de l'Histoire des Religions
0035-1431 Revue de l'Industrie Minerale *see* 0302-2129
0035-144X Revue de l'Infirmiere et de l'Assistante Sociale *changed to* Revue de l'Infirmiere
0035-1458 Revue de Linguistique Romane
0035-1466 Revue de Litterature Comparee
0035-1474 Revue de l'Occident Musulman et de la Mediterranee
0035-1482 Revue de Madagascar†
0035-1490 Flair
0035-1504 Revue de Mathematiques Speciales
0035-1512 Revue de Medecine
0035-1520 Revue de Medecine Aeronautique et Spatiale *changed to* Medicine Aeronautique et Spatial - Medicine Subaquatique et Hyperbare
0035-1539 Revue de Medecine Moderne
0035-1547 Revue de Medecine Psychosomatique
0035-1555 Revue de Medecine Veterinaire
0035-1563 Revue de Metallurgie
0035-1571 Revue de Metaphysique et de Morale
0035-158X Revue de Metrologie Pratique et Legale
0035-1598 Revue de Micropaleontologie
0035-1601 Revue de Musicologie
0035-161X Revue de Neuropsychiatrie de l'Ouest
0035-1628 Neuropsychiatrie de l'Enfance et de l'Adolescence
0035-1628 Revue de Neuropsychiatrie Infantile et d'Hygiene Mentale de l'Enfance *see* 0035-1628
0035-1636 Revue de Pathologie Comparee†
0035-1644 Revue de Pediatrie
0035-1652 Revue de Philologie, de Litterature et d'Histoire Anciennes
0035-1660 Revue de Phonetique Appliquee
0035-1679 Revue de Physiologie Subaquatique et Medecine Hyperbare†
0035-1687 Revue de Physique Appliquee
0035-1709 Revue de Psychologie Appliquee
0035-1717 Revue de Psychologie des Peuples *see* 0046-2608
0035-1725 Revue de Qumran
0035-1733 Revue de Science Criminelle et de Droit Penal Compare
0035-1741 Revue de Science Financiere†
0035-175X Revue de Statistique Appliquee
0035-1768 Revue de Stomatologie et de Chirurgie Maxillo-Faciale
0035-1776 Revue de Synthese
0035-1784 Revue de Theologie et de Philosophie
0035-1792 Revue de Tuberculose et de Pneumologie. *see* 0301-0279
0035-1806 Revue de Zoologie Agricole et de Pathologie Vegetale
0035-1814 Revue de Zoologie et de Botanique Africaines *changed to* Revue de Zoologie Africaine
0035-1822 Revue d'Ecologie et de Biologie du Sol
0035-1849 Revue d'Egyptologie
0035-1857 Revue d'Electroencephalographie et de Neurophysiologie Clinique
0035-1865 Revue d'Elevage et de Medecine Veterinaire des Pays Tropicaux
0035-1873 Lebanese Dental Journal
0035-1903 Revue des Agents de Police *changed to* Flute
0035-1911 Revue des Applications de l'Electricite *see* 0035-2926
0035-192X Revue des Assureurs-Vie *see* 0380-3147
0035-1938 Revue des Caisses d'Epargne
0035-1954 Revue des Corps de Sante des Armees *see* 0300-4937
0035-1962 Revue des Deux Mondes *changed to* Revue de Deux Mondes: Litterature, Histoire, Arts et Sciences
0035-1970 Revue des Disques et de la Haute Fidelite
0035-1989 Revue des Droits de l'Homme†
0035-1997 Revue des Ecoles
0035-2004 Revue des Etudes Anciennes
0035-2012 Revue des Etudes Augustiniennes
0035-2020 Revue des Etudes Cooperatives
0035-2039 Revue des Etudes Grecques
0035-2047 Revue des Etudes Italiennes
0035-2055 Revue des Etudes Juives
0035-2063 Revue des Etudes Sud-Est Europeennes
0035-2071 Revue des Fermentations et des Industries Alimentaires
0035-208X Revue des Finances Communales
0035-2098 Revue des Hotesses
0035-2101 Offrir *changed to* Offrir International
0035-211X Revue des Langues Vivantes
0035-2128 Revue des Lettres
0035-2136 Revue des Lettres Modernes
0035-2144 Revue des Materiaux de Construction et de Travaux Publics *changed to* Ciments, Betons, Platres, Chaux
0035-2152 Revue des P T T de France *changed to* Revue des Postes et Telecommunications de France
0035-2160 Revue des Questions Scientifiques
0035-2179 Cahiers des Ingenieurs Agronomes
0035-2195 Revue des Sciences Humaines
0035-2209 Revue des Sciences Philosophiques et Theologiques
0035-2217 Revue des Sciences Religieuses
0035-2241 Revue des Societes Savantes de Haute Normandie
0035-225X Revue des Tabacs
0035-2284 Revue Desjardins
0035-2292 Revue d'Esthetique
0035-2306 Revue d'Etudes Militaires, Aeriennes et Navales
0035-2314 Revue d'Histoire de la Deuxieme Guerre Mondiale
0035-2322 Revue d'Histoire de la Gaspesie *changed to* Gaspesie
0035-2330 Revue d'Histoire de la Medecine Hebraique
0035-2349 Revue d'Histoire de la Pharmacie
0035-2357 Revue d'Histoire de l'Amerique Francaise
0035-2365 Revue d'Histoire Diplomatique
0035-2373 Revue d'Histoire du Theatre
0035-2381 Revue d'Histoire Ecclesiastique
0035-239X Revue d'Histoire Economique et Sociale
0035-2403 Revue d'Histoire et de Philosophie Religieuses
0035-2411 Revue d'Histoire Litteraire de la France
0035-242X Revue d'Hygiene du Travail†
0035-2438 Revue d'Epidemiologie, Medecine Sociale et Sante Publique *see* 0398-7620
0035-2446 Revue d'Hygiene et Medecine Scolaire et Universitaire
0035-2462 Revue d'Informatique Medicale†
0035-2470 Revue d'Odonto-Stomatologie du Midi de la France
0035-2497 Revue d'Oto-Neuro-Ophtalmologie
0035-2500 Revue du Bois Detail†
0035-2527 Revue du Bouton†
0035-2535 Revue du Cethedec
0035-2543 Revue du Cinema International & TV†
0035-2551 Revue du Clerge Africain†
0035-256X Revue du Droit du Travail†
0035-2578 Revue du Droit Public et de la Science Politique en France et a l'Etranger
0035-2586 Revue du Genie Militaire *changed to* Bulletin Technique du Genie (1960)
0035-2594 Revue du Jouet
0035-2608 Revue du Louvre et des Musees de France
0035-2616 Revue du Marche Commun
0035-2624 Revue du Nord
0035-2632 Revue du Notariat
0035-2640 Revue du Praticien
0035-2659 Revue du Rhumatisme et des Maladies Osteoarticulaires
0035-2667 Revue du Rouergue
0035-2675 Revue du Son *changed to* Nouvelle Revue du Son
0035-2683 Asia Quarterly
0035-2705 Revue du Travail
0035-273X Revue du Vin de France
0035-2748 Revue du Vivarais
0035-2756 Acta Technica Belgica. Revue E: Electricite Courants Forts. Electrotechnique Generale et ses Applications
0035-2764 Revue Economique
0035-2772 Revue Economique et Sociale
0035-2780 Revue Economique Francaise
0035-2799 Revue Economique Franco Suisse
0035-2802 Revue Europeenne des Papiers Cartons-Complexes†
0035-2810 Revue Fiscale *changed to* Journal de Droit Fiscal
0035-2829 Revue Forestiere Francaise
0035-2845 Revue Francaise d'Allergologie *changed to* Revue Francaise d'Allergologie et Immunologie Clinique
0035-2853 Revue Francaise d'Apiculture
0035-2861 Revue Francaise de Bridge
0035-287X Revue Francaise de Droit Aerien
0035-2896 Revue Francaise de Gerontologie *changed to* Revue de Geriatrie
0035-290X Revue Francaise de Gynecologie et d'Obstetrique
0035-2918 Revue Francaise de l'Agriculture†
0035-2926 Revue Francaise de l'Electricite
0035-2934 Revue Francaise de l'Energie *see* 0303-240X
0035-2942 Revue Francaise de Psychanalyse
0035-2950 Revue Francaise de Science Politique
0035-2969 Revue Francaise de Sociologie
0035-2977 Revue Francaise de Transfusion *see* 0338-4535
0035-2985 Revue Francaise des Affaires Sociales
0035-2993 Revue Francaise des Bijoutiers Horlogers
0035-3000 Revue Francaise des Corps Gras
0035-3019 Revue Europeenne d'Etudes Cliniques et Biologiques *see* 0300-0893
0035-3027 Revue Francaise d'Etudes Politiques Africaines
0035-3035 Revue Francaise d'Informatique et de Recherche Operationnelle *see* 0399-0516
0035-3035 Revue Francaise d'Informatique et de Recherche Operationnelle *see* 0399-0559
0035-3035 Revue Francaise d'Informatique et de Recherche Operationnelle *see* 0399-0524
0035-3035 Revue Francaise d'Informatique et de Recherche Operationnelle *see* 0399-0532
0035-3035 Revue Francaise d'Informatique et de Recherche Operationnelle *see* 0399-0540
0035-3043 Revue Francaise d'Odonto-Stomatologie *see* 0300-9815
0035-3078 Revue Generale Belge *changed to* Revue Generale: Lettres, Arts et Sciences Humaines
0035-3086 Revue Generale de Droit
0035-3094 Revue Generale de Droit International Public
0035-3108 Revue Generale de l'Air et de l'Espace†
0035-3116 Revue Generale de l'Electricite
0035-3124 Revue Generale de l'Enseignement des Deficients Auditifs
0035-3132 Revue Generale de l'Etancheite et de l'Isolation
0035-3140 Revue Generale de l'Hotellerie, de la Gastronomie et du Tourisme
0035-3159 Revue Generale de Thermique
0035-3167 Revue Generale des Assurances Terrestres
0035-3175 Revue Generale des Caoutchoucs et Plastiques
0035-3183 Revue Generale des Chemins de Fer
0035-3191 Revue Generale des Routes et des Aerodromes
0035-3205 Revue Generale du Froid
0035-3213 Revue Geographique de l'Est
0035-3221 Revue Geographique des Pyrenees et du Sud-Ouest
0035-3248 Acta Technica Belgica. Revue H F: Electricite Courants Faibles. Electronique Telecommunications
0035-3256 Revue Hellenique de Droit International
0035-3264 Revue Historique
0035-3272 Revue Historique Ardennaise
0035-3280 Revue Historique de Droit Francais et Etranger
0035-3299 Revue Historique des Armees
0035-3302 Revue Horticole *see* 0031-5087
0035-3310 Revue Independante
0035-3329 Revue Internationale de Criminologie et de Police Technique†
0035-3337 Revue Internationale de Droit Compare
0035-337X Revue Internationale de la Propriete Industrielle et Artistique
0035-3396 Revue Internationale de Police Criminelle
0035-340X Revue Internationale de Psychologie Appliquee†
0035-3418 Comptabilite Economique Universelle-Scientifique
0035-3426 Revue Internationale des Fleuristes
0035-3434 Revue Internationale des Hautes Temperatures et des Refractaires
0035-3442 Revue Internationale des Industries Agricoles. Bulletin Analytique
0035-3469 Revue Internationale des Services de Sante des Armees de Terre, de Mer et de l'Air
0035-3485 Revue Internationale d'Ethnopsychologie Normale et Pathologique†
0035-3493 Revue Internationale d'Oceanographie Medicale
0035-3515 Revue Internationale du Droit d'Auteur
0035-3531 Revue Internationale du Trachome et des Maladies Oculaires des Pays Tropicaux et Sub Tropicaux *see* 0301-5017
0035-354X International Review for Business Education
0035-3566 Revue Juridique et Economique de Sud-Quest *changed to* Revue Economique du Sud-Ouest

0035-3574 Revue Juridique et Politique, Independance et Cooperation
0035-3582 Revue de l'Air Liquide†
0035-3590 Revue Laitiere Francaise
0035-3604 Revue Legale
0035-3620 Revue Mabillon
0035-3639 Revue Medicale de Bruxelles
0035-3655 Revue Medicale de la Suisse Romande
0035-3663 Revue Medicale de Liege
0035-368X Revue Militaire Suisse
0035-3698 Revue Moderne
0035-371X Revue-Moteur
0035-3728 Revue Municipale
0035-3736 Revue Musicale
0035-3744 Revue Musicale de Suisse Romande
0035-3752 Revue Nationale de le Chasse
0035-3779 Revue Neuchateloise
0035-3787 Revue Neurologique
0035-3795 R N D
0035-3809 Revue Nouvelle
0035-3825 Revue Penitentiaire et de Droit Penal
0035-3833 Revue Philosophique de la France et de l'Etranger
0035-3841 Revue Philosophique de Louvain
0035-385X Revue Politique et Parlementaire
0035-3868 Revue Pratique du Froid *changed to* Journal R P F
0035-3876 Revue Pratique des Questions Commerciales et Economiques
0035-3884 Societe Calviniste de France. Revue Reformee
0035-3892 Revue Roumaine des Sciences Sociales. Serie de Psychologie
0035-3906 Revue Romane
0035-3914 Revue Roumaine de Biologie. Serie Botanique *changed to* Revue Roumaine de Biologie. Serie Biologie Vegetale
0035-3922 Revue Roumaine de Biologie. Serie Zoologie *changed to* Revue Roumaine de Biologie. Serie Biologie Animale
0035-3930 Revue Roumaine de Chimie
0035-3957 Revue Roumaine de Linguistique
0035-3965 Revue Roumaine de Mathematiques Pures et Appliquees
0035-3973 Revue Roumaine de Medecine Interne *changed to* Revue Roumaine de Medecine. Serie Medecine Interne
0035-3981 Revue Roumaine de Neurologie et Psychiatrie *see* 0301-7303
0035-399X Revue Roumaine de Physiologie *changed to* Revue Roumaine de Morphologie, d'Embryologie et Physiologie. Serie Physiologie
0035-4007 Revue Roumaine de Morphologie, d'Embryologie et Physiologie. Serie Morphologie et Embryologie
0035-4015 Revue Roumaine d'Endocrinologie *changed to* Revue Roumaine de Medecine. Serie Endocrinologie
0035-4023 Revue Roumaine des Sciences Sociales. Serie de Sciences Juridiques
0035-4031 Revue Roumaine des Sciences Sociales. Serie de Philosophie et de Logique
0035-404X Revue Roumaine des Sciences Sociales. Serie de Sciences Economiques
0035-4066 Revue Roumaine des Sciences Techniques. Serie Electrotechnique et Energetique
0035-4074 Revue Roumaine des Sciences Techniques. Serie de Mecanique Appliquee
0035-4082 Revue Roumaine d'Inframicrobiologie *changed to* Revue Roumaine de Medecine. Serie Virologie
0035-4090 Revue Roumaine de Physique
0035-4104 Revue Scolaire†
0035-4112 Revue Senegalaise de Droit
0035-4120 Servir†
0035-4139 Revue Socialiste
0035-4147 Revue Stomato-Odontologique du Nord de la France
0035-4163 Revue Suisse de Numismatique
0035-4171 Revue Suisse de Viticulture et Arboriculture *changed to* Revue Suisse de Viticulture, Arboriculture et Horticulture
0035-418X Revue Suisse de Zoologie
0035-4198 Revue Suisse des Marches Agricoles *changed to* Schweizerisches Bauernverband. Information
0035-4201 Revue Suisse du Trafic Routier†
0035-421X Revue Syndicale Suisse
0035-4228 Revue Technique des Hotels, Restaurants, Bars, Brasseries, Limonadiers, Tabacs, Habitats Collectifs
0035-4252 Revue de la Technique Europeenne *changed to* Indicateur Industriel
0035-4260 Revue Technique Luxembourgeoise
0035-4279 Revue Technique Thomson-C S F
0035-4287 Revue Textile Melliand†
0035-4295 Revue Thomiste
0035-4317 Revue Trimestrielle de Droit Europeen
0035-4325 Revue Trimestrielle de Droit Sanitaire et Social
0035-4333 Revue Tunisienne de Sciences Sociales
0035-4341 Revue Universelle des Mines, de la Metallurgie, de la Mecanique, des Travaux Publics, des Sciences et des Arts Appliques a l'Industrie†
0035-435X Revue Universitaire de Science Morale *changed to* Reseaux
0035-4376 Revues Medicales Normandes†
0035-4384 Revue de Droit Penal et de Criminologie
0035-4406 Revuo Orienta
0035-4422 Rexevents
0035-4449 Rheinhessische Wirtschaft
0035-4457 Rheinisch-Westfaelische Boerse zu Duesseldorf. Amtliches Kursblatt
0035-4465 Rheinisch-Westfaelisches Institut fuer Wirtschaftsforschung. Mitteilungen
0035-4473 Rheinische Vierteljahrsblaetter
0035-4481 Rheinisches Aerzteblatt
0035-449X Rheinisches Museum fuer Philologie
0035-4511 Rheologica Acta
0035-452X Rheology Abstracts
0035-4538 Rheology Bulletin
0035-4546 Rheumatism
0035-4554 Rheumatologia, Balneologia, Allergologia
0035-4570 Rhode Island Business Quarterly *changed to* New England Journal of Business & Economics
0035-4589 Rhode Island College Alumni Association. Review *changed to* Rhode Island College Alumni Association. Alumni Review
0035-4597 Rhode Island. Department of State Library Services. Newsletter
0035-4600 Rhode Island. Department of Labor and Employment Security. Employment Bulletin *changed to* Rhode Island. Department of Employment Security. Employment Bulletin
0035-4619 Rhode Island History
0035-4627 Rhode Island Medical Journal *see* 0360-067X
0035-4635 Rhode Island Resources†
0035-4643 Rhode Island State Dental Society. Journal
0035-466X Rhodeo
0035-4678 Rhodes Newsletter *changed to* Rhodes Review
0035-4686 Rhodesia Agricultural Journal
0035-4694 Rhodesia and World Report
0035-4708 Rhodesia Calls *changed to* Africa Calls
0035-4716 Zimbabwe. National Archives. Occasional Papers
0035-4724 Rhodesia Railways Magazine *changed to* Zimbabwe Rhodesia Railways Magazine
0035-4732 Rhodesia Science News
0035-4759 Rhodesian Commentary *see* 0304-7628
0035-4775 Rhodesian Farmer *changed to* Farmer
0035-4791 Rhodesian Industrialist
0035-4805 Rhodesian Insurance Review *changed to* Insurance Review
0035-4813 Rhodesian Journal of Agricultural Research
0035-4821 Rhodesian Journal of Economics
0035-483X Rhodesian Law Journal
0035-4848 Rhodesian Librarian *changed to* Zimbabwe Librarian
0035-4864 Rhodesian Property & Finance
0035-4872 Rhodesian Railway Review *changed to* Railway Review
0035-4880 Rhodesian Tobacco Journal *changed to* Zimbabwe Tobacco Today
0035-4899 Rhodesian Viewpoint
0035-4902 Rhodora
0035-4929 Rhumatologie†
0035-4937 Rhythm
0035-4953 Ribarski List
0035-4961 Rice Journal
0035-497X Rice Review
0035-4988 Rice University Review†
0035-4996 Rice University Studies
0035-5011 Ricerca Scientifica
0035-502X Ricerche Bibliche e Religiose
0035-5038 Ricerche di Matematica
0035-5046 Ricerche Didattiche
0035-5054 Ricerche Economiche
0035-5062 Ricerche Filosofiche†
0035-5070 Ricerche Storiche
0035-5089 Richard Cotten's Conservative Viewpoint
0035-5097 Richesses de France
0035-5100 Greater Richmond Chamber of Commerce. Research Bulletin
0035-5119 Richmond County History
0035-5135 Richting
0035-5143 Ridge News
0035-516X Riding
0035-5186 Ridotto
0035-5194 Riechstoffe, Aromen, Koerperpflegemittel *see* 0341-440X
0035-5216 Rifle Magazine *see* 0162-3583
0035-5224 Rifleman
0035-5240 Riforma della Scuola
0035-5259 Riforma Medica
0035-5267 Rig
0035-5283 Rights
0035-5291 Rights & Reviews†
0035-5305 Rehabilitation
0035-5313 Rijk der Vrouw
0035-5321 Rijkstuinbouwconsulentschap. Mededelingen
0035-533X Rijksuniversiteit te Gent. Faculteit Landbouwwetenschappen. Mededelingen
0035-5348 Rijksuniversiteit te Groningen. Mededelingenblad *changed to* Universiteitskrant Groningen
0035-5356 St. Paul's Economic Review
0035-5372 Rimba Indonesia
0035-5380 Rinascita
0035-5402 Rinderproduktion *changed to* Industriemaessige Rinderproduktion
0035-5410 Ring
0035-5429 Ring
0035-5437 Ring-Rund†
0035-5445 Ringdoc Profile Booklets
0035-5453 Ringing World
0035-5461 Ringling Museums Newsletter
0035-5488 Folia Odontologica Practica
0035-550X Journal of Clinical Pediatrics
0035-5518 Ripley's Believe It or Not
0035-5526 Ripon Forum
0035-5534 Ripresa Nazionale
0035-5550 Rise Hvezd
0035-5569 Risiko *changed to* Weerwoord
0035-5585 Risk†
0035-5593 Risk Management
0035-5607 Risorgimento
0035-5615 Risparmio
0035-5623 Risveglio del Molise e del Mezzogiorno
0035-5631 Ritenour School District News *changed to* Ritenour News
0035-564X Intercom (Overland) *changed to* Ritenour Reporter
0035-5682 Riverlander
0035-5690 Riverside County Farm & Agricultural Business News *changed to* Riverside County Agriculture
0035-5720 Riviere
0035-5739 Rivista Abruzzese
0035-5747 Rivista Aeronautica - Missilistica *changed to* Rivista Aeronautica
0035-5755 Rivista Agricola dell'O C D E†
0035-5763 Rivista Amministrativa della Repubblica Italiana
0035-5771 Rivista Araldica
0035-5798 Rivista Biblica
0035-5801 Rivista Chirurgia Pediatrica†
0035-581X Rivista Critica di Storia della Filosofia
0035-5836 Rivista degli Infortuni e delle Malattie Professionali
0035-5844 Rivista degli Ospedali
0035-5852 Rivista dei Combustibili
0035-5860 Rivista del Catasto e dei Servizi Tecnici Erariari
0035-5879 Rivista del Cinematografo
0035-5887 Rivista del Diritto Commerciale E del Diritto Generale delle Obbligazioni
0035-5895 Rivista del Diritto della Navigazione†
0035-5917 Rivista del Nuovo Cimento
0035-5925 Rivista del Porto di Napoli
0035-595X Rivista della Guardia di Finanza
0035-5968 Rivista della Ortoflorofrutticoltura Italiana
0035-5976 Rivista della Proprieta' Industriale e della Concorrenza
0035-5984 Rivista della Proprieta Intellettuale Ed Industriale†
0035-5992 Rivista della Strada
0035-600X Consacrazione e Servizio
0035-6018 Rivista delle Societa
0035-6026 Rivista di Agricoltura Subtropicale e Tropicale
0035-6034 Rivista di Agronomia
0035-6042 Rivista di Archeologia Cristiana
0035-6050 Rivista di Biologia
0035-6069 Rivista di Chirurgia Pediatrica†
0035-6077 Rivista di Clinica Pediatrica *see* 0026-4946
0035-6085 Rivista di Cultura Classica e Medioevale
0035-6093 Rivista di Diritto Civile
0035-6107 Rivista di Diritto del Lavoro
0035-6115 Rivista di Diritto Economia e Tecnica della Pesca
0035-6123 Rivista di Diritto Europeo
0035-6131 Rivista di Diritto Finanziario e Scienza delle Finanze
0035-614X Rivista di Diritto Industriale
0035-6158 Rivista di Diritto Internazionale
0035-6166 Rivista di Diritto Internazionale e Comparato del Lavoro
0035-6174 Rivista di Diritto Internazionale Privato e Processuale
0035-6182 Rivista di Diritto Processuale
0035-6190 Rivista di Economia Agraria
0035-6204 Rivista di Emoterapia e Immunoematologia
0035-6212 Rivista di Estetica
0035-6220 Rivista di Filologia e di Istruzione Classica
0035-6239 Rivista di Filosofia
0035-6247 Rivista di Filosofia Neoscolastica
0035-6255 Rivista di Gastro-Enterologia
0035-6263 Ingegneria
0035-6271 Rivista di Legislazione Scolastica Comparata†
0035-628X Rivista di Lugano
0035-6298 Universita degli Studi di Parma. Rivista di Matematica
0035-6301 Rivista di Meccanica
0035-631X Rivista di Medicina Aeronautica e Spaziale
0035-6328 Rivista di Meteorologia Aeronautica
0035-6336 Rivista di Neurobiologia
0035-6344 Rivista di Neurologia
0035-6352 Rivista di Neuropsichiatria e Scienze Affini
0035-6360 Rivista di Organizzazione Aziendale†
0035-6379 Rivista di Ostetricia e Ginecologia†
0035-6387 Rivista di Parassitologia
0035-6395 Rivista di Pastorale Liturgica
0035-6409 Rivista di Patologia Clinica e Sperimentale
0035-6417 Rivista di Patologia e Clinica

1048 ISSN INDEX

0035-6425 Rivista di Patologia e Clinica della Tubercolosi *changed to* Rivista di Patologia e Clinica della Tubercolosi e di Pneumologia
0035-6433 Rivista di Patologia Nervosa e Mentale
0035-6441 Rivista di Patologia Vegetale
0035-645X Rivista di Politica Agraria
0035-6468 Rivista di Politica Economica
0035-6476 Rivista di Polizia
0035-6484 Rivista di Psichiatria
0035-6492 Rivista di Psicoanalisi
0035-6506 Rivista di Psicologia
0035-6514 Rivista di Scienze Preistoriche
0035-6522 Rivista di Servizio Sociale
0035-6530 Rivista di Sociologia†
0035-6549 Rivista di Statistica Applicata
0035-6557 Rivista di Storia della Chiesa in Italia
0035-6565 Rivista di Storia della Medicina
0035-6573 Rivista di Storia e Letteratura Religiosa
0035-6581 Rivista di Studi Classici
0035-659X Rivista di Studi Crociani
0035-6603 Rivista di Studi Liguri
0035-6611 Rivista di Studi Politici Internazionali
0035-662X Suinicoltura *changed to* Rivista di Suinicoltura
0035-6638 Rivista di Vita Spirituale
0035-6646 Rivista di Zootecnia *changed to* Rivista di Zootecnia e Veterinaria
0035-6654 Rivista Diocesana del Patriarcato di Venezia
0035-6662 Rivista Diocesana Rimini
0035-6689 Rivista Generale Italiana di Chirurgia
0035-6697 Rivista Geografica Italiana
0035-6700 Rivista Giuridica della Circolazione e dei Trasporti
0035-6719 Rivista Internazionale di Dialogo†
0035-6727 Rivista Internazionale di Filosofia del Diritto
0035-6735 Rivista Internazionale di Filosofia Politica e Sociale e Diritto Comparato†
0035-6743 Rivista Internazionale di Psicologia e Ipnosi
0035-6751 Rivista Internazionale di Scienze Economiche e Commerciali
0035-676X Rivista Internazionale di Scienze Sociali
0035-6778 Rivista Italiana del Petrolio†
0035-6786 Rivista Italiana del Tracoma e di Patologia Oculare Virale Ed Esotica†
0035-6794 Rivista Italiana della Saldatura
0035-6808 Rivista Italiana delle Sostanze Grasse
0035-6816 Impresa
0035-6824 Rivista Italiana di Diritto Sociale
0035-6832 Rivista Italiana di Economia Demografia E Statistica
0035-6840 Rivista Italiana di Ginecologia
0035-6859 Rivista Italiana di Medicina e Igiene della Scuola
0035-6867 Rivista Italiana di Musicologia
0035-6875 Rivista Italiana di Ornitologia
0035-6883 Rivista Italiana di Paleontologia e Stratigrafia
0035-6905 Rivista Italiana di Stomatologia
0035-6913 Rivista Italiana di Studi Napoleonici
0035-6921 Rivista Italiana d'Igiene
0035-6948 Rivista Italiana Essenze Profumi, Piante officianali, Aromi, Saponi, Cosmetici, Aerosol
0035-6956 Rivista Liturgica
0035-6964 Rivista Marittima
0035-6972 Revista della Citta di Trieste
0035-6980 Rivista Militare
0035-6999 Rivista Militare della Svizzera Italiana
0035-7022 Rivista Penale
0035-7030 Rivista Rosminiana di Filosofia e di Cultura
0035-7049 Rivista Siciliana della Tubercolosi e delle Malattie Respiratorie
0035-7057 Rivista Sperimentale di Freniatria
0035-7065 Rivista Storica del Mezzogiorno
0035-7073 Rivista Storica Italiana
0035-7081 Rivista Tecnica di Cinematografia
0035-709X Rivista Tributaria
0035-7103 Rivista Trimestrale†
0035-7111 Rivista Trimestrale di Scienza Politica e Dell Amministrazione
0035-7138 Riv'on Le'inyanei Misim/Quarterly Tax Journal *see* 0334-3065
0035-7146 Rizeni Ekonomiky v Socialistickych Zemich *changed to* Rizeni Ekonomiky
0035-7154 R. L. C.'s Museum Gazette
0035-7162 Australia. Bureau of Statistics. Road Accident Fatalities *changed to* Australia. Bureau of Statistics. Road Traffic Accidents Involving Fatalities
0035-7170 Road Ahead
0035-7189 Road & Track
0035-7200 Road Apple Review
0035-7219 Road International†
0035-7227 Road Maps of Industry *changed to* Economic Road Maps
0035-7235 Raad och Roen
0035-7243 Road Rider
0035-7251 Road Tar†
0035-726X Road Test/Dune Buggy†
0035-7308 Road Transporter *changed to* Road Transporter of Australia
0035-7316 Road Way
0035-7324 Roadrunner *changed to* Wow
0035-7340 Roads and Streets *see* 0362-0506
0035-7359 Roanoke Historical Society. Journal *changed to* Roanoke Valley Historical Society Journal
0035-7367 Roanoke Review
0035-7375 Roaring Twenties (Seabrook) *see* 0147-6165
0035-7383 Robert Dumm Piano Review
0035-7391 Robot
0035-7405 Rochester Engineer
0035-7413 Rochester History
0035-7421 Rochester Review
0035-743X Rock and Soul Songs
0035-7448 Rock Mechanics
0035-7456 Rock Mechanics Abstracts *see* 0148-9062
0035-7464 Rock Products
0035-7480 Rocket
0035-7502 Rocketeer *changed to* Rocketeer (1976)
0035-7510 Rockhurst Hawk
0035-7529 Rocks and Minerals
0035-7537 Rocks & Minerals in Canada
0035-7553 Rockwell Water Journal
0035-757X Rocky Mountain Druggist *changed to* Pharmacy West
0035-7596 Rocky Mountain Journal of Mathematics
0035-760X Rocky Mountain Medical Journal *see* 0199-7343
0035-7618 Rocky Mountain Mineral Law Review *see* 0148-6489
0035-7626 Rocky Mountain Modern Language Association. Bulletin *changed to* Rocky Mountain Review of Language and Literature
0035-7634 Rocky Mountain Social Science Journal *changed to* Social Science Journal
0035-7642 Western Association of Africanists. Newsletter
0035-7650 Rocky Mountain Union Farmer
0035-7669 Rocznik Historii Czasopismiennictwa Polskiego *see* 0137-2998
0035-7677 Roczniki Chemii
0035-7685 Roczniki Filozoficzne
0035-7715 Panstwowy Zaklad Higieny. Roczniki
0035-7723 Roczniki Teologiczno-Kanoniczne
0035-7766 Rodina a Skola
0035-7774 Digest of Science of Labour
0035-7782 Roedovre Avis
0035-7790 Roeh Hacheshbon
0035-7812 Roemische Quartalschrift fuer Christliche Altertumskunde und Kirchengeschichte
0035-7820 Roentgenpraxis
0035-7839 Roester i Radio-TV
0035-7847 Rohm and Haas Reporter
0035-7855 Rohre-Rohrleitungsbau-Rohrleitungstransport *changed to* 3 R-International
0035-7863 Rohstoff-Rundschau
0035-788X Roll Call
0035-7898 Roll Sign
0035-7901 Der Roller
0035-791X Rolling Stone
0035-7928 Rolling Stone of Tampa†
0035-7936 Rollins Sandspur
0035-7944 Rolls - Royce News†
0035-7952 Rolls Royce Owner
0035-7960 Roma e Provincia Attraverso la Statistica
0035-7979 Roman-Zeitung
0035-7995 Romance Notes
0035-8002 Romance Philology
0035-8029 Romania
0035-8037 Revista de Statistica
0035-8045 Romanian Books
0035-8053 Romanian Bulletin
0035-8061 Romanian Engineering
0035-807X Romanian Foreign Trade
0035-8088 Romanian Review
0035-8096 Romanian Scientific Abstracts
0035-810X Romanian Scientific Abstracts. Social Sciences†
0035-8118 Romanic Review
0035-8126 Romanische Forschungen
0035-8142 Romantikk
0035-8150 Media Records Report of Business Publication Advertising
0035-8150 Rome Report of Business Publication Advertising *see* 0035-8150
0035-8169 Rond de Tafel
0035-8177 Rondom het Boek
0035-8185 Ronzatore
0035-8193 Roofing Contractor
0035-8207 Rooi Rose
0035-8215 Roopa-Lekha
0035-8231 Ropa a Uhlie
0035-824X Rope News *changed to* Rope Newsletter
0035-8258 Rorinstallatoren *changed to* V V S-Forum
0035-8266 Rosacruz
0035-8274 Rosario de Maria
0035-8282 Rosario e la Nuova Pompei
0035-8290 Rosebank Record†
0035-8312 Rosenberg Library Bulletin
0035-8320 Roses and Gold from Our Lady of the Ozarks
0035-8339 Rosicrucian Digest
0035-8355 Ross Reports Television
0035-8363 Rossica Society of Russian Philately Journal
0035-8371 Rostlinna Vyroba
0035-838X Rotarian
0035-8401 Rotary
0035-8428 Rote Revue *changed to* Profil
0035-8444 Rothwell Advertiser
0035-8452 Rotor & Wing *see* 0191-6408
0035-8487 Rotterdam - Europoort - Delta
0035-8495 Rotunda
0035-8525 Rough Notes
0035-8533 Round Table
0035-8541 Round-up - Children's Services†
0035-855X Roundup
0035-8568 Route
0035-8584 Rowing
0035-8606 Royal Air Force College Journal
0035-8614 Royal Air Force News
0035-8630 Royal Air Forces Quarterly†
0035-8649 Royal Arch Mason
0035-8657 Royal Army Chaplains Department. Quarterly Journal *changed to* Great Britain. Royal Army Chaplains' Department. Journal
0035-8665 Royal Army Medical Corps. Journal
0035-8673 Royal Army Pay Corps Journal
0035-8681 Royal Army Veterinary Corps. Journal†
0035-869X Royal Asiatic Society of Great Britain and Ireland. Journal
0035-8711 Royal Astronomical Society. Monthly Notices
0035-872X Royal Astronomical Society of Canada. Journal
0035-8738 Royal Astronomical Society. Quarterly Journal
0035-8746 Royal Australian Chemical Institute. Proceedings *see* 0314-4240
0035-8762 Royal Australian Historical Society. Journal
0035-8770 Royal Bank of Canada. Monthly Letter *changed to* Royal Bank Letter
0035-8789 Royal Central Asian Society. Journal *see* 0306-8374
0035-8797 Royal College of General Practitioners. Journal
0035-8800 Royal College of Physicians and Surgeons of Canada. Annals
0035-8819 Royal College of Physicians of London. Journal
0035-8827 Royal College of Surgeons in Ireland. Journal. *changed to* Irish Colleges of Physicians and Surgeons. Journal
0035-8835 Royal College of Surgeons of Edinburgh. Journal
0035-8843 Royal College of Surgeons of England. Annals
0035-8851 Royal Commonwealth Society Library Notes
0035-886X Royal Commonwealth Society. Newsletter *changed to* Commonwealth Outlook
0035-8878 Royal Engineers Journal
0035-8894 Royal Entomological Society of London. Transactions *changed to* Ecological Entomology
0035-8908 Royal Gazette
0035-8916 Royal Historical Society of Queensland Bulletin
0035-8924 Royal Horticultural Society Journal *see* 0308-5457
0035-8932 R I B A Journal
0035-8940 Royal Institute of Chemistry Reviews *see* 0306-0012
0035-8967 Royal Institution of Naval Architects. Transactions
0035-8975 Royal Irish Academy. Proceedings. Section A: Mathematical, Astronomical and Physical Science
0035-8983 Royal Irish Academy. Proceedings. Section B: Biological, Geological and Chemical Sciences
0035-8991 Royal Irish Academy. Proceedings. Section C: Archaeology, Celtic Studies, History, Linguistics and Literature
0035-9009 Royal Meteorological Society. Quarterly Journal
0035-9017 Royal Microscopical Society. Proceedings
0035-9025 Royal Military Police Journal
0035-9033 Royal Naval Medical Service. Journal
0035-9041 Royal Naval Sailing Association Journal
0035-905X Royal Neighbor
0035-9068 Royal Nepal Economist†
0035-9076 Royal Pioneer
0035-9084 Royal Service
0035-9092 Royal Society International Scientific Information Services. Bulletin†
0035-9106 Royal Society of Antiquaries of Ireland. Journal
0035-9114 Royal Society of Arts. Journal
0035-9122 Royal Society of Canada. Transactions
0035-9130 Royal Society of Health Journal
0035-9149 Royal Society of London. Notes and Records
0035-9157 Royal Society of Medicine. Proceedings *see* 0141-0768
0035-9165 Royal Society of Medicine. Section of Odontology Proceedings†
0035-9173 Royal Society of New South Wales. Journal and Proceedings
0035-9181 Royal Society of New Zealand. Transactions *see* 0303-6758
0035-919X Royal Society of South Africa. Transactions
0035-9203 Royal Society of Tropical Medicine and Hygiene Transactions
0035-9211 Royal Society of Victoria. Proceedings
0035-922X Royal Society of Western Australia. Journal
0035-9238 Royal Statistical Society. Journal. Series A: General

ISSN	Title
0035-9246	Royal Statistical Society. Journal. Series B: Methodology
0035-9254	Royal Statistical Society. Journal. Series C: Applied Statistics
0035-9262	Royal Tehran Hilton
0035-9270	Royal Television Society. Journal see 0308-454X
0035-9289	Royal United Service Institution. Journal see 0307-1847
0035-9297	University of Malta. Faculty of Arts. Journal
0035-9300	Royalauto
0035-9319	Royale Federation Cololmbophile Belge. Bulletin Federal
0035-9327	Rozhl'adyt
0035-9335	Rozhlasova Prace
0035-9343	Rozhledy Matematicko-Fyzikalni
0035-9351	Rozhledy v Chirurgii
0035-9378	Narodni Technicke Muzeum. Rozpravy
0035-9386	Rozprawy Elektrotechniczne
0035-9394	Rozprawy Hydrotechniczne
0035-9408	Rozprawy Inzynierskie
0035-9416	Rozvoj Mistniho Hospodarstvi
0035-9424	Rtam
0035-9432	Rub-Off†
0035-9440	Rubber Age see 0146-0706
0035-9467	Rubber Chem Lines†
0035-9475	Rubber Chemistry and Technology
0035-9483	Rubber Developments
0035-9491	Rubber India
0035-9505	Rubber Journal see 0305-2222
0035-9513	Rubber News
0035-9521	Rubber Research Institute of Sri Lanka. Quarterly Journal changed to Rubber Research Institute of Sri Lanka. Journal
0035-953X	Rubber Research Institute of Malaysia. Journal
0035-9548	Rubber Statistical Bulletin
0035-9556	Rubber Statistical News Sheet†
0035-9564	Rubber Trends
0035-9572	Rubber World
0035-9580	Ruby
0035-9599	Ruch Filozoficzny
0035-9602	Ruch Literacki
0035-9610	Ruch Muzyczny
0035-9629	Ruch Prawniczy, Ekonomiczny i Socjologiczny
0035-9637	Rudarski Glasnik
0035-9645	Rudarsko-Metalurski Zbornik
0035-9653	Rudder changed to Sea
0035-9661	Ruedo
0035-9688	Rudy
0035-9696	Rudy i Metale Niezelazne
0035-970X	La rue
0035-9726	Rugby
0035-9742	Rugby League Week
0035-9750	Rugby News changed to Rugby (Year)
0035-9777	Rugby World
0035-9793	Rukovet
0035-9815	Romania Today
0035-9823	Ruminskii Biulleten Naucinoi Informatii. Estestvennie Nauki changed to Ruminskii Biulleten Naucinoi Informatii. Estestvennie Nauki. Meditsinskie Nauki
0035-9831	Ruminskii Biuleten Inorganicnoi Informatii. Obscestvennie Nauki†
0035-9866	Rundfunk- Fernseh- Grosshandel changed to Rundfunk - Fernseh - Wirtschaft
0035-9874	Rundfunk und Fernsehen
0035-9882	Rundfunkjournalistik in Theorie und Praxis
0035-9890	Rundfunktechnische Mitteilungen
0035-9904	Rundschau fuer den Deutschen Einzelhaendler
0035-9912	Rundschau fuer Internationale Damenmode
0035-9920	Hotel- und Gastgewerbe-Rundschau
0035-9939	Runner's World
0035-9955	Ruota Diorama
0035-9963	Rupambara
0035-998X	Ruperto-Carola
0035-9998	Rural & Urban Roads
0036-0007	Rural Councillor
0036-0015	Rural District Review see 0306-3240
0036-0023	Rural Education News changed to Rural-Regional Education News
0036-0058	Rural India
0036-0066	Rural Kentuckian
0036-0074	Rural Life
0036-0082	Rural Missions changed to T N T
0036-0090	C S I R O Rural Research
0036-0104	Rural Roundup
0036-0112	Rural Sociology
0036-0139	Ruralista
0036-0147	Ruritan
0036-0155	Rusky Jazyk changed to Rusky Jazyk ve Skole
0036-0163	Russell: The Journal of the Bertrand Russell Archives
0036-0171	Russell's Official National Motor Coach Guide
0036-018X	Russia Cristiana changed to Centro Studi Russia Cristiana. Rivista
0036-0201	Russian Castings Production†
0036-021X	Russian Chemical Reviews
0036-0228	Russian Engineering Journal see 0144-6622
0036-0236	Russian Journal of Inorganic Chemistry
0036-0244	Russian Journal of Physical Chemistry
0036-0252	Russian Language Journal
0036-0260	Russian Language Monthly†
0036-0279	Russian Mathematical Surveys
0036-0287	Russian Messenger
0036-0295	Russian Metallurgy
0036-0309	Russian Oil and Gas Bulletin
0036-0317	Russian Orthodox Journal
0036-0325	Russian Pharmacology and Toxicology
0036-0341	Russian Review
0036-035X	Russisch changed to Zielsprache Russisch
0036-0368	Russkaya Rech'
0036-0376	Russkii Yazyk v Shkole
0036-0384	Russkii Yazyk za Rubezhom
0036-0406	Russky Golos
0036-0414	Russland und Wir
0036-0422	Ruta Dominicana
0036-0430	Rutas de Pasion
0036-0449	Rutgers-Camden Law Journal
0036-0457	Rutgers Alumni Magazine
0036-0465	Rutgers Law Review
0036-0473	Rutgers University. Libraries. Journal
0036-0481	Rwanda-Carrefour d'Afrique changed to Releve
0036-049X	Rybnoe Khozyaistvo
0036-0503	Rybovodstvo i Rybolovstvo
0036-0511	Rydge's
0036-052X	Rynki Zagraniczne
0036-0538	Rehabilitation
0036-0546	Rythmes du Monde†
0036-0570	South African Banking
0036-0597	S A C O Tidningen see 0347-0342
0036-0600	South African Cerebral Palsy Journal
0036-0627	South African Chemical Processing see 0032-5937
0036-0643	South African Draughtsman
0036-0651	S A E - Australasia
0036-0678	S A E S T Transactions
0036-0708	S A F E - Nachrichten
0036-0716	S A F T O Exporter
0036-0724	South African Friesland Journal
0036-0740	S A H S Newsletter
0036-0759	S. A. Hairdressing and Beauty Culture
0036-0767	S A I P A
0036-0775	S A I S Review†
0036-0783	S A L A Newsletter
0036-0791	S A M A B
0036-0805	Advanced Management Journal
0036-0813	S A M P E Journal†
0036-0821	S A M P E Quarterly
0036-083X	S A M
0036-0848	South African Machine Tool Review
0036-0864	S A N B
0036-0872	S A N T A News
0036-0880	S A N T A Bantu changed to S A N T A Health Magazine
0036-0899	S. A. News for the Deaf†
0036-0929	S.A.R. & H. Employees' Review changed to Emplo Review/Tydskrif
0036-0945	S. A. Road Transport changed to S.A. Road Transport Journal
0036-0953	SASSAR
0036-097X	S A T I S†
0036-0988	S A U K-S A B C Bulletin changed to Family Radio & TV
0036-0996	Sweden. Statens Avtalsverk. Information Fraan S A V changed to Sweden. Statens Arbetsgivarverk. Arbetsgivarverket Informerar
0036-1003	South African Wool and Textile Research Institute. Bulletin
0036-1011	S. A. Worker
0036-102X	S B
0036-1038	S-B Gazette/Sutters Bourgeoisie Gazette see 0038-9900
0036-1062	Bibliotheque de Travail Supplement
0036-1070	S B Z - Sanitaer-Technik, Heizungs-, und Lueftungsbau see 0342-8184
0036-1089	S C A A Viewpoint†
0036-1097	S. C. A. R. Boletin
0036-1100	S C A T Bulletin see 0701-1024
0036-1119	S C A-Tidningen
0036-1127	S.C.E.T.A. Bulletin de Documentation changed to S C E T A Documentation
0036-1135	S C J
0036-1143	S C L A Data†
0036-116X	Santa Casa di Loreto. Messaggio
0036-1178	S. D. C. Bulletin
0036-1186	S D L Newsletter†
0036-1194	S D R-Kontakt
0036-1224	S E A G Boletin del Algodon changed to E A G Publicaciones
0036-1232	S E A G Boletin del Maiz†
0036-1232	S E A G Boletin del Maiz changed to E A G Publicaciones
0036-1240	S E A G. Boletin del Trigo†
0036-1240	S E A G Boletin del Trigo changed to E A G Publicaciones
0036-1267	S E D O C
0036-1275	S E H A Newsletter and Proceedings
0036-1291	S E M Newsletter
0036-1313	S E S A Proceedings
0036-1321	S E V Bulletin changed to Bulletin S E V/V S E
0036-1356	S F O Bladet changed to Stampersonel
0036-1364	S F W A Bulletin
0036-1372	Slovenska Akademia Vied. Geologicky Ustav D. Stura: Zbornik: Zapadne Karpaty
0036-1380	S H E N†
0036-1399	S I A M Journal on Applied Mathematics
0036-1402	S I A M Journal on Control see 0363-0129
0036-1410	S I A M Journal on Mathematical Analysis
0036-1429	S I A M Journal on Numerical Analysis
0036-1437	S I A M Newsletter changed to S I A M News
0036-1445	S I A M Review
0036-147X	Formerly; S I C A S H Newsletter changed to S I G L A S H Newsletter
0036-1488	Sida; Contributions to Botany
0036-1496	S. I. D. Proceedings
0036-150X	S I E C U S Newsletter see 0091-3995
0036-1518	S I E T Studies changed to S E D M E
0036-1526	S I G S P A C†
0036-1534	S I I/Socialist International Information see 0049-0946
0036-1542	S I L B I Bollettino
0036-1550	S I L News changed to Individual Liberty
0036-1569	S J M Bulletin/Scandinavian Steel and Metal News changed to Nordisk Skrottidning
0036-1577	S J T A News
0036-1585	S Z
0036-1607	Special Libraries Association. Geography and Map Division. Bulletin
0036-1615	S L F Tidningen†
0036-1631	S L R Camera
0036-164X	S M E A Maskin-Industrien
0036-1666	S.M.M.B. Bulletin see 0309-0809
0036-1682	S M P T E Journal
0036-1704	S. M. U. H. Bulletin see 0399-0966
0036-1720	S N E C M A Informations changed to S N E C M A Informations
0036-1763	S Nine Two Way Radio see 0145-4560
0036-178X	S O S Messenger
0036-1798	S. O. S. Soviet Jewry
0036-1801	S.O.S., U.S.A. Ship of State
0036-181X	S. P. A. Journal
0036-1836	Student Personnel Association for Teacher Education. Journal see 0362-9783
0036-1852	S P I C
0036-1860	S P I E Journal see 0091-3286
0036-1879	Sweden. Sjukvaardens och Socialvaardens Planerings- och Rationaliseringsinstitut. S P R I Litteraturtjaenst
0036-1887	S R F Resume changed to Resume
0036-1909	S S R C Newsletter
0036-1925	S S S Newsletter (Simulation in the Service of Society) see 0037-5497
0036-1933	S & T A-Scienza e Tecnologia degli Alimenti
0036-1941	S T A Educator†
0036-195X	S T A News
0036-1976	S T E L C O - Scope
0036-1984	S U C Bulletin
0036-1992	S U D A M. Biblioteca. Informa
0036-200X	S U D E NE. Boletim da Biblioteca†
0036-2018	S U H A F-Tidningen
0036-2034	Society of St. Vincent de Paul. Bulletin for Southern Africa
0036-2050	Czechoslovak Society of Arts and Sciences in America. Zpravy SVU
0036-2069	South West Africa Scientific Society. Newsletter
0036-2093	S Y R-Information med Fruktodlaren see 0348-7032
0036-2107	Commercial Transport changed to Commercial Transport
0036-2107	Commercial Transport changed to Freight World
0036-2115	Saarbruecker Hefte
0036-2123	Saastopankki
0036-2131	Sabah Society. Journal
0036-214X	Sabbath Recorder
0036-2158	Sabena Revue
0036-2174	Sabouraudia
0036-2182	Saco-Lowell Bulletin changed to Platt Saco Lowell Bulletin
0036-2190	Sacra Doctrina
0036-2204	Sacramento Business
0036-2212	Sacramento Observer
0036-2220	Sacramento Teacher†
0036-2247	Sacramento Valley Union Labor Bulletin
0036-2255	Sacred Music
0036-2263	Sacred Organ Journal
0036-228X	Sadelmager-og Tapetserer Tidende
0036-2298	Sadovodstvo
0036-231X	Holzindustrie†
0036-2328	Saenger- und Musikantenzeitung
0036-2336	Saenger-Zeitung
0036-2344	Saeugetierkundliche Mitteilungen
0036-2352	Safari
0036-2360	Safe and Security News
0036-2379	Safe Deposit Bulletin
0036-2387	Safe Driver
0036-2395	Safe Engineering†
0036-2409	Safeco Agent
0036-2417	Safer (Volkswagen) Motoring
0036-2425	Safer Oregon
0036-2433	Safety†
0036-2441	Safety at Sea International
0036-245X	Safety Briefs
0036-2468	Safety Digest changed to Safety Management
0036-2476	Safety Energizer†
0036-2484	Safety in Industry changed to Safety Management
0036-2492	Safety in Mines Abstracts see 0141-9803
0036-2506	Safety Journal

ISSN	Title
0036-2514	Environmental Control & Safety Management†
0036-2530	Safety Products News changed to Industrial Safety Product News
0036-2549	Safety Review†
0036-2557	Safety Standards see 0090-4589
0036-2565	Saga
0036-2573	Sagan-Sprottauer Heimatbriefe
0036-2581	Saguenay Medical
0036-259X	Saagverken
0036-2603	Sahakar changed to Satyachar
0036-2611	Sahakari Jagat
0036-262X	Sahamies
0036-2638	Sahara
0036-2646	Saharien
0036-2654	Sahifat Al-Tarbiya
0036-2670	Sahko-Elektriciteten i Finland
0036-2689	Journal of Accidental Medicine
0036-2700	Sail
0036-2719	Sailing
0036-2727	Sailing Industry News†
0036-2735	Sailplane and Gliding
0036-2743	Sainik Samachar
0036-2751	St. Andrews Review
0036-276X	St. Anthony Messenger
0036-2778	St. Bartholomew's Hospital Journal
0036-2794	Triomphe Saint-Cyr
0036-2808	St. Dunstan's Review
0036-2824	St. Francis Xavier University Contemporary and Alumni News changed to St. Francis Xavier University Alumni News
0036-2832	St. Gallen
0036-2840	Saint George's Hospital Gazette
0036-2859	St. Hallvard
0036-2867	Saint Hubert
0036-2875	St. Hubertus
0036-2883	St. John Review
0036-2891	St. John's Hospital Dermatological Society. Transactions changed to Clinical and Experimental Dermatology
0036-2905	St. John's Law Review
0036-2921	St. Jude's Magazine†
0036-293X	St. Louis Commerce
0036-2948	St. Louis Countian
0036-2956	St. Louis Genealogical Society Quarterly
0036-2964	St. Louis Jewish Light
0036-2972	St. Louis Journalism Review
0036-2980	St. Louis Park Medical Center. Bulletin
0036-2999	St. Louis Pharmacists' Association Magazine
0036-3014	Saint Louis University Research Journal
0036-3022	St. Louis Review
0036-3030	Saint Louis University Law Journal
0036-3057	Saint-Luc Medical
0036-3065	St. Lucas Allgemeine Glaserzeitung changed to Glas und Rahmen
0036-3081	St. Luke's Hospital Gazette†
0036-309X	St. Luke's Journal changed to St. Luke's Journal of Theology
0036-3103	St. Mark's Review
0036-3111	St. Martin's Review
0036-312X	St. Mary's Hospital Gazette
0036-3138	Saint Mary's University Journal
0036-3146	Saint Paul Area Chamber of Commerce Action†
0036-3154	St. Paul News
0036-3162	St. Poeltner Dioezesanblatt
0036-3170	St. Poeltner Kirchenzeitung changed to Kirche Bunt
0036-3189	St. Regis News, Southern Edition changed to St. Regis News
0036-3197	Saint Thomas More Political Science Journal
0036-3200	St. Thomas's Hospital Gazette see 0306-3860
0036-3219	Saint Vincent de Paul Record
0036-3227	St. Vladimir's Theological Quarterly
0036-3243	Sainte Therese de Lisieux. Annales
0036-3251	Saints' Herald
0036-326X	Sairaala
0036-3278	Sairaanhoitaja-Sjukskoterskan
0036-3286	Collecting and Breeding
0036-3294	Saison
0036-3316	Saiva Siddhanta
0036-3324	Saivite Light changed to Gracious Light
0036-3340	Sakharnaya Promyshlennost'
0036-3359	Sakharnaya Svekla
0036-3367	Sal†
0036-3375	Salamandra
0036-3383	Salem County Historical Society Newsletter
0036-3391	Sales†
0036-3413	Sales Management see 0163-7517
0036-3421	Sales Manager's Bulletin
0036-343X	Marketing World changed to Marketing Times
0036-3448	Sales/Promotion changed to Sales & Marketing Management in Canada
0036-3456	Sales Prospector
0036-3464	Sales/Slants
0036-3472	Sales Tax Advices
0036-3480	Salesian
0036-3502	Salesianum
0036-3510	Salesman's Opportunity Magazine
0036-3529	Salmagundi
0036-3537	Salmanticensis
0036-3545	Salmon and Trout Magazine
0036-3553	Salon Owner see 0095-1404
0036-3561	Salotto Culturale
0036-357X	Salpisma
0036-3596	Salt Lake Business changed to Doing Business in the Salt Lake Area
0036-360X	Salt Lick
0036-3618	Salt Water Sportsman
0036-3634	Salud Publica de Mexico
0036-3642	Salus Militiae
0036-3650	Salut les Copains changed to Salut
0036-3650	Salut les Copains
0036-3669	Salvage Bids
0036-3677	Salzburger Wirtschaft
0036-3693	Samaj Kalyan
0036-3707	Samaj Kalyan
0036-3715	Samarbete
0036-3723	Samaritano
0036-3731	Samaru Agricultural Newsletter changed to Noma
0036-374X	Samatat Prakashan
0036-3782	Samhaellsgemenskap
0036-3790	Samlarnytt
0036-3804	Sammelwerk Bauzentrumring†
0036-3820	Sammler Express
0036-3839	Samoa Times
0036-3847	Samostiina Ukrayina
0036-3855	Samouprava Zavarovancev†
0036-3871	Sampada
0036-388X	Samphire†
0036-3898	Sample Case
0036-391X	Samson Technology Trends†
0036-3928	Samtiden
0036-3944	Samvirke
0036-3952	San Antonian
0036-3960	San Antonio
0036-3979	San Antonio District Dental Society. Journal changed to San Antonio District Dental Society Newsletter
0036-3995	San Bernardino County Library Newsletter†
0036-4002	San Diego Business†
0036-4010	San Diego County Dental Society. Bulletin changed to San Diego County Dental Society. News
0036-4037	San Diego Law Review
0036-4045	San Diego
0036-4053	San Diego Numismatic Society. Bulletin
0036-4061	San Diego Physician
0036-407X	American Federation of Musicans Local 325
0036-4088	San Francisco
0036-4096	San Francisco Bay Guardian
0036-410X	San Francisco Business
0036-4118	San Francisco Camera
0036-4126	San Francisco Earthquake†
0036-4134	San Francisco Labor changed to Northern California Labor
0036-4142	San Francisco Medical Society. Bulletin changed to San Francisco Medicine
0036-4169	San Francisco Unified School District Newsletter†
0036-4185	San Jose Post-Record
0036-4215	San Luis Valley Historian
0036-4223	San Marino (Repubblica) Bollettino Ufficiale
0036-424X	San Salvatore da Horta
0036-4258	Sanatorio Sao Lucas. Boletim
0036-4266	Sand Castles†
0036-4282	Sandal Prints
0036-4290	Sandlapper
0036-4304	SANE World
0036-4312	Saneamento
0036-4320	Sangeet Kala Vihar changed to Indian Musicological Society. Journal
0036-4339	Sangeet Natak
0036-4355	Sangre
0036-4363	Sangue della Redenzione
0036-4371	Industrial and Technological Information of Yokkaichi City
0036-438X	Industrial Training
0036-4398	Industrial Vehicles
0036-4401	Sanitaer- und Heizungstechnik
0036-4428	University of California. Sanitary Engineering Research Laboratory. News Quarterly
0036-4436	Sanitary Maintenance
0036-4444	Sanity
0036-4460	Sannio Elegante
0036-4479	Sanomalehtimies
0036-4487	Sanop Kwa Kyongyong
0036-4517	Santa Clara County Historical & Genealogical Quarterly
0036-4525	Santa Clara County in Action†
0036-4541	Santa Fe Magazine
0036-455X	Santa Gertrudis Journal
0036-4568	Sante de l'Abeille
0036-4576	Sante et Sport
0036-4584	Sante, Liberte et Vaccination
0036-4606	Santo dei Voli
0036-4614	Santuario de Aparecida
0036-4622	Santuario della Madonna delle Rocche
0036-4630	Santuario di N.S.D. Grazie e di S. Maria Goretti
0036-4649	Sanyo Kasei News
0036-4657	Sao Paulo
0036-4665	Instituto de Medicina Tropical de Sao Paulo. Revista
0036-4681	Sapere
0036-469X	Sapeur-Pompier
0036-4703	Sapientia
0036-4711	Sapienza
0036-472X	Sapporo Medical Journal
0036-4738	Sarah Lawrence Journal†
0036-4746	S.L. Literary Review changed to Sarah Lawrence Review
0036-4754	Sarasvat
0036-4762	Sarawak Gazette
0036-4770	Sardegna Economica
0036-4789	Sardegna Informazioni
0036-4797	Sarika
0036-4819	S A R P changed to Servamus
0036-4827	Sarsia
0036-4835	Sarvodaya
0036-4843	Sash
0036-4851	Sask Tel News
0036-4878	Saskatchewan Archaeology Newsletter
0036-4886	Saskatchewan Bulletin
0036-4894	Saskatchewan Gazette
0036-4908	Saskatchewan History
0036-4916	Saskatchewan Law Review
0036-4924	Saskatchewan Library
0036-4940	Saskatchewan Motorist
0036-4975	Saturday Night
0036-4983	Saturday Review†
0036-4991	Satya Prakash
0036-5009	Sau og Geit
0036-5025	Saucers, Space & Science†
0036-5033	Sauna Nachrichten mit Sauna Archiv
0036-5041	Sauvegarde de l'Enfance
0036-505X	Sauvegarde des Chantiers
0036-5068	Savacou
0036-5076	Savannah State College Bulletin
0036-5084	Savant
0036-5092	Savez Omladine
0036-5106	Saving Health
0036-5114	Savings and Loan News
0036-5122	Savings Association News
0036-5130	Savings Bank Journal
0036-5149	Savita
0036-5157	Savoia
0036-5165	Savoir et Beaute
0036-5173	Savremena Praksa
0036-519X	Savremenik
0036-5203	Savremeno Domacinstvo
0036-5211	Saxons Veckotidning
0036-522X	Sbirka Soudnich Rozhodnuti a Stanovisek
0036-5238	Sbirka Zlepsovacich Navrhu a Pokrokovych Vyrobnich Zkusenosti see 0322-9564
0036-5246	Sbornik Archivnich Praci
0036-5254	Ceskoslovenska Spolecnost Zemepisna. Sbornik
0036-5270	Sbornik Geologickych Ved: Antropozoikum
0036-5289	Sbornik Geologickych Ved: Hydrogeologie, Inzenyrska Geologie
0036-5297	Sbornik Geologickych Ved: Paleontologie
0036-5300	Sbornik Geologickych Ved: Technologie, Geochemie
0036-5319	Sbornik Geologickych Ved: Uzita Geofyzika
0036-5327	Sbornik Lekarsky
0036-5335	Narodni Muzeum. Sbornik. Rada A: Historie
0036-5343	Narodni Muzeum. Sbornik. Rada B: Prirodni Vedy
0036-5351	Narodni Muzeum. Sbornik. Rada C: Literarni Historie
0036-536X	V S D a V u D Sobornik Praci†
0036-5378	Sbornik UVTIZ - Genetika a Slechteni
0036-5386	Sbornik UVTIZ - Meliorace
0036-5394	Sbornik UVTIZ - Ochrana Rostlin
0036-5408	Scabbard and Blade Journal
0036-5416	Scala International
0036-5424	Scale Modeler
0036-5432	Scale Models
0036-5467	Scan
0036-5475	Scan see 0306-2295
0036-5483	Scandia
0036-5491	Scandinavian Economic History Review
0036-5505	Scandinavian Journal of Rehabilitation Medicine
0036-5513	Scandinavian Journal of Clinical & Laboratory Investigation
0036-5521	Scandinavian Journal of Gastroenterology
0036-553X	Scandinavian Journal of Haematology
0036-5548	Scandinavian Journal of Infectious Diseases
0036-5556	Scandinavian Journal of Plastic and Reconstructive Surgery
0036-5564	Scandinavian Journal of Psychology
0036-5572	Scandinavian Journal of Respiratory Diseases changed to European Journal of Respiratory Diseases
0036-5580	Scandinavian Journal of Thoracic and Cardiovascular Surgery
0036-5599	Scandinavian Journal of Urology and Nephrology
0036-5602	Scandinavian Public Library Quarterly
0036-5610	Scandinavian Research Information Notes†
0036-5629	Scandinavian Shipping Gazette
0036-5637	Scandinavian Studies
0036-5661	Scanlan's Monthly†
0036-5696	Scautismo
0036-570X	Scelte del Consumatore†
0036-5718	Scen och Salong
0036-5726	Scena
0036-5734	Scena
0036-5742	Scena Illustrata
0036-5777	Scenes from Oceana†
0036-5793	Scenes et Pistes
0036-5815	Scenografie
0036-5831	Schach-Echo
0036-584X	Schachklub Hietzing Nachrichtenblatt
0036-5858	Schakel
0036-5882	Schakels†
0036-5890	Schakend Nederland

0036-5904 Schakt-Bladet
0036-5920 Scharnhorst Auslese
0036-5939 Das Schaufenster
0036-5947 Die Schaulade
0036-5955 Schedario
0036-5971 Scheepspraat *changed to* Fama
0036-5998 Scheppend Ambacht
0036-6005 Scherma
0036-6013 Schiedamse Gemeenschap†
0036-6021 Schienenfahrzeuge
0036-603X Schiff und Hafen *changed to* Schiff und Hafen /Kommandobruecke
0036-6048 Schiffbau-Normung
0036-6056 Schiffbauforschung
0036-6064 Schiffstechnik
0036-6072 Schilder *changed to* Intrex
0036-6080 Norda Schimmel Briefs *see* 0090-1903
0036-6099 Schip en Werf
0036-6102 Schippersblad†
0036-6110 Schism, a Journal of Divergent American Opinion†
0036-6129 Schizophrenia *see* 0317-0209
0036-6137 Schlager fuer Dich
0036-6145 Schlern
0036-6153 Schlesien
0036-6161 Schleswig-Holstein
0036-617X Schluessel
0036-6188 Der Schluessel
0036-6196 Schmalenbachs Zeitschrift fuer Betriebswirtschaftliche Forschung
0036-620X Schmalfilm *changed to* Schmalfilm und Videofilmen
0036-6218 Schmiertechnik und Tribologie
0036-6226 Schmierungstechnik
0036-6234 Schmollers Jahrbuch fuer Wirtschafts- und Sozialwissenschaften *see* 0342-1783
0036-6242 Informationsdienst Information/ Dokumentation
0036-6250 Schoeffe
0036-6269 Schoen - Visie
0036-6307 Schoenwereld
0036-6315 Schoevers Koerier
0036-6331 Scholarly Books in America†
0036-634X Scholarly Publishing
0036-6358 Scholars' Choice
0036-6366 Scholarships, Fellowships, Loans News Service
0036-6374 Scholarships for Foreign Students and University Graduates at Austrian Institutions of Higher Learning
0036-6382 Scholastic Coach
0036-6390 Scholastic Editor Graphics/ Communications *changed to* Scholastic Editor
0036-6404 Scholastic News Ranger
0036-6412 Scholastic Scope
0036-6439 School Administrator
0036-6447 School and Community
0036-6455 School and Society *see* 0161-7389
0036-6471 School Board†
0036-648X School Boards Newsletter *changed to* School Board Notes
0036-6498 School Buildings Equipment and Supplies *changed to* School Buildings Equipment and Supplies and School Government Chronicle
0036-6501 School Bus Fleet
0036-6536 School Counselor
0036-6544 School en Godsdienst
0036-6552 School Food Services Bulletin
0036-6560 School Government Chronicle *changed to* School Buildings Equipment and Supplies and School Government Chronicle
0036-6579 School Health Review *see* 0097-0050
0036-6587 School Law Review†
0036-6595 School Librarian
0036-6609 School Libraries *changed to* School Media Quarterly
0036-6617 School Library *changed to* School Media Centre
0036-6641 School Lunch Journal *see* 0160-6271
0036-6668 School Music News
0036-6676 School Musician Director and Teacher
0036-6684 School News†
0036-6692 School News *changed to* Ednews
0036-6706 Michigan State University. School of Labor and Industrial Relations. Newsletter
0036-6722 School of Theology at Claremont. Perspective
0036-6730 School Press Review
0036-6749 School Product News
0036-6765 School Research Information Service Quarterly *see* 0147-9741
0036-6773 School Review *changed to* American Journal of Education
0036-6781 School Safety *changed to* School Safety World
0036-679X School Science
0036-6803 School Science and Mathematics
0036-6811 School Science Review
0036-682X School Shop
0036-6838 School Tie *changed to* Education News
0036-6846 School Times†
0036-6854 School Trustee
0036-6862 School Yarn Magazine
0036-6870 Schoolbestuur
0036-6889 Schoolblad
0036-6897 Schoolgirl Story Magazine
0036-6900 Schools in Action†
0036-6919 Schott-Kurier *changed to* Schott Aktuell
0036-6943 Evangelischer Bund in Oesterreich. Schriftenreihe
0036-696X Schriftenreihe fuer Die Evangelische Frau
0036-6978 Geschichte der Naturwissenschaften, Technik und Medizin. Schriftenreihe
0036-6986 Das Schrifttum der Agrarwirtschaft
0036-6994 Schrifttumkartei Bauwesen *see* 0343-4494
0036-7001 Schrifttumkartei Beton†
0036-7001 Schrifttumkartei Beton *see* 0343-4494
0036-701X Schrifttumsuebersicht Laermminderung *see* 0344-7758
0036-7036 Schuh im Bild
0036-7044 Schuh-Kurier
0036-7052 Schuhtechnik A B C
0036-7060 Schuh-Zeitung
0036-7079 Schuhmarkt
0036-7087 Schuhwirtschaft
0036-7095 Schul- und Sportstaettenbau
0036-7117 Schule und Gesellschaft†
0036-7125 Schulfernsehen
0036-7133 Schutz und Wehr†
0036-715X Schwann Record & Tape Guide *changed to* Schwann-1 Record & Tape Guide
0036-7168 Schweineproduktion *changed to* Industriemaessige Schweineproduktion
0036-7176 Schweinezucht und Schweinemast
0036-7184 Schweissen und Schneiden
0036-7192 Schweisstechnik
0036-7206 Schweisstechnik
0036-7214 Schweizerische Arbeitslehrerinnen-Zeitung
0036-7230 Schweiz, Suisse, Svizzera, Switzerland
0036-7257 Schweizer Aluminium Rundschau
0036-7273 Schweizer Archiv fuer Neurologie, Neurochirurgie und Psychiatrie
0036-7281 Schweizer Archiv fuer Tierheilkunde
0036-729X Schweizer Auto-Verkehr†
0036-7303 Schweizer Baublatt
0036-7311 Schweizer Brauerei-Rundschau *changed to* Brauerei-Rundschau
0036-732X Schweizer Buch
0036-7338 Schweizer Buchhandel
0036-7346 Schweizer Frauenblatt
0036-7354 Schweizer Hundesport
0036-7362 Schweizer Illustrierte
0036-7370 Schweizer Journal
0036-7389 Schweizer Kavallerist
0036-7397 Schweizer Maschinenmarkt
0036-7400 Schweizer Monatshefte
0036-7419 Schweizer Musiker-Revue
0036-7427 Schweizer Naturschutz
0036-7443 Schweizer Schule
0036-746X Schweizer Treuhaender
0036-7478 Schweizer Uhr *changed to* Uhren Rundschau
0036-7486 Schweizerische Aerztezeitung
0036-7508 Schweizerische Apotheker-Zeitung
0036-7516 Schweizerische Arbeitgeber-Zeitung
0036-7524 Schweizerische Bauzeitung *changed to* Schweizer Ingenieur und Architekt
0036-7532 Schweizerische Beobachter
0036-7540 Schweizerische Bienen-Zeitung
0036-7559 Schweizerische Blatter fuer Heizung und Luftung
0036-7567 Schweizerische Drogistenzeitung
0036-7575 Schweizerische Entomologische Gesellschaft. Mitteilungen
0036-7583 Schweizerische Fachschrift fuer Buchbindereien *changed to* Bindetechnik
0036-7591 Schweizerische Gesellschaft der Offiziere des Munitionsdienstes. Bulletin
0036-7613 Schweizerische Juristen-Zeitung
0036-7621 Schweizerische Kartellkommission. Veroeffentlichungen
0036-763X Schweizerische Landwirtschaftliche Forschung
0036-7648 Schweizerische Landwirtschaftliche Monatshefte
0036-7656 Schweizerische Lehrerzeitung
0036-7664 Schweizerische Mechaniker-Zeitschrift
0036-7672 Schweizerische Medizinische Wochenschrift
0036-7680 Schweizerische Metzger-Zeitung
0036-7699 Schweizerische Mineralogische und Petrographische Mitteilungen
0036-7702 Schweizerische Monatsschrift fuer Zahnheilkunde
0036-7710 Schweizerische Musikzeitung
0036-7729 Schweizerische Nationalbank. Monatsbericht
0036-7737 Schweizerische Photorundschau
0036-7745 Schweizerische Schachzeitung
0036-7753 Schweizerische Schreinerzeitung
0036-7761 Schweizerische Uhrmacher Zeitung *changed to* Schweizerische Uhrmacher- und Goldschmiede-Zeitung
0036-777X Schweizerische Vereinigung fuer Atomenergie. Bulletin
0036-7788 Schweizerische Vereinigung fuer Klinische Chemie. Bulletin *changed to* Schweizerische Gesellschaft fuer Klinische Chemie. Bulletin
0036-7796 Schweizerische Weinzeitung
0036-780X Schweizerische Wirte-Zeitung
0036-7818 Schweizerische Zeitschrift fuer Forstwesen
0036-7826 Schweizerische Zeitschrift fuer Gemeinnuetzigkeit
0036-7834 Schweizerische Zeitschrift fuer Geschichte
0036-7842 Schweizerische Zeitschrift fuer Hydrologie
0036-7850 Schweizerische Zeitschrift fuer Musik-Handel und Industrie
0036-7869 Schweizerische Zeitschrift fuer Psychologie und ihre Anwendungen
0036-7877 Schweizerische Zeitschrift fuer Sozialversicherung
0036-7885 Schweizerische Zeitschrift fuer Sportmedizin
0036-7893 Schweizerische Zeitschrift fuer Strafrecht
0036-7907 Schweizerische Zeitschrift fuer Vermessung, Photogrammetrie und Kulturtechnik *changed to* Mensuration, Photogrammetrie, Genie Rural
0036-7923 Schweizerischer Zeitungsverleger-Verband. Bulletin
0036-7931 Schweizerisches Archiv fuer Verkehrswissenschaft und Verkehrs-Politik *changed to* Schweizerische Zeitschrift fuer Verkehrswirtschaft
0036-794X Schweizerisches Archiv fuer Volkskunde
0036-7958 Schweizerisches Gutenbergmuseum†
0036-7966 Schweizerisches Kaufmaennisches Zentralblatt
0036-7974 Schweizerisches Patent- , Muster- und Marken-Blatt
0036-7982 Schweizerisches Rotes Kreuz
0036-7990 Schweizerisches Zentralblatt fuer Staats- und Gemeindeverwaltung
0036-8008 G W A - Gas Wasser Abwasser
0036-8016 Schweizerjaeger
0036-8024 Schweizerische Zeitschrift fuer Militaermedizin *changed to* Schweizerische Zeitschrift fuer Militaer- und Katastrophenmedizin
0036-8032 Schwenkfeldian
0036-8040 Sci
0036-8059 Sci-Tech News
0036-8067 Sci/Tech Quarterly Index†
0036-8075 Science
0036-8083 Scienze
0036-8091 Physics Abstracts
0036-8105 Electrical & Electronic Abstracts
0036-8113 Computer & Control Abstracts
0036-8121 Science Activities
0036-813X Science Affairs†
0036-8148 Science and Children
0036-8156 Science and Culture
0036-8164 Science and Engineering
0036-8172 Doshisha University. Science and Engineering Review
0036-8180 Science and Industry
0036-8210 Science and Practice of Mushroom Growing
0036-8237 Science and Society
0036-8245 Science and Technology
0036-8253 Science Books *see* 0098-342X
0036-827X Science Citation Index
0036-8288 Science Curriculum Improvement Study Newsletter†
0036-8296 Science Digest
0036-830X Science Dimension
0036-8318 Science du Sol *see* 0335-1653
0036-8326 Science Education
0036-8334 Science Education News
0036-8342 Science et Nature
0036-8350 Science et Peche
0036-8369 Science et Vie
0036-8377 Science Fiction Review
0036-8407 Science in Parliament
0036-8423 Science News
0036-8458 Science of Mind
0036-8466 Science of the Soul
0036-8474 Science on the March *see* 0160-0664
0036-8482 Science Policy Reviews†
0036-8504 Science Progress
0036-8520 Science Review
0036-8539 Science Studies *changed to* Us
0036-8547 Science Teacher *changed to* C A S M E Journal
0036-8555 Science Teacher
0036-858X Science Today
0036-8598 Science Tools
0036-8601 Science World
0036-861X Sciences
0036-8628 Sciences & l'Enseignement des Sciences†
0036-8636 Sciences et Avenir
0036-8652 Sciences et Techniques
0036-8679 Scientia
0036-8687 Scientia
0036-8695 Scientia Electrica
0036-8709 Scientia Pharmaceutica
0036-8717 Scientiae
0036-8725 Scientiarum Historia†
0036-8733 Scientific American
0036-8741 S T A R
0036-875X Science and Australian Technology *see* 0310-9100
0036-8768 Scientific, Engineering, Technical Manpower Comments
0036-8776 Information-Part 1-News/Sources/ Profiles *see* 0360-5817
0036-8784 Scientific Information Notes
0036-8792 Industrial Lubrication & Tribology
0036-8806 Scientific Meetings
0036-8814 Scientific Progress
0036-8822 Scientific Research Council of Jamaica. Journal

ISSN	Title
0036-8830	Scientific Researches *changed to* Bangladesh Journal of Scientific and Industrial Research
0036-8857	Scientific World
0036-8865	Scienza dell'Alimentazione
0036-8873	Scienza e la Tecnica della Organizzazione Nella Pubblica Amministrazione *changed to* Rivista Trimestrale di Scienza della Amministrazione
0036-8881	Scienza e Tecnica Agraria
0036-889X	Scienza e Tecnica Lattiero-Casearia
0036-8903	Scienze Ed Il Loro Insegnamento *changed to* Scienze, la Matematica e Il Loro Insegnamento
0036-892X	Scierie & Charpente†
0036-8954	Scooter World
0036-8962	Scopcraeft†
0036-8970	Scope†
0036-8989	Scope *changed to* Health Student
0036-8997	Scope (Minneapolis)
0036-9012	Scope
0036-9020	Scopus
0036-9039	Score†
0036-9055	Scotland *changed to* Business Scotland
0036-9063	Scotland's Magazine†
0036-9071	Scots Independent
0036-908X	Scots Law Times
0036-911X	Scottish Art Review
0036-9128	Scottish Bankers Magazine
0036-9136	Scottish Baptist Magazine
0036-9144	Scottish Birds
0036-9152	Scottish Clubman *changed to* Motorscot
0036-9160	Scottish Curler
0036-9195	Scottish Farmer
0036-9209	Scottish Field
0036-9217	Scottish Forestry
0036-9225	Scottish Geographical Magazine
0036-9233	Scottish Grocer
0036-9241	Scottish Historical Review
0036-9276	Scottish Journal of Geology
0036-9284	Scottish Journal of Occupational Therapy†
0036-9292	Scottish Journal of Political Economy
0036-9306	Scottish Journal of Theology
0036-9314	Scottish Law Gazette
0036-9322	Scottish Licensed Trade News
0036-9330	Scottish Medical Journal
0036-9349	Scottish Miner
0036-9357	Scottish Pharmacist†
0036-9365	Scottish Plumbing and Heating Monthly *changed to* Plumbing and Heating
0036-9373	Scottish Primary Quarterly†
0036-939X	Scottish Schoolmaster†
0036-9411	Scottish Studies
0036-942X	Scottish Sunday School Teacher†
0036-9446	Scottish Women's Temperance News
0036-9462	Canadian Leader
0036-9470	Scout Pionnier
0036-9489	Scouting
0036-9500	Scouting Magazine
0036-9519	Scoutledaren
0036-9527	Scrap Age
0036-9535	Scraper
0036-9543	Screen
0036-9551	Screen
0036-956X	Screen Actor
0036-9586	Point of Sale News
0036-9594	Screen Printing
0036-9624	Screw
0036-9632	Scribblings†
0036-9640	Scriblerian *changed to* Scriblerian and Kit-Cats:
0036-9713	Scripta Mathematica
0036-9721	Scripta Medica
0036-973X	Scripta Mercaturae
0036-9748	Scripta Metallurgica
0036-9764	Scripta Theologica
0036-9772	Scriptorium
0036-9780	Scripture Bulletin
0036-9799	Scroll of Phi Delta Theta
0036-9802	Scugnizzo
0036-9810	Scuola Cattolica
0036-9837	Scuola di Base
0036-9845	Italy. Scuola di Guerra. Biblioteca. Bolletino
0036-9853	Scuola e Citta
0036-9861	Scuola e Didattica
0036-987X	Scuola e l'Uomo
0036-9888	Scuola Italiana Moderna
0036-9896	Scuola Media†
0036-990X	Scuola Normale Superiore di Pisa. Annali. Lettere, Storia e Filosofia *changed to* Scuola Normale Superiore di Pisa. Annali. Classe di Lettere e Filosofia
0036-9918	Scuola Normale Superiore di Pisa. Annali. Scienze, Fisiche e Matematiche *changed to* Scuola Normale Superiore di Pisa. Annali. Classe di Scienze
0036-9926	Scuola Viva
0036-9942	Sdelovaci Technika
0036-9950	Se Vuoi
0036-9969	Sea and Pacific Motor Boat *changed to* Sea
0036-9977	Sea Breezes
0036-9985	Sea Cadet *changed to* Navy News. Sea Cadet Edition
0036-9993	Sea Frontiers
0037-0002	Canadian Fisherman *see* 0317-2023
0037-0010	Sea Letter
0037-0029	Sea Secrets
0037-0037	Sea Spray
0037-0045	Maryland-Washington-Delaware Beverage Journal
0037-0053	Seaby's Coin and Medal Bulletin
0037-0061	Seacraft *see* 0005-0237
0037-007X	Seafarer
0037-0096	Seafarer's Log *see* 0160-2047
0037-010X	Seafood Export Journal
0037-0118	Seahorse
0037-0126	Seal†
0037-0142	Seaman
0037-0150	Seaports and the Shipping World
0037-0169	Seara Medica Neurocirurgica
0037-0177	Seara Nova
0037-0185	Search *see* 0022-6726
0037-0207	Search: Chemical Materials & Products Division†
0037-0215	Search: Coal, Coke & Mineral Tars Division†
0037-0223	Search: CPI Marketing & Statistics Division†
0037-0231	Search: Drugs Division†
0037-024X	Search: Dyes, Pigments & Coatings Division†
0037-0258	Search: Essential Oils, Soaps & Toiletries Division†
0037-0266	Search: Fertilizers Division†
0037-0274	Search: Foodstuffs Division†
0037-0282	Search: Inorganic Chemicals Division†
0037-0290	Search (Amherst) *changed to* Search-Flying Saucers
0037-0304	Search: Metals Division†
0037-0312	Search: Non-Metallic Minerals Division†
0037-0320	Search: Oils, Fats & Waxes Division†
0037-0339	Search: Organic Chemicals Division†
0037-0347	Search: Pesticides Division†
0037-0355	Search: Petroleum Division†
0037-0363	Search: Plastics & Resins Division†
0037-0371	Search: Pulp & Paper Division†
0037-038X	Search: Rubber Division†
0037-0398	Search: Textiles Division†
0037-0401	Searcher
0037-041X	Searcher
0037-0428	Seatrade
0037-0436	Seattle Audubon Society Notes
0037-0444	Seattle Business
0037-0452	Seattle-King County Dental Society. Journal
0037-0460	Seattle Folklore Society Newsletter
0037-0479	Seattle University Spectator
0037-0487	Seaway Review
0037-0495	Adhesion and Adhesives
0037-0517	Secolul 20
0037-0584	Secondary Raw Materials *changed to* Recycling Today
0037-0592	Secret Confessions
0037-0606	Secret Place
0037-0622	Secretary
0037-0649	Secrets
0037-0657	Securitas
0037-0665	Securities Regulation & Law Report
0037-0673	Securities Regulation and Transfer Report
0037-0681	Security Police Digest
0037-069X	Security Systems Digest
0037-0703	Security World
0037-0711	Sedia e Il Mobile
0037-0738	Sedimentary Geology
0037-0746	Sedimentology
0037-0754	See
0037-0762	See India
0037-0770	Seed and Nursery Trader
0037-0789	Seed Trade News
0037-0797	Seed World
0037-0800	Seedsmen's Digest
0037-0819	Seeing Eye Guide
0037-0827	Seek
0037-0843	Schiffahrt International /Seekiste *changed to* Schiffahrt International mit Seekiste und Nautilus
0037-0851	Seer (Inkprint Edition)
0037-086X	Seeverkehr†
0037-0878	Der Seewart
0037-0886	Seewirtschaft
0037-0894	Sefarad
0037-0916	Seglarbladet
0037-0924	Segnalatore Musicale delle Edizioni Carrara *changed to* Carrara
0037-0932	Segnalazioni Cinematografiche
0037-0940	Camera di Commercio Italiana per la Gran Bretagna e il Commonwealth. Segnalazioni
0037-0959	Segnalazioni Stradali *see* 0391-2019
0037-0967	Segretario del Comune e della Provincia†
0037-0975	Sehen und Hoeren
0037-0991	Seihin News
0037-1009	Bookbinding Industry
0037-1017	Japanese Biochemical Society. Journal
0037-1025	Life and Environment
0037-1033	Orthopedics and Traumatology
0037-1041	Seine et Paris†
0037-105X	Production Research
0037-1076	Tokyo Journal of Psychoanalysis†
0037-1084	Seishin Studies
0037-1092	Japanese Junior Red Cross
0037-1106	Seismological Society of America. Bulletin
0037-1114	Seismological Society of Japan. Journal
0037-1122	Seiva
0037-1130	Sejl og Motor
0037-1149	Sekretarska Praxe
0037-1157	Selbst Ist der Mann *changed to* Selbst mit 1000 Tips
0037-1165	Selbsthilfe
0037-1173	Sele Arte
0037-1181	Selecciones de Libros *changed to* Actualidad Bibliografica de Filosofia y Teologia
0037-119X	Selecciones de Teologia
0037-1203	Selecciones del Reader's Digest (Chilean Edition)
0037-1246	Selecciones del Reader's Digest (Iberian Edition)
0037-1262	Selecoes Zootecnicas†
0037-1297	Selected Abstracts of Non-U.S. Literature on Production and Industrial Uses of Radioisotopes†
0037-1300	University of California, Berkeley. Library School Library. Selected Additions to the Library School Library Collection
0037-1327	Crime and Delinquency Literature *see* 0146-9177
0037-1335	Selected Philippine Periodical Index†
0037-1343	Selected Rand Abstracts
0037-1351	Princeton University. Industrial Relations Sections Selected References
0037-136X	Selected Water Resources Abstracts
0037-1378	Selection du Reader's Digest (Canadian-French Edition)
0037-1386	Selection du Reader's Digest (French Edition)
0037-1394	Selection du Reader's Digest (Swiss-French Edition)
0037-1408	Selection du Reader's Digest (Belgian-French Edition)
0037-1416	Belgium. Office Belge du Commerce Exterieur. Informations du Commerce Exterieur
0037-1424	Selection of International Railway Documentation
0037-1432	Selective Abstracting Service: Welding and Allied Processes *see* 0340-4749
0037-1459	Selektsiya i Semenovodstvo
0037-1467	Selenium & Tellurium Abstracts
0037-1483	Selezione Dal Reader's Digest (Italian Edition)
0037-1491	Selezione di Picchiarello *changed to* Top Mix
0037-1505	Selezione per l'Avicoltore
0037-1513	Selezione Tessile
0037-1521	Selezione Veterinaria
0037-153X	Self
0037-1556	Self-Knowledge
0037-1564	Self-Realization
0037-1572	Self Service and Supermarket *changed to* Super Marketing
0037-1599	Selling
0037-1602	Selling Christmas Decorations
0037-1610	Selling Sporting Goods
0037-1629	Selling Today
0037-1637	Selmer Bandwagon
0037-1645	Sel'skii Mekhanizator
0037-1653	Sel'skoe Khozyaistvo za Rubezhom. Seriya: Rasteneivodstvo i Zhivotnovodstvo
0037-167X	Sel'skokhozyaistvennaya Biologiya
0037-1688	Sel'skokhozyaistvennaya Literatura S. S. S. R.
0037-1718	Selskostopanska Tekhnika
0037-1734	Semailles
0037-1750	Semaine Commerciale
0037-1769	Annales de Pediatrie
0037-1793	Semana
0037-1807	Semana Medica†
0037-1815	Semana Medica de Centroamerica y Panama
0037-1823	Semana Medica de Mexico
0037-184X	Semana Vitivinicola
0037-1858	Semanario Israelita
0037-1866	Sembrador
0037-1874	Semeador Baptista
0037-1882	Gemengo Textiel†
0037-1890	Sementi Elette
0037-1904	Semiconductor Diode & S C R D.A.T.A. Book *changed to* Diode D. A. T. A. Book
0037-1912	Semigroup Forum
0037-1939	Seminar
0037-1947	Seminar†
0037-1963	Seminars in Hematology
0037-198X	Seminars in Roentgenology
0037-1998	Semiotica
0037-2005	Seema
0037-2013	Semper Floreat *changed to* Gamut
0037-203X	Sempre Pronto
0037-2048	Sem'ya i Shkola
0037-2064	Textile Review
0037-2072	Japan Research Association for Textile End-Uses. Journal
0037-2080	S E R Tidningen
0037-2099	Senales
0037-2102	Senckenbergiana biologica
0037-2110	Senckenbergiana Lethaea
0037-2129	Sendbote des Herzens Jesu
0037-2145	Seneca Review
0037-2153	Senegal. Direction de la Statistique. Bulletin Statistique et Economique Mensuel
0037-2161	Senftenegger Monatsblatt fuer Genealogie und Heraldik†
0037-217X	Dyeing & Finishing
0037-2188	Sen'i to Kogyo†
0037-2196	Senior Citizens News *changed to* S R S News
0037-2218	Senior Golfer
0037-2226	Senior High Challenge *changed to* Senior High New Life Literature

ISSN	Title
0037-2234	Senior News
0037-2242	Senior Scholastic
0037-2250	Seniorscope†
0037-2269	Sent *changed to* Share
0037-2277	Miscellanea Bryologica et Lichenologica
0037-2285	Congenital Anomalies
0037-2315	Sentinel (Ottawa)
0037-2323	Sentinel (Hartford)
0037-234X	Sentinella Agricola
0037-2366	Separation Science *see* 0149-6395
0037-2374	Sepia†
0037-2390	Sept Jours de l'Economie Britannique *changed to* Semaine Economique et Financiere en Grande Bretagne
0037-2404	Sept Jours de l'Economie Francaise†
0037-2412	Sequences
0037-2420	Sequoia
0037-2439	Serafico Vessillo
0037-2447	Serials Bulletin
0037-2455	Journal of Sericultural Science of Japan
0037-2463	Series Haematologica†
0037-248X	Sermon Builder
0037-2498	Serpe
0037-2501	Serra d'Or
0037-251X	Serra-Post†
0037-2528	Serrurerie Constructions Metalliques
0037-2536	Serviam
0037-2544	Service
0037-2552	Service and Indemnity
0037-2560	Service de la Carte Geologique d'Alsace et de Lorraine. Bulletin *see* 0302-2692
0037-2579	Revue Technique Diesel
0037-2595	Service Economique & Financier "Secofi"
0037-2609	Service Employee
0037-2617	Service News
0037-2625	Service Protestant Francais de Presse et d'Information
0037-2633	Service Social
0037-2641	Service Social dans le Monde
0037-265X	Service Station
0037-2668	Service Station & Garage Management
0037-2676	Service Station Management and Merchandising *see* 0037-2668
0037-2684	Service World Reports *changed to* I/V 400 Chain Report
0037-2692	Servicio Nacional Tecnico del Carton Ondulado. Revista†
0037-2706	Servicios Publicos *see* 0099-1694
0037-2714	Portugal. Servico de Administracao Militar. Revista Mensal *changed to* Portugal. Servico de Administracao Militar. Revista Bimestral
0037-2722	Servico de Odontologia Santaria. Boletim *changed to* Equipe de Odontologia Sanitaria. Boletim
0037-2730	Portugal. Servicos Geologicos. Comunicacoes
0037-2749	Serving America
0037-2757	Servir Mieux
0037-2765	Servire
0037-2773	Servizio della Parola
0037-2781	Italy. Ministero dell'Interno. Rassegna degli Agchivi di Stato
0037-279X	Servizio Informazioni Avio
0037-2803	Servizio Migranti
0037-282X	Session Cases†
0037-2838	Sessuologia *changed to* Rivista di Sessuologia
0037-2846	Sestina Sveta v Obrazech†
0037-2862	Setimo Ceu
0037-2870	Seto Marine Biological Laboratory. Publications
0037-2889	Square Dancing
0037-2897	Settanta Anni di Calcio
0037-2900	Settegiorni
0037-2919	Settimana del Sordomuto *changed to* Settimana del Sordo
0037-2927	Settimana Medica
0037-2935	Settimanale di Diritto e Legislazione del Lavoro†
0037-2943	Seura *changed to* Seura (1979)
0037-2951	Seva-Bharati
0037-2986	Seven Arts†
0037-2994	Seven Arts Digest†
0037-3001	Seven Arts Guide†
0037-301X	Seventeen
0037-3028	Seventeenth-Century News
0037-3036	73 Amateur Radio *see* 0098-9010
0037-3044	Sewanee News
0037-3052	Sewanee Review
0037-3060	Sexology *see* 0199-7149
0037-3087	Sekstant
0037-3095	Sexual Behavior
0037-3117	S-Gravenhage *changed to* Den Haag
0037-3125	Shabistan Urdu Digest
0037-3133	Shade Tree
0037-3141	Shaded Room
0037-3168	Shaftesbury Review
0037-3176	Shaheen
0037-3184	Shahpar
0037-3214	Shakespeare Newsletter
0037-3222	Shakespeare Quarterly
0037-3230	Shakhmatnyi Byulleten'
0037-3249	Shakhmaty v S. S. S. R.
0037-3257	Shale Shaker
0037-3265	Shalom
0037-3273	Shama
0037-3281	Shankar's Weekly†
0037-329X	Shantih
0037-3303	Craftsmen's Technical Digest *see* 0360-6740
0037-3311	Shareholder
0037-3346	Shavian
0037-3354	Shaw Review *changed to* Shaw Annual
0037-3362	Shawcover
0037-3370	She
0037-3389	She†
0037-3400	Sheep and Goat Raiser
0037-3419	Sheep Breeder and Sheepman
0037-3427	Sheera Udyog†
0037-3435	Sheet-A-Week
0037-3451	Sheet Metal Industries
0037-3478	Sheet Metal Workers' Journal
0037-3494	Shejzat
0037-3508	Shelfmark
0037-3516	Shell Aviation News
0037-3524	Shell Bitumen Review
0037-3532	Shell Chronicle
0037-3540	Shell Dealer News
0037-3559	Shell Hausnachrichten
0037-3567	Shell Revue†
0037-3575	Shell Erdoel Informationen
	Shellfish Situation and Outlook *see* 0098-8014
0037-3583	Shenandoah
0037-3591	Shepherd *changed to* Shepherd and Sheep Raiser
0037-3605	Shepherd's Call
0037-3613	Shepherd's Magazine
0037-3621	Sherlock Holmes Journal
0037-3648	Shetkari
0037-3656	Sheviley Hahinuch
0037-3664	Audio-Visual Education
0037-3672	Shield
0037-3680	Shikoku Entomological Society. Transactions
0037-3699	Shikoku Acta Medica
0037-3702	Shikoku National Agricultural Experiment Station. Bulletin
0037-3710	Tokyo Dental College Society. Journal
0037-3729	Shilo Stag
0037-3737	New Flowers
0037-3745	New Nippon Electric Technical Review
0037-3761	New Cities
0037-377X	Shingle
0037-3788	Shinkan News for Readers
0037-3796	Nerve Chemistry *changed to* Japanese Neurochemical Society. Bulletin
0037-3818	Shinshu University. Faculty of Engineering. Journal
0037-3826	Shinshu Medical Journal
0037-3834	Ship & Boat International
0037-3842	Ship-Shape†
0037-3850	Shipbuilding and Shipping Record *see* 0306-347X
0037-3885	Shipping and Port Review†
0037-3907	Shipping Executive
0037-3915	Shipping Gazette
0037-3923	Shipping Register and Shipbuilder
0037-3931	Shipping World & Shipbuilder
0037-394X	Ships Monthly
0037-3958	Shipyard Review
0037-3966	Shire & Municipal Record
0037-3974	Shirley Link *see* 0306-0748
0037-3982	Shiryo Gaido†
0037-3990	Japanese Journal of Education of the Handicapped
0037-4008	Shituf
0037-4024	Shkola i Proizvodstvo
0037-4032	Shoe and Leather Journal *see* 0705-1433
0037-4040	Shoe and Leather News
0037-4067	Shoe Service Wholesaler
0037-4075	Shoe Workers' Journal†
0037-4083	Shoes on Parade
0037-4091	Plant Protection
0037-4105	Food Science
0037-4113	Journal of Child Health
0037-4121	Clinical Pediatrics
0037-413X	Shoorath
0037-4148	Shooting Industry
0037-4156	Shooting Sport
0037-4172	Shop Equipment & Shopfitting News
0037-4180	Shop Fitting and Equipment Monitor†
0037-4199	Shop Property
0037-4202	Shopfitting International
0037-4210	Shopping Center Directory *see* 0419-3512
0037-4229	Shopping Guide *changed to* Home Services
0037-4237	Shore and Beach
0037-4245	Short Story
0037-4253	Short-Term Economic Survey of Principal Enterprises in Japan
0037-4261	Short Wave Magazine
0037-427X	Shorthorn News
0037-4288	Shorthorn World†
0037-430X	Show-Business
0037-4318	Show Business
0037-4326	Show-Me Libraries
0037-4334	Show-Me Missouri Legionnaire
0037-4342	Showa Medical Association. Journal
0037-4350	Showcase
0037-4377	Japanese Journal of Pharmacognosy
0037-4385	Shreveport Magazine
0037-4393	Shropshire Magazine
0037-4407	Shubyo to Engei
0037-4423	Mercury Magazine Operation
0037-4431	Shveinaya Promyshlennost'
0037-444X	Si-De-Ka Magazine
0037-4466	Siberian Mathematical Journal
0037-4474	Sibirskii Matematicheskii Zhurnal
0037-4482	Sibylle
0037-4504	Sicher ist Sicher
0037-4512	Sichere Arbeit
0037-4520	Sicherheit Bergbau, Energiewirtschaft, Metallurgie *changed to* Sicherheit Bergbau, Energiewirtschaft, Geologie, Metallurgie
0037-4539	Sicherheit Zuerst
0037-4547	Sicherheitstechniker-Korrespondenz
0037-4563	Sicilia
0037-4571	Sicilia Archeologica
0037-458X	Siculorum Gymnasium
0037-4598	Sicurezza Sociale
0037-4601	Sidemount Reporter
0037-461X	7 Tage
0037-4628	Siecle a Mains
0037-4652	Siemens Data Report *changed to* Data Report
0037-4660	Siemens Electromedica *changed to* Electromedica
0037-4679	Siemens Electronic Components Bulletin *see* 0341-6569
0037-4687	Elektrodienst
0037-4695	Siemens Informationen Fernsprech-Vermittlungstechnik *see* 0340-2975
0037-4709	Siemens-Zeitschrift
0037-4717	Siempre
0037-4725	Sierra Club Bulletin *changed to* Sierra
0037-4741	Sierra Leone. Central Statistics Office. Quarterly Statistical Bulletin†
0037-475X	Sierra Leone Studies
0037-4768	Sierra Leone Trade Journal
0037-4792	Sifriya Laam
0037-4806	Sight and Sound
0037-4814	Sight & Sound Marketing
0037-4822	Sightsaving Review†
0037-4830	Sightlines
0037-4849	Sigma†
0037-4857	Sigma
0037-4865	Sigma-T
0037-4873	Sign (Union City)
0037-4903	Signa†
0037-4911	Signal†
0037-492X	Signal
0037-4938	Signal (Falls Church)
0037-4946	Signal
0037-4954	Signal
0037-4970	Signal International
0037-4997	Signal und Draht
0037-5004	Signal und Schiene
0037-5012	Signal 8-2
0037-5020	Signalman's Journal
0037-5039	Signature
0037-5047	Signs of the Times
0037-5055	Signs of the Times
0037-5063	Signs of the Times
0037-5071	Signs of the Times
0037-508X	Sigurnost
0037-5098	Siipikarja
0037-5101	Sika
0037-511X	Sikh Courier
0037-5128	Sikh Review
0037-5136	Sikio *changed to* Kenrail
0037-5136	Sikio *changed to* Tanzania Railways Corporation. Habari za Reli
0037-5144	Sikkim†
0037-5152	Sikorsky News
0037-5160	Siksha - O - Sahitya
0037-5179	Silarus
0037-5187	Silent Advocate
0037-5195	Silent Messenger
0037-5209	Silent Picture†
0037-5217	Silhouette
0037-5225	Silicates Industriels
0037-5233	Silikattechnik
0037-5241	Silikaty
0037-525X	Silk and Rayon Industries of India *changed to* Man-Made Textiles in India
0037-5268	Silk Screen
0037-5276	Silliman Christian Leader†
0037-5284	Silliman Journal
0037-5292	Silnicni Doprava *changed to* Silnicni Obzor
0037-5306	Silo
0037-5314	Silpakon
0037-5330	Silva Fennica
0037-5349	Silvae Genetica
0037-5357	Silver
0037-5365	Silver Screen
0037-5373	Silvicultura†
0037-539X	Simian
0037-5403	Simiente
0037-5411	Simiolus
0037-542X	Simmenthal Club†
0037-5438	Simmons Librarian
0037-5446	Simon Fraser University. Library. Information Bulletin†
0037-5454	Simon Stevin
0037-5462	Simon van der Stel Foundation. Bulletin *changed to* Restorica
0037-5470	Simon's Town Historical Society Bulletin
0037-5497	Simulation
0037-5500	Simulation & Games
0037-5519	Simulation Councils Proceedings
0037-5527	Sin Nombre
0037-5535	Sinai Hospital of Detroit. Bulletin
0037-5543	Sindacato Moderno
0037-556X	Sindicato Nacional de la Pesca Boletin de Informacion
0037-5594	Sinfonian Newsletter
0037-5608	Sinfonie Scacchistiche
0037-5616	Sinformation
0037-5624	Sing Out!
0037-5632	Singabout; Journal of Australian Folksong

ISSN	Title
0037-5640	Singapore. Department of Statistics. Monthly Digest of Statistics.
0037-5659	Singapore International Chamber of Commerce. Economic Bulletin
0037-5675	Singapore Medical Journal†
0037-5683	Singapore Paediatric Society. Journal†
0037-5705	Singapore Trade & Industry *changed to* Singapore Business
0037-5713	Singapore Travel News *see* 0129-5020
0037-5721	Singende Kirche
0037-573X	Singer Showcase *see* 0026-816X
0037-5748	Single Parent
0037-5756	Sinn und Form
0037-5764	Sino Azul
0037-5772	Sintese Politica, Economica e Social *changed to* Sintese
0037-5780	Sintesi Economica
0037-5799	Sintesis Informativa Economica y Financiera
0037-5802	Sintesis *changed to* Sintesis-A L A L C
0037-5810	Sion
0037-5829	Sioux City Journal Farm Weekly
0037-5837	Sipapu
0037-5845	Sir
0037-5853	Siren†
0037-5861	Standard
0037-5888	Sistematica
0037-5896	Sistemi e Automazione
0037-590X	Sisters Today
0037-5918	Situation Agricole en France *changed to* Situation Agricole
0037-5926	Situation Economique *changed to* Banque de France. Enquete Mensuelle de Conjoncture
0037-5934	Situation in Argentina†
0037-5942	Gesellschaft Naturforschender Freunde zu Berlin. Sitzungsberichte. Neue Folge
0037-5950	Sivam
0037-5969	Seventies
0037-5985	S J-Nytt
0037-5993	Sjaloom *changed to* Achtergrond
0037-6000	Sjoesport
0037-6019	Sjukgymnasten
0037-6027	Tidskrift foer Sveriges Sjukskoeterskor†
0037-6035	Skagerak
0037-6043	Skakbladet
0037-6051	Skakelblad
0037-606X	Skandinavisk Aktuarietidskrift *changed to* Scandinavian Actuarial Journal
0037-6078	Skandinavisk Emballage- och Transport-Tidskrift
0037-6086	Skandinavisk Motor Journal *changed to* Motor-Journalen Bilen
0037-6094	Skandinavisk Tidskrift for Faerg och Lack
0037-6108	Skandinaviska Banken. Quarterly Review *see* 0347-3139
0037-6124	Skate
0037-6132	Skating
0037-6140	Skeet Shooting Review
0037-6159	Ski
0037-6167	Ski
0037-6175	Ski Area Management
0037-6191	Ski Business
0037-6205	Helice *changed to* Cahiers du Yachting
0037-6213	Ski Racing
0037-6221	Ski Runner
0037-623X	Ski-Schweizer Skisport
0037-6248	Skier (Brattleboro)
0037-6264	Skiing
0037-6299	Skiing Trade News
0037-6310	Ringsport
0037-6329	Skillings' Mining Review
0037-6337	Skin & Allergy News
0037-6345	Skin Diver Magazine
0037-6353	Skipper
0037-6361	Skipsteknikk *changed to* Skipsnytt
0037-637X	Sklar a Keramik
0037-6388	Sko-Magasinet
0037-6396	Skogeieren
0037-640X	Skogen
0037-6418	S L A-Tidskriften†
0037-6426	Skogsaegaren†
0037-6434	Skogsbruket
0037-6442	Skol Vreizh- l'Ecole Bretonne
0037-6450	Skola Danas
0037-6469	Skolans Artikelservice
0037-6477	Barn och Kultur
0037-6485	Skolefilm†
0037-6515	Skolledaren
0037-6523	Skolska Televizija
0037-6531	Skolske Novine
0037-654X	Skolski Vjesnik
0037-5558	Skolta Mondo
0037-5566	Skolvaerlden
0037-6574	Skotoidetaljisten *changed to* SKO
0037-6582	Skov og So
0037-6590	Skraeddarmaestaren *changed to* Skraedderi
0037-6604	Sky and Telescope
0037-6612	Sky Diver
0037-6620	Skylights†
0037-6647	Skyscraper Management *changed to* Building Owner and Manager
0037-6671	Skyways
0037-668X	Slaboproudy Obzor
0037-6698	Slager
0037-6701	Slagerij *changed to* Vlees en Vleeswaren
0037-671X	Slagersambacht
0037-6736	Slavia
0037-6744	Slavia Orientalis
0037-6779	Slavic Review
0037-6787	Slavica Slovaca
0037-6795	Slavonic and East European Review
0037-6809	Sleep Bulletin *changed to* Sleep Bulletin (1978)
0037-6817	Sleep-Learning Association. Journal
0037-6825	Slevarenstvi
0037-6833	Slezsky Sbornik
0037-6841	Slijtersvakblad
0037-685X	Slingervel
0037-6868	Sloboda
0037-6884	Slobodna Rec
0037-6892	Sloejd och Ton
0037-6906	Slovenska Chemicka Spolocnost. Chemical Papers
0037-6914	Slovak Press Digest
0037-6922	Slovansky Prehled
0037-6930	Slovenska Akademia Vied. Biologicke Prace
0037-6949	Slovenska Archeologia
0037-6957	Slovenska Drzava
0037-6965	Slovenska Hudba†
0037-6973	Slovenska Literatura
0037-6981	Slovenska Rec
0037-699X	Slovenske Divadlo
0037-7007	Slovenske Pohlady na Literaturu a Umenie
0037-7015	Slovensky Hlas
0037-7023	Slovensky Narodopis
0037-7031	Slovo a Slovesnost
0037-704X	Slow Learning Child *changed to* Exceptional Child
0037-7058	Slowakei
0037-7074	Sluzba Bozja
0037-7082	Sluzba Lidu
0037-7090	Sluzben Glasnik na Sojuzot za Fizicka Kultura na Makedonija
0037-7104	Sluzbene Novine Opcine Karlovac
0037-7112	Opcina Podravska Slatina. Sluzbeni Glasnik
0037-7120	Sluzbeni Glasnik Opcine Rovinj
0037-7147	Sluzben Vesnik na Socijalisticka Republika Makedonija
0037-7155	Sluzbeni Vjesnik Opcine Buje, Novigrad i Umag
0037-7163	Sluzbeni Vjesnik Opcine Krizevci
0037-7171	Smaaskipsfart *changed to* Skipsnytt
0037-718X	Small Boat *changed to* Yacht and Boat Owner
0037-7198	Voice of Small Business
0037-7201	Small Offset Printing *changed to* Offset Printer
0037-721X	Small Pond
0037-7228	Small Press Review
0037-7244	Small Stock Magazine *see* 0363-8723
0037-7252	Small Trader & Wholesaler *changed to* Trader
0037-7260	Small World
0037-7279	Small World
0037-7287	Smit-las *changed to* Smitweld Reportage
0037-7309	Smith
0037-7317	Smith College Studies in Social Work
0037-7325	Smith's Trade News *changed to* C T N
0037-7333	Smithsonian
0037-7341	Smithsonian Torch
0037-735X	Smog
0037-7368	Smokeless Air *see* 0300-5143
0037-7376	Smuffeltje†
0037-7392	Snack
0037-7406	Snack Food
0037-7414	Snack Foods Merchandiser *see* 0026-7805
0037-7449	Sneha Sandesh†
0037-7457	Snips
0037-7473	Snowy Egret
0037-7481	Soap and Chemical Specialties *see* 0091-1372
0037-749X	Soap, Perfumery and Cosmetics
0037-7503	Soaring
0037-7511	Slaski Kwartalnik Historyczny "Sobotka"
0037-752X	Sobre Educacion Superior
0037-7538	Soccer News†
0037-7546	Soccer Star†
0037-7554	Soccer World
0037-7562	Soccorso Perpetuo di Maria
0037-7570	Sochi Gakkaishi
0037-7589	Sociaal-Economische Raad. Informatie- en Documentatie Bulletin
0037-7597	Sociaal-Economische Wetgeving *changed to* Tijdschrift voor Europees en Economisch Recht
0037-7600	Sociaal Maandblad Arbeid
0037-7619	Socialnytt
0037-7627	Social Action
0037-7635	Social Action *see* 0164-5528
0037-7643	Social and Economic Administration *changed to* Social Policy and Administration
0037-7651	Social and Economic Studies
0037-766X	Social Biology
0037-7678	Social Casework
0037-7686	Social Compass
0037-7694	Social Crediter
0037-7708	Social Debatt i Tidningar och Tidskrifter *changed to* Social Debatt
0037-7716	Social Defence
0037-7732	Social Forces
0037-7740	Social Health News *changed to* V D News
0037-7759	Social Horizon
0037-7767	Social Justice Review
0037-7775	Washington Bulletin *see* 0149-2578
0037-7791	Social Problems
0037-7805	Church and Society
0037-7813	Social Psychiatry
0037-7821	Social Questions Bulletin
0037-783X	Social Research
0037-7848	Social Science
0037-7856	Social Science and Medicine *see* 0271-7123
0037-7856	Social Science and Medicine *see* 0160-7995
0037-7856	Social Science and Medicine *see* 0160-7987
0037-7856	Social Science and Medicine *see* 0160-8002
0037-7864	Social Sciences Information
0037-7872	Social Science Record
0037-7880	Social Science Reporter and Public Relations Research Review†
0037-7899	Social Sciences & Humanities Index *see* 0094-4920
0037-7899	Social Sciences and Humanities Index *see* 0095-5981
0037-7902	Social Security Abstracts†
0037-7910	Social Security Bulletin
0037-7929	Social Security Rulings on Federal Old-Age, Survivors, Disability and Health Insurance, Supplemental Security Income, and Miners Benefits
0037-7937	Social Service†
0037-7945	Social Service Outlook†
0037-7953	Social Service Quarterly†
0037-7961	Social Service Review
0037-797X	Social Services in Wisconsin†
0037-7996	Social Studies
0037-8003	Social Studies Teacher†
0037-8011	Social Survey
0037-802X	Social Theory and Practice
0037-8038	Social Welfare
0037-8046	Social Work
0037-8054	Social Work
0037-8062	Social Work Education Reporter
0037-8070	Social Work Today
0037-8089	Social Worker
0037-8097	Sociale Wetenschappen
0037-8127	Socialisme
0037-8143	Socialismo Democratico *changed to* Umanita
0037-8151	Socialismo Settanta†
0037-816X	Socialist Action
0037-8178	Socialist Commentary
0037-8208	Socialist India
0037-8216	Sotsialisticheskii Trud
0037-8224	Socialist Leader *see* 0305-0297
0037-8232	Socialist Monitor†
0037-8240	Socialist Revolution *see* 0161-1801
0037-8259	Socialist Standard
0037-8275	Socialista
0037-8283	Socialista
0037-8291	Socialisticka Skola
0037-8305	Socialisticka Zakonnost
0037-8313	Socialisticke Zemedelstvi
0037-8321	Socialisticky Obchod
0037-833X	Socialmedicinsk Tidskrift
0037-8364	Sociedad Americana de Oftalmologia y Optometria. Archivos
0037-8380	Sociedad Argentina de Biologia. Revista
0037-8402	Sociedad Bolivariana de Venezuela. Revista
0037-8410	Sociedad Canaria de Pediatria. Boletin
0037-8429	Sociedad Castellano-Astur-Leonosa de Pediatria. Boletin
0037-8437	Sociedad Cientifica Argentina. Anales
0037-8445	Sociedad Colombiana de Endocrinologia. Revista
0037-8453	Sociedad Colombiana de Ortodoncia. Revista
0037-8461	Sociedad Colombiana de Quimicos Farmaceuticos. Boletin
0037-847X	Sociedad Cubana de Historia de la Medicina. Revista
0037-8488	Sociedad Cubana de Ingenieros. Revista†
0037-8496	Sociedad de Bibliotecarios de Puerto Rico. Boletin
0037-850X	Sociedad de Biologia de Concepcion. Boletin
0037-8518	Sociedad de Ciencias Naturales la Salle. Memoria
0037-8526	Sociedad de Cirugia de Rosario. Boletines
0037-8534	Sociedad de Medicina Veterinaria de Chile. Revista
0037-8542	Sociedad de Obstetricia y Ginecologia de Buenos Aires. Revista
0037-8550	Sociedad Espanola de Ceramica. Boletin *changed to* Ceramica y Vidrio
0037-8569	Sociedad Espanola de Socorros Mutuos y Beneficencia. Boletin
0037-8577	Sociedad Geografica de Colombia. Boletin
0037-8585	Sociedad Geografica de Lima, Peru. Boletin
0037-8593	Interamerican Planning Society. Revista *changed to* Revista Interamericana de Planificacion
0037-8607	Gazeta de Baixada
0037-8615	Sociedad Matematica Mexicana. Boletin
0037-8623	Sociedad Quimica del Peru. Boletin
0037-8631	Sociedad Rural Argentina. Anales
0037-864X	Sociedad Rural Argentina. Boletin
0037-8658	Sociedad Vasco-Navarra de Pediatria. Boletin
0037-8666	Sociedade Brasileira de Estudos Sobre Discos Voadores. Boletim
0037-8674	Sociedade Brasileira de Geografia. Boletim

0037-8682 Sociedade Brasileira de Medicina Tropical. Revista
0037-8712 Sociedade Paranaense de Matematica. Boletim
0037-8720 Societa Astronomica Italiana. Memorie
0037-8739 Societa di Studi Valdesi. Bollettino
0037-8747 Societa Entomologica Italiana. Bollettino e Memorie
0037-8755 Societa Geografica Italiana. Bollettino
0037-8763 Societa Geologica Italiana. Bollettino and Memorie
0037-8771 Societa Italiana di Biologia Sperimentale. Bollettino
0037-878X Societa Italiana di Cardiologia. Bollettino
0037-8798 Societa Italiana di Farmacia Ospedaliera. Bollettino
0037-8801 Societa Italiana di Fisica. Bollettino
0037-881X Societa Italiana di Fotogrammetria e Topografia. Bollettino
0037-8828 Societa Italiana di Mineralogia e Petrologia. Rendiconti
0037-8836 Societa Italiana di Pediatria. Notiziario
0037-8844 Societa Italiana di Scienze Naturali e del Museo Civico di Storia Naturale. Atti
0037-8852 Societa Medica Chirurgica, Cremona. Bollettino
0037-8879 Societas
0037-8887 Archivum Historicum Societatis Iesu
0037-8895 Societe Archeologique, Historique, Litteraire & Scientifique du Gers. Bulletin
0037-8909 Societe Belge de Geologie, de Paleontologie et d'Hydrologie. Bulletin *changed to* Societe Belge de Geologie. Bulletin
0037-8917 Societe Belge de Photogrammetrie. Bulletin Trimestriel
0037-8925 Societe Belge d'Etudes Geographiques. Bulletin
0037-8933 Societe Belge d'Etudes Napoleoniennes. Bulletin†
0037-8941 Societe Botanique de France. Bulletin *see* 0181-1797
0037-895X Societe Centrale d'Education et d'Assistance pour les Sourds-Muets en France. Bulletin d'Information†
0037-8968 Societe Chimique de France. Bulletin
0037-8984 Societe d'Anthropologie de Paris. Bulletin & Memoires
0037-8992 Bulletin d'Archeologie et de Statistique de la Drome *changed to* Revue Dromoise
0037-900X Societe d'Astronomie Populaire de Toulouse. Bulletin Mensuel *changed to* Pulsar
0037-9018 Societe de Biogeographie. Compte Rendu *changed to* Societe de Biogeographie. Compte Rendu des Seances
0037-9026 Societe de Biologie et de ses Filiales. Comptes Rendus des Seances
0037-9034 Societe de Botanique du Nord de la France. Bulletin
0037-9042 Societe de Chimie Biologique. Bulletin *see* 0300-9084
0037-9050 Societe de l'Histoire du Protestantisme Francais. Bulletin
0037-9069 Societe de Linguistique de Paris. Bulletin
0037-9077 Societe de Mythologie Francaise Bulletin
0037-9085 Societe de Pathologie Exotique et de ses Filiales. Bulletin
0037-9093 Societe de Pharmacie de Bordeaux. Bulletin
0037-9107 Societe de Pharmacie de Lyon. Bulletin des Travaux
0037-9115 Societe de Pharmacie de Montpellier. Travaux
0037-9123 Societe de Pharmacie de Nancy. Bulletin *see* 0301-0635
0037-9131 Societe de Pharmacie de Strasbourg. Bulletin
0037-914X Societe de Statistique de Paris. Journal *changed to* Societe de Statistique de Paris et de France. Journal
0037-9158 Societe d'Emulation du Bourbonnais. Bulletin
0037-9166 Societe des Africanistes. Journal *changed to* Journal des Africanistes
0037-9174 Societe des Americanistes. Journal
0037-9182 Societe des Amis de Montaigne. Bulletin
0037-9190 Societe des Antiquaires de l'Ouest. Bulletin
0037-9204 Societe des Antiquaires de Picardie. Quarterly Bulletin
0037-9212 Revue Francaise d'Histoire du Livre
0037-9220 Societe des Chirurgiens de Paris. Bulletin et Memoires†
0037-9247 Societe des Sciences Medicales du Grand-Duche de Luxembourg. Bulletin
0037-9255 Societe des Sciences Naturelles et Physiques du Maroc. Bulletin
0037-9263 Societe d'Etudes et d'Expansion. Revue *changed to* Etudes et Expansion
0037-9271 Societe Entomologique de France. Annales
0037-928X Societe Entomologique de France. Bulletin
0037-9298 Societe Entomologique de Mulhouse. Bulletin
0037-9301 Societe Entomologique du Quebec. Annales
0037-931X Societe Francaise de Ceramique. Bulletin. *see* 0019-9044
0037-9328 Societe Francaise de Mineralogie et de Cristallographie. Bulletin *see* 0180-9210
0037-9336 Societe Francaise de Mycologie Medicale. Bulletin
0037-9344 Societe Francaise de Numismatique. Bulletin
0037-9352 Societe Francaise de Philosophie. Bulletin
0037-9360 Societe Francaise de Physique. Bulletin
0037-9379 Societe Francaise d'Egyptologie. Bulletin
0037-9387 Societe Genealogique Canadienne-Francaise. Memoires
0037-9395 Societe Geologique de Belgique. Annales
0037-9409 Societe Geologique de France. Bulletin
0037-9417 Societe Geologique de France. Compte Rendu Sommaire des Seances *see* 0037-9409
0037-9425 Societe Historique et Archeologique du Perigord. Bulletin
0037-9441 Societe Industrielle de Mulhouse. Bulletin
0037-945X Societe Internationale de Chirurgie. Bulletin†
0037-945X Societe Internationale de Chirurgie. Bulletin *see* 0364-2313
0037-9468 Societe Internationale de Psycho-Prophylaxie Obstetricale. Bulletin Officiel
0037-9476 Societe Mathematique de Belgique. Bulletin
0037-9484 Societe Mathematique de France. Bulletin
0037-9492 Societe Medico-Chirurgicale des Hopitaux et Formations Sanitaires des Armees. Bulletin
0037-9506 Societe Paul Claudel. Bulletin
0037-9514 Societe Prehistorique Francaise. Bulletin
0037-9522 Societe Royale Belge de Gynecologie et d'Obstetrique. Bulletin
0037-9530 Societe Royale Belge des Electriciens. Bulletin
0037-9549 Societe Royale Belge des Ingenieurs et des Industriels. Revue
0037-9557 Societe Royale de Botanique de Belgique. Bulletin
0037-9565 Societe Royale des Sciences de Liege. Bulletin
0037-9573 Societe Royale Forestiere de Belgique. Bulletin
0037-9581 Societe Scientifique de Bretagne. Bulletin
0037-959X Societe Scientifiques de Bruxelles. Annales. Serie 1: Sciences Mathematiques,Astronomiques et Physiques *changed to* Societe Scientifique de Bruxelles. Annales. Sciences Mathematiques, Astronomiques et Physiques
0037-9603 Societe Vaudoise des Sciences Naturelles. Bulletin
0037-9611 Societe Vaudoise des Sciences Naturelles. Memoires
0037-962X Societe Zoologique de France. Bulletin
0037-9638 Societes Belges de Medecine Tropicale, de Parasitologie et de Mycologie. Annales *changed to* Societe Belge de Medecine Tropicale. Annales
0037-9646 Bulletin des Societes Chimiques Belges
0037-9662 Society and Culture
0037-9670 Society and Leisure†
0037-9689 Current Titles in Electrochemistry
0037-9697 Society for Analytical Chemistry. Proceedings *see* 0306-1396
0037-9700 Society for Army Historical Research. Journal
0037-9719 S C U P. News and Journal *changed to* Planning for Higher Education
0037-9727 Society for Experimental Biology and Medicine. Proceedings
0037-9735 Society for Historical Archaeology. Newsletter
0037-9743 Society for Italic Handwriting. Journal
0037-9751 Society for Psychical Research. Journal
0037-976X Society for Research in Child Development. Monographs
0037-9778 Society for the Bibliography of Natural History. Journal *changed to* Archives of Natural History
0037-9786 Society for the Study of State Governments. Journal
0037-9794 Society of Actuaries. Transactions
0037-9808 Society of Architectural Historians. Journal
0037-9816 Society of Archivists. Journal
0037-9824 Society of Chartered Property and Casualty Underwriters. Annals
0037-9832 Society of Cosmetic Chemists. Journal *see* 0142-5463
0037-9840 Society of Dairy Technology. Journal
0037-9859 Society of Dyers and Colourists. Journal
0037-9867 Society of Engineers. Journal and Transactions
0037-9875 Society of Fiber Science and Technology, Japan. Journal
0037-9883 Society of Film & Television Arts. Journal
0037-9905 Society of Health of Nigeria. Journal
0037-9913 Society of Independent Professional Earth Scientists. Newsletter
0037-9921 Society of Leather Trades' Chemists. Journal *see* 0144-0322
0037-993X Society of Malawi Journal
0037-9948 Society of Medalists. News Bulletin
0037-9956 Society of Medical Friends of Wine. Bulletin
0037-9964 Society of Mining Engineers of A I M E. Transactions†
0037-9972 Society of Occupational Medicine Transactions *see* 0301-0023
0037-9999 Society of Petroleum Engineers Journal
0038-0016 Society of Public Teachers of Law. Journal
0038-0024 Society of Research Administrators. Journal
0038-0032 Society of Rheology. Transactions *see* 0148-6055
0038-0059 Society of Photographic Science and Technology of Japan. Bulletin
0038-0067 Society of Women Engineers. Newsletter
0038-0075 Society Page
0038-0091 Socijalna Politika
0038-0105 Socijalni Rad
0038-0121 Socio-Economic Planning Sciences
0038-013X Sociocom Directory of Positions†
0038-0148 Sociologia†
0038-0156 Sociologia
0038-0164 Sociologia Internationalis
0038-0172 Netherlands' Journal of Sociology
0038-0172 Sociologia Neerlandica *see* 0038-0172
0038-0180 Sociologia Religiosa†
0038-0199 Sociologia Ruralis
0038-0202 Sociological Abstracts
0038-0210 S A
0038-0229 Sociological Bulletin
0038-0237 Sociological Focus
0038-0245 Sociological Inquiry
0038-0253 Sociological Quarterly
0038-0261 Sociological Review
0038-027X Sociological Symposium *see* 0273-2173
0038-0288 Sociologicky Casopis
0038-0296 Sociologie du Travail
0038-030X Sociologie et Societes
0038-0318 Sociologija
0038-0326 Sociologija Sela
0038-0334 Sociologische Gids
0038-0342 Sociologisk Forskning
0038-0350 Sociologiske Meddelelser
0038-0369 Sociologist
0038-0377 Sociologus
0038-0385 Sociology
0038-0393 Sociology and Social Research
0038-0407 Sociology of Education
0038-0415 Sociology of Education Abstracts
0038-0431 Sociometry *changed to* Social Psychology Quarterly
0038-044X Socionomen
0038-0458 Socioscoop
0038-0466 Socker Handlingar†
0038-0474 Sodobna Pedagogika
0038-0482 Sodobnost
0038-0490 Soedra Afrika. Informations Bulletin *see* 0346-9158
0038-0504 Soekaren
0038-0512 Soendags-B. T.
0038-0520 Soefart
0038-0547 Soft Drink Industry *see* 0148-6187
0038-0555 Soft Drink "Insider" Newsletter *see* 0148-6713
0038-0571 Soft Drinks *see* 0098-2318
0038-058X Soft Drinks Trade Journal
0038-0598 Soft Serve & Drive-in Field†
0038-061X Software Age
0038-0628 Software Central†
0038-0636 Software Digest
0038-0644 Software: Practice & Experience
0038-0652 Software World
0038-0660 Sogo Kango
0038-0687 Soil & Health Journal
0038-0695 Soil & Water
0038-0709 Soil Association. Journal *see* 0307-2576
0038-0717 Soil Biology and Biochemistry
0038-0725 Soil Conservation
0038-0741 Soil Mechanics and Foundation Engineering
0038-075X Soil Science
0038-0768 Soil Science & Plant Nutrition
0038-0776 Soil Science Society of America. Proceedings *see* 0361-5995
0038-0784 Soil Sense†
0038-0792 Soils and Fertilizers
0038-0806 Soils & Foundations
0038-0814 Soins
0038-0822 Sokol Polski
0038-0830 Geodetic Society of Japan. Journal
0038-0849 El Sol
0038-0857 Sol de Uruapan
0038-0865 Sol Institiae *changed to* Utrechts Universiteitsblad
0038-0881 Solaire Reflexen *changed to* Utrechts Universiteitsblad
0038-0903 Solanus
0038-092X Solar Energy
0038-0938 Solar Physics
0038-0946 Solar System Research
0038-0954 Soldado Argentino
0038-0962 Der Soldat
0038-0970 Soldat im Volk
0038-0989 Soldat und Technik
0038-0997 Soldaten Kurier†
0038-1004 Soldier
0038-1012 Soleil
0038-1039 Solia
0038-1047 Solicitors' Journal
0038-1055 Solid Fuel
0038-1063 Solid-Liquid Flow Abstracts
0038-108X Solid State Abstracts

0038-1098 Solid State Communications
0038-1101 Solid-State Electronics
0038-111X Solid State Technology
0038-1128 Solid Waste Report
0038-1136 Solid Wastes Management/Refuse Removal Journal *see* 0161-035X
0038-1152 Solidarity
0038-1160 Solidarity
0038-1195 Solothurner-Zeitung
0038-1209 Sols Africains
0038-1217 Sols-Soils
0038-1241 Solution *changed to* Amplifier
0038-125X Solvent Extraction Reviews†
0038-1268 Somali National Bank. Bulletin *changed to* Central Bank of Somali. Bulletin
0038-1276 Somborske Novine
0038-1284 Some/Thing†
0038-1292 Someni
0038-1314 Somerset Farmer
0038-1322 Somerset Gazette†
0038-1349 Something Else Newsletter†
0038-1357 Sonderschule
0038-1365 Song Hits
0038-1373 Songwriter's Review
0038-1381 Sonjog
0038-139X Sonntagspost
0038-1411 Sonntag
0038-142X Sonoma County Herald-Recorder *changed to* Sonoma County Daily Herald-Recorder
0038-1438 Sonorum Speculum *changed to* Key Notes
0038-1446 Sons of Italy News
0038-1454 Sons of Italy Times
0038-1462 Sons of Norway Viking
0038-1470 Sons of the American Revolution Magazine
0038-1489 Gosudarstvennyi Astronomicheskii Institut im. P. K. Shternberga. Soobshcheniya
0038-1497 Sooner
0038-1500 Sooner L P G Times
0038-1519 Sooner State Press†
0038-1527 Sophia
0038-1543 Sophia *changed to* Medicine Jug
0038-1551 Sorby Natural History Society Newsletter
0038-156X Sorrisi e Canzoni T.V. (Milan)
0038-1578 Japanese Journal of Phycology
0038-1578 Japanese Society of Phycology. Bulletin *see* 0038-1578
0038-1586 Japan Society for Technology of Plasticity. Journal
0038-1594 Sosiaalinen Aikakauskirja
0038-1608 Sosial Trygd
0038-1616 Sosialistinen Aikakauslehti
0038-1624 Sosialoekonomen
0038-1632 Sosialt Arbeid *changed to* Sosialt Forum/Sosialt Arbeid
0038-1659 Sot la Nape
0038-1667 Soteria
0038-1675 Sotilasaikakauslehti
0038-1683 Sotsiologicheski Problemi
0038-1691 Sotsialisticheskaya Zakonnost'
0038-1705 Sotsialistychna Kul'tura
0038-1713 Sotsial'noe Obespechenie
0038-173X Soudage et Techniques Connexes
0038-1748 Souder
0038-1756 Soul
0038-1764 Soul Force
0038-1799 Sound *see* 0300-5364
0038-1802 Sound & Image†
0038-1810 Sound and Vibration
0038-1829 Sound and Vision *see* 0305-3601
0038-1837 Sound Ideas
0038-1845 Sound & Communications
0038-1853 Soundings (Santa Barbara)
0038-1861 Soundings (Nashville)
0038-187X Sounds of Truth and Tradition
0038-1888 Source (Sacramento)
0038-1896 Source
0038-1934 South Africa. Department of Agricultural Technical Services. Science Bulletins
0038-1942 South Africa. Weather Bureau. Monthly Weather Report/Maandelikse Weerverslag
0038-1969 South African Archaeological Bulletin
0038-1985 South African Association for the Advancement of Science. Newsletter
0038-2000 South African Banker
0038-2019 South African Bee Journal
0038-2027 South African Builder
0038-2035 S. A. Building and Decorating Materials *see* 0007-3369
0038-2043 South African Cancer Bulletin
0038-206X S A C A
0038-2078 South African Chemical Institute. Journal *see* 0379-4350
0038-2094 South African Chessplayer
0038-2116 South African Citrus Journal *changed to* South African Citrus and Sub-Tropical Fruit Journal
0038-2132 South African Digest *changed to* South African Digest
0038-2140 South African Engineer *changed to* Electrical Engineer
0038-2159 South African Fire Services Institute. Quarterly
0038-2167 South African Forestry Journal
0038-2175 South African Garage and Motor Engineer *changed to* Motor World
0038-2183 South African Garden & Home
0038-2191 South African Hardware
0038-2205 S.A. Medical Equipment News *changed to* S.A. Hospital Supplies
0038-2213 South African Institute of Assayers and Analysts. Journal
0038-2221 South African Institute of Electrical Engineers. Transactions
0038-223X South African Institute of Mining and Metallurgy. Journal
0038-2256 South African Insurance Magazine
0038-2264 South African Jersey
0038-2272 S. A. Jewellery & Gifts†
0038-2280 South African Journal of Economics
0038-2299 South African Journal of Laboratory and Clinical Medicine†
0038-2302 South African Journal of Medical Laboratory Technology
0038-2310 South African Journal of Medical Sciences†
0038-2329 South African Journal of Obstetrics and Gynaecology†
0038-2329 South African Journal of Obstetrics and Gynecology *see* 0038-2469
0038-2337 South African Journal of Occupational Therapy
0038-2353 South African Journal of Science
0038-2361 South African Journal of Surgery
0038-237X South African Lapidary Magazine
0038-2388 South African Law Journal
0038-2396 South African Law Reports
0038-240X South African Libraries
0038-2418 South African Library. Quarterly Bulletin
0038-2442 South African Mechanical Engineer
0038-2450 S. A. Mechanised Handling Equipment *see* 0025-6579
0038-2469 South African Medical Journal
0038-2477 South African Mining & Engineering Journal
0038-2477 South African Mining Equipment *see* 0038-2477
0038-2493 South African Music Teacher
0038-2507 South African Nursing Journal *changed to* Nursing News
0038-2515 South African Observer
0038-2523 South African Outlook
0038-2531 S.A. Packaging *changed to* Pack & Print
0038-254X South African Panorama
0038-2558 South African Pharmaceutical Journal
0038-2566 South African Philatelist
0038-2574 South African Press Review *see* 0015-5055
0038-2582 S.A. Printer *changed to* Pack & Print
0038-2590 South African Racehorse
0038-2604 South African Red Cross News Digest *changed to* South African Red Cross Society (Cape Region). Newsletter
0038-2612 South African Refractionist
0038-2620 South African Reserve Bank. Quarterly Bulletin
0038-2639 South African Retail Chemist
0038-2647 South African Review†
0038-2655 South African Rider
0038-2671 South African Shipping News and Fishing Industry Review
0038-268X South African Soccer Monthly *changed to* Sharp Shoot Soccer
0038-2698 South Africa. Bureau of Standards. S A B S Bulletin
0038-2701 South African Stationery Trades Journal *changed to* Stationery
0038-271X South African Statistical Journal
0038-2728 South African Sugar Journal
0038-2736 South African Survey Journal
0038-2744 South African Table Tennis News
0038-2752 South African Tax Cases
0038-2760 South African Transport
0038-2779 South African Treasurer
0038-2787 South African Typographical Journal
0038-2795 South African Union Lantern
0038-2809 South African Veterinary Medical Association. Journal *see* 0301-0732
0038-2817 South African Yachting, Powerboats, Sailing, Waterski *changed to* South African Yachting, Sail, Power & Waterski
0038-2841 South Asian Review†
0038-285X South Asian Studies
0038-2876 South Atlantic Quarterly
0038-2892 South Australian Electrical Contractor
0038-2906 South Australian Government Gazette
0038-2922 South Australian Institute of Architects' Monthly Bulletin
0038-2949 Central Times
0038-2957 South Australian Motor
0038-2965 South Australian Naturalist
0038-2973 South Australian Ornithologist
0038-2981 South Australian Racing Calendar
0038-3015 South Australian Teachers Journal
0038-3023 South Australiana
0038-3031 South Bay Economic Review *changed to* Daily Breeze Economic Review
0038-304X South Carolina Economic Indicators
0038-3058 South Carolina Education Journal†
0038-3066 South Carolina Education News Emphasis *changed to* S C E A Emphasis
0038-3074 South Carolina Farmer-Grower†
0038-3082 South Carolina Historical Magazine
0038-3090 South Carolina History Illustrated†
0038-3104 South Carolina Law Review
0038-3112 South Carolina Librarian
0038-3120 South Carolina Magazine
0038-3139 South Carolina Medical Association. Journal
0038-3147 South Carolina Methodist Advocate
0038-3155 South Carolina Nursing†
0038-3163 South Carolina Review†
0038-3163 South Carolina Review
0038-3171 South Carolina Schools
0038-318X South Carolina. State Department of Education. Office of General Education Media Services Newsletter†
0038-3198 South Carolina Wildlife
0038-3201 South Carolina Young Farmer and Future Farmer
0038-321X South Central Bulletin
0038-3228 South Coast Herald
0038-3252 South Dakota Bird Notes
0038-3260 South Dakota Business Review
0038-3279 South Dakota Conservation Digest
0038-3287 South Dakota Dental Association. Newsletter
0038-3295 Farm & Home Research
0038-3309 South Dakota High Liner
0038-3317 South Dakota Journal of Medicine
0038-3325 South Dakota Law Review
0038-3333 South Dakota Motor Carrier
0038-3341 South Dakota Musician
0038-3368 South Dakota Review
0038-3376 South Dakota State Library Commission Bulletin†
0038-3384 South Dakota Stockgrower
0038-3406 South East Asia Journal of Theology
0038-3414 South-East Asia Treaty Organization. Economic Bulletin†
0038-3422 South East London & Kentish Mercury
0038-3430 South End
0038-3465 South India Churchman
0038-3473 South Indian Horticulture
0038-3481 South Indian Teacher
0038-349X South Pacific Bulletin
0038-3503 South Penn Motorist
0038-3511 Green Tree
0038-352X South Shore Record
0038-3538 South Street Reporter *changed to* Seaport Magazine
0038-3546 South Texas Law Journal
0038-3562 South Wales Institute of Architects. Journal†
0038-3570 South Wales Institute of Engineers. Proceedings
0038-3597 Southam Building Guide
0038-3600 Southeast Asia Quarterly *changed to* Southeast Asia Journal
0038-3619 Southeast Asian Journal of Tropical Medicine and Public Health
0038-3627 Southeast Furniture & Appliance News†
0038-3643 Southeastern Dairy Review
0038-3651 Southeastern Drug Journal *changed to* Southern Pharmacy Journal
0038-366X Southeastern Geographer
0038-3678 Southeastern Geology
0038-3686 Southeastern Librarian
0038-3694 Southeastern Peanut Farmer
0038-3708 Southeastern Poultry Times *see* 0048-4989
0038-3716 Southeasterner
0038-3724 Southend-on-Sea & District Chamber of Trade & Industry. Monthly Journal *changed to* Southend-on-Sea & District Chamber of Trade, Commerce & Industry. Monthly Journal
0038-3732 Southerly
0038-3791 Southern Africa Textiles
0038-3805 Southern and Southwestern Railway Club. Proceedings
0038-3813 Southern Association of Colleges and Schools. Proceedings
0038-3821 Southern Automotive Journal†
0038-383X Southern Banker
0038-3848 Southern Baptist Educator
0038-3856 Southern Bell Views
0038-3864 Southern Building
0038-3872 Southern California Academy of Sciences. Bulletin
0038-3899 Southern California Dental Hygienists' Association. Journal
0038-3902 Southern California Guide
0038-3910 Southern California Law Review
0038-3929 Southern California Quarterly
0038-3937 Southern California Rancher
0038-3945 Southern California Dental Laboratory Association. Bulletin
0038-3953 Southern California Teamster
0038-397X Southern Cemetery
0038-3988 Southern Connecticut Business Journal *see* 0300-7529
0038-4003 Southern Cooperator
0038-4011 Southern Cross
0038-402X Southern Dairy Products Journal
0038-4038 Southern Economic Journal
0038-4046 Southern Economist
0038-4054 Southern Engineer
0038-4062 Southern Engineering
0038-4070 Southern Exposure
0038-4089 Southern Exposure Library Staff Bulletin
0038-4097 Southern Farm Equipment *changed to* Southern Farm Equipment & Supply
0038-4097 Southern Farm Equipment *changed to* National Farm Equipment and Supply
0038-4100 Southern Farmer
0038-4119 Southern Florist and Nurseryman
0038-4127 Southern Folklore Quarterly
0038-4135 Southern Funeral Director
0038-4143 Southern Gardens
0038-4151 Southern Garment Manufacturer

0038-416X Southern Hardware
0038-4186 Southern Humanities Review
0038-4208 Southern Industrial Supplier
0038-4224 Southern Israelite
0038-4232 Southern Jeweler
0038-4240 Southern Jewish Weekly
0038-4259 Southern Journal of Business *changed to* Journal of Business Research
0038-4267 Southern Journal of Education Research
0038-4275 Southern Journal of Optometry
0038-4283 Southern Journal of Philosophy
0038-4291 Southern Literary Journal
0038-4305 Southern Living
0038-4313 Southern Lumberman
0038-4348 Southern Medical Journal
0038-4364 Southern Methodist University. Industrial Information Services. Newsletter
0038-4372 Southern Motor Cargo
0038-4380 Southern News and Views
0038-4399 Southern Outdoors/Gulf Coast Fisherman *changed to* Southern Outdoors
0038-4402 Southern Patriot *changed to* Southern Struggle
0038-4410 Southern Pharmaceutical Journal *changed to* Southern Pharmacy Journal
0038-4461 Southern Plumbing, Heating, Cooling
0038-447X Southern Poetry Review
0038-4488 Southern Pulp and Paper Manufacturer
0038-4496 Southern Quarterly
0038-450X Southern Railways
0038-4518 Southern Research Institute Bulletin
0038-4526 Southern Review
0038-4534 Southern Review
0038-4542 Southern Sawdust
0038-4577 Southern Sociologist
0038-4585 Southern Speech Journal *see* 0361-8269
0038-4593 Southern Stationer and Office Outfitter
0038-4607 Southern Textile News
0038-4615 U.S. Agricultural Research Service. Southern Regional Research Center. Publications and Patents
0038-4631 Southern Waterways
0038-464X Southern Wings
0038-4658 Southwest Advertising and Marketing *changed to* Adweek/Southwest Advertising News
0038-4666 Southwest Furniture News *changed to* Southwest Homefurnishings News
0038-4674 Southwest Jewish Chronicle
0038-4690 Southwest Kansas Register
0038-4704 Southwest News-Herald
0038-4712 Southwest Review
0038-4720 Southwest Water Works Journal *changed to* Southwest & Texas Water Works Journal
0038-4739 Southwestern Art *changed to* Art Insight/Southwest
0038-4747 Southwestern Association on Indian Affairs. Inc. Quarterly
0038-4763 Southwestern Collegian†
0038-478X Southwestern Historical Quarterly
0038-4801 Southwestern Journal of Anthropology *see* 0091-7710
0038-481X Southwestern Journal of Philosophy
0038-4828 Southwestern Journal of Theology
0038-4836 Southwestern Law Journal
0038-4844 Southwestern Lore
0038-4852 Southwestern
0038-4860 Southwestern Medicine†
0038-4879 Southwestern Miller *see* 0091-4843
0038-4887 Southwestern Minnesota Education Association Bulletin†
0038-4895 Southwestern Musician
0038-4909 Southwestern Naturalist
0038-4917 Southwestern News
0038-4925 Southwestern Philosophical Society. Newsletter
0038-4933 Southwestern Retailer
0038-4941 Social Science Quarterly
0038-495X Southwestern Veterinarian
0038-4968 Souvenirs and Novelties
0038-4976 Sou'wester
0038-4984 Sou'wester
0038-500X Sovetakan Arvest
0038-5018 Sovetakan Grakanutiun
0038-5026 Sovetakan Mankavarzh
0038-5034 Sovetskaya Arkheologiya
0038-5042 Sovetskaya Bibliografiya
0038-5050 Sovetskaya Etnografiya
0038-5069 Sovetskaya Geologiya
0038-5085 Sovetskaya Muzyka
0038-5093 Sovetskaya Pedagogika
0038-5107 Sovetskaya Torgovlya
0038-5123 Sovetskii Ekran
0038-5131 Sovetskii Krasnyi Krest
0038-514X Soviet Union
0038-5158 Sovetskii Shakhter
0038-5166 Sovetskie Arkhivy
0038-5174 Sovetskie Profsoyuzy
0038-5182 Sovetskoe Finnougrovedenie
0038-5190 Sovetskoe Foto
0038-5204 Sovetskoe Gosudarstvo i Pravo
0038-5220 Soviet Military Review
0038-5239 Sovetskoe Zdravookhranenie
0038-5247 Sovety Deputatov Trudyashchikhsya
0038-5255 Soviet Aeronautics
0038-5263 Soviet and Eastern European Foreign Trade
0038-5271 Soviet Antarctic Expedition Information Bulletin†
0038-528X Soviet Anthropology and Archaeology
0038-5298 Soviet Applied Mechanics
0038-5301 Soviet Astronomy A. J. *changed to* Soviet Astronomy
0038-531X Soviet Atomic Energy
0038-5328 Soviet Automatic Control
0038-5336 Soviet-Bloc Research in Geophysics, Astronomy, and Space *changed to* U S S R Report: Geophysics, Astronomy, and Space
0038-5344 Soviet Chemical Industry
0038-5360 Soviet Education
0038-5379 Soviet Electrical Engineering
0038-5387 Soviet Electrochemistry
0038-5395 Soviet Film
0038-5409 Soviet Genetics
0038-5417 Soviet Geography - Review and Translation *changed to* Soviet Geography
0038-5425 Soviet Hydrology: Selected Papers
0038-5441 Soviet Inventions Illustrated
0038-545X Soviet Jewish Affairs, a Journal on Jewish Problems in the USSR and Eastern Europe
0038-5468 Soviet Jewry Action Newsletter
0038-5484 Soviet Journal of Non-Ferrous Metals
0038-5492 Soviet Journal of Nondestructive Testing
0038-5506 Soviet Journal of Nuclear Physics
0038-5514 Soviet Journal of Optical Technology
0038-5522 Soviet Land
0038-5530 Soviet Law and Government
0038-5549 Soviet Life
0038-5557 Soviet Literature
0038-5565 Soviet Materials Science
0038-5573 Soviet Mathematics-Doklady
0038-5581 Soviet Mining Science
0038-559X Soviet Neurology and Psychiatry
0038-5603 Soviet News
0038-5611 Soviet Panorama *see* 0038-5549
0038-562X Soviet Physics - Acoustics
0038-5638 Soviet Physics - Crystallography
0038-5646 Soviet Physics - J E T P
0038-5654 Soviet Physics - Solid State
0038-5662 Soviet Physics - Technical Physics
0038-5670 Soviet Physics- Uspekhi
0038-5689 Soviet Physics-Doklady
0038-5697 Soviet Physics Journal
0038-5700 Soviet Physics-Semiconductors
0038-5719 Soviet Plant Physiology
0038-5727 Soviet Plastics†
0038-5735 Soviet Powder Metallurgy and Metal Ceramics
0038-5743 Soviet Progress in Chemistry
0038-5751 Soviet Psychology
0038-576X Soviet Radiochemistry
0038-5786 Soviet Review
0038-5794 Soviet Review
0038-5816 Soviet Science Review†
0038-5824 Soviet Sociology
0038-5832 Soviet Soil Science
0038-5840 Soviet Statutes and Decisions
0038-5859 Soviet Studies
0038-5867 Soviet Studies in History
0038-5875 Soviet Studies in Literature
0038-5883 Soviet Studies in Philosophy
0038-5891 Soviet Technology Bulletin†
0038-5905 Soviet Weekly
0038-5913 Soviet Woman
0038-5921 Sovietica†
0038-5948 Sovremennik
0038-5964 Sovremeno Pretprijatie
0038-5972 Sovremenost
0038-5980 Sower
0038-5999 Sowjetstudien†
0038-6006 Sowjetwissenschaft
0038-6014 Soybean Digest
0038-6030 Der Sozialdemokrat
0038-6049 Soziale Berufe
0038-6057 Soziale Selbstverwaltung
0038-6065 Soziale Sicherheit
0038-6073 Soziale Welt
0038-609X Sozialer Fortschritt
0038-6103 Der Sozialistische Akademiker
0038-6111 Sozialistische Arbeitswissenschaft
0038-6138 Sozialistische Demokratie†
0038-6146 Sozialistische Erziehung
0038-6154 Sozialistische Forstwirtschaft
0038-6162 Der Sozialistiche Kaempfer
0038-6170 Sozialkunde Heute†
0038-6189 Sozialpaedagogik
0038-6197 Sozialpolitik und Arbeitsrecht
0038-6200 Sozial Versicherung - Arbeitsschutz
0038-6227 Space†
0038-6235 Space Age Market Research
0038-6243 Space Business Daily News Service *changed to* Defense/Space Business Daily
0038-6251 Space Business Week
0038-6278 Space Letter
0038-6286 Space Life Sciences *see* 0302-1688
0038-6294 Space Propulsion *see* 0363-8219
0038-6308 Space Science Reviews
0038-6332 Space World
0038-6340 Spaceflight
0038-6367 Spafaswap
0038-6375 Spain. Departamento de Fomento y Difusion Internacional. Documentacion
0038-6391 Spain. Instituto Nacional de Estadistica. Boletin Mensual de Estadistica
0038-6405 Spain. Ministerio del Aire. Boletin Oficial
0038-6413 Spain. Ministerio de Industria. Registro de la Propreidad Industrial. Boletin Oficial
0038-6448 Span†
0038-6456 Spanish Cultural Index
0038-6464 Spanish Newsletter†
0038-6499 Spare Time
0038-6502 Sparebankbladet
0038-6510 Der Sparefroh
0038-6529 Sparekassetidende *changed to* Sparekassen
0038-6537 Sparer Magazin†
0038-6545 Sparfraemjaren *see* 0346-1602
0038-6553 Spark
0038-6561 Sparkasse
0038-657X Sparkling Gems†
0038-6588 Sparrow *changed to* Sparrow Poverty Pamphlets
0038-6618 Frosch†
0038-6626 Speaking of "Columbias"
0038-6634 Spear
0038-6650 Spearhead†
0038-6677 Spear's Special Situation Reports†
0038-6685 Specchio del Libro per Ragazzi
0038-6693 Special
0038-6707 Special Education *see* 0305-7526
0038-6723 Special Libraries
0038-6731 Special Libraries Association. Biological Sciences Division. Reminder†
0038-6766 Special Libraries Association. Metals/Materials Division News
0038-6782 Special Libraries Association. Publishing Division. Bulletin†
0038-6847 Specialia
0038-6855 Specialities†
0038-6863 Specializzazione
0038-6871 Specialty Advertising Report
0038-688X Specialty Baker's Voice
0038-6898 Specialty Foods Magazine†
0038-6901 Specialty Salesman and Franchise Opportunities *see* 0164-8233
0038-691X Specification Associate
0038-6936 Specijalna Skola
0038-6944 Spectacle du Monde
0038-6952 Spectator
0038-6960 Spectator†
0038-6995 Spectroscopia Molecular
0038-7002 Spectroscopical Society of Japan. Journal
0038-7010 Spectroscopy Letters
0038-7029 Spectrovision *changed to* Scan
0038-7061 Spectrum
0038-7088 Spectrum†
0038-7096 Spectrum der Herenmode
0038-710X Spectrum International
0038-7126 Speculator†
0038-7134 Speculum
0038-7142 Speech and Drama
0038-7150 Speech and Hearing Association of Virginia. Journal
0038-7169 Speech Monographs *see* 0363-7751
0038-7177 Speech Teacher *see* 0363-4523
0038-7185 Speed Age†
0038-7193 Speed & Custom Dealer *changed to* Specialty & Custom Dealer
0038-7207 Speed and Custom Equipment News *see* 0018-6023
0038-7215 Speed and Supercar†
0038-7223 Speed Mechanics†
0038-7231 Speedway Post†
0038-724X Speedway Star
0038-7258 D O E
0038-7266 Spejlet
0038-7274 Spektrum
0038-7282 S. P. E. L. D. Information
0038-7290 Speleologia Emiliana
0038-7304 Speleologist
0038-7312 Speleweit†
0038-7320 Speling
0038-7339 Spelling Progress Bulletin
0038-7347 Spenser Newsletter
0038-7355 Sperimentale
0038-738X Spettacolo
0038-7398 Spettatore Internazionale
0038-7401 Spettatore Musicale
0038-741X Sphincter
0038-7428 Sphinx
0038-7436 Sphinx-Magazin
0038-7444 Spica
0038-7452 Der Spiegel
0038-7460 Spiegel der Historie
0038-7479 Spiegel der Letteren
0038-7487 Spiegel Historiael
0038-7495 Spiegelreflex - Praxis Reflex *changed to* Reflex
0038-7509 Spiel und Theater
0038-7517 Der Spielplan
0038-7533 Spin
0038-7541 Spinner Weber Textilveredlung *see* 0340-4188
0038-755X Spinning Wheel
0038-7584 Spirit
0038-7592 Spirit & Life
0038-7606 Spiritual Book News
0038-7614 Spiritual Frontiers†
0038-7622 Spiritual Healer
0038-7630 Spiritual Life
0038-7649 Spiritualita
0038-7657 Spiritudsen- und Weinhandel
0038-7665 Spiritus
0038-7681 Spokane Affairs
0038-7703 Spokane Schools
0038-7711 Spokane, Washington. Official Gazette
0038-772X Spoken English
0038-7738 Spokeswoman
0038-7746 Spolem
0038-7754 Spoljnopoliticka Dokumentacija
0038-7770 Sport

ISSN INDEX

ISSN	Title
0038-7789	I u S Sport Bulletin
0038-7797	Sport
0038-7800	Sport Age†
0038-7819	Sport and Recreation *see* 0144-7181
0038-7827	Sport-Auto
0038-7835	Sport Aviation
0038-7851	Sport en Spel
0038-786X	Sport Fishery Abstracts
0038-7878	Sport Flying
0038-7894	Sport in de Pers
0038-7908	Sport in the USSR
0038-7916	Sport Italia
0038-7924	Sport- und Baederbauten
0038-7932	Sport und Technik
0038-7940	Sport World
0038-7959	Sportartikel - Sportmode *changed to* Sport - Spiel - Freizeit
0038-7967	Sportdykaren
0038-7991	Sportimes
0038-8017	Sporting Goods Dealer
0038-805X	Sporting News
0038-8076	Sporting Shooter†
0038-8084	Shooting Times
0038-8092	Sportivnaya Zhizn' Rossii
0038-8106	Sportivnye Igry
0038-8114	Sportovni a Umelecka Gymnastika *changed to* Sportovni-Moderni Gymnastika
0038-8122	Sportowiec
0038-8130	Sportparade
0038-8149	Sports Afield *changed to* Sports Afield
0038-8165	Sports Car Graphic†
0038-8165	Sports Car Graphic *see* 0027-2094
0038-8173	Sports Car World
0038-8181	Sports and Recreation Equipment†
0038-8211	Sportsfiskeren
0038-822X	Sports Illustrated
0038-8238	Sports Loisirs, Education Physique†
0038-8254	Sports Trader
0038-8270	Sportshelf News
0038-8289	Sportski Ribolov *changed to* Ribolov
0038-8297	Sportswear on Parade
0038-8300	Sportyvna Gazeta
0038-8319	Sposa
0038-8343	Spot News from Abroad
0038-8351	Spotlight†
0038-8386	Spotlight
0038-8408	Spotlight on South Africa†
0038-8416	P D C A 74 *see* 0099-0310
0038-8424	Spots and Stripes *see* 0163-416X
0038-8432	Spotted News
0038-8440	Spraakvaard
0038-8459	Sprachdienst
0038-8467	Die Sprache
0038-8475	Sprache im Technischen Zeitalter
0038-8483	Sprachkunst
0038-8491	Sprachlabor†
0038-8505	Der Sprachmittler
0038-8513	Sprachspiegel
0038-8521	Spraak og Spraakundervisning†
0038-853X	Sprawy Miedzynarodowe
0038-8548	Sprechsaal fuer Keramik, Glas, Email, Silikate *see* 0341-0676
0038-8556	Sprig of Shillelagh†
0038-8564	Spring Arbor College Bulletin *changed to* Spring Arbor College Update
0038-8572	Spring Thirty-One Hundred
0038-8580	Springfield-Illinois-Review of Business & Economic Conditions†
0038-8599	Springfield. Massachusetts. City Library Bulletin
0038-8602	Springfield Public Schools. News and Views
0038-8610	Springfielder *changed to* Concordia Theological Quarterly
0038-8629	Springs & Brakpan Advertiser
0038-8637	Sprinkler Bulletin
0038-8645	Sprog og Kultur
0038-8653	Spur *changed to* Young Country
0038-8688	Spur of Virginia *see* 0098-5422
0038-8696	Spurk
0038-870X	Der Spurkranz
0038-8718	Sputnik
0038-8726	Sputnik Junior
0038-8734	Square Dance *see* 0091-3383
0038-8750	Squilla
0038-8769	Squilla di S. Gerardo
0038-8777	Srecanja
0038-8785	Srednee Spetsial'noe Obrazovanie
0038-8793	Srpska Akademija Nauka i Umetnosti. Glasnik†
0038-8807	Sruth†
0038-8815	St Paul's Printer
0038-8823	Staal†
0038-884X	Der Staat
0038-8858	Staat und Recht
0038-8866	Staatsbibliothek Preussischer Kulturbesitz. Mitteilungen
0038-8874	Staatsbuerger
0038-8882	Staatspensioenen
0038-8890	Stacks
0038-8904	Stad Gods
0038-8912	Stadio Club†
0038-8920	Stadion
0038-8939	Stadlinger Post
0038-8947	Stads & Havneingenioeren
0038-8963	Stadsbyggnad
0038-8971	Stadt Linz
0038-898X	Stadt- und Gebaeudetechnik
0038-8998	Stadtbau-Informationen
0038-9005	Stadtehygiene†
0038-9013	Der Stadtverkehr
0038-9021	S I N Information†
0038-903X	Staedtebund *changed to* Staedte- und Gemeindebund
0038-9048	Der Staedtetag
0038-9056	Starch
0038-9064	Staff and Line *changed to* Inforcadre
0038-9072	Staff Spectator†
0038-9099	Stage and Television Today
0038-9102	Stage Centre *changed to* Manitoba Theatre Centre. House Programme
0038-9110	Stage in Canada†
0038-9129	Stagioni *changed to* Quattro Stagioni
0038-9145	Der Stahlbau
0038-9153	Stain Technology
0038-9161	Stained Glass
0038-917X	Stainless Steel
0038-9188	Stakker *changed to* Elvas-Krant
0038-9196	Stal†
0038-920X	Stal'
0038-9218	Steel in the U S S R
0038-9226	Stalactite
0038-9234	Stamboeker *changed to* Keurstamboeker
0038-9269	Stamp Collecting
0038-9277	Stamp Lover
0038-9293	Stamp News
0038-9307	Stamp Weekly†
0038-9315	Stamp Wholesaler
0038-9323	Stampa Medica
0038-934X	Stamping/Diemaking†
0038-9358	Stamps
0038-9366	Stand
0038-9374	Standard
0038-9382	Standard (Evanston)
0038-9390	Standard (Boston)
0038-9404	Standard (Amherst)
0038-9412	Standard and Poor's Security Owner's Stock Guide *changed to* Standard & Poor's Stock Guide
0038-9420	Standard & Poor's Stock Summary
0038-9439	Standard Bank Review *see* 0305-9553
0038-9447	Standard Bearer
0038-9455	Standard Rate and Data Service. Print Media Production Data
0038-9463	Standard Rate and Data Service. Direct Mail List Rates and Data
0038-9471	British Rate and Data
0038-948X	Standard Rate and Data Service. Business Publication Rates and Data
0038-9498	Standard Rate and Data Service. Canadian Advertising Rates and Data
0038-9501	Dati e Tariffe Pubblicitarie
0038-951X	Media Daten
0038-9528	Medios Publicitarios Mexicanos *changed to* Directorio M P M-Medios Impresos
0038-9536	Standard Rate and Data Service. Network Rates and Data
0038-9544	Standard Rate and Data Service. Newspaper Rates and Data
0038-9552	Standard Rate and Data Service. Spot Television Rates and Data
0038-9560	Standard Rate and Data Service. Spot Radio Rates and Data
0038-9579	Tarif Media
0038-9587	Standard Rate and Data Service. Weekly Newspaper Rates and Data *see* 0162-8887
0038-9595	Standard Rate and Data Service. Consumer Magazine and Farm Publication Rates and Data
0038-9609	Standard Rate and Data Service. Transit Advertising Rates and Data
0038-9617	Standard-Serie *changed to* Record-Serie
0038-9625	Standardisering
0038-9633	Standards Action
0038-9641	Standards and Specifications Information Bulletin
0038-965X	Standards/Canada
0038-9668	Standards Engineering
0038-9676	A N S I Reporter
0038-9684	Standards: Monthly Additions
0038-9692	Standarty i Kachestvo
0038-9706	Stander
0038-9714	Standing Conferences of Women's Organisations. Newsletter *changed to* Newsletter of Women's Forum and the Standing Conferences of Women's Organisations
0038-9722	Der Standpunkt
0038-9730	Standpunte
0038-9749	Stanford Alumni Almanac
0038-9757	Stanford Chaparral
0038-9765	Stanford Law Review
0038-9781	Stanford M. D
0038-979X	Stanford Observer
0038-9803	Stanford University. Graduate School of Business. Bulletin *changed to* Stanford G S B
0038-9811	Stanki i Instrumenty
0038-982X	Stanovnistvo
0038-9838	Staple Cotton Review *changed to* StaplReview
0038-9846	Star and Garter Magazine
0038-9862	Star & Style
0038-9870	Star of Zion
0038-9889	Star Serviceman
0038-9900	Star West
0038-9927	Starlights
0038-9927	International Typographical Union. Bulletin *see* 0041-4832
0038-9935	Start
0038-9943	Start & Speed
0038-9951	Start und Aufstieg
0038-996X	Startling Detective
0038-9978	Stash Capsules†
0038-9994	State
0039-0003	State Bank of India. Monthly Review
0039-0011	State Bank of Pakistan. Bulletin
0039-002X	State Bar of California. Journal *see* 0161-9241
0039-0038	State Bar of New Mexico. Bulletin and Advance Opinions
0039-0046	State Education Journal Index
0039-0054	State Engineer†
0039-0070	New Jersey School Boards Association. School Board Notes *changed to* New Jersey School Leader
0039-0089	State Geologists Journal
0039-0097	State Government
0039-0119	State Government News
0039-0143	State Principals Association. Bulletin
0039-0151	State Service
0039-016X	State Transport News *changed to* Journal of Transport Management
0039-0178	State Underwriter *changed to* Ohio Underwriter
0039-0186	State University of New York. College at Buffalo. Record
0039-0194	State University College of Arts & Science at Geneseo. School of Library Science. Newsletter *changed to* State University College of Arts & Science at Geneseo. School of Library and Information Science. Newsletter
0039-0208	State University of New York. Downstate Medical Center. Faculty Briefs
0039-0232	Staten Island Historian
0039-0240	Staten Island Institute of Arts & Sciences. Proceedings
0039-0259	Sweden. Statens Naturvaardsverk. Publikationer
0039-0267	Sweden. Statens Planverk. Statens Planverk Aktuellt
0039-0275	Statens Vaextskyddsanstalt. Meddelanden†
0039-0283	Stater
0039-0291	States†
0039-0305	Statesman
0039-0313	Statesman
0039-0321	Statesman Weekly
0039-0348	Stati Uniti d'Europa
0039-0356	Station Seismographique de Lisboa. Bulletin Seismique
0039-0372	Stationery Trade Review
0039-0380	Statistica
0039-0399	Statistica del Turismo
0039-0402	Statistica Neerlandica
0039-0410	U.S. Securities and Exchange Commission. Statistical Bulletin *see* 0272-7846
0039-0437	Statistical Methods in Linguistics *changed to* S M I L Quarterly Journal of Linguistic Calculus
0039-0445	Statistical News Summary†
0039-0453	Statistical Office of the European Communities. Foreign Trade: Monthly Statistics
0039-0461	Statistical Office of the European Communities. General Statistical Bulletin
0039-047X	Statistical Office of the European Communities. Industrial Statistics
0039-0488	Statistical Office of the European Communities. Social Statistics
0039-050X	Statistical Reporter
0039-0518	Statistical Theory and Method Abstracts
0039-0526	Statistician
0039-0534	Yugoslavia. Savezni Zavod za Statistiku. Statisticka Revija
0039-0542	Statisticki Pregled Socijalisticke Republike Bosne i Hercegovine
0039-0550	Revue Statistique du Quebec *changed to* Quebec (Province) Bureau of Statistiques Statistiques
0039-0569	State Bank of Pakistan. Statistics on Co-Operative Banks
0039-0577	State Bank of Pakistan. Statistics on Scheduled Banks
0039-0585	Austria. Bundeskammer der Gewerblichen Wirtschaft. Statistik und Dokumentation. Information
0039-0593	Statistika
0039-0607	Banking Statistics
0039-0615	Belgium. Institut National de Statistique. Statistique de la Navigation Maritime
0039-0623	Bourse de Paris. Statistiques Mensuelles
0039-0631	Statistische Hefte
0039-064X	Statistische Praxis
0039-0658	Denmark. Danmarks Statistik. Statistisk Tabelvaerk/Statistical Tables
0039-0674	Denmark. Danmarks Statistik. Statistiske Efterretninger
0039-0682	Denmark. Danmarks Statistik. Statistiske Undersogelser
0039-0690	Statisztikai Szemle
0039-0704	Statni Statky
0039-0712	Statsanstaelld
0039-0720	Statsoekonomisk Tidsskrift
0039-0747	Statsvetenskaplig Tidskrift
0039-0755	Status of Your Vestal Schools *changed to* Report from Your Vestal Schools
0039-0763	Statutes and Notifications†
0039-0771	Staub, Reinhaltung der Luft
0039-078X	Stavebnicky Casopis
0039-0798	Stavebnik
0039-0801	Stavivo

0039-081X Stazione Zoologica di Napoli. Pubblicazioni
0039-0828 Steam & Fuel Users' Journal
0039-0836 Steam and Heating Engineer *see* 0307-7950
0039-0844 Steamboat Bill
0039-0852 Steaua
0039-0879 Stedebouw en Volkshuisvesting
0039-0887 Stedfast Magazine
0039-0895 Industry Week
0039-0909 Steel Castings Abstracts
0039-0917 Steel Facts *changed to* Steel...(Year)
0039-0925 Steel Horizons *see* 0149-1997
0039-0941 Steel Labor
0039-095X Steel Times
0039-0968 Steel Trade
0039-0976 Steelwork in South Africa *see* 0010-6690
0039-100X Steinbeck Quarterly
0039-1018 Steinbruch und Sandgrube
0039-1026 Steine Sprechen
0039-1034 Steinmetz und Bildhauer
0039-1042 Steirische Berichte
0039-1050 Steirische Gemeinde-Nachrichten
0039-1085 Steirische Kriegsopfer Zeitung
0039-1093 Steirische Statistiken
0039-1107 Steirische Wirtschaft
0039-1115 Steklo i Keramika
0039-1131 Stelutis Alpinis
0039-1158 Stendhal Club. Quarterly
0039-1166 Stenografisk Tidsskrift
0039-1174 Der Stenopraktiker
0039-1182 Stephen Crane Newsletter†
0039-1190 Stephenson Locomotive Society Journal
0039-1204 Ster
0039-1212 Stereo Headphones
0039-1220 Stereo Review
0039-1239 Stern
0039-1247 Sterna†
0039-1255 Sterne
0039-1263 Sterne und Weltraum
0039-1271 Der Sternenbote
0039-128X Steroids
0039-1298 Steering Wheel
0039-1328 Stevens Indicator
0039-1344 Steward Anthropological Society. Journal
0039-1387 Paardesport in Ren en Draf
0039-1395 Stichting Stedelijke Raad voor Maatschappelijk Welzijn. Informatie-Bulletin
0039-1409 Wirtschaft und Wissenschaft†
0039-1417 Stiinta si Tehnica
0039-1425 Stijl *changed to* Women
0039-1433 Stil Novo
0039-1441 Stile Casa *changed to* Casa Stile
0039-1484 Stimme und Weg
0039-1492 Stimmen der Zeit
0039-1514 Stimulus
0039-1557 Stock and Crops *changed to* Zimbabwe Tobacco Today
0039-1565 Stock and Land
0039-1573 Stock Car-Hot Rod Journal†
0039-1581 Stock Exchange Journal†
0039-1611 Stock Exchange of New Zealand *changed to* Stock Exchange Journal of New Zealand
0039-162X Stock Journal
0039-1638 Stock Market Magazine
0039-1654 Stockholms Handelskammare. Meddelanden *see* 0345-4495
0039-1662 Stockton-San Joaquin County Public Library Newsletter†
0039-1670 Stokvis Expres *changed to* Inzicht
0039-1689 Stolica
0039-1697 Stoma *see* 0044-166X
0039-1700 Stomatologia
0039-1719 Revista de Chirurgie, Oncologie, O.R.L., Radiologie, Oftalmologie, Stomatologie. Stomatologie
0039-1727 Stomatologica
0039-1735 Stomatologiya
0039-1743 Stomatoloski Glasnik Srbije
0039-176X Stone
0039-1786 Stonehenge†
0039-1794 Stony Brook†
0039-1808 Stop
0039-1816 Stopanski Pregled
0039-1824 Stoperitidende
0039-1832 Storage Handling Distribution
0039-1840 Store Chat
0039-1859 Store Planning Service
0039-1867 Stores
0039-1875 Storia Contemporanea
0039-1883 Storia dell'Agricoltura
0039-1891 Storia e Nobilta
0039-1905 Storia e Politica
0039-1913 Storia Illustrata
0039-1921 Storie di Cucciolo†
0039-193X Storie di Tiramolla *changed to* Racolta Storie di Tiramolla
0039-1948 Storie e Fiabe†
0039-1956 Storkjoekken
0039-1972 Storm Data
0039-1980 Stormklockan
0039-1999 Story Art
0039-2006 Story Friends
0039-2014 Story of Life†
0039-2022 Discovery (Winona Lake)
0039-2030 Storyville
0039-2049 Strad
0039-2057 Strade Aperte
0039-2065 Strade e Traffico
0039-2073 Strahlentherapie
0039-2081 Straight *changed to* Now
0039-209X Straight Talk *changed to* Aryan
0039-2103 Strain
0039-212X Strandjaegeren
0039-2138 Strani Pravni Zivot. Serija D: Teorija, Zakonodavstvo, Praksa
0039-2146 Die Strasse
0039-2162 Strasse und Autobahn
0039-2170 Strasse und Nuechternheit *changed to* 0/00 Freie Fahrt
0039-2189 Strasse und Verkehr
0039-2197 Strassen- und Tiefbau *changed to* Strassen- und Tiefbau Vereinigt mit Strasse-Bruecke-Tunnel, Bitumen-Teere-Asphalts-Peche
0039-2200 Strassenbau-Technik *see* 0005-6634
0039-2219 Strassenverkehrstechnik
0039-2235 Strategie†
0039-2243 Strathclyde Telegraph
0039-2251 Straub Clinic Proceedings
0039-226X Street and Highway Lighting†
0039-2278 Streiflichter†
0039-2294 Stremez
0039-2308 Strength & Health Magazine
0039-2316 Strength of Materials
0039-2324 Streven
0039-2340 Stride
0039-2359 Strides of Medicine
0039-2375 Stroitel'
0039-2383 Stroitel'naya Mekhanika i Raschot Sooruzhenii
0039-2391 Stroitel'nye i Dorozhnye Mashiny
0039-2405 Stroitel'stvo i Arkhitektura
0039-2413 Stroitel'stvo i Arkhitektura Leningrada
0039-2421 Stroitel'stvo i Arkhitektura Moskvy
0039-2448 Stroitel'stvo Truboprovodov
0039-2456 Strojirenska Vyroba
0039-2464 Strojirenstvi
0039-2472 Strojnicky Casopis
0039-2480 Strojniski Vestnik
0039-2499 Stroke: a Journal of Cerebral Circulation
0039-2502 Association of Lunar and Planetary Observers. Journal
0039-2510 Strom und See
0039-2545 Strout World
0039-2553 Structural Engineer *changed to* Structural Engineer. Part A
0039-2553 Structural Engineer *changed to* Structural Engineer. Part B
0039-2561 Structural Mechanics *see* 0360-1218
0039-2588 Struggle
0039-260X Strumenti & Musica
0039-2618 Strumenti Critici
0039-2626 Stud & Stable *changed to* Pacemaker
0039-2634 Stud. Med.
0039-2650 Student (Sacramento)
0039-2669 Student†
0039-2677 Student
0039-2685 Student (Nashville)
0039-2693 Student
0039-2715 Student Advocate†
0039-2723 Student Federalist *changed to* World Citizen/Federalist Letter
0039-2731 Student Impact *see* 0195-153X
0039-274X Student Lawyer
0039-2758 Student Life
0039-2766 Student Life Highlights *see* 0094-0836
0039-2790 Student Times International
0039-2804 Student Voice
0039-2839 Danske Studerendes Faellesraad. Studenterbladet
0039-2847 Studentische Politik†
0039-2855 Studentravel Magazine
0039-2863 Students' Digest
0039-2871 Students Quarterly Journal *see* 0013-5127
0039-288X S L
0039-2898 Studi Biblici
0039-2901 Studi Cattolici
0039-291X Studi di Sociologia
0039-2928 Studi Economici
0039-2936 Studi Emigrazione
0039-2944 Studi Francesi
0039-2952 Studi Germanici
0039-2960 Studi Grafici
0039-2987 Studi Italiani di Filologia Classica
0039-2995 Studi Romani
0039-3002 Studi Salentini
0039-3010 Studi Senesi
0039-3037 Studi Storici
0039-3045 Studi Storici dell'Ordine dei Servi di Maria
0039-3053 Studi Sul Lavoro†
0039-3061 Studi Teatrali†
0039-307X Studi Urbinati. Serie A: Diritto
0039-3088 Studi Urbinati. Serie B: Letteratura, Storia, Filosofia
0039-310X Studia Canonica
0039-3118 Studia Croatica
0039-3126 Studia Cywilistyczne
0039-3134 Studia Demograficzne
0039-3142 Studia Filozoficzne
0039-3150 Studia Forestalia Suecica
0039-3169 Studia Geophysica et Geodaetica
0039-3177 Instytut Przemyslu Drobnego i Rzemiosla Studia i Informacje *changed to* Instytut Ekonomiki Uslug i Drobnej Wytworczosci. Studia i Informacje
0039-3185 Studia Leibnitiana
0039-3193 Studia Linguistica
0039-3207 Studia Liturgica
0039-3215 Studia Logica
0039-3223 Studia Mathematica
0039-3231 Studia Mediewistyczne
0039-324X Studia Metodologiczne. Dissertationes Methodologicae
0039-3258 Studia Monastica
0039-3266 Studia Musicologica Academiae Scientiarum Hungaricae
0039-3274 Studia Neophilologica
0039-3282 Studia Orientalia
0039-3290 Studia Papyrologica
0039-3304 Studia Patavina
0039-3312 Studia Prawnicze
0039-3320 Studia Psychologica
0039-3339 Studia Romanica et Anglica Zagrabiensia
0039-3347 Studia Rosenthaliana
0039-3363 Studia Slavica Academiae Scientiarum Hungaricae
0039-3371 Studia Socjologiczne
0039-338X Studia Theologica
0039-3398 Studia Universitatis "Babes-Bolyai". Biologia
0039-3401 Studia Universitatis "Babes-Bolyai". Chemia
0039-341X Studia Universitatis "Babes-Bolyai". Geologia. Geographia
0039-3428 Studia Universitatis "Babes-Bolyai". Historia
0039-3436 Studia Universitatis "Babes-Bolyai". Series Mathematica-Physica *changed to* Studia Universitatis "Babes-Bolyai". Mathematica
0039-3444 Studia Universitatis "Babes-Bolyai". Philologia
0039-3452 Studiekamraten
0039-3460 Studiemappen†
0039-3495 Studies
0039-3525 Studies in Adult Education
0039-3533 Studies in African Linguistics
0039-3541 Studies in Art Education
0039-3568 Studies in Bibliography and Booklore
0039-3576 Studies in Black Literature†
0039-3584 Studies in Burke and His Time *see* 0193-5380
0039-3592 Studies in Comparative Communism
0039-3606 Studies in Comparative International Development†
0039-3606 Studies in Comparative International Development
0039-3614 Studies in Comparative Local Government *changed to* Planning & Administration
0039-3622 Studies in Comparative Religion
0039-3630 Studies in Conservation
0039-3649 Studies in English Literature
0039-3657 Studies in English Literature 1500-1900
0039-3665 Studies in Family Planning
0039-3673 Studies in Germanics†
0039-3681 Studies in History and Philosophy of Science
0039-369X Studies in History and Society
0039-3703 Studies in Iowa History†
0039-3711 Studies in Islam
0039-3738 Studies in Philology
0039-3754 Studies in Race and Nations†
0039-3762 Studies in Romanticism
0039-3770 Studies in Scottish Literature
0039-3789 Studies in Short Fiction
0039-3797 Studies in Soviet Thought
0039-3800 Studies in the Humanities
0039-3819 Studies in the Literary Imagination
0039-3827 Studies in the Novel
0039-3835 Studies in the Twentieth Century†
0039-3851 Studies on Oriental Music
0039-386X Studies on the Soviet Union†
0039-3886 Studii si Cercetari de Antropologie
0039-3916 Studii si Cercetari de Documentare
0039-3940 Studii si Cercetari de Fizica
0039-3959 Studii si Cercetari de Fiziologie†
0039-3967 Studii si Cercetari de Geologie, Geofizica si Geografie. Geografie
0039-3983 Studii si Cercetari de Istoria Artei. Seria Arta Plastica
0039-3991 Studii si Cercetari de Istoria Artei. Seria Teatru-Muzica-Cinematografie
0039-4009 Studii si Cercetari de Istorie Veche *changed to* Studii si Cercetari de Istorie Veche si Arheologie
0039-4017 Studii si Cercetari de Mecanica Aplicata
0039-4041 Studii si Cercetari Juridice
0039-405X Studii si Cercetari Lingvistice
0039-4068 Studii si Cercetari Matematice
0039-4084 Studio
0039-4092 Studio†
0039-4106 Studio
0039-4114 Studio International
0039-4122 Studio Light/Commercial Camera
0039-4130 Studium
0039-4149 Studium Generale†
0039-4157 Study Encounter†
0039-4165 Stuekulturer
0039-4181 Stuff
0039-4203 Stuurwiel
0039-4211 Stuwing *changed to* Toorts
0039-422X Stvaranje
0039-4238 Style
0039-4246 Style
0039-4254 Style Auto
0039-4262 Style for Men†
0039-4270 Stylus (Chestnut Hill)
0039-4289 Stylus (Brockport)
0039-4297 Stylus (Sioux Falls)
0039-4300 Stylus (Ashland)
0039-4319 Styret *changed to* Cykelbranchen
0039-4335 Sub-Postmaster
0039-4351 Subject Index to Children's Magazines

ISSN	Title
0039-436X	Suboticke Novine
0039-4378	Subsidia Medica†
0039-4386	Subsidia Pataphysica *changed to* Organographes du Cymbalum Pataphysicum
0039-4394	Subterranean Sociology Newsletter
0039-4424	Success Unlimited
0039-4432	Successful Farming
0039-4440	Successo†
0039-4459	Succhi di Frutta e Bevande Gassate
0039-4467	Succulenta
0039-4491	Sucrerie Francaise
0039-4505	Sud Africa - Ieri, Oggi, Domani *changed to* Realta Sudafricana
0039-4521	Sudebnomeditsinskaya Ekspertiza
0039-453X	Sudene Informa
0039-4564	Sudhoffs Archiv
0039-4572	Suedost-Gesellschaft. Mitteilungen *see* 0340-174X
0039-4580	Sudostroenie
0039-4599	Suecana Extranea†
0039-4610	Suedamerika
0039-4629	Suedtirol in Wort und Bild
0039-4637	Suedwestfaelische Wirtschaft
0039-4653	Suesswaren
0039-4661	Suffolk Cooperative Library System. Newsletter†
0039-467X	Suffolk County Agricultural News
0039-4688	Suffolk County Dental Society. Bulletin
0039-4696	Suffolk University Law Review
0039-470X	Mathematics
0039-4726	Sugar Bulletin
0039-4734	Sugar Journal
0039-4742	Sugar y Azucar
0039-4750	Sugarbeet Grower
0039-4777	Sugarland
0039-4793	Suggestion Systems Quarterly *changed to* Performance (Chicago)
0039-4807	Suid-Afrikaanse Akademie vir Wetenskap en Kuns. Nuusbrief
0039-4815	Suid-Afrikaanse Tydskrif vir Die Pedagogiek
0039-4823	Suiker-Facetten *changed to* Kwartaalblad Suiker
0039-4858	Water Science
0039-4866	Fisheries World
0039-4874	Suisse Horlogere et Revue Internationale de l'Horlogerie *changed to* Suisse Horlogere et Revue Europeenne de l'Horlogerie-Bijouterie
0039-4882	Sukh Datta
0039-4890	Sulphur
0039-4904	Sulphur Institute Journal†
0039-4904	Sulphur Institute Journal *see* 0160-0680
0039-4912	Sulzer Technical Review
0039-4947	Sumarios de Odontologia
0039-4955	Sumitomo Bank Review
0039-4963	Sumitomo Light Metal Technical Reports
0039-4971	Summa
0039-498X	Summa Brasiliensis Mathematicae†
0039-4998	Summary of Available Applicants and Summary of Academic, Industrial, and Government Openings†
0039-5005	Summary of Labor Arbitration Awards
0039-5021	Summer Texan *changed to* Daily Texan
0039-5056	Summit
0039-5064	Summit County Labor News
0039-5072	Summons
0039-5080	Sun *changed to* Sun, Monthly
0039-5110	Sun & Health†
0039-5137	Sun Seeker†
0039-5145	Sunbelt Dairyman
0039-5153	Sunday†
0039-5161	Sunday
0039-517X	Sunday Companion†
0039-5188	Sunday Digest
0039-5196	Sunday Express
0039-520X	Sunday Gleaner
0039-5218	Sunday Independent
0039-5226	Sunday Mail
0039-5234	Sunday Mainichi
0039-5242	Sunday Mercury
0039-5250	Bible-in-Life Pix
0039-5277	Sunday Post
0039-5285	Sunday School Counselor
0039-5315	Sunday Sun
0039-5323	Sunday Times
0039-5358	Sunday Truth *changed to* Sunday Sun
0039-5366	Sundhedsbladet
0039-5374	Sun
0039-5382	Sunflower
0039-5390	Sunlore
0039-5404	Sunset
0039-5412	Sunshine
0039-5420	Sunshine
0039-5439	Sunshine & Health
0039-5447	Sunshine State Agricultural Research Report
0039-5455	Sunt Foernuft
0039-5463	Sunyata
0039-5471	Suo
0039-548X	Suomalainen
0039-5498	Suomalaiset B-Referaatit *changed to* R T-Uutiset
0039-5501	Suomen Elainlaakarilehti
0039-551X	Suomen Hammaslaakariseura. Toimituksia
0039-5528	Suomen Kalastuslehti
0039-5544	Suomen Kunnallislehti
0039-5552	Suomen Kuvalehti
0039-5560	Suomen Laakarilehti
0039-5579	Laakintavoimistelija
0039-5587	Suomen Lehdisto
0039-5595	Suomen Maataloustieteellisen Seuran Julkaisuja†
0039-5609	Suomen Osuustoimintalehti
0039-5617	Suomen Puutalous
0039-5625	Suomen Silta
0039-5633	Suomi Merella
0039-565X	Super Omnia Charitas†
0039-5668	Super Power Publications
0039-5676	Super Service Station
0039-5684	Superba
0039-5706	Super Sports
0039-5714	Superconducting Devices and Materials†
0039-5765	Superlove†
0039-5773	Supermachos
0039-5781	Supermarket
0039-579X	Supermarket Management
0039-5803	Supermarket News
0039-5811	Supermarketing *changed to* Supermarket Business
0039-582X	Supernovelas
0039-5846	Supertiendas†
0039-5854	Supervision
0039-5862	Supervisor *changed to* Supervisory Management
0039-5870	Supervisor Nurse
0039-5889	Supervisor's Bulletin
0039-5897	Supervisors Quarterly *changed to* Teacher Educator
0039-5919	Supervisory Management
0039-5927	Supplementary Service to European Taxation
0039-5935	Supply House Times
0039-596X	Supreme Court Notes
0039-5978	Supreme Court Practice
0039-5994	Sur l'Eau
0039-6001	Industrial Finishing and Surface Coatings *see* 0309-3018
0039-6028	Surface Science
0039-6036	Surfer
0039-6052	Surfing East
0039-6060	Surgery
0039-6087	Surgery, Gynecology & Obstetrics
0039-6095	Surgical Business
0039-6109	Surgical Clinics of North America
0039-6117	Surgical Journal of Delhi
0039-6125	Surgo
0039-6133	Surinaamse Landbouw
0039-6141	Suriname Zending *changed to* Hernhutter Suriname Zending
0039-6168	Surrealist Transformation
0039-6176	Surrey N.F.U. Journal *changed to* Central Southern Farmer
0039-6184	Sursum Corda
0039-6192	Survey
0039-6206	Survey of Anesthesiology
0039-6214	Survey of Current Affairs
0039-6222	Survey of Current Business
0039-6230	Survey of International Development†
0039-6249	Quarterly Survey of Japanese Finance and Industry *changed to* Japanese Finance and Industry: Quarterly Survey
0039-6257	Survey of Ophthalmology
0039-6265	Great Britain. Directorate of Overseas Surveys. Survey Review
0039-6273	Surveying and Mapping
0039-6303	Surveyor
0039-6303	Surveyor-Local Government Technology *see* 0039-6303
0039-6311	Surveys of the Work of British Writers *changed to* Writers & Their Work
0039-632X	Survival *see* 0702-3138
0039-6338	Survival
0039-6346	Survival Magazine
0039-6354	Survive *changed to* Journal of Civil Defense
0039-6362	Sus Hijos
0039-6370	Sushama
0039-6397	Sussex Life
0039-6419	Svedectvi
0039-6427	Sveiseteknikk
0039-6435	Svensk Bergs- och Brukstidning
0039-6443	Svensk Bokfoerteckning
0039-6451	Svensk Bokhandel
0039-646X	Svensk Botanisk Tidskrift
0039-6478	Svensk Bridge
0039-6486	Svensk Dam Tidning
0039-6494	Nord-Emballage
0039-6508	Svensk Export
0039-6516	Svensk Faerghandel
0039-6524	Svensk Farmaceutisk Tidskrift
0039-6532	Svensk Filatelistisk Tidskrift
0039-6540	Svensk Fotografisk Tidskrift
0039-6559	Svensk Guldsmeds-Tidning
0039-6567	Svensk Handel
0039-6575	Svensk Handelstidning Justita
0039-6591	Svensk Juristtidning
0039-6605	Kemisk Tidskrift
0039-6613	Svensk Lantmaeteritidskrift
0039-6621	Svensk Leksaksrevy
0039-663X	Svensk Litteraturtidskrift
0039-6648	Svensk Lokaltrafik
0039-6664	S M T
0039-6672	Svensk Omnibustidning
0039-6680	Svensk Papperstidning
0039-6699	Svensk Pastoral Tidskrift
0039-6702	Svensk Sjoefarts Tidning
0039-6702	Sveriges Riksbank. Aarsbok *see* 0348-7342
0039-6729	Svensk Snickeritidskrift *see* 0346-2846
0039-6737	Svensk Sparbankstidskrift *see* 0346-1602
0039-6745	Svensk Tandlaekare-Tidskrift *changed to* Swedish Dental Journal
0039-6753	Svensk Tapetserareteidning
0039-6761	Svensk Teologisk Kvartalskrift
0039-677X	Svensk Tidskrift
0039-6796	Svensk Traevaru- och Papersmassetidning
0039-680X	Svensk Ur- Optik Tidning
0039-6818	Svensk Valltidskrift†
0039-6826	Svensk Veckotidning
0039-6834	Gasnytt
0039-6842	Svenska Litteratursaellskapet i Finland. Skrifter
0039-6869	Svenska Mejeriernas Riksfoerening. Meddelande
0039-6877	Svenska Mejeritidningen *changed to* Nordisk Mejeriindustri
0039-6885	Svenska Museer
0039-6893	Sweden. Riksarkivet. Meddelanden
0039-6907	Svenska Tidningsartiklar
0039-6915	Svenska Tidskriftsartiklar
0039-6923	Svenska Vaegfoereningens Tidskrift
0039-6931	Svenska Kraftverksfoereningens Publikationer
0039-694X	Svenskt Fiske
0039-6958	Sverige-Nytt
0039-6966	Sveriges Flotta
0039-6974	Sveriges Natur
0039-6982	Tandlaekartidningen
0039-6990	Sveriges Utsadesfoerenings Tidskrift
0039-7008	Svet†
0039-7016	Svet Motoru
0039-7024	Svet Sovetu *changed to* Svet Socialismu
0039-7032	Svet v Obrazech
0039-7059	Svetlost
0039-7075	Svetova Literatura
0039-7083	Svetsaren
0039-7091	Svetsen
0039-7105	Zvezda
0039-7113	Svijet
0039-7121	Svijet
0039-713X	Svinovodstvo
0039-7148	Svisa Esperanto Revuo
0039-7148	Svisa Espero *see* 0039-7148
0039-7156	Svit/Light
0039-7180	Swap Shop *changed to* Administrator's Swap Shop Newsletter
0039-7199	Swarajya
0039-7202	Swatantra in Parliament†
0039-7210	Swatantra Newsletter†
0039-7229	Swaziland Recorder†
0039-7245	Sweden Now
0039-7253	Sweden. Statistiska Centralbyraan. Allmaan Maanadsstitistik
0039-7261	Sweden. Statistiska Centralbyraan. Statistisk Tidskrift
0039-727X	Sweden. Statistiska Centralbyraan. Utrikeshandel. Kvartalsstatistik
0039-7288	Sweden. Statistiska Centralbyraan. Utrikeshandel. Maanadsstatistik
0039-7296	Swedish Economy
0039-730X	Swedish Forestry Association. Magazine
0039-7318	Swedish Journal of Economics *changed to* Scandinavian Journal of Economics
0039-7326	Swedish Pioneer Historical Quarterly
0039-7342	Sweet Briar College. Alumnae Magazine
0039-7377	Swiat *see* 0031-6059
0039-7385	Swimming Pool Review *changed to* Swimming Pool
0039-7393	Swimming Pool Weekly and Swimming Pool Age
0039-7415	Swimming Technique
0039-7423	Swimming Times
0039-7431	Swimming World
0039-744X	Swing Journal
0039-7458	Swing Through the Air *changed to* Sportparachutist
0039-7466	Swiss Bank Corporation. Bulletin *see* 0304-2162
0039-7474	Swiss Journal
0039-7482	Swiss Observer
0039-7490	Swiss Review of World Affairs
0039-7504	Swiss Technics†
0039-7512	Swiss Watch†
0039-7520	Swiss Watch and Jewelry Journal
0039-7539	Sword & Trowel
0039-7547	Sword of the Lord
0039-7555	Swordsman Review
0039-7563	Sybarite Review
0039-7571	Sydan
0039-758X	Sydney Jewish News *changed to* Australian Jewish Times
0039-7598	Sydney Stock Exchange Limited Gazette *see* 0045-0901
0039-7601	Sydney Tourist Guide
0039-761X	Sydney Water Board Journal
0039-7628	Sykepleien
0039-7636	S Y L F Nytt
0039-7652	Sylvaply News *changed to* MacMillan Bloedel Building Materials News
0039-7660	Sylwan
0039-7679	Symbolae Osloenses
0039-7695	Symposium
0039-7709	Symposium
0039-7717	Syn og Segn
0039-7725	Synagogue School *changed to* Impact!
0039-7733	Synagogue Service†
0039-7741	Syndicalisme Hebdo *changed to* Syndicalisme C F D T
0039-775X	Syndicalisme C F T C
0039-7776	Syndicat des Critiques Litteraires. Bulletin

ISSN INDEX 1061

ISSN	Title
0039-7784	Syndicat National des Officers de la Marine Marchande C.F.D.T. Bulletin de Liaison
0039-7806	Syndrome
0039-7830	Synopsis Revue†
0039-7830	Synopsis†
0039-7849	Synpunkt
0039-7857	Synthese
0039-7873	Who Put the Bomp *changed to* Bomp
0039-7881	Synthesis
0039-789X	Synthesis in Inorganic and Metalorganic Chemistry *see* 0094-5714
0039-7903	Synthesis Microbiologica
0039-7911	Synthetic Communications
0039-792X	Syracuse Chemist
0039-7938	Syracuse Law Review
0039-7946	Syria
0039-7954	Syria. Central Bureau of Statistics. Summary of Foreign Trade Statistics *changed to* Syria. Central Bureau of Statistics. Monthly Summary of Foreign Trade
0039-7962	Syrie et Monde Arabe
0039-7989	Systematic Zoology
0039-8004	Systemation Service *see* 0563-0355
0039-8012	Systeme D
0039-8039	Systems Education Forum†
0039-8047	Systems Technology
0039-8055	Systems, Technology and Science for Law Enforcement and Security Newsletter *changed to* Systems, Technology and Science for Law Enforcement and Security
0039-8071	Szabadalmi Kozlony es Vedjegyertesito
0039-808X	Szamvitel - Ugyviteltechnika
0039-8098	Szazadok
0039-8101	Szemeszet
0039-811X	Szene
0039-8128	Szigma
0039-8136	Szinhaz
0039-8144	Szklo i Ceramika
0039-8152	Szpilki
0039-8160	T. I. T. Journal of Life Sciences
0039-8179	T A†
0039-8209	T A I C H News
0039-8217	T. A. Informations
0039-8225	T A L B Talks†
0039-8233	T A M S Journal
0039-8241	T A P P I
0039-8268	T A V R *changed to* Territorial Army Magazine
0039-8284	T C T A News
0039-8292	T E A News
0039-8306	T E A Newsletter
0039-8314	T E C Report
0039-8322	T.E.S.O.L. Quarterly
0039-8330	T F C Nieuws
0039-8349	T G A Cosmetic Journal *see* 0090-0591
0039-8357	Textile Institute and Industry
0039-839X	T. I. P. Informatie†
0039-8403	T I P R O Reporter
0039-8411	T I S C O Technical Journal
0039-842X	T N A News
0039-8438	T N C - Aktuellt
0039-8446	T N O-Nieuws *changed to* T N O-Project
0039-8454	T. P. A. Travelers
0039-8462	T P Annales
0039-8470	T. P. L. News
0039-8497	T. T. A
0039-8500	T T G International *changed to* T T G Europa
0039-8519	T V Communications *changed to* T V C
0039-8527	T V Comic
0039-8535	I V A†
0039-8543	T V Guide
0039-8551	T V Hebdo
0039-8578	T V Radio Mirror *changed to* T V Mirror
0039-8608	T V Times
0039-8624	T V Times
0039-8632	T W A Ambassador
0039-8640	T. W. A. U. News
0039-8659	T W U Express
0039-8667	T Z fuer Praktische Metallbearbeitung *changed to* T Z fuer Metallbearbeitung
0039-8675	Ta Kung Pao
0039-8683	Taag
0039-8691	Taal en Tongval
0039-8705	Taalgenoot
0039-8721	Tabak
0039-873X	Tabak
0039-8748	Tabak Journal International
0039-8756	Tabakpflanzer Oesterreichs
0039-8772	Tabakverschleisser Oesterreichs
0039-8780	Table et Cadeau
0039-8799	Table Tennis News
0039-8802	Tableau de Bord des Industries Francaises
0039-8829	Tables of Redemption Values for U.S. Savings Bonds, Series A-E
0039-8837	Tablet
0039-8845	Tablet
0039-8853	Tableware International & Pottery Gazette *changed to* Tableware International
0039-8861	Tabor
0039-8888	Tachydromos
0039-8896	Tactics†
0039-890X	Facultad de Medicina de Sevilla. Revista†
0039-8926	Formerly (1876-1975); Taeglicher Wetterbericht *see* 0341-2970
0039-8942	Tageszeitung fuer Brauerei
0039-8950	Tagus
0039-8969	Tahqiqat e Eqtesadi
0039-8977	Taide
0039-8993	Refractories
0039-9000	Japan Society of Air Pollution. Journal
0039-9019	Air Pollution News†
0039-9027	Tail-Wagger and Family Magazine†
0039-9043	Tailor and Men's Wear *changed to* Men's Wear
0039-9051	Taipei Pictorial
0039-906X	Japanese Journal of Physical Fitness
0039-9078	Taiwan†
0039-9086	Taiwan
0039-9094	Taiwan Chenglian
0039-9108	Taiwan Industrial Panorama
0039-9116	Taiwan Museum. Quarterly Journal
0039-9124	Taiwan Trade Monthly†
0039-9132	Take One
0039-9140	Talanta
0039-9159	Talespinner
0039-9175	Talim-O-Tarbiat
0039-9183	Talking Book Topics (Inkprint Edition)
0039-9191	Talking Machine Review *changed to* Talking Machine Review International
0039-9213	Talks and Tales
0039-9221	Taller
0039-9248	Talon
0039-9256	Tamarack Review
0039-9264	Tamarind Fact Sheets†
0039-9280	Tamil Arasu
0039-9299	Tamil Culture
0039-9310	Tamil Nadu Information
0039-9329	Tamil Nadu Police Journal
0039-9345	Tan *changed to* Black Stars
0039-9353	Tandlaegebladet
0039-9361	Tanecni Listy
0039-9388	Tangent†
0039-940X	Tangerine
0039-9418	Tank
0039-9434	Report of Coal Mine Safety†
0039-9450	Protein, Nucleic Acid, Enzyme
0039-9469	Tanzania. Bureau of Statistics. Quarterly Statistical Bulletin
0039-9477	Tanzania Education Journal
0039-9485	Tanzania Notes & Records
0039-9493	Tanzania Trade and Industry *changed to* Tanzania. Ministry of Trade. Foreign Trade News Bulletin
0039-9507	Tanzania Zamani
0039-9515	Das Tanzarchiv
0039-9531	Tape Record
0039-954X	Studio Sound *changed to* Studio Sound & Broadcast Engineering
0039-9566	Tapenzeitung Tapete und Bodenbeleg *changed to* T Z Tapenzeitung
0039-9574	Tapetsereren
0039-9582	Tapissier Decorateur
0039-9590	Taproots†
0039-9604	Taptoe
0039-9612	Tar Heel Economist
0039-9620	Tar Heel Nurse
0039-9639	Tar River Poets *changed to* Tar River Poetry
0039-9655	Target
0039-9663	Tarheel Banker
0039-968X	Tarheel Wheels
0039-9698	Tarikh
0039-971X	Tarsadalmi Szemle
0039-9728	Tartarino
0039-9736	Tarwewijk
0039-9760	Tasmanian Education Gazette
0039-9787	Tasmanian Fruitgrower & Farmer
0039-9795	Tasmanian Government Gazette
0039-9809	Tasmanian Historical Research Association. Papers and Proceedings
0039-9817	Tasmanian Journal of Agriculture
0039-9825	Tasmanian Journal of Education *see* 0314-2531
0039-9833	Australia. Bureau of Statistics. Tasmanian Office. Monthly Summary of Statistics
0039-9841	Tasmanian Motor News
0039-985X	Tasmanian Motor Trader
0039-9868	Tasmanian Teacher
0039-9914	Tatrzanski Orzel
0039-9922	Finland. Patentti- ja Rekisterihallitus. Tavaramerkkilehti/Varumarkestidning/Trademark Gazette
0039-9930	Tawow
0039-9949	Tax Administrators News
0039-9957	Tax Adviser
0039-9965	Tax Affairs
0039-9973	Tax Alert†
0039-999X	Tax Coordinator *see* 0163-996X
0040-0017	United States Tax Court Report
0040-0025	Tax Executive
0040-0041	Tax Law Review
0040-005X	Tax Lawyer
0040-0068	Philippines. National Tax Research Center. Tax Monthly
0040-0076	Tax News Service
0040-0084	Tax Planning
0040-0092	Tax Planning Ideas
0040-0106	Tax Policy†
0040-0114	Tax Review
0040-0122	Tax Times
0040-0130	Taxa Droske Tidende *changed to* Dansk Taxi Tidende
0040-0149	Taxation
0040-0157	Taxation
0040-0173	Taxation Record Journal
0040-0181	Taxes
0040-019X	Taxes and Estates
0040-0203	Taxes Interpreted
0040-0211	Taxi News Digest
0040-022X	Taxitrafiken
0040-0246	Taxicab Management
0040-0254	Taxinews
0040-0262	Taxon
0040-0270	Taxpayer
0040-0289	Taxpayer
0040-0297	Tchahert
0040-0300	Te Ao Hou†
0040-0319	Te Maori *changed to* Te Awatea
0040-0327	Te-ve Guia
0040-0343	Tea and Coffee Trade Journal
0040-0351	Tea Journal of Pakistan *changed to* Tea Journal of Bangladesh
0040-036X	Tea Quarterly & Annual Reports *changed to* Tea Quarterly
0040-0378	Tea Research Foundation of Central Africa. Quarterly Newsletter
0040-0386	Tea Room, Restaurant and Catering Journal†
0040-0394	Teach†
0040-0408	Teacher
0040-0416	Teacher
0040-0424	Teacher Education in New Countries†
0040-0440	Teacher of the Blind *changed to* Insight
0040-0459	Teacher of the Deaf
0040-0467	Teacher Paper†
0040-0475	Teachers College Record
0040-0483	Teachers' Journal
0040-0505	Message of the Teacher
0040-0521	Teacher's World
0040-053X	Teaching†
0040-0548	Teaching Adults
0040-0556	T A D *see* 0046-1482
0040-0564	Teaching All Nations
0040-0572	Teaching & Training
0040-0580	Teaching Beginners *changed to* Teaching Under 5s
0040-0599	Teaching Exceptional Children
0040-0602	Teaching History
0040-0610	Teaching History
0040-0629	Teaching Juniors *changed to* Teaching 7-10
0040-0645	Teaching Pictures for Bible Searchers
0040-0653	Teaching Primaries *changed to* Teaching 5-7
0040-0661	Milwaukee Public Schools Superintendent's Bulletin *changed to* Milwaukee Public Schools Staff Bulletin
0040-067X	Teaching Teenagers *see* 0308-356X
0040-0688	Teaching Tools for Consumer Ed *changed to* Teaching Tools for Consumer Reports
0040-0696	Team
0040-0718	Teamwork in Industry *changed to* Worklife
0040-0734	Crippled Children
0040-0769	Teatr
0040-0777	Teatr
0040-0785	Teatral'naya Zhizn'
0040-0793	Teatro
0040-0807	Teatro e Cinema†
0040-0815	Teatrul
0040-0823	Tebiwa *changed to* Tebiwa Miscellaneous Papers
0040-0831	Tech Air
0040-0858	Tech Talk *see* 0002-242X
0040-0866	Technica
0040-0874	Technical Association of Graphic Arts of Japan. Bulletin
0040-0882	Technical Association of Malaysia. Journal
0040-0890	Technical Book Review Index
0040-0904	Technical Co-Operation
0040-0912	Education and Training
0040-0920	Technical Education Abstracts
0040-0939	Technical Education Newsletter *changed to* A T E A Journal
0040-0947	Technical Film International Bulletin *changed to* Technical Film Cards/International Selection
0040-0955	T. I.
0040-0963	Technical Journal *see* 0308-1907
0040-0971	Technical Photography
0040-098X	Technical Progress in Israel†
0040-1005	Technical Survey
0040-1021	Technicien Belge en Prothese Dentaire
0040-103X	Technicien du Film
0040-1056	Technicka Praca
0040-1064	Technicky Tydenik
0040-1072	Technicuir
0040-1080	Techniek en Toepassing *changed to* Philips Professional Profile
0040-1099	Die Technik
0040-1102	Technik und Betrieb
0040-1110	Technika
0040-1137	Technika i Gospodarka Morska
0040-1145	Technika Lotnicza i Astronautyczna
0040-1153	Technika Motoryzacyjna
0040-1161	Technika Poszukiwan *changed to* Technika Poszukiwan Geologicznych
0040-117X	Technikgeschichte
0040-1188	Technion
0040-1226	Technique et Pratique Agricoles *changed to* Hommes et Agriculture
0040-1242	Technique Laitiere
0040-1250	Technique Moderne
0040-1269	Technique Pharmaceutique *changed to* Sciences et Technique Pharmaceutiques

ISSN	Title
0040-1277	Technique Routiere
0040-1285	Techniques†
0040-1293	Techniques C E M
0040-1307	Techniques de l'Air Comprimé†
0040-1315	Techniques de l'Habillement
0040-1331	Techniques Economiques
0040-1358	Techniques for Teachers of Adults
0040-1374	Techniques Hospitalieres, Medico-Sociales et Sanitaires
0040-1382	Techniques Nouvelles†
0040-1390	Technisch Gemeenteblad†
0040-1404	Technische Gids voor Ziekenhuis en Instelling
0040-1420	Technische Information Armaturen
0040-1439	Technische Mitteilungen
0040-1447	A E G-Telefunken. Technische Mitteilungen
0040-1455	R F Z. Technische Mitteilungen
0040-1463	Krupp Technische Mitteilungen. Forschungsberichte und Werksberichte
0040-1471	P T T Technische Mitteilungen
0040-148X	Technische Rundschau
0040-1498	T U Technische Ueberwachung see 0376-1185
0040-1501	Technische Universitaet Clausthal. Mitteilungsblatt
0040-151X	Schweizerische Technische Zeitschrift
0040-1528	Technische Hochschule Karl-Marx-Stadt. Wissenschaftliche Zeitschrift
0040-1536	Technischer Ansporn
0040-1544	Technischer Fortschritt (Duesseldorf)
0040-1552	Technischer Handel
0040-1560	Technisches Journal†
0040-1587	Technocracy Digest
0040-1595	Technocrat†
0040-1617	Technocratic Trendevents†
0040-1625	Technological Forecasting and Social Change
0040-1641	Technology changed to Fertilizer Technology
0040-165X	Technology and Culture
0040-1676	Technology Ireland
0040-1692	Technology Review
0040-1706	Technometrics
0040-1714	Tecnica
0040-1722	Tecnica de la Regulacion y Mando Automatico
0040-1730	Tecnica del Frio
0040-1749	Tecnica della Confezione changed to Tecnica della Confezione e della Maglieria
0040-1757	Tecnica dell'Aria Compressa†
0040-1765	Tecnica dell'Arte
0040-1773	Tecnica e Circolazione Autostradale
0040-1781	Tecnica e Industria
0040-179X	Tecnica e Invencion
0040-1803	Tecnica e Ricostruzione
0040-1811	Tecnica e Uomo
0040-182X	Tecnica Hospitalaria
0040-1838	Tecnica Industrial
0040-1846	Tecnica Italiana
0040-1854	Tecnica Mecanica†
0040-1862	Tecnica Molitoria
0040-1889	Tecnica Pecuaria en Mexico
0040-1897	Tecnica Sanitaria
0040-1900	Tecnica Textil Internacional
0040-1919	Tecnicas Financieras†
0040-1927	Tecniche dell'Automazione
0040-1943	Tecnologia Alimentaria
0040-1951	Tectonophysics
0040-196X	Tedenska Tribuna changed to I T D
0040-1978	Tednik
0040-1986	Teen Guide†
0040-1994	Teen Life†
0040-2001	Teen
0040-201X	Teen Pin-Ups
0040-2044	Teen World†
0040-2060	Teens' and Boys' Outfitter changed to Teens' and Boys' Magazine
0040-2079	Teenville
0040-2087	Teenways†
0040-2095	Tees-Side Journal of Commerce
0040-2109	Teg och Teknik
0040-2117	Tegel
0040-2125	Tegen de Tuberculose
0040-2133	Tegenwoordig
0040-2141	Tegl
0040-215X	Tegnikon
0040-2168	Tekhnicheska Misul
0040-2176	Tehnika
0040-2184	Teilhard Review
0040-2192	Teintex
0040-2222	Tekenen des Tijds†
0040-2249	Tekhnika Kino i Televideniya
0040-2257	Tekhnika - Moladezhi
0040-2265	Tekhnika v Sel'skom Khozyaistve
0040-2273	Journal of Labor Hygiene in Iron and Steel Industry
0040-2281	Tekenikens Varld Med Flying changed to Teknikens Vaerld
0040-2303	Tekniikka
0040-2311	Teknisk Information†
0040-232X	Teknisk Nyt
0040-2338	Teknisk Skoletidende
0040-2354	Teknisk Ukeblad-Teknikk
0040-2362	Teknikst Forum see 0533-070X
0040-2370	Tekstiililehti
0040-2389	Tekstilna Industrija
0040-2397	Tekstil'naya Promyshlennost'
0040-2400	Tel Hashomer Hospital Proceeding†
0040-2419	Tel Quel
0040-2427	TELE (Swedish Edition)
0040-2443	Telemagazine
0040-2451	Tele-Scout†
0040-2486	Telecommunication Journal of Australia
0040-2494	Telecommunications
0040-2508	Telecommunications and Radio Engineering
0040-2524	Teledyne Ryan Aeronautical Reporter†
0040-2532	Teleflora Spirit changed to Flowers &
0040-2540	Telefood Magazine
0040-2567	Telegrama Politico
0040-2575	Telegraph
0040-2583	Telegraph Worker Journal
0040-2591	Telekomunikace
0040-2605	Telekomunikacije
0040-2621	Telemetry Journal†
0040-263X	Telephone Engineer and Management
0040-2648	Telephone Review Magazine†
0040-2656	Telephony
0040-2672	Teleprograma
0040-2680	Telepulestudomanyi Kozlemenyek
0040-2699	Telerama
0040-2702	Telescope
0040-2710	Telesis
0040-2729	Telesna Vychova Mladeze
0040-2737	Telespazio
0040-2745	Telespiegel changed to Der Oesterreichische Schulfunk mit Telespiegel
0040-2753	Teleteknik. Danish Edition
0040-2788	Broadcast
0040-2818	Telhan Patrika
0040-2826	Tellus
0040-2834	Telonde
0040-2850	Telovychovny Pracovnik
0040-2869	Temas
0040-2877	Temas Administrativos see 0120-033X
0040-2885	Temas Contemporaneos
0040-2915	Temas Sociales
0040-2923	Temoignage Chretien
0040-2958	Temple Apothecary
0040-2966	Temple David Bulletin
0040-2974	Temple Law Quarterly
0040-2982	Tempo
0040-2990	Tempo†
0040-3008	Tempo
0040-3016	Tempo
0040-3024	Tempo
0040-3040	Tempo Economico
0040-3067	Temps Libre Informations changed to Enjeu
0040-3075	Temps Modernes
0040-3083	Tenant
0040-3113	Tenders
0040-3121	Tenneco
0040-313X	Tennessee Academy of Science. Journal
0040-3148	Tennessee Agricultural Experiment Station. Bulletin
0040-3156	Tennessee Alumnus
0040-3199	Tennessee Banker
0040-3202	Tennessee Conservationist
0040-3229	Tennessee Farm and Home Science
0040-3237	Tennessee Farm Bureau News
0040-3261	Tennessee Historical Quarterly
0040-327X	Tennessee Law Enforcement Journal
0040-3288	Tennessee Law Review
0040-3296	Tennessee Librarian see 0162-1564
0040-330X	Tennessee Life Insurance News see 0194-4312
0040-3318	Tennessee Medical Association. Journal
0040-3326	Tennessee Mockingbird
0040-3334	Tennessee Musician
0040-3342	Tennessee Nurses Association. Bulletin
0040-3350	Tennessee Planner†
0040-3369	Tennessee Poetry Journal†
0040-3377	Tennessee Public Welfare Record changed to Record (Nashville)
0040-3385	Tennessee Dental Association. Journal
0040-3393	Tennessee Survey of Business†
0040-3393	Tennessee Survey of Business see 0040-3393
0040-3407	Tennessee Teacher
0040-3415	Tennessee Town and City
0040-3423	Tennis
0040-3431	Tennis Tidningen
0040-3458	Golf Europeen
0040-3466	Tennis U. S. A.
0040-3474	Tennis World
0040-3482	Tenrikyo
0040-3490	Tenside - Detergents
0040-3504	Tensor
0040-3520	Tentoonstellingsagenda
0040-3539	Teollisuuslehti changed to Teollisuus
0040-3547	Teollisuustekniikka
0040-3555	Teologinen Aikakauskirja
0040-3563	Teoresi
0040-3571	Teoreticheskie Osnovy Khimicheskoi Tekhnologii
0040-358X	Teorie a Praxe Telesne Vychovy
0040-3598	Teorija in Praksa
0040-3601	Teoriya i Praktika Fizicheskoi Kul'tury
0040-361X	Teoriya Veroyatnostei i Ee Primenenie
0040-3628	Teosofi i Norden
0040-3636	Teploenergetika
0040-3644	Teplofizika Vysokikh Temperatur
0040-3652	Teramo
0040-3660	Terapevticheskii Arkhiv
0040-3679	Terapia†
0040-3687	Terapia†
0040-3695	Terapia Moderna
0040-3709	Teratology
0040-3717	Termeszet Vilaga
0040-3725	Termotecnica
0040-3741	Terra
0040-3768	Terra e Sole
0040-3776	Terra e Vita
0040-3784	Terra Santa
0040-3792	Terra Umbra†
0040-3806	Terrazzo Topics
0040-3814	Terre
0040-3822	Terre Cuite
0040-3830	Terre de Chez Nous
0040-3849	Terre des Jeunes changed to Francs-Jeux
0040-3865	Terre et la Vie
0040-389X	Terres Australes et Antarctiques Francaises†
0040-3903	Terveydenhoitolehti see 0355-1903
0040-3911	Terveys
0040-392X	Terzo Mondo
0040-3938	Tesoro Eucaristico
0040-3946	Test
0040-3954	Test Engineering & Management
0040-3962	Testigo†
0040-3970	Textil & Beklaednings†
0040-3989	Testimonianze
0040-3997	Testing, Instruments, and Controls changed to Non-Destructive Testing-Australia
0040-4004	Tete†
0040-4012	Tethys
0040-4020	Tetrahedron
0040-4039	Tetrahedron Letters
0040-4047	Railway Pictorial
0040-4055	Monthly Statistics of Actual Production of Railway Cars
0040-4071	Tevyne
0040-4101	Texaco Tempo†
0040-4128	Texas A & M University. College of Liberal Arts. Review†
0040-4136	Texas A & M University Library Notes
0040-4144	Texas Academy of Science. Newsletter
0040-4152	Texas Agriculture
0040-4160	Texas and Southwest Hotel-Motel Review
0040-4179	Texas Architect
0040-4187	Texas Bar Journal
0040-4195	Financial Trend
0040-4209	Texas Business Review
0040-4241	Texas Coach
0040-425X	Texas Concho Register
0040-4276	Texas Dental Hygienists' Association. Journal
0040-4314	Texas Fashions†
0040-4330	Texas Future Farmer
0040-4349	Texas Highways
0040-4357	Texas Hospitals
0040-4365	Texas Industrial Expansion
0040-4373	Texas Industry changed to T. A. B. Quarterly
0040-4381	Texas International Law Forum changed to Texas International Law Journal
0040-439X	Texas Jewish Post
0040-4403	Texas Journal of Science
0040-4411	Texas Law Review
0040-442X	Texas Lawman
0040-4438	Texas Libraries
0040-4454	Texas LP-Gas News
0040-4462	Texas Manpower Trends changed to Texas Labor Market Review
0040-4470	Texas Medicine
0040-4489	Texas Methodist changed to Texas Methodist/United Methodist Reporter
0040-4497	Texas Motorist changed to A A A Texas Motorist
0040-4519	Texas Observer
0040-4527	Texas Oil Jobber changed to Texas Oil Marketer
0040-4535	Texas Oil Journal†
0040-4543	Texas Ornithological Society. Bulletin
0040-4551	Texas Outlook
0040-4578	Texas Parent-Teacher changed to Texas P T A Communicator
0040-4586	Texas Parks and Wildlife Magazine
0040-4608	Texas Poultry and Egg News see 0048-4989
0040-4616	Texas Presbyterian changed to Presbyterian
0040-4624	Texas Press Messenger changed to T P A Messenger
0040-4632	Texas Professional Engineer
0040-4640	Texas Public Employee
0040-4659	Texas Quarterly†
0040-4675	Texas Reports on Biology and Medicine
0040-4683	Texas Schools changed to T S T A Texas Schools
0040-4691	Texas Studies in Literature and Language
0040-4705	Texas Study of Secondary Education Research Bulletin
0040-4721	Texas Techsan
0040-473X	Texas Town & City
0040-4748	Texas Transportation Researcher
0040-4756	Texas Veterinary Medical Journal
0040-4764	Technika Chronika
0040-4772	Texpress
0040-4780	Text
0040-4799	France. Institut National de Recherche et de Documentation Pedagogiques. Textes et Documents pour la Classe.
0040-4810	Textiel-Visie/Weekly
0040-4829	Textil
0040-4845	Textil och Konfektion
0040-4853	Textil Praxis International
0040-4861	Textil-Revue
0040-487X	Textil-Wirtschaft
0040-4888	Textilbranschen
0040-4896	Textile Bulletin†
0040-490X	Textile Chemist and Colorist
0040-4926	Textile Dyer and Printer

0040-4934 Textile Engineer *changed to* Ramifications
0040-4969 Textile History
0040-4977 Textile India
0040-4985 Textile Industries
0040-4993 Textile Industry & Trade Journal
0040-5000 Textile Institute. Journal
0040-5019 Textile Journal Australia
0040-5027 Textile Labor *changed to* Labor Unity
0040-5035 Textile Machinery
0040-5043 Textile Machinery Society of Japan. Journal (English Edition).
0040-5051 Textile Machinery Society of Japan. Proceedings *changed to* Textile Machinery Society of Japan. Journal (Japanese Edition).
0040-506X Textile Machinery Society of Japan. Transactions *changed to* Textile Machinery Society of Japan. Journal (Japanese Edition).
0040-5078 Textile Magazine
0040-5086 Textile Magazine
0040-5094 Textile Maintenance Reporter
0040-5116 Textile Month
0040-5124 Textile News
0040-5132 Textile Organon
0040-5140 Textile Panamericanos
0040-5167 Textile Progress
0040-5175 Textile Research Journal
0040-5191 Textile Technology Digest
0040-5205 Textile Trends
0040-5213 Textile World
0040-5221 Officiel du Pret a Porter
0040-523X Textiles of Ireland and Linen Trade Circular *changed to* Textile Times International.
0040-5248 Textiles Suisses
0040-5264 Textilia
0040-5280 Textilis *changed to* Tex-Textilis
0040-5299 Textilmesteren†
0040-5302 Textilreinigung
0040-5329 Text und Kritik
0040-5345 Thai Fisheries Gazette
0040-5353 Thai Journal of Development Administration
0040-5361 Thai Junior Red Cross Magazine
0040-537X Thailand Illustrated†
0040-5388 Thailand. National Statistical Office. Quarterly Bulletin of Statistics
0040-5396 Thames Valley Countryside *see* 0306-6614
0040-5418 Theater der Zeit
0040-5442 Theater-Rundschau
0040-5450 Theaternachrichten *changed to* Theater in Graz
0040-5469 Theatre Crafts
0040-5477 Theatre Design and Technology
0040-5485 Theatre Documentation†
0040-5493 Theatre en Pologne
0040-5507 Theater Heute
0040-5515 Theatre Information Bulletin
0040-5523 Theatre Notebook
0040-5531 Theatre Organ
0040-5558 Theatre Organ Review
0040-5566 Theatre Research *see* 0307-8833
0040-5574 Theatre Survey
0040-5604 Theatron
0040-5612 Theologia Reformata
0040-5620 Theological Education
0040-5639 Theological Studies
0040-5655 Theologie und Philosophie
0040-5663 Theologisch-Praktische Quartalschrift
0040-5671 Theologische Literaturzeitung
0040-568X Theologische Revue
0040-5698 Theologische Rundschau
0040-5701 Theologische Zeitschrift
0040-571X Theology
0040-5728 Theology Digest
0040-5736 Theology Today
0040-5744 Theoretica Chimica Acta
0040-5752 Theoretical and Applied Genetics
0040-5760 Theoretical and Experimental Chemistry
0040-5779 Theoretical and Mathematical Physics
0040-5787 Theoretical Chemical Engineering Abstracts
0040-5795 Theoretical Foundations of Chemical Engineering
0040-5809 Theoretical Population Biology
0040-5817 Theoria
0040-5833 Theory and Decision
0040-5841 Theory Into Practice
0040-585X Theory of Probability and Its Applications
0040-5868 Theosofia
0040-5876 Theosophical Journal
0040-5884 Theosophical Movement
0040-5892 Theosophist
0040-5906 Theosophy
0040-5914 Therapeutic Recreation Journal
0040-5922 Therapeutique†
0040-5930 Therapeutische Umschau
0040-5949 Therapia Hungarica
0040-5957 Therapie
0040-5965 Therapie der Gegenwart
0040-5973 Therapiewoche
0040-599X Thermal Abstracts *changed to* International Building Services Abstracts
0040-6007 Thermal Analysis Review *see* 0306-0438
0040-6015 Thermal Engineering†
0040-6015 Thermal Engineering
0040-6023 Thermiek
0040-6031 Thermochimica Acta
0040-604X Thesaurus
0040-6058 These Times
0040-6066 Theta
0040-6074 Theta†
0040-6082 Thin Films *see* 0305-3091
0040-6090 Thin Solid Films
0040-6104 Things to Watch & Watch For
0040-6112 Think†
0040-6120 Third Branch
0040-6139 Third Degree
0040-6147 Third Federal Savings & Loan Association of Cleveland, Ohio. News
0040-6155 Magazine of Metals Producing *see* 0149-1210
0040-6171 This England
0040-618X This Is Arkansas *changed to* Inside Arkansas
0040-6198 This Is London
0040-6201 This Is West Texas
0040-6228 This Magazine Is About Schools *see* 0381-3746
0040-6236 This Malta
0040-6244 This Month in London†
0040-6252 This Month in Your Library
0040-6279 Key-This Week in Chicago
0040-6295 This Week in Rome
0040-6309 This Week
0040-6317 This Week in the Nations' Capital
0040-6325 Thomist
0040-6341 Thomson C S F. Revue Technique
0040-6376 Thorax
0040-6384 Thoraxchirurgie - Vaskulaere Chirurgie *see* 0171-6425
0040-6392 Thoreau Journal Quarterly
0040-6406 Thoreau Society Bulletin
0040-6414 Thoroughbred Record and the Racing Calendar
0040-6430 Thoth
0040-6449 Thought†
0040-6457 Thought
0040-6465 Thought
0040-6473 Thought and the Spark
0040-649X Three Banks Review
0040-6511 Three Crafts Journal†
0040-652X Three Crowns
0040-6538 Three/Four *changed to* Vine
0040-6546 Three Hundred Thirty-Eight News
0040-6554 3M Panorama
0040-6562 Threshold
0040-6589 Throb
0040-6597 Thrombosis et Diathesis Haemorrhagica†
0040-6597 Thrombosis et Diathesis Haemorrhagica *see* 0340-6245
0040-6600 Through to Victory†
0040-6619 Thru the Garden Gate
0040-6635 Thunder
0040-6643 Thunderbolt
0040-6651 Thursday†
0040-666X Thyssenforschung *see* 0340-5060
0040-6686 Ti Saluto Fratello
0040-6694 Tibet im Exil†
0040-6708 Tibetan Review
0040-6716 Tic
0040-6732 Ticitl
0040-6740 Tiden
0040-6759 Tiden
0040-6767 Tidens Ekko†
0040-6775 Tidens Kvinder†
0040-6783 Tidewater Motorists
0040-6791 Tidings
0040-6805 Tidnings Nytt
0040-683X Tidskrift Foer Kustartilleriet
0040-6848 Tidskrift foer Schack
0040-6856 Tidskrift foer Yrkesutbildning
0040-6872 Tidskrift foer Dokumentation
0040-6880 Tidsskrift for Groenlands Retsvaesen
0040-6899 Tidskrift foer Svenska Folkhoegskolan *see* 0348-4769
0040-6902 Sveriges Advokatsamfund. Tidskrift
0040-6937 Tidskrift i Fortifikation
0040-6945 Tidskrift i Sjovasendet
0040-6953 Juridiska Foereningen i Finland. Tidskrift
0040-6961 Tidskriften Bostadsnaemnden
0040-6988 Tidskriften Heimdal
0040-6996 Tidskriften Laboratoriet
0040-7003 Tidskriften Landsstaten
0040-7011 Tidskriften Taxeringsnaemden
0040-702X Tidsskrift for Danske Sygehuse
0040-7038 Tidsskrift for Faareavl
0040-7046 Tidsskrift for Fjerkraeavl *see* 0045-9607
0040-7062 Tidsskrift for Hermetikindustri†
0040-7062 Tidsskrift for Hermetikkindustri *changed to* Naeringsmiddelindustrien og Tidsskrift for Hermetikkindustri
0040-7070 Tidsskrift for Industri *see* 0045-9623
0040-7089 Tidsskrift for Jordmoedre
0040-7100 Tidsskrift for Kortbolge Radio *changed to* OZ
0040-7119 Tidsskrift for Landokonomi
0040-7127 Naeringsmiddelindustrien *changed to* Naeringsmiddelindustrien og Tidsskrift for Hermetikkindustri
0040-7135 Tidsskrift for Planteavl
0040-7143 Tidsskrift for Rettsvitenskap
0040-7151 Tidsskrift for Revisjon og Regnskapsvesen *changed to* Revisjon og Regnskap
0040-716X Tidsskrift for Samfunnsforskning
0040-7178 Tidsskrift for Skogbruk
0040-7186 Tidsskrift for Soevaesen
0040-7194 Tidsskrift for Teologi og Kirke
0040-7208 Tidsskrift for Textilteknik *see* 0049-3236
0040-7216 Tidsskrift for Voksenopplaering
0040-7224 Tidsskriftet Ny Tid og Vi
0040-7232 Tie
0040-7240 Tiefbau, Ingenieurbau, Strassenbau
0040-7259 Tiefkuehl Praxis International *see* 0342-376X
0040-7267 Tielehti *see* 0355-7855
0040-7275 Tiempo
0040-7283 Tiempo de Cine
0040-7291 Tier
0040-7305 Tierreich
0040-7313 Tierfreund *changed to* Schweizer Tierschutz
0040-733X Tierra
0040-7348 Tierra y dos Mares†
0040-7356 Tiers Monde
0040-7372 Tiesa
0040-7380 Tiger Beat
0040-7402 Tiili
0040-7410 Vereniging Koniniklijke Nederlandsche Heide Maatschappij. Tijdschrift
0040-7429 Tijdschrift voor Architectuur en Beeldende Kunsten†
0040-7437 Tijdschrift voor Bestuurswetenschappen en Publiek Recht
0040-7445 Tijdschrift voor Chemie & Instrument *changed to* Chemie & Instrument
0040-7453 Tijdschrift voor Diergeneeskunde
0040-7461 Tijdschrift voor Economie *changed to* Tijdschrift voor Economie en Management
0040-747X Tijdschrift voor Economische en Sociale Geografie
0040-7488 Tijdschrift voor Effectief Directiebeleid†
0040-7496 Tijdschrift voor Entomologie
0040-750X Tijdschrift voor Filosofie
0040-7518 Tijdschrift voor Geschiedenis
0040-7526 Nederlands Geodetisch Tijdschrift
0040-7542 Tijdschrift voor Mattschappelijk Werk *changed to* T M W Welzijnsmaandblad
0040-7550 Tijdschrift voor Nederlandse Taal- en Letterkunde
0040-7577 Tijdschrift voor Opvoedkunde *changed to* Pedagogisch Tijdschrift
0040-7593 Tijdschrift voor Revalidatie *changed to* Revalidatie
0040-7607 Tijdschrift voor Sociale Geneeskunde
0040-7615 Tijdschrift voor Sociale Wetenschappen
0040-7623 Tijdschrift voor Vervoerswetenschap
0040-764X Tijdspiegel
0040-7658 Tilastollisia Kuukaustitietoja Helsingista†
0040-7658 Tilastollisia Kuukaustitietoja Helsingista *see* 0357-3362
0040-7666 Tile & Architectural Ceramics
0040-7674 Tile and Till
0040-7682 Till Rors (Med Segel och Motor) *changed to* Paa Kryss och till Rors
0040-7704 Tim *changed to* Maky
0040-7712 TIM
0040-7720 Timber *changed to* Timber and Timber Products
0040-7739 Timber and Plywood
0040-7739 Timber and Plywood *changed to* Timber Trades Journal and Wood Processing
0040-7755 Timber Development Association of India. Journal
0040-7763 Timber Grower
0040-7771 Timber Journal†
0040-778X Timber Supply Review
0040-7798 Timber Trades Journal and Woodworking Machinery *changed to* Timber Trades Journal and Wood Processing
0040-7798 Wood Based Panels International
0040-781X Time
0040-7836 Time & Tide
0040-7852 Time Machine
0040-7879 Times and Challenge
0040-7887 Times Educational Supplement
0040-7895 Times Literary Supplement
0040-7917 Times of the Americas
0040-7925 Timken
0040-7933 Timmerfabrikant
0040-7941 Tin and Its Uses
0040-795X Tin International
0040-7968 Tin News
0040-7976 Tin Printer and Box Maker *see* 0040-795X
0040-7984 Tintoria
0040-8018 Tip
0040-8026 Tip-O-Texan†
0040-8034 Tipperary Star
0040-8042 Tips and Topics in Home Economics
0040-8050 Y Tir and Welsh Farmer
0040-8069 Tir Sportif en France†
0040-8077 Tiramolla
0040-8085 Tire Review
0040-8093 Federacion Nacional del Tiro Olimpico Espanol. Revista Informativa *changed to* Federacion Nacional del Tiro Olimpico Espanol. Boletin Informativo
0040-8107 Tirol†
0040-8115 Tiroler Heimatblaetter
0040-8123 Tisch und Kueche *changed to* TuK Inform
0040-8131 Tischler
0040-814X Tischtennis-Schau
0040-8166 Tissue & Cell
0040-8174 Tissue Culture Abstracts
0040-8182 Titanic Commutator

ISSN	Title
0040-8190	Title News
0040-8204	Titogradska Tribina
0040-8212	Titular
0040-8239	Tlalocan
0040-8247	To Free Mankind *changed to* World Citizen/Federalist Letter
0040-8255	Nisaki Mas i Kea
0040-8263	Toastmaster
0040-8271	Tobacco
0040-828X	Tobacco†
0040-8298	Tobacco Abstracts
0040-8301	Tobacco Intelligence†
0040-8328	Tobacco Reporter *see* 0361-5693
0040-8336	Tobacco Retailers Journal *changed to* Retail Tobacconist
0040-8344	U.S. Department of Agriculture. Economics, Statistics, and Cooperatives Service. Tobacco Situation
0040-8352	Dialogue (Birmingham)†
0040-8360	Today
0040-8379	Today†
0040-8387	Today *changed to* Today in Africa
0040-8409	Today in Anaheim/Orange County
0040-8417	Today in France
0040-8433	Today in San Diego
0040-8441	Today's Catholic Teacher
0040-8468	Today's Child Newsmagazine
0040-8476	Today's Children†
0040-8484	Today's Education
0040-8492	Todays Family†
0040-8514	Today's Health *see* 0014-7249
0040-8522	Today's Housing Briefs†
0040-8549	Today's Parish
0040-8565	Today's Secretary
0040-8573	Today's Speech *see* 0146-3373
0040-8581	Today's Teens†
0040-859X	Today's Transport International
0040-8603	Todo
0040-8611	Todo es Historia
0040-8638	Toerist
0040-8646	Wudd
0040-8654	Toga Calabrese
0040-8670	Toho University Medical Society. Journal
0040-8689	Tohoku University. Research Institute for Scientific Measurements. Bulletin
0040-8697	Tohoku University. Institute for Agricultural Research. Bulletin
0040-8700	Tohoku Medical Journal
0040-8719	Tohoku Journal of Agricultural Research
0040-8727	Tohoku Journal of Experimental Medicine
0040-8735	Tohoku Mathematical Journal
0040-8743	Tohoku Psychologica Folia
0040-8751	Tohoku Archivo por Orthopedia Kej Akcidenta Hirurgio *changed to* Tohoku Archives of Orthopaedic Surgery and Traumatology
0040-876X	Tohoku University. Research Institute of Mineral Dressing and Metallurgy. Bulletin
0040-8778	Tohoku University. Science Reports. Series 1: Physics, Chemistry, Astronomy
0040-8786	Tohoku University. Science Reports. Series 4: Biology
0040-8794	Tohoku University. Science Reports. Series 5: Geophysics
0040-8808	Tohoku University. Science Reports of the Research Institutes. Series A: Physics, Chemistry, and Metallurgy
0040-8816	Tohoku University. Faculty of Engineering. Technology Reports
0040-8824	Toilers of the Deep
0040-8859	Tokai Regional Fisheries Research Laboratory
0040-8867	Toko-Ginecologia Practica
0040-8875	Tokushima Journal of Experimental Medicine
0040-8883	Tokushima University. Faculty of Engineering. Bulletin
0040-8891	Tokyo Dental College. Bulletin
0040-8905	Tokyo Medical College. Journal
0040-8913	Tokyo Journal of Climatology
0040-8921	Tokyo Medical and Dental University. Bulletin
0040-893X	Tokyo Municipal News
0040-8948	Tokyo National Museum News
0040-8956	Tokyo Medical Association. Journal
0040-8964	University of Tokyo. College of General Education. Scientific Papers
0040-8972	Tokyo University. Earthquake Research Institute. Bulletin†
0040-8980	University of Tokyo. Faculty of Science. Journal. Section 1A: Mathematics
0040-8999	University of Tokyo. Faculty of Science. Journal. Section 2: Geology, Mineralogy, Geography, Geophysics
0040-9006	University of Tokyo. Institute of Industrial Science. Report
0040-9014	Tokyo University of Fisheries. Journal
0040-9022	Tokyo Women's Medical College. Journal
0040-9030	Tolar Creek Syndicate†
0040-9049	Toldbladet
0040-9057	Toledo Business News
0040-9065	Toledo City Journal
0040-9081	Toledo Jewish News
0040-909X	Tolkien Journal
0040-9103	Tolpolski's Chronicle
0040-9111	Tolvmandsbladet
0040-912X	Tom Thumb
0040-9146	Tomorrow Through Research *changed to* Technology Today
0040-9154	Tomorrow's Man†
0040-9170	Toneel Teatraal
0040-9189	Tong-Tong *changed to* Moesson
0040-9219	Tooling Manufacturing Engineering and Management *see* 0361-0853
0040-9227	Tooling
0040-9243	Tooling & Production
0040-9251	Toonzaal†
0040-926X	Top Gear†
0040-9286	Top of the News
0040-9308	Topcu Dergisi†
0040-9324	Topical Dates & Facts Newsletter†
0040-9332	Topical Time
0040-9340	Topicator
0040-9367	Topics
0040-9375	Topique - Revue Freudienne
0040-9383	Topology
0040-9391	Tora Ya Tebelo
0040-9405	Torah Umesorah Report
0040-9413	Audio & Electronics
0040-944X	Torch (Chicago)
0040-9456	Torch of Knowledge†
0040-9472	Torfyanaya Promyshlennost'
0040-9499	Tornado
0040-9502	Foro Universitario
0040-9510	Metropolitan Toronto Board of Trade. Journal *changed to* Business Journal
0040-9529	Toronto Boys and Girls House Subscription Reviews†
0040-9537	Toronto Calendar Magazine
0040-9553	Toronto Railway Club. Official Proceedings
0040-9561	University of Toronto News *see* 0042-0212
0040-957X	Torque†
0040-9588	Torre
0040-9596	Torre Civica
0040-960X	Torre Davidica
0040-9618	Torrey Botanical Club. Bulletin
0040-9626	Illinois State Bar Association. Tort Trends
0040-9634	Tortenelmi Szemle
0040-9642	Toshiba Review
0040-9650	Japan Society of Library Science. Annals
0040-9669	Library World
0040-9677	Tot 'n Teen Fashions
0040-9693	Total Comfort Dealer
0040-9707	Total Energy
0040-9715	Total Translation in Science
0040-9723	Totem
0040-9731	Tour de Feu
0040-974X	Tourama *changed to* Hotel Tourama of Rhodesia
0040-9758	Touring
0040-9766	Touring Freizeit *changed to* Freizeit
0040-9782	Tourisme Informations
0040-9804	Tourist Time†
0040-9812	Tourists' Ceylon *changed to* Tourmaline
0040-9820	Tout pour Vous
0040-9839	Tout-Rouen
0040-9855	Toute l'Electronique
0040-9863	Toutou-Journal
0040-9898	Toward Freedom
0040-9901	Tower†
0040-991X	Tower Smiling *see* 0190-3284
0040-9928	Towers
0040-9952	Town and Country
0040-9960	Town and Country Planning
0040-9979	Town and Village
0040-9995	Town Planning and Local Government Guide
0041-0012	Town Planning Quarterly
0041-0020	Town Planning Review
0041-0039	Town Talk about Toronto
0041-0047	Towns & Cities Magazines†
0041-0055	Township
0041-0063	Towson State Journal of International Affairs
0041-0071	Toxicity Bibliography†
0041-008X	Toxicology and Applied Pharmacology
0041-0101	Toxicon
0041-011X	Toy & Hobby World
0041-0128	Toy Trader†
0041-0136	Toy Trader
0041-0144	Toyo Soda Manufacturing Company. Scientific Report
0041-0152	Toyoda Technical Review
0041-0160	Toys†
0041-0179	Toys *see* 0160-8010
0041-0195	Toys International *changed to* Toys International and the Retailer
0041-0209	Tozhil Udayam *changed to* Tozhil Uravu
0041-0233	Fomento del Trabajo Nacional. Economia Nacional, Internacional de la Empresa *changed to* Horizonte Empresarial
0041-0241	Trabajos de Estadistica e Investigacion Operativa
0041-025X	Trabajos de Hematologia y Hemoterapia†
0041-0276	Traces
0041-0284	Track & Field News
0041-0292	Track and Field Quarterly Review
0041-0306	Track Newsletter†
0041-0314	Track Technique
0041-0330	Tracker
0041-0349	Tracks
0041-0357	Tract Messenger
0041-0365	Trade-A-Plane
0041-0373	Trade and Industry
0041-0381	Trade and Industry of Japan *changed to* Focus Japan
0041-039X	Trade and Tours†
0041-0403	Trade Channel
0041-0411	Trade Chronicle
0041-042X	Trade Digest *changed to* World Fairs Guide
0041-0438	Trade Marks Journal
0041-0446	Trade Marks Journal
0041-0454	Trade Marks Journal
0041-0462	Trade of the Maltese Islands *changed to* Malta Trade Statistics
0041-0470	Trade Review of the Week†
0041-0489	Trade Trends
0041-0500	Trade Union Information
0041-0519	Trade Union News Bulletin from Norway
0041-0527	Trade Union Press *changed to* Flashes from the Trade Unions
0041-0535	Trade Union Record
0041-0543	Trade with Greece
0041-0551	Trade with Italy
0041-056X	Trademark Reporter
0041-0586	Trading Post
0041-0608	Tradition
0041-0624	Trae Nyt
0041-0632	Traeindustrien *see* 0105-8738
0041-0659	Traffic Bulletin
0041-0683	Traffic Engineering and Control
0041-0691	Traffic Management
0041-0705	Traffic Manager
0041-0713	Traffic Quarterly
0041-0721	Traffic Safety
0041-073X	Traffic World
0041-0748	Trail and Landscape
0041-0756	Trail and Timberline
0041-0764	Trailblazer†
0041-0772	Trailer-Body Builders
0041-0780	Trailer Life
0041-0799	Trailer Topics Magazine†
0041-0802	Trailer Travel Magazine *see* 0160-3000
0041-0829	Train Collectors Quarterly
0041-0837	Train Dispatcher
0041-0845	Train Sheet
0041-0853	Trained Men *changed to* Training Digest
0041-0861	Training and Development Journal *changed to* Training and Development Journal (1978)
0041-087X	Training Briefs†
0041-0888	Training Directors Newsletter
0041-0896	Training in Business and Industry *see* 0095-5892
0041-090X	Training Officer
0041-0918	Training School Bulletin†
0041-0926	Trainmaster
0041-0934	Trains
0041-0950	Traitement Thermique
0041-0969	Traktoeren
0041-0977	Traktor- og Landbrugsbladet
0041-0985	Traktor Aktuell
0041-1027	Tranciatura Stampaggio
0041-1035	Trans-Action-Social Science and Modern Society *see* 0147-2011
0041-1043	Transair
0041-1051	Transactional Analysis Bulletin *changed to* Transactional Analysis Journal
0041-106X	Transafrican Journal of History
0041-1078	Transatlantic Review†
0041-1086	Transatom Bulletin *see* 0378-6803
0041-1108	Transcultural Psychiatric Research Review
0041-1116	Transdex Index
0041-1124	Transformacion
0041-1132	Transfusion
0041-1159	Transistor D.A.T.A. Book
0041-1167	Transit of Chi Epsilon
0041-1175	Transit Postmark Collector
0041-1183	Transit Record
0041-1191	Transition *changed to* Ch'indaba
0041-1205	Transition
0041-1213	Transitrends†
0041-1221	Translation *changed to* In Other Words
0041-123X	Translation Talk†
0041-1256	Translations Register-Index
0041-1264	Translatoeren
0041-1272	Transmisiones
0041-1280	Transmission and Distribution
0041-1299	TransPacific
0041-1302	Transparent
0041-1310	Transpatent
0041-1337	Transplantation
0041-1345	Transplantation Proceedings
0041-1361	Transport
0041-137X	Transport
0041-1388	Transport and Communications
0041-1396	Transport & Communications Bulletin for Asia & the Far East
0041-140X	Transport Commercial
0041-1418	Transport-Communications Monthly Review *changed to* Indian Highways
0041-1426	Transport-Dienst
0041-1434	Transport Economics
0041-1442	Transport et Tourisme
0041-1450	Transport Theory and Statistical Physics
0041-1469	Transport History
0041-1477	Transport Industry and Trade Journal *changed to* Transport Industry and Trade Annual
0041-1493	Transport Journal of Australia
0041-1507	Transport-Journalen
0041-1523	Transport-Nytt
0041-1531	Transport Salaried Staff Journal
0041-154X	Transport Teknik
0041-1558	Transport Topics

ISSN	Title
0041-1566	Transport und Lager
0041-1574	Transport und Lagertechnik
0041-1582	Transport und Schiffahrt†
0041-1590	Transportation Ad Views†
0041-1604	Transportation Engineer
0041-1612	Transportation Journal
0041-1639	Translog
0041-1647	Transportation Research see 0191-2607
0041-1647	Transportation Research see 0191-2615
0041-1655	Transportation Science
0041-1663	Standard and Poor's Transportation Securities Weekly Outlook changed to Standard & Poor's Transportation Securities
0041-1671	Transportation Technology see 0308-1060
0041-168X	Transporte
0041-1698	Transporte Moderno
0041-1701	Transportnoe Stroitel'stvo
0041-171X	Transvaal Education Bulletin†
0041-1728	Transvaal Educational News
0041-1736	Transvaal Farmer
0041-1744	Transvaal Gardener
0041-1752	Transvaal Museum. Annals
0041-1760	Trap & Field
0041-1779	Trapani Nuova
0041-1787	Trasfusione del Sangue
0041-1795	Trasporti Aerei
0041-1809	Trasporti Industriali
0041-1817	Trasporti Pubblici
0041-1825	Trattamenti dei Metalli†
0041-1833	Trattamenti e Finitura
0041-1841	I M A Trattorista
0041-185X	Travail et Methodes
0041-1868	Travail Humain
0041-1876	Travailleur du Livre
0041-1892	Saagverken/Traevarunindustrin see 0036-259X
0041-1906	Travaux
0041-1914	Travaux de Peinture†
0041-1930	Travaux et Jours
0041-1965	Travel see 0161-7184
0041-1973	TravelAge West
0041-1981	Travel Agency
0041-199X	Travel Agent
0041-2007	Travel & Leisure
0041-2015	Travel Management Daily
0041-2023	Travel Marketing Newsletter
0041-2031	Travel Times†
0041-204X	Travel Times
0041-2058	Travel Trade Magazine see 0311-2179
0041-2066	Travel Trade
0041-2074	Travel Trade Gazette
0041-2082	Travel Weekly
0041-2090	Travel World†
0041-2104	TravelAge East
0041-2120	Travelling
0041-2139	Treasure
0041-2155	U. S. Treasury Department. Treasury Bulletin
0041-2163	Treasury Information Bulletin†
0041-2171	Tree
0041-2198	Tree-Ring Bulletin
0041-2201	Tree Talks
0041-221X	Trees
0041-2228	Trees
0041-2236	Trees in South Africa
0041-2244	Trefoil
0041-2252	Trefpunt
0041-2260	Trekker
0041-2279	Tremplin
0041-2287	Trend†
0041-2295	Trend
0041-2317	Trend in Engineering
0041-2325	Trenden
0041-2333	Standard & Poor's Trendline's Current Market Perspectives
0041-2341	Trends
0041-2368	Bauma-Trends
0041-2376	Trends (Arlington)†
0041-2384	Trends in Adjusting
0041-2406	Trends in Management-Stockholder Relations
0041-2414	Trends in Parks and Recreation changed to Trends
0041-2430	Trendway Advisory Service
0041-2449	Trenton
0041-2457	Trgovinski Glasnik
0041-2465	Tri-County Dental Society. Bulletin
0041-2473	Tri County News
0041-2481	Tri-Ology Technical Report
0041-249X	Tri-State Food News
0041-2503	Tri-State Trader
0041-2511	Triad
0041-252X	Triades
0041-2538	Trial
0041-2546	Trial Lawyer's Guide
0041-2554	Trial Lawyers Quarterly
0041-2562	Inklusief
0041-2570	Triangle
0041-2597	Triangle
0041-2600	Triangle of Mu Phi Epsilon
0041-2619	Triangle Pointer
0041-2627	Triangle Review
0041-266X	Tribina
0041-2678	Tribology see 0301-679X
0041-2694	Tribos-Tribology Abstracts
0041-2708	Tribritta
0041-2716	Tribuene
0041-2724	Tribuna
0041-2767	Tribuna Musical
0041-2775	Tribuna Odontologica†
0041-2783	Tribuna Politica
0041-2791	Tribuna Postale changed to Tribuna Postale e delle Telecomunicazioni
0041-2805	Tribunal de Justica do Estado do Rio Grande do Sul. Revista de Jurisprudencia
0041-2813	Tribunal Federal de Recursos. Revista
0041-2821	Tribuna
0041-283X	Tribune de l'Enfance
0041-2848	Tribune des Nations
0041-2864	Tribune Graphologique
0041-2872	Tribune Libre
0041-2899	Tributi Sugli Affari
0041-2902	Tricolor
0041-2910	Tricontinental - Edition Francais†
0041-2929	Trident†
0041-2945	Trierer Theologische Zeitschrift
0041-2961	Trim U Fit†
0041-2988	Trilobite
0041-3003	Trimestre Economico
0041-3011	Trimestre Economico
0041-302X	Trinaesti Maj
0041-3046	Trinidad and Tobago. Central Statistical Office. Quarterly Economic Report
0041-3054	Trinity College Record
0041-3062	Trinity News
0041-3097	TriQuarterly
0041-3119	Triton changed to Diver
0041-3135	Triveni
0041-3143	Trivsel†
0041-316X	Trompie changed to Student
0041-3178	Trons Segrar
0041-3186	Tropenlandwirt
0041-3208	Tropical Abstracts see 0304-5951
0041-3216	Tropical Agriculture
0041-3224	Tropical Agriculturist
0041-3240	Tropical Diseases Bulletin
0041-3259	Tropical Fish Hobbyist
0041-3267	Tropical Medicine
0041-3275	Tropical Medicine and Hygiene News
0041-3283	Tropical Products Quarterly†
0041-3291	Tropical Science
0041-3321	Tros-Kompas
0041-333X	Trottingbred†
0041-3348	Trotwaer
0041-3356	Trotzdem
0041-3364	Trout
0041-3372	Trout and Salmon
0041-3380	Truck and Bus Transportation
0041-3399	Truck Insider Newsletter
0041-3410	Trucking Business changed to Heavy Truck Business
0041-3429	Trucking News†
0041-3437	Trudbenik
0041-3445	Trudov Invalid
0041-3453	Gosudarstvennyi Astronomicheskii Institut im. P. K. Shternberga. Trudy
0041-3461	True†
0041-347X	True Confessions†
0041-3488	True Confessions
0041-3496	True Confidential Confessions
0041-350X	True Detective
0041-3518	True Experience†
0041-3534	True Life Secrets
0041-3542	True Love†
0041-3550	True Love
0041-3569	True Modern Romances
0041-3585	True Romance†
0041-3593	True Story†
0041-3607	Treasure World changed to Lost Treasure
0041-3615	True West
0041-3658	Truppendienst
0041-3666	Truppenpraxis
0041-3674	Trustee
0041-3682	Trusts and Estates
0041-3690	Truth
0041-3704	Truth about Communism†
0041-3712	Truth Seeker
0041-3720	Trybuna Spoldzielcza
0041-3739	Tryckluft
0041-3747	Trziste Povrca i Voca†
0041-3755	Trziste Stoke i Stochih Proizoda
0041-3763	T M P M
0041-3771	Tsitologiya
0041-378X	Tsopano News
0041-3798	Soil Mechanics and Foundation Engineering
0041-3801	Tsukumo Earth Science
0041-381X	Communication Industries
0041-3828	Tswelopele
0041-3836	Tu Cher Wen Cher Reader's Digest(Chinese Edition)
0041-3852	Tuatara†
0041-3860	Tuatara
0041-3879	Tubercle
0041-3887	Tuberkulozis es Tudobetegsegek
0041-3895	Tuberkulozis es Tudogyogyaszat Referalo Szemle
0041-3909	Tubular Structures
0041-3917	Tudomanyos es Muszaki Tajekoztatas
0041-3925	Turk Idare Dergisi
0041-3941	Tufts Dental Outlook†
0041-395X	Tufts Health Science Review
0041-3968	Tuiles et Briques changed to Connaissance des Ceramiques
0041-3976	Tuinbouwberichten changed to Boer en de Tuinder
0041-3984	Tuinderij
0041-3992	Tulane Law Review
0041-400X	Tulane Medicine Faculty and Alumni changed to Tulane Medicine
0041-4018	Tulane Studies in Geology and Paleontology
0041-4026	Tulanian
0041-4034	Tulimuld
0041-4042	Tulsa
0041-4050	Tulsa Law Journal
0041-4093	Tumor Research: Experimental and Clinical
0041-4107	Tungsram Technische Mitteilungen
0041-4115	Tunisia. Institut National de la Statistique. Bulletin Mensuel de Statistique
0041-4123	Tunisie Economique
0041-4131	La Tunisie Medicale
0041-414X	Tunnels & Tunnelling
0041-4158	Turf and Sport Digest
0041-4182	Turist
0041-4190	Turist
0041-4204	Turisticke Novine
0041-4212	Turisticni Vestnik
0041-4220	Turk Dili
0041-4239	Turk Kulturu
0041-4247	Turk Tarih Kurumu. Belgeler
0041-4255	Turk Tarih Kurumu. Belleten
0041-4263	Turkey. Devlet Istatistik Enstitusu. Aylik Istatistik Bulteni/Monthly Bulletin of Statistics
0041-4271	Turkey World
0041-4298	Turkish Digest†
0041-4301	Turkish Journal of Pediatrics
0041-431X	Turkish Medical Association. Journal/Turk Tip Cemiyeti Mecmuasi changed to Turk Tip Dernegi Dergisi
0041-4328	Turkish National Bibliography
0041-4336	Turkiye Cumhuriyet Merkez Bankasi. Aylik Bulten
0041-4344	Bibliography of Articles in Turkish Periodicals
0041-4352	Tumori
0041-4360	Turrialba
0041-4379	Tussen de Rails
0041-4395	Tutti Fotografi
0041-4409	Tuttitalia†
0041-4417	Tutto Cucciolo
0041-4441	Tuttosport
0041-445X	Tuttoville
0041-4468	Tuulilasi
0041-4476	T.V. changed to Science et Culture
0041-4484	T V and Movie Play†
0041-4492	T V and Movie Screen
0041-4506	T V Digest changed to T V Times
0041-4514	T V Publicity Outlets-Nationwide
0041-4522	Sorrisi e Canzoni T.V. (Rome)
0041-4549	Tvai
0041-4565	Tvorchestvo
0041-4573	Twainian
0041-4581	2 N
0041-459X	Twentieth Century†
0041-4611	Twentieth Century Fund. Newsletter
0041-462X	Twentieth Century Literature
0041-4638	Twentieth Century Studies†
0041-4646	Twigs see 0163-1209
0041-4654	Twin Circle
0041-4662	Two Bridges News†
0041-4670	Two Rivers
0041-4697	Two Wheeler
0041-4700	Two Wheels
0041-4719	Two Worlds
0041-4727	Tworczosc
0041-4743	Tijdschrift voor Vennootschappen, Verenigingen en Stichtingen changed to T.V.V.S. Maandblad voor Ondernemingsrecht
0041-4751	Tydskrif vir Geesteswetenskappe
0041-476X	Tydskrif vir Letterkunde
0041-4778	Journal for Secondary Education†
0041-4786	Tydskrif vir Natuurwetenskappe
0041-4794	Tydskrif vir Rasse-Aangeleenthede
0041-4808	Tygodnik Powszechny
0041-4816	Tyo-Terveys-Turvallisuus
0041-4824	Typetalks Magazine†
0041-4832	Typographical Journal
0041-4840	Typographische Monatsblaetter
0041-4859	Tyres and Accessories
0041-4867	Tsement
0041-4883	Tsitologiya i Genetika
0041-4891	Tsvetnye Metally
0041-4905	Tsvetovodstvo
0041-4913	Library of Congress Professional Association. Newsletter
0041-4921	U. A. L. Economic and Financial Review†
0041-493X	U A M P T†
0041-4948	Egypt. Ministry of Tourism. Statistical Bulletin
0041-4972	U A W Fair Practices Fact Sheet†
0041-4980	U A W Washington Report
0041-4999	U B C Alumni Chronicle
0041-5006	U B N
0041-5014	U C L A Graduate Journal†
0041-5030	U E C Journal
0041-5049	U E News (Don Mills)
0041-5057	U E G Boletim changed to Boletim U E R J
0041-5065	U E News (New York)
0041-5081	U F O-Nachrichten
0041-509X	U H S Bulletin changed to H I A S Bulletin
0041-5103	U.I.A.M.S. Informations
0041-5111	U I C C Bulletin
0041-512X	U I R Research Newsletter
0041-5146	U I T P Biblio-Index
0041-5154	U I T P Revue
0041-5162	U. I. U. Journal
0041-5170	U. K. Press Gazette
0041-5189	U L L I C O Bulletin
0041-5200	U M Profiles changed to Profiles

1066 ISSN INDEX

0041-5219 U N A F. Bulletin de Liaison *see* 0220-9926
0041-5227 U N C T A D Guide to Publications
0041-5243 UNESCO Bulletin for Libraries *changed to* Unesco Journal of Information Science, Librarianship and Archives Administration
0041-5251 Unesco. Oficina Regional de Educacion para America Latina y le Caribe. Boletin de Educacion
0041-526X Unesco Chronicle
0041-5278 Unesco Courier
0041-5286 Unesco Features
0041-5294 U N E S C O Philippines
0041-5308 U N H C R Report
0041-5316 U N H Magazine
0041-5324 U N I A P A C *changed to* U N I A P A C. International
0041-5340 Unicef News
0041-5359 U N I S A English Studies
0041-5367 U N Monthly Chronicle
0041-5375 U N U C I
0041-5383 U. P. A. Journal
0041-5391 U P College of Dentistry Journal
0041-5405 U P E N
0041-5421 University Review†
0041-543X U R S I Information Bulletin
0041-5448 Local 1010 Steelworker
0041-5456 U S A F Instructors Journal†
0041-5464 U S A Record
0041-5472 U S B W A Tip-Off
0041-5480 U S C O L D Newsletter
0041-5499 U S F & G Bulletin
0041-5502 U S G A Green Section Record
0041-5510 U S I U Doctoral Society Journal
0041-5537 U S News and World Report
0041-5545 U S S R and Third World
0041-5553 U S S R Computational Mathematics and Mathematical Physics
0041-5561 U S U Staff News
0041-557X U T
0041-5588 U. T. C
0041-5596 U. T. Dental Alumni News
0041-5618 U T U Transportation News *see* 0098-5937
0041-5626 Ubaqa *see* 0041-5634
0041-5634 Ubaqa Lwabantwana
0041-5642 Ubulum†
0041-5650 U C L A Law Review
0041-5669 Ude og Hjemme
0041-5677 Udenrigs Handel og Industri Information
0041-5685 Udenrigsministeriets Tidsskrift *changed to* U T
0041-5693 Udenrigspolitiske Skrifter
0041-5707 Uebersee Rundschau
0041-5715 Ufahamu
0041-5731 Ufficio Moderno - Pubblicita
0041-574X Uganda Journal
0041-5758 Uganda. Ministry of Planning and Economic Development. Statistics Division. Quarterly Economic and Statistical Bulletin
0041-5766 Uganda Teacher†
0041-5774 Ugeskrift for Agronomer *see* 0106-0546
0041-5782 Ugeskrift for Laeger
0041-5790 Ugol'
0041-5804 Ugol' Ukrainy
0041-5812 Uhli
0041-5820 Uhr *changed to* Uhren-Juwelen-Schmuck
0041-5847 Uhren und Schmuck
0041-5855 Uhrenjournal
0041-5863 Uit de Pluimveepers
0041-5871 Uit de Verf *changed to* Bouwvaria
0041-588X Uit Europoortkringen
0041-5898 Uit in Utrecht
0041-5901 Uit Ons Werk†
0041-591X Uitgelezen
0041-5936 Uitlotings-Archief
0041-5944 Uitzicht
0041-5952 Uj Iras
0041-5979 Ukiyo-e Art
0041-5987 Ukrainian Bulletin†
0041-5995 Ukrainian Mathematical Journal
0041-6002 Ukrainian News
0041-6010 Ukrainian Quarterly
0041-6029 Ukrainian Review
0041-6037 Ukrainian Voice
0041-6045 Ukrainski Khimicheskii Zhurnal
0041-6053 Ukrainskii Matematicheskii Zhurnal
0041-6061 Ukrains'kyi Istoryk
0041-607X Ukrainian Medical Association of North America. Journal
0041-6088 Ukraina
0041-6096 Ukrains'ka Mova i Literatura v Shkoli
0041-610X Ukrains'kyi Biokhimichnyi Zhurnal
0041-6118 Ukrains'kyi Botanichnyi Zhurnal
0041-6126 Ukrainskii Fizicheskii Zhurnal
0041-6134 Ukrains'kyi Istorychnyi Zhurnal
0041-6142 Ukrains'kyi Samostijnyk†
0041-6150 Ukulima Wa Kisasa
0041-6177 Finland. Tullihallituksen Kauppatilastotoimisto. Ulkomaankauppa-Kuukausijulkaisu/ Foreign Trade Monthly Bulletin *changed to* Finland. Tullihallitus. Ulkomaankauppa/Utrikeshandel/ Foreign Trade
0041-6185 Ulster Commentary
0041-6193 Ulster Medical Journal
0041-6207 Ulster Motorist
0041-6223 Ultima Moda
0041-624X Ultrasonics
0041-6258 Ultreya
0041-6266 Ulysses S. Grant Association. Newsletter†
0041-6274 Umafrika
0041-6282 Umana†
0041-6290 Umanesimo†
0041-6312 Umbria Agricola
0041-6320 Umetnost
0041-6339 Umpqua Trapper
0041-6347 Umschau in Wissenschaft und Technik
0041-6355 Umwelt
0041-6371 Economic Bulletin for Asia and the Far East *changed to* Economic Bulletin for Asia and the Pacific
0041-638X Economic Bulletin for Europe
0041-6398 Economic Bulletin for Latin America *changed to* C E P A L Review
0041-6401 Statistical Bulletin for Latin America *changed to* Statistical Yearbook for Latin America
0041-641X U N A Nursing Journal†
0041-6428 Una Sancta†
0041-6436 Unasylva
0041-6444 Unausforschlicher Reichtum
0041-6452 Unauthorized Practice News†
0041-6460 Under Glass
0041-6479 Under the Sign of Pisces: Anais Nin and Her Circle
0041-6487 Undergraduate Journal of Philosophy†
0041-6533 Undersea Technology *see* 0093-3651
0041-6541 Underseas Cable World†
0041-655X Understanding
0041-6576 Understanding Japan
0041-6584 Undervisning og Velferd
0041-6592 Underwater Letter
0041-6606 Underwater Naturalist
0041-6614 Underwater Journal and Information Bulletin *see* 0302-3478
0041-6622 Underwriters' Report
0041-6630 Underwriters Review
0041-6649 Unzer Weg†
0041-6657 Unga Oernar
0041-6681 Unicorn Folio†
0041-6703 Unidad†
0041-6711 Unidad Cristiana-Oriente Cristiano
0041-672X Uniform Commercial Code Law Journal
0041-6738 Uniforms and Accessories Review
0041-6746 Cinema Francais
0041-6754 Unijapan Film Quarterly†
0041-6762 Unilit
0041-6770 Union
0041-6797 Union
0041-6800 Union Agricultural Cooperative of Syra. Bulletin
0041-6819 Union Agriculture
0041-6827 Assemblee de l'Union de l'Europe Occidentale. Bulletin Mensuel d'Information
0041-6835 Union Democracy in Action *changed to* Union Democracy Review
0041-6843 Union des Aveugles de Guerre. Bulletin Mensuel
0041-6851 Union Douaniere et Economique de l'Afrique Centrale. Bulletin des Statistiques Generales
0041-686X Electrical Union World
0041-6878 Union Farmer
0041-6908 Union Industrial Uruguaya. Guia de Socios y de Productos *changed to* Products of Uruguay
0041-6916 U I A Information
0041-6924 Union Labor News
0041-6932 Union Matematica Argentina. Revista
0041-6940 Union Medicale Balkanique. Archives
0041-6959 Union Medicale du Canada
0041-6975 Leeds Student
0041-6991 Union Postal Clerk and Postal Transport Journal *see* 0044-7811
0041-7009 Union Postale
0041-7017 Union Recorder
0041-7025 Union Seminary Quarterly Review
0041-7033 Union Signal
0041-7041 Union Sociale
0041-705X Union Technique de l'Automobile du Motocycle et du Cycle. Bulletin Mensuel de Documentation
0041-7068 Union-Tribune Index of San Diego Business Activity
0041-7076 Unione degli Industriali della Provincia di Imperia. Notiziario†
0041-7084 Unione Matematica Italiana. Bolletino
0041-7092 Unionist
0041-7106 Unitholder *see* 0028-6052
0041-7122 Unitarian Universalist World
0041-7130 Unitas
0041-7149 Unitas
0041-7157 Unite Stenographique
0041-7165 United Arab Republic Journal of Veterinary Science *changed to* Egyptian Journal of Veterinary Science
0041-7173 United Asia
0041-7181 United Association Journal
0041-719X United Bible Societies. Bulletin
0041-7203 United Business Service *see* 0360-8662
0041-722X United Church Herald *changed to* United Church of Christ A.D.
0041-7238 United Church Observer
0041-7246 United Church Review†
0041-7262 United Evangelical
0041-7270 United Evangelical Action
0041-7289 United Kingdom Atomic Energy Authority. List of Publications Available to the Public
0041-7300 United Lutheran
0041-7319 United Methodist Periodical Index
0041-7327 United Mine Workers Journal
0041-7335 Asian Development Institute. Newsletter *changed to* A D I Quarterly News Letter
0041-7343 United Nations. Current Bibliographical Information
0041-7351 U N D E X
0041-736X Economic Bulletin for Africa
0041-7378 Quarterly Bulletin of Steel Statistics for Europe
0041-7386 International Social Development Review
0041-7394 United Nations Library. Geneva. Monthly List of Books Catalogued in the Library of the United Nations
0041-7408 United Nations Library. Monthly List of Selected Articles
0041-7416 United Nations. Population and Vital Statistics Report
0041-7424 U. N. Quarterly Housing Construction Summary for Europe *changed to* U. N. Annual Bulletin of Housing and Building Statistics for Europe
0041-7432 United Nations Statistical Office. Monthly Bulletin of Statistcs
0041-7440 United Neighborhood Houses. News
0041-7459 United Paper *see* 0363-6437
0041-7475 United Rubber Worker
0041-7483 U S A
0041-7491 United States Air Force Medical Service Digest
0041-7505 U. S. Army Natick Laboratories. Activities Report *changed to* Research & Development Associates for Military Food and Packaging Systems. Activities Report
0041-7513 U.S. Army Recruiting and Career Counseling Journal *see* 0192-6071
0041-753X United States Book Exchange Newsletter *changed to* U S B E News
0041-7548 U S Catholic
0041-7556 U. S. Chemical Patents†
0041-7564 U.S. Coast Guard. Merchant Marine Council. Proceedings *see* 0364-0981
0041-7572 U.S. Consumer *changed to* Consumer Newsweekly
0041-7610 U. S. Department of State. Bulletin
0041-7629 U.S. Department of State. Newsletter
0041-7637 U S Farm News
0041-7645 U. S. Federal Home Loan Bank Board. Journal
0041-7653 U S Fur Rancher *changed to* Fur Rancher
0041-7661 U S Glass, Metal & Glazing
0041-770X U. S. I. Journal
0041-7718 United States Investor *see* 0148-8848
0041-7726 L C Card Number Index to the National Union Catalog
0041-7734 U.S. Library of Congress. Accessions List: India†
0041-7742 U. S. Library of Congress. Accessions List: Indonesia, Malaysia, Singapore and Brunei *see* 0096-2341
0041-7769 U.S. Library of Congress. Accessions List: Middle East
0041-7777 U. S. Library of Congress. Accessions List: Pakistan†
0041-7785 U.S. Library of Congress. Books: Subjects *see* 0096-8803
0041-7793 U. S. Library of Congress Catalog-Music and Phonorecords *see* 0092-2838
0041-7807 U. S. Library of Congress Catalog-Motion Pictures and Filmstrips *see* 0091-3294
0041-7815 U.S. Copyright Office. Catalog of Copyright Entries. Third Series. Part 1. Books and Pamphlets *see* 0163-7290
0041-7815 U.S. Copyright Office. Catalog of Copyright Entries. Third Series. Part 1. Books and Pamphlets, Including Serials and Contributions to Periodicals *see* 0163-7304
0041-784X U.S. Copyright Office. Catalog of Copyright Entries. Third Series. Part 2. Periodicals *see* 0163-7304
0041-7858 U.S. Copyright Office. Catalog of Copyright Entries. Third Series. Parts 3-4. Drama and Works Prepared for Oral Delivery *see* 0163-7312
0041-7866 U.S. Copyright Office Catalog of Copyright Entries. Third Series. Part 5. Music *see* 0163-7312
0041-7874 U.S. Copyright Office. Catalog of Copyright Entries. Third Series. Part 6. Maps and Atlases *see* 0163-7347
0041-7882 U.S. Copyright Office. Catalog of Copyright Entries. Third Series. Parts 7-11A. Works of Art *see* 0163-7339
0041-7890 U.S. Library of Congress. Cataloging Service *see* 0160-8029
0041-7904 U. S. Library of Congress. Information Bulletin
0041-7912 U. S. Library of Congress. L. C. Classification - Additions and Changes
0041-7920 U.S. Library of Congress Pl-480 Newlsetter *see* 0095-0629
0041-7939 U. S. Library of Congress. Quarterly Journal

ISSN INDEX 1067

0041-7947 U. S. Library of Congress. Subject Headings Used in the Dictionary Catalogs of the Library of Congress *changed to* U. S. Library of Congress Subject Headings Supplement
0041-7955 United States Municipal News *changed to* Mayor
0041-7971 United States National Student Association Newsletter *see* 0098-5570
0041-798X U. S. Naval Institute. Proceedings
0041-7998 U.S. Navy Medical News Letter *see* 0364-6807
0041-8013 U. S. P. Boletim Informativo
0041-8021 U.S. Patent Office. Official Gazette *see* 0098-1133
0041-8021 U.S. Patent Office. Official Gazette *see* 0360-5132
0041-803X United States Patents Quarterly
0041-8048 U S Piper
0041-8056 United States Review†
0041-8072 Gosudarstvennaya Biblioteka S. S. S. R. im. V. I. Lenina. Informatsionnyi Byulleten' Novykh Inostrannykh Knig, Postupivshikh v Biblioteku. Seriya 1: Fiziko - Matematicheskie i Khimicheskie Nauki; Nauki o Zemle; Tekhnika i Tekhnicheskie Nauki
0041-8080 Gosudarstvennaya Biblioteka S. S. S. R. im. V. I. Lenina. Informatsionnyi Byulleten' Novykh Inostrannykh Knig, Postupivshikh v Biblioteku. Seriya 3: Obshchestvennye Nauki; Khudozhestvennaya Literatura; Iskusstvo
0041-8099 United States Ski News†
0041-8102 U S Steel News
0041-8110 U S Steel Quarterly
0041-8129 U S Tax Week
0041-8137 United States Tobacco Journal
0041-8153 United Synagogue Review
0041-8161 United Teacher *changed to* New York Teacher
0041-817X Uniter
0041-8188 Unity Daily Word
0041-820X Universal News *changed to* Pipeline Digest
0041-8218 Universalist
0041-8226 Universe
0041-8234 Universidad
0041-8242 Universidad
0041-8250 Universidad Argentina de la Empresa. Revista†
0041-8277 Universidad Autonoma de Santo Domingo. Biblioteca Central. Boletin de Adquisiciones
0041-8285 Universidad Central de Venezuela. Facultad de Agronomia. Revista
0041-8293 Universidad Central de Venezuela. Facultad de Derecho. Revista *changed to* Universidad Central de Venezuela. Facultad de Ciencias Juridicas y Politicas. Revista
0041-8307 Universidad Central de Venezuela. Facultad de Farmacia. Revista
0041-8323 Universidad de Antioquia. Instituto de Antropologia. Boletin de Antropologia *see* 0010-6364
0041-8331 Universidad de Buenos Aires. Facultad de Filosofia y Letras. Gaceta
0041-834X Universidad de Buenos Aires, Instituto Bibliotecologico. Boletin Informativo
0041-8358 Universidad de Chile. Anales†
0041-8366 Universidad de Chile. Biblioteca. Instituto de Economia. Boletin *changed to* Universidad de Chile. Facultad de Ciencias Economicas y Adinistrativas. Biblioteca. Lista de Memorias y Libros Seleccionados
0041-8390 Universidad de Cuenca. Anales
0041-8404 Universidad de Guadalajara. Instituto de Astronomia y Meteorologia. Informacion
0041-8412 Universidad de Guayaquil. Facultad de Ciencias Medicas. Revista
0041-8420 Universidad de la Habana. Publicacion
0041-8439 Universidad de la Republica. Facultad de Ciencias Economicas y Administracion. Instituto de Estadistica. Indice de Precios al Consumidor
0041-8447 Universidad de la Republica. Facultad de Humanidades y Ciencias. Publicaciones
0041-8455 Universidad de la Republica. Hospital de Clinicas. Informe Estatistico
0041-848X Universidad de Narino. Biblioteca Central. Boletin Informativo y Bibliograficas†
0041-8498 Universidad Autonoma de Nuevo Leon. Centro de Investigaciones Economicas. Boletin Bimestral
0041-851X Universidad de Puerto Rico. Escuela de Derecho. Revista Juridica
0041-8528 Universidad de Puerto Rico. Servicio de Extension Agricola. Boletin Ganadero†
0041-8536 Universidad de Yucatan. Revista
0041-8544 Universidad Externado de Colombia. Revista
0041-8552 Universidad Hispalense. Anales. Series: Filosofia y Letras, Derecho, Medicina, Ciencias y Veterinaria *changed to* Anales de la Universidad Hispalense. Serie: Filosofia y Letras
0041-8579 Universidad Industrial de Santander. Boletin Informativo†
0041-8587 Universidad Industrial de Santander. Revista *see* 0120-0852
0041-8595 Universidad Boliviana Mayor de San Andres. Facultad de Derecho Revista de Derecho
0041-8609 Universidad Mayor de San Andres. Gaceta Universitaria†
0041-8617 Universidad Boliviana Mayor de San Simon. Instituto de Estudios Sociales y Economicos. Revista
0041-8625 Universidad Nacional de la Plata. Revista
0041-8633 Boletin Mexicano de Derecho Comparado
0041-8641 Universidad Nacional de Cordoba. Biblioteca de Ciencias Economicas. Noticias†
0041-8641 Noticias de la Biblioteca
0041-865X Universidad Nacional de Cordoba. Instituto de Administracion. Revista *changed to* Revista de Ciencias Administrativas
0041-8668 Universidad Nacional de Cuyo. Facultad de Ciencias Economicas. Revista
0041-8676 Universidad Nacional de la Plata. Facultad de Agronomia. Revista
0041-8684 Universidad Nacional de Rosario. Facultad de Ciencias, Ingenieria y Arquitectura. Instituto de Fisiografia y Geologia. Publicaciones
0041-8714 Universidad Nacional Mayor de San Marcos. Boletin Universitario†
0041-8730 Universidad Pontificia Bolivariana†
0041-8749 Universidad Tecnica Federico Santa Maria. Boletin Informativo†
0041-8765 Universidade de Coimbra. Museum Zoologico. Memorias e Estudos *changed to* Ciencia Biologica: Biologia Molecular e Celular
0041-8781 Universidade de Sao Paulo. Hospital das Clinicas. Revista
0041-8803 Universidade de Sao Paulo. Museu de Arte Contemporanea. Boletim Informativo
0041-8811 Universidad del Zulia. Revistas
0041-8838 Universidade Federal de Minas Gerais. Escola de Engenharia. Revista
0041-8846 Universidade Federal de Santa Maria. Faculdade de Farmacia e Bioquimica. Revista
0041-8854 Arquivos de Ciencias do Mar
0041-8862 Revista de Ciencias Sociais
0041-8870 Universidade Federal do Ceara. Departamento de Ciencias Sociais e Filosofia. Documentos
0041-8889 Universidade Federal do Ceara. Faculdade de Medicina. Revista *changed to* Universidade Federal do Ceara. Faculdade de Medicina. Revista de Medicina
0041-8900 Universidade do Parana. Departamento do Botanica e Farmacognosia. Boletim *see* 0301-2123
0041-8919 Universidade Federal do Rio de Janeiro. Faculdade de Odontologia. Anais
0041-8927 Universidade Federal do Rio Grande do Norte. Instituto de Biologia Marinha. Boletim
0041-8935 Universidades
0041-8943 Universita degli Studi Perugia. Istituto di Anatomia e Istologia. Lavori†
0041-8951 Universita degli Studi di Cagliari. Facolta di Scienza. Seminario. Rendiconti
0041-896X Universita degli Studi di Firenze. Istituto di Statistica. Documentazione
0041-8978 Universita degli Studi di Genova. Istituto di Geologia. Atti
0041-8986 Universita degli Studi di Modena. Seminario Matematico e Fisico. Atti
0041-8994 Universita di Padova. Seminario Matematico. Rendiconti
0041-9001 Universita Urbinate. Notiziario Mensile†
0041-9036 Etudes Scientifiques
0041-9044 Universitario
0041-9060 Universitas
0041-9079 Universitas
0041-9087 Universitas Comeniana. Acta Pharmaceuticae
0041-9095 Universitas Medica
0041-9109 Universitatea "Al. I. Cuza" din Iasi. Analele Stiintifice. Sectiunea 1A: Matematica
0041-9117 Universitatea "Al. I. Cuza" din Iasi. Analele Stiintifice. Sectiunea 1c: Chimie
0041-9125 Universitatea "Al. I. Cuza" din Iasi. Analele Stiintifice. Sectiunea 3a: Istorie
0041-9133 Universitatea "Al. I. Cuza" din Iasi. Analele Stiintifice. Sectiunea 2a: Biologie
0041-9141 Universitatea "Al. I. Cuza" din Iasi. Analele Stiintifice Sectiunea 1b: Fizica
0041-915X Universite de Lausanne. Faculte des Lettres. Publications
0041-9168 Universite de Montreal. Institute Botanique. Contributions
0041-9176 Universite de Paris. Annales†
0041-9206 Universite d'Ottawa. Revue
0041-9214 Universite Laval. Fonds de Recherches Forestieres. Bulletin
0041-9222 Universite Moderne
0041-9230 Universities Quarterly *see* 0307-8612
0041-9249 University
0041-9257 University Affairs
0041-9265 University Bookman
0041-9273 University College Hospital Magazine
0041-9281 University College Quarterly
0041-929X University Engineer†
0041-9303 University Equipment
0041-9311 University Film Association. Journal
0041-932X University Jewish Voice†
0041-9346 University of Alabama in Birmingham. Medical Center Bulletin *changed to* University of Alabama, Birmingham. Medical Center
0041-9354 University of Alaska. Anthropological Papers
0041-9362 University of Alaska. Geophysical Institute. Report Series
0041-9370 University of Alberta. Department of Chemistry. Division of Theoretical Chemistry. Technical Report
0041-9389 University of Arizona. Agricultural Experiment Station. Technical Bulletin
0041-9397 University of Auckland Gazette *changed to* University of Auckland News
0041-9400 University of Auckland. Fine Arts Library. Bulletin
0041-9419 University of Baghdad. Faculty of Medicine. Journal
0041-9427 University of British Columbia Library. Asian Studies Division. List of Catalogued Books†
0041-9435 University of California U C News Clip Sheet *changed to* U C Clip Sheet
0041-9443 University of California. Institute of Governmental Studies Library. Accessions List
0041-946X University of California. Seismographic Stations. Bulletin
0041-9486 University of Chicago. Department & Graduate School of Education. Newsletter *changed to* Education on the Midway
0041-9494 University of Chicago Law Review
0041-9508 University of Chicago Magazine
0041-9516 University of Colorado Law Review
0041-9524 University of Dayton Review
0041-9532 University of Denver Alumni News *changed to* University of Denver News
0041-9559 Journal of Urban Law *changed to* University of Detroit Journal of Urban Law
0041-9567 University of Edinburgh Journal
0041-9583 University of Florida Law Review
0041-9605 University of Ghana Law Journal
0041-9613 University of Ibadan. Department of Linguistics and Nigerian Languages. Research Notes
0041-963X University of Illinois Law Forum
0041-9648 University of Iowa. School of Library Science. Newsletter
0041-9656 University of Iowa Studies in Natural History†
0041-9664 Washburn University. Department of Chemistry. Register
0041-9672 University of Kansas. Museum of Art. Register *changed to* University of Kansas. Helen Foresman Spencer Museum of Art. Register
0041-9680 University of Kansas Newsletter
0041-9702 University of Kansas School of Medicine and Medical Center. Bulletin *changed to* University of Kansas College of Health Sciences and Hospital. Bulletin
0041-9737 University of Leeds Review
0041-977X University of London. School of Oriental and African Studies. Bulletin
0041-9788 Library Review
0041-9796 University of Manila Law Gazette
0041-980X University of Manitoba Alumni Journal
0041-9818 University of Miami Law Review
0041-9826 University of Michigan Medical Center Journal
0041-9834 University of Michigan. Museum of Paleontology. Contributions
0041-9842 University of Michigan. Division of Research Development and Administration. Research News
0041-9850 Michigan Today
0041-9869 University of Minnesota Alumni News
0041-9877 University of Montana Law School News
0041-9885 University of Nebraska. Museum Notes
0041-9893 University of North Carolina School of Library Science. Alumni Association Bulletin. *changed to* News from Chapel Hill
0041-9907 University of Pennsylvania Law Review
0041-9915 University of Pittsburgh Law Review
0041-9923 University of Portland Review
0041-9931 University of Puerto Rico Dental School Newsletter†
0041-994X University of Puerto Rico. Journal of Agriculture
0041-9958 University of Queensland. Computer Centre. Computer Centre Bulletin
0041-9974 University of Rochester Library Bulletin
0041-9990 University of San Carlos. University Bulletin
0042-000X University of San Fernando Valley Law Review *changed to* San Fernando Valley Law Review

1068 ISSN INDEX

ISSN	Title
0042-0018	University of San Francisco Law Review
0042-0026	University of Saskatchewan. University News
0042-0034	University of Sheffield. Diary of Events *see* 0309-0191
0042-0042	University of South Carolina Education Report
0042-0050	University of South Carolina Governmental Review *changed to* Public Affairs Bulletin
0042-0069	University of South Dakota Bulletin
0042-0077	University of South Florida Language Quarterly
0042-0085	Trojan Family
0042-0093	University of Sydney. Australian Language Research Centre. Occasional Papers
0042-0107	University of Sydney. Gazette
0042-0115	University of Sydney. Postgraduate Committee in Medicine. Bulletin
0042-0123	University of Teheran. Faculty of Veterinary Medicine. Journal
0042-0131	University of Teheran. Faculty of Science. Quarterly Bulletin
0042-014X	University Medical
0042-0158	U E Business Review
0042-0174	University of the State of New York Bulletin†
0042-0182	University of the Witwatersrand, Johannesburg. University Gazette
0042-0190	University of Toledo Law Review
0042-0204	University of Toronto. Department of Computer Science. Technical Reports
0042-0212	University of Toronto Graduate
0042-0220	University of Toronto Law Journal
0042-0239	University of Toronto Medical Journal
0042-0247	University of Toronto Quarterly
0042-0255	University of Toronto Undergraduate Dental Journal
0042-0271	University of Virginia News Letter
0042-0298	University of Washington Business Review *see* 0194-0430
0042-0301	University of Washington. College of Education Record
0042-031X	University of Waterloo. Gazette
0042-0328	University of Western Australia Law Review
0042-0336	University of Western Ontario Medical Journal
0042-0344	University of Western Ontario. Alumni Gazette
0042-0352	University of Windsor Review
0042-0360	University (Philippines)
0042-0379	University Review *changed to* New Letters
0042-0387	University Seminar Directory†
0042-0395	University Vision†
0042-0409	Universo
0042-0417	Universum†
0042-0425	Univerzitet Danas
0042-0433	Uniwersytet Warszawski. Instytut Geograficzny. Katedra Klimatologii. Biuletyn
0042-0441	Unlisted Drugs
0042-045X	Unlisted Drugs on Cards
0042-0468	Unscheduled Events
0042-0476	Unsearchable Riches
0042-0484	Unser Neustadt
0042-0492	Unser Schaffen
0042-0506	Unser Tsait
0042-0549	Unsere Wirtschaft
0042-0565	Unterhaltungskunst
0042-0573	Unternehmensforschung/Operations Research/Recherche Operationnelle *see* 0340-9422
0042-0581	Der Unternehmer
0042-059X	Unternehmung
0042-0603	Unterricht Heute†
0042-0611	Unterrichtsblaetter fuer die Bundeswehrverwaltung
0042-0638	Unterstufe
0042-0646	Uomini e Idee
0042-0654	Uomini e Libri
0042-0662	Up against the Wall Street Journal
0042-07C0	Upholstering Industry
0042-0725	Upper Room
0042-0743	Uproar
0042-0778	Uradni Vestnik Obcin Ormoz in Ptuj
0042-0786	Ural-Altaische Jahrbuecher
0042-0794	Urania
0042-0816	Urban Affairs Quarterly
0042-0824	Urban and Rural Planning Thought
0042-0832	Urban and Social Change Review
0042-0840	Urban Crisis Monitor†
0042-0859	Urban Education
0042-0867	Urban Employment†
0042-0875	Urban Georgia
0042-0883	Urban History Newsletter†
0042-0891	Urban Land
0042-0905	Urban Lawyer
0042-0913	Urban Memo†
0042-0921	Urban Renewal and Low-Income Housing *see* 0383-3003
0042-0948	Urban Reporter†
0042-0956	Urban Research Bulletin/Bulletin de Recherches Urbaines *see* 0318-8140
0042-0964	Urban Research News†
0042-0972	Urban Review
0042-0980	Urban Studies
0042-1006	Urban World†
0042-1014	Urbanisme
0042-1022	Urbanistica
0042-1C30	Urbe
0042-1C57	Urdu Adab
0042-1065	Urdu Namah
0042-1073	Urim La-Orim
0042-1081	Urmager-Tidende *changed to* Ure og Optik
0042-1103	Urologe-Ausgabe A *see* 0340-2592
0042-1111	Urologe-Ausgabe B *changed to* Der Urologe. Section B
0042-112X	Urologia
0042-1138	Urologia Internationalis
0042-1146	Urological Survey
0042-1154	Urologiya i Nefrologiya
0042-1162	Urology and Nephrology *see* 0301-1623
0042-1170	Urology Digest *see* 0148-5172
0042-1189	Uruguay Filatelico
0042-1197	Urval
0042-1200	Urzica
0042-1219	U. S. Federal Register. (Microfiche Edition)
0042-1227	U S Medicine
0042-1235	Us Wurk
0042-1243	Use of English
0042-1251	Usine Automation†
0042-126X	Usine Nouvelle
0042-1286	Usines et Industries
0042-1294	Uspekhi Fizicheskikh Nauk
0042-1308	Uspekhi Khimii
0042-1316	Uspekhi Matematicheskikh Nauk
0042-1324	Uspekhi Sovremennoi Biologii
0042-1340	Eko-Index
0042-1359	Ustredni Ustav Geologicky. Vestnik
0042-1367	Ut de Smidte fan de Fryske Akademy
0042-1375	Utah Cattleman
0042-1383	Utah Construction Report
0042-1391	Utah Eagle
0042-1405	Utah Economic and Business Review
0042-1413	U E A Action
0042-1421	Utah Geological and Mineral Survey. Quarterly Review *see* 0362-6288
0042-143X	Utah Historical Quarterly
0042-1448	Utah Law Review
0042-1456	Utah Libraries
0042-1472	Utah P T A Bulletin *changed to* Sound-off
0042-1480	Utah Peace Officer *changed to* Code 10-5
0042-1499	Utah Publisher and Printer
0042-1502	Utah Science
0042-1529	Utah State Historical Society Newsletter
0042-1537	Utan Grans
0042-1553	Ute och Hemma
0042-157X	Uthon
0042-1596	Utility Supervision
0042-160X	Utrikespolitiska Institut. Archives *changed to* World Press Archives
0042-1618	Uttar Bharat Bhoogol Patrika
0042-1626	Uttar Pradesh. State Planning Institute. Quarterly Bulletin of Statistics
0042-1642	Uusi Maailma *see* 0355-3043
0042-1650	Uw Koninkrijk Kome
0042-1669	Uw Rijk Komet
0042-1685	Uzbekskii Biologicheskii Zhurnal
0042-1693	Uzbekskii Geologicheskii Zhurnal
0042-1707	Uzbekskii Khimicheskii Zhurnal
0042-1715	V A M Mededelingen
0042-1723	V A S L A
0042-1731	V D I/V D E Dokumentation Regelungstechnik *see* 0340-3955
0042-174X	V D I-Forschungshefte
0042-1758	V D I-Nachrichten
0042-1766	V D I-Z
0042-1774	V D K-Mitteilungen *changed to* V D K-Mitteilungen Sozialpolitische Fachzeitschrift
0042-1782	V D M A-Wirtschaftsbild
0042-1790	V E A News
0042-1820	V. F. W. Magazine
0042-1839	V I C A
0042-1847	V I P: The Playboy Club Magazine
0042-1871	V-Illustriert
0042-188X	V Mire Knig
0042-1898	V. G. R. O-Mededelingen†
0042-1901	Vereinigung Schweizerischer Petroleum-Geologen und -Ingenieure. Bulletin
0042-191X	V S S D A Newsletter *changed to* V S B A Newsletter
0042-1928	V S T Revue
0042-1944	V V S
0042-1952	V W *changed to* Auto Toeruit
0042-1960	V W D-Kaffee-Spezialdienst
0042-1979	V W D-Kaffee Uebersee Sonderdienst
0042-1987	V W D-Kakao-Spezialdienst
0042-1995	Va-Nytt
0042-2002	Vaar Bostad
0042-2010	Vaar Fana
0042-2029	Vaar Skole†
0042-2037	Vaart Vern
0042-2053	Vacature
0042-207X	Vacuum
0042-2088	Vado e Torno
0042-2126	Vaerksteds Nyt *see* 0106-0104
0042-2134	Vaerldshorisont
0042-2142	Vaerldsmarknad
0042-2150	Vaestgoetalitteratur
0042-2177	Vaeg- och Vattenbyggaren
0042-2185	Vaegnytt
0042-2193	Vagabond†
0042-2215	Vakblad voor Biologen
0042-2223	Vakblad voor de Bloemisterij
0042-2231	Vakblad voor de Meubelindustrie *see* 0165-4543
0042-224X	Vakblad voor Textielreiniging
0042-2258	Vakstudie Nieuws
0042-2266	Vakuum-Technik
0042-2274	Vale do Rio dos Sinos *changed to* Perspectiva Economica
0042-2290	Valitut Patat
0042-2304	Valle Santa di Rieti
0042-2312	Vallecchi Informa
0042-2339	Valley Views†
0042-2347	Enforcement Journal
0042-2363	Valparaiso University Law Review
0042-2371	Valsalva
0042-238X	Valuation Magazine
0042-2398	Value Line Convertible Survey *changed to* Value Line Option & Convertible Survey
0042-2401	Value Line Investment Survey
0042-241X	Valuer
0042-2428	Valuer
0042-2436	Valve Information Report *changed to* Impact-Valves
0042-2444	Nav-Chitrapat
0042-2452	Van der Werff & Hubrecht N.V. Beursoverzicht
0042-2460	Van Steenwyk News Letter
0042-2479	Vancouver Art Gallery. Bulletin *see* 0315-5226
0042-2487	Vancouver Historical Society. Newsletter
0042-2495	Vancouver Public Aquarium Newsletter *see* 0700-9275
0042-2509	Vand†
0042-2517	Vanderbilt Hustler
0042-2525	Vanderbilt International *see* 0090-2594
0042-2533	Vanderbilt Law Review
0042-2541	Vanfoerebladet
0042-255X	Vanguard (San Francisco)
0042-2568	Vanguard (Valparaiso)
0042-2584	Vanity Fair *see* 0018-4551
0042-2614	Vantaggio
0042-2622	Vanyajati
0042-2630	Vapor Trail's Competition News and Manufacturing Report *changed to* Vapor Trail's Boating News & International Yachting & Cruiser and Manufacturers Report
0042-2649	Vaar Faagelvaerld
0042-2657	Vaar Foeda
0042-2665	Var Konst
0042-2673	Vaar Kyrka
0042-2681	Var Naring
0042-269X	Vaara Hundar
0042-2703	Vaara Paelsdjur
0042-2711	Varazdinske Vijesti
0042-272X	Variator
0042-2738	Variety
0042-2754	Vaerldspolitikens Dagsfragor
0042-2762	Varlik
0042-2770	Varme og Sanitets Nyt
0042-2789	Varsity
0042-2797	Varsity
0042-2800	Vaart Foersvar
0042-2819	Vaart Roeda Kors
0042-2827	Vartavaha†
0042-2843	Vaskeri-Tidende *changed to* Vask-Rens-Rengoering
0042-2851	Vassar Quarterly
0042-286X	Vaste Goederen *changed to* Vastgoed
0042-2878	Vasudha Monthly
0042-2886	Vatten
0042-2908	Vauxhall Motorist†
0042-2924	Vcelarstvi
0042-2932	Ve Venezuela
0042-2940	Veckojournalen *changed to* Maanadsjournalen
0042-2959	Vector†
0042-2983	Vedanta Kesari
0042-2991	Vedecky Svet†
0042-3009	Vedetta†
0042-3017	Verkhovnyi Sovet S.S.S.R. Vedomosti
0042-3025	Vee-en Vleeshandel†
0042-3033	Bedrijfsontwikkeling. Editie Veehouderij *changed to* Bedrijfsontwikkeling
0042-3041	Veevoeding
0042-305X	Vega
0042-3068	Vegetable Crop Management
0042-3084	U.S. Department of Agriculture. Economics, Statistics, and Cooperatives Service. Vegetable Situation
0042-3092	Vegetables Newsletter
0042-3106	Vegetatio
0042-3114	Vehicle System Dynamics
0042-3122	Veilig Vliegen
0042-3130	Veilig Werken
0042-3149	Veiligheid
0042-3157	Veilingberichten
0042-3165	Veja
0042-3173	Vejen Frem
0042-3211	Vela e Motore
0042-322X	Velikogoricki List
0042-3238	Velki
0042-3254	Veltro
0042-3262	Veluws Kerkblad
0042-3297	Vend *see* 0042-3327
0042-3319	Vending Engineer†
0042-3327	Vending Times
0042-3343	Vene
0042-3351	Veneficus
0042-336X	Turismo in Italia *changed to* Italia Turistica
0042-3378	Venezuela. Archivo General de la Nacion. Boletin
0042-3394	Venezuela. Ministerio de Minas e Hidrocarburos. Carta Semanal *changed to* Venezuela. Ministerio de Energia y Minas. Carta Semanal

ISSN INDEX

0042-3408	Venezuela. Ministerio de Minas e Hidrocarburos. Informations *changed to* Venezuela. Ministerio de Energia y Minas. Informations
0042-3416	Venezuela. Ministerio de Minas e Hidrocarburos. Monthly Bulletin *changed to* Venezuela. Ministerio de Energia y Minas. Monthly Bulletin
0042-3424	Venezuela Odontologia
0042-3432	Venezuela Up-to-Date
0042-3440	Vent - Art
0042-3459	Ventana
0042-3467	Ventil
0042-3483	Venture
0042-3491	Ventura County Historical Society Quarterly
0042-3513	Venture
0042-3548	Venture
0042-3556	Venture-the Traveler's World†
0042-3564	Ventures†
0042-3572	Venturi
0042-3580	Venus: Japanese Journal of Malacology
0042-3599	Vera Giustizia Sociale
0042-3610	Anzeiger des Verbandes der Antiquare Oesterreichs
0042-3629	Verband der Bibliotheken des Landes Nordrhein-Westfalen. Mitteilungsblatt
0042-3637	Verband Oesterreichischer Landsmannschaften Nachrichten-und Mitteilungsblatt
0042-3645	Verband Schweizerischer Verkehrsvereine und der Verband Schweizerischer Kur- und Verkehrsdirektoren. Bulletin†
0042-3653	Verbraucher-Politische Korrespondenz
0042-3661	Verbraucher Rundschau
0042-367X	Verbrauchermarkt-Information *changed to* S B - Warenhaus
0042-3688	Verbum
0042-3696	Verbum
0042-370X	Communion/Verbum Caro
0042-3718	Verdad y Vida
0042-3726	Vysoka Skola Banska. Sbornik Vedeckych Praci: Rada Hutnicka
0042-3734	Verdi
0042-3750	Verein der Freunde Carnuntums. Mitteilungen
0042-3769	S.W.A. Scientific Society. Verein fuer Hochlenforschung. Arbeitsberichte†
0042-3777	Verein fuer Krebsforschung. Mitteilungen
0042-3785	V G B Mitteilungen *see* 0372-5715
0042-3807	Nachrichten V S B/S V D
0042-3815	Schweizerische Vereinigung der Versicherungsmathematiker. Mitteilungen
0042-3831	Verein Schweizerischer Lithographiebesitzer. Mitteilungen
0042-384X	Vereinte Nationen
0042-3858	Vereniging van Vrienden van de Nederlandse Ceramiek. Mededelingenblad *changed to* Nederlandse Vereniging van Vrienden van de Ceramiek. Mededelingenblad
0042-3866	Vereniging voor Naamkunde. Mededelingen *changed to* Naamkunde
0042-3874	Vereniging voor Nederlandse Muziekgeschiedenis. Tijdschrift
0042-3882	Vereniging voor Oppervlaktetechnieken van Metalen. Documentatieservice *changed to* Vereniging voor Oppervlaktetechnicken van Materialen. Documentatieservice
0042-3890	Verfahrenstechnische Berichte
0042-3904	Verfkroniek
0042-3912	Verge†
0042-3920	Vergleichende Paedagogik
0042-3939	Verhuetet Unfaelle
0042-3947	Veritas
0042-3955	Veritas
0042-3963	Veritas
0042-3971	Verite *changed to* Magnificat - la Verite
0042-398X	Verkeersrecht
0042-3998	Verkeerstechniek *changed to* Verkeerskunde
0042-4005	Verkehr und Technik
0042-4013	Verkehrsblatt
0042-4021	Verkehrsmedizin und ihre Grenzgebiete
0042-403X	Verkehrspraktiker *see* 0023-4443
0042-4048	Verkehrspsychologischer Informationsdienst
0042-4056	Verkstaederna
0042-4064	Verladen†
0042-4099	Der Vermessungsingenieur
0042-4102	Vermessungstechnik
0042-4110	Vermessungstechnische Rundschau (VR) *see* 0340-5141
0042-4129	Vermissa Herald
0042-4137	Vermont Blackboard *changed to* V E A Today
0042-4145	Vermont Catholic Tribune
0042-4161	Vermont History
0042-417X	Vermont Life
0042-4196	Vernieuwing van Opvoeding en Onderwijs *changed to* Vernieuwing van Opvoeding, Onderwijs en Maatschappij
0042-420X	Vero Dialogo
0042-4234	Verona Fathers Missions *changed to* Verona Missions
0042-4242	Verona Fedele
0042-4250	Wiener Boersekammer. Verordnungsblatt
0042-4269	Verpackung
0042-4277	Verpackung
0042-4293	Verpackungs Berater
0042-4307	Verpackungs-Rundschau
0042-4315	Verpakking
0042-4323	Verre Naasten Naderbij
0042-4331	Verres et Refractaires
0042-434X	Vers Demain
0042-4358	Versicherungswirtschaft
0042-4366	Versiones†
0042-4374	Verso l'Azzurro
0042-4382	Versorgungswirtschaft
0042-4390	Versuchsstation fuer das Gaerungsgewerbe in Wien. Mitteilungen
0042-4404	Vertebrata Palasiatica (China)
0042-4412	Vertegenwoordiger
0042-4420	Vertex
0042-4439	Vertical File Index
0042-4447	Vertice
0042-4455	Vertiflite
0042-4463	Vertragssystem *changed to* Wirtschaftsrecht
0042-4471	Vertriko Visie†
0042-448X	Vervoer *changed to* Vervoer en Transporttechniek
0042-4498	Die Verwaltung
0042-4501	Verwaltungsarchiv
0042-451X	Verwarming en Ventilatie
0042-4528	Verzekerings-Archief
0042-4536	Veseli Svet
0042-4544	Vesmir
0042-4552	Udruzenje Pravoslavnog Svestenstva SFR Jugoslavije. Glavni Savez. Vesnik
0042-4560	Vestes
0042-4579	Vestire
0042-4587	Vestnik
0042-4595	Ceskoslovenska Spolecnost Zoologicka. Vestnik
0042-4609	Vestnik Dermatologii i Venerologii
0042-4617	Vestnik Drevnei Istorii
0042-4625	Vestnik Khirurgii im. I. I. Grekova
0042-4633	Vestnik Mashinostroeniya
0042-4641	Federalni Ministerstvo Financi. Vestnik *see* 0322-9653
0042-465X	Vestnik Oftal'mologii
0042-4668	Vestnik Otorinolaringologii
0042-4676	Vestnik Rentgenologii i Radiologii
0042-4684	Vestnik Sel'skokhozyaistvennoi Nauki Kazakhstana
0042-4692	Vestnik Statistiki
0042-4706	Vestnik Svyazi
0042-4714	Urad pro Normalizaci a Mereni. Vestnik
0042-4749	Vsesoyuznyi Nauchno-Issledovatel'skii Institut Zheleznodorozhnogo Transporta. Vestnik
0042-4757	Vestnik Vysshei Shkoly
0042-4765	Veteran
0042-4773	Veteran and Vintage *changed to* Collector's Car
0042-4781	Veteran Car
0042-4811	Veterantics
0042-482X	Veterinaria Mocambicana†
0042-4838	Veterinario y la Industria
0042-4846	Veterinariya
0042-4854	Veterinary Bulletin
0042-4862	Veterinary Economics
0042-4870	Veterinary Institute, Pulawy. Bulletin
0042-4889	Veterinary Medicine/Small Animal Clinician
0042-4897	Veterinary Practice
0042-4900	Veterinary Record
0042-4919	Pionyr
0042-4935	Vetus Testamentum
0042-4943	Vi Bilaegare Med Hem och Hobby
0042-4951	Vi Menn
0042-4978	Via
0042-4986	Via Libera
0042-4994	Via Migliore
0042-5001	Via Port of New York *changed to* Via Port of New York-New Jersey
0042-5028	Vialidad
0042-5036	Viata Medicala - Cadre Superioare
0042-5044	Viata Militara
0042-5052	Viata Romineasca
0042-5060	Vibrations†
0042-5079	Vichiana
0042-5087	Vickers Voice
0042-5095	Victoria Government Gazette
0042-5109	Victoria Reports†
0042-5117	Victoria University of Wellington Law Review
0042-5125	Victorian
0042-5141	Victorian Dry Cleaner†
0042-515X	Victorian Farmer
0042-5184	Victorian Naturalist
0042-5206	Victorian Poetry
0042-5214	Victorian Reports
0042-5222	Victorian Studies
0042-5230	Victoria's Resources
0042-5265	Vida Pastoral *changed to* Pastoral Popular
0042-5281	Vide
0042-5303	Vidura
0042-5311	Vidya *changed to* Oriente e Occidente
0042-532X	Vidyodaya†
0042-5338	Vie Asistenziali *changed to* Promozione Sociale
0042-5346	Vie Canine
0042-5362	Vie Catholique du Berry
0042-5370	Vie Collective
0042-5400	Vie Communale et Departementale
0042-5419	Vie de la Douane
0042-5427	Vie de la Recherche Scientifique
0042-5435	Vie des Arts
0042-5451	Vie des Transports
0042-546X	Qui Touring
0042-5478	Vie du Rail
0042-5486	Vie et Bonte *see* 0301-0260
0042-5516	Vie et Milieu
0042-5524	Vie et Sante
0042-5532	Vie et Travail
0042-5567	Vie Judiciaire
0042-5575	Vie
0042-5583	Vie Medicale
0042-5591	Vie Musicale†
0042-5605	Vie Sociale
0042-5613	Vie Spirituelle
0042-5621	Vie Theresienne
0042-563X	Vie Urbaine
0042-5648	Vie Wallonne
0042-5656	Vient de Paraitre
0042-5672	Naturforschende Gesellschaft in Zuerich. Vierteljahresschrift
0042-5680	Vierteljahresschrift Wirtschaft und Verwaltung†
0042-5702	Vierteljahrshefte fuer Zeitgeschichte
0042-5710	Vietnam
0042-5729	Vietnam Bulletin
0042-5745	Vietnam International Information Bulletin *changed to* Vietnam/South East Asia International
0042-5788	Vietnambulletinen
0042-5796	Vieux Jardinier *changed to* Ami des Fleurs
0042-580X	View from the Bottom†
0042-5818	Viewpoints
0042-5834	Viewpoint
0042-5842	Viewpoint
0042-5850	Viewpoint†
0042-5869	Viewpoint (Indianapolis)
0042-5877	Viewpoints
0042-5877	I C A Viewpoint
0042-5893	Views†
0042-5907	Views and Ideas on Mankind
0042-5915	Views & Reviews
0042-5931	Viga en el Ojo
0042-594X	Vigencia
0042-5958	Vigilance
0042-5966	Vigilance†
0042-5974	Vigilancia
0042-6024	Vigilia
0042-6032	Vigiliae Christianae
0042-6040	Vignes & Raisins
0042-6059	Vigo County Public Library Staff Bulletin
0042-6075	Vigyan Pragati
0042-6083	Vijesti Muzealaca i Konzervatora Hrvatske
0042-6091	Vijnan Karmee
0042-6105	Vikan
0042-6113	Viikkosanomat†
0042-6121	Vikram
0042-613X	Vikrant
0042-6156	Villa & Hem i Sveriget†
0042-6164	Villa de Madrid
0042-6172	Village
0042-6180	Village Voice
0042-6199	Villager
0042-6202	Villager
0042-6210	Villamossag
0042-6229	Villanova Law Review
0042-6237	Ville-Giardini
0042-6253	Viltis
0042-6288	Vinduet
0042-6296	Vingehjulet *changed to* D S B Bladet
0042-630X	Vini d'Italia
0042-6318	Vinodelie i Vinogradarstvo S.S.S.R.
0042-6326	Vinohrad
0042-6334	Vins d'Alsace
0042-6369	Vintage Jazz Mart
0042-6385	Vinyl Technology Newsletter†
0042-6393	Vinzenzbote *changed to* Dienen und Helfen
0042-6407	Viola-Traedgardsvaerlden
0042-6415	Viomichaniki Epitheorissis
0042-6423	Virchows Archiv. Abteilung A: Pathologische Anatomie *see* 0340-1227
0042-6431	Virchows Archiv. Abt.B. Zellpathologie-Cell Pathology *see* 0340-6075
0042-644X	Virginia Accountant
0042-6458	Virginia Advocate
0042-6466	Virginia Agricultural Economics
0042-6474	Virginia Cavalcade
0042-6482	Virginia. Department of Agriculture. Bulletin
0042-6490	Virginia Economic Indicators
0042-6504	Virginia Forward†
0042-6512	Virginia Geographer
0042-6520	Virginia Health Bulletin
0042-6547	Virginia Highway Bulletin *changed to* Virginia Department of Highways and Transportation Bulletin
0042-6555	Virginia Historical Society. Occasional Bulletin
0042-6563	Virginia Journal of Education
0042-6571	Virginia Journal of International Law
0042-658X	Virginia Journal of Science
0042-6598	Kirkus Reviews
0042-6601	Virginia Law Review
0042-661X	Virginia Law Weekly
0042-6628	Virginia Librarian
0042-6636	Virginia Magazine of History and Biography
0042-6652	Virginia Minerals
0042-6660	Virginia Municipal Review

ISSN	Title
0042-6687	Virginia Museum of Fine Arts. Members Bulletin see 0363-3519
0042-6695	Virginia Nurse Quarterly changed to Virginia Nurse
0042-6709	Virginia P T A Bulletin
0042-6717	Virginia Pharmacist
0042-6725	Virginia Polytechnic Institute and State University. Extension News
0042-6733	Virginia Poultryman
0042-6741	Virginia Publisher and Printer changed to Virginia's Press
0042-675X	Virginia Quarterly Review
0042-6768	Virginia Record
0042-6776	Virginia School Boards Association Newsletter
0042-6784	Virginia Town & City
0042-6792	Virginia Wildlife
0042-6806	Virittaja
0042-6822	Virology
0042-6830	Virology Abstracts
0042-6857	Virus
0042-6865	Visages de l'Ain
0042-6873	Visao
0042-6881	Vishwakarma
0042-692X	Vision Magazine
0042-6938	Weyerhaeuser World changed to Weyerhaeuser Today
0042-6946	Vision and Voice†
0042-6954	Vision - Europe†
0042-6962	Vision Letter
0042-6970	Vision of India†
0042-6989	Vision Research
0042-6997	Visitors East
0042-7004	Visnyk
0042-7039	Vispera†
0042-7047	Visserij
0042-708X	Vista
0042-7098	Vista changed to In-Touch
0042-7101	Vista
0042-711X	Vista see 0094-5072
0042-7128	Vistazo
0042-7136	Visti Ukrayins'kykh Inzheneriv
0042-7152	Visual Education
0042-7160	Visual Medicine†
0042-7179	Visva - Bharati Patrika
0042-7187	Visva-Bharati Journal of Philosophy
0042-7195	Visva-Bharati Quarterly
0042-7209	Viswa Rachana
0042-7217	Viswasilpi
0042-7233	Vita Cattolica
0042-7241	Vita dell'Infanzia
0042-725X	Vita e Pensiero
0042-7268	Vita e Salute
0042-7276	Vita Giuseppina
0042-7284	Vita in Cristo e Nella Chiesa
0042-7292	Vida Italiana
0042-7306	Vita Latina
0042-7330	Vita Consacrata
0042-7349	Vita Scolastica
0042-7357	Vita Sindacale Bergamasca
0042-7365	Vita Sociale
0042-7381	Vital Christianity
0042-739X	Vital Issues
0042-7411	Vital Notes on Medical Periodicals
0042-742X	Vital Speeches of the Day
0042-7438	Vital Statistics Monthly Report†
0042-7446	Vitalita
0042-7470	Vitchyzna
0042-7489	Vitesse-Speed
0042-7497	Vitezna Kridla
0042-7500	Vitis
0042-7519	Vitreous Enameller
0042-7527	Vivant Univers
0042-7543	Vivarium
0042-756X	Vivienda
0042-7578	Vivir
0042-7586	Rivista del Clero Italiano
0042-7594	Vivliothiki Ghoneon
0042-7608	Vivre en Harmonie
0042-7616	Vizugyi Kozlemenyek
0042-7624	Vjesnik Komune
0042-7632	Vjesnik Rada
0042-7640	Vjesnik U Srijedu
0042-7659	Vjesnik Nadbiskupije Splitsko-Makarske
0042-7667	Vlaamse Chemische Vereniging. Mededelingen†
0042-7675	Vlaamse Gids
0042-7683	Vlaanderen
0042-7691	Vleesdistributie en Vleestechnologie
0042-7705	Vliegende Hollander
0042-7721	Foreign Trade
0042-773X	Vnitrni Lekarstvi
0042-7748	Voca Newsletter changed to County Voc- Tec News
0042-7756	Vocation
0042-7764	Vocational Guidance Quarterly
0042-7772	Vocations for Social Change changed to Workforce
0042-7780	Voce
0042-7802	Voce Bruzia
0042-7810	Voce degli Italiani
0042-7829	Voce del Tabaccaio
0042-7837	Voce della Fiera
0042-7845	Voce della Madonna delle Grazie
0042-7853	Voce di Ferrara
0042-7861	Voce di Siracusa
0042-787X	Voce Nuova changed to Voce della Regione
0042-7888	Voci Fraterne
0042-7896	Voci Nuove. Quaderni di Poesia Contemporanea
0042-790X	Vodohospodarsky Casopis
0042-7918	Vodosnabzhenie i Sanitarnaya Tekhnika
0042-7926	Voeding
0042-7934	Voedingsmiddelentechnologie
0042-7942	Voeest-Alpine Betriebeskurier
0042-7950	Voegel der Heimat
0042-7977	Voetbal International
0042-7985	Vogeljaar
0042-7993	Die Vogelwelt
0042-8000	Vogue
0042-8019	Vogue Australia
0042-8027	Vogue (Italy)
0042-8035	Vogue Living
0042-8043	Vogue Pattern Book International changed to Vogue Patterns
0042-8051	Queens Voice changed to New York Voice
0042-806X	National Institute of Rug Cleaning Voice changed to Voice (Arlington)
0042-8078	Voice of A G S
0042-8086	Voice of Ahinsa
0042-8094	Voice of Buddhism
0042-8108	Voice of Business†
0042-8116	Voice of Freedom
0042-8132	Voice of Islam
0042-8140	Voice of Jamaica
0042-8159	Voice of Liberty
0042-8167	Voice of Methodism
0042-8175	Voice of Missions
0042-8191	Voice of the Cement, Lime, Gypsum and Allied Workers
0042-8213	Voice of the Nazarene-a Universal Challenger
0042-8221	Voice of the People
0042-8248	Voice of the Unions†
0042-8256	Voice of Youth
0042-8264	Full Gospel Business Men's Voice
0042-8280	Voices International
0042-8299	Voicespondent
0042-8302	Phase Zero†
0042-8329	Voie de la Paix
0042-8337	Volk auf dem Weg
0042-837X	Voix des Enseignants
0042-8388	Voix du Silence
0042-8396	Voix et Visages
0042-840X	Vojni Glasnik
0042-8418	Vojnik
0042-8426	Vojno Delo
0042-8442	Vojnoistorijski Glasnik
0042-8450	Vojnosanitetski Pregled
0042-8469	Vojnotehnicki Glasnik
0042-8485	Vokrug Sveta
0042-8493	Volksgesundheit
0042-8507	Volkshochschule Brigittenau. Mitteilungsblatt†
0042-8515	Volkshochschule im Westen
0042-8531	Volkskunde in Oesterreich
0042-854X	Volksmacht
0042-8558	Volksmusik changed to Musikforum
0042-8574	Volkstuin
0042-8582	Wirtschaftswoche: Volkswirt changed to Wirtschaftswoche
0042-8590	Switzerland. Bundesamt fuer Industrie, Gewerbe und Arbeit. Volkswirtschaft
0042-8612	Volonte du Commerce et de l'Industrie changed to Volonte du Commerce, de l'Industrie et des Prestataires de Services
0042-8620	Volt
0042-8639	Volta Review
0042-8647	Voluntary Action
0042-8671	Volunteer
0042-868X	Volunteer Views changed to Volunteer in Education
0042-8698	Volunteer World see 0007-4942
0042-8701	Volunteer's Digest†
0042-871X	Vom S I H fuer Sie changed to S I H Bulletin
0042-8728	Voorligter
0042-8736	Voprosy Ekonomiki
0042-8744	Voprosy Filosofii
0042-8752	Voprosy Ikhtiologii
0042-8779	Voprosy Istorii
0042-8787	Voprosy Kurortologii, Fizioterapii i Lechebnoi Fizicheskoi Kul'tury
0042-8795	Voprosy Literatury
0042-8809	Voprosy Meditsinskoi Khimii
0042-8817	Voprosy Neirokhirurgii
0042-8825	Voprosy Okhrany Materinstva i Detstva
0042-8833	Voprosy Pitaniya
0042-8841	Voprosy Psikhologii
0042-885X	Voprosy Revmatizma
0042-8868	Voprosy Yazykoznaniya
0042-8884	Vorarlbergs Gewerbliche Wirtschaft changed to Vorarlbergs Wirtschaft aktuell
0042-8892	Vorschau Europa
0042-8914	Vorschau-Tabelle
0042-8922	Vorschriften fuer die Veterinaerverwaltung†
0042-8930	Vorwaerts
0042-8949	Vorwaerts
0042-8957	Vospitanie Shkol'nikov
0042-8965	Votre Beaute
0042-8973	Votre Maison
0042-8981	Vou
0042-899X	Vox Romanica
0042-9007	Vox Sanguinis
0042-9015	Vox Theologica†
0042-9031	Voyages
0042-904X	Voyageur
0042-9058	Voenno-Istoricheskii Zhurnal
0042-9066	Voennyi Vestnik
0042-9074	Voennye Znaniya
0042-9082	Voz de la Biblioteca Universitaria†
0042-9104	Vozhatyi
0042-9112	Vredesactie
0042-9139	Vriend
0042-9147	Vriend der Kinderen†
0042-9155	Vriend van Oud en Jong
0042-9163	Vrienden Kring
0042-9171	Vriendenkring van Het Rembrandthuis. Kroniek†
0042-9198	Vrishchik
0042-921X	Vrouw in Middenstand en Burgerij changed to Vrouw
0042-9228	Free State Educational News
0042-9236	Vsemirnoe Profsoyuznoe Dvizhenie
0042-9244	Vsesoyuznaya Akademiya Sel'skokhozyaistvennykh Nauk im. V. I. Lenina. Doklady
0042-9260	Vsesoyuznoe Mineralogicheskoe Obshchestvo. Zapiski
0042-9287	Vsesvit
0042-9287	Vu Par les Belges
0042-9309	Vukovarske Novine
0042-9317	Vuoriteollisus
0042-9325	Vyapar
0042-935X	Vynalezy changed to Vynalezy a Zlepsovaci Navrhy
0042-9368	Vysokomolekulyarnye Soedineniya
0042-9376	Vystavba a Architektura
0042-9384	Vytis
0042-9392	Vytvarnictvo, Fotografia, Film
0042-9406	Vyziva a Zdravie
0042-9414	Vyziva Lidu
0042-9422	Vyzvol'nyi Shlyakh
0042-9430	W. A. A. C. C. S. Motor Industry
0042-9449	W A C L Bulletin
0042-9465	W. A. Grower
0042-949X	W. A. Teachers' Journal changed to Western Teacher
0042-9503	W. A. V. A. E. News
0042-9511	W A W Newsletter
0042-952X	W & L
0042-9538	W & V
0042-9562	W B F O
0042-9570	W C L C Newsletter
0042-9589	W D
0042-9635	W E M Newsletter
0042-9643	W F L N Philadelphia Guide changed to W F L N Philadelphia Guide to Events and Places
0042-9651	Chicago Guide changed to Chicago
0042-966X	W G A Geschaeftsbericht
0042-9678	W G O - Monatshefte fuer Osteuropaeisches Recht
0042-9686	World Health Organization. Bulletin
0042-9694	W H O Chronicle
0042-9716	W I N
0042-9732	W I Z O Review
0042-9740	Indo-Iran Journal
0042-9767	W M O Bulletin
0042-9775	W N Y F
0042-9783	W P M Newletter
0042-9791	W R L News
0042-9805	Washington Recreation and Park Society. News changed to Washington Recreation and Park Association. Bulletin
0042-983X	W S D A News
0042-9864	Women Strike for Peace
0042-9872	W W I Mitteilungen changed to W S I Mitteilungen
0042-9899	W Z E Wissenschaftliche Zeitschrift der Elektrotechnik†
0042-9902	Wacht te Kooi
0042-9929	Waerme- und Stoffuebertragung
0042-9937	Waescherei- und Reinigungs-Praxis
0042-9945	Waffen- und Kostumkunde
0042-9953	Wagenbouwnieuws
0042-9961	Waggoner
0042-997X	Karosseriebauer und Wagner†
0042-9996	Die Wahrheit
0043-0005	Waiblinger Anzeigenblatt
0043-0013	Wakayama Medicine
0043-0021	Wakayama Prefecture. Monthly Report of Meteorology
0043-003X	Wake Forest Law Review
0343-0048	Die Waldarbeit
0043-0056	Wales
0043-0064	Walkabout†
0043-0072	Walker Watchword†
0043-0099	Wall Street Reports
0043-0102	Wall Street Transcript
0043-0129	Wallaces Farmer
0043-0137	Wallerstein Laboratories Communications†
0043-0145	Wallpaper and Wallcoverings†
0043-0153	Wallpaper, Paint & Wallcovering
0043-0161	Walls & Ceilings
0043-017X	Walt Whitman Review
0043-0188	Walters Art Gallery. Bulletin
0043-0196	Wanasan
0043-020X	War Communiques
0043-0218	War Cry
0043-0226	War Cry
0043-0234	War Cry
0043-0242	War Cry
0043-0250	War Cry
0043-0269	War on Hunger see 0161-1976
0043-0277	War/Peace Report see 0305-0629
0043-0307	Waratah
0043-0315	Ward's Auto World
0043-0323	Ward's Bulletin
0043-0331	Warenzeichenblatt. Teil 1: Angemeldete Zeichen
0043-034X	Warenzeichenblatt. Teil 2: Eingetragene Zeichen
0043-0358	Warmte†
0043-0374	Warship International

0043-0382 Balai Penyelidikan Perusahaan Perkebunan Gula. Warta Bulanan
0043-0404 Was Tun
0043-0412 Wascana Review
0043-0420 Washburn Law Journal
0043-0439 Washington Academy of Sciences. Journal
0043-0447 Washington Afro-American
0043-0455 Washington and Jefferson Literary Journal
0043-0463 Washington & Lee Law Review
0043-0471 Washington Atomic Energy Report and Guideletter *changed to* Washington Atomic Energy Report
0043-0501 Washington Coach
0043-051X Washington County Education News
0043-0544 Washington Diocese
0043-0552 Washington Education†
0043-0560 Washington Food Dealer Magazine
0043-0587 Washington Grange News
0043-0595 Washington Insurance Newsletter
0043-0609 Washington International Arts Letter
0043-0617 Washington Law Review
0043-0633 Washington Monthly
0043-0641 Washington Motorist
0043-065X Washington Music Educator *changed to* Voice of Washington Music Educators
0043-0684 Washington Newspaper
0043-0692 Washington Plumbing and Heating Contractor
0043-0706 Washington Purchaser
0043-0714 Washington Report
0043-0722 Washington Report
0043-0730 Washington Report on Medicine & Health
0043-0749 Science Trends
0043-0757 Washington Sounds†
0043-0765 Library Leads
0043-0773 Washington State Entomological Society Proceedings
0043-0781 Washington State Journal of Nursing
0043-0803 Washington State Research Council Monthly Report *changed to* Washington State Research Council Report
0043-0811 Washington State School Directors Association Newsletter *changed to* Signal (Olympia)
0043-082X Washington State University. Mathematics Notes
0043-0838 Washington State University. Research Studies
0043-0846 Washington State Voter
0043-0862 Washington University Law Quarterly
0043-0897 Washingtonian
0043-0927 Wasmann Journal of Biology
0043-0943 Wasser und Abwasser *changed to* Wasser und Abwasser / Bau-Intern
0043-0951 Wasser und Boden
0043-096X Wasser und Energiewirtschaft *changed to* Wasser, Energie, Luft
0043-0978 Die Wasserwirtschaft
0043-0986 Wasserwirtschaft-Wassertechnik (W W T)
0043-0994 Wasserwirtschaftliche Mitteilungen
0043-1001 Waste Age
0043-1028 Wastewater Works News
0043-1036 Wat Kan Ons Opvoer'
0043-1079 Watchmaker, Jeweller & Silversmith
0043-1087 Watchtower
0043-1117 Water and Pollution Control
0043-1125 Water and Sewage Works *changed to* Water/Engineering and Management
0043-1133 Water and Waste Treatment
0043-1141 Water and Wastes Digest
0043-115X Water and Wastes Engineering *changed to* Water/Engineering and Management
0043-1168 Water and Water Engineering *see* 0301-7028
0043-1176 Water Bodem Lucht†
0043-1184 Water Conditioning
0043-1192 Water Conditions in Wisconsin†
0043-1206 Water Desalination Report
0043-1222 Water in the News†
0043-1249 Water Law Newsletter
0043-1257 Water Management Bulletin†
0043-1265 Water News
0043-1273 Water Newsletter
0043-1281 Water Pollution Abstracts *see* 0306-6649
0043-129X Water Pollution Control
0043-1303 Water Pollution Control Federation. Journal
0043-1311 Water Polo Scoreboard
0043-1338 Water Power *changed to* Water Power and Dam Construction
0043-1346 U D S Water Quality Control Digest *changed to* Water Quality Control Digest
0043-1354 Water Research
0043-1362 Water Resources Abstracts *changed to* Hydro-Abstracts
0043-1370 Water Resources Bulletin
0043-1397 Water Resources Research
0043-1400 Water Resources Review
0043-1435 Water Spectrum
0043-1443 Water Well Journal
0043-1451 Waterkampioen
0043-146X Waterloo Campus *see* 0700-5105
0043-1486 Waterschapsbelangen
0043-1494 Watershed News
0043-1508 Watersheds†
0043-1516 Watersport†
0043-1524 Waterways Journal
0043-1532 Watsonia
0043-1540 Chalkboard
0043-1559 Wave Hill News†
0043-1567 Wavriensia
0043-1575 Way
0043-1583 Shlach
0043-1591 Way-Catholic Viewpoints *changed to* Way(San Francisco)
0043-1605 Way of Life
0043-1613 Wayne County Farm and Home News *changed to* Extension (Alton)
0043-1621 Wayne Law Review
0043-163X Wayne State University Alumni News
0043-1648 Wear
0043-1656 Weather
0043-1664 Weather Vane
0043-1672 Weatherwise
0043-1680 Webb Society Quarterly Journal
0043-1699 Webe Mit
0043-1710 Wee Wisdom (Inkprint Edition)
0043-1729 Weed Abstracts
0043-1737 Weed Research
0043-1745 Weed Science
0043-1753 Weeds, Trees and Turf
0043-177X Weekblad Cinema
0043-1788 Weekblad voor Bloembollencultuur *changed to* Bloembollencultuur
0043-1796 Weekblad voor Fiscaal Recht
0043-180X Weekend *changed to* Weekend News
0043-1818 Weekend
0043-1826 Weekend Magazine†
0043-1834 Weekly Letter Commentary†
0043-1842 Weekly Livestock Reporter
0043-1850 Weekly Market Bulletin
0043-1869 National Braille Press. Weekly News†
0043-1877 Weekly News *changed to* Sunday Herald
0043-1885 Weekly People *see* 0199-350X
0043-1893 Weekly Pharmacy Reports: The Green Sheet
0043-1907 National Promotion Audit
0043-1915 Weekly Review *see* 0307-188X
0043-1931 Weekly Summary of Countries Reporting Quarantinable Diseases *changed to* Weekly Summary of Countries with Areas Infected with Quarantinable Diseases
0043-194X Weekly Times
0043-1966 Weekly Underwriter
0043-1974 Weekly Weather and Crop Bulletin, National Summary†
0043-1982 Weekly Weather Report of Pakistan & Kashmir
0043-2008 Weekly Wool Chart *changed to* Wool Record Weekly Market Report
0043-2016 Weg en Waterbouw†
0043-2024 Weg und Ziel
0043-2032 Weg zur Gesundheit
0043-2040 Wege zum Menschen
0043-2059 Wege zur Sozialversicherung
0043-2067 Wegen
0043-2075 Gornictwo Odkrywkowe
0043-2083 Wegvervoer
0043-2091 Wegwijs in de Sportliteratuur
0043-2105 Wegwijzer
0043-2113 Wehr und Wirtschaft *changed to* Wehrtechnik, Vereinigt mit Wehr und Wirtschaft
0043-2121 Wehrausbildung in Wort und Bild
0043-2156 Wehrmedizinische Monatsschrift
0043-2164 Wehrpolitische Information
0043-2180 Weight Watchers
0043-2199 Weimarer Beitraege
0043-2202 Weiss-Blaue Rundschau
0043-2210 Welcome to Czechoslovakia
0043-2229 Welcome to Singapore†
0043-2237 Welder
0043-2245 Welding and Metal Fabrication
0043-2253 Welding Design and Fabrication
0043-227X Welding Engineer†
0043-227X Welding Engineer *see* 0043-2253
0043-2288 Welding in the World
0043-2296 Welding Journal
0043-230X Welding Production
0043-2318 Welding Research Abroad
0043-2326 Welding Research Council Bulletin
0043-2342 Welfare in Review *changed to* Human Needs
0043-2369 Welfare Reporter†
0043-2385 Welfarer†
0043-2407 Welldoer
0043-2415 Wells Fargo Bank Business Review
0043-2431 Welsh History Review
0043-244X Welsh Music
0043-2458 Welsh Nation
0043-2474 Welsh Secondary Schools Review
0043-2482 Welt der Arbeit
0043-2490 Die Welt der Buecher
0043-2512 Die Molkerei-Zeitung Welt der Milch
0043-2555 Welt-Spirale
0043-2563 Welt und Sport†
0043-258X Weltblick
0043-2598 Die Weltbuehne
0043-2601 Die Weltgewerkschaftsbewegung
0043-261X Weltkunst
0043-2628 Weltraumfahrt-Raketentechnik†
0043-2628 Weltraumfahrt - Raketentechnik *see* 0041-6347
0043-2636 Weltwirtschaftliches Archiv
0043-2644 Weltweite Hilfe
0043-2652 Die Weltwirtschaft
0043-2660 Weltwoche
0043-2679 Die Wende
0043-2687 Wendepunkt†
0043-2695 Wending
0043-2709 Werbegeschenk-Berater *see* 0341-5600
0043-2741 Wereldmarkt
0043-275X Wereldwijzer
0043-2776 Werkmeister und Techniche Arbeitsleiter/Contremaitre et Agent de Maistrise *changed to* Werkmeister
0043-2784 Werkpaedagogische Hefte†
0043-2792 Werkstatt und Betrieb
0043-2806 Werkstattstechnik *see* 0340-4544
0043-2814 Werkstoffe *changed to* Werkstoffe und Technik
0043-2822 Werkstoffe und Korrosion
0043-2830 Werkzeitung des Schweizerischen Industrie *changed to* W Z : Wirtschaftszeitung fuer Alle
0043-2849 Die Weser
0043-2857 Weserlotse
0043-2865 Wesfarmers News *changed to* Western Farmer and Grazier
0043-2873 Wesley Historical Society. Proceedings
0043-289X Wesleyan Advocate
0043-2911 Wesleyan News†
0043-292X Wessex Life†
0043-2938 West
0043-2954 West-Ost-Journal
0043-2962 West Africa
0043-2970 West African Builder and Architect
0043-2989 West African Journal of Biological and Applied Chemistry
0043-2997 West African Journal of Education
0043-3004 West African Medical Journal
0043-3020 West African Science Association Journal *see* 0029-0114
0043-3039 West African Technical Review ABC
0043-3047 West & East
0043-3071 West Bengal Labour Gazette
0043-3098 West Cameroon Monthly Digest of Statistics†
0043-3101 West Coast Druggist *changed to* Pharmacy West
0043-311X West Coast Review
0043-3128 West Country Homefinder *see* 0018-4160
0043-3136 West Georgia College Review
0043-3144 West Indian Medical Journal
0043-3152 West Indies Chronicle *changed to* Caribbean Chronicle
0043-3160 West Lancashire Evening Gazette
0043-3179 West Pakistan Journal of Agricultural Research *changed to* Journal of Agricultural Research
0043-3187 West Texas Register *changed to* West Texas Catholic
0043-3195 West Virginia Agriculture & Forestry
0043-3209 West Virginia Archaeologist†
0043-3217 West Virginia C.P.A
0043-3225 West Virginia Dental Journal
0043-3233 West Virginia Free Press
0043-3241 West Virginia Hillbilly
0043-325X West Virginia History
0043-3268 West Virginia Law Review
0043-3284 West Virginia Medical Journal
0043-3292 West Virginia Pharmacist†
0043-3306 West Virginia Progress†
0043-3314 West Virginia School Boards Association. Bulletin. *changed to* Communicator (Charleston)
0043-3322 West Virginia School Journal *see* 0274-8606
0043-3330 West Virginia. State Department of Health. Weekly Morbidity Report *changed to* State of the State's Health
0043-3349 West Virginia University Magazine *changed to* West Virginia University Alumni Magazine
0043-3357 WestArt
0043-3365 Westchester Business Journal
0043-3373 Westchester County Press
0043-339X Westchester Realtor
0043-342X Westerly
0043-3438 Westermanns Monatshefte
0043-3446 Westermanns Paedagogische Beitraege
0043-3454 Western
0043-3462 Western American Literature
0043-3470 Western Apparel Industry *changed to* Apparel Industry
0043-3489 Western Australia. Government Gazette
0043-3519 Western Banker
0043-3527 Western Buddhist†
0043-3535 Western Builder
0043-3551 Western Carolina University Journal of Education†
0043-356X Western City
0043-3578 Western Collector *changed to* Avon Collectors Newsletter
0043-3594 Western Confectioner and Tobacconist *changed to* American Buyer's Review
0043-3608 Western Conservation Journal
0043-3624 Western Construction & Industry
0043-3640 Western Economic Journal *see* 0095-2583
0043-3659 Western Electric Engineer
0043-3675 Western European Education
0043-3691 Western Farm Equipment
0043-3705 Western Fire Journal
0043-373X Western Folklore
0043-3764 Western Fruit Grower
0043-3780 Western Grocer and Food Store Manager *changed to* Western Grocer Magazine
0043-3799 Western Grower & Shipper
0043-3802 Western Heart

0043-3810 Western Historical Quarterly
0043-3829 Western Horizons
0043-3837 Western Horseman
0043-3845 Western Humanities Review
0043-3853 Western Illinois University Bulletin†
0043-3861 Western Landscaping News
0043-387X Western Livestock Journal *changed to* Livestock
0043-3888 Western Lumber & Building Materials Merchant *changed to* Merchant
0043-390X Western Manufacturing *changed to* Western Plant Operation
0043-3918 Western Meat Industry *see* 0099-2011
0043-3934 Western Miner
0043-3942 Western Mobile News
0043-3950 Western Motor Fleet
0043-3977 Western New York Motorist
0043-3985 Western Oil Reporter
0043-3993 Western Ontario History Nuggets†
0043-4000 Western Outdoors
0043-4019 Western Pacific Orthopaedic Association. Journal
0043-4027 Western Paint Review
0043-4035 Western Pennsylvania Historical Magazine
0043-4051 Western Plains Library System Newsletter
0043-4078 Western Political Quarterly
0043-4086 Western Printer & Lithographer†
0043-4094 Western Producer
0043-4108 Western Railroader *changed to* Western Railroader and Western Railfan
0043-4116 Western Railway Club. Official Proceedings
0043-4124 Western Real Estate News
0043-4132 Western Recorder
0043-4140 Case Western Reserve University. School of Dentistry. Dental Alumni Bulletin *changed to* Case Western Reserve University School of Dentistry: Dental Alumni News
0043-4175 Western School Law Review†
0043-4191 Western Socialist
0043-4205 Western Speech *changed to* Western Journal of Speech Communication
0043-4213 Western Stamp Collector *changed to* Stamp Collector
0043-4221 Western States Jewish Historical Quarterly
0043-423X Western Sun
0043-4256 Western Underwriter
0043-4280 Western Wear & Equipment
0043-4299 Western World Review
0043-4310 Westernews *see* 0191-5959
0043-4329 Western's World
0043-4345 Westhoek†
0043-4361 Westinghouse Engineer†
0043-437X Westminster Review
0043-4388 Westminster Theological Journal
0043-4396 Westmoreland Traveler
0043-440X Westport Historical Quarterly†
0043-4418 Der Westpreusse
0043-4426 Westsider *changed to* Manhattan Business
0043-4434 Westways
0043-4442 Wetenschap en Samenleving
0043-4450 Wetter und Leben
0043-4477 Whaley-Eaton Foreign Letter†
0043-4485 Wharton Quarterly†
0043-4493 What†
0043-4507 What Goes On in Medicine
0043-4523 What's Happening†
0043-454X What's New at Colgate *changed to* Colgate Scene
0043-4558 What's New in Advertising and Marketing
0043-4574 What's New in Co-Op Information†
0043-4582 What's New in Food and Drug Research†
0043-4590 What's New in Home Economics
0043-4612 What's News in Reinsurance
0043-4620 What's on for Young People†
0043-4639 What's on in Aberdeen *changed to* What's on and Where to Shop in Aberdeen
0043-4647 What's on in Calcutta
0043-4655 What's on in Glasgow
0043-4663 What's on in Jersey
0043-4671 What's on in London
0043-468X What's on in Ottawa
0043-4698 Australia. Bureau of Statistics. Wheat Industry *changed to* Australia. Bureau of Statistics. Wheat Statistics
0043-4701 Wheat Life
0043-471X Wheat Review†
0043-4728 Wheat Scoop
0043-4736 Wheat Situation *changed to* Australia. Bureau of Agricultural Economics. Wheat: Situation and Outlook
0043-4744 Wheel Clicks
0043-4752 Wheel of Delta Omicron
0043-4760 Wheeled Sportsman†
0043-4779 Wheels
0043-4787 Wheels Afield *see* 0027-2094
0043-4795 Whenever Whatever *changed to* Rainbow
0043-4809 Where
0043-4817 Where to Go in London & Around
0043-4825 Whereas†
0043-4841 Which?
0043-485X Whip
0043-4868 Whitaker's Books of the Month and Books to Come
0043-4876 White Collar
0043-4884 White Collar Management
0043-4892 White Collar Report
0043-4906 White County Heritage
0043-4922 White Fathers†
0043-4930 White Horse and Fleur de Lys *see* 0140-0991
0043-4957 White Power
0043-4965 White Ribbon Bulletin
0043-4973 White Ribbon Magazine
0043-4981 White Rose Motorist
0043-5007 White Wing Messenger
0043-5023 Whitley Bulletin
0043-5031 Whole Earth Catalog *see* 0095-134X
0043-504X Wholesale Commodity Prices
0043-5058 Wholesale Food Prices
0043-5066 Industrial Engineering Management Science *changed to* Industrial Business Management Technology
0043-5074 Wiadomosci
0043-5090 Wiadomosci Botaniczne
0043-5104 Wiadomosci Chemiczne
0043-5112 Wiadomosci Elektrotechniczne
0043-5120 Wiadomosci Gornicze
0043-5139 Wiadomosci Hutnicze
0043-5147 Wiadomosci Lekarskie
0043-5155 Wiadomosci Numizmatyczne
0043-5163 Wiadomosci Parazytologiczne
0043-5171 Wiadomosci Sluzby Hydrologicznej i Meteorologicznej *see* 0208-6263
0043-518X Poland. Glowny Urzad Statystyczny. Wiadomosci Statystyczne
0043-5198 Wiadomosci Telekomunikacyjne
0043-5201 Poland. Urzad Patentowy. Wiadomosci
0043-521X Wiadomosci Warsztatowe
0043-5228 Wichita
0043-5236 Wichtigste fuer den Chef *changed to* Chef
0043-5244 Widnokregi
0043-5252 Wiederbelebung-Organersatz-Intensivmedizin *see* 0303-6251
0043-5260 Wielewaal
0043-5295 Wiener Buecherbriefe
0043-5309 Wiener Entomologische Gesellschaft. Zeitschrift
0043-5317 Wiener Geschichtsblaetter
0043-5325 Wiener Klinische Wochenschrift
0043-5333 Wiener Library Bulletin
0043-5341 Wiener Medizinische Wochenschrift
0043-535X Wiener Tieraerztliche Monatsschrift
0043-5376 Wiener Zeitschrift fuer Innere Medizin und ihre Grenzgebiete. *see* 0303-8173
0043-5392 Wig & Hairgoods Business
0043-5406 Wigs & Hairpieces†
0043-5414 Wijsgerig Perspectief op Maatschappij en Wetenschap
0043-5430 Wilderness Camping
0043-5449 Wilderness Travel Magazine†
0043-5457 Wildlife Crusader
0043-5473 Wildlife Disease Association. Journal *see* 0090-3558
0043-5481 Wildlife in Australia
0043-549X Wildlife in North Carolina
0043-5503 Wildlife News *changed to* Wildlife Report: the Canadian Scene
0043-5511 Wildlife Review (Fort Collins)
0043-552X Wildlife Society News *see* 0091-7648
0043-5538 Wildlife Views†
0043-5546 Roux' Archiv fuer Entwicklungsmechanik der Organismen *see* 0340-0794
0043-5554 Willamette Bridge†
0043-5562 Willamette Law Journal *see* 0191-9822
0043-5570 Der Wille zur Form
0043-5589 William & Mary Law Review
0043-5597 William and Mary Quarterly
0043-5600 William and Mary Review
0043-5619 Comments on Current World Affairs *changed to* William Winter Comments-on Current World Affairs
0043-5627 Williams' Family Bulletin
0043-5635 Wilmington Public Schools. Profile†
0043-5643 Wilson Bulletin
0043-5651 Wilson Library Bulletin
0043-566X Wiltshire Farmer
0043-5678 Wimpel
0043-5686 Win Magazine *changed to* Wind
0043-5694 W I N B A N News†
0043-5708 Wind Bell
0043-5716 Windless Orchard
0043-5724 Window†
0043-5759 House & Garden (London)
0043-5775 Off Licence News
0043-5783 Wine-Butler *see* 0141-6014
0043-5791 Wine Magazine†
0043-5805 Wine Review
0043-5813 Wine, Spirit & Malt†
0043-5821 Wineletter
0043-583X Wines and Vines
0043-5848 Winged Arrow†
0043-5856 Winged Foot
0043-5864 Winged Head
0043-5880 Wings
0043-5899 Wings
0043-5902 Wings at Home *see* 0704-6804
0043-5910 Wings over Africa
0043-5929 Wingspan *changed to* British Caledonian International
0043-5937 Winner
0043-5953 Der Winzer
0043-5961 Wir Blenden Auf
0043-597X Wir Herbergs Freunde *changed to* Jugendherbergswerk
0043-5988 Wir und Unsere Welt
0043-5996 Wire
0043-6011 Wire Industry
0043-602X Wire Journal
0043-6046 Wire World International
0043-6062 Wireless World
0043-6070 Wireport
0043-6089 Wirkendes Wort
0043-6097 Wirkerei- und Strickerei-Technik
0043-6100 Wirtschaft
0043-6119 Die Wirtschaft: Ausgabe A
0043-6127 Die Wirtschaft: Ausgabe B
0043-6135 Wirtschaft und Recht
0043-6143 Wirtschaft und Statistik
0043-6151 Wirtschaft und Wettbewerb
0043-616X Wirtschaft und Wissen *changed to* Angestellten Magazin Wirtschaft und Wissen
0043-6186 Wirtschaftliche Mitteilungen
0043-6194 Wirtschaft und Investment
0043-6208 Wirtschaftsblaetter
0043-6216 Wirtschafts-Correspondent
0043-6240 Wirtschaftsbericht ueber die Lateinamerikanischen Laender sowie Spanien und Portugal *changed to* Wirtschaftsbericht Lateinamerika
0043-6259 Wirtschaftsberichte
0043-6275 Wirtschaftsdienst
0043-6283 Wirtschaftskonjunktur
0043-6291 Wirtschaftspolitische Blaetter
0043-6305 Wirtschaftspolitische Chronik
0043-6313 Die Wirtschaftspruefung
0043-6321 Der Wirtschaftstreuhaender
0043-633X Wirtschaftswissenschaft
0043-6348 Wisconsin A A A Motor News *see* 0162-3591
0043-6356 Wisconsin Agriculturist
0043-6364 Wisconsin Archeologist
0043-6380 Wisconsin Bar Bulletin
0043-6399 Wisconsin Beverage Journal
0043-6402 Wisconsin C P A
0043-6410 Wisconsin Conservation Bulletin *changed to* Wisconsin Natural Resources
0043-6437 Wisconsin Department of Public Instruction. Administrative Newsletter *see* 0148-5040
0043-6453 Wisconsin Engineer
0043-6488 Wisconsin Jewish Chronicle
0043-6496 Wisconsin Journal of Education†
0043-650X Wisconsin Law Review
0043-6526 Wisconsin Library Bulletin
0043-6534 Wisconsin Magazine of History
0043-6542 Wisconsin Medical Journal
0043-6550 Wisconsin Mental Hygiene Review†
0043-6569 Wisconsin Newsletter†
0043-6577 Wisconsin Parent Teacher Bulletin
0043-6585 Wisconsin Pharmacist
0043-6593 Wisconsin Pharmacy Extension Bulletin
0043-6607 Wisconsin Poetry Magazine Illustrated
0043-6615 Wisconsin Professional Engineer
0043-6623 Wisconsin Rehabilitation†
0043-6631 Wisconsin Review
0043-664X Wisconsin School Board News *changed to* Wisconsin School News
0043-6666 Wisconsin Sociologist
0043-6674 Wisconsin State Dental Society. Journal *see* 0091-4185
0043-6682 Wisconsin State Laboratory of Hygiene. Laboratory Newsletter
0043-6690 Wisconsin State Universities Report†
0043-6704 Wisconsinsuror *changed to* Wisconsin Insuror
0043-6712 Wisconsin Tales and Trails *see* 0095-4314
0043-6739 Wisconsin Then and Now *see* 0196-1306
0043-6747 Wisconsin's Health
0043-6755 Wise Owl News *changed to* Prevent Blindness News
0043-6763 Mitteilungen aus dem Wissenschaftlichen Bibliothekswesen der DDR
0043-678X Wissenschaft und Weisheit†
0043-6798 Wissenschaft und Weltbild
0043-6801 A E G-Telefunken. Wissenschaftliche Berichte
0043-6836 Friedrich-Schiller-Universitaet Jena Mathematisch-Naturwissenschaftliche Reihe. Wissenschaftliche Zeitschrift
0043-6844 Hochschule fuer Verkehrswesen "Friedrich List". Wissenschaftliche Zeitschrift
0043-6852 Humboldt-Universitaet zu Berlin. Wissenschaftliche Zeitschrift
0043-6860 Karl Marx Universitaet, Leipzig, Mathematisch Naturwissenschaftliche Reihe. Wissenschaftliche Zeitschrift
0043-6879 Karl-Marx-Universitaet Leipzig. Wissenschaftliche Zeitschrift
0043-6895 Paedagogischen Hochschule, Potsdam. Gesellschafts und Sprachwissenschaftliche u. Math. Nat. Reihe. Wissenschaftliche Zeitschrift†
0043-6909 Technische Hochschule Carl Schorlemmer Leuna-Merseburg. Wissenschaftliche Zeitschrift.
0043-6917 Technische Hochschule Ilmenau. Wissenschaftliche Zeitschrift
0043-6925 Technische Universitaet Dresden. Wissenschaftliche Zeitschrift
0043-6933 Rostock Universitaet, Wissenschaftliche Zeitschrift. Gesellschafts-und Sprachwissenschaftliche Reihe

ISSN	Title
0043-6941	Wissenschaftlicher Dienst fuer Ostmitteleuropa see 0340-3297
0043-695X	Wissenschaftlicher Dienst Suedosteuropa
0043-6968	Wissenschaftlicher Literaturanzeiger
0043-6976	Wissenschaftsrecht, Wissenschaftsverwaltung, Wissenschaftsfoerderung
0043-6984	With
0043-6992	Within Our Gates
0043-700X	Without Prejudice
0043-7018	Without the Camp changed to New Day
0043-7050	Witte Krant†
0043-7069	Witte Museum Quarterly†
0043-7077	Witterung in Oesterreich. Monatsuebersicht
0043-7085	Witterung in Uebersee
0043-7093	Wittgenstein
0043-7107	Wivenhoe Park Review
0043-7123	Woche in Australien
0043-7131	Wochenblatt fuer Papierfabrikation
0043-714X	Wofford Bibliopolist
0043-7158	Wohnen und Siedeln
0043-7166	Wohnungseigentum
0043-7182	Wojskowy Przeglad Historyczny
0043-7190	Wojskowy Przeglad Lotniczy†
0043-7220	Woman
0043-7239	Woman
0043-7255	Woman Bowler
0043-7263	Woman, Bride and Home†
0043-7271	Woman C P A
0043-728X	Woman Constitutionalist
0043-7298	Woman Engineer
0043-7301	Woman Golfer†
0043-731X	Woman Journalist
0043-7328	Woman's Day
0043-7336	Woman's Day
0043-7344	Woman's Journal
0043-7352	Woman's National Magazine
0043-7360	Woman's Own
0043-7379	Woman's Pulpit†
0043-7387	Woman's Realm
	Knitting changed to Sewing & Knitting
0043-7409	Woman's Way Weekly
0043-7417	Woman's Weekly
0043-7425	Woman's World†
0043-7433	Women: A Journal of Liberation
0043-7441	Women in Business
0043-745X	Women in Council†
0043-7468	Women Lawyers Journal
0043-7476	Women of the Whole World
0043-7492	Women-To-By-Of-and About†
0043-7506	Women Today
0043-7514	Women's American O R T Reporter
0043-7522	Women's Dress Buyers changed to Women's, Misses & Jr. Dress Buyers
0043-7530	Women's Employment
0043-7549	Women's Intimate Apparel Buyers
0043-7557	Women's League Outlook
0043-7565	Women's Sportswear Buyers changed to Women's, Misses & Jr. Sportswear Buyers
0043-7573	Women's Track and Field World changed to Women's Track World
0043-7581	Women's Wear Daily see 0149-5380
0043-759X	Women's World
0043-7603	Women's Zionist Council of South Africa. News and Views
0043-762X	Wood changed to Timber Trades Journal and Wood Processing
0043-7646	Wood & Equipment News
0043-7654	Wood and Fiber
0043-7662	Wood & Wood Products
0043-7670	Wood Construction and Building Materials†
0043-7689	Wood Heat Quarterly†
0043-7697	Wood Preserving see 0099-1716
0043-7700	Wood Science
0043-7719	Wood Science and Technology
0043-7727	Woodall's Trailer Travel see 0160-3000
0043-7743	Woodlands Papers†
0043-7743	Pulp and Paper Research Institute of Canada. Woodlands Papers†
0043-7751	Woodmen of the World Magazine
0043-776X	Woodworker
0043-7778	Woodworking & Furniture Digest
0043-7786	Woodworking Industry
0043-7808	Wool and Woolens of India
0043-7816	Wool Intelligence (and Fibres Supplement)†
0043-7824	Wool News
0043-7832	Wool Record & Textile World
0043-7840	Wool Sack
0043-7867	U.S. Department of Agriculture. Economic Research Service. Wool Situation changed to U.S. Department of Agriculture. Economics, Statistics, and Cooperatives Service. Cotton and Wool Situation
0043-7875	Wool Technology and Sheep Breeding
0043-7883	Woollens & Worsteds of India
0043-7891	Worcester Art Museum. News Bulletin and Calendar changed to Worcester Art Museum. Journal
0043-7913	Worcester Polytechnic Institute. Journal see 0148-6128
0043-7921	Worcester Punch†
0043-7948	Word
0043-7956	Word
0043-7980	Word Ways
0043-7999	On the Line
0043-8006	Wordsworth Circle
0043-8014	Work Boat
0043-8022	Work Study
0043-8030	Work Study and Management Services see 0307-6768
0043-8057	Workbench
0043-8065	Queensland Worker see 0045-0979
0043-809X	Workers World
0043-8103	Working for Boys
0043-8111	Workmen's Circle Call
0043-812X	Works†
0043-8146	Workshop see 0308-6283
0043-8154	World
0043-8162	World
0043-8170	Canada & the World
0043-8189	World Affairs
0043-8200	World Affairs
0043-8219	World Agricultural Economics and Rural Sociology Abstracts
0043-8227	World Agriculture
0043-8243	World Archaeology
0043-826X	World Aviation Directory
0043-8278	World Bowls
0043-8286	World Buddhism†
0043-8294	World Calendar of Forthcoming Meetings: Metallurgical and Related Fields
0043-8308	World Call see 0092-8372
0043-8324	World Christian Digest†
0043-8332	World Christian Education†
0043-8359	World Coins†
0043-8375	World Construction
0043-8383	World Convention Dates
0043-8391	World Crops
0043-8405	World Dredging & Marine Construction
0043-8413	World Encounter
0043-8421	World Farming
0043-843X	World Federalist changed to Transnational Perspectives
0043-8448	World Federation
0043-8464	World Fellowship of Buddhists Review
0043-8472	World Fisheries Abstracts†
0043-8480	World Fishing
0043-8502	World Health
0043-8510	World Health Statistics Report changed to World Health Statistics Quarterly
0043-8529	World Highways
0043-8561	World Industrial Reporter
0043-857X	World Informo
0043-8588	World Irrigation†
0043-8596	World Jewry†
0043-860X	World Journal of Psychosynthesis
0043-8634	World Leprosy News†
0043-8642	World Marxist Review
0043-8669	World Medicine
0043-8677	World Meetings: Outside United States and Canada
0043-8685	World Meetings: Social and Behavioral Sciences, Education and Management see 0194-6161
0043-8693	World Meetings: United States and Canada
0043-8707	World Mining
0043-874X	World News of the Week changed to World Newsmap of the Week
0043-8758	World Metal Statistics
0043-8766	World of Comic Art
0043-8782	World of Pretzels†
0043-8790	World Oil
0043-8804	World Order
0043-8812	New World Outlook
0043-8820	World Over
0043-8839	World Parish
0043-8847	World Petroleum†
0043-8855	International Oil News
0043-8871	World Politics
0043-888X	World Ports see 0161-6323
0043-8898	World-Product-Casts
0043-8901	World Progress
0043-891X	World Radio Bulletin†
0043-8928	World Refrigeration and Air Conditioning†
0043-8936	World-Regional-Casts
0043-8944	World Report on Technical Advancement
0043-8952	World Reporter
0043-8979	World Review of Animal Production
0043-8987	World Revolution†
0043-8995	World Scouting
0043-9002	World Scouting Newsletter
0043-9010	World Ships on Order
0043-9029	World Shopping changed to World Shopping Encyclopedia
0043-9037	World Soccer
0043-9045	World Space Directory Including Oceanology†
0043-9053	World Sports changed to Sportsworld
0043-9061	World Stamps
0043-907X	W S C F Newsletter†
0043-9088	World Surface Coatings Abstracts†
0043-9088	World Surface Coating Abstracts
0043-910X	World Tennis
0043-9118	World Textile Abstracts
0043-9126	World Tobacco
0043-9134	World Today
0043-9142	World Trade
0043-9150	World Trade Bulletin
0043-9169	World Travel
0043-9177	World Traveler†
0043-9185	World Union
0043-9215	World Vision
0043-9223	World War II Historical Association. Newsletter changed to World War Enthusiast 1939-1945
0043-9231	World Week see 0037-2242
0043-9258	World Wood
0043-9274	World Youth
0043-9282	Worldmission
0043-9290	World's Children
0043-9304	World's Fair
0043-9312	Worlds of If†
0043-9320	World's Paper Trade Review see 0306-8234
0043-9339	World's Poultry Science Journal
0043-9355	Worldwide Art Book Bibliography†
0043-9363	Worldwide Art Catalogue Bulletin
0043-9371	Worldwide Marketing Horizons
0043-9398	Worldwide Projects & Installation Planning see 0091-4800
0043-9401	Wormwood Review
0043-941X	Worship
0043-9428	Das Wort fuer Heute
0043-9444	Wort und Weg
0043-9452	Wrangler's Roost
0043-9460	Wrecking & Salvage Journal
0043-9479	Wrestler†
0043-9495	Wretched Mess News†
0043-9509	Wright Advisory Report changed to Wright Bankers' Service
0043-9517	Writer
0043-9525	Writer's Digest
0043-9533	Writers Guild of America, West. Newsletter
0043-9541	Writers Newsletter changed to J R G Newsletter
0043-955X	Writer's Notes and Quotes
0043-9568	Writer's Review see 0260-2776
0043-9576	Writers' World
0043-9592	Wszechswiat
0043-9606	Wuerttembergisches Wochenblatt fuer Landwirtschaft
0043-9614	Wuerzburg-Heute
0043-9622	Das Wuestenrot-Heim
0043-9630	Wychowanie Fizyczne i Sport. Studia i Materialy
0043-9649	Wynalazczosc; Racjonalizacja changed to TEMAT - Wynalazczosc i Racjonalizacja
0043-9657	Wynboer
0043-9665	Wyoming Archaeologist
0043-9673	Wyoming Beverage Analyst
0043-9681	Wyoming Education News
0043-969X	Wyoming Educator
0043-9703	Wyoming Employment Outlook
0043-9711	Wyoming Future Farmer
0043-972X	Wyoming History News
0043-9738	Wyoming Library Roundup
0043-9754	Wyoming P T A News
0043-9762	Wyoming Progress Reports changed to D E P A D Progress Reports
0043-9770	Wyoming Rural Electric News
0043-9789	Wyoming School Boards Bulletin
0043-9797	Pulse changed to Medical Wire
0043-9800	Wyoming Stockman Farmer
0043-9819	Wyoming Wildlife
0043-9827	Wyoming Wool Grower
0043-9851	X-Ray Fluorescence Spectrometry Abstracts
0043-986X	Xaloc
0043-9878	Xaverian†
0043-9886	Xaverian Weekly
0043-9924	Y W C A Magazine†
0043-9932	Die Yacht
0043-9940	Yachting
0043-9959	Yachting
0043-9975	Yachting Italiano-Altomare
0043-9983	Yachting Monthly
0043-9991	Yachting World
0044-0000	Yachts and Yachting
0044-0019	Yachtsman's Wife†
0044-0027	Yadernaya Fizika
0044-0035	Practical Pharmacy
0044-0043	Pharmacy Companion
0044-0051	Yale Alumni Magazine
0044-006X	Yale Economic Essays†
0044-0078	Yale French Studies
0044-0086	Yale Journal of Biology and Medicine
0044-0094	Yale Law Journal
0044-0108	Yale Literary Magazine see 0148-4605
0044-0116	Yale Medicine
0044-0124	Yale Review
0044-0132	Yale Review of Law and Social Action†
0044-0140	Yale Scientific Magazine see 0091-0287
0044-0159	Yale Speleological Society. Journal
0044-0167	Yale/Theatre see 0161-0775
0044-0175	Yale University Library Gazette
0044-0183	Yamashina Institute for Ornithology. Miscellaneous Reports
0044-0191	Yankee
0044-0213	Yaqeen International
0044-0221	Yardage
0044-023X	Yarn (Your Auckland Railway News)
0044-0256	Yavneh Studies
0044-0280	Rashut Ha-Nemalim Be-Yisrael, Yedion changed to Ha-Nemalim Be-Israel. Berashut
0044-0310	Yememhiran Dimts
0044-0329	Yememhiran Melkt
0044-0337	Yeni Sinema
0044-0345	Yeon-Gu Weolbo
0044-0353	Yes see 0315-467X
0044-0361	Yesodot
0044-037X	Yesteryears
0044-0388	Yevanhelskyj Ranok
0044-0396	Yhteishyva
0044-040X	Yid
0044-0418	Yiddishe Heim
0044-0426	Yiddishe Kultur
0044-0434	Yiddisher Kemfer
0044-0442	Yidishe Shprakh

ISSN INDEX 1073

0044-0450 Yidisher Kval
0044-0469 Yleiselektroniikka *changed to* Elektroniikkauutiset
0044-0477 Ymer
0044-0485 Yoga
0044-0493 Yoga Institute. Journal
0044-0507 Yoga-Mimamsa
0044-0515 Yojana
0044-0523 Yokohama Mathematical Journal
0044-0531 Yokohama Medical Bulletin
0044-0558 Yonago Medical Association. Journal
0044-0574 Yorker *changed to* Yorker (1976)
0044-0590 Bulletin of Economic Research
0044-0612 Yorkshire Journal
0044-0639 Yorkshire Ridings
0044-0647 Yorkshire Terrier Quarterly†
0044-0663 Monthly Statistics of Paper Distribution
0044-0671 Fish Culture
0044-068X You and Your World
0044-0698 Welcome to Cyprus
0044-0701 You†
0044-071X Young Ambassador
0044-0728 Young Children
0044-0736 Young Citizen
0044-0744 Young Citizen *changed to* News Citizen
0044-0752 Young Engineer & Scientist
0044-0760 Young Folk
0044-0787 Young Ideas
0044-0795 Young India
0044-0809 Young Israel Viewpoint
0044-0817 Young Judaean
0044-0833 Young Miss
0044-0841 Young Musicians
0044-0876 Young Scotland†
0044-0884 Young Socialist
0044-0892 Young Socialist-the Organizer *changed to* Young Socialist
0044-0906 Young Soldier
0044-0914 Young Sower *changed to* Search
0044-0922 Young Teen Power *changed to* Teen Power (1979)
0044-0973 Youngstown Jewish Times
0044-0981 Your Astrology†
0044-099X Your Business†
0044-1007 Your Child
0044-1015 Your Edmundite Missions News Letter
0044-1031 Your Garden
0044-104X Your Health
0044-1058 Your Library Presents†
0044-1074 Your New Baby†
0044-1082 Your Personal Astrology Magazine
0044-1090 International Rider and Driver *see* 0094-3355
0044-1104 Your Public Schools
0044-1112 Your Schools
0044-1120 Your Schools
0044-1139 You're the Critic†
0044-1155 Youth Aliyah Review
0044-1171 Youth and Nation
0044-118X Youth & Society
0044-1201 Youth Chronicle
0044-121X Youth Happiness *changed to* Young & Alive (Large Print Edition)
0044-1228 Youth Hosteller *see* 0306-8927
0044-1236 Youth in Action
0044-1244 Youth Life *changed to* Union of Yugoslav Youth. Newsletter
0044-1252 Youth Program Service *changed to* Emmaus Letter
0044-1260 Youth Review
0044-1309 Yritystalous *see* 0356-5327
0044-1317 Yrkesopplaering *see* 0332-5814
0044-1325 Yudhagama
0044-1333 Yugoslav Life
0044-135X Yugoslav Trade Unions
0044-1368 Yugoslavia Export
0044-1376 Yukon News
0044-1384 Yunak
0044-1392 Yunyi Naturalist
0044-1406 Yunyi Tekhnik
0044-1414 Yuvak
0044-1422 Z
0044-1449 Zeitschrift fuer Dialektologie und Linguistik
0044-1457 Informationsdienst Bibliothekwesen
0044-1465 Z I S Mitteilungen
0044-1473 Z Naszej Oficyny
0044-1481 Z Otchlani Wiekow
0044-149X Z Pola Walki
0044-1503 Z Prac Zakladu Nauk Ekonomicznych PAN
0044-1511 Z V und Z V
0044-152X Za Domovinu
0044-1538 Za i Przeciw
0044-1554 Za Rubezhom
0044-1562 Zaaier
0044-1570 Zacchia
0044-1589 Zadarska Revija
0044-1597 Zagadnienia Drgan Nieliniowych
0044-1600 Zagadnienia Ekonomiki Rolnej
0044-1619 Zagadnienia Naukoznawstwa
0044-1643 Zahnaerztliche Mitteilungen
0044-1651 Zahnaerztliche Praxis
0044-166X Z W R
0044-1678 Der Zahnarzt
0044-1686 Zahntechnik
0044-1694 Zahradnicke Listy
0044-1708 Zabrana Skod
0044-1716 Zajednica
0044-1724 Zambia Library Service Bulletin†
0044-1732 Zambia Mail *changed to* Zambia Daily Mail
0044-1783 Zapatos y Zapaterias
0044-1791 Zapiski Historyczne
0044-1813 Zapowiedzi Wydawnicze
0044-1821 Zaragoza
0044-183X Zaranie Slaskie
0044-1848 Zarja
0044-1856 Zashchita Metallov
0044-1864 Zashchita Rastenii
0044-1872 Zastita
0044-1880 Zastita Rada
0044-1899 Zastosowania Matematyki
0044-1902 Zavarivanje
0044-1910 Zavodskaya Laboratoriya
0044-1929 Zbior Dokumentow
0044-1937 Zbornik za Drustvene Nauke
0044-1945 Zdorov'e
0044-1953 Zdravie
0044-1961 Zdravookhranenie Belorussii
0044-197X Zdravookhranenie Rossiiskoi Federatsii
0044-1988 Zdravotni Technika a Vzduchotechnika
0044-1996 Zdravotnicke Noviny
0044-2011 Zdrowie Publiczne
0044-202X Zealandia
0044-2038 Zeichen der Zeit
0044-2046 Zeichnen in Technik, Architektur, Vermessung *changed to* Zeichnen Fachzeitschrift fuer Alle Bereiche Technischen Zeichnens
0044-2054 Zeiss Information
0044-2062 Zeiss-Mitteilungen ueber Fortschritte der Technischen Optik†
0044-2070 Die Zeit
0044-2089 Die Zeit im Buch
0044-2097 Zeit- und Kulturarchiv
0044-2100 ZeitBild
0044-2119 Zeitgeist†
0044-2127 Zeitschrift des Bernischen Juristenvereins
0044-2135 Deutscher Verein fuer Kunstwissenschaft. Zeitschrift
0044-2151 Zeitschrift fuer Acker- und Pflanzenbau
0044-216X Zeitschrift fuer Aegyptische Sprache und Altertumskunde
0044-2178 Zeitschrift fuer Aerztliche Fortbildung
0044-2186 Zeitschrift fuer Aesthetik und allgemeine Kunstwissenschaft
0044-2194 Deutsche Landwirtschafts-Gesellschaft. Mitteilungen der D L G *changed to* D L G - Mitteilungen
0044-2194 Zeitschrift fuer Agrargeschichte und Agrarsoziologie
0044-2208 Zeitschrift fuer allgemeine Mikrobiologie
0044-2216 Zeitschrift fuer Allgemeine Wissenschaftstheorie
0044-2224 Zeitschrift fuer Alternsforschung
0044-2232 Zeitschrift fuer Anatomie und Entwicklungsgeschichte *see* 0340-2061
0044-2240 Zeitschrift fuer Angewandte Entomologie
0044-2259 Zeitschrift fuer Angewandte Geologie
0044-2267 Zeitschrift fuer Angewandte Mathematik und Mechanik
0044-2275 Zeitschrift fuer Angewandte Mathematik und Physik
0044-2283 Zeitschrift fuer Angewandte Physik *see* 0340-3793
0044-2291 Zeitschrift fuer Angewandte Zoologie
0044-2305 Anglistik und Amerikanistik. Zeitschrift
0044-2313 Zeitschrift fuer Anorganische und Allgemeine Chemie
0044-2321 Zeitschrift fuer Arbeitsrecht und Sozialrecht
0044-233X Archaeologie. Zeitschrift
0044-2348 Zeitschrift fuer Auslaendisches Oeffentliches Recht und Voelkerrecht
0044-2356 Zeitschrift fuer Balkanologie
0044-2364 Zeitschrift fuer Bayerische Landesgeschichte
0044-2372 Zeitschrift fuer Betriebswirtschaft
0044-2380 Zeitschrift fuer Bibliothekswesen und Bibliographie
0044-2399 Zeitschrift fuer Bienenforschung *see* 0044-8435
0044-2402 Zeitschrift fuer Chemie
0044-2410 Zeitschrift fuer das gesamte Familienrecht
0044-2429 Zeitschrift fuer das Gesamte Genossenschaftswesen
0044-2437 Zeitschrift fuer das gesamte Handelsrecht und Wirtschaftsrecht
0044-2445 Zeitschrift fuer das Gesamte Kreditwesen
0044-2461 Zeitschrift fuer den Erdkundeunterricht
0044-247X Zeitschrift fuer den Lastenausgleich
0044-2496 Zeitschrift fuer Deutsche Philologie
0044-2518 Zeitschrift fuer Deutsches Altertum und Deutsche Literatur
0044-2526 Zeitschrift fuer die alttestamentliche Wissenschaft
0044-2534 Zeitschrift fuer die gesamte experimentelle Medizin einschliesslich experimenteller Chirurgie *see* 0300-9130
0044-2542 Zeitschrift fuer die Gesamte Innere Medizin und ihre Grenzgebiete
0044-2550 Zeitschrift fuer die Gesamte Staatswissenschaft
0044-2585 Zeitschrift fuer die gesamte Versicherungswissenschaft
0044-2593 Zeitschrift fuer die Geschichte der Juden†
0044-2615 Zeitschrift fuer die neutestamentliche Wissenschaft und die Kunde der Aelteren Kirche
0044-2623 Zeitschrift fuer die Zuckerindustrie *changed to* Zuckerindustrie
0044-2631 Zeitschrift fuer Erkrankungen der Atmungsorgane
0044-264X Zeitschrift fuer Ernaehrungswissenschaft
0044-2666 Zeitschrift fuer Ethnologie
0044-2674 Zeitschrift fuer Evangelische Ethik
0044-2682 Zeitschrift fuer Evangelische Rundfunk- und Fernseharbeit Medium *see* 0025-8350
0044-2690 Zeitschrift fuer Evangelisches Kirchenrecht
0044-2704 Zeitschrift fuer experimentelle Chirurgie
0044-2712 Zeitschrift fuer Experimentelle und Angewandte Psychologie
0044-2720 Zeitschrift fuer Fischerei und deren Hilfswissenschaften†
0044-2739 Zeitschrift fuer Flugwissenschaften
0044-2747 Zeitschrift fuer Franzoesische Sprache und Literatur
0044-2755 Zeitschrift fuer Fremdenverkehr
0044-2763 Zeitschrift fuer Ganzheitsforschung
0044-2771 Zeitschrift fuer Gastroenterologie
0044-278X Zeitschrift fuer Geburtshilfe und Gynakoologie *see* 0300-967X
0044-2801 Zeitschrift fuer Geophysik *see* 0340-062X
0044-281X Zeitschrift fuer Gerontologie
0044-2828 Geschichtswissenschaft. Zeitschrift
0044-2836 Zeitschrift fuer Gletscherkunde und Glazialgeologie
0044-2844 Zeitschrift fuer Haut- und Geschlechtskrankheiten *see* 0301-0481
0044-2852 Zeitschrift fuer Heereskunde
0044-2860 Zeitschrift fuer Hoergeraete Akustik
0044-2887 Zeitschrift fuer Jagdwissenschaft
0044-2895 Zeitschrift fuer katholische Theologie
0044-2909 Zeitschrift fuer Kinderchirurgie und Grenzgebiete *see* 0174-3082
0044-2925 Zeitschrift fuer Kirchengeschichte
0044-2933 Zeitschrift fuer klinische Chemie und klinische Biochemie
0044-2941 Zeitschrift fuer Krankenpflege
0044-295X Zeitschrift fuer Kreislaufforschung *see* 0300-5860
0044-2968 Zeitschrift fuer Kristallographie
0044-2976 Zeitschrift fuer Kulturaustausch
0044-2984 Zeitschrift fuer Kulturtechnik und Flurbereinigung
0044-2992 Zeitschrift fuer Kunstgeschichte
0044-300X Zeitschrift fuer Landeskultur†
0044-3018 Zeitschrift fuer Laryngologie, Rhinologie, Otologie und ihre Grenzgebiete *changed to* Laryngologie, Rhinologie, Otologie Vereingt mit Monatsschrift fuer Ohrenheilkunde
0044-3026 Zeitschrift fuer Lebensmittel Untersuchung und Forschung
0044-3034 Zeitschrift fuer Luftrecht und Weltraumrechtsfragen *see* 0340-8329
0044-3042 Zeitschrift fuer Markt-, Meinungs- und Zukunftsforschung
0044-3050 Mathematische Logik und Grundlagen der Mathematik. Zeitschrift
0044-3069 Zeitschrift fuer medizinische Labortechnik *see* 0323-5637
0044-3077 Zeitschrift fuer Medizinische Mikrobiologie und Immunologie *see* 0300-8584
0044-3085 Zeitschrift fuer Menschenkunde und Zentralblatt fuer Graphologie, Ausdruckswissenschaft und Charakterkunde *changed to* Zeitschrift fuer Menschenkunde. Zentralblatt fuer Schriftpsychologie und Schriftvergleichung
0044-3093 Zeitschrift fuer Metallkunde
0044-3107 Zeitschrift fuer Mikroskopisch-Anatomische Forschung
0044-3115 Zeitschrift fuer Militaergeschichte *changed to* Militaergeschichte
0044-3123 Zeitschrift fuer Missionswissenschaft und Religionswissenschaft
0044-3131 Zeitschrift fuer Morphologie der Tiere *changed to* Zoomorphology
0044-314X Zeitschrift fuer Morphologie und Anthropologie
0044-3158 Zeitschrift fuer Nationaloekonomie
0044-3166 Zeitschrift fuer Naturforschung. Ausgabe A *see* 0340-4811
0044-3174 Zeitschrift fuer Naturforschung. Ausgabe B. *see* 0340-5087
0044-3182 Zeitschrift fuer Naturheilkunde
0044-3190 Zeitschrift fuer Niederdeutsche Familienkunde
0044-3204 Zeitschrift fuer Oeffentliche Fuersorge
0044-3212 Zeitschrift fuer Organisation
0044-3220 Zeitschrift fuer Orthopaedie und ihre Grenzgebiete
0044-3239 Zeitschrift fuer Ostforschung
0044-3247 Zeitschrift fuer Paedagogik
0044-3255 Zeitschrift fuer Parasitenkunde
0044-3263 Zeitschrift fuer Pflanzenernaehrung und Bodenkunde
0044-3271 Zeitschrift fuer Pflanzenkrankheiten und Pflanzenschutz
0044-328X Zeitschrift fuer Pflanzenphysiologie
0044-3298 Zeitschrift fuer Pflanzenzuechtung
0044-3301 Zeitschrift fuer philosophische Forschung

0044-331X Zeitschrift fuer Phonetik, Sprachwissenschaft und Kommunikationsforschung
0044-3328 Zeitschrift fuer Physik. *see* 0340-2193
0044-3336 Zeitschrift fuer Physikalische Chemie
0044-3344 Zeitschrift fuer Physikalische Medizin†
0044-3360 Zeitschrift fuer Politik
0044-3379 Zeitschrift fuer Praeventivmedizin *changed to* Sozial- und Praeventivmedizin
0044-3387 Zeitschrift fuer Praktische Anaesthesie, Wiederbelebung und Intensivtherapie *changed to* Anaesthesie - Intensivtherapie - Notfallmedizin
0044-3395 Zeitschrift fuer Psycho-Somatische Medizin *see* 0340-5613
0044-3409 Zeitschrift fuer Psychologie
0044-3417 Zeitschrift fuer Psychotherapie und Medizinische Psychologie *see* 0173-7937
0044-3425 Zeitschrift fuer Radiaesthesie
0044-3433 Zeitschrift fuer Rechtsmedizin
0044-3441 Zeitschrift fuer Religions- und Geistesgeschichte
0044-345X Zeitschrift fuer Rheumaforschung *see* 0301-6382
0044-3468 Zeitschrift fuer Saeugetierkunde
0044-3476 Zeitschrift fuer Schweizerische Archaeologie und Kunstgeschichte
0044-3484 Zeitschrift fuer Schweizerische Kirchengeschichte
0044-3492 Zeitschrift fuer slavische Philologie
0044-3506 Zeitschrift fuer Slawistik
0044-3522 Zeitschrift fuer Sozialberatung†
0044-3530 Zeitschrift fuer Staatssoziologie
0044-3557 Zeitschrift fuer Therapie†
0044-3565 Zeitschrift fuer Tierphysiologie, Tierernaehrung und Futtermittelkunde
0044-3573 Zeitschrift fuer Tierpsychologie
0044-3581 Zeitschrift fuer Tierzuechtung und Zuechtungsbiologie
0044-359X Zeitschrift fuer Tropenmedizin und Parasitologie *see* 0303-4208
0044-3603 Zeitschrift fuer Unfallmedizin und Berufskrankheiten
0044-3611 Zeitschrift fuer Urologie und Nephrologie
0044-362X Zeitschrift fuer Vergleichende Physiologie *see* 0340-7594
0044-362X Zeitschrift fuer Vergleichende Physiologie *changed to* Journal of Comparative Physiology. B: Biochemical, Systematic, and Environmental Physiology
0044-3646 Zeitschrift fuer Vergleichende Sprachforschung
0044-3654 Zeitschrift fuer Verkehrssicherheit
0044-3662 Zeitschrift fuer Verkehrsrecht
0044-3670 Zeitschrift fuer Verkehrswissenschaft
0044-3689 Zeitschrift fuer Vermessungswesen
0044-3697 Zeitschrift fuer Versuchstierkunde
0044-3700 Zeitschrift fuer Volkskunde
0044-3719 Zeitschrift fuer Wahrscheinlichkeitstheorie und Verwandte Gebiete
0044-3727 Zeitschrift fuer Wasser- und Abwasserforschung
0044-3735 Zeitschrift fuer Wasserrecht
0044-3743 Zeitschrift fuer Wirtschaftliche Fertigung
0044-3751 Zeitschrift fuer Wirtschaftsgeographie
0044-376X Microscopica Acta
0044-3778 Zeitschrift fuer Wissenschaftliche Zoologie. Abteilung A†
0044-3786 Zeitschrift fuer Wuerttembergische Landesgeschichte
0044-3794 Zeitschrift fuer Zellforschung und Mikroskopische Anatomie *see* 0302-766X
0044-3808 Zeitschrift fuer Zoologische Systematik und Evolutionsforschung
0044-3816 Zeitschrift Interne Revision
0044-3824 Zeitschriftendienst Musik
0044-3832 Zeitungs- und Zeitschriftenhandel *changed to* Presse Report (PR)
0044-3840 Zeitwende/Die Neue Furche *changed to* Zeitwende
0044-3867 Zellstoff und Papier
0044-3875 Zemedelska Skola
0044-3883 Zemedelska Technika
0044-3891 Zemedelsky a Lesni Zamestnanec
0044-3905 Zement-Kalk-Gips *see* 0340-5095
0044-3905 Zement-Kalk-Gips *see* 0341-0560
0044-3913 Zemledelie
0044-3921 Zemlja Sovjeta
0044-3948 Zemlya i Vselennaya
0044-3956 Zen Bow *changed to* Zen Bow Newsletter
0044-3972 Zending *changed to* Vandaar
0044-3980 Zenit
0044-3999 Zenit†
0044-4006 Zenken Journal
0044-4014 Zentralblatt der Bulgarischen Wissenschaftlichen Literatur. Geschichte, Archaeologie und Ethnographie
0044-4022 Zentralblatt fuer Aero- und Astronautik†
0044-4030 Zentralblatt fuer Allgemeine Pathologie und Pathologische Anatomie
0044-4049 Zentralblatt fuer Arbeitsmedizin und Arbeitsschutz *see* 0340-7047
0044-4073 Zentralblatt fuer Bakteriologie, Parasitenkunde, Infektionskrankheiten und Hygiene. Abteilung 1: Referate
0044-4081 Zentralblatt fuer Bibliothekswesen
0044-409X Zentralblatt fuer Chirurgie
0044-4103 Zentralblatt fuer Didaktik der Mathematik
0044-4111 Zentralblatt fuer Die Gesamte Kinderheilkunde
0044-412X Zentralblatt fuer Die Gesamte Neurologie und Psychiatrie
0044-4138 Zentralblatt fuer Die Gesamte Ophthalmologie und ihre Grenzgebiete
0044-4146 Zentralblatt fuer Die Gesamte Radiologie
0044-4154 Zentralblatt fuer Die Gesamte Rechtsmedizin und ihre Grenzgebiete
0044-4170 Zentralblatt fuer Geologie und Palaeontologie. Teil 1: Allgemeine, Angewandte, Regionale und Historische Geologie
0044-4189 Zentralblatt fuer Geologie und Palaeontologie. Teil 2: Palaeontologie
0044-4197 Zentralblatt fuer Gynaekologie
0044-4200 Zentralblatt fuer Hals-, Nasen- und Ohrenheilkunde Sowie Deren Grenzgebiete *see* 0340-5214
0044-4219 Zentralblatt fuer Haut- und Geschlechtskrankheiten Sowie Deren Grenzgebiete /Dermatology *see* 0343-3048
0044-4227 Zentralblatt fuer Industriebau
0044-4235 Zentralblatt fuer Mathematik und ihre Grenzgebiete/Mathematics Abstracts
0044-4251 Zentralblatt fuer Neurochirurgie
0044-426X Zentralblatt fuer Phlebologie *see* 0301-1526
0044-4278 Zentralblatt fuer Sozialversicherung, Sozialhilfe und Versorgung
0044-4286 Zentralblatt fuer Verkehrs-Medizin, Verkehrs-Psychologie, Luft- und Raumfahrt-Medizin†
0044-4294 Zentralblatt fuer Veterinaermedizin *see* 0300-8711
0044-4294 Zentralblatt fuer Veterinaermedizin *see* 0514-7166
0044-4308 Zentralorgan fuer Die Gesamte Chirurgie und ihre Grenzgebiete
0044-4316 Zentralsparkasse der Gemeinde Wien. Information
0044-4324 Zentralverein der Wiener Lehrerschaft. Mitteilungen
0044-4383 Zeszyty Problemowe Gornictwa
0044-4391 Zeszyty Historyczne
0044-4405 Katolicki Uniwersytet Lubelski. Zeszyty Naukowe
0044-4413 Fasciculi Mathematici
0044-443X Zeszyty Teoretyczno-Polityczne *changed to* Prezentacje
0044-4448 Zheleznodorozhnyi Transport
0044-4456 Zhenshchiny Mira
0044-4464 Zhilishchnoe i Kommunal'noe Khozyaistvo
0044-4472 Zhilishchnoe Stroitel'stvo
0044-4480 Zhivotnovodstvo
0044-4499 Zhovten'
0044-4502 Zhurnal Analiticheskoi Khimii
0044-4510 Zhurnal Eksperimental'noi i Teoreticheskoi Fiziki
0044-4529 Zhurnal Evolyutsionnoi Biokhimii i Fiziologii
0044-4537 Zhurnal Fizicheskoi Khimii
0044-4545 Zhurnal Mod
0044-4553 Zhurnal Moskovskoi Patriarkhii
0044-4561 Zhurnal Nauchnoi i Prikladnoi Fotografii i Kinematografii
0044-457X Zhurnal Neorganicheskoi Khimii
0044-4588 Zhurnal Nevropatologii i Psikhiatrii im S.S. Korsakova
0044-4596 Zhurnal Obshchei Biologii
0044-460X Zhurnal Obshchei Khimii
0044-4618 Zhurnal Prikladnoi Khimii
0044-4626 Zhurnal Prikladnoi Mekhaniki i Tekhnicheskoi Fiziki
0044-4634 Zhurnal Strukturnoi Khimii
0044-4642 Zhurnal Tekhnicheskoi Fiziki
0044-4650 Zhurnal Ushnykh, Nosovykh i Gorlovykh Boleznei
0044-4669 Zhurnal Vychislitel'noi Matematiki i Matematicheskoi Fiziki
0044-4677 Zhurnal Vysshei Nervnoi Deyatel'nosti
0044-4693 Ziegelindustrie *see* 0341-0552
0044-4707 Ziekenfondsgids†
0044-4715 Ziekenhuis
0044-4723 Zimbabwe Review *changed to* Revolution
0044-4731 Zinc Abstracts
0044-4758 Zion
0044-4766 Zionist Collegiate
0044-4774 Zionist Literature
0044-4782 Zionist Record and S. A. Jewish Chronicle
0044-4790 Zion's Herald *changed to* Zion's Herald (1976)
0044-4812 Ziva
0044-4820 Ziviler Bevoelkerungsschutz. ZB†
0044-4839 Zivilverteidigung
0044-4847 Zivocisna Vyroba
0044-4855 Zivot i Skola
0044-4863 Zivotne Prostredie
0044-4871 Zlaty Maj
0044-488X Znak
0044-4898 Znamya
0044-4901 Znamya Rossiyi
0044-4928 Zobozdravstveni Vestnik
0044-4936 Zodiac†
0044-4944 Zodiac *changed to* Helix
0044-4952 Zodiaque
0044-4995 Zona: Revista de Comercio Latino-Americana
0044-5002 Zondagsmis
0044-5010 Zone
0044-5029 Zoo Anvers
0044-5037 Zoo
0044-5045 Zoolog *see* 0315-5064
0044-5053 Zoologia *see* 0301-2123
0044-5061 Ricerche di Zoologia Applicata alla Caccia *changed to* Ricerche di Biologia della Selvaggina
0044-5088 Zoologica
0044-5096 Zoologica Africana *changed to* South African Journal of Zoology
0044-510X Zoologica Poloniae
0044-5118 Zoological Magazine
0044-5126 Zoological Society of Southern Africa. News Bulletin *changed to* Zoological Society of Southern Africa. Newsletter
0044-5134 Zoologicheskii Zhurnal
0044-5142 Folia Zoologica
0044-5150 Zoologische Beitraege
0044-5169 Der Zoologische Garten
0044-5177 Zoologische Jahrbuecher. Abteilung fuer Anatomie und Ontogenie der Tiere
0044-5185 Zoologische Jahrbuecher. Abteilung fuer Allgemeine Zoologie und Physiologie der Tiere
0044-5193 Zoologische Jahrbuecher. Abteilung fuer Systematik, Oekologie und Geographie der Tiere
0044-5223 Zoologisches Museum Hamburg. Entomologische Mitteilungen
0044-5231 Zoologischer Anzeiger
0044-524X Zoologischer Zentral-Anzeiger
0044-5274 Zoon
0044-5282 Zoonooz
0044-5290 Zooprofilassi†
0044-5304 Zoo's Letter
0044-5312 Zootechnia
0044-5320 Zootecnia
0044-5339 Zorgenkind *changed to* Raakpunt
0044-5347 Shipbuilding
0044-5355 Zpravodaj VZLU
0044-5363 Divadelni Ustav. Zpravy
0044-5371 Zuchthygiene
0044-538X Zucker†
0044-538X Zucker *changed to* Zuckerindustrie
0044-5398 Die Zuckerruebe
0044-5401 Zuechtungskunde
0044-5428 Zuid-Afrika
0044-5436 Zuivelnieuws
0044-5452 Zukunft
0044-5460 Zukunft
0044-5479 Zulqarnain
0044-5487 Zum Nachdenken
0044-5509 Zur Geschichte der Pharmazie *see* 0341-0099
0044-5517 Zurita
0044-5525 Zvaranie
0044-5533 Zvezdina Revija
0044-555X Zvuk
0044-5576 Zwingli
0044-5584 Zycie i Mysl
0044-5592 A - Rivista Anarchica
0044-5614 A B C Decor
0044-5622 A B S E E S†
0044-5630 A C I I D
0044-5649 A D P Newsletter†
0044-5681 A I M
0044-569X A Is A Newsletter *changed to* A Is A
0044-5711 A R I S
0044-5746 Aboriginal Quarterly†
0044-5800 Abstracts of Hungarian Economic Literature
0044-5819 Abstracts on Health Effects of Environmental Pollutants
0044-5827 Abundance
0044-5843 Acadia Bulletin
0044-5851 Acadiensis: Journal of the History of the Atlantic Region
0044-586X Acarologia
0044-5878 Accident Prevention
0044-5894 Accion Empresarial
0044-5908 Accion Indigenista *changed to* Mexico Indigena
0044-5916 Accountants and Secretaries Educational Journal
0044-5924 Accountants" Washington Taxletter†
0044-5932 A C E
0044-5940 Acoma†
0044-5959 Acta Agronomica
0044-5967 Acta Amazonica
0044-5975 Acta Antiqua
0044-5983 Acta Botanica Neerlandica
0044-5991 Acta Histochemica et Cytochemica
0044-6009 Acta Hospitalia
0044-6017 Acta Medica del Valle
0044-6025 Acta Medica Iranica
0044-6033 Acta Physiologica Polonica†
0044-6041 Acta Socio-Medica Scandinavica *see* 0300-8037
0044-605X Acta Veterinaria Scandinavica
0044-6068 Action
0044-6092 Action Era Vehicle
0044-6106 Action Populaire
0044-6130 Actualidade Universitaria†
0044-6149 Actualite de la Medecine Officielle et Medecine Naturelle
0044-6157 Actualite Fiduciaire
0044-6165 Actualites Industrielles Lorraines
0044-6173 Aktuelle Traumatologie
0044-6181 Adam and Eve

ISSN INDEX

ISSN	Title
0044-6203	Alcoholism & Drug Addiction Research Foundation. Journal
0044-6211	Adelaide. National Gallery of South Australia *see* 0004-3206
0044-622X	Adelaide. Stock Exchange. Official Record†
0044-6238	Adelante (Orlando)
0044-6262	Administracion, Desarrollo, Integracion
0044-6289	A C O A
0044-6297	Administrative Court Digest
0044-6300	Administrative Scene
0044-6319	Administrator
0044-6327	Administrator
0044-6335	Adolescent Medicine
0044-6343	Adult & Child *see* 0092-4032
0044-636X	Advanced Technology Libraries
0044-6378	Advances in Urethane Science and Technology
0044-6386	Adventures in Experimental Physics
0044-6394	Adverse Drug Reaction Bulletin
0044-6408	Ad. Activities†
0044-6432	Aero News†
0044-6467	Affirm
0044-6475	Africa
0044-6483	Africa Confidential
0044-6491	Africa Letter
0044-6513	Africa Now *changed to* SIM Now
0044-653X	African Crescent
0044-6556	African Jewish Newspaper
0044-6564	African Journal of Pharmacy and Pharmaceutical Sciences
0044-6580	African Missionary *changed to* S M A-the African Missionary
0044-6602	African Religious Research†
0044-6610	African Studies Association of the West Indies. Bulletin
0044-6629	African Urban Notes *changed to* African Urban Studies
0044-6645	Africana i Nordiska Vetenskapliga. Bibliotek *changed to* Africana in the Library of the Scandinavian Institute of African Studies
0044-6661	Afrique et Parole
0044-667X	Afriscope
0044-670X	Afterthought
0044-6718	Agency Sales/With Agent and Representative *see* 0162-3656
0044-6726	Agora
0044-6734	Agra University. Bulletin
0044-6742	Agregation
0044-6750	Agri Sept
0044-6769	Agrichemical Age
0044-6785	Agricultura
0044-6793	Agricultura em Sao Paulo
0044-6807	Agricultural Engineering Society. Journal†
0044-6807	Agricultural Engineering Australia
0044-6823	Agriculture and Farming†
0044-6331	Agrifack
0044-684X	Agrologist
0044-6858	Agronomia Mocambicana
0044-6874	Agronomist
0044-6882	Agrosintesis
0044-6890	Agua
0044-6904	Ahead: Australian Health Advisory Digest†
0044-6912	Aichi-Gakuin Journal of Dental Science
0044-6920	Aikamerkki
0044-6963	Air Enthusiast *see* 0306-5634
0044-6971	Air et Cosmos
0044-698X	Air over Arizona†
0044-7005	Airfair Interline
0044-7013	Airline Passengers Association News *changed to* A P A Holiday
0044-7021	Airport Report
0044-703X	Laisve
0044-7048	Akron Business and Economic Review
0044-7064	Alaluz
0044-7072	Albania Today
0044-7080	Alberta Bowhunter and Archer
0044-7099	Alberta Builder†
0044-7102	Alberta Certified Nursing Aide Association. Newsletter *changed to* A R N A Pulse
0044-7129	Alberta Education Council. Newsletter†
0044-7137	A H E A Newsletter
0044-7145	Alberta Landrace Association. Newsletter
0044-7153	Alberta, Lands, Forests, Parks, Wildlife†
0044-7161	A M T A News Bulletin *see* 0709-4272
0044-717X	Alberta Pharmaceutical Association. A. Ph. A. Bulletin *see* 0382-4292
0044-7218	Alcheringa†
0044-7226	Alcoholism and Alcohol Education Newsletter
0044-7234	Alert
0044-7242	Alert (Crows Nest N. S. W.)
0044-7250	Alexandria Journal of Agricultural Research
0044-7269	A B N Bank. Economic Review
0044-7277	Alianza Federal de Pueblos Libres. Vox de la Alianza
0044-7293	All India Institute of Medical Sciences, New Delhi. Bulletin†
0044-7307	All India Ophthalmological Society. Journal *see* 0301-4738
0044-734X	Alliance
0044-7358	Allo Dix-Huit
0044-7382	Alternative *see* 0148-3184
0044-7412	Amanuensis†
0044-7439	Ambassador‡
0044-7447	Ambio
0044-7455	Ambulance *changed to* Ambulance Service Journal
0044-7463	Amenagement et Nature
0044-7471	Amerasia Journal
0044-748X	Latinskaya Amerika
0044-7498	American Academic Association for Peace in the Middle East. Bulletin *see* 0097-9791
0044-7501	American Alumni Council Commentary†
0044-751X	American Antiquarian Society. Proceedings
0044-7528	American-Arab Association for Commerce & Industry. Bulletin
0044-7536	A A M Bulletin *changed to* Aviso
0044-7544	American Baby
0044-7552	A B A Bulletin *see* 0045-1312
0044-7560	A L I-A B A/C L E Review
0044-7579	AMCHAM Journal *changed to* Business Journal
0044-7587	A C S Single Article Announcement
0044-7609	A C A Journal of Chiropractic
0044-7617	American Chronicle†
0044-7625	American Cinemeditor
0044-7633	American Classical Review
0044-7641	Nurses Association of the American College of Obstetricians and Gynecologists. Bulletin News *see* 0090-0311
0044-765X	American Cotton Grower
0044-7676	American Federation of Television and Radio Artists. A F T R A
0044-7684	American Film Institute Report†
0044-7692	American Fisheries Society Newsletter†
0044-7692	American Fisheries Society. Newsletter *see* 0363-2415
0044-7722	A S
0044-7730	American Journal of Therapeutics & Clinical Reports - Cases & Comments†
0044-7749	American Laboratory
0044-7757	A L A Zurnals
0044-7765	A M A Update†
0044-7773	American Notary
0044-7781	Nursing Research Report†
0044-779X	American Philological Association. Directory of Members
0044-7803	American Politics Quarterly
0044-7811	American Postal Worker
0044-782X	A P W A Washington Report *see* 0160-001X
0044-7838	American Revolution†
0044-7854	A S E A Newsletter†
0044-7889	A S M News
0044-7897	A S M News (Washington)
0044-7900	American Society for Neo-Hellenic Studies. Newsletter
0044-7919	A S P R Newsletter
0044-7927	A S T R Newsletter
0044-7935	American Society of Architectural Hardware Consultants. News and Views *see* 0361-5294
0044-7943	American Society of Cartographers. Bulletin
0044-7951	American Society of Civil Engineers. Engineering Mechanics Division. Journal
0044-796X	American Society of Civil Engineers. Hydraulics Division. Journal
0044-7978	American Society of Civil Engineers. Irrigation and Drainage Division. Journal
0044-7986	American Society of Civil Engineers. Sanitary Engineering Division. Journal *see* 0090-3914
0044-7994	American Society of Civil Engineers. Soil Mechanics and Foundation Division. Journal *see* 0093-6405
0044-8001	American Society of Civil Engineers. Structural Division. Journal
0044-801X	American Society of Civil Engineers. Transportation Engineering Division. Journal *see* 0569-7891
0044-8028	American Society of Civil Engineers. Waterways, Harbors, and Coastal Engineering Division. Journal *see* 0148-9895
0044-8044	American Society of Planning Officials. A S P O Planning Advisory Service *changed to* A P A Planning Advisory Service Reports
0044-8052	A S D A Newsletter *changed to* New Dentist
0044-8060	American Studies in Scandinavia
0044-8079	American Zionist Federation. News and Views
0044-8087	Ami de la Boulangerie *changed to* Nouvelles de la Boulangerie
0044-8095	Ami des Jardins et de la Maison
0044-8117	Ami du Charcutier, du Boucher et du Salaisonnier
0044-8125	Amino Acids, Peptide & Protein Abstracts *changed to* Biochemistry Abstracts, Part 3: Amino Acids, Peptides & Proteins
0044-8133	Amis d'Andre Gide. Bulletin
0044-815X	Ampute de Guerre
0044-8168	Amra
0044-8176	Analecta Linguistica
0044-8184	Anales de Ortopedia y Traumatologia
0044-8192	Analysen und Prognosen ueber die Welt von Morgen
0044-8206	Anapress
0044-8214	Anasthesiologische Praxis *see* 0303-6200
0044-8222	Ancestor
0044-8249	Angewandte Chemie
0044-8257	A.C.A. Review
0044-8265	Anglo-Soviet Journal
0044-8273	Anglo-Ukranian News†
0044-8281	Angola Bulletin *changed to* Amandla
0044-829X	Animal Defence League of Canada. News Bulletin
0044-832X	Annals of Economic and Social Measurement†
0044-8338	Annals of Immunology *changed to* Immunologia Polska
0044-8346	Irish Booklore
0044-8362	Antepasados
0044-8370	Anthropological Society of Oxford. Journal
0044-8389	Antioquia Medica
0044-8400	Apartment News *changed to* Apartment Owner-Builder
0044-8419	Apero†
0044-8427	Apiculture in Western Australia†
0044-8435	Apidologie
0044-8451	Applied Radiology *see* 0160-9963
0044-8486	Aquaculture
0044-8508	Aquarium Society of New South Wales, Monthly Journal
0044-8516	Aquatic Sciences & Fisheries Abstracts *see* 0140-5373
0044-8516	Aquatic Sciences & Fisheries Abstracts *see* 0140-5381
0044-8524	Aqui
0044-8540	Arab-Canada Newsletter *see* 0703-9018
0044-8559	Arab News†
0044-8575	West Virginia University. Department of Biology. Arboretum Newsletter *changed to* West Virginia University. Department of Biology. Core Arboretum Bulletin
0044-8591	Archaeology in Montana
0044-8605	Archeologicke Rozhledy
0044-8613	Archipel
0044-8621	Architect
0044-863X	Architectura
0044-8648	Architectural Association, London. A A Notes†
0044-8664	Architectuur en Beeldende Kunsten
0044-8672	Architekt
0044-8680	Architektura a Urbanizmus
0044-8699	Archiv Orientalni
0044-8702	Archives Medicales de Normandie
0044-8710	Archives of Child Health
0044-8729	Archives of Labor History and Urban Affairs Newsletter *changed to* Archives of Labor and Urban Affairs Newsletter
0044-8737	Archivio Storico Siracusano
0044-8745	Archivium Hibernicum
0044-8753	Archivum Mathematicum
0044-8761	Archiwum Procesow Spalania
0044-877X	Arctic Frontiers†
0044-8788	Areas of Concern
0044-8796	Arecanut and Spices Bulletin *changed to* Indian Arecanut, Spices & Cocoa Journal
0044-8818	Argosy Weekly
0044-8826	Argus *changed to* Argus Magazine
0044-8850	A S D M Newsletter
0044-8869	Arizona Safety Sad-Istics *see* 0147-3743
0044-8877	University of Arizona Library. Bibliographic Bulletin
0044-8885	Ark River Review†
0044-8885	Ark River Review
0044-8893	Arkansas LP News
0044-8907	Arkansas Poultry Times
0044-8915	Arkkitehtiuutiset
0044-8931	Armed Citizen News
0044-894X	Armenian Observer
0044-8958	Armidale, New South Wales. Teachers' College. Bulletin *changed to* Armidale College of Advanced Education. Bulletin
0044-8966	Armor
0044-8974	Armstrong Logic
0044-8982	Arquivos Fluminenses de Odontologia
0044-9008	Ars
0044-9016	Art Gallery of Greater Victoria. Bulletin *see* 0317-2031
0044-9024	Art Gallery of Ontario. Coming Events *see* 0709-8413
0044-9032	ARLIS Newsletter *see* 0307-4722
0044-9059	Art Teachers Association of Victoria. Journal *changed to* A C T A Magazine
0044-9067	Arte Nuova Oggi *changed to* Arte Nuova
0044-9075	Artefact
0044-9091	Arthur
0044-9105	Artificial Rainfall Newsletter
0044-913X	Artistic Pakistan†
0044-9148	Asahi Camera
0044-9164	Asia Focus†
0044-9172	Asia Research Bulletin
0044-9180	Asian Beacon
0044-9199	Asian Development Bank. Newsletter *changed to* A D B Quarterly Review
0044-9202	Asian Music
0044-9210	Asian Periodicals: a Selected List of Titles Received and Their Contents *changed to* Periodicals of Asia and Oceania
0044-9229	Asian Productivity Organization. A P O News

0044-9245 Asian Studies Professional Review†
0044-9253 Revista Astronomica
0044-9261 A I T I M Boletin de Informacion Tecnica
0044-9288 A. N. A. B. A. Boletin
0044-930X A N E C
0044-9318 Asociacion Peruana de Astronomia. Boletin
0044-9326 Asociacion Rural del Uruguay. Revista
0044-9342 Assessors Review
0044-9369 Associacao Brasileira de Educacao Agricola Superior. A B E A S Informa
0044-9393 A C A Reports *see* 0194-1305
0044-9407 Association Canadienne des Bibliothecaires de Langue Francaise. Nouvelles de l'A C B L F *see* 0316-0963
0044-9415 Association des Architects de la Province de Quebec. Bulletin *see* 0316-9200
0044-9423 Archives
0044-9458 A. F. E. A. S. Bulletin *see* 0705-3851
0044-9466 Association for Preservation Technology. Bulletin
0044-9474 Association for Retarded Children of British Columbia. Newsletter *see* 0702-7265
0044-9482 Association for the Advancement of Agricultural Sciences in Africa. Journal *changed to* African Journal of Agricultural Sciences
0044-9490 A I L A Bulletin
0044-9504 A I O S P Bulletin
0044-9539 Association of British Columbia Librarians. Newsletter†
0044-9547 Association of Canadian Distillers. A C D Bulletin†
0044-9555 Association of Canadian Faculties of Dentistry. Newsletter
0044-9563 A. C. U. Bulletin of Current Documentation (ABCD)
0044-9598 Association of Engineers, India. Journal
0044-9601 A G B Notes *changed to* A G B News Notes
0044-961X A G B Reports
0044-9628 Association of Law Teachers. Journal *see* 0306-9400
0044-9636 Association of New Jersey Conservation Commissions Newsletter *changed to* A N J E C Report
0044-9652 A R L Minutes
0044-9660 A S L A President's Newsletter
0044-9679 Association of Teachers of Mathematics of New York City. Summation
0044-9687 Association of Teachers of Social Studies. A. T. S. S. Bulletin
0044-9695 A U A Newsletter
0044-9709 Association pour l'Histoire de Belle-Ile-En-Mer. Bulletin Trimestriel
0044-9725 Association Senegalaise pour l'Etude du Quaternaire de l'Ouest African. Bulletin de Liaison *changed to* Association Senegalaise pour l'Etude du Quaternaire Africain. Bulletin de Liaison
0044-9733 Associazione Italiana di Cartografia. A I C Bolletino
0044-9741 A P A C Inform
0044-975X A I S C A T Informazioni
0044-9768 Astarte
0044-9776 Asthma Welfarer
0044-9792 Astrology and Athrishta
0044-9806 Astronomical Society of South Australia. Bulletin
0044-9814 Astronomical Society of Victoria. Journal
0044-9822 Astronomy & Space†
0044-9830 At Home & Abroad *see* 0306-9028
0044-9849 Atenea
0044-9857 Athanor
0044-9865 Athenes-Presse Libre
0044-9873 Athletic Administration
0044-9881 Atlantic Control States Beverage Journal
0044-989X Atlantic Provinces Economic Council. Newsletter
0044-9903 Atlantic Provinces Numismatic Association. Newsletter
0044-992X Atlantic Salmon Journal
0044-9954 Atomic Absorption Newsletter *see* 0195-5373
0044-9962 Attak *changed to* Buut
0044-9970 W R R I News Reports
0044-9989 Audience and Programme Research
0045-0006 Auditor's Computer Update Digest†
0045-0014 Audubon Leader
0045-0030 Auris
0045-0049 Ausbildung und Beratung in Land- und Hauswirtschaft
0045-0065 Australasian Amateur Athletics *changed to* Australasian Track & Field
0045-0073 Australasian Insurance Journal
0045-0081 Australasian Kennel Review and Dog News
0045-009X Australasian Model Railroad Magazine *changed to* Australian Model Railway Magazine
0045-0111 Australia. Bureau of Statistics. Balance of Payments
0045-012X Industrial Information Bulletin†
0045-0138 Australia. Department of National Development. Nat/Dev†
0045-0146 Australia. Department of the Northern Territory. Northern Territory Affairs†
0045-0170 A N Z A News
0045-0189 Australia. Northern Territory Division. Northern Territory Newsletter
0045-0197 Australia Now
0045-0200 Australia. Bureau of Agricultural Economics. Fibres Other Than Wool *see* 0311-2950
0045-0219 Australian and New Zealand Association for Medieval and Renaissance Studies. Bulletin†
0045-0235 Australian Angler *changed to* Australian Angler's Fishing World
0045-0243 Australian Apprenticeship Advisory Committee. Apprenticeship News†
0045-026X Australian Author
0045-0286 Australian Bankruptcy Bulletin
0045-0308 Australian Biblical Review
0045-0316 Australian Birdwatcher
0045-0324 Australian Boating Industry
0045-0332 Australian Bridge
0045-0340 Australian Chemical Industry Directory†
0045-0359 Australian Chiropractors Association. Journal
0045-0367 Australian Chit Chat *changed to* Postmarked OCEANIA
0045-0383 Australian Computer Society. Canberra Branch. Bulletin *changed to* Canberra Computer Bulletin
0045-0391 A C O S S Quarterly *changed to* Australian Social Welfare
0045-0391 A C O S S Quarterly *see* 0004-9557
0045-0405 Australian Current Law
0045-0413 Australian Current Law Review†
0045-0421 Australian Dental Journal
0045-043X Australian Environmental Report *see* 0311-0931
0045-0448 Australian Films
0045-0456 Australian Furnishing Trade Journal *changed to* Furnishing
0045-0472 Australian Goat World
0045-0480 Australian Government News†
0045-0499 Australian GP
0045-0510 Australian Hand Weaver and Spinner
0045-0537 Australian Home Gardener†
0045-0545 Australian Institute of Agricultural Science. Journal
0045-0553 Australian Institute of Dairy Factory Managers and Secretaries. Butter Fats and Solids
0045-0588 Australian Jersey Journal
0045-0596 Australian Journal of Advanced Education
0045-060X Australian Journal of Experimental Agriculture and Animal Husbandry
0045-0618 Australian Journal of Forensic Sciences
0045-0626 Australian Journal of Instrumentation and Control
0045-0634 Australian Journal of Mental Retardation *changed to* Australian Journal of Developmental Disabilities
0045-0642 Australian Journal of Optometry
0045-0650 Australian Journal of Sports Medicine
0045-0669 Australian Labor Party. A.L.P.
0045-0677 Australian Maps
0045-0685 Australian Mathematics Teacher
0045-0693 Australian Meat Board. Meat Producer and Exporter *changed to* Australian Meat and Livestock Corporation. Meat Producer and Exporter
0045-0707 A M D E L Bulletin
0045-0715 A.M.R.A. Journal
0045-0731 A N C O L D Bulletin
0045-074X Australian National Drycleaner
0045-0758 Australian Nurses' Journal
0045-0774 Australian O.C.C.A. Proceedings and News
0045-0782 Australian Orchid Review
0045-0820 Australian Retail Tobacconist
0045-0839 Australian Road Transport Federation. A. R. T. F. Digest
0045-0847 Australian Roads
0045-0855 Australian Science Teachers' Journal
0045-0863 Australian Sea Spray Weekly *see* 0311-7839
0045-0901 Australian Stock Exchange Journal
0045-091X Australian Teacher *changed to* Teachers Guild of New South Wales. Proceedings
0045-0928 Australian Technical Teacher
0045-0936 Australian Tobacco Journal†
0045-0944 Australian Trader
0045-0952 Australian Union of Students. Education Newsletter *see* 0312-8318
0045-0960 Australian Welding Research†
0045-0979 Australian Worker
0045-0995 Auto Accessory Retailer International *see* 0306-2899
0045-1002 Auto-Neige
0045-1010 Auto und Reise
0045-1053 Automobile & Tractor (Ancillary & Agri Equipment)
0045-107X Automotive Marketing *see* 0193-3264
0045-1088 Automotive Messenger
0045-110X Automotive Transport Labour Relations Association. Monthly Labour Bulletin†
0045-1118 Autonomi
0045-1126 Autotouring
0045-1142 Auvergne Economique
0045-1150 Avant-Scene Cinema
0045-1169 Avant Scene Theatre
0045-1177 Aviacion y Astronautica
0045-1185 Aviation Historical Society of Australia. Journal
0045-1193 International Aviation Mechanics Journal
0045-1207 Aviation Safety Digest
0045-1223 Aware†
0045-1231 Awareness†
0045-124X Ayn Rand Letter†
0045-1258 Azor *changed to* Cuadernos Literarios Azor
0045-1266 B E E
0045-1274 B P Shield International
0045-1282 Ba Shiru
0045-1290 Background to South African and World News†
0045-1304 Badger Herald
0045-1312 Badminton U.S.A.†
0045-1320 Baha'i World
0045-1347 Ballet-Hoo
0045-1355 Balloon *changed to* Atkinson Balloon
0045-1363 Baltimore Health News *changed to* Perspectives (Baltimore)
0045-1371 Baltistica
0045-138X Bamah
0045-1398 Banana Bulletin
0045-1401 Banco de Guatemala. Informe Economico
0045-1428 Bangladesh Journal of Biological and Agricultural Sciences *changed to* Bangladesh Journal of Biological Sciences
0045-1444 Bank Melli Iran. Bulletin
0045-1460 Bank of Canada. Review
0045-1479 Bank of Tanzania. Economic Bulletin
0045-1487 Bank Operations Report
0045-1495 Bank Pembangunan Indonesia Newsletter
0045-1509 Bank Street Reporting *changed to* Report from Bank Street
0045-1533 Banque Canadienne Nationale. Bulletin Mensuel†
0045-1541 Bar Executive Key Handbook†
0045-155X Barnet Marksman
0045-1576 Battle Line *see* 0145-1677
0045-1592 Beaverbrook Art Gallery
0045-1606 Bedriftsoekonomisk Informasjon *changed to* Oekonomisk Rapport
0045-1614 Bedryfsleiding/Business Management *see* 0378-9098
0045-1622 Beef & You†
0045-1649 Beer in Canada†
0045-1673 B R S Monthly Index
0045-1681 Beitraege zur Historischen Sozialkunde
0045-169X Beitraege zur Konfliktforschung
0045-1703 Belgium. Institut National de Statistique. Bulletin de Statistique
0045-172X Benefits International
0045-1738 Bensiini Uutiset
0045-1746 Bergens Privatbanks Kvartalsskrift *see* 0332-6756
0045-1762 Berliner Bauwirtschaft
0045-1770 Beseda Nasi Vesnice
0045-1789 Betrifft: Erziehung
0045-1797 Better Boating†
0045-1800 Better Business Bureau of Metropolitan New York. News Review†
0045-1819 Better Business Bureau of Metropolitan New York. Report to Business *changed to* Report to Business and Consumer Information
0045-1827 Beverly Hills Bar Association. Journal
0045-1843 Biblical Theology Bulletin
0045-1851 Biblio-Cal Notes
0045-186X Bibliografie van de Nederlandse Taal- en Literatuur Wetenschap
0045-1878 Bibliographic Society of Canada. Index Committee. Newsletter†
0045-1886 Bibliographie Nationale de la Tunisie†
0045-1894 Bibliographie Selective des Publications Officielles Francaise
0045-1908 Bibliographies of Chemists†
0045-1916 Bibliographische Informationen aus der Technik und Ihren Grundlagenwissenschaften†
0045-1924 Bibliography of Articles on Physical and Health Education, Sport and Allied Subjects *changed to* Bibliographical Index on Physical and Health Education, Sport and Allied Subjects
0045-1932 Bibliography on High Pressure Research
0045-1940 Biblionews and Australian Notes and Queries
0045-1959 Biblioteca Teatrale
0045-1967 Bibliotheque Nationale. Bulletin
0045-1975 Big Bike Magazine *changed to* Choppers & Big Bike Magazine
0045-1983 Big Book of Metalworking Machinery
0045-1991 Big Byte
0045-2009 Bil-Nyt *changed to* Motor-Journalen Bilen
0045-2025 Biochemical Systematics *see* 0305-1978
0045-2033 Biological Science
0045-205X Biologie in Unserer Zeit
0045-2068 Bioorganic Chemistry
0045-2076 Bird Keeping in Australia
0045-2084 Black Bag
0045-2114 Black Books Bulletin
0045-2165 Black Graphics International
0045-2181 Black Law Journal
0045-219X Black Lechwe
0045-2203 Black Lines: a Journal of Black Studies†
0045-222X Black Maria
0045-2238 Black News Digest
0045-2246 Black Oracle *changed to* Cinemacabre
0045-2270 Blackfish
0045-2289 Bleu et Rouge
0045-2297 Blues & Soul Music Review
0045-2300 Boardroom Reports

0045-2319 Bodyshop
0045-2351 Boian News Service
0045-236X BolaffiArte
0045-2378 Boletim de Materiais Dentarios
0045-2386 Boletim de Vulgarizacao Veterinaria
0045-2394 Boletin de Ciencias Politicas y Sociales
0045-2424 Bollettino di Magistratura Democratica
0045-2467 Bolsa de Cereales. Revista Institucional
0045-2483 Bonsai in Australia
0045-2505 Book Angles†
0045-2513 Book Trolley *see* 0305-9340
0045-2521 Bookplates in the News
0045-253X Books *changed to* Booknews
0045-2556 Books for Young People†
0045-2564 Books in Canada
0045-2572 Books in English
0045-2580 Border Business Digest *changed to* Cumbria Weekly Digest
0045-2599 Bosch Kurier†
0045-2602 Boston After Dark *changed to* Boston Phoenix
0045-2629 Botanica
0045-2637 Botaniste†
0045-2637 Botaniste *see* 0181-7582
0045-2653 Bouliste et le Petanquier *see* 0336-8424
0045-2688 Boys Village Report *changed to* Dellcrest Children's Centre Newsletter
0045-2696 Brannmannen
0045-270X Brasil Florestal
0045-2718 Brauer und Maelzer *see* 0341-7115
0045-2726 M A N
0045-2742 Brazil. Superintendencia do Desenvolvimento da Amazonia. S U D A M Documenta
0045-2769 Break Through†
0045-2777 Breakthrough
0045-2785 Breves Nouvelles de France *changed to* Nouvelles de France
0045-2793 Brian Bex Report *changed to* American Record
0045-2823 Bridge (New York)
0045-2831 Brigade
0045-2858 Bristol Diocesan Gazette *changed to* Bristol Diocesan News
0045-2866 Britain and Overseas
0045-2874 British Advent Messenger
0045-2890 British Caribbean Philatelic Journal
0045-2904 British Columbia Art Teachers' Association. Newsletter *see* 0316-1544
0045-2912 B. C. Association of Teachers of Classics. Newsletter *see* 0316-2508
0045-2947 British Columbia Counsellors' Association. Newsletter *see* 0705-8802
0045-2955 British Columbia English Teacher *see* 0316-0173
0045-2963 British Columbia Historical News
0045-2971 British Columbia Hotelman†
0045-2998 British Columbia Mountaineer
0045-3005 British Columbia Museums Association. Museum Round-Up
0045-3013 B C Outdoors
0045-3021 British Columbia Rancher
0045-303X British Columbia Snow Survey Bulletin
0045-3048 British Columbia Social Studies Teachers' Association. Newsletter *see* 0315-8527
0045-3056 British Columbia Tax Reports
0045-3064 British Columbia Thoroughbred
0045-3072 Phycological Newsletter
0045-3080 B.C. Voice
0045-3099 British Iron and Steel Research Association. Open Report List *changed to* British Steel Corporation. Corporate Development Laboratory. Open Report List
0045-3102 British Journal of Social Work
0045-3110 British Naturopathic Journal and Osteopathic Review
0045-3129 B N A Topics
0045-3145 British Society of Rheology. Bulletin
0045-3153 British Speleological Association. Bulletin *see* 0142-1832
0045-317X B M I: the Many Worlds of Music
0045-3188 Broadcasting Bibliophile's Booknotes *changed to* Mass Media Booknotes
0045-3226 Broken Spoke
0045-3234 Bromeletter
0045-3242 B.A.C.A. Calendar of Cultural Events
0045-3250 Bruce County Historical Notes†
0045-3269 Brush
0045-3277 Belgium. Institut Royal Meteorologique. Bulletin Mensuel: Pollution Atmospherique. Fumee et So Deux†
0045-3285 Buckeye Review
0045-3293 Buck's Safety Management AID†
0045-3315 Buddhist Quarterly
0045-3323 Budgerigar Bulletin
0045-3331 Museo Social Argentino. Boletin
0045-334X Buffalo
0045-3374 Buhiti
0045-3382 Builder
0045-3412 Building Ideas
0045-3420 Building News†
0045-3439 Building Specification
0045-3447 University of Stellenbosch. Bureau for Economic Research. Building Survey
0045-3455 Building with Steel
0045-348X Bullet
0045-3498 Bulletin Bibliographique de la Prevention *see* 0302-7651
0045-3501 Bulletin de l'Afrique Noire
0045-351X Bulletin Jugend und Literatur
0045-3536 Bulwark
0045-3544 Bureaucrat
0045-3552 Burning Spear
0045-3587 Business and Professional Woman
0045-3595 Business and Professional Woman
0045-3609 Business and Society Review
0045-3617 Business Aviation
0045-3625 Business Dynamics *changed to* B & P A
0045-3633 Business Ideas and Facts†
0045-3641 Business Venezuela
0045-3668 Businessman's Law
0045-3676 Bust†
0045-3676 Bust
0045-3684 Buyers' Market
0045-3692 Buzz
0045-3706 C I D X Messenger
0045-3714 Cable
0045-3730 Cahiers Bibliographiques des Lettres Quebecoise†
0045-3749 Cahiers de Litterature et de Linguistique Applique†
0045-3765 Cahiers d'Outre-Mer
0045-3773 Cahiers du Bilinguisme
0045-3781 Cahiers du Travailleur Intellectuel
0045-379X Cahiers Spartacus
0045-3803 University of Cairo. Faculty of Medicine. Medical Journal
0045-3811 Caisses et Emballages en Bois
0045-382X Calamus
0045-3838 Calcutta Gazette
0045-3846 Calcutta Review
0045-3854 Calcutta Weekly Notes
0045-3862 Calcuttan
0045-3870 Caledonian
0045-3889 Calgary Livestock Market Journal
0045-3900 California Builder and Engineer
0045-3919 C C A C Review *changed to* C C A C
0045-3927 California Condor *changed to* Raptor Report
0045-3935 California Grocers Advocate†
0045-3943 California Institute of Technology, Pasadena. Division of Geological and Planetary Sciences. Report on Geological and Planetary Sciences for the Year†
0045-3943 California Institute of Technology. Division of Geological and Planetary Sciences. Report on Geological and Planetary Sciences for the Year
0045-3951 California News Index†
0045-396X California News Reporter†
0045-3978 California Quarterly
0045-3986 University of California, Los Angeles. Chicano Studies Center. Creative Series
0045-3994 University of California, Los Angeles. Chicano Studies Center. Monographs
0045-4001 Caliper
0045-401X Call
0045-4036 Call and Post
0045-4044 Callboard
0045-4052 Calquarium
0045-4087 Cameroun Litteraire†
0045-4095 CAMmunique†
0045-4125 Camping
0045-4133 Campus (Toronto) *see* 0383-2406
0045-415X Statistics Canada Weekly *see* 0380-0547
0045-4168 Canada. Department of Agriculture. Forage Crops Division. Forage Notes
0045-4176 Canada. Department of Energy, Mines, and Resources. Departmental Map Library. Acquisitions of Maps, Atlases and Gazeteers†
0045-4192 Canada Gazette: Part 1: Government, Divorce, Bankruptcy Notices, Etc
0045-4206 Canada Gazette: Part 2: Statutory Orders and Regulations
0045-4214 Canada Japan Trade Council. Newsletter
0045-4230 Canada Supreme Court Reports
0045-4249 Canada-Svensken
0045-4257 Canada Today/d'Aujourd'hui
0045-4265 Canada Travel Digest
0045-4273 Canada Trust Bulletin†
0045-4281 Canada-U.K. Trade News
0045-429X Canada. Western Forest Products Laboratory. Information Reports *see* 0708-6172
0045-4303 Canada's Business Climate
0045-4311 Canadian Aberdeen-Angus News
0045-432X Canadian Agricultural Engineering
0045-4338 Canadian Air Comments
0045-4346 Canadian Collector
0045-4354 Canadian Association for Laboratory Animal Science Newsletter
0045-4362 Canadian Association of Exhibitions. Ex-Site
0045-4389 Canadian Assoication of Medical Clinics. Bulletin *changed to* Group Practice in Canada
0045-4397 Canadian Association of Medical Record Librarians. Bulletin *see* 0227-3748
0045-4419 Canadian Association of Social Workers. Newsletter†
0045-4427 Canadian Athletic Director and Coach
0045-4435 C. B. A. Bulletin
0045-4451 Canadian Barber and Men's Hairstylists *changed to* Canadian Men's Hairstylist and Barber
0045-446X Canadian Bee Journal†
0045-4486 Canadian Biographical Studies
0045-4494 Canadian Boating
0045-4508 Canadian Building News
0045-4524 Canadian Chamber of Commerce. Newsletter†
0045-4540 Canadian Chess Chat
0045-4567 Canadian Coach†
0045-4575 Canadian Coin Box
0045-4583 Canadian Community Publisher *see* 0380-8025
0045-4605 Canadian Council of Churches. Council Communicator
0045-4613 Canadian Council of Teachers of English. Newsletter
0045-4621 Canadian Courses and Seminars *changed to* Short Courses and Seminars
0045-463X Canadian Criminology and Corrections Association. Bulletin *see* 0705-9094
0045-4648 Canadian Curling News
0045-4656 Canadian Daily Stock Charts
0045-4680 Canadian Earnings Estimator
0045-4702 C E M A Newsletter *changed to* E E M A C Newsletter
0045-4729 C. F. C. F. News for the Canadian Camper *see* 0316-280X
0045-4737 Canadian Far Eastern Newsletter
0045-4745 Canadian Farmer
0045-477X Canadian Fiction
0045-4788 Canadian Field Hockey News
0045-4796 C O S S I P
0045-480X Canadian Film Institute. Bulletin *changed to* Images
0045-4834 Canadian Football News
0045-4850 Canadian Forces Dental Services Quarterly†
0045-4869 C. F. A. News
0045-4877 Canadian Forwarder
0045-4885 Canadian Fruitgrower
0045-4893 Canadian Government Programs and Services
0045-4907 Canadian Guernsey Breeders' Journal
0045-4915 Canadian Handgun
0045-4931 Canadian Imperial Bank of Commerce. Foreign Trade News†
0045-4958 Canadian India Times
0045-4966 Canadian Industrial Relations and Personnel Developments
0045-4974 Canadian Industrial Traffic League. Traffic Notes
0045-4982 C I C A Dialogue
0045-4990 Canadian Insurance Law Reports
0045-5008 Canadian Interline News†
0045-5024 Canadian Ionospheric Data
0045-5059 Canadian Jewish Outlook
0045-5067 Canadian Journal of Forest Research
0045-5075 Canadian Journal of Optometry
0045-5083 Canadian Journal of Otolaryngology *see* 0381-6605
0045-5091 Canadian Journal of Philosophy
0045-5105 Canadian Journal of Spectroscopy
0045-5121 Canadian Leathercraft
0045-5156 Canadian Manager
0045-5172 Canadian Music Educators Association. Newsletter
0045-5202 Canadian Numismatic Research Society. Transactions
0045-5229 Canadian Opera Guild. Guild News *changed to* Canadian Opera Guild. Overtures
0045-5237 Canadian Paper Money Journal
0045-5245 Canadian Parachutist *see* 0319-3896
0045-5253 Canadian Philatelist
0045-527X Canadian Red Book
0045-5288 Canadian Red Cross Society. Ontario Division. News Bulletin
0045-5296 C R H A Reporter
0045-530X Canadian Risk Management & Business Insurance
0045-5318 Canadian Sales and Credit Law Guide *changed to* Canadian Commercial Law Guide
0045-5326 Canadian Sales Tax Reports
0045-5334 Canadian Scene
0045-5342 Canadian Securities Law Reports
0045-5369 Canadian Society for Education through Art. Newsletter
0045-5377 Canadian Society of Laboratory Technologists. Bulletin
0045-5385 Canadian Sports Digest
0045-5393 Canadian Steam
0045-5407 Canadian Stock Market Point and Figure Summary
0045-5423 Canadian Swine
0045-5431 Canadian Teacher of the Deaf *see* 0382-7976
0045-544X Canadian Theosophist
0045-5458 CTM: the Human Element
0045-5458 Canadian Training Methods *see* 0045-5458
0045-5466 Canadian Transport
0045-5482 Canadian Travel News *see* 0319-7093
0045-5490 Canadian Travel Press
0045-5504 Canadian Trot Canadien *see* 0704-0733
0045-5512 Canadian Union of Public Employees. Journal *changed to* Canadian Union of Public Employees. The Public Employee
0045-5520 Canadian Vocational Journal
0045-5539 Canadian Warehousing Association. C W A Reporter†
0045-5555 Canadian Western Rider *see* 0702-9071
0045-5571 Canadian Wildlife and Fisheries Newsletter Bulletin *see* 0318-5133

ISSN	Title
0045-5598	Canadian Wool Grower and Sheep Breeder see 0319-7387
0045-5601	Canberra and District Historical Society. Journal see 0313-5977
0045-561X	Canberra Comments
0045-5628	Canberra Survey
0045-5660	Capella†
0045-5687	Capitol Studies changed to Congressional Studies
0045-5695	Caps and Flints
0045-5709	Car Buyer†
0045-5717	Car Tips†
0045-5725	Caravan Industry & Park Operator
0045-5733	Carbide Journal changed to Carbide and Tool Journal
0045-5741	Cardiac Rehabilitation
0045-575X	Cardiovascular & Metabolic Diseases†
0045-5776	Career Development†
0045-5792	Caribbean Business News
0045-5822	Caribbean News
0045-5830	Carleton Education Bulletin
0045-5857	Carolina Centerscope†
0045-5865	Carolina Tips
0045-5873	Carolinian
0045-5881	Cartologica
0045-592X	Castle Street Circular
0045-5938	Catalog of Selected Documents in Psychology
0045-5946	Catalogue of Replacement Books for Children's Library Collections†
0045-5954	Catalyst (Madison)
0045-5970	Catholic Agitator
0045-5989	Catholic Citizen
0045-5997	Cavalletto e Tavolozza
0045-6004	Caveat Emptor
0045-6020	Celebrity Bulletin
0045-6039	Cell Differentiation
0045-6047	Cent Blagues
0045-6055	C R R I Road Abstracts
0045-6063	Centre Canadien International de Recherches et d'Information sur l'Economie Publique et Cooperative. Revue du Canadien see 0384-8744
0045-608X	Centre de Recherche en Civilisation Canadienne-Francaise. Bulletin
0045-6098	C H I S S Cahiers
0045-6101	Centre International pour le Credit Communal changed to Local Finance
0045-611X	Ecuador. Centro de Desarrollo Industrial. Boletin Industrial
0045-6128	Centro de Estudios Educativos. Revista
0045-6136	Centro Latinoamericano de Demografia. Boletin Demografico
0045-6152	Ceramurgia
0045-6179	Cercles des Jeunes Naturalistes. Feuillets du Club
0045-6187	Ceskoslovensky Casopis Historicky
0045-6195	Ceylon Forester changed to Sri Lanka Forester
0045-6209	Ceylon Trade Journal†
0045-6217	Congress News
0045-6225	Chakra†
0045-6233	Challenge (Washington)
0045-625X	Challenge in Educational Administration
0045-6268	Challenger†
0045-6276	Chambre de Commerce, d'Agriculture, d'Industrie et des Mines du Gabon. Bulletin
0045-6292	Chambre de Commerce du Sud de la Tunisie. Bulletin Economique
0045-6306	Chambre de Commerce Francaise au Canada. Revue see 0318-7306
0045-6314	Champion
0045-6330	Channel (Wellesley)
0045-6349	Chaplin
0045-6365	Chat
0045-6381	Chelsea Speleological Society Newsletter
0045-639X	Chemical Industry Notes
0045-6403	Chemical Insight
0045-6411	C R C Critical Reviews in Biochemistry
0045-642X	C R C Critical Reviews in Bioengineering
0045-6446	C R C Critical Reviews in Toxicology
0045-6454	C R C Critical Reviews in Microbiology
0045-6470	Chemical Society, London. Journal. Section B: Physical Organic Chemistry
0045-6497	Chemical Take-Off
0045-6500	Chemical Weekly
0045-6519	Chemische Technik
0045-6527	Chemists' Quarterly
0045-6535	Chemosphere
0045-6543	Cherokee One Feather
0045-6551	Cherokee Times
0045-656X	Chesapeake Bay Magazine
0045-6578	Chess Canada
0045-6586	Sahovski Informator
0045-6594	Chess Player†
0045-6608	Chevre
0045-6616	C A G L A Newsletter changed to Chicago Area Group on Latin America. Occasional Papers
0045-6624	Chicagoland Development
0045-6632	Child Care Quarterly
0045-6640	Child Education Quarterly changed to Child Education Special
0045-6659	Child Welfare League Newsletter
0045-6667	Children's Aid Society News changed to Children's Aid Society Newsletter
0045-6675	C.A.S. Record see 0319-7468
0045-6691	Children's Apparel Merchandising Aids
0045-6705	Children's Libraries Newsletter changed to Orana
0045-6713	Children's Literature in Education
0045-6721	Chilton's Truck Repair Manual changed to Chilton's Truck and Van Repair Manual
0045-6756	China Monthly†
0045-6764	China Now
0045-6780	Christian Brothers of the Australian and New Zealand Provinces. Our Studies
0045-6799	Christian Communications Journal in Africa
0045-6802	Christian Graduate
0045-6810	Christian Institute for Ethnic Studies in Asia. Bulletin
0045-6829	Christian Patriot
0045-6845	Christian Research Institute. Newsletter changed to Forward (San Juan Capistrano)
0045-6861	Church and Clergy Finance
0045-687X	Church and School Equipment News
0045-6888	Ciencia Agronomica
0045-6896	Ciervo
0045-690X	Cine-Dossiers
0045-6926	Cinema
0045-6942	Circulo Odontologico de Cordoba. Revista
0045-6969	C L News
0045-6985	City and Suburban Travel
0045-6993	City College Alumnus
0045-7019	City of Ottawa Coin Club. Monthly Bulletin
0045-7027	Civic Affairs
0045-7035	Civil Affairs Journal & Newsletter
0045-7043	Civil & Military Law Journal
0045-7051	Civil Liberties
0045-706X	Civil Rights News Letter
0045-7116	Clave
0045-7159	Climbing
0045-7183	Clio Medica
0045-7191	Clown War
0045-7205	Club Management in Australia
0045-7213	Club Mirror
0045-723X	Coastal Zone Management
0045-7248	Cocina y Hogar
0045-7256	Cocoa Growers Bulletin
0045-7272	Coin Launderer and Cleaner
0045-7280	Coin Wholesaler
0045-7310	CODIA
0045-7329	Colegio Nacional de Enfermeras. Revista
0045-7337	Coleopterists Newsletter see 0010-065X
0045-7345	Collective Bargaining Settlements in New York State
0045-7353	Collector's Exchange
0045-7361	College Canada
0045-737X	College Law Digest
0045-7388	College of Physicians and Surgeons of Ontario. Semi-Annual Report
0045-7396	Collegiate
0045-740X	Colony changed to Question Mark
0045-7426	Colorado Journal of Educational Research
0045-7434	C T R C Newsletter
0045-7450	Cahiers de Combat pour la Paix
0045-7469	Combat pour l'Homme changed to Nouvel Humanisme
0045-7477	Combat Syndicaliste changed to Espoir
0045-7523	Comfort Engineering changed to Environmental Design
0045-754X	Commerce
0045-7558	Commerce et Distribution†
0045-7566	Commercial Bank of Australia. Economic Review
0045-7574	Commercial Bank of Ethiopia. Market Report
0045-7582	Commission des Ecoles Catholiques de Montreal. Bulletin d'Information†
0045-7620	Commonwealth and Colonial History Newsletter
0045-7639	Commonwealth Professional
0045-7647	Commonwealth Scientific and Industrial Research Organization. Industrial Research News
0045-7663	Communication
0045-7671	Communicator (Ann Arbor) changed to Great Lakes Communicator
0045-768X	Communicator of Technical Information see 0308-9580
0045-7698	Communika
0045-7701	Communitarian†
0045-7701	Communitarian changed to Communities; a Journal of Cooperative Living
0045-771X	Community changed to Community Focus
0045-7728	Community College Social Science Quarterly changed to Community College Social Science Journal
0045-7736	Community Education Journal†
0045-7787	Company Law Institute of India. Reports of Company Cases
0045-7809	Compass
0045-7817	Compulsory Military Service and the Objector†
0045-7825	Computer Methods in Applied Mechanics and Engineering
0045-7833	Computer Operations†
0045-7841	Computer Price Guide
0045-785X	Computer Program Abstracts
0045-7868	Computer Programs in Science and Technology
0045-7892	Computer Society of India. Journal
0045-7906	Computers & Electrical Engineering
0045-7930	Computers & Fluids
0045-7949	Computers & Structures
0045-7965	Computing Newsletter for Instructors of Data Processing
0045-7981	Comunita Mediterranea
0045-799X	Concerns
0045-8007	Concrete Abstracts
0045-8015	Concrete Pipe News
0045-8023	Confederation Nationale de la Construction. Annuaire
0045-804X	Conference Board of the Mathematical Sciences. Newsletter
0045-8058	Conference on Great Lakes Research. Proceedings see 0380-1330
0045-8066	Conflux†
0045-8082	Congiuntura Economica Lombarda
0045-8120	Connecticut Nutmegger
0045-8139	I P S Local Government Newsletter
0045-8155	Conservation Council of Ontario. Bulletin†
0045-8163	Consolidated Report of the Condition of Banks Operating in Puerto Rico
0045-8171	Consoliere†
0045-8198	Construction Metallique changed to C T I C M-Construction Metallique
0045-8201	Consultants News
0045-821X	Consulting
0045-8236	Consumer Comment
0045-8252	Consumer Interest†
0045-8260	Consumer News†
0045-8309	Contact in Urban and Regional Affairs changed to Contact (Waterloo)
0045-8317	Contacto
0045-8325	Contacts
0045-8333	Contemporary Indian Literature†
0045-835X	Content
0045-8368	Contents of Recent Economics Journals
0045-8384	Continuing Education Directory for Metropolitan Toronto
0045-8406	Contractspeler
0045-8414	Contrasts
0045-8422	Convenience Store News
0045-8430	C A I D Newsletter
0045-8449	Conventions, Meetings, Incentive World†
0045-8457	Cooperateur de France
0045-8465	C E I R (Cooperative Economic Insect Report) see 0363-0889
0045-8473	Cooperative Educational Abstracting Service
0045-849X	Cooperator†
0045-8503	Cooperator's Bulletin
0045-8511	Copeia
0045-8538	Core Teacher
0045-8546	Cormorant see 0362-9368
0045-8554	Cormorant News Bulletin
0045-8562	Cornell University. Libraries. Bulletin
0045-8570	Cornish Nation
0045-8597	Corporation Journal
0045-8635	Corrections Process see 0705-9094
0045-8643	Correio Portugues
0045-866X	Corriere Canadese
0045-8678	Corrosion Y Proteccion
0045-8686	Corse Mediterranee Medicale see 0302-9263
0045-8694	Cosmobiology International
0045-8716	Cosmarama
0045-8724	Cosmos
0045-8732	COSPAR Information Bulletin
0045-8740	Costa Rica. Instituto Geografico Nacional. Informe Semestral
0045-8759	Cotton Development
0045-8775	Council for Planning & Conservation. Newsletter
0045-8791	C P L Newsletter
0045-8813	Countdown (Wichita)†
0045-8821	Countdown
0045-8848	Country Bizarre
0045-8856	Country Life
0045-8864	Courier changed to B.C. Corrections Courier
0045-8872	C F B Cold Lake Courier
0045-8899	Courrier du Parlement
0045-8902	Courrier du Vietnam
0045-8910	Courrier Pedagogique changed to Courrier du Francais-Cadre
0045-8929	Coursing News changed to Greyhound Review
0045-8937	Cowan Investment Survey. Weekly Market Digest changed to Cowan Investment Survey. Midas
0045-897X	Creative Moment
0045-8988	Creative Teacher†
0045-8996	Creative Urge†
0045-9003	Credit Union National Association. Research and Economics Department. R E Statistical Bulletin changed to Credit Union National Association. Research Division. Research Bulletin
0045-9011	Creditalk
0045-902X	Crime and Delinquency Abstracts†
0045-9038	Criminal Justice Newsletter
0045-9062	Critic†
0045-9070	Critical Digest
0045-9089	Critique Socialiste
0045-9097	Critiques de l'Economie Politique
0045-9100	Cross Reference see 0190-0447
0045-9119	Crossroads
0045-9127	Crown
0045-9135	Crucible
0045-9143	Crusader: Justice for Hungary
0045-9151	Cryptogram†
0045-9178	Cuadernos de Historia de la Salud Publica

ISSN	Title
0045-9186	Cuadernos de Historia Economica de Cataluna
0045-9194	Cuadernos de Informacion Cientifica
0045-9208	Cuisine Collective
0045-9216	Cultivar
0045-9240	Culture and Education *changed to* Education for the Disadvantaged Child
0045-9259	Cultured Dairy Products Journal
0045-9267	Cultuurtechnisch Tijdschrift
0045-9275	Cumberland-Samford Law Review *see* 0360-8298
0045-9283	Current Citations on Communication Disorders *changed to* Current Citations on Communication Disorders: Hearing and Balance
0045-9283	Current Citations on Communication Disorders *changed to* Current Citations on Communications Disorders: Language, Speech, and Voice
0045-9291	Current Engineering Practice
0045-933X	Current Physics Advance Abstracts: Solid State†
0045-9348	Current Physics Microform
0045-9380	Current Problems in Pediatrics
0045-9399	Current Problems in Radiology *see* 0363-0188
0045-9429	Cyprus To-day
0045-9445	Czas
0045-9453	Czasopismo Geograficzne
0045-9461	Czechoslovak Economic Digest
0045-947X	Czechoslovak Science & Technology Digest
0045-9488	Czechoslovak Scientific and Technical Periodicals Contents
0045-9496	Dafni†
0045-9518	Dakota Territory
0045-9534	Dalhousie University. University News *changed to* Dalhousie University. University News This Week
0045-9542	Dalka
0045-9550	Dallas. Methodist Hospital. Bulletin of the Medical Staff
0045-9577	Dance /America
0045-9585	Danmarks Handels Tidende
0045-9593	Dansk Bygge Journal
0045-9607	Dansk Erhvervsfjerkrae
0045-9615	Dansk Handelsblad
0045-9623	Dansk Industri
0045-9631	Dansk Ungdom og Idraet
0045-964X	Danske Realskole *changed to* Tidens Skole
0045-9658	Darshak
0045-9666	Data
0045-9674	Data-Canada†
0045-9682	Data Communications User *see* 0362-4277
0045-9690	Data Processing Management Association. Magazine
0045-9704	Datapro Seventy
0045-9739	Davidsonia
0045-9747	De Nos Mains
0045-9755	De Rebus
0045-9771	Deacon
0045-9801	Deccan College. Postgraduate & Research Institute. Bulletin
0045-981X	Decennie 2†
0045-9836	Defending All Outdoors†
0045-9844	Delaware Basin Bulletin
0045-9852	Delaware Conservationist
0045-9879	Delikt en Delinkwent
0045-9887	Delinquency Prevention Reporter *see* 0092-5438
0045-9895	Delta del Parana
0045-9933	Dental Hygienist
0045-9941	Dental Radiography and Photography
0045-995X	Dental Student News†
0045-9968	Dentoscope†
0045-9984	Departements et Communes
0045-9992	Derecho Penal Contemporaneo
0046-001X	Desarrollo Economico
0046-0028	Desarrollo Rural en las Americas
0046-0036	Descent
0046-0044	Desert Rancher
0046-0060	Designer & Builder in Asia†
0046-0079	Despatch
0046-0087	Despatch *changed to* Service
0046-0095	Detective†
0046-0117	Deutsche Baecker Zeitung
0046-0141	Deutsche Vereinigung von Winnipeg. Mitteilungen
0046-015X	Deutsches Wirtschafts Institut, Leipzig. D W I Forschungshefte *changed to* I P W Forschungshefte
0046-0168	Deux-Tiers†
0046-0184	Devonport News
0046-0192	Diabetes
0046-0206	Dialogo Social
0046-0222	Diana's Bimonthly
0046-0249	Digest of Executive Opportunities
0046-0265	Dimension
0046-029X	Dinny's Digest
0046-0303	Dio e Popolo
0046-032X	Dire†
0046-032X	Dire
0046-0338	Direct from Cuba
0046-0346	Discussion *see* 0361-4751
0046-0362	Disposable Soft Goods *see* 0163-4429
0046-0370	Disposables International†
0046-0389	Dissonance†
0046-0435	Dixie Logger and Lumberman *see* 0192-7124
0046-0443	Djassin'foue
0046-0451	Doctor
0046-0478	Documentation Par l'Image
0046-0486	Documentos de Educacion Cooperativa *changed to* Tribuna Cooperativa
0046-0494	Doings†
0046-0508	Dokita
0046-0516	Dolphin
0046-0559	Dominion Companies Law Reports *changed to* Canada Corporations Law Reports
0046-0567	Dominion Tax Cases
0046-0575	Dominionaire
0046-0583	Domino *changed to* Schweizer Buch-Spiegel
0046-0591	Donna di Casa
0046-0605	Donnybrook Report: Photography†
0046-0621	Dorset
0046-063X	Doshisha Literature
0046-0648	Down Under
0046-0656	Downtown Athletic Club Journal
0046-0664	Downtown Developments†
0046-0672	Dravo Review
0046-0680	Dressage *see* 0147-796X
0046-0702	Drilling Contractor
0046-0710	Drive *changed to* Drive and Trial
0046-0737	Druckindustrie
0046-0753	Drug Forum†
0046-0788	Duckological
0046-0796	Duesseldorf
0046-080X	Duitse Boek *changed to* Deutsche Buecher
0046-0818	DukEngineer
0046-0826	Duodecimal Bulletin *changed to* Dozenal Bulletin
0046-0834	Du Pont Magazine
0046-0842	Dutch Quarterly Review of Anglo American Letters
0046-0869	E E
0046-0885	E I
0046-0915	Eagle's Eye
0046-0931	Earthquake Information Bulletin
0046-0966	East St. Louis Monitor
0046-0974	Eastern Film†
0046-0990	Easyriders
0046-1016	Eau Vive *changed to* Eau Vive (1978)
0046-1024	Eburnea
0046-1032	Ecclaire
0046-1040	Echo
0046-1059	Echo
0046-1067	Echo
0046-1083	Echo des Vieux de France *changed to* Echo
0046-1091	Echoes of History†
0046-1121	Ecology Law Quarterly
0046-113X	Economia
0046-1148	Economia Cafetera
0046-1180	Economic Research Corporation. Research Review†
0046-1199	Economic Analysis and Policy
0046-1202	Economie de l'Energie
0046-1229	Ecosources
0046-1237	Ecosphere
0046-1245	EdCentric
0046-1261	Editing Technology *see* 0364-5517
0046-127X	Editor's Newsletter
0046-1288	Edmonton Livestock Market News *see* 0383-2058
0046-1296	Edmonton Native News
0046-130X	Edmonton Report on Business and Industrial Development *changed to* Edmonton Report on Business and Travel Development
0046-1318	Edmonton Stamp Club Bulletin
0046-1326	Edseletter
0046-1334	Educacao
0046-1350	Educateurs Specialises *changed to* Action Educative Specialisee
0046-1369	Education
0046-1377	Education and Culture†
0046-1385	Education and Psychology Review
0046-1407	Education Commission of the States Bulletin†
0046-1415	Education Equipment Selector
0046-1423	Education in Eastern Africa
0046-1431	Education Mathematique
0046-144X	Education News from Metrologic
0046-1466	Educational & Industrial Television
0046-1474	Educational Broadcasting†
0046-1474	Educational Broadcasting *changed to* Instructional Broadcasting
0046-1482	Educational Digest
0046-1490	Education Exchange *changed to* Educational International
0046-1504	Educational Forum†
0046-1520	Educational Psychologist
0046-1539	Educational Reporter
0046-1547	E T S Developments
0046-1555	Educator *changed to* National Educator
0046-1571	Educators Negotiating Service
0046-158X	Educator's Purchasing Guide†
0046-1598	Effective Teaching with Programmed Instruction†
0046-1601	Eglise de Quebec *changed to* Pastorale-Quebec
0046-161X	Egyptian Journal of Genetics and Cytology
0046-1636	Eisenhower College Newsletter *changed to* Eisenhower
0046-1644	Election Archives
0046-1660	Electrical Contractor
0046-1679	Electrical Equipment Selector
0046-1695	Electrical Week
0046-1709	Electromagnetic Metrology Current Awareness Service
0046-1717	Electronic Equipment Monitor
0046-1725	Electronic Products *see* 0046-1717
0046-1733	Electronics Communicator
0046-1741	Electronics of America
0046-175X	Electronique et Microelectronique Industrielles *see* 0398-1851
0046-1776	Elektro-Handel
0046-1784	Elektromonteur *changed to* Elektrotechnik
0046-1792	Elements
0046-1806	Elements of Technology
0046-1814	Eletronica em Foco
0046-1822	Eleveur Maine Anjou
0046-1830	Ellipse
0046-1849	Eltern
0046-1865	Embassy of Switzerland Bulletin
0046-1881	Emily Dickinson Bulletin *see* 0164-1492
0046-1903	Employer
0046-1946	Enchantment
0046-1962	Enfance et la Mode
0046-1970	Enfant Exceptionnel *see* 0704-7517
0046-1997	Engineer in Education Newsletter†
0046-2004	Engineering and Construction†
0046-2012	Engineering Design Graphics Journal
0046-2020	Engineering Horizons†
0046-2039	Engineering in Medicine
0046-2055	Engineering News of India *changed to* Engineering & Metals Review
0046-2063	Engineering Opportunities *changed to* Factory & Industrial Equipment
0046-208X	English in Australia
0046-2098	English Usage in Southern Africa
0046-2101	Enseignants
0046-211X	Enseignement *see* 0315-4998
0046-2128	Ensemble - l'Information d'Action Sociale
0046-2136	Enterpriser
0046-2144	Entre-Nous
0046-2152	Enterprises Agricoles
0046-2187	Envers et l'Endroit†
0046-2217	Environment Improvement Case History Report Service†
0046-2225	Environmental Affairs *see* 0190-7034
0046-2241	G A T F Environmental Control Report
0046-225X	Environmental Entomology
0046-2268	Excerpta Medica. Section 46: Environmental Health *see* 0300-5194
0046-2276	Environmental Law
0046-2284	Environmental Law Reporter
0046-2306	Environmental Periodicals; Indexed Article Titles *see* 0145-3815
0046-2314	Environmental Quality Report†
0046-2322	Environmental Systems Industries *see* 0705-9272
0046-2349	Envoy†
0046-2357	Kruidenier
0046-2365	Epidemiologic Notes and Communicable Disease Morbidity Report†
0046-2373	Eprouvette
0046-2381	Equinox
0046-239X	Equipe
0046-2403	Era
0046-2411	Erasmus Review†
0046-242X	Erdoel-Dienst
0046-2438	Ergo
0046-2446	Ergonomics Abstracts
0046-2454	Ergot
0046-2462	Erie Motorist
0046-2489	Escutcheon
0046-2497	Espace Geographique
0046-2500	Esperanto - Interlangue Universelle
0046-2519	Esperanto Contact†
0046-2527	Esperanto Teacher
0046-2535	Espoir de la Nation Togolaise
0046-256X	Est-Ovest
0046-2578	Estrategia
0046-2586	Et la Lumiere Fut
0046-2608	Ethnopsychologie
0046-2616	Ethnologie Francaise
0046-2632	Etnia
0046-2640	Etudes Polemologiques†
0046-2659	Etudes Renaniennes Bulletin
0046-2667	Eureka
0046-2683	Europaeisches Bau-Forum
0046-2705	Europe Left
0046-273X	European Civil Engineering Abstracts *see* 0305-2176
0046-2756	European Demographic Information Bulletin
0046-2764	European Engineering
0046-2772	European Journal of Social Psychology
0046-2802	European Studies Newsletter
0046-2837	Translation News
0046-2853	Evangelical Magazine
0046-287X	Everybody's Money
0046-2888	Exclusive
0046-2896	Executive Review
0046-2926	Experimental Study of Politics
0046-2950	Export Times
0046-2977	Expression
0046-2985	Eye†
0046-2993	F. I. N. S.
0046-3000	F T Abstracts in Science & Technology†
0046-3019	F Y I
0046-3027	Fabbrica e Stato
0046-3035	Fabricator
0046-3043	Fabulous Las Vegas
0046-3051	Facets
0046-306X	Facets of Freshwater
0046-3086	Factory and Office Selector
0046-3116	Komitee Zuidelijk Afrika. Angola Comite. Facts and Reports
0046-3124	Facts, Figures and Film

ISSN INDEX

ISSN	Title
0046-3132	Facts File
0046-3140	Facts on Fish
0046-3159	F A C C C Bulletin
0046-3167	Fag Rag
0046-3175	Fairfield County
0046-3221	Audio-Digest Family Practice
0046-323X	Family Service Highlights†
0046-3248	Fanfare *changed to* Go
0046-3256	Fanfares
0046-3264	Far East Week by Week
0046-3272	Far Eastern Law Review
0046-3280	Der Farbenhaendler
0046-3299	Farm and Country
0046-3302	Farm and Food Research
0046-3329	Farm Supply Store†
0046-3337	Farmer's Digest
0046-337X	Fauna†
0046-3388	Fauna & Flora
0046-3418	Federal Labor-Management Consultant
0046-3426	Federal Librarian†
0046-3434	Federal Linguist
0046-3442	Federal Program Monitor†
0046-3450	Federal Reserve Bank of Chicago. Banking Briefs†
0046-3469	Federal Reserve Bank of Chicago. International Letter
0046-3523	Federation des Travaux Publics et des Transports. Revue
0046-3531	F. I. E. J. Bulletin
0046-354X	Federacion Odontologica Colombiana. Revista
0046-3558	F A H Review *see* 0148-9496
0046-3566	Federation of British Columbia Naturalists. Newsletter
0046-3574	Federation of Ontario Naturalists. Newsletter *changed to* Seasons
0046-3582	Federation of Victorian Film Societies. Federation News *see* 0158-3778
0046-3590	Federation Quebecoise de la Faune. Nouvelles
0046-3604	Feed and Farm Supply Dealer
0046-3639	Feline Practice
0046-3647	Feltornithologen
0046-3655	Femeia
0046-3663	Feminist Studies
0046-368X	Fernsehen und Film†
0046-3698	Ferrocarriles Argentinos
0046-3701	Fettesian
0046-3728	Fibre Market News
0046-3736	Fiction
0046-3760	Fighting Back†
0046-3787	Film Journal†
0046-3809	Film Review Index *see* 0094-6818
0046-3817	Films - Learning Corporation of America†
0046-3825	Films a l'Ecran
0046-3841	Revista Filologia Moderna *changed to* Filologia Moderna
0046-385X	Filozofia
0046-3876	Financial Daily *changed to* M/G Financial Weekly
0046-3892	Financial Management
0046-3906	Financne Studie
0046-3922	Finishing Highlights
0046-3957	First-Fleeters
0046-3965	Fish Trades Review
0046-3973	Fisheries Council of Canada. Bulletin
0046-399X	Fitofilo
0046-4015	Five Feathers News
0046-4031	Flame and Flavour
0046-404X	Flap Internacional
0046-4058	Flashpoint *see* 0308-1230
0046-4082	Florafacts
0046-4090	Florida Audiovisual Association. A V A News *changed to* Florida Media Quarterly
0046-4112	Florida Contractor
0046-4120	Florida. Department of Agriculture and Consumer Services. Market Bulletin *changed to* Florida Market Bulletin
0046-4139	Florida. Department of State. Division of Archives. Archives and History News
0046-4147	Florida Libraries
0046-4155	Florida Music Director
0046-4171	Florida Psychologist *changed to* F P
0046-4198	University of Florida. Communication Sciences Laboratory. Quarterly Progress Reports
0046-4201	Flow†
0046-421X	Flower Arranger
0046-4236	Flyer International
0046-4244	Flying Fish Newsletter
0046-4260	Focus
0046-4287	Focus *changed to* Tell
0046-4295	Focus on Asian Studies
0046-4317	Focus on Mental Health
0046-4325	Focus on Pakistan†
0046-4333	Folio (New Canaan)
0046-435X	Fontes Linguae Vasconum
0046-4368	Food Aid Bulletin†
0046-4384	Food and Nutrition
0046-4414	Food Industry Futures: a Strategy Service
0046-4422	Foodcorp Quarterly
0046-4449	Football Association News *see* 0306-1132
0046-4457	Football News†
0046-4473	For Adults Only
0046-4481	Forages
0046-449X	Forbruker-Rapporten
0046-4511	Force Ouvriere Hebdo
0046-4538	Ford World
0046-4546	U.S. Department of Agriculture. Economics, Statistics, and Cooperatives Service. Foreign Agricultural Trade of the United States
0046-4554	Foreign Investment News
0046-4570	Forensic Science Gazette
0046-4589	Forest Scene
0046-4597	Forestdale News *changed to* Bano Biggyan Patrika
0046-4600	Foret Privee
0046-4619	Forets de France et Action Forestiere
0046-4627	Formation Premilitaire et Physique
0046-4643	Foersvar i Nutid
0046-4651	Fort Concho Report
0046-466X	Fort Worth Como Monitor
0046-4678	Universidade do Ceara. Boletim
0046-4686	Forthcoming International Scientific and Technical Conferences
0046-4708	Forum for the Discussion of New Trends in Education
0046-4716	Forum Internationale†
0046-4732	Lutheran Forum. Forum Letter
0046-4759	Forward Atlanta
0046-4767	Foster Parent Nourricier *see* 0705-1123
0046-4775	Foto-Avisen
0046-4783	Foto und Film Rundschau†
0046-4791	Fotoarte
0046-4805	Fotografi
0046-4821	Foundry News
0046-4848	Fourth Estate
0046-4856	Fox†
0046-4864	Fra Ribe Amt
0046-4872	Francaise Frisonne Pie Noire
0046-4899	France Agricole
0046-4910	France Forum
0046-4929	France Genealogique
0046-4937	Annales d'Hydrobiologie†
0046-4945	France Pays-Bas Informations Rapides
0046-4961	Franklin County Historical Review
0046-497X	Frau im Spiegel
0046-4988	Fredonia Statement
0046-5003	Free Market†
0046-5011	Free Press†
0046-502X	Freedom from Hunger Campaign/Ideas and Action Bulletin *changed to* Freedom from Hunger Campaign/Action for Development
0046-5038	Freedom to Read Foundation News
0046-5046	Freight Forwarding
0046-5062	Frendz
0046-5070	Freshwater Biology
0046-5089	Fri Fagbevegelse
0046-5097	Friday Report
0046-5100	Friend International
0046-5119	Friendly Way†
0046-5135	Friidrott
0046-5143	Frivakt
0046-5151	Froid et la Climatisation
0046-516X	From the State Capitals. Taxes-Property†
0046-5178	Mibifnim
0046-5186	Front and Center
0046-5216	Frontiersman
0046-5224	Frugt, Groent og Blomster
0046-5240	Fruit Intelligence‡
0046-5259	Fulbright Newsletter
0046-5267	Full Tide
0046-5275	Fulton County (Illinois) Historical Society Newsletter *changed to* Fulton County (Illinois) Historical & Genealogical Society Newsletter
0046-5291	Fur, Feathers and Fins†
0046-5305	Furies†
0046-5313	Furniture and Furnishings†
0046-5321	Furniture Index†
0046-533X	Furniture News Journal
0046-5364	Gaceta Textil
0046-5372	Galvano Teknisk Tidsskrift
0046-5380	Gambia News Bulletin
0046-5399	Ganagrinco
0046-5402	Ganita
0046-5410	Gar
0046-5429	Garage and Transport Equipment *see* 0307-1154
0046-5437	Gartneryrket
0046-5445	Garuda
0046-5453	Garuda Indonesian Airways Magazine
0046-5461	Gas Chromatography-Mass Spectrometry Abstracts
0046-547X	Gastgewerbe *changed to* D G Deutsche Gaststaette/Deutsche Hotel-Zeitung Gastwirt und Hotelier
0046-5488	Gay
0046-5496	Gay Liberator†
0046-550X	Gay Sunshine
0046-5518	Gazdalkodas
0046-5526	Gazette des Hopitaux†
0046-5542	Gazette Officielle de la Peche
0046-5569	Gee Report†
0046-5577	Gemeentewerken
0046-5593	G E C Telecommunications Journal
0046-5607	General Practitioner
0046-5615	Generazione Zero
0046-5623	Genhinen
0046-5658	Geodex Retrieval System for Geotechnical Abstracts
0046-5666	Geographer
0046-5690	Geographical Review of India
0046-5704	Geographical Society of New South Wales. Geography Bulletin
0046-5712	Geographical View Point
0046-5720	Geologi
0046-5739	Geological Society of the Oregon Country. Geological Newsletter
0046-5755	Geometriae Dedicata
0046-5763	Geophysical Surveys
0046-578X	Georgia Journal of International and Comparative Law
0046-5798	Georgia Music News
0046-5801	Geoscience Information Society. Newsletter *changed to* G.I.S. Newsletter
0046-581X	Geoscope
0046-5828	Geotechnical Engineering
0046-5836	German-American Studies *changed to* Journal of German-American Studies
0046-5879	Getreide und Mehl *changed to* Getreide, Mehl und Brot
0046-5895	Ghala†
0046-5909	Ghana Bulletin of Theology†
0046-5917	Ghana Farmer†
0046-5917	Ghana Farmer
0046-5933	Giessereiforschung
0046-5941	Ginecologia Brasileira†
0046-5968	Giornale Italiano di Cardiologia
0046-5984	Giorni
0046-5992	Glas Kanadskin Srba
0046-600X	Glasgow Dental Journal†
0046-6018	Glassposten
0046-6026	Global Village
0046-6034	Glos Polski-Gazeta Polska
0046-6050	Goeteborgs-Koepmannen
0046-6069	Golden Gate North†
0046-6077	Golden Legacy
0046-6085	Golden Spike†
0046-6093	Das Goldene Blatt
0046-6115	Gonzaga Law Review
0046-6123	Good Gardening
0046-6131	Good Healthkeeping†
0046-614X	Good News†
0046-6158	Good Old Days
0046-6174	Goodfruit Grower
0046-6182	Goodfruit Grower. Supplement *changed to* Goodgrape Grower
0046-6190	Goool†
0046-6239	Grace
0046-6247	Graduado†
0046-6247	Graduado†
0046-6255	Grain Grower
0046-6263	Grains
0046-6271	Grande Sinal
0046-628X	Grands-Musees†
0046-6298	Granite
0046-6301	Granite State Libraries
0046-631X	Graphoscope
0046-6328	Grassroots (Carbondale) *see* 0017-3541
0046-6344	Great Lakes Sportsman
0046-6352	Greater World
0046-6379	Greek-American Trade
0046-6387	Greek Canadian Tribune
0046-6395	Green Egg†
0046-6409	Green Sheet
0046-6417	Green 'un
0046-6433	Gridweek *changed to* Gridweek (1979)
0046-6441	Grosshandelskaufmann *changed to* Handel
0046-645X	Ground Water Age
0046-6468	Group Process†
0046-6476	Grower
0046-6484	Growing Minds
0046-6492	Growing Older
0046-6506	Growing Point
0046-6514	Gruppendynamik
0046-6522	Guam Recorder
0046-6549	Guatemala Filatelica
0046-6565	Guest and Host
0046-659X	Gulf Coast Plumbing-Heating-Cooling News
0046-6603	Gullsmedkunst
0046-6638	Guppy Digest
0046-6646	Guyana Development Corporation. Industrial Review†
0046-6654	Guyana Journal
0046-6662	Guynews†
0046-6670	Gymnast *see* 0162-9867
0046-6689	Habit†
0046-6697	Hablemos de Cine
0046-6700	Hackney Journal
0046-6735	Halifax Board of Trade. Commercial News
0046-6743	Halifax Wildlife Association. Wildlife News
0046-6751	Royal Botanical Gardens, Hamilton, Ont. Gardens' Bulletin
0046-676X	Hamore
0046-6778	Handball
0046-6786	Handbook of Environmental Management Series†
0046-6794	Handchirurgie
0046-6808	Der Handelsvertreter und Handelsmakler
0046-6816	Haandverk og Industri
0046-6832	Happiness Holding Tank
0046-6840	Hardsyssels Aarbog
0046-6859	Harian's the Traveler's Newsletter†
0046-6875	Harris Survey Column Subscription *changed to* A B C News-Harris Survey
0046-6891	Harvard Dental Alumni Bulletin
0046-6905	Harvard University. Graduate School of Education Association. Bulletin
0046-6913	Haryana Electricity
0046-6921	Haryana Labour Journal
0046-693X	Haustechnischer Anzeiger *see* 0341-4817

1082 ISSN INDEX

ISSN	Title
0046-6948	Hawaii Farm Science†
0046-6964	Horticulture Digest
0046-6980	Headmasters Association Review *changed to* Secondary Heads Association Review
0046-6999	Headpiece†
0046-7006	Health
0046-7014	Health and Vision
0046-7022	Health Devices
0046-7057	Health for Life
0046-7065	Health in New Brunswick *changed to* New Brunswick. Department of Health. Happenings in Health / Actualites Sante
0046-7073	Health in New South Wales
0046-709X	Health Planning in Illinois†
0046-7103	Health Sciences TV Bulletin†
0046-7111	Heart Care
0046-7146	Heat Pipe Technology
0046-7154	Hebdo de la Blanchisserie-Teinturerie
0046-7170	Hedmark Slektshistorielags Tidsskrift
0046-7197	Helderberg Review†
0046-7235	Hemicrania†
0046-7243	Hemingway Notes†
0046-7251	Hemophilia Today
0046-726X	Henna
0046-7278	Her World
0046-7286	Heraldo del Cine
0046-7294	Here Now
0046-7316	Heron
0046-7324	Herz Kreislauf
0046-7332	Hi-Fidelity & Video Review†
0046-7340	Hi-Fi Newsletter†
0046-7359	Hibueras
0046-7367	High Fidelity Trade News
0046-7375	Higher Education in the States
0046-7383	Highway
0046-7391	Highway Engineering in Australia
0046-7405	Highway Users Federation. Federation Reporter
0046-7413	Hikobia
0046-7421	Hill Monitor†
0046-7448	Him
0046-7456	Himalayan Observer
0046-7472	Hiroshima University Dental Society. Journal
0046-7480	Hispania
0046-7499	Histoire au Pays de Matane
0046-7510	Histoire en Savoie
0046-7537	Historian†
0046-7545	Historical Journal of Barmera and District
0046-7553	Historical Musings†
0046-7553	Historical Musings
0046-7561	Historie
0046-757X	Historiens et Geographes
0046-7588	Historisk Aarbog for Skive og Omegn
0046-7596	Historisk Tidskrift foer Finland
0046-760X	History of Education
0046-7618	History of Medicine†
0046-7626	Hjemmet
0046-7634	Hjukrunarfelag Islands. Timarit *changed to* Hjukrun
0046-7642	Hobart and William Smith Colleges Official Publication *changed to* Hobart and William Smith Colleges Bulletin
0046-7650	Hobby
0046-7677	Hoch und Tiefbau
0046-7685	Hochzeit
0046-7693	Hockey Digest
0046-7707	Hockey World *changed to* Hockey Pictorial World
0046-7723	Hogar y la Moda
0046-774X	Holly Letter
0046-7766	Home Economics and Domestic Subjects Review *see* 0307-2053
0046-7774	Home Economics Research Journal
0046-7790	Homme
0046-7812	Homoeopathic World
0046-7820	Homoeopathy
0046-7839	Hon: a Book-Bin for Scholars
0046-7855	Honneur et Fidelite
0046-7863	Honourable Artillery Company Journal
0046-791X	Horizont
0046-7936	Horses
0046-7960	Hospital Engineering
0046-7995	Hospital Indicators†
0046-8010	Hospital Medical Practice
0046-8037	Hospitais Civis de Lisboa. Boletim Clinico
0046-8045	Hot Bike†
0046-8061	Hotuys
0046-8088	Houses for Sale *changed to* New Homes and Apartment Guide
0046-8096	Housing Australia *changed to* Housing Victoria
0046-8134	Human Behavior†
0046-8150	Human Design
0046-8169	Human Ecology (Park Ridge)
0046-8177	Human Pathology
0046-8185	Human Rights
0046-8193	Human Rights Bulletin
0046-8207	H R W Newsletter
0046-8215	Human Rights in U.S.S.R†
0046-8223	Human Rights News and Views *changed to* Human Rights News
0046-8231	Human Settlements *changed to* Habitat News
0046-824X	Humanistische Union. Mitteilungen
0046-8258	Humanitas
0046-8290	Hungarian Co-operation
0046-8304	Hungarian Library and Information Science Abstracts
0046-8312	Hunter Natural History
0046-8339	Husdjur
0046-8347	Husholdningslaereren (Copenhagen)
0046-8371	I E E E Publications Bulletin
0046-838X	I E E E Transactions. Manufacturing Technology *see* 0148-6411
0046-8398	I E T: Zeitschrift fuer Elektrische Informations- und Energietechnik
0046-8401	I S L A
0046-841X	I S M
0046-8428	I. W. K.
0046-8436	University of Ibadan. Library. Library Record
0046-8444	Ibero-Americana
0046-8460	Ici Radio Canada Television
0046-8487	Idaho Economic Indicators
0046-8495	I E A Reporter *changed to* I E A Reporter (1976)
0046-8509	Idaho School Trustees Newsletter
0046-8517	Ide
0046-8525	Ide og Form
0046-8533	Ideal
0046-8541	Idealistic Studies
0046-8568	Idiom
0046-8576	Idoles†
0046-8584	Ikkevold
0046-8592	Ikorok
0046-8606	Illinois Education News
0046-8622	Illinois State Genealogical Society Quarterly
0046-8630	Illinois. University. Department of Urban & Regional Planning. Research Bureau. Newsletter *changed to* Planning and Public Policy
0046-8665	Images du Transport *changed to* Magazine du Transport Routier
0046-869X	Impact†
0046-8703	Impact
0046-8711	Impegno Settanta
0046-872X	Impianti Manutenzione Trasporti†
0046-8754	In Re
0046-8762	In-Short
0046-8770	In Step with the Visiting Nurse Association of Brooklyn *changed to* V N A Newsletter
0046-8797	Inbavan Tanah Air
0046-8819	Inchiesta
0046-8827	Incorporated Swimming Teacher *see* 0306-0403
0046-8843	Independent Republic Quarterly
0046-8886	Index to Chinese Periodicals-Humanities and Social Sciences *changed to* Index to Chinese Periodicals
0046-8894	Index to Chinese Periodicals-Science and Technology *changed to* Index to Chinese Periodicals
0046-8908	Index to Current Urban Documents
0046-8916	Index to the American Banker *changed to* American Banker Index
0046-8924	Index to the Times *changed to* Times Index
0046-8932	India Abroad
0046-8940	India. Directorate of Jute Development. Jute Bulletin
0046-8959	India Weekly
0046-8967	Indian Affairs
0046-8975	Indian Archives
0046-8983	Indian Geotechnical Journal
0046-8991	Indian Journal of Microbiology
0046-9009	Indian Journal of Psychometry and Education
0046-9017	Indian Journal of Regional Science
0046-9025	Indian Manager
0046-9033	I P I R I Journal
0046-905X	Indian Roads Congress. Journal
0046-9068	Indian Tourist
0046-9076	Indian Trader
0046-9092	Indian Welding Journal
0046-9106	Indiana Law Review
0046-9114	Indiana. University. Libraries. Library Newsletter†
0046-9122	M E R P Memo
0046-9130	Indiana University. School of Medicine. Review†
0046-9149	Indien
0046-9157	Exceptional Parent
0046-9165	Indonesian Current Affairs Translation Bulletin†
0046-9173	Indonesian Review of International Affairs
0046-9181	Industria Lechera
0046-919X	Industrial Bookshelf *changed to* Business/Management Book Review
0046-9203	Industrial Informika
0046-9211	Industrial Launderer
0046-9246	Industrial Relations Review and Report
0046-9262	Industrial Wastes
0046-9270	Industrialist
0046-9289	Industrie- und Handelszeitung
0046-9297	Der Industriebackmeister
0046-9300	Industries de l'Alimentation Animale
0046-9319	Brewers Association of Canada. Industry Notes†
0046-9327	Informateur des Chefs d'Entreprises Libres
0046-9343	Information G
0046-9351	Information Historique
0046-936X	Information Immobiliere
0046-9378	Information-Part 2-Reports/Bibliographies *see* 0360-0971
0046-9386	Comite Belge de la Distribution. Information Specialisee
0046-9394	Informationen der Afrika-Studienstelle *changed to* I F o Mitteilungen der Abteilung Entwicklungslaender
0046-9408	Informationen zur Politischen Bildung
0046-9416	Informations Aerauliques et Thermiques†
0046-9432	Informations Laitieres
0046-9459	Informations Sociales
0046-9483	Informatologia Yugoslavica
0046-9491	Informazioni di Parapsicologia
0046-9505	Informer *changed to* Tourist Talks
0046-9513	Ingenieur-Constructeur†
0046-9556	Innenrikske Blad og Tidsskrifter *changed to* Avis- og Bladlista
0046-9564	Innovation World
0046-9572	Innovator
0046-9580	Inquiry
0046-9599	Inquisitor
0046-9610	Inside
0046-9629	Inside Canberra
0046-9653	Insight (St. Paul)
0046-9661	Insita *changed to* Ars Populi
0046-967X	Instant Research on Peace and Violence *see* 0356-7893
0046-9688	I F E P P Informations
0046-9696	Institut fuer Gesellschaftspolitik. Mitteilungen
0046-970X	I P W Berichte
0046-9718	I I E E Bulletin†
0046-9726	Belgium. Institut National d'Assurance Maladie Invalidite. I.N.A.M.I. Bulletin d'Information
0016-9734	Institut Panafricain pour le Developpement. Annuaire des Anciens Etudiants
0046-9742	I.A.P. Professional Photography in Australia
0046-9750	Institute of Brewing, London. Journal
0046-9769	I C B Review (Institute of Canadian Bankers) *see* 0315-6230
0046-9777	C F A Digest
0046-9785	Institute of Club Managers and Secretaries. Club Guide
0046-9793	Institute of Commerce, London. Magazine
0046-9807	Institute of Electrical Inspectors. I. E. I. Journal
0046-984X	Institute of Southeast Asian Studies. Library. Accessions List
0046-9858	Institution of Chemical Engineers. Transactions
0046-9866	Institution of Engineers, Australia. Brisbane Division. Technical Papers *changed to* Institution of Engineers, Australia Queensland Division. Technical Papers
0046-9874	Institution of Engineers Australia. South Australian Division. Bulletin†
0046-9882	Institution of Engineers, Jamaica. Journal
0046-9890	Instituto Agricola Catalan de San Isidro. Revista
0046-9912	Instituto Brasileiro de Mercado de Capitais. Boletim de Documentacao†
0046-9920	I C A Informa
0046-9939	Instituto de Pesca, Sao Paulo. Boletim
0046-9947	Instituto de Pesquisa Agropecuaria do l'Este. Pesquisa e Experimentos. Comunicado Technico
0046-9955	Instituto de Soldadura. Boletim
0046-9963	Instituto Estadual de Hematologia Arthur de Siqueira Cavalcanti. Boletim
0046-9971	Instituto Forestal Latinoamericano de Investigacion y Capacitacion. Boletin Bibliografico
0046-998X	Instituto Historico e Geografico Brasileiro. Revista
0046-9998	Pan American Institute of Geography and History. Commission on Cartography. Cartografia†
0047-0007	Institute for Latin American Integration. Boletin de la Integracion†
0047-0007	Boletin de la Integracion *changed to* Integracion Latinoamericana
0047-0333	Institutul National de Informare si Documentare Stiintifica si Technica. Revista de Titluri: Transport Intern. Ambalare. Depozitare.
0047-0368	Institutul National de Informare si Documentare Stiintifica si Tehnica. Revista de Titluri: Scientica. Cercetare. Proiectare. Estetica Indusriala
0047-0376	Instruments India†
0047-0376	Instruments India
0047-0384	Insurgent Sociologist
0047-0406	Intelligence Survey
0047-0414	Inter-Com; Washington Area Librarians
0047-0422	I M C O Bulletin *changed to* I M C O News
0047-0430	Interchange
0047-0449	Interchange†
0047-0457	Interchange (Portland)
0047-0465	Interchange (Washington)
0047-0473	Intercom†
0047-049X	Interior
0047-0503	Intermode
0047-0511	Intermountain Jewish News
0047-052X	Audio-Digest Internal Medicine
0047-0538	International Afro-American Museum. Newsletter *changed to* Afro-American Museum of Detroit. Newsletter
0047-0554	I A C P Law Enforcement Legislation and Litigation Report†

0047-0562 I A C P Law Enforcement Legislative Research Digest†
0047-0570 International Bank for Reconstruction and Development. Statement of Loans†
0047-0597 International Barbed Wire Gazette
0047-0619 International Book Year Newsletter
0047-0627 International Business Digest†
0047-0635 International Cataloguing
0047-0643 International Centre of Films for Children and Young People. News *changed to* Young Cinema International
0047-0651 I C M A Newsletter
0047-0678 International Commission of Jurists Journal†
0047-0678 International Commission of Jurists. Journal *see* 0020-6393
0047-0686 International Dostoevsky Society Bulletin
0047-0694 International Export Association. Export News
0047-0716 International Institute for Population Studies. Newsletter
0047-0724 International Journal of Government Auditing†
0047-0724 International Journal of Government Auditing
0047-0732 International Journal of Group Tensions
0047-0740 International Journal of Nuclear Medicine and Biology
0047-0759 International Journal of Radiation Engineering
0047-0767 International Journal of Sport Psychology
0047-0783 Co-operative Information†
0047-0791 International Labour Office. Minutes of the Governing Body
0047-0813 International Law News
0047-083X I M F Survey
0047-0856 I N I S Newsletter
0047-0864 International Oil Scouts Association. Official Publication
0047-0880 International Planned Parenthood Federation. Library Bulletin *see* 0309-6904
0047-0899 International Press Cutting Service: Modern Plastics and Engineering
0047-0902 International Press Cutting Service: Ceramics - Porcelain - Refractory - Cement - Glass
0047-0910 International Press Cutting Service: Chemical Process Engineering. Drugs - Pharmaceuticals
0047-0929 International Press Cutting Service: Dyestuff Industry and Chemicals
0047-0937 International Press Cutting Service: Electronics and Electricals Industry
0047-0945 International Press Cutting Service: Fermented Wines, Liquers, Brandy, Gin, Rum, Whisky, Beer and Alcoholic Drinks
0047-0953 International Press Cutting Service: Import-Export-Licenses
0047-0961 International Press Cutting Service: Jute, Gunny, Hessian, Burlap, Coir
0047-097X International Press Cutting Service: Labour Welfare - Industrial Legislation and Personnel Management
0047-0988 International Press Cutting Service: Leather - Hides - Skin - Footwear
0047-0996 International Press Cutting Service: Machine Tool and Iron Steel Industry
0047-1003 International Press Cutting Service: Mines & Minerals (Coal/Ores)
0047-1011 International Press Cutting Service: Non-Ferrous Metals - Aluminium
0047-102X International Press Cutting Service: Oils (Vegetable) Fats - Soap - Animalfeed
0047-1038 International Press Cutting Service: Paper - Pulp - Board/Straw
0047-1046 International Press Cutting Service: Petroleum - Petrochemicals - Fertilisers - Agricultural Chemistry
0047-1054 International Press Cutting Service: Plywood-Timber-Particle Board
0047-1062 International Press Cutting Service: Rubber and Rubber Technology
0047-1070 International Press Cutting Service: Scientific Instruments, Laboratory Equipment & Chemicals
0047-1089 International Press Cutting Service: Sugar-Gur-Khandasari
0047-1097 International Press Cutting Service: Taxation - Finance - Company Law
0047-1100 International Press Cutting Service: Tea and Coffee News
0047-1119 International Press Cutting Service: Textile News
0047-1127 International Press Cutting Service: Tender Notifications (Indian & Global)
0047-1135 International Press Cutting Service: Tobacco News
0047-1143 International Press Cutting Service: Wheat & Wheat Products (Rice/Food Grains)
0047-1151 International Press Cutting Service: Processed Food Products/Spices
0047-116X International Psychologist
0047-1178 International Relations
0047-1186 International Review
0047-1208 International Review of Music Aesthetics and Sociology *changed to* International Review of the Aesthetics and Sociology of Music
0047-1216 I T C C Review
0047-1224 International Telecommunication Union. Operational Bulletin
0047-1240 International Understanding at School
0047-1259 I. U. G. G. Chronicle
0047-1267 International Union of Geological Sciences. Geological Newsletter *see* 0705-3797
0047-1275 International Wealth Success Newsletter
0047-1291 Interprete
0047-1305 I F C O News
0047-1321 Intervention
0047-133X Inventus
0047-1348 Investa†
0047-1348 Investa *changed to* Kovoexport-Investa
0047-1356 Investor's Digest of Canada
0047-1372 Invitation to Snowmobiling†
0047-1399 Iowa Geographer *changed to* Geographical Perspectives
0047-1402 University of Iowa. Libraries. Newsletter
0047-1410 Iran Family Planning Bulletin
0047-1429 Iraq News Bulletin
0047-1437 Irish Ancestor
0047-1445 Irish Bacon News
0047-1461 Irish Hardware and Allied Trader
0047-147X Irish Medical Times
0047-1488 Irish Pulse†
0047-1496 Iron Man†
0047-150X Ironwood
0047-1518 Irrigation Journal
0047-1542 Islas
0047-1550 Isotype Titles *changed to* Zidis
0047-1569 Israel. Department of Antiquities and Museums. Archaeological News
0047-1577 Israel Gerontological Society. Information Bulletin
0047-1585 Israel Oil News
0047-1593 Israel Shipping Research Institute. Journal *see* 0334-2751
0047-1607 Issue
0047-1623 Istanbul Universitesi. Tip Fakultesi. Tip Fakultesi Mecmuasi *see* 0301-7362
0047-1631 I A I Informa
0047-164X It Ain't Me Babe†
0047-1658 Italian-Australian Bulletin of Commerce
0047-1666 Italix
0047-1674 Ivoire Dimanche
0047-1690 Jack O'Dwyer's Newsletter *changed to* Jack O'Dwyer's PR Newsletter
0047-1712 Jakemate
0047-1720 Jamaica Churchman
0047-1739 Janus†
0047-1755 Japan Chemical Week
0047-1763 Japan Dental Association. Journal
0047-1771 Japan Foreign Trade Journal†
0047-1798 Japan Society of Civil Engineers. Transactions
0047-181X Japanese Business Journal†
0047-1828 Japanese Circulation Journal
0047-1836 Japanese Journal for the Midwife
0047-1852 Japanese Journal of Clinical Medicine
0047-1860 Japanese Journal of Clinical Pathology
0047-1879 Japanese Journal of Industrial Health
0047-1887 Japanese Journal of Legal Medicine
0047-1895 Japanese Journal of Nurses' Education
0047-1909 Japanese Journal of Surgery
0047-1917 Japanese Journal of Veterinary Research
0047-1925 J N R Bulletin
0047-1933 Jasmin†
0047-1941 Javelin
0047-1968 Jeremiad†
0047-1976 Jeugd en Samenleving
0047-1984 Jeunesse Ouvriere
0047-1992 Jeunesse Ouvriere Chretienne *changed to* Equipe Ouvriere
0047-200X Jewish Radical
0047-2018 Jewish Veteran
0047-2034 Jobs in Social Work†
0047-2042 Johnstown Motorist *changed to* Motorist(Johnstown)
0047-2050 Joka Poika *see* 0355-4201
0047-2077 Jornal Brasileiro de Medicina
0047-2085 Jornal Brasileiro de Psiquiatria
0047-2093 Jornal de Letras
0047-2115 Journal Constructo
0047-2123 Journal de la Navigation
0047-2131 Journal de la Police Nationale†
0047-214X Journal de la Publicite et des Techniques de la Promotion et Publi-Magazine
0047-2158 Journal de Mathematiques Elementaires
0047-2166 Journal de Pharmacie de Belgique
0047-2174 Journal de Tanger
0047-2182 Journal des Caisses d'Epargne
0047-2204 Journal du Bricoleur
0047-2212 Journal for the Study of Judaism *changed to* Journal for the Study of Judaism in the Persian, Hellenistic and Roman Period
0047-2220 Journal of Applied Rehabilitation Counseling
0047-2239 Journal of Architectural Education
0047-2255 Journal of Canadian Fiction
0047-228X Journal of Clinical Child Psychology
0047-2298 Journal of Coated Fibrous Materials *see* 0093-4658
0047-2301 Journal of Collective Negotiations in the Public Sector
0047-231X Journal of College Science Teaching
0047-2328 Journal of Comparative Family Studies
0047-2336 Journal of Contemporary Asia
0047-2352 Journal of Criminal Justice
0047-2360 Journal of Development Administration
0047-2379 Journal of Drug Education
0047-2395 Journal of Educational Technology Systems
0047-2409 Journal of Entomology (A) *see* 0307-6962
0047-2417 Journal of Entomology (B) *see* 0307-6970
0047-2425 Journal of Environmental Quality
0047-2433 Journal of Environmental Systems
0047-2441 Journal of European Studies
0047-2468 Journal of Geometry
0047-2476 Journal of Geriatrics†
0047-2484 Journal of Human Evolution
0047-2506 Journal of International Business Studies
0047-2514 Journal of Irish Literature
0047-2522 Journal of Korean Affairs†
0047-2530 Journal of Legal Studies
0047-2549 Journal of Marketing and Economic Research
0047-2557 Journal of Mathematical and Physical Sciences
0047-2565 Journal of Medical Primatology
0047-2573 Journal of Medieval and Renaissance Studies
0047-2581 Journal of Mexican American History
0047-259X Journal of Multivariate Analysis
0047-2603 Journal of Neurosurgical Nursing
0047-262X Journal of Nursing
0047-2638 Journal of Operational Psychiatry
0047-2646 Journal of Organizational Communication
0047-2662 Journal of Phenomenological Psychology
0047-2670 Journal of Photochemistry
0047-2689 Journal of Physical and Chemical Reference Data
0047-2697 Journal of Political and Military Sociology
0047-2700 Journal of Political Studies
0047-2719 Journal of Popular Film *changed to* Journal of Popular Film and Television
0047-2727 Journal of Public Economics
0047-2735 Journal of Religious Studies
0047-2743 Journal of Remote Sensing†
0047-2751 Journal of Rural Development and Administration
0047-276X Journal of Russian Studies
0047-2778 Journal of Small Business Management
0047-2786 Journal of Social Philosophy
0047-2794 Journal of Social Policy
0047-2816 Journal of Technical Writing and Communication
0047-2824 Journal of Technology
0047-2840 Journal of the New Harbinger *see* 0190-2741
0047-2859 Journal of the Southern Confederacy
0047-2867 Journal of Theology for Southern Africa
0047-2875 Journal of Travel Research
0047-2883 Journal of Value Engineering†
0047-2891 Journal of Youth and Adolescence
0047-2905 Journal on the Handicapped Child†
0047-2913 Journal Pakistan†
0047-2921 Journal Thirty One
0047-293X Journalistes Francais
0047-2948 Jousi
0047-2956 Juco Review
0047-2972 Judges' Journal
0047-2980 Judo-Koerier *changed to* Budo Koerier
0047-2999 Jungle
0047-3030 K
0047-3049 K F Z-Betrieb und Automarkt
0047-3057 K-Kauppa Ja Myyja *see* 0355-3078
0047-3065 K-3 Bulletin of Teaching Ideas and Materials†
0047-3073 Kaeltetechnik-Klimatisierung *changed to* K I Klima, Kaelte, Heizung
0047-3081 Kainai News
0047-309X Kajian Veterinar
0047-3103 Kalakalpam
0047-3111 Kalakshetra *changed to* Kalakshetra Quarterly
0047-312X Kalori
0047-3138 Makerere University. Library. Library Bulletin and Accessions List
0047-3146 Kanadai Fuggetlen Hirlap
0047-3154 Kanadsky Slovak
0047-3189 Kansas State Engineer
0047-3197 Karachi. Chamber of Commerce and Industry. Trade Journal
0047-3200 Karaki†
0047-3219 Karavana
0047-3227 Die Karawane
0047-3235 Karibu Tanzania†
0047-3243 Karjantuote
0047-3251 Karjatalous
0047-326X Karnatak University, Dharwad, India. Bulletin†
0047-3278 Kart og Plan
0047-3286 Kasari†
0047-3294 Katholischer Digest
0047-3308 Kauneus ja Terveys
0047-3316 Kauppateknikko
0047-3340 Kenya Journal of Adult Education
0047-3359 Kerala Industry
0047-3367 Kerala Sabha
0047-3375 Keretapi
0047-3383 Kesatuan Bulletin
0047-3391 Keste Damena
0047-3405 Kettenwirk-Praxis
0047-3413 Keynote *see* 0272-6513
0047-343X Kirjakauppalehti
0047-3456 Kirkens Verden†
0047-3472 Kneipp-Bademeister†
0047-3480 Know
0047-3499 Knox Alumnus *changed to* Knox Now and the Knox Alumnus

ISSN INDEX

ISSN	Title
0047-3510	Koettbranschen
0047-3529	Kol Bo
0047-3537	Kommunalt Tidsskrift
0047-3553	Konfekturehandleren
0047-3561	Koninklijke Officiers Schermbond. Kos-Gebeuren
0047-3588	Korea Focus†
0047-3596	Korea Today†
0047-360X	Korean Medical Abstracts
0047-3618	Korean Nurse
0047-3626	Korps Komando *changed to* Mari Jo
0047-3634	Korrosjons-Nytt
0047-3650	Kosmos
0047-3677	Kotiseutu
0047-3685	Kotitalous
0047-3693	Krishnamurti Foundation. Bulletin
0047-3715	Kryds-Avisen†
0047-3731	Kulturen Zivot
0047-3766	Kunststoff-Journal
0047-3774	L. A. S. I. E
0047-3839	Labor Arbitration in Government
0047-3855	Laboratory Product News
0047-3863	Labores del Hogar
0047-3871	Labour *changed to* Labor Press and Information
0047-388X	Labour Research Department Fact Service
0047-3898	Lago
0047-3901	Lagos Librarian
0047-391X	Lakaskultura
0047-3928	Lambda Alpha Journal of Man
0047-3936	Lamp
0047-3944	Lamp in the Spine†
0047-3952	Land Reform, Land Settlement and Cooperatives
0047-3960	Landbonyt
0047-3979	Landesverband der Tonkuenstler und Musiklehrer. Mitteilungsblatt
0047-3995	Landmaschinen-Rundschau
0047-4002	Landwirt im Ausland *changed to* Entwicklung und Laendlicher Raum
0047-4010	Die Landwirtschaft
0047-4029	Landwirtschaftsblatt Weser-Ems
0047-4037	Language and Literature†
0047-4045	Language in Society
0047-4053	Lantern's Core
0047-4061	Lanzadera†
0047-407X	Lapsi Ja Nuoriso *see* 0355-3736
0047-4088	Lariat
0047-4096	Laser and Electro-Optic Reviews *see* 0092-0754
0047-410X	Laser-Raman Spectroscopy Abstracts *see* 0309-5320
0047-4126	Lasteblieieren
0047-4134	Latin American Literary Review
0047-4142	Literacy Advance
0047-4169	Law and Society Newsletter *changed to* Law and Society Quarterly
0047-4177	Law Council of Australia. Law Council Newsletter *changed to* Australian Law News
0047-4185	Law Report News†
0047-4193	Law Review Digest
0047-4207	Lawasia
0047-4215	LawLab Journal *changed to* Expert Witness Journal
0047-4231	Lazio Ieri e Oggi
0047-424X	Leadership
0047-4258	League of Pity Paper *changed to* Young N S P C C News
0047-4274	Leben und Erziehen
0047-4282	Lebensmittel-Kaufmann
0047-4290	Lebensmitteltechnik
0047-4304	Lecturas
0047-4312	Lederwaren-Zeitung
0047-4320	Leeds & West Riding Topic *changed to* Leeds & Yorkshire Topic
0047-4339	Leeds Weekly Citizen
0047-4355	Leichtathletik
0047-4363	Leisure
0047-438X	Leka Nuhou†
0047-4401	Ragioni Critiche
0047-441X	Letras da Provincia
0047-4428	Letras de Hoje
0047-4444	Levende Gedachten
0047-4452	Lex
0047-4460	Liberal
0047-4479	Liberalt Perspektiv *changed to* Populist
0047-4495	Liberation War
0047-4509	Libertarian Analyst†
0047-4517	Libertarian Forum
0047-4525	Library Action
0047-4533	Library Association of Australia. University and College Libraries Section. News Sheet†
0047-4541	Library Trustees Foundation of New York State. Newsletter
0047-4568	Libros Nuevos†
0047-4576	Les Nouvelles
0047-4584	Licht und Leben
0047-4592	Life Threatening Behavior *see* 0363-0234
0047-4614	Life in America†
0047-4630	Lifeliner
0047-4649	Light
0047-4657	Light
0047-4665	Lillit
0047-4681	Lincolnshire Agricultural and Industrial Sales and Wants
0047-469X	Linde Distributor Progress†
0047-4703	Lingua e Cultura
0047-4711	Lingua e Literatura
0047-4738	Link
0047-4746	Linnean Society of New South Wales. Proceedings
0047-4754	Liquified Petroleum Gas
0047-4762	Listening Index *changed to* A M P S Broadcast Media
0047-4770	Literacy: a Newsletter *changed to* Adult Education Information Notes
0047-4789	Literacy Documentation†
0047-4797	Literary Repository
0047-4800	Litterature
0047-4819	Little Flower Monthly
0047-4827	Liverpool Newsletter
0047-4835	Living City
0047-4843	Living Earth
0047-4851	Living Historical Farms Bulletin
0047-486X	Living in South Carolina
0047-4894	Llewellyn *see* 0145-885X
0047-4908	Lloyd's Weekly Casualty Reports
0047-4916	Lo Gai Saber *changed to* Gai Saber
0047-4924	Local Government in South Australia†
0047-4959	Locus
0047-4967	Logberg-Heimskringla
0047-4975	Logger†
0047-4983	Loggers World
0047-4991	Logistics and Transportation Review
0047-5009	Logistik Technik und Versorgung†
0047-5017	Loisirs Nautiques
0047-5025	London City Mission Magazine *changed to* Span
0047-5033	London Collector
0047-5041	L.I.L.C.O. Almanac *changed to* Long Island Almanac
0047-505X	Lost
0047-5068	W C N Commercial News
0047-5076	Los Angeles County Medical Association. Bulletin *see* 0162-7163
0047-5084	Los Angeles County Museum of Art. Graphic Arts Council. Newsletter
0047-5106	Louisiana Researcher†
0047-5122	Louisiana Tech Engineer
0047-5149	Loyalist Gazette
0047-5157	Ludd's Mill
0047-5165	Lugha Yetu
0047-519X	Lure of Litchfield Hills
0047-522X	Luton Commerce and Trade Journal
0047-5246	M D of Canada†
0047-5254	M-H Builders News *changed to* M H/R V Builders News
0047-5262	M I S
0047-5270	M. S. News
0047-5289	M S T English Quarterly
0047-5297	M. T. A. Journal
0047-5300	M U M
0047-5319	Maanmittaus
0047-5327	Maansiirto
0047-5335	Macdonald Journal
0047-5351	Machinery & Machine Tool Journal
0047-536X	Machines Production
0047-5378	Machinist
0047-5386	McKee-Pedersen Instruments. M P I Applications Notes†
0047-5394	McKinsey Quarterly
0047-5408	McLean Bulletin
0047-5416	Madagascar; Revue de Geographie
0047-5424	Made in Europe. Technical Equipment Catalog
0047-5467	Magic and Spells Quarterly†
0047-5475	Magic Carpet
0047-5505	Magnetohydrodynamics and Plasmas *see* 0361-3321
0047-5513	Magyar Elet
0047-5521	Magyar Hirlap†
0047-5548	Maine Trail
0047-5572	Mak†
0047-5599	Malayan Economic Review
0047-5610	Malaysia in History
0047-5629	Malaysian Digest
0047-5637	Mallee Horticulture Digest†
0047-5653	Management
0047-5661	Management by Objectives
0047-567X	Management Development Centre, Dacca. Quarterly Bulletin *see* 0378-7532
0047-5688	Management Education & Development
0047-570X	Management in Government
0047-5718	Management-Scope
0047-5726	Manager Magazin
0047-5734	University of Santo Tomas. Faculty of Civil Law. Law Review
0047-5742	University of Santo Tomas. Graduate School. Journal of Graduate Research
0047-5750	U.S.T. Library Bulletin†
0047-5769	Manitoba Journal of Education
0047-5785	Manpower and Vocational Education Weekly
0047-5793	Manpower Documentation
0047-5807	Mantenimiento Ingenieria de Fabricas *see* 0149-3566
0047-5815	Manufacturing Engineer *changed to* Industrial Technology and Machine Tools
0047-5823	Manx Star
0047-5831	Maoriland
0047-5858	Maquettes-Plastiques *changed to* Maquettes Plastique Magazine
0047-5866	Mar
0047-5874	Marathon
0047-5882	Marches du Poisson *changed to* France-Europeche et Marches du Poisson
0047-5890	Marches Europeens des Fruits et Legumes
0047-5904	Marelli
0047-5912	Marga
0047-5920	Mariemou
0047-5939	Marine and Outdoor Trades *see* 0705-8993
0047-5955	Marine Engineers Review
0047-5963	Maritime Express†
0047-5971	Maritime Tax Reports
0047-598X	Market Research in Benelux *see* 0308-3446
0047-5998	Market Research in Germany *see* 0308-3446
0047-6005	Market Research in Italy *see* 0308-3446
0047-6013	Marketing for Sales Executives
0047-603X	Marmi Graniti Pietre
0047-6048	Marquette University Education Review†
0047-6056	Marriage Counseling Quarterly *changed to* Marriage and Family Counselors Quarterly
0047-6064	Marturion
0047-6072	Marxistiskt Forum
0047-6080	Maryland Nurse
0047-6099	Maryland Researcher
0047-6102	Maskinmesteren
0047-6110	Mass Line
0047-6129	Massachusetts Correctional Association. Correctional Research Bulletin†
0047-6137	Massachusetts Journal of Mental Health†
0047-6145	Massachusetts Psychological Center. Bulletin
0047-6153	Massachusetts Researcher
0047-617X	Master Builder *changed to* Tectonics
0047-6188	Master Indicator of the Stock Market
0047-6196	Master Photographer
0047-620X	Match
0047-6234	Materials Handling and Storage
0047-6242	Mathematical Association of South Australia. S.A. Mathematics Teacher *changed to* Mobius
0047-6250	Mathematical Association of Tanzania. Bulletin *changed to* Tanzanian Mathematical Bulletin
0047-6269	Mathematics Education
0047-6277	Mathematische Operationsforschung und Statistik; Series Statistics *changed to* Statistics
0047-6277	Mathematische Operationsforschung und Statistik *changed to* Optimization
0047-6285	Matthew Bender Tax Letter *changed to* Washington Tax and Business Report
0047-6293	Mawazo
0047-6315	Me Jane
0047-6323	Measurement in Education
0047-6331	Meat and Allied Trades Federation of Australia. Western Australian Division. Meat Industry
0047-634X	Meat and Livestock Commission, Bucks, England. International Market Survey
0047-6358	Meat Packers Council of Canada. Facts, Figures, Comment
0047-6366	Meat Trades Journal of Australia *see* 0156-2681
0047-6374	Mechanisms of Ageing and Development
0047-6390	Medaille Militaire
0047-6404	Medecine d'Afrique Noire
0047-6412	Medecine et Chirurgie Digestives
0047-6420	Medecine et Collectivite
0047-6439	Media and Consumer *see* 0010-194X
0047-6447	Media Mix Newsletter *changed to* Media Mix
0047-6455	Medical Assistance†
0047-6463	Medical Chronicle Monthly†
0047-6471	M C G Today
0047-6498	Medical Equipment *changed to* Patient Management
0047-651X	Medical Journal of Zambia
0047-6528	Medical News Fortnightly
0047-6536	Medical News, Medicine and Law
0047-6544	Medical News-Tribune *changed to* Medical News
0047-6552	Medical Progress through Technology
0047-6560	Medical Research Council Newsletter
0047-6587	Medico-Legal Society of New South Wales. Proceedings
0047-6595	Medico-Legal Society of Victoria. Proceedings
0047-6609	Mediterraneo
0047-6617	Meditsinskaya Tekhnika
0047-6641	Meetings on Atomic Energy
0047-665X	Meie Elu
0047-6668	Mekong Monthly Bulletin *changed to* Mekong Bulletin
0047-6676	Melbourne. Royal Melbourne Hospital. Quarterly†
0047-6692	American Association of State Colleges and Universities. Memo: to the President
0047-6706	Memorial-Sloan Kettering Cancer Center. Clinical Bulletin
0047-6714	Memphis State University Law Review
0047-6730	Men's Week†
0047-6749	Mental Health News†
0047-6757	Mental Hygiene News†
0047-6773	Mercury
0047-6781	Merseyside Business News†
0047-679X	Message
0047-6803	Message of Life
0047-682X	Metal
0047-6838	Metal and Engineering†
0047-6854	M. T. I. A. News Bulletin
0047-6862	Metal Trades Journal *see* 0047-6838

ISSN INDEX

ISSN	Title
0047-6870	Metaletter
0047-6889	Metallbericht
0047-6897	Metals Australia *changed to* Metals Australasia
0047-6919	Methodist Church Music Society Bulletin
0047-6935	Metro Guide. Halifax-Dartmouth Current Events
0047-6943	Metro Teen Scene
0047-696X	Metropolitan Area Planning Council Regional Report
0047-6978	M A U D E P Newsletter
0047-6986	Metsastaja
0047-6994	Mexican Newsletter
0047-701X	C I A B Circular
0047-7028	Mexico Forestal
0047-7036	Mexico Ganadero
0047-7052	Michigan Academy of Science, Arts, and Letters. Academy Letter
0047-7060	Michigan Society for Respiratory Therapy. Journal
0047-7079	Michigan Association of Health and Physical Education. M.A.H.P.E.R. Journal
0047-7087	Michigan Civil Rights Commission Newsletter
0047-7095	Michigan Dental Hygienist Association. Bulletin
0047-7109	Michigan. Department of Commerce. Corporation & Securities Bureau. Securities Bulletin
0047-7117	Michigan Food News
0047-7125	Michigan Reading Journal
0047-7133	Michigan Researcher
0047-7141	Michigan State University. Center for International Programs. International Report†
0047-715X	Michigan State University. Latin American Studies Center. Newsletter
0047-7168	Summation
0047-7184	Microfilm Techniques†
0047-7192	Microinfo
0047-7206	Micron
0047-7214	Microwave Systems News *see* 0164-3371
0047-7222	Midden
0047-7230	Middle East Economic Digest
0047-7249	Middle East International
0047-7257	Middle East Observer
0047-7265	Middle East Research & Information Project Reports
0047-7273	Midi-Minuit Fantastique
0047-7281	Midland Cooperator
0047-729X	Midland History†
0047-729X	Midland History
0047-7311	Midwest Purchasing
0047-732X	Midwest Racing News
0047-7338	Migrant Echo
0047-7346	Militaertechnik
0047-7354	Militaer Teknisk Tidskrift
0047-7362	Militaerseelsorge
0047-7370	Military Collectors News
0047-7389	Military History of Texas and the Southwest
0047-7397	Voenno-Meditsinskii Zhurnal
0047-7400	Milk News
0047-7419	Milk Topics
0047-7427	Mill Trade Journal
0047-7443	Mineria y Metalurgia, Plasticos y Electricidad
0047-7478	Miniaturbahnen
0047-7494	Mining in Canada *see* 0008-4492
0047-7508	M L N Bulletin *changed to* M L N Bulletin-Newsletter
0047-7524	Mirror of the Month†
0047-7532	Mississippi Dental Association. Journal
0047-7540	Mississippi Housing Newsletter†
0047-7559	Mississippi Review
0047-7567	Missouri Highways†
0047-7575	U M K C Law Review
0047-7583	Mlezi
0047-7591	Mobil & Motor
0047-7605	Mobile Home and Trailer News *changed to* Mobile Home and R.V. News
0047-7648	Modelisme
0047-7664	Modern Astronomy†
0047-7672	Modern Athlete and Coach
0047-7699	Modern Farmer
0047-7702	Modern Greek Studies Association Bulletin
0047-7710	Modern Kemi†
0047-7729	Modern Language Studies
0047-7737	Modern Office *see* 0311-7731
0047-7753	Modern Unionist
0047-7761	Modern Woman
0047-777X	Moderna Organizacija *see* 0350-1531
0047-7788	Modersmaalet
0047-7796	Moebel-Kultur
0047-780X	Der Moebelspediteur
0047-7826	Molecular Sieve Abstracts†
0047-7834	Monarchist
0047-7842	Monatsschrift Deutscher Zahnaerzte *see* 0340-1766
0047-7850	Monde Arabe†
0047-7869	Mondo Occulto
0047-7877	Monete e Medaglie
0047-7885	Monika
0047-7893	Moniteurs *changed to* M.A.
0047-7907	Monographs for Teachers of French *changed to* Macquarie University French Monographs
0047-7923	Montagne et Alpinisme
0047-7931	Montana Food Distributor
0047-794X	Montana Oil Journal
0047-7958	Montana Post
0047-7966	Montana Public Affairs Report
0047-7974	Montana Rural Electric News *changed to* Rural Montana
0047-7982	Montana. State University. Library. Recent Acquisitions†
0047-7990	Montana Stockgrower
0047-8008	Montana's Treasure Acres†
0047-8016	Montevecchio†
0047-8032	Australia. Bureau of Statistics. South Australian Office. Monthly Summary of Statistics
0047-8040	Monthly Tax Features
0047-8059	Montreal Children's Hospital. Children's News
0047-8075	Montreal. Stock Exchange. Monthly Review
0047-8083	Moon Rainbow
0047-8105	Moreana
0047-8121	Morning Star People
0047-813X	Mortgage and Real Estate Executives Report
0047-8148	Mosca Profana
0047-8164	Mosella
0047-8172	Mother & Baby
0047-8180	Moto Revue
0047-8199	Motor
0047-8210	Motor Manual *changed to* Australian Motor Manual
0047-8261	Mountain & Plain History Notes *changed to* Colorado Heritage News
0047-8288	Movie/TV Marketing
0047-830X	Moving Out
0047-8318	Ms
0047-8326	Mufulira Mirror *changed to* Mining Mirror
0047-8342	Mundo Taquigrafico†
0047-8350	Munger Africana Library Notes
0047-8369	Municipal Engineer
0047-8377	Munnpleien
0047-8385	Murmur
0047-8407	Muscle Training Illustrated
0047-8415	Muscular Development
0047-8423	Music & Arts
0047-8431	Music and the Teacher
0047-844X	Music Educators National Conference. Contemporary Music Project. C M P Newsletter†
0047-8466	Musical Newsletter†
0047-8474	Der Musikmarkt
0047-8482	Mutter und Kind
0047-8490	Mutual Fund Performance Monthly
0047-8504	Mutual Funds Forum
0047-8512	Mylord†
0047-8539	Mysore Journal of Agricultural Sciences
0047-8555	Mythic Society Quarterly Journal
0047-8563	N P
0047-8598	Nachrichten zur Wirtschafts- und Sozialpolitik
0047-8601	Naering i Nord
0047-861X	Naftika Chronika
0047-8628	Nairang Da'ijist
0047-8636	Nairobi Handbook
0047-8644	Nande
0047-8660	Nashotah Review†
0047-8679	Nashville, Tennessee. Children's Museum. Museum Notes†
0047-8687	N C P C Newsletter†
0047-8695	Nassau Lawyer
0047-8717	N A R D A News
0047-8733	National Association of Conservation Districts. Tuesday Letter
0047-8741	N A J E Educator
0047-875X	National Auto Research Canada. Black Book *changed to* Black Book Official Used Car Market Guide
0047-8768	National Braille Mail
0047-8784	National Congress of American Indians. Bulletin
0047-8792	National Council of Women of Australia. Bulletin
0047-8830	National Democrat†
0047-8857	National Electronics Council. Review *see* 0305-2257
0047-8865	National Folk
0047-8881	N I C A Outlook *changed to* Insulation Outlook
0047-8903	National League of Cities. Congressional Report *changed to* N L C Washington Report to the Nations Cities
0047-8938	N L F A Feed-Lines *changed to* Beef Business Bulletin
0047-8946	National Maritime S A R Review *see* 0093-2124
0047-8962	British Israel World Federation. National Message
0047-8989	N O L P E School Law Journal
0047-8997	N O L P E Notes
0047-9012	National Parks Journal
0047-9020	N. P. A. Journal
0047-9047	National Police Journal†
0047-9055	National Research Council, Canada. Division of Mechanical Engineering and National Aeronautical Establishment. Quarterly Bulletin†
0047-9063	National Saver *see* 0047-9071
0047-9071	National Savings Newsletter†
0047-908X	N S S F N S News
0047-9101	N S A C Newsletter *changed to* Advocate (Albany)
0047-911X	National Times
0047-9128	National Trust of Australia (New South Wales) National Trust Bulletin *changed to* National Trust of Australia (New South Wales) National Trust Magazine
0047-9136	N T I Newsletter
0047-9152	Natural Health Bulletin
0047-9160	Natural Life Styles†
0047-9195	Nebraska Art Association Quarterly *changed to* Nebraska Art Association Newsletter
0047-9209	Nebraska Law Review
0047-9217	Nebraska Resources†
0047-9217	Nebraska Resources
0047-9233	Nederlands Tijdschrift voor Vacuumtechniek
0047-9241	Nederlandse Krijgsman
0047-925X	Needle Arts
0047-9268	Neerlandica Americana
0047-9276	Neerlandica Extra Muros†
0047-9284	Neerlands Voetbal *changed to* K N V Ber
0047-9292	Negotiations Management
0047-9306	Negro Lawmaker Journal†
0047-9322	Nelson Gallery and Atkins Museum. Gallery Events
0047-9349	Nepalese Perspective†
0047-9357	Nepriklausoma Lietuva
0047-9365	Netherlands Journal of Veterinary Science†
0047-9373	Network/Urban Coalition
0047-9381	Neue Apotheken Illustrierte
0047-939X	Neue Barke *see* 0007-3016
0047-9403	Neue Bergbautechnik
0047-9411	Neurocirugia
0047-942X	Neuroelectric News
0047-9438	Neuropsihijatrija *changed to* Neurologija
0047-9446	Neutron Activation Analysis Abstracts
0047-9454	Nevada Engineer
0047-9462	Nevada Historical Society Quarterly
0047-9470	Nevada Livestock and Agriculture Journal
0047-9489	Nevada Rancher
0047-9497	R C U Report
0047-9500	New Age
0047-9519	New American Electronics Literature and Technical Data
0047-9527	New Banner
0047-9543	New Brunswick Historical Society. Historical Review†
0047-9551	New Brunswick Naturalist
0047-956X	New Chislehurst Announcer
0047-9578	New Church Herald†
0047-9594	New Critic *changed to* Saturday Review Book Club News
0047-9608	New Diffusionist†
0047-9616	New Directions
0047-9624	New Electronics
0047-9640	N E A P Q News†
0047-9659	New England Marine Resources Information *changed to* New England Marine Advisory Services Information
0047-9683	New Focus *see* 0145-8361
0047-9691	New French Books†
0047-9705	New Frontiers in Education
0047-9721	New Hellas
0047-973X	New Human Services Newsletter *see* 0094-5129
0047-9756	New Jersey Environmental Times *changed to* New Jersey Outdoors
0047-9772	New Jersey Historical Commission Newsletter
0047-9810	New Mexico Transporter
0047-9829	New Patriot
0047-9837	New Priorities *see* 0305-0629
0047-9845	New Products Medical-Surgical *see* 0009-9325
0047-9853	New Promotions and Competitions
0047-987X	New Shetlander
0047-9888	Bush Fire Bulletin†
0047-990X	New South Wales. Fire Service. Fire News
0047-9918	New South Wales Journal of Optometry
0047-9926	New South Wales Pastoral Conditions *see* 0034-6616
0047-9934	New South Wales Police News
0047-9942	New Times(Phoenix) *changed to* New Times Weekly
0047-9950	New Unity
0047-9969	New Wave
0047-9977	New Ways
0047-9985	New Writing†
0047-9993	New York (City) Economic Development Administration. Office of Public Affairs. Economic and Other Indicators†
0048-0002	New York Denik
0048-0037	New York Liberty Dispatch†
0048-0045	New York State Migrant Center. Newsletter†
0048-0053	New York State Environment
0048-0061	New York (State) Office of Planning Coordination. O P C News Summary†
0048-0088	New York Times Biographical Edition *see* 0161-2433
0048-010X	New Zealand Bookseller and Publisher *changed to* New Zealand Bookworld
0048-0118	New Zealand Camera *changed to* Camera
0048-0134	New Zealand Journal of Forestry Science
0048-0142	New Zealand Sanitarian *see* 0110-4969
0048-0150	New Zealand Surveyor

0048-0169 New Zealand Veterinary Journal
0048-0177 Newfoundland Amateur†
0048-0185 Newfoundland. Department of Education. Newsletter *changed to* School World
0048-0193 Newfoundland Medical Association. Newsletter *see* 0705-6702
0048-0207 Newman
0048-0215 News and Farmer
0048-0223 News from Zambia†
0048-0231 News of the New World
0048-024X Newscope-Current Events Edition *changed to* Newscope-Middle/Intermediate/Junior High School Edition
0048-0258 Newscope-Science Edition *changed to* ScienceCope
0048-0266 Newscope-Secondary Current Events Edition *changed to* Newscope-High School/College Edition
0048-0274 Newshunter
0048-0282 Newsletter of Biomedical Safety & Standards
0048-0304 Newspeace
0048-0320 Niagara Frontier Purchaser
0048-0339 Niedersaechsischer Jaeger
0048-0355 Nieuwe Pockets en Paperbacks
0048-0363 Nigeria Confidential
0048-0371 Nigerian Accountant
0048-038X Nigerian Business Digest
0048-0398 Nigerian Insurance Monitor
0048-0401 Nigerian Journal of Contemporary Law
0048-041X Nile Gazette
0048-0428 Nippon Acta Radiologica
0048-0444 Nippon Medical School. Journal
0048-0452 Nippon Steel News
0048-0460 Niv Hamidrashia
0048-0479 Noir et Rouge†
0048-0495 Nordisk Jordbrugsforskning
0048-0509 Nordisk Tidsskrift for Specialpaedagogik
0048-0541 Norkontakt
0048-055X Norlin Library, University of Colorado. Occasional Notes
0048-0568 Norrona
0048-0576 Norsk Dampkjelforening. Meddelelser
0048-0584 Norsk Drosjeeierblad
0048-0592 Norsk Husflid
0048-0606 Norsk Skibsfoerertidende
0048-0614 Norsk Tidsskrift for Sjakk
0048-0630 N A C L A News *see* 0149-1598
0048-0657 North Carolina Bar *see* 0164-6850
0048-0665 North Carolina Researcher
0048-0673 N C I Catalyst
0048-0681 North Dakota Education News
0048-069X North Dakota Society of Medical Technologists. Newsletter
0048-0711 Northampton and County Independent
0048-0746 Northeastern Regional Antipollution Conference. Proceedings
0048-0754 Northern Air
0048-0770 Northern Ireland. Ministry of Education. Education Statistics
0048-0789 Northern Libraries Bulletin
0048-0797 Northern Teacher
0048-0800 Special Schools Bulletin *see* 0310-5709
0048-0835 Nos Chasses
0048-0843 Nos Maisons Familiales de Vacances
0048-0851 Nostalgia News
0048-086X Notes on New Books *changed to* Bibliographical Index on Physical and Health Education, Sport, and Allied Subjects
0048-0886 Noticias da Africa do Sul *changed to* S.A. Panorama
0048-0894 Noticiero del Plastico-Elastomeros
0048-0908 Noticiero Quimico
0048-0916 Notizie dall'Albania
0048-0924 Notre Comte
0048-0932 Notre Dame Journal
0048-0940 Nottingham Topic
0048-0967 Nouvelle Ecole
0048-0975 Nouvelle Revue Internationale
0048-0983 Nova Scotia Reports
0048-1009 Novum Testamentum
0048-1017 Nowi Dni
0048-1025 Nuclear Active
0048-1033 Nuclear Magnetic Resonance Spectrometry Abstracts
0048-1041 Nucleic Acids Abstracts *changed to* Biochemistry Abstracts, Part 2: Nucleic Acids
0048-105X Nucleonics Week
0048-1076 Nueva Cultura *see* 0011-2755
0048-1084 Nueva Narrativa Hispanoamericana†
0048-1106 Nuggets
0048-1114 Numismatic Messenger†
0048-1122 Nuova Tradotta
0048-1149 Nuovo Impegno
0048-1165 Nurse in Israel
0048-119X Nuwe Afrikaner
0048-1203 Ny Jord *see* 0332-5229
0048-1211 Nya Cyklisten
0048-122X Det Nye
0048-1238 Nye Boeger om Film *changed to* Nye Boeger om Film/TV
0048-1246 O A G Travel Planner *see* 0193-3299
0048-1254 O.R.L. Digest *see* 0198-7038
0048-1262 Oak Ridge National Laboratory Review
0048-1270 Oberflaeche
0048-1289 Objectif Monde Uni†
0048-1297 Obra de Cooperacion Sacerdotal Hispanoamericana. Mensaje Iberoamericano *changed to* Comision Episcopal de Misiones y Cooperacion Entre las Iglesias. Mensaje Iberoamericano
0048-1319 Observateur Africain
0048-1378 Occupational Health New Zealand *see* 0301-0384
0048-1386 Ocean Soundings *see* 0025-3324
0048-1394 Ochrana Fauny†
0048-1408 Odd Fellow
0048-1416 Oesterreichische Bau-Wirtschaft
0048-1424 Oesterreichische Buergermeister Zeitung
0048-1440 Oesterreichische Militaerische Zeitschrift
0048-1459 Oesterreichische Foto-Zeitung
0048-1467 Oesterreichische Schulfunk *changed to* Der Oesterreichische Schulfunk mit Telespiegel
0048-1475 Oesterreichische Tieraerztezeitung
0048-1483 Oesterreichische Touristenzeitung
0048-1491 Off Center
0048-1505 Official Karate
0048-153X Ohio Archaeologist
0048-1548 Ohio Insect Information†
0048-1556 Ohio Jersey News
0048-1564 Ohio Researcher†
0048-1572 Ohio State Law Journal
0048-1580 Oil Palm News
0048-1599 Oklahoma Farm Bureau Farmer
0048-1602 Oklahoma Highwayman†
0048-1610 Oklahoma Rural News
0048-1629 Okyeame
0048-1637 Old Cars *changed to* Old Cars Weekly
0048-1645 Old Contemptible
0048-1653 Old Time Music
0048-1661 Omicron Nu *changed to* Omicron Nu Newsletter
0048-1688 Once upon a Time
0048-1696 Onderwatersport
0048-170X One-Ten *see* 0092-5667
0048-1734 Ontario Amateur
0048-1742 Ontario Archaeological Society. Arch Notes
0048-1750 Ontario Companies Law Guide *changed to* Ontario Corporations Law Guide
0048-1769 Ontario Education Review *changed to* O E A Review
0048-1785 Ontario Forests
0048-1793 Ontario Association for Geographic & Environmental Education. Monograph
0048-1793 Ontario Geography Teachers Association Monograph *see* 0048-1793
0048-1815 Ontario Numismatist
0048-1823 Ontario Plumbing Inspectors Association. Bulletin
0048-1831 Ontario Research Foundation. Newsletter *changed to* Technology Today
0048-1858 Ontario Shade Tree Council. Newsletter
0048-1866 Ontario Tax Reports
0048-1882 Onward†
0048-1890 Op Safari
0048-1904 Open Access†
0048-1904 Open Access
0048-1912 Open Court Newsletter *changed to* Educator: Open Court Newsletter
0048-1920 Open Home†
0048-1939 Open Letter
0048-1947 Open Road
0048-1955 Ophthalmology Digest *see* 0149-4260
0048-1963 Audio-Digest Ophthalmology
0048-198X Opinion Economica
0048-2013 Optics *see* 0308-7670
0048-2021 Optikko
0048-203X Optometry Today
0048-2056 Opus International
0048-2064 Oral Implantology
0048-2080 Orben Comedy Letter†
0048-2099 Orben's Comedy Fillers
0048-2102 Orben's Current Comedy
0048-2110 Orbit Weekly†
0048-2129 Ordo
0048-2137 Oregon A S C D Curriculum Bulletin *changed to* Curriculum Bulletin
0048-2145 Oregon Environmental Council Newsletter *changed to* Earthwatch Oregon
0048-2153 Research and Development Perspectives *changed to* Center (Eugene)
0048-217X Organizacija i Kadrovi
0048-2196 Organized Farmer *see* 0383-2244
0048-2234 Origins
0048-2242 Orissa Homoeopathic Bulletin
0048-2269 Orthodox Church
0048-2277 Volund
0048-2285 Ospedale Psichiatrico
0048-2293 Osteopathic Hospitals
0048-2331 Ottawa Law Review
0048-234X University of Ottawa. Aesculapian Society. Medical Review†
0048-2358 A P M Bulletin
0048-2366 Ouest Medical
0048-2382 Our Children *changed to* Activnews
0048-2390 Our Local Sixty Six
0048-2404 Our Town
0048-2420 Outdoor Guide
0048-2447 Outdoorman†
0048-2455 Outdoorsman
0048-2463 Outlook
0048-2471 Outlook†
0048-2498 Ouvrier Senegalais
0048-251X Overseas Advertising
0048-2528 Overseas Books
0048-2536 Overseas Hindustan Times
0048-2544 Overseas Press Bulletin *changed to* Overseas Press Club Bulletin
0048-2560 Oxford Consumer
0048-2579 Oxford Mission
0048-2587 P D & D International†
0048-2595 P G/Prisonniers de Guerre *changed to* P G-C A T M
0048-2609 P R Reporter
0048-2617 Pacific Alert *changed to* California Chamber of Commerce Alert
0048-2625 P.A.T.A. Indonesia
0048-2633 Pacific Marketer
0048-2641 Pacific Sun
0048-265X Pacifist
0048-2676 Packaging News
0048-2684 Packaging Review
0048-2692 Pakistan Educational Review†
0048-2706 Pakistan Heart Journal
0048-2722 Pakistan Pediatric Journal
0048-2749 Pakistan Survey *changed to* Dakshinesia
0048-2757 Pakistan Textile Journal
0048-2765 Palabra†
0048-2773 Palette†
0048-2781 Palmetto Piper
0048-282X Panorama (Boston)
0048-2838 Panorama Aujourd'hui
0048-2846 Panorama des Entreprises†
0048-2854 Papel Impreso
0048-2862 Paperprintpack India
0048-2870 Papers on Far Eastern History
0048-2889 Papetier
0048-2897 Papier und Kunststoff Verarbeiter
0048-2919 Papua and New Guinea Education Gazette
0048-2935 Paragraphic
0048-2951 Parassitologia
0048-296X Paratracks
0048-2978 Parent Cooperative Preschools International Journal
0048-2986 Parenteral Drug Association. Bulletin *changed to* Parenteral Drug Association. Journal.
0048-2994 Parliamentary Journal
0048-3001 Parliamentary Studies *see* 0301-9047
0048-301X Parnassos
0048-3028 Parnassus: Poetry in Review
0048-3036 Parsiana
0048-3044 Partisan
0048-3079 National Asphalt Pavement Association. Paving Forum
0048-3087 Pax
0048-3095 Pazifische Rundschau
0048-3109 Pearl Gazette
0048-3117 Pecan Quarterly
0048-3133 Pediatric Clinics of India
0048-3141 Pediatric Portfolio
0048-3176 Die Pelzwirtschaft
0048-3192 Pennant
0048-3206 Pennsylvania Academy of Ophthalmology and Otolaryngology. Transactions
0048-3214 Pennsylvania Geology
0048-3230 Pennsylvania News
0048-3249 Pennsylvania Researcher
0048-3257 Pennsylvania Road Builder
0048-3281 Pensioners Voice
0048-329X People
0048-3303 People
0048-3311 People for Progress†
0048-332X People United to Save Humanity. P.U.S.H.-Operation Push
0048-3338 People Watching†
0048-3354 New Zealand People's Voice
0048-3362 People's Voice†
0048-3370 Periodista
0048-3397 Periscoop
0048-3400 Periscope
0048-3419 Faculdade de Odontologia de Pernambuco. Revista
0048-3435 Personal Injury Researcher
0048-3443 Personal Report for the Executive
0048-3451 Personnel Guide to Canada's Travel Industry
0048-3478 Personnel News for School Systems
0048-3486 Personnel Review
0048-3494 Perspective (Washington)
0048-3508 Perspectives (Washington)
0048-3524 Perspectives in Defense Management
0048-3532 Perspectives Syndicalistes *changed to* Pense et Lutte
0048-3540 Royal Perth Hospital. Journal†
0048-3559 Perth. Stock Exchange. Official Record
0048-3567 Pesquisa Medica
0048-3575 Pesticide Biochemistry and Physiology
0048-3583 Petersen's PhotoGraphic Magazine
0048-3591 Petroleum Gazette
0048-3605 Petts Wood Post
0048-3613 P.G. Football Newsletter
0048-3621 Pharmaceutical Salesman *changed to* Pharmaceutical Representative
0048-363X Pharmacognosy Titles†
0048-3648 Pharmascope
0048-3656 Pharmazeutische Praxis
0048-3664 Pharmazie in Unserer Zeit
0048-3672 Pharos
0048-3699 Phi Sigma Iota Newsletter *changed to* Phi Sigma Iota Forum
0048-3702 Philadelphia Tribune
0048-3710 Philatelic Journalist
0048-3729 P. T. S. Journal
0048-3737 Philatopic Magazine

0048-3745 Philippine Economy and Industrial Journal
0048-3753 Philippine Entomologist
0048-3761 Philippine Journal of Animal Industry
0048-377X Philippine Journal of Fisheries
0048-3796 Philippine Journal of Linguistics
0048-380X Philippine Journal of Mental Health
0048-3818 Philippine Journal of Nursing
0048-3826 Philippine Journal of Plant Industry
0048-3834 Philippine Journal of Soils
0048-3842 Philippine Mining & Engineering Journal
0048-3850 Philippine Planning Journal
0048-3869 Philippine Sugar Institute Quarterly
0048-3877 Philippines Quarterly
0048-3885 Philologica Pragensia
0048-3893 Philosophia
0048-3907 Philosophic Research and Analysis *changed to* Contemporary Philosophy
0048-3915 Philosophy and Public Affairs
0048-3923 Philosophy of Education Society of Great Britain. Proceedings *see* 0309-8249
0048-3931 Philosophy of the Social Sciences
0048-3958 Photo Gallery
0048-3966 Der Foto-Markt†
0048-3974 Photo-Memo
0048-3982 Photo Reporter
0048-3990 Photographe Professionnel†
0048-4008 Photographic Journal of the Sun
0048-4016 Photography North
0048-4024 Physical Review Abstracts
0048-4059 Physiological Plant Pathology
0048-4067 Physiology Canada
0048-4083 Physiotherapists' Quarterly
0048-4105 Piano-Tuners Quarterly
0048-4113 Pick's World Currency Report
0048-4121 Pictorial Education
0048-413X Pictorial Education Quarterly *changed to* Pictorial Education Special
0048-4148 Pielegniarka i Polozna
0048-4156 Pig Breeders Weekly
0048-4164 Pigeon Racing News & Gazette
0048-4172 Piltdown Newsletter†
0048-4180 Pink Sheet on the Left
0048-4199 Pioneer
0048-4202 Pioneer
0048-4210 Pipe Dream
0048-4229 Pirogue
0048-4237 Pisciculture Francaise
0048-4245 Pitture e Vernici
0048-4253 Place†
0048-4261 Placedart†
0048-427X Plaisirs de la Chasse
0048-4288 Planet
0048-4296 Planner's Notebook *changed to* Practicing Planner
0048-4296 Planner's Notebook *see* 0001-2610
0048-430X Planning Advisory Service Reports *changed to* A P A Planning Advisory Service Reports
0048-4318 Planning in Northeastern Illinois
0048-4326 P I B C News
0048-4334 Plant Genetic Resources Newsletter
0048-4350 Plaste und Kautschuk
0048-4369 Plastforum *changed to* Plastforum Scandinavia
0048-4385 Plastics Southern Africa
0048-4407 Play Ball New York
0048-4415 Playboard
0048-4423 Playfair Cricket Monthly†
0048-444X Plebeian†
0048-4466 P L E R U S
0048-4474 Ploughshares
0048-4482 Plural Societies
0048-4490 Plymothian
0048-4504 Pneumatik Digest
0048-4520 Poemes Inedits
0048-4547 Poesia Hispanica†
0048-4563 Poesie Presente
0048-4571 Poetics
0048-458X Poetry
0048-4598 Poetry Information
0048-4601 Poetry Miscellany
0048-4628 Poets' Guild
0048-4636 Point and Figure Digest
0048-4695 Police Nationale
0048-4709 Policia Espanola
0048-4717 Policlinico. Sezione Medica
0048-4725 Poliisimies
0048-4733 Polska Akademia Nauk. Wydzial Nauk Medycznych. Annals *changed to* Polska Akademia Nauk. Wydzial Nauk Medycznych. Acta Medica Polona
0048-4741 Polish Institute of Arts and Sciences in America. Information Bulletin†
0048-475X Politieke Dokumentatie
0048-4768 Polizeiblatt fuer das Land Baden-Wuerttemberg
0048-4776 Polizei und Verkehrsjournal *changed to* Polizei Journal
0048-4784 Pollution
0048-4806 Polymer India
0048-4822 Popular Culture Association Newsletter *changed to* Popular Culture Association. Newsletter and Popular Culture Methods
0048-4830 Popular Dogs†
0048-4849 Population Newsletter
0048-4857 Porfeydd
0048-4865 Port of Melbourne Quarterly
0048-4881 Portland
0048-489X Portside
0048-4903 Portugaliae Physica
0048-492X Posta si Telecomunicatii†
0048-4946 Postgraduate Medicine Quarterly Abstracts†
0048-4954 Pottery in Australia
0048-4970 Poultry Meat *see* 0007-2176
0048-4989 Poultry Times
0048-4997 Pour l'Enfant Vers l'Homme
0048-5004 Pourquoi
0048-5012 Powder Metallurgy International
0048-5020 Powder Metallurgy Science & Technology
0048-5039 Power
0048-5047 Power & Industry in Asia†
0048-5071 Practical Education and School Crafts
0048-508X Practical Forms and Precedents (New South Wales)
0048-511X Prairies Tax Reports†
0048-5128 Der Praktische Arzt
0048-5136 Praxis der Beregnungswirtschaft†
0048-5144 Precision Shooting
0048-5152 Preface
0048-5160 Premisa
0048-5179 Prensa Chilena y Sus Comentarios
0048-5195 Presence Francophone
0048-5209 Press Forum *changed to* Depthnews
0048-5233 Prevention
0048-5241 Prevention
0048-525X Preview Abstracts in Physics and Astronomy†
0048-5268 Preview of Bermuda
0048-5276 Prim-Aid†
0048-5284 Primary Education
0048-5292 Primary Industry Survey
0048-5306 Principality of Liechtenstein: a Documentary Handbook
0048-5314 Print-Equip News
0048-5322 Printers News
0048-5330 Printers News
0048-5349 Prism *changed to* Pratt Reports
0048-5357 Prisma
0048-5365 Prison Law Reporter†
0048-5373 Prisoners Rights Newsletter *see* 0048-5365
0048-5381 Pro Motion
0048-539X Probation *changed to* Probation Journal
0048-5403 Probleme und Ergebnisse der Psychologie
0048-5411 Problemi di Ulisse
0048-5438 Professional Engineer *see* 0158-3158
0048-5446 Professional Engineer in Industry Newsletter†
0048-5454 Professional Officer
0048-5489 Progreso
0048-5497 Progress in Fire Retardancy
0048-5500 Progress in Materials Science†
0048-5519 Progress in Physical Therapy†
0048-5535 Prometheus
0048-5543 Promise M/R†
0048-5551 Propeller Club Quarterly
0048-5578 Prophetic Expositor
0048-5586 Proscope
0048-5608 Prosperity
0048-5624 Protection Management
0048-5632 Proud
0048-5640 Proud Black Images
0048-5659 Proust Research Association Newsletter
0048-5667 Proverbium†
0048-5675 Przeglad Psychologiczny
0048-5683 PSI *changed to* I Am
0048-5691 Psicologia e Lavoro
0048-5713 Psychiatric Annals
0048-5721 Psychiatric Outpatient Services in Los Angeles County
0048-573X Psychic Observer & Chimes
0048-5748 Psychological Issues
0048-5756 Psychologie Medicale
0048-5764 Psychopharmacology Bulletin
0048-5772 Psychophysiology
0048-5799 Public Administration *changed to* Public Administration and Finance Newsletter
0048-5802 Public Affairs
0048-5810 Public Affairs Information Service Foreign Language Index
0048-5829 Public Choice
0048-5853 Public Finance Quarterly
0048-5888 Public Ledger
0048-5896 Public Relations Australia†
0048-5926 Public Service *changed to* Public Service-Staff Vacancies Weekly
0048-5942 Publishers' Auxiliary
0048-5950 Publius
0048-5977 Puhelin
0048-6000 Pulse
0048-6019 Punjab Agricultural University. Journal of Research
0048-6027 Punjab Punch
0048-6035 Purchasing Management Newsletter†
0048-6043 Pyrethrum Post
0048-6051 O and M Bulletin *see* 0307-8558
0048-606X Q E D Renaissance *changed to* Pittsburgh
0048-6078 Q I M A
0048-6086 Quaderni di Radiologia
0048-6094 Quaderni Piacentini
0048-6116 Quarry Mine and Pit *changed to* Resources Industry-Quarry Mine & Construction Equipment
0048-6124 Quarter Racing World *see* 0364-9237
0048-6132 Quarterly Bibliography of Computers and Data Processing *see* 0270-4846
0048-6159 Quarterly Bulletin of Statistics for Asia and the Far East *changed to* Quarterly Bulletin of Statistics for Asia and the Pacific
0048-6167 Quarterly Bulletin on Solar Activity
0048-6175 Quarterly Journal of Management Development *changed to* Organization & Administrative Sciences
0048-6183 Quarterly Market Projection†
0048-6191 Quarterly Statistical Bulletin for Africa
0048-6205 Quarto Mondo
0048-6213 Quasi
0048-6221 Que Pasa†
0048-623X Que Pasa in Puerto Rico *changed to* Que Pasa
0048-6248 Quebec Aujourd' Hui†
0048-6256 Quebec-Histoire†
0048-6299 Quebec Tax Reports
0048-6302 Queens County Bar Association. Queens Bar Bulletin
0048-6310 Queen's Intramural Law Journal *changed to* Queen's Law Journal
0048-6329 Queens Own Highlander
0048-6337 Queensland. Guidance and Special Education Branch. Special Schools Bulletin for Teachers of Exceptional Children *see* 0313-6728
0048-6345 Q. H. A. Review
0048-6353 Queensland Littoral Society. Newsletter *changed to* Operculum
0048-6361 Queensland Master Builder
0048-637X Queensland Master Plumber
0048-6388 Queensland Roads
0048-6396 Queensland Statistics; Monthly Summary
0048-6418 Administrators' Bulletin†
0048-6426 Quest for Higher Productivity *changed to* Australian Productivity Action
0048-6434 Quest in Education
0048-6442 Questo Nostro Ambiente†
0048-6450 Queyras
0048-6477 Journal de la Quincaillerie†
0048-6493 Quinzaine Litteraire
0048-6507 R E
0048-6523 Racehorse
0048-654X Radharc
0048-6574 R C A Engineer
0048-6582 R C A Plain Talk and Technical Tips *see* 0381-095X
0048-6590 RadioFernseh-Haendler
0048-6604 Radio Science
0048-6612 Rail Engineering International
0048-6639 Railroad Modeler
0048-6647 Railway Digest International
0048-6663 Rakennustaito
0048-668X Rally
0048-6698 Rama *changed to* Peoples Media Digest
0048-671X Ramus
0048-6728 Rapeseed Digest
0048-6736 Rassegna Alpina
0048-6744 Rassegna di Medicina del Traffico
0048-6760 Rassegna di Neuropsichiatria e Scienze Affini†
0048-6779 Rassegna Internazionale di Logica
0048-6787 Rassegna Odontotecnica
0048-6809 Ratcliffian
0048-6817 Rating and Valuation Reporter
0048-6825 Raum und Siedlung *changed to* Structur
0048-6833 Rautatieliikenne
0048-6841 Razon y Fabula
0048-685X Real Estate Institute of Queensland. Real Estate Journal
0048-6868 Real Estate Law Journal
0048-6884 Realist†
0048-6906 Reason
0048-6922 Recherche en Matiere d'Ecomomie des Transports *see* 0304-3320
0048-6930 Recherche Spatiale†
0048-6949 Rechte Lijn
0048-6957 Record *changed to* Record - Dossier
0048-6965 Records Management Report†
0048-6973 Recreation Property Ontario *changed to* Ontario Cottager
0048-6981 Recursos Hidricos
0048-699X Red Buffalo
0048-7007 Red Comb Poultry Journal *changed to* Red Comb Journal
0048-7023 Red Cross Quarterly
0048-7031 Red Cross Junior *changed to* Link-up
0048-7031 Red Cross Senior *changed to* Link-up
0048-7066 Reeves Journal
0048-7090 Regione Toscana
0048-7104 R N A B C News
0048-7112 R N A O News
0048-7120 Rehabilitacion
0048-7139 Rehabilitation Digest
0048-7155 Reign of the Sacred Heart
0048-7163 Universite de Reims. Institut de Geographie. Travaux
0048-7171 Reinsurance
0048-718X Relay Engineer *see* 0308-4213
0048-7198 Relazioni Clinico Scientifiche
0048-7201 Relevo
0048-7228 Remedes
0048-7236 Remedial Education *see* 0311-1954
0048-7252 Report from Washington *changed to* In Common
0048-7260 Report on Indian Legislation†
0048-7279 Reports on Rheumatic Diseases
0048-7287 Die Republik
0048-7295 R E T S Digest

0048-7317 Research Institute of America. Research Institute Recommendations
0048-7325 Research Journal of Philosophy
0048-7333 Research Policy
0048-7341 Researcher
0048-7368 Reserve Bank of Australia. Currency
0048-7376 Resources
0048-7384 Resources for American Literary Study
0048-7392 Respiratory Therapy
0048-7406 Restaurant News
0048-7422 Retail Operations News Bulletin
0048-7430 Rettung
0048-7449 Reumatismo
0048-7457 Reuse/Recycle
0048-7465 Review of Books and Religion *see* 0146-0609
0048-7473 Review of Contemporary Law
0048-7481 Review of Law & Social Change
0048-749X Review of Regional Studies
0048-7511 Reviews in American History
0048-752X Reviews in Analytical Chemistry
0048-7538 Reviews on Coatings and Corrosion
0048-7546 Reviews on Drug Interactions *see* 0334-2190
0048-7554 Reviews on Environmental Health
0048-7562 Reviews on Reactive Species in Chemical Reactions *see* 0162-7546
0048-7570 Reviews on Silicon, Germanium, Tin and Lead Compounds
0048-7589 Reviews on Deformation Behavior of Materials
0048-7597 Revista Agropecuaria
0048-7600 Revista Argentina de Cirurgia
0048-7619 Revista Argentina de Radiologia
0048-7627 Revista Argentina de Urologia y Nefrologia
0048-7635 Revista Brasileira Cardiovascular
0048-7643 Revista Brasileira de Tecnologia
0048-7651 Revista Chilena de Literatura
0048-766X Revista Chilena de Obstetrica y Ginecologia
0048-7678 Revista Cubana de Ciencias Veterinarias
0048-7694 Revista de Estudios Politicos
0048-7708 Revista de Geografia
0048-7716 Revista de la Sanidad Militar Argentina
0048-7724 Revista de Medicina Veterinaria y Parasitologia
0048-7732 Revista de Obstetricia y Ginecologia de Venezuela
0048-7740 Revista de Psicologia Normal e Patologica†
0048-7740 Revista de Psicologia Normal e Patologica
0048-7759 Revista de Soldadura
0048-7775 Revista Ecuatoriana de Higiene y Medicina Tropical
0048-7783 Revista Educativa†
0048-7813 L T R. Revista
0048-7848 Revista Medico-Chirurgicala
0048-7856 Revista Odonto-Estomatologica
0048-7864 Revista Paulista de Hospitais
0048-7872 Revista de Divulgacion Agropecuaria
0048-7880 Revista Portuguesa de Pediatria e Puericultura
0048-7902 Revue Avicole
0048-7910 Revue Belge du Feu
0048-7929 Revue de Droit et d'Economie Immobiliere *changed to* Revue d'Economie et de Droit Immobilier
0048-7937 Revue de Jurisprudence Commerciale
0048-7945 Revue de l'Atherosclerose†
0048-7953 Revue de l'Habitat Francais
0048-7988 Revue d'Histoire de l'Eglise de France
0048-7996 Revue d'Histoire des Sciences et de Leurs Applications
0048-8003 Revue d'Histoire Moderne et Contemporaine
0048-8011 Revue du Materiel d'Entreprise
0048-8038 Revue Economique Franco-Allemande
0048-8062 Revue Francaise d'Endocrinologie Clinique, Nutrition et Metabolisme
0048-8097 Revue Generale de Botanique
0048-8119 Revue Generale d'Etudes de la Police Francaise
0048-8143 Revue Internationale de Philosophie
0048-8151 Revue Internationale d'Onomastique
0048-816X Revue Ivoirienne de Droit
0048-8178 Revue Roumaine d'Etudes Internationales
0048-8186 Revue Technique du Batiment
0048-8194 Revue Technique du Feu
0048-8208 Revue Trimestrielle de Droit Commercial *changed to* Revue Trimestrielle de Droit Commercial et du Droit Economique
0048-8216 Rhode Island. University. U. R. I. Commercial Fisheries Newsletter†
0048-8224 Rhodes Report
0048-8232 Rhodesian Caravaner and Outdoor Life *changed to* Caravaner and Outdoor Life
0048-8267 Ricardian
0048-8275 Ricemill News
0048-8291 Ricerche di Automatica
0048-8305 Right On
0048-8321 Risques du Metier
0048-8348 Rivista del Colore
0048-8356 Rivista Di Anatomia Artistica
0048-8364 Rivista di Anatomia Patologica e di Oncologia
0048-8372 Rivista di Diritto Sportivo
0048-8399 Rivista di Idrobiologia
0048-8402 Rivista Italiana di Scienza Politica
0048-8410 Rivista Oto-Neuro-Oftalmologica
0048-8429 Rivista Tributaria Ticinese
0048-8437 Roan Antelope *changed to* Mining Mirror
0048-8445 Rock & Folk
0048-8453 Rock & Gem
0048-8461 Rocket
0048-847X Rockhound
0048-8488 Rocky Mountain Analgesia Society. Journal
0048-8496 Rod & Line
0048-850X Rodale's Environment Action Bulletin†
0048-8518 Roeien
0048-8526 Roerfag
0048-8534 Rogue Digger
0048-8542 Rolling Along
0048-8550 Romania Literara
0048-8577 Romanian Journal of Chemistry
0048-8593 Romantisme
0048-8623 Rosette
0048-8631 Rotary Down Under
0048-8658 Romania; Documents-Events
0048-8666 Roundabout
0048-8674 Rountree Report
0048-8690 Royal Canadian Legion's Coaching Review†
0048-8704 Royal Life Saving Society. Quarterly Journal
0048-8712 Royal National Institute for the Blind. School Magazine
0048-8720 R S P C A Today
0048-8739 Royal Town Planning Institute Journal *see* 0309-1384
0048-8747 Rubber, Plastic and Cable Industries Journal
0048-8755 Rund um den Pelz International
0048-8771 Running Board
0048-878X Rural Arkansas
0048-8798 Rural Education Review†
0048-8801 Rural Electric Missourian *see* 0164-8578
0048-881X Russian Literature Triquarterly
0048-8828 Russian Ultrasonics
0048-8836 Rutebiltidende
0048-8844 Rutgers Journal of Computers and the Law *changed to* Rutgers Journal of Computers, Technology and the Law
0048-8852 Rutland Historical Society Newsletter *changed to* Rutland Historical Society Quarterly
0048-8860 Rx Bulletin†
0048-8879 Ryde Recorder
0048-8887 Rydge's Construction, Civil Engineering and Mining Review *changed to* Rydge's C C E M-Construction, Civil Engineering and Mining
0048-8895 S F Greats†
0048-8917 S M/Sales Meetings *see* 0148-4052
0048-8933 Sabretache
0048-8941 Sackbut†
0048-895X Saddle and Striker
0048-8968 Safety Canada
0048-8976 Sage Professional Papers in International Studies†
0048-8984 Sahkourakoitsija
0048-8992 Saint Louis Chronicle
0048-900X St. Paul Dispatch & Pioneer Press Newspaper Index
0048-9018 Saisons d'Alsace
0048-9026 Salary and Merit
0048-9034 Sales and Marketing in Australia†
0048-9050 Salvage Locator
0048-9069 S A E
0048-9077 San Bernardino County Museum Association. Newsletter
0048-9093 San Gabriel Valley Dental Society. Bulletin
0048-9107 Sante Publique
0048-9115 Santiago
0048-9123 Santo Tomas Nursing Journal
0048-914X Saskatchewan Administrator
0048-9166 Saskatchewan Care
0048-9174 Saskatchewan Farm Science *see* 0707-7793
0048-9182 Saskatchewan Genealogical Society. Bulletin
0048-9190 Saskatchewan Guidance and Counseling Association. Guidelines
0048-9204 Saskatchewan Indian
0048-9212 Saskatchewan Journal of Educational Research and Development†
0048-9220 Saskatchewan Medical Quarterly†
0048-9239 Saturday Evening Post
0048-9247 Savings Banks Institute. Journal
0048-9263 Scandinavian-American Bulletin
0048-9271 Scandinavian Audiology
0048-928X Scandinavian Canadian Businessman
0048-9301 Scandinavian Refrigeration
0048-931X Scene
0048-9328 Schach
0048-9336 Scheidewege
0048-9344 Schietsport
0048-9352 Schiltrom†
0048-9360 Schizophrenics Anonymous International. Bulletin *see* 0318-8272
0048-9409 School Guidance Worker
0048-9417 School Health Bulletin
0048-9433 School Library Newsletter†
0048-9441 S M S G Newsletter
0048-945X School Nurse
0048-9476 School Services Curriculum Perspectives†
0048-9484 Schulverwaltungsblatt fuer Niedersachsen
0048-9492 Schuss
0048-9506 Die Schwalbe
0048-9514 Schweizer Hotel Journal
0048-9522 Schweizer Volkskunde
0048-9530 Schweizerische Zeitschrift fuer Nachwuchs und Ausbildung†
0048-9549 Schwestern Revue
0048-9581 Science and Government Report
0048-9603 Science Education News
0048-962X Science Fantasy†
0048-9646 Science Fiction Research Association Newsletter
0048-9654 Science Fiction Times
0048-9662 Science for the People
0048-9670 Science in Agriculture
0048-9689 Science of Man
0048-9697 Science of the Total Environment
0048-9700 Science Policy *see* 0302-3427
0048-9719 S T A News *see* 0381-6036
0048-9727 Sciences Medicales
0048-9735 Scope-Journal
0048-9743 Scope/Recreational Vehicle and Camping News
0048-9743 Recreational Vehicle & Camping News *see* 0380-8343
0048-9751 Scots Magazine
0048-976X Scottish Cooperator *changed to* Co-Operative News (Scottish Edition)
0048-9778 Scottish Institute of Missionary Studies Bulletin
0048-9786 S L A News
0048-9794 Scottish Literary News *see* 0305-0785
0048-9808 Scottish Transport
0048-9816 Scout Leader
0048-9824 Scrap and Waste Reclamation and Disposal†
0048-9832 Screenings
0048-9859 S G M News Digest
0048-9867 Sea Classics
0048-9875 Sea Grant Seventies
0048-9883 Sealandair
0048-9905 Sear
0048-9913 Search (Nashville)
0048-9921 Search (Washington, D.C.) *changed to* Urban Institute. Policy and Research Report
0048-9948 Seattle Centerstage
0048-9956 Second Coming
0048-9964 Second Order
0048-9980 Second Wave
0048-9999 Secondary Curriculum Letter *changed to* Curriculum Letter
0049-0008 Secularist
0049-0016 Security Distributing & Marketing
0049-0024 Security Gazette
0049-0032 Seed Producers Review *changed to* Australian Seed Producers Review
0049-0040 Seed Scoop
0049-0059 Seguranca
0049-0067 Selecciones Municipales
0049-0075 Selecoes Odontologicas
0049-0083 Select
0049-0091 Select Bibliography on Higher Education
0049-0105 Selected References on Environmental Quality as It Relates to Health†
0049-0113 Selective Service Law Reporter *see* 0193-3906
0049-0156 Semaine Juridique
0049-0164 Semina
0049-0172 Seminars in Arthritis & Rheumatism
0049-0199 Senior Citizens Today
0049-0202 Sentinel (Willowdale)
0049-0210 Srpski Arhiv za Celokupno Lekarstvo
0049-0229 Service to Business and Industry-BPL
0049-0237 Service World International
0049-0253 Sesame Street
0049-027X Seventeen's Make It!†
0049-0296 Severn and Wye Review†
0049-0318 Sex Problems Court Digest
0049-0326 Sexologie†
0049-0334 Shareholder and New Investor†
0049-0342 Shawensis†
0049-0369 Ship Repair and Maintenance *changed to* Shipcare & Maritime Management
0049-0385 Sh'ma
0049-0393 Shopping Center World
0049-0407 Shore Review
0049-0415 Shotgun News
0049-0423 Shuttle, Spindle & Dyepot
0049-0431 Sic†
0049-044X Sierra Club. National News Report
0049-0466 Sign World
0049-0490 Silent News
0049-0504 Sillon†
0049-0512 Simmons Review
0049-0520 S I A Journal
0049-0547 Singapore Undergrad
0049-0555 Singles-Mingles
0049-0563 Sinnets Helse
0049-0571 Sinopse de Cardiologia *changed to* Sinopse de Medicina Interna
0049-058X Sinopse de Gastrenterologia *changed to* Sinopse de Medicina Interna
0049-0598 Sintesis
0049-0601 Sinteza
0049-061X Sioniste
0049-0628 Sirjana
0049-0636 Sistema Nervoso†
0049-0652 Ski Scene†
0049-0660 Skolnytt *see* 0356-7842
0049-0679 Skotoey *changed to* SKO
0049-0687 Skylook *changed to* Mufon U F O Journal
0049-0709 Slavic Gospel News
0049-0733 Slice of Pizza

ISSN INDEX 1089

0049-075X Slimming & Nutrition *changed to* Slimming
0049-0776 Smoke Signals
0049-0806 Sno-Fari News Events *changed to* Colorado Outfitter
0049-0822 SnoTrack
0049-0849 Sobre los Derivados de la Cana de Azucar
0049-0857 Social Change
0049-0865 Social Dimension Newsletter†
0049-0881 Social Reformer
0049-089X Social Science Research
0049-0911 Social Sciences
0049-092X Social Sciences in Canada
0049-0938 Socialisme Quebecois
0049-0946 Socialist Affairs
0049-0954 Socialist Press Bulletin
0049-0962 Socialni Politika
0049-0970 Socialt Forum *see* 0347-5484
0049-0989 Boletin S A C M†
0049-0997 Sociedad Dominicana de Geografia Boletin†
0049-1004 Sociedad Mexicana de Geografia y Estadistica. Boletin
0049-1039 Sociedade de Lingua Portuguesa. Boletim
0049-1063 Societe d'Etudes et de Preparation aux Examens Publics et Prives. Revue d'Etudes
0049-108X Societe Francaise de Photogrammetrie. Bulletin *see* 0244-6014
0049-1098 Societe Historique Acadienne. Cahiers
0049-1101 Societe Medicale d'Afrique Noire de Langue Francaise. Bulletin
0049-111X Etudes Prehistoriques†
0049-1128 Societe Royale Belge d'Entomologie. Bulletin et Annales†
0049-1136 Societe Royale Zoologique de Belgique. Annales
0049-1144 S.A.M. News International
0049-1152 Society for Ancient Numismatics. S A N Journal
0049-1160 S A A D Digest
0049-1179 Society for the Study of Labour History. Bulletin
0049-1187 Society of Archer-Antiquaries. Newsletter
0049-1195 Society of Architectural Historians Newsletter
0049-1209 Society of Manufacturing Engineers. Technical Digest
0049-1217 Sociolinguistics Newsletter
0049-1225 Sociologia
0049-1233 Sociological Analysis *see* 0306-2481
0049-1241 Sociological Methods & Research
0049-125X Soenderjysk Maanedsskrift
0049-1276 Sol
0049-1292 Solidarite Ouvriere
0049-1306 Somerset and Dorset Notes and Queries
0049-1330 Sosialistisk Perspektiv
0049-1349 Sotainvalidi
0049-1357 Souffles
0049-1381 S.A. Athlete
0049-1403 South African Financial Gazette
0049-1411 South African Metrication News
0049-1438 South Australia. Department of Education. Education Gazette
0049-1446 South Australian Dairymen's Journal
0049-1454 South Australian Garden Guide†
0049-1470 South Australian State Reports
0049-1489 South Carolina Dental Journal
0049-1497 Medical University of South Carolina. Bulletin *changed to* Auctus Alumni Bulletin
0049-1519 South Coast Sun
0049-1527 South Eastern Latin Americanist
0049-1535 South Vietnam in Struggle
0049-1543 S.W.A. Boer
0049-1551 Southeast Asia†
0049-1616 Southern MotoRacing
0049-1624 Southern Purchasor
0049-1640 Southern Stars
0049-1659 Southern Utah News
0049-1667 Southwest Skier *changed to* Skier
0049-1675 Southwestern American Literature
0049-1683 Southwestern Journal of Social Education
0049-1691 S P R P C Reports *changed to* Omnibus
0049-1705 Sou'wester
0049-173X Soviet Journal of Developmental Biology
0049-1748 Soviet Journal of Quantum Electronics
0049-1756 Soviet Power Engineering
0049-1764 Soviet Progress in Polyurethanes
0049-1772 Sower *changed to* Sower (1979)
0049-1780 Space Adventures†
0049-1802 Spanish Today
0049-1810 Spastics News
0049-1829 Spear†
0049-1837 Special Education Newsletter
0049-1845 Special-Interest Autos
0049-1861 Spektrum
0049-187X Spoke Wheels†
0049-1888 Spokesman
0049-190X Sport Heroes *changed to* Hockey Illustrated
0049-1926 Sport und Mode
0049-1934 Sporting Investor Method Magazine†
0049-1942 Sporting Press
0049-1950 Sporting Star
0049-1985 Sports Merchandiser
0049-1993 Sportshandleren *changed to* Sport
0049-2000 Spotlight (Bath)
0049-2019 Sprachpflege
0049-2027 Squadron†
0049-2035 Stagione delle Arti, del Libro, e del Turismo
0049-2051 Stampa Sud
0049-206X Standard-Bearer
0049-2078 Standpunkte und Dokumente
0049-2086 Stanford Law School Journal
0049-2108 Stanford University Campus Report
0049-2116 Star
0049-2159 State Supplies
0049-2167 Statement of the Assets and Liabilities of the Chartered Banks of Canada
0049-2175 Statistical Indicators in ECAFE Countries *changed to* Statistical Indicators for Asia and the Pacific
0049-2183 Switzerland. Directorate General of Customs. Monthly Statistics
0049-2205 Steel Construction
0049-2213 Steel Pipe News†
0049-2221 Steroidologica *see* 0301-0163
0049-223X Der Steuerberater
0049-2248 Sti og Varde
0049-2280 Stockowners' Digest
0049-2302 Strada
0049-2310 Strategy and Tactics
0049-2329 Street Chopper
0049-2337 Street Level†
0049-2345 Strobe†
0049-2353 Stromata
0049-2361 Studi e Problemi di Critica Testuale
0049-237X Studies in Logic and the Foundations of Mathematics
0049-2388 University of Illinois. Department of Linguistics. Working Papers *changed to* Studies in the Linguistic Sciences
0049-2396 Studii si Cercetari de Biochimie
0049-2418 Sub-Normal Children's Welfare Association. Welfare News
0049-2426 Sub-Stance
0049-2434 S F M A Bulletin *changed to* F M A Bulletin
0049-2442 Success
0049-2450 Sud
0049-2469 Sudan Engineering Society. Journal
0049-2477 Sugar News
0049-2515 Sunday Funday
0049-2531 Sundet Rundt
0049-254X Bulletin of Sung and Yuan Studies
0049-2558 Sunstone Review
0049-2566 Suomen Invalidi
0049-2574 Super-8 Filmaker
0049-2590 Supermarket and Retailer
0049-2612 Supreme Court Researcher
0049-2620 Sur les Sentiers de l'Ecole Active†
0049-2639 Surface Wave Abstracts
0049-2647 Surgelation
0049-2655 Survie de l'Ame Humaine *see* 0151-4016
0049-2663 Svensk Idrott
0049-2671 Svensk Skidsport
0049-2698 Svensk Ishockeymagasin *see* 0345-4347
0049-2701 Swedish Journal of Agricultural Research
0049-2728 Swiss Canadian News
0049-2736 Syndicats de Roumanie
0049-2744 Syndicats Vietnamiens
0049-2752 Synergist
0049-2760 Synoptic
0049-2787 Terveystyo *see* 0356-3081
0049-2795 Systems
0049-2817 Taamuli
0049-2825 Die Tabak Zeitung
0049-2833 Tactile†
0049-2868 Take Over
0049-2876 Talent News and Views *changed to* Whitmark News & Views
0049-2906 Talk
0049-2914 Tallow Light†
0049-2922 Tambor
0049-2930 Tamkang Journal of Mathematics
0049-2949 Tamkang Review
0049-2957 Tangley Oaks Reading Guide†
0049-2973 Tanzania. Bureau of Statistics. Employment and Earnings *changed to* Tanzania. Bureau of Statistics. Survey of Employment
0049-3007 Tasmanian Association for the Teaching of English. Journal *see* 0311-1784
0049-3015 Tasmanian Fisheries Research
0049-3023 Tasmanian Hotel Review
0049-3058 Taxi Drivers Voice†
0049-3066 Tchad et Culture
0049-3074 Teacher *changed to* M T A Association A E M
0049-3082 Teacher in Wales†
0049-3090 Teacher-Librarian
0049-3112 Teacher Today†
0049-3139 Teachers World *see* 0309-3484
0049-3147 Teaching of English
0049-3155 Technical Communication
0049-3171 Technicka Knihovna
0049-3198 Technology Mart†
0049-321X Teenager Monthly
0049-3228 Teen's Star†
0049-3236 Teknisk Tidsskrift for Textil og Beklaedning
0049-3252 Tele Presse
0049-3287 Telecine†
0049-3295 Teleguide
0049-3309 Teletronics *see* 0310-6411
0049-3317 Television Sponsors Directory
0049-3325 TeleVizier
0049-3333 Temas de Orientacion Agropecuaria
0049-335X Tempo
0049-3368 Tempus†
0049-3376 Tenants Outlook†
0049-3392 Tennessee Parent-Teacher *changed to* Tennessee Parent-Teacher Bulletin
0049-3406 Tennessee School Board Bulletin
0049-3422 Tennessee Vo-Tech News†
0049-3430 Tenth
0049-3449 Teologia y Vida
0049-3473 Terre Africaine
0049-3481 Teton
0049-349X Texas Agricultural Progress
0049-3503 Texas Dental Assistants Association. Bulletin
0049-3511 Texas Farm & Ranch News
0049-352X Texas Metro
0049-3538 C R W R News
0049-3554 Textile Asia
0049-3562 Textile Labour/Canadian Edition *changed to* Labor Unity
0049-3589 Thai Journal of Agricultural Science
0049-3597 Theatre Enfance et Jeunesse
0049-3600 Theatre Quarterly
0049-3619 Theatre-Quebec†
0049-3635 Theologia
0049-3651 Theological Times
0049-366X Theologie und Glaube
0049-3678 Theoretical Physics Journal *see* 0361-3321
0049-3686 Theoria to Theory
0049-3694 Theosophy in Australia
0049-3708 Theosophy in New Zealand
0049-3716 Therapeutica Nova *changed to* Probatum Est
0049-3724 Thin-Layer Chromatography Abstracts
0049-3740 Third World Reports
0049-3759 This Fortnight in Pakistan
0049-3767 This Is Calgary *changed to* Calgary
0049-3783 This Week†
0049-3805 Thomas
0049-3813 T. P. S. Bulletin
0049-3821 Thoroughbred of California
0049-3848 Thrombosis Research
0049-3856 Sygeplejersken
0049-3864 Tieraerztliche Umschau
0049-3880 Tijdschrift voor Bejaarden- ,Kraam- en Ziekenverzorging
0049-3899 Tijdschrift voor Gastro-Enterologie†
0049-3910 Time Out
0049-3929 Times Higher Education Supplement
0049-3937 Tips
0049-3945 Tobacco International
0049-3953 Tobacco Review
0049-3961 Tobakk-Frukt-Sjokolade
0049-397X Tocher
0049-3988 Today in Mining†
0049-4003 Today's Girl†
0049-402X Tohoku Regional Fisheries Research Laboratory. Bulletin
0049-4038 Toike Oike
0049-4046 Tokyo Book Development Centre. Newsletter *changed to* Asian Book Development
0049-4054 Freshwater Fisheries Research Laboratory, Tokyo. Bulletin *changed to* National Research Institute of Aquaculture. Bulletin
0049-4062 Toledo Museum News
0049-4070 Tomorrow's Newspaper†
0049-4089 Tonnage Club Farm News†
0049-4100 Top Management Abstracts
0049-4119 Top of the News with Fulton Lewis†
0049-4127 Topic
0049-4135 Topical Stamp Handbooks
0049-4143 Torax
0049-416X Torch (Chicago)
0049-4178 Torch of Homoeopathy†
0049-4186 Toronto Jewish Press
0049-4194 Toronto Life
0049-4216 Toronto Stock Exchange Review
0049-4232 Toronto Vegetarian Association. Newsletter
0049-4283 Touristik Aktuell
0049-4291 Town and Countryside
0049-4313 T P I C News *see* 0708-5397
0049-4321 Trade and Commerce
0049-433X Trade Unions International of Workers in Commerce. Bulletin
0049-4348 Trade Winds from Japan†
0049-4356 Traedgaardsnytt
0049-4372 Tramway Museum Society. Journal
0049-4380 Trans Tasman
0049-4402 Transit News
0049-4410 Transit-Times
0049-4429 Transition
0049-4445 Transition *changed to* Perspective
0049-4461 Transport
0049-4488 Transportation
0049-4496 Transportation and Distribution Management†
0049-4518 Transportation Safety Association of Ontario. Bulletin
0049-4526 Transportation Safety Association of Ontario. Driver's News Letter
0049-4534 Travail Theatral
0049-4542 Travel and Camera *see* 0041-2007
0049-4577 Travelnews
0049-4585 TravLtips Freighter Bulletin *see* 0162-9816
0049-4593 Treasure
0049-4615 Trefoil Trail
0049-4623 Trend
0049-4631 Tribuna Farmaceutica
0049-464X Tribuna Italiana

ISSN	Title
0049-4658	Tribune-Post
0049-4666	Tribune Psychique
0049-4674	Tribune Socialiste†
0049-4682	Tricontinental
0049-4690	Trident
0049-4704	Universita degli Studi di Trieste. Istituto di Matematica. Rendiconti
0049-4712	Trinitarian Bible Society Quarterly Record
0049-4720	Tripura Review†
0049-4739	Troisieme Civilisation
0049-4747	Tropical Animal Health and Production
0049-4755	Tropical Doctor
0049-4763	Tropical Grasslands
0049-478X	Truck Trends
0049-481X	Tungsten News
0049-4828	Tungsten Statistics
0049-4836	Tupart Monthly Reports on the Underground Press†
0049-4852	Turkiye Muhendislik Haberleri
0049-4887	Tvaettnytt
0049-4909	Twilight
0049-4917	Two Tone
0049-4925	Two-Year College Mathematics Journal
0049-4933	Tydskrif vir Volkskunde en Volkstaal
0049-495X	Typog†
0049-4968	New York Typographical Union Number Six. Bulletin
0049-4976	U F O-Nyt
0049-4984	Unicef Information Bulletin
0049-500X	Ubique†
0049-5026	Uganda Schools Newsletter
0049-5034	Ugens Politik†
0049-5042	Uhrenfachgeschaeft
0049-5069	Uj Konyvek
0049-5077	Ukrainian Canadian
0049-5107	Ulster Tatler
0049-5123	Umeni
0049-5131	Umweltschutz
0049-514X	Unabashed Librarian
0049-5166	U E C A Publication
0049-5174	Underground Lamp Post
0049-5190	Une Semaine de Paris-Pariscope
0049-5204	Unesco. Centro de Documentacion Cultural, Havana. Informaciones Trimestriales
0049-5212	Unesco. Regional Centre for Book Development in Asia, Karachi. Newsletter *changed to* Unesco. Regional Office for Culture and Book Development in Asia. Newsletter
0049-5220	Unidad Latina†
0049-5239	Unifier
0049-524X	Union Herald
0049-5298	Manhattan-Bronx Postal Union. Union Mail *changed to* New York Metro Area Postal Union. Union Mail
0049-5301	Union Research Service†
0049-531X	Unitarian
0049-5328	U C O News *changed to* U C O Cornerstone
0049-5344	United Florists News *changed to* United Flowers-by-Wire Canada Journal
0049-5379	U N I D O Documents Checklist
0049-5387	U N I D O Newsletter
0049-5395	U N I T A R News
0049-5433	United Reformed Church History Society. Journal
0049-5441	United Senior Citizens of Ontario. Bulletin *see* 0382-0068
0049-5468	B N D D Bulletin *see* 0098-3470
0049-5484	U. S. National Clearinghouse for Poison Control Centers. Bulletin
0049-5506	Universe
0049-5514	Universita Karlova. Fakulta Vseobecneho Lekarstvi. Pobocka v Hradci Kralove. Sbornik Vedeckych Praci
0049-5522	Universita Karlova. Fakulta Vseobecneho Lekarstvi. Pobocka v Hradci Kralove. Sbornik Vedeckych Praci: Supplementum
0049-5530	Universitas
0049-5557	Unmuzzled Ox
0049-5581	Unser Kleeblatt
0049-559X	Unspeakable Visions of the Individual
0049-562X	Urania
0049-5638	Urban Affairs Today†
0049-5654	Urban Data Service Report
0049-5662	Urban Life and Culture *see* 0098-3039
0049-5689	Urban Rights†
0049-5697	Urbat *see* 0241-6794
0049-5700	Urethane Plastics and Products
0049-5719	Urogallo†
0049-5735	Utbildningstidningen
0049-576X	V E News *see* 0318-0867
0049-5778	V E 6
0049-5794	Valeurs Actuelles
0049-5808	Valiseesti
0049-5816	Vancouver Calendar Magazine
0049-5824	Vancouver Numismatic Society. News Bulletin
0049-5832	Vancouver Stock Exchange Review
0049-5867	Vaar Industri†
0049-5883	Vasama
0049-5891	Vasculum
0049-5905	Vegetarian Courier
0049-5913	Velocidad
0049-5921	Verbindungstechnik
0049-593X	Verdict
0049-5948	Verfahrenstechnik
0049-5956	Vermont Libraries†
0049-5956	Vermont Libraries†
0049-5964	Vern og Velferd
0049-5972	Vernice
0049-5980	Vers la Vie Nouvelle
0049-5999	Versandhausberater
0049-6006	Der Versicherungskaufmann
0049-6014	Versicherungsvermittlung
0049-6022	Vertical
0049-6030	Vesey Street Letter
0049-6057	Die Veterinaermedizin
0049-6065	Veterinary Doctor and Veterinary Digest†
0049-6073	Vibration
0049-6081	Vibrations *see* 0361-5359
0049-609X	Vickers News
0049-6103	Victoria. Department of Agriculture. Dairyfarming Digest†
0049-6111	Victoria, Australia. Education Department. Curriculum and Research Bulletin
0049-6138	Victorian Computer Bulletin
0049-6146	Victorian Horticulture Digest†
0049-6154	V. I. E. R. Bulletin
0049-6162	Australia. Bureau of Statistics. Victorian Office. Victorian Monthly Statistical Review *changed to* Australia. Bureau of Statistics. Victorian Office. Monthly Summary of Statistics - Victoria
0049-6170	Victorian Municipal Directory
0049-6189	Victorian Periodicals Newsletter *changed to* Victorian Periodicals Review
0049-6197	Victorian Railways Newsletter *changed to* Victorian Rail Ways
0049-6200	Victorian Tobacco Grower†
0049-6227	Vida Nostra *changed to* Vida Nostra Revolum
0049-6235	Video *see* 0310-6411
0049-6243	Videocassette Newsletter *changed to* Videocassette & CATV Newsletter
0049-6278	Vie du Rail Outremer *see* 0181-1878
0049-6294	Vie Publique
0049-6308	Viehhandel
0049-6316	Vieilles Maisons Françaises
0049-6340	Vietnam Digest
0049-6359	Vietnam Economic Report†
0049-6367	Vietnam: Yesterday and Today
0049-6375	Vietnam Youth
0049-6383	View from Ottawa *changed to* Ottawa Letter
0049-6405	Viewpoint†
0049-6421	Vigilante *changed to* Hotel and Catering
0049-643X	Vigneron Champenois
0049-6448	Viking
0049-6464	V I N A Quarterly
0049-6472	Virginia Dental Journal
0049-6480	Virginia Gazette
0049-6499	Virginia Researcher
0049-6510	Vision Index
0049-6529	Visite
0049-6545	Vista Femenina Centroamericana
0049-657X	Vivre†
0049-660X	Vivres-Voeding *changed to* Federation Belge des Enterprises de Distribution. Courrier Hebdomadaire
0049-6618	V F I Information Bulletin†
0049-6626	Voce dell'Africa
0049-6634	Voce d'Italia in Canada
0049-6650	Vogelwarte
0049-6669	Voice
0049-6677	Voix de la Construction†
0049-6685	Voix de la Resistance
0049-6693	Voix des Parents
0049-6707	Voix du Retraite
0049-6715	Volare Necesse Est
0049-6723	Volkswagen Greats *see* 0273-6748
0049-6731	Volley Kroniek *changed to* Volleybal
0049-674X	Volume Retail Merchandising†
0049-6758	Vrachebnoe Delo
0049-6812	Vrije Pers†
0049-6820	Wirtschaft und Technik im Transport *changed to* Foerdertechnik
0049-6847	A Wake Newslitter
0049-6855	Wakra
0049-6871	Wallonie Art et Histoire
0049-688X	War Cry
0049-6898	War Cry
0049-6901	Warrior
0049-691X	Washington International Business Report
0049-6928	Washington Researcher†
0049-6944	Washington University Librarian
0049-6952	Washington Wildlife†
0049-6960	Watchmakers of Victoria *changed to* Watchmakers of Australia
0049-6979	Water, Air, and Soil Pollution
0049-6987	Water Pollution Control Federation. Highlights
0049-6995	Water Rights and Quality News and Views *changed to* California Waterscape
0049-7002	Water Skier
0049-7010	Water Talk
0049-7029	Wayne Engineer
0049-7045	Wealth of Nations
0049-7053	Weather Timetable
0049-7061	Weekly Nation
0049-707X	Weekly Unity†
0049-7088	Weewish Tree
0049-710X	Weimaraner *see* 0162-315X
0049-7126	Weltbild
0049-7134	Weltgeschehen
0049-7142	Werk und Leben *changed to* Magazin fuer Mitarbeiter - Werk und Leben
0049-7150	Werk und Zeit
0049-7169	Wertpapier
0049-7177	West†
0049-7185	West Australian Gardener
0049-7193	West Bengal
0049-7207	Mechanical Engineering Bulletin
0049-7215	West Coast Poetry Review†
0049-7223	West End
0049-7231	West Indian Sportsman
0049-724X	West Texas Livestock Weekly *see* 0162-5047
0049-7258	West Virginia Economic Indicators
0049-7266	Westchester Historian
0049-7274	Westchester Law Journal
0049-7282	Western Association of Map Libraries. Information Bulletin
0049-7312	Western Australia. Education Department. Education Circular
0049-7320	Western Australia. Forests Department. Forest Focus
0049-7347	Western Australian Institute of Technology Gazette
0049-7371	Western Canadian Lumber Worker
0049-738X	Western Cleaner and Launderer
0049-7398	Western Floors
0049-7436	W I D News
0049-7460	Western Ontario Farmer
0049-7479	Western Outdoor News
0049-7487	Western Outfitter
0049-7495	Western Potter
0049-7517	Western Temperance Herald
0049-7525	Western Weekly Reports
0049-7533	What's New
0049-7541	Wheel
0049-755X	Wheel Extended
0049-7568	Wheelchair Competitor *changed to* Achievement
0049-7584	White Pelican
0049-7592	Whooper *changed to* S W F News
0049-7614	Widening Horizons
0049-7622	Wiesbadener Leben
0049-7630	Wilcox Report†
0049-7630	Wilcox Report
0049-7649	Wilmington Journal
0049-7657	Wind Rose
0049-7673	Window†
0049-7681	Windsor Sportsmen's News
0049-7703	Wirtschaft zwischen Nord- und Ostsee
0049-7711	Das Wirtschaftseigene Futter
0049-772X	W A V A Dispatch
0049-7746	Wisconsin Researcher†
0049-7754	Witches International Craft Associates. W I C A Newsletter
0049-7762	Wloptoonakun†
0049-7770	Woman Activist
0049-7797	Women and Film†
0049-7800	Women in Kenya
0049-7819	Women in Struggle
0049-7827	Women Speaking
0049-7835	Women Studies Abstracts
0049-7843	Women's Army Corps Journal†
0049-786X	Womens Press
0049-7878	Women's Studies
0049-7878	Women's Studies
0049-7886	Wood Duck
0049-7908	Wood Products Industry Abstracts Bulletin *see* 0360-3083
0049-7916	Wood Research
0049-7924	Wood World†
0049-7940	Woodworkers and Painters Journal *see* 0042-5842
0049-7959	Word and Way
0049-7967	Word Processing Report
0049-7975	Workers Action
0049-8017	World Agricultural Report
0049-8025	World Animal Review
0049-805X	World Ecology Two Thousand†
0049-8068	W F P A News *changed to* Animalia
0049-8076	W F D Y News
0049-8084	World Food Programme News
0049-8092	World Future Society Bulletin
0049-8106	World Gift Review Monthly Newsletter
0049-8114	Weekly Epidemiological Record
0049-8122	World Medical Journal
0049-8130	World Peace News
0049-8149	World Sugar News
0049-8157	World Tanker Fleet Review
0049-8165	World Tribune
0049-819X	Write-In, USA
0049-8203	Writing†
0049-8211	Writing Published *see* 0308-2024
0049-822X	Wyoming Valley Motorist *changed to* Valley Motorist
0049-8238	X-Ray on Current Affairs in Southern Africa
0049-8246	X-Ray Spectrometry
0049-8254	Xenobiotica
0049-8262	Xi Psi Phi Quarterly
0049-8289	Yatri
0049-8297	Yesterday
0049-8300	Yiddish Press
0049-8319	Yoga Life International†
0049-8335	Yokohama Plant Protection News
0049-8343	You†
0049-8351	Young Age
0049-836X	Young Alliance†
0049-8378	Young Indian
0049-8394	Your Church
0049-8432	Your Region in Action *changed to* Your Region
0049-8440	Youth Action†
0049-8459	Youth Mirror
0049-8467	Youth Report *see* 0160-9696
0049-8475	Yrke

0049-8483 Yugoslavia
0049-8505 Zahir
0049-8513 Zaire-Afrique
0049-8521 Zambia Farmer†
0049-853X Zambia Library Association Journal
0049-8572 Zdravotnicka Pracovnice
0049-8580 Zeitschrift fuer Analytische Psychologie und ihre Grenzgebiete *see* 0301-3006
0049-8599 Zeitschrift fuer Auslaendische Landwirtschaft
0049-8602 Zeitschrift fuer Bewaesserungswirtschaft
0049-8610 Zeitschrift fuer die Gesamte Hygiene und ihre Grenzgebiete
0049-8629 Zeitschrift fuer Eigenheimfreunde
0049-8637 Zeitschrift fuer Entwicklungspsychologie und Paedagogische Psychologie
0049-8645 Zeitschrift fuer Lateinamerika
0049-8653 LiLi
0049-8661 Zeitschrift fuer Romanische Philologie
0049-867X Zeitschrift fuer Sozialpsychologie
0049-8688 Zeitschrift fuer Werkstofftechnik *changed to* Zeitschrift fuer Werkstofftechnik, Materials Technology and Testing
0049-8696 Zentralblatt fuer Pharmazie, Pharmakotherapie und Laboratoriumsdiagnostik
0049-8718 Z P G National Reporter
0049-8726 Zhurnal Mikrobiologii, Epidemiologii i Immunobiologii
0049-8750 Zonneland
0049-8769 Zoological Society of India. Journal
0049-8777 Zootecnia e Veterinaria *see* 0020-0735
0049-8785 Zuidafrikaanse Koerier†
0052-2678 World Council of Young Mens Service Clubs. Minutes of the General Meeting
0065-0005 A B Bookman's Yearbook
0065-0013 A B C British Columbia Lumber Trade Directory and Year Book
0065-0021 A B C Directory
0065-003X A B C Europ Production
0065-0048 A B C of Book Trade
0065-0072 Ag Engineers Notebook
0065-0080 A. I. Voeikov Main Geophysical Observatory, Leningrad. Data of Measurements of Electric Field Strength of the Atmosphere at Various Altitudes by the Results of Soundings
0065-0099 A. I. Voeikov Main Geophysical Observatory, Leningrad. Results of Ground Observations of Atmospheric Electricity. Additional Issue
0065-0102 A V E in Japan
0065-0129 A. W. Mellon Lectures in the Fine Arts
0065-0137 Aachener Geschichtsverein. Zeitschrift
0065-0145 Aarbog for Dansk Skolehistorie
0065-017X Aarhus Universitet. Matematisk Institut. Lecture Notes Series
0065-0188 Aarhus Universitet. Matematisk Institut. Various Publications Series
0065-0196 Aarsbok foer Skolan
0065-020X Aarsbok foer Sveriges Kummuner
0065-0218 Norges Landbrukshoegskole. Institutt for Bygningsteknikk. Byggekostnadsindeks for Driftsbygninger i Jordbruket. Prisutviklingen
0065-0226 Norges Landbrukshoegskole. Institutt for Bygningsteknikk. Aarsmelding/Annual Report
0065-0234 Norges Landbrukshoegskole. Institutt for Bygningsteknikk. Melding
0065-0242 Norges Landbrukshoegskole. Institutt for Jordskifte og Eiendomsutforming. Melding
0065-0269 Hong Kong. Fisheries Research Station. Bulletin
0065-0277 University of Aberdeen. Department of Forestry. Economic Survey of Private Forestry
0065-0285 Aberystwyth Memoranda in Agricultural, Applied and Biometeorology
0065-0293 Wales. National Library. Handlist on Manuscripts in the National Library of Wales
0065-0307 Abhandlungen aus dem Gesamten Buergerlichen Recht, Handelsrecht und Wirtschaftsrecht
0065-0315 Abhandlungen Moderner Medizin
0065-0323 Abhandlungen und Materialen zur Publizistik
0065-0358 Abhandlungen zur Handels- und Sozialgeschichte
0065-0366 Abhandlungen zur Philosophie, Psychologie und Paedagogik
0065-0374 About Zambia
0065-0382 Abr-Nahrain
0065-0390 Abr-Nahrain. Supplements
0065-0412 Absorption Spectra in the Ultraviolet and Visible Region
0065-0420 Abstracts of Belgian Geology and Physical Geography
0065-0439 Abstracts of Gothenburg Dissertations in Science†
0065-0447 Academia Campinense de Letras. Publicacoes
0065-0455 Academia Espanola, Madrid. Anejos del Boletin
0065-0471 Academia Hondurena de la Lengua. Boletin
0065-048X Academia de Stiinte Sociale si Politice. Institutul de Istorie si Arheologie Cluj-Napoca. Anuarul
0065-0498 Institutul de Speologie Emil Racovitza. Travaux
0065-0501 Academia Scientiarum Fennica. Proceedings/Sitzungsberichte *see* 0356-6927
0065-051X Academic Underachiever†
0065-0544 Academie des Inscriptions et Belles-Lettres. Etudes et Commentaires
0065-0552 Academie des Sciences. Annuaire
0065-0560 Academie des Sciences. Index Biographique des Membres et Correspondants
0065-0579 Academie des Sports, Paris. Annuaire
0065-0587 Academie Francaise. Annuaire
0065-0595 Academie Royale de Medecine de Belgique. Memoires. Collection in 8 *changed to* Academie Royale de Medecine de Belgique. Bulletin et Memoires
0065-0609 Academie Royale des Sciences, des Lettres et des Beaux Arts de Belgique. Index Biographique des Membres, Correspondants et Associes
0065-0625 Academy for Educational Development. Academy Papers
0065-0633 Academy of American Franciscan History. Documentary Series
0065-0641 Academy of American Franciscan History. Monograph Series
0065-065X Academy of American Franciscan History. Propaganda Fide Series
0065-0668 Academy of Management. Proceedings
0065-0676 A N P H I Papers
0065-0684 Academy of Political Science. Proceedings
0065-0692 Academy of the Hebrew Language. Specialized Dictionaries
0065-0714 Accademia Musicale Chigiana. Quaderni.
0065-0722 Accademia dei Fisiocritici, Siena. Sezione Medico-Fisica *see* 0390-7783
0065-0730 Accademia Etrusca di Cortona. Annuario
0065-0749 Accademia Lucchese di Scienze, Lettere ed Arti. Atti. Nuova Serie
0065-0757 Accademia Nazionale Italiana di Entomologia. Rendiconti
0065-0765 Accademia Patavina di Scienze Lettere ed Arti. Collana Accademica
0065-0781 Accademia Toscana di Scienze e Lettere La Colombaria. Studi
0065-079X Accepted Dental Therapeutics
0065-082X Accidents in North American Mountaineering
0065-0838 Accidents to Aircraft on the British Register
0065-0846 Accounting Research Studies†
0065-0862 Accredited Institutions of Higher Education *see* 0361-9362
0065-0870 Acoustical Holography *changed to* Acoustical Imaging: Recent Advances in Visualization and Characterization
0065-0889 Acronyms and Initialisms Dictionary *changed to* Acronyms, Initialisms and Abbreviations Dictionary
0065-0897 Acta Academiae Regiae Gustavi Adolphi
0065-0900 Acta ad Archaeologiam et Artium Historiam Pertinentia
0065-0919 Acta Agraria et Silvestria. Series Agraria
0065-0927 Acta Agraria et Silvestria. Series Silvestris
0065-0935 Acta Agraria et Silvestria. Series Zootechnica
0065-0943 Acta Agriculturae Scandinavica. Supplementum *issued with* 0001-5121
0065-0951 Acta Agrobotanica
0065-096X Acta Allergologica. Supplementum *changed to* Allergy. Supplementum
0065-0986 Acta Archaeologica Lodziensia
0065-0994 Acta Archaelogica Lundensia: Monographs of Lunds Universitets Historiska Museum. Series in 8
0065-1001 Acta Archaelogica Lundensia: Monographs of Lunds Universitets Historiska Museum. Series in 4
0065-101X Acta Archaeologica
0065-1028 Acta Arctica
0065-1036 Acta Arithmetica
0065-1044 Acta Baltico-Slavica
0065-1052 Acta Bernensia: Beitraege zur Praehistorischen, Klassischen und Juengeren Archaeologie
0065-1060 Acta Bibliothecae Regiae Stockholmiensis
0065-1079 Acta Bibliothecae Universitatis Gothoburgensis
0065-1095 Acta Biologica Hellenica
0065-1109 Acta Borealia A. Scientia
0065-1125 Taiwania
0065-1133 Acta Chemica Scandinavica. Supplementum†
0065-1141 Acta Classica
0065-115X Acta Concilium Ophthalmologicum
0065-1168 Acta Criminologica *see* 0316-0041
0065-1176 Acta Dermatologica
0065-1184 Acta Embryologiae Experimentalis
0065-1192 Acta Endocrinologica Panamericana
0065-1206 Acta Facultatis Medicae Fluminensis
0065-1214 Godisen Zbornik na Medicinskiot Fakultet vo Skopje
0065-1222 Acta Geobotanica Barcinonensia *changed to* Acta Botanica Barcinonensia
0065-1230 Acta Geographica†
0065-1249 Acta Geographica Lodziensia
0065-1257 Acta Geographica Lovaniensia
0065-1265 Acta Geologica Taiwanica
0065-1273 Acta Germanica
0065-1281 Acta Histochemica
0065-129X Acta Historiae Neerlandicae
0065-1303 Acta Historica
0065-1311 Acta Historica Scientiarum Naturalium et Medicinalium
0065-132X Acta Hydrobiologica
0065-1338 Acta Hydrophysika
0065-1346 Acta Juridica
0065-1389 Acta Medicae Historiae Patavina
0065-1397 Acta Medicinae Legalis et Socialis
0065-1400 Acta Neurobiologiae Experimentalis
0065-1419 Acta Neurochirurgica. Supplement
0065-1427 Acta Neurologica Scandinavica. Supplementum
0065-1435 Acta Neuropathologica. Supplement
0065-1443 Acta Nuntiaturae Gallicae
0065-1451 Acta Ophthalmologica. Supplementum
0065-146X Acta Pacis Westphalicae
0065-1478 Acta Parasitologica Polonica
0065-1508 Acta Pharmacologica et Toxicologica. Supplementum
0065-1516 Acta Philologica
0065-1524 Acta Philologica
0065-1532 Acta Philologica Aenipontana
0065-1540 Acta Philosophica et Theologica
0065-1559 Acta Physica Austriaca. Supplement
0065-1567 Acta Phytomedica
0065-1575 Acta Phytotaxonomica Barcinonensia†
0065-1583 Acta Protozoologica
0065-1591 Acta Psychiatrica Scandinavica. Supplementum
0065-1605 Acta Psychologica-Gothoburgensia
0065-1613 Acta Psychologica Taiwanica
0065-1621 Acta Radiobotanika et Genetika
0065-1656 Acta Scientiarum Socialium
0065-1672 Acta Theologica Danica
0065-1699 Acta Veterinaria Scandinavica. Supplementum
0065-1710 Acta Zoologica Cracoviensia
0065-1729 Acta Zoologica Lilloana
0065-1737 Acta Zoologica Mexicana
0065-1753 Action in Pharmacy
0065-177X Action Universitaire
0065-1788 Activite Economique de la Haute-Normandie
0065-1796 Actrascope *see* 0315-484X
0065-180X Actua. Special Enfants
0065-1818 Actualite Rhumatologique, Presentee au Praticien
0065-1826 Actualites Endocrinologiques†
0065-1850 Adan E. Treganza Anthropology Museum. Papers
0065-1869 Adansonia. Memoires†
0065-1877 Adaptations Series
0065-1885 Addiction Research Foundation of Ontario. Bibliographic Series
0065-1907 Adelaide. Institute of Medical and Veterinary Science. Annual Report of the Council
0065-1915 Adelaide Law Review
0065-1923 Aden Magazine
0065-1931 Adhesives Red Book
0065-194X Adlai Stevenson Institute of International Affairs. Annual Report†
0065-1966 Kenya Institute of Administration. Journal
0065-1974 Administrator
0065-1982 Administrators in Action†
0065-1990 Admission Requirements of American Dental Schools *see* 0091-729X
0065-2008 Adolescent Psychiatry†
0065-2008 Adolescent Psychiatry
0065-2024 Zuerl's Adressbuch der Deutschen Luft- und Raumfahrt
0065-2032 Adressbuch fuer den Deutschsprachigen Buchhandels
0065-2067 Advance of Christianity through the Centuries†
0065-2075 Advanced Accountancy Seminar. Proceedings
0065-2091 Advances in Activation Analysis
0065-2113 Advances in Agronomy
0065-2121 Advances in Alicyclic Chemistry
0065-213X Advances in Alicyclic Chemistry. Supplement†
0065-2148 Advances in Analytical Chemistry and Instrumentation
0065-2156 Advances in Applied Mechanics
0065-2164 Advances in Applied Microbiology
0065-2172 Advances in Applied Microbiology. Supplement
0065-2180 Advances in Astronomy and Astrophysics†
0065-2199 Advances in Atomic and Molecular Physics
0065-2210 Advances in Biochemical Engineering
0065-2229 Advances in Biochemical Psychopharmacology
0065-2245 Advances in Biological and Medical Physics
0065-2253 Advances in Biology of Skin
0065-2261 Advances in Biomedical Engineering and Medical Physics†
0065-227X Advances in Biophysics
0065-2288 Advances in Blood Grouping†
0065-2296 Advances in Botanical Research
0065-230X Advances in Cancer Research
0065-2318 Advances in Carbohydrate Chemistry and Biochemistry

1092 ISSN INDEX

0065-2326 Advances in Cardiology
0065-2334 Advances in Cardiopulmonary Diseases†
0065-2342 Advances in Catalysis and Related Subjects *see* 0360-0564
0065-2350 Advances in Cell and Molecular Biology†
0065-2377 Advances in Chemical Engineering
0065-2385 Advances in Chemical Physics
0065-2393 Advances in Chemistry Series
0065-2407 Advances in Child Development and Behavior
0065-2415 Advances in Chromatography
0065-2423 Advances in Clinical Chemistry
0065-2431 Advances in Communication Systems†
0065-244X Advances in Comparative Physiology and Biochemistry
0065-2458 Advances in Computers
0065-2466 Advances in Control Systems *see* 0090-5267
0065-2474 Advances in Corrosion Science and Technology
0065-2482 Advances in Cryogenic Engineering
0065-2490 Advances in Drug Research
0065-2504 Advances in Ecological Research
0065-2539 Advances in Electronics and Electron Physics
0065-2547 Advances in Electronics and Electron Physics. Supplement
0065-2555 Advances in Engineering
0065-2563 Advances in Environmental Science and Technology
0065-2571 Advances in Enzyme Regulation
0065-258X Advances in Enzymology and Related Areas of Molecular Biology
0065-2598 Advances in Experimental Medicine and Biology
0065-2601 Advances in Experimental Social Psychology
0065-261X Advances in Fluorine Research and Dental Caries Prevention†
0065-2628 Advances in Food Research
0065-2636 Advances in Food Research. Supplement
0065-2644 Advances in Free Radical Chemistry†
0065-2652 Advances in Gas Chromatography†
0065-2660 Advances in Genetics
0065-2679 Advances in Genetics. Supplement
0065-2687 Advances in Geophysics
0065-2695 Advances in Geophysics. Supplement
0065-2709 Advances in Gerontological Research
0065-2717 Advances in Heat Transfer
0065-2725 Advances in Heterocyclic Chemistry
0065-2733 Advances in High Pressure Research†
0065-2741 Advances in High Temperature Chemistry
0065-275X Advances in Human Genetics
0065-2768 Advances in Hydroscience
0065-2776 Advances in Immunology
0065-2784 Advances in Information Systems Science
0065-2792 Advances in Inorganic Chemistry and Radiochemistry
0065-2806 Advances in Insect Physiology
0065-2814 Advances in Instrumentation
0065-2822 Advances in Internal Medicine
0065-2830 Advances in Librarianship
0065-2849 Advances in Lipid Research
0065-2857 Advances in Machine Tool Design and Research *see* 0020-7357
0065-2865 Advances in Macromolecular Chemistry†
0065-2873 Advances in Magnetic Resonance
0065-2881 Advances in Marine Biology
0065-2903 Advances in Metabolic Disorders
0065-2911 Advances in Microbial Physiology
0065-292X Advances in Microbiology of the Sea *see* 0161-8954
0065-2938 Advances in Microcirculation
0065-2946 Advances in Microwaves
0065-2954 Advances in Molten Salt Chemistry
0065-2962 Advances in Morphogenesis†
0065-2970 Advances in Nuclear Physics
0065-2989 Advances in Nuclear Science and Technology
0065-2997 Advances in Obstetrics and Gynaecology *see* 0304-4246
0065-3004 Advances in Ophthalmology *see* 0250-3751
0065-3012 Advances in Optical and Electron Microscopy
0065-3020 Advances in Oral Biology
0065-3039 Advances in Oral Surgery *changed to* Update in Oral Surgery
0065-3047 Advances in Organic Chemistry
0065-3055 Advances in Organometalic Chemistry
0065-3063 Advances in Orthodontics *changed to* Update in Orthodontics
0065-3071 Advances in Oto-Rhino-Laryngology
0065-308X Advances in Parasitology
0065-3098 Advances in Particle Physics†
0065-3101 Advances in Pediatrics
0065-311X Advances in Pedodontics†
0065-3128 Advances in Periodontics *changed to* Update in Periodontics
0065-3136 Advances in Pharmaceutical Sciences
0065-3144 Advances in Pharmacology and Chemotherapy
0065-3152 Advances in Photochemistry
0065-3160 Advances in Physical Organic Chemistry
0065-3179 Advances in Planned Parenthood
0065-3187 Advances in Plasma Physics†
0065-3195 Advances in Polymer Science
0065-3217 Advances in Probability
0065-3225 Advances in Prosthodontics†
0065-3233 Advances in Protein Chemistry
0065-3241 Advances in Psychobiology
0065-325X Advances in Psychological Assessment
0065-3268 Advances in Psychosomatic Medicine
0065-3276 Advances in Quantum Chemistry
0065-3284 Advances in Quantum Electronics
0065-3292 Advances in Radiation Biology
0065-3306 Advances in Radiation Chemistry†
0065-3314 Advances in Radio Research
0065-3322 Advances in Reproductive Physiology†
0065-3357 Advances in Solid State Physics
0065-3365 Advances in Space Science and Technology†
0065-3373 Advances in Space Science and Technology. Supplement
0065-3381 Advances in Stereoencephalotomy
0065-339X Advances in Steroid Biochemistry and Pharmacology *changed to* Advances in Steroid Biochemistry and Pharmacology (1978)
0065-3403 Advances in Structure Research by Diffraction Methods†
0065-3411 Advances in Surgery
0065-342X Advances in Teratology *see* 0306-2090
0065-3446 Advances in the Biosciences
0065-3454 Advances in the Study of Behavior
0065-3470 Advances in Theoretical Physics
0065-3500 Advances in Tuberculosis Research
0065-3519 Advances in Veterinary Science and Comparative Medicine
0065-3527 Advances in Virus Research
0065-3535 Advances in Water Pollution Research
0065-3543 Advancing Frontiers of Plant Sciences†
0065-3578 Advertiser's Annual
0065-3586 Ad Guide: an Advertiser's Guide to Periodicals†
0065-3586 Advertiser's Guide to Scholarly Periodicals
0065-3594 Advertising and Press Annual of Africa *changed to* Advertising and Press Annual of Southern Africa
0065-3640 Advertising Statistical Review†
0065-3659 Advertising Standards Authority, London. Annual Report
0065-3667 Aeldre Danske Tingboeger
0065-3675 Aerodynamics Deceleration Systems Conference. Papers Presented *see* 0065-8707
0065-3683 Aeromedical Reviews
0065-3691 Aeromodeller Annual
0065-3705 Aeronautics Bulletin
0065-3713 Aeronomica Acta
0065-3721 Aeroport de Paris. Rapport du Conseil d'Administration
0065-373X National Aerospace and Electronics Conference. Record
0065-3756 Aerospace Materials Buyers Guide†
0065-3764 Aerospace Medical Association. Annual Scientific Meeting; Preprints
0065-3772 Aerospace Safety Buyers Guide†
0065-3780 Aerospatiale
0065-3799 Affaires et Gens d'Affaires
0065-3802 Africa Annual†
0065-3829 Africa at a Glance: A Quick Reference of Facts and Figures on Africa
0065-3845 Africa Contemporary Record, Annual Survey and Documents
0065-3853 Africa Institute. Annual Report *changed to* Africa Institute. Chairman's Report
0065-3861 Africa Institute. Communications
0065-3888 Africa Institute. Special Publications *changed to* Africa Institute. Occasional Publications
0065-3896 Africa South of the Sahara
0065-3918 African Bibliographic Center, Washington, D.C. Biblioresearch Series†
0065-3926 African Bibliographic Center, Washington, D.C. Current Reading List Series
0065-3934 African Bibliographic Center, Washington, D.C. Special Bibliographic Series
0065-3942 African Bibliographic Center, Washington, D.C. Special Bibliographic Series: Labor in Africa†
0065-3985 African Language Studies
0065-4000 African Literature Today
0065-4019 African Music
0065-4043 African Social Security Series *see* 0379-7074
0065-4051 Indiana University. Research Center for the Language Sciences. African Studies *see* 0073-7062
0065-406X African Studies Series
0065-4086 African Wildlife News *changed to* Wildlife News
0065-4116 Africana Collectanea Series
0065-4140 Journal of African Studies
0065-4167 Afrique Industrie. Informations. *see* 0301-8520
0065-4191 Afro-Asian Peoples' Conference. Proceedings
0065-4213 Age of Firearms
0065-4248 Agence pour la Securite de la Navigation Aerienne en Afrique et a Madagascar. Direction de l'Exploitation Meteorologique. Publications. Serie 1
0065-4256 Agenda de la Quincaillerie
0065-4264 Agenda del Dirigente di Azienda
0065-4272 Agent's and Buyer's Guide
0065-4299 Agents and Actions
0065-4337 Agrarian Development Studies
0065-4345 Agrarmarkt-Studien
0065-4353 Agrarpolitik und Marktwesen
0065-4361 A S G Eingliederung Heimatvertriebener Landwirte auf Vollbauernstellen†
0065-437X Agrarsoziale Gesellschaft. Geschaefts- und Arbeitsbericht
0065-4388 Agrarsoziale Gesellschaft. Rundbriefe
0065-4396 Agri-Business Buyers Reference
0065-440X Agricultura Espanola *changed to* Agricultura Espanola en (Year)
0065-4418 North Carolina Agricultural Chemicals Manual
0065-4426 Agricultural Development Bank of Pakistan. Annual Report and Statement of Accounts
0065-4434 Agricultural Economics Bulletin for Africa
0065-4442 Michigan State University. Agricultural Economics Report
0065-4469 Agricultural Economist
0065-4477 Agricultural Engineers Yearbook
0065-4485 Canadian Pest Management Society Proceedings
0065-4485 Agricultural Pesticide Society. Annual Meeting. Proceedings *see* 0065-4485
0065-4493 Agricultural Progress
0065-4507 Great Britain. Institute of Animal Physiology. Report
0065-4515 Agricultural Research Council of Malawi. Annual Report *changed to* Malawi. Department of Agricultural Research. Annual Report
0065-4523 Agricultural Research Guyana
0065-4531 Agricultural Research Index
0065-454X Agricultural Society of Nigeria. Proceedings
0065-4558 Agricultural Statistics, England and Wales
0065-4566 Agricultural Statistics of Bangladesh
0065-4574 Agricultural Statistics of Greece
0065-4582 Agricultural Statistics, Scotland
0065-4590 Agricultural Statistics, United Kingdom
0065-4604 Cornell Agricultural Waste Management Conference. Proceedings
0065-4612 U.S. Department of Agriculture. Agriculture Handbook
0065-4639 U.S. Department of Agriculture. Agriculture Information Bulletin
0065-4647 Agro-Ecological Atlas of Cereal Growing in Europe†
0065-4655 Agro-Nouvelles
0065-4663 Agronomy: a Series of Monographs
0065-4671 Agronomy Abstracts
0065-468X Ahmadu Bello University. Centre of Islamic Legal Studies. Journal
0065-4698 Ahmadu Bello University. Department of Geography. Occasional Paper
0065-471X Ahmadu Bello University. Institute for Agricultural Research. Annual Report†
0065-4728 Ahmadu Bello University. Institute for Agricultural Research. Soil Survey Bulletin
0065-4744 Ahmadu Bello University. Institute of Administration. Traditional Land Tenure Surveys
0065-4752 Ahmadu Bello University. Institute of Education. Paper
0065-4760 Ahmadu Bello University. Northern History Research Scheme. Papers *changed to* Ahmadu Bello University. Northern History Research Scheme. Interim Report
0065-4779 Ahmedabad Textile Industry's Research Association. Proceedings of the Management Conference
0065-4787 Ailleurs et Demain; Classiques
0065-4809 Air Conditioning, Ventilating and Heating Equipment *changed to* H V A C Red Book of Heating, Ventilating and Air Conditioning Equipment
0065-4817 Air New Zealand. Annual Report
0065-4825 Air Officer's Guide
0065-4841 Air Safety Forum†
0065-485X Air Transport Association of Canada. Annual Report
0065-4868 Air Travel Bargains
0065-4876 Aircraft Accident Digest
0065-4892 Aircraft Engines of the World
0065-4906 Aircraft Owners and Pilots Association. A O P A Airport Directory *see* 0271-065X
0065-4914 Airline Guide to Stewardess & Stewards Career
0065-4930 Airway Pioneer; Yearbook of the Society of Airway Pioneers
0065-4949 Universite d'Aix-Marseille I. Centre d'Etudes des Societes Mediterraneennes. Cahiers
0065-4965 Universite d'Aix-Marseille III. Centre des Hautes Etudes Touristiques. Etudes et Memoires
0065-4973 Universite d'Aix-Marseille I. Faculte des Lettres et Sciences Humaines. Annales
0065-4981 Universite d'Aix-Marseille I. Centre d'Etudes et de Recherches Helleniques. Publications
0065-499X Universite d'Aix-Marseille. Faculte des Lettres et Sciences Humaines. Travaux et Memoires†
0065-5007 Universite d'Aix-Marseille III. Institut d'Histoire des Pays d'Outre-Mer. Etudes et Documents

ISSN INDEX 1093

ISSN	Title
0065-5015	Akademie der Wissenschaften der DDR. Geodaetisches Institut. Veroeffentlichungen *changed to* Akademie der Wissenschaften der DDR. Zentralinstitut fuer Physik der Erde. Veroeffentlichungen
0065-5023	Zentralinstitut fuer Physik der Erde. Seismologischer Dienst Jena. Seismologische Bulletin
0065-5066	Akademie der Wissenschaften. Berlin. Jahrbuch *see* 0304-2154
0065-5198	Akademie der Wissenschaften, Berlin. Sektion fuer Vor- und Fruehgeschichte. Schriften *changed to* Schriften zur Ur- und Fruehgeschichte
0065-5228	Akademie der Wissenschaften, Berlin. Volkskundliche Veroeffentlichungen *changed to* Veroeffentlichungen zur Volkskunde und Kulturgeschichte
0065-5236	Akademie der Wissenschaften der DDR. Zentralinstitut fuer Geschichte. Schriften
0065-5260	Akademie der Wissenschaften, Berlin. Zentralinstitut fuer Sprachwissenschaft. Schriften *changed to* Sprache und Gesellschaft
0065-5279	Akademie der Wissenschaften der DDR. Zentralinstitut fuer Wirtschaftswissenschaften. Schriften
0065-5287	Akademie der Wissenschaften, Goettingen. Nachrichten 1. Philologisch-Historische Klasse
0065-5295	Akademie der Wissenschaften, Goettingen. Nachrichten 2. Mathematisch-Physikalische Klasse
0065-5309	Deutsche Geodaetische Kommission. Veroeffentlichungen: Reihe A. Theoretische Geodaesie
0065-5317	Deutsche Geodaetische Kommission. Veroeffentlichungen: Reihe B. Angewandte Geodaesie
0065-5325	Deutsche Geodaetische Kommission. Veroeffentlichungen: Reihe C. Dissertationen
0065-5333	Deutsche Geodaetische Kommission. Veroeffentlichungen: Reihe D. Tafelwerke
0065-5341	Deutsche Geodaetische Kommission. Veroeffentlichungen: Reihe E. Geschichte und Entwicklung der Geodaesie
0065-535X	Oesterreichische Akademie der Wissenschaften, Vienna. Mathematisch-Naturwissenschaftliche Klasse. Anzeiger *changed to* Oesterreichische Akademie der Wissenschaften, Vienna. Mathematisch' Naturwissenschaftliche Klasse. Denkschriften
0065-5368	Oesterreichische Akademie der Wissenschaften. Philosophisch-Historische Klasse. Anzeiger
0065-5376	Oesterreichische Akademie der Wissenschaften. Praehistorische Kommission. Mitteilungen
0065-5384	Akademie fuer Fuehrungskraefte der Wirtschaft. Taschenbuecher zur Betriebspraxis
0065-5392	Akademie fuer Staatsmedizin, Duesseldorf. Jahrbuch *changed to* Akademie fuer Oeffentliches Gesundheitswesen. Schriftenreihe
0065-5503	Koninklijke Nederlandse Akademie van Wetenschapen. Afdeling Natuurkunde, Verhandelingen. Eerste Reeks
0065-5511	Koninklijke Nederlandse Akademie van Wetenschappen. Afdeling Letterkunde. Verhandelingen. Nieuwe Reeks
0065-552X	Koninklijke Nederlandse Akademie van Wetenschappen. Afdeling Natuurkunde. Verhandelingen. Tweede Reeks
0065-5538	Akademische Vortraege und Abhandlungen
0065-5554	Akiyoshi-dai Science Museum. Bulletin *changed to* Akiyoshi-dai Museum of Natural History. Bulletin
0065-5562	Aktion fuer Kultur und Politik *see* 0002-3760
0065-5589	Aktuelle Probleme in der Chirurgie *changed to* Aktuelle Probleme in Chirurgie Orthopaedie
0065-5597	Aktuelle Probleme in der Klinischen Biochemie *see* 0300-1725
0065-5600	Aktuelle Probleme in der Psychiatrie, Neurologie, Neurochirurgie
0065-5619	Aktuellt och Historiskt *changed to* Militaerhistorisk Tidskrift
0065-5627	Al-Hikma†
0065-5635	Alabama Geological Society. Guidebook for the Annual Field Trip
0065-5686	Alan Rogers' Selected Sites for Caravanning and Camping in Europe
0065-5694	Alaska Agricultural Statistics
0065-5708	Alaska. Department of Fish and Game. Annual Report
0065-5724	Alaska. Division of Geological and Geophysical Surveys. Annual Report
0065-5732	Alaska. Division of Geological and Geophysical Surveys. Geochemical Report†
0065-5759	Alaska. Division of Geological and Geophysical Surveys. Information Circular
0065-5767	Alaska. Division of Geological and Geophysical Surveys. Laboratory Note
0065-5775	Alaska. Division of Geological and Geophysical Surveys. Laboratory Report
0065-5783	Alaska. Division of Geological and Geophysical Surveys. Miscellaneous Paper†
0065-5805	Alaska. Employment Security Division. Workforce Estimates, by Industry and Area *see* 0362-4196
0065-5813	Alaska Petroleum and Industrial Directory
0065-5821	Annual Report of the Public Libraries of Alaska†
0065-583X	Alaska State Plan for the Construction of Hospitals and Medical Facilities†
0065-5848	Alaska Travel Guide
0065-5856	University of Alaska. Geophysical Institute. Bibliography of Publications
0065-5864	University of Alaska. Geophysical Institute. Contributions. Series A†
0065-5872	University of Alaska. Geophysical Institute. Contributions. Series B†
0065-5929	University of Alaska. Institute of Marine Sciences. Technical Report
0065-5937	Institute of Social, Economic and Government Research. Reports *changed to* Institute of Social and Economic Research. Reports
0065-5945	I S E G R Research Notes *changed to* I S E R Research Notes
0065-5953	University of Alaska. Institute of Water Resources. Annual Report
0065-5961	University of Alaska. Mineral Industry Research Laboratory. Report
0065-597X	Alberta. Department of Agriculture. Annual Report
0065-5988	Alberta Research Council. Highway Research
0065-5996	Alberta Poetry Yearbook†
0065-6003	Alberta Society of Petroleum Geologists. Geological Guide *changed to* Canadian Society of Petroleum Geologists. Bulletin
0065-6046	University of Alberta. Department of Agricultural Economics and Rural Sociology. Agricultural Economics and Rural Sociology Research Bulletin *changed to* University of Alberta. Department of Rural Economy. Bulletin
0065-6062	Alberta. University, Edmonton. Department of Computing Science. Publication *see* 0316-4683
0065-6070	University of Alberta. Faculty of Business Administration and Commerce. Research Studies in Business
0065-6097	Albertan Geographer
0065-6100	V. Graefes Archiv fuer Klinische und Experimentelle Opthalmologie
0065-6119	Addiction Research Foundation of Ontario. Annual Report
0065-6119	Alcoholism and Drug Addiction Research Foundation. Annual Report *see* 0065-6119
0065-6127	Alcoy; Fiesta de Moros y Cristianos
0065-6143	Aldrich Entomology Club. Newsletter
0065-6151	Alessandria, Italy. Centro Documentazione e Richerche Economico-Sociali. Quaderno
0065-616X	Alexander Lectures
0065-6186	Alfred Benzon Symposium. Proceedings
0065-6216	Alfred P. Sloan Foundation. Report
0065-6224	Algemene Bank Nederland. Annual Report
0065-6232	Observatoire Astronomique d'Alger. Annales
0065-6240	Algorytmy†
0065-6259	Aligarh Muslim University, Aligarh, India. Department of History. Publication
0065-6267	Alimentation et la Vie
0065-6275	Aliso
0065-6283	All India Crime Prevention Society. Annual Report and Audited Statement of Accounts
0065-6291	All India Government Travellers Bungalows Annual Recorder
0065-6305	All India Leather Directory†
0065-6313	All-Pakistan Income-Tax Reports and Returns and Income-Tax Revenue Statistics†
0065-6321	All Pakistan Women's Association. Annual Report†
0065-6348	Allam es Jogtudomany Uttoroi†
0065-6364	Allan Hancock Monographs in Marine Biology
0065-6372	Allergologicum; Transactions of the Collegium Internationale
0065-6410	Allied Artists of America. Exhibition Catalog
0065-6429	Allionia
0065-6453	Almanac of Hawaiiana
0065-6461	Almanac of the Pacific *changed to* Thrum's All About Hawaii
0065-647X	Almanac of World Military Power
0065-650X	Almanach du Peuple
0065-6526	Almanach Sceny Polskiej
0065-6534	Alpenvereins-Jahrbuch
0065-6542	Alpha Annual†
0065-6569	Alpine Journal
0065-6585	Alt-Thueringen
0065-6593	Altbabylonische Briefe im Umschrift und Uebersetzung
0065-6607	Altdeutsche Textbibliothek. Ergaenzungsreihe
0065-6623	Altech
0065-6631	Naturkundliches Museum "Mauritianum" Altenburg. Abhandlungen und Berichte
0065-6658	Aluminum Standards and Data
0065-6666	Aluminum Statistical Review
0065-6674	Amakusa Marine Biological Laboratory. Contributions
0065-6682	Amakusa Marine Biological Laboratory. Publications
0065-6690	Amateur Athletic Association. Handbook
0065-6704	Amateur Chamber Music Players. Directory
0065-6712	Percy Thrower's Guide to Modern Gardening *changed to* Amateur Gardening Guide
0065-6739	Amateur Softball Association of America. Official Guide and Rule Book
0065-6747	Amateur Trapshooting Association. Official Trapshooting Rules
0065-6755	Amazoniana; Limnologia et Oecologia Regionalis Systemae Fluminis Amazonas
0065-6763	America - Problema
0065-6771	America en Cifras†
0065-678X	America Votes
0065-6798	American Academy for Jewish Research. Proceedings of the A A J R
0065-6801	American Academy in Rome. Memoirs
0065-681X	American Academy in Rome. Papers and Monographs
0065-6836	American Academy of Arts and Letters. Proceedings *see* 0145-8493
0065-6844	American Academy of Arts and Sciences. Records of the Academy
0065-6852	American Academy of Child Psychiatry. Journal. Monograph†
0065-6860	American Academy of Environmental Engineers. Roster
0065-6879	A A M A Executive *changed to* Medical Administration Executive
0065-6887	American Academy of Optometry Series†
0065-6895	American Academy of Orthopaedic Surgeons. Committee on Instructional Courses. Instructional Course Lectures
0065-6909	American Academy of Pediatrics. Committee on Infectious Diseases. Report
0065-6917	American Academy of Political and Social Science. Monographs
0065-6925	American Alpine Journal
0065-6933	American Anthropological Association. Annual Report and Directory
0065-6941	American Anthropologist. Special Publication
0065-6968	American Art Directory
0065-6976	American Assembly (Background Papers and Final Report) *see* 0569-2245
0065-6984	American Association for Conservation Information. Yearbook†
0065-700X	A A H P E R Archery-Riding Guide *changed to* N A G W S Guide. Archery-Fencing
0065-7018	Basketball Guide, with Official Rules and Standards *see* 0362-3254
0065-7026	Field Hockey-Lacrosse Guide *changed to* N A G W S Guide. Field Hockey
0065-7034	Soccer-Speedball Guide *changed to* N A G W S Guide. Flag Football, Speedball, Speed-a-Way
0065-7042	Tennis-Badminton-Squash Guide *changed to* N A G W S Guide. Tennis
0065-7050	Volleyball Guide *changed to* N A G W S Guide. Volleyball
0065-7069	American Association for Textile Technology. Technical Review and Register
0065-7085	American Association for the Advancement of Science. Publications†
0065-7107	American Association of Cereal Chemists. Monograph Series
0065-7115	Standard Methods of Clinical Chemistry†
0065-7123	A A C T E Yearbook
0065-7131	American Assembly of Collegiate Schools of Business. Accredited Schools, Officers, Committees
0065-7158	American Association of Cost Engineers. Transactions of the Annual Meeting
0065-7182	American Association of Equine Practitioners. Proceedings of the Annual Convention
0065-7190	American Association of Foot Specialists. Program Journal
0065-7204	American Association of Genito-Urinary Surgeons. Transactions
0065-7239	American Association of Community and Junior Colleges. Governmental Affairs Special†
0065-7263	American Association of Medical Milk Commissions. Methods and Standards for the Production of Certified Milk

0065-7271 American Association of Motor Vehicle Administrators. Annual Conference. Proceedings
0065-728X American Association of Obstetricians and Gynecologists. Transactions
0065-7298 American Association of Pathologists and Bacteriologists. Symposium. Monographs
0065-731X American Association of Petroleum Geologists. Memoir
0065-7328 A A S A Convention Reporter†
0065-7344 A A S C U Studies
0065-7352 American Association of Textile Chemists and Colorists. Products Buyer's Guide *changed to* American Association of Textile Chemists and Colorists. Buyer's Guide
0065-7360 American Association of Theological Schools in the United States and Canada. Bulletin *see* 0362-1472
0065-7379 American Association of Theological Schools in the United States and Canada. Directory *changed to* Association of Theological Schools in the United States and Canada. Directory
0065-7395 American Association of Workers for the Blind. Proceedings
0065-7433 A A S Photo-Bulletin
0065-7441 American Bankers Association. National Automation Conference. Proceedings *see* 0095-5396
0065-745X American Bantam Association. Yearbook
0065-7468 American Baptist Education Association. Report†
0065-7476 Federal Government Legal Career Opportunities *changed to* Washington Want Ads
0065-7492 American Bar Association. Section of Labor-Relations Law. Report *changed to* American Bar Association. Section of Labor Relations Law. Committee Reports.
0065-7522 American Bar Association. Standing Committee on Legal Assistance for Servicemen. Occasional Newsletter *see* 0163-1373
0065-7549 American Bar Foundation. Research Contributions
0065-7565 American Blue Book of Funeral Directors
0065-759X American Book Trade Directory
0065-7603 American Broncho-Esophagological Association. Transactions
0065-7611 American Bureau of Metal Statistics. Year Book *see* 0360-9553
0065-762X American Camellia Yearbook
0065-7638 American Catholic Philosophical Association. Proceedings
0065-7646 American Cement Directory
0065-7654 American Ceramic Society. Special Publications
0065-7662 American Chamber of Commerce for Brazil. Annual Directory
0065-7670 American Chamber of Commerce in France. Directory
0065-7689 AMCHAM Morocco
0065-7697 American Chamber of Commerce of Venezuela. Yearbook and Membership Directory *changed to* Venezuelan-American Chamber of Commerce and Industry. Yearbook and Membership Directory
0065-7700 A C S Laboratory Guide *see* 0458-595X
0065-7719 A C S Monographs
0065-7727 American Chemical Society. Abstracts of Papers (at the National Meeting)
0065-7735 American Chemical Society. Abstracts of Papers (at the Regional Meetings)
0065-7743 Annual Reports in Medicinal Chemistry
0065-7778 American Clinical and Climatological Association. Transactions
0065-7786 American College of Apothecaries. Proceedings†
0065-7794 American College of Hospital Administrators. Directory
0065-7816 American College Public Relations Association. Directory *changed to* Council for Advancement and Support of Education. Membership Directory
0065-7832 A C T Monograph Series
0065-7840 A C T Research Service Report *see* 0569-3993
0065-7875 A C I Manual of Concrete Practice
0065-7883 A C I Monograph
0065-7891 American Concrete Institute. Special Publication
0065-7905 American Conference of Academic Deans. Proceedings
0065-7913 American Congress on Surveying and Mapping. Papers from the Annual Meetings *see* 0161-0945
0065-793X American Cooperation Yearbook
0065-7948 American Correctional Association. Annual Congress of Correction. Proceedings
0065-7956 State and Federal Correctional Institutions *see* 0362-9287
0065-7964 American Council of Independent Laboratories. Directory
0065-7980 Accredited Colleges of Pharmacy
0065-7999 American Country Life Association. Proceedings of the Annual Conference
0065-8006 American Crystallographic Association. Transactions
0065-8014 American Culture
0065-8022 American Dance Therapy Association. Proceedings of the Annual Conference†
0065-8030 Annual Report on Dental Education
0065-8049 Dental Students' Register *see* 0065-8030
0065-8057 American Dental Association. Council on Dental Education. Requirements and Registration Data: State Dental Examining Boards†
0065-8073 American Dental Directory
0065-8081 American Dexter Cattle Association. Herd Book
0065-809X American Doctoral Dissertations
0065-8103 American Drop-Shippers Directory
0065-8111 American Drug Index
0065-8138 American Theatre Association. Annual Directory of Members
0065-8146 American Enterprise Institute for Public Policy Research. Legislative and Special Analyses *changed to* American Enterprise Institute for Public Policy Research. Legislative Analyses
0065-8154 American Enterprise Institute for Public Policy Research. Long-Range Studies *see* 0149-9130
0065-8162 American Entomological Institute. Memoirs
0065-8170 American Entomological Society. Memoirs
0065-8189 American Ephemeris and Nautical Almanac *changed to* Astronomical Almanac
0065-8197 American Ethnological Society. Monographs
0065-8200 American Ethnological Society. Proceedings of Spring Meeting
0065-8219 American Exploration and Travel
0065-8308 American Film Review
0065-8316 American Folk Music Occasional
0065-8324 American Folklore Society. Bibliographical and Special Series†
0065-8332 American Folklore Society. Memoirs†
0065-8359 American Foundation for the Blind. Annual Report
0065-8367 A F B Research Bulletin *see* 0145-482X
0065-8375 American Foundrymen's Society. Transactions
0065-8391 Gas Utility and Pipeline Industry Projections†
0065-8405 American Gem Society. Member Suppliers
0065-8413 American Geographical Society of New York. Occasional Publication
0065-8421 American Geographical Society of New York. Research Series
0065-843X American Geographical Society of New York. Special Publication
0065-8448 American Geophysical Union. Geophysical Monograph Series
0065-8456 American Goat Society. Year Book
0065-8480 American Gynecological Society. Transactions of the A G S
0065-8499 American Heart Association. Monographs
0065-8502 American Heart Association. Scientific Sessions. Abstracts
0065-8510 American Helicopter Society. National Forum. Proceedings
0065-8529 American-Hellenic Chamber of Commerce. Business Directory *see* 0065-8537
0065-8537 American-Hellenic Chamber of Commerce. Business Directory. Special Issue
0065-8545 American Histadrut Cultural Exchange Institute. Annual Arden House Conference. Proceedings†
0065-8553 American Histadrut Cultural Exchange Institute. Round Table Pamphlet Series†
0065-8561 American Historical Association. Annual Report
0065-8588 American Home Economics Association. Textiles and Clothing Section. Textile Handbook
0065-8596 American Humane Association. National Humane Report *changed to* American Humane Association Annual Report
0065-860X American Imago
0065-8618 American Industrial Arts Association. Addresses and Proceedings of the Annual Convention
0065-8634 American Industrial Arts Association. Yearbook *see* 0084-6333
0065-8642 American Industrial Real Estate Association. Journal
0065-8650 American Institute for Marxist Studies. Bibliographic Series
0065-8669 American Institute for Marxist Studies. Historical Series
0065-8677 American Institute for Marxist Studies. Monograph Series
0065-8685 American Institute of Aeronautics and Astronautics. A I A A Los Angeles Section. Monographs
0065-8693 A I A A Roster
0065-8707 American Institute of Aeronautics and Astronautics. Paper
0065-8715 American Institute of Aeronautics and Astronautics. Selected Reprint Series
0065-8723 A I A Building Construction Legal Citator. Supplement†
0065-874X American Institute of Certified Public Accountants. Division of Federal Taxation. Statements on Responsibilities in Tax Practice
0065-8758 American Institute of Certified Public Accountants. Committee on Practice Review. Practice Review Bulletin†
0065-8766 American Institute of Certified Public Accountants. Management Advisory Services. Guideline Series
0065-8774 American Institute of Certified Public Accountants. Practical Accounting and Auditing Problems†
0065-8782 American Institute of Certified Public Accountants. Statements on Auditing Procedure†
0065-8790 A I Ch E Continuing Education Series
0065-8804 A I Ch E Monograph Series†
0065-8812 A I Ch E Symposium Series
0065-8820 American Institute of Graphic Arts. Journal†
0065-8847 American Institute of Islamic Studies. Bibliographic Series
0065-8855 American Institute of Musicology. Miscellanea
0065-8871 American Institute of Ultrasound in Medicine. Annual Scientific Conference. Program
0065-888X American Institute of Ultrasound in Medicine. Proceedings of Annual Meeting *see* 0098-0382
0065-8928 American Jewish Committee. Institute of Human Relations. Pamphlet Series. *changed to* American Jewish Committee. Institute of Human Relations. Paperback Series
0065-8936 American Jewish Communal History
0065-8944 American Jewish Historical Society. News *changed to* American Jewish Historical Society. Report
0065-8979 American Jewish Organizations Directory
0065-8987 American Jewish Yearbook
0065-8995 American Journal of Jurisprudence
0065-9010 A J S Information Report Series†
0065-9029 American Junior Colleges
0065-9037 American Laryngological, Rhinological and Otological Society. Transactions
0065-9045 American Law Institute. Annual Meeting. Proceedings
0065-907X A L A Studies in Librarianship
0065-9088 L T P Publications†
0065-9096 A L A Social Responsibilities Round Table Newsletter
0065-910X American Library Directory
0065-9118 American Life Collector's Annual†
0065-9142 American Literary Scholarship
0065-9150 American Littoral Society. Special Publications
0065-9169 American Malacological Union. Bulletin
0065-9185 American Management Association. Research Studies
0065-9193 American Management Association. Seminar Program
0065-9207 American Maritime Library
0065-9215 A M A Abstracts of Papers of the Conferences *see* 0065-9231
0065-9231 American Marketing Association. Proceedings
0065-924X American Marketing Association. Reprint Series†
0065-9258 American Mathematical Society. Colloquium Publications
0065-9266 American Mathematical Society. Memoirs
0065-9274 Selected Translations in Mathematical Statistics and Probability
0065-9282 Translations of Mathematical Monographs
0065-9290 American Mathematical Society. Translations. Series 2
0065-9304 A M A Drug Evaluations
0065-9312 Current Procedural Terminology *see* 0590-4129
0065-9320 Medical and Surgical Motion Pictures†
0065-9339 American Medical Directory
0065-9347 American Men and Women of Science. Physical and Biological Sciences
0065-9401 American Meteorological Society. Meteorological Monographs
0065-9436 American Midland Naturalist Monograph Series
0065-9444 A M S News Notes *changed to* A. M. S. Newsletter
0065-9452 American Museum of Natural History. Anthropological Papers
0065-9479 American Neurological Association. Transactions
0065-9487 A E C/A N S Monographs *changed to* Nuclear Science Technology Monograph Series
0065-9495 A N A Clinical Sessions†
0065-9509 American Nurses' Association. Conference for Members and Professional Employees of State Boards of Nursing and A N A Advisory Council. Proceedings

ISSN INDEX 1095

0065-9517 American Nurses' Association. House of Delegates. Reports
0065-9533 American Ophthalmological Society. Transactions
0065-9541 American Oriental Series
0065-955X American Orthoptic Journal†
0065-9576 American Osteopathic College of Radiology. Newsletter. *changed to* Viewbox
0065-9622 American Personnel and Guidance Association. Convention Abstracts
0065-9630 Thermodynamics Research Center. A P I 44. Hydrocarbon Project. Selected Values of Properties of Hydrocarbons and Related Compounds. Category A: Tables of Selected Values of Physical and Thermodynamic Properties of Hydrocarbons *changed to* Thermodynamics Research Center. Hydrocarbon Project. Selected Values of Properties of Hydrocarbons and Related Compounds. Category A: Tables of Selected Values of Physical and Thermodynamic Properties of Hydrocarbons
0065-9649 Thermodynamics Research Center. A P I 44. Hydrocarbon Project. Selected Values of Properties of Hydrocarbons and Related Compounds. Category B: Selected Infrared Spectral Data *changed to* Thermodynamics Research Center. Hydrocarbon Project. Selected Values of Properties of Hydrocarbons and Related Compounds. Category B: Selected Infrared Spectral Data
0065-9657 Thermodynamics Research Center. A P I 44. Hydrocarbon Project. Selected Values of Properties of Hydrocarbons and Related Compounds. Category C: Selected Ultraviolet Spectral Data *changed to* Thermodynamics Research Center. Hydrocarbon Project. Selected Values of Properties of Hydrocarbons and Related Compounds. Category C: Selected Ultraviolet Spectral Data
0065-9665 Thermodynamics Research Center. A P I 44. Hydrocarbon Project. Selected Values of Properties of Hydrocarbons and Related Compounds. Category D: Selected Raman Spectral Data *changed to* Thermodynamics Research Center. Hydrocarbon Project. Selected Values of Properties of Hydrocarbons and Related Compounds. Category D: Selected Raman Spectral Data
0065-9673 Thermodynamics Research Center. A P I 44. Hydrocarbon Project. Selected Values of Properties of Hydrocarbons and Related Compounds. Category E: Selected Mass Spectral Data *changed to* Thermodynamics Research Center. Hydrocarbon Project. Selected Values of Properties of Hydrocarbons and Related Compounds. Category E: Selected Mass Spectral Data
0065-9681 Thermodynamics Research Center. A P I 44. Hydrocarbon Project. Selected Values of Properties of Hydrocarbons and Related Compounds. Category F: Selected Nuclear Magnetic Resonance Data *changed to* Thermodynamics Research Center. Hydrocarbon Project. Selected Values of Properties of Hydrocarbons and Related Compounds. Category F: Selected Nuclear Magnetic Resonance Data
0065-9703 American Philological Association. Special Publications
0065-9711 American Philological Association. Transactions and Proceedings *see* 0362-9945
0065-9711 American Philological Association. Transactions and Proceedings *see* 0360-5949
0065-972X American Philosophical Association. Proceedings and Addresses
0065-9738 American Philosophical Society. Memoirs
0065-9746 American Philosophical Society. Transactions
0065-9762 American Philosophical Society. Yearbook
0065-9770 American Podiatry Association. Desk Reference and Directory with Catalogue of Audio-Visual, Informational and Educational Materials and Standard Podiatric Nomenclature
0065-9797 American Power Boat Association. A P B A Rule Book
0065-9800 American Printing House for the Blind, Louisville, Kentucky. Department of Educational Research. Annual Report
0065-9819 A P I C S Annual Conference Proceedings *see* 0191-1783
0065-9827 American Psychiatric Association. Biographical Directory
0065-9843 American Psychoanalytic Association. Journal. Monograph
0065-9851 American Psychological Association. Employment Bulletin
0065-9886 American Psychopathological Association. Publications
0065-9894 American Public Gas Association. Memorandum Bulletins *changed to* American Public Gas Association. Newsletter
0065-9932 American Public Works Association. Research Foundation. Special Reports
0065-9940 American Railway Bridge and Building Association. Proceedings
0065-9959 American Reference Books Annual
0065-9967 American Register of Exporters and Importers *changed to* American Export Register
0065-9975 American Register of Inter-Corporate Ownership *changed to* Directory of Inter-Corporate Ownership
0065-9991 American Research Center in Egypt. Journal
0066-0000 American Rose Annual
0066-0027 American School of Prehistoric Research. Bulletins
0066-0035 American Schools of Oriental Research. Annual
0066-0043 American Science Manpower†
0066-0051 American Series of Foreign Penal Codes
0066-006X American Society for Abrasive Methods. Technical Conference. Proceedings *see* 0363-8065
0066-0078 American Society for Artificial Internal Organs. Transactions
0066-0116 American Society for Horticultural Science. Tropical Region. Proceedings of the Annual Meeting
0066-0132 American Society for Neurochemistry. Transactions
0066-0159 American Society for Quality Control. Transactions of Annual Technical Conferences *see* 0360-6929
0066-0183 Annual Book of A S T M Standards. Part 1. Steel Piping, Tubing, and Fittings
0066-0191 Annual Book of A S T M Standards. Part 2. Ferrous Castings, Ferro-Alloys
0066-0205 Annual Book of A S T M Standards. Part 3. Steel Strip, Bar, Rod, Wire, Chain, and Spring: Wrought Iron; Metallic Coated Products; Ferrous Surgical Implants *changed to* Annual Book of A S T M Standards. Part 3. Steel Plate, Sheet, Strip and Wire; Metallic Coated Products
0066-0213 Annual Book of A S T M Standards. Part 4. Structural Steel; Concrete Reinforcing Steel; Pressure Vessel Plate; Steel Rails; Wheels, and Tires; Bearing Steel; Steel Forgings. *changed to* Annual Book of A S T M Standards. Part 4. Structural Steel; Concrete Reinforcing Steel; Pressure Vessel Plate and Forgings; Steel Rails, Wheels, and Tires; Steel Fasteners
0066-0221 Annual Book of A S T M Standards. Part 6. Copper and Copper Alloys (Including Electrical Conductors)
0066-023X Annual Book of A S T M Standards. Part 7. Die-Cast Metals; Light Metals and Alloys (Including Electrical Conductors)
0066-0248 Annual Book of A S T M Standrads. Part 7. Nonferrous Metals and Alloys (Including Corrosion Tests); Electrodeposited Metallic Coatings; Metal Powders; Surgical Implants. *changed to* Annual Book of A S T M Standards. Part 8. Nonferrous Metals--Nickel, Lead, and Tin Alloys, Precious Metals, Primary Metals; Reactive Metals
0066-0256 Annual Book of A S T M Standards. Part 9. Cement; Lime; Gypsum *changed to* Annual Book of A S T M Standards. Part 13. Cement; Lime; Ceilings and Walls (Including Manual of Cement Testing)
0066-0264 Annual Book of A S T M Standards. Part 14. Concrete and Mineral Aggregates (Including Manual of Concrete Testing)
0066-0272 Annual Book of A S T M Standards. Part 11. Bituminous Materials for Highway Construction, Waterproofing and Roofing: Soil and Rock; Skid Resistance *changed to* Annual Book of A S T M Standards. Part 15. Road and Paving Materials; Bituminous Materials for Highway Construction, Waterproofing and Roofing, and Pipe; Skid Resistance
0066-0280 Annual Book of A S T M Standards. Part 12. Chemical-Resistant Nonmetallic Materials; Clay and Concrete Pipe and Tile; Masonry Mortars and Units; Asbestos-Cement Products; Natural Building Stones *changed to* Annual Book of A S T M Standards. Part 16. Chemical-Resistant Nonmetallic Materials. Vitrified Clay and Concrete Pipe and Tile; Masonry Mortars and Units; Asbestos-Cement Products
0066-0299 Annual Book of A S T M Standards. Part 17. Refractories, Glass and Other Ceramic Materials; Manufactured Carbon and Graphite Products
0066-0302 Annual Book of A S T M Standards. Part 18. Thermal and Cryogenic Insulating Materials; Building Seals and Sealants; Fire Tests; Building Constructions; Environmental Acoustics
0066-0310 Annual Book of A S T M Standards. Part 15. Paper; Packaging; Cellulose; Casein; Flexible Barrier Materials; Carbon Paper; Leather *changed to* Annual Book of A S T M Standards. Part 20. Paper; Packaging; Business Copy Products
0066-0329 Annual Book of A S T M Standards. Part 22. Wood; Adhesives
0066-0337 Annual Book of A S T M Standards. Part 17. Petroleum Products - Fuels; Solvents; Burner Fuel Oils; Lubricating Greases; Hydraulic Fluids *changed to* Annual Book of A S T M Standards. Part 23. Petroleum Products and Lubricants (1)
0066-0345 Annual Book of A S T M Standards. Part 18. Petroleum Products - Measurement and Sampling; Liquefied Petroleum Gases; Light Hydrocarbons; Plant Spray Oils; Aerospace Materials; Sulfonates; Crude Petroleum; Petroleum; Wax; Graphite *changed to* Annual Book of A S T M Standards. Part 24. Petroleum Products and Lubricants (2)
0066-0353 Annual Book of A S T M Standards. Part 26. Gaseous Fuels; Coal and Coke *changed to* Annual Book of A S T M Standards. Part 26. Gaseous Fuels; Coal and Coke; Atmospheric Analysis
0066-0361 Annual Book of A S T M Standards. Part 20. Paint, Varnish, Lacquer, and Related Products - Materials Specifications and Tests; Naval Stores; Industrial Aromatic Hydrocarbons and Related Chemicals *changed to* Annual Book of A S T M Standards. Part 29. Paint - Fatty Oils and Acids, Solvents, Miscellaneous; Aromatic Hydrocarbons; Naval Stores
0066-037X Annual Book of A S T M Standards. Part 27. Paint - Tests for Formulated Products and Applied Coatings
0066-0388 Annual Book of A S T M Standards. Part 30. Soap; Engine Coolants; Polishes; Halogenated Organic Solvents; Activated Carbon; Industrial Chemicals
0066-0396 Annual Book of A S T M Standards. Part 23. Water; Atomspheric Analysis *changed to* Annual Book of A S T M Standards. Part 31. Water
0066-040X Annual Book of A S T M Standards. Part 32. Textiles--Yarn, Fabrics, and General Test Methods
0066-0418 Annual Book of A S T M Standards. Part 33. Textiles--Fibers, Zippers; High Modulus Fibers
0066-0426 Annual Book of A S T M Standards. Part 26. Plastics - Specifications; Methods of Testing Pipe, Film, Reinforced and Cellular Plastics *changed to* Annual Book of A S T M Standards. Part 36. Plastics--Materials, Film, Reinforced and Cellular Plastics; High Modulus Fibers and Their Composites
0066-0434 Annual Book of A S T M Standards. Part 35. Plastics - General Test Methods; Nomenclature
0066-0442 Annual Book of A S T M Standards. Part 28. Rubber; Carbon Black; Gaskets *changed to* Annual Book of A S T M Standards. Part 38. Rubber Products, Industrial--Specifications and Related Test Methods; Gaskets; Tires
0066-0450 Annual Book of A S T M Standards. Part 39. Electrical Insulating Materials--Test Methods *changed to* Annual Book of A S T M Standards. Part 39. Electrical Insulation--Test Methods: Solids and Solidifying Fluids
0066-0469 Annual Book of A S T M Standards. Part 41. General Test Methods (Nonmetal); Statistical Methods; Space Simulation; Particle Size Measurement; Deterioration of Nonmetallic Materials *changed to* Annual Book of A S T M Standards. Part 41. General Test Methods, Nonmetal; Statistical Methods; Space Simulation; Particle Size Measurement; General Laboratory Apparatus; Durability of Nonmetallic Materials; Metric Practice
0066-0477 Annual Book of A S T M Standards. Part 31. Metals - Physical, Mechanical, Nondestructive, and Corrosion Tests, Metallography, Fatigue, Effect of Temperature. *changed to* Annual Book of A S T M Standards. Part 10. Metals - Mechanical, Fracture, and Corrosion Testing; Fatigue; Erosion; Effect of Temperature
0066-0485 Annual Book of A S T M Standards. Part 12. Chemical Analysis of Metals; Sampling and Analysis of Metal Bearing Ores

1096 ISSN INDEX

0066-0493 Annual Book of A S T M Standards. Part 48. Index
0066-0507 Annual Book of A S T M Standards. Part 8. Magnetic Properties; Metallic Materials for Thermostats and Contacts Materials for Electron Devices and Microelectronics *changed to* Annual Book of A S T M Standards. Part 44. Magnetic Properties and Magnetic Materials; Metallic Materials for Thermostats and for Electrical Resistance, Heating, and Contacts; Temperature Measurement; Illuminating Standards
0066-0515 A S T M Proceedings
0066-0523 American Society for Testing and Materials. Compilation of A S T M Standards in Building Codes
0066-0531 American Society for Testing and Materials. Data Series Publications
0066-054X American Society for Testing and Materials. Five-Year Index to A S T M Technical Papers and Reports
0066-0553 American Society for Testing and Materials. Special Technical Publications
0066-0566 American Society of Agronomy. A S A Special Publication
0066-0582 American Society of Bakery Engineers. Proceedings of the Annual Meeting
0066-0590 C L U Forum Report
0066-0604 American Society of Civil Engineers. Transactions
0066-0612 American Society of Civil Engineers. Urban Water Resources Research Program. Technical Memorandum
0066-0620 A S H R A E Handbook & Product Directory
0066-0639 American Society of International Law. Newsletter
0066-0647 American Society of International Law. Proceedings
0066-0655 American Society of Ophthalmologic and Otolaryngologic Allergy. Transactions
0066-0663 American Society of Photogrammetry. Technical Papers from the Annual Meeting
0066-068X American Society of Sanitary Engineering. Year Book
0066-0698 American Society of Traffic and Transportation, Ohio Chapter. Proceedings of the Annual Seminar†
0066-0701 American Society of University Composers. Proceedings
0066-071X A S H A Monographs†
0066-0736 American Statistical Association. Business and Economic Statistics Section. Proceedings
0066-0752 American Statistical Association. Social Statistics Section. Proceedings
0066-0760 American Stock Exchange. AMEX Databook
0066-0779 American Stock Exchange. Annual Report
0066-0795 American Studies Research Centre. Newsletter
0066-0809 American Studies Series†
0066-0825 American Suffolk Sheep Society. Breeders List
0066-0833 American Surgical Association. Transactions
0066-0868 American Theological Library Association. Conference. Summary of Proceedings
0066-0884 American Trail Series
0066-0892 American Trucking Associations Report *changed to* American Trucking Trends
0066-0922 American Universities and Colleges
0066-0930 American Universities Field Staff. Reports. Central and Southern Africa Series *changed to* Fieldstaff Reports. Central and Southern Africa Series
0066-0949 American Universities Field Staff. Reports. East Africa Series *changed to* Fieldstaff Reports. East Africa Series
0066-0973 American Universities Field Staff. Reports. Mexico and Caribbean Area *changed to* Fieldstaff Reports. North America Series
0066-0981 American Universities Field Staff. Reports. North Africa Series *changed to* Fieldstaff Reports. North Africa Series
0066-104X American Universities Field Staff. Reports. Southeast Europe Series *changed to* Fieldstaff Reports. Southeast Europe Series
0066-1058 American Universities Field Staff. Reports. West Africa Series *changed to* Fieldstaff Reports. West Africa Series.
0066-1082 American Universities Field Staff. Annual Report of the Executive Director
0066-1104 American Universities Field Staff. List of Publications
0066-1112 American Universities Field Staff. Select Bibliography: Asia, Africa, Eastern Europe, Latin America. Supplement†
0066-1147 American Veterinary Medical Association. Directory
0066-1155 American Veterinary Radiology Society. Journal *see* 0196-3627
0066-1171 American Water Resources Conferences. Annual Proceedings
0066-118X American Waterways Series†
0066-1201 American Youth Hostels Guide and Handbook *changed to* A Y H Handbook
0066-121X Americans Before Columbus
0066-1228 A C A Index
0066-1236 Americans for Constitutional Action. Report
0066-1244 Amino Acides, Peptides, Proteines. Cahier†
0066-1260 AMLI Studies in Music Bibliography
0066-1279 Amoeba
0066-1287 Rijksinstituut voor Oorlogsdocumentatie. Documenten
0066-1295 Rijksinstituut voor Oorlogsdocumentatie. Monografieen
0066-1309 Amsterdam-Rotterdam Bank. Annual Report
0066-1317 Universiteit van Amsterdam. Fysisch Geografisch en Bodemkundig Laboratorium. Publikaties
0066-1325 Universiteit van Amsterdam. Zoologisch Museum. Bulletin
0066-1333 Anadolu Sanati Arastirmalari
0066-1341 Anaesthesiology and Resuscitation *changed to* Anaesthesiologie und Intensivmedizin
0066-135X Analecta Biblica. Investigationes Scientificae in Res Biblicas
0066-1368 Analecta Boerhaaviana
0066-1376 Analecta Gregoriana
0066-1392 Analecta Romana Instituti Danici
0066-1406 Analecta Romana Instituti Danici. Supplementum
0066-1414 Analecta Vaticano-Belgica. Deuxieme Serie. Section A: Nonciature de Flandre
0066-1422 Analecta Vaticano-Belgica. Deuxieme Serie. Section B: Nonciature de Cologne
0066-1430 Analecta Vaticano-Belgica. Deuxieme Serie. Section C: Nonciature de Bruxelles
0066-1449 Analecta Vaticano-Belgica. Premiere Serie: Documents Relatifs aux Anciens Dioceses de Cambrai, Liege, Therouanne et Tournai
0066-1465 Anales de Cirugia
0066-1473 Anales de Moral Social y Economica
0066-1481 Analog: Stories Selected from Analog Science Fact and Science Fiction†
0066-149X Analyses of Natural Gases of the United States
0066-152X Analyst
0066-1538 Analytical Calorimetry
0066-1546 Anatolian Studies
0066-1554 Anatolica
0066-1562 Anatomische Gesellschaft. Verhandlungen
0066-1589 Anciens Pay et Assemblees d'Etats
0066-1600 Ancient Pakistan†
0066-1619 Ancient Society
0066-1627 Anderson Hospital and Tumor Institute, Houston, Texas. General Report
0066-1635 Anderson Hospital and Tumor Institute, Houston, Texas. Research Report
0066-1651 Andhra Pradesh, India. Department of Archaeology. Epigraphy Series *changed to* Andhra Pradesh, India. Department of Archaeology and Museums. Epigraphy Series
0066-166X Andhra Pradesh, India. Department of Archaeology. Museum Series *changed to* Andhra Pradesh, India. Department of Archaeology and Museums. Museum Objects and Numismatics Series
0066-1678 Andhra University Humanities and Sciences Series†
0066-1686 Andhra University Memoirs in Oceanography
0066-1694 Andrew W. Mellon Foundation. Report
0066-1708 Andrews University. Monographs
0066-1724 Anesthesiologie Europeenne et Mediterraneenne. Annuaire†
0066-1732 Anesthesiologie Francaise. Annuaire†
0066-1759 Angewandte Botanik
0066-1767 Angewandte Forschung in der Bundesrepublik Deutschland†
0066-1783 Anglers' Annual *changed to* Fishing Waters
0066-1791 Anglica Germanica. British Studies in Germanic Languages and Literatures†
0066-1805 Anglistica
0066-1848 Angola. Direccao dos Servicos de Estatistica. Estatisticas do Comercio Externo
0066-1872 Animal Health Yearbook
0066-1899 Canada. Agriculture Canada. Animal Research Institute. Research Report
0066-1910 Anleitung fuer die Chemische Laboratoriumspraxis
0066-1937 Annales Academiae Medicae Cracoviensis. Index Dissertationum Editarum
0066-1945 Annales Academiae Medicae Stetinensis
0066-1953 Annales Academiae Scientiarum Fennicae. Series A, 1: Mathematica
0066-1961 Annales Academiae Scientiarum Fennicae. Series A, 2: Chemica
0066-197X Annales Academiae Scientiarum Fennicae. Series A, 3: Geologica-Geographica
0066-1988 Annales Academiae Scientiarum Fennicae. Series A, 4: Biologica†
0066-1996 Annales Academiae Scientiarum Fennicae. Series A, 5: Medica
0066-2003 Annales Academiae Scientiarum Fennicae. Series A, 6: Physica
0066-2011 Annales Academiae Scientiarum Fennicae. Series B
0066-2054 Annales de Chirurgie Thoracique et Cardio-Vasculaire
0066-2062 Annales de Demographie Historique
0066-2070 Annales de Gastroenterologie et d'Hepatologie
0066-2119 Annales d'Esthetique
0066-2127 Annales d'Ethiopie†
0066-2135 Annales d'Etudes Internationales†
0066-2143 Annales Francaises de Chronometrie et de Micromecanique *see* 0221-0665
0066-216X Annales Malgaches. Series Lettres et Sciences Humaines *changed to* Universite de Madagascar. Annales. Serie Lettres et Sciences Humaines
0066-2186 Annales Moreau de Tours
0066-2194 Annales Odonto-Stomatologiques
0066-2216 Annales Polonici Mathematici
0066-2224 Annales Silesiae
0066-2232 Annales Universitatis Mariae Curie-Sklodowska. Sectio C. Biologia
0066-2240 Annales Universitatis Mariae Curie-Sklodowska. Sectio D. Medicina
0066-2259 Annali del Mezzogiorno†
0066-2267 Annali di Laringologia, Otologia, Rinologia, Faringologia
0066-2275 Annali di Sociologia
0066-2283 Quaderni Internazionali di Storia Economica e Sociale
0066-2291 Annals of Clinical Research. Supplementum
0066-2348 Annee Epigraphique; Revue des Publications Epigraphiques Relatives a l'Antiquite Romaine
0066-2356 Annee Politique†
0066-2364 Annee Politique Africaine
0066-2372 Annee Politique Suisse
0066-2380 Universite Libre de Bruxelles. Institut de Sociologie. Annee Sociale
0066-2399 Annee Sociologique
0066-2402 Annee Therapeutique en Ophtalmologie *see* 0301-4495
0066-2410 Annotated Bibliography and Index of the Geology of Zambia
0066-2445 Annotated Guide to Taiwan Periodical Literature
0066-2453 Annuaire Administratif de la Republique du Mali
0066-2461 Annuaire Administratif et Judiciaire de Belgique
0066-247X Annuaire Biographique du Cinema et de la Television en France et en Belgique
0066-2488 Annuaire Catholique de France
0066-2518 Annuaire de la Chapellerie et de la Mode
0066-2526 Annuaire de la Chaussure et des Cuirs
0066-2534 Annuaire de la France Rurale dans le Marche Commun
0066-2542 Annuaire de la Maree
0066-2550 Annuaire de la Marine Marchande
0066-2569 Annuaire de la Noblesse de France et d'Europe
0066-2577 Annuaire de la Papeterie Francaise *changed to* Annuaire de la Papeterie
0066-2585 Annuaire de la Presse et de la Publicite
0066-2593 Annuaire de l'Activite Nucleaire Francaise
0066-2607 Annuaire de l'Afrique du Nord
0066-2615 Annuaire de l'Ameublement *changed to* Annuaire de l'Ameublement et des Industries s'y Rattachant
0066-2623 Annuaire de l'Armement a la Peche
0066-264X Annuaire de l'Eclairage
0066-2658 Annuaire de Legislation Francaise et Etrangere
0066-2674 Annuaire de l'Industrie du Caoutchouc et de ses Derives
0066-2704 Annuaire de l'U. R. S. S. *see* 0397-8249
0066-2712 Annuaire Dentaire
0066-2720 Annuaire des Annuaires
0066-2739 Annuaire des Arachnologistes Mondiaux
0066-2747 Annuaire des Architectes
0066-2763 Annuaire des Boissons et des Liquides Alimentaires
0066-2771 Annuaire des Chercheurs Francais du Fonds de Bourses de Recherche Scientifique et Technique de l'Organisation du Traite de l'Atlantique Nord
0066-278X Annuaire des Caisses d'Epargne; France et Outre-Mer
0066-2798 Annuaire des Chambres de Commerce et d'Industrie
0066-281X Annuaire des Docteurs (Lettres) de l'Universite de Paris et Autres Universites Francaises
0066-2828 Annuaire des Entreprises d'Outre-Mer, des Organismes Officiels et Professionels d'Outre-Mer, des Organismes de Cooperation Francais, Entrangers et Internationaux *changed to* Annuaire des Entreprises et Organismes d'Outre-Mer

0066-2844 Annuaire des Geographes de la France et de l'Afrique Francophone *changed to* Repertoire des Geographes de France
0066-2860 Annuaire des Instituts de Religieuses en France
0066-2909 Annuaire des Negociants en Combustibles†
0066-2917 Annuaire des Organismes d'Habitat Rural *changed to* Guide de l'Habitat et de l'Amenagement Rural
0066-2933 Groupement des Societes Immobilieres d'Investissement. Annuaire
0066-2941 Annuaire des Stations Hydro-Minerales, Climatiques, et Balneaires de France et des Etablissements Medicaux *changed to* Annuaire des Stations Thermales et Climatiques et des Etablissements Medicaux Francais
0066-295X Annuaire Diplomatique et Consulaire de la Republique Francaise
0066-2968 Annuaire du Cinema et Television
0066-2976 Annuaire du Corps Interministeriel des Ingenieurs des Telecommunications
0066-300X Annuaire du Marketing
0066-3018 Annuaire du Quebec
0066-3026 Annuaire du Spectacle
0066-3042 Annuaire Economique de la Tunisie
0066-3069 Guide Europeen de l'Amateur d'Art, de l'Antiquaire et du Bibliophile
0066-3077 Annuaire Europeen des Directeurs Commerciaux et de Marketing
0066-3085 Annuaire Francais de Droit International
0066-3107 Annuaire Franco-Asiatique†
0066-3115 Annuaire Franco-Italien
0066-3123 Annuaire Franco-Suisse
0066-3131 Annuaire Fructidor
0066-314X Annuaire General Automobile *changed to* Annuaire National Automobile
0066-3158 Annuaire General de la Pharmacie Francaise
0066-3174 Jaarboek der Schone Kunsten
0066-3182 Annuaire General des Cooperatives Francaises et de Leurs Fournisseurs; France, Afrique et Marche Commun
0066-3204 Guide de l'Organisation et de la Modernisation des Industries et Collectives *changed to* Guide de l'Organisation de l'Informatique et de la Formation
0066-3212 Annuaire-Guide International de l'Energie Atomique et des Autres Energies *see* 0337-2219
0066-3247 Annuaire International des Dix-Huitiemistes
0066-3255 Annuaire International des Jus de Fruits
0066-3263 Annuaire International des Ventes
0066-328X Annuaire Luxembourgeois; Annuaire LUX pour l'Industrie, le Commerce et l'Artisant†
0066-3298 Annuaire Medical de l'Hospitalisation Francaise.
0066-3301 Annuaire National de la Kinesitherapie
0066-331X Annuaire National de la Musique†
0066-3328 Annuaire National de l'Aviculture
0066-3352 Annuaire National des Beaux-Arts
0066-3379 Annuaire National des Fournisseurs des Administrations Francaises
0066-3387 Annuaire National des Lettres
0066-3395 Annuaire National des Specialistes en Gynecologie-Obstetrique et des Competents Exlusifs en Gynecologie et Obstetrique
0066-3417 Annuaire National des Specialistes Qualifies en Chirurgie
0066-3425 Annuaire National des Specialistes Qualifies Exclusifs des Maladies de l'Appareil Digestif
0066-345X Annuaire National des Specialistes Qualifies Exclusifs en Dermatologie et Venereologie
0066-3468 Annuaire National des Specialistes Qualifies Exclusifs en Electroradiologie
0066-3476 Annuaire National des Specialistes Qualifies Exclusifs en Neuropsychiatrie
0066-3514 Annuaire National des Specialistes Qualifies Exclusifs en Pediatrie
0066-3522 Annuaire National des Specialistes Qualifies Exclusifs en Rhumatologie
0066-3549 Annuaire National des Transports
0066-3557 Annuaire National du Verre
0066-3565 Annuaire O. G. M.
0066-3581 Annuaire Paris: Bijoux
0066-362X Annuaire Protestant; la France Protestante et les Eglises de Langue Francaise
0066-3638 Quatre Mille Imprimeries Francaises
0066-3646 Annuaire Statistique de la Belgique
0066-3654 Annuaire Statistique de la France
0066-3689 Annuaire Statistique de la Tunisie
0066-3697 Annuaire Statistique de l'Industrie Francaise du Jute
0066-3719 Annuaire Statistique du Maroc
0066-3727 Annuaire Suisse de Science Politique
0066-3743 Annuaires Francais et Listes d'Adresses Susceptibles d'Interesser le Commerce et l'Industrie
0066-376X Annual Banff Regional Conference for School Administrators. Report†
0066-3778 Annual Basic Hobby Industry Trade Directory *changed to* Craft, Model & Hobby Industry Annual Trade Directory
0066-3786 Annual Bibliography of English Language and Literature
0066-3794 Annual Bibliography of Indian Archaeology
0066-3808 Annual Bulletin of Coal Statistics for Europe
0066-3816 Annual Bulletin of Electric Energy Statistics for Europe
0066-3824 Annual Bulletin of Gas Statistics for Europe
0066-3832 Annual Bulletin of Historical Literature
0066-3859 Annual Bulletin of Transport Statistics for Europe
0066-3883 Annual Conference of Model Reporting Area for Blindness Statistics. Proceedings†
0066-3891 Annual Development Plan of Madhya Pradesh
0066-3913 Annual Directory of Booksellers in the British Isles Specialising in Antiquarian and Out-Of-Print Books
0066-3921 Annual Dog Watch *changed to* Dog Watch
0066-3964 Annual Estimates of the Population of Scotland
0066-3972 N U T Guide to Careers Work
0066-4014 Annual of Advertising, Editorial and Television Art and Design *changed to* Annual of Advertising, Editorial & Television Art & Design with the Annual Copy Awards
0066-4030 Annual Progress in Child Psychiatry and Child Development
0066-4049 Annual Register of Grant Support
0066-4057 Annual Register World Events
0066-4065 Oklahoma. Department of Libraries. Annual Report and Directory of Libraries in Oklahoma
0066-409X Annual Reports in Organic Synthesis
0066-4103 Annual Reports on N M R Spectroscopy
0066-412X Hawaii Vistors Bureau. Annual Research Report
0066-4138 Annual Review in Automatic Programming
0066-4146 Annual Review of Astronomy and Astrophysics
0066-4154 Annual Review of Biochemistry
0066-4162 Annual Review of Ecology and Systematics
0066-4170 Annual Review of Entomology
0066-4189 Annual Review of Fluid Mechanics
0066-4197 Annual Review of Genetics
0066-4200 Annual Review of Information Science and Technology
0066-4219 Annual Review of Medicine *changed to* Annual Review of Medicine: Selected Topics in the Clinical Sciences
0066-4227 Annual Review of Microbiology
0066-4235 Annual Review of N M R Spectroscopy
0066-4243 Annual Review of Nuclear Science *see* 0163-8998
0066-4251 Annual Review of Pharmacology *see* 0362-1642
0066-426X Annual Review of Physical Chemistry
0066-4278 Annual Review of Physiology
0066-4286 Annual Review of Phytopathology
0066-4294 Annual Review of Plant Physiology
0066-4308 Annual Review of Psychology
0066-4332 Silver Market
0066-4340 Annual Review of United Nations Affairs
0066-4359 Annual Safety Education Review†
0066-4367 Annual Statistical Review: The Distilled Spirits Industry
0066-4375 Annual Summary of Business Statistics, New York State
0066-4383 Annual Summary of Information on Natural Disasters
0066-4391 Annual Summary of Merchant Ships Launched in the World *changed to* Annual Summary of Merchant Ships Launched/Completed in the World
0066-4405 Annual Survey of African Law
0066-4413 Annual Survey of American Law
0066-443X Annual Survey of Psychoanalysis†
0066-4456 Annuale Mediaevale
0066-4464 Annuario Cattolico d'Italia
0066-4472 Annuario Ceramica
0066-4480 Annuario della Comunita Lombarda†
0066-4499 Annuario dell' Industria Italiana della Gomma
0066-4510 Annuario Politecnico Italiano
0066-4545 Annuario Statistico Italiano
0066-4553 Anorganische und Allgemeine Chemie in Einzeldarstellungen *changed to* Inorganic Chemistry Concepts
0066-4596 Anschriften Deutscher Verlage und Auslaendischer Verlage mit Deutschen Auslieferungen
0066-460X Anschriften Deutschsprachiger Zeitschriften *see* 0419-005X
0066-4618 Anson G. Phelps Lectureship on Early American History
0066-4626 Antarctic Bibliography
0066-4634 Antarctic Research Series
0066-4642 Antemurale
0066-4677 Anthropological Forum
0066-4685 Anthropologie
0066-4693 Anthropologische Gesellschaft, Vienna. Mitteilungen
0066-4723 Anthropos
0066-4758 Antibiotics and Chemotherapy
0066-4766 Antichita Classica e Cristiana
0066-4774 Antichthon
0066-4782 Antike Kunst. Beihefte
0066-4804 Antimicrobial Agents and Chemotherapy
0066-4812 Antipode: A Radical Journal of Geography
0066-4839 Antiquitas. Reihe 1. Abhandlungen zur Alten Geschichte
0066-4847 Antiquitas. Reihe 2. Abhandlungen aus dem Gebiete der Vor- und Fruehgeschichte
0066-4855 Antiquitas. Reihe 3. Abhandlungen zur Vor- und Fruehgeschichte, zur Klassischen und Provinzial-Roemischen Archaeologie und zur Geschichte des Altertums
0066-4863 Antiquitas. Reihe 4. Beitraege zur Historia-Augusta-Forschung
0066-4871 Antiquites Africaines
0066-488X Israel. Ministry of Education and Culture. Department of Antiquities and Museums. Atiqot (English Series)
0066-4928 Antologia del Folklore Musical Chileno†
0066-4936 Antologias del Pensamiento Politico
0066-4979 Kunsthistorische Musea, Antwerp. Schone Kunsten
0066-5010 Anuario Bibliografico Costarricense
0066-5045 Anuario Colombiano de Historia Social y de la Cultura
0066-5053 Anuario de Cinema
0066-5061 Anuario de Estudios Medievales
0066-507X Anuario de Filologia
0066-510X Anuario de Relojeria y Arte en Metal para Espana e Hispanoamerica
0066-5118 Anuario del Comercio Exterior Latino-Americano
0066-5126 Anuario de Psicologia
0066-5169 Mexico. Direccion General de Estadistica. Anuario Estadistico Compendiado†
0066-5177 Anuario Estadistico de Espana
0066-5185 Anuario Estadistico de Los Andes; Venezuela
0066-5193 Angola. Direccao dos Servicos de Estatistica. Anuario Estatistico
0066-5207 Anuario F.H.I. Argentina: Frutas y Hortalizas Industriarizadas y Frescas
0066-5215 Anuario Filosofico
0066-5223 Anuario Geografico del Peru
0066-5231 Anuario Industrial de Minas Gerais *changed to* Guia Economico e Industrial do Estado de Minas Gerais
0066-524X Anuario Martiano *changed to* Centro de Estudios Martianos. Anuario
0066-5274 Yearbook for Inter-American Musical Research†
0066-5282 Anzeiger fuer Slavische Philologie
0066-5304 Aphidologists' Newsletter†
0066-5320 Apocrypha Novi Testamenti
0066-5339 Apollonia
0066-5347 Apotheker-Jahrbuch
0066-5363 Financial Review
0066-5371 Appalachian Gas Measurement Short Course, West Virginia University. Proceedings
0066-538X Appalachian Underground Corrosion Short Course, West Virginia University. Proceedings
0066-5398 Appel Service; Repertoire d'Adresses Utiles pour le Commerce et l'Industrie
0066-5401 Appliance Technical Conference. Preprints
0066-541X Applied Chemistry Series
0066-5452 Applied Mathematical Sciences
0066-5460 North-Holland Series in Applied Mathematics and Mechanics
0066-5479 Applied Mathematics and Mechanics
0066-5487 Applied Mineralogy. Technische Minerologie
0066-5495 Applied Optics. Supplement
0066-5509 Applied Physics and Engineering
0066-5517 Applied Polymer Symposium. Papers
0066-5533 Applied Solid State Science
0066-5568 Appreciation of the Arts
0066-5576 Approaches to Semiotics
0066-5606 Aqui
0066-5614 Aquinas Lecture Series
0066-5622 Arab and Afro-Asian Monograph Series *changed to* Institute for Arab Studies. Publications and Studies
0066-5630 Arab Book Annual
0066-5665 Arbeiten aus dem Paul-Ehrlich-Institut, dem Georg-Speyer-Haus und dem Ferdinand-Blum-Institut
0066-5673 Arbeiten zur Angewandten Statistik
0066-5681 Arbeiten zur Geschichte des Antiken Judentums und des Urchristentums
0066-569X Arbeiten zur Paedagogik
0066-5703 Arbeiten zur Rechtsvergleichung
0066-5711 Arbeiten zur Theologie. Reihe 1
0066-572X Arbeiten zur Theologie. Reihe 2†
0066-5738 Arbeitsblaetter fuer Restauratoren
0066-5746 A R D - Jahrbuch
0066-5754 Rheinisch-Westfaelische Akademie der Wissenschaften. Veroeffentlichungen
0066-5770 Arbeitsgemeinschaft zur Verbesserung der Agrarstruktur in Hessen. A V A-Beratungsunterlagen†
0066-5789 Arbeitsgemeinschaft zur Verbesserung der Agrarstruktur in Hessen. A V A-Hefte†
0066-5797 Arbeitsgemeinschaft zur Verbesserung der Agrarstruktur in Hessen. A V A-Materialsammlungen†

0066-5800 Arbeitsgemeinschaft zur Verbesserung der Agrarstruktur in Hessen. A V A-Sonderhefte†
0066-5819 Arbeitsgemeinschaft zur Verbesserung der Agrarstruktur in Hessen. A V A Bezugshefte†
0066-5827 Arbeitshefte zur Gemeinschaftskunde
0066-5843 Arbeitsmedizin
0066-5851 Arbeitsmedizinische Fragen in der Ophthalmologie†
0066-586X Arbeitsrecht der Gegenwart
0066-5878 Arboretum Kornickie
0066-5886 Archaeo-Physika
0066-5894 Archaeologia Cantiana
0066-5908 Archaeologia Geographica
0066-5916 Archaeologia Hungarica. Series Nova
0066-5924 Archaeologia Polona
0066-5932 Archaeologica Slovaca. Catalogi
0066-5940 Archaeologica Slovaca. Fontes
0066-5967 Archaeological Bibliography for Great Britain and Ireland
0066-5975 Archaeological Exploration of Sardis. Monographs
0066-5983 Archaeological Journal
0066-6009 Archaeologische Funde und Denkmaeler des Rheinlandes
0066-6017 Archaeologische Gesellschaft Koeln. Schriftenreihe†
0066-6025 Archeologische Kaarten van Belgie
0066-6033 Archaeologische Mitteilungen aus Iran. Neue Folge
0066-6041 Archeion
0066-605X Archeologia
0066-6068 Archeologie et Civilisation†
0066-6084 Archeologie Mediterraneenne
0066-6092 Archigram
0066-6106 Archimede. Quaderni
0066-6114 Architect and Contractors Yearbook
0066-6122 Architectes
0066-6149 Architects, Builders and Contractors Pocket Book†
0066-6157 Architects, Contractors & Engineers Guide to Construction Costs
0066-6165 Architect's Detail Library†
0066-6173 Architect's Handbook of Professional Practice
0066-6181 Architects Standard Catalogues
0066-619X Architects' Year Book
0066-6203 Architectural and Archaeological Society of Durham and Northumberland. Transactions. New Series
0066-6211 Architectural Association, London. Papers†
0066-622X Architectural History
0066-6238 Architecture at Rice University†
0066-6262 Architecture in Greece
0066-6270 Architectura
0066-6297 Archiv fuer Diplomatik, Schriftgeschichte, Siegel- und Wappenkunde
0066-6327 Archiv fuer Geschichte des Buchwesens
0066-6335 Archiv fuer Geschichte von Oberfranken
0066-636X Archiv fuer Hessische Geschichte und Altertumskunde
0066-6378 Archiv fuer Kinderheilkunde. Beihefte *see* 0373-3165
0066-6386 Archiv fuer Liturgiewissenschaft
0066-6394 Archiv fuer Meteorologie, Geophysik und Bioklimatologie. Series A. Meteorology and Geophysics. Supplement
0066-6416 Archiv fuer Meteorologie, Geophysik und Bioklimatologie. Series A. Meteorologie und Geophysik
0066-6424 Archiv fuer Meteorologie, Geophysik und Bioklimatologie. Series B. Klimatologie, Umweltmeteorologie Strahlungschung
0066-6432 Archiv fuer Mittelrheinische Kirchengeschichte
0066-6440 Archiv fuer Orientforschung
0066-6459 Archiv fuer Papyrusforschung und Verwandte Gebiete
0066-6475 Archiv fuer Psychologie
0066-6491 Archiv fuer Schlesische Kirchengeschichte
0066-6505 Archiv fuer Sozialgeschichte
0066-6513 Archiv fuer Voelkerkunde
0066-6521 Archivalia Medica
0066-653X Archives and the User
0066-6548 Archives Bakounine
0066-6556 Archives Claudeliennes
0066-6564 Archives de Philosophie du Droit
0066-6572 Archives des Lettres Canadiennes
0066-6580 Archives d'Ethnologie Francaise
0066-6599 Archives in Trade Union History and Theory Series†
0066-6602 Archives Internationales de Finances Publiques†
0066-6610 Archives Internationales d'Histoire des Idees
0066-6629 Archives of Archaeology†
0066-6637 Archives of Asian Art
0066-6645 Archives of Maryland†
0066-6653 Archives Suisses d'Anthropologie Generale
0066-6661 Archivio del Teatro Italiano
0066-667X Archivio di Oceanografia e Limnologia
0066-6688 Archivio Italiano per la Storia della Pieta
0066-6696 Archivio Linguistico Veneto. Quaderni.
0066-670X Archivio Putti di Chirurgia degli Organi di Movimento
0066-6718 Archivio Storico Italiano. Biblioteca
0066-6734 Archivo Epistolar Colombiano
0066-6742 Archivo Espanol de Arqueologia
0066-6750 Archivos Argentinos de Dermatologia
0066-6769 Archivos de Investigacion Medica
0066-6777 Archivos de Oftalmologia de Buenos Aires
0066-6785 Archivum Historiae Pontificae
0066-6793 Archivum; Revue Internationale des Archives
0066-6807 Archivum Romanicum. Biblioteca. Serie 1: Storia Letteratura-Paleografia
0066-6815 Archivum Romanicum. Biblioteca. Serie 2: Linguistica
0066-6823 Archiwum Akustyki
0066-6831 Archiwum Dziejow Oswiaty
0066-684X Archiwum Energetyki
0066-6858 Archiwum Etnograficzne
0066-6866 Archiwum Filologiczne
0066-6874 Archiwum Historii Filozofii i Mysli Spolecznej
0066-6882 Archivum Iuridicum Cracoviense
0066-6890 Archiwum Kryminologii
0066-6904 Archiwum Literackie
0066-6912 Archiwum Mineralogiczne
0066-6939 Arctic Anthropology
0066-6947 Arctic Bibliography†
0066-6955 Arctic Institute of North America. Annual Report†
0066-6963 Arctic Institute of North America. Newsletter *see* 0315-2561
0066-6971 Arctic Institute of North America. Research Paper
0066-698X Arctic Institute of North America. Technical Paper
0066-6998 Arctos; Acta Philologica Fennica. Supplementum†
0066-7005 Argentina. Consejo Federal de Inversiones. Bibliografia Sobre el Desarrollo Economico Nacional†
0066-7021 Argentina. Departamento de Estadistica Educativa. Boletin Informativo.
0066-703X Argentina. Departamento de Estudios Historicos Navales. Serie A: Cultura Nautica
0066-7048 Argentina. Departamento de Estudios Historicos Navales. Serie B: Historia Naval Argentina
0066-7056 Argentina. Departamento de Estudios Historicos Navales. Serie C: Biografias Navales Argentinas
0066-7080 Argentina. Departamento de Estudios Historicos Navales. Serie J: Libros y Impresos Raros
0066-7099 Argentina. Direccion de Investigaciones Forestales. Misceleneas Forestales
0066-7102 Argentina. Direccion de Investigaciones Forestales. Notas Silvicolas
0066-7110 Argentina. Direccion de Investigaciones Forestales. Notas Tecnologicas Forestales *changed to* Argentina. Direccion de Investigaciones Forestales. Folleto Tecnico Forestal
0066-7129 Argentina. Direccion de Investigaciones Forestales. Planificacion del Desarrollo Forestal†
0066-7145 Argentina. Servicio Nacional Minero Geologico. Anales
0066-7153 Argentina. Servicio Nacional Minero Geologico. Boletin
0066-7161 Argentina. Servicio Nacional Minero Geologico. Estadistica Minera
0066-717X Argentina. Servicio Nacional Minero Geologico. Revista
0066-7188 Argentina. Instituto Nacional de Derecho Aeronautico y Espacial
0066-7196 Argentina. Instituto Nacional de Estadistica y Censos. Informe Serie E: Edificacione
0066-7242 Argentina. Estacion Experimental Agropecuaria Manfredi. Serie Informacion Tecnica
0066-7269 Argentina. Junta Nacional de Carnes. Sintesis Estadistica
0066-7277 Argentina. Oficina Sectorial de Desarrollo de Energia. Anuarios Estadisticos: Combustible
0066-7285 Argentina. Oficina Sectorial de Desarrollo de Energia. Anuarios Estadisticos. Energia Electrica
0066-7293 Argentina. Secretaria de Guerra. Direccion de Estudios Historicos. Boletin Bibliografico
0066-7331 Argentina. Servicio de Inteligencia Naval. Bibliotecas de la Armada. Boletin Bibliografico.
0066-734X Argus de la Poesie Francaise
0066-7358 Arheologia Moldovei
0066-7366 Arid Zone Research
0066-7382 Arizona. Department of Public Safety. Annual Report
0066-7390 Arizona. Department of Public Safety. Statistical Reviews *see* 0066-7382
0066-7404 Arizona Forestry Notes
0066-7412 Arizona Geological Society Digest
0066-7439 Arizona Land Surveyors Conference. Proceedings
0066-7447 Arizona Model United Nations
0066-7455 Arizona State University. Bureau of Educational Research and Services. Educational Services Bulletin.
0066-7463 Arizona State University. Bureau of Educational Research and Services. Research and Services Bulletin.
0066-748X Arizona State University, Tempe. Institute of Public Administration. Monograph. *changed to* Arizona State University. Center for Public Affairs. Monograph.
0066-7501 University of Arizona. Anthropological Papers
0066-751X University of Arizona. College of Education. Monograph Series
0066-7536 University of Arizona. Department of English. Graduate English Papers
0066-7560 E E S Series Report†
0066-7587 University of Arizona. Laboratory of Tree-Ring Research. Papers
0066-7609 University of Arizona. Optical Sciences Center. Newsletter†
0066-7617 University of Arizona. Optical Sciences Center. Technical Report†
0066-7641 Continuing Education in Business Administration†
0066-7668 Arkiv for Nordisk Filologi
0066-7684 Arlington Historical Magazine
0066-7706 University of New England. Department of Geography. Monograph Series in Geography
0066-7714 University of New England. Department of Geography. Research Series in Applied Geography†
0066-7730 University of New England. Exploration Society. Report†
0066-7749 Armorial†
0066-7765 Arnamagnaean Institute. Bulletin *changed to* Arnamagnaean Institute and Dictionary. Bulletin
0066-7781 Arnoldia Rhodesia
0066-7803 Arqueologicas
0066-7811 Arquivo de Anatomia e Antropologia
0066-782X Arquivos Brasileiros de Cardiologia
0066-7846 Arquivos de Cirurgia Clinica e Experimental
0066-7854 Arquivos de Patologia Geral e Anatomia Patologica
0066-7862 Arquivos de Tisiologia†
0066-7870 Arquivos de Zoologia
0066-7900 Ars Quatuor Coronatorum
0066-7919 Ars Suecica
0066-7927 Art and Artists of the Monterey Peninsula
0066-7935 Art Bulletin of Victoria
0066-7943 Art Directors Club Milano
0066-7951 Art et les Grandes Civilisations
0066-796X Art Gallery of South Australia. Special Exhibitions
0066-7978 Art in Its Context: Studies in Ethno-Aesthetics. Field Reports†
0066-7986 Art in Its Context: Studies in Ethno-Aesthetics. Museum Series†
0066-8036 Arthropods of Florida and Neighboring Land Areas
0066-8044 Arthur Holmes Society. Journal
0066-8079 Universidade de Lisboa. Faculdade de Ciencias. Instituto Botanico. Artigo de Divulgacao
0066-8095 Arts
0066-8133 Arts Council of Great Britain. Annual Report and Accounts
0066-815X Arts of Mankind†
0066-8168 Arts Patronage Series
0066-8176 Arv
0066-8184 Arvernia Biologica: Botanique
0066-8192 Arznei-Telegramm
0066-8222 Ascidian News
0066-8230 Asia-Africa World Trade Register
0066-8249 Centro de Estudios Orientales. Anuario
0066-8265 Asia Monograph Series
0066-8281 Asian and African Studies†
0066-8281 Asian and African Studies
0066-829X Asian and Pacific Archaeology Series
0066-8303 Asian and Pacific Council. Cultural and Social Centre. Annual Report
0066-8311 A S P A C Seminar on Audio-Visual Education. Proceedings
0066-8346 Asian and Pacific Marketing Conference. Proceedings†
0066-8362 Asian Book Trade Directory
0066-8370 Asian Development Bank. Annual Report
0066-8389 Asian Development Bank. Board of Governors. Summary of Proceedings (of the) Annual Meeting
0066-8397 Asian Development Bank. Occasional Papers
0066-8419 Asian Journal of Pharmacy
0066-8435 Asian Perspectives
0066-8443 Asian Philosophical Studies†
0066-8451 Asian Population Studies Series
0066-846X A P O Annual Report
0066-8478 Asian Social Science Bibliography with Annotations and Abstracts
0066-8486 Asian Studies at Hawaii Monograph Series
0066-8508 Asien - Afrika - Lateinamerika *changed to* Asien - Afrika - Lateinamerika. Jahrbuch
0066-8524 Aslib Membership List
0066-8532 Aslib Occasional Publications
0066-8540 Asociacion Espanola Contra el Cancer. Memoria de la Assemblea General *changed to* Asociacion Espanola Contra el Cancer. Memoria Tecnico-Administrativa
0066-8567 Asociacion Nacional del Cafe. Departamento de Asuntos Agricolas. Informe Anual

ISSN INDEX 1099

0066-8591 Asociacion Venezolana de Archiveros. Coleccion Doctrina
0066-8613 Asociacion Venezolana de Enfermeras Profesionales. Boletin
0066-8672 Aspects of Education
0066-8699 Assembly Directory and Handbook *see* 0066-8702
0066-8702 Assembly Engineering Master Catalog
0066-8710 Associated Church Press. Directory
0066-8729 Associated Colleges of Illinois. Report
0066-8753 Associated Public Schools Systems. Yearbook
0066-8761 Bibliography of Publications of University Bureaus of Business and Economic Research
0066-877X Associated Western Universities. Annual Report *changed to* Associated Western Universities. Biennial Report
0066-8796 Association Belge pour l'Etude, l'Essai et l'Emploi des Materiaux. Publication A.B.E.M
0066-880X Association Belge pour l'Etude, l'Essai et l'Emploi des Materiaux. Publication Groupement†
0066-8818 Association Belge pour l'Etude, l'Essai et l'Emploi des Materiaux. Proces Verbal de l'Assemblee Generale Ordinaire
0066-8826 Association Canadienne des Bibliothecaires de Langue Francaise. Rapport *see* 0316-0955
0066-8842 Association Canadienne-Francaise pour l'Avancement des Sciences. Annales
0066-8850 Association Canadienne-Francaise pour l'Avancement des Sciences. Bulletin
0066-8877 Association de l'Ecole Nationale Superieure des Bibliothecaires. Annuaire
0066-8893 Association des Amis d'Alfred de Vigny. Bulletin
0066-8907 Association des Amis de Pierre Teilhard de Chardin. Bulletin
0066-8915 Association des Anatomistes. Bulletin
0066-8923 Association of Attenders and Alumni of the Hague Academy of International Law. Yearbook
0066-8931 Association des Bibliothecaires Francais. Annuaire
0066-894X Documents A B F
0066-8958 Association des Bibliotheques Ecclesiastiques de France. Bulletin de Liaison
0066-8982 I C A M Annuaire
0066-8990 Association des Institutions d'Enseignement Secondaire. Annuaire
0066-9008 Association des Societes et Fonds Francais d'Investissement. Annuaire
0066-9016 Association des Traducteurs et Interpretes de l'Ontario. Annuaire
0066-9024 Association des Universites Partiellement Ou Entierement de Langue Francaise. Cahiers†
0066-9032 Association des Universites Partiellement Ou Entierement de Langue Francaise. Colloques et Congres. Comptes Rendus†
0066-9040 Association Euratom-Ital. Annual Report
0066-9059 Association for Asian Studies. Monographs
0066-9075 Association for Childhood Education International. Yearbook†
0066-9083 Association for Commonwealth Literature and Language Studies. Bulletin
0066-9091 Association for Computing Machinery. Proceedings of National Conference
0066-9105 Association for Education of the Visually Handicapped. Selected Papers from A E V H Biennial Conferences
0066-9156 A S C U S Annual-Teaching Opportunities for You
0066-9164 A S C U S Directory of Membership and Subject Field Index
0066-9172 Association for Social Anthropology in Oceania. Monograph Series
0066-9210 A D B S Annuaire
0066-9229 Association Francaise des Ingenieurs du Caoutchouc et des Plastiques. Annuaire
0066-9245 Association Francaise des Ingenieurs et Techniciens de l'Aeronautique et de l'Espace. Annuaire *changed to* Association Aeronautique et Astronautique de France. Annuaire
0066-9253 Association Francaise des Relations Publiques. Annuaire
0066-927X Association Francaise des Techniciens et Ingenieurs de Securite et des Medecins du Travail. Annuaire
0066-9288 Association Francaise d'Experts de la Cooperation Technique Internationale. Annuaire
0066-9296 Association Francaise d'Informatique et de Recherche Operationnelle. Annuaire *changed to* Association Francaise pour la Cybernetique Economique et Technique. Annuaire
0066-9318 Association Nationale de la Recherche Technique. Information et Documentation†
0066-9350 Association of American Geographers. Commission on College Geography. General Series Publications†
0066-9369 Association of American Geographers. Resource Papers
0066-9393 Association of American Geographers. Monograph Series
0066-9407 Association of American Law Schools. Proceedings
0066-9423 Medical School Admission Requirements, U. S. A. and Canada
0066-9431 Association of American Pesticide Control Officials. Official Publication
0066-944X Association of American Pesticide Control Officials. Pesticide Chemicals Official Compendium†
0066-9458 Association of American Physicians. Transactions
0066-9466 Association of Asphalt Paving Technologists. Proceedings
0066-9474 Association of Canadian Map Libraries. Annual Conference Proceedings *see* 0318-2851
0066-9482 Association of Canadian Map Libraries. Newsletter *see* 0318-2851
0066-9490 Association of Canadian Schools of Business. Proceedings of the Annual Conference *see* 0318-5036
0066-9539 Association of Colleges for Further and Higher Education. Year Book
0066-9547 Association of European Paediatric Cardiologists. Proceedings *see* 0301-4711
0066-9555 Association of Faculties of Pharmacy of Canada. Proceedings
0066-9563 Association of Graduate Schools in Association of American Universities. Journal of Proceedings and Addresses†
0066-9571 Association of Island Marine Laboratories of the Caribbean. Proceedings
0066-958X Association of Japanese Geographers. Special Publication
0066-9598 Association of Life Insurance Medical Directors of America. Transactions
0066-9601 Association of Midwest Fish and Game Commissioners Proceedings *changed to* Association of Midwest Fish and Wildlife Commissioners. Proceedings
0066-961X Association of Official Analytical Chemists. Official Methods of Analysis
0066-9628 Association of Pacific Coast Geographers. Yearbook
0066-9644 Association of Registered Professional Foresters of New Brunswick. Papers and Reports
0066-9652 A R L Newsletter
0066-9679 A S A Monographs
0066-9687 Association of Southeast Asian Institutions of Higher Learning. Handbook: Southeast Asian Institutions of Higher Learning
0066-9695 A S A I H L. Seminar Reports
0066-9709 A T M Occasional Papers
0066-9717 Association of the Russian-American Scholars in U.S.A. Zapiski Russkoi Akademicheskoi Gruppy v S. Sh. A. Transactions
0066-9725 Association of Universities and Colleges of Canada. Annual Meeting. Proceedings
0066-9741 Association of University Evening Colleges. Proceedings *changed to* Association for Continuing Higher Education. Proceedings
0066-975X Association of University Summer Sessions. Summary Report
0066-9768 A. V. S. Journal
0066-9776 T.A. Documents
0066-9784 A.E.T.F.A.T. Index
0066-9792 Association Scientifique de la Precontrainte. Sessions d'Etudes
0066-9806 Association Technique de l'Industrie du Gaz en France. Compte Rendu du Congres
0066-9814 Association Technique Maritime et Aeronautique, Paris. Bulletin
0066-9822 Associazione Elettrotecnica Ed Elettronica Italiana. Rendiconti della Riunione Annuale
0066-9830 Associazione Genetica Italiana. Atti
0066-9857 Associazione Internazionale della Stampa Medica. Bollettino Bibliografico†
0066-9865 Associazione Italiana Laringectomizzati. Atti (Del) Convegno Nazionale
0066-9873 Associazione Medica Chirurgica di Tivoli e della Val d'Aniene. Atti e Memorie
0066-989X Assurances Generales de France. Informations
0066-9903 Assyriological Studies
0066-9911 Asterisks†
0066-992X Asticou
0066-9938 Astrology and Horse Racing†
0066-9946 Astronautics Year†
0066-9962 Astronomical Ephemeris *changed to* Astronomical Almanac
0066-9970 Astronomical Ephemeris of Geocentric Places of Planets
0066-9997 Astronomical Society of Australia. Proceedings
0067-0006 Astronomical Society of Victoria. Yearbook
0067-0014 Astronomische Grundlagen fuer den Kalender
0067-0022 Astronomy and Astrophysics Abstracts
0067-0030 Astrophysica Norvegica
0067-0049 Astrophysical Journal. Supplement Series
0067-0057 Astrophysics and Space Science Library
0067-0065 At the Court of St. James's
0067-0073 Athens Center of Ekistics. Research Report
0067-009X Mongrafie della Scuola Archeologica di Atene e delle Missioni Italiane in Oriente
0067-0103 Centre des Sciences Sociales d'Athenes. Publications†
0067-012X Athletisme Francais
0067-0138 Israel. Ministry of Education and Culture. Department of Antiquities and Museums. Atiqot (Hebrew Series)
0067-0162 Atlantic Provinces Economic Council. Annual Report
0067-0197 Atlantic Provinces Inter-University Committee on the Sciences. Annual Report
0067-0200 Atlantic Provinces Studies
0067-0219 Atlantic Yearbook†
0067-0227 Atlantide Report. Scientific Results of the Danish Expedition to the Coasts of Tropical West Africa
0067-0235 Atlantische Tijdingen *changed to* Atlantisch Perspektief
0067-0243 Atlas Arqueologico de la Republica Mexicana
0067-0251 Atlas de la Economia Colombiana†
0067-026X Atlas d'Attraction Urbaine.†
0067-0294 Atlas Flory Polskiej i Ziem Osciennych
0067-0308 Atlas of External Diseases of the Eye
0067-0316 Atlas Polskich Strojow Ludowych
0067-0324 Atlas Rozmieszczenia Drzew i Krzewow w Polsce
0067-0332 Atlas Rozmieszczenia Roslin Zarodnikowych w Polsce. Seria Iv. Watrobowce. Hepaticae†
0067-0340 Colorado State University. Atmospheric Science Paper
0067-0367 A E C L Report Series
0067-0383 Atomic Energy of Canada. Annual Report
0067-0405 Atomic Energy of Canada. List of Publications
0067-0421 Auburn Forestry Forum†
0067-043X Auburn University. Water Resources Research Institute. Annual Report
0067-0456 Auckland Institute and Museum. Bulletin
0067-0464 Auckland Institute and Museum. Records
0067-0480 University of Auckland Historical Society. Annual
0067-0499 University of Auckland. Library. Bibliographical Bulletin
0067-0510 Auckland University Law Review
0067-0537 Audarena Stadium Guide and International Directory
0067-0545 Audio Annual *changed to* Hi Fi News & Record Review Annual
0067-0553 Audiovisual Market Place; A Multimedia Guide
0067-057X Augustana Library Publications
0067-0588 Augustana Historical Society, Rock Island, Illinois. Publications
0067-0618 Aus dem Schweizerischen Landesmuseum
0067-0634 Buecher fuer Alle *changed to* Buecher
0067-0642 Aus Forschung und Kunst
0067-0669 Auslaendische Aktiengesetze
0067-0685 Ausruestung in Luft- und Raumfahrt
0067-0707 University of Texas, Austin. Center for Neo-Hellenic Studies. Bulletin†
0067-0715 Australasian Corrosion Directory†
0067-0731 Australia. Bureau of Statistics. Banking and Currency Bulletin†
0067-074X Australia. Bureau of Statistics. Building and Construction Bulletin†
0067-0758 Australia. Bureau of Statistics. Commonwealth Finance†
0067-0766 Australia. Bureau of Statistics. Causes of Death
0067-0774 Australia. Bureau of Statistics. Commonwealth Taxation Assessment Bulletin†
0067-0782 Australia. Bureau of Statistics. Demography (Population and Vital) Bulletin†
0067-0790 Australia. Bureau of Statistics. Insurance and Other Private Finance Bulletin†
0067-0804 Australia. Bureau of Statistics. Imports Cleared for Home Consumption
0067-0812 Australia. Bureau of Statistics. Labour Report *changed to* Australia. Bureau of Statistics. Labour Statistics
0067-0820 Australia. Bureau of Statistics. Manufacturing Commodities Bulletin†
0067-0839 Australia. Bureau of Statistics. Manufacturing Industry Bulletin†
0067-0847 Australia. Bureau of Statistics. Non-Rural Primary Industries†
0067-0855 Australia. Bureau of Statistics. Northern Territory Statistical Summary
0067-0863 Australia. Bureau of Statistics. Overseas Trade Bulletin
0067-0871 Australia.Bureau of Statistics. Rural Industries Bulletin†
0067-088X Australia. Bureau of Statistics. South Australian Office. Births
0067-0898 Australia. Bureau of Statistics. South Australian Office. Deaths
0067-0901 Australia. Bureau of Statistics. South Australian Office. Divorce

1100 ISSN INDEX

0067-091X Australia. Bureau of Statistics. South Australian Office. Divisional Statistics
0067-0928 Australia. Bureau of Census and Statistics. South Australian Office. Factories *see* 0310-0871
0067-0936 Australia. Bureau of Statistics. South Australian Office. General Insurance†
0067-0944 Australia. Bureau of Statistics. South Australian Office. Livestock. *changed to* Australia. Bureau of Statistics. South Australian Office. Livestock and Livestock Products
0067-0952 Australia. Bureau of Statistics. South Australian Office. Marriages
0067-0979 Australia. Bureau of Statistics. South Australian Office. Projections of Population†
0067-0987 Australia. Bureau of Statistics. South Australian Office. Rural Production
0067-1002 Australia. Bureau of Statistics. Transport and Communication Bulletin†
0067-1010 Australia. Bureau of Statistics. Tasmanian Office. Building Industry
0067-1029 Australia. Bureau of Statistics. Tasmanian Office. Demography
0067-1037 Australia. Bureau of Statistics. Tasmanian Office. Finance *see* 0312-7850
0067-1045 Australia. Bureau of Statistics. Tasmanian Office. Labour, Wages and Prices
0067-1053 Australia. Bureau of Statistics. Tasmanian Office. Primary Industries (Excluding Mining) *see* 0314-1659
0067-1061 Australia. Bureau of Statistics. Tasmanian Office. Social *see* 0314-1705
0067-107X Australia. Bureau of Statistics. Tasmanian Office. Trade and Shipping
0067-1088 Australia. Bureau of Statistics. Victorian Office. Causes of Death
0067-1096 Australia. Bureau of Statistics. Victorian Office. Demography
0067-1118 Australia. Bureau of Statistics. Victorian Office. General Statistics of Local Government Areas
0067-1126 Australia. Bureau of Statistics. Victorian Office. Hospital Morbidity†
0067-1134 Australia. Bureau of Statistics. Victorian Office Industrial Accidents and Workers Compensation. Statistics *changed to* Australia. Bureau of Statistics. Victorian Office. Industrial Accidents and Workers Compensation
0067-1142 Australia. Bureau of Statistics. Victorian Office. Government Finance *changed to* Australia. Bureau of Statistics. Victorian Office. Local Government Finance
0067-1150 Australia. Bureau of Statistics. Victorian Office. Primary and Secondary Education
0067-1169 Australia. Bureau of Statistics. Value of Production Bulletin†
0067-1185 Australia. Bureau of Statistics. Victorian Office. Road Traffic Accidents Involving Casualties
0067-1193 Australia. Bureau of Statistics. Victorian Office. Tertiary Education†
0067-1207 Australia. Bureau of Statistics. Victorian Office. Victorian Pocket Yearbook
0067-1215 Australia. Bureau of Statistics. Victorian Office. Victorian Statistical Publications
0067-1223 Australia. Bureau of Statistics. Victorian Office. Victorian Yearbook
0067-1231 Australia. Bureau of Statistics. Western Australian Office. Agricultural and Pastoral Statistics *changed to* Australia. Bureau of Statistics. Western Australian Office. Agricultural Statistics (General Summary)
0067-124X Australia. Bureau of Statistics. Western Australian Office. Abstract of Statistics of Local Government Areas.
0067-1266 Australian Bureau of Statistics. Western Australian Office. Industrial Accidents *changed to* Australia. Bureau of Statistics. Western Australian Office. Industrial Accidents. Series A: Absence from Work for One Day or More
0067-1282 Australia. Bureau of Statistics. Western Australian Office. Local Government Revenue and Expenditure: Budget Estimates†
0067-1290 Australia. Bureau of Statistics. Western Australian Office. Population, Dwellings and Vital Statistics
0067-1312 Australia. Bureau of Meteorology. Bulletin
0067-1320 Australia. Bureau of Meteorology. Meteorological Study
0067-1339 Australia. Bureau of Mineral Resources, Geology and Geophysics. Pictorial Index of Activities†
0067-1347 Australia. Department of Customs and Excise. Review of Activities *changed to* Australia. Department of Police and Customs. Review of Activities
0067-1355 Australia. Department of Education. A.C.T. Education Directory†
0067-1444 Australia. Department of the Treasury. Income Tax Statistics
0067-1452 Australia. Forestry and Timber Bureau. Bulletins *changed to* Commonwealth Scientific and Industrial Research Organization. Division of Forest Research. Bulletins
0067-1460 Australia. Forestry and Timber Bureau. Forest Resources Newsletter *changed to* Australian Forest Resources
0067-1479 Australia. Forestry and Timber Bureau. Leaflets *changed to* Commonwealth Scientific and Industrial Research Organization. Division of Forest Research. Leaflets
0067-1495 Australia Handbook
0067-1509 Australia Mineral Industry Review *see* 0084-7488
0067-1517 Australia. National Capital Development Commission. Annual Report
0067-155X Australian Academy of Science. Records
0067-1568 Australian Academy of Science. Reports
0067-1576 Australian Academy of Science. Science and Industry Forum Reports
0067-1584 Australian Academy of Science. Year Book
0067-1592 Australian Academy of the Humanities. Proceedings
0067-1606 Australian Advertising Rate and Data Service
0067-1622 Australian and New Zealand Law List and Legal Compendium *changed to* Australian and New Zealand Law List
0067-1630 Australian Association of Adult Education. Monograph
0067-1649 Australian Association of Adult Education. Proceedings of the National Conference
0067-1657 Australia.Atomic Energy Commission. Research Establishment. A A E C/E
0067-1665 Australia.Atomic Energy Commission. Research Establishment. A A E C/M
0067-1703 Australian Biochemical Society. Proceedings
0067-172X Australian Books in Print
0067-1738 Australian Books; Select List
0067-1754 Australia. Bureau of Statistics. Australian Capital Territory. Statistical Summary
0067-1762 Australian Coal Industry Research Laboratories. Annual Report
0067-1770 Australian College of Education. Proceedings of the Annual Conference and Annual Report *see* 0311-4775
0067-1789 Australian College of Ophthalmologists Transactions. *see* 0310-1177
0067-1819 Australian Computer Society. Council. Report
0067-1835 Australian Council for Educational Research. Occasional Papers
0067-1843 Australian Digest
0067-186X Australia. Bureau of Statistics. Australian Exports Bulletin *changed to* Australia. Bureau of Statistics. Australian Exports, Country by Commodity
0067-1878 Australian Government Publications
0067-1886 Australian Hereford Annual *see* 0311-2144
0067-1894 Australian Honey Board. Annual Report
0067-1916 Australia. Bureau of Statistics. Australian Imports Bulletin *changed to* Australia. Bureau of Statistics. Australian Imports, Country by Commodity
0067-1924 Australian Journal of Botany
0067-1940 Australian Journal of Marine and Freshwater Research
0067-1959 Australian Market Guide
0067-1967 Australian Museum, Sydney. Memoirs
0067-1975 Australian Museum, Sydney. Records
0067-1983 Australian National Accounts. National Income and Expenditure†
0067-2017 Australian National University, Canberra. Department of International Relations. Documents and Data Paper†
0067-2025 Australian National University, Canberra. Department of International Relations. Workpaper†
0067-2033 Australian National University, Canberra. Department of Political Science. Occasional Paper. *changed to* Australian National University, Canberra. Research School of Social Sciences. Department of Political Science. Occasional Papers
0067-2041 Australian National University, Canberra. Faculty of Asian Studies. Occasional Papers
0067-2076 Australian Photography Directory
0067-2084 Australian Physiological and Pharmacological Society. Proceedings
0067-2106 Rural Industry Directory
0067-2130 Australian Society for Medical Research. Proceedings
0067-2149 Australian Society of Animal Production. Proceedings
0067-2165 Australian Studies in Health Service Administration
0067-2173 Australian Sugar Year Book
0067-2181 Australian Telecommunication Monographs
0067-219X Australian Water Resources Council. Hydrological Series
0067-222X Australian Wool *see* 0311-9882
0067-2238 Australian Zoologist
0067-2246 Australiana Facsimile Editions
0067-2254 Austria. Bundeskammer fuer die Gewerbliche Wirtschaft
0067-2262 Austria. Bundesministerium fuer Land- und Forstwirtschaft. Taetigkeitsbericht
0067-2270 Austria. Bundesministerium fuer Unterricht und Kunst. Erziehung, Wissenschaft, Forschung *changed to* Austria. Bundesministerium fuer Unterricht und Kunst. Schriftenreihe
0067-2289 Austria. Bundesministerium fuer Unterricht und Kunst. Jahresbericht
0067-2297 Oesterreichisches Staatsarchiv. Mitteilungen
0067-2300 Austria. Statistisches Zentralamt. Die Wohnbautaetigkeit
0067-2319 Beitraege zur Oesterreichischen Statistik
0067-2327 Austria. Statistisches Zentralamt. Ergebnisse der Landwirtschaftlichen Statistik
0067-2335 Austria. Statistisches Zentralamt. Die Natuerliche Bevoelkerungsbewegung
0067-2343 Oesterreichische Hochschulstatistik
0067-2351 Austria. Zentralanstalt fuer Meteorologie und Geodynamik. Jahrbuch
0067-236X Austrian Historical Bibliography
0067-2378 Austrian History Yearbook
0067-2386 Author's and Writer's Who *see* 0143-8263
0067-2408 Auto Racing Guide
0067-2416 Auto-Universum
0067-2424 Autocatalogue
0067-2432 Autocourse†
0067-2491 Automatic Support Systems Symposium for Advanced Maintainability. Proceedings *changed to* Autotestcon
0067-2521 Automobile Buyers' Guide†
0067-253X Automobile Facts and Figures *see* 0146-9932
0067-2548 Automobile News Annual
0067-2572 Automotive Mass Marketer *see* 0702-8318
0067-2580 Automotive News Almanac *changed to* Automotive News Market Data Book
0067-2610 Avant-Siecle
0067-2629 Aventure des Civilisations†
0067-2637 Aves del Arca
0067-2653 Aviation et Astronautique†
0067-2661 Aviation Medical Education Series
0067-267X Aviation Week & Space Technology. Marketing Directory.
0067-2696 Ayer Directory of Newspapers, Magazines, and Trade Publications *see* 0145-1642
0067-270X Azania
0067-2734 B B A Library
0067-2742 B. G. Rudolph Lectures in Judaic Studies
0067-2777 American Society for Microbiology. Abstracts of the Annual Meeting
0067-2793 Badania z Dziejow Spolecznych i Gospodarczych
0067-2807 Badania Fizjograficzne nad Polska Zachodnia. Seria A. Geografia Fizyczna
0067-2815 Badania Fizjograficzne nad Polska Zachodnia. Seria B. Biologia
0067-2823 Badania Nad Dziejami Przemyslu i Klasy Robotniczej W Polsce†
0067-2831 Kommission fuer Geschichtliche Landeskunde in Baden-Wuerttemberg. Veroeffentlichungen. Reihe A. Quellen
0067-284X Staatliche Kunstsammlungen in Baden-Wuerttemberg. Jahrbuch
0067-2858 Badischer Landesverein fuer Naturkunde und Naturschutz, Freiburg. Mitteilungen. Neue Folge
0067-2866 Badlands Natural History Association. Bulletin
0067-2874 Badman†
0067-2882 Badminton Association of England. Official Handbook
0067-2890 University of Baghdad. Biological Research Centre. Bulletin
0067-2904 University of Baghdad. College of Science. Bulletin *changed to* Iraqi Journal of Science
0067-2912 Bahamas Handbook and Businessman's Annual
0067-2947 Baily's Hunting Directory
0067-2955 Baja California Travel Series
0067-2963 Baker and Bakery Management Handbook and Buyers Guide†
0067-298X Balance of Payments of Japan†
0067-2998 Balance of Payments of Sierra Leone
0067-3005 Balance of Payments of Trinidad and Tobago
0067-3013 Balanza de Pagos de Chile†
0067-3021 Balanza de Pagos de Espana
0067-303X Baldwin Lectures in Teacher Education
0067-3048 Bale Catalogue of Israel Stamps *see* 0305-4039
0067-3064 Baltica
0067-3072 Baltimore College of Dental Surgery, Journal
0067-3080 Baltimore Museum of Art. Annual†
0067-3099 Baltische Studien
0067-3102 Baltisches Recht; das Recht Estlands, Lettlands und Litauens in Vergangenheit und Gegenwart†

0067-3110 Chambre de Commerce et d'Industrie du Mali. Precis Fiscal, Commercial, des Changes et des Echanges
0067-3129 Bampton Lectures in America
0067-3161 Banca d'Italia. Assemblea Generale Ordinaria dei Partecipanti.
0067-3188 Somali National Bank. Report and Balance Sheet *changed to* Central Bank of Somali. Annual Report and Statement of Accounts
0067-3196 Banco Central de Chile, Santiago. Memoria Anual
0067-320X Banco Central de Costa Rica. Memoria Anual
0067-3218 Banco Central de Honduras. Memoria
0067-3226 Banco Central de Nicaragua. Informe Anual
0067-3234 El Salvador. Superintendencia de Bancos y Otras Instituciones Financieras. Estadisticas: Seguros, Finanzas, Capitalizacion *changed to* El Salvador. Superintendencia de Bancos y Otras Instituciones Financieras. Estadisticas: Seguros, Fianzas, Bancos
0067-3250 Banco Central de Venezuela. Informe Economico
0067-3269 Banco Central de Venezuela. Memoria
0067-3277 Banco Central del Ecuador. Memoria del Gerente General
0067-3285 Banco Central del Paraguay. Memoria
0067-3315 Banco de Espana. Informe Anual
0067-3323 Banco de la Republica Cuentas Nacionales†
0067-3331 Banco de la Republica Disposiciones†
0067-334X Guia para el Inversionista.†
0067-3366 Banco de la Republica Series Estadisticas y Graficos.†
0067-3374 Banco de Mexico. Informe Anual
0067-3390 Banco Nacional de Fomento, Tegucigalpa. Memoria Anual
0067-3412 Bancroftiana
0067-3439 Indian Statistical Institute. Documentation Research and Training Centre. Annual Seminar
0067-3455 University of Agricultural Sciences, Bangalore. Annual Report
0067-3463 University of Agricultural Sciences, Bangalore. Research Series
0067-3471 U A S Extension Series
0067-348X U A S Miscellaneous Series
0067-3498 Bangkok, Thailand. College of Education. Thesis Abstract Series
0067-3501 Bank Administration Institute. Accounting Bulletins
0067-351X Bank Administration Institute. Annual Report
0067-3528 Bank Officer Salary Survey *see* 0525-4620
0067-3536 Bank Administration Institute. Personnel Policies and Practices *changed to* Biennial Survey of Bank Personnel Policies and Practices
0067-3544 Bank Administration Institute. Security Bulletins
0067-3560 Bank for International Settlements. Annual Report
0067-3587 Bank of Canada. Annual Report
0067-3595 Bank of Canada. Staff Research Studies
0067-3617 Central Bank of Ceylon. Report and Accounts†
0067-3617 Bank of Ceylon. Report and Accounts *changed to* Bank of Ceylon. Annual Report and Accounts
0067-3625 Bank of England. Report *see* 0308-5279
0067-3633 Hawaii Annual Economic Review
0067-3641 Bank of Israel. Main Points of the Annual Report
0067-365X Bank of Israel. Annual Report
0067-3668 Bank of Jamaica. Report and Statement of Accounts
0067-3676 Bank of Japan. Annual Report of the Policy Board
0067-3684 Bank of Japan. Business Report
0067-3692 Bank of Japan. Economic Research Department. B O J Special Paper
0067-3706 Bank of Korea. Annual Report
0067-3714 Bank of Libya. Annual Report of the Board of Directors
0067-3722 Bank of Mauritius. Annual Report
0067-3730 Bank of Sierra Leone. Annual Report *changed to* Bank of Sierra Leone. Annual Report and Accounts
0067-3749 Bank of Sudan. Report
0067-3757 Bank of Tanzania. Economic and Operations Report
0067-3765 Bank of Tanzania. Economic Report *see* 0067-3757
0067-3773 Bank of Thailand. Annual Economic Report
0067-3781 Der Bankangestellte
0067-379X Bankers Almanac and Year Book
0067-3803 Bankers' Who's Who
0067-3811 Banking Statistics of Pakistan
0067-382X Bankwirtschaftliche Forschungen
0067-3838 Bankwirtschaftliche Studien
0067-3846 Banque Centrale de Syrie. Bulletin Periodique *changed to* Central Bank of Syria. Quarterly Bulletin
0067-3854 Banque Centrale de Tunisie. Bulletin
0067-3862 Banque Centrale de Tunisie. Rapport d'Activite
0067-3889 Banque Centrale des Etats de l'Afrique de l'Ouest. Rapport Annuel
0067-3897 Banque Centrale des Etats de l'Afrique de l'Ouest. Rapport d'Activite.
0067-3900 Banque des Etats de l'Afrique Centrale. Rapport d'Activite
0067-3919 Banque de Bruxelles. Rapport Annuel
0067-3927 Banque de France. Compte- Rendu.
0067-3935 Banque de la Republique du Burundi. Rapport Annuel
0067-3943 Banque de l'Union Europeenne. Informations Economiques et Financieres. *changed to* Banque de l'Union Europeenne. Chiffres et Commentaires
0067-3951 Banque des Mots
0067-396X Banque du Maroc. Rapport Annuel
0067-3978 Banque Nationale de Belgique. Rapport sur les Operations
0067-4001 Banque Nationale du Congo. Rapport Annuel *see* 0300-1172
0067-401X Banque Nationale Malagasy de Developpement. Rapport d'Activite
0067-4028 Banque Populaire Suisse. Information
0067-4036 Banque Togolaise de Developpement. Rapport Annuel *changed to* Banque Togolaise de Developpement. Rapport d'Activites
0067-4044 Bantu Treasury
0067-4052 Baptist Handbook†
0067-4060 Baptist Missionary Society, London. Annual Report
0067-4079 Baptist Missionary Society, London. Official Report and Directory of Missionaries
0067-4087 Baptist Union of Western Canada. Year Book
0067-4095 Baptist World Alliance. Congress Reports
0067-4109 Bar-Ilan: Annual of Bar-Ilan University
0067-4125 Barbados. Statistical Service. Overseas Trade Report
0067-4141 Universidad de Barcelona. Biblioteca Central. Catalogos de la Produccion Editorial Barcelona
0067-4168 Patronato Municipal de la Vivienda de Barcelona. Memoria
0067-4176 Universidad de Barcelona. Facultad de Farmacia. Memoria
0067-4184 Universidad de Barcelona. Instituto de Arqueologia y Prehistoria. Publicaciones Eventuales
0067-4206 Die Barke
0067-4222 Baroque
0067-4230 Barque's Pakistan Trade Directory and Who's Who
0067-4257 Baseball Annual
0067-4265 Baseball Dope Book *see* 0162-5411
0067-4273 Baseball Guide
0067-4281 Baseball Register *see* 0162-542X
0067-4303 Gewerbemuseum Basel. Schriften†
0067-4311 Oeffentliche Kunstsammlung. Jahresbericht
0067-4338 Basic Auto Repair Manual
0067-4362 Basic Bodywork and Painting
0067-4370 Basic Cams, Valves and Exhaust Systems
0067-4389 Basic Carburetion and Fuel Systems
0067-4397 Basic Chassis, Suspension and Brakes
0067-4400 Basic Clutches and Transmissions
0067-4419 Basic Facts about the United Nations
0067-4427 Basic Ignition and Electrical Systems
0067-4443 Basic Science Symposium Series†
0067-446X Basis
0067-4478 Basler Beitraege zur Ethnologie†
0067-4486 Basler Beitraege zur Geographie
0067-4494 Basler Drucke
0067-4508 Basler Studien zur Deutschen Sprache und Literatur
0067-4524 Basler Veroeffentlichungen zur Geschichte der Medizin und der Biologie
0067-4532 Basler Wirtschaftswissenschaftliche Vortraege
0067-4540 Basler Zeitschrift fuer Geschichte und Altertumskunde
0067-4575 Bau und Baustoff Handbuch†
0067-4583 Baubeschlag-Taschenbuch
0067-4591 Bauernhaeuser der Schweiz
0067-4605 Bauhinia
0067-463X Bausteine zur Geschichte des Neuhochdeutschen *changed to* Bausteine zur Sprachgeschichte des Neuhochdeutschen
0067-4648 Instituto Nacional de la Pesca de Cuba. Centro de Investigaciones Pesqueras. Boletin de Divulgacion Tecnica†
0067-4656 Centro de Investigaciones. Pesqueras. Contribuciones *see* 0138-8452
0067-4664 Bauwelt Katalog
0067-4672 Bayer-Symposien
0067-4702 Bayerisches Beamten-Jahrbuch
0067-4710 Bayerisches Forstdienst-Taschenbuch
0067-4729 Bayerisches Jahrbuch fuer Volkskunde
0067-4745 Beaufortia
0067-4761 Bed and Breakfast in South and Southwest England *changed to* Bed and Breakfast in Britain
0067-477X Bed and Breakfast in Wales, Northern England and Scotland *changed to* Bed and Breakfast in Britain
0067-4788 Bedford Institute of Oceanography. A O L Data Series *changed to* Bedford Institute of Oceanography. Data Report
0067-4796 Atlantic Oceanographic Laboratory. A O L Report
0067-480X Bedford Institute of Oceanography. Biennial Review *changed to* Bedford Institute of Oceanography Review
0067-4826 Bedfordshire Historical Record Society. Publications
0067-4834 Bedrijfschap voor de Lederwarenindustrie. Jaarverslag
0067-4885 Behring-Werke. Mitteilungen *see* 0301-0457
0067-4893 Beihefte der Bonner Jahrbuecher
0067-4907 Sonderbaende zur Theologischen Zeitschrift
0067-4915 Beilsteins Handbuch der Organischen Chemie. Fourth Supplement
0067-4931 Beiruter Texte und Studien
0067-4966 Beitraege zum Rundfunkrecht
0067-4974 Technische Beitraege zur Archaeologie
0067-4982 Current Topics in Nutritional Sciences
0067-5008 Beitraege zur Geologie von Thueringen
0067-5016 Beitraege zur Gerichtlichen Medizin
0067-5024 Beitraege zur Geschichte der Philosophie und Theologie des Mittelalters Neue Folge
0067-5032 Beitraege zur Geschichte des Alten Moenchtums und des Benediktinerordens
0067-5040 Geschichte des Buchwesens. Beitraege
0067-5059 Beitraege zur Geschichte des Religioesen und Wissenschaftlichen Denkens
0067-5067 Beitraege zur Harmonikalen Grundlagenforschung
0067-5075 Beitraege zur Heilpaedagogik und Heilpaedagogischen Psychologie
0067-5083 Beitraege zur Hygiene und Epidemiologie
0067-5091 Beitraege zur Inkunabelkunde. Dritte Folge
0067-5105 Beitraege zur Kinderpsychotherapie
0067-5113 Krebsforschung. Beitraege†
0067-5121 Beitraege zur Kunst des Christlichen Ostens
0067-5148 Beitraege zur Meereskunde
0067-5156 Beitraege zur Neurochirurgie
0067-5164 Beitraege zur Oberpfalzforschung
0067-5172 Beitraege zur Oekumenischen Theologie
0067-5180 Beitraege zur Praktischen Medizin†
0067-5199 Beitraege zur Rheumatologie
0067-5202 Beitraege zur Romanischen Philologie des Mittelalters
0067-5210 Beitraege zur Sexualforschung
0067-5237 Beitraege zur Strafvollzugswissenschaft
0067-5245 Beitraege zur Ur- und Fruehgeschichtlichen Archaeologie des Mittelmeerkulturraumes
0067-5253 Beitraege zur Wehrforschung
0067-5261 Beitraege zur Westfaelischen Familienforschung
0067-527X Brazil. Instituto de Pesquisas Agropecuarias do Norte. Boletim Tecnico†
0067-5288 Instituto de Pesquisas Agropecuarias do Norte. Circular†
0067-5296 Instituto de Pesquisas Agropecurarias do Norte. Communicado Tecnico†
0067-5342 Belfast and Northern Ireland Directory
0067-5369 Belgium. Administration des Eaux et Forets. Station de Recherches des Eaux et Forets. Travaux. Serie D. Hydrobiologie
0067-5385 Belgium. Conseil National du Travail. Rapport du Secretariat sur l'Activite du Conseil
0067-5393 Belgium. Conseil Superieur des Classes Moyennes. Rapport Annuel du Secretaire General
0067-5407 Belgium. Fonds National de la Recherche Scientifique. Rapport Annuel
0067-5415 Activities des Aerodromes Belges *changed to* Belgium. Institut National de Statistique. Statistiques des Transports
0067-5423 Belgium. Institut National de Statistique. Annuaire Statistique de l'Enseignement *changed to* Belgium. Ministere de l'Education Nationale et de la Culture Francaise. Annuaire Statistique de l'Enseignement
0067-5431 Belgium. Institut National de Statistique. Annuaire Statistique de Poche
0067-544X Belgium. Institut National de Statistique. Batiments et Logements *changed to* Belgium. Institut National de Statistique. Statistiques de la Construction et du Logement
0067-5458 Belgium. Institut National de Statistique. Mouvement de la Population des Communes†
0067-5466 Belgium. Institut National de Statistique. Statistique Agricole *changed to* Belgium. Institut National de Statistique. Statistiques Agricoles
0067-5482 Belgium. Institut National de Statistique. Statistique Annuelle du Trafic International des Ports *changed to* Belgium. Institut National de Statistique. Statistique du Trafic International des Ports
0067-5490 Belgium. Institut National de Statistique. Statistiques Demographiques

0067-5504 Belgium. Institut National de Statistique. Statistique des Accidents de la Circulation sur la Voie Publique
0067-5512 Belgium. Institut National de Statistique. Statistique des Accidents de Roulage *see* 0067-5504
0067-5520 Belgium. Institut National de Statistique. Statistique de la Navigation du Rhin
0067-5539 Belgium. Institut National de Statistique. Statistique de la Navigation Interieure
0067-5547 Belgium. Institut National de Statistique. Statistique du Tourisme et de l'Hotellerie
0067-5555 Belgium. Institut National de Statistique. Statistique des Vehicules a Moteur Neufs Mis en Circulation
0067-5563 Belgium. Institut National de Statistique. Statistiques Sociales
0067-5571 Belgium. Ministere de la Prevoyance Sociale. Annuaire Statistique de la Securite Sociale/Statistisch Jaarboek van de Sociale Zeherheid†
0067-558X Belgium. Ministere de la Prevoyance Sociale. Rapport General sur la Securite Sociale/Algemeen Verslag over de Sociale Zekerheid
0067-5598 Belgium. Ministere de l'Education Nationale et de la Culture Francaise. Rapport Annuel
0067-5601 Bibliotheque Africaine. Catalogue des Acquisitions. Catologus van de Aanwinsten
0067-561X Belgium. Office Belge du Commerce Exterieur. Bijvoegsel B B H. Reeks B
0067-5628 I C E Supplement. Serie C
0067-5644 Belgium. Office National de l'Emploi. Rapport Annuel
0067-5652 Societe National du Logement. Rapport Annuel
0067-5660 Vojni Muzej, Belgrade. Vesnik
0067-5687 Universidade Federal de Minas Gerais. Instituto de Pesquisas Radioativas. Relatorios Anuais
0067-5695 Beloit Poetry Journal. Chapbook
0067-5709 B E M A Engineering Directory
0067-5717 Benjamin F. Fairless Lectures
0067-5725 Benn's Hardware Directory
0067-5733 Bent
0067-5768 Berg- und Huettenmaennische Monatshefte. Supplement
0067-5792 Bergischer Geschichtsverein. Zeitschrift
0067-5806 Berichte des Vereins Natur und Heimat und des Naturhistorischen Museums zu Luebeck
0067-5814 Nursing Journal of Singapore
0067-5822 Berkeley Analyses of Molecular Spectra†
0067-5830 Berkeley Journal of Sociology
0067-5849 Biologische Bundesanstalt fuer Land- und Forstwirtschaft, Berlin-Dahlem. Mitteilungen
0067-5857 Historische Kommission zu Berlin. Einzelverdeffentlichungen
0067-5865 Berlin. Freie Universitaet. Institut fuer Statistik und Versicherungsmathematik. Berichte *see* 0066-5673
0067-5873 Freie Universitaet Berlin. Osteuropa-Institut. Berichte
0067-5881 Freie Universitaet Berlin. Osteuropa-Institut. Bibliographische Mitteilungen
0067-589X Freie Universitaet Berlin. Osteuropa-Institut. Erziehungswissenschaftliche Veroeffentlichungen
0067-5903 Freie Universitaet Berlin. Osteuropa-Institut. Historische Veroeffentlichungen
0067-5911 Freie Universitaet Berlin. Osteuropa-Institut. Philosophische und Soziologische Veroeffentlichungen
0067-592X Freie Universitaet Berlin. Osteuropa-Institut. Slavistische Veroeffentlichungen
0067-5938 Freie Universitaet Berlin. Osteuropa-Institut. Wirtschaftswissenschaftliche Veroeffentlichungen
0067-5954 Hochschule fuer Oekonomie "Bruno Leuschner" Berlin. Wissenschaftliche Zeitschrift
0067-5962 Museum fuer Voelkerkunde, Berlin. Veroeffentlichungen. Neue Folge. Abteilung: Afrika
0067-5989 Museum fuer Voelkerkunde, Berlin. Veroeffentlichungen. Neue Folge. Abteilung: Suedsee
0067-5997 R I A S-Funkuniversitaet, Berlin. Forschung und Information
0067-6004 Staatliche Museen zu Berlin. Jahrbuch. Forschungen und Berichte
0067-6039 Technische Universitaet Berlin. Institut fuer Sozialoekonomie der Agrarentwicklung. Taetigkeitsbericht *changed to* Technische Universitaet Berlin. Institut fuer Sozialoekonomie der Agrarentwicklung. Jahresbericht
0067-6047 Berlin, Theater und Drama
0067-6055 Berliner Byzantinistische Arbeiten
0067-6063 Berliner Handelsregister Verzeichnis
0067-6071 Berliner Historische Kommission. Veroeffentlichungen
0067-6098 Berliner Tierpark-Buch
0067-6128 Berner Beitraege zur Nationaloekonomie
0067-6136 Berner Beitraege zur Soziologie
0067-6144 Berner Kriminologische Untersuchungen
0067-6152 Berner Studien zum Fremdenverkehr
0067-6160 Bernice Pauahi Bishop Museum, Honolulu. Occasional Papers
0067-6179 Bernice Pauahi Bishop Museum, Honolulu. Special Publications
0067-6195 Berytus: Archeological Studies
0067-6209 Besonders Wertvoll. Kurzfilme
0067-6217 Besonders Wertvoll. Langfilme
0067-6225 Best American Plays *changed to* John Gassner's Best American Plays
0067-6233 Best American Short Stories
0067-625X Best Detective Stories of the Year
0067-6276 Borestone Mountain Poetry Awards†
0067-6284 Best Short Plays
0067-6292 Best Sports Stories
0067-6306 Bestands-Statistik der Kraftfahrzeuge in Oesterreich
0067-6314 Bestimmungsbuecher zur Bodenfauna Europas
0067-6330 Bestsellers du Monde Entier†
0067-6349 Bestuurlike Informasie
0067-6357 Beta Phi Mu Chapbook
0067-6365 Beton- und Fertigteil-Jahrbuch
0067-6381 Schriftenreihe Betriebswirtschaftiche Beitraege zur Organisation und Automation
0067-639X Betriebswirtschaftliche Mitteilungen
0067-6411 Betriebswirtschaftliches Periskop *changed to* Der Volks- und Betriebswirt
0067-642X Better Building Bulletin
0067-6454 Bharat Krishak Samaj. Year Book
0067-6462 Basic Road Statistics of India
0067-6470 Bialostockie Towarzystwo Naukowe. Prace
0067-6489 Akademia Medyczna, Bialystok. Rocznik
0067-6543 Bibliografi over Danmarks Offentlige Publikationer
0067-6551 Bibliografia Analitica a Periodicelor Romanesti
0067-656X Bibliografia Bibliotecologica Argentina
0067-6578 Bibliografia Boliviana *changed to* Bio-Bibliografia Boliviana
0067-6586 Bibliografia Brasileira de Botanica
0067-6594 Bibliografia Brasileira de Ciencias Agricolas
0067-6608 Bibliografia Brasileira de Ciencias Sociais
0067-6616 Bibliografia Brasileira de Direito
0067-6624 Bibliografia Brasileira de Documentacao
0067-6632 Bibliografia Brasileira de Educacao
0067-6640 Bibliografia Brasileira de Fisica
0067-6659 Bibliografia Brasileira de Livros Infantis†
0067-6667 Bibliografia Brasileira de Matematica
0067-6675 Bibliografia Brasileira de Medicina
0067-6683 Bibliografia Brasileira de Quimica *see* 0100-0756
0067-6691 Bibliografia Brasileira de Zoologia
0067-6705 Bibliografia Cubana
0067-6721 Bibliografia Historii Polskiej
0067-6748 Bibliografia Oficial Colombiana†
0067-6756 Bibliografia Portuguesa de Construcao Civil
0067-6764 Bibliografia Sobre a Economia Portuguesa
0067-6772 Bibliografia Ticinese
0067-6780 Bibliograficky Zbornik
0067-6799 Bibliografija Medicinske Periodike Jugoslavije
0067-6802 Bibliographia Medica Cechoslovaca
0067-6829 Bibliographia Scientiae Naturalis Helvetica
0067-6837 Bibliographic Annual in Speech Communication†
0067-6853 Bibliographica Judaica
0067-6861 Bibliographical Selection of Museological Literature *changed to* Selected Bibliography of Museological Literature
0067-687X Bibliographical Society of Canada. Facsimile Series
0067-6888 Bibliographical Society of Canada. Monographs
0067-6896 Bibliographical Society of Canada. Papers
0067-6918 Bibliographie Annuelle de l'Histoire de France
0067-6926 Bibliographie Annuelle de Madagascar
0067-6934 Bibliographie Cartographique Internationale†
0067-6942 Bibliographie de la Litterature Francaise du Moyen Age a Nos Jours
0067-6950 Bibliographie der Chemisch-Archaeologischen Literatur†
0067-6969 Bibliographie der Paedagogischen Veroeffentlichungen in der Deutschen Demokratischen Republik
0067-6977 Bibliographie der Sozialethik
0067-6985 Bibliographie en la Langue Francaise d'Histoire du Droit de 987 a 1875
0067-6993 Bibliographie Geographique Internationale
0067-7000 Bibliographie Internationale de l'Humanisme et de la Renaissance
0067-7027 Bibliographie Programmierter Unterricht *see* 0523-2678
0067-7043 Bibliographie zur Geschichte Luxemburgs
0067-706X Bibliographie zur Symbolik, Ikonographie und Mythologie
0067-7094 Bibliographies in Paint Technology
0067-7116 Bibliographies on the Near East†
0067-7132 Bibliography and Reference Series†
0067-7159 Bibliography of Asian Studies
0067-7175 Bibliography of Canadian Bibliographies
0067-7183 Bibliography of Developmental Medicine and Child Neurology. Books and Articles Received
0067-7191 Bibliography of Historical Works Issued in the United Kingdom
0067-7205 Bibliography of Interlingual Scientific and Technical Dictionaries
0067-7213 Bibliography of Old Norse-Icelandic Studies
0067-7221 Bibliography of Published Papers of the Atomic Bomb Casualty Commission *changed to* Bibliography of Published Papers of the Radiation Effects Research Foundation
0067-7256 Bibliography of South African Government Publications
0067-7264 Bibliography of Surgery of the Hand
0067-7272 Bibliography of the Geology of Missouri
0067-7280 Bibliography of the History of Medicine
0067-7302 Bibliography of the Middle East
0067-7310 Bibliography of Works by Polish Scholars and Scientists Published outside Poland in Languages Other Than Polish
0067-7329 Bibliography on Foreign and Comparative Law : Books and Articles in English.
0067-7353 Bibliography on Satellite Geodesy and Related Subjects *changed to* International Association of Geodesy. Central Bureau for Satellite Geodesy. Bibliography
0067-7361 Bibliography on Smoking and Health
0067-737X Bibliohrafichnyi Pokazhczyk Ukrains'koi Presy Poza Mezhamy Ukrainy
0067-7388 Biblioteca de Arheologie
0067-7396 Biblioteca de Cultura Vasca
0067-740X Biblioteca de Teologia
0067-7418 Biblioteca di Bibliografia Italiana
0067-7434 Biblioteca di Labeo
0067-7442 Biblioteca di Storia Toscana Moderna e Contemporanea Studi e Documenti
0067-7450 Biblioteca di Studi Etruschi
0067-7469 Biblioteca do Educador Profissional
0067-7477 Bibliotheca Germanica. Handbuecher, Texte und Monographien aus dem Gebiete der Germanischen Philologie
0067-7493 Biblioteca Istorica
0067-7507 Biblioteca Praehistorica Hispana
0067-7515 Bibliotheca Romanica
0067-7523 Biblioteca Storica Toscana *changed to* Biblioteca Storica Toscana. Serie I
0067-7531 Biblioteconomia e Bibliografia. Saggi e Studi
0067-754X Biblioteczka Ateisty
0067-7558 Biblioteka Kopernikanska
0067-7582 Biblioteczka Wiedzy O Slasku. Seria Archeologiczna†
0067-7590 Biblioteczka Wiedzy O Slasku. Seria Etnograficzna†
0067-7604 Biblioteczka Wiedzy O Slasku. Seria Historyczna†
0067-7612 Biblioteczka Wiedzy O Slasku. Seria Literatura Ludowa†
0067-7620 Biblioteczka Wiedzy O Slasku. Seria Przyrodnicza†
0067-7639 Biblioteka Archeologiczna
0067-7655 Biblioteka Etnografii Polskiej
0067-7671 Biblioteka Klasykow Pedagogiki
0067-768X Biblioteka Kornicka. Pamietnik
0067-7698 Biblioteka Krakowska
0067-7701 Biblioteka Mechaniki Stosowanej
0067-7728 Biblioteka Nawigatora
0067-7736 Biblioteka Pisarzow Polskich *see* 0519-8631
0067-7752 Biblioteka Polska. Seria Tomistyczna
0067-7760 Biblioteka Popularnonaukowa
0067-7779 Biblioteka Sluchacza Koncertowego. Seria Wprowadzajaca
0067-7787 Towarzystwo Literackie im. A. Mickiewicza. Biblioteka
0067-7795 Biblioteka Wiadomosci Statystycznych
0067-7809 Biblioteka Zagadnien Gospodarczych Polski†
0067-7817 Bibliotheca Aegyptiaca
0067-7825 Bibliotheca Africana Droz
0067-7833 Bibliotheca Anatomica
0067-7841 Bibliotheca Arnamagnaeana
0067-785X Bibliotheca Arnamagnaeana. Supplementum
0067-7868 Bibliotheca Athena
0067-7876 Bibliotheca Australiana
0067-7884 Bibliotheca Bibliographica Aureliana
0067-7892 Bibliotheca Botanica
0067-7906 Bibliotheca Cardiologica
0067-7914 Bibliotheca Celtica
0067-7922 Bibliotheca del Planeamiento Educativo
0067-7930 Bibliotheca Emblematica
0067-7957 Bibliotheca Haematologica
0067-7965 Bibliotheca Helvetica Romana
0067-7981 Bibliotheca Historica Romaniae. Studies
0067-799X Bibliotheca Historica Romaniae. Monographies
0067-8007 Bibliotheca Hungarica Antiqua
0067-8015 Bibliotheca Ibero-Americana
0067-8023 Bibliotheca Indonesica
0067-8031 Bibliotheca Latina Medii et Recentiori Aevi
0067-8058 Bibliotheca Microbiologia *see* 0301-3081
0067-8066 Bibliotheca Mycologica
0067-8082 Bibliotheca Oeconomica
0067-8090 Bibliotheca Ophthalmologica *see* 0250-3751

0067-8104 Bibliotheca Orientalis Hungarica
0067-8112 Bibliotheca Phycologica
0067-8120 Bibliotheca Phonetica
0067-8139 Bibliotheca Primatologica *see* 0301-4231
0067-8147 Bibliotheca Psychiatrica
0067-8155 Bibliotheca Radiologica
0067-8163 Bibliotheca Seraphico-Capuccina
0067-8198 Bibliotheca Nutritio et Dieta
0067-8201 Bibliothek der Klassischen Altertumswissenschaften. Neue Folge
0067-8228 Bibliothek fuer das Gesamtgebiet der Lungenkrankheiten
0067-8236 Bibliothek und Wissenschaft
0067-8260 Bibliotheque de la Mer
0067-8279 Bibliotheque de la Revue d'Histoire Ecclesiastique
0067-8295 Bibliotheque de Sciences Religieuses†
0067-8309 Bibliotheque des Cahiers Archeologiques
0067-8325 Bibliotheque d'Etudes Balkaniques
0067-8333 Bibliotheque Europeenne†
0067-8341 Bibliotheque Francaise et Romane. Serie A: Manuels et Etudes Linguistiques
0067-835X Bibliotheque Francaise et Romane. Serie B: Editions Critiques de Textes
0067-8368 Bibliotheque Francaise et Romane. Serie C: Etudes Litteraires
0067-8376 Bibliotheque Francaise et Romane. Serie D: Initiation, Textes et Documents
0067-8384 Bibliotheque Francaise et Romane. Serie E: Langue et Litterature Francaises au Canada
0067-8406 Bibliotheque Historique Vaudoise
0067-8414 Bibliotheque Ideale†
0067-8422 Bibliotheque Introuvable
0067-8457 Bibliotheque Rencontre des Lettres Anciennes et Modernes†
0067-8473 Bidrag til H. C. Andersens Bibliografi
0067-8481 Bidrag till Kaennedom av Finlands Natur och Folk
0067-849X Biennale Internationale de la Tapisserie
0067-8538 Bijdragen tot de Bibliotheckwetenschap
0067-8546 Bijdragen tot de Dierkunde
0067-8554 Bijdragen tot de Geschiedenis van Arnhem
0067-8562 Bilateral Studies in Private International Law
0067-8570 Bild des Menschen in der Wissenschaft†
0067-8589 Bildungsplanung in Oesterreich
0067-8597 Campus Attractions *changed to* International Talent and Touring Directory
0067-8600 Billboard's International Buyer's Guide of the Music-Record-Tape Industry
0067-8627 International Directory of Recording Studios *changed to* International Recording Equipment and Studio Directory
0067-8643 Die Binnengewaesser
0067-8651 Binsted'S Directory of Food Trade Marks and Brand Names
0067-866X Bio-Information
0067-8678 Biochemistry of Disease
0067-8686 Biochemical Preparations†
0067-8694 Biochemical Society Symposia
0067-8716 Biogeographical Society of Japan. Bulletin
0067-8724 Biograficke Studie
0067-8732 Biographical Encyclopedia of Pakistan
0067-8740 Biographies de Personnalites Francaises Vivantes
0067-8767 Biologia Pesquera
0067-8775 Biological Macromolecules Series
0067-8783 B S C S Bulletin Series†
0067-8791 B S C S Special Publication†
0067-8805 Biologie du Sol *see* 0378-181X
0067-8821 Biomathematics
0067-8848 Biomedical Engineering Series of Monographs *changed to* Biomedical Engineering and Health Systems: A Wiley-Interscience Series
0067-8856 Biomedical Sciences Instrumentation
0067-8864 Biomembranes
0067-8899 Verzeichnis Lieferbarer Buecher
0067-8902 Biometeorology; Proceedings
0067-8910 Biophysical Society. Abstracts
0067-8929 Biophysics Series†
0067-8937 Biosis: List of Serials *changed to* Serial Sources for the Biosis Data Base
0067-8945 Bird Control Seminar. Proceedings
0067-8953 University of Birmingham. Centre for Urban and Regional Studies. Occasional Papers
0067-8961 University of Birmingham. Centre for Urban and Regional Studies. Urban and Regional Studies
0067-897X Bituminous Coal Data *see* 0145-417X
0067-8988 Bituminous Coal Facts *changed to* Coal Facts
0067-8996 Biuletyn Fonograficzny
0067-9003 Biuletyn Geologiczny
0067-902X Biuletyn Polonistyczny
0067-9038 Biuletyn Peryglacjalny
0067-9070 Black Experience in Children's Books
0067-9100 Black Orpheus
0067-9119 Black Review†
0067-9178 Blick hinter die Fassade
0067-9186 Blindness
0067-9194 National Museum, Bloemfontein. Memoirs
0067-9208 National Museum, Bloemfontein. Navorsinge/Researches
0067-9216 University of the Orange Free State. Opsommings van Proefskrifte en Verhandelinge. Abstracts of Dissertations and Theses
0067-9224 Bloodstock Breeders' Review
0067-9232 Bloomsbury Geographer
0067-9240 Blue Book: Leaders of the English-Speaking World
0067-9275 Blue Book of Occupational Education *see* 0360-5434
0067-9283 Blue Book of Optometrists
0067-9321 Boat Owners Buyers Guide *changed to* Yachting's Boat Buyers Guide
0067-933X Boat World
0067-9399 Boating Guide
0067-9402 B I A Certification Handbook
0067-9453 Bochumer Universitaetsreden†
0067-9461 Bodendenkmalpflege in Mecklenburg
0067-947X Bydgoskie Towarzystwo Naukowe. Wydzial Nauk Humanistycznych. Prace. Seria D: (Sztuka)
0067-9488 Bodleian Library Record
0067-9496 Boersen- und Wirtschaftshandbuch
0067-9518 Colombia. Observatorio Astronomico Nacional. Publicaciones
0067-9526 Universidad Nacional de Colombia. Centro de Estudios Folkloriques. Annuario†
0067-9534 Universidad Nacional de Colombia. Centro de Estudios Folkloricos. Monografias
0067-9542 Bois-Chantiers†
0067-9550 Bol og By
0067-9585 Boletim Climatologico
0067-9593 Boletim de Ciencias do Mar
0067-9607 Boletim de Engenharia de Producao
0067-9615 Boletim de Industria Animal
0067-9623 Boletim de Zoologia e Biologia Marinha. Nova Serie *changed to* Boletim de Zoologia
0067-9631 Boletim Oficial de Angola
0067-964X Boletim Paranaense de Geociencias
0067-9666 Boletin de Estudios Medicos y Biologicos
0067-9674 Boletin de Filologia
0067-9690 Boletin de Literatura Argentina e Iberoamericana†
0067-9720 Boletin Genetico
0067-9747 Boletin Hidrologico
0067-981X Bolivia Information Handbook
0067-9828 Bolivia. Servicio Geologico. Boletin
0067-9836 Bolivia. Servicio Geologico. Circulare
0067-9844 Bolivia. Servicio Geologico. Informe
0067-9852 Bolivia. Servicio Geologico. Serie Mineralogica. Contribucione
0067-9860 B R A D S
0067-9879 Bolletino dell'Atlante Linguistico Mediterraneo
0067-9887 Universita degli Studi di Bologna. Osservatorio Astronomico. Notizie e Rassegne†
0067-9895 Universita degli Studi di Bologna. Osservatorio Astronomico. Pubblicazioni
0067-9909 Bolsilibros
0067-9917 Bombay Labour Journal
0067-9925 Bombay Technologist
0067-9941 Institut "Finanzen und Steuern." Gruene Briefe
0067-995X Institut "Finanzen und Steuern." Schriftenreihe
0067-9968 Rheinisches Landesmuseum, Bonn. Schriften
0067-9976 Rheinisches Landesmuseum in Bonn. Bonner Jahrbuecher
0068-001X Bonner Arbeiten zur Deutschen Literatur
0068-0028 Bonner Beitraege zur Bibliotheks- und Buecherkunde
0068-0036 Bonner Beitraege zur Kunstwissenschaft
0068-0044 Bonner Beitraege zur Soziologie
0068-0052 Bonner Geschichtsblaetter
0068-0087 Station Biologique de Bonnevaux (Doubs). Section de Biologie et d'Ecologie Animales. Publications
0068-0095 Book Auction Records
0068-0109 Book Dealers in North America
0068-0117 Book of Bantams
0068-0125 Book of the States
0068-0133 Bookman's Guide to Americana
0068-0141 Bookman's Price Index
0068-0168 Books about Canada†
0068-0176 Books about Singapore
0068-0184 Books for Secondary School Libraries
0068-0192 Books for the Teen Age
0068-0206 Books from Pakistan
0068-0214 Books in Print
0068-0222 Books of the Theatre Series†
0068-0249 Booksellers Association of Great Britain and Ireland. List of Members
0068-0257 Booksellers Association of Great Britain and Ireland. Trade Reference Book
0068-0265 Bord Iascaigh Mhara. Tuarascail Agus Cuntaisi
0068-0273 Universite de Bordeaux. Collection Sinologique
0068-0281 Boreal Institute, Edmonton. Annual Report *see* 0316-7828
0068-029X Boreal Institute, Edmonton. Miscellaneous Publications
0068-0303 Boreal Institute, Edmonton. Occasional Publications
0068-0338 Boston College. Bureau of Public Affairs. Community Analysis and Action Series. Monograph†
0068-0346 Boston Studies in the Philosophy of Science
0068-0354 Bostwick Paper
0068-0370 Botanica Gothoburgensia
0068-0397 Botany as a Profession *changed to* Careers in Botany
0068-0400 Botanical Society of America. Yearbook *changed to* Botanical Society of America. Directory
0068-0419 Botanical Society of South Africa. Journal *changed to* Veld & Flora
0068-0427 Botanische Studien†
0068-0443 Botschaft des Alten Testaments
0068-0451 Botswana. Annual Statements of Accounts
0068-046X Botswana. Commissioner of the Police. Annual Report
0068-0478 Botswana. Ministry of Agriculture. Annual Report
0068-0486 Botswana. Forest Department. Report
0068-0494 Bottin International
0068-0508 Bottlers Year Book
0068-0524 Boundary Historical Society. Report
0068-0532 Boutique
0068-0540 Bowker Annual
0068-0559 Bowling and Billiard Buyers Guide
0068-0567 Bowling Guide
0068-0575 Boys Baseball. Blue Book *changed to* Pony Baseball. Blue Book
0068-0605 Boys' Brigade, London. Annual Report
0068-0613 Svenska Riksbyggen. Byggteknisk Information
0068-063X Bradford's Directory of Marketing Research Agencies and Management Consultants in the United States and the World
0068-0672 Brandeis University. Society of Bibliophiles. Publications
0068-0699 Brasil Industrial *see* 0005-4585
0068-0702 Brassey's Annual - the Armed Forces Year-Book *see* 0305-6155
0068-0710 Brauereien und Maelzereien in Europa
0068-0729 Technische Universitaet Braunschweig. Pharmaziegeschichtlichen Seminar. Veroeffentlichungen
0068-0745 Braunschweigisches Jahrbuch
0068-0761 Technion-Israel Institute of Technology. Braverman Memorial Lecture
0068-0788 Brazil. Diretoria do Patrimonio Historico e Artistico Nacional. Revista
0068-0796 Centro de Pesquisas Ictiologicas. Boletim Tecnico
0068-0834 Brazil. Ministerio das Relacoes Exteriores. Biblioteca. Bibliografia Anual *changed to* Brazil. Ministerio das Relacoes Exteriores. Biblioteca. Aquisicoes Bibliograficas
0068-0850 Brazil. Servico de Piscicultura. Publicacao
0068-0877 Breifne
0068-0885 Uebersee-Museum, Bremen. Veroeffentlichungen. Reihe A: Naturwissenschaften
0068-0893 Uebersee-Museum, Bremen. Veroeffentlichungen. Reihe B: Voelkerkunde
0068-0907 Bremer Archaeologische Blaetter
0068-0915 Institut fuer Meeresforschung, Bremerhaven. Veroeffentlichungen
0068-0931 Brewery Manual *see* 0305-8123
0068-094X Brewing and Malting Barley Research Institute. Annual Report
0068-0958 Brewing Industry Survey†
0068-0982 Bridge†
0068-1008 Brigham Young University. College of Engineering Sciences and Technology. Annual Engineering Symposium. Abstracts
0068-1016 Brigham Young University. Department of Geology. Geology Studies
0068-1032 Bristol and Gloucestershire Archaeological Society, Bristol, England. Transactions
0068-1040 Bristol Naturalists' Society. Proceedings
0068-1075 Britain: An Official Handbook
0068-1105 Britain in the World Today
0068-113X Britannia
0068-1148 Britannica Atlas
0068-1156 Britannica Book of the Year
0068-1180 A C T F L Annual Review of Foreign Language Education
0068-1199 Britannica Yearbook of Science and the Future *see* 0096-3291
0068-1210 British Aid Statistics; Statistics of Economic Aid to Developing Countries
0068-1229 Great Britain. British Airports Authority. Annual Report and Accounts
0068-1245 British and Foreign State Papers†
0068-1288 British Archaeological Association. Journal
0068-1296 Who's Who in Industrial Editing *changed to* B. A. I. E. Membership Directory
0068-130X British Astronomical Association. Handbook
0068-1318 British Astronomical Association. Memoirs†
0068-1326 British Athletics
0068-1334 British Authors Series

0068-1350 British Books in Print
0068-1377 British Broadcasting Corporation. B B C Handbook
0068-1385 British Bryological Society. Transactions. *see* 0373-6687
0068-1407 British Catalogue of Music
0068-1415 British Chamber of Commerce in France. Year Book
0068-1423 British Columbia. Cancer Foundation. Annual Report
0068-1431 University of British Columbia. Department of Geophysics and Astronomy. Publications†
0068-144X British Columbia. Ministry of Energy, Mines and Petroleum Resources. Bulletin
0068-1458 British Columbia. Department of Recreation and Conservation. Annual Report
0068-1466 British Columbia. Department of Human Resources. Annual Report *see* 0317-4670
0068-1490 British Columbia. Forest Service. Annual Report *changed to* British Columbia. Ministry of Forests. Annual Report
0068-1520 British Columbia. Forest Service. Research Notes *changed to* British Columbia. Ministry of Forests. Research Notes.
0068-1539 British Columbia. Forest Service. Research Review *changed to* British Columbia. Ministry of Forests. Research Review
0068-1555 British Columbia Fruit Growers Association. Horticultural Conference Proceedings *see* 0701-757X
0068-1563 British Columbia Fruit Growers Association. Minutes of the Proceedings of the Annual Convention
0068-1571 British Columbia Geographical Series: Occasional Papers in Geography
0068-158X British Columbia Hospitals' Association. Proceedings of the Annual Conference *changed to* B. C. Health Association. Proceedings of the Annual Conference
0068-1598 British Columbia Insurance Directory. Insurance Companies, Agents and Adjusters
0068-1601 British Columbia Lumberman's Greenbook
0068-161X British Columbia Municipal Yearbook
0068-1652 British Columbia Research Council. Annual Report *changed to* B. C. Research. Annual Report
0068-1687 University of British Columbia Library. Asian Studies Division. List of Catalogued Books. Supplement
0068-1695 University of British Columbia. Center for Continuing Education. Occasional Papers in Continuing Education
0068-1709 University of British Columbia. Department of Civil Engineering. Report. Soil Mechanics Series
0068-1725 University of British Columbia. Department of Geophysics and Astronomy. Annual Report
0068-1733 University of British Columbia. Department of Geology. Report
0068-1768 University of British Columbia. Faculty of Education. Journal of Education†
0068-1776 University of British Columbia. Faculty of Foresty. Foresty Bulletin *see* 0318-9171
0068-1784 University of British Columbia. Faculty of Forestry. Research Notes
0068-1792 University of British Columbia. Faculty of Forestry. Research Papers
0068-1806 University of British Columbia. Faculty of Forestry. Translations
0068-1849 University of British Columbia Law Review
0068-1857 University of British Columbia Library. Reference Publication
0068-1873 British Columbia. Department of Lands, Forests and Water Resources. Water Resources Service. Report
0068-1903 British Commonwealth Stamp Catalogue
0068-1938 British Cycling Federation. Handbook
0068-1970 British Exports *changed to* British Exports
0068-1989 British Federation of Master Printers. Master Printers Annual *see* 0308-1443
0068-1997 British Film and T.V. Yearbook *changed to* Screen International Film and T.V. Yearbook
0068-2004 British Film Fund Agency. Annual Report
0068-2012 British Friesian Herd Book
0068-2020 British Glass Industry Research Association. Annual Report
0068-2039 British Goat Society. Herd Book
0068-2047 British Goat Society. Year Book
0068-2098 British Hospitals Contributory Schemes Association. Directory of Hospitals Contributory Scheme Benefits
0068-2101 British Hospitals Contributory Schemes Association. Report
0068-211X British Hospitals Home and Overseas†
0068-2128 B H R C A Guide to Hotels and Restaurants *see* 0307-062X
0068-2152 British Institute in Eastern Africa. Annual Report
0068-2160 British Institute of International and Comparative Law. Comparative Law Series
0068-2179 British Institute of International and Comparative Law. International Law Series
0068-2195 British International Law Cases
0068-2217 British Journal of Photography Annual
0068-2268 British Middle Market Directory *changed to* Guide to Key British Enterprises I and II
0068-2292 British Museum (Natural History) Bulletin. Botany
0068-2306 British Museum (Natural History) Bulletin. Historical
0068-2314 British Orthoptic Journal
0068-2322 British Paper and Board Industry Federation. Technical Division. Fundamental Research International Symposia
0068-2330 British Paper and Board Industry Federation. Technical Section. Technical Papers
0068-2349 British Paper and Board Industry Federation. Technical Section. Yearbook
0068-2381 Europlastics Year Book *see* 0306-5502
0068-239X British Printer Specification Manual *changed to* British Printer Dataguide
0068-2403 British Pteridological Society. Newsletter *see* 0301-9195
0068-242X British Railways Board. Report and Statement of Accounts
0068-2446 British Rowing Almanack
0068-2454 British School at Athens. Annual
0068-2462 British School at Rome. Papers. Archaeology
0068-2519 British Society for the History of Pharmacy. Transactions
0068-2578 British Standards Year Book
0068-2586 British Steel Corporation. Annual Report and Accounts
0068-2616 British Tourist Authority. Digest of Tourist Statistics
0068-2624 B T M A Directory
0068-2632 British Trades Alphabet *changed to* B T A Studycards
0068-2640 British Transport Commission. Annual Report and Accounts†
0068-2659 British Transport Docks Board. Annual Report and Accounts
0068-2667 British Tourist Authority. Annual Report
0068-2675 British Trust for Ornithology. Annual Report
0068-2683 British Waterways Board. Annual Report and Accounts
0068-2691 British Year Book of International Law
0068-2705 Universita J. E. Purkyne. Filosoficka Fakulta. Sbornik Praci
0068-2713 Broadcasting Yearbook *changed to* Broadcasting/Cable Yearbook
0068-2721 Broadman Comments; International Sunday School Lessons
0068-273X Broads Book
0068-2748 Broadside (New York, 1940)
0068-2780 Brookfield Bandarlog
0068-2799 Brookhaven Symposia in Biology
0068-2810 Brookings Institution. Reprint *changed to* Brookings Pamphlet Series
0068-2829 Brookings Research Report†
0068-2829 Brookings Research Report Series *changed to* Brookings Pamphlet Series
0068-2853 Brookside Monographs
0068-2861 Brown and Haley Lecture Series
0068-2888 Brown's Directory of North American Gas Companies *see* 0197-8098
0068-290X Brown's Nautical Almanac
0068-2918 Brunei Museum Journal
0068-2926 Bibliotheque Royale Albert 1er. Catalogue Collectif des Periodiques Etrangers
0068-2942 Annuaire et Statistique de l'Enseignement Catholique
0068-2985 Universite Libre de Bruxelles. Institut de Sociologie. Cahiers
0068-2993 Universite Libre de Bruxelles. Institut d'Etudes Europeennes. Enseignement Complementaire. Nouvelle Serie
0068-3000 Universite Libre de Bruxelles. Institut d'Etudes Europeennes. Theses et Travaux Economiques
0068-3019 Universite Libre de Bruxelles. Institut d'Etudes Europeennes. Theses et Travaux Juridiques
0068-3035 Bryn Mawr-Haverford Review
0068-3043 Das Buch der Jugend
0068-3051 Buch und Buchhandel in Zahlen
0068-306X Institutul de Geologie si Geofizica. Dari de Seama ale Sedintelor
0068-3078 Muzeul de Istorie Naturala "Gr. Antipa." Travaux
0068-3086 Observatorul Astronomic din Bucuresti. Anuarul
0068-3094 Observatorul Astronomic din Bucuresti. Observations Solaires
0068-3108 Analele Universitatii Bucuresti. Fizica†
0068-3116 Universitatea Bucuresti. Analelf. Acta Logica
0068-3124 Analele Universitatii Bucuresti. Biologie Animala†
0068-3132 Analele Universitatii Bucuresti. Biologie Vegetala†
0068-3140 Analele Universitatii Bucuresti. Chimie†
0068-3159 Analele Universitatii Bucuresti. Estetica†
0068-3167 Analele Universitatii Bucuresti. Filologie†
0068-3175 Analele Universitatii Bucuresti. Filozofie†
0068-3183 Analele Universitatii Bucuresti. Geologie†
0068-3191 Analele Universitatii Bucuresti. Geografie†
0068-3205 Analele Universitatii Bucuresti. Istorie†
0068-3213 Analele Universitatii Bucuresti. Limbi Clasice†
0068-3221 Analele Universitatii Bucuresti. Limbi Germanice†
0068-323X Analele Universitatii Bucuresti. Limbi Romanice†
0068-3248 Analele Universitatii Bucuresti. Limbi Slave†
0068-3256 Analele Universitatii Bucuresti. Limba si Literatura Romana†
0068-3264 Analele Universitatii Bucuresti. Literatura Universala si Comparata†
0068-3272 Analele Universitatii Bucuresti. Matematica-Mecanica†
0068-3280 Analele Universitatii Bucuresti. Pedagogie†
0068-3299 Analele Universitatii Bucuresti. Psihologie†
0068-3302 Analele Universitatii Bucuresti. Sociologie†
0068-3310 Analele Universitatii Bucuresti. Stiinte Juridice†
0068-3329 Acta Botanica Horti Bucurestiensis
0068-3337 Budapest Varostorteneti Monografiai
0068-3345 Buddhist Publication Society. Report†
0068-3361 Buecherei des Augenarztes
0068-337X Buecherei des Frauenarztes
0068-3388 Buecherei des Orthopaeden
0068-3396 Ein Buechertagebuch
0068-340X Buenos Aires. Centro de Investigacion de Biologia Marina. Contribucion Cientificia
0068-3418 Buenos Aires. Instituto de Fitotecnia. Boletin Informativo
0068-3485 Universidad del Salvador. Anales
0068-3493 Universidad de Buenos Aires Instituto Bibliotecologico. Publicacion
0068-3507 B and C J Directory
0068-3523 Building Board Directory
0068-3531 Building Construction Cost Data
0068-354X Great Britain. Building Research Establishment. Annual Report
0068-3566 Building Societies. Year Book
0068-3612 National Free Library of Rhodesia. Annual Report *changed to* National Free Library Service. Annual Report
0068-3620 Bulgarska Akademiia na Naukite. Arkheologicheski Institut Izvestiia
0068-3639 Astronomicheski Kalendar na Observatoriiata v Sofia
0068-3655 Bulgarska Akademiia na Naukite. Botanicheski Institut. Izvestiia
0068-3671 Bulgarska Akademiia na Naukite. Tsentralna Biblioteka. Izvestiia
0068-3701 Bulgarska Akademiia na Naukite, Sofia. Tsentralnata Laboratoriia po Geodeziia. Izvestiia *changed to* Geodesy
0068-371X Bulgarska Akademiia na Naukite. Tsentralna Khelmintologichna Laboratoriia. Izvestiia
0068-3736 Bulgarska Akademiia na Naukite. Geofizichni Institut. Izvestiia
0068-3744 Bulgarska Akademiia na Naukite. Geografski Institut. Izvestiia
0068-3779 Bulgarska Akademiia na Naukite. Institut za Istoriia. Izvestiia
0068-3787 Bulgarska Akademiia na Naukite. Institut za Bulgarski Ezik. Izvestiia
0068-3817 Bulgarska Akademiia na Naukite. Institut po Morfologiia. Izvestiia
0068-3841 Bulgarska Akademiia na Naukite, Institut po Obshta i Sravnitelna Patalogiia. Izvestiia
0068-385X Bulgarska Akademiia na Naukite. Institut po Tekhnicheska Kibernetika. Izvestiia
0068-3876 Bulgarska Akademiia na Naukite. Institut po Khidrologiia i Meteorologiia. Izvestiia
0068-3884 Bulgarska Akademiia na Naukite. Institut za Pravni Nauki. Izvestiia
0068-3949 Bulgarian Academy of Sciences, Sofia. Mathematical Institute. Bulletin†
0068-3957 Bulgarska Akademiia na Naukite. Mikrobiologichni Institut. Izvestiia
0068-3965 Bulgarska Akademiia na Naukite. Institut za Muzikoznanie. Izvestiia
0068-3973 Bulgarska Akademiia na Naukite. Institut po Filosofiia. Izvestiia
0068-3981 Bulgarska Akademiia na Naukite, Sofia. Zoologicheski Institut S Muzei. Izvestiia *changed to* Acta Zoologica Bulgarica
0068-4007 Institut de Recherches Agronomiques Tropicales et des Cultures Vivrieres. Bulletin Agronomique†
0068-4015 Bulletin d'Archeologie Marocaine

0068-4023 Bulletin de Philosophie Medievale
0068-4031 Bulletin des Jeunes Romanistes
0068-4058 Bulletin d'Histoire Economique et Sociale de la Revolution Francaise
0068-4066 Bulletin Linguistique et Ethnologique
0068-4090 Bulletin of Sugar Beet Research. Supplement
0068-4104 Bulletin of Suicidology†
0068-4112 Bulletin of Suicidology. Supplements†
0068-4120 Bulletin of the European Communities. Supplement
0068-4139 Bulletin of Thermodynamics and Thermochemistry *see* 0149-2268
0068-4155 Bulletin Socialiste *changed to* Le Poing et la Rose
0068-4171 Institut National des Industries Extractives. Bulletin Technique: Securite et Salubrite†
0068-4201 Bullinger's Postal and Shippers Guide for the United States and Canada
0068-421X Bundesanstalt fuer Pflanzenbau und Samenpruefung, Vienna. Jahrbuch
0068-4236 Bureau International de l'Heure. Rapport Annuel
0068-4287 Burt Franklin American Classics in History and Social Sciences
0068-4295 Burt Franklin Art History and Art Reference Series
0068-4309 Burt Franklin Bibliography and Reference Series
0068-4317 Burt Franklin Essays in History, Economics, and Social Sciences
0068-4325 Burt Franklin Essays in Literature and Criticism
0068-4333 Monographs in Philosophy and Religious History
0068-4341 Burt Franklin Research and Source Works Series
0068-4376 Buses Annual
0068-4384 Business Almanac Series
0068-4392 West Virginia University. Business and Economic Studies
0068-4406 Business Blue-Book of Southern Africa *changed to* Blue-Book of S.A. Business
0068-4414 Business Education Index
0068-4430 University of New Mexico. Bureau of Business and Economic Research. Business Information Series
0068-4449 Business Monitor: Miscellaneous Series. M2 Cinemas
0068-4457 Business Monitor: Miscellaneous Series. M3 Company Finance
0068-4465 Business Monitor: Miscellaneous Series. M4 Overseas Transactions
0068-449X Business Science Monographs
0068-4503 Business Who's Who of Australia
0068-452X Butterworths Tax Handbook *changed to* Butterworths Yellow Tax Handbook
0068-4562 Buying and Selling United States Coins
0068-4570 Bydgoskie Towarzystwo Naukowe. Wydzial Nauk Humanistycznych. Prace. Seria B (Jezyk i Literatura)
0068-4589 Bydgoskie Towarzystwo Naukowe. Wydzial Nauk Humanistycznych. Prace. Seria C (Historia i Archeologia)
0068-4597 Bydgoskie Towarzystwo Naukowe. Wydzial Nauk Technicznych. Prace. Seria Z: (Prace Zbiorowe)
0068-4600 Byers National Industrial Directory
0068-4635 Muzeum Gornoslaskie w Bytomiu. Rocznik. Seria Archeologia
0068-4643 Muzeum Gornoslaskie w Bytomiu. Rocznik. Seria Etnografia
0068-4651 Muzeum Gornoslaskie w Bytomiu. Rocznik. Seria Historia
0068-466X Muzeum Gornoslaskie w Bytomiu. Rocznik. Seria Przyroda
0068-4678 Muzeum Gornoslaskie w Bytomiu. Rocznik. Seria Sztuka
0068-4694 C A T V and Station Coverage Atlas and 35-Mile Zone Maps *changed to* Cable and Station Coverage Atlas and 35-Mile Zone Maps
0068-4708 C. C. Williamson Memorial Lecture
0068-4716 C E Cost Guide *changed to* Engelsman's General Construction Cost Guide
0068-4775 Cadastro Brasileiro de Materias-Primas Farmaceuticas, Por Produto, Por Fabricante
0068-4791 Centre de Geomorphologie, Caen. Bulletin
0068-4805 Universita degli Studi di Cagliari. Istituto di Storia Medioevale. Publicazioni
0068-4813 Economies et Societes. Serie F. Developpement, Croissance, Progres des Pays en Voie de Developpement
0068-4821 Economies et Societes. Serie AB. Economie du Travail
0068-483X Economies et Societes. Serie G. Economie Planifiee
0068-4848 Economies et Societes. Serie L. Economie Regionale†
0068-4856 Economies et Societes. Serie S. Etudes de Marxologie
0068-4864 Economies et Societes. Serie AF. Histoire Quantitative de l'Economie Francaise
0068-4872 Economies et Societies. Serie T. Information - Recherche Innovation
0068-4880 Economies et Societes. Serie M. Philosophie - Sciences Sociales Economie
0068-4899 Economies et Societes. Serie AG. Progres et Agriculture
0068-4902 Economies et Societes. Serie P. Relations Economiques Internationales
0068-4953 Cahiers Bretons
0068-4961 Cahiers Canadiens Claudel
0068-4996 Cahiers d'Allemand; Revue de Linguistique et de Pedagogie
0068-5011 Cahiers de Civilisation Medievale. Supplement
0068-5038 Cahiers de la Quatrieme Internationale
0068-5054 Cahiers de Micropaleontologie
0068-5070 Cahiers de Psychomecanique de Langage
0068-5089 Cahiers de Saint-Michel de Cuxa
0068-5097 Cahiers de Sciences Sociales
0068-5119 Cahiers des Universites Francaises
0068-5143 Cahiers du Pacifique *see* 0180-9954
0068-5151 Cahiers du Tourisme
0068-516X Cahiers Ferdinand de Saussure
0068-5194 Cahiers Nepalais
0068-5208 Cahiers O.R.S.T.O.M. Serie Biologie
0068-5224 Cahiers Rouge. Nouvelle Serie Internationale
0068-5259 Cain
0068-5267 Cairngorm Club Journal
0068-5275 Egyptian National Museum. Library. Catalogue
0068-5283 Societe d'Archeologie Copte. Bibliotheque de Manuscrits
0068-5291 Societe d'Archeologie Copte. Bulletin
0068-5305 Societe d'Archeologie Copte. Textes et Documents
0068-5313 University of Cairo. Herbarium. Publications
0068-5356 Calcutta Management Association. Annual Report
0068-5364 Calcutta Research Series†
0068-5372 School of Tropical Medicine, Calcutta. Bulletin
0068-5380 University of Calcutta. Centre of Advanced Study in Ancient Indian History and Culture. Lectures
0068-5399 University of Calcutta. Centre of Advanced Study in Ancient Indian History and Culture. Proceedings of Seminars
0068-5410 Calendars of American Literary Manuscripts†
0068-5437 University of Calgary. Archaeological Association. Paleo-Environmental Workshop. Proceedings
0068-5453 Universidad del Valle Biblioteca. Publicaciones *changed to* Universidad del Valle. Departamento de Biliotecas. Boletin de Adquisiciones
0068-5461 California Academy of Sciences. Occasional Papers
0068-547X California Academy of Sciences. Proceedings
0068-5488 California. Administrative Office of the California Courts. Annual Report
0068-5496 California. Air Resources Board. Annual Report
0068-5518 Preservation, Organization and Display of State of California's Historic Documents: Report to the California State Legislature†
0068-5526 Annotated Bibliography of Research in Economically Important Species of California Fish and Game. Supplement†
0068-5542 California Design
0068-5550 California. Department of Parks and Recreation. Archaeological Report *changed to* California Archaeological Reports
0068-5569 California. Department of Forestry. Range Improvement Studies
0068-5577 California. Department of Forestry. State Forest Notes
0068-5585 California Environmental Law: A Guide†
0068-5607 California Government Notes†
0068-5615 California Handbook
0068-5631 California Insect Survey. Bulletin
0068-564X California Institute of International Studies. Report *see* 0090-7103
0068-5658 California Institute of Technology. Division of Engineering and Applied Science. Report of Research and Other Activities *changed to* California Institute of Technology. Division of Engineering and Applied Science. Annual Report
0068-5682 U.S. National Aeronautics and Space Administration. Jet Propulsion Laboratory. Technical Memorandum†
0068-5739 California Manufacturers Register
0068-5755 California Natural History Guides
0068-5763 California Newspaper Directory *changed to* California Newspaper Publishers' Association. Directory and Rate Book
0068-5771 California Public School Directory
0068-5798 California Slavic Studies
0068-5801 California. State Board of Equalization. Annual Report
0068-581X Taxable Sales in California (Sales and Use Tax)
0068-5836 San Diego State University. Bureau of Business and Economic Research. Monographs
0068-5844 San Diego State University. Bureau of Business and Economic Research. Research Studies and Position Papers
0068-5860 San Francisco State University. Audio-Visual Center. Media Catalog
0068-5879 California County Law Library Basic List
0068-5887 California Transportation and Public Works Conference. Proceedings
0068-5895 California Studies in Classical Antiquity
0068-5909 California Studies in the History of Art
0068-5917 California Studies in Urbanization and Environmental Design†
0068-5933 University of California, Berkeley. Archaeological Research Facility. Contributions
0068-5968 University of California, Berkeley. Center for Real Estate and Urban Economics. Reprint Series
0068-5976 University of California, Berkeley. Center for Real Estate and Urban Economics. Research Report
0068-5984 University of California, Berkeley. Center for Real Estate and Urban Economics. Special Report
0068-5992 University of California, Berkeley. Center for Real Estate and Urban Economics. Technical Report
0068-600X University of California. Center for South and Southeast Asia Studies. Occasional Papers
0068-6018 University of California. Center for South and Southeast Asia Studies. Research Monograph Series
0068-6069 I B E R Special Publications
0068-6077 University of California. Institute of Business and Economic Research. Publications
0068-6085 University of California, Berkeley. Institute of Human Development. Annual Report
0068-6093 University of California, Berkeley. Institute of International Studies. Research Series
0068-6115 University of California, Berkeley. Institute of Transportation Studies. Library References
0068-6123 University of California. Institute of Transportation Studies. Selected List of Recent Acquisitions of the Transportation Library
0068-6131 University of California, Irvine. Center for Pathobiology. Miscellaneous Publications
0068-614X University of California, Irvine. Museum of Systematic Biology. Research Series
0068-6158 University of California, San Diego. Institute of Marine Resources. Annual Report *changed to* University of California, San Diego. Institute of Marine Resources. Biennial Report.
0068-6166 University of California, Santa Barbara. Library. Annual Report†
0068-6174 University of California, Berkeley. School of Criminology. San Francisco Project. Research Report
0068-6182 University of California, Los Angeles. Institute of Archaeology. Archaeological Survey. Annual Report†
0068-6190 University of California, Los Angeles. African Studies Center. Occasional Paper
0068-6204 University of California, Los Angeles. Institute of Archaeology. Archaeological Survey. Special Monograph Series *changed to* University of California, Los Angeles. Institute of Archaeology. Monograph Series
0068-6212 University of California, Los Angeles. Biotechnology Laboratory. Progress Report†
0068-6220 University of California, Los Angeles. Center for Medieval and Renaissance Studies. Publications
0068-6239 University of California, Los Angeles. Center for Medieval and Renaissance Studies. Contributions
0068-6247 University of California, Los Angeles. Center for the Study of Comparative Folklore and Mythology. Publications
0068-6255 University of California, Los Angeles. Institute of Industrial Relations. Monograph Series
0068-6263 University of California, Los Angeles. Latin American Center. Reference Series
0068-628X University of California, Los Angeles. Museum of Cultural History. Occasional Papers
0068-6298 University of California, Davis. Water Resources Center. Annual Report
0068-6301 University of California, Davis. Water Resources Center. Contributions
0068-631X University of California Engineering and Physical Sciences Extension Series
0068-6336 University of California Publications. Anthropological Records
0068-6344 University of California Publications. Classical Studies

0068-6352 University of California Publications. English Studies†
0068-6360 University of California Publications. Folklore Studies *changed to* University of California Publications. Folklore & Mythology Studies
0068-6379 University of California Publications in Anthropology
0068-6387 University of California Publications in Automatic Computation†
0068-6387 University of California Publications in Automatic Computation†
0068-6395 University of California Publications in Botany
0068-6409 University of California Publications in Contemporary Music
0068-6417 University of California Publications in Entomology
0068-6433 University of California Publications in Egyptian Archaeology†
0068-6441 University of California Publications in Geography
0068-645X University of California Publications in Geological Sciences
0068-6468 University of California Publications in History†
0068-6476 University of California Publications in Librarianship
0068-6484 University of California Publications in Linguistics
0068-6492 University of California Publications in Modern Philology
0068-6506 University of California Publications in Zoology
0068-6514 University of California Publications. Near Eastern Studies
0068-6522 University of California Publications. Occasional Papers
0068-6530 Californians in Congress
0068-6549 Calwer Hefte†
0068-6557 Calwer Predigthilfen *changed to* Neue Calwer Predigthilfen
0068-659X Cambridge Air Surveys
0068-6603 Cambridge Authors' and Printers' Guides *changed to* Cambridge Authors' and Publishers' Guides
0068-6611 Cambridge Bibliographical Society. Transactions
0068-662X Cambridge Bibliographical Society. Transactions. Monograph Supplements
0068-6638 Cambridge Classical Texts and Commentaries
0068-6654 Cambridge Geographical Studies
0068-6689 Cambridge Latin American Studies
0068-6697 Cambridge Monographs in Experimental Biology
0068-6719 Cambridge Papers in Social Anthropology
0068-6727 Cambridge Papers in Sociology
0068-6735 Cambridge Philological Society. Proceedings
0068-6743 Cambridge Philological Society. Proceedings. Supplement
0068-6751 Cambridge Studies in International and Comparative Law
0068-676X Cambridge Studies in Linguistics
0068-6786 Cambridge Studies in Medieval Life and Thought. Third Series
0068-6794 Cambridge Studies in Social Anthropology
0068-6808 Cambridge Studies in Sociology
0068-6816 Cambridge Texts and Studies in the History of Education
0068-6824 Cambridge Tracts in Mathematics and Mathematical Physics *changed to* Cambridge Tracts in Mathematics
0068-6832 Cambridge University. Department of Applied Economics. Monographs
0068-6840 Cambridge University. Department of Applied Economics. Occasional Papers
0068-6883 Cambridge University. Institute of Criminology. Bibliographical Series
0068-6891 Cambridge University. Oriental Publications
0068-6905 Camden Fourth Series
0068-6913 Camper's Digest
0068-693X Campground Guide for Tent and Trailer Tourists†
0068-6948 Camping Caravanning and Sports Equipment Trades Directory
0068-6956 Camping Club of Great Britain and Ireland. Year Book with List of Camp Sites *changed to* Camping Club Handbook and Sites List
0068-6964 Camping Guide
0068-6980 Camping Sites in Britain and France *changed to* Practical Camper's Sites Guide
0068-7014 Can Manufacturers Institute. Annual Metal Cans Shipment Report
0068-7057 Canada. Statistics Canada. Aviation Statistics Centre. Service Bulletin/Bulletin de Service du Centre des Statistiques de l'Aviation
0068-7065 Canada. Grain Commission. Marketings, Distribution and Visible Carry-over of Canadian Grain in and Through Licensed Elevators *see* 0380-8718
0068-7073 Canada. Statistics Canada. Aggregate Productivity Trends/Tendances de la Productivite des Agregats *see* 0317-7882
0068-7103 Canada. Statistics Canada. Crude Petroleum and Natural Gas Industry/Industrie du Petrole Brut et du Gaz Naturel
0068-7111 Canada. Statistics Canada. Dairy Statistics/Statistique Laitiere†
0068-712X Canada. Statistics Canada. Farm Net Income/Revenu Net Agricole
0068-7138 Canada. Statistics Canada. Placer Gold Mines, Gold Quartz Mines and Copper-Gold-Silver Mines/Placers d'Or Mines de Quartz Aurifere et Mines de Cuivre-Or-Argent *see* 0380-4968
0068-7146 Canada. Statistics Canada. Index of Farm Production/Indice de la Production Agricole
0068-7154 Canada. Statistics Canada. Livestock and Animal Products Statistics/Statistique du Betail et des Produits Animaux
0068-7162 Canada. Statistics Canada. Petroleum Refineries/Raffineries de Petrole
0068-7189 Canada. Statistics Canada. Production of Poultry and Eggs/Production de Volaille et Oeufs
0068-7200 Canada. Statistics Canada. Retail Trade/Commerce de Detail†
0068-7227 Canada. Statistics Canada. Survey of Production/Releve de la Production
0068-7251 Canada Commerce
0068-7278 Canada. Department of Agriculture. Analytical Chemistry Research Service. Research Report†
0068-7286 Canada. Agriculture Canada. Economics Branch. Trade in Agricultural Products
0068-7294 Canada. Department of Agriculture. Engineering Research Service, Ottawa. Research Report *changed to* Canada. Department of Agriculture. Engineering & Statistical Research Institute, Ottawa. Research Report
0068-7308 Canada. Agriculture Canada. Food Research Institute, Ottawa. Research Report
0068-7316 Canada. Agriculture Canada. Health of Animals Branch. Bovine Tuberculosis and Brucell0sis
0068-7324 Canada. Agriculture Canada. Livestock Market Review
0068-7340 Canada. Agriculture Canada Publications
0068-7375 Canada. Fisheries and Environment Canada. Annual Report
0068-7383 Canada. Department of Insurance. Report. Co-Operative Credit Associations
0068-7391 Canada. Department of Insurance. Report. Trust and Loan Companies
0068-7405 Canada. Department of Insurance. Report of the Superintendent of Insurance
0068-7413 Canada. Department of Insurance. Report. Small Loans Companies and Money-Lenders
0068-743X Canada. Labour Canada. Wage Rates, Salaries and Hours of Labour
0068-7448 Canada. Women's Bureau. Women in the Labour Force: Facts and Figures
0068-7456 Canada. Department of National Health and Welfare. Annual Report
0068-7472 Canada. Agriculture Canada. Research Station, Melfort, Saskatchewan. Research Highlights. Annual Publications
0068-7480 Canada. Experimental Farm, St. John's West, Newfoundland. Research Report
0068-7499 Canada. Fisheries & Marine Service Annual. *changed to* Canada. Fisheries Research Board Annual
0068-7510 Canada. Fisheries and Marine Service. Biological Station, St. Andrews, New Brunswick. General Series Circular
0068-7537 Canada. Fisheries and Marine Service Bulletin Series.
0068-7545 Canada. Fisheries and Marine Service Review.†
0068-7553 Canada. Fisheries and Marine Service. Technical Report Series
0068-7561 Canada. Forest Fire Research Institute. Bibliography. Supplement
0068-757X Canada. Forest Fire Research Institute. Information Report (FF-X)
0068-7588 Canada. Department of the Environment. Forest Insect and Disease Survey. Annual Report *see* 0226-9759
0068-7626 Canada. Geological Survey. Bulletin
0068-7634 Canada. Geological Survey. Memoir
0068-7642 Canada. Geological Survey. Miscellaneous Report
0068-7650 Canada. Geological Survey. Paper
0068-7669 Canada. Hydrographic Service. Water Levels
0068-7677 Canada in the Atlantic Economy
0068-7685 Canada in World Affairs
0068-7693 Canada Land Inventory. Report
0068-7715 Canada. Atmospheric Environment Service. Climatological Studies
0068-7723 Canada. Atmospheric Environment Service. Ice Observations: Canadian Arctic†
0068-7731 Canada. Atmospheric Environment Service. Ice Observations: Canadian Inland Waterways†
0068-774X Canada. Atmospheric Environment Service. Ice Observations: Eastern Canadian Seaboard†
0068-7758 Canada. Atmospheric Environment Service. Ice Summary and Analysis, Canadian Arctic
0068-7766 Canada. Atmospheric Environment Service. Ice Summary and Analysis, Eastern Canadian Seaboard
0068-7774 Canada. Atmospheric Environment Service. Ice Summary and Analysis, Hudson Bay and Approaches
0068-7782 Canada. Atmospheric Environment Service. Meteorological Translations
0068-7790 Canada. Atmospheric Environment Service. Snow Cover Data. Canada
0068-7804 Canada. Atmospheric Environment Service. Technical Memoranda
0068-7812 Canada. Mineral Resources Branch. Mineral Information Bulletin. *changed to* Canada. Mineral Policy Sector. Mineral Information Bulletin
0068-7820 Canada. Mineral Resources Branch. Mineral Report *changed to* Canada. Mineral Policy Sector. Mineral Report.
0068-7839 Canada. Mineral Resources Branch. Mineral Survey *changed to* Canada. Mineral Policy Sector. Mineral Survey
0068-7847 Canada. Mines Branch. Information Circular†
0068-7847 Canada. Centre for Mineral and Energy Technology. Information Circular†
0068-7863 Canada. Department of Energy, Mines and Resources. Monographs†
0068-7871 Canada. Mines Branch. Research Report *changed to* Canada. Centre for Mineral and Energy Technology. Technology Series Reports
0068-7898 Canada. Committee on Pesticide Use in Agriculture. Pesticide Research Report
0068-7901 Canada. National Energy Board. Annual Report
0068-791X Canada. National Energy Board. Staff Papers
0068-7928 Canada. National Harbours Board. Annual Report *changed to* Canada. National Harbours Board. Port Directory
0068-7987 Canada. National Museums, Ottawa. Publications in Botany
0068-7995 Canada. National Museums, Ottawa. Publications in Biological Oceanography
0068-8002 Canada. National Museums, Ottawa. Publications in Ethnology†
0068-8010 Canada. National Museums, Ottawa. Publications in History†
0068-8037 Canada. National Museums, Ottawa. Publications in Zoology
0068-8061 Canada. Oceanographic Data Centre. Data Record Series†
0068-807X Canada. Research Institute, London, Ontario. Research Report *changed to* Canada. Agriculture Canada. Research Institute. Research Branch Report
0068-8088 Canada. Public Archives. Register of Post Graduate Dissertations in Progress in History and Related Subjects
0068-8096 Canada. Agriculture Canada. Research Station, Beaverlodge, Alberta. Research Report *changed to* Canada. Agriculture Canada. Research Branch. Annual Report
0068-8134 Canada Who's Who of the Poultry Industry
0068-8142 Canada Yearbook†
0068-8150 Canada's Meat Industry
0068-8185 Canadian Agricultural Insect Pest Review
0068-8193 Canadian Almanac and Directory
0068-8207 Canadian Alpine Journal
0068-8215 Canadian Annual Review *see* 0315-1433
0068-8231 Canadian Architecture Yearbook *changed to* Canadian Architect Yearbook
0068-824X Canadian Archivist *see* 0318-6954
0068-8258 C.A.R. Scope
0068-8274 C A A E Annual Report
0068-8312 Canadian Association of Geographers. Newsletter *changed to* Canadian Association of Geographers. Directory
0068-8320 Canadian Association of Management Consultants. Annual Report
0068-8339 Canadian Association of Physicists. Annual Report
0068-8347 Canadian Bankruptcy Reports
0068-8398 Canadian Books in Print
0068-8401 C B C Engineering Review
0068-841X Canadian Building Series
0068-8428 Canadian Bureau for International Education. Bulletin *see* 0319-7778
0068-8436 Canadian Cancer Research Conference. Proceedings†
0068-8444 Canadian Ceramic Society. Journal
0068-8452 Canadian Chemical, Pharmaceutical and Product Directory
0068-8487 Canadian Conference of the Arts. Miscellaneous Reports
0068-8495 Canadian Conference on Research in the Rheumatic Diseases. Proceedings†

0068-8509 Canadian Conference on Social Welfare. Proceedings/Compte Rendu *changed to* Canadian Conference on Social Development. Proceedings/Compte Rendu
0068-8517 Canadian Conference on Uranium and Atomic Energy. Proceedings *see* 0706-1293
0068-8525 Canadian Controls & Instrumentation Control/Instrumentation Buyers' Guide *changed to* Canadian Controls & Instruments Control/Instruments Buyers' Guide
0068-855X Canadian Correspondence Courses for University Credit
0068-8584 Canadian Council on Social Development. Annual Report/Rapport Annuel
0068-8622 Canadian Dental Association. Directory
0068-8630 Canadian Dental Association. Transactions
0068-8649 Canadian Depreciation Guide
0068-8657 C E A Handbook
0068-8665 Canadian Engineering & Industrial Year Book
0068-8681 Canadian Federation of Biological Societies. Canadian Federation News of the Annual Meeting
0068-869X Canadian Federation of Biological Societies. Proceedings *changed to* Canadian Federation of Biological Societies. Programme and Proceedings of the Annual Meeting
0068-8703 Canadian Federation of Biological Societies. Programme of the Annual Meeting *changed to* Canadian Federation of Biological Societies. Programme and Proceedings of the Annual Meeting
0068-8711 Canadian Federation and Municipalities. Annual Conference and Proceedings *see* 0708-9511
0068-872X Canadian Filmography Series†
0068-8746 Canadian Folk Music Journal
0068-8754 Canadian Food and Packaging Directory
0068-8762 Canadian Footwear & Leather Directory
0068-8770 Canadian Fruit Wholesalers' Association. Yearbook
0068-8789 Canadian Furniture & Furnishings Directory
0068-8797 Canadian Gas Association. Manufacturers' Section. Manufacturers Directory
0068-8800 Canadian Gas Association. Statistical Summary of the Canadian Gas Industry
0068-8819 Canadian Geophysical Bulletin
0068-8827 Canadian Good Roads Associations. Annual Conference Proceedings *see* 0703-7090
0068-8835 Canadian Government Series
0068-8843 Canadian Gunner
0068-8851 Canadian Heart Foundation. Annual Report
0068-886X Canadian Historical Association. Historical Booklets. Brochures Historiques
0068-8878 Canadian Historical Association. Historical Papers
0068-8908 Canadian Horticultural Council. Annual Meeting Reports
0068-8916 Canadian Horticultural Council. Committee on Horticultural Research. Annual Reports
0068-8932 Canadian Hospital Directory
0068-8940 Canadian Housing Statistics
0068-8967 Canadian Industry Shows and Exhibitions
0068-8975 Canadian Institute of Actuaries. Yearbook
0068-8983 C I C A Handbook
0068-8991 Canandian Institute of Forestry. Annual Report *issued with* 0015-7546
0068-8991 Canadian Institute of Forestry. Annual Report
0068-9009 C. I. M. Directory
0068-9025 Canadian Insurance. Annual Statistical Issue
0068-9033 Canadian Insurance Law Bulletin Service
0068-9041 Canadian Jewellery & Giftware Directory
0068-905X Canadian Labour Terms
0068-9068 Canadian Library Association. Annual Reports†
0068-9092 Canadian Library Association. Occasional Papers
0068-9106 Canadian Library Association. Proceedings†
0068-9130 C L A Organization Handbook and Membership List *changed to* C L A Directory
0068-9157 Canadian Life Insurance Facts
0068-9165 Canadian Local Histories to 1950. A Bibliography. Histoires Locales et Regionales Canadiennes des Origines A 1950
0068-919X Canadian Mathematical Congress. Proceedings†
0068-9203 Canadian Medical Directory
0068-9211 Canadian Mental Health Association. Annual Report
0068-9246 Canadian Meteorological Memoirs
0068-9254 Canadian Meteorological Society. Annual Congress
0068-9270 Canadian Minerals Yearbook
0068-9289 Canadian Mines Handbook
0068-9297 Canadian Mines Register of Dormant and Defunct Companies
0068-9300 Canadian Mines Register of Dormant and Defunct Companies. Supplement
0068-9319 Canadian Mining Manual *see* 0315-9140
0068-9335 Canadian Music Industry Directory
0068-9378 Canadian National Institute for the Blind. National Annual Report
0068-9386 Canadian Nurses Association. Biennial Meeting. Folio of Reports
0068-9394 Canadian Oil Register
0068-9424 Canadian Paraplegic Association. Annual Report
0068-9440 Canadian Phytopathological Society. Proceedings
0068-9459 Canadian Plastics Directory and Buyer's Guide
0068-9467 Canadian Ports and Seaways Directory
0068-9491 Canadian Pulp and Paper Association. Newsprint Data.
0068-9505 Canadian Pulp and Paper Association. Pulp and Paper Report
0068-9521 Canadian Pulp and Paper Association. Technical Section. Proceedings
0068-9548 Canadian Pulp and Paper Association. Woodlands Section. Publications
0068-9556 Canada. Radio-Television Commission. Annual Report *changed to* Canada. Canadian Radio-Television and Telecommunications Commission. Annual Report
0068-9564 Canadian Real Estate Annual *changed to* Real Estate Development Annual
0068-9572 Canadian Red Cross Society. Annual Report
0068-9580 Canadian Rehabilitation Council for the Disabled. Annual Report
0068-9610 Canadian Seed Growers Association. Annual Report
0068-9629 Automotive Service Data Book
0068-9637 Canadian Skater
0068-9645 Canadian Society for Education through Art. Annual Journal
0068-9653 Canadian Society for Immunology. Bulletin
0068-9688 Canadian Society of Agronomy. Annual Meeting. Proceedings
0068-9696 Canadian Society of Animal Production. Proceedings
0068-970X Canadian Society of Biblical Studies. Bulletin
0068-9718 Canadian Society of Rural Extension. Meeting and Convention. Proceedings
0068-9734 Canadian Special Truck Equipment Manual
0068-9777 Canadian Studies in Criminology
0068-9793 Canadian Studies in History and Government
0068-9807 Canadian Studies in Sociology†
0068-9815 Canadian Tax Foundation. Annual Report†
0068-9823 Canadian Tax Foundation. Provincial Finances *see* 0317-946X
0068-984X Canadian Technical Asphalt Association. Proceedings of the Annual Conference
0068-9858 Canadian Textile Directory
0068-9874 Canadian Theses
0068-9882 Canadian Tide and Current Tables
0068-9890 Canadian Toy Fair. Trade Show Directory *see* 0317-9443
0068-9904 Canadian Trade Index
0068-9912 Canada. Transport Commission. Annual Report
0068-9939 Canadian Tuberculosis and Respiratory Disease Association. Annual Report *changed to* Canadian Lung Association. Bulletin
0068-9955 Canadian Variety & Merchandise Directory
0068-9963 Who's Who, The Canadian *changed to* Canadian Who's Who
0069-0015 Canadian Wildlife Service. Monograph Series
0069-0023 Canadian Wildlife Service. Progress Notes
0069-0031 Canadian Wildlife Service. Report Series
0069-0058 Canadian Yearbook of International Law
0069-0066 Canals Book
0069-0082 Australia. National Library. Annual Report of the Council
0069-0104 Canberra Papers on Strategy and Defense†
0069-0147 Cancer Facts and Figures
0069-0155 Cancer Incidence in Sweden
0069-0163 Cancer Institute, Tokyo. Selected Papers†
0069-0171 Cancer Seminar Proceedings
0069-018X Canned Food Pack Statistics
0069-0198 Canterbury Archaeological Society. Occasional Papers
0069-0201 Canterbury Engineering Journal
0069-021X Cape Cod Compass†
0069-0228 University of Cape Town. Department of Gynaecology. Annual Report *changed to* University of Cape Town. Department of Obstetrics and Gynaecology. Annual Report
0069-0244 Capuchin Annual†
0069-0260 Car and Driver Yearbook *changed to* Car and Driver Buyers Guide
0069-0295 Caravan Manual and Tourist Park Guide
0069-0309 Caravan Sites and Mobile Home Parks *changed to* Caravan Sites
0069-0317 Caravan & Chalet Sites Guide
0069-0333 Caravan Yearbook *changed to* Caravan Factfinder
0069-035X Cardiff Medical Society. Scientific Proceedings†
0069-0368 Cardinal O'Hara Series†
0069-0384 Cardiovascular Clinics
0069-0392 Cardiovascular Review; a Medical World News Publication†
0069-0406 Cardiovascular Surgery
0069-0422 Careers for School Leavers
0069-0430 Careers in Banking, Insurance, Finance†
0069-0449 Careers in Depth
0069-0457 Caribbean Conference Series
0069-0465 Caribbean Bibliography
0069-0473 Caribbean Documents
0069-0481 Caribbean Economic Almanac
0069-0503 Caribbean Islands Research Institute. Annual Report *changed to* Caribbean Research Institute. Report
0069-0511 Caribbean Monograph Series
0069-052X Caribbean Scholars' Conference. Proceedings
0069-0538 Caribbean Series
0069-0546 Caridad, Ciencia y Arte
0069-0554 Caritas Internationalis. International Yearbooks
0069-0562 Caritas Internationalis. Reports of General Assemblies
0069-0570 Caritas; Jahrbuch des Deutschen Caritasverbandes
0069-0597 Carl X Gustaf-Studier†
0069-0600 Carleton Mathematical Series
0069-0619 Carleton University, Ottawa. Department of Geology. Geological Papers
0069-0635 Carnegie Corporation of New York. Annual Report
0069-0643 Carnegie Endowment for International Peace in the 1970's
0069-0643 Carnegie Endowment for International Peace Report *see* 0069-0643
0069-0651 Carnegie Foundation for the Advancement of Teaching. Report
0069-066X Carnegie Institution of Washington. Year Book
0069-0686 Carnegie United Kingdom Trust. Annual Report
0069-0694 Carnet des Arts†
0069-0708 Carnival Glass Price Guide
0069-0724 Carolina Population Center. Monograph
0069-0732 Carotenoids Other Than Vitamin A
0069-0740 Carpet and Rug Institute. Directory and Report *changed to* Carpet and Rug Institute. Directory
0069-0767 Carpet Annual
0069-0783 Carson and Newman College, Jefferson City, Tennessee. Faculty Studies
0069-0805 Cartography
0069-0813 Carus Mathematical Monographs
0069-0821 Institut des Peches Maritimes. Bulletin
0069-0848 Case Studies in Library Science†
0069-0872 Cases Decided in the Court of Claims of the United States
0069-0880 Cass Library of African Studies. Africana Modern Library
0069-0899 Cass Library of African Studies. General Studies
0069-0902 Cass Library of African Studies. Researches and Travels
0069-0910 Cass Library of African Studies. South African Studies
0069-0929 Cass Library of African Studies. Travels and Narratives
0069-0937 Cass Library of Industrial Classics
0069-0945 Cass Library of Science Classics
0069-0961 Cassal Bequest Lectures
0069-097X Cassell's Directory of Publishing in Great Britain, The Commonwealth, Ireland and South Africa *changed to* Cassell and Publishers Association Directory of Publishing in Great Britain, the Commonwealth, Ireland, South Africa and Pakistan
0069-0988 Castle's Guide to the Fruit, Flower, Vegetable and Allied Trades
0069-0996 Castle's Town and County Trades Directory
0069-1003 Cat Fanciers Association. Year Book
0069-102X Catalog of Modern World Coins
0069-1038 Catalog of Selected Films for Mental Health Education *changed to* Mental Health Media Center Film Catalog
0069-1046 Catalogo de Publicaciones Latinoamericanas Sobre Formacion Profesional
0069-1054 Catalogo dei Libri Italiani in Commercio *changed to* Catalogo dei Libri in Commercio
0069-1062 Catalog of Reprints in Series†
0069-1089 Catalogue de l'Edition Francaise *changed to* Livres Disponibles
0069-1097 Catalogue des Catalogues Automobile
0069-1100 Catalogue des Produits Agrees Par Qualite-France
0069-1119 Catalogue General. Radio, Television, Electrophones, Magnetophones, Haute-Fidelite, Stereophonie, Audio-Visuel
0069-1135 Catalogue of Reproductions of Paintings Prior to 1860
0069-1143 Catalogue of Reproductions of Paintings, 1860-1973

0069-1151 Catalogue of Indian Chemical Plants *changed to* Guide to Indian Chemical Plants and Equipment
0069-116X Catalogus Musicus
0069-1178 Cataluna Exporta
0069-1186 Universita degli Studi di Cantania. Istituto di Storia delle Tradizioni Popolari. Studi e Testi
0069-1194 Catering & Hotel Management Year Book & Diary
0069-1208 Catholic Almanac
0069-1216 Catholic Central Union of America. Proceedings
0069-1224 Catholic Directory
0069-1232 Catholic Directory for the Clergy and Laity in Scotland *see* 0306-5677
0069-1240 Catholic Directory of Eastern Africa
0069-1267 Catholic Theological Society of America. Proceedings
0069-1291 Cavalcade and Directory of Fairs *see* 0361-4255
0069-1305 Cave Research Group of Great Britain. Transactions. *see* 0305-859X
0069-1313 Cave Studies
0069-1321 University of San Carlos. Series A: Humanities
0069-133X University of San Carlos. San Carlos Publications. Series B: Natural Sciences†
0069-1348 University of San Carlos. San Carlos Publications. Series C: Religion†
0069-1356 University of San Carlos. Series D: Occasional Monographs
0069-1372 Celebrity Service International Contact Book
0069-1399 Celtica
0069-1402 Cement Industry Technical Conference. Record
0069-1429 Census of Industrial Production in Zambia
0069-1437 Census of U.S. Civil Aircraft
0069-1445 Center for Inter-American Relations. Review
0069-1461 Centers of Civilization Series
0069-147X Central African Power Corporation. Annual Report and Accounts
0069-1488 Central Asiatic Studies†
0069-1496 Central Bank of Ceylon. Annual Report
0069-150X Central Bank of China, T'ai-Pei. Annual Report
0069-1518 Central Bank of Cyprus. Annual Report
0069-1526 Central Bank of Egypt. Board of Directors. Report *changed to* Central Bank of Egypt. Annual Report
0069-1534 Central Bank of Iraq, Baghdad. Report
0069-1542 Central Bank of Ireland. Report
0069-1550 Central Bank of Jordan. Annual Report
0069-1569 Central Bank of Kenya. Annual Report
0069-1577 Central Bank of Nigeria. Annual Report and Statement of Accounts
0069-1585 Central Bank of the Philippines. Annual Report
0069-1593 Central Bank of Trinidad and Tobago. Report
0069-1607 Central Conference of American Rabbis. Yearbook
0069-1615 Central Conference of Teamsters. Officers' Report
0069-1623 Central Electric Railfans' Association. Bulletin
0069-1631 Central Institute of Research and Training in Public Cooperation, New Delhi. Publications
0069-164X Central Literary Magazine
0069-1674 Central Naugatuck Valley Regional Planning Agency. Annual Report
0069-1690 Central Road Research Institute, New Delhi. Road Research Paper
0069-1704 Scandinavian Institute of Asian Studies. Annual Newsletter
0069-1712 Scandinavian Institute of Asian Studies. Monograph Series
0069-1720 Centre Culturel Francais, Algiers. Rencontres Culturelles
0069-1739 Centre Culturel International de Cerisy-La-Salle. Decades. Nouvelle Serie†
0069-1747 Centre de Cartographie Phytosociologique. Communications *changed to* Centre d'Ecologie Forestiere et Rurale. Communications
0069-1755 Centre International de Documentation et Sociale Africaine. Enquetes Bibliographiques
0069-1763 Centre International de Documentation Economique et Sociale Africaine. Monographies Documentaires
0069-1771 French-Canadian Civilization Research Center. Cahiers
0069-1798 France. Centre de Recherches sur les Zones Arides. Publications. Serie Geologie *changed to* Centre Geologique et Geophysique de Montpellier. Publications. Serie Geologie
0069-1801 Centre d'Ecologie Forestiere. Notes Techniques *changed to* Centre d'Ecologie Forestiere et Rurale. Notes Techniques. B: Herbageres
0069-1801 Centre d'Ecologie Forestiere. Notes Techniques *changed to* Centre d'Ecologie Forestiere et Rurale. Notes Techniques. A: Forestieres
0069-1836 Centre d'Etude du Sud-Est Asiatique et de l'Extreme-Orient. International Working Sessions. Proceedings†
0069-1844 Centre d'Etudes et de Documentation Europeennes. Cahiers. Annals
0069-1852 Centre d'Etudes Pratiques d'Informatique et d'Automatique. Collection†
0069-1879 Centre d'Information des Services Medicaux d'Entreprises et Interentreprises. Annuaire
0069-1895 Centre Europeen d'Etudes Burgondo-Medianes. Publication
0069-1909 C E L O S Bulletins†
0069-1917 Centre for Environmental Studies, London. Conference Paper
0069-1925 Centre for Environmental Studies, London. Information Paper
0069-1968 Centre National de Documentation Scientifique et Technique. Rapport d'Activite
0069-1976 Centre National de la Recherche Scientifique. Colloques Internationaux. Sciences Humaines
0069-1984 Centre National d'Archeologie et d'Histoire du Livre. Publication
0069-1992 Centre National de Recherches Archeologiques en Belgique. Repertoires Archeologiques. Serie A: Repertoires Bibliographiques
0069-200X Centre National de Recherches Archeologiques en Belgique. Repertoires Archeologiques. Serie B: Repertoires des Collections
0069-2018 Centre National de Recherches Archeologiques en Belgique. Repertoires Archeologiques. Serie C: Repertoires Divers
0069-2026 C R I C Rapport de Recherche
0069-2034 Centre National d'Etudes Spatiales. Rapport d'Activite
0069-2050 Centre Regional de Recherche et de Documentation Pedagogiques de Lyon. Annales.
0069-2069 Centre Regional de Documentation Pedagogique de Toulouse. Annales
0069-2077 Centres of Art and Civilization†
0069-2085 Centro Brasileiro de Pesquisas Fisicas. Monografias†
0069-2093 Centro Brasileiro de Pesquisas Fisicas. Notas Tecnicas†
0069-2107 Tropical Science Center, Costa Rica. Occasional Paper
0069-214X Centro de Investigaciones en Administracion Publica. Documentos de Trabajo *changed to* Centro de Estudios de Estado y Sociedad. Estudios Sociales
0069-214X Centro de Investigaciones en Administracion Publica. Documentos de Trabajo *changed to* Centro de Estudios de Estado y Sociedad. Documentos de Trabajo
0069-2166 Centro de Salud "Max Arias Schreiber", Lima. Congreso Nacional de Tuberculosis y Enfermedades Respiratorias
0069-2204 Centro Studi per la Magna Grecia, Naples. Pubblicazioni Proprie
0069-2212 Center for Agricultural Publishing and Documentation. Agricultural Research Reports
0069-2220 Ceramic Plants in Canada
0069-2239 Ceramics and Glass Series
0069-2247 Cercle d'Etudes Numismatiques. Travaux
0069-2255 Cerebral Vascular Diseases. Conference *see* 0146-6917
0069-2263 Ceredigion
0069-228X Ceskoslovenska Akademie Ved. Rozpravy. MPV: Rada Matematickych a Prirodnich Ved
0069-2298 Ceskoslovenska Akademie Ved. Rozpravy. SV: Rada Spolecenskych Ved
0069-2301 Ceskoslovenska Akademie Ved. Rozpravy. TV: Rada Technickych Ved
0069-231X Ceskoslovenska Gynekologie
0069-2328 Ceskoslovenska Pediatrie
0069-2336 Ceskoslovenska Psychiatrie
0069-2344 Ceskoslovenska Radiologie
0069-2352 Sri Lanka. Department of National Museums. Translations Series†
0069-2360 Sri Lanka Export Directory
0069-2379 Ceylon Journal of Science. Biological Sciences
0069-2387 Chain Shoe Stores and Leased Shoe Department Operators
0069-2395 Chain Store Age Supermarket Sales Manual
0069-2417 Chalmers Tekniska Hoegskola. Handlingar†
0069-2441 Survey of Local Chambers of Commerce
0069-245X Chamber of Mines of South Africa. Research Review†
0069-2476 Chambers Trades Register. Lancashire, Cheshire, and North Wales *see* 0309-5649
0069-2484 Chambers Trades Register. Midlands†
0069-2492 Chambers Trades Register of Scotland *see* 0309-5630
0069-2506 Chambers Trades Register. South Wales and South West England†
0069-2514 Chambers Trades Register. Yorkshire Northumberland and Durham†
0069-2522 Chambre de Commerce d'Agriculture et d'Industrie de Bamako, Mali. Annuaire Statistique *see* 0076-3411
0069-2530 Chambre de Commerce, d'Industrie et des Mines du Cameroun. Rapport Annuel
0069-2549 Chambre de Commerce et d'Industrie d'Alger. Centre d'Etudes Economiques. Publication†
0069-2557 Chambre de Commerce Franco-Asiatique. Annuaire des Membres
0069-2573 Chambre de Commerce Suedoise en France. Annuaire
0069-2581 Chambre Officielle Franco Allemande de Commerce et d'Industrie. Liste des Membres
0069-259X Chambre Syndicale des Mines de Fer de France. Rapport d'Activite
0069-2603 Chambre Syndicale Nationale des Entreprises et Industries de l'Hygiene Publique. Annuaire
0069-2611 Chambre des Ingenieurs-Conseils de France. Annuaire
0069-2646 Champlain Society, Toronto. Report
0069-2654 Chanakya Defence Annual
0069-2662 Chandler and Boatbuilder Trade Directory *see* 0306-3593
0069-2697 Charbonnages de France. Rapport *changed to* Charbonnages de France. Rapport d'Activite
0069-2727 Charles E. Merrill Monograph Series in the Humanities and Social Sciences
0069-2735 Charles F. Kettering Foundation. Annual Report
0069-2751 Charles W. Hunt Lecture
0069-276X Charles Warren Center for Studies in American History. Annual Report†
0069-2778 Chart
0069-2786 Charter
0069-2794 Chartered Insurance Institute, London. Journal *see* 0309-4928
0069-2808 Chartered Insurance Institute, London. Yearbook *see* 0309-4928
0069-2824 Checklists in the Humanities and Education
0069-2840 Chefs-d'Oeuvre de la Science-Fiction†
0069-2867 Chelates in Analytical Chemistry: A Collection of Monographs
0069-2875 ChemBooks†
0069-2883 Chemical Analysis
0069-2891 Chemical Buyers Guide
0069-2921 Chemical Engineering Progress. Reprint Manuals
0069-293X Chemical Engineering Progress. Safety in Air and Ammonia Plants *see* 0360-7011
0069-2948 Chemical Engineering Progress Symposium Series *see* 0065-8812
0069-2956 Chemical Engineering Progress. Technical Manuals
0069-2964 Chemical Guide to Europe†
0069-2972 Chemical Guide to the United States†
0069-2980 Chemical Industry Directory
0069-3022 Chemical Society, London. Annual Reports on the Progress of Chemistry. Section A: General, Physical and Inorganic Chemistry *see* 0308-6003
0069-3030 Chemical Society, London. Annual Reports on the Progress of Chemistry. Section B: Organic Chemistry
0069-3073 Chemie, Physik und Technologie der Kunststoffe in Einzeldarstellungen *changed to* Polymers-Properties and Applications
0069-3111 Chemistry and Biochemistry of Amino Acids, Peptides, and Proteins
0069-312X Chemistry and Industry Buyers' Guide
0069-3138 Chemistry and Physics of Carbon: A Series of Advances
0069-3146 Chemistry of Functional Groups
0069-3154 Chemistry of Heterocyclic Compounds
0069-3162 Chemistry of Natural Products
0069-3197 Chess Book List
0069-3219 Chiba University. Faculty of Horticulture. Transactions†
0069-3227 Chiba University. Faculty of Horticulture. Technical Bulletin
0069-3235 Art Institute of Chicago. Museum Studies
0069-3243 Chicago Buyers' Guide
0069-3251 Chicago, Cook County and Illinois Industrial Directory
0069-326X Chicago Crime Commission. Annual Report†
0069-3278 Chicago History of American Civilization
0069-3286 Chicago Lectures in Mathematics
0069-3294 Chicago Lectures in Physics
0069-3316 University of Chicago. Center for Health Administration Studies. Research Series†
0069-3324 University of Chicago. Center for Middle Eastern Studies. Publications†
0069-3332 University of Chicago. Center for Studies in Criminal Justice. Annual Report
0069-3340 University of Chicago. Department of Geography. Research Papers
0069-3359 University of Chicago. Graduate School of Business. Selected Papers
0069-3367 University of Chicago Oriental Institute. Publications

0069-3375 University of Chicago Studies in Library Science
0069-3391 Chigiana
0069-3405 C A D U Publications *changed to* A R D U Publication
0069-3413 Child Health in Israel
0069-3456 Children Welcome!
0069-3464 Children's Books; a List of Books for Preschool through Junior High School Age
0069-3472 Children's Books: Awards and Prizes
0069-3480 Children's Books in Print
0069-3502 Suggested as Holiday Gifts *changed to* Children's Books: One Hundred Titles for Reading and Sharing
0069-3510 Chile. Comision de Planeamiento Integral de la Educacion. Bibliografia de Investigaciones y Estudios en Educacion†
0069-3529 Chile. Comision de Planeamiento Integral de la Educacion. Publicacion†
0069-3537 Chile. Servicio Agricola y Ganadero. Division Proteccion Pesquera. Anuario Estadistico *changed to* Chile. Servicio Nacional de Pesca. Anuario Estadistico de Pesca
0069-3545 Chile. Superintendencia de Educacion Publica. Cuadernos†
0069-3553 Universidad de Chile. Departamento de Astronomia. Publicaciones
0069-3561 Universidad de Chile. Departamento de Geologia. Serie Apartado
0069-357X Universidad de Chile. Departamento de Geologia. Serie Communicaciones
0069-3588 Universidad de Chile. Departamento de Geologia. Serie Publicaciones†
0069-3596 Universidad Catolica de Chile. Facultad de Teologia. Anales
0069-3634 Chilton's Auto Repair Manual
0069-3642 Chimes
0069-3677 China Glass and Tableware Red Book Directory
0069-3693 China Research Monographs
0069-3715 Chiron
0069-3723 Chittagong Port Trust. Yearbook of Information *changed to* Chittagong Port Authority. Yearbook
0069-3758 Chord and Discord
0069-3774 University of Canterbury. Department of Psychology and Sociology. Research Projects
0069-3790 Lincoln College. Agricultural Economics Research Unit. Research Report
0069-3804 Lincoln College. Agricultural Economics Research Unit. Technical Paper†
0069-3820 Lincoln College. Department of Horticulture. Bulletin
0069-3839 Lincoln College. Farmers' Conference. Proceedings
0069-3855 Christian Camping Internatioal Directory *changed to* Guide to Christian Camps
0069-3863 Christian Endeavour Year Book *changed to* Christian Endeavour Topic Book
0069-3871 Christian Periodical Index
0069-388X Christian School Directory
0069-3898 Christian Service Training Series
0069-391X Handbook for Christian Writers *changed to* Successful Writers and Editors Guidebook
0069-3928 Christmas: An American Annual of Christmas Literature and Art
0069-3936 Chromatographic Science Series†
0069-3944 Chromosomes Today†
0069-3952 Chronologie des Communautes Europeennes
0069-3960 Chronology of the United Nations†
0069-3979 Church and Society Series
0069-3987 Church of England Yearbook
0069-3995 Church of Scotland. Yearbook
0069-4002 Church Pulpit Year Book
0069-4029 Churchman's Pocket Book and Diary *changed to* Church Pocket Book and Diary
0069-4037 CIBA Foundation. Study Groups†
0069-4045 CIBA Zeitschriften†
0069-4053 Ciencia e Sociedade: Temas e Debates†
0069-4061 Cincinnati Art Museum. Bulletin
0069-4088 Cincinnati Classical Studies. Supplementary Monograph†
0069-4096 Cincinnati Dental Society Bulletin
0069-410X Excavations of the University of Cincinnati: Guide Book†
0069-4118 Cine Club del Uruguay. Cuadernos
0069-4134 Cineguia
0069-4150 Cinema Studies
0069-4177 Circe
0069-4185 Circulation Research. Supplement
0069-4193 Circulation. Supplement
0069-4215 Circum-Spice
0069-4258 Civic Municipal Reference Manual and Purchasing Guide *changed to* Civic Public Works Reference Manual and Buyer's Guide
0069-4266 University of Illinois at Urbana-Champaign. Civil Engineering Studies. Construction Research†
0069-4274 University of Illinois at Urbana-Champaign. Civil Engineering Studies. Structural Research Series
0069-4290 Civilisations et Societes
0069-4304 Civilization of the American Indian
0069-4312 Civilta Asiatiche
0069-4339 Civilta Veneziana. Dizionari Dialettali e Studi Linguistici
0069-4347 Civilta Veneziana. Fonti e Testi. Serie Terza
0069-4355 Civilta Veneziana. Fonti e Testi. Serie Prima: Fonti e Testi per la Storia dell'Arte Veneta
0069-4371 Civilta Veneziana. Saggi
0069-438X Civilta Veneziana. Studi
0069-4401 Clark Guidebooks†
0069-441X Clarke Institute of Psychiatry. Monograph Series
0069-4444 Clasicos Colombianos
0069-4452 Classic European Historians†
0069-4460 Classical Association. Proceedings
0069-4479 Classici Greci e Latini
0069-4487 Classics in Anthropology
0069-4495 Classics in Education†
0069-4509 Classics of British Historical Literature
0069-4517 Classified Business Directory of the State of Connecticut
0069-4525 Classified Directory of Wisconsin Manufacturers
0069-4533 Classiques de la Pensee Politique
0069-4541 Classiques de la Renaissance en France. Premiere Serie†
0069-4592 Clay Resources Bulletin
0069-4606 Clean Air Year Book *see* 0140-6795
0069-4614 Clegg's International Directory of the World'S Book Trade
0069-4630 Poultry Health and Management Short Course. Proceedings
0069-4649 Clemson University Review of Industrial Management and Textile Science
0069-4657 Clemson University. Water Resources Research Institute. Report
0069-4665 Catalogue des Theses de Pharmacie Soutenues en France *see* 0458-5747
0069-4665 Catalogue des Theses de Pharmacie Soutenues en France. Quinquennial Cumulation
0069-4681 Universite de Clermont-Ferrand II. Annales Scientifiques. Serie Biologie Animale
0069-469X Universite de Clermont-Ferrand II. Annales Scientifique. Serie Biologie Vegetale
0069-4703 Universite de Clermont-Ferrand II. Annales Scientifique. Serie Chemie
0069-4711 Universite de Clermont-Ferrand II. Annales Scientifiques. Serie Geologie et Mineralogie
0069-472X Universite de Clermont-Ferrand II. Annales Scientifiques. Serie Mathematique
0069-4738 Universite de Clermont-Ferrand II. Annales Scientifiques. Serie Physique
0069-4746 Universite de Clermont-Ferrand II. Annales Scientifiques. Serie Physiologie Animale
0069-4754 Cles de l'Entreprise†
0069-4770 Clin-Alert
0069-4789 University of Illinois at Urbana-Champaign. Clinic on Library Applications of Data Processing. Proceedings
0069-4797 Clinical Approaches to the Problems of Childhood: The Langley Porter Child Psychiatry Series†
0069-4800 Clinical Conference on Cancer. Papers†
0069-4819 Clinical Endocrinology†
0069-4827 Clinical Neurosurgery; Proceedings
0069-4835 Clinics in Developmental Medicine
0069-4851 Co-Operation†
0069-4886 Coach Tours in Britain & Ireland
0069-4894 Coal Mines in Canada
0069-4916 Coal Traffic Annual
0069-4924 Coates's Herd Book (Beef)
0069-4932 Coates's Herd Book (Dairy)
0069-4983 Coins Market Values
0069-4991 Coke Oven Managers' Association. Year Book
0069-5009 Cold Spring Harbor Laboratory. Annual Report
0069-5017 Colecao Filosofia†
0069-5025 Coleccion Aberri ta Azkatasuna
0069-5033 Coleccion "Aniversarios Culturales"
0069-505X Coleccion Canonica
0069-5068 Coleccion Ciencia Urbanistica
0069-5076 Coleccion Filosofica
0069-5084 Coleccion "Foros y Seminarios." Serie Foros
0069-5092 Coleccion "Foros y Seminarios." Serie Seminarios
0069-5106 Coleccion Historica
0069-5114 Coleccion "Humanism y Ciencia"
0069-5122 Coleccion Juridica
0069-5130 Coleccion Monografica Africana†
0069-5149 Coleccion Pensamiento Argentino
0069-5165 Collana di Cultura
0069-5203 Collana di Studi e Saggi
0069-5246 Collana "Insegnare"
0069-5254 Collana Ricciana. Fonti
0069-5262 Collect British Stamps
0069-5270 Collectanea Historiae Musicae
0069-5300 Collected Studies in Criminological Research *changed to* Criminology, Criminal Law, Penology
0069-5319 Collected Works on Cardio-Pulmonary Disease
0069-5335 Collection de Sociologie Generale et de Philosophie Sociale
0069-5343 Collection d'Histoire Contemporaine
0069-5351 Collection Dictionnaires des Idees dans les Litteratures Occidentales. Litterature Francaise†
0069-5378 Collection Etudes et Travaux de la Revue "Mediterranee"
0069-5386 Figures de Wallonie
0069-5416 Collection "Pilotes"†
0069-5440 Collection PSI
0069-5459 Litteratures Anciennes
0069-5467 Collection U. Serie Droit des Affaires et de l'Economie
0069-5475 Collection U. Serie Droit des Communautes Europeennes
0069-5483 Collection U. Serie Etudes Allemandes
0069-5491 Collection U. Serie Histoire Ancienne
0069-5505 Collection U. Serie Relations et Institutions Internationales
0069-5513 Collections: Les Idees du Jour
0069-5521 Collectors Club Handbooks
0069-553X College and Adult Reading *changed to* N C R A Yearbook
0069-5548 Football Guide
0069-5572 College Blue Book
0069-5580 College de France. Annuaire
0069-5599 College des Medecins et Chirurgiens de la Province de Quebec. Bulletin *see* 0315-2979
0069-5602 Baccalaureate Education in Nursing: Key to a Professional Career in Nursing
0069-5688 College Facts Chart
0069-5696 College Music Symposium
0069-570X College of Dairy Agriculture, Hokkaido. Journal *see* 0388-001X
0069-5718 College of Insurance. General Bulletin
0069-5726 College of Physicians and Surgeons of British Columbia. Medical Directory
0069-5734 College Placement Annual
0069-5750 College Theology Society. Proceedings
0069-5777 Collezione di Filosofia
0069-5793 Collier's Yearbook
0069-5807 Colloque de Metallurgie
0069-5815 Colloques Internationaux d'Histoire Maritime. Travaux
0069-5823 Colloquium on Scottish Studies. Proceedings *changed to* Scottish Tradition
0069-5831 Colloquium on the Law of Outer Space. Proceedings
0069-584X Colloquim Series on Transportation. Proceedings *see* 0076-3993
0069-5858 Bibliothekar-Lehrinstitut des Landes Nordrhein-Westfalen. Arbeiten aus dem B L I
0069-5866 Bibliothekar-Lehrinstitut des Landes Nordrhein-Westfalen. Bibliographische Hefte
0069-5874 Universitaet zu Koeln. Geologiches Institut. Sonderveroeffentlichungen
0069-5882 Universitaet zu Koeln. Institut fuer Geophysik und Meteorologie. Mitteilungen
0069-5890 Universitaet Zu Koeln. Jahrbuch
0069-5904 Banco de la Republica Estadisticas Basicas.†
0069-5920 Universidad Nacional de Colombia. Centro de Bibliografia y Documentacion. Boletin Informativo *changed to* Universidad Nacional de Colombia. Biblioteca Central. Boletin de Adquisiciones
0069-5939 Colombo Law Review
0069-5947 Colombo Plan Bureau. Technical Cooperation under the Colombo Plan. Report
0069-5963 Colombo Plan for Co-Operative Economic Development in South and South-East Asia; Report of the Consultative Committee. *changed to* Colombo Plan for Co-operative Economic and Social Development in Asia and the Pacific. Consultative Committee. Report
0069-5971 Colonial Williamsburg Archaeological Series
0069-598X Coloquio de Estudos Luso Brasileiros. Anais
0069-5998 Color Photography
0069-6005 Colorado Cooperative Wildlife Research Unit. Special Scientific Reports. Technical Papers
0069-6013 Colorado. Department of Highways. Traffic Volume Study
0069-6048 Colorado Rail Annual
0069-6056 Colorado School of Mines. Professional Contributions
0069-6064 Colorado School of Mines. Research
0069-6072 Colorado Springs Fine Arts Center. Report
0069-6099 Colorado State University. Fluid Mechanics Papers†
0069-6110 Colorado State University. Hydrology Papers
0069-6129 Colorado State University. Sanitary Engineering Papers†
0069-6145 University of Colorado. Institute of Arctic and Alpine Research. Occasional Papers
0069-6161 University of Colorado Libraries. Report
0069-6277 Colston Research Society, Bristol, England. Proceedings of the Symposium. Colston Research Papers
0069-6285 Columbia Biological Series
0069-6293 Columbia County History (Oregon)

0069-6307 Columbia Essays in International Affairs. The Dean's Papers†
0069-6315 Columbia Essays on Modern Writers†
0069-6323 Columbia Essays on the Great Economists
0069-6331 Columbia Studies in Economics
0069-634X Columbia University-Presbyterian Hospital School of Nursing. Alumnae Association. Magazine
0069-6358 Columbia University Studies in International Organization†
0069-6366 Columbia University Studies in Jewish History, Culture, and Institutions†
0069-6412 Comitatus; a Journal of Medieval and Renaissance Studies
0069-6439 Marine Marchand: Etudes et Statistiques *changed to* Transport Maritime: Etudes et Statistiques
0069-6498 Comite International des Poids et Mesures. Comite Consultatif pour la Definition du Metre. Travaux†
0069-651X Comite National de l'Organisation Francaise. Annuaire
0069-6528 Comite National Francais de Geodesie et Geophysique. Comptes-Rendus
0069-6536 Comite National Francais de Geodesie et Geophysique. Rapport National Francais a l'U G G I
0069-6552 Petrole(Year)
0069-6579 Commentationes Biologicae†
0069-6587 Commentationes Humanarum Litterarum
0069-6609 Commentationes Physico-Mathematicae
0069-6625 Annuaire du Commerce Franco-Italien
0069-6633 Commerce in Nigeria
0069-6676 Commercial Transport Handbook and Buyer's Guide for S.A. *changed to* Transport Manager's Handbook
0069-6692 Commission of the European Communities. Etudes: Serie Aide au Developpement
0069-6706 Commission of the European Communities. Etudes: Serie Concurrence- Rapprochement des Legislations
0069-6714 Commission of the European Communities. Etudes: Serie Energie
0069-6722 Commission of the European Communities. Etudes: Serie Informations Internes sur l'Agriculture
0069-6730 Commission of the European Communities. Etudes: Serie Politique Sociale
0069-6749 General Report on the Activities of the European Communities
0069-6757 Commission of the European Communities. Investments in the Community Coalmining and Iron and Steel Industries. Report on the Survey
0069-6765 Commission of the European Communities. Studies: Agricultural Series
0069-6773 Commission of the European Communities. Studies: Economic and Financial Series
0069-679X Commission of the European Communities. Studies: Transport Series
0069-6811 Commissione Italiana per la Geofisica. Pubblicazioni. Serie I Q S Y†
0069-682X C E D Newsletter
0069-6838 Committee for International Cooperation in Information Retrieval Among Patent Offices. Bulletin.†
0069-6846 Committee for International Cooperation in Information Retrieval Among Patent Offices. Proceedings of Annual Meetings†
0069-6854 Committee on Institutional Cooperation. Annual Report
0069-6862 Commodity Year Book
0069-6870 Commonwealth Acoustic Laboratories, Sydney. Annual Report *see* 0311-8983
0069-6897 Commonwealth Agricultural Bureaux. List of Research Workers
0069-6919 Commonwealth Bureau of Animal Breeding and Genetics. Technical Communications
0069-6927 Commonwealth Bureau of Animal Health. Review Series
0069-6935 Commonwealth Bureau of Nutrition. Annotated Bibliographies
0069-6943 Commonwealth Bureau of Nutrition. Technical Communications
0069-6986 Commonwealth Bureau of Horticulture and Plantation Crops. Horticultural Review
0069-6994 Commonwealth Bureau of Horticulture and Plantation Crops. Research Review
0069-7001 Commonwealth Bureau of Horticulture and Plantation Crops. Technical Communications
0069-701X Commonwealth Bureau of Pastures and Field Crops. Bulletin
0069-7036 Commonwealth Bureau of Soils. Technical Communications
0069-7044 Commonwealth Entomological Conference. Report
0069-7052 Commonwealth Forestry Bureau Annotated Bibliographies
0069-7060 Commonwealth Forestry Bureau. Technical Communication
0069-7109 Commonwealth Institute, London. Annual Report
0069-7125 Commonwealth Institute of Biological Control. Technical Communications
0069-7133 Commonwealth Law Reports
0069-7141 Commonwealth Mycological Institute. Phytopathological Papers
0069-7168 Commonwealth Press Union. Book of Quinquennial Conference†
0069-7184 Commonwealth Scientific and Industrial Research Organization. Annual Report
0069-7192 C. S. I. R. O. Film Catalogue
0069-7222 Commonwealth Scientific and Industrial Research Organization. Division of Applied Geomechanics. Report†
0069-7249 Commonwealth Scientific and Industrial Research Organization. Division of Applied Geomechanics. Technical Report
0069-7257 Commonwealth Scientific and Industrial Research Organization. Division of Applied Geomechanics. Technical Paper
0069-7265 Commonwealth Scientific and Industrial Research Organization. Division of Applied Geomechanics. Technical Memorandum†
0069-7273 Commonwealth Scientific and Industrial Research Organization. Division of Animal Health. Annual Report
0069-7281 Commonwealth Scientific and Industrial Research Organization. Division of Animal Physiology. Report. *see* 0155-7742
0069-729X Commonwealth Scientific and Industrial Research Organization. Division of Building Research. Building Study†
0069-732X Commonwealth Scientific and Industrial Research Organization. Division of Entomology. Report
0069-7338 Commonwealth Scientific and Industrial Research Organization. Division of Entomology. Technical Paper
0069-7346 Commonwealth Scientific and Industrial Research Organization. Division of Fisheries and Oceanography. Fisheries Synopsis
0069-7370 Commonwealth Scientific and Industrial Research Organization. Division of Fisheries and Oceanography. Report
0069-7397 Commonwealth Scientific and Industrial Research Organization. Division of Fisheries and Oceanography. Annual Report
0069-7419 Commonwealth Scientific and Industrial Research Organization. Division of Food Research. Report of Research
0069-7427 Commonwealth Scientific and Industrial Research Organization. Division of Food Research. Technical Paper
0069-7435 Commonwealth Scientific and Industrial Research Organization. Division of Horticultural Research. Report
0069-7443 Commonwealth Scientific and Industrial Research Organization. Division of Irrigation Research. Report†
0069-746X Commonwealth Scientific and Industrial Research Organization. Division of Land Use Research. Technical Paper
0069-7486 Commonwealth Scientific and Industrial Research Organization. Division of Mechanical Engineering. Circular
0069-7494 Commonwealth Scientific and Industrial Research Organization. Division of Mechanical Engineering. Engineering Development Reports *changed to* Commonwealth Scientific and Industrial Research Organization. Division of Mechanical Engineering. Technical Reports
0069-7508 Commonwealth Scientific and Industrial Research Organization. Division of Mechanical Engineering. Report
0069-7524 Commonwealth Scientific and Industrial Research Organization. Division of Mathematical Statistics. Technical Paper
0069-7540 Commonwealth Scientific and Industrial Research Organization. Division of Plant Industry. Annual Repot *changed to* Commonwealth Scientific and Industrial Research Organization. Division of Plant Industry. Report
0069-7567 Commonwealth Scientific and Industrial Research Organization. Division of Plant Industry. Technical Paper
0069-7575 Commonwealth Scientific and Industrial Research Organization. Division of Radiophysics. Report
0069-7583 Commonwealth Scientific and Industrial Research Organization. Division of Soils. Biennial Report
0069-7591 Commonwealth Scientific and Industrial Research Organization. Division of Soils. Soil Publications†
0069-7613 Commonwealth Scientific and Industrial Research Organization. Division of Tropical Pastures. Technical Paper *changed to* Commonwealth Scientific and Industrial Research Organization. Division of Tropical Crops and Pastures. Technical Paper
0069-763X Commonwealth Scientific and Industrial Research Organization. Division of Wildlife Research. Technical Paper
0069-7648 Commonwealth Scientific and Industrial Research Organization. Land Research Series
0069-7680 Commonwealth Scientific and Industrial Research Organization. Wheat Research Unit. Report
0069-7699 Commonwealth Secretariat. Commodities Division. Dairy Produce†
0069-7702 Commonwealth Secretariat. Commodities Division. Fruit†
0069-7710 Commonwealth Secretariat. Commodities Division. Meat†
0069-7729 Commonwealth Secretariat. Commodities Division. Plantation Crops†
0069-7737 Commonwealth Secretariat. Commodities Division. Vegetable Oils and Oilseeds†
0069-7745 Commonwealth Universities Yearbook
0069-7761 Annuaire des Communautes d'Enfants
0069-777X Communications Handbook
0069-7788 Communist China Problem Research Series
0069-7796 Communist China Yearbook Series
0069-7818 Community Council of Greater New York. Budget Standard Service. Annual Price Survey and Family Budget Costs†
0069-7842 Community Improvement Corporation. Annual Report
0069-7850 Community Mental Health Journal Monograph Series†
0069-7893 Comparative Juridical Review
0069-7907 Comparative Studies in Society and History
0069-794X Comparazione dei Salari e del Costo del Lavoro in Europa
0069-7958 Compendio Statistico Italiano
0069-7966 Compendium of Pharmaceuticals and Specialties
0069-7974 Complete Book of Engines†
0069-7982 Complete Chevrolet Book†
0069-7990 Complete Ford Book†
0069-8008 Complete Volkswagen Book
0069-8016 Composers of the Americas
0069-8024 Wilson & Wilson's Comprehensive Analytical Chemistry
0069-8032 Comprehensive Biochemistry
0069-8040 Comprehensive Chemical Kinetics
0069-8067 Comprehensive Media Guide: Korea
0069-8075 Comptes Nationaux de la Belgique
0069-8091 Compton Yearbook
0069-8105 Computer Applications in the Natural and Social Sciences *see* 0308-4221
0069-8121 Computer Index†
0069-8148 Association for Computing Machinery. Annual Computer Personnel Research Conference Proceedings†
0069-8164 Computer Service Buyers Guide†
0069-8180 Computer Yearbook
0069-8202 Comunidad Latinoamericana de Escritores. Boletin *changed to* Comunidad Latinoamericana de Escritores. Revista
0069-8210 Comunidad. Suplementos†
0069-8245 Concise Statistical Yearbook of Greece
0069-827X Concrete Industries Yearbook
0069-8288 Concrete Year Book
0069-8296 Condon Lectures†
0069-830X Confederation des Industries Ceramiques de France. Annuaire
0069-8326 Confederation Nationale des Groupes Folkloriques Francais. Annuaire†
0069-8342 Conference Board in Canada. Canadian Studies
0069-8350 Conference Board. Cumulative Index
0069-8369 Conference Board. Report on Company Contributions *changed to* Conference Board. Annual Survey of Corporate Contributions
0069-8393 Conference in Reading. Proceedings†
0069-8407 Conference in the Study of Twentieth-Century Literature, Michigan State University. Proceedings
0069-8474 Conference of State Sanitary Engineers. Report of Proceedings
0069-8490 Advances in X-Ray Analysis
0069-8512 Conference on Biological Sonar and Diving Mammals. Proceedings†
0069-8520 Perugia Quadrennial International Conferences on Cancer. Proceedings
0069-8547 Conference on Frontiers in Education. Digest
0069-8555 Conference on Human Relations in Industry. Proceedings
0069-8563 Conference on Labor, New York University. Proceedings†
0069-8571 Conference on Land Surveying, Purdue University. Proceedings†
0069-858X Conference on Laser Engineering and Applications *see* 0099-121X
0069-8598 Conference on Latin American History. Publications†
0069-8601 Conference on United Nations Procedures. Report
0069-8636 Conference on Radar Meteorology. Preprints
0069-8644 Conference on Remote Systems Technology. Proceedings
0069-8652 Conference on Research in Income and Wealth
0069-8679 Conference on Severe Local Storms. Preprints

ISSN INDEX 1111

0069-8687 National Tax Association-Tax Institute of America. Proceedings of the Annual Conference
0069-8695 Conference on Teacher Education in the Eastern Caribbean. Report *changed to* Eastern Caribbean Standing Conference on Teacher Education. Report
0069-8733 Conference on the United Nations of the Next Decade. Report *changed to* United Nations of the Next Decade Conference. Report
0069-8741 Conference on Trace Substances in Environmental Health. Proceedings
0069-875X Conference on Underground Transmission and Distribution. Record.
0069-8768 Conference on Veterans Administration Studies in Mental Health and Behavioral Sciences. Highlights
0069-8784 Conferencias de Bioquimica
0069-8792 Conflict Studies
0069-8814 Confluence. Etats des Recherches en Sciences Sociales: Surveys of Research in the Social Sciences†
0069-8830 Zaire. Direction de la Statistique et des Etudes Economiques. Annuaire des Statistiques du Commerce Exterieur *see* 0304-5692
0069-8849 United Reformed Church in England and Wales. United Reformed Church Year Book
0069-8857 Congregational Council for World Mission. Annual Report *changed to* C W M Report
0069-8881 Congres Archeologique de France (Publication.)
0069-889X Congres National des Peches et Industries Maritimes. Compte Rendu
0069-8903 Congress for Recreation and Parks. Proceedings
0069-8911 Congres National de Speleologie. Actes
0069-892X Congressional Record Digest and Tally of Roll Call Votes
0069-8938 Congressional Staff Directory
0069-8946 Coniectanea Biblica. New Testament Series
0069-8954 Coniectanea Biblica. Old Testament Series
0069-8970 Connecticut Academy of Arts and Sciences. Memoirs
0069-8989 Connecticut Academy of Arts and Sciences. Transactions
0069-8997 Storrs Agricultural Experiment Station. Research Report
0069-9012 Connecticut College Monograph
0069-9020 Connecticut. Department of Community Affairs. Division of Research and Program Evaluation. Construction Activity Authorized by Building Permits. Summary *changed to* Housing Units in Connecticut. Annual Summary
0069-9039 Connecticut Master Transportation Plan
0069-9047 University of Connecticut. Center for Real Estate and Urban Economic Studies. General Series
0069-9055 Connecticut Urban Research Report
0069-9063 University of Connecticut. Institute of Water Resources. Report Series
0069-908X Connolly's Suppressed Writings
0069-9101 U.S. Department of the Interior. Conservation Bulletins†
0069-911X Conservation Directory
0069-9128 Fish and Wildlife Facts
0069-9136 Conservation of Library Materials
0069-9144 Conservation of Nature and Natural Resources *changed to* Nature and Environment Series
0069-9152 U.S. Department of the Interior. Conservation Yearbook.†
0069-9160 Consortium for the Study of Nigerian Rural Development†
0069-9179 Consortium for the Study of Nigerian Rural Development. C S N R D Working Paper
0069-9187 Construction in Hawaii
0069-9195 Israel. Central Bureau of Statistics. Construction in Israel
0069-9209 C I R I A Annual Report
0069-9217 Construction Writers Association. Newsletter
0069-9225 Consulting Engineer Who's Who and Year Book
0069-9233 U. S. Federal Trade Commission. Consumer Bulletins†
0069-9276 U.S. National Bureau of Standards. Consumer Information Series
0069-9284 Consumers Directory
0069-9292 Contabilidad Nacional de Espana
0069-9306 Contact†
0069-9314 Containerization: A Bibliography
0069-9322 Contamination Control Directory†
0069-9330 Contemporary African Monographs
0069-9357 Contemporary American History Series
0069-9381 Contemporary Drama Series
0069-942X Contemporary Issues Series
0069-9446 Contemporary Neurology Series
0069-9454 Contemporary Neurology Symposia†
0069-9527 Continental Camping & Caravan Sites
0069-9535 Continental Research Series
0069-956X Continuing Engineering Studies Series *changed to* C I E C Proceedings
0069-9578 Contract Carpeting
0069-9616 Contributii Botanice
0069-9624 Contributions in Afro-American and African Studies
0069-9632 Contributions in Anthropology
0069-9640 Texas A & M University. Department of Oceanography. Contributions in Oceanography.
0069-9659 Contributions to Indian Sociology
0069-9683 Contributions to Library Literature
0069-9691 Contributions to Marine Science
0069-9705 Contributions to Sensory Physiology
0069-9713 Contributions to the History of Science and Technology in Baltics
0069-973X Control Magazine
0069-9748 Convegno di Studi Sulla Magna Grecia. Atti
0069-9764 Convegno Nazionale dei Commercianti de Mobili. Atti e Relazioni
0069-9772 Convegno Nazionale per la Civilta del Lavoro. Atti.
0069-9780 Cooper Monographs on English and American Language and Literature
0069-9799 Cooperador Dental
0069-9810 Cooperative Education Association Membership Directory
0069-9829 C I C R I S Directory and Guide to Resources
0069-9837 Cooperative Trade Directory for Southeast Asia
0069-9845 Coordination Chemistry
0069-9861 Danmarks Biblioteksskole. Skrifter
0069-987X Geoteknisk Institut, Copenhagen. Bulletin
0069-9888 Handelshoejskolen i Koebenhavn. Instituttet for Udenrigshandel. Smaaskrifter
0069-9896 Denmark. Kongelige Bibliotek. Fund og Forskning
0069-9918 Koebenhavns Universitet. Filosofiska Fakultet. Extracts†
0069-9950 Copyright Law Symposium
0069-9969 Copyright Laws and Treaties of the World. Supplements
0069-9977 Coral Gables Conference on Fundamental Interactions at High Energy. (Proceedings)
0069-9993 Corn Annual
0070-0002 Cornell Biennial Electrical Engineering Conference
0070-0010 Cornell International Agricultural Development Mimeographs *changed to* Cornell International Agriculture Mimeographs
0070-0029 Cornell International Industrial and Labor Relations Reports
0070-0053 Cornell Studies in Industrial and Labor Relations
0070-0061 Cornell University. Center for Housing and Environmental Studies. Research Reports *changed to* Cornell University. Program in Urban and Regional Studies. Research Reports
0070-0096 Cornell University. Modern Indonesia Project. Bibliography Series†
0070-0118 Tree Fruit Production Recommendations *changed to* Cornell Recommendations for Commercial Tree-Fruit Production
0070-0126 Cornell University. New York State School of Industrial and Labor Relations. Annual Institute for Training Specialists. (Publication)†
0070-0134 New York State School of Industrial and Labor Relations. Bulletin
0070-0142 Industrial and Labor Relations Bibliography Series
0070-0177 I L R Paperbacks
0070-0185 New York State School of Industrial and Labor Relations. Key Issues Series
0070-0207 Cornell University. New York State School of Industrial and Labor Relations. Technical Monograph Series†
0070-0215 Cornell University. Southeast Asia Program. Data Papers
0070-0223 Cornell University. Thailand Project. Interim Reports Series
0070-024X Cornish Archaeology
0070-0258 Cornwall Archaeological Society. Field Guide
0070-0282 Corporate Management Tax Conference
0070-0290 Corporate Pension Fund Seminar. Proceedings
0070-0304 Corporation des Ingenieurs Forestiers du Quebec. Congres Annuel. Texte des Conferences *changed to* Ordre des Ingenieurs Forestiers du Quebec. Congres Annuel. Texte des Conferences
0070-0312 Corpus Antiquitatum Americanensium
0070-0320 Corpus Catholicorum
0070-0339 Corpus der Romanischen Kunst im Saechsisch-Thueringischen Gebiet†
0070-0347 Corpus Medicorum Graecorum
0070-0355 Corpus Medicorum Latinorum†
0070-0363 Corpus Mensurabilis Musicae
0070-038X Corpus Palladianum
0070-0398 Corpus Scriptorum Christianorum Orientalium: Aethiopica
0070-0401 Corpus Scriptorum Christianorum Orientalium: Arabica
0070-041X Corpus Scriptorum Christianorum Orientalium: Armeniaca
0070-0428 Corpus Scriptorum Christianorum Orientalium: Coptica
0070-0436 Corpus Scriptorum Christianorum Orientalium: Iberica
0070-0444 Corpus Scriptorum Christianorum Orientalium: Subsidia
0070-0452 Corpus Scriptorum Christianorum Orientalium: Syriaca
0070-0460 Corpus Scriptorum de Musica
0070-0479 Corpus Vasorum Antiquorum. Italia†
0070-0479 Corpus Vasorum Antiquorum. Italia
0070-0495 Corpus Vasorum Antiquorum. Poland†
0070-0509 Correctional Literature Published in Canada†
0070-0517 Correspondance d'Orient
0070-0533 Cosmetic Formulary†
0070-0576 Costa Rica. Ministerio de Hacienda Oficina del Presupesto. Informe
0070-0584 Universidad de Costa Rica. Serie Agronomia†
0070-0592 Universidad de Costa Rica. Serie Bibliotecologia†
0070-0606 Universidad de Costa Rica. Series Ciencias Juridicas y Sociales†
0070-0614 Universidad de Costa Rica. Serie de Filosofia†
0070-0622 Universidad de Costa Rica. Serie Educacion†
0070-0630 Universidad de Costa Rica. Serie Economia y Estadistica†
0070-0649 Universidad de Costa Rica. Serie Economia y Estadistica. Estadistica Universitaria†
0070-0657 Universidad de Costa Rica. Serie Historia y Geografia†
0070-0665 Universidad de Costa Rica. Serie Textos Universitarios†
0070-0673 Cotton International
0070-0681 Cotton Ginnings in the United States
0070-069X Council for Basic Education. Occasional Papers
0070-072X Council for Old World Archaeology: C O W A Surveys and Bibliographies. Area 1: British Isle†
0070-0738 Council for Old World Archaeology: C O W A Surveys and Bibliographies. Area 2: Scandinavia†
0070-0746 Council for Old World Archaeology: C O W A Surveys and Bibliographies. Area 3: Western Europe: Part 1†
0070-0754 Council for Old World Archaeology: C O W A Surveys and Bibliographies. Area 3: Western Europe: Part 2†
0070-0762 Council for Old World Archaeology: C O W A Surveys and Bibliographies. Area 4: Western Mediterranean†
0070-0797 Council for Old World Archaeology: C O W A Surveys and Bibliographies. Area 7: Eastern Mediterranean†
0070-0800 Council for Old World Archaeology: C O W A Surveys and Bibliographies. Area 8: European Russia†
0070-0819 Council for Old World Archaeology: C O W A Surveys and Bibliographies. Area 9: Northeast Africa†
0070-0827 Council for Old World Archaeology: C O W A Surveys and Bibliographies. Area 10. Northwest Africa†
0070-0835 Council for Old World Archaeology: C O W A Surveys and Bibliographies. Area 11. West Africa†
0070-0843 Council for Old World Archaeology: C O W A Surveys and Bibliographies. Area 12. Equatorial Africa†
0070-0851 Council for Old World Archaeology: C O W A Surveys and Bibliographies. Area 13. South Africa†
0070-086X Council for Old World Archaeology: C O W A Surveys and Bibliographies. Area 14. East Africa†
0070-0878 Council for Old World Archaeology: C O W A Surveys and Bibliographies. Area 15. Western Asia†
0070-0886 Council for Old World Archaeology: C O W A Surveys and Bibliographies. Area 16. Southern Asia†
0070-0894 Council for Old World Archaeology: C O W A Surveys and Bibliographies. Area 17. Far East†
0070-0916 Council for Old World Archaeology: C O W A Surveys and Bibliographies. Area 18. Northern Asia†
0070-0924 Council for Old World Archaeology: C O W A Surveys and Bibliographies. Area 19. Southeast Asia†
0070-0932 Council for Old World Archaeology: C O W A Surveys and Bibliographies. Area 20. Indonesia†
0070-0940 Council for Old World Archaeology: C O W A Surveys and Bibliographies. Area 21. Pacific Islands†
0070-0959 Council for Old World Archaeology: C O W A Surveys and Bibliographies. Area 22. Australia†
0070-1009 Council of Europe. Consultative Assembly. Documents; Working Papers/Documents de Seance *changed to* Council of Europe. Parliamentary Assembly. Documents; Working Papers/Documents de Seance

0070-1017	Council of Europe. Consultative Assembly. Orders of the Day, Minutes of Proceedings/Ordres du Jour, Proces Verbaux *changed to* Council of Europe. Parliamentary Assembly. Orders of the Day, Minutes of Proceedings/Ordres du Jour, Proces Verbaux
0070-1033	Council of Europe. Consultative Assembly. Texts Adopted by the Assembly/Textes Adoptes Par l'Assemblee *changed to* Council of Europe. Parliamentary Assembly. Texts Adopted by the Assembly/Textes Adoptes Par l'Assemblee
0070-105X	Council of Europe. European Treaty Series
0070-1076	Council of Graduate Schools in the United States. Proceedings of the Annual Meeting
0070-1106	Council of Organizations Serving the Deaf. Annual Forum Proceedings†
0070-1114	Council of Organizations Serving the Deaf. Council Membership Directory†
0070-1157	Suggested State Legislation
0070-1165	Whole World Handbook: a Student Guide to Work, Study and Travel Abroad
0070-1181	Council on Library Resources Report *changed to* Council on Library Resources Annual Report
0070-1203	Council on the Teaching of Hebrew. Bulletin
0070-1211	Councils, Committees and Boards
0070-1238	Countdown: Canadian Nursing Statistics†
0070-1262	Country Dance and Song
0070-1270	Country Life Annual†
0070-1300	County and Municipal Year Book for Scotland *see* 0305-6562
0070-1327	County Louth Archaeological and Historical Journal
0070-136X	Course Guide for High School Theatre *changed to* Course Guide in the Theatre Arts at the Secondary School Level
0070-1386	Court of Justice of the European Communities. Recueil de la Jurisprudence
0070-1394	Courtenay Library of Reformation Classics
0070-1408	Courtenay Studies in Reformation Theology
0070-1416	Cranbrook Institute of Science, Bloomfield Hills, Michigan. Bulletin
0070-1424	Cranfield Fluidics Conference. Proceedings
0070-1467	Credit Manual of Commercial Laws
0070-1475	Cremation Society of Great Britain. Conference Report
0070-1483	Cri du Peuple
0070-1505	Crime and Delinquency Issues, Monographic Series *changed to* Crime and Delinquency Topics, Monograph Series
0070-1521	Criminal Appeal Reports
0070-153X	Critical Essays in Modern Literature
0070-1548	Critical Review Melbourne *changed to* Critical Review
0070-1556	Critiques de Notre Temps Et...
0070-1572	Croissance Urbaine et Progres des Nations
0070-1580	Croner's Reference Book for Employers
0070-1599	Croner's Reference Book for Exporters
0070-1602	Croner's Reference Book for Importers
0070-1610	Croner's Road Transport Operation
0070-1629	Croner's World Directory of Freight Conferences
0070-167X	Crystal Structures†
0070-1688	Cuadernos de Historia del Arte
0070-1696	Cuadernos de Historia del Islam. Serie Monografica Islamica Occidentalia *changed to* Cuadernos de Historia del Islam
0070-170X	Cuadernos de Orientacion
0070-1718	Cuadernos de Pedagogia
0070-1726	Cuadernos de Sintesis†
0070-1734	Cuadernos de Sociologia
0070-1750	Cuadernos del Mexico Prehispanico
0070-1785	Cuadernos para Estudiantes: Los Poetas
0070-1793	Cumulative Index to Nursing Literature, Nursing Subject Headings *see* 0146-5554
0070-1815	Universidade do Parana. Departamento de Historia. Boletim
0070-184X	Current Australian Serials
0070-1858	Current British Directories
0070-1866	Current Caribbean Bibliography
0070-1882	Current Coins of the World
0070-1890	Current Concepts in Clinical Nursing
0070-1947	Index of Current Equine Research
0070-1955	Current European Directories
0070-1971	Current Issues in Higher Education
0070-198X	Current Issues in Music Education
0070-1998	Current Legal Problems
0070-2005	Current Medical Information and Terminology
0070-203X	Current Practice in Orthopaedic Surgery
0070-2064	Current Problems in Dermatology
0070-2080	Current Psychiatric Therapies
0070-2099	Nebraska Symposium on Motivation (Publication)
0070-2110	Current Therapy in Dentistry
0070-2129	Current Topics in Bioenergetics
0070-2137	Current Topics in Cellular Regulation
0070-2145	Current Topics in Clinical and Community Psychology
0070-2153	Current Topics in Developmental Biology
0070-2161	Current Topics in Membranes and Transport
0070-217X	Current Topics in Microbiology and Immunology
0070-2188	Current Topics in Pathology
0070-2196	Current Topics in Surgical Research
0070-2234	Cusanus-Gesellschaft. Buchreihe
0070-2242	Cushman Foundation for Foraminiferal Research. Special Publication
0070-2250	Custom House Guide
0070-2277	Cycle Buyers Guide
0070-2307	Cyprus. Agricultural Research Institute. Annual Report
0070-2315	Cyprus. Agricultural Research Institute. Technical Bulletin
0070-2323	Cyprus. Budget: Estimates of Revenue and Expenditure
0070-2331	Cyprus Chamber of Commerce and Industry Directory
0070-234X	Cyprus. Department of Agriculture. Soils and Plant Nutrition Section. Report
0070-2366	Cyprus. Department of Antiquities. Monographs
0070-2374	Cyprus. Department of Antiquities. Annual Report
0070-2390	Cyprus. Ministry of Labour and Social Insurance. Annual Report
0070-2404	Cyprus. Department of Social Welfare Services. Annual Report
0070-2412	Cyprus. Department of Statistics and Research. Economic Report
0070-2420	Cyprus. Department of Statistics and Research. Statistics of Imports and Exports
0070-2439	Cyprus. Department of Statistics and Research. Shipping Statistics
0070-2463	Cytobiologie *see* 0171-9335
0070-2471	Czasopismo Prawno-Historyczne
0070-248X	Czechoslovakia. Federalni Statisticky Urad. Statisticka Rocenka
0070-2498	D A T A Book of Discontinued Transistors
0070-251X	Dacia; Revue d'Archeologie et d'Histoire Ancienne
0070-2528	Daedalus
0070-2536	Daedalus Library
0070-2544	Daffodils
0070-2587	Dairy Industries Catalog
0070-2617	Institut Fondamental d'Afrique Noire. Catalogues et Documents
0070-2625	Institut Fondamental d'Afrique Noire. Initiations et Etudes Africaines
0070-2633	Institut Fondamental d'Afrique Noire. Memoires
0070-2668	Dana-Report
0070-2676	Dance Directory
0070-2684	Dance Magazine Annual
0070-2692	Dance World
0070-2714	Dania Polyglotta
0070-2730	Danish Review of Game Biology
0070-2749	Danish Yearbook of Philosophy
0070-2765	Danmarks Folkeminder
0070-2781	Danmarks Vareindfoersel og- Udfoersel
0070-279X	Dans le Fantastique
0070-2803	Dansk Elvaerksstatistik *changed to* Dansk Elforsyning
0070-2811	Danske Bogauktioner med en Oversigt over Bogpriserne
0070-282X	Danske Forlaeggerforening. Faelleslagerkatalog
0070-2838	Danske Landmandsbank. Annual Report *changed to* Danske Bank af 1871. Annual Report
0070-2846	Danske Magazin
0070-2854	Danske Reklamebureauers Brancheforening. Oplagstal og Markedstal
0070-2862	Dante Studies
0070-2889	Data Processing in Medicine†
0070-2897	Datos y Cifras de la Ensenanza en Espana
0070-2900	David Davies Memorial Institute of International Studies, London. Annual Memorial Lecture
0070-2927	University of Toronto. David Dunlap Observatory. Publications
0070-2943	Davison's Knit Goods Trade
0070-2951	Davison's Textile Blue Book
0070-296X	Davison's Textile Catalog and Buyer's Guide *changed to* Davison's Textile Buyer's Guide
0070-2978	Davison's Textile Directory for Executives and Salesmen *see* 0363-5252
0070-2986	Davy's Devon Herd Book
0070-3001	Dawn Song and All Day
0070-3028	Dayton Art Institute. Annual Report
0070-3044	University of Dayton. School of Education. Abstracts of Research Projects
0070-3052	University of Dayton. School of Education. Workshop Proceedings
0070-3060	De Proprietatibus Litterarum. Series Major
0070-3079	De Proprietatibus Litterarum. Series Minor
0070-3087	De Proprietatibus Litterarum. Series Practica
0070-3095	Dead Sea Works, Beersheba, Israel. Report of the Directors
0070-3141	December
0070-315X	Dechema Monographien
0070-3176	Decisions of the United States Courts Involving Copyrights
0070-3192	Decorating Contractor Annual Directory
0070-3206	Decorative Art and Modern Interiors
0070-3222	Deems Lectureship†
0070-3230	Defects in Cristalline Solids *changed to* Defects in Solids
0070-3249	Deiches Fund Studies of Public Library Service†
0070-3257	Dein Kind†
0070-3265	Delaware Directory of Commerce and Industry
0070-3273	Delaware Geological Survey Bulletins
0070-3281	Delaware Nurse *changed to* Delaware Nurses' Association Reporter
0070-329X	Delaware. Department of Highways and Transportation. Traffic Summary
0070-3303	Delegations to the United Nations
0070-3311	Institute of Economic Growth, Delhi. Census Studies
0070-3338	Delphica
0070-3346	Democrat
0070-3354	Demographie et Sciences Humaines
0070-3362	Demographie et Societes
0070-3370	Demography
0070-3389	Demokratische Existenz Heute
0070-3419	Denken, Schauen, Sinnen
0070-3427	Denkmaeler des Rheinlandes†
0070-3435	Denmark. Danmarks Fiskeri- og Havundersoegelser. Meddeleser *see* 0106-553X
0070-346X	Denmark. Danmarks Statistik. Arbejdsloesheden/Unemployment
0070-3478	Denmark. Danmarks Statistik. Befolkningens Bevaegelser
0070-3486	Danmarks Skibe og Skibsfart
0070-3494	Denmark. Danmarks Statistik. Ejendoms- og Personbeskatingen i Skattearet *changed to* Denmark. Danmarks Statistik. Ejendoms- og Selskabsbeskatningen i Skatteaaret
0070-3508	Denmark. Danmarks Statistik. Ejendomssalg/Sales of Real Property
0070-3516	Denmark. Danmarks Statistik. Faerdselsuheld
0070-3524	Denmark. Danmarks Statistik. Indkomstansaettelser Til Staten *changed to* Denmark. Danmarks Statistik. Indkomster og Formver Ved Slutligningen
0070-3532	Denmark. Danmarks Statistik. Industristatistik/Industrial Statistics
0070-3540	Denmark. Danmarks Statistik. Kriminalstatistik
0070-3559	Denmark. Danmarks Statistik. Landbrugsstatistik Herunder Gartneri og Skovbrug/Statistics on Agriculture, Gardening and Forestry
0070-3567	Denmark. Danmarks Statistik. Statistisk Aarbog/Statistical Yearbook
0070-3583	Denmark. Danmarks Statistik. Statistik Tiars-Oversigt
0070-3605	Denmark. Fiskeriministeriet. Forsoegslaboratorium. Aarsberetining/Annual Report
0070-3621	Denmark. Statens Filmcentral. S F C Film
0070-3656	Dental Guide
0070-3664	Dental Images
0070-3672	Dental Laboratorie Bladet
0070-3699	Dental Practitioner Handbook
0070-3702	Dental Products Annual Report
0070-3729	Tenth District Dental Society of the State of New York. Bulletin
0070-3737	Dentistry in Japan
0070-3745	Denver Museum of Natural History. Museum Pictorial†
0070-3753	Denver Museum of Natural History. Proceedings†
0070-3761	University of Denver. College of Business Administration. Occasional Studies
0070-377X	University of Denver. College of Business Administration. Special Publication
0070-3788	Derbyshire Archaeological Journal
0070-3826	Description and Analysis of Contemporary Standard Russian
0070-3834	Design and Industries Association. Year Book and Membership List *see* 0306-6185
0070-3869	Dessinateurs, Peintres et Sculpteurs de Belgique *see* 0066-3174
0070-3877	Detroit Dental Spectrum *changed to* Detroit Mirror and Explorer
0070-3885	Detroit Studies in Music Bibliography
0070-3893	Deutsch-Slawische Forschungen zur Namenkunde und Siedlungsgeschichte
0070-3907	Deutsche Akademie der Landwirtschaftswissenschaften, Berlin. Jahrbuch†
0070-3915	Akademie fuer Aerztliche Fortbildung der DDR. Bibliographie
0070-3923	Deutsche Akademie fuer Sprache und Dichtung. Jahrbuch
0070-394X	Deutsche Bundesbank. Geschaeftsbericht
0070-3966	D F V L R Jahresbericht
0070-3974	Deutsche Forschungsgemeinschaft. Denkschriften zur Lage der Deutschen Wissenschaft

0070-3982 Deutsche Forschungsgemeinschaft. Forschungsberichte
0070-3990 Deutsche Forschungsgemeinschaft. Kommissionen. Mitteilungen
0070-4040 Deutsche Gesellschaft fuer Chronometrie. Jahrbuch
0070-4075 Deutsche Gesellschaft fuer Kreislaufforschung. Verhandlungen
0070-4083 D. G. L. R. Jahrbuecher
0070-4091 Deutsche Gesellschaft fuer Orthopaedie und ihre Grenzgebiete *see* 0044-3220
0070-4105 Deutsche Gesellschaft fuer Ostasienkunde. Koordinierungstelle fuer Gegenwartsbezogene Ostasienforschung Mitteilungen *changed to* Deutsche Gesellschaft fuer Ostasienkunde. Koordinierungsstelle fuer Gegenwartsbezogene Ost- und Suedostasienforschung. Mitteilungen
0070-4113 Deutsche Gesellschaft fuer Pathologie. Verhandlungen
0070-4121 Deutsche Gesellschaft fuer Rheumatologie. Verhandlungen.
0070-413X Deutsche Gesellschaft fuer Urologie. Verhandlungsbericht
0070-4148 Die Deutsche Handelsflotte
0070-4164 Deutsche Hydrographische Zeitschrift. Ergaenzungsheft. Reihe A
0070-4172 Deutsche Hydrographische Zeitschrift. Ergaenzungsheft. Reihe B
0070-4199 Deutsche Keramische Gesellschaft. Fachausschussberichte
0070-4210 Deutsche Kraftfahrtforschung und Strassenverkehrstechnik
0070-4229 Deutsches Krebsforschungszentrum. Veroeffentlichungen
0070-4237 Die Deutsche Lebensversicherung
0070-4245 Duetsche Luft- und Raumfahrt. Forschungsberichte *changed to* D F V L R-Forschungsberichte und D F V L R-Mitteilungen
0070-4253 Deutsche Luft- und Raumfahrt. Mitteilungen†
0070-4261 DIN-Taschenbuecher
0070-427X Deutsche Ophthalmologische Gesellschaft. Zusammenkunft. Bericht
0070-4296 Deutsche Papierwirtschaft
0070-430X Deutsche Physikalische Gesellschaft. D P G - Nachrichten†
0070-4318 Deutsche Schiller-Gesellschaft. Jahrbuch
0070-4326 Deutsche Shakespeare-Gesellschaft West. Jahrbuch
0070-4334 Deutsche Texte des Mittelalters
0070-4342 Deutsche Zoologische Gesellschaft. Verhandlungen
0070-4377 Deutscher Kuesten-Almanach
0070-4423 Deutsches Beamten-Jahrbuch; Bundesausgabe
0070-4431 Deutsches Buehnen-Jahrbuch
0070-4458 Deutsches Hydrographisches Institut. Jahresbericht
0070-4490 Deutsches Institut fuer Puppenspiel. Forschung und Lehre
0070-4504 Deutsches Jahrbuch der Musikwissenschaft *changed to* Jahrbuch Peters
0070-4512 Deutsches Universitaets-Handbuch†
0070-4563 Developments in Industrial Microbiology
0070-4571 Developments in Sedimentology
0070-458X Developments in Solid Earth Geophysics
0070-4598 Developments in Theoretical and Applied Mechanics†
0070-461X Devon and Cornwall Holidays in the Sun *changed to* Holidays in the Sun, Devon, Cornwall, Somerset and Dorset
0070-4628 Central Mining Research Station, Dhanbad. Progress Report
0070-4652 Diabetes-Related Literature Index by Authors and Key Words in the Title
0070-4660 Diagnostische Informationen fuer die aerztliche Praxis *see* 0300-8096
0070-4687 Diatomeenschalen im Elektronenmikroskopschen Bild
0070-4695 Dichter und Zeichner
0070-4709 Dictionary of African Biography†
0070-4717 Dictionary of Canadian Biography
0070-4733 Dictionary of Latin American and Caribbean Biography
0070-475X Dictionnaire des Parfums de France et des Lignes pour Hommes
0070-4768 Dictionnaire des Produits de Beaute et de Cosmetologie *changed to* Dictionnaire des Produits de Soins de Beaute
0070-4776 Dictionnaire des Valeurs des Meubles et Objets d'Art
0070-4792 Didactica Classica Gandensia
0070-4806 Diderot Studies
0070-4814 Diebeners Goldschmiede- und Uhrmacher-Jahrbuch
0070-4822 Diesel and Gas Turbine World Wide Catalog
0070-4830 Diesel Locomotive Question & Answer Manual
0070-4849 Digest of Health Statistics for England and Wales *changed to* Health and Personal Social Services Statistics
0070-4857 Digest of Legal Activities of International Organizations and Other Institutions
0070-4865 Digest of Literature on Dielectrics
0070-4873 Digest of World Events
0070-4881 Dimension: Languages
0070-4903 Dine Israel
0070-492X Diplomaciai Iratok Magyarorszag Kulpolitikajahoz
0070-4938 Diplomatarium Danicum
0070-4946 Diplomatic Corps of Belgrade
0070-4962 Diplomat's Annual†
0070-4970 Direct Selling
0070-4997 Directories of Science Information Sources, International Bibliography†
0070-5012 Directory for Exceptional Children
0070-5020 Directory for the Nonwoven Fabrics and Disposable Soft Goods Industries *see* 0095-683X
0070-5039 Directory Iron and Steel Plants
0070-5047 Directory of Accredited Camps for Boys and Girls *changed to* Parents' Guide to Accredited Camps. Midwest Edition
0070-5047 Directory of Accredited Camps for Boys and Girls *changed to* Parents' Guide to Accredited Camps. Northeast Edition
0070-5047 Directory of Accredited Camps for Boys and Girls *changed to* Parents' Guide to Accredited Camps. West Edition
0070-5047 Directory of Accredited Camps for Boys and Girls *changed to* Parents' Guide to Accredited Camps. South Edition
0070-5055 Directory of Accredited Private Home Study Schools *changed to* Directory of Accredited Home Study Schools
0070-5063 Directory of American College Theatre
0070-5071 Directory of American Firms Operating in Foreign Countries
0070-508X Directory of American Philosophers
0070-5098 Directory of American Savings and Loan Associations
0070-5101 Directory of American Scholars
0070-5152 Directory of British Associations
0070-5179 Directory of Brush and Allied Trades
0070-5187 Directory of Business Schools *changed to* Directory of Accredited Institutions
0070-5195 Directory of Buying Offices and Accounts
0070-5217 Directory of Canadian Map Collections
0070-5225 Directory of Canadian Trust Companies
0070-5233 Directory of Catholic Schools and Colleges
0070-5241 Directory of Central Atlantic States Manufacturers. Maryland, Delaware, Virginia, West Virginia, North Carolina, South Carolina
0070-525X Directory of Chemical Engineering Research in Canadian Universities
0070-5268 Directory of Church of England Social Services
0070-5276 Directory of College and University Libraries in New York State
0070-5284 Directory of College Placement Offices *changed to* Directory of Career Planning and Placement Offices
0070-5292 Directory of Communication Organizations *see* 0094-2588
0070-5306 Directory of Community Services in Maryland
0070-5314 Directory of Companies and Their Subsidiaries in the Wine, Spirit and Brewing Trades *changed to* Off Licence News Directory
0070-5322 Directory of Company Secretaries
0070-5330 Directory of Computerized Information in Science and Technology
0070-5357 Directory of Cooperative Education
0070-5365 Directory of Corporate Affiliations
0070-5373 Directory of Correctional Institutions and Agencies of the United States of America, Canada, and Great Britain *see* 0362-9287
0070-5381 Directory of Correctional Services in Canada / Repertoire des Services de Correction du Canada *see* 0225-4115
0070-539X Directory of Current Research in Israel: Physical and Life Sciences *see* 0301-4657
0070-5403 Directory of Current Scientific Research Projects in Pakistan†
0070-5411 Directory of Dealers in Secondhand and Antiquarian Books in the British Isles
0070-542X Directory of Directors
0070-5438 Directory of Directors
0070-5446 Directory of Discount Centers *changed to* Directory of Discount Department Stores
0070-5454 Directory of Education Studies in Canada
0070-5462 Directory of Engineering College Research and Graduate Study *changed to* Engineering College Research and Graduate Study.
0070-5470 Directory of Engineering Societies and Related Organizations
0070-5489 Directory of Engineers *changed to* Institution of Engineers of Ireland. Register of Chartered Engineers and Members
0070-5497 Directory of Nature Centers and Related Environmental Education Facilities
0070-5500 Directory of European Associations. Part 1: National Industrial Trade & Professional Associations
0070-5527 Directory of Farmers' Organizations and Marketing Boards in Canada
0070-5543 Directory of Foreign Firms Operating in the United States
0070-556X Directory of Franchising Organizations
0070-5586 Directory of Government Agencies Safeguarding Consumer and Environment†
0070-5616 Directory of Graduate Programs in the Speech Communication Arts and Sciences
0070-5624 Directory of Grant-Making Trusts
0070-5632 Hawaii's Scientific Resources Directory†
0070-5640 Directory of Health, Welfare and Recreation Services of Greater Montreal *see* 0319-258X
0070-5659 Directory of Historical Societies and Agencies in the United States and Canada
0070-5675 Directory of Institutions of Higher Education in Missouri
0070-5691 Directory of Insurance Companies Licensed in New York State
0070-5705 Directory of Israeli Merchants and Manufacturers *changed to* Directory of Israel
0070-5721 Directory of Kansas Manufacturers and Products
0070-573X Directory of Law Teachers
0070-5756 Directory of Lawyer Referral Services, Legal Aid and Defender Offices and Legal Assistance Offices of the Armed Forces†
0070-5772 Directory of Machine Tools and Related Products
0070-5799 Directory of Maryland Exporters-Importers
0070-5802 Directory of Maryland Manufacturers
0070-5810 Directory of Medical Libraries in New York State
0070-5829 Directory of Medical Specialists
0070-5837 Directory of Mental Health Resources in Florida†
0070-5845 Directory of Michigan Manufacturers
0070-5861 Directory of Mineral Producers in Oklahoma†
0070-5888 Directory of Municipal Officials of New Mexico
0070-5896 Directory of National and International Labor Unions in the United States *see* 0090-4163
0070-5918 National Trade and Professional Associations of the United States and Labor Unions *see* 0094-8284
0070-5926 Directory of Nebraska Manufacturers
0070-5934 Directory of New Mexico Manufacturing and Mining
0070-5950 Directory of New York State Public Library Systems
0070-5969 Directory of Oceanographers in the United States *changed to* Directory of Marine Scientists in the United States
0070-5977 Directory of Official Architects and Planners *changed to* Directory of Official Architecture and Planning
0070-5985 Directory of Ohio Manufacturers *changed to* Ohio Industrial Directory
0070-5993 Directory of Oil Marketing and Wholesale Distributors
0070-6000 Directory of On-Going Research in Smoking and Health
0070-6019 Directory of Opportunities for Graduates
0070-6035 Directory of Organizations and Personnel in Educational Management
0070-6051 Directory of Overseas Summer Jobs
0070-606X Directory of Pakistani Scholars Abroad
0070-6078 Directory of Pakistan's Periodicals in Social Sciences†
0070-6086 Directory of Pathology Training Programs
0070-6094 Directory of Periodicals Publishing Articles on English and American Literature and Language
0070-6124 Directory of Premium and Incentive Buyers *changed to* Directory of Premium, Incentive and Travel Buyers
0070-6140 Directory of Professional Photography
0070-6167 Directory of Public Refrigerated Warehouses
0070-6175 Directory of Quarries and Pits†
0070-6183 Directory of Reference and Research Library Resources Systems in New York State
0070-6205 Directory of Regional Councils *see* 0095-1455
0070-6213 Directory of Research Reports Relating to Produce Packaging and Marketing
0070-623X Directory of Scholarly and Research Publishing Opportunities *changed to* Directory of Publishing Opportunities in Journals and Periodicals
0070-6256 Directory of Science Resources for Maryland
0070-6264 Directory of Scientific and Technical Associations and Institutes in Israel *see* 0334-2824
0070-6272 Directory of Scientific Directories
0070-6280 Directory of Scientific Research in Nigeria
0070-6302 Directory of Serials in Pure and Applied Science and Economics Published in Israel†
0070-6310 Directory of Shipowners, Shipbuilders and Marine Engineers
0070-6337 Directory of Singapore Manufacturers
0070-6345 Directory of Service Organizations.†

0070-6361 Directory of Special Libraries and Information Centers in the U.S. & Canada
0070-637X Directory of Special Libraries in Israel
0070-6396 Directory of Special Libraries in Montreal
0070-640X Directory of State and Federal Funds Available for Business Development
0070-6418 Directory of State Arts Councils†
0070-6426 Directory of Steel Foundries in the United States, Canada and Mexico
0070-6442 Tennessee Directory of Manufacturers *see* 0360-5477
0070-6450 Directory of Texas Manufacturers
0070-6477 Directory of the Forest Products Industry
0070-6515 Directory of Travel Agencies
0070-6523 Directory of United Funds and Community Health and Welfare Councils *changed to* United Way of America. International Directory
0070-6531 Directory of United States Importers
0070-654X Directory of U.S. Institutions of Higher Education *changed to* Education Directory. (School Year): Colleges and Universities
0070-6558 Directory of United States Standardization Activities
0070-6566 Directory of Utah Manufacturers
0070-6574 Directory of Virginia Manufacturing and Mining
0070-6582 Directory of Visiting Scholars in the United States Awarded Grants Under the Mutual Educational and Cultural Exchange Act (the Fulbright-Hays Act) *see* 0098-1508
0070-6604 Directory to the Furnishing Trade
0070-6612 Diretorio Brasileiro de Industria Farmaceutica
0070-6639 D I S A Information. Measurement and Analysis
0070-6655 Disc Collector *see* 0360-8700
0070-6663 Discourse Units in Human Communication for Librarians
0070-668X Discoveries in the Judaean Desert of Jordan
0070-6698 Discovery Reports
0070-6701 Dispersion and Unity *changed to* Forum
0070-671X Disquisitiones Mathematicae Hungariae
0070-6728 Dissertationes Botanicae
0070-6736 U S C Annual Distinguished Lecture Series Monographs in Special Education and Rehabilitation
0070-6760 Dix-Huitieme Siecle
0070-6779 Do-It-Yourself. Annual
0070-6787 Do-It-Yourself Gardening Annual
0070-6795 Doblingers Verlagsnachrichten†
0070-6809 Doctoral Dissertations on Transportation
0070-6817 Documentologie†
0070-6825 Documenta Romaniae Historica. Serie A: La Moldavie
0070-6833 Documenta Romaniae Historica. Serie B: La Valachie
0070-6841 Documentacion Bibliotecologica
0070-685X Documentatio Didactica Classica
0070-6868 Documentation du Batiment
0070-6884 Documente Istorice
0070-6892 Documente si Manuscrise Literare
0070-6906 Documenti Sulle Arti del Libro
0070-6922 Documentos Latino Americanos†
0070-6957 Documents et Recherches sur l'Economie des Pays Byzantins, Islamiques et Slaves et Leurs Relations Commerciales au Moyen Age†
0070-6973 Documents on American Foreign Relations *changed to* American Foreign Relations-a Documentary Record
0070-7007 Dod's Parliamentary Companion
0070-7015 Dog World Annual
0070-7023 Dokumentation Verschleiss, Reibung und Schmierung *see* 0340-3475
0070-7031 Dokumente zur Deutschlandpolitik
0070-704X Dollars and Cents of Shopping Centers
0070-7058 Domestic Oceanborne and Great Lakes Commerce of the United States *changed to* Domestic Waterborne Trade of the United States
0070-7066 Dominican Republic. Secretaria de Obras Publicas y Comunicaciones. Estadistica *changed to* Dominican Republic Secretaria de Estado de Obras Publicas y Comunicaciones. OPC
0070-7074 Donauschwaebisches Schrifttum
0070-7082 Hewitt-Donlon Catalog of United States Small Size Paper Money
0070-7112 Dorset Natural History and Archaeological Society. Proceedings
0070-7120 Dorset Worthies
0070-7139 Dossiers d'Education Familiale
0070-7155 Dossiers du Cinema
0070-7171 Downdraft
0070-718X Downhill Only Journal
0070-7198 Dramascripts Series
0070-7201 Landesmuseum fuer Vorgeschichte, Dresden. Veroeffentlichungen
0070-721X Medizinische Akademie "Carl Gustav Carus" Dresden. Schriften
0070-7228 Staatliches Museum fuer Mineralogie und Geologie, Dresden. Abhandlungen†
0070-7244 Staatliches Museum fuer Tierkunde in Dresden. Entomologische Abhandlungen
0070-7252 Staatliches Museum fuer Tierkunde in Dresden. Faunistische Abhandlungen
0070-7260 Staatliches Museum fuer Tierkunde in Dresden. Malakologische Abhandlungen
0070-7279 Reichenbachia
0070-7287 Staatliches Museum fuer Tierkunde in Dresden. Zoologische Abhandlungen
0070-7295 Staatliches Museum fuer Voelkerkunde Dresden. Abhandlungen und Berichte
0070-7325 Droit Polonais Contemporain
0070-7333 Drosophila Information Service
0070-7341 Drug Abuse Law Review†
0070-735X Drug Abuse Papers
0070-7368 Drug Dependence†
0070-7376 Drug Topics Redbook
0070-7392 Drugs in Current Use and New Drugs
0070-7406 Drugs of Choice
0070-7414 Dublin Institute for Advanced Studies. Communications. Series A
0070-7422 Dublin Institute for Advanced Studies. School of Cosmic Physics. Geophysical Bulletin
0070-7430 Dudley, England (West Midlands) Public Libraries. Archives Department. Transcripts
0070-7457 Universitaet Duesseldorf. Jahrbuch
0070-7473 Duke University. Commonwealth-Studies Center. Publications
0070-7481 Duke University. Cooperative Oceanographic Program. Progress Report
0070-7546 Dumbarton Oaks Papers
0070-7554 Dumbarton Oaks Studies
0070-7562 Dumbarton Oaks Texts
0070-7589 Electronic Marketing Directory
0070-7597 Dun and Bradstreet Metalworking Directory
0070-7600 Dun & Bradstreet Middle Market Directory *changed to* Dun and Bradstreet Million Dollar Directory. Vol. 2
0070-7619 Dun and Bradstreet Million Dollar Directory. Vol. 1
0070-7627 Dun and Bradstreet Reference Book of Corporate Managements
0070-7635 Dun & Bradstreet Register *changed to* Dun & Bradstreet Standard Register
0070-7643 Dunsink Observatory. Publications
0070-7694 Duquesne Studies. Philological Series *changed to* Duquesne Studies. Language and Literature
0070-7708 Duquesne Studies. Philosophical Series
0070-7716 Duquesne Studies. Psychological Series
0070-7732 Duquesne Studies. Theological Series
0070-7740 University of Durban-Westville. Journal
0070-7759 University of Natal. Institute for Social Research. Annual Report
0070-7767 Durch Stipendien Studieren
0070-7783 Dutch Studies in Russian Literature†
0070-7791 Dzieje Polskiej Granicy Zachodniej
0070-7805 E D P Conference for Retailers†
0070-7821 E I A Guide
0070-7864 Early English Text Society. Publications. Extra Series
0070-7872 Early English Text Society. Publications. Original Series
0070-7880 Early English Text Society. Publications. Supplementary Texts
0070-7902 Earth and Extraterrestrial Sciences *see* 0146-2970
0070-7910 Earth Sciences Series
0070-7945 East African Academy. Proceedings *changed to* Kenya National Academy for Advancement of Arts and Sciences. Proceedings
0070-7953 East African Freshwater Fisheries Research Organization. Annual Report
0070-7961 East African Geographical Review
0070-7988 Maktaba
0070-8003 East African Railways. Annual Report†
0070-8011 East African Research Information Centre. E A R I C Information Circular *changed to* Kenya National Academy for Advancement of Arts and Sciences. Research Information Circulars
0070-8038 East African Wildlife Journal *see* 0141-6707
0070-8062 University of Kansas. Center for East Asian Studies. International Studies: East Asian Series. Research Series
0070-8070 University of Kansas. Center for East Asian Studies. International Studies: East Asian Series. Reference Series
0070-8089 East Carolina University Publications in History
0070-8097 East Europe in German Books
0070-8100 East Europe Monographs
0070-8127 East Lakes Geographer
0070-8135 Bangladesh. Education Directorate. Report on Pilot Project on Adult Education
0070-8143 Bangladesh. Directorate of Agricultural Marketing. Agricultural Marketing Series
0070-8151 Bangladesh. Directorate of Agriculture. Season and Crop Report
0070-8178 Bangladesh Research and Evaluation Centre. Report
0070-8186 Bangladesh University of Engineering and Technology, Dacca. Technical Journal
0070-8208 East Yorkshire Local History Series
0070-8224 Eastern Hemisphere Petroleum Directory *changed to* European Petroleum Directory
0070-8224 Eastern Hemisphere Petroleum Directory *changed to* Africa-Middle East Petroleum Directory
0070-8224 Eastern Hemisphere Petroleum Directory *changed to* Asia-Pacific Petroleum Directory
0070-8232 Eastern New Mexico University. Contributions in Anthropology
0070-8259 University of Eastern Philippines. Research Center. Report
0070-8275 Eaton Electronics Research Laboratories. Technical Report
0070-8305 Echos des Charites de St. Vincent de Paul *changed to* Equipes St Vincent
0070-8321 Ecole Francaise des Attaches de Presse. Association des Anciens Eleves. Annuaire
0070-833X Tall Timbers Conference on Ecological Animal Control by Habitat Management. Proceedings
0070-8348 Ecological Society of Australia. Proceedings
0070-8356 Ecological Studies; Analysis and Synthesis
0070-8364 Ecologie Marina†
0070-8372 Ecology and Conservation Series
0070-8399 Economia *changed to* Revista de Economia
0070-8402 Economia e Storia
0070-8437 Economic and Scientific Research Foundation, New Delhi. Annual Report
0070-8453 National Institute of Economic and Social Research, London. Economic and Social Studies
0070-847X Economic Council of Canada. Annual Report
0070-8488 Economic Council of Canada. Annual Review
0070-8518 Economic Development Programme for the Republic of South Africa
0070-8534 Economic Education Experiences of Enterprising Teachers
0070-8550 Economic Handbook of the Machine Tool Industry
0070-8593 Economic Picture of Japan†
0070-8615 Economic Questions for Illinois Agriculture
0070-8623 Economic Research Studies†
0070-8631 Economic Review
0070-864X Economic Review of World Tourism
0070-8666 Bank of Japan. Economic Statistics Annual
0070-8674 Economic Studies†
0070-8690 Economic Survey of Asia and the Far East *changed to* Economic and Social Survey of Asia and the Pacific
0070-8704 Bangladesh Economic Survey *changed to* Bamladesa Arthanaitika Jaripa
0070-8712 Economic Survey of Europe
0070-8720 Economic Survey of Latin America
0070-8739 Economic Survey of Rhodesia
0070-8747 Economic Yearbook of Tunisia
0070-8755 Economic and Social Research Institute. Publications Series. Paper
0070-8763 Economics of Fruit Farming
0070-8771 Economie Belge et Internationale
0070-878X Economie de la Tunisie en Chiffres
0070-8798 Economie et Finances Agricoles
0070-8801 Economie et Societe
0070-881X Luxembourg. Service Central de la Statistique et des Etudes Economiques. Cahiers Economiques. Serie A: Economie Luxembourgeoise
0070-8836 Economisch Instituut voor Het Midden-en Kleinbedrijf. Verslag
0070-8852 Economy and History†
0070-8860 Ecrits Libres
0070-8879 Ecriture
0070-8887 Ecuador. Centro de Desarrollo Industrial. Informe de Labores
0070-8895 Ecuador. Instituto Nacional de Estadistica y Censos. Anuario de Estadisticas Hospitalarias†
0070-8909 Ecuador. Instituto Nacional de Estadistica y Censos. Anuario de Estadisticas Vitales†
0070-8917 Ecuador. Instituto Nacional de Estadistica y Censos. Estadistica del Trabajo
0070-8925 Ecuador Economico
0070-8933 Ecuador. Servicio Nacional de Meteorologia e Hidrologia. Anuario Hidrologico *changed to* Ecuador.Instituto Nacional de Meteorologia e Hidrologia. Anuario Hidrologico
0070-8941 Ecuador. Servicio Nacional de Meteorologia e Hidrologia. Anuario Meteorologico *changed to* Ecuador. Instituto Nacional de Meteorologia e Hidrologia. Anuario Meteorologico
0070-8976 Edgar Brookes Academic and Human Freedom Lecture
0070-8992 University of Edinburgh. Architecture Research Unit. Report

ISSN	Title
0070-9018	University of Edinburgh. Publications. Language and Literature†
0070-9034	University of Edinburgh. Publications. Science†
0070-9069	Editiones Arnamagnaeanae. Series A
0070-9077	Editiones Arnamagnaeanae. Series B
0070-9085	Editiones Arnamagnaeanae. Supplementum
0070-9093	Editori Librai Cartolibrai e Biblioteche d'Italia†
0070-9107	Editorial Offices in the West†
0070-9115	Education and Science
0070-9131	Education Authorities' Directory and Annual
0070-9158	Education Committees Year Book *changed to* Education Year Book
0070-9166	Education for Nursing: The Diploma Way
0070-9182	Education in Europe. Section 1: Higher Education and Research
0070-9190	Education in Europe. Section 2: General and Technical Education
0070-9204	Education in Europe. Section 3: Out-Of-School Education
0070-9212	Education in Europe. Section 4 (General)
0070-9220	Education in Japan; A Graphic Presentation
0070-9239	Education in Large Cities Series†
0070-9263	Educational and Psychological Interactions
0070-931X	Educational/Instructional Broadcasting Buyers Guide†
0070-9344	Educational Studies and Documents
0070-9352	Educational Technology Bibliography Series
0070-9360	Educational Theatre Journal. Supplement†
0070-9379	Educational Therapy
0070-9387	Educators Grade Guide to Free Teaching Aids
0070-9395	Educators Guide to Free Films
0070-9409	Educators Guide to Free Filmstrips
0070-9417	Educators Guide to Free Guidance Materials
0070-9425	Educators Guide to Free Science Materials
0070-9433	Educators Guide to Free Social Studies Materials
0070-9441	Educators Guide to Free Tapes, Scripts, and Transcriptions *see* 0160-1296
0070-945X	Edward Shann Memorial Lecture in Economics†
0070-9468	Egon Ronay's Dunlop Guide to Hotels and Restaurants in the British Isles *changed to* Egon Ronay's Lucas Guide to Hotels, Restaurants and Inns in Great Britain and Ireland
0070-9484	Egyptian Dental Journal
0070-9492	Egyptian Religious Texts and Representation†
0070-9506	Egyptian Society of Endocrinology and Metabolism. Journal
0070-9514	Eidgenoessische Zukunft: Bausteine fuer Die Kommende Schweiz
0070-9522	Einfuehrung in die Information und Dokumentation
0070-9530	Einkaufsfuehrer durch die Pelz- und Ledermode
0070-9557	Ekologia Polska
0070-9565	El Hi Textbooks in Print
0070-9573	El Paso Archaeological Society. Special Reports
0070-959X	Eldridge Reeves Johnson Foundation for Medical Physics. Colloquium. Proceedings
0070-9603	Electeur
0070-9638	Electrical and Electronic Trader Year Book
0070-9646	Electrical and Electronics Trades Directory
0070-9654	Electrical Contractors' Year Book *changed to* E C A Year Book Desk Diary
0070-9662	Electrical Engineering Research Abstracts. Canadian Universities
0070-9670	Electrical Engineer's Pocket Book†
0070-9697	Electrical Electronics Insulation Conference. Record
0070-9719	Electrical Process Heating in Industry. Technical Conference. Record
0070-9735	Electricite de France. Rapport d'Activite
0070-9751	Electricite de France. Statistiques de la Production et de la Consommation
0070-976X	Electricity Supply Handbook
0070-9778	Electroanalytical Chemistry: A Series of Advances
0070-9808	Electron, Ion and Laser Beam Technology Conference. Record *see* 0099-121X
0070-9816	Electron Technology
0070-9832	Electronics Components Conference. Record *see* 0569-5503
0070-9840	Electronic Connection Techniques and Equipment†
0070-9867	Electronic Market Data Book
0070-9875	Electronic News Financial Fact Book and Directory
0070-9913	Electronics in Japan
0070-9956	Elektro-Jahr
0070-9964	Elektryfikacja i Mechanizacja Gornictwa i Hutnictwa
0070-9972	Elementa Ad Fontium Editiones
0070-9980	Elementary Teachers Guide to Free Curriculum Materials
0070-9999	Elements de Mathematique†
0071-0008	Elements du Bilan Economique
0071-0024	Elizabethan Stamp Catalogue
0071-0032	Elizabethan Theatre
0071-0067	Elsner; Handbuch fuer Strassenbau und Strassenverkehrstechnik *changed to* Elsners Handbuch fuer Strassenwesen
0071-0075	Elsners Taschenbuch der Eisenbahntechnik
0071-0091	Empire State Historical Publications
0071-0113	E R E A C Directory *changed to* E-R-C Directory
0071-013X	Employment and Earnings Statistics for the United States *changed to* Employment and Earnings: United States
0071-0148	Employment Opportunities for Advanced Post-Graduate Scientists and Engineers
0071-0156	En Direct Avec l'Histoire
0071-0164	Encore
0071-0180	Encyclopaedia Chimica Internationalis†
0071-0199	Encyclopaedic Dictionary of Physics. Supplement†
0071-0202	Encyclopedia of Associations
0071-0210	Encyclopedia of Business Information Sources
0071-0229	Encyclopedia of Materials Handling. Supplement†
0071-0237	Encyclopedia of Social Work
0071-027X	American University. Energy Institute. Proceedings
0071-0288	Engineer Buyers Guide
0071-0318	Engineering Geology and Soils Engineering Symposium. Proceedings
0071-0326	Engineering Geology Case Histories
0071-0334	Engineering in Medicine and Biology Conference. Record
0071-0342	Engineering Industries Association. Classified Directory and Buyers Guide
0071-0350	Engineering Laboratories Series
0071-0369	Tennessee Valley Authority. Engineering Laboratory. Research in the Fields of Civil Engineering, Mechanical Engineering, Instrumentation†
0071-0377	Engineering Sciences Data Index *changed to* Engineering Sciences Data Unit Index
0071-0385	Engineers Joint Council. Engineering Manpower Commission. Demand for Engineers and Technicians *changed to* Engineers Joint Council. Engineering Manpower Commission. Demand for Engineers
0071-0393	American Association of Engineering Societies. Engineering Manpower Commission. Engineering and Technology Degrees
0071-0407	Engineering and Technology Enrollments *changed to* American Association of Engineering Societies. Engineering Manpower Commission. Engineering Enrollment Data.
0071-0415	American Association of Engineering Societies. Engineering Manpower Commission. Engineers' Salaries: Special Industry Report.
0071-0423	American Association of Engineering Societies. Engineering Manpower Commission. Professional Income of Engineers.
0071-0431	Prospects of Engineering and Technology Graduates *changed to* American Association of Engineering Societies. Engineering Manpower Commission. Placement of Engineering and Technology Graduates.
0071-0474	Salaries of Engineering Technicians *changed to* American Association of Engineering Societies. Engineering Manpower Commission. Salaries of Engineering Technicians and Technologists.
0071-0490	English and American Studies in German
0071-0547	English Ceramic Circle. Transactions
0071-0555	English Church Music *changed to* World of Church Music
0071-0571	English Guernsey Herd Book
0071-058X	English Historical Documents
0071-0598	English Institute. Selected Essays
0071-0601	English Language and Orientation Programs in the United States
0071-061X	English Little Magazines
0071-0628	English Monarch Series
0071-0636	English Place-Name Society
0071-0644	English Studies Series
0071-0660	English Translations of German Standards
0071-0679	Ensayo y Testimonio
0071-0687	Ente Nazionale Idrocarburi. Report and Statement of Accounts
0071-0695	Entertainment Industry Series
0071-0709	Entomological Society of Alberta. Proceedings
0071-0717	Entomological Society of America. Miscellaneous Publications
0071-0725	Entomological Society of Australia (N.S.W.) Journal *see* 0158-0760
0071-0741	Entomological Society of Canada. Bulletin
0071-075X	Entomological Society of Canada. Memoirs
0071-0768	Entomological Society of Ontario. Proceedings
0071-0776	Entomological Society of Pennsylvania. Newsletter
0071-0784	Societe Entomologique du Quebec. Memoires
0071-0792	Entomologicke Problemy
0071-0822	Entretiens sur l'Antiquite Classique
0071-0830	Environment Law Review *changed to* Land Use and Environment Law Review
0071-0857	Environmental Geology
0071-0873	Environmental Health Engineering Series
0071-089X	Environmental Health Series: Air Pollution
0071-0911	Environmental Health Series: Radiological Health
0071-092X	Environmental Hygiene for the Public Health Inspector *see* 0316-0661
0071-0946	Environmental Wastes Control Manual *see* 0163-9730
0071-0954	Kentron Epistemonikon Ereunion. Epeteris
0071-0962	Ephemeris of the Sun, Polaris and Other Selected Stars with Companion Data and Tables
0071-0989	Epigraphische Studien
0071-1004	Epimeleia: Beitraege zur Philosophie†
0071-1039	Equal Opportunity; the Minority Student Magazine
0071-1055	Eranos Yearbook. Papers†
0071-1063	Erasmus in English
0071-108X	Eretz-Israel. Archaeological, Historical and Geographical Studies
0071-1098	Advances in Anatomy, Embryology and Cell Biology
0071-111X	Ergebnisse der Inneren Medizin und Kinderheilkunde. New Series
0071-1128	Ergebnisse der Limnologie
0071-1136	Ergebnisse der Mathematik und Ihrer Grenzgebiete
0071-1160	Erlanger Geologische Abhandlungen
0071-1179	Ernaehrungsforschung
0071-1187	Ernest Bloch Lectures
0071-1195	Ernest Bloch Society. Bulletin
0071-1217	Ernst-Mach-Institut, Freiburg. Wissenschaftlicher Bericht *see* 0340-8833
0071-1233	Ertekezesek a Torteneti Tudomanyok Korebol. Uj Sorozat
0071-125X	Erziehung und Unterricht
0071-1268	Esakia
0071-1276	Universidade de Sao Paulo. Escola Superior de Agricultura "Luis de Queiroz." Anais
0071-1284	Universidade de Sao Paulo. Escola Superior de Agricultura "Luis de Queiroz." Boletim Didactico†
0071-1292	Universidade de Sao Paulo. Escola Superior de Agricultura "Luis de Queiroz." Boletim de Divulgacao
0071-1306	Universidade de Sao Paulo. Escola Superior de Agricultura "Luis de Queiroz." Boletim Tecnico-Cientifico†
0071-1314	Escuela Interamericana de Bibliotecologia. Estadisticas
0071-1330	Esprit et Liberte
0071-1357	Essays and Studies
0071-1365	Essays in Biochemistry
0071-1373	Essays in Chemistry
0071-139X	Essays in French Literature
0071-1411	Essays in History
0071-142X	Essays in International Finance
0071-1438	Essays in Physics
0071-1446	Essays in Toxicology
0071-1462	Essener Bibliographie
0071-1470	Essential Articles
0071-1489	Essex Naturalist
0071-1497	Estadistica de la Ensenanza Media en Espana *changed to* Estadistica de la Ensenanza en Espana
0071-1500	Estadistica de la Primaria y de las Escuelas Magisterio en Espana *changed to* Estadistica de la Ensenanza en Espana
0071-1519	Estadistica de la Ensenanza Superior en Espana *changed to* Estadistica de la Ensenanza en Espana
0071-1527	Estadistica del Comercio Exterior de Espana
0071-1543	Mexico. Direccion General de Estadistica. Estadistica Industrial Anual
0071-156X	Estadisticas Minera y Metalurgica de Espana
0071-1578	Estate Planning, Quick Reference Outline†
0071-1586	Estates Gazette Digest of Land and Property Cases
0071-1594	Mid-Year Estimates of Population of New Mexico Counties†
0071-1616	Current Population Reports; Population Estimates and Projections. Estimates of the Population of the United States and Components of Population Change

ISSN INDEX 1115

0071-1624 Current Population Reports, P-25: Population Estimates and Projections. Estimates of the Population of the United States by Age, Color, and Sex *changed to* Current Population Reports: Population Estimates and Projections. Estimates of the Population of the United States by Age, Sex and Race
0071-1632 Coleccion Estructuras y Formas
0071-1640 Estudios de Arte Moderno†
0071-1659 Estudios de Arte y Estetica
0071-1667 Estudios de Cultura Maya
0071-1675 Universidad Nacional Autonoma de Mexico. Instituto de Investigaciones Historicas. Serie de Cultura Nahuatl. Estudios de Cultura Nahuatl
0071-1683 Estudios de Folklore
0071-1691 Estudios de Literatura
0071-1705 Estudios de Literatura Contemporanea
0071-1713 Estudios Filologicos
0071-1721 Estudios Filologicos. Anejo
0071-173X Estudios Oceanologicos†
0071-1748 Estudios y Fuentes del Arte en Mexico
0071-1772 Ethiopian Publications: Books, Pamphlets, Annuals and Periodical Articles
0071-1780 Ethnic Chronology Series
0071-1837 Ethnographica
0071-1845 Ethnologia
0071-1853 Ethnomedizin
0071-1861 Etnografia Polska
0071-187X Etudes Africaines
0071-1888 Etudes d'Anglais
0071-1896 Etudes de Cas de Conflits Internationaux
0071-190X Etudes de Linguistique Appliquee
0071-1918 Etudes de Litterature Etrangere et Comparee *see* 0035-1466
0071-1926 Etudes de Philologie, d'Archeologie et d'Histoire Ancienne
0071-1934 Etudes de Philologie et d'Histoire
0071-1942 Etudes de Pollution Atmospherique a Paris et dans les Departments Peripheriques
0071-1969 Etudes d'Histoire de l'Art
0071-1977 Etudes d'Histoire Economique et Sociale
0071-1993 Etudes d'Histoire Africaine
0071-2027 Etudes et Travaux d'Archeologie Marocaine
0071-2035 Etudes Ethnologiques
0071-2043 Etudes Europeennes†
0071-2051 Etudes Finno-Ougriennes
0071-206X Etudes Foreziennes
0071-2078 Etudes Gobiniennes
0071-2086 Etudes Gregoriennes
0071-2108 Etudes Historiques
0071-2124 Etudes Linguistiques
0071-2140 Etudes Picardes
0071-2191 Studies on Taxation and Economic Development
0071-2213 Etudes Universitaires sur l'Integration Europeenne
0071-2221 Eucarpia
0071-223X Eugenics Society Symposia
0071-2248 Eureka; the Archimedean's Journal
0071-2264 European Company for the Financing of Railway Rolling Stock. Annual Report
0071-2272 Europa Camping und Caravaning. Internationaler Fuehrer
0071-2299 Europa. Revue de Presse Europeenne
0071-2302 Europa Year Book
0071-2329 Europaeische Schriften
0071-2388 European and Mediterranean Plant Protection Organization. E P P O Bulletin/Bulletin O E P P
0071-2396 European and Mediterranean Plant Protection Organization. Publications. Series B: Plant Health Newsletter
0071-240X European and Mediterranean Plant Protection Organization. Publications. Series C: Reports of Working Parties *see* 0071-2388
0071-2418 European and Mediterranean Plant Protection Organization. Publications. Series D: Miscellaneous†
0071-2426 European Art Exhibitions. Catalog
0071-2477 European Association for Animal Production. Publications
0071-2485 European Association for Animal Production. Symposia on Energy Metabolism
0071-2493 European Association for Personnel Management. Congress Reports
0071-2507 European Association for Potato Research. Proceedings of the Triennial Conference *changed to* E A P R Abstracts of Conference Papers
0071-2523 European Bookdealers
0071-2531 European Brewery Convention. Proceedings of the International Congress
0071-2558 European Civil Aviation Conference (Report of Session)
0071-2566 European Commision of Human Rights. Collection of Decisions/Recueil de Decisions *changed to* European Commission of Human Rights. Decisions and Reports
0071-2574 Comite Europeen du Beton. Bulletin d'Information *changed to* Comite Euro-International du Beton. Bulletin d'Information
0071-2582 European Companies
0071-2612 European Conference of Local Authorities. Documents *changed to* European Conference of Local and Regional Authorities. Documents
0071-2620 European Conference of Local Authorities. Official Reports of Debates *changed to* European Conference of Local and Regional Authorities. Official Reports of Debates
0071-2639 European Conference of Local Authorities. Texts Adopted *changed to* European Conference of Local and Regional Authorities. Texts Adopted
0071-2647 European Congress on Electron Microscopy
0071-2655 European Conference on Microcirculation. Proceedings
0071-2671 European Congress of Anaesthesiology. Proceedings
0071-268X European Congress of Neurological Surgery. (Papers) *see* 0001-6268
0071-2698 European Congress of Perinatal Medicine. Proceedings
0071-2701 European Convention on Human Rights. Yearbook *changed to* Yearbook of Human Rights
0071-271X European Coordination Centre for Research and Documentation in Social Sciences. Publications
0071-2728 European Curriculum Studies
0071-2787 European Federation of Finance House Associations. Annual Report
0071-2795 European Federation of Finance House Associations. Conference Proceedings
0071-2817 Confederation Europeene pour la Therapie Physique. Congress Reports
0071-2825 European Grassland Federation. Proceedings of the General Meeting
0071-2868 European Investment Bank. Annual Report
0071-2884 European League for Economic Cooperation. Publications
0071-2892 European League for Economic Cooperation. Reports of the International Congress
0071-2906 European Leather Guide *changed to* Leather Guide
0071-2930 European Marketing Data and Statistics
0071-2965 European Ophthalmological Society. Congress. Abstracts
0071-2981 European Organization for Quality Control. Conference Proceedings
0071-3015 Debates of the European Parliament
0071-3023 European Parliament. Documents de Seance
0071-3090 European Society for the Study of Drug Toxicity. Proceedings *changed to* European Society of Toxicity. Proceedings
0071-3104 European Southern Observatory. Bulletin†
0071-3112 European Symposium on Chemical Reaction Engineering. Proceedings
0071-3120 European Passenger Timetable Conference Minutes
0071-3139 European Yearbook
0071-3155 Europinion
0071-3171 E T S Bulletin *see* 0360-8808
0071-321X Evasion†
0071-3236 Everyman's Income Tax†
0071-3244 Everyman's United Nations
0071-3252 Evolution de l'Economie des Pays Sud-Americains
0071-3260 Evolutionary Biology
0071-3279 Excavaciones Arqueologicas en Espana
0071-3287 Excavations at Dura-Europos
0071-3295 Exceptional Infant
0071-3309 Executive Directory of the U.S. Pharmaceutical Industry
0071-3333 Experiences in Faith†
0071-335X Experientia. Supplementum
0071-3376 Experiment in International Living. President's Report *changed to* Experiment in International Living. Annual Report
0071-3384 Experimental Biology and Medicine
0071-3392 Experimental Botany; An International Series of Monographs
0071-3422 Experimental Mechanics; Proceedings
0071-3430 Experimentelle Medizin, Pathologie und Klinik†
0071-3473 Exploration Geophysics
0071-3481 Explorations in Education
0071-3503 Export-Import Bank of Japan. Annual Report
0071-3511 Export-Import Bank of the United States. Summary of Operations
0071-3546 Exporters' Encyclopaedia-World Marketing Guide *see* 0149-8118
0071-3554 Export Data
0071-3554 Export Data Exporters Year Book *see* 0071-3554
0071-3570 Fabian Society. Annual Report
0071-3597 Facet Books. Biblical Series†
0071-3600 Facet Books. Historical Series†
0071-3619 Facet Books. Social Ethics Series†
0071-3627 Fachliteratur zum Buch- und Bibliothekswesen
0071-3635 Facts About Israel
0071-3643 Facts about New England Colleges, Universities and Institutes
0071-3651 Facts about Nursing
0071-3678 Facts and Figures on Government Finance
0071-3686 Faculty of Actuaries in Scotland. Transactions
0071-3716 Fairchild's Financial Manual of Retail Stores
0071-3724 Fallout in Norway†
0071-3740 Family Holiday Guide
0071-3759 Family Planning Association of Pakistan. Annual Report *changed to* F P A P Biennial Report
0071-3791 Far East and Australasia
0071-3821 Far Eastern Economic Review. Yearbook *changed to* Asia Yearbook
0071-3848 Farm Classification in England and Wales
0071-3864 Farm Credit Corporation. Annual Report
0071-3872 Farm Credit Corporation. Federal Farm Credit Statistics/Statistiques du Credit Agricole Federal
0071-3880 Farm and Garden Equipment Guide
0071-3899 Farm Equipment Directory/Annuaire†
0071-3910 Farm Incomes in England and Wales
0071-3937 Farm Machinery Yearbook
0071-3945 Farm Management *see* 0311-8665
0071-3961 Farming in the East Midlands
0071-397X Lincoln College. Department of Farm Management and Rural Valuation. Farm Management Papers†
0071-3988 Lincoln College. Department of Farm Management and Rural Valuation. Farm Management Studies†
0071-4003 Farm Real Estate Taxes *changed to* U. S. Department of Agriculture, Economics, Statistics, and Cooperatives Service. Farm Real Estate Taxes, Recent Trends and Developments
0071-402X Farnborough Air Show (Public Programme)
0071-4038 Fasciculi Historici
0071-4046 Fastener Standards
0071-4054 Fauna Fennica
0071-4062 Fauna of the Clyde Sea Area†
0071-4070 Fauna Republicii Socialiste Romania†
0071-4089 Fauna Slodkowodna Polski
0071-4097 Fawley Foundation Lectures
0071-4100 Feature Films on 8mm and 16mm *changed to* Feature Films on 8mm, 16mm and Videotape
0071-4119 Federacion Espanola Galguera. Anuario y Memoria Deportiva
0071-4127 Federal Employees Almanac
0071-4135 Federal Graduated Withholding Tax Tables
0071-4143 Federal Tax Return Manual
0071-4151 Federatie van Bedrijfsverenigingen. Jaarverslag
0071-416X Federation d'Associations de Techniciens des Industries des Peintures, Vernis, Emaux et Encres d'Imprimerie de l'Europe Continentale. Annuaire Officiel. Official Yearbook. Amtliches Jahrbuch
0071-4178 Federation des Industries Belges. Rapport Annuel *changed to* Federation des Entreprises de Belgique. Rapport Annuel
0071-4186 F. F. M. Annuaire Officiel
0071-4194 Federation Francaise de Natation. Annuaire
0071-4232 Federation Francaise des Sports Equestres. Annuaire Officiel
0071-4240 Federation Francaise et Europeenne du Commerce, de l'Industrie et de l'Epargne. Revue
0071-4259 Federation Horlogere Suisse. Annual Report
0071-4267 Federation Internationale de Rugby Amateur. Annuaire
0071-4283 Federation Internationale Motocycliste. Annuaire
0071-4291 Federation Nationale de l'Industrie de la Chaussure de France. Annuaire
0071-4305 Federation Nationale des Agences de Presse. Annuaire
0071-4348 Federation Nationale des Conseils Juridiques et Fiscaux. Cahiers
0071-4356 Annuaire de la Cooperation F.N.C.C.
0071-4364 Federation Nationale es Foyers Ruraux de France. Informations et Liaisons *see* 0180-2410
0071-4399 Federation of American Societies for Experimental Biology. Council on Biological Sciences Information. Working Documents†
0071-4402 Federation of European Biochemical Societies. (Proceedings of Meeting)
0071-4410 Federation of Migros Cooperatives. Abridged Report
0071-4429 Federation of Pakistan Chambers of Commerce Industry. Brief Report of Activities
0071-4437 Federation of Societies for Paint Technology. Yearbook *changed to* Federation of Societies for Coatings Technology. Yearbook and Annual Membership Directory
0071-450X Feed Additive Compendium
0071-4518 Feed Industry Red Book

ISSN INDEX 1117

0071-4542 Universita degli Studi di Ferrara. Istituto di Geologia, Paleontologia e Paleontologia Umana. Annali. Sezione 15. Paleontologia Umana e Paleontologia *changed to* Universita degli Studi di Ferrara. Istituto di Geologia. Annali. Sezione 15. Paleontologia Umana e Paletnologia
0071-4550 Universite degli Studi di Ferrara. Istituto di Geologia, Paleontologia e Paleontologia Umana. Annali. Sezione 9. Scienze Geologiche *changed to* Universita degli Studi di Ferrara. Istituto di Geologia. Annali. Sezione 9. Scienze Geologiche
0071-4569 Universita degli Studi di Ferrara. Istituto di Geologia, Paleontologia e Paleontologia Umana. Memorie Geopaleontologiche†
0071-4577 Universita degli Studi di Ferrara. Istituto di Geologia, Paleontologia e Paleontologia Umana. Pubblicazioni *changed to* Universita degli Studi di Ferrara. Istituto di Geologia. Pubblicazioni
0071-4585 Der Fertighaus-Katalog
0071-4615 Fertilizer Industry Series
0071-4623 Fertilizer Science and Technology Series
0071-4631 Fertilizer Trends
0071-464X Fertilizers: an Annual Review of World Production, Consumption and Trade *see* 0084-6546
0071-4658 Festival Film Guide *changed to* American Film Festival Guide
0071-4674 Feuerwehr-Jahrbuch
0071-4682 Fiber Science Series
0071-4690 Fibrinolysis, Thrombolysis, and Blood Clotting; a Bibliography *see* 0360-7607
0071-4704 Fiches Analytiques de la Presse Technique Francaise
0071-4712 Fiches Typologiques Africaines
0071-4739 Fieldiana: Anthropology
0071-4755 Fielding's Guide to the Caribbean Plus the Bahamas *changed to* Fielding's Caribbean
0071-4763 Fielding's Quick Currency Guide for Europe†
0071-4771 Fielding's Quick Currency Guide for Far, Near and Middle East Including Russia and China†
0071-478X Fielding's Selective Shopping Guide to Europe
0071-4798 Fielding's Super Economy Europe *see* 0095-6406
0071-481X Figura. Nova Series
0071-4828 Fiji. Bureau of Statistics. Annual Statistical Abstract
0071-4844 Fiji. Ministry of Agriculture & Fisheries. Annual Report
0071-4852 Filipiniana Book Guild. Publications
0071-4860 Film: An Anthology by the National Society of Film Critics†
0071-4879 Film-Echo Filmwoche. Verleih-Katalog
0071-4887 Film-English/Humanities Association. Journal
0071-4917 Film Review
0071-4925 Filmaarsboken
0071-4933 Spielfilmliste
0071-4941 Filmstatistisches Taschenbuch
0071-495X Filologia
0071-4968 Filologia e Critica
0071-4976 Filologos Colombianos
0071-4984 Filozofiai Irok Tara
0071-4992 Filozofiai Tanulmanyok
0071-5042 Financial Post Directory of Directors
0071-5050 Financial Post Survey of Industrials
0071-5077 Financial Post Survey of Markets *changed to* Financial Post Canadian Markets
0071-5085 Financial Post Survey of Mines *see* 0227-1656
0071-5115 Financial Reporting in Canada
0071-5131 Financial Times of Canada. Economic Forecast and Top Hundred *changed to* Top Hundred
0071-5166 Financing Higher Education in Canada.†
0071-5182 Finishing Handbook and Directory
0071-5190 Finnish Meteorological Institute. Contributions
0071-5204 Finland. Ilmatieteen Laitos. Tiedonantoja
0071-5212 Magnetic Results from Nurmijarvi Geophysical Observatory
0071-5220 Finnish Meteorological Institute. Observations of Radioactivity
0071-5239 Finnish Meteorological Institute. Soil Temperature Measurements
0071-5247 Finland. Kansanelakelaitos. Tilastollinen Vuosikirja
0071-5255 Finland. Kansantalousosasto. Kansantalouden Kehitysarvio. Summary: National Budget for Finland
0071-5271 Finland. Kansantalousosasto. Taloudellinen Katsaus. Economic Survey
0071-528X Finland. Ulkoasiainministerio. Ulkapolititisija Lausuntoja ja Asiakirjoja
0071-5298 Finland. Posti- ja Lennatinlaitos. Kotimaisten Sanomalehtien Hinnasto. Inhemsk Tidningstaxa
0071-5301 Finland. Posti-ja Lennatinlaitos. Ulkomaisten Sanomalehtien Hinnasto. Utlandsk Tidningstaxa
0071-531X Finland. Rakennushallitus. Tutkimus-ja Kehitystoiminnan. Tiedote
0071-5328 Finland. Sosiaalihallitus. Sosiaalihuoltotilaston Vuosikirja
0071-5336 Finland. Sosiaali- ja Terveysministerio. Sosiaalisia Erikoistutkimuksia
0071-5344 Finland. Tilastokeskus. Teollisuustilasto
0071-5360 Finland. Valtakunnansuunnittelutoimisto. Julkaisuja. Sarja A *see* 0355-8878
0071-5379 Great Britain. Department of the Environment. Fire Research Station. Fire Notes *changed to* Great Britain. Building Research Establishment. Reports
0071-5387 Crime and Fire Prevention *see* 0049-0024
0071-5395 Fire Prevention News
0071-5409 Fire Protection Directory
0071-5417 Fire Protection Handbook
0071-5425 Fire Protection Handbook Study Guide
0071-5433 Fire Research Annual Reports *see* 0068-354X
0071-545X Great Britain. Department of the Environment. Fire Research Station. Technical Papers *changed to* Great Britain. Building Research Establishment. Reports
0071-5468 Fire Yearbook
0071-5484 National Bureau of Economic Research. Fiscal Studies
0071-5492 Fish Disease Leaflets
0071-5506 U. S. Environmental Protection Agency. Fish Kills Caused by Pollution
0071-5522 Fisheries and Wildlife Paper. Victoria
0071-5530 Fisheries Circular, Victoria†
0071-5549 Fisheries Contribution, Victoria†
0071-5581 Fisheries Statistics of Japan
0071-5603 Fishery Statistics of the United States *changed to* Fisheries of the United States
0071-5611 Fresh Water Fishing Guide
0071-5638 Fisken og Havet
0071-5654 Fitzgerald/Hemingway Annual
0071-5662 British Librarianship & Information Science
0071-5670 Fix Your Chevrolet
0071-5689 Fix Your Ford
0071-5697 Fix Your Volkswagen
0071-5735 Flood Damage Prevention; an Indexed Bibliography
0071-5751 Flora Ecologica de Restingas do Sudeste do Brasil
0071-576X Flora et Vegetatio Mundi
0071-5786 Flora Malesiana. Series 2: Pteridophyta
0071-5794 Flora Neotropica. Monographs
0071-5808 Flora of Texas†
0071-5816 Flora Polska; Rosliny Naczyniowe Polski i Ziem Osciennych
0071-5824 Flora Polska: Rosliny Zarodnikowe Polski i Ziem Osciennych
0071-5840 Flora Slodkowodna Polski
0071-5867 Flore du Cambodge, du Laos et du Vietnam
0071-5875 Flore du Cameroun
0071-5883 Flore du Gabon
0071-5948 Florida. Division of Plant Industry. Biennial Report
0071-5999 Florida Requirements for Teacher Certification
0071-6006 Florida Speleological Society. Special Papers
0071-6014 Florida State Documents *see* 0430-7801
0071-6022 Florida Statistical Abstract
0071-6030 University of Florida. Bureau of Economic and Business Research. Population Studies
0071-6057 University of Florida. Communication Sciences Laboratory. Annual Report *see* 0046-4198
0071-6065 University of Florida. Department of Accounting. Accounting Series†
0071-609X University of Florida. Institute of Food and Agricultural Sciences. Annual Research Report†
0071-6103 University of Florida. Center for Gerontology. Studies and Programs.
0071-6111 Southern Conference on Gerontology Report†
0071-6138 University of Florida. Libraries. Technical Processes Department. Caribbean Acquisitions
0071-6146 University of Florida. School of Forestry. Cooperative Forest Genetics Research Program. Progress Report *changed to* University of Florida. School of Forest Resources & Conservation. Cooperative Forest Genetics Research Program. Progress Report.
0071-6154 Florida State Museum. Bulletin. Biological Series *changed to* Florida State Museum. Bulletin. Biological Sciences
0071-6162 Florida State Museum. Contributions. Social Sciences *changed to* Florida State Museum. Contributions. Anthropology and History
0071-6170 University of Florida. University College Series
0071-6189 University of Florida Monographs. Humanities
0071-6197 University of Florida Monographs. Social Sciences
0071-6235 Flotation Index
0071-6243 Flour Milling and Baking Research Association. Annual Report and Accounts
0071-6278 Fluid Power Symposium. Proceedings
0071-6286 Flying Annual and Pilots' Guide *see* 0163-1144
0071-6294 Focus on Dance
0071-6308 Focus (Drink and Gambling) *changed to* C O A D Words
0071-6316 Focus Series†
0071-6340 Fodor's Austria
0071-6359 Fodor's Belgium and Luxembourg
0071-6367 Fodor's Czechoslovakia
0071-6375 Fodor's Guide to Europe
0071-6383 Fodor's France
0071-6391 Fodor's Germany *see* 0192-0952
0071-6405 Fodor's Great Britain
0071-6413 Fodor's Greece
0071-6421 Fodor's Hawaii
0071-643X Fodor's Holland
0071-6456 Fodor's India *changed to* Fodor's India & Nepal
0071-6464 Fodor's Ireland
0071-6472 Fodor's Italy
0071-6480 Fodor's Japan and East Asia *see* 0098-1613
0071-6480 Fodor's Japan and East Asia *see* 0160-8991
0071-6499 Fodor's Mexico
0071-6510 Fodor's Portugal
0071-6529 Fodor's Scandinavia
0071-6537 Fodor's South America
0071-6545 Fodor's Spain
0071-6553 Fodor's Switzerland
0071-6561 Fodor's Guide to the Caribbean, Bahamas, and Bermuda *see* 0098-2547
0071-657X Fodor's Yugoslavia
0071-6588 Fodor's Israel
0071-6596 Fodor's London
0071-660X Fodor's Rome: A Companion Guide†
0071-6618 Fodor's Turkey
0071-6634 Foerderungsgemeinschaft fuer Absatz- und Werbeforschung. Schriften *changed to* Aus dem Schrifttum ueber Werbung
0071-6642 Foldrajzi Monografiak
0071-6650 Foldrajzi Tanulmanyok
0071-6677 Folia Forestalia Polonica. Series A. Lesnictwo
0071-6685 Folia Forestalia Polonica. Series B. Drzewnictwo
0071-6693 Folia Geographica Danica
0071-6707 Folia Geographica. Geographica-Oeconomica
0071-6715 Folia Geographica. Geographica-Physica
0071-6723 Folia Historiae Artium
0071-6731 Folia Medica Lodziensia†
0071-674X Folia Oeconomica Cracoviensia
0071-6766 Folklivsskildringar och Bygdesstudier
0071-6774 Folklore Americano
0071-6782 Folklore Annual
0071-6804 Folktales of the World
0071-6847 Fonds de Developpment Economique et Social. Conseil de Direction. Rapport
0071-6855 Fonetica si Dialectologie
0071-6863 Fontes Archaeologici Posnanienses
0071-6871 Fontes Rerum Austriacarum. Reihe 1. Scriptores
0071-688X Fontes Rerum Austriacarum. Reihe 2. Diplomataria et Acta
0071-6898 Fontes Rerum Austriacarum. Reihe 3. Fontes Juris
0071-6901 Fonti Sui Comuni Rurali Toscani
0071-6928 Food and Agriculture Organization of the United Nations. Commodity Policy Studies
0071-6944 Food and Agriculture Organization of the United Nations Conference. Report
0071-6952 Food and Agriculture Organization of the United Nations. Commodity Reference Series†
0071-6960 F A O Agricultural Development Papers
0071-6979 F A O Atomic Energy Series†
0071-6987 F A O Agricultural Studies
0071-7002 F A O Commodity Review and Outlook
0071-7010 F A O Food Additive Control Series
0071-7029 F A O Forestry Development Papers
0071-7037 F A O Fisheries Studies
0071-7045 F A O Legislative Series
0071-7061 F A O Manuals in Fisheries Science
0071-707X F A O Nutrition Meetings Report Series
0071-7088 F A O Nutritional Study
0071-7096 F A O Rice Report†
0071-710X Food and Agriculture Organization of the United Nations. National Grain Policies
0071-7118 Food and Agriculture Organization of the United Nations. Production Yearbook
0071-7126 Food and Agriculture Organization of the United Nations. Trade Yearbook
0071-7142 Philippines. Food and Nutrition Center. Annual Report *changed to* Philippines. Food and Nutrition Research Institute. Annual Report

1118 ISSN INDEX

0071-7150 Kansas State University. Food and Feed Grain Institute. Technical Assistance in Food Grain Drying, Storage, Handling and Transportation *changed to* Kansas State University. Food and Feed Grain Institute. Technical Assistance in Grain Storage, Processing and Marketing, and Agribusiness Development

0071-7185 Food Industries of S.A. Buyers' Guide *changed to* Food Industries Yearbook and Buyers' Guide

0071-7193 Food Industry Studies

0071-7207 Food Processing and Packaging Directory *changed to* Food Processing Industry Directory

0071-7215 Food Processing Review *see* 0093-0075

0071-7223 Food Science Series

0071-7231 Food Trades Directory, Food Buyer's Yearbook

0071-724X Football Association Year Book

0071-7258 Football Register

0071-7266 For Younger Readers, Braille and Talking Books

0071-7274 Ford Foundation Annual Report

0071-7282 Forecast

0071-7312 Foreign Area Studies Series†

0071-7320 Foreign Consular Offices in the United States

0071-7339 Foreign Liabilities, Assets and Foreign Investments in Pakistan†

0071-7355 Foreign Relations of the United States

0071-7371 Annual Foreign Trade Statistics of Bangladesh

0071-738X Foreign Trade of Greece *changed to* Commerce Exterieur de la Grece

0071-7398 Foreign Trade Statistics of Africa. Series A: Direction of Trade

0071-7401 Foreign Trade Statistics of Africa. Series B: Trade by Commodity

0071-7428 Foreign Trade Statistics of Pakistan

0071-7436 Foreningen til Norske Fortidsminnesmerkers Bevaring. Aarbok

0071-7444 Forest Engineering Symposium. Proceedings

0071-7452 Forest Farmer. Manual Edition

0071-7479 U.S. Forest Service. Forest Insect Conditions in the Northern Region *changed to* U.S. Forest Service. Forest Insect and Disease Conditions in the Northern Region

0071-7487 Forest Insect Conditions in the United States

0071-7495 Canada. Department of the Environment. Forest Management Institute. Program Review

0071-7509 Forest Pest Leaflets *changed to* Forest Insect and Disease Leaflets

0071-7533 Forest Research in India

0071-7541 Forest Research News for the South *changed to* U.S. Forest Service. Southern Forest Experiment Station. Research Accomplished

0071-755X Forest Resources Reports *see* 0090-239X

0071-7568 Forest Science Monographs

0071-7576 Forest Tree Nurseries in the United States

0071-7584 Forestry Abstracts. Leading Article Reprint Series

0071-7592 Formal Linguistics Series

0071-7614 Etudes Mathematiques en Vue des Applications: Formulaire de Mathematiques a l'Usage des Physiciens et des Ingenieurs

0071-7622 Formulaire Thera

0071-7630 Forretnings- og Bedriftslederen

0071-7649 Forschung und Konstruktion im Stahlbau

0071-7657 Forschungen aus Staat und Recht

0071-7665 Forschungen zur Antiken Sklaverei

0071-7673 Forschungen zur Mittelalterlichen Geschichte

0071-7681 Forschungen zur Romanischen Philologie

0071-769X F I W - Schriftenreihe

0071-7703 Forschungsprobleme der Vergleichenden Literaturgeschichte

0071-7711 Forschungsstelle fuer Jagdkunde und Wildschadenverhuetung. Schriftenreihe

0071-772X Forstwissenschaftliche Forschungen

0071-7738 Fort Belknap Genealogical Association. Bulletin

0071-7754 Fort Burgwin Research Center. Publications

0071-7762 Fort Hays Studies. New Series. Art†

0071-7770 Fort Hays Studies. New Series. Bibliography†

0071-7789 Fort Hays Studies. New Series. Economics†

0071-7800 Fort Hays Studies. New Series. Literature†

0071-7819 Fort Hays Studies. New Series. Music†

0071-7827 Fort Hays Studies. New Series. Science†

0071-7835 Fortbildung und Praxis

0071-7843 Gastroenterologische Fortbildungskurse fuer die Praxis†

0071-7851 Fortbildungskurse fuer Rheumatologie

0071-786X Fortschritte der Arzneimittelforschung

0071-7878 Fortschritte der Botanik *see* 0340-4773

0071-7886 Fortschritte der Chemie Organischer Naturstoffe

0071-7894 Fortschritte der Chemischen Forschung *changed to* Topics in Current Chemistry

0071-7908 Immunology Reports and Reviews

0071-7916 Fortschritte der Kiefer- und Gesichts-Chirurgie

0071-7924 Fortschritte der Physikalischen Chemie

0071-7932 Fortschritte der Praktischen Dermatologie und Venerologie

0071-7940 Fortschritte der Psychoanalyse

0071-7975 Fortschritte der Urologie und Nephrologie

0071-7991 Fortschritte der Zoologie

0071-8009 Fortschritte in der Geologie von Rheinland und Westfalen

0071-8017 Progress in Colloid and Polymer Science

0071-8025 Forum der Psychiatrie

0071-8033 Forum des Transports Publics *see* 0397-6521

0071-8041 Forum on Fundamental Surgical Problems

0071-805X Forum on Homemaker-Home Health Aide Service. Report†

0071-8068 Fotogrammetriska Meddelanden

0071-8076 Fotointerpretacja w Geografii

0071-8084 Foulsham's Original Old Moore's Almanack

0071-8092 Foundation Directory

0071-8106 Foundation for the Study of Cycles. Research Bulletin

0071-8122 Foundations of Language Supplementary Series†

0071-8130 Foundry Directory and Register of Forges

0071-8157 Fowler's Mechanical Engineers Pocket Book†

0071-8165 Fowler's Mechanics and Machinists Pocket Book†

0071-8173 Fraenkische Geographische Gesellschaft. Mitteilungen

0071-8181 France-Allemagne

0071-819X France. Archives Nationales. Centre d'Information de la Recherche Historique en France. Bulletin

0071-8211 France. Service du Traitement de l'Information et des Statistiques Industrielles. Annuaire de Statistique Industrielle

0071-822X Annuaire de l'Administration et du Corps des Mines

0071-8246 France. Bureau de Recherches Geologiques et Minieres. Memoires

0071-8254 France. Caisse Nationale de Credit Agricole. Rapport sur le Credit Agricole Mutuel

0071-8262 France. Service de Documentation et de Cartographie Geographiques. Memoires et Documents.

0071-8270 Centre National de la Recherche Scientifique. Seminaire d'Econometrie. Monographies

0071-8289 Centre d'Etudes Sociologiques. Travaux et Documents

0071-8297 France. Centre National de Coordination des Etudes et Recherches sur la Nutrition et l'Alimentation. Cahiers Techniques

0071-8300 Centre National de la Recherche Scientifique. Colloques Internationaux. Sciences Mathematiques, Physico-Chimiques, Biologiques et Naturelles *changed to* Centre National de la Recherche Scientifique. Colloques Internationaux. Sciences Mathematiques, Physiques, Chimiques, Biologiques et Medicales

0071-8319 France. Centre National de la Recherche Scientifique. Colloques Nationaux

0071-8327 Centre National de la Recherche Scientifique. Rapport d'Activite

0071-8335 Centre National de la Recherche Scientifique. Rapport National de Conjoncture Scientifique

0071-8343 Centre National de la Recherche Scientifique. Seminaire d'Econometrie. Cahiers

0071-8351 Centre National de la Recherche Scientifique. Tableau de Classement des Chercheurs

0071-836X Centre National du Commerce Exterieur. Annuaire

0071-8378 Chambre Syndicale des Commissionaires pour le Commerce Exterieur. Annuaire Officiel

0071-8386 France-Collectivites: Guide National des Chefs des Services d'Achats et des Fournisseurs de Collectivites

0071-8394 France. Comite des Travaux Historiques et Scientifiques. Bulletin Archeologique.

0071-8408 France. Comite des Travaux Historiques et Scientifiques. Bulletin Philologique et Historique (Jusqu'a 1610)

0071-8416 France. Comite des Travaux Historiques et Scientifiques. Section d'Archeologie. Actes du Congres National des Societes Savantes

0071-8424 Comite des Travaux Historiques et Scientifiques. Section de Geographie. Actes du Congres National des Societes Savantes

0071-8432 France. Comite des Travaux Historiques et Scientifiques. Section de Geographie. Bulletin

0071-8440 France. Comite des Travaux Historiques et Scientifiques. Section d'Histoire Moderne et Contemporaine. Actes du Congres National des Societes Savantes

0071-8459 France. Comite des Travaux Historiques et Scientifiques. Section d'Histoire Moderne et Contemporaine. Bulletin

0071-8467 France. Commissariat a l'Energie Atomique. Annual Report

0071-8483 France. Commission Centrale des Marches. Guide du Fournisseur de l'Etat et des Collectivites Locales

0071-8491 France. Commission Nationale de l'Amenagement du Territoire. Rapport

0071-8505 France. Commission Technique des Ententes. Economiques Rapports

0071-8513 France. Conseil National de la Comptabilite. Rapport d'Activite

0071-853X France. Delegation Generale a la Recherche Scientifique et Technique. Recherche dans le Domaine de l'Eau: Repertoire des Laboratoires

0071-8548 France. Delegation Generale a la Recherche Scientifique et Technique. Repertoire National des Laboratoires; la Recherche Universitaire; Sciences Exactes et Naturelles. Tome 2: Biologie

0071-8556 France. Delegation Generale a la Recherche Scientifique et Technique. Repertoire National des Laboratoires; la Recherche Universitaire; Sciences Exactes et Naturelles. Tome 3: Chimie

0071-8564 France. Delegation Generale a la Recherche Scientifique et Technique. Repertoire National des Laboratoires; la Recherche Universitaire; Sciences Exactes et Naturelles. Tome 4: Mathematiques, Sciences de l'Espace et de la Terre

0071-8572 France. Delegation Generale a la Recherche Scientifique et Technique. Repertoire National des Laboratoires; la Recherche Universitaire; Sciences Exactes et Naturelles. Tome 1: Physique

0071-8629 France. Direction Generale des Douanes et Droits Indirects. Annuaire†

0071-8637 France. Direction Generale des Douanes et Droits Indirects. Annuaire Abrege de Statistiques

0071-8645 France. Direction Generale des Douanes et Droits Indirects. Commentaires Annuels des Statistiques du Commerce Exterieur

0071-8653 France. Direction Generale des Douanes et Droits Indirects. Navigation Maritime Internationale de la France (Tableaux Generaux)†

0071-8661 France. Direction Generale des Douanes et Droits Indirects. Statistiques du Commerce Exterieur. Transit Direct†

0071-8688 France. Direction Generale des Douanes et Droits Indirects. Statistiques du Commerce Exterieur: Importations-Exportations. Nomenclature: N.G.P. (Nomenclature Generale des Produits)

0071-8696 France. Direction Generale des Douanes et Droits Indirects. Statistiques du Commerce Exterieur: Importations-Exportations. Nomenclature C.T.C.I. (Classification Type pour le Commerce International)†

0071-870X France. Direction Generale de la Concurrence et des Prix. Bulletin Officiel des Services des Prix

0071-8718 France. Direction Nationale des Douanes et Droits Indirects. Transport du Commerce Exterieur

0071-8726 France. Direction Nationale des Douanes et Droits Indirects. Tableau General des Transports

0071-8734 France en Poche. Total Guide

0071-8742 France. Inspection Generale des Finances. Annuaire

0071-8793 Annuaire Statistique des Territoires d'Outre Mer

0071-8815 France. Institut National de la Statistique et des Etudes Economiques. Tendances de la Conjoncture

0071-8823 France. Institut National d'Etudes Demographiques. Cahiers de Travaux et Documents

0071-884X France. Institut Pedagogique National. Dossiers Pedagogiques de la Radio-Television Scolaire†

0071-8866 France. Ministere de la Sante Publique et de la Securite Sociale. Annuaire Statistique de la Sante et de l'Action Sociale *changed to* France. Ministere de la Sante et de la Securite Sociale. Tableaux Statistiques "Sante et Securite Sociale"

0071-8882 France. Ministere de la Sante. Note d'Information *changed to* France. Ministere de la Sante et de la Securite Sociale. Notes d'Information

0071-8890 France. Ministere de l'Economie et des Finances. Balance des Paiements Entre la France et l'Exterieur

0071-8904 France. Ministere du Budget. Budget

0071-8912 France. Ministere de l'Economie et des Finances. Rapport du President de la Republique Francaise sur les Operations des Caisses d'Epargne Ordinaires. *changed to* France. Ministere de l'Economie et des Finances. Statistiques et Etudes Financieres. Finance Publique. Serie Bleue
0071-8920 France. Ministere de l'Economie. Rapport du Conseil de Direction du Fonds de Developpement Economique et Social
0071-8963 France. Institut National de Recherche et de Documentation Pedagogiques. Repertoire d'Etablissements Publics d'Enseignement et de Services
0071-8971 France. Ministere des Affaires Etrangeres. Recueil des Traites et Accords de la France
0071-8998 O.R.S.T.O.M. Annales Hydrologiques
0071-9005 Memoires O.R.S.T.O.M.
0071-9013 Office de la Recherche Scientifique et Technique Outre-Mer. Rapport d'Activite
0071-9021 Office de la Recherche Scientifique et Technique Outre-Mer. Initiations Documentations Techniques
0071-903X France. Office National d'Immigration. Statistiques de l'Immigration
0071-9048 France-Peinture
0071-9056 France Plastiques
0071-9064 France Protestante
0071-9072 France. Direction Generale de l'Aviation Civile. Annuaire†
0071-9080 France. Ministere de l'Agriculture et du Developpement Rural. Service Central des Enquetes et Etudes Statistiques. Statistique Agricole Annuelle *changed to* France. Ministere de l'Agriculture. Enquete Communautaire sur la Structure des Exploitations Agricoles
0071-9102 France-Sports
0071-9129 Tribunal de Commerce, Paris. Annuaire
0071-917X Franco British Trade Directory
0071-9188 Archiv Ungedruckter Wissenschaftlicher Schriften†
0071-9196 Institut fuer Angewandte Geodaesie. Mitteilungen
0071-920X Nachrichten aus dem Karten- und Vermessungswesen *see* 0469-4236
0071-9218 Frankfurt am Main. Statistisches Amt und Wahlamt. Statistisches Jahrbuch
0071-9226 Frankfurter Beitraege zur Germanistik
0071-9234 Frankfurter Geographische Hefte
0071-9277 Fraser's Canadian Trade Directory
0071-9285 Frater of Psi Omega
0071-9293 Fraternal Actuarial Association. Proceedings
0071-9307 Free and Inexpensive Learning Materials
0071-9315 Free China *see* 0304-1204
0071-9331 Free-World Trends in Passenger-Car Production and Engines *changed to* World Trends in Passenger-Car Production and Engines
0071-934X Freedom from Hunger Campaign. Basic Studies
0071-9366 Freedom of Speech Yearbook *changed to* S C A Free Speech Yearbook
0071-9382 Freer Gallery of Art, Washington, D.C. Occasional Papers
0071-9390 Freiberger Forschungshefte. Montanwissenschaften: Reihe A. Bergbau und Geotechnik, Arbeitsschutz und Sicherheitstechnik, Grundstoff-Verfahrenstechnik, Maschinen- und Energietechnik
0071-9404 Freiberger Forschungshefte. Montanwissenschaften: Reihe C. Geowissenschaften
0071-9420 Freiberger Forschungshefte. Montanwissenschaften: Reihe B. Metallurgie *changed to* Freiberger Forschungshefte. Montanwissenschaften: Reihe B. Metallurgie und Werbstofftechnik
0071-9439 Freiburger Geographische Arbeiten†
0071-9447 Freiburger Geographische Hefte
0071-9463 Freies Deutsches Hochstift, Frankfurt am Main. Jahrbuch
0071-9471 Freight Industry Yearbook
0071-948X Fremdenverkehr in Oesterreich
0071-9498 Fremdenverkehrswissenschaftliche Reihe†
0071-9536 Fresh Water and Salmon Fisheries Research (Scotland)†
0071-9544 Fifth District Dental Society. Bulletin *changed to* Thirtieth District Dental Society, Fresno, California. Bulletin
0071-9552 Universite de Fribourg. Paedagogisches Institut. Studien und Forschungsberichte†
0071-9560 F C L Action
0071-9587 Friends Historical Society. Journal
0071-9609 Friends Service Council. Annual Report *see* 0260-9584
0071-9617 American Friends Service Committee. Annual Report
0071-9625 Fringe Benefit Costs in Canada *see* 0701-1539
0071-9633 Frontera Oberta
0071-9641 Frontier Military Series
0071-965X Frontiers of Biology†
0071-9676 Frontiers of Radiation Therapy and Oncology
0071-9684 Frozen Food Factbook and Directory
0071-9692 Frozen Foods Year Book
0071-9706 Fruehmittelalterliche Studien
0071-9730 Fuchsia Annual
0071-9749 Fuehrer durch die Technische Literatur
0071-9757 Fuehrer zu Vor- und Fruegeschichtlichen Denkmaelern
0071-9765 Fuehrung und Organisation der Unternehmung
0071-9773 Fuentes Indigenas de la Cultura Nahuatl
0071-9781 Fukui University. Faculty of Education. Memoirs. Series 2: Natural Science
0071-979X Fulcrum
0071-982X Fundacion Bariloche. Boletin *changed to* Universitaet Zuerich. Soziologisches Institut. Bulletin
0071-9838 Fundacion Bariloche. Departamento de Sociologia. Documentos de Trabajo *changed to* Fundacion Bariloche. Desarrollos Sinergicos. Publicaciones
0071-9846 Fundacion Bariloche. Programa de Recursos Naturales y Energia. Publicaciones *changed to* Fundacion Bariloche. Instituto de Economia de la Energia. Publicaciones
0071-9862 Fundamentals of Educational Planning
0071-9870 Fundamentals of Educational Planning. Lecture-Discussion Series
0071-9889 Fundberichte aus Hessen
0071-9897 Fundberichte aus Schwaben, Neue Folge *changed to* Fundberichte aus Baden-Wuerttemberg
0071-9900 Fundheft fuer Arbeitsrecht
0071-9919 Fundheft fuer Oeffentliches Recht
0071-9927 Fundheft fuer Zivilrecht
0071-9951 Funspots Directory *changed to* Funparks Directory
0071-996X Furnished Holiday Homes & Caravans
0071-9994 Furniture Forum†
0072-0003 Further Aspects of Piaget's Work†
0072-0038 Fysiatricky a Reumatologicky Vestnik
0072-0046 G; Documentation Technique et Commerciale des Vendeurs de Gaz
0072-0062 G Q, Guide to Fashion Sources†
0072-0070 Gabinetto Disegni e Stampe degli Uffizi. Cataloghi.
0072-0089 Galerie Nierendorf, Berlin. Kunstblaetter
0072-0100 Gallia Prehistoire. Supplement
0072-0119 Gallia. Supplement
0072-0127 Galpin Society Journal
0072-0143 Gandhi Memorial Lectures
0072-0151 Gann Monographs
0072-016X Ganterie Francaise†
0072-0178 Gardens' Bulletin, Singapore
0072-0186 Gardens of England and Wales Open to the Public *see* 0141-2361
0072-0208 Gas and Fuel Corporation of Victoria. Annual Report
0072-0216 British Gas Corporation. Report and Accounts
0072-0232 Gas Industry Directory *see* 0307-3084
0072-0240 Gas Journal Directory *see* 0307-3084
0072-0259 Gas Marketing Pocket Book and Diary
0072-0267 Gas Turbine Catalog *changed to* Turbomachinery Catalog and Workbook
0072-0291 Gaster; l'Annuaire de Gastro-Enterologie
0072-0313 Gaz de France. Rapport Annuel†
0072-0321 Gaz de France. Secretariat General. Schema d'Organisation Profor
0072-033X Gazdasagtorteneti Ertekezesek
0072-0348 Gazeteer of India
0072-0356 Gazeto
0072-0364 Politechnika Gdanska. Zeszyty Naukowe. Fizyka
0072-0372 Politechnika Gdanska. Zeszyty Naukowe. Matematyka
0072-0380 Politechnika Gdanska. Zeszyty Naukowe. Mechanika
0072-0410 Gdanskie Towarzystwo Naukowe. Wydzial I. Nauk Spolecznych i Humanistycznych. Komisja Archeologiczna. Prace
0072-0429 Gdanskie Towarzystwo Naukowe. Wydzial I. Nauk Spolecznych i Humanistycznych. Seria Popularnonaukowa "Pomorze Gdanskie"
0072-0437 Gdanskie Towarzystwo Naukowe. Wydzial I. Nauk Spolecznych i Humanistycznych. Seria Zrodel
0072-0445 Gdanskie Towarzystwo Naukowe. Wydzial III. Nauk Matematyczno-Przyrodniczych. Rozprawy
0072-0453 Uniwersytet Gdanski. Wydzial Humanistyczny. Zeszyty Naukowe. Filozofia i Socjologia
0072-0461 Uniwersytet Gdanski. Wydzial Humanistyczny. Zeszyty Naukowe. Historia
0072-047X Uniwersytet Gdanski. Wydzial Humanistyczny. Zeszyty Naukowe. Pedagogika, Psychologia, Historia Wychowania
0072-0488 Uniwersytet Gdanski. Wydzial Humanistyczny. Zeszyty Naukowe. Prace Historyczno-Literackie
0072-0496 Morski Instytut Rybacki, Gdynia. Prace. Seria A: Oceanograficzno - Ichtiologiczna
0072-050X Morski Instytut Rybacki, Gdynia. Prace. Seria B: Technika Rybacka i Technologia Ryb
0072-0518 Morski Instytut Rybacki, Gdynia. Prace. Seria C: Ekonomika Rybacka
0072-0526 Gebbie House Magazine Directory *changed to* Internal Publications Directory
0072-0534 Gegenwartsfragen der Ost-Wirtschaft
0072-0542 Geiriadur Prifysgol Cymru
0072-0550 Geistige Begegnung
0072-0577 Gemeinschaft der Selbst-Verwirklichung. Jahresheft
0072-0585 Genava
0072-0607 Life Agency Management Program Brochure
0072-0615 General Agreement on Tariffs and Trade. G A T T Activities in (Year)
0072-0623 General Agreement on Tariffs and Trade. Basic Instruments and Selected Documents Series. Supplement
0072-064X General Agreement on Tariffs and Trade. International Trade
0072-0658 General Catalogue of Unesco and Unesco-Sponsored Publications
0072-0666 General Conference of the New Church. Yearbook
0072-0674 General Dental Council. Dentists Register
0072-0682 General Dental Council. Minutes of the Proceedings
0072-0690 General Directory of the Press and Periodicals in Jordan and Kuwait
0072-0704 General Directory of the Press and Periodicals in Syria
0072-0712 General Atomic Company. Library. Journal of Holdings of the Library
0072-0720 General Education Reading Material Series
0072-0739 General Encyclopedias in Print *see* 0361-1094
0072-0747 General Fisheries Council for the Mediterranean. Proceedings and Technical Papers. Debats et Documents Techniques
0072-0755 General Fisheries Council for the Mediterranean. Reports of the Sessions
0072-0763 General Medical Council, London. Medical Register
0072-0771 General Semantics Bulletin
0072-078X General Stud Book. Supplement
0072-0798 General Systems Yearbook
0072-0801 Geneseo Studies in Library and Information Science
0072-081X Genetics Lectures†
0072-0828 Musee d'Ethnographie de la Ville de Geneve. Bulletin Annuel
0072-0836 Universite de Geneve. Section d'Histoire. Documents
0072-0844 Genie Industriel; Catalogue de l'Ingenierie
0072-0852 Universita degli Studi di Genova. Istituto di Filologia Classica e Medievale. Pubblicazioni
0072-0860 Universita degli Studi di Genova. Istituto di Paleografia e Storia Medievale. Collana. Storica di Fonti e Studi
0072-0879 Gentes Herbarum
0072-0887 Genuine Irish Old Moore's Almanac
0072-0909 Geographer
0072-0917 Geografinis Metrastis
0072-0925 Geographical Observer
0072-0941 Geographische Gesellschaft, Munich. Mitteilungen
0072-095X Geographisches Jahrbuch
0072-0968 Geographisches Taschenbuch
0072-0976 Geografija ir Geologija
0072-0984 Geography of New Zealand†
0072-0992 Geologia Colombiana
0072-100X Geologia Sudetica
0072-1018 Geologica et Palaeontologica
0072-1026 Geologica Ultraiectina
0072-1042 Geological Association of Canada. Special Paper
0072-1050 Geological Journal
0072-1069 Geological Society of America. Memoirs
0072-1077 Geological Society of America. Special Papers
0072-1085 Geological Society of Australia. Special Publication
0072-1093 Geological Society of Malaysia. Bulletin
0072-1107 Geologie des Aires Oceaniques†
0072-1115 Universitaet Hamburg. Geologisch-Palaeontologisches Institut. Mitteilungen
0072-1174 Geophysica Norvegica
0072-1182 Geofizicheskii Byulleten'
0072-1190 George Ernest Morrison Lectures in Ethnology
0072-1212 Georgetown University. Institute of Languages and Linguistics. Report of the Annual Round Table Meeting on Linguistics and Language Studies *see* 0196-7207
0072-1220 Georgia Congress of Parents and Teachers. Annual Summer Institute. Handbook for P T A Leaders *changed to* Georgia Congress of Parents and Teachers. Annual Leadership Training Conference. Workshop for P T A Leaders

ISSN	Title
0072-1247	Georgia State University. Hospital Administration Program. Occasional Publication *see* 0093-8041
0072-1255	University of Georgia. Anthropology Curriculum Project. Occasional Paper Series
0072-1263	University of Georgia. College of Business Administration. Travel Research Series
0072-1271	University of Georgia. College of Agriculture Experiment Stations. Bulletin
0072-128X	University of Georgia. College of Agriculture Experiment Stations. Research Reports
0072-131X	University of Georgia Libraries. Miscellanea†
0072-1344	University of Georgia. School of Pharmacy. Pharmaceutical Services for Small Hospitals and Nursing Homes
0072-1379	Georgia Vital and Morbidity Statistics *see* 0362-0662
0072-1395	Geoscience and Man *see* 0191-6122
0072-1409	Geoscience Information Society. Proceedings
0072-1417	Geoserials *changed to* Geosources
0072-1433	German Arab Trade
0072-145X	German Motor Tribune
0072-1476	German Research Service
0072-1484	Germanica†
0072-1492	Germanistische Linguistik
0072-1506	Germany (Democratic Republic, 1949-) Meteorologischer Dienst. Abhandlungen
0072-1549	D B Report
0072-1557	Germany (Federal Republic,1949-) Bundesministerium fuer Arbeit und Sozialordnung. Hauptergebnisse der Arbeits-und Sozialstatistik
0072-1565	Germany (Federal Republic,1949-) Bundesministerium fuer Ernaehrung, Landwirtschaft und Forsten. Agrarbericht der Bundesregierung
0072-1581	Statistisches Jahrbuch ueber Ernaehrung, Landwirtschaft und Forsten der Bundesrepublik Deutschland
0072-159X	Germany (Federal Republic, 1949-) Sachverstaendigenrat zur Begutachtung der Gesamtwirtschaftlichen Entwicklung. Jahresgutachten
0072-1603	Deutscher Wetterdienst. Seewetteramt. Einzelveroeffentlichungen
0072-1611	Germany (Federal Republic, 1949-) Statistiches Bundesamt Arbeiten *changed to* Survey of German Federal Statistics
0072-162X	Das Arbeitsgebiet der Bundesstatistik
0072-1638	Germany (Federal Republic, 1949-) Statistisches Bundesamt. Alphabetisches Laenderverzeichnis fuer die Aussenhandelsstatistik
0072-1646	Germany (Federal Republic, 1949-) Statistisches Bundesamt. Fachserie 7, Reihe 1: Zusammenfassende Uebersichten fuer den Aussenhandel
0072-1654	Germany (Federal Republic, 1949-) Statistisches Bundesamt. Fachserie 7, Reihe 2: Aussenhandel nach Waren und Laendern (Spezialhandel)
0072-1662	Germany (Federal Republic, 1949-) Statistisches Bundesamt. Fachserie 7, Reihe 3: Aussenhandel Nach Laendern und Warengruppen (Spezialhandel)
0072-1697	Germany (Federal Republic, 1949-) Statistisches Bundesamt. Fachserie 7, Reihe 6: Durchfuhr im Seeverkehr und Seeumschlag
0072-1700	Germany (Federal Republic, 1949-) Statistisches Bundesamt. Aussenhandel. Reihe 7: Sonderbeitraege
0072-1719	Germany (Federal Republic, 1949-) Statistisches Bundesamt. Ausgewaehlte Zahlen fuer die Bauwirtschaft
0072-1727	Germany(Federal Republic, 1949-) Statishes Bundesamt. Fachserie 4, Reihe 5: Beschaeftigung, Umsatz, Investitionen und Kosten Struktur in Baugewerbe *changed to* Germany(Federal Republic, 1949-) Statistisches Bundesamt. Fachserie 4, Reihe 5.
0072-1735	Germany (Federal Republic, 1949-) Statistisches Bundesamt. Fachserie 5, Reihe 1: Bautaetigkeit
0072-1743	Germany (Federal Republic, 1949-) Statistisches Bundesamt. Fachserie 5, Reihe 2: Bewilligungen im Sozialen Wohnungsbau
0072-1751	Germany (Federal Republic, 1949-) Statistisches Bundesamt. Fachserie 5, Reihe 3: Bestand an Wohnungen
0072-1778	Germany (Federal Republic, 1949-) Statistisches Bundesamt. Fachserie 11: Bildung und Kultur
0072-1786	Germany (Federal Republic, 1949-) Statistisches Bundesamt. Fachserie 1, Reihe 1: Gebiet und Bevoelkerung
0072-1794	Germany (Federal Republic, 1949-) Statistisches Bundesamt. Fachserie 1, Reihe 2: Bevoelkerungsbewegung
0072-1808	Germany (Federal Republic, 1949-) Statistisches Bundesamt. Fachserie 1, Reihe 2.3: Wanderungen
0072-1832	Germany (Federal Republic, 1949-) Statistisches Bundesamt. Fachserie 1, Reihe 4: Erwerbetaetigkeit
0072-1840	Germany (Federal Republic, 1949-) Statistisches Bundesamt. Fachserie 12, Reihe 1: Ausgewaehlte Zahlen fuer das Gesundheitswesen
0072-1859	Germany (Federal Republic, 1949-) Statistisches Bundesamt. Fachserie 10. Rechtspflege
0072-1867	Bevoelkerungsstruktur und Wirtschaftskraft der Bundeslaender
0072-1964	Germany (Federal Republic, 1949-) Statistisches Bundesamt. Fachserie 6, Reihe 1: Grosshandel
0072-1972	Germany (Federal Republic, 1949-) Statistisches Bundesamt. Fachserie 6, Reihe 3: Einzelhandel
0072-1980	Germany (Federal Republic, 1949-) Statistisches Bundesamt. Fachserie 6, Reihe 6: Wahrenverkehr mit der Deutschen Demokratischen Republik und Berlin (Ost)
0072-1999	Germany (Federal Republic, 1949-) Statistisches Bundesamt. Fachserie 6, Reihe 7: Reiseverkehr
0072-2014	Germany (Federal Republic, 1949-) Statistisches Bundesamt. Fachserie 9, Reihe 1: Boden- und Kommunalkreditinstitute†
0072-2022	Germany (Federal Republic, 1949-) Statistisches Bundesamt. Geld und Kredit. Reihe 2: Aktienkurse *changed to* Germany (Federal Republic, 1949-) Statistisches Bundesamt. Fachserie 9, Reihe 2: Aktienmaerkte
0072-2030	Germany (Federal Republic, 1949-) Statistisches Bundesamt. Fachserie 2, 4: Zahlungsschwierigkeiten
0072-2073	Germany (Federal Republic, 1949-) Statistisches Bundesamt. Fachserie 4, Reihe S: Sonderbeitraege
0072-209X	Germany (Federal Republic, 1949-) Statistisches Bundesamt. Fachserie 4, Reihe 2: Indices des Auftragseingangs in Ausgewaehlten Industriezweigen und im Bauhauptgewerbe *changed to* Germany (Federal Republic, 1949-) Statistisches Bundesamt. Fachserie 4, Reihe 2.2: Indices des Auftragseingangs, des Umsatzes und des Auftragsbestands fuer das Verarbeitende Gewerbe und fuer das Bauhaupt Gewerbe
0072-2103	Germany (Federal Republic, 1949-) Statistisches Bundesamt. Fachserie 4, Reihe 7: Handwerk
0072-3673	Germany (Federal Republic, 1949-) Statistisches Bundesamt. Fachserie 3, Reihe 4.5: Fischerei
0072-3681	Germany (Federal Republic, 1949-) Statistisches Bundesamt. Fachserie 3, Reihe 2: Betriebs-, Arbeits- und Einkommensverhaeltnisse
0072-3754	Germany (Federal Republic, 1949-) Statistisches Bundesamt. Fachserie 13, Reihe 2,3: Sozialhilfe; Kriegsopferfuersorge
0072-3762	Germany (Federal Republic, 1949-) Statistisches Bundesamt. Fachserie 13, Reihe 6: Oeffentliche Jugendhilfe
0072-3789	Germany (Federal Republic, 1949-) Statistisches Bundesamt. Fachserie 16, Reihe 2: Unternehmerverdienste in Industrie und Handel
0072-3797	Germany (Federal Republic, 1949-) Statistisches Bundesamt. Fachserie 16, Reihe 3: Arbeiterverdienste im Handwerk
0072-3827	Germany (Federal Republic, 1949-) Statistisches Bundesamt. Fachserie 17, Reihe 10: Internationaler Vergleich der Preise fuer die Lebenserhaltung
0072-3843	Germany (Federal Republic, 1949-) Statistisches Bundesamt. Fachserie 16, Reihe 4: Tarifloehne und Tarifgehaelter
0072-386X	Germany(Federal Republic, 1949-) Statistisches Bundesamt. Fachserie 15, Reihe 1: Wirtschaftsrechnungen *changed to* Germany (Federal Republic, 1949-) Statistisches Bundesamt. Fachserie 15, Reihe 1: Einnahmen und Ausgaben Ausgewaehlter Privater Haushalte
0072-3878	Germany (Federal Republic, 1949-) Statistisches Bundesamt. Fachserie 17, Reihe 3: Index der Grundstoffrpreise
0072-3886	Germany (Federal Republic, 1949-) Statistisches Bundesamt. Fachserie 17, Reihe 2: Preise und Preisindizes fuer Industrielle Produkte. Erzeugerpreise *changed to* Germany (Federal Republic, 1949-) Statistisches Bundesamt. Fachserie 17, Reihe 2: Preise und Preisindizes fuer Gewerbliche Produkte. Erzeugerpreise
0072-3894	Germany (Federal Republic, 1949-) Statistisches Bundesamt. Fachserie 17, Reihe 1: Preise und Preisindizes fuer die Land- und Forstwirtschaft
0072-3908	Germany(Federal Republic, 1949-) Statistisches Bundesamt. Preise, Loehne, Wirtschaftsrechnungen. Reihe 5: Preise und Preisindices fuer Bauwerke und Bauland *changed to* Germany (Federal Republic, 1949--) Statistisches Bundesamt. Fachserie 17, Reihe 5: Kaufwerte fuer Bauland
0072-3916	Germany (Federal Republic, 1949-) Statistisches Bundesamt. Fachserie 17, Reihe 7: Preise und Preisindizes der Lebenserhaltung
0072-3924	Germany (Federal Republic, 1949-) Statistisches Bundesamt. Fachserie 17, Reihe 9: Preise fuer Verkehrsleistungen
0072-3940	Germany (Federal Republic, 1949-) Statistisches Bundesamt. Auslandsstatistik, Reihe 5: Preise und Preisindizes im Ausland
0072-3967	Studies on Statistics
0072-3975	Germany (Federal Republic, 1949-) Statistisches Bundesamt. Unternehmen und Arbeitsstaetten. Reihe 1: Die Kostenstruktur in der Wirtschaft†
0072-4009	Germany (Federal Republic, 1949-) Statistisches Bundesamt. Fachserie 18, Reihe 1: Konten und Standardtabellen
0072-4025	Germany (Federal Republic, 1949-) Statistisches Bundesamt. Fachserie 8, Reihe 5: Seeschiffahrt
0072-4033	Germany (Federal Republic, 1949-) Statistisches Bundesamt. Fachserie 8, Reihe 6: Luftverkehr
0072-405X	Germany (Federal Republic, 1949-) Statistisches Bundesamt. Fachserie 8, Reihe 3: Strassenverkehr
0072-4068	Germany (Federal Republic, 1949-) Statistisches Bundesamt. Fachserie 8, Reihe 3.3: Strassenverkehrsunfaelle
0072-4106	Germany (Federal Republic, 1949-) Statistisches Bundesamt. Warenverzeichnis fuer die Aussenhandelsstatistik
0072-4114	Germany (Federal Republic, 1949-) Statistisches Bundesamt. Zahlenkompass
0072-4122	Annalen der Meteorologie. Neue Folge
0072-4130	Deutscher Wetterdienst. Berichte
0072-4149	Deutscher Wetterdienst. Bibliographien
0072-4157	Geron
0072-4165	Gesamtverzeichnis Oesterreichischer Dissertationen
0072-4173	Geschichte der Ethik†
0072-4203	Geschichtliche Landeskunde
0072-4211	Geselecteerde Agrarische Cijfers van de E E C *changed to* E E G Vademecum
0072-422X	Gesellschaft fuer die Geschichte und Bibliographie des Brauwesens. Jahrbuch
0072-4246	Gesellschaft fuer Physiologische Chemie, Mosbach. Colloquium *changed to* Gesellschaft fuer Biologische Chemie, Mosbach. Colloquium
0072-4254	Gesellschaft fuer Schleswig-Holsteinische Geschichte. Zeitschrift
0072-4262	Wiener Gesellschaft fuer Theaterforschung. Jahrbuch
0072-4270	Gesellschaft pro Vindonissa. Jahresbericht
0072-4289	Gesellschaft pro Vindonissa. Veroeffentlichungen
0072-4327	Geyer's Who Makes It Directory
0072-4335	Ghana. Central Bureau of Statistics. Economic Survey
0072-436X	Ghana Law Reports
0072-4378	Ghana National Bibliography
0072-4408	Ghana. Railway and Ports Administration. Report
0072-4416	University of Ghana. Institute of Statistical, Social and Economic Research. Technical Research Monographs *changed to* University of Ghana. Institute of Statistical, Social and Economic Research. Technical Publication Series
0072-4432	Rijksuniversiteit Te Gent. Sterrenkundig Observatorium. Mededelingen: Astronomie
0072-4440	Rijksuniversiteit te Gent. Sterrenkundig Observatorium. Mededelingen: Meteorologie en Geofysica
0072-4459	Giannini Foundation of Agricultural Economics. Research Report
0072-4467	Gids bij de Prijscourant
0072-4483	Universitaet Giessen. Bibliothek. Berichte und Arbeiten
0072-4491	Universitaet Giessen. Bibliothek. Kurzberichte aus den Papyrus-Sammlungen
0072-4505	Gift and Decorative Accessories Buyers Directory
0072-4513	Gifu University. Faculty of Agriculture. Research Bulletin

ISSN INDEX 1121

0072-4521 Gifu University. School of Medicine. Archives
0072-4548 Gioventu Passionista
0072-4556 Girios Aidas
0072-4564 Girls School Year Book
0072-4610 University of Glasgow. Social and Economic Studies. Occasional Papers
0072-4629 University of Glasgow. Social and Economic Research Studies
0072-4637 Glass Containers
0072-4645 Glass/Metal Catalog *see* 0147-300X
0072-4661 Glaxo Volume; an Occasional Contribution to the Science and Art of Medicine†
0072-467X Glenbow Foundation. Occasional Paper†
0072-467X Glenbow-Alberta Institute. Occasional Paper
0072-4688 Politechnika Slaska. Zeszyty Naukowe. Elektryka
0072-4696 Politechnika Slaska. Zeszyty Naukowe. Inzynieria Sanitarna
0072-470X Politechnika Slaska. Zeszyty Naukowe. Matematyka-Fizyka
0072-4718 Politechnika Slaska. Zeszyty Naukowe. Nauki Spoleczne
0072-4742 Global Focus Series
0072-4750 Glossaria Interpretum†
0072-4769 Glottodidactica; an International Journal of Applied Linguistics
0072-4777 Glove News
0072-4793 Goeteborger Germanistische Forschungen
0072-4807 Acta Regiae Societatis Scientiarum et Litterarum Gothoburgensis. Zoologica
0072-4815 Acta Regiae Societatis Scientiarum et Litterarum Gothoburgensis. Geophysica
0072-4823 Acta Regiae Societatis Scientiarum et Litterarum Gothoburgensis. Humaniora
0072-4831 Goeteborgs Tandlaekare Saellskap. Aarsbok
0072-484X Goethe-Gesellschaft. Jahrbuch *changed to* Goethe-Jahrbuch
0072-4858 Goethe-Institut zur Pflege Deutscher Sprache und Kultur im Ausland. Jahrbuch
0072-4866 Niedersaechsische Staats- und Universitaetsbibliothek, Goettingen. Arbeiten
0072-4874 Goettinger Abhandlungen zur Soziologie
0072-4882 Goettinger Jahrbuch
0072-4890 Goff's Guide to Motels in Great Britain and Europe *changed to* Goff's Guide to Motels and Motorways in Great Britain and Ireland
0072-4904 Going-To-College Handbook
0072-4912 Gokhale Institute of Politics and Economics. Studies
0072-4920 Gold†
0072-4939 All-Asia Guide
0072-4947 Golf Course Superintendents Association of America. Proceedings of the International Conference and Show
0072-4955 Golf Guide
0072-4963 Golf Rules Illustrated
0072-4971 Golfer's Digest
0072-498X Golfer's Handbook
0072-4998 Gondwana Newsletter
0072-5005 Good Food Guide
0072-5013 Gornoslaskie Studia Socjologiczne
0072-5021 Gorog es Latin Irok Tara
0072-503X Gothenburg Studies in English
0072-5048 Gothenburg Studies in Philosophy†
0072-5056 Gothenburg Studies in Physics†
0072-5064 Demografiska Forskargruppen, Goeteborg. Reports†
0072-5072 Oceanografiska Institutet, Goeteborg. Meddelanden *changed to* Goeteborgs Universitet. Oceanografiska Institutionen. Reports
0072-5080 Goeteborgs Universitet. Economisk-Historiska Institutionen. Meddelanden
0072-5099 Goeteborgs Universitet. Sociologiska Institutionen. Forsknings-Rapport
0072-5102 Goeteborgs Universitet. Sociologiska Institutionen. Monografier
0072-5110 Goeteborgs Universitet. Statistiska Institutionen. Skriftserie. Publications
0072-5129 Sell's Government and Municipal Contractors Register *see* 0140-5764
0072-5145 Government Contracts Guide†
0072-5153 Government Contracts Monographs
0072-5161 Government Finance Brief. New Series
0072-517X Government in Hawaii
0072-5188 Government Reference Books
0072-5196 Arizona State University. Governmental Finance Institute. Proceedings *see* 0078-9151
0072-520X Governmental Research Association Directory
0072-5250 Graduate Fellowship Awards Announced by National Science Foundation
0072-5277 Graduate Study in Psychology
0072-5285 Graduate Texts in Mathematics
0072-5315 Grafton Fashions for Men†
0072-534X Grain Crops†
0072-5358 Grain Trade of Canada†
0072-5382 Universidad de Granada. Colleccion Monografica
0072-5404 Grandes Figures de la Charite
0072-5439 Grandes Todos
0072-5455 Grands Courants de la Pensee Mondiale Contemporaine†
0072-5471 Grants Register
0072-548X Graphic Arts Japan
0072-5498 Graphic Arts Trade Directory and Register *see* 0147-1651
0072-5501 Graphic Directory†
0072-551X Graphic Guide to Consumer Markets *see* 0072-8314
0072-5528 Graphis Annual
0072-5536 Graphis Packaging
0072-5544 Grass
0072-5552 Grassland Research Institute, Hurley, England (Berkshire) Technical Reports
0072-5560 Grassland Soceity of Southern Africa. Proceedings of the Annual Congresses
0072-5579 Great Black Athletes†
0072-5587 Great Britain. Admiralty Advisory Committee Reports: Structural Steel†
0072-5595 Great Britain. Aeronautical Research Council. Current Paper Series
0072-5609 Great Britain. Aeronautical Research Council. Reports and Memoranda Series
0072-5617 Great Britain. Air Transport Licensing Board. Report *see* 0306-3569
0072-5625 Ancient Monuments Board for England. Annual Report
0072-5633 Great Britain. Department of Trade. Bankruptcy: General Annual Report
0072-5641 Great Britain. Civil Aviation Authority. Civil Aviation Publications
0072-565X Great Britain. Department of Trade. Companies: General Annual Report
0072-5668 Great Britain. Department of Trade. Export of Works of Art
0072-5676 Great Britain. Department of Trade. Import Duties Act 1958. Annual Report
0072-5684 Great Britain. Board of Trade. Insurance Business: Annual Report *see* 0308-499X
0072-5692 Great Britain. Department of Trade. Particulars of Dealers in Securities and of Trust Units
0072-5706 Great Britain. Department of Trade. Patents, Design and Trade Marks(Annual Report)
0072-5714 Great Britain. Central Health Services Council. Report
0072-5722 Great Britain. Central Office of Information. Reference Division. Reference Pamphlets
0072-5730 Great Britain. Central Statistical Office. Annual Abstract of Statistics
0072-5749 Great Britain. Central Statistical Office Abstracts of Regional Statistics *see* 0261-1783
0072-5757 Great Britain. Central Statistical Office. Research Series
0072-5765 Great Britain. Central Statistical Office. Social Trends
0072-5773 Great Britain. Cinematograph Films Council. Annual Report
0072-579X Great Britain. Commission on Industrial Relations. Reports†
0072-5803 Great Britain. Department of the Environment. Committee on Synthetic Detergents. Progress Report
0072-5811 Great Britain. Committee on Tribology. Report†
0072-582X Great Britain. Department of Education and Science. Computer Board for Universities and Research Councils. Report
0072-5838 Great Britain. Consumer Council. Report†
0072-5846 Annual Statement of the Overseas Trade of the United Kingdom
0072-5870 Great Britain. Department of Education and Science. Building Bulletins
0072-5889 Great Britain. Department of Education and Science. Education Planning Paper†
0072-5897 Great Britain. Department of Education and Science. Education Surveys
0072-5900 Great Britain. Department of Education and Science. Statistics of Education
0072-5919 Great Britain. Department of Education and Science. Science Policy Studies
0072-5927 Great Britain. Department of Employment. Family Expenditure Survey
0072-5935 Great Britain. Department of Employment and Productivity. Safety, Health and Welfare. New Series Booklets†
0072-5943 Great Britain. Department of Employment. Training Information Papers†
0072-596X Great Britain. Department of Health and Social Security. Annual Report
0072-5978 Great Britain. Department of Health and Social Security. Capricode Capital Projects Code. Hospital Building Procedure Notes
0072-5994 Great Britain. Department of Health and Social Security. Hospital Building Bulletins†
0072-6001 Great Britain. Department of Health and Social Security. Hospital Building, England and Wales: Progress Report†
0072-601X Great Britain. Department of Health and Social Security. Hospital Building Notes *changed to* Great Britain. Department of Health and Social Security. Health Building Notes
0072-6028 Great Britain. Department of Health and Social Security. Hospital Equipment Notes *see* 0141-1403
0072-6036 Great Britain. Department of Health and Social Security. Hospital In-Patient Inquiry
0072-6044 Great Britain. Department of Health and Social Security. Hospital Organization and Methods Service Reports†
0072-6052 Great Britain. Department of Health and Social Security. Health Service Design Notes†
0072-6060 Great Britain. Department of Health and Social Security. Hospital Technical Memoranda†
0072-6087 Great Britain. Department of Health and Social Security. ON the State of the Public Health
0072-6125 Great Britain. Department of Health and Social Security. Statistical Report Series *changed to* Great Britain. Department of Health and Social Security. Statistical and Research Report Series
0072-6141 Scotland. Directorate of Fisheries Research. Annual Report *see* 0140-5012
0072-6168 Great Britain. Foreign and Commonwealth Office. Antigua. Report†
0072-6184 Great Britain. Foreign and Commonwealth Office. Bahamas. Report†
0072-6192 Great Britain. Foreign and Commonwealth Office. Bermuda. Report†
0072-6230 Great Britain. Foreign and Commonwealth Office. Colonial Numbered Series†
0072-6249 Great Britain. Foreign and Commonwealth Office. Dominica. Report†
0072-6257 Great Britain. Foreign and Commonwealth Office. Falkland Islands. Report†
0072-6303 Great Britain. Foreign and Commonwealth Office. Montserrat. Report†
0072-632X Great Britain. Foreign and Commonwealth Office. Overseas Research Publications†
0072-6338 Great Britain. Foreign and Commonwealth Office. St. Christopher-Nevis-Anguilla. Report†
0072-6354 Great Britain. Foreign and Commonwealth Office. St. Lucia. Report†
0072-6362 Great Britain. Foreign and Commonwealth Office. Seychelles. Report†
0072-6370 Great Britain. Foreign and Commonwealth Office. St. Vincent. Report†
0072-6397 Great Britain. Foreign and Commonwealth Office. Treaty Series
0072-6400 Great Britain. General Register Office. Studies on Medical and Population Subjects
0072-6435 Great Britain. Home Office. Research Studies
0072-6443 Great Britain. Home Office. Studies in the Causes of Delinquency and the Treatment of Offenders
0072-646X Great Britain. Industrial Coal Consumers' Council. Report *changed to* Great Britain. Domestic Coal Consumers' Council. Annual Report
0072-6478 Great Britain. Industrial Reorganization Corporation. Report and Accounts†
0072-6486 Great Britain. Pest Infestation Control Laboratory. Report
0072-6494 Great Britain. Institute of Geological Sciences. Memoirs of the Geological Survey of Great Britain
0072-6508 Great Britain. Iron and Steel Consumers' Council. Report†
0072-6516 Great Britain. Keeper of Public Records. Annual Report of the Keeper of Public Records on the Work of the Public Record Office and the Report of the Advisory Council on Public Records
0072-6524 Great Britain. Laboratory of the Government Chemist. Annual Report of the Government Chemist
0072-6532 Great Britain. Manpower Research Unit. Manpower Studies
0072-6559 Great Britain. Medical Research Council. Monitoring Report Series. Assay of Strontium - 90 in Human Bone in the United Kingdom *changed to* Great Britain. Medical Research Council. Special Report Series
0072-6567 Great Britain. Medical Research Council. Report *changed to* Great Britain. Medical Research Council. Annual Report
0072-6567 National Institute for Medical Research. Report

1122 ISSN INDEX

0072-6575 Great Britain. Medical Research Council. Special Report Series†
0072-6583 Great Britain. Medical Research Council. Memoranda†
0072-6591 Great Britain. Mercantile Navy List
0072-6605 Great Britain. Meteorological Office. Annual Report
0072-6613 Great Britain. Meteorological Office. Geophysical Memoirs
0072-6621 Great Britain. Meteorological Office. Scientific Paper
0072-653X Great Britain. Ministry of Power. Annual Report on Electricity *changed to* Great Britain. Department of Energy. Electricity: Annual Report
0072-6664 Great Britain. Ministry of Agriculture, Fisheries and Food. Animal Disease Surveys†
0072-6672 Great Britain. Ministry of Agriculture. Fisheries and Food. Fatstock Guarantee Scheme
0072-6680 Great Britain. Ministry of Agriculture. Fisheries and Food. Fishery Investigations. Series II: Sea Fisheries†
0072-6699 Great Britain. Ministry of Agriculture, Fisheries and Food. Laboratory Leaflet
0072-6729 Great Britain. Ministry of Agriculture, Fisheries and Food. Technical Bulletin
0072-677X Great Britain. Ministry of Housing and Local Government. Handbook of Statistics†
0072-6796 Great Britain. Ministry of Housing and Local Government. Planning Bulletin *changed to* Great Britain. Department of the Environment. Housing and Construction. Planning Bulletin
0072-680X Great Britain. Ministry of Housing and Local Government. Report†
0072-6818 Great Britain. Department of the Environment. Statistics for Town and Country Planning. Series 1
0072-6826 Great Britain. Department of the Environment. Statistics for Town and Country Planning. Series 2
0072-6842 Great Britain. Department of the Environment. Archaeological Reports
0072-6850 Great Britain. Department of the Environment. Engineering Specifications
0072-6869 Great Britain. Department of the Environment. Metrication in the Construction Industry
0072-6893 Great Britain. Department of Transport. Highway Statistics
0072-6907 Great Britain. National Advisory Council on Art Education. Report†
0072-6923 Great Britain. National Agricultural Advisory Service. Experimental Husbandry Farms and Experimental Horticulture Stations. Progress Report†
0072-694X Great Britain. National Economic Development Office. Monographs
0072-6958 Great Britain. National Film Finance Corporation. Annual Report
0072-6966 Great Britain. National Health Service. Hospital Costing Returns *changed to* Great Britain. National Health Service. Health Service Costing Returns
0072-7008 Great Britain. Natural Environment Research Council. Report
0072-7016 Great Britain. Public Record Office. Handbooks
0072-7032 Great Britain. Public Works Loan Board. Report
0072-7059 Great Britain. Road Research Laboratory. Technical Papers†
0072-7067 Great Britain. Royal Commission on the Ancient and Historical Monuments and Constructions of England. Interim Report
0072-7075 Great Britain. Royal Commission on the Ancient and Historical Monuments and Constructions of Wales and Monmouthshire. Interim Report
0072-7083 Great Britain. Royal Commission on Historical Manuscripts. Commissioners' Reports to the Crown
0072-7091 Great Britain. Royal Commission on Historical Manuscripts. Joint Publication
0072-7105 Great Britain. Royal Mint. Annual Report
0072-7113 Great Britain. Schools Council Publications. Curriculum Bulletins
0072-7121 Great Britain. Schools Council Publications. Examinations Bulletins
0072-713X Great Britain. Schools Council Publications. Working Papers
0072-7148 Great Britain. Science Research Council. Report
0072-7172 Great Britain. Soil Survey of England and Wales. Memoirs†
0072-7180 Great Britain. Soil Survey of England and Wales. Records
0072-7199 Great Britain. Soil Survey of England and Wales. Report
0072-7202 Great Britain. Soil Survey of England and Wales. Special Surveys
0072-7210 Great Britain. Soil Survey of England and Wales. Technical Monographs
0072-7229 Great Britain Specialised Stamp Catalogue
0072-7237 Great Britain. University Grants Committee. Annual Survey
0072-7245 Great Britain. Water Resources Board. Publication
0072-7253 Great Britain. Water Resources Board. Report
0072-7261 Great Britain. White Fish Authority. Annual Report and Accounts
0072-7288 Great Ideas Today
0072-7296 Great Lakes Fishery Commission (United States and Canada) Annual Report
0072-730X Great Lakes Fishery Commission (United States and Canada) Technical Report
0072-7318 Great Lakes Red Book
0072-7326 Great Lakes Research Checklist
0072-7334 Great Ormond Street Gazette†
0072-7342 Great West and Indian Series
0072-7350 Greater London Papers
0072-7385 Greek National Committee for Astronomy. Annual Reports of the Astronomical Institutes of Greece
0072-7393 Greece. National Statistical Service. Annual Industrial Survey
0072-7407 Greece. National Statistical Service. Annuaire Statistique de l'Enseignement *changed to* Greece. National Statistical Service. Education Statistics
0072-7415 Greece. National Statistical Service. Annual Statistical Survey of Mines, Quarries and Salterns
0072-7423 Greece. National Statistical Service. Shipping Statistics
0072-7431 Greece. National Statistical Service. Statistical Yearbook of Public Finance *changed to* Greece. National Statistical Service. Public Finance Statistics
0072-744X Greek Coins in North American Collections *changed to* Ancient Coins in North American Collections
0072-7458 State of Greek Industry in (Year)
0072-7466 Greek Mathematical Society. Bulletin
0072-7474 Greek, Roman and Byzantine Monographs
0072-7482 Greek, Roman and Byzantine Studies. Scholarly Aids
0072-7490 Greenwood'S Guide to Great Lakes Shipping
0072-7504 Greifswald. Universitaet. Wissenschaftliche Zeitschrift. Gesellschafts- und Sprachwissenschaftliche Reihe
0072-7512 Greifswald. Universitaet. Wissenschaftliche Zeitschrift. Mathematisch-Naturwissenschaftliche Reihe
0072-7520 Bibliotheque Universitaire, Grenoble. Publications
0072-7539 Universite des Sciences Sociales de Grenoble. Centre de Recherche d'Histoire Economique, Sociale et Institutionnelle. Collection. Serie Histoire Institutionnelle†
0072-7547 Universite des Sciences Sociales de Grenoble. Centre de Recherche d'Histoire Economique, Sociale et Institutionnelle. Collection. Serie Histoire Sociale†
0072-7555 Universite des Sciences Sociales de Grenoble. Centre de Recherche Economique et Sociale. Collection. Serie Agriculture et Devenir Social†
0072-7563 Universite des Sciences Sociales de Grenoble. Centre de Recherche Economique et Sociale. Collection. Serie Economie du Financement†
0072-7571 Universite des Sciences Sociales de Grenoble. Centre de Recherche Economique et Sociale. Collection. Serie Etudes d'Economie de l'Energie†
0072-758X Universite des Sciences Sociales de Grenoble. Centre de Recherche Economique et Sociale. Collection. Serie Economie du Developpement†
0072-7598 Universite des Sciences Sociales de Grenoble. Centre de Recherche Juridique. Collection. Serie Droit de la Propriete Industrielle†
0072-7601 Universite des Sciences Sociales de Grenoble. Centre de Recherche Juridique. Collection. Serie Droit du Tourisme†
0072-761X Universite des Sciences Sociales de Grenoble. Centre de Recherche Juridique. Collection. Serie Droits Etrangers et Droit Compare†
0072-7628 Universite des Sciences Sociales de Grenoble. Collection Generale†
0072-7636 Universite des Sciences Sociales de Grenoble. Institut d'Etudes Politiques. Serie Essais et Travaux†
0072-7644 Universite des Sciences Sociales de Grenoble. Institut d'Etudes Politiques. Serie Textes et Documents†
0072-7652 Universite de Grenoble. Institut Francais de Florence. Publication. Serie 1: Collection d'Etudes d'Histoire
0072-7660 Universite de Grenoble. Institut Francais de Florence. Publication. Serie 2: Collection d'Etudes Bibliographiques
0072-7687 Gripper†
0072-7695 Grocer Directory of Multiples and Co-Operatives *changed to* Grocer Marketing Directory
0072-7717 Der Grosse Gartenkatalog
0072-7725 Grosse Heimatbuecher
0072-7741 Grosse Naturforscher
0072-775X Group for the Advancement of Psychiatry. Report *changed to* Group for the Advancement of Psychiatry. Publication
0072-7792 Groupement des Directeurs Publicitaires de France. Annuaire
0072-7806 Groupement des Entreprises Francaises dans la Lutte Contre le Cancer. Bulletin National de Liaison
0072-7814 Growth of Crystals
0072-7822 Grundlagen der Kriminalistik
0072-7830 Grundlehren der Mathematischen Wissenschaften in Einzeldarstellungen
0072-7865 Guam Business Directory
0072-7873 Guam. Department of Revenue and Taxation. Report
0072-7903 Guia de Editores y de Libreros de Espana
0072-792X Guida Camping d'Italia
0072-7946 Guidance Control and Flight Mechanics Conference. Proceedings *see* 0065-8707
0072-7954 Guide Analytique du Pharmacien d'Officine
0072-7962 Guide Annuaire du Commerce Franco-Allemand
0072-7970 Guide de la Papeterie†
0072-7989 Guide de la Parfumerie
0072-8020 Guide des Prix Litteraires
0072-8039 Guide des Sports†
0072-8047 Guide du Feu et de la Protection Civile *see* 0337-5781
0072-8055 Guide du Petrole, Gaz, Chimie *changed to* Guide du Petrole, Gaz, Petrochimie
0072-8063 Guide du Show-Business; Guide Professionnel du Spectacle
0072-8071 Guide du Slaviste†
0072-808X Guide Europeen de l'Immobilier†
0072-8098 Guide for Laboratory Animal Facilities and Care *changed to* Guide for the Care and Use of Laboratory Animals
0072-8101 Guide for Planning Educational Facilities
0072-8128 Guide International de l'Energie Atomique et des Etudes Spatiales *see* 0337-2219
0072-8136 Guide International des Machines, Appareils, Outils†
0072-8144 Guide Medical et Hospitalier
0072-8187 Guide National des Douanes et Droits Indirects
0072-8209 Guide Rosenwald: Annuaire Medical et Pharmaceutique
0072-8217 Guide Sommaire des Ouvrages de Reference en Sciences Sociales†
0072-8225 Guide to American Educational Directories
0072-8276 Guide to Business & Investment Books *see* 0361-3917
0072-8284 Guide to College Courses in Film and Television
0072-8314 Guide to Consumer Markets†
0072-8322 Guide to Correspondence Studies in Colleges and Universities *see* 0149-1083
0072-8330 Guide to Europe†
0072-8403 Guide to Fluorescence Literature
0072-8411 Guide to Foreign Government-Loan Film (16 MM) *changed to* Guide to Free Loan Films About Foreign Lands
0072-842X Guide to Foreign Legal Materials Series
0072-8438 Guide to Free-Loan Training Films (16 MM)
0072-8446 Guide to Gas Chromatography Literature
0072-8454 Guide to Government in Hawaii
0072-8462 Guide to Government-Loan Films Volume 1: the Civilian Agencies
0072-8497 Guide to Graduate Departments of Geography in the United States and Canada
0072-8500 Guide to Graduate Study in Botany for the United States and Canada
0072-8519 Guide to Graduate Study: Programs Leading to the Ph.D. Degree†
0072-8527 Guide to Hotels and Restaurants in Great Britain *changed to* Hotels and Restaurants in Britain
0072-8551 Guide to Japanese Taxes
0072-8586 Guide to Military-Loan Films *changed to* Guide to Government-Loan Films
0072-8608 Guide to National Bibliographical Information Centres
0072-8616 Guide to New Zealand Income Tax Practice
0072-8624 Guide to Reference Books
0072-8632 Guide to Reference Books. Supplement†
0072-8640 Guide to Reference Material
0072-8659 Guide to Refinery Operating Costs†
0072-8667 Guide to Reprints
0072-8705 Guide to Summer Camps and Summer Schools
0072-8713 Guide to the Coalfields
0072-8721 Guide to the National Merit Scholarship Program
0072-873X Guide to the Performing Arts†
0072-8748 Guide to the Press of the World
0072-8756 Guide to the Social Services
0072-8764 Guide to the World's Training Facilities in Documentation and Information Work.†

0072-8772 Travel Routes Around the World: Guide to Traveling Around the World by Passenger-Carrying Freighters†
0072-8802 Guidebook of English Coins, Nineteenth and Twentieth Centuries
0072-8810 Guidebook of Modern United States Currency
0072-8829 Guidebook of United States Coins
0072-8837 Guidebook to California Taxes
0072-8845 Guidebook to Illinois Taxes
0072-8853 Guidebook to Labor Relations
0072-8861 Guidebook to Massachusetts Taxes
0072-887X Guidebook to Michigan Taxes
0072-8888 Guidebook to New Jersey Taxes
0072-8896 Guidebook to New York Taxes
0072-890X Guidebook to Pennsylvania Taxes
0072-8918 Guidelines for Teachers
0072-8934 Guides to Information Sources in Science and Technology†
0072-8950 Guid'Ouest Africain†
0072-8977 Guild of Prescription Opticians of America. Reference List
0072-8985 Guildhall Miscellany *see* 0306-3194
0072-8993 Guillaume Apollinaire
0072-9019 Gulf and Caribbean Fisheries Institute. Annual Proceedings
0072-9027 Gulf Research Reports
0072-9043 Gun Digest
0072-9051 Gumma University. Faculty of Education. Annual Report: Art and Technology Series
0072-906X Guns and Ammo Annual
0072-9078 Guns Illustrated
0072-9086 Perspectives in Virology
0072-9094 Gutenberg-Jahrbuch
0072-9108 Guyana. Geological Survey Department.Annual Reports *changed to* Guyana. Geology & Mines Commission. Annual Report
0072-9124 Guyana. Geological Survey Department. Mineral Resources Pamphlet *changed to* Guyana. Geology & Mines Commission. Mineral Resources Pamphlet
0072-9140 H. R. Macmillan Lectureship in Forestry
0072-9159 H. Rowan Gaither Lectures in Systems Science†
0072-9167 H.S.M.A. Hotel-Motel Directory and Facilities Guide *changed to* H.S.M.A. Hotel Facilities Digest
0072-9175 Habelts Dissertationsdrucke. Reihe Alte Geschichte
0072-9183 Habelts Dissertationsdrucke. Reihe Klassische Archaeologie
0072-9191 Habelts Dissertationsdrucke. Reihe Klassische Philologie
0072-9205 Habelts Dissertationsdrucke. Reihe Kunstgeschichte
0072-9213 Habelts Dissertationsdrucke. Reihe Mittelalterliche Geschichte
0072-9221 Hacettepe Fen ve Muhendislik Bilimleri Dergisi
0072-923X Hadassah Medical Organization. Report
0072-9248 Hadassah Vocational Guidance Institute. Report
0072-9264 Hafenbautechnische Gesellschaft. Jahrbuch
0072-9272 Hague Conference on Private International Law. Actes et Documents
0072-9280 Hahn-Meitner-Institut fuer Kernforschung Berlin. Bericht *changed to* Hahn-Meitner-Institut fuer Kernforschung Berlin. Jahresbericht
0072-9302 T. A. E. Report
0072-9310 M E D Report†
0072-9329 Israel Institute of Technology. President's Report and Reports of Other Officers *changed to* Technion-Israel Institute of Technology. President's Report
0072-9345 Addis Ababa University. Geophysical Observatory. Contributions
0072-9361 Addis Ababa University. Institute of Ethiopian Studies. Qene Collections†
0072-9388 Addis Ababa University. University Testing Center. Technical Report
0072-9396 Hakluyt Society. Works in the Ordinary Series. Second Series
0072-940X Landesmuseum fuer Vorgeschichte, Halle. Veroeffentlichungen
0072-9418 Hals-, Nasen- und Ohrenheilkunde
0072-9426 Analysen
0072-9469 Hamburgisches Museum fuer Voelkerkunde. Mitteilungen
0072-9493 Forschungstelle fuer Voelkerrecht und Auslaendisches Oeffentliches Recht. Werkhefte *see* 0341-3241
0072-9507 Hamburger Abhandlungen
0072-9515 Hamburger Beitraege fuer Russischlehrer
0072-9523 Hamburger Beitraege zur Numismatik
0072-954X Hamburger Hafen Handbuch†
0072-9558 Hamburger Historische Studien
0072-9566 Hamburger Jahrbuch fuer Wirtschafts- und Gesellschaftspolitik
0072-9574 Hamburger Oeffentlich-Rechtliche Nebenstunden
0072-9582 Hamburger Philologische Studien
0072-9604 Hamburger Studien zur Philosophie
0072-9612 Hamburgisches Zoologisches Museum und Institut. Mitteilungen
0072-9639 Art Gallery of Hamilton. Annual Exhibition *changed to* Art Gallery of Hamilton. Annual Winter Exhibition
0072-9647 Royal Botanical Gardens, Hamilton, Ont. Special Bulletin
0072-9655 Royal Botanical Gardens, Hamilton, Ont. Technical Bulletin
0072-9663 Hammarskjold Forum. Working Paper and Proceedings†
0072-9671 Hampstead Clinic Psychoanalytic Library†
0072-968X Hand
0072-9698 Handball und Faustball in Oesterreich
0072-9728 Handbook of Basic Statistics of Maharashtra State
0072-9736 Handbook of Biochemistry *changed to* C R C Handbook of Biochemistry and Molecular Biology
0072-9787 Handbook of Denominations in the U.S.
0072-9795 Handbook of Electronic Materials
0072-9809 Handbook of Fiji
0072-9817 Handbook of Geochemistry†
0072-9825 Official Handbook of Ghana
0072-9833 Handbook of Latin American Studies: A Selected and Annotated Guide to Recent Publications
0072-985X Handbook of Ocular Therapeutics and Pharmacology *changed to* Ocular Therapeutics and Pharmacology
0072-9868 Handbook of Papua and New Guinea *changed to* Papua New Guinea Handbook
0072-9876 Handbook of Physiology
0072-9884 Handbook of Private Schools
0072-9892 Handbook of Securities of the United States Government and Federal Agencies and Related Money Market Instruments
0072-9906 Handbook of Sensory Physiology
0072-9914 Handbook of Servicemen's and Veterans' Benefits *changed to* Handbook of Service Members' and Veterans' Benefits
0072-9922 Handbook of the Northern Wood Industries
0072-9930 Handbook of the Universities of Pakistan†
0072-9949 Handbook of United States Coins
0072-9965 Handbook on International Study *changed to* Handbook on U.S. Study for Foreign Nationals
0072-9981 Handbook on U. S. Luminescent Stamps
0073-0009 Handbuch der Analytischen Chemie. Part 2: Qualitative Nachweisverfahren†
0073-0017 Handbuch der Analytischen Chemie. Part 3: Quantitative Bestimmungs- und Trennungsmethoden†
0073-0025 Europaeische Volksmusikinstrumente. Handbuch
0073-0033 Handbuch der Experimentellen Pharmakologie
0073-0068 Handbuch der Grossunternehmen
0073-0076 Handbuch der Internationalen Kautschukindustrie
0073-0084 Handbuch der Internationalen Kunstoffindustrie
0073-0092 Handbuch der Justiz
0073-0106 Handbuch der Klassifikation
0073-0114 Handbuch der Mikroskopischen Anatomie des Menschen
0073-0122 Handbuch der Rationalisierung
0073-0130 Handbuch der Stratigraphischen Geologie
0073-0149 Handbuch der Sudetendeutschen Kulturgeschichte
0073-0157 Handbuch fuer Berufskraftfahrer
0073-0165 Handbuch fuer den Werbenden Buch- und Zeitschriftenhandel
0073-0173 Handbuch fuer die Druckindustrie Berlin
0073-0181 Handbuch fuer die Sanitaetsberufe Oesterreich
0073-019X Handbuch Oeffentlicher Verkehrsbetriebe
0073-0203 Statistik des Hamburgischen Staates
0073-0211 Handloader's Digest
0073-022X Haney Foundation Series
0073-0238 Hank Seale Oil Directory: Central United States *changed to* Armstrong Oil Directory: Central United States
0073-0254 Hank Seale Oil Directory: Louisiana, Mississippi, Arkansas, Texas Gulf Coast and East Texas *changed to* Armstrong Oil Directory: Louisiana, Mississippi, Arkansas, Texas Gulf Coast and East Texas
0073-0262 Hank Seale Oil Directory: Texas Including Southeast New Mexico *changed to* Armstrong Oil Directory: Texas Including Southeast New Mexico
0073-0270 Voelkerkundliche Abhandlungen
0073-0289 Technische Universitaet Hannover. Lehrstuhl fuer Stahlbau. Schriftenreihe *changed to* Universitaet Hannover. Lehrstuhl fuer Stahlbau. Schriftenreihe
0073-0300 Technische Universitaet Hannover. Institut fuer Statistik. Mitteilungen *changed to* Universitaet Hannover. Institut fuer Statistik. Mitteilungen
0073-0319 Technische Universitaet Hannover. Institut fuer Siedlungswasserwirtschaft. Veroeffentlichungen
0073-0327 Hansische Geschichtsblaetter
0073-036X Hardware Merchandising's Hardware Handbook *changed to* Hardware Merchandising's Canadian Hardware Handbook
0073-0378 Hardy's Encyclopaedia Guide to Agra, Jaipur, Delhi, Varanasi
0073-0386 Hardy's Encyclopaedia Hotels of India and Nepal
0073-0394 Harmon Memorial Lectures in Military History
0073-0408 Harpers Directory and Manual of the Wine and Spirit Trade *changed to* Harpers Directory of the Wine and Spirit Trade
0073-0416 Harpers Guide to Sports Trade
0073-0424 Harry S. Truman Research Institute, Jerusalem. Publications†
0073-0432 Hartford Studies in Linguistics
0073-0459 Harvard Armenian Texts and Studies
0073-0467 Harvard Books in Biology
0073-0475 Harvard Books in Biophysics
0073-0483 Harvard East Asian Monographs
0073-0491 Harvard East Asian Series
0073-0505 Harvard Economic Studies
0073-0513 Harvard English Studies
0073-0521 Harvard Historical Monographs
0073-053X Harvard Historical Studies
0073-0548 Harvard Journal of Asiatic Studies
0073-0564 Harvard Librarian
0073-0572 Harvard Middle Eastern Monographs
0073-0580 Harvard Middle Eastern Studies
0073-0599 Harvard Oriental Series
0073-0602 Harvard Paperbacks
0073-0610 Harvard Papers in Theoretical Geography
0073-0629 Harvard Publications in Music
0073-0637 Harvard Semitic Monographs
0073-0645 Harvard Semitic Series
0073-067X Harvard Studies in Business History
0073-0688 Harvard Studies in Classical Philology
0073-0696 Harvard Studies in Comparative Literature
0073-070X Harvard Studies in East Asian Law *changed to* Studies in East Asian Law, Harvard University
0073-0718 Harvard Studies in Romance Languages
0073-0726 Harvard Theological Studies
0073-0734 Harvard University. Center for International Affairs. Annual Report
0073-0742 Harvard University. Center for Studies in Education and Development. Annual Report†
0073-0769 Harvard University. Computation Laboratory. Mathematical Linguistics and Automatic Translation; Report to National Science Foundation
0073-0777 Harvard University. Graduate School of Business Administration. Baker Library. Kress Library of Business and Economics. Publications
0073-0785 Harvard University. Graduate School of Business Administration. Program for Management Development. Publication
0073-0793 Harvard University. Law School. Library. Annual Legal Bibliography
0073-0807 Harvard University. Museum of Comparative Zoology. Department of Mollusks. Occasional Papers on Mollusks
0073-0815 Harvard University. Program on Regional and Urban Economics. Discussion Paper†
0073-0831 Harvard University. Russian Research Center. Russian Research Center Studies
0073-084X Harvard-Yenching Institute. Monograph Series
0073-0858 Harvard-Yenching Institute. Studies
0073-0866 Harvest
0073-0874 Harvey Lectures
0073-0882 Harz-Zeitschrift
0073-0904 Hat Life Year Book *changed to* Hat Life Year Book & Directory
0073-0912 Hattori Botanical Laboratory. Journal
0073-0939 Hautes Etudes du Monde Greco-Romain
0073-0947 Hautes Etudes Islamiques et Orientales d'Histoire Comparee
0073-0955 Hautes Etudes Medievales et Modernes
0073-0963 Hautes Etudes Numismatiques
0073-0971 Hautes Etudes Orientales
0073-098X Hawaii Agricultural Experiment Station, Honolulu. Research Bulletin
0073-0998 Hawaii Agricultural Experiment Station, Honolulu. Research Report
0073-1005 Hawaii Agricultural Experiment Station, Honolulu. Technical Bulletin
0073-1013 Hawaii. Children's Health Services Division. Crippled Children Branch Report *changed to* Hawaii. Family Health Services Division. Crippled Children Services Branch. Report
0073-1021 Hawaii Dental Association. Transactions
0073-103X Hawaii. Department of Education. Office of Library Services. Report
0073-1048 Hawaii. Department of Health. Mental Health Statistical Section Psychiatric Outpatient Program *changed to* Hawaii. Department of Health. Mental Health Statistical Section. Psychiatric Outpatient, Inpatient and Community Programs
0073-1056 Hawaii, Department of Health Research and Planning Statistical Office. (Report on) Waimano Training School and Hospital *changed to* Hawaii. Department of Health. Waimano Training School and Hospital Division (Report)

0073-1072 Hawaii. Department of Planning and Economic Development. Annual Report
0073-1080 State of Hawaii Data Book
0073-1102 Hawaii Economic Review. Market Annual†
0073-1110 Hawaii. Insurance Division. Report of the Insurance Commissioner of Hawaii
0073-1129 Hawaii International Conference on System Sciences. Proceedings
0073-1137 Hawaii. Office of the Ombudsman. Report
0073-1145 Hawaii Series
0073-1153 Hawaii Topical Conference in Particle Physics. Proceedings
0073-1161 University of Hawaii. College of Tropical Agriculture. Cooperative Extension Service. Circular
0073-117X University of Hawaii. College of Tropical Agriculture. Cooperative Extension Service Leaflet
0073-1188 University of Hawaii. College of Tropical Agriculture. Cooperative Extension Service. Miscellaneous Publication
0073-1196 University of Hawaii. Counseling and Testing Center. Report
0073-1226 University of Hawaii. Industrial Relations Center. Occasional Publications
0073-1277 Hawaii. Legislative Reference Bureau. Report
0073-1293 University of Hawaii. Water Resources Research Center. Collected Reprints
0073-1307 University of Hawaii. Water Resources Research Center. Technical Report
0073-1315 Meteorological Monographs†
0073-1331 Hawaii Institute of Marine Biology. Technical Reports
0073-1358 Hawaiian Planters' Record
0073-1366 Hawaiian Sugar Planters' Association Experiment Station. Annual Report
0073-1382 Nathaniel Hawthorne Journal
0073-1390 Haydn Yearbook. Haydn Jahrbuch
0073-1404 Hayes Directory of Dental Supply Houses
0073-1412 Hayes Directory of Physician and Hospital Supply Houses
0073-1420 Hayes Druggist Directory
0073-1439 University of Iowa. Graduate Program in Hospital and Health Administration. Health Care Research Series
0073-1455 Health Education Monographs *changed to* Health Education Quarterly
0073-1498 Health Physics Society. Newsletter
0073-1501 Health Statistics of India†
0073-151X Heat Bibliography†
0073-1552 Heating and Ventilating Year Book *see* 0306-3585
0073-1560 Hebbel-Jahrbuecher
0073-1579 Hegel-Jahrbuch
0073-1587 Hegel-Studien
0073-1595 Heidelberg Science Library
0073-1625 Heidelberger Akademie der Wissenschaften. Mathematisch-Naturwissenschaftliche Klasse. Sitzungsberichte
0073-1633 Heidelberger Arbeitsbuecher
0073-1641 Heidelberger Jahrbuecher
0073-165X Heidelberger Rechtswissenschaftliche Abhandlungen. Neue Folge
0073-1676 Heidelberger Sociologica
0073-1684 Heidelberger Taschenbuecher
0073-1692 Heine-Jahrbuch
0073-1714 Helps for Students of History
0073-1730 Helsingin Yliopisto Keskussairaala. Psykiatria Klinika. Julkaisusarja *see* 0355-7693
0073-179X University of Helsinki. Institute of Education. Research Bulletin
0073-1803 Helvetica Odontologica Acta. Supplementum *see* 0036-7702
0073-1811 Helvetica Paediatrica Acta. Supplementum
0073-182X Helvetia Politica
0073-1846 Henrietta Szold Institute. Report on Activities†
0073-1897 Heraldisch-Genealogische Gesellschaft Adler. Jahrbuch
0073-1900 Heraldo Dental
0073-1927 Herbert Read Series
0073-1943 Herd Book of Hereford Cattle
0073-1951 Hereford Breed Journal
0073-196X Herforder Jahrbuch; Beitraege zur Geschichte der Stadt und des Stiftes Herford
0073-1978 Heritage†
0073-1986 Heritage of Sociology
0073-1994 University of Queensland. Great Barrier Reef Committee: Heron Island Research Station. Papers†
0073-2001 Hessisches Jahrbuch fuer Landesgeschichte
0073-201X Heutiges Deutsch. Reihe I: Linguistische Grundlagen
0073-2044 Hi-Fi Sound Annual *changed to* Hi-Fi Test Annual
0073-2060 Hi-Fi Year Book
0073-2095 High Fidelity. Records in Review†
0073-2109 High Polymers
0073-2141 Highlights of V A Medical Research *changed to* Medical Research in the V.A.
0073-215X Nation on the Move†
0073-2176 Highway Planning Notes
0073-2184 U.S. Federal Highway Administration. Highway Planning Technical Reports
0073-2206 Highway Research Record *see* 0361-1981
0073-2214 Highway Safety Literature Annual Cumulations†
0073-2222 Highway Safety Literature Indexes†
0073-2230 Hilgardia
0073-2273 Hind Mazdoor Sabha. Report of the Annual Convention
0073-2281 Hindu Astronomical and Mathematical Text Series
0073-229X Hirosaki University. Faculty of Agriculture. Bulletin
0073-2303 Hiroshima University. Department of Geology. Geological Report
0073-2311 Hiroshima University. Faculty of Engineering. Memoirs
0073-232X Hiroshima University. Research Institute for Nuclear Medicine and Biology. Proceedings
0073-2338 Histochemische-Methoden†
0073-2354 Histoire de l'Europe†
0073-2362 Histoire de la Pensee
0073-2370 Histoire de la Philosophie Europeenne†
0073-2389 Histoire des Personnages Mysterieux et des Societes Secretes†
0073-2397 Histoire des Idees et Critique Litteraire
0073-2400 Histoire et Civilisation Arabe
0073-2419 Histoire et Civilisation du Livre
0073-2435 Historia
0073-2443 Historia†
0073-2451 Historia del Arte en Mexico†
0073-2486 Historia y Cultura
0073-2494 Historia y Filosofia de la Ciencia. Serie Mayor. Encuadernada
0073-2508 Historia y Filosofia de la Ciencia. Serie Menor. Rustica
0073-2516 Historiae Musicae Cultores Biblioteca
0073-2524 Historiae Naturalis Classica
0073-2532 Historiae Scientiarum Elementa
0073-2540 Historiallinen Arkisto
0073-2559 Historiallisia Tutkimuksia
0073-2567 Historic Houses, Castles and Gardens *changed to* Historic Houses, Castles and Gardens in Great Britain and Ireland
0073-2591 Historical Association, London. Aids for Teachers
0073-2605 Teaching of History
0073-2613 Historical Conservation Society. Publications
0073-2621 Historical Problems: Studies and Documents
0073-2648 Historical Society of Ghana. Transactions
0073-2656 Historical Statistics of the Gas Industry
0073-2664 Historical Statistics of the United States
0073-2672 Historical Studies in the Physical Sciences†
0073-2680 Historischer Verein der Pfalz. Mitteilungen
0073-2699 Historischer Verein Dillingen an der Donau. Jahrbuch
0073-2702 Historiska och Litteraturhistoriska Studier
0073-2710 History and Structure of Languages
0073-2745 Chicago History of Science and Medicine
0073-2753 History of Science
0073-277X Historyka; Studia Metodologiczne
0073-2788 Hitotsubashi Journal of Arts and Sciences
0073-2796 Hitotsubashi Journal of Law and Politics
0073-280X Hitotsubashi Journal of Social Studies
0073-2818 Hobart Papers
0073-2842 Hochschulbuecher fuer Mathematik
0073-2850 Hochschulbuecher fuer Physik
0073-2877 Hoehnea
0073-2885 E.T.A. Hoffmann-Gesellschaft. Mitteilungen
0073-2893 United States & Canadian Mailing Lists
0073-2907 Hofstra University Yearbook of Business
0073-2915 Hokkaido Dental Association. Journal
0073-2923 Hokkaido National Agricultural Experiment Station. Soil Survey Report
0073-2931 Hokkaido University. Institute of Low Temperature Science. Series A. Physical Science
0073-294X Hokkaido University. Institute of Low Temperature Science. Series B. Biological Science
0073-2958 Holiday Book†
0073-2966 Holiday Camps Directory and Magazine *changed to* Holiday Camps and Centres Directory
0073-2982 Holiday Chalets and Caravans Directory Magazine
0073-3024 Holidays in Britain
0073-3032 Holland Exports
0073-3059 Hollis Press and Public Relations Annual
0073-3075 U.S. Department of Agriculture. Home and Garden Bulletin
0073-3091 Home Economics Education Association. Bulletin *changed to* Home Economics Education Association, Newsletter
0073-3105 Home Economics in Institutions Granting Bachelors or Higher Degrees
0073-3113 U.S. Department of Agriculture. Home Economics Research Report
0073-3121 Home Gunsmithing Digest
0073-3148 Home University Library†
0073-3156 Four Things Every Woman Should Know *changed to* Homemaker's Handbook
0073-3164 Homing World Stud Book
0073-3180 Homme Face a la Nature
0073-3202 Hommes et la Terre
0073-3210 Hong Kong Catholic Directory and Year Book
0073-3229 Hong Kong. Census and Statistics Department. Annual Departmental Reports†
0073-3237 Hong Kong Library Association. Journal
0073-3245 Hong Kong Manufacturers and Exporters Register
0073-3253 Hong Kong Nursing Journal
0073-3261 Hong Kong Trade Directory
0073-327X Hontanar
0073-3288 Hood College, Frederick, Maryland. Monograph†
0073-3296 Hoover Institution on War, Revolution, and Peace. Publications Series
0073-330X Hoover Institution Studies Series
0073-3326 Actualites Nephrologiques
0073-3342 Hoppenstedt Vademecum der Investmentfonds
0073-3350 Hoppenstedt Versicherungs-Jahrbuch
0073-3369 Horace M. Albright Conservation Lectureship
0073-3385 Horizon
0073-3407 Hornero
0073-3415 Horse and Hound Year Book†
0073-3431 Hoseasons Holidays Boats and Bungalows Hire
0073-3458 Sell's Hospital and Surgical Supplies *see* 0140-5748
0073-3466 Hospital Statistics of New Zealand *see* 0110-1900
0073-3474 Hospitals & Health Services Year Book and Directory of Hospital Suppliers
0073-3482 Hot Rod Yearbook†
0073-3490 Hotel and Motel Red Book
0073-3504 Sell's Hotel, Restaurant and Canteen Supplies *see* 0142-1824
0073-3512 Hotels and Restaurants in Britain
0073-3539 Hotels de la France et d'Outre-Mer *changed to* Hotels de la France
0073-3563 House Beautiful's Gardening and Outdoor Living
0073-3571 House Beautiful's Houses and Plans
0073-3601 Households with Television Sets in the United States
0073-361X House's Guide to the Building Industry *changed to* House's Guide to the Construction Industry (1979)
0073-3652 Housing and Urban Development Legislation in New York State
0073-3741 Howard Journal of Penology and Crime Prevention
0073-375X Hsin-Ya Hsueh Pao
0073-3768 Atlas of Mammalian Chromosomes†
0073-3776 Hudson Institute. Report to the Members
0073-3792 Hueber Hochschulreihe
0073-3806 University of Hull. Institute of Education. Aids to Research
0073-3814 University of Hull. Institute of Education. Research Monographs
0073-3822 Human Basics Library
0073-3865 Human Resources Research Organization. Bibliography of Publications
0073-3873 Human Resources Research Organization. Professional Papers
0073-389X Human Resources Research Organization. Technical Report
0073-3903 European Court of Human Rights. Publications. Series A: Judgments and Decisions
0073-3911 European Court of Human Rights. Publications. Series B: Pleadings, Oral Arguments and Documents
0073-3938 Humanities, Christianity and Culture
0073-3946 Humanities Research Council of Canada. Report *changed to* Canadian Federation for the Humanities. Annual Report
0073-4012 Egeszsegneveles Szakkonyvtara
0073-4020 Hungary. Kozponti Statisztikai Hivatal. Demografiai Evkonyv
0073-4039 Statisztikai Evkonyv
0073-4055 Magyar Orszagos Leveltar Kiadvanyai. 2. Forraskiadvanyok†
0073-4063 Orszagos Muemleki Felugyeloseg. Kiadvanyok
0073-411X Hurricane Annual†
0073-4128 Hvalraadets Skrifter
0073-4136 Hybrid Microelectronics Symposium. (Papers)
0073-4144 National Geophysical Research Institute. Publications
0073-4160 Hydraulic Research in the United States *see* 0094-1832
0073-4179 Hydraulics Conference. Proceedings†
0073-4187 Great Britain. Hydraulics Research Station. Reports
0073-4217 Hydrological Yearbook of Israel
0073-425X Hypertension Series
0073-4268 I F O Institut fuer Wirtschaftsforschung. Studien zu Handelsfragen *see* 0170-5695
0073-4284 I N F A Press and Advertisers Year Book

0073-4292 I N U F A: Internationaler Nutzfahrzeug-Katalog/International Catalogue for Commercial Vehicles
0073-4314 University of Ibadan. Institute of Education. Occasional Publications
0073-4322 University of Ibadan. Library. Annual Report
0073-4330 University of Ibadan. Library. Bibliographical Series
0073-4349 Ibero-Americana
0073-4365 Ibsen Aarboken
0073-4373 Icefield Ranges Research Project Scientific Results
0073-4381 J. L. B.Smith Institute of Ichthyology. Ichthyological Bulletin
0073-439X Icones Fungorium Maris†
0073-4403 Icones Plantarum Africanarum
0073-4411 Iconographia Mycologia
0073-442X Idaho. Bureau of Mines and Geology. Bulletin
0073-4446 Idaho. Bureau of Mines and Geology. Information Circular
0073-4462 Idaho. Bureau of Mines and Geology. Pamphlet†
0073-4497 Idaho Education Association. Proceedings
0073-4527 Idaho. Department of Fish and Game. Federal Aid Investigation Projects. Progress Reports and Publications
0073-4551 Idaho State University Museum. Occasional Papers *changed to* Idaho Museum of Natural History. Occasional Papers
0073-456X Idaho Statistical Abstract
0073-4586 University of Idaho. Forest, Wildlife and Range Experiment Station, Moscow. Station Bulletin
0073-4594 University of Idaho. Forest, Wildlife and Range Experiment Station, Moscow. Station Note
0073-4608 University of Idaho. Forest, Wildlife and Range Experiment Station, Moscow. Station Paper†
0073-4616 University of Idaho. Water Resources Research Institute. Annual Report
0073-4624 Ideas for Management
0073-4640 Dictionnaires du Savoir Moderne
0073-4675 Idesia
0073-4691 Iheringia. Serie Antropologia
0073-4705 Iheringia. Serie Botanica
0073-4713 Iheringia. Serie Geologia
0073-4721 Iheringia. Serie Zoologia
0073-4748 Illinois Biological Monographs
0073-4756 Illinois. Board of Higher Education. Report
0073-4772 Illinois. Department of Mental Health. Annual Report *see* 0361-3534
0073-4799 Illinois Directory and Suppliers Listing *changed to* Illinois Dealer Directory and Buyer's Guide
0073-4810 Illinois. Department of Conservation. Technical Bulletin†
0073-4837 Illinois Government. *see* 0195-7783
0073-4853 Illinois. State Geological Survey. Industrial Mineral Notes *see* 0094-9442
0073-487X Illinois Law Enforcement Commission. Annual Report
0073-490X Illinois. Natural History Survey. Biological Notes
0073-4918 Illinois. Natural History Survey. Bulletin
0073-4926 Illinois. Natural History Survey. Circular
0073-4934 Northern Illinois University. Center for Southeast Asian Studies. Special Report Series
0073-4942 Southern Illinois University, Carbondale. Business Research Bureau. Regional Studies in Business and Economics. Monographs
0073-4950 Southern Illinois University, Carbondale. Department of Geography. Discussion Paper
0073-4969 Southern Illinois University, Carbondale. Occasional Paper Series in Geography
0073-4977 Southern Illinois University, Carbondale. University Libraries. Bibliographic Contributions
0073-4985 Southern Illinois University. University Museum Studies
0073-4993 Southern Illinois University, Edwardsville. Center for Urban and Environmental Research and Services. C U E R S. Report
0073-5000 Illinois State Bar Association. Antitrust Law Newsletter
0073-5027 Illinois State Bar Association. Federal Tax Section Newsletter
0073-5035 Illinois State Bar Association. Local Government Law Newsletter
0073-5043 Illinois State Bar Association. Patent, Trademark, and Copyright Newsletter
0073-5051 Illinois. State Geological Survey. Bulletins
0073-506X Illinois. State Geological Survey. Circulars
0073-5078 Illinois. State Geological Survey. Educational Series
0073-5086 Illinois. State Geological Survey. Environmental Geology Notes
0073-5094 Illinois. State Geological Survey. Guidebook Series
0073-5108 Illinois. Environmental Protection Agency. Semi-Annual Report
0073-5116 Illinois. State Geological Survey. Mineral Economic Briefs *see* 0094-9442
0073-5124 Illinois. State Geological Survey. Reports of Investigations†
0073-5167 Illinois Studies in Anthropology
0073-5175 Illinois Studies in Language and Literature
0073-5183 Illinois Studies in the Social Sciences
0073-5191 University of Illinois at Urbana-Champaign. Center for International Education and Research in Accounting. Monograph
0073-5205 University of Illinois at Urbana-Champaign. College of Agriculture. Special Publication
0073-5213 University of Illinois at Urbana-Champaign. Department of Agricultural Economics. Agricultural Finance Program Report
0073-5221 University of Illinois at Urbana-Champaign. Department of Agricultureal Economics. Bulletin†
0073-523X University of Illinois at Urbana-Champaign. Department of Agricultural Economics. Research Report
0073-5256 University of Illinois at Urbana-Champaign. Department of Art. Newsletter
0073-5264 T & A M Report
0073-5272 University of Illinois at Urbana - Champaign. Engineering Experiment Station. Bulletin
0073-5280 University of Illinois at Urbana-Champaign. Engineering Experiment Station. Summary of Engineering Research
0073-5299 University of Illinois at Urbana-Champaign. College of Agriculture. Agricultural Communications Research Report
0073-5302 University of Illinois at Urbana-Champaign. Graduate School of Library Science. Monograph Series
0073-5310 University of Illinois at Urbana-Champaign. Graduate School of Library Science. Occasional Papers
0073-5353 University of Illinois at Urbana-Champaign. Institute of Labor and Industrial Relations. Reprint Series
0073-5361 University of Illinois at Urbana-Champaign. Graduate School of Library Science. Library Research Center. Annual Report
0073-5388 University of Illinois at Urbana-Champaign. Office of Instructional Resources. Measurement and Research Division. Research Report
0073-5396 University of Illinois. Small Homes Council. Building Research Council. Circulars *changed to* University of Illinois. Small Homes Council. Building Research Council. Council Notes
0073-540X University of Illinois. Small Homes Council. Building Research Council. Research Report
0073-5426 University of Illinois. Small Homes Council. Building Research Council. Technical Notes
0073-5434 University of Illinois at Urbana-Champaign. Water Resources Center. Annual Report
0073-5442 University of Illinois at Urbana-Champaign. Water Resources Center. Research Report
0073-5450 Illinois Water Quality Network. Summary of Data
0073-5469 I E S Lighting Handbook
0073-5477 Illustrators; The Annual of American Illustration
0073-5515 Image; Illustrierte Zeitschrift fuer Aerzte und Apotheken†
0073-5531 Immunopathology
0073-5566 Implement & Tractor Product File
0073-5574 Implement & Tractor Red Book
0073-5582 Import Car Buyer's Guide†
0073-5604 Importers and Exporters Trade Promotion Guide
0073-5612 Imports into Pakistan under U.S. Economic Aid†
0073-5620 Imprimatur; Jahrbuch fuer Buecherfreunde. Neue Folge
0073-5639 Infact Medical School Information System
0073-5655 In Vitro
0073-5671 Income, Estate and Gift Tax Provisions: Internal Revenue Code
0073-568X U. S. Bureau of the Census. Income (in Year) of Families in the United States *changed to* Current Population Reports: Consumer Income. Income in (Year) of Families and Persons in the United States
0073-5698 Money Income (in Year) of Families, Unrelated Individuals and Persons in the United States *changed to* Current Population Reports: Consumer Income. Money Income (in Year) of Families and Persons in the United States
0073-5701 Incontri e Testimonianze†
0073-571X Restrictive Practices Reports *see* 0306-2163
0073-5728 Incorporated Law Society of Sri Lanka. Annual Report
0073-5736 Incorporated Law Society of Sri Lanka. Journal
0073-5752 Incunabula Graeca
0073-5760 I P A C Petroleum News
0073-5779 Independent Schools Association of the Southwest. Membership List
0073-5787 Index Hepaticarum
0073-5817 Index of Articles on Jewish Studies
0073-5825 Index of Graduate Theses in Baptist Theological Seminaries
0073-5884 Index of Psychoanalytic Writings
0073-5892 Index to Book Reviews in the Humanities
0073-5914 Index to Early American Periodical Literature, 1728-1870
0073-5930 Index to How to Do It Information
0073-5949 Index to Little Magazines†
0073-5957 Index to New Zealand Periodicals
0073-5973 Index to Periodical Articles by and About Negroes *see* 0161-8245
0073-5981 Index to Periodicals of the Church of Jesus Christ of Latter-Day Saints. Cumulative Edition
0073-599X Index to Philippine Periodicals
0073-6023 Index to Reviews, Symposia Volumes and Monographs in Organic Chemistry†
0073-6031 U.S. Bureau of Outdoor Recreation. Index to Selected Outdoor Recreation Literature†
0073-604X Index to Textile Auxiliaries
0073-6066 Index to Theses Accepted for Higher Degrees in the Universities of Great Britain and Ireland
0073-6074 Index Translationum
0073-6082 Indexes of Output per Person Employed and per Man-Hour in Canada, Commercial Industries *see* 0317-7882
0073-6090 India. A Reference Annual
0073-6120 India. Central Board of Revenue. Central Excise Manual
0073-6139 India. Central Statistical Organization. Annual Survey of Industries
0073-6147 India. Central Statistical Organization. Estimates of National Income *changed to* India. Central Statistical Organization. National Accounts Statistics
0073-6155 India. Central Statistical Organization. Statistical Abstract
0073-6163 India. Central Statistical Organization. Sample Surveys of Current Interest in India; Report
0073-6171 India. Central Vigilance Commission. Report
0073-618X India. Department of Atomic Energy. Annual Report
0073-6198 India. Khadi and Village Industries Commission. Report *changed to* K V I C Annual Report
0073-6201 India. Ministry of Education and Social Welfare. Department of Education. Report *changed to* India. Ministry of Education and Social Welfare. Department of Education. Report
0073-6236 India. Union Public Service Commission Report
0073-6244 India Who's Who
0073-6252 Indian Adult Education Association. National Seminar. Report†
0073-6260 I A S L I C Technical Pamphlets
0073-6279 I A S L I C Special Publication
0073-6287 Indian Books; Bibliography of Indian Books Published or Reprinted in the English Language *changed to* B E P I
0073-6295 Indian Chemical Directory *issued with* Guide to Indian Chemical Plants and Equipment
0073-6295 Indian Chemical Directory
0073-6309 Indian Council of Medical Research. Annual Report†
0073-6317 Indian Council of Medical Research. Report of the Advisory Committees†
0073-6325 Indian Council of Medical Research. Special Report Series†
0073-6333 Indian Engineering Association. Handbook of Statistics *changed to* Association of Indian Engineering Industry. Handbook of Statistics
0073-6341 C. A. S. N. P. Bulletin
0073-635X Indian Forest Bulletin (New Series)
0073-6368 Indian Forest Leaflets (New Series)
0073-6376 Indian Forest Records (New Series) Botany
0073-6384 Indian Forest Records (New Series) Composite Wood
0073-6392 Indian Forest Records (New Series) Entomology
0073-6406 Indian Forest Records (New Series) Forest Pathology
0073-6414 Indian Forest Records (New Series) Logging
0073-6422 Indian Forest Records (New Series) Silviculture
0073-6430 Indian Forest Records (New Series) Statistical
0073-6449 Indian Forest Records (New Series) Timber Mechanics
0073-6465 Indian Institute of Advanced Study. Transactions and Monographs
0073-6473 Indian Institute of Foreign Trade. Report

1126 ISSN INDEX

0073-649X Indian Institute of Sugarcane Research, Lucknow. Annual Report
0073-6503 Indian Institute of Technology, Bombay. Series
0073-6511 Indian Institute of Technology, Madras. Annual Report
0073-652X Indian Institute of Technology, Madras. Technical Communications†
0073-6546 I I T C Directory
0073-6554 Indian Journal of Engineers. Annual Foundry Number
0073-6562 Indian Jute Mills Association. Annual Summary of Jute and Gunny Statistics
0073-6570 Indian Jute Mills Association. Loom and Spindle Statistics
0073-6589 Indian Linguistics Monograph Series
0073-6597 I M E Directory: Mines, Minerals, Equipment
0073-6600 Indian National Science Academy. Proceedings
0073-6619 Indian National Science Academy. Year Book
0073-6627 I N S D O C Union Catalogue Series
0073-6635 Indian Pharmaceutical Guide
0073-6643 Indian Roads Congress. Road Research Bulletin *see* 0376-4788
0073-6651 Indian Rubber Statistics
0073-666X Indian School of International Studies *see* 0075-3548
0073-6678 Indian Society of International Law. Publications
0073-6686 Indian Statistical Institute. Annual Report
0073-6694 Indian Statistical Institute. Econometric and Social Sciences Series. Research Monographs
0073-6708 Indian Statistical Institute. Library. Bibliographic Series
0073-6716 Indian Statistical Institute. Statistics and Probability Series. Research Monographs
0073-6724 Indian Statistical Series
0073-6732 Indian Voice
0073-6759 Indiana Academy of Science. Monograph
0073-6767 Indiana Academy of Science. Proceedings
0073-6775 Indiana. Aeronautics Commission. Annual Report
0073-6783 Indiana. Agricultural Experiment Station. Inspection Report
0073-6791 Indiana. Agricultural Experiment Station. Research Bulletin
0073-6821 Ball State Monographs
0073-6856 Indiana. Civil Rights Commission. Annual Report *changed to* Indiana. Civil Rights Commission. Triennial Report
0073-6872 Indiana. Division of Fish and Wildlife. Annual Report
0073-6880 Indiana Historical Collections
0073-6899 Indiana Historical Society. Prehistory Research Series
0073-6902 Indiana Historical Society. Publications
0073-6910 Indiana Industrial Directory
0073-6937 Indiana State University. Department of Geography and Geology. Professional Papers
0073-6945 Indiana Studies in Prediction *changed to* Indiana Studies in Higher Education
0073-6953 Indiana University. Department of Geography. Geographic Monograph Series
0073-6961 University of Indiana. Department of Geography. Occasional Publication.†
0073-6996 Indiana University. Folklore Institute. Monograph Series
0073-702X Indiana University Monograph Series in Adult Education
0073-7038 Indiana University Art Museum. Publications
0073-7062 Indiana University. Research Center for Language and Semiotic Studies. African Series
0073-7097 Indiana University. Research Center for Language and Semiotic Studies. Uralic and Altaic Series
0073-7119 Indiana University. School of Dentistry. Alumni Bulletin
0073-7127 Indiana University. Sesquicentennial Series on Insurance
0073-7151 Indice Agricola Colombiano
0073-7178 Indice General de Publicaciones Periodicas Latinoamericanas; Humanidades y Ciencias Sociales†
0073-7186 Indices of Urban Land Prices and Construction Cost of Wooden Houses in Japan
0073-7194 Indices Verborum Linguae Mongoliae Monumentis Traditorum
0073-7208 Indices zur Deutschen Literatur
0073-7224 Indo-Iranian Monographs†
0073-7240 Indo-Pacific Mollusca
0073-7275 Industria del Petrolio in Italia
0073-7283 Industria International *see* 0039-7245
0073-7291 Industria Italiana del Ciclo e del Motociclo. Annuario
0073-7305 Industrial Accident Prevention Association. Annual Report
0073-7313 Industrial Accident Prevention Association. Guide to Safety
0073-7321 Industrial Alabama *see* 0145-4048
0073-733X Industrial and Commercial Power Systems and Electrical Space Heating and Air Conditioning Joint Technical Conference. Record
0073-7356 Industrial Bank of Sudan. Board of Directors. Annual Report
0073-7364 Industrial Catering
0073-7372 Industrial Development Bank of India. Annual Report
0073-7380 Industrial Development Bank of Israel Limited. Report
0073-7399 Industrial Development Bank of Pakistan. Report
0073-7402 Industrial Development Bank of Turkey. Annual Statement
0073-7410 Foundation for Business Responsibilities. Discussion Paper
0073-7429 Foundation for Business Responsibilities. Occasional Papers
0073-7437 Foundation for Business Responsibilities. Research Paper
0073-7445 Industrial Engineering Conference. Proceedings
0073-7453 Industrial Fibres†
0073-747X International Finishing Industries Manual *changed to* Finishing Diary
0073-7488 Industrial Health Foundation. Chemical-Toxicological Series. Bulletin
0073-7496 Industrial Health Foundation. Engineering Series. Bulletin
0073-750X Industrial Health Foundation. Legal Series Bulletin.
0073-7518 Industrial Health Foundation. Medical Series. Bulletin
0073-7526 Industrial Hygiene Foundation. Nursing Series. Bulletins *changed to* Industrial Health Foundation. Nursing Series. Bulletins
0073-7542 Industrial Hygiene Highlights *changed to* Industrial Environmental Health
0073-7550 Industrial Intelligence; Industrial Yearbook†
0073-7569 Industrial Locations in Canada
0073-7577 Industrial Planning and Programming Series
0073-7593 Industrial Relations Research in Canada
0073-7615 Industrial Research in United Kingdom
0073-7623 Industrial Research Laboratories of the U. S
0073-7658 Industrial South Africa
0073-7666 Industrial Structure of Rajasthan
0073-7682 Industrial Waste Conference, Purdue University, Lafayette, Indiana. Proceedings
0073-7704 Industrie-Adresboek voor Zuid-Holland *changed to* Adreslijst van de Zuid-Hollandse Industrie
0073-7712 Industrie Compass Oesterreich
0073-7720 Industrie de la Manutention dans les Ports Francais
0073-7739 Industrie et Artisanat
0073-7747 Industrie Francaise des Moteurs a Combustion Interne
0073-7755 Industrieabwaesser
0073-7763 Industries Directory, Capitals
0073-7771 Industries Directory, Delhi
0073-7798 Industries Directory, Northern India
0073-7801 Industry-Engineering Education Series†
0073-7801 Industry-Engineering Education Series *changed to* C I E C Proceedings
0073-781X Industry in East Africa
0073-7828 Inedits Russes
0073-7844 Information Display Buyers Guide†
0073-7860 Information Please Almanac
0073-7879 Information Processing Association of Israel. National Conference on Data Processing. Proceedings
0073-7887 Information Series in Agricultural Economics
0073-7887 Information Series on Agricultural Economics *changed to* Giannini Foundation of Agricultural Economics. Information Series
0073-7895 Information Service of the European Communities. Newsletter on the Common Agricultural Policy
0073-7909 Trade Union News from the European Community
0073-7909 Information Service of the European Communities. Trade Union News
0073-7917 Informations Annuelles de Caryosystematique et Cytogenetique
0073-7925 Informations et Etudes Socialistes
0073-7941 Informatique *changed to* Zero-Un Informatique
0073-7976 Informatique Industrielle *changed to* Automatique et Informatique Industrielles
0073-7984 Informatore Farmaceutico
0073-7992 Ingenieria. Boletin Informativo
0073-800X Inglis Lecture
0073-8018 Initiation a la Linguistique. Serie A. Lectures
0073-8026 Initiation a la Linguistique. Serie B. Problemes et Methodes
0073-8034 Initiation. Serie Textes, Bibliographies
0073-8042 Inland Printer/American Lithographer Buyer's Guide†
0073-8077 Inorganic Syntheses Series
0073-8085 Chimica Acta Reviews *see* 0020-1693
0073-8093 Canada. Insect Pathology Research Institute. Program Review†
0073-8115 Insects of Micronesia
0073-8123 Insights
0073-8131 Institut Belge de Science Politique. Bibliotheque. Nouvelle Serie
0073-814X Institut Belge de Science Politique. Bibliotheque. Serie Documents
0073-8158 Institut Belge de Science Politique. Documents
0073-8166 Institut Belge d'Information et de Documentation. Repertoire de l'Information
0073-8174 Institut Collegial Europeen. Bulletin
0073-8182 Institut de Droit International. Annuaire
0073-8190 Institut de France. Annuaire
0073-8212 Institut de Recherche et d'Histoire des Textes, Paris. Documents, Etudes et Repertoires
0073-8220 Institut Armoricain de Recherches Historiques, Rennes. (Publication) *changed to* Universite de Rennes. Institut Armoricain de Recherches Economiques et Humaines. (Publication)
0073-8239 Institut de Science Economique Appliquee. Rapport d'Activite *changed to* Institut de Sciences Mathematiques et Economiques Appliquees. Rapport d'Activite
0073-8247 Institut d'Emission d'Outre Mer, Paris. Rapport d'Activite
0073-8255 Institut d'Emission Malgache. Rapport d'Activite *changed to* Banque Centrale de la Republique Malgache. Rapport d'Activite
0073-8263 Institut des Etudes Occitanes. Publications
0073-8271 Institut des Hautes Etudes de l'Amerique Latine. Cahiers†
0073-828X Institut des Hautes Etudes de l'Amerique Latine. Centre d'Etudes Politiques, Economiques et Sociales. Publications Multigraphiees.
0073-8298 Institut des Hautes Etudes de l'Amerique Latine. Travaux et Memoires
0073-8301 Institut des Hautes Etudes Scientifiques, Paris. Publications Mathematiques
0073-8336 Institut Francais de Pondichery. Section Scientifique et Technique. Travaux
0073-8344 Institut Francais de Pondichery. Section Scientifique et Technique. Travaux. Hors Serie
0073-8352 Institut Francais d'Indologie. Publications
0073-8360 Institut Francais du Petrole. Collection Colloques et Seminaires
0073-8379 Institut Francais du Petrole. Rapport Annuel
0073-8387 Institut fuer Asienkunde. Schriften
0073-8417 Institut fuer den Wissenschaftlichen Film. Publikationen zu Wissenschaftlichen Filmen. Sektion Biologie
0073-8433 Institut fuer den Wissenschaftlichen Film. Publikationen zu Wissenschaftlichen Filmen. Sektion Technische Wissenschaften, Naturwissenschaften
0073-8441 Publikationen zu Wissenschaftlichen Filmen. Sektion Geschichte, Paedagogik *see* 0341-5937
0073-8468 Institut fuer Gewerbeforschung, Vienna. Taetigkeitsbericht
0073-8484 Institut fuer Oesterreichische Geschichtsforschung. Mitteilungen
0073-8492 Institut fuer Ostrecht. Studien
0073-8522 Institut Historique Belge de Rome. Bibliotheque
0073-8530 Institut Historique Belge de Rome. Bulletin
0073-8549 Institut Historique et Archeologique Neerlandais de Stamboull. Publications
0073-8557 Institut Jules Destree. Etudes et Documents
0073-8565 Institut Michel Pacha. Annales
0073-8573 Institut Pasteur de Lille. Annales
0073-859X Universite de Geneve. Institut Universitaire de Hautes Etudes Internationales. Etudes et Travaux
0073-8603 Universite de Geneve. Institut Universitaire de Hautes Etudes Internationales. Publication
0073-8611 Instituta et Monumenta. Series I: Monumenta
0073-862X Institute for Balkan Studies. Publications
0073-8638 Institute for Clinical Science. Proficiency Test Service. Report
0073-8646 I C R Studies
0073-8654 Institute for Defense Analyses. Papers
0073-8662 Institute for Defense Analyses. Reports
0073-8670 Institute for Defense Analyses. Studies
0073-8697 I/D/E/A Monographs
0073-8700 I/D/E/A Occasional Papers
0073-8751 Institute for Fermentation, Osaka. Research Communications
0073-8778 Institute for Monetary Research. Monographs
0073-8786 Institute for Palestine Studies. Anthology Series†
0073-8794 Institute for Palestine Studies. Basic Documents Series
0073-8808 Institute for Palestine Studies. International Annual Documentary Series
0073-8816 Institute for Palestine Studies. Monograph Series

ISSN INDEX 1127

0073-8832 Institute for Petroleum Research and Geophysics, Holon, Israel. Report
0073-8875 Institute for Psychoanalysis. Report *changed to* Institute for Psychoanalysis. Newsletter
0073-8921 I S M A Papers
0073-893X I S M A Occasional Papers
0073-8948 Institut fuer Iberoamerika-Kunde. Schriftenreihe
0073-8972 Institute of Actuaries of Australia and New Zealand. Transactions *changed to* Institute of Actuaries of Australia. Transactions
0073-8980 Institute of Actuaries. Year Book
0073-8999 Institute of Bankers in Pakistan. Council. Report and Accounts
0073-9006 Institute of British Geographers. Special Publication
0073-9014 Institute of Building. Year Book and Directory of Members
0073-9030 Institute of Chartered Accountants in England and Wales. Management Information Series
0073-9049 Institute of Chartered Accountants in England and Wales. Practice Administration Series, Exposure Drafts and Statements of Standard Accounting Practice
0073-9057 Institute of Chartered Accountants of Scotland. Official Directory
0073-9065 C F A Monograph Series†
0073-9073 Institute of Clerk of Works' of Great Britain Incorporated. Year Book
0073-909X Institute of Economic Affairs. Occasional Papers
0073-9103 Institute of Economic Affairs. Research Monographs
0073-9138 I E E E International Convention and Exhibition. Record
0073-9146 I E E E Membership Directory
0073-9154 I E E E Power Engineering Society. Winter Meeting. Preprints
0073-9162 I E E E Standards
0073-9170 I E E E Region 3 Conference. Record
0073-9189 I E E E Region 6. Technical Conference. Record *changed to* I E E E Region 6. Conference. Proceedings
0073-9197 I E E E Region 5 Conference. Record
0073-9200 Institution of Engineers. Technical Journal
0073-9219 Institution of Engineers. Year Book
0073-9227 Institute of Environmental Sciences. Annual Meeting. Proceedings
0073-9251 Institute of Environmental Sciences. Tutorial Series
0073-926X Institute of European Studies. Announcements
0073-9278 Institute of European Studies. Papers and Addresses of the Annual Conference and Academic Council
0073-9286 I F T World Directory and Guide
0073-9294 Institute of Forest Genetics, Suwon, Korea. Research Report
0073-9308 Great Britain. Institute of Geological Sciences. Annual Report
0073-9316 Great Britain.Institute of Geological Sciences. Geomagnetic Bulletins
0073-9324 Great Britain. Institute of Geological Sciences. Geophysical Papers†
0073-9332 Great Britain. Institute of Geological Sciences. Overseas Geology and Mineral Resources
0073-9340 Institute of Geological Sciences, London. Overseas Geology and Mineral Resources. Supplement Series†
0073-9359 Great Britain.Institute of Geological Sciences. Report
0073-9367 Institute of Geological Sciences, London. Statistical Summary of the Mineral Industry *changed to* World Mineral Statistics
0073-9375 Great Britain. Institute of Geological Sciences. Water Supply Papers†
0073-9383 Great Britain. Institute of Geological Sciences. Water Supply Papers. Research Reports†
0073-9391 Great Britain. Institute of Geological Sciences. Water Supply Papers. Technical Communications†
0073-9413 Institute of Judicial Administration. Calendar Status Study†
0073-9421 Institute of Labor and Industrial Relations. Policy Papers in Human Resources and Industrial Relations
0073-943X Institute of Labor and Industrial Relations. Reprint Series
0073-9448 Institute of Medical Laboratory Technology. London. Annual Report *changed to* Institute of Medical Laboratory Sciences. London, Annual Report
0073-9456 Institute of Mennonite Studies Series
0073-9464 Institute of Metals. Monograph and Report Series†
0073-9472 Institute of Nuclear Materials Management. Proceedings of Annual Meeting
0073-9480 Institute of Paper Chemistry. Bibliographic Series
0073-9502 Institute of Pastoral Psychology. Proceedings *see* 0079-0141
0073-9529 Institute of Petroleum, London. Report of the Summer Meeting†
0073-9537 I P C Monographs
0073-9545 I P C Papers
0073-9561 Institute of Psychophysical Research. Proceedings
0073-957X Institute of Public Administration, Dublin. Administrative Procedure Series†
0073-9588 Institute of Public Administration, Dublin. Annual Report
0073-9596 Institute of Public Administration, Dublin. Administration Yearbook and Diary
0073-960X Institute of Public Administration, Dublin. Research Series†
0073-9618 Institute of Public Administration, Khartoum. Occasional Papers
0073-9626 Institute of Public Administration, Khartoum. Proceedings of the Annual Round Table Conference
0073-9650 Institute of Purchasing and Supply. Yearbook
0073-9669 Institute of Quantity Surveyors. Year Book
0073-9677 Institute of Refrigeration, London. Proceedings
0073-9693 Institute of Social Studies, The Hague. Publications. Paperback Series†
0073-9707 Institute of Social Studies, The Hague. Publications. Series Major†
0073-9723 Institute of Southeast Asian Studies. Library Bulletin
0073-9731 Institute of Southeast Asian Studies. Occasional Paper
0073-9766 I E E Monograph Series
0073-9782 Institution of Engineers (India). Directory
0073-9790 Institution of Engineers of Ireland. Transactions
0073-9804 Institution of Municipal Engineers, London. Annual Conference. Proceedings†
0073-9812 Institution of Nuclear Engineers. Year Book†
0073-9839 Institution of Railway Signal Engineers. Proceedings
0073-9847 Institution of Structural Engineers. Yearbook
0073-9855 Instituto Adolfo Lutz. Revista
0073-9863 Instituto Antartico Chileno. Boletin
0073-9871 Instituto Antartico Chileno. Contribution. Serie Cientifica
0073-988X Instituto Brasileiro do Cafe. Departamento Economico. Anuario Estatistico do Cafe. *changed to* Instituto Brasileiro do Cafe. Departamento Economico. Anuario Estatistico do Cafe
0073-9901 Instituto Butantan. Memorias
0073-991X Instituto Caro y Cuervo. Serie Bibliografica
0073-9928 Instituto Caro y Cuervo. Serie Minor
0073-9936 Instituto Centro Americano de Investigacion y Tecnologia Industrial. Publicaciones Geologicas
0073-9944 Instituto Centroamericano de Administracion Publica. Serie 100. Aspectos Humanos de la Administracion
0073-9952 Instituto Centroamericano de Administracion Publica. Serie 200. Ciencia de la Administracion
0073-9960 Instituto Centroamericano de Administracion Publica. Serie 300: Investigacion
0073-9979 Instituto Centroamericano de Administracion Publica. Serie 400: Economia y Finanzas
0073-9995 Instituto Centroamericano de Administracion Publica. Serie 600: Informes de Seminarios
0074-0004 Instituto Centroamericano de Administracion Publica. Serie 700: Materiales de Informacion
0074-0012 Instituto Centroamericano de Administracion Publica. Serie 800: Metodologia de la Administracion
0074-0020 Instituto Centroamericano de Administracion Publica. Serie 900: Miscelaneas
0074-0039 Instituto Costarricense de Cultura Hispanica. Publicacion
0074-0047 Informe de Operacion de las Principales Empresas Productoras y Distribuidoras de Energia Electrica de Costa Rica
0074-0063 Instituto de Ciencia Politica Rafael Bielsa. Anuario
0074-008X Instituto de Investigacao Cientifica de Angola. Bibliograficas Tematicas
0074-0098 Instituto de Investigacao Cientifica de Angola. Memorias e Trabalhos
0074-0144 Instituto de Tecnologia de Alimentos. Instrucoes Praticas
0074-0152 Instituto de Tecnologia de Alimentos. Instrucoes Tecnicas
0074-0195 Instituto Espanol de Oceanografia. Boletin
0074-0209 Instituto Espanol de Oceanografia. Trabajos
0074-0233 Instituto Hondureno de Seguridad Social. Departamento de Estadistica y Procesamiento de Datos. Anuario Estadistico
0074-025X Fundacion Miguel Lillo. Miscelanea
0074-0268 Instituto Nacional de Seguros. Informe Anual *changed to* Instituto Nacional de Seguros Memoria Anual
0074-0276 Instituto Oswaldo Cruz, Rio de Janeiro. Memorias
0074-0292 I T A Humanidades†
0074-0306 Instituto Tecnologico y de Estudios Superiores. Publicaciones. Serie: Catalogos de Biblioteca
0074-0330 Instituto Torcuato di Tella. Centro de Estudios Urbanos Regionales. Documentos de Trabajo
0074-0349 Instituto Torcuato di Tella. Centro de Investigaciones Economicas. Documentos de Trabajo
0074-0357 Instituto Torcuato di Tella. Centro de Investigaciones Sociales. Documentos de Trabajo
0074-0373 Institutul de Cercetari Pentru Cultura Cartofului si Sfeclei de Zahar, Brasov. Anale. Cartoful
0074-0381 Institutul de Cercetari Pentru Cultura Cartofului si Sfeclei de Zahar, Brasov. Anale. Sfecla de Zahar
0074-039X Institutul de Istorie si Arheologie "A. D. Xenopol". Anuarul
0074-0411 Instituut voor Cultuurtechniek en Waterhuishouding. Mededeling
0074-042X Instituut voor Cultuurtechniek en Waterhuishouding. Technical Bulletin
0074-0438 Instituut voor Cultuurtechniek en Waterhuishouding. Verspreide Overdrukken
0074-0446 Instituut voor Plantenziektenkundig Onderzoek. Jaarverslag
0074-0462 Koninklijk Instituut voor Taal-, Land- en Volkenkunde. Bibliographical Series
0074-0470 Koninklijk Instituut voor Taal-, Land- en Volkenkunde. Translation Series
0074-0489 Instituut voor Veevoedingsonderzoek "Hoorn" Jaarverslag *changed to* Instituut voor Veevoedingsonderzoek Jaarverslag
0074-0497 Instrument and Control Systems Buyers Guide
0074-0500 I S A Transducer Compendium
0074-0527 Instrument Society of America. Standards and Practices for Instrumentation
0074-0543 Instrumentation in Nuclear Medicine
0074-0551 Instrumentation in the Chemical and Petroleum Industry
0074-056X Instrumentation in the Power Industry
0074-0578 Instruments, Electronics and Automation Purchasing Directory *changed to* Directory of Instruments, Electronics, Automation
0074-0586 Instytut Gospodarki Wodnej. Prace
0074-0616 Instytut Slaski. Kommunikaty. Seria Niemcoznawcza
0074-0632 Instytut Slaski. Wydawnictwa
0074-0640 Instytut Badan Jadrowych. Zaklad Radiobiologii i Ochrony Zdrowia. Prace Doswiadczaine
0074-0659 Insulation /Circuits Directory / Encyclopedia *changed to* Insulation/ Circuits Desk Manual
0074-0675 Insurance Almanac; Who, What, When and Where in Insurance
0074-0683 Insurance Casebook
0074-0691 Insurance Directory and Year Book
0074-0705 Israel. Central Bureau of Statistics. Insurance in Israel
0074-0713 Insurance Facts
0074-0721 Insurance Institute of Canada. Report
0074-073X Insurance Periodicals Index
0074-0748 Asociacion Interamericana de Bibliotecarios y Documentalistas Agricolas. Boletin Especial
0074-0756 Asociacion Interamericana de Bibliotecarios y Documentalistas Agricolas. Boletin Tecnico†
0074-0764 Inter-American Commission of Women. Special Assembly. Final Act
0074-0780 Inter-American Commission on Human Rights. Report on the Work Accomplished During Its Special Sessions†
0074-0799 Inter-American Conference of Ministers of Labor on the Alliance for Progress. Final Act†
0074-0802 Inter-American Conference on Community Development. Final Act†
0074-0810 Inter-American Conference on Indian Life. Acta
0074-0829 Inter-American Council for Education, Science, and Culture. Final Report
0074-0837 Work Accomplished by the Inter-American Juridicical Committee During Its Meeting
0074-0861 Inter-American Development Bank. Board of Governors. Proceedings of the Meeting
0074-087X Inter-American Development Bank. Annual Report
0074-0888 Socio-Economic Progress in Latin America; Annual Report *see* 0095-2850
0074-0918 Inter-American Economic and Social Council. Final Report of the Annual Meeting at the Ministerial Level

0074-0926 Inter-American Institute of Agricultural Sciences. Center for Training and Research. Bibliotecologia y Documentacion *see* 0301-438X
0074-0942 Inter-American Nuclear Energy Commission. Final Report
0074-0950 Inter-American Port and Harbor Conferences. Final Act†
0074-0969 Inter-American Statistical Conferences. Final Report†
0074-0985 Inter-American Travel Congresses. Final Act†
0074-0993 Inter-American Tropical Tuna Commission. Bulletin
0074-1000 Inter-American Tropical Tuna Commission. Informe Anual. Annual Report
0074-1019 Inter-Documentation Company. Newsletter
0074-1027 Inter-Guiana Geological Conference. Proceedings
0074-1035 Inter-Nord; Revue Internationale d'Etudes Arctiques et Nordiques
0074-1043 Chronicle of Parliamentary Elections *changed to* Chronicle of Parliamentary Elections and Developments
0074-1051 Inter-Parliamentary Union. Conference Proceedings
0074-106X Inter-University Case Program. Case Study
0074-1078 Inter-university Consortium for Political and Social Research. Annual Report
0074-1086 Interamerican Conference on Materials Technology. (Proceedings)†
0074-1116 Interavia A B C
0074-1132 Interdisciplinary Topics in Gerontology
0074-1140 Interferences, Arts, Lettres
0074-1175 Intergovernmental Oceanographic Commission. Technical Series
0074-1191 Design in Greece
0074-1205 Internal Revenue Guide to Your Federal Income Tax
0074-1213 Internal Trade of Iran
0074-123X International Academy of Indian Culture. Report
0074-1248 International Academy of Legal Medicine and of Social Medicine. (Congress Reports)
0074-1256 International Academy of Oral Pathology. Proceedings
0074-1264 International Actuarial Congress. Transactions
0074-1272 Biennial Survey of Advertising Expenditures Around the World *see* 0568-0301
0074-1329 International Air Transport Association. Bulletin *changed to* International Air Transport Association. Annual Report
0074-1337 International Air Transport Association. Symposium Papers from the Annual General Meeting†
0074-1353 International Anatomical Congress. Proceedings
0074-137X International Archery Federation. Bulletin Officiel
0074-1388 International Arthurian Society. Bibliographical Bulletin
0074-1396 International Arthurian Society. Report of Congress
0074-140X International Association for Bridge and Structural Engineering. Bulletin/ Mitteilungen†
0074-1418 International Association for Bridge and Structural Engineering. Final Report (of Congress)
0074-1434 International Association for Bridge and Structural Engineering. Preliminary Report (of Congress)
0074-1442 International Association for Bridge and Structural Engineering. Reports of the Working Commissions
0074-1450 International Association for Cereal Chemistry. Working and Discussion Meetings Reports
0074-1469 International Association for Classical Archaeology. Proceedings of Congress
0074-1477 International Association for Hydraulic Research. Congress Proceedings
0074-1507 International Association for Statistics in Physical Sciences. Proceedings (of Meetings)†
0074-1515 I A A E E Reprint
0074-1523 I A A E E Monographs
0074-154X International Association for the Advancement of Educational Research. Congress Reports *changed to* World Association for Educational Research. Congress Reports
0074-1574 International Association of Applied Psychology. Proceedings of Congress
0074-1582 International Association of Chain Stores. Report of Plenary Session
0074-1604 International Association of Democratic Lawyers. Congress Report
0074-1612 International Association of Engineering Geology. Bulletin
0074-1655 International Association of Logopedics and Phoniatrics. Reports of Congress
0074-1663 International Association of Meteorology and Atmospheric Physics. Report of Proceedings of General Assembly
0074-1671 International Association of Milk Control Agencies. Proceedings of Annual Meetings
0074-168X International Association of Museums of Arms and Military History. Congress Reports
0074-1698 A. I. J. P. Yearbook
0074-1701 International Association of Philatelic Journalists. Bulletin
0074-171X International Association of Philatelic Journalists. Minutes of Annual Congresses
0074-1728 International Association of Physical Education and Sports for Girls and Women. Proceedings of the International Congress
0074-1736 International Association of Seed Crushers. Proceedings of the Annual Congress
0074-1744 International Association of State Lotteries. (Reports of Congress)
0074-1760 International Association of Thalassotherapy. Congress Reports
0074-1787 International Association of Workers for Maladjusted Children. Congress Reports
0074-1795 International Astronautical Congress. Proceedings *see* 0304-8705
0074-1809 International Astronomical Union. Proceedings of Symposia
0074-1833 International Atomic Energy Agency. Bibliographical Series†
0074-1841 I A E A Laboratory Activities†
0074-185X I A E A Research Contracts†
0074-1868 International Atomic Energy Agency. Legal Series
0074-1876 International Atomic Energy Agency. Panel Proceedings Series
0074-1884 International Atomic Energy Agency. Proceedings Series
0074-1892 International Atomic Energy Agency. Safety Series
0074-1906 International Atomic Energy Agency. Technical Directories
0074-1914 International Atomic Energy Agency. Technical Report Series
0074-1922 International Auction Records
0074-1973 International Baccalaureate Office. Annual Bulletin
0074-1981 International Badminton Federation. Annual Handbook *changed to* International Badminton Federation. Annual Statute Book
0074-199X World Bank Staff Occasional Papers
0074-2007 International Beekeeping Congress. Reports
0074-2015 International Bibliography of Historical Sciences
0074-2031 International Bibliography of Rice Research
0074-204X International Bibliography of Studies on Alcohol
0074-2066 International Biennial Exhibition of Prints in Tokyo
0074-2074 I B P Handbooks†
0074-2082 International Biometeorological Congress. Summaries and Reports Presented to the Congress
0074-2090 International Botanical Congress. Abstracts of Papers
0074-2104 International Bureau of Fiscal Documentation. Annual Report
0074-2112 International Bureau of Fiscal Documentation. Publication
0074-2147 International Catalogue of Occupational Safety and Health Films
0074-2155 International Cemetery Directory
0074-2163 International Centre for Settlement of Investment Disputes. Annual Report
0074-2171 International Centre of Fertilizers. World Congress. Acts
0074-218X International Ceramic Congress. Proceedings
0074-221X International Civil Aviation Association. Aeronautical Agreements and Arrangements. Annual Supplement
0074-2228 International Civil Aviation Organization. (Panel On) Application of Space Techniques Relating to Aviation. Report of Meeting
0074-2244 International Civil Aviation Organization. Airworthiness Committee. Report of Meeting
0074-2252 International Civil Aviation Organization. Automated Data Interchange Systems Panel. Report of Meeting
0074-2287 International Civil Aviation Organization. Air Navigation Plan. Africa-Indian Ocean Region
0074-2295 International Civil Aviation Organization. Air Navigation Plan. Caribbean and South American Regions. *changed to* International Civil Aviation Organization. Air Navigation Plan. Caribbean Region
0074-2309 International Civil Aviation Organization. Air Navigation Plan. European Region
0074-2317 International Civil Aviation Organization. Air Navigation Plan. Middle East and South East Asia Regions
0074-2325 International Civil Aviation Organization. Air Navigation Plan. North Atlantic, North American and Pacific Regions
0074-2333 International Civil Aviation Organization. All-Weather Operations Panel. Report of Meeting
0074-235X International Civil Aviation Organization. Assembly. Resolutions
0074-2368 International Civil Aviation Organization. Assembly. Report and Minutes of the Legal Commission
0074-2376 International Civil Aviation Organization. Assembly. Report of the Economic Commission
0074-2384 International Civil Aviation Organization. Assembly. Report of the Technical Commission
0074-2422 International Civil Aviation Organization. Digests of Statistics. Series AT. Airport Traffic
0074-2430 International Civil Aviation Organization. Digests of Statistics. Series F. Financial Data
0074-2449 International Civil Aviation Organization. Digests of Statistics. Series FP. Fleet, Personnel
0074-2457 International Civil Aviation Organization. Digests of Statistics. Series R. Civil Aircraft on Register
0074-2465 International Civil Aviation Organization. Digests of Statistics. Series T. Traffic
0074-2481 I C A O Circulars
0074-249X International Civil Aviation Organization. Indexes to I C A O Publications. Annual Cumulation
0074-2503 International Civil Aviation Organization. Legal Committee. Minutes and Documents (of Sessions)
0074-252X International Civil Aviation Organization. Obstacle Clearance Panel. Report of Meeting
0074-2546 International Civil Aviation Organization. Report of the Air Navigation Conference
0074-2562 International Civil Aviation Organization. Sonic Boom Panel. Report of the Meeting
0074-2570 International Civil Aviation Organization. Technical Panel on Supersonic Transport. Report of Meeting
0074-2589 International Civil Aviation Organization. Visual Aids Panel. Report of Meeting
0074-2597 International Clay Conference. Proceedings
0074-2600 International College of Dentists. India Section. Newsletter
0074-2627 International Commission for the Northwest Atlantic Fisheries. Annual Proceedings *see* 0704-4798
0074-2635 International Commission for the Northwest Atlantic Fisheries. List of Fishing Vessels *see* 0250-7811
0074-2643 International Commission for the Northwest Atlantic Fisheries. Redbook *see* 0250-6416
0074-2651 Journal of Northwest Atlantic Fishery Science
0074-2651 International Commission for the Northwest Atlantic Fisheries. Research Bulletin *see* 0074-2651
0074-266X International Commission for the Northwest Atlantic Fisheries. Statistical Bulletin *see* 0250-6394
0074-2694 International Commission of Agricultural Engineering. Reports of Congress
0074-2708 International Commission of Sugar Technology. Proceedings of the General Assembly
0074-2724 International Commission on Illumination. Proceedings
0074-2732 International Commission on Irrigation and Drainage. Congress Reports
0074-2759 International Commission on Radiological Protection. Report
0074-2775 International Organizing Committee of World Mining Congresses. Report *changed to* World Mining Congress. Report
0074-2783 International Committee for Historical Science. Bulletin d'Information
0074-2791 International Committee of Onomastic Sciences. Congress Proceedings
0074-2805 International Committee on Laboratory Animals. Proceedings of Symposium *changed to* International Council for Laboratory Animal Science. Proceedings of the Symposium
0074-2813 International Comparative Literature Association. Proceedings of the Congress
0074-283X International Computer Bibliography
0074-2848 International Computer Technical Conference. Record *changed to* I E E E Computer Society International Conference. Digest of Papers
0074-2856 International Confederation for Agricultural Credit. Assembly and Congress Reports
0074-2872 International Confederation of Free Trade Unions. World Congress Reports

ISSN INDEX 1129

0074-2899 International Confederation of Societies of Authors and Composers
0074-2902 International Conference of Agricultural Economists. Proceedings
0074-2961 International Conference of Social Work. Conference Proceedings
0074-297X International Conference of Sociology of Religion
0074-3011 International Conference on Cloud Physics. Proceedings
0074-3038 International Conference on Congenital Malformations. Proceedings
0074-3054 International Conference on Endodontics. Transactions
0074-3062 International Conference on Engineering in the Ocean Environment. Digest
0074-3089 International Conference on Fluid Sealing. Proceedings
0074-3097 International Conference on Global Impacts of Applied Microbiology. Proceedings
0074-3100 International Conference on Health and Health Education. Proceedings
0074-3135 International Conference on Intra-Uterine Contraception. Proceedings
0074-3143 International Conference on Phenomena in Ionized Gases. Proceedings
0074-3151 International Conference on Large High Voltage Electric Systems. Proceedings
0074-316X International Conference on Lead. Proceedings
0074-3216 International Conference on Oral Biology. Proceedings
0074-3240 International Conference on Physics of Semiconductors. Proceedings
0074-3259 International Conference on Planned Parenthood. Proceedings†
0074-3275 International Conference on Education. Proceedings *changed to* International Conference on Education. Final Report
0074-3305 International Conference on Social Welfare. Proceedings
0074-3313 International Conference on Soil Mechanics and Foundation Engineering. Proceedings
0074-333X International Conference on the Physics of Electronic and Atomic Collisions. Papers
0074-3356 International Commission on Trichinellosis. Proceedings
0074-3372 International Congress for Child Psychiatry. Proceedings
0074-3380 International Congress for Cybernetics. Proceedings. Actes
0074-3402 International Congress for Logic, Methodology and Philosophy of Science. Proceedings
0074-3429 International Congress for Papyrology. Proceedings
0074-3437 International Congress for Stereology. Proceedings
0074-3445 International Congress of Acarology. Proceedings
0074-3453 International Congress of Allergology. Proceedings
0074-347X International Congress of Angiology. Proceedings
0074-3488 International Congress of Animal Production. Proceedings†
0074-3496 International Congress of Anthropological and Ethnological Sciences. Proceedings
0074-3518 International Congress of Archives. Proceedings
0074-3526 International Congress of Automatic Control. Proceedings
0074-3534 International Congress of Biochemistry. Proceedings
0074-3542 International Congress for Byzantine Studies. Acts
0074-3550 International Congress of Cell Biology. Summaries of Reports and Communications
0074-3577 International Congress of Chemotherapy. Proceedings
0074-3615 International Congress of Cybernetic Medicine. Proceedings
0074-3631 International Congress of Electroencephalography and Clinical Neurophysiology (Proceedings)
0074-364X International Congress of Entomology
0074-3666 International Congress of Food Science and Technology. Proceedings
0074-3682 International Congress of Hematology. Proceedings
0074-3690 International Congress of Histochemistry and Cytochemistry. Proceedings
0074-3712 International Congress of Home Economics. Report
0074-3747 International Congress of Life Assurance Medicine. Proceedings
0074-3755 International Congress of Linguists. Proceedings
0074-378X International Congress of Nephrology. Proceedings
0074-3801 International Congress of Neurological Surgery. Abstracts of Papers
0074-3828 International Congress of Occupational Therapy. Proceedings
0074-3860 International Congress of Parasitology. Proceedings
0074-3879 International Congress of Pharmaceutical Sciences. Proceedings†
0074-3879 International Congress of Pharmaceutical Sciences. Proceedings
0074-3887 International Congress of Physical Medicine. Abstracts of Papers Presented
0074-3895 International Congress of Primatology. Proceedings
0074-3917 International Congress of Psychotherapy. Proceedings/Verhandlungen/Comptes Rendus
0074-3925 International Congress of Pure and Applied Chemistry. (Lectures)
0074-3933 International Congress of Radiology. (Reports)
0074-3968 International Congress of Sugarcane Technologists. Proceedings
0074-3984 Transplantation Today
0074-3992 International Congress of University Adult Education. Journal
0074-400X International Conference on Acoustics. Reports
0074-4026 International Congress on Animal Reproduction and Artificial Insemination. Proceedings
0074-4034 International Congress on Canned Foods. Report
0074-4042 International Congress on Clinical Chemistry. Abstracts
0074-4050 International Congress on Clinical Chemistry. Proceedings
0074-4069 International Congress on Clinical Chemistry. Papers
0074-4077 International Congress on Combustion Engines. Proceedings
0074-4107 International Congress on Hormonal Steroids. Abstracts of Papers Presented
0074-4115 International Commission on Large Dams. Transactions
0074-4123 International Congress on Metallic Corrosion. (Proceedings)
0074-4131 International Congress on Occupational Health. Proceedings
0074-4190 International Congress on the History of Art. Proceedings
0074-4212 International Congresses on Tropical Medicine and Malaria. (Proceedings)
0074-4220 International Convocation on Immunology. Papers
0074-4239 International Cooperation Council. Directory *changed to* Directory for a New World
0074-4247 International Cooperative Alliance. Congress Report
0074-4255 International Cooperative Alliance. Cooperative Series
0074-4263 International Council for Bird Preservation. British Section. Report
0074-4271 International Council for Bird Preservation. Proceedings of Conferences
0074-428X International Council for Building Research, Studies and Documentation. Congress Reports
0074-4298 International Council for Philosophy and Humanistic Studies. General Assembly. Compte Rendu *changed to* International Council for Philosophy and Humanistic Studies. Bulletin
0074-431X International Council for the Exploration of the Sea. Cooperative Research Reports
0074-4328 I C E S Oceanographic Data Lists *changed to* I C E S Oceanographic Data Lists and Inventories
0074-4336 International Council for the Exploration of the Sea. Rapports et Proces-Verbaux des Reunions
0074-4360 International Council of Homehelp Services. Reports of Congress
0074-4387 International Council of Scientific Unions. Year Book
0074-4395 International Council of Voluntary Agencies. Documents Series
0074-4409 International Council of Voluntary Agencies. General Conference. Record of Proceedings
0074-4417 I C H P E R Congress Reports *changed to* I C H P E R Congress Proceedings
0074-4425 International Council on Social Welfare. European Symposium. Proceedings
0074-445X International Court of Justice. Yearbook
0074-4468 Credit Union Yearbook
0074-4476 International Customs Journal
0074-4484 International Dairy Federation. Annual Bulletin
0074-4522 International Diabetes Federation. Proceedings of Congress
0074-4557 S D C E International Die Casting Congress. Transactions
0074-4565 International Directory of Arts
0074-4573 International Directory of Biological Deterioration Research†
0074-4581 International Directory of Computer and Information System Services†
0074-4603 International Directory of Philosophy and Philosophers
0074-4611 International Directory of Programs in Business and Commerce
0074-462X International Directory of 16MM Film Collectors
0074-4638 International District Heating Association. Proceedings
0074-4646 International Economic Association. Proceedings of the Conferences and Congresses
0074-4670 International Electron Devices Meeting. Abstracts
0074-4697 International Electrotechnical Commission. Report on Activities
0074-4700 International Encyclopedia of Food and Nutrition *see* 0306-0632
0074-5766 International Encyclopedia on Packaging Machines
0074-5774 International Engineering Directory
0074-5790 International Falcon Movement. Conference Reports
0074-5804 F.I.D./C.R. Report Series
0074-5812 International Federation for Documentation. Proceedings of Congress
0074-5820 F I D Annual Report†
0074-5839 F I D Yearbook *see* 0379-3680
0074-5847 International Federation for Medical Psychotherapy. Congress Reports
0074-5855 International Federation for Modern Languages and Literature. Congress Reports
0074-5863 International Federation of Agricultural Producers. General Conference Proceedings
0074-588X International Federation of Asian and Western Pacific Contractors' Associations. Proceedings of the Annual Convention
0074-5898 International Federation of Associations of Textile Chemists and Colorists. Reports of Congress
0074-5952 International Federation of Fruit Juice Producers. Proceedings of Congress. Compte-Rendu du Congres
0074-5960 I F I Information†
0074-5979 International Federation of Journalists and Travel Writers. Official List/Repertoire Officiel
0074-5987 I F L A Annual
0074-6002 I F L A Directory
0074-6037 International Federation of Medical Students' Associations. Reports of General Assembly
0074-6045 International Federation of Prestressing. Congress Proceedings
0074-6053 International Film Guide
0074-6061 International Finance Corporation. Report
0074-6096 International Folk Music Council. Yearbook
0074-610X International Football Book
0074-6126 International Gas Union. Proceedings of Conferences
0074-6134 International Geographical Union. Report of Congress
0074-6142 International Geophysics Series
0074-6169 International Graphical Federation. Conference. Proceedings *see* 0018-9782
0074-6177 International Graphical Federation. Report of Activities
0074-6185 International Grassland Congress. Proceedings
0074-6193 International Green Book
0074-6207 International Group for Scientific Research in Stomatology. Bulletin
0074-6215 International Handbook of Universities and Other Institutions of Higher Education
0074-6223 International Hop Growers Convention. Report of Congress
0074-6231 International Horticultural Congress. Proceedings
0074-624X International Hotel Guide
0074-6258 International Humanist and Ethical Union. Proceedings of the Congress
0074-6274 International Hydrographic Conference. Reports of Proceedings
0074-6282 International Hydrographic Bureau. Yearbook *changed to* International Hydrographic Organization. Yearbook
0074-6320 International Indian Ocean Expedition. Collected Reprints
0074-6401 International Institute for Educational Planning. Occasional Papers
0074-641X International Institute for Labour Studies. International Educational Materials Exchange. List of Available Materials
0074-6428 International Institute for Land Reclamation and Improvement. Annual Report
0074-6436 International Institute for Land Reclamation and Improvement. Bibliography
0074-6444 International Institute for Land Reclamation and Improvement. Bulletin
0074-6452 International Institute for Land Reclamation and Improvement. Publication
0074-6460 International Institute for Sugar Beet Research. Reports of the Winter Congress
0074-6479 International Institute of Administrative Sciences. Reports of the International Congress
0074-6487 International Institute of Differing Civilizations. (Session Papers)

0074-6495 International Institute of Ibero-American Literature. Congress Proceedings. Memoria

0074-6509 International Institute for Labour Studies. Publications

0074-6525 International Institute of Philosophy. Actes

0074-6533 International Institute of Public Finance. Papers and Proceedings

0074-6541 International Institute of Refrigeration. Proceedings of Commission Meetings

0074-655X International Institute of Seismology and Earthquake Engineering. Bulletin

0074-6568 International Institute of Seismology and Earthquake Engineering. Earthquake Report

0074-6584 International Institute of Seismology and Earthquake Engineering. Lecture Note

0074-6592 International Institute of Seismology and Earthquake Engineering. Progress Report

0074-6606 International Institute of Seismology and Earthquake Engineering. Report of Individual Study by Participants to I I S E E

0074-6614 International Institute of Seismology and Earthquake Engineering. Year Book

0074-6622 International Institute on the Prevention and Treatment of Alcoholism. Selected Papers

0074-6673 International Labour Conference. Reports to the Conference and Record of Proceedings

0074-6738 International Law Association. Reports of Conferences

0074-6746 International League of Liberal Christian Women. Newsletter *changed to* International Association of Liberal Religious Women. Newsletter

0074-6754 International League of Societies for the Mentally Handicapped. World Congress Proceedings.

0074-6762 International Leprosy Congress. Abstracts and Papers *changed to* International Leprosy Congress. Transactions

0074-6770 International Lesson Annual

0074-6797 International Linguistic Association. Monograph

0074-6800 International Linguistic Association. Special Publications

0074-6819 International Literary and Artistic Association. Proceedings and Reports of Congress

0074-6827 International Literary Market Place

0074-6835 International Machine Tool Design and Research Conference. Proceedings

0074-6843 International Magnetics Conference. Digest

0074-6878 International Maize and Wheat Improvement Center. Research Bulletin

0074-6908 International Market Guide - Continental Europe

0074-6916 International Measurement Conference. Proceedings. Acta IMEKO *changed to* Acts IMEKO

0074-6932 International Medical Congress. Year Book

0074-6940 International Medieval Bibliography. Annual Subject Guide

0074-6959 International Meeting of Animal Nutrition Experts. Proceedings

0074-6975 International Meeting on Cattle Diseases. Reports

0074-6983 International Metalworkers' Congress. Reports

0074-7009 International Microwave Symposium Digest

0074-7017 International Mineralogical Association. Proceedings of Meetings

0074-7025 International Monetary Fund. Summary Proceedings of the Annual Meeting of the Board of Governors

0074-7033 International Monographs on Advanced Biology and Biophysics

0074-7041 International Monographs on Advanced Chemistry

0074-705X International Monographs on Advanced Mathematics and Physics

0074-7068 International Monographs on Studies in Indian Economics

0074-7084 International Motion Picture Almanac

0074-7114 International Narcotic Conference. Report: Proceedings of Annual Conference

0074-7122 International Naturist Guide

0074-7157 International North Pacific Fisheries Commission. Bulletin

0074-7165 International North Pacific Fisheries Commission. Annual Report

0074-7173 International Olive Growers Federation. Congress Reports

0074-7181 International Olympic Academy. Report of the Sessions

0074-719X International Organization for the Study of the Old Testament. Proceedings of the International Congress

0074-7203 International Organization of Citrus Virologists. Proceedings of the Conference

0074-722X International P. E. N. Congress. Report

0074-7238 International Pacific Halibut Commission (U.S. and Canada). Annual Report

0074-7246 International Pacific Halibut Commission (U.S. and Canada). Scientific Reports

0074-7254 International Pacific Salmon Fisheries Commission. Annual Report

0074-7262 International Pacific Salmon Fisheries Commission. Bulletin

0074-7270 International Pacific Salmon Fisheries Commission. Progress Report

0074-7289 I P R A Studies in Peace Research

0074-7297 International Peace Research Association. Proceedings of the Conference

0074-7343 International Philatelic Federation. General Assembly. Proces-Verbal

0074-7351 International Photobiological Congress. Proceedings

0074-7386 International Planned Parenthood Federation. Proceedings of the Conference of the Europe and near East Region†

0074-7394 International Planned Parenthood Federation. Working Papers†

0074-7408 International Association of Plant Breeders for the Protection of Plant Varieties. Congress Reports

0074-7416 International Playground Association. Conference Report

0074-7432 International Polar Motion Service. Annual Report

0074-7459 International Political Science Association. Circular *changed to* Participation

0074-7467 International Political Science Association. World Conference. Proceedings *changed to* International Political Science Association. World Congress

0074-7475 International Poplar Commission. Session Reports

0074-7483 International Poster Annual†

0074-7491 International Potash Institute. Colloquium. Compte Rendu

0074-7505 International Potash Institute. Congress Report

0074-7513 International Powder Metallurgy Conference. Proceedings-Modern Developments in Powder Metallurgy

0074-7521 International Pressure Die Casting Conferences. Report *changed to* International Pressure Die Casting Conferences. Proceedings

0074-753X International Psycho-Analytical Association. Bulletin *issued with* 0020-7578

0074-7548 International Psycho-Analytical Library

0074-7556 International Publishers Association. Proceedings of Congress

0074-7564 I R T S Gold Medal Annual

0074-7572 International Railway Progress *see* 0309-1465

0074-7580 International Railway Statistics. Statistics of Individual Railways

0074-7599 International Rayon and Synthetic Fibres Committee. Statistical Yearbook

0074-7602 International Rayon and Synthetic Fibres Committee. Technical Conference. Reports

0074-7610 International Rayon and Synthetic Fibres Committee. World Congress. Report

0074-7637 International Real Estate Federation. Reports of Congress

0074-7645 International Reference Annual for Building and Equipment of Sports, Tourism, Recreation Installations

0074-7653 International Reference Handbook of Services, Organizations, Diplomatic Representation, Marketing and Advertising Channels *changed to* International Reference Handbook of Marketing, Management and Advertising Organizations.

0074-7661 International Reinforced Plastics Conference. Papers and Proceedings. *see* 0306-3607

0074-767X International Review of Connective Tissue Research

0074-7688 International Review of Criminal Policy

0074-7696 International Review of Cytology

0074-770X International Review of Cytology. Supplement

0074-7718 International Review of Experimental Pathology

0074-7726 International Review of Forestry Research†

0074-7734 International Review of General and Experimental Zoology

0074-7742 International Review of Neurobiology

0074-7750 International Review of Research in Mental Retardation

0074-7777 International Review of Tropical Medicine

0074-7785 International Reviews in Aerosol Physics and Chemistry†

0074-7793 I R R I Annual Report

0074-7815 International Road Congresses. Proceedings

0074-7823 International Rubber Study Group. Summary of Proceedings of the Group Meetings and Assemblies

0074-784X International School of Physics "Enrico Fermi." Proceedings

0074-7858 International School of Physics "Ettore Majorana," Erice, Italy. Proceedings

0074-7866 International Science Review Series

0074-7874 International Seaweed Symposium. Proceedings

0074-7882 International Society for Performing Arts. Libraries and Museums. Congress Proceedings

0074-7890 International Security Directory

0074-7904 International Sedimentological Congress. Guidebook

0074-7920 International Seminar on Reproductive Physiology and Sexual Endocrinology. Proceedings

0074-7939 International Seminar on Special Education. Proceedings

0074-7947 International Series of Monographs in Aeronautics and Astronautics. Division 1. Solid and Structural Mechanics *changed to* International Series in Aeronautics and Astronautics. Division 1. Solid and Structural Mechanics

0074-7955 International Series of Monographs in Aeronautics and Astronautics. Division 2. Aerodynamics *changed to* International Series in Aeronautics and Astronautics. Division 2. Aerodynamics and Astronautics

0074-7963 International Series of Monographs in Aeronautics and Astronautics. Division 3. Propulsion Systems Including Fuels *changed to* International Series in Aeronautics and Astronautics. Division 3. Propulsion Systems Including Fuels

0074-7998 International Series of Monographs in Aeronautics and Astronautics. Division 7. Astronautics *changed to* International Series in Aeronautics and Astronautics. Division 7. Astronautics

0074-8005 International Series of Monographs in Aeronautics and Astronautics. Division 9. Symposia *changed to* International Series in Aeronautics and Astronautics. Division 9. Symposia

0074-8021 International Series on Chemical Engineering

0074-803X International Series of Monographs in Electrical Engineering

0074-8056 International Series of Monographs in Mechanical Engineering†

0074-8064 International Series in Natural Philosophy

0074-8080 International Series on Automation and Automatic Control

0074-8099 International Series on Analytical Chemistry

0074-8129 International Series on Electronics and Instrumentation

0074-8137 International Series of Monographs on Experimental Psychology

0074-820X International Series in Library and Information Sciences

0074-8234 International Series on Oral Biology

0074-8242 International Series on Organic Chemistry

0074-8269 International Series of Monographs on Pure and Applied Biology. Division: Biochemistry *changed to* International Series on Pure and Applied Biology. Biochemistry Division

0074-8277 International Series of Monographs on Pure and Applied Biology. Division: Botany *changed to* International Series on Pure and Applied Biology. Botany Division

0074-8285 International Series of Monographs on Pure and Applied Biology. Division: Modern Trends in Physiological Sciences *changed to* International Series on Pure and Applied Biology. Modern Trends in Physiological Science Division

0074-8293 International Series of Monographs on Pure and Applied Biology. Division: Plant Physiology *changed to* International Series on Pure and Applied Biology. Plant Physiology Division

0074-8307 International Series of Monographs on Pure and Applied Biology. Division: Zoology *changed to* International Series on Pure and Applied Biology. Zoology Division

0074-8315 International Series on Semiconductors

0074-834X International Shade Tree Conference. Proceedings *changed to* Journal of Arboriculture

0074-8358 International Shipping and Shipbuilding Directory

0074-8404 International Social Science Council. Publications

0074-8439 International Social Security Association. Technical Reports of Assemblies

0074-8447 International Society for Cell Biology. Symposia†

0074-8471 International Society for Research on the Moors. Report of Congress

0074-848X International Society for Rock Mechanics. Congress. Proceedings

0074-8498 International Society for Terrain-Vehicle Systems. Proceedings of International Conference

0074-8528 International Society of Blood Transfusion. Proceedings of the Congress
0074-8536 International Society of Geographical Pathology. Proceedings of the Conference
0074-8544 International Society of Internal Medicine. Congress Proceedings
0074-8552 International Society of Orthopaedic Surgery and Traumatology. Proceedings of Congresses
0074-8560 International Society of Surgery. Comptes-Rendus†
0074-8579 International Society of Urology. Reports of Congress
0074-8587 International Solid State Circuits Conference. Digest
0074-8609 International Statistical Institute. Bulletin. Proceedings of the Biennial Sessions
0074-8617 International Statistical Yearbook of Large Towns†
0074-8684 International Studies in Sociology and Social Anthropology
0074-8706 International Sugar Organization. Annual Report
0074-8714 International Superphosphate and Compound Manufacturers Association Limited. Technical Meeting. Proceedings
0074-8722 International Symposia on Comparative Law. Proceedings
0074-8757 International Symposium on Aerobiology. Proceedings
0074-8765 International Symposium on Atherosclerosis. Proceedings
0074-8803 International Symposium on Crop Protection. Communications *changed to* International Symposium on Crop Protection. Proceedings
0074-8811 International Symposium on Electromagnetic Compatibility. Record
0074-882X International Symposium on Fault-Tolerant Computing. Digest *see* 0363-8928
0074-8897 International Symposium on Regional Development. Papers and Proceedings
0074-8927 International Symposium on the Continuous Cultivation of Microorganisms. Proceedings
0074-8935 International Symposium on the Reactivity of Solids. Proceedings†
0074-8951 International T N O Conference. (Proceedings)
0074-9001 List of Cables Forming the World Submarine Network
0074-901X List of Destination Indicators and Telex Identification Codes
0074-9028 List of International Telephone Routes
0074-9044 International Telecommunication Union. List of Telegraph Offices Open for International Service
0074-9052 Table of International Telex Relations and Traffic
0074-9087 International Textile Machinery
0074-9095 International Thyroid Conference. Proceedings
0074-9109 International Tin Council. Statistical Supplement. Tin, Tinplate Canning *changed to* Tin Statistics
0074-9117 International Tin Council. Statistical Yearbook *changed to* Tin Statistics
0074-9125 International Tin Research Council. Annual Report
0074-9133 International Touring Alliance. Minutes of the General Assembly
0074-9141 International Tracts in Computer Science and Technology and Their Application†
0074-915X I T C - Publications. Series A (Photogrammetry)
0074-9184 International Travel Statistics *changed to* World Travel Statistics
0074-9192 International Union against Cancer. Manual
0074-9206 International Union against Cancer. Proceedings of Congress
0074-9214 International Union against Cancer. U I C C Monograph Series†
0074-9222 U I C C Technical Report Series
0074-9230 International Union Against the Veneral Diseases and the Treponematoses. Proceedings of Assemblies *see* 0007-134X
0074-9249 International Union against Tuberculosis. Bulletin
0074-9265 I U C N Yearbook *changed to* I U C N Annual Report
0074-9273 I U C N Publications. New Series†
0074-9281 International Union for Conservation of Nature and Natural Resources. Proceedings and Papers of the Technical Meeting
0074-929X International Union for Conservation of Nature and Natural Resources. Proceedings of the General Assembly
0074-9311 International Union for Inland Navigation. Annual Report
0074-932X International Union for Quaternary Research. Congress Proceedings
0074-9338 International Population Conference. Proceedings
0074-9346 Union Academique Internationale. Compte Rendu de la Session Annuelle du Comite
0074-9362 International Union of Biological Sciences. Reports of General Assemblies *changed to* International Union of Biological Sciences. General Assemblies. Proceedings
0074-9370 International Union of Building Societies and Savings Associations. Congress Proceedings
0074-9389 International Union of Crystallography. Abstracts of the Triennial Congress
0074-9397 International Union of Crystallography. Structure Reports
0074-9400 International Union of Forest Research Organizations. Congress Proceedings/ Rapports du Congres/Kongressberichte
0074-9419 International Union of Geodesy and Geophysics. Proceedings of the General Assembly
0074-9427 Commission for the Geological Map of the World. Bulletin
0074-9443 International Union of Local Authorities. Reports of Congress
0074-9451 International Union of Official Travel Organizations. Minutes of the IUOTO General Assemblies†
0074-946X International Union of Physiological Sciences. Proceedings of Congress
0074-9478 International Union of Prehistoric and Protohistoric Sciences. Proceedings of Congress
0074-9486 International Union of Producers and Distributors of Electrical Energy. (Congress Proceedings)
0074-9494 International Union of Public Transport. Reports and Proceedings of the International Congress *changed to* International Union of Public Transport. Proceedings of the International Congress
0074-9508 International Union of Pure and Applied Chemistry. Comptes Rendus of IUPAC Conference†
0074-9516 International Union of Radio Science. Proceedings of General Assemblies
0074-9524 International Union of School and University Health and Medicine. Congress Reports
0074-9532 International Union of Students. Congress Resolutions
0074-9540 Congres International d'Histoire des Sciences. Actes
0074-9575 International Water Conference. Proceedings
0074-9583 International Water Supply Congress. Proceedings
0074-9591 International Whaling Commission. Report
0074-9613 International Who's Who
0074-9621 International Year Book and Statesmen's Who's Who
0074-963X International Association for Child Psychiatry and Allied Professions. Yearbook
0074-9648 International Yearbook of the Underwater World
0074-9664 International Zoo Yearbook
0074-9672 Internationale Bibliographie der Fachadressbuecher
0074-9702 Internationale Bibliographie der Fachwoerterbuecher *changed to* Fachwoerterbuecher und Lexika. Ein Internationales Verzeichnis
0074-9729 Internationale Gesellschaft fuer Geschichte der Pharmazie. Veroeffentlichungen. Neue Folge
0074-9737 Internationale Volkskundliche Bibliographie
0074-9745 Internationale Zeitschriftenschau fuer Bibelwissenschaft und Grenzgebiete†
0074-9753 Internationaler Campingfuehrer *changed to* ADAC-Campingfuehrer. Band 1: Suedeuropa
0074-977X Internationaler Spitalbedarf
0074-9796 Internationales Firmenregister der Brauindustrie, Malzerien, Mineralwasser und Erfrischungsgetranke *changed to* International Brewers' Directory and Soft Drink Guide
0074-980X Internationales Forschungszentrum fuer Grundfragen der Wissenschaften, Salzburg. Forschungsgespraeche
0074-9834 Internationales Jahrbuch fuer Geschichts und Geographieunterricht
0074-9850 Internationales Jahrbuch fuer Religionssoziologie
0074-9877 Internationales Verlagsadressbuch
0074-9931 Interscience Monographs and Texts in Physics and Astronomy
0074-994X Interscience Tracts in Pure and Applied Mathematics *changed to* Pure and Applied Mathematics: A Wiley Interscience Series of Texts, Monographs and Tracts
0074-9958 Interscience Tracts on Physics and Astronomy
0074-9966 Interstate Commission on the Potomac River Basin. Technical Bulletin *changed to* Interstate Commission on the Potomac River Basin. Technical Reports
0074-9974 North American Conference on Labor Statistics. Selected Papers
0075-0018 Inventaire General des Monuments et des Richesses Artistiques de la France
0075-0026 Inventari dei Manoscritti delle Biblioteche d'Italia
0075-0034 Inventaria Archaeologica Belgique
0075-0042 Inventaria Archaeologica Ceskoslovensko
0075-0050 Inventaria Archaeologica Denmark
0075-0069 Inventaria Archaeologica Deutschland
0075-0077 Inventaria Archaeologica Espana
0075-0085 Inventaria Archaeologica France
0075-0093 Inventaria Archaeologica Great Britain
0075-0107 Inventaria Archaeologica Italia
0075-0115 Inventaria Archaeologica Jugoslavija
0075-0123 Inventaria Archaeologica Norway
0075-0131 Inventaria Archaeologica Oesterreich
0075-014X Inventaria Archaeologica Pologne
0075-0158 Inventaria Archaeologica Ungarn
0075-0166 Inventaris van Het Kunstpatrimonium van Oost-Vlaanderen
0075-0174 Inventory of Programs in Maryland'S Private and Public Universities and Colleges†
0075-0204 Investigaciones Antropologicas
0075-0220 Investigations in Physics†
0075-0247 Investissements Etrangers en Belgique
0075-0255 I B A Occasional Paper
0075-0263 Securities Industry Association. State and Local Pension Funds
0075-0271 Investment Companies
0075-028X Investment Dealers' Association of Canada. Canada and Canadian Provinces: Funded Debts Outstanding *see* 0317-607X
0075-0301 Invitation to Photography
0075-0328 Ion Exchange; a Series of Advances *see* 0092-0193
0075-0336 Ionenaustauscher in Einzeldarstellungen
0075-0344 I A S Bulletin
0075-0352 Iowa English Yearbook *changed to* Iowa English Bulletin
0075-0360 Iowa Development Commission. Digest
0075-0379 Directory of Iowa Manufacturers
0075-0387 Iowa Nurses' Association. Bulletin
0075-0395 Iowa Publications in Philosophy
0075-0409 Iowa State Engineering Research *see* 0149-0605
0075-0425 Iowa State University. Library. Annual Report
0075-0433 Iowa State University. Engineering Research Institute. Engineering Research Report
0075-045X University of Iowa. Center for Labor and Management. Monograph Series *see* 0578-6371
0075-0468 I P E K
0075-0476 Iran Almanac and Book of Facts
0075-0484 Iran. Geological Survey. Report
0075-0492 Foreign Trade Statistics of Iran. Yearbook
0075-0506 Iranian Industrial Statistics
0075-0514 Iranian Mineral Statistics
0075-0522 Iranian National Bibliography
0075-0530 Iraqi Journal of Agricultural Science
0075-0549 Ireland (Eire) Central Statistics Office. Crops and Livestock Numbers. *changed to* Ireland (Eire) Central Statistics Office. Crops and Pasture and Numbers of Livestock
0075-0557 Ireland (Eire) Central Statistics Office. Estimates of the Quantity and Value of Agricultural Output *changed to* Ireland (Eire) Central Statistics Office. Estimated Gross and Net Agricultural Output
0075-0565 Ireland (Eire) Central Statistics Office. External Trade Statistics *changed to* Trade Statistics of Ireland
0075-0573 Ireland (Eire) Central Statistics Office. Hire-Purchase and Credit Sales
0075-0581 Ireland (Eire) Central Statistics Office. Inquiry into Advertising Agencies Activities
0075-059X Ireland (Eire) Central Statistics Office. Livestock Numbers
0075-0603 Ireland (Eire) Central Statistics Office. National Income and Expenditure
0075-0611 Ireland (Eire) Central Statistics Office. Statistics of Wages, Earnings and Hours of Work†
0075-062X Ireland (Eire) Central Statistics Office. Tuarascail Ar Staidreamh Beatha. Report on Vital Statistics
0075-0638 Ireland (Eire) Central Statistics Office. Trend of Employment and Unemployment
0075-0646 Ireland (Eire) Department of Agriculture and Fisheries. Annual Report
0075-0654 Ireland (Eire) Department of Agriculture and Fisheries. Journal
0075-0662 Ireland (Eire) Department of Education. Liosta de Iar-Bhunscoileanna Aitheanta. List of Recognised Post-Primary Schools
0075-0670 Ireland (Eire) Department of Finance. Financial Statement of the Minister for Finance
0075-0697 Ireland (Eire) National Industrial Economic Council. Report†
0075-0700 Iris Year Book

1132 ISSN INDEX

0075-0719 Irish Agricultural Organization Society. Annual Report *changed to* Irish Cooperative Organization Society. Annual Report
0075-0727 Irish Baptist Historical Society. Journal
0075-0735 Irish Catholic Directory
0075-0751 Irish Creamery Managers' Association. Creamery Yearbook and Diary *changed to* Irish Creamery Managers' Association. Creamery Directory and Diary
0075-076X Irish Drama Series†
0075-0778 Irish Geography
0075-0816 Irish Play Series
0075-0824 Irodalom - Szocializmus
0075-0832 Irodalomelmelet Klasszikusai
0075-0840 Irodalomtorteneti Fuzetek
0075-0859 Irodalomtorteneti Konyvtar
0075-0867 Iron and Steel. Annual Statistics for the United Kingdom
0075-0875 Iron and Steel Works of the World
0075-0921 Islam in Paperback
0075-093X Islamic Surveys
0075-0948 Islamic World†
0075-0956 Israel Academy of Sciences and Humanities. Section of Sciences. Proceedings†
0075-0964 Israel. Agricultural and Settlement Planning and Development Center. Statistical Series for the Agricultural Year *changed to* Israel. Rural Planning and Development Authority. Agricultural and Rural Economic Report
0075-0972 Israel Annual Conference on Aviation and Astronautics. Proceedings
0075-0980 Israel. Atomic Energy Commission. IA-Reports
0075-0999 Israel. Central Bureau of Statistics. Causes of Death
0075-1006 Israel. Central Bureau of Statistics. Criminal Statistics
0075-1014 Israel. Central Bureau of Statistics. Diagnostic Statistics of Hospitalized Patients
0075-1022 Israel. Central Bureau of Statistics. Juvenile Delinquency
0075-1030 Israel. Central Bureau of Statistics. Judicial Statistics
0075-1049 Israel. Central Bureau of Statistics. Labour Force Surveys
0075-1057 Israel. Central Bureau of Statistics. Motor Vehicles
0075-1065 Israel. Central Bureau of Statistics. Schools and Kindergartens
0075-1073 Israel. Central Bureau of Statistics. Strikes and Lock-Outs
0075-1081 Israel. Central Bureau of Statistics. Students in Academic Institutions
0075-109X Israel. Central Bureau of Statistics. Survey of Housing Conditions
0075-1103 Israel. Central Bureau of Statistics. Trade Survey
0075-1111 Israel. Central Bureau of Statistics. Vital Statistics
0075-1138 Israel. Department of Surveys. Geodetic Papers
0075-1146 Israel Discount Bank. Report
0075-1162 Israel Film-Making Plus *changed to* Filmmaking in Israel
0075-1189 Israel. Ministry of Agriculture. Department of Fisheries. Israel Fisheries in Figures
0075-1200 Israel. Geological Survey. Bulletin
0075-1219 Israel. Hydrological Service. Hydrological Paper†
0075-1227 Israel Institute of Applied Social Research. Research Report
0075-1235 Israel Institute of Productivity. Report of Activities†
0075-1243 Israel Journal of Entomology
0075-1251 Israel Medical Bibliography
0075-126X Israel. Meteorological Service. Annual Rainfall Summary. Series B (Observational Data)
0075-1278 Israel. Meteorological Service. Series A (Meteorological Notes)
0075-1286 Israel. Meteorological Service. Annual Weather Report. Series B (Observational Data)
0075-1294 Israel. Agricultural and Settlement Planning and Development Center. Statistical Series of the Budgetary Year *changed to* Israel. Rural Planning and Development Authority. Agricultural and Rural Economic Report
0075-1308 Israel. Ministry of Communications. Statistics
0075-1324 National Insurance Institute, Jerusalem. Full Actuarial Report
0075-1340 National Insurance Institute, Jerusalem. Statistical Abstract
0075-1367 Israel Petroleum and Energy Year Book
0075-1383 Israel Society for Rehabilitation of the Disabled. Annual
0075-1391 Israel Studies in Criminology
0075-1405 Israel Tourist Statistics
0075-1413 Israel Yearbook
0075-1421 Israel. Central Bureau of Statistics. Israel's Foreign Trade
0075-143X Issues†
0075-1472 Studi Etruschi†
0075-1480 Istituto di Studi Pirandelliani e Sul Teatro Contemporaneo
0075-1499 Istituto e Museo di Storia della Scienza. Biblioteca
0075-1502 Istituto Ellenico di Studi Bizantini e Postbizantini, Venice. Biblioteca
0075-1510 Istituto Italiano di Idrobiologia. Memorie
0075-1529 Istituto Mobiliare Italiano. Annual Report
0075-1537 Istituto Nazionale per l'Assicurazione Contro le Malattie, Rome. Bilancio Consuntivo†
0075-1545 Istituto Siciliano di Studi Bizantini e Neoellenici. Quaderni
0075-1553 Istituto Siciliano di Studi Bizantini e Neoellenici. Testi e Monumenti. Testi
0075-1561 Istituto Storico della Resistenza in Modena e Provincia. Quaderni
0075-157X Istituto Storico della Resistenza in Modena e Provincia. Rassegna Annuale†
0075-1588 Istituto Universitario Navale, Naples. Annali
0075-1596 Istituzioni e Monumenti dell' Arte Musicale Italiana Nuova Serie
0075-160X Istoria Limbii Romane
0075-1626 Istorie si Civilizatie
0075-1634 Italian Studies
0075-1642 Italy: An Economic Profile
0075-1650 Italy. Direzione Generale delle Fonti di Energia e delle Industrie di Base. Bilanci Energetici
0075-1669 Italy. Istituto Centrale di Statistica. Annuario di Statistica Agraria
0075-1677 Italy. Istituto Centrale di Statistica. Annuario delle Statistiche Culturali
0075-1685 Italy. Istituto Centrale di Statistica. Annuario di Statistiche Demografiche
0075-1693 Annuario di Statistiche del Lavoro e dell'Emigrazione *see* 0390-6450
0075-1707 Italy. Istituto Centrale di Statistica. Annuario di Statistica Forestale
0075-1715 Italy. Istituto Centrale di Statistica. Annuari di Statistiche Giudiziarie
0075-1723 Italy. Istituto Centrale di Statistica. Annuario di Statistiche Industriali
0075-1731 Italy. Istituto Centrale di Statistica. Annuario di Statistiche Meteorologiche
0075-1758 Italy. Istituto Centrale di Statistica. Annuario di Statistiche Sanitarie
0075-1774 Italy. Istituto Centrale di Statistica. Annuario Statistiche Zootecniche *see* 0390-6426
0075-1782 Italy. Istituto Centrale di Statistica. Annuario Statistico del Commercio Interno
0075-1790 Italy. Istituto Centrale di Statistica. Annuario Statistico dell'Assistenza e della Previdenza Sociale
0075-1863 Italy. Istituto Centrale di Statistica. Popolazione e Movimento Anagrafico dei Comuni
0075-1871 Italy. Istituto Centrale di Statistica. Statistica Annuale del Commercio con l'Estero *see* 0390-6558
0075-1871 Italy. Istituto Centrale di Statistica. Statistica Annuale del Commercio con l'Estero *see* 0390-6566
0075-1898 Italy. Istituto Centrale di Statistica. Annuario Statistico della Navigazione Marittima
0075-1901 Istituto di Fisica dell'Atmosfera, Rome. Bibliografia Generale.
0075-191X Istituto di Fisica dell'Atmosfera, Rome. Contributi Scientifici: Pubblicazioni di Fisica dell'Atmosfera e di Meteorologia.
0075-1928 Istituto di Fisica dell' Atmosfera, Rome. Pubblicazioni Didattiche
0075-1936 Istituto di Fisica dell'Atmosfera, Rome. Pubblicazioni Scientifiche
0075-1944 Istituto di Fisica dell'Atmosfera, Rome. Pubblicazioni Varie.
0075-1952 Istituto di Fisica dell'Atmosfera, Rome. Rapporti Interni Provvisori Adiffusione Limitata
0075-1960 Istituto di Fisica dell'Atmosfera, Rome. Rapporti Scientifici
0075-1979 Istituto di Fisica dell'Atmosfera, Rome. Rapporti Tecnici
0075-1987 Italy. Istituto Nazionale per Lo Studio della Congiuntura. Quaderni Analitici
0075-1995 Italy. Ministero del Bilancio e della Programmazione Economica. Relazione Generale Sulla Situazione Economica del Paese
0075-2002 Itinera Romana
0075-2010 Itsuu Laboratory, Tokyo. Annual Report
0075-2029 Ius Romanum in Helvetia†
0075-2037 Ius Romanum Medii Aevi
0075-2045 J. Anderson Fitzgerald Lecture
0075-2053 Miller's Sporting Annual and Athletic Record†
0075-2061 J. K. Lasser's Your Income Tax, Professional Ed
0075-207X J. L. B. Smith Institute of Ichthyology. Occasional Paper†
0075-2088 J. L. B. Smith Institute of Ichthyology. Special Publication
0075-210X J. T. Stewart Lecture in Planning
0075-2118 Jaarbericht "Ex Oriente Lux"
0075-2142 Jacob Blaustein Lectures in International Affairs
0075-2150 Jaeger's Intertravel
0075-2193 Jahrbuch der Auktionspreise
0075-2207 Jahrbuch der Berliner Museen
0075-2215 Jahrbuch der Bibliotheken, Archive und Informationstellen der Deutschen Demokratischen Republik
0075-2223 Jahrbuch der Deutschen Bibliotheken
0075-224X Jahrbuch der Export- und Versandtleiter
0075-2266 Graphische Unternehmungen Oesterreichs. Jahrbuch
0075-2274 Jahrbuch der Hamburger Kunstsammlungen
0075-2282 Jahrbuch des Heeres
0075-2312 Kunsthistorische Sammlungen in Wien. Jahrbuch
0075-2320 Jahrbuch der Luftwaffe
0075-2347 Jahrbuch der Oeffentlichen Meinung *changed to* Allensbacher Jahrbuch der Demoskopie
0075-2355 Oesterreichische Byzantinistik. Jahrbuch
0075-2363 Jahrbuch der Psychoanalyse
0075-2371 Raabe- Gesellschaft. Jahrbuch
0075-238X Jahrbuch der Schiffart†
0075-2398 Jahrbuch der Schleiff-, Hon-, Laepp- und Poliertechnik *changed to* Jahrbuch Schleiffen, Honen, Laeppen und Polieren, Verfahren und Maschinen
0075-2401 Deutscher Turner-Bund. Jahrbuch der Turnkunst
0075-241X Jahrbuch der Wehrmedizin
0075-2428 Jahrbuch der Wehrtechnik
0075-2436 Jahrbuch des Baltischen Deutschtums
0075-2479 Jahrbuch des Eisenbahnwesens
0075-2487 Jahrbuch des Elektrischen Fernmeldewesens†
0075-2509 Jahrbuch des Kameramanns
0075-2517 Jahrbuch des Oeffentlichen Rechts der Gegenwart
0075-2533 Jahrbuch fuer Amerikastudien *see* 0340-2827
0075-2541 Jahrbuch fuer Antike und Christentum
0075-255X Jahrbuch fuer Bergbau, Energie, Mineraloel und Chemie
0075-2568 Jahrbuch fuer Berlin-Brandenburgische Kirchengeschichte
0075-2576 Jahrbuch fuer Bundesbahnbeamte
0075-2584 Jahrbuch fuer Christliche Sozialwissenschaften
0075-2592 Jahrbuch fuer das Textil-Reinigungs-Gewerbe: Waescherei und Chemischreinigung†
0075-2606 Jahrbuch fuer den Oesterreichischen Tierarzt
0075-2622 Erziehungs- und Schulgeschichte Jahrbuch
0075-2630 Exlibriskunst und Gebrauchsgraphik. Jahrbuch
0075-2649 Jahrbuch fuer Fremdenverkehr
0075-2665 Geschichte der Sozialistischen Laender Europas. Jahrbuch
0075-2673 Jahrbuch fuer Geschichte von Staat, Wirtschaft und Gesellschaft Lateinamerikas.
0075-2681 Jahrbuch fuer Liturgik und Hymnologie
0075-269X Jahrbuch der Luftfahrt und Raumfahrt *changed to* Reuss Jahrbuch der Luft- und Raumfahrt
0075-2703 Jahrbuch fuer Musikalische Volks- und Voelkerkunde
0075-2711 Jahrbuch fuer Numismatik und Geldgeschichte
0075-272X Jahrbuch fuer Optik und Feinmechanik
0075-2738 Jahrbuch fuer Ostdeutsche Volkskunde
0075-2746 Jahrbuch fuer Ostrecht
0075-2754 Jahrbuch fuer Salesianische Studien
0075-2762 Jahrbuch fuer Schlesische Kirchengeschichte
0075-2770 Jahrbuch fuer Sozialwissenschaft
0075-2789 Jahrbuch fuer Volksliedforschung
0075-2800 Jahrbuch fuer Wirtschaftsgeschichte
0075-2819 Jahrbuch Oberflaechentechnik
0075-2827 Jahrbuch zur Alkohol- und Tabakfrage *changed to* Jahrbuch zur Frage der Suchtgefahren
0075-2835 Jahresbericht der Bayerischen Bodendenkmalpflege
0075-2851 Jahresbericht ueber die Deutsche Fischwirtschaft
0075-286X Deutsche Geschichte. Jahresberichte
0075-2878 Jahresberichte ueber Holzschutz†
0075-2886 Jahresfachkatalog Recht-Wirtschaft-Steuern
0075-2894 Jahreshefte fuer Karst- und Hoehlenkunde
0075-2908 Jahreskatalog Kybernetik, Automation, Informatik *changed to* Kybernetik Jahreskatalog
0075-2916 Jahreskatalog Philosophie
0075-2924 Jahreskatalog Psychologie
0075-2932 Mitteldeutsche Vorgeschichte. Jahresschrift
0075-2940 Jahresverzeichnis der Deutschen Hochschulschriften *changed to* Jahresverzeichnis der Hochschulschriften der DDR, der BRD und Westberlins
0075-2959 Jahresverzeichnis der Musikalien und Musikschriften
0075-2967 Jahresverzeichnis des Deutschen Schrifttums *see* 0300-8436
0075-2983 Jamaica. Department of Statistics. Annual Abstract of Statistics *changed to* Jamaica. Department of Statistics. Statistical Abstract
0075-2991 Jamaican National Bibliography
0075-3009 James Terry Duce Memorial Series
0075-3017 Jane's All the World Aircraft

ISSN INDEX 1133

0075-3025 Jane's Fighting Ships
0075-3033 Jane's Freight Containers
0075-305X Jane's Surface Skimmers
0075-3068 Jane's Weapon Systems
0075-3084 Jane's World Railways
0075-3092 Janua Linguarum. Series Critica
0075-3106 Janua Linguarum. Series Didactica
0075-3114 Janua Linguarum. Series Major
0075-3122 Janua Linguarum. Series Minor
0075-3130 Janua Linguarum. Series Practica
0075-3157 Japan Annual of Law and Politics
0075-3165 Japan Anti-Tuberculosis Association. Reports on Medical Research Problems
0075-3173 Japan. Bureau of Statistics. Annual Report on Family Income and Expenditures
0075-3181 Japan. Bureau of Statistics. Employment Status Survey
0075-319X Japan Chemical Annual
0075-3203 Japan Chemical Directory
0075-3211 Japan Company Directory *changed to* Japan Company Handbook
0075-322X Japan Directory
0075-3238 Japan Economic Research Center. Center Paper Series
0075-3246 Japan Economic Year Book
0075-3270 Japan. Ministry of Health and Welfare. Statistics and Information Department. Vital Statistics
0075-3289 Japan Census of Manufactures: Report by Commodities
0075-3300 Japan P.E.N. News *changed to* Japanese Literature Today
0075-3319 Japan Road Association. Annual Report of Roads
0075-3327 Japan Society for Cancer Therapy. Proceedings of the Congress
0075-3335 Japan Statistical Yearbook
0075-3343 Japanese Antarctic Research Expedition Data Reports.
0075-3351 Japanese Antarctic Research Expedition, 1956-1962. Scientific Reports. Series A: Aeronomy *see* 0386-5517
0075-336X Japanese Antarctic Research Expedition, 1956-1962. Scientific Reports. Series B: Meteorology *see* 0386-5525
0075-3378 Japanese Antarctic Research Expedition, 1956-1962. Scientific Reports. Series C: Earth Sciences. *see* 0386-5533
0075-3386 Japanese Antarctic Research Expedition, 1956-1962. Scientific Reports. Series D: Oceanography *changed to* National Institute of Polar Research . Memoirs. Series D: Oceanography
0075-3394 Japanese Antarctic Research Expedition, 1956-1962. Scientific Reports. Series E. Biology *see* 0386-5541
0075-3408 Japanese Antarctic Research Expedition, 1956-1962. Scientific Reports. Series F: Logistic *see* 0386-555X
0075-3424 Japanese Journal of Botany†
0075-3432 Japanese Journal of Mathematics†
0075-3440 Japanese Miniature Electronic Components Data†
0075-3459 Japanese Phonograph Records of Folk Songs, Classical and Popular Music
0075-3467 Japanese Progress in Climatology
0075-3475 Japan's Iron and Steel Industry
0075-3491 Jarlibro
0075-3505 Institutul Agronomic "Ion Ionescu de la Brad". Lucrari Stiintifice. I. Agronomie - Horticultura
0075-3513 Institutul Agronomic "Ion Ionescu de la Brad" Lucrari Stiintifice II Zootehnie - Medicina Veterinara
0075-3521 Universitatea "Al. I. Cuza" din Iasi. Analele Stiintifice. Sectiunea 2B: Geologie
0075-353X Universitatea "Al. I. Cuza" din Iasi. Analele Stiintifice. Sectiunea 3b: Stiinte Filozofice
0075-3548 Jawaharlal Nehru University. School of International Studies Series
0075-3572 Jazzforschung
0075-3580 Jean-Paul-Gesellschaft. Jahrbuch
0075-3599 Jefferson Memorial Lecture Series
0075-3602 Jehovah's Witnesses Yearbook
0075-3610 Jerome Lectures
0075-3629 Jersey Herd Book and Directory of the U.K. *changed to* Jersey Herd Book and Members Directory
0075-3637 Hebrew University of Jerusalem. Authority for Research Report. Medicine, Pharmacy, Dental Medicine *changed to* Hebrew University of Jerusalem. Authority for Research and Development. Current Research
0075-3645 Hebrew University of Jerusalem. Authority for Research and Development. Research Report: Humanities, Social Sciences, Law, Education, Social Work, Library *changed to* Hebrew University of Jerusalem. Authority for Research and Development. Current Research
0075-3653 Hebrew University of Jerusalem. Authority for Research and Development. Research Report. Science and Agriculture *changed to* Hebrew University of Jerusalem. Authority for Research and Development. Current Research
0075-3661 Hebrew University of Jerusalem. Folklore Research Center. Studies
0075-3696 Jerusalem Symposia on Quantum Chemistry and Biochemistry
0075-3726 Jewish Book Annual
0075-3734 Jewish Federations, Welfare Funds and Community Councils Directory *see* 0161-2638
0075-3742 Jewish Social Service Yearbook
0075-3750 Jewish Travel Guide
0075-3769 Jewish Year Book
0075-3777 Jobson's Mining Year Book
0075-3785 Jobson's Year Book of Public Companies of Australia and New Zealand
0075-3793 Johannesburg Stock Exchange. Handbook
0075-3807 University of the Witwatersrand, Johannesburg. Library. Annual Report of the University Librarian
0075-3815 John Alexander Monograph Series on Various Phases of Thoracic Surgery
0075-384X John E. Owens Memorial Foundation. Publications†
0075-3858 Johns Hopkins Oceanographic Studies
0075-3866 Johns Hopkins Series in Integration and Community Building in Eastern Europe
0075-3874 Johns Hopkins Symposia in Comparative History
0075-3890 Johns Hopkins University Studies in Geology
0075-3904 Johns Hopkins University Studies in Historical and Political Science
0075-3920 Johnsonia
0075-3939 Joint Automatic Control Conference. Record
0075-3947 Joint Center for Urban Studies. Publications
0075-3955 Joint Engineering Societies Management Conference. Proceedings *changed to* Joint Engineering Management Conference. Conference Record
0075-3963 Joint F A O/W H O Expert Committee on Food Additives Report
0075-3971 Joint F A O/W H O Expert Committee on Nutrition. Report
0075-398X Joint Power Generation Technical Conference. Preprint *changed to* Joint Power Generation Conference. Conference Record
0075-3998 Joint Railroad Technical Conference. Preprint *changed to* Joint Railroad Conference. Conference Record
0075-4005 Ahmedabad Textile Industry's Research Association. Joint Technological Conferences. Proceedings
0075-4013 Jordan. Department of Statistics. Annual Statistical Yearbook
0075-4021 Jordan. Department of Statistics. External Trade Statistics
0075-403X Sweden. Sveriges Geologiska Undersoekning. Jordmagnetiska Publikationer/Geomagnetic Publications
0075-4056 Jouets et Jeux
0075-4064 Journal Belge de Radiologie (Monographie)
0075-4072 Journal de Biologie et de Medicine Nucleaires†
0075-4080 Journal des Oiseaux du Monde
0075-4099 Journal for the Protection of All Beings
0075-4102 Journal fuer die Reine und Angewandte Mathematik
0075-4110 Journal of Ancient Indian History
0075-4129 Journal of Animal Science. Supplement
0075-4145 Journal of Behavioural Science *see* 0081-2463
0075-4161 Journal of Byelorussian Studies
0075-417X Journal of Child Psychotherapy
0075-4188 Journal of Civil Procedure
0075-4196 Journal of Commerce Annual Review†
0075-4218 Journal of Croatian Studies
0075-4242 Journal of English Linguistics
0075-4250 Journal of Glass Studies
0075-4269 Journal of Hellenic Studies
0075-4277 Journal of Juristic Papyrology
0075-4285 Journal of Maltese Studies
0075-4293 Journal of Mathematics
0075-4307 Journal of Natural Science
0075-4315 Journal of Nuclear Medicine. Supplement†
0075-4323 Journal of Neuro-Visceral Relations. Supplement *see* 0303-6995
0075-4331 Journal of Periodontal Research. Supplementum
0075-434X Journal of Rhodesian History *changed to* Zimbabwean History
0075-4358 Journal of Roman Studies
0075-4366 Hiroshima University. Journal of Science. Series B. Division 2. Botany
0075-4374 Hiroshima University. Journal of Science. Series C. Geology and Mineralogy
0075-4390 Journal of the Warburg and Courtauld Institutes
0075-4404 Journal of Ultrastructure Research. Supplement
0075-4412 Journalism Abstracts
0075-4420 Journee de Reeducation
0075-4439 Journees Annuelles de Diabetologie de l'Hotel Dieu
0075-4455 Journees de Physiologie Appliquee au Travail Humain
0075-4463 Acquisitions Medicales Recentes.†
0075-4471 Journees Parisiennes de Pediatrie
0075-4501 Judean Desert Studies
0075-4528 Jugendherbergs-Verzeichnis
0075-4536 Jugoslovenska Investiciona Banka. Annual Report
0075-4544 Sir Moses Montefiore Collections des Juifs Celebres
0075-4552 Community, Junior, and Technical College Directory
0075-4552 Community and Junior College Directory *see* 0075-4552
0075-4560 Junior High School Association of Illinois. Study
0075-4579 Juntendo University, Tokyo. Medical Ultrasonics Research Center. Annual Report
0075-4587 Just B'twx Us: An Interlibrary Loan Service Newsletter *changed to* Just B'twx Us: an Interlibrary Loan Newsletter
0075-4609 Universitaet Giessen. Ergebnisse Landwirtschaftlicher Forschung
0075-4617 Liebigs Annalen der Chemie
0075-4625 Jyvaskyla Studies in Education, Psychology and Social Research
0075-4633 Jyvaskyla Studies in the Arts
0075-4641 Jyvaskylan Yliopisto. Matematiikan Laitos. Report
0075-465X Jyvaskylan Yliopisto. Department of Physics. Research Report
0075-4668 Kaiser Foundation Medical Care Program. Annual Report
0075-4676 Kakteen. Gesamtdarstellung (Monographie) der Eingefuehrten Arten nebst Anzucht- und Pflege
0075-4684 Kalastuspaikkaopas
0075-4722 Makerere University. Department of Geography. Occasional Paper
0075-4730 Makerere University. Faculty of Agriculture. Handbook
0075-4773 Makerere University. Faculty of Agriculture. Technical Bulletin
0075-4781 Makerere University. Faculty of Law. Handbook
0075-4854 Makerere University. Library. Makerere Library Publications
0075-4900 Kansainvalinen Automatkailu *see* 0355-2896
0075-4919 Kansas Linguistics Conference. Papers *changed to* Mid-America Linguistics Conference. Papers
0075-4927 Kansas Geological Survey. Computer Contribution
0075-4935 Kansas Geological Survey. Short Papers in Research
0075-4951 Kansas State University. Library Bibliography Series
0075-4986 University of Kansas. Center for Latin American Studies. Graduate Studies on Latin America
0075-4994 University of Kansas. Department of Geology. Special Publications†
0075-5001 University of Kansas Libraries. Library Series.
0075-501X University of Kansas. Museum of Art. Miscellaneous Publications *changed to* University of Kansas. Spencer Museum of Art. Miscellaneous Publications
0075-5028 University of Kansas. Museum of Natural History. Miscellaneous Publications
0075-5036 University of Kansas. Museum of Natural History. Publications
0075-5044 University of Kansas. Paleontological Contributions. Articles
0075-5052 University of Kansas. Paleontological Contributions. Papers
0075-5060 Kappa Tau Alpha Yearbook
0075-5079 Karachi. Chamber of Commerce and Industry. Report
0075-5095 Karachi Law Journal
0075-5109 Karachi Port Trust. Year Book of Information, Port of Karachi, Pakistan
0075-5125 Wyzsza Szkola Ekonomiczna. Zeszyty Naukowe *changed to* Akademia Ekonomiczna, Krakow. Zeszyty Naukowe
0075-5133 Staatliche Kunsthalle Karlsruhe. Bildhefte
0075-5141 Staatliche Kunsthalle Karlsruhe. Graphik-Schriftenreihe
0075-515X Karnatak University, Dharwad, India. Journal. Humanities
0075-5168 Karnatak University, Dharwad, India. Journal. Science
0075-5176 Karnatak University, Dharwad, India. Journal. Social Sciences
0075-5184 Karthago. Collection Epigraphique
0075-5192 Kasetsart Journal
0075-5206 Kasetsart University, Bangkok, Thailand. Faculty of Fisheries. Notes
0075-5222 Kasmera
0075-5230 Katalog Fauny Pasozytniczej Polski
0075-5249 Katalog Fauny Polski
0075-5257 Katalog Zabytkow Sztuki w Polsce
0075-5265 Katherine Asher Engel Lectures
0075-5273 Katholisches Leben und Kirchenreform im Zeitalter der Glaubensspaltung
0075-5281 Wyzsza Szkola Pedagogiczna, Katowice. Zeszyty Naukowe. Sekcja Jezykoznawstwa
0075-529X Kazakhskii Nauchno-issledovatel'skii Institut Onkologii i Radiologii. Trudy
0075-5303 Keeping Track, Current News from the Department of Agricultural Economics at Purdue

0075-5311 Keepsake
0075-532X Keilschrifturkunden aus Boghazkoei
0075-5338 Keilschrifttexte aus Boghazkoi
0075-5346 Keio Monographs of Business and Commerce
0075-5354 Kekkaku No Kenkyu. *changed to* Hokkaido University. Institute of Immunological Science. Bulletin
0075-5370 Kelly's Manufacturers and Merchants Directory
0075-5389 Kelly's Post Office London Directory
0075-5397 Kemia Ujabb Eredmenyei
0075-5400 Kempe's Engineers Year Book
0075-5419 Kemps Directory
0075-5427 Kemps Film and Television Year Book (International) *changed to* Kemps International Film and Television Year Book
0075-5443 Kemp's Jersey Holiday Guide†
0075-5451 Kemps Music and Record Industry Year Book *changed to* Kemps International Music and Record Yearbook
0075-546X Kent Studies in Anthropology and Archaeology†
0075-5494 Kentucky Directory of Manufacturers
0075-5508 Kentucky Folklore Series
0075-5516 Kentucky Industrial Directory *see* 0075-5494
0075-5524 Kentucky Nature Studies
0075-5532 Kentucky Personal Income *changed to* Kentucky Personal Income Report
0075-5559 University of Kentucky. Geological Survey. Series X. Bulletin
0075-5567 University of Kentucky. Geological Survey. Series XI. County Report
0075-5575 University of Kentucky. Geological Survey. Guidebook to Geological Field Trips
0075-5583 University of Kentucky. Geological Survey. Series XI. Information Circular
0075-5591 University of Kentucky. Geological Survey. Series X. Report of Investigations
0075-5605 University of Kentucky. Geological Survey. Reprints
0075-5613 University of Kentucky. Geological Survey. Series XI. Special Publication
0075-5621 University of Kentucky. Geological Survey. Series XI. Thesis Series
0075-5761 K I A Occasional Papers
0075-580X Kenya. Mines and Geological Department. Annual Report
0075-5818 Kenya. Ministry of Economic Planning and Development. Statistics Division. Development Estimates *changed to* Kenya. Central Bureau of Statistics. Development Estimates
0075-5826 Kenya. Ministry of Economic Planning and Development. Estimates of Revenue Expenditures *changed to* Kenya. Central Bureau of Statistics. Estimates of Revenue Expenditures
0075-5834 Kenya. Ministry of Economic Planning and Development. Statistics Division. Estimates of Recurrent Expenditures *changed to* Kenya. Central Bureau of Statistics. Estimates of Recurrent Expenditures
0075-5842 Kenya. Ministry of Economic Planning and Development. Economic Survey *changed to* Kenya. Central Bureau of Statistics. Economic Survey
0075-5850 Kenya. Ministry of Economic Planning and Development. Statistics Division. Statistical Abstract *changed to* Kenya. Central Bureau of Statistics. Statistical Abstract
0075-5869 Kenya. Ministry of Education. Annual Report
0075-5877 Kenya. Ministry of Health and Housing. Annual Report *changed to* Kenya. Ministry of Housing. Annual Report
0075-5885 Kenya. Ministry of Information. Annual Report *changed to* Kenya. Ministry of Information and Broadcasting. Annual Report
0075-5915 Kenya. National Irrigation Board. Reports and Accounts
0075-5923 Kenya. National Library Service Board. Annual and Audit Report
0075-5931 Kenya. Public Accounts Committee. Annual Report
0075-594X Kenya. Public Service Commission. Annual Report
0075-5966 Keswick Week†
0075-5974 Kew Bulletin
0075-5982 Kew Bulletin. Additional Series
0075-5990 Canadian Electronics Engineering Annual Buyers' Guide and Catalog Directory *changed to* Canadian Electronics Engineering Components and Equipment Directory
0075-6008 Keys to Music Bibliography†
0075-6040 Kime's International Law Directory
0075-6067 Kinetics and Mechanisms of Polymerization†
0075-6083 Kings of Tomorrow Series
0075-6091 Queen's University at Kingston. Department of Electrical Engineering. Research Report
0075-6105 Queen's University at Kingston. Department of Mathematics. Research Report *see* 0079-8797
0075-6113 Queen's University at Kingston. Douglas Library. Occasional Papers
0075-6121 Queen's University. Engineering Society. Proceedings†
0075-613X Queen's University at Kingston. Industrial Relations Centre. Bibliography Series
0075-6148 Queen's University at Kingston. Industrial Relations Centre. Report of Activities
0075-6156 Queen's University at Kingston. Industrial Relations Centre. Reprint Series
0075-6164 Queen's University. Industrial Relations Centre. Research Series *see* 0317-2546
0075-6199 Kirchenmusikalisches Jahrbuch
0075-6202 Kirchenreform†
0075-6210 Kirchliches Jahrbuch fuer die Evangelische Kirche in Deutschland
0075-6229 Kirin Brewery Company, Tokyo. Research Laboratory. Report
0075-6245 Kirtlandia
0075-6261 Kjelberg-e SAB-Schriften; Erfahrungsberichte ueber Lichtbogen-Schweisstechnik *changed to* Svetsaren
0075-627X Klasings Bootsmarkt International; Yachten und Boote Zubehoer, Ausruestung, Motoren
0075-6288 Klassieken Nederlandse Letterkunde†
0075-6318 Kleine Deutsche Prosadenkmaeler des Mittelalters
0075-6326 Kleine Museumshefte
0075-6334 Klio
0075-6342 Klucze do Oznaczania Kregowcow Polski†
0075-6350 Klucze do Oznaczania Owadow Polski
0075-6369 Kniznicny Zbornik
0075-6385 Knotty Problems of Baseball
0075-6407 Kobe Economic and Business Review
0075-6415 Kobe Economic and Business Research Series
0075-6423 Kobe University Law Review. International Edition
0075-6431 Kobe University Medical Journal
0075-6458 Koedoe
0075-6466 Koedoe. Monographs
0075-6474 Koehlers Flottenkalender. Jahrbuch fuer Schiffahrt und Haefen
0075-6482 Koeln
0075-6490 Koelner Ethnologische Mitteilungen
0075-6512 Koelner Jahrbuch fuer Vor- und Fruehgeschichte
0075-6520 Koelner Romanistische Arbeiten
0075-6547 Koleopterologische Rundschau
0075-6555 Kolloid-Gesellschaft. Verhandlungsberichte
0075-6563 Kolloquium ueber Spaetantike und Fruehmittelalterliche Skulptur
0075-6601 Kommunikation und Kybernetik in Einzeldarstellungen *see* 0340-0034
0075-661X Kompas Danmark
0075-6628 Kompass Australia
0075-6636 Kompass Belgium/Luxembourg
0075-6644 Kompass Espana
0075-6652 Annuaire Industriel. Repertoire Generale de la Production Francaise *see* 0337-5714
0075-6660 Kompass Holland
0075-6679 Kompass Hong Kong
0075-6687 Kompass Italia
0075-6695 Kompass Maroc
0075-6709 Kompass Norge
0075-6717 Kompass Schweiz/Liechtenstein
0075-6725 Kompass Sverige
0075-6733 Kompass United Kingdom/CBI *changed to* Kompass United Kingdom
0075-6741 Koninklijk Nederlands Geologisch Mijnbouwkundig Genootschap. Verhandelingen
0075-675X Konjunkturberichte ueber das Handwerk *see* 0341-0978
0075-6768 Konstruktionsbuecher
0075-6776 Kontrollraadet foer Betongvaror. Meddelande
0075-6784 Konyvtartudomanyi Tanulmanyok
0075-6792 Koranyi Sandor Tarsasag. Tudomanyos Ulesek
0075-6806 Korea Development Bank; Its Functions and Activities
0075-6814 Korea Directory
0075-6822 Korea (Republic) Bureau of Statistics. Annual Report on the Family Income and Expenditure Survey
0075-6830 Korea (Republic) Bureau of Statistics. Annual Report of the Price Survey
0075-6849 Korea (Republic) Bureau of Statistics. Report on Mining and Manufacturing Survey
0075-6857 Korea (Republic) Bureau of Statistics. Wholesale and Retail Trade Census Report
0075-6865 Korea (Republic) Office of Rural Development. Agricultural Research Report
0075-6873 Korea Statistical Yearbook
0075-6881 Korean Publications Yearbook
0075-6911 Korosi Csoma Kiskonyvtar
0075-6938 Korrosion†
0075-6946 Korunk Tudomanya
0075-6954 Kosten en Financiering van de Gezondheidzorg in Nederland
0075-6962 Koszen es Koolaj Anyagismereti Monografiak
0075-6970 Kothari's World of Reference Works
0075-6989 Kozgazdasagi Ertekezesek
0075-6997 Akademia Gorniczo-Hutnicza im. Stanislawa Staszica. Zeszyty Naukowe. Gornictwo
0075-7004 Akademia Gorniczo-Hutnicza Im. Stanislawa Staszica. Zeszyty Naukowe. Hutnictwo
0075-7020 Krakow Dawniej i Dzis
0075-7039 Muzeum Archeologiczne, Krakow. Materialy Archeologiczne
0075-7047 Obserwatorium Krakowski. Rocznik Astronomiczny. Dodatek Miedzynarodowy
0075-7055 Politechnika Krakowska. Zeszyty Naukowe. Chemia
0075-7063 Jahrbuch Krankenhaus
0075-7071 Krankenhaus-Apotheke *see* 0173-7597
0075-708X Krankenhaus-Probleme der Gegenwart
0075-7098 Krebsforschung und Krebsbekaempfung†
0075-7101 Beitraege zur Kardiologie und Angiologie
0075-711X Kresge Foundation. Annual Report
0075-7136 Kriminologische Gegenwartsfragen
0075-7144 Kriminologie. Abhandlungen ueber abwegiges Sozialverhalten
0075-7152 Kriminologische Abhandlungen
0075-7160 Kryptadia: Journal of Erotic Folklore
0075-7179 Ksiazka w Dawnej Kulturze Polskiej
0075-7209 Kulturpflanze
0075-7217 Kumamoto University. Institute of Constitutional Medicine. Bulletin. Supplement
0075-7225 University of Science and Technology. Journal
0075-7233 Kungliga Skogs- och Lantbruksakademiens, Tidskrift. Supplement *issued with* 0023-5350
0075-7241 Kunst-Katalog: Auktionen
0075-725X Kunst und Altertum am Rhein
0075-7268 Kunstdenkmaeler des Rheinlandes. Beihefte†
0075-7276 Kunststoff-Industrie und ihre Helfer
0075-7292 Kunststoffe im Lebensmittelverkehr
0075-7306 Kuratorium fuer Verkehrssicherheit. Kleine Fachbuchreihe
0075-7322 Kurzauszuege Oesterreichischer Dissertationen: Geistes- und Sozialwissenschaften†
0075-7330 Kurzuaszuege Oesterreichischer Dissertationen: Naturwissenschaften und Technik†
0075-7349 Kush
0075-7357 Kyoto University. Institute for Virus Research. Annual Report
0075-7365 Kyoto University. Research Activities in Civil Engineering and Related Fields
0075-7373 Kyoto Prefectural University. Scientific Reports: Agriculture
0075-7381 Kyoto Prefectural University. Scientific Reports: Humanities
0075-739X Kyoto Prefectural University. Scientific Reports: Natural Science, Domestic Science and Social Welfare *changed to* Kyoto Prefectural University. Scientific Reports: Natural Science and Living Science
0075-7403 Universidad Nacional Agraria. Programa Cooperativo de Investigaciones en Maiz. Boletin†
0075-742X Universidad Nacional de la Plata. Instituto de Estudios Sociales y del Pensamiento Argentino. Cuadernos de Extension Universitaria
0075-7446 Lab World. Labstracts. Annual Reference Guide†
0075-7470 University of Pennsylvania. Wharton School of Finance and Commerce. Labor Relations and Public Policy Series. Reports
0075-7489 Labor Relations Yearbook
0075-7500 Laboratory Guide†
0075-7535 Laboratory Techniques in Biochemistry and Molecular Biology
0075-756X Labour Literature: A Bibliography
0075-7578 Directory of Labour Organizations in Canada
0075-7586 Labour Standards in Canada. Normes du Travail au Canada
0075-7608 Lafayette Clinic Handbooks in Psychiatry
0075-7616 Lafayette Clinic Monographs in Psychiatry
0075-7640 Lagos Notes and Records
0075-7659 University of Lagos. Inaugural Lecture Series
0075-7667 University of Lagos. Continuing Education Centre. Occasional Papers
0075-7675 University of Lagos. Humanities Series
0075-7691 University of Lagos. Law Series†
0075-7705 University of Lagos. Library. Annual Report
0075-7713 University of Lagos. Scientific Monograph Series
0075-7721 Universidad de la Laguna. Facultad de Ciencias. Anales
0075-773X Universidad de la Laguna. Facultad de Derecho. Anales
0075-7748 Lake Carriers' Association. Annual Report
0075-7772 Lamar Lecture Series
0075-7780 Lammergeyer
0075-7799 Lancashire Dialect Society. Journal

0075-7810 University of Lancaster. Library. Occasional Papers†
0075-7837 Land Economics Monographs
0075-7853 Landbrukets Aarbok. Jordbruk, Hagebruk, Skogbruk
0075-7861 Landbrukets Aarbok. Skogbruk *see* 0075-7853
0075-787X Landolt-Boernstein, Zahlenwerte und Funktionen aus Naturwissenschaften und Technik. Neue Serie. Group 3: Crystal Physics
0075-7888 Landolt-Boernstein, Zahlenwerte und Funktionen aus Naturwissenschaften und Technik. Neue Serie. Group 1: Nuclear Physics
0075-7896 Landolt-Boernstein, Zahlenwerte und Funktionen aus Naturwissenschaften und Technik. Neue Serie. Group 6: Astronomy
0075-790X Landolt-Boernstein, Zahlenwerte und Funktionen aus Naturwissenschaften und Technik. Neue Serie. Group 5: Geophysics
0075-7918 Landolt-Boernstein, Zahlenwerte und Funktionen aus Naturwissenschaften und Technik. Neue Serie. Group 2: Atomic Physics
0075-7926 Landolt-Boernstein, Zahlenwerte und Funktionen aus Naturwissenschaften und Technik. Neue Serie. Group 4: Macroscopic and Technical Properties of Matter
0075-7942 Landschaftsverband Westfalen-Lippe. Volkskundliche Kommission. Schriften
0075-7950 Language Monographs†
0075-7969 Language Science Monographs
0075-7985 Langues et Styles
0075-7993 Langues et Litteratures de l'Afrique Noire†
0075-8019 Lares. Biblioteca
0075-8027 Laser Focus Buyers' Guide
0075-8035 Lasers: A Series of Advances
0075-8108 Latin American Monographs
0075-8116 Latin American Petroleum Directory
0075-8124 Latin American Political Guide†
0075-8132 University of California, Los Angeles. Latin American Center. Latin American Studies Series
0075-8140 University of Pittsburgh. Center for International Studies: Latin American Studies. Occasional Papers
0075-8159 Latin American Travel and Pan American Highway Guide *changed to* Latin American Travel Guide & Pan American Highway Guide (Mexico-Central-South America)
0075-8167 Latin American Urban Research†
0075-8175 Latin Language Mathematicians Group. Actes et Travaux du Congres
0075-8191 Universite de Lausanne. Ecole des Sciences Sociales et Politiques. Publications
0075-8213 World Legal Directory†
0075-8221 Law Books in Print
0075-823X Law in Eastern Europe
0075-8256 Law Reprints. Trade Regulation Series *changed to* B N A's Law Reprints: Trade Regulation
0075-8264 Pre-Law Handbook. Official Law School Guide
0075-8272 Lazy Man's Guide to Holidays Afloat
0075-8310 Leading Advertisers in Business Publications†
0075-8329 Leahy's Hotel-Motel Guide and Travel Atlas†
0075-8337 Learning Disorders
0075-8345 Leather Buyers Guide and Leather Trade Marks
0075-8353 Lebanese Industrial and Commercial Directory
0075-8361 Year-Book of the Lebanese Joint-Stock Companies
0075-837X Lebanon. Direction Centrale de la Statistique. Comptes Economiques
0075-8388 Lebanon. Direction Centrale de la Statistique. Recueil de Statistiques Libanaises
0075-8396 LeBaron Russell Briggs Prize Honors Essays in English
0075-8418 Lebensdarstellungen Deutscher Naturforscher
0075-8426 Lectura Dantis Romana
0075-8434 Lecture Notes in Mathematics
0075-8442 Lecture Notes in Economics and Mathematical Systems
0075-8450 Lecture Notes in Physics
0075-8469 Lecture Notes in Pure and Applied Mathematics
0075-8485 Lectures in Applied Mathematics
0075-8493 Lectures in Biblical Studies†
0075-8523 Lectures on Mathematics in the Life Sciences
0075-8531 Lectures on the History of Religions. New Series
0075-854X University of Leeds. Institute of Education. Papers
0075-8558 University of Leeds. Research Institute of African Geology. Annual Report
0075-8566 Leeds Studies in English
0075-8574 Leeds Texts and Monographs
0075-8582 Legal Almanac Series
0075-8590 Legal Medicine Annual
0075-8612 Lehrer-Briefe zur Verkehrserziehung
0075-8620 Leicester University Geographical Journal *changed to* Confluence
0075-8639 Leidse Geologische Mededelingen
0075-8647 Leidse Romanistische Reeks
0075-8655 Sportmedizinische Schriftenreihe
0075-8663 Museum fuer Voelkerkunde, Leipzig. Jahrbuch
0075-8671 Museum fuer Voelkerkunde, Leipzig. Veroeffentlichungen
0075-871X Leitende Maenner der Wirtschaft
0075-8728 Stamm Leitfaden Durch Presse und Werbung
0075-8736 Lekarske Prace
0075-8744 Leo Baeck Institute. Year Book
0075-8760 Leonardo
0075-8779 Lepetit Colloquia on Biology and Medicine. Proceedings†
0075-8787 Lepidoptera
0075-8795 Lepidopterists' Society. Memoirs
0075-8809 Leprosy Mission, London. Annual Report
0075-8817 Lesotho. Treasury. Report on the Finances and Accounts
0075-8825 Lessico Intellettuale Europeo
0075-8833 Lessing Yearbook
0075-8841 Letopis Pamatnika Slovenskej Literatury *changed to* Literarno-Muzejny Letopis
0075-8868 Let's Go: the Student Guide to Europe.
0075-8876 Let's Halt Awhile in Great Britain
0075-8892 Lettere Italiane. Biblioteca
0075-8906 La Lettre†
0075-8914 Levant
0075-8949 Leybold-Kontakt *changed to* Contact
0075-8957 Liaisons Financieres en France *changed to* Collection Radiographie du Capital - les Liaisons Financieres
0075-8973 Librarians, Censorship and Intellectual Freedom
0075-899X Libraries, Museums and Art Galleries Year Book
0075-9007 Library and Documentation Journals†
0075-9031 Library Association. Library History Group. Occasional Publication†
0075-904X Library Association of Alberta. Occasional Papers
0075-9058 Library Association. Reference, Special and Information Section. North Western Group. Occasional Papers†
0075-9066 Library Association. Year Book
0075-9074 Library Buildings *see* 0307-9767
0075-9082 Library Journal Book Review
0075-9104 Library of Exact Philosophy
0075-9120 Library of Law and Contemporary Problems
0075-9155 Library of Scandinavian Literature
0075-9201 Libros y Material de Ensenanza
0075-921X Bank of Libya. Balance of Payments
0075-9228 Libya. Census and Statistical Office. External Trade Statistics
0075-9236 Libya. Census and Statistical Office. General Population Census
0075-9244 Libya. Census and Statistical Office. Industrial Census
0075-9252 Libya. Census and Statistical Office. Report of the Annual Survey of Large Manufacturing Establishments
0075-9260 Libya. Census and Statistical Office. Report of the Annual Survey of Petroleum Mining Industry
0075-9279 Libya. Census and Statistical Office. Report of the Survey of Licensed Construction Units
0075-9287 Libya. Census and Statistical Office. Statistical Abstract
0075-9295 Libya. Census and Statistical Office. Wholesale Prices in Tripoli Town
0075-9309 Libyan Travel Series *changed to* Libya Past and Present Series
0075-9325 Lick Observatory. Publications
0075-9333 Universite de Liege. Faculte des Sciences Appliquees. Collection des Publications
0075-9341 Universite de Liege. Institut de Pharmacie. Recueil des Conferences Organisees Par le Cercle A. Gilkinet *changed to* Journee Scientifique de Mars. Conferences et Communications
0075-935X Universite de Liege. Institut de Pharmacie. Travaux Publies
0075-9368 Universite de Liege. Laboratoire d'Analyse Statistique des Langues Anciennes. Travaux Publies†
0075-9376 Lieux et les Dieux
0075-9384 Life around Us: A Commercial Directory†
0075-9392 Life Insurance Agency Management Association. Proceedings of the Annual Meeting *changed to* Life Insurance Marketing and Research Association. Proceedings of the Annual Meeting
0075-9406 Life Insurance Fact Book
0075-9414 Life Insurers Conference. Annual Proceedings
0075-9422 Life Sciences and Space Research *see* 0273-1177
0075-9465 Ligue Antituberculeuse de Quebec. Rapport
0075-9473 Institut de Medecine Legale et de Medecine Sociale. Archives
0075-9481 Lilloa
0075-949X Lilies and Other Liliaceae
0075-9511 Limnologica
0075-9554 Lindley Lecture
0075-9597 Linguistic Circle of Manitoba and North Dakota. Proceedings
0075-9600 Linguistic Society of America. Meeting Handbooks
0075-9627 Linguistic Society of India. Bulletin
0075-9635 Linguistic Structures†
0075-9643 Academy of the Hebrew Language. Linguistic Studies *changed to* Academy of the Hebrew Language. Texts & Studies
0075-9651 Linguistics in Documentation; Current Abstracts†
0075-9678 Linguistique Balkanique
0075-9686 Linguistische Reihe
0075-9694 Linnaean Society of New York. Proceedings
0075-9708 Linnaean Society of New York. Transactions
0075-9724 Linzer Hochschulschriften *changed to* Linzer Universitaetsschriften
0075-9732 Linzer Jahrbuch fuer Kunstgeschichte *changed to* Kunstjahrbuch der Stadt Linz
0075-9740 Hebrew University of Jerusalem. Lionel Cohen Lectures
0075-9759 L P-Gas Market Facts
0075-9767 Instituto de Higiene e Medicina Tropical. Anais
0075-9775 Lisbon. Universidade. Faculdade de Ciencias. Revista. Serie 2. Seccao B. Ciencias Fisicq-Quimicas†
0075-9813 List Bio-Med; Biomedical Serials in Scandinavian Libraries
0075-9821 L I S T†
0075-983X List of Grants and Awards Available to American Writers *see* 0092-5268
0075-9864 Listening Library of LP Recordings
0075-9872 Literarny Archiv
0075-9880 Literary and Library Prizes
0075-9899 Literary Market Place
0075-9902 Literary Monographs
0075-9929 Literary Prizes in Pakistan
0075-9937 Literatur und Wirklichkeit
0075-9945 Literatura Piekna. Adnotowany Rocznik Bibliograficzny
0075-9961 Literatures of the World in English Translation: A Bibliography†
0075-997X Literaturwissenschaftliches Jahrbuch. Neue Folge
0075-9988 Litomericko
0075-9996 Litterature. Science. Ideologie. *see* 0335-9190
0076-0013 Little Red Book, Classified to All Public Transport Fleet Owners and Operators and Vehicle Manufacturers
0076-003X University of Notre Dame. Department of Theology. Liturgical Studies
0076-0048 Liturgiewissenschaftliche Quellen und Forschungen
0076-0056 University of Liverpool. Department of Geography. Research Paper
0076-0072 Living History of the World†
0076-0080 Living Word Commentary†
0076-0102 Livre Contemporain et les Bibliophiles Francosuisses†
0076-0110 Livre de Langue Francaise-Repertoire des Editeurs *changed to* Repertoire International des Editeurs et Diffuseurs de Langue Francaise
0076-0129 Livre et Societes†
0076-0137 Bulletin Bibliographique Thematique
0076-0145 Livres de l'Annee/BIBLIO†
0076-0153 Livres et Auteurs Quebecois
0076-0188 Llen Cymru
0076-0196 Lloyd's Calendar & Nautical Book *changed to* Lloyd's Nautical Yearbook & Calendar
0076-020X Lloyd'S Maritime Atlas, Including a Comprehensive List of Ports and Shipping Places of the World
0076-0226 Lloyd's Register of American Yachts *see* 0163-285X
0076-0234 Lloyd'S Register of Shipping. Statistical Tables
0076-0242 Local Government Reports of Australia
0076-0269 Locations of Industries in Gujarat State
0076-0277 Lockwood's Directory of the Paper and Allied Trades
0076-0285 Locomotive Maintenance Officers Association. Annual Proceedings
0076-0293 Locomotive Maintenance Officers Association. Preconvention Report
0076-0315 Muzeum Archeologiczne i Etnograficzne, Lodz. Prace i Materialy. Seria Etnograficzna
0076-0323 Politechnika Lodzka. Zeszyty Naukowe. Budownictwo
0076-0331 Politechnika Lodzka. Zeszyty Naukowe. Wlokiennictwo
0076-034X Uniwersytet Lodzki. Prace
0076-0358 Uniwersytet Lodzki. Zeszyty Naukowe. Seria 1. Nauki Humanistyczno-Spoleczne†
0076-0366 Uniwersytet Lodzki. Zeszyty Naukowe. Seria 2: Nauki Matematyczno-Przyrodnicze
0076-0374 Uniwersytet Lodzki. Zeszyty Naukowe. Seria 3: Nauki Ekonomiczne *changed to* Acta Universitatis Lodziensis. Zeszyty Naukowe. Seria 3: Nauki Ekonomiczne
0076-0382 Lodzkie Studia Etnograficzne
0076-0390 Lodzkie Towarzystwo Naukowe. Komisji Jezykowej. Rozprawy

0076-0404 Lodzkie Towarzystwo Naukowe. Wydzial I. Prace
0076-0412 Lodzkie Towarzystwo Naukowe. Wydzial III. Nauk Matematyczno-Przyrodniczych. Prace
0076-0420 Lodzkie Towarzystwo Naukowe. Wydzial IV. Nauk Lekarskich. Prace
0076-0439 Lodzkie Towarzystwo Naukowe. Wydzial V. Nauk Technicznych. Prace
0076-0447 Log
0076-0455 Log of the Star Class
0076-0471 Logos
0076-048X Loi de l'Impot sur le Revenu, Canadienne
0076-0498 London Red Guide
0076-0501 London and Middlesex Archaeological Society. Transactions
0076-051X London Bibliography of the Social Sciences
0076-0528 London Chamber of Commerce & Industry. Annual Report & Annual Directory *changed to* London Chamber of Commerce & Industry. Directory
0076-0536 London Divinity Series. New Testament
0076-0544 London History Studies
0076-0552 London Mathematical Society. Lecture Note Series
0076-0560 London Mathematical Society. Monographs
0076-0579 London Naturalist
0076-0587 University of Western Ontario. Centre for Radio Science. Annual Report
0076-0595 University of Western Ontario. D. B. Weldon Library. Library Bulletin
0076-0609 University of Western Ontario. Museums. Museum Bulletin†
0076-0633 London Papers in Regional Science
0076-0641 London School of Economics and Political Science. Department of Geography. Geographical Papers
0076-0668 L S E Research Monographs
0076-0684 Stock Exchange, London. Stock Exchange Official Year Book
0076-0692 University of London Historical Studies
0076-0714 University of London Legal Series
0076-0722 University of London. Institute of Archaeology. Bulletin
0076-0730 University of London. Institute of Classical Studies. Bulletin
0076-0749 University of London. Institute of Classical Studies. Bulletin Supplement
0076-0765 University of London. Institute of Commonwealth Studies. Commonwealth Papers
0076-0773 University of London. Institute of Commonwealth Studies. Collected Seminar Papers
0076-0781 University of London. Institute of Commonwealth Studies. Annual Report
0076-079X University of London. Institute of Education. Library. Education Libraries Bulletin Supplements
0076-0803 University of London. Institute of Germanic Studies. Library Publications
0076-082X University of London. Institute of Historical Research Bulletin. Special Supplement
0076-0846 University of London. Institute of Latin American Studies. Monographs
0076-0854 University of London. Royal Postgraduate Medical School. Report
0076-0862 Looking for Leisure†
0076-0889 Looking into Leadership Series
0076-0897 Lorentzia
0076-0900 Natural History Museum of Los Angeles County. Contributions in Science
0076-0927 Natural History Museum of Los Angeles County. Contributions in History
0076-0935 Natural History Museum of Los Angeles County. Science Bulletin†
0076-0943 Natural History Museum of Los Angeles County. Science Series
0076-096X Los Angeles Geographical Society. Publication
0076-1001 Lost Play Series
0076-101X Lotus; a Review of Contemporary Architecture
0076-1028 Louisiana Directory of Manufacturers
0076-1044 Louisiana Tech University. Division of Life Sciences Research. Research Bulletin.
0076-1052 Louisiana State University. Animal Science Department. Livestock Producers' Day Report
0076-1060 Louisiana State University. Division of Engineering Research. Engineering Research Bulletin
0076-1087 Louisiana State University. Law School. Institute on Mineral Law. Proceedings
0076-1095 Louisiana State University. School of Forestry and Wildlife Management. Annual Forestry Symposium. Proceedings
0076-1109 L S U Wood Utilization Notes
0076-1168 Instituto de Investigacao Cientifica de Mocambique. Memorias. Series A (Ciencias Biologicas)†
0076-1176 Instituto de Investigacao Cientifica de Mocambique. Memorias. Serie B (Ciencias Geograficas-Geologicas)†
0076-1184 Instituto de Investigacao Cientifica de Mocambique. Memorias. Serie C (Ciencias Humanas)†
0076-1192 Centre Belge Histoire Rurale. Publications
0076-1206 Universite Catholique de Louvain. Centre d'Etudes Politiques. Working Group "American Foreign Policy." Cahier
0076-1230 Universite Catholique de Louvain. Facultes de Theologie et de Droit Canonique. Travaux de Doctorat en Theologie et en Droit Canonique. Nouvelle Serie
0076-1265 Universite Catholique de Louvain. Institut Orientaliste. Publications
0076-1281 Universite Catholique de Louvain. Laboratoire de Pedagogie Experimentale. Cahiers de Recherches
0076-1311 Universite Catholique de Louvain. Recueil de Travaux d'Histoire et de Philologie
0076-132X Lovejoy's College Guide
0076-1346 Lovejoy's Career and Vocational School Guide
0076-1354 Lovoe Geomagnetic Observatory Yearbook
0076-1370 Loewdin Symposia; Proceedings of the International Symposium on Atomic, Molecular, and Solid-State Theory and Quantum Biology
0076-1370 International Symposium on Atomic, Molecular and Solid-State Theory and Quantum Biology. Proceedings *changed to* International Symposium on Atomic, Molecular and Solid-State Theory, Collision Phenomena and Computational Methods. Proceedings
0076-1389 Lower Palaeozic Rocks of the New World
0076-1397 Loyola University. Center for Urban Policy. Studies
0076-1400 National Botanic Gardens, Lucknow. Annual Report *changed to* National Botanic Gardens, Lucknow. Progress Report
0076-1419 National Botanic Gardens, Lucknow. Bulletin
0076-1427 Lucknow Law Journal†
0076-1435 Lud
0076-1443 Lueneburger Blaetter†
0076-1451 Lund Studies in English
0076-146X Lund Studies in Geography. Series A. Physical Geography
0076-1478 Lund Studies in Geography. Series B. Human Geography
0076-1486 Lund Studies in Geography. Series C. General and Mathematical Geography
0076-1494 Lund Studies in International History
0076-1508 Lusitania Sacra
0076-1516 Lustracje Dobr Krolewskich XVI-XVIII Wieku
0076-1524 Lute Society of America. Journal
0076-1532 L E A Yearbook
0076-1540 Lutheran World Federation. Proceedings of the Assembly
0076-1559 Luxembourg. Ministere des Finances. Budget de l'Etat
0076-1567 Luxembourg. Office National du Travail. Rapport Annuel *changed to* Luxembourg. Administration de l'Emploi. Rapport Annuel
0076-1575 Luxembourg. Service Central de la Statistique et des Etudes Economiques. Annuaire Statistique
0076-1583 Luxembourg. Service Central de la Statistique et des Etudes Economiques. Bulletin du STATEC
0076-1591 Luxembourg. Service Central de la Statistique et des Etudes Economiques. Collection D et M: Definitions et Methodes
0076-1613 Luxembourg. Service Central de la Statistique et des Etudes Economiques. Collection RP: Recensements de la Population
0076-163X Lychnos-Bibliotek. Studies och Kaellskrifter Udgivna av Laerdomshistoriska Samfundet. Studies and Sources Published by the Swedish History of Science Society
0076-1648 Lychnos-Laerdomshistoriska Samfundets Aarsbok. Annual of the Swedish History of Science Society
0076-1656 Universite Claude Bernard. Departement de Mathematiques. Publications
0076-1664 Universite de Lyon. Faculte de Droit et des Sciences Economiques. Annales *changed to* Universite Jean Moulin. Annales
0076-1699 Lyrical Iowa
0076-1710 Sweden Institute of Marine Research. Series Biology. Reports *see* 0346-8666
0076-1729 M.L. Seidman Memorial Town Hall Lecture Series
0076-1745 Asta-Press
0076-1753 M T P International Review of Science. Inorganic Chemistry, Series 1
0076-1761 M T P International Review of Science. Organic Chemistry
0076-177X M T P International Review of Science. Physical Chemistry
0076-1818 Universita degli Studi di Macerata. Facolta di Lettere e Filosofia. Annali
0076-1842 McGill University, Montreal. Department of Meteorology. Publication in Meteorology
0076-1850 McGill University, Montreal. Axel Heiberg Island Research Reports
0076-1877 McGill University, Montreal. Brace Research Institute. Annual Report
0076-1893 McGill University, Montreal. Centre for Developing-Area Studies. Annual Report
0076-1907 McGill University, Montreal. Centre for Developing-Area Studies. Occasional Paper Series *see* 0702-8431
0076-1915 McGill University, Montreal. Centre for Developing-Area Studies. Reprint Series†
0076-1931 McGill University, Montreal. Department of Geography. Climatological Research Series
0076-194X McGill University, Montreal. Industrial Relations Centre. Annual Conference Proceedings
0076-1966 McGill University, Montreal. Mechanical Engineering Research Laboratories. Report
0076-1974 McGill University, Montreal. Mechanical Engineering Research Laboratories. Technical Note
0076-1982 McGill Sub-Arctic Research Papers
0076-1990 McGoldrick's Handbook of Canadian Customs Tariff and Excise Duties
0076-2016 McGraw-Hill Yearbook of Science and Technology
0076-2032 Machine Intelligence Workshop
0076-2040 Machinery's Annual Buyer's Guide *see* 0305-3121
0076-2059 McMaster University, Hamilton, Ontario. Institute for Materials Research. Annual Report
0076-2067 MacRae's Blue Book
0076-2075 Macromolecular Chemistry
0076-2083 Macromolecular Reviews
0076-2091 Macromolecular Syntheses
0076-2105 Made in Austria
0076-213X Madison Avenue Europe†
0076-2148 Madison Avenue Handbook
0076-2156 Madison Avenue London†
0076-2164 Madison Avenue Paris†
0076-2180 Madison Avenue West Germany†
0076-2202 University of Madras. Archaeological Series
0076-2210 University of Madras. Endowment Lectures
0076-2229 University of Madras. Historical Series
0076-2237 University of Madras. Kannada Series
0076-2245 University of Madras. Malayalam Series
0076-2253 University of Madras. Philosophical Series
0076-2261 University of Madras. Sanskrit Series
0076-227X University of Madras. Tamil Series
0076-2288 University of Madras. Telugu Series
0076-2296 University of Madras. Urdu Series
0076-230X Casa de Velaquez, Madrid. Melanges
0076-2318 Real Conservatorio Superior de Musica. Anuario
0076-2326 Maerchen der Europaeischen Voelker
0076-2334 Magazine
0076-2342 Magazine of Albemarle County History
0076-2350 Magenta Frog
0076-2369 Magon. Serie Scientifique
0076-2377 Magon. Serie Technique
0076-2385 Magyar Irodalomtortenetiras Forrasai; Fontes Ad Historiam Litterariam Hungariae Spectantes
0076-2393 Magyar Konyv
0076-2407 Magyar Kozlony
0076-2415 Magyar Munkasmozgalmi Muzeum. Evkonyv
0076-2423 Magyar Tudomanyos Akademia. Agrartudomanyok Osztalya. Monografiasorozat
0076-2431 Magyar Tudomanyos Akademia. Mikrobiologiai Kutato Intezet. Proceedings
0076-244X Studia Biologica Academiae Scientiarum Hungaricae
0076-2458 Studia Historica Academiae Scientiarum Hungaricae
0076-2466 Studia Philosophica Academiae Scientiarum Hungaricae
0076-2474 Magyarorszag Allatvilaga
0076-2482 Magyarorszag Kulturfloraja
0076-2490 Magyarorszag Muemleki Topografiaja
0076-2504 Magyarorszag Regeszeti Topografiaja
0076-2512 Magyarorszag Tajfoldrajza
0076-2520 Maharaja Sayajirao University of Baroda. Department of Archaeology and Ancient History. Archaeology Series
0076-2539 Maharashtra: an Economic Review *changed to* Economic Survey of India
0076-2547 Maharashtra Archives Bulletin
0076-2555 Maharashtra State Budget in Brief
0076-2563 Maharashtra State Financial Corporation. Annual Report
0076-2571 Mahratta
0076-258X Maia†
0076-2636 Maine. Department of Sea and Shore Fisheries. General Bulletin *changed to* Maine. Department of Marine Resources. Fisheries Circulars
0076-2652 Maine Heritage Series

0076-2679 Maine Pocket Data Book *see* 0093-724X
0076-2695 Maine Recreation Authority. Annual Report *changed to* Maine Guarantee Authority. Annual Report
0076-2709 Maine That Was Series†
0076-2717 Maine Writers' Conference Chapbook
0076-2725 Mainfraenkisches Jahrbuch fuer Geschichte und Kunst
0076-2733 Roemisch-Germanisches Zentralmuseum, Mainz. Ausstellungskataloge
0076-2741 Roemisch-Germanisches Zentralmuseum, Mainz. Jahrbuch
0076-275X Roemisch-Germanisches Zentralmuseum, Mainz. Kataloge Vor- und Fruehgeschichtlicher Altertuemer
0076-2776 Mainzer Philosophische Forschungen
0076-2784 Mainzer Reihe
0076-2792 Mainzer Zeitschrift
0076-2806 Maison des Sciences de l'Homme. Collection de Reeditions†
0076-2814 Maisons d'Enfants et d'Adolescents de France. Album-Annuaire National
0076-2822 Maitres-Cuisiniers de France
0076-2849 Major League Baseball
0076-289X Makedonika
0076-2989 Mala Biblioteka Baletowa
0076-2997 Malacologia
0076-3004 Malacological Review
0076-3012 Malawi Year Book *changed to* Malawi. Department of Information. Year in Review
0076-3020 Malawi. Accountant General. Report
0076-3047 Malawi. Department of Agriculture. Annual Report *changed to* Malawi. Department of Agricultural Research. Annual Report
0076-3055 Malawi. Department of Civil Aviation. Annual Report
0076-3063 Malawi. Department of Customs and Excise. Annual Report†
0076-3071 Malawi. Department of Forestry and Game. Report
0076-308X Malawi. Police Force. Annual Report
0076-3101 Malawi Economic Report
0076-311X Malawi. Geological Survey. Annual Report
0076-3128 Malawi. Geological Survey. Bulletin
0076-3136 Malawi. Geological Survey. Memoir
0076-3144 Malawi. Geological Survey. Records
0076-3152 Malawi. Judicial Department. Annual Report†
0076-3160 Malawi. Ministry of Justice. Annual Report
0076-3179 Malawi. Lands Department. Annual Report†
0076-3195 Malawi. Ministry of Finance. Budget Statement
0076-3225 Malawi. Ministry of Local Government. Annual Report
0076-3233 Malawi. Ministry of Works and Supplies. Annual Report†
0076-3241 Malawi. National Statistical Office. Annual Survey of Economic Activities
0076-325X Malawi. National Statistical Office. Annual Statement of External Trade
0076-3268 Malawi. National Statistical Office. Compendium of Statistics *changed to* Malawi Statistical Yearbook
0076-3276 Malawi. National Statistical Office. Household Income and Expenditure Survey
0076-3284 Malawi. National Statistical Office. National Accounts Report
0076-3292 Malawi. National Statistical Office. National Sample Survey of Agriculture
0076-3306 Malawi. National Statistical Office. Population Census Final Report
0076-3314 Malawi. Office of the Auditor General. Report
0076-3322 Malawi. Post Office Savings Bank. Annual Report
0076-3330 Malawi Railways. Annual Reports and Accounts
0076-3349 Malawi. Registrar of Insurance. Report
0076-3357 Malawi Treaty Series
0076-3365 Malawi. Department of Veterinary Services and Animal Industry. Annual Report
0076-3373 Malaysia Official Year Book
0076-3381 National Archives of Malaysia. Annual Report
0076-339X Malaysia Year Book *changed to* Information Malaysia
0076-3411 Mali. Service de la Statistique Generale, de la Comptabilite Nationale et de la Mecanographie. Annuaire Statistique
0076-342X Malignant Intrigue
0076-3438 University of Lund. School of Dentistry. Faculty of Odontology. Annual Publications
0076-3446 Malta Trade Directory *changed to* Malta Chamber of Commerce. Trade Directory
0076-3454 Malta. Office of Statistics. Census of Agriculture *changed to* Malta. Central Office of Statistics. Census of Agriculture and Fisheries
0076-3462 Malta. Central Office of Statistics. Census of Production Report
0076-3470 Malta. Central Office of Statistics. Demographic Review
0076-3489 Malta. Central Office of Statistics. Education Statistics
0076-3519 Mammalian Species
0076-3578 Management Aids for Small Manufacturers *see* 0190-3225
0076-3586 Management and Labor Studies. English Series†
0076-3616 Management, Fonctions, Methodes, Experiences†
0076-3624 Management Guide to N C
0076-3640 Management Monographs *changed to* L R I Guides to Management. Monographs
0076-3667 Management Advisory Services Technical Study†
0076-3705 Manchester Association of Engineers. Transactions
0076-3713 Manchester Guardian Society for the Protection of Trade. Annual Report
0076-3721 Manchester Literary and Philosophical Society. Memoirs and Proceedings
0076-3748 La Mandragore Qui Chante
0076-3756 National Museum of the Philippines. Annual Report
0076-3764 National Museum of the Philippines. Museum Publications (Pamphlet Series)
0076-3772 National Museum of the Philippines. Monograph Series
0076-3780 Philippine Normal College. Language Study Center. Occasional Paper
0076-3802 Manitoba Cancer Treatment and Research Foundation. Report
0076-3810 Manitoba Entomologist
0076-3829 Manitoba Historical Society. Transactions†
0076-3853 Manitoba Labour-Management Review Committee. Annual Report
0076-3861 Manitoba Law Journal
0076-387X Manitoba. Mining Engineering Division. Geological Paper *changed to* Manitoba. Mineral Resources Division. Geological Paper
0076-3888 Manitoba Museum of Man and Nature. Biennial Report
0076-3896 Manitoba Record Society. Publications
0076-390X Manitoba Trade Directory
0076-3918 University of Manitoba. Center for Settlement Studies. Publication Series†
0076-3926 University of Manitoba. Center for Settlement Studies. Series 1. Annual Reports†
0076-3934 University of Manitoba. Center for Settlement Studies. Series 2. Research Report†
0076-3942 University of Manitoba. Center for Settlement Studies. Series 3. Bibliography and Information†
0076-3950 University of Manitoba. Center for Settlement Studies. Series 4. Proceedings†
0076-3969 University of Manitoba. Center for Settlement Studies. Series 5. Occasional Papers†
0076-3977 University of Manitoba. Center for Transportation Studies. Occasional Paper
0076-3993 University of Manitoba. Center for Transportation Studies. Seminar Series on Transportation. Proceedings
0076-4000 University of Manitoba. Department of Agricultural Economics and Farm Management. Occasional Papers
0076-4035 University of Manitoba. Department of Slavic Studies. Readings in Slavic Literature
0076-4051 University of Manitoba. Faculty of Agriculture. Progress Report on Agricultural Research and Experimentation
0076-4108 University of Manitoba. Medical Journal
0076-4116 Mankind Monographs
0076-4124 Manna†
0076-4140 Manpower/Automation Research Notices†
0076-4167 Materials Handling Buyers Guide
0076-4167 Manual of Materials Handling and Ancilliary Equipment *see* 0076-4167
0076-4175 Mutual Funds Almanac
0076-4205 Manuels Pratiques d'Economie†
0076-4213 Manufacturers' Agents' Guide
0076-423X Manufacturing Chemists Association. Statistical Summary†
0076-4248 Canada. Statistics Canada. Manufacturing Industries of Canada: Type of Organization and Size of Establishment/Industries Manufacturieres du Canada: Forme d'Organisation et Taille des Etablissements†
0076-4256 Manufacturing Management Series†
0076-4264 Manx Museum, Douglas, Isle of Man. Journal
0076-4280 Maori Education Foundation. Annual Report
0076-4299 Instituto de Biologia Marina. Boletin†
0076-4302 Instituto di Biologia Marina. Serie Contribuciones *see* 0325-6790
0076-4310 Instituto de Biologia Marina. Memoria Anual†
0076-4337 Universidad Nacional del Zulia. Facultad de Humanidades y Educacion. Artes y Letras
0076-4345 Universidad Nacional del Zulia. Facultad de Humanidades y Educacion. Conferencias y Coloquios
0076-4353 Universidad Nacional del Zulia. Facultad de Humanidades y Educacion. Fuera de Serie
0076-4361 Universidad Nacional del Zulia. Facultad de Humanidades y Educacion. Manuales de la Escuela de Educacion
0076-437X Universidad Nacional del Zulia. Facultad de Humanidades y Educacion. Monografias y Ensayos
0076-4418 Marconi's International Register
0076-4434 Marian Library Studies. New Series
0076-4442 Marine Biology; Proceedings of the Interdisciplinary Conference
0076-4450 Marine Catalog
0076-4469 Marine Engineering/Log Annual Maritime Review and Yearbook Issue
0076-4477 Morskaya Geologiya i Geofizika
0076-4485 Marine Marchande
0076-4493 Marine Research
0076-4507 Marine Science Affairs *changed to* Reports on Marine Science Affairs
0076-4515 Maritime Bank of Israel. Annual Report
0076-4523 Market Research Society. Yearbook
0076-4531 Market Statistics Key Plant Directory *see* 0098-1397
0076-4566 Marketing et Developpement Industriel *changed to* Marketing Industriel
0076-4582 Marketing Guide to the Chemical Industry *changed to* Kline Guide to the Chemical Industry
0076-4590 Marketing Guide to the Packaging Industries *changed to* Kline Guide to the Packaging Industry
0076-4604 Marketing Guide to the Paint Industry *changed to* Kline Guide to the Paint Industry
0076-4612 Marketing Guide to the Paper and Pulp Industry *changed to* Kline Guide to the Paper and Pulp Industry
0076-4620 Marketing Research Techniques Series†
0076-4647 Markets Year Book
0076-4655 Maroc en Chiffre
0076-4671 Marquette Slavic Studies
0076-4701 Marsyas
0076-471X Martin Classical Lectures
0076-4728 Mary C. Richardson Lecture†
0076-4736 Maryland. Council for Higher Education. Annual Report *see* 0361-140X
0076-4744 Maryland. Department of Juvenile Services. Annual Statistical Report *changed to* Maryland. Juvenile Services Administration. Annual Statistical Report
0076-4752 Maryland. Department of State Planning. Activities Report
0076-4779 Maryland. Geological Survey. Bulletin
0076-4787 Maryland. Geological Survey. Educational Series
0076-4795 Maryland. Geological Survey. Information Circular
0076-4809 Maryland. Geological Survey. Report of Investigations
0076-4817 Maryland. Geological Survey. Water Resources Basic Data Report
0076-4825 University of Maryland. Institute for Fluid Dynamics and Applied Mathematics. Public Lecture Series
0076-4833 University of Maryland. College of Library and Information Services. Conference Proceedings
0076-4841 University of Maryland. College of Library and Information Services. Student Contribution Series
0076-4884 Massachusetts. Advisory Committee on Correction. Annual Report
0076-4892 Massachusetts Audubon Newsletter *see* 0272-8966
0076-4906 Massachusetts. Department of Mental Health. Newsletter†
0076-4922 Massachusetts. Division of Employment Security. Employment and Wages in Establishments Subject to the Massachusetts Employment Security Law. State Summary
0076-4930 Massachusetts. Division of Employment Security. Annual Planning Report
0076-4949 Massachusetts. Division of Employment Security. Statistical Digest
0076-4957 Massachusetts. Division of Fisheries and Game. Annual Report
0076-4981 Massachusetts Historical Society. Proceedings
0076-499X Massachusetts Housing Finance Agency. Annual Report
0076-5066 University of Massachusetts. Department of Anthropology. Research Reports
0076-5082 Master Plan for Higher Education in Illinois *changed to* Master Plan for Postsecondary Education in Illinois
0076-5104 Masters Education; Route to Opportunities in Modern Nursing *changed to* Masters Education: Route to Opportunities in Contemporary Nursing
0076-5112 Master's Theses in Education
0076-5139 Material Culture Monographs (American Indian)
0076-5147 Materiale si Cercetari Arheologice
0076-5163 Materiali per Una Storia della Cultura Giuridica
0076-5171 Materialien zur Roemisch-Germanischen Keramik

0076-5201 Materials Science Research
0076-521X Materialy i Prace Antropologiczne
0076-5228 Materialy i Studia do Historii Prasy i Czasopismiennictwa Polskiego†
0076-5236 Materialy Zachodnio-Pomorskie
0076-5244 Materialy Zrodlowe do Dziejow Kosciola W Polsce
0076-5287 Materiaux pour l'Histoire du Socialisme International. Serie 2. Essais Bibliographiques†
0076-5295 Materiaux pour l'Histoire du Socialisme International. Serie 1. Textes et Documents†
0076-5333 Mathematical Expositions
0076-5341 University of Notre Dame. Department of Mathematics. Mathematical Lectures†
0076-5376 Mathematical Surveys
0076-5384 Mathematical Table Series
0076-5392 Mathematics in Science and Engineering
0076-5406 Mathematiques et Sciences de l'Homme
0076-5414 Mathematische Forschungsberichte†
0076-5430 Mathematische Lehrbuecher und Monographien. Abteilung: Mathematische Monographien.
0076-5449 Mathematische Schuelerbuecherei
0076-5473 Maurice Falk Institute for Economic Research in Israel. Report
0076-5481 Mauritius. Archives Department. Annual Report
0076-549X Mauritius. Customs and Excise Department. Annual Report
0076-5503 Mauritius. Legislative Assembly. Sessional Paper
0076-5511 Mauritius. Meteorological Services. Report
0076-552X Mauritius. Ministry of Housing, Lands and Town and Country Planning. Annual Reports
0076-5538 Mauritius. Ministry of Social Security. Annual Report
0076-5554 Mauritius. Ministry of Works and Internal Communications. Report
0076-5562 Mauritius. Public Accounts Committee. Report
0076-5589 Max C. Fleischmann College of Agriculture. Publications. B (Series)
0076-5597 Max C. Fleischmann College of Agriculture. Publications. C (Series)
0076-5600 Max C. Fleischmann College of Agriculture. Publications. R (Series)
0076-5619 Max C. Fleischmann College of Agriculture. Publications. T (Series)
0076-5627 Max-Planck-Institut fuer Bildungsforschung, Berlin. Studien und Berichte
0076-5635 Max-Planck-Gesellschaft zur Foerderung der Wissenschaften. Jahrbuch
0076-5643 Max-Planck-Institut fuer Aeronomie. Mitteilungen
0076-5651 Max-Planck-Institut fuer Auslaendisches Oeffentliches Recht und Voelkerrecht. Fontes *changed to* Max-Planck-Institut fuer Auslaendisches Oeffentliches Recht und Voelkerrecht. Fontes Iuris Gentium
0076-566X Max-Planck-Institut fuer Silikatforschung, Wuerzburg. Veroeffentlichungen†
0076-5678 Mitteilungen aus dem Max-Planck-Institut fuer Stroenmungsforschung und der Aerodynamischen Versuchsansalt *see* 0374-1257
0076-5694 Max-Reger-Institut, Bonn. Mitteilungen†
0076-5716 Meat and Livestock Commission, Bucks, England. Index of Research
0076-5732 Mechanical Engineering Monographs†
0076-5783 Mechanics *see* 0191-8885
0076-5791 Mechanisms of Molecular Migrations†
0076-5805 Politechnika Poznanska. Zeszyty Naukowe. Mechanizacja i Elektryfikacja Rolnictwa *see* 0137-6918
0076-5813 Electro-Radiologiste Qualifie de France. Annuaire *changed to* Medecin Electro-Radiologiste Qualifie de France
0076-5821 Media Scandinavia
0076-583X Medieval Academy of America. Publications *changed to* Medieval Academy Books
0076-5856 Mediaeval Philosophical Texts in Translation
0076-5864 Mediaeval Scandinavia
0076-5872 Mediaeval Studies
0076-5880 Mediaevalia Philosophica Polonorum
0076-5899 Medical Annual
0076-5902 Medical Art *see* 0094-2499
0076-5929 Medical Books in Print *see* 0000-0574
0076-5945 Medical Library Association. Publication†
0076-5953 Medical Physics Series
0076-5961 Medical Protection Society. Annual Report
0076-5988 Medical Research Centre, Nairobi. Annual Report
0076-5996 Medical Research Council (Ireland). Report
0076-6003 Medical Research Index
0076-6011 Medical Society of London. Transactions
0076-6038 Medical Ultrasonics†
0076-6046 Medicina
0076-6054 Medicinal Chemistry
0076-6062 Medicinal Research: A Series of Monographs
0076-6070 Medicine and Sport
0076-6097 Medieval Archaeology
0076-6100 Medieval Iberian Penninsula
0076-6119 Medieval India; a Miscellany
0076-6135 Medium Aevum Monographs†
0076-6143 Medium Industry Bank, Seoul. Report *changed to* Small and Medium Industry Bank, Seoul. Annual Report
0076-6151 Medizinische Laenderkunde. Geomedical Monograph Series
0076-616X Medizinische Praxis
0076-6178 Medizinische Radiographie und Photographie†
0076-6186 Sozialmedizinische und Paedagogische Jugendkunde
0076-6194 Meet the U. S. A†
0076-6208 Meier-Dudy
0076-6216 Meister des Puppenspiels
0076-6224 Melanderia
0076-6232 Melbourne Historical Journal
0076-6240 Science Museum of Victoria. Report of Activities
0076-6259 Melbourne Monographs in Germanic Studies†
0076-6267 Melbourne Slavonic Studies
0076-6275 Melbourne Studies in Education
0076-6283 University of Melbourne. Institute of Applied Economic and Social Research. Monographs
0076-6291 University of Melbourne. Institute of Applied Economic and Social Research. Technical Papers
0076-6313 Melland Schill Lectures on International Law
0076-6321 Melsheimer Entomological Series
0076-633X Melville Society Newsletter *changed to* Melville Society Extracts
0076-6348 Melville Society. Special Publication *changed to* Melville Society Extracts
0076-6356 Membranes: A Series of Advances
0076-6364 Memoires de Photo-Interpretation
0076-6372 Memorabilia Zoologica
0076-6380 Junta de Estudios Historicos de Mendoza. Revista
0076-6399 Universidad Nacional de Cuyo. Biblioteca Central. Boletin Bibliografico
0076-6402 Universidad Nacional de Cuyo. Biblioteca Central. Cuadernos de la Biblioteca
0076-6429 Mennonite History Series
0076-6437 Men's Wear Year Book and Diary
0076-6453 Mental Health Statistics for Illinois
0076-6461 Mental Measurements Yearbook
0076-650X Merchant Vessels of the United States
0076-6518 Merck Index; an Encyclopedia of Chemicals and Drugs
0076-6526 Merck Manual; a Handbook of Diagnosis and Therapy
0076-6542 Merck Veterinary Manual; a Handbook of Diagnosis and Therapy for the Veterinarian
0076-6550 Universidad de los Andes. Facultad de Derecho. Anuario
0076-6569 Universidad de Los Andes. Instituto de Geografia y Conservacion de Recursos Naturales. Cuadernos Geograficos
0076-6577 Merite du Defricheur. Rapport de l'Ordre du Merite du Defricheur *changed to* Merite du Defricheur. Rapport de l'Ordre du Merite Agricole
0076-6607 Mesoamerican Studies†
0076-6615 Mesopotamia
0076-6623 Universita degli Studi di Messina. Istituto di Filologia Moderna. Biblioteca Letteraria
0076-6631 Universita degli Studi di Messina. Istituto di Storia Medievale e Moderna. Pubblicazioni
0076-664X Metal Bulletin Handbook
0076-6658 Metal Statistics
0076-6690 Metallurgical Reviews *see* 0308-4590
0076-6704 Metallurgical Works in Canada, Nonferrous and Precious Metals
0076-6712 Metallurgical Works in Canada, Primary Iron and Steel
0076-6720 Metaphysische Rundschau
0076-6739 Meteorological Yearbook of Finland. Part 1B: Climatological Data from Jokioinen and Sodankyla Observatories
0076-6747 Meteorological Yearbook of Finland. Part 1A: Climatological Data
0076-6755 Meteorological Yearbook of Finland. Part 2: Precipitation and Snow Cover Data
0076-6763 Meteorological Yearbook of Finland. Part 4: Measurements of Radiation and Bright Sunshine
0076-6771 Methodensammlung der Elektronenmikroskopie
0076-681X Methods and Achievements in Experimental Pathology
0076-6828 Methods and Models in the Social Sciences
0076-6836 Methods and Techniques in Geophysics†
0076-6852 Methods in Cancer Research†
0076-6852 Methods in Cancer Research
0076-6860 Methods in Computational Physics: Advances in Research and Applications
0076-6879 Methods in Enzymology
0076-6887 Methods in Free-Radical Chemistry†
0076-6895 Methods in Geochemistry and Geophysics
0076-6909 Methods in Hydroscience *see* 0065-2768
0076-6917 Methods in Immunology and Immunochemistry
0076-6925 Methods in Neurochemistry†
0076-6933 Methods in Virology
0076-6941 Methods of Biochemical Analysis
0076-695X Methods of Experimental Physics
0076-6984 Metodicke Prirucky Experimentalni Botaniky
0076-700X Metro Building Industry Directory
0076-7018 METRO; New York Metropolitan Reference and Research Library Agency. METRO Miscellaneous Publications Series
0076-7050 Metropolitan Library Service Agency. Annual Report
0076-7077 Metropolitan Milwaukee Association of Commerce. Economic Studies *changed to* Metropolitan Milwaukee Economic Fact Book
0076-7085 Metropolitan Politics†
0076-7093 Metropolitan Toronto
0076-7107 Metropolitan Washington Council of Governments. Annual Report
0076-7115 Metropolitan Washington Council of Governments. Regional Directory
0076-7131 Instituto Nacional de Cancerologia, Mexico. Revista
0076-7158 Museu Nacional de Antropologia. Cuadernos
0076-7166 Universidad Nacional Autonoma de Mexico. Centro de Estudios Mayas. Cuadernos
0076-7174 Universidad Nacional Autonoma de Mexico. Instituto de Biologia. Anales
0076-7182 Universidad Nacional Autonoma de Mexico. Instituto de Geofisica. Anales
0076-7190 Universidad Nacional Autonoma de Mexico. Instituto de Geografia. Boletin
0076-7204 Universidad Nacional Autonoma de Mexico. Instituto de Geofisica. Monografias
0076-7212 Universidad Nacional Autonoma de Mexico. Instituto de Investigaciones Historicas. Serie de Cultura Nahuatl. Fuentes
0076-7239 Universidad Nacional Autonoma de Mexico. Instituto de Investigaciones Esteticas. Anales
0076-7247 Universidad Nacional Autonoma de Mexico. Instituto de Investigaciones Esteticas. Anales. Suplemento†
0076-7255 Universidad Nacional Autonoma de Mexico. Instituto de Investigaciones Esteticas. Publicaciones Especiales†
0076-7263 Universidad Nacional Autonoma de Mexico. Instituto de Investigaciones Antropologicas. Cuadernos Serie Antropologica
0076-7271 Universidad Nacional Autonoma de Mexico. Instituto de Investigaciones Historicas. Cuadernos Serie Documental
0076-7298 Universidad Nacional Autonoma de Mexico. Instituto de Investigaciones Antropoligicas. Serie Antropologica
0076-7301 Universidad Nacional Autonoma de Mexico. Instituto de Investigaciones Historicas. Serie Bibliografica
0076-731X Universidad Nacional Autonoma de Mexico. Instituto de Investigaciones Historicas. Serie Documental
0076-7328 Universidad Nacional Autonoma de Mexico. Instituto de Investigaciones Historicas. Serie de Cultures Mesoamericanas
0076-7344 Universidad Nacional Autonoma de Mexico. Instituto de Investigaciones Historicas. Serie de Cultura Nahuatl. Monografias
0076-7352 Universidad Nacional Autonoma de Mexico. Instituto de Investigaciones Historicas. Serie de Historia General
0076-7379 Universidad Nacional Autonoma de Mexico. Instituto de Investigaciones Historicas. Serie de Historia Novohispana *changed to* Estudios de Historia Novohispana
0076-7387 Universidad Nacional Autonoma de Mexico. Instituto de Investigaciones Historicas. Serie de Historiadores y Cronistas
0076-7441 Universidad Nacional Autonoma de Mexico. Instituto de Matematicas. Anales
0076-7468 Universidad Nacional Autonoma de Mexico. Seminario de Investigaciones Bibliotecologica. Publicaciones. Serie B. Bibliografia
0076-7476 Instituto Nacional de Energia Nuclear. Publication
0076-7492 Mexico. Secretaria de Programacion y Presupuesto
0076-7506 Instituto Nacional de Antropologia e Historia. Departamento de Monumentos Coloniales. (Publicaciones)
0076-7514 Instituto Nacional de Antropologia e Historia. Departamento de Monumentos Prehispanicos. (Publicaciones)†

0076-7530 Mexico. Direccion General de Prensa, Memorias, Bibliotecas y Publicaciones. Coleccion: Documentos Economicos de la Administracion Publica
0076-7549 Instituto Nacional de Antropologia e Historia. Sociedad de Alumnos. (Publicaciones)
0076-7557 Instituto Nacional de Antropologia e Historia. Anales
0076-7565 Instituto Nacional de Antropologia e Historia. Coleccion Breve
0076-7573 Instituto Nacional de Antropologia e Historia. Investigaciones
0076-759X Instituto Nacional de Antropologia e Historia. Memorias†
0076-7603 Instituto Nacional de Antropologia e Historia. Obras Varias
0076-7611 Instituto Nacional de Antropologia e Historia. Serie Cientifica
0076-762X Instituto Nacional de Antropologia e Historia. Serie Culturas del Mundo
0076-7670 Meyers Grosses Jahreslexikon
0076-7689 Meyniana
0076-7697 Miami Linguistic Series†
0076-7719 University of Miami Hispanic-American Studies†
0076-7727 Michel-Briefmarken-Kataloge
0076-7735 Camping, Caravaning in France
0076-7743 Michelin Red Guide Series: Benelux
0076-7751 Michelin Red Guide Series: Germany
0076-776X Michelin Red Guide Series: Spain & Portugal
0076-7778 Michelin Red Guide Series: France
0076-7786 Michelin Red Guide Series: Italy
0076-7794 Michelin Red Guide Series: Paris
0076-7808 Michigan Abstracts of Chinese and Japanese Works on Chinese History
0076-7824 Michigan Beef Cattle Day Report
0076-7832 Michigan Business Cases
0076-7840 Michigan Business Papers
0076-7859 Michigan Business Reports
0076-7867 Michigan Business Studies
0076-7875 Michigan. Civil Rights Commission. Report *changed to* Michigan. Civil Rights Commission. Annual Report
0076-7905 Michigan. Department of Natural Resources. Institute for Fisheries Research. Miscellaneous Publication
0076-7913 Michigan. Division of Vocational Education. Report
0076-7948 Michigan Geographical Publications
0076-7956 Michigan Governmental Studies
0076-7964 Michigan. Department of Natural Resources. Institute for Fisheries Research. Lake Inventory Summary†
0076-7972 Michigan International Business Studies
0076-7999 Michigan International Labor Studies
0076-8014 Michigan Municipal League. Municipal Legal Briefs
0076-8057 Michigan Natural Resources Council. Scientific Advisory Committee. Annual Report
0076-8065 Michigan Papers in Chinese Studies
0076-8073 Michigan. Plant Industry Division. Plant Pest Control Programs†
0076-8081 Michigan Library Directory & Statistics
0076-809X Michigan Science in Action
0076-8103 Michigan Slavic Contributions
0076-8111 Michigan State Plan for Construction of Community Mental Health Facilities†
0076-812X Michigan State University. Asian Studies Center. Occasional Papers: East Asian Series
0076-8138 Michigan State University. Asian Studies Center. Occasional Papers: South Asian Series
0076-8146 Michigan State University. Department of Physics. Cyclotron Project
0076-8189 Michigan State University. Latin American Studies Center. Monograph Series
0076-8197 Michigan State University.Latin American Studies Center. Occasional Papers†
0076-8200 Michigan State University. Latin American Studies Center. Research Reports
0076-8227 Michigan State University. Museum Publications. Biological Series
0076-8235 Michigan State University. Museum Publications. Cultural Series
0076-8243 Michigan State University. Public Administration Program. Research Report
0076-8251 Michigan State University. Rural Manpower Center. R M C Mimeograph *changed to* Michigan State University. Center for Rural Manpower & Public Affairs. Mimeograph
0076-826X Michigan State University. Rural Manpower Center. R M C Report *changed to* Michigan State University. Center for Rural Manpower & Public Affairs. Report
0076-8278 Michigan State University. Rural Manpower Center. R M C Special Paper *changed to* Michigan State University. Center for Rural Manpower & Public Affairs. Special Paper
0076-8308 Michigan Statistical Abstract
0076-8316 Michigan Technological University. Library. Serial Holdings List
0076-8324 Michigan Technological University. Library. Library Publication
0076-8332 University of Michigan. Graduate School of Business Administration. Leadership Award Lecture
0076-8340 University of Michigan. Center for Japanese Studies. Bibliographical Series
0076-8359 University of Michigan. Center for Japanese Studies. Occasional Papers
0076-8367 University of Michigan. Museum of Anthropology. Anthropological Papers.
0076-8375 University of Michigan. Museum of Anthropology. Memoirs
0076-8391 University of Michigan. Museum of Art. Bulletin *see* 0270-1642
0076-8405 University of Michigan. Museum of Zoology. Miscellaneous Publications
0076-8413 University of Michigan. Museum of Zoology. Occasional Papers
0076-8421 University of Michigan Observatories. Publications
0076-843X University of Michigan. School of Dentistry. Alumni Bulletin
0076-8480 Microfiche Foundation. Newsletter
0076-8502 Middle East and North Africa
0076-8510 Middle East Economic Papers†
0076-8529 Middle East Record
0076-8537 Middle Eastern Monographs
0076-857X University of Chicago . Midwest Administration Center. Monograph Series
0076-8588 Midwest Electrical Buyers' Guide†
0076-8596 Midwest Monographs. Series 1 (Drama)
0076-860X Midwest Monographs. Series 2 (Poetry)
0076-8618 Midwest Monographs. Series 3 (Graphic Works)
0076-8626 Midwest Monographs. Series 4 (Translation)
0076-8634 Midwest Monographs. Series 5 (Culture and Criticism)
0076-8642 Mikrochimica Acta. Supplement
0076-8650 Istituto di Ricerche Agrarie, Milan. Contributi†
0076-8669 Universita Cattolica del Sacro Cuore, Milan. Contributi. Serie Terza. Scienze Storiche†
0076-8677 Universita Cattolica del Sacro Cuore, Milan. Contributi. Serie Terza. Scienze Filosofiche†
0076-8685 Universita Cattolica del Sacro Cuore, Milan. Contributi. Serie Terza. Scienze Filologiche e Letteratura†
0076-8693 Universita Cattolica del Sacro Cuore, Milan. Contributi. Serie Terza. Scienze Psicologiche†
0076-8707 Universita Cattolica del Sacro Cuore, Milan. Istituto di Archeologia. Contributi†
0076-8715 Universita Cattolica del Sacro Cuore, Milan. Saggi e Ricerche. Serie Terza. Scienze Filologiche e Letteratura†
0076-8723 Universita Cattolica del Sacro Cuore, Milan. Saggi e Ricerche. Serie Terza. Scienze Filosofiche†
0076-8731 Universita Cattolica del Sacro Cuore, Milan. Saggi e Ricerche. Serie Terza. Scienze Geografiche†
0076-874X Universita Cattolica del Sacro Cuore, Milan. Saggi Ericerche. Serie Terza. Scienze Psicologiche†
0076-8758 Universita Cattolica del Sacro Cuore, Milan. Saggi e Ricerche. Serie Terza. Scienze Storiche†
0076-8766 Mildex Motor Book†
0076-8782 Military Year Book
0076-8790 Milla Wa-Milla
0076-8812 Millesime
0076-8820 Milton Studies
0076-8839 Milu; Wissenschaftliche und Kulturelle Mitteilungen aus dem Tierpark Berlin
0076-8847 M I M S Desk Reference
0076-8855 Brazil. Tribunal Regional do Trabalho. Tercera Regiao. Revista
0076-8863 Universidade Federal de Minas Gerais. Escola de Veterinaria. Arquivos
0076-8871 Universidade Federal de Minas Gerais. Revista†
0076-8901 Mindolo News Letter
0076-891X M W V /A E V Jahresbericht
0076-8944 Minerals, Rocks and Inorganic Materials *changed to* Minerals and Rocks
0076-8952 U.S. Bureau of Mines. Minerals Yearbook
0076-8960 Minerva; Jahrbuch der Gelehrten Welt *changed to* Minerva; Internationales Verzeichnis Wissenschaftlicher Institutionen
0076-8987 Mining in Rhodesia *changed to* Mining in Zimbabwe
0076-8995 Mining Annual Review
0076-9010 Zambia Mining Yearbook
0076-9029 Minkus Austria, Switzerland, Lichtenstein Stamp Catalog†
0076-9037 Minkus British Commonwealth Stamp Catalog†
0076-9045 Minkus Germany and Colonies Stamp Catalog†
0076-9053 Minkus Italy and Colonies, San Marino and Vatican Stamp Catalog†
0076-9061 Minkus New American Stamp Catalog
0076-907X Minkus New World Wide Stamp Catalog
0076-9088 Minkus Russia, Poland, Hungary, Romania, Czechoslovakia Stamp Catalog†
0076-9096 Minneapolis Institute of Arts. Annual Report
0076-910X Minneapolis Institute of Arts. Bulletin
0076-9118 Minnesota. Department of Human Rights. Biennial Report
0076-9126 Minnesota. Department of Manpower Services. Annual Report *changed to* Minnesota. Department of Economic Security. Annual Report
0076-9134 Minnesota. Division of Game and Fish. Technical Bulletin *changed to* Minnesota. Division of Fish & Wildlife. Technical Bulletin
0076-9142 Minnesota Drama Editions
0076-9150 Minnesota Fisheries Investigations
0076-9169 Minnesota. Geological Survey. Bulletin†
0076-9177 Minnesota. Geological Survey. Report of Investigations
0076-9185 Minnesota. Geological Survey. Special Publication Series†
0076-9215 Minnesota Monographs in the Humanities
0076-9223 Minnesota Private College Fund. Report
0076-9258 Minnesota Studies in the Philosophy of Science
0076-9266 Minnesota Symposia on Child Psychology
0076-9274 University of Minnesota. Audio-Visual Library Service. Educational Resources Bulletin
0076-9282 University of Minnesota. Center for Research in Human Learning. Report *changed to* University of Minnesota. Center for Research in Human Learning. Report and Fellowship Offerings
0076-9290 University of Minnesota. Graduate School Research Center. Inventory of Faculty Research†
0076-9312 University of Minnesota Studies in Economics and Business.†
0076-9347 Miscellanea Byzantina Monacensia
0076-9355 Miscellanea Musicologica
0076-9371 Mision Arqueologica Espanola en Nubia. Memorias
0076-9401 Missions to Seamen Handbook *changed to* Missions to Seamen Annual Report
0076-941X Missionswissenschaftliche Abhandlungen und Texte
0076-9428 Missionswissenschaftliche Forschungen
0076-9460 Mississippi Congress of Parents and Teachers. Proceedings
0076-9479 Mississippi Congress of Parents and Teachers. Yearbook
0076-9509 Mississippi State University. Forest Products Utilization Laboratory. Information Series
0076-9517 Mississippi State University. Christian Student Center. Annual Lectureship
0076-9525 M V C Bulletin
0076-9533 Mississippi Water Resources Conference. Proceedings
0076-9541 Missouri Archaeological Society. Memoir Series
0076-955X Missouri Archaeological Society. Newsletter
0076-9576 Missouri Archaeologist
0076-9606 Missouri. Division of Geological Survey and Water Resources. Engineering Geology Series
0076-9614 Missouri. Division of Geological Survey and Water Resources. Water Resources Report
0076-9630 Missouri Handbook Series
0076-9649 Missouri Literary Frontiers Series
0076-9657 University of Missouri, St. Louis. Center for International Studies. Monograph
0076-9665 University of Missouri, Columbia. Mathematical Sciences Technical Reports
0076-969X University of Missouri. College of Business and Public Administration. Office of Research, Annual Report†
0076-9703 University of Missouri Studies
0076-9711 University of Missouri, Columbia. Veterinary Medical Diagnostic Laboratory. Annual Report
0076-9754 Mittellateinische Studien und Texte
0076-9762 Mittellateinisches Jahrbuch
0076-9770 Moana; Estudios de Antropologia Oceanica
0076-986X Current Population Reports, P-20: Population Characteristics. Mobility of the Population of the United States *changed to* Current Population Reports: Population Characteristics. Geographic Mobility
0076-9878 Moccasin Telegraph
0076-9894 Modern America
0076-9908 Modern Analytic and Computational Methods in Science and Mathematics
0076-9916 Modern Approaches to the Diagnosis and Instruction of Multi-Handicapped Children
0076-9924 Modern Aspects of Electrochemistry
0076-9932 Modern Brewery Age Blue Book
0076-9959 Modern Drug Encyclopedia and Therapeutic Index
0076-9967 Modern Filologiai Fuzetek

0076-9983 Modern Humanities Research Association. Monograph *changed to* Modern Humanities Research Association. Publications
0076-9991 Modern Machine Shop N C Guidebook and Directory *changed to* Modern Machine Shop NC/CAM Guidebook
0077-0000 Modern Materials. Advances in Development and Applications
0077-0027 Modern Middle East Series
0077-0035 Modern Packaging Encyclopedia
0077-0043 Modern Perspectives in Psychiatry
0077-0078 Modern Problems in Ophthalmology *see* 0250-3751
0077-0086 Modern Problems in Paediatrics
0077-0094 Modern Problems of Pharmacopsychiatry
0077-0108 Modern Publicity
0077-0159 Modern Trends in Orthopaedics
0077-0167 Modern Vocational Trends Reference Handbook†
0077-0175 Modern Wood *changed to* Treated Wood Perspectives
0077-0205 Moebel-Industrie und Ihre Helfer
0077-0221 Molecular Biology, Biochemistry and Biophysics
0077-023X Molecular Biology; Proceedings of the International Conference
0077-0264 University of the West Indies, Jamaica. Department of Geography. Occasional Publications Series†
0077-0272 University of the West Indies, Jamaica. Department of Geography. Research Notes Series†
0077-0280 Monarchist Book Review
0077-0299 Monarchist Press Association. Historical Series
0077-0353 Centre pour l'Etude des Problemes de Monde Musulman Contemporain. Initiations
0077-0361 Mondo†
0077-0396 Mongolia Society. Occasional Papers
0077-040X Monitor
0077-0418 Monks Wood Experimental Station. Report *changed to* Great Britain. Institute of Terrestrial Ecology. Report
0077-0426 Great Britain. Monks Wood Experimental Station. Symposia *changed to* Great Britain. Institute of Terrestrial Ecology. Symposia
0077-0434 Monnaies, Prix, Conjoncture
0077-0442 Monografias de Filosofia Juridica y Social
0077-0469 Monografias de Psicologia, Normal y Patologica
0077-0485 Monografie Biochemiczne
0077-0493 Monografie di Archeologia Libica
0077-0507 Monografie Matematyczne
0077-0515 Monografie Psychologiczne
0077-0523 Monografie Slaskie Ossolineum
0077-0531 Monografie Slawistyczne
0077-054X Monografie z Dziejow Nauki i Techniki
0077-0558 Monografie z Dziejow Oswiaty
0077-0574 Monograph Series in Probability and Statistics†
0077-0582 Monograph Series in World Affairs
0077-0612 Monograph Series on Languages and Linguistics *see* 0196-7207
0077-0620 Monograph Series on Schizophrenia
0077-0639 Monographiae Biologicae
0077-0647 Monographiae Biologicae Canarienses
0077-0655 Monographiae Botanicae
0077-0663 Monographie der Flaumeichen-Buschwaelder
0077-0671 Monographien aus dem Gesamtgebiete der Psychiatrie - Psychiatry Series
0077-0698 Monographien zur Angewandten Entomologie
0077-0701 Monographies de l'Industrie et du Commerce en France
0077-071X Monographies Francaises de Psychologie
0077-0728 Monographies Juridiques
0077-0744 Monographs and Textbooks in Material Science
0077-0752 Monographs and Texts in the Behavioral Sciences
0077-0760 Monographs in Allergy
0077-0795 Monographs in Chemistry in Non-Aqueous Ionizing Solvents
0077-0809 Monographs in Clinical Cytology
0077-0817 Monographs in Computer Science and Computer Applications
0077-0825 Monographs in Developmental Biology
0077-0833 Monographs in Electroanalytical Chemistry and Electrochemistry
0077-085X Monographs in Geology and Paleontology
0077-0868 Monographs in Hormone Research *see* 0301-3073
0077-0876 Monographs in Human Genetics
0077-0884 Monographs in Macromolecular Chemistry
0077-0892 Monographs in Oral Science
0077-0906 Monographs in Organic Functional Group Analysis *changed to* Analysis of Organic Materials: an International Series of Monographs
0077-0914 Monographs in Paediatrics
0077-0922 Monographs in Pathology
0077-0930 Monographs in Population Biology
0077-0949 Monographs in Statistical Physics and Thermodynamics†
0077-0965 Monographs in Virology
0077-099X Monographs on Atherosclerosis
0077-1007 Monographs on Education
0077-1015 Monographs on Endocrinology
0077-1023 Monographs on Immunology
0077-1031 Monographs on Linguistic Analysis
0077-104X Monographs on Oceanographic Methodology
0077-1074 London School of Economics Monographs on Social Anthropology
0077-1090 Montana. Bureau of Mines and Geology. Bulletin
0077-1104 Montana. Bureau of Mines and Geology. Directory of Mining Enterprises
0077-1112 Montana. Bureau of Mines and Geology. Ground Water Reports *see* 0077-1090
0077-1120 Montana. Bureau of Mines and Geology. Memoir
0077-1139 Montana. Bureau of Mines and Geology. Special Publications
0077-1147 Montana Journalism Review
0077-1155 University of Montana. Forest and Conservation Experiment Station, Missoula. Bulletin.
0077-1163 University of Montana. Forest and Conservation Experiment Station, Missoula. Research Notes.
0077-118X University of Montana. Department of Antropology. Contributions to Anthropology
0077-1198 Montana Vital Statistics
0077-1201 Montana. Water Resources Board. Inventory Series
0077-1228 Instituto Tecnologico y de Estudios Superiores. Publicaciones. Serie Historia
0077-1236 Instituto Tecnologico y de Estudios Superiores. Publicaciones. Serie Letras
0077-1244 Museo Nacional de Historia Natural. Communicaciones Antropologicas
0077-1252 Universidad de Uruguay. Departamento de Literatura Iberoamericana Publicaciones
0077-1260 Universidad de Uruguay. Facultad de Agronomia. Boletin
0077-1279 Universidad de la Republica. Facultad de Agronomia. Publicacion Miscelanea
0077-1287 Universidad de la Republica. Instituto de Administracion. Cuaderno
0077-1295 Universidad de Uruguay. Instituto de Mathematica y Estadistica. Publicaciones Didacticas
0077-1309 Montre Suisse. Annuaire
0077-1317 Jardin Botanique de Montreal. Annuelles et Legumes†
0077-1325 Jardin Botanique de Montreal. Memoire
0077-1341 Universite de Montreal. Ecole de Bibliotheconomie. Publications
0077-1376 Monumenta Aegyptiaca
0077-1384 Monumenta Americana
0077-1392 Monumenta Antiquitatis Extra Fines Hungariae Reperta Quae in Museo Artium Hungarico Aliisque Museis et Collectionibus Hungaricis Conservantur
0077-1406 Monumenta Artis Romanae
0077-1414 Monumenta Chartae Papyraceae Historiam Illustrantia
0077-1430 Monumenta Historica Budapestinensia
0077-1449 Monumenta Historica Ordinis Minorum Capuccinorum
0077-1457 Monumenta Iuris Canonici
0077-1465 Monumenta Musicae in Polonia
0077-1473 Monumenta Musicae Suecicae
0077-1481 Monumenta Paedagogica
0077-149X Monumenta Serica
0077-1503 Monuments of Renaissance Music
0077-152X Moravske Numismaticke Zpravy
0077-1546 Mortgage Banking: Financial Statements and Operating Ratios
0077-1554 Moscow Mathematical Society. Transactions
0077-1562 Gosudarstvennyi Muzei Izobrazitel'nykh Iskusstv im. Pushkina. Soobshcheniya
0077-1570 Motocyclo Catalogue
0077-1589 Motor Cycle Diary
0077-1597 Motor Industry of Great Britain
0077-1600 Motor Manual
0077-1619 Motor Traffic in Sweden
0077-1643 Motor Truck Facts *see* 0146-9932
0077-166X Motorboote und Yachten
0077-1678 Motorcycle Buyer's Guide
0077-1694 Motoring in Malaya
0077-1716 Motor Parts and Time Guide
0077-1724 Motor Truck & Diesel Repair Manual *see* 0098-3624
0077-1740 Mount Zion Hospital and Medical Center, San Francisco. Bulletin
0077-1759 Mountain World†
0077-1767 Movimento Natural de la Poblacion de Espana
0077-1775 Moyens de la Recherche Scientifique et Technique en Haute-Normandie.†
0077-1791 Instituto de Investigacao Agronomica de Mocambique. Centro de Documentacas Agraria. Memorias
0077-1805 Mozart-Jahrbuch
0077-1813 Muelleria
0077-1864 Muenchner Entomologische Gesellschaft. Mitteilungen
0077-1872 Muenchner Germanistische Beitraege
0077-1880 Muenchener Indologische Studien
0077-1899 Muenchner Jahrbuch der Bildenden Kunst
0077-1902 Muenchner Studien zur Sozial- und Wirtschaftsgeographie
0077-1910 Muenchener Studien zur Sprachwissenschaft
0077-1929 Universitaet Muenster. Astronomisches Institut. Mitteilungen
0077-1937 Universitaet Muenster. Astronomisches Institut. Sonderdrucke
0077-1945 Universitaet Muenster. Institut fuer Christliche Sozialwissenschaften. Schriften†
0077-1953 Fontes et Commentationes†
0077-197X Universitaet Muenster. Institut fuer Missionswissenschaft. Veroeffentlichungen
0077-1996 Muenstersche Beitraege zur Deutschen Literaturwissenschaft
0077-2003 Muenstersche Beitraege zur Vor- und Fruehgeschichte
0077-2011 Muensterschwarzacher Studien
0077-202X Multihull International Catalogue Annual†
0077-2046 Multilingual Forestry Terminology Series
0077-2054 Mundo Antiguo
0077-2062 Statistisches Jahrbuch Muenchen
0077-2070 Bayerische Staatssammlung fuer Palaeontologie und Historische Geologie. Mitteilungen
0077-2089 Technische Universitaet Muenchen. Jahrbuch†
0077-2100 Universitaet Muenchen. Geophysikalisches Observatorium, Fuerstenfeldbruck. Veroeffentlichungen. Serie B
0077-2119 Westfaelische Wilhelms-Universitaet Muenster. Institut fuer Kreditwesen. Schriftenreihe
0077-2127 Universitaet Muenchen. Wirtschaftsgeographisches Institut. "W G I"-Berichte zur Regionalforschung
0077-2135 Zoologische Staatssammlung, Muenchen. Veroeffentlichungen
0077-2143 Municipal Association of Victoria. Minutes of Proceedings of Annual Session
0077-2151 Municipal Index
0077-216X Michigan Municipal League. Salaries, Wages and Fringe Benefits for Michigan Villages and Cities 1000-4000 Population
0077-2178 Municipal Waste Facilities in the U. S
0077-2186 Municipal Year Book
0077-2194 Muse
0077-2208 Museion
0077-2216 Museu Paraense Emilio Goeldi. Boletim Botanica. Nova Serie
0077-2224 Museu Paraense Emilio Goeldi. Boletim Zoologia. Nova Serie
0077-2240 Museu Paraense Emilio Goeldi. Publicacoes Avulsas
0077-2267 Museums and Galleries *see* 0141-6723
0077-2275 Museum Boymans-van Beuningen. Agenda-Diary
0077-2291 Museum fuer Ur- und Fruehgeschichte Thueringens. Veroeffentlichungen
0077-2313 Museum Publications†
0077-233X Museums and Monuments Series
0077-2348 Museums Journal of Pakistan
0077-2356 Insects†
0077-2364 Mushroom Science
0077-2372 Music Handbook
0077-2402 Music Educators National Conference. Selective Music List: Vocal Solos and Ensembles
0077-2410 Music in Higher Education
0077-2429 Music Indexes and Bibliographies
0077-2445 Music Library Association. Index Series *see* 0094-6478
0077-2461 Musica Disciplina
0077-247X Musica Medii Aevi
0077-2488 Musicologica Hungarica. Neue Folge
0077-2496 Musicological Studies and Documents
0077-250X Musicology
0077-2518 Musik i Sverige
0077-2526 Musikalische Denkmaeler
0077-2542 Musk-Ox
0077-2577 Muzea Walki
0077-2615 Mystic Seaport Manuscripts Inventory
0077-2623 N A S A-University Conference on Manual Control (Papers)
0077-2631 N H K Technical Monograph
0077-264X Nagoya University. Research Institute of Atmospherics. Proceedings
0077-2658 Nagyuzemi Gazdalkodas Kerdesei
0077-2666 Nairobi Airport. Annual Report
0077-2690 Names in South Carolina
0077-2704 Namn och Bygd
0077-2712 Universite de Nancy II. Centre de Recherches et d'Applications Pedagogiques en Langues. Melanges
0077-2720 Universite de Nancy II. Centre Europeen Universitaire. Memoires
0077-2739 Nanta Mathematica
0077-2747 Nanyang University Journal†
0077-2755 Napao: A Saskatchewan Anthropology Journal
0077-2763 Istituto Universitario Orientale di Napoli. Annali. Sezione Germanica
0077-2771 Istituto Universitario Orientale di Napoli. Annali. Sezione Slava
0077-2798 National Bank of Yugoslavia. Annual Report
0077-2801 Narradores de Arca

0077-281X University of Rhode Island. Narragansett Marine Laboratory. Collected Reprints *changed to* University of Rhode Island. Graduate School of Oceanography. Collected Reprints
0077-2828 University of Rhode Island. Narragansett Marine Laboratory. Occasional Publication
0077-2836 Narragansett Marine Laboratory. Technical Reports *changed to* University of Rhode Island. Graduate School of Oceanography. Marine Technical Reports
0077-2844 Narrativa Latinoamericana
0077-2879 Nassau Review
0077-2887 Nassauische Annalen
0077-2895 Natal Regional Survey. Additional Report†
0077-2925 National Academy of Sciences. Annual Report
0077-2933 National Academy of Sciences. Biographical Memoirs
0077-2941 National Accounts and Balance of Payments of Rhodesia *changed to* National Accounts of Rhodesia
0077-295X National Accounts of the Maltese Islands
0077-2968 Catalogue of N A L Technical Translations
0077-2976 National Aeronautical Laboratory. Annual Report
0077-300X National Aeronautical Laboratory. Technical Note
0077-3085 National Aeronautics and Space Administration. N A S A Factbook
0077-3093 N A S A Facts
0077-3115 U.S. National Aeronautics and Space Administration. Research and Technology Program Digest. Flash Index *changed to* U.S. National Aeronautics and Space Administration. Research and Technology Operating Plan (RTOP) Summary
0077-3131 National Aeronautics and Space Administration. Technical Notes
0077-314X National Aeronautics and Space Administration. Technical Reports
0077-3158 National Aeronautics and Space Administration. Technical Translations
0077-3166 List of Accredited Schools of Architecture *changed to* Accredited Programs in Architecture
0077-3174 National Art Education Association. Research Monograph
0077-3190 N A F S A Directory
0077-3204 National Association for Physical Education of College Women. Biennial Record†
0077-3212 N A A C P Annual Report
0077-3220 National Association for the Care and Resettlement of Offenders. Papers and Reprints†
0077-3255 National Association of Animal Breeders Annual Proceedings
0077-3263 National Association of Boards of Pharmacy. Proceedings
0077-328X National Association of College Deans and Registrars. Proceedings
0077-3298 N A E S P Convention Reporter†
0077-3336 N A I A Handbook
0077-3344 N A I A Official Record Book
0077-3352 National Association of Jewish Center Workers. Conference Papers
0077-3360 N A M F Accounting Manual
0077-3379 N A M F Management Manual
0077-3387 National Association of Regulatory Utility Commissioners. Proceedings
0077-3409 National Association of Schools of Music. Proceeding of the Annual Meeting
0077-3417 N A S S P Convention Reporter†
0077-3425 National Association of State Universities and Land-Grant Colleges. Appropriations of State Tax Funds for Higher Education
0077-3433 National Association of State Universities and Land-Grant Colleges. Proceedings
0077-3441 National Association of Suggestion Systems. Statistical Report
0077-345X National Association of Teachers' Agencies. List of the Accredited Members
0077-3468 Coordinator
0077-3476 National Association of Training Schools and Juvenile Agencies. Proceedings
0077-3506 National Bank of Ethiopia. Local Prices
0077-3514 National Bank of Greece. Annual Report
0077-3522 National Bank of Pakistan. Report and Statement of Accounts
0077-3549 National Baseball Congress. Official Baseball Annual *changed to* N B C Official Yearbook
0077-3557 National Bible Society of Scotland. Annual Report
0077-3573 National Budget of Norway
0077-3581 National Building Research Institute. Complete List of N B R I Publications
0077-359X National Building Studies (Great Britain) Research Papers†
0077-3603 National Building Studies (Great Britain) Special Reports†
0077-3611 National Bureau of Economic Research. Annual Report
0077-3638 National Bureau of Economic Research. General Series
0077-3654 National Bureau of Economic Research. Technical Papers†
0077-3662 National Cancer Center. Collected Papers
0077-3670 National Cancer Conference. Proceedings
0077-3689 National Cancer Institute of Canada. Report
0077-3719 National Center for Audio Tapes. Catalog
0077-376X National Coal Board (Great Britain). Annual Report and Accounts. Vol. 2, Accounts and Statistical Tables *see* 0307-7691
0077-3786 National Coal Board. Report and Accounts
0077-3794 National Collegiate Athletic Association. Annual Reports.
0077-3808 National Collegiate Athletic Association. Convention Proceedings
0077-3816 National Collegiate Athletic Association. Manual
0077-3824 National Collegiate Championships
0077-3832 National Colloquium on Oral History. Proceedings *see* 0094-0798
0077-3840 National Committee for Audio-Visual Aids in Education. Experimental Development Unit. Report†
0077-3859 National Committee for Audio-Visual Aids in Education. Occasional Paper†
0077-3913 National Conference on Aerospace Meteorology. Proceedings *changed to* Conference on Atmospheric Environment of Aerospace Systems and Applied Meteorology. Preprints
0077-3956 National Conference on Weather Modification. Preprints *changed to* Conference on Planned and Inadvertent Weather Modification. Preprints
0077-3964 National Conference on Weights and Measures. Report
0077-3980 National Congress of Parents and Teachers. Proceedings of Annual Convention *changed to* National Congress of Parents and Teachers. Convention Digest
0077-4006 National Consumer Credit Counseling Service. Proceedings†
0077-4014 Selected and Annotated Bibliography of Reference Materials in Consumer Credit
0077-4022 National Cottonseed Products Association. Trading Rules
0077-4030 National Council for Geographic Education. Yearbook *changed to* National Council for Geographic Education. Pacesetter Series
0077-4065 N C A E R Occasional Papers†
0077-4073 National Council of Churches. Division of Education and Ministry. Audio-Visual Resource Guide†
0077-4081 National Council of Engineering Examiners. Proceedings
0077-409X National Council of Social Service. Annual Report *changed to* National Council for Voluntary Organizations. Annual Report
0077-4103 National Council of Teachers of Mathematics. Yearbook
0077-4111 National Council of the Churches of Christ in the United States of America. Church World Service. Annual Report *changed to* National Council of the Churches of Christ in the U.S.A. Triennial Report
0077-412X National Council of the Churches of Christ in the United States of America. Division of Overseas Ministries. Overseas Ministries
0077-4146 National Council of the Paper Industry for Air and Stream Improvement. Report to Members
0077-4162 National Council on Family Relations. Annual Meeting Proceedings†
0077-4189 National Dahlia Society Annual
0077-4219 National Distribution Directory *changed to* Warehousing/Distribution Directory
0077-4235 U.S. Food and Drug Administration. National Drug Code Directory
0077-4243 National Education Association of the United States. Addresses and Proceedings *see* 0190-7662
0077-4413 National Electronics Conference. Proceedings *changed to* National Electronics Conference-National Communications Forum. Proceedings
0077-4421 National Electronics Conference. Record
0077-443X National Engineering Laboratory, East Kilbridge, Scotland. Annual Report†
0077-4448 National Equine (and Smaller Animals) Defence League. Annual Report
0077-4456 N A L G O Annual Report
0077-4472 National Faculty Directory
0077-4480 National Federation of Plastering Contractors. Year Book
0077-4499 National Federation of Retail Newsagents. National Federation Yearbook†
0077-4510 National Fertilizer Development Center. Annual Report
0077-4529 National Finances; an Analysis of the Revenues and Expenditures of the Government of Canada
0077-4537 National Fire Prevention Gazette
0077-4545 National Fire Protection Association. National Fire Codes
0077-4553 N F P A Technical Committee. Report
0077-457X National Fisherman. Yearbook Issue
0077-4588 National Football League. Record Manual
0077-4596 National Foundation for Education Research in England and Wales. Occasional Publication Series†
0077-4618 National Geographic Books (Series)
0077-4626 National Geographic Society Research Reports
0077-4634 National Governors' Conference. Proceedings of the Annual Meeting *see* 0191-3441
0077-4642 National Guild of Piano Teachers. Guild Syllabus
0077-4685 National Heart Foundation of Australia. Research-In-Progress
0077-4723 National Income Statistics of Thailand
0077-474X National Institute for Architectural Education. Yearbook
0077-4758 National Institute for Personnel Research. Annual Report
0077-4766 National Institute for Personnel Research. List of N I P R Publications
0077-4774 National Institute Social Services Library
0077-4782 National Institute of Agricultural Botany, Cambridge, England. Annual Report of the Council and Accounts
0077-4790 National Institute of Agricultural Botany, Cambridge, England. Journal
0077-4812 National Institute of Agricultural Engineering, Silsoe, England. Translations
0077-4820 National Institute of Agricultural Sciences, Tokyo. Bulletin. Series A (Physics and Statistics)
0077-4839 National Institute of Agricultural Sciences, Tokyo. Bulletin. Series B (Soils and Fertilizers)
0077-4847 National Institute of Agricultural Sciences, Tokyo. Bulletin. Series C (Plant Pathology and Entomology)
0077-4855 National Institute of Agricultural Sciences, Tokyo. Bulletin. Series D (Physiology and Genetics)
0077-4863 National Institute of Agricultural Sciences, Tokyo. Bulletin. Series H (Farm Management, Land Utilization, Rural Life)
0077-4871 National Institute of Agricultural Sciences, Tokyo. Miscellaneous Publication
0077-488X National Institute of Animal Industry, Chiba, Japan. Bulletin
0077-4898 National Institute of Animal Industry, Chiba, Japan. Bulletin Summaries
0077-491X National Institute of Economic and Social Research. Annual Report
0077-4928 National Institute of Economic and Social Research, London. Occasional Papers
0077-4936 National Institute of Economic and Social Research, London. Regional Studies *changed to* National Institute of Economic and Social Research, London. Regional Papers
0077-4944 N I F P General Series
0077-4952 N I F P Manual Series
0077-4960 N I F P Monograph Series
0077-4979 N I F P Report Series
0077-4987 N I F P Technical Paper Series
0077-4995 National Institute of Genetics, Mishima, Japan. Annual Report
0077-5002 National Institute of Hygienic Sciences. Bulletin
0077-5037 Israeli Life Table
0077-5053 Jamaica. National Insurance Scheme. Annual Reports *changed to* Jamaica. Ministry of Social Security. Report
0077-5061 National Investment Bank, Ghana. Report of the Directors *changed to* National Investment Bank, Ghana. Annual Report
0077-507X National Jewish Welfare Board. Yearbook
0077-5088 National Junior Horticultural Association. Newsletter
0077-5096 National Kidney Foundation. Annual Report
0077-5118 National League for Nursing. Associate Degree Education for Nursing
0077-5134 National League for Nursing. League Exchange
0077-5177 National List of Advertisers
0077-5185 National Maritime Board. (Great Britain) Year Book
0077-5193 Sefunim
0077-5223 National Microfilm Association. Proceedings of the Annual Convention *changed to* National Micrographics Association. Proceedings of the Annual Conference
0077-5231 National Minority Business Directory *changed to* Try Us
0077-524X National Observer Index†

0077-5266 National Opinion Research Center. Newsletter
0077-5274 National Opinion Research Center. Report
0077-5282 National Party Platforms. Supplement
0077-5290 National Physical Laboratory, Teddington, England. Annual Report†
0077-5312 National Pig Breeders' Association Herd Book
0077-5320 National Planning Association Center for Development Planning. Planning Methods Series†
0077-5339 National Psychological Association for Psychoanalysis. Bulletin
0077-5347 National Publishing Directory
0077-5355 N R M C A Publication
0077-5371 National Register of Prominent Americans and International Notables
0077-538X National Register of Scholarships and Fellowships†
0077-5401 National Relay Conference. Proceedings
0077-541X Natonal Reprographic Centre for Documentation, Hertford, England. Technical Evaluation Reports
0077-5428 National Research Council, Canada. Associate Committee on Geotechnical Research. Technical Memorandum
0077-5452 National Research Council, Canada. Division of Building Research. Bulletin†
0077-5460 National Research Council, Canada. Division of Building Research. Building Research Note
0077-5479 National Research Council, Canada. Division of Building Research. Computer Program
0077-5487 National Research Council, Canada. Division of Building Research. Fire Research Note†
0077-5495 National Research Council, Canada. Division of Building Research. Fire Study†
0077-5509 National Research Council, Canada. Division of Building Research. Housing Note†
0077-5517 National Research Council, Canada. Division of Building Research. Research Program
0077-5525 National Research Council, Canada. Division of Building Research. Research Paper†
0077-5533 National Research Council, Canada. Division of Building Research. Technical Paper†
0077-5541 National Research Council, Canada. National Aeronautical Establishment. Aeronautical Report (L R Series)
0077-555X National Research Council, Canada. National Aeronautical Establishment. Mechanical Engineering Reports
0077-5568 National Research Council, Canada. National Aeronautical Establishment. Publications List and Supplements
0077-5576 National Science Library of Canada. Annual Report *see* 0703-0320
0077-5584 National Research Council, Canada. Publications
0077-5592 National Research Council, Canada. Space Research Facilities Branch. Report. (SRFB Series)
0077-5606 National Research Council, Canada. Technical Translation
0077-5614 National Cooperative Highway Research Program Reports
0077-5622 Highway Research Board Special Publication *see* 0360-859X
0077-5630 Atoll Research Bulletin
0077-5657 National Rural Electric Cooperative Association. Government Relations Department. Research Division. Research Papers and Circulars.
0077-5673 N S G A Circular
0077-569X National School Boards Association. Yearbook
0077-5703 National Securities and Research Corporation. Annual Forecast
0077-5711 National Shellfisheries Association. Proceedings
0077-5738 National Skeet Shooting Association. Records Annual
0077-5754 National Society for Prevention of Cruelty to Children. Annual Report
0077-5762 National Society for the Study of Education. Yearbook
0077-5770 National Society of Public Accountants. Proceedings of the Annual Professional Institute
0077-5789 National Soybean Processors Association. Yearbook
0077-5819 National Taiwan University. College of Agriculture. Memoirs
0077-5827 National Taiwan University. College of Engineering. Memoirs†
0077-5835 National Taiwan University. College of Law. Journal of Social Science
0077-5843 National Taiwan University. Department of Archaeology and Anthropology. Bulletin
0077-5851 National Taiwan University Journal of Sociology
0077-586X National Tank Truck Carrier Directory
0077-5886 Tire Dealers Survey *see* 0027-7045
0077-5894 National Trade-Index of Southern Africa
0077-5908 Learning Resources Corporation. Selected Reading Services
0077-5916 National Trust for Scotland Yearbook
0077-5932 N U S Yearbook
0077-5940 National Union of Teachers. Annual Report
0077-5959 National University Extension Association. Proceedings†
0077-5975 Nationale-Nederlanden. Annual Report
0077-5983 Nationwide Directory of Men's and Boys Wear Buyers (Exclusive of New York Metropolitan Area)
0077-5991 Nationwide Directory of Women's and Children's Wear Buyers (Exclusive of New York Metropolitan Area)
0077-6009 Nationwide Major Mass Market Merchandisers (Exclusive of New York Metropolitan Area)
0077-6017 Native American Arts†
0077-6025 Natur und Mensch; Jahresmitteilungen der Naturhistorischen Gesellschaft Nuernberg
0077-6033 Natura Jutlandica
0077-6041 Natural Gas Processing Plants in Canada
0077-6084 Natural Resources Law Newsletter
0077-6092 Natural Resources Research
0077-6106 Naturegraph Ocean Guidebooks†
0077-6114 Mouvement Naturel de la Population de la Grece
0077-6122 Naturforschende Gesellschaft in Basel. Verhandlungen
0077-6130 Naturforschende Gesellschaft in Bern. Mitteilungen
0077-6149 Naturhistorische Gesellschaft Nuernberg. Abhandlungen
0077-6157 Naturwissenschaftliche Rundschau. Buecher der Zeitschrift
0077-6165 Naturwissenschaftlicher Verein fuer Schleswig-Holstein. Schriften
0077-6173 Nauheimer Fortbildungs-Lehrgaenge
0077-6181 Nauka dla Wszystkich
0077-619X Nautical Almanac
0077-6211 Nautisches Jahrbuch, oder Ephemeriden und Tafeln
0077-6238 U. S. Naval Institute. Naval Review
0077-6262 Navigation
0077-6270 Navis
0077-6289 Maritime Survey†
0077-6297 Nawpa Pacha
0077-6300 Near and Middle East Series
0077-6319 Near East Foundation. Annual Report
0077-6343 Nebraska Academy of Sciences. Proceedings
0077-6351 Nebraska Academy of Sciences. Transactions
0077-636X Nebraska. Equal Opportunity Commission. Annual Report†
0077-6378 University of Nebraska. School of Journalism. Depth Report
0077-6386 University of Nebraska Studies. New Series
0077-6394 Nebraska Water Resources Research Institute, University of Nebraska. Annual Report of Activities
0077-6408 Nebula Award Stories *see* 0162-3818
0077-6416 Nederlands-Zuidafrikaanse Vereniging. Jaarverslag
0077-6432 Nederlandse Malacologische Vereniging. Correspondentieblad
0077-6440 Nederlandse Vereniging voor Internationaal Recht. Mededelingen
0077-6467 Negev Institute for Arid Zone Research, Beer-Sheva, Israel. Report for Year *changed to* Ben-Gurion University of the Negev. Research and Development Authority. Scientific Activities.
0077-6475 Negro American Biographies and Autobiographies
0077-6483 Negro in the Congressional Record
0077-6513 Nelson Gallery and Atkins Museum. Bulletin
0077-6521 Neo-Hellenika
0077-653X Neodidagmata
0077-6548 Nepal Industrial Development Corporation. Annual Report
0077-6556 Nepal Industrial Development Corporation. Industrial Digest
0077-6564 Nepal Industrial Development Corporation. Statistical Abstracts
0077-6572 Nepal Law Translation Series *changed to* Nepal Miscellaneous Series
0077-6580 Nepal Rastra Bank. Report of the Board of Directors *changed to* Nepal Rastra Bank. Annual Report
0077-6599 Neprajzi Ertesito
0077-6602 Neprajzi Tanulmanyok
0077-6610 Nerthus†
0077-6645 Jaarstatistiek van de in-en Uitvoer per Land van de Nederlandse Antillen
0077-6653 Jaarstatistiek van de in-en Uitvoer per Goederensoort van de Nederlandse Antillen
0077-6661 Netherlands Antilles. Bureau voor de Statistiek. Statistisch Jaarboek
0077-667X Netherlands Antilles. Bureau voor de Statistiek. Statistiek van de Meteorologische Waarnemingen in de Nederlandse Antillen
0077-6688 Netherlands. Centraal Bureau voor de Statistiek. Bezoek aan Vermakelijkheidsinstellingen. Attendance at Public Entertainments
0077-670X Belastingdruk in Nederland
0077-6718 Netherlands. Centraal Bureau voor de Statistiek. Beleggingen van Institutionele Beleggers. Investments of Institutional Investors
0077-6726 Netherlands. Centraal Bureau voor de Statistiek. Bibliografie van Regionale Onderzoekingen Op Sociaalwetenschappelijk Terrein. Bibliography of Regional Studies in the Social Sciences
0077-6734 Netherlands. Centraal Bureau voor de Statistiek. Criminele Statistiek. Criminal Statistics
0077-6742 Netherlands. Centraal Bureau voor de Statistiek. Diagnosestatistiek Bedrijfsverenigingen (Omslagleden). Social Insurance Sickness Statistics
0077-6750 Nederlandse Jeugd en Haar Onderwijs
0077-6769 Ontwikkeling van het Onderwijs in Nederland
0077-6777 Sportaccommodatie in Nederland
0077-6785 Netherlands. Centraal Bureau voor de Statistiek. Voorziening in de Behoefte aan Onderwijzers Bij het Lager Onderwijs. Supplying the Need for Teachers in Elementary Education
0077-6793 Netherlands. Centraal Bureau voor de Statistiek. Faillissementsstatistiek. Bankruptcies
0077-6815 Netherlands. Centraal Bureau voor de Statistiek. Gevangenisstatistiek. Statistics of Prisons
0077-6823 Netherlands. Centraal Bureau voor de Statistiek. Hypotheken en Hypotheekbanken. Statistics of Mortgages *changed to* Netherlands. Centraal Bureau voor de Statistiek. Hypotheken. Statistics of Mortgages
0077-684X Netherlands. Centraal Bureau voor de Statistiek. Justitiele Statistiek. Judicial Statistics
0077-6858 Statistical Yearbook of the Netherlands
0077-6866 Netherlands. Centraal Bureau voor de Statistiek. Nationale Rekeningen. National Accounts
0077-6874 Nederlandse Schadeverzekeringsmaatschappijen
0077-6882 Netherlands. Centraal Bureau voor de Statistiek. Naamlijsten voor de Statistiek van de Buitenlandse Handel. List of Goods for the Statistics of Foreign Trade
0077-6890 Netherlands. Centraal Bureau voor de Statistiek. Naamlijsten voor de Statistiek van de Buitenlandse Handel. Supplement. List of Goods for the Statistics of Foreign Trade. Supplement
0077-6904 Omvang der Vakbeweging in Nederland
0077-6912 Netherlands. Centraal Bureau voor de Statistiek. Produktiestatistieken. Production Statistics of Individual Industries†
0077-6947 Netherlands. Centraal Bureau voor de Statistiek. Statistisch Bulletin
0077-6955 Netherlands. Centraal Bureau voor de Statistiek. Statistiek der Branden. Fire Statistics
0077-6963 Netherlands. Centraal Bureau voor de Statistiek. Statistiek der Lonen in de Landbouw. Statistics of Wages in Agriculture
0077-698X Netherlands. Centraal Bureau voor de Statistiek. Statistiek der Motorrijtuigen *changed to* Netherlands. Centraal Bureau voor de Statistiek. Statistiek der Motorvoertuigen. Statistics of Motor Vehicles
0077-6998 Statistiek der Rijksfinancien
0077-7005 Netherlands. Centraal Bureau voor de Statistiek. Statistiek der Spaarbanken. Statistical View of the Savings Banks†
0077-7013 Netherlands. Centraal Bureau voor de Statistiek. Statistiek der Verkiezingen. Gemeenteraden. Election Statistics. Municipal Councils
0077-7021 Netherlands. Centraal Bureau voor de Statistiek. Statistiek der Verkiezingen. Provinciale Staten. Election Statistics. Provincial Councils
0077-703X Netherlands. Centraal Bureau voor de Statistiek. Statistiek der Verkiezingen. Tweede Kamer der Staten-Generaal. Election Statistics. Second Chamber of the States-General
0077-7048 Netherlands. Centraal Bureau voor de Statistiek. Statistische en Econometrische Onderzoekingen. Statistical and Econometric Studies *changed to* Netherlands. Centraal Bureau voor de Statistiek. Statistische Onderzoekingen
0077-7056 Speur- en Ontwikkelingswerk in Nederland
0077-7064 Netherlands. Centraal Bureau voor de Statistiek. Statistical Studies
0077-7072 Netherlands. Centraal Bureau voor de Statistiek. Statistiek van de Algemene Bijstand. Statistics of Public Assistance
0077-7099 Netherlands. Centraal Bureau voor de Statistiek. Statistiek van de Bejaardenoorden. Homes for the Aged

ISSN	Title
0077-7102	Netherlands. Centraal Bureau voor de Statistiek. Statistiek van de Internationale Binnenvaart. Statistics of the International Inland Shipping
0077-7110	Netherlands. Centraal Bureau voor de Statistiek. Statistiek van de Investeringen in Vaste Activa in de Industrie *changed to* Netherlands. Centraal Bureau voor de Statistiek. Statistiek van de Investeringen in Vaste Activa in de Nijverheid. Statistics on Fixed Capital Formation in Industry
0077-7129	Netherlands. Centraal Bureau voor de Statistiek. Statistiek van de Koopvaardijvloot. Statistics of the Merchant Marine
0077-7137	Netherlands. Centraal Bureau voor de Statistiek. Statistiek van de Luchtvaart. Civil Aviation Statistics
0077-7145	Netherlands. Centraal Bureau voor de Statistiek. Statistiek van de Land- en Tuinbouw. Statistics of Agriculture
0077-7161	Statistiek van de Scheepvaartbeweging in Nederland
0077-7188	Netherlands. Centraal Bureau voor de Statistiek. Statistiek van de Uitgaven der Overheid voor Onderwijs. Statistics of the Expenditure of the State, the Provinces and the Municipalities on Education
0077-7196	Netherlands.Centraal Bureau voor de Statistiek. Statistiek van de Uitgaven der Overheid voor Cultuur en Recreatie *changed to* Netherlands. Centraal Bureau voor de Statistiek. Statistiek van de Inkomsten en Uitgaven der Overheid voor Cultuur en Recreatie. Statistics of Government Expenditure on Culture and Recreation
0077-720X	Netherlands. Centraal Bureau voor de Statistiek. Statistiek van de Uitgaven der Overheid voor Onderwijs, Wetenschap en Cultuur. Statistics of the Expenditure of the State, the Provinces and the Municipalities on Education, Science and Culture†
0077-7218	Netherlands. Centraal Bureau voor de Statistiek. Statistiek van de Voorlichting Bij Beroepskeuze. Statistics of Vocational Guidance and Selection of Personnel *changed to* Netherlands. Centraal Bureau voor de Statistiek. Statistiek van de Voorlichting Bij Scholen en Beroepskeuze. Statistics of Vocational Guidance
0077-7226	Netherlands. Centraal Bureau voor de Statistiek. Statistiek van de Gemeentewege per Leerling Beschikbaar Gestelde Bedragenter Bestrijding van de Materiele Exploitatiekosten der Lagere Scholen. Statistics of the Amounts per Pupil Provided by the Municipality to Meet the Material Cost of Elementary Education *changed to* Netherlands. Centraal Bureau voor de Statistiek. Per Leerling Beschikbaar Gestelde Bedragen voor het Lager Onderwijs. Amounts per Pupil Provided for Primary Education
0077-7234	Netherlands. Centraal Bureau voor de Statistiek. Statistiek van de Verkeersongevallen op de Openbare Weg. Statistics of Road-Traffic Accidents
0077-7242	Netherlands. Centraal Bureau voor de Statistiek. Statistiek van de Visserij. Statistics of Fisheries
0077-7250	Netherlands. Centraal Bureau voor de Statistiek. Statistiek van de Zeevaart. Statistics of Seaborne Shipping
0077-7269	Netherlands. Centraal Bureau voor de Statistiek. Statistiek van Het Binnenlands Goederenvervoer. Statistics of Internal Goods Transport in the Netherlands
0077-7285	Netherlands. Centraal Bureau voor de Statistiek. Statistiek van het Beroepsonderwijs *changed to* Netherlands. Centraal Bureau voor de Statistiek. Statistiek van het Beroepsonderwijs: Technisch en Nautisch Onderwijs. Statistics on Vocational Training
0077-7293	Netherlands. Centraal Bureau voor de Statistiek. Statistiek van Het Internationaal Goederenvervoer. Statistics of the International Goods Traffic
0077-7307	Netherlands. Centraal Bureau voor de Statistiek. Statistiek van het Kunstonderwijs. Statistics on Art Colleges *changed to* Netherlands. Centraal Bureau voor de Statistiek. Statistiek van het Beroepsonderwijs: Kunstonderwijs. Art Colleges
0077-7315	Netherlands. Centraal Bureau voor de Statistiek. Statistiek van Het Kleuteronderwijs. Statistics of Nursery Schools†
0077-7323	Netherlands. Centraal Bureau voor de Statistiek. Statistiek van het Kweekschoolonderwijs. Statistics on Teacher Training Colleges *changed to* Netherlands. Centraal Bureau voor de Statistiek. Statistiek van het Beroepsonderwijs: Opleidingsscholen Kleuterleidsters en Pedagogische Academies
0077-7331	Netherlands. Centraal Bureau voor de Statistiek. Statistiek van het Land- en Tuinbouwonderwijs. Statistics Concerning Agricultural and Horticultural Education *changed to* Netherlands. Centraal Bureau voor de Statistiek. Statistiek van het Beroepsonderwijs: Agrarisch Onderwijs
0077-734X	Netherlands. Centraal Bureau voor de Statistiek. Statistiek van het Nijverheidsonderwijs *changed to* Netherlands. Centraal Bureau voor de Statistiek. Statistiek van het Beroepsonderwijs: Huishoud- en Nijverheidsonderwijs
0077-7358	Netherlands. Centraal Bureau voor de Statistiek. Statistiek van Het Personenvervoer. Statistics of Passenger Transport
0077-7366	Netherlands. Centraal Bureau voor de Statistiek. Statistiek van het Schriftelijk Onderwijs. Statistics on Correspondence Courses *changed to* Netherlands. Centraal Bureau voor de Statistiek. Statistiek van het Erkende Schriftelijk Onderwijs. Statistics on Correspondence Courses
0077-7374	Netherlands. Centraal Bureau voor de Statistiek. Statistiek van het Sociaal-Pedagogisch Onderwijs. Statistics on Socio-Pedagogic Training *changed to* Netherlands. Centraal Bureau voor de Statistiek. Statistiek van het Beroepsonderwijs: Sociaal-Pedagogisch Onderwijs
0077-7382	Netherlands. Centraal Bureau voor de Statistiek. Statistiek van Het Toneel. Statistics on Theatre Performances†
0077-7390	Netherlands. Centraal Bureau voor de Statistiek. Statistiek van Het Uitgebreid Lager Onderwijs. Statistics of Continued Elementary Education†
0077-7404	Netherlands. Centraal Bureau voor de Statistiek. Statistiek van het Voorbereidend Hoger en Middelbaar Onderwijs: Leraren. Statistics of Secondary Education: Teachers *changed to* Netherlands. Centraal Bureau voor de Statistiek. Statistiek van het W V O, H A V O en M A V O; Instroom, Doorstroom en Uitstroom van Leerlingen
0077-7439	Netherlands. Centraal Bureau voor de Statistiek. Statistiek van Het Wetenschappelijk Onderwijs. Statistics of University Education
0077-7447	Netherlands. Centraal Bureau voor de Statistiek. Statistiek Vreemdelingenverkeer. Tourism Statistics
0077-7463	Netherlands. Centraal Bureau voor de Statistiek. Statistisch Zakboek. Pocket Yearbook
0077-7471	Netherlands. Centraal Bureau voor de Statistiek. Toepassing der Kinderwetten. Application of Juvenile Law *changed to* Netherlands. Centraal Bureau voor de Statistiek. Justiciele Kinderbescherming
0077-748X	Netherlands. Centraal Bureau voor de Statistiek. Toepassing der Wegenverkeerswet. Statistics of the Application of the Road Traffic Act
0077-7498	Netherlands. Centraal Bureau voor de Statistiek. Vermogensverdeling. Regionale Gegevens. Distribution of Personal Wealth. Regional Data
0077-7501	Vakantiebesteding van de Nederlandse Bevolking *changed to* Netherlands. Centraal Bureau voor de Statistiek. Vakantieonderzoek
0077-751X	Netherlands. Centraal Bureau voor de Statistiek. Winststatistiek der Grotere Naamloze Vennootschappen. Profit-Statistics of the Limited Liability Companies
0077-7528	Netherlands. Centraal Bureau voor de Statistiek. Zuivelstatistiek. Dairy Statistics *changed to* Netherlands. Centraal Bureau voor de Statistiek. Productie Statistiek van de Zuivelindustrie. Production Statistics of the Dairy Industry
0077-7536	Netherlands. Centraal Planbureau. Central Economic Plan
0077-7552	Netherlands. Commissie Zeehavenoverleg. Jaarverslag
0077-7560	Netherlands Investment Bank for Developing Countries. Annual Report
0077-7579	Netherlands Journal of Sea Research
0077-7587	Yearbook Geomagnetism: Paramaribo, Surinam
0077-7595	Netherlands Nitrogen Technical Bulletin
0077-7609	Produktschap voor Siergewassen. Jaarverslag *changed to* Produktschap voor Siergewassen. Jaarverslag/Statistiek
0077-7617	Netherlands. Rijks Geologische Dienst. Jaarverslag
0077-7625	Netherlands. Rijkscommissie voor Geodesie. Publications on Geodesy. New Series
0077-7633	Universite de Neuchatel. Faculte des Lettres. Recueil de Travaux
0077-7641	Universite de Neuchatel. Seminaire de Geometrie. Publications. Serie 1. Courtes Publications *changed to* Centre de Recherches en Mathematiques Pures. Publications. Serie 1
0077-765X	Universite de Neuchatel. Seminaire de Geometrie. Publications. Serie 2. Monographies *changed to* Centre de Recherches en Mathematiques Pures. Publications. Serie 2. Monographies
0077-7668	Neudrucke Deutscher Literaturwerke
0077-7676	Neudrucke Deutscher Literaturwerke. Sonderreihe
0077-7684	Neue Beitraege zur Englischen Philologie
0077-7706	Neue Muenstersche Beitraege zur Geschichtsforschung
0077-7714	Neue Musikgeschichtliche Forschungen
0077-7730	Neues aus der Mariahilfer Strasse†
0077-7749	Neues Jahrbuch fuer Geologie und Palaeontologie. Abhandlungen
0077-7757	Neues Jahrbuch fuer Mineralogie. Abhandlungen
0077-7765	Neues Trierisches Jahrbuch *changed to* Neues Trierisches Jahrbuch fuer Heimatpflege und Heimatgeschichte
0077-7773	Neumanns Jahrbuch der Deutschen Versicherungswirtschaft. Teil 1: Personenversicherung (Lebens- und Krankenversicherung)
0077-7781	Neumanns Jahrbuch der Deutschen Versicherungswirtschaft. Teil 2: Schaden- und Rueckversicherung
0077-779X	Neumanns Jahrbuch der Deutschen Versicherungswirtschaft. Teil 3: Institutionen, Uebersichten und Anschriften
0077-7803	Neuro-Ophthalmology
0077-7838	Neuroradiology Workshop
0077-7846	Neuroscience Research
0077-7862	Neusser Jahrbuch fuer Kunst, Kulturgeschichte und Heimatkunde
0077-7870	Nevada. Department of Highways. Planning Survey Division. Status of Road Systems *changed to* Nevada. Department of Transportation. Planning Division. Status of Road Systems
0077-7889	Nevada. Division of Personnel. Biennial Report
0077-7897	Nevada. State Museum, Carson City. Anthropological Papers
0077-7900	Nevada. State Museum, Carson City. Natural History Publications
0077-7919	Nevada. State Museum, Carson City. Occasional Papers
0077-7927	Nevada. State Museum, Carson City. Popular Series
0077-7935	Nevada Studies in History and Political Science
0077-7943	University of Nevada. Bureau of Business and Economic Research. Research Report
0077-7951	Desert Research Institute Publications in the Social Sciences
0077-796X	University of Nevada. Desert Research Institute. Technical Report
0077-7986	New Acronyms and Initialisms *changed to* New Acronyms, Initialisms and Abbreviations
0077-7994	New African Literature and the Arts
0077-801X	New Babylon: Studies in the Social Sciences
0077-8036	New Brunswick Department of Fisheries. Annual Report
0077-8052	New Brunswick. Department of Labour and Manpower. Annual Report
0077-8052	New Brunswick. Department of Labour. Annual Report *see* 0077-8052
0077-8060	New Brunswick. Department of Municipal Affairs. Report
0077-8079	New Brunswick. Department of Youth. Report
0077-8087	New Brunswick. Liquor Control Commission. Report
0077-8109	New Brunswick. Mineral Resources Branch. Report of Investigations
0077-8117	New Brunswick. Research and Productivity Council. Report
0077-8141	University of New Brunswick. Law Journal
0077-8168	New Campus
0077-8206	N D T
0077-8222	New England Guide
0077-8230	New England Papers on Education†
0077-8281	New England Road Builders Association. N E R B A Annual Directory *changed to* Construction Directory
0077-832X	New Hampshire. Agricultural Experiment Station, Durham. Research Reports

1144 ISSN INDEX

0077-8338 New Hampshire. Agricultural Experiment Station, Durham. Station Bulletins
0077-8346 New Hampshire Archeologist
0077-8354 New Hampshire Camping Guide
0077-8362 New Hampshire. Fish and Game Department. Biennial Report
0077-8370 New Hampshire. Fish and Game Department. Management and Research. Biological Survey Series
0077-8389 New Hampshire. Fish and Game Department. Management and Research. Technical Circular Series
0077-8397 New Hampshire. Fish and Game Department. Management and Research. Biological Survey Bulletin
0077-8400 University of New Hampshire. Institute of Natural and Environmental Resources. Research Reports
0077-8419 New Hampshire Vacation Guide *changed to* New Hampshire Recreation Vacation Guide
0077-8427 New Hampshire Winter Holidays†
0077-8435 New Hebrides. Anglo-French Condominium Geological Survey. Annual Reports. *changed to* New Herbrides. Condominium Geological Survey. Annual Reports
0077-8443 New Hebrides. Condominium Geological Survey. Reports
0077-8451 New Jersey Clean Air Council. Report
0077-846X New Jersey. Department of Agriculture. Highlights of the Annual Report
0077-8478 New Jersey. Economic Policy Council. Annual Report of Economic Policy Council and Office of Economic Policy
0077-8508 New Jersey Public Employer-Employee Relations
0077-8516 New Jersey Speech and Hearing Association. Newsletter
0077-8540 New Mexico Agricultural Statistics
0077-8559 New Mexico. Employment Security Commission. Annual Rural Manpower Service Report *changed to* New Mexico. Employment Services Department. Annual Rural Manpower Service Report
0077-8567 New Mexico Geological Society. Guidebook, Field Conference
0077-8575 New Mexico Statistical Abstract
0077-8583 University of New Mexico Art Museum. Bulletin
0077-8591 New Official Guide: Japan
0077-8605 New Orleans Academy of Ophthamology. Transactions
0077-8613 New Perspectives in Political Science†
0077-8621 New Poetry
0077-8656 New South Wales. Board of Architects. Architects Roll
0077-8664 New South Wales. Department of Mines. Annual Report *changed to* New South Wales. Department of Mineral Resources and Development. Annual Report
0077-8672 New South Wales. Department of Mines. Chemical Laboratory. Report
0077-8680 New South Wales. Department of Mines. Coalfields Branch. Reports
0077-8699 New South Wales. Geological Survey. Memoirs: Palaeontology
0077-8699 New South Wales. Department of Mines. Memoirs: Palaeontology *see* 0077-8699
0077-8710 New South Wales. Geological Survey. Memoirs: Geology
0077-8729 New South Wales. Geological Survey. Mineral Industry Series
0077-8737 New South Wales. Geological Survey. Mineral Resources Series
0077-8753 New South Wales National Herbarium. Contributions *see* 0312-9764
0077-8761 Flora of New South Wales.
0077-8788 New South Wales. State Fisheries. Research Bulletin†
0077-8796 University of New South Wales. School of Civil Engineering. U N I C I V Reports. Series I
0077-880X University of New South Wales. School of Civil Engineering. U N I C I V Reports. Series R
0077-8818 University of New South Wales. Water Research Laboratory, Manly Vale. Laboratory Research Reports
0077-8826 New Teacher
0077-8842 New Testament Tools and Studies
0077-8869 New Trade Names in the Rubber and Plastics Industries
0077-8877 New Trends in Biology Teaching
0077-8885 New Trends in Chemistry Teaching
0077-8893 New Trends in Mathematics Teaching
0077-8907 New Trends in Physics Teaching
0077-8931 New York Botanical Garden. Memoirs
0077-894X City College Papers
0077-8958 Metropolitan Museum Journal
0077-8966 New York Agricultural Statistics
0077-8974 New York Crop Reporting Service. Statistics Relative to the Dairy Industry in New York State *changed to* New York Dairy Statistics
0077-9008 New York Psychoanalytic Institute. Kris Study Group. Monograph
0077-9016 New York Public Library. Films
0077-9024 New York Publicity Outlets
0077-9059 New York State Archeological Association. Occasional Papers
0077-9067 New York State Archeological Association. Researches and Transactions
0077-9083 New York State Business Fact Book. Part 1: Business and Manufacturing
0077-9091 New York State Business Fact Book. Part 2: Population and Housing
0077-9105 New York State Business Fact Book. Supplement
0077-9148 New York (State) Crime Victims Compensation Board. Report
0077-9156 New York (State) Department of Commerce. Research Bulletin†
0077-9172 College and University Degrees Conferred, New York State
0077-9180 College and University Enrollment in New York State *see* 0147-5894
0077-9210 Distribution of High School Graduates and College Going Rate, New York State
0077-9229 Public School Professional Personnel Report, New York State
0077-9245 New York (State) Education Department. Public School Professional Personnel Report *changed to* Public School Enrollment and Staff, New York State
0077-9253 Nonpublic School Enrollment and Staff, New York State
0077-9296 New York. State Library, Albany. Checklist of Official Publications of the State of New York
0077-930X New York. State Library, Albany. Division of Library Development. Excerpts from New York State Education Law, Rules of the Board of Regents, and Regulations of the Commissioner of Education Pertaining to Public and Free Association Libraries, Library Systems, Trustees and Librarians
0077-9318 New York. State Library, Albany. Division of Library Development. Institution Libraries Statistics
0077-9326 New York. State Library, Albany. Division of Library Development. Public and Association Libraries Statistics
0077-9334 New York (State) Division of the Budget. New York State Statistical Yearbook
0077-9342 Analysis of School Finances, New York State School Districts
0077-9350 State University of New York at Albany. Faculty Senate. Annual Faculty Assembly Proceedings
0077-9407 New York (State) Upstate Medical Center, Syracuse. Library. Faculty Bibliography†
0077-9415 New York (State) Upstate Medical Center, Syracuse. Library. Library Guide†
0077-9423 New York State Urban Development Corporation. Annual Report
0077-944X New York University. Comparative Criminal Law Project. Publications
0077-9458 New York University. Criminal Law Education and Research Center. Monograph Series
0077-9466 New York University. Institute of Finance. Bulletin *changed to* New York University. Center for the Study of Financial Institutions. Bulletin; Monograph Series in Finance and Economics
0077-9490 New York University. Libraries. Bulletin of the Tamiment Library
0077-9504 New York University Studies in Comparative Literature
0077-9520 New Zealand Agricultural Engineering Institute. Annual Report
0077-9539 Lincoln College. New Zealand Agricultural Engineering Institute. Extension Bulletin†
0077-9563 Lincoln College. New Zealand Agricultural Engineering Institute. Research Publication†
0077-9571 New Zealand Business Who's Who
0077-958X New Zealand. Central Advisory Committee on the Appointments and Promotion of Primary Teachers. Report to the Minister of Education
0077-9601 New Zealand. Department of Scientific and Industrial Research. Annual Report
0077-961X New Zealand. Department of Scientific and Industrial Research. Bulletin
0077-9628 New Zealand. Department of Scientific and Industrial Research. Geological Survey. Bulletin
0077-9636 New Zealand. Department of Scientific and Industrial Research. Information Series
0077-9644 New Zealand. Soil Bureau. Bulletin
0077-9652 New Zealand. Department of Statistics. Annual Report of the Government Statistician
0077-9660 New Zealand. Department of Statistics. Exports
0077-9679 New Zealand. Department of Statistics. Imports
0077-9687 New Zealand. Department of Statistics. Population Census: Ages and Marital Status
0077-9695 New Zealand. Department of Statistics. Population Census: Dwellings
0077-9709 New Zealand. Department of Statistics. Population Census: Education
0077-9717 New Zealand. Department of Statistics. Population Census: General Report
0077-9725 New Zealand. Department of Statistics. Population Census: Households *changed to* New Zealand. Department of Statistics. Population Census: Households, Families & Fertility
0077-9733 New Zealand. Department of Statistics. Population Census: Incomes
0077-9741 New Zealand. Department of Statistics. Population Census: Industries and Occupations
0077-975X New Zealand. Department of Statistics. Population Census: Maori Population and Dwellings
0077-9768 New Zealand. Department of Statistics. Population Census: Provisional Report on Population and Dwellings *changed to* New Zealand. Department of Statistics. Population Census: Provisional Population and Dwelling Statistics
0077-9776 New Zealand. Department of Statistics. Population Census: Race *changed to* New Zealand. Department of Statistics. Population Census: Birthplaces and Ethnic Origin
0077-9784 New Zealand. Department of Statistics. Population Census: Religious Professions
0077-9792 New Zealand. Department of Statistics. Population Census: Increase and Location of Population *changed to* New Zealand. Department of Statistics. Population Census. Location and Increase of Population. Part A: Population Size and Distribution
0077-9792 New Zealand. Department of Statistics. Population Census: Increase and Location of Populaion *changed to* New Zealand. Department of Statistics. Population Census. Location and Increase of Population. Part B: Population Density
0077-9806 New Zealand. Department of Statistics. Report and Analysis of External Trade
0077-9822 New Zealand. Department of Statistics. Statistical Report of Farm Production *see* 0110-4624
0077-9865 New Zealand. Department of Statistics. Industrial Production†
0077-989X New Zealand. Department of Statistics. National Income and Expenditure *see* 0110-344X
0077-9903 New Zealand. Department of Statistics. Statistical Report of Population, Migration and Building. *see* 0110-375X
0077-9911 New Zealand. Department of Statistics. Price, Wages and Labour *see* 0110-5019
0077-9954 New Zealand Economic Papers
0077-9962 New Zealand Entomologist
0077-9997 New Zealand. Forest Research Institute. Report
0078-0006 New Zealand. Forest Research Institute. Technical Paper
0078-0014 New Zealand. Forest Service. Report of the Director General of Forests
0078-0022 New Zealand Geographical Society. Miscellaneous Series
0078-0030 New Zealand Geography Conference Proceedings Series
0078-0049 New Zealand Institute of Economic Research. Discussion Paper
0078-0057 New Zealand Institute of Economic Research. Report
0078-0065 New Zealand Institute of Economic Research. Research Paper
0078-0073 New Zealand Institute of Economic Research. Technical Memorandum
0078-0081 New Zealand Law Register
0078-009X New Zealand Library School, Wellington. Bibliographical Series†
0078-0103 New Zealand Library School, Wellington. Occasional Papers†
0078-0111 New Zealand. Marine Department. Annual Report on Fisheries†
0078-0138 New Zealand. Meat and Wool Boards' Economic Service. Annual Review of the Sheep Industry
0078-0146 New Zealand Medical Records Officers' Association. Conference Proceedings†
0078-0154 New Zealand. National Research Advisory Council. Senior and Post Doctoral Research Fellowship Awards for Research in New Zealand Government Departments
0078-0162 New Zealand. National Research Advisory Council. Report
0078-0170 New Zealand Official Year-Book
0078-0189 New Zealand Pottery and Ceramics Research Association. Technical Report
0078-0197 New Zealand Poultry Board. Report and New Zealand Marketing Authority Report and Statement of Accounts

0078-0219 New Zealand Wheat Review
0078-0243 Newcastle History Monographs
0078-0251 University of Newcastle-Upon-Tyne. Philosophical Society. Proceedings
0078-026X University of Newcastle-Upon-Tyne. Department of Geography. Research Series
0078-0278 Newfoundland and Labrador. Department of Education. Statistical Supplement to the Annual Report†
0078-0286 Newfoundland and Labrador Who's Who
0078-0294 Newfoundland. Department of Social Services. Annual Report
0078-0308 Newfoundland. Mineral Development Division. Geological Survey. Bulletin
0078-0316 Newfoundland Medical Directory
0078-0340 Newfoundland. Mineral Development Division. Information
0078-0359 Newfoundland. Mineral Development Division. Information Circular.
0078-0367 Newfoundland. Mines Branch. Annual Report Series
0078-0375 Newfoundland. Mines Branch. Geological Survey of Newfoundland. Bulletin Series
0078-0383 Newfoundland. Mines Branch. Geological Survey of Newfoundland. Report Series
0078-0421 Newsletters on Stratigraphy
0078-043X Newspaper Press Directory *see* 0141-1772
0078-0448 Israel. Goverment Press Office. Newspapers and Periodicals Appearing in Israel
0078-0502 Niagara Parks Commission. Annual Report
0078-0510 Nicaragua. Direccion General de Aduanas. Memoria
0078-0537 Niederdeutsche Beitraege zur Kunstgeschichte
0078-0545 Niederdeutsches Wort
0078-0561 Niedersaechsisches Jahrbuch fuer Landesgeschichte
0078-057X Nigeria Annual and Trading Directory
0078-0588 Nigeria Assistance Programs of U.S. Non-Profit Organizations†
0078-0596 Nigeria Business Directory
0078-0626 Nigeria. Federal Office of Statistics. Annual Abstract of Statistics
0078-0634 Nigeria. Federal Office of Statistics. Review of External Trade
0078-0642 Nigeria. Federal Office of Statistics. Trade Report
0078-0650 Nigeria Trade Summary†
0078-0677 University of Nigeria. Report on Research†
0078-0685 Nigeria Year Book
0078-0707 Nigerian Chamber of Mines. Annual Review
0078-0715 Nigerian Institute for Oil Palm Research. Journal
0078-0723 Nigerian Institute of International Affairs. Digest of Selected Articles on International Questions†
0078-0731 Nigerian Institute of International Affairs. Lecture Series
0078-074X Nigerian Institute of Social and Economic Research. Annual Report
0078-0758 Nigerian Institute of Social and Economic Research. Information Bulletin *changed to* Nigerian Institute of Social and Economic Research. Bulletin
0078-0758 Nigerian Institute of Social and Economic Research. Information Bulletin†
0078-0766 Nigerian Institute of Social and Economic Research. Library. List of Accessions
0078-0774 Nigerian Law Journal
0078-0782 Nigerian Medical Directory
0078-0804 Nigerian National Advisory Council for the Blind. Annual Report
0078-0820 Nigerian Tobacco Company. Report *changed to* Nigerian Tobacco Company. Annual Report and Accounts
0078-0839 Nippon Veterinary and Zootechnical College. Bulletin
0078-0855 Nityanand Universal Series
0078-0863 Nivel de la Economia Argentina
0078-088X N M R
0078-0898 NMR Data Table for Organic Compounds†
0078-091X Noble Official Catalog of Canada Precancels
0078-0928 Noble Official Catalog of United States Bureau Precancels
0078-0936 Noctes Romanae
0078-0944 Noda Institute for Scientific Research. Report
0078-0952 Nomenclator Zoologicus
0078-0960 Nomenclature des Entreprises Nationales a Caractere Industriel ou Commercial et des Societies d'Economie Mixte d'Interet National
0078-0979 Nomos
0078-0987 Non-Ferrous Metal Works of the World
0078-0995 Non-Metallic Solids
0078-1002 Nonaligned Third World Annual
0078-1029 Nord-Norge Naeringsliv og Oekonomi
0078-1037 Nordelbingen
0078-1045 Nordfriesisches Jahrbuch
0078-1053 Nordicana
0078-1061 Nordisk Medicinhistorisk Aarsbok
0078-107X Nordisk Numismatisk Aarsskrift
0078-1088 Nordisk Statistisk Aarsbok
0078-110X Nordiska Afrikainstitutet. Skriftserie†
0078-1126 N K B Skriftserie
0078-1134 Nordistica Gothoburgensia
0078-1142 Norfolk Broads Holidays Afloat *changed to* Blakes Holidays Afloat
0078-1150 Norfolk Holiday Handbook
0078-1169 Norfolk Record Society. Publications
0078-1185 Norges Bank. Report and Accounts
0078-1193 Norges Geotekniske Institutt. Publikasjon
0078-1207 Norwegian Geotechnical Institute. Technical Report
0078-1215 Norges Handels-Kalender
0078-1223 Norges Landbruksoekonomiske Institutt. Driftsgranskinger i Jordbruker *changed to* Norges Landbruksoekonomiske Institutt. Driftsgranskinger i Jord- og Skogbruk
0078-1231 Norges Teknisk-Naturvitenskapelige Forskningsraad. Aarsberetning
0078-124X Norges Teknisk-Naturvitenskapelige Forskningsraad. Transportoekonomisk Institutt. Aarsberetning *changed to* Transportoekonomisk Institutt. Aarsberetning
0078-1266 Norsk Litteraer Aarbok
0078-1274 North American Association of Alcoholism Programs. Meeting. Selected Papers *changed to* A D P A Selected Papers of Annual Meetings
0078-1282 North American Association of Alcoholism Programs. N A A P Facilities Directory *see* 0092-3826
0078-1304 North American Fauna
0078-1312 North American Flora
0078-1320 North American Forest Soils Conference. Proceedings
0078-1339 North American Protestant Ministries Overseas *see* 0093-8130
0078-1347 North American Radio-T V Guide
0078-1355 North American Wildlife and Natural Resources Conference. Transactions
0078-1371 North Carolina. Division of Health Services. Public Health Statistics Branch. North Carolina Vital Statistics
0078-138X North Carolina. Department of Revenue. Franchise Tax and Corporate Income Tax Bulletins for Taxable Years
0078-1398 North Carolina . Division of Mineral Resources. Special Publication *changed to* North Carolina. Geological Survey Section. Special Publication
0078-1428 North Carolina State University. Development Council. Report
0078-1444 North Carolina State University. School of Design. (Student Publication)
0078-1452 University of North Carolina, Chapel Hill. Graduate School of Business Administration. Technical Papers
0078-1460 University of North Carolina, Greensboro. Faculty Publications
0078-1495 University of North Carolina, Chapel Hill. Institute of Statistics. Mimeo Series
0078-1517 North Carolina State University. Department of Crop Science. Research Report
0078-1525 North Carolina State University. Water Resources Research Insitute. Report
0078-1541 North Dakota Crop and Livestock Statistics
0078-155X North Dakota. Employment Security Bureau. Annual Report
0078-1568 North Dakota. Employment Security Bureau. Biennial Report to the Governor
0078-1576 North Dakota. Geological Survey. Miscellaneous Series
0078-1592 North-Holland Linguistic Series
0078-1622 North Pacific Fur Seal Commission. Proceedings of the Annual Meeting
0078-1630 North Queensland Naturalist
0078-1649 North Staffordshire Journal of Field Studies
0078-1665 Northeast Conference on the Teaching of Foreign Languages. Reports of the Working Committees
0078-1673 Northeast Electronics Research and Engineering Meeting. Record
0078-1681 Northeast Folklore
0078-169X Northeastern University Studies in Rehabilitation
0078-1703 Northeastern Weed Science Society. Proceedings
0078-1711 Northern Cavern and Mine Research Society. Occasional Publications *changed to* Northern Mine Research Society. Occasional Publications
0078-172X Northern History
0078-1746 Northern Ireland. Department of Agriculture. Annual Report on Research and Technical Work
0078-1754 Northern Ireland. Department of Agriculture. Record of Agricultural Research
0078-1762 North-Central State. Ministry of Works. Report *changed to* Kaduna State. Ministry of Works. Report
0078-1770 Northern Virginia Planning District Commission. Annual Report†
0078-1789 Northwest Historical Series
0078-1797 Northwest Wood Products Clinic. Proceedings
0078-1800 Northwestern-Iowa Dealer Reference Manual
0078-1835 Norway. Arbeidsdirektoratet. Aarsmelding
0078-1843 Norway. Fiskeridirektoratet. Skrifter. Serie Fiskeri†
0078-186X Norway. Fiskeridirektoratet. Skrifter. Serie Teknologiske Undersoekelser†
0078-1878 Norway. Statistisk Sentralbyraa. Arbeidsmarkedstatistikk/Labour Market Statistics
0078-1886 Norway. Statistisk Sentralbyraa. Industristatistikk/Industrial Statistics
0078-1894 Norway. Statistisk Sentralbyraa. Jordbruksstatistikk/Agricultural Statistics
0078-1908 Norway. Statistisk Sentralbyraa. Kredittmarked Statistikk/Credit Market Statistics
0078-1916 Norway. Statistisk Sentralbyraa. Loennsstatistikk/Wage Statistics
0078-1924 Norway. Statistisk Sentralbyraa. Oekonomisk Utsyn/Economic Survey
0078-1932 Norway. Statistisk Sentralbyraa. Statistisk Aarbok/Statistical Yearbook
0078-1940 Norway. Statistisk Sentralbyraa. Utenrikshandel/External Trade
0078-1959 Norway. Statistisk Sentralbyraa. Varehandelsstatistikk/Wholesale and Retail Trade Statistics
0078-1967 Norwegian-American Historical Association. Newsletter
0078-1975 Norwegian American Historical Association. Travel and Description Series
0078-1983 Norwegian-American Studies
0078-1991 Norwegian Studies in English
0078-2009 Notas de Algebra y Analisis
0078-2017 Notas de Logica Matematica
0078-2025 Notes for Medical Catalogers
0078-2041 Notes in Anthropology
0078-205X Noticiario Arqueologico Hispanico
0078-2076 University of Notre Dame. Department of Economics. Union-Management Conference. Proceeding
0078-2084 Geographical Field Group (Nottingham). Regional Studies
0078-2106 University of Nottingham. School of Agriculture. Report†
0078-2114 Town and Country Planning Summer School; Report of Proceedings
0078-2122 Nottingham Medieval Studies
0078-2130 O. R. S. T. O. M. Recueil de Travaux. Oceanographie
0078-2157 Nouveautes Techniques Maritimes
0078-2165 Nouvelle Bibliotheque Nervalienne
0078-2211 Nouvelles Economiques
0078-2238 Nova Hedwiga, Beihefte
0078-2246 Nova Kepleriana. Neue Folge
0078-2254 Instituto de Investigacao Agronomica de Angola. Relatorio
0078-2262 Instituto de Investigacao Agronomica de Angola. Serie Cientifica
0078-2270 Instituto de Investigacao Agronomica de Angola. Serie Tecnica
0078-2300 Nova Scotia Community Planning Conference Proceedings
0078-2319 Nova Scotia. Department of Bacteriology. Annual Report†
0078-2351 Nova Scotia. Department of Pathology. Annual Report†
0078-236X Nova Scotia. Department of Public Health. Nutrition Division. Annual Report
0078-2378 Nova Scotia. Emergency Measures Organization. Report
0078-2386 Nova Scotia Fruit Growers Association. Annual Report and Proceedings
0078-2459 Nova Scotia Power Corporation. Annual Report
0078-2483 Nova Scotia Research Foundation. Bulletin†
0078-2491 Nova Scotia Technical College. School of Architecture. Report Series *changed to* Technical University of Nova Scotia. School of Architecture. Report Series
0078-2521 Nova Scotian Institute of Science. Proceedings
0078-253X Novarien
0078-2564 Novos Taxa Entomologicos†
0078-2599 Nuclear Engineering
0078-2602 Nuclear Medicine Seminar†
0078-2610 Nuclear News Buyers Guide
0078-2637 Nuclear Science and Applications
0078-2653 Nuernberger Forschungen
0078-2696 Numismatic Chronicle and Journal
0078-270X Numismatic Literature. Supplement†
0078-2718 Numismatic Notes and Monographs
0078-2726 Numismatica Moravica
0078-2734 Numismatiska Meddelanden
0078-2742 Nuntiaturberichte aus Deutschland Nebst Ergaenzenden Aktenstuecken
0078-2750 Nuova Dirigenza
0078-2769 Nuovi Saggi
0078-2777 Stadtbibliothek Nuernberg. Ausstellungskatalog
0078-2785 Beitraege zur Geschichte und Kultur der Stadt Nuernberg

0078-2807 SIN-Staedtebauinstitut. Schriftenreihe
0078-2815 SIN-Staedtebauinstitut. Studienhefte
0078-2823 SIN-Staedtebauinstitut. Werkberichte
0078-2831 Nursing Education Monographs†
0078-284X Nutrition News in Zambia
0078-2858 Nyelveszeti Tanulmanyok
0078-2866 Nyelvtudomanyi Ertekezesek
0078-2874 O. I. G. G.†
0078-2882 O. P. Market
0078-2890 Oak Ridge Associated Universities. Medical Division. Research Report
0078-2904 Oak Ridge Associated Universities. Report
0078-2920 Oberhessische Gesellschaft fuer Natur- und Heilkunde, Giessen. Berichte
0078-2939 Oberrheinische Geologische Abhandlungen
0078-2947 Oberrheinischer Geologischer Verein. Jahresberichte und Mitteilungen
0078-2963 Obraz Literatury Polskiej
0078-2971 Observation
0078-3005 Occasional Papers in Anthropology
0078-3013 Occasional Papers in Economic and Social History
0078-303X Occasional Papers in English Local History
0078-3048 Occasional Papers in Estate Management
0078-3056 Occasional Papers in Geography
0078-3064 Occasional Papers in Industrial Relations
0078-3072 Occasional Papers in International Affairs *changed to* Harvard Studies in International Affairs
0078-3080 Occasional Papers in Librarianship
0078-3099 Occasional Papers in Modern Languages
0078-3129 Occupational Safety and Health Series
0078-3137 Ocean Engineering Information Series
0078-3153 Ocean Technology†
0078-3161 Oceana Docket Classics†
0078-317X Oceana Docket Series†
0078-3188 Oceanic Linguistics. Special Publications
0078-320X Oceanographic Research Institute, Durban. Investigational Report
0078-3218 Oceanography and Marine Biology
0078-3226 Elsevier Oceanography Series
0078-3234 Oceanologia
0078-3250 Ochrona Przyrody
0078-3269 Octagon Lectures†
0078-3277 Odense University Slavic Studies
0078-3285 Odense University Studies in Art History
0078-3293 Odense University Studies in English
0078-3307 Odense University Studies in History and Social Sciences
0078-3315 Odense University Studies in Linguistics
0078-3323 Odense University Studies in Literature
0078-3331 Odense University Studies in Scandinavian Languages and Literatures
0078-3358 Odontologiska Samfundet i Finland. Aarsbok
0078-3366 Odrodzenie w Polsce†
0078-3374 O'Dwyers Directory of Public Relations Firms
0078-3390 Oekonometrie und Unternehmensforschung
0078-3404 Oekonomische Studientexte
0078-3412 Oenologie Pratique†
0078-3420 Oerlikon Schweissmitteilungen
0078-3439 Oesterreichisches Ost- und Suedosteuropa Institut. Schriftenreihe
0078-3447 Oesterreichische Akademie der Wissenschaften. Almanach
0078-3455 Das Oesterreichische Buch
0078-3463 Oesterreichische Gesellschaft fuer Aussenpolitik und Internationale Beziehungen. Schriftenreihe†
0078-3471 Oesterreichische Gesellschaft fuer Musik. Beitraege
0078-3501 Oesterreichische Komponisten des XX. Jahrhunderts
0078-351X Oesterreichische Moorforschung
0078-3528 Oesterreichische Nationalbank. Bericht ueber das Geschaeftsjahr mit Rechnungsabschluss
0078-3536 Oesterreichische Schriften zur Entwicklungshilfe
0078-3544 Oesterreichische Schul-Statistik†
0078-3552 Oesterreichische Zeitschrift fuer Oeffentliches Recht. Supplement
0078-3560 Oesterreichischer Buchklub der Jugend. Jahrbuch
0078-3579 Oesterreichisches Archaeologisches Institut. Jahreshefte: Grabungen *changed to* Oesterreichisches Archaeologisches Institut. Jahreshefte
0078-3595 Oesterreichisches Wirtschaftsinstitut fuer Strukturforschung und Strukturpolitik. Schriftenreihe
0078-3617 Oesterreichisches Institut fuer Raumplanung. Taetigkeitsbericht
0078-3625 Oesterreichisches Institut fuer Raumplanung. Veroeffentlichungen
0078-3633 Oesterreichisches Jahrbuch fuer Exlibris und Gebrauchsgraphik
0078-3641 Oesterreichisches Kulturinstitut, Rom. Abteilung fuer Historische Studien. Publikationen I. Abteilung: Abhandlungen
0078-365X Oesterreichisches Kulturinstitut, Rom. Abteilung fuer Historische Studien. Publikationen Ii. Abteilung: Quellen
0078-3692 Offshore Europe†
0078-3706 Off-Shore Technology Conference. Record
0078-3714 Offa-Jahrbuch; Vor- und Fruehgeschichte
0078-3722 Office des Communications Sociales, Montreal. Cahiers d'Etudes et de Recherches
0078-3730 Office des Communications Sociales, Montreal. Selection de Films pour Cine Clubs. *changed to* Office des Communications Sociales, Montreal. Selection de Films in 16 MM
0078-3749 Rydge's Office Equipment Buyers Guide
0078-3773 France. Office National d'Etudes et de Recherches Aerospatiales. Activities
0078-3781 France. Office National d'Etudes et de Recherches Aerospatiales. Notes Techniques
0078-379X France. Office National d'Etudes et de Recherches Aerospatiales. Publications
0078-3803 Office Universitaire de Recherche Socialiste. Cahiers
0078-3811 Officer's Guide *see* 0148-6799
0078-382X Official American Basketball Association Guide†
0078-3838 Official Baseball Guide
0078-3846 Official Baseball Rules
0078-3854 Official Catholic Directory
0078-3862 Official National Basketball Association Guide
0078-3889 Official Talent & Booking Directory
0078-3897 Official Touring Guide to East Africa *changed to* A A Guide to Motoring in Kenya
0078-3900 Official World Series Records
0078-3919 Official Directory of the Catholic Church of Australia and Papua-New Guinea, New Zealand and the Pacific Islands *changed to* Official Directory of the Catholic Church of Australia and New Zealand
0078-3927 Official Year Book of the Commonwealth of Australia *changed to* Australia. Bureau of Statistics. Year Book Australia
0078-3943 D C C-Camping Fuehrer Europa
0078-3951 Ohio Agricultural Research and Development Center, Wooster. Research Bulletin
0078-396X Ohio Agricultural Research and Development Center, Wooster. Research Circular
0078-3978 Ohio Agricultural Research and Development Center, Wooster. Research Summary†
0078-3986 Ohio Biological Survey. Biological Notes
0078-3994 Ohio Biological Survey. Bulletin. New Series
0078-4001 Ohio. Division of State Personnel. Annual Report
0078-401X Ohio. Division of Mines. Report
0078-4028 Ohio Fish Monographs *see* 0085-4468
0078-4036 Ohio Game Monographs *see* 0085-4468
0078-4052 Ohio Speech Journal
0078-4087 Ohio State University. College of Administrative Science. Monograph†
0078-4095 Ohio State University. College of Law. Law Forum Series
0078-4109 Ohio State University. Disaster Research Center. D R C - T R *see* 0164-1875
0078-4133 Ohio State University. Disaster Research Center. Report Series
0078-415X Ohio State University. Institute of Polar Studies. Report Series
0078-4184 Kent State University. Center for Business and Economic Research. Comparative Administration Research Institute Series
0078-4192 Kent State University. Center for Business and Economic Research. Labor and Industrial Relations Series
0078-4206 Kent State University. Center for Business and Economic Research. Printed Series
0078-4214 Kent State University. Center for Business and Economic Research. Research Papers
0078-4222 Kent State University. Libraries. Occasional Paper
0078-4230 Ohio University. Center for Educational Research and Service. Pupil Services Series
0078-4265 Oikos. Supplementum†
0078-429X Okayama University. Research Laboratory for Surface Science. Reports
0078-4303 Oklahoma Academy of Science. Proceedings
0078-4311 Oklahoma Academy of Science. Annals†
0078-432X Oklahoma Anthropological Society. Bulletin
0078-4338 Oklahoma Anthropological Society. Newsletter
0078-4362 Oklahoma. Department of Public Welfare. Annual Report *changed to* Oklahoma. Department of Institutions, Social and Rehabilitative Services. Annual Report
0078-4370 Oklahoma. Fishery Research Laboratory, Norman. Bulletin
0078-4389 Oklahoma. Geological Survey. Bulletin
0078-4397 Oklahoma. Geological Survey. Circular
0078-4400 Oklahoma. Geological Survey. Guidebook
0078-4427 Oklahoma State University. College of Business Administration. Extension Service. Business Papers *changed to* Oklahoma State University. College of Business Administration. Working Papers
0078-4435 University of Oklahoma. Center for Economic and Management Research. Monograph Series†
0078-4508 Oklahoma's Grand River Dam Authority. Annual Report
0078-4516 Old Farmer's Almanac
0078-4540 Old Salem Gleaner
0078-4559 Old Sturbridge Village Booklet Series
0078-4583 Wyzsza Szkola Rolnicza, Olsztyn. Zeszyty Naukowe *see* 0324-9204
0078-4591 Ombres de l'Histoire
0078-4605 Official Baseball Record Book
0078-463X Onoma
0078-4648 Onomastica
0078-4664 Ontario. Agricultural Research Institute. Report
0078-4672 Ontario Archaeology
0078-4680 Ontario Association for Curriculum Development. Annual Conference (Report)
0078-4699 Ontario Cancer Treatment and Research Foundation. Annual Report *see* 0315-9884
0078-4702 Ontario Catholic Directory
0078-4745 Ontario. Ministry of Transportation and Communications. Research and Development Division. Research Report†
0078-4753 Ontario. Division of Forests. Research Library. Research Report *see* 0381-3924
0078-4826 Ontario Federation of Labour. Report of Proceedings
0078-4834 Ontario Field Biologist
0078-4850 Ontario Geography
0078-4869 Ontario Historical Society. Bulletin
0078-4885 Ontario. Ministry of Housing. Annual Report
0078-4893 Ontario. Ministry of the Environment. Industrial Waste Conference. Proceedings
0078-5032 Ontario Joint Highway Research Programme. Report *see* 0078-4745
0078-5040 Ontario Petroleum Institute. Annual Conference Proceedings
0078-5059 Ontario. Ministry of Natural Resources. Petroleum Resources Branch. Drilling and Production Report, Oil and Natural Gas
0078-5067 Ontario Planning *see* 0318-4552
0078-5083 Ontario Research Foundation. Annual Report
0078-5091 Ontario Series
0078-5105 Ontario Speech and Hearing Association. Journal†
0078-5113 Ontario Statistical Review *changed to* Ontario Statistics
0078-5148 Ontario. Ministry of the Environment. Pollution Control Branch. Research Publication
0078-5156 Ontario. Ministry of the Environment. Ground Water Bulletin
0078-5164 Open Door International for the Emancipation of the Woman Worker. Report of Congress
0078-5172 Open Doors
0078-5237 Opera Botanica
0078-5245 Opera Lilloana
0078-5288 Operations and Policy Research. Institute for the Comparative Study of Political Systems. Political Study Series
0078-530X Operations and Policy Research. Institute for the Comparative Study of Political Systems. Election Analysis Series
0078-5318 Operations Research-Verfahren
0078-5326 Ophelia
0078-5334 Ophthalmological Societies of the United Kingdom. Transactions
0078-5342 Ophthalmological Society of Egypt. Bulletin
0078-5458 Opportunities Abroad for Teachers *changed to* U.S. Office of Education. Opportunities for Teachers Abroad
0078-5466 Optica Applicata
0078-5474 Optical Industry and Systems Directory
0078-5482 Optical Physics and Engineering
0078-5504 Optics and Spectroscopy. Supplement
0078-5512 Optik und Feinmechanik in Einzeldarstellungen†
0078-5520 Opuscula Atheniensia
0078-5539 Opuscula - aus Wissenschaft und Dichtung
0078-5547 Orange Free State. Director of Hospital Services. Report
0078-5555 Orbis Antiquus
0078-5563 Orbis Artium
0078-5571 Orbis Pictus†
0078-5601 Ordre des Geometres-Experts. Annuaire
0078-5679 Oregon School Directory
0078-5709 Oregon. State Department of Geology and Mineral Industries. Bulletin

0078-5717 Oregon. State Department of Geology and Mineral Industries. G M I Short Papers
0078-5725 Oregon. State Department of Geology and Mineral Industries. Miscellaneous Papers
0078-5733 Oregon. State Department of Geology and Mineral Industries. Miscellaneous Publications
0078-5741 Oregon. State Department of Geology and Mineral Industries. Oil and Gas Investigations
0078-575X Oregon State Plan for the Construction and Modernization of Hospitals, Public Health Centers and Medical Facilities†
0078-5768 Oregon State Monographs. Bibliographic Series
0078-5776 Oregon State Monographs. Studies in Botany
0078-5784 Oregon State Monographs. Studies in Economics
0078-5792 Oregon State Monographs. Studies in Education and Guidance
0078-5806 Oregon State Monographs. Studies in Entomology
0078-5814 Oregon State Monographs. Studies in Geology
0078-5822 Oregon State Monographs. Studies in History
0078-5830 Oregon State Monographs. Studies in Zoology
0078-5849 Oregon State University. Water Resources Research Institute. Water Research Summary
0078-5857 Oregon State University. Annual Biology Colloquium. Proceedings
0078-5865 Oregon State University. Forest Research Laboratory. Annual Report
0078-5903 Oregon State University. Forest Research Laboratory. Research Bulletin
0078-5911 Oregon State University. Forest Research Laboratory. Research Note
0078-592X Oregon State University. Forest Research Laboratory. Research Paper
0078-5938 Oregon State University. School of Engineering. Graduate Research and Education
0078-5946 Oregon State University. School of Engineering. Research Activities
0078-5962 University of Oregon. Bureau of Business Research. Research Studies†
0078-5970 University of Oregon. Bureau of Governmental Research and Service. Information Bulletin
0078-5989 University of Oregon. Bureau of Governmental Research and Service. Legal Bulletin
0078-5997 University of Oregon. Bureau of Governmental Research and Service. Local Government Notes and Information: Policy and Practice Series
0078-6004 University of Oregon. Center for the Advanced Study of Educationl Administration. Monographs *changed to* University of Oregon. Center for Educational Policy and Management. Monographs
0078-6012 University of Oregon. Center for the Advanced Study of Educational Administration. Occasional Papers *changed to* University of Oregon. Center for Educational Policy and Management. Occasional Papers
0078-6020 University of Oregon. Center for Educational Policy and Management. Technical Reports†
0078-6039 University of Oregon. Library. Occasional Paper†
0078-6047 University of Oregon. Museum of Natural History. Bulletin
0078-6063 University of Oregon. Bureau of Business Research. Business Publications†
0078-6071 University of Oregon Anthropological Papers
0078-608X Orestes Brownson Series on Contemporary Thought and Affairs
0078-6098 Organ Yearbook
0078-611X Organic Chemistry
0078-6128 Organic Directory
0078-6136 Organic Electronic Spectral Data
0078-6144 Organic Photochemical Syntheses
0078-6152 Organic Photochemistry: A Series of Advances
0078-6160 Organic Reaction Mechanisms. Annual Survey
0078-6179 Organic Reactions
0078-6187 Organic Substances of Natural Origin
0078-6209 Organic Syntheses
0078-6217 Organic Syntheses Collective Volumes
0078-6225 Organische Chemie in Einzeldarstellungen
0078-6233 Afro-Asian Peoples' Solidarity Organization. Council. Documents of the Session
0078-6241 Review of Fisheries in OECD Member Countries
0078-625X Organization for Economic Cooperation and Development. Nuclear Energy Agency. Activity Report
0078-6276 O E C D High Temperature Reactor Project Dragon†
0078-6284 O E C D Halden Reactor Project
0078-6292 List of Research Institutes and Scientists in O. E. C. D. Member Countries†
0078-6306 O A U Review†
0078-6322 Organization of American States. Department of Scientific Affairs. Serie de Fisica: Monografias
0078-6330 Organization of American States. Department of Scientific Affairs. Serie de Matematica: Monografias
0078-6357 Organization of American States. Department of Cultural Affairs. Cuadernos Bibliotecologicos†
0078-6373 Organization of American States. Department of Cultural Affairs. Estudios Bibliotecarios
0078-6381 Organization of American States. Department of Cultural Affairs Manuales del Bibliotecario
0078-6403 O A S. General Secretariat. Annual Report
0078-642X Organization of American States. Official Records. Indice y Lista General
0078-6438 Organization of American States. Permanent Council. Decisions Taken at Meetings (Cumulated Edition)
0078-6489 Organometallic Compounds of the Group IV Elements
0078-6497 Organometallic Reactions Series *changed to* Organometallic Reactions and Syntheses
0078-6500 Organon
0078-6527 Oriens
0078-6543 Oriental Notes and Studies
0078-6551 Oriental Studies
0078-656X Orientalia Gothoburgensia
0078-6578 Orientalia Suecana
0078-6586 Original Manuscript Music for Wind and Percussion Instruments
0078-6594 Ornithological Monographs
0078-6608 Orthodontie Francaise
0078-6624 Orton Society. Bulletin
0078-6632 Center for Adult Diseases, Osaka. Annual Report
0078-6640 Osaka City University Economic Review
0078-6659 Osaka City University. Faculty of Engineering. Memoirs
0078-6667 Osaka Medical School, Takatsuki. Bulletin. Supplement†
0078-6675 Osaka Museum of Natural History. Bulletin
0078-6683 Osaka Museum of Natural History. Occasional Papers
0078-6691 Osaka University Dental Society. Journal
0078-6705 Osaka University. Institute for Protein Research. Memoirs
0078-6713 Norges Veterinaerhoegskole. Aarsberetning
0078-673X Norway. Statens Institutt for Alkoholforskning. Skrifter
0078-6748 Universitetet i Oslo. Etnografiske Museum. Aarbok†
0078-6764 Universitetet i Oslo. Institutt for Bibelvitenskap. Smaaskrifter†
0078-6772 Universitetet i Oslo. Institutett for Statsvitenskap. Skrifter†
0078-6780 Physica Mathematica Universitatis Osloensis
0078-6799 Osram-Gesellschaft. Technisch-Wissenschaftliche Abhandlungen
0078-6845 Ostbairische Grenzmarken
0078-687X Osteuropa Institut, Munich. Veroeffentlichungen. Reihe Geschichte
0078-6888 Osteuropastudien der Hochschulen des Landes Hessen. Reihe 1. Giessener Abhandlungen zur Agrar- und Wirtschaftsforschung des Europaeischen Ostens
0078-6896 Ostpanorama
0078-690X Otago Geographer
0078-6918 Otago Law Review
0078-6926 Other Lands, Other Peoples†
0078-6950 Victoria, British Columbia. Dominion Astrophysical Observatory. Publications
0078-6977 National Gallery of Canada. Annual Review *changed to* National Gallery of Canada. Annual Bulletin
0078-6985 National Gallery of Canada. Library. Canadiana in the Library of the National Gallery of Canada: Supplement
0078-6993 National Gallery of Canada. Library. Checklist of Canadian Artists' Files *changed to* Artists in Canada
0078-7000 National Library of Canada. Annual Report
0078-7027 University of Ottawa. Library. Annual Report
0078-7035 Ou Monter a Cheval
0078-7094 Outline of Japanese Tax
0078-7108 Overseas Development Council. Monograph Series
0078-7116 O D I Review
0078-7124 Overseas Directories, Who's Who, Press Guides, Year Books and Overseas Periodical Subscriptions
0078-7132 Overseas Media Guide
0078-7159 Overseas Newspapers and Periodicals
0078-7167 Owen's Commerce and Travel and International Register
0078-7175 Oxford Bibliographical Society. Occasional Publications
0078-7183 Oxford Bibliographical Society. Publications. New Series
0078-7191 Oxford German Studies
0078-7205 Oxford Historical Series
0078-7221 Oxford History of English Literature
0078-723X Oxford Paperbacks University Series
0078-7248 Oxford Science Research Papers
0078-7264 Oxford Studies of Composers
0078-7272 Oxford Theological Monographs
0078-7353 P A S Reporter†
0078-7388 P I /L T; Occasional Papers on Programmed Instruction and Language Teaching
0078-740X Pacific Anthropological Records
0078-7418 Pacific Anthropologists†
0078-7426 Pacific Botanists†
0078-7442 Pacific Coast Obstetrical and Gynecological Society. Transactions
0078-7469 Pacific Coast Philology
0078-7507 Pacific History Series†
0078-7515 Pacific Insects Monographs
0078-7523 Pacific Islands Year Book
0078-7531 Pacific Linguistics. Series A: Occasional Papers
0078-754X Pacific Linguistics. Series B: Monographs
0078-7558 Pacific Linguistics. Series C: Books
0078-7566 Pacific Linguistics. Series D: Special Publications
0078-7574 Pacific Marine Fisheries Commission. Annual Report
0078-7582 Pacific Marine Fisheries Commission. Bulletin
0078-7590 Pacific Marine Fisheries Commission. Newsletter
0078-7604 Pacific Marine Station, Dillon Beach, California. Research Report
0078-7612 Pacific Northwest Conference on Foreign Languages. Proceedings *see* 0363-8391
0078-7620 Pacific Northwest Conference on Higher Education. Proceedings
0078-7647 Pacific Science Association. Congress Proceedings *changed to* Pacific Science Association. Congress and Inter-Congress Proceedings
0078-7663 Pacific Trollers Association Newsletter
0078-768X Packaging Directory
0078-7698 Packaging Machinery Manufacturers Institute. Official Packaging Machinery Directory
0078-7701 Papua New Guinea. Bureau of Statistics. Rural Industries
0078-771X Universita degli Studi di Padova. Centro per la Storia della Tradizione Artistotelica nel Veneto. Saggi e Testi
0078-7728 Universita degli Studi di Padova. Facolta di Lettere e Filosofia. Opuscoli Accademici
0078-7736 Universita degli Studi di Padova. Facolta di Lettere e Filosofia. Pubblicazioni
0078-7744 Universita degli Studi di Padova Istituto di Storia Antica. Pubblicazioni
0078-7752 Universita degli Studi di Padova. Istituto per la Storia. Contributi
0078-7760 Universita degli Studi di Padova. Istituto per la Storia. Quaderni
0078-7779 Universita degli Studi di Padova. Scuola di Perfezionamento in Filosofia. Pubblicazioni
0078-7787 Paedagogica Europaea *see* 0141-8211
0078-7795 Paediatrische Fortbildungskurse fuer die Praxis
0078-7809 Paideuma
0078-7817 Polymers Paint and Colour Year Book
0078-7833 Painting Holidays
0078-785X Pakistan Annual Law Digest
0078-7868 Pakistan Archaeology
0078-7884 Pakistan Banking Directory
0078-7892 Pakistan Basic Facts
0078-7914 Pakistan. Central Bureau of Education. Educational Statistics Bulletin Series
0078-7922 Pakistan. Central Bureau of Education. Yearbook *see* 0078-8287
0078-7930 Pakistan Central Cotton Committee. Agricultural Survey Report
0078-7949 Pakistan Central Cotton Committee. Technological Bulletin. Series A
0078-7957 Pakistan Central Cotton Committee. Technological Bulletin. Series B
0078-7965 Pakistan. Central Statistical Office. Census of Electricity Undertakings†
0078-7973 Pakistan. Central Statistical Office. Consumer Price Index Numbers for Industrial Workers†
0078-7981 Pakistan. Statistics Division. Consumer Price Index: Scope and Limitations
0078-799X Pakistan. Statistics Division. Key to Official Statistics
0078-8007 Pakistan. Statistics Division. N S S Series
0078-8015 Pakistan. Central Statistical Office. Some Socio-Economic Trends†
0078-8023 Pakistan. Central Statistical Office. Statistical Yearbook *changed to* Pakistan. Statistics Division. Statistical Yearbook
0078-804X Pakistan Council of Scientific and Industrial Research. Report
0078-8058 Pakistan Customs Tariff
0078-8082 Pakistan Economic Survey
0078-8090 Pakistan Export Directory
0078-8104 Pakistan. Export Promotion Bureau. Export Guide Series

0078-8112 Pakistan. Export Promotion Bureau. Fresh Fruits
0078-8139 Pakistan. Food and Agriculture Division. Yearbook of Agricultural Statistics
0078-8147 Pakistan Forest Institute, Peshawar. Annual Progress Report
0078-8155 Pakistan. Geological Survey. Memoirs; Paleontologia Pakistanica
0078-8163 Pakistan. Geological Survey. Records
0078-8171 Pakistan Historical Society. Memoir
0078-818X Pakistan Historical Society. Proceedings of the Pakistan History Conference
0078-8198 Pakistan Industrial Credit and Investment Corporation. Report
0078-8201 Pakistan Industrial Development Corporation. Report
0078-821X Pakistan Institute of Development Economics. Report
0078-8228 Pakistan Institute of Development Economics. Research Report
0078-8236 Pakistan Insurance Year Book
0078-8252 Pakistan Leather Year Book†
0078-8287 Pakistan. Ministry of Education. Yearbook
0078-8295 Pakistan. Ministry of Finance. Basic Facts About the Budget *see* 0078-7892
0078-8309 Pakistan. Ministry of Finance. Budget in Brief *changed to* Pakistan. Finance Division. Budget in Brief
0078-8317 Pakistan. Ministry of Finance. Budget of the Central Government *changed to* Budget of the Government of Pakistan. Demands for Grants and Appropriations
0078-8325 Pakistan. Ministry of Finance. Economic Analysis of the Central Government *changed to* Pakistan. Finance Division. Economic Analysis of the Budget
0078-8333 Pakistan. National Assembly. Debates. Official Report
0078-835X Lists of P A N S Doc Bibliographies *changed to* Lists of P A S T I C Bibliographies
0078-8368 P A N S D O C Translations *changed to* P A S T I C Translations
0078-8376 Pakistan Nursing and Health Review
0078-8392 Pakistan. Office of the Economic Adviser. Government Sponsored Corporations and Other Institutions
0078-8406 Pakistan Philosophical Congress. Proceedings
0078-8414 Pakistan. Planning and Development Division. Development Programme
0078-8422 Pakistan Postage Stamps
0078-8430 Pakistan Science Conference. Proceedings
0078-8457 Pakistan Standards Institution. Report
0078-8473 Pakistan Statistical Association. Proceedings
0078-8481 Pakistan. Survey of Pakistan. General Report
0078-849X Bangladesh Tea Board. Annual Review†
0078-8511 Pakistan Western Railway. Yearbook of Information *changed to* Pakistan Railways. Yearbook of Information
0078-852X Pakistan's Balance of Payments
0078-8538 Palaeoecology of Africa and the Surrounding Islands and Antarctica
0078-8546 Palaeontographica Americana
0078-8554 Palaeontologia Africana
0078-8562 Palaeontologia Polonica
0078-8570 Paleoecologia†
0078-8589 Paleontological Bulletins
0078-8597 Paleontological Society. Memoir
0078-8600 Zentrales Geologisches Institut. Palaeontologische Abhandlungen
0078-8619 Universita degli Studi di Palermo. Istituto di Entomologia Agraria. Bollettino
0078-8627 Universita degli Studi di Palermo. Istituto di Filologia Greca. Quaderni
0078-866X Pamietnik Slowianski
0078-8686 Universidad de Navarra. Instituto de Ciencias de la Educacion. Coleccion I C E
0078-8708 Universidad de Navarra. Instituto de Estudios Superiores de la Empresas. Coleccion I E S E. Serie L *changed to* Empresa y Su Entorno. Serie L
0078-8716 Universidad de Navarra. Instituto de Estudios Superiores de la Empresas. Coleccion I E S E. Serie AC *changed to* Empresa y Su Entorno. Serie AC
0078-8724 Universidad de Navarra. Facultad de Ciencias de la Informacion. Cuadernos de Trabajo
0078-8732 Universidad de Navarra. Escuela de Arquitectura. Manuales: Arquitectura
0078-8740 Universidad de Navarra. Escuela de Bibliotecarias. Manuales: Bibliotecarias
0078-8759 Universidad de Navarra. Departamento de Derecho Canonico. Manuales: Derecho Canonico
0078-8767 Universidad de Navarra. Manuales: Derecho Notarial Espanol *changed to* Universidad de Navarra. Manuales de Derecho
0078-8783 Universidad de Navarra. Facultad de Ciencias de la Informacion. Manuales: Periodismo
0078-8805 Pan American Highway Congresses. Final Acts†
0078-8813 Pan American Institute of Geography and History. Commission on History. Bibliografias
0078-8821 Pan American Institute of Geography and History. Commission on History. Guias
0078-883X Pan American Institute of Geography and History. Commission on History. Historiografias Americanas
0078-8848 Pan American Institute of Geography and History. Commission on History. Historiadores de America
0078-8856 Pan American Institute of Geography and History. Commission on History. Monumentos Historicos y Arqueologicos
0078-8864 Pan American Medical Women's Alliance. Newsletter
0078-8899 Panama Canal Company. Meteorological and Hydrographic Branch. Climatological Data: Canal Zone and Panama
0078-8902 Estadistica Panamena. Seccion 221. Movimento de Problacion *see* 0378-6749
0078-8937 Panama. Direccion de Estadistica y Censo. Estadistica Panamena. Serie F. Industrias-Encuestas *see* 0378-2557
0078-8961 Panama. Direccion de Estadistica y Censo. Estadistica Panamena Serie M: Empleo *changed to* Estadistica Panamena. Situacion Social. Seccion 441-Trabajo y Salarios. Estadisticas del Trabajo
0078-897X Estadistica Panamena. Estadistica Electoral
0078-8996 Panama en Cifras
0078-9038 Papermakers' and Merchants' Directory of All Nations *see* 0079-158X
0078-9054 Papers in Anthropology
0078-9062 Papers in Australian Linguistics
0078-9070 Papers in Borneo Linguistics
0078-9100 Papers in International Studies: Africa Series
0078-9119 Papers in International Studies: Southeast Asia Series
0078-9127 Papers in Linguistics of Melanesia
0078-9135 Papers in New Guinea Linguistics
0078-9143 Papers in Philippine Linguistics
0078-9151 Papers in Public Administration
0078-916X Papers in Public Administration
0078-9178 Papers in South East Asian Linguistics
0078-9194 Papers on Formal Linguistics
0078-9216 Papers on Modern Japan†
0078-9224 London School of Economics Papers in Soviet and East European Law, Economics and Politics
0078-9232 Papiermusterheft†
0078-9240 Papiri Greci e Latini
0078-9259 Papua New Guinea. Bureau of Statistics. Statistical Bulletin: Capital Expenditure by Private Businesses
0078-9267 Papua New Guinea. Bureau of Statistics. Workers' Compensation Statistics *changed to* Papua New Guinea. Bureau of Statistics. Workers' Compensation Claims
0078-9283 Papua New Guinea. Bureau of Statistics. Private Overseas Investment
0078-9291 Papua New Guinea. Bureau of Statistics. Overseas Trade Statistics *changed to* Papua New Guinea. Bureau of Statistics. International Trade Statistics.
0078-9313 Papua New Guinea. Bureau of Statistics. Secondary Industries (Factories and Works). Preliminary Statement
0078-9321 Papua New Guinea. Bureau of Statistics. Rural Industries. Preliminary Statement
0078-933X Papua New Guinea. Bureau of Statistics. Secondary Industries
0078-9356 Papua New Guinea. Bureau of Statistics. Statistics of Religious Organisations
0078-9372 Papua New Guinea. Bureau of Statistics. Taxation Statistics. Preliminary Bulletin
0078-9399 Papua New Guinea. Public Service Board. Report.
0078-9402 Papyrologica Bruxellensia
0078-9410 Papyrologica Coloniensia
0078-9429 Paralogue
0078-9437 Parapsychological Monographs
0078-947X Aeroport de Paris. Service Statistique. Statistique de Trafic
0078-9496 Paris-Bijoux Exportation
0078-950X Bureau Universitaire de Recherche Operationnelle.Cahiers
0078-9518 Societe de l'Ecole des Chartes. Memoires et Documents
0078-964X Ecole Pratique des Hautes Etudes. Quatrieme Section. Historiques et Philologiques. Annuaire
0078-9666 France. Imprimerie Nationale. Annuaire.
0078-9674 Institut de Recherches Agronomiques Tropicales et des Cultures Vivrieres. Bulletin Scientifique.†
0078-9682 Institut Oceanographique. Annales
0078-9704 Musee Guimet, Paris. Bibliotheque d'Etudes
0078-9712 Musee Guimet, Paris. Etude des Collections du Musee
0078-9720 Museum National d'Histoire Naturelle, Paris. Annuaire
0078-9739 Museum National d'Histoire Naturelle, Paris. Archives
0078-9747 Museum National d'Histoire Naturelle, Paris. Memoires. Nouvelle Serie. Serie A. Zoologie
0078-9755 Museum National d'Histoire Naturelle, Paris. Memoires. Nouvelle Serie. Serie B. Botanique
0078-9763 Museum National d'Histoire Naturelle, Paris. Memoires. Nouvelle Serie. Serie C. Sciences de la Terre
0078-9771 Museum National d'Histoire Naturelle, Paris. Memoires. Nouvelle Serie. Serie D. Sciences Physico-Chimiques
0078-9887 Universite de Paris. Faculte des Lettres et Sciences Humaines. Publications. Serie Acta
0078-9895 Universite de Paris. Faculte des Lettres et Sciences Humaines. Publications. Serie Recherches
0078-9909 Universite de Paris VI (Pierre et Marie Curie). Institut Henri Poincare. Seminaire Choquet. Initiation a l'Analyse†
0078-995X Institut d'Etudes Politiques de Paris. Livret
0078-9968 Institut d'Etudes Slaves, Paris. Annuaire†
0078-9976 Institut d'Etudes Slaves, Paris. Bibliotheque Russe
0078-9984 Institut d'Etudes Slaves, Paris. Collection de Grammaires
0078-9992 Institut d'Etudes Slaves, Paris. Collection de Manuels
0079-0001 Institut d'Etudes Slaves, Paris. Collection Historique
0079-001X Institut d'Etudes Slaves, Paris. Textes
0079-0028 Institut d'Etudes Slaves, Paris. Travaux
0079-0036 Universite de Paris VI (Pierre et Marie Curie). Institut Henri Poincare. Seminaire Lions†
0079-0044 Parker Directory of Attorneys *changed to* Parker Directory of California Attorneys
0079-0052 Parkes Library Pamphlets
0079-0060 Parkinson's Disease and Related Disorders. Cumulative Bibliography
0079-0079 Parkinson's Disease and Related Disorders: Citations from the Literature
0079-0087 Parklands Poets Series
0079-0095 Parliament House Book
0079-0117 Partners in Learning
0079-0125 Passaic County Dental Society. Bulletin
0079-0133 Passenger Transport in Great Britain *changed to* Transport Statistics Great Britain
0079-0141 Pastoral Psychology Series
0079-015X Patent and Trademark Institute of Canada. Annual Proceedings
0079-0168 Patent Law Review *changed to* Intellectual Property Law Review
0079-0184 Pathology Annual
0079-0192 Patterns of American Prejudice Series
0079-0206 Patterns of Literary Criticism†
0079-0214 Patterns of Religious Commitment†
0079-0222 Patterson Smith Series in Criminology, Law Enforcement and Social Problems
0079-0230 Patterson's American Education
0079-0249 Paul Anthony Brick Lectures
0079-0257 Paul Carus Lectures
0079-0265 Universita degli Studi di Pavia. Istituto Botanico. Atti
0079-0273 Paving Conference. Proceedings
0079-0281 Pax Romana
0079-029X Peabody Museum of Archaeology and Ethnology. Memoirs
0079-0303 Peabody Museum of Archaeology and Ethnology. Papers
0079-032X Peabody Museum of Natural History. Bulletin
0079-0338 Peabody Museum of Natural History. Special Publication
0079-0354 Pearce-Sellards Series
0079-0362 Pears Cyclopaedia
0079-0370 Paedagogica Belgica Academica
0079-0400 Pediatrics; a Medical World News Publication†
0079-0435 Marine Research in Indonesia
0079-0451 Penn State Studies
0079-046X Pennsylvania Crop and Livestock Annual Summary
0079-0478 Pennsylvania Crop Reporting Service. C.R.S. *see* 0079-046X
0079-0486 P. E. L. State Bulletin
0079-0494 Indiana University of Pennsylvania. Annual Research Bulletin†
0079-0508 Pennsylvania School Study Council. Reports
0079-0524 Millersville State College. Contributions to Research: Faculty and Student Publications†
0079-0540 Pennsylvania State University. College of Business Administration. Center for Research. Occasional Papers
0079-0567 Pennsylvania State University. College of Engineering. Engineering Research Bulletin†
0079-0583 Pennsylvania State University. Council on Research. Research Publications and Other Contributions *see* 0093-7568
0079-0591 Pennsylvania State University. Earth and Mineral Sciences Experiment Station. Bulletin

ISSN INDEX 1149

0079-0605 Pennsylvania State University. Earth and Mineral Sciences Experiment Station. Bulletin. Mineral Conservation Series. Paper
0079-0613 Pennsylvania State University. Earth and Mineral Sciences Experiment Station. Circular
0079-0621 Pennsylvania State University. Institute for Research on Land and Water Resources. Information Reports
0079-063X Pennsylvania State University. Institute for Research on Land and Water Resources. Research Publication
0079-0656 Pennsylvania State University. Libraries. Bibliographic Series
0079-0672 University of Pennsylvania. Department of Linguistics. Transformations and Discourse Analysis Papers
0079-0680 University of Pennsylvania. Institute for Environmental Studies. City Planning Series
0079-0699 University of Pennsylvania. Institute for Environmental Studies. Report
0079-0710 Penrose Annual
0079-0729 People from the Past Series.
0079-0737 Peoples' Appalachia†
0079-0745 Peoria Academy of Science. Proceedings
0079-0753 Peptides†
0079-0761 Per Jacobsson Foundation. Proceedings
0079-077X Per Jacobsson Memorial Lecture *see* 0079-0761
0079-0788 Performance Data on Architectural Acoustical Materials *changed to* Acoustical and Board Products. Bulletin
0079-0818 Pergamon General Psychology Series
0079-0826 Pergamon Mathematical Tables Series
0079-0834 Pergamon Series of Monographs in Laboratory Techniques†
0079-0842 Pergamon Series of Monographs on Furniture and Timber†
0079-0869 Pergamon Unified Engineering Series
0079-0877 Periodicals in East African Libraries: a Union List *changed to* Periodicals in Eastern African Libraries: a Union List
0079-0885 Periscope 2000†
0079-0893 Persica
0079-0907 Personal Income in Counties of New York State
0079-0931 Personality and Psychopathology
0079-0958 Perspecta; The Yale Architectural Journal
0079-0966 Perspective†
0079-0982 Perspectives de l'Economique. Serie 1. les Fondateurs de l'Economie
0079-0990 Perspectives in American History
0079-1008 Perspectives in Criticism†
0079-1008 Perspectives in Criticism
0079-1016 Perspectives in Jewish Learning *changed to* Solomon Goldman Lectures
0079-1032 Perspectives in Powder Metallurgy *changed to* New Perspectives in Powder Metallurgy
0079-1040 Perspectives in Social Work
0079-1059 Perspectives in Structural Chemistry†
0079-1067 Perth Observatory. Communications
0079-1075 Peru - Problema
0079-1083 Instituto Nacional de Enfermedades Neoplasicas. Trabajos de Investigacion Clinica y Experimental
0079-1091 Sociedad Geologica del Peru. Boletin
0079-1148 Pesticide Review
0079-1156 Petersen's Pro Football Annual *see* 0079-5526
0079-1288 Petroleum and Chemical Industry Technical Conference. Record
0079-1296 Petroleum Refineries in Canada
0079-130X Pets Welcome
0079-1334 Pflanzenschuetzer†
0079-1342 Pflanzenschutz-Nachrichten Bayer
0079-1350 Phaenomenologica
0079-1369 Phanerogamarum Monographiae
0079-1393 Pharmaceutical Historian
0079-1407 Pharmacopeia of the United States of America *changed to* United States Pharmacopeia-National Formulary
0079-1423 Philippine Education Abstracts†
0079-1458 Philippine Men of Science†
0079-1466 Philippine Scientist
0079-1490 Philippines Nuclear Journal
0079-1504 Philippines. Board of Investments. Annual Report
0079-1512 Philippines. Bureau of Agricultural Economics. Crop, Livestock and Natural Resources Statistics *changed to* Philippines. Bureau of Agricultural Economics. Crop and Livestock Statistics
0079-1520 Philippines. Bureau of Agricultural Economics. Report
0079-1539 Philippines. Department of Commerce and Industry. Annual Report *changed to* Philippines. Ministry of Trade. Annual Report
0079-1547 Philippines. National Tax Research Center. Report
0079-158X Phillips' Paper Trade Directory- Europe- Mills of the World
0079-1598 Philologen-Jahrbuch
0079-1628 Philological Monographs
0079-1636 Philological Society Transactions
0079-1644 Philologische Beitraege zur Suedost- und Osteuropaforschung
0079-1687 Philosophia Antiqua
0079-1695 Philosophical Society of the Sudan. Proceedings of the Annual Conference
0079-1717 Philosophische Studientexte
0079-1733 Philosophy of Education Society. Proceedings of the Annual Meetings
0079-175X PHILSOM
0079-1768 Phineas L. Windsor Lecture in Librarianship†
0079-1776 Phoenix
0079-1784 Phoenix. Supplementary Volumes
0079-1806 Photochemistry
0079-1814 Photoelectric Spectrometry Group Bulletin *changed to* U.V. Spectrometry Group. Bulletin
0079-1830 Photographis
0079-1849 Photography Annual
0079-1857 Photography Directory and Buying Guide
0079-1865 Photography Year Book
0079-1873 Physical Acoustics: Principles and Methods
0079-1881 Physical Chemistry
0079-189X Physical Education around the World. Monograph
0079-1903 Physical Education Association of Great Britain and Northern Ireland. Report
0079-1911 Physical Education Year Book†
0079-1938 Physics and Chemistry in Space
0079-1946 Physics and Chemistry of the Earth
0079-1954 Physics and Chemistry of the Organic Solid State
0079-1970 Physics of Thin Films; Advances in Research and Development
0079-1989 Physik und Technik†
0079-1997 Physikalisch-Chemische Trenn- und Messmethoden
0079-2012 Physiologia Plantarum. Supplementum†
0079-2020 Physiological Society. Monographs
0079-2047 Phyton. Annales Rei Botanicae
0079-2055 Pianeta Fresco
0079-2063 Pick's Currency Yearbook
0079-2071 Pilot Studies Approved for State Aid in Public School Systems in Virginia
0079-208X Pion Applied Physics Series
0079-211X Pisarze Slascy XIX i XX Wieku
0079-2128 Pit and Quarry Handbook and Purchasing Guide *changed to* Pit & Quarry Handbook and Buyers Guide
0079-2144 Pittsburgh Studies in Library and Information Sciences†
0079-2179 L R D C News†
0079-2217 Planning, Programming, Budgeting for City, State, County Objectives. P P B Note Series
0079-2225 Plant Breeding Institute, Cambridge. Annual Report
0079-2233 Plant Monograph: Reprints
0079-2241 Plant Physiology. Supplement
0079-225X Plant Protection Abstracts. Supplement
0079-2276 Planung und Kontrolle in der Unternehmung
0079-2284 Planungsstudien
0079-2306 Plastics, Paint and Rubber Buyers' Guide for S.A. *changed to* Plastics and Rubber Yearbook and Buyers' Guide of S.A.
0079-2314 Playfair Cricket Annual
0079-2322 Playfair Football Annual
0079-2349 Playthings Directory
0079-2373 Poche-Couleurs Larousse
0079-2381 Pocket Book of Transport Statistics of India
0079-239X Australia. Bureau of Statistics. Pocket Compendium of Australian Statistics *changed to* Australia. Bureau of Statistics. Pocket Year Book of Australia
0079-2403 Pocket Data Book, USA
0079-2411 Pocket Digest of New Zealand Statistics
0079-242X Pocket Library of Studies of Art
0079-2438 Pocket Poets Series
0079-2446 Pocket Year Book of South Australia
0079-2462 Poesia
0079-2470 Poetes et Prosateurs du Portugal
0079-2500 Poeti e Prosatori Tedeschi
0079-2519 Poetry Eastwest†
0079-2527 Poetyka. Zarys Encyklopedyczny
0079-2535 Points. Films
0079-2543 Points for Emphasis; International Sunday School Lessons in Pocket Size
0079-256X Universite de Poitiers. Centre d'Etudes Superieures de Civilisation Medievale. Publications
0079-2586 Poland. Glowny Urzad Statystyczny. Atlas Statystyczny. Statistical Atlas
0079-2594 Poland. Glowny Urzad Statystyczny. Budzet Panstwa. State Budget
0079-2608 Poland. Glowny Urzad Statystyczny. Maly Rocznik Statystyczny. Concise Statistical Yearbook
0079-2616 Poland. Glowny Urzad Statystyczny. Rocznik Demograficzny
0079-2632 Poland. Glowny Urzad Statystyczny. Rocznik Statystyczny Budownictwa. Yearbook of Construction Statistics
0079-2640 Poland. Glowny Urzad Statystyczny. Rocznik Statystyczny Finansow. Yearbook of Finance Statistics
0079-2659 Poland. Glowny Urzad Statystyczny. Rocznik Statystyczny Gospodarski Mieszkaniowej i Komunalnej
0079-2667 Poland. Glowny Urzad Statystyczny. Rocznik Statystyczny Gospodarki Morskiej. Yearbook of Sea Economy Statistics
0079-2675 Poland. Glowny Urzad Statystyczny. Rocznik Statystyczny Gornictwa. Yearbook of Mining Statistics
0079-2683 Poland. Glowny Urzad Statystyczny. Rocznik Statystyczny Handlu Wewnetrznego/Yearbook of International Trade Statistics
0079-2691 Poland. Glowny Urzad Statystyczny. Rocznik Statystyki Handlu Zagranicznego
0079-2705 Poland. Glowny Urzad Statystyczny. Rocznik Statystyczny Inwestycji i Srodkow Trwalych. Yearbook of Investment and Fixed Assets Statistics
0079-2713 Poland. Glowny Urzad Statystyczny. Kultura *changed to* Poland. Glowny Urzad Statystyczny. Rocznik Statystyczny Kultury. Statistical Yearbook of Culture
0079-2721 Poland. Glowny Urzad Statystyczny. Rocznik Statystyczny Lesnictwa. Yearbook of Forestry Statistics
0079-273X Poland. Glowny Urzad Statystyczny. Rocznik Statystyki Miedzynarodowej. Yearbook of International Statistics
0079-2748 Poland. Glowny Urzad Statystyczny. Rocznik Statystyczny Ochrony Zdrowia. Yearbook of Public Health Statistics
0079-2756 Poland. Glowny Urzad Statystyczny. Rocznik Statystyczny Powiatow. Statistical Yearbook of Counties
0079-2764 Poland. Glowny Urzad Statystyczny. Rocznik Statystyczny Przemyslu. Yearbook of Industry Statistics
0079-2772 Poland. Glowny Urzad Statystyczny. Rocznik Statystyczny Pracy. Yearbook of Labour Statistics
0079-2780 Poland. Glowny Urzad Statystyczny. Rocznik Statystyczny. Statistical Yearbook
0079-2799 Poland. Glowny Urzad Statystyczny. Rocznik Statystyczny Szkolnictwa. Yearbook of Education Statistics
0079-2802 Poland. Glowny Urzad Statystyczny. Rocznik Statystyczny Transportu. Yearbook of Transport Statistics
0079-2810 Poland. Glowny Urzad Statystyczny. Rolniczy Rocznik Statystyczny. Yearbook of Agricultural Statistics *changed to* Poland. Glowny Urzad Statystyczny. Rocznik Statystyczny Rolnictwai Gospodarki Zywnosciowej. Yearbook of Agricultural Statistics
0079-2829 Poland. Glowny Urzad Statystyczny,. Zeszyty Metodyczne
0079-2837 Poland. Glowny Urzad Statystyczny. Statystyka Zegluci Srodladowej i Drog Wodnych Srodladowych
0079-2845 Poland. Glowny Urzad Statystyczny. Studia i Prace Statystyczne
0079-2853 Poland. Glowny Urzad Statystyczny. Ubezpieczenia Majatkowe i Osobowe. Property and Personal Insurance
0079-2861 Poland. Glowny Urzad Statystyczny. Uzytkowanie Gruntow i Powierzchnia Zasiewow Oraz Zwierzeta Gospodarskie
0079-287X Poland. Glowny Urzad Statystyczny. Wypadki Drogowe
0079-2888 Poland. Glowny Urzad Statystyczny. Wypadki Przy Pracy. Accidents at Work
0079-2896 Poland. Glowny Urzad Statystyczny. Zatrudnienie w Gospodarce Narodowej
0079-290X Poland. Glowny Urzad Statystyczny. Zwierzeta Gospodarskie. Livestock
0079-2918 Polar Notes†
0079-2926 Polemologische Studien
0079-2950 Police Yearbook
0079-2985 Polish Journal of Soil Science
0079-2993 Polish Psychological Bulletin
0079-3000 Polish Round Table
0079-3027 Politica
0079-3035 Political Handbook and Atlas of the World *changed to* Political Handbook of the World
0079-3043 Political Science Annual†
0079-3051 Maharaja Sayajirao University of Baroda. Political Science Series†
0079-3078 Politics†
0079-3094 Politics of Modernization Series†
0079-3108 Politique Belge†
0079-3116 Pollution Technology Review
0079-3124 K-W Probe†
0079-3132 Polonia Typographica Saeculi Sedecimi
0079-3140 Polska Akademia Nauk. Biblioteka, Krakow. Rocznik
0079-3159 Academie Polonaise des Sciences. Centre Scientifique, Paris. Conferences
0079-3167 Conferenze
0079-3175 Polska Akademia Nauk. Centrum Obliczeniowe. Prace *changed to* Polish Academy of Sciences. Institute of Computer Science. Reports
0079-3183 Sredniowiecze.Studia o Kulturze
0079-3205 Polska Akademia Nauk. Instytut Maszyn Przeplywowych. Prace

ISSN	Title
0079-323X	Polish Academy of Sciences. Institute of Fundamental Technological Research. Scientific Activities
0079-3256	Polska Akademia Nauk. Oddzial w Krakowie Komisja Archeologiczna. Prace
0079-3264	Polska Akademia Nauk. Oddzial w Krakowie. Komisja Ceramiczna. Prace: Ceramika
0079-3272	Polska Akademia Nauk. Oddzial w Krakowie. Komisja Filologii Klasycznej. Prace
0079-3280	Polska Akademia Nauk. Oddzial w Krakowie. Komisja Gorniczo-Geodezyjna. Prace: Gornictwo
0079-3299	Polska Akademia Nauk. Oddzial w Krakowie. Komisja Gorniczo-Geodezyjna. Prace: Geodezja
0079-3302	Polska Akademia Nauk. Oddzial w Krakowie. Komisja Historycznoliteracka. Rocznik
0079-3310	Polska Akademia Nauk. Oddzial w Krakowie. Komisja Jezykoznawstwa. Prace
0079-3329	Polska Akademia Nauk. Oddzial w Krakowie. Komisja Jezykoznawstwa. Wydawnictwa Zrodlowe
0079-3337	Polska Akademia Nauk. Oddzial w Krakowie. Komisja Mechaniki Stosowanej. Prace: Mechanika
0079-3345	Polska Akademia Nauk. Oddzial w Krakowie. Komisja Metalurgiczno-Odlewnicza. Prace: Metalurgia
0079-3353	Polska Akademia Nauk. Oddzial w Krakowie. Komisja Nauk Ekonomicznych. Prace
0079-3361	Prace Geologiczne
0079-337X	Polska Akademia Nauk. Oddzial w Krakowie. Komisja Nauk Historycznych. Materialy
0079-3388	Polska Akademia Nauk. Oddzial w Krakowie. Komisja Nauk Historycznych. Prace
0079-3396	Polska Akademia Nauk. Oddzial w Krakowie. Komisja Nauk Mineralogicznych. Prace Mineralogiczne
0079-340X	Polska Akademia Nauk. Oddzial w Krakowie. Komisja Nauk Pedagogicznych. Prace
0079-3418	Polska Akademia Nauk. Oddzial w Krakowie. Komisja Nauk Pedagogicznych. Rocznik
0079-3426	Polska Akademia Nauk. Oddzial w Krakowie. Komisja Orientalistyczna. Prace
0079-3434	Polska Akademia Nauk. Oddzial w Krakowie. Komisja Slowianoznawstwa. Prace
0079-3442	Polska Akademia Nauk. Oddzial w Krakowie. Komisja Socjologiczna. Prace
0079-3450	Polska Akademia Nauk. Oddzial w Krakowie. Komisja Urbanistyki i Architektury. Teka
0079-3477	Polska Akademia Nauk. Komitet Gospodarki Wodnej. Prace i Studia
0079-3485	Prace Jezykoznawcze
0079-3493	Polska Akademia Nauk. Komitet Przestrzennego Zagospodarowania Kraju. Biuletyn
0079-3507	Polska Akademia Nauk. Komitet Przestrzennego Zagospodarowania Kraju. Studia
0079-3531	Polska Akademia Nauk. Oddzial w Krakowie. Rocznik
0079-354X	Polska Akademia Nauk. Oddzial w Krakowie. Komisja Naukowych. Sprawozdania z Posiedzen
0079-3558	Polska Akademia Nauk. Wydzial Nauk Medycznych. Rozprawy
0079-3566	Polska Akademia Nauk. Zaklad Archeologii Srodziemnomorskiej. Etudes et Travaux
0079-3574	Polska Akademia Nauk. Instytut Geofizyki. Materialy i Prace
0079-3582	Polska Adakemia Nauk. Centrum Badan Naukowych w Wojewodztwie Katowickim. Prace i Studia
0079-3590	Polska Bibliografia Literacka
0079-3612	Polska Piesn i Muzyka Ludowa. Zrodla i Materialy
0079-3620	Polska 2000
0079-3647	Polskie Archiwum Weterynaryjne
0079-3655	Polskie Towarzystwo Cybernetyczne. Biuletyn see 0137-3595
0079-3663	Polskie Towarzystwo Geologiczne. Rocznik
0079-368X	Polskie Towarzystwo Matematyczne. Roczniki. Seria I: Commentationes Mathematicae. Prace Matematyczne
0079-3698	Polskie Towarzystwo Matematyczne. Roczniki. Seria II. Wiadomosci Matematyczne
0079-3701	Mechanika Teoretyczna i Stosowana
0079-371X	Polskie Towarzystwo Naukowe na Obczyznie. Rocznik
0079-3728	Polymer Engineering and Technology Series
0079-3736	Polymer Reviews
0079-3795	Pomologia Republicii Socialiste Romania†
0079-3809	University of Poona. Centre of Advanced Study in Sanskrit. Publications
0079-3825	Poor's Register of Corporations, Directors and Executives
0079-3833	Popes through History†
0079-3841	Popular Lectures in Mathematics Series
0079-3868	Population Census of Papua New Guinea. Population Characteristics Bulletin Series
0079-3876	Population Council, New York. Country Profiles†
0079-3892	Population Council, New York. Reports on Population/Family Planning†
0079-3906	Population Estimates of Arizona
0079-3922	University of California, Berkeley. Institute of International Studies. Population Monograph Series†
0079-3930	Population of the Municipalities of the Netherlands
0079-3957	University of Port Elizabeth. Publications. General Series
0079-3965	University of Port Elizabeth. Publications. Research Papers
0079-3973	University of Port Elizabeth. Publications. Symposia and Seminars *changed to* University of Port Elizabeth. Publications. Symposia, Seminars, and Lectures
0079-3981	Port of Baltimore Handbook
0079-399X	Port of Piraeus Authority. Statistical Bulletin *changed to* Port of Piraeus Authority. Statistical Report
0079-4058	Universidade do Rio Grande do Sul. Instituto de Ciencias Naturais. Boletim *changed to* Universidade Federal do Rio Grande do Sul. Instituto de Biociencias. Boletim
0079-4066	Ports of the World
0079-4082	Portugal. Instituto Nacional de Estatistica. Centro de Estudos Demograficos. Revista
0079-4104	Portugal. Instituto Nacional de Estatistica. Anuario Demografico. *changed to* Portugal. Instituto Nacional de Estatistica. Estatisticas Demograficas
0079-4112	Portugal. Instituto Nacional de Estatistica. Anuario Estatistico
0079-4120	Portugal. Instituto Nacional de Estatistica. Estatististicas das Contribucoes e Impostos
0079-4139	Portugal. Instituto Nacional de Estatistica. Estatisticas Agricolas
0079-4147	Portugal. Instituto Nacional de Estatistica. Estatisticas do Comercio Externo
0079-4155	Portugal. Instituto Nacional de Estatistica. Estatisticas de Educacao
0079-4163	Portugal. Instituto Nacional de Estatistica. Estatisticas das Organizacoes Sindicais
0079-4171	Portugal. Instituto Nacional de Estatistica. Estatisticas das Financas Publicas
0079-418X	Portugal. Instituto Nacional de Estatistica. Estatistica Industrial
0079-4201	Portugal. Ministerio das Financas. Relatorio do Orcamento Geral do Estado
0079-421X	Portugiesische Forschungen der Goerresgesellschaft. Reihe 1: Aufsaetze zur Portugiesischen Kulturgeschichte
0079-4228	Portugiesische Forschungen der Goerresgesellschaft. Reihe 2: Monographien
0079-4236	Post-Medieval Archaeology
0079-4244	Postage Stamps of the United States
0079-4252	Postepy Mikrobiologii
0079-4260	Postepy Napedu Elektrycznego
0079-4279	Postepy Pediatrii
0079-4295	Postilla
0079-4309	Potato Marketing Board, London. Annual Report and Accounts
0079-4317	Abstracts of Theses and Dissertations Accepted for Higher Degrees in the Potchefstroom University for Christian Higher Education
0079-4325	Union Catalogue of Theses and Dissertations of the South African Universities
0079-4333	Potchefstroom University for Christian Higher Education. Wetenskaplike Bydraes. Reeks A: Geesteswetenskappe
0079-4341	Potchefstroom University for Christian Higher Education. Wetenskaplike Bydraes. Reeks B: Natuurwetenskappe. Series
0079-4376	Museum fuer Ur- und Fruehgeschichte des Bezirkes Potsdam, Frankfurt/Oder und Cottbus. Veroeffentlichungen
0079-4384	Potsdam. Paedagogische Hochschule. Wissenschaftliche Zeitschrift
0079-4414	Power Conditioning Specialists Conference. Record *changed to* I E E E Power Electronics Specialists Conference. Record
0079-4422	Power Farming Technical Annual
0079-4430	Power Industry Computer Applications Conference. Record
0079-4457	Power Sources Symposium. Proceedings
0079-4465	Powstanie Styczniowe. Materialy i Dokumenty
0079-4473	Politechnika Poznanska. Zeszyty Naukowe. Chemia Techniki Zastosowan see 0137-6896
0079-4481	Politechnika Poznanska. Materialy Historyczno-Metodyczne. Studia Filozoficzne *changed to* Materialy Historyczno-Metodyczne
0079-449X	Politechnika Poznanska. Zeszyty Naukowe. Budownictwo Ladowe *changed to* Politechnika Poznanska. Zeszyty Naukowe. Budownictwo
0079-4503	Politechnika Poznanska. Zeszyty Naukowe. Elektryka
0079-4511	Politechnika Poznanska. Zeszyty Naukowe. Fizyka
0079-452X	Politechnika Poznanska. Zeszyty Naukowe. Matematyka see 0044-4413
0079-4538	Politechnika Poznanska. Zeszyty Naukowe. Mechanika
0079-4546	Akademia Ekonomiczna, Poznan. Zeszyty Naukowe .Seria 1
0079-4554	Akademia Ekonomiczna, Poznan. Zeszyty Naukowe. Seria 2. Prace Habilitacyjne i Doktorskie
0079-4570	Societe des Amis des Sciences et des Lettres de Poznan. Bulletin. Serie D: Sciences Biologiques
0079-4589	Poznanskie Towarzystwo Przyjaciol Nauk. Komisja Automatyki. Prace *changed to* Studia z Automatyki
0079-4597	Poznanskie Towarzystwo Przyjaciol Nauk. Komisja Budownictwa i Architektury. Prace
0079-4619	Poznanskie Towarzystwo Przyjaciol Nauk. Komisja Biologiczna. Prace
0079-4627	Poznanskie Towarzystwo Przyjaciol Nauk. Komisja Elektrotechniki. Prace
0079-4635	Poznanskie Towarzystwo Przyjaciol Nauk. Komisja Filozoficzna. Prace
0079-4643	Poznanskie Towarzystwo Przyjaciol Nauk. Komisja Geograficzno-Geologiczna. Prace
0079-4651	Poznanskie Towarzystwo Przyjaciol Nauk. Komisja Historyczna. Prace
0079-466X	Poznanskie Towarzystwo Przyjaciol Nauk. Komisja Historii Sztuki. Prace
0079-4678	Poznanskie Towarzystwo Przyjaciol Nauk. Komisja Jezykoznawcza. Prace
0079-4686	Poznanskie Towarzystwo Przyjaciol Nauk. Komisja Matematyczno-Przyrodnicza. Prace
0079-4708	Poznanskie Towarzystwo Przyjaciol Nauk. Komisja Nauk Rolniczych i Komisja Nauk Lesnych. Prace
0079-4716	Poznanskie Towarzystwo Przyjaciol Nauk. Komisja Nauk Spolecznych. Prace
0079-4724	Poznanskie Towarzystwo Przyjaciol Nauk. Komisja Technologii Drewna. Prace
0079-4740	Lingua Posnaniensis
0079-4759	Prace i Materialy Etnograficzne
0079-4767	Prace Literackie
0079-4775	Prace Onomastyczne
0079-4783	Prace Orientalistyczne
0079-4791	Prace Polonistyczne
0079-4805	Prace Popularnonaukowe
0079-4821	Practical Table Series
0079-4848	Praehistorische Zeitschrift
0079-4856	Prague Studies in Mathematical Linguistics†
0079-4872	Prakseologia
0079-4880	Praktische Betriebswirtschaft
0079-4899	Praktische Chirurgie
0079-4902	Prameny Ceske a Slovenske Lingvistiky. Rada Ceska
0079-4929	Pravnehistoricke Studie
0079-4937	Pravoslavny Theologicky Sbornik
0079-4945	Praxis der Klinischen Psychologie
0079-4953	Prediction Annual
0079-4961	Predigtstudien
0079-497X	Prehistoric Society, London. Proceedings
0079-4988	Preparative Inorganic Reactions†
0079-4996	Presbyterian Church in Canada. General Assembly. Acts and Proceedings
0079-502X	Press Braille, Adult
0079-5046	Press Radio and T.V. Guide
0079-5054	Pressure Gauge
0079-5062	Pretoria College for Advanced Technical Education. Annual/Jaarblad†
0079-5089	Primary Socialization, Language, and Education†
0079-5100	Primates
0079-5119	Primates in Medicine
0079-5127	Primatologia
0079-5143	Prince Edward Island. Department of Fisheries. Annual Report
0079-5151	Prince Edward Island. Public Utilities Commission. Annual Report
0079-5178	Princeton-Cambridge Studies in Chinese Linguistics *changed to* Princeton-Cambridge Series in Chinese Linguistics
0079-5186	Princeton Essays in Literature
0079-5194	Princeton Mathematical Series
0079-5208	Princeton Monographs in Art and Archaeology
0079-5216	Princeton Series in Physics
0079-5240	Princeton Studies in Mathematical Economics
0079-5259	Princeton Studies in Music

0079-5267 Princeton University. Center of International Studies Policy Memorandum
0079-5275 Princeton University. Committee for the Excavation of Antioch. Publications†
0079-5283 Princeton University. Computer Sciences Laboratory. Technical Report
0079-5291 Princeton University. Econometric Research Program. Research Memorandum
0079-5305 Princeton University. Industrial Relations Section. Research Report
0079-5313 Prindle, Weber and Schmidt Complementary Series in Mathematics
0079-5321 Printing Historical Society. Journal
0079-533X Printing Magazine Purchasing Guide†
0079-5348 Printing Trades Blue Book. New York Edition
0079-5356 Printing Trades Blue Book. Northeastern Edition
0079-5364 Printing Trades Blue Book. Southeastern Edition
0079-5372 Printing Trades Directory
0079-5399 Private Independent Schools
0079-5402 Private Press Books
0079-5453 Prize Stories; The O. Henry Awards
0079-550X Pro and Amateur Hockey Guide
0079-5518 Pro Basketball Guide *changed to* Basketball Guide
0079-5526 Pro Football
0079-5534 Pro Football
0079-5550 Pro Helvetia†
0079-5569 N.H.L. Pro Hockey
0079-5577 Pro Hockey Guide
0079-5593 Pro Mundi Vita. Special Notes *changed to* Pro Mundi Vita Dossiers
0079-5607 Probability and Mathematical Statistics
0079-5615 Probation and Parole
0079-5631 Probe
0079-564X Probleme der Festkoerperelektronik
0079-5666 Problemes Actuels d'Endocrinologie et de Nutrition
0079-5682 Problemi e Ricerche de Storia Antica
0079-5690 Problemi Economici d'Oggi†
0079-5739 Problems in Mathematical Analysis Report
0079-5763 Problems of the Contemporary World
0079-5771 Problems of the North
0079-578X Problemy Ekonomiczne
0079-5798 Problemy Polonii Zagranicznej
0079-5801 Problemy Rad Narodowych. Studia i Materialy
0079-581X Problemy Rejonow Uprzemyslawianych
0079-5836 Prodei
0079-5852 Produccion Rural Argentina
0079-5860 Produce Marketing Association. Yearbook *changed to* Produce Marketing Almanac
0079-5895 Producto Neto de la Agricultura Espanola
0079-5925 Professional and Trade Organisations in India
0079-5933 Professional School Psychology
0079-595X Profitability of Cotton Growing in Israel
0079-5968 Profitability of Poultry Farming in Israel
0079-5976 Profitability of Sugarbeet Growing in Israel
0079-5984 Profits
0079-6018 Accredited Programs in Journalism *changed to* Accredited Journalism Education
0079-6026 Progress in Aeronautical Sciences *see* 0376-0421
0079-6034 Progress in Allergy
0079-6042 Progress in Analytical Chemistry
0079-6050 Progress in Astronautics and Aeronautics Series
0079-6077 Progress in Bio-Organic Chemistry
0079-6085 Progress in Biochemical Pharmacology
0079-6107 Progress in Biophysics and Molecular Biology
0079-6115 Progress in Boron Chemistry†
0079-6123 Progress in Brain Research
0079-614X Progress in Ceramic Science†
0079-6158 Progress in Chemical Toxicology
0079-6166 Progress in Clinical Cancer
0079-6174 Progress in Clinical Pathology
0079-6182 Progress in Clinical Psychology
0079-6212 Progress in Control Engineering†
0079-6247 Progress in Elementary Particle and Cosmic Ray Physics†
0079-6255 Progress in Experimental Personality Research
0079-6263 Progress in Experimental Tumor Research
0079-6271 Progress in Gastroenterology
0079-628X Progress in Geophysics
0079-6298 Progress in Gynecology
0079-6301 Progress in Haematology
0079-631X Progress in Heat and Mass Transfer†
0079-6328 Progress in High Temperature Physics and Chemistry†
0079-6336 Progress in Histochemistry and Cytochemistry
0079-6344 Progress in Immunobiological Standardization *see* 0301-5149
0079-6379 Progress in Inorganic Chemistry
0079-6387 Progress in Learning Disabilities
0079-6409 Progress in Liver Diseases
0079-6417 Progress in Low Temperature Physics
0079-6425 Progress in Materials Science
0079-645X Progress in Medical Virology
0079-6468 Progress in Medicinal Chemistry†
0079-6468 Progress in Medicinal Chemistry
0079-6484 Progress in Molecular and Subcellular Biology
0079-6492 Progress in Neurological Surgery
0079-6506 Progress in Neurology and Psychiatry†
0079-6514 Progress in Nuclear Energy. Series 3-Process Chemistry *see* 0149-1970
0079-6530 Progress in Nuclear Energy. Series 9-Analytical Chemistry *see* 0149-1970
0079-6557 Progress in Nuclear Energy. Series 3-Process Chemistry *see* 0149-1970
0079-6565 Progress in Nuclear Magnetic Resonance Spectroscopy
0079-6573 Progress in Nuclear Medicine
0079-6581 Progress in Nuclear Medicine *see* 0163-6170
0079-659X Progress in Nuclear Physics *see* 0146-6410
0079-6603 Progress in Nucleic Acid Research and Molecular Biology
0079-6611 Progress in Oceanography
0079-6638 Progress in Optics
0079-6646 Progress in Pediatric Radiology
0079-6654 Progress in Pediatric Surgery
0079-6662 Progress in Physical Organic Chemistry
0079-6670 Progress in Physiological Psychology *changed to* Psychobiology and Physiological Psychology
0079-6689 Progress in Phytochemistry
0079-6697 Progress in Polarography†
0079-6700 Progress in Polymer Science
0079-6719 Progress in Powder Metallurgy
0079-6727 Progress in Quantum Electronics
0079-6735 Progress in Radiation Therapy
0079-6743 Progress in Reaction Kinetics
0079-6751 Progress in Respiration Research
0079-6786 Progress in Solid State Chemistry
0079-6794 U. S. Fish and Wildlife Service. Progress in Sport Fishery Research *see* 0362-0700
0079-6808 Progress in Stereochemistry†
0079-6816 Progress in Surface Science
0079-6824 Progress in Surgery
0079-6832 Progress in the Chemistry of Fats and Other Lipids *see* 0163-7827
0079-6840 Progress in the Science and Technology of the Rare Earths†
0079-6859 Progress in Theoretical Biology
0079-6883 Progress Polimernoi Khimii
0079-6891 Progress of Public Education in the United States *changed to* Progress of Education in the United States of America
0079-6913 Progress Report on Clays and Shales of Montana†
0079-6921 Progressive Grocer's Marketing Guidebook
0079-6956 Project Skywater. Annual Report
0079-6972 Promotrans
0079-6980 Proof: The Yearbook of American Bibliographical and Textual Studies†
0079-6999 Proportions†
0079-7006 Proprietary Association. Committee on Scientific Development. Annual Research and Scientific Development Conference. Proceedings
0079-7014 Prospects for America
0079-7022 Prospezioni Archeologiche†
0079-7049 Protein Synthesis: a Series of Advances
0079-7065 Protides of the Biological Fluids
0079-7073 Protoplasmologia; Handbuch der Protoplasmaforschung *changed to* Cell Biology Monographs
0079-709X Provinzialinstitut fuer Westfaelische Landes- und Volksforschung. Veroeffentlichungen
0079-7111 Pruefen und Entscheiden
0079-7138 Przeglad Archeologiczny
0079-7154 Przeglad Naukowej Literatury Rolniczej i Lesnej. Gleboznawstwo. Chemia Rolna. Ogolna Uprawa Roli i Roslin i Siedliska Lesne
0079-7162 Przeglad Naukowej Literatury Zootechnicznej
0079-7170 Przeglad Zagranicznej Literatury Geograficznej
0079-7189 Przeszlosc Demograficzna Polski. Materialy i Studia
0079-7197 Pseudepigrapha Veteris Testamenti Graece
0079-7227 Psychiatria Fennica
0079-726X Psychiatrie de l'Enfant
0079-7278 Psychiatry; a Medical World News Publication†
0079-7286 Psychiatry and Art
0079-7294 Psychoanalytic Study of Society
0079-7308 Psychoanalytic Study of the Child
0079-7324 Psychologen Adresboek
0079-7332 Psychologia Africana
0079-7340 Psychologia Africana. Monograph Supplement†
0079-7359 Psychological Issues. Monograph
0079-7383 Psychological Studies. Major Series *changed to* Psychological Studies
0079-7391 Psychological Studies. Minor Series†
0079-7405 Psychologie und Person
0079-7413 Psychologische Praxis
0079-7421 Psychology of Learning and Motivation: Advances in Research and Theory
0079-743X Psychopharmacology Handbook: Animal Research in Psychopharmacology†
0079-7448 Psychotheque
0079-7456 Pszichologia a Gyakorlatban
0079-7464 Pszichologiai Tanulmanyok
0079-7472 Pubblicita in Italia
0079-7499 Public Administration in Israel and Abroad†
0079-7537 Public and Preparatory Schools. Yearbook
0079-7545 Public Continuing and Adult Education Almanac
0079-7561 Sweden. Riksrevisionsverket. Statens Finanser
0079-7588 Public Health Conference on Records and Statistics. Proceedings
0079-7596 Public Health Monograph
0079-7618 University of Kansas Libraries. Annual Public Lecture on Books and Bibliography†
0079-7626 Public Papers of the Presidents of the United States
0079-7634 Public Policy Issues in Resource Management
0079-7642 Public Affairs Manual for the Bench and Bar of California†
0079-7650 Public Schools Careers Guide†
0079-7669 S I L Publications in Linguistics and Related Fields
0079-7685 Publications in Medieval Science
0079-7707 Publications in Near and Middle East Studies. Series A
0079-7715 Publications in Near and Middle East Studies. Series B
0079-7731 Publications in Psychology
0079-774X Publications in Seismology
0079-7758 Publications in Tropical Geography Savanna Research Series
0079-7766 Publications in Water Research at Oregon State University
0079-7782 Publications on Asia
0079-7790 Publications on Russia and Eastern Europe
0079-7804 Publications on Social History
0079-7812 Publications Romanes et Francaises
0079-7820 Publishers and Printers of Israel; a Select List *changed to* Israel Book Trade Directory
0079-7839 Publishers in the United Kingdom and Their Addresses
0079-7847 Publishers International Yearbook†
0079-7855 Publishers' Trade List Annual
0079-7863 Puerto Rico. Negociado del Presupuesto. Resoluciones Conjuntas del Presupuesto General y de Presupuestos Especiales
0079-7871 Puerto Rico. Department of the Treasury. Economy & Finances
0079-788X Universidad de Puerto Rico. Institute of Caribbean Studies. Special Studies
0079-7901 Puku
0079-7936 Canada's Pulp and Paper Business Directory *see* 0317-3550
0079-7944 Pulp and Paper Industry Technical Conference. Record *see* 0190-2172
0079-7952 Pulp & Paper Magazine of Canada's Reference Manual & Buyers' Guide *changed to* Pulp and Paper, Canada's Reference Manual & Buyers' Guide
0079-7960 Pulp and Paper Research Institute of Canada. Annual Report
0079-8029 University of the Punjab. Arabic and Persian Society. Journal
0079-8045 University of the Punjab. Department of Zoology. Bulletin. New Series
0079-8061 Pupila: Libros de Nuestro Tiempo
0079-807X Purdue Opinion Panel, Lafayette, Indiana. Report†
0079-8096 Purdue University. Civil Engineering Reprints
0079-810X Purdue University. Engineering Experiment Station. Joint Highway Research Project. Research Reports
0079-8126 Materials Research in Science and Engineering at Purdue University. Progress Report
0079-8134 Purdue University. Office of Manpower Studies. Manpower Report
0079-8142 Purdue University. Road School. Proceedings of Annual Road School
0079-8150 Pure and Applied Cryogenics†
0079-8169 Pure and Applied Mathematics
0079-8177 Pure and Applied Mathematics Series
0079-8185 Pure and Applied Mathematics; a Series of Texts and Monographs *changed to* Pure and Applied Mathematics: A Wiley Interscience Series of Texts, Monographs and Tracts
0079-8193 Pure and Applied Physics
0079-8207 University of Pittsburgh. Pymatuning Laboratory of Ecology. Special Publication
0079-8215 Pyrenae: Cronica Arqueologica
0079-8223 Pyttersen's Nederlandse Almanak
0079-824X Quaderni dei Padri Benedettini di San Giorgio Maggiore
0079-8258 Quaderni di Archeologia della Libia
0079-8274 Quaderni di Poesia Neogreca
0079-8282 Quaderni e Guide di Archeologia†
0079-8304 Quality of Surface Waters of the United States†
0079-8312 Quarterly Journal of Studies on Alcohol. Supplement *see* 0363-468X
0079-8347 Universite Laval. Centre d'Etudes Nordiques. Travaux et Documents
0079-8355 Universite Laval. Departement d'Exploitation et Utilisation des Bois. Note de Recherches

1152 ISSN INDEX

0079-8363 Universite Laval. Departement d'Exploitation et Utilisation des Bois. Note Technique
0079-838X Universite Laval. Fonds de Recherches Forestieres. Contribution
0079-8398 Universite Laval. Institut d'Histoire. Cahiers
0079-8428 Quebec Library Association. Newsletter
0079-8738 Quebec (Province) Department of Natural Resources. Geological Reports
0079-8746 Quebec (Province) Ministere des Richesses Naturelles. Travaux sur le Terrain
0079-8754 Quebec (Province) Marine Biological Station, Grande-Riviere. Rapport *see* 0318-8779
0079-8762 Quebec (Province) Marine Biological Station, Grande-Riviere. Cahiers d'Information *changed to* Quebec (Province) Direction Generale des Peches Maritimes Cahiers d'Information
0079-8770 Quebec (Province) Office de la Langue Francaise. Cahiers
0079-8789 Queen's Medical Review
0079-8797 Queen's Papers on Pure and Applied Mathematics
0079-8800 Queensland. Geological Survey. Publications
0079-8819 Geological Survey of Queensland. Report
0079-8827 Queensland Law Almanac *changed to* Queensland Legal Directory
0079-8835 Queensland Museum, Brisbane. Memoirs
0079-8843 Queensland Naturalist
0079-8851 Queensland Society of Sugar Cane Technologists. Proceedings *changed to* Australian Society of Sugar Cane Technologists. Proceedings.
0079-886X University of Queensland. Computer Centre. Papers
0079-8878 University of Queensland. Department of Agriculture. Papers†
0079-8886 University of Queensland. Department of Architecture. Papers†
0079-8894 University of Queensland. Department of Accountancy. Papers *changed to* University of Queensland. Department of Commerce. Papers
0079-8908 University of Queensland. Department of Botany. Papers†
0079-8916 University of Queensland. Department of Entomology. Papers†
0079-8924 University of Queensland. Departments of Government and History. Paper†
0079-8932 University of Queensland. Department of Geology. Papers†
0079-8940 University of Queensland. Department of Social Sciences. Papers†
0079-8959 University of Queensland. Department of Zoology. Papers†
0079-8975 University of Queensland. Faculty of Arts. Papers†
0079-8983 University of Queensland. Faculty of Education. Papers†
0079-8991 University of Queensland. Faculty of Law. Papers†
0079-9009 University of Queensland. Faculty of Medicine. Papers†
0079-9017 University of Queensland. Faculty of Veterinary Science. Papers†
0079-9033 University of Queensland Inaugural Lectures
0079-9041 Queensland'S Health†
0079-905X Quellenkataloge zur Musikgeschichte
0079-9068 Quellen und Forschungen aus Italienischen Archiven und Bibliotheken
0079-9076 Quellen und Forschungen zur Basler Geschichte
0079-9084 Quellen und Forschungen zur Wuerttembergischen Kirchengeschichte
0079-9114 Quellen und Studien zur Geschichte Osteuropas
0079-9130 Quellen und Untersuchungen zur Geschichte der Deutschen und Oesterreichischen Arbeiterbewegung. Neue Folge†
0079-9149 Quellenschriften zur Westdeutschen Vor- und Fruehgeschichte
0079-9157 Quellenwerke zur Alten Geschichte Amerikas
0079-919X Question
0079-9211 Quetico-Superior Wilderness Research Center, Ely, Minnesota. Annual Report
0079-922X Quetico-Superior Wilderness Research Center, Ely, Minnesota. Technical Notes
0079-9238 University of the Philippines. Asian Center. Monograph Series
0079-9246 University of the Philippines. Community Development Research Council. Study Series
0079-9254 University of the Philippines. Institute of Public Administration. (Publication)
0079-9262 Qui Represente Qui
0079-9270 Qui Vend et Achete Quoi?
0079-9289 Quick Frozen Foods Directory of Frozen Food Processors
0079-9300 R I C
0079-9327 Universidade Federal de Minas Gerais. Corpo Discente. Revista Literaria.
0079-9335 R L S: Regional Language Studies... Newfoundland
0079-9343 R. M. Bucke Memorial Society for the Study of Religious Experience. Newsletter-Review
0079-9351 R. M. Bucke Memorial Society for the Study of Religious Experience. Proceedings of the Conference
0079-936X Rabbinical Assembly, New York. Proceedings
0079-9386 Rabindranath Tagore Memorial Lectureship†
0079-9394 Raceform up-to-Date
0079-9408 Racehorses
0079-9416 Racial Policies of American Industry. Reports†
0079-9424 Racing and Football Outlook: Racing Annual
0079-9440 Radio Amateur's Handbook
0079-9467 Radio Handbook
0079-9475 R S G B Amateur Radio Call Book
0079-9483 Radiochemical and Radioanalytical Letters
0079-9491 Radner Lectures
0079-9513 Railway Directory and Yearbook
0079-9521 Railway Fuel and Operating Officers Association. Proceedings
0079-9548 Railway Technical Review
0079-9556 Rajasthan, India. Directorate of Economics and Statistics. Budget Study
0079-9564 Rajasthan, India. Directorate of Economics and Statistics. Basic Statistics
0079-9572 Rajasthan Year Book and Who's Who
0079-9580 Rak v Sloveniji. Tabele
0079-9599 Rampenlicht
0079-9602 Ranchi University Mathematical Journal
0079-9610 Rand McNally Campground and Trailer Park Guide
0079-9629 Rand McNally National Park Guide
0079-9637 Rand McNally Discover Historic America
0079-9645 Rand McNally Travel Trailer Guide *see* 0079-9610
0079-967X Ranganathan Series in Library Science†
0079-9688 Rapport Annuel sur l'Economie Arabe
0079-9696 Rapport Annuel sur l'Economie Syrienne
0079-9726 Rassegna Internazionale del Film Scientifico - Didattico†
0079-9815 Raymond Dart Lecture
0079-9823 Reaction Mechanisms in Organic Chemistry
0079-9831 Reader's Digest Almanac and Yearbook
0079-984X Readex Microprint Publications
0079-9858 University of Reading. Graduate School of Contemporary European Studies. Occasional Publication
0079-9866 Reading University Studies on Contemporary Europe
0079-9874 Readings in Political Economy *see* 0305-814X
0079-9890 Real Estate Reports
0079-9912 Recent Advances in Food Science†
0079-9939 Recent Advances in Plasma Diagnostics
0079-9947 Recent Developments in the Chemistry of Natural Carbon Compounds
0079-9955 Recent Developments of Neurobiology in Hungary
0079-9963 Recent Progress in Hormone Research. Proceedings of the Laurentian Hormone Conference
0079-9971 Recent Progress in Surface Science
0079-998X Recent Publications in the Social and Behavioral Sciences. A B S Guide Supplement†
0080-0015 Recent Results in Cancer Research
0080-0023 Recent Sociology
0080-0031 Recherches Africaines†
0080-0058 Recherches de Psychologie Experimentale et Comparee†
0080-0074 Recherches et Documents d'Art et d'Archeologie
0080-0090 Recherches Mediterraneennes. Bibliographies†
0080-0139 Recherches sur la Musique Francaise Classique
0080-0155 Recht und Wettbewerb†
0080-0163 Rechts- und Staatswissenschaften
0080-018X Rechtspflege Jahrbuch
0080-0228 Universidade Federal de Pernambuco. Instituto de Antibioticos. Revista
0080-0236 Universidade Federal de Pernambuco. Instituto Oceanografico. Trabalhos *see* 0374-0412
0080-0244 Universidad Federal de Pernambuco. Instituto de Geosciencias. Serie B: Estudos e Pesquisas
0080-0252 Recommended Wayside Inns of Britain
0080-0260 Reconstruction Surgery and Traumatology
0080-0287 Records of Civilization. Sources and Studies
0080-0295 Records of Oceanographic Works in Japan. New Series†
0080-0309 Recueil Complet des Budgets de la Syrie
0080-0333 Recueil des Instructions Donnees aux Ambassadeurs et Ministres de France
0080-0341 Recurring Bibliography, Education in the Allied Health Professions
0080-0384 American National Red Cross. Annual Report *changed to* American Red Cross. Annual Report
0080-0392 New Zealand Red Cross Society. Report
0080-0414 Reducing Your Income Tax
0080-0422 Reed's Nautical Almanac
0080-0430 Reference and Subscription Books Reviews
0080-0449 Reference Book - Argentina
0080-0457 Reference Book - Republic of South Africa
0080-0473 Reformationsgeschichtliche Studien und Texte
0080-0481 Reformed Church of America. Historical Series
0080-049X Refractory Materials
0080-0503 Refrigeration and Air Conditioning Directory *see* 0305-0777
0080-0511 Refrigeration Annual
0080-0538 Regency International Directory
0080-0554 Regesta Regum Scottorum
0080-0562 Regi Magyar Dallamok Tara
0080-0570 Regi Magyar Prozai Emlekek
0080-0589 Regional Conference on Water Resources Development in Asia and the Far East. Proceedings
0080-0619 Regional Science Research Institute, Philadelphia. Bibliography Series
0080-0627 Regional Science Research Institute, Philadelphia. Monograph Series
0080-066X Registre Aeronautique International
0080-0678 Registre International de Classification de Navires et d'Aeronefs *changed to* Registre Maritime
0080-0686 Registry of Accredited Facilities and Certified Individuals in Orthotics and Prosthetics
0080-0708 Rehabilitation der Entwicklungsgehemmten
0080-0724 Rehabilitation Industries Corporation. Annual Report
0080-0759 Rehovot Conference on Science in the Advancement of New States. (Proceedings)†
0080-0783 Reilly-Lake Shore Graphics. R O P Color Requirements Report *changed to* Newspaper Requirements
0080-0791 Reine und Angewandte Metallkunde in Einzeldarstellungen *changed to* Materials Research and Engineering
0080-0813 Reliability and Maintainability†
0080-0821 Reliability Physics Symposium Abstracts
0080-0848 Religion and Reason; Method and Theory in the Study and Interpretation of Religion
0080-0864 Religion et Sciences de l'Homme
0080-0872 Religion, Wissenschaft, Kultur. Jahrbuch
0080-0880 Remains, Historical and Literary, Connected with the Palatine Counties of Lancaster and Chester
0080-0899 Remedia Hoechst
0080-0910 Renderers' Yearbook *changed to* Spectrum
0080-0929 Universite de Haute Bretagne. Centre d'Etudes Hispaniques, Hispano-Americaines et Luso-Bresiliennes. Travaux
0080-0937 Commission Belge de Bibliographie. Repertoire Annuel des Comptes-Rendus de Congres Scientifiques
0080-0945 Repertoire Complementaire Alphabetique des Valeurs Mobilieres Francaises et Etrangeres Non Cotees en France
0080-0953 Bulletin Signaletique. Part 530: Repertoire d'Art et d'Archeologie. Nouvelle Serie
0080-097X Repertoire des Cooperatives du Quebec
0080-0988 Annuaire des Entreprises du Mali
0080-1003 Repertoire des Livres de Langue Francaise Disponibles *changed to* Livres Disponibles
0080-1011 Repertoire des Principaux Textes Legislatifs et Reglementaires Promulgues en Republique du Mali
0080-102X Repertoire des Productions de l'Industrie Cotonniere Francaise
0080-1038 France. Delegation Generale a la Recherche Scientifique et Technique. Repertoire des Scientifiques Francais. Tome 3: Biologie
0080-1046 France. Delegation Generale a la Recherche Scientifique et Technique. Repertoire des Scientifiques Francais. Tome 4: Chimie
0080-1062 France. Delegation Generale a la Recherche Scientifique et Technique. Repertoire des Scientifiques Francais. Tome 5: Physique
0080-1070 Repertoire des Societes de Commerce Exterieur Francaises
0080-1089 Repertoire Dictionnaire Industriel
0080-1100 Syndicat National de la Librairie Ancienne et Moderne. Repertoire *changed to* Guide a l'Usage des Amateurs de Livres
0080-1127 Repertoire General Alphabetique des Valeurs Cotees en France et des Valeurs Non Cotees
0080-1135 Repertoire General des Clubs Sportifs de France
0080-1151 Repertoire International des Medievistes
0080-116X France. Delegation Generale a la Recherche Scientifique et Technique. Repertoire National des Chercheurs: Sciences Sociales et Humaines. Tome 1: Ethnologie, Linguistique, Psychologie, Psychologie Sociale, Sociologie

ISSN INDEX 1153

0080-1186 France. Delegation Generale a la Recherche Scientifique et Technique. Repertoire Permanent de l'Administration Francaise
0080-1194 Repertoire Pratique de la Publicite
0080-1216 Repertorio delle Industrie Siderurgiche Italiane
0080-1224 Repertorium van Werken, in Vlaanderen Uitgegeven, of Door Monopoliehouders Ingevoerd
0080-1240 Report and Studies in the History of Art *see* 0091-7338
0080-1259 Report of Forest and Windbarrier Planting in the United States *changed to* Report of Forest Planting, Seeding and Silvical Treatments in the United States
0080-1267 Report of Milk Utilization in Montana
0080-1283 Fisheries of Scotland Report
0080-1305 Zambia. Central Statistical Office. Agricultural and Pastoral Production *changed to* Zambia. Central Statistical Office. Agricultural and Pastoral Production (Commercial and Non-Commercial)
0080-1305 Zambia. Central Statistical Office. Agricultural and Pastoral Production *changed to* Zambia. Central Statistical Office. Agricultural and Pastoral Production (Non-Commercial)
0080-1305 Zambia. Central Statistical Office. Agricultural and Pastoral Production *changed to* Zambia. Central Statistical Office. Agricultural and Pastoral Production (Commercial Farms)
0080-1313 Israel. Ministry of Labour. Registrar of Cooperative Societies. Report on the Cooperative Movement in Israel
0080-1321 Development of Education in Pakistan
0080-133X Reportages Fantastiques
0080-1348 Reports and Papers in the Social Sciences
0080-1356 Reports and Papers on Mass Communications
0080-1364 Reports of Patent, Design, Trade Mark and Other Cases
0080-1372 International Astronomical Union. Transactions and Highlights
0080-1380 Reprints in International Finance
0080-1429 Requirements for Certification of Teachers, Counsellors, Librarians, Administrators for Elementary Schools, Secondary Schools, Junior Colleges
0080-1453 Research and Clinical Studies in Headache
0080-147X Register of Research and Investigation in Adult Education
0080-1488 Research and Publications in New York State History
0080-1518 Research Centers Directory
0080-1526 Alberta Research Council. Annual Report
0080-1534 Alberta Research Council. Contribution Series
0080-1542 Alberta Research Council. Hail Studies Reports *changed to* Alberta Research Council. Atmospheric Sciences Reports
0080-1550 Alberta Research. Highways and River Engineering Reports *changed to* Alberta Research Council. River Engineering and Surface Hydrology Reports
0080-1569 Alberta Research Council. List of Publications
0080-1577 Alberta Research Council. Memoirs
0080-1593 Alberta Research Council. Preliminary Reports. Soil Surveys
0080-1607 Research Council of Alberta. Report *changed to* Alberta Research Council. Reports
0080-1623 Research Group for European Migration Problems. Publications
0080-1631 Research in Economics/Business Administration
0080-1658 Research in Protozoology
0080-1666 Research in Surface Forces
0080-1674 Research in the History of Education: A List of Theses for Higher Degrees in the Universities of England and Wales
0080-1704 Research Relating to Children. Bulletins
0080-1739 Research Studies in Library Science
0080-1763 Resena de Literatura, Arte, y Espectaculos
0080-1771 Reserve Bank of Australia. Annual Report
0080-178X Reserve Bank of Australia. Occasional Papers
0080-1798 Reserve Bank of Australia. Statistical Bulletin. Supplement
0080-1801 Reserve Bank of India. Annual Report
0080-181X Residue Reviews
0080-1828 Resources of Music
0080-1836 Restaurator. Supplement†
0080-1844 Results and Problems in Cell Differentiation
0080-1852 Retail Credit Federation Membership Directory *changed to* Consumer Credit Association of the United Kingdom. Membership Directory
0080-1860 Retail Wages and Salaries in Canada
0080-1933 Review of Accidents on Indian Government Railways
0080-1992 Review of the Economy of Rhodesia *see* 0070-8739
0080-2018 Reviews in Engineering Geology
0080-2026 U. S. National Science Foundation. Reviews of Data on Science Resources
0080-2042 Reviews of Physiology, Biochemistry and Experimental Pharmacology
0080-2050 Reviews of Plasma Physics
0080-2069 Revista Agronomica del Noroeste Argentino
0080-2085 Revista Cartografica
0080-2093 Revista Chilena de Historia Y Geografia
0080-2107 Revista de Administracao
0080-2115 Revista de Biologia Marina
0080-2123 Revista de Ciencias Agronomicas. Serie A†
0080-2131 Revista de Ciencias Agronomicas. Serie B†
0080-214X Revista de Ciencias Biologicas. Serie A†
0080-2158 Revista de Ciencias Biologicas. Serie B†
0080-2166 Revista de Ciencias do Homem. Serie A†
0080-2174 Revista de Ciencias do Homen. Serie B†
0080-2182 Revista de Ciencias Geologicas. Serie A†
0080-2190 Revista de Ciencias Geologicas. Serie B†
0080-2204 Revista de Ciencias Matematicas. Serie A†
0080-2212 Revista de Ciencias Matematicas. Serie B†
0080-2220 Revista de Ciencias Medicas. Serie A†
0080-2239 Revista de Ciencias Medicas. Serie B†
0080-2247 Revista de Ciencias Veterinarias. Serie A†
0080-2255 Revista de Ciencias Veterinarias. Serie B†
0080-2263 Revista de Fisica, Quimica e Engenharia. Serie A†
0080-2271 Revista de Fisica, Quimica e Engenharia. Serie B†
0080-228X Revista de Humanidades†
0080-2352 Revista de Letras
0080-2360 Revista de Matematica y Fisica Teorica. Serie A
0080-2387 Revista Humanidades
0080-2425 Revista Peruana de Entomologia
0080-2433 Revista Portuguesa de Filologia
0080-2441 Revista Scriitorilor Romani
0080-2476 Revolutionary Cuba: A Bibliographical Guide†
0080-2484 Revue Bibliographique de Sinologie
0080-2506 Revue Francaise de Cooperation Economique Avec Israel
0080-2514 Revue de Droit Compare
0080-2530 Revue des Archaeologues et Historiens d'Art de Louvain
0080-2557 Revue des Etudes Slaves
0080-2581 Revue Economique de Madagascar†
0080-259X Egyptian Review of International Law
0080-2603 Revue Hittite et Asiatique
0080-2611 Revue Internationale d'Histoire de la Banque
0080-262X Revue Roumaine d'Histoire de l'Art. Serie Beaux-Arts
0080-2638 Revue Roumaine d'Histoire de l'Art. Serie Theatre, Musique, Cinematographie
0080-2646 Revue Roumaine des Sciences Sociales. Serie de Sociologie
0080-2654 Revue Theologique de Louvain
0080-2662 Rhein-Mainische Forschungen
0080-2670 Rheinische Lebensbilder
0080-2689 Rheinische Schriften
0080-2697 Rheinisches Jahrbuch fuer Volkskunde
0080-2700 Rheumatism Review
0080-2719 Rheumatismus
0080-2727 Rheumatology
0080-2743 Rhode Island Directory of Manufacturers and List of Commercial Establishments *changed to* Rhode Island Directory of Manufacturers
0080-2751 Rhode Island Education Association. Journal
0080-2778 University of Rhode Island. Bureau of Government Research. Information Series
0080-2786 University of Rhode Island. Bureau of Government Research. Metropolitan Series†
0080-2794 University of Rhode Island. Bureau of Government Research. Research Series
0080-2808 University of Rhode Island. Law of the Sea Institute. Occasional Paper Series†
0080-2832 Zimbabwe. Ministry of Water Development. Hydrological Summaries
0080-2840 Zimbabwe. Ministry of Water Development. Hydrological Year Book
0080-2859 Zimbabwe. Ministry of Education. African Education Report
0080-2875 Zimbabwe-Rhodesia. Tobacco Research Board. Annual Report and Accounts
0080-2883 Rhodesian Nurse†
0080-2891 Rhododendrons, with Magnolias and Camellias
0080-2905 Rhododendron Information†
0080-293X Ricerche di Storia della Lingua Latina
0080-2948 Ricerche Filosofiche†
0080-2964 Ricerche Sulle Dimore Rurali in Italia
0080-2972 Richard J. Gonzalez Lecture
0080-3006 University of Richmond. Institute for Business and Community Development. Newsletter†
0080-3014 Rickia
0080-3022 Rickia. Suplemento
0080-3057 Instituut voor Rassenonderzoek van Landbouwgewassen. Jaarverslag *changed to* Rijksinstituut voor het Rassenonderzoek van Cultuurgewassen. Jaarverslag
0080-3065 Instituut voor Rassenonderzoek van Landbouwgewassen. Mededelingen *changed to* Rijksinstituut voor het Rassenonderzoek van Cultuurgewassen. Mededelingen
0080-3073 Rinascimento
0080-309X Ring Index: A List of Ring Systems Used in Organic Chemistry. Supplement
0080-3103 Colegio Militar do Rio de Janeiro. Revista Didactica
0080-3111 Museu Nacional, Rio de Janeiro. Arquivos
0080-312X Museu Nacional, Rio de Janeiro. Boletim. Nova Serie. Zoologia
0080-3138 Observatorio Nacional, Rio de Janeiro. Relatorios Preliminares†
0080-3146 Observatorio Nacional, Rio de Janeiro. Servico Astronomico. Publicacoes†
0080-3154 Observatorio Nacional, Rio de Janeiro. Servico Gravimetrico. Publicacoes†
0080-3162 Observatorio Nacional, Rio de Janerio. Servico Magnetico. Publicacoes†
0080-3189 Museu Nacional, Rio de Janeiro. Boletim. Nova Serie. Antropologia
0080-3197 Museu Nacional, Rio de Janeiro. Boletim. Nova Serie. Botanica
0080-3200 Museu Nacional, Rio de Janeiro. Boletim. Nova Serie. Geologie
0080-3227 River Bend Library System. Report of the Director
0080-3235 Rivista Archeologica dell'Antica Provincia e Diocesi di Como
0080-3243 Rivista di Chirurgia della Mano†
0080-3251 Rivista di Cultura Classica e Medioevale. Quaderni
0080-3278 Road Builder's Clinic. Proceedings
0080-3286 Road Facts India†
0080-3294 Road Notes
0080-3308 Road Research *changed to* Transport and Road Research
0080-3316 Roadmasters and Maintenance of Way Association of America. Proceedings
0080-3324 Roads and Transportation Association of Canada. Proceedings *see* 0703-7090
0080-3340 R M A Annual Statement Studies
0080-3359 Rochester Conference on Programmed Instruction in Medical Education. Proceedings
0080-3367 Rock Magazine
0080-3375 Rock Mechanics/Felsmechanik/ Mechanique des Roches. Supplement
0080-3383 Rockbridge Historical Society, Lexington, Virginia. Proceedings
0080-3391 Rockefeller Foundation. Annual Report
0080-3405 Rockefeller University, New York. Annual Report *changed to* Rockefeller University, New York. Scientific and Educational Programs
0080-3413 Rocket and Space Science Series
0080-3421 Rocznik Bialostocki
0080-343X Rocznik Ekonomiczny
0080-3448 Rocznik Elektrycznosci Atmosferycznej i Meteorologii
0080-3456 Rocznik Gdanski
0080-3464 Rocznik Grudziadzki
0080-3472 Rocznik Historii Sztuki
0080-3480 Rocznik Jeleniogorski
0080-3499 Rocznik Krakowski
0080-3502 Rocznik Lodzki
0080-3510 Rocznik Lubelski
0080-3537 Rocznik Olsztynski
0080-3545 Rocznik Orientalistyczny
0080-3561 Rocznik Sadecki
0080-357X Polskie Towarzystwo Botaniczne. Sekcja Dendrologiczna. Rocznik
0080-3588 Rocznik Slawistyczny
0080-3618 Rocznik Wroclawski
0080-3626 Roczniki Biblioteczne
0080-3634 Roczniki Dziejow Spolecznych i Gospodarczych
0080-3642 Roczniki Gleboznawcze
0080-3650 Roczniki Nauk Rolniczych. Seria A. Produkcja Roslinna
0080-3669 Roczniki Nauk Rolniczych. Seria B. Zootechniczna
0080-3677 Roczniki Nauk Rolniczych. Seria C.Technika Rolnicza
0080-3685 Roczniki Nauk Rolniczych. Seria D. Monografie
0080-3693 Roczniki Nauk Rolniczych. Seria E. Ochrona Roslin
0080-3707 Roczniki Nauk Rolniczych. Seria F. Melioracji i Vzytkow Zielonych
0080-3715 Roczniki Nauk Rolniczych. Seria G. Ekonomika Rolnictwa
0080-3723 Roczniki Nauk Rolniczych. Seria H. Rybactwo
0080-3731 Roczniki Socjologii Wsi. Studia i Materialy
0080-374X Roczniki Technologii i Chemii Zywnosci *changed to* Acta Alimentaria Polonica
0080-3758 Rodd's Chemistry of Carbon Compounds
0080-3782 Roemische Bronzen aus Deutschland
0080-3790 Roemische Historische Mitteilungen
0080-3820 Romance Languages and Their Structures. First Series. F: (French)†

0080-3839 Romance Languages and Their Structures. First Series. R: (Rumanian) †
0080-3847 Romance Languages and Their Structures. First Series. S: (Spanish)†
0080-3855 Romanica Gandensia
0080-3863 Romanica Gothoburgensia
0080-3871 Romanica Helvetica
0080-388X Romanische Bibliographie
0080-3898 Romanistisches Jahrbuch
0080-391X Istituto Giapponese di Cultura, Rome. Annuario.
0080-3928 Istituto Giapponese di Cultura, Rome. Notiziario.
0080-3936 Museo dell'Impero Romano. Studi e Materiali.
0080-3960 Pontificia Universita Gregoriana. Istituto di Scienze Sociali Studia Socialia.
0080-3979 Pontificia Universita Gregoriana. Miscellanea Historiae Pontificiae
0080-3987 Pontificia Universita Gregoriana. Studia Missionalia
0080-3995 Documenta Missionalia
0080-4010 Universita degli Studi di Roma. Istituto di Economia Politica. Collana di Studi
0080-4029 Universita degli Studi di Roma. Scuola di Filologia Moderna. Pubblicazioni
0080-4037 Roofing
0080-4045 U. P. Irrigation Research Institute. General Annual Report
0080-4053 U.P. Irrigation Research Institute. Technical Memorandum
0080-4088 Rothmans Football Yearbook
0080-4134 Royal Agricultural Society of England. Journal
0080-4185 Royal Architectural Institute of Canada. Allied Arts Catalogue. Catalogue des Arts Connexes†
0080-4193 Royal Astronomical Society of Canada. Observer's Handbook
0080-4274 Notes from the Royal Botanic Garden, Edinburgh
0080-4282 Royal Caledonian Curling Club. Annual
0080-4290 Royal Canadian Academy of Arts. Annual Exhibition. Catalogue
0080-4304 Royal Canadian Institute. Proceedings
0080-4312 Royal Canadian Institute. Transactions
0080-4320 Royal College of Organists. Year Book
0080-4339 Royal Dublin Society. Scientific Proceedings Series A
0080-4347 Royal Dublin Society. Scientific Proceedings. Series B
0080-4355 Royal Entomological Society of London. Proceedings *see* 0140-1890
0080-4363 Royal Entomological Society of London. Symposia
0080-4371 Great Britain. Royal Greenwich Observatory. Annals
0080-4398 Royal Historical Society. Guides and Handbooks
0080-4401 Royal Historical Society. Transactions. Fifth Series
0080-441X R. H. S. Gardener's Diary
0080-4428 Chemical Society, London, Monographs for Teachers
0080-4436 Royal Institute of Philosophy. Lectures
0080-4444 Royal Institute of the Architects of Ireland. Yearbook
0080-4452 Royal Musical Association, London. Proceedings
0080-4460 Royal Musical Association, London. R. M. A. Research Chronicle
0080-4479 Royal National Institute for the Blind. Information Leaflets
0080-4495 Royal School of Mines, London. Journal
0080-4509 R S P B Annual Report and Accounts
0080-4517 Royal Society of Canada. Proceedings
0080-4541 Royal Society of Edinburgh. Proceedings. Section A. Mathematical and Physical Sciences *see* 0308-2105
0080-455X Royal Society of Edinburgh. Proceedings. Section B. Biology *changed to* Royal Society of Edinburgh. Proceedings. (Biological Sciences)
0080-4568 Royal Society of Edinburgh. Transactions. (Earth Sciences)
0080-4576 Royal Society of Edinburgh. Year Book
0080-4606 Royal Society of London. Biographical Memoirs of Fellows of the Royal Society
0080-4614 Royal Society of London. Philosophical Transactions. Series A. Mathematical and Physical Sciences
0080-4622 Royal Society of London. Philosophical Transactions. Series B. Biological Sciences
0080-4630 Royal Society of London. Proceedings. Series A. Mathematical and Physical Sciences
0080-4649 Royal Society of London. Proceedings. Series B. Biological Sciences
0080-4673 Royal Society of London. Year Book
0080-469X Royal Society of Queensland, St. Lucia. Proceedings
0080-4703 Royal Society of Tasmania, Hobart. Papers and Proceedings
0080-4711 Royal Society of Tropical Medicine and Hygiene, London. Yearbook
0080-472X Royal Society of Ulster Architects. Year Book
0080-4738 Royal Western Australian Historical Society. Journal and Proceedings
0080-4754 Rozprawy z Dziejow Oswiaty
0080-4762 Rubber and Plastics Industry Technical Conference. Record
0080-4770 Rubber Directory of Great Britain *see* 0306-414X
0080-4789 Rudolf Steiner Publications
0080-4797 Rudolf Virchow Medical Society in the City of New York. Proceedings
0080-4800 Ruestungsbeschraenkung und Sicherheit†
0080-4819 Ruff's Guide to the Turf and The Sporting Life Annual
0080-4827 Rugby Football League Official Guide
0080-4835 Rumanian Journal of Sociology†
0080-4843 Runa: Archivo para las Ciencias del Hombre†
0080-4851 Rural Development Research Paper
0080-4878 Russian and East European Series†
0080-4886 Russian and East European Studies
0080-4916 Russian Series on Social History
0080-4924 Rutgers Banking Series†
0080-4940 Rutgers Series on Systems for the Intellectual Organization of Information†
0080-4967 Rutgers University. Bureau of Biological Research. Research Conference. Research Conferences of the Bureau of Biological Research (Proceedings)†
0080-4975 Rutgers University.Bureau of Engineering Research. Annual Report
0080-4983 Rutgers University. Center of Alcohol Studies. Monograph
0080-5009 Rutherglen, Australia. Research Station. Digest of Recent Research
0080-5033 Rwanda. Direction Generale de la Documentation et de la Statistique. Rapport Annuel *changed to* Rwanda. Direction Generale de la Statistique. Rapport Annuel
0080-505X Ryland'S Directory
0080-5076 South African Fishing Industry Handbook and Buyer's Guide
0080-5084 S I A M - A M S Proceedings
0080-5092 S. J. Hall Lectureship in Industrial Forestry
0080-5122 S W A T H
0080-5130 S.A. Mechanised Handling Equipment Buyer's Guide†
0080-5149 SAAB Technical Notes
0080-5157 Saalburg-Jahrbuch
0080-5165 Annales Universitatis Saraviensis. Reihe: Mathematisch-Naturwissenschaftliche Fakultaet
0080-5173 Universitaet des Saarlandes. Jahresbibliographie
0080-5181 Saarbruecker Beitraege zur Altertumskunde
0080-519X Saarbruecker Studien zur Musikwissenschaft
0080-5203 Sabah. Department of Statistics. Annual Bulletin of Statistics
0080-5211 Sabah. Forest Department. Annual Report
0080-522X Sabah. Marine Department. Annual Report
0080-5246 Sacred Books of the East†
0080-5262 Saechsische Akademie der Wissenschaften, Leipzig. Jahrbuch
0080-5270 Saechsische Akademie der Wissenschaften, Leipzig. Mathematisch-Naturwissenschaftliche Klasse. Sitzungsberichte
0080-5289 Saechsische Akademie der Wissenschaften, Leipzig. Mathematisch-Naturwissenschaftliche Klasse. Abhandlungen
0080-5297 Saechsische Akademie der Wissenschaften, Leipzig. Philologisch-Historische Klasse. Abhandlungen
0080-5300 Saechsische Akademie der Wissenschaften, Leipzig. Philologisch-Historische Klasse. Sitzungsberichte
0080-5319 Saeculum
0080-5335 Sagamore Army Materials Research Conference. Proceedings†
0080-5343 Sage Professional Papers in Comparative Politics†
0080-5351 Sage Readers in Cross-National Research†
0080-536X Sage Research Progress Series on War, Revolution and Peacekeeping
0080-5378 Sage Series on Armed Forces and Society
0080-5386 Sage Series on Politics and the Legal Order†
0080-5394 Saggi e Memorie di Storia dell'Arte
0080-5408 Sagittarius *changed to* Schuetz-Jahrbuch
0080-5416 Sahitya Akademi, New Delhi. Report
0080-5432 Saint Bonaventure University. Franciscan Institute. Philosophy Series
0080-5440 Saint Bonaventure University. Franciscan Institute. Text Series
0080-5459 Franciscan Studies
0080-5467 Saint Bonaventure University. Science Studies
0080-5483 St. Louis University. Pius XII Library. Publications†
0080-5513 Science Museum of Minnesota. Museum Observer†
0080-5521 Science Museum of Minnesota. Scientific Publications *see* 0161-4452
0080-5548 Michigan Municipal League. Salaries, Wages, and Fringe Benefits in Michigan Municipalities over 4,000 Population
0080-5572 Saling Aktienfuehrer
0080-5661 El Salvador. Direccion General de Estadistica y Censos. Anuario Estadistico
0080-567X Salvation Army Year Book
0080-5696 Salzburger Jahrbuch fuer Philosophie
0080-570X Salzburger Patristische Studien†
0080-5718 Salzburger Studien zur Anglistik und Amerikanistik†
0080-5726 Salzburger Studien zur Philosophie
0080-5734 Salzburger Universitaetsreden
0080-5769 Samaru Miscellaneous Paper
0080-5777 Samaru Research Bulletin
0080-5793 Sammlung Chemischer und Chemisch-Technischer Beitraege. Neue Folge†
0080-5807 Sammlung Dalp
0080-5815 Sammlung Dialog†
0080-5823 Sammlung Geltender Staatsangehoerigkeitsgesetze
0080-5831 Sammlung Lebensmittelrechtlicher Entscheidungen
0080-584X Sammlung Meusser
0080-5858 Sammlung Wissenschaft und Gegenwart†
0080-5866 Samos
0080-5882 San Diego Business Survey
0080-5890 San Diego. Museum of Man. Ethnic Technology Notes
0080-5904 San Diego. Museum of Man. Papers
0080-5920 San Diego Society of Natural History. Memoirs
0080-5939 San Diego Society of Natural History. Occasional Papers
0080-5947 San Diego Society of Natural History. Transactions
0080-5955 Instituto y Observatorio de Marina. Observaciones Meteorologicas, Magneticas y Sismicas. Anales
0080-5963 Almanaque Nautico
0080-5971 Instituto y Observatorio de Marina. Efemerides Astronomicas
0080-598X San Mateo County Dental Society. Bulletin
0080-6013 Water Quality Conference.Proceedings *changed to* Public Water Supply Engineers Conference (Proceedings)
0080-6021 Sanitation Industry Yearbook
0080-603X Hochschule St. Gallen fuer Wirtschafts- und Sozialwissenschaften. Forschungsinstitut fuer Absatz und Handel. Schriftenreihe
0080-6048 Sankt Galler Beitraege Zum Fremdenverkehr und zur Verkehrswirtschaft: Reihe Verkehrswirtschaft
0080-6056 Sankt Gallische Naturwissenschaftliche Gesellschaft. Bericht ueber Die Taetigkeit
0080-6064 Sankyo Research Laboratories. Annual Report
0080-6099 Santa Fe. Centro de Documentacion e Informacion Educativa. Boletin de Informacion Educativa
0080-6137 Santakuti Vedic Research Series
0080-6145 Universidad Internacional Menendez Pelayo. Publicaciones
0080-6153 Santiago de Chile. Instituto de Fomento Pesquero Publicacion *changed to* Instituto de Fomento Pesquero. Informes Pesquero
0080-6234 Universidade de Sao Paulo. Escola de Enfermagem. Revista
0080-6250 Universidade de Sao Paulo. Faculdade de Direito. Revista
0080-6374 Universidade de Sao Paulo. Museu Paulista. Anais
0080-6382 Museu Paulista. Colecao *changed to* Universidade de Sao Paulo. Museu Paulista. Colecao. Serie de Etnologia
0080-6382 Museu Paulista. Colecao *changed to* Universidade de Sao Paulo. Museu Paulista. Colecao. Serie de Historia
0080-6382 Museu Paulista. Colecao *changed to* Universidade de Sao Paulo. Museu Paulista. Colecao. Serie de Numismatica
0080-6382 Museu Paulista. Colecao *changed to* Universidade de Sao Paulo. Museu Paulista. Colecao. Serie de Mobiliario
0080-6382 Museu Paulista. Colecao *changed to* Universidade de Sao Paulo. Museu Paulista Colecao. Serie de Geografia
0080-6382 Museu Paulista. Colecao *changed to* Universidade de Sao Paulo. Museu Paulista. Colecao. Serie de Arqueologia
0080-6390 Universidade de Sao Paulo. Museu Paulista. Revista
0080-6404 Coordenadoria de Saude Mental, Sao Paulo. Arquivos
0080-6412 Sao Paulo, Brazil (State) Observatorio. Anuario Astronomico *changed to* Universidade de Sao Paulo. Instituto Astronomico e Geofisico. Anuario Astronomico
0080-6420 Sarawak. Department of Agriculture. Research Branch. Annual Report
0080-6439 Annual Statistical Bulletin Sarawak
0080-6447 Sarawak Vital Statistics
0080-6455 Sarawak External Trade Statistics
0080-6471 Sarvadanand Universal Series
0080-648X Saskatchewan. Department of Agriculture. Family Farm Improvement Branch. Technical Bulletin

0080-6498 Saskatchewan. Department of Industry and Commerce. Report for the Fiscal Year
0080-6501 Saskatchewan. Department of Mineral Resources. Core Index†
0080-6528 Saskatchewan. Department of Natural Resources. Forestry Branch. Technical Bulletins *changed to* Saskatchewan. Department of Tourism and Renewable Resources. Technical Bulletins
0080-6536 Saskatchewan Manufacturers Guide
0080-6544 Saskatchewan. Medical Care Insurance Commission. Annual Report
0080-6552 Saskatchewan Natural History Society. Special Publications
0080-6560 Saskatchewan Poetry Book
0080-6579 Saskatchewan Professional Engineer
0080-6587 Saskatchewan Research Council. Annual Report
0080-6595 Saskatchewan Research Council. Geology Division. Circular†
0080-6609 Saskatchewan. Research Council. Geology Division. Report†
0080-6633 Saskatchewan Telecommunications. Annual Report
0080-665X University of Saskatchewan. Institute for Northern Studies. Annual Report
0080-6676 Saskatchewan's Financial and Economic Position
0080-6684 Sather Classical Lectures
0080-6706 Scandinavian Institute of African Studies. Annual Seminar Proceedings
0080-6714 Scandinavian Institute of African Studies. Research Report
0080-6722 Scandinavian Journal of Haematology. Supplementum
0080-6730 Scandinavian Journal of Respiratory Diseases. Supplementum *changed to* European Journal of Respiratory Diseases. Supplementum
0080-6757 Scandinavian Political Studies
0080-6765 Scando-Slavica
0080-6773 Scavi di Spina. *changed to* Scavi di Luni
0080-679X Schiffahrtmedizinisches Institut der Marine, Kiel. Veroeffentlichungen
0080-6803 Schiffbautechnische Gesellschaft. Jahrbuch
0080-6811 Embroidery Directory
0080-6838 Schoenste Schweizer Buecher
0080-6854 Scholae Adriani de Buck Memoriae Dicatae
0080-6897 Schools
0080-6900 Schools Abroad
0080-6919 Schools of England, Wales, Scotland and Ireland
0080-6927 Schools of English in Great Britain *see* 0143-2214
0080-6935 Schopenhauer-Jahrbuch
0080-6943 Schowalter Memorial Lecture Series
0080-6951 Monumenta Germaniae Historica. Schriften
0080-696X Schriften und Quellen der Alten Welt
0080-6994 Schriften zur Geschichte und Kultur des Alten Orient
0080-7001 Schriften zur Handelsforschung
0080-701X Schriften zur Jugendlektuere
0080-7028 Schriften zur Kooperationsforschung. Berichte
0080-7036 Schriften zur Kooperationsforschung. Studien
0080-7044 Schriften zur Kooperationsforschung. Vortraege
0080-7052 Schriften zur Kunstgeschichte†
0080-7060 Schriften zur Rechtslehre und Politik
0080-7079 Schriften zur Sozialpsychologie
0080-7087 Schriftenreihe zur Theoretischen und Angewandten Betriebswirtschaftslehre
0080-7117 Schriftenreihe des Buchklubs der Jugend
0080-7125 Deutsch-Auslaendische Beziehungen. Schriftenreihe
0080-7133 Schriftenreihe fuer Laendliche Sozialfragen
0080-7141 Schriftenreihe fuer Sportwissenschaft und Sportpraxis *see* 0342-457X
0080-715X Schriftenreihe Neurologie/Neurology Series
0080-7168 Schriftenreihe zur Geschichte und Politischen Bildung
0080-7176 Schrifttum zur Deutschen Kunst
0080-7192 Schrijvers Prentenboek
0080-7206 Schweich Lectures
0080-7214 Schweizer Anglistische Arbeiten
0080-7230 Schweizer Buchhandels-Adressbuch
0080-7249 Publicus
0080-7257 Switzerland. Schweizerische Anstalt fuer das Forstliche Versuchswesen. Mitteilungen *changed to* Switzerland. Eidgenoessische Anstalt fuer das Forstliche Versuchswesen. Mitteilungen
0080-7273 Schweizerische Beitraege zur Altertumswissenschaft
0080-7281 Schweizerische Botanische Gesellschaft. Berichte
0080-729X Schweizerische Geisteswissenschaftliche Gesellschaft. Schriften
0080-7311 Schweizerische Gesellschaft fuer Ur- und Fruehgeschichte. Institut fuer Ur- und Fruehgeschichte der Schweiz. Jahrbuch
0080-732X Schweizerische Gesellschaft fuer Volkskunde. Schriften
0080-7338 Schweizerische Meteorologische Zentralanstalt. Annalen
0080-7346 Schweizerische Meteorologische Zentralanstalt. Veroeffentlichungen
0080-7354 Schweizerische Musikforschende Gesellschaft. Publikationen. Serie II
0080-7362 Schweizerische Naturforschende Gesellschaft. Verhandlungen *changed to* Schweizerische Naturforschende Gesellschaft. Jahrbuch
0080-7389 Schweizerische Palaeontologische Abhandlungen
0080-7397 Schweizerische Zeitschrift fuer Geschichte. Beihefte
0080-7400 Schweizerisches Medizinisches Jahrbuch
0080-7419 Schweizerisches Sozialarchiv
0080-7427 T.M.
0080-746X Science and Technology
0080-7540 Science Nouvelle
0080-7559 Science of Advanced Material and Process Engineering Series
0080-7575 Science of Ceramics
0080-7591 Science Policy Studies and Documents
0080-7605 Science Record†
0080-7613 Science Surveys†
0080-7621 Science Year
0080-763X Sciences
0080-7648 Sciences de l'Education†
0080-7672 Sciences Secretes
0080-7680 Scientific and Learned Societies of Great Britain†
0080-7702 Scientific and Technical Periodicals Published in South Africa
0080-7710 Scientific and Technical Societies in South Africa
0080-7737 Scientific Horticulture
0080-7745 Scientific Research in British Universities and Colleges†
0080-7753 Israel. National Council for Research and Development. Scientific Research in Israel
0080-7761 Scientific Research Organizations in South Africa
0080-777X Scientists Forum
0080-7788 Scotland by Road†
0080-7796 Great Britain. Department of Agriculture and Fisheries for Scotland. Advisory Bulletins†
0080-7826 Scotland for Coarse Fishing *changed to* Angler's Guide to Scottish Waters
0080-7834 Scotland for Fishing *changed to* Angler's Guide to Scottish Waters
0080-7834 Scotland for Fishing
0080-7842 Scotland-Home of Golf
0080-7850 Scotland. Department of Agriculture and Fisheries. Red Deer Commission. Annual Report
0080-7869 Scotland. Registrar General. Annual Report
0080-7885 Scotland. Scottish Home and Health Department. Hospital Design in Use†
0080-7915 Great Britain. Scottish Law Commission. Annual Report
0080-7923 Scotland Tomorrow *changed to* Scotlink
0080-7931 Scottish Castles and Historic Houses *changed to* Scotland: 1001 Things to See
0080-7966 Scottish Agricultural Economics; Some Studies of Current Economic Conditions in Scottish Farming
0080-7974 Scottish Bakers' Year Book
0080-8008 Scottish Council for Research in Education. Publications
0080-8016 Scottish Episcopal Church Yearbook
0080-8024 Scottish Gaelic Studies†
0080-8032 Scottish Graduate
0080-8059 Scottish Hardware and Drysalters Association. Yearbook
0080-8075 Scottish Journal of Science
0080-8083 Scottish Law Directory
0080-8091 Scottish Libraries
0080-8105 Scottish Licensed Trade Association. Annual Handbook†
0080-8113 Scottish Licensed Trade Directory†
0080-8121 S. M. B. A. Collected Reprints
0080-813X Scottish Mountaineering Club. Journal
0080-8148 Scottish National Register of Classified Trades
0080-8164 Scottish Postmark Group. Handbook
0080-8202 Scottish Sea Fisheries Statistical Tables
0080-8210 Scottish Society for Prevention of Vivisection. Annual Pictorial Review
0080-8229 Scottish Sports Holidays *changed to* Scotland for Youth
0080-8245 Scottish Typographical Annual Report†
0080-8253 Scottish Universities' Summer School in Physics. Proceedings
0080-8288 Screen World
0080-830X Scripps Clinic and Research Foundation. Annual Report
0080-8318 Scripps Institution of Oceanography. Bulletin
0080-8326 Scripps Institution of Oceanography. Contributions
0080-8334 Scripps Institution of Oceanography. Deep Sea Drilling Project. Initial Reports.
0080-8350 Scripta Artis Monographia
0080-8369 Scripta Hierosolymitana
0080-8377 Scripta Mongolica
0080-8385 Scriptores Byzantini
0080-8393 Scriptores Latini; Collana di Scrittori Latini ad Uso Accademico
0080-8415 Seabird Report
0080-8423 Seaports and the Shipping World. Annual Issue
0080-8474 Securities Law Review
0080-8482 Sediment Data for Selected Canadian Rivers
0080-8504 Seed Trade Buyer's Guide
0080-8512 Seeker's Guide
0080-8539 Kihara Institute for Biological Research. Report
0080-8547 Seishin-Igaku Institute of Psychiatry, Tokyo. Bulletin
0080-858X Selected Documents of the International Petroleum Industry
0080-8628 Selected Studies on Indonesia†
0080-8636 Selected Topics in Solid State Physics
0080-8644 Selected Trade and Professional Associations in Texas *changed to* Texas Trade and Professional Associations and Other Selected Organizations
0080-8660 Selective Organic Transformations†
0080-8679 Self Catering Holidays
0080-8695 Sell's British Aviation *see* 0143-1145
0080-8709 Sell's British Exporters *see* 0140-5772
0080-8717 Sell's Building Index
0080-8725 Sell's Directory of Products & Services *changed to* Sell's Directory
0080-875X Selysia
0080-8768 Semainier Beaux Pays de France
0080-8784 Semiconductors and Semimetals
0080-8792 Seminaire Belge de Perfectionnement aux Affaires. Exposes
0080-8806 Seminar de Fizica Teoretica
0080-8814 Seminar on Canadian-American Relations (Papers)
0080-8830 Seminar on Integrated Surveys of Environment. Proceedings *changed to* I T C-U N E S C O International Seminar. Proceedings
0080-8849 Seminar on the Acquisition of Latin American Library Materials. Final Report and Working Papers
0080-8857 Seminar on the Acquisition of Latin American Library Materials. Microfilming Projects Newsletter
0080-8881 Semitic Texts with Translations
0080-889X Senckenbergiana Maritima. Zeitschrift fuer Meeresgeologie und Meeresbiologie
0080-8903 Sennacieca Revuo
0080-8938 Serie Afrique Noire
0080-8946 Universidad de Costa Rica Serie Ciencias Naturales†
0080-8954 Series Entomologica
0080-8962 Series in Decision and Control
0080-8970 Series in the Philosophy of Science
0080-8997 Series on Company Approaches to Industrial Relations
0080-9004 Series on Rock and Soil Mechanics
0080-9012 Series Paedopsychiatrica
0080-9020 Service de la Carte Geologique d'Alsace et de Lorraine. Memoires *see* 0302-2684
0080-9039 Service d'Echange d'Informations Scientifiques. Serie A: Bibliographies†
0080-9047 Service d'Echange d'Informations Scientifiques. Serie B: Guides et Repertoires†
0080-9055 Service d'Echange d'Informations Scientifiques. Serie C: Catalogues et Inventaires†
0080-9063 Service d'Echange d'Informations Scientifiques. Serie D: Methodes et Techniques†
0080-9071 Servitor di Piazza†
0080-9098 Seto Marine Biological Laboratory. Special Publications
0080-9101 Universidad de Sevilla. Seminario de Antropologia Americana. Publicaciones
0080-911X Seyd's Commercial Lists *changed to* Dun & Bradstreet Standard Register
0080-9128 Shakespeare-Jahrbuch
0080-9144 Shakespeare Research and Opportunities; Report of the Modern Language Association of America Conference
0080-9152 Shakespeare Survey
0080-9160 Shalom
0080-9209 University of Sheffield. Metallurgical Society. Journal
0080-9233 Shepard's Acts and Cases by Popular Names, Federal and State
0080-9241 Sherborn Fund Facsimiles
0080-9268 Shipping and Aviation Statistics of the Maltese Islands
0080-9284 Shipping Marks on Timber
0080-9292 Ships and Aircraft of the United States Fleet
0080-9314 Shivaji University, Kolhapur, India. Journal. Humanities and Sciences
0080-9322 Shri Chhatrapati Shivaji University. Report
0080-9330 Shoe Buyers Guide†
0080-9349 Shoe Trades Directory
0080-9381 Shop Equipment & Shopfitting Directory *changed to* Shop Equipment & Materials Guide
0080-939X Short Oxford History of the Modern World
0080-9403 Short Play Series
0080-9411 Short Studies in Political Science†
0080-9497 Siemens-Entwicklungsberichte *see* 0370-9736
0080-9500 Siemens-Mitteilungen

0080-9519 Sierra Club Exhibit Format Series
0080-9527 Chamber of Commerce of Sierra Leone. Journal
0080-9535 Sierra Leone in Figures
0080-9551 Sierra Leone. Ministry of Education. Report
0080-956X Sigma
0080-9578 Sigma Zetan
0080-9594 Silesia Antiqua
0080-9608 Sinclair Lewis Newsletter†
0080-9616 University of Sind. Research Journal. Arts Series: Humanities and Social Sciences
0080-9640 Singapore Accountant
0080-9659 Singapore Book World
0080-9667 University of Singapore. Chinese Society. Journal
0080-9675 Singapore. Department of Statistics. Report on the Census of Industrial Production
0080-9683 Singapore. Economic Development Board. Annual Report
0080-9691 Singapore Facts and Pictures
0080-9705 Singapore Law Review
0080-9713 Singapore National Bibliography
0080-9721 Singapore. National Library. Annual Report
0080-973X Singapore. National Library. Board Report†
0080-9748 Sinologica†
0080-9756 Sinopsis Dun - Brazil
0080-9772 Sintesis Bibliografica
0080-9780 Sir George Earle Memorial Lecture on Industry and Government
0080-9799 Sir Thomas Browne Instituut. Publications. General Series *changed to* Sir Thomas Browne Instituut. Publications. General Series and Special Series
0080-9810 Site Selection Handbook
0080-9829 Situation Economique de Cote d'Ivoire
0080-9837 Situation Economique de l'Algerie†
0080-9845 Situation Economique du Maroc
0080-9853 Situation Economique du Senegal
0080-9888 Sjoefartshistorisk Aarbok
0080-9918 Skier's Guide
0080-9950 Skolens Aarbok
0080-9985 SLAM: Trade Year Book of Africa
0080-9993 Slavia Antiqua
0081-0002 Slavia Occidentalis
0081-0010 Slavica Gothoburgensia
0081-0029 Slavistic Printing and Reprintings
0081-0045 Sloan-Kettering Institute for Cancer Research. Progress Report
0081-0053 Slog-Europa†
0081-0061 Slovaci v Zahranici
0081-007X Slovanske Historicke Studie
0081-0088 Slovenska Numizmatika
0081-0118 Small Business Management Series
0081-0142 Family Hotel and Guest House†
0081-0193 Smith College Studies in History
0081-0207 Smithsonian Annals of Flight†
0081-0223 Smithsonian Contributions to Anthropology
0081-0231 Smithsonian Contributions to Astrophysics
0081-024X Smithsonian Contributions to Botany
0081-0258 Smithsonian Studies in History and Technology
0081-0266 Smithsonian Contributions to Paleobiology
0081-0274 Smithsonian Contributions to the Earth Sciences
0081-0282 Smithsonian Contributions to Zoology
0081-0304 Smithsonian Institution. Astrophysical Observatory. Central Bureau for Astronomical Telegrams. Circular
0081-0312 International Association of Geodesy. Central Bureau for Satellite Geodesy. Information Bulletin
0081-0320 Smithsonian Institution. Astrophysical Observatory. S A O Special Report
0081-0339 Smithsonian Opportunities for Research and Study in History Art Science
0081-0355 Smoker's Handbook
0081-0363 Smoking and Health Bulletin
0081-038X Soccer Year Book for Northern Ireland
0081-0398 Sociaal-Geografische Studien
0081-0401 Sociaal-Historische Studien
0081-041X Social and Economic Studies. New Series†
0081-0444 Great Britain. Social Science Research Council. Report
0081-0452 Social Science Research Council of Canada. Report *changed to* Social Science Federation of Canada. Annual Report
0081-0460 Social Science Studies
0081-0487 Social Scientist
0081-0495 Social Security Handbook
0081-0533 Zambia. Department of Social Welfare. Social Welfare Research Monographs
0081-055X Social Work and Social Issues
0081-0568 Social Work Practice†
0081-0584 Denmark. Socialforskningsinstituttet. Beretning om Socialforskningsinstituttes Virksomhed
0081-0606 Socialist Register
0081-0630 Sociedad Rural Argentina. Memoria
0081-0649 Sociedad Uruguaya
0081-0657 Sociedade Broteriana. Boletim
0081-0665 Sociedade Broteriana. Memorias
0081-0681 Societa di Studi Romagnoli. Guide
0081-0703 S.I.S.F. Documenti
0081-0711 Societatis Scientiarum Lodziensis. Acta Chimica
0081-072X Societe Academique des Arts Liberaux de Paris. Anthologie de Societaires *changed to* Societe Academique des Arts Liberaux de Paris. Collection
0081-0738 Societe Astronomique de Bordeaux. Bulletin
0081-0746 Societe Belge d'Ophtalmologie. Bulletin
0081-0754 Societe Chateaubriand. Bulletin. Nouvelle Series
0081-0770 Societe de Chimie Physique. Annuaire†
0081-0789 Societe de Geographie de Marseille. Bulletin
0081-0797 Societe de l'Industrie Minerale. Annuaire
0081-0819 Societe d'Emulation Historique et Litteraire d'Abbeville. Bulletin
0081-0835 Societe d'Ergonomie de Langue Francaise. Actes du Congres
0081-0843 Societe des Auteurs, Compositeurs, Editeurs pour la Gerance des Droits de Reproduction Mecanique. (Bulletin)
0081-086X Societe des Explorateurs et des Voyageurs Francais. Annuaire General
0081-0878 Societe des Francs-Bibliophiles. Annuaire
0081-0886 Societe des Ingenieurs Civils de France. Annuaire
0081-0894 Societe des Oceanistes. Publications
0081-0908 Societe des Poetes Francais. Annuaire
0081-0916 Societe des Professeurs Francais en Amerique. Bulletin Annuel
0081-0924 Bulletin S.E.D.E.I.S†
0081-0940 Societe d'Histoire de France. Annuaire
0081-0959 Societe d'Histoire et d'Archaeologie de Geneve. Bulletin
0081-0967 Societe d'Histoire et d'Archeologie de la Goele. Bulletin d'Information
0081-0975 Societe d'Histoire Moderne. Annuaire
0081-0983 Societe Entomologique d'Egypte. Bulletin
0081-0991 Societe Entomologique d'Egypte. Bulletin. Economic Series
0081-1033 Societe Francaise de Chirurgie Orthopedique et Traumatologique. Conferences d'Enseignement
0081-1068 Societe Francaise de Microbiologie. Annuaire
0081-1076 Societe Francaise de Physique. Annuaire
0081-1084 Societe Francaise des Ingenieurs d'Outre-Mer. Annuaire†
0081-1106 Societe Franco-Japonaise de Biologie. Bulletin†
0081-1114 Societe Generale de Belgique. Rapport/Report
0081-1122 Bulgarsko Istorichesko Druzhestvo. Izvestiia
0081-1130 Societe Historique de Quebec. Textes
0081-1181 Societe Nationale des Antiquaires de France. Bulletin
0081-119X Societe Nationale des Chemins de Fer Belges. Rapport Annuel
0081-1203 Societe Odonto-Stomatologique du Nord-Est. Revue Annuelle
0081-1211 Mededelingen "Ex Oriente Lux" *changed to* Vooraziatisch-Egyptisch Genootschap "Ex Oriente Lux". Mededelingen en Verhandelingen
0081-122X Societe Phycologique de France. Bulletin *see* 0181-15[illegible]
0081-1238 Bibliotheque de la S E L A [illegible]
0081-1262 Federation Nationale des Societes d'Economie Mixte de Construction, d'Amenagement et de Renovation. Annuaire
0081-1270 Societe d'Ophtalmologie de France. Bulletin
0081-1289 Societes et Fournisseurs d'Afrique Noire et de Madagascar. Guide Economique Noire
0081-1297 Society for African Church History. Bulletin
0081-1300 Society for American Archaeology. Memoirs
0081-1319 Asian Music Publications. Series A: Bibliographic and Research Aids
0081-1327 Asian Music Publications. Series B. Translations
0081-1335 Asian Music Publications. Series C: Reprints
0081-1343 Asian Music Publications. Series D: Monographs
0081-136X Society for Endocrinology (Great Britain) Memoirs
0081-1386 Society for Experimental Biology. Symposia
0081-1394 Society for General Microbiology. Symposium
0081-1416 Society for International Development. World Conference Proceedings
0081-1424 Society for Italian Historical Studies. Newsletter
0081-1432 Society for New Testament Studies. Monograph Series
0081-1440 Society for Old Testament Study. Book List
0081-1459 Society for Pediatric Research. Program and Abstracts *changed to* American Pediatric Society and Society for Pediatric Research. Program and Abstracts
0081-1475 Society for Psychical Research. Proceedings
0081-1483 Society for the Advancement of Food Service Research. Proceedings
0081-1491 Society for the History of Technology. Monograph Series
0081-1513 Society for the Promotion of Nature Reserves. Technical Publications *changed to* Society for the Promotion of Nature Conservation. Technical Publications
0081-153X Society for the Study of Human Biology. Symposia
0081-1556 National S A M P E Technical Conference Series. N S T C Preprint Series
0081-1564 Society of Antiquaries of Scotland. Proceedings
0081-1572 Society of Chemical Industry, London. Reports on the Progress of Applied Chemistry†
0081-1580 Society of Cypriot Studies. Bulletin
0081-1599 Society of Exploration Geophysicists. Yearbook†
0081-1602 Society of Glass Decorators. Papers Presented at Annual Seminar
0081-1637 Society of Manufacturing Engineers. Collected Papers and Technical Papers Presented at Southeastern Engineering and Tool Exposition†
0081-1645 Society of Manufacturing Engineers. Collected Papers and Technical Papers Presented at Western Metal and Tool Exposition and Conference
0081-1653 Society of Manufacturing Engineers. Technical Papers
0081-1661 Society of Naval Architects and Marine Engineers. Transactions
0081-1688 Society of Petroleum Engineers of American Institute of Mining, Metallurgical and Petroleum Engineers. Petroleum Transactions Reprint Series
0081-1696 Society of Petroleum Engineers of American Institute of Mining, Metallurgical and Petroleum Engineers. Transactions
0081-170X Society of Plant Protection of North Japan. Annual Report
0081-1718 Society of Professional Well Logging Analysts. S P W L A Annual Logging Symposium Transactions
0081-1734 Sociologia I†
0081-1742 Sociologia II
0081-1750 Sociological Methodology
0081-1769 Sociological Review. Monograph
0081-1777 Sociological Yearbook of Religion in Britain†
0081-1807 Sociologist
0081-1823 Sofiiski Universitet. Biologicheski Fakultet. Godishnik
0081-1831 Sofiiski Universitet. Fakultet po Slavianska Filologiia. Godishnik
0081-184X Sofiiski Universitet. Filosofski Fakultet. Godishnik
0081-1858 Sofiiski Universitet. Fakultet po Matematika i Mekhanika. Godishnik
0081-1866 Sofiiski Universitet. Iuridicheski Fakultet. Godishnik
0081-1882 Soil Conservation Society of America. Proceedings of the Annual Meeting†
0081-1890 Books in Soils and the Environment
0081-1904 S S S A Special Publication Series
0081-1912 Soils and Land Use Series
0081-1939 Preparation and Properties of Solid State Materials
0081-1947 Solid State Physics; Advances in Research and Applications
0081-1955 Solid State Physics; Advances in Research and Applications. Supplement
0081-1963 Solid State Physics Literature Guides
0081-1971 Solid State Surface Science
0081-203X Some Statistics on Baccaluareate and Higher Degree Programs in Nursing *changed to* N L N Nursing Data Book: Statistical Information on Nursing Education & Newly Licensed Nurses
0081-2048 Somerset Birds
0081-2056 Somerset Archaeology and Natural History
0081-2080 Soundings: A Music Journal
0081-2110 Sources in Ancient History
0081-2129 Sources of Supply/Buyers Guide
0081-2137 South Africa. Bureau of Standards. S A B S Yearbook
0081-2145 South Africa. Department of Agricultural Technical Services. Agricultural Research
0081-2153 South Africa. Department of Agricultural Technical Services. Report of the Secretary for Agricultural Technical Services
0081-2161 South Africa. Department of Agricultural Technical Services. Special Publication
0081-217X South Africa. Department of Agricultural Technical Services. Technical Communication
0081-2188 South Africa. Department of Bantu Education. Annual Report
0081-2196 South Africa. Department of Customs and Excise. Foreign Trade Statistics
0081-220X South Africa. Department of Higher Education. Annual Report

ISSN INDEX 1157

0081-2218 Formerly; South Africa. Division of Sea Fisheries. Annual Report *changed to* South Africa. Sea Fisheries Branch. Annual Report
0081-2234 South Africa. Division of Sea Fisheries. Investigational Report *changed to* South Africa. Sea Fisheries Institute. Investigational Report
0081-2250 University of South Africa. Communications†
0081-2307 South Africa. Weather Bureau. Notos†
0081-2315 South Africa. Weather Bureau. Radiosonde Rawin Data
0081-2323 South Africa. Weather Bureau. Report on Meteorological Data of the Year/ Verslag Oor Weerkundige Data van die Jaar
0081-2331 South Africa. Weather Bureau. W.B. Series
0081-234X South African Association for Marine Biological Research. Bulletin
0081-2382 C S I R Annual Report
0081-2390 C S I R Organization and Activities
0081-2412 Report to S C A R on South African Antarctic Research Activities
0081-2420 S.A. Engineer and Electrical Review *changed to* Electrical Engineer
0081-2439 South African Institute of International Affairs. Annual Report†
0081-2455 South African Journal of Antarctic Research
0081-2463 South African Journal of Psychology
0081-2471 South African Speech and Hearing Association. Journal *changed to* South African Journal of Communication Disorders
0081-248X South African Medical Research Council. Annual Report
0081-2498 South African Mining and Engineering Yearbook
0081-2501 S A N T A Annual Report
0081-251X South African Pollen Grains and Spores
0081-2528 South African Reserve Bank. Annual Economic Report
0081-2536 South African Society of Animal Production. Proceedings. Handelinge *changed to* South African Journal of Animal Science
0081-2544 South African Statistics
0081-2552 S A F T O Annual Report
0081-2560 S A W T R I Technical Report
0081-2579 South American Handbook
0081-2587 South and Southeast Asia Urban Affairs Bi-Annuals†
0081-2595 South Asia Church Aid Newsletter *changed to* South Asia Church Aid Association. Annual
0081-2633 South Australia. Libraries Board. Annual Report
0081-2641 South Australia. Libraries Board. Books for Young People
0081-2676 South Australian Museum, Adelaide. Records
0081-2684 South Carolina Arts Commission. Annual Report
0081-2692 South Carolina State Plan for Franchising, Construction and Modernization of Hospital and Related Medical Facilities
0081-2706 University of South Carolina. Libraries. Report of the Director of Libraries
0081-2714 University of South Carolina. School of Education. Proceedings of the Reading Conference†
0081-2722 South Central Research Library Council. Library Directory *changed to* Directory of Libraries and Library Resources in the South Central Research Library Council Region
0081-2773 South Dakota State Historical Society. Collections
0081-2811 South Pacific Commission. Handbook
0081-282X South Pacific Commission. Information Circular
0081-2838 South Pacific Commission. Information Document
0081-2846 South Pacific Commission. Report of S P C Technical Meetings
0081-2854 South Pacific Commission. South Pacific Report *changed to* South Pacific Commission. Annual Report
0081-2862 South Pacific Commission. Technical Paper
0081-2889 South Seas Society. Journal
0081-2897 South Seas Society. Monograph
0081-2935 University of Southampton. Library. Automation Project Report
0081-2943 Southeastern Association of Game and Fish Commissioners. Proceedings of the Annual Conference *changed to* Southeastern Association of Fish and Wildlife Agencies. Proceedings
0081-2951 S E C O L A S Annals
0081-2986 Southern Angler's and Hunter's Guide
0081-2994 Southern Anthropological Society. Proceedings
0081-3001 Southern Baptist Convention. Annual
0081-301X Southern Baptist Convention. Historical Commission. Microfilm Catalogue
0081-3028 Southern Baptist Periodical Index
0081-3036 Southern Historical Publications†
0081-3044 Southern Illinois Studies†
0081-3052 Southern Journal of Agricultural Economics
0081-3060 S R E B Educational Board. Annual Report
0081-3079 S R E B Research Monograph Series†
0081-3087 Southern Regional Education Board. State Legislation Affecting Higher Education in the South
0081-3109 Southern Water Resources and Pollution Control Conference. Proceedings†
0081-3141 Southwestern Profiles†
0081-315X Southwestern Studies. Monographs
0081-3192 Sovietica. Monographs *changed to* Sovietica. Publications and Monographs
0081-3206 Sovietica. Publication *changed to* Sovietica. Publications and Monographs
0081-3214 Sovremennoe Polskoe Pravo
0081-3222 Soybean Digest Blue Book *changed to* Soya Bluebook
0081-3249 Soziale Sicherheit
0081-3257 Textausgaben zur Fruehen Sozialistischen Literatur in Deutschland
0081-3265 Soziologische Gegenwartsfragen. Neue Folge
0081-3338 Spain. Instituto Nacional de Estadistica. Estadistica del Movimento de Viajeros en Alojamientos Hoteleros y Acampamentos Turisticos *changed to* Estadisticas de Turismo
0081-3346 Spain. Instituto Nacional de Estadistica. Estadistica de Transporte†
0081-3354 Spain. Instituto Nacional de Estadistica. Estadistica Industrial
0081-3362 Spain. Instituto Nacional de Estadistica. Industrias Derivadas de la Pesca
0081-3370 Spain. Instituto Nacional de Estadistica. Informe Sobre la Distribucion de las Rentas
0081-3389 Spain. Instituto Nacional de Estadistica. Poblacion Activa
0081-3397 Informes J. E. N.
0081-3435 Spain. Ministerio de Hacienda. Informacion Estadistica
0081-3443 Spain. Ministerio de Hacienda. Memoria *changed to* Spain. Ministerio de Hacienda. Direccion General de Seguros. Balances y Cuentas
0081-3451 Spain. Instituto de Credito Oficial. Memoria del Credito Oficial
0081-346X Spain. Ministerio de Informacion y Turismo. Estadisticas de Turismo *changed to* Spain. Ministerio de Comercio y Turismo. Estadisticas de Turismo
0081-3478 Spain. Servicio de Extension Agraria. Serie Tecnica
0081-3486 Spanische Forschungen der Goerresgesellschaft. Reihe 1: Gesammelte Aufsaetze zur Kulturgeschichte Spaniens
0081-3494 Spanische Forschungen der Goerresgesellschaft. Reihe 2: Monographien
0081-3516 Spanish Institute. Annual Report
0081-3532 Special Education and Rehabilitation Monograph Series *changed to* Syracuse Special Education and Rehabilitation Monograph Series
0081-3540 Special Libraries Association. Washington D.C. Chapter. Chapter Notes
0081-3559 Special Papers in International Economics
0081-3567 Specification
0081-3575 Specola Astronomica Vaticana, Castel Gandolfo, Italy. Annual Report
0081-3583 Specola Astronomica Vaticana, Castel Gandolfo, Italy. Miscellanea Astronomica
0081-3591 Specola Astronomica Vaticana, Castel Gandolfo, Italy. Ricerche Astronomiche
0081-3605 Specola Astronomica Vaticana, Castel Gandolfo, Italy. Ricerche Spettroscopiche
0081-3648 Speech Communication Association. Directory *changed to* Speech Communication Directory
0081-3656 Speech Index
0081-3672 Spezial
0081-3680 Spezialbibliographien zu Fragen des Staates und des Rechts
0081-3699 Spezielle Pathologische Anatomie
0081-3702 Spiegel Deutscher Buchkunst *changed to* Die Schoensten Buecher der Deutschen Demokratischen Republik
0081-3729 Spirituosen-Jahrbuch
0081-3745 Spolia Zeylanica
0081-3761 Sporting Chronicle "Horses in Training"
0081-377X Raceform up-to-Date Form Book Annual
0081-3788 Sporting News' National Football Guide†
0081-3788 Sporting News' National Football Guide
0081-3818 Sprache und Denken; Finnische Beitrage zur Philosophie und Sprachwissenschaft†
0081-3826 Sprache und Dichtung. Neue Folge
0081-3834 Sprawozdania Archeologiczne
0081-3842 Sprechplatten Katalog†
0081-3850 Sprenger Instituut. Jaarverslag/Annual Report
0081-3869 Springer Tracts in Modern Physics
0081-3877 Springer Tracts in Natural Philosophy
0081-3885 Squash Rackets Association. Handbook
0081-3907 Sri Venkateswara University. Oriental Journal
0081-3915 Sri Venkateswara University. Department of Sanskrit. Symposium
0081-394X Srpska Akademija Nauka i Umetnosti. Odeljenje Drustvenih Nauka. Glas
0081-3958 Srpska Akademija Nauka i Umetnosti. Odeljenje Jezika i Knjizevnosti. Glas
0081-3966 Srpska Akademija Nauka i Umetnosti. Odeljenje Medicinskih Nauka. Glas
0081-3974 Srpska Akademija Nauka i Umetnosti. Odeljenje Tehnickih Nauka. Glas
0081-3982 Srpska Akademija Nauka i Umetnosti. Odeljenje Drustvenih Nauka. Posebna Izdanja
0081-3990 Srpska Akademija Nauka i Umetnosti. Odeljenje Jezika i Knjizevnosti. Posebna Izdanja
0081-4008 Srpska Akademija Nauka i Umetnosti. Odelenje Likovne i Muzicke Umetnosti. Posebna Izdanja
0081-4016 Srpska Akademija Nauka i Umetnosti. Odeljenje Medicinskih Nauka. Posebna Izdanja
0081-4024 Srpska Akademija Nauka i Umetnosti. Odeljenje Prirodno-Matematickih Nauka. Posebna Izdanja
0081-4032 Srpska Akademija Nauka i Umetnosti Spomenica
0081-4040 Srpska Akademija Nauka i Umetnosti. Odeljenje Tehnickih Nauka. Posebna Izdanja
0081-4059 Srpska Akademija Nauka i Umetnosti. Odeljenje Drustvenih Nauka. Spomenik
0081-4067 Srpski Etnografski Zbornik. Naselja i Poreklo Stanovnistva
0081-4075 Srpski Etnografski Zbornik. Rasprave i Gradja
0081-4083 Srpski Etnografski Zbornik. Srpske Narodne Umotvorine
0081-4091 Srpski Etnografski Zbornik. Zivot i Obicaji Narodni
0081-4105 Staat und Politik
0081-4113 Staatlicher Mathematisch-Physikalischer Salon, Dresden. Veroeffentlichungen
0081-4148 Stadler Genetics Symposium. Proceedings
0081-4172 Stahl und Form
0081-4180 Stahleisen Kalender
0081-4210 Stamps of the World
0081-4229 Standard Directory of Advertisers
0081-4237 Standard Education Almanac
0081-4245 Standard Lesson Commentary
0081-427X Standard Nomenclature of Athletic Injuries
0081-430X Standards Engineers Society. Proceedings of Annual Meeting
0081-4318 National Conference of Standards Laboratories. Proceedings
0081-4326 Stanford Journal of International Studies
0081-4342 Stanford Studies in Germanics and Slavics†
0081-4350 Stanford University. Publications. Geological Sciences
0081-4369 Stanstead County Historical Society. Journal
0081-4377 Star Almanac for Land Surveyors
0081-4385 Starfish Book of Farm and Country Holidays
0081-4407 Stars and Stellar Systems†
0081-4423 State-Approved Schools of Nursing - L. P. N./L. V. N.
0081-4431 State-Approved Schools of Nursing - R. N
0081-444X State Bank of Pakistan. Annual Report†
0081-4458 State Bank of Pakistan. Department of Research. Report on Currency and Finance†
0081-4466 State Bank of Pakistan. Index Numbers of Stock Exchange Securities
0081-4474 State Constitutional Convention Studies†
0081-4482 State Court Systems†
0081-4504 State Government Undertakings in Gujarat
0081-4520 State of British Agriculture†
0081-4539 State of Food and Agriculture
0081-4563 State of Nevada Wage Report *changed to* Nevada Wage Survey
0081-4571 State of the Air Transport Industry
0081-4598 State Tax Handbook
0081-4601 Statesman's Year Book
0081-461X Stationery Trade Reference Book and Buyer Guide
0081-4628 Statistical Abstract for Bangladesh
0081-4636 Statistical Abstract of Sri Lanka
0081-4644 Statistical Abstract of Higher Education in North Carolina
0081-4652 Statistical Abstract of Iceland
0081-4660 Statistical Abstract of Ireland
0081-4679 Israel. Central Bureau of Statistics. Statistical Abstract of Israel
0081-4687 Statistical Abstract of Latin America
0081-4695 Statistical Abstract of Louisiana
0081-4709 Statistical Abstract of Maharashtra State
0081-4717 Statistical Abstract of Rajasthan
0081-4725 Syria. Central Bureau of Statistics. Statistical Abstract
0081-4733 Malta. Central Office of Statistics. Annual Abstract of Statistics
0081-4741 Statistical Abstract of the United States
0081-475X Statistical Abstract of Virginia†

0081-4768 Statistical Analysis of World's Merchant Fleets Showing Age, Size, Speed and Draft by Frequency Groupings
0081-4776 Statistical and Social Inquiry Society of Ireland. Journal
0081-4784 Statistical Guides in Educational Research†
0081-4792 Statistical Handbook of Japan
0081-4806 Statistical Handbook of Korea
0081-4814 Statistical Handbook of Sarawak
0081-4822 Statistical Handbook of Thailand
0081-4857 Statistical Office of the European Communities. Associes Statistique du Commerce Exterieur. Annuaire
0081-4865 Statistical Office of the European Communities. Balances of Payments Yearbook
0081-4873 Statistical Office of the European Communities. Basic Statistics
0081-4881 Statistical Office of the European Communities. Commerce Exterieur: Products C E C A
0081-489X Statistical Office of the European Communities. Energy Statistics. Yearbook
0081-4903 Statistical Office of the European Communities. Foreign Trade: Standard Country Classification
0081-4911 Statistical Office of the European Communities. National Accounts. Yearbook
0081-492X Statistical Office of the European Communities. Overseas Associates. Annuaire Statistiques des Etats Africains et Malgache
0081-4938 Statistical Office of the European Communities. Recettes Fiscales. Annuaire
0081-4946 Statistical Office of the European Communities. Statistique Agricole
0081-4954 Statistical Office of the European Communities. Siderurgie Annuaire
0081-4962 Statistical Office of the European Communities. Statistiques des Transports. Annuaire
0081-4970 Statistical Office of the European Communities. Statistiques Industrielles Annuaire
0081-4989 Statistical Office of the European Communities. Statistiques Sociales. Annuaire
0081-4997 Statistical Office of the European Communities. Yearbook Regional Statistics
0081-5004 Statistical Pocket-Book of Pakistan
0081-5012 Statistical Pocket Book: India
0081-5020 Statistical Research Monographs
0081-5039 Statistical Review of the World Oil Industry
0081-5047 Statistical Survey of Economy of Japan
0081-5063 Suomen Tilastollinen Vuosikirja
0081-5071 Statistical Yearbook of Greece
0081-508X Statisticians and Others in Allied Professions *changed to* Directory of Statisticians
0081-5098 Statistics - Africa
0081-5101 Statistics - Europe
0081-511X Statistics for Iron and Steel Industry in India
0081-5128 U.S. Department of Agriculture. Farmer Cooperative Service. Statistics of Farmer Cooperatives *changed to* U.S. Department of Agriculture. Economics, Statistics and Cooperatives Service. Statistics of Farmer Cooperatives
0081-5136 Statistics of Foreign Trade of Syria
0081-5144 India (Republic) Ministry of Shipping and Transport. Statistics of Water Transport Industries *changed to* Water Transport Statistics of India
0081-5152 Statistics of Indiana Libraries
0081-5160 Statistics of Road Traffic Accidents in Europe
0081-5179 Statistics of the Communications Industry in the United States
0081-5195 Statistics of World Trade in Steel
0081-5209 Statistics on Japanese Industries
0081-5217 Statistics on Social Work Education *see* 0091-7192
0081-5225 Statistiek van de Gasvoorziening in Nederland
0081-5233 Austria. Statistisches Zentralamt. Statistik der Aktiengesellschaften in Oesterreich
0081-5241 Statistik der Kommunalen Oeffentlichen Bibliotheken der Bundesrepublik†
0081-525X Switzerland: Directorate General of Customs. Annual Statistics
0081-5268 Statistique Criminelle de la Belgique
0081-5276 Statistique du Commerce Exterieur de Cote d'Ivoire
0081-5292 Statistiques du Commerce Exterieur de la Tunisie
0081-5306 Statistiques du Commerce Exterieur de Madagascar
0081-5314 Statistisches Handbuch fuer die Republik Oesterreich
0081-5322 Statistisches Jahrbuch Berlin
0081-5330 Statistisches Jahrbuch der Schweiz
0081-5357 Statistisches Jahrbuch fuer die Bundesrepublik Deutschland
0081-5365 Statistisches Jahrbuch der Eisen- und Stahlindustrie
0081-5381 Statistisk Aarsbok foer Sverige
0081-539X Statni Banka Ceskoslovenska. Bulletin
0081-5403 Statsvetenskapliga Foereningen i Uppsala. Skrifter†
0081-5411 Steam-Electric Plant Factors *changed to* Steam-Electric Plant Factors (1978)
0081-542X Steam Passenger Service Directory
0081-5438 Steklov Institute of Mathematics. Proceedings
0081-5446 Stellenbosch, South Africa. University. Bureau for Economic Research. Economic Prospects. Ekonomiese Vooruitsigte†
0081-5454 University of Stellenbosch. Bureau for Economic Research. Survey of Contemporary Economic Conditions and Prospects
0081-5462 Steppenwolf†
0081-5470 Stereo/Hi-Fi Directory *see* 0090-6786
0081-5519 Steuerberater-Jahrbuch
0081-5535 Der Stickstoff
0081-5551 Stifterverband fuer die Deutsche Wissenschaft. Jahrbuch *changed to* Stifterverband fuer die Deutsche Wissenschaft. Taetigkeitsbericht
0081-5578 Stiftung Preussische Kulturbesitz. Jahrbuch
0081-5586 Still: Yale Photography Annual
0081-5594 Stille Schar
0081-5608 Stimmen Indianischer Voelker
0081-5624 Stock Values and Dividends for Tax Purposes
0081-5632 Ethnographical Museum of Sweden. Monograph Series
0081-5640 Flygtekniska Foersoeksanstalten. Meddelande/Report
0081-5659 Ingenioersvetenskapsakademien. Transportforskningskommissionen. Meddelanden†
0081-5667 Ingenioersvetenskapsakademien. Transportforskningskommissionen. Utredningsrapporter†
0081-5675 Musikhistoriska Museet, Stockholm. Skrifter
0081-5683 Sweden. Nationalmuseum. Skriftserie
0081-5691 Museum of Far Eastern Antiquities. Bulletin
0081-5705 Statens Geotekniska Institut. Proceedings *changed to* Statens Geotekniska Institut. Rapports
0081-573X Tekniska Nomenklaturcentralen Publikationer
0081-5756 Stockholms Universitet. Psykologiska Institutionen. Report Series
0081-5772 Stone and Cox General Insurance Year Book *changed to* Stone and Cox General Insurance Register
0081-5780 Stone and Cox Life Insurance Tables
0081-5799 Stones of Pittsburgh
0081-5802 Storage Battery Manufacturing Industry Yearbook
0081-5810 Stores and Shops Retail Directory
0081-5829 Stores of the World Directory
0081-5837 Storia, Costumi e Tradizioni
0081-5845 Storia della Miniatura. Studi e Documenti
0081-5861 Stories from the Hills
0081-5896 Strahovska Knihovna
0081-590X Observatoire de Strasbourg. Publication
0081-5918 Universite de Strasbourg II. Centre de Philologie et Litteratures Romanes. Actes et Colloques
0081-5926 Universite de Strasbourg. Centre de Recherche et de Documentation des Institutions Chretiennes. Bulletin du CERDIC
0081-5934 Universite de Strasbourg II. Institut de Phonetique. Travaux
0081-5942 Strategy for Peace Conference. Report *changed to* Strategy for Peace U.S. Foreign Policy Conference. Report
0081-5950 Stratford International Film Festival†
0081-5977 Street and Highway Manual *see* 0163-9730
0081-5985 Strikes and Lockouts in Canada
0081-5993 Structure and Bonding
0081-6000 Structure of Glass
0081-6027 Structurist
0081-6043 Stubbs Buyers Guide *changed to* Stubbs Directory
0081-6051 Stubs (Metro N.Y.)
0081-606X Student Guide: North America†
0081-6078 Student Journalist Guide Series
0081-6086 Student London†
0081-6116 Studi Albanesi. Studi e Testi
0081-6124 Studi Classici e Orientali
0081-6140 Studi d'Architettura Antica
0081-6159 Studi di Metrica Classica
0081-6175 Studi e Materiali di Storia delle Religioni. Quaderni†
0081-6183 Studi e Testi di Papirologia
0081-6205 Studi Romagnoli
0081-6213 Studi Romagnoli. Estratti di Sezione
0081-6221 Studi Romagnoli. Quaderni
0081-6248 Studi Secenteschi
0081-6256 Studi Tassiani
0081-6264 Studi Veneziani
0081-6272 Studia Anglica Posnaniensia; an International Review of English Studies
0081-6280 Studia Archaeologica
0081-6299 Studia Archaeologica
0081-6302 Studia Archeologiczne
0081-6310 Studia Aristotelica
0081-6329 Studia Balcanica
0081-6337 Studia Biophysica
0081-6345 Studia Caucasica
0081-6353 Studia Celtica
0081-637X Studia Estetyczne
0081-6388 Studia et Documenta Historiae Musicae: Bibliotheca
0081-6396 Studia Francisci Scholten Memoriae Dicata
0081-640X Studia Geograficzne
0081-6418 Studia Geograficzno-Fizyczne z Obszaru Opolszczyzny
0081-6426 Studia Geologica Polonica
0081-6434 Studia Geomorphologica Carpatho-Balcanica
0081-6442 Studia Germanica Gandensia
0081-6450 Studia Graeca et Latina Gothoburgensia
0081-6469 Studia Grammatica
0081-6477 Studia Hibernica
0081-6485 Studia Historiae Oeconomica
0081-6493 Studia Historica
0081-6507 Studia Historica
0081-6515 Studia Historica Gothoburgensia
0081-6523 Studia Historica Jyvaskylaensia
0081-6531 Studia Historica Upsaliensia
0081-654X Studia i Materialy do Dziejow Wielkopolski i Pomorza
0081-6566 Studia i Materialy do Teorii i Historii Architektury i Urbanistyki
0081-6574 Studia i Materialy z Dziejow Nauki Polskiej. Seria A. Historia Nauk Spolecznych
0081-6582 Studia i Materialy z Dziejow Nauki Polskiej. Seria B. Historia Nauk Biologicznych i Medycznych
0081-6590 Studia i Materialy z Dziejow Nauki Polskiej. Seria C. Historia Nauk Matematycznych, Fizyko-Chemicznych i Geologiczno-Geograficznych
0081-6604 Studia i Materialy z Dziejow Nauki Polskiej. Seria D. Historia Techniki i Nauk Technicznych
0081-6612 Studia i Materialy z Dziejow Nauki Polskiej. Seria E. Zagadnienia Ogolne
0081-6620 Studia i Materialy z Dziejow Polski w Okresie Oswiecenia
0081-6647 Studia i Materialy z Dziejow Teatru Polskiego *changed to* Studia i Materialy do Dziejow Teatru Polskiego
0081-6663 Studia Irenica
0081-6671 Studia Iuridica
0081-668X Studia Judaica†
0081-6698 Studia Juridica
0081-6701 Studia Copernicana
0081-6736 Studia Moralia
0081-6744 Studia Musicologica Upsaliensia. Nova Series
0081-6752 Studia nad Zagadnieniami Gospodarczymi i Spolecznymi Ziem Zachodnich
0081-6760 Studia Naturae *changed to* Studia Naturae. Seria A. Wydawnictwa Naukowe
0081-6760 Studia Naturae *changed to* Studia Naturae. Seria B. Wydawnictwa Popularno-Naukowe
0081-6779 Studia Numismatica et Medailistica
0081-6787 Studia Palmyrenskie
0081-6795 Studia Pedagogiczne
0081-6809 Studia Philologiae Scandinavicae Upsaliensia
0081-6817 Studia Philologica†
0081-6825 Studia Philosophica†
0081-6833 Studia Philosophica Gandensia *see* 0379-8402
0081-6841 Studia Prawno - Ekonomiczne
0081-685X Studia Psychologiczne
0081-6884 Studia Rossica Posnaniensia
0081-6892 Studia Scientiae Paedagogicae Upsaliensia *see* 0347-1314
0081-6906 Studia Scientiarum Mathematicarum
0081-6914 Studia Semitica Neerlandica
0081-6922 Studia Slovenica. Special Series
0081-6930 Studia Spoleczno-Ekonomiczne
0081-6949 Studia Staropolskie
0081-6957 Studia Theodisca
0081-7015 Studia Uralica et Altaica Upsaliensia
0081-7023 Studia Warszawskie
0081-704X Studia z Dziejow Gornictwa i Hutnictwa†
0081-7058 Studia z Dziejow Osadnictwa
0081-7082 Studia z Dziejow ZSRR i Europy Srodkowej
0081-7090 Studia z Filologii Polskiej i Slowianskiej
0081-7104 Studia z Historii Sztuki
0081-7112 Studia z Okresu Oswiecenia
0081-7120 Studia z Teorii Filmu†
0081-7139 Studia z Zakresu Budownictwa *changed to* Studia z Zakresu Inzynierii
0081-7147 Studia Zrodloznawcze
0081-7155 Studiecentrum voor Kernenergie. Annual Scientific Report
0081-7163 Centre d'Etude de l'Energie Nucleaire. Index of S.C.K. /C.E.N. Papers†
0081-718X Studien zu Religion, Geschichte und Geisteswissenschaften†
0081-7198 Studien zur Agrarwirtschaft
0081-721X Studien zur Begabungsforschung und Bildungsfoerderung†
0081-7228 Studien zur Deutschen Kunstgeschichte
0081-7236 Studien zur Deutschen Literatur
0081-7244 Studien zur Englischen Philologie, Neue Folge
0081-7252 Studien zur Europaeischen Geschichte
0081-7260 Studien zur Evangelischen Ethik†
0081-7279 Studien zur Finanzpolitik

ISSN INDEX 1159

0081-7287 Studien zur Geschichte Asiens, Afrikas und Lateinamerikas. *changed to* Studien ueber Asien, Afrika und Lateinamerika
0081-7295 Studien zur Geschichte der Katholischen Moraltheologie
0081-7309 Studien zur Geschichte des Neunzehnten Jahrhunderts
0081-7317 Studien zur Geschichte Osteuropas
0081-7325 Studien zur Kunst des Neunzehnten Jahrhunderts
0081-7333 Studien zur Medizingeschichte des Neunzehnten Jahrhunderts
0081-7341 Studien zur Musikgeschichte des Neunzehnten Jahrhunderts
0081-735X Studien zur Philosophie und Literatur des Neunzehnten Jahrhunderts
0081-7368 Studien zur Rhetorik des Neunzehnten Jahrhunderts†
0081-7376 Studien zur Wissenschaftstheorie im Neunzehnten Jahrhundert
0081-7384 Studienbuecherei
0081-7392 Studienhefte Psychologie in Erziehung und Unterricht
0081-7406 Studientage fuer Die Pfarrer
0081-7414 Studier i Nordisk Arkeologi
0081-7449 Studies and Reports in Hydrology Series
0081-7465 University of Texas, Austin. Bureau of Business Research. Studies in Accounting
0081-749X Studies in African History, Anthropology, and Ethnology†
0081-7503 Studies in American History
0081-7511 Studies in American Jewish History
0081-752X Studies in American Literature
0081-7538 Studies in Anabaptist and Mennonite History
0081-7546 Studies in Ancient History
0081-7554 Studies in Ancient Oriental Civilization
0081-7562 Studies in Art†
0081-7570 University of Texas, Austin. Bureau of Business Research. Studies in Banking and Finance
0081-7589 Studies in Biblical Theology†
0081-7597 Studies in Biblical Theology. Second Series†
0081-7600 Studies in Bibliography
0081-7619 Studies in British History and Culture
0081-7627 University of New Mexico. Bureau of Business and Economic Research. Studies in Business and Economics†
0081-7635 Studies in Business and Society
0081-7643 Studies in Business Cycles
0081-766X Studies in Capital Formation and Financing
0081-7686 Studies in Chinese Communist Terminology *changed to* Studies in Chinese Terminology.
0081-7694 Studies in Chinese Government and Politics†
0081-7724 Studies in Classical Literature
0081-7732 Studies in Communism, Revisionism and Revolution†
0081-7767 Studies in Comparative Literature
0081-7775 Studies in Comparative Literature
0081-7783 Studies in Compulsory Education
0081-7791 Studies in Consumer Instalment Financing
0081-7805 Studies in Corporate Bond Financing
0081-7813 Studies in Development Progress†
0081-783X Finnish Meteorological Institute. Studies on Earth Magnetism
0081-7856 Studies in Economics
0081-7872 Studies in Economics and Business Administration†
0081-7880 University of Mississippi Studies in English
0081-7899 Studies in English Literature
0081-7902 Studies in Ethnomusicology
0081-7910 Studies in European History
0081-7929 Studies in Federal Taxation. Tax Study
0081-7937 Studies in French Literature
0081-7945 Studies in General and Comparative Literature
0081-7953 Studies in General Anthropology
0081-7961 Studies in Geography in Hungary
0081-797X Studies in German Literature
0081-7988 Studies in Higher Education in Canada
0081-7996 Studies in Historical and Political Science. Extra Volumes
0081-8011 Studies in Industrial Economics†
0081-802X Studies in International Affairs
0081-8046 Studies in International Affairs
0081-8054 Studies in International Communism
0081-8062 Studies in International Economic Relations
0081-8070 Studies in International Finance
0081-8097 Studies in Irish History
0081-8100 Studies in Irish History. Second Series†
0081-8119 Studies in Italian Literature
0081-8127 Studies in Japanese Culture
0081-8135 University of Texas, Austin. Bureau of Business Research. Studies in Latin American Business
0081-8143 Studies in Latin Literature and Its Influence *changed to* Greek and Latin Studies Series
0081-8151 Studies in Librarianship
0081-8178 Studies in Manuscript Illumination
0081-8186 University of Texas, Austin. Bureau of Business Research. Studies in Marketing
0081-8194 Studies in Mathematical and Managerial Economics
0081-8208 Studies in Mathematics
0081-8216 Studies in Mathematics
0081-8224 Studies in Medieval and Renaissance History
0081-8232 Studies in Mediterranean Archaeology. Monograph Series
0081-8259 Studies in Museology
0081-8267 Studies in Music
0081-8275 Studies in Mycenaean Inscriptions and Dialect
0081-8291 Studies in Near Eastern Civilization
0081-8305 Studies in Neuro-Anatomy†
0081-8313 Great Britain. Central Statistical Office. Studies in Official Statistics
0081-8321 Studies in Oriental Culture
0081-8348 University of Texas, Austin. Bureau of Business Research. Studies in Personnel and Management
0081-8364 Studies in Personnel Psychology†
0081-8380 Studies in Philosophy
0081-8399 Studies in Philosophy
0081-8402 Studies in Political Development†
0081-8437 University of Pennsylvania. Wharton School of Finance and Commerce. Studies in Quantitative Economics
0081-8453 Studies in Rural Land Use
0081-8461 Studies in Semitic Languages and Linguistics
0081-8496 Studies in Social Anthropology
0081-850X Studies in Social History
0081-8518 Studies in Social Life
0081-8534 Studies in Spanish Literature
0081-8542 Studies in Statistical Mechanics†
0081-8542 Studies in Statistical Mechanics
0081-8569 Studies in the Economic Development of India†
0081-8577 Studies in the Foundations, Methodology and Philosophy of Science
0081-8585 Studies in the Geography of Israel
0081-8593 Studies in the Germanic Languages and Literatures
0081-8607 Studies in the History of Christian Thought
0081-8615 Studies in the History of Discoveries
0081-8623 Studies in the Humanities†
0081-8631 Studies in the Modern Russian Language
0081-864X Studies in the National Income and Expenditure of the United Kingdom
0081-8658 Studies in the Renaissance *see* 0034-4338
0081-8666 Studies in the Romance Languages and Literatures *changed to* North Carolina Studies in the Romance Languages and Literatures.
0081-8674 Studies in the Social Sciences
0081-8682 West Georgia College Studies in the Social Sciences
0081-8690 Studies in the Structure of Power: Decision Making in Canada
0081-8704 Studies in the Theory of Science
0081-8720 Studies in Tropical Oceanography
0081-8747 Studies in Vermont Geology
0081-8771 Studies of Developing Countries
0081-878X Studies of Negro Employment
0081-8798 Studies of Northern Peoples†
0081-8801 Studies of Urban Society
0081-8844 Studii Clasice
0081-8852 Studii de Literatura Universala si Comparata
0081-8860 Studii de Slavistica
0081-8879 Studii si Cercetari de Bibliologie. Serie Noua
0081-8887 Studii si Cercetari de Numismatica
0081-8909 Studium Biblicum Franciscanum. Analecta
0081-8917 Studium Biblicum Franciscanum. Collectio Major
0081-8925 Studium Biblicum Franciscanum. Collectio Minor
0081-8933 Studium Biblicum Franciscanum. Liber Annuus
0081-8941 Studium Niemcoznawcze
0081-895X Study Abroad
0081-8992 Bibliothek fuer Zeitgeschichte, Stuttgart. Jahresbibliographie
0081-900X Bibliothek fuer Zeitgeschichte, Stuttgart. Schriften
0081-9050 Sudan. National Planning Commission. Economic Survey *changed to* Sudan. Ministry of Finance and National Economy. Economic and Financial Research Section. Economic Survey
0081-9077 Suedost-Forschungen
0081-9085 Suedostdeutsches Archiv
0081-9093 Suedostdeutsches Kulturwerk, Munich. Kleine Suedostreihe
0081-9107 Suedostdeutsches Kulturwerk, Munich. Schriftenreihen. Reihe A. Kultur und Dichtung
0081-9115 Suedostdeutsches Kulturwerk, Munich. Schriftenreihen. Reihe B. Wissenschaftliche Arbeiten
0081-9123 Suedostdeutsches Kulturwerk, Munich. Schriftenreihen. Reihe C. Erinnerungen und Quellen
0081-9131 Suedosteuropa-Bibliographie
0081-914X Suedosteuropa-Jahrbuch
0081-9158 Suedosteuropa-Schriften
0081-9166 Suedosteuropa-Studien
0081-9174 Suesswaren Jahrbuch
0081-9204 Sugar Technology Reviews
0081-9212 Sugar y Azucar Yearbook
0081-9220 Suid-Afrikaanse Guernsey
0081-9255 Sulphur Institute. Technical Bulletin
0081-9271 Sumer
0081-928X Sumitomo Bulletin of Industrial Health
0081-9301 Summary of Floods in the United States†
0081-931X Summary of State Laws and Regulations Relating to Distilled Spirits
0081-9352 Summer Employment Directory of the United States
0081-9379 Summer Study Abroad *changed to* Learning Traveler. Vacation Study Abroad
0081-9387 Summer Theatre Directory
0081-9395 Suomen Aikakauslehti-Indeksi
0081-9417 Suomen Historiallinen Seura. Kasikirjoja
0081-9425 Suomen Historian Laehteitae
0081-9433 Suomen Naishammaslaakarit Ryhma. Julkaisu
0081-9441 Suomen Osallistuminen Yhdistyneiden Kansakuntien Toimintaan
0081-945X Bank of Finland. Annual Statement
0081-9468 Bank of Finland. Yearbook
0081-9476 Suomen Pankki Taloustieteellinen Tutkimuslaitos. Julkaisuja. Series A: Taloudellisia Selvityksia *see* 0355-6034
0081-9484 Finlands Bank. Institut foer Ekonomisk Forskning. Publikationer *see* 0357-4776
0081-9492 Suomen Pankki. Julkaisuja. Serie C
0081-9506 Suomen Pankki Series D. Mimeographed Series *see* 0355-6042
0081-9514 Suomen Pankki. Taloustieteellinen Tutkimuslaitos. Julkaisuja. Series Kasvututkimuksia *see* 0355-6050
0081-9522 Facts About New Super Markets
0081-9530 Supermarket Industry Speaks *see* 0190-3349
0081-9557 Supreme Court Review
0081-9573 Surface and Colloid Science†
0081-9581 Surface Water Supply of the United States†
0081-959X Surface Water Year Book of Great Britain
0081-9603 Surfactant Science Series
0081-9611 Surfboard Builders' Yearbook
0081-9638 Surgery Annual
0081-9646 Surgical Pathology
0081-9654 Surgical Trade Buyers Guide
0081-9662 Surplus Dealers Directory
0081-9670 Surrey Papers in Economics
0081-9697 Survey of Biological Progress
0081-9727 Survey of Consumer Finances *see* 0085-3410
0081-9743 Israel. Ministry of Commerce and Industry. Surveys and Development Plans of Industry in Israel
0081-9751 Survey of London
0081-976X Survey of Progress in Chemistry
0081-9778 Survey of Race Relations in South Africa
0081-9794 Svensk Foersaekrings-Aarsbok
0081-9816 Svensk Tidskrift foer Musikforskning
0081-9859 Svenska Bokfoerlaeggarefoereningen. Matrikel
0081-9867 Svenska Filminstitutet. Dokumentationsavdelningen. Skrifter
0081-9905 Cement- och Betonginstitutet. Utredningar. Applied Studies†
0081-9913 Svenska Handelsbanken. Annual Report
0081-9921 Svenska Institutet i Athen. Skrifter
0081-993X Svenska Institutet i Rom. Skrifter. Acta Series Prima
0081-9956 Kungliga Svenska Vetenskapsakademien. Bidrag till Kungliga Vetenskapsakademiens Historia
0081-9964 Sveriges Jaernvaegar
0081-9980 Swansea Geographer
0081-9999 Swaziland. Geological Survey and Mines Department. Annual Report
0082-0008 Swaziland. Geological Survey and Mines Department. Bulletin
0082-0016 Sweden. Sveriges Geologiska Undersoekning.Serie Ca. Avhandlingar och Uppsatser i Kvarto/Notices in Quarto and Folio
0082-0024 Sweden. Sveriges Geologiska Undersoekning. Serie C. Avhandlingar och Uppsatser/Memoirs and Notices
0082-0032 Institute of Freshwater Research, Drottningholm. Report
0082-0040 Kungliga Skogshoegskolan. Institutionen foer Virkeslaera. Rapporter *see* 0348-4599
0082-0059 Kungliga Skogshoegskolan. Institutionen foer Virkeslaera. Uppsatser *changed to* Sveriges Lantbruksuniversitet. Institution foer Virkeslaera. Uppsatser
0082-0067 Sweden. Konjunkturinstitutet. Occasional Paper
0082-0075 Sweden. Riksfoersaekringsverket. Allmaen Foersaekring
0082-0083 Swedish Social Security Scheme
0082-0091 Sweden. Riksgaeldskontoret. Aarsbok
0082-0105 Sweden. Sjukvaardens och Socialvaardens Planerings- och Rationaliseringsinstitut. S P R I Specifikationer
0082-0113 Sweden. Sjukvaardens och Socialvaardens Planerings- och Rationaliseringsinstitut. S P R I Raad
0082-0121 Sweden. Statens Institut foer Konsumentfraagor. Meddelar *see* 0035-7235

0082-0121 Sweden. Statens Institut foer Konsumentfraagor. Meddelar
0082-0156 Sweden. Statistiska Centralbyraan. Befolkningsfoeraendringar
0082-0164 Sweden. Statistiska Centralbyraan. Folkmaengd
0082-0172 Sweden. Statistiska Centralbyraan. Industri
0082-0180 Sweden. Statistiska Centralbyraan. Information i Prognosfragor/Forecasting Information
0082-0199 Sweden. Statistiska Centralbyraan. Jordbruksstatistisk Aarsbok
0082-0202 Sweden. Statistiska Centralbyraan. Kommunal Personal
0082-0210 Sweden. Statistiska Centralbyraan. Loener
0082-0229 Sweden. Statistiska Centralbyraan. Meddelanden i Samordningsfraagor
0082-0237 Sweden. Statistiska Centralbyraan. Statistiska Meddelanden. Subgroup Am (Labor Market)
0082-0245 Sweden. Statistiska Centralbyraan. Statistiska Meddelanden. Subgroup Be (Population)
0082-0261 Sweden. Statistiska Centralbyraan. Statistiska Meddelanden. Subgroup H (Trade)
0082-027X Sweden. Statistiska Centralbyraan. Statistiska Meddelanden. Subgroup I (Manufacturing)
0082-0288 Sweden. Statistiska Centralbyraan. Statistiska Meddelanden. Subgroup J (Agriculture)
0082-0296 Sweden. Statistiska Centralbyraan. Statistiska Meddelanden. Subgroup N (National Accounts and Finance)
0082-030X Sweden. Statistiska Centralbyraan. Statistiska Meddelanden. Subgroup P (Prices and Price Indices)
0082-0318 Sweden. Statistiska Centralbyraan. Statistiska Meddelanden. Subgroup R (Judicial Statistics. Law and Social Welfare)
0082-0326 Sweden. Statistiska Centralbyraan. Statistiska Meddelanden. Subgroup S (Social Welfare Statistics)
0082-0334 Sweden. Statistiska Centralbyraan. Statistiska Meddelanden. Subgroup T (Transport and Other Forms of Communication)
0082-0342 Sweden. Statistiska Centralbyraan. Statistiska Meddelanden. Subgroup U (Education and Culture)
0082-0350 Sweden. Statistiska Centralbyraan. Urval Skriftseries/Selection Series
0082-0369 Sweden. Statistiska Centralbyraan. Utrikeshandel/Foreign Trade
0082-0377 Sweden. Universitetskanslersaembetet. Research and Development in Post-Secondary Education *see* 0347-4976
0082-0393 Swedish Budget
0082-0415 Swedish Nutrition Foundation. Symposia
0082-0423 Swedish Theological Institute, Jerusalem. Annual
0082-0431 Sweet's Canadian Construction Catalogue File
0082-044X Swiatowit
0082-0458 Rocznik Magnetyczny
0082-0466 Swimming Pool Weekly/Age - Data and Reference Annual
0082-0482 Swiss Society of Plastic and Reconstructive Surgeons. Proceedings (of) Annual Meeting
0082-0490 Switching and Automata Theory Conference. Record
0082-0504 Switzerland. Bundesamt fuer Sozialversicherung. Spezialitaeten-Liste/Liste des Specialites/Elenco delle Specialita
0082-0512 Sydney Law Review
0082-0520 Sydney Studies in Literature
0082-0547 University of Sydney. Basser Department of Computer Science. Technical Report
0082-0555 University of Sydney. Department of Agriculture Economics. Mimeographed Report. *changed to* University of Sydney. Department of Agricultural Economics. Research Report.
0082-0563 University of Sydney. Department of Agricultural Economics. Research Bulletin
0082-0571 University of Sydney. Department of Architectural Science. Reports
0082-0598 Sydowia: Annales Mycologici
0082-061X Sylloge Nummorum Graecorum Deutschland
0082-0628 Sylloge of Coins of the British Isles
0082-0644 Symbolae Botanicae Upsalienses
0082-0660 Symbolon
0082-0695 Symposia Biologica Hungarica
0082-0725 Symposia Mathematica
0082-0733 Symposia on Fundamental Cancer Research. Papers
0082-0741 Symposia on Naval Structural Mechanics. Proceedings†
0082-075X Symposia on Theoretical Physics and Mathematics
0082-0768 Symposia Series in Immunobiological Standardization *see* 0301-5149
0082-0776 International Television Symposium and Technical Exhibit, Montreux. (Papers)
0082-0784 Symposium (International) on Combustion
0082-0806 Symposium on Advanced Propulsion Concepts. Proceedings
0082-0814 Symposium on Applications of Walsh Functions. Record
0082-0830 Symposium on Information Display. Digest of Technical Papers *see* 0097-966X
0082-0849 Symposium on Naval Hydrodynamics. Proceedings
0082-0857 Symposium on Nondestructive Evaluation of Components and Materials in Aerospace, Weapons Systems and Nuclear Applications
0082-0865 Symposium on Nondestructive Testing of Aircraft and Missile Components *see* 0082-0857
0082-0873 Symposium on Ocular Therapy†
0082-089X Symposium on Particleboard. Proceedings
0082-0903 Symposium on Physics and Nondestructive Testing, San Antonio. Proceedings *changed to* Symposium on Nondestructive Evaluation. Proceedings
0082-0911 Institute of Management Sciences. Symposium on Planning. Proceedings
0082-092X Symposium on Reliability. Proceedings
0082-0954 Symposium on Special Ceramics, Stoke-On-Trent, England. Special Ceramics, Proceedings
0082-0970 Symposium on the Nondestructive Testing of Wood. Proceedings†
0082-0989 Symposium on Thermophysical Properties. Proceedings
0082-1012 Symposium on Water Resources Research. Proceedings
0082-1020 Syndicat des Industries de Material Professionnel Electronique et Radioelectrique. Annuaire *changed to* S P E R Annuaire
0082-1047 Syndicat General de l'Industrie Cotonniere Francaise. Annuaire
0082-1055 Syndicat General des Impots. Guide National de l'Enregistrement et des Domaines *changed to* Syndicat General des Impots. Guide Fonciers
0082-1098 Syndromes de la Douleur†
0082-1101 Synopses of the British Fauna
0082-111X Synthese Historical Library
0082-1128 Synthese Library
0082-1136 Synthetic Methods of Organic Chemistry
0082-1144 Synthetic Organic Chemicals, United States Production and Sales
0082-1152 Synthetic Procedures in Nucleic Acid Chemistry†
0082-1160 Syracuse Geographical Series
0082-1179 Syracuse University Publications in Continuing Education. Occasional Papers
0082-1195 System of Ophthalmology
0082-1209 Systemes-Decisions. Section II. Gestion Financiere et Comptabilite
0082-1217 Systems Engineering of Education Series
0082-1233 Akademia Rolnicza, Szczecin. Zeszyty Naukowe
0082-1241 Szczecinskie Towarzystwo Naukowe. Sprawozdania
0082-125X Szczecinskie Towarzystwo Naukowe. Wydzial Nauk Lekarskich. Prace
0082-1268 Szczecinskie Towarzystwo Naukowe. Wydzial Nauk Matematyczno Technicznych. Prace
0082-1276 Szczecinskie Towarzystwo Naukowe. Wydzial Nauk Przyrodniczo-Rolniczych. Prace
0082-1284 Szczecinskie Towarzystwo Naukowe. Wydzial Nauk Spolecznych. Prace
0082-1292 Szczecinskie Towarzystwo Naukowe. Wydzial Nauk Spolecznych. Wydawnictwa
0082-1306 Szilikatkemiai Monografiak
0082-1322 Szociologiai Tanulmanyok
0082-1330 T. B. Davie Memorial Lecture
0082-1357 T V Feature Film Source Book
0082-1365 T V-Film Filebook
0082-1373 T V Film Source Book. Series, Serials and Packages *changed to* Series, Serials, and Packages
0082-1381 T V "Free" Film Source Book†
0082-139X T V in Psychiatry Newsletter
0082-1403 Table Ronde Francaise. Annuaire
0082-1411 Tables of Constants and Numerical Data†
0082-1438 Tableware and Pottery Gazette Reference Book *changed to* Tableware Reference Book
0082-1446 Taccuino dell'Azionista
0082-1454 Tagore Studies
0082-1470 Taiwan Buyers' Guide
0082-1489 Taiwan. Fisheries Research Institute, Keelung. Bulletin
0082-1497 Taiwan. Fisheries Research Institute, Keelung. Laboratory of Fishery Biology. Report
0082-1519 Talking Books, Adult
0082-1527 Tall Timbers Fire Ecology Conference. Proceedings
0082-156X Tamagawa University. Faculty of Agriculture. Bulletin
0082-1578 Tamil Nadu. Department of Statistics. Annual Statistical Abstract
0082-1586 Tamil Nadu. Department of Statistics. Season and Crop Report
0082-1594 Tamil Nadu. Legislative Council. Quinquennial Review
0082-1608 Tamworth Annual
0082-1624 Universite de Madagascar. Annales. Serie Sciences de la Nature et Mathematiques†
0082-1632 Tanulmanyok a Nevelestudomany Korebol
0082-1659 Review of the Mineral Industry in Tanzania
0082-1675 National Museum of Tanzania. Annual Report
0082-1713 Tarbell's Teacher's Guide
0082-173X Tariff Schedules of the United States Annotated
0082-1748 Tarsadalomtudomanyi Kismonografiak
0082-1764 Taschenbuch der Fernmelde-Praxis
0082-1772 Taschenbuch der Giesserei-Praxis
0082-1799 Taschenbuch der Pflanzenarztes
0082-1802 Taschenbuch der Werbung *changed to* Deutscher Werbekalender
0082-1810 Taschenbuch der Werkzeugmaschinen und Werkzeuge
0082-1829 Taschenbuch des Oeffentlichen Lebens
0082-1837 Taschenbuch des Textileinzelhandels
0082-1845 Taschenbuch fuer Agrarjournalisten
0082-1853 Taschenbuch fuer den Buchhalter *changed to* Jahrbuch fuer Praktiker des Rechnungswesens
0082-1861 Taschenbuch fuer den Fernmeldedienst
0082-187X Taschenbuch fuer Liturgie und Kirchenmusik
0082-1888 Taschenbuch fuer den Oeffentlichen Dienst
0082-1896 Taschenbuch fuer die Textil-Industrie
0082-190X Taschenbuch der Post- und Fernmelde-Verwaltung
0082-1918 Taschenbuch fuer Ingenieure und Techniker in Industrie und Wirtschaft
0082-1926 Taschenbuch fuer Ingenieure und Techniker im Oeffentlichen Dienst
0082-1934 Taschenbuch fuer Kriminalisten
0082-1942 Taschenbuch fuer Logistik
0082-1950 Taschenbuchreihe Geschichte
0082-1969 Taschenbuecher zur Musikwissenschaft
0082-1985 Information about Investment in Tasmania
0082-1993 Tasmania. Department of Agriculture. Annual Report
0082-2043 Tasmania. Department of Mines. Geological Survey Bulletins
0082-2051 Tasmania. Department of Mines. Geological Survey Record†
0082-206X Tasmania. Department of Mines. Geological Survey Reports†
0082-2078 Tasmania. Department of Mines. Technical Reports
0082-2086 Tasmania. Department of Mines. Underground Water Supply Papers†
0082-2094 Tasmania. Metropolitan Water Board. Report
0082-2108 University of Tasmania Law Review
0082-2116 Australia. Bureau of Statistics. Tasmanian Office. Tasmanian Year Book
0082-2124 Tatura, Australia. Horticultural Research Station. Annual Research Report
0082-2132 Tatzlil
0082-2159 Tax Foundation, New York. Research Publications. New Series
0082-2167 Taxation in Western Europe
0082-2175 Taxation Tables
0082-2183 Taylor's Encyclopedia of Government Officials. Federal and State
0082-2191 Tbilisi Universitet. Institut Prikladnoi Matematiki. Seminar. Annotatsii Dokladov
0082-2205 Teacher Education
0082-2213 Teachers' Associations. Associations d'Enseignants. Asociaciones de Personal Docente
0082-223X Teaching
0082-2256 Teatro Clasico de Mexico. Boletin. Notas y Comentarios†
0082-2272 Technical and Scientific Books in Print†
0082-2299 T A G A Proceedings
0082-2310 Technical Papers in Hydrology Series
0082-2329 Technical Service Data (Automotive)
0082-2353 Technician Education Yearbook
0082-2361 Technikgeschichte in Einzeldarstellungen
0082-240X Technique of Organic Chemistry *see* 0082-2531
0082-2418 Techniques and Applications in Organic Synthesis
0082-2434 Techniques and Methods of Polymer Evaluation
0082-2442 Techniques Artisanales Modernes
0082-2450 Techniques Avancees†
0082-2469 Techniques d'Aujourd'Hui
0082-2477 Techniques Economiques Modernes. Analyse Economique
0082-2485 Techniques Economiques Modernes. Espace Economique†
0082-2493 Techniques Economiques Modernes. Histoire et Pensee Economique†
0082-2507 Techniques Economiques Modernes. Production et Marches†
0082-2515 Techniques in Pure and Applied Microbiology
0082-2523 Techniques of Biochemical and Biophysical Morphology
0082-2531 Techniques of Chemistry

ISSN INDEX

ISSN	Title
0082-254X	Techniques of Electrochemistry
0082-2558	Techniques of Metals Research†
0082-2566	Technische Fortschrittsberichte†
0082-2590	Technische Physik in Einzeldarstellungen
0082-2604	Technology and Democratic Society *changed to* Organisations, People, Society/O P S
0082-2612	Etudes Teilhardiennes
0082-2620	Museum of Antiquities of Tel-Aviv-Yafo. Publications
0082-2639	Tel Aviv-Yafo. Research and Statistical Department. Special Surveys *changed to* Tel Aviv-Yafo. Center for Economic and Social Research. Research and Surveys Series
0082-2647	Telemetry Journal Buyers Guide†
0082-2655	Telephone Engineer and Management Directory
0082-2663	Telephone Tickler for Insurance Men *changed to* Telephone Tickler for Insurance Men and Women
0082-2671	Telphony's Directory of the Telephone Industry *changed to* Telephony's Directory & Buyer's Guide for the Telephone Industry
0082-268X	Television Factbook
0082-2701	Coleccion Temas de Arquitectura Actual
0082-2744	East Tennessee State University. Research Development Committee. Publications
0082-2752	Tennessee. State Planning Office. State Planning Office Publication
0082-2760	Tennessee Statistical Abstract
0082-2779	Tennessee Tech Journal
0082-2787	Tennessee Valley Authority. Annual Report
0082-2795	Tennessee Valley Authority. Power Annual Report *changed to* Tennessee Valley Authority. Power Program Summary
0082-2809	Tennessee Valley Authority. Technical Monographs
0082-2817	Tennessee Valley Authority. Technical Reports
0082-2825	Tennis for Travelers†
0082-2833	Tennis Guide
0082-2841	Tennyson Research Bulletin
0082-285X	Tennyson Society, Lincoln, England. Monographs
0082-2868	Tennyson Society, Lincoln, England. Report
0082-2884	Terrae Incognitae
0082-2922	Texas A & M Oceanographic Studies
0082-2930	Texas Archeological Society. Bulletin
0082-2949	Texas Archeology
0082-2957	Texas Archeology Salvage Project. Papers†
0082-2973	Texas Christian University Monographs in History and Culture
0082-29?1	Texas. Coordinating Board. Texas College and University System. C B Annual Report
0082-9?X	Texas. Coordinating Board. Texas College and University System. C B Policy Paper
0082-30?	Texas. Coordinating Board. Texas College and University System. C B Study Paper
008?-501?	Texas Folklore Society. Paisano Series†
008?-30?	Texas Folklore Society. Publications
0082-3031	Texas. Forest Service. Cooperative Forest Tree Improvement Program. Progress Report
0082-304X	Texas Forestry Papers
0082-3058	Texas. Governor's Committee on Aging. Biennial Report
0082-3066	Texas Industry Series
0082-3074	Texas Memorial Museum. Bulletin
0082-3082	Texas Memorial Museum. Miscellaneous Papers
0082-3090	Texas Memorial Museum. Notes Series†
0082-3104	Texas Mineral Producers†
0082-3120	Texas Public Library Statistics
0082-3139	Texas Research Foundation, Renner. Contributions
0082-3163	Texas Special Libraries Directory
0082-318X	Stephen F. Austin State University. School of Forestry. Bulletin
0082-3198	Texas Tech University. Graduate Studies
0082-3201	African and Afro-American Studies and Research Center. Occasional Publication†
0082-3228	University of Texas, Austin. Bureau of Business Research. Area Economic Survey
0082-3236	University of Texas, Austin. Bureau of Business Research. Bibliography
0082-3244	University of Texas, Austin. Bureau of Business Research. Business Guide
0082-3279	University of Texas, Austin. Bureau of Business Research. Research Monograph *changed to* University of Texas, Austin. Bureau of Business Research. Research Report Series
0082-3287	University of Texas, Austin. Bureau of Economic Geology. Annual Report
0082-3309	University of Texas, Austin. Bureau of Economic Geology. Geological Circular
0082-3333	University of Texas, Austin. Bureau of Economic Geology. Mineral Resource Circulars
0082-335X	University of Texas, Austin. Bureau of Economic Geology. Report of Investigations
0082-3384	University of Texas, Austin. Natural Fibers Economic Research. Research Report
0082-3392	Texas Cotton Review
0082-3406	University of Texas, Austin. County Auditors' Institute. Proceedings†
0082-3414	University of Texas, Austin. Department of Anthropology. Anthropology Series†
0082-3422	University of Texas, Austin. Governmental Accounting and Finance Institute. Proceedings†
0082-3430	University of Texas, Austin. Institute for Tax Assessors. Proceedings†
0082-3449	University of Texas. Institute of Marine Science. Contributions *changed to* Contributions in Marine Science
0082-3546	University of Texas Monographs in Astronomy
0082-3554	Texas. Water Development Board. Biennial Report†
0082-3562	Texas. Water Development Board. Report *changed to* Texas. Department of Water Resources. Report
0082-3570	Texas. Water Quality Board. Biennial Report†
0082-3589	Texte und Untersuchungen zur Geschichte der Altchristlichen Literatur
0082-3597	Texte zur Kirchen- und Theologiegeschichte
0082-3627	Textil-Industrie und ihre Helfer
0082-3635	Textile Chemistry†
0082-3651	Textile Industry Technical Conference. Record *see* 0094-9884
0082-366X	Textile Japan
0082-3708	Textiles Suisses/Interieur
0082-3732	Texts and Studies in the History of Mediaeval Education
0082-3759	Texts from Cuneiform Sources
0082-3767	Textus
0082-3775	Textus Patristici et Liturgici
0082-3791	Thailand. National Statistical Office. Statistical Bibliography
0082-3805	Thames Book
0082-3821	Theatre Annual
0082-383X	Theatre Ouvert
0082-3848	Theatre Student Series
0082-3856	Theatre World
0082-3880	Theodor-Storm-Gesellschaft. Schriften
0082-3899	Theokratia; Jahrbuch des Institutum Judaicum Delitzschianum
0082-3902	Theologische Dissertationen
0082-3945	Theoretical and Experimental Biology
0082-3953	Theoretical and Experimental Biophysics: A Series of Advances†
0082-3961	Theoretical Chemistry
0082-3988	Theorie de la Production
0082-4003	Theriaca
0082-4011	Thermal Analysis Series†
0082-402X	Thermodynamics Research Center Data Project. Selected Values of Properties of Chemical Compounds. Category B. Selected Infrared Spectral Data
0082-4038	Thermodynamics Research Center Data Project. Selected Values of Properties of Chemical Compounds. Category D. Selected Raman Spectral Data *changed to* Thermodynamics Research Center. Hydrocarbon Project. Selected Values of Properties of Hydrocarbons and Related Compounds. Category D: Selected Raman Spectral Data
0082-4046	Thermodynamics Research Center Data Project. Selected Values of Properties of Chemical Compounds. Category A. Tables of Selected Values of Physical and Thermodynamic Properties of Chemical Compounds
0082-4054	Thermodynamics Research Center Data Project. Selected Values of Properties of Chemical Compounds. Category C. Selected Ultraviolet Spectral Data†
0082-4062	Thermodynamics Research Center Data Project. Selected Values of Properties of Chemical Compounds. Category E. Selected Mass Spectral Data†
0082-4070	Thermodynamics Research Center Data Project. Selected Values of Properties of Chemical Compounds. Category F. Selected Nuclear Magnetic Resonance Spectral Data
0082-4089	Silumine Fizika
0082-4097	Thesaurismata
0082-4119	Theses in Germanic Studies
0082-4127	University of London. Institute of Germanic Studies. Theses in Progress at British Universities *see* 0260-5929
0082-4151	Thomas Grocery Register
0082-416X	Thomas Hardy Year Book
0082-4178	Thomas Jefferson Center for Political Economy. Research Monographs.†
0082-4186	Thomas Mann Gesellschaft. Blaetter
0082-4208	St. Thomas More Lectures
0082-4216	Thomas Register of American Manufacturers *changed to* Thomas Register of American Manufacturers and Thomas Register Catalog File
0082-4224	Thom's Commercial Directory
0082-4232	Thoresby Society, Leeds, England. Publications
0082-4240	Thoroughbred Racing Associations. Directory and Record Book
0082-4267	Thruway-Interstate Highway Guide
0082-4283	Thunder Bay Historical Museum Society. Papers and Records
0082-4305	Tierwelt Deutschlands
0082-4313	Tijdschrift voor Privaatrecht
0082-433X	Timber and Plywood. Board News Annual
0082-4364	Timber Trades Journal. Annual Special Issue
0082-4372	Timber Trades Directory
0082-4399	Times Guide to the House of Commons
0082-4410	Times Literary Supplement. T.L.S; Essays and Reviews
0082-4429	Times 1000
0082-4437	Times of India Annual
0082-4445	Times of India Directory and Yearbook Including Who's Who
0082-4453	Universitatea din Timisoara. Analele. Stiinte Fizico-Chimice
0082-4461	Universitatea din Timisoara. Analele. Stiinte Filologice
0082-4496	Tire and Rim Association. Standards Year Book
0082-450X	Tiryns
0082-4518	Tissue Culture Studies in Japan: The Annual Bibliography
0082-4526	Titles in Series
0082-4534	Titles of Dissertations and Theses Completed in Home Economics
0082-4542	Tjaenstemaennens Centralorganisation. Aaret
0082-4550	Tlatoani†
0082-4569	Tlatoani. Suplemento†
0082-4585	Sources of Contemporary Jewish Thought
0082-4593	Tobacco Associates. Annual Report
0082-4607	Tobacco Research Council. Research Papers†
0082-4615	Tobacco Research Council. Review of Activities†
0082-4623	Tobacco Science Yearbook
0082-4631	Tobacco Trade Year Book and Diary
0082-464X	Tohoku University. Institute of Geology and Paleontology. Science Reports. Second Series
0082-4658	Tohoku University. Institute of Geology and Paleontology. Contributions
0082-4666	Tohoku University. Research Institutes. Science Reports. Series D: Agriculture *changed to* Tohoku University. Institute for Agricultural Research. Reports
0082-4674	Tokai-Kinki National Agricultural Experiment Station, Tsu, Japan. Bulletin†
0082-4690	Tokyo Astronomical Bulletin. Second Series
0082-4704	Tokyo Astronomical Observatory. Annals. Second Series
0082-4712	Tokyo Astronomical Observatory. Reprints
0082-4720	Tokyo Metropolitan Agricultural Experiment Station, Itsukaichi Office. Forestry Experimental Bulletin
0082-4739	Tokyo Medical and Dental University. Institute for Medical and Dental Engineering. Reports
0082-4747	Tokyo Metropolitan University. Faculty of Technology. Memoirs
0082-4755	National Science Museum. Memoirs
0082-4763	Snow Brand Milk Products Co., Ltd. Research Laboratory. Reports
0082-4771	Tokyo Metropolitan Research Laboratory of Public Health, Annual Report
0082-478X	University of Tokyo. Department of Geography. Bulletin
0082-4798	University of Tokyo. Institute for Solid State Physics. Technical Report. Series A
0082-4801	University of Tokyo. Institute for Solid State Physics. Technical Report. Series B
0082-481X	University of Tokyo. Institute of Applied Microbiology. Reports
0082-4828	University of Tokyo. Institute of Space and Aeronautical Science. Report
0082-4836	Tokyo University of Fisheries. Journal. Special Edition *changed to* Tokyo University of Fisheries. Transactions
0082-4844	Tokyo University of Foreign Studies. Summary
0082-4852	Toledo Area Artists Exhibition
0082-4895	Tonga. Minister of Health. Report
0082-495X	Topics in Inorganic and General Chemistry
0082-4968	Topics in Lipid Chemistry†
0082-4992	Topics in Phosphorous Chemistry
0082-500X	Topics in Stereochemistry
0082-5018	Art Gallery of Ontario. Annual Report
0082-5034	Hospital for Sick Children, Toronto. Research Institute. Annual Report
0082-5042	Toronto Medieval Bibliographies
0082-5050	Toronto Mediaeval Latin Texts
0082-5077	Royal Ontario Museum. Art and Archaeology. Occasional Papers†
0082-5077	Royal Ontario Museum. Art and Archaeology. Occasional Papers
0082-5093	Royal Ontario Museum. Life Sciences. Miscellaneous Publications
0082-5107	Royal Ontario Museum. Life Sciences. Occasional Papers

0082-5115 Royal Ontario Museum. Annual Report
0082-5123 Toronto Semitic Texts and Studies
0082-514X University of Toronto. Department of Electrical Engineering. Research Report
0082-5158 University of Toronto. Department of English. Studies and Texts†
0082-5166 Natural Hazard Research Working Papers
0082-5174 University of Toronto. Department of Geography. Research Publications
0082-5182 University of Toronto. Department of Mechanical Engineering. Technical Publication Series
0082-5190 University of Toronto. Faculty of Forestry. Technical Reports
0082-5239 University of Toronto. Institute for Aerospace Studies. Progress Report
0082-5247 University of Toronto. Institute for Aerospace Studies. Review
0082-5255 University of Toronto. Institute for Aerospace Studies. Report
0082-5263 University of Toronto. Institute for Aerospace Studies. Technical Note
0082-5271 University of Toronto. Institute for the Quantitative Analysis of Social and Economic Policy. News Letter *changed to* University of Toronto. Institute for Policy Analysis. Annual Report
0082-5298 University of Toronto. Institute for the Quantitative Analysis of Social and Economic Policy. Reprint Series *changed to* University of Toronto. Institute for Policy Analysis. Reprint Series
0082-5301 University of Toronto. Institute for the Quantitative Analysis of Social and Economic Policy. Working Paper Series *changed to* University of Toronto. Institute for Policy Analysis. Working Paper Series
0082-531X University of Toronto. Library. Annual Report
0082-5328 Pontifical Institute of Mediaeval Studies. Studies and Texts
0082-5336 University of Toronto Romance Series
0082-5344 Torquay Natural History Society. Transactions and Proceedings
0082-5352 Torry Research Station, Aberdeen, Scotland. Annual Report
0082-5360 Tottori University. Faculty of Agriculture. Journal
0082-5379 Tottori University Forests. Bulletin
0082-5395 Universite de Toulouse-le Mirail. Faculte des Sciences. Annales†
0082-5409 France-Iberie Recherche. Etudes et Documents
0082-5417 France-Iberie Recherche. Theses et Documents
0082-5433 T'oung Pao
0082-5441 Touring with Towser
0082-545X Tourism in Greece
0082-5468 Tourist Bibliography *changed to* Tourism Compendium
0082-5484 Toute la Boisson. International
0082-5506 Towarzystwo Naukowe w Toruniu. Fontes
0082-5514 Towarzystwo Naukowe w Toruniu. Komisja Historii Sztuki. Teka
0082-5522 Towarzystwo Naukowe w Toruniu. Roczniki
0082-5530 Studia Societatis Scientiarum Torunensis. Sectio B (Chemia)
0082-5549 Studia Societatis Scientiarum Torunensis. Sectio C (Geografia et Geologia)
0082-5557 Studia Societatis Scientiarum Torunensis. Sectio D (Botanika)
0082-5565 Studia Societatis Scientiarum Torunensis. Sectio E (Zoologia)
0082-5573 Studia Societatis Scientiarum Torunensis. Sectio F. (Astronomia)
0082-5581 Studia Societatis Scientiarum Torunensis. Sectio G (Physiologia)
0082-5611 Toy Trader Year Book
0082-562X Oriental Library. Research Department. Memoirs
0082-5638 Trabajos de Prehistoria. Nueva Serie
0082-5646 Trabrennen
0082-5662 Tractocatalogue
0082-5689 Trade Associations and Professional Bodies of the United Kingdom
0082-5697 Trade Directory of Malta
0082-5735 Trade Directory of the Republic of the Sudan
0082-5743 Trade Directory Wine and Spirit *changed to* Off Licence News Directory
0082-5751 Trade Index of Iran
0082-5778 Trade of China
0082-5786 Trade-Mark Register of the United States
0082-5794 Trader Handbook *changed to* Motor Trader Directory
0082-5808 Trades Register of London *changed to* London Directory of Industry and Commerce
0082-5824 Trado; Asian-African Directory of Exporters, Importers and Manufacturers
0082-5859 Traffic Laws Commentary
0082-5867 Traffic Report of the St. Lawrence Seaway
0082-5891 Railway World Annual
0082-5913 Transit Fact Book *see* 0706-7658
0082-5921 Transition Metal Chemistry: A Series of Advances
0082-593X Translations and Reprints from the Original Sources of European History *changed to* Middle Ages
0082-5948 Transplantation Reviews *see* 0105-2896
0082-5956 Transportation Statistics in the United States
0082-5964 Transportieren Umschlagen Lagern
0082-5980 Transtelel; Transmissions, Telecommunications, Electronique en France
0082-6006 Trattati di Architettura
0082-6022 Travaux de Droit, d'Economique de Sociologie et de Sciences Politiques
0082-6049 Travaux de Linguistique
0082-6057 Travaux de Linguistique et de Litterature
0082-6073 Travaux d'Histoire Ethico-Politique
0082-6081 Travaux d'Humanisme et Renaissance
0082-609X Travaux sur les Pecheries du Quebec
0082-6103 Travel Abroad: Frontier Formalities
0082-612X Travel Industry Association of Canada. Convention Report *changed to* Tourism Industry Association of Canada. Convention Report
0082-6146 Travel Industry Personnel Directory
0082-6197 Travel Research Journal
0082-6200 Travel Trends in the United States and Canadian Provinces *changed to* Travel Trends in the United States and Canada
0082-6219 Travel World Year Book and Diary
0082-6243 Treatise on Analytical Chemistry. Part 1: Theory and Practice of Analytical Chemistry
0082-6251 Treatise on Analytical Chemistry. Part 2: Analytical Chemistry of the Elements; Analytical Chemistry of Organic and Inorganic Compounds
0082-626X Treatise on Analytical Chemistry. Part 3: Analytical Chemistry in Industry
0082-6278 Treatise on Coatings†
0082-6286 Trends in Developing Countries†
0082-6316 Trends in Southeast Asia
0082-6324 Trends in the International Petroleum-Refining Industry
0082-6340 Treubia
0082-6359 Tri-State Transportation Commission. Public Transport Services to Non C/B/D Employment Concentrations; Progress Report
0082-6367 T R I U M F, Vancouver, British Columbia. Report
0082-6391 Tribolium Information Bulletin
0082-6405 Tribology Convention. Proceedings
0082-6413 Tribus
0082-643X Trierer Grabungen und Forschungen
0082-6448 Istituto Sperimentale Talassografico, Trieste. Annuario.
0082-6456 Instituto Sperimentale Talassografico, Trieste. Pubblicazione
0082-6464 Universita di Trieste. Istituto di Chimica Biologica. Publicazioni†
0082-6472 Universita degli Studi di Trieste. Istituto di Chimica Farmaceutica. Pubblicazioni†
0082-6480 Universita degli Studi di Trieste. Istituto di Pedagogia. Quaderni
0082-6499 Trinc's Blue Book of the Trucking Industry
0082-6502 Trinidad and Tobago. Central Statistical Office. Annual Statistical Digest
0082-6510 Trinidad and Tobago. Central Statistical Office. Digest of Statistics on Education
0082-6529 Trinidad and Tobago. Central Statistical Office. Financial Statistics
0082-6537 Trinidad and Tobago. Central Statistical Office. International Travel Report
0082-6545 Trinidad and Tobago. Central Statistical Office. Overseas Trade. Annual Report
0082-6553 Trinidad and Tobago. Central Statistical Office. Population and Vital Statistics; Report
0082-6561 Trinidad and Tobago Today
0082-657X Trinidad and Tobago Trade Directory
0082-6588 Trinitarian Bible Society. Annual Report
0082-6596 Trinity University Studies in Religion
0082-6618 Universitetet i Trondheim. Norges Tekniske Hoegskole. Vassdrags- og Havnelaboratoriet. Meddelelse
0082-6642 Tropical Pesticides Research Institute. Annual Report
0082-6669 Tuberkulose-Jahrbuch†
0082-6677 Tuberkulose und ihre Grenzgebiete in Einzel-Arstellungen†
0082-6693 Universidad Nacional de Tucuman. Instituto de Ingenieria Electrica. Revista
0082-6707 Tudomanyszervezesi Fuzetek
0082-6715 Tudomanytorteneti Tanulmanyok
0082-6731 Tuebinger Rechtswissenschaftliche Abhandlungen
0082-674X Tufting Year Book
0082-6758 Tulane Studies in English *changed to* T S E: Tulane Studies in English
0082-6766 Tulane Studies in Philosophy
0082-6774 Tulane Studies in Political Science
0082-6782 Tulane Studies in Zoology and Botany
0082-6790 Howard-Tilton Memorial Library. Report
0082-6812 University of Tulsa. Department of English. Monograph Series
0082-6820 Tunisia. Ministere du Plan. Budget Economique
0082-6839 Tunisia. Institut National de la Statistique. Statistiques Industrielles *changed to* Tunisia. Institut National de la Statistique. Recensement des Activites Industrielles
0082-6847 Turcica; Revue d'Etudes Turques
0082-6855 Institut Universitaire d'Etudes Europeennes de Turin. Annuaire†
0082-6863 Museo Egizio, Turin. Catalogo. Serie Prima: Monumenti e Testi.
0082-6871 Universita Delgi Studi di Torino. Facolta di Scienze Agrarie. Annali
0082-688X Universita degli Studi di Torino. Istituto di Storia. Collana†
0082-6898 Turkish Review of Ethnography
0082-6901 Turkey. Devlet Istatistik Enstitusu. Dis Ticaret Yillik Istatistik/Statistique Annuelle du Commerce Exterieur/Annual Foreign Trade Statistics
0082-691X Turkiye Istatistik Yilligi
0082-6928 Turkey. Devlet Istatistik Enstitusu. Tarim Istatistikleri Ozeti/Summary of Agricultural Statistics
0082-6936 Turkey. Devlet Istatistik Enstitusu. Tarimsal Yapi ve Uretim/Agricultural Structure and Production
0082-6944 Turkey. Devlet Planama Teskilati. Yili Programi Ucuncu Bes Yil/Annual Program of the Five Year Development Plan
0082-6952 Turkish Trade Directory & Telex Index
0082-6979 Turun Yliopisto. Julkaisuja. Sarja A. II. Biologica- Geographica- Geologica
0082-6987 Turun Yliopisto. Julkaisuja. Sarja B. Humaniora
0082-6995 Turun Yliopisto. Julkaisuja. Sarja C. Scripta Lingua Fennica Edita
0082-7002 Turun Yliopisto. Julkaisuja. Sarja A. I. Astronomica-Chemica-Physica-Mathematica
0082-7010 Turun Yliopisto. Kirjasto. Julkaisuja
0082-7029 Turun Yliopisto. Klassillisen Filologian Laitos. Opera Ex Instituto Philologiae Classicae Universitatis Turkuensis Edita
0082-7037 Turun Yliopisto. Psykologian Laitos. Reports *changed to* University of Turku Psychological Reports
0082-7037 Turun Yliopisto. Psykologian Laitos. Reports *changed to* Turun Yliopisto Psykologian Tutkimuksia
0082-7088 Twentieth Century Legal Philosophy Series
0082-710X St. Paul, Minnesota. Metropolitan Transit Commission. Annual Report *changed to* St. Paul, Minnesota. Twin Cities Area Metropolitan Transit Commission. Annual Report
0082-7118 Tyndale Bulletin
0082-7126 U C L A Business Forecast for the Nation and California
0082-7134 U C L A Forum in Medical Sciences
0082-7142 U K Trade Names
0082-7150 Ub'†
0082-7169 Uganda. Geological Survey and Mines Department. Memoirs†
0082-7177 Uganda. Forestry Department. Annual Report
0082-7185 Uganda. Forestry Department. Bulletins†
0082-7193 Uganda. Forestry Department. Technical Notes
0082-7215 Uganda. Geological Survey and Mines Department. Annual Report
0082-7231 Uganda. Ministry of Planning and Economic Development. Statistics Division. Background to the Budget
0082-724X Uganda. Ministry of Planning and Economic Development. Statistics Division. Enumeration of Employees
0082-7282 Uhrmacher-Jahrbuch†
0082-7290 Uhrmacher-Jahrbuch fuer Handwerk und Handel
0082-7312 Uj Magyar Nepkoltesi Gyujtemeny
0082-7347 Ulster Folklife
0082-7355 Ulster Journal of Archaeology
0082-7363 Ulster-Scot Historical Series
0082-7371 Ulster Year Book
0082-7444 Underwater Acoustics†
0082-7452 Underwriting Results in Canada
0082-7460 Unesco Bibliographical Handbooks *changed to* Documentation, Libraries and Archives: Bibliographies and Reference Works
0082-7479 Unesco Earthquake Study Missions
0082-7487 Unesco Handbook of International Exchanges
0082-7495 Unesco Manuals for Libraries *changed to* Documentation, Libraries and Archives: Studies and Research
0082-7509 Unesco. Records of the General Conference. Proceedings
0082-7517 Unesco. Records of the General Conference. Resolutions
0082-7525 Unesco. Report of the Director-General on the Activities of the Organization
0082-7533 Unesco Statistical Reports and Studies
0082-7541 Unesco Statistical Yearbook
0082-755X Ungarn-Jahrbuch
0082-7584 Uniform Building Code

0082-7592 Uniform Crime Reports for the United States
0082-7630 Union List of Publications in Opaque Microforms†
0082-7649 Union List of Scientific and Technical Periodicals Held in the Principal Libraries of East Africa†
0082-7657 Union List of Scientific Serials in Canadian Libraries
0082-7681 Union List of Serials in the Wayne State University Libraries *changed to* Union List of Selected Serials of Michigan
0082-7711 Union Nationale de l'Enseignement Agricole Prive. Annuaire
0082-7746 Union of British Columbia Municipalities. Minutes of Annual Convention
0082-7762 Union of Nova Scotia Municipalities. Proceedings of the Annual Convention
0082-7770 Union Professionnelle Feminine. Annuaire
0082-7789 Index to Titles of English News Releases of Hsinhua News Agency
0082-7797 Unitarian and Free Christian Churches. Yearbook of the General Assembly *changed to* Unitarian and Free Christian Churches. Handbook and Directory of the General Assembly
0082-7800 Unitarian Historical Society, London. Transactions
0082-7819 Unitarian Historical Society. Proceedings
0082-7827 Unitarian Universalist Directory
0082-7835 Egypt. Service des Antiquites. Annales
0082-7843 United Baptist Convention of the Atlantic Provinces. Yearbook
0082-786X United Church of Canada. Committee on Archives. Bulletin. Records and Proceedings
0082-7878 United Church of Canada. General Council. Record of Proceedings
0082-7886 United Church of Canada. Year Book
0082-7894 United Community Funds and Councils of America. Addresses Delivered at the United Way Staff Conference†
0082-7908 United Free Church of Scotland. Handbook
0082-7916 United Graphic Guide
0082-7932 Travel Trade Directory, U K and Ireland
0082-7940 United Kingdom Atomic Energy Authority. Annual Report
0082-7959 United Kingdom Fire and Loss Statistics *changed to* United Kingdom Fire Statistics
0082-7967 Meat Trade Yearbook
0082-7983 United Methodist Church (United States) Division of Education. Adult Planbook.
0082-8009 United Nations and What You Should Know about It
0082-8025 United Nations Congress on the Prevention of Crime and the Treatment of Offenders. Report
0082-8041 Demographic Yearbook
0082-805X Population Studies
0082-8076 United Nations. Disarmament Commission. Official Records
0082-8084 United Nations. Economic and Social Council. Index to Proceedings
0082-8092 United Nations. Economic and Social Council. Official Records
0082-8106 United Nations Economic and Social Commission for Asia and the Pacific. Development Programming Techniques Series
0082-8114 United Nations Economic and Social Commission for Asia and the Pacific. Mineral Resources Development Series
0082-8122 United Nations Economic and Social Commission for Asia and the Pacific. Regional Economic Cooperation Series
0082-8130 Water Resources Development Series
0082-8157 United Nations. General Assembly. Index to Proceedings
0082-8211 Resolutions of the General Assembly of the United Nations
0082-8289 United Nations. International Law Commission. Yearbook
0082-8297 United Nations Juridical Yearbook
0082-8300 United Nations Legislative Series
0082-8319 United Nations. Multilateral Treaties in Respect of Which the Secretary-General Performs Depositary Functions
0082-8327 Estimated World Requirements of Narcotic Drugs, Supplement
0082-8335 Estimated World Requirements of Narcotic Drugs
0082-8343 United Nations. Permanent Central Narcotics Board. Report to the Economic and Social Council on the Work of the Permanent Central Narcotics (Opium) Board *changed to* United Nations. Permanent Central Narcotics (Opium) Board. Report of the International Narcotics Control Board on Its Work
0082-836X United Nations Regional Cartographic Conference for Asia and the Far East. Proceedings of the Conference and Technical Papers
0082-8408 United Nations. Security Council. Index to Proceedings
0082-8416 United Nations. Security Council. Official Records
0082-8459 United Nations. Statistical Yearbook
0082-8475 United Nations. Trade and Development Board. Official Records
0082-8483 United Nations. Trade and Development Board. Official Records. Supplements
0082-8491 United Nations. Trusteeship Council. Index to Proceedings
0082-8505 United Nations. Trusteeship Council. Official Records
0082-8513 United Nations. Trusteeship Council. Official Records. Supplements
0082-8521 United Nations. Yearbook
0082-8548 United Presbyterian Church in the United States of America. Minutes of the General Assembly
0082-8556 U S O Annual Report
0082-8564 United Society for Christian Literature. Annual Report *changed to* U S C L Bulletin
0082-8599 U S A Oil Industry Directory
0082-8602 U S College-Sponsored Programs Abroad. Academic Year *changed to* Learning Traveler. U.S. College-Sponsored Programs Abroad: Academic Year
0082-8637 U. S. Agency for International Development. Proposed Foreign Aid Program, Summary Presentation to Congress†
0082-8661 Tables on Hatchery and Flock Participation in the National Poultry Improvement Plan
0082-867X U. S. Agricultural Research Service. Animal Science Research Division. Tables on Hatchery and Flock Participation in the National Turkey Improvement Plan *see* 0082-8661
0082-8688 U.S. Air Force Academy Assembly. Proceedings
0082-8696 U. S. Air Force Academy Library. Special Bibliography Series
0082-870X U.S. Air Force Cambridge Research Laboratories. AFCRL (Series) *changed to* U.S. Air Force Geophysics Laboratory. AFGL (Series)
0082-8742 United States and Canadian Publications on Africa†
0082-8750 United States Animal Health Association. Proceedings of the Annual Meeting
0082-8769 U. S. Arms Control and Disarmament Agency. Annual Report to Congress
0082-8793 World Military Expenditures and Related Data *changed to* World Military Expenditures and Arms Transfers
0082-8815 U. S. Atomic Energy Commission. Annual Report to Congress†
0082-8823 U. S. Atomic Energy Commission. Annual Report to Congress. Supplement. Atomic Energy Research Reports†
0082-8831 U. S. Atomic Energy Commission. Division of Plans and Reports. Fundamental Nuclear Energy Research†
0082-884X U. S. Atomic Energy Commission. Safety and Fire Protection Technical Bulletins†
0082-8939 U. S. Bureau of International Commerce. Annual Reports
0082-8947 Export Control Regulations *see* 0094-8411
0082-8963 U. S. Bureau of International Commerce. Trade Lists
0082-9013 U. S. Bureau of Labor Statistics. Analysis of Work Stoppages
0082-9021 U. S. Bureau of Labor Statistics. Bulletins
0082-903X U. S. Bureau of Labor Statistics. B L S Staff Paper
0082-9048 U.S. Bureau of Labor Statistics. Employment and Earnings Statistics for States and Areas *changed to* U. S. Bureau of Labor Statistics. Employment and Earnings: States and Areas
0082-9056 U. S. Bureau of Labor Statistics. Handbook of Labor Statistics
0082-9064 U. S. Bureau of Labor Statistics. Industry Wage Surveys
0082-9099 U.S. Bureau of Labor Statistics. Union Wages and Hours Surveys
0082-9102 U.S. Bureau of Labor Statistics. Wage Chronologies
0082-9110 U. S. Bureau of Land Management. Public Land Statistics
0082-9129 U. S. Bureau of Mines. Bulletin
0082-9137 U. S. Bureau of Mines. Commodity Data Summaries
0082-9250 U. S. Bureau of Radiological Health. Seminar Paper Series†
0082-9307 U.S. Bureau of the Census. Annual Survey of Manufactures
0082-9315 U. S. Bureau of the Census. Census of Agriculture
0082-9323 U.S. Bureau of the Census. Census of Business *changed to* U.S. Bureau of the Census. Census of Retail Trade, Wholesale Trade and Selected Service Industries
0082-934X U. S. Bureau of the Census. Census of Construction Industries
0082-9358 U. S. Bureau of the Census. Census of Governments
0082-9366 U. S. Bureau of the Census. Census of Housing
0082-9374 U. S. Bureau of the Census. Census of Manufactures
0082-9382 U. S. Bureau of the Census. Census of Mineral Industries
0082-9390 U. S. Bureau of the Census. Census of Population
0082-9404 U. S. Bureau of the Census. Census of Transportation
0082-9412 U. S. Bureau of the Census. Census Tract Manual
0082-9420 U.S. Bureau of the Census. Recurrent Reports on Governments (Series G F-7) Chart Book on Government Finances and Employment *see* 0360-2508
0082-9439 Current Governments Reports: City Government Finances
0082-9447 U. S. Bureau of the Census. Congressional District Data Book
0082-9455 U. S. Bureau of the Census. County and City Data Book
0082-9463 U. S. Bureau of the Census. County Business Patterns
0082-9471 Current Population Reports
0082-948X Current Population Reports: Population Characteristics. Household and Family Characteristics
0082-9498 Current Population Reports: International Population Reports
0082-9501 Current Population Reports, P-20: Population Characteristics. Marital Status and Family Status *changed to* Current Population Reports: Populaion Characteristics. Marital Status and Living Arrangements
0082-951X U. S. Bureau of the Census. Current Population Reports: Negro Population *changed to* Current Population Reports: Population Characteristics. Social and Economic Characteristics of the Black Population
0082-9528 U. S. Bureau of the Census. Current Population Reports: School Enrollment: October (Year) *changed to* Current Population Reports: Population Characteristics. School Enrollment: Social and Economic Characteristics of Students
0082-9536 U. S. Bureau of the Census. Technical Notes
0082-9544 U. S. Bureau of the Census. Technical Paper
0082-9552 U. S. Bureau of the Census. Working Papers
0082-9560 United States Catholic Missionary Personnel Overseas *changed to* United States Catholic Mission Council. Handbook
0082-9609 U. S. Civil Aeronautics Board. Aircraft Operating Cost and Performance Report
0082-9625 U. S. Coast Guard. Oceanographic Reports (CG-373 Series)
0082-9641 U.S. Commission on Civil Rights. Clearinghouse Publications
0082-965X World Refugee Report
0082-9706 United States Cross-Country and Distance Running Coaches Association. Proceedings *changed to* United States Cross-Country Coaches Association. Annual Business Meeting. Minutes
0082-9714 U.S. Department of Agriculture. Agricultural Statistics
0082-9722 Hatcheries and Dealers Participating in the National Poultry Improvement Plan
0082-9765 U.S. Department of Agriculture. Farmer Cooperative Service. Information (Series) *changed to* U.S. Department of Agriculture. Economics, Statistics and Cooperatives Service. Cooperative Information Report
0082-9781 U.S. Department of Agriculture. Marketing Research Report
0082-979X U.S. Department of Agriculture. Production Research Reports
0082-9803 U. S. Department of Agriculture. Report of the Secretary of Agriculture
0082-9811 U.S. Department of Agriculture. Technical Bulletin
0082-9846 U.S. Bureau of Domestic and International Business Administration. Overseas Business Reports
0082-9862 U. S. Department of Defense. Defense Program and Defense Budget
0082-9889 U. S. Department of Health, Education, and Welfare. Catalog of H E W Assistance Providing Financial Support and Service to States, Communities, Organizations, Individuals†
0082-9897 U. S. Department of Health, Education and Welfare. Health, Education and Welfare Trends†
0082-9900 U.S. Social and Rehabilitation Service. Juvenile Court Statistics

0082-9935 U. S. Department of Health, Education and Welfare. Statistics on Public Institutions for Delinquent Children *changed to* Children in Custody
0082-9943 U. S. Department of Justice. Annual Report of the Attorney General of the United States
0082-9951 U. S. Department of Justice. Opinions of Attorney General
0082-9994 Manpower Research Projects *changed to* U.S. Department of Labor. Employment and Training Administration. Manpower Research and Development Projects
0083-0003 U. S. Department of State. African Series
0083-0011 U. S. Department of State. Biographic Register
0083-002X U. S. Department of State. Commercial Policy Series
0083-0038 U. S. Department of State. Department and Foreign Service Series
0083-0054 U. S. Department of State. East Asian and Pacific Series
0083-0062 U. S. Department of State. Economic Cooperation Series
0083-0070 U. S. Department of State. European and British Commonwealth Series
0083-0089 Far Eastern Series *see* 0083-0054
0083-0097 U. S. Department of State. General Foreign Policy Series
0083-0119 U. S. Department of State. International Information and Cultural Series
0083-0127 U. S. Department of State. International Organization and Conference Series
0083-0135 U. S. Department of State. International Organization Series
0083-0143 U. S. Department of State. Inter-American Series
0083-0151 U.S. Department of State. Near and Middle Eastern Series *changed to* U.S. Department of State. Near East and South Asian Series
0083-0186 U. S. Department of State. Treaties and Other International Acts Series
0083-0194 U. S. Department of State. Treaties in Force
0083-0208 United States Participation in the United Nations.
0083-0305 U.S. Army. Corps of Engineers. Port Series
0083-0313 U.S. Army. Corps of Engineers. Technical Reports, T R (Series)
0083-0321 U.S. Department of the Interior.Annual Report *see* 0069-9152
0083-0364 U. S. Department of the Interior. Safety Conference Guides†
0083-0380 U. S. Department of Transportation. Bibliographic Lists
0083-0399 U.S. Department of Transportation. Annual Report on High Speed Ground Transportaion Act *changed to* U.S. Department of Transportation. Report on the High Speed Ground Transportation Act of 1965
0083-0429 United States Dispensatory and Physicians Pharmacology *changed to* United States Dispensatory
0083-0445 U.S. Department of Agriculture. Agricultural Economics Report
0083-050X Sewage Facilities Construction
0083-0518 U. S. Environmental Protection Agency. Pesticides Enforcement Division. Notices of Judgement under Federal Insecticide, Fungicide, and Rodenticide Act
0083-0526 U.S. Equal Employment Opportunity Commission. Annual Report
0083-0534 U. S. Excise Tax Guide
0083-0542 U.S. Farm Credit Administration. Annual Report of the Farm Credit Administration on the Work of the Cooperative Farm Credit System *changed to* U.S. Farm Credit Administration. Annual Report of the Farm Credit Administration and the Cooperative Farm Credit System
0083-0585 U. S. Federal Communications Commission. Annual Report
0083-0607 U. S. Federal Communications Commission. I N F Bulletins
0083-0615 U. S. Federal Communications Commission. Rules and Regulation
0083-0631 U. S. Federal Council for Science and Technology. Interdepartmental Committee for Atmospheric Sciences. I C A S Reports†
0083-064X U.S. Federal Crop Insurance Corporation. Annual Report to Congress
0083-0658 U. S. Federal Deposit Insurance Corporation. Annual Report
0083-0666 U. S. Federal Deposit Insurance Corporation. Bank Operating Statistics
0083-0674 U. S. Federal Deposit Insurance Corporation. Changes Among Operating Banks and Branches
0083-0682 U. S. Federal Fire Council. Federal Fire Experience for Fiscal Year†
0083-0690 U. S. Federal Fire Council. Minutes of Annual Meeting†
0083-0704 U. S. Federal Fire Council. Recommended Practices†
0083-0720 U. S. Federal Home Loan Bank Board. Report
0083-0747 U. S. Federal Home Loan Bank Board. Trends in the Savings and Loan Field
0083-0755 U. S. Federal Maritime Commission. Annual Report
0083-0771 U. S. Federal Mediation and Conciliation Service. Annual Report
0083-078X U. S. Federal Power Commission. Annual Report†
0083-0828 Statistics of Electric Utilities in the United States. Classes A and B Privately Owned Companies *see* 0161-9004
0083-0852 Steam-Electric Plant Construction Cost and Annual Production Expenses
0083-0887 U. S. Federal Reserve System. Annual Report
0083-0917 U. S. Federal Trade Commission. Annual Report
0083-0925 U. S. Federal Trade Commission. Federal Trade Commission Decisions, Findings, Orders and Stipulations
0083-0933 U.S. Federal Trade Commission. Statutes and Court Decisions Pertaining to the Federal Trade Commission. Supplements *changed to* U. S. Federal Trade Commission. Court Decisions Pertaining to the Federal Trade Commission
0083-0941 U. S. Fish and Wildlife Service. Research Reports
0083-0968 United States Foamed Plastic Markets and Directory
0083-0976 U. S. Foreign Agricultural Service. Food and Agricultural Export Directory
0083-0984 Foreign Agriculture Reports†
0083-0992 U. S. Foreign Agricultural Service. Miscellaneous Reports
0083-1018 U.S. Forest Service. Forest Products Laboratory, Madison, Wisconsin. Report of Research at the Forest Products Laboratory.
0083-1026 U.S. Forest Service. Annual Fire Report for National Forests
0083-1034 U.S. Forest Service. Division of Cooperative Fire Protection. Forest Fire Statistics *see* 0360-8034
0083-1042 U. S. Forest Service. National Forest Areas *changed to* U. S. Forest Service. National Forest System Areas
0083-1077 U. S. Forest Service. Technical Equipment Reports
0083-1093 U. S. Geological Survey. Bulletin
0083-1107 U. S. Geological Survey. Circular
0083-1131 U. S. Geological Survey. Water Supply Papers
0083-1166 U. S. Government Films for Public Educational Use†
0083-1174 United States Government Organization Manual *see* 0092-1904
0083-1220 U. S. Immigration and Naturalization Service. Administrative Decisions under Immigration and Nationality Laws
0083-1239 U. S. Immigration and Naturalization Service. Administrative Decisions under Immigration and Nationality Laws. Interim Decisions of the Department of Justice
0083-1247 U. S. Immigration and Naturalization Service. Annual Report
0083-1263 United States Import Duties Annotated
0083-128X United States in World Affairs *changed to* American Foreign Relations-a Documentary Record
0083-1298 United States Independent Telephone Association. Annual Statistical Volume
0083-1328 U. S. Industrial College of the Armed Forces. Monograph Series
0083-1336 U. S. Industrial College of the Armed Forces. Research Project Abstracts
0083-1344 U. S. Industrial Outlook
0083-1425 U.S. Institute of Tropical Forestry. Annual Report†
0083-1468 U.S. Forest Service. Annual Report *changed to* U.S. Forest Service. Intermountain Forest and Range Experiment Station. Recent Reports
0083-1476 U. S. Internal Revenue Service. Annual Report
0083-1484 U. S. Internal Revenue Service. Tax Guide for Small Business
0083-1506 U. S. Interstate Commerce Commission. Advance Bulletin of Interstate Commerce Acts Annotated
0083-1514 U. S. Interstate Commerce Commission. Annual Report
0083-1522 U. S. Interstate Commerce Commission. Interstate Commerce Acts Annotated
0083-1530 U. S. Interstate Commerce Commission. Interstate Commerce Commission Reports. Decisions of the Interstate Commerce Commission of the United States
0083-1557 United States Lawn Tennis Association. Yearbook
0083-1565 U. S. Library of Congress. Annual Report of the Librarian of Congress
0083-1573 Dewey Decimal Classification Additions, Notes and Decisions
0083-1581 U. S. Library of Congress. Hispanic Foundation. Bibliographic Series
0083-1603 U. S. Library of Congress. Library of Congress Publications in Print
0083-1611 U. S. Library of Congress. Manuscript Division. Register of Papers
0083-1646 Newspapers Currently Received and Permanently Retained in the Library of Congress
0083-1670 U. S. Maritime Administration. Annual Report
0083-1697 U. S. Maritime Administration. Technical Report Index, Maritime Administration Research and Development
0083-1700 U. S. Master Tax Guide
0083-1786 U.S. National Bureau of Standards. Applied Mathematics Series
0083-1794 U. S. National Bureau of Standards. Building Science Series
0083-1808 U.S. National Bureau of Standards. Commercial Standards *changed to* U.S. National Bureau of Standards. Voluntary Product Standards
0083-1840 U.S. National Bureau of Standards. National Standard Reference Data Series
0083-1859 U.S. National Bureau of Standards. Product Standards *changed to* U.S. National Bureau of Standards. Voluntary Product Standards
0083-1905 Technical Highlights of the National Bureau of Standards *changed to* U.S. National Bureau of Standards. Annual Report
0083-1913 U. S. National Bureau of Standards. Technical Notes
0083-1921 U. S. National Cancer Institute. Monograph
0083-1956 U. S. National Center for Health Statistics. Health Resources Statistics
0083-1964 U.S. National Center for Health Care Statistics. Vital and Health Statistics. Series 12. Data from the Institutional Population Surveys *changed to* U.S. National Center for Health Statistics. Vital and Health Statistics. Series 13. Data on Health Resources Utilization
0083-1972 U. S. National Center for Health Statistics. Vital and Health Statistics. Series 10. Data from the Health Interview Survey
0083-1980 U.S. National Center for Health Statistics. Vital and Health Statistics. Series 11. Data from the Health Examination Survey *changed to* U.S. National Center for Health Statistics. Vital and Health Statistics. Series 11. Data from the Health and Nutrition Examination Survey
0083-1999 U. S. National Center for Health Statistics. Vital and Health Statistics. Series 14. Data on Health Resources: Manpower and Facilities
0083-2006 U.S. National Center for Health Care Statistics. Vital and Health Statistics. Series 13. Data from the Hospital Discharge Survey *changed to* U.S. National Center for Health Statistics. Vital and Health Statistics. Series 13. Data on Health Resources Utilization
0083-2014 U. S. National Center for Health Statistics. Vital and Health Statistics. Series 1. Programs and Collection Procedures
0083-2022 U. S. National Center for Health Statistics. Vital and Health Statistics. Series 20. Data on Mortality
0083-2030 U. S. National Center for Health Statistics. Vital and Health Statistics. Series 21. Data on Natality, Marriage, and Divorce
0083-2049 U.S. National Center for Health Statistics. Vital and Health Statistics. Series 22. Data on Natality and Mortality Surveys *see* 0083-2022
0083-2049 U.S. National Center for Health Statistics. Vital and Health Statistics. Series 22. Date on Natality and Mortality Surveys *see* 0083-2030
0083-2057 U. S. National Center for Health Statistics. Vital and Health Statistics. Series 2. Data Evaluation and Methods Research
0083-2065 U.S. National Center for Health Statistics. Vital and Health Statistics. Series 3. Analytical Studies
0083-2073 U.S. National Center for Health Statistics. Vital and Health Statistics. Series 4. Documents and Committee Report
0083-209X N C R P Report
0083-2103 U. S. National Endowment for the Arts. Annual Report
0083-2111 National Endowment for the Humanities. Annual Report
0083-2200 U. S. National Labor Relations Board. Annual Report
0083-2219 U. S. National Labor Relations Board. Court Decisions Relating to the National Labor Relations Act
0083-2243 U.S. National Library of Medicine. Annual Report *see* 0093-0393
0083-2251 National Library of Medicine. Literature Search Series

0083-2278 U. S. National Mediation Board. (Reports of Emergency Boards)
0083-2286 U. S. National Mediation Board. Annual Report
0083-2294 National Medical Audiovisual Center. Catalog†
0083-2308 U.S. National Park Service. Archaeological Research Series *changed to* Publications in Archaelogy
0083-2316 U. S. National Park Service. Historical Handbook Series
0083-2324 U. S. National Park Service. Source Books Series
0083-2332 U. S. National Science Foundation. Annual Report
0083-2359 U.S. National Science Foundation. Federal Funds for Science *changed to* U.S. National Science Foundation. Federal Funds for Research, Development, and Other Scientific Activities
0083-2375 U. S. National Science Foundation. N S F Factbook
0083-2383 U. S. National Science Foundation. Research and Development in Industry
0083-2405 U. S. National Science Foundation. Surveys of Science Resources Series
0083-2421 Astronomical Phenomena
0083-243X U. S. Naval Observatory. Astronomical Papers Prepared for Use of American Ephemeris and Nautical Almanac
0083-2448 U. S. Naval Observatory. Publications. Second Series
0083-2472 U. S. Forest Service. North Central Forest Experiment Station, St. Paul, Minnesota. Annual Report *changed to* U.S. Forest Service. North Central Forest Experiment Station. List of Publications
0083-2618 U. S. Office of Education. Accredited Higher Institutions†
0083-2634 U.S. National Center for Education Statistics. Digest of Educational Statistics *changed to* U.S. National Center for Education Statistics. Degest of Education Statistics
0083-2650 Education Directory: Education Associations *see* 0160-0508
0083-2677 Education Directory. Public Schools *changed to* Education Directory. Local Education Agencies
0083-2715 U. S. Office of Education. Guide to Organized Occupational Curriculums in Higher Education†
0083-2723 U. S. Office of Education. International Teacher Development Program. Annual Report to Bureau of Education and Cultural Affairs, Department of State†
0083-2758 Opening Fall Enrollment in Higher Education *changed to* U.S. National Center for Education Statistics. Fall Enrollment in Higher Education
0083-2774 U. S. Office of Education. Public School Finance Program†
0083-2790 U. S. Office of Education. Residence and Migration of College Students, Analytic Report†
0083-2855 U. S. Office of Education. Studies in Comparative Education. Education in (Country)†
0083-288X U. S. Office of Education. Title VII: New Educational Media News and Reports†
0083-2898 U. S. Office of Education. Vocational and Technical Education, Annual Report†
0083-2901 U. S. Office of Saline Water. Desalting Plants Inventory Report†
0083-291X U. S. Office of Saline Water. Saline Water Conversion Report†
0083-2960 U. S. Office of the Federal Register. Code of Federal Regulations
0083-2979 U. S. Office of the Federal Register. Guide to Record Retention Requirements
0083-2987 U.S. Forest Service. Pacific Northwest Forest and Range Experiment Station. Annual Report†
0083-2995 U.S. Forest Service. Pacific Southwest Forest and Range Experiment Station. Annual Report†
0083-3002 U.S. Patent and Trademark Office. Annual Report of the Commissioner of Patents
0083-3010 U.S. Patent and Trademark Office. Classification Bulletins
0083-3029 General Information Concerning Trademarks
0083-3037 U. S. Patent Office. Index of Patents Issued from the United States Patent Office *see* 0362-0719
0083-3045 Index of Trademarks Issued from the United States Patent Office *see* 0099-0809
0083-307X U.S. Patent Office. Trademark Rules of Practice of the Patent Office with Forms and Statutes *changed to* U.S. Patent and Trademark Office. Trademark Rules of Practice of the Patent and Trademark Office with Forms and Statutes
0083-3088 U. S. Peace Corps. Annual Report
0083-3118 United States Polo Association. Yearbook
0083-3134 U. S. Renewal Assistance Administration. Technical Guides†
0083-3142 U. S. Renewal Assistance Administration. Urban Renewal Project Characteristics†
0083-3150 U. S. Renewal Assistance Administration. Urban Renewal Service Bulletins†
0083-3169 U.S. Rocky Mountain Forest and Range Experiment Station. Annual Report of Research at the Station†
0083-3177 U. S. Rural Electrification Administration. Annual Statistical Report. Rural Electrification Borrowers
0083-3185 U. S. Rural Electrification Administration. Annual Statistical Report. Rural Telephone Program
0083-3193 U. S. Rural Electrification Administration. Report of the Administrator of the Rural Electrification Administration
0083-3207 U. S. Saint Lawrence Seaway Development Corporation. Annual Report
0083-3215 U. S. Securities and Exchange Commission. Annual Report
0083-3223 U. S. Securities and Exchange Commission. Decisions and Reports
0083-3231 U. S. Securities and Exchange Commission. Judicial Decisions
0083-324X United States SERVAS Committee. Newsletter *changed to* U S SERVAS News
0083-3258 United States Ski Association. Directory
0083-3274 U. S. Small Business Administration. Annual Report
0083-3282 S B I C Industry Review *changed to* U.S. Small Business Administration. SBIC Digest
0083-3304 U. S. Soil Conservation Service. National Engineering Handbook
0083-3320 U. S. Soil Conservation Service. Soil Survey Investigation Reports
0083-3339 U. S. Soil Conservation Service. Technical Publications
0083-3398 United States Squash Raquets Association. Official Year Book
0083-3401 United States Statutes at Large
0083-3428 U.S. Tariff Commission. Annual Report *changed to* U.S. International Trade Commission. Annual Report
0083-3436 U.S. International Trade Commission. Imports of Benzenoid Chemicals and Products
0083-3444 U.S. International Trade Commission. Operation of the Trade Agreements Program
0083-3479 United States Tobacco Journal Supplier Directory
0083-3487 United States Treaties and Other International Agreements
0083-3495 Sires and Dams *changed to* U S T A Sires and Dams
0083-3509 Trotting and Pacing Guide
0083-3517 U S T A Year Book
0083-3533 U. S. Veterans Administration. Annual Report
0083-355X U. S. Veterans Administration. Medical Research Program.
0083-3568 U. S. Veteran's Administration. Spinal Cord Injury Conference. Conference Proceedings
0083-3576 U. S. Veterans Administration. V A Fact Sheets
0083-3592 United States Volleyball Association. Official Volleyball Guide and Rule Book
0083-3622 Handbook on Women Workers
0083-3665 United Way of America. Directory *changed to* United Way of America. International Directory
0083-3673 Univers Historique
0083-369X Universal Business Directories, Brisbane and Suburban Business and Trade Directory *changed to* Universal Business Directories, Brisbane and Suburban Business and Street Directory
0083-3703 Universal Business Directories Combined Central and Southern New South Wales Business and Trade Directory†
0083-3711 Universal Business Directories, Combined New England, North and North West New South Wales Business and Trade Directory *changed to* Universal Business Directories, New South Wales Business and Street Directory
0083-372X Universal Business Directories. East Victoria Country Trade Directory *changed to* Universal Business Directories, Victoria Country Trade Directory
0083-3746 Universal Business Directories Melbourne and Suburban Business and Trade Directory
0083-3754 Universal Business Directories North Territory Business and Trade Directory†
0083-3762 Universal Business Directories, Northern Queensland Business and Trade Directory *changed to* Universal Business Directories, Northern Queensland Business and Street Directory
0083-3789 Universal Business Directories Perth and Fremantle and Suburbs Business and Trade Directory
0083-3797 Universal Business Directories, Adelaide and South Australia Country Trade and Business Directory *changed to* Universal Business Directories, Adelaide Business and Street Directory
0083-3800 Universal Business Directories, Southern Queensland Business and Trade Directory *changed to* Universal Business Directories, Southern Queensland Business and Street Directory
0083-3819 Universal Business Directories, Sydney and Suburban Business and Trade Directory *changed to* Universal Business Directories, Sydney and Suburban Business and Street Directory
0083-3827 Universal Business Directories, Tasmania Business and Trade Directory *changed to* Universal Business Directories, Tasmania Business and Street Directory
0083-3835 Universal Business Directories West Victoria Country Business and Trade Directory†
0083-3843 Universal Business Directories Western Australia Country Business and Trade Directory
0083-3851 Kongresa Libro
0083-3878 Union Postale Universelle
0083-3886 Universalist Historical Society. Journal†
0083-3932 Universities and Colleges of Canada *see* 0706-2338
0083-3940 Universities-National Bureau Conference Series
0083-3967 U C E A Case Series in Educational Administration
0083-3975 University Geographer
0083-4017 University of Illinois at Chicago Circle. Center for Urban Studies. Occasional Paper Series *changed to* University of Illinois at Chicago Circle. College of Urban Sciences. Occasional Paper Series
0083-4025 University of Kansas Law Review
0083-4041 University of Queensland Law Journal
0083-405X University of Singapore Science Journal†
0083-4068 University of West Los Angeles Law Review
0083-4106 Univerzita Komenskeho. Filozoficka Fakulta. Zbornik: Ethnologia Slavica
0083-4114 Univerzita Komenskeho. Filozoficka Fakulta. Zbornik: Graecolatina et Orientalia
0083-4122 Univerzita Komenskeho. Filozoficka Fakulta. Zbornik: Historica
0083-4130 Univerzita Komenskeho. Filozoficka Fakulta. Zbornik: Musaica
0083-4165 Univerzita Komenskeho. Filozoficka Fakulta. Zbornik: Paedagogica
0083-4173 Univerzita Komenskeho. Filozoficka Fakulta. Zbornik: Philologica
0083-4181 Univerzita Komenskeho. Filozoficka Fakulta. Zbornik: Philosophica
0083-419X Univerzita Komenskeho. Filozoficka Fakulta. Zbornik: Psychologica
0083-4211 Univerzita Komenskeho. Oddelenie Liecebnej a Specialnej Pedagogiky. Zbornik: Paedagogica Specialis
0083-422X Univerzita Komenskeho. Filozoficka Fakulta. Zbornik: Zurnalistika
0083-4238 Uniwersytet im. Adama Mickiewicza w Poznaniu. Wydzial Biologii i Nauk o Ziemi. Prace. Seria Geologia
0083-4246 Uniwersytet im. Adama Mickiewicza w Poznaniu. Wydzial Filozoficzno-Historyczny. Prace. Seria Filozofia-Logika *changed to* Filozofia-Logika
0083-4254 Uniwersytet im. Adama Mickiewicza w Poznaniu. Wydzial Historyczny. Prace. Seria Psychologia-Pedagogika *changed to* Psychologia-Pedagogika
0083-4262 Uniwersytet im. Adama Mickiewicza w Poznaniu. Wydzial Prawa. Prace *changed to* Prawo
0083-4270 Historia Sztuki
0083-4289 Uniwersytet Jagiellonski. Zeszyty Naukowe. Prace Geograficzne. Prace z Geografii Ekonomicznej
0083-4300 Uniwersytet Jagiellonski. Zeszyty Naukowe. Prace Archeologiczne
0083-4319 Uniwersytet Jagiellonski. Zeszyty Naukowe. Prace Chemiczne
0083-4327 Uniwersytet Jagiellonski. Zeszyty Naukowe. Prace Etnograficzne
0083-4335 Uniwersytet Jagiellonski. Zeszyty Naukowe. Prace Fizyczne
0083-4343 Uniwersytet Jagiellonski. Zeszyty Naukowe. Prace Geograficzne
0083-4351 Uniwersytet Jagiellonski. Zeszyty Naukowe. Prace Historyczne
0083-436X Uniwersytet Jagiellonski. Zeszyty Naukowe. Prace Historycznoliterackie
0083-4378 Uniwersytet Jagiellonski. Zeszyty Naukowe. Prace Jezykoznawcze

1166 ISSN INDEX

0083-4386 Uniwersytet Jagiellonski. Zeszyty Naukowe. Prace Matematyczne
0083-4394 Uniwersytet Jagiellonski. Zeszyty Naukowe. Prace Prawnicze
0083-4408 Uniwersytet Jagiellonski. Zeszyty Naukowe. Prace Psychologiczno-Pedagogiczne
0083-4416 Uniwersytet Jagiellonski. Zeszyty Naukowe. Prace Zoologiczne
0083-4424 Uniwersytet Jagiellonski. Zeszyty Naukowe. Prace z Historii Sztuki
0083-4432 Uniwersytet Jagiellonski, Krakow. Zeszyty Naukowe. Prace z Logiki *changed to* Reports on Mathematical Logic
0083-4467 Uniwersytet Mikolaja Kopernika, Torun. Nauki Humanistyczno-Spoleczne. Archeologia *see* 0137-6616
0083-4475 Uniwersytet Mikolaja Kopernika, Torun. Nauki Humanistyczno-Spoleczne. Filozofia *see* 0208-564X
0083-4483 Uniwersytet Mikolaja Kopernika, Torun. Nauki Humanistyczno-Spoleczne. Filologia Polska *see* 0208-5321
0083-4491 Uniwersytet Mikolaja Kopernika, Torun. Nauki Humanistyczno-Spoleczne. Historia *see* 0137-5830
0083-4513 Uniwersytet Mikolaja Kopernika, Torun. Nauki Humanistyczno-Spoleczne. Prawo *see* 0208-5283
0083-4521 Uniwersytet Mikolaja Kopernika, Torun. Nauki Matematyczno-Przyrodnicze. Biologia *see* 0208-4449
0083-4548 Unternehmung und Unternehmungsfuehrung
0083-4564 Untersuchungen zur Deutschen Literaturgeschichte
0083-4572 Untersuchungen zur Deutschen Staats- und Rechtsgeschichte. Neue Folge
0083-4580 Untersuchungen zur Sprach- und Literaturgeschichte der Romanischen Voelker
0083-4610 Upper Midwest Economic Study. Progress Report
0083-4637 Upper Midwest Economic Study. Technical Paper
0083-4645 Upper Midwest Economic Study. Urban Report
0083-4661 Uppsala Universitet. Institutionen foer Nordiska Spraak. Skrifter†
0083-4688 Urban Affairs Annual Reviews
0083-4696 Urban Environment
0083-470X Urban Land Institute. Research Report†
0083-4718 Urban Land Institute. Technical Bulletin†
0083-4726 Urban Planning/Development Series *changed to* University of Washington. College of Architecture and Urban Planning. Development Series
0083-4769 Uro-Nephro; Annuaire de l'Urologie et de la Nephrologie
0083-4785 Universidad de la Republica. Facultad de Odontologia. Anales
0083-4793 Uruk-Warka: Abhandlungen der Deutschen Orient-Gesellschaft
0083-4807 Used Book Price Guide
0083-4823 Utah Academy of Science, Arts and Letters. Proceedings *changed to* Encyclia
0083-484X Utah Geological Association. Annual Guidebook
0083-4858 Utah State University of Agriculture and Applied Science. Monograph Series†
0083-4912 University of Utah. Institute of Industrial Relations. Bulletin
0083-4920 University of Utah. Office of Institutional Studies. Statistical Summaries
0083-4947 University of Utah Anthropological Papers
0083-4963 Utrecht Micropaleontological Bulletins
0083-4998 Disputationes Rheno-Trajectinae†
0083-5013 Uttar Pradesh, India. Scientific Research Committee Monograph Series
0083-5021 V W Z
0083-5056 Vacuum Metallurgy Conference. Transactions *changed to* Vacuum Metallurgy Conference. Proceedings
0083-5072 Vade-Mecum
0083-5080 Vademecum Deutscher Lehr- und Forschungsstaetten
0083-5102 Vaikunth Mehta National Institute of Cooperative Management. Publications
0083-5137 Value Engineering Association. Proceedings†
0083-5145 Van Nostrand Mathematical Studies†
0083-5161 Vancouver Art Gallery. Annual Report
0083-517X Vancouver. Board of Trade. Annual Report
0083-5196 Vancouver Neurological Centre. Annual Reports
0083-520X Vancouver Stock Exchange. Annual Report
0083-5218 Vanderbilt Rubber Handbook
0083-5226 Vanderbilt Sociology Conference. Proceedings
0083-5234 Vanderbilt University. Center for Latin American Studies. Occasional Papers
0083-5242 Varia
0083-5250 VARTA Fuehrer durch Deutschland, Westlicher Teil und Berlin
0083-5269 Vascular Flora of Ohio
0083-5277 Vaskohaszati Enciklopedia
0083-5293 Vatican Observatory Publications
0083-5307 Vegetable Growers Association of Manitoba. Technical and Scientific Papers Presented at the Annual Meeting *changed to* Vegetable Growers Association of Manitoba. Technical and Scientific Papers Presented at Horticultural Industry Days
0083-5315 Vegetarian Handbook *changed to* International Vegetarian Health Food Handbook
0083-5323 Vegetation Ungarischer Landschaften
0083-5331 Vehicle Builders and Repairers Association. Yearbook *changed to* Vehicle Builders & Repairers Association. Directory of Members & Buyers Guide
0083-534X Veiligheidsjaarboek
0083-5358 Vejtransporten i Tal og Tekst
0083-5366 Venezuela. Ministerio de Agricultura y Cria. Direccion de Economica y Estadistica Agropecuaria. Anuario Estadistico Agropecuario
0083-5374 Venezuela. Ministerio de Minas e Hidrocarburos. Memoria y Cuenta *changed to* Venezuela. Ministerio de Energia y Minas. Memoria y Cuenta
0083-5382 Venezuela. Ministerio de Minas e Hidrocarburos. Oficina de Economia Minera. Hierro y Otros Datos Estadisticos *changed to* Hierro
0083-5390 Venezuela. Ministerio de Minas e Hidrocarburos. Oficina de Economia Petrolera. Petroleo y Otros Datos Estadisticos *changed to* Venezuela. Ministerio de Energia y Minas. Petroleo y Otros Datos Estadisticos
0083-5412 Universidad Central de Venezuela. Facultad de Derecho. Coleccion Tesis de Doctorado†
0083-5420 Universidad Central de Venezuela. Instituto de Estudios Politicos. Cuadernos
0083-5439 Universidad Central de Venezuela. Consejo de Desarrollo Cientifico y Humanistico. Catalogo de la U. C. V.
0083-5447 Musei Civici Veneziani. Bollettino
0083-5455 Venture Capital†
0083-5463 Ver Sacrum; Neue Hefte fuer Kunst und Literatur
0083-5471 Verband der Automobilindustrie. Taetigkeitsbericht *changed to* Verband der Automobilindustrie. Jahresbericht
0083-548X Tatsachen und Zahlen aus der Kraftverkehrswirtschaft
0083-5501 Verband der Versicherungsunternehmungen Oesterreichs. Bericht ueber das Geschaeftsjahr *changed to* Verband der Versicherungsunternehmungen Oesterreichs. Geschaeftsbericht
0083-5536 Varbergs Museum. Aarsbok
0083-5544 Verdensmarkedet og Danmark†
0083-5560 V D I-Berichte
0083-5579 Verein fuer Geschichte der Stadt Nuernberg. Mitteilungen
0083-5587 Verein fuer Hamburgische Geschichte. Zeitschrift
0083-5609 Verein fuer Luebeckische Geschichte und Altertumskunde. Zeitschrift
0083-5625 Verein zum Schutze der Alpenpflanzen und Tiere. Jahrbuch *changed to* Verein zum Schutz der Bergwelt. Jahrbuch
0083-5633 Vereinigte Evangelisch-Lutherische Kirche Deutschlands. Amtsblatt
0083-5641 Vereinigung Pro Sihltal. Blaetter
0083-565X Vereinigung Freunde der Universitaet Mainz. Jahrbuch
0083-5676 Verfassung und Verfassungswirklichkeit
0083-5684 Verhandlungen des Deutschen Geographentages
0083-5692 Verified Directory of Manufacturers' Representatives
0083-5706 Vermont. Agricultural Experiment Station, Burlington. Research Report
0083-5714 Vermont. Agricultural Experiment Station, Burlington. Station Bulletin Series
0083-5722 Vermont. Agricultural Experiment Station, Burlington. Station Pamphlet Series
0083-5730 Vermont. Commissioner of Banking and Insurance. Annual Report of the Bank Commissioner
0083-5757 Vermont. Geological Survey. Bulletin
0083-5765 Vermont. Geological Survey. Special Publication
0083-5781 Vermont Year Book
0083-579X Vermont's Game Annual†
0083-5803 Verpackungs-Magazin†
0083-5811 Verpackungsfolien/Verpackungspapiere†
0083-582X Verse Speaking Anthology†
0083-5846 Verstaendliche Wissenschaft
0083-5862 Veterinaer-Medizinische Nachrichten
0083-5870 Veterinary Annual†
0083-5889 Vetus Testamentum. Supplements
0083-5897 Viator
0083-5900 Great Britain. Victoria and Albert Museum. Illustrated Booklets
0083-5919 Great Britain. Victoria and Albert Museum. Monographs
0083-5927 Victoria and Albert Museum, South Kensington. Yearbook†
0083-5935 Victoria, Australia. Department of Agriculture. Agricultural Economics Branch. Contract Rates†
0083-5943 Victoria, Australia. Department of Agriculture. Agricultural Economics Branch. Farm Credit (Sources and Terms)†
0083-5951 Victoria, Australia. Department of Agriculture. Pig Industry Branch. Pig Farm Management Study
0083-596X Victoria, Australia. Department of Agriculture. Poultry Branch. Poultry Farm Management Study
0083-5978 Victoria, Australia. Forests Commission. Forestry Technical Papers
0083-5986 Victoria, Australia. National Museum of Victoria. Memoirs
0083-601X Victoria League for Commonwealth Friendship. Annual Report
0083-6028 Victoria University of Manchester. Faculty of Arts. Publications
0083-6036 Victoria University of Wellington. Awards Handbook
0083-6060 Victoria University of Wellington Zoology Publications
0083-6079 Victorian Society. Annual
0083-6087 Victorian Society. Conference Reports
0083-6095 Vie des Affaires
0083-6109 Vie Musicale en France Sous les Rois Bourbons. Serie 1: Etudes
0083-6117 Vie Musicale en France Sous les Rois Bourbons. Serie 2: Recherches sur la Musique Classique Francaise
0083-6125 Informationen zu Aktuellen Fragen der Sozial- und Wirtschaftpolitik
0083-6133 Naturhistorisches Museum in Wien. Annalen
0083-6141 Naturhistorisches Museum in Wien. Flugblatt†
0083-6176 Vienna. Universitaet. Institut fuer Theaterwissenschaft. Wissenschaftliche Reihe *changed to* Wiener Forschungen zur Theater und Medienwissenschaft
0083-6184 Assemblees de Dieu de France. Annuaire
0083-6230 Viewpoints in Biology†
0083-6257 Viking Society for Northern Research. Text Series
0083-6265 Vilagtortenet
0083-6273 Villa Guide
0083-6281 Vincentian Studies†
0083-629X Virgil Society. Proceedings
0083-6311 Virginia Baptist Register
0083-632X Virginia. Division of Mineral Resources. Information Circular *changed to* Virginia. Division of Mineral Resources. Publications
0083-6338 Virginia. Division of Mineral Resources. Resources Report *changed to* Virginia. Division of Mineral Resources. Publications
0083-6346 Virginia. Division of Mineral Resources. Report of Investigations *changed to* Virginia. Division of Mineral Resources. Publications
0083-6354 Virginia Educational Directory
0083-6370 Virginia Highway Conference. Procceedings *changed to* Virginia Highway and Transportation Conference. Proceedings
0083-6389 Virginia Historical Society. Documents
0083-6397 Virginia Institute of Marine Science, Gloucester Point. Translation Series.
0083-6419 Virginia Institute of Marine Science, Gloucester Point. Data Reports
0083-6427 Virginia Institute of Marine Science, Gloucester Point. Educational Series
0083-6435 Virginia Institute of Marine Science, Gloucester Point. Marine Resources Advisory Series
0083-6443 Virginia Institute of Marine Science, Gloucester Point. Special Scientific Report
0083-6451 Virginia Military Institute, Lexington. Publications, Theses, and Dissertations of the Staff and Faculty
0083-646X Virginia Place Name Society. Occasional Papers
0083-6508 Virginia Polytechnic Institute and State University. Wood Research and Wood Construction Laboratory. Special Report
0083-6516 Virginia Port Authority. Foreign Trade Annual Report: The Ports of Virginia
0083-6524 Virginia. State Library. Publications
0083-6532 Virginia Port Authority. Board of Commissioners. Annual Report
0083-6540 Virginia Union List of Biomedical Serials
0083-6575 Virginia's Supply of Public School Instructional Personnel
0083-6591 Virology Monographs
0083-6613 Vishveshvaranand Indological Paper Series
0083-6621 Vishveshvaranand Indological Series
0083-6656 Vistas in Astronomy
0083-6672 Visiti Iz Sarseliu
0083-6680 Visual Education Yearbook†
0083-6710 Vital Statistics of the United States
0083-6729 Vitamins and Hormones: Advances in Research and Applications

0083-6737 Kungliga Vitterhets- , Historie- och Antikvitets Akademien. Antikvariskt Arkiv
0083-6745 Kungliga Vitterhets- , Historie- och Antikvitets Akademien. Filologiskt Arkiv
0083-6753 Kungliga Vitterhets- , Historie- och Antikvitets Akademien. Historiskt Arkiv
0083-6761 Kungliga Vitterhets- , Historie- och Antikvitets Akademien. Handlingar. Antikvariska Serien
0083-677X Kungliga Vitterhets- , Historie- och Antikvitets Akademien. Handlingar. Filologisk-Filosofiska Serien
0083-6788 Kungliga Vitterhets- , Historie- och Antikvitets Akademien. Handlingar. Historiska Serien
0083-6796 Kungliga Vitterhets- , Historie- och Antikvitets Akademien. Aarsbok
0083-6826 Voix dans le Monde
0083-6842 Agricultural Research Organization, Rehovot. Bulletin *changed to* Agricultural Research Organization. Pamphlet
0083-6877 Volkstum der Schweiz
0083-6893 Vollschlank
0083-6907 Voluntary Social Services
0083-6915 Vom Wasser
0083-6923 Vorreformationsgeschichtliche Forschungen
0083-6931 Vortraege aus der Praktischen Chirurgie *see* 0079-4899
0083-694X Vulkaniseur-Jahrbuch
0083-6982 Waermelehre und Waermewirtschaft in Einzeldarstellungen†
0083-6990 Landbouwhogeschool, Wageningen. Miscellaneous Papers
0083-7016 Tasmanian Almanac
0083-7024 Walden's A B C Guide and Paper Production Yearbook
0083-7059 Walia
0083-7067 Walker's Old Moore's Almanac
0083-7075 Wall Street Journal Index
0083-7091 Wallace Wurth Memorial Lecture†
0083-7105 Wallraf-Richartz-Jahrbuch; Westdeutsches Jahrbuch fuer Kunstgeschichte
0083-7113 Wirtschaftswissenschaftliche und Wirtschaftsrechtliche Untersuchungen
0083-7121 Walter Lynwood Fleming Lectures in Southern History
0083-713X Walter Prescott Webb Memorial Lectures
0083-7148 Walter W. S. Cook Alumni Lecture
0083-7156 Walters Art Gallery. Journal
0083-7172 Wanderlust†
0083-7199 Warburg Institute. Studies
0083-7210 Ward-Phillips Lectures in English Language and Literature
0083-7229 Ward's Automotive Yearbook
0083-7261 Biblioteka Narodowa. Rocznik
0083-7288 Akademia Rolnicza, Warsaw. Zeszyty Naukowe. Ogrodnictwo
0083-7296 Akademia Rolnicza, Warsaw. Zeszyty Naukowe. Seria Historyczna
0083-730X Szkola Glowna Planowania i Statystyki. Zeszyty Naukowe†
0083-7326 Uniwersytet Warszawski. Instytut Geograficzny. Prace i Studia.
0083-7334 Uniwersytet Warszawski. Katedra Klimatologii. Prace i Studia
0083-7342 Uniwersytet Warszawski. Roczniki
0083-7350 Warwick Economic Research Papers
0083-7369 Warwick Research Industrial and Business Studies *changed to* Warwick Industrial Economic and Business Research Papers
0083-7393 Washington
0083-7407 Textile Museum Journal
0083-7431 Washington State Dental Journal
0083-7474 Washington (State) Department of Fisheries. Technical Report
0083-7482 Washington (State) Office of Program Planning and Fiscal Management. Population and Enrollment Section. Population Trends *changed to* Washington (State) Office of Financial Management. Forecasting and Support Division. Population Trends
0083-7490 Washington (State) Parks and Recreation Commission. Annual Report *see* 0090-2497
0083-7504 Washington State University. Bureau of Economic and Business Research. Study
0083-7512 Washington State University. College of Engineering. Annual Report *see* 0033-6327
0083-7520 University of Washington. Department of Oceanography. Contribution
0083-7539 University of Washington. Department of Oceanography. Fishery Report†
0083-7547 University of Washington. Department of Oceanography. Special Report†
0083-7555 Research in Fisheries
0083-7563 Washington. State University, Pullman. Library Staff Association. L S A Open Stacks
0083-7571 University of Washington Publications in Biology†
0083-758X Washington (State) Utilities and Transportation Commission. Transportation Report†
0083-7598 Washington (State) Water Research Center, Pullman. Report
0083-761X Waste Management Research Abstracts
0083-7628 Watchmaker, Jeweller and Silversmith Directory of Trade Names and Punch Marks
0083-7636 Water
0083-7644 Water Engineer's Handbook *see* 0307-1782
0083-7652 Water in Biological Systems
0083-7660 Water Pollution Research
0083-7679 Water Pollution Research Laboratory, Stevenage, England. Technical Papers
0083-7717 Water Works Manual *see* 0163-9730
0083-7725 Waterborne Commerce of the United States
0083-7733 Waterloo Historical Society. Report
0083-7741 Wayne State University. Center for the Study of Cognitive Processes. Dissertations in Cognitive Processes
0083-775X Wayne State University. Medical Library. Report *changed to* Wayne State University, Detroit. Medical School Library. Report
0083-7776 Health and Welfare of Andhra Pradesh Series *changed to* Social Sciences Research Series
0083-7792 Webbia; Raccolta di Scritti Botanici
0083-7822 Wehrwissenschaftliche Berichte *changed to* Bernard und Graefe Aktuell
0083-7849 Weizmann Institute of Science, Rehovot, Israel. Scientific Activities
0083-7873 Wellesley Edition Cantata Index Series
0083-7881 Wellesley Edition
0083-789X New Zealand Oceanographic Institute. Collected Reprints
0083-7903 New Zealand Oceanographic Institute. Memoir
0083-7911 Welsh Bibliographical Society. Journal
0083-7938 Welsh Soils Discussion Group. Report
0083-7946 Welsh Studies in Education Series
0083-7954 Weltstaedte der Kunst. Edition Leipzig
0083-7989 Wenner Gren Center International Symposium Series
0083-7997 Wenner-Gren Foundation for Anthropological Research. Report
0083-8012 Werbung in Deutschland *changed to* Jahrbuch der Werbung
0083-8047 Werken und Wohnen
0083-8055 Werkstattbuecher fuer Betriebsfachleute Konstrukteure und Studenten *changed to* Fertigung und Betrieb
0083-8063 Werte Unserer Heimat
0083-811X Wessex Cave Club Occasional Publication
0083-8136 Wessex Geographical Year
0083-8144 West Africa Annual
0083-8160 West African Journal of Archaeology
0083-8187 West African Religion
0083-8195 West Canadian Research Publications of Geology and Related Sciences
0083-8217 West Coast Reliability Symposium
0083-8233 West Indies and Caribbean Year Book *see* 0705-2731
0083-8241 West Midland Bird Report
0083-8292 Pakistan. Directorate of Livestock Farms. Report
0083-8306 Pakistan. Directorate of Rural Works Programme. Evaluation Report
0083-8349 Pakistan. Water and Power Development Authority. Report
0083-8381 West Virginia. Agricultural Experiment Station, Morgantown. Current Report
0083-839X West Virginia Business Index. Annual Review Number
0083-8403 West Virginia University. Center for Appalachian Studies and Development. Information Series†
0083-8411 West Virginia University. Center for Appalachian Studies and Development. Research Series *changed to* West Virginia University. Center for Extension and Continuing Education. Research Series
0083-842X West Virginia Coal Mining Institute. Proceedings
0083-8438 West Virginia. Commission on Aging. Annual Progress Report
0083-8446 West Virginia. Commission on Mental Retardation. Annual Report†
0083-8454 West Virginia. Department of Commerce. Annual Report
0083-8462 West Virginia. Department of Mines. Directory of Mines
0083-8470 West Virginia Geological Survey. Newsletter *see* 0163-2825
0083-8489 West Virginia Geological Survey. Archaeological Series†
0083-8497 West Virginia Geological Survey. Basic Data Reports *changed to* West Virginia River Basin Basic Data Reports
0083-8500 West Virginia Geological Survey. Bulletin†
0083-8519 West Virginia Geological Survey. Circulars†
0083-8527 West Virginia Geological Survey. Geological Publications. Volumes†
0083-8535 West Vignia Geological Survey. Archaeological Investigations *changed to* West Virginia Reports of Archaeological Investigations
0083-8543 West Virginia Geological Survey. Reports of Investigations *changed to* West Virginia Reports of Geologic Investigations
0083-856X West Virginia Geological Survey. River Basin Bulletins *changed to* West Virginia River Basin Bulletins
0083-8578 West Virginia Geological Survey. State Park Bulletins *changed to* West Virginia State Park Geology Bulletins
0083-8586 West Virginia Government†
0083-8594 West Virginia. Human Rights Commission. Report
0083-8608 West Virginia University. Bureau for Government Research. Publications†
0083-8640 West Virginia University. Engineering Experiment Station. Bulletin
0083-8659 West Virginia University. Engineering Experiment Station. Report
0083-8667 Western Apparel Industry National Suppliers and Contractors Directory *changed to* National Apparel Suppliers and Contractors Directory
0083-8675 Western Australia. Department of Agriculture. Technical Bulletin
0083-8683 Western Australia. Fisheries and Fauna Department. Bulletin *changed to* Western Australia. Department of Fisheries and Wildlife. Fisheries Research Bulletin
0083-8691 Western Australia. Office of Director General of Transport. Annual Report
0083-8705 University of Western Australia. Institute of Agriculture. Research Report: Agricultural Economics†
0083-8713 University of Western Australia. Library. Report on the Library
0083-8721 Western Australia Museum, Perth. Report of the Museum Board *changed to* Western Australian Museum, Perth. Annual Report
0083-873X Western Australian Museum, Perth. Special Publication
0083-8748 Western Australian Naturalists' Club, Perth. Handbook *changed to* Western Australian Naturalist Scientific Journal
0083-8756 Western Australian Pocket Yearbook
0083-8764 Western Australian Reports
0083-8772 Western Australian Yearbook. New Series
0083-8810 Western Canadian Society for Horticulture. Report of Proceedings of Annual Meeting
0083-8829 Western Canadian Studies in Modern Languages and Literature†
0083-8837 W E S C O N Technical Papers *changed to* W E S C O N Conference Record
0083-8853 Assembly of Western European Union. Proceedings
0083-887X Western Frontier Library
0083-8888 Western Frontiersmen Series
0083-8934 Western Lands and Waters Series
0083-8942 Western Market Almanac†
0083-8950 Western Ontario Law Review *changed to* University of Western Ontario Law Review
0083-8969 Western Pharmacology Society. Proceedings
0083-8977 W P S Professional Handbook Series
0083-8985 Western Reserve Historical Society, Cleveland. Publications
0083-9000 Western Thoroughbred
0083-9019 Westernlore Ghost Town Series
0083-9027 Westfaelische Forschungen
0083-9043 Westfaelische Zeitschrift
0083-906X Westminster Series
0083-9078 Weyers Flottentaschenbuch
0083-9086 Whales Research Institute, Tokyo, Japan. Scientific Reports
0083-9094 University of Pennsylvania. Wharton School of Finance and Commerce. Industrial Research Unit. Studies
0083-9108 What Every Veteran Should Know
0083-9116 What Research Says to the Teacher Series
0083-9132 What You Should Know about Taxes in Puerto Rico
0083-9167 Where America's Large Foundations Make Their Grants
0083-9175 Where to Buy
0083-9205 Where to Eat in London
0083-9213 Where to Golf in Europe
0083-9221 Where to Stay in Scotland *changed to* Scotland: Where to Stay, Hotels and Guest Houses
0083-9221 Where to Stay in Scotland *changed to* Scotland: Where to Stay, Bed and Breakfast
0083-923X Which University *changed to* Which Degree
0083-9248 Whidden Lectures
0083-9256 Whitaker's Almanack
0083-9272 White Paper on Japan's Forest Industries
0083-9299 Wer Baut Maschinen
0083-9302 Who Owns Whom. Continental Europe
0083-9310 Who Owns Whom, North America
0083-9329 Who Owns Whom. United Kingdom *see* 0140-4040
0083-9337 Who Represents Whom†
0083-937X Who's Who; an Annual Biographical Dictionary
0083-9396 Who's Who in America
0083-9450 Who's Who in Canada

0083-9477 Who's Who in Communist China
0083-9485 Who's Who in Consulting
0083-9493 Who's Who in East Africa†
0083-9507 Who's Who in Electronics
0083-9523 Who's Who in Finance and Industry
0083-9531 Who's Who in France
0083-9558 Who's Who in Indian Engineering and Industry
0083-9566 Who's Who in Indian Science
0083-9574 Who's Who in Insurance
0083-9590 Who's Who in Israel
0083-9612 Who's Who in Lebanon
0083-9620 Who's Who in Malaysia and Singapore
0083-9639 Who's Who in Movies
0083-9647 Who's Who in Music and Musicians' International Directory *see* 0307-2894
0083-9655 Who's Who in New Zealand
0083-9671 Who's Who in Pakistan
0083-9701 Who's Who in Soviet Science and Technology†
0083-971X Who's Who in Soviet Social Sciences, Humanities, Art and Government†
0083-9728 Who's Who in Space
0083-9736 Who's Who in Switzerland
0083-9744 Agricultural Institute of Canada. Membership Directory
0083-9752 Who's Who in the Arab World
0083-9760 Who's Who in the East
0083-9779 Who's Who in the Gas Industry *see* 0307-3084
0083-9787 Who's Who in the Midwest
0083-9809 Who's Who in the South and Southwest
0083-9817 Who's Who in the West
0083-9825 Who's Who in the World
0083-9833 Who's Who in the Theatre
0083-9841 Who's Who of American Women
0083-985X Who's Who of British Engineers†
0083-9868 Who's Who of Rhodesia, Mauritius, Central and East Africa *changed to* Who's Who of Southern Africa Including Mauritius, South West Africa, Zimbabwe-Rhodesia and Neighboring Countries
0083-9876 Who's Who of Southern Africa *changed to* Who's Who of Southern Africa Including Mauritius, South West Africa, Zimbabwe-Rhodesia and Neighboring Countries
0083-9892 Widener Library Shelflist
0083-9906 Wiener Arbeiten zur Deutschen Literatur
0083-9914 Wiener Beitraege zur Englischen Philologie
0083-9922 Wiener Beitraege zur Kulturgeschichte und Linguistik
0083-9930 Wiener Beitraege zur Theologie
0083-9957 Wiener Geographische Schriften
0083-9965 Wiener Humanistische Blaetter
0083-9973 W I S T-Informationen
0083-9981 Wiener Jahrbuch fuer Kunstgeschichte
0083-999X Wiener Jahrbuch fuer Philosophie
0084-0009 Wiener Katholische Akademie. Studien
0084-0017 Wiener Musikhochschule. Publikationen
0084-0025 Wiener Rechtswissenschaftliche Studien
0084-0033 Wiener Romanistische Arbeiten
0084-0041 Wiener Slavistisches Jahrbuch
0084-005X Wiener Studien. Zeitschrift fuer Klassische Philologie und Patristik
0084-0068 Wiener Voelkerkundliche Mitteilungen
0084-0076 Wiener Zeitschrift fuer die Kunde des Morgenlandes
0084-0084 Wiener Zeitschrift fuer die Kunde Suedasiens und Archiv fuer Indische Philosphie
0084-0092 Wiener Zeitschrift fuer Nervenheilkunde und deren Grenzgebiete. Supplement
0084-0106 Wijsgerige Teksten en Studies
0084-0114 Wilderness Report
0084-0122 Wildlife Behavior and Ecology
0084-0130 Alaska. Department of Fish and Game. Wildlife Booklet Series
0084-0149 Wildlife Circular, Victoria†
0084-0157 Victoria, Australia. Fisheries and Game Department. Wildlife Contributions *changed to* Wildlife Contribution, Victoria
0084-0165 U. S. Fish and Wildlife Service. Wildlife Leaflets
0084-0173 Wildlife Monographs
0084-0181 Wiley American Republic Series
0084-019X Wiley Series on Systems Engineering and Analysis
0084-0203 Wiley Series on the Science and Technology of Materials
0084-0238 William-Frederick Poets Series
0084-0246 William K. McInally Lecture
0084-0254 William Morris Society. Journal
0084-0270 William Morris Society. Report
0084-0297 Williamsburg in America Series
0084-0300 Williamsburg Research Studies
0084-0327 Wilmington Society of the Fine Arts. Report *changed to* Delaware Art Museum. Annual Report
0084-0335 Wiltshire Archaeological and Natural History Magazine *see* 0309-3476
0084-0335 Wiltshire Archaeological and Natural History Magazine *see* 0309-3468
0084-0343 Wine and Spirit Trade Review Directory *changed to* Off Licence News Directory
0084-0351 Wines and Vines-Annual Directory of the Wine Industry *changed to* Wines and Vines: Directory of the Wine Industry in North America
0084-036X Child Guidance Clinic of Winnipeg. Annual Report†
0084-0386 Winter Sports in Scotland
0084-0394 Winter's Tales
0084-0408 Winterthur Conference Report *see* 0084-0416
0084-0416 Winterthur Portfolio
0084-0424 Wire Industry Yearbook
0084-0432 Wire Review *changed to* Wire Industry Machinery Guide
0084-0440 Wireless Pioneer *changed to* Sparks
0084-0459 Wireless World Diary
0084-0467 Wirkung der Literatur
0084-0483 Wirtschaft im Ostseeraum *changed to* Ostseejahrbuch
0084-0505 Wisconsin Academy of Sciences, Arts and Letters, Transactions
0084-0513 Wisconsin Business Monographs
0084-0521 Wisconsin Business Papers†
0084-053X Wisconsin China Series
0084-0548 Wisconsin. Commissioner of Securities. Annual Report *changed to* Wisconsin. Commissioner of Securities. Biennial Report
0084-0564 Wisconsin. Department of Natural Resources. Technical Bulletin
0084-0572 Wisconsin. Department of Transportation. Division of Planning and Budget. Highway Mileage Data
0084-0580 Wisconsin. Department of Transportation. Division of Planning. Highway Traffic
0084-0599 Wisconsin Economy Studies
0084-0602 Wisconsin. Governor's Advocacy Committee on Children and Youth Annual Report†
0084-0610 Wisconsin Project Reports†
0084-0629 Wisconsin Research and Development Center for Cognitive Learning. Practical Papers *changed to* Wisconsin Research and Development Center for Individualized Schooling. Practical Papers
0084-0637 Wisconsin Research and Development Center for Cognitive Learning. Theoretical Papers *changed to* Wisconsin Research and Development Center for Individualized Schooling. Theoretical Papers
0084-0645 Wisconsin Research and Development Center for Cognitive Learning. Technical Reports *changed to* Wisconsin Research and Development Center for Individualized Schooling. Technical Reports
0084-067X Wisconsin State Historical Society. Urban History Group. Newsletter
0084-0734 University of Wisconsin, Madison. Applied Population Laboratory. Population Notes
0084-0742 University of Wisconsin, Madison. Applied Population Laboratory. Population Series
0084-0769 University of Wisconsin, Madison. Institute for Research on Poverty. Reprint Series
0084-0785 Land Tenure Center. Newsletter
0084-0793 Land Tenure Center. Paper
0084-0807 University of Wisconsin, Madison. Land Tenure Center. Reprint
0084-0815 Land Tenure Center. Research Paper
0084-0823 University of Wisconsin, Madison. Land Tenure Center. Training and Methods Series
0084-0831 University of Wisconsin, Milwaukee. Language and Area Center for Latin America. Discussion Papers. *see* 0146-258X
0084-084X University of Wisconsin, Milwaukee. Center for Latin America. Essay Series
0084-0858 University of Wisconsin, Milwaukee. Language and Area Center for Latin America. Special Studies Series *changed to* University of Wisconsin, Milwaukee. Center for Latin America. Special Studies Series
0084-0890 University of Wisconsin. Mathematical Research Center Series
0084-0904 Wisdom†
0084-0912 Wissenschaftliche Alpenvereinshefte
0084-0939 Wissenschaftliche Gesellschaft fuer Personenstandswesen und Verwandte Gebiete. Schriftenreihe. Neue Folge
0084-0947 Wissenschaftliche Normung†
0084-0955 Wissenschaftliche Redaktion
0084-0963 Wissenschaftliche Taschenbuecher. Reihe Biologie
0084-0971 Wissenschaftliche Taschenbuecher. Reihe Chemie
0084-098X Wissenschaftliche Taschenbuecher. Reihe Mathematik, Physik
0084-0998 Wissenschaftliche und Angewandte Photographie
0084-1005 Wissenschaftliche Vereinigung der Augenoptiker. Fachvortraege der Jahrestagungen *changed to* Wissenschaftliche Vereinigung fuer Augenoptik und Optometrie. Fachvortraege des WVAO - Jahreskongresses
0084-1013 Wistar Institute Symposium Monograph†
0084-103X Wolfman Report on the Photographic Industry in the United States
0084-1056 Women's Accessories Directory; New York Metropolitan Area
0084-1064 Women's Coats and Suits Directory; New York Metropolitan Area
0084-1072 Woningbouwstudies
0084-1080 Wood & Wood Products Reference Data/Buying Guide *changed to* Wood & Wood Products Reference Buying Guide
0084-1102 Woodall's Mobile-Modular Living *see* 0163-4313
0084-1110 Woodall's Trailering Parks and Campgrounds *see* 0146-1362
0084-1137 Woodrow Wilson National Fellowship Foundation. Newsletter
0084-1145 Woodrow Wilson National Fellowship Foundation. Report
0084-117X Woodstock Papers: Occasional Essays for Theology†
0084-1188 Woodworker *changed to* Woodworker Projects & Techniques
0084-1196 Woodworker Annual
0084-120X Woodworking Industry /Directory *changed to* Woodworking Industry / Buyers' Guide
0084-1218 Wool Review
0084-1226 Woolhope Naturalists' and Archaeologists Field Club, Herefordshire. Transactions *changed to* Woolhope Naturalists' Field Club, Herefordshire. Transactions
0084-1234 Woolknit Annual
0084-1242 Woolner Indological Series
0084-1250 Words: Wai-Te-Ata Studies in Literature†
0084-1285 Work of Aslib: Annual Report
0084-1307 Working Conditions in Canadian Industry
0084-1323 Working Press of the Nation
0084-1358 U.S. Department of Agriculture. Economics, Statistics, and Cooperatives Service. World Agricultural Situation
0084-1366 World Air Transport Statistics
0084-1374 World Airline Record
0084-1382 World Almanac and Book of Facts
0084-1404 World Association for the Advancement of Veterinary Parasitology. Proceedings of Conference
0084-1412 World Association of Girl Guides and Girl Scouts. Report of Conference
0084-1439 World Book Year Book
0084-1455 WorldBusiness Perspectives
0084-1463 World Cars
0084-1471 World Cartography
0084-148X World Coal Trade *changed to* International Coal
0084-1498 World Collectors Annuary
0084-1501 World Commerce Annual
0084-151X World Confederation for Physical Therapy. Proceedings of the Congress
0084-1528 W C O T P Annual Report
0084-1544 Trade Unions International of Chemical, Oil and Allied Workers. International Trade Conference. Documents
0084-1552 World Conference on Animal Production. Proceedings
0084-1560 World Conference on Earthquake Engineering. Proceedings†
0084-1595 World Congress of Anaesthesiologists. Proceedings
0084-1609 World Congress of Psychiatry. Proceedings
0084-1625 World Congress of the Deaf. Lectures and Papers
0084-1641 World Congress on Fertility and Sterility. Proceedings
0084-165X World Congress on the Prevention of Occupational Accidents and Diseases. Proceedings
0084-1668 World Council of Churches. Commission on World Mission and Evangelism. Research Pamphlets†
0084-1676 World Council of Churches. General Assembly. Assembly-Reports
0084-1684 World Council of Churches. Minutes and Reports of the Central Committee Meeting
0084-1692 World Council of Churches. World Council Studies†
0084-1706 World Crafts Council. General Assembly. Proceedings of the Biennial Meeting
0084-1714 World Economic Survey
0084-1722 World Energy Conference. Plenary Conferences. Transactions
0084-1730 World Energy Conference. Survey of Energy Resources
0084-1749 World Energy Supplies
0084-1757 World Federation for Mental Health. Proceedings of Annual Meetings
0084-1781 World Fellowship of Buddhists. Book Series
0084-179X World Food Problems
0084-182X World Grain Trade Statistics
0084-1854 World Jersey Cattle Bureau. Conference Reports
0084-1870 World List of Social Science Periodicals
0084-1889 World List of Universities, Other Institutions of Higher Education and University Organizations

ISSN INDEX 1169

0084-1897 World Medical Association. General Assembly. Proceedings
0084-1900 World Meteorological Association. Regional Associations. Abridged Final Reports *changed to* World Meteorological Organization. Reports of Sessions of Regional Associations
0084-1919 World Meteorological Association. Technical Commissions Abridged Final Reports *changed to* World Meteorological Organization. Reports of Sessions of Technical Commissions
0084-1927 World Meteorological Congress. Abridged Report with Resolutions
0084-1935 World Meteorological Congress. Proceedings
0084-1943 World Meteorological Organization. Basic Documents, Records and Reports *changed to* World Meteorological Organization. Basic Documents and Official Reports
0084-196X World Meteorological Organization. Executive Committee Sessions: Abridged Reports with Resolutions *changed to* World Meteorological Organization. Executive Committee Reports: Abridged Reports with Resolutions
0084-1978 Global Atmospheric Research Programme. Publication Series
0084-1986 Global Atmospheric Research Programme. G A R P Special Reports
0084-1994 World Meteorological Organization. Annual Reports
0084-2001 World Meteorological Organization. Report on Marine Science Affairs
0084-201X World Meteorological Organization. Technical Notes
0084-2028 World Money Guide†
0084-2036 World Motor Vehicle Production and Registration†
0084-2044 World Movement of Mothers. Reports of Meetings
0084-2052 World Muslim Conference. Proceedings
0084-2060 World Muslim Gazetteer
0084-2117 World of Learning
0084-2141 World Peace through Law Center. Pamphlet Series†
0084-2168 World Perspectives
0084-2184 World Ploughing Contest. Official Handbook
0084-2206 World Psychiatric Association. Bulletin†
0084-2214 World Record Marine Fishes *changed to* World Record Game Fishes
0084-2230 World Review of Nutrition and Dietetics
0084-2257 U.S. Department of State. World Strength of the Communist Party Organizations. Annual Report.†
0084-2265 World Survey of Climatology
0084-2273 World Tobacco Directory
0084-2281 World Today Series: Africa
0084-229X World Today Series: Far East and Southwest Pacific
0084-2303 World Today Series: Latin America
0084-2311 World Today Series: Middle East and South Asia
0084-232X World Today Series: Soviet Union and Eastern Europe
0084-2338 World Today Series: Western Europe
0084-2370 World Trade Union Congress. Reports†
0084-2400 World Union of Organizations for the Safeguard of Youth *changed to* World Union for the Safeguard of Youth. Conference Proceedings
0084-2419 World University Service. Annual Report
0084-2427 World University Service. Programme of Action
0084-2435 World Veterinary Association. Catalogue of Veterinary Films and Films of Veterinary Interest
0084-2443 World Veterinary Congress. Proceedings
0084-2451 World Weather Watch Planning Reports
0084-2478 World Wide Chamber of Commerce Directory
0084-2486 World Wide Register of Adult Education
0084-2494 World Wildlife Series†
0084-2508 World Yearbook of Education
0084-2516 World Zionist Organization. General Council. Addresses, Debates, Resolutions
0084-2532 World's Poultry Science Association. Report of the Proceedings of International Congress
0084-2540 World'S Woman's Christian Temperance Union. Convention Report
0084-2559 Worldview
0084-2567 Worldwide Directory of National Technical Information Services†
0084-2575 Worldwide Offshore Contractors Directory *see* 0475-1310
0084-2583 Worldwide Petrochemical Directory
0084-2591 Worldwide Refining and Gas Processing
0084-2605 Wormley, England (Surrey) National Institute of Oceanography. Collected Reprints *see* 0309-7463
0084-2613 Der Wormsgau
0084-2621 Wormsloe Foundation. Publications
0084-263X Woytinsky Lectures
0084-2648 Wrightia
0084-2664 Writers' and Artists' Yearbook
0084-2680 Writers' and Photographers' Marketing Guide; Directory of Australian and New Zealand Literary and Photo Markets
0084-2699 Writers Directory
0084-2710 Writer's Handbook
0084-2729 Writer's Market
0084-2737 Writer's Yearbook
0084-2745 Writing
0084-2753 Writings on British History
0084-277X Akademia Medyczna, Wroclaw. Prace Naukowe
0084-2788 Instytut Automatyki Systemow Energetycznych. Prace
0084-2796 Muzeum Etnograficzne, Wroclaw. Zeszyty Etnograficzne
0084-280X Politechnika Wroclawska. Instytut Technologii Elektronowej. Prace Naukowe. Monografie
0084-2818 Politechnika Wroclawska. Instytut Chemii i Technologii Nafty i Wegla. Prace Naukowe. Studia i Materialy
0084-2826 Politechnika Wroclawska. Instytut Energoelektryki. Prace Naukowe. Studia i Materialy
0084-2834 Politechnika Wroclawska. Instytut Geotechniki. Prace Naukowe. Monografie
0084-2842 Politechnika Wroclawska. Instytut Geotechniki. Prace Naukowe. Studia i Materialy
0084-2850 Politechnika Wroclawska. Instytut Inzynierii Chemicznej i Urzadzen Cieplnych. Prace Naukowe. Monografie
0084-2869 Politechnika Wroclawska. Instytut Inzynieri Ochrony Srodowska. Prace Naukowe. Monografie
0084-2877 Politechnika Wroclawska. Instytut Inzynierii Ochrony Srodowiska. Prace Naukowe. Studia i Materialy
0084-2885 Politechnika Wroclawska. Instytut Technologii Elektronowej. Prace Naukowe. Studia i Materialy
0084-2893 Politechnika Wroclawska. Instytut Technologii Nieorganicznej i Nawozow Mineralnych. Prace Naukowe. Konferencje
0084-2907 Politechnika Wroclawska. Instytut Technologii Nieorganicznej i Nawozow Mineralnych. Prace Naukowe. Monografie
0084-2915 Politechnika Wroclawska. Instytut Technologii Nierorganicznej i Nawozow Mineralnych. Prace Naukowe. Studia i Materialy
0084-294X Politechnika Wroclawska. Instytut Ukladow Elektromaszynowych. Prace Naukowe. Studia i Materialy
0084-2958 Politechnika Wroclawska. Instytut Metrologii Elektrycznej. Prace Naukowe. Studia i Materialy
0084-2974 Wroclawski Rocznik Ekonomiczny
0084-2982 Wroclawskie Towarzystwo Naukowe. Komisja Historii Sztuki. Rozprawy
0084-2990 Wroclawskie Towarzystwo Naukowe. Komisja Jezykowa. Rozprawy
0084-3008 Litteraria
0084-3016 Wroclawskie Towarzystwo Naukowe. Prace. Seria A. Humanistyka
0084-3024 Wroclawskie Towarzystwo Naukowe. Prace. Seria B. Nauki Scisle
0084-3032 Wspolczesne Malarstwo Wroclawskie
0084-3040 Wuerttembergischer Pferdeuchtverband. Mitteilungen†
0084-3067 Wuerttembergisch Franken
0084-3083 Wuerzburger Wehrwissenschaftliche Abhandlungen
0084-3091 Technische Akademie Wuppertal. Berichte
0084-3113 Wykeham Science Series
0084-3121 Wykeham Technological Series
0084-313X Wyoming. Agricultural Experiment Station, Laramie. Bulletin
0084-3148 Wyoming. Agricultural Experiment Station, Laramie. Research Journal
0084-3156 Wyoming. Agricultural Experiment Station, Laramie. Science Monograph
0084-3164 Wyoming Nurses Newsletter *changed to* Wyoming Nurse
0084-3180 University of Wyoming. Natural Resources Research Institute. Information Circular†
0084-3199 University of Wyoming Publications
0084-3210 University of Wyoming. Water Resources Research Institute. Water Resources Series
0084-3229 Xavier University. Museum and Archives Publications
0084-3237 Yachting Belge
0084-3253 Yachting World Handbook†
0084-3261 Yachtsman's Guide to the Caribbean
0084-327X Yachtsman's Guide to the Great Lakes
0084-3288 Yad Vashem News†
0084-3296 Yad Vashem Studies on the European Jewish Catastrophe and Resistance *changed to* Yad Vashem Studies
0084-330X Yale Classical Studies
0084-3318 Yale College Series
0084-3326 Yale Fastbacks
0084-3334 Yale Germanic Studies
0084-3342 Yale Historical Publications (Manuscripts and Edited Texts)†
0084-3350 Yale Historical Publications (Miscellany)
0084-3369 Yale Judaica Series
0084-3377 Yale Mathematical Monographs
0084-3385 Yale Near Eastern Researches
0084-3393 Yale Publications in American Studies
0084-3407 Yale Publications in Religion
0084-3415 Yale Publications in the History of Art
0084-3423 Yale Romanic Studies. Second Series
0084-3431 Yale Russian and East European Studies
0084-344X Yale Scene; University Series
0084-3458 Yale Series of Younger Poets
0084-3466 Yale Southeast Asia Studies
0084-3482 Yale Studies in English
0084-3490 Yale Studies in Political Science
0084-3504 Yale Studies in the History of Music
0084-3512 Yale Studies in the History of Science and Medicine
0084-3520 Yale Studies of the City
0084-3539 Yale University Art Gallery. Bulletin
0084-3555 Yale Western Americana Paperbounds†
0084-3563 Yale Western Americana Series
0084-358X Yearbook and Directory of Osteopathic Physicians
0084-3601 Yearbook of Adult Education
0084-3628 U.S. Department of Agriculture. Yearbook of Agriculture
0084-3644 Yearbook of American and Canadian Churches
0084-3652 Year Book of Anesthesia
0084-3660 Yearbook of Astronomy
0084-3679 Year Book of Cancer
0084-3687 Yearbook of Cardiovascular Medicine and Surgery *see* 0145-4145
0084-3695 Yearbook of Comparative and General Literature
0084-3709 Yearbook of Comparative Criticism
0084-3717 Year Book of Dentistry
0084-3733 Year Book of Drug Therapy
0084-3741 Year Book of Endocrinology
0084-375X Yearbook of Fishery Statistics
0084-3768 Yearbook of Forest Products
0084-3784 Yearbook of Higher Education
0084-3806 Yearbook of International Congress Proceedings
0084-3814 Yearbook of International Organizations
0084-3822 Yearbook of International Trade Statistics
0084-3830 Yearbook of Israel Ports Statistics
0084-3857 Year Book of Labour Statistics.
0084-3865 Yearbook of Manitoba Agriculture
0084-3873 Year Book of Medicine
0084-3881 Yearbook of National Accounts Statistics
0084-3903 Year Book of Nuclear Medicine
0084-3911 Year Book of Obstetrics and Gynecology
0084-392X Year Book of Ophthalmology
0084-3938 Year Book of Orthopedics and Traumatic Surgery
0084-3946 Year Book of Pathology and Clinical Pathology
0084-3954 Year Book of Pediatrics
0084-3962 Year Book of Plastic and Reconstructive Surgery
0084-3970 Year Book of Psychiatry and Applied Mental Health
0084-3989 Year Book of Radiology *see* 0098-1672
0084-3997 Yearbook of Railroad Facts
0084-4020 Yearbook of Technical Education and Training for Industry *see* 0309-5290
0084-4047 Yearbook of the Commonwealth
0084-4055 Year Book of the Ear, Nose and Throat *changed to* Year Book of Otolaryngology
0084-4071 Year Book of Urology
0084-408X Yearbook of World Affairs
0084-4098 Yearbook on Human Rights
0084-4101 Yearbook on International Communist Affairs
0084-411X Yearbook on Jute
0084-4128 Yearbooks in Christian Education
0084-4144 Year's Work in English Studies
0084-4152 Year's Work in Modern Language Studies
0084-4160 Yeats Centenary Papers *changed to* New Yeats Papers
0084-4179 Yerkes Regional Primate Research Center. Newsletter
0084-4195 Yeshiva University. Belfer Graduate School of Science. Monographs†
0084-4209 Yivo Annual of Jewish Social Science
0084-4217 Yivo Bleter
0084-4225 Finnish Broadcasting Company. Section for Long-Range Planning. Research Reports
0084-4241 York University. Toronto. Institute of Behavioural Research. Bulletin *changed to* York University, Toronto. Institute for Behavioural Research. Newsletter
0084-4268 York University, Toronto. Molecular Psycho-Biology Laboratory. Report†
0084-4276 Yorkshire Archaeological Journal
0084-4292 Y M C A Yearbook and Official Roster
0084-4306 Young Women's Christian Association of the United States of America. The Printout
0084-4314 J. K. Lasser's Your Income Tax
0084-4322 Your United Nations
0084-4349 Yugoslav Export-Import Directory
0084-4357 Demografska Statistika
0084-4365 Yugoslavia. Savenzi Zavod za Statistiku. Statisticki Bilten
0084-4373 Statistika Spoljne Trgovine SFR Jugoslavije

0084-439X Yuval
0084-4411 Z Dziejow Form Artystycznych w Literaturze Polskiej
0084-442X Z Dziejow Muzyki Polskiej
0084-4446 Zagadnienia Rodzajow Literackich
0084-4454 Zagadnienia Eksploatacji Maszyn
0084-4462 Zahnaerztliche Fortbildung
0084-4489 Zambia. Central Statistical Office. Annual Statement of External Trade
0084-4497 Zambia. Office of the Auditor-General. Report of the Auditor-General
0084-4500 Zambia. Central Statistical Office. Employment and Earnings
0084-4519 Zambia. Central Statistical Office. Financial Statistics of Public Corporations
0084-4527 Zambia. Central Statistical Office. Government Sector Accounts (Economic and Functional Analysis) *changed to* Zambia. Central Statistical Office. Financial Statistics of Government Sector (Economic and Functional Analysis)
0084-4535 Zambia. Central Statistical Office. Insurance Statistics†
0084-4543 Zambia. Central Statistical Office. Migration Statistics
0084-4551 Zambia. Central Statistical Office. Statistical Year Book
0084-456X Zambia. Central Statistical Office. Vital Statistics
0084-4586 Zambia. Commission for the Preservation of Natural and Historical Monuments and Relics. Annual Report
0084-4608 Zambia. Department of Community Development. Report
0084-4616 Zambia. Department of Forestry. Report
0084-4632 Zambia. Department of Labour. Report
0084-4659 Zambia. Prisons Department. Report
0084-4657 Zambia. Department of Social Welfare. Report
0084-4675 Zambia. Department of Taxes. Annual Report of the Commissioner of Taxes
0084-4683 Zambia. Department of the Administrator-General and Official Receiver. Report
0084-4705 Zambia. Department of Water Affairs. Report
0084-4713 Fisheries Research Bulletin of Zambia
0084-473X Zambia. Geological Survey. Annual Reports
0084-4748 Zambia. Geological Survey. Economic Reports
0084-4756 Zambia. Geological Survey. Occasional Papers
0084-4764 Zambia. Geological Survey. Reports
0084-4802 Zambia. Immigration Department. Report
0084-4810 Zambia. Information Services. Annual Report
0084-4853 Zambia. Ministry of Agriculture. Annual Report
0084-487X Zambia. Ministry of Education. Annual Report
0084-4896 Zambia. Ministry of Finance. Annual Report *changed to* Zambia. Ministry of Planning and Finance. Annual Report
0084-4942 National Archives of Zambia. Annual Report
0084-4950 Zambia. National Council for Scientific Research. Annual Report
0084-4969 Zambia. National Food and Nutrition Commission. Annual Report
0084-4977 Zambia. National Museums Board. Report
0084-4993 Zambia. Natural Resources Board. Annual Report *changed to* Zambia. Natural Resources Department. Annual Report
0084-5000 Zambia. Pneumoconiosis Medical and Research Bureau and Pneumoconiosis Compensation Board. Annual Reports
0084-5019 Zambia. General Post Office. Annual Report of the Postmaster-General *changed to* Zambia. Posts and Telecommunications Corporation. Annual Report
0084-5035 Zambia. Public Service Commission. Report
0084-506X Zambia. Sports Directorate. Report
0084-5078 Zambia. Survey Department. Report
0084-5086 Zambia. Teaching Service Commission. Annual Report
0084-5108 University of Zambia. Institute for African Studies. Communication
0084-5116 Zambian Industrial Directory.
0084-5124 Zambian Papers
0084-5132 Escuela de Gerentes de Cooperativas. Cartillas de Cooperacion
0084-5159 Escuela de Gerentes de Cooperativas. Coleccion Textos
0084-5167 Escuela de Gerentes de Cooperativas. Cuadernos de Practicas
0084-5175 Escuela de Gerentes de Cooperativas. Serie Especial
0084-5183 Zbornik Istorije Knjizevnosti
0084-5191 Zbornik za Istoriju, Jezik i Knjizevnost Srpskog Naroda. Fontes Rerum Slavorum Meridionalium
0084-5205 Zbornik za Istoriju, Jezik i Knjizevnost Srpskog Naroda. Spomenici na Srpskom Jeziku
0084-5213 Zbornik za Istoriju, Jezik i Knjizevnost Srpskog Naroda. Spomenici na Tudjim Jezicima
0084-5221 Ze Skarbca Kultury
0084-523X Zeichenwerk
0084-5264 Savigny-Stiftung fuer Rechtsgeschichte. Zeitschrift. Germanistische, Romanistische und Kanonistische Abteilung
0084-5272 Zeitschrift fuer Alternsforschung. Supplementbaende
0084-5280 Zeitschrift fuer Angewandte Baeder- und Klimaheilkunde
0084-5299 Zeitschrift fuer Assyriologie und Vorderasiatische Archaeologie
0084-5302 Zeitschrift fuer Celtische Philologie
0084-5310 Zeitschrift fuer die gesamte Strafrechtswissenschaft
0084-5337 Zeitschrift fuer Ernaehrungswissenschaft. Supplementa
0084-5345 Zeitschrift fuer Klinische Psychologie - Forschung und Praxis
0084-5353 Zeitschrift fuer Krebsforschung und Klinische Onkologie *see* 0171-5216
0084-5361 Zeitschrift fuer Meteorologie
0084-5388 Zeitschrift fuer Papyrologie und Epigraphik
0084-5396 Zeitschrift fuer Romanische Philologie. Beihefte
0084-540X Zeitschrift fuer Schweizerisches Recht
0084-5442 Zenith *changed to* Zenith Science Magazine
0084-5477 Zeszyty Problemowe Postepow Nauk Rolniczych
0084-5485 Ziegeleitechnisches Jahrbuch
0084-5493 Ziema Kozielska. Studia i Materialy
0084-5507 Ziemie Zachodnie. Studia i Materialy
0084-5515 Jimbun
0084-5523 Zionism; Studies in the History of the Zionist Movement and of the Jews in Palestine
0084-5531 Zionist Year Book
0084-554X Zonarida
0084-5558 Zondervan Pastor's Annual
0084-5566 Zoning Digest *see* 0094-7598
0084-5574 ZooBooks†
0084-5582 Zoologia†
0084-5590 Zoologica Gothoburgensia†
0084-5604 Zoological Record
0084-5612 Zoological Society of London. Symposia
0084-5620 Zoological Society of London. Transactions
0084-5639 Zoologisch-Botanische Gesellschaft, Vienna. Abhandlungen
0084-5647 Zoologisch-Botanische Gesellschaft, Vienna. Verhandlungen
0084-5655 Zoology of Iceland
0084-5663 Zoophysiology and Ecology *changed to* Zoophysiology
0084-5671 Shipbuilding Yearbook†
0084-568X Zrodla do Dziejow Bydgoszczy
0084-5698 Zrodla do Dziejow Mysli Pedagogicznej
0084-5701 Zrodla do Dziejow Nauki i Techniki
0084-571X Zrodla do Historii Muzyki Polskiej
0084-5736 Zuckerwirtschaftliches Taschenbuch
0084-5744 Eidgenoessische Technische Hochschule Zuerich. Mitteilungen. Aerodynamik
0084-5752 Eidgenoessische Technische Hochschule Zuerich. Mitteilungen. Photoelastizitaet
0084-5760 Eidgenoessische Technische Hochschule Zuerich. Mitteilungen. Textilmaschinenbau und Textilindustrie
0084-5779 Eidgenoessische Technische Hochschule Zuerich. Institut fuer Geophysik.Schweizerische Erdbebendienst. Jahresbericht
0084-5809 Zur Lage der Schweiz
0084-5817 Zweisprachige Reihe
0084-5825 Zwierzeta Laboratoryjne†
0084-5833 A D C A; American Directory Collections Agencies
0084-5841 A M A
0084-5884 Accountancy Research Foundation, Melbourne. Accounting and Auditing Research Committee. Research Studies *changed to* Australian Accounting Research Foundation. Research Studies
0084-5892 Achter het Boek
0084-5906 Acta Botanica Venezuelica
0084-5914 Acta Phytogeographica Suecica
0084-5922 Adelaide City Council Municipal Yearbook *changed to* Adelaide City Council Municipal Reference Book
0084-5930 Advances in Cyclic Nucleotide Research
0084-5949 Advances in Cytopharmacology
0084-5957 Advances in Nephrology from the Necker Hospital
0084-5965 Adventure Trip Guide *changed to* Adventure Travel (New York)
0084-5981 African and Oriental Holiday *changed to* African, Mediterranean and Oriental Travel
0084-6015 Agence pour la Securite de la Navigation Aerienne en Afrique et a Madagascar. Direction de l'Exploitation Meteorologique. Publications. Serie 2
0084-6023 Agenda Memento des Cadres et Maitrises de l'Imprimerie, de l'Edition et des Industries Graphiques *changed to* Agenda Memento des Protes
0084-6031 Agricultural Technologist
0084-6066 Agricultural Wages in India
0084-6082 Akademie der Wissenschaften, Goettingen. Jahrbuch
0084-6090 Bayerische Akademie der Wissenschaften. Jahrbuch
0084-6104 Akademie der Wissenschaften und der Literatur, Mainz. Jahrbuch
0084-6112 Alabama Linguistic and Philological Series†
0084-6120 Alaska Science Conference. Proceedings
0084-6139 Alaska. State Library, Juneau. Historical Monographs
0084-6147 University of Alaska. Institute of Marine Science. Occasional Publication
0084-6163 Alberta. Department of Health and Social Development. Annual Report *see* 0381-4327
0084-6171 Alberta Motor Transport Directory
0084-618X University of Alberta. Department of Animal Science. Annual Feeders' Day Report
0084-6198 ALGOL Bulletin
0084-6201 All Sports International
0084-621X University of Allahabad. Education Department. Researches and Studies
0084-6236 Almanaque Salvadoreno
0084-6244 Aloha Aina†
0084-6252 Altern und Entwicklung
0084-6260 Alternatives Newsmagazine *changed to* Communities; a Journal of Cooperative Living
0084-6279 Aluminium Development Council of Australia. Technical Papers
0084-6287 A A R Studies in Religion
0084-6309 American Association of Stratigraphic Palynologists. Proceedings of the Annual Meeting *see* 0191-6122
0084-6317 A B F Research Reporter
0084-6325 A C I Bibliography
0084-6333 American Council on Industrial Arts Teacher Education. Yearbook
0084-6341 American Educational Research Association. Annual Meeting Paper and Symposia Abstracts
0084-635X American Frozen Food Institute. Membership Directory
0084-6368 American Institute for Marxist Studies. Occasional Papers
0084-6376 American Institute of Chemists. Membership Directory
0084-6384 A I G A Children's Books Show†
0084-6414 National Formulary *changed to* United States Pharmacopeia-National Formulary
0084-6422 American Philosophical Quarterly. Monograph Series†
0084-6430 American Philosophical Society. Library Publications
0084-6449 American Society of Hospital Pharmacists. Membership Directory†
0084-6465 Anderseniana
0084-6473 Annee Balzacienne
0084-6481 Annuaire de la Photographie Professionnelle
0084-6511 Annuaire des Institutions d'Enseignement Secondaire *see* 0066-8990
0084-652X Annuaire National des Industries de la Conserve
0084-6538 Annuaire National du Lait
0084-6546 Annual Fertilizer Review
0084-6554 Annual Report on Dental Auxiliary Education
0084-6570 Annual Review of Anthropology
0084-6589 Annual Review of Biophysics and Bioengineering
0084-6597 Annual Review of Earth and Planetary Sciences
0084-6600 Annual Review of Materials Science
0084-6619 Annuario Amministrativo Italiano
0084-6627 Annuario Generale Italiano
0084-6635 Annuario Italiano delle Imprese Assicuratrici
0084-6651 Apartment Building Income-Expense Analysis *changed to* Income-Expense Analysis: Apartments
0084-666X Apocalypse†
0084-6678 Apparel Plant Wages and Personnel Policies *changed to* Apparel Plant Wages Survey
0084-6678 Apparel Plant Wages and Personnel Policies *changed to* Personnel Policies and Benefits for the Apparel Industry
0084-6708 Architects, Builders, and Contractors Blue-Book†
0084-6724 Archiv fuer Religionspsychologie
0084-6732 Armidale and District Historical Society. Journal and Proceedings
0084-6740 University of New England. Bulletin *see* 0156-1006
0084-6759 University of New England. Faculty of Agricultural Economics. Farm Case Study†
0084-6767 University of New England. Faculty of Agricultural Economics. Farm Management Report†
0084-6775 Arquivos Brasileiros de Nutricao
0084-6783 Art at Auction; the Year at Sotheby's and Parke-Bernet
0084-6805 Asia in the Modern World Series†
0084-6813 Asian Institute Translations†
0084-6821 Asian Population Programme News
0084-683X A T A V E Boletin Informativo

0084-6848 Asociacion Venezolano Britanica de Comercio e Industria. Anuario *changed to* Camara Venezolano Britanica de Comercio e Industria. Anuario
0084-6899 Association of Consulting Engineers of Canada. Specialization Typical Projects *see* 0317-6525
0084-6902 Center for Chinese Research Materials. Bibliographical Series
0084-6953 Australasian Bandsman
0084-6961 Australasian Commercial Teachers' Association. Journal
0084-697X A. I. J. Manual of Australasian Life Assurance
0084-6988 Australasian Methodist Historical Society. Journal and Proceedings *changed to* Church Heritage
0084-6996 Australasian Society of Engineers. Engineers Handbook
0084-7011 Australia. Bureau of Agricultural Economics. Beef Situation *see* 0311-0885
0084-702X Australia. Bureau of Agricultural Economics. Coarse Grains and Oilseeds Situation *see* 0311-0788
0084-702X Australia. Bureau of Agricultural Economics. Coarse Grains and Oilseeds Situation *changed to* Australia. Bureau of Agricultural Economics. Oilseeds: Situation and Outlook
0084-7038 Australia. Bureau of Agricultural Economics. Dairy Situation *changed to* Australia. Bureau of Agricultural Economics. Dairy Products: Situation and Outlook
0084-7046 Australia. Bureau of Agricultural Economics. Egg Situation *changed to* Australia. Bureau of Agricultural Economics. Eggs: Situation and Outlook
0084-7054 Australia. Bureau of Agricultural Economics. Mutton and Lamb Situation *see* 0311-0885
0084-7089 Australia. Bureau of Mineral Resources, Geology and Geophysics. Bulletin
0084-7097 Australia. Bureau of Mineral Resources, Geology and Geophysics. Petroleum Search Subsidy Acts. Publications†
0084-7100 Australia. Bureau of Mineral Resources, Geology and Geophysics. Reports
0084-7135 Australia. Department of Foreign Affairs. International Treaties and Conventions
0084-7208 Australian and New Zealand Hospitals and Health Services Yearbook *see* 0312-5599
0084-7216 A. A. T. E. Guide to English Books
0084-7224 Australian Association of Neurologists Proceedings *see* 0158-1597
0084-7232 Australian Aviation Yearbook
0084-7259 Australian Catholic Historical Society. Journal
0084-7267 Australian Coin Catalogue
0084-7275 Australian Communist
0084-7283 A C F Newsletter
0084-7291 Australian Cricket Yearbook
0084-7305 Australian Directory of Exports *changed to* Australian Exports
0084-7348 Australian Economy; Business Forecast *changed to* Management Reports on the Australian Economy
0084-7356 Australian Fisheries Paper
0084-7364 Australian Gliding Yearbook
0084-7402 Australian Horse Racing Annual
0084-7410 Australian Hospital Newsletter *changed to* Hospital Brief
0084-7429 Australian House and Garden Annual†
0084-7445 Australian Industrial Law Review
0084-7453 Australian Insurance Institute. Journal
0084-747X Australian Journal of Biblical Archaeology
0084-7488 Australian Mineral Industry. Annual Review
0084-7496 Australian National University, Canberra. Department of Engineering Physics. Publication Ep-Rr
0084-750X Australian National University, Canberra. Geology Department. Publication
0084-7518 Australian National University, Canberra. Research School of Physical Sciences. Research Paper
0084-7526 Australian Packaging and Materials Handling Yearbook and Buyers Guide *changed to* Australian Packaging Buyers Guide
0084-7534 A. P. E. A. Journal
0084-7550 Australian Poetry†
0084-7585 Australian Science Fiction Association. Journal *see* 0156-6342
0084-7593 Australian Ski Yearbook
0084-7607 Australian Society for Limnology. Bulletin†
0084-7623 Australian Welder *changed to* Australian and New Zealand Welder
0084-7631 Australian Welding Research Association. Bulletin
0084-764X Australian Wool Corporation. Statistical Analysis *see* 0311-9882
0084-7658 Australian Yearbook of International Law
0084-7674 Automobile Year
0084-7682 Bach-Jahrbuch
0084-7690 Forstatistisches Jahrbuch
0084-7704 Band Music Guide
0084-7712 Battelle Memorial Institute. Published Papers and Articles
0084-7739 Baustatistisches Jahrbuch
0084-7747 Bean Improvement Cooperative. Annual Report
0084-7755 Bed, Breakfast and Evening Meal
0084-7763 Beecham Society Bulletin
0084-7771 Belgica Selecta; Nouveau Livres Belges†
0084-778X University of Bergen. Department of Applied Mathematics. Report
0084-7798 Musikwissenschaftliche Arbeiten in der DDR. Bericht†
0084-7801 Beyond the Age Barrier: Newsletter for Adult Students at Iowa State University
0084-781X Indian Agriculture in Brief
0084-7828 Bibliografia Internationala Cinema
0084-7836 Bibliographia Internationalis Spiritualitatis
0084-7844 Bibliographia Musicologica
0084-7852 Bibliographical Society of Australia and New Zealand. Bulletin
0084-7860 Bibliographie de la Cote d'Ivoire
0084-7879 Bibliography of Electrical Recordings in the CNS and Related Literature
0084-7887 Bibliography on the Hypothalamic-Pituitary-Gonadal System
0084-7895 Biological Society of Nevada. Occasional Papers and Memoirs
0084-7925 Blantyre Water Board. Annual Report and Statement of Accounts
0084-7941 Boletin de Informacion Estadistica Sobre Cafe
0084-7968 Bolsa de Cereales. Revista Institucional. Numero Estadistico
0084-7976 Bornholmske Samlinger
0084-7984 Borough of Twickenham Local History Society. Papers
0084-7992 Bowdoin College. Museum of Art. Occasional Papers
0084-800X Bradea
0084-8018 B B C Music Guides
0084-8026 British Building Products Catalogue
0084-8034 British Columbia. Library Development Commission. Public Libraries, Statistics *changed to* British Columbia Public Libraries, Statistics
0084-8050 University of British Columbia Library. Serial Holdings†
0084-8069 University of British Columbia. Research Forest Annual Report
0084-8085 Checklist of British Official Serial Publications
0084-8093 Broadcasting and Television Year Book *changed to* B & T Year Book
0084-8107 Bromeliads
0084-8115 Bruce County Historical Society. Year Book
0084-8123 Brunei Annual Report
0084-8131 Brunei Museum. Special Publication
0084-814X Building and Engineering Review
0084-8182 Bulletin of Zoo Management
0084-8204 Buyer's Guide to Microfilm Equipment, Products, and Services *see* 0362-0131
0084-8212 By og Bygd
0084-8220 Cahiers Amitie Franco-Vietnamienne
0084-8239 Cahiers Paul-Louis Courier
0084-8263 California. Department of Water Resources. Bulletin
0084-8271 California Government & Politics Annual
0084-828X California Savings and Loan Data Book
0084-8298 University of California, Davis. Institute of Governmental Affairs. Environmental Quality Series†
0084-831X University of California, Los Angeles. School of Engineering and Applied Science. Research Development, and Public Service Activities
0084-8328 Cambrian Law Review
0084-8336 Cambridge Studies in Early Modern History
0084-8352 Camena†
0084-8379 Canada. Department of Agriculture. Library. Current Periodicals. Periodiques en Cours
0084-8387 Canada. Earth Physics Branch. Seismological Series
0084-8425 Canadian Catholic Conference. National Bulletin on Liturgy *changed to* Canadian Conference of Catholic Bishops. National Bulletin on Liturgy
0084-8565 Canadian Ladies' Golf Association. Year Book
0084-8573 Canadian Law List
0084-859X Caracterologie†
0084-8603 Cardiologisches Bulletin
0084-862X Catalog of Dealers' Prices for Marine Shells
0084-8638 Catholic International Education Office. Bulletin Trimestriel *changed to* O I E C Bulletin
0084-8646 Universidade Federal do Ceara. Escola de Agronomia. Departamento de Fitotecnia. Relatoria Tecnico
0084-8654 Center for Consumer Education Services. Monographs
0084-8662 Central Valley Project (California) Annual Report *changed to* U.S. Bureau of Reclamation. Mid-Pacific Region. Report
0084-8689 Centro de Investigaciones Agricolas de Tamaulipas. Circular CIAT
0084-8697 Centro de Investigaciones Agricolas de Tamaulipas. Informe Anual de Labores
0084-8700 Channel Islands Annual Anthology *changed to* Channel Islands Anthology
0084-8719 Chapel Hill Conference on Combinatorial Mathematics and Its Applications. Proceedings
0084-8727 Charles C. Moskowitz Lectures
0084-8735 Chiasma
0084-8743 Chilton's Import Car Repair Manual *changed to* Chilton's Import Automotive Repair Manual
0084-8751 Chitty's Ontario Annual Practice *changed to* Ontario Annual Practice
0084-876X Chromosome Atlas: Fish, Amphibians, Reptiles and Birds
0084-8786 CIBA Collection of Medical Illustrations
0084-8794 Ciencia
0084-8808 Coburger Landesstiftung. Jahrbuch
0084-8816 Cold-Drill
0084-8824 Cold Spring Harbor Laboratory. Abstracts of Papers Presented at Meetings
0084-8859 C.T.T.S. Annual
0084-8875 Colorado. Division of Wildlife. Special Report
0084-8883 Colorado. Division of Wildlife. Technical Publication
0084-8891 Colorado Ski and Winter Recreation Statistics
0084-8905 Colorado State University Libraries. Publication
0084-893X Comentarios Bibliograficos Americanos. Anuario *changed to* Anuario - C B A - Yearbook
0084-8948 Comitato Glaciologico Italiano. Bollettino†
0084-8956 Commentary
0084-8964 Committee for Economic Development. Supplementary Paper†
0084-8972 Council of Ontario Universities Biennial Review *see* 0315-9590
0084-8999 Commonwealth Scientific and Industrial Research Organization. Minerals Research Laboratories. Investigation Report *see* 0156-9953
0084-9014 Commonwealth Scientific and Industrial Research Organization. Division of Animal Physiology. Technical Report *changed to* Commonwealth Scientific and Industrial Research Organization. Division of Animal Production Technical Report
0084-9073 Commonwealth Scientific and Industrial Research Organization. Division of Wildlife Research. Technical Memorandum
0084-9081 Communications
0084-909X Company of Master Mariners of Australia. Journal
0084-9103 Texas Tech University. Interdepartmental Committee on Comparative Literature. Proceedings of the Comparative Literature Symposium
0084-9138 Conference for College and University Leaders in Continuing Education. Proceedings
0084-9146 Conference on Artificial Insemination of Beef Cattle. Proceedings
0084-9154 Conference on Bank Structure and Competition. Proceedings
0084-9162 Conference on Electrical Insulation and Dielectric Phenomena. Annual Report
0084-9170 Conference on the Economics of Education. Proceedings
0084-9189 Conimbriga
0084-9197 Conseil Superieur du Livre. Annuaire
0084-9219 Contributions in American History
0084-9227 Contributions in American Studies
0084-9235 Contributions in Economics and Economic History
0084-9243 Contributions in Librarianship and Information Science
0084-9251 Contributions in Military History
0084-926X Contributions in Philosophy
0084-9278 Contributions in Sociology
0084-9294 Convenience Store Industry Report
0084-9308 Denmark. Nationalmuseet. Arbejdsmarkt
0084-9324 Cosmetics Handbook
0084-9332 COSPAR Technique Manual
0084-9340 COSPAR Transactions
0084-9359 Costs and Curves†
0084-9405 Cover
0084-9413 Cowles Foundation for Research in Economics at Yale University. Monographs *changed to* Cowles Foundation Monographs
0084-9421 Coyote
0084-943X Criminal Justice Review†
0084-9456 Criticism and Interpretation
0084-9499 Current Biography Yearbook
0084-9502 Curtain, Drapery and Bedspread National Buyers Guide
0084-9510 Cyprus. Development Estimates
0084-9529 Dacotah Territory
0084-9537 Dada/Surrealism
0084-9545 Dairy Credit Book *see* 0085-0780
0084-9553 Danforth News and Notes†
0084-9561 Danmarks Adels Aarbog
0084-957X Biblioteksaarbog
0084-9588 Dansk Medicinhistorisk Aarbog

0084-9596 Dansk Periodicafortegnelse. Supplement
0084-960X University of Dar es Salaam. Bureau of Resource Assessment and Land Use Planning. Annual Report
0084-9626 University of Dar es Salaam. Bureau of Resource Assessment and Land Use Planning. Research Paper
0084-9634 University of Dar es Salaam. Bureau of Resource Assessment and Land Use Planning. Research Report
0084-9642 Delaware. Department of Natural Resources and Environmental Control. Annual Report
0084-9650 Delaware Museum of Natural History. Monograph Series
0084-9669 Delaware Museum of Natural History. Reproduction Series
0084-9677 Delaware Museum of Natural History. Special Publications
0084-9685 Delaware. State Treasurer. Annual Report
0084-9693 Denmark Exports†
0084-9707 Denmark. Folketinget. Folketingsaarbog
0084-9715 Denmark. Rigsbibliotekarembedet. Accessionskatalog
0084-9723 Dental Register of Ireland
0084-974X Designers in Britain
0084-9758 Deutsche Gesellschaft fuer Hygiene und Mikrobiologie. Berichte ueber Tagungen†
0084-9766 Deutsche Messen und Ausstellungen - Ein Zahlenspiegel
0084-9774 Gezeitentafeln
0084-9782 Institut der Deutschen Wirtschaft. Gewerkschaftsreport
0084-9790 Deutschlandfunk. Jahrbuch
0084-9804 Dialectic
0084-9820 Dimensions of Radio†
0084-9839 Dimensions of Television†
0084-9855 Directory of Bankers Schools
0084-9863 Directory of Canadian Community Funds and Councils *changed to* United Way of Canada. Directory of Members
0084-9871 Directory of Canadian Welfare Services
0084-988X Directory of College Stores
0084-9898 Directory of Colorado Manufacturers
0084-991X Directory of Educational Institutions in New Mexico
0084-9936 Directory of Fulbright Alumni
0084-9944 Directory of Governments in Metropolitan Toronto
0084-9952 Directory of Incorporated (Registered) Companies in Nigeria
0084-9960 Directory of Iranian Periodicals
0084-9979 Directory of Little Magazines, Small Presses and Underground Newspapers *see* 0092-3974
0084-9987 Directory of National Organizations Concerned with Land Pollution Control
0084-9995 Directory of Pakistan Commerce and Industry†
0085-0004 Directory of Registered Dentists and Registered Dental Hygienists in Connecticut†
0085-0012 Directory of Social and Health Agencies of New York City
0085-0020 Directory of the College Student Press in America
0085-0039 Directory of the Public Aquaria of the World
0085-0071 Drexel Research Conference. Summary Report
0085-008X Drexel University Research Review
0085-011X Earth and You
0085-0128 Earth's Wild Places†
0085-0144 Economic Aspects of Public Education in Pennsylvania†
0085-0160 Economic Survey of Indian Agriculture
0085-0187 Edubba
0085-0225 Elizabethan Club Series
0085-025X English around the World
0085-0268 Enterprise
0085-0276 Enzyklopaedie der Rechts- und Staatswissenschaft. New Series. Staatswissenschaft†
0085-0284 Universidade Federal do Espirito Santo. Comissao de Planejamento. Documentario Estatistico Sobre a Situacao Educacional
0085-0292 Universidade Federal do Espirito Santo. Comissao de Planejamento. Documentario Estatistico sobre a Situacao Educacional. Supplemento
0085-0306 Universidade Federal do Espirito Santo. Comissao de Planejamento. Vestibulandos†
0085-0314 Estimates of Area and Production of Principal Crops in India. Summary Tables
0085-0322 Etudes Haguenoviennes†
0085-0330 Eurail Guide
0085-0349 Europa Handbuch der Werbegesellschaften
0085-0357 Evangelische Zentralstelle fuer Weltanschauungsfragen. Materialdienst
0085-0365 Excerpta Historica Nordica
0085-0373 Explore Canada *changed to* Guide to Canada
0085-039X Expression
0085-042X Universidade Federal do Rio Grande do Sul. Faculdade de Medicina. Anais
0085-0438 Farm and Ranch Vacation Guide *see* 0147-3867
0085-0462 Federal Law Reports
0085-0489 Federation des Industries Chimiques de Belgique. Rapport
0085-0497 Federation Nationale des Chambres de Commerce, d'Industrie et d'Agriculture de la Republique du Zaire. Circulaire d'Information *changed to* Association Nationale des Entreprises Zairoises. Circulaire d'Information
0085-0500 Felix Ravenna; Rivista di Antichita Ravennati, Cristiane e Bizantine
0085-0519 Fer-Blanc en France et dans le Monde
0085-0535 Film and TV Festival Directory†
0085-0543 Financial Aids to Illinois Students
0085-0551 Financial Stock Guide Service. Directory of Obsolete Securities
0085-0586 Flinders Asian Studies Lecture
0085-0608 Florida. Bureau of Geology. Geological Bulletins
0085-0616 Florida. Bureau of Geology. Information Circulars
0085-0624 Florida. Bureau of Geology. Map Series
0085-0632 Florida. Bureau of Geology. Report of Investigations
0085-0640 Florida. Bureau of Geology. Special Publications
0085-0659 Florida. Bureau of Historic Sites and Properties. Bulletin
0085-0683 Memoirs of the Hourglass Cruises
0085-0748 Folia Mendeliana *changed to* Acta Musei Moraviae. Scientia Naturales 3: Folia Mendeliana
0085-0756 Folk; Dansk Etnografisk Tidsskrift
0085-0764 Folklivsstudier
0085-0780 Food Credit Book
0085-0802 Foreign Investment Opportunities in the Philippines
0085-0829 Foreign Medical School Catalogue
0085-0837 Forstlige Forsoegsvaesen i Danmark
0085-0845 Fra Als og Sundeved
0085-0853 Fra Viborg Amt. Aarbog
0085-0888 French XX Bibliography; Critical and Biographical References for the Study of French Literature since 1885
0085-0896 Frodskaparrit; Annales Societatis Scientiarum Faeroensis
0085-090X Fruit World Annual and Orchardists Guide
0085-0918 Fynske Aarboeger
0085-0934 Genealogisches Handbuch des Bayerischen Adels
0085-0942 Observatoire de Geneve. Publications. Serie A
0085-0950 Universita degli Studi di Genova. Bolletino dei Musei degli Istituti Biologici
0085-0969 Geographical Education
0085-0977 Geography Teachers Association of Queensland. Journal *see* 0314-3457
0085-0985 Geological Survey of Ireland. Bulletin
0085-0993 Geological Survey of Ireland. Information Circulars
0085-1000 Geological Survey of Ireland. Memoirs
0085-1019 Geological Survey of Ireland. Special Papers
0085-1027 Geology, Exploration, and Mining in British Columbia *changed to* Exploration in British Columbia
0085-1043 Georgia Statistical Abstract
0085-1051 University of Georgia. College of Business Administration. Research Monograph Series
0085-106X Gesellschaft zur Foerderung Tiefenpsychologischer und Psychotherapeutischer Forschung und Weiterbildung, Munich. Beitraege und Berichte†
0085-1078 Rijksuniversiteit te Gent. Laboratorium voor Experimentele, Differentiele en Genetische Psychologie. Mededlingen en Werkdocumenten
0085-1108 Goettinger Universitaetsreden
0085-1124 Good Health†
0085-1132 Graduate Careers Directory *see* 0311-4201
0085-1140 Grain†
0085-1167 Great Britain. Commission of Inquiry on Small Firms. Research Report†
0085-1191 Great Britain. Ministry of Housing and Local Government. Design Bulletin *changed to* Great Britain. Department of the Environment. Housing and Construction. Design Bulletin
0085-1205 University of Northern Colorado. Museum of Anthropology. Occasional Publications in Anthropology. Ethnology Series
0085-1213 University of Northern Colorado. Museum of Anthropology. Occasional Publications in Anthropology. Miscellaneous Series
0085-1221 University of Northern Colorado. Museum of Anthropology. Occasional Publications in Anthropology. Archaeology Series
0085-123X University of Northern Colorado. Museum of Anthropology. Occasional Publications in Anthropology. Linguistics Series
0085-1264 Universite de Grenoble. Institut de Phonetique. Manuels. Serie A *changed to* Universite de Grenoble III. Institut de Phonetique. Travaux: Serie A: Manuals
0085-1272 Universite de Grenoble III. Institut de Phonetique. Travaux. Serie B: Etudes Linguistiques
0085-1280 Growth
0085-1299 Grundbegriffe der Modernen Biologie.
0085-1302 Gruppenpsychotherapie und Gruppendynamik. Beihefte
0085-1310 Guam Statistical Annual Report
0085-1329 University of Guelph. Department of Land Resource Science. Progress Report
0085-1337 Guia de los Caballos Verificadas en Espana
0085-1345 Guidance and Counselling *see* 0306-9885
0085-1353 Guide to Biomedical Standards
0085-1361 Hafnia; Copenhagen Papers in the History of Art
0085-140X Handbuch der Physik†
0085-1418 Handels- og Soefartsmuseet paa Kronborg. Aarbog
0085-1434 Hard Core News
0085-1442 Harris Survey Yearbook of Public Opinion†
0085-1450 Health Physics Research Abstracts
0085-1469 Hefte zur Unfallheilkunde
0085-1477 Herald Caravanning Guide
0085-1485 Herald Motel Guide
0085-1493 Here and Now
0085-1523 Higher Education Monograph Series†
0085-1531 Hippocrene
0085-154X History Teacher
0085-1558 History Teachers Association of New South Wales. Newsletter
0085-1566 Hockey Association. Official Handbook
0085-1574 Home Appliance Blue Book *changed to* Home Appliance Trade-in Blue Book
0085-1582 Hoover Institution Bibliographies Series
0085-1590 Hoover Institution on War, Revolution and Peace. Library Surveys
0085-1612 Hotel and Motel Directory *changed to* Hotel, Motel and Travel Directory
0085-1620 How to Avoid Financial Tangles: Section A. Elementary Property Problems and Financial Relationships
0085-1639 How to Avoid Financial Tangles: Section B. Wills and Trusts, Taxes, and Help for the Widow
0085-1647 How to Avoid Financial Tangles: Section C. The Harvest Years Financial Plan†
0085-1663 Hunter Valley Research Foundation. Monographs
0085-1671 Hypomnemata
0085-1698 Icographic†
0085-1701 Idaho Pea and Lentil Commission. Annual Report
0085-1728 Illinois Labor History Society Reporter
0085-1736 Illustrated Human Embryology†
0085-1760 Index of Art in the Pacific Northwest
0085-1779 India. Committee on Science and Technology. Annual Report
0085-1787 Indian Agricultural Statistics†
0085-1795 F M U Occasional Lectures
0085-1809 Indian Livestock Census†
0085-1817 Indian Science Congress Association. Proceedings
0085-1833 Industrial Cities News Service
0085-1876 Informator Archeologiczny
0085-1884 Inlet
0085-1892 Institut Royal de Patrimoine Artistique. Bulletin
0085-1914 Instituto Boliviano del Petroleo. Boletin†
0085-1922 Instituto de la Patagonia. Anales
0085-1930 Insurance Life/Non-Life Annual Statistics
0085-1949 Inter-American Institute of Agricultural Sciences. Bibliografias *see* 0301-438X
0085-1965 S T P Notes
0085-1981 Intergovernmental Council for Automatic Data Processing. Proceedings of Conference
0085-199X I A T A News Review *see* 0376-642X
0085-2007 International Association for Scientific Study of Mental Deficiency. Proceedings of International Congress
0085-2015 I A S L Newsletter
0085-2023 International Atomic Energy Agency. Annual Report
0085-204X International Bibliography of the Social Sciences. Economics
0085-2058 International Bibliography of the Social Sciences. Political Science
0085-2066 International Bibliography of the Social Sciences. Sociology
0085-2074 International Bibliography of the Social Sciences. Social and Cultural Anthropology
0085-2082 I B M Research Symposia Series
0085-2090 International Clean Air Congress. Proceedings
0085-2104 International Conference on Chemical Vapor Deposition. Proceedings†
0085-2112 International Congress of Psychology. Proceedings
0085-2120 International Council for Scientific Management. Proceedings of World Congress
0085-2147 International Court of Justice. Bulletin†

ISSN INDEX 1173

0085-2163 International Monetary Fund. Annual Report on Exchange Restrictions *changed to* International Monetary Fund. Annual Report on Exchange Arrangements and Exchange Restrictions
0085-2171 International Monetary Fund. Annual Report of the Executive Directors *changed to* International Monetary Fund. Annual Report of the Executive Board
0085-218X International Percussion Reference Library. Catalog
0085-2198 International Press Institute. Survey
0085-2201 International Telecommunication Union. Report on the Activities
0085-221X Memento de l'O.I.V.
0085-2228 Inventory of Continuing Education Activities in Pennsylvania Secondary School Districts *changed to* Inventory of Continuing Education Activities in the Public School Districts of Pennsylvania
0085-2252 Iowa State Archaeologist. Report
0085-2260 Iraq Natural History Research Centre. Publication *changed to* Iraq Natural History Research Centre and Museum. Publication
0085-2287 Istituto Storico Artistico Orvietano. Bollettino
0085-2295 Italia Dialettale
0085-2309 Italy. Laboratorio di Studi sulla Ricerca e sulla Documentazione. Note di Bibliografia e Documentazione Scientifica *changed to* Italy. Istituto di Studi sulla Ricerca e Documentazione Scientifica. Note Bibliografia e Documentazione Scientifica
0085-2317 Giunta Centrale per gli Studi Storici, Rome. Bibliografia Storica Nazionale
0085-2325 Iwate University. Faculty of Engineering. Technology Reports
0085-2341 Jahrbuch fuer Regionalgeschichte
0085-2368 Jewish Boston
0085-2376 Journal of Arabic Literature
0085-2384 Journal of Astrological Studies
0085-2392 Journal of Development Planning
0085-2406 Journal of Drug Research of Egypt
0085-2414 Journal of Northwest Semitic Languages†
0085-2422 Joyous Struggle: a Women's Newsletter *changed to* University of New Mexico. Women's Center Newsletter
0085-2430 Juvenile Court Digest *see* 0162-5055
0085-2449 Kalamies
0085-2457 University of Kansas. Department of Anthropology. Publications in Anthropology
0085-2465 University of Kansas. Museum of Natural History. Monographs
0085-2473 University of Kansas Humanistic Studies
0085-2481 Karate International Annual
0085-249X Kariba Studies
0085-2503 Kerry Archaeological and Historical Society. Journal
0085-2511 Key to Finland†
0085-2538 Kidney International
0085-2546 King's Gazette
0085-2554 Kirkon Nuoriso-Pistis *see* 0356-794X
0085-2562 Knitting Times Yearbook
0085-2570 Kobe University. School of Business Administration. Annals
0085-2589 Kongelig Dansk Hof- og Statskalender; Statshaandbog for Kongeriget Danmark
0085-2597 Kontrast
0085-2600 Kultaseppien Lehti
0085-2619 Kyrkohistorisk Aarsskrift
0085-2627 Kyushu University. Faculty of Science. Memoirs Series B: Physics
0085-2635 Kyushu University. Faculty of Science. Memoirs. Series C: Chemistry
0085-2643 France. Laboratoires des Ponts et Chausees. Rapport de Recherche
0085-266X Land Laws Service
0085-2678 Langue et Cultures
0085-2686 Langue Internationale
0085-2694 Latin American Studies in the Universities of the United Kingdom
0085-2708 Latin American Studies in the Universities of the United Kingdom. Staff Research in Progress or Recently Completed in the Humanities and the Social Sciences
0085-2724 L I R I Research Bulletin
0085-2740 Report by the Auditor General on the Accounts of Lesotho
0085-2759 Louisiana State University. Library. Library Lectures
0085-2767 Library Lit
0085-2775 Light Age Directory; The Buyers Guide to Lamps. Lighting Fixtures, Accessories and Shades†
0085-2783 Centre International de Documentation Arachnologiques. Liste des Travaux Arachnologiques
0085-2805 Livestock and Poultry in Latin America. Annual Conference
0085-2821 Local Government Finances in Maryland
0085-283X London Record Society. Occasional Publications
0085-2848 London Record Society. Publications
0085-2856 University of London. School of Oriental and African Studies. Contemporary China Institute. Publications
0085-2899 Lozania
0085-2902 Luksave
0085-2910 Lyman's Canada-British North America Standard Postage Stamp Retail Catalogue *see* 0227-1699
0085-2929 M. Oliver Newsletter
0085-2937 Made in Europe Buyers' Guide
0085-2945 Madras. Government Museum. Bulletin. New Series
0085-2953 Mail Order Business Directory
0085-297X Maine. Soil and Water Conservation Commission. Biennial Report†
0085-3003 Malawi. National Statistical Office. Balance of Payments
0085-3011 Malawi. National Statistical Office. Compendium of Agricultural Statistics
0085-302X Malawi. National Statistical Office. Tourist Report *changed to* Malawi Tourism Report
0085-3038 University of Malawi.Library. Report to the Senate on the University Libraries
0085-3046 Malaysia. Department of Statistics. Survey of Construction Industries: Peninsular Malaysia
0085-3054 Management Monographs (New York)
0085-3070 Manitoba. Mining Engineering Division. Publication *changed to* Manitoba. Mineral Resources Division. Publication
0085-3100 Mario Negri Institute for Pharmacological Research. Monographs
0085-3119 Marken-Handbuch der Werbung und Etatbetreuung
0085-3135 Maryland. Police Training Commission. Annual Report *changed to* Maryland. Police and Correctional Training Commissions. Report to the Governor, the Secretary of Public Safety and Correctional Services, and Members of the General Assembly
0085-3143 Massachusetts Correctional Institution, Norfolk, Norfolk Colony School. Report
0085-3178 Mathematics Annual *see* 0317-8579
0085-3186 Matrix†
0085-3194 Mauritius Directory of the Diplomatic Corps
0085-3208 Ny Carlsberg Glyptotek. Meddelelser
0085-3224 Melbourne Journal of Politics
0085-3232 Melbourne Notes on Agricultural Extension
0085-3240 University of Melbourne. Department of Civil Engineering. Departmental Report
0085-3259 University of Melbourne. Department of Electrical Engineering. Research Report
0085-3267 University of Melbourne. Faculty of Agriculture and Forestry. Agricultural Economics Report†
0085-3275 University of Melbourne. Gazette
0085-3283 Melbourne University Magazine
0085-3291 Memo of Current Books in the Brain Sciences
0085-3321 M. T. I. A. Annual Report
0085-3356 Michigan. Department of Education. Bulletin†
0085-3364 Michigan. Geological Survey Division. Miscellany†
0085-3372 Michigan Mineral Producers Annual Directory:
0085-3380 Michigan Police Journal
0085-3410 Surveys of Consumers
0085-3429 Michigan's Oil and Gas Fields: Annual Statistical Summary
0085-3445 Mineral Industry of Michigan Annual Statistical Summary:
0085-3453 Mine and Quarry Mechanisation
0085-3461 Ministerialtidende for Kongeriget Danmark: Section A & B
0085-347X Minnesota Medical Assistance Biennial Report *changed to* People. Biennial Report
0085-3488 Minority Students Opportunities in United States Medical Schools
0085-3496 Missouri. Department of Conservation. Annual Report
0085-350X Missouri Journal of Research in Music Education
0085-3518 Modern Plastics Encyclopedia
0085-3526 Modern Teaching
0085-3534 Monmouth Reviews; Journal of the Literary Arts
0085-3542 Monographs in Modern Concepts of Philosophy†
0085-3550 Montana. Governor's Annual Report
0085-3577 Movie/TV Marketing Global Motion Picture Year Book
0085-3585 Municipal Association of Tasmania. Session. Minutes of Proceedings
0085-3607 Music and Life
0085-3623 Musikalier i Danske Biblioteker
0085-364X N U M U S Numismatica, Medalhistica, Argueologia
0085-3658 NADA
0085-3674 Natalia
0085-3682 National Civic Council. Facts
0085-3747 National Education Society of Sri Lanka. Journal
0085-3755 National Health Council. Annual Report
0085-3763 National Incinerator Conference. Proceedings *changed to* National Waste Processing Conference. Proceedings
0085-378X National Institute for Educational Research. Research Bulletin
0085-3798 National Institute for Research in Dairying. Biennial Report *see* 0302-0851
0085-3801 National Institute for Research in Dairying. Biennial Reviews†
0085-381X National Opera Association. Membership Directory
0085-3828 National Research Council, Canada. Division of Building Research. Bibliography
0085-3836 National Science Council (Ireland). Register of Scientific Research Personnel
0085-3860 Nature/Science Annual†
0085-3879 Nebraska. Agricultural Experiment Station, North Platte. Fall Crops and Irrigation Field Day
0085-3887 Nemouria; Occasional Papers of the Delaware Museum of Natural History
0085-3909 Network
0085-3917 Neue Hefte fuer Philosophie
0085-3925 University of Nevada. Anthropology Department. Student Papers in Anthropology†
0085-3933 N E H T A Newsletter *see* 0028-4912
0085-395X New Jersey. Department of Transportation. Report of Operations *changed to* New Jersey. Department of Transportation. Annual Report
0085-3968 University of New Mexico. Institute of Meteoritics. Special Publication
0085-3976 New South Wales. Department of Education. School Management Bulletin
0085-3984 New South Wales. Forestry Commission. Research Notes
0085-400X New South Wales. Law Reform Commission. Report
0085-4018 University of New South Wales. Metallurgical Society. Metallurgical Review
0085-4026 New South Wales Veterinary Proceedings
0085-4042 New York Pro Musica Instrumental Series
0085-4077 Annual Educational Summary, New York State
0085-4093 Racial/Ethnic Distribution of Public School Students and Staff, New York State
0085-4123 New Zealand. Ministry of Transport. Annual Report
0085-414X New Zealand. Water and Soil Division. Hydrological Research Annual Report & Series†
0085-4158 University of Newcastle. Department of Electrical Engineering. Technical Report EE
0085-4166 News from the Rare Book Room
0085-4174 Newsletter on Contemporary Japanese Prints
0085-4190 Nigerian Office and Quarters Directory *changed to* Nigerian Office and Residential Directory
0085-4204 Nimrod
0085-4212 Nordisk Ekumenisk Aarsbok
0085-4220 Nordiske Domme i Sjofartsanliggender
0085-4247 Universitetet i Trondheim. Norges Tekniske Hoegskole. Biblioteket. Literaturliste
0085-4263 N I B R Rapport
0085-4271 Norsk Polarinstitutt. Aarbok
0085-428X North Carolina Communicable Disease Morbidity Statistics
0085-4301 Norway. Forsvarets Forskningsinstitutt. N D R E Report
0085-431X Norway. Statistisk Sentralbyraa. Artikler/Articles
0085-4344 Norway. Statistisk Sentralbyraa. Samfunnsoekonomiske Studier/Social Economic Studies
0085-4352 Norwegian-American Historical Association. Topical Studies
0085-4387 Noticiero Tuberosas
0085-4395 Nova Scotia. Fire Marshal. Annual Report
0085-4409 Nucleus
0085-4417 Nuytsia
0085-4433 Oesterreichs Volkseinkommen
0085-4441 Official Year Book of New South Wales
0085-445X Oficina; Revista de Equipos para Oficinas
0085-4468 Ohio Fish and Wildlife Report
0085-4484 Oklahoma Art Center. Annual Eight State Exhibition of Painting and Sculpture Catalog
0085-4506 Oondoona
0085-4514 Opera Slavica†
0085-4522 Orientalia Lovaniensia Periodica
0085-4530 Der Orthpaede
0085-4557 Osler Library Newsletter
0085-4565 Oslo Boers. Beretning
0085-4573 Ostracodologist
0085-4581 P I E
0085-459X Pacific Islands Studies and Notes
0085-4603 Paedagogica†
0085-4611 Palaeontographica. Supplementbaende

0085-4638 Pan American Health Organization. Bulletin
0085-4654 Panama. Ministerio de Agricultura y Ganaderia. Boletin Tecnico
0085-4662 Papers on Islamic History
0085-4670 Papers on the History of Bourke
0085-4689 Papua and New Guinea Law Reports
0085-4697 Papua and New Guinea Scientific Society. Annual Report and Proceedings
0085-4700 Papua and New Guinea Scientific Society. Transactions
0085-4719 Papua New Guinea. Department of Labour. Industrial Review.†
0085-4735 University of Papua New Guinea. Department of Physics. Technical Paper
0085-4743 Paraguay. Ministerio de Industria y Comercio. Division de Registro y Estadistica Industrial. Encuesta Industrial
0085-4751 Pardon Me, But
0085-476X Museum National d'Histoire Naturelle, Paris. Bibliotheque Centrale. Liste des Periodiques Francais et Etrangers.Supplement
0085-4778 Cartes Synoptiques de la Chromosphere Solaire *changed to* Cartes Synoptiques de la Chromosphere Solaire et Catalogues des Filaments et des Centres d'Activite
0085-4786 Documents de Linguistique Quantitative
0085-4794 Partiojohtaja
0085-4808 Peace Research Laboratory. Annual Report
0085-4816 Pennsylvania. Department of Education. Our Colleges and Universities Today
0085-4824 Pennsylvania. Office of the Budget. Program Budget
0085-4840 Peru. Oficina Regional de Desarrollo del Norte. Analisis General de Situacion de la Region Norte
0085-4859 Petroleum Search in Australia†
0085-4867 Phi Sigma Iota News Notes *changed to* Phi Sigma Iota Forum
0085-4875 Philippine Mining and Engineering Journal. Mining Annual and Directory
0085-4883 Philippines Today†
0085-4905 Plumbers Friend
0085-4921 Pocket Yearbook of New South Wales
0085-493X Australia. Bureau of Statistics. Tasmanian Office. Pocket Year Book of Tasmania
0085-4956 Teki Historyczne
0085-4980 Politique de la Science
0085-4999 Polk's World Bank Directory. International Edition
0085-5006 Population Profile *see* 0146-7646
0085-5014 P R B Selection *see* 0146-7646
0085-5022 University of Port Elizabeth. Publications. Inaugural and Emeritus Addresses
0085-5030 Port of New Orleans Annual Directory
0085-5065 Practical Welder
0085-5073 Praxis der Kinderpsychologie und Kinderpsychiatrie. Beihefte
0085-5081 Precinct Returns for Major Elections in South Dakota
0085-5103 Prescriber's Journal *changed to* Australian Prescriber
0085-512X Prince Edward Island. Department of Labour. Annual Report
0085-5138 Prince Edward Island. Department of the Environment. Annual Report
0085-5154 Privates Bausparwesen
0085-5170 Progress and Growth of Papua New Guinea†
0085-5189 Progress in Atomic Medicine *see* 0163-6170
0085-5197 Progress in Land Reform
0085-5219 International Personnel Management Association. Annual Report†
0085-5227 Publications in the American West
0085-5235 Quaternaria
0085-5243 Universite Laval. Archives de Folklore
0085-526X Queen Alexandra Solarium for Crippled Children Annual Report *changed to* Queen Alexandra Hospital for Children. Annual Report
0085-5278 Queen Victoria Museum and Art Gallery. Launceston, Tasmania. Records
0085-5286 Queensland. Bureau of Sugar Experiment Stations. Technical Communication†
0085-5308 Queensland Historical Review†
0085-5308 Queensland Historical Review
0085-5316 Queensland Pocket Yearbook
0085-5324 Queensland Police Journal
0085-5332 Queensland Primary Producers' Co-Operative Association. Primary Producers' Guide
0085-5359 Queensland Yearbook
0085-5367 Quellen und Studien zur Geschichte der Pharmazie
0085-5375 Quirindi and District Historical Notes
0085-5383 Randschriften; a Newsletter for the Guild of Carilloneurs *changed to* Carillon News
0085-5391 Readings in Literary Criticism†
0085-5405 Real Estate Trends in Metropolitan Vancouver
0085-5413 Notas e Communicacoes de Matematica
0085-5421 Record Houses†
0085-543X Recueil des Films
0085-5456 Register of Companies in New South Wales†
0085-5499 Repertoire Bibliographique des Livres Imprimes en France
0085-5510 Report on Australian Universities
0085-5529 Report on the World Health Situation
0085-5545 Research and Development in Ireland
0085-5553 Research in Phenomenology
0085-5561 Respiratory Therapy Buyers Guide and Ordering Catalog†
0085-5596 Review of Economic Situation of Air Transport
0085-560X Review of Maritime Transport
0085-5626 Revista Brasileira de Entomologia
0085-5642 Revistero
0085-5677 Rhodesia National Bibliography *changed to* Zimbabwe National Bibliography
0085-5685 Zimbabwe. Central Statistical Office. Census of Population.
0085-5693 Zimbabwe. Department of Meteorological Services. Rainfall Report
0085-5707 Zimbabwe. Department of Meteorological Services. Report
0085-5715 Riddell's Australian Purchasing Yearbook *changed to* Business Who's Who Australian Buying Reference
0085-5723 Rivista di Antropologia
0085-5731 Rivista di Etnografia
0085-5774 Royal Asiatic Society. Hong Kong Branch. Journal
0085-5782 Royal Automobile Association of South Australia. Accommodation Guide *changed to* Australian Accommodation Guide
0085-5790 Royal Geographical Society of Australasia. South Australian Branch. Proceedings
0085-5804 Royal Historical Society of Queensland. Journal
0085-5812 Royal Society of South Australia. Transactions
0085-5820 Royal Zoological Society of New South Wales. Proceedings *changed to* Koolewong
0085-5839 Rural Africana
0085-5855 St. John's University, Collegeville, Minnesota. Monastic Manuscript Microfilm Library. Project Progress Report†
0085-588X Sammlung Musikwissenschaftlicher Abhandlungen
0085-5898 San Francisco Bay Conservation and Development Commission. Annual Report
0085-5901 Universidade Federal de Santa Maria. Centro de Ciencias Rurais. Revista
0085-591X Scandinavian Journal of Clinical and Laboratory Investigation. Supplement
0085-5928 Scandinavian Journal of Gastroenterology. Supplement
0085-5936 Scandinavian Studies in Criminology
0085-5944 Scandinavian Studies in Law
0085-5952 Schmankerl
0085-5960 Schriftenreihe fuer Vegetationskunde
0085-5979 Science Fiction Book Review Index
0085-5995 Scientific, Technical and Related Societies of the United States
0085-6002 Scottish Building & Civil Engineering Year Book
0085-6010 Search†
0085-6029 Seminario Matematico Garcia de Galdeano. Publicaciones
0085-6037 Semitica
0085-6045 Setting National Priorities. the (Year) Budget†
0085-6053 Seychelles. Labour Department. Annual Report†
0085-6061 Shaw's Directory of Courts in England and Wales
0085-607X Sheller's Directory of Clubs, Books, Periodicals and Dealers
0085-6096 Sindicato Nacional del Metal, Madrid. Informe-Economico y Social
0085-610X University of Singapore. History Society. Journal
0085-6118 Singapore Libraries
0085-6126 Skandinavisk Tidskrift for Faerg och Lack. Aarsbok
0085-6134 Slovenski Jezuiti V Kanade. Year Book
0085-6142 Smithsonian Institution. Center for Short Lived Phenomena. Annual Report
0085-6169 Snoeck's Almanach
0085-6177 Snoeck's; Literatuur Kunst Film Toneel Mode Reizen
0085-6193 Social, Economic and Political Studies of the Middle East
0085-6207 Social History of Canada
0085-6223 Sociedad Mexicana de Micologia. Boletin
0085-6231 Societa Storica Valtellinese. Bollettino
0085-624X Societe d'Etude du Vingtieme Siecle. Bulletin
0085-6258 Societe d'Histoire de la Guadeloupe. Bulletin
0085-6266 Societe Historique et Archeologique dans le Limbourg. Publications
0085-6282 Societe Royale des Sciences de Liege. Memoires in 8†
0085-6304 Society for the Study of Midwestern Literature. Newsletter
0085-6312 Real Estate Agents & Valuers Society. Land and Building
0085-6320 Socioloski Pregled
0085-6339 Soelleroedbogen
0085-6347 Source (Ann Arbor)
0085-6355 Investment Sources and Ideas *changed to* S I E Sophisticated Investor
0085-6363 South African Biographical and Historical Studies
0085-6371 South African Jewish Frontier†
0085-638X South African Journal of African Affairs *changed to* Africa Insight
0085-6398 South African Journal of Photogrammetry
0085-6401 South Asia; Journal of South Asian Studies
0085-6428 South Australian Yearbook
0085-6444 Industrial Directory of South Carolina *changed to* South Carolina Industrial Directory
0085-6452 University of South Carolina. Institute of International Studies. Essay Series
0085-6460 South Dakota. Department of Revenue. Annual Statistical Report
0085-6479 South Dakota Geological Survey. Bulletin
0085-6487 South Dakota Geological Survey. Circular
0085-6495 South Dakota Geological Survey. Reports of Investigation
0085-6509 Southeast Asian Archives
0085-6525 Southern Indian Studies
0085-6533 Soviet Affairs Symposium
0085-6541 Spain. Direccion General de Capacitacion y Extension Agrarias Resumen de Actividades
0085-655X Spain. Direccion General de Trafico. Anuario Estadistico de Accidentes. Boletin Informativo
0085-6568 Spain. Direccion General de Trafico. Anuario Estadistico General.
0085-6584 Spektrum des Geistes
0085-6592 S F I Bulletin
0085-6606 Standard Australian Coin Catalogue
0085-6614 Standard Directory of Advertising Agencies
0085-6622 Standard Directory of Newsletters†
0085-6630 Standard Periodical Directory
0085-6657 Standards for Australian Aluminium Mill Products
0085-6665 Stanford Museum
0085-6673 Stanford Occasional Papers in Linguistics
0085-6703 New South Wales State Reports *see* 0312-1674
0085-6711 Statistical Yearbook for Asia and the Far East *changed to* Statistical Yearbook for Asia and the Pacific
0085-672X Statistics on the Developing South *changed to* Southeastern Historical Statistics
0085-6738 Status
0085-6746 Steinbeck Monograph Series
0085-6762 Stockholm Studies in Politics
0085-6770 Stratford Festival
0085-6789 Stratford Festival Story
0085-6800 Student Mathematics
0085-6819 Studi Americani
0085-6827 Studi e Saggi Linguistici
0085-6835 Studia Fennica: Revue de Linguistique et d'Ethnologie Finnoises
0085-6843 Studies in Anthropology
0085-6851 University of Texas, Austin. Bureau of Business Research. Studies in Insurance and Actuarial Science†
0085-686X Studies in Jewish Jurisprudence
0085-6878 Studies in Medieval Culture
0085-6886 Studies in Polish Civilization†
0085-6894 Studies in Romance Languages
0085-6908 Studies on Selected Development Problems in Various Countries in the Middle East
0085-6916 Universitaet Stuttgart. Institut fuer Steuerungstechnik der Werkzeugmaschinen und Fertigungseinrichtungen. i S W Berichte
0085-6932 Suomen Geodeettisen Laitoksen. Julkaisuja
0085-6940 Suomen Kalatalous
0085-6967 Cement- och Betonginstitutet. Handlingar. Proceedings†
0085-6975 Cement- och Betonginstitutet. Meddelanden. Bulletins†
0085-6983 Svenska Traeforskningsinstitutet. Meddelande. Series A
0085-6991 Sweden. Statistiska Centralbyraan. Statistiska Meddelanden. Subgroup Bo (Housing and Construction)
0085-7009 Sydney Observatory Papers
0085-7017 Sydney Speleological Society. Communications *changed to* Sydney Speleological Society. Occasional Paper
0085-7025 University of Sydney Economics Society. Economic Review
0085-7033 University of Sydney. Institute of Criminology. Proceedings
0085-7041 University of Sydney Medical Journal†
0085-7068 Symposium on Coal Mine Drainage Research. Papers
0085-7076 Symposium on the Physiology and Pathology of Human Reproduction *changed to* Harold C. Mack Symposium. Proceedings

0085-7092 University of Texas, Austin. Tarlton Law Library. Legal Bibliography Series
0085-7106 Tasmanian State Reports
0085-7114 Teachers of History in the Universities of the United Kingdom
0085-7130 Telektronikk
0085-7149 Television Blue Book *changed to* Television Trade-in Blue Book
0085-7157 Television News Index and Abstracts
0085-7165 Tennessee Civilian Work Force Estimates *changed to* Tennessee Annual Average Labor Force Estimates
0085-7246 Thailand. Division of Agricultural Chemistry. Report on Fertilizer Experiments and Soil Fertility Research
0085-7262 Thorvaldsen Museum. Meddelelser
0085-7289 Tokyo. Polar Research Center. Antarctic Record *changed to* Antarctic Record
0085-7297 Topics in Ocean Engineering
0085-7327 Transport och Hanteringsekonomi *see* 0346-2773
0085-7335 Travaux Linguistiques de Prague†
0085-7351 Better Homes and Gardens Travel Ideas†
0085-7378 Treewell
0085-7386 Trilobite News
0085-7394 Tromsoe Museum. Skrifter
0085-7408 True to Life
0085-7416 T R U K-P A C T
0085-7432 Turkiyat Mecmuasi
0085-7440 Turun Historiallinen Arkisto
0085-7467 Annuaire U N I T†
0085-7475 United Nations Association of Australia. United Nations Reporter
0085-7491 United Nations. Division of Narcotic Drugs. Information Letter
0085-7513 United Nations Economic and Social Commission for Asia and the Pacific. Social Development Division. Social Work Training and Teaching Materials Newsletter
0085-7580 Dairy Herd Improvement *changed to* Dairy Herd Improvement Letter
0085-7602 Union Postale Universelle. Statistique des Services Postaux
0085-7629 University of Newcastle Historical Journal
0085-7645 Vendsyssel Aarbog
0085-7653 Venezuela. Ministerio de Agricultura y Cria. Direccion de Economia y Estadistica Agropecuaria. Division de Estadistica. Plan de Trabajo
0085-7661 Verbaende, Behoerden, Organisationen der Wirtschaft
0085-767X Museo Civico di Storia Naturale, Verona. Memorie
0085-770X Victoria, Australia. Department of Agriculture. Technical Bulletin†
0085-7718 Vegetable Growers Digest†
0085-7726 Victoria, Australia. Education Department. Curriculum and Research Branch. Research Reports
0085-7742 Victoria, Australia. Forests Commission. Bulletin
0085-7750 Victoria, Australia. Geological Survey. Bulletin
0085-7769 Victoria, Australia. Geological Survey. Memoirs
0085-7823 Vietnamese Studies
0085-7831 Viridian Starfire *changed to* Square Balloon
0085-784X Vocational Training in New York City. . . Where to Find It†
0085-7858 Wagga Wagga and District Historical Society. Journal
0085-7866 Waigani Seminar. Papers
0085-7874 Walter Neurath Memorial Lectures
0085-7882 W R I Newsletter
0085-7904 Washington Center for Metropolitan Studies. Metropolitan Bulletin†
0085-7920 University of Washington Publications in Anthropology†
0085-7939 University of Washington Publications in Fisheries
0085-7947 University of Washington Publications on Language and Literature†
0085-798X Washington University. Institute for Urban and Regional Studies. Working Paper
0085-8013 Water Research Foundation of Australia. Bulletin *see* 0085-8021
0085-8021 Water Research Foundation of Australia. Reports
0085-803X Weed Society of New South Wales. Proceedings
0085-8048 Welcome to Finland
0085-8056 Welcome to Greenland *changed to* North Atlantic
0085-8064 Welcome to Iceland *changed to* North Atlantic
0085-8072 Welcome to the Faroes *changed to* North Atlantic
0085-8080 West Malaysia Annual Statistics of External Trade
0085-8099 West Virginia Education Directory
0085-8102 Western Association of State Game and Fish Commissioners. Proceedings *changed to* Western Association of Fish and Wildlife Agencies. Proceedings
0085-8110 Western Australia. Aboriginal Affairs Planning Authority. Newsletter *changed to* Western Australia. Department of Aboriginal Affairs. Newsletter
0085-8129 Western Australia. Forests Department. Bulletin
0085-8137 Western Australia. Geological Survey. Bulletin
0085-8145 Western Australia. Geological Survey. Report
0085-8153 Western Australia. Government Chemical Laboratories. Report of Investigations
0085-8161 Western Australia Law Almanac
0085-8188 Western Canadian Steam Locomotive Directory
0085-8196 Wheat Australia
0085-820X Whiteacre
0085-8226 Wisconsin. Department of Administration. Annual Fiscal Report
0085-8242 Wisconsin Women Newsletter
0085-8250 Witchcraft Digest
0085-8285 World Health Organization. Work of W H O
0085-8307 World Motor Vehicle Data
0085-8315 World Population Data Sheet
0085-8331 Wyoming Work Injury Report *see* 0093-1241
0085-834X Yamagata University. Bulletin
0085-8366 Yokohama National University. Science Reports. Section I: Mathematics, Physics, Chemistry
0085-8374 York Journal of Convocation
0085-8382 Your Australian Garden
0085-8390 Your Texas Ancestors
0085-8412 Zeitschrift fuer Psychosomatische Medizin und Psychoanalyse. Beihefte
0085-8420 Eidgenoessische Sternwarte, Zurich. Astronomische Mitteilungen
0090-0036 American Journal of Public Health
0090-0044 National Union Catalog of Manuscript Collections
0090-0079 MEDI-KWOC Index†
0090-0141 Directory of Dental Educators
0090-0176 Japanese Studies in the History of Science
0090-0214 Nuclear Data Tables *see* 0092-640X
0090-0222 Great Lakes Entomologist
0090-0311 J O G N Nursing
0090-0443 Current Concepts in Nutrition
0090-046X Medical Communications
0090-0486 Environment Film Review
0090-0494 Obesity & Bariatric Medicine
0090-0508 Current Contents/Agriculture, Biology & Environmental Sciences
0090-0575 International Bibliography on Burns
0090-0591 C T F A Cosmetic Journal
0090-0613 U.S. National Meteorological Center. Long Range Prediction Group. Average Monthly Weather Outlook
0090-0664 North Carolina State University. School of Forest Resources. Technical Report.
0090-0672 Union Catalog of Medical Periodicals *changed to* U C M P Quarterly
0090-0702 Maternal-Child Nursing Journal
0090-0710 Hospital Medical Staff
0090-0737 Pennsylvania Crop Reporting Service. Pennsylvania Orchard and Vineyard Survey†
0090-0753 Index of Tissue Culture†
0090-077X New Jersey. Developmental Disabilities Council. Annual Report
0090-0834 Optical Management
0090-0842 Consensus†
0090-0869 O A G Travel Planner & Hotel/Motel Guide *see* 0193-3299
0090-0877 Immunological Communications
0090-0893 N F A I S Newsletter
0090-0907 Chemical Marketing Reporter
0090-0923 Family Planning/Population Reporter
0090-0931 New Mexico State Records Center and Archives. Publications Filed
0090-0958 Institute for the Development of Indian Law. Education Journal *see* 0145-7993
0090-1032 Harvard Political Review
0090-1059 Oregon. Department of Education. Racial and Ethnic Survey
0090-1083 Annual Review of Allergy
0090-1091 Journal of Clinical Computing
0090-1156 U.S. Center for Disease Control. Brucellosis Surveillance: Annual Summary
0090-1164 Current Citations on Strabismus, Amblyopia, and Other Diseases of Ocular Motility
0090-1180 Administration in Mental Health
0090-1210 A S T M Standardization News
0090-1229 Clinical Immunology & Immunopathology
0090-1237 Claudel Studies
0090-1245 Index of Dermatology†
0090-1326 Recurring Bibliography of Hypertension
0090-1377 Cumulated Abridged Index Medicus
0090-1407 Cerebrovascular Bibliography
0090-144X Psychotherapy
0090-1482 Journal of Alcohol and Drug Education
0090-1520 Florida. Legislature. Joint Legislative Management Committee. Summary of General Legislation
0090-1601 Foundation Grants Index; Subjects on Microfiche *changed to* Comsearch Printouts: Subjects
0090-1628 Zoos & Aquariums in the Americas *changed to* Zoological Parks & Aquariums in the Americas
0090-1652 Biology of Brain Dysfunction†
0090-1660 Committee of Interns and Residents Bulletin *changed to* C I R News
0090-1741 National Roster of Realtors
0090-1768 Municipal Research and Services Center of Washington. Information Bulletins
0090-1881 American Psychiatric Association. Scientific Proceedings in Summary Form
0090-1903 Norda Briefs
0090-1911 Vibrational Spectra and Structure
0090-192X Key Systems Guide†
0090-1938 Journal of Erie Studies
0090-1954 Symposium on Creation†
0090-1989 Directory: North Dakota City Officials
0090-1997 Florida Symposium on Automata and Semigroups†
0090-2047 Oui
0090-2055 U. S. Environmental Protection Agency. Office of Research and Development. Bibliography of Water Quality Research Reports *changed to* U. S. Environmental Protection Agency. Office of Research and Development. Indexed Bibliography
0090-2063 Photographica
0090-2071 Proteus
0090-208X Official Associated Press Almanac *changed to* Hammond Almanac
0090-2136 Q P Herald *see* 0146-5023
0090-2144 Motor Racing Year.
0090-2209 Newspaper Guild. Annual T.N.G. Convention Officers' Report
0090-2225 In-Service Training and Education *see* 0160-7006
0090-2233 Hawaii. Commission on Aging. Report of Achievements of Programs for the Aging
0090-225X Foreign Newspaper Report *see* 0190-9819
0090-2268 Lectures in Heterocyclic Chemistry
0090-2292 Hockey Register
0090-2381 I E E E Power Processing and Electronics Specialists Conference. Record *changed to* I E E E Power Electronics Specialists Conference. Record
0090-239X U.S. Forest Service. Forest Service Research Accomplishments
0090-2403 U.S. National Cancer Institute. Report of the Carcinogenesis Program
0090-2411 A. E. Legal Newsletter
0090-2446 Field and Stream Camping on Wheels *changed to* Field & Stream Guide to Camping on Wheels
0090-2454 Product Management†
0090-2454 Product Management *changed to* Product Marketing
0090-2497 Washington (State) Natural Resources and Recreation Agencies. Annual Report
0090-2500 Adit†
0090-2519 Contamination Control/Biomedical Environments†
0090-2535 Guidebook of Catholic Hospitals
0090-2578 Sunset Christmas Ideas and Answers
0090-2594 Vanderbilt Journal of Transnational Law
0090-2608 Illinois State Bar Association. Individual Rights and Responsibilities Newsletter
0090-2616 Organizational Dynamics
0090-2756 Connecticut. Department of Correction. Publications
0090-2810 World Currency Charts
0090-2845 U. S. Copyright Office. Annual Report of the Register of Copyrights
0090-2861 Microfilm Source Book *changed to* International Micrographics Source Book
0090-287X Annual Review of the Schizophrenic Syndrome
0090-290X Subject Guide to Microforms in Print
0090-2918 U.S. Health Resources Administration. Public Health Reports
0090-2934 Dialysis & Transplantation
0090-2969 Alcohol and Health Notes *see* 0364-0531
0090-2977 Neurophysiology
0090-2985 Carnival & Circus Booking Guide
0090-2993 Cavalcade and Directory of Acts & Attractions
0090-3000 Cinemagic
0090-3019 Surgical Neurology
0090-3051 Delaware. Division of Social Services. Annual Report
0090-3159 Contemporary Ob/Gyn
0090-3167 Learning
0090-3191 United Way of America. Information Center. Digest of Current Reports *changed to* United Way of America. Information Center. Digest of Selected Reports
0090-3213 Planetarian
0090-3221 State of Nebraska Uniform Crime Report
0090-323X Miami Malacological Society. Quarterly
0090-3248 Illinois. Housing Development Authority. Annual Report

1176 ISSN INDEX

0090-3256 Good Sam Club's Recreational Vehicle Owners Directory *see* 0093-4283
0090-3272 Communications in Statistics *see* 0361-0926
0090-3280 Non-G P O Imprints Received in the Library of Congress†
0090-3329 American Dental Association. Annual Reports and Resolutions
0090-3353 Rock Scene
0090-3361 Keyboard Arts†
0090-337X Countryside and Small Stock Journal *see* 0363-8723
0090-3477 Journal of Non-Metals *see* 0309-5991
0090-3485 Engage/Social Action *see* 0164-5528
0090-3493 Critical Care Medicine
0090-3515 A R L I S /N A Newsletter
0090-3558 Journal of Wildlife Diseases
0090-3604 American Academy of Psychoanalysis. Journal
0090-3612 Puerto Rico Official Industrial Directory
0090-3647 American Bar Association. Section of Administrative Law. Annual Reports of Committees
0090-3655 Semiconductor Application Notes D.A.T.A Book
0090-3663 Music World Magazine†
0090-3671 Year Book of Surgery
0090-371X U. S. Library of Congress. Accessions List: Eastern Africa
0090-3736 U.S. Library of Congress. Accessions List: Sri Lanka†
0090-3744 U.S. Library of Congress. Accessions List: Nepal†
0090-3752 Nuclear Data Sheets
0090-3779 Appalachian Journal
0090-3809 Montana State Plan for Alcohol Abuse and Alcoholism Prevention, Treatment and Rehabilitation
0090-3825 Management World
0090-3833 Destination: Philadelphia
0090-3841 Recreational Vehicle Retailer *changed to* Recreational Vehicle Dealer
0090-3884 Steam Electric Fuels *changed to* Steam-Electric Plant Factors (1978)
0090-3892 Comparative Urban Research
0090-3906 Oregon. Mass Transit Division. Annual Report *changed to* Public Transportation in Oregon
0090-3914 American Society of Civil Engineers. Environmental Engineering Division. Journal
0090-3949 Cross-Talk
0090-3965 National Association of College Admissions Counselors. Membership Directory
0090-3973 A S T M Journal of Testing and Evaluation
0090-3981 High Fidelity's Test Reports
0090-399X Realty Bluebook
0090-4007 Country Music
0090-4023 Successful Ventures in Contemporary Education in Oklahoma
0090-4058 Franklin Mint. Numismatic Issues *changed to* Franklin Mint. Limited Editions
0090-4066 Directory of Corporate Urban Affairs Officers
0090-4074 National Directory of Providers of Psychiatric Services to Religious Institutions
0090-4082 Outstanding Elementary Teachers of America†
0090-4104 Journal of Soviet Mathematics
0090-4112 Critiques
0090-4155 Behaviorism
0090-4163 Directory of National Unions and Employee Associations†
0090-4171 Stations†
0090-418X Who's Who in the Securities Industry
0090-4201 Journal of Sports Medicine *see* 0363-5465
0090-4236 Annual Editions: Readings in Sociology
0090-4244 Mountain Plains Journal of Adult Education
0090-4260 Literature/Film Quarterly
0090-4295 Urology
0090-4309 Annual Editions: Readings in Business
0090-4325 Montana. Office of the Legislative Auditor. Department of Institutions Reimbursements Program; Report on Audit
0090-4341 Archives of Environmental Contamination and Toxicology
0090-4368 G. H. S. Foot-Notes
0090-4376 Cable Tech
0090-4384 Annual Editions: Readings in Biology
0090-4392 Journal of Community Psychology
0090-4406 Photography Year
0090-4414 Amateur Athletic Union of the United States. Official A A U Basketball Handbook†
0090-4422 Economics: Encyclopedia
0090-4430 Annual Editions: Readings in Economics
0090-4449 Evaluation and Change
0090-4473 American Association of Zoological Parks and Aquariums. Proceedings. Annual A A Z P A Conference
0090-4481 Pediatric Annals
0090-449X Clark County History
0090-4511 Annual Editions: Readings in American History
0090-452X Catskills†
0090-4546 Virginia Woolf Quarterly
0090-4570 Rag Times
0090-4589 Job Safety and Health†
0090-4600 Tax Management International Journal
0090-466X Journal of Pharmacokinetics and Biopharmaceutics
0090-4716 New York (State) Department of Social Services. Bureau of Data Management and Analysis. Program Analysis Report
0090-4759 Soviet Journal of Particles and Nuclei
0090-4848 Human Resource Management
0090-4856 Iowa Wildlife Research Bulletin
0090-4872 Directory - Juvenile Adult Correctional Institutions and Agencies of the United States of America, Canada, and Great Britain *see* 0362-9287
0090-4910 Retirement Living *see* 0163-2027
0090-4945 Directory of Consulting Specialists†
0090-4961 Sunday Clothes†
0090-4988 American Psychiatric Association. Membership Directory
0090-4996 Animal Learning & Behavior
0090-5003 China Medical Reporter
0090-502X Memory and Cognition
0090-5046 Physiological Psychology
0090-5054 Psychonomic Society. Bulletin
0090-5070 Ground Water Newsletter
0090-5089 K A F P Journal
0090-5119 Health, Physical Education and Recreation Microform Publications Bulletin
0090-5151 Woodall's Campground Directory. Florida Campgrounds Edition
0090-5178 E M: Heavy Duty Equipment & Maintenance
0090-5186 Madison County Genealogist
0090-5224 Poe Studies
0090-5232 L C Science Tracer Bullet
0090-5259 Scene†
0090-5259 Current Governments Reports, GF - Government Finance
0090-5267 Control and Dynamic Systems: Advances in Theory and Applications
0090-5291 Electronics Buyers' Guide
0090-5305 Pocket Playboy†
0090-5313 Fire Marshals Association of North America. Year Book
0090-5348 Annual Editions: Readings in Human Development
0090-5364 Annals of Statistics
0090-5380 Symphony News *see* 0271-2687
0090-5402 Paint Red Book
0090-5461 Journal of Non-White Concerns in Personnel and Guidance
0090-547X Annual Editions: Readings in American Government
0090-5488 Biomaterials, Medical Devices and Artificial Organs
0090-5496 Oregon. State Board of Education. ESEA Title III State Plan†
0090-5526 Small Group Behavior
0090-5542 Basic Life Sciences
0090-5550 Rehabilitation Psychology
0090-5569 Selected Abstracts on Animal Models for Biomedical Research†
0090-5577 Directory of North Dakota Manufacturers
0090-5593 California. Teachers Retirement Board. State Teacher's Retirement System; Annual Report to the Governor and the Legislature
0090-5607 Ultrasonics Symposium. Proceedings
0090-5631 Meat Science Institute. Proceedings
0090-5674 Paideuma
0090-5720 Journal of Behavioral Economics
0090-5747 Sage Urban Studies Abstracts
0090-5895 Current Governments Reports: State Government Finances
0090-5917 Political Theory
0090-5968 California State Water Project
0090-5992 Nationalities Papers
0090-600X Wheelers Trailer Resort and Campground Guide *changed to* Wheelers Recreational Vehicle Resort and Campground Guide: Easterner Edition
0090-6034 Cricket
0090-6077 Connecticut. Department on Aging. Report to the Governor and General Assembly
0090-6093 Cowan Clan United. Newsletter
0090-6107 Maine. Law Enforcement Planning & Assistance Agency. Progress Report *changed to* Maine. Criminal Justice Planning & Assistance Agency. Progress Report
0090-6263 Annual Report of Federal Civilian Employment by Geographic Area *changed to* Federal Civilian Work Force Statistics. Annual Report of Employment by Geographic Area
0090-628X Nebraska. Accounting Division. Annual Report of Receipts and Disbursements State of Nebraska
0090-6352 Assessment and Valuation Legal Reporter
0090-6360 Atomic Physics
0090-6409 Oregon. Department of Forestry. Biennial Report of the State Forester *see* 0015-7449
0090-6425 Minnesota. State Board of Health. Biennial Report
0090-6433 Better Homes and Gardens Hundreds of Ideas
0090-645X Billboard International Tape Directory *changed to* Billboard Tape/Audio/Video Sourcebook
0090-6484 Directory of Executive Recruiters
0090-6514 Telos (St. Louis)
0090-6549 Infectious Disease Reviews.
0090-6557 Tennessee Pocket Data Book
0090-6581 Cosmetics and Perfumer *see* 0361-4387
0090-6611 Popular Computing
0090-662X Yearbook of Drug Abuse.
0090-6654 Evaluations of Drug Interactions
0090-6662 Hospital Statistics; Data from American Hospital Association Annual Survey
0090-6689 Medical Instrumentation
0090-6700 Official Museum Directory
0090-6735 Oregon. State Board of Accountancy. Certified Public Accountants, Public Accountants, Professional Corporations, and Accountants Authorized to Conduct Municipal Audits in Oregon
0090-6743 Montana. Department of Public Instruction. Descriptive Report of Program Activities for Vocational Education†
0090-6778 I E E E Transactions. Communications
0090-6786 Stereo Directory & Buying Guide
0090-6808 U.S. Environmental Protection Agency. Office of Research and Development. Selected Irrigation Return Flow Quality Abstracts
0090-6816 U S A N and the U S P Dictionary of Drug Names
0090-6883 Synthesis (Cambridge)
0090-6905 Journal of Psycholinguistic Research
0090-6913 Letters in Applied and Engineering Sciences *see* 0020-7225
0090-693X Community-Clinical Psychology Series
0090-6964 Annals of Biomedical Engineering
0090-6980 Prostaglandins
0090-7103 World Affairs Report
0090-7111 Census of Maine Manufactures
0090-7197 Black Photographers Annual
0090-7227 Federal Civilian Manpower Statistics. Monthly Release *see* 0163-8270
0090-7235 L O M A Literature on Modern Art *see* 0300-466X
0090-7286 Topical New Issues
0090-7294 I E E E International Convention Digest
0090-7324 R S R
0090-7383 Conference on Data Systems Languages. Data Base Task Group. Report
0090-7421 Journal of Allied Health
0090-7480 Best's Safety Directory
0090-760X Missouri Life
0090-7618 U.S. National Center for Education Statistics. Expenditures and Revenues for Public Elementary and Secondary Education *changed to* U.S. National Center for Education Statistics. Revenues and Expenditures for Public Elementary and Secondary Education
0090-7626 Sweet's Industrial Construction Catalog File *see* 0092-8763
0090-7634 B & P-Brass & Percussion *see* 0098-4574
0090-7782 A H M E Journal
0090-7790 Black Perspective in Music
0090-7812 Directory of Missouri's Regional Planning System *changed to* Directory of Missouri's Regional Planning Commissions
0090-7820 Bonnes Feuilles
0090-7847 Railroad History
0090-7855 P A A B S Revista†
0090-7863 U.S. National Credit Union Administration. N C U A Quarterly
0090-788X Let's Go: the Student Guide to the United States and Canada
0090-7944 Columbia Human Rights Law Review
0090-7987 Children's Book Review Service
0090-7995 Rhodes Directory of Black Dentists Registered in the United States
0090-8002 U.S. Emergency Loan Guarantee Board. Annual Report†
0090-8029 Auto Racing Digest
0090-8088 GreenAmerica
0090-8118 National Society for Programmed Instruction. Newsletter *changed to* Performance & Instruction
0090-8177 Minnesota. Department of Natural Resources. Biennial Report
0090-8185 Dirt Bike Buyer's Guide†
0090-8258 Gynecologic Oncology
0090-8266 Graduate & Professional School Opportunities for Minority Students†
0090-8274 Hawaii Literary Review *see* 0093-9625
0090-8282 Insect World Digest†
0090-8290 Canadian-American Slavic Studies
0090-8304 U.S. Library of Congress. Accessions List. Bangladesh†
0090-8312 Energy Sources
0090-8320 Ocean Development and International Law
0090-8339 Coastal Zone Management Journal
0090-8347 Energy Systems and Policy
0090-8363 Chemical Abstracts - Applied Chemistry and Chemical Engineering Sections
0090-8371 U.S. Copyright Office. Catalog of Copyright Entries. Third Series. Parts 12-13. Motion Pictures and Filmstrips *see* 0163-7320
0090-838X Alcohol Health and Research World

0090-8401 Michigan. Employment Security Commission. Annual Planning Report
0090-8401 Michigan. Employment Security Commission. Labor Market Analysis Section. Annual Manpower Planning Report: Detroit Labor Market Area *see* 0090-8401
0090-8479 Venereal Disease Bibliography†
0090-8517 Connecticut River Valley Covered Bridge Society. Bulletin
0090-8541 U.S. National Bureau of Standards. Methods of Measurement for Semiconductor Materials, Process Control, and Devices; Quarterly Report *changed to* U.S. National Bureau of Standards. Semiconductor Measurement Technology
0090-8584 Current Topics in Comparative Pathobiology
0090-8592 Behavior of Nonhuman Primates: Modern Research Trends†
0090-8614 A L A Sights to See Book
0090-8630 Family Circle's Home Decorating Guide *changed to* Decorating Made Easy
0090-8649 Southern Regional Education Board. State and Local Revenue Potential
0090-8657 Tire Science and Technology†
0090-8673 O C L C. Annual Report
0090-8738 Bromeliad Society Journal
0090-8746 Library Scene
0090-8800 Contemporary Topics in Molecular Immunology
0090-8843 Alabama Marine Resources Bulletin
0090-8878 Household & Personal Products Industry†
0090-8886 Infectious Diseases
0090-8932 Render
0090-8967 Illinois Institute for Environmental Quality. Annual Report
0090-9009 Swizzle Stick
0090-9033 Buyer's Guide to the World of Tape *see* 0161-4371
0090-905X Iowa Genealogical Society. Surname Index
0090-9076 American Psychological Association. Biographical Directory *see* 0196-6545
0090-9084 Journal of Police Science and Administration
0090-9092 Art Psychotherapy
0090-9114 Americana
0090-9130 Index of American Periodical Verse
0090-919X Corporation Finance and New Issue Weekly *changed to* Corporate Financing Week
0090-9203 H I S S News-Journal
0090-9211 Art Investment Report *see* 0161-1232
0090-9238 Insight on Site
0090-9300 Maryland Geographer†
0090-9319 Woman's Day 101 Gardening & Outdoor Ideas
0090-9386 Maine. Criminal Justice Planning & Assistance Agency. Criminal Justice Intership Program. Report and Evaluation
0090-9416 Latin American Index
0090-9440 Hawaii. Department of Education. Office of Business Services. Report on Federally Connected Pupils: Hawaii Public Schools
0090-9467 Foreign Economic Trends and Their Implications for the United States
0090-9475 Exporter's Encyclopedia-United States Marketing Guide†
0090-9491 Stochastics
0090-9521 Architecture Plus†
0090-9556 Drug Metabolism and Disposition
0090-9580 International Journal of Cooperative Development†
0090-9599 R F Illustrated
0090-9688 U.S. Department of Agriculture. Food and Home Notes
0090-9718 Focus: Technical Cooperation†
0090-9742 Private Investors Abroad
0090-9750 University of Maryland. Natural Resources Institute. N. R. I. Special Report
0090-9785 M R I S Bulletin *see* 0147-572X
0090-9815 North Dakota Crop and Livestock Reporting Service. Wheat Varieties, North Dakota†
0090-9866 Clergy's Federal Income Tax Guide *see* 0163-1241
0090-9882 Journal of Applied Communications Research
0090-9912 Montana. Office of the Legislative Auditor. State of Montana Board of Investments. Report on Examination of Financial Statements
0090-9955 Directory of Polish Officials
0090-9963 Maryland. Correctional Training Commission. Annual Report *changed to* Maryland. Police and Correctional Training Commissions. Report to the Governor, the Secretary of Public Safety and Correctional Services, and Members of the General Assembly
0090-9971 Executive Compensation Service. Reports on International Compensation. Puerto Rico
0090-998X Audio Journal Review: General Surgery
0091-0031 U.S. Center for Disease Control. Morbidity and Mortality Weekly Report
0091-004X Pediatric Conferences with Sydney Gellis†
0091-0120 Current Packaging Abstracts
0091-0155 Enzyme Technology Digest†
0091-018X Food Management
0091-0198 Grain and Farm Service Centers *changed to* Grain & Feed Journals
0091-0260 Public Personnel Management
0091-0279 Veterinary Clinics of North America *changed to* Veterinary Clinics of North America: Small Animal Practice
0091-0279 Veterinary Clinics of North America *changed to* Veterinary Clinics of North America: Large Animal Practice
0091-0287 Yale Scientific
0091-0376 Prairie Naturalist
0091-0392 Bank Protection Bulletin *changed to* Banking Insurance and Protection Bulletin
0091-0406 Nebraska State Publications Checklist
0091-0430 Lawyer-to-Lawyer Consultation Panel
0091-0449 D M G-D R S Journal: Design Research and Methods *see* 0147-1147
0091-0457 Montana. Environmental Quality Council. Annual Report
0091-0465 Annual Guide to Undergraduate Study *see* 0147-8451
0091-0473 Collectable Old Advertising
0091-0538 A P L A Quarterly Journal
0091-0546 Oregon. Public Utility Commissioner. Statistics of Electric, Gas, Steam Heat, Telephone, Telegraph and Water Companies
0091-0562 American Journal of Community Psychology
0091-0600 International Journal of Psychoanalytic Psychotherapy
0091-0627 Journal of Abnormal Child Psychology
0091-0651 Field & Stream Sportsman†
0091-0678 Maine. State Planning Office. Annual Report
0091-0716 Guide to Nebraska State Agencies
0091-0724 Poverty in South Dakota
0091-0724 Annual Causes & Conditions of Poverty in South Dakota *see* 0091-0724
0091-0732 Idaho. Department of Employment. Annual Farm Labor Report *changed to* Idaho. Department of Employment. Annual Rural Employment Report
0091-0759 Maine. State Library. Special Subject Resources in Maine
0091-0767 New York (State) Department of Labor. Division of Research and Statistics. Employment Statistics
0091-0775 Kentucky School Directory
0091-0813 Potentially Reactive Carbonate Rocks; Progress Report
0091-0848 Texas. Water Quality Board. Agency Publication†
0091-0864 American Fabrics & Fashions
0091-0899 Dairy Scope†
0091-0988 Western Economic Indicators
0091-0996 Montana. Department of Social and Rehabilitation Services. Annual Report
0091-1003 Directory. Diocesan Agencies of Catholic Charities. United States, Puerto Rico and Canada
0091-1054 Oklahoma Pontotoc County Quarterly
0091-1062 S.A.M.P.E. Journal
0091-1097 Missouri Annual Highway Safety Work Program *changed to* Missouri. Division of Highway Safety. Highway Safety Plan
0091-1186 Guidebook to North Carolina Taxes
0091-1305 FarmFutures
0091-1372 Soap/Cosmetics/Chemical Specialties
0091-1402 Statehouse Observer
0091-1410 Transportation. Current Literature
0091-1429 United States Earthquakes
0091-1488 Bachy
0091-1518 S I O: a Report on the Work and Programs of Scripps Institution of Oceanography
0091-1526 Wall Street Review of Books
0091-1550 Texas Livestock Statistics
0091-1607 A-Ki-Ki
0091-1615 Working Papers for a New Society
0091-1658 American Statistics Index
0091-1666 Chicago Dental Society Review
0091-1674 Clinical Social Work Journal
0091-1704 Current Contents/Clinical Practice
0091-1712 Environmental Education Report *see* 0199-6916
0091-1720 Public Science Newsletter†
0091-1747 Syndrome Identification†
0091-1798 Annals of Probability
0091-181X Marine Behavior and Physiology
0091-1887 Underwater Photographer
0091-1909 Journal of Urban Analysis
0091-2026 Atmospheric Technology
0091-2085 Documents to the People
0091-2093 North Dakota. Consumer Credit Division. Consolidated Annual Report of Licensees
0091-2131 Ethos
0091-2166 Hearing Aid Journal
0091-2174 International Journal of Psychiatry in Medicine
0091-2182 Journal of Nurse-Midwifery
0091-2220 Best Editorial Cartoons of the Year
0091-2263 Population and the Population Explosion: a Bibliography†
0091-2271 U. S. Army Infantry Center. History; Annual Supplement
0091-231X Missouri. Division of Mental Health. Annual Report *changed to* Missouri. Department of Mental Health. Annual Report
0091-2328 Investment Adviser Directory
0091-2360 Today's Chiropractic
0091-2379 Nursing Care *changed to* Journal of Nursing Care
0091-2387 National Spokesman
0091-2468 Transportation Research Forum. Proceedings: Annual Meeting
0091-2492 U.S. Executive Office of the President. International Economic Report of the President
0091-2573 Potomac Review
0091-2611 Corrective and Social Psychiatry and Journal of Applied Behavior Therapy *see* 0093-1551
0091-262X Iowa. Department of Job Service. Research and Statistics Division. Annual Manpower Planning Report
0091-2646 U. S. Labor-Management Services Administration. Decisions and Reports on Rulings of the Assistant Secretary of Labor for Labor-Management Relations
0091-2662 Drug Abuse Council. Public Policy†
0091-2670 Prism†
0091-2697 Manuscript
0091-2700 Journal of Clinical Pharmacology
0091-2743 Baptist Missionary Association of America. Directory and Handbook
0091-2751 Journal of Clinical Ultrasound
0091-2786 American Gas Association. Research and Development
0091-2859 Regional Institute of Social Welfare Research. Annual Report
0091-2905 Commanders' Conference Information Exchange Program. Report
0091-3057 Pharmacology, Biochemistry and Behavior
0091-3065 Review of Child Development Research
0091-3103 Medicaid Statistics: Medical Assistance (Medicaid) Financed Under Title XIX of the Social Security Act
0091-3154 Who's Who in Ecology†
0091-3219 Journal of Ethnic Studies
0091-3235 Directory of A S U Latin Americanists
0091-3235 Directory of Latin Americanists *see* 0091-3235
0091-3243 Directory of Secondary Schools with Occupational Curriculums, Public and Nonpublic *changed to* Occupational Education: Enrollments and Programs in Noncollegiate Post Secondary Schools
0091-3251 New York (State). Department of Audit and Control. Index to the Public Schools†
0091-3286 Optical Engineering
0091-3294 Films and Other Materials for Projection
0091-3367 Journal of Advertising
0091-3383 American Squaredance
0091-3391 Amateur Athletic Union of the United States. Athletic Library. Official A A U Gymnastics Handbook†
0091-3405 Amateur Athletic Union of the United States. Official Handbook of the A A U Code
0091-3413 Amateur Athletic Union of the United States. Athletic Library. Official Rules for Competitive Swimming
0091-3421 Contemporary Literary Criticism Series
0091-3448 Georgia. State Economic Opportunity Office. Annual Report
0091-3464 Georgia Labor Market Trends
0091-3464 Georgia Manpower Trends *see* 0091-3464
0091-3472 Robert Wood Johnson Foundation. Annual Report
0091-3499 Building Cost File
0091-3502 U.S. Department of Agriculture. Economics, Statistics, and Cooperatives Service. Agricultural Finance Statistics
0091-3553 U. S. Community Services Administration. Federal Outlays in Summary
0091-3588 State of Iowa Scholarships, Tuition Grants. Biennium Report *changed to* Iowa. College Aid Commission. Biennium Report
0091-3634 Deeds and Data
0091-3642 Fruit Varieties Journal
0091-3685 National Journal Reports *see* 0360-4217
0091-3707 Social Sciences Citation Index
0091-3715 Political Science Reviewer
0091-3723 Journal of Chinese Linguistics
0091-3731 Print Review
0091-3774 Motorcycle Blue Book
0091-3782 Northwest Missouri State University Studies
0091-3804 American Bankers Association. Committee on Uniform Security Identification Procedures. C U S I P Directory: Corporate Directory
0091-3839 U S P Guide to Select Drugs.
0091-3847 Physician and Sportsmedicine
0091-3855 Cost of Personal Borrowing in the United States.
0091-3901 Illustrated Digest of Baseball†
0091-3952 Advances in Neurology
0091-3960 American Journal of Acupuncture
0091-3995 S I E C U S Report

0091-4010 Guidebook to Ohio Taxes
0091-4029 Hofstra Law Review
0091-4037 International Journal of Polymeric Materials
0091-4045 Nutritional Update *changed to* Nutritional Update
0091-4061 S E C Docket
0091-407X U S /Japan Outlook†
0091-4118 Pennsylvania. Crime Commission. Report
0091-4150 International Journal of Aging & Human Development
0091-4169 Journal of Criminal Law & Criminology
0091-4185 Wisconsin Dental Association. Journal
0091-4266 History of Childhood Quarterly *see* 0145-3378
0091-4312 Washington (State). Human Resources Agencies. Annual Report
0091-4347 Lietuviu Tautos Praeitis
0091-4371 American Horseman
0091-4428 Cutter and Chariot Racing World *see* 0194-8814
0091-4452 Journal of Color and Appearance†
0091-4460 M A F E S Research Highlights
0091-4479 Association of Research Libraries. University Library Management Studies Office. Occasional Paper
0091-4487 Western Society of Weed Science. Proceedings
0091-4509 Contemporary Drug Problems
0091-4541 Illinois. Environmental Protection Agency. Water Pollution Control Plan
0091-4576 Consumer Guide Photographic Equipment Test Reports Quarterly *changed to* Consumer Guide Photo Annual
0091-4630 U.S. Office of Minority Business Enterprise. Minority Enterprise Progress Report
0091-4655 Lawn & Garden Marketing
0091-4673 Texas Small Grains Statistics
0091-469X I E E E Symposium on Computer Software Reliability. Record *changed to* International Conference on Reliable Software.(Proceedings)
0091-4711 Louisiana Labor Market
0091-4738 C V P
0091-4789 Colorado County and City Retail Sales by Standard Industrial Classification
0091-4800 Worldwide Projects
0091-4843 Milling & Baking News
0091-4916 Journal of Nuclear Medicine Technology
0091-4924 Flannery O'Connor Bulletin
0091-4932 U.S. Federal Housing Administration. F H A Homes
0091-4967 Washington (State). Transportation Agencies. Annual Report
0091-4975 Corporate Reports on File†
0091-5041 Geological Society of America. Memorials
0091-5114 Pennsylvania State Plan for the Administration of Vocational-Technical Education Programs
0091-5122 American Association of State Highway and Transportation Officials. Sub-Committee on Computer Technology. Proceedings. National Conference
0091-519X Criminal Justice News†
0091-5203 Gravure Environmental and O S H A Newsletter
0091-522X Envios
0091-5246 Select Data on Students, Alabama Institutions of Higher Learning
0091-5254 Wisconsin Population Projections
0091-5270 C A L L
0091-5300 Veterinary Toxicology *changed to* Veterinary and Human Toxicology
0091-5319 C I S Annual
0091-536X Conservation Foundation Letter
0091-5440 University of Baltimore Law Review
0091-5459 Union Labor Report
0091-5491 American Marine Register
0091-5513 West Virginia Coal Facts
0091-5521 Community College Review
0091-553X A D & D; Tax Interpretations†
0091-5564 Delaware Reporter
0091-5580 Review of Special Education
0091-5599 Survey of Salaries and Employee Benefits of Private and Public Employers in Arizona. *changed to* Joint Governmental Salary Survey : Arizona
0091-5610 American Universities Field Staff. Population: Perspective
0091-5629 Illinois. Governor's Office of Human Resources. Annual Report†
0091-5637 Journal of South Asian Literature
0091-5645 Coda
0091-5653 Monthly Checklist of Kentucky State Publications
0091-5661 Personal Income Tax in Oregon†
0091-5688 Access (Washington)
0091-5696 Quality of Life in Iowa
0091-5793 Motorcycle Facts
0091-5823 Colorado. Department of Social Services. Research and Statistics Section. Research Report AFDC†
0091-584X University of Alaska. State Wide Bulletin†
0091-5858 Multi Media Reviews Index *see* 0363-7778
0091-5882 Idaho. State Board for Vocational Education. Annual Descriptive Report of Program Activities for Vocational Education
0091-5939 Housing and Development Reporter
0091-6056 U. S. Federal Highway Administration. Motor Vehicle Registrations by Standard Metropolitan Statistical Areas
0091-6080 Wisconsin. Department of Transportaion. Traffic Planning Section. Automatic Recorder Station Traffic Data
0091-6099 Illinois. Department of Public Aid. Annual Report
0091-6102 West Virginia Research League. Statistical Handbook
0091-6129 Pennsylvania Manufacturing Exporters *see* 0360-8859
0091-6137 Magazine of New York Business *changed to* Manhattan Business
0091-6145 Progress in Extractive Metallurgy
0091-6188 Delaware. Department of Public Instruction. Educational Personnel Directory
0091-6196 West Virginia's State System of Higher Education; Annual Report, Current Operating Revenues and Expenditures
0091-620X Saturday Review
0091-6234 U. S. General Accounting Office. Social Development Activities in Latin America Promoted by the Inter-American Foundation: Report to the Congress by the Comptroller General of the United States†
0091-6242 U.S. General Services Administration. Management Report
0091-6269 A O A Newsbriefs†
0091-6277 Surgical Team
0091-6293 Hoover Institution on War, Revolution, and Peace. Report
0091-6315 Mental Retardation and Developmental Disabilities
0091-6323 Soul Journey†
0091-6331 Exercise and Sport Sciences Reviews
0091-634X American Academy of Psychiatry and the Law. Bulletin
0091-6358 Astronomy
0091-6390 Northwestern and Mississippi Valley Lumberman *see* 0092-0681
0091-6439 Midwest Genealogical Society. Surname Index *changed to* Midwest Historical and Genealogical Society. Quarterly
0091-6455 Trails and Tales
0091-6471 Journal of Psychology and Theology
0091-6501 California Mosquito Control Association. Proceedings and Papers of the Annual Meeting *changed to* California Mosquito and Vector Control Association. Proceedings and Papers of the Annual Meeting
0091-6528 Society for Neuroscience. Annual Meeting. Conference Report
0091-6536 C R C Critical Reviews in Clinical Radiology and Nuclear Medicine *see* 0147-6750
0091-6544 Family Therapy
0091-6595 Annual Review of Behavior Therapy Theory & Practice
0091-6617 Fiber Producers Buyers Guide *see* 0361-4921
0091-6633 Missouri State Government Publications
0091-6641 Studio Potter
0091-6676 Irvine Humanities Review†
0091-6684 Navajo Historical Publications. Biographical Series
0091-6706 Wood - Woods Family Magazine
0091-6722 Radiation Data and Reports†
0091-6730 Nebraska Medical Journal
0091-6749 Journal of Allergy and Clinical Immunology
0091-6765 E H P
0091-6773 Behavioral Biology *changed to* Behavioral and Neural Biology
0091-679X Methods in Cell Biology
0091-6811 Research Futures†
0091-6846 Strategic Review
0091-6854 Spectrum One: Stock Holdings Survey
0091-6862 Spectrum Two: Investment Company Portfolios
0091-6900 Kansas Agriculture Report *changed to* Kansas. State Board of Agriculture. Annual Report with Farm Facts
0091-6919 U. S. Department of Defense. Defense Department Report
0091-6935 Who's Who in National High School Football
0091-6943 Vintage Airplane
0091-6978 New Jersey Airport Directory
0091-7036 International Journal of Computer and Information Sciences
0091-7052 Guide to Graduate Departments of Sociology
0091-7168 Eastern Association of Student Financial Aid Administrators. Directory
0091-7176 Ancient Times
0091-7192 Statistics on Social Work Education in the United States
0091-7206 E D P Performance Review
0091-7214 Mathematics International
0091-7222 National Gallery of Art. Annual Report
0091-7257 Vertex (Los Angeles)†
0091-7265 Washington (State). Department of Social and Health Services. Jail Inspection Report†
0091-7281 Learning Today
0091-729X Admission Requirements of U.S. and Canadian Dental Schools
0091-7311 Washington Report on Long Term Care *changed to* Long Term Care
0091-732X Review of Research in Education
0091-7338 Studies in the History of Art
0091-7346 Index to Literature on the American Indian
0091-7354 U.S. Department of Transportation. Office of Policy Review. Working Paper†
0091-7370 Annals of Clinical and Laboratory Science
0091-7389 American Psychopathological Association. Proceedings of the Annual Meeting
0091-7397 Current Topics in Experimental Endocrinology
0091-7419 Journal of Supramolecular Structure
0091-7427 American Medical Women's Association. Journal
0091-7435 Preventive Medicine
0091-7443 Association for Research in Nervous and Mental Disease. Research Publications
0091-7451 Cold Spring Harbor Laboratory. Symposia on Quantitative Biology
0091-746X Institute of Medicine of Chicago. Proceedings
0091-7516 Quarter Racing Record
0091-7605 Food Purity Perspectives
0091-7613 Geology
0091-763X Professional Communications: Libraries
0091-7648 Wildlife Society Bulletin
0091-7664 Whiskey, Women, And...†
0091-7699 Instrument Society of America. I S A Final Control Elements Symposium. Final Control Elements; Proceedings
0091-7710 Journal of Anthropological Research
0091-7729 Science-Fiction Studies
0091-7737 Technical Association of the Pulp and Paper Industry. Directory
0091-780X Colorado. Department of Social Services. Research and Statistics Section. Research Report W P M†
0091-7818 Colorado. Department of Social Services. Research and Statistics Section. Research Report W I N†
0091-7842 Colorado. Department of Social Services. Research and Statistics Section. Research Report A D M†
0091-7885 Technology Book Guide *see* 0360-2761
0091-7907 Conference Publications Guide *see* 0360-2729
0091-7915 Government Publications Guide *see* 0360-2796
0091-7958 University of Kansas. Museum of Natural History. Occasional Papers.
0091-8059 Headlights
0091-8075 Statistical Profile of the U.S. Exchange Program
0091-8083 Studies in American Fiction
0091-8105 Food Fish Market Review and Outlook
0091-8113 University of California, Berkeley. Serials Key Word Index *see* 0363-7026
0091-8121 Honolulu. Mayor's Committee on the Status of Women. Annual Report
0091-8164 Medicaid Statistics
0091-8180 Colorado. Department of Social Services. Research and Statistics Section. Report A D C†
0091-8245 Guidelines for Improving Practice. Architects and Engineers Professional Liability
0091-8253 Washington (State) Legislature. Pictorial Directory
0091-8261 U.S. Bureau of Labor Statistics. Employee Compensation in the Private Nonfarm Economy
0091-8296 Missiology
0091-830X Best's Recommended Independent Insurance Adjusters
0091-8369 Journal of Homosexuality
0091-8377 Industrial Machinery and Equipment Pricing Guide
0091-8385 Techniques of Marriage and Family Counseling†
0091-8393 U S Medical Directory
0091-8415 Fixed Income Investor
0091-844X Nebraska. Department of Roads. Traffic Analysis Unit. Continuous Traffic Count Data and Traffic Characteristics on Nebraska Streets and Highways
0091-8482 Workshop for Child Care Staff of Florida's Child Caring Facilities. Report
0091-8512 U.S. National Oceanic and Atmospheric Administration. National Climatic Center. Marine Climatological Summaries
0091-861X Cooking for Profit
0091-8644 U.S. Department of Transportation. Climatic Impact Assessment Program Office. Technical Abstract Report†
0091-8660 Ebony Jr
0091-8695 Report on Federal Funds Received in Iowa
0091-8725 U. S. National Weather Service. Data Acquisition Division. Marine Surface Observations

ISSN	Title
0091-8784	Oregon Education Biennial Report†
0091-8792	Arizona. State Advisory Council for Vocational Education. Annual Report
0091-8806	Cincinnati. Division of Police. Annual Report
0091-8822	Motor Sport Yearbook†
0091-8830	Southwest Art Magazine see 0192-4214
0091-8857	Watauga Association of Genealogists. Bulletin
0091-8873	Alaska State Chamber of Commerce. Membership Directory†
0091-8938	Student Enrollment Report; West Virginia Institutions of Higher Education
0091-8954	National Safety Council. Product Safety UP TO Date
0091-8962	Iowa. Department of Public Instruction. Summary of Federal Programs
0091-8970	Indiana. State Advisory Council for Vocational Technical Education. Annual Report
0091-8989	Educational Testing Service Annual Report
0091-9004	North Dakota. Geological Survey. Educational Series
0091-9020	Washington Folk Strums
0091-9039	U. S. Department of Commerce. Publications; a Catalog and Index
0091-9047	Michigan Business and Economic Research Bibliography
0091-908X	K-Bar-T Country Roundup changed to Country Music Roundup
0091-9101	Election Laws of Hawaii
0091-9128	Nebraska. Commission on Law Enforcement and Criminal Justice. Criminal Justice Comprehensive Plan†
0091-9144	Centrum
0091-9152	Chain Store Guide Directory: Food Service Distributors
0091-9187	New Jersey. Office of Demographic and Economic Analysis. Population Estimates for New Jersey
0091-9195	Nebraska. Commission on Law Enforcement and Criminal Justice. Criminal Justice Action Plan†
0091-9209	Current Governments Reports: City Employment
0091-9225	Air Defense Magazine
0091-9225	Air Defense Trends see 0091-9225
0091-9233	Puerto Rico. Department of Labor. Bureau of Labor Statistics. Employment Hours and Earnings in the Manufacturing Establishments Promoted by the Economic Development Administration of the Puerto Rican Industrial Development Company
0091-9268	Johns Hopkins University. Population Information Program. Population Report. Series C. Sterilization (Female)
0091-9276	Johns Hopkins University. Population Information Program. Population Report. Series G. Prostaglandins
0091-9284	Johns Hopkins University. Population Information Program. Population Report. Series F. Pregnancy Termination
0091-9357	American Book Prices Current
0091-9381	American Baptist Churches in the U.S.A. Directory
0091-9403	U.S. Bureau of Labor Statistics. Employment and Wages.
0091-942X	Nebraska. Office of Athletic Commissioner. Report
0091-9446	North Dakota. Milk Stabilization Board. Annual Report of Administrative Activities
0091-9489	Lawrence Berkeley Laboratory. Research Highlights
0091-9500	U. S. National Oceanographic Data Center. Key to Oceanographic Records Documentation
0091-9519	Electronic Industries Association. Trade Directory and Membership List
0091-9527	Catholic Schools in the United States see 0147-8044
0091-9535	Alaska. Office of the Governor. Governor's Manpower Plan
0091-956X	Report from N J D A†
0091-9586	Kansas Country Living
0091-9632	Guide to Graduate Study in Political Science.
0091-9640	Currituck County Historical Society. Journal
0091-9659	Northwest Journal of African and Black American Studies†
0091-9675	Semiconductor Diode D.A.T.A. Book changed to Diode D. A. T. A. Book
0091-9683	To the World's Oboists changed to International Double Reed Society (Publication)
0091-9691	Utah Bar Journal
0091-9748	U. S. Advisory Council on Historic Preservation. Newsletter see 0098-4035
0091-9756	Metropolitan Atlanta Business Directory changed to Terminus Business Directory
0091-9764	Huntsville Association of Folk Musicians. Newsletter
0091-9772	Journal of Primal Therapy changed to Primal Institute Newsletter
0091-9780	Art Dealer & Framer changed to Art Business News
0091-9802	Kansas. State Department of Education. Administration and Finance Division. Annual Statistical Report
0091-9837	Environmental Defense Fund. Annual Report
0091-9845	Hawaii Observer†
0091-9918	Conference Board. Monthly Business Review see 0362-5435
0091-9942	Florida. Governor. Annual Report on State Housing Goals
0091-9977	Street and Smith's Official Yearbook: College Football
0091-9993	No-Till Farmer
0092-0002	International Decade of Ocean Exploration. Progress Report†
0092-0037	Ag Chem & Commercial Fertilizer see 0092-0053
0092-0053	Farm Chemicals
0092-0150	Modern Pharmacology see 0098-6925
0092-0177	Florida. Division of Motor Vehicles. Tags and Revenue
0092-0193	Ion Exchange and Solvent Extraction
0092-0258	Stanford Review†
0092-0290	University of California, Berkeley. Office of Institutional Research . Campus Statistics.
0092-0320	U.S. Coast Guard. Polluting Incidents in and Around U.S. Waters
0092-0371	A. A. M. C. Curriculum Directory
0092-038X	Current Business Reports: Monthly Selected Services Receipts
0092-0436	Disc and That
0092-0444	Apartment Life changed to Metropolitan Home
0092-0479	Powder Coating Conference
0092-0487	Faxon Librarians' Guide to Periodicals see 0146-2660
0092-0495	Carpet and Rug Institute. Review--State of the Industry changed to Carpet and Rug Institute. Industry Review
0092-0509	Powder Diffraction File Search Manual. Alphabetical Listing. Inorganic
0092-0517	Journal of Country Music
0092-0525	Jazz Digest
0092-0525	Jazznytt
0092-0541	Solid Waste Management: Abstracts from the Literature
0092-055X	Teaching Sociology
0092-0576	Powder Diffraction File Search Manual. Organic
0092-0592	Grapevine (Saratoga)
0092-0606	Journal of Biological Physics.
0092-0614	Directory of Louisiana Cities, Towns and Villages
0092-0622	Aqueduct
0092-0673	Louisiana Annual Rural Manpower Report†
0092-0681	Northwestern Lumberman
0092-0703	Academy of Marketing Science. Journal
0092-0711	A.D. United Church Herald Edition changed to United Church of Christ A.D.
0092-072X	Christian Association for Psychological Studies. Proceedings see 0147-7978
0092-0754	Science Research Abstracts Journal, Part B: Laser and Electro-Optic Reviews; Quantum Electronics; Unconventional Energy Sources
0092-0789	Devil's Box
0092-0908	World Directory of Environmental Organizations
0092-0959	Baldwin's Ohio Legislative Service
0092-0983	Folklore Newsletter
0092-1009	Air Pollution Effects Surveillance Network Data Report changed to Air Quality Data for Arizona.
0092-1025	Outstanding Secondary Educators of America†
0092-1033	Minnesota. Department of Corrections. Research, Information and Data Systems Unit. Characteristics of Populations Under Supervision of the Institutions and Field Services. changed to Minnesota. Department. of Corrections. Characteristics on Institutional Populations
0092-105X	Soviet Aerospace
0092-1068	American Hunter
0092-1084	Nevada. Commission on Crime, Delinquency and Corrections. Comprehensive Law Enforcement Plan
0092-1122	Battelle Memorial Institute. Research Outlook see 0145-8477
0092-1149	Monograph Abstracts changed to Research Abstracts
0092-1157	Journal of Biological Standardization
0092-1270	Virgin Islands Register
0092-1297	Commercial Directory of Puerto Rico-Virgin Islands changed to Commercial Buyer's Guide Puerto Rico-Virgin Islands
0092-1300	Powder Diffraction File Search Manual. Fink Method. Inorganic
0092-1319	Powder Diffraction File Search Manual. Hanawalt Method. Inorganic
0092-1327	American Art Review
0092-1335	Annual Reports in Inorganic and General Syntheses
0092-1343	California Enviromental Yearbook & Directory see 0148-0324
0092-1432	Employment Relations Abstracts: Subject Heading List
0092-1459	New Jersey Covered Employment Trends by Geographical Areas of the State
0092-1483	Directory-Hardware and Home Improvement Center Chains, Auto Supply Chains see 0094-8667
0092-1505	Nebraska. Commission on Law Enforcement and Criminal Justice. Legislative Reporter†
0092-153X	Texas Field Crop Statistics
0092-1548	Brookhaven Highlights
0092-1602	New Jersey. Division of Water Resources. Special Report
0092-1645	U.S. Federal Railroad Administration. Office of Safety. Accident Bulletin see 0163-4674
0092-1661	Symposium on Incremental Motion Control Systems and Devices. Proceedings
0092-1696	Nebraska. Fisheries Production Division. Annual Report
0092-1726	North Carolina. Secretary of State. North Carolina Elections
0092-1734	New Fishing
0092-1777	Hawaii. Department of Education. Educational Directory: State & District Office
0092-1785	U. S. Agricultural Research Service. A R S-N C
0092-1793	Fremontia
0092-1807	Journal of Spanish Studies: Twentieth Century
0092-1815	International Journal of Instructional Media
0092-1858	Alaska Blue Book
0092-1866	Intercultural Studies Information Service
0092-1874	Directory of Registered Federal and State Lobbyists see 0146-0323
0092-1904	United States Government Manual (1973)
0092-1912	Fiction International
0092-1920	Incentive Travel Manager
0092-1939	U. S. Agricultural Research Service. A R S-S
0092-198X	South Dakota. Department of History. Report and Historical Collections see 0081-2773
0092-2013	Teaching Political Science
0092-2056	U. S. Office of Federal Coordinator for Meteorological Services and Supporting Research. National Hurricane Operations Plan
0092-2102	Interfaces
0092-2145	California and Western States Grape Grower
0092-2242	University of California, Los Angeles. Latin American Center. Latin American Activities and Resources†
0092-2293	Verdict Reports
0092-2307	H I S S Titles and Review
0092-2315	American Journal of Criminal Law
0092-2323	Journal of Indo-European Studies
0092-2358	Tri-State Regional Planning Commission. Annual Regional Report changed to Tri-State Regional Planning Commission. Annual Regional Report
0092-2374	Utah Export Directory
0092-2382	Journal of World Education changed to Association for World Education. Journal
0092-2463	New Times (New York)†
0092-2471	Chicagoan†
0092-2498	Criminal Justice (Chicago)
0092-2528	Oklahoma Water Resources Research Institute. Annual Report
0092-2633	National Peach Council. Proceedings
0092-2684	Colorado Water Resources Circulars
0092-2765	U. S. Postal Service. Support Group. Revenue and Cost Analysis
0092-2803	Rand Report Series
0092-2803	Rand Paper Series see 0092-2803
0092-2811	American Coin-Op
0092-282X	Pickup, Van & 4WD
0092-2838	Music, Books on Music and Sound Recordings
0092-2870	Air Freight Directory
0092-2889	Arkansas Average Covered Employment and Earnings by County and Industry
0092-2900	Perspectives in Nephrology and Hypertension
0092-2935	National Roster of Black Elected Officials
0092-2986	Midwest History of Education Society. Journal
0092-3052	Homosexual Counseling Journal†
0092-3060	Oregon. Office of Community Health Services. Local Health Services Annual Summary
0092-3079	New Jersey. Violent Crimes Compensation Board. Annual Report†
0092-3117	U. S. Department of Transportation. Fiscal Year Budget in Brief
0092-3206	U. S. Bureau of East-West Trade. Office of Export Administration. Export Administration Report see 0198-6570
0092-3214	Street and Smith's Official Yearbook: Pro Football
0092-3257	Directory of Facilities for the Learning Disabled see 0093-7703

0092-3281 Illinois Air Sampling Network Report *changed to* Illinois. Division of Air Pollution Control. Annual Air Quality Report
0092-3311 New Jersey. Department of Environmental Protection. Annual Report
0092-332X U. S. Geological Survey. Water Resources Investigations
0092-3362 Massachusetts. Division of Mineral Resources. Annual Report†
0092-3389 U.S. Federal Highway Administration. Highway Transportation Research and Development Studies
0092-3419 Native American Rights Fund. Catalogue *changed to* National Indian Law Library. Catalogue
0092-3427 Tennessee Thrusts†
0092-3435 Occupational Safety and Health Decisions
0092-346X N A S A Report to Educators
0092-3478 American Baptist Churches in the U. S. A. Yearbook
0092-3486 Annual Index to Popular Music Record Reviews
0092-3524 Iustitia (Bloomington)†
0092-3540 Texscope; U S A Textile Industry Overview
0092-3559 Texas Southern University Law Review
0092-3583 Washington (State). Department of Motor Vehicles. Research and Technology. Research Report
0092-3591 Overview of the F A A Engineering & Development Programs
0092-3745 Texas. State Board of Landscape Architects. Annual Roster
0092-3761 Data on Iowa's Area Schools
0092-380X Washington State†
0092-3826 Alcoholism Treatment Facilities Directory: United States and Canada†
0092-3850 Woman's Day Gifts You Can Make for Christmas
0092-3877 Bar†
0092-394X Newsletter for Research in Mental Health & Behavioral Sciences†
0092-394X U.S. Veterans Administration. Newsletter for Research in Mental Health and Behavioral Sciences
0092-3974 International Directory of Little Magazines and Small Presses
0092-4032 Medical Challenge†
0092-4067 Directory of Missouri Libraries
0092-4075 U. S. General Accounting Office. Financial Status of Selected Major Weapon Systems, Department of Defense
0092-4091 Present Tense
0092-4113 W.P.A.S.Museletter
0092-4164 Where the Trails Cross
0092-4180 Better Homes and Gardens Crafts & Sewing†
0092-4199 Day Care and Early Education
0092-4202 Directory of Private Trade, Technical and Art Schools
0092-4210 Investment Statistics: Capital Investment Conditions *see* 0361-4239
0092-4229 Speed†
0092-4245 Wesleyan Theological Journal
0092-4253 California Job Development Corporation Law Executive Board. Annual Report *changed to* California Job Creation Program Board. Annual Report
0092-4261 Woodrow Wilson International Center for Scholars. Annual Report
0092-427X Arctic Bulletin†
0092-4288 University of Nevada. Seismological Laboratory. Bulletin
0092-430X Pepperdine Law Review
0092-4318 Platte Valley Review
0092-4326 American Society for Engineering Education. Review and Directory *changed to* A S E E Profile
0092-4334 B I S Conference Report
0092-4407 Managers†
0092-444X Intercom (Washington)
0092-4466 Hearing Instruments
0092-4539 Youth Correctional Institution, Bordentown, N.J. Annual Report
0092-4555 Federal Aviation Administration. National Aviation System Policy Summary *changed to* U.S. Federal Aviation Administration. National Aviation System: Challenges of the Decade Ahead
0092-4563 Syntax and Semantics
0092-4571 Border States
0092-4598 Who's Who in Training and Development
0092-4601 N.A.D.A. Recreation Vehicle Appraisal Guide
0092-461X Facts About Maryland Public Education
0092-4652 Criminal Justice Plan for New Jersey
0092-4679 National Security Traders Association. Traders' Annual
0092-4695 Soviet Business & Trade
0092-4725 Browning Institute Studies
0092-4733 Michigan State University. Institute for Community Development and Services. Population Report. Community Development Series†
0092-4768 American Institute of Certified Public Accountants. Committee on Minority Recruitment and Equal Opportunity. Report†
0092-4857 M E I Marketing Economics Guide
0092-4865 R E I T Handbook of Member Trusts†
0092-489X Artes Visuales
0092-4954 Credit Union Directory and Buyers' Guide
0092-4962 Classified Index of National Labor Relations Board Decisions and Related Court Decisions *changed to* Classified Index of N.L.R.B. and Related Court Decisions
0092-4970 Directory of Electric Light and Power Companies
0092-4989 International Directory of Executive Recruiters
0092-5039 Franklin Mint Almanac
0092-5055 Annual of Psychoanalysis
0092-5071 Colorado Business
0092-508X D.A.T.A. Book of Discontinued Thyristors
0092-511X Street and Smith's College & pro Official Basketball Yearbook *see* 0149-7103
0092-5144 Vermont Facts and Figures
0092-5187 N E M A Bulletin
0092-5268 Grants and Awards Available to American Writers
0092-5306 Best of National Lampoon
0092-5322 Fusilier (La Puente)†
0092-5349 Michigan. State Library Services. Catalog of Books on Magnetic Tape
0092-542X Safety Science Abstracts *see* 0160-1342
0092-5438 Youth Reporter†
0092-5454 Countrywide Annual Year Book
0092-5462 Data Resources Review *see* 0197-6966
0092-5470 Developments in Human Services Series
0092-5489 National Directory of College Athletics (Women)
0092-5489 National Directory of Women's Athletics *see* 0092-5489
0092-5497 Paper Conservation News
0092-5519 American Folklife
0092-5535 Panjandrum Poetry Journal
0092-5543 Washington (State). Vocational Rehabilitation Services Division. State Facilities Plan *changed to* Washington (State). Vocational Rehabilitation Services Division. State Facilities Development Plan
0092-5594 U.S. Center for Disease Control. Congenital Malformations Surveillance
0092-5632 American Journal of Roentgenology and Radium Therapy *see* 0361-803X
0092-5659 American Lung Association. Bulletin
0092-5667 Healthnews†
0092-5675 Academy Awards Oscar Annual
0092-5691 National Education Association of the United States. Annual Summative Evaluation Report
0092-5756 Bibliography of Noise
0092-5764 Connecticut Walk Book
0092-5799 O.S.H.A. Compliance Letter
0092-5810 Vermont's Fisheries Annual†
0092-5845 Food Service Marketing
0092-5853 American Journal of Political Science.
0092-5896 U.S. Department of Agriculture. Bimonthly List of Publications and Visuals
0092-590X American History and Culture†
0092-5934 Attorneys and Agents Registered to Practice Before the U.S. Patent Office *see* 0361-3844
0092-5950 N M R I Compensation in Mass Retailing, Salaries and Incentives
0092-5969 Popular Sports Face-off†
0092-6000 Current Literature in Family Planning
0092-6019 Immunology: an International Series of Monographs and Treatises
0092-606X Degrees Conferred by West Virginia Institutions of Higher Education
0092-6086 Inter Alia
0092-6108 Title Varies†
0092-6132 Directory of the Mutual Savings Banks of the United States
0092-6175 Transportation and Products Legal Directory
0092-6213 Circulatory Shock
0092-6221 High School Behavioral Science†
0092-623X Journal of Sex & Marital Therapy
0092-6248 Lawrence Berkeley Laboratory. Inorganic Materials Research Division. Annual Report *changed to* Lawrence Berkeley Laboratory. Materials and Molecular Research Division. Annual Report
0092-6256 Aurora AFX Road Racing Handbook
0092-6280 Association for Educational Data Systems. Handbook and Directory
0092-6299 Iowa. Bureau of Labor. Occupational Injuries and Illnesses Survey
0092-6302 Semiconductor Heat Sink, Socket & Associated Hardware D.A.T.A. Book
0092-6345 Iowa State Journal of Research
0092-6361 Current Contents/Social & Behavioral Sciences
0092-640X Atomic Data and Nuclear Data Tables
0092-6442 Nebraska. Natural Resources Commission. State Water Plan Publication (Lincoln)
0092-6485 American Medical Technologists. Offical Journal *see* 0002-9963
0092-6507 Auerbach Annual: Best Computer Papers†
0092-6531 Federal Estate and Gift Taxes Explained, Including Estate Planning
0092-654X Illustrated Digest of Pro Football†
0092-6558 Interdenominational Theological Center, Atlanta. Journal
0092-6566 Journal of Research in Personality
0092-6639 Women's Organizations & Leaders Directory
0092-6647 Foreign Newspaper and Gazette Report *see* 0190-9819
0092-6655 Personal Income Tax Analysis
0092-6698 New Writers (New York) *changed to* New Writing and Writers
0092-6736 Alaska. Department of Revenue. State Investment Portfolio
0092-6841 Nevada. Office of Legislative Auditor. Biennial Report
0092-6841 Nevada. Office of Fiscal Analyst. Annual Report *see* 0092-6841
0092-6868 Aspen Leaves *see* 0362-9554
0092-6876 Automatic Taxfinder and Tax Preparer's Handbook
0092-6884 Daily Tax Report
0092-6930 Cajal Club. Proceedings
0092-7082 Sports Afield Almanac *see* 0190-1249
0092-7120 Sierra Sourcebook: Electronics Industry Market Data
0092-7147 Daily Bread
0092-718X Letters & Papers on the Social Sciences: an Undergraduate Review
0092-7201 Linear Integrated Circuits and M.O.S. Devices†
0092-721X R C A Corporation. Solid State Division. R. F. Power Devices†
0092-7228 Thyristors, Rectifiers, and Diacs†
0092-7287 U.S. National Center for Health Statistics. Current Listing and Topical Index to the Vital and Health Statistics Series
0092-735X Continuing Education for the Family Physician
0092-7368 Early Childhood Development in Texas
0092-7384 I A B C News
0092-7384 I A B C Journal *see* 0092-7384
0092-7392 Index to the Contemporary Scene†
0092-7449 Direction
0092-7473 Tennis Trade *changed to* Tennis/ Racquet Trade
0092-7481 Urban Institute. Annual Report
0092-749X Walker's Manual of Western Corporations
0092-7643 Overseas Development Council. Annual Report
0092-7651 Archives of Podiatric Medicine and Foot Surgery†
0092-7678 Asian Affairs: an American Review
0092-7686 Booklegger
0092-7694 Cason Quarterly
0092-7708 Conch Review of Books
0092-7724 Past and Likely Future of 58 Research Libraries, 1951-1980: a Statistical Study of Growth and Change†
0092-7732 Product Safety & Liability Reporter
0092-7759 Social and Rehabilitation Record *changed to* U.S. Health Care Financing Administration Record
0092-7767 Predicasts. Source Directory
0092-7783 Illinois Community College Board. Biennial Report
0092-7783 Illinois. Junior College Board. Annual Report *see* 0092-7783
0092-7813 Children's Hospital National Medical Center. Clinical Proceedings
0092-7856 Architecture Schools in North America
0092-7864 Commodity Journal
0092-7872 Communications in Algebra
0092-7899 Mississippi Educational Directory *see* 0363-874X
0092-7929 Annual of New Art and Artists†
0092-7937 Pennsylvania. Citizens Advisory Council to the Department of Environmental Resources. Annual Report
0092-7945 Missouri River Basin Commission. Annual Report
0092-7953 Genealogical Society of Old Tryon County. Bulletin
0092-7961 Better Homes and Gardens Furnishings and Decorating Ideas
0092-797X Keeping up with Orff-Schulwerk in the Classroom
0092-7996 Texas Yearbook
0092-8003 S.O.S. Directory
0092-8089 Adsorption and Adsorbents
0092-8119 Best Science Fiction Stories of the Year
0092-8208 Children's Literature (New Haven)
0092-8216 Cord Sportfacts: Hunting
0092-8240 Bulletin of Mathematical Biology
0092-8313 Prairie Scout
0092-833X Libraries of Maine; Directory and Statistics
0092-8364 District of Columbia. City Council. Annual Report
0092-8372 Disciple (St. Louis)
0092-8380 Encyclopedia of Governmental Advisory Organizations
0092-8410 N. A. C. D. S. Lilly Digest
0092-8429 U.S. Library of Congress. Processing Department. Newsletter
0092-8437 Physics

0092-847X University of Wisconsin, Madison. Institute for Research on Poverty. Research Report
0092-8488 State Planning Issues
0092-8518 Directory: Who's Who in Nuclear Energy
0092-8526 Directory Listing Curriculums Offered in the Community Colleges of Pennsylvania
0092-8550 U.S. General Accounting Office. Office of the General Counsel. Quarterly Digest of Unpublished Decisions of the Comptroller General of the United States; Procurement Law†
0092-8615 Drug Information Journal
0092-8623 Journal of Mental Health Administration
0092-8631 St. Luke's Hospital. Medical Staff Journal
0092-8658 A.P.S.A. Directory of Department Chairpersons
0092-8658 A.P.S.A. Directory of Department Chairmen *see* 0092-8658
0092-8666 Bell Tower
0092-8674 Cell
0092-8704 Jacksonville Genealogical Society. Magazine. *see* 0149-6867
0092-8763 Sweet's System for the Industrial Construction & Renovation Market
0092-8763 Sweet's Plant Engineering Extension Industrial Construction and Renovation File *see* 0092-8763
0092-881X College Football Modern Record Book *changed to* N.C.A.A. Football Records
0092-8828 P B X Systems Guide
0092-8836 Reference Data on Socioeconomic Issues of Health
0092-8887 Creative Guitar International†
0092-8917 U. S. National Oceanic and Atmospheric Administration. Manned Undersea Science and Technology Program; Report
0092-8933 Police and Law Enforcement
0092-8941 Puerto Rico Highway Improvement Program
0092-9018 Inspiration Three
0092-914X American Real Estate and Urban Economics Association. Journal
0092-9158 California. Department of Water Resources. Inventory of Waste Water Production and Waste Water Reclamation Practices in California
0092-9166 Creation Research Society Quarterly
0092-9174 Directory of San Francisco Attorneys
0092-9190 Hawaii. State Commission on the Status of Women. Annual Report
0092-9212 Michigan State Employees' Retirement System Financial and Statistical Report
0092-9301 Memory and Learning - Neural Correlates in Animals *changed to* Memory and Learning - Research in the Nervous System
0092-9336 Osteopathic Annals
0092-9344 Johns Hopkins University. Population Information Program. Population Report. Series B. Intrauterine Devices
0092-9395 G P S A Journal
0092-9425 Schist†
0092-9433 U.S. Environmental Protection Agency. Clean Water; Report to Congress
0092-9441 Urban Telecommunications Forum†
0092-945X C & P Warrant Analysis
0092-9468 U. S. National Cancer Program. Report of the National Cancer Advisory Board Submitted to the President of the United States for Transmittal to the Congress of the United States
0092-9506 Fielding's Selected Favorites: Hotels and Inns, Europe *see* 0191-0329
0092-9522 Abortion Bibliography
0092-9530 U.S. Department of Agriculture. Economics, Statistics and Cooperatives Service. Cost of Storing and Handling Cotton at Public Storage Facilities
0092-9549 Oswego County Historical Society. Journal
0092-9565 Current Geological and Geophysical Studies in Montana
0092-9638 Utah. Forestry and Fire Control. R C and D Release†
0092-9654 U.S. Forest Service. General Technical Report INT
0092-9670 National Air Monitoring Program Air Quality and Emissions Trends. Report *changed to* National Air Quality Emissions Trends. Report
0092-9689 U. S. Environmental Protection Agency. Upgrading Metal-Finishing Facilities to Reduce Pollution
0092-9727 Popular Periodical Index
0092-9751 Nuclear Industry Status
0092-9778 National Issues Outlook *see* 0360-4217
0092-9794 Massachusetts Agricultural Statistics
0092-9824 F A S Public Interest Report
0092-9832 Bergen County Dental Society. Journal
0092-9867 Toxicological and Environmental Chemistry Reviews
0092-9913 Oregon. Motor Vehicles Division. Oregon Motorcycle Accidents
0092-993X Nuclear Fuel Status and Forecast
0092-9948 Nuclear Powerplant Performance
0092-9980 Oklahoma. Aeronautics Commission. Annual Report
0093-0040 Utah. State Board of Education. Opinions of the Utah State Superintendent of Public Instruction
0093-0075 Food Technology Review
0093-0083 Clemson University. Department of Forestry. Forestry Bulletin
0093-0164 Lyons Teacher-News
0093-0245 Business Radio/Action
0093-0253 Computational Musicology Newsletter
0093-0261 Energy Users Report
0093-0288 1810 Overture
0093-0296 R C A Corporation. Solid State Division. Power Transistors and Power Hybrid Circuits†
0093-0334 Hastings Center Report
0093-0393 National Library of Medicine. Programs and Services
0093-0407 Sleep Research
0093-0415 Western Journal of Medicine
0093-0431 Children's Literary Almanac
0093-044X Crime Prevention Review†
0093-0458 Dimensions (Washington)
0093-0466 Highway Loss Data Institute. Automobile Insurance Losses Collision Coverages Variations by Make and Series
0093-0482 Meetings & Expositions†
0093-0490 Radio Free Jazz
0093-0512 Energy Pipelines and Systems *changed to* Chilton's Oil & Gas Energy
0093-0520 Maryland. State Department of Legislative Reference. Synopsis of Laws Enacted by the State of Maryland
0093-0539 Summary of Ground Water Data for Tennessee
0093-0563 U.S. Library of Congress. Library of Congress Name Headings with References
0093-0571 Monographic Series
0093-061X Government Publications Review *see* 0196-335X
0093-061X Government Publications Review *see* 0196-3368
0093-0687 Louisiana Fairs and Festivals
0093-0709 Syracuse Journal of International Law & Commerce
0093-0717 Arizona Business
0093-0741 Missouri. Public Service Commission. Regulated Electric Study†
0093-0776 Something Else Yearbook†
0093-0881 Association-Sterling Films. Free Loan Films *changed to* Association Films. Free Loan Films
0093-0903 Tennessee. State Advisory Council on Vocational Education. Annual Evaluation Report
0093-0938 Better Homes and Gardens Building Ideas
0093-1004 Biological Psychology Bulletin
0093-1039 Alaska Bar Brief
0093-1047 Harris Auction Galleries. Collectors' Auction
0093-1063 Florida Law Revision Commission. Annual Report *changed to* Florida Law Revision Council. Annual Report.
0093-1071 Florida. State Board of Independent Colleges and Universities. Report
0093-1098 New Jersey Public Libraries. Statistics
0093-111X Pretrial Justice Quarterly†
0093-1160 Association of Trial Lawyers of America. Newsletter *see* 0364-8125
0093-1179 Atlanta Constitution: a Georgia Index
0093-1195 Official Motor Home Trade-in Guide
0093-1241 Wyoming. Department of Labor and Statistics. Survey of Occupational Injuries and Illnesses
0093-125X Marketing Guide
0093-1284 American Annals of the Deaf and Dumb *see* 0002-726X
0093-1330 American Bell Association. Directory
0093-1365 Photo Information Almanac
0093-1454 American Marketing Association. Directory of Marketing Services and Membership Roster
0093-1551 Corrective and Social Psychiatry and Journal of Behavioral Technology Methods and Therapy
0093-1659 Purchasing World
0093-1713 Excited States
0093-173X Hospital Topics and Buyer's Guide *see* 0018-5868
0093-1748 Journal of Legal Medicine *see* 0190-2350
0093-1799 Official Port of Detroit World Handbook
0093-1853 Journal of Psychiatry and Law
0093-1861 American Artist Business Letter
0093-1896 Critical Inquiry
0093-190X Babson's Investment Digest†
0093-1918 Classic Collector†
0093-1926 I.R.C.A. Foreign Log
0093-1942 Conference of State Employment Security Personnel Officers. Report
0093-2094 American Indian Media Directory†
0093-2124 On Scene
0093-2132 Product Digest *see* 0146-5023
0093-2205 International Journal of Occupational Health & Safety *see* 0362-4064
0093-2213 Pavlovian Journal of Biological Science
0093-2248 P.M.B.R. Physician's Medical Book Reference
0093-2302 Minicomputer Review
0093-2310 Serials Updating Service
0093-2329 Serials Updating Service Quarterly
0093-2388 U.S. Federal Railroad Administration. Bibliography of Published Research Reports *see* 0097-0042
0093-2485 Economic Books: Current Selections
0093-2515 Drug Abuse Bibliography
0093-2531 McLean Guide to Kennels of America†
0093-254X Photographic Historical Society of New York. Membership Directory
0093-2558 Minnesota Alcohol Programs for Highway Safety†
0093-2582 St. Croix Review
0093-304X Columbia Law Alumni Observer
0093-3058 Duquesne Law Review
0093-3066 American Chemical Society. Division of Environmental Chemistry. Preprints of Papers.
0093-3074 U. S. National Park Service. Public Use of the National Park System; Fiscal Year Report
0093-3082 Montana. Animal Health Division. Statistical Data *changed to* Montana. Animal Health Division. Statistical Summary
0093-3090 Southern California Business Directory and Buyers Guide
0093-3139 College Literature
0093-3155 Forest H. Belt's Yearbook of Consumer Electronics†
0093-3163 Grants and Awards Available to Foreign Writers†
0093-3171 Journal of Family Counseling *see* 0192-6187
0093-318X Monday *see* 0145-1677
0093-3236 E C & M's Electrical Products Yearbook
0093-3252 Hastings Center Studies *see* 0093-0334
0093-3279 Alcoholism Digest Annual
0093-3287 Environment Abstracts
0093-3295 Pesticides Abstracts
0093-3317 Studies on the Development of Behavior and the Nervous System
0093-3414 College and University Employees, New York State
0093-3430 U.S. Department of Health, Education and Welfare. Annual Report to the Congress of the United States on Services Provided to Handicapped Children in Project Head Start
0093-3465 Opportunities in Iowa's Area Schools
0093-3481 Hawaii. Department of Health. Research and Statistics Office. R & S Report
0093-3503 Your Business and the Law *changed to* You and the Law
0093-3546 Cardiovascular Diseases
0093-3589 Industrial Pharmacology
0093-3619 Year Book of Dermatology
0093-3627 Yearbook of Dermatology and Syphilology *see* 0093-3619
0093-3643 N E C Newsletter *see* 0098-1664
0093-3651 Sea Technology
0093-366X U. S. Civil Service Commission. Personnel Research and Development Center. Technical Study
0093-3686 Journal of Jazz Studies
0093-3716 U. S. Department of the Interior. Office of Personnel Management. Annual Manpower Personnel Statistics†
0093-3813 I E E E Transactions. Plasma Science
0093-3821 List of Journals Indexed in Index Medicus
0093-3864 Land Use Planning Reports
0093-3945 U. S. Office of Saline Water. Catalog of Research Projects†
0093-3961 Journal of Financial Education
0093-397X Legal Notes for Education†
0093-3996 Pacific Tropical Botanical Garden. Bulletin
0093-4038 California and Western Medicine *see* 0093-0415
0093-4054 Contemporary Topics in Immunobiology
0093-4062 American Automobile Association. Digest of Motor Laws
0093-4089 Florida Senate
0093-416X Computer Review
0093-4240 New School for Social Research. Philosophy Department. Graduate Faculty Philosophy Journal
0093-4267 Battelle Memorial Institute. Columbus Laboratories. Report on National Survey of Compensation Paid Scientists and Engineers Engaged in Research and Development Activities
0093-4283 Trailer Life's Recreational Vehicle Campground and Services Guide
0093-4429 Peanut Market News
0093-4437 Anesthesiology Review
0093-4445 Journal of Long Term Care Administration
0093-4461 Physicians' Desk Reference
0093-4488 Johns Hopkins University. Population Information Program. Population Report. Series D. Sterilization (Male)
0093-4496 Johns Hopkins University. Population Information Program. Population Reports. Series H. Barrier Methods
0093-4518 American Society for Preventive Dentistry Journal†
0093-4526 Journal of Zoo Animal Medicine
0093-4585 Guide to the Recommended Country Inns of New England
0093-4593 Leisure Home Living†

0093-4615 Council on Foreign Relations. President's Report *changed to* Council on Foreign Relations. Annual Report
0093-4623 University of Michigan. Graduate School of Business Administration. Proceedings of the Annual Business Conference†
0093-4631 U.S. Fish and Wildlife Service. Selected List of Federal Laws and Treaties Relating to Sport Fish and Wildlife
0093-4658 Journal of Coated Fabrics
0093-4666 Mycotaxon
0093-4674 Criminal Law Commentator (New York) †
0093-4682 Family Law Commentator (New York)
0093-4690 Journal of Field Archaeology
0093-4712 American Journal of Pharmacy *see* 0163-464X
0093-4755 Evolutionary Theory
0093-4763 Groups: a Journal of Group Dynamics and Psychotherapy
0093-4771 Methods in Membrane Biology
0093-4909 Lackawanna-Wayne-Pike-Susquehanna Farm & Home News
0093-4992 Energy Resources Report *see* 0162-3958
0093-500X Energy Today
0093-5018 Europe Basic Oil Law & Concession Contracts
0093-5026 Good News of Tomorrow's World *see* 0032-0420
0093-5034 New York (State) Department of Labor. Division of Research and Statistics. Labor Research Report
0093-5050 Skeptic *see* 0160-4929
0093-5069 U.S. Division of Wildlife Services. Annual Report†
0093-5107 Journal of Real Estate Taxation
0093-5166 Contemporary Problems in Cardiology
0093-5220 Insiders' Guide to the Colleges
0093-5239 U. S. Bureau of Sport Fisheries and Wildlife. Report to the Fish Farmer†
0093-5255 Business Week Letter *changed to* Personal Finance Letter
0093-5271 Doane's Agricultural Report
0093-528X Hennepin County Library Cataloging Bulletin
0093-5301 Journal of Consumer Research
0093-531X Perspectives in Religious Studies
0093-5336 Recon†
0093-5336 Recon
0093-5352 Retirement Letter
0093-5387 Undersea Biomedical Research
0093-5417 Budd Gore Media Mix Newsletter
0093-5530 Wyoming. Division of Planning, Evaluation and Information Services. Statistical Report Series
0093-5557 Benchmark Papers in Human Physiology
0093-5603 Population Analysis of the Illinois Adult Prison System†
0093-5654 U. S. Bureau of Radiological Health. Research Grants Program†
0093-5700 Geothermal Energy
0093-5735 Engineering, Scientific and Technical Salary Survey
0093-5751 Financial Reporting Trends: Fire and Casualty Insurance *changed to* Financial Reporting Trends: Property/Casualty Insurance
0093-5786 Amateur Athletic Union of the United States. Official Rules for Water Polo
0093-5794 Word Processing World *see* 0279-7992
0093-5816 Directory of Published Proceedings. Series PCE: Pollution Control & Ecology
0093-5832 Farmland News
0093-5891 Toxic Materials News
0093-6049 Foresight (Washington)†
0093-609X Origins, N C Documentary Service
0093-6138 Florida Speech Communication Journal
0093-6332 Vanderbilt University. Department of Environmental and Water Resources Engineering. Technical Reports
0093-6391 Endocrine Research Communications
0093-6405 American Society of Civil Engineers. Geotechnical Engineering Division. Journal.
0093-6413 Mechanics Research Communications
0093-6472 Montana Advisory Council for Vocational Education. Annual Report
0093-6502 Communication Research
0093-6510 Findings and Forecasts
0093-6553 Cost of Picking and Hauling Florida Citrus Fruits
0093-6626 Biography News†
0093-6642 Monographs on Music in Higher Education†
0093-6685 United States Trade Associations
0093-6693 Washington (State). Attorney General's Office. Directory of Charitable Organizations and Trusts Registered with the Office of Attorney General *changed to* Washington (State). Attorney General's Office. Charitable Trust Directory
0093-6715 Florida. Division of Family Services. Annual Statistical Report
0093-674X Federal Telephone Directory†
0093-6758 Film Literature Index
0093-6766 International Bonds *changed to* International Bond Guide
0093-6774 Michigan. Department of Social Services. Public Assistance Statistics
0093-6782 Motorboat
0093-6901 Oceanic Abstracts
0093-691X Theriogenology
0093-6995 Tax Management Executive Compensation Journal *see* 0148-690X
0093-7002 American Journal of Optometry and Physiological Optics
0093-7053 Modern Healthcare (Long-Term Care) *see* 0160-7480
0093-7061 Modern Healthcare (Short-Term Care) *see* 0160-7480
0093-707X Persimmon Hill
0093-7134 Idaho's Comprehensive Plan for Criminal Justice
0093-7142 Montana Manual of State and Local Government†
0093-7223 Idaho. State Superintendent of Public Instruction. Annual Report. State of Idaho Johnson-O'Malley Program
0093-7231 Juvenile Justice *see* 0161-7109
0093-724X Maine Economic Data Book†
0093-7274 Woodall's Directory of Mobile Home Communities *see* 0163-4313
0093-7282 Audio Journal of Podiatric Medicine
0093-7290 Data Channels
0093-7347 New Jersey Dental Association. Journal
0093-7363 National Medical Audiovisual Center Motion Picture and Videotape Catalog *see* 0083-2294
0093-7398 Population Sciences: Index of Biomedical Research†
0093-7401 A S A Refresher Courses in Anesthesiology
0093-7436 University of Alaska Museum. Annual Report
0093-7452 Arkansas. Department of Mental Retardation. Annual Report
0093-7487 Multinational Executive Travel Companion
0093-7495 Origins
0093-7525 California. Department of Industrial Relations. Division of Labor Statistics and Research. Building Trades Wage Rates†
0093-7568 Pennsylvania State University. Research Publications and Professional Activities
0093-7630 F E P Guidelines
0093-7673 People(New York) *changed to* People Weekly
0093-7703 Directory of Educational Facilities for the Learning Disabled
0093-7711 Immunogenetics
0093-7754 Seminars in Oncology
0093-7797 American Bar Association. Special Committee on Environmental Law. Quarterly Newsletter *changed to* Environmental Law
0093-7800 Compliance and Legal Seminar. Proceedings
0093-7819 Illinois. Department of Mental Health. Drug Abuse Program. Progress Report
0093-7835 Michigan. Department of Social Services. Program Statistics
0093-7843 North Dakota State Plan for Rehabilitation Facilities and Workshops
0093-7851 Petroleo Internacional
0093-786X Deseret News Church Almanac
0093-7886 Maine. Bureau of Labor and Industry. Occupational Wage Survey
0093-7924 U.S. National Advisory Council on Indian Education. Annual Report to the Congress of the United States
0093-8025 Basebook
0093-8041 Georgia State University. Institute of Health Administration. Occasional Publication
0093-8076 Clinical Laboratory Reference
0093-8130 Mission Handbook: North American Protestant Ministries Overseas
0093-8149 Public Telecommunications Review (PTR)†
0093-8157 Reviews in Anthropology
0093-8203 North Dakota. Department of Agriculture. Annual Report *changed to* North Dakota. Department of Agriculture. Biennial Report
0093-8246 Montana. Department of Business Regulation. Annual Report
0093-8262 Federal Reserve Bank of San Francisco. Business Review *see* 0363-0021
0093-8270 C O S/M O S Digital Integrated Circuits†
0093-8327 Industrial Fishery Products; Market Review and Outlook
0093-8343 Engineering Issues *changed to* Issues in Engineering
0093-8378 Bioengineering Abstracts
0093-8394 Energy Conservation Abstracts†
0093-8408 Energy Abstracts
0093-8416 Energy Conversion Abstracts *see* 0093-8408
0093-8440 Soldiers
0093-8475 Folklore Feminists Communication†
0093-8505 Railway History Monograph
0093-8548 Criminal Justice & Behavior
0093-8572 National Patterns of R. & D. Resources; Funds & Manpower in the United States
0093-8599 U. S. National Clearinghouse for Drug Abuse Information. Report Series
0093-8610 Criminal Defense
0093-8637 Guidebook to Florida Taxes
0093-8645 Guidebook to Wisconsin Taxes
0093-8653 Annual Public Defenders' Workshop. Handbook†
0093-8688 Journal of College and University Law
0093-8696 Learning and the Law†
0093-870X Minnesota. Department of Education. Biennial Report†
0093-8726 Industrial Fishery Products
0093-8742 Educational Research Service. Salaries Scheduled for Administrative and Supervisory Personnel in Public Schools†
0093-8750 Executive Compensation Service. Technician Report
0093-8785 U.S. Health Resources Administration. Health Resources News
0093-8823 Direct Levies on Gaming in Nevada
0093-8831 Fact Book and Report of the West Virginia State System of Higher Education
0093-884X Physical Facilities at Institutions of Higher Education in West Virginia
0093-8858 Pro Se†
0093-8874 Teaching English to the Deaf
0093-8912 California. Council on Criminal Justice. Comprehensive Plan for Criminal Justice
0093-8920 Latvija Sodien
0093-8939 Illinois. Judicial Inquiry Board. Report
0093-8955 Utah. State Archives and Records Service. Administrative Rule Making Bulletin *changed to* Utah. State Archives and Records Service. Utah State Bulletin
0093-9021 National Environmental Research Center. Annual Report†
0093-9048 Montana Law Enforcement Academy. Annual Report to the Governor of Montana†
0093-9102 Missouri. Air Conservation Commission. Annual Report†
0093-9137 Michigan. Advisory Council for Vocational Education. Annual Report
0093-9161 Public Sector Arbitration Awards
0093-9188 Alternatives in Print
0093-9277 Education Bulletin (Missoula)
0093-9285 Sociology of Work and Occupations
0093-9293 Southern Voices†
0093-934X Brain & Language
0093-9374 Leica Manual
0093-9382 United Methodists Today†
0093-9382 United Methodists Today
0093-9390 Michigan. Office of Criminal Justice. Comprehensive Law Enforcement and Criminal Justice Plan
0093-9404 Overview of Blood
0093-9412 U.S. National Marine Fisheries Service. Report
0093-9447 Media Guide International. Newspapers/Newsmagazines Edition
0093-9501 Directory of Special Programs for Minority Group Members; Career Information Services, Employment Skills, Banks, Financial Aid Sources
0093-951X Directory of Trust Institutions
0093-9528 Dun & Bradstreet Reference Book of Transportation
0093-9552 Illinois State and Regional Economic Data Book
0093-9560 M.H.S. Review
0093-9579 Semiotext(e)
0093-9587 Special Libraries Directory of Greater New York
0093-9595 Nevada. Advisory Council for Manpower Training and Career Education. Annual Evaluation Report *changed to* Nevada. Advisory Council for Vocational-Technical Education. Annual Evaluation Report
0093-9625 Hawaii Review
0093-9633 U S Export Weekly
0093-9692 U.S. Department of Commerce. Effects of Pollution Abatement on International Trade†
0093-9706 Guide to Dental Materials and Devices *changed to* Dentist's Desk Reference
0093-9714 Research Advances in Alcohol & Drug Problems
0093-9722 Urology Times
0093-9730 North Carolina. Council on State Goals and Policy. Annual Report *changed to* North Carolina. State Goals and Policy Board. Annual Report
0093-9811 Parrott Talk
0093-982X E M Bibliography for Consumers†
0093-9854 Heart of Texas Records
0093-9889 Tennessee. State Board for Vocational Education. Information Series
0093-9897 U.S. Department of Transportation. Year-End Report†
0093-9951 Roster of Black Elected Officials in the South
0093-996X Tape Recording and Buying Guide *changed to* Stereo Review's Tape Recording & Buying Guide
0093-9978 Noise Control Engineering
0093-9986 New Jersey. Legislature. Office of Fiscal Affairs. Annual Report
0093-9994 I E E E Transactions. Industry Applications
0094-0003 Physical Review Index
0094-002X American Indian Law Review
0094-0054 Camper's Guide to Area Campgrounds
0094-0100 Advanced Biomedical Technology *see* 0147-2682

0094-0119 Biomedical Inventions Reporter *see* 0147-2682
0094-0127 Government Documents Review *see* 0147-2682
0094-0135 Health Care Statistics Report *see* 0147-2682
0094-0143 Urologic Clinics of North America
0094-0151 Reference Guide & Comprehensive Catalog of International Serials *changed to* Librarians' Guide to Back Issues of International Periodicals
0094-0178 Old-House Journal
0094-0186 Off-Lead
0094-0194 New York Culture Review
0094-0208 N A E P Newsletter
0094-0224 Lawyer's Newsletter
0094-0232 Imprint: Oregon
0094-0240 First Friday
0094-0267 Addictive Diseases
0094-0283 Genealogy
0094-0291 Hiking (Highland Park)†
0094-0305 McCall's Cooking School
0094-033X New German Critique
0094-0348 Population Mobility in Hawaii
0094-0364 Multitype Library Cooperative News
0094-0372 Cockshaw's Construction Labor News & Opinion
0094-0399 Your School and the Law
0094-0402 Annual Report of the Arts Activities in Alabama
0094-0488 Arkansas Nurse†
0094-0496 American Ethnologist
0094-050X S C A G Annual Report
0094-0526 Blair & Ketchum's Country Journal
0094-0534 Consumers Index to Product Evaluations and Information Sources
0094-0585 Journal of Carbohydrates-Nucleosides-Nucleotides
0094-0593 Journal of Corporate Taxation
0094-0607 Journal of Voluntary Action Research
0094-0615 Law & Liberty
0094-0623 Legal Notes for Insurance
0094-064X Planning Review
0094-0658 Sage International Yearbook of Foreign Policy†
0094-0658 Sage International Yearbook of Foreign Policy Studies
0094-0712 Arizona. Department of Economic Security. Annual Report
0094-0763 Huber Law Survey
0094-0771 Middle School Journal
0094-078X Northwestern Tour Book *see* 0363-2695
0094-0798 Oral History Review
0094-0801 University of Florida. Growth Conference. Prepared Papers
0094-0836 Student Advocate
0094-0844 Thorny Trail
0094-0852 Explorations in Economic Research†
0094-0887 Far-Western Forum†
0094-0895 Biofeedback Society of America. Proceedings of the Annual Meeting
0094-0933 U.S. Center for Disease Control. Abortion Surveillance. Annual Summary
0094-095X Directory of Continuing Education Opportunities in New York City
0094-0968 University of Chicago. Law School. Law Alumni Journal
0094-0984 Ohio's Comprehensive Criminal Justice Plan
0094-100X Directory of Municipal Bond Dealers of the United States
0094-1050 Curriculum Improvement
0094-1069 Michigan. Office of Highway Safety Planning. Annual Highway Safety Work Plan. *changed to* State of Michigan's Annual Highway Safety Plan.
0094-1093 Administrative Law Newsletter†
0094-1115 Basic Economic Data for Idaho
0094-1123 Nevada State Plan for Vocational Education *changed to* Nevada. State Board for Vocational Education. Annual Program Plan for Vocational Education
0094-1131 Official Truck Camper Trade-in Guide
0094-114X Mechanisms and Machine Theory
0094-1174 Alaska. Division of Family and Children Services. Annual Report
0094-1182 Civil War Collectors' Dealer Directory
0094-1190 Journal of Urban Economics
0094-1204 National Investor Relations Institute. Proceedings of the Annual National Conference *changed to* National Investor Relations Institute. Executive Summary of the Annual National Conference
0094-1220 Social Services in North Dakota
0094-1247 Nebraska. State Patrol. Annual Report
0094-1255 Book of Names†
0094-1271 Idaho Agricultural Statistics.
0094-128X Northeast Pacific Pink and Chum Salmon Workshop. Proceedings
0094-1298 Clinics in Plastic Surgery
0094-1336 Comprehensive Health Plan for New Jersey
0094-1344 Country Music World
0094-1352 IndustriScope
0094-1360 Jeffersonian Review†
0094-1409 Minnesota. Office of Ombudsman for Corrections. Annual Report
0094-1417 Astrograph
0094-1468 Florida. Department of Education. Florida Statewide Assessment Program: Capsule Report
0094-1476 Philadelphia Association for Psychoanalysis. Journal
0094-1484 Magyar Naptar (New York)
0094-1492 Materials Performance
0094-1506 Michigan State Plan for Vocational Education
0094-1514 Motor Handbook
0094-1522 N. C. F. A. Office Manual
0094-1557 Georgia. Department of Education. Statistical Report
0094-1565 University of Toledo. Business Research Center. Working Papers in Operations Analysis
0094-1611 Internationales Verzeichnis der Wirtschaftsverbaende
0094-162X Tenth Muse
0094-1638 Sociology: Reviews of New Books
0094-1646 Industerial Energy *see* 0194-2468
0094-1670 Conservation in Kansas
0094-1689 American Cartographer
0094-1697 Minnesota. Governor. Annual Report on the Quality of the Environment
0094-1700 Journal of Sport History
0094-1719 Academy of Sciences of the Lithuanian SSR. Mathematical Transactions *see* 0363-1672
0094-1727 Minnesota Statutes. Supplement
0094-1735 International Monetary Fund. Selected Decisions of the International Monetary Fund and Selected Documents
0094-176X W V E A School Journal *see* 0274-8606
0094-1786 Alaska. State Board of Registration for Architects, Engineers and Land Surveyors. Directory of Architects, Engineers and Land Surveyors
0094-1816 North Dakota. State Department of Health. Report
0094-1824 Society of Pharmacological and Environmental Pathologists. Bulletin *see* 0192-6233
0094-1832 Hydraulic Research in the United States and Canada
0094-1840 International Contact Lens Clinic
0094-1859 Journal of Afro-American Issues†
0094-1875 National Traffic Law News
0094-1891 Woodall's Mobile Home Park Directory *see* 0163-4313
0094-1921 Campaign Law Reporter
0094-1948 Forum (Baltimore) *see* 0360-2044
0094-1956 Journal of Instructional Psychology
0094-1964 Paintbrush
0094-1972 Review of Applied Urban Research
0094-2006 University of Washington Medicine
0094-2057 California School Law Digest
0094-2065 Communio
0094-2073 Minnesota. Governor's Commission on Crime Prevention and Control. Comprehensive Plan *changed to* Minnesota. Crime Control Planning Board. Comprehensive Plan
0094-209X Directories of Hawaii
0094-2200 South Dakota. Department of Labor. Research and Statistics. Annual Report on State and Area Occupational Requirements for Vocational Education
0094-2227 American College Testing Program. Handbook for Financial Aid Administrators
0094-2235 Illinois Student Lawyer
0094-2243 Cincinnati Bar Association. Journal
0094-2251 Virginia State Bar. Young Lawyers Conference. Newsletter
0094-2251 Virginia State Bar. Younger Members Conference. Newsletter *see* 0094-2251
0094-226X Newsletter & Digest of Selected Opinions of State Attorneys General†
0094-2278 Railway Passenger Car Annual
0094-2294 Florida. Mental Health Program Office. Statistical Report of Hospitals
0094-2308 Supply and Demand: Educational Personnel in Delaware
0094-2316 World of Politics
0094-2324 Community Development Digest
0094-2332 Criminal Justice Digest†
0094-2367 Everyman
0094-2375 Fantasiae (Los Angeles)
0094-2383 Journal of Abstracts in International Education
0094-2391 Journal of Agronomic Education
0094-2405 Medical Physics
0094-2413 Juvenile Justice Digest
0094-2421 Celebration: a Creative Worship Service
0094-243X A I P Conference Proceedings
0094-2448 Bead Journal *see* 0148-3897
0094-2464 Small Businessman's Clinic
0094-2499 Journal of Biocommunication
0094-2502 Business Regulation Law Report†
0094-2510 Marketing California Dried Fruits: Prunes, Raisins, Dried Apricots & Peaches
0094-2553 United States Judicial Reporter
0094-2561 Disclosure Record
0094-257X Weekly Record (New York)
0094-2588 Communication Directory
0094-260X A A B C Newsletter
0094-2626 Library Statistics of Illinois Colleges and Universities: Institutional Data†
0094-2634 Index to Foreign Market Reports
0094-2677 Ohio Juvenile Court Statistics
0094-2715 Inscape
0094-2766 Monthly Summary of Texas Natural Gas
0094-2782 New Mexico Forest Products Directory
0094-2790 Movement of California Fruits and Vegetables by Rail, Truck, and Air
0094-2820 Washington Geologic Newsletter
0094-2863 Soviet Union
0094-2871 U.S. Environmental Protection Agency. Office of Air Quality Planning and Standards. State Air Pollution Implementation Plan Progress Report†
0094-288X Russian History
0094-2898 Southeastern Symposium on System Theory. Proceedings
0094-291X Rhode Island. Department of Mental Health, Retardation and Hospitals. Mental Health, Retardation and Hospitals
0094-2987 Illinois. Department of Public Instruction. Publications Resource Manual†
0094-3002 Broker-Dealer Directory
0094-3029 Carnegie Endowment for International Peace. Financial Report
0094-3037 East Central Europe
0094-3061 Contemporary Sociology
0094-3096 American Metric Journal *changed to* American Metric Journal S I Metricpac
0094-310X Barrister Bulletin *see* 0162-2900
0094-3142 U.S. Environmental Protection Agency. Summaries of Foreign Government Environmental Reports
0094-3231 Environmental Information Systems Directory
0094-324X International Academy of Preventive Medicine. Journal
0094-3320 13th Moon
0094-3339 East-West Markets†
0094-3347 Eutrophication†
0094-3355 Horse and Horseman
0094-3452 Places†
0094-3460 National Association for Women Deans, Administrators and Counselors. Journal
0094-3479 Michigan. Department of Commerce. Annual Report Summary
0094-3495 Journal of Social Welfare
0094-3509 Journal of Family Practice
0094-3517 I C T A Roster *changed to* I C T A Directory
0094-3568 Arts in Alaska
0094-3576 Arkansas. Bureau of Vital Statistics. Annual Report of Births, Deaths, Marriages and Divorces as Reported to the Bureau of Vital Statistics
0094-3614 Southern Europe Travel Guide *changed to* Travel Guide to Europe
0094-3630 Missouri. Division of Fisheries. Abstracts of Fishery Research Reports†
0094-3649 Drum Corps Review
0094-3657 Central Europe and Scandinavia Travel Guide *changed to* Travel Guide to Europe
0094-3673 Behavior Science Research
0094-3681 Chem Sources - Europe
0094-369X Guthrie Bulletin
0094-372X South Dakota Indian Recipients of Social Welfare
0094-3738 Journal of Peace Science *changed to* Conflict Management and Peace Science
0094-3746 Glass Dealer
0094-3754 Michigan. Deparment of Education. College Admissions & Financial Assistance Handbook *changed to* Michigan Postsecondary Admissions & Financial Assistance Handbook
0094-3800 California Plant Pathology
0094-3894 Recipe Index Series†
0094-3924 Wyoming. State of Wyoming Annual Report
0094-3932 Advances in Fire Retardants†
0094-3975 Fundamentals of Aerospace Instrumentation
0094-3983 Minnesota Pocket Data Book†
0094-3991 Narcotics and Drug Abuse A-Z
0094-4033 Union Catalog of Maps†
0094-4076 Emory Law Journal
0094-4084 International Directory of Behavior and Design Research
0094-4106 U.S. Veterans Administration. Manpower Planning Data
0094-4114 Nantucket Review
0094-4211 G.A.I.U. Handbook of Wages, Hours and Fringe Benefits
0094-422X American Society of Pension Actuaries. Transcribings. Annual Conference
0094-4246 Arizona Legislative Service
0094-4262 Facts About South Dakota†
0094-4270 I.C.C. Supplemental Reports
0094-4289 Journal of Engineering Materials and Technology
0094-4327 California. State Board of Cosmetology. Rules and Regulations.
0094-4335 Statistics for Water Utilities Including Water Authorities in Pennsylvania
0094-4424 U.S. Center for Disease Control. Family Planning Services: Annual Summary
0094-4459 National Collegiate Athletic Association. Proceedings of the Special Convention
0094-4467 Southeastern Europe
0094-4491 Maryland Manual

0094-4505 Guide to American Scientific and Technical Directories
0094-4548 Letters in Heat and Mass Transfer
0094-4610 Visual Merchandising
0094-4629 Maryland. Bureau of Air Quality Control. State-Local Cooperative Air Sampling Program Yearly Data Report *changed to* Maryland Air Quality Programs. Data Report
0094-467X Securities Investor Protection Corporation. Annual Report
0094-4696 Atmospheric Turbidity and Precipitation Chemistry Data for the World
0094-4742 World Environmental Directory
0094-4831 Bibliography of Society, Ethics and the Life Sciences
0094-484X Dental Research in the United States, Canada, and Great Britain *see* 0147-264X
0094-4858 Fresh Fruit and Vegetable Market News: Weekly Summary, Shipments-Unloads
0094-4904 Canine Practice
0094-4920 Social Sciences Index
0094-4998 Point of Reference
0094-5013 L A M A's Travel Digest for Latin America
0094-5048 Maine. Department of Transportation. Annual Report
0094-5056 Eastern Economic Journal
0094-5072 Inter Dependent
0094-5080 Journal of Forest History
0094-5099 Music Library Association. Technical Reports
0094-5102 Journal of Marriage and Family Counseling *see* 0194-472X
0094-5129 New Human Services Review†
0094-5145 Journal of Community Health
0094-5196 U.S. National Oceanic and Atmospheric Administration. Report to the Congress on Ocean Dumping and Other Man-Induced Changes to Ocean Ecosystems *see* 0098-4922
0094-5218 Official Railway Guide. North American Passenger Travel Edition *see* 0273-9658
0094-5226 Official National Collegiate Athletic Association Football Rules & Interpretations
0094-5234 Official National Collegiate Athletic Association Basketball Rules *changed to* N C A A Basketball Rules and Interpretations
0094-5242 Official Meeting Facilities Guide
0094-5277 Barrister
0094-5307 Advances in Satellite Meteorology
0094-5323 Augustinian Studies
0094-534X Ohio Northern University Law Review
0094-5358 Solid Waste Systems *see* 0190-7808
0094-5366 Bilingual Review
0094-5390 Directory of Oklahoma Airports
0094-5404 Essays in Literature
0094-5420 Judicial Education News†
0094-5439 Maine Prosecutor Bulletin
0094-5447 Metallurgy-Materials Education Yearbook
0094-5455 North Dakota Academic Library Statistics. *changed to* North Dakota Library Statistics
0094-5463 Product Safety & the Law†
0094-5471 Directory of Women Physicians in the U.S.
0094-5498 Journal of Altered States of Consciousness *changed to* Imagination, Cognition and Personality
0094-5528 Agricultural Situation in Africa and West Asia *see* 0148-7094
0094-5587 Community Leaders and Noteworthy Americans
0094-5617 Hastings Constitutional Law Quarterly
0094-5625 Le-Torah ve-Hora Ah
0094-5633 Measuring Mormonism
0094-5641 Minnesota Health Statistics
0094-5668 Ohio Journal of Religious Studies
0094-5676 Oppositions
0094-5714 Synthesis and Reactivity in Inorganic and Metalorganic Chemistry
0094-5749 Indiana. Environmental Management Board. Annual Report
0094-5765 Acta Astronautica
0094-579X Stone Soup
0094-5803 University of Wisconsin, Madison. Bureau of Business Research and Service. Research in the School of Business†
0094-582X Latin American Perspectives
0094-5846 Fundamentals of Cosmic Physics
0094-5862 Family Album
0094-5897 Arnold Newsletter *see* 0160-4848
0094-5900 Syracuse University. Libraries. Annual Report†
0094-5978 Illinois. Cities and Villages Municipal Problems Commission. Annual Report to the Session of the General Assembly
0094-601X Annual Handbook for Group Facilitators
0094-6028 Computer Medicine
0094-615X L A C U N Y *changed to* Urban Academic Librarian
0094-615X L A C U N Y Occasional Papers
0094-6176 Seminars in Thrombosis and Hemostasis
0094-6184 Serial Handbook of Modern Psychiatry
0094-6192 Continuing Education in Nursing Home Administration *see* 0160-6980
0094-6206 Origins of Behavior Series
0094-6230 Oklahoma. Department of Highways. Sufficiency Rating Report and Needs Study: Oklahoma State Highways *changed to* Oklahoma. Department of Transportation. Sufficiency Rating Report and Needs Study: Oklahoma State Transportation
0094-6249 Chemical Reference Manual
0094-6265 Maryland. State Highway Administration. Traffic Trends
0094-6281 Energy Index
0094-6303 Global Directory of Gas Companies†
0094-6311 Lake Michigan Shore and Open Water Report
0094-6338 South Carolina Vital and Morbidity Statistics
0094-6346 Directory of Selected Illinois State Agencies
0094-6354 A A N A Journal
0094-6427 Susquehanna River Basin Commission. Annual Report
0094-6435 Florida. Division of Corrections. Financial Report
0094-6451 Economics Working Papers: Bibliography
0094-6451 Economic Working Papers
0094-6478 Music Library Association. Index and Bibliography Series
0094-6494 Illinois. Department of Public Health. Poison Control Program Report
0094-6508 Ohio. Department of Mental Health and Mental Retardation. Annual Financial and Statistical Report
0094-6516 Legal Bibliographic Data Service Weekly Subject Listing *see* 0360-7151
0094-6532 Early Years
0094-6575 Emergency Medical Services
0094-6591 Orthopaedic Review
0094-6605 U.S. Center for Disease Control. Tetanus Surveillance; Report
0094-6648 Graduate School Programs in Public Affairs and Public Administration
0094-6745 Institutions/Volume Feeding *changed to* Institutions
0094-6761 Current Topics in Molecular Endocrinology
0094-6818 International Index to Multi Media Information
0094-6842 Systems and Management Annual†
0094-6893 Federal Reserve Bank of Richmond. Economic Review
0094-6907 Cantwell Tapestry
0094-6915 Backtracker
0094-6958 Sage Public Administration Abstracts
0094-7008 U.S. National Marine Fisheries Service. Grant-in-Aid for Fisheries: Program Activities
0094-7024 S S I E Science Newsletter
0094-7032 Advances in Image Pickup and Display
0094-7032 Advances in Image Pickup and Display. Supplements
0094-7040 Aldine Crime and Justice Annual†
0094-7091 Geokhimiya Translations
0094-7148 Report of Cases Determined in the Supreme Court and Court of Appeals of the State of New Mexico
0094-7156 Federal Home Loan Mortgage Corporation. Report
0094-7172 Research in Parapsychology
0094-7202 Nassau County Medical Center. Proceedings *changed to* N C M C Proceedings
0094-7245 Clinical Engineering News *see* 0149-290X
0094-727X Connecticut. Commission to Study and Investigate the Problems of Deaf and Hearing-Impaired Persons. Annual Report *changed to* Connecticut. Commission on the Deaf and Hearing-Impaired. Annual Report
0094-7288 Engineering and Society Series
0094-7296 Federal Aid Fact Book†
0094-730X Journal of Fluency Disorders
0094-7326 New Mexico. Veterans' Service Commission. Report
0094-7342 Journal of Mormon History
0094-7393 Highway User Quarterly†
0094-7466 International Symposium on Transport and Handling of Minerals. Minerals Transportation; Proceedings
0094-7474 Summer Computer Simulation Conference. Proceedings
0094-7482 Status of the Market Nuclear Fuel Fabrication
0094-7504 Annual Statistical Report of the Colorado Judiciary
0094-7512 Directory of Counseling Services
0094-7520 Foreign Trade Reports. General Imports of Cotton Manufactures
0094-7547 New York (City) Mayor. Schedules Supporting the Executive Budget
0094-7555 Banking Legislation in the Congress
0094-7571 Crime and Social Justice
0094-7598 Land Use Law and Zoning Digest
0094-7628 New Hampshire Comprehensive Law Enforcement Plan *changed to* New Hampshire Comprehensive Criminal Justice Plan
0094-7660 Illinois Insurance
0094-7679 Journalism History
0094-7687 New Hampshire Annual Rural Manpower Report
0094-7695 National Federation of Independent Business. Quarterly Economic Report *see* 0362-3548
0094-7733 Society of General Physiologists Series
0094-775X Folk Mass and Modern Liturgy *see* 0363-504X
0094-7768 International Studies Notes
0094-7776 U.S. Occupational Safety and Health Review Commission. Administrative Law Judge and Commission Decisions
0094-7814 Inventory of Marriage and Family Literature
0094-7822 Theatre/Drama & Speech Index *changed to* Theatre/Drama Abstracts
0094-7857 U.S. National Science Foundation. Division of Environmental Systems and Resources. Summary of Awards†
0094-7881 U.S. National Science Foundation. Graduate Science Education Student Support and Postdoctorals
0094-789X Executive Compensation Journal *see* 0148-690X
0094-7911 Delaware Statistical Abstract
0094-792X C P A Letter
0094-7954 A P S A Departmental Services Program Survey of Departments
0094-7962 University of California, Davis. Food Protection and Toxicology Center. Summary Report
0094-7989 Bergen County History
0094-8012 Firelands Arts Review *changed to* Firelands Review
0094-8039 Journal of Muscle Shoals History
0094-8055 Peace Science Society (International). Papers
0094-8063 Energy Review
0094-8071 Flammability News Bulletin†
0094-8071 Flammability Institute. News Bulletin *see* 0094-8071
0094-8101 Outboard Boating Handbook†
0094-8128 Journal of Combustion Toxicology
0094-8136 Yachting Year Book of Northern California
0094-8187 Surgery Update†
0094-8233 Alloys Index
0094-825X Sweet's Industrial Construction & Renovation File with Plant Engineering Extension Market List
0094-8268 Summary of Expenditure Data for Michigan Public Schools
0094-8276 Geophysical Research Letters
0094-8284 National Trade and Professional Associations of the United States and Canada and Labor Unions
0094-8306 North Dakota. State Advisory Council for Vocational Education. Annual Evaluation Report
0094-8314 Utah. State Board of Education. Annual Report of the State Superintendent of Public Instruction
0094-8322 Illinois. Board of Higher Education. Directory of Higher Education
0094-8373 Paleobiology
0094-8381 Air Force Law Review
0094-8403 Directory of Colorado Libraries
0094-8411 U.S. Bureau of East-West Trade. Export Administration Regulations
0094-8446 Kelley Blue Book R V Guide
0094-8454 Official Southern California Ports Maritime Directory and Guide
0094-8470 Progress in Radiation Protection
0094-8535 Florida Bank Monitor
0094-8543 American Arabic Speaking Community Almanac†
0094-8551 Florida. Bureau of Local Government Finance. Annual Local Government Financial Report
0094-8594 Journal of Purchasing & Materials Management
0094-8616 Consumer Price Index
0094-8616 U.S. Bureau of Labor Statistics. Consumer Price Index *see* 0095-926X
0094-8632 Eastern Europe Travel Guide *changed to* Travel Guide to Europe
0094-8640 Evaluations of Drug Interactions. Supplement
0094-8667 Directory: Home Centers & Hardware Chains, Auto Supply Chains
0094-8675 Homeowners How to Handbook
0094-8675 Homeowners Handbook *see* 0094-8675
0094-8705 Journal of Philosophy of Sport
0094-8705 Journal of the Philosophy of Sport
0094-873X Montana Library Directory, with Statistics of Montana Public Libraries
0094-8764 Association of American Plant Food Control Officials. Official Publication
0094-8829 Library Development in Alaska: Long Range Program
0094-8837 Selected Tables in Mathematical Statistics.
0094-8845 St. Lawrence University. Conference on the Adirondack Park (Proceedings)
0094-8853 Council of Better Business Bureaus. Annual Report
0094-890X New Jersey. State Library. Union List of Serials†
0094-8934 Folk Harp Journal
0094-8950 Monographs in Lipid Research
0094-8969 Guide to the Health Care Field
0094-8977 Non Solus
0094-9000 Theory of Probability and Mathematical Statistics
0094-9019 Wyoming. Department of Revenue and Taxation. Annual Report

0094-9027 Young Students Encyclopedia Yearbook
0094-9043 Ohio Geographers: Recent Research Themes
0094-9086 Hopkins Quarterly
0094-9108 Physical Fitness Research Digest†
0094-9183 Annual Editions: Readings in Social Problems
0094-9191 A.P.C.A. Directory and Resource Book *changed to* Directory of Governmental Air Pollution Agencies
0094-9205 University of Georgia. Institute of Ecology. Annual Report
0094-9264 Principles and Techniques of Human Research and Therapeutics†
0094-9302 Concise Clinical Neurology Review
0094-9329 Modern Sawmill Techniques
0094-9337 International Journal of Sulfur Chemistry. Part A. Original Articles, Notes and Communications *see* 0308-664X
0094-9345 International Journal of Sulfur Chemistry. Part B. Quarterly Reports *see* 0308-664X
0094-9353 International Journal of Sulfur Chemistry. Part C. Mechanisms of Reactions of Sulfur Compound *see* 0308-664X
0094-9426 Book Forum
0094-9442 Illinois Minerals Notes
0094-9477 Previews of Heat and Mass Transfer
0094-9515 Joint Federal-State Land Use Planning Commission for Alaska. Annual Report *changed to* Alaska's Land
0094-9531 Shepard's Federal Law Citations in Selected Law Reviews
0094-9582 U.S. National Institute of Neurological Diseases and Stroke. Research Program Reports
0094-9604 Medical Group Management Association. International Directory
0094-9620 American Optometric Association News
0094-9655 Statistical Computation and Simulation
0094-9655 Journal of Statistical Computation and Simulation
0094-9671 Conference on Ground Water. Proceedings
0094-9701 Ha-Mesivta
0094-9744 Basenji
0094-9779 Geothermal World Directory
0094-9787 Olympian
0094-9795 Illinois. Legislative Investigating Commission. Annual Report
0094-9884 Annual Textile Industry Technical Conference. (Publication)
0094-9914 Your Highway Department, Arkansas
0094-9922 Transportation USA
0094-9930 Journal of Pressure Vessel Technology
0094-9973 Best's Agents Guide to Life Insurance Companies
0095-0025 Job Corps Happenings
0095-0033 Data Base
0095-0084 Business Digest
0095-0092 Business Monthly *changed to* Managing
0095-0106 Communique (Boston)†
0095-0149 Environmental Quality Abstracts†
0095-0157 Florida Marine Research Publications
0095-0165 Homegrown
0095-019X Osiris
0095-0203 Personal Finance Letter†
0095-0211 Real Estate Investor
0095-0254 U.S. National Heart and Lung Institute. Annual Report of the Director of the National Heart and Lung Institute *changed to* U. S. National Heart, Lung, and Blood Institute. Report of the Director
0095-0262 U.S. National Heart and Lung Advisory Council. Annual Report *changed to* U. S. National Heart, Lung, and Blood Advisory Council. Report
0095-036X Texas Nursing
0095-0386 Mort's Guide to Low-Cost Vacations & Lodgings on College Campuses
0095-0475 Practical Psychology for Physicians *see* 0162-6957
0095-0491 Catfish Farmer and World Aquaculture News *see* 0199-1388
0095-053X National Library Reporter†
0095-0556 Car Classics *changed to* Car Collector and Car Classics
0095-0564 Wisconsin. Division of Corrections. Bureau of Planning, Development and Research. Work Release-Study Release Program *changed to* Wisconsin. Division of Corrections. Office of Information Management. Work Release-Study Release Program
0095-0580 Hospital/Health Care Training Media Profiles
0095-0629 L C Foreign Acquisitions Newsletter†
0095-0637 Fact Book. Alabama Institutions of Higher Education, Universities and Colleges
0095-0645 Minnesota. Department of Revenue. Biennial Report
0095-0653 Collegiate Career Woman's Magazine
0095-0653 Collegiate Woman's Career Magazine *see* 0095-0653
0095-067X WoodenBoat
0095-0688 Manhattan Directory of Commercial & Industrial Properties
0095-0696 Journal of Environmental Economics and Management
0095-0726 Commerce Reporter†
0095-0750 Doctoral Scientists and Engineers in the United States. Profile *changed to* Science, Engineering, and Humanities Doctorates in the United States: Profile
0095-084X Electrical Installation & Repair Projects†
0095-0858 Social Psychiatry
0095-0866 Western Pennsylvania Genealogical Quarterly
0095-0890 Foreign Trade Reports. U.S. Waterborne Exports and General Imports
0095-0963 Automedica
0095-0971 Bio-Medical Scoreboard
0095-0998 Medical School Rounds
0095-1005 Search and Seizure Law Report
0095-1013 Lifestyle†
0095-1021 I. F. T. Journal
0095-1048 Footwear Manual
0095-1072 U.S. Library of Congress. Chinese Cooperative Catalog
0095-1080 Africana Journal
0095-1102 New Hampshire Occupational Outlook
0095-1137 Journal of Clinical Microbiology
0095-1145 Psychology†
0095-1188 Women Law Reporter†
0095-1250 Water Resources Research in Virginia, Annual Report
0095-1269 Alabama World Trade Directory
0095-1285 Alabama. Commission on Higher Education. Biennial Report to the Governor and the Legislature
0095-134X CoEvolution Quarterly
0095-1358 Fodor's Soviet Union
0095-1374 R.E.I.T. Fact Book
0095-1382 Vermont. Department of Employment Security. Statistical Tables
0095-1390 Albion
0095-1404 American Hairdresser/Salon Owner
0095-1420 Artbibliographies Current Titles
0095-1439 Central Kentucky Researcher
0095-1447 Cinefan†
0095-1455 National Association of Regional Councils. Directory
0095-148X American Venereal Disease Association. Journal *see* 0148-5717
0095-1498 Kentucky Local Debt Report
0095-1528 Urban Planning Quarterly†
0095-1536 Women (Washington)†
0095-1544 Journal of Cyclic Nucleotide Research
0095-1579 British Isles and Ireland Travel Guide *changed to* Travel Guide to Europe
0095-1587 Foster Natural Gas Report
0095-1625 Rider
0095-1633 North Dakota. Social Service Board. Statistics
0095-165X El Dorado
0095-1676 Indiana. Division of Fish and Wildlife. Management Series
0095-1684 American Poetry and Poetics
0095-1692 Civil Engineering Report Series *changed to* Water Resources Report Series
0095-1714 Imprint†
0095-1730 Seems
0095-1811 American Clean Car
0095-182X American Indian Quarterly
0095-1846 Virginia. Law Enforcement Officers Training Standards Commission. Biennial Report *changed to* Virginia. Criminal Justice Services Commission. Annual Report
0095-1870 Industrial Contact List for North Carolina Communities
0095-1900 Texas. Department of Corrections. Research and Development Division. Research Report
0095-1951 Procedures in Computer Sciences
0095-1978 Virginia. State Water Control Board. Annual Report
0095-1994 Tennessee. Department of Safety. Annual Report
0095-2028 National College of the State Judiciary
0095-2060 Florida. Department of Transportation. Annual Report
0095-2087 I M P Directory†
0095-2109 U.S. Office of Technology Assessment Annual Report to the Congress
0095-2125 Energy: a Continuing Bibliography with Indexes
0095-2141 U.S. Bureau of Health Resources Development. Division of Nursing. Special Project Grants and Contracts Awarded for Improvement in Nurse Training
0095-2184 Integrity: Gay Episcopal Forum *changed to* Integrity Forum
0095-2214 Chromatography Newsletter
0095-2222 Consumers' Research
0095-2273 N Y S S A Sphere
0095-2338 Journal of Chemical Information and Computer Sciences
0095-2346 Drugs in Health Care
0095-2397 Advent Review and Sabbath Herald *see* 0161-1119
0095-2427 Harvard Magazine
0095-2443 Journal of Elastomers and Plastics
0095-2583 Economic Inquiry
0095-2591 International Netsuke Collectors Society Journal
0095-2656 Transportation Research News
0095-2699 Agricultural Libraries Information Notes
0095-2702 Serials Updating Service Annual
0095-2729 National Paint and Coatings Association. Annual Report
0095-2826 American Society for Personnel Administration. Personnel and Industrial Relations Colleges
0095-2842 Handbook of Illinois Government
0095-2850 Economic and Social Progress in Latin America; Annual Report
0095-2869 Directory of American Book Specialists
0095-2885 Current Topics in Classroom Instruction Series
0095-2893 Illinois. State Museum. Inventory of the Collections
0095-2907 Dickson Mounds Museum Anthropological Studies†
0095-2915 Illinois. State Museum. Research Series. Papers in Anthropology
0095-2923 Insurance Forum
0095-294X Forecaster
0095-2958 Biology Digest
0095-2966 Resources
0095-2974 New World Communications†
0095-2990 American Journal of Drug and Alcohol Abuse
0095-3024 Minnesota. Department of Revenue. Petroleum Division. Annual Report
0095-3075 Virginia. Employment Commission. Manpower Research Division. Economic Assumptions
0095-3105 Nebraska Statistical Report of Abortions
0095-3113 National Directory of State Agencies
0095-3121 Family Planning Programs in Oklahoma
0095-3148 Illinois. State Board of Investment. Investment Transactions
0095-3237 Occupational Safety & Health Report
0095-3245 Fleet Maintenance and Specifying
0095-3253 Washington (State) Game Department. Applied Research Section. Bulletin
0095-327X Armed Forces and Society
0095-3318 Alaska. Office of Alcoholism. Report
0095-3342 Federal Funding Guide for Elementary and Secondary Education
0095-3369 Digest of the United States Practice in International Law
0095-3377 College Board. Admissions Testing Program. National Report on College-Bound Seniors
0095-3415 Alaska. Violent Crimes Compensation Board. Annual Report
0095-3423 Commerce Business Daily
0095-3431 Alabama's Vital Events
0095-3474 A.C.A. Industry Guide to Hearing Aids. International Edition
0095-3490 Statistics of Virginia Public Libraries *changed to* Statistics of Virginia Public Libraries and Institutional Libraries
0095-3547 Geological Society of America. Yearbook
0095-3555 West Coast Review of Books
0095-3601 Cal-Neva Wildlife; Transactions
0095-361X Alabama. Public Library Service. Basic State Plan and Annual Program *changed to* Alabama. Public Library Service. Annual Report
0095-3628 Microbial Ecology
0095-3679 Peanut Science
0095-3741 Current Governments Reports: Governmental Finances
0095-3784 Abstracts of Instructional and Research Materials in Vocational and Technical Education *changed to* Resources in Vocational Education
0095-3814 Topics in Health Care Financing
0095-3830 Economic Outlook U.S.A.
0095-3865 Alaska. Legislature. Budget and Audit Committee. Annual Report.
0095-389X Wyoming. Employment Security Commission. Research and Analysis Section. Farm Labor Report
0095-3911 St. Clair County Historical Society. Journal
0095-392X State University of New York at Buffalo. Law Library. Law Library Periodicals†
0095-3962 Sales Training & Development *see* 0193-2136
0095-3997 Administration and Society
0095-4004 Wisconsin. Division of Corrections. Bureau of Planning, Development, and Research. Adult Probation Admissions
0095-4012 American Journal of I.V. Therapy *changed to* American Journal of Intravenous Therapy & Clinical Nutrition
0095-4020 Massachusetts. Department of Public Welfare. State Advisory Board. Annual Report
0095-4047 New York (State). Division of Criminal Justice Service. Annual Report
0095-4063 Communications World
0095-4098 Library Resources Notes
0095-4101 Popular Music Periodicals Index
0095-411X Production and Marketing California Grapes, Raisins and Wine *see* 0527-2181
0095-4128 Propylene Annual.
0095-4144 Executive Compensation Service. Reports on International Compensation. Argentina
0095-4209 Hawaii. State Law Enforcement and Juvenile Delinquency Planning Agency. Annual Action Program
0095-4225 Power Semiconductors
0095-425X Christianity Applied†
0095-4306 Wisconsin. Division of Corrections. Office of Informatiom Management. Juvenile Probation Admissions

0095-4306 Wisconsin. Division of Corrections. Bureau of Planning, Development and Research. Probation and Parole Terminations *changed to* Wisconsin. Division of Corrections. Office of Information Management. Probation and Parole Terminations
0095-4314 Wisconsin Trails
0095-4322 World Mines Register
0095-4330 Washington Agricultural Statistics
0095-4365 U.S. National Climatic Center. Climatological Data; National Summary
0095-442X Oklahoma. Conservation Commission. Biennial Report
0095-4438 Columban Mission
0095-4470 Journal of Phonetics
0095-4489 Studies in Browning and His Circle
0095-4527 Cytology and Genetics
0095-4535 Advances in Environmental Sciences *see* 0065-2563
0095-4543 Primary Care: Clinics in Office Practice
0095-4594 Corrections Magazine
0095-4616 Applied Mathematics and Optimization
0095-4624 Connecticut. Council on Environmental Quality. Annual Report
0095-4632 A. D. F. &. G. Technical Data Report
0095-4659 West Virginia. Department of Natural Resources. Annual Report on the Comprehensive Water Resources Plan
0095-4667 Alaska Medicaid Status Report
0095-4675 Alaska. Division of Medical Assistance. Medicaid Annual Status Report *see* 0095-4667
0095-4683 Airline Handbook
0095-4721 L.S.C.A. Annual Program, Hawaii State Library System
0095-4748 National Treasury Employees Union. Bulletin
0095-4772 Pensions & Investments *changed to* Pension & Investment Age
0095-4799 South Carolina's Manpower in Industry
0095-4802 South Dakota Vital Statistics Annual Report
0095-4810 Southwest New Mexico Council of Governments. Annual Work Program
0095-4837 U.S. Bureau of Labor Statistics. Chartbook on Prices, Wages, and Productivity†
0095-4853 I R M
0095-4861 Clinical and Biochemical Analysis
0095-4888 Directory of Minnesota's Area Mental Health, Mental Retardation, Inebriety Programs
0095-490X Intercollegiate Bibliography. New Cases in Administration
0095-4918 Journal of Portfolio Management
0095-4942 North Carolina. Department of Human Resources. Annual Plan of Work
0095-4977 Curriculum Materials Clearinghouse. Index and Curriculum Briefs
0095-4993 Journal of African Studies
0095-5019 Illinois. Department of Transportation. Annual Report
0095-5108 Clinics in Perinatology
0095-5175 Florida. Department of Administration. Budget in Brief
0095-5183 Drug Development Communications *see* 0363-9045
0095-5191 Directory of Investor-Owned Hospitals and Hospital Management Companies
0095-5221 Interest-Adjusted Index
0095-5248 New Frontiers (Seattle)†
0095-5264 Nevada. Bureau of Mines and Geology. Report
0095-5310 Arizona. Department of Education. Annual Report of the Superintendent of Public Instruction
0095-5329 Consolidated Report on Elementary and Secondary Education in Colorado
0095-5337 Illinois Handcrafts Directory
0095-537X Weighing & Measurement
0095-5396 American Bankers Association. National Operations & Automation Conference. Proceedings
0095-5418 Strictly U.S.
0095-5493 Foreign Trade Reports. U.S. General Imports - Schedule A - Commodity by Country
0095-5523 New Hampshire Vital Statistics
0095-5558 Country Place†
0095-5558 Country Place *see* 0147-4928
0095-5582 Annual Editions: Readings in Anthropology
0095-5590 New York (State) Consumer Protection Board. Annual Report
0095-5655 Gallaudet Almanac†
0095-5663 New York Times School Microfilm Collection Index by Reels *changed to* New York Times School Microfilm Collection Index
0095-5698 Access (Syracuse)†
0095-5698 Access (Syracuse)
0095-571X Semeia
0095-5744 Viking
0095-5760 Alaska Hunting Guide†
0095-5787 Annual Editions: Readings in Education
0095-5833 Criminal Victimization in the United States
0095-585X Montana Federal Grants-in-Aid Report†
0095-5876 San Diego Biomedical Symposium. Proceedings
0095-5884 Louisiana. State Board of Nurse Examiners. Report
0095-5892 Training
0095-5930 N A C L A's Latin America & Empire Report *see* 0149-1598
0095-5981 Humanities Index
0095-599X Drug Interactions
0095-6082 Washington (State) Legislature. Transportation Committee. Report
0095-6120 North Dakota. Judicial Council. Statistical Compilation and Report *changed to* North Dakota. Judicial Council. Annual Report
0095-6139 Ethnicity
0095-6155 Annual Editions: Readings in Marriage and Family
0095-6201 Georgia Archive
0095-6236 Rangeman's Journal *changed to* Rangelands
0095-6325 North Dakota. Social Service Board. Report
0095-6333 North Dakota. Social Service Board. Area Social Service Centers
0095-6384 Kentucky Law Enforcement Council. Annual Report
0095-6406 Fielding's Low-Cost Europe
0095-6422 Delaware. Department of Health and Social Service. Annual Report
0095-6430 State of Florida Comprehensive Manpower Plan
0095-6449 Computer Design's Data Sheet Directory of Digital Electronics†
0095-6457 Carpet Specifier's Handbook
0095-6465 California Historical Courier
0095-6481 National Conference on Power Transmission. Proceedings
0095-6538 N.A.D.A. Mobile Home Appraisal Guide
0095-6562 Aviation, Space, and Environmental Medicine
0095-6619 Hawaii. Legislative Reference Bureau. Digest and Index of Laws Enacted
0095-6627 Pet Mass Marketing *changed to* Pets/Supplies/Marketing
0095-6686 Illinois. Department of Transportation. Physical Research Report
0095-6694 O.S.S.C. Bulletin
0095-6775 Damon Runyon-Walter Winchell Cancer Fund. Annual Report
0095-6783 Mississippi Marine Resources Council. Annual Report
0095-683X International Directory of the Nonwoven Fabrics Industry
0095-6848 Journal of Japanese Studies
0095-6880 National Computer Conference and Exposition. (Proceedings)
0095-6910 Homegrown†
0095-6937 V.D. Fact Sheet
0095-6945 Intersections
0095-6953 N.A.D.A. Motorcycle Appraisal Guide
0095-702X Rendezvous of Western Art†
0095-7100 B N A Pension Reporter
0095-7119 Best Science Fiction of the Year
0095-7143 O.T.S.: off-the-Shelf Catalog of Electro Products
0095-7151 Convenience Store Merchandiser
0095-7186 Election Index
0095-7216 Hip
0095-7232 Reviews in European History†
0095-7240 World Almanac Guide to Pro Hockey
0095-7267 California. Office of Criminal Justice Planning. Bulletin
0095-7275 Electronics and Equipment Market Abstracts *see* 0161-8032
0095-7291 Foreign Tax Law Bi-Weekly Bulletin
0095-733X Michigan. Department of Management and Budget. Annual Report
0095-7348 Minnesota and Environs Weather Almanac *changed to* Weather Guide Calendar
0095-7356 Monthly Energy Review
0095-7364 New England Journal on Prison Law
0095-7526 Electric Vehicle News
0095-7577 Journal of Space Law
0095-7607 European Parliament Digest†
0095-7615 Grumman Aerospace Horizons
0095-7755 Software Briefs†
0095-7771 Foreign Trade Reports. U.S. Airborne Exports and General Imports
0095-781X National Savings and Loan League Journal
0095-7917 Current Contents/Engineering, Technology & Applied Sciences
0095-795X U. S. Library of Congress. Accessions List: Brazil
0095-7976 Materials Performance Buyer's Guide
0095-7984 Journal of Black Psychology
0095-8050 Massachusetts. Rehabilitation Commission. Expenditures Report
0095-8107 New Harbinger; a Journal of the Cooperative Movement *see* 0190-2741
0095-8115 Discography Series
0095-8174 Virginia. Department of Labor and Industry. Division of Research and Statistics. Occupational Injuries and Illnesses by Industry
0095-8247 Illinois. Fire Protection Personnel Standards and Education Commission. Annual Report
0095-8301 Diabetes Forecast
0095-8387 Del-Chem Bulletin
0095-8956 Journal of Combinatorial Theory. Series B.
0095-8964 Journal of Environmental Education
0095-8972 Journal of Coordination Chemistry
0095-926X U.S. Bureau of Labor Statistics. CPI Detailed Report
0095-9286 New Silver Technology
0095-9294 National Center for the Study of Collective Bargaining in Higher Education. Annual Conference Proceedings
0095-9626 Journal of Morphology and Physiology *see* 0362-2525
0095-9650 American Society of Agronomy. Journal *see* 0002-1962
0095-9782 Journal of Solution Chemistry
0095-9782 Journal of Solid-Phase Biochemistry *see* 0273-2289
0095-9960 Ceramic Abstracts
0096-0179 Connecticut State Medical Journal *see* 0010-6178
0096-0551 Computer Languages
0096-0764 Fluid Mechanics - Soviet Research
0096-0772 Foote Prints
0096-0802 Heat Transfer - Japanese Research
0096-1159 Graphic Arts Technical Foundation. Research Project Report
0096-1191 Journal of Foraminiferal Research
0096-1221 International Pacific Halibut Commission. Report *see* 0579-3920
0096-1248 Tennessee Valley Authority. Division of Land and Forest Resources. Technical Note
0096-1337 Journal of Undergraduate Psychological Research†
0096-1353 Ford's Deck Plan Guide
0096-140X Aggressive Behavior
0096-1442 Journal of Urban History
0096-1469 Ashleys of America Quarterly *changed to* Ashleys of America
0096-1507 A I D Research and Development Abstracts
0096-1515 Journal of Experimental Psychology: Human Learning and Memory (JEP: HLM)
0096-1523 Journal of Experimental Psychology: Human Perception and Performance (JEP: HPP)
0096-1736 J O M
0096-2023 Ice Cream Review *changed to* Dairy Field
0096-2031 Ice Cream Trade Journal *changed to* Dairy Field
0096-2279 Colorado-Wyoming Academy of Sciences Journal
0096-2333 Rubber Age and Tire News *see* 0146-0706
0096-2341 U.S. Library of Congress. Accessions List: Southeast Asia
0096-2546 Ice Cream Field *changed to* Dairy Field
0096-2651 Fieldiana: Geology
0096-2708 Horizons in Biochemistry and Biophysics
0096-2716 Contact Lens Journal
0096-2732 Journal of Preventive Dentistry *see* 0163-9633
0096-2740 Perspective on Aging
0096-3003 Applied Mathematics and Computation
0096-3054 Nebraska. Office of Mental Retardation. Directory of Community-Based Mental Retardation Services
0096-3070 Florida State University Law Review
0096-3089 Geochimica†
0096-3135 Politeia
0096-3143 Orange County Bar Journal
0096-3259 Translator Referral Directory†
0096-3291 Yearbook of Science and the Future
0096-3364 Current Aviation Statistics
0096-3402 Bulletin of the Atomic Scientists
0096-3445 Journal of Experimental Psychology: General (JEP: GEN)
0096-3518 I E E E Transactions. Acoustics, Speech & Signal Processing
0096-3925 Moscow University Biological Sciences Bulletin
0096-3941 Eos
0096-4077 Tulane Studies in Geology *see* 0041-4018
0096-4417 American Horticulturist
0096-5332 Advances in Carbohydrate Chemistry *see* 0065-2318
0096-591X Textile Colorist and Converter *see* 0002-8266
0096-7033 Lying-in *see* 0024-7758
0096-736X S A E Transactions
0096-7750 Academy of Natural Sciences of Philadelphia. Monographs
0096-7807 Soviet Journal of Ecology
0096-848X Yearbook of Physical Anthropology (Washington)
0096-8684 Begonian
0096-8765 Systems-Computers-Controls
0096-8803 U.S. Library of Congress. Subject Catalog
0096-882X Journal of Studies on Alcohol
0096-8846 Italian Americana
0096-8870 Gas Processors Association. Annual Convention. Proceedings
0096-9877 U.S. Bureau of the Census. Data User News
0096-9907 International Economic Indicators and Competitive Trends
0097-0042 Railroad Research Bulletin
0097-0050 Health Education
0097-0085 Medicolegal News
0097-0220 Keyword Index in Internal Medicine

ISSN INDEX 1187

0097-0247 Journal of Fire & Flammability/Fire Retardant Chemistry *see* 0362-1693
0097-0549 Neuroscience and Behavioral Physiology
0097-0638 American Fisheries Society. Special Publications
0097-109X Progress in Cardiology
0097-1138 Absolute Sound
0097-1146 Anima
0097-1162 Journal of Fire & Flammability/ Consumer Product Flammability Supplement *see* 0362-1677
0097-1170 Journal of Physical Education and Recreation *changed to* Journal of Physical Education, Recreation and Dance
0097-1189 State O'Maine Facts
0097-1510 Virginia Polytechnic Institute and State University. Research Division. Report
0097-2126 American Power Conference. Proceedings.
0097-2509 International Pulp & Paper Directory
0097-3157 Academy of Natural Sciences of Philadelphia. Proceedings
0097-3165 Journal of Combinatorial Theory. Series A
0097-3254 Academy of Natural Sciences of Philadelphia. Special Publications
0097-3289 Milk Dealer *changed to* Dairy Field
0097-3599 Journal of Medical Research *see* 0002-9440
0097-4145 American Concrete Institute. Proceedings
0097-4463 Carnegie Museum of Natural History. Annals of (the) Carnegie Museum
0097-4536 Cross Ties
0097-4943 Computers & Mathematics with Applications
0097-5184 Nineteenth Century
0097-5192 Official Airline Guide. International Edition *see* 0364-3875
0097-5257 Pediatric Nephrology†
0097-5427 Wadley Medical Bulletin *see* 0162-9360
0097-6075 Creativity
0097-6156 A C S Symposium Series
0097-6164 Advocate (Springfield) *changed to* I E A/N E A Advocate
0097-6172 America: History and Life. Part B: Index to Book Reviews
0097-6180 American Congress on Surveying and Mapping. Bulletin
0097-6237 Florida Journal of Commerce/American Shipper *see* 0160-225X
0097-627X American Dance Therapy Association. Monographs†
0097-6326 U. S. Office of the Federal Register. Federal Register
0097-6482 Analog Sounds
0097-6539 Hype
0097-7004 Modern China
0097-7209 Crystal Mirror
0097-7268 North Cal - Neva Resource Conservation and Development Project. Annual Work Plan
0097-7314 International Tax Journal
0097-7330 Magnetic Resonance Review: A Quarterly Literature Review Journal
0097-739X Wyoming Area Manpower Review
0097-7403 Journal of Experimental Psychology: Animal Behavior Processes (JEP: ABP)
0097-7519 Water Quality Monitoring Data for Georgia Streams
0097-7675 West Virginia Economic Profile
0097-7721 G T E Journal of Research and Development†
0097-7764 U.S. Civil Service Commission. Manpower Statistics Division. Study of Employment of Women in the Federal Government†
0097-7799 U. S. Office of Management and Budget. Catalog of Federal Domestic Assistance
0097-7829 Copper *see* 0163-4186
0097-7977 U.S. Administrative Office of the United States Courts. Report on Applications for Orders Authorizing or Approving the Interception of Wire or Oral Communications
0097-8035 Paid My Dues
0097-8043 Restaurant Business
0097-8078 Water Resources
0097-8124 Babe Ruth Baseball's Athletes of the Year†
0097-8140 Creative Computing
0097-8159 Energy Communications
0097-8167 Washington Post. Newspaper Index *see* 0195-6361
0097-8175 Gebbie Press All-in-One Directory
0097-8213 New Settler's Guide for Washington, D.C. and Communities in Nearby Maryland and Virginia
0097-8256 Record and Tape Reviews Index†
0097-8337 Consumer Guide Magazine: Auto
0097-8345 Credit (Washington)
0097-8353 Current Concepts in Ophthalmology
0097-8388 I & S M
0097-8396 I C P Software Directory
0097-840X Journal of Human Stress
0097-8434 New Jersey Municipal Bond News
0097-8442 Ancient Interface
0097-8485 Computers & Chemistry
0097-8493 Computers & Graphics
0097-8507 Language (Baltimore)
0097-8523 European Labor and Working Class History Newsletter *see* 0147-5479
0097-8620 Current Prescribing†
0097-8779 O A G Worldwide Cruise & Shipline Guide
0097-8884 Bittersweet
0097-8892 Journal of Developmental Disabilities†
0097-8930 Computer Graphics
0097-8957 Consumer Guide Magazine: Stereo & Tape Equipment Test Reports
0097-8965 International Studies Newsletter
0097-9007 Government Reports Announcements and Index
0097-9031 J N M *see* 0161-5505
0097-9074 Johns Hopkins University. Population Information Program. Population Report. Series A. Oral Contraceptives
0097-9082 Johns Hopkins University. Population Information Program. Population Report. Series E. Law and Policy
0097-9090 Johns Hopkins University. Population Information Program. Population Report. Series I. Periodic Abstinence
0097-9104 Johns Hopkins University. Population Information Program. Population Report. Series K. Injectables and Implants
0097-9171 Wisconsin. Employment Relations Commission. Reporter
0097-9325 Nebraska Statistical Handbook
0097-9376 U.S. Mining Enforcement and Safety Administration. Informational Report
0097-9473 Ohio. Division of Geological Survey. Guidebook
0097-952X Cultural Information Service
0097-9546 Orchid Advocate
0097-9554 Securities Regulation Law Journal
0097-9562 Soroptimist of the Americas
0097-9627 Newspapers in Microform
0097-966X S I D International Symposium. Digest of Technical Papers
0097-9716 Journal of Dermatologic Surgery *see* 0148-0812
0097-9740 Signs
0097-9759 Cooperative Housing Bulletin
0097-9783 Human Life Review
0097-9791 Middle East Review
0097-9805 Pediatric Nursing
0097-9813 Litigation
0097-9953 Arizona. Advisory Commission on Arizona Environment. Annual Report *changed to* Arizona. Governor's Commission on Arizona Environment. Annual Report
0098-0005 List of Legal Investments for Savings Banks in Connecticut
0098-0110 Missouri. State Division of Youth Services. Annual Report *changed to* Missouri. Division of Youth Services. Annual Report
0098-0129 Transportation Focus†
0098-0161 Advances in Sex Hormone Research
0098-0234 U.S. Federal Highway Administration Research and Development Program
0098-0242 Foreign Trade Reports. U.S. Exports - Schedule B - Commodity by Country *see* 0190-499X
0098-0269 Illinois. Department of Public Instruction. Annual State of Education Message *changed to* Illinois. State Board of Education. Annual Report
0098-0285 New Jersey. Department of Labor and Industry. Division of Planning and Research. Commercial and Industrial Construction Plans Approved; Annual Summary†
0098-0307 Michigan Labor Market Review
0098-0331 Journal of Chemical Ecology
0098-0366 Somatic Cell Genetics
0098-0382 Ultrasound in Medicine
0098-0404 Air Carrier Traffic Statistics
0098-0471 Film Review Digest†
0098-051X North Carolina. Division of Social Services. Statistical Journal
0098-0579 Human Rights Organizations & Periodicals Directory
0098-0730 Soul in Review
0098-0757 Alcohol, Tobacco and Firearms Bulletin
0098-079X Maine Prosecutor, Criminal Legislation Manual
0098-0846 Wyoming. Water Quality Division. Wyoming State Plan
0098-0889 Radioassay News
0098-0897 Resources in Education
0098-0900 Center for Hermeneutical Studies in Hellenistic and Modern Culture. Protocol Series of the Colloquies
0098-096X Directory of Occupational Education Programs in New York State
0098-1052 Texas Family Physician
0098-1109 Directory of U. S. Government Audiovisual Personnel
0098-1133 Official Gazette of the United States Patent and Trademark Office. Patents
0098-1176 Chicago Tribune. Newspaper Index *see* 0195-6353
0098-1184 Index to the Christian Science Monitor
0098-1192 Los Angeles Times. Newspaper Index *see* 0195-6418
0098-1206 New Orleans Times-Picayune. Newspaper Index *see* 0195-640X
0098-1214 Asia Society. Annual Report
0098-1222 Insects of Virginia
0098-1230 Bicycle Bibliography *see* 0193-8584
0098-1273 Journal of Polymer Science. Polymer Physics Edition
0098-1354 Computers & Chemical Engineering
0098-1389 Social Work in Health Care
0098-1397 Marketing Economics Key Plants
0098-1435 California Employer
0098-1451 National Directory of Summer Interships for Undergraduate Students
0098-1508 Directory of Visiting Fulbright Scholars in the United States
0098-1524 Emergency Physician Legal Bulletin
0098-1532 Medical and Pediatric Oncology
0098-1540 Microbiology (Washington)
0098-1575 Practical Guide to Individual Income Tax Return Preparation *changed to* 1040 Preparation
0098-1605 Anthropology Newsletter
0098-1613 Fodor's Japan and Korea
0098-163X History in Newspaper Front Pages
0098-1664 Student Activities Programming
0098-1672 Year Book of Diagnostic Radiology
0098-1729 Income Tax Guide for Military Personnel
0098-1745 Motor's Auto Repair Manual
0098-1753 Pension World
0098-180X Hospital Infection Control
0098-1850 Abstracts of Doctoral Dissertations in Anthropology
0098-1974 Missouri Vital Statistics
0098-2067 Policy Analysis
0098-2091 National Basic Intelligence Factbook
0098-2113 Currents in Theology and Mission
0098-2121 De-Acquisitions Librarian *see* 0146-2679
0098-213X Forecast
0098-2164 Academy of Sciences of the U S S R. Biology Bulletin
0098-2180 Emergency Product News *see* 0162-5942
0098-2199 John Berryman Studies†
0098-2202 Journal of Fluids Engineering
0098-2210 Metal Distribution
0098-2245 F & O S *see* 0160-4570
0098-2318 Beverage World
0098-2326 Hebert's Catalogue of Used Plate Number Singles *changed to* Hebert's Catalogue of Plate Number Singles
0098-2369 Brand X International
0098-2377 American Group Practice Association Directory
0098-2423 Sexual Law Reporter
0098-2466 Dun & Bradstreet's Guide to Your Investments
0098-2512 Washington Report on Health Legislation
0098-2547 Fodor's Caribbean, Bahamas and Bermuda
0098-2571 Automotive Engineering
0098-2601 Eighteenth Century Life
0098-261X Justice System Journal
0098-2644 Yearbook of Herpetology
0098-2741 M G World *changed to* M G International
0098-275X Studies in Modern European History and Culture
0098-2784 Bibliography and Index of Geology
0098-2806 Fate of Drugs in the Organism; a Bibliographic Survey
0098-2814 APhArmacy Weekly
0098-2822 Art and Architecture Book Guide *see* 0360-2699
0098-2830 Federal Home Loan Bank of San Francisco. Annual Report.
0098-2857 National Bar Examination Digest
0098-2865 N A H B Journal-Scope *changed to* NA H B Builder
0098-2873 Estate Planning Review
0098-2881 Council on Anthropology and Education Quarterly *see* 0161-7761
0098-2997 Molecular Aspects of Medicine
0098-3004 Computers & Geosciences
0098-3039 Urban Life
0098-3047 C S A Specs Buying Guide for Store Planners
0098-3063 I E E E Transactions. Consumer Electronics
0098-308X U.S. National Capital Planning Commission. Quarterly Review of Commission Proceedings
0098-311X Health Consequences of Smoking
0098-3209 U. S. Department of Transportation. Annual Report on Highway Safety Improvement Programs
0098-3284 Graduate
0098-3292 Hospitality, Restaurant *see* 0147-9989
0098-3322 Yellow Book of Funeral Directors & Services
0098-3373 Newark Museum Quarterly
0098-3403 Maryland Historical Trust. Annual Report
0098-342X Science Books & Films
0098-3446 Medical Electronics & Data *changed to* Medical Electronics
0098-3462 Health and Rehabilitative Library Services News *changed to* H R L S D Journal
0098-3470 Drug Enforcement
0098-3497 Current Governments Reports: Local Government Employment in Selected Metropolitan Areas and Large Counties

1188 ISSN INDEX

0098-3500 A C M Transactions on Mathematical Software
0098-3519 Cruising World
0098-3527 Dulcimer Players News
0098-3543 American Association of Veterinary Laboratory Diagnosticians. Proceedings of Annual Meeting
0098-3551 I E E E Vehicular Technology Conference. Record
0098-356X Schwann-1, Records and Tapes *changed to* Schwann-1 Record & Tape Guide
0098-3608 Labor Rates for the Construction Industry
0098-3616 Medicaid Recipient Characteristics and Units of Selected Medical Services
0098-3624 Motor Truck Repair Manual
0098-3675 Urban Anthropology Newsletter
0098-3888 U. S. Department of Defense. Report of Secretary of Defense to the Congress
0098-3896 U. S. Treasury Department. Bureau of Government Financial Operations. Report on Foreign Currencies Held by the U. S. Government
0098-3942 Federal Communications Commission Reports
0098-4000 U.S. Department of Agriculture. Economics, Statistics, and Cooperatives Service. Agricultural Situation in Eastern Europe
0098-4027 United States. Defense Property Disposal Service. Annual Historical Summary†
0098-4035 U. S. Advisory Council on Historic Preservation. Report†
0098-4094 I E E E Transactions. Circuits and Systems
0098-4108 Journal of Toxicology and Environmental Health
0098-4132 State Directory of Higher Education Institutions and Agencies in Maryland†
0098-4485 Doctoral Dissertations on Asia
0098-4507 Sav-on-Hotels
0098-4574 Woodwind World-Brass & Percussion
0098-4582 Columbia Journal of Environmental Law
0098-4590 Florida Scientist
0098-4604 Index to U.S. Government Periodicals
0098-4612 Journal of Political Science (Clemson)
0098-4752 Condition of Education
0098-4760 Old Fort Log
0098-4779 Equipment Market Abstracts *see* 0161-8032
0098-4817 National Sculpture Society, New York. Annual Exhibition
0098-4825 Utah Geological and Mineral Survey. Bulletin
0098-4833 Medical Law Letter for Physicians, Surgeons & Health Professionals
0098-4841 Copper State Bulletin
0098-4922 U.S. National Oceanic and Atmospheric Administration. Report to the Congress on Ocean Pollution, Overfishing, and Offshore Development
0098-4981 American Portuguese Society. Journal
0098-5058 Wyoming. Governor's Office of Highway Safety. Annual Report
0098-5082 Wisconsin. Division of Highway Safety Coordination. Highway Safety Report to the Legislature
0098-5104 Energy Abstracts for Policy Analysis
0098-5139 Ohio. Advisory Council for Vocational Education. Annual Report
0098-5147 California Private School Directory
0098-5244 Joint Center for Urban Studies. Research Report from M I T-Harvard
0098-5279 Data Book on Illinois Higher Education
0098-5368 Pennsylvania Chamber of Commerce. Directory of State, Regional and Commercial Organizations
0098-5376 Equipment & Technology International†
0098-5422 Spur
0098-5430 American Paint & Coatings Journal
0098-5449 Faith & Reason
0098-5481 Backstage TV Film/Tape & Syndication Directory
0098-5554 Current Christian Books. Authors and Titles *changed to* Current Christian Books
0098-5562 Current Christian Books. Titles, Authors, and Publishers *changed to* Current Christian Books
0098-5570 United States National Student Association. N S A Magazine†
0098-5589 I E E E Transactions. Software Engineering
0098-5597 Review of Education
0098-5619 Training Resources
0098-5651 Oklahoma Health Statistics
0098-5708 Hawaii. Criminal Injuries Compensation Commission. Annual Report.
0098-5716 Idaho. Department of Agriculture. Annual Report
0098-5910 Society of Wireless Pioneers. Yearbook
0098-5929 Working Papers on Language Universals†
0098-5937 U T U News
0098-5961 Law and Psychology Review
0098-597X Journal of Computer-Based Instruction
0098-5988 Basketball Digest
0098-6054 Romanian Sources
0098-6062 Index to St. Louis Newspapers
0098-6089 Advances in Neurochemistry
0098-6127 Artery
0098-616X Psychopharmacology Communications†
0098-6186 Connecticut State Industrial Directory
0098-6194 Maine State Industrial Directory
0098-6208 Vermont State Industrial Directory
0098-6216 New Hampshire State Industrial Directory
0098-6224 New Jersey State Industrial Directory
0098-6232 Delaware Valley Regional Planning Commission. Biennial Report *changed to* Delaware Valley Regional Planning Commission. Annual Report
0098-6240 Medical Tribune and Medical News *see* 0279-9340
0098-6275 S A L A L M Newsletter
0098-6283 Teaching of Psychology
0098-6291 Teaching English in the Two-Year College
0098-6305 E N R Directory of Design Firms
0098-6356 Academic Year Abroad in Europe-Africa-Australia
0098-6399 New Jersey. Department of Human Services. Community Mental Health Projects Summary Statistics
0098-6445 Chemical Engineering Communications
0098-6453 E N R Directory of Contractors
0098-6461 Mideast Markets†
0098-647X Research Opportunities in Renaissance Drama
0098-6569 Catheterization and Cardiovascular Diagnosis
0098-6615 Ecology U S A
0098-6623 U.S. Center for Disease Control. Foodborne & Waterborne Disease Outbreaks. Annual Summary
0098-6631 Golden Gate Law Review *see* 0363-0307
0098-6658 Microelectronics *see* 0363-8529
0098-6739 Kentucky Vital Statistics *see* 0145-5990
0098-6755 Delaware State Minority Business Directory
0098-678X Current Governments Reports: County Government Finances
0098-681X U. S. Federal Trade Commission. Quarterly Financial Report for Manufacturing, Mining and Trade Corporations
0098-6828 Arizona. State Dental Board. Report.
0098-6925 Modern Pharmacology-Toxicology
0098-6976 Wisconsin Journal of Public Instruction†
0098-6984 Wyoming. Department of Health and Social Services. Annual Report
0098-7077 New Mexico. Bureau of Mines and Mineral Resources. Progress Report
0098-7093 Coldspring Journal
0098-7174 Pennsylvania Police Criminal Law Bulletin
0098-7182 Flight Safety Facts & Reports
0098-7239 Issues in Media Management
0098-7298 Journal of Applied Photographic Engineering
0098-7301 Perspectives on Contemporary Literature
0098-7336 Bankruptcy Court Decisions
0098-7379 Annual Review of English Books on Asia *changed to* Review of English Books on Asia
0098-7387 Arizona Commission on the Arts & Humanities. Report to the Governor.
0098-7409 New Jersey. Division of Banking. Annual Report *changed to* New Jersey. Department of Banking. Annual Report
0098-7484 J A M A: the Journal of the American Medical Association
0098-7530 Product Safety Letter
0098-7557 Downtown Malls *see* 0364-586X
0098-7565 Creative Child and Adult Quarterly
0098-7573 Devices & Diagnostics Letter
0098-7611 B A R-B R I Bar Review. Torts
0098-762X B A R-B R I Bar Review. Contracts
0098-7638 B A R-B R I Bar Review. Constitutional Law
0098-7689 Genealogy Digest†
0098-7719 International Law Perspective
0098-7735 National Urban League Progress Report *changed to* National Urban League Annual Report
0098-7778 Package Printing and Diecutting *see* 0163-9234
0098-7786 Modern Paint and Coatings
0098-7840 Mississippi. State Game and Fish Commission. Annual Report to the Regular Session of the Mississippi Legislature
0098-7875 Michigan. Office of the Court Administrator. Judicial Statistics
0098-7913 Serials Review
0098-7921 Population and Development Review
0098-793X Allied Landscape Industry Member Directory
0098-7956 Historical Evaluation and Research Organization. Combat Data Subscription Service†
0098-7980 Bay Area Review Course. Legal Ethics *changed to* B A R-B R I Bar Review. Professional Responsibility
0098-7999 B A R-B R I Bar Review. Remedies
0098-8014 Shellfish Market Review and Outlook
0098-8049 B A R-B R I Bar Review. Criminal Law
0098-8073 New Jersey. Division of Savings and Loan Associations. Annual Report *changed to* New Jersey. Department of Banking. Annual Report
0098-8111 U.S. President's Committee on Mental Retardation. Mental Retardation and the Law
0098-8138 Connecticut. Judicial Department. Report
0098-8162 N C C C Chronicles
0098-8170 Fish and Wildlife Reference Service Newsletter
0098-8243 Comprehensive Therapy
0098-826X Nebraska. Governor's Conference on Human Resource Development Report†
0098-8278 I A S S W Directory; Member Schools and Associations
0098-8332 California. Employment Data and Research Division. Taxable and Total Wages, Regular Benefits Paid, Employer Contributions Earned, and Average Covered Employment, by Industry
0098-8340 Canto Libre
0098-8359 Export-Import Bank of the United States. Cumulative Records†
0098-8383 Marine Science Communications *changed to* Ocean Science and Engineering
0098-8405 U.S. Administration on Aging. Annual Report
0098-8472 Environmental and Experimental Botany
0098-8510 Pennsylvania. Department of Public Welfare. Public Welfare Annual Statistics
0098-8537 Homicide in California
0098-8561 Idaho. Department of Health and Welfare. Bureau of Research and Statistics. Research Report *changed to* Idaho. Department of Health and Welfare. Bureau of Research and Statistics. Quarterly Welfare Statistical Bulletin
0098-857X Scandinavian Review
0098-8588 American Journal of Law & Medicine
0098-860X Birth and the Family Journal
0098-8650 Bike World
0098-8669 Down River *see* 0161-052X
0098-8685 Nordic World *changed to* Skier's World
0098-8707 Soccer World†
0098-8731 North Carolina Review of Business and Economics
0098-874X Florida Administrative Weekly
0098-8766 Maryland. Commission on Intergovernmental Cooperation. Annual Report
0098-8782 North Dakota. Social Service Board Statistics, Juvenile Court and State Youth Authority *changed to* North Dakota. Social Service Board. Juvenile Court and State Youth Authority. Delinquency, Dependency and Neglect. Special Proceedings
0098-8820 Ohio. Attorney General's Office. Report
0098-8847 Earthquake Engineering and Structural Dynamics
0098-8855 Alternatives†
0098-8863 Exposure
0098-8898 Employee Relations Law Journal
0098-8901 Land Use Planning Abstracts
0098-891X Lending Law Forum
0098-8928 Marketing California Pears for Fresh Market
0098-8936 Real Estate Directory of Manhattan
0098-8944 United States League of Savings Associations. Annals
0098-8952 School Student and the Courts *changed to* Schools and the Courts
0098-8960 Upshaw Family Journal
0098-8987 Texas Lawyers' Weekly Digest
0098-9010 73 Magazine for Radio Amateurs
0098-9037 Country Music News
0098-9053 Linguistic Analysis
0098-9061 Quarterly Survey of Judicial Salaries in State Court Systems *changed to* Survey of Judicial Salaries in State Court Systems
0098-907X Optics News
0098-910X U.S. International Trade Commission. Quarterly Report to the Congress and the East-West Foreign Trade Board on Trade Between the United States and the Nonmarket Economy Countries
0098-9134 Journal of Gerontological Nursing
0098-9142 R C. Respiratory Care *changed to* Respiratory Care (1980)
0098-9169 Assets Protection
0098-9193 Southeast Louisiana Historical Association. Papers
0098-9207 Qualified Remodeler
0098-9215 Radio Control Buyers Guide
0098-9223 Reflections
0098-924X Centerpoint
0098-9355 French Forum
0098-9363 Ascent
0098-9371 Children's Book Showcase. Catalog†
0098-9398 Media Guide International. Business Publications Edition *see* 0164-1743
0098-9444 Biblical Archaeology Review
0098-9452 Chariton Review
0098-9487 I. A. J. R. C. Journal
0098-9495 Journal of Education Finance
0098-9509 Marxism and the Mass Media
0098-9517 Sabbath Watchman
0098-9525 Union (Cranford)
0098-9533 National Journal of Criminal Defense
0098-9541 New Jersey Orchard and Vineyard Survey
0098-955X Quest (Washington)

0098-9568 Real Estate Valuation Cost File
0098-9584 Journal of School Social Work†
0098-9665 Index to Scientific Reviews. Guide and Journal Lists†
0098-972X U.S. National Institute of Mental Health. Mental Health Statistical Notes
0098-9738 Aha Ilono
0098-9770 Kentucky. Council on Public Higher Education. Origin of Enrollments, Accredited Colleges and Universities
0098-9819 Current Physics Index
0098-9827 Educational opportunity Program Notes†
0098-9835 Guide to Professional Development Opportunities for College and University Administrators: Seminars, Workshops, Conferences, and Internships
0098-9886 International Journal of Circuit Theory & Applications
0099-0027 Professional Safety
0099-0035 National Bluegrass News
0099-0043 Engravers Journal
0099-0051 Bowling-Fencing Guide *changed to* N A G W S Guide. Bowling-Golf
0099-006X Council of State Governments. Southern Legislative Conference. Summary, Annual Meeting
0099-0086 College and Research Libraries News
0099-0094 Environmental Geology
0099-0108 Connecticut. Treasury Department. Annual Report
0099-0159 Goldenseal
0099-0167 Schwann-2, Records and Tapes *changed to* Schwann-2 Record & Tape Guide
0099-0205 N A A Where to Stay Book
0099-0213 Grant Information System
0099-0248 C R C Critical Reviews in Food Science and Nutrition
0099-0256 Accreditation
0099-0264 Moons and Lion Tailes
0099-0299 Nebraska Library Commission. Annual Report
0099-0302 Pennsylvania. Department of Education. Special Education Programs-Services
0099-0310 Professional Decorating & Coating Action
0099-0329 Western Society for French History. Proceedings of the Annual Meeting
0099-0353 Commercial Fish Farmer and Aquaculture News *see* 0199-1388
0099-037X Progress in Behavior Modification
0099-0396 Time Barrier Express
0099-0418 Bay Area Review Course. Conflicts of Law†
0099-0442 Nebraska Highway Statistics: State and Local Construction Mileage *changed to* Nebraska. Department of Roads. Highway Statistics: State and Local Road and Street Data for (Year)
0099-0450 Plastics Manufacturing Capabilities in Mississippi
0099-0604 Harmony (Harmony)
0099-0671 W.V.O.E.S. Annual Report
0099-0728 Kansas Educational Directory
0099-0809 Index of Trademarks Issued from the U.S. Patent and Trademark Office
0099-085X Southeastern Library Network. Annual Report *changed to* Solinet. Annual Report
0099-0868 Common Ground (Hanover)
0099-0876 Index to Pravda
0099-0906 New Dimensions Science Fiction
0099-1015 County Year Book†
0099-1023 Indiana Public Management
0099-1031 Bar Leader
0099-1058 State Bar of Arizona. Newsletter
0099-1066 U.S. Department of Agriculture. Economics, Statistics, and Cooperatives Service. Agricultural Outlook
0099-1090 I F P A Communicator
0099-1112 Photogrammetric Engineering and Remote Sensing
0099-1147 Advances in Pathobiology
0099-121X I E E E/O S A Conference on Laser Engineering and Applications. Digest of Technical Papers
0099-1236 B A R-B R I Bar Review. Corporations
0099-1244 B A R-B R I Bar Review. Civil Procedure
0099-1279 Wyoming. Department of Environmental Quality. Annual Report
0099-1333 Journal of Academic Librarianship
0099-135X Detroit College of Law Review
0099-1546 Progress in Anesthesiology
0099-1554 Training Directory of the Rehabilitation Research and Training Centers
0099-166X Defense Survey and Directory *changed to* Defense & Economy World Report & Survey
0099-1694 Desarrollo Nacional-Servicios Publicos
0099-1716 A/E Concepts in Wood Design
0099-1759 Faith for the Family
0099-1767 J E N
0099-1791 Luptonian
0099-1821 N C R R Bulletin
0099-183X Social Thought
0099-1848 Collier Bankruptcy Cases
0099-1864 Martin Family Quarterly
0099-1872 Industrial Growth in Tennessee, Annual Report
0099-1929 Louisiana. Department of Agriculture. Analysis of Official Pesticide Samples; Annual Report
0099-2011 Meat Industry
0099-2100 State Health Benefits Program of New Jersey. Annual Report
0099-2224 Management Research (Amherst)
0099-2240 Applied and Environmental Microbiology
0099-2267 U.S. Department of Transportation. Office of University Research. Awards to Academic Institutions by the Department of Transportation
0099-2305 South Dakota. State Department of Public Welfare. Research and Statistics Annual Report
0099-2313 Sunset Ideas for Improving Your Home
0099-2356 Mid-South Folklore *changed to* Mid-America Folklore
0099-2399 Journal of Endodontics
0099-2445 Financial Analysis of the Motor Carrier Industry
0099-2453 Human Resources Abstracts
0099-4480 Illuminating Engineering Society. Journal
0099-8745 Na Okika O Hawaii
0100-0195 Revista Medica do Estado do Rio de Janeiro
0100-0217 Revista Pernambucana de Desenvolvimento
0100-0233 Revista Baiana de Saude Publica
0100-0551 Pesquisa e Planejamento Economico
0100-0705 Bibliografia Brasileira de Engenharia
0100-0756 Bibliografia Brasileira de Quimica e Quimica Tecnologica
0100-0829 Universidade Federal de Minas Gerais. Escola de Biblioteconomia. Revista
0100-0888 Revista Letras
0100-0977 Amazonia - Bibliografia
0100-123X Brazil. Servico Nacional de Levantamento e Conservacao de Solos. Boletim Tecnico
0100-1248 Navigator
0100-1876 Brazil. Biblioteca Nacional. Boletim Bibliografico
0100-1922 Brazil. Biblioteca Nacional. Anais
0100-1949 Bahia, Brazil (State). Centro de Pesquisas e Desenvolvimento. Boletim Tecnico
0100-1965 Ciencia da Informacao
0100-204X Pesquisa Agropecuaria Brasileira
0100-2716 Periodicos Brasileiros de Cultura *see* 0100-2767
0100-2767 Periodicos Brasileiros de Ciencias e Tecnologia
0100-3151 Instituto Florestal. Boletim Tecnico
0100-3364 Informe Agropecuario
0100-350X Instituto de Tecnologia de Alimentos. Coletanea
0100-3593 Energia Nuclear e Agricultura
0100-3941 Rede Ferroviaria Federal. Lista de Artigos Selecionados
0100-4271 Brasil(Year)
0100-4298 Agroanalysis
0100-4409 Sao Paulo, Brazil (State). Instituto de Economia Agricola. Informacoes Economicas
0100-4700 Natureza em Revista
0100-5146 Universidade de Sao Paulo. Instituto Oceanografico. Publicacao Especial
0100-5146 Universidade de Sao Paulo. Instituto Oceanografico. Relatorio Interno
0100-5162 Precos Medios do Boi Gordo e La
0100-5197 Universidade de Sao Paulo. Instituto Oceanographico. Relatorio de Cruzeiros
0100-5219 Precos Recebidos Pelos Agricultores
0100-526X Prognostico
0100-5316 Prognostico Regiao Centro-Sul
0100-560X Acompanhamento da Situcao Agropecuaria do Parana
0100-6266 Bibliografia Brasileira de Odontologia
0100-7912 Geografia
0105-001X Acta Linguistica *see* 0374-0463
0105-0168 Automatik
0105-0257 Kopenhagener Beitraege zur Germanistischen Linguistik
0105-032X L O-Bladet
0105-0656 Acta Pathologica et Microbiologica Scandinavica. Section B: Microbiology. Supplementum
0105-0834 Dansk Pelsdyrblad *see* 0011-6424
0105-1024 Folk og Kultur
0105-1040 Dansk Geologisk Forening. Meddelelser *see* 0011-6297
0105-1393 Psykologisk Litteratur i Danske Forskningsbiblioteker
0105-1423 Historia Medicinae Veterinariae
0105-1504 Alrune
0105-1873 Contact Dermatitis
0105-1938 Carlsberg Research Communications
0105-2373 Aktuel Elektronik
0105-2454 Welcome to Norway†
0105-2896 Immunological Reviews
0105-3094 Miljoe-Projekter
0105-3507 Groenlands Geologiske Undersoegelse. Bulletin
0105-3574 Entomologica Scandinavica. Supplementum
0105-4260 Forsikring
0105-4503 I W G I A Documents
0105-4538 Allergy
0105-4570 Landinspektoeren
0105-5216 Humaniora
0105-6492 N A A
0105-6603 D P A
0105-6611 Nordisk Tidsskrift for Rensning og Vask
0105-6654 Levnedsmiddelbladet-Supermarkedet
0105-7154 Historiske Studier fra Fyn
0105-7510 Orbis Litterarum
0105-7669 Contact with Denmark
0105-8010 Nordisk Kunst og Design
0105-810X Scanshore
0105-8401 Currero International de Interlingua
0105-8738 Trae og Industri
0105-9211 Fisk og Hav
0105-922X Polytekniske Laereanstalt, Danmarks Tekniske Hoejskole. Afdelingen for Baerende Konstruktioner. Rapport R
0105-9327 Holarctic Ecology
0105-9556 Skolebiblioteket
0105-9629 Installations Nyt
0105-9998 New Religious Movements Up-Date
0106-0104 Produktions Nyt
0106-0120 Dansk Fagpresse
0106-0279 Hjemkundskab
0106-0473 Auto Nyt
0106-0481 Kongelige Danske Videnskabernes Selskab. Historisk-Filosofiske Meddelelser
0106-0546 Ugeskrift for Jordbrug
0106-0627 1066 Tidsskrift for Historisk Forskning
0106-0864 Denmark. Jordbrugsoekonomisk Institut. Undersoegelse
0106-0953 Paedagogik
0106-1003 International Council for the Exploration of the Sea. Annales Biologiques
0106-1291 Denmark. Jordbrugsoekonomisk Institut. Landbrugets Oekonomi
0106-1348 ICO-Iconographisk Post
0106-147X Dansk Artikelindeks: Aviser og Tidsskrifter
0106-1585 Plast Nyt
0106-164X Elektronik Nyt
0106-1658 Agro Nyt
0106-1666 Virksomheds Nyt
0106-1887 Denmark. Statens Husholdningsraad. Pjecer
0106-2689 Denmark. Jordbrugsoekonomisk Institut. Meddelelse
0106-2891 Denmark. Ministeriet for Groenland. Statistisk Kontor. Meddelelser
0106-3014 U Vejviser
0106-3642 Denmark. Jordbrugsoekonomisk Institut. Memorandum
0106-3715 Bygningsstatiske Meddelelser
0106-4762 Denmark. Forskningensekretariatet. Forskningen og Samfundet
0106-4967 Denmark. Jordbrugsoekonomisk Institut. Aarsberetning
0106-519X Denmark. Jordbrugsoekonomisk Institut. Beretning
0106-5351 Lokalhistorisk Journal
0106-553X Denmark. Danmarks Fiskeri- og Havundersoegelser. Dana
0106-7265 Nordeuropaeisk Mejeri-Tidsskrift
0106-8881 V V S-Installatoeren
0106-9543 Liver
0107-055X Nordic Journal of Botany
0110-0068 Miorita
0110-0076 New Quarterly Cave *see* 0110-3970
0110-0084 Outrigger
0110-0262 New Zealand International Review
0110-0394 Soccer News
0110-0483 Country Side of Music
0110-070X Butterworths Current Law
0110-0831 New Zealand Annual
0110-084X Farming Statistics
0110-0858 Islands
0110-1048 What's New in Forest Research
0110-1153 Horticulture in N.Z.
0110-1277 New Zealand Administrative Reports
0110-1625 Turnbull Library Record
0110-1668 New Zealand Energy Journal
0110-1749 New Zealand. Ministry of Agriculture and Fisheries. Fisheries Research Division. Bulletin.
0110-1900 New Zealand. Department of Health. Hospital Management Data
0110-344X New Zealand. Department of Statistics. System of National Accounts
0110-3458 New Zealand. Department of Statistics. Transport Statistics
0110-3466 New Zealand. Department of Statistics. Local Authority Statistics
0110-3474 New Zealand, Department of Statistics. Insurance Statistics
0110-3482 New Zealand. Department of Statistics. Justice Statistics.
0110-375X New Zealand. Department of Statistics. Population and Migration Part A: Population
0110-3768 New Zealand. Department of Statistics. Population and Migration. Part B: External Migration
0110-3776 New Zealand. Department of Statistics. Incomes and Income Tax Statistics
0110-392X New Zealand Household Survey
0110-3970 Pacific Quarterly Moana
0110-4055 New Zealand. Department of Statistics. Quarterly Population Bulletin
0110-4373 Library Life
0110-4519 New Zealand. Ministry of Agriculture and Fisheries. Fisheries Research Division: Information Leaflet
0110-4527 Entomological Society of New Zealand. Bulletin
0110-4586 New Zealand. Department of Statistics. Vital Statistics
0110-4616 New Zealand. Department of Statistics. Balance of Payments

1190 ISSN INDEX

0110-4624 New Zealand. Department of Statistics. Agricultural Statistics
0110-4772 New Zealand Economist
0110-4969 New Zealand Environmental Health Inspector
0110-5019 New Zealand. Department of Statistics. Part A: Prices.
0110-5027 New Zealand. Department of Statistics. Part B: Wages and Labour
0110-5132 Book Trade Monthly
0110-5760 Royal New Zealand Institute of Horticulture. Annual Journal
0110-5787 New Zealand Listener
0110-585X English in New Zealand
0110-6007 New Zealand Cartographic Journal
0110-604X Wildlife - a Review
0110-6112 New Zealand. Department of Scientific and Industrial Research. Geophysics Division. Report
0110-6155 Rails
0110-618X N Z O I Records
0110-6376 S E T: Research Information for Teachers
0110-6392 New Zealand Operational Research
0110-666X Directory of Australian Associations
0110-7011 Blue Water
0110-7089 New Zealand. Department of Scientific and Industrial Research. Geophysics Division. Technical Note
0110-7720 Lincoln College. Agricultural Economics Research Unit. Discussion Paper
0110-7844 Forest Industries Review
0111-0470 New Zealand Planning Council. Planning Paper
0111-0829 New Zealand Agricultural Engineering Institute. Current Publications
0111-2821 N Z C E R Newsletter
0115-0243 Philippine Quarterly of Culture and Society
0115-0456 FORPRIDE Digest
0115-0553 Kalikasan
0115-0944 International Rice Research Newsletter
0115-0960 Canopy
0115-1142 International Rice Research Institute. Research Highlights
0115-1207 Philippine Astronomical Handbook
0115-1274 Philippine Science Index
0115-138X Integrated Bar of the Philippines. Journal
0115-1843 Builder of Progress
0115-2157 Trends in Technology
0115-2173 Philippine Journal of Veterinary and Animal Sciences
0115-2394 Trade Post
0115-2408 Journal of Northern Luzon
0115-2467 I R R I Reporter
0115-2521 University of Baguio Journal
0115-2661 Social Development News
0115-2742 Mindanao Journal
0115-2777 Technology Journal
0115-2971 Homelife
0115-3307 Philippines. Atmosphere, Geophysical and Astronomical Services Administration. Table of Sunrise, Sunset, Twilight, Moonrise and Moonset
0115-3676 Evergreen
0115-3757 Atomedia
0115-3862 I R R I Research Paper Series
0115-4575 I C L A R M Newsletter
0120-0216 Aleph
0120-0283 Universidad Industrial de Santander. Boletin de Geologia
0120-033X Revista E A F I T-Temas Administrativos
0120-0747 Estudios Rurales Latinoamericanos
0120-0798 Revista Acodal
0120-0852 Universidad Industrial de Santander. Revista - Investigaciones
0120-0887 C E R L A L: Noticias sobre el Libro y Bibliografia
0120-0909 Universidad Industrial de Santander. Revista - Medicina
0120-095X Universidad Industrial de Santander. Revista - Humanidades
0120-0976 Revista Interamericana de Bibliotecologia
0120-100X Universidad Industrial de Santander. Revista - Ion.
0120-1085 Museo de Arte Moderno. Boletin Informativo
0120-1131 Resumenes de la Literatura Medica Colombiana
0120-1158 Noticias CERLAL
0120-1263 Escritos
0120-1425 Boletin Geologico
0120-1468 Franciscanum
0120-1557 Revista de Egresados
0120-1603 Revista Universidad Tecnologica
0120-162X Educar
0120-1875 Informativo Juridico
0120-1921 Informativo Fasecolda
0120-1972 Fasecolda
0120-2278 Revista Cafetera de Colombia
0120-2499 Revista Centro Interamericano de Fotointerpretacion
0120-2669 Universidad Nacional de Colombia. Facultad de Arquitectura. Revista
0120-2758 Colombia. Observatorio Astronomico Nacional. Anuario
0125-0000 Thai Abstracts, Series A. Science and Technology
0125-0191 Thai-American Business
0125-1759 Journal of Ferrocement
0125-4529 Scientific Serials in Thai Libraries
0125-4537 List of Scientific and Technical Literature Relating to Thailand
0125-5606 N I D A Bulletin
0125-5827 Index to Thai Periodical Literature
0125-9008 Baca
0125-9229 Warta Ekonomi Maritim Review for Entrepreneurs
0125-9318 Menara Perkebunan
0126-0057 Trubus
0126-1282 Indeks Berita Surat Kabar
0126-1568 Atom Indonesia
0126-2319 Indonesia. Central Bureau of Statistics. Economic Indicator Bulletin
0126-2874 Nusa
0126-4273 Tempo
0126-5040 Malaysian Periodicals Index
0126-5156 Foram Pembangunan
0126-5210 Malaysian National Bibliography
0126-527X Malaysian Panorama
0126-5520 U M B C Economic Review
0126-5539 Geological Society of Malaysia. Newsletter *changed to* Warta Geologi
0126-5547 Timah
0126-5628 Malaysia. Geological Survey. Annual Report
0126-5849 Rubber Research Institute of Malaysia. Planters Conference Proceedings
0126-625X Accounting Journal
0126-6268 Surveyor
0126-6330 Directory of Timber Trade
0126-6586 Around Malaysia
0126-6705 Malaysian Mathematical Society. Bulletin
0126-690X Foreign Affairs Malaysia
0126-7558 Kuala Lumpur Stock Exchange. Companies Handbook
0126-7590 Southeast Asian Ministers of Education Organisation. Regional Centre for Education in Science and Mathematics. Library Accession List
0126-7612 R E C S A M News
0126-7663 Journal of Science and Mathematics Education in Southeast Asia
0126-771X Maskayu
0126-7809 Majallah Perpustakaan Malaysia
0126-8155 Southeast Asian-Ministers of Education Organisation. Regional Centre for Education in Science and Mathematics. Governing Board Meeting. Final Report
0126-8279 Rubber Research Institute of Malaysia. Annual Report
0126-8864 Malaysia. Meteorological Service. Summary of Observations for Malaysia
0126-8872 Monthly Abstract of Meteorological Observations of Malaysia
0129-2056 Asian Mass Communications Bulletin
0129-279X Singapore. National Statistical Commission. Statistical News
0129-2900 A S E A N Business Quarterly
0129-3117 Singapore Literature
0129-3214 Shaonian Yuekan
0129-4024 Asian Journal of Infectious Diseases
0129-4172 Asian Journal of Pharmaceutical Sciences
0129-5020 Singapore Travel
0129-508X Students' Literature
0129-6639 Young Generation
0129-6736 Harapan
0129-6787 New Worker
0129-6884 Singapore Arts
0133-0152 Magyar Kozgazdasagi Irodalom
0133-1655 Tajekoztato a Kulfoldi Kozgazdasagi Irodalomrol. Series B
0133-1736 Reaction Kinetics and Catalysis Letters
0133-2074 Szociologiai Informacio
0133-2929 Nehezipari Muszaki Egyetem, Miskolc. Publications. Series D: Natural Sciences
0133-297X Nehezipari Muszaki Egyetem, Miskolc. Publications. Series C: Machinery
0133-3046 Studia Comitatensia
0133-3267 Temadokumentacios Kiadvanyok
0133-3755 Kincskereso
0133-381X Szoleszet es Boraszat
0133-3852 Analysis Mathematica
0133-4751 Eletunk
0133-4875 Mezogazdasagi es Elelmiszeripari Konyvtarosok Tajekoztatoja
0133-5502 Hungarian Academy of Sciences. Central Research Institute for Physics. Yearbook
0133-5707 Muszaki es Gazdasagi Fejlodes Fo Iranyai
0133-6622 Folia Historica
0133-6673 Ars Decorativa
0133-6894 Magyar Nemzeti Bibliografia Idoszaki Kiadvanyok Repertoriuma
0133-736X Magyar Konyvtari Szakirodalom Bibliografiaja
0133-7505 Hungarika Irodalmi Szemle
0133-7769 Trends in World Economy
0133-8684 Hungary. Kozponti Statisztikai Hivatal. Ipari Zsebkonyv
0133-9133 Hungary. Kozponti Statisztikai Hivatal. Kulkereskedelmi Statisztikai Evkonyv
0134-0719 Journal of Radioanalytical Chemistry
0134-1103 Nemzetkozi Szemle
0134-1138 Hungary. Kozponti Statisztikai Hivatal. Belkereskedelmi Evkonyv
0134-1510 Informacio a Konyvtari Munka Eszkozeirol es Berendezeseirol
0137-1096 Acta Universitatis Wratislaviensis. Prace Pedagogiczne
0137-1215 Politechnika Wroclawska. Prace Naukoznawcze i Prognostyczne
0137-1223 Systems Science
0137-1339 Materials Science
0137-1398 Politechnika Wroclawska. Instytut Technologii Organicznej i Tworzyw Sztucznych. Prace Naukowe. Konferencje
0137-1983 Annales Universitatis Mariae Curie-Sklodowska. Sectio B. Geographia, Geologia, Mineralogia et Petrographia
0137-2025 Annales Universitatis Mariae Curie-Sklodowska. Sectio I. Philosophia-Sociologia
0137-2033 Annales Universitatis Mariae Curie-Sklodowska. Sectio F. Humaniora
0137-219X Eksploatacya Kolei
0137-284X Drogi Kolejowe
0137-2858 Automatyka Kolejowa
0137-2939 Polska Akademia Nauk. Oddzial w Krakowie. Osrodek Dokumentacji Fizjograficznej. Studia
0137-2963 Trakja i Wagony
0137-2998 Kwartalnik Historii Prasy Polskiej
0137-3013 Humanizacja Pracy
0137-303X Przeglad Polonijny
0137-3080 Estudios Latinoamericanos
0137-3404 Studia o Ksiazce
0137-3501 Rocznik Kaliski
0137-3595 Postepy Cybernetyki
0137-3943 Paideia
0137-4079 Ethnologia Polona
0137-4389 Studia Polono-Slavica Orientalia. Acta Litteraria
0137-4435 Transport Museums
0137-4885 Polish Archaeological Abstracts
0137-5326 Szkice Legnickie
0137-5806 Oeconomica Polona
0137-5830 Acta Universitatis Nicolai Copernici. Historia
0137-6217 Politechnika Wroclawska. Biblioteka Glowna i Osrodek Informacji Naukowo-Technicznej. Prace Naukowe. Konferencje
0137-6225 Politechnika Wroclawska. Biblioteka Glowna i Osrodek Informacji Naukowo-Technicznej. Prace Naukowe. Studia i Materialy
0137-6241 Politechnika Wroclawska. Instytut Budownictwa. Prace Naukowe. Studia i Materialy
0137-6284 Politechnika Wroclawska. Instytut Ukladow Elektromaszynowych. Prace Naukowe. Monografie
0137-6292 Politechnika Wroclawska. Instytut Ukladow Elektromaszynowych. Prace Naukowe. Przemysl
0137-6306 Politechnika Wroclawska. Osrodek Badan Prognostycznych. Prace Naukowe. Konferencje
0137-6322 Politechnika Wroclawska. Osrodek Badan Prognostycznych. Prace Naukowe. Studia i Materialy
0137-6330 Politechnika Wroclawska. Osrodek Badan Prognostycznych. Prace Naukowe. Wspolpraca.
0137-6349 Politechnika Wroclawska. Studium Praktycznej Nauki Jezykow Obcych. Prace Naukowe. Studia i Materialy
0137-6365 Studia Geotechnica et Mechanica
0137-6608 Studia Semiotyczne
0137-6616 Acta Universitatis Nicolai Copernici. Archeologia
0137-6896 Politechnika Poznanska. Zeszyty Naukowe. Chemia Techniki Zastosowan
0137-690X Politechnika Poznanska. Zeszyty Naukowe. Ekonomika i Organizacja Przemyslu
0137-6918 Politechnika Poznanska. Zeszyty Naukowe. Maszyny Robocze i Pojazdy
0137-6969 Politechnika Czestochowska. Zeszyty Naukowe. Nauki Techniczne. Mechanika
0137-6977 Politechnika Czestochowska. Zeszyty Naukowe. Nauki Techniczne. Elektrotechnika
0137-9585 Rocznik Pedagogiczny
0137-9860 Studies on the Developing Countries
0138-8452 Revista Cubana de Investigaciones Pesqueras
0139-4045 Marx Karoly Kozgazdasagtudomanyi Egytem. Egyetemi Szemle/University Review
0139-4533 Hungary. Kozponti Statisztikai Hivatal. Belkereskedelmi es Idegenforgalmi Adatok
0139-5106 Novinky Literatury: Biologie
0139-5203 Novinky Literatury: Ekonomie
0139-5351 Novinky Literatury: Chemie
0139-5408 Novinky Literatury: Matematika. Fyzika
0139-5459 Novinky Literatury: Novinky Knihovnicke Literatury
0139-6765 Vodni Sporty
0139-7915 Zakladni a Rekreacni Telesna Vychova
0139-8571 Biologizace a Chemizace Zivocisne Vyroby-Veterinaria
0140-0053 Emergency Services News
0140-0118 Medical & Biological Engineering & Computing
0140-0525 Hazards Bulletin
0140-0649 International Communist

0140-0673 Creativity Network
0140-072X International Advances in Nondestructive Testing
0140-0851 Folk News
0140-0991 Kingsman
0140-1300 Traveller's Guide to Africa
0140-1319 Traveller's Guide to the Middle East
0140-1599 Acoustics Letters
0140-1750 Journal of Social and Biological Structures
0140-1874 Arab Business Yearbook
0140-1890 Antenna
0140-2188 C B I News
0140-2285 Jazz Journal International
0140-2382 West European Politics
0140-2390 Journal of Strategic Studies
0140-2447 New Literature on Old Age
0140-2722 British Medicine
0140-2773 Interlending Review: Journal of the British Library Lending Division
0140-2935 Envoy International
0140-3028 Medical Laboratory World
0140-315X Concetto
0140-3230 Education Equipment, Primary & Middle School Edition *changed to* Primary & Middle School Equipment
0140-3273 Health Education Index
0140-332X Historic Society of Lancashire and Cheshire. Transactions
0140-3397 Quinquereme
0140-3435 Which Computer?
0140-3494 Browne Records
0140-3664 Computer Communications
0140-3826 Zero†
0140-4040 Who Owns Whom. United Kingdom and Republic of Ireland
0140-4067 Nuclear Energy
0140-4113 British Library of Political and Economic Science. Quarterly List of Additions in Russian and East European Languages
0140-4156 R A P R A Recent Literature on Hazardous Environments in Industry
0140-4202 Birmingham & Warwickshire Archaeological Society. Transactions
0140-427X Map Collector
0140-4288 IMS Pharmaceutical Marketletter
0140-4296 World Pharmaceutical Introductions
0140-4415 M I M S Africa
0140-4539 Treasure Hunting
0140-4547 Bike
0140-458X Climate Monitor
0140-4741 IMS Monitor Report: Europe *changed to* IMS Monitor Report
0140-4768 Rural Development Abstracts
0140-4776 Rural Extension, Education and Training Abstracts
0140-4784 Forest Products Abstracts
0140-4822 Agricultural Supply Industry
0140-4857 Bio-Medical Applications of Polymers
0140-489X Economic Outlook
0140-4962 People's Dispensary for Sick Animals. Guild News†
0140-4989 Sheffield and North Derbyshire Topic *changed to* Sheffield & South Yorkshire Topic
0140-5004 Scotland. Department of Agriculture and Fisheries. Freshwater Fisheries Triennial
0140-5012 Scotland. Department of Agriculture and Fisheries. Triennial Review of Research
0140-5039 E. A. R.
0140-511X Journal of Audiovisual Media in Medicine
0140-5136 Alembic
0140-5179 Sales Management
0140-525X Behavioral and Brain Sciences
0140-5268 Offshore Petroleum Exploration Service
0140-5284 European Journal of Science Education
0140-5373 Aquatic Sciences & Fisheries Abstracts. Part 1: Biological Sciences & Living Resources
0140-5381 Aquatic Sciences & Fisheries Abstracts. Part 2: Ocean Technology, Policy and Non-Living Resources
0140-5500 International Accounting and Financial Report
0140-5578 Shoe Retailers Manual
0140-5721 Country Music Round up
0140-5748 Health Service Buyers Guide
0140-5764 Government and Municipal Contractors
0140-5772 British Exporters
0140-5810 Scottish Women's Liberation Journal
0140-5977 Gem Craft *changed to* Popular Crafts
0140-6000 Darts World
0140-6078 Musica Asiatica
0140-6116 Afrique
0140-6450 World Airline Fleets Monthly
0140-6566 Molecular Crystals and Liquid Crystals. Letters
0140-6701 Fuel and Energy Abstracts
0140-671X Journal of Sources in Educational History
0140-6728 Westminster Studies in Education
0140-6736 Lancet
0140-6795 N. S. C. A. Reference Book
0140-6981 Leicester Topic
0140-7007 International Journal of Refrigeration
0140-7503 Essex Family Historian
0140-7554 International Association of Orientalist Librarians. Newsletter *see* 0161-7397
0140-7597 Iron
0140-7635 Economics Selections
0140-7724 Postgraduate Doctor: Middle East
0140-7732 School Technology
0140-7740 Animations
0140-7767 Pellison's Researcher
0140-7775 Journal of Fish Diseases
0140-7783 Journal of Veterinary Pharmacology and Therapeutics
0140-7791 Plant, Cell and Environment
0140-7805 Books in the Earth Sciences
0140-7813 British Geological Literature
0140-7821 Zapis
0140-7953 Middle East Living Costs
0140-7961 Matter of Degree
0140-8003 Private Post
0140-8011 Arab Business
0140-8046 Reed's Special Ships
0140-8089 Leeds Medieval Studies
0140-8186 Coventry Chamber of Commerce & Industry Directory
0140-8313 Middle East Transport
0140-8321 Middle East Travel
0140-833X New African
0140-8399 Minor Metals Survey
0140-8402 Iron & Manganese Ores Survey
0140-8410 Revealer Cassettes
0140-8429 Flintshire Historical Society. Publications, Journal and Record Series
0140-8445 Powder Coatings Bulletin
0140-8453 Chief Executive
0140-8461 Maritime Management *changed to* Shipcare & Maritime Management
0140-878X Scholarships at Independent Schools
0140-8798 Waterborne & High Solids Coatings Bulletin
0140-895X Irish Literary Studies
0140-9050 World Water
0140-9069 Rabies Magazine
0140-9115 Annual Reports on Fermentation Processes
0140-9131 Northamptonshire Past and Present
0140-9174 Management Research News
0140-9301 Leicestershire Family History Circle. Newsletter
0140-9352 Aggie Weston's
0140-9506 New Equals
0140-976X Municipal Entertainment *see* 0143-8980
0140-9816 Business Location File
0140-9883 Energy Economics
0140-9948 Clothing Research Journal
0141-0008 University of Nottingham. Department of Adult Education. Bulletin of Local History, East Midlands Region
0141-0164 Rice Abstracts
0141-0172 Soyabean Abstracts
0141-0180 Seed Abstracts
0141-0296 Engineering Structures
0141-030X Studies in Welsh History
0141-0423 Journal of Research in Reading
0141-0547 Harpers & Queen
0141-0555 Cosmopolitan: English Edition
0141-0571 Current Literature on Health Services
0141-061X Electronic Technology
0141-0687 Cargo Handling Abstracts
0141-0768 Royal Society of Medicine. Journal
0141-0792 Liszt Society. Journal
0141-0814 Society for Underwater Technology. Journal
0141-0822 Veterinary Review
0141-0962 Forensic Photography
0141-1004 Studies in Operations Research
0141-1020 American Business Overseas†
0141-1047 European and Middle East Tax Report
0141-1063 Tax Haven & Shelter Report *changed to* Tax Haven & Investment Report
0141-108X Durham and Newcastle Research Review
0141-1136 Marine Environmental Research
0141-1144 Company
0141-1152 Oxford Theatre Texts
0141-1179 Dramau'r Byd
0141-1187 Applied Ocean Research
0141-1195 Advances in Engineering Software
0141-1241 Global Tapestry Journal
0141-1268 National Maritime Museum. Occasional Lecture Series
0141-1314 I D S Research Report
0141-1381 Diesel Engines for the World
0141-1403 Great Britain. Department of Health and Social Security. Health Equipment Notes
0141-142X Harpers Sports
0141-142X Harpers Sports and Camping *see* 0141-142X
0141-1594 Phase Transitions
0141-1667 State Research
0141-1772 Benn's Press Directory
0141-187X Chartered Institute of Public Finance and Accountancy. Leisure Estimate Statistics
0141-1918 International Power Generation
0141-1926 British Educational Research Journal
0141-2159 Direction Line
0141-2175 Planned Innovation
0141-2183 Publications Review: Management & Technology & Policy *changed to* Publications Review
0141-2361 Gardens Open to the Public in England and Wales
0141-2442 Socialist Review
0141-2604 Great Britain. Departments of the Environment and Transport. Library Services. Annual List of Publications
0141-2698 Stanley Link in Design and Craft Education
0141-2701 Thomas Cook International Timetable (1980) *see* 0144-7475
0141-2701 Thomas Cook International Timetable *see* 0144-7467
0141-2760 Journal of Clinical & Laboratory Immunology
0141-2876 British Tax Report
0141-2930 B C I R A Abstracts of International Foundry Literature
0141-2949 Police Studies
0141-3228 Financial Times Oil and Gas International Year Book
0141-3236 Financial Times Who's Who in World Oil and Gas
0141-3244 Financial Times Mining International Year Book
0141-3279 Great Britain. Warren Spring Laboratory. Annual Review
0141-3287 Natural Energy & Living
0141-3317 Journal of Chronic Diseases and Therapeutics Research
0141-3341 Africa Year Book and Who's Who
0141-3368 Current Topics in Immunology
0141-3406 Information Privacy
0141-3589 Talbotania
0141-3619 Open Earth
0141-3910 Polymer Degradation and Stability
0141-3929 African Business
0141-4100 Scan
0141-4151 Seatrade Guide to Arab Shipping
0141-4348 London Bird Report
0141-4585 Seatrade Guide to EEC Shipping
0141-4607 Agricultural Wastes
0141-4690 Ferro-Alloys Survey
0141-4836 International Environment and Safety
0141-4925 Development Research Digest
0141-5050 Writers of Wales
0141-5263 Industrial Minerals Directory
0141-5271 International Zinc & Galvanizing Directory
0141-5298 Stainless Steel World Guide
0141-5301 Tinplate World Survey
0141-531X Aluminum World Survey
0141-5352 Quaker Peace & Service
0141-5387 European Journal of Orthodontics
0141-5433 Practical Computing
0141-5468 Chartered Institute of Public Finance and Accountancy. Financial General & Rating Statistics
0141-5492 Biotechnology Letters
0141-5530 International Journal of Materials in Engineering Applications *changed to* Materials in Engineering
0141-5867 Law Notes
0141-5956 Aspects of Educational Technology
0141-5964 Perspectives on Academic Gaming & Simulation
0141-5972 British Qualifications
0141-6014 Decanter
0141-6022 Primary Education Review
0141-6197 British Insurance Broker
0141-6251 A. B. C. Hotel Guide
0141-6278 A B C Guide to International Travel
0141-6340 Nomina
0141-6359 Precision Engineering
0141-6383 A. S. L. G. Newsletter
0141-6421 Journal of Petroleum Geology
0141-6456 Bibliofem
0141-6529 A B C Air Cargo Guide
0141-6707 African Journal of Ecology
0141-6723 Museums and Galleries in Great Britain and Ireland
0141-6790 Art History
0141-6936 B Q S F Review
0141-6952 New Ecologist *changed to* Ecologist (1979)
0141-7258 Commercial Laws of Europe
0141-7266 European Commercial Cases
0141-7568 Occupational Hygiene Monographs
0141-7711 Neurosciences Abstracts†
0141-772X Pharmacology Abstracts†
0141-7835 Chartered Institute of Public Finance and Accountancy. Water Services Charges Statistics
0141-8033 Journal of Social Welfare Law
0141-8130 International Journal of Biological Macromolecules
0141-8149 Oxford German Studies Book Supplement
0141-8211 European Journal of Education
0141-8246 Health & Safety at Work
0141-8505 University of London. Institute of Archaeology. Occasional Publication
0141-8513 Commonwealth Currents
0141-8734 Combustion Research Digest
0141-8955 Journal of Inherited Metabolic Disease
0141-898X Rural Technology Guide
0141-9307 Social Work Service
0141-9382 Displays
0141-9412 International Theatrelog
0141-948X M/F
0141-9498 Great Britain. Civil Aviation Authority. Library Bulletin
0141-9536 Africa Health
0141-9544 North Middlesex Family History Society. Journal
0141-9803 H S L Abstracts
0141-9846 Journal of Developmental Physiology
0141-9854 Clinical and Laboratory Haematology
0141-9862 Fisheries Management
0141-9870 Ethnic and Racial Studies
0141-9889 Sociology of Health and Illness
0141-9897 In Fact
0141-9927 Buses Extra

0141-9935 Trains Illustrated/Express Trains *changed to* Trains Illustrated/Railway Preservation
0142-0097 Craft and Hobby Trade Directory
0142-0356 Journal of Chemical Technology and Biotechnology
0142-0364 Command
0142-0453 Journal of Automatic Chemistry
0142-0496 Computer Fraud and Security Bulletin
0142-050X Product Liability Bulletin
0142-0534 Clothing and Footwear Journal
0142-0615 International Journal of Electrical Power and Energy Systems
0142-064X Journal for the Study of the New Testament
0142-0755 Publican
0142-0798 Hali
0142-095X International Journal of Cement Composites *changed to* International Journal of Cement Composites and Lightweight Concrete
0142-0968 International Journal of Lightweight Concrete *changed to* International Journal of Cement Composites and Lightweight Concrete
0142-0976 International Journal of Wood Preservation
0142-0992 Zimbabwe Information Group Bulletin
0142-1123 International Journal of Fatigue
0142-128X Urbane Gorilla
0142-1468 Chartered Institute of Public Finance and Accountancy. Water and Sewage Treatment and Disposal Statistics. Actuals
0142-1484 Chartered Institute of Public Finance and Accountancy. Charges for Leisure Services
0142-1531 Pharmaceutical Medicine
0142-162X Financial Times World Business Weekly
0142-1794 Sports Documentation Monthly Bulletin
0142-1824 Hotel, Restaurant and Catering Supplies
0142-1832 Caves & Caving
0142-1883 Fruit and Tropical Products
0142-1891 Hides and Skins
0142-1913 Tobacco Quarterly
0142-193X Tsetse and Trypanosomiasis Information Quarterly
0142-2146 N H R National Newsletter
0142-2383 Network†
0142-2391 Resource Management and Optimization
0142-2405 Radioactive Waste Management
0142-2413 Surveys in High Energy Physics
0142-2456 Community Medicine
0142-2499 Aquatic Environment Monitoring Report
0142-2529 Industrial Relations News
0142-2545 Food Books Review
0142-2553 British Shipping Review
0142-2774 Journal of Occupational Behavior
0142-2782 Biopharmaceutics & Drug Disposition
0142-3215 Metal Detecting *see* 0140-4539
0142-3304 Historical Metallurgy
0142-3363 Board of Celtic Studies. Bulletin
0142-3371 Efrydiau Athronyddol
0142-3460 Family History Newsletter
0142-3630 Building Services
0142-4319 Journal of Muscle Research and Cell Motility
0142-4688 Southern History
0142-4696 Armed Forces
0142-4742 Caribbean Insight
0142-4769 Directory of Export Buyers in the U.K.
0142-4823 Currency Forecasting Service
0142-484X I R C S Medical Science: Key Reports in Cell and Molecular Biology
0142-4858 I R C S Medical Science: Key Reports in Human and Animal Physiology
0142-4874 International Education Newsletter
0142-4904 Ciba-Geigy Technical Notes
0142-498X Year Book of Agricultural Co-Operation
0142-4998 Agricultural Co-Operation in the United Kingdom: Summary of Statistics
0142-5005 Plunkett Foundation for Co-Operative Studies. Study Series
0142-5056 Seatrade U.S. Yearbook
0142-5064 Seatrade Guide to Latin American Shipping
0142-5072 City of London Directory & Livery Companies Guide
0142-5218 British Alternative Theatre Directory
0142-5242 Grass and Forage Science
0142-5307 Paper and Packaging Bulletin
0142-5455 Employee Relations
0142-5463 International Journal of Cosmetic Science
0142-5498 Arena
0142-5587 Narrow Gauge
0142-5595 Narrow Gauge News
0142-5625 Channel Islands Specialised Catalogue
0142-5641 Coins and Medals
0142-5692 British Journal of Sociology of Education
0142-5854 Communication Technology Impact
0142-5862 Hazards Review
0142-5978 Good Camps Guide
0142-601X London Studies on South Asia
0142-6028 Studies on Asian Topics
0142-6044 Exchange Rate Outlook
0142-6168 Highways & Public Works
0142-6184 Defence
0142-6222 Warship
0142-6265 Insurance Age
0142-6419 C B I Members Bulletin *see* 0140-2188
0142-6427 C B I Education and Training Bulletin
0142-6435 C B I Industrial Trends Survey
0142-646X West European Living Costs
0142-6575 Socialist Challenge
0142-6591 Animal Health Trust. Annual Report
0142-6699 Air Cushion Review
0142-694X Design Studies
0142-7067 I P R A Review
0142-7113 C A A T Newsletter
0142-7164 Applied Psycholinguistics
0142-7245 Minerals and the Environment
0142-7253 Archaeoastronomy
0142-7318 Aliphatic and Related Natural Product Chemistry
0142-7326 Live Rail
0142-7474 Conference Britain
0142-7547 Society for General Microbiology Quarterly
0142-761X Fast Food
0142-7660 Bonny Moor Hen
0142-7830 Commonwealth Catalogue of Queen Elizabeth Stamps
0142-7865 Photography/Politics
0142-7946 Postgraduate Doctor: Africa
0142-7954 U. H. Stamp Digest
0142-8004 Biological Rhythms
0142-8047 Cell Membranes
0142-8055 Cyclic Amp
0142-8071 Enzyme Regulation
0142-8128 Immunoassay
0142-8136 Immunohistochemistry
0142-8225 Nerve Cell Biology
0142-8241 Neurophysiology
0142-8314 Releasing Hormones
0142-8322 Ribosomes
0142-8357 Renal Transplantation and Dialysis
0142-8950 Hampshire Field Club and Archaeological Society Proceedings
0142-8977 Royal Observatory, Edinburgh. Communications
0142-9256 Quantitative Sociology Newsletter
0142-9272 Nigeria Newsletter
0142-9280 Middle East Newsletter
0142-9302 Saudi Arabia Newsletter
0142-9310 Egypt Newsletter
0142-9353 Rubber & Plastics Fire & Flammability Bulletin
0142-9361 Simulation/Games for Learning
0142-9418 Polymer Testing
0142-9523 Book Dealers' and Collectors' Year-Book and Diary
0142-9612 Biomaterials
0142-9671 Mackintosh European Electronics Companies File
0142-971X Runnymede Trust Bulletin
0142-9981 Journal of Morphanalysis
0143-0084 Res Mechanica
0143-0149 Pope Teaches
0143-0181 Revelation
0143-0246 Argo (Oxford)
0143-0270 Bookdealers in India, Pakistan and Sri Lanka
0143-0343 School Psychology International
0143-036X New Magic Lantern Journal
0143-053X U K S T U Newsletter
0143-0599 U. K. I. R. T. Newsletter
0143-0602 International Journal of Masonry Construction
0143-067X Auto Export
0143-0696 Mackintosh European Electronics Companies Bulletin *see* 0142-9671
0143-0750 Journal of Ambient Energy
0143-0807 European Journal of Physics
0143-0815 Clinical Physics and Physiological Measurement
0143-084X Journal of Industrial Affairs
0143-1005 Helicopter Magazine
0143-103X Return of Outstanding Debt
0143-1064 Syzygy
0143-1080 European Medical Ultrasonics
0143-1102 D P International
0143-1145 Aviation Europe
0143-1153 Sell's Marine Market
0143-1218 Journal of Biodynamic Psychology
0143-1234 Scottish Wildlife
0143-1269 Elgar Society. Journal
0143-1285 Books in Scotland
0143-1307 West African Farming & Food Processing
0143-1404 Bio-Control News & Information
0143-1471 Environmental Pollution. Series A: Ecological and Biological
0143-148X Environmental Pollution. Series B: Chemical and Physical
0143-1749 Secondary Education Journal
0143-1927 Ambassador
0143-1935 British Alternative Press Index†
0143-2028 Cosmos Newsletter
0143-2044 Cryo-Letters
0143-2060 Environmental Technology Letters
0143-2087 Optimal Control Applications and Methods
0143-2095 Strategic Management Journal
0143-2214 Where to Learn English in Great Britain
0143-2443 Water Research Centre. Annual Report
0143-2516 Tourism Management
0143-2680 Bargaining Report
0143-2745 Worker Writer
0143-280X Rowland's Tax Guide
0143-2885 International Endodontic Journal
0143-2958 European Distributor Directory *changed to* European Electronic Component Distributor Directory
0143-2974 Local Population Studies
0143-3083 Research and Clinical Forums
0143-3105 Latin American Newsletters. Book News
0143-3180 Journal of Clinical and Hospital Pharmacy
0143-3334 Carcinogenesis
0143-3369 International Journal of Vehicle Design
0143-3385 A L L C Journal
0143-3512 Business Matters
0143-3563 Nova Hrvatska
0143-3598 Fouling Prevention Research Digest
0143-3598 Fouling Prevention Research Digest
0143-3628 Geriatric Medicine
0143-3636 Nuclear Medicine Communications
0143-3768 Landscape History
0143-3857 Ergodic Theory and Dynamical Systems
0143-4063 Air Transport (London)
0143-4136 National Association for the Teaching of English. Newsletter
0143-4160 Cell Calcium
0143-4381 Vending International Manual
0143-4659 Worcestershire Archaeology and Local History Newsletter
0143-4748 Youth Service Scene
0143-5000 Drydock
0143-5108 Journal for the Study of the New Testament. Supplement Series
0143-5124 Library Management
0143-5183 Microprocessors at Work
0143-523X Latin America Regional Reports-Caribbean
0143-5248 Latin America Regional Reports-Andean Group
0143-5256 Latin America Regional Reports-Southern Cone
0143-5264 Latin America Regional Reports-Mexico & Central America
0143-5272 Latin America Regional Reports-Brazil
0143-5280 Latin America Weekly Report
0143-5299 Latin America Informe Semanal
0143-540X Chartered Institute of Public Finance and Accountancy. Local Authority Airports. Accounts and Statistics
0143-5485 Coin *changed to* Coin Monthly(1980)
0143-5604 Douglas DC-3
0143-5698 International Tree Crops Journal
0143-5914 Anthroposophical Review
0143-6058 Educational Computing
0143-6112 Contraceptive Delivery Systems
0143-6147 Tropical Pest Management
0143-6236 Social Science Information Studies
0143-6368 Arid Land Abstracts
0143-6392 Which Word Processor?
0143-6481 Noise and Vibration Control-Worldwide
0143-6538 Tibet News Review
0143-6570 Managerial and Decision Economics
0143-6619 WestIndian Digest
0143-683X Historical Geography Research Series
0143-6872 Who's Who in Steel
0143-7011 Stamps
0143-7038 I E E Proceedings Part B: Electric Power Applications
0143-7097 I E E Proceedings Part H: Microwaves, Optics and Antennas
0143-7208 Dyes and Pigments
0143-7410 Reports Index
0143-7496 International Journal of Adhesion and Adhesives
0143-7607 Metal Traders of the World
0143-7720 International Journal of Manpower
0143-7739 Leadership and Organisation Development Journal
0143-7844 Sheet Metal Industries International
0143-8123 Comments on Molecular and Cellular Biophysics
0143-8131 Artistes and Their Agents
0143-814X Journal of Public Policy
0143-8158 West Midlands Archives Newsletter
0143-8166 Optics and Lasers in Engineering
0143-8174 Reliability Engineering
0143-8190 Countryside Planning Yearbook
0143-8263 International Author's and Writer's Who's Who
0143-8425 Drawing Paper
0143-8441 Food: Flavouring Ingredients Processing & Packaging
0143-8484 Plunkett Development Series
0143-8557 Solids Handling
0143-8565 Yesteryear Transport
0143-8654 School of Agriculture, Aberdeen. Annual Report
0143-8980 Entertainment and Arts Management
0143-9014 Pig News & Information
0143-926X Cosmatom
0143-9359 Administrative Accounting
0143-9405 China Business Report
0143-960X I W P C Newsletter
0143-9642 Computer Performance
0143-9669 Re Report
0143-9677 Tax Haven & Shelter Report-North American Edition†
0143-9685 Historical Journal of Film, Radio and Television
0143-9693 Sussex Genealogist and Local Historian
0143-9766 World Gas Report
0144-0322 Society of Leather Technologists and Chemists. Journal
0144-0497 Middle Thames Naturalist
0144-1655 Modern Tramway and Light Rail Transit
0144-221X Natural History Society of Northumbria. Transactions
0144-2368 Beacon House Bulletin
0144-2449 Zeolites
0144-2570 U K C I S Newsletter
0144-2848 T. O. P. S.-The Old Police Station
0144-2880 Polymer Photochemistry
0144-2902 Christian Jewish Relations

0144-3070 Occasional Papers in Modern Dutch Studies
0144-3127 Studies in Language Disability and Remediation
0144-333X International Journal of Sociology and Social Policy
0144-3410 Educational Psychology
0144-3577 International Journal of Operations and Production Management
0144-3585 Journal of Economic Studies
0144-364X Birdwatcher's Yearbook
0144-3704 Hospitality
0144-3879 Animal Disease Occurrence - Data Tables
0144-4379 Paper Bag
0144-4425 Paint Titles
0144-4565 Biomass
0144-4611 Awards for Commonwealth University Academic Staff
0144-462X Grants for Study Visits by University Administrators and Librarians
0144-5138 History of Universities
0144-5251 Dairyman's Yearbook
0144-574X About Books for Children
0144-5871 High Performance Textiles
0144-6045 Plastics and Rubber Processing and Applications
0144-610X Chartered Institute of Public Finance and Accountancy. Personal Social Services Estimate Statistics
0144-6118 Enterprise
0144-6193 Journal of Construction Industry Economics and Management
0144-624X Recreation Management Handbook
0144-6320 What Camera Weekly
0144-6428 Slade Magazine
0144-6533 Legion
0144-6622 Soviet Engineering Research
0144-6630 New Age
0144-6657 British Journal of Clinical Psychology
0144-6665 British Journal of Social Psychology
0144-686X Ageing and Society
0144-7106 Trade Union Studies Journal
0144-7149 Chronicle (London)
0144-7181 Sport and Leisure
0144-7440 Political Studies Association of the United Kingdom. Newsletter
0144-7467 Thomas Cook Overseas Timetable
0144-7475 Thomas Cook Continental Timetable (1980)
0144-7831 Res Mechanica Letters
0144-8099 Tourism
0144-8153 Evangelical Review of Theology
0144-8285 Catholic Commission for Racial Justice. Notes & Reports
0144-8404 Spon's Landscape Pricebook
0144-8412 Artery
0144-8455 Postgraduate Doctor: Asia
0144-8587 Chartered Institute of Building. Construction Papers
0144-8676 Royal Society of Medicine. Annual Report of the Council
0144-8684 Current Topics in Anaesthesia
0144-8765 Biological Agriculture and Horticulture
0144-9486 University College of Swansea. Centre for Development Studies. Monograph Series
0144-9494 University College of Swansea. Centre for Development Studies. Occasional Papers Series
0144-9508 United Society for the Propagation of the Gospel. Annual Report/Review
0144-9621 B A S C A News
0144-9753 Asian Digest
0144-9850 University of London. Institute of Germanic Studies. Bithell Memorial Lectures
0144-9893 Corporate Crime
0144-9907 Security Report
0144-9915 Chartered Institute of Public Finance and Accountancy. Police Statistics. Estimates
0145-0085 Electronic Connector Study Group. Annual Connector Symposium. Proceedings
0145-0093 Kansas State University. Center for Energy Studies. Report
0145-0344 Weekly Government Abstracts. Civil & Structural Engineering *changed to* Weekly Government Abstracts. Civil Engineering
0145-062X Public Documents Highlights
0145-0689 River Currents
0145-0743 American Society of Civil Engineers. Water Resources Planning and Management Division. Journal
0145-0786 International Poetry Review
0145-1014 Aviation Monthly
0145-1030 Money Management Digest†
0145-1065 National Institute on Drug Abuse Statistical Series; Quarterly Report
0145-1073 Surface Warfare
0145-109X Boating Safety Newsletter *see* 0198-1501
0145-1146 Vessel Safety Review
0145-1227 Fireword
0145-1391 Epoch (Ithaca)
0145-1405 Atlanta Historical Bulletin *see* 0162-5721
0145-1413 Museum Notes (New York)
0145-1421 East-West Technology Digest
0145-1456 Soviet Journal of Marine Biology
0145-1472 College Student and the Courts
0145-1499 Authors in the News
0145-160X Washington Spectator/Between the Lines
0145-1642 Ayer Directory of Publications
0145-1677 First Monday
0145-1707 Finance and Development
0145-1715 Downtown Planning & Development Annual†
0145-1715 Downtown Planning & Development Annual†
0145-1731 Caligrafree Scribe
0145-188X Industrial Relations Law Journal
0145-191X Guide to Catholic Literature *see* 0008-8285
0145-2037 Educational Commission for Foreign Medical Graduates. Annual Report
0145-2061 Thrust (Burlingame)
0145-207X Engineering Index. Notes & Comment
0145-2096 Diplomatic History
0145-210X Songsmith's Journal
0145-2118 Design Abstracts International
0145-2126 Leukemia Research
0145-2134 Child Abuse & Neglect
0145-224X Nuclear Track Detection *see* 0191-278X
0145-2258 African Economic History
0145-2355 Sources: a Guide to Print and Nonprint Materials Available from Organizations, Industry, Government Agencies, and Specialized Publishers
0145-2363 Anales de la Narrativa Espanola Contemporanea
0145-2371 Alpine Information
0145-2517 Music & Musicians: Instructional Disc Recordings Catalog
0145-2525 Music & Musicians: Instructional Cassette Recordings Catalog
0145-2584 International Countermeasures Handbook
0145-2665 Speedway Sports Pictorial News
0145-2681 De Colores
0145-2835 Cleveland
0145-2843 Jazz
0145-3017 Corporate Buyers of Design Services/U S A
0145-3041 Social Services U.S.A.
0145-305X Developmental and Comparative Immunology
0145-3068 Journal of Bioengineering *see* 0090-6964
0145-3084 Bibliography Newsletter
0145-3130 Music & Musicians: Braille Scores Catalog - Piano
0145-3149 Music & Musicians: Braille Scores Catalog - Organ
0145-3157 Music & Musicians: Braille Scores Catalog - Voice
0145-3173 Music & Musicians: Braille Scores Catalog - Choral
0145-319X N A S A Tech Briefs *changed to* N T I S Tech Notes
0145-3351 Association for the Care of Children in Hospitals. Journal *changed to* Children's Health Care Journal
0145-3378 Journal of Psychohistory
0145-3416 Immigration Newsletter
0145-3483 Cinegram
0145-370X International Opthalmological Reporter
0145-3726 Progress in Cancer Research and Therapy
0145-3815 Environmental Periodicals Bibliography: Indexed Article Titles
0145-3831 Swimming & Diving Case Book *see* 0163-2884
0145-3920 American Postcard Journal
0145-3939 Extra
0145-3971 Review of Regional Economics and Business
0145-403X Cardiovascular Medicine
0145-4048 Alabama Directory of Mining and Manufacturing
0145-4064 Firehouse
0145-4072 Exchange (Columbia)
0145-4129 Health Lawyers News Report
0145-4145 Year Book of Cardiology
0145-417X Coal Data
0145-4250 American Handgunner
0145-4331 Foundational Studies
0145-4455 Behavior Modification
0145-4471 Powder
0145-448X New York Law School Law Review
0145-4498 Current Concepts in Emergency Medicine
0145-4560 C B Radio/S9
0145-4676 U.S. National Bureau of Standards. Semiconductor Measurement Technology. Quarterly Report *changed to* U.S. National Bureau of Standards. Semiconductor Measurement Technology
0145-4692 Evaluation Quarterly *see* 0193-841X
0145-482X Journal of Visual Impairment and Blindness
0145-4927 Manufacturers' Export Sales and Orders of Durable Goods
0145-5028 Woven Fabrics. Production Inventories, and Unfilled Orders
0145-5168 Fats and Oils. Oilseed Crushings
0145-5176 Fats and Oils. Production, Consumption, and Factory and Warehouse Stocks
0145-5273 Package Development & Systems *see* 0274-4996
0145-5281 Circus Maximus†
0145-5303 Phantasm
0145-5311 Recently Published Articles
0145-5338 Benchmark Papers in Analytical Chemistry
0145-5397 Library Developments
0145-5400 G. P. U. News
0145-546X Mountain Review
0145-5508 Journal of Pedodontics
0145-5532 Social Science History
0145-5605 Earth Resources; a Continuing Bibliography with Indexes
0145-5613 Ear, Nose & Throat Journal
0145-5664 Current Business Reports: Canned Food
0145-5672 I U P A C Information Bulletin *see* 0193-6484
0145-5680 Cellular & Molecular Biology
0145-5699 Communications in Psychopharmacology
0145-5702 Mazingira†
0145-5753 Rohmer Review
0145-5761 Working Woman
0145-5818 Criminal Justice Periodical Index
0145-5869 Foodservice Distributor Salesman
0145-5885 Florida Environmental and Urban Issues
0145-5990 Kentucky. Department for Human Resources. Selected Vital Statistics and Planning Data
0145-6008 Alcoholism: Clinical and Experimental Research
0145-6016 Hobby Artist News†
0145-6024 Country Messenger†
0145-6032 Cinefantastique
0145-6059 English Genealogist
0145-6075 White Book of U.S. Ski Areas *see* 0163-9684
0145-6105 American Historical Society of Germans from Russia. Work Paper *see* 0162-8283
0145-613X Daiwa Fishing Annual
0145-6180 M P L A Newsletter
0145-6210 Body Forum
0145-6237 Guitar Foundation of America Soundboard *changed to* Soundboard
0145-6261 Feed/back
0145-627X Book Talk
0145-6288 International Plant Protection Center. Infoletter
0145-6318 China Exchange News
0145-6342 A L I-A B A Course Materials Journal
0145-6431 Orlando-Land
0145-6466 Indian Opinion†
0145-6571 Law Officer's Bulletin
0145-6644 Fund Sources in Health and Allied Fields
0145-6776 Auto Index
0145-6792 Glassworks
0145-6822 A C T News *see* 0163-7908
0145-6830 Society for Slovene Studies Newsletter *changed to* Slovene Studies
0145-6857 Alabama's Health
0145-6881 C N L/Quarterly World Report
0145-692X Corporate Profiles for Executives & Investors
0145-7071 Business People in the News
0145-7217 Diabetes Educator
0145-7233 Concordia Journal
0145-7241 Artnewsletter
0145-7322 Criminal Law Outline
0145-7365 Christian Science Quarterly (Inkprint Edition)
0145-7616 Computed Axial Tomography *see* 0149-936X
0145-7624 Death Education
0145-7632 Heat Transfer Engineering
0145-7659 Privacy Journal
0145-7667 Liberty Bell
0145-7675 Other Side
0145-7861 Society for South India Studies. Newsletter
0145-7888 Studies in Twentieth Century Literature
0145-7918 Blaisdell Institute. Journal.†
0145-7950 Orthodox Church in America. Yearbook and Church Directory
0145-7969 New Pulpit Digest *see* 0160-838X
0145-7985 W I N News
0145-7993 American Indian Journal
0145-8035 Guide to Graduate and Professional Study†
0145-8043 Student Aid Manual *see* 0190-339X
0145-8116 Black Art(Jamaica)
0145-8124 Election Administration Reports
0145-8264 Journal of the Milking Shorthorn and Illawarra Breeds
0145-8299 Feminist Press. News/Notes
0145-8302 Grantechs
0145-8361 Seeker Newsletter
0145-837X Pharmaceutical Trends
0145-8388 New Laurel Review
0145-8396 Institute for Studies in American Music. Newsletter
0145-840X Korean Studies
0145-8418 Eastern Electrical Buyers' Guide†
0145-8426 Southern Electrical Buyers' Guide†
0145-8442 Customer Service Newsletter
0145-8477 Battelle Today
0145-8493 American Academy and Institute of Arts and Letters. Proceedings
0145-871X Consultant's Coin Report
0145-8752 Moscow University Geology Bulletin
0145-8779 Marianne Moore Newsletter
0145-8787 Pulp
0145-8795 Joint Conference
0145-8809 Astrology Now†
0145-8825 Greater Llano Estacado Southwest Heritage
0145-8833 Vantage Conference Report
0145-8841 Stanley Foundation. Occasional Paper

0145-885X Gnostica†
0145-8868 Llewellyn's Astrological Calendar
0145-8876 Journal of Food Process Engineering
0145-8884 Journal of Food Biochemistry
0145-8892 Journal of Food Processing and Preservation
0145-8930 Hospital Libraries
0145-8973 Chasqui
0145-899X Combinations
0145-9007 Maine Marketing Directory
0145-9023 VideoNews
0145-9031 Carnegie Museum of Natural History. Special Publication
0145-904X Racing Cars
0145-9058 Carnegie Museum of Natural History. Bulletin
0145-9066 D I S C A R
0145-9074 Business Law Review
0145-9090 World Coin News
0145-9104 Gaysweek
0145-918X Ski Competition East
0145-9198 American Oil & Gas Reporter
0145-9244 Materials and Components in Fossil Energy Applications and E R D A Newsletter *changed to* Materials and Components in Fossil Energy Applications
0145-9317 Near East and North Africa Report
0145-935X Child & Youth Services
0145-9384 Texas Farmer-Stockman
0145-9392 Oklahoma Farmer-Stockman
0145-9406 Security Management
0145-9457 B P Report
0145-9473 Joyer Travel Report
0145-9481 Sahel Bibliographic Bulletin/Bulletin Bibliographique.
0145-949X Chairman's Chat *see* 0163-0253
0145-952X U.S. Social Security Administration. Office of Research and Statistics. Public Assistance Statistics
0145-9570 Coach: Women's Athletics *see* 0160-2624
0145-9635 Independent School
0145-9651 Media Report to Women
0145-9678 Clements' International Report
0145-9686 Clements' Encyclopedia of World Governments
0145-9740 Medical Anthropology (Pleasantville)
0145-9759 Psychocultural Review
0145-9767 N A G W S Guide. Team Handball, Racquetball, Orienteering *changed to* N A G W S Guide. Team Handball, Orienteering
0145-9783 Man and Medicine
0145-9791 Horse Illustrated
0145-983X Weid: the Sensibility Revue†
0146-0005 Seminars in Perinatology
0146-0013 Quarterly Review of Film Studies
0146-0072 Pay TV Newsletter
0146-0080 Cablecast
0146-0099 Multicast
0146-0102 Cable T V Regulation
0146-0110 Broadcast Investor
0146-0129 In a Nutshell
0146-0137 Technical Education News
0146-0145 International Flash†
0146-0153 Photomethods
0146-020X Agenda
0146-0234 International Society for Labor Law and Social Legislation. United States National Committee. Bulletin *see* 0147-9202
0146-0234 International Society for Labor Law and Social Legislation. United States National Committee. Bulletin *see* 0147-9202
0146-0269 Graves Family Newsletter
0146-0315 Santa Clara Law Review
0146-0323 Directory of Registered Lobbyists and Lobbyist Legislation
0146-0404 Investigative Ophthalmology and Visual Science
0146-0412 Journal of Energy
0146-0498 Indiana Speech Journal
0146-0501 Pesticide & Toxic Chemical News
0146-0595 Real Estate Issues
0146-0609 New Review of Books and Religion†
0146-0625 B M W E Railway Journal
0146-0641 Journal of Solid-Phase Biochemistry†
0146-0706 Elastomerics
0146-0722 Advances in Pain Research and Therapy
0146-0749 Microbiological Reviews
0146-0781 American Motor Carrier Directory: Illinois-Missouri Edition
0146-079X American Motor Carrier Directory: Southeastern Edition
0146-0803 American Motor Carrier Directory: Middle Atlantic Edition
0146-0811 American Motor Carrier Directory: New England Edition
0146-0838 Checklist of Official New Jersey Publications
0146-0846 Series in Clinical and Community Psychology
0146-0854 Series in Thermal and Fluids Engineering
0146-0862 Issues in Comprehensive Pediatric Nursing
0146-0889 Sporting Goods Business
0146-0897 Catalog Showroom Business
0146-0900 Bank Systems & Equipment
0146-0919 Multi Housing News
0146-0951 National Purchasing Review
0146-0978 Conservative Digest
0146-0994 Japanese Philately
0146-1001 Alternative Sources of Energy
0146-1044 Sexuality and Disability
0146-1052 Journal of Population *changed to* Population and Environment
0146-1052 Population (New York) *changed to* Population and Environment
0146-1087 New Jersey Poetry Monthly *changed to* New Jersey Poetry
0146-1095 Channel D L S
0146-1109 Mid-Continental Journal of Archaeology
0146-1117 Council Notes
0146-1125 Factory Outlet Shopping Guide for New Jersey and Rockland County
0146-1133 Women's Coaching Clinic
0146-1141 International Foundation of Employee Benefit Plans. Digest
0146-115X Career Education Workshop
0146-1168 Guidance Clinic
0146-1176 Reading Clinic
0146-1184 Slow Learner Workshop†
0146-1214 Technology & Conservation
0146-1362 Woodall's Campground Directory. North American/Canadian Edition
0146-1397 Stone Country
0146-1559 Tox-Tips
0146-1672 Personality and Social Psychology Bulletin
0146-1710 Yale Italian Studies†
0146-1737 Production Engineering
0146-1745 International Review of Natural Family Planning
0146-1842 News for South Carolina Libraries
0146-1869 Rio Grande History
0146-1885 Rockingchair
0146-1907 Summary of Rate Schedules of Natural Gas Pipeline Companies as Filed with the Federal Power Commission *see* 0190-2997
0146-1990 Bryant Backtrails
0146-2059 Structural Mechanics Software Series
0146-2067 Stony Hills
0146-2083 Tuumba
0146-2091 Media Digest
0146-2105 Star-Web Paper
0146-2113 Affirmative Action Register
0146-2156 Summary of Congress
0146-2199 Cape Rock
0146-2202 J'adoube!
0146-2229 Utah Genealogical Association. Genealogical Journal
0146-2237 P L A Report
0146-2334 Lilith
0146-2350 E D C News†
0146-2377 Konglomerati
0146-2520 In Situ
0146-2547 Second Republic Newsletter
0146-2555 G S M Quarterly
0146-2571 University of California, Los Angeles. Graduate School of Management. Annual Report
0146-258X University of Wisconsin, Milwaukee. Center for Latin America. Discussion Papers
0146-2598 University of Wisconsin-Milwaukee. Center for Latin America. Special Papers Series
0146-2628 Super Chevy
0146-2660 Faxon Librarians' Guide
0146-2679 Collection Management
0146-2725 L B L Newsmagazine
0146-275X Long-Term Care Administrator
0146-2806 Current Problems in Cardiology
0146-2857 Factory Outlet Newsletter
0146-2865 Factory Outlet Shopping Guide for New York, Long Island, Westchester
0146-2873 Factory Outlet Shopping Guide for Washington D.C., Maryland, Delaware, Virginia
0146-2881 Factory Outlet Shopping Guide for North and South Carolina
0146-2903 Factory Outlet Shopping Guide for Pennsylvania
0146-2970 Comments on Astrophysics
0146-2997 Arizona Mining and Manufacturing
0146-3071 Journal of Seed Technology
0146-308X Audio Journal Review: Ophthalmology
0146-3128 PharmChem Newsletter
0146-3225 Chowder Review
0146-3284 Soccer Corner†
0146-3365 C A O Times
0146-3373 Communication Quarterly
0146-339X Off Belay†
0146-3403 Optical Index
0146-3411 Heresies
0146-3489 Relix
0146-3527 Pulp, Paper and Board *see* 0164-095X
0146-3535 Progress in Crystal Growth and Characterization
0146-3586 Studies in Human Rights
0146-3608 Contributions in Labor History
0146-3640 Older American Reports
0146-3659 Plants Alive
0146-3721 American Journal of Dance Therapy
0146-3764 L. S. B. Leakey Foundation News
0146-3772 Hang Glider Weekly *see* 0164-3452
0146-3780 Food Publications Round-up
0146-3799 Copy Cornucopia *changed to* Creative Forum
0146-3810 Advances in General and Cellular Pharmacology
0146-390X World Issues
0146-3934 College Student Journal
0146-3942 Institute of Mathematics and its Applications. Bulletin
0146-3942 Institute of Mathematical Statistics. Bulletin
0146-4094 Hebrew Studies
0146-4116 Automatic Control and Computer Sciences
0146-4124 Topology Proceedings
0146-4124 Topology Proceedings
0146-4140 Journal of Ballistics
0146-4167 Colloquia in Anthropology
0146-423X Columbia Today
0146-4329 School Universe Data Book *see* 0162-9646
0146-437X New York History
0146-4566 International Solar Energy Society. American Section. Annual Meeting. Proceedings
0146-4574 Polo
0146-4582 Red Book of Ophthalmology
0146-4604 Radiation Curing
0146-4639 Product Safety Watchdog Service *changed to* Regulatory Safety Watchdog Service
0146-4647 I T A News Digest
0146-4671 Petersen's Hunting
0146-4701 Audio Critic
0146-4744 Business Assistance Monograph Series
0146-4752 High Solids Coatings
0146-4760 Journal of Analytical Toxicology
0146-4779 Journal of Environmental Pathology and Toxicology
0146-4795 Thyristor D.A.T.A. Book
0146-4817 Noise Control Report
0146-4825 D.A.T.A. Book of Discontinued Integrated Circuits *see* 0271-0129
0146-4833 Computer Communication Review
0146-4965 African Literature Association Newsletter
0146-4981 International Journal of Fusion Energy
0146-5007 Basketball Clinic
0146-5015 Salaries of Scientists, Engineers and Technicians
0146-5023 Motion Picture Product Digest
0146-5031 U V Curing Buyer's Guide
0146-5090 Journal of Cybernetics and Information Science
0146-5104 Handbook for Recruiting at the Historically Black Colleges
0146-5376 Contemporary China
0146-5422 Online (Weston)
0146-5473 Public Works News
0146-5546 Jump Cut
0146-5554 Cumulative Index to Nursing & Allied Health Literature
0146-5554 Nursing and Allied Health Literature Index
0146-5562 Interracial Books for Children. Bulletin
0146-5643 Idaho Heritage†
0146-5678 Nonferrous Castings
0146-5716 New Periodicals Index
0146-5724 Radiation Physics and Chemistry
0146-5759 Crime in Virginia
0146-5783 Association for Gravestone Studies. Newsletter
0146-5864 Solar Thermal Energy Utilization *see* 0160-3671
0146-5864 Solar Thermal Energy Utilization *see* 0148-4397
0146-5864 Solar Thermal Energy Utilization *see* 0160-368X
0146-5945 Policy Review
0146-5996 Home Improvement Contractor
0146-6143 Dixie Gun Works Muzzleloaders' Annual
0146-6216 Applied Psychological Measurement
0146-6283 Cereal Foods World
0146-6321 A H C A Weekly Notes
0146-6364 Chinese Astronomy *see* 0275-1062
0146-6372 Journal of Enterprise Management
0146-6380 Organic Geochemistry
0146-6399 Materials and Society
0146-6402 Advances in Behavior Research and Therapy
0146-6410 Progress in Particle and Nuclear Physics
0146-6429 Society of Vector Ecologists. Bulletin
0146-6453 I C R P Annals
0146-6518 International Journal for Housing Science and Its Applications
0146-6534 Dow Jones-Irwin Business Almanac
0146-6607 Crafts 'n Things
0146-6615 Journal of Medical Virology
0146-664X Computer Graphics & Image Processing
0146-678X Oriental Institute Communications
0146-6798 Materials and Studies for Kassite History
0146-6801 Toll Free Business
0146-6917 Princeton Conference on Cerebrovascular Diseases
0146-695X Monthly Poetry Anthology
0146-7042 Big Deal
0146-7085 Directory Information Service
0146-7166 Christian Science Bible Lessons(Braille Edition)
0146-7190 Powell Monetary Analyst
0146-7204 Powell Gold Industry Guide & International Mining Analyst
0146-7212 Ancram Standard
0146-7220 Eudora Welty Newsletter
0146-7239 Motivation and Emotion
0146-7336 Directory of Research Grants
0146-7611 Investigative and Cell Pathology *changed to* Diagnostic Histopathology

ISSN INDEX 1195

0146-7638 Keeping Abreast Journal *see* 0164-7083
0146-7646 P R B Report†
0146-7743 Insight (New York)
0146-7832 New Thought (Scottsdale)
0146-7891 Nineteenth Century French Studies
0146-7980 I L Z R O Lead Research Digest
0146-7999 I L Z R O Zinc Research Digest
0146-8006 Struggle *changed to* New York Alliance
0146-8030 Fiber and Integrated Optics
0146-809X Southern Exposure (Chapel Hill)
0146-8170 New Thought Bulletin *see* 0146-7832
0146-8197 International Series on Biomechanics
0146-8294 Artist's & Photographer's Market *see* 0161-0546
0146-8294 Artists & Photographer's Market *see* 0147-247X
0146-8510 Uroboros
0146-8537 Comentarios Sobre el Desarrollo Internacional†
0146-8677 Queens College Studies in Librarianship
0146-8693 Journal of Pediatric Psychology
0146-8707 Baxter's Eurailpass Travel Guide
0146-8790 Advances in the Management of Clinical Heart Disease
0146-8812 Fighting Woman News
0146-8901 C O M P Newsletter
0146-8995 Canto
0146-9061 Universitas
0146-9096 Kettering Abstracts of Available Literature on the Biological and Related Aspects of Lead and Its Compounds
0146-9126 Ocean Resources Engineering
0146-9177 Criminal Justice Abstracts
0146-9223 Market Scope
0146-9231 Electronics Foreign Trade
0146-9231 Leningrad University. Vestnik. Mathematics
0146-9282 Educational Considerations
0146-9290 Coatings Adlibra
0146-9304 Foods Adlibra
0146-9312 Sea History
0146-9339 Mythlore *issued with* 0146-9347
0146-9339 Mythlore
0146-9347 Mythprint
0146-9398 Ala-Arts
0146-9428 Journal of Food Quality
0146-9436 M A S K C Komondor News
0146-9568 Toledot
0146-9584 Journal of Legislation
0146-9592 Optics Letters
0146-9606 American Artist Directory of Art Schools & Workshops
0146-9673 Employment and Training Reporter
0146-9738 Dental Lab Products
0146-9770 A I C P A Washington Report
0146-9924 Circuit Rider
0146-9932 M V M A Motor Vehicle Facts and Figures
0146-9959 Meteor News
0146-9967 Longest Revolution
0146-9983 Postal History U.S.A
0146-9991 Colorado Express
0147-0019 Brown Family
0147-0035 Data Entry Digest and Distributed Processing *changed to* Data Entry Digest
0147-006X Annual Review of Neuroscience
0147-0078 Recent Researches in American Music
0147-0086 Recent Researches in the Music of the Classical Era
0147-0302 Motor Skills: Theory into Practice
0147-0310 Association of American Publishers. Exhibits Directory
0147-0353 Health Values: Achieving High Level Wellness
0147-0396 Rebis Chapbook Series
0147-0493 C C L P: Contents of Current Legal Periodicals *see* 0279-5787
0147-0515 N.I.A.A.A.-R.U.C.A.S. Alcoholism Treatment Series
0147-0590 Regulation (Washington, 1977)
0147-0604 Michigan State University. Library. Africana: Select Recent Acquisitions
0147-0612 Michigan State University. Library. Latin America: Select Recent Acquisitions†
0147-0620 Michigan State University. Library. Asia: Select Recent Acquisitions†
0147-0655 Focus: Human Sexuality *see* 0163-836X
0147-071X Advances in Behavioral Pharmacology
0147-0728 Gay Community News
0147-0787 Books at Brown
0147-0833 Journal of Equine Medicine and Surgery
0147-0906 Linguistics in Literature
0147-0965 Curwood Collector
0147-0981 Fletcher Forum
0147-1023 Contributions in Family Studies
0147-1031 Contributions in Intercultural and Comparative Studies
0147-104X Contributions in Women's Studies
0147-1058 Contributions in Medical History
0147-1066 Contributions in Political Science
0147-1066 Contributions to the Study of Religion
0147-1074 Contributions in Legal Studies
0147-1082 Contemporary Problems of Childhood
0147-1090 New Directions in Librarianship
0147-1104 Studies in Population and Urban Demography
0147-1112 Dax Money-Maker Newsletter
0147-1120 Association of College Unions-International. Proceedings of the Annual Conference
0147-1139 Dignity
0147-1147 Design Methods and Theories
0147-1155 Cancer Focus
0147-1201 M A I N
0147-121X Light
0147-1260 Child Protection Report
0147-1465 Washington Review of Strategic and International Studies *see* 0163-660X
0147-149X Cottonwood Review
0147-1503 Thermodynamics Research Center. International Data Series. Selected Data on Mixtures. Series A. Thermodynamic Properties of Non-reacting Binary Systems of Organic Substances
0147-1570 CompFlash
0147-1619 Corporation Law and Tax Report
0147-1627 Calyx
0147-1651 Graphic Arts Green Book.
0147-1678 Directory of Fee-Based Information Services
0147-1686 Floating Island
0147-1694 Contemporary Jewry
0147-1740 Urban League Review
0147-1759 Women & Literature
0147-1767 International Journal of Intercultural Relations
0147-1775 International Journal of Family Counseling *see* 0192-6187
0147-1783 Washington (State) Division of Geology and Earth Resources. Information Circular
0147-1821 Graduate Programs: Physics, Astronomy, and Related Fields
0147-1902 Georgia Museum of Art Bulletin
0147-1937 Real Analysis Exchange
0147-1961 Florida Banker
0147-197X Current Problems in Anesthesia and Critical Care Medicine†
0147-1988 Current Problems in Obstetrics and Gynecology
0147-1996 Year Book of Family Practice
0147-2003 Southwest Regional Conference for Astronomy and Astrophysics. Proceedings
0147-2011 Society
0147-2135 A R L Statistics
0147-2208 Laventhol and Horwath Perspective
0147-2275 Seriatim
0147-2291 American Medical Association. Directory of Accredited Residencies
0147-2313 Screen Achievement Records Bulletin *see* 0163-5123
0147-2399 Travel Research Bulletin *see* 0047-2875
0147-2429 Plastics in Building Construction
0147-2453 Curriculum Review
0147-2461 Art & Crafts Market *changed to* Craftworker's Market
0147-2461 Cartoonists' Market *see* 0161-0546
0147-247X Photographer's Market
0147-2488 Richardson Family Researcher and Historical News
0147-2496 E R
0147-2526 Dance Chronicle
0147-2550 Massachusetts Music News
0147-2593 Lion & the Unicorn
0147-2615 Abstracts of Popular Culture
0147-2631 Hollow Spring Review of Poetry
0147-264X Dental Research in the United States and Other Countries
0147-2682 Biomedical Technology Information Service
0147-2704 Seventh Ray
0147-2747 N S P I Journal(1976) *changed to* Performance & Instruction
0147-281X West Point Museum Bulletin
0147-2828 Black Press Information Handbook
0147-2917 Comparative Medicine East and West *changed to* American Journal of Chinese Medicine
0147-2992 Interface Age
0147-300X International Glass/Metal Catalog
0147-3085 Celestinesca
0147-3204 I E E E Transactions. Cable Television
0147-3247 Nuestro
0147-328X Liquid Chromatography Literature-Abstracts and Index
0147-3301 Cablelines
0147-345X Notes from Eastman (1979)
0147-3522 Ocean Engineering *see* 0146-9126
0147-3565 Porsche Panorama
0147-3646 A.P.S. Writers Unit Number Thirty News Bulletin
0147-3743 Safety Sadistics†
0147-3751 Americans Abroad†
0147-3786 Quest (Year)
0147-3867 Country Vacations U.S.A.
0147-4006 Carcinogenesis
0147-4022 Journal of Divorce
0147-4030 How to Fly for Less
0147-4049 Bright Lights
0147-4057 Newsounds
0147-409X Export Grafics U S A
0147-4243 Economic Analysis of North American Ski Areas
0147-4308 Israel Securities Review Monthly Magazine *see* 0147-4316
0147-4316 Israel Securities Review
0147-4375 A A E S P H Review (American Association for the Education of the Severely-Profoundly Handicapped) *changed to* Association for the Severely Handicapped. Journal
0147-4391 B I A Education Research Bulletin
0147-4413 American Liszt Society. Journal
0147-4502 West Coast Plays
0147-4642 Communication Yearbook
0147-4650 Checklist of Official Publications of the State of Oregon
0147-4693 On the Line Magazine
0147-4707 Chicago Library System Communicator
0147-4804 World Wide Printer
0147-4820 A A S H T O Quarterly Magazine
0147-4863 Advances in Microbial Ecology
0147-4871 Feedback
0147-4928 Country Gentleman
0147-4936 Invisible City
0147-5045 Ars Semeiotica
0147-507X First World
0147-510X Us(New York, 1977)
0147-5185 American Journal of Surgical Pathology
0147-5207 Mon-Khmer Studies
0147-5231 Somatics
0147-5363 Project Management Quarterly
0147-538X New York Times Index
0147-5401 Industrial Hygiene News
0147-5428 West Coast Writer's Conspiracy
0147-5436 Aloha
0147-5460 Journal of Hispanic Philology
0147-5479 International Labor and Working Class History
0147-5533 Billboard's International Disco Sourcebook *changed to* Billboard's International Club and Disco Equipment Sourcebook
0147-5630 Index to Free Periodicals
0147-572X M R I S Abstracts
0147-5754 Intermedia Magazine
0147-5762 Alive & Kicking
0147-5770 Finders International Newsletter
0147-5843 E M T Journal
0147-5894 College and University Admissions and Enrollment, New York State
0147-5916 Cognitive Therapy and Research
0147-5924 Info Franchise Newsletter
0147-5967 Journal of Comparative Economics
0147-5975 Experimental Mycology
0147-6165 Roaring Twenties, Gay Nineties†
0147-6254 Bedside Care
0147-6335 Korean Studies Forum
0147-6491 Bibliographic Guide to North American History
0147-6513 Ecotoxicology and Environmental Safety
0147-6521 Energy Information Abstracts
0147-653X E I C Energy Directory Update Service
0147-6548 New Atlantean Journal
0147-6580 Federal Reserve Bank of New York. Quarterly Review
0147-6629 Seattle Review
0147-6726 Journal for Medicaid Management†
0147-6742 Medical Ultrasound
0147-6750 C R C Critical Reviews in Diagnostic Imaging
0147-6890 Fiscal Observer†
0147-6939 Fatal Accident Reporting System; Annual Report
0147-698X Journal of Powder & Bulk Solids Technology
0147-6998 D E/Domestic Engineering
0147-7013 Moravian Music Foundation. Bulletin
0147-7129 Attic Press
0147-7137 Urban Futures Idea Exchange
0147-7188 Managing the Leisure Facility
0147-7218 Law and Behavior†
0147-7226 Hope Reports Perspective
0147-7307 Law and Human Behavior
0147-7366 International Review of Biochemistry
0147-7439 Satellite Communications
0147-7447 Orthopedics (Thorofare)
0147-7463 Human Nature†
0147-7471 Adventure Travel (Seattle)
0147-7544 Dialogue in Instrumental Music Education
0147-7625 New Realities
0147-7633 Chilton's Review of Optometry
0147-7668 Aerophile
0147-7676 High Fidelity's Buying Guide to Speaker Systems
0147-7684 Car Care Handbook†
0147-7706 Short Story International
0147-782X International Psychic Register
0147-7862 Hart Crane Newsletter
0147-7870 U.S. Department of Housing and Urban Development. Statistical Yearbook
0147-7889 A S C Newsletter
0147-7927 Perinatology/Neonatology
0147-7943 District Lawyer
0147-7951 Dressage and Combined Training *see* 0147-796X
0147-796X Dressage & CT
0147-7978 Christian Association for Psychological Studies. Bulletin
0147-8001 Urban Systems *see* 0198-9715
0147-8044 N C E A Ganley's Catholic Schools in America
0147-8168 Southern Review of Public Administration
0147-8176 Fodor's Egypt
0147-8222 Illinois Journal of Pharmacy
0147-8265 Who's Who in Chiropractic, International

0147-829X Social Psychology *changed to* Social Psychology Quarterly
0147-8311 Conditions
0147-832X House & Garden Kitchen & Bath Guide
0147-8354 Adult Literacy and Basic Education
0147-8389 P A C E
0147-8451 Peterson's Annual Guide to Undergraduate Study
0147-8478 U.S. Geological Survey. Annual Report *see* 0162-9484
0147-8591 House & Garden Gardening Guide
0147-8656 Fodor's Southwest
0147-8680 Fodor's South
0147-8745 Fodor's U.S.A.
0147-877X Business Officer
0147-8818 Ham Radio Horizons *see* 0148-5989
0147-8869 Cuba Review
0147-8885 Journal of Histotechnology
0147-8893 Diagnostic Medicine
0147-8907 Video
0147-8923 Marine Business
0147-9024 Journal of New World Archaeology
0147-9156 Contemporary French Civilization
0147-9202 Comparative Labor Law†
0147-9202 Comparative Labor Law
0147-9245 Digital Design
0147-9253 Intermedia Arts and Communication Resource Newsletter†
0147-9288 American Alpine News
0147-9296 Association for Educational Data Systems. Annual Convention Proceedings
0147-9415 Computer Terminals Review
0147-9466 Directory of African and Afro-American Studies in the United States
0147-9512 Global Political Assessment
0147-9563 Heart and Lung
0147-9571 Comparative Immunology, Microbiology and Infectious Diseases
0147-958X Clinical and Investigative Medicine
0147-9733 Colorado Libraries
0147-9741 Center on Evaluation, Development and Research. Quarterly
0147-992X McElroy Family Newsletter
0147-9989 Restaurant Hospitality
0148-0057 Measurements and Control
0148-0065 Directory of East Asian Collections in North American Libraries
0148-0162 Raccoon
0148-0227 J G R: Journal of Geophysical Research *see* 0196-6928
0148-0227 J G R: Journal of Geophysical Research *see* 0196-6936
0148-0243 American Go Journal
0148-0324 California Environmental Directory
0148-0375 International Petroleum Encyclopedia
0148-0537 Fusion (New York)
0148-0545 Drug and Chemical Toxicology
0148-0561 Kxe6s Verein Newsletter
0148-057X Kxe6s Verein Chess Society. Advisory Board Record
0148-0650 Illinois Health Sciences Libraries Serials Holdings List
0148-0685 Women's Studies International Quarterly
0148-0766 Lodging Hospitality
0148-0812 Journal of Dermatologic Surgery and Oncology
0148-0847 Social Work Research and Abstracts
0148-1037 Minority Voices
0148-1045 Media Law Reporter
0148-107X Employment Discrimination Digest
0148-1096 Zetetic *changed to* Skeptical Inquirer
0148-1150 N A G W S Rules. Skiing
0148-1177 Pacific Boating Almanac. Pacific Northwest & Alaska
0148-1827 Ore Bin *see* 0164-3304
0148-186X Administration of the Marine Mammal Protection Act of 1972 *see* 0196-4690
0148-1886 Massachusetts Archaeological Society. Bulletin
0148-1959 Interdisciplinary Perspectives
0148-2033 Specialty Advertiser
0148-2076 19th Century Music
0148-2092 Freebies
0148-2165 Lifelong Learning: the Adult Years
0148-2173 Pig American
0148-2181 Journal of Pension Planning and Compliance
0148-3218 Best's Insurance Report: Property-Casualty
0148-3250 Louisville Review
0148-3331 Christianity and Literature
0148-3366 Municipal Law Docket
0148-3390 Illinois Magazine
0148-3471 Surgical Techniques Illustrated
0148-3641 Directory of Washington Manufacturers *see* 0148-5687
0148-3668 American Preservation
0148-3706 Golf Business
0148-3897 Ornament
0148-3900 Journal of Interdisciplinary Modeling and Simulation
0148-3919 Journal of Liquid Chromatography
0148-3927 Clinical and Experimental Hypertension
0148-396X Neurosurgery
0148-4036 Pennsylvania Mennonite Heritage
0148-4052 Successful Meetings
0148-4079 Job Safety & Health (Silver Spring)
0148-4087 Public Transit Report
0148-4095 Solar Energy Intelligence Report
0148-4109 Federal Research Report
0148-4125 Sludge Newsletter
0148-415X New International Review
0148-4184 Accounting Historians Journal
0148-4214 Missouri Area Labor Trends
0148-4265 Current Nephrology
0148-432X American Educator
0148-4397 Solar Thermal Components
0148-4443 Pipeline (Houston)
0148-4451 Serials in Transition
0148-4478 Chilton's Food Engineering International
0148-4532 Yale Lit *see* 0148-4605
0148-4605 Yale Literary Magazine (1977)
0148-4648 International Drug Report
0148-4761 Health Labor Relations Reports
0148-477X Special Education Report
0148-4818 U S Pharmacist
0148-4958 Foodservice Equipment Specialist
0148-4982 Judicial Function Outline
0148-5016 Archives of Andrology
0148-5040 Wisconsin. Department of Public Instruction. Newsletter
0148-5059 Wisconsin Public School Directory
0148-5113 Geographical Survey
0148-5121 International File of Micrographics Equipment & Accessories
0148-5164 Ob/Gyn Digest (1980)
0148-5164 Journal of Continuing Education in Obstetrics & Gynecology *see* 0148-5164
0148-5172 Urology Digest (1980)
0148-5172 Journal of Continuing Education in Urology *see* 0148-5172
0148-5180 Journal of Continuing Education in O.R.L. & Allergy *see* 0198-7038
0148-5199 Cardiology Digest (1980)
0148-5199 Journal of Continuing Education in Cardiology *see* 0148-5199
0148-530X U. S. Bureau of Labor Statistics. Publications
0148-5385 Health Facilities Court Digest
0148-5407 Disabled USA
0148-5431 D M: Data Management
0148-5512 Federal Index
0148-558X Journal of Accounting Auditing & Finance
0148-5598 Journal of Medical Systems
0148-5628 Climatological Data for Amundsen-Scott, Antarctica
0148-5644 U.S. Library of Congress. Accessions List: Afghanistan†
0148-5652 Delaware State Industrial Directory
0148-5660 Maryland State Industrial Directory
0148-5679 Rhode Island State Industrial Directory
0148-5687 Washington Manufacturers Register
0148-5717 Sexually Transmitted Diseases
0148-5733 Pacific Information Service on Street-Drugs
0148-5741 Yale Forest School News
0148-5792 Jobber/Retailer
0148-5806 E C & T J
0148-5903 American Bookseller
0148-5989 Ham Radio Magazine
0148-6039 Accident Facts
0148-6055 Journal of Rheology
0148-6101 R I P E H The Review of Iranian Political Economy & History
0148-6128 W P I Journal
0148-6179 Black American Literature Forum
0148-6187 Beverage Industry
0148-6195 Journal of Economics and Business
0148-6225 Association for Asian Studies. Committee on East Asian Libraries. Bulletin
0148-6381 Who's Who Among Vocational and Technical Students in America
0148-6403 Head & Neck Surgery
0148-6411 I E E E Transactions. Components, Hybrids and Manufacturing Technology
0148-642X Catalog of Fossil Spores and Pollen
0148-6489 Public Land & Resources Law Digest
0148-6535 Studies in Economics
0148-6543 Studies in History and Philosophy. Pamphlet Series
0148-6551 Studies in Law
0148-656X Studies in Social Theory
0148-6586 Index to Mormonism in Periodical Literature
0148-6616 Genealogical Society of Okaloosa County, Florida. Journal
0148-6659 Roots
0148-6675 Fire Technology Abstracts
0148-6713 Leisure Beverage Insider Newsletter
0148-6721 Car Dealer Insider Newsletter
0148-673X Trumpeter
0148-6748 Europe Today (Augusta)
0148-6799 Army Officer's Guide
0148-6802 Invest Yourself
0148-6845 Violin Society of America. Journal
0148-690X Compensation Planning Journal
0148-6934 E E O Review
0148-7043 Annals of Plastic Surgery
0148-7078 Motel/Hotel Insider Newsletter
0148-7094 U.S. Department of Agriculture. Economics, Statistics, and Cooperatives Service. Africa and West Asia Agricultural Situation
0148-7175 Afro-American Journal
0148-7280 Gamete Research
0148-7299 American Journal of Medical Genetics
0148-7442 Directory of Michigan Municipal Officials
0148-7469 Air Cargo Magazine
0148-7469 O A G Air Cargo Guide
0148-7558 Massachusetts State Industrial Directory
0148-7566 Get Ready Sheet
0148-7604 D A T A Book of Discontinued Semiconductor Diodes
0148-7639 A D F L Bulletin
0148-7671 Polar Geography *changed to* Polar Geography and Geology
0148-771X Grass Roots Perspectives on American History
0148-7736 Texas Monthly
0148-7868 Africana Libraries Newsletter
0148-7876 Texas. Department of Water Resources. Library. Bulletin.
0148-7876 Texas. Department of Water Resources. Library Bulletin
0148-7922 Family Law Reporter
0148-7930 Retail/Services Labor Report
0148-7949 Government Manager
0148-7957 Noise Regulation Reporter
0148-7965 B N A's Patent, Trademark & Copyright Journal
0148-7973 Chemical Regulation Reporter
0148-7981 Labor Arbitration Reports
0148-7981 Labor Relations Reporter
0148-799X Dynamic Years
0148-8066 Association of Departments of Foreign Languages. Bulletin *see* 0148-7639
0148-8139 United States Law Week
0148-8147 Affirmative Action Compliance Manual for Federal Contractors
0148-8155 Daily Report for Executives
0148-8279 Lithuanian Mathematical Transactions *see* 0363-1672
0148-8287 Journal of Thermal Insulation
0148-8295 Tax Management Memorandum
0148-8295 Washington Tax Review
0148-8317 Environmental Impact News†
0148-8325 South Dakota. Department of Social Services. Annual Medical Report
0148-8376 Journal of Social Service Research
0148-8384 International Journal of Family Therapy
0148-8414 American Spectator
0148-8430 Press
0148-8465 M R I S Current Awareness Service
0148-849X National Research Council. Transportation Research Board. Bibliography
0148-8619 U S Journal of Drug and Alcohol Dependence
0148-8627 Ensayistas
0148-8740 Motorboat & Equipment Directory
0148-8821 Marriage and Divorce Today
0148-883X Sexuality Today
0148-8848 United States Banker
0148-8880 Financial Reporting Trends: Life Insurance
0148-8996 Biblioscan Q-Z
0148-9011 Biblioscan H-L
0148-9062 International Journal of Rock Mechanics and Mining Sciences and Geomechanics Abstracts
0148-9100 American Art & Antiques *see* 0195-8208
0148-9119 Plastics Compounding
0148-9127 Crafts
0148-9151 Jackson Magazine
0148-916X International Journal of Leprosy and Other Mycobacterial Diseases
0148-9232 Indiana. Office of Community Services Administration. Annual Report
0148-9267 Computer Music Journal
0148-9364 Fanfare
0148-9410 Auto Reports†
0148-9437 Gift and Tableware Reporter. Gift Guide
0148-9496 Federation of American Hospitals. Review
0148-9526 U.S. Department of Agriculture Economics, Statistics and Cooperatives Service. Outlook for U.S. Agricultural Exports
0148-9666 Driftwood East
0148-9798 National Collegiate Championships Record Book *see* 0077-3824
0148-9801 Fueloil & Oil Heat & Solar Systems
0148-9836 Northeast Gulf Science
0148-9895 American Society of Civil Engineers. Waterway, Port, Coastal and Ocean Division. Journal
0148-9917 Journal of Ambulatory Care Management
0149-015X Studies in the American Renaissance
0149-0206 Working Craftsman
0149-0214 Gambling Times
0149-0265 Journal of Continuing Education in Psychiatry *changed to* Psychiatry Digest (1980)
0149-0273 Journal of Continuing Education in Family Medicine
0149-0281 Who Audits America
0149-0354 Barataria
0149-0362 East West Journal
0149-0389 Terrorism
0149-0397 Marine Mining
0149-0400 Leisure Sciences
0149-0419 Marine Geodesy
0149-0427 Acoustical Imaging and Holography *changed to* Imaging Science
0149-0451 Geomicrobiology Journal
0149-046X Membrane Biochemistry
0149-0508 Peace & Change
0149-0516 Pequod
0149-0532 Women's Agenda
0149-0605 Engineering Research Highlights
0149-0672 Equus
0149-0680 Sports Wise: New York
0149-0699 Self (New York)

0149-0729 Mahogany
0149-0737 News Media and the Law
0149-0796 African Index
0149-0907 Bioresearch Today: Pesticides
0149-0915 Bioresearch Today: Population, Fertility & Birth Control
0149-0923 Bioresearch Today: Industrial Health & Toxicology
0149-0931 Bioresearch Today: Human Ecology
0149-094X Bioresearch Today: Human and Animal Parasitology
0149-0958 Bioresearch Today: Food Additives & Residues
0149-0966 Bioresearch Today: Human & Animal Aging
0149-0974 Bioresearch Today: Food Microbiology
0149-0982 Bioresearch Today: Birth Defects
0149-0990 Bioresearch Today: Bio-Engineering & Instrumentation
0149-1008 Bioresearch Today: Addiction
0149-1016 Bioresearch Today: Cancer A-Cancerogenesis
0149-1024 Bioresearch Today: Cancer B-Anticancer Agents
0149-1032 Bioresearch Today: Cancer C-Immunology
0149-1040 New York Literary Forum
0149-1083 Guide to Independent Study Through Correspondence Instruction
0149-1091 O'Dwyer's Directory of Corporate Communications
0149-1148 Comprehensive Immunology
0149-1172 Washington Journalism Review
0149-1199 A C M Guide to Computing Literature
0149-1202 Bibliography and Subject Index of Current Computing Literature *see* 0149-1199
0149-1210 33 Metal Producing
0149-1288 Fodor's Paris
0149-1423 A A P G Bulletin
0149-1482 Reading Today International
0149-1598 N A C L A Report on the Americas
0149-1695 Legal Briefs for Editors, Publishers and Writers†
0149-1776 Glaciological Data
0149-1784 Journal of South Asian and Middle Eastern Studies
0149-1938 Sunworld
0149-1970 Progress in Nuclear Energy(New Series)
0149-1997 Allegheny Ludlum Horizons
0149-2004 Aletheia
0149-2047 Community Health Studies
0149-2063 Journal of Management
0149-2268 Bulletin of Chemical Thermodynamics (1977)
0149-2276 Competitivedge
0149-2357 Modern Electronics
0149-2373 Strike
0149-2381 Chemical Times & Trends
0149-2438 Tufts Kinsmen
0149-2446 A C S A News
0149-2454 Current Concepts in Radiology
0149-2462 Georgia. Water Resources Survey. Hydrologic Report
0149-2489 A F L-C I O American Federationist
0149-2578 Washington Social Legislation Bulletin
0149-2632 Hospital Peer Review
0149-290X Clinical Engineering
0149-2926 Sexual Medicine Today
0149-3361 Indiana Writes
0149-337X American City & County
0149-3442 Tack 'n Togs Merchandising
0149-3450 ELHI Funding Sources Newsletter
0149-3566 Industria Internacional
0149-3752 Illinois Issues Annual
0149-399X Asia Mail
0149-4007 Land Use and Transportation
0149-4147 Turbomachinery International
0149-4236 Chaplaincy
0149-4244 New Oxford Review
0149-4252 Chaplaincy Letter
0149-4260 Ophthalmology Digest (1980)
0149-4465 Diesel and Gas Turbine Worldwide
0149-449X Iowa. Department of Job Service. Annual Report
0149-4511 American Transportation Builder
0149-4600 Industrial Development's Site Selection Handbook *see* 0080-9810
0149-466X Players
0149-4732 Advances in Clinical Child Psychology
0149-4856 Airline Executive
0149-4872 Sociological Observations
0149-4880 Papers in International Studies: Latin America Series
0149-4899 Plastics Machinery and Equipment
0149-4902 M O T A
0149-4910 N A C T A Journal
0149-4929 Marriage & Family Review
0149-5011 Overtones
0149-5046 Heard Heritage
0149-5054 Computer Peripherals Review
0149-5070 Western New York Magazine
0149-5135 Sufi Times *see* 0161-6331
0149-516X Southern Accents
0149-5240 Equipment Guide News
0149-5283 Mine Regulation & Productivity Report
0149-5348 Current Bibliography of Plastic & Reconstructive Surgery
0149-5364 Federal Reserve Bank of Dallas. Review
0149-5372 Checklist of Human Rights Documents
0149-5380 W W D
0149-5437 Olson
0149-5534 Industry Mart
0149-5585 International Construction Week
0149-5712 Maarav
0149-5720 Numerical Heat Transfer
0149-5739 Journal of Thermal Stresses
0149-5747 Advanced Lighter-Than-Air Review
0149-578X Coal Week
0149-5879 Sewage Treatment Construction Grants Manual
0149-5887 Tiger Report†
0149-5895 Food, Drug & Cosmetic Manufacturing
0149-5909 Convenience Store News-Executive/Store Manager Edition
0149-5917 Inspiration (Los Angeles)
0149-5925 Vans & Pickups†
0149-5933 Comparative Strategy
0149-5941 Conflict
0149-5976 Monthly Detroit
0149-5992 Diabetes Care
0149-6026 Inner Paths
0149-6085 Journal of Food Safety
0149-6093 Good Ideas for Decorating
0149-6115 Geotechnical Testing Journal
0149-614X Together (New York) *see* 0199-7149
0149-6158 Together Sexology *see* 0199-7149
0149-6166 Index to Federal Tax Articles (Supplement)
0149-6352 Hospital Week
0149-6395 Separation Science and Technology
0149-6425 Rodeo News
0149-6441 West Branch
0149-6549 Health Practitioner *changed to* Physician Assistant/Health Practitioner
0149-6573 Environmental Comment
0149-6581 Directory of Companies Required to File Annual Reports with the Securities and Exchange Commission Under the Securities Exchange Act of 1934
0149-6646 Alaska. Department of Natural Resources. Annual Report
0149-6700 Studies in History of Biology
0149-6719 Cardiopulmonary Medicine
0149-6727 Medical Imaging†
0149-6743 Nutrition Planning
0149-676X American Wine Society Manual
0149-6778 American Wine Society. Bulletin
0149-6832 V U Marketplace
0149-6840 Folklife Center News
0149-6859 Cross Reference
0149-6867 Jacksonville Genealogical Society Quarterly
0149-6891 Unearth
0149-6948 Case Analysis in Social Science n Social Therapy
0149-6956 Crain's Chicago Business
0149-6964 International Review of Food & Wine
0149-6972 Far West
0149-6980 Media & Values
0149-7014 On Location
0149-7081 Women Artist News
0149-709X R F D
0149-7103 Street & Smith's Official Yearbook: Basketball
0149-712X Journal of Reform Judaism
0149-7162 Down's Syndrome
0149-7189 Evaluation and Program Planning
0149-7197 Retired Military Almanac
0149-7316 Runner
0149-7324 Impresario†
0149-7332 Somos
0149-7448 Regulators
0149-7499 Floral Underawl & Gazette Times
0149-7510 Job Safety & Health (Washington)
0149-7537 Who's Who in Engineering
0149-7545 Engineers of Distinction *see* 0149-7537
0149-7634 Neuroscience and Biobehavioral Reviews
0149-7642 Red Book of Housing Manufacturers
0149-7677 Dance Research Journal
0149-7820 Beehive
0149-7847 Directory of Conservative and Libertarian Serials, Publishers, and Freelance Markets
0149-7863 Pushcart Prize: Best of the Small Presses
0149-7901 Journal of Applied Management
0149-7944 Current Surgery
0149-7952 German Studies Review
0149-7995 Arizona Manpower Review
0149-8037 Willing Water (Denver) *see* 0273-3218
0149-8088 Index to Scientific & Technical Proceedings
0149-810X Subject Guide to Reprints
0149-8118 Dun & Bradstreet Exporters' Encyclopaedia-World Marketing Guide
0149-8142 Dunsworld Marketing Management
0149-8231 New York Business Change Service
0149-824X New Jersey Business Change Service
0149-838X A E I Defense Review *see* 0163-9927
0149-8398 Ecolibrium
0149-8428 Religion Index One: Periodicals
0149-8436 Religion Index Two: Multi-Author Works
0149-8444 Keystone Folklore
0149-8487 Gratz College Annual of Jewish Studies
0149-8681 Marxist Perspectives†
0149-8711 Omni
0149-8738 International Environment Reporter
0149-8797 Public Administration Times
0149-8827 Corporation Law Review
0149-8924 Sourcebook of Equal Educational Opportunity
0149-8932 Interview (New York)
0149-9114 Kansas History
0149-9130 Contemporary Economic Problems
0149-9157 Public Opinion
0149-922X A E I Studies on Contemporary Economic Problems *see* 0149-9130
0149-9262 Access (Washington, 1975)
0149-9289 Ningas-Cogon *changed to* Ningas
0149-9300 Micrographics Today
0149-936X C T, the Journal of Computed Tomography
0149-9386 Energy
0149-9408 American Book Review
0149-9483 Advances in Nutritional Research
0149-953X Prana Yoga Life
0149-9556 Data/Comm Industry Report
0149-9572 Minority Group Media Guide *changed to* Minority/Ethnic Media Guide
0149-9602 Health Foods Business
0149-970X Chicago Catholic
0149-9912 Physician's Guide to Practical Gastroenterology *see* 0163-7894
0149-9939 National Library of Medicine Audiovisuals Catalog
0149-9963 American Statistical Association. Statistical Computing Section. Proceedings (of the Annual Meeting)
0150-1011 Israel & Palestine
0150-1399 Bibliographie de la France. Supplement 1: Publications en Serie
0150-1402 Bibliographie de la France. Livres
0150-4428 Lys Rouge
0150-536X Journal of Optics/Nouvelle Revue d'Optique
0150-5467 Feuillet Rapide Fiscal Social
0150-5955 Bibliographie de la France. Supplement 2: Publications Officielles
0150-5971 Bibliographie de la France. Supplement 3: Musique
0150-5998 Bibliographie de la France. Supplement 4: Atlas, Cartes et Plans
0150-6463 Petrole Informations
0150-651X Maille Informations
0150-7516 Revue des Ingenieurs
0150-7540 Toutes les Nouvelles de l'Hotellerie et du Tourisme
0150-8695 Bulletin Signaletique. Part 528: Bibliographie Internationale de Science Administrative
0151-0479 Cahiers C E R T-C I R C E
0151-0509 Academie des Sciences. Comptes Rendus Hebdomadaires des Seances. Serie 1: Mathematiques
0151-0592 B.O.P.I. Abreges
0151-2943 Indicateur Bertrand
0151-3605 Visages du Vingtieme Siecle
0151-4016 Renaitre 2000
0151-4695 Jardineries
0151-5772 Royaliste
0151-5845 Psychomotricite
0151-685X Sciences et Tecniques Biomedicales
0151-6973 Techniques et Sciences Municipales Eau
0151-7341 Alsace Historique
0151-7791 Fou Parle
0151-783X Phot 'argus(Edition Professionnelle)
0151-7848 Phot 'argus (Edition Generale)
0151-8720 Societe Generale pour Favoriser de Developpement du Commerce et de l'Industrie en France. Bulletin
0151-9638 Annales de Dermatologie et de Venereologie
0151-9808 Ethnopsychiatrica
0152-7886 Phreatique
0153-226X Energie Solaire Actualites
0153-3401 Mostakbal
0153-3614 Argus International
0153-3673 Monuments Historiques
0153-4270 Mediatheques Publiques
0153-4351 Histoire pour Tous
0153-4602 Escargot Folk?
0153-4742 Lettre Medicale
0153-5021 Etudes sur l'Egypte et le Soudan Anciens
0153-5048 Cahiers de Philologie
0153-6133 Association Francaise des Amis d'Albert Schweitzer. Cahiers
0153-9019 Marche de l'Innovation
0153-9396 Electro-Negoce
0153-9620 Vagabondages
0153-9884 Interets Prives
0153-9930 Institut Europeen de Formation des Techniciens des Circuits Imprimes. Informations
0153-999X Catalogue National du Genie Climatique-Chauffage et Conditionnement d'Air
0154-0009 Tequi Electricite Electronique
0154-0033 Bulletin Officiel du Ministere de l'Environnement et du Cadre de Vie et du Ministere des Transports
0154-0041 Recapitulatif Mensuel des Signalements d'Origine CEDOCAR. Series 1: Documents Rediges en Langue Francaise
0154-0041 Recapitulatif Mensuel des Signalements d'Origine CEDOCAR. Series 2: Documents d'Origine Etrangere
0154-0157 Institut d'Etudes Slaves. Lexiques
0154-0165 Plan de Classement PASCAL
0154-0238 Groupe d'Etudes des Rythmes Biologiques. Bulletin
0154-6902 Semiotique et Bible
0154-7550 France Clima
0155-0187 University of New South Wales. Biomedical Library. Newsletter
0155-0306 Social Alternatives
0155-0438 Corella
0155-0489 Development News Digest *changed to* Development Dossier

0155-0543 Musicological Society of Australia. Newsletter
0155-0837 Dairy Topics
0155-1264 Trolley Wire
0155-2090 C A I News
0155-218X Reading Time
0155-2589 Industrial Arbitration Reports, New South Wales
0155-3070 A. A. P. A. Newsletter
0155-3089 A. A. P. A. Technitopics
0155-3372 New South Wales. Geological Survey. Records
0155-5111 Indonesian News Selections
0155-5561 New South Wales. Geological Survey. Bulletin
0155-6282 Monash University. Department of Civil Engineering. Civil Engineering Research Report
0155-6894 Word in Life
0155-7009 Australian Importers
0155-7742 Commonwealth Scientific and Industrial Research Organization. Division of Animal Production Report
0155-7785 Speculations in Science and Technology
0155-9044 Helix
0155-9222 Primary Industry Newsletter
0155-9443 Australian Renewable Energy Resources Index
0155-977X Social Analysis
0156-0115 Hostel Yarn
0156-0352 Food and Liquor Retailer
0156-1006 U N E Convocation Bulletin & Alumni News
0156-1383 Bird Behaviour
0156-1596 Inside Asean
0156-160X A N S O L Bibliography Series
0156-1650 Religious Traditions
0156-191X Bulletin of Christian Affairs
0156-2681 Australian Meat Industry Bulletin
0156-2703 Inpharma
0156-3726 Pacific Aviation Yearbook
0156-4420 Studies in Society
0156-4714 Health Education News and Views
0156-4919 Pursuit
0156-6148 Western Intelligence Report
0156-6342 Science Fiction News
0156-6717 Guidelines
0156-7446 Quarterly Review of the Rural Economy
0156-7594 Rationalist News
0156-8760 New South Wales. Department of Technical and Further Education. T A F E Quarterly
0156-9945 Commonwealth Scientific and Industrial Research Organization. Institute of Earth Resources. Technical Communication.
0156-9953 Commonwealth Scientific and Industrial Research Organization. Institute of Earth Resources. Investigation Report.
0157-1532 Australian Journal of Audiology
0157-2431 Railway Digest
0157-244X Australian Science Education Research Association. Research in Science Education
0157-308X Australian Littoral Society. Bulletin
0157-3470 Release
0157-3977 Hosteller
0157-6429 Australian Marine Sciences Association. Bulletin
0157-7271 Reactions
0157-809X Queensland. Department of Forestry. Research Paper
0157-8200 Australia. National Information Service on Drug Abuse. Technical Information Bulletin
0158-0760 General and Applied Entomology
0158-0876 Incite
0158-1589 Victorian Government Directory
0158-1597 Clinical and Experimental Neurology
0158-3158 P E News
0158-3778 Filmviews
0158-3921 Victorian Fiction Research Guides
0158-3999 Australian Standard
0158-4154 Cantrills Filmnotes
0158-4197 Emu
0158-4243 Comet
0158-4960 Australian Journal of Medical Laboratory Science
0158-7765 Zinc Today
0159-1088 Instep
0159-1096 Contact (Sydney)
0159-110X Now
0159-2033 Lab-Talk
0159-3803 Quest
0159-950X Monash Review
0160-001X Washington Report
0160-0168 Bulletin of Research in the Humanities
0160-0176 International Regional Science Review
0160-0281 American Journal of Trial Advocacy
0160-0303 Graphic Communications Marketplace
0160-0311 Military Journal
0160-0338 Texas Woman
0160-0346 Logging Management
0160-0354 Spiritual Community Guide
0160-0419 French-American Review
0160-0508 Directory of Education Associations
0160-063X Face the Nation (Annual)
0160-0664 Collections (Buffalo)
0160-0680 Sulphur in Agriculture
0160-0699 Umbrella (Glendale)
0160-0850 Fiddle and a Bow
0160-0885 United Methodist Church. Curriculum Plans
0160-0893 Cornell Review
0160-0923 Helios (Lubbock)
0160-0974 Colorado. Water Conservation Board. Ground Water Series. Circular *see* 0092-2684
0160-1059 E V/Battery Technology
0160-1075 New Directions for Women
0160-1083 Growth Industry News
0160-1148 Electronotes
0160-127X Interface (Carmel)
0160-1296 Educators Guide to Free Audio and Video Materials
0160-1342 Safety Science Abstracts Journal
0160-1504 D I S C U S Facts Book
0160-1512 International Energy Biweekly Statistical Review
0160-1725 Historical Geography Newsletter
0160-1741 U. S. National Bureau of Standards. Journal of Research
0160-1792 Arise
0160-1830 Sports Afield Deer
0160-1997 Health and Society
0160-2047 Log
0160-2071 Micropaleontology Special Publications
0160-208X Journal of Jewish Art
0160-2098 Journal of Juvenile Law
0160-2144 Great River Review
0160-2179 Advances in Polyamine Research
0160-2217 New Brooklyn
0160-2233 South Florida Ports Handbook
0160-2241 Jacksonville Port Handbook
0160-225X American Shipper
0160-2365 American Musical Instrument Society. Newsletter
0160-242X Comprehensive Endocrinology
0160-2438 E E G Interpretation†
0160-2446 Journal of Cardiovascular Pharmacology
0160-2454 M D Anderson Clinical Conferences on Cancer
0160-2462 Membrane Transport Processes
0160-2470 Nutrition in Health and Disease
0160-2489 Seminars in Neurological Surgery
0160-2527 International Journal of Law and Psychiatry
0160-2543 Cynegeticus
0160-2551 Critical Care Quarterly
0160-256X Association for Women in Science. Newsletter
0160-2578 American Bench-Judges of the Nation
0160-2624 Coaching: Women's Athletics
0160-2659 Kansas Water Resources Research Institute. Annual Report
0160-2675 Policy Grants Directory
0160-2713 Journal of African-Afro-American Affairs
0160-2748 Neurotoxicology
0160-2780 Urbanism Past & Present
0160-2853 Georgetown University Papers on Languages and Linguistics
0160-2896 Intelligence
0160-3000 Woodall's Trailer & R V Travel
0160-3078 University of Oklahoma. Archaeological Research and Management Center. Project Report Series
0160-3086 University of Oklahoma. Archaeological Research and Management Center. Research Series
0160-3094 Public Accounting Report
0160-323X State and Local Government Review
0160-3329 Backpacker
0160-337X Enhanced Oil-Recovery Field Reports
0160-3450 American Pharmacy
0160-3469 Sociological Forum *see* 0273-2173
0160-3477 Journal of Post Keynesian Economics
0160-3493 Hispano-Italic Studies
0160-3515 Pulpit Preaching *see* 0160-838X
0160-3566 Black Sociologist
0160-3574 S P E C Flyer
0160-3604 Energy Research Abstracts
0160-3671 Solar Thermal Power Generation
0160-368X Solar Thermal Heating and Cooling
0160-3728 Who's Who in Religion
0160-3779 Mineral Economics Abstracts
0160-3825 Student Press Law Center Report
0160-3876 Musical Heritage Review Magazine
0160-3914 Fodor's Cruises Everywhere
0160-3930 N I T A
0160-4074 Industrial Research/Development
0160-4090 Zip
0160-4112 Fatigue of Engineering Materials and Structures
0160-4120 Environment International
0160-4139 Progress in Analytical Atomic Spectroscopy
0160-4147 Downtown Implementation Guide
0160-4163 Conference of Insurance Legislators
0160-4201 V O Y A
0160-4309 Exceptional Child Education Resources
0160-4317 Freshwater and Marine Aquarium
0160-449X Labor Studies Journal
0160-4570 F & O S. Motor Carrier Annual Report
0160-4767 Pizzazz†
0160-4848 The Arnoldian
0160-4880 Fiction Catalog
0160-4929 Politics Today
0160-4953 Collection Building
0160-5119 Florida Friends of Bluegrass Society. Newsletter
0160-5178 Commercial Finance Journal
0160-5402 Journal of Pharmacological Methods
0160-5534 Perekrestki
0160-5569 School Psychology Review
0160-5607 Construction News
0160-5682 Operational Research Society. Journal
0160-5704 Horse, of Course!
0160-5720 M L A Newsletter
0160-5739 Florida Retirement Living
0160-5895 House & Garden Decorating Guide
0160-5976 Humanity & Society
0160-5992 In These Times
0160-6042 Lawn Care Industry
0160-6077 Directory of Library Reprographic Services
0160-6107 Van Life and Family Trucking *see* 0164-503X
0160-6123 Information Manager
0160-6131 McCall's Working Mother
0160-614X Made in U S A
0160-6158 Standard (New York)
0160-6166 Club Living
0160-6174 Diamond Report
0160-6271 School Foodservice Journal
0160-628X Blake: an Illustrated Quarterly
0160-6352 P T J. Passenger Train Journal *see* 0160-6913
0160-6360 Chemical New Product Directory
0160-6379 Family and Community Health
0160-6433 Timber Harvesting
0160-6476 National Zip Code Directory *see* 0191-6971
0160-6557 N J E B, Nebraska Journal of Economics and Business
0160-6565 Guest Author
0160-6662 National Conference on Individual Onsite Wastewater Systems. Proceedings
0160-6689 Journal of Clinical Psychiatry
0160-6824 Golf Industry
0160-6891 Research in Nursing & Health
0160-6913 Passenger Train Journal
0160-6980 Continuing Education for Health Care Providers†
0160-7006 Health Care Education
0160-7049 Conference of Presidents of Major American Jewish Organizations. Annual Report *see* 0160-7057
0160-7057 Conference of Presidents of Major American Jewish Organizations. Report
0160-7065 Diesel Car Digest
0160-7146 Jacob Marschak Interdisciplinary Colloquium on Mathematics in the Behavioral Sciences
0160-7219 Perinatal Press
0160-7243 Stone in America
0160-7278 Army/Navy Store & Outdoor Merchandiser
0160-7308 Trial Diplomacy Journal
0160-7332 Amateur Boxer
0160-7340 Guide to Manufactured Homes
0160-7375 Frank Lloyd Wright Newsletter
0160-7383 Annals of Tourism Research
0160-7391 West Virginia State Industrial Directory
0160-7405 Utah State Industrial Directory
0160-7413 Compost Science/Land Utilization *changed to* Bio Cycle
0160-7472 International Telephone Directory of the Deaf
0160-7480 Modern Healthcare (1977)
0160-7545 Ellen Glasgow Newsletter
0160-757X Infusion
0160-7618 Health & Medical Care Services Review
0160-7626 Infertility
0160-7677 Slackwater Review
0160-7685 Dermatology Digest (1980)
0160-7685 Journal of Continuing Education in Dermatology *see* 0160-7685
0160-7693 Journal of Continuing Education in Pharmacy
0160-7707 Journal of Continuing Education in Orthopedics
0160-7715 Journal of Behavioral Medicine
0160-7731 Bill of Rights in Action
0160-7766 Journal of Continuing Education in Orthopedics *changed to* Orthopedics Digest (1980)
0160-7766 Journal of Continuing Education in Pediatrics *changed to* Pediatrics Digest (1979)
0160-7774 Journal of Supervision and Training in Ministry
0160-7782 Geothermal Resources Council. Bulletin
0160-7847 Fundamenta Scientiae
0160-788X Reclamation Review
0160-7901 Psychology U S S R
0160-791X Technology in Society
0160-7952 Metals Forum
0160-7960 Counseling and Values
0160-7979 Social Science and Medicine. Part A: Medical Psychology and Sociology *see* 0271-7123
0160-7987 Social Science & Medicine. Part B: Medical Anthropology
0160-7995 Social Science & Medicine. Part C: Medical Economics
0160-8002 Social Science & Medicine. Part D: Medical Geography
0160-8010 Toys, Hobbies & Crafts
0160-8029 U.S. Library of Congress. Cataloging Service Bulletin
0160-8037 Developing Country Courier
0160-8045 Latin American Indian Literatures
0160-8053 Food, Nutrition & Health Newsletter
0160-8126 Public Education Directory
0160-8134 Executive Female Digest *see* 0199-2880
0160-8177 Practical Law Books Review
0160-8223 Market & Credit Interchange Report
0160-8320 Athletic Training
0160-8347 Estuaries

ISSN INDEX 1199

0160-838X Pulpit Digest (1978)
0160-8398 Viewpoints in Teaching and Learning
0160-8460 Annotation
0160-8495 Pennsylvania Law Journal (Philadelphia, 1977)
0160-8665 Mime, Mask & Marionette
0160-8673 World of Opera
0160-8703 Literary Onomastics Studies
0160-8827 Financial Reporting Trends: Savings and Loan
0160-8843 American Association of Stratigraphic Palynologists. Contributions Series
0160-8908 Claude Hall's International Radio Report
0160-8916 Computer Dealer
0160-8932 Key (Goreville)
0160-8991 Fodor's Southeast Asia
0160-9009 Frontiers: a Journal of Women Studies
0160-9211 U.S. Library of Congress. National Library for the Blind and Physically Handicapped. News
0160-9289 Clinical Cardiology
0160-9300 Chronicle College Counseling for Transfers *changed to* Chronicle Guide for Transfers
0160-9327 Endeavour
0160-9394 Folia Slavica
0160-9416 Newsfront International
0160-9475 Spina Bifida Therapy
0160-9513 Social Work with Groups
0160-9572 Seybold Report on Word Processing
0160-9602 Northeastern Nevada Historical Society Quarterly
0160-9645 Ancient World
0160-967X Addiction and Substance Abuse Report
0160-9688 Criminal Justice and the Public
0160-9696 Success with Youth Report
0160-970X Book Industry Trends
0160-9734 Grants Magazine
0160-9742 Network Planning Paper
0160-9769 High Performance
0160-9807 Focus: Unexplored Deviance
0160-9815 Focus: Urban Society
0160-984X Palestine-Israel Bulletin
0160-9939 Marathoner
0160-9947 Future Life
0160-9963 Applied Radiology(1976)
0160-998X Index to Audio Visual Serials in the Health Sciences
0161-0155 Broward Life
0161-0287 Practice Digest
0161-0295 T I M S/O R S A Bulletin
0161-0325 Highway & Vehicle/Safety Report
0161-0333 Together (Washington, 1975) *see* 0193-3922
0161-035X Solid Wastes Management
0161-0376 Analytical & Enumerative Bibliography
0161-0384 Business International Money Report
0161-052X River World
0161-0546 Artist's Market(1979)
0161-0562 Current Career and Occupational Literature
0161-0619 Housing
0161-0627 Iran Economic News
0161-0724 American Universities Field Staff Reports
0161-0775 Theater (New Haven)
0161-0945 American Congress on Surveying and Mapping. Proceedings
0161-1089 State and Mind
0161-1119 Adventist Review
0161-1127 Government R and D Report
0161-1178 American Family
0161-1186 Cum Notis Variorum
0161-1194 Cryptologia
0161-1232 Art/Antiques Investment Report
0161-1267 Bottom Line
0161-1372 Surgical Rounds
0161-1380 Integral Yoga
0161-1402 A S I L S International Law Journal
0161-1577 Brilliant Corners
0161-164X New Women's Times
0161-1674 U.S. Department of Energy. Office of State and Local Programs. Annual Report to the President and the Congress on the State Energy Conservation Program
0161-1704 Music O C L C Users Group. Newsletter
0161-1739 Mail Order Counselor
0161-1798 Velo-News
0161-1801 Socialist Review (San Francisco)
0161-1828 Overseas Outlook
0161-1836 Birding
0161-1895 I.D.E.A.S.
0161-1976 Agenda (Washington)
0161-1992 Brides
0161-200X House & Garden Building & Remodeling Guide
0161-2018 Street & Smith's Official Yearbook: Baseball
0161-2042 Successful Business
0161-2085 Whole Earth Papers
0161-2158 International Association of Fire Chiefs. Official Publication
0161-2190 Vogue Beauty & Health Guide
0161-2328 Analog Science Fiction-Science Fact
0161-2336 House & Garden Plans Guide
0161-2387 Federal Reserve Bank of Kansas City. Economic Review
0161-2395 Delta Nu Alphian *changed to* Alphian
0161-2433 New York Times Biographical Service
0161-2492 Callaloo
0161-2506 Bloodroot (Grand Forks)
0161-2514 Aging and Work
0161-2549 Gallimaufry
0161-2638 Directory of Jewish Federations, Welfare Funds and Community Councils
0161-2719 Tull Tracing
0161-2778 Journal of Personality and Social Systems
0161-2786 Earnshaw's Infants, Girls and Boys Wear Review
0161-2832 Boston College International and Comparative Law Journal
0161-2840 Issues in Mental Health Nursing
0161-2875 World Meetings: Medicine
0161-3065 American Journal of Intravenous Therapy *changed to* American Journal of Intravenous Therapy & Clinical Nutrition
0161-3081 Tune up
0161-326X A J O T: The American Journal of Occupational Therapy
0161-3332 International Association of Fish and Wildlife Agencies. Proceedings of the Convention
0161-3448 Satellite News
0161-3464 Dax Dynamic Showcase
0161-3499 Veterinary Surgery
0161-357X McGraw-Hill's Construction Contracting *see* 0270-1588
0161-4002 Annual Institute on Securities Law and Regulations. Proceedings
0161-4010 Copyright Management
0161-4126 Communication Outlook
0161-4223 Lightworks
0161-4274 U.S. Department of Agriculture. Economics, Statistics, and Cooperatives Service. National Food Review
0161-4282 Seminars
0161-4312 Racquetball Illustrated
0161-4320 Moped Dealer
0161-4339 Farm Industry News/West
0161-4347 Farm Industry News/South
0161-4355 ASIA (New York)
0161-4371 High Fidelity's Buying Guide to Tape Systems
0161-4428 Focus on Alcohol and Drug Issues
0161-4452 Science Museum of Minnesota. Scientific Publications, New Series
0161-4576 Journal of Sex Education and Therapy
0161-4630 Prostaglandins and Medicine
0161-4738 North Carolina State Industrial Directory
0161-4754 Journal of Manipulative and Physiological Therapeutics
0161-4835 Death
0161-4843 Casino-East
0161-4851 Gas Digest
0161-486X Columbia
0161-4908 Asian Theatre Reports
0161-4924 Annual New Mexico Water Conference. Proceedings
0161-4932 Florida Genealogist
0161-5114 Re-View
0161-522X Marine Recreational Fisheries
0161-5238 Brethren Missionary Herald
0161-5246 Issues in Health Care of Women
0161-5319 Frontiers of Power Technology Conference. Proceedings
0161-5378 Highlander
0161-5386 Taxation with Representation Newsletter
0161-5394 A M A Management Digest
0161-5408 AG Alert
0161-5440 Historical Methods
0161-5491 Journal of Holistic Health
0161-5505 Journal of Nuclear Medicine (1978)
0161-5556 Book-Mart
0161-5653 School Social Work Journal
0161-5653 School Social Work Journal
0161-5661 Graduate Woman
0161-570X Alternative Lifestyles
0161-5785 Printing Paper
0161-5823 Broadcasting & the Law
0161-5866 Money Business: Grants and Awards for Creative Artists
0161-5874 Health Science
0161-5882 National Association of Realtors. Existing Home Sales
0161-5890 Molecular Immunology
0161-5947 Chorister *changed to* Young Chorister
0161-5971 Songwriter's Market
0161-5998 Academy of Management Newsletter
0161-6005 A P I C Journal *see* 0196-6553
0161-6080 Successful Dealer
0161-6129 Police Magazine
0161-6234 Linn's Stamp News
0161-6277 U.S. Environmental Protection Agency. Grants Administration Division. Awards Register, Grants Assistance Programs
0161-6293 B P C
0161-6315 Cost Engineering
0161-6323 American Seaport
0161-6331 Wings†
0161-6412 Neurological Research
0161-6420 Ophthalmology
0161-6439 Journal of Otolaryngology and Head and Neck Surgery *see* 0194-5998
0161-6463 American Indian Culture and Research Journal
0161-6528 Atlas World Press Review
0161-6587 Boston College Law Review
0161-6595 Energy Conservation News
0161-6684 Human Rights and the U.S. Foreign Assistance Program
0161-6706 Sports 'n Spokes
0161-6730 Virginia Road Builder
0161-6773 Long Term Care and Health Services Administration Quarterly†
0161-6781 Health Manpower Report *see* 0362-3165
0161-682X Romantist
0161-6838 Teacher Information Exchange
0161-6846 Public Library Quarterly
0161-6862 Computer Products
0161-7001 Best Buys in Print
0161-7109 Juvenile & Family Court Journal
0161-7133 Missionary Monthly
0161-7184 Travel/Holiday
0161-7184 Travel Incorporating Holiday *see* 0161-7184
0161-7222 Studia Mystica
0161-7230 Research in Political Economy
0161-7249 Research in Philosophy and Technology
0161-7257 Current Construction Costs
0161-7311 Producer Prices and Price Indexes
0161-7346 Ultrasonic Imaging
0161-7389 U S A Today
0161-7397 International Association of Orientalist Librarians. Bulletin
0161-7400 School Social Work Quarterly
0161-7419 Fairfield County Executive
0161-7427 Microelectronic Manufacturing and Testing
0161-7435 George Herbert Journal
0161-746X Florida Pharmacy Journal
0161-7478 Forum on Medicine
0161-7486 Harvard Medical School Health Letter
0161-7508 Datacomm and Distributed Processing Report
0161-7567 Journal of Applied Physiology: Respiratory, Environmental and Exercise Physiology
0161-7605 CableLibraries
0161-7710 Bflo
0161-7745 Best's Review. Property-Casualty Insurance Edition
0161-7753 Arkansas Educator
0161-7761 Anthropology & Education Quarterly
0161-7796 U.S. Environmental Protection Agency. Radiation Protection Activities
0161-780X Current Neurology
0161-7818 Current Radiology
0161-7826 D Magazine
0161-7869 I E E E Geoscience Electronics Society Newsletter
0161-7885 Illinois Horizons
0161-8032 Predicasts Overview of Markets and Technologies
0161-8091 Energy Developments in Japan
0161-8105 Sleep
0161-813X Neurotoxicology
0161-8229 Sales Training *see* 0193-2136
0161-8245 Index to Periodical Articles by and About Blacks
0161-8318 Assembling
0161-8342 Antique Trader Weekly
0161-8423 Theodore Roosevelt Association Journal
0161-8458 Journal of Mechanical Design
0161-8490 E P A Activities Under the Resource Conservation and Recovery Act of 1976
0161-8563 Alabama State Industrial Directory
0161-8571 Georgia State Industrial Directory
0161-8644 Bilalian News
0161-8768 Officemation Reports *changed to* Officemation Product Reports
0161-8784 Realities (Horsham)
0161-8792 Perspectives in Ophthalmology
0161-8938 Journal of Policy Modeling
0161-8954 Advances in Aquatic Microbiology
0161-9004 Statistics of Privately Owned Electric Utilities in the United States
0161-9020 Football Notes
0161-9055 Home Video Report
0161-9225 I & L
0161-9241 California State Bar Journal
0161-9268 Advances in Nursing Science
0161-9276 Clergy Tax Tips
0161-9284 Magazine Antiques
0161-9330 In Public Service
0161-9373 Maritime Newsletter
0161-9500 Executive Educator
0161-9640 Clinical Chemistry News
0161-9713 Textile Week
0161-973X RetailWeek
0161-9896 Highlands Voice
0162-0029 Garcia Lorca Review
0162-0045 Food Monitor
0162-007X Physical Education/Sports Index
0162-0088 Contributions to Music Education
0162-0088 World Wide Shipping Guide
0162-0126 Cinemonkey
0162-0177 C R: Centennial Review
0162-0223 Media Index
0162-0266 History News
0162-0290 Directory and Statistics of Oregon Libraries
0162-0304 Greenhouse Review
0162-0363 Catholic Sentinel (Diocese of Baker)
0162-0401 Frets Magazine
0162-0436 Qualitative Sociology
0162-0525 Journal of Juvenile & Family Courts *see* 0161-7109
0162-0533 Builder (Washington) *changed to* N A H B Builder
0162-0606 E E Report *see* 0199-6916
0162-069X X, a Journal of the Arts *changed to* Cumberland Journal
0162-0800 Olmste/A/D'S Geneaology Recorded
0162-0843 Health Sciences Serials

0162-0878 South Carolina State Industrial Directory
0162-0886 Reviews of Infectious Diseases
0162-0894 Tamarack
0162-0908 Year Book of Sports Medicine
0162-0916 Where to Write for Marriage Records: United States and Outlying Areas
0162-0932 Verbatim
0162-1017 Tamarisk
0162-1025 Fleet Owner: Small Fleet Edition
0162-1041 El Paso Business Review
0162-1149 Gargoyle (Washington)
0162-122X Products Liability Reporter
0162-1262 Texas Business & Texas Parade
0162-1424 Home Health Care Services Quarterly
0162-1432 A S A I O Journal
0162-1440 Tree Tracers
0162-153X American Shotgunner
0162-1564 T L, Tennessee Librarian
0162-1599 New England States Limited
0162-184X Center for Southern Folklore Newsletter *see* 0195-4903
0162-1858 Exchange: the Organizational Behavior Teaching Journal
0162-1890 Evangel
0162-1912 Western Journal of Agricultural Economics
0162-1939 Illinois. State Museum. Guidebooklet Series
0162-1963 General Science Index
0162-2102 Catholic Sentinel (Archdiocese of Portland, Oregon)
0162-2110 World of Rodeo and Western Heritage
0162-217X Charles Redd Monographs in Western History
0162-2188 Ischia Mondo
0162-220X Cancer Nursing
0162-2226 Professional Remodeling
0162-2234 Assemblies of God Home Missions
0162-2242 Sportstyle
0162-2250 Journal of Commerce & Industry
0162-2269 Clinical Behavior Therapy Review
0162-234X Philosopher's Annual
0162-2404 Soviet World Outlook
0162-2439 Science, Technology, & Human Values
0162-2463 Guide to Graduate Management Education
0162-2471 F E W's News & Views
0162-2498 Book Collector's Market *see* 0196-5654
0162-2714 Coal Outlook
0162-2714 Coal, Quarterly Reports: Demonstration Plants
0162-2730 Fuel Oil Week†
0162-2749 International Family Planning Perspectives and Digest *see* 0190-3187
0162-2757 Detroit in Perspective
0162-2765 Goodfellow Review of Crafts
0162-2773 L A E Journal†
0162-2811 Communication Abstracts
0162-2870 October
0162-2889 International Security
0162-2897 California History (San Francisco)
0162-2900 Los Angeles Lawyer
0162-296X Orpheus
0162-2978 Adobe Today
0162-2994 Washington Drug and Device Letter *see* 0194-1291
0162-3036 Engineering Index Monthly and Author Index
0162-3052 L A E News
0162-3109 Immunopharmacology
0162-3125 Bacon's Publicity Checker
0162-3141 U.S. Army Recruiting and Re-Enlisting Journal *see* 0192-6071
0162-315X Weimaraner Magazine
0162-3192 Journal of Guidance and Control
0162-3214 Petersen's 4 Wheel & Off-Road
0162-3230 Flower and Garden. Southern Edition
0162-3249 Flower and Garden. Northern Edition
0162-3257 Journal of Autism and Developmental Disorders
0162-3273 Computer Graphics (Eugene) *changed to* Computer Graphics World
0162-3281 Related Patent Index
0162-329X Dual Dictionary to Petroleum Abstracts
0162-3346 Perspectives (Pittsburgh)
0162-3354 Periodical Update
0162-3362 Prep
0162-3389 Actuator Systems
0162-3400 Savor
0162-3559 P S B A Bulletin
0162-3583 Rifle
0162-3591 A A A Traveler Magazine
0162-3613 B S C S Journal
0162-3656 Agency Sales Magazine
0162-3664 Young World *see* 0009-3971
0162-3761 Contemporary Pharmacy Practice
0162-3796 Campground Management
0162-3818 Nebula Winners
0162-3958 Energy Resources & Technology
0162-3974 Neighbors
0162-4024 Continuum(Washington D.C.)
0162-4040 Financial Review (New York)
0162-4067 World Naturopathic Journal†
0162-4075 Concrete International: Design & Construction
0162-4237 Cemetery Business & Legal Guide
0162-461X Children's Leadership
0162-4687 Bible Discoverers: Teacher
0162-4962 Biography
0162-5047 Livestock Weekly
0162-5055 Juvenile Law Digest
0162-5136 Candy Wholesaler
0162-5152 Insiders' Chronicle
0162-5160 Pennsylvania Township News
0162-5233 Washington Food Report
0162-5306 Action Line
0162-5330 Ceramic Mold Mart
0162-5403 Alaska Review of Social and Economic Conditions
0162-5411 Official Baseball Dope Book
0162-542X Official Baseball Register
0162-5446 Dermatology
0162-5454 Seminars in Infectious Disease
0162-5519 Hadronic Journal
0162-5578 F T Fastener Technology *see* 0191-8508
0162-5594 Intercontinental Press Combined with Inprecor
0162-5616 Florida Folk Arts Directory *changed to* Florida Festival Arts Directory
0162-5632 Miniature Magazine
0162-5691 Corporate Practice Series
0162-5721 Atlanta Historical Journal
0162-573X Daisy
0162-5764 Licensing Law and Business Report
0162-5810 Alembic†
0162-5853 Computer Business News
0162-5861 Dining In & Out
0162-5918 Alpha
0162-5942 Emergency
0162-5950 On-Your-Own Guide to Asia
0162-5977 C S P Directory of Suppliers of Educational Foreign Language Materials
0162-5993 D I S C U S Newsletter
0162-6108 Frozen Fishery Products. Annual Summary
0162-6175 Coke and Coal Chemicals
0162-6191 Constructor
0162-6205 Highway Safety Highlights
0162-6256 Sanitary Services in Tennessee
0162-6272 Opiniones Latinoamericanas *changed to* Opiniones
0162-6280 Folklore and Mythology Studies
0162-6302 New York(State) Department of Social Services. Bureau of Data Management and Analysis. Program Brief
0162-6329 Defenders of Wildlife Magazine *see* 0162-6337
0162-6337 Defenders
0162-6345 Footwear Focus
0162-6353 Carolinas Companies
0162-637X Chemical Worker
0162-6396 Sexology (1978) *see* 0199-7149
0162-6418 20th Century Christian
0162-6426 Library of Congress
0162-6493 Infectious Disease Practice
0162-654X U S Hockey Biz *changed to* American Hockey & Arena
0162-6566 American Journal of Proctology, Gastroenterology & Colon & Rectal Surgery
0162-6574 Journal of Experiential Learning and Simulation
0162-6604 Aftermarket Executive
0162-6620 Action in Teacher Education
0162-6639 Index of N L M Serial Titles
0162-6663 Handy Andy
0162-6760 Spirituality Today
0162-6817 Market Logic
0162-6876 Sharing (Rockville)
0162-6906 Monographs in Developmental Pediatrics
0162-6957 Behavioral Medicine
0162-6973 Cadence (Redwood)
0162-704X Conference Papers Index
0162-7155 Journal of Obstetrics and Gynecology of the Republic of China
0162-7163 L A C M A Physician
0162-7171 Synopsis of Family Therapy Practice
0162-7295 Legal Times of Washington
0162-7325 National Law Journal
0162-7333 New York Theatre Annual *changed to* American Theatre Annual
0162-7341 Journal of Sport Behavior
0162-735X O A G Travel Planner & Hotel/Motel Guide. European Edition
0162-7376 Woodall's Campground Directory. Texas Edition
0162-7384 Woodall's Campground Directory. Arizona Edition
0162-7392 Woodall's Campground Directory. California Edition
0162-7406 Woodall's Campground Directory. Eastern Edition
0162-7414 Woodall's Campground Directory. Western Edition
0162-7422 Bank Loan Officers Report
0162-7430 Bank Marketing Report
0162-7449 Bank Personnel Report
0162-7465 Bank Tax Report
0162-7473 Bank Teller's Report
0162-749X Effective Manager
0162-7503 Executive Compensation Report *changed to* Executive Compensation and Employee Benefits Report
0162-7511 Kess Tax Practice Report
0162-7546 Reviews of Chemical Intermediates
0162-7600 European Journal of Cellular Plastics
0162-7635 Yachtsman's Guide to the Greater Antilles
0162-766X Middle East: Abstracts and Index
0162-766X Middle East: Abstracts and Index
0162-7910 A A H E Bulletin
0162-7961 Social Work in Education
0162-7996 Antitrust
0162-8003 Advances in Archaeological Method and Theory
0162-8046 U F O Annual
0162-8127 Horse Care
0162-816X Medical Equipment Classified
0162-8208 Altadena Review
0162-8216 Communication Theory in the Cause of Man
0162-8267 Heritage Review
0162-8283 American Historical Society of Germans from Russia. Journal
0162-8291 Sea World†
0162-8305 Galileo (Boston)
0162-8321 Monographs of Marine Mollusca
0162-833X Journal of the New Alchemists
0162-8356 Confluencia
0162-8402 Hydrogen Progress
0162-8445 Arts & Humanities Citation Index
0162-8453 Journal of Curriculum Theorizing
0162-8488 Pre-Raphaelite Review
0162-8496 Mail Order Product Newsletter
0162-8534 Electrical Business
0162-8585 American Hispanist
0162-8658 Small Business Tax Control
0162-8712 California Sociologist
0162-8739 A Different Drummer
0162-8801 Home and Auto
0162-881X Flooring
0162-8836 Housewares
0162-8887 Standard Rate and Data Service. Community Publication Rates and Data
0162-8895 Standard Rate and Data Service. Weekly Newspaper and Shopping Guide Rates and Data *see* 0162-8887
0162-8917 Sassy
0162-8933 Character
0162-8941 Equine Practice
0162-895X Political Psychology
0162-8968 Inc.
0162-8976 Prairie Sun
0162-9050 New Issues
0162-9069 Nursing Job News: Nursing Job Guide to over 7000 Hospitals
0162-9077 Home Lighting & Accessories
0162-9085 Nahuatzen
0162-9093 Communications and the Law
0162-9107 Januz Direct Marketing Letter
0162-9123 Workbasket
0162-9131 Energy User News
0162-9158 H F D-Retailing Home Furnishings
0162-9174 University of Dayton Law Review
0162-9301 Bible and Spade
0162-9360 Journal of Clinical Hematology and Oncology
0162-9379 Orthopaedic Transactions
0162-945X Update (Arlington)
0162-9468 Textile Products and Processes
0162-9484 U. S. Geological Survey. Yearbook
0162-9638 S N M Newsline
0162-9646 C I C's School Directories
0162-9719 Journal of Materials for Energy Systems
0162-976X A A B S Newsletter
0162-9794 Forum on Taxing & Spending
0162-9816 TravLtips
0162-9824 Nathaniel Hawthorne Society. Newsletter
0162-9867 International Gymnast
0162-9875 Extension Review
0162-9972 Hotel and Travel Index
0163-0016 Working Papers in Applied Linguistics
0163-0067 Information World†
0163-0075 Cincinnati Medicine
0163-0083 Woodall's Campground Directory. New England States Edition
0163-0105 Woodall's Campground Directory. Wisconsin Edition
0163-0113 Woodall's Campground Directory. New Jersey/New York Edition
0163-0121 Woodall's Campground Directory. Michigan Edition
0163-013X Dash
0163-0229 Korean Review
0163-0253 Life Lines
0163-030X Chilton's I A M I Iron Age Metalworking International
0163-0350 Latin American Music Review
0163-0369 New Farm
0163-0458 Health Devices Alerts
0163-0466 Index to New England Periodicals
0163-0504 Genealogical Forum of Portland, Oregon. Bulletin *see* 0433-3179
0163-0512 Facets
0163-0539 Genealogical Society of Portland, Oregon. Monthly Bulletin *see* 0433-3179
0163-0563 Numerical Functional Analysis and Optimization
0163-0571 Journal of Immunopharmacology
0163-0652 Limited Partners Letter
0163-0660 Allergy Information Exchange *see* 0192-995X
0163-0679 Chilton's Control Equipment Master
0163-0741 Wind Technology Journal
0163-075X Kenyon Review
0163-0768 Forum Linguisticum
0163-0911 Antiques World
0163-092X Portfolio
0163-0938 Fashion Rage
0163-0946 Odyssey
0163-0954 Icarus(Baltimore)
0163-1004 Fuego de Aztlan†
0163-1020 U S News Washington Letter

0163-1101 Shepard's Military Justice Citations
0163-1136 Connecticut
0163-1144 Flying Annual & Buyers' Guide
0163-1152 Maine Historical Society. Quarterly
0163-1187 Chronicles of Culture
0163-1209 Cumberlands
0163-1241 Abingdon Clergy Income Tax Guide
0163-1268 Small Business Computers
0163-1276 New York Production Manual
0163-1284 Platt's Oilgram News
0163-1322 Hospital Purchasing Management
0163-1365 American Jewish Congress. Congress Monthly
0163-1373 L A M P Occasional Newsletter
0163-1411 Massachusetts Law Review
0163-1489 Procurement Systems Digest
0163-1578 Advances in Asthma & Allergy†
0163-1640 18 Almanac
0163-1667 Texas. Department of Health Resources. Biennial Report
0163-1675 Cardiology Update
0163-1691 Dermatology Update
0163-1748 Professional Salesman's Letter *changed to* Creative Selling
0163-1764 Oil Report
0163-1780 World Traveling
0163-1799 Today's Christian Woman
0163-1810 American Institute of Industrial Engineers. Fall Industrial Engineering Conference. Proceedings
0163-1853 Polamerica
0163-1861 Kent Collector
0163-1926 Cat World
0163-1950 Woodall's Campground Directory. Ohio/Pennsylvania Editions
0163-1977 Manufactured Housing Dealer
0163-2027 50 Plus
0163-206X Steel Industry Review
0163-2078 Judicial Newsletter
0163-2116 Digestive Diseases and Sciences
0163-2124 National Contract Management Quarterly Journal *changed to* National Contract Management Journal(1980)
0163-2175 Gifts & Tableware(New York)
0163-2183 Synerjy
0163-2205 L I N K S
0163-2213 C A R C H News
0163-223X Nursing Job News
0163-2280 Censored
0163-2396 Studies in Symbolic Interaction
0163-240X Woodall's Campground Directory. Ontario Edition
0163-2469 Milford Series
0163-2485 Woodall's Campground Directory. Illinois/Indiana Edition
0163-2493 Woodall's Campground Directory. Idaho/Oregon/Washington Edition
0163-2566 E D F Letter
0163-2582 Physical Fitness/Sports Medicine
0163-2647 Universal Human Rights *see* 0275-0392
0163-2655 Psychiatric Opinion†
0163-2728 Patterson's American Educational Directory *see* 0079-0230
0163-2787 Evaluation and the Health Professions
0163-2809 Children's Language
0163-2817 Official National Collegiate Athletic Association Basketball Rules and Interpretations *changed to* N C A A Basketball Rules and Interpretations
0163-2825 Mountain State Geology
0163-2833 S A R Statistics
0163-2841 Modern Psychotherapy
0163-285X North American Yacht Register
0163-2876 Commercial and Financial Chronicle
0163-2884 Swimming and Diving Rules
0163-2914 State Laws and Regulations
0163-2922 State, Local, and Urban Law Newsletter
0163-2965 Studia Africana
0163-299X Today's Professionals
0163-3023 Commonsense
0163-3058 Magill's Literary Annual
0163-3155 Current Contents/Arts & Humanities
0163-321X Shooting Commercials
0163-321X R.F. Design
0163-3228 Diagnosis
0163-3252 Journal of Studies in Technical Careers
0163-3295 Urthkin
0163-3384 Developments in Statistics
0163-3392 Current Issues and Research in Advertising
0163-3449 Organic Gardening
0163-3457 E D A Research Review
0163-3562 Dynamite
0163-3651 Art Teacher *see* 0004-3125
0163-366X West Virginia University Alumni Quarterly *changed to* West Virginia University Alumni Magazine
0163-3716 Palestine Perspectives
0163-3813 Contributions in Comparative Colonial Studies
0163-3821 Contributions in Drama and Theatre Studies
0163-3848 Edward Sapir Monograph Series in Language, Culture, and Cognition
0163-3864 Journal of Natural Products
0163-3872 Porch
0163-3929 Historical Journal of Western Massachusetts
0163-3937 Books of the Times
0163-3945 National Guard
0163-3996 Health Law Project Library Bulletin
0163-4070 Soccer America
0163-4089 American Demographics
0163-4100 Chronicle Annual Vocational School Manual *changed to* Chronicle Vocational School Manual
0163-4119 Feed and Grain Times
0163-4143 Studies in Contemporary Satire
0163-416X ZooGoer
0163-4186 Copper: Quarterly Report
0163-4267 N A G W S Guide. Synchronized Swimming
0163-4275 Environmental Ethics
0163-4313 Woodall's Florida & Southern States Retirement & Resort Communities Directory
0163-4321 Woodall's Senior Exchange
0163-433X Journal of Sport Psychology
0163-4348 Science Fiction & Fantasy Book Review
0163-4356 Therapeutic Drug Monitoring
0163-4399 Formed Fabrics Industry *see* 0163-4429
0163-4429 Nonwovens Industry
0163-4437 Media Culture and Society
0163-4445 Journal of Family Therapy
0163-4453 Journal of Infection
0163-4461 Humanities in Society
0163-447X B C & T News
0163-4488 Supermarket Trends
0163-4526 Journal of Water Borne Coatings
0163-4534 Polyphony
0163-4542 Powder Coatings
0163-4631 Precisely
0163-464X Pharmacy Management†
0163-4674 U.S. Federal Railroad Administration. Office of Safety. Accident/Incident Bulletin
0163-4712 Florida State Industrial Directory
0163-4747 N A G W S Guide. Soccer
0163-4763 Soccer Rules
0163-4828 Weekly Reader Eye
0163-4852 Senior Weekly Reader
0163-4860 Weekly Reader News Parade
0163-4879 Weekly Reader News Patrol
0163-4887 My Weekly Reader Surprise
0163-4895 Buddy's Weekly Reader
0163-4909 Weekly Reader News Hunt
0163-4941 Aeronautical Engineering; a Special Bibliography with Indexes
0163-4976 Iowa. Crop and Livestock Reporting Service. Planting to Harvest. Weather and Field Crops *changed to* Iowa Crop and Livestock Reporting Service. Planting to Harvest. Weather and Field Crops
0163-4984 Biological Trace Element Research
0163-4992 Cell Biophysics: an International Journal
0163-5026 Impact Two
0163-5069 Film Criticism
0163-5077 Labor Relations and Employment *see* 0193-5739
0163-5093 Information Moscow
0163-5123 Annual Index to Motion Picture Credits
0163-514X Journal of Prevention
0163-5158 Ageing International
0163-5182 Human Factors Society Annual Meeting. Proceedings
0163-5255 Rockford Papers
0163-5271 Mixed Pickles
0163-528X Folk Dance Directory
0163-5298 Journal of Continuing Education in Radiology
0163-531X Business (Atlanta)
0163-5328 Woodall's Campground Directory. Arkansas/Missouri Edition
0163-5336 Woodall's Campground Directory. Kentucky/Tennessee Edition
0163-5344 Woodall's Campground Directory. Colorado Edition
0163-5352 Woodall's Campground Directory. North Carolina/South Carolina Edition
0163-5379 Advances in Instructional Psychology
0163-5387 Persuasion at Work
0163-5425 Focus: Teaching English Language Arts
0163-5433 Wyoming Issues
0163-545X Environmental Law Newsletter
0163-5468 Field & Stream Bass Fishing Annual
0163-5476 Middle East Contemporary Survey
0163-5484 Northeastern Agricultural Economics Council. Journal
0163-5506 Public Libraries
0163-5514 Federal Controls†
0163-5530 Writing (La Mesa)†
0163-5549 Journal of Integral Equations
0163-5573 American Institute of Industrial Engineers. Proceedings of the Spring Annual Conference
0163-5581 Nutrition and Cancer
0163-559X International Society of Magnetic Resonance. Bulletin
0163-5662 Energy Guidebook
0163-5689 Progress in Communication Sciences
0163-6057 Soviet Union
0163-6065 Directory of Blood Establishments Registered Under Section 510 of the Food, Drug, and Cosmetic Act
0163-6170 Recent Advances in Nuclear Medicine
0163-6197 Electronic Business
0163-6200 Football Case Book
0163-626X Voice of Z-39
0163-6278 Current Chemical Reactions
0163-6359 Wildlifer
0163-6383 Infant Behavior and Development
0163-6413 Durak
0163-6480 Moral Education Forum
0163-6499 Urban Innovation Abroad
0163-6529 Urban Transit Abroad *changed to* Urban Transportation Abroad
0163-6545 Radical History Review
0163-657X Stanford French Review
0163-6588 Research in Law and Sociology *changed to* Research in Law, Deviance and Social Control
0163-660X Washington Quarterly: A Review of Strategic and International Studies
0163-6618 P/S/R/O Reports
0163-6626 Interface: the Computer Education Quarterly
0163-6642 Family Practice Recertification
0163-6650 Eberly's Michigan Journal
0163-6715 Gospel Teacher
0163-6766 Biomass Digest
0163-6774 Acronyms
0163-6782 Savings and Loan Market Study
0163-6855 Eastern Finance Association. Proceedings of the Annual Meeting
0163-6952 People and Energy†
0163-7010 Oxbridge Directory of Newsletters
0163-7029 Modern Technics in Surgery. Cardiac/Thoracic Surgery
0163-7037 Modern Technics in Surgery. Neurosurgery
0163-7088 Notes on Teaching English
0163-710X Family Advocate
0163-7134 Sawyer's Gas Turbine International *see* 0149-4147
0163-7169 China Business Review
0163-7193 Industrial Gas and Energy Utilization *see* 0164-4262
0163-7207 Boating Registration Statistics
0163-7258 Pharmacology and Therapeutics
0163-7266 Railfan & Railroad
0163-7282 Exetasis
0163-7290 U.S. Copyright Office. Catalog of Copyright Entries. Fourth Series. Part 1: Nondramatic Literary Works
0163-7304 U.S. Copyright Office. Catalog of Copyright Entries. Fourth Series. Part 2: Serials and Periodicals
0163-7312 U.S. Copyright Office. Catalog of Copyright Entries. Fourth Series. Part 3: Performing Arts
0163-7320 U.S. Copyright Office. Catalog of Copyright Entries. Fourth Series. Part 4: Motion Pictures and Filmstrips
0163-7339 U.S. Copyright Office. Catalog of Copyright Entries. Fourth Series. Part 5: Visual Arts Excluding Maps
0163-7347 U.S. Copyright Office. Catalog of Copyright Entries. Fourth Series. Part 6: Maps
0163-7355 U.S. Copyright Office. Catalog of Copyright Entries. Fourth Series. Part 7: Sound Recordings
0163-7363 U.S. Copyright Office. Catalog of Copyright Entries. Fourth Series. Part 8: Renewals
0163-7452 Board & Sail Magazine
0163-7460 Art Product News
0163-7517 S and M M
0163-7525 Annual Review of Public Health
0163-755X M E L U S
0163-7606 Federal Communications Law Journal
0163-7622 Milwaukee History
0163-7673 Reviews in Biochemical Toxicology
0163-769X Endocrine Reviews
0163-7789 Bulletin Exterieur
0163-7827 Progress in Lipid Research
0163-7843 Pacific Horticulture
0163-7851 Horticultural Reviews
0163-786X Research in Social Movements, Conflicts and Change
0163-7878 Research in Population Economics
0163-7894 Primary Care Physician's Guide to Practical Gastroenterology
0163-7908 Re: Act
0163-7916 Untitled
0163-8211 American Rag
0163-822X Illinois School Research and Development
0163-8246 N M A L: Notes on Modern American Literature
0163-8262 Impact (Syracuse)
0163-8270 Federal Civilian Work Force Statistics. Monthly Release
0163-8297 Public Welfare Directory
0163-8300 American Public Welfare Association. W-Memo
0163-836X Annual Editions: Readings in Human Sexuality
0163-8459 Topics
0163-8475 Community Review
0163-8483 World Higher Education Communique
0163-8491 Holistic Health Review
0163-8505 Sociological Practice
0163-8548 Human Studies
0163-8602 President's National Urban Policy Report
0163-898X O C L C Newsletter
0163-8998 Annual Review of Nuclear and Particle Science
0163-903X Washington Review
0163-9048 Human Rights Internet Newsletter *changed to* Human Rights Internet Reporter
0163-9234 Package Printing
0163-9250 Darkroom Photography
0163-9269 Behavioral & Social Sciences Librarian
0163-9277 Goodstay: Your Hospital Stay Magazine

0163-9358 Emergency Medical Services Quarterly *changed to* Emergency Health Services Quarterly
0163-9366 Journal of Nutrition for the Elderly
0163-9404 Feature
0163-9528 Supermarket Shopper
0163-9536 Impact: American Distilled Spirits Market Review and Forecast
0163-9544 Impact: the American Wine Market Review and Forecast
0163-9609 U.S. National Diabetes Advisory Board. Annual Report
0163-9625 Deviant Behavior
0163-9633 Clinical Preventive Dentistry
0163-9641 Infant Mental Health Journal
0163-9684 White Book of Ski Areas. U.S. and Canada
0163-9706 View (Oakland)
0163-9730 Public Works Manual
0163-9803 Bioethics Quarterly
0163-9897 Gay Insurgent
0163-9900 Herb Quarterly
0163-9927 A E I Foreign Policy and Defense Review
0163-9951 Clan MacNeil Association of America. Galley
0163-996X Federal Tax Coordinator
0163-9994 Research Institute Lawyers Tax Alert
0164-0046 Advances in Space Exploration *see* 0273-1177
0164-0070 Carolina Planning
0164-0089 Chilton's Instruments & Control Systems
0164-016X National Center Reporter *see* 0190-1168
0164-0178 American Jewish History
0164-0186 Better Homes and Gardens Bedroom and Bath Decorating Ideas
0164-0259 Knowledge: Creation, Diffusion and Utilization
0164-0305 Journal of Behavioral Assessment
0164-0356 50 State Legislative Review
0164-0534 Topics in Clinical Nursing
0164-0542 Group Health News
0164-0593 Associated Equipment Distributors. Rental Rates Compilation
0164-0674 Catholic Near East Magazine
0164-0704 Journal of Macroeconomics
0164-0739 Microforms in Print. Supplement
0164-0747 Guide to Microforms in Print. Author, Title
0164-0763 Library Research
0164-0771 Philosophy Research Archives
0164-078X Psychotherapy Digest
0164-0828 Bank Note Reporter (Iola)
0164-0836 Car Exchange
0164-0925 A C M Transactions on Programming Languages and Systems
0164-095X Forest Products Review
0164-0968 Task Force on Environmental Cancer and Heart and Lung Disease. Annual Report to Congress
0164-1085 Silverfish Review
0164-1212 Journal of Systems and Software
0164-1220 Futurics
0164-1247 Comparative Studies in Sociology
0164-1255 Fundamental Concepts of Estate Administration
0164-1336 Michigan Health Educator
0164-1352 Checklist of State Publications *changed to* State Publications Index
0164-1360 Notes on Modern American Literature *see* 0163-8246
0164-1433 South Jersey
0164-1441 Bostonia
0164-145X Higginson Journal
0164-1484 Periodically Speaking
0164-1492 Dickinson Studies
0164-1662 Florida Journal of Anthropology
0164-1689 Transportation Law Seminar. Papers and Proceedings
0164-1743 Media Guide International. Business/Professional Publications Edition
0164-176X P I P E R
0164-1867 D R C Historical and Comparative Disasters Series
0164-1875 D R C Book & Monograph Series
0164-1883 Trouser Press
0164-1905 Artes Graficas U S A
0164-2103 Cosecha/Harvest *see* 0145-2681
0164-2111 Fantastica *changed to* Fangoria
0164-212X Occupational Therapy in Mental Health
0164-2340 Topics in Emergency Medicine
0164-2472 Social Text
0164-2790 Analysis of Jewish Policy Issues
0164-2839 Design News. Materials
0164-2855 University of Arkansas at Little Rock Law Journal
0164-2863 Air Gun
0164-2871 Design News. Fluid Power
0164-288X Forum (College Park)
0164-3010 Springfield/Hartford
0164-3150 American Organist
0164-3169 Perspectiva Mundial
0164-3177 New England Review
0164-3207 Democratic Left
0164-324X Fiberarts
0164-3304 Oregon Geology
0164-3371 M S N Microwave Systems News
0164-3452 Hang Glider Magazine
0164-3495 Emmy
0164-3525 Economic World
0164-3746 Gulf Coast Fisherman
0164-3754 South-West Foodservice
0164-3762 Electronic Field Engineer
0164-386X Sheet Music
0164-3959 K E A News
0164-4092 Aviation Engineering & Maintenance†
0164-4262 Modern Industrial Energy
0164-4289 Kennel Review
0164-4327 Reproductions Review and Methods *see* 0198-9065
0164-4386 Nephrology Nurse
0164-4483 Siberian World
0164-4556 Southwest Magazine
0164-4645 Glaucoma
0164-4742 Words
0164-4777 Jordan (Washington)
0164-503X Motorhome Life (1978)
0164-5080 American Auditory Society. Journal
0164-5196 Police Product News
0164-5218 Black Odyssey
0164-5226 Rainbow (Minneapolis)
0164-5242 Specifying Engineer
0164-5331 California-Arizona Farm Press
0164-5412 Michigan Real Estate Magazine
0164-5420 A P A News
0164-5455 Compendium on Continuing Education for the Small Animal Practitioner
0164-5528 E/S A
0164-5560 Classic Film/Video Images *see* 0275-8423
0164-5609 Council of Biology Editors. Newsletter *changed to* C B E Views
0164-5617 Motor Inn Journal *see* 0018-6082
0164-5757 A L I Reporter
0164-582X Ideal Beef Memo
0164-5846 Recreational Computing
0164-5889 Subway
0164-5897 Pizza Maker
0164-5951 O W N
0164-6028 Update (Minneapolis)
0164-6044 Muffler Digest
0164-6052 Mergers and Corporate Policy
0164-6079 Human Services Reporter
0164-6168 Texas Thoroughbred
0164-6249 Real Estate Washington
0164-632X Ocean World
0164-6338 Pro Sound News
0164-6346 Dairymen's Digest: Southern Region Edition
0164-6532 Twin Cities
0164-6540 Snowmobile West
0164-6583 Community Planning Report
0164-6613 Evener
0164-6699 Mississippi Magazine
0164-6753 Expo (Philadelphia) *see* 0199-7602
0164-6850 North Carolina State Bar Quarterly
0164-694X Jogger
0164-6974 Nordic Skiing
0164-7059 Business Viewpoint
0164-7083 Keeping Abreast Journal of Human Nurturing
0164-7202 Nutrition Health Review
0164-7296 Municipal Management: a Journal
0164-7695 Hardware Retailing
0164-7768 Personal Finance: The Inflation Survival Letter
0164-7792 Muscle Digest
0164-7830 Calculators/Computers Magazine†
0164-7857 Current Concepts in Hospital Pharmacy Management
0164-7970 New Directions for Student Services
0164-7989 New Directions for Program Evaluation
0164-8047 Arena News
0164-8071 Atlanta Business Chronicle
0164-8098 New York Theatre Review
0164-8136 American Firearms Industry
0164-8152 New Hampshire Business Review
0164-8233 Specialty Salesman and Business Opportunities
0164-8276 Texas & Southern Quarter Horse Journal
0164-8578 Rural Missouri
0164-8756 Computer/Law Journal
0164-8780 Ranch & Coast
0164-887X Oil Patch
0164-8969 Journal of Genealogy
0164-9175 VocEd
0164-9183 Bowlers Journal
0164-9248 Circus Weekly *changed to* Circus (1979)
0164-9345 Kentucky Bench & Bar
0164-9566 Library P R News
0164-9612 Diving World
0164-9655 Millimeter
0164-9698 Financial Planning Today
0164-9728 G/C/T
0164-9787 Houston Engineer
0164-9876 Marketing Bestsellers
0164-9914 Chain Drug Review
0164-9922 Spray *changed to* Spray's Water Ski
0164-999X Broadcast Communications
0165-0009 Climatic Change
0165-005X Culture, Medicine and Psychiatry
0165-0068 Urban Law and Policy
0165-0076 Proces
0165-0106 Erkenntnis
0165-0114 Fuzzy Sets and Systems
0165-0122 Tijdschrift voor de Politie
0165-0157 Linguistics and Philosophy
0165-0165 Journal of Comparative Corporate Law and Securities Regulation
0165-019X Z T
0165-0203 Natural Resources Forum
0165-022X Journal of Biochemical and Biophysical Methods
0165-0254 International Journal of Behavioral Development
0165-0270 Journal of Neuroscience Methods
0165-0424 Aquatic Insects
0165-0475 Journal of Clinical Neuropsychology
0165-0505 Bijdragen en Mededelingen Betreffende de Geschiedenis der Nederlanden
0165-0521 Studies on the Neotropical Fauna and Environment
0165-0572 Resources and Energy
0165-0653 International Journal for the Advancement of Counselling
0165-0807 Moon and the Planets
0165-1005 Core Journals in Ophthalmology
0165-1056 Core Journals in Clinical Neurology
0165-1269 International Journal of Invertebrate Reproduction
0165-148X Overzicht-Internationale Universitaire Samenwerking
0165-1633 Solar Energy Materials
0165-1684 Signal Processing
0165-1730 Current Bibliography of Agriculture in China
0165-1765 Economics Letters
0165-1838 Journal of the Autonomic Nervous System
0165-2125 Wave Motion
0165-2222 Excerpta Medica. Section 51: Leprosy and Related Subjects
0165-2273 Geo-Processing
0165-2281 Health Policy and Education
0165-232X Cold Regions Science and Technology
0165-2370 Journal of Analytical and Applied Pyrolysis
0165-2427 Veterinary Immunology and Immunopathology
0165-2478 Immunology Letters
0165-2575 Esperanto Documents. New Series
0165-2672 Language Problems and Language Planning
0165-2818 Outlook on Research Libraries
0165-4101 Journal of Accounting and Economics
0165-4543 Meubel
0165-4608 Cancer Genetics & Cytogenetics
0165-5515 Journal of Information Science
0165-5515 Journal of Information Science: Principles & Practice
0165-5701 International Ophthalmology
0165-5752 Systematic Parasitology
0165-6090 Thymus
0165-716X Amsterdam Studies in the Theory and History of Linguistic Science. Series 2: Classics in Psycholinguistics
0165-7267 Amsterdam Studies in the Theory and History of Linguistic Science. Series 5: Library and Information Sources in Linguistics
0165-7666 Vicus Cuadernos: Linguistica
0165-7712 Linguistic & Literary Studies in Eastern Europe
0165-7763 Studies in Language Companion Series
0165-8042 Lover
0165-8182 Zeewezen
0165-859X Marine Biology Letters
0165-8646 Photobiochemistry and Photobiophysics
0165-8743 Purdue University Monographs in Romance Language
0165-9545 Milieudefensie
0166-0616 Studies in Mycology
0166-0829 Linguistik Aktuell
0166-137X Betoniek
0166-5162 International Journal of Coal Geology
0166-5316 Performance Evaluation
0166-574X Demografie
0166-610X Penitentiaire Informatie
0166-6231 Criminology & Penology Abstracts
0166-6258 Pragmatics and Beyond
0166-6282 Police Science Abstracts
0166-6622 Colloids and Surfaces
0166-8595 Photosynthesis Research
0166-8641 Topology and Its Applications
0166-9966 Bibliografie van Nederlandse Proefschriften
0167-093X Linksaf
0167-1731 Fertilizer Research
0167-2231 Carnegie-Rochester Conference Series on Public Policy
0167-2681 Journal of Economic Behavior & Organization
0167-2940 Trends in Analytical Chemistry
0167-3696 Ins and Outs
0167-4757 Selected Annotated Bibliography of Population Studies in the Netherlands
0167-5265 Information Services and Use
0170-0189 Bacillaria
0170-026X Zeitschrift fuer Arabische Linguistik
0170-0456 Die Chemische Produktion
0170-0561 Genetik.Grundlagen und Perspektiven
0170-057X Gestalt Theory
0170-0839 Polymer Bulletin
0170-0847 Oesterreichisches Jahrbuch fuer Politik
0170-0863 Biologica Didactica
0170-1541 Mathematica Didactica
0170-155X Technica Didactica *changed to* Didaktik-Arbeit, Technik, Wirtschaft
0170-1711 Elektrotechnische Zeitschrift
0170-1916 Bochumer Materialen zur Entwicklungsforschung und Entwicklungspolitik
0170-2025 Jahrbuch fuer Westdeutsche Landesgeschichte
0170-2408 Hiersemanns Bibliographische Handbuecher
0170-2416 Uebersee-Museum, Bremen. Veroeffentlichungen. Reihe E: Human-Oekologie
0170-303X La Technique du Roulement

0170-3056 La Tecnica de los Rodamientos
0170-3080 Deutsche Handelsakten des Mittelalters und der Neuzeit
0170-3099 Universitaet Frankfurt. Seminar fuer Voelkerkunde. Arbeiten
0170-3102 Bibliotheca Islamica
0170-3137 Beitraege zur Suedasien Forschung
0170-3153 Deutsche Sprache in Europa und Uebersee
0170-3188 Erdwissenschaftliche Forschung
0170-3196 Aethiopistische Forschungen
0170-3242 Alt- und Neu-Indische Studien
0170-3250 Geoecological Research
0170-3285 Freiburger Islamstudien
0170-3307 Freiburger Altorientalische Studien
0170-3315 Beitraege zur Literatur des 15-18. Jahrhunderts
0170-3447 Veroeffentlichungen zur Geschichte des Glases und der Glashuetter in Deutschland
0170-3455 Glasenapp-Stiftung
0170-3463 Industriegewerkschaft Druck und Papier. Schriftenreihe fuer Betriebsrate
0170-348X Uebersetzungen Auslaendischer Arbeiten zur Antiken Sklaverei
0170-3544 Studien zur Kulturkunde
0170-3560 Mainzer Studien zur Sprach- und Volksforschung
0170-3579 Wissenschaftliche Paperbacks
0170-3595 Quellen und Studien zur Geschichte des Oestlichen Europa
0170-3617 I F O Spiegel der Wirtschaft
0170-3633 Verschollene und Vergessene
0170-365X Institut fuer Europaeische Geschichte, Mainz. Veroeffentlichungen. Abteilung Universalgeschichte. Beihefte
0170-3668 Muenchener Ostasiatische Studien
0170-3676 Muenchener Ostasiatische Studien. Sonderreihe
0170-3684 Studien zur Ostasiatischen Schriftkunst
0170-3692 Universitaet zu Koeln. Kunsthistorisches Institut. Abteilung Asien. Publikationen
0170-3706 Sinologica Coloniensia
0170-4478 Betriebswirtschaftlicher Informationsdienst
0170-4761 Kritik
0170-5091 Basler Afrika Bibliographien. Mitteilungen
0170-5105 Buchhandelsgeschichte. Zweite Folge
0170-5334 Anaesthesiologie und Intensivmedizin
0170-5598 Arbeitsgemeinschaft der Parlaments-und Behoerden Bibliotheken. Mitteilungen
0170-5695 I F O Institut fuer Wirtschaftsforschung. Studien zu Handels- und Dienstleistungsfragen
0170-6012 Informatik-Spektrum
0170-7434 Physics Briefs
0170-7671 Agrarsoziale Gesellschaft. Kleine Reihe
0170-7809 Z M P Bilanz Getreide-Futtermittel
0170-7922 Schulleiter Handbuch
0170-8791 N Z
0170-8929 Muenchner Zeitschrift fuer Balkanologie
0170-902X Das Band
0170-9526 V D I Informationsdienst. Blechbearbeitung
0170-9550 V D I Informationsdienst. Kaltmassivumformung
0170-9569 V D I Informationsdienst. Elektrisch Abtragende Fertigungsverfahren
0170-9739 Zeitschrift fuer Physik. Section C: Particles and Fields
0170-9925 Archives of Gynecology
0171-0087 Basler Afrika Bibliographien. Nachrichten
0171-1091 Urologic Radiology
0171-1547 Forschung Stadtverkehr: Sonderreihe
0171-1555 B B A Planen und Bauen
0171-1660 Beitraege zur Afrikakunde
0171-1687 Geomethodica
0171-1741 European Journal of Applied Microbiology and Biotechnology
0171-2268 Uni Hannover
0171-3434 Psychosozial
0171-3647 V D I Informationsdienst. Schmieden und Pressen
0171-4279 Labor Praxis in der Medizin
0171-4910 Goettinger Orientforschungen. Reihe: Grundlagen und Ergebnisse
0171-5216 Journal of Cancer Research and Clinical Oncology
0171-5747 Atomkernenergie/Kerntechnik
0171-6042 Made in Europe. Furniture and Interiors
0171-6425 Thoracic and Cardiovascular Surgeon
0171-6468 Operations Research Spektrum
0171-6530 Aurora-Buchreihe
0171-7243 Amusement-Industrie
0171-791X Praxis der Psychotherapie und Psychosomatik
0171-8096 Technisches Messen - T M
0171-8177 Entomologia Generalis
0171-9262 Wirtschaftsschutz *changed to* Wirtschaftsschutz und Sicherheitstechnik
0171-9335 European Journal of Cell Biology
0171-953X Journal fuer Geschichte
0171-967X Calcified Tissue International
0171-9718 Behindertenhilfe Durch Erziehung, Unterricht und Therapie
0172-0473 Blumen
0172-0643 Pediatric Cardiology
0172-5599 Zentralblatt fuer Bakteriologie, Parasitenkunde, Infektionskrankheiten und Hygiene. Originale Reihe A: Medizinische Mikrobiologie und Parasitologie
0172-5602 Zentralblatt fuer Bakteriologie, Parasitenkunnde, Infektionskrankheiten und Hygiene-Krankenhaushygiene-Praeventive Medizin-Betriebshygiene
0172-8083 Current Genetics
0172-8113 Der Pathologe
0172-8172 Rheumatology International
0172-8199 Haustechnik, Bauphysik, Umwelttechnik
0172-9314 Cargoworld
0173-0843 Dokumente zum Hochschulsport
0173-1890 Pharmazeutische Verfahrenstechnik Heute
0173-5500 Seifen, Oele, Fette, Wachse
0173-7597 Krankenhauspharmazie
0173-783X Beitraege zur Tabakforschung International
0173-7872 Z S Magazin
0173-7937 Psychotherapie - Psychosomatik - Medizinische Psychologie
0173-8046 A I T
0174-304X Neuropediatrics
0174-3082 Zeitschrift fuer Kinderchirurgie
0174-3511 Kunstpreis-Jahrbuch
0174-3597 Helgolaender Meeresuntersuchungen
0180-0817 Urgence
0180-2410 Federation Nationale des Foyers Ruraux de France. Bulletin d'Information
0180-4103 Notes Bibliographiques Caraibes
0180-5738 Chirurgie Pediatrique
0180-6734 Combustibles et Carburants
0180-8095 Panorama de l'Energie
0180-8214 Commentaire
0180-9210 Bulletin de Mineralogie
0180-9296 Bulletin Signaletique. Part 527: Histoire et Sciences des Religions
0180-9555 Documents Pedozoologiques
0180-9822 Voies†
0180-9849 Revue de Droit Immobilier
0180-989X Annuaire des Marees pour l'An... Tome 1. Ports de France
0180-9938 Avis aux Navigateurs
0180-9954 Cahiers de l'Indo-Pacifique†
0180-9962 Annuaire des Marees pour l'An, Tome 2. Ports d'Outre Mer
0180-9970 Recueil des Corrections de Cartes (Year)
0180-9989 Bulletin Signaletique. Part 361: Reproduction. Embryologie. Endocrinologie
0181-0006 Bulletin Signaletique. Part 364: Protozoaires et Invertebres. Zoologie Generale et Appliquee
0181-0014 Bulletin Signaletique. Part 365: Zoologie des Vertebres. Ecologie Animale. Physiologie Appliquee Humaine
0181-0030 Bulletin Signaletique. Part 380: Produits Alimentaires
0181-1304 Universite Rene Descartes. Bulletin
0181-1347 Alpes - Region
0181-1525 Musee National d'Art Moderne. Cahiers
0181-1568 Cryptogamie: Algologie
0181-1576 Cryptogamie: Bryologie et Lichenologie
0181-1584 Cryptogamie: Mycologie
0181-1789 Actualites Botaniques
0181-1797 Lettres Botaniques
0181-1878 Le Rail et le Monde
0181-1894 Bulletin Signaletique. Part 525: Prehistoire et Protohistoire
0181-1916 Reproduction, Nutrition, Developpement
0181-2874 Action Juridique (Paris, 1978)
0181-3048 Connaissance des Temps
0181-4141 Filmechange
0181-5210 Paris Voices
0181-5512 Journal Francais d'Ophtalmologie
0181-561X Universite de Haute Bretagne. Centre d'Etudes Irlandaises. Cahier
0181-687X 4 Taxis
0181-7582 Revue de Cytologie et de Biologie Vegetales-la Botaniste
0181-8120 Entretien des Textiles
0181-9224 Champion d'Afrique
0181-9801 Feuillets de Radiologie
0182-1377 Medecine et 3eme Age
0182-2322 Afrique Defense
0182-2411 Histoire
0182-3329 Batiment International
0182-4295 Fondation Louis de Broglie. Annales
0182-5887 Verbum
0183-0139 Le van et le Camping-Car
0183-3189 Pour la Danse
0183-3634 Philatelie Francaise
0183-3898 Tout le Tricot - le Crochet et le Tricot d'Art
0183-3901 Tout le Tricot
0183-391X Tout le Tricot - Ouvrages au Crochet
0183-3928 Tout le Tricot - Tricot d'Art
0183-3944 Toute la Broderie - Point de Croix
0183-4037 Chambre de Commerce et d'Industrie d'Auxerre. Documentation Economique
0183-4150 Dossiers Histoire de la Mer
0183-4738 Toute la Broderie - Tous les Ouvrages
0183-5688 Societe de Biometrie Humaine. Revue
0183-7591 Etudes sur Pezenas et l'Herault
0183-8490 Cartes Postales et Collections
0183-9187 Revue de Nematologie
0184-7783 Population et Societes
0185-0008 Ciencia y Desarrollo
0185-0105 C B
0185-0601 Comercio Exterior
0185-0903 C L A S E
0185-1004 Periodica. Indice de Revistas Latinoamericanas en Ciencias
0185-1357 Naturaleza
0190-0005 City Hall Digest
0190-0226 Boarding Kennel Proprietor
0190-0234 Inklings
0190-0242 Children's Rights Report
0190-0447 Cross-Reference on Human Resources Management
0190-0471 Analytical and Quantitative Cytology
0190-0536 Philosophical Investigations
0190-0684 Journal of Civil Engineering Design
0190-0684 Journal of Civil Engineering Design
0190-0692 International Journal of Public Administration
0190-0870 St. Louis Labor Tribune
0190-0943 I T E M
0190-1028 Behavioral Counseling Quarterly
0190-1052 American Society for Engineering Education. Annual Conference Proceedings
0190-1133 Survey of Retirement, Thrift and Profit Sharing Plans Covering Salaried Employees of the 50 Largest U. S. Industrial Companies
0190-1141 U.S. Department of Energy. Fossil Energy Research and Development Program
0190-1168 New Spirit
0190-1192 Community Association Law Reporter
0190-1206 Cancer Clinical Trials
0190-1249 Sports Afield Outdoor Almanac
0190-1281 Research in Economic Anthropology
0190-129X Louisiana State Industrial Directory
0190-1311 Tennessee State Industrial Directory
0190-132X Virginia State Industrial Directory
0190-1338 Michigan State Industrial Directory
0190-1346 Mississippi State Industrial Directory
0190-1354 Kentucky State Industrial Directory
0190-1362 Indiana State Industrial Directory
0190-1370 Electrical Apparatus
0190-1397 Forge
0190-1400 Photoletter
0190-1427 A J S Update
0190-1435 Dr. Dobb's Journal of Computer Calisthenics & Orthodontia
0190-1451 Laser Focus with Fiberoptic Communications *see* 0275-1399
0190-1516 Energy Regulation Digest
0190-1559 Banjo Newsletter
0190-1567 Free Stock Photography Directory
0190-1575 International Advances in Surgical Oncology
0190-1737 Street Magazine
0190-177X Amoxcalli Newsletter
0190-1974 Learning Resources (Washington)
0190-1982 C B S News Review
0190-1990 New York Times Current Events Edition
0190-2040 Patient Counseling and Health Education
0190-2067 Journal of the History of Sociology
0190-2148 Experimental Lung Research
0190-2172 I E E E Annual Pulp and Paper Industry Technical Conference. Conference Record
0190-2180 Humanities Report
0190-2210 State Consumer Action
0190-2229 Pacific Coast Council on Latin American Studies. Proceedings
0190-2253 Gusto
0190-2261 Journal of Fee-Based Information Services
0190-2288 Design News Annual. Fastening Edition *see* 0190-2296
0190-2296 Design News. Fastening
0190-230X Family and Child Mental Health
0190-2334 Regional Council Directory *see* 0095-1455
0190-2342 Chutzpah
0190-2350 Legal Aspects of Medical Practice
0190-2423 Agri-Fieldman and Consultant
0190-2458 In Business
0190-2563 Corrections Today
0190-2709 Academy of Sciences of the U S S R. Special Astrophysical Observatory-North Caucasus. Bulletin
0190-2717 Academy of Sciences of the U S S R. Crimean Astrophysical Observatory. Bulletin
0190-2733 Examiner (Dayton)
0190-2741 Co-Op (Ann Arbor)
0190-275X H U D Statistical Yearbook *see* 0147-7870
0190-2911 MidAmerica (East Lansing)
0190-292X Policy Studies Journal
0190-2946 Academe (Washington, 1979)
0190-2954 U. S. Office of Consumer Affairs. Directory: Federal, State, County, and City Government Consumer Offices *see* 0190-2962
0190-2962 U. S. Office of Consumer Affairs. Directory: Federal, State, and Local Government Consumer Offices
0190-2970 Current Topics in Eye Research
0190-2989 Health Sciences Audiovisual Resource List
0190-2997 Summary of Rate Schedules of Natural Gas Pipeline Companies as Filed with the Federal Energy Regulatory Commission and the National Energy Board of Canada

0190-3012 Northern New England Review
0190-3047 Directory of Manufacturers, State of Hawaii
0190-3055 Rhode Island Genealogical Register
0190-3071 Encyclopedia of American Associations *see* 0071-0202
0190-3101 Truck & Van Buyer's Guide
0190-3136 World Food Situation *see* 0084-1358
0190-3160 Community and Junior College Journal
0190-3187 International Family Planning Perspectives
0190-3225 Management Aids for Small Business Annual
0190-3233 Virginia Polytechnic Institute and State University. Review
0190-3233 Review (Charlottesville)
0190-3241 Future Survey
0190-3276 Copley Mail Order Advisor
0190-3284 Zero
0190-3292 N A S A Activities
0190-3306 Faceplate
0190-3314 Green Feather
0190-3349 Food Marketing Industry Speaks
0190-3357 Foundation Center. Annual Report
0190-339X Chronicle Student Aid Annual
0190-3640 Sez
0190-3659 Boundary 2
0190-373X U.S. Community Services Administration. Annual Report of Community Services Administration
0190-3748 Food Topics *changed to* Supermarket Business
0190-3799 National Municipal Review *see* 0027-9013
0190-3896 U.S. Administration on Aging. Elderly Population: Estimates by County
0190-4019 American Journal of Clinical Biofeedback
0190-4094 Chemical, Biomedical & Environmental Instrumentation
0190-4124 Platt's Oil Regulation Report *changed to* Platt's Oil Policy and Regulation Report
0190-4132 International Conference on Lasers. Proceedings
0190-4167 Journal of Plant Nutrition
0190-4175 Electric Vehicle Progress
0190-4183 Practical Parenting
0190-4205 St. Louis Home/Garden
0190-4302 Material Handling and Industrial Engineer *changed to* American Institute of Industrial Engineers. Material Handling Institute. Proceedings
0190-4523 Duke Divinity School Bulletin *see* 0012-7078
0190-4655 Cooperative Education Quarterly
0190-4663 Chronicle Career Index Annual
0190-4752 Paragraph
0190-4817 Advances in Cancer Chemotherapy
0190-485X Counter Pentagon
0190-4876 Energy Research Reports
0190-4906 Black Review
0190-4914 Business Owner
0190-4930 Plans for the Implementation of the Post-Vietnam Era Veterans' Educational Assistance Act of 1977
0190-4981 Combined Cumulative Index to Pediatrics
0190-499X Foreign Trade Reports. U.S. Exports - Schedule E - Commodity by Country
0190-5074 International Psoriasis Bulletin
0190-521X Political Science Discussion Papers
0190-5422 U.S. National Arthritis Advisory Board. Annual Report
0190-5589 Semi-Annual Electric Power Survey *see* 0190-5600
0190-5600 Annual Electric Power Survey
0190-5619 Electric Power Survey *see* 0190-5600
0190-5740 Government Procurement Newsletter
0190-5821 I L A Newsletter
0190-5848 Frontiers in Education Conference. Proceedings
0190-5872 Meeting Site Selector
0190-597X SciQuest
0190-602X China Facts & Figures Annual
0190-6100 Wesleyan Methodist *see* 0043-289X
0190-6275 Business Today *changed to* Business America
0190-647X Culture and Language Learning Newsletter *changed to* Culture Learning Institute Report
0190-6569 Light' n' Heavy
0190-6577 Folk Music Magazine
0190-6593 Western New England Law Review
0190-6631 A C H Newsletter
0190-6690 Official Intermodal Equipment Register
0190-6704 Official Railway Guide. North American Freight Service Edition
0190-6739 R V Aftermarket
0190-678X Format
0190-6798 Speedy Bee
0190-7034 Boston College Environmental Affairs Law Review
0190-7077 Bibliography of Agricultural Bibliographies
0190-7409 Children and Youth Services Review
0190-7654 Financial Education *see* 0093-3961
0190-7662 National Education Association of the United States. Proceedings of the Annual Meeting
0190-7743 Isthmus
0190-7808 National Waste News
0190-8049 National Arts Guide
0190-8189 Folk and Kinfolk of Harris County
0190-8227 Applewood Journal
0190-8340 A P I C S International Technical Conference Proceedings *see* 0191-1783
0190-8553 Commercial Kitchen & Institutional Dining Room
0190-9177 Journal of Heat Treating
0190-9185 Monitoring the Future
0190-9320 Political Behavior
0190-9622 American Academy of Dermatology. Journal
0190-9819 National Preservation Report
0190-986X Lens' on Campus
0190-9940 Archaeoastronomy
0191-0132 Asian Wall Street Journal Weekly
0191-0310 Statistical Abstract of Oklahoma
0191-0329 Fielding's Favorites: Hotels & Inns, Europe
0191-0574 Index to Social Science & Humanities Proceedings
0191-0760 Gravida
0191-0833 C N I Weekly Report
0191-1031 Kentucky Review
0191-118X Analysis of Workers' Compensation Laws
0191-1295 Library Computer Equipment Review
0191-1295 Library Computer Equipment Review
0191-135X Sealift†
0191-1554 Performing Woman
0191-1562 Minnesota Statutes
0191-1600 Developmental Disabilities Abstracts†
0191-1643 Fact Book on Higher Education in the South
0191-1686 Nuclear Science Applications - Section A - Short Reviews, Research Papers, and Comments
0191-1759 National Health
0191-1767 Foundry World
0191-1783 American Production and Inventory Control Society. Annual Conference Proceedings
0191-183X Florida Business Publications Index
0191-1953 Full Blast
0191-1961 Missouri Review
0191-2186 Focus on Poverty Research *changed to* FOCUS (Madison)
0191-2259 Black Box
0191-2283 High/Low Report
0191-2321 Fodor's Australia, New Zealand and the South Pacific
0191-2607 Transportation Research. Part A: General
0191-2615 Transportation Research. Part B: Methodological
0191-2690 Ballet News
0191-2763 Loss Prevention and Control
0191-2771 Metabolic and Pediatric Ophthalmology
0191-278X Nuclear Tracks
0191-2836 Arthritis Foundation. Annual Report
0191-2917 Plant Disease
0191-2925 Stamp Show News & Philatelic Review
0191-2933 Plants, Sites & Parks
0191-2941 Nature and System
0191-3026 Research in Marketing
0191-3085 Research in Organizational Behavior
0191-3123 Ultrastructural Pathology
0191-328X Alaska Today
0191-3352 Agni Review
0191-3387 Pacific Basin Quarterly
0191-3441 National Governors' Association. Annual Meeting. Proceedings
0191-3468 Sunset Western Travel Adventures
0191-3522 Man at Arms
0191-3557 Journal of California and Great Basin Anthropology
0191-3654 Turtle
0191-3727 How to Evaluate Health Programs†
0191-3794 Cancer Control Journal
0191-3875 Desert Tortoise Council. Proceedings of Symposium
0191-3905 Draper Fund Report
0191-4006 Business Library Newsletter
0191-4138 Man in the Northeast
0191-4146 University Publishing
0191-426X Argosy(1979)
0191-4502 Oxbridge Directory of Religious Periodicals
0191-4634 Web
0191-4898 Broadcast Programming and Production
0191-491X Studies in Educational Evaluation
0191-5061 Family Finder
0191-5096 Journal of Sociology and Social Welfare
0191-5142 South Bay
0191-5215 Enterprise (Washington, 1977)
0191-524X Virginia Federation of Business and Professional Women's Clubs. Federation Notes
0191-5258 Georgia Disabled American Veterans
0191-5355 West Virginia State Firemen's Association Journal
0191-5371 Ion-Selective Electrode Reviews
0191-538X Advances in Earth-Oriented Applications of Space Technology
0191-5398 Environmental Professional
0191-5401 Behavioral Assessment
0191-5592 Colorado Woman
0191-5606 MobileTimes
0191-5614 Live and Invest
0191-5622 Solubility Data Series
0191-5630 Project (Elmsford)
0191-5657 High Country News
0191-5681 Behavioral Group Therapy
0191-5738 Lawman
0191-5835 Racquetball Industry
0191-5851 Tennis Industry
0191-5886 Journal of Nonverbal Behavior
0191-5959 Grain & Feed Review (Des Moines)
0191-5967 Magnolia L P N
0191-5975 Maryland's Highlights
0191-5983 Palmetto Licensed Practical Nurse
0191-5991 Senior Circle
0191-6017 Spyglass
0191-6025 Tennessee Fireman
0191-6084 T.L.P.N.A. Bulletin
0191-6122 Palynology
0191-6408 Rotor & Wing International
0191-6505 Maryland Magazine of Genealogy
0191-6599 History of European Ideas
0191-6769 C I R A Scope
0191-6777 Heavy-Duty Distribution
0191-6793 N/C Commline
0191-6807 Northern Hardware Trade
0191-6815 Outlook (Kansas City)
0191-6823 Professional Carwashing
0191-6939 Generations (Baltimore)
0191-6971 National Zip Code & Post Office Directory
0191-7587 Drug Store News
0191-765X Evaluation in Education-International Progress
0191-7706 Equine Events
0191-7714 Eastern - Western Quarter Horse Journal
0191-7870 Clinical Biomechanics
0191-8095 Snow Goer
0191-8141 Journal of Structural Geology
0191-815X Nuclear and Chemical Waste Management
0191-8176 Wisconsin Trillium
0191-8206 Latitude 20
0191-8257 Urban Health
0191-8273 Printing Journal
0191-8427 Archery Retailer
0191-8443 Design Professional Product Bulletin Directory
0191-8508 Fastener Technology
0191-8745 Landscape West & Irrigation News
0191-8753 World of Golf-Tennis & Resorts
0191-880X Stockton's Port Soundings
0191-8826 Apartment Owner
0191-8834 Pig International. Europe, Asia, Africa, Latin America and Oceania Edition
0191-8842 Biopsychosocial Health
0191-8850 Learning and Society
0191-8869 Personality and Individual Differences
0191-8877 Substance and Alcohol Misuse *changed to* Substance and Alcohol Action/Misuse
0191-8885 Mechanics Today
0191-8923 Westchester Illustrated
0191-9008 I S A Directory of Instrumentation
0191-9016 North Central Journal of Agricultural Economics
0191-9040 Insect Science & Its Application
0191-9059 Physicochemical Hydrodynamics
0191-9067 Space Solar Power Review *see* 0273-1177
0191-9067 Space Solar Power Review
0191-9075 Electronic Distributing
0191-9113 Alabama & Gulf Coast Retailing News
0191-9121 Georgia Retailing News
0191-9202 Physical Education Index
0191-9245 Syracuse Magazine
0191-9474 Greater Salt Lake Builder
0191-9482 Mountainwest Magazine
0191-9512 Ozone
0191-9520 Composites Science and Engineering
0191-9539 Journal of Engineering & Applied Sciences
0191-9768 Mobile/Manufactured Home Merchandiser
0191-9776 Computer and Information Systems Abstract Journal
0191-9792 Working Arts
0191-9822 Willamette Law Review
0191-9873 Contemporary Administrator
0192-0103 G A T N
0192-0561 International Journal of Immunopharmacology
0192-0596 Training and Development Alert
0192-0618 c/o: Journal of Alternative Human Services
0192-0790 Journal of Clinical Gastroenterology
0192-0812 Research in Community and Mental Health
0192-0863 Pecan South
0192-0952 Fodor's Germany: West and East
0192-1118 Plant Energy Management
0192-1193 Journal of Clinical and Experimental Gerontology
0192-1223 N A P S A C News
0192-1266 Biomedical Products
0192-1290 Engineer's Digest
0192-1304 20/20
0192-1312 Development Communication Report
0192-1460 MacNeil/Lehrer Report
0192-1541 Electronic Engineering Times
0192-1622 American Inventor
0192-1975 Leisure Cooking
0192-2238 Petersen's Pro Basketball
0192-2262 Hospital Materiel Management Quarterly
0192-2319 New Magazine Review
0192-2327 Restaurant Employee
0192-2408 New Pacific
0192-2467 Ohio Valley Retailer
0192-2475 Retail Reporter

0192-253X Developmental Genetics
0192-2718 Military Clubs & Recreation
0192-2807 Meat Plant Magazine
0192-2858 Annals of Scholarship
0192-2874 Book Production Industry and Magazine Production *see* 0273-8724
0192-2882 Theatre Journal
0192-2890 Dreamworks
0192-2920 Let's Go: the Budget Guide to Italy
0192-2963 Physician East
0192-3021 I D: Industrial Design
0192-3048 Golf Course Management
0192-3056 Missouri Beef Cattleman
0192-3064 Industry and Commerce
0192-3072 Simmental Shield
0192-3080 Topeka Magazine
0192-3102 Bay Views (San Rafael)
0192-3153 Renews (Deerfield)
0192-3161 Animal Hospital Product News
0192-3196 PhotographiConservation
0192-334X Discographies
0192-3412 Fodor's New England
0192-3420 Kite Tales *see* 0192-3439
0192-3439 KiteLines
0192-3498 Florida Hotel & Motel News
0192-3706 Decorating & Craft Ideas
0192-3730 Fodor's Far West
0192-3757 Black Collegian (New Orleans)
0192-382X Port of New Orleans. Weekly Bulletin
0192-3838 Louisiana Pharmacist
0192-3846 Marina Management/Marketing
0192-3951 Rocky Mountain Construction(South Edition)
0192-396X Buddhist Research Information
0192-3978 Construction Equipment
0192-3994 I T S Review
0192-401X O R T E S O L Journal
0192-4044 Journal of Superstition & Magical Thinking
0192-4168 Southern Tier Town & Country Living
0192-4176 Bradford-Tioga-Sullivan-Potter-Wyoming Farm & Home News
0192-4184 Seven County Farm and Home News
0192-4214 Southwest Art
0192-429X Journal of Electronic Defense
0192-4311 Purchasing Administration
0192-4389 Gulf Coast Lumberman
0192-4486 Carpet & Rug Industry
0192-4745 Mine Safety & Health Reporter
0192-4893 New Homes Magazine
0192-4923 Minicomputer News *changed to* Computer Times
0192-5059 Plantation Society in the Americas
0192-5199 Truck Tracks
0192-5210 Yankee Horsetrader
0192-5237 Farm and Ranch
0192-5245 Antiques Observer
0192-527X Capital District Business Review
0192-5326 Fielding's Europe
0192-5482 Athletic Purchasing and Facilities
0192-5490 Personal Computing
0192-5539 Friendscript
0192-5571 Fodor's Midwest
0192-5709 American Tool, Die & Stamping News
0192-5717 Ann Arbor Observer
0192-5725 Ann Arbor Scene Magazine
0192-5776 Amicus Journal
0192-5784 Official (Los Angeles)
0192-592X T.H.E. Journal
0192-6071 All Volunteer
0192-6152 Legal Memorandum
0192-6160 Practitioner
0192-6179 Mineral & Energy Resources
0192-6187 American Journal of Family Therapy
0192-6233 Toxicologic Pathology
0192-6365 N A S S P Bulletin
0192-6411 Kentucky Sports World
0192-6675 Healthways Magazine Digest
0192-6772 National Home Center News
0192-6845 W A A
0192-7000 N O O N
0192-7027 My Little Salesman
0192-7124 Logger and Lumberman
0192-7132 Processed Prepared Food
0192-7140 Stockman Farmer
0192-7159 Pacific Coast Nurseryman and Garden Supply Dealer
0192-7248 Graphics (Hollis)
0192-7256 Graphics (Kissimmee) *see* 0274-774X
0192-7272 American Association of Stratigraphic Palynologists. Abstracts of Papers Presented at the Annual Meetings.
0192-7299 American Association of Stratigraphic Palynologists. Newsletter
0192-7329 National Independent Coal Leader
0192-7345 Voice (Honolulu)
0192-7396 Small Boat Journal
0192-740X Gerontopics *changed to* Gerotopics: A Forum of the Aging Network
0192-7590 Building Construction News
0192-7639 Domestic and International Commercial Loan Charge-Offs *changed to* Report on Domestic and International Commercial Loan Charge-Offs
0192-7868 On the Upbeat
0192-7973 Metropolitan Purchasor
0192-818X Music Retailer
0192-8457 Insulator's Guide
0192-8473 Accent/Grand Rapids *changed to* West Michigan
0192-8481 Porsche Uber Alles
0192-8562 American Journal of Pediatric Hematology/Oncology
0192-8651 Journal of Computational Chemistry: Organic and Inorganic
0192-8651 Journal of Computational Chemistry
0192-8716 Pikestaff Forum
0192-8724 Pikestaff Review
0192-8929 Wind Sock
0192-8953 Iowa Snowmobiler
0192-8961 Minnesota Snowmobiler
0192-8988 Sunflower (Fargo)
0192-902X Mining Equipment International
0192-9240 Detroit Industrial Market News
0192-9259 Chevy 4 x 4
0192-9283 Publications Image
0192-9399 Money Making Opportunities
0192-9488 Baltimore Purchaser
0192-950X Midwest Dairyman
0192-9526 Agri-Equipment Today
0192-9828 Chinese Studies in Archaeology
0192-9925 Fodor's California
0192-995X Living with Allergies
0193-0184 Gothic
0193-0257 Michigan Banking & Business News
0193-0265 New England Sportsman
0193-0281 Progress (Framingham)
0193-032X Ophthalmology Times
0193-0400 Hardhat
0193-0648 What's New in Plant Physiology
0193-0818 Research Communications in Substance Abuse
0193-0869 New Ventures
0193-0982 Special Topics in Endocrinology and Metabolism
0193-1091 American Journal of Dermatopathology
0193-1199 Chain Store Age Executive with Shopping Center Age
0193-1350 Chain Store Age General Merchandise Edition
0193-1350 Chain Store Age General Merchandise Group *see* 0193-1350
0193-1369 Chain Store Age Supermarkets
0193-1466 Sikh Religious Studies Information
0193-1504 Whole Foods
0193-1814 News Circle
0193-1830 A M H C A Journal
0193-1849 American Journal of Physiology: Endocrinology and Metabolism
0193-1857 American Journal of Physiology: Gastrointestinal and Liver Physiology
0193-189X Mideast Business Exchange
0193-1962 Aircraft Owners Bulletin. Kansas-Missouri-Southern Illinois Edition
0193-1997 Heart of America Aquarium Society News
0193-2012 Horses Unlimited
0193-2020 Kansas City
0193-2039 Mid-Continent Purchaser
0193-2047 Mid-America Commerce & Industry
0193-2055 Modern Jeweler. South-East
0193-2063 Modern Jeweler. North Central
0193-2071 Modern Jeweler. South-Central
0193-208X Modern Jeweler. National Executive
0193-2098 Modern Jeweler. Western
0193-2101 Modern Jeweler. North-East
0193-211X Pilot News
0193-2128 Service Reporter
0193-2136 Training World
0193-2284 Cigar Magazine†
0193-2551 Giftware News
0193-2586 Inside Contracting
0193-2683 Home Health Review
0193-2691 Journal of Dispersion Science and Technology
0193-2713 Operant Subjectivity
0193-2799 Truck Stop Management
0193-2810 Photography Index
0193-2993 Rancho Bernardo
0193-3086 O D L Source
0193-3108 New Florida
0193-3140 Aquaculture Digest
0193-3221 Business Opportunities Journal
0193-3248 Chilton's Distribution Worldwide *see* 0195-7244
0193-3264 Chilton's Automotive Marketing
0193-3299 O A G Travel Planner & Hotel/Motel Guide. North American Edition
0193-3469 Revolution
0193-3469 Communist
0193-3485 Revolutionary Worker
0193-3507 Pacific Boating Almanac. Southern California, Arizona, Baja
0193-3515 Pacific Boating Almanac. Northern California & Nevada
0193-3906 Military Law Reporter
0193-3914 Pulpit Helps
0193-3922 Journal for Specialists in Group Work
0193-3949 Printing Trades Blue Book. Delaware Valley-Ohio Edition
0193-418X Schools & Civil Rights News
0193-4201 Significant Issues Facing Directors
0193-4279 Directorship
0193-4309 Tar Heel Libraries
0193-4414 Business Advocate
0193-4503 Navajo Education Newsletter *changed to* Navajo Area Newsletter
0193-4600 Blue Chip Economic Indicators
0193-4783 Across the Seas
0193-4929 Reviews in Organic Chemistry
0193-497X Wine Spectator
0193-5135 P R N Radio Guide
0193-5151 American Petroleum Institute. Central Abstracting and Indexing Service. Thesaurus
0193-5321 St. Louis Bowling Review
0193-533X Gazette (New York)
0193-5380 Eighteenth Century: Theory and Interpretation
0193-5615 Anthropology and Humanism Quarterly
0193-5739 Labor & Employment Law
0193-5771 Tax Angles
0193-578X A I T Newsletter
0193-5798 Enclitic
0193-5895 Research in Law and Economics
0193-600X International Association of Buddhist Studies. Journal
0193-6131 Junior Eagle
0193-614X Chilton's Electronic Component News
0193-6301 Black Warrior Review
0193-645X Lighting Supply & Design
0193-6468 Econoscope View
0193-6484 Chemistry International
0193-6794 Neighborhood & Rehab Report
0193-6808 Managing Housing Letter
0193-6832 Buss
0193-6859 American Popular Culture
0193-6867 Art Reference Collection
0193-6875 Contributions to the Study of Science Fiction and Fantasy
0193-6883 Denominations in America
0193-6891 Contributions to the Study of Music and Dance
0193-6891 Popular Culture Bio-Bibliographies
0193-7308 A I P R
0193-7375 Counseling and Human Development
0193-7383 Editorial Eye
0193-7391 Publishing in the Output Mode
0193-7472 Builder Architect-Contractor Engineer
0193-7480 Arizona Business/Industry
0193-7758 I R B: a Review of Human Subjects Research
0193-7782 A F T A
0193-7871 World Eagle
0193-8207 American Indian Libraries Newsletter
0193-841X Evaluation Review
0193-855X Anthropology
0193-8576 Electron Device Letters
0193-8584 Bicycle Resource Guide
0193-8630 Hub Rail
0193-8703 Contemporary Marxism
0193-905X Index to International Public Opinion
0193-919X Convenience Stores *changed to* C-Store Business
0193-922X Gilbert Law Summaries. Criminal Procedure
0193-9297 Consumer Complaint Contact System, Annual Report
0193-9629 University of Wisconsin, Madison. Engineering Experiment Station. Annual Report
0193-970X Public Administration Series: Bibliography
0193-9777 Irish Renaissance Annual
0193-9866 Military Images Magazine
0194-0147 Water Pollution Control
0194-0430 Journal of Contemporary Business
0194-0449 Unite (Chicago)
0194-0546 Conference Papers Annual Index
0194-0767 National Employment Listing Service for the Criminal Justice System. Bulletin
0194-0775 National Employment Listing Service for Human Services. Bulletin
0194-0775 N E L S Human Services Bulletin
0194-0805 National Employment Listing Service for the Criminal Justice System. Special Edition: Education Opportunities
0194-0813 National Employment Listing Service for the Criminal Justice System. Police Employment Guide
0194-083X Green Book of Home Improvement Contractors
0194-0910 National Hardwood Magazine
0194-0929 Rice Farming and Rice Industry News
0194-0937 Southeast Farm Press
0194-1186 Import/Export Wood Purchasing News
0194-1240 Tennessee Journal
0194-1259 Tennessee Attorneys Memo
0194-1291 Washington Drug Letter (Washington, 1979)
0194-1305 American Arts
0194-1321 Home Center Magazine
0194-1356 Architecture Series: Bibliography
0194-1429 Specialty Food Merchandising
0194-1461 M & C: Measurement & Control News
0194-150X Log Trucker
0194-1607 Media Science Newsletter
0194-1682 California Correctional News
0194-1704 National Employment Listing Service for the Criminal Justice System. Federal Employment Information Directory
0194-2158 Journal of Community Communications
0194-2174 Dispensing Optician
0194-2212 Equal Opportunity in Higher Education
0194-2212 Student Aid News
0194-2239 Higher Education Daily
0194-2247 Federal Grants & Contracts Weekly
0194-2255 Education of the Handicapped
0194-2263 Nation's Schools Report
0194-2271 School Law News
0194-228X Tax Exempt News
0194-231X Education and Work
0194-2352 Health Grants & Contracts Weekly
0194-2360 Labor Relations in Education
0194-2468 Gas Industries
0194-2557 Cardiac Alert
0194-2603 Los Angeles Business Journal
0194-2859 Teacher Update

0194-2875 Industrial Organization Review
0194-2913 California Communities
0194-2948 Puppetry in Education News
0194-2972 Price Trends of Food Ingredients Newsletter
0194-2980 Food Packaging and Labeling Newsletter
0194-2999 Watermark
0194-3294 Vette'n U S A
0194-3448 American Journal of Theology & Philosophy
0194-3502 Crossroad
0194-3510 Leaders
0194-3588 D M News
0194-360X Furniture /Today
0194-3650 Harvard Architecture Review
0194-3812 Dog Groomers Gazette
0194-3936 T A P
0194-3960 Research in Human Capital and Development
0194-4118 Newscribes
0194-4134 Computer Law Monograph Series
0194-4282 Beefmaster Cowman
0194-4312 Lifetimes
0194-4320 North American Hunter
0194-4339 Filmmakers' Monthly
0194-4347 Dental Graduate
0194-4363 American Planning Association. Journal
0194-438X New Wine
0194-4517 Earth Shelter Digest & Energy Report
0194-4525 Midlands Business Journal
0194-4584 Africa Update
0194-4592 Fashions Magazine
0194-4622 Great Lakes Sailing Scanner
0194-4655 P.R.O.'s Magazine
0194-472X Journal of Marital and Family Therapy
0194-4746 Electrical Energy Management
0194-4800 Florida Administrative Law Reports
0194-4851 TypeWorld
0194-4908 Abstracts of Health Care Management Studies
0194-5017 National Mall Monitor
0194-5343 Health Foods Communicator
0194-5351 Pool & Spa News
0194-5408 Intermountain Golf News
0194-5467 Photographer's Forum
0194-5475 Writing
0194-5572 Current Energy and Ecology
0194-570X Van, Pickup and Offroad World
0194-5866 Electronic Industry Weekly
0194-5874 H P M *changed to* Heating and Plumbing Product News
0194-5955 Timber Mart-South
0194-598X Missouri Police Chief
0194-5998 Otolaryngology and Head and Neck Surgery
0194-6161 World Meetings: Social & Behavioral Sciences, Human Services and Management
0194-6226 Solar Engineering Magazine
0194-6277 Michigan Food & Beverage
0194-7060 Southern California Contractor
0194-7176 A H E A Action
0194-7257 Landscape Contractor
0194-7419 Heavy Duty Aftermarket Exchange
0194-7435 Arizona Professional Engineer
0194-7885 Defense Electronics
0194-7990 Amerikai Magyar Szo
0194-827X Aircraft Owners Bulletin. Eastern Nebraska-Iowa-Western Illinois Edition
0194-8652 A/C Flyer
0194-8814 Horse & Chariot†
0194-8822 Tax, Financial and Estate Planning for the Owner of a Closely-Held Corporation
0194-8849 A E A Advocate
0194-9071 A I Art Insight *changed to* Art Insight/Southwest
0194-911X Hypertension
0194-9268 N A H R O Monitor
0194-9314 Surfing (San Clemente)
0194-9535 Esquire (1979)
0194-9543 Angus Journal
0194-9845 Impact: Information Technology
0194-9977 Space Gamer
0195-0118 Textile Rental
0195-0673 Washington Agricultural Record
0195-1017 Film News(1979)
0195-153X S N E A Impact: The Student Voice of the United Teaching Profession
0195-1696 Obscenity Law Bulletin
0195-1793 Minnesota
0195-1874 Home Energy Digest & Wood Burning Quarterly
0195-2250 Global Communications
0195-2358 Informer (Washington)
0195-2390 Equal Employment News
0195-3346 F C X Carolina Cooperator
0195-3354 Nursing Abstracts
0195-3370 Technology Tomorrow
0195-3389 Education Tomorrow
0195-3443 Maryland Documents
0195-3478 Inside Sports
0195-3508 Channel (Los Angeles)
0195-3532 San Francisco Business Journal
0195-3567 Computer Law Bibliography
0195-3591 C F T C Databook
0195-363X A L L-O-Grams
0195-3761 Checklist of Congressional Hearings and Committee Prints
0195-3974 World Trade & Business Digest
0195-3982 Griffith Observer
0195-4121 County Lines
0195-4156 Careers (Saratoga)
0195-4202 Oxbridge Directory of Ethnic Periodicals
0195-4326 Design Directory
0195-4474 Energy Conservation Digest
0195-4490 Daily Traffic World
0195-4865 Association of Food and Drug Officials. Quarterly Bulletin
0195-4903 Center for Southern Folklore Magazine
0195-5314 Pennmarva
0195-5365 Science Fiction Chronicle
0195-5373 Atomic Spectroscopy
0195-539X Who's Who in California Business and Finance
0195-5632 Army Motors
0195-5926 Pediatric Social Work
0195-6140 People's Computers *see* 0164-5846
0195-6183 Woman Poet
0195-6353 Index to the Chicago Tribune
0195-6361 Index to Washington Post
0195-6396 Index to the San Francisco Chronicle
0195-640X Index to the New Orleans Times-Picayune
0195-6418 Index to the Los Angeles Times
0195-6426 Index to the Detroit News
0195-6426 Index to the Houston Post
0195-6426 Index to the American Banker
0195-6434 Index to the Denver Post
0195-6442 Index to the Chicago Sun-Times
0195-654X Home Fashion Textiles
0195-6582 Rodale's New Shelter
0195-6612 Communications and Information Handling Equipment & Services: Semi-Annual Directory/Index†
0195-6728 Discotheque Magazine
0195-6752 Journal of Historical Review
0195-6760 Swim Swim
0195-6779 Media History Digest
0195-6787 International Journal of Oral History
0195-7031 C I S Highlights
0195-7082 Arizona State Industrial Directory
0195-7112 Minnesota State Industrial Directory
0195-7120 Montana State Industrial Directory
0195-7139 Nevada State Industrial Directory
0195-7147 Oregon State Industrial Directory
0195-7155 Wisconsin State Industrial Directory
0195-7244 Chilton's Distribution
0195-7260 Papers in Romance
0195-7279 Pleasures of Cooking
0195-7287 E F T Report
0195-7384 Je Me Souviens
0195-7430 C M J Progressive Media
0195-7473 Political Communication and Persuasion
0195-7589 U S Import Weekly
0195-7600 New Roots
0195-7740 National Council on Radiation Protection and Measurements. Proceedings of the Annual Meeting
0195-7783 Illinois Government Research
0195-7910 American Journal of Forensic Medicine and Pathology
0195-8054 Silver and Gold Report
0195-8127 Journal of Psychiatric Treatment and Evaluation
0195-8208 Art & Antiques
0195-8461 Blue Book of Major Home Builders
0195-847X Gold Book of Multi Housing
0195-8496 Plumbers Ink
0195-8550 Economic Forum (Salt Lake City)
0195-878X Advances in Shock Research
0195-9131 Medicine and Science in Sports and Exercise
0195-914X Abraham Lincoln Association. Papers
0195-9255 Environmental Impact Assessment Review
0195-9271 International Journal of Infrared and Millimeter Waves
0195-928X International Journal of Thermophysics
0195-9298 Journal of Nondestructive Evaluation
0195-9301 International Journal of Policy Analysis and Information Systems
0195-931X Western Wood Products Association. Statistical Yearbook
0195-9336 Destination of Shipments of Western Wood Species by State
0195-9344 Quarterly Injury & Illness Incidence Report
0195-9379 Starship
0195-9395 Lumber Price Index. Inland Mills
0195-9409 Monthly F.O.B. Price Summary, Past Sales. Inland Mills
0195-9425 Journal of Security Adminstration
0195-9646 Packet
0195-9700 Education's Federal Funding Alert
0195-9735 Contest Hotline
0195-9883 Journal of Enterostomal Therapy
0196-0148 New Book of Knowledge Annual
0196-0555 Directory of World Chemical Producers
0196-058X Occupational Health & Safety Letter
0196-0598 Environmental Health Letter
0196-0644 Annals of Emergency Medicine
0196-0660 Franchise Adviser
0196-0709 American Journal of Otolaryngology
0196-0784 Congressional Insight
0196-0806 U.S. Federal Highway Administration. Monthly Motor Gasoline Reported by States
0196-0873 Mission (Washington)
0196-0881 Mapline
0196-1004 C P C Salary Survey
0196-1152 Research in Social Problems and Public Policy
0196-1276 Overseas Private Investment Corporation. Annual Report
0196-1306 Columns
0196-1454 Platt's O H A Digest
0196-1772 Sulfur Reports
0196-1799 L I T A Newsletter
0196-1888 Geo
0196-1918 Modern Technics in Surgery. Abdominal Surgery
0196-1942 Association Trends
0196-1977 Library Insights, Promotion & Programs
0196-2116 Corporate Director
0196-2221 Anthology of Magazine Verse and Yearbook of American Poetry
0196-2256 J G R: Journal of Geophysical Research. C: Oceans and Atomospheres
0196-2280 University of Hartford Studies in Literature
0196-2604 Moody Street Irregulars
0196-2884 San Fernando Poetry Journal
0196-2892 I E E E Transactions. Geoscience and Remote Sensing
0196-3031 J Q. Journalism Quarterly
0196-335X Government Publications Review. Part A: Research Articles
0196-3368 Government Publications Review. Part B: Acquisitions Guide to Significant Government Publications at All Levels
0196-3597 Armed Forces Journal International
0196-3627 Veterinary Radiology
0196-3821 Research in Finance
0196-3929 New Mexico Blue Book
0196-3988 Pacific Basin Economic Indicators
0196-4003 National Association of Regional Councils. Washington Report
0196-4240 Native Self-Sufficiency
0196-4283 Journal of Food Service Systems
0196-4305 Industrial & Engineering Chemistry Process Design and Development
0196-4313 Industrial & Engineering Chemistry Fundamentals
0196-4321 Product R & D
0196-4453 Community Property Journal
0196-447X Index to Book Reviews in the Sciences
0196-4542 Annual Editions: Readings in Environment
0196-4690 Marine Mammal Protection Act of 1972 Annual Report
0196-5204 S I A M Journal on Scientific and Statistical Computing
0196-5212 S I A M Journal on Algebraic and Discrete Methods
0196-5530 Quarterly Index to Current Contents/ Life Sciences
0196-5549 3-Wheeling
0196-5581 Biological Oceanography Journal
0196-5603 Institute Scholar
0196-5654 American Book Collector
0196-5816 E D A M Newsletter
0196-5875 Art Ink
0196-5964 Engineering Thermophysics in China
0196-6219 Ceramic Engineering and Science Proceedings
0196-6227 Cashflow Magazine
0196-626X G M P Letter
0196-6324 American Journal of Mathematical and Management Sciences
0196-6332 Group Health Journal
0196-6545 American Psychological Association. Directory
0196-6553 American Journal of Infection Control
0196-6693 Synfuels Week
0196-6715 Education Law and the Public Schools. Bulletin and Update Subscription Service
0196-691X Artful Dodge
0196-6928 J G R: Journal of Geophysical Research. A: Space Physics
0196-6936 J G R: Journal of Geophysical Research. B: Solid Planets
0196-6960 Exceptional Education Quarterly
0196-6979 Instructional Innovator
0196-7150 Air Pollution Control
0196-7207 Georgetown University Round Table on Languages and Linguistics
0196-7223 B R S Bulletin
0196-755X List of Serials and Monographs Indexed for Online Users
0196-7967 Sonneck Society Newsletter
0196-8009 Who's Who in American Jewry
0196-8017 Mass Communication Review Yearbook
0196-8092 Lasers in Surgery and Medicine
0196-8211 Materials Management & Physical Distribution Abstracts
0196-822X Practices of the Wind
0196-8432 Magic Changes
0196-8858 Advances in Applied Mathematics
0196-8904 Energy Conversion and Management
0196-9323 Peter Dag Investment Letter
0196-9536 Revenue Sharing Bulletin
0196-9617 Diagnostic Gynecology and Obstetrics
0196-9722 Cybernetics and Systems
0197-0062 Electric Company Magazine
0197-0178 I D P Report
0197-0186 Neurochemistry International
0197-0208 Stolen Art Alert
0197-0690 Research in Health Economics *changed to* Advances in Health Economics and Health Services Research
0197-0747 Acquisitive Librarian
0197-0771 Campaigns and Elections
0197-1042 Philosophy Teacher's Handbook
0197-1468 Genealogist (New York)
0197-1646 Directory of on-Line Information Resources
0197-2243 Information Society
0197-2367 Collector-Investor
0197-3428 Tributaries
0197-3479 Ski Industry Letter

ISSN INDEX 1207

0197-3592 Ostaro's Market Newsletter
0197-3606 Free-Lance West
0197-3622 U M A P Journal
0197-3657 Ear Research Institute. Progress Report
0197-3762 Visual Resources
0197-3851 Prenatal Diagnosis
0197-3975 Habitat International
0197-4041 Ligand Review
0197-4637 Multinational Monitor
0197-5080 Research in Sociology of Education and Socialization
0197-5579 C A A S Newsletter
0197-5617 Farm Bureau News
0197-5986 Modern Photography's Guide to the World's Best Cameras
0197-6052 Reporter's Report
0197-6060 Ragan Report
0197-6524 Information Management
0197-6729 Journal of Advanced Transportation
0197-6753 T M R Travel Marketing Report
0197-680X Phantasmagoria
0197-6818 Snippets
0197-6826 Pastiche
0197-6931 North American Archaeologist
0197-6966 Data Resources Review of the U. S. Economy
0197-7032 National Right to Work Newsletter
0197-7083 Donoghue's Moneyletter
0197-7091 Donoghue's Money Fund Report of Holliston, MA 01746
0197-7717 Behavioral Medicine Abstracts
0197-8098 Brown's Directory of North American and International Gas Companies
0197-8454 Clinical Lab Letter
0197-8462 Bioelectromagnetics
0197-8527 Hawaii on 25 Dollars a Day
0197-890X Tendril
0197-9140 Water Pollution Research Journal of Canada
0197-9280 Industrial Robots International
0197-9337 Earth Surface Processes and Landforms
0197-9388 ScriptWriter News
0197-9477 Fastfacts U.S.A. Hotel Motel Locator
0198-0106 M A S C A Journal
0198-0149 Deep-Sea Research. Part A: Oceanographic Research Papers
0198-0149 Deep-Sea Research. Part B: Oceanographic Literature Review
0198-022X Mail Order Information Seller
0198-1501 Safe Boating
0198-6228 International Advertiser
0198-6503 Federal Reporter
0198-6570 U.S. Bureau of Trade Regulation. Office of Export Administration. Export Administration Report
0198-6597 Sports Collectors Directory
0198-6945 Just Pulp
0198-7038 O.R.L. & Allergy Digest
0198-7097 Radiology Management
0198-7208 Ohio Monitor
0198-7275 Melliand Textilberichte (English Edition)
0198-7356 Bartonia
0198-7518 Annual Editions: Educating Exceptional Children
0198-7593 Journal of Heat Recovery Systems
0198-7623 Career World 2
0198-8190 Sportsguide for Team Sports
0198-831X Colorado Shakespeare Festival Annual *changed to* On-Stage Studies
0198-8778 Specialty Law Digest: Health Care
0198-8840 C O I N T Reports
0198-9006 Quarterly Strategic Bibliography
0198-9065 In-Plant Reproductions
0198-912X Annual Editions: Readings in Personal Growth and Adjustment
0198-9375 Gateway Heritage
0198-9456 Videodisc/Teletext
0198-9618 Mariner's Catalog
0198-9715 Computers, Environment and Urban Systems
0198-9855 Sing Heavenly Muse!
0199-0349 Hispanic Business
0199-0918 Ohio P T A News
0199-1388 Aquaculture Magazine
0199-1639 Wisconsin Master Plumber
0199-2066 Chicago Nurse
0199-2333 Kind
0199-2511 Word Processing Systems *see* 0279-7992
0199-2880 Executive Female
0199-3313 Keyboard World
0199-350X People (Palo Alto)
0199-4239 Holstein World
0199-4433 Mission Journal
0199-4557 New Jersey Interact
0199-5103 Group Practice Journal
0199-5421 Mainline Modeler
0199-5510 Nutrition Action
0199-5553 Museum Magazine
0199-6290 Back Home in Kentucky
0199-6312 Hospital Risk Management
0199-6584 M D A Journal *see* 0273-3463
0199-6916 Environmental Education Report (1980)
0199-7149 Sexology Today
0199-719X Astrology(Year)
0199-7211 Military Police Journal
0199-7343 Colorado Medicine
0199-7602 Inside (Philadelphia)
0199-8218 Current Lifestudies
0199-8226 Farmstead Magazine
0199-8323 Contact High
0199-8994 N C E E Registration Bulletin
0199-9249 Internos
0199-9303 Los Angeles Home and Garden Magazine
0199-9583 Huguenot Historian
0199-9664 Nebraska State Historical Society Historical Newsletter
0199-9745 Video Programs Retailer
0199-9885 Annual Review of Nutrition
0199-9974 Weekly Government Abstracts. Health Planning & Health Services Research
0208-4333 Bibliotekarz
0208-4449 Acta Universitatis Nicolai Copernici. Biologia
0208-5267 Acta Universitatis Nicolai Copernici. Socjologia Wychowania
0208-5283 Acta Universitatis Nicolai Copernici. Prawo
0208-5321 Acta Universitatis Nicolai Copernici. Filologia Polska
0208-564X Acta Universitatis Nicolai Copernici. Filozofia
0208-6263 Instytut Meteorologii i Gospodarki Wodnej. Wiadomosci
0209-4010 Hungary. Kozponti Statisztikai Hivatal. Beruhazasi-Epitoipari Adatok
0210-0002 Revistas Espanolas en Curso de Publicacion
0210-0177 Actualidad Bibliografica Iberoamericana
0210-0347 Boletin Informativo de Medio Ambiente
0210-0592 Sumario Actual de Revistas
0210-0614 Revista Espanola de Documentacion Cientifica
0210-069X Spain. Servicio Social de Higiene y Seguridad del Trabajo. Boletin Bibliografico
0210-086X Cuadernos de Geografia
0210-0975 Instituto de Estudios de Administracion Local. Secretariado Iberoamericano de Municipios. Boletin de Informacion
0210-1173 Hacienda Publica Espanola
0210-1203 Edicion
0210-1297 Escuela Tecnica Superior de Ingenieros de Montes. Biblioteca. Boletin Bibliografico y Documental
0210-1343 Anuario de Filologia
0210-1610 Manresa
0210-1793 Facultad de Medicina de Barcelona. Departamento de Psiquiatria. Revista
0210-1831 Boletin Merksa de Estudios de Mercado
0210-2056 Energia
0210-2064 Ingenieria Quimica
0210-2153 Luz y Fuerza
0210-2196 Revista Quirurgica Espanola
0210-220X Jano "Medicina y Humanidades"
0210-2331 Perspectiva Escolar
0210-2404 Revista de Economia y Hacienda Local
0210-2412 Revista Espanola de Financiacion y Contabilidad
0210-2420 Revista Jurisdiccion Contencioso-Administrativa
0210-2595 Comercio e Industria. Suplemento Quincenal
0210-329X Spain. Instituto Nacional de Investigaciones Agrarias. Comunicaciones. Serie: Produccion Vegetal
0210-3303 Spain. Instituto Nacional de Investigaciones Agrarias. Comunicaciones. Serie: Produccion Animal
0210-3338 Spain. Instituto Nacional de Investigaciones Agrarias. Anales. Serie: Recursos Naturales
0210-4245 Nueva Estetica
0210-4326 Parapsicologia†
0210-4466 Asclepio
0210-4822 Real Academia Espanola. Boletin
0210-5454 Universidad de Granada. Boletin
0210-5462 Cuadernos Geograficos
0210-5578 Diario de Congresos Medicos
0210-5705 Gastroenterologia y Hepatologia
0210-5713 American Journal of Medicine (Spanish Edition)
0210-5721 Pediatrics
0210-573X Clinica e Investigacion en Ginecologia y Obstetricia
0210-5977 Presupuesto y Gasto Publico
0210-685X Deformacion Metalica
0210-6868 Piscinas
0210-7023 Alerta Informativa. Serie E: Economia de la Empresa
0210-7953 Estudios de Filologia Inglesa
0210-8488 Indice Espanol de Humanidades
0210-8852 F A C: Revista Practica de Medicina
0210-9603 Anuario de Historia Moderna y Contemporanea
0220-2387 Danse
0220-5157 Plume Limousine
0220-5270 Revue de l'Offshore†
0220-5424 Bulletin des Consommateurs
0220-5610 Cahiers Victoriens et Edouardiens
0220-6102 Tiers-Monde Engineering *changed to* Tiers-Monde Ingenierie
0220-9926 Realites Familiales
0221-0665 Annales Francaises de Chronometrie et de Microtechnique
0221-301X Presse du Vin-Vinetec
0221-5047 Institut Maurice Thorez. Cahiers d'Histoire
0222-0377 Charcuterie et Gastronomie
0222-3856 Audition et Parole
0222-5069 International Journal of Microsurgery
0222-5956 Cahiers Confrontation
0223-0127 Videoglyphes
0223-1077 A B C D S
0223-3398 B.O.P.I. Dessins & Modeles
0223-3401 B.O.P.I. Marques
0223-4092 B.O.P.I. Listes
0223-4238 Bulletin Signaletique. Part 381: Sciences Agronomiques. Productions Vegetales
0223-4246 Bulletin Signaletique. Part 891: Industries Mecaniques
0223-4254 Bulletin Signaletique. Part 892: Batiment. Travaux Publics. Transports
0223-4718 Revue Fiduciaire
0223-4734 Croire Aujourd'hui
0223-5145 Enterprise et Formation Permanente
0223-9159 Bibliographie Internationale des Industries Agro-Alimentaires
0223-9434 Lettre du Psychiatre
0224-1196 Special Motoculteurs et Tondeuses a Gazon
0224-2435 Syndicat General des Commerces et Industries du Caoutchouc et des Plastiques. Guide
0224-2478 Annuaire Repertoire de la Motoculture de Plaisance Jardinage
0224-5027 Boulanger-Patissier, Confiseur, Glacier
0225-1485 Canadian Heritage
0225-1701 Insurance Institute of Ontario. Newsletter
0225-1760 U T L A S Newsletter
0225-2112 Feuillet Biblique
0225-3488 Western Hog Journal
0225-3550 S P E A Q Journal
0225-3895 Medicine North America
0225-4115 Justice-Directory of Services
0225-4123 Studies in Land Use History and Landscape Change
0225-4565 Agent West Weekly
0225-4913 Horses All
0225-5383 Moving to Saskatchewan
0225-5642 Canada. Statistics Canada. List of Canadian Hospitals and Special Care Facilities/Liste des Hopitaux Canadiens et des Etablissements de Soins Speciaux
0225-5847 Canadian Legislative Report
0225-7270 Theodolite
0225-7351 Chess Canada Echecs
0225-8013 Economic Council of Canada. Discussion Paper
0225-851X Professional Engineer
0225-9036 Index to Commonwealth Legal Periodicals
0226-0336 Canada Mortgage and Housing Corporation. Annual Report
0226-0344 Cottager Magazine
0226-0786 Forintek Canada Corporation, Western Laboratory. Review Reports
0226-0808 Advanced Financial Accounting Notes
0226-093X Canadian Homeowner
0226-1170 Forintek Canada Corporation, Western Laboratory. Special Publications
0226-1480 M I M I
0226-1928 Ethnocultural Directory of Ontario
0226-224X Economic Council of Canada. Au Courant
0226-3343 Canada. Earth Physics Branch. Library. Library News
0226-3440 U. C. Review
0226-5702 Ontario Water Skier
0226-5761 Theatre History in Canada
0226-577X Canadian Amateur Softball Association. Facts & Figures
0226-6156 Brayon
0226-6326 Guelph This Week
0226-6342 Canada. Department of the Environment. Information Reports Digest
0226-661X Inter-Church Committee on Human Rights in Latin America. Newsletter
0226-6822 Financial Accounting Problems with Detailed Solutions
0226-7004 Summer Breezes
0226-7101 Kingston Business Review
0226-7209 Toronto Historical Board. Year Book
0226-7276 Moving to Vancouver & B.C.
0226-7365 Quality of Working Life
0226-7454 Universities
0226-7462 Whiskey Jack
0226-7470 Canadian Nuclear Society. Transactions
0226-7500 Meetings Canada
0226-7527 Carleton University. Library. Serials List
0226-7551 Shopping Centre Canada
0226-773X Federation of Canadian Archers. Rules Book
0226-7829 Moving to Toronto & Area
0226-7837 Moving to Ottawa/Hull
0226-8264 Canadian Real Estate Journal
0226-8760 Canadian Network Papers
0226-9759 Canada. Department of the Environment. Insect and Disease Conditions in Canada.
0227-1001 Wood Technology Notes
0227-1230 Juice & Cookie
0227-1265 Tax Principles to Remember
0227-1427 Coordinating Council on Deafness of Nova Scotia. Newsletter *see* 0227-1435
0227-1435 Access (Halifax)
0227-1524 North American Anarchist
0227-1532 Newfoundland TV Topics
0227-1559 U F O Update
0227-1656 Financial Post Survey of Mines and Energy Resources
0227-1699 Lyman's Standard Catalogue of Canada-BNA Postage Stamps

1208 ISSN INDEX

0227-1796 Canada. Statistics Canada. Estimation of Population by Marital Status, Age and Sex, Canada and Provinces/ Estimations de la Population Suivant l'Etat Matrimonial, l'Age et le Sexe, Canada et Provinces
0227-1834 Soccer Canada
0227-1907 Canadian Nuclear Society. Annual Conference Proceedings
0227-2083 Professional Circle *see* 0227-2091
0227-2091 Circle
0227-227X Liaison
0227-2636 L M G Report on Data and Word Processing
0227-2865 National Bank of Canada. Economic Review
0227-2865 Economic Review
0227-3748 Canadian Health Record Association. Recorder
0227-8731 Micro-Scope
0227-9363 Journal de Radiologie
0228-0108 Supreme Court Law Review
0228-1244 Ennui
0228-1546 Growing up Whole
0228-2194 Nicola Indian
0228-2356 Aspen
0228-2518 In Summary
0228-5843 Noticias do Canada
0228-8397 Canadian Association of African Studies. Bulletin
0228-863X Directory of Alcohol and Drug Treatment Sources in Ontario
0228-8648 Substance Abuse Book Review Index
0228-9989 Canada. Forestry Service Research Notes
0229-2947 Projection
0240-3803 Special Scies a Moteur et Accessoires
0240-5407 Tour de l'Orle d'Or
0240-6411 Avenir et Sante
0240-642X Acta Endoscopica
0240-8368 Epimenides
0240-8376 Epidecides Lunaires
0240-8430 Perspectives Mediterraneennes
0240-9925 Inter Regions
0241-0109 Journal International de Medecine
0241-1407 Revue de Geologie Dynamique et de Geographie Physique
0241-6794 Cahiers Techniques du Batiment
0241-8185 A-YA
0243-1203 Journal Europeen de Radiotherapie
0243-7651 Acta Oecologica-Oecologia Plantarum
0243-766X Acta Oecologica-Oecologia Generalis
0243-7678 Acta Oecologica-Oecologia Applicata
0244-2019 Isolation
0244-6014 Societe Francaise de Photogrammetrie et de Teledetection. Bulletin
0245-5552 Journal d'Echographie et de Medecine Ultrasonore
0245-5811 Journal de Traumatologie
0245-5919 Motricite Cerebrale: Readaptation Neurologie du Developpement.
0245-6001 Messages des P T T
0248-0018 Journal d'Urologie
0248-1758 Psychiatrie du Practicien
0249-5619 Recherches d'Histoire et de Sciences Sociales
0250-0019 Dyers Dyegest
0250-1163 Johannesburg Historical Foundation. Journal
0250-1333 South African Shoemaker and Leather Review
0250-1619 Centre d'Etudes et de Documentation Africaines. Cahiers
0250-1643 National Science Council, Republic of China. Proceedings
0250-1651 National Science Council Monthly
0250-216X University of Cape Town. Department of Geology. Precambrian Research Unit. Bulletin
0250-2402 Barclays Business Brief
0250-3190 Revista A I B D A
0250-3697 Societe pour le Developpement Minier de la Cote d'Ivoire. Rapport Annuel
0250-3751 Developments in Ophthalmology
0250-4987 Revue Celinienne
0250-538X Maadini
0250-5983 Indian Academy of Sciences. Proceedings (Engineering Sciences)
0250-5991 Journal of Biosciences
0250-6009 Indian Institute of Tropical Meteorology. Research Report
0250-6017 Indian Institute of Tropical Meteorology. Annual Report
0250-6114 Chiefs of State and Cabinet Ministers of the American Republics
0250-6173 Juventud
0250-6211 Organization of American States. Directory
0250-6270 Inter-American Review of Bibliography
0250-6289 Organization of American States. Statistical Bulletin
0250-6394 N A F O Statistical Bulletin
0250-6416 N A F O Scientific Council Meeting Reports
0250-6424 N A F O Sampling Yearbook
0250-6432 N A F O Scientific Council Studies
0250-6513 Semillas
0250-6793 Stem Cells
0250-6807 Annals of Nutrition and Metabolism
0250-7161 Revista Latinoamericana de Estudios Urbano Regionales
0250-7536 Organization of American States. Regional Scientific and Technological Program. Newsletter
0250-7544 Organization of American States. Department of Scientific Affairs. Newsletter.
0250-7609 Geosur
0250-779X United Nations Educational, Scientific and Cultural Organization
0250-7811 N A F O List of Fishing Vessels
0260-0005 Serials in the British Library
0260-0447 Current Transnational Corporations Bibliography
0260-0471 Great Britain. Department of Education and Science. Architects and Building Branch. Broadsheet
0260-0498 Eurovet Bulletin
0260-0749 Financial Aid for First Degree Study at Commonwealth Universities
0260-1508 Exhibitor's Handbook
0260-1745 Kitchens
0260-2474 Aspis
0260-2776 Writer
0260-3055 Annals of Glaciology
0260-3233 Vegetarian(1981)
0260-3306 Great Britain. Advisory Council for Adult and Continuing Education. Annual Report
0260-3675 Transit Packaging
0260-3993 Vive la Difference
0260-4027 World Futures
0260-4043 Ultrasound Patents & Papers
0260-406X Chartered Institute of Public Finance and Accountancy. Housing Rents. Statistics
0260-4078 Chartered Institute of Public Finance and Accountancy. Housing Revenue Accounts. Actuals Statistics
0260-4086 Chartered Institute of Public Finance and Accountancy. Housing Estimate Statistics
0260-4426 West of Scotland Visitor
0260-4868 European Human Rights Reports
0260-4876 I. P. Reports from Socialist Countries
0260-4922 Engineering Distributor
0260-5511 Abstracts on Hygiene and Communicable Diseases
0260-5546 Chartered Institute of Public Finance and Accountancy. Rate Collection Statistics. Actuals
0260-583X Kingston History Society. Papers
0260-5929 University of London. Institute of Germanic Studies. Research in Germanic Studies
0260-6437 Offshore Oil & Gas Yearbook
0260-6593 Current Technology Index
0260-664X Austin Healey Year Book
0260-7387 List of Shipowners
0260-7409 International Packaging Abstracts
0260-7468 European Racehorse
0260-7476 Journal of Education for Teaching
0260-7522 I C S A Bulletin
0260-7603 Chartered Institute of Public Finance and Accountancy. Waste Collection Statistics. Actuals
0260-7964 Irish Drama Selections
0260-8391 Caraher Family History Society. Journal
0260-8642 Chartered Institute of Public Finance and Accountancy. Planning and Development Statistics. Actuals
0260-9061 Weekender
0260-9088 Soil Survey and Land Evaluation
0260-9096 British Journal of Administrative Management
0260-910X Visit California with Fyfe Robertson
0260-9320 Studies in Joint Disease
0260-9460 Biblical Creation
0260-9584 Quaker Peace and Service. Annual Report
0260-9983 U. K. I. R. T. Report
0261-0094 Anbar Management Publications Joint Index
0261-0108 Anbar Management Publications Bibliography
0261-1783 Great Britain. Central Statistical Office. Regional Trends
0261-1791 Great Britain. Central Statistical Office. Guide to Official Statistics
0261-3107 Philatelic Magazine (1980)
0270-0255 Mathematical Modelling
0270-0352 F M I Monthly Index Service
0270-059X University of Tennessee. Library Lectures
0270-0662 News from the Hill (Washington)
0270-1146 Metalsmith
0270-1421 Kentucky Economy: Review & Perspective
0270-1588 Construction Contracting
0270-1642 University of Michigan. Museums of Art and Archaeology. Bulletin
0270-2010 Journal of Soviet Laser Research
0270-2029 Girls Gymnastics Rules
0270-2088 Controversies in Nephrology
0270-2282 North American Human Rights Directory
0270-2398 Travelore Report
0270-2487 Government Union Review
0270-2614 Skenectada
0270-272X William Mitchell Law Review
0270-2738 International Data Networks News
0270-2894 Continental Birdlife
0270-3092 Applied Research in Mental Retardation
0270-3211 Teratogenesis, Carcinogenesis, and Mutagenesis
0270-322X Pediatric Pharmacology
0270-3424 Legal Connection: Corporations and Law Firms
0270-353X Political Finance/Lobby Reporter
0270-3580 Gizeh
0270-3750 Dictionary, Encyclopedia & Handbook Review
0270-4013 Advances in Special Education
0270-4021 Advances in Early Education and Day Care
0270-4048 Jazz Rag
0270-4056 Advances in Myocardiology
0270-4234 National Society to Prevent Blindness. Report
0270-4331 Kansas. Legislative Research Department. Report on Kansas Legislative Interim Studies
0270-4447 Safety News (Denver)
0270-448X Commuter Air Carrier Traffic Statistics
0270-4676 Bulletin of Science, Technology and Society
0270-4684 Analysis and Intervention in Developmental Disabilities
0270-4846 Computer Literature Index
0270-5230 Topics in Health Record Management
0270-5346 Camera Obscura
0270-5508 Szivarvany
0270-5524 Sea Heritage News
0270-5540 Energy News Digest
0270-6296 Journal of Soviet Oncology
0270-630X Journal of Soviet Cardiovascular Research
0270-6733 Occupational Safety and Health Compliance Manual
0270-675X Toxic Substances Reporter
0270-6776 P C A S Newsletter
0270-7306 Molecular and Cellular Biology
0270-7314 Journal of Futures Markets
0270-7446 China International Business
0270-7543 Directors Encyclopedia of Newspapers
0270-787X Fodor's Budget Italy
0270-8183 Fodor's Central America
0270-823X Energy Research Digest
0270-854X John Marshall Law Review
0270-8981 Dance Films Association. Bulletin
0270-9015 Command Policy†
0270-9171 Dancer's Digest *changed to* Dancer's Digest & Off Broadway
0270-9287 United Methodist Board of Higher Education and Ministry. Quarterly Review
0270-935X National Center for a Barrier Free Environment. Report
0270-9368 Shaker Messenger
0271-0129 Discontinued Integrated Circuit D.A.T.A. Book
0271-0137 Journal of Mind and Behavior
0271-0560 New Directions for Higher Education
0271-0579 New Directions for Institutional Research
0271-0587 New Directions for Institutional Advancement
0271-0595 New Directions for Experiential Learning
0271-0641 Arizona State University Anthropological Research Papers
0271-065X A O P A's Airports U.S.A.
0271-0730 Arba Sicula
0271-0838 Photograph Collector
0271-0986 Hispanic Journal
0271-0994 New Publications for Architecture Libraries
0271-1079 N C ShopOwner
0271-1141 Intelligence Reports in Cardiovascular Disease
0271-1206 Topics in Hospital Pharmacy Management
0271-1222 Topics in Health Care Planning and Marketing Quarterly
0271-1249 New Directions for Methodology of Social & Behavioral Science
0271-1427 Southwest Folklore
0271-1443 Weekly Reader Funday
0271-1478 Chemical Substances Control
0271-1494 Topics in Learning and Learning Disabilities
0271-1575 Journal of Neurological and Orthopaedic Surgery
0271-1966 Classical Calliope
0271-2091 International Journal for Numerical Methods in Fluids
0271-258X Real Estate Appraiser and Analyst
0271-2601 Hazardous Waste Report
0271-2636 Petersen's Pro Hockey
0271-2687 Symphony Magazine
0271-3225 Stepparent News
0271-3993 Sylloge Nummorum Graecorum
0271-4299 Columbia Road Review
0271-5090 Woodstove, Coalstove, Fireplace & Equipment Directory
0271-521X Ibro Neuroscience Calendar
0271-5309 Language and Communication
0271-5317 Nutrition Research
0271-5384 Social Science & Medicine. Part E: Medical Psychology
0271-5392 Social Science & Medicine. Part F: Medical Ethics
0271-6100 Florida Keys Magazine
0271-6585 Cell Motility
0271-6771 A V S Biomedical Bulletin
0271-6925 Ripley P. Bullen Monographs in Anthropology and History
0271-7085 Enhanced Energy Recovery News
0271-7107 Applied Genetics News
0271-7123 Social Science & Medicine. Part A: Medical Sociology
0271-8014 Entertainment Industry Directory

ISSN INDEX 1209

0271-8057 Journal of Tissue Culture Methods
0271-8189 Best of Micro
0271-8197 New Pages
0271-8219 Modern Technics in Surgery. Head and Neck Surgery
0271-8294 Topics in Language Disorders
0271-9002 Micro
0271-9142 Journal of Clinical Immunology
0271-9843 Power Station Practice U.S.S.R.
0271-9940 Dance Book Forum
0271-9983 Clinical Respiratory Physiology
0272-0493 Wise Giving Bulletin
0272-0582 Psychological Cinema Register
0272-0884 Technicalities
0272-1902 New Hearer
0272-2135 Directory of College Recruiting Personnel
0272-2801 Research in the Interweave of Social Roles: Women and Men
0272-3646 Physical Geography
0272-3751 Pets and People of the World
0272-4316 Journal of Early Adolescence
0272-4626 European Applied Research Reports
0272-4790 Advances in Drying
0272-4804 Series in Computational Methods in Mechanics and Thermal Sciences
0272-5371 Western Bank Directory
0272-5541 Masson Today
0272-6343 Electromagnetics
0272-6513 Connections (New York)
0272-6750 Democracy
0272-6955 Your Patient & Cancer
0272-7145 Children's Digest (1980)
0272-7374 Journal of Housing
0272-7846 S E C Monthly Statistical Review
0272-846X Journal of Clinical Neuro-Ophthalmology
0272-8494 Folklore Bibliography for (Year)
0272-880X International Centre for Heat and Mass Transfer. Proceedings
0272-8966 Sanctuary
0272-9032 Genetic Technology News
0273-0278 Postgraduate Radiology
0273-0278 Postgraduate Radiology
0273-1177 Advances in Space Research
0273-2173 Sociological Spectrum
0273-2289 Applied Biochemistry and Biotechnology
0273-236X Employee Benefit Cases
0273-2904 Biofuels Report
0273-3218 A W W A Mainstream
0273-3463 Missouri Dental Association Journal
0273-429X Chinese Physics
0273-6748 V W & Porsche
0273-7183 Global Church Growth Bulletin
0273-7582 Children's Digest and Children's Playcraft *see* 0272-7145
0273-7590 Humpty Dumpty's Magazine
0273-8589 Diver
0273-8724 Book and Magazine Production
0273-9658 Official Railway Guide. North American Travel Edition
0274-4996 Packaging Technology
0274-6328 Ad Forum
0274-6549 Oregon Optometry
0274-7529 Discover
0274-774X Southern Graphics
0274-8606 W V School Journal (West Virginia)
0274-8614 Equitable Distribution Reporter
0274-8622 Minnesota Sportsman
0275-0031 Wise Giving Guide
0275-0392 Human Rights Quarterly
0275-0503 Professional Liability
0275-0589 Gamut
0275-0945 Best Sellers & Best Choices (Year)
0275-1062 Chinese Astronomy and Astrophysics
0275-1356 American Council on Consumer Interests. Proceedings of the Annual Conference
0275-1399 Laser Focus with Fiberoptic Technology
0275-2107 Specialty Law Digest: Education
0275-3510 Death Education and Thanatology
0275-3677 P R Casebook
0275-3774 Minerals Report
0275-4924 Focus: on the Center for Research Libraries
0275-7427 Top 1,500 Private Companies
0275-7435 Top 1,500 Companies
0275-7443 Second 1,500 Companies
0275-7451 Zip Code Business Patterns
0275-746X Congressional District Business Patterns
0275-8423 Classic Images
0275-8717 Progress in Cybernetics and Systems Research
0276-0770 Journal of Religious Education of the African Methodist Episcopal Church
0276-1459 Multiphase Science and Technology
0276-2374 Empirical Study of the Arts
0276-2374 Imagination, Cognition and Personality
0276-3362 Hemingway Review
0276-749X Computer Aided Design Report
0276-8585 Ecological and Life Chemistry
0276-8747 OP
0277-0288 Library Systems Newsletter
0277-3082 New E R A Newsletter
0277-612X For Parents
0279-5787 Legal Contents
0279-585X Science and Electronics
0279-5957 Rural Sociologist
0279-6198 Watch and Clock Review
0279-6430 A E D C Journal
0279-6570 Pharmaceutical Executive
0279-7992 Word Processing and Information Services
0279-9308 Flying Safety
0279-9340 Medical Tribune (1980)
0279-9596 Scriptwriter News
0300-0087 Anali di Ostetricia Ginecologia Medicina Perinatale
0300-0109 Archivio e Rassegna Italiana di Ottalmologia
0300-0249 Canada. Statistics Canada. Tobacco Products Industries/Industrie du Tabac
0300-0265 Canada. Statistics Canada. Wool Production and Supply/Production et Stocks de Laine
0300-0273 Canadian Statistical Review. Weekly Supplement/Supplement Hebdomadaire de la Revue Statistique du Canada
0300-0443 Psychological Reader's Guide
0300-0486 Society of Biological Chemists. Proceedings
0300-0508 Physiotherapy Canada
0300-0524 Rendiconti Romani di Gastro-Enterologia *see* 0300-0877
0300-0583 Caraibe Medical
0300-0605 Journal of International Medical Research
0300-0621 Steroids and Lipids Research *see* 0301-0163
0300-0664 Clinical Endocrinology
0300-0672 Rassegna Italiana d'Ottalmologia *see* 0300-0109
0300-0702 Mises a Jour Cardiologiques
0300-0877 Rendiconti di Gastroenterologia†
0300-0893 Biomedecine
0300-0923 W H O Food Additives Series†
0300-0990 Arbeitsgemeinschaft fuer Juristisches Bibliotheks- und Dokumentationswesen. Mitteilungen
0300-1016 Versuchstierkunde
0300-1067 Studia Phonologica
0300-1164 Bulletin Mensuel de la Normalisation Francaise
0300-1172 Banque du Zaire. Rapport Annuel
0300-1199 Canada. Statistics Canada. Household Furniture Manufacturers/Industrie des Meubles de Maison
0300-1202 Canada. Statistics Canada. Wool Yarn and Cloth Mills/Filature et Tissage de la Laine
0300-1237 European Journal of Forest Pathology
0300-1245 Paediatrician
0300-1261 Chemoreception Abstracts
0300-1342 New Zealand Journal of Dairy Science and Technology
0300-1385 Cocoa Research Institute. Annual Report
0300-1407 Carbohydrate Chemistry and Metabolism Abstracts†
0300-1547 Annual Reports on Competition Policy in O E C D Member Countries
0300-1555 South Africa. Prisons Department. Report of the Commissioner of Prisons/Verslag van die Kommissaris van Gevangenisse
0300-1628 International Tax Report
0300-1652 Nigerian Medical Journal
0300-1679 Guinness Book of Records *changed to* Guinness Book of World Records
0300-1695 Pilot
0300-1725 Current Problems in Clinical Biochemistry
0300-1881 Nigeria. Federal Ministry of Trade. Quarterly Information Bulletin
0300-1954 Letopis na Statiite ot Bulgarskite Vestnitsi
0300-1962 Letopis na Statiite ot Bulgarskite Spisaniia i Sbornitsi
0300-1997 Tiroler Verkehswirtschaftliche Zahlen
0300-2012 Wolfenbuettler Beitraege
0300-208X Who's Notable in Mexico
0300-2144 Management Journal
0300-2233 European Law Newsletter *changed to* European Law Letter
0300-2241 Liberia. Department of State. Newsletter
0300-225X World Peace
0300-2373 Kenya. Central Bureau of Statistics. Agricultural Census (Large Farm Areas)
0300-2403 Nigeria. Federal Department of Forest Research. Research Paper
0300-2497 Neki Pokazatelji Tehnickog Razvoja Privrede Jugoslavije
0300-2519 U N I S I S T Newsletter
0300-2527 Drustveni Proizvod i Narodni Dohodak
0300-2535 Licni Dohoci
0300-2594 Institut d'Etudes Slaves, Paris. Documents Pedagogiques
0300-2608 Enseignement du Russe
0300-2667 Management Information Service
0300-2713 Oriental Insects Supplements Series
0300-2721 Insaat Muhendisleri Odasi. Teknik Bulten
0300-2772 Austria. Bundesministerium fuer Wissenschaft und Forschung. Bericht der Bundesregierung an den Nationalrat
0300-2829 Arable Farming
0300-287X Bibliothekspraxis
0300-2896 Archivos de Bronoconeumologia
0300-3000 I S D S Bulletin
0300-3094 Nordisk Statutsamling
0300-3108 Travelgram
0300-3124 Teollisuussanomat *changed to* Teollisuus
0300-3132 Tavola Rotonda†
0300-3159 Tekawennake
0300-3167 Umformtechnik
0300-3175 Valori Umani
0300-3183 Vida Hospitalar
0300-3205 Voice of Malta
0300-3213 Voxair
0300-3221 Work-Environment-Health *see* 0355-3140
0300-3256 Zoologica Scripta
0300-3264 Young Soldier
0300-3272 Talyllyn News
0300-3280 Swing *changed to* On the Agenda
0300-3302 Sun Yat-Sen Cultural Foundation Bulletin/Chung Shan Hsueh Shu Wen Hua Chi Kan
0300-3310 Skip
0300-3329 Sicherheitsingenieur
0300-3337 Sicherheitsbeauftragter
0300-3361 Science Chelsea
0300-337X Scottish Genealogist
0300-3388 Salamandra
0300-3396 Rheumatology and Rehabilitation
0300-340X Rivista Storica dell'Antichita
0300-3426 Revista de Microscopia Electronica
0300-3434 Renal Physiology
0300-3442 Hospital Career†
0300-3450 Rechentechnik-Datenverarbeitung
0300-3469 Reader
0300-3477 Razza Bovina Piemontese
0300-3485 Rassegna di Diritto Legislazione e Medicina Legale Veterinaria
0300-3493 Foreign Compound Metabolism in Mammals
0300-3507 Rank and File
0300-3515 Rally
0300-3523 Protee
0300-3558 Prison Service Journal
0300-3566 Prezzi dei Materiali e delle Opere Edili in Ferrara
0300-3574 Pollustop
0300-3582 Plastics & Polymers†
0300-3582 Plastics and Polymers *see* 0309-4561
0300-3604 Photosynthetica
0300-3612 University of the Philippines. Institute of Library Science. Newsletter
0300-3620 Philippines. Civil Service Commission. Civil Service Reporter
0300-3655 Personalhistorisk Tidsskrift
0300-3663 Periodex
0300-368X Nigerian Agricultural Journal
0300-3701 Orquidea (Mexico)
0300-371X Notes on the Science of Building
0300-3728 Nova Scotia Historical Quarterly
0300-3736 New Spectator *changed to* Church & Nation
0300-3752 New Linguist†
0300-3760 Mining Technical Digest
0300-3779 Muchachas
0300-3787 Mundo Electronico
0300-3809 Natun Thikana
0300-3817 Magyar Tortenelmi Szemle
0300-3825 Medico†
0300-3868 Medical Technician *see* 0309-2666
0300-3884 Mundo Financiero
0300-3906 Mindanao Mail
0300-3914 Mitsubishi Bank Review
0300-3922 Multinational Business
0300-3930 Local Government Studies
0300-3957 Kerala Homoeo Journal
0300-3965 Interdit *changed to* Diplomes
0300-3973 Informazione Radio TV
0300-3981 Informationen zur Orts- , Regional- und Landesplanung *changed to* Dokumente und Informationen zur Schweizerischen Orts- ,Regional- und Landesplanung
0300-4007 Indranil
0300-4015 Korean Journal of Physiology
0300-4023 Indochina
0300-4031 In Terris
0300-4058 International Law Reporter
0300-4074 Kanara Chamber of Commerce & Industry Journal
0300-4112 Forstarchiv
0300-4139 Germinal
0300-4155 Impact
0300-4163 I P P F - S E A O R News *changed to* Concern
0300-4171 I D E
0300-418X Hong Kong Monthly Digest of Statistics
0300-421X Flour Milling and Baking Research Association Abstracts
0300-4228 Fleet Street Letter
0300-4236 Evangelische Kommentare
0300-4252 European Federation of Finance House Associations. Newsletter
0300-4260 English Golf Union. News & Fixtures *changed to* Golf News & Fixtures
0300-4279 Education Three-Thirteen
0300-4287 Economics
0300-4309 Dhandha
0300-4317 Desarrollo del Tropico Americano
0300-4325 British Clayworker *see* 0305-7623
0300-4333 University of Calgary Gazette
0300-4341 Business Japan
0300-435X Canadian Guider
0300-4368 Charadista
0300-4384 Concord
0300-4414 Dejiny Ved a Techniky
0300-4422 Deputazione di Storia Patria per l'Umbria. Bollettino
0300-4430 Early Child Development and Care
0300-4465 Cooperator†
0300-4473 Cidade†
0300-4481 Cerveza y Malta
0300-449X Transport and Tourism Journal

0300-4503 Case Studies in Atomic Physics *see* 0370-1573
0300-4511 Canada Rides
0300-452X Camouflage Air Journal
0300-4538 Cahiers de la Presse Francaise
0300-4554 B I P
0300-4562 British Lichen Society Bulletin
0300-4570 British Ceramic Abstracts
0300-4589 Bollettino di Collegamento
0300-4600 Athletic Echo
0300-4619 Brewing Industry Research Foundation. Bulletin of Current Literature *changed to* Brewing Research Foundation. Bulletin of Current Literature
0300-4627 Blatt fuer Sortenwesen
0300-4651 African
0300-466X Artbibliographies Modern
0300-4678 Action
0300-4686 Acrida
0300-4708 A M A Gazette
0300-4716 Canada Manpower Review *see* 0318-4099
0300-4724 A und O der Hausfrau *see* 0340-238X
0300-4732 Dansk Forsikrings Tidende/ Assurandoeren *see* 0105-4260
0300-4740 Cayman Islands. Legislative Assembly. Minutes
0300-483X Toxicology
0300-4864 Journal of Neurocytology
0300-4899 Dokumentationsdienst Lateinamerika
0300-4910 Annales d'Immunologie
0300-4937 Medecine et Armees
0300-4953 Artes de Mexico
0300-4961 Rocky Mountain Social Science Association. Newsletter *changed to* Western Social Science Association Newsletter
0300-4988 Chester Zoo News
0300-5038 I A R C Scientific Publications
0300-5062 Actas Luso-Espanolas de Neurologia Psiquiatria y Ciencias Afines
0300-5089 Clinics in Gastroenterology
0300-5127 Biochemical Society, London. Transactions
0300-5143 Clean Air
0300-5186 Monographs in Neural Sciences
0300-5194 Excerpta Medica. Section 46: Environmental Health and Pollution Control
0300-5232 Society of Chemical Industry. Bulletin
0300-5275 Ontario Dentist
0300-5283 Medical Journal of Malaysia
0300-5305 Architektura C S R
0300-5321 Excerpta Medica. Section 36: Health Economics and Hospital Management
0300-533X Institute of Child Health, Calcutta, Annals†
0300-5356 Arhitectura
0300-5364 British Journal of Audiology
0300-5372 Excerpta Medica. Section 29: Clinical Biochemistry
0300-5402 Acta Universitatis Carolinae: Geographica
0300-5410 Annales de Microbiologie
0300-5429 Environmental Physiology & Biochemistry†
0300-5453 New Al-Hoda
0300-5461 Hospital and Health Service Purchasing
0300-5488 Studies on the Fauna of Suriname and Other Guyanas
0300-550X Agricultural Association of China. Journal
0300-5526 Intervirology
0300-5577 Journal of Perinatal Medicine
0300-5607 Courses et Elevage
0300-5623 Urological Research
0300-5658 Eperon
0300-5704 Aktuelle Gerontologie
0300-5712 Journal of Dentistry
0300-5720 Hospital Development
0300-5747 South Africa. Maize Board. Report on Grain Sorghum and Buckwheat for the Financial Year
0300-5755 Alimentaria
0300-5763 Biological Membrane Abstracts *changed to* Biochemistry Abstracts, Part 1: Biological Membranes
0300-5771 International Journal of Epidemiology
0300-5801 Biodeterioration Research Titles
0300-581X Arbeitsmedizin, Sozialmedizin, Praeventivmedizin
0300-5852 Behavioural Biology Abstracts, Section A: Animal Behaviour *see* 0301-8695
0300-5860 Zeitschrift fuer Kardiologie
0300-5879 Medical Technologist *see* 0309-2666
0300-5925 Public Health Engineer
0300-5992 Terpenoids and Steroids
0300-600X Venture Management†
0300-6018 New Dimensions in Legislation *see* 0146-9584
0300-6026 Trends in Housing
0300-6034 Consumer Credit and Truth-In-Lending Compliance Report
0300-6050 Texas State and Region Newsletter†
0300-6069 New Jersey Register
0300-6107 California Teachers Association. Chapter News Service†
0300-6115 New Jersey Savings League Guide *changed to* New Jersey Savings League News
0300-6123 Rubber & Plastics News
0300-6131 San Diego County Planning Department Population and Housing *changed to* San Diego County Integrated Planning Office Population and Housing
0300-6158 Miesiecznik Franciszkanski
0300-6166 T A A Newsletter *changed to* Sister City News
0300-6182 South Dakota Municipalities
0300-6190 Tube Topics
0300-6204 Business & Government Insider Newsletter†
0300-6212 Svithiod Journal
0300-6239 Southern Tobacco Journal
0300-6247 Talking Leaf
0300-6271 Pregled Review
0300-6298 Teacher Advocate
0300-6301 Motor North
0300-6328 Rawhide Press
0300-6336 Union W.A.G.E.
0300-6379 Rainbow
0300-6387 Sports Car
0300-6409 N A H R O Letter *see* 0194-9268
0300-6433 T E P S A Journal
0300-6441 Regional Plan Association Library Acquisitions *changed to* Regional Plan Association Selected Library Acquisitions
0300-645X Virginia Genealogist
0300-6468 Rhode Island Statewide Planning Program Monthly Progress Report
0300-6476 Rodniye Dali
0300-6484 Palestine Digest
0300-6506 Transportation Business Report†
0300-6549 Walker's Manual Supplement
0300-6557 Trailer Boats
0300-6565 Whispering Wind
0300-6573 Whitmore Investment Letter†
0300-659X Womanpower *see* 0195-2390
0300-6603 Twin Cities Courier
0300-6611 Women's Advocate
0300-662X Western Mining News
0300-6638 Voluntary Action News *changed to* Voluntary Action Leadership
0300-6646 National On-Campus Report
0300-6654 Vital Signs
0300-6670 N S A A Newsletter *changed to* N S A A News
0300-6689 N A T E News
0300-6700 Technology and Human Affairs *changed to* I I T Technology and Human Affairs
0300-6719 Owens Valley Indian Education Center Monthly Newsletter
0300-6727 North Carolina Agribusiness
0300-6743 Noticiero Obrero Norteamericano
0300-676X Oshkosh Advance-Titan
0300-6778 Nichols Alumnus *changed to* Nichols News
0300-6786 Post Eagle
0300-6794 Nostalgia Newsletter†
0300-6808 Ute Bulletin
0300-6816 P A A Affairs
0300-6824 Northwest Investment Review
0300-6832 North Dakota Publisher
0300-6840 Northwest Investment Tablistics *changed to* Northwest Stock Guide
0300-6859 Urban Affairs Abstracts
0300-6867 W E A L Washington Report
0300-6883 I A L News
0300-6891 A.D. Presbyterian Life Edition *changed to* United Presbyterian A.D.
0300-6905 Highway Safety Literature
0300-6913 Voice of Brotherhood
0300-6921 Chicago Reporter
0300-6948 Arts in Common *see* 0194-1305
0300-6956 Current Programs *see* 0162-704X
0300-6964 Augsburg College Now
0300-6972 U.S. Center for Disease Control. Abortion Surveillance Report
0300-6999 Federation Forum *changed to* Planning and Action
0300-7006 World Education Reports
0300-7014 Feminist Art Journal†
0300-7030 Concerned Business Students' Report†
0300-7049 Inside Industry
0300-7057 Video Publisher *see* 0161-9055
0300-7065 A C A Word from Washington *changed to* UpDate (New York)
0300-7073 Family Practice News
0300-7081 Chicago. Municipal Reference Library. Recent Additions
0300-7103 Essecondsex†
0300-7111 Fashion Newsletter
0300-712X Chicago. Municipal Reference Library. Checklist of Publications Issued by the City of Chicago
0300-7138 Du Pont Context
0300-7154 Michael Reese Hospital & Medical Center. Medical Staff Newsletter *changed to* Rounds
0300-7162 Diacritics
0300-7170 Environmental Pollution Control Journal†
0300-7189 Dependable's List Letter
0300-7197 Drywall Newsmagazine *changed to* Construction Dimensions Magazine
0300-7200 Medic Alert Newsletter
0300-7219 American Challenge
0300-7227 Bibliography and Index of Micropaleontology
0300-7235 Bay View†
0300-7278 American Indian News†
0300-7308 Metric Association Newsletter *changed to* U S Metric Association Newsletter
0300-7316 Discovery (Richmond)
0300-7324 Dow Theory Forecasts
0300-7340 D C A T Bulletin
0300-7359 Media Ecology Review†
0300-7375 Consumer Newsweek *changed to* Consumer Newsweekly
0300-7391 Contents of Current Legal Periodicals *see* 0279-5787
0300-7405 Intermountain Logging News
0300-7413 Civitan
0300-7421 American University Report *changed to* American
0300-743X CORE Magazine
0300-7456 Mayo Alumnus
0300-7472 Afterimage
0300-7480 Beer Marketer's Insights
0300-7499 Buffalo Spree
0300-7502 Maryland Travel Scene
0300-7529 Connecticut Business Journal
0300-7553 Margins†
0300-7561 Crab
0300-757X Inside R & D
0300-7588 Inter-Society Color Council Newsletter *changed to* Inter-Society Color Council News
0300-7596 Vie Collegienne
0300-7618 Poblacion†
0300-7626 American White Water
0300-7634 Correio Operario Norteamericano
0300-7650 M A T Y C Journal
0300-7669 Your Clipping Analyst
0300-7677 Indian Legal Information Development Service Legislative Review *see* 0145-7993
0300-7693 Performance Guide Publications. Mutual Funds and Timing
0300-7707 M A S C D Newsletter *changed to* Focus Magazine (Detroit)
0300-7715 Payment Systems Newsletter
0300-7723 Photo Industry Newsletter
0300-7731 Plus-Profit Publicity
0300-7766 Popular Music & Society
0300-7782 Headlines
0300-7790 New Yorkers for Abortion Law Repeal. Newsletter
0300-7804 Live Steam Magazine *see* 0364-5177
0300-7812 Goddard Journal†
0300-7820 Suomi-Opiston Viesti
0300-7839 Human Ecology
0300-7855 Laging Una
0300-7898 New York (State) University. Division of Continuing Education. Newsletter†
0300-7901 Know News Service
0300-7928 Ripon College Magazine
0300-7936 Robinson Jeffers Newsletter
0300-7952 Kitchen Planning
0300-7960 Shmuessen mit Kinder Un Yugent
0300-7995 Current Medical Research and Opinion
0300-8029 Inforasia†
0300-8037 Scandinavian Journal of Social Medicine
0300-8053 International Jugglers Association Newsletter
0300-8096 D T. I
0300-810X Italian Heritage Newsletter
0300-8126 Infection
0300-8134 Journal of Human Ergology
0300-8169 Medicina e Historia†
0300-8177 Molecular and Cellular Biochemistry
0300-8185 Pakistan Journal of Biochemistry
0300-8207 Connective Tissue Research
0300-824X Environmental Quality and Safety: Chemistry, Toxicology and Technology
0300-8258 Connecticut Fireside
0300-8282 E D V in Medizin und Biologie
0300-8320 Helminthological Abstracts. Series B: Plant Nematology
0300-8339 Helminthological Abstracts. Series A: Animal and Human Helminthology
0300-8347 Health & Social Service Journal
0300-8355 Gem City News *changed to* Idaho Cities
0300-8371 Neue Muenchner Beitraege zur Geschichte der Medizin und Naturwissenschaften. Medizinhistorische Serie
0300-838X Microbiology Abstracts. Section A. Industrial & Applied Microbiology
0300-8398 Microbiology Abstracts. Section B. Bacteriology
0300-8436 Jahresverzeichnis der Verlagsschriften und Einer Auswahl der ausserhalb des Buchhandels Erschienenen Veroeffentlichungen der DDR, der BRD und Westberlins sowie der Deutschsprachigen Werke Anderer Laender
0300-8452 Forecast FM *changed to* Forecast (Silver Spring)
0300-8495 Australian Family Physician
0300-8509 Fore
0300-8584 Medical Microbiology and Immunology
0300-8592 Roentgen Blaetter
0300-8622 Leber Magen Darm
0300-8630 Klinische Paediatrie
0300-8665 Verein fuer Wasser-, Boden- und Lufthygiene. Schriftenreihe
0300-869X Zeitschrift fuer Klinische Psychologie und Psychotherapie
0300-8703 Studebaker Story
0300-8711 Zentralblatt fuer Veterinaermedizin. Series A

ISSN INDEX 1211

0300-872X Zeitschrift fuer Immunitaetsforschung, Experimentelle und Klinische Immunologie *see* 0340-904X
0300-8754 Housing and Community Development News *see* 0194-2913
0300-8819 Neurobiology†
0300-8819 Neurobiology†
0300-8827 Acta Orthopaedica Scandinavica. Supplementum
0300-8851 Herold der Wahrheit
0300-8908 Nevada Planner
0300-8924 Acta Vitaminologica et Enzymologica†
0300-8959 New Alaskan
0300-8967 Acta Psychiatrica Belgica
0300-9009 Acta Neurologica Belgica
0300-9033 Acta Gastroenterologica Latinoamericana
0300-9084 Biochimie
0300-9130 Research in Experimental Medicine
0300-922X Chemical Society, London. Journal: Perkin Transactions 1
0300-9238 Chemical Society, London. Journal: Faraday Transactions 2
0300-9246 Chemical Society, London. Journal: Dalton Transactions
0300-9254 National Science Council of Sri Lanka. Journal
0300-9262 Bulletin Signaletique-Bibliographie des Sciences de la Terre. Section 220. Mineralogie, Geochimie, Geologie Extraterrestre
0300-9270 Bulletin Signaletique-Bibliographie des Sciences de la Terre. Section 221. Cahier B. Gitologie, Economie Miniere *changed to* Bulletin Signaletique-Bibliographie des Sciences de la Terre. Section 221. Gisements Metalliques et Non Metalliques. Economie Miniere
0300-9289 Bulletin Signaletique-Bibliographie des Sciences de la Terre. Section 222. Roches Cristallines
0300-9297 Bulletin Signaletique-Bibliographie des Sciences de la Terre. Section 223. Roches Sedimentaires, Geologie Marine
0300-9300 Bulletin Signaletique-Bibliographie des Sciences de la Terre. Section 224. Stratigraphie, Geologie, Regionale et Geologie Generale
0300-9319 Bulletin Signaletique-Bibliographie des Sciences de la Terre. Section 225. Tectonique
0300-9327 Bulletin Signaletique-Bibliographie des Sciences de la Terre. Section 226. Hydrologie, Geologie de l'Ingenieur, Formations Superficielles
0300-9335 Bulletin Signaletique - Bibliographie des Sciences de la Terre. Section 227. Paleontologie
0300-9351 France. Bureau de Recherches Geologiques et Minieres. Bulletin. Section 2. Geologie Appliquee-Chronique des Mines *changed to* France. Bureau de Recherches Geologiques et Minieres. Bulletin. Section 2: Geologie des Gites Mineraux
0300-936X France. Bureau de Recherches Geologiques et Minieres. Bulletin. Section 3: Hydrogeologie-Geologie de l'Ingenieur
0300-9432 Forensic Science *see* 0379-0738
0300-9467 Chemical Engineering Journal
0300-9475 Scandinavian Journal of Immunology
0300-9483 Boreas
0300-9513 Revue Francaise d'Histoire d'Outre-Mer
0300-9564 Journal of Neural Transmission
0300-9572 Resuscitation
0300-9580 Chemical Society, London. Perkin Transactions 2
0300-9599 Chemical Society, London. Journal: Faraday Transactions 1
0300-9629 Comparative Biochemistry and Physiology. Part A: Comparative Physiology
0300-9637 Biochemistry, General and Molecular *see* 0024-3205
0300-9653 Life Sciences. Part 1: Physiology and Pharmacology *see* 0024-3205
0300-967X Zeitschrift fuer Geburtshilfe und Perinatologie
0300-970X Acta Hepato-Gastroenterologica *changed to* Hepato-Gastroenterology
0300-9718 Revista de Quimica Textil
0300-9734 Upsala Journal of Medical Sciences
0300-9742 Scandinavian Journal of Rheumatology
0300-9750 Acta Endocrinologica Congress. Advance Abstracts
0300-9777 Journal of Oral Pathology
0300-9785 International Journal of Oral Surgery
0300-9815 Revue d'Odonto-Stomatologie
0300-9831 Internationale Zeitschrift fuer Vitamin- und Ernaehrungsforschung
0300-984X Archiv fuer Genetik†
0300-9858 Veterinary Pathology
0300-9920 Journal of Tropical Pediatrics and Environmental Child Health *changed to* Journal of Tropical Pediatrics
0300-9947 Nursing Bibliography
0300-9955 Science, Medicine and Man *see* 0271-5392
0300-9963 Selected Annual Reviews of the Analytical Sciences
0300-9998 International Journal of Chronobiology
0301-0015 Journal of Physics A-Mathematical, Nuclear and General *see* 0305-4470
0301-0023 Society of Occupational Medicine. Journal
0301-0066 Perception
0301-0074 Organometallic Chemistry
0301-0082 Progress in Neurobiology
0301-0104 Chemical Physics
0301-0112 Abstracts on Police Science *see* 0166-6282
0301-0139 Pigment Cell
0301-0147 Haemostasis
0301-0155 Frontiers of Matrix Biology
0301-0163 Hormone Research
0301-0171 Cytogenetics and Cell Genetics
0301-018X Australasian Nurses Journal
0301-0244 Polish Journal of Pharmacology and Pharmacy
0301-0260 Presence Croix-Rouge
0301-0279 Revue Francaise des Maladies Respiratoires
0301-0287 Psychiatries
0301-0295 Bulletin Signaletique. Part 320: Biochimie. Biophysique
0301-0309 Bulletin Signaletique. Part 101: Sciences de l'Information. Documentation
0301-0333 Kenya Nursing Journal
0301-035X Bangladesh Medical Journal
0301-0368 Asian Archives of Anaesthesiology and Resuscitation
0301-0376 Modern Medicine of Asia
0301-0384 Health of the People
0301-0422 Public Health Reviews
0301-0430 Clinical Nephrology
0301-0449 Pediatric Radiology
0301-0457 Behring Institut. Mitteilungen
0301-0481 Zeitschrift fuer Hautkrankheiten H und G
0301-0481 Sozialversicherungs-Beamte und -Angestellte *see* 0301-0481
0301-049X Food Irradiation Information
0301-0503 Journal of Maxillofacial Surgery
0301-0511 Biological Psychology
0301-0546 Allergologia et Immunopathologia
0301-0554 Malaysian Journal of Science
0301-0597 Ceskoslovenska Neurologie a Neurochirurgie
0301-0635 Sciences Pharmaceutiques et Biologique de Lorraine
0301-0643 Epoch
0301-0708 Biosynthesis
0301-0716 Radiochemistry
0301-0724 Folia Veterinaria Latina
0301-0732 South African Veterinary Association. Journal
0301-0740 World Health Organization. World Health Assembly and the Executive Board. Handbook of Resolutions and Decisions.
0301-0791 Cahiers de Chirurgie†
0301-0813 F.N.I.B.
0301-0821 Queen's Nursing Journal†
0301-0864 Anaesthesia, Resuscitation and Intensive Therapy†
0301-0996 Goeteborg Psychological Reports
0301-102X John Rylands University Library of Manchester. Bulletin
0301-1208 Indian Journal of Biochemistry and Biophysics
0301-1216 Indian Journal of Preventive and Social Medicine
0301-133X Bulletin Signaletique. Part 349: Anesthesie.Reanimation
0301-1402 Klassische Homoeopathie
0301-1445 Giornale di Batteriologia, Virologia ed Immunologia ed Annali dell'Ospedale Maria Vittoria di Torino. Parte 2. Sezione Clinica
0301-1453 Giornale di Batteriologia, Virologia Ed Immunologia Ed Annali dell'Ospedale Maria Vittoria di Torino. Parte 1. Microbiologia
0301-1518 La Nouvelle Presse Medicale
0301-1526 Vasa
0301-1534 Vie Medicale au Canada Francais
0301-1569 O R L
0301-1607 Z W R - Zahnaerztliche Welt, Zahnaerztliche Rundschau *see* 0044-166X
0301-1623 International Urology and Nephrology
0301-2115 European Journal of Obstetrics, Gynecology and Reproductive Biology
0301-2123 Acta Biologica Paranaense
0301-2190 Hospital and Health Administration *changed to* Australian Hospital
0301-2204 Gynecologie
0301-2255 Anali Klinicke Bolnice "Dr. M. Stojanovic"
0301-228X British Journal of Orthodontics
0301-2328 Microbiology Abstracts. Section C. Algology, Mycology & Protozoology
0301-2425 Biofizika Zhivoi Kletki
0301-2689 Berichte ueber Landwirtschaft. Sonderhefte
0301-2697 Naturwissenschaftlicher Verein in Hamburg. Abhandlungen und Verhandlungen
0301-2719 Gaertnerische Berufspraxis
0301-2727 Fortschritte der Pflanzenzuechtung
0301-2735 Fortschritte im Acker- und Pflanzenbau
0301-2743 Fortschritte in der Tierphysiologie und Tierernaehrung
0301-2778 Mammalia Depicta
0301-2794 Fortschritte der Veterinaermedizin
0301-2808 Fortschritte der Verhaltensforschung
0301-2891 Calendar of International and Regional Congresses of Medical Sciences
0301-2980 Datenverarbeitung im Recht
0301-2999 Vierteljahresschrift fuer Sozialrecht
0301-3006 Analytische Psychologie
0301-3014 Perspectives in Medicine
0301-3057 Monographs on Drugs†
0301-3073 Frontiers of Hormone Research
0301-3081 Contributions to Microbiology and Immunology
0301-309X International Symposium on Brain-Endocrine Interaction. Proceedings
0301-3146 Canadian Society for Immunology. International Symposium. Proceedings
0301-3243 Infusionstherapie und Klinische Ernaehrung *see* 0378-0791
0301-326X European Ophthalmological Society. Congress Acta
0301-3308 Bulletin Signaletique. Part 140: Electrotechnique *changed to* Bulletin Signaletique. Part 140: Eldoc-Electrotechnique
0301-3316 Bulletin Signaletique. Part 145: Electronique *changed to* Bulletin Signaletique. Part 145: Eldoc-Electronique
0301-3324 Bulletin Signaletique. Part 346: Ophtalmologie
0301-3332 Bulletin Signaletique. Part 160: Physique de l'Etat Condense
0301-3340 Bulletin Signaletique. Part 161. Cristallographie *see* 0304-1298
0301-3359 Bulletin Signaletique. Part 165: Atomes et Molecules. Plasmas
0301-3375 Bulletin Signaletique. Part 347: Oto-Rhino-Laryngologie, Stomatologie, Pathologie Cervicofaciale
0301-3383 Bulletin Signaletique. Part 348: Dermatologie - Venereologie
0301-3391 Bulletin Signaletique. Part 352: Maladies de l'Appareil Respiratoire du Coeur et des Vaisseaux - Chirurgie Thoracique et Vasculaire
0301-3405 Bulletin Signaletique. Part 354: Maladies de l'Appareil Digestif. Chirurgie Abdominale
0301-3413 Bulletin Signaletique. Part 355: Maladies des Reins et des Voies Urinaires - Chirurgie de l'Appareil Urinaire
0301-3421 Bulletin Signaletique. Part 356: Maladies du Systeme Nerveux Myopathies-Neurochirurgie
0301-343X Bulletin Signaletique. Part 357: Maladies des Os et des Articulations - Chirurgie Orthopedique - Traumatologie
0301-3448 Bulletin Signaletique. Part 359: Maladies du Sang
0301-3456 Bulletin Signaletique. Part 360. Biologie Animale. Physio-Pathologie des Invertebres. Ecologie *see* 0181-0006
0301-3464 Bulletin Signaletique. Part 363: Genetique
0301-3472 Bulletin Signaletique. Part 365. Physiologie des Vertebres *see* 0181-0014
0301-3480 Bulletin Signaletique. Part 745: Soudage, Brasage et Techniques Connexes
0301-3499 Bulletin Signaletique. Part 885: Nuisances
0301-3537 Bulletin Signaletique. Part 110: Informatique-Automatique-Recherche Operationnelle-Gestion *changed to* Bulletin Signaletique. Part 110: Informatique-Automatique-Recherche Operationnelle-Gestion-Economie
0301-3693 Nuovo Archivio Italiano di Otologia, Rinologia e Laringologia
0301-374X New Techniques in Biophysics and Cell Biology
0301-3782 Basel Institute for Immunology. Annual Report
0301-3863 Minerva Ecologica e Idroclimatologica *see* 0391-1624
0301-388X Gas and Liquid Chromatography Abstracts
0301-3901 Institut d'Hygiene des Mines. Revue
0301-3952 Journal de Biologie Buccale
0301-4150 A G E Current Awareness Series
0301-4193 Contributions to Human Development
0301-4207 Resources Policy
0301-4215 Energy Policy
0301-4223 New Zealand Journal of Zoology
0301-4231 Contributions to Primatology
0301-4355 Instituto Interamericano de Ciencios Agricolas de la O E A. Documentos Oficiales
0301-438X Inter-American Centre for Agricultural Documentation and Information. Documentacion e Informacion Agricola
0301-4428 Theoretical Linguistics
0301-4436 R & D Projects in Documentation and Librarianship
0301-4444 Annales de Medecine de Reims Champagne- Ardennes†
0301-4460 Annals of Human Biology
0301-4495 Annee Therapeutique et Clinique en Ophtalmologie
0301-4606 Bangladesh Pharmaceutical Journal
0301-4614 Bibliographie der Bibliographien
0301-4622 Biophysical Chemistry
0301-4657 Current Research and Development Projects in Israel: Natural Sciences and Technology

1212 ISSN INDEX

0301-4665 Deutsche Bibliographie. Hochschulschriften-Verzeichnis
0301-4681 Differentiation
0301-469X Eastern Archives of Ophthalmology
0301-4703 Essays in Fundamental Immunology
0301-4711 European Journal of Cardiology
0301-472X Experimental Hematology
0301-4738 Indian Journal of Ophthalmology
0301-4746 Industrial Safety Chronicle
0301-4797 Journal of Environmental Management
0301-4800 Journal of Nutritional Science and Vitaminology
0301-4827 Kerala Medical Journal
0301-4835 Die Krankenversicherung
0301-4843 Kupat-Holim Yearbook
0301-4851 Molecular Biology Reports
0301-486X Mycopathologia
0301-5017 Revue Internationale du Trachome
0301-5068 Egyptian Journal of Pharmaceutical Sciences
0301-5076 United Arab Republic Journal of Pharmaceutical Sciences *see* 0301-5068
0301-5092 Veterinaria Mexico
0301-5106 Who's Who in India
0301-5149 Developments in Biological Standardization
0301-536X Frontiers of Oral Physiology
0301-5521 New Zealand Journal of Experimental Agriculture
0301-5548 European Journal of Applied Physiology and Occupational Physiology
0301-5564 Histochemistry
0301-5572 British Journal of Sexual Medicine
0301-5580 International Hospital Equipment
0301-5610 Nucleic Acids Research
0301-5629 Ultrasound in Medicine & Biology
0301-5645 People
0301-5661 Community Dentistry and Oral Epidemiology
0301-567X Tropische Landwirtschaft und Veterinaermedizin. Beitraege
0301-5696 Faraday Symposia
0301-5718 Update
0301-5769 Schmuck†
0301-5785 Australian Outlook
0301-584X Kongresszentralblatt fuer die Gesamte Innere Medizin. Sektion A: Zentralblatt Praktische Innere Medizin und Grenzgebiete/Internal Medicine
0301-5858 Kongresszentralblatt fuer die Gesamte Innere Medizin. Sektion B: Zentralblatt Kardiologie-Nephrologie/Cardiology-Nephrology
0301-5866 Kongresszentralblatt fuer die Gesamte Innere Medizin. Sektion C: Zentralblatt Pneumonologie-Tuberkulose/Pneumonology-Tuberculosis
0301-5874 Kongresszentralblatt fuer die Gesamte Innere Medizin. Sektion D: Zentralblatt Gastroenterologie-Stoffwechsel-Endokrinologie/Gastroenterology-Metabolism-Endocrinology
0301-5882 Kongresszentralblatt fuer die Gesamte Innere Medizin Sektion E: Zentralblatt Immunologie-Transplantation/Immunology-Transplantation
0301-5912 Biotelemetry *see* 0378-309X
0301-6129 Acta Diurna Historica
0301-620X Journal of Bone and Joint Surgery: British Volume
0301-6226 Livestock Production Science
0301-6269 Indonesian Indicator
0301-634X Radiation and Environmental Biophysics
0301-6366 Mensuel du Medecin Acupuncteur
0301-6374 N. G. M.
0301-6382 Zeitschrift fuer Rheumatologie
0301-6412 Neurolinguistics
0301-6536 Building Services Engineer *see* 0142-3630
0301-6587 Anthropologica
0301-6625 Central Bank of Yemen. Annual Report
0301-6676 Boletin de Estudios Latinoamericanos y del Caribe
0301-6722 Universidade Federal do Para. Revista†
0301-679X Tribology International
0301-6811 Zeitschrift fuer Kinder-und Jugendpsychiatrie
0301-6897 Matematicheskie Problemy Geofiziki
0301-6900 Lingvisticheskie Issledovaniya
0301-6919 Voprosy Fiziki Tverdogo Tela
0301-701X Teoria y Praxis
0301-7028 Water Services
0301-7036 Problemas del Desarrollo
0301-7095 Malaysia in Brief
0301-7214 Guitar
0301-7249 Faraday Discussions
0301-7257 Byron Journal
0301-7265 Community Medicine†
0301-7303 Revue Roumaine de Medecine. Serie Neurologie et Psychiatrie
0301-7338 Revista de Igiena, Bacteriologie, Virusologie, Parazitologie, Pneumoftiziologie. Bacteriologie, Virusologie, Parazitologie, Epidemiologie
0301-7362 Istanbul Medical Faculty. Medical Bulletin
0301-7443 Anuario Financiero y de Sociedades Anonimas de Espana
0301-7478 Survey of Construction Activities of the Private Sector in Urban Areas of Iran
0301-7516 International Journal of Mineral Processing
0301-7524 Greater London Council. Housing Facts and Figures†
0301-7559 Financial Statistics of Education in Cyprus
0301-7567 Guia de Reuniones Cientificas y Tecnicas en la Argentina
0301-7575 Electron Spin Resonance Spectroscopy Abstracts
0301-7605 Critique
0301-7621 Almanak Jakarta
0301-7729 Universidade Federal de Minas Gerais. Faculdade de Medicina. Anais
0301-7737 Annales Universitatis Mariae Curie-Sklodowska. Sectio DD. Medicina Veterinaria
0301-7753 Cameroon Year Book
0301-7761 Daily Mail Year Book
0301-7788 Iter†
0301-7796 Facts and Figures
0301-7818 Argentina. Biblioteca del Congreso. Boletin Legislativo
0301-7877 Finish Digest†
0301-8059 Sociedade Entomologica do Brasil. Anais
0301-8105 South Africa. Department of Statistics. Census of Electricity, Gas and Steam
0301-8121 Journal of Chinese Philosophy
0301-8156 Rio Grande do Sul, Brazil. Fundacao de Economia e Estatistica. Indicadores Sociais
0301-8423 Gambia. Produce Marketing Board. Annual Report
0301-8520 Afrique Industrie Infrastructures
0301-861X Contraception-Fertilite-Sexualite
0301-8636 Archives Belges de Dermatologie†
0301-8660 Egyptian Journal of Physiological Science
0301-8695 Animal Behaviour Abstracts
0301-8768 Intergeo *see* 0396-5880
0301-8849 Egyptian Journal of Bilharziasis
0301-8881 Let's Square Dance
0301-8938 Fluorocarbon and Related Chemistry
0301-9004 In
0301-9020 Botswana
0301-9039 Clean Air Conference (Gt. Brit.)
0301-9047 Democratic World
0301-9055 Democratic Forum
0301-9063 Derecho
0301-908X Finnish Fisheries Research
0301-9101 Ideas
0301-9195 British Pteridological Society. Bulletin
0301-9217 Exports of the Republic of China
0301-9225 Handbuch der Oeffentlichen Bibliotheken
0301-9233 Ironmaking and Steelmaking
0301-9268 Precambrian Research
0301-9322 International Journal of Multiphase Flow
0301-9349 Confederacion General de la Industria. Memoria y Balance General
0302-0231 Japan Map Center News
0302-0282 Nihon No Minken Kyoiku
0302-0479 Kanazawa University. College of Liberal Arts. Annals of Science
0302-0622 Euro Cooperation; Economic Studies on Europe
0302-0657 Gesamtverzeichnis der Zeitschriften und Serien in Bibliotheken der Bundesrepublik Deutschland Einschliesslich Berlin (West)
0302-0665 Frontiers of Gastrointestinal Research
0302-0665 Bibliotheca Gastroenterologica *see* 0302-0665
0302-0681 South Africa; Official Yearbook of the Republic of South Africa
0302-072X Journal de Physique - Lettres
0302-0738 Journal de Physique
0302-0762 Hot Buttered Soul†
0302-0851 National Institute for Research in Dairying. Report
0302-086X Mauri Ora
0302-1173 Koinonike Epitheoresis
0302-1254 Big Beat
0302-1289 Energy Conservation
0302-1440 Study of Nursing Care: Research Project Series
0302-1475 Sign Language Studies
0302-1599 Himalangue
0302-1610 Indian Journal of Psychiatric Social Work
0302-167X P T A Heute
0302-1688 Origins of Life
0302-1742 Crystal Structure Communications
0302-184X Ocean Management
0302-1998 National Children's Bureau. Annual Review
0302-2013 Bank Indonesia. Data Kredit Perbankan†
0302-203X Forest Products Trade Statistics of Indonesia *changed to* Indonesian Statistics on Trade of Forest Products
0302-2048 Schweizerische Gesellschaft fuer Marktforschung. Geschaeftsbericht
0302-2056 National Accounts of Botswana
0302-2129 Industrie Minerale
0302-2137 Medical Biology
0302-2277 Observatorio Astronomico Municipal de Rosario. Boletin
0302-2293 Monographs on Standardization of Cardioangiological Methods
0302-2358 Archives Internationales Claude Bernard
0302-2366 Advances in Neurosurgery
0302-2374 Statistical Yearbook of Bangladesh
0302-2404 Postgraduate Institute of Medical Education and Research. Bulletin
0302-2420 Estudios Interdisciplinarios
0302-2439 Universidade de Sao Paulo. Departamento de Botanica. Boletim de Botanica
0302-2471 Chemical Senses and Flavour *changed to* Chemical Senses
0302-248X Archiv for Pharmaci og Chemi. Scientific Edition
0302-2536 Revue Siemens
0302-2587 G E C Journal of Science & Technology
0302-2684 Sciences Geologiques - Memoires
0302-2692 Sciences Geologiques. Bulletin
0302-2706 R A D I A L S Bulletin
0302-2773 Applied Neurophysiology
0302-2803 Child's Brain
0302-2811 Mental Health and Society†
0302-282X Neuropsychobiology
0302-2838 European Urology
0302-2846 British Book Design & Production
0302-2870 Pumps and Other Fluids Machinery Abstracts
0302-2935 Malaysian Forester
0302-2951 Geoteborg. Stadskontor. Statistiska Meddelanden
0302-3052 Mondes en Developpment
0302-3060 Journal of Social Science
0302-3176 Ayrshire Collections
0302-3184 Baptist Union Directory
0302-3249 Institute of Trading Standards Administration Monthly Review
0302-329X Civil Service Year Book
0302-3338 Human Experimentation & Toxicology Abstracts
0302-3354 Liquid Scintillation Counting.†
0302-3427 Science and Public Policy
0302-3451 Audiovisual Librarian
0302-3478 Underwater Information Bulletin
0302-3494 Summary of Postgraduate Diplomas and Courses in Medicine
0302-3524 Estuarine and Coastal Marine Science
0302-4091 Who Owns Whom. Australasia and Far East
0302-4148 Merseyside Chamber of Commerce and Industry. Directory
0302-4172 M I M S Middle East
0302-4180 Paper Review of the Year
0302-4199 Oxford Chemistry Series
0302-4210 Photographic Techniques in Scientific Research
0302-4261 East African Journal of Medical Research
0302-427X Annales de Kinesitherapie
0302-4326 Maternidade Dr. Alfredo da Costa, Lisbon. Arquivo Clinico
0302-4342 Anales Espanoles de Pediatrica
0302-4350 Aktuelle Neurologie
0302-4369 Acta Chemica Scandinavica. Series B: Organic Chemistry and Biochemistry
0302-4377 Acta Chemica Scandinavica. Series A: Physical and Inorganic Chemistry
0302-4466 Acta Dermatovenerologica Iugoslavica
0302-4520 Egyptian Journal of Animal Production
0302-4555 Sugar Technologists' Association of Trinidad and Tobago. Proceedings.
0302-4598 Bioelectrochemistry and Bioenergetics
0302-4725 Stomatologie der D D R
0302-4814 Universite de Brazzaville. Annales
0302-4822 Mexico. Comison Nacional de los Salarios Minimos. Informe de Labores
0302-4881 Rajasthan State Tanneries Limited. Annual Report
0302-5047 Zambia. Meteorological Department. Totals of Monthly and Annual Rainfall
0302-5063 Quarto Potere
0302-508X N C E R T Newsletter
0302-511X European Congress on Ballistocardiography and Cardiovascular Dynamics. Proceedings
0302-5128 Sleep
0302-5136 International College of Psychosomatic Medicine. Proceedings of the Congress
0302-5144 Contributions to Nephrology
0302-5152 International Congress of Psychosomatic Medicine in Obstetrics and Gynaecology. Proceedings
0302-5160 Historiographia Linguistica
0302-5195 Precos Pagos Pelos Agricultores
0302-5233 Ecuador. Instituto Nacional de Estadistica y Censos. Encuesta Anual de Manufactura y Mineria
0302-5268 Investigacion e Informacion Textil y de Tensioactivos
0302-5349 Dansk Maskinhandlerforening. Handbog
0302-5403 Kongeriget Danmarks Handels-Kalender
0302-5489 We Represent in Israel and Abroad.
0302-5640 Cultures au Zaire et en Afrique
0302-5691 Antartida
0302-5705 Argentina. Servicio Nacional de Parques Nacional. Anales
0302-5756 L E M I T. Anales
0302-5802 Timber Trade Review
0302-6248 Karka
0302-6256 Vedere-International
0302-6477 Galvano-Organo *changed to* Galvano-Organo-Traitements de Surface
0302-6574 Review of Economics and Business
0302-6620 States of Malaya Chamber of Mines. Council Report
0302-6655 Revista Juridica Panamena
0302-6671 Management Heute und Marktwirtschaft
0302-668X Management Heute *see* 0302-6671
0302-6701 Egyptian Journal of Soil Science

0302-671X Bonner Zoologische Monographien
0302-6736 Makerere Institute of Social Research. Research Abstracts and Newsletter†
0302-6744 Indian Records
0302-6795 Bank Ekspor Impor Indonesia. Annual Report/Laporan Tahunan
0302-6809 Barclays National Review *see* 0250-2402
0302-6957 Anales de Ciencias Humanas
0302-6965 Anuario del Arte Espanol
0302-7368 Acta Alimentaria
0302-7406 Instituto Antituberculoso Francisco Moragas. Publicaciones
0302-7503 Deutsche Wochen-Zeitung
0302-7546 I C S S R Journal of Abstracts and Reviews: Sociology, Social Anthropology
0302-7546 I C S S R Journal of Abstracts and Reviews *see* 0302-7546
0302-7554 Indian Biologist
0302-7562 Indian Journal of Zoology
0302-7600 Praktische Anaesthesie *changed to* Anaesthesie - Intensivtherapie - Notfallmedizin
0302-7651 C I S Abstracts
0302-766X Cell and Tissue Research
0302-7678 Chemical Industry Developments
0302-7724 Cuadernos de Realidades Sociales
0302-7902 World Transport Data
0302-7937 M I T Research Journal *changed to* U S M Research Journal
0302-8003 Revista E A C
0302-8070 Balneologia Bohemica
0302-8127 Immanuel
0302-8143 Adrikhalut *changed to* A-A
0302-8178 Bay Zikh
0302-8194 BIAF-Israel Aviation and Space Magazine
0302-8267 Israel. Ministry of the Interior. City and Region
0302-8429 Academie des Sciences. Comptes Rendus Hebdomadaires des Seances. Serie A. Sciences Mathematiques *see* 0151-0509
0302-8437 Academie des Sciences. Comptes Rendus Hebdomadaires des Seances. Serie B. Sciences Physiques *see* 0151-0509
0302-847X Muzykal'noe Vospitanie v Shkole
0302-8585 Uniwersytet Jagiellonski. Zeszyty Naukowe. Prace Botaniczne
0302-8844 Addab Journal
0302-8852 Revisor
0302-8933 Archives of Microbiology
0302-8984 Pschotherapie und Medizinische Psychologie *see* 0173-7937
0302-9069 Liteinoe Proizvodstvo, Metallovedenie i Obrabotka Metallov Davleniem
0302-9085 Issledovania po Teorii Algorifmov i Matematicheskoi Logike
0302-9263 Mediterranee Medicale
0302-9336 Jamaica. Department of Statistics. Consumer Price Indices
0302-9336 Consumer Price Indices (Bulletin)
0302-9379 Laryngologie, Rhinologie, Otologie und ihre Grenzgebiete *changed to* Laryngologie, Rhinologie, Otologie Vereingt mit Monatsschrift fuer Ohrenheilkunde
0302-9417 Tropische und Subtropische Pflanzenwelt
0302-9468 B G S
0302-9530 Archives of Oto-Rhino-Laryngology
0302-9611 Banco de la Republica. Registros de Exportacion e Importacion
0302-9794 Novum Gebrauchsgraphik/International Advertising Art
0302-9840 Vincent†
0303-111X Sovetskie Ljudi Segodnja
0303-1179 Asterisque
0303-1187 Institut Henri Poincare and Societe Mathematique de France. Circulaire d'Informations
0303-1241 Betriebs- und Marktwirtschaft im Gartenbau
0303-125X One World
0303-1268 Euromicro Journal
0303-1276 Bulletin de Liaison de la Recherche en Informatique et Automatique
0303-1829 Centro Latinoamericano de Demografia. Notas de Poblacion
0303-190X Philippine National Bibliography
0303-223X Bilten Dokumentacije. Savremena Organizacija i Ekonomika Radnih Organizacija
0303-2361 Itogi Nauki i Tekhniki: Tekhnologiia Organicheskikh Veshchestv
0303-240X Revue de l'Energie
0303-2434 I T C Journal
0303-2485 Kuukausikatsaus Suomen Ilmastoon
0303-2493 Informationen zur Raumentwicklung
0303-254X Monographs in Anaesthesiology
0303-2582 Indian Journal of Clinical Psychology
0303-2590 Roentgen Technology
0303-2647 Biosystems
0303-2728 Al-Ahram Index
0303-2876 Indonesia. Badan Tenaga Atom Nasional. Majalah B A T A N
0303-2906 Prayasa
0303-2949 Gunakesari†
0303-3007 International Journal of Korean Studies
0303-3171 Man and Society
0303-321X Sangkakala Peradilan
0303-3309 I S O Catalogue
0303-3317 I S O Annual Review
0303-3848 Brass Bulletin
0303-3856 Revolutionary World
0303-3899 Educational Documentation and Information†
0303-3902 Interface
0303-3910 Irish Journal of Psychology
0303-3929 Mathematical Programming Studies
0303-4100 Finnish Chemical Letters
0303-4151 International Commission for the Northwest Atlantic Fisheries. Annual Report *see* 0704-4798
0303-4208 Tropenmedizin und Parasitologie
0303-4259 Psychiatrische Praxis
0303-4283 Leben und Umwelt
0303-4305 Innere Medizin
0303-4461 Oesterreichische Krankenpflegezeitschrift
0303-4550 Bulletin of Reprints
0303-4569 Andrologia
0303-4577 I M B I S
0303-5220 Reproduccion
0303-5344 Hungary. Kozponti Statisztikai Hivatal. Teruleti Statisztikai Evkonyv
0303-5980 Studia Leibnitiana. Supplementa
0303-6200 Intensivmedizinische Praxis
0303-6251 Intensivmedizin
0303-6758 Royal Society of New Zealand. Journal
0303-6812 Journal of Mathematical Biology
0303-6847 Blood Vessels
0303-691X West African Journal of Pharmacology and Drug Research
0303-6936 Hydrological Sciences Bulletin
0303-6979 Journal of Clinical Periodontology
0303-6987 Journal of Cutaneous Pathology
0303-6995 Journal of Neural Transmission. Supplement
0303-7002 Kerrygold International
0303-7207 Molecular and Cellular Endocrinology
0303-7479 Groupement Europeen pour la Recherche Scientifique en Stomatologie et Odontologie. Bulletin
0303-7584 Instituto de Tonantzintla. Boletin
0303-7657 Revista Brasileira de Saude Ocupacional
0303-7932 Majalah Kedokteran Surabaya
0303-805X I S O Bulletin
0303-8106 Audiology Japan
0303-8157 Poznan Studies in the Philosophy of the Sciences and the Humanities†
0303-8173 Acta Medica Austriaca
0303-8300 Social Indicators Research
0303-8432 Folia Allergologica et Immunologica Clinica
0303-8971 Institut Economique Agricole. Cahiers
0303-9021 Vlaams Diergeneeskundig Tijdschrift
0303-903X Belgium. Rijksstation voor Sierplantenteelt. Mededelingen
0303-9056 Belgium. Rijksstation voor Landbouwtechniek. Mededelingen
0303-9072 Belgium. Rijksstation voor Zeevisserij. Mededelingen
0303-9099 Annales de Gembloux
0303-9145 Institut Belge pour l'Amelioration de la Betterave. Publication Trimestrielle
0303-9153 Jardin Botanique National de Belgique. Bulletin
0303-9676 Estudios Sociales Centroamericanos
0304-0003 LIAS; Sources and Documents Relating to the Early Modern History of Ideas.
0304-0062 U N I S I S T Boletin de Informacion
0304-0070 U N I S I S T Newsletter. Russian Edition
0304-0089 Yearbook of World Problems and Human Potential
0304-0100 I I C A en America
0304-0119 Indice Agricola de America Latina y el Caribe
0304-0313 Patologia e Clinica Ostetrica e Ginecologica
0304-0704 Planeur
0304-0712 Amsterdam Studies in the Theory and History of Linguistic Science. Series 1: Amsterdam Classics in Linguistics, 1800-1925
0304-0720 Amsterdam Studies in the Theory and History of Linguistic Science. Series 3: Studies in the History of Linguistics
0304-0763 Amsterdam Studies in the Theory and History of Linguistic Science. Series 4: Current Issues in Linguistic Theory
0304-078X Cultures
0304-095X Bangladesh Development Studies
0304-1131 Agriculture and Environment
0304-1158 Indian School of Mines. Annual Report
0304-1204 Free China Today†
0304-1263 Iceland Review
0304-1298 Bulletin Signaletique. Part 161: Structure de l'Etat Condense. Cristallographie
0304-1301 Bulletin Signaletique-Bibliographie des Sciences de la Terre. Section 221. Gisements Metalliques et Non Metalliques *changed to* Bulletin Signaletique-Bibliographie des Sciences de la Terre. Section 221. Gisements Metalliques et Non Metalliques. Economie Miniere
0304-131X Acta Pathologica et Microbiologica Scandinavica. Section B: Microbiology
0304-1328 Acta Pathologica et Microbiologia Scandinavica. Section C: Immunology
0304-1409 Atheist
0304-162X Times of India. Index
0304-1743 Norwegian Maritime Research
0304-1786 Prospect
0304-2154 Akademie der Wissenschaften der DDR. Jahrbuch
0304-2162 Mois Economique et Financier
0304-2170 Indonesian Quarterly
0304-2251 Malaysian Branch of the Royal Asiatic Society Journal
0304-2308 Pesquisa e Planejamento *see* 0100-0551
0304-2421 Theory and Society
0304-2499 Tecnica Pesquera
0304-2502 Pastizales
0304-2529 Actividades en Turrialba
0304-2553 Bangladesh Economic Review *see* 0304-095X
0304-2685 Ciencia & Tropico
0304-2839 Documentacion e Informacion para el Desarrollo Agricola†
0304-2863 Colloquium Internationale
0304-2871 European Organization for Nuclear Research. Liste des Publications Scientifiques/List of Scientific Publications
0304-288X C E R N Courier
0304-2898 C E R N School of Computing. Proceedings
0304-2901 C E R N Annual Report
0304-324X Gerontology
0304-3282 Organization for Economic Cooperation and Development. Guide to Legislation on Restrictive Business Practices. Supplements
0304-3312 Organization for Economic Cooperation and Development. Labour Statistics/Statistiques de la Population Active
0304-3320 Research on Transport Economics/Recherche en Matiere d'Economie des Transports
0304-3371 O E C D Financial Statistics
0304-3479 Russian Literature
0304-3568 Experimental Cell Biology
0304-3584 Actualidades Biologicas
0304-3681 Extern
0304-3738 Organization for Economic Cooperation and Development. Quarterly National Accounts Bulletin/Bulletin des Comptes Nationaux Trimestriels
0304-3746 Agro-Ecosystems
0304-3754 Alternatives: A Journal of World Policy
0304-3762 Applied Animal Ethology
0304-3770 Aquatic Botany
0304-3797 European Journal of Engineering Education
0304-3800 Ecological Modelling
0304-3835 Cancer Letters
0304-3843 Hyperfine Interactions
0304-3851 Journal of Applied Science and Engineering Section A. Electrical Power and Information Systems†
0304-386X Hydrometallurgy
0304-3878 Journal of Development Economics
0304-3886 Journal of Electrostatics
0304-3894 Journal of Hazardous Materials
0304-3908 Journal of Industrial Aerodynamics *changed to* Journal of Wind Engineering Industrial Aerodynamics
0304-3924 Landscape Planning
0304-3932 Journal of Monetary Economics
0304-3940 Neuroscience Letters
0304-3959 Pain
0304-3967 Resource Recovery and Conservation *changed to* Resource and Conservation
0304-3975 Theoretical Computer Science
0304-3991 Ultramicroscopy
0304-4009 Urban Ecology
0304-4017 Veterinary Parasitology
0304-4025 Wave Electronics
0304-4033 Revista Centroamericana de Nutricion y Ciencias de Alimentos†
0304-4041 Excerpta Medica. Section 40: Drug Dependence
0304-405X Journal of Financial Economics
0304-4068 Journal of Mathematical Economics
0304-4076 Journal of Econometrics
0304-4092 Dialectical Anthropology
0304-4114 Mass Emergencies†
0304-4130 European Journal of Political Research
0304-4130 European Journal of Operational Research
0304-4149 Stochastic Processes and Their Applications
0304-4157 B B A-Reviews on Biomembranes
0304-4165 B B A-General Subjects
0304-4173 B B A Reviews on Bioenergetics
0304-4181 Journal of Medieval History
0304-419X B B A-Reviews on Cancer
0304-4203 Marine Chemistry
0304-4211 Plant Science Letters
0304-4238 Scientia Horticulturae
0304-4246 Contributions to Gynecology and Obstetrics
0304-4254 Pediatric and Adolescent Endocrinology
0304-4262 Progress in Reproductive Biology
0304-4270 INSEAD Address Book
0304-4289 Pramana
0304-4556 Iranian Journal of Public Health
0304-5102 Journal of Molecular Catalysis
0304-5161 Instituto de Investigaciones Pesqueras. Informes Tecnicos
0304-5242 Journal of Plantation Crops
0304-5250 Indian Journal of Ecology

0304-5307 National Museums and Monuments of Rhodesia. Occasional Papers. Series A: Human Sciences. *changed to* National Museums and Monuments Administration. Occasional Papers. Series A: Human Sciences
0304-5315 National Museums and Monuments of Rhodesia. Occasional Papers. Series B: Natural Sciences *changed to* National Museums and Monuments Administration. Occasional Papers. Series B: Natural Sciences
0304-5323 Museum Memoir
0304-5374 Comparative Animal Nutrition
0304-5439 C I M M Y T Report on Wheat Improvement
0304-5447 C I M M Y T Today
0304-5463 C I M M Y T Review
0304-548X C I M M Y T Report on Maize Improvement
0304-551X C I M M Y T Information Bulletin
0304-5609 Ciencia e Investigacion Agraria
0304-5617 Investigacion Agricola
0304-5692 Zaire. Institut National de la Statistique. Annuaire des Statistiques du Commerce Exterieur
0304-5714 Institut Oceanographique. Memoires
0304-5757 Conjonction
0304-5765 Tropical Grain Legume Bulletin
0304-5935 Abstracts of Geochronology and Isotope Geology
0304-5951 Abstracts on Tropical Agriculture
0304-5978 Gewestelijke Economische Raad voor Vlaanderen. Activiteitsverslag
0304-6125 Afghanistan Journal
0304-6133 Afghanistan Republic Annual
0304-615X Africanus
0304-6184 Madhya Pradesh. Directorate of Agriculture. Agricultural Statistics
0304-6214 A I I S Quarterly Newsletter
0304-6451 Association of Urban Authorities. Annual Bulletin
0304-6729 Arab Fund for Economic and Social Development. Annual Report
0304-6818 Central Sericultural Research and Training Institute. Annual Report
0304-6907 Cotton Corporation of India. Annual Report
0304-6966 Deposit Insurance Corporation. Annual Report: Directors' Report, Balance Sheet and Accounts
0304-7032 Indian Council of Historical Research. Annual Report
0304-7067 Indian Veterinary Research Institute. Annual Report
0304-7083 Institute of Secretariat Training and Management. Annual Report
0304-7091 International Centre for Theoretical Physics. Annual Report
0304-7164 Jammu & Kashmir Minerals Limited. Annual Report
0304-7245 Madhya Pradesh State Agro-Industries Development Corporation Ltd. Annual Report
0304-727X Liberia. Ministry of Finance. Annual Report
0304-7296 Liberia. Ministry of Lands and Mines. Annual Report
0304-730X Liberia. Ministry of Local Government, Rural Development & Urban Reconstruction. Annual Report
0304-7326 Liberia. Ministry of Public Works. Annual Report
0304-7423 Israel Oceanographic and Limnological Research. Annual Report
0304-7628 Focus on Rhodesia
0304-8101 Punjab National Bank. Annual Report
0304-8594 Architects Trade Journal
0304-8608 Archives of Virology
0304-8632 Art Spectrum *see* 0004-3230
0304-8683 Asiryada
0304-8705 Astronautical Research
0304-8713 Austria Today
0304-8721 Automobil
0304-8845 P T L†
0304-8853 Journal of Magnetism and Magnetic Materials
0304-8942 Food and Nutrition
0304-9272 Brahmana-Gaurava
0304-9558 Indian Institute of History of Medicine. Bulletin
0304-9566 Osmania Medical College. Institute of History of Medicine. Bulletin *see* 0304-9558
0304-9701 International Forum on Information and Documentation
0304-971X Revista de Biologia del Uruguay
0305-0009 Journal of Child Language
0305-0017 Geocom Programs *see* 0098-3004
0305-0033 Aslib Information
0305-0041 Cambridge Philosophical Society. Mathematical Proceedings.
0305-005X Emergency Post
0305-0068 Comparative Education
0305-0076 Review of Applied Entomology. Series A: Agricultural
0305-0084 Review of Applied Entomology. Series B: Medical and Veterinary
0305-0165 Current Clinical Chemistry
0305-0254 Sun at Work in Britain
0305-0262 Waste Materials Biodegradation Research Titles
0305-0270 Journal of Biogeography
0305-0297 Labour Leader†
0305-0319 Cosmetic World News
0305-0351 C.I.H. Descriptions of Plant-Parasitic Nematodes
0305-036X Arabian Studies
0305-0424 News from Victoria, Australia
0305-0440 Historical Breechloading Smallarms Association. Journal
0305-0467 Freezer Foods
0305-0483 Omega
0305-0491 Comparative Biochemistry and Physiology. Part B: Comparative Biochemistry
0305-0513 Offshore Abstracts
0305-0548 Computers & Operations Research
0305-0602 Power & Sail
0305-0629 International Interactions
0305-0653 Work Study & O and M Abstracts
0305-0661 Marketing & Distribution Abstracts
0305-067X Personnel & Training Abstracts
0305-0734 Middle East
0305-0777 Refrigeration and Air Conditioning Year Book
0305-0785 Scottish Literary Journal
0305-0904 Thomas Cook News *changed to* World of Thomas Cook
0305-0920 Appropriate Technology
0305-0963 Radical Science Journal
0305-0998 Norwegian Chamber of Commerce. Year Book and Directory of Members
0305-1129 Stock Exchange, London. Members and Firms of the Stock Exchange
0305-1137 L B A Handbook
0305-1471 N M M News
0305-1498 Oxford Literary Review *changed to* Oxford Literary Review: A Post-Structuralist Journal
0305-1536 Home and School
0305-1552 Commonwealth Bureau of Agricultural Economics. Annotated Bibliographies Series A
0305-1552 Commonwealth Bureau of Agricultural Economics. Annotated Bibliographies. Series B: Agricultural Policy and Rural Development in Africa
0305-165X Librarians for Social Change
0305-1668 Systems International
0305-1706 Film Dope
0305-1714 British Library Research and Development Newsletter
0305-1811 Journal of Immunogenetics
0305-182X Journal of Oral Rehabilitation
0305-1838 Mammal Review
0305-1846 Neuropathology and Applied Neurobiology
0305-1862 Child: Care, Health and Development
0305-1870 Clinical and Experimental Pharmacology and Physiology
0305-1897 Geo Abstracts A (Landforms & the Quaternary)
0305-1900 Geo Abstracts B (Climatology and Hydrology)
0305-1919 Geo Abstracts C (Economic Geography)
0305-1927 Geo Abstracts D(Social & Historical Geography)
0305-1935 Geo Abstracts E (Sedimentology)
0305-1943 Geo Abstracts F (Regional and Community Planning)
0305-1951 Geo Abstracts G (Remote Sensing Photogrammetry and Cartography)
0305-196X Ecological Abstracts
0305-1978 Biochemical Systematics and Ecology
0305-2001 Royal Observatory, Edinburgh. Publications
0305-215X Engineering Optimization
0305-2176 I.C.E. Abstracts
0305-2222 European Rubber Journal
0305-2230 Incentive Marketing & Sales Promotion
0305-2249 Audio Visual
0305-2257 National Electronics Review
0305-2303 South East Hampshire Geneaological Society. Journal *see* 0306-6843
0305-2346 Institute of Physics, London. Conference Series. Proceedings
0305-2524 Commonwealth Bureau of Soils. Annotated Bibliographies
0305-2680 Descriptions of Plant Viruses
0305-2729 C I H Keys to the Nematode Parasites of Vertebrates
0305-3040 Applied Ecology Abstracts *changed to* Ecology Abstracts
0305-3091 Electrocomponent Science & Technology
0305-3105 Water
0305-3121 Machinery's Buyers' Guide
0305-3199 Adhesives Directory
0305-3210 Middle East Review
0305-3253 Higher Education Exchange *changed to* Educational International
0305-3504 MINTEL
0305-3555 Fabian Research Series
0305-3601 Communication & Broadcasting
0305-3679 Essex County Library. Essex Union List of Serials
0305-3695 Corporate Planning Journal *changed to* Local Government Policy Making
0305-3709 Bulk: Storage, Movement, Control
0305-3849 Par Golf
0305-3873 Surface and Defect Properties of Solids *changed to* Chemical Physics of Solids and Their Surfaces
0305-4039 Bale Catalogue of Palestine and Israel Postage Stamps
0305-408X C I R I A Report
0305-411X Council of Legal Education. Calendar
0305-4136 Hospital Update
0305-4179 Burns
0305-4233 Communication
0305-4322 Ditchley Journal
0305-4349 Druglink
0305-439X Processing
0305-4403 Journal of Archaeological Science
0305-4438 Music and Liturgy
0305-4470 Journal of Physics A: Mathematical and General
0305-4543 Spon's Mechanical & Electrical Services Price Book
0305-4608 Journal of Physics F: Metal Physics
0305-4616 Journal of Physics G: Nuclear Physics
0305-4624 Physics in Technology
0305-4659 Northamptonshire Archaeology
0305-4756 Camden History Review
0305-4829 Heat Treatment of Metals
0305-4934 Ornamental Horticulture
0305-4985 Oxford Review of Education
0305-5000 Dental Update
0305-5167 British Library Journal
0305-5183 British Library. Lending Division. Index of Conference Proceedings Received
0305-5280 Council for British Archaeology. Current Offprints and Reports
0305-5426 Programming Index†
0305-5698 Educational Studies
0305-5728 Vine
0305-5752 Property Studies in the U.K. and Overseas
0305-5795 Devon Archaeological Society. Proceedings
0305-5892 Register of Thoroughbred Stallions
0305-5914 Geographical Papers
0305-5981 Omnibus
0305-6104 Independent Broadcasting
0305-6147 Radical Education
0305-6155 R. U. S. I. and Brassey's Defence Yearbook
0305-6198 Saturated Heterocyclic Chemistry
0305-6252 Minority Rights Group. Reports
0305-635X Office Equipment Index
0305-6473 Civil Engineering (London)
0305-6481 I R C S Journal of Medical Science
0305-649X I R C S Medical Science: Classified List
0305-6503 B L L Review *see* 0140-2773
0305-652X Pick
0305-6562 Scotlands Regions
0305-6589 Laxton's Building Price Book
0305-6651 I R C S Medical Science: Library Compendium
0305-666X I R C S Medical Science: Immunology and Allergy
0305-6678 I R C S Medical Science: Alimentary System
0305-6686 I R C S Medical Science: Anatomy and Human Biology
0305-6694 I R C S Medical Science: Anesthetics†
0305-6708 I R C S Medical Science: Biochemistry
0305-6716 I R C S Medical Science: Biomedical Technology
0305-6724 I R C S Medical Science: Cancer
0305-6732 I R C S Medical Science: Cardiovascular System
0305-6740 I R C S Medical Science: Cell and Membrane Biology
0305-6759 I R C S Medical Science: Clinical Pharmacology and Therapeutics
0305-6767 I R C S Medical Science: Connective Tissue, Skin and Bone
0305-6775 I R C S Medical Science: Dentistry and Oral Biology
0305-6783 I R C S Medical Science: Endocrine System
0305-6791 I R C S Medical Science: The Eye
0305-6805 I R C S Medical Science: Hematology
0305-6813 I R C S Medical Science: Kidneys and Urinary System
0305-6821 I R C S Medical Science: Metabolism and Nutrition
0305-683X I R C S Medical Science: Microbiology, Parasitology and Infectious Diseases
0305-6848 I R C S Medical Science: Neurobiology and Neurophysiology†
0305-6856 I R C S Medical Science: Neurology and Neurosurgery†
0305-6864 I R C S Medical Science: Pediatrics†
0305-6872 I R C S Medical Science: Pharmacology
0305-6880 I R C S Medical Science: Physiology
0305-6899 I R C S Medical Science: Psychiatry and Clinical Psychology†
0305-6902 I R C S Medical Science: Psychology†
0305-6910 I R C S Medical Science: Radiology and Nuclear Medicine†
0305-6929 I R C S Medical Science: Reproduction, Obstetrics and Gynecology
0305-6937 I R C S Medical Science: Respiratory System
0305-6945 I R C S Medical Science: Social and Occupational Medicine
0305-6953 I R C S Medical Science: Surgery and Transplantation
0305-6961 I R C S Medical Science: Veterinary Science†
0305-697X Inorganic Chemistry of the Main Group Elements
0305-6996 B K S T S Journal
0305-7054 Consumer Education *see* 0307-2053
0305-7070 Journal of Southern African Studies
0305-7100 Kemps Music and Record Industry Year Book International *changed to* Kemps International Music and Record Yearbook

0305-716X Journal of Flour & Animal Feed Milling *changed to* Milling Feed and Fertiliser
0305-7178 Music Trades International.
0305-7224 Psychoenergetic Systems
0305-7232 Cancer Biochemistry - Biophysics
0305-7240 Journal of Moral Education
0305-7259 Mathematics in School
0305-7291 Education for Development
0305-7321 Brushes International
0305-733X Blinds and Shutters
0305-7348 Ideas†
0305-7356 Psychology of Music
0305-7372 Cancer Treatment Reviews
0305-7399 Clinical Oncology
0305-7429 Modern China Studies. International Bulletin
0305-7445 International Journal of Nautical Archaeology and Underwater Exploration
0305-7453 Journal of Antimicrobial Chemotherapy
0305-7488 Journal of Historical Geography
0305-7496 Educational Administration
0305-750X World Development
0305-7526 Special Education: Forward Trends
0305-7623 Ceramic Industries Journal
0305-7631 British Journal of in-Service Education
0305-764X Cambridge Journal of Education
0305-7658 Conference
0305-7666 Studies in Design, Education and Craft *changed to* Studies in Design, Education and Craft
0305-7682 British Exports. Export Services. *changed to* British Exports
0305-7712 Environmental Chemistry
0305-7755 Teaching English
0305-7798 Sheet Metal Industries Year Book
0305-781X Association of British Theological and Philosophical Libraries. Bulletin
0305-7828 Aether
0305-7844 Fire Prevention Science and Technology
0305-7860 Therapeutic Education†
0305-7879 Vocational Aspect of Education
0305-7887 British Library. Board. Annual Report
0305-7917 Spectrum
0305-7925 Compare
0305-795X Scottish Journal of Adult Education
0305-7984 University of Manchester. School of Education. Gazette
0305-7992 Proof
0305-8018 Teaching Geography
0305-8026 British Journal of International Studies
0305-8069 C B I Overseas Reports
0305-8077 A B C Air/Rail Europe
0305-8107 Journal of Occupational Psychology
0305-8123 Brewery Manual and Who's Who in British Brewing
0305-8131 B C R A Review
0305-814X Reading in Political Economy
0305-8174 Offshore Fishing
0305-8182 Jabberwocky
0305-8190 University of Oxford. School of Geography. Research Papers
0305-8220 Regular Savings Plans *changed to* Unit-Linked Savings Plans
0305-8255 Inorganic Reaction Mechanisms
0305-8298 Millennium
0305-8336 N E R C News Journal
0305-8344 New Review
0305-8468 Focus on International and Comparative Librarianship
0305-8476 European Law Digest
0305-8549 Devon Historian
0305-859X British Cave Research Association. Transactions
0305-862X African Research and Documentation
0305-8646 University of Glasgow. Institute of Latin American Studies. Occasional Papers
0305-8670 Common Market News
0305-8697 Awards for Commonwealth University Staff *see* 0144-4611
0305-8751 Home and Freezer Digest
0305-876X Offshore Engineer
0305-8913 British Journal of Teacher Education *see* 0260-7476
0305-8921 Tolley's Income Tax
0305-8964 Tropical Storage Abstracts *see* 0564-3325
0305-8972 M I R A Abstracts *see* 0309-0817
0305-8980 Glasgow Archaeological Journal
0305-9006 Progress in Planning
0305-9014 Public Finance and Accountancy
0305-9022 Guslar
0305-9049 Oxford Bulletin of Economics and Statistics
0305-9154 Plant Growth Regulator Abstracts
0305-9162 Maize Quality Protein Abstracts
0305-9189 State Librarian
0305-9219 Viking Society for Northern Research. Saga Book
0305-9235 Fluid Flow Measurement Abstracts
0305-9243 Omnibus Magazine
0305-9251 Theatrefacts *changed to* Theatrefacts/Theatrelogs
0305-926X Housman Society Journal
0305-9286 Association of Christian Teachers. Digest.
0305-9324 Fellowship for Freedom in Medicine. Newsletter
0305-9332 Industrial Law Journal
0305-9340 Health and Welfare Libraries Quarterly
0305-9367 Insurance†
0305-9421 Quarry Management and Products
0305-9456 Civil Engineering Hydraulics Abstracts
0305-9499 Applecon
0305-9529 New Internationalist
0305-9529 New Internationalist
0305-9537 Cremation Society Handbook and Directory of Crematoria
0305-9545 Carbonization Research Report
0305-9553 Standard Chartered Review
0305-9561 Eurolaw Commercial Intelligence
0305-9596 I E E Medical Electronics Monographs
0305-9642 Hospital Life
0305-9669 Family Practitioner Services
0305-9707 Alkaloids
0305-9715 Aromatic and Heteroaromatic Chemistry
0305-9723 Colloid Science
0305-9731 Chemical Thermodynamics
0305-974X Dielectric and Related Molecular Processes
0305-9758 Electron Spin Resonance
0305-9766 Electronic Structure & Magnetism of Inorganic Compounds
0305-9774 Inorganic Chemistry of the Transition Elements
0305-9782 Molecular Spectroscopy
0305-9790 Molecular Structure by Diffraction Methods
0305-9804 Nuclear Magnetic Resonance
0305-9812 Organic Compounds of Sulphur, Selenium and Tellurium
0305-9839 Hard Cheese
0305-9855 A L L C Bulletin
0305-988X Modern Purchasing
0305-9898 Borthwick Institute Bulletin
0305-9960 Statistical Mechanics
0305-9979 Electrochemistry
0305-9987 Mass Spectrometry
0305-9995 Theoretical Chemistry
0306-0004 Amino-Acids, Peptides and Proteins
0306-0012 Chemical Society, London. Reviews
0306-0020 Mantatoforos
0306-0039 I S M E C Bulletin
0306-0128 Dance Gazette
0306-0152 Great Britain. Property Services Agency. Construction References
0306-0160 Leicestershire, Northamptonshire & Rutland Farmer
0306-0179 Engineering Capacity
0306-0195 Poetry Post
0306-0209 Naval Architect
0306-0233 Health Services Manpower Review
0306-0241 Dundee Tayside
0306-0284 Bibliography of Insecticide Materials of Vegetable Origin†
0306-0322 African Book Publishing Record
0306-0349 Airtrade
0306-0357 Organ Club Journal
0306-039X Pharmacology and Therapeutics. Part B. General and Systematic Pharmacology *see* 0163-7258
0306-0403 Swimming Teacher
0306-042X B M S -Biomedical Mass Spectrometry
0306-0438 Thermal Analysis Abstracts
0306-0462 Craft Teacher News *changed to* Craft, Design & Technology News
0306-0497 Self & Society
0306-0519 Furniture Manufacturer
0306-056X Street Research Bulletin
0306-0586 High-Speed Ground Transportation and Urban Rapid Transit Systems Bibliography Service
0306-0594 Air-Cushion and Hydrofoil Systems Bibliography Service
0306-0624 University of York. Institute of Advanced Architectural Studies. Research Papers
0306-0632 Progress in Food & Nutrition Science
0306-0691 Screen Education
0306-0748 Textiles
0306-0772 Facts
0306-0837 Llafur
0306-0845 Urban History Yearbook
0306-0861 Scottish Small Presses
0306-087X Theological and Religious Index
0306-090X Civic Trust News
0306-0942 Service Point
0306-1000 B A I E News
0306-1043 Great Britain. Departments of the Environment and Transport. Library. Library Bulletin.
0306-1051 Antiques Trade Gazette
0306-1078 Early Music
0306-1124 Commonwealth Bibliographies
0306-1132 Football News
0306-1140 Romford Record
0306-1256 Gallery
0306-1264 A B L C News
0306-1280 Lancashire
0306-1353 Annual Reports on Analytical Atomic Spectroscopy
0306-1353 Society for Analytical Chemistry. Annual Reports on Analytical Atomic Spectroscopy
0306-1396 Chemical Society. Analytical Division. Proceedings
0306-140X Pennine Platform
0306-1426 Women's Report†
0306-1450 B I A S Journal
0306-1477 Voices of North Devon
0306-154X After the Battle
0306-1582 Poultry Abstracts
0306-1620 S W
0306-1639 Digest of English-Language Textile Literature *changed to* Textile Digest
0306-1701 Emigrante
0306-1728 Schedule of Postgraduate Courses in United Kingdom Universities
0306-1736 Scholarships Guide for Commonwealth Postgraduate Students
0306-1841 EuroClay
0306-1884 New Towns Bulletin
0306-1892 Workers' Control Bulletin
0306-1914 Current Information in the Construction Industry
0306-1922 Procurement Weekly
0306-1973 Literature & History
0306-1981 I L E A Contact
0306-2015 Children's Literature Abstracts
0306-204X European Glass Directory and Buyer's Guide
0306-2074 Spore Research
0306-2082 Journal of Musicological Research
0306-2090 Experimental Embryology and Teratology†
0306-2104 Liquid Chromatography Abstracts
0306-2163 Industrial Cases Reports
0306-2279 European Industrial & Commercial Review
0306-2295 Outlook
0306-2309 Offshore Services *changed to* Offshore Services & Technology
0306-2392 Undercurrents
0306-2406 Certified Accountant
0306-2414 Natural Gas for Commerce†
0306-2465 A T L A Abstracts
0306-2473 Yearbook of English Studies
0306-2481 Sociological Analysis & Theory
0306-252X Paper Technology and Industry
0306-2597 Liquid Crystals Abstracts†
0306-2619 Applied Energy
0306-2643 International Review of Psycho-Analysis
0306-2686 Plant Foods for Man *changed to* Journal of Plant Foods
0306-2708 Society for General Microbiology Proceedings *see* 0142-7547
0306-2740 Queen Mary College. Department of Geography. Occasional Papers
0306-283X Quaker Service *see* 0141-5352
0306-2864 Diagnostics Index
0306-2880 Reprographics Quarterly
0306-2899 Auto Accessory Retailer & Automotive Parts Review
0306-2899 Auto Accessory Retailer *see* 0306-2899
0306-2910 I B C A M Journal
0306-2945 Lloyd's Maritime & Commercial Law Quarterly
0306-2988 Stainless Steel Industry
0306-3003 Intestinal Absorption
0306-3046 Spon's Architects' & Builders' Price Book
0306-3054 Spon's Landscape Handbook *see* 0144-8404
0306-3062 Recreation Management Yearbook *see* 0144-624X
0306-3070 Journal of General Management
0306-3089 Financial Times Tax Newsletter
0306-3127 Social Studies of Science
0306-3151 Gwynedd Archives Service. Bulletin
0306-3194 Building Trades Journal
0306-3194 Guildhall Studies in London History
0306-3224 Contents Pages in Management
0306-3240 District Councils Review
0306-3275 Biochemical Journal. Part 2: Molecular Aspects
0306-3283 Biochemical Journal. Part 1: Cellular Aspects
0306-3291 Current Advances in Ecological Sciences
0306-3313 N. A. P. V. Newsletter
0306-3321 Guerrilheiro†
0306-333X Electronic Production
0306-3372 Bibliography of Vertebrate Paleontology and Related Subjects *changed to* Bibliography of Vertebrate Paleontology
0306-3380 British Geomorphological Research Group. Technical Bulletin
0306-3410 Jane's Infantry Weapons
0306-3429 Career Accountant
0306-3437 Footwear World†
0306-3453 Metal Science
0306-3461 Meridian†
0306-347X Marine Week
0306-3534 European Plastics News
0306-3569 Great Britain. Civil Aviation Authority. Annual Report and Accounts
0306-3577 Great Britain. Civil Aviation Authority. C A A Monthly Statistics
0306-3585 Heating, Ventilating and Air Conditioning Year Book
0306-3593 Boat Equipment Buyers' Guide
0306-3593 Boatbuilders' & Chandlers' Directory of Suppliers *see* 0306-3593
0306-3607 Reinforced Plastics Congress
0306-3623 General Pharmacology
0306-3631 Journal of Commonwealth & Comparative Politics
0306-364X Renewable Energy Bulletin
0306-3666 Men of Achievement
0306-3674 British Journal of Sports Medicine
0306-3704 British Journal of Law and Society
0306-3712 Brass Band Review†
0306-3763 N C A V A E. E D U. Technical Reports
0306-3860 St. Thomas's Gazette
0306-3879 Double Glazing - Domestic, Industrial & Commercial
0306-3909 Creative Camera International Year Book *changed to* Creative Camera Collection
0306-3933 Hambro Euromoney Directory

0306-395X Petroleum Economist
0306-3968 Race and Class
0306-3992 Equals *see* 0140-9506
0306-400X International Water Power and Dam Construction
0306-4018 I P P F News
0306-4034 University of Birmingham. Centre for Urban and Regional Studies. Research Memorandum
0306-4069 Hydraulic Pneumatic Mechanical Power
0306-4077 Bindery Data Index†
0306-4107 British Theatre Directory
0306-4123 Board Manufacture & Processing
0306-414X European Rubber Directory
0306-4212 Foundry Yearbook
0306-4220 Index on Censorship
0306-4336 International Tourism Quarterly
0306-4379 Information Systems
0306-4395 English Harpsichord Magazine
0306-4395 Harpsichord Magazine
0306-4484 Current Advances in Plant Science
0306-4492 Comparative Biochemistry and Physiology. Part C: Comparative Pharmacology
0306-4522 Neuroscience
0306-4530 Psychoneuroendocrinology
0306-4549 Annals of Nuclear Energy
0306-4565 Journal of Thermal Biology
0306-4573 Information Processing and Management
0306-4581 Ethics in Science and Medicine *see* 0271-5392
0306-4603 Addictive Behaviors
0306-462X Life and Health†
0306-4824 World Trade Union Movement
0306-4859 Society for Lincolnshire History and Archaeology. Annual Report and Statement of Accounts
0306-4867 Motor Cycle and Cycle Trader Year Book
0306-4875 Chemical Society, London, Annual Report of Council and Accounts
0306-4964 Foundation
0306-4980 I D F Bulletin
0306-5030 Manchester Free Press
0306-5065 British Mensa Newsletter
0306-5103 Collect Channel Islands Stamps
0306-512X New Humanist
0306-5154 Shirley Institute Publications. S: Series
0306-5162 European Market Report†
0306-5197 Chigwell Local History Society. Transactions
0306-5251 British Journal of Clinical Pharmacology
0306-526X Metallurgist & Materials Technologist
0306-5278 Northern Scotland
0306-5286 Road Traffic Reports
0306-5332 Museums Association Information Sheets
0306-5413 Great Britain. Commission on Industrial Relations. Annual Report
0306-5456 British Journal of Obstetrics & Gynaecology
0306-5480 H. G. Wells Society Newsletter
0306-5499 Institute of United States Studies Monographs
0306-5502 European Plastics Buyers Guide
0306-5529 Prospect
0306-5537 Key Abstracts - Solid State Devices
0306-5553 Key Abstracts - Systems Theory
0306-5561 Key Abstracts - Power Transmission & Distribution
0306-557X Key Abstracts - Electronic Circuits
0306-5588 Key Abstracts - Communications Technology
0306-5596 Key Abstracts - Industrial Power & Control Systems
0306-5618 Sales Engineering *see* 0140-5179
0306-5626 Revolutionary Communist
0306-5634 Air International
0306-5677 Catholic Directory for Scotland
0306-5693 Esperanto News
0306-5707 Challenge†
0306-5723 Outdoors
0306-5758 Manchester Chamber of Commerce and Industry. Yearbook
0306-5766 References to Scientific Literature on Fire
0306-5774 Mackintosh Yearbook of West European Electronics Data
0306-5790 Anglesey Antiquarian Society Transactions
0306-5839 Mobile Home & Holiday Caravan
0306-5928 British Music Yearbook
0306-6061 Political Social Economic Review
0306-610X Crafts
0306-6118 Security Surveyor
0306-6142 C A T M O G
0306-6150 Journal of Peasant Studies
0306-6185 D I A Yearbook - Design Action
0306-6193 Educational Yearbook†
0306-624X International Journal of Offender Therapy and Comparative Criminology
0306-6274 Motor Report International
0306-6304 Language Teaching and Linguistics Abstracts
0306-6312 750 Bulletin
0306-6444 Gas Engineering & Management
0306-6452 Highway Engineer
0306-6479 New Law Journal
0306-6495 Practical Hi-Fi & Audio
0306-6509 Solid Wastes
0306-6517 International Flavours and Food Additives *see* 0143-8441
0306-6541 Pram and Nursery Trader Year Book *see* 0082-5611
0306-6568 Sea Angler
0306-6614 Bucks and Berks Countryside
0306-6649 W R C Information
0306-6673 Personnel and Training Management Yearbook
0306-672X Hertfordshire Countryside
0306-6746 Progress in Water Technology
0306-6800 Journal of Medical Ethics
0306-6843 Hampshire Family Historian
0306-6886 Computer Report
0306-6908 Middle East Week
0306-7041 British Airways Executive
0306-7068 Monotype Pictorial†
0306-7076 British Ceramic Review
0306-719X Farm Business Review
0306-7262 Reform
0306-7297 Journal of Human Movement Studies
0306-7319 International Journal of Environmental Analytical Chemistry
0306-7327 Irrigation and Drainage Abstracts
0306-7335 Challenger Society. Newsletter
0306-7351 Ocean Energy†
0306-7408 University of Strathclyde, Fraser of Allander Institute for Research on the Scottish Economy. Research Monograph
0306-7432 Association of Teachers of Russian.Newsletter
0306-7440 Traditional Music
0306-7475 Antiquarian Book Monthly Review
0306-7556 Crop Physiology Abstracts
0306-7564 Dynamica
0306-7580 Small-Animal Abstracts
0306-7602 Broadcast
0306-7645 Just Peace
0306-7696 International Newsletter on Chemical Education
0306-770X Oil World Statistics
0306-7734 International Statistical Review
0306-7858 Tape Teacher
0306-7866 University of Strathclyde. Fraser of Allander Institute for Research on the Scottish Economy. Quarterly Economic Commentary
0306-7920 Lawn Tennis†
0306-7920 Lawn Tennis *changed to* Tennis
0306-7947 British Model Soldier Society. Bulletin
0306-7963 L A G Bulletin
0306-7971 Spare Rib
0306-798X B U F O R A Journal
0306-7998 Jewish Historical Society of England. Annual Report and Accounts for the Session
0306-8099 Opera North†
0306-8129 Forestry and Home Grown Timber *see* 0308-7638
0306-8145 Canada Today *changed to* Canada Today/D'Aujourd'hui
0306-817X Art Design Photo
0306-8234 Paper
0306-8285 Industrial Pollution Control Yearbook†
0306-8293 International Journal of Social Economics
0306-8374 Asian Affairs
0306-8404 Bandersnatch
0306-8412 Africa Currents
0306-8463 Postal History International
0306-8471 Eugenics Society Bulletin
0306-848X Radnorshire Society. Transactions
0306-8536 Manxman
0306-8552 Electrotechnology
0306-8560 Livestock International
0306-8781 Amon Hen
0306-879X Italiano†
0306-882X Flora
0306-8838 Bradwell Abbey Field Centre for the Study of Archaeology, Natural History & Environmental Studies. Occasional Papers
0306-8919 Optical and Quantum Electronics
0306-8927 Hostelling News
0306-8943 Stainless
0306-9001 Northamptonshire & Bedfordshire Life
0306-9028 Window
0306-9079 Cornish Banner
0306-9192 Food Policy - Economics, Planning and Politics of Food and Agriculture
0306-9192 Guide to British Offshore Suppliers
0306-9206 North Cheshire Family Historian
0306-9338 Bangor Occasional Papers in Economics
0306-9346 B B C Modern English
0306-9397 Conferences and Exhibitions *changed to* Conferences and Exhibitions International
0306-9400 Law Teacher
0306-9419 International Journal of Forensic Dentistry
0306-9427 Welding Research International
0306-9435 Transport Manager's Handbook
0306-9486 Communications on Physics†
0306-9486 Maritime Studies and Management *see* 0308-8839
0306-9516 African Books in Print
0306-9524 Index Islamicus
0306-9540 M E N
0306-9559 Chartered Institute of Transport. Handbook
0306-9567 Report on Czechoslovak Jewry
0306-9699 Midwife, Health Visitor and Community Nurse
0306-977X Ilkeston and District Local History Society. Occasional Paper
0306-9788 City of London Law Review
0306-9869 Electron Microscopy Abstracts
0306-9877 Medical Hypotheses
0306-9885 British Journal of Guidance and Counselling
0306-9915 U F O Research Review
0307-0018 Cranes Today
0307-0026 European Spectroscopy News
0307-0042 University of Wales. Board of Celtic Studies. Social Science Monographs
0307-0107 External Walls
0307-0131 Byzantine and Modern Greek Studies
0307-0220 Fairplay International Shipping Weekly
0307-0255 F A S Journal
0307-0360 London Currency Report
0307-0379 International Economic Data Service
0307-0387 Middle East Currency Reports
0307-0395 Young Drama†
0307-0409 Anbar Yearbook
0307-0417 Greater London Arts Association. Annual Report and Yearbook *see* 0309-1945
0307-0441 Local Government Trends
0307-0468 Chartered Institute of Public Finance and Accountancy. Housing Maintenance & Management. Actuals Statistics
0307-0506 Chartered Institute of Public Finance and Accountancy. Local Health & Social Services Statistics *see* 0309-653X
0307-0514 Chartered Institute of Public Finance and Accountancy. Education Estimates Statistics
0307-0522 Chartered Institute of Public Finance and Accountancy. Public Library Statistics. Estimates
0307-0565 International Journal of Obesity
0307-0573 Chartered Institute of Public Finance and Accountancy. Fire Service Statistics. Estimates
0307-0603 Digest of United Kingdom Energy Statistics
0307-062X Official Guide to Hotels & Restaurants in Great Britain, Ireland and Overseas
0307-0654 University of Durham. Center for Middle Eastern and Islamic Studies. Occasional Papers Series.
0307-0697 Power and Works Engineering
0307-0719 Institute of Jewish Studies. Bulletin
0307-076X National Institute for Medical Research. Scientific Report *see* 0072-6567
0307-0778 Paper and Board Abstracts
0307-0786 Ostrich
0307-0794 Marketing Abstracts *see* 0308-2172
0307-0808 Studies in Library Management
0307-0832 Navin Weekly
0307-093X Social Services Yearbook
0307-1006 Discourse Analysis Monographs
0307-1022 Social History
0307-109X Theses in Latin American Studies at British Universities in Progress and Completed
0307-112X Immunology Abstracts
0307-1146 Great Britain. Electricity Council. Report and Accounts
0307-1154 Garage and Transport
0307-1219 British Combustion
0307-1294 Chartered Institute of Public Finance and Accountancy. Police Estimates Statistics. Actuals *see* 0144-9915
0307-1308 Chartered Institute of Public Finance and Accountancy. Housing Part 1: Rents. Actuals Statistics *see* 0260-406X
0307-1316 Chartered Institute of Public Finance and Accountancy. Housing Part 2: Revenue Accounts. Actuals Statistics *see* 0260-4078
0307-1375 Arboricultural Journal
0307-1391 S S R C Survey Archive Bulletin
0307-1448 Donizetti Society. Journal
0307-1596 Food Machinery and Ingredients Export News†
0307-1634 E A A Review
0307-1642 Thomas Hardy Society. Review
0307-1677 Industrial Past
0307-1693 Metals Technology
0307-174X International Polymer Science and Technology
0307-1782 Water Services Handbook
0307-1790 Youth in Society
0307-1804 Locomotives Illustrated
0307-1847 R U S I
0307-1847 Royal United Service for Defence Studies. Journal *see* 0307-1847
0307-188X Intelligence Digest Weekly Review
0307-1901 E S S R A Magazine†
0307-191X Pensions World
0307-1936 Contact (London, 1973)
0307-2029 Calgacus
0307-2053 Home Economics
0307-2061 British National Association for Soviet and East European Studies. Information Bulletin
0307-2118 FItech
0307-2169 Black Music & Jazz Review
0307-2274 Association of Commonwealth Universities. Annual Report of the Council Together with the Accounts of the Association
0307-2312 Teaching over 13s
0307-2363 Retail and Distribution Management
0307-2401 Electronics Industry
0307-2444 Studies for Trade Unionists
0307-2525 Museums Bulletin

0307-2568 Sussex Archaeological Society Newsletter
0307-2576 Soil Association. Quarterly Review
0307-2606 Locke Newsletter
0307-2614 S. E. E. Journal
0307-2630 U K Plant Hire Guide *changed to* Contract Journal(1979)
0307-2649 Journal of A T E *changed to* Test
0307-2657 B S B I Abstracts
0307-2770 New German Studies
0307-2827 C H E C News
0307-2851 Midland Ancestor
0307-2894 International Who's Who in Music and Musicians' Directory
0307-2916 Fireweed
0307-2991 What Car?
0307-3025 Corporate Planner's Yearbook
0307-3084 Gas Directory and Who's Who
0307-3149 Jane's Ocean Technology
0307-3262 Iberian Studies
0307-3289 Institute of Health Education. Journal
0307-3319 Great North Review
0307-3408 Bard
0307-3424 Tass Journal *changed to* Tass News and Journal
0307-3513 Youth Social Work Bulletin *see* 0307-1790
0307-353X Insight: Soviet Jews
0307-3572 Tennyson Society, Lincoln, England. Occasional Papers
0307-3580 Management Review & Digest
0307-4293 New Fiction
0307-434X British Directory of Little Magazines and Small Presses
0307-4358 Managerial Finance
0307-4412 Biochemical Education
0307-4463 Population Trends
0307-4536 Greek Review
0307-4552 Barclays Country Reports
0307-4617 Screen International
0307-4625 Centerpiece
0307-4722 Art Libraries Journal
0307-4730 British Journal of Clinical Equipment
0307-4757 Policy Publications Review *changed to* Publications Review
0307-4803 New Library World
0307-4870 Journal of Planning and Environment Law
0307-5079 Studies in Higher Education
0307-5087 Contrebis
0307-5095 Journal of Electrophysiological Technology
0307-5133 Journal of Egyptian Archaeology
0307-5281 Watford and District Industrial History Society. Journal
0307-5354 S P E L
0307-5400 European Law Review
0307-5451 History of Technology
0307-546X Tangent
0307-5494 Microbios Letters
0307-5508 Community Care
0307-5583 Cromwelliana
0307-5591 Industrial Relations Law Reports
0307-5656 Institute of Medical Laboratory Sciences. Gazette
0307-580X Jeweller
0307-5826 Library Association. Rare Books Group. Newsletter
0307-5966 Journal of Meteorology
0307-5974 Religion in Communist Lands
0307-5982 Together
0307-6008 India Office Library and Records Newsletter
0307-6032 Who's Who in Finance
0307-6067 Community Work
0307-6075 Dissertation Abstracts International. Section C: European Abstracts
0307-6091 Federation of Children's Book Groups. Yearbook *see* 0144-574X
0307-6164 British Plastics and Rubber
0307-6334 Church Music Quarterly
0307-6490 Automotive Engineer
0307-6539 Commonwealth Magistrates' Conference. Report
0307-6547 Great Britain. Department of Energy. Report on Research and Development
0307-6571 Coin Yearbook
0307-6628 Cheshire Archaeological Bulletin
0307-6652 Notes on Water Research
0307-6679 Stamp Magazine
0307-6687 Tolley's Tax Tables
0307-6695 New Aspects of Breast Cancer
0307-6717 Criminal Statistics, Scotland.
0307-6741 Toy Retailing News†
0307-6768 Management Services
0307-6776 R A I N: Royal Anthropological Institute News
0307-6822 Road Accidents in Great Britain
0307-6857 International Planned Parenthood Federation. Annual Report *changed to* I P P F in Action
0307-689X Directory of Agricultural Co-Operatives in the United Kingdom
0307-6903 S. C. O. C. L. I. S. News
0307-692X Australian Journal of Ecology
0307-6938 Clinical and Experimental Dermatology
0307-6946 Ecological Entomology
0307-6962 Physiological Entomology
0307-6970 Systematic Entomology
0307-7004 Triticale Abstracts
0307-7039 Politics Today
0307-7098 Collect Isle of Man Stamps
0307-7144 Lore and Language
0307-7195 Printing Industries
0307-7225 Church of England. General Synod. Report of Proceedings
0307-7276 Weyfarers
0307-7349 Soviet Non-Ferrous Metals Research
0307-7365 Surfacing Journal
0307-7411 Air Extra
0307-7497 Occasional Papers in German Studies
0307-7535 Fabian Tract
0307-7543 Trade Union Register
0307-7640 Medical Informatics
0307-7667 Quarterly Review of Marketing
0307-7675 Museums Yearbook
0307-7683 New Civil Engineer
0307-7691 National Coal Board Statistical Tables
0307-7713 Civil Engineering Technician
0307-7772 Clinical Otolaryngology and Allied Sciences
0307-7780 Securitech
0307-7861 Accountants Weekly
0307-7896 Metal Construction
0307-7942 Energy World
0307-7950 Heating and Air Conditioning Journal
0307-7969 Key Abstracts - Physical Measurements and Instrumentation
0307-7977 Key Abstracts - Electrical Measurements and Instrumentation
0307-8000 Comparison
0307-8051 Courtauld Institute Illustration Archives. Archive 1
0307-806X Courtauld Institute Illustration Archives. Archive 2
0307-8078 Courtauld Institute Illustration Archives. Archive 3
0307-8086 Courtauld Institute Illustration Archives. Archive 4
0307-8140 Northumberland & Durham Family History Society. Journal
0307-8329 Chartered Institute of Public Finance and Accountancy. Planning Estimates Statistics. Actuals *see* 0260-8642
0307-8337 English Language Teaching Journal
0307-8353 Institution of Civil Engineers. Proceedings. Part 1: Design and Construction
0307-8361 Institution of Civil Engineers. Proceedings. Part 2: Research and Theory
0307-8515 Clothing Institute Year Book and Membership Register *changed to* Clothing and Footwear Institute Year Book and Membership Register
0307-8523 Music Trades Directory
0307-8531 Rare Earth Bulletin
0307-8558 Management Services in Government
0307-8590 Maritime Monographs and Reports
0307-8604 Coop Marketing & Management
0307-8612 New Universities Quarterly
0307-8647 Bar Quarterly†
0307-8698 Ringing and Migration
0307-8833 Theatre Research International
0307-8965 Computing Europe *changed to* Computing
0307-9007 NR Technology
0307-9023 Research Intelligence *see* 0141-1926
0307-904X Applied Mathematical Modelling
0307-9082 Great Britain. Centre for Overseas Pest Research. Report
0307-9112 London Mystery Selection
0307-9163 Association of Art Historians. Bulletin
0307-9201 Sage Race Relations Abstracts
0307-9252 Communicator†
0307-9341 Lakeland Dialect Society. Bulletin
0307-9481 British Library News
0307-9562 Thames Poetry
0307-9570 Moonshine
0307-9589 Great Britain. Civil Service Department. Report
0307-9597 Scottish Social Work Statistics†
0307-9732 International Yearbook of Educational & Instructional Technology
0307-9767 New Library Buildings
0307-9813 Gay Left
0307-9864 Annual Bibliography of Scottish Literature
0308-003X Tape and Hi-Fi Test†
0308-0110 Medical Education
0308-0129 English Philological Studies
0308-0137 Rural Recreation and Tourism Abstracts *changed to* Leisure, Recreation and Tourism Abstracts
0308-0161 Pressure Vessels and Piping
0308-0188 Interdisciplinary Science Reviews
0308-0234 Hospital and Health Services Review
0308-0455 Business Graduates Association Address Book
0308-0501 Fire and Materials
0308-0528 Middle East Construction
0308-0587 Modern English Teacher
0308-0617 Catholic Life
0308-0633 Contact (London,1961)
0308-065X Interfish
0308-0676 Warfare
0308-0765 Human Rights Review
0308-082X Town and Country Planning Association. Annual Report
0308-0838 Fern Gazette
0308-0862 British Plumbing and Heating *changed to* Plumbing and Heating
0308-0889 Four Decades†
0308-0900 London Facts and Figures
0308-0935 Fishing Prospects
0308-0943 Skinner's British Textile Register†
0308-0951 Charles Lamb Bulletin
0308-1060 Transportation Planning and Technology
0308-1079 International Journal of General Systems
0308-1087 Linear and Multilinear Algebra
0308-1206 Comments on Solid State Physics
0308-1222 Energy Trends
0308-1230 On Target
0308-1265 Brewing & Distilling International
0308-1273 Netherlands-British Trade Directory
0308-129X Royal Society of Edinburgh. Communications, Physical Sciences
0308-1397 Wellsian
0308-1400 International Dredging Abstracts
0308-1419 Great Britain. Department of Employment. New Earnings Survey
0308-1443 Printing Industries Annual
0308-1451 Royal Institution of Chartered Surveyors Year Book
0308-146X Great Britain. Central Statistical Office. Regional Statistics *see* 0261-1783
0308-1516 Onearth
0308-1540 Society for Latin America Studies. Bulletin
0308-1656 Akhbar-e-Watan Urdu Newsweekly
0308-1729 Savings Market
0308-1745 Great Britain. Department of the Environment. Local Government Financial Statistics: England and Wales
0308-180X Natural History Book Reviews
0308-1907 N A T F H E Journal
0308-1958 Impact of Tax Changes on Income Distribution†
0308-1990 Footnote
0308-2024 Writing
0308-2075 Occasional Papers in Linguistics and Language Learning
0308-2091 Artefact
0308-2105 Royal Society of Edinburgh. Proceedings. (Mathematics)
0308-2113 Royal Society of Edinburgh. Proceedings. (Natural Environment) *changed to* Royal Society of Edinburgh. Proceedings. (Biological Sciences)
0308-213X International Planned Parenthood Federation. Report to Donors, Programme Development & Financial Statements
0308-2172 Management and Marketing Abstracts
0308-2199 British Mining
0308-230X British Library. Bibliographic Services Division. Newsletter
0308-2342 Journal of Chemical Research
0308-244X British Journal of Music Therapy
0308-2636 P N Review
0308-2741 Society for Lincolnshire History and Archaeology. Newsletter
0308-2776 Prospice
0308-2792 New Age Concern Today *see* 0144-6630
0308-2857 Survival International Review
0308-2938 International Marketing Data and Statistics
0308-2962 Tropical Oil Seeds Abstracts
0308-2970 Sorghum and Millets Abstracts
0308-2997 Feeding-Weight and Obesity Abstracts†
0308-3047 Market Research Great Britain
0308-308X Elektor
0308-3268 Horticulture Industry
0308-3276 S. I. S. Review
0308-3306 Farming Industry
0308-3314 Database Journal
0308-3314 Small Systems Software *changed to* Mini Micro Software
0308-3381 Bananas
0308-342X Surrey Archaeological Society. Research Volumes
0308-3446 Market Research Europe
0308-3535 Royal College of Art, Journal *changed to* Ark (1978)
0308-356X Teaching 10-13
0308-3586 Focus on Political Repression in South Africa
0308-3586 Focus (London)
0308-3594 Local Council Review
0308-3616 Medical Laboratory Sciences
0308-3713 Japanese Patents Gazette. Part 1: Chemical
0308-373X Plumbing and Heating Equipment News
0308-3756 Pali Buddhist Review
0308-3764 Court
0308-4035 South East Asia Library Group Newsletter
0308-4086 Journal of Crystal and Molecular Structure
0308-4094 B L L D Announcement Bulletin *changed to* British Reports, Translations and Theses
0308-4159 I C E Yearbook
0308-4205 Professional Printer
0308-4213 Cable Television Engineering
0308-4221 Computer Applications
0308-423X I B A Technical Review
0308-4272 Radiological Protection Bulletin
0308-4329 Journal of Human Nutrition
0308-4353 Consumer Europe
0308-4388 Halsbury's Laws of England Annual Abridgment
0308-4426 Journal of Maternal & Child Health *changed to* Maternal & Child Health
0308-4450 West African Journal of Sociology and Political Science
0308-4485 Offset Data Index†
0308-4507 Carpet Review Weekly
0308-454X Television (London, 1931)

0308-4558 Royal Historical Society. Annual Bibliography of British and Irish History
0308-4590 International Metals Reviews
0308-4620 World Patents Index Gazette Section P: General
0308-4639 World Patents Index Gazette Section Q: Mechanical
0308-4647 World Patents Index Gazette Section R: Electrical
0308-4655 World Patents Index Gazette. Section Ch: Chemical
0308-4698 British Country Music Association. Yearbook
0308-4752 Omens
0308-4787 Limestone Literary Magazine
0308-4795 Diesel Engineering
0308-4809 Northumbriana
0308-4892 Committee on Invisible Exports. Annual Report
0308-4922 British Paedodontic Society. Proceedings
0308-4930 A & S
0308-4949 Royal British Legion. Journal.
0308-499X Great Britain. Department of Trade. Insurance Business: Annual Report
0308-5074 Royal Greenwich Observatory Bulletins
0308-5082 Great Britain. Institute of Geological Sciences. Seismological Bulletins
0308-5090 United Kingdom Mineral Statistics
0308-5147 Economy and Society
0308-518X Environment and Planning A
0308-5198 Defence Materiel
0308-5201 Maritime Defence
0308-5201 Maritime Defense International *see* 0308-5201
0308-521X Agricultural Systems
0308-5252 C W I Herald
0308-5279 Bank of England. Report and Accounts
0308-5325 Great Britain. Institute of Geological Sciences. Overseas Memoirs
0308-5333 Great Britain. Institute of Geological Sciences. Mineral Assessment Report
0308-5368 Great Britain. Institute of Geological Sciences. Well Inventory Series. Metric Units *changed to* Great Britain. Institute of Geological Sciences. Metric Well Inventory
0308-5376 B U F C Newsletter
0308-5384 Biological Structure and Function
0308-5414 Pollution Monitor
0308-5457 Royal Horticultural Society. Garden Journal
0308-5538 Documents on International Affairs†
0308-5554 Sounding Brass
0308-5562 Oxoniensia
0308-5589 Great Britain. Ministry of Agriculture, Fisheries and Food. Fisheries Research Technical Report
0308-5597 A A R P
0308-5651 Buildings Maintenance & Services
0308-5694 Imago Mvndi
0308-5732 Agricultural Engineer
0308-5759 Adoption and Fostering
0308-5791 British Flower
0308-5864 I D S Discussion Paper
0308-5872 I D S Bulletin
0308-5899 Fortean Times
0308-5910 Annual Art Sales Index: Oil Paintings, Drawings and Watercolours
0308-5953 Microprocessors *changed to* Microprocessors & Microsystems
0308-5961 Telecommunications Policy
0308-597X Marine Policy
0308-6003 Chemical Society, London. Annual Reports on the Progress of Chemistry. Section A: Physical and Inorganic Chemistry
0308-602X Chest, Heart and Stroke Journal†
0308-6100 Craft & Hobby Dealer
0308-6119 University of London. Contemporary China Institute. Research Notes and Studies
0308-616X Housing Outlook
0308-6259 Commercial Food Information
0308-6283 New Poetry†
0308-6348 Nottinghamshire Historian
0308-6380 Marfleet Society Newsletter
0308-650X General Engineer
0308-6534 Journal of Imperial and Commonwealth History
0308-6569 Anglo-American Law Review
0308-6577 Cotton and Tropical Fibres Abstracts
0308-6593 Journal of Clinical Pharmacy *see* 0143-3180
0308-664X Phosphorus and Sulfur and the Related Elements
0308-6666 Great Britain. Central Statistical Office. Monthly Digest of Statistics
0308-6674 Mallorn
0308-6712 British Toys & Hobbies
0308-6747 Architecture West Midlands
0308-678X Africa Guide
0308-6801 J C A T S *changed to* C. A. T. S. Reports
0308-6860 Ethnic Groups
0308-6887 Amnesty International Newsletter
0308-6895 A T P A S Printing Education & Training Journal
0308-6909 C O R E
0308-6925 Communicator of Scientific and Technical Information
0308-6992 Geographers
0308-7018 Cassell's Directory of Publishing in Great Britain, The Commonwealth, Ireland, South Africa and Pakistan *changed to* Cassell and Publishers Association Directory of Publishing in Great Britain, the Commonwealth, Ireland, South Africa and Pakistan
0308-7026 Gas Marketing
0308-7107 Sell's Health Service Buyers Guide *see* 0140-5748
0308-7174 Electrical Contractor
0308-7298 History of Photography
0308-731X Cherwell
0308-7344 Potato Abstracts
0308-7379 Scottish Diver
0308-7395 Quarterly Index Islamicus
0308-7417 Historical Research for University Degrees in the United Kingdom. Part 1: Theses Completed
0308-7425 Historical Research for University Degrees in the United Kingdom. Part 2: Theses in Progress
0308-745X Partners
0308-7484 Registered Accountant
0308-7506 Tertiary Research Group. Special Papers
0308-7565 Canoeing
0308-762X International Newsletter
0308-7638 Forestry and British Timber
0308-7646 Gifts
0308-7670 Scottish Ophthalmic Practitioner
0308-7778 Brands and Alloys
0308-7786 European Scrap Directory
0308-7794 Metallurgical Plantmakers of the World
0308-7816 Residential Social Work†
0308-7840 Community Home Schools Gazette *changed to* Community Homes Gazette
0308-7883 Income Tax Digest and Accountants' Review
0308-7948 Whillan's Tax Tables and Tax Reckoner *changed to* Whillans's Tax Tables
0308-7980 Oncology Abstracts†
0308-7980 Toxicology Abstracts
0308-7999 Gazelle Review of Literature on the Middle East
0308-8006 Steel Traders of the World
0308-8030 Simon's Tax Cases *changed to* Simon's Weekly Tax Service
0308-8073 Institute of Building. Estimating Information Service
0308-8081 Institute of Building. Site Management Information Service
0308-8111 INSPEC Reports
0308-812X Ley Hunter
0308-8146 Food Chemistry
0308-8197 Dairy Industries International
0308-8219 Bar List of the United Kingdom
0308-8227 Rights!
0308-8359 Materials Handling Index
0308-8367 Laboratory Equipment Index
0308-8375 Electronic Engineering Index
0308-8383 Engineering Components and Materials Index
0308-8391 Chemical Engineering Index
0308-8405 Manchester United Football Book
0308-8456 Archaeology in Britain (Year)
0308-8464 Financial Times World Hotel Directory
0308-8480 C A B News
0308-8561 Domestic Heating Plus Plumbing: Bathrooms-Kitchens
0308-8669 Labour Weekly
0308-8677 L A N S A
0308-8774 Latest Literature in Family Planning
0308-8839 Maritime Policy and Management
0308-8855 World Cement Technology
0308-8863 Agricultural Engineering Abstracts
0308-888X Essays in Poetics
0308-8987 Kitchin's Road Transport Law
0308-9002 Interest Rate Service
0308-9037 Kent Family History Society. Record Publication
0308-9126 N D T International
0308-9142 Iron and Steel International
0308-9231 Intercommunity - International Community Education *changed to* Youth International
0308-9274 A G M Service
0308-9290 Research Fields in Physics at United Kingdom Universities and Polytechnics
0308-9304 A B C Freight Guide
0308-9347 Music Master
0308-9398 Footwear Industry Statistical Review
0308-9533 Highways & Road Construction International *see* 0142-6168
0308-9541 Journal of Applied Systems Analysis
0308-9568 L A C News
0308-9584 Agent's Hotel Gazetteer: Tourist Cities
0308-9614 Domestic Heating and Air Conditioning
0308-9649 Tertiary Research
0308-9657 Liberal Party Organisation. Study Paper *changed to* Liberal Publication Department. Study Paper
0308-9665 Building Management Abstracts
0308-9703 Epilepsy News
0308-9762 Classical Music Weekly *changed to* Classical Music
0308-9770 Iron and Steel Industry: Monthly Statistics
0308-9789 I M M Bulletin
0308-9819 Great Britain. Department of the Environment. Housing and Construction Statistics
0309-0019 Performing Right News
0309-0108 Royal Observatory, Edinburgh. Annual Report
0309-0132 Great Britain. Medical Research Council. Handbook
0309-0167 Histopathology
0309-0175 Independent Broadcasting Authority. Annual Report and Accounts
0309-0191 University of Sheffield. Newsletter Diary
0309-0248 B S R I A Technical Notes
0309-0256 Media Reporter
0309-0329 Canada-U.K. Year Book
0309-0388 Commonwealth Diary of Coming Events *see* 0141-8513
0309-0396 Shaw Newsletter
0309-0531 Nutrition Information Centre. Bulletin†
0309-0558 Managerial Law
0309-0566 European Journal of Marketing
0309-0574 Recommended Recordings
0309-0582 Management Bibliographies and Reviews
0309-0655 British Library. Lending Division. Current Serials Received
0309-0728 Industrial Archaeology Review
0309-0787 Journal for the Study of the Old Testament. Supplement Series
0309-0809 Milk Bulletin
0309-0817 M I R A Automobile Abstracts
0309-0884 Performing Right Year Book
0309-0892 Journal for the Study of the Old Testament
0309-099X Royal Observatory, Edinburgh. Occasional Reports
0309-1031 Dog News and Family Pets
0309-1112 Family Planning Today
0309-118X InterMedia
0309-1252 Bristow's Book of Yachts
0309-1287 Protozoological Abstracts
0309-1295 Nutrition Abstracts and Reviews. Series A: Human and Experimental
0309-1309 Mervyn Peake Review
0309-1317 International Journal of Urban and Regional Research
0309-1325 Progress in Human Geography
0309-1333 Progress in Physical Geography
0309-135X Nutrition Abstracts and Reviews. Series B: Livestock Feeds and Feeding
0309-1376 Meccano Magazine
0309-1384 Planner
0309-1414 Police Review
0309-1422 Waterways World
0309-1449 British Quarrying & Slag Federation. Technical Review *see* 0141-6936
0309-1465 Developing Railways
0309-1473 I R C S Medical Science: Environmental Biology and Medicine
0309-1481 I R C S Medical Science: Clinical Biochemistry
0309-149X I R C S Medical Science: Developmental Biology and Medicine
0309-1503 I R C S Medical Science: Drug Metabolism and Toxicology
0309-1511 I R C S Medical Science: Pathology
0309-152X I R C S Medical Science: Psychology and Psychiatry
0309-1546 I R C S Medical Science: Clinical Medicine
0309-1554 I R C S Medical Science: Nervous System
0309-1562 I R C S Medical Science: Experimental Animals
0309-1600 Institution of Water Engineers and Scientists. Journal
0309-1619 Powys Review
0309-1635 British Journal of Alcohol & Alcoholism
0309-166X Cambridge Journal of Economics
0309-1708 Advances in Water Resources
0309-1740 Meat Science
0309-1783 Hobart Paperbacks
0309-1813 Atomic Absorption & Emission Spectrometry Abstracts
0309-1821 Guinea-Pig News Letter
0309-1848 Rat News Letter
0309-1902 Journal of Medical Engineering & Technology
0309-1929 Geophysical and Astrophysical Fluid Dynamics
0309-1945 Greater London Arts Association. Annual Report
0309-1953 Heat Transfer & Fluid Flow Digest
0309-1961 Lectures in Commercial Diplomacy
0309-2143 Converter Directory
0309-2216 International Copper Information Bulletin
0309-2232 Library Research Occasional Paper *see* 0143-5124
0309-2275 Oxfordshire Family Historian
0309-233X Vision
0309-2356 U K Chemical Industry Statistics Handbook
0309-2402 Journal of Advanced Nursing
0309-2445 Publishing History
0309-2526 Hands off Ireland
0309-2534 Advances in Raman Spectroscopy†
0309-2658 Action (Horsham)
0309-2666 Medical Technologist and Scientist
0309-2984 History Workshop
0309-300X Latin America Commodities Report†
0309-300X Latin America Commodities Report
0309-3018 Finishing Industries
0309-3077 LP Gas Review
0309-3093 Berkshire Archaeological Journal
0309-3115 United Kingdom Temperance Alliance. Alliance News
0309-314X On-Line Review

0309-3204 Council for British Archaeology. Newsletter and Calendar of Excavations
0309-3247 Journal of Strain Analysis for Engineering Design
0309-3263 Reading Geographer
0309-331X Coffee International *changed to* Coffee & Cocoa International
0309-3328 Counterpoint
0309-3336 What Hi-Fi?
0309-345X African Environment Special Reports
0309-3468 Wiltshire Natural History Magazine
0309-3476 Wiltshire Archaeological Magazine
0309-3484 Junior Education
0309-3492 Third Way
0309-3557 Recycling and Waste Disposal†
0309-3646 Prosthetics and Orthotics International
0309-3700 Liverpool Classical Monthly
0309-3891 Journal of Consumer Studies & Home Economics
0309-3913 African Journal of Medicine & Medical Sciences
0309-3948 Institute of Marine Engineers Technical Reports
0309-4006 Scottish Journal of Sociology
0309-4073 Leveller
0309-409X Chelsea Speleological Society. Records
0309-426X Advances in Infrared and Raman Spectroscopy†
0309-4332 Geophysical Abstracts
0309-4359 Gramophone Popular Catalogue
0309-4367 Gramophone Classical Catalogue
0309-4472 Institute of Oceanographic Sciences. Annual Report
0309-4545 Fertility and Contraception†
0309-4561 Plastics and Rubber International
0309-457X Maghreb Review
0309-4693 Social Service Abstracts
0309-474X European Bulletin and Press
0309-4928 C I I Journal
0309-4944 International Petroleum Abstracts
0309-4960 Worldwide Marketing Opportunities Digest
0309-4995 Employment Digest
0309-510X Practical Self-Sufficiency
0309-5134 Daily Mail Skier's Holiday Guide
0309-5150 Optics Abstracts†
0309-5207 Journal of Beckett Studies
0309-524X Wind Engineering
0309-5290 Directory of Technical and Further Education
0309-5304 L G O R U Transportation News
0309-5312 X-Ray Diffraction Abstracts
0309-5320 Laser Raman & Infrared Spectroscopy Abstracts
0309-5339 Directory of European Associations. Part 2: National Learned, Scientific & Technical Societies
0309-5355 Popular Hi-Fi & Sound *changed to* Popular Hi-Fi
0309-5371 Statistics - Asia & Australasia: Sources for Market Research
0309-5444 Microcomputer Analysis *changed to* Microcomputer News International
0309-5452 Statistics - America
0309-5460 Current African Directories
0309-5495 Newsrelease
0309-5606 Quarry and Mining News
0309-5614 Chartered Institute of Public Finance and Accountancy. Education Statistics. Actuals
0309-5630 Chambers Trades Register of Scotland and North East England†
0309-5649 Chambers Trades Register of the Wirral to the Wash†
0309-5770 Catalysts in Chemistry
0309-586X Agricultural Administration
0309-5878 Medicine (London)
0309-5991 Semiconductors and Insulators
0309-5991 Semiconductors and Insulators
0309-6149 Croydon Natural History & Scientific Society. Bulletin
0309-622X Chartered Institute of Public Finance and Accountancy. Fire Service Statistics. Actuals
0309-6254 Nautical Review *changed to* Lloyd's Ship Manager
0309-6270 Logophile: the Cambridge Journal of Words and Language
0309-653X Chartered Institute of Public Finance and Accountancy. Personal Social Services Statistics. Actuals
0309-6629 Chartered Institute of Public Finance and Accountancy. Public Library Statistics. Actuals
0309-6858 International Association of Dentistry for Children. Journal
0309-6866 Fire Prevention
0309-6890 Gas Kinetics and Energy Transfer
0309-6904 I P P F Co-Operative Information Service
0309-7234 European Industrial Relations Review
0309-7242 Purchasing and Supply
0309-7285 Cienfuegos Press Anarchist Review
0309-7323 Scottish Opera News
0309-7374 North West Industrial Development Association. Newsletter
0309-7463 Institute of Oceanographic Sciences. Collected Reprints
0309-751X Financial Times World Insurance Year Book
0309-7552 Science Bulletin
0309-7676 International Business Lawyer
0309-7714 Journal of Environmental Planning and Pollution Control
0309-7765 Bronte Society Transactions
0309-7803 Surrey Archaeological Collections
0309-7854 Economic Bulletin(London)
0309-7951 Texture of Crystalline Solids
0309-7951 Texture of Crystalline Solids
0309-8168 Capital and Class
0309-8222 Modern Tramway
0309-8230 Noise Control, Vibration and Insulation *see* 0143-6481
0309-8249 Journal of Philosophy of Education
0309-8265 Journal of Geography in Higher Education
0309-8273 East Coast Digest *changed to* Coast and Country
0309-8346 Huguenot Society of London. Proceedings
0309-8354 Huguenot Society of London, Quarto Series
0309-8486 Northamptoniana
0309-8524 Tourism International Research/Caribbean†
0309-8559 Family History News and Digest
0309-8567 Tourism International Policy†
0309-8575 Tourism International History†
0309-8591 Croydon Bibliographies for Regional Survey
0309-8613 Tourism International Research/Pacific†
0309-8621 Tourism International Airletter
0309-8648 Dozenal Review
0309-8656 Croydon Natural History & Scientific Society. Proceedings and Transactions
0309-877X Journal of Further and Higher Education
0309-8885 Computing Journal Abstracts
0309-9105 Scottish Fisheries Information Pamphlets
0309-9156 Ideology and Consciousness
0309-9210 Thoroton Society of Nottinghamshire. Transactions
0309-9253 New Vegetarian *see* 0260-3233
0309-9334 Business Traveller
0310-0049 Australian Mammalogy
0310-0081 Droughtmaster Digest
0310-0103 New South Wales. Higher Education Board. Higher Education Handbook†
0310-0138 Massada Quarterly *changed to* Kivun
0310-0189 Space
0310-0308 F. A. A. Journal
0310-0316 Impact
0310-0367 Water
0310-0391 Bookmark
0310-0634 Audio Visual Australia
0310-0677 Australia†
0310-0871 Australia. Bureau of Statistics. South Australian Office. Manufacturing Establishments
0310-1010 Autosafe†
0310-1045 Australian Association of Permanent Building Societies. National Newsletter
0310-1053 Australian Business Law Review
0310-1118 Australian Family Circle
0310-1177 Australian Journal of Ophthalmology
0310-1347 Australian Superannuation and Employee Benefits Planning in Action *changed to* Australian Superannuation and Employee Benefits Guide
0310-138X Australian Veterinary Practitioner
0310-1398 Australian Wool Corporation. Bi-Monthly Market Report *changed to* Australian Wool Corporation. Wool Market News: Monthly Perspectives
0310-1444 Bell Bryant News
0310-1452 Belle†
0310-1584 Cabbages and Kings
0310-1649 Canberra Papers in Continuing Education
0310-1797 Cleo
0310-186X New South Wales. Department of Agriculture. Commodity Bulletin
0310-1878 C. C. E. A. Newsletter
0310-1886 Commonwealth Police Officers' Association Journal
0310-1894 Commonwealth Scientific and Industrial Research Organization. Division of Applied Geomechanics. Abstracts of Published Papers
0310-1908 Commonwealth Scientific and Industrial Research Organization. Division of Atmospheric Physics. Annual Report
0310-1967 Comworks Technical Bulletin *changed to* Australia. Department of Housing and Construction. Technical Bulletin
0310-2076 Cosmopolitan
0310-2084 Australia. Department of Agriculture. Marketing Division. Cotton Market News *changed to* Australia. Department of Primary Industry. Cotton Market News
0310-2157 Deed†
0310-2165 Digger
0310-2173 Australia. Repatriation Department. Directory of Ex-Service Organisations *changed to* Australia. Department of Veterans Affairs. Directory of Ex-Service Organisations
0310-222X Earth Garden
0310-2246 Economic Newsletter†
0310-2467 Bronze Swagman Book of Bush Verse
0310-270X Environmental Control†
0310-2815 Furnishing Cyclopaedia
0310-2890 Grass Roots
0310-2920 Guide to Book Outlets in Australia†
0310-3048 In Print
0310-3064 Australian Council of Employers Federation. Economic Newsletter *see* 0155-2090
0310-3137 Jaguar Journal of Australia
0310-3145 Keep Australia Beautiful News†
0310-3242 Learning Exchange
0310-334X Manifest
0310-3471 Minie News
0310-3625 National Water Well Association Journal
0310-3684 New South Wales. Attorney-General. Bureau of Crime Statistics and Research. Statistical Report
0310-3706 New South Wales Clayworker
0310-3714 New South Wales Dairyman
0310-3773 Niugini Caver
0310-3781 N. A. G. Newsletter†
0310-3811 Australia. Chamber of Industries, Northern Territory. Northern Territory Business Journal
0310-4036 Priorities†
0310-4044 Probe
0310-4079 Queensland. Department of Education. Research and Curriculum Branch. Curriculum Paper
0310-4087 Queensland. Department of Education. Research and Curriculum Branch. Document *changed to* Queensland. Department of Education. Information and Publications Branch. Document
0310-4095 Queensland. Department of Education. Research and Curriculum Branch. Reporting Research *changed to* Queensland. Department of Education. Research Branch. Reporting Research
0310-4141 R. M. C. Historical Journal
0310-4168 Refractory Girl
0310-4184 P E X: Australia's Petroleum Exploration Newsletter
0310-4230 Australia. Department of the Treasury. Round-up of Economic Statistics
0310-4257 Rydge's CCEM Industry Report and Buyers Guide
0310-4273 Saturday Club Book of Poetry *see* 0313-685X
0310-4303 Science in New Guinea
0310-4389 Something on Paper
0310-4575 Tasmanian Chamber of Industries. Service Bulletin
0310-4591 Tasmanian Official Publications†
0310-4605 Teaching Religion Today†
0310-4664 Training and Development in Australia
0310-4729 University of Sydney. Archives Record
0310-4923 Rural Reconstruction Authority of Western Australia. Annual Report
0310-5083 Ploughman's Lunch *see* 0310-6837
0310-5121 Queensland. Department of Education. Research and Curriculum Branch. Information Statement *changed to* Queensland. Department of Education. Information and Publications Branch. Information Statement
0310-5202 South Australia. Education Department. School Libraries Branch. Review
0310-5296 Australian Labor Party (NSW Branch). Labor Year Book
0310-5415 Current Australian and New Zealand Legal Literature Index
0310-544X Australian Department of Social Security. Social Security Quarterly
0310-5466 Sydney Town Express
0310-5571 International Association for the Evaluation of Educational Achievement (Australia). Newsletter
0310-558X I. E. A. (Australia) Report
0310-5601 Urbanology
0310-5652 Feedback†
0310-5695 Monash University. Higher Education Advisory and Research Unit. Notes on Higher Education
0310-5709 Developing Education
0310-5725 Environment Control News
0310-5814 Ancient Society; Resources for Teachers
0310-5822 Aboriginal Child at School
0310-5857 Ekstasis
0310-5865 Australian Computer Weekly *changed to* Pacific Computer Weekly
0310-589X National Greyhound News
0310-5903 Australian Weight Lifting Journal
0310-5938 Gredzens
0310-5946 New South Wales Horizons†
0310-5989 Australian Disc and Tape Review
0310-6012 Australia. National Drug Information Service. Technical Information Bulletin *see* 0157-8200
0310-6020 Filter: a Paper for Science Teachers
0310-608X Association of Teachers of English as a Foreign Language. Bulletin
0310-6152 Australia's External Aid *see* 0312-9217
0310-6217 Tube
0310-6276 Australia. Environment Housing and Community Development. Farm Holidays†
0310-6330 Western Australia. Main Roads Department. Technical Report
0310-6357 Mathsnews *changed to* P R I M E
0310-6381 Australian Theatre Review†
0310-639X Gentle Folk and Other Creatures
0310-6403 Australasian Stud and Stable *see* 0311-8215
0310-6411 Video-Tronics
0310-6462 M. C. B. Newsletter *changed to* M. C. B. News
0310-6500 Australian Comparative Education Society. Newsletter

1220 ISSN INDEX

0310-6578 Cities Commission Bulletin†
0310-6632 Newsletter on Soviet and East European Studies in Australia and New Zealand†
0310-6659 Indonesian Acquisitions List
0310-6721 Meatworker
0310-6748 Ball Bearing Journal
0310-6756 New South Wales. National Parks and Wildlife Service. Parks and Wildlife
0310-6837 Ploughman†
0310-6861 St. Thomas More Society. Journal
0310-6969 Welcare
0310-7078 South Australian Canine Journal
0310-7175 Independent Education
0310-7213 Wedgwood News
0310-723X Aboriginal News
0310-7299 Albury/Wodonga
0310-7345 Official Publications of Western Australia
0310-740X Serbian Bulletin
0310-7442 Spectrum†
0310-7531 Tasmanian Transport Bulletin
0310-7582 Steel Spiel
0310-7787 W A P E T Journal
0310-7809 Women's Electoral Lobby. Newsletter
0310-7817 Australian Federal Tax Reporter
0310-7833 Australian Wildlife Research
0310-7841 Australian Journal of Plant Physiology
0310-785X Australian Labor Party. A. C. T. Branch. Newsletter
0310-8031 International Telex Directory. International Service
0310-8147 Papua New Guinea. Department of Social Development and Home Affairs. Social Science Research†
0310-8163 C. S. I. R. O. Sheep and Wool Research†
0310-818X Scout Association of Australia. Review of Progress
0310-8198 Victoria, Australia. Department of Education. News Exchange
0310-8228 Consequences
0310-8252 Australian Marxist Review
0310-8341 Aboriginal Medical Service. Newsletter
0310-8368 Australian Speedway Yearbook *changed to* Peter Webster's International Speedway Review
0310-8465 Interprobe
0310-8546 Victoria, Australia. Directory of Government Departments and Authorities *see* 0158-1589
0310-8554 Graduate Careers Council of Australia. Digest of Research†
0310-8562 Australian Estate and Gift Duty Reporter†
0310-8651 Executive Briefing
0310-8740 J E T R O Information Bulletin *changed to* J E T R O News Digest
0310-8783 Australasian Athletics *changed to* Australasian Track & Field
0310-8813 Australian Corporate Affairs Reporter
0310-8856 Australian Advisory Council on Bibliographical Services. Library Services for Australia
0310-8880 Irrigation Farmer
0310-8902 Australian Hi-Fi Annual
0310-8937 Informed Opinion†
0310-897X Western Australia. Department of Agriculture. Rangeland Management Section. Rangeland Bulletin
0310-9054 A. P. E. A. News†
0310-9070 C. S. I. R. O. Food Research Quarterly
0310-9100 Science and Technology†
0310-9143 Retrieval
0310-9178 Artificial Breeding News *changed to* T H I O News!
0310-9186 Iris and Res Novissimae
0310-933X Australian Process Engineering *changed to* Process Engineering
0310-9356 Cricket Quadrant
0310-9399 Soaring in the A.C.T.
0310-9496 W. E. L. (Victoria) Papers
0310-9534 B. N. I. A. *changed to* Build
0310-9569 A. C. E. S. Review
0310-9585 A S I F
0310-9593 Tariff Insight
0310-964X Liberation
0310-9658 Ecology Action Newsletter
0310-9666 Murray Grey World
0310-9674 M. L. T. A. News
0310-9704 Marine Board of Hobart. Newsletter†
0310-9879 Australian and Pacific Book Prices Current†
0310-9968 Gegenschein
0311-0001 Caspa
0311-0087 Art Craft Teachers Association Magazine
0311-0095 Artviews
0311-015X Steel Fabrication Journal
0311-0184 Pharmaceutical Society of Victoria. Bulletin
0311-0192 Insurance and Banking Record *changed to* Insurance Record of Australia & New Zealand
0311-0222 Pivot†
0311-0230 Electronics News
0311-0265 Australian Securities Law Reporter
0311-0273 Mitsui News
0311-029X Credit Scene *changed to* Credo
0311-0311 I. F. A. P. News
0311-032X Moonbi
0311-0346 Australian Racing Drivers Club Journal
0311-0370 Agribusiness Decision
0311-0389 Company Directors Association of Australia. Directors Law Reporter
0311-0400 Australian Golf Instructional *changed to* Australian Golf (1978)
0311-0419 Kabar
0311-046X Craft Australia
0311-0478 Society for Mass Media and Resource Technology. Journal
0311-0486 Challenge
0311-0559 Flautist
0311-0567 Impact†
0311-0621 I M U Canberra Circular
0311-0699 Dental Anaesthesia and Sedation
0311-0702 South Australia. Department of Labour and Industry. Guide to Legislation
0311-0710 University of Sydney. Department of Architectural Science. General Reports†
0311-0737 Checkpoint
0311-0745 Nature Conservation Council of N. S. W. Bulletin
0311-0753 Plain Turkey
0311-0761 Dane Digest
0311-0788 Australia. Bureau of Agricultural Economics. Coarse Grains: Situation and Outlook
0311-0826 Pacific Travel Directory
0311-0842 A. M. R. C. Review
0311-0850 Canberra Bulletin†
0311-0885 Australia. Bureau of Agricultural Economics. Meat: Situation and Outlook
0311-0931 Australian and New Zealand Environmental Report†
0311-094X Australian Tax Review
0311-0982 C A T Newsletter†
0311-1008 Engineering Associate *changed to* Engineers Australia
0311-1016 Nurungi
0311-1032 A. B. O. A. Newsletter
0311-1172 Your Chamber Reporting†
0311-1180 Concrete Masonry Association of Australia. Project Review
0311-1199 Australian Speedway†
0311-1229 Caesarian
0311-1237 Australia. Department of Manufacturing Industry. Technical Newsletter†
0311-1245 Cor Serpentis
0311-127X V. C. M. File
0311-1342 Primary Journal
0311-1385 Baker & Millers' Journal
0311-1431 Farming Forum
0311-1490 Pen
0311-175X Big League
0311-1784 Words and Windmills
0311-1806 Modern Cleaning
0311-1822 Prod†
0311-1873 Nexus†
0311-1881 Australian Entomological Magazine
0311-1903 Chartered Builder
0311-1911 Power Farming
0311-1946 Country Shows Annual *changed to* Agricultural Shows Annual
0311-1954 Australian Journal of Remedial Education
0311-1962 Polycom
0311-1989 Intervention
0311-2144 Hereford Quarterly
0311-2160 Manufacturing News in Australia *changed to* Factory Management
0311-2179 Travel Consultant†
0311-2195 Tourism Australia†
0311-2209 Australia. Department of Manufacturing Industry. Bulletin *changed to* Australia. Department of Industry and Commerce. Bulletin
0311-2225 Adbrief
0311-2233 Studium
0311-2349 Q. I. E. R. Journal
0311-2373 Serials in Education in Australian Libraries: a Union List
0311-2381 New Products Bulletin†
0311-2497 Cordell's Building Cost Book and Estimating Guide. New South Wales *changed to* Cordell's Building Cost Book. New Construction
0311-2519 Business Outlook†
0311-2659 Gay Liberation Press *see* 0312-7915
0311-2667 Australian Key Business Directory
0311-2764 Australian Composer
0311-2772 Teacher Feedback *see* 0013-1156
0311-2780 Mitchell Business Review
0311-2810 Poets of Australia
0311-290X Southeast Asian Research Materials Group. Newsletter
0311-2926 Ark
0311-2934 Australian Copyright Council. Bulletin
0311-2950 Australia. Bureau of Agricultural Economics. Fibre Review
0311-2969 Hospitality Yearbook *changed to* Hospitality Buyers Guide
0311-3000 Australian Council on Awards in Advanced Education. Bulletin
0311-3078 South Australia. State Library. Reference Services Branch. Reference Services Bibliographies
0311-3140 Monash University Law Review
0311-323X Australian Audio-Visual Reference Book
0311-3248 A. N. Z. H. E. S. Journal
0311-3531 Earth Science and Related Information
0311-354X Municipal Engineering in Australia
0311-3558 Waste Disposal and Water Management in Australia
0311-3655 Chart Book of the Melbourne Share Price Index
0311-368X Community†
0311-4015 Goodwill†
0311-4023 Impact†
0311-4031 Play
0311-404X Splashdown†
0311-4074 Australia. Department of Aboriginal Affairs. Western Australian Office. Newsletter†
0311-4198 Hecate
0311-4201 Graduate Careers†
0311-4511 Administration for Development
0311-4546 Ecos
0311-4775 Unicorn
0311-5518 Alcheringa
0311-5836 C. S. I. R. O. Index
0311-628X Australian Transport
0311-6603 Australian Institute of Criminology. Information Bulletin *changed to* Information Bulletin of Australian Criminology
0311-6999 Australian Education Researcher
0311-7057 Scarlet Letter
0311-7189 Australia. Environment Housing and Community Development. Annual Report†
0311-7731 Modern Office & Data Management
0311-7839 Australian Sea Spray
0311-7979 A W R C Activities†
0311-7987 Australian Water Resources Council. Water Resources Newsletter
0311-7995 Australian Foreign Affairs Record
0311-8215 Stud and Stable
0311-8223 Australian Parks & Recreation
0311-8665 Australian Farm Management Society Newsletter
0311-8924 Historical Journal
0311-8975 Australia. Bureau of Statistics. Mineral Production
0311-8983 National Acoustic Laboratories, Sydney. Annual Report†
0311-905X Current Therapeutics
0311-9491 Queensland. Department of Local Government. Conference of Local Authority Engineers. Proceedings
0311-9882 Australian Wool Sale Statistics. Statistical Analysis. Part A & B
0312-0007 University of Wollongong. Calendar
0312-0112 Australasian Small Press Review†
0312-0325 Australian Women's Wear†
0312-1356 Australia. Bureau of Statistics. Tasmanian Office. Public Justice
0312-1437 Australia. Bureau of Statistics. Trade Union Statistics: Australia
0312-1658 Queensland Lawyer
0312-1674 New South Wales Law Reports
0312-2115 Australian Road Index
0312-259X Australia. National Library. Acquisitions Newsletter
0312-3162 Western Australian Museum, Perth. Records
0312-3685 Mathematical Scientist
0312-4029 Industrial Arbitration Service
0312-407X Australian Social Work
0312-4134 A F C O Quarterly
0312-4746 Official Year Book of Australia *changed to* Australia. Bureau of Statistics. Year Book Australia
0312-5599 Australian Hospitals and Health Services Yearbook
0312-5963 Clinical Pharmacokinetics
0312-620X Rebuild
0312-6242 Australia. Bureau of Statistics. Value of Primary Production, Excluding Mining, and Indexes of Quantum and Unit Gross Value of Agricultural Production *changed to* Australia. Bureau of Statistics. Value of Agricultural Commodities Produced
0312-6250 Australia. Bureau of Statistics. Australian National Accounts - National Income and Expenditure
0312-6269 Australia. Bureau of Statistics. Western Australian Office. Western Australia: Artificial Fertiliser Used on Rural Holdings
0312-6447 Australia. Bureau of Statistics. Dairying Industry *changed to* Australia. Bureau of Statistics. Dairying and Dairy Products
0312-7850 Australia. Bureau of Statistics. Tasmanian Office. Local Government Finance
0312-7907 Australia. Bureau of Statistics. Western Australian Office. Hospital in-Patient Statistics
0312-7915 Working Papers in Sex, Science and Culture†
0312-7923 Royal Australian College of Dental Surgeons. Annals *changed to* Royal Australasian College of Dental Surgeons. Annals
0312-7990 Australia. Bureau of Statistics. Western Australian Office. Road Traffic Accident Statistics
0312-827X Australian Journal for Health, Physical Education and Recreation
0312-8318 AUS Education Information
0312-844X Australia. Bureau of Statistics. Western Australian Office. Sheep, Lambing and Wool Clip
0312-875X Modern Medicine
0312-9217 Australia's Overseas Development Assistance

ISSN INDEX 1221

0312-9225 Commonwealth Scientific and Industrial Research Organization. Division of Chemical Technology. Research Review
0312-9608 B M R Journal of Australian Geology and Geophysics
0312-9616 Media Information Australia
0312-9764 Telopea
0312-9837 Petroleum Newsletter
0313-122X Western Australian Museum, Perth. Records. Supplement
0313-1459 Span
0313-2080 Theatre Australia
0313-2919 Health Action
0313-3192 Australian Plant Introduction Review
0313-3311 Australian Computer Society. Conference Proceedings
0313-4075 Ports of New South Wales
0313-4253 Queensland Law Society Journal
0313-427X University of New South Wales. Library. Annual Report
0313-5047 Tomorrow's Business Decisions *see* 0313-5055
0313-5055 McCabe-McMiles Letter
0313-5977 Canberra Historical Journal
0313-6221 Parergon
0313-6620 Australian Citizen Limited
0313-6728 Queensland. Department of Education. Division of Special Education. Special Education Bulletin
0313-6744 Tableaus
0313-685X S C O P P
0313-6906 University of Wollongong. Annual Report
0313-704X A E S I S Quarterly
0313-7384 Australian Society of Endodontology. Newsletter
0313-7864 Enterprise, Western Australia
0313-8143 Queensland Education Digest
0313-8704 University of Sydney. Department of Agricultural Economics. Agricultural Extension Bulletin
0313-8747 Explore
0313-8860 Western Geographer
0313-9050 Australian Computer Bulletin
0313-9220 Australian Journal of Geodesy, Photogrammetry & Surveying
0313-9603 Australian Commonwealth Specialists' Catalogue
0313-9611 Australian Banknote Catalogue
0313-9921 University of Wollongong. Research Bulletin
0313-9948 Australia. National Capital Development Commission. Technical Papers
0314-0377 Australasian Shipping Record
0314-1039 Defence Force Journal
0314-1160 Criminal Law Journal
0314-1586 Metal & Engineering Industry Year Book
0314-1659 Australia. Bureau of Statistics. Tasmanian Office. Agricultural Industry
0314-1667 Australia. Bureau of Statistics. Tasmanian Office. Fruit Production *changed to* Australia. Bureau of Statistics. Tasmanian Office. Fruit
0314-1705 Australia. Bureau of Statistics. Tasmanian Office. Education
0314-1721 Australia. Bureau of Statistics. Tasmanian Office. Industrial Accident Statistics
0314-2531 Panorama
0314-2868 Australian Congress of Trade Unions. Bulletin
0314-3171 Australian Institute of Petroleum. Annual Report
0314-3457 Queensland Geographer
0314-4240 Chemistry in Australia
0314-4321 Monitor
0314-4607 Mining Review
0314-464X Australian Musician
0314-5514 Life: Be in It /Y S R News
0314-7134 Victoria, Australia. Women's Bureau. Women and Work Newsletter
0314-7487 Energy
0314-7533 Asian Studies Association of Australia. Review
0314-755X National Bank of Australasia. National Bank Monthly Summary
0314-7894 Candy Family History Newsletter
0314-8009 Compass
0314-9099 Canberra Anthropology
0315-0003 Accessible *see* 0027-9633
0315-0054 Dalhousie University. School of Library Service. Newsletter
0315-0062 Canadian Frontier
0315-0097 Encounter
0315-0143 Urban Focus
0315-0208 Spear
0315-033X Around the North
0315-0380 E C O /L O G Week
0315-0496 Stuffed Crocodile†
0315-0518 Recreation Property *changed to* Ontario Cottager
0315-0534 Montreal Calendar Magazine
0315-0542 Outdoor Canada
0315-0550 Cuttings and Comments†
0315-0607 Articles et Commentaires†
0315-0623 Lodgistiks†
0315-0720 Titmouse Review *changed to* Titmouse Annual
0315-0771 Ottawa Ethnic Groups Directory
0315-0836 Canadian Theatre Review
0315-0860 Historia Mathematica
0315-0879 Canadian Key Business Directory
0315-0887 Volleyball Technical Journal
0315-0895 Guide to Departments of Sociology and Anthropology in Canadian Universities
0315-0909 Canadian Amateur Boxing News
0315-0917 Beal's Letter
0315-0941 Geoscience Canada
0315-095X Y Canada
0315-100X Conventions & Meetings-Canada
0315-1042 On Continuing Practice
0315-1174 T. S. Eliot Newsletter *see* 0704-5700
0315-1182 AudioScene Canada
0315-1204 Cooperateur Agricole
0315-1298 Heritage Canada *see* 0225-1485
0315-1301 Cosmetics
0315-1409 Canadian and International Education
0315-1433 Canadian Annual Review of Politics and Public Affairs
0315-1468 Canadian Journal of Civil Engineering
0315-162X Journal of Rheumatology
0315-1654 Energy Analects
0315-1700 World Directory of Historians of Mathematics
0315-1840 L S M News†
0315-1859 Charlatan
0315-1867 Consommateur Canadien
0315-1972 Civic
0315-2022 Western Geographical Series
0315-2057 Production Machinery & Equipment
0315-2081 Eau du Quebec
0315-2146 Entomological Society of Manitoba. Proceedings
0315-2235 Venture Forth
0315-226X Corporation Professionnelle des Medecins du Quebec. Annuaire Medical
0315-2286 Canadian Bar National
0315-2340 Documentation et Bibliotheques
0315-2359 Beaux-Arts
0315-2456 File
0315-2561 Information North
0315-257X C P I Management Service *changed to* Corpus Chemical Report
0315-260X Quebec Chasse et Peche
0315-2685 Jewish Dialogue
0315-2693 Canadian Library Progress: a Selection of the Best Writings from Canadian Library Publications
0315-2804 Raincoast Chronicles
0315-2979 Corporation Professionnelle des Medecins du Quebec. Bulletin
0315-3010 Westwater
0315-3037 Ego
0315-3088 Where to Eat in Canada
0315-3118 Skimania†
0315-3223 Biomass Energy Institute. Newsletter *see* 0708-1936
0315-3290 Creative Canada
0315-3339 Accelerator
0315-3371 History Collection: Canadian Catholic Church†
0315-3452 Canadian Layman
0315-3495 Canadian Defence Quarterly
0315-3525 Canadian Rehabilitation Council for the Disabled. Employment Bulletin
0315-3541 Canadian Association of University Schools of Music. Journal *changed to* Canadian University Music Society Review
0315-355X Alberta-Westmorland-Kent Regional Library. Extension Department. News†
0315-3606 Body Politic
0315-3630 Northern Journey†
0315-3673 Strategie
0315-369X Reporting Classroom Research
0315-3754 Capilano Review
0315-3770 Event
0315-3800 Alberta Hog Journal *see* 0225-3488
0315-3819 E D P in-Depth Reports
0315-3835 British Columbia Genealogist
0315-3843 C R E A Reporter *changed to* Canadian Real Estate
0315-3932 Waves
0315-3959 Canadian Dancers News
0315-3967 Cahiers Linguistiques d'Ottawa
0315-3975 Video-Presse
0315-4025 Cahier de Linguistique *see* 0710-0167
0315-4114 Concern International
0315-4149 International Fiction Review
0315-4254 C B Newsletter†
0315-4297 Journal of Canadian Art History
0315-4351 Comment on Education
0315-4459 Forgotten People
0315-4661 Computernews
0315-467X Chien d'Or
0315-4785 Arctic and Northern Development Digest *see* 0704-4836
0315-4793 Better Vending & Catering
0315-484X Actrascope News†
0315-4874 Landscape/Paysage Canada
0315-4998 Ligne Directe
0315-5064 Manitoba Nature
0315-5226 Vanguard
0315-5463 Canadian Institute of Food Science and Technology. Journal
0315-5943 Repertoire de l'Edition au Quebec
0315-5986 I N F O R Journal
0315-6168 Canadian Parliamentary Guide
0315-6230 Canadian Banker and I C B Review
0315-6877 Canadian Society for Horticultural Science. Journal
0315-6915 Shaver Focus
0315-694X Mark II *changed to* Sales & Marketing Management in Canada
0315-6966 Motion
0315-7083 Corpus Almanac of Canada
0315-727X C S S E Yearbook
0315-7288 Guide to Periodicals and Newspapers in the Public Libraries of Metropolitan Toronto
0315-7326 Sixteen Mm Films Available in the Public Libraries of Metropolitan Toronto
0315-7423 Grain
0315-7466 Atlantic Sport News†
0315-758X Next Year Country *changed to* Next Year Country Journal
0315-758X Next Year Country *changed to* Next Year Country News
0315-7601 Canada: an Historical Magazine†
0315-761X Canadian Archaeological Association. Bulletin *see* 0705-2006
0315-7784 Black Images†
0315-7911 City Magazine
0315-7997 Historical Reflections
0315-8020 Kateri (Edition Francaise)
0315-8098 Corporate Insurance in Canada
0315-8101 Mennonite Mirror
0315-8179 Ascent
0315-8233 Canadian Gas Association. Membership Directory
0315-8349 Directory of Gas Utilities *see* 0576-5269
0315-8527 Horizon
0315-8691 Foreign Focus†
0315-8705 Canadian Ethnic Studies Association. Bulletin
0315-8748 A I M E†
0315-8756 Log House
0315-8888 Emergency Librarian
0315-8934 Automatic Control Theory and Applications
0315-8977 Canadian Society for Mechanical Engineering. Transactions
0315-9000 Council of Ontario Universities. Annual Review *see* 0315-9590
0315-9027 Discovery Through Art
0315-906X Classmate
0315-9124 Manitoba School Library Audio Visual Association Journal
0315-9140 Canadian Mining Journal's Reference Manual & Buyers' Guide
0315-9159 Manitoba Science Teacher
0315-9183 Plant Management and Engineering
0315-9248 Development Journal
0315-9337 Canadian Micrographic Society. Micro Notes
0315-9388 Educational Planning†
0315-940X Universities Art Association of Canada. Journal
0315-9523 O H P A Market Place
0315-9566 Humanities Research Council of Canada. Bulletin *see* 0707-8048
0315-9590 Council of Ontario Universities Triennial Review
0315-985X Canadian Chemical Register
0315-9884 Cancer in Ontario
0315-9906 R A C A R
0315-9922 About Unions
0315-9930 Argus
0315-9981 I D R C Reports
0316-0033 Probe *see* 0381-646X
0316-0041 Criminologie
0316-0114 National Research Council, Canada. Associate Committee on Scientific Criteria for Environmental Quality. Status Report
0316-0149 Canadian Theses on Microfiche (Supplement)
0316-0173 British Columbia English Teachers' Association. Journal
0316-0297 Directory of Federally Supported Research in Universities
0316-0300 Essays on Canadian Writing
0316-0386 Notes on Unions
0316-0602 Lifeline *changed to* Writer's Lifeline
0316-0661 Environmental Management for the Public Health Inspector
0316-0688 Dalhousie Labour Institute for the Atlantic Provinces. Proceedings
0316-0696 Canadian Essay and Literature Index
0316-0734 Directory of Associations in Canada
0316-0769 Subsidia Mediaevalia
0316-0874 Mediaeval Sources in Translation
0316-0955 Association pour l'Avancement des Sciences et des Techniques de la Documentation. Rapport
0316-0963 Association pour l'Avancement des Sciences et des Techniques de la Documentation. Nouvelles de l'A S T E D
0316-0963 A. S. T. E. D. Nouvelles
0316-1218 Canadian Journal of Higher Education
0316-1269 Royal Ontario Museum. History, Technology and Art Monographs
0316-1277 Royal Ontario Museum. Ethnography Monograph
0316-1285 Royal Ontario Museum. Archaeology Monographs
0316-1323 Canadian Theatre Review Yearbook
0316-1544 British Columbia Art Teachers' Association. Journal
0316-1552 Alberta History
0316-1609 Room of One's Own
0316-1617 Ontario Government Publications, Monthly Checklist

0316-1862 Canada. National Museum of Man. Mercury Series. Canadian Ethnology Service. Papers
0316-1897 Canada. National Museum of Man. Mercury Series. Canadian Centre for Folk Culture Studies. Papers
0316-1900 Canada. National Museum of Man. Mercury Series. History Division. Papers
0316-1919 Canada. National Museum of Man. Mercury Series. Canadian War Museum. Papers
0316-2281 Mining in Canada - Facts & Figures
0316-2494 Tailspinner
0316-2508 Vexillum
0316-2516 Sound Heritage
0316-2540 Talespinner *see* 0316-2494
0316-2672 Etudes Francaises dans le Monde *see* 0226-7454
0316-2702 Grand Manan Historian
0316-280X Canadian Camper
0316-2907 Canadian Gideon
0316-2915 Torch and Trumpet *see* 0316-2907
0316-2923 Philosophiques
0316-3040 Come and See
0316-313X Social Development
0316-3210 Echo
0316-327X PSST†
0316-3334 Perspectives
0316-3393 L A W G Letter
0316-3423 Profitable Outdoor Occupations *see* 0316-3431
0316-3431 Outdoor Careers
0316-3458 Winnipeg Industrial Topics†
0316-3547 Canadian Gas Facts
0316-3571 Canadian Tax Foundation. Tax Conference. Report of Proceedings
0316-3768 Writ
0316-3903 O T F/F E O Interaction
0316-3938 Canadian Locations of Journals Indexed in Index Medicus *changed to* Canadian Locations of Journals Indexed for Medline
0316-4004 Pulp & Paper Canada
0316-4047 National Research Council, Canada. Annual Report on Scholarships and Grants in Aid of Research
0316-4055 Ontario Review
0316-4241 Canadian Pulp and Paper Association. Annual Newsprint Supplement
0316-4454 Rehabilitation Institute of Montreal. Bulletin
0316-4543 Canadian Association of University Business Officers. Bulletin
0316-4608 Profile Index to Canadian and Municipal Government Publications *see* 0707-3135
0316-4616 Royal Society of Canada. Proceedings and Transactions
0316-4675 University of Western Ontario. Department of Psychology. Research Bulletin
0316-4683 University of Alberta. Department of Computing Science. Technical Reports
0316-4853 Pulp and Paper Research Institute of Canada. Logging Research Reports†
0316-4896 Black Book Vehicle Identification Guide
0316-4969 History and Social Science Teacher
0316-5019 C F F S Index of Feature Length Films
0316-5078 Queen's University. Institute for Economic Research. Discussion Paper
0316-5116 Insurance Institute of Canada. Newsletter
0316-5310 Law Society of Upper Canada. Special Lectures
0316-5329 Nineteenth Century Theatre Research
0316-5345 Science et Esprit
0316-5515 Canadian Film Digest Yearbook
0316-5973 Modernist Studies: Literature and Culture, 1920-1940
0316-5981 Atlantic Provinces Book Review
0316-6325 Nova Scotia Law News
0316-6368 Universite de Moncton. Revue
0316-6546 Institute of Chartered Accountants of Alberta. Monthly Statement
0316-6570 McGill University, Montreal. Centre for Developing-Area Studies. Bibliography Series
0316-6597 Serials Holdings in the Libraries of Memorial University of Newfoundland, St. John's Public Library and College of Trades and Technology
0316-6600 Memorial University of Newfoundland. Library. Serials Holdings in the Libraries of Memorial University of Newfoundland and St. John's Public Library *see* 0316-6597
0316-6724 Charlottes
0316-7437 Books in Bengali
0316-7518 New Canadian Stories *see* 0703-9476
0316-7631 Canadian Export Association. Export News Bulletin
0316-7771 Canadian Sporting Goods & Playthings. Directory
0316-7828 Boreal Institute, Edmonton. Report of Activities
0316-7917 Canadian Journal of Research in Semiotics
0316-7933 Canadian Urban Transit Association. Proceedings
0316-7941 Canadian Transit Association. Proceedings *see* 0316-7933
0316-7984 University of Manitoba. Center for Transportation Studies. Research Report
0316-800X Lutheran Churches in Canada. Directory
0316-8131 Canadian and Provincian Golf Records
0316-8174 National Hockey League. Guide
0316-8212 Royal Canadian Golf Association. National Tournament Records *see* 0316-8131
0316-8433 News News News
0316-8484 Canadian Children's Annual
0316-8549 Ontario Directory of Education
0316-8565 Canadian Journal of Social Work Education
0316-859X Canadian Logger & Pulpwood Contractor
0316-8603 German-Canadian Yearbook
0316-8670 Words from Inside
0316-8743 Canadian Religious Conference. Bulletin
0316-8840 Revolting Librarian
0316-8913 My Brother and I
0316-8956 Canadian Information Processing Society. Computer Census
0316-9014 Humane Viewpoint
0316-9200 Ordre des Architectes du Quebec. Bulletin
0316-9235 Art & Literary Review *see* 0316-9243
0316-9243 Muskeg Review†
0316-9375 Canadian Construction Association. Documentation de Reference
0316-9448 Current Canadian Books
0316-9537 Blue Book of Food Store Operators & Wholesalers
0317-0209 Journal of Orthomolecular Psychiatry
0317-0349 Ontario Education Dimensions†
0317-0403 All About Boating†
0317-0500 Chesterton Review
0317-0713 Cahiers de Psychologie et de Reeducation†
0317-0802 English Studies in Canada
0317-0845 Repository
0317-0861 Canadian Public Policy
0317-0926 C I M Bulletin
0317-1272 Insurance Marketer
0317-1280 R T A C News
0317-1493 Consensus
0317-1655 Jewish Historical Society of Western Canada. Annual Publication
0317-1663 Dalhousie Law Journal
0317-1671 Canadian Journal of Neurological Sciences
0317-1817 Fisheries Fact Sheet.
0317-2023 Canadian Fisherman & Ocean Science
0317-2031 Arts Victoria
0317-204X Canadian American Review of Hungarian Studies
0317-2147 Chelsea Journal
0317-2244 Canada. National Museum of Man. Mercury Series. Archaeological Survey of Canada. Papers
0317-2317 Journal of Leisurability
0317-2333 Cinema Quebec
0317-2481 Flypaper
0317-2546 Queen's University. Industrial Relations Centre. Research and Current Issues Series
0317-266X Evangelical Baptist Churches in Canada. Fellowship Yearbook
0317-2678 Guide de Reussite dans le Carriere d'Assureur-Vie
0317-2686 Guide d'Une Carriere a Succes *see* 0317-2678
0317-2716 Canada. National Museum of Man. Mercury Series. Communications Division. Papers
0317-2775 Canadian Urban Sources *see* 0707-3135
0317-2791 Canadian Pool and Patio
0317-2961 Vernon's City of Guelph (Ontario) Directory
0317-297X British Columbia Provincial Judges' Association. Annual Conference
0317-3119 University of Alberta. Department of Sociology. Population Research Laboratory. Alberta Series Report
0317-3348 University of Waterloo Biology Series
0317-3445 Canada. Statistics Canada. Railway Freight Traffic/Trafic Marchandises Ferroviaire
0317-3518 Emergency Planning Digest
0317-3526 Nova Scotia. Environmental Control Council. Annual Report
0317-3550 Pulp & Paper Canada's Business Directory
0317-3720 Canada. Statistics Canada. Surgical Procedures and Treatments/Interventions Chirurgicales et Traitements
0317-3798 Autosport Canada
0317-3925 Alberta Statistical Review
0317-3925 Alberta Statistical Review
0317-3992 Ontario School Counsellors' Association. Newsletter *see* 0383-9931
0317-4018 Svetovy Kongres Slovakov. Bulletin.
0317-4026 Canadian Business Review
0317-4085 Canada. Northern Natural Resources and Environment Branch. Oil and Mineral Division. North of 60: Oil and Gas Technical Reports
0317-4336 Social Services in Nova Scotia
0317-4344 Saskatchewan. Department of Culture and Youth. Annual Report
0317-4514 In Search
0317-4522 Living
0317-4530 Prince Edward Island. Department of Health. Annual Report
0317-4611 Saskatchewan. Department of the Environment. Annual Report
0317-4654 Canadian Materials
0317-4670 Services for People
0317-4697 Canada. Department of Manpower and Immigration. Strategic Planning and Research. Supply, Demand and Salaries: New Graduates of Universities and Community Colleges. Offre, Demande et Salaires.: Nouveaux Diplomes d'Universites et de Colleges.†
0317-4859 Reports of Family Law
0317-4921 Public Libraries in Canada†
0317-4956 Germano-Slavica
0317-5006 A C M C Forum
0317-5065 Cahiers des Etudes Anciennes
0317-5375 Canada. Statistics Canada. Exports-Merchandise Trade/Exportations-Commerce de Merchandises
0317-543X Canadian Society for Legal History. Newsletter†
0317-5642 National Museum of Natural Sciences. Natural History Series†
0317-5685 Canadian Communications Research Information Centre. Newsletter†
0317-5693 Canadian Commission for UNESCO. Annual Report
0317-5766 National Science Library. Health Sciences Resources Centre. Conference Proceedings in the Health Sciences Held by the National Science Library/Comptes Rendus des Conferences sur les Sciences de la Sante Qui Se Trouvent a la Bibliotheque Scientifique Nationale†
0317-5839 Conservation News *see* 0383-6479
0317-5960 Touring Directory of the Performing Arts in Canada *changed to* Touring Artists Directory
0317-5979 Tournees de Spectacles
0317-6045 C M A Gazette
0317-607X Bond Record
0317-6126 Ahoy
0317-6193 Captain George's Penny Dreadful
0317-6282 Prairie Forum
0317-6525 Consulting Engineers-Canada-Ingenieurs-Conseils
0317-6649 Canada Business Corporations Act with Regulations
0317-6673 Conservation Canada
0317-6738 Travel Between Canada and Other Countries
0317-6789 Economic Council of Canada. Economic and Social Indicators†
0317-6878 C A Magazine
0317-6908 Canada. Forestry Service. Bi-Monthly Research Notes *see* 0228-9989
0317-6983 Maltese Directory: Canada, United States
0317-7076 Decks Awash
0317-7173 Cartographica
0317-7254 Carleton Germanic Papers
0317-7262 Manitoba. Horse Racing Commission. Annual Report
0317-7335 Saskatchewan Labour Report
0317-7645 Dimensions in Health Service
0317-7785 Canadian Rodeo News
0317-7882 Canada. Statistics Canada. Aggregate Productivity Measures/Mesures Globales de Productivite
0317-7904 Canadian Review of Studies in Nationalism
0317-7920 Canadian Art Auction Record†
0317-8064 Chess Federation of Canada. Bulletin *see* 0225-7351
0317-8161 Ontario. Ministry of Consumer and Commercial Relations. Statistical Review
0317-851X En Eglise
0317-8536 Directory of Libraries in Manitoba
0317-8552 Free Press Report on Farming
0317-8579 Alberta Teachers Association. Mathematics Monograph
0317-8633 University of Waterloo. Division of Environmental Studies. Occasional Paper *changed to* University of Waterloo. Faculty of Environmental Studies. Occasional Paper
0317-8765 Anglican Year Book
0317-8781 Scott's Industrial Directory. Western Section *see* 0317-879X
0317-879X Scott's Industrial Directories - Western
0317-882X Canadian Pulp & Paper Association. Technical Section. Transactions
0317-9044 Canadian Drama
0317-9087 Canadian Council on International Law. Proceedings of the Annual Conference
0317-9281 Bridge Digest *see* 0707-9524
0317-9311 U F O - Quebec
0317-9443 Toy and Decoration Fair
0317-946X Canadian Tax Foundation. Provincial and Municipal Finances
0317-9508 Mining-What Mining Means to Canada
0317-9672 Canada. Statistics Canada. Production and Value of Maple Products/Production et Valeur des Produits de l'Erable
0317-9893 University of Toronto. Department of Geography. Discussion Paper Series
0318-000X Indian Education Newsletter
0318-0069 Cable Communications

ISSN INDEX

ISSN	Title
0318-0077	Learning Resources
0318-0123	Donum Dei
0318-0247	O L A Focus
0318-0344	Fraser's Construction & Building Directory
0318-0433	H P E C Runner see 0707-3186
0318-0468	Water & Pollution Control. Directory and Handbook
0318-0492	Quebec Astronomique
0318-0522	Canadian Structural Engineering Conference. Proceedings
0318-0646	Professional Institute of the Public Service of Canada. Communications
0318-0794	Canadian Environmental Control Newsletter
0318-0859	Canadian Process Equipment & Control News
0318-0867	Canadian Amateur
0318-0913	Simmental Scene
0318-0948	Reviewing Librarian
0318-1006	Nursing Papers: Perspectives on Nursing
0318-1049	Meetings & Incentive Travel
0318-1235	University of Toronto-York University Joint Program in Transportation. Newsletter
0318-1251	University of Toronto-York University. Joint Program in Transportation. Annual Report
0318-1340	Liaison
0318-1723	N A P E News changed to Communicator
0318-174X	University of Victoria (B.C.) Library. Serials Holdings Catalogue
0318-1944	Canadian Information Processing Society. Canadian Salary Survey
0318-1960	C. A. H. P. E. R. News
0318-2037	Current Soviet Leaders
0318-2126	Association of New Brunswick Land Surveyors.Annual Report
0318-2274	Canada. Statistics Canada. Private and Public Investment in Canada. Outlook/Investissements Prives et Publics au Canada. Perspectives
0318-2452	Femme
0318-2789	Canadian Conservation Directory
0318-2851	Association of Canadian Map Libraries. Bulletin
0318-3270	Introductions from an Island see 0706-8093
0318-3610	Matrix
0318-3874	Canada. Statistics Canada. Salaries and Qualifications of Teachers in Public, Elementary and Secondary Schools/Traitements et Qualifications des Enseignants des Ecoles Publiques, Primaires et Secondaires
0318-3912	Manitoba. Water Services Board. Annual Report
0318-3971	Alberta Opportunity Company. Annual Report
0318-4099	Canada Manpower and Immigration Review
0318-4137	Recherches Amerindiennes au Quebec
0318-4277	Canadian Forest Industries
0318-4315	Institute of Canadian Bankers. Educational Programs
0318-4390	Touring & Travel
0318-4552	Housing Ontario
0318-4684	Saskatchewan. Department of Tourism and Renewable Resources. Annual Report
0318-4757	Alberta. Department of Transportation. Annual Report
0318-4943	Alberta Fishing Guide
0318-5036	Canadian Association of Administrative Sciences. Proceedings, Annual Conference/Rapport, la Conference Annuelle
0318-5133	Canadian Society of Environmental Biologists Newsletter
0318-5176	Alberta Modern Language Journal
0318-5184	Canada. Statistics Canada. Survey of Canadian Nursery Trades Industry/Enquete sur l'Industrie des Pepinieres Canadiennes
0318-5273	Canada. Statistics Canada. Household Facilities and Equipment/L'Equipment Menager
0318-5311	Issues in Canadian Science Policy†
0318-5729	Amigo
0318-5737	Amisol
0318-5753	Amber
0318-6075	Cross Country
0318-6210	Training Aids Action Service
0318-6229	Careers for Graduates
0318-6342	T. S. Eliot Review see 0704-5700
0318-6385	Metric Message
0318-6415	Manitoba Community Reports
0318-658X	Agronews
0318-6644	Artmagazine
0318-6717	Canadian Business Periodicals Index changed to Canadian Business Index
0318-675X	Canadian Government Publications: Catalogue
0318-6830	C U S O Forum
0318-6954	Archivaria
0318-7020	Parachute (Montreal)
0318-708X	Canada. Statistics Canada. National Income and Expenditure Accounts/Comptes Nationaux des Revenus et des Depenses
0318-7128	Canada. Statistics Canada. Sawmills and Planing Mills and Shingle Mills/Scieries et Ateliers de Rabotage et Usines de Bardeaux
0318-7179	University and College Libraries in Canada†
0318-7306	Action Canada France
0318-7306	Action Canada France
0318-7403	Dalhousie University. School of Library Service. Occasional Papers
0318-742X	C G A Magazine
0318-7446	Land see 0700-1770
0318-7454	Forestalk see 0700-1770
0318-7551	Eskimo
0318-7632	Hiballer Magazine see 0708-2169
0318-7721	Hospitality Canada
0318-7888	Canada. Statistics Canada. Report on Fur Farms/Rapport sur les Fermes a Fourrure
0318-7985	Italian Chamber of Commerce Bulletin
0318-8116	L U A C Monitor
0318-8140	Urban Forum
0318-8272	Huxley Institute-C.S.F. Newsletter
0318-8329	Inventory of Research into Higher Education in Canada
0318-8647	Indian-ed changed to Canadian Journal of Native Education
0318-8655	Black Moss
0318-8752	Franchise Annual
0318-8779	Quebec (Province) Direction Generale des Peches Maritimes. Direction de la Recherche. Rapport Annuel
0318-8787	Canada. Statistics Canada. Selected Financial Statistics of Charitable Organizations/Certaines Statistiques Financieres des Oeuvres de Charite†
0318-8809	Canada. Statistics Canada. Building Permits/Permis de Batir
0318-8841	Canada. Statistics Canada. Contract Drilling for Petroleum and Other Contract Drilling/Forage de Puits de Petrole a Forfait et Autre Forage a Forfait†
0318-8868	Canada's International Investment Position/Bilan Canadien des Investissements Internationaux
0318-8876	Canada. Statistics Canada. Provincial Government Finance, Assets, Liabilities, Sources and Uses of Funds/Finances Publiques Provinciales, Actif, Passif, Sources et Utilisations des Fonds
0318-8914	Canada. Statistics Canada. Shipping Report. Part 1: International Seaborne Shipping (by Country) /Transport Maritime. Partie 1: Transport Maritime International (Par Pays)†
0318-8930	Canada. Statistics Canada. Shipping Report. Part 3: Coastwise Shipping/Transport Maritime. Partie 3: Navigation Nationale†
0318-8949	Canada. Statistics Canada. Shipping Report. Part 5: Origin and Destination for Selected Commodities/Transport Maritime. Partie 5: Origine et Destination de Certaines Marchandises†
0318-9007	Canada. Statistics Canada. Estimates of Labour Income/Estimations du Revenu du Travail
0318-9090	Canadian Journal of University Continuing Education
0318-9171	University of British Columbia. Faculty of Forestry. Bulletin
0318-9201	Voix et Images
0318-9368	Black Book Used Truck Guide
0318-952X	Current Industrial Relations Scene in Canada
0318-9600	Canadian Aural/Oral History Association. Bulletin see 0383-6576
0318-9651	Apartment & Building
0318-9937	American Society for Information Science, Western Canada Chapter. Annual Meeting Proceedings
0319-003X	Atlantic Canada Economics Association. Annual Conference: A C E A Papers
0319-0080	Canadian Children's Literature
0319-0161	Computing Canada
0319-034X	Educational ABC of Canadian Industry
0319-0358	North Shore Numismatic Society. Bulletin see 0380-8866
0319-0382	Venereal Diseases in Canada
0319-0382	Canada. Epidemiology Division. Venereal Disease in Canada see 0319-0382
0319-0404	British Columbia. Labour Relations Board. Annual Report
0319-0412	British Columbia Economic Outlook Survey see 0701-757X
0319-051X	Canadian Review of Comparative Literature
0319-0552	York Dance Review†
0319-0595	Harlequint
0319-0684	B C S T A Convention Reporter see 0703-766X
0319-0994	Women Can see 0319-1001
0319-1001	Pedestal
0319-1095	Interuniversity Centre for European Studies. Bulletin
0319-1214	Pangnirtung
0319-1915	Canadian Gladiolus Society. Annual
0319-1974	Canadian Research
0319-2008	Uncertified Human
0319-2148	Canadian Office
0319-2148	Canadian Office Redbook
0319-2156	Connection
0319-2431	Canadian Tax News
0319-2571	Canadian Archer
0319-258X	Directory of Community Services of Greater Montreal
0319-2636	Order of Nurses of Quebec. News and Notes
0319-2644	Canadian Public Health Association. Proceedings of the Annual Meeting
0319-2709	Mart
0319-2822	Cycle Canada
0319-2962	Canada News
0319-3098	Jardin Botanique de Montreal. Annuelles et Legumes: Resultats des Cultures d'Essai
0319-3101	Jardin Botanique de Montreal. Annuelle see 0319-3098
0319-3225	Canadian Funeral Director
0319-3233	Canadian Export Association. Review & Digest Bulletin
0319-3322	Canadian Business Law Journal
0319-3535	Alberta Hail and Crop Insurance Corporation. Annual Report
0319-3608	Environment News see 0701-9637
0319-3799	Canada. Statistics Canada. Honey Production/Production de Miel
0319-3896	CANPARA
0319-4019	Monarchy Canada
0319-4027	Industrial Manager see 0045-5156
0319-423X	Alberta. Alcoholism and Drug Abuse Commission. Annual Report
0319-4434	Canadian Journal of Radiography, Radiotherapy, Nuclear Medicine.
0319-4477	Canadian Newsletter of Research on Women see 0707-8412
0319-4558	A P T Communique
0319-4604	R N A N S Bulletin
0319-4639	Cape Breton's Magazine
0319-4728	Centre Stage
0319-485X	Religious Studies Review
0319-4930	Canada. Statistics Canada. Labour Costs in Canada: Finance, Insurance and Real Estate/Couts de la Main-d'Oeuvre au Canada: Finances, Assurances, et Immeuble
0319-4957	Canada. Statistics Canada. Feldspar and Quartz Mines/Mines de Feldspath et de Quartz†
0319-5023	Action
0319-5376	Canadian Association of Law Libraries. Newsletter
0319-5465	Sanavik Cooperative. Baker Lake Prints
0319-5724	Canadian Journal of Statistics
0319-5759	Energy Processing/Canada
0319-583X	Canada North Almanac
0319-5864	National Gallery of Canada. Journal
0319-616X	Floor Covering News
0319-6267	Canadian Premiums & Incentives
0319-6348	Canadian Quarter Horse Journal
0319-6356	Canadian Music Teacher
0319-6771	Environmental Health Review
0319-681X	Cegepropos
0319-6879	C V 2
0319-6887	Bharati
0319-6984	Alerte au Quebec
0319-7018	Building Management Maintenance News
0319-7093	Canadian Travel News Weekly
0319-7107	Canadian Travel News
0319-7336	Hume Studies
0319-7387	Canadian Wool Grower
0319-7468	Communique
0319-7581	Corinthian
0319-7697	Manitoba Moods†
0319-7778	Communications
0319-7832	Craftnews
0319-7840	Craftsman changed to Ontario Craft
0319-7980	Alberta Decisions, Civil and Criminal Cases
0319-7999	Saskatchewan Decisions, Civil and Criminal Cases
0319-8014	Canada. Statistics Canada. Hospitals Section. List of Canadian Hospitals and Related Institutions and Facilities/Liste des Hopitaux Canadiens et des Etablissements et Installations Connexes see 0225-5642
0319-8227	Canada. Statistics Canada. Statistics of Criminal and Other Offences/Statistique de la Criminalite†
0319-8251	Canada. Statistics Canada. Construction Price Statistics. Quarterly Report/Statistiques des Prix de la Construction Rapport Trimestriel†
0319-8278	Canada. Statistics Canada. Housing Starts and Completions/Logements Mis en Chantier et Paracheves
0319-8294	Industrial Business Management changed to Industrial Business Management Technology
0319-8316	Ontario. Ministry of Labour. Research Library. Library Selection see 0705-517X
0319-8340	Dimensions
0319-8413	Design Product News
0319-8480	Discovery
0319-8499	Saskatchewan Registered Nurses' Association. Bulletin
0319-8561	Cross Trail News
0319-8588	Dome
0319-8650	Envers du Decor
0319-8693	Asia Times
0319-8715	Canadian India Star

ISSN	Title
0321-186X	Leningradskii Universitet. Vestnik. Seriya Biologiya
0322-7243	Metodicky Zpravodaj Cs. Soustavy Vedeckych, Technickych a Ekonomickych Informaci
0322-8959	Novinky Literatury: Geologie-Geografie
0322-9378	Novinky Literatury: Jazykoveda. Literarni Veda
0322-9564	Prumyslove Informace
0322-9653	Financni Zpravodaj
0323-1283	Hudebni Nastroje
0323-1364	Atletika
0323-1445	Lyzarstvi
0323-1569	Bibliograficky Katalog C S S R: Ceske Hudebniny a Gramofonove Desky
0323-1615	Bibliograficky Katalog C S S R: Ceske Knihy
0323-1763	Bibliograficky Katalog C S S R: Ceske Knihy. Zvlastni Sesit. Ceske Disertace
0323-214X	Myslivost
0323-3308	Agrartechnik
0323-3553	D E T
0323-374X	Deutsches Buecherverzeichnis
0323-3804	Textiltechnik
0323-410X	Frisur und Kosmetik
0323-4290	Zidis-Information *changed to* Zidis
0323-4614	D D R-Medizin-Report
0323-4983	Anaesthesiologie und Reanimation
0323-5386	Medizin Aktuell
0323-5637	Zeitschrift fuer medizinische Laboratoriumsdiagnostik
0323-8776	Z F I-Mitteilungen
0324-3451	Hungarian Book Review
0324-4628	Nehezipari Muszaki Egyetem, Miskolc. Publications. Series A: Mining
0324-4652	Neohelicon
0324-4679	Nehezipari Muszaki Egyetem, Miskolc. Publications. Series B: Metallurgy
0324-6957	Acta Marxistica Leninistica. Tudomanyos Szocializmus Tanulmanyok
0324-6957	Acta Marxistica Leninistica. Filozofiai Tanulmanyok
0324-6957	Acta Marxistica Leninistica. Politikai Gazdasagtan Tanulmanyok
0324-7341	Modszertani Kiadvanyok
0324-7473	New Hungarian Exporter
0324-8003	Kartkowy Katalog Nowosci
0324-802X	Politechnika Slaska. Zeszyty Naukowe. Hutnictwo
0324-8046	Politechnika Slaska. Zeszyty Naukowe. Organizacja
0324-8208	Teksty
0324-8240	Szpitalnictwo Polskie
0324-8283	Studies on International Relations
0324-8453	Magazyn Fotograficzny FOTO
0324-8461	Archiwum Ochrony Srodowiska
0324-8739	Prace Przemyslowego Instytutu Maszyn Rolniczych
0324-8828	Environment Protection Engineering
0324-9050	Wyzsza Szkola Pedagogiczna, Opole. Zeszyty Naukowe. Filologia Polska
0324-9182	Mechanika i Budownictwo Ladowe
0324-9204	Akademia Rolniczo-Techniczna. Zeszyty Naukowe
0324-931X	Politechnika Wroclawska. Instytut Ukladow Elektromaszynowych. Prace Naukowe. Konferencje
0324-9328	Politechnika Wroclawska. Instytut Telekomunikacji i Akustyki. Prace Naukowe. Monografie
0324-9336	Politechnika Wroclawska. Instytut Telekomunikacji i Akustyki. Prace Naukowe. Studia i Materialy
0324-9344	Politechnika Wroclawska. Instytut Telekomunikacji i Akustyki. Prace Naukowe. Konferencje
0324-9360	Politechnika Wroclawska. Instytut Technologii Budowy Maszyn. Prace Naukowe. Studia i Materialy
0324-9379	Politechnika Wroclawska. Instytut Technologii Budowy Maszyn. Prace Naukowe. Konferencje
0324-9387	Politechnika Wroclawska. Instytut Techniki Cieplnej i Mechaniki Plynow. Prace Naukowe. Monografie
0324-9395	Politechnika Wroclawska. Instytut Techniki Cieplnej i Mechaniki Plynow. Prace Naukowe. Konferencje
0324-9409	Politechnika Wroclawska. Instytut Techniki Cieplnej i Mechaniki Plynow. Prace Naukowe. Studia i Materialy
0324-9441	Politechnika Wroclawska. Instytut Podstaw Elektrotechniki i Elektrotechnologii. Prace Naukowe. Konferencje
0324-945X	Politechnika Wroclawska. Instytut Podstaw Elektrotechniki i Elektrotechnologii. Prace Naukowe. Monografie
0324-9468	Politechnika Wroclawska. Instytut Organizacji i Zarzadzania. Prace Naukowe. Studia i Materialy
0324-9484	Politechnika Wroclawska. Instytut Organizacji i Zarzadzania. Prace Naukowe. Konferencje
0324-9492	Politechnika Wroclawska. Instytut Organizacji i Zarzadzania. Prace Naukowe. Monografie
0324-9506	Politechnika Wroclawska. Instytut Nauk Spolecznych. Prace Naukowe. Monografie
0324-9514	Politechnika Wroclawska. Instytut Nauk Spolecznych. Prace Naukowe. Studia i Materialy
0324-9530	Politechnika Wroclawska. Instytut Metrologii Elektrycznej. Prace Naukowe. Przemysl
0324-9549	Politechnika Wroclawska. Instytut Metrologii Elektrycznej. Prace Naukowe. Monografie
0324-9557	Politechnika Wroclawska. Instytut Metrologii Elektrycznej. Prace Naukowe. Konferencje
0324-9565	Politechnika Wroclawska. Instytut Materialoznawstwa i Mechaniki Technicznej. Prace Naukowe. Monografie
0324-9573	Politechnika Wroclawska. Instytut Materialoznawstwa i Mechaniki Technicznej. Prace Naukowe. Konferencje
0324-9603	Politechnika Wroclawska. Instytut Matematyki. Prace Naukowe. Monografie
0324-9611	Politechnika Wroclawska. Instytut Matematyki. Prace Naukowe. Studia i Materialy
0324-962X	Politechnika Wroclawska. Instytut Konstrukcji i Eksploatacji Maszyn. Prace Naukowe. Monografie
0324-9638	Politechnika Wroclawska. Instytut Konstrukcji i Eksploatacji Maszyn. Prace Naukowe. Studia i Materialy
0324-9646	Politechnika Wroclawska. Instytut Konstrukcji i Eksploatacji Maszyn. Prace Naukowe. Konferencje
0324-9654	Politechnika Wroclawska. Instytut Historii Architektury, Sztuki i Techniki. Prace Naukowe. Studia i Materialy
0324-9670	Politechnika Wroclawska. Instytut Gornictwa. Prace Naukowe. Konferencje
0324-9689	Politechnika Wroclawska. Instytut Gornictwa. Prace Naukowe. Monografie
0324-9697	Politechnika Wroclawska. Instytut Fizyki. Prace Naukowe. Studia i Materialy
0324-9719	Politechnika Wroclawska. Instytut Inzynierii Ochrony Srodowiska. Prace Naukowe. Konferencje
0324-9727	Politechnika Wroclawska. Instytut Inzynierii Ladowej. Prace Naukowe. Monografie
0324-9743	Politechnika Wroclawska. Instytut Inzynierii Ladowej. Prace Naukowe. Konferencje
0324-9751	Politechnika Wroclawska. Instytut Inzynierii Chemicznej i Urzadzen Cieplnych. Prace Naukowe. Studia i Materialy
0324-976X	Politechnika Wroclawska. Instytut Energoelektryki. Prace Naukowe. Monografie
0324-9778	Politechnika Wroclawska. Instytut Energoelektryki. Prace Naukowe. Konferencje
0324-9786	Politechnika Wroclawska. Instytut Cybernetyki Technicznej. Prace Naukowe. Monografie
0324-9794	Politechnika Wroclawska. Instytut Cybernetyki Technicznej. Prace Naukowe. Konferencje
0324-9808	Politechnika Wroclawska. Instytut Cybernetyki Technicznej. Prace Naukowe. Studia i Materialy
0324-9816	Politechnika Wroclawska. Instytut Chemii Organicznej i Fizycznej. Prace Naukowe. Monografie
0324-9824	Politechnika Wroclawska. Instytut Chemii Organicznej i Fizycznej. Prace Naukowe. Konferencje
0324-9832	Politechnika Wroclawska. Instytut Chemii Nieorganicznej i Metalurgii Pierwiastkow Rzadkich. Prace Naukowe. Konferencje
0324-9840	Politechnika Wroclawska. Instytut Chemii Nieorganicznej i Metalurgii Pierwiastkow Rzadkich. Prace Naukowe. Monografie
0324-9859	Politechnika Wroclawska. Instytut Chemii i Technologii Nafty i Wegla. Prace Naukowe. Monografie
0324-9867	Politechnika Wroclawska. Instytut Chemii i Technologii Nafty i Wegla. Prace Naukowe. Konferencje
0324-9875	Politechnika Wroclawska. Instytut Budownictwa. Prace Naukowe. Monografie
0324-9883	Politechnika Wroclawska. Instytut Budownictwa. Prace Naukowe. Konferencje
0324-9891	Politechnika Wroclawska. Instytut Architektury i Urbanistyki. Prace Naukowe. Studia i Materialy
0324-9905	Politechnika Wroclawska. Instytut Architektury i Urbanistyki. Prace Naukowe. Konferencje
0325-0075	Archivos Argentinos de Pediatria *see* 0325-3767
0325-0210	Ceramica y Cristal (1961) *see* 0325-0229
0325-0229	Ceramica y Cristal
0325-0245	Tesis Presentadas a la Universidad de Buenos Aires
0325-0431	C L A C S O Boletin
0325-0474	Revista Latinoamericana de Ingenieria Quimica y Quimica Aplicada
0325-058X	Revista de la Union Industrial†
0325-0598	Liberacion y Derecho†
0325-0601	Revista de Ciencias Juridicas Sociales
0325-0725	Revista Latinoamericana de Filosofia
0325-0806	Revista de Ciencias Economicas. Temas de Administracion (1971-1972) *see* 0325-0814
0325-0814	Administracion
0325-0822	Revista de Ciencias Economicas. Temas de Economia (1971-1972) *see* 0325-0830
0325-0830	Economia
0325-1071	Universidad de Cordoba. Facultad de Odontologia. Revista
0325-1209	Universidad de Buenos Aires. Instituto de Historia Antigua Oriental. Revista
0325-1276	Revista de la Bolsa de Cereales *see* 0045-2467
0325-1306	Centro de Investigacion y Accion Social. Revista
0325-1799	Estacion Experimental Region Agropecuaria Pergamino. Informe Tecnico
0325-1799	Pergamino, Argentina. Estacion Experimental Regional Agropecuaria. Informe Tecnico
0325-1950	Argentina. Instituto Nacional de Estadistica y Censos. Boletin de Estadistica y Censos
0325-1969	Argentina. Instituto Nacional de Estadistica y Censos. Boletin Estadistico Trimestral
0325-2868	Archivo General de la Nacion. Revista
0325-3767	Pediatria
0325-4453	Nudos en la Cultura Argentina
0325-4615	Summa
0325-5387	Ethos
0325-6251	Bibliotecologia y Documentacion Argentina
0325-6278	Argentina. Instituto Nacional de Tecnologia Industria. Boletin Tecnico
0325-6375	Instituto Nacional de Investigacion y Desarrollo Pesquero. Revista
0325-6790	Instituto Nacional de Investigacion y Desarrollo Pesquero. Serie Contribuciones
0325-6987	Instituto Nacional de Investigacion y Desarrollo Pesquero. Memoria
0325-7479	Circulo Argentino de Odontologia. Revista
0325-8238	Folia Historica del Nordeste
0325-934X	I N T I
0331-0094	Nigerian Journal of Entomology
0331-0361	Nigerian Economic Society. Proceedings of the Annual Conference
0331-0388	Association for Teacher Education in Africa. Western Council. Report of the Annual Conference
0331-0515	West African Journal of Educational and Vocational Measurement
0331-0531	West African Journal of Modern Languages
0331-1481	Nsukka Library Notes
0331-2151	Nigeria Bulletin on Foreign Affairs
0331-3468	Muse
0331-3646	Nigerian Journal of International Affairs
0331-6254	Nigerian Institute of International Affairs. Monograph Series
0331-8400	Marketing in Nigeria
0331-8494	Healthy Living
0332-0006	Dublin. National Library of Ireland. Council of Trustees Report
0332-0235	GLASRA
0332-1711	Engineers Journal
0332-5024	Studia Musicologica Norvegica
0332-5040	Vaeret
0332-5121	Gyldendals Aktuelle Magasin†
0332-5202	A M S-Skrifter
0332-5210	European Offshore Petroleum Newsletter
0332-5229	Jord og Myr
0332-5237	Northern Offshore *see* 0305-876X
0332-5326	Plan og Bygg
0332-5334	Scandinavian Oil Gas Magazine
0332-544X	Noroil
0332-5466	Norsk Advokatblad
0332-5474	Norsk Landbruk
0332-5490	Norsk Oljerevy
0332-5520	Tekstilforum
0332-5571	Ur
0332-5598	Penger og Kreditt
0332-5814	Videregaaende Opplaering
0332-5865	Nordic Journal of Linguistics
0332-5938	Teknikk og Miljoe
0332-5997	Tradisjon
0332-611X	Ingenioer - Nytt
0332-6128	Moderne Transport
0332-6136	Norsk Plast
0332-6144	North Sea Observer
0332-6152	Byggherren
0332-6306	A M S-Varia
0332-6411	A M S-Smaatrykk
0332-6527	Nordisk Statistisk Skriftserie
0332-656X	Synopsis
0332-6578	Norske Arkitektkonkurranser
0332-6756	Bergen Banks Kvartalsskrift
0332-6802	Personal-Opplaering
0332-7205	Fortidsvern
0332-7299	Norsk Utenrikspolitisk Aarbok

0332-7841 Hjelpepleieren
0332-8201 Kontor og Datateknikk
0332-8244 Forum for Utviklingsstudier
0332-8988 Samferdsel
0333-0656 Stavanger Museum. Aarbok
0333-0664 Stavanger Museum. Skrifter
0333-5526 United States-Israel Binational Science Foundation. Project-Report Abstracts
0333-5879 Technion-Israel Institute of Technology. Faculty of Agricultural Engineering. Publications
0333-8487 Herodote
0334-200X Yad la-Kore
0334-2190 Reviews on Drug Metabolism and Drug Interactions
0334-2212 Kidma
0334-2344 Reviews on Powder Metallurgy
0334-2468 Current Research in Behavioral Sciences in Israel
0334-2565 Iyunim Bi-Hinukh
0334-2581 Hebrew University of Jerusalem. News
0334-2751 Sapanut
0334-2808 Mid-East and World Shipping News(Information Paper) *changed to* Mediterranean and World Shipping News (Information Paper)
0334-2824 Directory of Scientific and Technical Associations in Israel
0334-2875 Directory of Research Institutes and Industrial Research Units in Israel *changed to* Directory of Research Institutes and Industrial Laboratories in Israel
0334-3065 Ha'Rivon Ha'Israeli Le'Misim
0334-3162 Israel. Environmental Protection Agency. Ekhut Ha-Sevivah Be-Yisrael. Duakh Shnati
0334-326X Argamon
0334-3715 Levantina
0334-4266 Modern Hebrew Literature
0334-4347 Reviews in Inorganic Chemistry
0334-4762 Social Research Review
0334-4800 Jerusalem Quarterly
0335-0274 I.N.R.S. Bulletin de Documentation
0335-0290 Association Francaise d'Amite et de Solidarite avec les Peuples d'Afrique. Bulletin d'Information *see* 0339-9958
0335-0800 Journal of Neuroradiology
0335-0894 Migrants Formations
0335-1653 Association Francaise pour l'Etude du Sol. Bulletin/Science du Sol
0335-1971 Numismatique & Change
0335-2013 Relations Internationales
0335-2021 Construction Neuve et Ancienne
0335-2986 Gymnastique Volontaire
0335-3559 Repertoire de Materiaux et Elements Controles du Batiment
0335-377X Pulp and Paper/Pates et Papiers
0335-394X Guide de l'Acheteur NF
0335-3958 Quercy Recherche
0335-5012 Assemblee Nouvelle
0335-5047 Droit et Pratique du Commerce International
0335-5160 Societe Geologique de Normandie et des Amis du Museum du Havre. Bulletin Trimestriel
0335-5276 Courrier de l'Industriel du Bois et de l'Ameublement
0335-5322 Actes de la Recherche en Sciences Sociales
0335-5330 Documents de Cartographie Ecologique
0335-704X Escargot *see* 0153-4602
0335-7163 Centre de Promotion de la Presse Industrielle et Scientifique Francaise. Revue des Sommaires†
0335-752X Nouvelles du Livre Ancien
0335-7619 Tribune Medicale
0335-8259 France. Centre National pour l'Exploitation des Oceans. Colloques. Actes
0335-9190 L.S.I.
0335-9395 Combat pour la Paix *see* 0045-7450
0336-1357 Universite de Lyon III. Faculte de Droit. Annales *changed to* Universite Jean Moulin. Annales
0336-1551 Penant
0336-1578 Revue des Sciences Sociales de la France de l'Est
0336-1667 Architecture Mouvement Continuite *see* 0336-1675
0336-1675 A M C
0336-1721 Pluriel
0336-2086 A G E C O P Liaison
0336-2698 Archontes†
0336-3112 France. Centre National pour l'Exploitation des Oceans. Centre Oceanologique de Bretagne. Recueil des Travaux
0336-3686 International Copyright Information Centre. Information Bulletin
0336-4402 Ingenieurs des Villes de France *see* 0336-4410
0336-4410 I V F - Ingenieurs des Villes de France
0336-4437 A.F.C. *see* 0395-2096
0336-4895 Recherche, Pedagogie et Culture
0336-5522 Travaux et Documents de Geographie Tropicale
0336-6324 Maghreb, Machrek, Monde Arabe
0336-6979 France. Institut National de la Statistique et des Etudes Economiques. Documents Divers
0336-8300 Societe Versaillaise des Sciences Naturelles. Bulletin
0336-8424 Bouliste
0336-8653 Nouveaux Echos de la Medecine
0336-9420 Combat Socialiste
0336-9455 Connaissance du Pays d'Oc
0336-9609 Revue Sexpol
0336-9730 Traverses
0336-9749 Babillard *see* 0338-5922
0337-1883 Haut-Parleur
0337-1891 Hifi Stereo
0337-2014 Paradoxes
0337-2219 Industrie du Petrole dans le Monde - Gaz - Petrochimie *changed to* Industrie du Petrole - Gaz - Chimie
0337-2219 Guide International de l'Energie Nucleare
0337-3126 Connexions Psychosociologie Sciences Humaines
0337-4092 Actualite, Combustibles, Energie
0337-5714 Repertoire General de la Production Francaise
0337-5781 Guide du Feu
0337-5927 Annuaire National M.K.D.E. France *see* 0337-5935
0337-5935 Annuaire National des Masseurs Kinesitherapeutes
0337-5978 Mots en Liberte, Bulletin d'Etudes Lexicales†
0337-5986 Lexique Dernier†
0337-6176 Centre Universitaire de la Reunion. Cahier
0337-6729 Informatique Nouvelle
0337-7393 Revue de Jurisprudence Fiscale
0337-8659 Eclats de Rire
0337-8888 Nostra
0337-9353 Loisirs Service-Sports Europe
0337-9736 Revue d'Orthopedie Dento-Faciale
0337-9965 Technicien Biologiste
0338-0181 Khamsin
0338-1439 Cahiers Medicaux
0338-1552 Nouveau Pouvoir Judiciaire
0338-1684 Diabete & Metabolisme
0338-1757 Solidaires
0338-1900 Oeuvres et Critiques
0338-2397 Psychanalyse a l'Universite
0338-2842 H
0338-4187 D F Actualites
0338-4446 Bibliotheque Nationale. Bulletin
0338-4535 Revue Francaise de Transfusion et Immuno-Hematologie
0338-5922 France. Secretariat d'Etat aux Universities. Service des Bibliotheques. Division de la Cooperation et de l'Automatisation. Bulletin de la DICA
0338-7070 Centre Lyonnais d'Acupuncture de Saint-Luc. Bulletin de Liaison
0338-8190 Inconnu
0338-9529 Handicapes Mechants
0339-0047 Secrets de l'Histoire†
0339-0055 Presence de l'Enseignement Agricole Prive
0339-0462 Foi et Developpement
0339-0608 Collections et Monnaies *see* 0183-8490
0339-0861 Echo du Lagon
0339-0934 Citoyen
0339-1116 Centre Auvergne Gadz'arts. Bulletin Trimestriel des Ingenieurs Arts et Metiers de la Region Auvergne
0339-1337 Livre d'Art et d'Essai
0339-1493 Photoroman d'Amour
0339-1507 Sol et Murs Magazine
0339-1558 Composants Mecaniques, Electriques et Electroniques
0339-2171 Cahiers d'Etudes et de Recherche Victoriennes *see* 0220-5610
0339-2899 France. Centre National pour l'Exploitation des Oceans. Publications. Serie: Rapports Scientifiques et Techniques
0339-2902 France. Centre National pour l'Exploitation des Oceans. Publications. Serie: Resultats des Campagnes a la Mer
0339-2910 France. Centre National pour l'Exploitation des Oceans. Publications. Serie: Rapports Economiques et Juridiques
0339-2945 France. Departement d'Economie et de Sociologie Rurales. Bulletin d'Information
0339-3070 Faire
0339-3097 Cahiers de l'Analyse des Donnees
0339-4212 I N E S Informations
0339-5081 Unites Petrochimiques en Europe de l'Ouest
0339-6460 Notes d'Informations Communautaires
0339-6851 Actes
0339-686X Champ Social
0339-6886 Revoltes Logiques
0339-705X Association France-Malte
0339-7068 Association France-Malte. Bulletin *see* 0339-705X
0339-722X S.T.A.L: Sciences et Techniques de l'Animal de Laboratoire
0339-7238 Association des Techniciens d'Animaux de Laboratoire. Bulletin Trimestriel *see* 0339-722X
0339-7963 Cuisine Chez Sol
0339-8390 Fleurs de France
0339-8498 Belisane
0339-8811 Universite de Paris VII. Groupe de Linguistique Japonaise. Travaux *changed to* Travaux de Linguistique Japonaise
0339-8943 Cinema Different
0339-8978 Changer le Cinema
0339-9052 Cheval Hebdo
0339-9702 Mecanisation Forestiere
0339-9958 Aujourd'hui l'Afrique
0340-000X Bibliotheksforum Bayern
0340-0026 International Journal of Clinical Pharmacology and Biopharmacy
0340-0034 Communication and Cybernetics
0340-0050 International Classification
0340-0077 Technische Universitaet Hannover. Franzius-Institut fuer Wasserbau und Kuesteningenieurwesen. Mitteilungen *changed to* Universitaet Hannover. Franzius-Institut fuer Wasserbau und Kuesteningenieurwesen. Mitteilungen
0340-0093 Medizinische Psychologie
0340-0107 Zeitungs-Index
0340-0131 International Archives of Occupational and Environmental Health
0340-0158 Communications
0340-0174 Zeitschrift fuer Historische Forschung
0340-0220 Exakt†
0340-0255 Friedens-Warte
0340-031X Wissenschaftliche Forschungsberichte. Reihe 1. Grundlagenforschung und Grundlegende Methodik. Abt. C. Psychologie
0340-0352 I F L A Journal
0340-0409 Bibliographia Cartographica
0340-0425 Leviathan
0340-045X International Journal of Law Libraries.
0340-0476 Materialien zur Politischen Bildung
0340-0522 International Bulletin for Research on Law in Eastern Europe.
0340-062X Journal of Geophysics
0340-0700 Staatsbibliothek Preussischer Kulturbesitz. Ausstellungskataloge
0340-0727 Psychological Research
0340-0751 Deutsche Forschungsberichte *changed to* Forschungsberichte aus Technik und Naturwissenschaften
0340-0778 Stereo
0340-0794 Roux' Archives of Developmental Biology
0340-0816 Auszuege aus den Offenlegungsschriften. Teil 1. Grund- und Rohstoffindustrie, Chemie und Huettenwesen, Bauwesen, Bergbau
0340-0824 Zeitschrift fuer Archaeologie des Mittelalters
0340-0840 Funktionsanalyse Biologischer Systeme
0340-0867 Auszuege aus den Offenlegungsschriften. Teil 2. Elektrotechnik, Physik, Feinmechanik und Optik, Akustik
0340-0905 Waking and Sleeping
0340-0913 Auszuege aus den Offenlegungsschriften. Teil 3. Uebrige Verarbeitungsindustrie und Arbeitsverfahren, Maschinen- und Fahrzeugbau, Ernaehrung, Landwirtschaft
0340-0921 Frontal
0340-0956 Sportwissenschaftliche Dissertationen
0340-1057 Biophysics of Structure and Mechanism
0340-1162 Immunitaet und Infektion
0340-1200 Biological Cybernetics
0340-1227 Virchows Archiv. Section A: Pathological Anatomy and Histology
0340-1294 Bergwelt
0340-1332 Handbuch der Internationalen Dokumentation und Information
0340-1502 Rassegna Tecnica A E G-Telefunken
0340-1553 Datenverarbeitung A E G-Telefunken *see* 0040-1447
0340-1588 Laryngologie, Rhinologie, Otologie und ihre Grenzgebiete Vereinigt mit Monatsschrift fuer Ohrenheilkunde *changed to* Laryngologie, Rhinologie, Otologie Vereingt mit Monatsschrift fuer Ohrenheilkunde
0340-160X Die Dritte Welt†
0340-1618 RoeFo. Fortschritte auf dem Gebiete der Roentgenstrahlen und der Nuklearmedizin
0340-1626 Kunst Magazin
0340-1650 WISt
0340-1669 Monatsschrift fuer Unfallheilkunde *see* 0341-5694
0340-1677 Psychologie Heute
0340-174X Suedosteuropa-Mitteilungen
0340-1758 Zeitschrift fuer Parlamentsfragen
0340-1766 Der Freie Zahnarzt
0340-1790 Bayerisches Staatsministerium fuer Arbeit und Sozialordnung. Amtsblatt.
0340-1804 Zeitschrift fuer Soziologie
0340-1812 Monatsschrift fuer Deutsches Recht
0340-1901 Aktuelle Probleme der Intensivmedizin
0340-1952 F und M, Feinwerktechnik und Messtechnik
0340-1960 Colloid and Polymer Science
0340-2002 C.I.I.A. Symposia
0340-2037 Divice†
0340-2061 Anatomy and Embryology
0340-2088 Chimica Didactica
0340-2096 Anatomia, Histologia, Embryologia
0340-210X Aktuelle Probleme der Polymer-Physik
0340-2118 European Journal of Applied Microbiology *see* 0171-1741
0340-2134 Physica Didactica
0340-2150 Praxis der Sozialpsychologie
0340-2185 B T†
0340-2193 Zeitschrift fuer Physik. Section A: Atoms and Nuclei
0340-2207 Der Fremdsprachliche Unterricht
0340-2215 Studien zur Altaegyptischen Kultur

0340-224X Zeitschrift fuer Physik. Section B. Quanta and Matter *changed to* Zeitschrift fuer Physik. Section B: Condensed Matter
0340-2258 Der Deutschunterricht
0340-2266 Entomologica Germanica *see* 0171-8177
0340-2274 Staatsbibliothek Preussischer Kulturbesitz. Jahresbericht
0340-2304 Sozialwissenschaftliche Informationen fuer Unterricht und Studium
0340-2355 Suedwestdeutsche Schulblaetter
0340-238X A und O - Magazin der Hausfrau
0340-2444 Zeitschrift fuer Arbeitswissenschaft
0340-2479 Zeitschrift fuer Unternehmens- und Gesellschaftsrecht
0340-2495 Denkmalpflege in Baden-Wuerttemberg
0340-2509 Spezielle Anorganische Chemie
0340-2541 Aktuelle Dermatologie
0340-2592 Der Urologe. Section A
0340-2649 Unfallchirurgie
0340-269X Phytocoenologia
0340-2703 Wissenschaftliche Forschungsberichte. Reihe 2. Anwendungstechnik und Angewandte Wissenschaft
0340-272X Allgemeine juedische Wochenzeitung
0340-2827 Amerikastudien
0340-2924 Surface and Vacuum Physics Index
0340-2940 Technik in der Medizin
0340-2967 F und I-Bau
0340-2975 Telefon Report
0340-2975 Technology Index for Plasma Physics Research and Fusion Reactors
0340-3017 Zahnaerzteblatt Baden-Wuerttemberg
0340-3068 Ibero-Amerikanishes Archiv
0340-3130 Akupunktur: Theorie und Praxis
0340-3157 Acta Pharmaceutica Technologica
0340-3238 Dokumentation Arbeitsmedizin
0340-3270 Landesversicherungsanstalt Wuerttemberg. Mitteilungen
0340-3289 Der Versorgungsbeamte
0340-3297 Dokumentation Ostmitteleuropa
0340-3343 Chemiefasern /Textil-Industrie
0340-3440 A B T Informationen
0340-3475 Dokumentation Tribologie
0340-3491 Buero und EDV
0340-3505 Baden-Wuerttembergische Verwaltungspraxis
0340-3513 Elektrowaerme International. Part A: Elektrowaerme im Technischen Ausbau
0340-3521 Elektrowaerme International. Part B: Industrielle Elektrowaerme
0340-3572 Fernwaerme International
0340-3637 Der Gemeindetag
0340-367X Der Sozialversicherungs-Beamte und -Angestellte bsba
0340-3688 Die Alte Stadt
0340-3696 Archives of Dermatological Research
0340-3793 Applied Physics
0340-3858 D G S
0340-3912 Architektur und Wohnwelt *see* 0173-8046
0340-3955 Dokumentation Regelungstechnik
0340-398X K I *changed to* K I Klima, Kaelte, Heizung
0340-3998 Forschung im Strassenwesen
0340-4137 Management Wissen
0340-4188 Textilbetrieb
0340-4242 Germany(Federal Republic, 1949-). Bundesanstalt fuer Gewaesserkunde. Hydrologische Bibliographie
0340-4277 Beitraege zur Naturkunde Niedersachsens
0340-4285 Transition Metal Chemistry
0340-434X Regelungstechnik
0340-4439 Der Sanitaerinstallateur und Heizungsbauer
0340-448X Die Neue Hochschule
0340-4528 Internationales Archiv fuer Sozialgeschichte der Deutschen Literatur
0340-4544 Werkstattstechnik- WT
0340-4552 Promet
0340-4684 Blood Cells
0340-4730 Regelungstechnische Praxis
0340-4749 Referate Organ: Schweissen und Verwandte Verfahren
0340-4773 Progress in Botany
0340-4781 Osnabruecker Naturwissenschaftliche Mitteilungen
0340-4803 Stahl und Eisen
0340-4811 Zeitschrift fuer Naturforschung. Section A: Physics, Physical Chemistry, Cosmic Physics
0340-4897 Mathematisch-Physikalische Semesterberichte *changed to* Mathematische Semesterberichte
0340-4900 Literaturberichte ueber Wasser, Abwasser, Luft und Feste Abfallstoffe
0340-4951 Zeitschriften- und Buecherschau "Stahl und Eisen"
0340-5044 Die Bautechnik. Ausgabe A
0340-5060 Thyssen Technische Berichte
0340-5087 Zeitschrift fuer Naturforschung. Section B: Inorganic and Organic Chemistry
0340-5095 Zement-Kalk-Gips. Edition A
0340-5133 Sprechsaal fuer Keramik, Glas, Baustoffe *see* 0341-0676
0340-5141 Vermessungswesen und Raumordnung (VR)
0340-5176 Deutsches Gewaesserkundliches Jahrbuch. Donaugebiet
0340-5184 Deutsches Gewaesserkundliches Jahrbuch. Kuestengebiet der Nort- und Ostsee
0340-5214 Zentralblatt fuer Hals-, Nasen- und Ohrenheilkunde, Plastische Chirurgie an Kopf und Hals
0340-5354 Journal of Neurology
0340-5362 Bremer Aerzteblatt
0340-5400 Research in Molecular Biology
0340-5419 Karl-August-Forster-Lectures
0340-5443 Behavioral Ecology and Sociobiology
0340-5508 Medizinisch-Orthopaedische Technik
0340-5532 Arzt- und Arzneimittelrecht
0340-5559 Dokumentation Impfschaeden-Impferfolge
0340-5613 Zeitschrift fuer Psychosomatische Medizin und Psychoanalyse
0340-5664 Chirurgia Plastica
0340-5702 Aerztliche Kosmetologie
0340-5710 Deutschland in Geschichte und Gegenwart
0340-5753 Die Rentenversicherung
0340-5761 Archives of Toxicology
0340-577X Modernes Leben-Natuerliches Heilen
0340-5796 Afrika
0340-5818 Welt der Schule
0340-5826 Blaetter fuer Lehrerfortbildung
0340-5958 Studien zur Franzoesischen Philosophie des Zwanzigsten Jahrhunderts
0340-5982 Kybernetik - Datenverarbeitung - Recht
0340-6040 Stahl-Report Lernen und Leisten
0340-6075 Virchows Archiv. Section B: Cell Pathology
0340-6083 Goettinger Predigtmeditationen
0340-6091 Frohe Botschaft
0340-613X Geschichte und Gesellschaft
0340-6172 Die Gestalt
0340-6180 Zeitschrift fuer Kunstpaedagogik
0340-6199 European Journal of Pediatrics
0340-6210 Luther
0340-6245 Thrombosis and Haemostasis
0340-6253 Match
0340-6261 Freiburger Beitraege zur Indologie
0340-627X Enchoria
0340-6318 Wolfenbuetteler Barock-Nachrichten
0340-6326 Goettinger Orientforschungen. Reihe I: Syriaca
0340-6334 Goettinger Orientforschungen. Reihe III: Iranica
0340-6342 Goettinger Orientforschungen. Reihe IV: Aegypten
0340-6350 Goettinger Orientforschungen. Reihe VI: Hellenistica
0340-6369 Giorgio Levi della Vida Conferences
0340-6377 Bonner Orientalistische Studien†
0340-6385 Neuindische Studien
0340-6407 Oriens Christianus
0340-6423 Societas Uralo-Altaica. Veroeffentlichungen
0340-6490 Schriften zur Geistesgeschichte des Oestlichen Europa
0340-6628 Materialien zur Psychoanalyse und analytisch orientierten Psychotherapie
0340-6644 Die Fotowirtschaft
0340-6644 Forward
0340-6679 Submarin
0340-6687 Ruhr-Universitaet Bochum. Ostasien Institut. Veroeffentlichungen
0340-6717 Human Genetics
0340-6717 Human Genetics. Supplement
0340-6725 Zoomorphologie *changed to* Zoomorphology
0340-6792 Studies in Oriental Religions
0340-6997 European Journal of Nuclear Medicine
0340-7004 Cancer Immunology and Immunotherapy
0340-7047 Zentralblatt fuer Arbeitsmedizin, Arbeitsschutz und Prophylaxe
0340-7063 Die Schaltung
0340-7071 Strassenbahn Magazin
0340-7217 Soziale Forschung und Praxis
0340-7322 Anzeiger fuer Schaedlingskunde, Pflanzen- und Umweltschutz *see* 0340-7330
0340-7330 Anzeiger fuer Schaedlingskunde, Pflanzenschutz, Umweltschutz
0340-7349 Public International Law
0340-739X Eurosport und Freizeitmode
0340-7462 Propellants and Explosives
0340-7489 Baurecht
0340-7497 Zeitschrift fuer Miet- und Raumrecht
0340-7519 Strom Praxis
0340-7594 Journal of Comparative Physiology. A: Sensory, Neural, and Behavioral Physiology
0340-7616 Journal of Comparative Physiology. B. Systematic, and Environmental Physiology *changed to* Journal of Comparative Physiology. B: Biochemical, Systematic, and Environmental Physiology
0340-7632 Current Contents Africa
0340-7756 Informationen Jugendliteratur und Medien-Jugendschriften-Warte
0340-7810 V D L-Nachrichten
0340-7829 Die Pirsch - der Deutsche Jaeger
0340-7837 Land Aktuell
0340-7845 Notfallmedizin
0340-7853 Bibliothek der Griechischen Literatur
0340-7888 Literarischer Verein in Stuttgart. Bibliothek
0340-7918 Betriebs-Berater
0340-7926 Recht der Internationalen Wirtschaft
0340-7969 Allgemeine Zeitschrift fuer Philosophie
0340-7993 Paepste und Papsttum
0340-8035 Monumenta Germaniae Historica. Staatsschriften des Spaeteren Mittelalters
0340-8051 Bibliothek des Buchwesens (B B)
0340-8094 Indices Naturwissenschaftlich-Medizinischer Periodica bis 1850
0340-8140 Mendelssohn Studien
0340-8221 Chemische Analyse
0340-8248 Sozialforschung und Gesellschaftspolitik
0340-8280 Renovatio
0340-8329 Zeitschrift fuer Luft- und Weltraumrecht
0340-837X Technisches Messen - A T M *see* 0171-8096
0340-8388 Dokumentation Rheologie
0340-8396 Deutsches Mittelalter, Kritische Studientexte der Monumenta Germaniae Historica
0340-840X Agrarrecht
0340-8434 Arbeit und Sozialpolitik
0340-8442 Kunststoffberater, -Rundschau, -Technik *see* 0023-5520
0340-8450 Records of the Ancient Near East
0340-8515 Physik und Didaktik. die Zeitschrift Fure Zeitgemaessen Physikunterricht
0340-8590 Demokratie und Recht
0340-8604 Deutsche Notar-Zeitschrift
0340-8728 Vierteljahrschrift fuer Sozial- und Wirtschaftsgeschichte
0340-8833 Ernst-Mach-Institut, Freiburg. Bericht
0340-8906 Grundrechte; die Rechtsprechung in Europa *see* 0341-9800
0340-904X Zeitschrift fuer Berufs- und Wirtschaftspaedagogik
0340-904X Zeitschrift fuer Immunitaetsforschung-Immunobiology
0340-9058 Zeitschrift fuer Sportpaedagogik *changed to* Sportpaedagogik
0340-9201 Sozialisation und Kommunikation
0340-9244 Politikwissenschaftliche Forschung
0340-9279 Betriebliches Vorschlagswesen
0340-9341 Deutsche Sprache
0340-9422 Z O R - Zeitschrift fuer Operations Research
0340-949X Beitraege zur Umweltgestaltung. Reihe B.
0340-9716 Beitraege zur Umweltgestaltung. Reihe A
0340-9767 Kritikon Litterarum
0340-9783 Hohenheimer Arbeiten
0340-9821 Veroeffentlichungen der Astronomischen Institute der Univeritaet Bonn
0340-9929 Suedkurs
0340-997X Hospital-Hygiene
0341-0056 Historia. Einzelschriften
0341-0064 Hermes-Einzelschriften
0341-0099 Beitraege zur Geschichte der Pharmazie
0341-0110 Apotheker und Kunst
0341-0137 Deutsche Morgenlaendische Gesellschaft. Zeitschrift
0341-0277 E I
0341-0382 Zeitschrift fuer Naturforschung. Section C: Biosciences
0341-0455 Altenpflege
0341-0463 Archiv fuer Eisenbahntechnik
0341-0498 Grundlagen und Fortschritte der Lebensmitteluntersuchung und Lebensmitteltechnologie
0341-051X Aktuelle Rheumatologie
0341-0528 Germany (Federal Republic, 1949-) Bundesanstalt fuer Materialpruefung. Jahresbericht
0341-0552 Z I International
0341-0560 Zement-Kalk-Gips. Edition B
0341-0609 Kopfklinik
0341-0668 Rundschau fuer Fleischuntersuchung und Lebensmittelueberwachung
0341-0676 Sprechsaal
0341-0730 Medizin in Unserer Zeit†
0341-0765 Studia Leibnitiana. Sonderhefte
0341-0773 Sudhoffs Archiv. Beihefte
0341-0781 Melliand Textilberichte /International Textile Reports
0341-079X Archiv fuer Rechts- und Sozialphilosophie. Beihefte. Neue Folge
0341-0803 Deutsche Morgenlaendische Gesellschaft. Zeitschrift. Supplementa
0341-0811 Zeitschrift fuer Franzoesische Sprache und Literatur. Beihefte.Neue Folge
0341-082X Das Wort in der Welt
0341-0838 Zeitschrift fuer Dialektologie und Linguistik. Beihefte
0341-0846 Vierteljahrschrift fuer Sozial-und Wirtschaftsgeschichte. Beihefte
0341-0854 Acta Pharmaceutica Technologica. Supplementa
0341-0862 Hamburger Hafen-Nachrichten
0341-0935 Betriebsverpflegung
0341-0951 Forschung Stadtverkehr
0341-0978 Die Konjunktur im Handwerk
0341-0986 Internationales Jahrbuch fuer Kartographie
0341-1052 Die Bautechnik. Ausgabe B
0341-1060 Braunkohle
0341-1206 Umweltmagazin
0341-1230 Aurora
0341-1567 Umwelt-Report
0341-1869 I K O - Innere Kolonisation - Land und Gemeinde
0341-1915 Neue Juristische Wochenschrift
0341-2040 Lung
0341-2091 Deutscher Gartenbau
0341-2253 Wolfenbuetteler Notizen zur Buchgeschichte

0341-2334 Zeitschrift fuer Verkehrserziehung
0341-2350 Der Klinikarzt
0341-2431 Dokumentation zur Raumentwicklung†
0341-244X Forschungen zur Raumentwicklung
0341-2474 Denkmaeler der Buchkunst
0341-2512 Referteblatt zur Raumentwicklung
0341-2520 Agraringenieur und Agrarmanager
0341-2598 Kongresszentralblatt fuer die Gesamte Innere Medizin. Sektion F: Zentralblatt Haematologie-Klinische Onkologie/ Haematology-Clinical Oncology
0341-2601 C C B
0341-2695 International Orthopaedics
0341-2717 Baumarkt
0341-275X Vereinigung von Afrikanisten in Deutschland. Schriften
0341-2784 Architektur und Wettbewerbe
0341-2903 Psycho
0341-2911 Medizin *see* 0344-5836
0341-2954 Steuer und Wirtschaft
0341-2970 Europaeischer Wetterbericht
0341-311X Fenno-Ugrica
0341-3136 Universitaet Bonn. Institut fuer Kommunikationsforschung und Phonetik. Forschungsberichte
0341-3144 Forum Phoneticum
0341-3152 Hamburger Beitraege zur Archaeologie
0341-3179 Hamburger Juristische Studien
0341-3187 Hamburger Phonetische Beitraege
0341-3195 Papiere zur Textlinguistik
0341-3209 Romanistik in Geschichte und Gegenwart
0341-3217 Bibliotheca Russica
0341-3225 Linguarum Minorum Documenta Historiographica
0341-3233 Universitaet Hamburg. Institut fuer Internationale Angelegenheiten. Veroeffentlichungen
0341-3241 Universitaet Hamburg. Institut fuer Internationale Angelegenheiten. Werkhefte
0341-3276 Dokumente zur Deutschlandpolitik. Beihefte
0341-3403 Atem und Mensch
0341-3667 Bank und Markt
0341-3675 Deutsch Lernen
0341-3772 Scripta Geobotanica
0341-3780 Goettinger Geographische Abhandlungen
0341-3861 Praxis Geographie. Beiheft
0341-3896 B I
0341-3918 Bayerische Vorgeschichtsblaetter
0341-4175 Elo
0341-4183 Bibliothek Forschung und Praxis
0341-4191 Studien zur Indologie und Iranistik
0341-440X R A K - Riechstoffe, Aromen, Kosmetica
0341-4434 Arzt und Auto
0341-468X Kraftfahrt-Bundesamt. Statistische Mitteilungen
0341-471X Schulbibliothek Aktuell
0341-4728 Schnellstatistik Allgemeiner Oeffentlicher Bibliotheken
0341-4817 Haustechnik
0341-4949 Blatt fuer Patent-, Muster- und Zeichenwesen
0341-5163 Nachrichten aus Chemie, Technik und Laboratorium
0341-5244 Bus-Fahrt
0341-5309 Lebensmittel und Gerichtliche Chemie
0341-5449 D S W R
0341-549X D F Z Wirtschaftsmagazin
0341-5570 Techno-Tip
0341-5589 Elektronikpraxis
0341-5600 Werbeartikel-Berater
0341-5627 Autofachmann
0341-5694 Unfallheilkunde
0341-5724 Textilkunst
0341-5759 Du und das Tier
0341-5775 Maschinenmarkt
0341-5783 Europa Industrie Revue
0341-5910 Institut fuer den Wissenschaftlichen Film. Publikationen zu Wissenschaftlichen Filmen. Sektion Ethnologie
0341-5929 Institut fuer den Wissenschaftlichen Film. Publikationen zu Wissenschaftlichen Filmen. Sektion Medizin
0341-5937 Institut fuer den Wissenschaftlichen Film. Publikationen zu Wissenschaftlichen Filmen. Sektion Geschichte, Publizistik
0341-6097 Export-Markt
0341-6208 Bankhistorisches Archiv
0341-633X Lecture Notes in Biomathematics
0341-6399 Geologisches Jahrbuch. Reihe A: Allgemeine und Regionale Geologie B.R. Deutschland und Nachbargebiete, Tektonik, Stratigraphie, Paleontologie
0341-6402 Geologisches Jahrbuch. Reihe B: Regionale Geologie Ausland
0341-6410 Geologisches Jahrbuch. Reihe C: Hydrogeologie. Ingenieurgeologie
0341-6429 Geologisches Jahrbuch. Reihe D: Mineralogie. Petrographie, Geochemie, Lagerstaettenkunde
0341-6437 Geologisches Jahrbuch. Reihe E: Geophysik
0341-6445 Geologisches Jahrbuch. Reihe F: Bodenkunde
0341-6569 Components Report
0341-6593 D T W - Deutsche Tieraerztliche Wochenschrift
0341-6615 Konstruieren und Giessen
0341-6631 China Aktuell
0341-6836 Meeresforschung
0341-6860 Medien & Erziehung
0341-695X Agrartechnik International
0341-7115 Brauindustrie
0341-7212 Aesthetik und Kommunikation
0341-7492 Beiheft zu Leistlingssport
0341-759X Meister-Zeitung
0341-7603 Schule und Museum
0341-7638 Journal of Literary Semantics
0341-7743 Musikbibliothek Aktuell†
0341-7816 Finnisch-ugrische Mitteilungen
0341-8022 Dokumentation Gefaehrdung Durch Alkohol, Rauchen, Drogen, Arzneimittel
0341-8235 Schul-Management
0341-8243 Lehrmittel Aktuell
0341-8332 Archiv fuer Angewandte Sozialpaedagogik
0341-8448 Iconographia Ecclesiae Orientalis
0341-8634 Museum
0341-8642 Indiana
0341-8669 Umsatzsteuer-Rundschau
0341-8812 Diabetes-Journal
0341-8960 Religionsunterricht an hoeheren Schulen
0341-9258 Uebersee-Museum, Bremen. Veroeffentlichungen. Reihe C: Geographie *changed to* Deutsche Geographische Blaetter
0341-9274 Uebersee-Museum, Bremen. Veroeffentlichungen. Reihe D: Voelkerkundliche Monographien
0341-938X Psychologie und Gesellschaft
0341-9622 Bremisches Jahrbuch
0341-9681 K F Z Anzeiger
0341-9754 Arzt und Krankenhaus†
0341-9800 Europaeische Grundrechtte Zeitschrift
0341-9835 Zeitschrift fuer Allgemeinmedizin
0342-0221 Bayerische Staatsbibliothek, Munich. Jahresbericht
0342-0477 Sprache - Stimme - Gehoer
0342-0671 Erziehung und Wissenschaft
0342-0795 Dokumentation Medizin im Umweltschutz
0342-0817 Betriebskrankenkasse
0342-0884 Linguistica Biblica
0342-0930 Der Langfristige Kred1t
0342-0957 D M I-die Medizinische Information
0342-1082 Frankfurter Turkologische Arbeitsmittel
0342-1104 Hannoversche Geschichtsblaetter
0342-1120 Algological Studies
0342-1589 Diskussion Deutsch
0342-1694 Archiv fuer Arzneitherapie
0342-1783 Zeitschrift fuer Wirtschafts- und Sozialwissenschaften
0342-1791 Physics and Chemistry of Minerals
0342-1821 Rechtsprechung zum Wiedergutmachungsrecht
0342-183X Psychologie in Erziehung und Unterricht
0342-1945 Recht der Arbeit
0342-2259 Der Landkreis
0342-2534 Verwaltungsrechtsprechung in Deutschland
0342-2852 Zeitschrift fuer Unternehmensgeschichte
0342-2895 Franzoesisch Heute
0342-2968 Kosmetik Journal
0342-3247 Mikrofauna des Meeresbodens
0342-328X Z F A
0342-3476 Z L R -Zeitschrift fuer das Gesamte Lebensmittelrecht
0342-3557 Gesetz und Verordnungsblatt fuer das Land Hessen
0342-376X G V-Praxis mit Tiefkuehlpraxis
0342-393X Zeitschrift fuer Individualpsychologie
0342-3956 Zeitschrift fuer Unternehmensgeschichte. Beihefte
0342-3964 Bibliographie Sozialisation und Sozialpaedagogik
0342-4022 Abwassertechnik mit Abfalltechnik
0342-4030 Universitaetssternwarte zu Wien. Annalen
0342-4162 Geolit
0342-4340 Wolfenbuetteler Renaissance Mitteilungen
0342-4553 Schauspielfuehrer
0342-457X Sportwissenschaft und Sportpraxis
0342-4634 I S B N Review
0342-4642 Intensive Care Medicine
0342-4774 Der Fremdenverkehr und das Reisebuero
0342-4898 Hoergeschaedigten-Paedagogik
0342-4960 Informationsdienst fuer den Kfz-Zubehoer Fachhandel und -Ersatzteile
0342-507X Halbjaehrliches Verzeichniss Taschenbuecher
0342-5258 Unsere Jugend
0342-5622 Oil Gas
0342-5665 Energy Developments
0342-5789 Antimilitarismus Information
0342-5843 Zeitschrift fuer Verbraucherpolitik
0342-5991 Bayerische Akademie der Wissenschaften. Philosophisch-Historische Klasse. Sitzungsberichte
0342-6017 Wirtschaft und Gesellschaft im Unterricht
0342-6173 Zielsprache Englisch
0342-6203 Zielsprache Franzoesisch
0342-6300 Jahrbach Deutsch Als Fremdsprache
0342-6335 Weltkonjunkturdienst
0342-6408 S T S - Sheet Metal - Tubes - Sections
0342-6610 Uebersee-Museum Bremen. Veroeffentlichungen. Reihe G: Bremer Suedpazifik-Archiv
0342-6785 Alexander von Humbolt-Stiftung. Jahresbericht
0342-6947 European Petroleum Yearbook
0342-7145 Theorie und Praxis der Sozialpaedagogik
0342-7188 Irrigation Science
0342-7196 Cardiovascular Radiology *changed to* Cardiovascular and Interventional Radiology
0342-7498 Praxis und Klinik der Pneumologie
0342-7978 Zeitschrift fuer Plastische Chirurgie
0342-8184 S B Z - Sanitaer-, Heizungs- und Klimatechnik
0342-9512 Lebensmittel Zeitung
0342-958X Microscopica Acta. Supplementa
0342-9601 Medizinische Monatsschrift fuer Pharmazeuten
0342-9857 Neue Praxis
0343-0510 Bergbau-Berufsgenossenschaft. Geschaeftsbericht
0343-1002 Medizin Bibliothek Dokumentation
0343-1657 Literatur fuer Leser
0343-2009 Saecula Spiritalia
0343-2092 Gas
0343-2246 K K - die Kaelte und Klimatechnik
0343-2432 Dermatosen in Beruf und Umwelt
0343-2521 GeoJournal
0343-2734 Suesswaren-Markt
0343-3048 Zentralblatt fuer Haut- und Geschlechtskrankheiten Sowie Deren Grenzgebiete/Dermatology-Venerology-Andrology
0343-3129 Kunststoffe im Bau
0343-3137 Deutsche Zeitschrift fuer Mund- , Kiefer- und Gesichtschirurgie
0343-317X Das Rechenzentrum
0343-3226 Selbstbedienung--Dynamik im Handel
0343-3366 Lady International
0343-3528 Primate Report
0343-3560 Schadenprisma
0343-3838 Der Deutsche Badebetrieb
0343-3846 Deutsche Bauern-Korrespondenz
0343-4109 Soziologische Revue
0343-4125 Contributions to Sedimentology
0343-4494 Schrifttum Bauwesen: Gesamtausgabe
0343-5202 Sprache und Datenverarbeitung
0343-5334 Didaktik der Mathematik die Zeitschrift fuer Methodisch-Didaktische Forschung und Unterrichtspraxis
0343-5539 German Chemical Engineering
0343-5563 Deutsche Universitaetszeitung
0343-5571 Film und TV Kameramann
0343-6098 Anatomia Clinica (English Edition)
0343-6993 Mathematical Intelligencer
0343-7051 Abhandlungen aus dem Gebiet der Auslandskunde. Series B & C
0343-7183 Packung und Transport in der Chemischen Industrie
0343-7477 Germany(Federal Republic, 1949-) Bundesministerium fuer Ernaehrung, Landwirtschaft und Forsten. Jahresbericht. Forschung im Geschaeftsbereich des Bundesministers fuer Ernaehrung, la Wirtschaft und Forsten
0343-7647 A Z-Nachrichten
0343-785X Ozean und Technik
0343-7868 Informationen - Bildung, Wissenschaft
0343-8651 Current Microbiology
0343-9321 P K V Informationdienst
0344-0338 Pathology, Research and Practice
0344-0354 Alexander von Humboldt-Stiftung. Mitteilungen
0344-0591 Sammlung Groos
0344-1415 Die Frauenfrage in Deutschland. Bibliographie
0344-1849 Institut fuer Konfliktforschung. Schriftenreihe
0344-2934 Deutscher Hugenotten-Verein E.V. Geschichtsblaetter
0344-4317 Uebersee-Museum, Bremen. Veroeffentlichungen. Reihe F: Bremer Afrika-Archiv
0344-4325 Springer Seminars in Immunopathology
0344-4376 Kueche
0344-4422 Restaurant and Hotel Management
0344-4430 Informationsaufnahme und Informationsverarbeitung im Lebenden Organismus
0344-449X Materialia Turcica
0344-4686 Backtechnik
0344-5399 Jazz Index
0344-5550 Staat und Wirtschaft in Hessen
0344-5607 Neurosurgical Review
0344-5690 Kultur and Technik
0344-5704 Cancer Chemotherapy and Pharmacology
0344-5712 Agrarsoziale Gesellschaft. Materialsammlung
0344-5836 Moderne Medizin
0344-5909 Germanistische Mitteilungen
0344-5933 Klinikarzt mit Medizinstudent. Ausgabe B
0344-7030 Ost-Wirtschaftsreport
0344-7758 Informationsdienst Laerm
0344-8444 Archives of Orthopaedic and Traumatic Surgery
0344-8614 Sielmanns Tierwelt
0344-9270 Die Voliere
0344-9416 Medizintechnik
0344-9777 Zeitschrift fuer Oeffentliche und Gemeinwirtschaftliche Unternehmen
0344-984X Die Schiefertafel
0345-0074 Striae
0345-0112 Text

0345-021X Stockholms Universitet. Psykologiska Institutionen. Reports. Supplement Series
0345-0295 Aneks
0345-0635 Aktuellt i Politiken
0345-0732 Alkohol och Narkotika
0345-1135 B i S
0345-1453 Biblicum
0345-1593 Blaaklint. Livlinan
0345-181X Broed-Konditorn
0345-1941 Byggreferat
0345-2131 Dans
0345-2581 Entre
0345-2719 Svenska Bankfoereningen. Ekonomiska Meddelanden
0345-3251 Fasaden
0345-3278 Fastighetsmaeklaren
0345-3286 F B R Aktuellt†
0345-3685 Frihetlig Socialistisk Tidskrift
0345-3979 Golv till Tak
0345-4347 Hockey
0345-4495 Handelskammartidningen
0345-4789 Haeften foer Kritiska Studier
0345-4843 Haent i Veckan
0345-4983 Invandrartidningen Information
0345-4991 Invandrartidningen
0345-4991 Easy Swedish edition *issued with* 0345-4991
0345-5300 Information-Ekonomi och Miljoe, Vetenskap och Humanism
0345-5440 International Union of Tenants. International Information
0345-5564 Journal of Traffic Medicine
0345-5653 Jefferson
0345-6005 Kvaekartidskrift
0345-7001 Lantbruksnytt
0345-7133 Leveranstidningen Entreprenad
0345-7389 Luthersk Barntidning
0345-7699 Musiktidningen
0345-7737 Moebler och Miljoe
0345-7788 MaskinKontakt
0345-7982 Bygd och Natur
0345-8199 M S-Brevet *changed to* Handikapp-Reflex
0346-0762 S C C News
0346-1025 Ship Abstracts
0346-1300 Skohandlaren
0346-1351 Skorstensfejarmaestaren
0346-1602 Sparbankerna
0346-2064 Svensk Fastighetstidning *see* 0348-5552
0346-2099 Svensk Froetidning
0346-2250 Svensk Veterinaertidning
0346-2471 Svinskoetsel
0346-251X System
0346-2773 Transport och Hantering
0346-2846 Traeindustrin
0346-329X Tonfallet
0346-3605 Undervisningsteknologi
0346-363X Ung Vaerld
0346-3788 Utsikt
0346-4687 Vaar Ponny
0346-5020 Didakometry and Sociometry
0346-5764 L M V-Information
0346-5837 Sweden. Medicinalvaesendet. Foerfattningssamling *see* 0346-6000
0346-5837 Sweden. Medicinalvaesendet. Foerfattningssamling *see* 0346-6019
0346-6000 Sweden. Socialstyrelsen. Foerfattningssamling: Medical
0346-6019 Sweden. Socialstyrelsen. Foerfattningssamling: Social
0346-6159 Paa Fritid
0346-6175 Sweden. Universitetskanslersaembetet. Educational Development *see* 0347-4976
0346-640X Dagens Industri
0346-6728 NORNA - Rapporter
0346-6906 C B I Forskning/Research
0346-7090 Svenska Traeskyddinstitutet. Meddelanden
0346-7236 Lantbrukshoegskolan Institutionen foer Vaextodling. Rapporter och Arhandlingar *changed to* Sveriges Lantbruksuniversitet. Institutionen foer Vaextodling. Rapporter och Arhandlingar
0346-8240 C B I Rapporter/Reports
0346-3445 Sweden. Sjukvaardens och Socialvaardens Planerings- och Rationaliseringsinstitut. S P R I Informerar
0346-8666 Sweden. Fishery Board. Institute of Marine Research. Report
0346-895X L O-Tidningen
0346-9158 Afrikabulletinen
0346-9212 Nya Antik & Auktion
0346-9468 Current Business in Sweden
0346-9670 Foereningsbankerna
0347-030X Railway Scene
0347-0342 S A C O/S R-Tidningen
0347-1314 Uppsala Studies in Education
0347-1748 Kullagertidningen
0347-2205 World Armaments and Disarmament: S I P R I Yearbook
0347-3139 Skandinaviska Enskilda Banken Quarterly Review
0347-3236 Vaextskyddsrapporter
0347-3449 Registreringstidning foer Varumaerken. Part A (Publications for Opposition) *see* 0348-324X
0347-3457 Registreringstidning foer Varumaerken. Part C (Renewals, Changes of Ownership) *see* 0348-3266
0347-3465 Registreringstidning foer Varumaerken. Part B (Publications of Registrations) *see* 0348-3258
0347-4135 Tidningsteknik
0347-416X Svensk Kyrkomusik. (Edition AB for Church Musicians)
0347-4178 Svensk Kyrkomusik (Edition B for Choir Members)
0347-4240 A I C A R C Bulletin
0347-4275 Yrkesfiskaren
0347-4585 R A-Nytt
0347-4917 Acta Regiae Societatis Scientiarum et Litterarum Gothoburgensis. Botanica
0347-4925 Acta Regiae Societatis Scientiarum et Litterarum Gothoburgensis. Interdisciplinaria
0347-4976 R & D in Higher Education
0347-5484 Kommun-Aktuelt
0347-5719 Documenta
0347-6030 Sweden. Statens Vaeg- och Trafikinstitut. Rapport
0347-6057 Sweden. Statens Vaeg- och Trafikinstitut. Verksamhetsberaettelse
0347-6154 Konsumentraett och Ekonomi
0347-8173 Sweden. Statens Naturvaardsverk. Naturvaardsverkets Aarsbok
0347-884X Goeteborgs Universitet. Universitetsbibliotek. Aarsberaettelse
0347-9331 Lill-Allers
0348-0356 Aakeri och Transport
0348-1964 Studies of Law in Social Change and Development
0348-2219 Goeteborgs Universitet. Institutionen foer Praktisk Pedagogik. Rapport
0348-2251 Sweden. Luftfartsverket. Aarsbok
0348-2480 Accessionskatalog over Utlaendsk Litteratur i Svenska Forskningshibliotek
0348-2790 C B I Rekommendationer/ Recommendations
0348-324X Svensk Varumaerkestidning/Swedish Trademark Journal. Part A (Publications for Opposition)
0348-3258 Svensk Varumaerkestidning/Swedish Trademark Journal. Part B (Publications of Registrations)
0348-3266 Svensk Varumaerkestidning/Swedish Trademark Journal. Part C (Renewals, Changes of Ownership)
0348-4076 Gothenburg Studies in Social Anthropology
0348-4114 Gothenburg Studies in Art and Architecture
0348-4386 Striolae
0348-4599 Sveriges Lantbruksuniversitet. Institutionen foer Virkeslaera. Rapporter
0348-4769 Folkhoegskolan
0348-5153 Sveriges Riksbank. Kredit- och Valutaoeversikt
0348-5552 Fastighetstidningen
0348-6087 Civilingenjoeren
0348-6613 Foeredrag vid Pyroteknikdagen
0348-6788 Gothenburg Studies in the History of Science and Ideas
0348-7032 Tidskrift foer Frukt- och Baerodling
0348-7342 Sveriges Riksbank. Statistisk Aarsbok
0348-7962 Ny Litteratur om Kvinnor: En Bibliografi
0348-9221 Byggnormindex
0350-0012 Wissenschaftliche Mitteilungen des Bosnisch-Herzegowinischen Landesmuseums. Naturwissenschaft
0350-0039 Akademija Nauka i Umjetnosti Bosne i Hercegovine. Odeljenje Drustvenih Nauka. Radovi
0350-0055 Bilten Dokumentacije. Zavarivanje
0350-0063 Zdravstveni Vestnik
0350-0071 Akademija Nauka i Umjetnosti Bosne i Hercegovine. Odeljenje Medicinskih Nauka. Radovi
0350-0101 Bilten Dokumentacije. Analiticka Hemija
0350-011X Naucni i Strucni Skupovi u Jugoslavii i u Inostranstvu
0350-0152 Bilten Dokumentacije. Otpadne Vode i Zagadjenje Vazduha
0350-0179 Balcanoslavica
0350-0209 Bilten Dokumentacije. Iskoriscenje Otpadaka
0350-0233 Folia Anatomica Iugoslavica
0350-025X Bilten Tehnickih Informacija Iz Oblasti Industrije Gume
0350-0306 Bilten Dokumentacije. Zastita na Radu
0350-0357 Bilten Dokumentacije. Informatika
0350-0365 Vestnik Instituta za Javno Upravo
0350-0403 O A P. Automatska Obrada Podataka. Bibliografija
0350-0454 Bilten Dokumentacije. Drzavni Organi. Drustvene Politicke Zajednice. Privreda. Drustvene Sluzbe. Pravo
0350-0470 Zbornik za Slavistiku
0350-0594 Tehnicka Fizika
0350-1019 Komercijalist
0350-1272 Dijalektika
0350-140X Univerzitet u Novom Sadu. Prirodno - Matematicki Fakultet. Zbornik Radova
0350-1450 Bibliografija Domacih i Stranih Knjiga
0350-1531 Organizacija in Kadri
0350-154X Revija za Socijologiju
0350-1698 Makedonska Akademija na Naukite i Umetnostite. Oddelenie za Opstestveni Nauki. Prilozi
0350-1701 Gradjevinski Fakultet. Institut za Materijale i Konstrukcije. Zbornik Istrazivackih Radova
0350-1728 Makedonski Arhivist
0350-2155 Jugoslovensko Vocarstvo
0350-2252 Yugoslav Law
0350-2619 Nase Gradevinarstvo
0350-2627 Rudarstvo - Geologija - Metalurgija
0350-2651 Kinematografija u Srbiji *changed to* Kinematografija u Srbiji - Uporedo SFRJ
0350-2856 Arhivist
0350-2953 Savremena Poljoprivredna Tehnika
0350-3089 Macedonian Review
0350-3097 Sveuciliste u Zagrebu. Fakultet Strojarstva i Brodogradnje. Zbornik Radova
0350-3283 University of Beograd. Faculty of Sciences. Department of Astronomy. Publications
0350-3569 Narodna in Univerzitetna Knjiznica, Ljubljana. Zbornik
0350-3577 Obvestila Republiske Matisne Knjiznice
0350-3585 Slovenska Bibliografija
0350-3658 Acta Parasitologica Iugoslavica
0350-3666 Arhitektura
0350-6525 Mostovi
0350-820X Science of Sintering
0350-9508 Yugoslav Information Bulletin
0351-0999 Zito Hleb
0351-3947 Obnovljeni Zivot
0355-0001 Suomen Kirjallisuus Vuosiluettelo
0355-001X Suomen Kirjallisuus
0355-0036 Signum
0355-0079 Yearbook of Finnish Foreign Policy
0355-0133 Union Bank of Finland. Annual Report
0355-0206 N I F Newsletter
0355-0214 Suomalais-Ugrilaisen Seura. Aikakauskirja
0355-0303 Kanava
0355-0346 Business Contacts in Finland
0355-0451 Maamies
0355-0532 Mejeritidskrift foer Finlands Svenskbygd
0355-0648 Riista- ja Kalatalouden Tutkimuslaitos. Kalantutkimusosasto. Tiedonantoja
0355-0699 Kuluttajatietoa
0355-0982 Finland. Vestientutkimuslaitos. Julkaisuja
0355-1008 International Peat Society. Bulletin
0355-113X Annales Academiae Scientiarum Fennicae. Dissertationes Humanarum Litterarum
0355-1350 Helsingin Yliopisto. Kirjasto. Julkaisuja
0355-1466 Valokuva
0355-1628 Kemia-Kemi
0355-1717 Finland. Ilmatieteen Laitos. Tutkimusseloste
0355-1733 Finnish Meterological Institute. Technical Report
0355-1792 Acta Philosophica Fennica
0355-1849 Paasikivi-Society. Mimeograph Series
0355-1865 Pientalo-Omakoti†
0355-1873 Tee Itse†
0355-189X Suur-Seura *changed to* Seura (1979)
0355-1903 TH-Kotilaakari
0355-1911 Non Stop†
0355-192X Muoti & Kauneus
0355-2004 Finnish Meteorological Institute. Observations of Satellites. Visual Observations of Artificial Earth Satellites in Finland
0355-2063 Finland. Tilastokeskus. Kasikirjoja
0355-2071 Finland. Tilastokeskus. Tutkimuksia
0355-208X Finland. Tilastokeskus. Tilastollisia Tiedonantoja
0355-2098 Suuri Kasityokerho
0355-2101 Aku Ankka
0355-211X Finland. Tilastokeskus. Tulo- Ja Omaisuustilasto
0355-2128 Finland. Tilastokeskus. Kuolleisuus- Ja Eloonjaamistauluja
0355-2136 Finland. Tilastokeskus. Vaestolaskenta
0355-2144 Finland. Tilastokeskus. Kuolemansyyt
0355-2152 Finland. Tilastokeskus. Asuntotuotanto
0355-2187 Finland. Tilastokeskus. Tuomioistuinten Toiminta
0355-2209 Finland. Tilastokeskus. Kansanedustajain Vaalit
0355-2217 Finland. Tilastokeskus. Kunnallisvaalit
0355-2225 Finland. Tilastokeskus. Korkeakoulut
0355-2233 Finland. Tilastokeskus. Tutkimustoiminta
0355-239X Finland. Tilastokeskus. Indeksitiedotus RK. Rakennuskustannusindeski/ Byggnadskostnadsindex/Building Cost Index
0355-2446 Finland. Tilastokeskus. Yleissivistavat Oppilaitokset
0355-2454 Finland. Tilastokeskus. Pankit
0355-256X Commentationes Scientiarum Socialium
0355-2624 Vaasan Kauppakorkeakoulu. Julkaisuja. Opetusmonisteita *changed to* Vaasan Korkeakoulu. Julkaisuja. Opetusmonisteita
0355-2632 Vaasan Kauppakorkeakoulu. Julkaisuja. Tutkimuksia *changed to* Vaasan Korkeakoulu. Julkaisuja. Tutkimuksia
0355-2667 Acta Wasaensia
0355-2691 Suomen Autolehti
0355-2705 Acta Polytechnica Scandinavica. Civil Engineering and Building Construction Series
0355-2713 Acta Polytechnica Scandinavica. Mathematics and Computer Science Series

ISSN INDEX 1229

0355-2721	Acta Polytechnica Scandinavica. Applied Physics Series	0355-6042	Suomen Pankki. Julkaisuja. Serie D
0355-2764	Jermu	0355-6050	Suomen Pankki. Julkaisuja. Kasvututkimuksia
0355-2772	Seksi	0355-6395	Valtion Teknillinen Tutkimuskeskus. Metallilaboratorio. Tiedonanto
0355-2896	Autolla Ulkomaille	0355-6735	Radiokauppias
0355-2950	Avotakka	0355-6832	Joensuun Korkeakoulu. Julkaisuja. Sarja B2
0355-2969	Katso	0355-6999	Kenkalusikka
0355-2977	Elamani Tarinat†	0355-7073	Liikuntakasvatus
0355-2985	Eeva	0355-726X	Toimiupseeri
0355-2993	Nakke	0355-7286	Ammattiautoilija
0355-3000	Ravi ja Ratsastus†	0355-7421	Kotiteollisuus
0355-3027	Eevaneule	0355-7588	Kelloseppae
0355-3043	U M: Uusi Maailma†	0355-7596	Metsanhoitaja
0355-3051	Apu	0355-7693	Psychiatria Fennica. Julkaisuserja
0355-3078	Kauppias	0355-7707	Psychiatria Fennica. Monografiasarja
0355-3086	Rautaviesti	0355-7839	Muoviuutiset†
0355-3140	Scandinavian Journal of Work, Environment & Health	0355-7855	Tie ja Liikenne
0355-3256	Myyntineuvoja	0355-7871	Navigator
0355-337X	Technical Research Centre of Finland. Publication. Building Technology and Community Development†	0355-7858	Teksi
		0355-8878	Finland. Valtioneuvoston Kanslian. Julkaisuja
0355-3388	Technical Research Centre of Finland. Publication. Materials and Processing Technology†	0355-8991	Tekstiiliopettaja-Textilaren
		0355-9076	Valtion Teknillinen Tutkimuskeskus. Sairaalatekniikan Laboratorio. Tiedonanto
0355-3396	Technical Research Centre of Finland. Publication. Electrical and Nuclear Technology†	0355-9483	Turun Yliopisto. Julkaisuja. Sarja D. Medica-Odontologica
0355-3434	Valtion Teknillinen Tutkimuskeskus. Kojetekniikan Laboratorio. Tiedonanto	0355-9521	Annales Chirurgiae et Gynaecologiae
		0355-953X	Puumies
0355-3450	Valtion Teknillinen Tutkimuskeskus. Geotekniikan Laboratorio. Tiedonanto	0355-9610	Aja
		0355-9912	Uudistova Konttori
0355-3477	Valtion Teknillinen Tutkimuskeskus. Maankayton Laboratorio. Tiedonanto	0356-004X	Valtion Teknillinen Tutkimuskeskus. A T K-Palvelutoimisto. Tiedonanto
0355-3485	Valtion Teknillinen Tutkimuskeskus. Palotekniikan Laboratorio. Tiedonanto	0356-0805	Leirinta ja Retkeily
		0356-1062	Biological Research Reports from the University of Jyvaskyla
0355-354X	Valtion Teknillinen Tutkimuskeskus. Biotekniikan Labboratorio. Tiedonanto	0356-1364	University of Helsinki. Department of Cooperative Studies. Publications
0355-3558	Valtion Teknillinen Tutkimuskeskus. Elintarvikelabboratorio. Tiedonanto	0356-1704	Vappa-Aika-Eurosport
		0356-276X	Savon Luonto
0355-3566	Valtion Teknillinen Tutkimuskeskus. Graafinen Laboratorio. Tiedonanto	0356-3014	Mallas ja Olut
		0356-3081	Syopa
0355-3574	Valtion Teknillinen Tutkimuskeskus. Kemian Laboratorio. Tiedonanto	0356-3189	Savonia
		0356-343X	Metsatilastollinen Vuosikirja
0355-3590	Valtion Teknillinen Tutkimuskeskus. Poltti- ja Voiteluainelaboratorio. Tiedonanto	0356-3472	P.S.†
		0356-4096	Projektio
		0356-4827	Auto ja Liikenne
0355-3639	Valtion Teknillinen Tutkimuskeskus. Tekstiililaboratorio. Tiedonanto	0356-5092	Hinnat ja Kilpailu
		0356-5327	Tehokas Yritys
0355-3663	Valtion Teknillinen Tutkimuskeskus. Reaktorilaboratorio. Tiedonanto	0356-6110	Rakennusviesti *changed to* Meidantalo
0355-3671	Valtion Teknillinen Tutkimuskeskus. Sahkotekniikan Laboratorio. Tiedonanto	0356-6927	Academia Scientiarum Fennica. Yearbook
		0356-7133	Aqua Fennica
0355-368X	Valtion Teknillinen Tutkimuskeskus. Teletekniikan Laboratorio. Tiedonanto	0356-7753	Finnish Boatbuilding Industry
		0356-780X	Institute for Migration, Turku. Migration Studies *changed to* Migration Institute. Migration Studies
0355-3698	Valtion Teknillinen Tutkimuskeskus. Ydinvoimatekniikan Laboratorio. Tiedonanto	0356-7818	Kemistin Kalenteri
		0356-7826	Suomen Vakuutusvuosikirja
0355-3701	Valtion Teknillinen Tutkimuskeskus. Teknillinen Informaatiopalvelulaitos. Tiedonanto	0356-7842	Laeraren
		0356-7850	Liikearkisto
		0356-7869	Maankaytto
0355-3736	Lapset ja Yhteiskunta	0356-7915	Current Research on Peace and Violence
0355-3752	Tuottavuus	0356-7923	Markkinointi *see* 0357-2862
0355-3795	Kuva ja Aani	0356-7931	Muusikko
0355-3817	E	0356-794X	Osto ja Materialitalous
0355-3913	Suomen Antropologi	0356-8067	Pistis
0355-3949	Help!†	0356-8075	Tahti
0355-3957	Joensuun Korkeakoulu. Julkaisuja. Sarja B *see* 0355-6832	0356-8083	Valokuvauksen Vuosikirja
		0356-8091	Vaatturi
0355-3965	Opettaja	0356-8105	Valtionyhtiot
0355-4031	Aabo Akademi. Statsvetenskapliga Fakulteten. Meddelanden. Serie A *changed to* Aabo Akademi. Statsvetenskapliga Fakulteten. Meddelanden	0356-827X	U I T B B Information
		0357-0312	Finland
		0357-1076	S F S Catalogue
		0357-1831	Finnish Marine Research
0355-4201	J P: Joka Poika		Valtion Teknillinen Tutkimuskeskus. Metallurgian ja Mineraalitekniikan Laboratorio. Tiedonanto
0355-4236	Jaana		
0355-4465	Aabo Akademi. Statsvetenskapliga Fakulteten. Meddelanden. Serie B *changed to* Aabo Akademi. Statsvetenskapliga Fakulteten. Meddelanden	0357-2714	Koululainen
		0357-2862	Mark Uusi Markkinointilehti
		0357-3362	Helsinki. Tilastokeskus. Neljannesvuosikatsaus
0355-4481	Finland. Patentti- ja Rekisterihallitus. Mallioikeuslehti/ Moensterraettstidning/Design Gazette	0357-3486	Vaasa School of Economics. Proceedings. Discussion Papers *changed to* University of Vaasa. Proceedings. Discussion Papers
0355-4503	Elektroniikka		
0355-4651	Suomen Hammaslaekariseura. Toimituksia. Supplementa	0357-3737	Valtion Teknillinen Tutkimuskeskus. Betoni- ja Silikaattitekniikan Laboratorio. Tiedonanto
0355-4813	Finland. Kansanelakelaitos. Julkaisuja. Sarja AL	0357-4776	Suomen Pankki. Julkaisuja. Serie B
0355-4821	Finland. Kansanelakelaitos. Julkaisuja. Sarja M	0357-7031	Valtion Teknillinen Tutkimuskeskus. Rakennetekniikan Laboratorio. Tiedonanto
0355-483X	Finland. Kansanelakelaitos. Julkaisuja. Sarja ML	0357-8747	Elainmaailma
0355-4848	Finland. Kansanelakelaitos. Julkaisuja. Sarja E	0357-8755	Roope-Seta
		0357-9387	V T T Symposium
0355-4856	Finland. Kansanelakelaitos. Julkaisuja. Sarja EL	0357-9921	Jyvaskyla Studies in Computer Science, Economics and Statistics
0355-5003	Finland Kansanelakelaitos. Toiminta Kertomus	0358-2671	Finland. Ilmatieteen Laitos. Ilmasahkohavaintoja
0355-5011	Tuberculosis and Respiratory Diseases Yearbook	0360-0017	Multiple Sclerosis Indicative Abstracts
		0360-0025	Sex Roles: A Journal of Research
0355-502X	Philatelia Fennica	0360-0053	Maine Fish and Wildlife
0355-5054	Rondo	0360-0114	Florida Bar News
0355-550X	Rakentajain Kalenteri	0360-0165	Concerned Demography
0355-5534	Rakennusalan Suomalaisen Kirjallisunden Kuukausikatsaus *changed to* R T-Uutiset	0360-0270	Illinois. State Museum. Reports of Investigations
		0360-0289	Illinois. State Museum. Story of Illinois Series
0355-578X	Acta Academiae Aboensis. Series A: Humaniora	0360-0297	Illinois. State Museum. Popular Science Series
0355-5798	Aabo Akademi. Aarsskrift		
0355-5895	4H -Tiedotuksia	0360-0300	A C M Computing Surveys
0355-6034	Suomen Pankki. Julkaisuja. Serie A		

0360-0319	Street Drug Survival *see* 0361-5359
0360-0327	Soviet Astronomy Letters
0360-0335	Soviet Journal of Low Temperature Physics
0360-0343	Soviet Journal of Plasma Physics
0360-0467	Areito
0360-0521	U.S. Department of Agriculture. Economic Research Service. Sugar and Sweetener Situation *see* 0362-9511
0360-0556	Civil Engineering A S C E
0360-0564	Advances in Catalysis
0360-0572	Annual Review of Sociology
0360-0637	Ebsco Bulletin of Serials Changes
0360-067X	R.I. Medical Journal
0360-0726	Rehabilitation/World
0360-0815	National Panorama of American Youth
0360-0939	A C A Bulletin
0360-0971	Information Reports and Bibliographies
0360-1005	Mandate Magazine
0360-1013	Ohio Review
0360-1021	Archaeology of Eastern North America
0360-1048	New Mexico Almanac *changed to* New Mexico Digest
0360-1056	North Carolina Genealogical Society Journal
0360-120X	Soviet Technical Physics Letters
0360-1218	Journal of Structural Mechanics
0360-1226	Journal of Environmental Science and Health. Part A: Environmental Science and Engineering
0360-1234	Journal of Environmental Science and Health. Part B: Pesticides, Food Contaminants, and Agricultural Wastes
0360-1250	Current Book Review Citations
0360-1269	Earth Surface Processes *see* 0197-9337
0360-1277	Educational Gerontology
0360-1285	Progress in Energy and Combustion Science
0360-1293	Acupuncture and Electro-Therapeutics Research
0360-1315	Computers & Education
0360-1323	Building and Environment
0360-1358	Contact and Intraocular Lens Medical Journal
0360-1390	Suicide *see* 0363-0234
0360-1420	Journal of Christian Reconstruction
0360-1447	Legal Economics
0360-1455	New River Review†
0360-151X	Brigham Young University Law Review
0360-1560	Lumberman and Wood Industries *see* 0015-7430
0360-1617	C.A.C. Document
0360-165X	American Enterprise Institute for Public Policy Research. Review, Session of the Congress
0360-1676	Florida State Dental Society. Journal *see* 0015-3990
0360-1684	National Association of Chiropodists. Journal *see* 0003-0538
0360-1714	Nucleic Acids Literature
0360-1722	Ongoing Current Bibliography of Plastic & Reconstructive Surgery *see* 0149-5348
0360-1757	E I A Electronics Multimedia Handbook†
0360-1765	Leviathan and Kinnikinnik
0360-1773	Market Chronicle
0360-1846	Great Lakes Review-Journal of Midwest Culture
0360-1889	Astrologia
0360-1897	Pacific Theological Review
0360-1927	Journal of Latin American Lore
0360-1935	Main Title†
0360-1943	Music Book Guide *see* 0360-2753
0360-196X	Corrections Court Digest
0360-1978	Richmond Historian†
0360-2044	Forum Law Journal
0360-2109	Paul's Record Magazine
0360-2133	Metallurgical Transactions A-Physical Metallurgy and Materials Science
0360-215X	Dictionary of Contemporary Quotations
0360-2206	Balkanistica
0360-2230	Plymouth Colony Genealogical Helper *changed to* Plymouth Colony Genealogist
0360-2257	Connecticut. Energy Advisory Board. Annual Report to the Governor and General Assembly. Executive Summary
0360-2265	E P A Reports Bibliography Quarterly *changed to* E P A Publications Bibliography Quarterly Abstracts Bulletin
0360-2273	Popular Mechanics Do-It-Yourself Yearbook
0360-2397	Harper's Weekly†
0360-2400	Management Contents
0360-2451	Catalysis Reviews: Science and Engineering
0360-2508	Current Governments Reports: Chart Book on Government Data. Organization, Finances and Employment
0360-2516	Billboard Index†
0360-2532	Drug Metabolism Reviews
0360-2540	Separation and Purification Methods
0360-2559	Polymer Plastics Technology & Engineering
0360-2672	Scree
0360-2699	Bibliographic Guide to Art and Architecture
0360-2702	Bibliographic Guide to Business and Economics
0360-2710	Bibliographic Guide to Black Studies

0360-2729 Bibliographic Guide to Conference Publications
0360-2737 Bibliographic Guide to Dance
0360-2745 Bibliographic Guide to Law
0360-2753 Bibliographic Guide to Music
0360-2761 Bibliographic Guide to Technology
0360-277X Bibliographic Guide to Psychology
0360-2788 Bibliographic Guide to Theatre Arts
0360-2796 Bibliographic Guide to Government Publications
0360-280X Bibliographic Guide to Government Publications-Foreign
0360-2834 Maryland Register
0360-2877 Concrete Pipe Industry Statistics
0360-2915 Trinity Studies *see* 0360-3032
0360-3016 International Journal of Radiation: Oncology - Biology - Physics
0360-3024 Family Motor Coaching
0360-3032 Trinity Journal
0360-3059 Vermont. Agency of Environmental Conservation. Biennial Report†
0360-3083 Wood Industry Abstracts
0360-3091 Portland Review Magazine
0360-3164 Plating and Surface Finishing
0360-3199 International Journal of Hydrogen Energy
0360-3245 U.S. Federal Bureau of Investigation. Bomb Summary
0360-3326 New York State Sea Grant Program. Annual Report *changed to* New York Sea Grant Institute. Annual Report
0360-3342 Liberty, Then and Now†
0360-3350 L A D O C
0360-3385 Tristania
0360-3520 Body Fashions/Intimate Apparel
0360-3539 Calling the World *changed to* World's Telephones
0360-3571 E R D A Energy Research Abstracts *see* 0160-3604
0360-3598 Family in Historical Perspective *see* 0363-1990
0360-3601 Genesis III†
0360-361X A.D. United Church of Christ Edition *changed to* United Church of Christ A.D.
0360-3628 A.D. United Presbyterian Edition *changed to* United Presbyterian A.D.
0360-3636 Arithmoi†
0360-3679 Institutes of Religion and Health. Institutes Reporter†
0360-3687 A I I S Annual Report
0360-3695 Film & History
0360-3709 American Poetry Review
0360-3717 A.M.E. Zion Quarterly Review
0360-3725 A. M. E. Church Review
0360-3733 Theological Currents†
0360-3741 Black Church†
0360-3768 Candler Review†
0360-3784 E F T S Report
0360-3814 Performing Arts Resources
0360-3857 Virginia Bar Association Journal
0360-3881 Alaska. Division of Geological and Geophysical Surveys. Special Report
0360-389X Adventist Heritage
0360-392X U.S. National Transportation Safety Board. Briefs of Accidents Involving Midair Collisions, U.S. General Aviation†
0360-3938 Business Outlook
0360-3954 U. S. National Transportation Safety Board. Listing of Aircraft Accidents-Incidents by Make and Model, U.S. Civil Aviation†
0360-3989 Human Communication Research
0360-3997 Inflammation
0360-4012 Journal of Neuroscience Research
0360-4020 Association of Military Dermatologists. Journal
0360-4039 Nursing (Jenkintown)
0360-4055 C S Journal
0360-4071 Quality Rock Reader
0360-4098 U.S. Department of Agriculture. Economics, Statistics, and Cooperatives Service. Agricultural Situation in the Soviet Union
0360-4209 Journal of Legislation *see* 0146-9584
0360-4217 National Journal (1975)
0360-4225 Visual Dialog
0360-4233 A S P A News and Views *see* 0149-8797
0360-4357 D.P.I. Yellow Pages
0360-4365 In Theory Only
0360-439X Tobacco Stocks
0360-4438 Appalachian Notes
0360-4519 Irish Genealogical Helper *changed to* Irish-American Genealogist
0360-4527 Fleet Specialist
0360-4543 U.S. Department of the Interior. Oil Shale Environmental Advisory Panel. Annual Report
0360-4594 U.S. Food and Nutrition Service. Food and Nutrition Programs
0360-473X Directions (New York, 1975)
0360-4837 Washington (State). Indian Assistance Division.Indian Economic Employment Assistance Program. Annual Report
0360-487X U.S. Social and Rehabilitation Service. Annual Report of Welfare Programs
0360-4918 Presidential Studies Quarterly
0360-4969 American Health Care Association. Journal
0360-4977 Topics in Infectious Diseases
0360-4985 Inforum: Environmental Report Data System *changed to* Inforum: Energy-Environment Information System
0360-5027 Journal of Teaching and Learning
0360-506X Retailing Today
0360-5094 Midwestern Advocate *changed to* Hamline Law Review
0360-5108 Looking Back to Those Wonderful Days Gone by
0360-5132 Official Gazette of the United States Patent and Trademark Office. Trademarks
0360-5159 Metal Industry (New York) *see* 0026-0576
0360-5167 American Hospital Association. House of Delegates. Proceedings
0360-523X Conference Board. Utility Investment Statistics. Utility Appropriations
0360-5248 Who's Who Among Students in American Vocational and Technical Schools *see* 0148-6381
0360-5272 Rail Transit Directory†
0360-5280 Byte
0360-5302 Communications in Partial Differential Equations
0360-5361 N A D L Journal
0360-537X Good and Inexpensive Books for Children *changed to* Bibliography of Books for Children
0360-5388 Ais-Eiri
0360-5434 Occupational Education
0360-5442 Energy (Oxford)
0360-5450 Vertica
0360-5477 Tennessee Manufacturers Directory
0360-5531 Old Northwest
0360-554X Uniformed Services Almanac. Special Reserve Forces Edition *see* 0363-860X
0360-5558 Alaska. Department of Natural Resources. Division of Oil and Gas. Statistical Report *changed to* Alaska. Oil and Gas Conservation Commission. Statistical Report
0360-5590 Texas Tech Journal of Education
0360-5612 Loon†
0360-5639 Home Horticulture
0360-5701 Freeing the Spirit
0360-5779 Chronicle (Greensburg) *see* 0015-8992
0360-5809 Information News and Sources *see* 0360-5817
0360-5817 Information Hotline
0360-5825 Financial Corporate Bond Transfer Service
0360-5841 Inventory of Agricultural Research
0360-5906 R T S D Newsletter
0360-5930 A C E S Bulletin
0360-5949 American Philological Association. Transactions
0360-5973 Journal of Psychiatric Nursing and Mental Health Services
0360-6031 Yearbook of Cardiovascular Medicine *see* 0145-4145
0360-6058 Bricklayers', Masons' and Plasterers' International Union of America. Journal *see* 0362-3696
0360-6112 Buddhist Text Information
0360-618X Center for Process Studies. Newsletter
0360-6244 Living Worship
0360-6325 L D & A
0360-6333 African Economic History Review *see* 0145-2258
0360-6376 Journal of Polymer Science. Polymer Chemistry Edition
0360-6384 Journal of Polymer Science. Polymer Letters Edition
0360-649X Copts
0360-6503 Process Studies
0360-6511 Personal Growth
0360-652X Patristics
0360-6538 Annotated Bibliography of New Publications in the Performing Arts
0360-6724 Obsidian: Black Literature in Review
0360-6740 Review of the Graphic Arts
0360-683X Nebraska. Indian Commission. Report
0360-6848 U.S. Social Security Administration. Applications and Case Dispositions for Public Assistance
0360-6864 Columbia River Water Management Report
0360-6929 American Society for Quality Control. Annual Technical Conference Transactions
0360-6945 Lutheran Journal
0360-6953 Liberalist
0360-697X A A C S B Newsline
0360-6996 A R T B A Officials and Engineers Directory, Transportation Agency Personnel
0360-7011 Ammonia Plant Safety and Related Facilities
0360-7046 M S U U Newsletter
0360-7100 American Institute for Decision Sciences. Southeast Section. Proceedings
0360-7119 Reporter (St. Louis. 1975)
0360-7135 Creative World
0360-7151 Legal Bibliographic Data Service: Weekly Listing†
0360-716X Navy Supply Corps Newsletter
0360-7178 A A M O A Reports
0360-7216 Functional Photography (Hempstead)
0360-7232 Mentalis
0360-7283 Health and Social Work
0360-7348 Replay
0360-7364 Sergeants
0360-7372 Survey of Law Reviews *see* 0279-5787
0360-7410 Renaissance Two; Journal of Afro-American Studies
0360-7437 A A M C Directory of American Medical Education
0360-7453 Violations of Human Rights in Soviet Occupied Lithuania
0360-7461 Arizona. Water Commission. Bulletin.
0360-7496 Canoe
0360-750X U. S. Urban Mass Transportation Administration Report to Congress Concerning the Demonstration of Fare-Free Mass Transportation†
0360-7569 Current Concepts in Psychiatry
0360-7577 Engineering in Medicine
0360-7607 Hemostasis and Thrombosis; a Bibliography
0360-7690 Nuclear Regulation Reports
0360-7739 Amicus Curiae
0360-7860 Revista Chicano-Riquena
0360-7887 Rackham Literary Studies
0360-7941 National Development-Modern Government
0360-795X Journal of Corporation Law
0360-800X Utah. Division of Wildlife Resources. Biennial Report
0360-8034 U.S. Forest Service. Cooperative Fire Protection. Wildfire Statistics
0360-8085 Best in Posters *changed to* Best in Covers and Posters
0360-814X American Water Works Association. Proceedings, A W W A Annual Conference
0360-8166 U.S. National Advisory Council on Extension and Continuing Education. Annual Report
0360-8174 I S I's Who Is Publishing in Science *changed to* Current Bibliographic Directory for the Arts & Sciences
0360-8182 Uniquest *changed to* International Journal for Logotherapy
0360-8212 Radical Religion
0360-8247 People Soup
0360-8263 Best in Advertising Campaigns *changed to* Best in Advertising
0360-8271 Best in Environmental Graphics
0360-8298 Cumberland Law Review
0360-8352 Computers & Industrial Engineering
0360-8360 Current Advances in Genetics†
0360-8409 ICarbS
0360-8417 International Defense Business *changed to* Defense & Economy World Report & Survey
0360-8425 American Foreign Service Journal *see* 0015-7279
0360-8476 Search at the State University of New York†
0360-8484 Matthay News
0360-8557 Engineering Index Annual
0360-8581 Engineering Management Review
0360-859X Transportation Research Board Special Report
0360-862X C A S E Currents
0360-8654 Guide to Micrographic Equipment
0360-8662 United Business & Investment Report
0360-8670 Aviation Quarterly
0360-8689 Best in Packaging
0360-8697 Country Music Explorer
0360-8700 Disc Collector Newsletter
0360-8727 R I d I M-R C M I Newsletter
0360-8743 Best in Annual Reports
0360-8751 Stream Improvement Technical Bulletin
0360-8778 Atmospheric Quality Improvement Technical Bulletin
0360-8786 Current Register of American Leaders
0360-8808 Evangelical Theological Society. Journal
0360-8816 Northeast Rising Sun
0360-8832 International Symposium on Atomic, Molecular and Solid-State Theory and Quantum Statistics. Proceedings *changed to* International Symposium on Atomic, Molecular and Solid-State Theory, Collision Phenomena and Computational Methods. Proceedings
0360-8840 American Accounting Association. Southeast Regional Group. Collected Papers of the Annual Meeting
0360-8859 Pennsylvania Exporters Directory
0360-8867 Marine Geotechnology
0360-8905 Journal of Polymer Science. Polymer Symposia Edition
0360-8913 International Conference on Cybernetics and Society. Proceedings
0360-8921 Argus F. C. & S. Chart
0360-8980 U.S. Department of Transportation. Summary of National Transportation Statistics *changed to* U.S. Department of Transportation. National Transportation Statistics. Annual
0360-8999 Foundry Management & Technology
0360-9006 Hastings Center. Recent Activities†
0360-9049 Hebrew Union College Annual
0360-9081 American Archivist
0360-912X Shocks
0360-9146 Uniform Crime Report for the State of Michigan
0360-9154 Alaska Accident Statistics
0360-9162 Illinois Air Quality Report *changed to* Illinois. Division of Air Pollution Control. Annual Air Quality Report
0360-9170 Language Arts

0360-9197 American Association of Blood Banks. Bulletin *see* 0041-1132
0360-9235 Lodging
0360-9278 Hearing Rehabilitation Quarterly
0360-9286 Highlights *see* 0360-9278
0360-9294 American Audiology Society. Journal *see* 0164-5080
0360-9316 Survey of Hospital Charges *see* 0090-6662
0360-9421 Pope Family Register
0360-9464 U.S. Veterans Administration. Annual Report on Relief from Administrative Error
0360-9553 Non-Ferrous Metal Data
0360-9561 Zoning Reporter
0360-9588 Adherent
0360-9642 N I D A Supported Drug Treatment Programs
0360-9669 Horizons (Villanova)
0360-9693 Military Chaplains' Review
0360-9731 Nevada Government Today
0360-9766 Annual Editions: Readings in Health
0360-9782 United Church of Christ. Pension Boards (Annual Report)
0360-9790 Lektos
0360-991X Z.C.L.A. Journal *changed to* Zen Writings
0360-9928 Marathon Handbook†
0360-9936 Quality (Wheaton)
0360-9960 Advances in Bioengineering
0360-9987 Directory of Diesel Fuel Stations Coast to Coast *changed to* Diesel Fuel Guide
0361-0004 Modern Recording *changed to* Modern Recording & Music
0361-0020 Retailing in Tennessee
0361-0047 Foreign Trade Reports. Summary of U.S. Export and Import Merchandise Trade
0361-0128 Economic Geology and the Bulletin of the Society of Economic Geologists
0361-0144 American Humanities Index
0361-0152 Newspaper and Gazette Report *see* 0190-9819
0361-0160 Sixteenth Century Journal
0361-0179 Aging (New York)
0361-0195 Health Systems Management
0361-0233 Progress in Chemical Fibrinolysis and Thrombolysis
0361-025X Tests in Print
0361-0268 T C A Manual *see* 0271-8057
0361-0365 Research in Higher Education
0361-0373 War and Society
0361-0438 Commerce America *changed to* Business America
0361-0462 International Brain Research Organization Monograph Series
0361-0470 American Society of Brewing Chemists. Journal
0361-0519 Ohio. Division of Geological Survey. Miscellaneous Report
0361-0527 Perspectives in Cardiovascular Research
0361-0551 Theoretical Chemistry: Advances and Perspectives
0361-056X Campaign Practices Reports
0361-0640 Rubber Red Book
0361-073X Experimental Aging Research
0361-0748 Society of Photo-Optical Instrumentation Engineers. Proceedings
0361-0772 American Nurses' Association. House of Delegates. Summary Proceedings
0361-0802 Pilgrimage
0361-0845 Coin World Almanac
0361-0853 Manufacturing Engineering
0361-0861 Southern School Law Digest
0361-0896 Celebrate
0361-090X Cancer Detection and Prevention
0361-0918 Communications in Statistics. Part B: Simulation and Computation
0361-0926 Communications in Statistics. Part A: Methods and Techniques
0361-0942 Video Systems
0361-0977 Formal Linguistics
0361-1043 Motorhome Life and Camper Coachman *see* 0164-503X
0361-1094 Encyclopedia Buying Guide
0361-1108 Bricker's International Directory of University-Sponsored Executive Development Programs
0361-1116 Abortion Research Notes
0361-1124 J A C E P *see* 0196-0644
0361-1175 Western Society of Malacologists. Annual Report
0361-1213 Microstructural Science
0361-1221 National Endowment for the Humanities. Program Announcement
0361-1302 Samizdat Bulletin
0361-1353 Alaska Geographic
0361-1361 Milepost: All-the-North Travel Guide
0361-137X Selected Alaska Hunting & Fishing Tales†
0361-1388 Sweet's Engineering Catalog File. Summary Edition: Mechanical, Sanitary and Related Products
0361-140X Maryland. Council for Higher Education. Annual Report and Recommendations†
0361-1434 I E E E Transactions. Professional Communication
0361-1442 Computers and People
0361-1493 Directory of Drug Information and Treatment Organizations†
0361-1507 National Institute of Education. Career Education Program: Program Plan
0361-1515 Grassroots (Madison)
0361-1582 Federal Grant-in-Aid Activity in Florida: a Summary Report
0361-1612 Council for Tobacco Research--U.S.A. Report
0361-1663 Abraxas
0361-1671 Milwaukee County Historical Society. Historical Messenger *see* 0163-7622
0361-168X New Boston Review
0361-1817 Nurse Practitioner
0361-1833 American Association for the Advancement of Science. Meeting Program.
0361-185X Selbyana
0361-1906 Journal of Theology
0361-1981 Transportation Research Record
0361-1981 National Research Council. Transportation Research Board. Record
0361-204X New York Folklore
0361-2066 Best in Covers *changed to* Best in Covers and Posters
0361-2112 Dress
0361-2120 Wisconsin. Educational Communications Board. Biennial Report
0361-2147 Antique Phonograph Monthly
0361-2163 A C M Annual Workshop on Microprogramming. Conference Record
0361-218X Worldwide Lodging Industry
0361-2198 U. S. Lodging Industry
0361-221X A A U Baton Twirling Rules and Regulations
0361-2228 Directory of Physics & Astronomy Staff Members
0361-2279 National Research Council. Committee on Polar Research. Report on United States Antarctic Research Activities
0361-2295 North Carolina Governor's Highway Safety Program. Summary of Activities *changed to* North Carolina. Department of Transportation. Office of Highway Safety. Summary of Activities
0361-2309 Corporate Examiner
0361-2317 Color Research and Application
0361-2325 Political Intelligence†
0361-2333 Prospects
0361-2376 Congregational Journal
0361-2449 U.S. Forest Service. Research Note NC
0361-2481 Wind
0361-249X Ophthalmic Seminars†
0361-2562 Resources Recovery/Energy Review†
0361-2570 Sales & Marketing Management *see* 0163-7517
0361-2597 Texas. Industrial Commission. Annual Report
0361-2635 Micropublishers' Trade List Annual
0361-2643 U.S. Social and Rehabilitation Service. Office of Management. Quality Control, States' Corrective Action Activities
0361-2651 U.S. Department of the Army. Projects Recommended for Deauthorization, Annual Report
0361-2678 Viewpoint (Columbus)
0361-2759 History: Reviews of New Books
0361-2767 Empirical Research in Theatre
0361-2783 Auerbach Guide to Computing Equipment Specifications†
0361-2791 C T A Quarterly
0361-2805 National Ocean Survey. Collected Reprints
0361-2813 Home Improvement and Repair *see* 0362-6520
0361-2821 Mechanical Properties *changed to* Mechanical and Corrosion Properties
0361-2848 Wisconsin Library Service Record
0361-2899 Official A A U Trampoline and Tumbling Handbook
0361-2929 Health Facilities Directory
0361-2961 Advances in Holography
0361-297X Alabama. Department of Industrial Relations. Annual Manpower Planning Report *changed to* Alabama. Department of Industrial Relations. Annual Planning Information
0361-2988 Complete Handbook of Pro Football
0361-2996 Directory of Manufacturers in Arkansas *changed to* Directory of Arkansas Manufacturers
0361-3011 Field & Stream Hunting Annual
0361-3038 N.E.S.F.A. Index: Science Fiction Magazines and Anthologies
0361-3054 Scripps Clinic and Research Foundation. Scientific Report
0361-3062 Germanic Genealogical Helper *see* 0363-9169
0361-3313 Electronics and Communications Abstracts Journal
0361-3321 Science Research Abstracts Journal, Part A: Superconductivity; Magnetohydrodynamics & Plasmas; Theoretical Physics
0361-333X Western Reserve Magazine
0361-3372 Practical Cardiology
0361-3399 I J A L Native American Texts Series
0361-3410 Toxicology Annual
0361-3445 Directory of State Government Energy-Related Agencies†
0361-3453 Fine Woodworking
0361-3461 South Dakota Highway Safety Work Program
0361-347X A A U Official Track and Field Handbook, Rules and Records
0361-3488 International Journal of Powder Metallurgy & Powder Technology
0361-3496 Environmental Psychology and Nonverbal Behavior *see* 0191-5886
0361-3518 Gas Turbine World
0361-3534 Illinois. Department of Mental Health and Developmental Disabiliities. Annual Report
0361-3550 Maine. Bureau of Property Taxation. Biennial Report
0361-3577 Loblolly
0361-3593 Southwest Directory of Advertising and Public Relations Agencies
0361-3658 Conservation & Recycling
0361-3666 Disasters
0361-3682 Accounting, Organizations and Society
0361-3712 Arlington Catholic Herald
0361-3747 Welding & Joining Digest
0361-3763 A B A Lawyers' Title Guaranty Funds Newsletter
0361-3771 Directory of Psychosocial Investigators†
0361-3798 Mental Retardation and Developmental Disabilities Abstracts *see* 0191-1600
0361-3801 Fine Print
0361-381X Bicycle Dealer Showcase
0361-3828 Breast: Diseases of the Breast
0361-3836 Annual Editions: Readings in Personality and Adjustment *see* 0198-912X
0361-3844 Attorneys and Agents Registered to Practice Before the U.S. Patent and Trademark Office
0361-3895 National Income and Product Accounts of the United States: Statistical Tables
0361-3917 S I E Guide to Business and Investment Books
0361-3968 Asian Thought & Society: an International Review
0361-3976 Women's International Bowling Congress. Playing Rules
0361-3984 Alaska Fishing Guide†
0361-4018 New York State Medical Care Facilities Finance Agency. Annual Report
0361-4034 Grocery Distribution
0361-4050 Employee Benefits Journal
0361-4166 Rehabilitation Gazette
0361-4190 Xerox Disclosure Journal
0361-4204 U.S. Federal Highway Administration. Federally Coordinated Program of Highway Research and Development
0361-4239 Conference Board. Manufacturing Investment Statistics. Capital Appropriations
0361-4247 Buyer's Directory of Suppliers for General Merchandise Buyers†
0361-4255 Directory of North American Fairs and Expositions
0361-4336 Children Today
0361-4344 F D A Drug Bulletin
0361-4387 Cosmetics and Toiletries
0361-4425 Yale University. School of Forestry. Bulletin
0361-4433 Geodesy, Mapping and Photogrammetry
0361-4441 Cuban Studies
0361-4476 Journal of Energy Resources Technology
0361-4506 California. State Water Resources Control Board. Annual State Strategy *changed to* California. State Water Resources Control Board. Program Guide
0361-4514 U.S. Office of Education. Determination of Basic Grant Eligibility Index†
0361-4522 U.S. Food and Drug Administration. Pesticide-P C B in Foods Program. Evaluation Report
0361-4530 U.S. Solicitor for the Department of the Interior. Solicitor's Review†
0361-4565 Wire Technology
0361-4654 A A U Junior Olympic Handbook
0361-4662 Bottomline†
0361-4670 European Skinny†
0361-4689 R & D Review (Schenectady)
0361-4735 Current Biographies of Leading Archaeologists
0361-4751 American Film Magazine(Washington)
0361-476X Contemporary Educational Psychology
0361-4794 Current Mathematical Publications
0361-4921 Fiber Producer
0361-4948 Tourbook: Alabama, Louisiana, Mississippi
0361-4956 Tourbook: Georgia, North Carolina, South Carolina
0361-4964 Tourbook: Kentucky, Tennessee
0361-4972 Electrical Consultant
0361-4999 Ithacagun Hunting & Shooting Annual†
0361-5006 Annual Symposium on Pulmonary Diseases
0361-5049 Educational Catalyst
0361-5057 Abbott, Langer & Associates. College Recruiting Report
0361-5065 Buoyant Flight
0361-5170 Victimology
0361-5227 Modern Psychoanalysis
0361-5235 Journal of Electronic Materials
0361-526X Serials Librarian
0361-5294 Doors and Hardware
0361-5332 Utah. Department of Transportation. Highway Safety Program, Annual Report
0361-5359 Drug Survival News
0361-5383 Billboard's on Tour *changed to* International Talent and Touring Directory

1232 ISSN INDEX

0361-5391 Wisconsin Secondary School Administrators Association. Bulletin *changed to* Association of Wisconsin School Administrators. Bulletin
0361-5413 History in Africa
0361-5421 M P, the Microprocessor
0361-5472 Orb (Harvard)
0361-5502 Hispanic American Periodical Index
0361-5537 North Carolina Medical Society. Transactions
0361-5545 C B S News Almanac *changed to* Hammond Almanac
0361-5553 Clarinet
0361-5650 Air Quality in Minnesota
0361-5669 A R L Annual Salary Survey
0361-5685 Dance Life in New York *changed to* Dance Life
0361-5693 T R
0361-574X Historic Madison. Journal
0361-5774 Bluegrass Reflections
0361-5782 Journal of Management *see* 0149-7901
0361-5820 Contemporary Keyboard *changed to* Keyboard
0361-5855 Recorder Review†
0361-591X Kentucky Deskbook of Economic Statistics
0361-5960 Cancer Treatment Reports
0361-5995 Soil Science Society of America. Journal
0361-6029 American Schools of Oriental Research. Newsletter
0361-6061 Face-to-Face (New York)
0361-607X Artist's Market *see* 0161-0546
0361-6118 Reading Abstracts
0361-6193 East Tennessee Historical Society's Publications
0361-6207 South Carolina Historical Association. Proceedings
0361-6266 Abstracts in Human Evolution†
0361-6274 Health Care Management Review
0361-6290 W W II Journal†
0361-6304 Who's Who in P/M
0361-6347 New Titles in Bioethics
0361-638X Woman's Day Home Decorating Ideas
0361-6398 Boston Bruins Official Yearbook
0361-6428 Journal of Radiation Curing
0361-6436 New York (State) Department of Social Services. Bureau of Research. Program Brief. *see* 0162-6302
0361-6525 Sociobiology
0361-6576 Journal of Economics
0361-6534 Kronos
0361-6606 O.O.B.A. Guidebook of Theatres
0361-6622 Selected Reports in Ethnomusicology
0361-6657 Comprehensive Dissertation Index. Supplement
0361-6665 Wage-Price Law & Economics Review
0361-6673 U.S. Environmental Protection Agency. Office of General Counsel. a Collection of Legal Opinions
0361-6681 Public Productivity Review
0361-6797 U.S. Civil Service Commission. Bureau of Personnel Management Evaluation. Evaluation Methods Series
0361-6843 Psychology of Women Quarterly
0361-6851 Alternative Higher Education
0361-686X Abba
0361-6886 Acta Geologica Sinica (English Edition) †
0361-6916 Bibliography, Corporate Responsibility for Social Problems *changed to* Bibliography of Corporate Social Responsibility
0361-6959 World of Work Report
0361-6967 Electric Machines and Electromechanics
0361-6975 Community/Junior College Research Quarterly
0361-6983 Detroit News. Newspaper Index *see* 0195-6426
0361-7025 California Optometrist *changed to* California Optometry
0361-7092 Notes on Urban-Industrial Mission, Literature and Training
0361-7122 South Central Research Library Council. Report
0361-7157 English Genealogical Helper *see* 0145-6059
0361-7165 Family Heritage Series†
0361-7173 Jewish Art Quarterly
0361-7181 Journal of California Anthropology *see* 0191-3557
0361-719X N A G W S Guide. Aquatics
0361-7203 Computer Law & Tax Report
0361-722X Film Reader
0361-7238 Modern Plywood Techniques
0361-7246 Journal of Historical Studies (Washington)
0361-7300 Army Administrator
0361-7327 Directory of California Justice Agencies Serving Juveniles and Adults
0361-7440 U.S. National Commission for Manpower Policy. Annual Report to the President and the Congress
0361-7467 P P F Survey
0361-7483 World Coal
0361-753X R & D Management Digest
0361-7629 Iowa. Geological Survey. Annual Report of the State Geologist to the Geological Board
0361-7653 Business and Public Administration Student Review
0361-7688 Programming and Computer Software
0361-7742 Progress in Clinical and Biological Research
0361-7823 Facts About Alaska *changed to* Alaska Almanac: Facts About Alaska
0361-7874 American Association for the Advancement of Science. Handbook; Officers, Organization, Activities
0361-7882 International Journal of African Historical Studies
0361-7947 Theatre Profiles
0361-8013 Federal Reserve Bank of Minneapolis. Annual Report
0361-803X American Journal of Roentgenology
0361-8188 Lake Michigan Water Quality Report
0361-8269 Southern Speech Communication Journal
0361-8374 Cablevision
0361-8382 Fire Protection Reference Directory
0361-8412 Malpractice Lifeline
0361-8528 Schoharie County Historical Review
0361-8560 South Dakota State Library Newsletter
0361-8587 Perfumer & Flavorist
0361-8609 American Journal of Hematology
0361-865X Mass Media Newsletter
0361-865X Mass Media Bi-Weekly Newsletter *see* 0361-865X
0361-8676 South Dakota History
0361-8714 Federal Reserve Bank of Boston Conference Series
0361-8773 J C T, Journal of Coatings Technology
0361-8854 Context
0361-8927 Guide to Four-Year College Databook *changed to* Chronicle Four-Year College Databook
0361-8935 Loyola Lawyer†
0361-8994 Career World
0361-9001 Chinese Science
0361-9087 U.S. Environmental Protection Agency. Eastern Environmental Radiation Facility. Annual Report
0361-9095 California Livestock Statistics
0361-9117 Women Artist Newsletter *see* 0149-7081
0361-915X Bell Journal of Economics
0361-9168 American Society of Magazine Photographers. Bulletin
0361-9230 Brain Research Bulletin
0361-9249 Current Practice in Obstetric and Gynecological Nursing
0361-9257 Current Practice in Pediatric Nursing
0361-9273 Guidebook of U.S. & Canadian Postdoctoral Dental Programs
0361-929X M C N: American Journal of Maternal Child Nursing
0361-9362 Accredited Institutions of Postsecondary Education
0361-9397 Chilton's Motor-Age Professional Labor Guide and Parts Manual
0361-9419 Poor Richard's Record
0361-9451 Wisconsin Sportsman
0361-946X Mediaevalia
0361-9478 W I L C O Newsletter†
0361-9486 American Bar Foundation. Research Journal
0361-9591 Means Construction Cost Indexes
0361-9613 Society for the Study of Pre-Han China. Newsletter *see* 0362-5028
0361-9621 Explicacion de Textos Literarios
0361-9729 Girls & Boys Together.
0361-9737 U.S. National Park Service. Public Use of the National Park System; Calendar Year Report
0361-9966 Seminar on the Acquisition of Latin American Library Materials. Resolutions and Lists of Commitees†
0362-0050 Notebook of Empirical Petrology†
0362-0085 Theologia 21
0362-0131 Buyer's Guide to Micrographic Equipment, Products, and Services
0362-0247 Four Zoas
0362-028X Journal of Food Protection
0362-0298 Behavioral Engineering
0362-0425 Ironcaster
0362-0506 Highway and Heavy Construction
0362-0557 Pilgrim State Newsletter
0362-0565 Underground Space
0362-0603 Theological Markings
0362-062X Journal of Reprints of Documents Affecting Women
0362-0662 Georgia Vital and Health Statistics
0362-0689 Dow Jones Commodities Handbook
0362-0700 U. S. Fish and Wildlife Service. Sport Fishery and Wildlife Research
0362-0719 Index of Patents Issued from the United States Patent and Trademark Office
0362-0794 N I C M Journal for Jews and Christians in Higher Education
0362-0808 M S S
0362-0824 Bioethics Northwest *see* 0163-9803
0362-0867 Explor
0362-0875 Film & Broadcasting Review
0362-0905 Focus Chicago *changed to* Facets Features
0362-0913 Quintessence of Dental Technology
0362-0999 Microform Market Place
0362-1006 Micrographics Equipment Review
0362-1014 Microlist *see* 0164-0739
0362-1057 A J S Joint Enterprise *see* 0190-1427
0362-1065 Abstracts of Book Reviews in Current Legal Periodicals
0362-1138 Nebraska. Department of Economic Development. Annual Economic Report
0362-1146 New West
0362-1162 Audiovideo International
0362-1170 Foundation Center Source Book *changed to* Foundation Center Source Book Profiles
0362-1197 Human Physiology
0362-1219 Gone Soft *changed to* Soundings East
0362-1243 California. Division of Oil and Gas. Annual Report of the State Oil and Gas Supervisor
0362-1251 Compact New York Times Magazine
0362-1278 Financial Industry
0362-1294 Literary Research Newsletter
0362-1324 Electric Comfort Conditioning News
0362-1332 F D A Consumer
0362-1383 Massachusetts Advocacy Center. Annual Report
0362-1391 Georgia Genealogist
0362-1405 Financial Industry Number Standard Directory
0362-1421 Arizona. Department of Health Services. Annual Report
0362-1472 Association of Theological Schools in the United States and Canada. Bulletin
0362-1480 Islamic Studies
0362-1510 News from the Congregational Christian Historical Society
0362-1529 Traditio
0362-1588 Houston Journal of Mathematics
0362-1596 Parabola
0362-1618 N E L B Link
0362-1626 Annual Review of Energy
0362-1642 Annual Review of Pharmacology and Toxicology
0362-1650 Atherosclerosis Reviews
0362-1677 Journal of Consumer Product Flammability
0362-1693 Journal of Fire Retardant Chemistry
0362-188X Air Force Engineering & Services Quarterly
0362-1898 Massachusetts. Board of Public Accountancy. Annual Report
0362-191X Commodity Drain Report of Florida's Primary Forest Industries
0362-1979 J. Paul Getty Museum Journal
0362-2428 Research Communications in Psychology, Psychiatry and Behavior
0362-2436 Spine
0362-2452 Body Fashions-Intimate Apparel Directory
0362-2487 Enjine!-Enjine!
0362-2525 Journal of Morphology (1931)
0362-2606 Personal Communications
0362-2606 Merchandising 2-Way Radio *see* 0362-2606
0362-2622 Occasional Papers in Entomology
0362-2630 American Indian Art
0362-2711 B & M Bulletin
0362-2770 Options
0362-2800 San Francisco Bay Area Rapid Transit District. Annual Report
0362-2827 Tab†
0362-2843 Southern California Rapid Transit District. Annual Report
0362-2894 Arnold Schoenberg Institute. Journal
0362-2908 Association of Feminist Consultants. Directory of Members†
0362-2916 Carrier Case Reports†
0362-2940 Hawaii. Office of Instructional Services. Special Programs Branch. Annual Performance Report on Adult Education
0362-2967 New Jersey Area Library Directory
0362-2983 Study of Federal Tax Law. Income Tax Volume: Business Enterprises
0362-3122 Transportation Terminal Techniques†
0362-3165 Health Planning and Manpower Report
0362-3173 Lactation Review
0362-3211 Toxicology Research Projects Directory
0362-3238 C B S News Index
0362-3246 Survey of Sources Newsletter
0362-3254 N A G W S Guide. Basketball
0362-3270 Official Field Hockey Rules for School Girls
0362-3289 Idaho. Department of Water Resources. Annual Report
0362-3416 E P R I Journal
0362-3432 Tennessee Valley Authority. Operations: Municipal and Cooperative Distributors of T.V.A. Power *changed to* Tennessee Valley Authority. Power Program Summary
0362-3459 Guide to Minority Business Directories *changed to* Guide to Obtaining Minority Business Directories
0362-3475 Southeast Michigan Council of Governments. Annual Report
0362-3513 Indiana. Geological Survey. Annual Report of the State Geologist
0362-3548 N F I B Quarterly Economic Report for Small Business
0362-3572 Recent Researches in the Music of the Middle Ages and Early Renaissance
0362-3599 Tourbook: Arizona, New Mexico
0362-3602 Tourbook: Western Canada and Alaska
0362-3610 Understanding Financial Support of Public Schools
0362-3661 Virginia. Division of Product and Industry Regulation. Inspection Service Section. Annual Report
0362-3688 New York Times Film Reviews
0362-3696 International Union of Bricklayers and Allied Craftsmen. Journal
0362-370X MESA
0362-3750 Who's Who Among Music Students in American High Schools

0362-3777 Corvette, the Sensuous American *changed to* Corvette, Sportscar of America
0362-3793 Labor Force Status of Indiana Residents
0362-3815 Transport 2000
0362-3823 Woodall's Campground Directory *see* 0146-1362
0362-3823 Woodall's Campground Directory *see* 0162-7414
0362-3823 Woodall's Campground Directory *see* 0162-7406
0362-3831 Monograph Abstracts
0362-3890 Facts & Figures on Footwear *see* 0095-1048
0362-3904 Georgia. State Data Center. City Population Estimates
0362-3912 Idaho. Department of Labor and Industrial Services. Annual Report
0362-3920 Merchandising
0362-4021 Group (New York, 1977)
0362-403X Issues in Child Mental Health *see* 0190-230X
0362-4048 American Rehabilitation
0362-4064 Occupational Health & Safety
0362-4102 Photo-Image
0362-4110 California. Department of the Youth Authority. Affirmative Action Statistics
0362-4129 California. Department of Industrial Relations. Annual Report
0362-4145 Children's Literature Review
0362-4196 Alaska. Employment Security Division. Labor Force Estimates by Industry and Area.
0362-420X Guide to Two-Year College Majors and Careers *changed to* Chronicle Two-Year College Databook
0362-4250 Bestways Magazine
0362-4277 Datacomm User
0362-4285 Federal Funding Guide for Local Governments
0362-4293 Lost in Canada?
0362-4366 Directory: Community Development Education and Training Programs Throughout the World
0362-4412 Journal of Vertigo
0362-4439 Pharmaceutical News Index
0362-4463 Southern Weed Science Society. Proceedings
0362-448X L J Special Reports
0362-4498 International Microfilm Source Book *changed to* International Micrographics Source Book
0362-451X D, the Magazine of Dallas *see* 0161-7826
0362-4536 I E E E Student Papers
0362-4544 Sun and Moon
0362-4544 Journal Holdings in the Washington-Baltimore Area
0362-4552 M I M C Microforms Annual
0362-4595 Chicago. Department of Planning, City and Community Development. Planning and Development Review *changed to* Chicago. Department of Planning, City and Community Development. Planning in Review
0362-4633 National Institute for Campus Ministries. National Newsletter *changed to* National Institute for Campus Ministries. Associates Newsletter
0362-4641 Moslem World *see* 0027-4909
0362-4668 Interdependence
0362-4706 University of Chicago Record
0362-4722 Consumer Electronics
0362-4730 D R I European Review
0362-4749 Gun World Hunting Guide *changed to* Gun World Annual
0362-4765 Political Science Utilization Directory
0362-4803 Journal of Labelled Compounds and Radiopharmaceuticals
0362-4846 Three Rivers Poetry Journal
0362-4889 Low Vision Abstracts
0362-4994 American Gas Association. Operating Section. Proceedings
0362-5001 A M J
0362-501X Corporate Systems
0362-5028 Early China
0362-5044 French Periodical Index
0362-5079 Population and Occupied Dwelling Units in Southeast Michigan
0362-5168 Knickerbocker Club. Club Book
0362-5214 Pig Iron
0362-5230 Study of Federal Tax Law. Income Tax Volume: Individuals
0362-5249 Supreme Court Historical Society. Yearbook
0362-5354 Wisconsin. Department of Natural Resources. Annual Water Quality Report to Congress
0362-5419 Gloria Vanderbilt Designs for Your Home
0362-5435 Conference Board. Quarterly Business Review†
0362-5451 Rx: R I A for Physicians†
0362-5451 Frontiers in Immunoassay
0362-546X Nonlinear Analysis
0362-5478 Pharmacology and Therapeutics. Part A. Chemotherapy, Toxicology and Metabolic Inhibitors *see* 0163-7258
0362-5486 Pharmacology and Therapeutics. Part C. Clinical Pharmacology and Therapeutics *see* 0163-7258
0362-5524 Illinois. Board of Higher Education. Statewide Space Survey
0362-5567 Fishing Guide†
0362-5664 Clinical Neuropharmacology
0362-5699 Reviews in Perinatal Medicine
0362-5710 Directory of Delaware Schools
0362-5729 Local Government Law Bulletin
0362-5737 Truck Broker Directory
0362-5745 Army Communicator
0362-5753 Who's Who Among Black Americans
0362-580X Journal of Social and Political Studies
0362-5818 E E O Today
0362-5834 Youth Magazine
0362-5907 A G O Times *see* 0164-3150
0362-5915 A C M Transactions on Database Systems
0362-5923 Activity Programmers Sourcebook†
0362-5931 Georgia Legislative Review
0362-594X Geographic Origin and Distribution of Students, Missouri Institutions of Higher Education†
0362-5958 New Jersey. Department of Education. Educational Assessment Program State Report
0362-5982 South
0362-6016 Policy Studies Directory
0362-6059 Accent
0362-6075 Andover Review†
0362-6180 Buyers' Guide for the Mass Entertainment Industry
0362-6199 Data Resources U.S. Long-Term Bulletin
0362-6210 New York (State). Environmental Quality Research and Development Unit. Technical Paper
0362-6245 U & L C
0362-6288 Utah Geological and Mineral Survey. Survey Notes
0362-6296 Hawaii. Department of Health. Division of Mental Health. Children's Health Services *changed to* Hawaii. Department of Health. Waimano Training School and Hospital Division (Report)
0362-6296 Hawaii. Department of Health. Mental Health Services for Children and Youth
0362-630X High Times
0362-6334 Texas Public School Law Bulletin
0362-6369 Washington (State). Department of Ecology. Water Quality Assessment Report
0362-6385 Field & Stream Fishing Annual
0362-6415 Red River Valley Historical Review
0362-6466 Food and Drug Letter
0362-6490 Virginia. Agricultural Opportunities Development Program. Annual Report†
0362-6520 Hudson Home Guides
0362-6547 Red River Valley Historical Journal of World History
0362-6563 California Department of Parks and Recreation. a Stewardship Report†
0362-6644 Health Quarterly
0362-6660 Kids Fashions Magazine
0362-6679 Summary of Kentucky Education Statistics
0362-6741 United States Investor/Eastern Banker *see* 0148-8848
0362-6784 Curriculum Inquiry
0362-6830 Monthly Catalog of United States Government Publications
0362-6849 Alaska Native Medical Center. Annual Report
0362-6881 Bentley Library Annual
0362-6911 Frontiers of Economics†
0362-6962 Alaska. Division of Game. Annual Report of Survey-Inventory Activities
0362-7047 Latvju Maksla
0362-7063 California. Department of Education. Office of Program Evaluation and Research. Innovative Programs for Child Care: Evaluation Report
0362-708X Academy
0362-7098 Louisiana. Division of Mental Health. Annual Performance Report and Continuation of the State Plan for Drug Abuse Prevention
0362-7152 Country Scene†
0362-7179 Directory of Services for Migrant Families
0362-7284 Alaska. Criminal Investigation Bureau. Annual Report
0362-7330 Gospel Music Association. Annual Directory and Yearbook *changed to* Gospel Music Association. Annual Directory
0362-7403 Analog Annual
0362-742X Public Welfare in California
0362-7462 Washington (State). Department of Revenue. Forest Tax Report
0362-7470 Wisconsin. Division of Corrections. Bureau of Planning, Development and Research. Releases from Juvenile Institutions *changed to* Wisconsin. Division of Corrections. Office of Information Management. Releases from Juvenile Institutions
0362-7489 Report of Probation Supervision Workload
0362-7705 Schoolhouse *changed to* E F L Reports
0362-7799 Petroleum Marketer
0362-7888 Harvest
0362-7942 F A A General Aviation News
0362-7969 Painted Bride Quarterly
0362-8205 S A E Handbook
0362-8213 Sound Approach to the Railroad Market
0362-823X Business Research Bulletin
0362-8302 Jam to-Day
0362-8353 Criminal Justice Plan (Richmond)
0362-8493 Across the Table
0362-8507 U.S. Advisory Commission on Intergovernmental Relations. Intergovernmental Perspective
0362-8523 Poor Joe's Pennsylvania Almanac
0362-854X University of Texas. General Libraries. Newsletter
0362-8558 Journal of Dialysis
0362-8566 Self Reliance
0362-8671 Index to Book Reviews in Historical Periodicals
0362-8701 Best's Insurance Securities Research Service
0362-8736 Inter-University Consortium for Political and Social Research. Guide to Resources and Services.
0362-8744 New York Metropolitan Reference & Research Library Agency. Directory of Members
0362-8787 Delaware. State Board of Education. Report of Educational Statistics
0362-8795 Illinois. Environmental Protection Agency. Operator Certification Section. Digester
0362-8817 Insurance Industry
0362-8833 N R E C A-A P P A Legal Reporting Service
0362-8841 Mother Jones
0362-885X Manufacturing and Engineering
0362-8868 Louisiana. Health and Human Resources Administration Comprehensive Annual Services Program Plan for Social Services Under Title 20
0362-8906 Washington (State). Natural Areas Advisory Committee. Biennial Report
0362-8914 American Journal of Ancient History
0362-8922 Gnostica News *see* 0145-885X
0362-8930 School Library Journal
0362-8973 Information Processing Journal *see* 0191-9776
0362-9066 F P S: a Magazine of Young People's Liberation
0362-9074 History of Anthropology Newsletter
0362-9090 Human Factor (New York)
0362-9163 U.S. Office of Management and Budget. Special Analysis: Budget of the United States Government
0362-9198 Maryland. Division of Correction. Report
0362-9279 Idaho. Department of Health and Welfare. Annual Summary of Vital Statistics
0362-9287 Directory - Juvenile and Adult Correctional Departments, Institutions, Agencies, and Paroling Authorities of the United States and Canada
0362-9368 Packard Cormorant
0362-9376 Plastics Design Forum
0362-9406 School Security†
0362-9457 American Society of Arms Collectors. Bulletin
0362-9473 Iowa Detailed Report of Vital Statistics *changed to* Vital Statistics of Iowa
0362-9481 N A G W S Guide. Track and Field
0362-9503 Connecticut. Auditors of Public Accounts. Report on Department of Transportation, Bureau of Rail and Motor Carrier Services
0362-9511 U.S. Department of Agriculture. Economics, Statistics and Cooperatives Service. Sugar and Sweetener Reports
0362-9554 Aspen Anthology
0362-9708 Manufacturing Investment Statistics: Capital Investment and Supply Conditions *see* 0361-4239
0362-9716 Ohio Inventory of Business and Industrial Change
0362-9759 Wheelers Recreational Vehicle Resort and Campground Guide: North American Edition
0362-9783 Humanist Educator
0362-9791 Journal of Educational Statistics
0362-9805 Legislative Studies Quarterly
0362-9821 Tourbook: Colorado, Utah
0362-9902 C. F. O. Journal
0362-9910 Fortitudine
0362-9945 American Philological Association. Proceedings†
0363-0021 Federal Reserve Bank of San Francisco. Economic Review
0363-0048 Preview of United States Supreme Court Cases
0363-0129 S I A M Journal on Control and Optimization
0363-0153 Archives of Pathology and Laboratory Medicine
0363-0161 Bibliography of Bioethics
0363-0188 Current Problems in Diagnostic Radiology
0363-020X Health Services Manager
0363-0234 Suicide and Life Threatening Behavior
0363-0242 Women & Health
0363-0250 Action for Libraries
0363-0269 Hemoglobin
0363-0277 Library Journal
0363-0307 Golden Gate University Law Review
0363-0358 National Association of Insurance Commissioners. Proceedings
0363-0366 Medical and Health Annual
0363-0404 Journal of Products Liability
0363-0447 First Principles

0363-0471 Hispamerica
0363-0617 Parks
0363-065X Access: the Index to Little Magazines
0363-079X Shout in the Street
0363-0889 C P P R
0363-0927 Guide to External and Continuing Education†
0363-0994 Unified World
0363-1028 Whistle Stop
0363-1079 Indochina Chronicle *changed to* Southeast Asia Chronicle
0363-1133 Women's Studies Newsletter
0363-1168 Virgin Islands Archaeological Society. Journal
0363-1192 Utah Geology
0363-1230 Webster Review
0363-1249 America: History and Life. Part C: American History Bibliography
0363-1257 METRO C.A.P. Catalog
0363-132X Graphics Today
0363-1621 Contact Lens Forum
0363-1672 Lithuanian Mathematical Journal
0363-1737 National Metalworking Blue Book
0363-1788 Tourbook: Atlantic Provinces and Quebec
0363-1818 Consumer Life
0363-1850 Eureka Review
0363-1869 Harris Michigan Manufacturers Industrial Directory *changed to* Harris Michigan Industrial Directory
0363-1877 Headmaster U.S.A. *changed to* Private School Quarterly
0363-1907 Journal of Psychiatric Education
0363-1915 Cable File
0363-1923 Illinois Classical Studies
0363-194X Pennsylvania Illustrated
0363-1990 Journal of Family History
0363-2024 Urban Anthropology
0363-2067 Vermont Industrial Development Authority. Annual Report
0363-2083 E M Complaint Directory for Consumers
0363-2091 Eastern Canada Campbook
0363-2148 University of Dayton Intramural Law Review *see* 0162-9174
0363-2164 Laughing Bear
0363-2245 Sean O'Casey Review
0363-2318 Appalachian Heritage
0363-2369 Kidney Disease and Nephrology Index†
0363-2377 Allegorica
0363-2393 Chilton's Motor-Age Professional Automotive Service Manual
0363-2407 Executive's Tax Review
0363-2415 Fisheries
0363-2431 T F News
0363-2490 Legal Malpractice Reporter
0363-2504 N A G W S Guide. Softball
0363-2512 North Dakota. Geological Survey. Oil and Gas Production Statistics
0363-2539 American Bankers Association. Operations and Automation Division. Results of the National Operations & Automation Survey
0363-2547 Audiotapes Reprints Publications†
0363-258X Electronic Warfare *see* 0194-7885
0363-2598 Improving College and University Teaching Yearbook†
0363-2601 Innovative Graduate Programs Directory
0363-261X International Nautical Index
0363-2628 Journal of Personalized Instruction
0363-2636 Lens Magazine
0363-2644 Metric Bulletin
0363-2679 Oklahoma Journal of Forensic Medicine
0363-2695 Tourbook: Idaho, Montana, Wyoming
0363-2717 Historical Abstracts. Part A: Modern History Abstracts, 1450-1914
0363-2725 Historical Abstracts. Part B: Twentieth Century Abstracts, 1914 to the Present
0363-2792 Image (Indianapolis)
0363-2822 Access: the Index to Little Magazines microform edition of 0363-065X
0363-2830 Downtown Promotion Reporter
0363-2849 International Trumpet Guild. Journal
0363-2857 I T G Newsletter
0363-2865 Jerusalem Journal of International Relations
0363-2873 Journal of Libertarian Studies
0363-2881 Marine Hobbyist News
0363-2903 Arete
0363-2911 Art & Cinema
0363-2962 Toll Free Digest
0363-2970 American Type Culture Collection. Catalogue of Strains Algae, Bacteria, Bacteriophages, Fungi and Protozoa
0363-2989 American Type Culture Collection. Catalogue of Viruses, Rickettsiae, Chlamydiae *changed to* American Type Culture Collection. Catalogue of Cells, Viruses, Rickettsiae, Chlamydiae
0363-311X Tibet Society Newsletter
0363-3195 Social Indicators Newsletter
0363-3268 Research in Economic History
0363-3276 Wilson Quarterly
0363-3284 New Collector's Directory
0363-3519 Virginia Museum Bulletin
0363-3586 Biofeedback & Self Regulation
0363-3624 Nurse Educator
0363-3640 Journal of Library & Information Science
0363-3659 Maledicta: the International Journal of Verbal Aggression
0363-373X Better Schools (Chicago) *see* 0194-2468
0363-3764 Bus Ride: Bus Industry Directory
0363-3780 En Passant Poetry Quarterly *changed to* En Passant/Poetry
0363-3799 Sensory Processes
0363-3810 Union of American Hebrew Congregations. State of Our Union
0363-3918 International Review of Physiology
0363-4132 University of Texas, Austin. Bureau of Economic Geology. Guidebook
0363-4140 Astrology Annual Reference Book *changed to* Astrology Reference Book
0363-4205 Journal of New Jersey Poets
0363-4337 Action (Little Rock)
0363-4396 Tax Planning Review
0363-440X Carolinas Genealogical Society. Bulletin
0363-4426 Multinational Marketing & Employment Directory
0363-4493 Chestnut Tree
0363-4507 Iowa Comprehensive State Plan for Drug Abuse Prevention: Annual Performance Report
0363-4523 Communication Education
0363-454X Brass Research Series
0363-4558 Edward H. Tarr Series
0363-4566 Texas School Directory
0363-4574 Cornfield Review
0363-4590 Seeker (Pittsburg)
0363-4639 Vintage Auto Almanac
0363-468X Journal of Studies on Alcohol. Supplement
0363-4728 Child Behavior Therapy
0363-4744 Housing Market Report
0363-4779 T.U.B.A. Newsletter *see* 0363-4787
0363-4787 T.U.B.A. Journal
0363-4795 World Military and Social Expenditures
0363-4817 Pacific Area Destination Handbook *changed to* Pacific Destinations Handbook
0363-4833 Western School Law Digest
0363-4841 Encomia
0363-4922 Security Letter
0363-4965 N A S B O Newsletter†
0363-5023 Journal of Hand Surgery
0363-504X Modern Liturgy
0363-5058 In Common
0363-5090 South Carolina Metalworking Directory
0363-5104 Primary Cardiology
0363-5120 Fast Service
0363-5171 Great Lakes Fisherman
0363-5198 Kentucky Directory of Selected Industrial Services
0363-5236 Bye Cadmos
0363-5244 Pro Musica Magazine†
0363-5252 Davison's Salesman's Book
0363-5260 American National Metric Council. Annual Report
0363-5341 Minnesota. Division of Fish and Wildlife, Environment Section. Special Publication
0363-535X American Executive Travel Companion
0363-5376 Alaska. Office of Ombudsman. Report of the Ombudsman
0363-5406 Window & Wall Decorating Ideas
0363-5414 Dikta
0363-5422 Federal Budget: Focus and Perspectives.
0363-5430 Foreign Exchange Rates and Restrictions†
0363-5465 American Journal of Sports Medicine
0363-5538 Bob Zwirz' Fishing Annual
0363-5570 Harvard Ukrainian Studies
0363-5600 Comprehensive Annual Services Program Plan for the State of California
0363-5643 State of Washington Comprehensive Plan for Crime Control and the Administration of Justice.
0363-566X American Business
0363-5694 American Society for Church Architecture. Journal
0363-5708 International Trombone Association Series
0363-5732 Abstract Journal in Earthquake Engineering
0363-5767 Casting & Jewelry Craft†
0363-5775 Los Angeles County Department of Regional Planning. Quarterly Bulletin
0363-5783 Gavel
0363-5821 Electronic Technician/Dealer
0363-5872 Recent Advances in Studies on Cardiac Structure and Metabolism *see* 0270-4056
0363-5880 House & Garden Guide to American Tradition†
0363-5910 Gay Nineties *see* 0147-6165
0363-5937 National/International Sculpture Conference. Proceedings
0363-5953 Readings in Educational Psychology: Contemporary Perspectives
0363-6003 Solar Engineering *see* 0194-6226
0363-6046 Complete Handbook of Soccer
0363-6100 American Journal of Physiology: Endocrinology, Metabolism and Gastrointestinal Physiology *see* 0193-1849
0363-6100 American Journal of Physiology: Endocrinology, Metabolism and Gastrointestinal Physiology *see* 0193-1857
0363-6119 American Journal of Physiology: Regulatory, Integrative and Comparative Physiology
0363-6127 American Journal of Physiology: Renal, Fluid and Electrolyte Physiology
0363-6135 American Journal of Physiology: Heart and Circulatory Physiology
0363-6143 American Journal of Physiology: Cell Physiology
0363-6275 Braddock's Federal-State-Local Government Directory
0363-6380 Invention Management
0363-6399 Data Communications
0363-6437 Paperworker
0363-6445 Systematic Botany
0363-647X Annals of Phenomenological Sociology
0363-6488 Philadelphia Photo Review
0363-650X Connecticut. Advisory Council on Vocational and Career Education. Vocational Education Evaluation Report
0363-6518 Books for Kansas Schools
0363-6526 Current Concepts in Gastroenterology
0363-6550 Midwest Studies in Philosophy
0363-6569 Pastoral Music
0363-6666 Journal of Comparative Cultures
0363-6712 Sea Boating Almanac. Southern California, Arizona, Baja *see* 0193-3507
0363-6720 Fact Book on Higher Education *changed to* Fact Book for Academic Administrators
0363-6771 General Dentistry
0363-678X Commercial News for the Foreign Service *changed to* Commercial News U S A
0363-6798 Foreign Trade Reports. Bunker Fuels
0363-6828 U.S. Geological Survey. Board on Geographic Names. Decisions of Geographic Names in the United States
0363-6836 Current Population Reports: Population Characteristics
0363-6895 Catholic Periodical Index *see* 0008-8285
0363-6941 J E G P. Journal of English and Germanic Philology
0363-6968 New Life
0363-700X Manufacturing Engineering Transactions
0363-7026 Berkeley Serials Union List
0363-7107 Harvard Library Notes *see* 0017-8136
0363-7123 International Organisations in World Politics Yearbook
0363-7158 Tennessee Public Library Statistics
0363-7166 Federal Programs, State of Arizona
0363-7190 Empire State Report
0363-7190 Empire State Report
0363-7220 U S S R and Eastern Europe Scientific Abstracts: Geophysics, Astronomy, and Space *changed to* U S S R Report: Geophysics, Astronomy, and Space
0363-7239 U.S. Congress. Congressional Record
0363-7360 Osteopathic Medicine
0363-7417 Weekly Government Abstracts. Urban Technology *changed to* Weekly Government Abstracts. Urban and Regional Technology and Development
0363-745X C U Directory
0363-7476 Commerce Clearing House. Compliance Guide for Plan Administrators
0363-7484 California. Department of Health. Annual Evaluation Report Program Information
0363-7565 Monumenta Archaeologica (Los Angeles)
0363-762X Viol
0363-7689 Blindness, Visual Impairment, Deaf-Blindness
0363-7700 Sea Boating Almanac. Northern California and Nevada *see* 0193-3515
0363-7751 Communication Monographs
0363-7778 Media Review Digest
0363-7816 San Francisco Chronicle. Newspaper Index *see* 0195-6396
0363-7824 Houston Post. Newspaper Index *see* 0195-6426
0363-7840 Farm Tax Saver
0363-7891 Soviet Physics-Collection
0363-7905 Mini-Micro Computer Report
0363-7972 Doll Castle News
0363-7980 Central School Law Digest†
0363-7999 Sea Boating Almanac. Pacific Northwest and Alaska *see* 0148-1177
0363-8006 Recent Developments in Maryland Law
0363-8057 Gradiva
0363-8065 Abrasive Engineering Society. Abrasive Usage Conference. Proceedings
0363-8138 Custom Bike
0363-8170 Coordination Directory of State and Federal Agency Water and Land Resources Officials
0363-8197 Texas Business *see* 0162-1262
0363-8200 Diplomatic World Bulletin and Delegates World Bulletin
0363-8219 Aerospace Propulsion
0363-8227 Helicopter News
0363-8235 Computerized Tomography
0363-826X Gayellow Pages
0363-8286 Current Housing Reports: Market Absorption of Apartments
0363-8294 Current Construction Reports: Value of New Construction Put in Place
0363-8340 National Property Law Digests
0363-8391 Pacific Northwest Council on Foreign Languages. Proceedings
0363-8448 Current Business Reports: Monthly Retail Trade, Sales and Accounts Receivable
0363-8464 U.S. Department of Defense. Index of Specifications and Standards

ISSN INDEX 1235

0363-8472 Music & Musicians: Large-Print Scores and Books Catalog
0363-8529 Soviet Microelectronics
0363-8537 Current Construction Reports: New One Family Homes Sold and for Sale
0363-8553 Current Business Reports: Monthly Wholesale Trade
0363-8561 U.S. Crop Reporting Board. Crop Production
0363-8588 Uniformed Services Almanac. National Guard Edition *see* 0363-8618
0363-860X Reserve Forces Almanac
0363-8618 National Guard Almanac
0363-8715 Journal of Computer Assisted Tomography
0363-8723 Countryside (Waterloo)
0363-874X Educational Directory of Mississippi Schools
0363-8782 Texas Speech Communication Journal
0363-8790 Current Construction Reports: Housing Authorized by Building Permits and Public Contracts
0363-8812 Federal Design Matters
0363-8820 Energy Reporter
0363-8847 Hudson Family Association, South. Bulletin
0363-8855 Journal of Clinical Engineering
0363-8863 Library Employee Relations Newsletter
0363-891X Psychohistory Review
0363-8928 International Symposium on Fault-Tolerant Computing. Proceedings
0363-8952 Psychiatry and the Humanities
0363-8960 Old Time Songs and Poems (Seabrook)†
0363-8987 Financial Studies of the Small Business
0363-9029 Cassette Books
0363-9037 Maledicta Press Publications
0363-9045 Drug Development and Industrial Pharmacy
0363-9061 International Journal for Numerical and Analytical Methods in Geomechanics
0363-907X International Journal of Energy Research
0363-910X B A I Index of Bank Performance
0363-9169 Germanic Genealogist
0363-9185 Help (Washington)
0363-9207 Ohio. Commission on Aging. Annual Report
0363-9282 N A G W S Guide. Gymnastics
0363-9290 Republican Almanac
0363-9347 International League for Human Rights. Annual Report
0363-9401 S.C.A., State & County Administrator†
0363-9428 American Journal of Small Business
0363-9444 Impact: Wine and Spirits Newsletter
0363-9452 Grand Jury Report
0363-9460 Confrontation-Change Review
0363-9479 C L S I Newsletter
0363-9487 T V Season†
0363-9495 South Carolina School Directory
0363-9509 Community College Frontiers
0363-9525 37 Design & Environment Projects
0363-9568 Nursing Administration Quarterly
0363-9762 Clinical Nuclear Medicine
0363-9797 Human Factors Society. Proceedings of the Annual Meeting *see* 0163-5182
0363-9819 U.S. Environmental Protection Agency. Radiological Quality of the Environment in the United States
0363-9991 Interstate
0364-0000 Cutting Edge
0364-0027 Oregon. State Advisory Council for Career and Vocational Education. Annual Evaluation Report
0364-0035 Special Education Directory
0364-0078 Country Style
0364-0086 Tourbook: Mid-Atlantic
0364-0094 A J S Review
0364-0116 E D I S†
0364-0205 Monthly Petroleum Statistics Report
0364-0213 Cognitive Science
0364-023X Flea Market Trader
0364-0302 Libertarian Review
0364-0337 Missouri. Disaster Operations Office. Newsletter
0364-0396 U.S. National Center for Health Statistics. Monthly Vital Statistics Report
0364-040X U.S. Social Security Administration. Monthly Benefit Statistics
0364-0426 Advisor, Navy Civilian Manpower Management
0364-0531 N I A A A Information and Feature Service
0364-0671 Drug Abuse
0364-068X Loka
0364-071X Colt American Handgunning Annual
0364-0728 Arkansas Vital Statistics
0364-0736 U.S. Department of Agriculture. Economics, Statistics, and Cooperatives Service. Farmer Cooperatives
0364-0752 Financial Stock Guide Service. Directory of Active Stocks
0364-0760 Charities U S A
0364-0779 Institute for Socioeconomic Studies. Journal
0364-0868 Biweekly Cryogenics Current Awareness Service†
0364-0930 U.S. Department of Housing and Urban Development. Office of International Affairs. Foreign Publications Accessions List†
0364-0981 U.S. Coast Guard Marine Safety Council. Proceedings
0364-099X Grain Market News
0364-1066 Correspondent
0364-1074 E I S: Key to Environmental Impact Statements *changed to* E I S: Digests of Environmental Impact Statements
0364-1082 Group & Organization Studies
0364-1112 Stress and Anxiety
0364-118X E L C
0364-1198 Female Patient
0364-1228 Current Index to Statistics
0364-1236 Library Resources for the Blind and Physically Handicapped
0364-1287 Army Lawyer
0364-1414 U.S. Federal Supply Service. Index of Federal Specifications and Standards
0364-152X Environmental Management (New York)
0364-1546 Dirt Bike
0364-1554 New Baby Talk *changed to* Baby Talk Magazine
0364-1597 A L A Yearbook
0364-1678 Federal Government
0364-1724 Law Enforcement News
0364-1732 Simplicity Home Catalog *changed to* Simplicity Today Incorporating Home Catalog
0364-1805 Copper-Base Mill and Foundry Products
0364-2003 Fusion Energy Foundation Newsletter *see* 0148-0537
0364-2011 E T A Interchange
0364-202X U.S. Crop Reporting Board. Cattle on Feed
0364-2046 Feed Market News
0364-2151 Environment Midwest
0364-216X Aesthetic Plastic Surgery
0364-2178 Occasional Bulletin of Missionary Research *changed to* International Bulletin of Missionary Research
0364-2194 Barbeque Planet†
0364-2216 Journal of the Graduate Music Students at the Ohio State University
0364-2267 U.S. Securities and Exchange Commission. Official Summary of Security Transactions and Holdings
0364-2313 World Journal of Surgery
0364-2321 Soviet Physics-Lebedev Institute Reports
0364-2348 Skeletal Radiology
0364-2356 Gastrointestinal Radiology
0364-2410 M E L A Notes
0364-2429 Money Digest
0364-2437 Afro-Americans in New York Life and History
0364-2569 Monographs in Pharmacology and Physiology
0364-2577 Guidelines to Metabolic Therapy
0364-2615 Tennessee Valley Perspective
0364-2801 P A A B S Symposium Series
0364-2968 Journal of Germanic Philology *see* 0363-6941
0364-2976 Journal of the Hellenic Diaspora
0364-3093 Offender Rehabilitation *changed to* Journal of Offender Counseling, Services & Rehabilitation
0364-3107 Administration in Social Work
0364-3115 Grantsmanship Center News
0364-3190 Neurochemical Research
0364-3263 Combat Fleets of the World
0364-3301 Corrosion Prevention/Inhibition Digest
0364-3344 Box 749
0364-3352 Current Bibliographic Survey of National Defense *see* 0198-9006
0364-3379 Artists of the Rockies and the Golden West
0364-3484 Mass Transit
0364-3549 English Fiction in Transition *see* 0013-8339
0364-359X Dragonfly
0364-3735 Private Higher Education
0364-3824 Taste
0364-3875 Official Airline Guide. World Wide Edition
0364-3921 Nevada Public Affairs Report
0364-3999 Micropublishing of Current Periodicals
0364-4014 Spirit That Moves Us
0364-4022 Poesie-U.S.A.
0364-4103 J S A E Review
0364-4529 Ninth District Quarterly *changed to* Federal Reserve Bank of Minneapolis. Quarterly Review
0364-474X Electric Perspectives
0364-4782 Journal of Human Services Abstracts
0364-491X U.S. Bureau of Labor Statistics. Employment Situation
0364-4928 Weekly Government Abstracts. Materials Sciences
0364-4936 Weekly Government Abstracts. Environmental Pollution & Control
0364-4944 Weekly Government Abstracts. Communication
0364-4952 Weekly Government Abstracts. Biomedical Technology & Engineering *changed to* Weekly Government Abstracts. Biomedical Technology & Human Factors Engineering
0364-4979 Weekly Government Abstracts. Natural Resources *changed to* Weekly Government Abstracts. Natural Resources & Earth Sciences
0364-5134 Annals of Neurology
0364-5177 Live Steam
0364-5193 Bioethics Digest
0364-5274 Energy Daily
0364-5479 Informer(Los Angeles)
0364-5487 Peters Notes
0364-5517 Seybold Report
0364-5533 Infosystems
0364-5541 Journal of Mental Imagery
0364-555X Russian-English Translators Exchange
0364-5568 Professional Translator†
0364-5711 Standard & Poor's International Stock Report†
0364-586X Downtown Mall Annual & Urban Design Report†
0364-5916 CALPHAD
0364-6408 Library Acquisitions: Practice and Theory
0364-6424 Weekly Government Abstracts. Ocean Technology & Engineering
0364-6432 Weekly Government Abstracts. Medicine & Biology
0364-6440 Weekly Government Abstracts. N A S A Earth Resources Survey Program
0364-6459 Weekly Government Abstracts. Problem-Solving Information for State and Local Governments
0364-6467 Weekly Government Abstracts. Library & Information Sciences
0364-6475 N E I S S News *changed to* N E I S S Data Highlights
0364-6483 Weekly Government Abstracts. Industrial & Mechanical Engineering
0364-6491 Weekly Government Abstracts. Government Inventions for Licensing
0364-6505 Edebiyat
0364-6653 Transportation Topics for Consumers *changed to* Transportation Consumer
0364-6696 U.S. Office of the Secretary of the Treasury. Treasury Papers
0364-6718 S E C News Digest
0364-6742 International Notices to Airmen
0364-6807 U. S. Navy Medicine
0364-6998 Solar Energy Update
0364-7064 U.S. National Cartographic Information Center. Newsletter
0364-7072 U.S. National Earthquake Information Service. Preliminary Determination of Epicenters, Monthly Listing
0364-7129 U.S. Railroad Retirement Board. Monthly Benefit Statistics
0364-7145 Maintenance
0364-7161 South Central Camping *changed to* South Central Campbook
0364-717X Minnesota. Department of Employment Services. Annual Report *changed to* Minnesota. Department of Economic Security. Annual Report
0364-720X Lake Superior Review
0364-7234 World Economic Conditions in Relation to Agricultural Trade†
0364-7358 Manpower Planning
0364-7390 Evaluation Studies Review Annual
0364-7471 American Druggist Blue Book
0364-7501 Musical Mainstream
0364-7609 Primavera
0364-7625 Access Reports
0364-765X Mathematics of Operations Research
0364-7714 Water Supply and Management
0364-7722 Progress in Neuro-Psychopharmacology
0364-796X Weekly Government Abstracts. Computers, Control & Information Theory
0364-7978 Weekly Government Abstracts. Business & Economics
0364-7986 Weekly Government Abstracts. Administration and Management
0364-8044 Panama Canal Spillway
0364-8125 A T L A Law Reporter
0364-815X Marquee (Norwalk)
0364-8184 New Horizon-Polish American Review
0364-8265 U.S. General Accounting Office. Monthly List of GAO Reports
0364-8591 Old Testament Abstracts
0364-8893 Associated Equipment Distributors. Rental Compilation *see* 0164-0593
0364-8958 International Fire Chief *see* 0161-2158
0364-8966 Directory of U.S. and Canadian Marketing Surveys and Services
0364-9008 Defense Business *changed to* Defense & Economy World Report & Survey
0364-9024 Journal of Graph Theory
0364-9059 I E E E Journal of Oceanic Engineering
0364-9156 Directors & Boards
0364-9210 Ethnodisc Journal of Recorded Sound
0364-9229 Astronomy Quarterly
0364-9237 Speedhorse
0364-9253 Estates, Gifts and Trusts Journal
0364-930X Alfa Owner
0364-9342 Mini-Micro Systems
0364-9407 Th-Bao Ga *changed to* Vietnam Quarterly
0364-9490 Delaware Journal of Corporate Law
0364-9539 National Distribution Directory of Local Cartage-Short Haul Carriers Warehousing *changed to* Warehousing/Distribution Directory
0364-9695 American Concrete Institute. Journal microform edition of 0002-8061
0364-9709 Water Supply Management microform edition of 0012-6233
0364-9733 Saturday Evening Post microform edition of 0048-9239
0364-9814 American City & County microform edition of 0149-337X
0364-9849 A A P G Bulletin microform edition of 0149-1423
0364-9857 Research Quarterly for Exercise and Sport microform edition of
0364-9865 American Artist microform edition of 0002-7375

0364-9873 American Anthropologist microform edition of 0002-7294
0364-989X America microform edition of 0002-7049
0364-9903 Lifelong Learning: the Adult Years microform edition of
0364-9911 Adult Education microform edition of 0001-8481
0364-992X Adolescence microform edition of 0001-8449
0364-9962 A S H R A E Journal microform edition of 0001-2491
0365-0138 Astronomy and Astrophysics Supplement Series
0365-1029 Annales Universitatis Mariae Curie-Sklodowska. Sectio A. Mathematica
0365-1118 Annales Universitatis Mariae Curie-Sklodowska. Sectio E. Agricultura
0365-2017 Annales de l'Est
0365-2726 Agronomico
0365-2807 Chile. Instituto de Investigaciones Agropecuarias. Agricultura Tecnica
0365-2807 Agricultura Tecnica
0365-4184 Acta Pathologica et Microbiologica Scandinavica. Section A: Pathology
0365-4478 Acta Medica Medianae
0365-4877 Analusis
0365-5563 Acta Pathologica et Microbiologica Scandinavica *see* 0304-131X
0365-5563 Acta Pathologica et Microbiologica Scandinavica: Section B: Microbiology and Immunology *see* 0304-1328
0365-5571 Acta Pathologica et Microbiologica Scandinavica. Section B: Microbiology and Immunology *see* 0304-131X
0365-5571 Acta Pathologica et Microbiologica Scandinavica. Section A: Pathology. Supplementum
0365-7000 Senckenbergische Naturforschende Gesellschaft. Abhandlungen
0365-8414 Atomwirtschaft - Atomtechnik
0365-9356 British Columbia. Ministry of Energy, Mines and Petroleum Resources. Annual Report
0365-9542 Deutsche Keramische Gesellschaft. Berichte
0365-9623 Cancer Research Campaign. Annual Report
0365-9631 Deutsche Botanische Gesellschaft. Berichte
0366-0281 Instituto de Tecnologia de Alimentos. Boletin
0366-2284 Bios
0366-3612 Kongelige Danske Videnskabernes Selskab. Biologiske Meddelelser†
0366-4198 Great Britain. Institute of Geological Sciences. Bulletin of the Geological Survey of Great Britain†
0366-5232 Caldasia
0366-5690 C E R N-H E R A Reports
0366-600X Cuadernos de Geologia
0366-6778 Clinica
0366-6824 Collective Phenomena
0366-7022 Chemistry Letters
0366-757X CODATA Bulletin
0366-8258 Academie Internationale d'Histoire des Sciences. Collection des Travaux
0367-0244 Ecology of Food and Nutrition
0367-1119 Energy Digest
0367-150X Environmental Pollution Management
0367-3812 Gaceta Veterinaria
0367-4061 Gunma Journal of Liberal Arts and Sciences
0367-4444 Glasnik Hemicara i Tehnologa Bosne i Hercegovine
0367-4983 Prirodnjacki Muzej u Beogradu. Glasnik. Serija A: Minerologija, Geologija, Paleontologija
0367-5807 Korean Journal of Animal Sciences
0367-598X Hemijska Industrija
0367-6439 Hirosaki University. Faculty of Science. Science Reports
0367-8377 International Journal of Peptide and Protein Research
0367-9012 Indian Journal of Medical Research, Supplement
0368-0770 International Association of Theoretical and Applied Limnology. Proceedings
0368-1327 Agricultural Society of Trinidad & Tobago. Journal
0368-2048 Journal of Electron Spectroscopy and Related Phenomena
0368-2188 Hokkaido University. Faculty of Science. Journal. Series 6: Zoology
0368-2307 Gesellschaft fuer Naturkunde in Wuerttemberg. Jahreshefte
0368-2315 Journal de Gynecologie Obstetrique et Biologie de la Reproduction
0368-2323 Geochemical Society of India. Journal
0368-2595 Institution of Nuclear Engineers. Journal *changed to* Nuclear Engineer
0368-5039 Kyoto University. Institute of Atomic Energy. Bulletin
0368-7171 Kongelige Veterinaer- og Landbohoejskole. Aarskrift
0368-7368 Lab Instrumenten
0368-945X Metallurgia and Metal Forming *changed to* Metallurgia: the Journal of Metals Technology, Metal Forming and Thermal Processing
0369-0512 Kyushu Institute of Technology. Memoirs: Engineering
0369-1233 Monatsschrift fuer Brauerei
0369-1632 Mine and Quarry
0369-1829 Royal Astronomical Society, England. Memoirs†
0369-4577 Chemical Society of Japan. Chemistry and Industrial Chemistry. Journal
0369-5387 Nippon Kagaku Zasshi *see* 0369-4577
0369-6464 Nutrition News
0369-9420 Pigment and Resin Technology
0369-9560 Photographe
0369-9641 Photo-Cine-Revue
0369-979X Pharmazie Heute *see* 0173-1890
0370-0755 Politechnika Wroclawska. Instytut Chemii Nieorganicznej i Metalurgii Pierwiastkow Rzadkich. Prace Naukowe. Studia i Materialy
0370-081X Politechnika Wroclawska. Instytut Chemii Organicznej i Fizycznej. Prace Naukowe. Studia i Materialy
0370-0828 Politechnika Wroclawska. Instytut Fizyki. Prace Naukowe. Monografie
0370-0836 Politechnika Wroclawska. Instytut Geotechniki. Prace Naukowe. Konferencje
0370-0844 Politechnika Wroclawska. Instytut Inzynierii Ladowej. Prace Naukowe. Studia i Materialy
0370-0852 Politechnika Wroclawska. Instytut Podstaw Elektrotechniki i Elektrotechnologii. Prace Naukowe. Studia i Materialy
0370-0879 Politechnika Wroclawska. Instytut Technologii Organicznej i Tworzyw Sztucznych. Prace Naukowe. Monografie
0370-0879 Politechnika Wroclawska. Instytut Technologiii Organicznej i Tworzyw Sztucznych. Prace Naukowe. Studia i Materialy
0370-0887 Politechnika Wroclawska. Instytut Technologii Elektronowej. Prace Naukowe. Konferencje
0370-0917 Politechnika Wroclawska. Instytut Materialoznawstwa i Mechaniki Technicznej. Prace Naukowe. Studia i Materialy
0370-1158 Polymers Paint and Colour Journal
0370-1573 Physics Reports
0370-1859 Process Engineering
0370-2030 Agricultural Society of Trinidad & Tobago. Proceedings *see* 0368-1327
0370-2529 Problems of Control and Information Theory
0370-5048 Revue Generale des Colloides *see* 0021-7689
0370-5331 Reviews on High-Temperature Materials
0370-7288 Sociedad Geologica Argentina. Revista *see* 0004-4822
0370-9736 Siemens Forschungs- und Entwicklungsberichte
0371-4098 Suomen Kemistilehti A *see* 0355-1628
0371-4101 Suomen Kemistilehti B *see* 0303-4100
0371-4756 Wroclawskie Towarzystwo Naukowe. Sprawozdania. Seria A
0371-7453 Institution of Mining and Metallurgy. Transactions. Section B: Applied Earth Sciences
0371-7844 Institution of Mining and Metallurgy. Transactions. Section A: Mining Industry
0371-9553 Institution of Mining and Metallurgy. Transactions. Section C: Mineral Processing & Extractive Metallurgy
0372-0187 Newcomen Society for the Study of the History of Engineering and Technology. Transactions
0372-5715 V G B Kraftwerkstechnik,
0372-8854 Zeitschrift fuer Geomorphologie
0372-9494 Politechnika Slaska. Zeszyty Naukowe. Chemia
0372-9508 Politechnika Slaska. Zeszyty Naukowe. Gornictwo
0372-9699 Politechnika Czestochowska. Zeszyty Naukowe. Nauki Techniczne. Hutnictwo
0372-9796 Politechnika Slaska. Zeszyty Naukowe. Energetyka
0373-0204 Zucker- und Suesswaren Wirtschaft
0373-0468 Bonner Geographische Abhandlungen
0373-0514 Bulletin Francais de Pisciculture
0373-0956 Universite Scientifique et Medicale de Grenoble. Institut Fourier. Annales
0373-1537 Bedi Kartlisa
0373-1944 Travail et Securite
0373-2045 International Council for the Exploration of the Sea. Bulletin Statistique
0373-2134 Prirodnjacki Muzej u Beogradu. Glasnik. Serija B: Bioloske Nauke
0373-2525 Saussurea
0373-2630 Revue d'Economie Politique
0373-3033 Accademia delle Scienze di Torino. Memorie. Part I. Classe di Scienze Fisiche, Matematiche e Naturali
0373-3165 Buecherei des Paediaters
0373-353X Vsesoyuznoe Geograficheskoe Obshchestvo. Izvestiya
0373-3629 Annales Hydrographiques
0373-403X Chmelarstvi
0373-4064 Metal Bulletin Monthly
0373-4285 Recherche et Architecture
0373-4331 Betonwerk und Fertigteil-Technik
0373-4854 Auroral Observatory. Magnetic Observations
0373-529X Royal Institution of Naval Architects. Supplementary Papers
0373-5346 Railway Gazette International
0373-5354 Tudomanyos Tajekoztatas Elmelete es Gyakorlata
0373-5524 Universidade de Sao Paulo. Instituto Oceanografico. Boletim
0373-580X Sociedad Argentina de Botanica. Boletin
0373-580X Sociedad Argentina de Botanica. Boletin
0373-6369 Bibliografija Jugoslavije. Serija A. Drustvene Nauke
0373-6377 Bibliografija Jugoslavije. Serija C. Umetnost, Sport, Filologija, Knjizevnost i Muzikalije
0373-6385 Kyushu University. Faculty of Science. Memoirs. Series A: Mathematics
0373-6547 Polska Akademia Nauk. Instytut Geografii i Przestrzennego Zagospodarowania. Prace Geograficzne
0373-6687 Journal of Bryology
0373-6873 Societas pro Fauna et Flora Fennica. Memoranda
0373-7187 Arbeiten zur Rheinischen Landeskunde
0373-7349 Association Nationale d'Etude et de Lutte Contre les Fleaux Atmospheriques. Rapport de Campagne
0373-7632 Floristisch-Soziologische Arbeitsgemeinschaft. Mitteilungen
0373-7640 Bayerische Botanische Gesellschaft. Berichte
0373-7772 Condizionamento dell'Aria
0373-9066 Museo Argentino de Ciencias Naturales Bernardino Rivadavia. Instituto Nacional de Investigacion des las Ciencias Naturales. Revista. Zoologia.
0373-9627 Zitteliana
0374-0412 Universidade Federal de Pernambuco. Departamento de Oceanografia. Centro de Tecnologia. Trabalhos Oceanograficas
0374-0463 Acta Linguistica Hafniensia
0374-1257 Mitteilungen aus dem Max-Planck-Institut fuer Stroemungsforschung
0374-2261 Le Trefile
0374-2490 Aviation Review *changed to* Aerospace & Defence Review
0374-2636 Bauelemente der Elektrotechnik *changed to* Elektronik Entwicklung
0374-2806 Comments on Plasma Physics and Controlled Fusion
0374-3225 Fluid: Apparecchiature Idrauliche e Pneumatiche
0374-3268 Geos
0374-356X Society of Environmental Engineers. Journal
0374-3659 Kent Technical Review†
0374-4353 Research Disclosure
0374-4361 Radio & Electronics Constructor
0374-4795 Works Management
0374-4809 X-Ray Focus†
0374-4965 Acta Anaesthesiologica Italica
0374-5791 Istituto Sperimentale per l'Enologia Asti. Annali
0374-633X British Journal of Mental Subnormality
0374-8774 Kerala Journal of Veterinary Science
0374-9444 Monitore Zoologico Italiano. Supplemento
0374-9894 Nature Canada
0375-0299 Palaeontographica. Abt. B: Palaeophytologie
0375-0442 Palaeontographica. Abt. A: Palaeozoologie - Stratigraphie
0375-5452 Acta Humboldtiana. Series Geologica, Palaeontologica et Biologica
0375-605X Canadian Rock Mechanics Symposium. Proceedings
0375-6505 Geothermics
0375-6742 Journal of Geochemical Exploration
0375-7471 Quartaer
0375-7587 Scripta Geologica
0375-8591 Arhiv za Higijenu Rada i Toksikologiju
0375-9210 Journal of Applied Chemistry and Biotechnology *see* 0142-0356
0375-9229 Journal of Bone and Joint Surgery *see* 0021-9355
0376-0421 Progress in Aerospace Sciences
0376-1185 T U - Sicherheit und Zuverlaessigkeit in Wirtschaft, Betrieb, Verkehr
0376-2793 Museo Argentino de Ciencias Naturales Bernardino Rivadavia. Instituto Nacional de Investigacion de las Ciencias Naturales. Revista. Botanica.
0376-4001 Utrechtse Geografische Studies
0376-4230 Contributions to Vertebrate Evolution
0376-4249 Current Topics in Critical Care Medicine
0376-4788 Indian Roads Congress. Highway Research Board Bulletin
0376-4826 Steirische Beitraege zur Hydrogeologie
0376-4842 Current Awareness in Particle Technology
0376-4885 Council of Europe. Documentation Centre for Education in Europe. Newsletter/Faits Nouveaux
0376-5016 O P T I M A Newsletter
0376-5024 Asociacion de Escribanos del Uruguay. Revista
0376-5032 Print Letter
0376-5040 Core Journals in Pediatrics
0376-5059 Core Journals in Obstetrics/Gynecology
0376-5067 Trends in Biochemical Sciences
0376-5075 Computer Networks
0376-5091 Excerpta Medica. Section 37: Drug Literature Index
0376-5423 Meghalaya Industrial Development Corporation. Annual Report

0376-5512 Andhra Pradesh State Trading Corporation Limited. Annual Report
0376-5725 Reserve Bank of Malawi. Financial and Economic Review
0376-6039 Books Ireland
0376-6349 Journal of Occupational Accidents
0376-6357 Behavioural Processes
0376-6381 World Index of Scientific Translations and List of Translations Notified to the International Translation Centre *see* 0378-6803
0376-6411 Terra et Aqua
0376-642X I A T A Review
0376-6438 Organization for Economic Cooperation and Development. Economic Surveys: New Zealand
0376-7213 Construction and Property News
0376-7221 Irish Motor Industry
0376-7272 Vaare Veger
0376-804X Andhra Pradesh Small Scale Industrial Development Corporation. Annual Report
0376-818X Dengue Newsletter for the Americas
0376-8600 Directory of Special Libraries in Indonesia
0376-8716 Drug and Alcohol Dependence
0376-9852 Indian Journal of Engineers
0376-9984 Indonesia Statistics
0377-0141 International Journal of Critical Sociology
0377-0257 Journal of Non-Newtonian Fluid Mechanics
0377-0273 Journal of Volcanology and Geothermal Research
0377-0273 Dynamics of Atmospheres and Oceans
0377-046X Journal of Molecular Medicine
0377-0486 Journal of Raman Spectroscopy
0377-0850 Law and Progress
0377-0907 Legal History
0377-0974 Libros Espanoles I S B N
0377-144X Barbados. Legislature. House of Assembly. Minutes of Proceedings
0377-1458 Barbados. Legislature. Senate. Minutes of Proceedings
0377-1792 Norsk Sykehustidende
0377-2586 Pakistan Pictorial
0377-2969 Pakistan Academy of Sciences. Proceedings.
0377-3205 Qualitas Plantarum
0377-3574 Contributions to Epidemiology and Biostatistics
0377-5135 Sciences, Techniques, Informations C R I A C
0377-5380 Social and Labour Bulletin
0377-628X Revista de Filologia y Linguistica
0377-6549 Warta Kesehatan *changed to* Warta Dinas Kesehatan
0377-6883 Diffusion and Defect Data
0377-7243 I A B S E Periodica
0377-7251 I A B S E Surveys *see* 0377-7243
0377-726X I A B S E Journal *see* 0377-7243
0377-7278 I A B S E Proceedings *see* 0377-7243
0377-7286 I A B S E Structures *see* 0377-7243
0377-7294 I A B S E Bulletin *see* 0377-7243
0377-7316 Anuario de Estudios Centroamericanos
0377-7340 Indian Electronics Directory
0377-7669 North Atlantic Treaty Organization. Expert Panel on Air Pollution Modeling. Proceedings
0377-7928 Singapore Periodicals Index
0377-8282 Drugs of the Future
0377-8320 Psicodeia
0377-8398 Marine Micropaleontology
0377-8401 Animal Feed Science and Technology
0377-841X Engineering and Process Economics *changed to* Engineering Costs and Production Economics
0377-8657 Purchasing South Africa
0377-8711 Corrosion and Coatings
0377-8886 Norway. Statistisk Sentralbyraa. Legestatistikk *changed to* Norway. Statistisk Sentralbyraa. Helsepersonellstatistikk
0377-8967 Review of Population Reviews
0377-919X Journal of Palestine Studies
0377-9211 Arabian Journal for Science and Engineering
0377-9424 Agronomia Costarricense
0377-9688 Limnological Society of Southern Africa. Journal
0377-9890 Journal of Educational Media Science
0378-0392 Mineral and Electrolyte Metabolism
0378-0473 Kanina
0378-0643 Poesie
0378-0651 Muziek en Onderwijs
0378-066X Entretiens d'Actualite
0378-0791 Infusionstherapie und Klinische Ernaehrung - Forschung und Praxis
0378-0880 Communication and Cognition
0378-1070 C O M L A Newsletter
0378-1097 F E M S-Microbiology Letters
0378-1100 Contemporary Crises
0378-1119 Gene
0378-1127 Forest Ecology and Management
0378-1135 Veterinary Microbiology
0378-1771 Central Bank of Barbados. Quarterly Report
0378-178X Central Bank of Barbados. Economic and Financial Statistics
0378-181X Pedofauna
0378-1909 Environmental Biology of Fishes
0378-195X Metro: a Bibliography
0378-1968 International Statistical Handbook of Urban Public Transport
0378-1976 International Union of Public Transport. Technical Reports of the Congresses
0378-2158 Kenya Uhuru Yearbook
0378-2166 Journal of Pragmatics
0378-2522 Estadistica Panamena. Situacion Economica. Seccion 351. Indice de Precios al por Mayor y al Consumidor
0378-2530 Estadistica Panamena. Situacion Economica. Seccion 351. Precios Pagados por el Productor Agropecuario
0378-2557 Estadistica Panamena. Situacion Economica. Seccion 314, 321, 323, 324, 325. Industria
0378-2573 Estadistica Panamena. Situacion Economica. Seccion 312. Superficie Sembrada y Cosecha de Cafe, Tabaco y Cana de Azucar
0378-2581 Estadistica Panamena. Situacion Economica. Seccion 312. Produccion Pecuaria
0378-259X Estadistica Panamena. Situacion Politica, Administrativa y Justicia. Seccion 631. Justicia
0378-2603 Estadistica Panamena. Situacion Economica. Seccion 342. Cuentas Nacionales
0378-2611 Estadistica Panamena. Situacion Economica: Seccion 351-Precios Recibidos por el Productor Agropecuario
0378-262X Estadistica Panamena. Situacion Social. Seccion 431. Asistencia Social
0378-2689 University of Hong Kong. Centre of Asian Studies. Occasional Papers and Monographs
0378-2697 Plant Systematics and Evolution
0378-3073 Oesterreichische Zeitschrift fuer Oeffentliches Recht und Voelkerrecht
0378-309X Biotelemetry and Patient Monitoring
0378-3472 Euro Abstracts Section II. Coal and Steel
0378-3588 Statistical Office of the European Communities. Crop Production
0378-3758 Journal of Statistical Planning and Inference
0378-3766 North-Holland/T I M S Studies in the Management Sciences
0378-3774 Agricultural Water Management
0378-3782 Early Human Development
0378-3790 Inorganic Perspectives in Biology and Medicine†
0378-3804 Journal of Mechanical Working Technology
0378-3812 Fluid Phase Equilibria
0378-3820 Fuel Processing Technology
0378-3839 Coastal Engineering
0378-4029 Geological Survey of India. News
0378-4037 International Bulletin of Sports Information
0378-4045 Progress in Clinical Neurophysiology
0378-4150 German Language and Literature Monographs
0378-4169 Lingvisticae Investigationes
0378-4177 Studies in Language
0378-4207 Eurostat News
0378-4266 Journal of Banking and Finance
0378-4274 Toxicology Letters
0378-4282 Animal Regulation Studies
0378-4290 Field Crops Research
0378-4304 Analytica Chimica Acta-Computer Techniques and Optimization
0378-4312 Veterinary Science Communications *changed to* Veterinary Research Communications
0378-4320 Animal Reproduction Science
0378-4339 Protection Ecology
0378-4347 Journal of Chromatography-Biomedical Applications
0378-4371 Physica
0378-4487 Advances in Molecular Relaxation and Interaction Processes
0378-4525 Zambian Ornithological Society. Bulletin
0378-4533 Zambian Ornithological Society. Newsletter
0378-469X Balafon
0378-4754 Mathematics and Computers in Simulation
0378-4789 Independent Journal of Philosophy
0378-4797 Africa Index
0378-4843 F C T L
0378-4940 Estadistica Panamena. Indicadores Economicos y Sociales. Seccion 011. Indicadores Economicos y Sociales
0378-4967 Estadistica Panamena. Situacion Cultural. Seccion 511. Educacion
0378-4975 Estadistica Panamena. Situacion Demografica. Seccion 231. Migracion Internacional
0378-4991 Estadistica Panamena. Situacion Economica. Seccion 352. Hoja de Balance de Alimentos
0378-5068 Vocational Training
0378-5122 Maturitas
0378-5165 International Journal of Political Education
0378-5173 International Journal of Pharmaceutics
0378-5327 South African Geographer
0378-5467 Labor Education
0378-5726 Etudes Mesoamericaines
0378-584X Onkologie
0378-5858 Renal Physiology
0378-5866 Developmental Neuroscience
0378-5882 International Labour Office. Official Bulletin. Series A
0378-5890 International Labour Office. Official Bulletin. Series B
0378-5904 I L O Publications
0378-5912 Trends in Neurosciences
0378-5939 Journal of Research Communication Studies
0378-5955 Hearing Research
0378-5963 Applications of Surface Science
0378-620X Integral Equations and Operator Theory
0378-6218 Resultate der Mathematik
0378-6501 Methods and Findings in Experimental and Clinical Pharmacology
0378-651X Financial Market Trends
0378-6536 Organization for Economic Cooperation and Development. Quarterly Oil Statistics
0378-6714 Statistical Office of the European Communities. Selling Prices of Vegetable Products
0378-6722 Statistical Office of the European Communities. Selling Prices of Animal Products
0378-6730 Estadistica Panamena. Situacion Economica. Seccion 343-344. Hacienda Publica y Finanzas
0378-6749 Estadistica Panamena. Situacion Demografica. Seccion 221. Estadisticas Vitales - Cifras Preliminares
0378-6757 Estadistica Panamena. Situacion Fisica. Seccion 121-Clima. Meteorologia
0378-6765 Estadistica Panamena. Situacion Social. Seccion 451. Accidentes de Transito
0378-6803 World Transindex
0378-6900 Advances in Cardiovascular Physics
0378-6935 Dialog
0378-7192 E U D I S E D R & D Bulletin
0378-7206 Information and Management
0378-7346 Gynecologic and Obstetric Investigation
0378-7354 Advances in Biological Psychiatry
0378-7389 Estadistica Panamena. Situacion Economica. Secciones 333 y 334. Transportes y Comunicaciones
0378-7397 Estadistica Panamena. Situacion Economica. Seccion 341. Balanza de Pagos
0378-746X I R E B I
0378-7478 Research in Tourism
0378-7494 Creative Book Selection Index
0378-7508 Library History Review
0378-7516 Asian Journal of European Studies
0378-7524 History of Agriculture
0378-7532 Management Development
0378-7656 International Federation for Documentation. P-Notes
0378-7680 Ciencia y Sociedad
0378-7753 Journal of Power Sources
0378-7761 Fire Research *see* 0379-7112
0378-777X Environmental Policy and Law
0378-7788 Energy and Buildings
0378-7796 Electric Power Systems Research
0378-780X Current Titles in Electrochemistry
0378-7931 Deviance et Societe
0378-7966 European Journal of Drug Metabolism and Pharmacokinetics
0378-7974 Revista de Estudios Hispanicos
0378-8059 Sudanow
0378-8350 Langues et Terminologies
0378-8490 Karger Highlights: Nephrology
0378-8512 Korean Journal of Biochemistry
0378-8733 Social Networks
0378-8741 Journal of Ethnopharmacology
0378-892X Instituut voor Hygiene en Epidemiologie. Reseau Soufre-Fumee/Zwavel-Rook Meetnet
0378-9098 South African Journal of Business Management
0378-9837 Diagnostic Imaging
0378-9853 Karger Highlights: Cardiology
0378-9861 Human Gene Mapping
0378-9977 International Background
0378-9993 Industry and Environment
0379-0037 Indian Journal of Applied Linguistics
0379-0258 Automatic Data Processing Information Bulletin
0379-0290 Current Research in Social Security
0379-0568 Indian Society of Desert Technology and University Centre of Desert Studies. Transactions
0379-0622 Zambezia: the Journal of the University of Zimbabwe
0379-0649 Penpals
0379-0738 Forensic Science International
0379-0827 Cyprus. Agricultural Research Institute. Agricultural Economics Report
0379-0932 Cyprus. Agricultural Research Institute. Technical Paper
0379-0940 Americas
0379-1068 Karger Highlights: Gerontology
0379-1734 I L O Information
0379-1998 Karger Highlights: Oncology
0379-2005 Karger Highlights: Oral Science
0379-220X O H O L O Biological Conferences (Proceedings)
0379-2811 International Association of Lighthouse Authorities. I.A.L.A. Bulletin
0379-2862 China Letter
0379-2870 Philippine Letter
0379-2889 Japan Letter
0379-3079 Euroforum
0379-3133 European File
0379-3168 Pure and Applied Mathematika Sciences
0379-3338 World Union for the Safeguard of Youth. Bulletin

ISSN INDEX

ISSN	Title
0379-3486	European Communities Trade with ACP States and the South Mediterranean States
0379-363X	Paracelsus
0379-3664	Schweizerische Zeitschrift fuer Soziologie
0379-3680	F I D Directory
0379-3915	Studies in History of Medicine
0379-3982	Tecnologia en Marcha
0379-4016	Trinidad Naturalist
0379-4032	Islam and the Modern World
0379-4040	Agri-Week
0379-4121	Annual Drug Data Report
0379-4350	South African Journal of Chemistry
0379-4369	South African Journal of Wildlife Research
0379-4377	South African Journal of Physics
0379-4474	Karger Highlights: Medical Imaging see 0250-6432
0379-4636	Caravan and Outdoor Life
0379-4792	Transport and Road Digest
0379-5268	Mana
0379-5721	Food and Nutrition Bulletin
0379-606X	Revue A T E E Journal
0379-6086	University of Stellenbosch. Bureau for Economic Research. Consumer Survey
0379-6124	National Institute for Transport and Road Research. Annual Report
0379-6175	South African Journal of Physiotherapy
0379-6191	University of Stellenbosch. Bureau for Economic Research. Trends
0379-6205	Journal for Studies in Economics and Econometrics
0379-6485	Ars Nova
0379-6779	Synthetic Metals
0379-6787	Solar Cells
0379-704X	Social Security Documentation: African Series
0379-7074	African News Sheet
0379-7112	Fire Safety Journal
0379-8305	Developmental Pharmacology and Therapeutics
0379-8402	Philosophica
0379-8577	Curationis
0379-8607	Schweizerische Akademie der Medizinischen Wissenschaften. Bulletin
0379-8658	Greenhill Journal of Administration
0379-9786	Christian Education Advance
0379-9867	Contree
0379-9921	Custos
0380-0008	Manitoba Decisions, Civil and Criminal Cases
0380-0067	Eastern Ontario Farmer
0380-0121	Mennonite Reporter
0380-013X	Canadian Mennonite Reporter see 0380-0121
0380-0172	Manitoba Motorist
0380-0180	Marketing Social
0380-0326	L. B. M. A. O. Reporter
0380-0334	Canada. Statistics Canada. Transportation and Communications Division. Communications Service Bulletin/Communications-Bulletin de Service
0380-0342	Canada. Statistics Canada. Water Transportation/Transport Par Eau
0380-0482	Expression
0380-0547	Canada. Statistics Canada. Infomat
0380-0741	Canada. Statistics Canada. Consumer Credit/Credit a la Consummation†
0380-1039	Vintage Canada
0380-1330	Journal of Great Lakes Research
0380-1349	Canada. Statistics Canada. Imports-Merchandise Trade
0380-1462	Teaching Positions Available†
0380-1470	Trellis
0380-1616	Ontario Genealogy Society. Newsleaf
0380-1799	Orchestra Canada
0380-1861	Registered Nursing Orderly
0380-1888	Ontario Society of Medical Technologists. Newsletter changed to Ontario Medical Technologist
0380-1969	Ontario Technologist
0380-2019	C T M Weekly Bulletin
0380-2051	Journal du Nord-Ouest
0380-2108	Canada. Statistics Canada. Labour Costs in Canada: Education, Libraries and Museums/Couts de la Main d'Oeuvre au Canada. Enseignement, Bibliotheques et Musees
0380-2221	Canadian Financial E-Z Directory
0380-2264	Canadian Association Executive
0380-2361	Canadian Journal of Education
0380-2469	Anglican Church of Canada. General Synod. Journal of Proceedings
0380-2604	Tab International
0380-2639	F M Compilation of the Statutes of Canada
0380-2795	Ontario Campus Culture Association. Newsletter†
0380-2841	N. E. R. L. S. Newsletter see 0708-9066
0380-285X	Onion
0380-2892	In a Nutshell
0380-2906	M P A News see 0380-2892
0380-2914	Adagio
0380-2957	Inside
0380-2973	Talking Books in the Public Library Systems of Metropolitan Toronto
0380-3147	L U A C Forum
0380-321X	Foret-Conservation
0380-3279	Alberta Museums Review
0380-3333	Greenmaster
0380-352X	Feather Fancier
0380-3554	Jr. Rider
0380-3651	Hog Marketplace Quarterly
0380-3945	I.F.†
0380-3988	Institute of Public Administration of Canada. Bulletin
0380-4011	Institute of Chartered Accountants of Guyana. Newsletter
0380-4194	Adaptation (Montreal)
0380-4208	Land Compensation Reports
0380-4275	Reserves of Coal, Province of Alberta
0380-4305	Schedule of Wells Drilled for Oil and Gas, Province of Alberta
0380-4496	Conservation in Alberta
0380-450X	Alberta. Environment Conservation Authority. Annual Report†
0380-4623	Museogramme
0380-4933	International Commission for the Northwest Atlantic Fisheries. Selected Papers see 0250-6432
0380-4968	Canada. Statistics Canada. Gold Quartz and Copper-Gold-Silver Mines/Mines de Quartz Aurifere et Mines de Cuivre-Or-Argent†
0380-5107	Manpower and Immigration Review: Quebec Region
0380-5131	Music Scene
0380-531X	Canada. Department of Employment and Immigration. Strategic Policy and Planning Division. Forward Occupational Imbalance Listing/Liste Anticipative des Desequilibres Par Profession
0380-5476	Voice of Tourism†
0380-5522	Northern Perspectives
0380-5689	Nova Scotia. Department of Labour. Annual Report
0380-5727	Red Deer College. Learning Resources Centre. What's the Use...?
0380-5921	Canadian Mathematical Congress. Research Committee. Report
0380-6073	TeleSemaine
0380-6197	Thunder Bay Camping Guide
0380-6294	Canada. Statistics Canada. Motion Picture Theatres and Film Distributors/Cinemas et Distributeurs de Films
0380-6308	Canada. Statistics Canada. Railway Carloadings/Chargements Ferroviaires
0380-6693	Sift
0380-6804	Canada. Statistics Canada. Labour Force/Population Active
0380-6847	Canada. Statistics Canada. Coal and Coke Statistics/Statistique du Charbon et du Coke
0380-691X	Canada. Statistics Canada. Consumer Prices and Price Indexes/Prix a la Consommation et Indices des Prix
0380-6928	Canada. Statistics Canada. Commercial Failures/Faillites Commerciales†
0380-6936	Canada. Statistics Canada. Employment, Earnings and Hours/Emploi, Gaines et Duree du Travail
0380-6952	Canada. Statistics Canada. Miscellaneous Non-Metal Mines/Mines Non Metalliques Diverses†
0380-6979	Makara
0380-6987	Canadian Automobile Association. Communique
0380-6995	Studies in Canadian Literature
0380-7053	Canada. Statistics Canada. Investment Statistics Service Bulletin/Bulletin de Service sur la Statistique des Investissements
0380-7150	Q L A Bulletin
0380-7177	Canada. Statistics Canada. Merchandising Inventories/Stocks Commerciaux
0380-7223	Canada. Statistics Canada. Gypsum Products/Produits de Gypse
0380-7525	Canada. Statistics Canada. Industrial Corporations Financial Statistics/Societes Industrielles Statistique Financiere
0380-7533	Canada. Statistics Canada. Causes of Death, Provinces by Sex and Canada by Sex and Age/Causes de Deces, Par Provinces Selon le Sexe et le Canada Selon le Sexe et l'Age
0380-7541	Canada. Statistics Canada. Index Numbers of Farm Prices of Agricultural Products/Nombres-Indices des Prix des Produits Agricoles
0380-7797	Canada's Mineral Production, Preliminary Estimate
0380-7878	Canada. Statistics Canada. Retail Chain Stores/Magasins de Detail a Succursales
0380-7894	Canada. Statistics Canada. Wholesale Trade/Commerce de Gros
0380-7967	Post see 0709-1370
0380-7975	Perceptual Post see 0709-1370
0380-8025	Publisher
0380-8041	S L I S Newsletter
0380-8068	Georgian Bay Regional Library System. Directory-Member Libraries
0380-8114	Random Thoughts
0380-8203	Canada. Statistics Canada. Mineral Wool/Laine Minerale
0380-8297	Saskatchewan. Advisory Council on the Status of Women. Publication
0380-8335	Scope/Woodall's Canadian Campgrounds Directory see 0380-8343
0380-8343	Scope/Wheelers Canadian Campground Guide
0380-8475	Catholic Hospital Association of Canada. Directory changed to Catholic Health Association of Canada. Directory
0380-8491	Alberta Teachers' Association. Learning Resources Council. Newsletter
0380-8505	Alberta Teachers' Association. School Library Council. Newsletter see 0380-8491
0380-8513	Alberta Teachers' Association. Audio-Visual Council. Newsletter see 0380-8491
0380-8599	N B C / N F C News
0380-8688	Canadian Scout Executive see 0380-8696
0380-8696	Scout Executive
0380-8718	Canada. Grain Commission. Economics and Statistics Division. Visible Grain Supplies and Disposition
0380-8823	Repertoire des Theses de Doctorat Soutenues Devant les Universites de Langue Francaise†
0380-8858	Toronto News†
0380-8866	Shore Line
0380-8890	Econrifleux†
0380-8920	A T A News Bulletin see 0709-4272
0380-903X	Imperial Oil Limited. Review
0380-9099	Business Life
0380-9102	A T A Magazine
0380-9218	Canadian Journal of Information Science
0380-9242	Nova Scotian Surveyor
0380-9366	Neologie en Marche. Serie A. Langue Generale
0380-9420	Canadian Journal of Political & Social Theory
0380-9455	Canada on Stage: Canadian Theatre Review Yearbook
0380-951X	Canada. Statistics Canada. Electric Power Statistics Volume 1: Annual Electric Power Survey of Capability and Load/Statistique de l'Energie Electrique. Volume 1: Enquete Annuelle sur la Puissance Maximale et sur la Charge des Reseaux
0380-9633	Megadrilogica
0380-9668	B. C. Hotelman
0380-9676	University of Saskatchewan. Library. Notable Works and Collections
0380-9773	Orienteering see 0382-8255
0380-979X	Manitoba. Environmental Council. Studies
0380-9803	Manitoba. Environmental Council. Annual Report
0380-9854	C C I Journal
0381-0100	Conference Board in Canada. Quarterly Provincial Forecast
0381-0380	Eglise de Montreal
0381-0410	University of British Columbia. Department of Economics. Resources Paper
0381-0569	Interlude†
0381-0739	Modicum
0381-0925	Continuum
0381-095X	Communicator
0381-0976	Canada. Information Canada. Municipal Report
0381-0984	Journal of Natural Resource Management and Interdisciplinary Studies
0381-1352	F C M Forum
0381-1387	Learning
0381-1603	Political Economy Series
0381-1638	University of Toronto. Faculty of Law. Review
0381-1794	Society
0381-2022	Newfoundland and Labrador Provincial Libraries. Newsletter
0381-2049	Legal Aid New Brunswick Annual Report
0381-209X	Newfoundland and Labrador Regional Libraries. Newsletter see 0381-2022
0381-2146	Canada. Environmental Protection Service. Canada-Ontario Agreement Research Report
0381-2278	Saskatchewan. Alcoholism Commission. Annual Report
0381-2294	Alberta. Utilities Division. Annual Report
0381-2421	Farmers' Market
0381-2472	Grain Facts
0381-2510	British Columbia. Law Reform Commission. Annual Report
0381-2561	Canada Health Manpower Inventory
0381-260X	British Columbia Institute of Technology. Annual Report see 0707-3291
0381-2669	Chalk River Nuclear Laboratories. Chemistry and Materials Division. Progress Report
0381-2677	Chalk River Nuclear Laboratories. Biology and Health Physics Division. Progress Report
0381-2898	British Columbia. Department of Labour. Annual Report see 0705-9698
0381-2995	Canada. Air Pollution Control Directorate. Annual Summary: National Air Pollution Surveillance New Brunswick
0381-3134	Nouveau-Brunswick Aujourd'hui see 0381-3134
0381-3142	Manitoba. Pension Commission. Annual Report
0381-3215	

ISSN INDEX 1239

0381-3223 Saskatchewan Farmers' Markets Annual Report
0381-3258 Trends in Collective Bargaining Settlements in Nova Scotia
0381-3711 Employers of New Community College Graduates: Directory
0381-372X Employers of New University Graduates: Directory
0381-3738 Directory of Employers Offering Employment to New University Graduates *see* 0381-372X
0381-3746 This Magazine: Education, Culture, Politics
0381-3886 Heartline
0381-3924 Ontario. Ministry of Natural Resources. Forest Research Report
0381-3932 Clover Leaflet
0381-3967 New Brunswick Industrial Safety Council. Newsletter *see* 0381-3975
0381-3975 Working Safely
0381-4319 National Research Council, Canada. Division of Building Research. D B R Paper
0381-4327 Alberta. Department of Social Services and Community Health. Annual Report
0381-4432 Canada. Statistics Canada. New Surveys/Nouvelles Enquetes
0381-4556 Telephone Echo
0381-4831 Bedford Institute of Oceanography. Computer Note
0381-4874 International Perspectives
0381-5013 Canadian Oldtimers' Hockey News
0381-5250 H R I Observations *changed to* Observations
0381-5447 Canadian Spectroscopic News
0381-551X Manual of the Textile Industry of Canada
0381-5528 Outdoor Power Products†
0381-565X Computing Services Bulletin
0381-5730 Canadian Music Directory
0381-5765 Canadian Hotel, Restaurant, Institution & Store Equipment Directory
0381-5781 Association des Traducteurs et Interpretes de l'Ontario. Informatio
0381-579X Yes, There Is Canadian Music†
0381-5900 Maritime Psychological Association. Bulletin *see* 0004-6833
0381-5919 Information *see* 0707-7793
0381-5927 Agricultural Science *see* 0707-7793
0381-596X Brasier
0381-5978 British Columbia School Trustees Association. Newsletter
0381-6036 B. C. Science Teacher
0381-6060 Anglican Church of Canada. Division of National and World Program. Bulletin *see* 0381-6079
0381-6079 Anglican Church of Canada. Bulletin†
0381-6133 Canadian Association of Slavists Newsletter
0381-6206 Brome County Historical Society. Publication
0381-6303 Alberta Wilderness Arts and Recreation *see* 0705-3150
0381-646X Environment Probe
0381-6486 C-Core News
0381-6524 Journal of Our Time
0381-6532 Guide to a Successful Life Insurance Career
0381-6591 Poetry Toronto Newsletter
0381-6605 Journal of Otolaryngology
0381-6745 Beverage Canada
0381-6826 N A P E Journal *changed to* Communicator
0381-6834 Beef Today *changed to* Canadian Livestock Journal
0381-6885 Harrowsmith
0381-6907 Quebec (Province) Centrale des Bibliotheques. Bulletin de Bibliographie†
0381-7024 Dalhousie University. Institute of Public Affairs. Occasional Papers
0381-7059 Canadian Amateur Photographer
0381-7245 Blue Book of Canadian Business
0381-727X Author-Publisher News & Views
0381-730X Tidings
0381-7695 Harness World
0381-7717 Native Perspective†
0381-7857 Interest
0381-7962 Public Employees Journal
0381-7970 New Brunswick Public Employees Association. News Letter
0381-8004 Ontario Industrial Arts Association. Bulletin
0381-8012 O I A A Bulletin *see* 0381-8004
0381-8047 Crucible
0381-8160 Farm Equipment Quarterly
0381-8179 Sanford Evans Gold Book of Used Car Prices
0381-8187 Scope
0381-8225 Revue des Fermieres
0381-8284 Transportation Research in Canada *changed to* Transportation R & D in Canada
0381-8357 Archaic Notes *changed to* Ottawa Archaeologist
0381-8535 Fur Trade Journal
0381-856X Caledonian
0381-8802 Canada. Statistics Canada. Hospital Statistics: Preliminary Annual Report/Statistique Hospitaliere: Rapport Annuel Preliminaire
0381-8845 Canada. Statistics Canada. Tuberculosis Statistics. Volume 2: Institutional Facilities, Services and Finances/La Statistique de la Tuberculose, Volume 2: Installations, Services et Finance des Etablissements†
0381-8888 Estates and Trusts Quarterly
0381-890X Prelude
0381-8918 Bravura *see* 0381-890X
0381-8950 Deutsche Katholik in Kanada
0381-8977 Sporting Goods Canada
0381-9000 S T O P Newsletter *see* 0383-6347
0381-9027 Silahis
0381-9043 International Yoga Life and Yoga Vacations *see* 0708-076X
0381-9116 Special Education *see* 0381-9124
0381-9124 Special Education in Canada
0381-9132 Olifant
0381-9140 New Review of East-European History
0381-9159 Canadian Band Directors Association. Newsletter
0381-9175 C B C: Coiffure-Beaute-Charme
0381-9191 Herstory†
0381-9256 Canada. Statistics Canada. Miscellaneous Non-Metallic Mineral Products Industries/Industries des Produits Mineraux Non-Metalliques Divers
0381-9280 Sporting Goods Trade
0381-9345 Atlantic Provinces Transportation Commission. Tips & Topics
0381-9361 Teiresias
0381-9388 Societe Historique Nicolas Denys Revue d' Histoire
0381-9418 Status of Women News
0381-9507 Canadian L P & Tape Catalogue
0381-9515 Artviews
0381-9612 Trust
0381-9663 Alberta Construction Industry Directory. Purchasing Guide
0381-9825 Montreal Special Libraries Association. Bulletin *changed to* Special Libraries Association. Eastern Canada Chapter/Section de l'Est du Canada. Bulletin
0381-9833 Special Libraries Association. Montreal Chapter. Bulletin *changed to* Special Libraries Association. Eastern Canada Chapter/Section de l'Est du Canada. Bulletin
0381-9868 Motive Power International†
0381-9884 Jewish Public Library Bulletin
0381-9930 Toys & Games
0381-9957 Association des Traducteurs et Interpretes de l'Ontario. Bulletin de l'A T I O *see* 0381-9965
0381-9965 Association des Traducteurs et Interpretes de l'Ontario. Translatio†
0382-0068 Voice of United Senior Citizens of Ontario
0382-0122 Vietnam Report
0382-0130 Ishtar Newsletter *see* 0382-0149
0382-0149 Ishtar News
0382-0157 Western Ontario Historical Notes
0382-0203 Village Squire
0382-0289 Vista
0382-0327 Voice of Radom
0382-0335 Jeu
0382-036X View *see* 0700-4400
0382-0424 Vision
0382-0467 Arctic in Colour
0382-0718 Vector
0382-0726 British Columbia Association of Mathematics Teachers. Newsletter *see* 0382-0718
0382-0734 Hollinger Mines Limited. Annual Report
0382-0750 Transition†
0382-0769 I D E E S
0382-0831 Westmorland Historical Society. Newsletter
0382-084X Lettres Quebecoises
0382-0912 Town and Country Librarian
0382-0920 Canada. Statistics Canada. Enrollment in Community Colleges/Effectifs des Colleges Communautaires
0382-0939 Canada. Statistics Canada. for-Hire Trucking Survey/Enquete sur le Transport Routier de Marchandises pour Compte d'Autrui
0382-0971 Canada. Statistics Canada. Concrete Products Manufacturers/Fabricants de Produits en Beton
0382-098X Canada. Statistics Canada. Principal Taxes and Rates: Federal, Provincial and Local Governments *see* 0382-0998
0382-0998 Canada. Statistics Canada. Principal Taxes in Canada†
0382-1048 Novia Scotia. Department of Labour and Manpower. Monthly Summary of Activities-Industrial Relations Division
0382-1102 Current Labour Force Statistics for Nova Scotia
0382-1161 Canada. Commissioner of Official Languages. Annual Report
0382-1315 Education Nova Scotia
0382-1463 Canada. Law Reform Commission. Annual Report
0382-1587 Canada. Pension Review Board. Reports
0382-1838 Saskatchewan Universities Commission. Annual Report
0382-1889 Labour Research Bulletin
0382-2028 Manitoba Grassland Projects
0382-2249 Annual Statistical Review of Canadian Fisheries
0382-2273 C F D C Annual Report
0382-232X Canada Diseases Weekly Report
0382-2788 Environment Ontario Legacy
0382-2834 Ontario Hydro. Statistical Yearbook
0382-3814 Education Quebec
0382-392X Canada. Anti-Inflation Board. Consumer Information
0382-4012 Manufacturing Industries of Canada: Sub-Provincial Areas
0382-4020 Canada. Statistics Canada. Manufacturing Industries Division. Potash Mines/Mines de Potasse†
0382-4039 Young Communist *see* 0382-4047
0382-4047 Young Worker
0382-408X Teacher
0382-411X Canada. Statistics Canada. Educational Staff in Community Colleges/Personnel d'Enseignement des Colleges Communautaires†
0382-4128 Canada. Statistics Canada. Statistical Profiles of Educational Staff in Community Colleges/Profiles Statistiques sur le Personnel d'Enseignement des Colleges Communautaires *see* 0382-411X
0382-4292 Alberta Pharmaceutical Association. A. Ph. A. Communications
0382-4306 Anglican Crusader *see* 0382-4314
0382-4314 Crusader (Toronto)
0382-4365 Avec "Lui"
0382-4373 Aim
0382-4438 Athletica
0382-4500 Arrow†
0382-4527 Action
0382-4535 Swim Signals *see* 0382-4527
0382-4543 Red Cross Youth *see* 0382-4527
0382-4551 Volunteer *see* 0382-4527
0382-456X Advocate
0382-4756 Banque de Commerce Canadienne Imperiale. Lettre Commerciale
0382-4764 Canadian Historical Association. Newsletter
0382-4926 Vie Montante. Edition Canadienne
0382-5027 Current Index to Commonwealth Legal Periodicals *see* 0225-9036
0382-5078 Criteria†
0382-5124 Ateliers
0382-5191 Alberta English
0382-5205 Urban Reader
0382-5264 Branching out
0382-5272 British Columbia Monthly
0382-5272 B. C. Monthly
0382-5302 Bulletin - S V P *changed to* Environnement
0382-5310 Societe pour Vaincre la Pollution. Bulletin de Liaison *changed to* Environnement
0382-5493 Teaching Mathematics†
0382-5507 B. C. A. M. T. Journal *see* 0382-5493
0382-5566 N B A R N News *see* 0382-5574
0382-5574 Info (Fredericton)
0382-5604 Bouscueil†
0382-5655 Blue Bill
0382-5728 Miners' Voice
0382-5795 Canadian Hackney Stud Book
0382-5868 Long Time Coming†
0382-5876 Canadian Funeral News
0382-5876 Canadian Golden West
0382-5906 Ontario Real Estate Law Guide
0382-5914 Repertoire des Cours d'Ete
0382-5949 Contact *see* 0410-3882
0382-6031 Canadian Manhood
0382-6120 Audio Marketnews
0382-6295 Amnesty International (Toronto Group) Newsletter
0382-6384 Beacon
0382-6406 Canadian Jersey Herd Record
0382-6414 Canadian Jersey Cattle Club. Record *see* 0382-6406
0382-6627 Owl
0382-6651 Clansman
0382-6996 Heating, Plumbing, Air Conditioning Buyers' Guide
0382-7038 C L U Comment (English Edition)
0382-7046 Commentaires (Don Mills)
0382-7054 United Cooperatives of Ontario. News *changed to* U C O Cornerstone
0382-7062 United Co-operatives of Ontario. Directors' Newsletter *see* 0382-7070
0382-7070 U C O Leader
0382-7437 Canadian Practitioner *see* 0382-7453
0382-7453 Canadian Practitioner and Review
0382-7577 Big Country Voice
0382-7887 Calgary Chamber of Commerce. Business News *see* 0707-8064
0382-7976 A. C. E. H. I. Journal
0382-8042 Canadian Miner *see* 0029-3164
0382-8115 Canada Crafts
0382-8255 C O F Newsletter
0382-8409 Challenge (Winnipeg)
0382-8476 Nurscene
0382-8522 South of Tuk *changed to* Sequel
0382-8557 Ciao
0382-8727 Christian Bus Driver
0382-876X Iconomatrix†
0382-8824 Laomedon Review
0382-8832 Cultural Horizons of the Deaf in Canada
0382-8980 Deaf Herald†
0382-909X Descant
0382-912X Council of Ontario Universities. Research Division. Application Statistics
0382-9391 Diocesan Times

0383-008X Canada. Statistics Canada. Fruit and Vegetable Production/Production de Fruits et de Legumes
0383-0101 Canadian Nurses Association. Library. Periodical Holdings
0383-0152 Rhythme de Notre Eglise
0383-0187 Guide to Film and Television Courses in Canada
0383-0470 Cite Libre *see* 0009-7489
0383-0640 Stationery & Office Products†
0383-0721 Ecouri Romanesti
0383-0861 Aube Arabe *see* 0383-087X
0383-087X Arab Dawn
0383-090X Metalworking Production & Purchasing
0383-1280 Canadian Music Library Association. Newsletter *see* 0383-1299
0383-1299 C A M L Newsletter
0383-1310 Catholic Dutch Canadian Association. C D C A Nieuws *see* 0383-1329
0383-1329 Nieuwe Weg (Montreal)
0383-1418 Eastern Light
0383-1493 Mandate
0383-1620 Catholic Register
0383-2031 Waters
0383-2058 Western Livestock & Agricultural News
0383-2244 Farm Trends
0383-2368 Guide Camping *see* 0705-8314
0383-2406 Canadian Campus Career Directory
0383-2430 Building Supply Dealers Association. Survey
0383-2538 Ievanhel's'kyi Holos
0383-2708 Focus on Vancouver
0383-2759 International Migration Newsletter *see* 0383-2767
0383-2767 International Newsletter on Migration
0383-2813 Canada-Mongolia Review
0383-2848 Carleton University, Ottawa. Norman Paterson School of International Affairs. Bibliography Series
0383-2945 Canadian Weekly Stock Charts: Industrials
0383-2953 Canadian Weekly Stock Charts: Mines & Oils
0383-2961 Nouvelle Revue Canadienne *see* 0547-0749
0383-3003 Living Places†
0383-3402 Electricity Today
0383-3437 Labour Organizations in Nova Scotia
0383-3585 Rural Real Estate Values in Alberta *see* 0701-7502
0383-3615 Alberta. Health Care Insurance Commission. Annual Report *changed to* Alberta. Health Care Insurance Plan. Annual Report
0383-3712 Alberta. Legislature Library. Annual Report
0383-3739 Alberta. Department of the Environment. Annual Report
0383-3925 Manitoba. Health Services Commission. Annual Report
0383-3933 Manitoba. Health Services Commission. Statistical Supplement to the Annual Report
0383-414X Canada. National Farm Products Marketing Council. Annual Report
0383-4239 Costume Society of Ontario. Newsletter
0383-4352 Saskatchewan Trading Corporation. Annual Report
0383-4379 Canada. Correctional Investigator. Annual Report
0383-4514 Documents in the History of Canadian Art
0383-4638 Canada. Department of National Defence. Defence
0383-4654 Cooperation Canada
0383-5154 Canada. Department of Industry, Trade and Commerce. Annual Report.
0383-5391 Masterpieces in the National Gallery of Canada
0383-5405 Canadian Artists Series
0383-5472 Water Quality Data for Ontario Streams & Lakes
0383-5588 Manitoba. Human Rights Commission. Annual Report
0383-5766 Canada. Statistics Canada. Passenger Bus and Urban Transit Statistics/Statistique du Transport des Voyageurs Par Autobus et du Transport Urbain
0383-6029 Manitoba Square Dancer *see* 0383-6037
0383-6037 Manisquare
0383-6061 Intercom
0383-6096 Manitoba Educational Research Council. Newsletter *changed to* Manitoba Educational Research Council. Research Bulletin
0383-6266 Artswest
0383-6312 Smallholder
0383-6347 S O S Montreal
0383-641X Comeback†
0383-6436 Countdown
0383-6479 Ontario Conservation News
0383-6509 Caledonia Diocesan Times
0383-6576 Canadian Oral History Association. Bulletin†
0383-6649 A I M Magazine
0383-669X Barreau du Quebec. Revue
0383-6894 Canadian Oral History Association. Journal
0383-7300 Gift Magazine
0383-7319 ComputerData
0383-7319 Canadian Data Processing Directory
0383-7521 Derives
0383-7645 Presbyterian Comment
0383-7653 Prairie Harvesters
0383-770X Canadian Book Review Annual
0383-7769 Main Deck
0383-7920 Canadian Rental Service
0383-7939 Bluenose Magazine
0383-8021 Condominium
0383-8358 Directory of Law Teachers
0383-8447 Ecole de Medecine Veterinaire, Saint-Hyacinthe, Quebec. Annuaire *see* 0383-8455
0383-8455 Universite de Montreal. Ecole de Medecine Veterinaire. Annuaire
0383-8714 Actualite
0383-9133 Lillooet District Historical Society. Bulletin
0383-9168 Newslitter
0383-9184 Metric Fact Sheets
0383-9230 Ontario Credit Union News
0383-9257 Landscape Ontario
0383-9338 Broadcast Equipment Today *see* 0709-9797
0383-9494 Criminal Reports (Third Series)
0383-9567 Nova Scotia Bird Society. Newsletter
0383-9737 Commerce Journal
0383-9745 Southam Business†
0383-9931 O S C A Reports
0384-0174 Critere
0384-0298 Colombien
0384-0360 Financial Post Magazine
0384-0417 Parapet
0384-0425 Simgames
0384-0433 Contemporary Poetry of British Columbia
0384-059X McGill University, Montreal. Centre for Developing-Area Studies. Working Papers
0384-0816 Mon Bebe
0384-093X Marsh and Maple
0384-0972 P D B
0384-0999 Canadian Yachting
0384-1006 P A C T
0384-1014 Norman Mackenzie Art Gallery. Newsletter *changed to* N-MAG
0384-1022 N M A G Review *changed to* N-MAG
0384-1405 Todays Generation *changed to* Teen Generation
0384-1480 Canadian Wolf Defenders. Newsletter
0384-1642 Newspacket
0384-1677 Canadian Power Engineer†
0384-1898 Newfoundland and Labrador Engineer
0384-191X Calgary Archaeologist
0384-2126 Discussion†
0384-2282 Noticiario de Canada
0384-2304 Hebdo Canada
0384-2312 Canada Weekly
0384-2355 Who's Who: A Guide to Federal and Provincial Departments and Agencies, Their Funding Programs, and the People Who Head Them
0384-2843 Canada. Statistics Canada. Cane and Beet Sugar Processors/Traitement du Sucre de Canne et de Betteraves
0384-2967 Canada. Statistics Canada. Foundation Garment Industry/Industrie des Corsets et Soutiens-Gorge
0384-3300 Canada. Statistics Canada. Leather Glove Factories/Fabriques de Gants en Cuir†
0384-3343 Canada. Statistics Canada. Knitting Mills/Bonneterie
0384-3696 Canada. Statistics Canada. Miscellaneous Food Processors/Traitment des Produits Alimentaires Divers
0384-3769 Canada. Statistics Canada. Miscellaneous Clothing Industries/Industries Diverses de l'Habillement
0384-3912 Canada. Statistics Canada. Manufacturers of Soap and Cleaning Compounds/Fabricants de Savon et de Produits de Nettoyage
0384-4080 Canada. Statistics Canada. Office Furniture Manufacturers/Industrie des Meubles de Bureau
0384-4161 Canada. Statistics Canada. Electric Lamp and Shade Manufacturers/Industrie des Lampes Electriques et des Abat-Jour
0384-4242 Canada. Statistics Canada. Scientific and Professional Equipment Industries/Fabrication de Materiel Scientifique et Professionnel
0384-4420 Canada. Statistics Canada. Fruit and Vegetable Processing Industries/Preparation de Fruits et de Legumes
0384-4498 Canada. Statistics Canada. Women's and Children's Clothing Industries/Industries des Vetements pour Dames et pour Enfants
0384-4633 Canada. Statistics Canada. Pulp and Paper Mills/Usines de Pates et Papiers
0384-465X Canada. Statistics Canada. Corrugated Box Manufacturers/Fabricants de Boites en Carton Ondule
0384-4811 Canada. Statistics Canada. Miscellaneous Leather Products Manufacturers/Fabricants d'Articles Divers en Cuir
0384-4951 Canada. Statistics Canada. Slaughtering and Meat Processors/Abattage et Conditionnement de la Viande
0384-5052 Ontario Folkdancer
0384-5060 Computers and Medieval Data Processing
0384-5087 Conference Catholique Canadienne. Bulletin National de Liturgie
0384-5133 Musique Liturgique†
0384-5184 Canadian Children's Magazine†
0384-5753 Canadian Bar Association. British Columbia Branch. Program Report
0384-5958 Foresight
0384-661X Communicate
0384-6628 Focus on Winnipeg Schools *see* 0384-6636
0384-6636 Our Schools
0384-6903 Canadian Directory of Railway Museums and Displays
0384-6970 Rapports de Pratique de Quebec
0384-7322 Fraser's Potato Newsletter
0384-7411 University of Ottawa. Vanier Library. List of Serials
0384-7446 Livre Canadien *changed to* Nos Livres
0384-7500 Pulse for Jaycee Executives *see* 0008-3895
0384-756X O V C Bulletin *see* 0384-7578
0384-7578 Ontario Veterinary College. Alumni Association. Alumni Bulletin
0384-7802 Blue Book of CBS Stock Reports
0384-7810 Plein Soleil
0384-8116 Dalhousie University. Computer Centre. Newsletter
0384-8159 Royal Ontario Museum. Life Sciences. Contributions
0384-8175 Island Magazine
0384-8434 Canadian Black Book *changed to* Black Book Official Used Car Market Guide
0384-8523 Alchemist
0384-868X Versus
0384-8701 C I L Contact
0384-8744 Canadian Journal of Public and Cooperative Economy
0384-8833 Essence
0384-9120 Regards sur Israel
0384-9147 New Directions
0384-9155 Resources Exchange Project Newsletter *see* 0384-9163
0384-9163 R E P Newsletter
0384-9252 Canada Report
0384-9694 Journal of Religious Ethics
0384-9813 Publicat Index to Canadian Federal Publications *see* 0707-3135
0384-9821 Urban Canada *see* 0707-3135
0384-983X Canadian Newspaper Index *changed to* Canadian News Index
0384-9856 Camping Canada
0384-9988 Conference Board in Canada. Technical Papers
0385-0110 Japanese Association of Periodontology. Journal
0385-0188 Special Libraries
0385-0234 Kawasaki Medical Journal
0385-0447 A E U
0385-1176 J A F S A Library News
0385-1621 Japanese Society of Soil Mechanics and Foundation Engineering. Journal
0385-2350 D K B Economic Report
0385-2423 National Science Museum. Bulletin. Series A: Zoology
0385-2431 National Science Museum. Bulletin. Series B: Botany
0385-244X National Science Museum. Bulletin. Series C: Geology & Paleontology
0385-3039 National Science Museum. Bulletin. Series D: Anthropology
0385-325X Japan. National Diet Library. Annual Report
0385-3284 Japanese National Bibliography
0385-3292 Japanese National Bibliography Weekly List
0385-3330 Monthly List of Selected Atomic Energy Publications
0385-4418 J E O L News - Analytical Instruments/Application *changed to* J E O L News: Analytical Instrumentation
0385-4426 J E O L News - Electron Optics Instruments/Application *changed to* J E O L News: Electron Optics Instrumentation
0385-5023 Dokkyo Journal of Medical Sciences
0385-5082 Journal of Law and Political Science
0385-5414 Heterocycles
0385-5694 Geijutsu Shunju
0385-6151 Hakkokogaku
0385-6321 Soka Gakkai News
0385-6380 Journal of Fermentation Technology
0385-6437 J A E R I Reports Abstracts
0385-6658 Computer Report
0385-6747 Contents
0385-7360 Diamond's Industria
0385-7530 Japan Indexers Association. Journal
0385-7832 Research Laboratory of Precision Machinery and Electronics. Bulletin
0386-0752 Kyoto University. Institute of Atomic Energy. Research Activities
0386-1112 I A T S S Research
0386-1465 Furusato Tembo
0386-2143 Chemical Abstracts
0386-300X Acta Medica Okayama
0386-3425 Snake
0386-3980 Japanese Journal of Leprosy
0386-426X Tohokai
0386-4294 Gumma University. Faculty of Education. Annual Report: Cultural Science Series
0386-5517 National Institute of Polar Research. Memoirs. Series A: Aeronomy
0386-5525 National Institute of Polar Research. Memoirs. Series B: Meteorology
0386-5533 National Institute of Polar Research. Memoirs. Series C: Earth Sciences

0386-5541 National Institute of Polar Research. Memoirs. Series E. Biology and Medical Science
0386-555X National Institute of Polar Research. Memoirs. Series F: Logistics
0386-6157 Society of Powder Technology, Japan. Journal.
0386-8362 World Livestock Industry
0386-8710 Tokyo Metropolitan University. Department of Geography. Geographical Reports
0387-1061 Konkuriito Kogaku
0387-2432 Mitsubishi Juko Giho
0387-2882 Journal of Law and Politics
0387-3935 Japan English Magazine Directory
0387-4753 Seijo University Economic Papers
0387-480X Osaka University. Faculty of Pharmaceutical Sciences. Memoirs
0387-8503 Japanese Periodicals Index. Medical Sciences and Pharmacology
0387-9348 Heron
0388-001X College of Dairying. Journal; Natural Science
0388-0028 College of Dairying. Journal; Cultural and Social Sciences
0388-0605 Monthly Finance Review
0388-1865 World Traders
0390-0037 Chronobiologia
0390-0355 Terzo Occhio
0390-0444 Colture Protette
0390-0460 Micologia Italiana
0390-0479 VigneVini
0390-0487 Zootechnica e Nutrizione Animale
0390-0541 Industrie delle Bevande
0390-0711 Medioevo Romanzo
0390-0991 Lavoro e Sindacato
0390-1106 Giornale di Astronomia
0390-1246 Ambiente Naturale e Urbano
0390-2153 Forme del Significato
0390-2439 Informatica & Documentazione
0390-346X Psicologia Contemporanea
0390-492X Memorie di Biologia Marina e di Oceanografia
0390-5748 Ricerca in Clinica e in Laboratorio
0390-6035 Materials Chemistry
0390-6078 Haematologica
0390-640X Compendio Statistico *see* 0069-7958
0390-6426 Italy. Istituto Centrale di Statistica. Annuario Statistico della Zootecnia, della Pesca e della Caccia
0390-6434 Italy. Istituto Centrale di Statistica. Bolletino Mensile di Statistica
0390-6450 Italy. Istituto Centrale di Statistica. Annuario di Statistiche del Lavoro
0390-6558 Italy. Istituto Centrale di Statistica. Statistica Annuale del Commercio con l'Estero. Tomo I
0390-6566 Italy. Istituto Centrale di Statistica. Statistica Annuale del Commercio con l'Estero. Tomo II
0390-6620 Italy. Istituto Centrale di Statistica. Indicatori Mensili
0390-6736 Montanaro d'Italia-Monti e Boschi
0390-6779 Cooperation in Education
0390-7783 Accademia delle Scienze di Siena Detta de Fisiocritici. Atti
0390-8542 Diritto e Societa (Naples)
0391-1527 Cronache Pompeiane
0391-1535 Cronache Ercolanesi
0391-1551 Rivista di Biologia Normale e Patologica
0391-1624 Minerva Ecologica Idroclimatologica Fisicosanitaria
0391-1632 Monitore Zoologico Italiano. Monografie
0391-1926 Contributi di Sociologia
0391-1934 Capitalismo e Socialismo
0391-1942 Strumenti Linguistici
0391-2019 H P Trasporti
0391-2515 Giornale Storico di Psicologia Dinamica
0391-3104 Quaderni del Vittoriale
0391-3163 Anthropos
0391-3171 Contributi di Sociologia. Readings
0391-321X Istituzioni Culturali
0391-3236 Quaderni di Analisi Matematica
0391-3244 Scienze della Materia
0391-3252 Serie di Matematica e Fisica
0391-3260 Societa e Diritto di Roma
0391-3279 Collana di Storia Moderna e Contemporanea
0391-3295 Teorie Economiche
0391-3457 Dossier Europa-Emigrazione
0391-4186 Verifiche
0391-4631 I.M.E.
0391-464X Carte d'Acquisto
0391-5018 Doc; Documentazione
0391-5360 Energie Alternative: Habitat, Territorio, Energia
0391-5492 Migranti-Press
0391-6030 Forme Materiali e Ideologie del Mondo Antico
0391-6049 Nuovo Medioevo
0391-6065 Dossiers di le Monde Diplomatique
0391-609X Societa e la Scienza
0391-6103 Studi d'Economia
0391-769X Fiuggi
0391-7797 Prospettiva Sindacale
0391-7983 Spezia Oggi
0391-8580 I.C.U. Papers
0395-000X Ordinaire du Psychanalyste
0395-0840 Animation et Education
0395-1294 France Transports†
0395-1766 En Equipe au Service de l'Evangile
0395-2061 Guide Europeen des Produits Logiciels
0395-2096 Forum Chirurgical
0395-2975 Habitation-Cahiers de l'UNIL *changed to* Union Nationale Interprofessionnelle du Logement. Cahiers
0395-3491 Sports Equestres
0395-3599 Courses Hippiques
0395-367X Technic Hebdo
0395-3890 Bulletin Europeen de Physiopathologie Respiratoire *see* 0271-9983
0395-403X Societe Francaise de Cardiologie. Bulletin d'Informations
0395-4374 Bulletin de Medecine Legale, Urgence Medicale, Centre Anti-Poisons *changed to* Journal de Medecine Legale
0395-4382 Karate Cinema
0395-451X Bulletin Rapide de Droit des Affaires
0395-7276 France. Ministere de l'Economie et des Finances. Bulletin de Liaison et d'Information *changed to* France. Ministere de l'Economie. Bulletin de Liaison et d'Information
0395-7349 Medecine, Sciences et Documents
0395-7519 Centre de Recherches Zootechniques et Veterinaires de Theix. Bulletin Technique
0395-7594 Federation Francaise de Sports pour Handicaps Physiques. Informations *changed to* Federation Francaise Handisport. Informations
0395-7691 Education Rurale
0395-773X Traduire
0395-7837 Chantiers de Pedagogie Mathematique
0395-7845 Chants des Peuples
0395-8183 Charolais
0395-8272 Economie Champenoise
0395-9066 Sport de l'Esprit
0395-9090 P.E.V.H. *see* 0048-4997
0395-9260 Journal de Microscopie et de Biologie Celluaire *see* 0399-0311
0395-9279 Journal de Microscopie et de Spectroscopie Electroniques
0395-9295 A.D.M.A: la Vie Musicale en Aquitaine
0395-9481 Actuel Developpement
0395-9600 France Transports
0396-0382 Syndicat General des Industries Medico - Chirurgicales et Dentaires. Annuaire
0396-0595 Courrier de l'Exploitant Forestier et du Scieur
0396-0625 Annuaire des Fournisseurs de Laboratoires Pharmaceutiques et Cosmetiques
0396-1214 Catalogue National du Traitement des Surfaces de l'Anticorrosion et des Traitements Thermiques
0396-2024 Connaissance de l'Ouest
0396-2318 Annuaire des Avocats
0396-2393 Union des Superieures Majeurs de France. Annuaire
0396-2458 Promotion
0396-2644 Unites Petrochimiques dans les Pays de l'OPEP et de l'OPAEP
0396-2679 Caribbean Archives
0396-2687 Bulletin des Centres de Recherches Exploration-Production ELF Aquitaine
0396-437X Chroniques d'Actualite de la S.E.D.E.I.S.
0396-4388 Port Autonome du Havre. Bulletin Analytique de Documentation Generale
0396-4396 Port Autonome du Havre. Bulletin Analytique de Documentation Technique
0396-4817 De l'Atlantique au Pacifique
0396-4957 Encyclopedie d'Utovie
0396-5880 Intergeo-Bulletin
0396-7107 Therapeutiques Naturelles
0396-7115 Groupement National pour l'Organisation de la Medecine Auxiliaire. Bulletin de Liaison *see* 0396-7107
0396-714X Commerce Moderne
0396-7360 Jeunesse du Quart Monde
0396-9657 Recherches Geographiques a Strasbourg
0396-969X Esprit Saint
0396-9975 Informations d'Ile de France
0397-0280 Unions Sexuelles
0397-0736 Echanges
0397-1511 Journal du Mineur
0397-2836 Biologie et Ecologie Mediterraneene
0397-2844 Geologie Mediterraneenne
0397-3816 Manutention - Stockage
0397-4715 Expomat Actualites
0397-474X Transport Public
0397-5754 Marches Agricoles-l'Echo des Halles
0397-6424 Hi Fi Magazine
0397-6491 Science Film
0397-6505 Secretaires d'Aujourd'hui
0397-6513 T. E. C.
0397-6521 Transports Urbains
0397-7153 Biologie du Comportement
0397-7730 Bulletin Signaletique. Part 360: Biologie Animale. Physiologie et Pathologie des Protozoaires et des Invertebres *see* 0181-0006
0397-7730 Bulletin Signaletique. Part 780: Polymeres. Peintures. Bois. Cuirs
0397-7757 Bulletin Signaletique. Part 130: Physique Mathematique, Optique, Acoustique, Mechanique, Chaleur
0397-7870 Revue Francaise d'Etudes Americaines
0397-8079 Revue de l'Embouteillage et des Industries du Conditionnement, Traitement, Distribution Transport *changed to* Revue Conditionnement des Liquides-Embouteillage
0397-8249 Annuaire de l'URSS et des Pays Socialistes Europeens
0397-8389 Economie Familiale
0397-8435 Centre National de la Cinematographie. Bulletin d'Information
0397-8702 Film Francais
0397-9180 Pediatre (Paris)
0397-944X Migrants Nouvelles
0397-9873 Revue Trimestrielle de Droit Civil
0398-0006 Paris Madame
0398-0049 Theatre et Animation
0398-0499 Journal des Maladies Vasculaires
0398-074X Astrolab
0398-1851 Electronique et Applications Industrielles
0398-3218 Geophysique
0398-3765 Centre International de Documentation Occitane. Serie Etudes
0398-7620 Revue d'Epidemiologie et de Sante Publique
0398-8287 Institut Technique de l'Aviculture. Tendances des Marche
0398-8341 Sport Bowling
0398-9372 Nouveau Photocinema
0398-9453 Biza Neira (Bise Noire)
0398-9690 News from France
0398-9836 Nouveau Journal de Chimie
0398-9941 Bulletin Signaletique. Part 310: Genie Biomedical. Informatique Biomedicale
0398-995X Bulletin Signaletique. Part 890: Industries Mecaniques-Batiment-Travaux Public-Transports *see* 0223-4246
0398-9968 Bulletin Signaletique. Part 165: Atomes et Molecules. Physiques des Fluides et Plasmas *see* 0301-3359
0399-0087 Septentrion
0399-0265 Services d'Aide Medicale Urgente. Revue
0399-0281 France. Ministere de l'Amenagement du Territoire, de l'Equipement, du Logement et des Transports. Bulletin Officiel
0399-0311 Biologie Cellulaire
0399-0435 Journal Francais de Biophysique et Medecine Nucleaire *changed to* Journal de Biophysique et Medecine Nucleaire
0399-0443 Universite de Bordeaux III. Centre de Recherches sur l'Amerique Anglophone. Annales
0399-0516 R A I R O Analyse Numerique/Numerical Analysis
0399-0524 R A I R O Automatique/Systems Analysis and Control
0399-0532 R A I R O Informatique/Computer Science
0399-0540 R A I R O Informatique Theorique/Theoretical Informatics
0399-0559 R A I R O Recherche Operationnelle/Operations Research
0399-0575 Revue Bryologique et Lichenologique *see* 0181-1576
0399-0648 Thesindex Medical
0399-0656 Thesindex Dentaire
0399-0834 Tunnels et Ouvrages Souterrains
0399-0842 Journal de Mecanique Appliquee
0399-0966 Planification, Habitat, Information
0399-1121 Amitie Henri Bosco. Cahiers
0399-1148 Revue Pratique de Droit Social
0399-1156 Vie des Collectivites Ouvrieres *changed to* Revue des Comites d'Entreprise
0399-1164 Vie Ouvriere
0399-1245 Analyses de la S.E.D.E.I.S.
0399-1253 Peuples Mediterraneens - Mediterranean Peoples
0399-127X Universite Scientifique et Medicale de Grenoble. Institut des Sciences Nucleaires. Rapport Annuel
0399-1415 Cahiers Leopold Delisle
0399-1571 Bulletin Signaletique. Part 166: G A P H Y O R. Atomes, Molecules, Gaz Neutres et Ionises
0399-1784 Oceanologica Acta
0399-1989 Recherches Germaniques
0399-2322 Bella
0399-5070 Actuels
0399-5569 France. Comite des Travaux Historiques et Scientifiques. Bulletin Philologique (Jusqu'a 1715) *see* 0071-8408
0399-7081 Dico - Plus
0399-7596 Creatis
0399-7715 Caravanier
0399-8223 Nouveau Guide Gault-Millau
0399-8320 Gastro-Enterologie Clinique et Biologique
0399-9726 France. Comite des Travaux Historiques et Scientifiques. Section d'Histoire Moderne et Contemporaine (Depuis 1610). Bulletin *see* 0071-8459
0399-9734 Bulletin du Bibliophile et du Bibliothecaire *see* 0399-9742
0399-9742 Bulletin du Bibliophile
0400-0439 A C E I Newsletter *changed to* A C E I Branch Exchange
0400-048X A C O G Newsletter
0400-132X A. M. I. F
0400-227X Aarbok for den Norske Kirke

1242 ISSN INDEX

0400-4043 Acta Humboldtiana. Series Geographica et Ethnographica
0400-471X Actualities Sociales Hebdomadaires
0400-5104 Adesso†
0400-7719 Agricoltore di Terra di Lavoro
0400-8510 Air Currents
0401-331X Algemeen Werkloosheidsfonds. Jaarverslag
0401-345X Algeria. Service Geologique. Bulletin
0401-3689 Alhambra
0401-3956 Printing Times
0401-5576 Aluminum Light
0401-6351 American Association for Automotive Medicine. Proceedings
0401-636X Aquatics Guide *see* 0361-719X
0402-4621 Annales de Medecine Physique
0402-5563 Anregung
0402-6233 Antoinette
0402-6802 Anwaltsverzeichnis
0402-7493 Arab Horse Society News
0402-852X Archaeologia Japonica
0402-9054 Archivos de Pediatria
0402-9283 Arena
0403-0133 Argentina. Ministerio de Trabajo y Seguridad Social. Boletin de Biblioteca
0403-0699 Arizona. State Land Department. Water Resources Report *see* 0360-7461
0403-1792 Arkansas Highways
0403-3884 Arzt und Christ†
0403-5542 Aspas de la Patata
0403-8894 Atomic Energy Guideletter *changed to* Washington Atomic Energy Report
0403-9114 Chalk River Nuclear Laboratories. Physics Division. Progress Report
0403-9319 Atoms in Japan
0404-3529 Automobil
0404-6811 Balik ve Balikcilik
0404-6919 Ballroom Dancing Year Book
0404-7710 Banco de la Republica. Biblioteca Luis Angel Arango. Boletin Cultural y Bibliografico
0404-8997 Bar North *changed to* North Dakota Stockman
0405-0738 Pflanzenschutz-Kurier
0405-1033 Der Beamten-Bund
0405-1157 Beauty & Barber Dealers World
0405-119X Beauty School World
0405-6485 Betriebs- und Arbeitswirtschaft in der Praxis
0405-6590 Better Homes and Gardens Christmas Ideas
0405-668X Better Nutrition
0405-6701 Betteravier Francais
0405-721X Bibliografia Brasileira de Quimica Tecnologia *see* 0100-0756
0405-9212 Biblioteca Promocion del Pueblo
0406-3597 Plant Protection Bulletin
0406-3678 Bitumes Actualites
0406-5948 Boletin de Londres†
0406-6987 Tata Institute of Fundamental Research. Lectures on Mathematics and Physics. Mathematics *changed to* Tata Institute Lecture Notes
0407-2294 University of British Columbia. Forest Club. Research Note
0407-5439 Buchwissenschaftliche Beitraege†
0407-5501 Bucks County Law Reporter
0407-7202 Building and Allied Trades Official Handbook *changed to* Building and Allied Industries Official Handbook
0407-8985 B D I-Mitteilungen
0407-923X Bunte Illustrierte *changed to* Bunte
0408-0904 Japanese Hospital Directory
0408-2133 Bahrain News
0408-215X Bahrain Trade Directory
0408-3075 Banca y Seguros
0408-3164 Banco Central de Costa Rica. Informacion de Estadistica Mensual *changed to* Banco Central de Costa Rica. Boletin Estadistico Bimestral
0408-3172 Banco Central de Costa Rica. Informacion Economica Semanal
0408-4012 Bancos y Bancarios de Colombia
0408-4284 Bank for International Settlements. Monetary and Economic Department. International Commodity Position. General Survey
0408-4632 Bank Pembangunan Indonesia. Annual Report
0408-568X Bargain Paradises of the World *changed to* Retirement Paradises of the World
0408-6392 Bastions de Geneve
0408-7496 Beauterama
0408-8107 Beitraege zum Buch- und Bibliothekswesen
0408-8344 Beitraege zur Geschichte der Reichskirche in der Neuzeit
0408-8379 Beitraege zur Geschichte der Universitaet Mainz
0408-8514 Beitraege zur Mittelamerikanischen Voelkerkunde
0408-9006 Commission Belge de Bibliographie. Bulletin
0408-9189 Belgium. Ministere de l'Emploi et du Travail. Bibliotheque. Bulletin Bibliographique Mensuel
0408-9235 Belgium. Ministere des Affaires Economiques. Direction Generale des Etudes et de la Documentation. Apercu de l'Evolution Economique
0409-0179 Belgrade. Univerzitet. Elektrotehnicki Fakultet. Publikacije. Serija: Telekomunikacije i Elektronika *changed to* Beogradski Univerzitet. Elektrotehnicki Fakultet. Publikacije. Serija: Elektronika, Telekomunikacije, Automatika
0409-0314 Zavod za Zdravstvenu Zastitu SR Srbije. Glasnik
0409-2163 Bermuda Historical Society. Occasional Publications
0409-2570 Best Jewish Sermons†
0409-2694 Beton-Litteratur Referater
0409-2740 Betontechnische Berichte
0409-2791 Betriebstechnik
0409-3453 Bibliografia Pomorza Zachodniego
0409-3747 Bibliographia Belgica
0409-6568 C. A. F. Bulletin Mensuel
0409-7734 Cactus
0409-8757 Cahiers Medico-Sociaux
0409-9192 Caja de Ahorros y Monte de Piedad de las Baleares. Memoria
0410-2894 California F P
0410-3556 California Teacher
0410-3882 Calvinist Contact
0410-5389 Canada. Statistics Canada. Grain Milling Statistics/Statistiques de Mouture des Grains†
0410-5869 Canada. Statistics Canada. Road and Street Mileage and Expenditure/Voies Publiques: Longueur et Depenses *see* 0706-3105
0410-5877 Canada. Statistics Canada. Sales Financing/Financement des Ventes†
0410-904X Canadian Jewish Congress. Information and Comment, Social and Economic Studies: Fundamental Rights and Freedoms in Canada. Progress Reports†
0411-275X Catholic Truth
0411-5023 Centro de Historia del Tachira. Boletin
0411-5562 Cercle Ernest Renan. Bulletin *see* 0008-0098
0411-8634 Chemia w Szkole
0411-8871 Chemical Spotlight
0412-2658 Chirugia Generale
0412-2968 Christ in Our Home
0412-3131 Christian Librarian
0412-5568 Cineromanzo
0412-6300 Citrus Engineering Conference. Transactions
0412-7994 Clinical Medicine *changed to* Journal of Continuing Education in Rural and Community Medicine
0413-7647 Colorado's Annual Highway Report
0413-8384 Columbia University. Bureau of Applied Social Research. Bureau Reporter†
0413-9593 Comite du Folklore Champenois. Bulletin
0414-1105 Communes d'Europe
0414-2713 Concretezza†
0414-4406 Congress International Medical de Pays de Langue Francaise de l'Hemisphere Americain. Rapports et Communications
0414-7790 Contemporary Philosophy Series
0414-8126 Contractor *changed to* Merit Shop Contractor
0415-1798 Deine Gesundheit
0415-6552 Deutscher Arbeitsamtskalender
0415-7508 B D I Deutschland Liefert
0415-9241 Directory of Blood Transfusion Facilities and Services *see* 0419-2206
0415-9764 Directory of Oil Well Drilling Contractors
0415-9772 Directory of Oil Well Supply Companies
0416-0371 Discussione
0416-7287 Politechnika Gdanska. Zeszyty Naukowe. Budownictwo Okretowe
0416-7295 Politechnika Gdanska. Zeszyty Naukowe. Budownictwo Wodne
0416-7309 Politechnika Gdanska. Zeszyty Naukowe. Chemia
0416-928X Delpinoa
0416-9336 Delta Pi Epsilon. Research Bulletin
0416-9565 Democrazia e Diritto
0417-2051 Deutsche Gesellschaft fuer Musik des Orients. Mitteilungen
0417-3228 Deutscher Sozialversicherungs- Kalender
0417-3635 Deutsches Soldatenjahrbuch
0417-3937 Dharmayug
0417-5522 Directory of American Horticulture
0417-5662 British Commonwealth Collections of Micro-Organisms. Directory of Collections and List of Species Maintained in Australia†
0417-5751 Directory of Conventions
0417-5905 Directory of Geophysical and Oil Companies Who Use Geophysical Service
0417-5964 Directory of Indian Engineering Exporters
0417-6383 Directory of Professional Electrologists
0417-6766 Diritto e Pratica nell'Assicurazione
0417-688X Discipline
0417-9382 Dominica. Ministry of Finance and Development. Annual Overseas Trade Report
0417-9994 Dortmunder Beitraege zur Zeitungsforschung
0418-2057 Dwarf Iris Society Portfolio
0418-2693 Daily Labor Report
0418-3304 Danish Films
0418-3614 Politechnika Gdanska. Zeszyty Naukowe. Elektronika
0418-3746 University of Dar es Salaam. Economic Research Bureau. Papers
0418-3770 Dar es Salaam University Law Journal
0418-3975 Geography Publications at Dartmouth
0418-4297 Daugavas Vanagu Menesraksts
0418-5013 Defense Indicators†
0418-5021 Defense Industry Bulletin *see* 0011-7595
0418-5633 I.A.M.R. Reports
0418-582X University of Delhi. Library. Documentation List: Africa
0418-6303 Denki Kagaku Newsletter *changed to* Electrochemistry and Industrial Physical Chemistry
0418-6443 Denmark. Atomenergikommissionens Forsoegsanslaeg, Risoe. Risoe Report
0418-6559 Groenlands Geologiske Undersoegelse. Rapport
0418-6745 Denmark Review
0418-7598 Desert Bighorn Council. Transactions
0418-761X Desert Locust Control Organization for Eastern Africa. Annual Report
0418-7717 Designed in Finland
0418-7830 Detalle
0418-8381 Das Deutsche Firmen-Alphabet
0418-842X Deutsche Forschungsgemeinschaft. Mexiko-Projekt
0418-8802 Der Deutsche Lehrer im Ausland
0418-9140 Deutsche Studien
0419-005X Deutschsprachige Zeitschriften Deutschland - Oesterreich - Schweiz
0419-0254 Developments in Geotectonics
0419-0432 Hukerikar Memorial Lecture Series
0419-0637 Dialog der Gesellschaft
0419-0890 Dianoia
0419-1137 Dictionary of International Biography
0419-1153 Dictionnaire Vidal
0419-1188 Didaskalos†
0419-1285 Digest of Commercial Laws of the World
0419-1293 Digest of Current Industrial and Labour Law
0419-2052 Directors Guild of America. Directory of Members
0419-2109 Directory of Alcoholism Treatment Facilities, Domiciliary Houses and State and Provincial Alcoholism *see* 0092-3826
0419-2206 Directory of Blood Banking and Transfusion Facilities and Services†
0419-2281 C I B Directory of Building Research Information and Development Organizations
0419-229X Directory of California Services for Juvenile and Adult Offenders *see* 0361-7327
0419-2370 Directory of Collections and List of Species Maintained in Canada†
0419-2400 Directory of Communicators in Agriculture
0419-2443 Directory of Cooperative Organisations in South-East Asia†
0419-2559 Directory of Educational Opportunities in Georgia *changed to* Directory: a Guide to Colleges, Vocational-Technical and Diploma Schools of Nursing
0419-2648 Directory of Fire Research in the United States *changed to* Directory of Fire Research
0419-2818 Directory of Jewish Health and Welfare Agencies
0419-2923 Directory of Mailing List Houses
0419-3040 Directory of Music Faculties in American Colleges and Universities *changed to* Directory of Music Faculties in Colleges & Universities U.S. and Canada
0419-3253 Directory of Physics and Astronomy Faculties in North American Colleges & Universities *see* 0361-2228
0419-3512 Directory of Shopping Centers
0419-3733 Directory of the Cultural Organizations of the Republic of China
0419-3806 Directory of the Turf
0419-3857 Directory of Washington State Manufacturers, Products, Industry, Location *see* 0148-5687
0419-3865 Directory of Water Pollution Research Laboratories
0419-3903 Direktor
0419-3911 Dirigente Municipal
0419-4187 Dispatch
0419-4209 Dissertation Abstracts International. Section A: Humanities and Social Sciences
0419-4241 Dissertationes Archaeologicae Gandenses
0419-4357 Distribution of Physicians, Hospitals, Hospital Beds in the U. S. *changed to* Physician Distribution & Medical Licensure in the U. S.
0419-4632 Dizionario Bibliografico delle Riviste Giuridiche Italiane
0419-537X Documentation sur l'Europe Centrale
0419-5612 Review of International Affairs
0419-5728 Documents pour la Carte de la Vegetation des Alpes *see* 0335-5330
0419-747X Droit de l'Espace†
0419-764X Drug Topics Health & Beauty Aids Directory
0419-7674 Drum (South Africa)

0419-7682 Drum (Nigerian Edition)
0419-7925 Dubrovacki Horizonti
0419-8050 Duke Endowment. Annual Report
0419-8093 Duke University. Council on Aging and Human Development. Proceedings of Seminars
0419-8735 Dwon Lwak
0419-8816 Dzieje Lublina
0419-8824 Dzieje Najnowsze
0419-9081 Diagramm
0419-9154 Directory of Textile Plant Processes†
0419-9472 Danmarks 500 Stoerste Virksomheder *changed to* Danmarks 2000 Stoerste Virksomheder
0420-0098 Design Automation Workshop. Proceedings *changed to* Design Automation Conference.(Proceedings)
0420-011X Designers West Resource Directory
0420-0195 Deutsche Physikalische Gesellschaft. Verhandlungen
0420-0632 Directory of Law Enforcement Professors†
0420-0942 Test Yourself for Science†
0420-1078 Dutch Archaeological and Historical Society. Studies
0420-2384 Dydaktyka Szkoly Wyzszej
0420-2392 Dziko
0420-3690 Eastern Indiana Farmer *changed to* Farmweek
0420-9397 Electric Power Industry in Japan
0421-4935 Est Industriel et Commercial
0421-4986 Estadisticas de la Aviacion Civil en Espana
0421-5370 Estudios Internacionales *changed to* Estudios Politicos
0421-6423 Europe Service
0421-7527 European Congress of Cardiology. Abstracts of Papers
0421-9090 Exile
0421-9724 Extension *see* 0020-4919
0421-9910 Analysis of Public Utility Financing
0422-017X ERB-Dom†
0422-1540 Eastern Industrial World *changed to* Northeastern Industrial World
0422-2482 Echoes from the East Tennessee Historical Society
0422-2504 Echos des Communications
0422-2555 Eco
0422-2628 Eco Motori
0422-2733 Economia Colombiana
0422-2954 Economic Research Institute. Economic Bulletin
0422-4108 I. E. (Chicago)
0422-5740 Edinburgh Tatler
0422-6186 Editur
0422-6690 Educational Council for Foreign Medical Graduates. Annual Report *see* 0145-2037
0422-6739 Educational Quest
0422-8707 Electrical Distributor
0422-9053 Electronic Industry Telephone Directory
0422-9576 Elelmiszervizsgalati Kozlemenyek
0422-9878 Elsevier Lexica†
0422-9932 Elu Local
0423-104X Endokrynologia Polska†
0423-1163 Energiewirtschaft
0423-4243 Espresso
0423-4847 Estudios de Deusto
0423-5037 Estudios Turisticos
0423-5509 Etnoloski Pregled
0423-5673 Etudes Eburneennes
0423-6831 European Coal and Steel Community. Consultative Committee. Yearbook
0423-6955 Commission of the European Communities. Collection du Droit du Travail
0423-7242 European Congress of Cardiology. (Proceedings)
0423-7269 European Cotton Industry Statistics
0423-7781 European Organization for Nuclear Research. Repertoire des Communications Scientifiques. Index of Scientific Publications *see* 0304-2871
0423-7846 European Parliament. Bulletin
0423-8044 European Purchasing Conference. (Proceedings)
0423-8346 Evangelisch-Lutherische Landeskirche Sachsens. Amtsblatt
0423-9938 E E M
0424-0227 E U M E N Action
0424-0928 East African Studies
0424-0944 East Asia Travel Association. Proceedings of the General Meeting
0424-1088 East Midland Archaeological Bulletin
0424-1401 East Pakistan Medical Journal *see* 0301-035X
0424-1851 Eastern Nigerian School Libraries Association. Bulletin *changed to* School Libraries Bulletin
0424-2033 Eau Pure
0424-2068 Ecclesiastical Court Digest
0424-2238 Ecole des Parents
0424-2483 Economia Politica
0424-2769 Economic Education Bulletin
0424-3145 Economie Agricole
0424-3331 Economist Intelligence Unit. E I U World Outlook
0424-3374 Economista Mexicano†
0424-480X Year-End Summary of the Electric Power Situation in the United States
0424-4923 Editor & Publisher International Year Book
0424-5059 Edmund's Used Car Prices
0424-5385 Education Court Digest
0424-5393 Education des Adultes *see* 0018-8891
0424-5407 Education Development Center. Annual Report
0424-5504 Education in the Americas Information Series; Bulletin†
0424-5512 Education in the North
0424-6241 Educators Guide to Free Health, Physical Education & Recreation Materials
0424-7558 Ekonomski Pregled
0424-7701 Electra
0424-7760 Electrical Engineering in Japan
0424-8201 Electron Microscopy Society of America. Proceedings
0424-8287 Electronic Production Aids Catalog *changed to* Electronic Packaging and Production Vendor Selection Issue
0424-8368 Electronics and Communications in Japan
0424-8384 Electronics Hobbyist
0424-8775 Elements de Bibliographie
0424-9283 Empirical Research in Accounting; Selected Studies *changed to* Journal of Accounting Research. Supplement
0424-9402 Commercial Bank of Greece. Report of the Chairman of the Board of Directors
0425-0494 English in Education
0425-0508 English in Africa
0425-0575 English Miscellany
0425-1067 Entomological Society of Nigeria. Bulletin *see* 0331-0094
0425-1466 Ephemerides Mariologicae
0425-1644 Equine Veterinary Journal
0425-1741 Erdkundliches Wissen
0425-2772 Espanol Actual
0425-3442 Estudios Agrarios
0425-3698 Estudios Empresariales
0425-3752 Estudios Lulianos
0425-4082 Estudos Universitarios
0425-4309 Ethiopia. Customs Head Office. External Trade Statistics
0425-4414 Ethiopian Journal of Education
0425-4597 Ethnologia Europaea
0425-4791 Etudes Bernanosiennes
0425-4937 Commission of the European Communities. Collection Physiologie et Psychologie du Travail
0425-497X Conseil Oecumenique des Eglises. Etudes†
0425-5054 Etudes et Sports Sous-Marins
0425-5089 F A O Nutrition Meeting for Europe. Report.†
0425-5291 F I S Bulletin
0425-5860 Fact Finder *changed to* C O A D Words
0425-7111 Far East Film News *see* 0047-8288
0425-7170 Far East Reporter *changed to* Far East Traveler
0425-9076 Federation des Industries Chimiques de Belgique. Annuaire
0426-3383 Fizyka w Szkole
0426-8261 Footprints
0426-844X For Men Only†
0426-9373 Forestal
0426-9918 Forschungsgesellschaft fuer das Strassenwesen. Arbeitsgruppe Asphalt- und Teerstrassen. Schriftenreihe
0427-0576 Foto
0427-7554 Fundacao Getulio Vargas. Boletim Informativo *changed to* Fundacao Getulio Vargas. Informativo
0427-8070 F A O Regional Conference for Asia and the Far East. Report
0427-8089 F A O Regional Conference for the Near East. Report
0427-8186 F B W-Information
0427-8321 F I F A Official Bulletin *changed to* F I F A News
0427-8879 Facts
0427-8968 Yugoslav Facts and Views
0427-9107 Faerg och Fernissa
0427-959X Family Fare
0427-9638 Family Law Newsletter *see* 0163-710X
0427-9824 Fantasmagie
0428-061X Fauna Japonica
0428-1039 Federacion Sudamericana de Asociaciones Cristianas de Jovenes. Noticias *changed to* Confederacion Latinoamericana de Asociaciones Cristianas de Jovenes. Carta
0428-1128 Federal Economic Review *changed to* Journal of Economic Studies
0428-1365 Federal Savings and Loan Insurance Corporation. List of Member Institutions
0428-1659 Federation Internationale de Gymnastique. Bulletin
0428-1845 Federation of Kenya Employers. Newsletter
0428-2779 Feuillets de Biologie
0428-304X Field Studies
0428-3341 Filatelia
0428-4666 Fire Control Notes
0428-4836 First Days
0428-4879 Citibank. Foreign Information Service. Annual Summary of Exchange and Foreign Trade Regulations†
0428-5018 Fischwirt
0428-5387 Museum of Northern Arizona Glen Canyon Series†
0428-5395 Museum of Northern Arizona Technical Series
0428-6766 Florida State University. Publications of the Faculty.
0428-7738 Fluid Power Handbook & Directory
0428-8211 Folger Shakespeare Library Annual Report
0428-8254 Folia Antropologica
0428-903X Fontes Iuris Gentium
0428-9374 Food and Agriculture Organization of the United Nations. Forestry Occasional Paper†
0428-9390 Food and Agriculture Organization of the United Nations. Index of Agricultural Institutions in Europe†
0428-9447 Nutrition Newsletter *see* 0304-8942
0428-9552 Food and Agriculture Organization of the United Nations. Animal Health Branch. Animal Health Monograph†
0428-9625 F A O Papers on Demand Analysis†
0428-9749 Food and Agriculture Organization of the United Nations. Plant Protection Committee for Southeast Asia and Pacific Region. Quarterly Newsletter
0428-9765 Food and Agriculture Organization of the United Nations. Plant Protection Committee for Southeast Asia and Pacific Region. Technical Document
0429-0208 Footwear News Fact Book
0429-0550 Forefront: News from New Zealand
0429-0917 Forest Products News
0429-1573 Forschungen zur Innsbrucker Universitaetsgeschichte
0429-1816 Forschungsgesellschaft fuer das Strassenwesen. Arbeitsgruppe Betonstrassen. Schriftenreihe
0429-2405 P I D C Journal *changed to* Civil Aviation in Pakistan: Half-Yearly Newsletter
0429-288X Fragmenta Entomologica
0429-3843 France. Direction du Gaz et de l'Electricite. Statistiques Officielles de l'Industrie Gaziere en France *changed to* Statistiques de l'Industrie Gaziere en France
0429-4092 B.O.P.I. Statistiques
0429-5412 France-Horizon
0429-7539 Frodskaparrit; Annales Societatis Scientiarum Faeronsis. Supplementa
0429-7725 Frontiers in Physics
0429-8284 Fuji Electric Review
0429-8918 Fundamenty
0429-9329 F A O Fisheries Circulars
0429-9337 F A O Fisheries Reports
0429-9345 F A O Fisheries Technical Paper
0429-9353 F A O Regional Conference for Africa
0429-9388 F A O/W H O Expert Panel on Veterinary Education. Report of the Meeting†
0429-9442 F D A Clinical Experience Abstracts
0429-9574 Faba
0429-9639 Fabulous Mexico
0429-9655 Fachbibliographischer Dienst Bibliothekswesen
0430-0610 Far East Scouting Bulletin *changed to* Asia-Pacific Scouting
0430-0661 Far Western Philosophy of Education Society. Proceedings *see* 0094-1050
0430-0750 Farm Chemicals Handbook
0430-084X Farm Management Notes for Asia and the Far East
0430-1188 Faulkner Facts and Fiddlings
0430-1536 Federacion Latinoamericana de Bancos. Revista *changed to* Revista FELABAN
0430-1919 Federal Reserve Bank of Chicago. Seventh District Statistics†
0430-1943 Federal Reserve Bank Reviews†
0430-2222 Congress F A T I P E C
0430-2419 Federation Internationale des Syndicats Chretiens d'Ouvriers Agricoles. Travailleur de la Terre†
0430-2583 Federation of Insurance Counsel. Quarterly
0430-2990 Femina
0430-327X Fertiliser Association of India. Fertiliser Statistics
0430-4055 Fikr-o-Nazar
0430-4497 Filmoteca Ultramarina Portuguesa. Boletim
0430-4578 Il Filo Metallico
0430-4748 Financial Aid News
0430-5205 Finland. Kansanelakelaitos. Julkaisuja. Sarja A
0430-5272 Finland. Tilastokeskus. Liikennetilastollinen Vuosikirja
0430-5280 Finland. Tyoviomaministerio. Tyovoimakatsaus
0430-5299 Finland. Laakintohallitus. Laakarit, Hammaslaakarit, Sairaalat *changed to* Finland. Laakintohallitus. Laakarit, Hammaslaakarit/Lakare, Tandlaekare
0430-5329 Finland. Board of Agriculture. Statistical Office. Monthly Review of Agricultural Statistics
0430-5566 Finland. Tilastokeskus. Kuntien Finanssitilasto
0430-5604 Finland. Tilastokeskus. Talonrakennustilasto
0430-5612 Finland. Tilastokeskus. Vaestonmuutokset *changed to* Finland. Tilastokeskus. Vaesto
0430-6090 Fishermen's Digest
0430-6155 Fitopatologia
0430-635X Museum of Northern Arizona Ceramic Series

1244 ISSN INDEX

0430-6457 Fleet Street Patent Law Reports *changed to* Fleet Street Reports
0430-666X Flore de la Nouvelle Caledonie et Dependances
0430-7291 Florida State University. Slavic Papers *changed to* Florida State University. Center for Yugoslav-American Studies, Research, and Exchanges. Proceedings and Reports of Seminars and Research
0430-7313 Florida State University. Educational Media Center. Educational Motion Pictures *changed to* Florida State University. Instructional Support Center. Film
0430-7658 Florida Economic Indicators
0430-7690 Florida F L Reporter
0430-7801 Florida Public Documents
0430-8247 Focus (Waterloo)
0430-8603 Folia Entomologica Mexicana
0430-862X Folia Linguistica
0430-8778 Folk Life
0430-9928 Galloway Journal
0431-1930 GeoChile
0431-1981 Geografia nelle Scuole
0431-8315 Ghana. Meteorological Department. Monthly Summary of Rainfall
0431-8323 Ghana. Meteorological Department. Monthly Weather Report
0431-8943 Gioventu al Lavoro
0431-915X Glades Star
0432-2924 R E M E Journal
0432-6105 Greece
0432-7454 Grundlagen und Fortschritte der Lebensmitteluntersuchung *see* 0341-0498
0432-9120 Guida Nazionale del Commercio Con l'Estero
0433-0730 Gaceta Bibliotecaria del Peru
0433-0854 Gaceta Indigenista
0433-0919 Garden Life
0433-230X Gdanskie Towarzystwo Naukowe. Wydzial I. Nauk Spolecznych i Humanistycznych. Seria Monografii
0433-3179 Genealogical Forum of Portland, Oregon. Quarterly Bulletin
0433-3519 General Fisheries Council for the Mediterranean. Studies and Reviews
0433-4035 Nuclear Engineering
0433-4515 Geographical Outlook *see* 0046-5712
0433-5473 Georgia. Geological Survey. Information Circular
0433-6054 Georgia Operator
0433-6305 German Business Weekly
0433-6844 Statistiches Taschenbuch der DDR
0433-6933 Zentralinstitut fuer Bibliothekswesen. Mitteilungen und Materialien
0433-762X Germany (Federal Republic, 1949-) Deutscher Bundestag. Wissenschaftliche Dienste. Bibliographien
0433-860X Gesellschaft fuer Bibliothekswesen und Dokumentation des Landbaues. Mitteilungen
0433-969X Ghana Year Book
0434-0035 Giessener Schriftenreiche Tierzucht und Haustiergenetik
0434-040X Giurisprudenza Agraria Italiana
0434-0760 Politechnika Slaska. Zeszyty Naukowe. Automatyka
0434-0779 Politechnika Slaska. Zeszyty Naukowe. Budownictwo
0434-0817 Politechnika Slaska. Zeszyty Naukowe. Mechanika
0434-1066 Glyndebourne Festival Programme Book
0434-2151 Gospodarka i Administracja Terenowa *changed to* Rada Narodowa, Gospodarka, Administracja
0434-3336 Le Grand Baton
0434-3581 Grands Naturalistes Francais
0434-5975 Greater Minneapolis
0434-8850 Guide to Employment Abroad
0434-9245 Guild of Book Workers Journal
0435-1096 Gamma Field Symposia
0435-1312 Gas Turbine International *see* 0149-4147
0435-1339 Gastroenterologia Japonica
0435-1568 Gdanski Rocznik Kulturalny *changed to* Rocznik Kulturalny Ziemi Gdanskiej
0435-1754 Gekkan Shakaito
0435-1835 Geldgeschichtliche Nachrichten
0435-1924 Geltende Seekriegsrecht in Einzeldarstellungen *changed to* Das Geltende Seevoelkerrecht in Einzeldarstellungen
0435-219X Gendai no Me
0435-2866 Studies on Voltaire and the Eighteenth Century
0435-2874 I I L S Bulletin *changed to* Labour and Society
0435-2939 Observatoire de Geneve. Publications. Serie B
0435-3048 Universita degli Studi di Genova. Facolta di Giurisprudenza. Annali
0435-3676 Geografiska Annaler. Series A. Physical Geography
0435-3684 Geografiska Annaler. Series B. Human Geography
0435-3730 Geographia Medica
0435-382X Aardrijkskunde/Geographie *changed to* Ardrijkskunde
0435-3951 Special Issues
0435-401X Geological Society of Jamaica Journal
0435-4311 Geonews
0435-5113 University of Georgia. Geography Curriculum Project Publications
0435-5253 Georgia Advocate
0435-5261 Georgia Alert
0435-5385 Georgia Genealogical Magazine
0435-5482 Georgia Manufacturing Directory
0435-7183 Bundesinstitut fuer Ostwissenschaftliche und Internationale Studien. Berichte
0435-7329 Germany (Federal Republic, 1949-) Bundesministerium fuer das Post-und Fernmeldewesen. Jahresrechnung, Nachweisung ueber die Einnahmen und Ausgaben der Deutschen Bundespost
0435-7442 Gesamtstatistik der Kraftfahrtversicherung
0435-7590 Germany (Federal Republic, 1949-) Deutscher Bundestag. Wissenschaftliche Dienste. Materialien
0435-7965 Deutscher Wetterdienst. Monatlicher Witterungsbericht
0435-852X Gesundheitstechnik *changed to* Umweltschutz Gesundheitstechnik
0435-8805 External Trade Statistics of Ghana
0435-8864 Ghana. Central Bureau of Statistics. Quarterly Digest of Statistics
0435-9348 Ghana Commercial Bank. Annual Report
0435-9380 Ghana Journal of Sociology
0435-9437 Ghana Radio and Television Times *changed to* G B C Radio and T V Times
0435-950X Rijksuniversiteit te Gent. Centrum voor Onkruidonderzoek. Mededeling
0436-0257 Giving U.S.A. Bulletin
0436-0265 Gizi Indonesia
0436-029X Gladius
0436-0605 Glenbow Foundation. Archives Series *changed to* Glenbow Museum. Archives Series
0436-0664 Globusfreund
0436-1121 Goeteborg Studies in Educational Sciences
0436-113X Goeteborgs Kungliga Vetenskaps- och Vitterhets-Samhaellet
0436-1202 Universitaet Goettingen. Jahresbericht
0436-1326 Gokhale Institute Mimeograph Series
0436-1474 Golf Course Superintendents Association of America. Membership Directory
0436-1571 Good Tidings
0436-2616 Gradina
0437-133X Heating and Ventilating Research Association. Technical Notes *see* 0309-0248
0437-5602 Hispania Antiqua Epigraphica
0437-8768 Horizon
0438-1629 Human Factors Society Bulletin
0438-2013 Hungarian Travel Magazine
0438-2242 Budapest Statisztikai Zsebkonyve
0438-4555 Protokolle zur Fischereitechnik
0438-5004 Handakten fuer die Standesamtliche Arbeit
0438-5403 Handel Wewnetrzny
0438-8887 Heating and Ventilating Research Association. Laboratory Reports *changed to* B S R I A Application Guides. Technical Notes
0438-895X Hebrew Abstracts *see* 0146-4094
0439-1292 Highway
0439-1365 Comparative Law Journal
0439-1705 Hirosaki University. Faculty of Literature and Science. Science Reports *see* 0367-6439
0439-2116 Historia Junior
0439-2183 Historian Aitta
0439-237X Historical Society of Michigan. Newsletter
0439-2795 Hitachi Zosen News
0439-3465 Hokkaido University. Research Institute of Applied Electricity. Monograph Series
0439-3511 Hokkaido University. Faculty of Fisheries. Data Record of Oceanographic Observations and Exploratory Fishing
0439-3678 Holiday Time in Thailand
0439-4208 Homiletica
0439-4291 Homo Faber
0439-5794 Horseshit: the Offensive Review
0439-6162 Hospitalisation Privee
0439-6383 House and Garden Remodeling Guide *see* 0161-200X
0439-9080 Hungarian P.E.N
0439-9714 Husserliana
0440-0607 Haematologie und Bluttransfusion
0440-1352 Hallmark†
0440-1875 Handboek van de Nederlandse Pers en Publiciteit
0440-193X Handbook on International Study: for Foreign Nationals *changed to* Handbook on U.S. Study for Foreign Nationals
0440-1948 Handbook on International Study for U.S. Nationals. Vol. 2: Study in the American Republics Area
0440-2103 Handbuch des Oeffentlichen Lebens in Oesterreich
0440-2278 Handjuawg
0440-2316 Hanging Loose
0440-2863 Hans-Pfitzner-Gesellschaft. Mitteilungen
0440-3428 Harvard Germanic Studies†
0440-3452 Harvard Monographs in Applied Science
0440-3509 Harvard Studies in World Religions
0440-4122 Haskins & Sells. Selected Papers
0440-4947 Directory of State, County , and Federal Officials
0440-5145 Hawaiian Journal of History
0440-5323 Haydn-Studien
0440-5730 Heartbeat†
0440-5749 Heat Transfer - Soviet Research
0440-5757 Heather Society. Yearbook
0440-601X Universitaet Heidelberg. Suedasien-Institut. Schriftenreihe
0440-6087 Heilige in Bild und Legende
0440-6230 Heimatgruss
0440-6826 Hemijski Pregled
0440-7881 Higher Education in New England
0440-8152 Hillside Hospital Journal *changed to* Hillside Journal of Clinical Psychiatry
0440-9213 Historical Archaeology
0440-9221 Historical Arms Series
0440-9264 Historical Association of Tanzania. Papers
0440-9426 Chronicle (Ann Arbor)
0440-9515 Historicke Studie
0440-9558 Historische Forschungen
0440-9736 Historisches Jahrbuch der Stadt Linz
0440-9884 History of Economic Thought Newsletter
0441-067X Hokkaido University. Faculty of Science. Journal. Series 7: Geophysics
0441-0734 Japan. Government Industrial Development Laboratory, Hokkaido. Reports
0441-1196 Almanakh Gomonu Ukrainy
0441-1900 University of Hong Kong. Centre of Asian Studies. Bibliographies and Research Guides
0441-2044 Honolulu
0441-2516 Radioactivity Survey Data in Japan
0441-2613 Hospital and Nursing Yearbook of Southern Africa
0441-2745 Hospital Medicine
0441-3016 House and Garden Building Guide *see* 0161-200X
0441-389X Hudson's Washington News Media Contacts Directory
0441-4004 University of Hull. Department of Geography. Miscellaneous Series in Geography
0441-4128 Human Relations
0441-4144 Humanidad
0441-4446 Hungarian Musical Guide
0441-4675 Hungary. Kozponti Statisztikai Hivatal. Mezogazdasagi Adatok
0441-4683 Hungary. Kozponti Statisztikai Hivatal. Mezogazdasagi Statisztikai Zsebkonyu
0441-5302 Hydronymia Germaniae
0441-537X Hyogo-ken Gan Senta Nenpo *changed to* Hyogo Cancer Hospital. Bulletin
0441-5833 Hi Fi Aarbogen
0441-5973 Hungarian Music News
0441-6058 Hacettepe Bulletin of Social Sciences and Humanities†
0441-6619 Heraldry in Canada
0441-6813 Hofmannsthal-Blaetter
0441-6910 Huguenot Trails
0441-7445 Home Study
0441-7461 Horticultural Research International
0441-7895 Honolulu's Annual Area Manpower Review *changed to* Hawaii. Department of Labor and Industrial Relations. Sub-Area Review
0441-7933 Health and Physical Education Bulletin for Teachers in Secondary Schools *changed to* Physical Education and Health
0441-8026 Historica Carpatica
0441-9057 International Recreation Association. Bulletin *changed to* World Leisure & Recreation Association Journal
0442-3054 Illustrierter Motorsport
0442-736X Indian Silk and Rayon
0442-8102 Indiana Rural News
0443-2460 Insel-Almanach
0443-3173 Institut Geographique du Zaire. Rapport Annuel
0443-8604 International Congress of Allergology. Abstracts of Reports of Discussion and of Communications
0444-0978 Periodic Bulletin of the International Office of Cocoa and Chocolate and the International Sugar Confectionary Manufacturers' Association
0444-4566 Iowa Documents
0444-4736 Iowa School Board Bulletin *see* 0021-0668
0444-6801 Israel. Meteorological Service. Series C (Miscellaneous Papers)
0445-0485 I C E A News
0445-0698 I F C A T I Directory *changed to* I T M F Directory
0445-1821 Ich Schreibe
0445-2216 Ideas and Action Bulletin
0445-2429 Medical Libraries
0445-2577 Kleine Ikonenbuecherei
0445-3387 Illinois. State Museum. Handbook of Collections
0445-3395 Illinois. State Museum. Scientific Papers Series
0445-4529 Imagen y Sonida *changed to* Eikonos
0445-5150 Incontri Con la Pubblicita†
0445-6289 Trade Unions in India
0445-6653 Press in India
0445-6831 India. Parliament. Public Accounts Committee. Report on the Accounts
0445-7706 Indian Journal of Occupational Therapy
0445-7854 Indian Machine Tools Journal

0445-7897 Indian Minerals Year Book
0445-801X Indian Press
0445-8192 Indian Tobacco *changed to* Tobacco News
0445-8206 Town and Country Planning Association Quarterly Journal
0446-0243 Industria dei Farmaci
0446-1266 Industries of Japan
0446-2378 Ingenieria
0446-2424 Ingenieria Sanitaria
0446-2491 Ingenioeren Indkoebsbog
0446-3161 Installation Specialist *changed to* Installation & Cleaning Specialist
0446-4648 Geological Society of Egypt. Annual Meeting. Abstracts of Papers
0446-5059 Japan. Meteorological Agency. Seismological Bulletin
0446-5458 Japan. Ministry of Agriculture and Forestry. Annual Report
0446-6217 Japan Hotel Guide
0446-6667 Japan's Bicycle Guide
0446-7310 Jersey at Home
0446-7965 Jezyki Obce w Szkole
0446-9577 Joseph Haas Gesellschaft. Mitteilungensblatt
0447-2276 J L C News
0447-2462 Jacksonville Seafarer
0447-2500 Jagriti
0447-2624 Jahrbuch der Wittheit zu Bremen
0447-2713 Jahrbuch fuer die Gefluegelwirtschaft
0447-3086 Jamaica. Department of Statistics. Quarterly Abstract of Statistics
0447-3280 Jamaica Annual
0447-3728 Japan. Maritime Safety Agency. Hydrographic Department. Notices to Mariners
0447-3892 Japan. Meteorological Agency. Volcanological Bulletin
0447-5240 Japan Agricultural Coop News
0447-5321 Japan Cotton Statistics and Related Data
0447-6441 Jemna Mechanika a Optika
0447-8053 Information Processing Society of Japan. Journal
0447-8452 Joint Meeting of the Members of the Consultative Assembly of the Council of Europe and of the Members of the European Parliamentary Assembly. Official Report of Debates
0447-8819 Jornal do Exercito
0447-9181 Transportation Telephone Tickler
0447-9645 Journalismus†
0447-9823 Association Internationale pour l'Histoire du Verre. Bulletin
0448-021X News-Jugoslavija Film
0448-1143 Jadavpur Journal of Comparative Literature
0448-150X Jahrbuch fuer den Kreis Pinneberg
0448-1690 Rajasthan University Studies in English
0448-1712 University of Rajasthan. Studies in Sanskrit and Hindi
0448-2174 Jamaica Library Association. Annual Bulletin *changed to* Jamaica Library Association. Bulletin
0448-2433 Jammu and Kashmir. Legislative Council. Committee on Privileges. Report
0448-3294 Annual Statistics of Maritime Safety
0448-3758 Japan. Meteorological Agency. Annual Report
0448-6072 Finance
0448-858X Japan Chemical Review
0448-8709 Japan Science Review: Economic Sciences
0448-8938 Japanese Railway Engineering
0448-8954 Japanese Religions
0448-9241 Jazykovedne Studie
0449-0193 Local Government Review
0449-0495 Job/Scope
0449-0576 Jokull
0449-0738 Johari za Kiswahili
0449-122X Joint F A O/W H O Codex Alimentarius Commission. Report of the Session
0449-1343 J I L A Information Center. Report
0449-1483 Jordan. Department of Statistics. External Trade Statistics and Shipping Activities in Aqaba Port
0449-1491 Jordan Economy in Figures
0449-1513 Jordan. Department of Statistics. National Accounts
0449-1602 Jordan Lectures in Comparative Religion
0449-1971 Journal des Agreges
0449-2099 Journal Mondial de Pharmacie†
0449-2145 Journal of African and Asian Studies
0449-2153 Journal of Alabama Archaeology
0449-2285 Egyptian Journal of Chemistry
0449-2560 Journal of Geosciences
0449-2722 Journal of Long Island History
0449-2986 Journal of Polymer Science. Part B Polymer Letters *see* 0360-6384
0449-2994 Journal of Polymer Science. Part C: Polymer Symposia *see* 0360-8905
0449-3060 Japan Radiation Research Society. Journal
0449-3109 Journal of Schizophrenia *see* 0317-0209
0449-3168 Journal of Social Sciences
0449-3362 Journalism Scholarship Guide *changed to* Journalism Career and Scholarship Guide
0449-3540 Judaisme Sephardi†
0449-3648 Jugoslavenska Akademija Znanosti i Umjetnosti. Historijski Institut, Dubrovnik. Anali.
0449-4156 Japan Society of Lubrication Engineers. Journal
0449-4342 Juristische Abhandlungen
0449-4555 Juventud Tecnica
0449-4636 Japan Economic Review
0449-4733 Journal de l'Annee
0449-4741 Journal of Contemporary Revolutions†
0449-4830 Japan Atomic Energy Commission. Annual Report
0449-4881 Jerusalem Historical Medical Publications
0449-5225 Jahrbuch der Wirtschaft Osteuropas
0449-5314 Japan. Bureau of Statistics. News Bulletin
0449-5705 Journal of Bioenergetics *changed to* Journal of Bioenergetics and Biomembranes
0449-5721 Journal of Plant and Machinery
0449-7554 Kansai University Economic Review
0449-7953 Kansas. State Department of Public Instruction. Bulletin *changed to* Kansas. State Department of Education. Bulletin
0449-8429 Kansas Law Review
0450-0261 Kemps Harrow and District Local Directory†
0450-6235 Kochpraxis und Gemeinschaftsverpflegung
0450-7169 Kommunalwirtschaft
0451-0887 Kunsterziehung
0451-1646 K-Mitteilungen
0451-1980 National Research Institute of Police Science. Report
0451-2030 Chemical Factory
0451-243X K V Convertible Fact Finder Service
0451-3991 Kansas City Genealogist
0451-4041 Kansas Farmer-Stockman
0451-5978 Management Science (Keiei- Kagaku) *changed to* Operations Research
0451-6001 Light Metal Statistics in Japan
0451-6109 National Research Laboratory of Metrology. Bulletin
0451-6222 Economic Theory
0451-7059 Kentucky Economic Outlook *changed to* Kentucky Council of Economic Advisors. Quarterly Report
0451-9396 Mechanical Engineering
0451-9930 Kirkia
0452-2834 Engineering Materials
0452-3687 Norway. Komite for Romforskning. N.S.R.C. Report *changed to* Space Activity in Norway
0452-5914 Korean Stamps
0452-621X Kosmos Bibliothek
0452-7208 Kristofer Lehmkuhl Forelesning
0452-7739 Die Kueste
0452-9650 Annual Report of Educational Psychology in Japan
0452-9995 Kyoto University. Research Institute for Food Science. Memoirs
0453-0047 Kyoto Technical University. Faculty of Industrial Arts. Memoirs: Science and Technology
0453-0314 Kyushu University. Contributions from the Department of Fisheries and the Fishery Research Laboratory
0453-0349 Kyushu Institute of Technology. Bulletin: Humanities, Social Sciences
0453-0357 Kyushu Institute of Technology. Bulletin: Science and Technology
0453-0535 Japan. National Institute of Animal Health. Annual Report
0453-0667 National Research Institute of Police Science. Annual Report
0453-0675 National Research Institute of Police Science. Data
0453-0691 Japan Association for Philosophy of Science. Annals
0453-0853 Kagoshima University. Faculty of Agriculture. Memoirs
0453-1515 Yearbook of Pulp and Paper Statistics
0453-1981 Kanazawa University. Faculty of Law and Literature. Studies and Essays
0453-2198 Kansai University Technology Reports
0453-2384 Kansas. State Soil Conservation Committee. Soil Conservation in Kansas *see* 0094-1670
0453-2406 Library School Review
0453-2805 Kansas Sportsman
0453-3283 Karlsruher Juristische Bibliographie
0453-3429 Karthago
0453-4387 Keats-Shelley Journal
0453-4484 Keidanren Geppo
0453-4557 Keio Business Review
0453-4778 Economic Journal
0453-4867 Kellogg World *changed to* Kelloggram
0453-512X Kennedy Quarterly
0453-5723 Kentucky Genealogist
0453-5944 Kenya. Dairy Board. Annual Report
0453-6002 Kenya Statistical Digest
0453-6525 Kenya, Uganda, Tanzania, Zambia, Malawi and Ethiopia Directory; Trade and Commercial Index *changed to* Kenya, Uganda, Tanzania, East African Community Directory; Trade Commerce Index
0453-7440 Kerala; an Economic Review
0453-767X Kernkraft Zentrale, Gundremmingen. Jahresberichte
0453-8129 Sudan Research Information Bulletin
0453-9222 National Research Institute for Metals. Transactions
0453-9249 Kiplinger California Letter
0453-9478 Kiruna Geophysical Data
0454-1111 Kobe University Economic Review
0454-1723 Kokugakuin University. Faculty of Law and Politics. Journal
0454-191X Foreign Aero-Space Literature
0454-1944 Japan. National Diet Library. Monthly List of Foreign Scientific and Technical Publications
0454-2029 National Institute for Leprosy Research. Annual Report
0454-2150 Asian Cultural Studies
0454-255X Kommunale Dienstleistungen
0454-3343 Konstitutsiya i Svoista Mineralov
0454-3491 Konyvtari es Dokumentacios Szakirodalom
0454-4196 Korean Trade Unions
0454-448X Kosmosophie
0454-5265 Kriminalwissenschaftliche Abhandlungen
0454-5508 Krugozor
0454-6059 Kultuurpatronen
0454-7543 Korea (Republic) Economic Planning Board. Annual Report on the Economically Active Population
0454-7659 Kyoto University. Abuyama Seismological Observatory. Seismological Bulletin
0454-7675 Kyoto University. Disaster Prevention Research Institute. Bulletin
0454-7802 Kyoto University. Faculty of Science. Memoirs. Series of Biology
0454-7810 Kyoto University. Faculty of Science. Memoirs. Series of Geology and Mineralogy
0454-7845 Kyoto University. Research Institute for Mathematical Sciences. Publications: Series A *see* 0034-5318
0454-7985 Kyoto University African Studies†
0454-8132 Kyushu American Literature Studies
0454-8221 Kyushu Institute of Technology. Bulletin: Mathematics, Natural Science
0454-949X Kenya Newsletter
0455-0374 Kernenergie Forschungsschiff "Otto Hahn". Jahresbericht†
0455-0463 Knjizevna Smotra
0455-2342 Landarbeit und Technik
0456-3867 Canadian Hardware, Electrical & Building Supply Directory
0456-4804 Ramsay Society of Chemical Engineers. Journal
0456-7463 Louisiana English Journal
0456-9814 Laboratorio
0457-0715 Landeskundliche Luftbildauswertung im Mitteleuropaeischen Raum
0457-1673 Universidad Nacional de la Plata. Instituto de la Produccion. Serie Contribuciones
0457-4184 Lejeunia
0457-7019 County Newsletter†
0457-7817 South Staffordshire Archaeological and Historical Society. Transactions
0457-9976 Liste des Societes Savantes et Litteraires
0458-063X Liturgy
0458-1520 Muzeum Archeologiczne i Etnograficzne, Lodz. Prace i Materialy. Seria Archeologiczna
0458-1547 Politechnika Lodzka. Zeszyty Naukowe. Zeszyt Specjalny
0458-1555 Politechnika Lodzka. Zeszyty Naukowe. Chemia
0458-1563 Politechnika Lodzka. Zeszyty Naukowe. Mechanika
0458-1822 Lok Magazin
0458-2314 Memorial Hospital of Long Beach. Quarterly Bulletin *changed to* Memorial Mercury
0458-4201 Lower Cape Fear Historical Society. Bulletin
0458-4317 Annales Universitatis Mariae Curie-Sklodowska. Sectio G. Ius
0458-497X Lutheran Digest
0458-5143 Lutte de Classe
0458-5674 L P V- Listos para Vencer
0458-5747 Labo - Pharma Problemes et Techniques
0458-5860 France. Laboratories des Ponts et Chaussees. Bulletin de Liaison
0458-5860 Laboratoires des Ponts et Chaussees. Bulletin de Liaison
0458-5933 Laboratory Animal Handbooks
0458-595X Laboratory Guide to Instruments, Equipment and Chemicals
0458-6026 Labour Law Cases†
0458-6123 Ladenbau
0458-6506 Lalit Kala
0458-6972 Landmark
0458-7014 Landscape Research News *changed to* Landscape Research
0458-7367 Language Research in Progress†
0458-7766 Instituto del Mar del Peru. Boletin
0458-7774 Instituto del Mar del Peru. Informe.
0458-7871 Laser and Unconventional Optics Journal
0458-8592 Law in Society
0458-8711 Law Society of Scotland. Journal
0458-8983 Leads: a Fact Sheet
0458-9564 Legal Bulletin
0458-9599 Legal Legislative Reports. News Bulletin
0458-9971 Leidse Germanistische en Anglistische Reeks
0458-998X Leidse Historische Reeks
0458-9998 Leidse Juridische Reeks
0459-0007 Leidse Wijsgerige Reeks

0459-004X Deutsche Buecherei. Jahrbuch
0459-0805 Leningradskii Universitet. Uchenye Zapiski. Seriya Geologicheskikh Nauk
0459-0953 Lens and Speaker
0459-1356 Letras Nacionales
0459-2182 Liberia. Ministry of Planning and Economic Affairs. Annual Report to the Session of the Legislature of the Republic of Liberia
0459-2298 Liberian Naturalist *changed to* U. L. Science Magazine
0459-2476 Y L G News†
0459-3030 Libyca
0459-3650 American Council of Life Insurance. Economic and Investment Report
0459-3774 Life Sciences
0459-3871 Ligue Internationale Contre la Concurrence Deloyale. Annuaire
0459-388X Ligue Internationale Contre la Concurrence Deloyale. Communication
0459-4487 Lincolnshire History and Archaeology
0459-4541 Lines Review
0459-4835 Lipunan Journal
0459-4851 Repertorio das Publicacoes Periodicas Portuguesas†
0459-5009 List of Current Periodical Publications in Ethiopia†
0459-5084 Liszt Society, London. Newsletter *see* 0141-0792
0459-6137 Living Bird
0459-6730 Lock Haven Review†
0459-682X Politechnika Lodzka. Zeszyty Naukowe. Elektryka
0459-6854 Societe des Sciences et des Lettres de Lodz. Bulletin
0459-7222 Military Balance
0459-7230 Strategic Survey
0459-7354 University of London Classical Studies
0459-7400 Bartlett Society. Transactions
0459-8474 Louisiana. Geological Survey. Water Resources Bulletin
0459-889X Louisiana Cancer Reporter
0459-8962 Louisiana Folklore Miscellany
0459-925X Lovejoy's Prep School Guide
0459-9586 Annales Universitatis Mariae Curie-Sklodowska. Sectio H. Oeconomia
0460-007X Lute Society Journal
0460-024X Lutheran Church in America. Western Canada Synod. Minutes of the Annual Convention
0460-1297 Little Lamp
0460-1327 Locator
0460-1408 Land Resource Bibliography
0460-1424 Denmark. Landoekonomiske Driftsbureau. Meddelelse *see* 0106-2689
0460-2048 Leidse Kunsthistorische Reeks
0460-2099 Lesotho. Ministry of Foreign Affairs. Diplomatic and Consular List
0460-2374 Luftverunreinigung
0460-2390 M & B Pharmaceutical Bulletin
0460-3060 Macao. Servico Meterologico. Resultados das Observacoes Meteorologicas de Macau
0460-3400 McGraw-Hill Series in Missile and Space Technology
0460-6736 Maine Geological Survey. Mineral Resources Index Series†
0460-8518 Malaysian Veterinary Journal
0461-0040 Manual of Excellent Management†
0461-2531 Masinstvo
0461-5298 Denmark. Rigsbibliotekaren. Meddelelser
0461-6529 Medizinstudent *see* 0344-5933
0461-7398 Men and Women of Hawaii
0462-1069 Mexico News
0462-3134 Advocacy Institute. Proceedings
0462-4874 Military Digest
0463-1935 Monographien zur Rheinisch-Westfaelischen Kunst der Gegenwart
0463-6457 Motor Club News
0463-6635 Motor Vehicle Statistics of Japan
0464-1973 M P S A Newsletter
0464-3755 Escuela Diplomatica. Cuadernos
0464-5030 Maharaja Sayajirao University of Baroda. Department of History Series
0464-5820 Maine Historical Society. Newsletter *see* 0163-1152
0464-591X Mainly Marketing
0464-7734 Male†
0464-7777 Der Maler und Lackierermeister
0464-8072 Mammillaria Journal
0464-882X Manual Azucarero Mexicano
0464-9567 March of the Nation†
0464-9605 Marche Financier de Paris
0464-9974 Market Bulletin
0465-0166 Marktforscher *changed to* Marktforschung
0465-1499 Commerce Digest†
0465-2592 Maszyny i Ciagniki Rolnicze
0465-2886 Materials Selector
0465-3750 Mathematik in der Schule
0465-4773 Universidad de Medellin. Facultad de Ciencias Administrativas. Revista
0465-5818 Revue de Politique Internationale
0465-7004 N R A News
0466-1478 Official National Collegiate Athletic Association Baseball Guide *changed to* N C A A Baseball Annual Guide
0466-1761 N.C.A.I. News Bulletin *see* 0047-8784
0466-3276 National Institute of Sciences of India. Mathematical Tables *changed to* Indian National Science Academy. Mathematical Tables
0466-499X Safety Newsletter: Occupational Health Nursing Section
0466-5007 Safety Newsletter: Public Utilities Section
0466-6046 Nature in Cambridgeshire
0466-6054 Nature in Wales
0466-7530 Netherlands Federation of Trade Unions. Information Bulletin *changed to* F N V News
0467-1872 New Caducean
0468-1835 Nielsen Newscast
0468-5067 Groundwater Bulletin
0468-6853 Northeastern Tour Book *changed to* Tourbook: Connecticut, Massachusetts, Rhode Island
0468-6853 Northeastern Tour Book *changed to* Tourbook: Maine, New Hampshire, Vermont
0469-0281 Nova Trgovina
0469-2071 Nukada Institute for Medical and Biological Research. Reports
0469-2454 Nuova Rivista Pedagogica
0469-323X N A S B I C News
0469-337X N B S Publications Newsletter
0469-4007 N U S A S Newsletter *changed to* Dissent
0469-4236 Nachrichten aus dem Karten- und Vermessungswesen. Reihe 1: Originalbeitraege
0469-4759 Nagoya University. Research Institute of Environmental Medicine. Annual Report
0469-4783 Nagoya Port Statistics Annual
0469-8029 National Automotive Directory
0469-9130 National Council for Geographic Education. Do It This Way
0470-0384 National Forest Products Association. Fingertip Facts & Figures
0470-0929 National Geographer
0470-1380 National Institute of Sciences of India. N I S I Monographs *changed to* Indian National Science Academy. Monographs
0470-2824 Safety Newsletter: Aerospace Section
0470-2832 Safety Newsletter: Air Transport Section
0470-2840 Safety Newsletter: Public Employee Section
0470-3219 National Stripper Well Survey
0470-3901 Naturkundliches Jahrbuch der Stadt Linz
0470-5017 Proceedings of the Section of Mathematics, Natural Science and Medicine *changed to* Shevchenko Scientific Society. Proceedings of the Section of Mathematics and Physics
0470-5017 Proceedings of the Section of Mathematics, Natural Sciences and Medicine *changed to* Shevchenko Scientific Society. Proceedings of the Section of Chemistry, Biology and Medicine
0470-5661 Nebraska Optometric Association. Journal
0470-6021 Nederlandse Chemische Industrie†
0470-6641 Netherlands. Centraal Bureau voor de Statistiek. Conjunctuurtest
0470-6684 Netherlands. Centraal Bureau voor de Statistiek. Maandstatistiek van de Industrie
0470-8105 Neurologia Medico-Chirurgica
0471-0320 Odziez
0471-1424 Office Equipment Exporter
0471-380X Oil & Gas Directory
0471-3850 Oil Directory of Alaska
0471-3877 Oil Directory of Houston, Texas
0471-492X Oklahoma Employment Security Review
0471-7376 Orafo Italiano
0471-7708 Ordine dei Medici. Bollettino
0471-8356 Oregon. State Board of Accountancy. Roster of Accountants Authorized to Conduct Municipal Audits *see* 0090-6735
0471-9174 Oregon Cattleman
0471-9336 Oregon Psychological Association. Newsletter.
0472-0490 Orient
0472-0784 Orientamenti Pastorali
0472-0989 Orissa, India. Finance Department. White Paper on Departmental Activities, Government of Orissa *changed to* Orissa, India. Finance Department. White Paper on the Economic Conditions and the Developmental Activities in Orissa
0472-2191 Oswiata Doroslych
0472-2744 Ouranos
0472-3325 Oxford Library of the Physical Sciences
0472-397X Ob-Gyn Collected Letters
0472-5263 Oeil
0472-5859 Oesterreichisches Forschungsinstitut fuer Sparkassenwesen. Schriftenreihe
0472-6685 Ohio. Division of Geological Survey. Educational Leaflet
0472-6979 Ohio State University. Institute of Polar Studies. Contribution Series
0472-7584 Oil and Australia
0472-7711 Oil Directory of Companies Outside the U.S. and Canada
0472-8637 Olam Hadash
0472-8807 Oleo-Semenal
0472-8874 Oljyposti
0472-948X Ondas
0472-9986 Ontario. Labour Relations Board. Decisions *changed to* Ontario. Labour Relations Board. Reports. A Monthly Series of Decisions
0473-0062 Ontario Cancer Treatment and Research Foundation. Clinical Conference. Proceedings†
0473-0658 Instituto de Botanica "Dr. Goncalo Sampaio". Publicacoes. 3 Serie
0473-0917 Optique†
0473-1174 Orafo Italiano nel Mundo
0473-3657 Organization of African Unity. Health, Sanitation and Nutrition Commission. Proceedings and Report
0473-4548 Osaka Daigaku Keizaigaku (Vol. 24) *changed to* Osaka Daigaku Keizaigaku-Osaka Economic Papers
0473-4580 Osaka University. Laboratory of Nuclear Studies. Report
0473-4637 University of Osaka Prefecture. Bulletin. Series D: Sciences of Economy, Commerce and Law
0473-5277 Frankfurter Abhandlungen zur Slavistik
0473-6788 Organization for Economic Cooperation and Development. Reviews of Manpower and Social Policies
0473-7490 Occasional Papers in Political Science†
0473-7733 Ochrona przed Korozja
0473-8322 Das Oesterreichische Papier
0473-8624 Oesterreichisches Volksliedwerk. Jahrbuch
0473-8837 Studies on Current Health Problems
0473-9787 O C W R U Quarterly Report
0474-0114 Oil Directory of Canada
0474-0157 Oita University Economic Review
0474-0696 Oklahoma Anthropological Society. Memoir
0474-070X Oklahoma Economic Indicators
0474-0750 Oklahoma Ornithological Society. Bulletin
0474-1382 On View†
0474-1560 Ontario. Ministry of Agriculture and Food. Seasonal Fruit and Vegetable Report
0474-2125 O L A Newsletter *see* 0318-0247
0474-2389 Open Places
0474-2893 Opolskie Roczniki Ekonomiczne
0474-3253 Oral History Association. Newsletter
0474-3326 Orbit (New York)
0474-3369 Orcrist
0474-4039 Public Welfare in Oregon *changed to* Adult and Family Services in Oregon
0474-4535 Oregon Historical Society. News
0474-4616 Oregon Recreation Briefs
0474-4829 Organisation of European Aluminum Smelters. Economic Situation of the Aluminum Smelters in Europe *changed to* Aluminum Smelters
0474-5086 Organization for Economic Cooperation and Development. Catalogue of Publications
0474-5124 Organization for Economic Cooperation and Development. Economic Surveys: Austria
0474-5132 Organization for Economic Cooperation and Development. Economic Surveys: Belgium-Luxembourg Economic Union
0474-5140 Organization for Economic Cooperation and Development. Economic Surveys: Canada
0474-5159 Organization for Economic Cooperation and Development. Economic Surveys: Denmark
0474-5167 Organization for Economic Cooperation and Development. Economic Surveys: France
0474-5175 Organization for Economic Cooperation and Development. Economic Surveys: Germany
0474-5183 Organization for Economic Cooperation and Development. Economic Surveys: Greece
0474-5191 Organization for Economic Cooperation and Development. Economic Surveys: Iceland
0474-5205 Organization for Economic Cooperation and Development. Economic Surveys: Ireland
0474-5213 Organization for Economic Cooperation and Development. Economic Surveys: Italy
0474-5221 Organization for Economic Cooperation and Development. Economic Surveys: Japan
0474-523X Organization for Economic Cooperation and Development. Economic Surveys: Netherlands.
0474-5248 Organization for Economic Cooperation and Development. Economic Surveys: Norway
0474-5256 Organization for Economic Cooperation and Development. Economic Surveys: Portugal
0474-5264 Organization for Economic Cooperation and Development. Economic Surveys: Socialist Federal Republic of Yugoslavia
0474-5272 Organization for Economic Cooperation and Development. Economic Surveys: Spain
0474-5280 Organization for Economic Cooperation and Development. Economic Surveys: Sweden

0474-5299 Organization for Economic Cooperation and Development. Economic Surveys. Switzerland
0474-5302 Organization for Economic Cooperation and Development. Economic Surveys: Turkey
0474-5310 Organization for Economic Cooperation and Development. Economic Surveys: United Kingdom
0474-5329 Organization for Economic Cooperation and Development. Economic Surveys: United States
0474-5337 Organization for Economic Cooperation and Development. Employment of Special Groups
0474-5353 Organization for Economic Cooperation and Development. Survey of Electric Power Equipment. Enquete sur l'Equipment Electrique
0474-537X Food Consumption in the O. E. C. D. Countries
0474-5434 Geographical Distribution of Financial Flows to Less Developed Countries. (Disbursements)
0474-5442 Organization for Economic Cooperation and Development. Historical Statistics. Statistiques Retrospectives
0474-5450 Organization for Economic Cooperation and Development. Industrial Production. Production Industrielle
0474-5469 Organization for Economic Cooperation and Development. Industrial Statistics. Statistiques Industrielles
0474-5477 Organization for Economic Cooperation and Development. Electricity Supply Industry. l'Industrie de l'Electricite
0474-5485 Pulp and Paper Industry in the O E C D Member Countries and Finland
0474-5493 Organization for Economic Cooperation and Development. Cement Industry. Industrie du Ciment
0474-5515 Organization for Economic Cooperation and Development. Labour Force Statistics (Yearbook) /Statistiques de la Population Active
0474-5523 Organization for Economic Cooperation and Development. Main Economic Indicators/Principaux Indicateurs Economiques
0474-5574 O E C D Economic Outlook
0474-5620 Organization for Economic Cooperation and Development. Wages and Labour Mobility Supplement†
0474-5655 Organization for Economic Cooperation and Development. Council. Code de la Liberation des Mouvements de Capitaux. Code of Liberalisation of Capital Movements
0474-5663 Organization for Economic Cooperation and Development. Development Assistance Committee. Report by the Chairman on the Annual Review
0474-585X Hides, Skins and Footwear Industry in O E C D Countries.†
0474-5868 Organization for Economic Cooperation and Development. Library. Special Annotated Bibliography; Automation. Bibliographie Speciale Analytique
0474-5884 Organization for Economic Cooperation and Development. Maritime Transport Committee. Maritime Transport
0474-5892 Organization for Economic Cooperation and Development. Social Affairs Division. Developing Job Opportunities
0474-5922 Organization for Economic Cooperation and Development. Social Affairs Division. Employment of Special Groups
0474-5973 Organization for Economic Cooperation and Development. Special Committee for Iron and Steel. Iron and Steel Industry
0474-6007 Organization for Economic Cooperation and Development. Special Committee for Oil. Oil Statistics. Supply and Disposal
0474-6023 Textile Industry in O E C D Countries
0474-6171 Organization of African Unity. Scientific Technical and Research Commission. Publication
0474-6317 Organization of the Petroleum Exporting Countries. Annual Review and Record
0474-635X Organizzarsi
0474-6376 Organo
0474-781X Osaka University. College of General Education. Science Reports
0474-7844 University of Osaka Prefecture. Bulletin. Series A: Engineering and Natural Sciences
0474-7852 University of Osaka Prefecture. Bulletin. Series B: Agriculture and Biology
0474-8042 Norsk Polarinstitutt. Polarhaandbok
0474-8603 Otago Museum. Records. Anthropology
0474-8611 Otago Museum. Records. Zoology
0474-9030 Our Heritage
0475-0071 Okayama University. School of Engineering. Memoirs
0475-0608 Organization of the Petroleum Exporting Countries. Annual Statistical Bulletin
0475-0926 Oklahoma. Attorney General's Office. Opinions of the Attorney General
0475-1310 Offshore Contractors and Equipment Directory
0475-1388 Old Athlone Society Journal
0475-1582 Organophosphorus Chemistry
0475-1671 Oyez
0475-171X Oceans
0475-1876 Old Car Value Guide
0475-1906 Optimum
0475-2015 Organizational Directory of the Government of Thailand
0475-2058 Osaka Dental University. Journal
0475-2112 Owner Operator
0475-9141 Patre
0476-0069 Pediatria Internazionale
0476-1103 Pennsylvania Statistical Abstract
0476-1960 P C T E Newsletter
0476-3475 Die Personalvertretung
0476-5532 Philippine Government Rulings
0476-9465 Plana
0477-244X Politica dei Trasporti
0477-6801 Ports and Dredging & Oil Report *changed to* Ports and Dredging
0477-7166 Boletim Actinometrico
0477-8685 Pozemni Stavby
0478-1376 Presenza
0478-1392 Preservation Progress
0478-1546 Presse
0478-1805 Previdenza Sociale nell'Agricoltura
0478-4049 Asbestos Producer
0478-4251 Products Finishing Directory
0478-6378 Proyeccion
0478-6726 Przemysl Drzewny
0479-0790 Pacific Hotel Directory & Travel Guide
0479-1290 Padova
0479-2327 Pakistan Cotton Bulletin *see* 0030-9699
0479-3013 Pan
0479-4346 Panorama Economico
0479-8244 Pembrokeshire Historian
0479-8775 Pennsylvania. Department of Public Welfare. Public Welfare Report *see* 0098-8510
0480-0257 Performing Arts Magazine (San Francisco Edition)
0480-0516 Permanent International Association of Navigation Congresses. Bulletin
0480-2160 Petroleum Intelligence Weekly
0480-2780 Philadelphia Association for Psychoanalysis. Bulletin *see* 0094-1476
0480-2853 Philanthropic Digest
0480-3981 Series of Philippine Scientific Bibliographies†
0480-8207 Quotidiano Minerva Medica
0481-0023 Quellen zur Geschichte des Islamischen Aegyptens
0481-0112 Quelques Donnees Statistiques sur l'Industrie Francaise des Pates, Papiers, Cartons *changed to* Statistiques de l'Industrie Francaise des Pates. Papiers et Cartons
0481-1275 Quantum Physics and Its Applications
0481-2085 Quarterly Journal of Engineering Geology
0481-2158 Quarterly Medical Review
0481-2786 Quebec (Province) Department of Tourism, Fish and Game. Annual Report
0481-2875 Quebec (Province). Liquor Board. Rapport Annuel *changed to* Societe des Alcools du Quebec. Rapport Annuel
0481-3375 Queensland. Registrar of Co-Operative and Other Societies. Report
0481-4118 Quimica e Derivados†
0481-5084 R F D News
0481-5475 Rachunkowosc
0481-6684 Revista de Chirurgie, Oncologie, O.R.L., Radiologie, Oftalmologie, Stomatologie. Radiologie
0481-6722 Radionic Quarterly
0481-6781 Radiotecnica TV
0481-9306 Recht der Jugend *see* 0034-1312
0481-9403 Rechtspraak Sociale Verzekering
0482-1319 Day's Register of Registrars
0482-2803 Report on Credit Unions
0482-5020 Revista Cailor Ferate Romane†
0482-5209 Revista de Administracion Publica
0482-5276 Revista de Ciencias Sociales
0482-5527 Revista de Educacao e Cultura
0482-5772 Revista de Ingenieria
0482-6558 Revista Iberica
0482-6876 Revista Mexicana de Seguridad Social
0482-8062 Revue du Travail
0483-2027 Robotnik
0483-3686 Rose Annual
0483-7738 R P A Bulletin *changed to* R P A News
0483-9218 Rajshahi University Studies
0483-9722 Rassegna di Diritto e Tecnica Doganale e delle Imposte di Fabbricazione
0484-0305 Readaptation
0484-0828 Recent Researches in the Music of the Baroque Era
0484-1506 Recording for the Blind. Catalog of Recorded Books
0484-2235 Referativnyi Zhurnal. Fotokinotekhnika
0484-2286 Referativnyi Zhurnal. Kommunal'noe, Bytovoe i Torgovoe Oborudovanie
0484-2472 Referativnyi Zhurnal. Stroitel'nye i Dorozhnye Mashiny
0484-2502 Referativnyi Zhurnal. Teploenergetika
0484-2537 Referativnyi Zhurnal. Vodnyi Transport
0484-2561 Referativnyi Zhurnal. Vozdushnyi Transport
0484-2596 Referativnyi Zhurnal. Zheleznodorozhnyi Transport
0484-2650 Reflection (Spokane)
0484-6796 Revista de Ciencias Economicas; Economia, Financas, Administracao, Estatistica *changed to* Ciencias Economicas
0484-6885 Revista de Derecho Financiero y de Hacienda Publica
0484-6923 Revista de Derecho Social Ecuatoriano
0484-8578 Revue de Mycologie *see* 0181-1584
0484-8594 Revue de Podologie
0484-8764 Revue Francaise de Comptabilite
0484-8934 Revue Metapsychique
0484-8942 Revue Numismatique
0484-9035 Reynard
0485-2044 Rio Grande Valley Horticultural Society. Journal
0485-2400 Rivista di Istochimica Normale e Patologica *changed to* Basic and Applied Histochemistry
0485-2435 Rivista Giuridica dell' Edilizia
0485-2877 Rocket News
0485-3091 Rocznik Pilski *see* 0557-2088
0485-3504 Rodzina i Szkola
0485-3695 Rolls-Royce Owners' Club, Directory and Register
0485-5140 Roundup *changed to* New Roundup
0485-5175 Roving Commissions
0485-7828 University of the Ryukyus. College of Agriculture. Science Bulletin
0485-8182 R I S S; National Magazine for Residents, Interns, and Senior Students *see* 0018-5795
0485-8255 Regional Science Research Institute, Philadelphia. Discussion Paper Series
0485-9561 Rajasthan Medical Journal
0485-9790 Rand Corporation. Index of Selected Publications *see* 0037-1343
0485-9960 Random Lengths Yearbook
0486-0306 Rassegna Geriatrica
0486-0349 Rassegna Italiana di Sociologia
0486-0373 Rassegna Parlamentare
0486-0748 Reactive Intermediates in Organic Chemistry
0486-0845 University of Reading. Department of Agricultural Economics. Miscellaneous Studies
0486-1019 Realidade†
0486-1019 Realidade
0486-106X Realites Gabonaises
0486-123X Recent Researches in the Music of the Renaissance
0486-1345 Recherches Internationales a la Lumiere du Marxisme
0486-1426 Recherches Voltaiques
0486-1493 Recht und Geschichte
0486-1558 Rechtswissenschaft und Sozialpolitik
0486-2236 Referativnyi Zhurnal. Astronomiya
0486-2252 Referativnyi Zhurnal. Avtomobil'nye Dorogi
0486-2260 Referativny Zhurnal. Biologicheskaya Khimiya *see* 0034-2300
0486-2279 Referativnyi Zhurnal. Dvigateli Vnutrennego Sgoraniya
0486-2287 Referativnyi Zhurnal. Elektronika i ee Primenenie
0486-2295 Referativnyi Zhurnal. Elektrosvyaz'
0486-2309 Referativnyi Zhurnal. Geologiya
0486-2325 Referativnyi Zhurnal. Khimia
0486-2333 Referativnyi Zhurnal. Kibernetika
0486-235X Referativnyi Zhurnal. Informatika
0486-2384 Referativnyi Zhurnal. Rastenievodstvo (Biologicheskie Osnovy)
0486-252X Reformed Journal
0486-2902 Regional Science Association. Papers
0486-3720 Renaissance and Modern Studies
0486-3739 Renaissance Drama
0486-3887 Renewal of Town and Village†
0486-4271 Repertorium Plantarum Succulentarum
0486-4514 Diplomatic Corps and Consular and Other Representatives in Canada. Corps Diplomatique et Representants Consulaires et Autres au Canada
0486-4700 Res Publica
0486-4867 Research Corporation Quarterly Bulletin
0486-5111 Research Progress in Organic, Biological and Medicinal Chemistry†
0486-5383 Reserve Bank of Malawi. Report and Accounts
0486-5588 Responsa Meridiana
0486-6134 Review of Radical Political Economics
0486-6460 Revista Camoniana
0486-8323 Safe Driver
0487-1596 I C A P Lista de Nuevas Adquisiciones
0487-3750 Guida Sardegna d'Oggi
0487-4013 Saskatchewan. Geodata Statistics and Research Branch. Weekly Drilling and Land Report *see* 0707-9788
0487-6830 School Sister of Notre Dame
0488-2644 Sempex Pharmaceutique
0488-3721 Servex
0488-6720 Shipmate
0488-7115 Show Business Who's Where *see* 0508-6795
0488-728X Free Albanian
0489-1376 Literarny Almanach Slovaka V Amerike†
0489-2089 Norsk Etnologisk Gransking. Smaaskrifter
0489-2992 Netherlands. Sociale Verzekeringsraad. Verslag van de Stand der Ziekengeldverzekering
0489-5606 Engineering Know-How in Engine Design
0489-5967 Socijalizam

0490-0200 Southern Illinois Labor Tribune
0490-1274 Soviet Export
0490-1606 Soziale Arbeit
0490-3323 Spain. Ministerio de la Vivienda . Boletin Oficial
0490-334X Spain. Ministerio de Obras Publicas. Boletin de Informacion *changed to* Obras Publicas
0490-4176 Spex Speaken
0490-5113 Sport Universitario
0490-5326 Sports Afield Gun Annual
0490-6381 Sri Lanka
0490-6659 Srpska Akademija Nauka i Umetnosti. Odeljenje Likovne i Muzicke Umetnosti. Muzicka Izdanja
0490-8287 State Agencies Cooperating with the U.S. Department of Agriculture Forest Service in Administration of Various Forestry Programs
0491-0869 Stockholm Studies in History of Literature
0491-0877 Stockholm Studies in Philosophy
0491-1520 Street and Smith's Baseball Yearbook *see* 0161-2018
0491-2705 Studia Ethnographica Upsaliensia
0491-3310 Studies in Public Opinion†
0491-3418 Studii de Muzicologie†
0491-4481 Sudan Medical Journal
0491-6204 Surmach
0491-6441 Svarochnoe Proizvodstvo
0492-004X Transportarbetaren
0492-0716 T V Star Annual
0492-1712 Taiwan Sugar
0492-3901 Taylor Talk
0492-4134 Teachers of the World
0492-4851 Technik Wlokienniczy
0492-5408 Teen Talk
0492-6471 Temas Sociales
0492-6749 Tempo Medico
0492-746X Tennessee Magazine
0493-3656 Today's Art
0493-4091 Tokyo College of Economics. Journal/ Tokyo Keidai Gakkai-Shi *changed to* Tokyo Keizai University. Journal
0493-4253 University of Electro-Communications. Report
0493-4334 University of Tokyo. Faculty of Science. Misaki Marine Biological Station. Contributions
0493-5284 Torch: U.S.
0493-5306 Torino Motori
0493-8348 Trelleborgs Nyheter
0493-9042 Tribune
0494-2884 Turkey Today
0494-5336 Taiwan Exports
0494-612X Taminga
0494-6944 Tap Roots
0494-8203 Source References for Facts and Figures on Government Finance
0494-9501 Tecnica e Metodologia Economale
0494-9870 Tehran Economist
0495-0127 TELE (English Edition)
0495-0615 Temas Economicos
0495-0658 Temi Romana
0495-145X Industrial Development in the T.V.A. Area
0495-257X Texas Vital Statistics
0495-2634 University of Texas, Austin. Bureau of Business Research. Publications
0495-2944 Texas Archeological Society. Special Publication
0495-369X Textile World Buyer's Guide/Fact File
0495-5773 Tierras de Leon
0495-6753 Tobacco Trade Barometer
0495-7725 Maison Franco-Japonaise. Bulletin
0495-7814 University of Tokyo. Institute for Nuclear Study. INS-J
0495-7822 University of Tokyo. Institute for Nuclear Study. Report
0495-8012 Journal of Humanities and Natural Sciences
0495-8020 Tokyo Institute of Technology. Bulletin
0495-8055 Tokyo Institute of Technology. Research Laboratory of Resources Utilization. Report
0495-8667 Toomey J Gazette *see* 0361-4166
0496-1021 Transportes
0496-1102 Transvaal Museum. Bulletin
0496-1803 Tri-City Genealogical Society. Bulletin
0496-3547 Tsuda Review
0496-4845 Turista
0496-7046 Taiwan Financial Statistics Monthly *changed to* Financial Statistics Monthly, Taiwan District, Republic of China
0496-8018 Universite de Madagascar. Centre d'Etudes des Coutumes. Cahiers†
0496-8018 Universite de Madagascar. Centre d'Etudes des Coutumes. Cahiers *changed to* Cahiers d'Histoire Juridique et Politique
0496-8026 Tane
0496-8360 C A F R A D News
0496-8492 Appropriation Accounts, Revenue Statements, Accounts of the Funds and Other Public Accounts of Tanzania
0496-8859 Taraxacum
0496-8913 Tar Heel Junior Historian
0496-9472 Tata Institute of Fundemental Research. Lectures on Mathematics and Physics. Physics *changed to* Tata Institute Lecture Notes
0496-974X Tax Foundation's Research Bibliography
0496-9944 Teacher's Arts & Crafts Workshop†
0497-0489 Technical Translation Bulletin
0497-1000 University of Teheran. Central Library. Library Bulletin
0497-1035 Tehnika Podmazivanja i Primjena Goriva *changed to* Goriva i Maziva
0497-1388 Telecommunications
0497-1507 Television Digest
0497-2384 Tennessee Studies in Literature
0498-2002 U.S. Agricultural Marketing Service. Dairy Division. Federal Milk Order Market Statistics
0498-7845 U.S. Bureau of Mines. Mineral Industry Surveys
0498-8442 Current Construction Reports: Housing Starts
0498-8450 Current Housing Reports: Housing Characteristics
0498-8469 Current Housing Reports: Housing Vacancies
0498-8477 Current Industrial Reports
0498-8485 Current Population Reports: Special Studies
0499-0994 U.S. Department of Commerce. Library. United States Department of Commerce Publications. Supplement *see* 0091-9039
0499-9320 National Aeronautics and Space Administration. Technical Memorandums
0500-5922 Universitas Belgica. Communication/ Mededeling *changed to* Universitas Belgica
0500-7720 Utah Vital Statistics Annual Report
0501-0659 Ulkopolitiikka
0501-1213 International Conference of Building Officials. Uniform Housing Code
0501-1590 Union of European Football Associations. Bulletin
0501-3615 Race Question in Modern Science
0501-4697 U S D A-D H I A Cow Performance Index List†
0501-7041 U.S. Bureau of Labor Statistics. National Survey of Professional, Administrative, Technical and Clerical Pay
0501-7467 U.S. Bureau of Reclamation. Engineering and Research Center. Research Reports *changed to* U.S. Water and Power Resources Service. Engineering and Research Center. Research Reports
0501-7718 Current Governments Reports, GT Quarterly Summary of State and Local Tax Revenue
0501-8390 U.S. Center for Disease Control. Malaria Surveillance Report
0501-9117 U.S. Department of Agriculture. Economics, Statistics, and Cooperatives Service. Agricultural Finance Outlook
0501-915X U.S. Department of Agriculture. Economics, Statistics, and Cooperatives Service. Rice Situation
0501-9257 U.S. Department of Agriculture. Economics, Statistics, and Cooperatives Service. Agricultural Situation in the Western Hemisphere
0502-3238 World Marketing
0502-4994 U.S. Forest Service. Research Note RM
0502-5001 U.S. Forest Service. Research Paper RM
0502-5842 United States-Italy Trade Directory
0502-6660 Latinamericanist†
0502-9554 Unesco Source Books on Curricula and Methods
0502-9767 U S Oil Week
0503-1036 Komitet' Ukrainstsiv Kanady. Biuleten'
0503-1966 Uniform Commercial Code Law Letter
0503-1982 Uniformed Services Almanac
0503-2032 Unima France *changed to* U N I M A-France Marionettes
0503-2334 Union Mondiale des Organisations Syndicales sur Bases Economique et Sociale Liberales. Conferences: Rapport
0503-2407 Collection of Documents for the Study of International Non-Governmental Relations
0503-2628 Unit Trust Yearbook
0503-3551 United Methodist Church. General Minutes of the Annual Conferences
0503-356X United Methodist Directory
0503-3772 Half-Yearly Bulletin of Electric Energy Statistics for Europe
0503-3934 United Nations. Regional Centre for Demographic Training and Research in Latin America. Serie A
0503-3942 United Nations. Regional Centre for Demographic Training and Research in Latin America. Serie C
0503-3950 United Nations. Regional Centre for Demographic Training and Research in Latin America. Serie D
0503-4299 Unesco Technical Papers in Marine Science
0503-440X Selected List of Catalogues for Short Films and Filmstrips
0503-4434 Unesco. Regional Office for Science and Technology for Africa
0503-4442 Unesco. Regional Centre for the Training of Educational Planners, Administrators and Supervisors in Asia. Publication†
0503-4450 Unesco. Regional Office for Education in Asia.Bulletin. *changed to* Unesco. Regional Office for Education in Asia and Oceana. Bulletin
0503-4469 Unesco Regional Office for Education in Asia. Regional Conference Reports *changed to* Population Education in Asia Newsletter
0503-5422 Appalachian Regional Commission. Annual Report
0504-0523 Veselye Kartinki
0504-0779 Veterans' Voices
0504-426X Virginia English Bulletin
0504-6556 Voix des Jeunes
0505-0146 Vanidades Continental
0505-0448 Vector
0505-3838 Vesitalous
0505-4753 Vidya
0505-5164 Naturhistorisches Museum in Wien. Veroeffentlichungen. Neue Folge
0505-7523 Vishva Jyoti
0506-306X V D G S A News
0506-3590 Yearbook of Population Research in Finland
0506-3876 Finnish State Railways
0506-3973 Vancouver Historical Journal†
0506-4155 Varia *changed to* Varia Beladiri
0506-4252 Varstvo Narave
0506-4406 Veckans Affaerer
0506-4414 Vector Genetics Information Service†
0506-6913 Verde Olivo
0506-7286 Verfassung und Recht in Uebersee
0506-7294 Vergilius
0506-7472 Vermont Labor Force
0506-7847 Vertebratologicke Zpravy
0506-7936 Verzeichnis der Orientalischen Handschriften in Deutschland
0506-7944 Verzeichnis der Orientalischen Handschriften in Deutschland. Supplementbaende
0506-8339 Vi i Norden
0506-872X Vida Escolar
0506-9122 Materialien zur Sozial- und Wirtschaftspolitik
0507-0252 Viola da Gamba Society of America Journal
0507-102X Virginia State Publications in Print
0507-1259 Virginia Polytechnic Institute and State University. Department of Geological Sciences. Geological Guidebooks.
0507-1410 Vishveshvaranand Indological Journal
0507-1690 Vita Evangelica
0507-2298 Voice of P S E A
0507-3952 Voprosy Teatra
0507-4150 Vorgaenge
0507-570X Universidad Central de Venezuela. Instituto de Ciencias Penales y Criminologicas. Anuario.
0507-6714 Verein Deutscher Zementwerke. Forschungsinstitut der Zementindustrie. Taetigkeitsbericht
0507-6773 Vertebrate Pest Conference. Proceedings
0507-6986 Vajra Bodhi Sea
0507-7184 Vida Pastoral
0507-7206 Wirtschaftsuniversitaet Wien. Dissertationen
0508-0924 Washington Report on Legislation for Children and What You Can do About It *changed to* Washington Report on Federal Legislation for Children
0508-0959 Washington Spectator *see* 0145-160X
0508-1254 Wasserrecht und Wasserwirtschaft
0508-2757 Welt der Arbeit
0508-6205 Wettbewerb in Recht und Praxis
0508-6795 Who's Where
0508-7104 Wiadomosci Tytoniowe
0508-8445 Wir vom Konsum
0508-850X Guide to Broadcasting
0509-5166 W. C. J. Meredith Memorial Lectures
0509-5190 W E M A Directory *changed to* American Electronics Association Directory
0509-5832 Waksman Foundation of Japan. Report
0509-6057 Walter E. Edge Lectures†
0509-6529 Centralny Osrodek Badan i Rozwoju Techniki Drogowej. Prace *changed to* Instytut Badawczy Drog i Mostow. Prace
0509-7053 Przemyslowy Instytut Elektroniki. Prace
0509-7134 Szkolna Glowna Gospodarstwa Wiejskiego. Zeszyty Naukowe. Zootechnika *changed to* Akademia Rolnicza, Warsaw. Zeszyty Naukowe. Zootechnika
0509-769X Environmental Radiation Surveillance in Washington State; Annual Report
0509-7703 Washington (State). Department of Institutions. Jail Inspection Report *see* 0091-7265
0509-7967 Washington State Traffic Accident Facts
0509-8262 Manufacturers and Distributors Directory of the Washington, D.C. Area
0509-9498 Weekly Crusader *changed to* Christian Crusade
0510-1492 West Virginia Geological Survey. Educational Series *changed to* West Virginia Geologic Education Series
0510-243X Western Material Handling/Packaging/ Shipping
0510-3746 Belaruski Instytut Navuki Mactatstva. Zapisy
0510-4130 Who's Who in the Egg and Poultry Industries
0510-4262 Wiadomosci Melioracyjne i Lekarskie
0510-4270 Wiadomosci Naftowe†
0510-4882 William Nelson Cromwell Foundation. Legal Studies†

0510-5315 Die Wirbelsaeule in Forschung und Praxis
0510-5528 Bilanz
0510-5609 Wirtschaftszahl
0510-6966 Wissenschaft und Fortschritt
0510-7350 Women's Comfort
0510-7385 Women's Household
0510-8055 World Branches Conference of the English Speaking Unions. Principal Addresses and Summary of the Proceedings†
0510-8225 World Congress in Public Park Administration. Reports *changed to* Congress in Park and Recreation Administration. Reports
0510-8233 World Congress in Public Park Administration. Programme *changed to* Congress in Park and Recreation Administration. Programme
0510-8292 World Congress of the Deaf. Proceedings.
0510-8837 World Health Organization. Regional Office for Africa. Report of the Regional Director
0510-8845 World Health Organization. Regional Office for the Western Pacific. Report on the Regional Seminar on the Role of the Hospital in the Public Health Programme
0510-9175 World O R T Union. Congress Report
0510-9477 World Veterinary Association. News Items
0510-9744 Wspotczesnosc *changed to* Literatura
0510-9833 Wuerzburger Geographische Arbeiten
0510-9868 Wychowanie Fizyczne i Higiena Szkolna
0510-9884 Wychowanie Techniczne w Szkole
0511-0653 Waelzlagertechnik
0511-0688 Instituut voor Cultuurtechniek en Waterhuishouding. Jaarverslag
0511-0726 A A G Bijdragen
0511-084X Wakayama Medical Reports
0511-1145 Warehouse Distributor News
0511-1927 Waseda University. Casting Research Laboratory. Report
0511-196X Waseda Political Studies
0511-2141 Washington (State) Department of Fisheries. Information Booklet†
0511-2400 Washington Economic Indicators†
0511-2834 University of Washington. College of Business Administration. Occasional Paper†
0511-3040 University Resources in the United States for Linguistics and the Teaching of English as a Foreign Language *changed to* Guide to Programs in Linguistics
0511-3172 Washington Financial Reports
0511-3180 Washington Highway News *changed to* Transpo News
0511-3202 Washington Library Letter
0511-3520 Wasser-Kalender
0511-3555 Water & Pollution Control Directory *see* 0318-0468
0511-392X Selected List of Biomedical Serials in Metropolitan Detroit *changed to* Union List of Selected Serials of Michigan
0511-4063 Wedgwood Society of London. Proceedings
0511-411X Weed Control Manual and Herbicide Guide
0511-4144 Weed Society of America. Abstracts *changed to* Weed Science Society of America. Abstracts
0511-4187 U.S. Office of the Federal Register. Weekly Compilation of Presidential Documents
0511-4365 Welding Data Book
0511-4934 Wesleyan Poetry Program
0511-5493 West Bengal. Bureau of Applied Economics and Statistics. Statistical Handbook
0511-568X West-European Symposia on Clinical Chemistry†
0511-6147 West Pakistan Cooperative Review *changed to* Pakistan Cooperative Review
0511-6775 West Virginia Statistical Handbook
0511-6848 Western Association of Graduate Schools. Proceedings of the Annual Meeting
0511-6910 Western Australia. Major Investment Projects, Public and Private, Current and Proposed
0511-6996 Western Australia. Geological Survey. Annual Report
0511-750X Western Forest Fire Committee. Proceedings *changed to* Western Forestry Conference. Executive Summaries of Proceedings
0511-7518 Western Forest Pest Committee. Proceedings *changed to* Western Forestry Conference. Executive Summaries of Proceedings
0511-7526 Western Reforestation Coordinating Committee. Proceedings *changed to* Western Forestry Conference. Executive Summaries of Proceedings
0511-7704 Western Lumber Facts
0511-8107 Western Society of Weed Science. Research Progress Report
0511-8255 Barometer (Portland)
0511-8298 Monthly F.O.B. Price Summary, Past Sales. Coast Mills
0511-8484 Westpreussen-Jahrbuch
0511-8654 What's New in Chemical Processing Equipment *changed to* Chemical Industry Products News
0511-8662 What's New in Forensic Sciences
0511-8719 Where to Retire on a Small Income
0511-8794 Whitmark Directory
0511-8824 Whitney Review
0511-8832 Whittier Newsletter
0511-8891 Who's Who Among Students in American Junior Colleges
0511-8905 Who's Who in Advertising
0511-8948 Who's Who in California
0511-8964 Who's Who in Floriculture
0511-9022 Who's Who in Public Relations (International)
0511-9162 Wiadomosci Historyczne
0511-9510 Wildlife Review
0511-9715 William L. Bryant Foundation American Studies. Report†
0511-9723 William L. Hutcheson Memorial Forest. Bulletin
0512-0624 Wisconsin. Division of Highways. System Planning Section. Highway Traffic in Wisconsin Cities *see* 0084-0580
0512-0640 Wisconsin. Geological and Natural History Survey. Information Circulars
0512-0659 Wisconsin. Geological and Natural History Survey. Special Report
0512-0918 University of Wisconsin. Bureau of Business Research and Service. Monographs *see* 0084-0513
0512-1175 Wisconsin Academy Review
0512-1213 Wisconsin English Journal
0512-1523 Universitaet Frankfurt. Wissenschaftliche Gesellschaft. Sitzungsberichte
0512-1817 Women of Korea
0512-1825 Women of Vietnam
0512-2368 World Airline Record Newsletter *see* 0002-2748
0512-2457 World Bank Atlas
0512-2511 World Confederation of Organizations of the Teaching Profession. Occasional Papers†
0512-252X W C O T P Theme Study
0512-2589 Faith and Order Papers
0512-2732 World Directory of Dental Schools
0512-2740 World Directory of Mathematicians
0512-2759 World Directory of Medical Schools
0512-2767 World Directory of Post-Basic and Post-Graduate Schools of Nursing
0512-2775 World Directory of Schools of Pharmacy
0512-2783 World Directory of Schools of Public Health
0512-2791 World Directory of Veterinary Schools
0512-2953 World Fertilizer Atlas
0512-3011 Vaccination Certificate Requirements for International Travel
0512-3038 World Health Organization. Monograph Series
0512-3054 W H O Technical Report Series
0512-3070 World Health Organization. Regional Office for Africa. Report of the Regional Committee. Minutes of the Plenary Session *changed to* World Health Organization. Regional Office for Africa. Report of the Regional Committee.
0512-3089 World Health Organization. Regional Office for the Eastern Mediterranean. Annual Report of the Regional Director *changed to* World Health Organization. Regional Office for the Eastern Mediterranean. Biennial Report of the Regional Director
0512-3135 World Hospitals
0512-3186 World Land Use Survey. Occasional Papers†
0512-3194 World Land Use Survey. Regional Monograph†
0512-3453 World Peace Through Law Center. Report of the Director-General†
0512-350X Estatistica Brasileira de Energia
0512-3739 World Trade Annual
0512-3747 World Trade Annual Supplement
0512-3844 World Wheat Statistics
0512-3879 World-Wide Summer Placement Directory
0512-4077 Wrangler
0512-4255 Wychowanie Myzyczne w Szkole
0512-4263 Wychowanie Obywatelskie
0512-4395 Wyoming Statistical Review
0512-4409 Wyoming. Employment Security Commission. Research and Analysis Section. Labor Force Trends
0512-4638 W. A. Cargill Memorial Lectures in Fine Art
0512-4743 West Virginia Union List of Serials
0512-4859 William D. Carmichael Jr. Lecture Series
0512-4921 World Health Organization. Regional Office for the Western Pacific. Annual Report of the Regional Director to the Regional Committee for the Western Pacific
0512-5030 Wasser und Abwasser in Forschung und Praxis
0512-5235 Western Catholic Reporter
0512-5278 What's Happening on the Chinese Mainland
0512-5405 Wire Journal Directory/Catalog
0512-5456 Wisconsin Studies in Vocational Rehabilitation. Monographs†
0512-5472 Works in Progress
0512-5804 What They Said
0512-5898 Eutrophication Abstracts *see* 0094-3347
0512-5901 Woman's Day Christmas Ideas for Children
0512-6355 Occupational Opportunities Information for Wisconsin
0513-0794 Yugoslavia. Savezni Zavod za Statistiku. Saobracaj i Veze
0513-0832 Yugoslavia. Savezni Zavod za Statistiku. Ucenici u Privredi
0513-0883 Yugoslavia. Savezni Zavod za Statistiku. Zaposleno Osoblje
0513-0891 Yugoslavia. Savezni Zavod za Statistiku. Zaposlenost
0513-1405 Yale Law School Studies
0513-1545 Western Historical Series
0513-2088 Yearly Digest of Criminal Cases
0513-2592 Yokohama National University. Faculty of Engineering. Bulletin
0513-2711 York Pioneer.
0513-2762 Yorkshire Dialect Society. Summer Bulletin
0513-3297 Youth *see* 0013-1482
0513-4242 Pharmaceutical Society of Korea. Journal
0513-4412 Yale Linguistic Series
0513-4501 Yale Southeast Asia Studies. Monograph Series
0513-5303 Yeni Yayinlar
0513-5613 Yokohama National University. Science Reports. Section II: Biological Sciences *changed to* Yokohama National University. Science Reports. Section II: Biological and Geological Sciences
0513-5621 Yokohama National University. Humanities. Section 1: Philosophy and Social Sciences
0513-5656 Yokohama National University. Educational Sciences
0513-5710 Yonago Acta Medica
0513-5974 Young East
0513-5982 Young Fabian Pamphlet
0513-6032 World Alliance of Y M C A's Directory
0513-6121 Young Socialist Forum *see* 0044-0884
0513-7926 Zahntechnik
0513-9147 Zeitschrift fuer Theologie und Kirche
0513-9295 Zeleznicni Technika
0513-9481 Zena
0513-9856 Zhinochyi Svit
0514-0668 Eidgenoessische Technische Hochschule Zuerich. Bibliothek. Schriftenreihe
0514-2253 Japanese Periodicals Index. Science and Technology *see* 0387-8503
0514-2482 Zeal
0514-2571 Zeitschrift fuer Beamtenrecht
0514-2733 Zeitschrift fuer Philosophische Forschung. Beihefte
0514-2938 Zement-Taschenbuch
0514-342X Zeszyty "Argumentow"
0514-5171 Japan Congress on Materials Research. Proceedings
0514-5236 Zambezia; a Journal of Social Studies in Southern and Central Africa *see* 0379-0622
0514-5392 Zambia. Central Statistical Office. Transport Statistics
0514-5430 Zambia. Department of Cooperatives. Annual Report
0514-5457 Zambia. Educational and Occupational Assessment Service. Annual Report
0514-5724 Zane Grey Collector†
0514-616X Zbornik Zastite Spomenika Kulture
0514-6321 Zeitschrift fuer allgemeine und textile Marktwirtschaft
0514-6364 Zeitschrift fuer Bibliothekswesen und Bibliographie. Sonderhefte
0514-6496 Zeitschrift fuer Rechtspolitik
0514-7115 Zentralblatt fuer Mineralogie. Teil 1: Kristallographie, Mineralogie
0514-7123 Zentralblatt fuer Mineralogie. Teil 2: Petrographie, Technische Mineralogie, Geochemie und Lagerstaettenkunde
0514-7166 Zentralblatt fuer Veterinaermedizin. Series B
0514-7352 Zeri i Rinise
0514-7441 Zhivotnovudni Nauki
0514-7972 Zoonosis
0514-809X Z M P D. Kwartalny Biuletyn Informacyjny
0514-857X Zentralasiatische Studien
0514-8731 Zambia. Central Statistical Office. Fisheries Statistics (Natural Waters)
0514-8863 American Crystallographic Association. Monographs
0514-9061 A D L Nachrichten *changed to* Online - A D L Nachrichten
0514-9142 A E G Newsletter
0514-9193 Arte Fotografico
0514-9797 A N A P
0514-9886 A O K Gesundheitsblatt *changed to* A O K Aktuell
0515-0361 Astin Bulletin
0515-2003 Academy of American Poets. Lamont Poetry Selections
0515-2089 Academy Reporter *see* 0360-3679
0515-2178 Accademia Italiana di Scienze Forestali. Annali
0515-2720 Acta Anaesthesiologica Scandinavica. Supplementum
0515-2925 Acta Medica et Sociologica
0515-3085 Acta Politecnica Mexicana
0515-3700 Actualites Pharmaceutiques

0515-4510 Advance
0515-6327 Afro-Asian Publications
0515-6610 Aggiornamenti Su Malattie Infettive Ed Immunologia
0515-6912 Agricoltore Bresciano
0515-698X Agricultura†
0515-7420 Agriculture Teachers Directory and Handbook
0515-7935 Vleugel en Wiel
0515-8125 Air Freight Directory of Points in the United States Served Directly by Air and by Pick-up and Delivery Service and by Connecting Motor Carriers *see* 0092-2870
0515-8672 Agriculture Asia
0516-3145 Akademiska Dzive
0516-4303 Alaska. Department of Fish and Game. Informational Leaflet
0516-4850 Alaska Farm Production *see* 0065-5694
0516-5504 Albuquerque Bar Journal†
0516-5849 Alexandria Medical Journal
0516-6950 Cotton Textile Statistics†
0516-8635 Amateur Hockey Association of the United States. Official Guide
0516-866X Amateur Skating Union of the United States. Offical Handbook
0516-8856 American Academy of Orthopaedic Surgeons. Directory
0516-9240 American Association for the Advancement of Slavic Studies. Directory of Members
0516-9313 American Association of Colleges for Teacher Education. Directory
0516-9445 Reference Book of Highway Personnel
0516-9518 A A V S O Bulletin
0516-9550 American Astrology Digest
0516-9623 American Atheist
0516-9631 American Authors and Critics Series
0516-9674 Tourbook: Florida
0517-0648 American College Public Relations Association. Newsletter†
0517-0680 American College Testing Program. Annual Report
0517-0745 American Concrete Institute. Compilation
0517-1024 Facts About States for the Dentist Seeking a Location
0517-2306 American Industrial Arts Association. Monograph Series
0517-3833 A M S. Proceedings of the National Seminar
0517-3868 Anthropological Handbook
0517-404X Numismatic Studies
0517-5178 American Society of Clinical Hypnosis. Directory
0517-5208 American Society of Clinical Pathologists. Summary Report
0517-5356 American Society of Mechanical Engineers. Machine Design Division. Papers
0517-564X American Trade Schools Directory
0517-5666 Truck Taxes by States
0517-6298 Ammo House Bulletin *changed to* C.A.C. Sporting Bulletin
0517-6816 Anales de Medicina. Cirugia
0517-6824 Anales de Medicina. Medicina
0517-6832 Anales de Medicina. Especialidades
0517-6956 Analisis de la Situacion Agricola de Sinaloa
0517-7731 Anglican
0517-8045 Ancient Iranian Cultural Society. Publication
0517-8452 Annales Bogorienses
0517-855X Annales des Antilles
0517-8991 Annuaire des Fournisseurs de Laboratoires Pharmaceutiques *see* 0396-0625
0518-0147 Handbuch Holz
0518-0937 Anuario dos Criadores
0518-1852 Arab World
0518-2220 Arbeitsgemeinschaft der Parlaments- und Behoerdenbibliotheken. Arbeitshefte
0518-2840 Arche
0518-3618 Archivo
0518-3979 Arena, Auditorium, Stadium Guide *see* 0067-0537
0518-4142 Argentina. Instituto Forestal Nacional. Anuario de Estadistica Forestal
0518-4614 Argentina. Direccion General de Parques Nacionales. Anales de Parques Nacionales *see* 0302-5705
0518-4673 Argentina. Direccion Nacional de Estadistica y Censos. Boletin Mensual de Estadistica *see* 0325-1950
0518-5378 Aristo - Mitteilungen fuer Ingenieur- und Hochschulen
0518-6242 Arizona Statistical Review
0518-6374 Water Resources Summary
0518-6544 University of Arkansas. Industrial Research and Extension Center. Annual Report
0518-7648 Art et Poesie
0518-794X Arthritis Foundation. Conference Series
0518-8857 Asian Conference on Occupational Health. Proceedings
0518-8881 Asian News Sheet
0518-9519 Asociacion Latinoamericana de Libre Comercio. Informe de las Actividades†
0519-1505 Association of Private Camps. Buyers Guide and Camp Directory *changed to* Association of Independent Camps. Buyers Guide and Camp Directory
0519-153X Association of Professors of Missions. Biennial Meeting. Proceedings
0519-1572 Bank Holding Company Facts
0519-2048 Associazione Italiana Biblioteche. Quaderni del Bollettino d'Informazioni
0519-3125 Atlantic Mail
0519-3273 Atlas Histoire *changed to* Atlas-Air France
0519-3389 Atomic Energy Clearinghouse
0519-4997 Australia. Bureau of Statistics. Instalment Credit for Retail Sales
0519-5373 Australia. Bureau of Statistics. Tasmanian Office. Potato Statistics *changed to* Australia. Bureau of Statistics. Tasmanian Office. Potato Production
0519-5659 Commonwealth Scientific and Industrial Research Organization. Division of Fisheries and Oceanography. Circular
0519-5950 Australia. Department of Foreign Affairs. Select Documents on International Affairs
0519-6035 Australia. Department of the Treasury. Taxation Branch. Taxation Statistics
0519-7201 Biblioteca Romanica Hispanica. Estudios y Ensayos *changed to* Biblioteca Romanica Hispanica
0519-8631 Biblioteka Pisarzow Polskich. Seria A
0519-8658 Biblioteka Pisarzy Reformacyjnych
0519-9514 Bibliotekovedenie i Bibliografiya za Rubezhom
0519-9603 Bibliotheca Archaeologica
0520-1802 Biological Council. Coordinating Committee for Symposia on Drug Action. Symposium Proceedings
0520-1810 Biological Journal of Okayama University
0520-1985 Biophysical Society. Symposium Proceedings *see* 0067-8910
0520-2795 Bliss Classification Bulletin
0520-2949 Blue Book, Official Inboard/Outdrive Boat Trade-in Guide
0520-2973 Blue Book of Junior College Athletics
0520-3015 Bluebell News
0520-3325 Bodhi Leaves
0520-4895 Bollettino delle Ricerche Sociali†
0520-5441 Bombay Cooperator†
0520-6294 Borzoi Books on Latin America
0520-6790 Bourne Society Local History Records
0520-6804 Bouwmarkt
0520-9048 Brennstoffstatistik der Waermekraftwerke fuer die Oeffentliche Elektrizitaetsversorgung in Oesterreich
0520-9404 Breve
0520-9455 Breviora Geologica Asturica
0521-1573 British Schools Exploring Society. Report
0521-4211 Marx Karoly Kozgazdasagtudomanyi Egyetem: Doktori Ertekezesek
0521-4882 Budapest Statisztikai Evkonyve
0521-6680 Bulgarski Tiutiun
0521-7091 Federation Belgo-Luxembourgeoise des Industries du Tabac. Bulletin F E D E T A B
0521-713X Bulletin Historique et Artistique du Calais
0521-7237 Bulletin of Brewing Science
0521-7903 Journal of Cultural Sciences
0521-8195 Burgense
0521-9477 British Broadcasting Corporation. B B C Lunchtime Lectures†
0521-9590 Library Association of Trinidad and Tobago. Bulletin
0521-9744 Babel
0521-9884 Kommission fuer Geschichtliche Landeskunde in Baden-Wuerttemberg. Veroeffentlichungen. Reihe B: Forschungen
0522-0629 Ball and Roller Bearing Engineering
0522-0653 Ballet Review
0522-0777 Banaras Hindu University. Darshana Series†
0522-0939 Banco Central de Bolivia. Boletin Estadistico
0522-098X Banco Central de Costa Rica. Estadisticas Economicas
0522-1153 Banco Central de Venezuela. Seccion A.L.A.L.C. Algunas Estadisticas de los Paises de ALALC
0522-1315 Banco de Bilbao. Informe Economico
0522-1986 Banco Nacional de Panama. Cuadernos
0522-2079 Banco Regional de Desenvolvimento do Extremo Sul. Relatorio da Directoria
0522-246X Bank of Sudan. Foreign Trade Statistical Digest
0522-2478 Bank Auditing and Accounting Report
0522-2494 Bank Director's Report
0522-2508 Bank Executive's Report
0522-2818 Bank of New South Wales Review
0522-2931 Banker
0522-2958 Current Business Picture
0522-2974 Investment Outlook *changed to* Credit and Capital Markets
0522-3199 Banque de France. Direction de la Conjoncture. Structure et Evolution Financiere des Regions de Province
0522-327X Banque Marocaine du Commerce Exterieur. Monthly Bulletin of Information *changed to* Banque Marocaine du Commerce Exterieur. Monthly Information Review
0522-3822 Colegio de Agentes de Cambio y Bolsa de Barcelona. Servicio de Estudios e Informacion. Boletin Financiero
0522-4314 Burqab
0522-4497 International Peace Research Institute. Basic Social Science Monographs
0522-4810 Battelle Research Outlook *see* 0145-8477
0522-4950 Bauingenieur-Praxis
0522-5337 Bayerische Verwaltungsblaetter
0522-5949 Beethoven-Jahrbuch
0522-604X Behoerden und Organisationen der Land- Forst- und Ernaehrungswirtschaft
0522-6201 Beitraege zum Buechereiwesen. Reihe B: Quellen und Texte†
0522-6562 Beitraege zur Geschichte der Universitaet Erfurt (1392-1816)
0522-6570 Beitraege zur Geschichte der Wissenschaft und der Technik
0522-6643 Beitraege zur Geschichte des Parlementarismus und der Politischen Parteien
0522-6759 Beitraege zur Japanologie
0522-7216 Beitraege zur Wirtschaftspolitik
0522-7291 Museu Paraense Emilio Goeldi. Boletim Antropologia. Nova Serie
0522-7496 Belgium. Commission Royale des Monuments et des Sites. Bulletin
0522-764X Belgium. Institut National de Statistique. Statistiques du Commerce et des Transports *changed to* Belgium. Institut National de Statistique. Statistiques du Commerce
0522-7690 Annuaire Statistique de la Sante Publique
0522-8557 Zavod za Fiziku. Radovi *see* 0350-0594
0522-8603 Belize. Weekly Newsletter†
0522-8670 Bellman Memorial Lecture *changed to* Bellman Lecture
0522-8883 Benedictine Yearbook
0522-8948 Benelux Economic Union. Conseil Consultatif Economique et Social Rapport du Secretaire Concernant les Activites du Conseil *changed to* B E N E L U X Economic Union. Conseil Central de l'Economie. Rapport du Secretaraire sur l'Activite du Conseil
0522-8980 Patrika *changed to* Bamla Ekademi Gabeshana Patrika
0523-1051 Better Beef Business
0523-1159 Bevolking en Gezin
0523-1639 Bibliografi Nasional Indonesia
0523-1698 Bibliografia Argentina de Psicologia
0523-218X Bibliografija Jugoslavije. Serija B. Prirodne i Primenjene Nauke
0523-2201 Bibliografija Jugoslavije. Knjige, Brosure i Muzikalije
0523-2392 Bibliographie de l'Algerie
0523-2449 Bibliographie der Deutschen Sprach- und Literaturwissenschaft
0523-2465 Bibliographie der Franzoesischen Literaturwissenschaft
0523-2678 Bibliographie Paedagogik
0523-302X Bibliography on Irrigation, Drainage, River Training and Flood Control
0523-5154 Biblische Untersuchungen
0523-6150 Bilten za Hematologiju i Transfuziju
0523-7238 Black Panther
0523-7688 Blue Shield (Chicago)
0523-7785 Boarding School Directory of the United States†
0523-8226 Boethius
0523-9095 Boletin del Cemento Portland
0523-9141 C E N D E S. Boletin Industrial
0524-0166 Bombay Civic Journal
0524-0182 Bombay Hospital Journal
0524-045X Bonner Mathematische Schriften
0524-0581 Book Review Index: Annual Clothbound Cumulations
0524-0913 Borthwick Institute of Historical Research. Borthwick Papers
0524-1014 Bosques *changed to* Bosques y Fauna
0524-112X Boston College Studies in Philosophy
0524-1448 Botswana. Estimates of Revenue and Expenditure
0524-1561 Bottin Europe†
0524-2444 Braunschweiger Geographische Studien
0524-4714 Briefs (Lexington)†
0524-5141 British Ceramic Society. Proceedings
0524-5168 British Club Year Book
0524-5370 British Columbia. Ministry of Economic Development. Monthly Bulletin of Business Activity
0524-5508 Schedule of Wells Drilled for Oil and Natural Gas in British Columbia
0524-5672 British Columbia Energy Board. Annual Report *see* 0703-086X
0524-5826 British Fern Gazette *see* 0308-0838
0524-7624 Bibliotheque Royale Albert 1er. Acquisitions Majeures
0524-7632 Bibliotheque Royale de Belgique. Bulletin *changed to* Bibliotheque Royal Albert 1er. Bulletin Bimestriel d'Information
0524-7764 Belgium. Institut Royal Meteorologique. Annuaire: Magnetisme Terrestre/ Jaarboek: Aardmagnetisme
0524-7780 Belgium. Institut Royal Meteorologique. Annuaire: Rayonnement Solaire/ Jaarboek: Zonnestraling
0524-8655 Magyar Allami Eotvos Lorand Geofizikai Intezet. Evi Jelentes

0524-8868 Orszagos Szechenyi Konyvtar. Evkonyv
0524-9481 Museo Argentino de Ciencias Naturales "Bernardino Rivadavia." Instituto Nacional de Investigacion de las Ciencias Naturales. Revista. Ecologia
0524-949X Museo Argentina de Ciencias Naturales "Bernardino Rivadavia." Instituto Nacional de Investigacion de las Ciencias Naturales. Revista. Entomologia
0524-9503 Museo Argentino de Ciencias Naturales "Bernardino Rivadavia." Instituto Nacional de Investigacion de las Ciencias Naturales. Revista. Hidrobiologia
0524-9511 Museo Argentino de Ciencias Naturales "Bernardino Rivadavia." Instituto Nacional de Investigacion de las Ciencias Naturales. Revista. Paleontologia
0524-952X Museo Argentino de Ciencias Naturales "Bernardino Rivadavia." Instituto Nacional de Investigacion de las Ciencias Naturales. Revista. Parasitologia
0524-9864 Buenos Aires (Province). Archivo Historico. Publicaciones. Sexta Serie
0525-1443 Bulletin of Epizootic Diseases of Africa *changed to* Bulletin of Animal Health and Production in Africa
0525-1524 Bulletin of Volcanic Eruptions
0525-1737 Germany (Federal Republic, 1949-) Bundesaufsichtsamt fuer das Versicherungswesen. Geschaeftsbericht
0525-1931 Bunseki Kagaku
0525-2156 Bulletin to Management
0525-2539 Burundi. Ministere du Plan. Departement des Statistiques. Bulletin de Statistique *changed to* Burundi. Departement des Etudes et Statistiques. Bulletin Trimestriel.
0525-2989 Buss Handbuch Europaeischer Produktenboersen
0525-3063 Butterworths Budget Tax Tables
0525-3675 Bibliografia Espanola
0525-3772 University of Birmingham. Faculty of Commerce and Social Science. Discussion Papers: Series F: Birmingham Society and Politics†
0525-4205 British National Committee on Large Dams. News and Views
0525-4507 Byzantina Neerlandica
0525-4620 Bank Administration Institute. Personnel Administration Commission. Biennial Survey of Bank Officer Salaries
0525-4663 Basketball Case Book
0525-4736 Beitraege zur Landesentwicklung
0525-4752 Belgium. Administration des Mines. Service: Statistiques. Siderurgie, Houille, Agglomeres, Cokes *changed to* Belgium. Administration des Mines. Statistiques: Houille, Cokes, Agglomeres Metallurgie, Carrieres/ Statistieken: Steenkolen, Cokes, Agglomeraten, Metallnijverheid, Groeven
0525-5090 Botswana Notes and Records
0525-6402 Cooperative News Digest
0525-6844 Koebenhavns Universitet. Historiske Institut. Skrifter
0525-8693 Accidentes de Transito en Costa Rica
0526-4375 Current & Forthcoming Offprints on Archaeology in Great Britain & Ireland *see* 0305-5280
0526-5053 Analysis of Cyprus Foreign Trade
0526-5096 Cyprus. Department of Statistics and Research. Statistical Summary
0526-6513 C.I.C.A.E. Bulletin d'Information
0526-7994 Cahiers de la Resistance
0526-8133 Cahiers des Explorateurs
0526-9288 California State Plan for Hospitals and Related Health Facilities *changed to* California State Health Plan
0526-9970 California. Division of Forestry. Conservation Camp Program†
0527-0189 California Property Tax Laws Annotated, Including Regulations
0527-2181 California Fruit and Nut Acreage
0527-3277 California Tomato Grower
0527-446X Camping Journal (New York)
0527-4834 Canada. Statistics Canada. Boatbuilding and Repair/Construction et Reparation d'Embarcations
0527-4869 Canada. Statistics Canada. Breweries/ Brasseries
0527-4893 Canada. Statistics Canada. Carpet, Mat and Rug Industry/Industrie des Tapis, des Carpettes et de la Moquette
0527-4915 Canada. Statistics Canada. Coffin and Casket Industry/Industrie des Cercueils
0527-494X Canada. Statistics Canada. Communications Equipment Manufacturers/Fabricants d'Equipement de Telecommunication
0527-4974 Construction in Canada
0527-4990 Canada. Statistics Canada. Cordage and Twine Industry /Corderie et Ficellerie (Fabrication)
0527-5016 Canada. Statistics Canada. Cotton Yarn and Cloth Mills/Filature et Tissage du Coton
0527-5024 Canada. Statistics Canada. Distilleries
0527-5148 Canada. Statistics Canada. Federal Government Employment in Metropolitan Areas/Emploi dans l'Administration Federale Regions Metropolitaines
0527-5172 Canada. Statistics Canada. Fish Products Industry/Industrie de la Transformation du Poisson
0527-5318 Canada. Statistics Canada. Gas Utilities (Transport and Distribution Systems) / Services de Gaz (Reseaux de Transport et de Distribution)
0527-5504 Canada. Statistics Canada. Manufacturers of Electric Wire and Cable/Fabricants de Fils et de Cables Electriques
0527-5539 Canada. Statistics Canada. Manufacturers of Industrial Chemicals/ Fabricants de Produits Chimiques Industriels
0527-5679 Canada. Statistics Canada. Men's Clothing Industries/Industrie des Vetements pour Hommes
0527-5717 Canada. Statistics Canada. Smelting and Refining/Fonte et Affinage
0527-5822 Canada. Statistics Canada. Motor Vehicle, Part 1, Rates and Regulations/ Vehicules a Moteur, Partie 1, Charges Fiscales et Reglementation†
0527-5830 Canada. Statistics Canada. Motor Vehicle. Part 2. Motive Fuel Sales/ Vehicules a Moteur. Partie 2. Ventes des Carburants *see* 0703-654X
0527-5849 Canada. Statistics Canada. Motor Vehicle, Part 4, Revenues/Vehicules a Moteur, Partie 4, Recettes†
0527-5865 Canada. Statistics Canada. Motor Vehicle Traffic Accidents/Accidents de la Circulation Routiere†
0527-5881 Canada. Statistics Canada. New Manufacturing Establishments in Canada/Nouveaux Etablissements Manufacturiers au Canada†
0527-5911 Canada. Statistics Canada. Oils and Fats/Huiles et Corps Gras
0527-5997 Canada. Statistics Canada. Ornamental and Architectural Metal Industry/ Industrie des Produits Metalliques d'Architecture et d'Ornement
0527-608X Canada. Statistics Canada. Provincial Government Employment /L'Emploi dans les Administrations Provinciales
0527-6144 Canada. Statistics Canada. Shipbuilding and Repair/Construction et Reparation de Navires
0527-6160 Canada. Statistics Canada. Shipping Statistics/Statistiques Maritime†
0527-6179 Canada. Statistics Canada. Shorn Wool Production/Production de Laine Tondue
0527-6403 Canada. Statistics Canada. Vegetable Oil Mills/Moulins a Huile Vegetale
0527-6411 Canada. Statistics Canada. Vending Machine Operators/Exploitants de Distributeurs Automatiques
0527-6497 Canadian Civil Aircraft Register
0527-6624 Marketing Boards in Canada
0527-9275 Directory of Canadian Chartered Accountants
0528-1458 Carl Newell Jackson Lectures
0528-1865 Carta Economica del Ecuador
0528-2152 Case Studies of International Conflict†
0528-2187 Cases in Practical Politics
0528-2438 Catalogo de la Industria de Madrid *changed to* Guia del Comercio y de la Industria de Madrid
0528-2594 Catalogus Translationem et Commentatorium
0528-2950 Catholic International Education Office. Bulletin Documentaire†
0528-3280 Caucho
0528-4759 Centre International de Liaison des Ecoles de Cinema et de Television. Bulletin d'Informations
0528-5984 Cerberus Alarm
0528-757X Ceylon Economist
0528-7618 Ceylon Journal of Social Work
0528-8231 Chambre Francaise de Commerce et d'Industrie du Maroc. Revue de Conjoncture
0528-9254 Politechnika Lodzka. Zeszyty Naukowe. Chemia Spozywcza
0528-9432 Chemicke Vlakna
0528-953X Chemmunique
0529-0775 Institute of Gas Technology. Technical Reports†
0529-0937 University of Chicago. Industrial Relations Center. Occasional Papers *changed to* University of Chicago. Human Resources Center. Occasional Papers
0529-1607 Current Publications: Serials *changed to* Catalogue of Japanese Periodicals
0529-1674 Child Welfare League of America. Directory of Member Agencies and Associates *changed to* Child Welfare League of America. Directory of Member Agencies and Associate Agencies Listing
0529-4975 Chroniques de Port-Royal
0529-7451 Cina
0529-8016 Cites Unies
0529-9160 Classroom Teacher Series in Health, Education, Recreation and Safety†
0529-9853 Club Filatelico de Caracas. Revista
0530-0495 Coir
0530-0657 Colecao de Estudos Juridicos
0530-749X Commission of the European Communities. Collection d'Hygiene et de Medecine du Travail
0530-8836 Collection Panorama
0530-9867 Istituto Internazionale di Studi Liguri. Collezione di Monografie Preistoriche Ed Archeologiche
0531-0008 Colligite†
0531-0318 Universitaet zu Koeln. Institut fuer Handelsforschung. Mitteilungen. Sonderhefte
0531-1926 Etudes Orientales
0531-1934 Etudes Philosophiques et Litteraires
0531-1950 Etudes Preliminaires aux Religions Orientales dans l'Empire Romain
0531-2051 Etudes Togolaises
0531-206X Etudes Vietnamiennes
0531-2248 Eurocontrol
0531-2485 Europarecht
0531-2663 European Aspects, Social Studies Series
0531-2671 European Aspects, Law Series
0531-2701 E A A A Newsletter
0531-2728 European Association of Exploration Geophysicists. Constitution and By-Laws, Membership List.
0531-2922 European Coal and Steel Community. Organe Permanent pour la Securite dans les Mines de Houille. Rapport *see* 0588-702X
0531-3015 Commission of the European Communities. Collection d'Economie du Travail
0531-3023 Commission of the European Communities. Collection d'Economie et Politique Regionale
0531-304X Commission of the European Communities. Conjoncture Energetique dans la Communaute
0531-3120 Fontes et Aciers
0531-3198 Commission of the European Communities. Collection Objectifs Generaux Acier
0531-3724 Commission of the European Communities. Expose sur l'Evolution Sociale dans la Communaute
0531-4119 E F T A Trade
0531-4127 European Free Trade Association. Annual Report
0531-4283 C E R N School of Physics. Proceedings
0531-4321 European Parliament. Informations
0531-4496 European Southern Observatory. Annual Report
0531-4518 European Space Research Organization. General Report†
0531-4526 European Space Research Organization. Report†
0531-4798 Evangelische Mission Jahrbuch
0531-495X Everyman's Science
0531-5131 International Congress Series
0531-5174 European Council of Jewish Community Services. Exchange Information Service *changed to* European Council of Jewish Community Services. Exchange
0531-5360 Exhibits Schedule
0531-5565 Experimental Gerontology
0531-5824 Herold Export-Adressbuch von Oesterreich
0531-5980 Chemicals and Allied Products Export Promotion Council. Exporters Directory
0531-6723 Egyptian Library Journal
0531-674X Ehe- und Familienrechtliche Entscheidungen
0531-6863 Electronics and Aerospace Systems Convention. E A S C O N Record
0531-7436 European League for Economic Cooperation. Report of the Secretary General on the Activities of E. L. E. C.
0531-7444 European Organisation for Civil Aviation Electronics. General Assembly. Annual Report
0531-7452 European Space Research Organization. Scientific Memorandum†
0531-7460 European Space Research Organization. Scientific Note†
0531-7479 Europhysics News
0531-755X Explotacion Agraria†
0531-786X Ecumene
0531-7886 Edmund's Foreign Car Prices
0531-8203 Economia Politica
0531-8327 Educating the Disadvantaged
0531-8432 Ecology *see* 0096-7807
0531-8955 Economic Review
0531-9153 Ele e Ela
0531-9218 Elektroniker
0531-9315 E R I C Clearinghouse for Junior Colleges. Topical Paper Series
0531-9323 Statistische Studien
0531-9455 Etudes Baudelairiennes
0531-9684 Folk Music Journal
0532-0194 Food and Agriculture Organization of the United Nations. Agricultural Planning Studies
0532-0208 Food and Agriculture Organization of the United Nations. Basic Texts
0532-0283 F A O Forestry and Forest Products Studies
0532-0291 F A O Library List of Recent Accessions
0532-0305 F A O Nutrition Special Reports†

0532-0313 F A O Terminology Bulletin
0532-0348 Food and Agriculture Organization of the United Nations. Interamerican Meeting on Animal Production and Health. Report†
0532-0402 Meeting of International Organizations for the Joint Study of Programs and Activities in the Field of Agriculture in Europe. Report.
0532-0437 Food and Agriculture Organization of the United Nations. Soils Bulletins
0532-0488 Food and Agriculture Organization of the United Nations. World Soil Resources Reports
0532-0623 F A O African Regional Meeting on Animal Production and Health. Report of the Meeting.
0532-0666 Food and Agriculture Organization of the United Nations. Forest Tree Seed Directory
0532-0690 Food and Agriculture Organization of the United Nations. Forestry and Forest Products Division. World Forest Products Statistics†
0532-0747 Forestry Newsletter of the Asia-Pacific Region
0532-0941 Food Quality Control *changed to* F D C Control Newsletter
0532-1042 Footwear and Leather Abstracts†
0532-2189 Forschungen zur Kunstgeschichte und Christlichen Archaeologie
0532-2731 Fortschritte der Verfahrenstechnik
0532-3010 Fotomuveszet
0532-5781 Francis Thompson Society. Journal *changed to* Eighteen Nineties Society.Journal
0532-6370 Freedom from Hunger Campaign. F F H C Report
0532-7091 F C L Newsletter
0532-7334 From the Sourdough Crock
0532-7466 Frontiers in Neuroendocrinology
0532-7776 Real Estate Research
0532-8942 Furniture Production
0532-9175 A.A.'s Far East Businessman's Directory
0532-9396 Food and Agriculture Organization of the United Nations. European Inland and Fisheries Advisory Commission. E I F A C Newsletter
0532-9841 Film Special
0533-005X Foundry Catalog File
0533-0327 Federacion Panamericana de Associaciones de Facultades de Medicina. Boletin
0533-0386 Universita degli Studi di Ferrara. Annali. Sezione 14. Fisica Sperimentale e Teorica
0533-0653 All of Mexico at Low Cost
0533-070X Forum foer Ekonomi och Teknik
0533-0866 France - Pays Arabes
0533-0939 Family Findings
0533-0963 Federal Aviation Regulations for Pilots
0533-1072 Barron's Profiles of American Colleges. Vol. 2: Index to Major Areas of Study
0533-196X Great Lakes Commission. Report to the States†
0533-2869 Greyfriar/Siena Studies in Literature
0533-3164 Group Analysis: International Panel and Correspondence
0533-3180 Colloques A M P E R E†
0533-3431 Grundschule
0533-4179 Instituto de Nutricion de Centro America y Panama. Informe Anual
0533-4500 Guia de la Industria del Caucho
0533-4675 Turismo, Guia Peuser *changed to* Guia Peuser de Turismo Argentina y Sudamericana
0533-5248 Guide to American Directories
0533-5388 Guide to Microreproduction Equipment *see* 0360-8654
0533-540X Guide to Radio Electronics & Components Trade and Industry in India *changed to* Guide to Electronics Industry in India
0533-5426 Guide to Scientific Instruments *changed to* Science Guide to Scientific Instruments
0533-5450 Guide to Hotels in South Africa *changed to* C V R Travel and Hotel Guide to Southern Africa
0533-5485 Guide to Traffic Safety Literature
0533-5620 Guides to Jewish Subjects in Social and Humanistic Research
0533-5701 Journal Officiel de Guinee
0533-649X Gujarat State Financial Corporation. Annual Report
0533-6724 Gumma Symposia on Endocrinology
0533-7275 Genealogical Reference Builders Newsletter
0533-7291 Generation (Windsor)
0533-7356 Geologic Field Trip Guidebooks of North America; a Union List Incorporating Monographic Titles
0533-7526 German Patents Gazette. Section 1: Chemical
0533-7534 German Patents Gazette. Section 2: Electrical
0533-7542 German Patents Gazette. Section 3: Mechanical and General
0533-8301 Geological Society of Iraq. Journal
0533-8387 Georgia Welcome Center. Research Report
0533-8646 University of Ghana. Institute of African Studies. Local Studies Series
0533-8859 Govor
0533-9235 Gaudeamus Information. English Edition
0533-9286 Geografia Urbana
0533-9685 Great Britain. Royal Commission on Historical Manuscripts.Secretary's Report to the Commissioners
0533-991X Guyana. Statistical Bureau. Annual Account Relating to External Trade
0534-0012 Genetika
0534-042X Laerarhoegskolan i Goeteborg. Pedagogiska Institutionen. Rapport *see* 0348-2219
0534-0489 G R I Newsletter
0534-0500 Great Britain. Department of Employment. Changes in Rates of Wages and Hours of Work
0534-2104 Chartered Institute of Public Finance and Accountancy. Crematoria Statistics. Actuals
0534-3364 Instituto de Estudios Tarraconenses Ramon Berenguer IV. Publicacion
0534-3844 Spain. Instituto Nacional de Industria. Direccion Financiera. Boletin de Informacion Financiera
0534-4050 Kjeller Report
0534-4859 Inter-African Phyto-Sanitary Commission. Publication
0534-607X Intercity Truck Tonnage *changed to* Motor Carrier Statistical Summary
0534-6509 International Aeronautic Federation. General Conference Minutes(of the) Business Meetings *changed to* International Aeronautic Federation. Annual Information Bulletin
0534-655X International African Seminar. Studies Presented and Discussed
0534-6622 International Amateur Basketball Federation. Official Report of the World Congress
0534-7319 I A E A Library Film Catalog
0534-7793 International Cargo Handling Coordination Association. Rapports des Comites Nationaux
0534-8021 International Children's Centre. Paris. Travaux et Documents
0534-8242 International Commission of Jurists. Bulletin *see* 0020-6393
0534-8293 International Commission on Large Dams. Bulletin
0534-8811 International Conference on Shielding Around High Energy Accelerators. Papers
0534-9044 International Congress of Graphoanalysts. Proceedings
0534-9109 International Congress of Neurological Sciences. Abstracts and Descriptions of Contributions of the Scientific Program
0534-9168 International Congress of Psychopathological Art. Program. Programme
0534-9257 International Congress on Canned Foods. Texts of Papers Presented and Resolutions
0534-9907 International Electrotechnical Commission. Central Office Report *see* 0074-4697
0535-0182 International Federation of Fruit Juice Producers. Proceedings. Berichte. Rapports
0535-0492 International Financial Statistics. Supplement†
0535-1405 International Medical News
0535-1588 International North Pacific Fisheries Commission. Statistical Yearbook
0535-1626 Report of the General Assembly of the Members of the International Office of Cocoa and Chocolate and the International Sugar Confectionary Manufacturers' Association
0535-1774 World List of Family Planning Agencies
0535-2479 International Skating Union. Minutes of Congress
0535-3114 International Symposium on Submarine and Space Medicine. Proceedings†
0535-4358 Internationales Handbuch fuer Rundfunk und Fernsehen
0535-4676 Interstate Commission on the Potomac River Basin. Proceedings
0535-5079 Inventare Nichtstaatlicher Archive
0535-5133 Investigacion Clinica
0535-899X Istruzione Tecnica e Professionale
0535-9821 Italy. Istituto Centrale di Statistica. Statistica Mensile del Commercio con l'Estero
0536-1095 I A G A News
0536-1184 I B M Medical Symposium. Proceedings
0536-132X I S C U Bulletin *changed to* I S C U Newsletter
0536-1362 I.D.
0536-1486 I E E E International Conference on Communications. Conference Record
0536-1966 I R C D Bulletin
0536-2067 I S O Memento
0536-2113 I T C Information Booklets
0536-2121 I T V Guide to Independent Television *changed to* Television & Radio
0536-2512 Ibero-American Bureau of Education. Information and Publications Department Series V: Technical Seminars and Meetings
0536-2571 I C A C H
0536-2733 Idaho Employment
0536-3055 Idaho Farm Labor Bulletin
0536-3713 Illinois. Administrative Office of Illinois Courts. Annual Report to the Supreme Court of Illinois
0536-4604 University of Illinois at Urbana-Champaign. Graduate School of Library Science. Allerton Park Institute. Papers
0536-5139 Illinois Teacher of Home Economics
0536-6518 Index of Reviews in Organic Chemistry
0536-7506 India. Office of the Comptroller and Auditor-General. Report: Union Government (Posts and Telegraphs)
0536-8014 India. Department of Economic Affairs. Quarterly Statistics on the Working of Capital Issues Control
0536-9029 India (Republic). Meteorological Department Report on Seismology *changed to* National Report for India: Seismology and Physics of the Earth's Interior
0536-9061 Import Trade Control Policy
0536-9290 India. Ministry of Finance. Budget *changed to* India. Finance Department. Budget of the Central Government
0536-9657 Bulletin for Metalliferous Mines in India
0536-9983 Import Trade Control: Handbook of Rules and Procedures
0537-0035 India. Office of the Registrar General. Newsletter *changed to* India. Ministry of Home Affairs. Vital Statistics Division. Sample Registration Bulletin
0537-0744 India. Zoological Survey. Annual Report
0537-0922 India Today
0537-1120 Survey of India's Exports
0537-1198 Indian Council for Africa. Library. Monthly Index of Important Articles and Editorials on Africa
0537-1546 Indian Ephemeris and Nautical Almanac *changed to* Indian Astronomical Ephemeris
0537-166X Indian Foreign Affairs
0537-197X Indian Journal of Agronomy
0537-1996 Indian Journal of Extension Education
0537-2003 Indian Journal of Fisheries
0537-202X Indian Journal of Homoeopathy *see* 0019-5243
0537-2410 Indian Phytopathological Society. Bulletin
0537-2429 Indian Police Journal
0537-2704 Indian Yearbook of International Affairs
0537-3638 Indo-Iranian Reprints†
0537-3654 Indo-Pacific Fisheries Council. Regional Studies
0537-3808 Statistical Pocketbook of Indonesia
0537-4685 I E R
0537-4715 Indus
0537-5126 Industrial Development in Arizona: Manufacturing *see* 0146-2997
0537-5215 Industrial Hygiene Foundation. Chemical-Toxicological Series. Bulletin *see* 0073-7488
0537-5223 Industrial Hygiene News Report
0537-5355 Industrial Relations Aspects of Manpower Policy†
0537-5452 Industrial Review of Japan
0537-6149 Information and Systems Theory
0537-6173 Information Circular on Insecticide Resistance. Insect Behaviour and Vector Genetics†
0537-6211 Societe Saint-Jean-Baptiste de Montreal. Information Nationale
0537-6246 Information Processing in Japan†
0537-6297 Documentation Europeenne - Serie Agricole
0537-667X Informator Nauki Polskiej
0537-6858 Informazione Scientifica
0537-7137 Journal of Humanistic Studies
0537-779X Institut Francais d'Archeologie d'Istanbul. Bibliotheque Archeologique et Historique
0537-7919 Institut fuer Europaeische Geschichte, Mainz. Veroeffentlichungen. Abteilung Universitaetsgeschichte und Abteilung fuer Abendlaendische Religionsphilosophie *changed to* Institut fuer Europaeische Gesichte, Mainz. Veroeffentlichungen. Abteilung Universalgeschichte und Abteilung Religionsgeschichte
0537-7927 Institut fuer Europaeische Geschichte, Mainz. Vortraege. Abteilung Universalgeschichte und Abteilung fuer Abendlaendische Religionsphilosophie *changed to* Institut fuer Europaeische Geschichte, Mainz. Vortraege. Abteilung Universalgesschichte und Abteilung Religionsgeschichte
0537-9024 Studies in Biology
0537-9202 I. D. E. Occasional Papers Series
0537-9679 Institute of Town Planners, India. Journal
0537-9768 University of Miami, Coral Gables. Law Center. Annual Institute on Estate Planning
0538-0022 British Institution of Radio Engineers. Journal *see* 0033-7722
0538-0057 Institution of Engineers, Malaysia, Journal
0538-009X Institution of Surveyors. Journal *changed to* Indian Surveyor
0538-0391 Instituto Colombiano Agropecuario. Boletin Tecnico

0538-0898 Instituto de Investigacion de Recursos Naturales. Publicacion
0538-1126 Instituto Forestal Latinoamericano de Investigacion y Capacitacion. Boletin
0538-1347 Instituto Latinoamericano de Mercadeo Agricola. I L M A - RR†
0538-1355 Instituto Latinoamericano de Mercadeo Agricola. Information Bulletin†
0538-1428 Instituto Mexicano del Petroleo. Revista
0538-2629 Insurance Market Place
0538-2769 Organization of African Unity. Inter-African Bureau for Soils. Bibliographie
0538-2912 Inter-American Commission of Women. News Bulletin
0538-2920 Inter-American Commission of Women. Noticiero
0538-3048 Inter-American Council of Commerce and Production. Uruguayan Section. Publicaciones
0538-3110 Inter-American Development Bank. Institute for Latin American Integration. Annual Report
0538-3277 Inter-American Institute of Agricultural Sciences. Informe Anual
0538-3307 Inter- American Institute of Agricultural Sciences. Reunion Anual de la Junta Directiva. Informe *issued with* 0301-4355
0538-3579 Inter-American Statistical Institute. Committee on Improvement of National Statistics. Report
0538-3609 Inter-American Tropical Tuna Commission. Data Report
0538-3641 Interbank
0538-4028 Intermediate Technology Development Group. Bulletin *see* 0305-0920
0538-4141 I A A World Directory of Marketing Communications Periodicals†
0538-4168 International Advertising Association. United Kingdom Chapter. Concise Guide to International Markets
0538-4257 International Alban Berg Society. Newsletter
0538-4281 International Animated Film Association. Bulletin
0538-4400 International Association for Shell and Spatial Structures. Bulletin
0538-4427 International Association for the Exchange of Students for Technical Experience. Annual Report
0538-4524 International Association of Law Libraries. Bulletin *see* 0340-045X
0538-4680 International Association of Theoretical and Applied Limnology. Communications
0538-4850 International Atomic Energy Agency. Radiation Data for Medical Use; Catalogue *changed to* Radiation Dosimetry Data; Catalogue
0538-4893 International Atomic Energy Agency. Law Library. Books and Articles in the I A E A Law Library. List†
0538-4915 International Audiology *see* 0020-6091
0538-5342 International Centre for African Social and Economic Documentation. (Bibliographical Index Cards)†
0538-5415 International Centre for Theoretical Physics. Report *see* 0304-7091
0538-5466 International Chamber of Commerce. United States Council. Report
0538-5482 International Children's Center. Courrier
0538-5490 International Children's Centre. Paris. Report of the Director-General to the Executive Board
0538-5520 International Christian Democratic Study and Documentation Center. Bulletin International *changed to* Christian Democratic World Union. Information Bulletin
0538-5539 International Christian Democratic Study and Documentation Center. Cahiers d'Etudes *changed to* Christian Democratic Study and Documentation Center. Cahiers d'Etudes
0538-5555 International Christian Democratic Study and Documentation Center. Informations *changed to* Panorama Democrate Chretien
0538-5644 International Colloquium on Rapid Mixing and Sampling Techniques Applicable to the Study of Biochemical Reactions. Proceedings
0538-5687 International Commission for the Scientific Exploration of the Mediterranean Sea. Bulletin de Liaison des Laboratoires†
0538-5768 International Commission on Irrigation and Drainage. Report
0538-5865 International Committee on Urgent Anthropological and Ethnological Research. Bulletin
0538-5946 International Confederation of Free Trade Unions. Features
0538-6039 International Conference of Social Work. Japanese National Committee. Progress Report *changed to* Japanese Report to the International Council on Social Welfare
0538-611X International Conference on Liquefied Natural Gas. Proceedings *changed to* International Conference on Liquefied Natural Gas. Papers
0538-6128 International Conference on Lighthouses and Other Aids to Navigation. (Reports)
0538-6381 International Congress for the Study of Pre-Columbian Cultures of the Lesser Antilles. Proceedings
0538-6462 International Congress of Endocrinology. Proceedings
0538-6586 International Congress of Radiation Research. Proceedings
0538-6640 International Congress on Catalysis. Proceedings
0538-6772 International Congress Science Series
0538-6829 International Cotton Industry Statistics
0538-6918 CODATA Newsletter
0538-7043 International Crop Improvement Association. Production Publication *changed to* Association of Official Seed Certifying Agencies. Production Publication
0538-7051 International Cryogenics Monograph Series
0538-7078 International Dairy Federation. Annual Memento
0538-7086 International Dairy Federation. Catalogue of I D F Publications. Catalogue des Publications de la F I L
0538-7094 International Dairy Federation. International Standard
0538-7159 International Directory of Antiquarian Booksellers
0538-7191 International Directory of Prisoners' Aid Agencies
0538-7205 International Directory of Research and Development Scientists *changed to* Current Bibliographic Directory for the Arts & Sciences
0538-7302 F I D Publications Catalogue†
0538-7353 I A G Communications
0538-740X International Federation of Film Archives. Annuaire. Yearbook†
0538-7442 International Federation of Operational Research Societies. Airline Group (A G I F O R S) Proceedings
0538-7477 International Federation of Plantation, Agricultural and Allied Workers. Report of the Secretariat to the I F P A A W World Congress
0538-7639 International Geographical Union. Newsletter *see* 0018-9804
0538-7736 International Histological Classification of Tumours
0538-7779 Internationale Hydrologische Dekade: Jahrbuch der Bundesrepublik Deutschland
0538-7965 Worldwide Bibliography of Space Law and Related Matters†
0538-8066 International Journal of Chemical Kinetics
0538-8082 International Journal of Comparative Sociology
0538-8333 International Labour Office. Special Report of the Director-General on the Application of the Declaration Concerning the Policy of Apartheid of the Republic of South Africa
0538-8643 International Maritime Committee. Documentation *changed to* C M I News Letter
0538-8643 International Maritime Committee. Documentation *changed to* C M I Year Book
0538-8732 International Military Sports Council Academy. Technical Brochure *changed to* International Military Sports Council. Technical Brochure
0538-8759 International Monetary Fund. Pamphlet Series
0538-8783 I M Z Information *see* 0019-0071
0538-8791 International Music Council. German Committee. Referate Informationen
0538-8880 International Oceanographic Tables
0538-8988 International Organization of Consumers Unions. Proceedings
0538-9089 Family Planning in Five Continents
0538-9275 International Quantum Electronics Conference. Digest of Technical Papers
0538-933X International Reading Association. Annual Report
0538-9461 International Rescue Committee Annual Report
0538-9550 International Rice Commission. Newsletter
0538-9755 International Secretariat of Entertainment Trade Unions. Newsletter
0538-9771 International Sedimentary Petrographical Series
0538-978X International Seismological Centre. P-Nodal Solutions for Earthquakes†
0538-9887 International Series on Civil Engineering
0538-9895 International Series on Heating, Ventilation and Refrigeration
0538-9968 International Series on Cerebrovisceral and Behavioral Psychology and Conditioned Reflexes
0538-9984 International Series on Earth Sciences
0538-9992 International Series on Electromagnetic Waves
0539-0125 International Series in Pure and Applied Mathematics
0539-0133 International Series in Solid State Physics
0539-0168 International Skating Union. Bestimmungen ueber das Eistanzen
0539-0230 I E S A Information
0539-0281 International Society for Rock Mechanics. News
0539-032X International Society of Criminology. Bulletin
0539-0338 International Society of Food Service Consultants. Directory†
0539-0346 International Society of Plant Morphologists. Yearbook
0539-0370 International Sporting Press Association. Bulletin. N.S.
0539-0559 International Symposium on Comparative Endocrinology. Proceedings
0539-0761 International Television Almanac
0539-0893 I T C Publications. Series B. Photo-Interpretation
0539-0915 International Transport Workers' Federation Report on Activities
0539-0990 Commission on Crystallographic Apparatus†
0539-1016 International Union of Geodesy and Geophysics. Monograph
0539-1083 I U L A (Publication)
0539-1113 International Union of Physiological Sciences. Newsletter
0539-113X International Union of Public Transport. Transports Publics dans les Principales Villes du Monde *see* 0378-1968
0539-1148 International Union of Pure and Applied Chemistry. Information Bulletin *see* 0193-6484
0539-1199 News Service
0539-1296 International Wheat Council. Report for Crop Year *changed to* International Wheat Council. Annual Report
0539-130X International Wheat Council. Record of Operations of Member Countries
0539-1318 International Wheat Council. Review of the World Grains Situation *changed to* Review of the World Wheat Situation
0539-1326 International Wheat Council. Secretariat Papers
0539-1342 International Who's Who in Poetry
0539-1512 Internationale Gesellschaft fuer Urheberrecht. Yearbook
0539-1539 Zahlestafeln der Physikalisch-Chemischen Untersuchungen des Rheins sowie der Mosel
0539-2047 Potomac River Water Quality Network *changed to* Potomac River Basin Water Quality Reports
0539-2063 Legal Report of Oil and Gas Conservation Activities
0539-2306 Inventaria Archaeologica Roumanie†
0539-239X Investigacion y Progreso Agricola†
0539-3337 Mens en Gemeenskap
0539-3728 Mercado Mundial
0539-3876 Merchandise Mart Directory *changed to* Merchandise Mart Buyers Guide
0539-3973 Mereni a Regulace
0539-5429 Metropolitan Washington Council of Governments. Regional Report *changed to* Region (Washington)
0539-6115 Hospital Infantil de Mexico. Boletin Medico
0539-6387 Mexico (City). Universidad Nacional. Observatorio Astronomico, Tacubaya. Boletin de los Observatorios Tonantzintla y Tacubaya *see* 0303-7584
0539-7413 Michigan Health Statistics
0539-8703 Michigan Aviation
0539-998X Mie Prefectural University. Faculty of Fisheries. Bulletin
0540-0694 Milford Historical Society Newsletter
0540-0961 Milton Society of America. Proceedings
0540-3847 Mississippi State University Abstracts of Theses and Dissertations
0540-3847 Mississippi State University Abstracts of Theses *see* 0540-3847
0540-410X Mississippi's Health
0540-4193 Missouri's New and Expanding Industries
0540-469X Mitsubishi Technical Bulletin
0540-4924 Miyazaki University. Faculty of Engineering. Memoirs
0540-5556 Modern Surgical Monographs
0540-6471 Mongol Nyelvemlektar *changed to* Monumenta Linguae Mongolicae Collecta
0540-8962 Mortgage Market†
0541-4385 Musizi
0541-4393 Muskeg Research Conference. Proceedings
0541-4873 Mwana Shaba
0541-5357 M B I's Indian Industries Annual
0541-5462 M.I.I. Series
0541-5489 M L A News
0541-5632 Mitzion Tetzeh Torah. M.T.T.
0541-5896 Maccabi News Bulletin *changed to* Maccabi World Union. Newsletter
0541-6159 McGill Journal of Business
0541-623X Keith Callard Lecture Series†
0541-6256 McGill University, Montreal. Department of Geography. Climatological Bulletin
0541-6299 McGill University, Montreal. Marine Sciences Centre. Annual Report
0541-6388 Machine Building Industry
0541-6434 Machine Tool Engineer
0541-6507 Mackinac History

1254 ISSN INDEX

0541-8836 Magazin Polovnika
0541-9220 Magyar Kulpolitikai Evkonyv
0541-9344 Magyar Szo Naptara
0542-0938 Mahasagar
0542-1136 Maine Geological Survey. Special Economic Studies Series†
0542-1462 Mainstream
0542-1470 Maintenant†
0542-1551 Mainzer Romanistische Arbeiten
0542-1594 Maison de Marie Claire
0542-1748 Egyptian Statistical Journal
0542-2108 Makedonski Folklor
0542-3570 Malaysia. Department of Statistics. Annual Bulletin of Statistics
0542-3686 Monthly Statistical Bulletin of West Malaysia
0542-397X Malaysian Chinese Association. Annual Report
0542-5395 Manitoba Crop Insurance Corporation. Annual Report
0542-559X Manitoba Library Association Bulletin
0542-5794 Manpower Information Service *see* 0146-9673
0542-5808 Manpower Journal
0542-6243 Map Collectors Circle†
0542-626X Maps†
0542-6375 Universidad del Zulia. Facultad de Medicina. Revista
0542-6480 Marburger Abhandlungen zur Politischen Wissenschaft
0542-6685 Marches Publics
0542-6758 Mare Balticum
0542-6766 International Association of Geodesy. Commission Permanente des Marees Terrestres. Marees Terrestres Bulletin d'Information
0542-7029 Marine Resources of the Atlantic Coast
0542-7363 Marketing Forum *see* 0307-7667
0542-7770 Marxistische Blaetter
0542-8343 Maryland English Journal
0542-8351 Maryland Genealogical Society Bulletin
0542-836X Maryland Lawyer's Manual
0542-9307 University of Massachusetts. School of Engineering. Annual Report
0542-9951 Informatyka
0543-0313 Materials Management Journal of India
0543-0941 Mathematics and Its Applications†
0543-1433 Mauritania. Direction de la Statistique et des Etudes Economiques. Bulletin Mensuel Statistique
0543-1565 Mauritius. Director of Audit. Report
0543-1719 Max Freiherr von Oppenheim-Stiftung. Schriften
0543-1735 Veroeffentlichungen des Max-Reger-Institutes
0543-1786 Ma'yanot
0543-1972 Measurement Techniques
0543-2146 Med-Events†
0543-2243 Medecine de l'Homme
0543-3657 Medjunarodna Politika
0543-3770 Meeting on Soil Correlation for North America. (Report)
0543-3789 Meeting on Soil Survey Correlation and Interpretation for Latin America. Report
0543-5056 Merchant Explorer
0543-5099 Mercurius†
0543-5900 "Meteor" Forschungsergebnisse. Reihe A. Allgemeines, Physik und Chemie des Meeres
0543-5919 "Meteor" Forschungsergebnisse. Reihe B. Meteorologie und Aeronomie
0543-5919 "Meteor" Forschungsergebnisse. Reihe C. Geologie und Geophysik
0543-5935 "Meteor" Forschungsergebnisse. Reihe D. Biologie
0543-6095 Methodology and Science
0543-615X Metmenys
0543-6206 Metodistkyrkans i Sverige. Aarsbok
0543-6915 Principales Indicadores Economicos de Mexico
0543-758X Anuario de Letras
0543-7741 Mexico
0543-8497 Michigan. Geological Survey Division. Bulletin
0543-940X University of Michigan. Great Lakes Research Division. Special Report
0543-9833 Michigan Jewish History
0543-9930 Michigan Slavic Materials
0544-0327 Mid-Atlantic Industrial Waste Conference Proceedings
0544-1153 Migraine News
0544-1188 Migration Today
0544-1374 Fondazione Giangiacomo Feltrinelli. Annali
0544-2540 Mineralogical Journal
0544-2648 Giornale di Fisica Sanitaria e Protezione Contro le Radiazioni-Minerva Fisiconucleare
0544-3105 Minnesota. Geological Survey. Information Circulars
0544-3512 Minnesota Economic Data: Countries and Regions
0544-3520 Minnesota English Newsletter
0544-358X Minnesota History News
0544-408X Miscelanea de Estudios Arabes y Hebraicos
0544-4136 Miscellanea Musicologica
0544-439X Missions Digest and Year Book *see* 0317-266X
0544-5094 Missouri Archaeological Society. Research Series
0544-5396 U M R Journal†
0544-5779 Mitsubishi Electric Engineer†
0544-6511 Modern Concepts of Medical Virology, Oncology and Cytology†
0544-7178 Modern's Market Guide
0544-7526 Momento
0544-7763 Mondo della Musica
0544-8417 Monographs in Semiconductor Physics
0544-8433 Monographs in the Economics of Development
0544-845X Monographs on American Art
0544-9189 Uruguay. Biblioteca Nacional. Revista
0545-0209 Moody's Handbook of Corporate Managements *see* 0070-7627
0545-0217 Moody's Industrial Manual
0545-0233 Moody's Municipal & Government Manual
0545-0241 Moody's Public Utility Manual
0545-0373 Morgannwg
0545-0489 Morocco. Direction de la Statistique. Bulletin Mensuel des Statistiques
0545-2252 New Jersey. Division of Water Resources. Water Resources Circulars
0545-6061 New York City Trade Union Handbook
0545-7041 New Zealand. Dairy Production and Marketing Board. Annual Report and Statement of Accounts *changed to* New Zealand. Dairy Board. Annual Report and Statement of Accounts
0545-7157 New Zealand. Department of Statistics. External Trade. Country Analyses†
0545-7289 New Zealand. Government Printing Office. Government Publications
0545-7297 New Zealand. Lottery Board of Control. Report *changed to* New Zealand Lottery Board. Report
0545-7785 New Zealand News Review
0545-7866 New Zealand Shipping Directory
0545-9249 Universidad Nacional Autonoma de Nicaragua. Biblioteca Central. Boletin
0545-9516 Niger. Service de la Statistique. Bulletin Trimestriel de Statistique *changed to* Niger. Direction de la Statistique et des Comptes Nationaux. Bulletin Trimestriel de Statistique
0545-9532 Niger; Fraternite-Travail-Progres
0545-9923 Nigeria. Meteorological Service. Agrometeorological Bulletin
0546-0719 Japan Printing Art Annual
0546-0786 Commodity Classification for Foreign Trade Statistics: Japan
0546-093X Japanese National Railways. Facts and Figures
0546-109X Annual Report of the Development of Agriculture in Japan
0546-126X Japan Steel Works Technical Review
0546-2347 Noise and Smog News
0546-3432 Norman Ford's Florida
0546-4552 E S E Notes
0546-4854 North Carolina Music Teacher
0546-5370 Northeast Folklore Society Newsletter
0546-5427 Northeastern Forest Fire Protection Commission. Compact News
0546-5559 Northern Dog News *see* 0164-4483
0546-6210 Northwest Ruralite *changed to* Ruralite
0546-9937 Nutmeg Shelf *changed to* Provisioner
0547-034X N.A.S.S.P. Newsletter
0547-051X N E C Research and Development
0547-0730 N P A News
0547-0749 N R C - Nouvelle Revue Canadienne
0547-1435 Collected Papers on Sciences of Atmosphere and Hydrosphere
0547-1567 Nagoya University. Institute of Plasma Physics. Annual Review
0547-1788 University of Nairobi. Institute for Development Studies. Discussion Papers
0547-1796 University College, Nairobi. Institute for Development Studies. Occasional Papers *changed to* University of Nairobi. Institute for Development Studies. Occasional Paper
0547-3101 Nase Gospodarstvo
0547-3101 Nase Teme
0547-3616 National Agricultural Society of Ceylon. Journal
0547-4175 National Association of Schools of Music. Directory
0547-4205 National Association of Secondary School Principals. Curriculum Report
0547-4728 National Business Education Yearbook
0547-485X National Catholic Educational Association. Calendar of Meetings of National and Regional Educational Associations†
0547-5090 Comitetul National Pentru Apararea Pacii din Republica Socialista Romania. Information Bulletin
0547-5570 National Cooperative Highway Research Program Synthesis of Highway Practice
0547-5619 C O S E R V Newsletter (National Council for Community Services to International Visitors) *changed to* N C I V Newsletter
0547-5643 National Council for Geographic Education. Special Publications
0547-616X National Directory of College Athletics (Men's Edition)
0547-6658 National Endowment for the Arts. Guide to Programs
0547-6844 Birth Defects Original Article Series
0547-7115 National Guild of Catholic Psychiatrists. Bulletin
0547-7204 Consumer Attitudes and Buying Plans
0547-7212 Consumer Market Indicators†
0547-7271 National Industrial Conference Board. Investment Statistics. Capital Appropriations *see* 0361-4239
0547-7301 Conference Board. Investment Statistics. Utility Appropriations *see* 0360-523X
0547-7557 National Institute of Sciences of India. Biographical Memoirs of Fellows *changed to* Indian National Science Academy. Biographical Memoirs of Fellows
0547-7573 National Institute of Sciences of India. Yearbook *see* 0073-6619
0547-8448 National Register of Microform Masters
0547-8626 Animals for Research
0547-8804 Financial and Operating Results of Department and Specialty Stores
0547-8847 N R E C A Legal Reporting Service *see* 0362-8833
0547-888X Fleet Safety Newsletter - Motor Transportation
0548-0523 Nautologia
0548-0906 University of Nebraska. Department of Agricultural Education. Report
0548-1163 Nederlandsche Entomologische Vereniging. Monographs
0548-1384 Need a Lift?
0548-1643 Annual of Advertising Art in Japan
0548-1910 Netherlands. Centraal Bureau voor de Statistiek. Maandcijfers van de Invoer, Uitvoer en Assemblage van Motorrijtuigen.
0548-1937 Netherlands. Centraal Bureau voor de Statistiek. Maandstatistiek Politie en Justitie
0548-2674 Neue Arzneimittel und Spezialitaeten
0548-2801 Neue Heimat
0548-3093 Neues von Rohde und Schwarz
0548-4065 New Brunswick Development Corporation. Annual Report†
0548-4081 New Brunswick Home Economics Association. Newsletter
0548-4162 New Canadian Film
0548-4340 New Directions in Psychology†
0548-4456 New England Electrical Blue Book
0548-4537 New Era *changed to* Nave Parva
0548-5150 New Jersey. Bureau of Statistical Analysis and Social Research. Schools for the Mentally Retarded
0548-5924 New Management
0548-5967 New Mexico. Agricultural Experiment Station. Research Report
0548-5975 New Mexico. Bureau of Mines and Mineral Resources. Memoir
0548-6599 New River News
0548-6793 New South Wales District Court Reports
0548-6831 University of New South Wales, Kensington. Research and Publications
0548-7269 Foundation Center. Report *see* 0190-3357
0548-7390 New York Stock Exchange Monthly Review *changed to* New York Stock Exchange. Statistical Highlights
0548-7900 School Business Management Handbook†
0548-9040 New York State English Council. Monograph Series
0548-9067 New York State Industrial Directory
0548-9415 Cancer Data: Deaths and Cases Reported (Wellington)
0548-9911 Mortality and Demographic Data
0548-992X Mental Health Data
0548-9938 Hospital and Selected Morbidity Data
0548-9962 New Zealand. Customs Department. Customs Bulletin
0549-0014 New Zealand. Road Research Unit. Newsletter
0549-0030 New Zealand. Road Research Unit. Bulletin
0549-0219 New Zealand Concrete Construction
0549-0294 New Zealand Federation of Labour. Bulletin
0549-110X News from the Ukraine
0549-2351 Nigeria. Federal Ministry of Labour. Quarterly Review.
0549-2513 Nigeria. Federal Department of Petroleum Resources. Monthly Petroleum Information *changed to* Nigerian National Petroleum Corporation. Monthly Petroleum Information
0549-2629 Nigeria and the Classics *changed to* Museum Africum
0549-2734 Nigerian Industrial Development Bank. Annual Report and Accounts
0549-2998 Nihon University. Research Institute of Science and Technology. Report
0549-317X Balance of Payments Monthly
0549-3811 Japan Society for Aeronautical and Space Sciences. Transactions
0549-4192 Japanese Political Science Association. Yearbook
0549-4540 Mathematical Society of Japan. Publications
0549-4826 Niigata University. Faculty of Agriculture. Memoirs
0549-6179 Norddeutsche Studentenzeitung
0549-6330 Scandinavian Institute of African Studies. Newsletter
0549-7000 Norske Veritas Classification and Registry of Shipping. Publication
0549-7078 North American Mentor
0549-7175 N A T O Handbook

0549-7728 North Carolina State Library Newsletter *see* 0193-4309
0549-8333 North Dakota Securities Bulletin
0549-8368 North Dakota Growth Indicators
0549-8899 Northeast Asia Journal of Theology
0550-0567 Norway. Statistisk Sentralbyraa. Statistisk Ukehefte/Weekly Bulletin of Statistics
0550-0850 Ukrainian Art Digest
0550-0923 Notes et Documents Voltaiques
0550-0958 Notes from Eastman *see* 0147-345X
0550-0990 Notes on Cardiovascular Diseases
0550-1067 Noticias de Galapagos
0550-1091 Noticias Sobre Reforma Agraria†
0550-1105 Noticiero del Cafe
0550-1156 Notiziario Chimico e Farmaceutico
0550-1555 Nova Americana†
0550-1741 Nova Scotia. Department of Labour. Economics and Research Division. Wage Rates, Salaries and Hours of Labour in Nova Scotia
0550-2241 Prirodni Vedy. Rada Biologicka *see* 0139-5106
0550-225X Prirodni Vedy. Rada Chemicke *see* 0139-5351
0550-3132 Nuclear Law Bulletin
0550-3205 Nuclear Physics
0550-3213 Nuclear Physics, Section B
0550-3248 Nuclear Science Abstracts of Japan *see* 0029-5620
0550-4082 Nuttall Ornithological Club. Publications
0550-4112 Nya Perspektiv
0550-4333 National Association of Real Estate Investment Funds N A R E I F Handbook of Member Trusts *see* 0092-4865
0550-4376 N.C.A.I. Sentinel *changed to* Sentinel (Washington, D.C.)
0550-4791 N E I W P C C Aqua News
0550-5054 New York University Education Quarterly
0550-5666 National Braille Association. Bulletin
0550-5682 N C E A Notes
0550-5755 Classroom Practices in Teaching English
0550-6565 New York Botanical Garden Newsletter†
0550-6638 New York (State). Department of Labor. Statistics on Operations
0550-6743 New Zealand National Society for Earthquake Engineering. Bulletin
0550-6891 Niger
0550-7006 North Carolina. Laws, Statutes, Etc. Planning Legislation in North Carolina
0550-712X Northian Newsletter
0550-7138 Northland Newsletter†
0550-7170 Norway. Statistisk Sentralbyraa. Folkemengden Etter Alder og Ekteskapelig Status/Population by Age and Marital Status
0550-7421 National Association of Independent Schools. Annual Report
0550-7448 National Bibliography of Cases in Business Administration†
0550-824X Trends in Health and Health Services
0550-8398 Non-Ionizing Radiation
0550-8401 Non-Profit Organization Tax Letter
0550-8525 North of Scotland College of Agriculture, Aberdeen. Annual Report *see* 0143-8654
0550-8843 N A F A Conference Brochure & Reference Book *changed to* N A F A Annual Reference Book
0550-9483 New Mexico Labor Market Trends *changed to* New Mexico Manpower Review
0550-9955 Nova Scotia Labour-Management Study Conference. Proceedings
0551-0503 Plastics Age
0551-0910 Plunkett Foundation for Co-Operative Studies. Occasional Papers
0551-3464 Politisk Revy
0551-651X Politechnika Poznanska. Zeszyty Naukowe. Bibliografia
0551-6625 Uniwersytet im. Adama Mickiewicza w Poznaniu. Wydzial Matematyki, Fizyki i Chemii. Prace. Seria Matematyka *changed to* Matematyka
0551-9039 Pravnicke Studie
0551-9276 Predi-Briefs
0552-1734 Problemes de l'Europe
0552-2005 Problems of the Baltic
0552-2188 Problemy Opiekunczo- Wychowawcze
0552-4199 Przeglad Kolejowy Przewozowy *see* 0137-219X
0552-4245 Przeglad Zachodnio - Pomorski
0552-5276 Census of Manufacturing Industries of Puerto Rico
0552-5934 Pulsen†
0552-6426 Pure Life Society. Annual Report
0552-6450 Push Pin Graphic
0552-6981 Publizistik Wissenschaftlicher Referatedienst
0552-7252 Pacific Coast Archaeological Society Quarterly
0552-7325 Pacific Dairyman *changed to* Utah Farmer-Stockman
0552-7333 Pacific Geology
0552-7635 Packaging Machinery Catalog *changed to* Package Engineering Annual Buyers Guide
0552-7775 Paedagogische Studien
0552-8100 World Peace Through Law Center. Bulletin†
0552-8259 Pakistan's Key Economic Indicators
0552-8968 Pakistan Hotel Guide
0552-9034 Pakistan Journal of Agricultural Sciences
0552-9050 Pakistan Journal of Scientific Research
0552-9115 Pakistan Petroleum Limited. Annual Report
0552-9395 Palante
0552-9506 Osservatorio Regionale per le Malattie della Vite. Osservazioni di Meteorologia, Fenologia e Patologia della Vite
0552-9638 Palingenesia
0552-9913 Pan American Development Foundation. Annual Report
0553-0067 Pan American Highway Congress. Boletin Informativo†
0553-013X Pan American Institute of Geography and History. Commission on History. Bulletin†
0553-0237 Studies in Export Promotion
0553-027X Pan American Union. Department of Educational Affairs. Bulletin of Information *changed to* Organization of American States. Department of Educational Affairs. Bulletin of Information
0553-0296 Pan American Union. Department of Educational Affairs. Resena Analitica *changed to* Organization of American States. Department of Educational Affairs. Resena Analitica
0553-0326 Pan American Associations in the United States; A Directory with Supplementary Lists of Other Associations. Inter-American and General
0553-0334 Pan American Union. Department of Scientific Affairs. Report of Activities. *changed to* Organization of American States. Department of Scientific Affairs. Report of Activities
0553-0342 Organization of American States. Department of Scientific Affairs. Serie de Biologia: Monografias
0553-0377 Organization of American States. Department of Scientific Affairs. Serie de Quimica: Monografias
0553-0385 Estudio Social de America Latina†
0553-0407 Pan American Union. Department of Social Affairs. Studies and Monographs†
0553-058X Inter-American Briefs†
0553-0601 Pan Am's World Guide
0553-0644 University of Malaya. Chinese Language Society. Journal
0553-0660 Estadistica Panamena. Situacion Economica. Seccion 331-Comercio. Comercio Exterior
0553-0946 Panchayati Raj *see* 0023-5660
0553-1454 Grocers Bags and Grocers Sacks
0553-2361 Materiaux pour le Manuel de l'Histoire des Song†
0553-2507 Musee de l'Homme, Paris. Catalogues. Serie B: Afrique Blanche et Levant
0553-2515 Musee de l'Homme, Paris. Catalogues. Serie G: Arctiques
0553-3066 Park News
0553-3104 Parking Progress *see* 0362-3122
0553-3864 Patent Law Annual-Southwestern Legal Foundation
0553-4054 Patterson's Schools Classified
0553-4283 Peace Research Reviews
0553-4917 Penguin Modern Poets†
0553-5743 Foreign Policy Research Institute. Research Monograph Series *changed to* Foreign Policy Research Institute. Monograph Series
0553-5816 University of Pennsylvania. Population Studies Center. Analytical and Technical Report
0553-6065 Pennsylvania State Industrial Directory
0553-6812 Permanent International Committee of Linguists. Committe on Linguistic Statistics. Publication†
0553-6855 General Treaty for Central American Economic Integration. Permanent Secretariat. Carta Informativa
0553-6863 Convenios Centroamericanos de Integration Economica.
0553-6898 General Treaty for Central American Economic Integration. Permanent Secretariat. Newsletter
0553-738X Perspective
0553-8467 Pesquisas: Publicacoes de Antropologia
0553-8475 Pesquisas: Publicacoes de Botanica
0553-8491 Pesquisas: Publicacoes de Historia
0553-8505 Pesquisas: Publicacoes de Zoologia
0553-8572 Pet Dealer
0553-9196 Pharmaceutical Chemistry Journal
0553-9323 Pharmacien Biologiste
0553-9382 Pharmacopoeia Internationalis
0553-9978 Philippine Atomic Energy Commission. Annual Report
0554-0186 Philippines. National Census and Statistics Office. Vital Statistical Report
0554-2537 Planiranje i Analiza Poslovanja
0554-2626 Planning News
0554-2693 Plant Engineering Directory & Specifications Catalog
0554-2731 Plant Location
0554-291X Plasticos
0554-3037 Play Index
0554-3045 Plays. A Classified Guide to Play Selection
0554-4084 Poeziya(Kiev)
0554-4246 Pointer
0554-498X Polish Yearbook of International Law
0554-5196 Political Science Review
0554-5455 Politische Bildung
0554-5749 Polska Akademia Nauk. Instytut Geografii. Prace Geograficzne *see* 0373-6547
0554-579X Polska Akademia Nauk. Oddzial w Krakowie. Komisja Historycznoliteracka. Prace
0554-7555 Ports and Harbors
0554-7598 Portsmouth Papers
0554-8063 Uniwersytet im. Adama Mickiewicza w Poznaniu. Wydzial Biologii i Nauk o Ziemi. Zeszyty Naukowe. Geografia *changed to* Geografia
0554-839X Postepy Astronautyki
0554-873X Pount
0554-890X Power Transmission & Bearing Handbook *changed to* Power Transmission Design Handbook
0554-9221 Rocenka Povetrnostnich Pozorovani Observatore Karlov
0554-9256 Naprstkovo Muzeum Asijskych, Africkych a Americkych Kultur. Annals
0554-9884 Prajna
0554-9906 Prakit Jain Institute Research Publication Series
0555-0025 Zeszyty Prasoznawcze
0555-0572 Presbyterian Layman
0555-0963 Preventive Law Newsletter
0555-1501 Princeton University. Center of International Studies. Research Monograph Series
0555-2176 Problemas Brasileiros
0555-3407 Professional Pilot Magazine
0555-3989 Progress in Industrial Microbiology†
0555-3989 Progress in Industrial Microbiology
0555-4276 Progress in Solid Mechanics†
0555-4349 Progress of Medical Parasitology in Japan
0555-4810 Prospettive dell'Industria Italiana
0555-5027 Protokolle
0555-5264 Przemysl Fermentacyjny i Rolny
0555-5620 Psychological Research Bulletin
0555-5795 Psychopathology and Pictorial Expression†
0555-5914 Public Affairs
0555-6015 Public Health Papers
0555-6023 Public Library Abstracts†
0555-6031 Public Library Reporter
0555-621X Public Works in Canada
0555-6392 Publishing, Entertainment and Advertising and Allied Fields Law Quarterly
0555-6511 Puerto Rico. Division of Demographic Registry and Vital Statistics. Annual Vital Statistics Report
0555-6562 Puerto Rico. Planning Board. Statistics Coordination Section. Programas Estadisticos
0555-6635 Empleo y Desempleo en Puerto Rico
0555-6945 Pulse
0555-7666 University of the Punjab. Journal of Research: Humanities
0555-7860 Puranam
0555-8158 Pushto
0555-8786 Pakistan. Ministry of Finance Estimates of Foreign Assistance *changed to* Pakistan. Finance Division. Estimates of Foreign Assistance
0556-0152 Phyllis Schlafly Report
0556-056X Police Research Bulletin
0556-0691 Pomarania Antiqua
0556-1442 Pressure Research Notes†
0556-1515 Printing Historical Society Newsletter *changed to* Printing Historical Society Bulletin
0556-171X Problemy Prochnosti
0556-1906 Progress of Science in India
0556-2791 Physical Review A (General Physics)
0556-2805 Physical Review B (Solid State) *changed to* Physical Review B (Condensed Matter)
0556-2813 Physical Review C (Nuclear Physics)
0556-2821 Physical Review D (Particles and Fields)
0556-3100 Problems in Education and Nation Building†
0556-3321 Pakistan Journal of Botany
0556-3488 Partio
0556-350X Pasquim
0556-3585 Exports by Pennsylvania Manufacturers
0556-3593 Pennsylvania. Department of Commerce. Bureau of Statistics. Statistics by Industry and Size of Establishment
0556-3615 Pennsylvania. Department of Commerce. Bureau of Statistics, Research and Planning. Statistics for Manufacturing Industries
0556-3860 Photochemistry
0556-431X Psychosocial Process *see* 0190-230X
0556-5006 Photofact Annual Index
0556-5367 Antique Trader. Price Guide to Antiques and Collectors' Items
0556-543X Produktschap voor Siergewassen. Statistiek *changed to* Produktschap voor Siergewassen. Jaarverslag/ Statistiek
0556-5693 Revista de Derecho
0556-5987 Revista de Historia de las Ideas
0556-5995 Revista de Historia de Rosario

0556-6177 Universidad de Navarra. Revista de Medicina
0556-6436 Revista del Folklore Ecuatoriano
0556-6703 Revista Interamericana de Ciencias Sociales†
0556-6908 Revista Paraguaya de Microbiologia
0556-6916 Revista Paranaense de Desenvolvimento
0556-7238 Revue Bibliographique des Ouvrages de Droit, de Jurisprudence, d'Economie Politique, de Science Financiere, de Sociologie, d'Histoire et de Philosophie
0556-7262 Revue Camerounaise de Pedagogie
0556-7335 Revue Annuelle d'Histoire du Quatorzieme Arrondissement de Paris
0556-7343 Revue d'Histoire et de Civilisation du Maghreb
0556-7793 Revue Francaise de Dietetique
0556-7807 Revue Francaise de Pedagogie
0556-7963 Revue Juridique Themis
0556-8099 Revue Roumaine de Geologie, Geophysique et Geographie. Geographie
0556-8102 Revue Roumaine de Geologie, Geophysique et Geographie. Geologie
0556-8110 Revue Roumaine de Geologie, Geophysique et Geographie. Geophysique
0556-8587 Rhode Island Audubon Report
0556-8609 Rhode Island Jewish Historical Notes
0556-8692 Zimbabwe. Registrar of Insurance. Report
0556-8706 Zimbabwe. Central Statistical Office. Monthly Digest of Statistics
0556-9605 Rhodesiana
0557-0352 Japan. Government Forest Experiment Station, Tokyo. Annual Report *changed to* Japan. Forestry and Forest Products Research Institute. Annual Report
0557-0395 Japan. Government Forest Experiment Station. Kyushu Branch. Annual Report
0557-0506 Bolsa de Valores do Rio de Janeiro. Resumo Anual
0557-1391 Rivista Italiana di Diritto e Procedura Penale
0557-1413 Rivista Italiana di Piscicultura e Ittiopatologia
0557-1464 Rivista Trimestrale di Diritto Pubblico
0557-1693 Rocenka Odborara
0557-2088 Rocznik Nadnotecki
0557-2282 Rodna Gruda
0557-2614 Romanfuehrer
0557-3122 Universita degli Studi di Roma. Seminario di Archeologia e Storia dell'Arte Greca e Romana. Studi Miscellanei
0557-319X Central Building Research Institute. Building Digests
0557-322X Central Building Research Institute. List of Publications
0557-3254 University of Roorkee Research Journal†
0557-4242 Royal Western Australian Historical Society. Newsletter
0557-532X Russian Orthodox Greek Catholic Church of America. Yearbook and Church Directory *see* 0145-7950
0557-5737 Fer de Lance
0557-644X Retreader's Journal
0557-6601 Royal New Zealand Institute of Horticulture. Journal *see* 0110-5760
0557-661X R. Y. A. News
0557-6911 University of Reading. Department of Agricultural Economics and Management. Farm Business Data
0557-6989 Recherches Anglaises et Americaines
0557-7330 Research into Disease
0557-7527 Review of Plant Protection Research
0557-7705 Revue Archeologique de Narbonnaise
0557-7713 Revue d'Acoustique
0557-7853 Rheinische Ausgrabungen
0557-8019 Rivista di Studi Salernitani†
0557-8183 Rural Advance
0557-8280 Readings in Development Economics
0557-8558 Revista Interamericana de Sociologia
0557-8639 University of Rhode Island. Law of the Sea Institute. Special Publications†
0557-9147 Record Exchanger
0557-9430 Riabilitazione
0558-0293 S I A M Series in Applied Mathematics†
0558-1613 Shakhs
0558-2431 Saitama University. Science Reports. Series A: Mathematics
0558-2431 Saitama University. Science Reports. Series A: Mathematics, Physics and Chemistry *see* 0558-2431
0558-244X Saitama University. Science Reports. Series B: Biology and Earth Sciences†
0558-3489 Salzburger Beitraege zur Paracelsusforschung
0558-3918 San Diego Economic Bulletin *changed to* Economic Bulletin (San Diego)
0558-4477 San Marino (Republica). Segretaria di Stato per gli Affari Esteri. Notiziario *changed to* San Marino (Republica). Segretaria di Stato per gli Affari Esteri. Notizia
0558-4779 Industry and Commerce
0558-6976 Saskatchewan Economic Review
0558-7220 Saudi Arabian Monetary Agency. Annual Report
0558-9746 Schriftenreihe fuer Raumforschung und Raumplanung.
0559-1414 Scientia et Praxis
0559-1422 Scientia Iuridica
0559-1791 Scottish Fisheries Bulletin
0559-2674 Sedar
0559-5258 Serial Slants *see* 0024-2527
0559-698X Social Development Research Institute. Organization and Activities
0559-8540 Shinrin Boeki Nyusu *changed to* Forest Protection
0559-8621 Shinshu University. Faculty of Textile Science and Technology. Journal. Series C: Chemistry
0559-9091 Shopping Center Newsletter
0559-9822 Sieboldia Acta Biologica
0560-0391 Silence
0560-0871 Sind University Journal of Education
0560-3641 Sociaal-Economische Raad. Verslag
0560-4168 Boletin de la Sociedad Cientifica del Paraguay y del Museo Etnografico
0560-5296 Societe des Etudes Juives. Memoires†
0560-6152 Society of Archer-Antiquaries. Journal
0560-8325 Songwriter's Annual Directory
0560-8996 Sources in Western Political Thought
0560-9208 South Africa. Geological Survey. Handbook
0560-9941 South African Wool and Textile Research Institute. Annual Report
0561-3663 Anejos de Archivo Espanol de Arqueologia
0561-4619 Spain. Ministerio de Educacion y Ciencia. Junta Nacional Contra el Analfabetismo. Boletin
0561-4902 Spain. Ministerio de la Vivienda. Estadistica de la Industria de la Construccion
0561-5062 Evolucion de la Economia Espanola†
0561-5313 Spain-U.S. Trade Bulletin
0561-7383 Srpska Akademija Nauka i Umetnosti. Predavanja
0561-7855 Stahlbau-Rundschau
0561-8630 State Administrative Officials (Classified by Functions)
0561-8738 State Bank of Pakistan. State Bank News
0561-922X Statistical Notes of Japan
0561-9440 Statistics & Facts About Nebraska Schools
0561-9998 University of Stellenbosch. Bureau for Economic Research. Opinion Survey Report
0562-0953 Statens Geotekniska Institut. Saertryck och Preliminaera Rapporter *changed to* Statens Geotekniska Institut. Rapports
0562-1887 Strojarstvo
0562-2719 Studia Anglistica Upsalienses
0562-4649 Subsidia Scientifica Franciscalia
0562-5033 Sudan Cotton Bulletin
0562-5068 Sudan Cotton Review
0562-5092 Sudan News Agency. English Daily Bulletin *changed to* SUNA
0562-5130 Sudan Society
0562-7087 Survivre *see* 0384-7810
0562-7451 Svenska Arkivsamfundet. Skriftserie
0562-8490 Sweden. Fisheries Board. Series Hydrography. Reports *see* 0346-8666
0562-861X Sweden. Riksfoersaekringsverket. Yrkesskador
0562-9020 Nouvelles Economiques de Suisse
0563-0355 Systemation Letter
0563-0924 S C A U L Newsletter
0563-1491 Universitaet des Saarlandes. Geographisches Institut. Arbeiten
0563-1637 Terre Malgache†
0563-1742 Archives d'Ethnographie *changed to* Musee Royal de l'Afrique Centrale. Archives d'Anthropologie
0563-1874 Test Collection Bulletin *changed to* News on Tests
0563-2153 Teva Va-Aretz
0563-2595 University of Texas. Humanities Research Center. Tower Bibliographical Series
0563-2625 Texas Biannual of Electronics Research *changed to* Texas Annual of Electronics Research
0563-3400 Thai Chamber of Commerce. Business Directory
0563-3737 Thailand Year Book
0563-4040 Theatre News
0563-4245 Au Coeur de l'Afrique
0563-4407 Theorie des Systemes
0563-4458 Theorie und Praxis der Koerperkultur
0563-4660 Things *see* 0440-2316
0563-4725 33 Magazine *see* 0149-1210
0563-4784 This Is Malawi
0563-4806 This Week in Public Health†
0563-5446 Timber Tax Journal
0563-5489 Timeless Fellowship
0563-6140 Tobacco Bibliography
0563-6191 Tax Burden on Tobacco
0563-6523 Tohoku University. Science Reports. Series 7: Geography
0563-6590 Tohoku University. Research Institute for Strength and Fracture of Materials. Reports
0563-7848 University of Tokyo. Institute for Nuclear Study. INS-PT
0563-7856 University of Tokyo. Institute for Nuclear Study. INS-TCA†
0563-7864 University of Tokyo. Institute for Nuclear Study. INS-TCB†
0563-7872 University of Tokyo. Institute for Nuclear Study. INS-TH
0563-7880 University of Tokyo. Institute for Nuclear Study. INS-TL
0563-7902 Strong-Motion Earthquake Records in Japan
0563-7937 University of Tokyo. Faculty of Engineering. Journal: Series B
0563-8054 University of Tokyo. Institute of Social Science. Annals
0563-8372 Tokyo University of Fisheries. Report
0563-8887 Tools and Tillage
0563-8895 Top Companies
0563-9425 Torreia
0563-9727 Universite des Sciences Sociales de Toulouse. Annales
0563-9743 Homo
0563-9751 Litteratures
0563-9786 Via Domitia
0563-9794 Universite de Toulouse II (le Mirail). Institut d'Art Prehistorique. Travaux
0564-0334 Trabajo
0564-0342 Trabalho
0564-0482 Trade Directories of the World
0564-0490 Trade Directory and Guide Book to Ethiopia
0564-089X Training Research Abstracts *changed to* Training and Development Journal (1978)
0564-1373 Transports
0564-1632 Travel Market Yearbook *changed to* Travel Market Yearbook (1980)
0564-1829 Tree Planters' Notes
0564-2159 Tribal Research and Development Institute. Bulletin
0564-2477 Universita degli Studi di Trieste. Istituto di Storia dell'Arte (Pubblicazioni)
0564-2612 Trinidad and Tobago. Central Statistical Office. Continuous Sample Survey of Population
0564-3287 Trooper
0564-3295 Tropical Ecology
0564-3325 Tropical Stored Products Information
0564-3392 Truck Data Book
0564-4070 Universidad Nacional de Tucuman. Facultad de Filosofia y Letras. Cuadernos de Humanitas
0564-4232 Tuebinger Geographische Studien
0564-4402 Tulane Tax Institute
0564-5093 Turk Kulturu Arastirmalari
0564-5409 Handelshoegeskolan vid Aabo Akademi. Ekonomisk-Geografiska Institutionen. Memoranda *changed to* Aabo Akademi. Ekonomisk-Geografiska Institutionen. Memoranda
0564-5409 Handelshoegeskolan vid Aabo Akademi. Ekonomisk-Geografiska Institutionen. Meddelanden *changed to* Aabo Akademi. Ekonomisk-Geografiska Institutionen. Meddelanden
0564-5654 Twentieth Century Series†
0564-6278 Tilburg Studies in Economics
0564-6294 Topics in Astrophysics and Space Physics
0564-6545 Tanzania.Central Statistical Bureau. Survey of Industrial Production *changed to* Tanzania. Bureau of Statistics. Survey of Industrial Production
0564-6723 Tea Research Association. Scientific Annual Report
0564-6758 Tecnologia de Alimentos
0564-6855 University of Texas. Humanities Research Center. Bibliographical Monograph Series
0564-6898 University of Tokyo. Ocean Research Institute. Bulletin
0564-7169 T A I U S
0564-724X Tanzania Directory of Trades
0564-7630 University of Tokyo. Research Institute of Logopedics and Phoniatrics. Annual Bulletin
0564-7975 C. E. R. E. S. Cahiers. Serie Linguistique
0564-836X Report on Tourism Statistics in Tanzania
0564-8602 Memphis State University. Anthropological Research Center. Occasional Papers
0564-8742 University of Tokyo. Computer Center. Report
0564-9048 25 Weekend Build-It Projects†
0564-9498 U. S. National Credit Union Administration. Research Report
0565-0704 U. S. Fish and Wildlife Service. Investigations in Fish Control
0565-0828 U.S. Bureau of the Census. Census Bureau Methodological Research
0565-0909 Current Business Reports: Monthly Retail Trade *see* 0363-8448
0565-0917 Current Population Reports: Federal-State Cooperative Program for Population Estimates
0565-0933 U. S. Bureau of the Census. Guide to Foreign Trade Statistics
0565-0941 Foreign Trade Reports. Highlights of U.S. Export and Import Trade
0565-1034 Current Business Reports: Monthly Department Store Sales for Selected Areas
0565-1190 U. S. Imports for Consumption and General Imports; Tariff Schedules Annotated by Country
0565-1204 Foreign Trade Reports. U.S. Trade with Puerto Rico and U.S. Possessions
0565-1530 U.S. Coast Guard Boating Statistics

ISSN INDEX 1257

0565-1603 U.S. Coastal Engineering Research Center. Bulletin and Progress Reports†
0565-1980 Poultry Market Statistics
0565-2820 U. S. Department of Housing and Urban Development. Annual Report
0565-5560 U.S. Foreign Broadcast Information Service. Daily Reports: Soviet Union
0565-6311 U S I T T Newsletter
0565-6567 U. S. Law Enforcement Assistance Administration. Annual Report
0565-7199 Management (Baltimore)
0565-744X U.S. National Center for Education Statistics. Earned Degrees Conferred
0565-7717 U. S. National Highway Traffic Safety Administration. Motor Vehicle Safety Defect Recall Campaigns
0565-811X Medical Subject Headings
0565-8454 Where to Write for Divorce Records: U.S. and Outlying Areas
0565-8462 Where to Write for Marriage Records *see* 0162-0916
0565-8543 Gulfstream
0565-8721 U. S. Forest Service. Research Paper NC
0565-873X U.S. Forest Service. Resource Bulletin NC
0565-9442 U. S. Office of Water Resources Research. Annual Report *changed to* U. S. Office of Water Research and Technology. Annual Report
0565-9582 Directory of Registered Patent Attorneys and Agents *see* 0361-3844
0566-0327 U.S. Social Security Administration. Research and Statistics Notes
0566-0335 U.S. Social Security Administration. Research Report
0566-0963 United Steelworkers of America. Information
0566-201X Universite de Yaounde. Faculte des Sciences. Annales
0566-2389 University of Richmond Law Review
0566-2680 Untei
0566-4152 Utah. Juvenile Court. Annual Report
0566-5655 U.S. General Services Administration. Management Improvement and Cost Reduction Goals
0566-6201 Unesco Asian Fiction Series
0566-7038 U.S. National Institute of Mental Health. Report Series on Mental Health Statistics. Series C: Methodology Reports
0566-7631 Census of Traffic on Main International Traffic Arteries *changed to* Census of Motor Traffic on Main International Traffic Arteries
0566-7658 United Nations. International Narcotics Control Board. Statistics on Narcotic Drugs Furnished by Governments in Accordance with the International Treaties and Maximum Levels of Opium Stocks
0566-8549 Selected United States Government Publications
0566-8654 Univers des Sciences et Techniques
0566-8719 University of Kentucky Research Foundation. Annual Report
0566-9197 Music News Bulletin
0566-9502 U.S. Department of Agriculture. Economics, Statistics, and Cooperatives Service. Agricultural Situation in the Far East and Oceania
0567-1469 Handelsrechtliche Entscheidungen
0567-1477 Austria. Oberlandesgericht Wien im Leistungsstreitverfahren Zweiter Instanz der Sozialversicherung (SSV). Entscheidungen
0567-168X Austrian Trade Bulletin
0567-2317 Automotive Rebuilder
0567-2392 Autopista
0567-2848 Avicultura Tecnica
0567-4069 A Ph A Newsletter *see* 0098-2814
0567-4263 A T A Professional Services Directory
0567-428X A U C A
0567-4565 Aarets Fotboll
0567-4573 Aarets Idrott
0567-4980 Abhandlungen fuer die Kunde des Morgenlandes
0567-5782 Academia de Ciencias de Cuba. Instituto de Oceanologia. Serie Oceanologica
0567-5871 Academia Dominicana de la Historia. Publicaciones
0567-6029 Academia Provincial de la Historia. Boletin
0567-6304 Revista de Istorie
0567-6541 Academie des Sciences. Comptes Rendus Hebdomadaires des Seances. Series C: Sciences Chimiques *changed to* Academie des Sciences. Comptes Rendus Hebdomadaires des Seances. Series 2: Mecanique, Physique, Chimie, Sciences de la Terre, Sciences de l'Univers
0567-655X Academie des Sciences. Comptes Rendus Hebdomadaires des Seances. Series D: Sciences Naturelles *changed to* Academie des Sciences. Comptes Rendus Hebdomadaires des Seances. Series 3: Sciences de la Vie
0567-6584 Academie Royale de Langue et de Litterature Francaises. Annuaires
0567-6592 Academie Royale des Sciences d'Outre Mer. Revue Bibliographique†
0567-6630 Academy of American Franciscan History. Bibliographical Series
0567-7254 Acta Asiatica
0567-7289 Acta Baltica
0567-7394 Acta Crystallographica. Section A: Crystal Physics, Diffraction, Theoretical and General Crystallography
0567-7408 Acta Crystallographica. Section B: Structural Crystallography and Crystal Chemistry
0567-7408 Acta Crystallographica *see* 0567-7408
0567-7467 Acta Universitatis Szegediensis de Attila Jozsef Nominatae. Acta Geographica
0567-7475 Acta Geographica Dedrecina
0567-7505 Acta Geologica Hispanica
0567-7513 Acta Geologica Lilloana
0567-753X Acta Herediana
0567-7572 Acta Horticulturae
0567-7599 Acta Humboldtiana. Series Historica
0567-7661 Acta Litteraria
0567-7734 Acta Medica et Biologica
0567-7785 Acta Mexicana de Ciencia y Tecnologia
0567-784X Acta Neophilologica
0567-7874 Acta Organologica
0567-7920 Acta Palaeontologica Polonica
0567-7947 Acta Physica et Chimica Debrecina
0567-8056 Acta Radiologica. Series 1: Diagnosis
0567-8064 Acta Radiologica. Series 2: Therapy, Physics, Biology *changed to* Acta Radiologica. Series 2: Oncology, Radiation Therapy, Physics and Biology
0567-8250 Acta Universitatis Carolinae: Medica
0567-8412 Action *see* 0093-0245
0567-8587 Organization of American States. Department of Educational Affairs. Actualidades†
0567-932X Adelphi Papers
0567-9907 Advances in Electrochemistry and Electrochemical Engineering
0568-0204 Advances in Test Measurement
0568-0301 World Advertising Expenditures
0568-0352 Advertising Research Foundation. Conference Proceedings†
0568-0476 Aegyptologische Abhandlungen
0568-0530 Aero West
0568-0581 University of Illinois at Urbana-Champaign. Department of Electrical Engineering. Aeronomy Laboratory. Aeronomy Report
0568-0743 Die Berliner Aerztekammer
0568-1138 Africa Institute of South Africa. Bulletin *changed to* Africa Institute Bulletin
0568-1308 African Development Bank. Report by the Board of Directors
0568-1332 African Historian
0568-2517 Agricultura Tecnica en Mexico
0568-3025 Agrociencia
0568-3114 Agrotecnia de Cuba
0568-3343 Ailleurs
0568-3424 Air Canada. Annual Report
0568-3653 Air Quality Monograph Series
0568-3866 Airplane, Missile and Spacecraft Structure Series†
0568-3939 Aisthesis
0568-4447 Akademie der Wissenschaften und der Literatur, Mainz. Orientalische Kommission. Veroeffentlichungen
0568-5230 Academy of Sciences of the U S S R. Division of Chemical Sciences. Bulletin
0568-6245 Glyatsiologiya
0568-6776 Akademiya Nauk S. S. S. R. Sibirskoe Otdelenie Uralskii Nauchnyi Tsentr. Institut Elektrkhimii. Trudy
0568-7276 Der Akademiker in Wirtschaft und Verwaltung
0568-7594 Aktuelle Fragen des Landbaues
0568-7632 Aktuelle Schaufenster *changed to* Das Schaufenster
0568-8442 Alaska. State Library, Juneau. State and Local Publications Received-Alaska
0568-9074 University of Alberta. Faculty of Agriculture. Agriculture Bulletin *changed to* University of Alberta. Agriculture and Forestry Bulletin
0568-9848 Revue Algerienne du Travail
0569-0196 All India Central Land Development Bank Cooperative Union. Journal *changed to* Land Bank Journal
0569-0838 Almanac for Geodetic Engineers
0569-0870 Almanach Africain
0569-096X Almanach Moderne
0569-1346 Altamura
0569-1796 Amateur Wrestling News
0569-1966 America by Car
0569-2229 American Antiquarian Society. News-Letter
0569-2245 American Assembly. Report
0569-230X School Nursing Monographs
0569-2393 American Association for the Advancement of Science. Committee on Desert and Arid Zone Research. Contributions
0569-2482 Report on the Credit Given by Educational Institutions *changed to* Transfer Credit Practices by Selected Education Institutions
0569-2628 A A F M Proceedings of Annual Meeting
0569-2679 American Association of Medical Clinics. Directory *see* 0098-2377
0569-292X American Bank Directory
0569-2954 American Bankers Association. Committee on Uniform Security Identification Procedures. C U S I P Directory
0569-3098 American Bar Association. Section of Administrative Law. Annual Reports of Divisions and Committees *see* 0090-3647
0569-3497 American Bibliography of Slavic and East European Studies
0569-3667 American Chamber of Commerce in Italy. Directory
0569-3845 American Christmas Tree Journal
0569-3950 A C O G Technical Bulletin
0569-3993 A C T Research Report
0569-4043 Industrial Ventilation; a Manual of Recommended Practice
0569-4108 American Council of Polish Cultural Clubs. Quarterly Review *changed to* Quarterly Review of Polish Heritage
0569-4221 American Crystallographic Association. Program & Abstracts
0569-4353 American Educational Research Association. Directory of Members†
0569-4450 American Entomological Institute. Contributions
0569-4833 American Foundation for the Study of Man. Publications
0569-5341 A I A Emerging Techniques
0569-5376 Research Problems in Biology
0569-5473 A I Ch E Equipment Testing Procedures
0569-5503 Electronic Components Conference. Proceedings
0569-5554 A I I E Transactions
0569-5716 Physics Manpower - Education and Employment Statistics
0569-5961 American Italian Historical Association. Newsletter
0569-6275 Financial Assistance for Library Education
0569-6348 American Lutheran Church. Yearbook
0569-6356 American Motor Carrier Directory: National Edition *changed to* American Motor Carrier Directory: North American Edition
0569-6364 American Motor Carrier Directory: Specialized Services Edition
0569-6534 American Medical Association. Directory of Officials and Staff
0569-6666 American Musicological Society. Greater New York Chapter. Publications
0569-6720 American Numismatic Society. Annual Report
0569-6763 A O A News Review *see* 0091-6269
0569-6852 American Petroleum Institute. Division of Statistics and Economics. Annual Statistical Review *changed to* Basic Petroleum Data Book
0569-6909 American Petroleum Institute. Division of Refining. Proceedings
0569-6917 Pharmaceutical Directory
0569-6992 American Phytopathological Society. Monographs
0569-714X American Psychological Association. Membership Register
0569-7344 American Review of Art and Science
0569-7468 Symposium on the Art of Glassblowing Proceedings.
0569-776X American Society for Training and Development. Membership Directory *see* 0092-4598
0569-7832 American Society of Animal Science. Western Section Proceedings
0569-7840 A S A Monograph
0569-7859 American Society of Appraisers. Appraisal and Valuation Manual
0569-7891 Transportation Engineering Journal
0569-7948 American Society of Civil Engineers. Construction Division. Journal
0569-8030 American Society of Civil Engineers. Power Division. Journal *changed to* American Society of Civil Engineers. Energy Division. Journal
0569-8057 Reinforced Concrete Research Council. Bulletins
0569-8073 American Society of Civil Engineers. Surveying and Mapping Division. Journal
0569-8081 American Society of Civil Engineers. Urban Planning and Development Division. Journal
0569-8154 American Dowser
0569-8154 American Society of Dowsers. Quarterly Digest *see* 0569-8154
0569-8219 American Society of Mammalogists. Special Publications
0569-8243 Reports on Diesel and Gas Engines Power Costs†
0569-8553 A S H A Reports
0569-8561 A S H A Directory
0569-9053 American Wedgwoodian
0569-9096 American Wildlife Region Series
0569-9258 Amerique Latine
0569-9460 Amministrazione della Difesa†
0569-9479 Amministrazione Tributi e Finanze
0569-9495 Amnesty International Annual Report *changed to* Amnesty International Report
0569-9789 Analecta Calasanctiana
0569-9827 Analecta Musicologia
0569-9843 Analecta Praehistorica Leidensia
0569-986X Analecta Romanica
0569-9894 Anales de Anatomia
0569-9908 Anales del Desarrollo

0570-023X	Ancient Peoples and Places†
0570-0655	Andhra Pradesh
0570-0973	Angol Filologiai Tanulmanyok
0570-1538	Annales Agriculturae Fenniae
0570-1724	Annales Malgaches. Droit *changed to* Universite de Madagascar. Annales. Serie Droit
0570-1791	Annals of Arid Zone
0570-1864	Annals of Regional Science
0570-2070	Union of European Football Associations. Handbook of U E F A
0570-2194	Geneva International Year Book†
0570-2658	Annual Survey of Commonwealth Law†
0570-2666	Annual Survey of Indian Law
0570-2674	Annual Survey of Massachusetts Law
0570-2976	Anthropological Studies
0570-3697	Antropologia Social
0570-393X	Anuario Bibliografico Colombiano
0570-3956	Anuario Brasileiro de Propaganda
0570-3980	Anuario Comercial Iberoamericano
0570-4006	Anuario Cultural del Peru
0570-4022	Anuario da Provincia de Mocambique *changed to* Anuario do Estado de Mocambique
0570-4200	Anuario del Desarrollo de la Educacion, la Ciencia y la Cultura en America Latina†
0570-4251	Anuario Ecuatoriano de Derecho Internacional
0570-426X	Anuario Estadistico Centroamericano de Comercio Exterior
0570-4324	Anuario Iberoamericano
0570-4359	Anuario Latinomamericano
0570-4723	Die Apothekenhelferin
0570-4839	Applied Economic Papers
0570-4898	Journal of Applied Polymer Science. Symposia
0570-4928	Applied Spectroscopy Reviews
0570-4979	Approach
0570-5029	Approdo Letterario†
0570-507X	Al-Aqlam Journal
0570-5258	Arab Observer†
0570-5886	Arbeitsmethoden der Medizinischen und Naturwissenschaftlichen Kriminalistik
0570-6068	Archaeologia Zambiana
0570-6270	Archeologia
0570-6483	Architectural Index
0570-6602	Architektur Aktuell
0570-6769	Archiv fuer Musikwissenschaft. Beihefte
0570-6793	Archiv fuer Vergleichende Kulturwissenschaft
0570-6955	Archives Medicales de l'Ouest
0570-7196	Archivos Venezolanos de Folklore
0570-7242	Archivum Bibliographicum Carmelitanum
0570-7293	Arco
0570-734X	Arctos; Acta Philologica Fennica
0570-7439	Arena†
0570-751X	Areopag
0570-8621	Argentine Republic. Mercado Nacional de Hacienda. Memoria *changed to* Argentina. Mercado Nacional de Hacienda. Anuario
0570-8915	Argus de la Legislation Libanaise
0570-8966	Arheoloski Vestnik
0570-9601	Arizona State University. Faculty of Industrial Engineering. Industrial Engineering Research Bulletin
0571-0111	Arizona Political Almanac
0571-0278	Arkansas. Geological Commission. Water Resources Circulars
0571-0731	Arkivinformation
0571-1223	Arquivo de Bibliografia Portuguesa
0571-1371	Ars Orientalis
0571-1509	Art de Basse Normandie
0571-205X	Artificial Satellites
0571-2742	Asian and African Studies
0571-2912	A.P.D.S.A. Journal
0571-2920	Asian Peoples' Anti-Communist League. China. Pamphlet
0571-2939	Asian Peoples' Anti-Communist League. Charts About Chinese Communists on the Mainland
0571-3005	Asian Productivity Organization. Review of Activities of National Productivity
0571-3161	Asiatic Society, Calcutta. Journal
0571-320X	Asiatische Forschungen
0571-3218	Asilomar Conference on Circuits and Systems. Conference Record
0571-3609	Asociacion de Investigacion Textil Algodonera. Coleccion de Manuales Tecnicos
0571-3684	A S E L F
0571-3692	Asociacion Espanola de Orientalistas. Boletin
0571-3846	Anuario de los Paises de A L A L C *see* 0066-5118
0571-3854	Asociacion Latinoamericana de Libre Comercio. Boletin Bibliografico†
0571-3870	Asociacion Latinoamericana de Libre Comercio. Comercio Exterior. Argentina. Exportacion *changed to* Asociacion Latinoamericana de Libre Comercio. Estadisticas de Comercio Exterior--Serie A-Exportaciones
0571-3889	Asociacion Latinoamericana de Libre Comercio. Comercio Exterior Argentina. Importacion *changed to* Asociacion Latinoamericana de Libre Comercio. Estadisticas de Comercio Exterior-Serie B-Importaciones
0571-3897	Asociacion Latinoamericana de Libre Comercio. Comercio Exterior Brasil. Exportacion†
0571-3897	Asociacion Latinoamericana de Libre Comercio. Comercio Exterior Brasil. Importacion *changed to* Asociacion Latinoamericana de Libre Comercio. Estadisticas de Comercio Exterior - Serie C - Importaciones Zonales
0571-3919	Asociacion Latinoamericana de Libre Comercio. Documentacion A L A L C†
0571-3927	Asociacion Latinoamericana de Libre Comercio. Indice Alfabetico de Mercaderias†
0571-3935	Asociacion Latinoamericana de Libre Comercio. Lista Consolidada de Concesiones
0571-396X	Asociacion Latinoamericana de Libre Comercio. Lista Nacional de Brasil
0571-3978	Asociacion Latinoamericana de Libre Comercio. Lista Nacional de Chile
0571-3986	Asociacion Latinoamericana de Libre Comercio. Lista Nacional de Colombia
0571-3994	Asociacion Latinoamericana de Libre Comercio. Lista Nacional de Ecuador
0571-4001	Asociacion Latinoamericana de Libre Comercio. Lista Nacional de la Republica Argentina *changed to* Asociacion Latinoamericana de Libre Comercio. Lista Nacional de Argentina
0571-401X	Asociacion Latinoamericana de Libre Comercio. Lista Nacional de Mexico
0571-4028	Asociacion Latinoamericana de Libre Comercio. Lista Nacional de Paraguay
0571-4036	Asociacion Latinoamericana de Libre Comercio. Lista Nacional de Peru
0571-4044	Asociacion Latinoamericana de Libre Comercio. Lista Nacional de Uruguay
0571-4052	Asociacion Latinoamericana de Libre Comercio. Listas de Concesiones Arancelarias para Ecuador y Paraguay†
0571-4079	Asociacion Latinoamericana de Libre Comercio. Serie Estadistica†
0571-4087	Asociacion Latinoamericana de Libre Comercio. Serie Instrumentos
0571-5520	Association for Asian Studies. Committee on East Asian Libraries. Newsletter *see* 0148-6225
0571-5644	A R E Journal
0571-5857	International Association for Byzantine Studies. Bulletin d'Information et de Coordination
0571-5865	International Association of French Studies. Cahiers
0571-5873	Association Internationale du Droit Commercial et du Droit Affaires. Groupe Francais. Travaux
0571-5962	Association of American Geographers. Handbook - Directory
0571-6098	Association of American University Presses Directory
0571-6241	Association of Commonwealth Universities. Report of the Council Together with the Accounts of the Association *see* 0307-2274
0571-625X	Compendium of University Entrance Requirements for First Degree Courses in the United Kingdom
0571-6322	Association of Institutes for European Studies. Annuaire
0571-6330	Association of Institutes for European Studies. Year-Book
0571-6357	A I L/Doc
0571-6519	Academic Library Statistics *see* 0147-2135
0571-7760	Crisis Papers†
0571-7795	Atlantic Papers
0571-7817	Atlantic Provinces Checklist†
0571-7868	Atlantic Series†
0571-8236	Attakapas Gazette
0571-8597	Attack†
0571-8600	Audio-Digest Anesthesiology
0571-8619	Audio-Digest General Practice *see* 0046-3221
0571-8635	Audio-Digest Obstetrics-Gynecology
0571-8643	Audio-Digest Pediatrics
0571-8651	Audio-Digest Surgery
0571-8678	Audio-Technik
0571-8724	Audiology *see* 0303-8106
0571-8759	Audio-Visual Equipment Directory
0571-9291	Australasian Conference on Hydraulics and Fluid Mechanics. Proceedings
0571-9518	Australia. Bureau of Statistics. Life Insurance
0571-9844	Australia. Bureau of Statistics. Tasmanian Office. Wool Production Statistics *changed to* Australia. Bureau of Statistics. Tasmanian Office. Wool Production and Disposal
0572-0400	Australia. Department of Civil Aviation. Civil Aviation Report *see* 0311-628X
0572-0494	Australia. Department of Territories. Territory of Norfolk Island; Report
0572-1431	Australian Road Research Board. Proceedings
0572-2241	Automatika
0572-3221	Agricultural Science Hong Kong *changed to* Agriculture Hong Kong
0572-4171	Asian Industrial Development News
0572-4198	Asian Institute of Technology. Research Summary
0572-4287	Association for the Advancement of Baltic Studies. Publications
0572-4295	Association of American Geographers. Proceedings†
0572-4325	Association of Southeast Asian Institutions of Higher Learning. Newsletter
0572-4953	American Association of Law Libraries. Newsletter
0572-5534	Brazil. Superintendencia da Borracha. Annuario Estatistico. Mercado Estrangeiro
0572-5860	Baas Becking Geobiological Laboratory. Annual Report
0572-5933	Bank Automation Newsletter
0572-5941	National Income of Iran
0572-5968	Bank of Jamaica. Statistical Digest
0572-6042	Barbados Nursing Journal
0572-6557	Biology and Behavior Series†
0572-6565	Biotechnology & Bioengineering Symposia
0572-6654	Bochumer Schriften zur Entwicklungsforschung und Entwicklungspolitik
0572-6921	Brigham Young University. Center for Thermochemical Studies. Contributions
0572-7146	Bruecke-Archiv
0572-7529	Bureau International des Societes Gerant les Droits d'Enregistrement et de Reproduction Mecanique. Bulletin
0572-7545	Business Asia
0572-7669	Colorado School Law Review
0572-9327	Comite International de Dachau. Bulletin
0572-9750	Common Market Reports
0573-0872	Commonwealth Space-Flight Symposium. Proceedings
0573-0910	Communes de France
0573-5661	Congress of International Congress Organizers and Technicians. Proceeding
0573-715X	Conservation Topics
0573-7869	Contacts Influential Business Reference Directory: Seattle, Washington
0573-7877	Contacts Influential Business Reference Directory: Denver, Colorado
0573-8555	Contributions to Economic Analysis
0573-8636	Control de Publicidad y Ventas
0573-9543	Cooperation Mediterraneenne pour l'Energie Solaire. Bulletin *changed to* Revue Internationale d'Heliotechnique
0574-0681	Cornell University. Modern Indonesia Project. Translations†
0574-1181	Corporate Diagrams and Administrative Personnel of the Chemical Industry
0574-1602	Corriere Nuova Europa
0574-2315	Cotton and Allied Textile Industries *changed to* International Textile Manufacturing
0574-2323	Cotton Farming
0574-2374	Cotton Statistics Monthly
0574-248X	Calendar of Regional Congresses of Medical Sciences *see* 0301-2891
0574-3370	Courrier Consulaire de la Haute Volta
0574-3680	Covered Wagon
0574-475X	Cronache e Opinioni
0574-5101	Cruzada Espanol
0574-6132	Anuario Estadistico de Cuba
0574-6817	Internationales Institut fuer den Frieden. Cultural Anniversaries Series
0574-7120	Curious Naturalist
0574-8135	Cycle
0574-8259	Cyprus. Geological Survey Department. Memoirs
0574-8267	Cyprus. Geological Survey Department. Annual Report
0574-8305	Cyprus. Loan Commissioners. Accounts and Statistics for the Year
0574-8399	Cyprus. Department of Statistics and Research. Motor Vehicles and Road Accidents
0574-9069	Politechnika Czestochowska. Zeszyty Naukowe. Nauki Podstawowe
0574-9077	Politechnika Czestochowska. Zeszyty Naukowe. Nauki Spoleczno-Ekonomiczne
0574-9468	C.I.A. Revue
0574-9549	C I S
0574-9700	C R C Handbook of Tables for Mathematics *changed to* C R C Handbook of Mathematical Sciences
0575-0415	Cahiers Charles du Bos
0575-0466	Cahiers d'Analyse Textuelle
0575-0563	Cahiers de Biotherapie
0575-0571	Cahiers de Bruges
0575-108X	Cahiers Ligures de Prehistoire et d'Archeologie
0575-1632	Caisse Centrale de Cooperation Economique. Rapport d'Activite *changed to* Caisse Centrale de Cooperation Economique. Rapport Annuel
0575-206X	University of Calgary. Department of Mathematics and Computing Science. Research Papers *changed to* University of Calgary. Department of Mathematics and Statistics. Research Papers
0575-2124	Caliban
0575-2221	California State Plan for Hospitals *changed to* California State Health Plan
0575-2426	California Economic Indicators
0575-2906	Characteristics of the California Youth Authority Parole Caseload†
0575-3368	Administrative Law Bulletin
0575-4208	Giannini Foundation of Agricultural Economics. Monograph

0575-6863 Cambridge South Asian Studies
0575-6871 Cambridge Studies in the History and Theory of Politics
0575-7258 Activites Mineres au Cameroun
0575-7894 Canada. Statistics Canada. Annual Report of Notifiable Diseases/Rapport Annuel sur les Maladies a Declaration Obligatoire†
0575-7975 Canada. Statistics Canada. Building Permits. Annual Summary/Permis de Batir
0575-8254 Canada. Statistics Canada. Consolidated Government Finance/Finances Publiques Consolidees
0575-8440 Canada. Statistics Canada. Estimates of Production and Disappearance of Meats/Estimation de la Production et de la Disparition des Viandes†
0575-8491 Canada. Statistics Canada. Federal Government Employment/Emploi dans l'Administration Publique Federale
0575-8521 Canada. Statistics Canada. Federal Government Finance/Finances Publiques Federales
0575-8548 Canada. Statistics Canada. Field Crop Reporting Series/Serie de Rapports sur les Grandes Cultures
0575-8645 Canada. Statistics Canada. General Review of the Mineral Industries/Revue Generale sur les Industries Minerales
0575-8661 Canada. Statistics Canada. Glass and Glass Products Manufacturers/Fabricants de Verre et d'Articles en Verre
0575-8807 Canada. Statistics Canada. Industrial Research and Development Expenditures in Canada/Depenses au Titre de la Recherche et du Developpement Industriels au Canada†
0575-884X Canada. Statistics Canada. Iron and Steel Mills/Siderurgie
0575-9021 Canada. Statistics Canada. Miscellaneous Manufacturing Industries/Industries Manufacturieres Diverses
0575-9048 Canada. Statistics Canada. Miscellaneous Metal Mines/Mines Metalliques Diverses.†
0575-9072 Canada. Statistics Canada. Motor Carriers Freight Quarterly/Entrepreneurs en Camionnage†
0575-9137 Canada. Statistics Canada. Moving and Storage Household Goods†
0575-917X Canada. Statistics Canada. Murder Statistics/Statistique de l'Homicide *see* 0706-2788
0575-9331 Canada. Statistics Canada. Police Administration Statistics/Statistique de l'Administration Policiere†
0575-934X Population Estimates by Marital Status, Age & Sex, Canada and Provinces/Estimations de la Population Suivant l'Etat Matrimonial, l'Age et le Sexe, Canada et Provinces *see* 0227-1796
0575-9455 Canada. Statistics Canada. Products Shipped by Canadian Manufacturers/Produits Livres Par les Fabricants Canadiens
0575-9463 Canada. Statistics Canada. Provincial Government Enterprise Finance/Finances des Entreprises Publiques Provinciales
0575-9501 Canada. Statistics Canada. Provincial Government Finance, Revenue and Expenditure (Estimates) /Finances Publiques Provinciales, Revenus et Defenses (Previsions)
0575-9560 Canada. Statistics Canada. Radio and Television Broadcasting/Radiodiffusion et Television
0575-9633 Sales of Toilet Preparations in Canada†
0575-9757 Canada. Statistics Canada. Shipping Report. Part 4: Origin and Destination for Selected Ports/Transport Maritime. Partie 4: Orgine et Destination pour Certains Ports†
0575-979X Canada. Statistics Canada. Sporting Goods and Toy Industries/Fabrication d'Articles de Sport et de Jouets
0575-9846 Canada. Statistics Canada. Stone Quarries/Carrieres†
0575-996X Canada. Statistics Canada. Training Schools/Etablissements de Protection de la Jeunesse†
0575-9978 Canada. Statistics Canada. Trusteed Pension Plans-Financial Statistics/Regimes de Pensions en Fiducie Statistique Financiere
0576-0046 Canada. Statistics Canada. Urban Transit/Transport Urbain†
0576-0070 Canada. Statistics Canada. Wooden Box Factories/Fabriques de Boites en Bois
0576-0097 Canada. Statistics Canada. Mechanical Contracting Industry/Les Entrepreneurs d'Installations Mecaniques
0576-016X Canada. Statistics Canada. Health Manpower Section. Annual Salaries of Hospital Nursing Personnel/Traitements Annuels du Personnel Infirmier des Hopitaux†
0576-1174 Canada. Department of Manpower and Immigration. Quarterly Immigration Bulletin†
0576-1999 Gazetteer of Canada
0576-4157 Unemployment Insurance Canada. Annual Report
0576-4300 Canada Council Annual Report and Supplement
0576-470X Canadian Book Prices Current
0576-5161 Canadian Electrical Association. Engineering and Operating Division. Transactions
0576-5234 Canadian Folk Music Society. Newsletter
0576-5269 Canadian Gas Utilities Directory
0576-5528 Canadian Jewish Archives (New Series)
0576-5625 Canadian Legal Studies Series
0576-5803 Canadian Notes & Queries
0576-6176 Canadian Symposium on Water Pollution Research. Water Pollution Research in Canada. Proceedings
0576-6885 University of Cape Town. Libraries. Statistical Report
0576-6931 Capilla Alfonsina. Boletin
0576-7172 Carbohydrate Chemistry
0576-7296 Career Index *see* 0190-4663
0576-7598 Caribbean Monthly Bulletin
0576-7954 Carnegie Quarterly
0576-808X Carolina Comments
0576-8519 Casa, Arredamento e Giardino
0576-8861 Catalogo Bolaffi d'Arte Moderna *changed to* Catalogo Nazionale Bolaffi d'Arte Moderna
0576-8888 Catalogo Bolaffi del Cacciatore e delle Armi
0576-8942 Catalogo de Filmes Brasileiros *changed to* Brasil Cinema
0576-9280 Catgut Acoustical Society Newsletter
0576-9787 Cellulose Chemistry and Technology
0576-9922 C R I Abstracts
0577-0335 C E N T O Newsletter†
0577-036X Central Africa Historical Association. Local Series Pamphlets *changed to* Historical Association of Zimbabwe. Local Series Pamphlets
0577-0653 Central Bank of Malta. Annual Report
0577-084X Central Marine Fisheries Research Institute. Bulletin
0577-1056 C E B E D E A U. Tribune
0577-1331 Centre d'Etudes Ethnologiques. Publications. Serie 1: Rapports et Comptes Rendus
0577-1730 Centre International d'Etude des Problems Humains. Bulletins
0577-1765 Universite Catholique de Louvain. Centre International de Dialectologie Generale. Travaux
0577-2168 Centro Camuno di Studi Preistorici. Bollettino
0577-2176 Centro Camuno di Studi Preistorici. Publicazioni†
0577-2451 Centro de Estudios Monetarios Latinoamericanos. Ensayos
0577-2907 Centro Interamericano de Investigacion y Documentacion Sobre Formacion Profesional. Boletin
0577-2915 C I N T E R F O R - Documentacion
0577-2931 C I N T E R F O R. Estudios y Monografias
0577-3334 Ceramica de Cultura Maya
0577-3490 Ceska Bibliografie
0577-4691 Ceylon Historical Journal
0577-4772 Ceylon Rationalist Ambassador
0577-5132 Challenge (White Plains)
0577-5183 Analysis of Workmen's Compensation Laws *see* 0191-118X
0577-5574 Charioteer
0577-571X Capital Investments of the World Petroleum Industry
0577-5728 Chases' Calendar of Annual Events
0577-7240 Chicago Linguistic Society. Papers from the Regional Meetings
0577-7259 Chicago Mercantile Exchange Yearbook
0577-800X Chile. Instituto Nacional de Estadisticas. Sintesis Estadistica *changed to* Chile. Instituto Nacional de Estadisticas. Informativo Estadistico
0577-8131 Chile. Servicio de Impuestos Internos. Memoria
0577-8832 China Informatie
0577-9065 Chinese Historical Society of America. Bulletin
0577-9081 Chinese Journal of Physics†
0578-0152 Christian Science Monitor. Cumulated Index *see* 0098-1184
0578-2228 Chuo University. Faculty of Science and Engineering. Bulletin
0578-3097 Circle K Magazine
0578-3283 Citizen (Jackson)
0578-3364 Citizens Conference on State Legislatures. Research Memorandum†
0578-3828 Civil Service Digest *see* 0381-7962
0578-3917 Civilisation Malgache
0578-4131 Clanky v Slovenskych Casopisoch *changed to* Slovenska Narodna Bibliografia Seria C: Clanky
0578-4182 Claretianum
0578-4247 Clark University (Worcester, Mass.) Dissertations and Theses
0578-4565 Classification Society Bulletin
0578-4573 Classified Bibliography on Graph Theory†
0578-5294 Clothing Institute Journal *see* 0142-0534
0578-5464 Studia Universitatis "Babes-Bolyai" Iurisprudentia
0578-5472 Studia Universitatis "Babes-Bolyai." Oeconomica.
0578-5480 Studia Universitatis "Babes-Bolyai". Philosophia
0578-5502 Studia Universitatis Babes-Bolyai. Psychologia-Pedagogia *see* 0578-5480
0578-5634 Coastal Engineering in Japan
0578-5677 Coastal Research Notes *changed to* Coastal Research
0578-6258 Iowa State University. Iowa Agriculture and Home Economics Experiment Station. Special Report
0578-6371 University of Iowa. Center for Labor and Management. Research Series.
0578-6533 Iowa Advocate
0578-655X Iowa Archeological Society. Newsletter
0578-6959 Iran. Ministry of Economy. Report on Commencement and Operation Permits for Industrial Establishments
0578-8056 Islamic Education
0578-8250 Israel. Department of Customs and Excise. Journal
0578-9427 Israels Aussenhandel
0578-9761 Sarkiyat Mecmuasi
0579-174X Itogi Nauki: Stratigrafiya. Paleontologiya *changed to* Itogi Nauki i Tekhniki: Stratigrafiya, Paleontologiya
0579-1766 Itogi Nauki: Tekhnologiya Organicheskikh Veshchestv *see* 0303-2361
0579-2290 Al-Ittihad
0579-2428 Ius Commune
0579-2983 Izvestiya Vysshikh Uchebnykh Zavedenii. Seriya Energetika
0579-3238 India. Department of Labour and Employment. Annual Report *changed to* India. Ministry of Labour. Annual Report
0579-3599 Instituto Argentino de Ciencias Genealogicas. Boletin Interno
0579-3718 Sociedad Interamericana de Planificacion. Correo Informativo/Newsletter
0579-3742 International Association for Mass Communication Research. Letter from the President
0579-3785 International Congress of Plastic and Reconstructive Surgery. Transactions
0579-3866 International Federation of Catholic Universities. General Assembly. (Report)
0579-3912 International Organization for Medical Cooperation. General Assembly. Report *changed to* International Organization for Cooperation in Health Care. General Assembly. Report
0579-3920 International Pacific Halibut Commission (U.S. and Canada). Technical Reports
0579-4234 I E E E International Symposium on Circuit Theory. Symposium Digest. Summaries of Papers *changed to* I E E E International Symposium on Circuits and Systems. Proceedings
0579-4374 Immigration History Newsletter
0579-4757 Indian Agricultural Index†
0579-5109 Institut Maurice Thorez. Conferences†
0579-5192 Instituto Latinoamericano de Mercadeo Agricola. Actividades del I L M A†
0579-5206 Instituto Latinoamericano de Mercadeo Agricola. Informes Sobre Comercializacion†
0579-5214 Instituto Latinoamericano de Mercadeo Agricola. Sistemas de Mercadeo de Productos Agricolas en Medellin†
0579-529X Insurance Stock Review
0579-5362 International Association of Volcanology and Chemistry of the Earth's Interior. Newsletter
0579-5427 I C I D Bulletin
0579-5486 Management Datamatics†
0579-5567 International Police Association. Meeting of the International Executive Council
0579-5613 I S O Information *changed to* Organ Building Periodical
0579-5621 U.I.A.M.S. Bulletin Trimestriel
0579-5664 Intersociety Energy Conversion Conference. Proceedings
0579-6059 Index to the Science Fiction Magazines *see* 0361-3038
0579-6105 India. Ministry of Education and Social Welfare. Provisional Statistics of Education in the States
0579-6407 Ingenieur Digest
0579-6695 Inter-American Press Association. Committee on Freedom of the Press. Report
0579-6733 International Association of Hydrogeologists. Memoires
0579-6881 International Police Association. Travel Scholarships
0579-6903 I. P. T. C. Newsletter
0579-692X International Union of Official Travel Organizations. Technical Bulletin *changed to* World Tourism Organization. Collection of Technical Bulletins
0579-7195 University of Ife. Faculty of Agriculture. Annual Research Report
0579-7772 Universitaet Innsbruck. Medizinische Fakultaet. Arbeiten
0579-7780 Universitaet Innsbruck. Theologische Fakultaet. Studien und Arbeiten

0579-7918 International Institute for the Unification of Private Law. Rapport sur l'Activite de l'Institut†
0579-7926 Tunisia. Institut National Scientifique et Technique d'Oceanographie et de Peche. Bulletin
0579-8140 International Directory of Occupational Safety and Health Services and Institutions
0579-8256 Through Europe by Train
0579-8299 International Union of Food and Allied Workers' Associations. Meeting of the Executive Committee. I. Documents of the Secretariat. II. Summary Report
0579-8302 International Union of Food and Allied Workers' Associations. Tobacco Workers' Trade Group Board. Meeting
0579-8337 Inter-Parliamentary Union. Series: "Reports and Documents"
0579-8388 Inventor
0580-0412 Motion Picture, TV & Theatre Directory
0580-0420 Motive
0580-0714 Mountain-Plains in Books *see* 0145-6180
0580-1540 Westfaelische Wilhelms-Universitaet Muenster. Slavisch-Baltisches Seminar†
0580-1583 Muenstersche Studien zur Kunstgeschichte
0580-1737 Multiple Sclerosis Abstracts *see* 0360-0017
0580-2652 Museums Calendar *see* 0307-7675
0580-289X Music Library Association. Newsletter
0580-2954 Musica Britannica
0580-308X Musical America Annual Directory Issue *changed to* Musical America International Directory of the Performing Arts
0580-3403 Musteranlagen der Energiewirtschaft
0580-3713 Muzica
0580-373X Muzikoloski Zbornik
0580-3780 My Golden West *see* 0382-5876
0580-4396 Mysore Orientalist
0580-4485 Minoseg es Megbizhatosag
0580-468X Universidad de Madrid. Departamento de Botanica y Fisiologia Vegetal. Trabajos
0580-4981 Makedonska Akademija na Naukite i Umetnostite. Oddelenie za Prirodno-Matematicki Nauki. Prilozi
0580-535X Agassiz Center for Water Studies. Research Report
0580-6097 University of Michigan. Herbarium. Contributions
0580-6976 University of Missouri, Columbia. Museum of Anthropology. Museum Briefs
0580-7247 M L O
0580-7727 Massachusetts. Division of Employment Security. Quarterly Survey of Unfilled Job Openings - Boston *changed to* Massachusetts. Division of Employment Security. Survey of Unfilled Job Openings - Boston
0580-8162 Modern Photography Annual
0580-8421 M D
0580-8650 Universidad de Madrid. Seminario de Metafisica. Anales
0580-8898 Manager and Entrepreneur
0580-9320 Medicina Termale e Climatologia
0580-9746 Michigan State University. Institute of Water Research. Technical Report
0581-0000 Mineral Statistics of India
0581-0086 Minnesota Genealogist
0581-0558 Musicologica Slovaca
0581-0892 Malawi Housing Corporation. Annual Report and Accounts
0581-0906 Malawi. National Library. Annual Report *changed to* Malawi. National Library Service. Annual Report
0581-1023 Marketing
0581-1058 Marxist Miscellany
0581-1155 Mathematical Chronicle
0581-2011 Mujeres
0581-2674 Safaho-Monographs
0581-2739 Safety†
0581-295X Saguenayensia
0581-3018 Sahitya Sahakar†
0581-3115 Sailboat Directory *changed to* Sailboat & Sailboat Equipment Directory
0581-3263 Information Veterinaire
0581-3999 Salt Research & Industry
0581-4111 El Salvador. Ministerio de Planificacion y Coordinacion del Desarrollo Economico y Social. Indicadores Economicos y Sociales
0581-4480 Samiske Samlinger
0581-4758 Sanskriti
0581-4790 Samvadadhvam
0581-6076 Universidade Federal de Santa Catarina. Museu de Antropologia. Anais
0581-6106 Santa Clara Lawyer *see* 0146-0315
0581-6866 Universidade de Sao Paulo. Faculdade de Odontologia. Revista
0581-7501 Zemaljski Muzej Bosne i Hercegovine. Glasnik. Arheologija
0581-751X Zemaljski Muzej Bosne i Hercegovine. Glasnik. Etnologija
0581-7528 Zemaljski Muzej Bosne i Hercegovine. Glasnik. Prirodne Nauke
0581-8079 Travel on Saskatchewan Highways
0581-8109 Saskatchewan. Department of Mineral Resources. Annual Report
0581-8389 Saskatchewan Fur Marketing Service. Annual Report
0581-8443 Saskatchewan Natural History Society. Newsletter
0581-8532 Satapitaka. Indo-Asian Literatures
0581-8672 Saudi Arabian Monetary Agency. Statistical Summary
0581-8761 Savings and Loan Fact Book
0581-8850 Savremena Poljoprivreda
0581-9172 Sbornik Geologickych Ved: Geologie
0581-9180 Sbornik Geologickych Ved: Loziskova Geologie, Mineralogie
0581-9423 Scandinavian Building Research
0581-9431 Scandinavian Corrosion Congress. Proceedings
0581-9911 School Activities and the Library†
0582-0421 Beitraege zur Politischen Wissenschaft
0582-138X Schrifttumnachweis Bau-, Wohnungs- und Siedlungswesen†
0582-1487 Schwann Artist Catalog
0582-1592 Societe Suisse des Americanistes.Bulletin
0582-1673 Biblische Beitraege
0582-2343 Scientia Agriculturae Bohemoslovaca
0582-2351 Scientia Paedagogica Experimentalis
0582-2637 Scissortail
0582-3692 Secondary Education *see* 0013-1482
0582-3730 Secular Democracy
0582-3978 Segnalazioni Assofarma
0582-4192 Seikei Ronso (Journal of the Faculty of Politics, Law, and Economics) *changed to* Kokugakuin University Economic Review
0582-4206 Japan Society of Precision Engineering. Bulletin
0582-4524 Journal of Classical Studies
0582-4532 World
0582-4761 Selbstbedienung und Supermarkt *see* 0343-3226
0582-4788 Selden Society, London. Supplementary Series
0582-4818 Selecciones Avicolas
0582-4877 Selecta
0582-6314 Seminarium
0582-7094 Cerro Tololo Interamerican Observatory (La Serena, Chile). Contributions
0582-8155 Series on Contemporary Javanese Life
0582-8201 Astrometriya i Astrofizika
0582-8759 Sestante†
0582-8929 Universidad de Sevilla. Instituto Garcia Oviedo. Publicaciones
0582-9399 Shakespeare Studies
0582-9402 Shakespeare Studies
0582-9860 Torch of Victory
0583-0362 Shimane Law Review
0583-0648 Shinshu University. Faculty of Textile Science and Technology. Journal. Series A: Biology
0583-0664 Shinshu University. Faculty of Textile Science and Technology. Journal. Series D: Arts
0583-0923 Shizuoka University. Faculty of Science. Reports
0583-1024 Shock and Vibration Digest
0583-1296 Shout
0583-1776 Siberian Husky Club of America Newsletter
0583-1881 Side Effects of Drugs
0583-2268 Sierra Leone. Library Board. Report
0583-239X Sierra Leone Geographical Journal
0583-2594 Signpost
0583-3132 Silvicultura Em Sao Paulo
0583-3736 Singapore International Chamber of Commerce. Report
0583-3981 Stock Exchange of Singapore. Handbook
0583-4279 Sino-British Trade Review
0583-4449 Siskiyou Pioneer and Yearbook
0583-4961 Institut za Nacionalna Istorija, Skopje. Glasnik
0583-5623 Slovakia
0583-564X Slovanske Studie
0583-6263 Slovo na Storozhi
0583-6948 Great Britain. Social Science Research Council. Research Supported by the Social Science Research Council
0583-7022 Social Welfare Court Digest
0583-7065 Social Work Forum
0583-7405 Sociedad de Historia Natural de Baleares. Boletin
0583-7480 Sociedad Espanola de Historia de la Medicina. Boletin
0583-7693 Sociedad Quimica de Mexico. Revista
0583-7774 Sociedad Venezolana de Planificacion. Cuadernos
0583-8045 Limba si Literatura
0583-8177 Societe Botanique de Geneve. Travaux *see* 0373-2525
0583-8193 Societe d'Archeologie et d'Histoire de la Manche. Departement de la Manche. Revue.
0583-8622 Societe Geographique de Liege. Bulletin
0583-8894 Analytical Sciences Monographs
0583-8916 Society for Applied Anthropology. Monographs
0583-8975 S C E H Newsletter
0583-9009 Society for Developmental Biology. Symposium
0583-9181 Society for the Preservation of Long Island Antiquities. Newsletter
0583-9246 Water Treatment and Examination†
0583-9270 S.A.W.E. Journal
0583-9572 S P I E Seminar Proceedings *see* 0361-0748
0584-0252 Sofiiski Universitet. Fakultet po Zapadni Filologii. Godishnik
0584-0651 Solar Energy Progress in Australia and New Zealand†
0584-1070 Something
0584-1739 Textile Information Sources and Resources†
0584-195X South Africa. Department of Statistics. Road Traffic Accidents
0584-2166 South Africa. Department of Coloured Relations and Rehoboth Affairs. Annual Report
0584-2352 South Africa. Geological Survey. Annals
0584-2360 Bibliography and Subject Index of South African Geology
0584-3073 South African Reserve Bank. Monthly Release of Money and Banking Statistics
0584-3170 South Asian Studies
0584-4088 Southeast Asia Treaty Organization. Secretary General. S E A T O Report†
0584-4118 S E C A C Review and Newsletter *changed to* Southeastern College Art Conference Review
0584-4207 Renaissance Papers
0584-4266 S E W R P C Newsletter
0584-455X Southern Office
0584-6374 Instituto de Estudios Madrilenos. Anales
0584-6544 Spain. Direccion General de Aduanas. Informe Mensuel Sobre el Comercio Exterior
0584-7109 Documentacion Iberoamericana
0584-8016 Span
0584-8067 Spanner
0584-8164 Speaker and Gavel
0584-8539 Spectrochimica Acta. Part A: Molecular Spectroscopy
0584-8547 Spectrochimica Acta. Part B: Atomic Spectroscopy
0584-8555 Spectroscopic Properties of Inorganic & Organometallic Compounds
0584-8652 Speculum Juris
0584-9144 Spores
0584-9217 Sport Parachutist
0584-9667 Springs
0585-0444 Standard Trade Index of Japan
0585-086X Stapp Car Crash Conference Proceedings
0585-0991 State Bank of India. Report of the Central Board of Directors
0585-1009 State Bank of Pakistan. Export Receipts
0585-1149 State Communities Aid Association Annual Report
0585-1289 State of South Africa
0585-1432 Statistical Compendium of the Americas†
0585-1580 Statistical Office of the European Communities. Quarterly Bulletin of Energy Statistics
0585-1777 Statistical Pocket Book of Ceylon *changed to* Statistical Pocket Book of the Democratic Socialist Republic of Sri Lanka
0585-198X Statistics Sources
0585-2471 Stephen Wilson Annual Pharmacy Seminar. Report
0585-2544 Stereophile
0585-2730 Great Britain. Warren Spring Laboratory. Investigation of Air Pollution: National Survey, Smoke and Sulphur Dioxide
0585-3273 Studia Missionalia Upsaliensia†
0585-3400 Sweden. Statens Raad foer Byggnadsforskning. Informationsblad
0585-3923 Straits Times Annual
0585-3931 Straits Times Directory of Malaysia and Singapore *changed to* N S T Directory of Malaysia
0585-3931 Straits Times Directory of Malaysia and Singapore *changed to* Straits Times Directory of Singapore
0585-4393 Struktura i Rol' Vody v Zhivom Organizme *changed to* Molekulyarnaya Fizika i Biofizika Vodnykh Sistem
0585-4555 Student Aid Annual *see* 0190-339X
0585-4768 Studi di Letteratura Francese
0585-4911 Studi Genuensi
0585-492X Studi Ispanici
0585-5098 Studia Entomologica†
0585-5462 Studia Philologica Jyvaskylaensia
0585-5500 Studia Post-Biblica
0585-5543 Studia Slovenica
0585-5578 Studia Sumiro-Hungarica
0585-5721 Studiecentrum voor Jeugdmisdadigheid. Publikatie
0585-5837 Studien und Texte zur Geistesgeschichte des Mittelalters
0585-5853 Studien zu den Bogazkoy-Texten
0585-6094 Studien zur Japanologie
0585-6175 Studien zur Publizistik. Bremer Reihe
0585-6515 Studies in Anglesey History
0585-6523 Studies in Anthropological Method
0585-6795 Studies in Inter-American Laws
0585-6833 Studies in Judaica
0585-6884 Studies in Managerial Economics†
0585-6914 Studies in Medieval and Reformation Thought
0585-6965 Studies in Philosophy & the History of Philosophy
0585-7023 Studies in Pre-Columbian Art and Archaeology
0585-7031 Studies in Public Communication
0585-718X Studies in Speleology
0585-7260 Studies in the History of Religions
0585-7694 Study Centre for Yugoslav Affairs. Review

0585-7856 Universitaet Stuttgart. Institut fuer Geologie und Palaeontologie Arbeiten Neue Folge
0585-8488 Sudan. Department of Statistics. Foreign Trade Statistics
0585-8631 Sudan Law Journal and Reports
0585-9328 Sunday School Senior Adults
0585-9581 Suomen Obligaatiokirja
0585-9794 Supreme Court Monthly Review
0585-9840 Surfaces(Paris)
0585-9980 Surrey Archaeological Society. Bulletin
0586-0431 Svensk Tidskriftsfoerteckning
0586-0709 Svenskt Musikhistoriskt Arkiv. Bulletin
0586-1357 Swaziland. Central Statistical Office. Annual Statistical Bulletin
0586-1691 Sweden. Sjukvaardens och Socialvaardens Planerings- och Rationaliseringsinstitut. S P R I Rapport
0586-2000 Swedish Archaeological Bibliography
0586-2779 Drug-Induced Diseases
0586-3031 U S Symposium on Rock Mechanics. Proceedings
0586-3260 Synteza
0586-3414 Syracuse University. Program of East African Studies. East African Bibliographic Series†
0586-3422 Syracuse University. Program of East African Studies. Occasional Bibliographies†
0586-3430 Syracuse University. Program of East African Studies. Occasional Papers†
0586-3783 Szep Versek
0586-4607 Slovenska Akademia Vied. Geofyzikalny Ustav. Contributions
0586-4925 Statistical Office of the European Communities. Aussenhandel: Analitische Ubersichten. Foreign Trade: Analytical Tables
0586-500X Strictly Wholesaling†
0586-5050 Studies in Accounting Research
0586-5107 Studies in Urban Geography
0586-5395 Saisons de la Danse
0586-5522 Saskatchewan. Water Supply Board. Annual Report
0586-5581 Scanning Electron Microscope Symposium. Proceedings *changed to* Scanning Electron Microscopy
0586-5751 Scientific Directory of Hong Kong
0586-6766 Sweden. Statens Raad foer Byggnadsforskning. Document
0586-6898 Studies and Documents on Cultural Policies
0586-6928 Studies in Language and Linguistics
0586-7282 Salt Lake City Messenger
0586-7614 Schizophrenia Bulletin
0586-7746 Scientific and Technical Societies of Canada
0586-8440 Council for Scientific and Industrial Research, Ghana. Forest Products Research Institute. Annual Report
0586-8491 Southern Wholesalers' Guide *changed to* National Hardware Wholesalers' Guide
0586-9145 Symposia Otorhinolaryngologica Iugoslavica
0586-9668 Science and Archaeology
0586-9889 Serie Vie Locale
0587-0631 Southeast Asia Treaty Organization. Secretary General. Record of Progress *see* 0584-4088
0587-1131 Storia dell'Arte
0587-1433 Swedish Natural Science Research Council. Ecological Bulletins
0587-1514 Szamitastechnika
0587-1689 Arbeitsmarkt Politik
0587-1948 Association for Institutional Research. Annual Forum on Institutional Research. Proceedings
0587-1956 A R S C Bulletin
0587-2006 Journalists' International Association for Studying Problems of Overseas Peoples. Annuaire†
0587-2138 Australasian Tax Reports
0587-2421 Acta Europaea Fertilitatis
0587-2871 American Animal Hospital Association Journal
0587-2936 American Bar Association. Section of Local Government Law. Committee Reports.
0587-3053 American Nurses' Association. A N A in Action *changed to* American Nurse
0587-3428 Aquila
0587-3452 Arch Plus
0587-3533 Arkansas Archeological Survey. Publications on Archeology. Popular Series
0587-3584 Art-Language
0587-3606 Asia Foundation. President's Review
0587-3746 Assure Social
0587-4076 Aarbok for Telemark
0587-4394 Advances in Metabolic Disorders. Supplements
0587-4793 All India Architects Directory
0587-5196 Anuario del Cuento Costariccense
0587-5447 Arte y Arqueologia
0587-5455 Arti Musices
0587-5471 Asian Pacific Congress of Cardiology. Symposia
0587-5560 Bulletin de l'ANECLA
0587-5781 Australia. Bureau of Statistics. Bee Farming. *changed to* Australia. Bureau of Statistics. Bee Keeping
0587-5846 Australian Conservation Foundation. Annual Report
0587-5919 Automobile Electronic Equipment
0587-5943 Codex Committee on Pesticide Residues. Report of the Meeting
0587-5994 Co-Existence
0587-6435 Colecao de Estudos Filologicos
0588-2583 Collectionneur Francais
0588-2990 Colleges Classified†
0588-3024 Collegium Musicum: Yale University
0588-3253 Colloquium Geographicum
0588-3598 Colombia. Direccion General del Presupuesto. Proyecto de Presupuesto *changed to* Colombia. Direccion General del Presupuesto. Proyecto de Presupuesto
0588-4543 Colorado. State Department of Public Health. Annual Progress Report. State Migrant Plan for Public Health Services
0588-5094 Colour Society. Journal
0588-5477 Columbia University. Russian Institute. Studies
0588-621X Comite International des Poids et Mesures. Comite Consultatif de Photometrie et Radiometrie.(Rapport et Annexes)
0588-6228 Comite International des Poids et Mesures. Comite Consultatif pour la Definition de la Seconde. (Rapport et Annexes)
0588-6236 Comite International des Poids et Mesures. Comite Consultatif pour la Definition du Metre (Rapport et Annexes)
0588-6244 Comite International des Poids et Mesures. Comite Consultatif pour les Etalons des Mesure des Radiations Ionisantes(Rapport et Annexes) *changed to* Comite International des Poids et Mesures. Comite Consultatif pour les Etalons des Mesure des Rayonnements Ionisants (Rapport et Annexes)
0588-6694 Commercial Bank of Ethiopia. Annual Report
0588-6783 Commision for Technical Co-Operation in Africa. Joint Project†
0588-6953 Commission of the European Communities. Expose Annuel sur les Activities d'Orientation Professionnelle dans la Communaute
0588-702X Mines Safety and Health Commission. Report
0588-7356 C O R D News *see* 0149-7677
0588-7445 Common Market Law Reports
0588-7712 Abstracts of Papers on Geology of the United Kingdom *changed to* Abstracts of Current Information on Geology and Mineral Resources
0588-7720 Commonwealth Geological Liaison Office. Liaison Report
0588-7739 Commonwealth Geological Liaison Office. Newsletter
0588-7755 Commonwealth Geological Liaison Office. Report (on) Resources of the British Commonwealth†
0588-7763 Commonwealth Geological Liaison Office. Special Publication
0588-7933 Commonwealth Trade†
0588-8018 Communications
0588-8093 Communicator†
0588-8360 Community
0588-8611 Easter Commemoration Digest†
0588-9049 Comparative Education Society in Europe. Proceedings of the General Meeting
0588-912X Compendio Estadistico Centroamericano
0588-9278 Comprehensive Education
0588-9405 Computer Programs for Chemistry†
0588-9545 Comunicaciones - Revista Tecnica
0588-9979 Confederacao Nacional do Comercio. Divisao de Divulgacao. Carta Mensal
0589-1019 Alliance for Engineering in Medicine and Biology. Proceedings of the Annual Conference
0589-3496 Connaissance de l'Orient. Collection Unesco d'Oeuvres Representatives
0589-400X Connecticut Water Resources Bulletin.
0589-4301 Consejo Superior Universitario Centroamericano. Actas de la Reunion Ordinaria
0589-4360 Consejo Superior Universitario Centroamericano. Publicaciones
0589-4468 Conservation Court Digest
0589-4522 Conservative Journal
0589-4735 Construction-Amenagement
0589-4867 Consultation on Church Union. Digest
0589-5065 Contact Lens Society of America Journal *see* 0096-2716
0589-5081 Contacto
0589-512X Contacts Influential Business Reference Directory: East Bay Area
0589-5286 Contemporary Music Newsletter
0589-7300 Cornell University. Modern Indonesia Project. Monographs
0589-7351 Cornell University. Library. Wason Collection. Southeast Asia Accessions List *changed to* Cornell University. Library. John M. Echols Collection on Southeast Asia. Accessions List
0589-7688 Ecuador. Comision de Valores. Corporacion Financiera Nacional. Memoria *changed to* Ecuador. Corporacion Financiera Nacional. Memoria
0589-7742 Corporacion Nacional de Fertilizantes. Memoria Anual
0589-7920 Corporate Report Fact Book
0589-7939 Corporation Counsel's Law and Tax Report *see* 0147-1619
0589-8056 Corpus Hispanorum de Pace
0589-8218 Correctional Psychologist *see* 0093-8548
0589-8366 Corriere Africano
0589-8544 Costa Rica. Direccion General de Estadistica y Censos. Inventario de las Estadisticas Nacionales
0589-8617 Costa Rica. Ministerio de Transportes. Memoria *changed to* Costa Rica. Ministerio de Obras Publicas y Transportes. Memorias
0589-8765 Costruttori Italiani nel Mondo
0589-9087 Council for Financial Aid to Education. C.F.A.E. Corporation Support of Higher Education
0589-915X Calendar of International Congresses of Medical Sciences *see* 0301-2891
0589-9362 Council of Europe. Exchange of Information Between the Member States on Their Legislative Activity and Regulations (New Series)
0589-9478 Council of Europe. Council for Cultural Cooperation. Annual Report
0589-9508 Council of Europe. Concise Handbook
0589-9575 European Co-Operation
0589-9591 Council of Europe Film Weeks
0589-9788 State Headlines
0590-0239 Courrier des Pays de l'Est
0590-0727 Creditanstalt-Bankverein. Wirtschaftsberichte
0590-1111 Cronache Meridionali†
0590-1243 Crop Protection Courier (International)
0590-1871 Cuadernos de Etnologia y Etnografia de Navarra
0590-2525 Cuadernos Republicanos
0590-2568 Cuadernos Uruguayos de Filosofia
0590-2916 Cuba Azucar
0590-3343 Universidad de Oriente. Instituto Oceanografico Biblioteca. Boletin Bibliografico
0590-3351 Universidad de Oriente. Instituto Oceanografico. Cuadernos Oceanograficos
0590-3408 Cumulated Index Medicus
0590-3831 Current Concepts of Cerebrovascular Disease: Stroke
0590-3955 Current Issues in Psychiatry
0590-4129 C P T
0590-417X Current Research in British Studies by American and Canadian Scholars
0590-4641 Cycle Guide Road Test Annual
0590-4846 Cyprus. Department of Statistics and Research. Demographic Report
0590-4854 Cyprus. Department of Statistics and Research. Annual Industrial Production Survey
0590-4862 Cyprus. Department of Statistics and Research. Statistical Abstract
0590-5001 Czechoslovak Economic Papers
0590-501X Dokumentacni Prehled CTK
0590-5214 Veterinarni Medicina
0590-5702 Canada. Statistics Canada. Direct Selling in Canada/Vente Directe au Canada
0590-580X Canada. Northern Natural Resources and Environment Branch. Mining Section. North of 60: Mines and Minerals, Activities
0590-6008 Catholic International Education Office. Etudes et Documents†
0590-6105 Informes Latinoamericanos de Fisica†
0590-6342 Cimbebasia. Series A: Natural History
0590-6563 Commission of the European Communities. Community Law
0590-6571 Commission of the European Communities. Financial Report
0590-6776 Cord Sportfacts Guns Guide
0590-7136 Council of Europe. European Committee on Crime Problems. International Exchange of Information Bills and Draft Regulations on Penal Matters. *changed to* European Committee on Crime Problems. Bulletin on Legislative Activities
0590-7225 Cours et Documents de Biologie
0590-7233 Bibliographie de Jurisprudence Europeenne Concernant les Decisions Judiciares Relatives aux Traites Institutant les Communautes Europeennes
0590-7853 Canada West
0590-8191 C R C Critical Reviews in Clinical Laboratory Sciences
0590-8434 Cleveland and Teesside Local History Society. Bulletin
0590-8655 Computer Newsfront
0590-8760 Consumer Communique *changed to* Consumer Contact
0590-8876 Costume
0590-9325 Market Research Handbook
0590-9775 British Shipping Statistics†
0590-9783 Charities Digest
0590-9945 Coin Bulletin

1262 ISSN INDEX

0591-0110 Commission of the European Communities. Expose Annuel sur les Activities des Services de Main-d'Ouvre des Etats Membres de la Communaute
0591-0129 Committee for Economic Development of Australia. C E D A Occasional Papers†
0591-0188 Comentarios Economico†
0591-0471 Courrier de l'Extreme-Orient
0591-0633 Cahiers Marxistes
0591-0986 Catalogue of Little Press Books in Print Published in the UK
0591-1036 Centrale Nucleare Garigliano. Relazione Annuale
0591-1044 Centrale Elletronucleare Latina. Relazione Annuale
0591-1281 Chips and Ships†
0591-1710 Commerce Yearbook of Public Sector
0591-1737 Commission of the European Communities. Etudes: Serie Industrie
0591-1745 Commission of the European Communities. Directory
0591-2237 Country Music People
0591-2296 Crux of the News
0591-2334 Custom Car
0591-2369 Zycie Literackie
0591-2377 Zycie Szkoly Wyzszej
0700-0278 Canada. Statistics Canada. Canvas Products and Cotton and Jute Bag Industries/Industrie des Articles en Grosse Toile et des Sacs de Coton et de Jute
0700-0324 Canada. Statistics Canada. Flour and Breakfast Cereal Products Industry/Meunerie et Fabrication de Cereales de Table
0700-0731 Canada. Statistics Canada. Felt and Fibre Processing Mills/Industrie du Feutre et du Traitement des Fibres
0700-138X Canada. Statistics Canada. Therapeutic Abortions/Avortements Therapeutiques
0700-141X Canada. Statistics Canada. Continuing Education: Universities/Education Permanente: Universites†
0700-1444 Canada. Statistics Canada. Continuing Education: Elementary-Secondary/Education Permanente: Niveau Elementaire-Secondaire†
0700-1681 Quebec (Province) Ministere du Travail et de la Main d'Oeuvre. Jurisprudence en Droit du Travail: Tribunal du Travail
0700-1770 ForesTalk(1978)
0700-205X Canada. Statistics Canada. Quarterly Estimates of Trusteed Pension Funds/Estimations Trimestrielles Relatives aux Caisses de Pensions en Fiducie
0700-2092 Public Sector
0700-2181 Canada. Statistics Canada. University Financial Statistics/Universites Statistiques Financieres†
0700-2408 Metric Monitor
0700-2645 Alberta. Department of Energy and Natural Resources. Annual Report
0700-2661 Who Does What: A Guide to National Associations, Service Organizations and Unions Operating in Most Areas of the Arts
0700-284X Coal in Canada, Supply and Demand
0700-2866 Canada. Grains Council. Annual Report
0700-2971 Manitoba Statistical Review
0700-3048 Dialogue (Ottawa)
0700-3161 Conserver Society Notes *see* 0705-7768
0700-3226 Korean Journal
0700-3269 Kodaly Institute of Canada. Notes
0700-3617 Overview
0700-365X Estuaire
0700-3684 Manitoba Library Association. Newsline
0700-3722 Information-Status of Women
0700-3730 Ontario. Advisory Council on the Physically Handicapped. Annual Report
0700-3749 Quebec (Province) Ministere des Terres et Forets. Conseil Consultatif des Reserves Ecologiques. Rapport Annuel
0700-3838 Music Research News
0700-3862 Labour
0700-3900 A l'Ecoute
0700-3919 Solitude-Inflexion *see* 0706-0556
0700-3986 U.S. Activities Report
0700-4400 International View
0700-463X Intralogue
0700-4982 London Community Services Directory
0700-5008 Marquee
0700-5032 Angler and Hunter in Ontario
0700-5040 Habitabec
0700-5105 Laurier Campus
0700-5199 Szamadas
0700-5202 Slavna Nadele
0700-5245 Conseil Canadien de Protection des Animaux, Ressource
0700-527X Northern Life
0700-5296 Book Trade in Canada
0700-5318 Opus
0700-5350 World Literacy of Canada. Newsletter
0700-5369 Literacy
0700-5482 Quest for a Common Denominator *see* 0702-7575
0700-5539 Canadian Business Service Investment Reporter
0700-558X Eureka *see* 0705-0348
0700-5768 Aerospace Canada
0700-5989 Association of Ontario Land Surveyors. Annual Report
0700-6004 Reseau
0700-6365 Glenbow Foundation. Occasional Paper *see* 0072-467X
0700-7388 Boating News
0700-7426 Sphere
0700-8007 Purchasing Management Digest
0700-8104 Early Canadian Life
0700-9216 Canadian Electrical Engineering Journal
0700-9275 Sea Pen
0700-9283 Records of Early English Drama Newsletter
0700-9712 Community Information Service. Newsletter
0700-9771 A R C Arabic Journal
0700-9801 Journal of Psychology and Judaism
0700-9844 Ontario Safety League. News
0700-9895 Outdoor Crest Newsletter *see* 0700-9909
0700-9909 Outdoor Crest
0700-9925 Proletarian Unity
0700-9976 Gastown and Vancouver Today
0701-001X Coach *see* 0705-7504
0701-0184 Culture & Tradition
0701-0214 Draudzes Vestis
0701-0419 Bookings
0701-0524 University of Toronto. Centre of Criminology Library. Acquisitions List
0701-0710 C I M Reporter
0701-0745 Grand Slam
0701-0788 Catholic Quote
0701-0796 Downtown Action
0701-080X Engineering Forum
0701-1008 Etudes Inuit Studies
0701-1024 Alberta Science Education Journal
0701-1075 Canadian Angling and Boating
0701-1156 About Women
0701-1237 Alberta Teachers' Association. Religious Studies & Moral Education Council. Newsletter
0701-1245 Equipment Trader
0701-1369 Wings Magazine of Canada
0701-144X County Magazine
0701-1539 Employee Benefit Costs in Canada
0701-1547 Action (Winnipeg)
0701-158X Annals of Air and Space Law
0701-161X Committee on Canadian Labour History. Journal†
0701-1687 Produits pour l'Industrie Quebecoise
0701-1733 Canadian Cases on the Law of Torts
0701-1784 Canadian Water Resources Journal
0701-1792 Journal of Ukrainian Graduate Studies *changed to* Journal of Ukrainian Studies
0701-1989 Revue 2
0701-2748 Periodics†
0701-4155 Journal Europeen du Collectionneur d'Ordres et Decorations
0701-4309 Canadian Council of Churches. Record of Proceedings
0701-4945 Phenomena
0701-5208 National Research Council, Canada. Division of Building Research. Special Technical Publication
0701-5216 National Research Council, Canada. Division of Building Research. Building Practice Note
0701-5488 Pension Plans in Canada
0701-7243 Inter-National
0701-7391 Canada. Ministry of State for Science and Technology. Federal Science Programs
0701-7502 Agricultural Real Estate Values in Alberta
0701-757X British Columbia Fruit Growers Association. Horticultural Forum Proceedings
0701-757X British Columbia Economic Activity
0701-7758 Ontario Science Center. Center News
0701-7995 Neologie en Marche. Serie B. Langues de Specialities
0701-8002 Natural Life
0701-8185 Hunter Training and Conservation. Instructor Newsletter
0701-8533 Ontario Business News
0701-8681 C I P S Review
0701-8746 Lutte Ouvriere
0701-8878 Relatively Speaking
0701-8894 Dalhousie University. School of Library Service. Y-A Hotline
0701-8983 Canadian Industrial Health & Safety News *changed to* Canadian Occupational Health & Safety News
0701-9637 Environment Views
0702-0066 Alberta. Department of Advanced Education and Manpower. Post-Secondary Education Programs
0702-0333 Canada-Japan, the Export-Import Picture
0702-0481 International Journal of Mini and Microcomputers
0702-0627 Monitor (Ottawa)
0702-1437 Bakka Magazine
0702-2735 Independent Forester
0702-3138 Alberta Disaster Services News & Notes
0702-3162 Canadian Coin News
0702-3855 Hrvatski Put
0702-4894 Wee Giant
0702-5459 On-Site
0702-5785 In the Driver's Seat
0702-6005 Foreign Investment Review
0702-634X Basilian Historical Bulletins
0702-6587 Canada. Statistics Canada. Security Transactions with Non-Residents/Operations avec des Non-Residents sur des Valeurs Mobilieres
0702-6633 Economic Council of Canada. Bulletin *see* 0226-224X
0702-6803 Magook
0702-6943 Quebec at a Glance
0702-7001 Atlantic Issues
0702-7060 Industrial Management
0702-7206 Municipal and Planning Law Reports
0702-7222 Progressive Conservative Party of Canada. Leader's Report
0702-7265 British Columbia Reporter
0702-7354 Alberta Square and Round Dance Federation. Newsletter
0702-7524 Boating Business
0702-7532 New Literature and Ideology
0702-7575 Mamashee
0702-7958 C. S. P. World News
0702-8075 B.C. Market News
0702-8083 Canada. Statistics Canada. Electrical Contracting Industry/Entrepreneurs d'Installations Electriques
0702-8091 Canada. Statistics Canada. Law Enforcement, Judicial and Correctional Statistics Service Bulletin/La Statistique Policiere, Judiciaire, et Correctionnelle, Bulletin de Service†
0702-8318 Automotive Marketer
0702-8431 McGill University, Montreal. Centre for Developing-Area Studies. Occasional Monograph Series
0702-844X End-Time News
0702-8458 Edmonton Revival Centre. News *see* 0702-844X
0702-8520 Dime Bag: Fiction Issue
0702-858X Monde des Loisirs
0702-8733 Canadian Highway Carriers Guide
0702-9063 Emmenager a Ottawa/Hull *see* 0226-7837
0702-9071 Canadian Rider
0702-9179 Moving to Toronto *see* 0226-7829
0702-9187 Moving to Vancouver/Victoria *see* 0226-7276
0702-9233 Jewish Historical Society of Canada. Journal *see* 0706-3547
0702-9284 Recreation Research Review
0702-9888 Selected Labour Statistics for Nova Scotia
0703-0169 Saskatchewan. Department of Labour. Research and Planning Branch. Wage Adjustments in Collective Bargaining Agreements
0703-0312 EnRoute
0703-0320 Canada Institute for Scientific and Technical Information. Annual Report
0703-0428 Urban History Review
0703-0606 New Brunswick Museum. Journal
0703-0665 British Columbia. Ministry of Labour. Research and Planning Branch. Negotiated Working Conditions
0703-0827 Manitoba. Lotteries Commission. Annual Report
0703-086X British Columbia. Energy Commission. Annual Report
0703-0878 B. C. Labour Directory
0703-1157 Chem Thirteen News
0703-1211 Legal Medical Quarterly
0703-1440 Big Country Cariboo Magazine
0703-1831 Cicada
0703-1874 Europa: a Journal of Interdisciplinary Studies
0703-1890 Bois Ouvre
0703-2048 Saskatchewan Reporter
0703-2129 Canadian Lawyer
0703-2234 Canada Folk Bulletin
0703-2358 Alberta Petroleum Marketing Commission. Annual Report
0703-2633 Canada. Statistics Canada. Annual Report/Rapport Annuel
0703-2684 Canada. Statistics Canada. Historical Labour Force Statistics, Actual Data, Seasonal Factors, Seasonally Adjusted Data/Statistiques Chronologiques sur la Population Active, Chiffres Reels, Facteurs Saisonniers et Donnees Desaisonnalisees
0703-2749 Canada. Statistics Canada. Local Government Finance: Revenue and Expenditure, Assets and Liabilities, Actual/Finances Publiques Locales: Revenus et Depenses, Actif et Passif, Chiffres Reels
0703-3117 Alberta Law Reports (2nd Series)
0703-3249 Canadian Conference on Information Science. Proceedings
0703-4520 Forge
0703-4563 Review Ottawa
0703-4598 Centre
0703-4660 National Museum of Natural Sciences. Natural History Notebook Series
0703-4687 Real Property Reports
0703-4857 Canada. Statistics Canada. Farm Income and Prices Section. Farm Cash Receipts/Recettes Monetaires Agricoles†
0703-4873 Canada. Statistics Canada. Employment, Earnings and Hours. Seasonally-Adjusted Series/Emploi, Remunerations et Heures; Series Desaisonnalisees
0703-5330 International Review of Slavic Linguistics

ISSN INDEX

ISSN	Title
0703-5357	Atlantic Co-Operator
0703-5411	International Atlantic Salmon Foundation. Newsletter.
0703-5500	Victorian Studies Association of Western Canada. Newsletter
0703-5527	P C L A Newsletter
0703-5551	Business Law Reports
0703-5608	Aviation Quebec
0703-5640	Theatre Canada. Special Bulletin
0703-5764	Diabetes Dialogue
0703-6078	Canada Council. Touring Office. Bulletin
0703-6337	Revue d'Integration Europeenne
0703-654X	Canada. Statistics Canada. Road Motor Vehicles-Fuel Sales/Vehicules Automobiles-Ventes de Carburants
0703-6566	New Brunswick. Department of Tourism. Annual Report
0703-6892	E & M Newsletter
0703-7090	R T A C Forum
0703-7139	Possibles
0703-7163	MoneyLetter
0703-7228	Katimavik†
0703-7244	Canada. Statistics Canada. Cable Television/Teledistribution
0703-7252	Canada. Statistics Canada. Telecommunications Statistics/Statistique des Telecommunications
0703-7295	Canada. Statistics Canada. Non-Residential General Building Contracting Industry/Industrie des Entreprises Generales en Construction Non Domiciliaire
0703-7333	Canada. Statistics Canada. Stocks of Frozen Meat Products/Stocks de Viandes Congelees
0703-7368	Canada. Statistics Canada. Family Incomes(Census Families)/Revenus des Famille (Familles de Recensement)
0703-7384	Corpus Administrative Index
0703-7406	Canada. Statistics Canada. Silver-Cobalt Mines and Silver-Lead-Zinc Mines/Mines d'Argent-Cobalt et Mines d'Argent-Plomb-Zinc†
0703-766X	A G M Reporter
0703-7732	Benefits Canada
0703-8240	International Journal of Women's Studies
0703-8372	Canadian Association of Pathologists. Newsletter
0703-895X	Canadian Token
0703-8968	Briar Patch
0703-8984	Electronics Today
0703-9018	Arab Review
0703-9085	A I B C Forum
0703-9115	Promises
0703-9158	Dairy Goat Gazette and Lively Vivid Escapades see 0708-6164
0703-9328	Canada. Statistics Canada. Financial Statistics of Education/Statistiques Financieres de l'Education
0703-9409	New Brunswick Anglican
0703-9468	Artisan Nouvelles
0703-9476	Best Canadian Stories
0703-9484	Auxiliaire
0703-9514	Furniture Production & Design Meubles
0703-9905	Marketing Voyages
0704-0059	Antiques see 0704-0067
0704-0067	Antique News (Toronto)
0704-0083	Acorn
0704-0288	Advocates Quarterly
0704-0407	Hospital Trustee
0704-0547	Silangan
0704-0598	N G R C Forum
0704-0601	Conference Board in Canada. Executive Bulletin
0704-061X	Cineclube
0704-0717	Canadian Workshop
0704-0733	Trot
0704-0857	Canadian Community Law Journal
0704-0873	Bulletin sur les Relations du Travail
0704-0970	New Brunswick. Forest Products Commission. Progress Report
0704-1217	L A R U Studies
0704-1225	Canadian Journal of Family Law
0704-1349	Palliser Wheat Growers Association. Newsletter
0704-1543	Commission d'Energie du Nord Canadien. Revue de l'Exploitation see 0704-1551
0704-1551	Northern Canada Power Commission. Annual Review
0704-173X	Your Home
0704-1950	Societe Quebecoise d'Ethnographie et de Folklore. Bulletin
0704-2590	Ontario Geological Survey Study
0704-2671	Education Manitoba
0704-2701	Ocean Dumping Report
0704-2728	Information C B
0704-2752	Ontario. Geological Survey. Annual Report of the Regional and Resident Geologist
0704-3139	Canada. Hydrographic Service. Annual Report
0704-3724	Canadian Occupational Safety & Health Law
0704-4062	E C O L/O G Information Services
0704-4771	N A F O Meeting Proceedings
0704-4798	N A F O Annual Report
0704-4836	Northern Development
0704-4860	Hearsay, for Dalhousie Law Graduates changed to Hearsay
0704-5263	Perception
0704-5387	Canada. Statistics Canada. Public Warehousing/Entreposage Public†
0704-5646	Canadian Poetry (London, Ont.)
0704-5697	Y E R Monograph Series
0704-5700	Yeats Eliot Review
0704-576X	National Museum of Natural Sciences. Syllogeus
0704-6138	A C M E Newsletter
0704-6359	Hospitalite
0704-6383	Image des Laurentides
0704-6391	Canadian Firefighter
0704-6588	Crosscurrents
0704-6596	Canada. Statistics Canada. Elementary-Secondary School Enrolment/Effectifs des Ecoles Primaires et Secondaires
0704-6790	South Central Ontario Construction Industry Directory. Purchasing Guide
0704-6804	Airforce
0704-7002	Polyphony
0704-7223	Taxipresse
0704-7290	Intrinsic
0704-7312	Whiskey Jack
0704-7517	Apprentissage et Socialisation
0704-7584	International Development Research Centre. Annual Report
0704-7673	Canada. Northern Forest Research Centre. Information Report
0704-769X	Canada. Maritimes Forest Research Centre, Fredericton, New Brunswick. Information Report M-X
0704-7886	Lundi
0704-7916	Arts Atlantic
0704-7940	Repertoire des Produits Fabriques au Quebec
0704-7975	Gardenland
0704-8017	Edmonton Chamber of Commerce. Commerce News
0704-8025	Reports on Separatism
0704-8475	Virus Montreal
0704-8734	Alberta. Government Libraries Council. Annual Reviews
0704-8785	York-Simcoe Ontario Construction Industry Directory. Purchasing Guide
0704-9056	Alberta Art Foundation. Annual Report
0704-9145	Alberta Genealogical Society. Surnames Register changed to Alberta Genealogical Society. Ancestor Index
0704-9153	Ovo Magazine
0704-9226	Halton Farm News
0704-9463	This Is Entertainment
0704-9528	Administrateur Hospitalier
0704-9536	Film Edmonton
0704-9722	Canadian Journal of Criminology
0704-982X	Quebec (Province) Conseil Superieur de l'Education. Conseil-Education
0705-0038	Children's Book News
0705-0119	Descent
0705-0348	Crux Mathematicorum
0705-0445	Theatre du Trident see 0705-0453
0705-0453	Theatre
0705-0585	Decor a Coeur
0705-064X	Development Directions
0705-0852	Journal de la Majorite
0705-1026	Federation des Associations de Parents et Instituteurs Langues Francaise de l'Ontario. Liaison
0705-1093	Decoration Chez-Soi
0705-1123	Echo (Ottawa)
0705-1131	Family Law Review
0705-1212	S T O P Press see 0383-6347
0705-1328	Journal of Canadian Poetry
0705-1433	Canadian Footwear Journal
0705-1530	Canadian Stereo Guide
0705-1727	Canadian Weightlifting Journal
0705-176X	Canadian Wrestler
0705-1867	Vani
0705-1883	Books in Finnish
0705-1905	Saint John Today
0705-1913	Review of Architecture and Landscape Architecture
0705-1980	Shearwater Warrior see 0707-8056
0705-2006	Canadian Journal of Archaeology
0705-2022	Working Teacher
0705-209X	C J L Foundation. Newsletter see 0705-2103
0705-2103	Committee for Justice and Liberty. Newsletter
0705-212X	Lawn & Garden Trade
0705-2294	Books in Dutch
0705-2304	Discovery
0705-2316	Books in Chinese
0705-2332	Books in Danish
0705-2367	Coal Miner
0705-2669	Manitoba Archaeological Quarterly
0705-2731	Caribbean Year Book
0705-288X	Water Pollution Research in Canada see 0197-9140
0705-3002	Canadian Journal of Italian Studies
0705-3010	Canadian Apparel Manufacture
0705-3150	Wilderness Arts and Recreation
0705-3193	Canadian Controls & Instruments
0705-3436	Loisir et Societe
0705-3754	Crescent International
0705-3797	Episodes
0705-3851	Femmes d'Ici
0705-3894	Free Throw
0705-3932	Canadian Renewable Energy News
0705-4009	Music Magazine
0705-4319	Control and Sale of Alcoholic Beverages in Canada/Controle et la Vente des Boissons Alcooliques au Canada
0705-4343	Canada. Statistics Canada. Air Passenger Origin and Destination. Canada-United States Report/Origine et Destination des Passagers Aeriens. Rapport sur le Trafic Canada-Etat Unis
0705-436X	Canada. Statistics Canada. Coal Mines/Mines de Charbon
0705-4572	Chinook
0705-4580	Canadian Journal of Regional Science
0705-503X	Canada. Great Lakes Forest Research Centre. Survey Bulletin
0705-5064	Canadian Theatre Checklist
0705-5137	Canadian Report
0705-517X	Ontario. Ministry of Labour. Library. Library Bulletin
0705-5196	C A N M E T Report
0705-520X	Canada. Great Lakes Forest Research Centre. Forestry Newsletter
0705-5242	Canada. Statistics Canada. Report on Livestock Surveys: Cattle, Sheep/Rapport des Enquetes sur le Betail: Bovins, Moutons†
0705-5331	Canada: Official Handbook of Present Conditions and Recent Progress†
0705-548X	Canadian Film Series
0705-5587	Canada Addictions Foundation. Directory
0705-5617	Coaching Review
0705-5757	British Columbia. Ministry of Agriculture. Nursery Production Guide
0705-5765	Canada. Statistics Canada. Canadian Statistical Review. Annual Supplement to Section 1/Revue Statistique du Canada. Supplement Annuel de la Section 1.
0705-5811	Alberta. Environment Council of Alberta. Annual Report
0705-5900	Atmosphere - Ocean
0705-596X	Alberta. Office of the Superintendent of Insurance and Real Estate. Annual Report
0705-6028	Canada. Advisory Council on the Status of Women. Annual Report
0705-6109	Misleading Advertising Bulletin
0705-6249	Directory of Canadian Orchestras and Youth Orchestras
0705-6435	Health in Schools
0705-6494	Books in Hungarian
0705-6591	Canadian Society for the Prevention of Cruelty to Children. Journal
0705-6605	Televiews
0705-6680	Canadian Perspective
0705-6702	Newfoundland Medical Association Journal
0705-6761	Embouteilleur Quebecois
0705-6931	Leadline
0705-7091	Financial Post Survey of Energy Resources see 0227-1656
0705-7156	Books in Spanish
0705-7172	Books in Arabic
0705-7199	Geographie Physique et Quaternaire
0705-7504	Canadian Soccer Association. Technical Manual
0705-7520	Gite
0705-7768	New Conserver Society Notes
0705-7814	Wise Owl News (Toronto)
0705-7822	Nayer Dor
0705-7970	Liban au Canada
0705-8063	Vandance
0705-8160	Directory of Courses. Tourism-Hospitality-Recreation
0705-8209	Books in Armenian
0705-825X	Books in Urdu
0705-8292	Conseil de la Jeunesse Scientifique. Bottin
0705-8314	Guide du Camping
0705-8330	Canadian Business Economics
0705-8373	Books in Hindi
0705-8454	A S T I S Current Awareness Bulletin
0705-856X	Facts
0705-8616	Algonkian's see 0707-3143
0705-8748	Farm Gate
0705-8799	Trade News North
0705-8802	British Columbia School Counsellors' Association. Newsletter
0705-8829	World Literacy of Canada, News and Views see 0700-5350
0705-887X	City of Toronto Planning Board. City Planning
0705-8993	Marine Trades
0705-9094	Canadian Association for the Prevention of Crime. Bulletin
0705-9175	Movie Works Weekly
0705-9213	Australian Road Research in Progress
0705-9272	Environment Systems & Industries
0705-9698	British Columbia. Ministry of Labour. Annual Report
0706-0114	Datafacts
0706-0203	About Arts and Craft
0706-0300	Bicycling News Canada
0706-0556	Esplumoir
0706-0661	Canadian Journal of Plant Pathology
0706-067X	Canada. Statistics Canada. Road Motor Vehicles-Registrations/Vehicules Automobiles-Immatriculations
0706-0726	Health Care in Canada changed to Health Care
0706-1293	Canadian Nuclear Association. Annual International Conference Proceedings
0706-1447	Alberta Energy Resource Industries, Monthly Statistics
0706-1706	Labour, Capital and Society

0706-2273 Quebec (Province) Centrale des Bibliotheques. Choix Jeunesse; Documentation Audiovisuelle
0706-2338 Directory of Canadian Universities
0706-2419 Parlure
0706-2451 Canada. Statistics Canada. Highway, Road, Street and Bridge Contracting Industry/Entrepreneurs de Grande Route, Chemin, rue et Pont
0706-246X Institute of Man and Resources Reports
0706-2788 Canada. Statistics Canada. Homicide Statistics/Statistique de l'Homicide
0706-280X Canadian Jewish Herald
0706-2893 British Columbia Police Journal
0706-2907 School Library Association
0706-3105 Canada. Statistics Canada. Road and Street Length and Financing/Voies Publiques, Longueur et Financement†
0706-3369 Alberta. Horticultural Research Center. Annual Report
0706-3547 Canadian Jewish Historical Society Journal
0706-3601 B. C. Economic Development
0706-3679 Education in Canada
0706-3792 Manitoba. Municipal Employees Benefits Board. Annual Report
0706-3857 Fireweed
0706-3962 TRANSPO
0706-4053 Monthly Record, Meteorological Observations in Eastern Canada
0706-4071 Monthly Record, Meteorological Observations in Western Canada
0706-408X Monthly Record, Meteorological Observations in Northern Canada
0706-4152 C C I Technical Bulletins
0706-4403 Prince Edward Island. Department of Municipal Affairs. Annual Report
0706-4772 School Libraries Newsletter *see* 0706-2907
0706-4926 Saskatchewan. Department of Labour. Wages and Working Conditions by Occupation
0706-5000 College Media Director Newsletter
0706-5019 Occupational Health and Safety Law
0706-506X Automotive Review
0706-5086 N F A Journal
0706-5132 Diver Magazine
0706-5159 British Columbia Housing Quarterly†
0706-5264 Producteur Agricole
0706-5302 Vancouver Gastronomic
0706-5310 Calgary Gastronomic
0706-5337 Chaos
0706-5388 Carswell's Practice Cases
0706-5469 E C S Newsletter
0706-5531 Nicola Valley Archives Association. Newsletter. Historical Work Paper
0706-5582 Canadian Journal of Life Insurance
0706-5590 Mission Magazine
0706-5604 Thalia
0706-5639 Debacle†
0706-5647 Family Law Reform Reporter
0706-5655 Estates & Trusts Reports
0706-585X Ravings
0706-6007 Canada. Treasury Board Secretariat. Federal Expenditure Plan
0706-652X Canadian Journal of Fisheries and Aquatic Sciences
0706-6600 Canadian Taxation
0706-6910 Atlantic Provinces Linguistic Association Journal
0706-7054 Earthcare Information Centre. Newsletter
0706-716X Reed Career Magazine
0706-7372 En Avant
0706-7410 SonEcran
0706-7437 Canadian Journal of Psychiatry
0706-7542 Scrumdown
0706-7623 Canadian Bluegrass Review
0706-7658 Transit Fact Book & Membership Directory
0706-7682 Great Expeditions
0706-7747 Forest Times
0706-7798 Manitoba. Public Library Services. Newsletter
0706-7852 Benefits for Saskatchewan Industry from Resource Development
0706-7860 Direction (Regina)
0706-7909 Canada & Arab World
0706-7917 Arab Directory
0706-795X Livres et des Jeunes
0706-7984 New Music
0706-7992 Subject to Change
0706-8018 Contact (Willowdale, Ont.)
0706-8042 Animals Canada
0706-8069 Canadian Churchman and Crosstalk
0706-8085 Reaching the Manitoba Market
0706-8093 From an Island
0706-8107 Canadian Review of Art Education Research
0706-8204 Canadian Women's Studies
0706-8328 Annuaire de l'Eglise du Quebec
0706-8441 Labour History
0706-8662 What's New in Publications
0706-8921 NorAct
0706-8956 Dunhill Insurance Law Report
0706-8964 Dunhill Liability Loss Report
0706-9006 Stoney Monday
0706-9014 Borealis
0706-9278 Canadian Emergency Services News
0706-9391 Saskatchewan Research Council. Physics Division. Annual Climatic Summary
0706-9758 Canadian Student Traveller
0706-9820 Unican†
0706-9839 Alberta Teachers' Association. Members' Handbook
0707-0047 Directory of Lifestyle Change Services
0707-0152 Saskatchewan. Prescription Drug Plan. Annual Report
0707-0195 Provincial Council of Women of British Columbia Newsletter
0707-0349 National P C President
0707-0365 Saskatchewan Motor Transport Guide
0707-0462 British Columbia. Medical Services Plan. Physician's Newsletter
0707-0756 Touchstone
0707-0780 Heritage Seekers
0707-0926 Open Interest
0707-0934 M S Ontario
0707-0942 Directory to Co-Operative Naturalists' Projects in Ontario.
0707-1000 Energy and Natural Resources Library Journals
0707-1027 Of Steam and Stone
0707-1434 Alberta. Health and Social Services Disciplines Committee. Annual Report
0707-1442 Ontario Tourism News
0707-1868 Pentecostal Assemblies of Canada. Cell Pak
0707-1884 B I D S
0707-1892 Business Information Data Services *see* 0707-1884
0707-1949 Business & Government News†
0707-1965 Maintenance Management
0707-2031 Videorecordings Available in the Public Libraries of Metropolitan Toronto
0707-2279 Worldwind
0707-2287 Eidos
0707-2392 Common Cents Magazine
0707-2570 Saskatchewan. Department of Mineral Resources. Statistical Yearbook
0707-2597 McSweeney Report on Canada
0707-2783 Alberta. Fish and Wildlife Division. Fisheries Pollution Report
0707-2791 Alberta. Fish and Wildlife Division. Pollution Report *see* 0707-2783
0707-2899 Economics in Canadian Schools
0707-2945 Canadian Muslim
0707-2996 Canada. Geological Survey. Index of Publications of the Geological Survey of Canada
0707-3062 C E C Newsletter
0707-3135 Microlog Index
0707-3143 Ontario Indian
0707-3151 Algoma Outdoors
0707-3186 Runner
0707-3232 Canadian Genealogist
0707-3240 B. C. Runner
0707-3291 B C I T: The Career Campus
0707-3364 Northland Today
0707-3372 Arab News of Toronto
0707-3380 Asian Tribune
0707-3542 Rollcall
0707-3739 British Columbia. Ministry of the Environment. Northeast Coal Study Preliminary Environmental Report
0707-3747 C O N S E R Microfiche
0707-3941 Halton Consumer
0707-4409 Calgary Magazine
0707-4611 Chickadee
0707-4808 Canadian Agricultural Economics Society. Proceedings of the Workshop
0707-4875 Current Law Notes *see* 0707-4883
0707-4883 Current Law Newsletter
0707-4891 Aikamme
0707-5014 British Columbia Motor Transport Directory
0707-5065 Socialist Albania
0707-5103 Con Brio
0707-5138 After Stonewall
0707-5162 Atlantic Salmon Directory
0707-5316 Montreal Writers' Forum
0707-5324 Lusitano
0707-5332 International History Review
0707-5405 Newfoundland and Labrador Recreation Advisory Council for Special Groups. Newsletter
0707-5456 Directory of Canadian Plays and Playwrights
0707-5723 Analysis
0707-5987 Cancer Comment *see* 0707-5995
0707-5995 Canadian Cancer Society, Manitoba Division. Communique
0707-6150 Canadian Life Insurance Association. Directory
0707-6401 Tele Communicator
0707-6894 Southeast Regional Library (Sask.) Library Directory
0707-705X Alberta Historical Resources Foundation. News & Views
0707-7106 Swamp Gas Journal
0707-7114 B. C. Agent
0707-7130 Connections
0707-7165 Envol
0707-7319 Breathing
0707-7327 Alberta Council of College Librarians. Newsletter
0707-7351 Management Consulting Institute. Bulletin
0707-7459 Igalaaq
0707-7718 Canada. Parks Canada. (Western Region). Library Information Bulletin
0707-7777 P E. M. C. Catalogue: Supplement
0707-7785 British Columbia. Provincial Educational Media Centre. Videotape Supplement *see* 0707-7777
0707-7793 Agricultural Science Bulletin
0707-7904 Dairy Industry Research Report
0707-7920 Confluent Education Newsletter
0707-7955 Canadian Association of University Research Administrators. Research Bulletin
0707-8021 Point de Mire
0707-803X Outwest Magazine
0707-8048 Canadian Federation for the Humanities. Bulletin
0707-8056 Warrior
0707-8064 Calgary Commerce
0707-820X Blackwell Newsletter
0707-8412 Resources for Feminist Research
0707-8897 Kaleidoscope Canada
0707-9087 Teaching of Adults Series
0707-9184 Snowmobile Accidents, Manitoba
0707-9524 Canadian Bridge Digest
0707-9559 Canada. Statistics Canada. Private and Public Investment in Canada, Mid-Year Review/Investissements Prives et Publics au Canada. Revue de la Mi-Annee
0707-9664 Astro-Directory News
0707-9699 International Review of Community Development
0707-9788 Monthly Summary Report of Saskatchewan Minerals
0707-9818 Alberta Rural Development Studies
0707-9834 Nova Scotia. Commission on Drug Dependency. Annual Report
0707-994X Alberta Authors Bulletin
0708-0263 At a Glance
0708-028X Saskatchewan Rail Committee. News Bulletin
0708-0719 B. C. Technologist
0708-0727 Canadian Shipping Project Newsletter
0708-0743 Recreation Saskatchewan
0708-076X International Sivananda Yoga Life and Yoga Vacations
0708-0840 B. C. News *see* 0708-0859
0708-0859 B. C. Peace News
0708-0999 Canadian Cancer Society. B. C. and Yukon Division. Newsletter
0708-1006 Physioquebec
0708-1030 Canadian Cancer Society. B.C. and Yukon Division. Provincial News *see* 0708-0999
0708-1065 Register of On-Going Labour Research
0708-1073 Construction Sightlines
0708-109X Standout Magazine
0708-1332 Export Canada
0708-1375 New Brunswick Construction Products Directory
0708-1936 Bio-Joule Newsletter
0708-1987 Etape
0708-2169 Hiballer Forest Magazine
0708-2177 Restoration
0708-2193 Directory of University Correspondence Courses
0708-2398 Etudes Creoles
0708-2495 36 Manieres
0708-2673 Alberta Health Education Programs
0708-2770 S A A Bulletin
0708-2800 S A A Newsletter *see* 0708-2770
0708-3017 Processing & Manufacturing Guide
0708-3025 Agricultural Processing & Manufacturing Guide *see* 0708-3017
0708-3041 Small Business News
0708-3106 Alberta. Department of Education. Early Childhood Services Program Highlights
0708-319X Etienne Gilson Series
0708-3629 Nova Scotia Fisherman
0708-3637 New Brunswick. Department of Social Services. Quarterly Statistical Bulletin
0708-3793 Spectrum
0708-3882 Saskatchewan. Department of Social Statistics. Annual Report
0708-3963 Consumer Bulletin
0708-4331 High Flight
0708-448X Datum
0708-4625 Free: The Newsletter of Free Materials and Services
0708-5052 Baha'i Studies
0708-5397 C I P Forum
0708-6113 Directory of Sports, Recreation and Physical Education
0708-6164 Dairy Goat Gazette
0708-6172 Forintek Canada Corporation, Western Laboratory. Technical Reports
0708-6180 About Women
0708-7012 Canada. Statistics Canada. Estimates of Population for Canada and the Provinces/Estimations de la Population du Canada et des Provinces
0708-9066 Ex Libris
0708-9104 Atlantic Life
0708-918X Planetary Association for Clean Energy. Newsletter
0708-9325 Canada. Prairie Farm Rehabilitation Administration. Library. Newsletter/Nouvelles de la Bibliotheque
0708-9511 Federation of Canadian Municipalities. Annual Conference Proceedings
0708-9635 Canadian Musician
0709-0412 Government of Canada Publications Quarterly Catalogue
0709-0706 Children's Aid Society of Ottawa. Information Bulletin *see* 0705-1123
0709-1370 National
0709-1532 Western Sportsman
0709-2016 Le Temps
0709-2652 Arctic Seas
0709-3373 Poetry Canada Review

ISSN INDEX

ISSN	Title
0709-4272	Pyramid
0709-4434	A-V Canada
0709-5341	Motor Vehicle Reports
0709-5368	Transpotech
0709-5597	Executive Compensation Service. Professional, Scientific, Technical Remuneration, Canada
0709-7115	Select Home Designs: Cottage Country
0709-7123	Select Home Designs: Home Design & Decor
0709-7751	Language and Society
0709-776X	B. C. Sea Angling Guide
0709-7778	B. C. Fresh Water Fishing Guide
0709-8006	F. A. P. U. Q. Nouvelles Universitaires
0709-8413	Art Gallery of Ontario. The Gallery
0709-8987	University of Toronto. Library Automation Systems. New Publications Awareness List
0709-9797	Broadcast Technology
0710-0167	Revue Quebecoise de Linguistique
0720-101X	Elektronik-Applikation
0720-6259	Pastoraltheologie - Monatsschrift fuer Wissenschaft und Praxis in Kirche und Gesellschaft
1661-2434	Teamwork
2306-2525	Family Planning International Assistance Newsletter

Title Index

Page numbers in italics refer to location of main entries, those in roman type refer to location of subject cross references. The country code and assigned ISSN appear below each entry.

A A A S Selected Symposia Series (American Association for the Advancement of Science) (US) *778*

A A C T E Yearbook (American Association of Colleges for Teacher Education) (US ISSN 0065-7123) *333*

A A F M Proceedings of Annual Meeting (American Association of Feed Microscopists) (US ISSN 0569-2628) *124*, 626

A A/G B Road Atlas (Automobile Association - Great Britain) (UK) *882*

A A Guide to Motoring in Kenya (Automobile Association of East Africa) (KE) *882*

A: a Journal of Contemporary Literature (US) *558*, 578

A A L S Library Statistics (Association of American Law Schools) (US) *507*, 525

A. A. M. C. Curriculum Directory (Association of American Medical Colleges) (US ISSN 0092-0371) *347*, 591

A A M C Directory of American Medical Education (Association of American Medical Colleges) (US ISSN 0360-7437) *333*, 591

A A M Handbook see Motoring in Malaya 889

A A R Dissertation Series (American Academy of Religion) (US) *762*

A A R P Monographs (Art and Archaeology Research Papers) (UK) *56*, 71

A A R Studies in Religion (American Academy of Religion) (US ISSN 0084-6287) *762*

A A R Texts and Translations (American Academy of Religion) (US) *762*

A A S C U Studies (American Association of State Colleges and Universities) (US ISSN 0065-7344) *333*

A.A.'s Far East Businessman's Directory (Artists Associates) (HK ISSN 0532-9175) *234*

A. A. T. E. Guide to English Books (Australian Association for the Teaching of English) (AT ISSN 0084-7216) *325*, 577

A A U Baton Twirling Rules and Regulations (Amateur Athletic Union of the United States) (US ISSN 0361-221X) *818*

A A U Code see Amateur Athletic Union of the United States. Official Handbook of the A A U Code 819

A A U Junior Olympic Handbook (Amateur Athletic Union of the United States) (US ISSN 0361-4654) *257*, 818

A A U Official Boxing Rules and Guide (Amateur Athletic Union of the United States) (US) *819*

A A U Official Handbook: Baton Twirling see A A U Baton Twirling Rules and Regulations 818

A A U Official Handbook: Trampoline & Tumbling see Official A A U Trampoline and Tumbling Handbook 821

A A U Official Rules: Swimming see Amateur Athletic Union of the United States. Athletic Library. Official Rules for Competitive Swimming 819

A A U Official Track and Field Handbook, Rules and Records (Amateur Athletic Union of the United States) (US ISSN 0361-347X) *819*

A A U Official Weightlifting Rules and Guide (Amateur Athletic Union of the United States) (US) *819*

A A V S O Bulletin (American Association of Variable Star Observers) (US ISSN 0516-9518) *80*

A A V S O Report (US) *81*

A B A Lawyers' Title Guaranty Funds Newsletter (American Bar Association) (US ISSN 0361-3763) *508*

A B Bookman's Yearbook (US ISSN 0065-0005) *757*

A B C - Arab Trade Reference: Arab & Middle East Countries (UA) *192*

A B C Blue-Book see Architects, Builders, and Contractors Blue-Book 904

A B C British Columbia Lumber Trade Directory and Year Book (CN ISSN 0065-0013) *412*

A B C der Deutschen Wirtschaft (GW) *234*

A B C Directory (US ISSN 0065-0021) *134*

A B C Europ Production (GW ISSN 0065-003X) *192*

A B C Freight Guide (UK ISSN 0308-9304) *881*

A B C Goods Transport Guide see A B C Freight Guide 881

A B C Newsletter (Africa Bibliographic Center) (KE) *87*

A B C of Book Trade (US ISSN 0065-0048) *757*

A B C Privrede Jugoslavije (YU) *234*

A B C's of Canadian Industry see Educational ABC of Canadian Industry 144

A B P A Bulletin see Acoustical and Board Products. Bulletin 68

A B T Informationen (Arbeitsberichte zur Bibliothekstechnik) (GW ISSN 0340-3440) *525*

A B's Guide to Souvenirs and Novelties see Buyers' Guide for the Mass Entertainment Industry 828

A C A Bulletin (Association for Communication Administration) (US ISSN 0360-0939) *558*

A C A Index (Americans for Constitutional Action) (US ISSN 0066-1228) *707*

A.C.A. Industry Guide to Hearing Aids. International Edition (Acoustic Corporation of America) (US ISSN 0095-3474) *286*, 706

A.C.A. Review (Anglers Cooperative Association) (UK ISSN 0044-8257) *274*, 395

A C B M Nouvelles see C A M L Newsletter 658

A C I Bibliography (American Concrete Institute) (US ISSN 0084-6325) *87*

A C I L see Amsterdam Studies in the Theory and History of Linguistic Science. Series 1: Amsterdam Classics in Linguistics, 1800-1925 540

A C I Manual of Concrete Practice (American Concrete Institute) (US ISSN 0065-7875) *134*

A C I Monograph (American Concrete Institute) (US ISSN 0065-7883) *134*

A C I Year Book (Australian Cat Federation, Inc.) (AT) *682*

A C M Administrative Directory of College and University Computer Science/Data Processing Programs and Computer Facilities (Association for Computing Machinery, Inc.) (US) *269*, 330

A C M Annual Workshop on Microprogramming. Conference Record (Association for Computing Machinery) (US ISSN 0361-2163) *270*

A C M E Newsletter (Academy of Country Music Entertainment) (CN ISSN 0704-6138) *656*

A C M Guide to Computing Literature (US ISSN 0149-1199) *274*

A C M Monograph Series (Association for Computing Machinery) (US) *270*

A C M Symposium on the Theory of Computing (Association for Computing Machinery) (US) *270*

A C S A Faculty Directory see Architecture Schools in North America 68

A C S Laboratory Guide see Laboratory Guide to Instruments, Equipment and Chemicals 247

A C S Monographs (American Chemical Society) (US ISSN 0065-7719) *245*

A C S Symposium Series (American Chemical Society) (US ISSN 0097-6156) *245*

A C T F L Annual Review of Foreign Language Education (American Council on the Teaching of Foreign Languages) (US ISSN 0068-1180) *347*

A C T Handbook for Financial Aid Administrators see American College Testing Program. Handbook for Financial Aid Administrators 343

A C T Monograph Series (American College Testing Program) (US ISSN 0065-7832) *333*

A C T Research Report (American College Testing Program) (US ISSN 0569-3993) *333*

A C T Research Service Report see A C T Research Report 333

A D B S Annuaire (Association Francaise des Documentalistes et des Bibliothecaires Specialises) (FR ISSN 0066-9210) *525*

A D C A; American Directory Collections Agencies (US ISSN 0084-5833) *168*

A. D. C. Reprints (Agricultural Development Council Inc.) (US) *11*

A.D.C. Staff Papers (Agricultural Development Council Inc.) (US) *26*

A. D. F. & G. Technical Data Report (Department of Fish and Game) (US ISSN 0095-4632) *395*

A D I O N Bulletin see Association pour le Developpement International de l'Observatoire de Nice. Bulletin 81

1268   A D

A D P A Selected Papers of Annual Meetings (Alcohol and Drug Problems Association of North America) (US) 286

A D T V - Nachrichten (Allgemeiner Deutscher Tanzlehrer Verband) (GW ISSN 0001-0979) 285

A D U K (Adresar Ukraintsiv u Vilnomu Sviti) (FR) 719

A E (SW) 361, 365, 701

A E C/A N S Monographs see Nuclear Science Technology Monograph Series 704

A E C L Report Series (Atomic Energy of Canada, Ltd.) (CN ISSN 0067-0367) 361, 701

A E I Forums see American Enterprise Institute for Public Policy Research. A E I Forums 708

A E I Hoover Policy Studies (American Enterprise Institute for Public Policy Research) (US) 707

A E I Review, Session of the Congress and Index of A E I Publications see American Enterprise Institute for Public Policy Research. Review, Session of the Congress 739

A E I Studies on Contemporary Economic Problems see Contemporary Economic Problems 741

A E M S Seminar (Papers) (American Engineering Model Society) (US) 134, 365

A.E.T.F.A.T. Index (Association pour l'Etude Taxonomique de la Flore d'Afrique Tropicale) (BE ISSN 0066-9784) 1, 109

A F A Europa Frimaerkekatalog see A F A Vesteuropa Frimaerkekatalog 478

A F A Europe Frimaerkekatalog see A F A Oesteuropa Frimaerkekatalog 478

A F A Oesteuropa Frimaerkekatalog (Aarhus Frimaerkehandel) (DK) 478

A F A Vesteuropa Frimaerkekatalog (Aarhus Frimaerkehandel) (DK) 478

A F R O Technical Papers (Regional Office for Africa) (UN) 750

A F T Issues Bulletin (American Federation of Teachers) (US) 313, 506

A G E Digest (Asian Information Center for Geotechnical Engineering) (TH) 288, 365

A G M Reporter (CN ISSN 0703-766X) 343

A G S Dairy Goat Yearbook see American Goat Society. Year Book 43

A. G. S. Guides (Alpine Garden Society) (UK) 414

A G V A News see A G V A Newsletter 506

A G V A Newsletter (American Guild of Variety Artists) (US) 506

A H A Health Services Monographs (Australian Hospital Association) (AT) 480

A I A A/A S M E/S A E Structures, Structural Dynamics, and Materials Conference. Proceedings (US) 6

A I A A Atmospheric Flight Mechanics Conference Proceedings (American Institute of Aeronautics and Astronautics) (US) 6

A I A A Communications Satellite Systems Conference. Technical Papers (American Institute of Aeronautics and Astronautics) (US) 6, 263

A I A A Roster (American Institute of Aeronautics and Astronautics) (US ISSN 0065-8693) 6

A I A A Symposium on the Aero/Hydronautics of Sailing. Proceedings see Ancient Interface 877

A I A Emerging Techniques (American Institute of Architects) (US ISSN 0569-5341) 68

A I A Energy Notebook (American Institute of Architects) (US) 68, 361

A I C P A Professional Standards (American Institute of Certified Public Accountants) (US) 167

A I Ch E Continuing Education Series (American Institute of Chemical Engineers) (US ISSN 0065-8790) 333, 372

A I Ch E Equipment Testing Procedures (American Institute of Chemical Engineers) (US ISSN 0569-5473) 372, 612

A I Ch E Symposium Series (American Institute of Chemical Engineers) (US ISSN 0065-8812) 372

A I I E. Industrial and Labor Relations Monograph Series (American Institute of Industrial Engineers, Inc.) (US) 205, 365

A I I S Annual Report (American Institute of Indian Studies) (US ISSN 0360-3687) 441

A. I. J. Manual of Australasian Life Assurance (Australasian Insurance Journal) (AT ISSN 0084-697X) 497

A. I. J. P. Yearbook (International Association of Philatelic Journalists) (FR ISSN 0074-1698) 478

A I L/Doc (Association of International Libraries) (EI ISSN 0571-6357) 525

A I M S Monograph Series (Australian Institute of Marine Science) (AT) 309

A I P Conference Proceedings (American Institute of Physics) (US ISSN 0094-243X) 695

A I Recommends (Associated Industries of New York State, Inc.) (US) 707

A I S E Yearbook (Association of Iron and Steel Engineers) (US) 626

A. I. Voeikov Main Geophysical Observatory, Leningrad. Data of Measurements of Electric Field Strength of the Atmosphere at Various Altitudes by the Results of Soundings (UR ISSN 0065-0080) 303

A. I. Voeikov Main Geophysical Observatory, Leningrad. Results of Ground Observations of Atmospheric Electricity. Additional Issue (UR ISSN 0065-0099) 303

A Is A (US) 555

A Is A Libertarian Directory (US) 903

A Is A Newsletter see A Is A 555

A J A S: Australian Journal of American Studies (AT) 465

A J S Review (Association for Jewish Studies) (US ISSN 0364-0094) 390, 770

A L A L C Carta Informativa (UY) 192

A L A Sights to See Book (Automobile Legal Association) (US ISSN 0090-8614) 882

A L A Studies in Librarianship (American Library Association) (US ISSN 0065-907X) 525

A L A Washington Newsletter (US ISSN 0001-1746) 525

A L A Yearbook (American Library Association) (US ISSN 0364-1597) 525

A L R C Report Series (Australia Law Reform Commission) (AT) 508

A.L.Z.A. Conference Series (US) 100, 591

A la Premiere Personne (FR) 96

A M A Drug Evaluations (American Medical Association) (US ISSN 0065-9304) 683

A M A Management Report Briefings (American Management Associations) (US) 213

A M A Papers of the Conferences see American Marketing Association. Proceedings 217

A M A Survey Reports (American Management Associations) (US) 213

A M A: Women in African and American Worlds (US) 900

A M D E L Bulletin (Australia Mineral Development Laboratories) (AT ISSN 0045-0707) 290, 641

A M S. Proceedings of the National Seminar (American Montessori Society) (US ISSN 0517-3833) 313

A M S Asian Studies (US) 441

A M S Directory of Office Salaries (Administrative Management Society) (US) 205, 213

A M S Guide to Management Compensation (Administrative Management Society) (US) 205, 213

A M S Occasional (Arthur Machen Society) (US) 558

A M S-Skrifter (NO ISSN 0332-5202) 56

A M S-Smaatrykk (Arkeologisk Museum i Stavanger) (NO ISSN 0332-6411) 56

A M S-Varia (Arkeologisk Museum i Stavanger) (NO ISSN 0332-6306) 56

A M U Press Alaskana Series (Alaska Methodist University) see A P U Press Alaskana Series 430

A N A Clinical Sessions (American Nurses Association) (US ISSN 0065-9495) 903

A N E P see European Petroleum Yearbook 474

A N E S see Columbia University. Ancient Near Eastern Society. Journal 669

A N S O L Bibliography Series (Australian National Social Sciences Library) (AT ISSN 0156-160X) 795

A N U Historical Journal (Australian National University) (AT ISSN 0001-2068) 447

A. N. Z. A. S. A. Bulletin see A J A S: Australian Journal of American Studies 465

A.O.E. Directory (Association of Overseas Educators, Inc.) (US) 313

A O P A's Airports U.S.A. (Aircraft Owners and Pilots Association) (US ISSN 0271-065X) 867

A P C A Directory see Directory of Governmental Air Pollution Agencies 385

A.P.C.A. Directory and Resource Book see Directory of Governmental Air Pollution Agencies 385

A.P.C.A. Proceedings Digest (Air Pollution Control Association) (US) 383

A.P.D.S.A. Journal (Asian Pacific Dental Student Association) (JA ISSN 0571-2912) 608

A. P. E. A. Journal (Australian Petroleum Exploration Association) (AT ISSN 0084-7534) 290, 677

A P G A Annual/A P K V Jaarblad (Apricot, Peach and Pear Growers' Association) (SA) 414

A P I C E Journal see Revista A P I C E 322

A P I C S Annual Conference Proceedings see American Production and Inventory Control Society. Annual Conference Proceedings 214

A P I Joint Conference on Prevention and Control of Oil Spills. Proceedings see Conference on Prevention and Control of Oil Spills. Proceedings 385

A P K V Jaarblad see A P G A Annual 414

A P O Annual Report (Asian Productivity Organization) (JA ISSN 0066-846X) 199, 220

A.P.R. see Algemene Practische Rechtverzameling 508

A P S A Departmental Services Program Survey of Departments (American Political Science Association) (US ISSN 0094-7954) 707

A.P.S.A. Directory of Department Chairmen see A.P.S.A. Directory of Department Chairpersons 707

A.P.S.A. Directory of Department Chairpersons (American Political Science Association) (US ISSN 0092-8658) 707

A P S Directory (Alternative Press Syndicate, Inc.) (US) 504

A P U Press Alaskana Series (Alaska Pacific University Press) (US) 47, 313, 430, 558

A Q (GW) 71

A R D - Jahrbuch (GW ISSN 0066-5746) 266

A R D U Publication (Arussi Rural Development Unit) (ET) 11

A R I S (Art Research in Scandinavia) (SW ISSN 0044-5711) 68, 71

A R L Annual Salary Survey (Association of Research Libraries) (US ISSN 0361-5669) 525

A R L Statistics (Association of Research Libraries) (US ISSN 0147-2135) 538

A R S C Bulletin (Association for Recorded Sound Collections) (US ISSN 0587-1956) 656

A R S Legislative Service see Arizona Legislative Service 509

A.R.S. N.C. Agricultural Research Service. North Central Region see U. S. Agricultural Research Service. A R S-N C 21

A.R.S. S. Agricultural Research Service. Southern Region see U. S. Agricultural Research Service. A R S-S 21

A R T A N E S see Aids and Research Tools in Ancient Near Eastern Studies 474

A R T B A Officials and Engineers Directory, Transportation Agency Personnel (American Road and Transportation Builders Association) (US ISSN 0360-6996) 374, 874

A.S.A. Bulletin and A.I.C.A. Bulletin see Australian Society of Accountants. Bulletin 167

A S A I H L. Seminar Reports (Association of Southeast Asian Institutions of Higher Learning) (TH ISSN 0066-9695) 333, 441

A S A Monograph (American Society of Appraisers) (US ISSN 0569-7840) 761

A S A Monographs (UK ISSN 0066-9679) 47

A S A Papers (African Studies Association) (US) 390

A S A Refresher Courses in Anesthesiology (American Society of Anesthesiologists) (US ISSN 0093-7401) 604

A S A Review of Books (African Studies Association) (US) 390

A S C A P Biographical Dictionary (American Society of Composers, Authors and Publishers) (US) 96, 558, 656

A S C U S Annual-Teaching Opportunities for You (Association for School, College and University Staffing) (US ISSN 0066-9156) 343

A S C U S Directory of Membership and Subject Field Index (US ISSN 0066-9164) 343

A S E E Profile (American Society for Engineering Education) (US) 365

A S H A Directory (American Speech-Language-Hearing Association) (US ISSN 0569-8561) 286, 345, 617

A S H A Reports (American Speech-Language-Hearing Association) (US ISSN 0569-8553) 286, 345, 617

A S H R A E Guide and Data Book. Fundamentals and Equipment see A S H R A E Handbook & Product Directory 429

A S H R A E Handbook & Product Directory (American Society of Heating, Refrigerating and Air-Conditioning Engineers Inc.) (US ISSN 0066-0620) 429

A S H R A E Handbook of Fundamentals see A S H R A E Handbook & Product Directory 429

A.S.I. Communications (African Studies Institute) (SA) 438

A S I F (Anarcho Surrealist Insurrectionary Feminists Collective) (AT ISSN 0310-9585) 47

A S I L S International Law Journal (Association of Student International Law Societies) (US ISSN 0161-1402) 333, 508

A S L S Newsletter (Association for Scottish Literary Studies) (UK) 558

A S M. Bibliography Series (American Society for Metals) (US ISSN 0001-2556) 1, 631

A S M Bookshelf Series (Association for Systems Management) (US) 213

A S P A C Seminar on Audio-Visual Education. Proceedings (Asian and Pacific Council) (KO ISSN 0066-8311) *441*
A S P C A Yellow Pages (US) *903*
A S T D Consultant Directory *see* Training Resources *211*
A. S. T. E. D. Nouvelles (CN ISSN 0316-0963) *525*
A S T M Proceedings (American Society for Testing and Materials) (US ISSN 0066-0515) *377*
A T A Professional Services Directory (American Translators Association) (US ISSN 0567-4263) *539*
A T A V E Boletin Informativo (Asociacion de Tecnicos Azucareros de Venezuela) (VE ISSN 0084-683X) *403*
A T F Annual Report (Australian Teachers' Federation) (AT) *313, 506*
A T F Monthly Report *see* A T F Annual Report *313*
A T L A Bibliography Series (American Theological Library Association) (US) *762*
A T L A Monograph Series (American Theological Library Association) (US) *762*
A T M Occasional Papers (Association of Teachers of Management) (UK ISSN 0066-9709) *213, 333*
A T V-H *see* Akademiet for de Videnskaber. Handbog *850*
A U B E R Bibliography *see* Bibliography of Publications of University Bureaus of Business and Economic Research *153*
A.V.C.D. - Annuaire de l'Audiovisuel (FR) *263, 347*
A V E in Japan (Japan Audio-Visual Education Association) (JA ISSN 0065-0102) *347*
A. V. S. Journal (Association of Veterinary Students of Great Britain and Ireland) (IE ISSN 0066-9768) *893*
A W A Technical Review (Amalgamated Wireless (Australasia) Ltd.) (AT ISSN 0001-2920) *903*
A. W. Mellon Lectures in the Fine Arts(US ISSN 0065-0129) *71*
A W R C Activities (Australian Water Resources Council) (AT ISSN 0311-7979) *903*
A Y H Handbook (American Youth Hostels, Inc.) (US) *882*
Aabo Akademi. Aarsskrift (FI ISSN 0355-5798) *333*
Aabo Akademi. Ekonomisk-Geografiska Institutionen. Meddelanden (FI) *141*
Aabo Akademi. Ekonomisk-Geografiska Institutionen. Memoranda (FI) *141*
Aabo Akademi. Statsvetenskapliga Fakulteten. Meddelanden (FI) *795*
Aabo Akademi. Statsvetenskapliga Fakulteten. Meddelanden. Serie A *see* Aabo Akademi. Statsvetenskapliga Fakulteten. Meddelanden *795*
Aabo Akademi. Statsvetenskapliga Fakulteten. Meddelanden. Serie B *see* Aabo Akademi. Statsvetenskapliga Fakulteten. Meddelanden *795*
Aachener Beitraege zur Komparatistik (GW) *558*
Aachener Geschichtsverein. Zeitschrift (GW ISSN 0065-0137) *448*
Aarbog for Dansk Skolehistorie (DK ISSN 0065-0145) *313*
Aarbog for Erhvervsuddannelserne i Danmark (DK) *328*
Aarbok for den Norske Kirke (NO ISSN 0400-227X) *762*
Aarbok for Telemark (NO ISSN 0587-4076) *448*
Aarets Bandy (SW) *819*
Aarets Fotboll (SW ISSN 0567-4565) *823*
Aarets Idrott (SW ISSN 0567-4573) *819*
Aarets Ishockey (SW) *819*
Aarhus Frimaerkehandel Oesteuropa Frimaerkekatalog *see* A F A Oesteuropa Frimaerkekatalog *478*

Aarhus Frimaerkehandel Vesteuropa Frimaerkekatalog *see* A F A Vesteuropa Frimaerkekatalog *478*
Aarhus Universitet. Matematisk Institut. Lecture Notes Series (DK ISSN 0065-017X) *583*
Aarhus Universitet. Matematisk Institut. Memoirs (DK) *583*
Aarhus Universitet. Matematisk Institut. Various Publications Series (DK ISSN 0065-0188) *583*
Aarsberetning Vedkommende Norges Fiskerier (NO) *395*
Aarsbok foer Skolan (SW ISSN 0065-0196) *313*
Aarsbok foer Sveriges Kummuner (SW ISSN 0065-020X) *747*
Ab Intra (US) *578*
Abba (US ISSN 0361-686X) *762*
Abbott, Langer & Associates. College Recruiting Report (US ISSN 0361-5057) *666*
Abe Bailey Institute of Inter-Racial Studies. Annual Report *see* Centre for Intergroup Studies. Annual Report *812*
Das Abendland (GW) *489*
Aberdeen-Angus Herd Book (UK) *43*
Aberdeen-Angus Review (UK ISSN 0001-317X) *43*
Abertay Historical Society. Series of Monographs (UK) *448*
Aberystwyth Memoranda in Agricultural, Applied and Biometeorology (UK ISSN 0065-0285) *11*
Abhandlungen aus dem Gebiet der Auslandskunde. Series B & C (GW ISSN 0343-7051) *778*
Abhandlungen aus dem Gesamten Buergerlichen Recht, Handelsrecht und Wirtschaftsrecht (GW ISSN 0065-0307) *508*
Abhandlungen fuer die Kunde des Morgenlandes (GW ISSN 0567-4980) *668*
Abhandlungen Moderner Medizin (GE ISSN 0065-0315) *591*
Abhandlungen und Materialen zur Publizistik (GW ISSN 0065-0323) *504*
Abhandlungen zur Handels- und Sozialgeschichte (GE ISSN 0065-0358) *448*
Abhandlungen zur Kunst- , Musik- und Literaturwissenschaft (GW) *71, 555, 656*
Abhandlungen zur Philosophie, Psychologie und Paedagogik (GW ISSN 0065-0366) *313, 687*
Abingdon Clergy Income Tax Guide (US ISSN 0163-1241) *226, 762*
Abortion Bibliography (US ISSN 0092-9522) *87, 133*
About Books for Children (UK ISSN 0144-574X) *257, 558*
About Zambia (ZA ISSN 0065-0374) *438*
Abr-Nahrain (NE ISSN 0065-0382) *668*
Abr-Nahrain. Supplements (NE ISSN 0065-0390) *668*
Abraham Flexner Lectures in Medicine (US) *591*
Abraham Lincoln Association. Papers (US ISSN 0195-914X) *707*
Abrasive Engineering Society. Abrasive Usage Conference. Proceedings (US ISSN 0363-8065) *365*
Absorption Spectra in the Ultraviolet and Visible Region (HU ISSN 0065-0412) *254, 705*
Abstract Journal in Earthquake Engineering (US ISSN 0363-5732) *1, 371*
Abstract System Theory Monographs (US) *778*
Abstracting and Indexing Services in Special Libraries in Israel (IS) *525*
Abstracts of Belgian Geology and Physical Geography (BE ISSN 0065-0420) *1, 290*
Abstracts of Doctoral Dissertations in Anthropology (US ISSN 0098-1850) *1, 601*

Abstracts of Efficiency Studies in the National Health Service *see* Great Britain. Department of Health and Social Security. Notes on Good Practices *480*
Abstracts of Health Care Management Studies (US ISSN 0194-4908) *1, 481*
Abstracts of Hospital Management Studies *see* Abstracts of Health Care Management Studies *481*
Abstracts of Japanese Literature in Forest Genetics and Related Fields. Part A (JA) *109, 412*
Abstracts of Japanese Literature in Forest Genetics and Related Fields. Part B (JA) *109, 412*
Abstracts of Theses Accepted by the Graduate School of Louisiana Tech University (US) *333*
Abstracts of Theses and Dissertations Accepted for Higher Degrees in the Potchefstroom University for Christian Higher Education (SA ISSN 0079-4317) *333*
Abu Dhabi. Department of Planning. Statistical Abstract and Yearbook (TS) *739*
Abu Dhabi Offical Gazette (TS) *739*
Academia Alfonso X el Sabio. Cuadernos Bibliograficos (SP) *87*
Academia Campinense de Letras. Publicacoes (BL ISSN 0065-0447) *558*
Academia de Ciencias de Cuba. Instituto de Geologia. Resumenes, Communicaciones y Notas del Consejo Cientifico (CU) *290*
Academia de Ciencias de Cuba. Instituto de Geologia. Resumenes del Consejo Cientifico *see* Academia de Ciencias de Cuba. Instituto de Geologia. Resumenes, Communicaciones y Notas del Consejo Cientifico *290*
Academia de Ciencias de Cuba. Instituto de Geologia. Serie Geologica (CU) *290*
Academia de Ciencias de Cuba. Instituto de Investigaciones Fundamentales en Agricultura Tropical. Informe Cientifico-Tecnico (CU) *11*
Academia de Ciencias de Cuba. Instituto de Oceanologia. Informes Cientificos Tecnicos (CU) *309*
Academia de Ciencias de Cuba. Instituto de Oceanologia. Serie Oceanologica (CU ISSN 0567-5782) *309*
Academia de Ciencias de Cuba. Instituto de Oceanologia. Tablas de Mareas (CU) *309*
Academia de Ciencias de Cuba. Instituto de Zoologia. Informe Cientifico-Tecnico (CU) *126*
Academia de Ciencias de Cuba. Instituto de Zoologia. Miscelanea Zoologica (CU) *126*
Academia de Ciencias Politicas y Sociales. Boletin. (VE) *707, 795*
Academia de Stiinte Sociale si Politice. Institutul de Istorie si Arheologie Cluj-Napoca. Anuarul (RM ISSN 0065-048X) *56, 448*
Academia Dominicana de la Historia. Publicaciones (DR ISSN 0567-5871) *465*
Academia Espanola, Madrid. Anejos del Boletin (SP ISSN 0065-0455) *558*
Academia Hondurena de la Lengua. Boletin (HO ISSN 0065-0471) *539*
Academia Mexicana de la Historia. Memorias (MX) *465*
Academia Nacional de Bellas Artes. Anuario (AG) *71*
Academia Nacional de Ciencias Morales y Politicas. Anales (AG) *707*
Academia Nacional de la Historia. Biblioteca. Serie: Estudios Monografias y Ensayos (VE) *465*
Academia Norteamericana de la Lengua Espanola. Boletin (US) *558*
Academia Paulista de Direito. Revista (BL) *508*
Academia Paulista de Letras. Revista (BL ISSN 0001-3846) *539, 558*

Academia Pernambucana de Letras. Revista (BL) *558*
Academia Portuguesa da Historia. Anais (PO) *448*
Academia Provincial de la Historia. Boletin (AG ISSN 0567-6029) *466*
Academia Republicii Socialiste Romania. Institutul de Speologie Emil Racovitza. Travaux *see* Institutul de Speologie Emil Racovitza. Travaux *304*
Academia Scientiarum Fennica. Proceedings/Sitzungsberichte *see* Academia Scientiarum Fennica. Yearbook *778*
Academia Scientiarum Fennica. Yearbook/Suomalainen Tiedeakatemia. Vuosikirja (FI ISSN 0356-6927) *778*
Academia Sinica. Institute of Chemistry. Bulletin (CH ISSN 0001-3927) *245*
Academia Sinica. Institute of Modern History. Bulletin/Chung Yang Yen Chiu Yuan. Chiu Tai Shih Yen Chiu So Chi K'an (CH) *430*
Academia Sinica. Institute of Physics. Annual Report (CH) *695*
Academiae Aboensis, Series B: Mathematics, Science, Engineering (FI ISSN 0001-5105) *583, 778*
Academic Collective Bargaining Information Service. Monographs (US) *343*
Academic Collective Bargaining Information Service. Research Summary (US) *343*
Academic Collective Bargaining Information Service. Special Reports (US) *343*
Academic Courses in Great Britain Relevant to the Teaching of English to Speakers of Other Languages (UK) *347, 539*
Academic Library Statistics *see* A R L Statistics *538*
Academic Life *see* Akademiska Dzive *391*
Academic Press Series in Cognition and Perception (US) *734*
Academic Year Abroad in Europe-Africa-Australia (US ISSN 0098-6356) *342*
Academica Helvetica (SZ) *333*
Academie de France a Rome. Correspondance des Directeurs. Nouvelle Serie (IT) *448*
Academie de Marine. Communications/ Marine Academie. Mededelingen (BE) *876*
Academie des Inscriptions et Belles-Lettres. Etudes et Commentaires (FR ISSN 0065-0544) *56, 430, 539*
Academie des Sciences. Annuaire (FR ISSN 0065-0552) *778*
Academie des Sciences. Index Biographique des Membres et Correspondants (FR ISSN 0065-0560) *778*
Academie des Sciences Morales et Politiques, Montreal. Travaux et Communications (CN) *555*
Academie des Sports, Paris. Annuaire (FR ISSN 0065-0579) *819*
Academie Francaise. Annuaire (FR ISSN 0065-0587) *558*
Academie Internationale d'Histoire des Sciences. Collection des Travaux (GW ISSN 0366-8258) *430, 778*
Academie Polonaise des Sciences. Centre Scientifique, Paris. Conferences (PL ISSN 0079-3159) *778*
Academie Royale de Langue et de Litterature Francaises. Annuaires (BE ISSN 0567-6584) *539, 555*
Academie Royale des Sciences d'Outre Mer. Revue Bibliographique/ Koninklijke Akademie voor Overzeese Wetenschappen. Bibliografisch Overzicht (BE ISSN 0567-6592) *903*
Academie Royale des Sciences, des Lettres et des Beaux-Arts de Belgique. Annuaire (BE) *489, 778*
Academie Royale des Sciences, des Lettres et des Beaux-Arts de Belgique. Classe des Beaux-Arts. Memoires (BE) *489*

Academie Royale des Sciences, des Lettres et des Beaux-Arts de Belgique. Classe des Lettres et des Science Morales et Politiques. Memoires (BE) 489
Academie Royale des Sciences, des Lettres et des Beaux Arts de Belgique. Classe des Sciences. Memoires (BE) 778
Academie Royale des Sciences, des Lettres et des Beaux Arts de Belgique. Index Biographique des Membres, Correspondants et Associes (BE ISSN 0065-0609) 87
Academy Awards Oscar Annual (US ISSN 0092-5675) 648
Academy for Educational Development. Academy Papers (US ISSN 0065-0625) 313
Academy of American Franciscan History. Bibliographical Series (US ISSN 0567-6630) 773
Academy of American Franciscan History. Documentary Series (US ISSN 0065-0633) 773
Academy of American Franciscan History. Monograph Series (US ISSN 0065-0641) 773
Academy of American Franciscan History. Propaganda Fide Series (US ISSN 0065-065X) 773
Academy of American Poets. Lamont Poetry Selections (US ISSN 0515-2003) 578
Academy of Country Music Entertainment Newsletter see A C M E Newsletter 656
Academy of Management. Proceedings (US ISSN 0065-0668) 213
Academy of Natural Sciences of Philadelphia. Monographs (US ISSN 0096-7750) 778
Academy of Natural Sciences of Philadelphia. Proceedings (US ISSN 0097-3157) 778
Academy of Natural Sciences of Philadelphia. Special Publications (US ISSN 0097-3254) 778
Academy of Political Science. Proceedings (US ISSN 0065-0684) 707
Academy of Sciences of the U S S R. Crimean Astrophysical Observatory. Bulletin (US ISSN 0190-2717) 81
Academy of Sciences of the U S S R. Special Astrophysical Observatory-North Caucasus. Bulletin (US ISSN 0190-2709) 81
Academy of the Hebrew Language. Linguistic Studies see Academy of the Hebrew Language. Texts & Studies 539
Academy of the Hebrew Language. Specialized Dictionaries (IS ISSN 0065-0692) 539
Academy of the Hebrew Language. Texts & Studies (IS) 539
Academy of the Social Sciences in Australia. Annual Report (AT) 795
Accademia dei Cinquecento per le Arti, Lettere, Scienze e Cultura. Anali (IT) 489
Accademia dei Concordi Rovigo. Collana di Musiche (IT) 656
Accademia dei Fisiocritici, Siena. Sezione Medico-Fisica see Accademia delle Scienze di Siena Detta de Fisiocritici. Atti 591
Accademia delle Scienze di Siena Detta de Fisiocritici. Atti (IT ISSN 0390-7783) 11, 591
Accademia Etrusca di Cortona. Annuario (IT ISSN 0065-0730) 448
Accademia Italiana di Scienze Forestali. Annali (IT ISSN 0515-2178) 407
Accademia Ligure di Scienze e Lettere. Atti (IT) 489, 778
Accademia Lucchese di Scienze, Lettere ed Arti. Atti. Nuova Serie (IT ISSN 0065-0749) 71, 778
Accademia Medica Lombarda. Atti (IT ISSN 0001-4427) 591
Accademia Medica Pistoiese "Filippo Pacini". Bolletino (IT) 591
Accademia Musicale Chigiana. Quaderni. (IT ISSN 0065-0714) 71, 558

Accademia Nazionale di Ragionera Papers on Business Administration (IT) 903
Accademia Nazionale di San Luca. Annuario (IT) 333
Accademia Nazionale Italiana di Entomologia. Rendiconti (IT ISSN 0065-0757) 120
Accademia Patavina di Scienze Lettere ed Arti. Collana Accademica (IT ISSN 0065-0765) 778
Accademia Toscana di Scienze e Lettere La Colombaria. Studi (IT ISSN 0065-0781) 778
Accepted Dental Remedies see Accepted Dental Therapeutics 608
Accepted Dental Therapeutics (US ISSN 0065-079X) 608
Access Reference Service (US) 718
Access: the Index to Little Magazines (US ISSN 0363-065X) 1
Accessions List. Afghanistan see U.S. Library of Congress. Accessions List: Afghanistan 915
Accessoirex (FR) 591, 683
Accident Facts (US ISSN 0148-6039) 750
Accident/Incident Bulletin see U.S. Federal Railroad Administration. Office of Safety. Accident/Incident Bulletin 874
Accidentes de Transito en Costa Rica (CR ISSN 0525-8693) 874
Accidents in North American Mountaineering (US ISSN 0065-082X) 828
Accidents to Aircraft on the British Register (UK ISSN 0065-0838) 867
Accountancy Research Foundation, Melbourne. Accounting and Auditing Research Committee. Research Studies see Australian Accounting Research Foundation. Research Studies 167
Accountants' Index (US) 1, 151
Accountants International Studies (US) 167
Accounting Journal (MY ISSN 0126-625X) 167
Accredited Colleges of Pharmacy (US ISSN 0065-7980) 683
Accredited Institutions of Postsecondary Education (US ISSN 0361-9362) 330
Accredited Institutions of Postsecondary Education and Programs see Accredited Institutions of Postsecondary Education 330
Accredited Journalism Education (US) 330, 504
Accredited Programs in Architecture (US) 68
Accredited Schools of Architecture see Accredited Programs in Architecture 68
Accumulative Veterinary Index (US) 1, 895
Achter het Boek (NE ISSN 0084-5892) 558, 651
Acopel (CK) 540, 558
Acoustic Corporation of America Industry Guide to Hearing Aids. International Edition see A.C.A. Industry Guide to Hearing Aids. International Edition 286
Acoustical and Board Products. Bulletin(US) 68
Acoustical Holography see Acoustical Imaging: Recent Advances in Visualization and Characterization 706
Acoustical Imaging: Recent Advances in Visualization and Characterization (US) 692, 706
Acronyms and Initialisms Dictionary see Acronyms, Initialisms and Abbreviations Dictionary 540
Acronyms, Initialisms and Abbreviations Dictionary (US) 540
Acta Academiae Aboensis. Series A: Humaniora (FI ISSN 0355-578X) 489
Acta Academiae Aboensis. Series B: Mathematica et Physica see Academiae Aboensis, Series B: Mathematics, Science, Engineering 583
Acta Academiae Regiae Gustavi Adolphi (SW ISSN 0065-0897) 401

Acta ad Archaeologiam et Artium Historiam Pertinentia (IT ISSN 0065-0900) 56
Acta Adriatica (YU ISSN 0001-5113) 309, 395
Acta Agraria et Silvestria. Series Agraria (PL ISSN 0065-0919) 32
Acta Agraria et Silvestria. Series Silvestris (PL ISSN 0065-0927) 407
Acta Agraria et Silvestria. Series Zootechnica (PL ISSN 0065-0935) 43
Acta Agrobotanica (PL ISSN 0065-0951) 11, 112
Acta Allergologica. Supplementum see Allergy. Supplementum 903
Acta Anaesthesiologica Scandinavica. Supplementum (DK ISSN 0515-2720) 604
Acta Archaelogica Lundensia: Monographs of Lunds Universitets Historiska Museum. Series in 4 (SW ISSN 0065-1001) 56
Acta Archaelogica Lundensia: Monographs of Lunds Universitets Historiska Museum. Series in 8 (SW ISSN 0065-0994) 56
Acta Archaeologica (DK ISSN 0065-101X) 56
Acta Archaeologica Carpathica (PL ISSN 0001-5229) 56
Acta Archaeologica Lodziensia (PL ISSN 0065-0986) 56
Acta Archaeologica Lovaniensia (BE) 56
Acta Arctica (DK ISSN 0065-1028) 778
Acta Arithmetica (PL ISSN 0065-1036) 584
Acta Baltica (GW ISSN 0567-7289) 448
Acta Baltico-Slavica (PL ISSN 0065-1044) 448
Acta Bernensia: Beitraege zur Praehistorischen, Klassischen und Juengeren Archaeologie (SZ ISSN 0065-1052) 56
Acta Bibliothecae Gothoburgensis see Acta Bibliothecae Universitatis Gothoburgensis 525
Acta Bibliothecae Regiae Stockholmiensis (SW ISSN 0065-1060) 525
Acta Bibliothecae Universitatis Gothoburgensis (SW ISSN 0065-1079) 525
Acta Biologica (PL) 100
Acta Biologica Hellenica (GR ISSN 0065-1095) 100
Acta Borealia A. Scientia (NO ISSN 0065-1109) 288, 849
Acta Botanica see Acta Botanica Slovaca 112
Acta Botanica Barcinonensia (SP) 112
Acta Botanica Cuba (CU) 112
Acta Botanica Horti Bucurestiensis (RM ISSN 0068-3329) 112, 414
Acta Botanica Slovaca (CS) 112
Acta Botanica Taiwanica see Taiwania 118
Acta Botanica Venezuelica (VE ISSN 0084-5906) 112
Acta Carsologica/Krasoslovni Zbornik (YU) 288
Acta Chemica Scandinavica. Supplementum (DK ISSN 0065-1133) 903
Acta Chirurgiae Maxillo-Facialis (GE) 624
Acta Classica (SA ISSN 0065-1141) 540
Acta Colloquii Didacticii Classici (BE) 313, 540
Acta Concilium Ophthalmologicum (FR ISSN 0065-115X) 615
Acta Endocrinologica Congress. Advance Abstracts (DK ISSN 0300-9750) 611
Acta Endocrinologica Panamericana (AG ISSN 0065-1192) 611
Acta Entomologica (CS) 120
Acta Ethnologica Slovaca (CS) 47, 401
Acta Facultatis Forestalis, Zvolen/Vysoka Skola Lesnicka a Drevarska vo Zvolene. Lesnicka Fakulta. Zbornik Vedeckych Prac (CS) 407

Acta Facultatis Medicinae Skopiensis see Godisen Zbornik na Medicinskiot Fakultet vo Skopje 595
Acta Facultatis Pharmaceuticae Bohemoslovenicae see Universitas Comeniana. Acta Pharmaceuticae 686
Acta Facultatis Politico-Juridicae Universitatis Scientiarum Budapestiensis de Rolando Eotvos Nominatae (HU) 508, 707
Acta Forestalia Fennica (FI ISSN 0001-5636) 407
Acta Geobotanica Barcinonensia see Acta Botanica Barcinonensia 112
Acta Geographica Dedrecina (HU ISSN 0567-7475) 290, 419, 631
Acta Geographica Lodziensia (PL ISSN 0065-1249) 419
Acta Geographica Lovaniensia (BE ISSN 0065-1257) 419
Acta Geologica Lilloana (AG ISSN 0567-7513) 290
Acta Geologica Taiwanica (CH ISSN 0065-1265) 291
Acta Germanica (SA ISSN 0065-1273) 540
Acta Gerontologica Japonica see Yokufukai Geriatric Journal 428
Acta Herediana (PE ISSN 0567-753X) 419
Acta Historiae Neerlandicae (NE ISSN 0065-129X) 448
Acta Historica (IT ISSN 0065-1303) 448
Acta Historica Leopoldina (GE ISSN 0001-5857) 591, 778
Acta Historica Scientiarum Naturalium et Medicinalium (DK ISSN 0065-1311) 778
Acta Historico-Oeconomica Iugoslaviae (YU) 191
Acta Horticulturae (NE ISSN 0567-7572) 414
Acta Humboldtiana. Series Geographica et Ethnographica (GW ISSN 0400-4043) 47, 419
Acta Humboldtiana. Series Geologica, Palaeontologica et Biologica (GW ISSN 0375-5452) 100, 291
Acta Humboldtiana. Series Historica (GW ISSN 0567-7599) 430
Acta Hydrobiologica (PL ISSN 0065-132X) 100
Acta Juridica (SA ISSN 0065-1346) 508
Acta Marxistica Leninistica. Filozofiai Tanulmanyok (HU ISSN 0324-6957) 687
Acta Marxistica Leninistica. Politikai Gazdasagtan Tanulmanyok (HU ISSN 0324-6957) 141
Acta Marxistica Leninistica. Tudomanyos Szocializmus Tanulmanyok (HU ISSN 0324-6957) 687
Acta Mediaevalia (PL) 448, 773
Acta Medica et Sociologica (FR ISSN 0515-2925) 694, 811
Acta Medicae Historiae Patavina (IT ISSN 0065-1389) 591
Acta Medicinae Legalis et Socialis (BE ISSN 0065-1397) 612
Acta Mexicana de Ciencia y Tecnologia(MX ISSN 0567-7785) 778
Acta Musei Apulensis see Apulum 449
Acta Musei Moraviae. Scientia Naturales 3: Folia Mendeliana (CS) 122
Acta Neophilologica (YU ISSN 0567-784X) 558
Acta Neurochirurgica. Supplement (US ISSN 0065-1419) 618, 624
Acta Neurologica Scandinavica. Supplementum (DK ISSN 0065-1427) 618
Acta Neuropathologica. Supplement (US ISSN 0065-1435) 618
Acta Neurovegetativa. Supplement see Journal of Neural Transmission. Supplement 620
Acta Nuntiaturae Gallicae (VC ISSN 0065-1443) 773
Acta Oceanographica Taiwanica (CH) 309
Acta Ophthalmologica. Supplementum (DK ISSN 0065-1451) 615

Acta Ordinis Sancti Augustini (IT ISSN 0001-642X) 773
Acta Organologica (GW ISSN 0567-7874) 656
Acta Orientalia (DK ISSN 0001-6438) 668
Acta Ornithologica (PL ISSN 0001-6454) 124
Acta Orthopaedica Scandinavica. Supplementum (DK ISSN 0300-8827) 616
Acta Pacis Westphalicae (GW ISSN 0065-146X) 448
Acta Parasitologica Iugoslavica (YU ISSN 0350-3658) 126, 607
Acta Parasitologica Polonica (PL ISSN 0065-1478) 123
Acta Pathologica et Microbiologica Scandinavica. Section A: Pathology. Supplementum (DK ISSN 0365-5571) 100, 591
Acta Pathologica et Microbiologica Scandinavica. Section B: Microbiology. Supplementum (DK ISSN 0105-0656) 100, 123
Acta Pathologica et Microbiologica Scandinavica. Section C: Immunology. Supplementum (DK) 603
Acta Pharmaceutica Technologica. Supplementa (GW ISSN 0341-0854) 683
Acta Pharmacologica et Toxicologica. Supplementum (DK ISSN 0065-1508) 683
Acta Philologica (IT ISSN 0065-1516) 540
Acta Philologica (PL ISSN 0065-1524) 540
Acta Philologica Aenipontana (AU ISSN 0065-1532) 540
Acta Philologica Scandinavica (DK ISSN 0001-6691) 540
Acta Philosophica et Theologica (IT ISSN 0065-1540) 687, 762
Acta Physica Austriaca. Supplement (US ISSN 0065-1559) 695
Acta Physica et Chimica Debrecina (HU ISSN 0567-7947) 245, 695
Acta Physiologiae Plantarum (PL) 11
Acta Phytogeographica Suecica (SW ISSN 0084-5914) 112, 419
Acta Phytomedica (GW ISSN 0065-1567) 112
Acta Polytechnica Scandinavica. Applied Physics Series (FI ISSN 0355-2721) 701
Acta Polytechnica Scandinavica. Chemistry Including Metallurgy Series (FI ISSN 0001-6853) 245, 626
Acta Polytechnica Scandinavica. Civil Engineering and Building Construction Series (FI ISSN 0355-2705) 134, 374
Acta Polytechnica Scandinavica. Electrical Engineering Series (FI ISSN 0001-6845) 351
Acta Polytechnica Scandinavica. Mathematics and Computer Science Series (FI ISSN 0355-2713) 270, 584
Acta Polytechnica Scandinavica. Mathematics and Computing Machinery Series see Acta Polytechnica Scandinavica. Mathematics and Computer Science Series 584
Acta Polytechnica Scandinavica. Mechanical Engineering Series (FI ISSN 0001-687X) 381
Acta Polytechnica Scandinavica. Physics Including Nucleonics Series see Acta Polytechnica Scandinavica. Applied Physics Series 701
Acta Psychiatrica Scandinavica. Supplementum (DK ISSN 0065-1591) 618
Acta Psychologica-Gothoburgensia (SW ISSN 0065-1605) 734
Acta Psychologica Taiwanica (CH ISSN 0065-1613) 734
Acta Radiobotanika et Genetika/Hoshasen Ikushujo Kenkyu Hokoku (JA ISSN 0065-1621) 100, 122
Acta Regiae Societatis Scientiarum et Litterarum Gothoburgensis. Botanica (SW ISSN 0347-4917) 112

Acta Regiae Societatis Scientiarum et Litterarum Gothoburgensis. Geophysica (SW ISSN 0072-4815) 303
Acta Regiae Societatis Scientiarum et Litterarum Gothoburgensis. Humaniora (SW ISSN 0072-4823) 489
Acta Regiae Societatis Scientiarum et Litterarum Gothoburgensis. Interdisciplinaria (SW ISSN 0347-4925) 489, 778
Acta Regiae Societatis Scientiarum et Litterarum Gothoburgensis. Zoologica (SW ISSN 0072-4807) 126
Acta Rei Cretariae Romanae Fautorum. Supplementa (GW) 56
Acta Sagittariana (GW ISSN 0001-6942) 656
Acta Scientiarum Socialium (IT ISSN 0065-1656) 811
Acta Seminarii Neotestamentici Upsaliensis see Coniectanea Biblica. New Testament Series 764
Acta Semiotica et Linguistica (BL) 540
Acta Sociologica. Serie Promocion Social (MX) 811
Acta Theologica Danica (NE ISSN 0065-1672) 762
Acta Universitatis Carolinae: Biologica (CS ISSN 0001-7124) 100
Acta Universitatis Nicolai Copernici. Archeologia (PL ISSN 0137-6616) 56
Acta Universitatis Nicolai Copernici. Biologia (PL ISSN 0208-4449) 100
Acta Universitatis Nicolai Copernici. Filologia Polska (PL ISSN 0208-5321) 540
Acta Universitatis Nicolai Copernici. Filozofia (PL ISSN 0208-564X) 687
Acta Universitatis Nicolai Copernici. Historia (PL ISSN 0137-5830) 448
Acta Universitatis Nicolai Copernici. Prawo (PL ISSN 0208-5283) 508
Acta Universitatis Nicolai Copernici. Socjologia Wychowania (PL ISSN 0208-5267) 313
Acta Universitatis Szegediensis de Attila Jozsef Nominatae. Acta Bibliothecaria (HU ISSN 0001-7175) 313, 525
Acta Universitatis Szegediensis de Attila Jozsef Nominatae. Acta Geographica (HU ISSN 0567-7467) 419
Acta Universitatis Wratislaviensis. Prace Pedagogiczne (PL ISSN 0137-1096) 313
Acta Veterinaria Scandinavica. Supplementum (DK ISSN 0065-1699) 893
Acta Visbyensia (SW) 448
Acta Wasaensia (FI ISSN 0355-2667) 191
Acta Zoologica Bulgarica (BU) 126
Acta Zoologica Cracoviensia (PL ISSN 0065-1710) 127
Acta Zoologica Lilloana (AG ISSN 0065-1729) 127
Acta Zoologica Mexicana (MX ISSN 0065-1737) 127
Actas del Cabildo Colonial de Guayaquil (EC) 466
Action Committee Against Narcotics. Annual Report (HK) 286
Activite Economique de la Haute-Normandie (FR ISSN 0065-1788) 178
Activites Mineres au Cameroun (CM ISSN 0575-7258) 641
Activities of O E C D: Report by the Secretary General see Organization for Economic Cooperation and Development. Activities of O E C D: Report by the Secretary General 200
Activities of the Astronomical Observatory on Skalnate Pleso see Prace Astronomickeho Observatoria na Skalnatom Plese 83
Activity Holidays in Britain (UK) 882
Activity Programmers Sourcebook (US ISSN 0362-5923) 903
Acts IMEKO (HU) 636
Actualidades (VE) 555

Actualidades de la Ingenieria Agronomica (CU) 32
Actualitates (DK) 540
Actualite Rhumatologique, Presentee au Praticien (FR ISSN 0065-1818) 623
Actualites Bibliographiques en Medecine, Pharmacie et Sciences Biomedicales (FR) 87, 591
Actualites Nephrologiques (FR ISSN 0073-3326) 625
Actualites Protozoologiques (US) 119, 127
Acute Myocardial Infarction Symposium. Proceedings. (US) 606
Ad Guide see Advertiser's Guide to Scholarly Periodicals 4
ADAC-Campingfuehrer. Band 1: Suedeuropa (GW) 828, 882
ADAC-Campingfuehrer. Band 2: Deutschland, Mittel- und Nordeuropa (GW) 828, 882
ADAC-Schriftenreihe. Jugendverkehrserziehung (GW) 869
Adan E. Treganza Anthropology Museum. Papers (US ISSN 0065-1850) 47
Adaptations Series (US ISSN 0065-1877) 558
Addab Journal (SJ ISSN 0302-8844) 489
Addiction Research Foundation of Ontario. Annual Report (CN ISSN 0065-6119) 286
Addiction Research Foundation of Ontario. Bibliographic Series (CN ISSN 0065-1885) 288
Addis Ababa University. Geophysical Observatory. Contributions (ET ISSN 0072-9345) 303
Addis Ababa University. University Testing Center. Technical Report (ET ISSN 0072-9388) 313
Adelaide. Institute of Medical and Veterinary Science. Annual Report of the Council (AT ISSN 0065-1907) 591, 893
Adelaide City Council Municipal Reference Book (AT) 748
Adelaide City Council Municipal Yearbook see Adelaide City Council Municipal Reference Book 748
Aden Magazine/Magallat Aden (YS ISSN 0065-1923) 441
Adhesives Directory (UK ISSN 0305-3199) 849
Adhesives Red Book (US ISSN 0065-1931) 706
Administracion, Desarrollo, Integracion (CR ISSN 0044-6262) 739
Administracion y Desarrollo (CK ISSN 0001-8309) 707, 739
Administratief en Gerechtelijk Jaarboek voor Belgie see Annuaire Administratif et Judiciaire de Belgique 739
Administration Federale du Canada see Organization of the Government of Canada 745
Administration in Kenya see Kenya Institute of Administration. Journal 743
Administration of the Marine Mammal Protection Act of 1972 see Marine Mammal Protection Act of 1972 Annual Report 277
Administrative Digest Business Directory (CN) 213
Administrative Directory of College and University Computer Science Departments and Computer Centers see A C M Administrative Directory of College and University Computer Science/Data Processing Programs and Computer Facilities 330
Administrative Management Society Directory of Office Salaries see A M S Directory of Office Salaries 205
Administrative Management Society Guide to Management Compensation see A M S Guide to Management Compensation 205
Administrator (CN ISSN 0065-1974) 263, 739
Admission Requirements of American Dental Schools see Admission Requirements of U.S. and Canadian Dental Schools 609

Admission Requirements of U.S. and Canadian Dental Schools (US ISSN 0091-729X) 330, 609
Adolescent Psychiatry (US ISSN 0065-2008) 618
Adresar Ukraintsiv u Vilnomu Sviti see A D U K 719
Adreslijst van de Zuid-Hollandse Industrie (NE) 220
Adressbuch fuer den Deutschsprachigen Buchhandels (GW ISSN 0065-2032) 757
Adult & Community Education Organizations & Leaders Directory (US) 328
Advance Locator for Capitol Hill (US) 707
Advance of Christianity through the Centuries (US ISSN 0065-2067) 903
Advanced Accountancy Seminar. Proceedings (NZ ISSN 0065-2075) 167
Advanced Financial Accounting Notes (CN ISSN 0226-0808) 167
Advanced Series in Agricultural Sciences (US) 11
Advanced Techniques in Failure Analysis Symposium. Proceedings (US) 351
Advanced Textbooks in Economics (NE) 141
Advanced Water Conference. Proceedings. (US) 895
Advances and Technical Standards in Neurosurgery (US) 618, 624
Advances in Activation Analysis (US ISSN 0065-2091) 249
Advances in Aerosol Physics (US) 695
Advances in Agronomy (US ISSN 0065-2113) 11
Advances in Agronomy and Crop Science see Fortschritte im Acker- und Pflanzenbau 35
Advances in Alicyclic Chemistry (US ISSN 0065-2121) 252
Advances in Analytical Chemistry and Instrumentation (US ISSN 0065-2148) 249
Advances in Anatomy, Embryology and Cell Biology (US ISSN 0071-1098) 100, 119
Advances in Animal Physiology and Animal Nutrition see Fortschritte in der Tierphysiologie und Tierernaehrung 44
Advances in Antimicrobial and Antineoplastic Chemotherapy (US) 110
Advances in Applied Mechanics (US ISSN 0065-2156) 377, 700
Advances in Applied Microbiology (US ISSN 0065-2164) 123
Advances in Applied Microbiology. Supplement (US ISSN 0065-2172) 123
Advances in Aquatic Microbiology (US ISSN 0161-8954) 123
Advances in Archaeological Method and Theory (US ISSN 0162-8003) 56
Advances in Asthma, Allergy and Pulmonary Diseases see Advances in Asthma & Allergy 903
Advances in Asthma & Allergy (US ISSN 0163-1578) 903
Advances in Atomic and Molecular Physics (US ISSN 0065-2199) 701
Advances in Behavioral Pediatrics (US) 617
Advances in Behavioral Pharmacology (US ISSN 0147-071X) 683
Advances in Biochemical Engineering (US ISSN 0065-2210) 110, 365
Advances in Biochemical Psychopharmacology (US ISSN 0065-2229) 618, 683
Advances in Bioengineering (US ISSN 0360-9960) 100, 365
Advances in Biological and Medical Physics (US ISSN 0065-2245) 112, 591
Advances in Biological Psychiatry (SZ ISSN 0378-7354) 618
Advances in Biology of Skin (US ISSN 0065-2253) 610
Advances in Biomedical Engineering and Medical Physics (US ISSN 0065-2261) 903

ADVANCES IN

Advances in Biophysics (JA ISSN 0065-227X) *112*
Advances in Botanical Research (UK ISSN 0065-2296) *113*
Advances in Cancer Chemotherapy (US ISSN 0190-4817) *683*
Advances in Cancer Research (US ISSN 0065-230X) *604*
Advances in Carbohydrate Chemistry *see* Advances in Carbohydrate Chemistry and Biochemistry *252*
Advances in Carbohydrate Chemistry and Biochemistry (US ISSN 0065-2318) *110*, *252*
Advances in Cardiology (SZ ISSN 0065-2326) *606*
Advances in Cardiovascular Physics (SZ ISSN 0378-6900) *606*
Advances in Catalysis (US ISSN 0360-0564) *254*
Advances in Ceramics Processing (IT) *244*
Advances in Chemical Engineering (US ISSN 0065-2377) *372*
Advances in Chemical Physics (US ISSN 0065-2385) *254*, *695*
Advances in Chemistry Series (US ISSN 0065-2393) *245*
Advances in Child Development and Behavior (US ISSN 0065-2407) *617*, *734*
Advances in Chromatography (US ISSN 0065-2415) *249*
Advances in Clinical Chemistry (US ISSN 0065-2423) *110*, *683*
Advances in Clinical Child Psychology (US ISSN 0149-4732) *734*
Advances in Comparative Physiology and Biochemistry (US ISSN 0065-244X) *110*, *125*
Advances in Computers (US ISSN 0065-2458) *270*
Advances in Control Systems *see* Control and Dynamic Systems: Advances in Theory and Applications *7*
Advances in Corrosion Science and Technology (US ISSN 0065-2474) *377*
Advances in Cryogenic Engineering (US ISSN 0065-2482) *365*, *700*
Advances in Cyclic Nucleotide Research (US ISSN 0084-5930) *110*
Advances in Cytopharmacology (US ISSN 0084-5949) *119*, *683*
Advances in Drug Research (UK ISSN 0065-2490) *683*
Advances in Drying (US ISSN 0272-4790) *365*
Advances in Early Education and Day Care (US ISSN 0270-4021) *313*
Advances in Ecological Research (UK ISSN 0065-2504) *383*
Advances in Econometrics (US) *141*
Advances in Electrochemistry and Electrochemical Engineering (US ISSN 0567-9907) *251*, *372*
Advances in Electronics and Electron Physics (US ISSN 0065-2539) *351*, *695*
Advances in Electronics and Electron Physics. Supplement (US ISSN 0065-2547) *351*, *695*
Advances in Engineering (US ISSN 0065-2555) *869*
Advances in Environmental Science and Engineering (US) *383*, *849*
Advances in Environmental Science and Technology (US ISSN 0065-2563) *383*
Advances in Enzyme Regulation (US ISSN 0065-2571) *125*, *591*
Advances in Enzymology and Related Areas of Molecular Biology (US ISSN 0065-258X) *110*
Advances in Enzymology and Related Subjects of Biochemistry *see* Advances in Enzymology and Related Areas of Molecular Biology *110*
Advances in Ethology *see* Fortschritte der Verhaltensforschung *128*
Advances in Experimental Medicine and Biology (US ISSN 0065-2598) *110*, *591*
Advances in Experimental Social Psychology (US ISSN 0065-2601) *734*, *811*

Advances in Family Intervention Assessment and Theory (US) *734*, *811*
Advances in Fisheries Oceanography (JA) *127*, *309*
Advances in Food Research (US ISSN 0065-2628) *403*
Advances in Food Research. Supplement (US ISSN 0065-2636) *403*
Advances in General and Cellular Pharmacology (US ISSN 0146-3810) *683*
Advances in Genetics (US ISSN 0065-2660) *122*
Advances in Genetics. Supplement (US ISSN 0065-2679) *122*
Advances in Geophysics (US ISSN 0065-2687) *303*
Advances in Geophysics. Supplement (US ISSN 0065-2695) *303*
Advances in Gerontological Research (US ISSN 0065-2709) *428*
Advances in Health Economics and Health Services Research (US) *694*
Advances in Heat Transfer (US ISSN 0065-2717) *700*
Advances in Heterocyclic Chemistry (US ISSN 0065-2725) *252*
Advances in High Temperature Chemistry (US ISSN 0065-2741) *254*
Advances in Holography (US ISSN 0361-2961) *692*, *695*
Advances in Human Genetics (US ISSN 0065-275X) *122*
Advances in Hydroscience (US ISSN 0065-2768) *307*
Advances in Image Pickup and Display (US ISSN 0094-7032) *351*
Advances in Image Pickup and Display. Supplements (US ISSN 0094-7032) *351*
Advances in Immunology (US ISSN 0065-2776) *603*
Advances in Inflammation Research (US) *591*
Advances in Information Systems Science (US ISSN 0065-2784) *525*
Advances in Inorganic Chemistry and Radiochemistry (US ISSN 0065-2792) *245*, *251*
Advances in Insect Physiology (UK ISSN 0065-2806) *120*
Advances in Instructional Psychology (US ISSN 0163-5379) *734*
Advances in Instrumentation (US ISSN 0065-2814) *496*
Advances in Internal Medicine (US ISSN 0065-2822) *591*
Advances in Internal Medicine and Pediatrics *see* Ergebnisse der Inneren Medizin und Kinderheilkunde. New Series *595*
Advances in Librarianship (US ISSN 0065-2830) *525*
Advances in Lifelong Education (US) *313*
Advances in Lipid Research (US ISSN 0065-2849) *110*
Advances in Liquid Crystals (US) *250*
Advances in Magnetic Resonance (US ISSN 0065-2873) *351*, *695*
Advances in Manufacturing Systems, Research and Development (US) *850*
Advances in Marine Biology (UK ISSN 0065-2881) *110*, *309*
Advances in Medical Social Science: Health and Illness as Viewed by Anthropology, Geography, History, Psychology and Sociology (US) *591*, *795*
Advances in Mental Handicap Research(UK) *618*, *734*
Advances in Metabolic Disorders (US ISSN 0065-2903) *611*
Advances in Metabolic Disorders. Supplements (US ISSN 0587-4394) *611*
Advances in Microbial Ecology (US ISSN 0147-4863) *123*
Advances in Microbial Physiology (US ISSN 0065-2911) *123*
Advances in Microbiology of the Sea *see* Advances in Aquatic Microbiology *123*
Advances in Microcirculation (SZ ISSN 0065-2938) *606*

Advances in Microwaves (US ISSN 0065-2946) *351*, *695*
Advances in Microwaves. Supplements (US) *351*, *695*
Advances in Molten Salt Chemistry (US ISSN 0065-2954) *251*
Advances in Myocardiology (US ISSN 0270-4056) *606*
Advances in Nephrology from the Necker Hospital (US ISSN 0084-5957) *625*
Advances in Neurochemistry (US ISSN 0098-6089) *110*, *618*
Advances in Neurology (US ISSN 0091-3952) *618*
Advances in Neurosurgery (US ISSN 0302-2366) *618*, *624*
Advances in Nuclear Physics (US ISSN 0065-2970) *702*
Advances in Nuclear Science and Technology (US ISSN 0065-2989) *365*, *702*
Advances in Nutritional Research (US ISSN 0149-9483) *665*
Advances in Obstetrics and Gynaecology *see* Contributions to Gynecology and Obstetrics *615*
Advances in Ophthalmology *see* Developments in Ophthalmology *615*
Advances in Optical and Electron Microscopy (UK ISSN 0065-3012) *124*
Advances in Oral Biology (US ISSN 0065-3020) *609*
Advances in Oral Surgery *see* Update in Oral Surgery *916*
Advances in Organic Chemistry (US ISSN 0065-3047) *252*
Advances in Organic Coatings Science and Technology (US) *252*
Advances in Organometalic Chemistry (US ISSN 0065-3055) *252*
Advances in Orthodontics *see* Update in Orthodontics *916*
Advances in Oto-Rhino-Laryngology (SZ ISSN 0065-3071) *617*
Advances in Pain Research and Therapy (US ISSN 0146-0722) *618*
Advances in Parapsychological Research (US) *676*
Advances in Parasitology (UK ISSN 0065-308X) *127*
Advances in Pathobiology (US ISSN 0099-1147) *100*
Advances in Pediatrics (US ISSN 0065-3101) *617*
Advances in Periodontics *see* Update in Periodontics *916*
Advances in Pharmaceutical Sciences (US ISSN 0065-3136) *683*
Advances in Pharmacology and Chemotherapy (US ISSN 0065-3144) *683*
Advances in Photochemistry (US ISSN 0065-3152) *254*
Advances in Physical Geochemistry (US) *291*
Advances in Physical Organic Chemistry (UK ISSN 0065-3160) *254*
Advances in Plant Breeding *see* Fortschritte der Pflanzenzuechtung *35*
Advances in Polyamine Research (US ISSN 0160-2179) *110*, *591*
Advances in Polymer Science/ Fortschritte der Hochpolymeren-Forschung (US ISSN 0065-3195) *252*, *372*
Advances in Probability (US ISSN 0065-3217) *584*
Advances in Prostaglandin and Thromboxane Research (US) *611*
Advances in Protein Chemistry (US ISSN 0065-3233) *110*
Advances in Psychobiology (US ISSN 0065-3241) *100*, *734*
Advances in Psychological Assessment (US ISSN 0065-325X) *734*
Advances in Psychosomatic Medicine (SZ ISSN 0065-3268) *618*
Advances in Quantum Chemistry (US ISSN 0065-3276) *245*
Advances in Quantum Electronics (US ISSN 0065-3284) *351*
Advances in Radiation Biology (US ISSN 0065-3292) *112*

Advances in Radio Research (UK ISSN 0065-3314) *266*
Advances in Sex Hormone Research (US ISSN 0098-0161) *611*
Advances in Sleep Research (US) *125*, *618*
Advances in Solid State Physics (US ISSN 0065-3357) *695*
Advances in Space Science and Technology. Supplement (US ISSN 0065-3373) *6*
Advances in Special Education (US ISSN 0270-4013) *345*
Advances in Spore Pollen Research (II) *113*
Advances in Stereoencephalotomy (SZ ISSN 0065-3381) *618*
Advances in Steroid Biochemistry *see* Advances in Steroid Biochemistry and Pharmacology (1978) *110*
Advances in Steroid Biochemistry and Pharmacology (1978) (US) *110*, *683*
Advances in Surgery (US ISSN 0065-3411) *624*
Advances in Test Measurement (US ISSN 0568-0204) *496*, *636*
Advances in the Biosciences (US ISSN 0065-3446) *110*, *591*
Advances in the Economics of Energy and Resources (US) *361*
Advances in the Management of Cardiovascular Disease (US) *606*
Advances in the Management of Clinical Heart Disease (US ISSN 0146-8790) *606*
Advances in the Study of Behavior (US ISSN 0065-3454) *734*
Advances in the Study of Communication and Affect. (US) *734*, *811*
Advances in Theoretical Physics (US ISSN 0065-3470) *695*
Advances in Tuberculosis Research (SZ ISSN 0065-3500) *623*
Advances in Veterinary Medicine *see* Fortschritte der Veterinaermedizin *894*
Advances in Veterinary Science and Comparative Medicine (US ISSN 0065-3519) *894*
Advances in Virology (JA) *123*
Advances in Virus Research (US ISSN 0065-3527) *123*, *608*
Advances in Water Pollution Research (US ISSN 0065-3535) *383*
Advances in X-Ray Analysis (US ISSN 0069-8490) *377*, *626*
Adventure Travel (New York) (US) *882*
Adventure Trip Guide *see* Adventure Travel (New York) *882*
Adventures in Poetry (US) *558*, *578*
Adventures in Western New York History (US ISSN 0001-883X) *313*, *466*
Advertiser's Annual (UK ISSN 0065-3578) *4*
Advertiser's Guide to Scholarly Periodicals (US ISSN 0065-3586) *4*, *757*
Advertising and Press Annual of Africa *see* Advertising and Press Annual of Southern Africa *506*
Advertising and Press Annual of Southern Africa (SA) *506*
Advertising Directions *see* Creativity *5*
Advertising Law Anthology (US) *4*, *508*
Advertising Research Foundation. Yearbook (US) *4*
Advertising Specialty Register: Product Research and Source Data (US) *4*
Advertising Standards Authority, London. Annual Report (UK ISSN 0065-3659) *4*
Advocacy Institute. Proceedings (US ISSN 0462-3134) *508*
Advocate (CN ISSN 0382-456X) *508*
Adyar Library Bulletin *see* Brahmavidya *669*
Aegyptica Helvetica (SZ) *56*
Aegyptologische Abhandlungen (GW ISSN 0568-0476) *474*
Aegyptologische Forschungen (US) *56*, *71*, *474*
Aeldre Danske Tingboeger (DK ISSN 0065-3667) *448*
Aeolian-Harp (US) *578*

Aero (BL) 6
Aero Philatelist Annals (US) 478
Aerodynamics Deceleration Systems Conference. Papers Presented see American Institute of Aeronautics and Astronautics. Paper 7
Aeromedical Reviews (US ISSN 0065-3683) 591
Aeromodeller Annual (UK ISSN 0065-3691) 475
Aeronautics Bulletin (US ISSN 0065-3705) 6
Aeronavegacion Comercial Argentina (AG) 6
Aeronomica Acta (BE ISSN 0065-3713) 6
Aeroport de Paris. Rapport du Conseil d'Administration (FR ISSN 0065-3721) 867
Aeroport de Paris. Service Statistique. Statistique de Trafic (FR ISSN 0078-947X) 867
Aerospace Industry Yearbook (JA) 7
Aerospace Medical Association. Annual Scientific Meeting; Preprints (US ISSN 0065-3764) 591
Aerospace Research Index (UK) 1, 11
Aerospaco (BL) 7
Aether (UK ISSN 0305-7828) 11
Aethiopistische Forschungen (GW ISSN 0170-3196) 668
Affaires et Gens d'Affaires (FR ISSN 0065-3799) 168, 448
Affirmation (US ISSN 0001-9674) 771
Afghanische Studien (GW) 441
Afghanistan. Ministry of Justice. Official Gazette/Rasmi Jaridah (AF) 508
Afghanistan Republic Annual (AF ISSN 0304-6133) 442
Africa at a Glance: A Quick Reference of Facts and Figures on Africa (SA ISSN 0065-3829) 438
Africa Bibliographic Center Newsletter see A B C Newsletter 87
Africa Contemporary Record, Annual Survey and Documents (US ISSN 0065-3845) 438
Africa Guide (UK ISSN 0308-678X) 141, 707
Africa in the Modern World (US) 438, 795
Africa Institute. Annual Report see Africa Institute. Chairman's Report 438
Africa Institute. Chairman's Report (SA) 438
Africa Institute. Communications (SA ISSN 0065-3861) 182, 438
Africa Institute. Occasional Publications (SA) 182, 439
Africa Institute. Special Publications see Africa Institute. Occasional Publications 439
Africa Institute of South Africa. Chairman's Report see Africa Institute. Chairman's Report 438
Africa Institute of South Africa. Communications see Africa Institute. Communications 438
Africa Institute of South Africa. Occasional Papers see Africa Institute. Occasional Publications 439
Africa International (KE) 439
Africa-Middle East Petroleum Directory (US) 677
Africa Pulse (US) 763
Africa South of the Sahara (UK ISSN 0065-3896) 182, 419, 439
Africa South of the Sahara; Index to Periodical Literature. Supplements (US) 437
Africa Year Book and Who's Who (UK ISSN 0141-3341) 390
African-American Heritage Series (US) 391, 466
African-American Library Series (US) 391
African and Oriental Holiday see African, Mediterranean and Oriental Travel 882
African Bibliographic Center, Washington, D.C. Current Reading List Series (US ISSN 0065-3926) 87, 437

African Bibliographic Center, Washington, D.C. Special Bibliographic Series (US ISSN 0065-3934) 437
African Bibliography Series (US) 87, 437
African Biographies (GW) 96, 439
African Book World and Press: A Directory (UK) 757
African Books in Print (UK ISSN 0306-9516) 87
African Colonial Studies (US) 719
African Companies see Current African Directories 154
African Development Bank. Annual Report see African Development Bank. Report by the Board of Directors 199
African Development Bank. Report by the Board of Directors/Banque Africaine de Developpement. Rapport du Conseil d'Administration(IV ISSN 0568-1308) 199
African Development Fund. Annual Report/Fonds Africain de Developpement. Rapport Annuel (IV) 199
African Development Research Annual/ Annuaire des Recherches Africaines sur les Problemes de Developpement (SG) 199
African Documents Series (US) 439
African Environment. Occasional Papers/Etudes et Recherches (SG) 383
African Environment Special Reports (UK ISSN 0309-345X) 383
African Freedom. Annual (SA) 439, 707
African Historian (NR ISSN 0568-1332) 439
African Historical Dictionaries (US) 439
African Institute for Economic Development and Planning. Programme (SG) 199
African Institute for Economic Development and Planning. Series in Economic and Social Development/ Institut Africain de Developpement Economique et de Planification. Collection d'Etudes sur le Developpement Economique et Social (SG) 199
African Language Studies (UK ISSN 0065-3985) 439, 540
African Literature Today (US ISSN 0065-4065) 558
African, Mediterranean and Oriental Travel (HK) 882
African Music (SA ISSN 0065-4019) 656
African Music Society. Newsletter see African Music 656
African News Sheet (SZ ISSN 0379-7074) 497
African Philosophical Journal see Cahiers Philosophiques Africains 687
African Research Studies (US) 439
African Series see Indiana University. Research Center for Language and Semiotic Studies. African Series 545
African Social Security Series see African News Sheet 497
African Studies (CH) 439
African Studies Association Papers see A S A Papers 390
African Studies Association Review of Books see A S A Review of Books 390
African Studies Bulletin see African Studies Review 391
African Studies Review (US ISSN 0002-0206) 391
African Studies Series (UK ISSN 0065-406X) 439
Africana Collectanea Series (SA ISSN 0065-4116) 439
Africana Gandensia (BE) 47
Africana Society of Pretoria. Yearbook/ Africana Vereniging van Pretoria. Jaarboek (SA) 439
Africana Vereniging van Pretoria. Jaarboek see Africana Society of Pretoria. Yearbook 439
Africanus (SA ISSN 0304-615X) 707, 739

Afrikano-Aziatski Problemi (BU) 439, 442
Afrique et Moyen-Orient see Annuaire Economique d'Afrique et du Moyen-Orient 719
Afro-American Music Opportunities Association. Resource Papers (US) 656
Afro-Asia (BL ISSN 0002-0591) 430, 540, 668
Afro-Asian Peoples' Conference. Proceedings (UA ISSN 0065-4191) 439, 442
Afro-Asian Peoples' Solidarity Organization. Council. Documents of the Session (UA ISSN 0078-6233) 439, 442
Afro-Asian Publications (UA ISSN 0515-6327) 439
Afro Technical Papers see A F R O Technical Papers 750
Afroasiatic Dialects (US) 540
Afroasiatic Linguistics (US) 540
Afurika Kenkyu see Journal of African Studies 440
Agassiz Center for Water Studies. Research Report (CN ISSN 0580-535X) 895
Age of Firearms (US ISSN 0065-4213) 828
Agence pour la Securite de la Navigation Aerienne en Afrique et a Madagascar. Direction de l'Exploitation Meteorologique. Publications. Serie 1 (SG ISSN 0065-4248) 631
Agence pour la Securite de la Navigation Aerienne en Afrique et a Madagascar. Direction de l'Exploitation Meteorologique. Publications. Serie 2 (SG ISSN 0084-6015) 631
Agency Publication - Texas Water Quality Board see Texas. Water Quality Board. Agency Publication 915
Agenda de la Quincaillerie (FR ISSN 0065-4256) 626
Agenda del Dirigente di Azienda (IT ISSN 0065-4264) 141
Agenda des Armees (FR) 638
Agenda dos Criadores e Agricultores (BL) 11
Agenda Edizione Guida Monaci. S.p.A.(IT) 213
Agenda Estadistica (MX) 832
Agenda Memento des Cadres et Maitrises de l'Imprimerie, de l'Edition et des Industries Graphiques see Agenda Memento des Protes 733
Agenda Memento des Protes (FR) 675, 733
Agenda Nautica (IT) 876
Agenda Vinicola & delle Industrie Alimentari (IT) 85, 407
Agent's and Buyer's Guide (US ISSN 0065-4272) 497
Agent's Hotel Gazetteer: America (UK) 482, 882
Agent's Hotel Gazetteer: Resorts (UK) 482, 882
Agent's Hotel Gazetteer: Tourist Cities (UK ISSN 0308-9584) 482
Agevolazioni e Vantaggi per i Pescatori Federati (IT) 828
Agglomeration Bruxelloise (BE) 811
Aging (New York) (US ISSN 0361-0179) 428
Aging and Development see Altern und Entwicklung 428
AgLink (NZ) 11
Agora (Ravenna) (IT) 687, 811
Agrarian Development Studies (UK ISSN 0065-4337) 26
Agrarmarkt-Studien (GW ISSN 0065-4345) 26
Agrarpolitik and Marktwesen (GW ISSN 0065-4353) 26
Agrarsoziale Gesellschaft. Kleine Reihe (GW ISSN 0170-7671) 11, 811
Agrarsoziale Gesellschaft. Arbeitsbericht see Agrarsoziale Gesellschaft. Geschaefts- und Arbeitsbericht 811
Agrarsoziale Gesellschaft. Geschaefts- und Arbeitsbericht (GW ISSN 0065-437X) 11, 811

AGRICULTURAL RESEARCH

Agrarsoziale Gesellschaft. Materialsammlung (GW ISSN 0344-5712) 11, 811
Agri-Business Buyers Reference (US ISSN 0065-4396) 26, 202
Agri Educator (US) 11, 313
Agricoltore Veronese (IT) 11
Agricultura e Industrias Agropecuarias y Pesca (CL) 401
Agricultura Espanola see Agricultura Espanola en (Year) 11
Agricultura Espanola en (Year) (SP) 11
Agricultural Co-Operation in the United Kingdom: Summary of Statistics (UK ISSN 0142-4998) 26
Agricultural Commodities Index (US) 11, 87
Agricultural Development and Marketing Corporation. Annual Report see Agricultural Development and Marketing Corporation. Annual Report and Statement of Accounts 26
Agricultural Development and Marketing Corporation. Annual Report and Statement of Accounts (MW) 26
Agricultural Development Bank of Pakistan. Annual Report and Statement of Accounts (PK ISSN 0065-4426) 26, 168
Agricultural Development Corporation. Balance Sheet and Accounts see Agricultural Development and Marketing Corporation. Annual Report and Statement of Accounts 26
Agricultural Development Council. Research and Training Network A.D.C.-R.T.N. (US) 11
Agricultural Development Council Inc. Reprints see A. D. C. Reprints 11
Agricultural Development Council Inc. Staff Papers see A.D.C. Staff Papers 26
Agricultural Directory of Malaysia (MY) 11
Agricultural Economics Bulletin for Africa (UN ISSN 0065-4434) 26
Agricultural Economist (PK ISSN 0065-4469) 26
Agricultural Engineers Yearbook (US ISSN 0065-4477) 32
Agricultural Experiment Station Surinam. Annual Report see Landbouwproefstation Suriname. Jaarverslag 17
Agricultural Finance Review see U.S. Department of Agriculture. Economics, Statistics, and Cooperatives Service. Agricultural Finance Review 30
Agricultural Finance Review Supplement see U.S. Department of Agriculture. Economics, Statistics, and Cooperatives Service. Agricultural Finance Statistics 26
Agricultural Finance Statistics see U.S. Department of Agriculture. Economics, Statistics, and Cooperatives Service. Agricultural Finance Statistics 26
Agricultural Institute of Canada. Membership Directory/Institut Agricole du Canada. Liste des Membres (CN ISSN 0083-9744) 11, 96
Agricultural Pesticide Society. Annual Meeting. Proceedings see Canadian Pest Management Society Proceedings 33
Agricultural Processing & Manufacturing Guide see Processing & Manufacturing Guide 30
Agricultural Production Levels in Bangladesh (BG) 26
Agricultural Progress (UK ISSN 0065-4493) 26
Agricultural Real Estate Values in Alberta (CN ISSN 0701-7502) 11, 761
Agricultural Research Center. Annual Report (US) 32
Agricultural Research Center. Proceedings of the Annual Meeting (US) 11

Agricultural Research Council of Malawi. Annual Report *see* Malawi. Department of Agricultural Research. Annual Report *17*
Agricultural Research Guyana (GY ISSN 0065-4523) *11*
Agricultural Research Index (UK ISSN 0065-4531) *11*
Agricultural Research Organization. Pamphlet (IS) *11*
Agricultural Research Organization, Rehovot. Bulletin *see* Agricultural Research Organization. Pamphlet *11*
Agricultural Science *see* Agricultural Science Bulletin *11*
Agricultural Science and Technology *see* AgLink *11*
Agricultural Science Bulletin (CN ISSN 0707-7793) *11*
Agricultural Science Hong Kong *see* Agriculture Hong Kong *12*
Agricultural Science in the Netherlands(NE) *11*
Agricultural Shows Annual (AT) *12*
Agricultural Situation in Africa and West Asia *see* U.S. Department of Agriculture. Economics, Statistics, and Cooperatives Service. Africa and West Asia Agricultural Situation *30*
Agricultural Society of Nigeria. Proceedings (NR ISSN 0065-454X) *12*
Agricultural Statistics, England and Wales (UK ISSN 0065-4558) *12*
Agricultural Statistics, Madhya Pradesh *see* Madhya Pradesh. Directorate of Agriculture. Agricultural Statistics *25*
Agricultural Statistics, Massachusetts *see* Massachusetts Agricultural Statistics *17*
Agricultural Statistics of Bangladesh (BG ISSN 0065-4566) *12*
Agricultural Statistics of Greece (GR ISSN 0065-4574) *23, 832*
Agricultural Statistics of Sabah (MY) *26*
Agricultural Statistics of Sarawak (MY) *26*
Agricultural Statistics, Scotland (UK ISSN 0065-4582) *12*
Agricultural Statistics, United Kingdom (UK ISSN 0065-4590) *12*
Agricultural Wages in India (II ISSN 0084-6066) *26, 205*
Agriculture Asia/Ajia Nogyo (JA ISSN 0515-8672) *12*
Agriculture Hong Kong (HK) *12*
Agriculture in Scotland (UK) *12*
Agriculture Teachers Directory and Handbook (US ISSN 0515-7420) *12, 313*
Agro Chemie-Koerier (NE) *32*
Agro-Nouvelles (CN ISSN 0065-4655) *12*
Agroborealis (US ISSN 0002-1822) *12*
Agrofizichni Izsledovaniia (BU) *12*
Agronomia Mocambicana (MZ ISSN 0044-6858) *12, 113*
Agronomy: a Series of Monographs (US ISSN 0065-4663) *12*
Agronomy Abstracts (US ISSN 0065-4671) *1, 23*
Agrupacion de Periodistas de Informacion Economica. Informe (SP) *141, 504*
Agrupacion Sindical Nacional de Empresas de Financiacion. Censo (SP) *168*
Ahmadu Bello University. Centre for the Study of Nigerian Languages. Harsunan Nijeriya *see* Harsunan Nijeriya *544*
Ahmadu Bello University. Centre of Islamic Legal Studies. Journal (NR ISSN 0065-468X) *769*
Ahmadu Bello University. Department of Geography. Occasional Paper (NR ISSN 0065-4698) *419*
Ahmadu Bello University. Institute for Agricultural Research. Soil Survey Bulletin (NR ISSN 0065-4728) *32*
Ahmadu Bello University. Institute of Administration. Traditional Land Tenure Surveys (NR ISSN 0065-4744) *26*
Ahmadu Bello University. Institute of Education. Paper (NR ISSN 0065-4752) *314*
Ahmadu Bello University. Northern History Research Scheme. Interim Report (NR) *439*
Ahmadu Bello University. Northern History Research Scheme. Papers *see* Ahmadu Bello University. Northern History Research Scheme. Interim Report *439*
Ahmedabad Textile Industry's Research Association. Joint Technological Conferences. Proceedings (II ISSN 0075-4005) *854*
Ahmedabad Textile Industry's Research Association. Proceedings of the Management Conference (II ISSN 0065-4779) *854*
Aichi-ken Kyodo Shiryo Sogo Mokuroku (JA) *87*
Aids and Research Tools in Ancient Near Eastern Studies (US) *474*
Aids for Industry-North West England (UK) *220*
Aids Index to How to do It Information *see* Index to How to Do It Information *476*
Aids to the Study of Religion (US) *763*
Aieee (US) *555*
Ailleurs et Demain; Classiques (FR ISSN 0065-4787) *558*
Aiolika Grammata (GR) *558*
Air Canada. Annual Report (CN ISSN 0568-3424) *7*
Air Conditioning, Ventilating and Heating Equipment *see* H V A C Red Book of Heating, Ventilating and Air Conditioning Equipment *429*
Air New Zealand. Annual Report (NZ ISSN 0065-4817) *867*
Air Officer's Guide (US ISSN 0065-4825) *638*
Air Pollution Control Association Proceedings Digest *see* A.P.C.A. Proceedings Digest *383*
Air Pollution Effects Surveillance Network Data Report *see* Air Quality Data for Arizona *383*
Air Quality Data for Arizona. (US) *383*
Air Quality in Minnesota (US ISSN 0361-5650) *383*
Air Quality Instrumentation (US) *383, 496*
Air Quality Monograph Series (US ISSN 0568-3653) *383*
Air Rhodesia Annual Report *see* Air Zimbabwe Annual Report *867*
Air Safety Forum (US ISSN 0065-4841) *903*
Air Transport (US) *867*
Air Transport (London) (UK ISSN 0143-4063) *7, 867*
Air Transport and Travel Industry Training Board. Report and Statement of Accounts. (UK) *867*
Air Transport Association. Annual General Meeting Reports and Proceedings *see* International Air Transport Association. Annual Report *868*
Air Transport Association of Canada. Annual Report (CN ISSN 0065-485X) *867*
Air Transportation Annual (CN) *867*
Air Travel Answers (US) *867, 882*
Air Travel Bargains (US ISSN 0065-4868) *882*
Air Zimbabwe Annual Report (RH) *867*
Aircraft Accident Digest (UN ISSN 0065-4876) *7*
Aircraft Engines of the World (US ISSN 0065-4892) *7*
Aircraft Illustrated Annual (UK) *7*
Aircraft Owners and Pilots Association. A O P A Airport Directory *see* A O P A's Airports U.S.A. *867*
Aircraft Owners and Pilots Association Airports U.S.A. *see* A O P A's Airports U.S.A. *867*
Airline Guide to Stewardess & Stewards Career (US ISSN 0065-4914) *666, 867*
Airline Handbook (US ISSN 0095-4683) *867*
Airman's Information Manual (Fallbrook) (US) *7, 867*
Airway Pioneer; Yearbook of the Society of Airway Pioneers (US ISSN 0065-4930) *867*
Ais-Eiri (US ISSN 0360-5388) *391*
Aisthesis (CL ISSN 0568-3939) *71, 314, 687*
Ajia Nogyo *see* Agriculture Asia *12*
Ajuris (BL) *508*
Akademia Ekonomiczna, Krakow. Zeszyty Naukowe (PL) *141*
Akademia Ekonomiczna, Poznan. Zeszyty Naukowe. Seria 1 (PL ISSN 0079-4546) *141*
Akademia Ekonomiczna, Poznan. Zeszyty Naukowe. Seria 2. Prace Habilitacyjne i Doktorskie (PL ISSN 0079-4554) *141*
Akademia Ekonomiczna we Wroclawiu. Prace Naukowe (PL) *141*
Akademia Gorniczo-Hutnicza im. Stanislawa Staszica. Instytut Ceramiki Specjalnej i Ogniotrwalej. Prace Naukowe (PL) *244*
Akademia Gorniczo-Hutnicza im. Stanislawa Staszica. Instytut Gornictwa Podziemnego. Prace (PL) *641*
Akademia Gorniczo-Hutnicza im. Stanislawa Staszica. Instytut Maszyn Hutniczych i Automatyki. Prace (PL) *626*
Akademia Gorniczo-Hutnicza im. Stanislawa Staszica. Zeszyty Naukowe. Gornictwo (PL ISSN 0075-6997) *641*
Akademia Gorniczo-Hutnicza Im. Stanislawa Staszica. Zeszyty Naukowe. Hutnictwo (PL ISSN 0075-7004) *626*
Akademia Medyczna, Bialystok. Rocznik (PL ISSN 0067-6489) *591*
Akademia Rolnicza, Krakow. Rolnictwo(PL) *12*
Akademia Rolnicza, Poznan. Rocznik. Algorytmy Biometryczne i Statystyczne (PL) *584*
Akademia Rolnicza, Poznan. Rocznik. Lesnictwo (PL) *407*
Akademia Rolnicza, Poznan. Rocznik. Melioracje Wodne (PL) *32*
Akademia Rolnicza, Poznan. Rocznik. Ogrodnictwo (PL) *414*
Akademia Rolnicza, Poznan. Rocznik. Ornitologia Stosowana (PL) *124*
Akademia Rolnicza, Poznan. Rocznik. Prace Habilitacyjne (PL) *12*
Akademia Rolnicza, Poznan. Rocznik. Rolnictwo (PL) *12*
Akademia Rolnicza, Poznan. Rocznik. Technologia Rolno-Spozywcza (PL) *403*
Akademia Rolnicza, Poznan. Rocznik. Zootechnika (PL) *43*
Akademia Rolnicza, Szczecin. Zeszyty Naukowe (PL ISSN 0082-1233) *12, 113*
Akademia Rolnicza, Warsaw. Zeszyty Naukowe. Ogrodnictwo (PL ISSN 0083-7288) *414*
Akademia Rolnicza, Warsaw. Zeszyty Naukowe. Seria Historyczna (PL ISSN 0083-7296) *12*
Akademia Rolnicza, Warsaw. Zeszyty Naukowe. Technologia Drewna (PL) *141*
Akademia Rolnicza, Warsaw. Zeszyty Naukowe. Zootechnika (PL) *127*
Akademia Rolnicza, Wroclaw. Rolnictwo (PL) *12*
Akademia Rolniczo-Techniczna. Zeszyty Naukowe (PL ISSN 0324-9204) *12*
Akademie der Wissenschaften. Berlin. Jahrbuch *see* Akademie der Wissenschaften der DDR. Jahrbuch *778*
Akademie der Wissenschaften, Berlin. Sektion fuer Vor- und Fruehgeschichte. Schriften *see* Schriften zur Ur- und Fruehgeschichte *435*
Akademie der Wissenschaften, Berlin. Volkskundliche Veroeffentlichungen *see* Veroeffentlichungen zur Volkskunde und Kulturgeschichte *403*
Akademie der Wissenschaften, Berlin. Zentralinstitut fuer Sprachwissenschaft. Schriften *see* Sprache und Gesellschaft *551*
Akademie der Wissenschaften der DDR. Abhandlungen. Abteilung Mathematik, Naturwissenschaften, Technik (GE) *795*
Akademie der Wissenschaften der DDR. Geodaetisches Institut. Veroeffentlichungen *see* Akademie der Wissenschaften der DDR. Zentralinstitut fuer Physik der Erde. Veroeffentlichungen *419*
Akademie der Wissenschaften der DDR. Institut fuer Geographie und Geoeekologie. Wissenschaftliche Veroeffentlichungen *see* Beitraege zur Geographie *420*
Akademie der Wissenschaften der DDR. Jahrbuch (GE ISSN 0304-2154) *778*
Akademie der Wissenschaften der DDR. Zentralinstitut fuer Geschichte. Schriften (GE ISSN 0065-5236) *448*
Akademie der Wissenschaften der DDR. Zentralinstitut fuer Physik der Erde. Veroeffentlichungen (GE) *419*
Akademie der Wissenschaften der DDR. Zentralinstitut fuer Wirtschaftswissenschaften. Schriften (GE ISSN 0065-5279) *141*
Akademie der Wissenschaften, Goettingen. Jahrbuch (GW ISSN 0084-6082) *778*
Akademie der Wissenschaften, Goettingen. Nachrichten 1. Philologisch-Historische Klasse (GW ISSN 0065-5287) *430, 540*
Akademie der Wissenschaften, Goettingen. Nachrichten 2. Mathematisch-Physikalische Klasse (GW ISSN 0065-5295) *584, 695*
Akademie der Wissenschaften und der Literatur. Geistes- und Sozialwissenschaftliche Klasse. Abhandlungen (GW ISSN 0002-2977) *489*
Akademie der Wissenschaften und der Literatur, Mainz. Jahrbuch (GW ISSN 0084-6104) *489, 778*
Akademie der Wissenschaften und der Literatur, Mainz. Klasse der Literatur. Abhandlungen (GW ISSN 0002-2985) *558*
Akademie der Wissenschaften und der Literatur, Mainz. Mathematisch-Naturwissenschaftliche Klasse. Abhandlungen (GW ISSN 0002-2993) *584*
Akademie der Wissenschaften und der Literatur, Mainz. Orientalische Kommission. Veroeffentlichungen (GW ISSN 0568-4447) *668*
Akademie fuer Aerztliche Fortbildung der DDR. Bibliographie (GE ISSN 0070-3915) *601*
Akademie fuer Fuehrungskraefte der Wirtschaft. Taschenbuecher zur Betriebspraxis (GW ISSN 0065-5384) *213*
Akademie fuer Oeffentliches Gesundheitswesen. Schriftenreihe (GW) *750*
Akademie fuer Staatsmedizin, Duesseldorf. Jahrbuch *see* Akademie fuer Oeffentliches Gesundheitswesen. Schriftenreihe *750*
Akademiet for de Videnskaber. Handbog (DK) *850*
Akademija Nauka i Umjetnosti Bosne i Hercegovine. Centar za Balkanoloska Ispitivanja. Godisnjak (YU) *448*
Akademija Nauka i Umjetnosti Bosne i Hercegovine. Odeljenje Drustvenih Nauka. Radovi (YU ISSN 0350-0039) *795*
Akademija Nauka i Umjetnosti Bosne i Hercegovine. Odeljenje Medicinskih Nauka. Radovi (YU ISSN 0350-0071) *591*
Akademija Nauka i Umjetnosti Bosne i Hercegovine. Odjeljenje Istorijsko Filoloskih Nauk. Djela (YU) *448, 540*
Der Akademiker in Wirtschaft und Verwaltung (GW ISSN 0568-7276) *666*

Akademische Vortraege und Abhandlungen (GW ISSN 0065-5538) *778*
Akademiska Dzive/Academic Life (US ISSN 0516-3145) *391, 448*
Akademiya Nauk Azerbaidzhanskoi S.S.R. Muzei Istorii. Trudy (UR) *656*
Akademiya Nauk Belarusskoi SSR. Belarusskii Etnograficheskii Sbornik. Seriya Fol'klora i Etnografii (UR) *401*
Akademiya Nauk CSSR. Vostochno-Sibirskii Filial, Irkutsk. Institut Geokhimii. Geokhimya Endogennych Protsessov (UR) *288*
Akademiya Nauk CSSR. Vostochno-Sibirskii Filial, Irkutsk. Institut Geokhimii. Geokhimicheskie Metody Poiskov, Metody Analiza (UR) *288*
Akademiya Nauk Kazakhskoi S.S.R. Astrofizicheskii Institut. Trudy (UR) *81*
Akademiya Nauk Kazakhskoi S.S.R. Institut Khimicheskikh Nauk. Trudy (UR) *252*
Akademiya Nauk Kazakhskoi S.S.R. Institut Metallurgii i Obogashcheniya. Trudy (UR) *626*
Akademiya Nauk Kazakhskoi S.S.R. Institut Organicheskogo Kataliza i Elektrokhimii. Trudy (UR) *251*
Akademiya Nauk Latviiskoi S. S. R. Elektronikas un Skaitlosanas Tehnikas Instituts. Raspoznavanie Obrazov (UR) *778*
Akademiya Nauk S.S.S.R. Institut Arkheologii. Kratkie Soobshcheniya (UR) *56*
Akademiya Nauk S.S.S.R. Institut Etnografii. Polevye Issledovaniya. (UR) *47*
Akademiya Nauk S.S.S.R. Institut Paleontologii. Trudy (UR) *673*
Akademiya Nauk S.S.S.R. Sibirskoe Otdelenie. Limnologichesku Institut. Trudy (UR) *307*
Akademiya Nauk S. S. S. R. Sibirskoe Otdelenie Uralskii Nauchnyi Tsentr. Institut Elektrkhimii. Trudy (UR ISSN 0568-6776) *251*
Akademiya Nauk S. S. S. R. Sibirskoe Otdelenie. Vostochno- Sibirskii Filial. Institut Geokhimii. Ezhegodnik (UR) *291*
Akiyoshi-dai Museum of Natural History. Bulletin (JA) *651*
Akiyoshi-dai Science Museum. Bulletin *see* Akiyoshi-dai Museum of Natural History. Bulletin *651*
Akkerbouw (NE) *26*
Aktual'nye Problemy Leksikologii i Slovoobrazovaniya (UR) *540*
Aktuelle Fragen des Landbaues (GW ISSN 0568-7594) *12*
Aktuelle Probleme der Intensivmedizin/ Current Topics in Intensive Care Medicine (GW ISSN 0340-1901) *591*
Aktuelle Probleme der Polymer-Physik (GW ISSN 0340-210X) *252, 372*
Aktuelle Probleme in Chirurgie Orthopadie (SZ) *616*
Aktuelle Probleme in der Chirurgie *see* Aktuelle Probleme in Chirurgie Orthopadie *616*
Aktuelle Probleme in der Klinischen Biochemie *see* Current Problems in Clinical Biochemistry *111*
Aktuelle Probleme in der Psychiatrie, Neurologie, Neurochirurgie (SZ ISSN 0065-5600) *618*
Aktuellt och Historiskt *see* Militaerhistorisk Tidskrift *457*
Akustyka (PL) *706*
Al Safarim ve-Korim/On Books and Readers (IS) *525*
Alabama. Commission on Higher Education. Biennial Report to the Governor and the Legislature (US ISSN 0095-1285) *333*
Alabama. Department of Industrial Relations. Annual Manpower Planning Report *see* Alabama. Department of Industrial Relations. Annual Planning Information *205*
Alabama. Department of Industrial Relations. Annual Planning Information (US) *205*

Alabama. Public Library Service. Annual Report (US) *525*
Alabama. Public Library Service. Basic State Plan and Annual Program *see* Alabama. Public Library Service. Annual Report *525*
Alabama Archaeological Society. Special Publication (US) *56*
Alabama County Data Book (US) *739*
Alabama Department of Education. Library Media Output (US) *525*
Alabama Directory of Mining and Manufacturing (US ISSN 0145-4048) *178*
Alabama Economic Outlook (US) *182*
Alabama Geological Society. Guidebook for the Annual Field Trip (US ISSN 0065-5635) *291*
Alabama Historical Quarterly (US ISSN 0002-4236) *466*
Alabama Institutions of Higher Education, Universities and Colleges *see* Fact Book. Alabama Institutions of Higher Education, Universities and Colleges *336*
Alabama Linguistic and Philological Series (US ISSN 0084-6112) *903*
Alabama, Louisiana, Mississippi TourBook *see* Tourbook: Alabama, Louisiana, Mississippi *891*
Alabama Planning Resource Checklist (US) *483*
Alabama State Industrial Directory (US ISSN 0161-8563) *234*
Alabama World Trade Directory (US ISSN 0095-1269) *234*
Alabama's Distinguished (US) *903*
Alabama's Vital Events (US ISSN 0095-3431) *832*
Alahli Bank of Kuwait K.S.C. Annual Report and Balance Sheet (KU) *168*
Alan Rogers' Selected Sites for Caravanning and Camping in Europe(UK ISSN 0065-5686) *828, 883*
Alaska. Criminal Investigation Bureau. Annual Report (US ISSN 0362-7284) *280*
Alaska. Department of Fish and Game. Annual Report (US ISSN 0065-5708) *274*
Alaska. Department of Fish and Game. Commercial Operators (US) *395*
Alaska. Department of Fish and Game. Game Division. Interior Moose and Moose Disease Studies (US) *903*
Alaska. Department of Fish and Game. Game Division. Interior Moose Studies *see* Alaska. Department of Fish and Game. Game Division. Interior Moose and Moose Disease Studies *903*
Alaska. Department of Fish and Game. Informational Leaflet (US ISSN 0516-4303) *275*
Alaska. Department of Fish and Game. Wildlife Booklet Series (US ISSN 0084-0130) *275*
Alaska. Department of Health and Social Services. Quarterly (US) *903*
Alaska. Department of Natural Resources. Annual Report (US ISSN 0149-6646) *275*
Alaska. Department of Revenue. State Investment Portfolio (US ISSN 0092-6736) *202, 226*
Alaska. Department of Revenue. Treasury Division. Annual Financial Report *see* Treasury Alaska *848*
Alaska. Division of Family and Children Services. Annual Report (US ISSN 0094-1174) *803*
Alaska. Division of Game. Annual Report of Survey-Inventory Activities(US ISSN 0362-6962) *828*
Alaska. Division of Geological and Geophysical Surveys. Annual Report (US ISSN 0065-5724) *291, 303*
Alaska. Division of Geological and Geophysical Surveys. Information Circular (US ISSN 0065-5759) *291, 303*
Alaska. Division of Geological and Geophysical Surveys. Laboratory Note (US ISSN 0065-5767) *291, 303*

Alaska. Division of Geological and Geophysical Surveys. Laboratory Report (US ISSN 0065-5775) *291, 303*
Alaska. Division of Geological and Geophysical Surveys. Special Report (US ISSN 0360-3881) *291, 303*
Alaska. Division of Medical Assistance. Medicaid Annual Status Report *see* Alaska Medicaid Status Report *497*
Alaska. Division of Oil and Gas Conservation. Statistical Report *see* Alaska. Oil and Gas Conservation Commission. Statistical Report *682*
Alaska. Employment Security Division. Labor Force Estimates by Industry and Area. (US ISSN 0362-4196) *205*
Alaska. Employment Security Division. Workforce Estimates, by Industry and Area *see* Alaska. Employment Security Division. Labor Force Estimates by Industry and Area *205*
Alaska. Legislature. Budget and Audit Committee. Annual Report. (US ISSN 0095-3865) *739*
Alaska. Office of Alcoholism. Report (US ISSN 0095-3318) *286*
Alaska. Office of Ombudsman. Report of the Ombudsman (US ISSN 0363-5376) *739*
Alaska. Office of the Governor. Governor's Manpower Plan (US ISSN 0091-9535) *205*
Alaska. Oil and Gas Conservation Commission. Statistical Report (US) *682*
Alaska. State Board of Registration for Architects, Engineers and Land Surveyors. Directory of Architects, Engineers and Land Surveyors (US ISSN 0094-1786) *68, 365*
Alaska. State Library, Juneau. Historical Monographs (US ISSN 0084-6139) *466*
Alaska. State Library, Juneau. State and Local Publications Received-Alaska (US ISSN 0568-8442) *748*
Alaska. Violent Crimes Compensation Board. Annual Report (US ISSN 0095-3415) *280*
Alaska Accident Statistics (US ISSN 0360-9154) *864*
Alaska Agricultural Statistics (US ISSN 0065-5694) *23*
Alaska Almanac: Facts About Alaska (US) *883*
Alaska Blue Book (US ISSN 0092-1858) *79*
Alaska Economy; Year-End Performance Report *see* Performance Report of the Alaska Economy *189*
Alaska Fisheries Commercial Operators. *see* Alaska. Department of Fish and Game. Commercial Operators *395*
Alaska Fishing Guide (US ISSN 0361-3984) *903*
Alaska Forest Products Newsletter (US) *412*
Alaska Hunting Guide (US ISSN 0095-5760) *903*
Alaska Libraries and Library Personnel Directory (US) *525*
Alaska Medicaid Status Report (US ISSN 0095-4667) *497*
Alaska Native Medical Center. Annual Report (US ISSN 0362-6849) *480, 803*
Alaska Pacific University Press Press Alaskana Series *see* A P U Press Alaskana Series *430*
Alaska Petroleum and Industrial Directory (US ISSN 0065-5813) *677*
Alaska Petroleum Directory *see* Alaska Petroleum and Industrial Directory *677*
Alaska Science Conference. Proceedings(US ISSN 0084-6120) *778*
Alaska State Industrial Directory (US) *234*
Alaska State Plan for the Construction of Hospitals and Medical Facilities (US ISSN 0065-583X) *903*
Alaska Today (US ISSN 0191-328X) *419*
Alaska Travel Guide (US ISSN 0065-5848) *883*

ALBERTA ENGLISH   1275

Alaska's Health and Social Services *see* Alaska. Department of Health and Social Services. Quarterly *903*
Alaska's Land (US) *275, 383*
Albania Report (US ISSN 0002-4651) *182, 707*
Albany Bulletin on Health and Welfare Legislation (US) *508, 750, 803*
Albany Series of Plays (SA) *858*
Albarregas (VE) *314, 489*
Alberta. Alcoholism and Drug Abuse Commission. Annual Report (CN ISSN 0319-423X) *286*
Alberta. Department of Advanced Education and Manpower. Post-Secondary Education Programs (CN ISSN 0702-0066) *329*
Alberta. Department of Agriculture. Annual Report (CN ISSN 0065-597X) *12*
Alberta. Department of Education. Early Childhood Services Program Highlights (CN ISSN 0708-3106) *256, 314*
Alberta. Department of Energy and Natural Resources, Annual Report (CN ISSN 0700-2645) *361, 677*
Alberta. Department of Health and Social Development. Annual Report *see* Alberta. Department of Social Services and Community Health. Annual Report *803*
Alberta. Department of Social Services and Community Health. Annual Report (CN ISSN 0381-4327) *750, 803*
Alberta. Department of the Environment. Annual Report (CN ISSN 0383-3739) *383*
Alberta. Department of Transportation. Annual Report (CN ISSN 0318-4757) *861*
Alberta. Energy Resources Conservation Board. Operations Report (CN) *275, 361*
Alberta. Environment Council of Alberta. Annual Report (CN ISSN 0705-5811) *384*
Alberta. Fish and Wildlife Division. Fisheries Pollution Report (CN ISSN 0707-2783) *384, 395*
Alberta. Fish and Wildlife Division. Pollution Report *see* Alberta. Fish and Wildlife Division. Fisheries Pollution Report *384*
Alberta. Government Libraries Council. Annual Reviews (CN ISSN 0704-8734) *525*
Alberta. Health and Social Services Disciplines Committee. Annual Report (CN ISSN 0707-1434) *750, 803*
Alberta. Health Care Insurance Commission. Annual Report *see* Alberta. Health Care Insurance Plan. Annual Report *497*
Alberta. Health Care Insurance Plan. Annual Report (CN) *497*
Alberta. Horticultural Research Center. Annual Report (CN ISSN 0706-3369) *414*
Alberta. Legislature Library. Annual Report (CN ISSN 0383-3712) *525*
Alberta. Office of the Superintendent of Insurance and Real Estate. Annual Report (CN ISSN 0705-596X) *497, 761*
Alberta. University, Edmonton. Department of Computing Science. Publication *see* University of Alberta. Department of Computing Science. Technical Reports *274*
Alberta. Utilities Division. Annual Report (CN ISSN 0381-2294) *739*
Alberta. Water Resources Division Annual Report *see* Alberta. Department of Agriculture. Annual Report *12*
Alberta Art Foundation. Annual Report(CN ISSN 0704-9056) *71*
Alberta Authors Bulletin (CN ISSN 0707-994X) *558*
Alberta Construction Industry Directory. Purchasing Guide (CN ISSN 0381-9663) *134, 234*
Alberta Decisions, Civil and Criminal Cases (CN ISSN 0319-7980) *508*
Alberta English (CN ISSN 0382-5191) *347, 540*

ALBERTA FISHING

Alberta Fishing Guide (CN ISSN 0318-4943) *828*
Alberta Genealogical Society. Ancestor Index (CN) *416*
Alberta Genealogical Society. Surnames Register *see* Alberta Genealogical Society. Ancestor Index *416*
Alberta Hail and Crop Insurance Corporation. Annual Report (CN ISSN 0319-3535) *32, 497*
Alberta Health Education Programs (CN ISSN 0708-2673) *347, 694*
Alberta Historical Resources Foundation. News & Views (CN ISSN 0707-705X) *466*
Alberta Landrace Association. Newsletter (CN ISSN 0044-7145) *43*
Alberta Motor Transport Directory (CN ISSN 0084-6171) *881*
Alberta Opportunity Company. Annual Report (CN ISSN 0318-3971) *168*
Alberta Petroleum Marketing Commission. Annual Report (CN ISSN 0703-2358) *217, 677*
Alberta Professional Engineer *see* Pegg/Professional Engineer, Geologist, Geophysicist *369*
Alberta Research. Highways and River Engineering Reports *see* Alberta Research Council. River Engineering and Surface Hydrology Reports *374*
Alberta Research Council. Annual Report (CN ISSN 0080-1526) *778, 850*
Alberta Research Council. Atmospheric Sciences Reports (CN) *778, 850*
Alberta Research Council. Bulletins (CN ISSN 0034-5172) *291*
Alberta Research Council. Contribution Series (CN ISSN 0080-1534) *182*
Alberta Research Council. Earth Science Reports (CN) *288*
Alberta Research Council. Hail Studies Reports *see* Alberta Research Council. Atmospheric Sciences Reports *778*
Alberta Research Council. Highway Research (CN ISSN 0065-5988) *374, 874*
Alberta Research Council. Information Series (CN ISSN 0034-5180) *677*
Alberta Research Council. List of Publications (CN ISSN 0080-1569) *538*
Alberta Research Council. Memoirs (CN ISSN 0080-1577) *778, 850*
Alberta Research Council. Preliminary Reports. Soil Surveys (CN ISSN 0080-1593) *32*
Alberta Research Council. Reports (CN) *778, 850*
Alberta Research Council. River Engineering and Surface Hydrology Reports (CN) *307, 374*
Alberta Rural Development Studies (CN ISSN 0707-9818) *12*
Alberta Shippers Guide *see* Alberta Motor Transport Directory *881*
Alberta Statistical Review (CN ISSN 0317-3925) *832*
Alberta Teachers' Association. Audio-Visual Council. Newsletter *see* Alberta Teachers' Association. Learning Resources Council. Newsletter *347*
Alberta Teachers' Association. Learning Resources Council. Newsletter (CN ISSN 0380-8491) *347*
Alberta Teachers Association. Mathematics Monograph (CN ISSN 0317-8579) *347, 584*
Alberta Teachers' Association. Members' Handbook (CN ISSN 0706-9839) *314*
Alberta Teachers' Association. Religious Studies & Moral Education Council. Newsletter (CN ISSN 0701-1237) *314*
Alberta Teachers' Association. School Library Council. Newsletter *see* Alberta Teachers' Association. Learning Resources Council. Newsletter *347*
Alberta 4-H Club News *see* Clover Leaflet *408*
Albertan Geographer (CN ISSN 0065-6097) *419*
Album Slavnych Sportovcov (CS) *819*

Album van Draf- en Rensport (NE) *827*
Albury/Wodonga (AT ISSN 0310-7299) *483*
Alcohol and Drug Problems Association of North America Selected Papers of Annual Meetings *see* A D P A Selected Papers of Annual Meetings *286*
Alcohol in Our Society (US) *286*
Alcoholism and Drug Addiction Research Foundation. Annual Report *see* Addiction Research Foundation of Ontario. Annual Report *286*
Alcoholism Digest Annual (US ISSN 0093-3279) *286*
Alcoholism Review (CN ISSN 0002-5038) *286*
Alcoy; Fiesta de Moros y Cristianos (SP ISSN 0065-6127) *401*
Alcuin (UK) *771*
Aldrich Entomology Club. Newsletter (US ISSN 0065-6143) *120*
Alembic (UK ISSN 0140-5136) *578*
Alessandria, Italy. Centro Documentazione e Richerche Economico-Sociali. Quaderno (IT ISSN 0065-6151) *182*
Aletheia (US ISSN 0149-2004) *687*
Alexander Lectures (CN ISSN 0065-616X) *558*
Alexander von Humbolt-Stiftung. Jahresbericht (GW ISSN 0342-6785) *489*
Alfa (BL ISSN 0002-5216) *540, 558*
Alfred A. Knopf Books in Economics (US) *141*
Alfred Benzon Symposium. Proceedings (DK ISSN 0065-6186) *125, 591*
Alfred P. Sloan Foundation. Report (US ISSN 0065-6216) *489*
Algemeen Jaarboek der Schone Kunsten *see* Jaarboek der Schone Kunsten *75*
Algemeen Werkloosheidsfonds. Jaarverslag (NE ISSN 0401-331X) *497*
Algemene Bank Nederland. Annual Report (NE ISSN 0065-6224) *168*
Algemene Practische Rechtverzameling (BE) *508*
Algeria. Institut National Algerien du Commerce Exterieur. Annuaire des Exportateurs (AE) *192*
Algeria. Service Geologique. Bulletin (AE ISSN 0401-345X) *291*
Algodon Hace Sus Cuentas (SP) *854*
ALGOL Bulletin (UK ISSN 0084-6198) *270*
Algoma Outdoors (CN ISSN 0707-3151) *883*
Aligarh Journal of English Studies (II) *558*
Aligarh Muslim University, Aligarh, India. Department of History. Publication (US ISSN 0065-6259) *442*
Alimentaria (MX) *403*
Aliso (US ISSN 0065-6275) *113*
Alkaloids (UK ISSN 0305-9707) *252*
Alkmaarse Historische Reeks (NE) *448*
All About Arizona, the Healthful State (US) *883*
All About Christmas *see* Holiday Book *765*
All About Hawaii *see* Thrum's All About Hawaii *891*
All About Snowmobiles (US) *828*
All Africa Conference of Churches. Refugee Department. Progress Report (KE) *763*
All Africa Conference of Churches. Refugee Department. Project List (KE) *763*
All-Asia Guide (HK ISSN 0072-4939) *419*
All-in-One Directory *see* Gebbie Press All-in-One Directory *264*
All India Architects Directory (II ISSN 0587-4793) *68, 96*
All-India Conference of Linguists. Proceedings (II) *540*
All-India Conference of Linguists. Souvenir (II) *540*
All India Crime Prevention Society. Annual Report and Audited Statement of Accounts (II ISSN 0065-6283) *280*

All India Government Travellers Bungalows Annual Recorder (II ISSN 0065-6291) *883*
All India Handloom Exporters Guide (II) *854*
All India Magic Circle Bulletin (II) *475*
All India Ophthalmological Society. Proceedings (II) *615*
All-India Oriental Conference. Summaries of Papers (II) *668*
All India Report on Agricultural Census (II) *12*
All of Mexico at Low Cost (US ISSN 0533-0653) *883*
All Pakistan Textile Mills Association. Annual Report (PK) *220, 854*
All Pakistan Women's Association. Triennial Conference Report (PK) *900*
All South Carolina Football Annual (US) *823*
Allan Hancock Monographs in Marine Biology (US ISSN 0065-6364) *100*
Allensbacher Almanach (GW) *448*
Allensbacher Jahrbuch der Demoskopie (GW) *811*
Allergologicum; Transactions of the Collegium Internationale (SZ ISSN 0065-6372) *603*
Allergy. Supplementum (DK) *903*
Allertonia (US) *113, 414*
Allgaeuer Geschichtsfreund (GW) *448*
Allgemeine Gastarife in der Bundesrepublik Deutschland (GW) *677*
Allgemeiner Caecilien-Verband. Schriftenreihe (GW) *656, 773*
Allgemeiner Deutscher Tanzlehrer Verband Nachrichten *see* A D T V -Nachrichten *285*
Alliance for Engineering in Medicine and Biology. Proceedings of the Annual Conference (US ISSN 0589-1019) *100, 365, 591*
Alliance Review (US ISSN 0002-6093) *314, 763*
Allied Artists of America. Annual Exhibition (Bulletin) (US) *651*
Allied Artists of America. Exhibition Catalog (US ISSN 0065-6410) *651*
Allied Health Education Directory (US) *330, 591*
Allied Landscape Industry Member Directory (US ISSN 0098-793X) *414*
Allied Medical Education Directory *see* Allied Health Education Directory *330*
Allionia (IT ISSN 0065-6429) *113*
Allis-Chalmers Engineering Review (US ISSN 0002-6123) *903*
Almanac for Computers (US) *81*
Almanac for Geodetic Engineers (PH ISSN 0569-0838) *81*
Almanac of Business and Industrial Financial Ratios (US) *168, 202*
Almanac of Hawaiiana (US ISSN 0065-6453) *466*
Almanac of the Cities (US) *360*
Almanac of the Pacific *see* Thrum's All About Hawaii *891*
Almanac of World Military Power (US ISSN 0065-647X) *638*
Almanacco Calcistico Svizzero (SZ) *823*
Almanacco Repubblicano (IT) *360*
Almanacco Roulotte (IT) *828*
Almanach Africain (FR ISSN 0569-0870) *439*
Almanach der Oesterreichischen Forschung (AU) *778*
Almanach des Organisations Suisses de la Politique de la Science et de l'Enseignement *see* Almanach Wissenschafts- und Bildungspolitischer Organisationen der Schweiz *708*
Almanach du Peuple (CN ISSN 0065-650X) *96, 360*
Almanach du Vieux Geneve *see* Revue du Vieux Geneve *460*
Almanach Moderne (CN) *234*
Almanach Moderne (CN ISSN 0569-096X) *360*
Almanach Moderne Eclair *see* Almanach Moderne *360*
Almanach Sceny Polskiej (PL ISSN 0065-6526) *858*

Almanach Wissenschafts- und Bildungspolitischer Organisationen der Schweiz/Almanach des Organisations Suisses de la Politique de la Science et de l'Enseignement (SZ) *708*
Almanahul Cinema (RM) *648*
Almanak Jakarta (IO ISSN 0301-7621) *360*
Almankh Gomonu Ukrainy (CN ISSN 0441-1196) *360, 391*
Almanaque (UY) *309*
Almanaque (BL) *555*
Almanaque Boricua (PR) *466*
Almanaque Creditario (CK) *26*
Almanaque del Peru (PE) *466*
Almanaque Misal (SP) *467*
Almanaque Nautico (SP ISSN 0080-5963) *81*
Almanaque Puertorriqueno (Year) (PR) *360*
Almanaque Salvadoreno (ES ISSN 0084-6236) *631*
Almanzar's Coins of the World (US) *477*
Almogaren (AU) *47, 56*
Aloka Bharati (II) *418*
Alon le-Technologyah Be-Khinukh *see* Israel. Ministry of Education and Culture. Department of Educational Technology. Bulletin *349*
Alpeninstitut. Schriftenreihe (GW) *779*
Alpenpaesse Alpenstrassen (GW) *883*
Alpenvereins-Jahrbuch (GW ISSN 0065-6534) *828*
Alpha News (US) *347*
Alpha Psi Omega: Playbill (US) *263, 858*
Alpine Garden Society Guides *see* A. G. S. Guides *414*
Alpine Journal (UK ISSN 0065-6569) *419*
Alt-Hildesheim (GW) *903*
Alt-Katholisches Jahrbuch (GW) *776*
Alt-Thueringen (GE ISSN 0065-6585) *47, 448*
Alt- und Neu-Indische Studien (GW ISSN 0170-3242) *442*
Alta Direccion. Monografias (SP) *213*
Altamura (IT ISSN 0569-1346) *652*
Altbabylonische Briefe im Umschrift und Uebersetzung (NE ISSN 0065-6593) *668*
Altdeutsche Textbibliothek. Ergaenzungsreihe (GW ISSN 0065-6607) *558*
Alte Abenteuerliche Reiseberichte (GW) *558*
Altech (II ISSN 0065-6623) *850*
Altern und Entwicklung/Aging and Development (GW ISSN 0084-6252) *428*
Alternate Routes (CN) *47, 795*
Alternative England and Wales (UK) *360*
Alternative London *see* Alternative England and Wales *360*
Alternative Press Syndicate, Inc. Directory *see* A P S Directory *504*
Alternatives in Print (US ISSN 0093-9188) *558, 802*
Altes Handwerk (GW) *401*
Altorientalische Forschungen (GE) *474, 668*
Aluminium Development Council of Australia. Technical Papers (AT ISSN 0084-6279) *626*
Aluminium Intern: Aluminium und Automobil (GW) *626*
Aluminum Smelters (GW) *641*
Aluminum Standards and Data (US ISSN 0065-6658) *626*
Aluminum Standards and Data-Metric (US) *626*
Aluminum Statistical Review (US ISSN 0065-6666) *626*
Aluminum World Survey (UK ISSN 0141-531X) *626*
Alumni Publications: a Catalogue (II) *87*
Am I Eligible? The Easy Way to Calculate the B E O G Index (US) *333*
Amakusa Marine Biological Laboratory. Contributions (JA ISSN 0065-6674) *100*
Amakusa Marine Biological Laboratory. Publications (JA ISSN 0065-6682) *100*

Amalgamated Wireless (Australasia) Ltd. Technical Review see A W A Technical Review *903*
Amateur Athletic Association. Handbook (UK ISSN 0065-6690) *819*
Amateur Athletic Union of the United States. Athletic Library. Official Rules for Competitive Swimming (US ISSN 0091-3413) *819*
Amateur Athletic Union of the United States. Official A A U Basketball Handbook (US ISSN 0090-4414) *903*
Amateur Athletic Union of the United States. Official A A U Judo Rules. see Official A A U Judo Rules *821*
Amateur Athletic Union of the United States. Official Handbook of the A A U Code (US ISSN 0091-3405) *819*
Amateur Athletic Union of the United States. Official Rules for Water Polo (US ISSN 0093-5786) *819*
Amateur Athletic Union of the United States Baton Twirling Rules and Regulations see A A U Baton Twirling Rules and Regulations *818*
Amateur Athletic Union of the United States Junior Olympic Handbook see A A U Junior Olympic Handbook *818*
Amateur Athletic Union of the United States Official A A U Diving Rules see Official A A U Diving Rules *821*
Amateur Athletic Union of the United States Official A A U Synchronized Swimming Handbook see Official A U Synchronized Swimming Handbook *821*
Amateur Athletic Union of the United States Official A A U Trampoline and Tumbling Handbook see Official A A U Trampoline and Tumbling Handbook *821*
Amateur Athletic Union of the United States Official A A U Wrestling Handbook see Official A A U Wrestling Handbook *821*
Amateur Athletic Union of the United States Official Boxing Rules and Guide see A A U Official Boxing Rules and Guide *819*
Amateur Athletic Union of the United States Official Track and Field Handbook, Rules and Records see A A U Official Track and Field Handbook, Rules and Records *819*
Amateur Athletic Union of the United States Official Weightlifting Rules and Guide see A A U Official Weightlifting Rules and Guide *819*
Amateur Chamber Music Players. Directory (US ISSN 0065-6704) *656*
Amateur Gardening Guide (UK) *903*
Amateur Hockey Association of the United States. Official Guide (US ISSN 0516-8635) *819*
Amateur Hockey Association of the United States. Rule Book (US) *819*
Amateur Skating Union of the United States. Offical Handbook (US ISSN 0516-866X) *819*
Amateur Softball Association of America. Official Guide and Rule Book (US ISSN 0065-6739) *823*
Amateur Trapshooting Association. Official Trapshooting Rules (US ISSN 0065-6747) *828*
Amateur Wrestling News (US ISSN 0569-1796) *819*
Amateurfilm Journal (SZ) *648*
Amazonia - Bibliografia (BL ISSN 0100-0977) *87*
Amazoniana; Limnologia et Oecologia Regionalis Systemae Fluminis Amazonas (GW ISSN 0065-6755) *100*
Ambio. Special Reports (NO) *384*
AMCHAM Morocco (American Chamber of Commerce in Morocco) (MR ISSN 0065-7689) *178*
Amenagement du Territoire et Developpement Regional (FR) *182*
America by Car (US ISSN 0569-1966) *883*
America en Cifras (US ISSN 0065-6771) *903*

America: History and Life. Part C: American History Bibliography (US ISSN 0363-1249) *437*
America Latina (BL ISSN 0002-709X) *795*
America Latina. Boletin (PE) *773*
America - Problema (PE ISSN 0065-6763) *811*
America Votes (US ISSN 0065-678X) *708*
American Academy and Institute of Arts and Letters. Proceedings (US ISSN 0145-8493) *489*
American Academy for Jewish Research. Proceedings of the A A J R (US ISSN 0065-6798) *770*
American Academy in Rome. Memoirs (IT ISSN 0065-6801) *258*
American Academy in Rome. Papers and Monographs (IT ISSN 0065-681X) *258*
American Academy of Allergy. Pollen and Mold Committee. Statistical Report (US) *603*
American Academy of Arts and Letters. Proceedings see American Academy and Institute of Arts and Letters. Proceedings *489*
American Academy of Arts and Sciences. Records of the Academy (US ISSN 0065-6844) *71, 779*
American Academy of Environmental Engineers. Roster (US ISSN 0065-6860) *365, 384*
American Academy of Orthopaedic Surgeons. Committee on Instructional Courses. Instructional Course Lectures (US ISSN 0065-6895) *616*
American Academy of Orthopaedic Surgeons. Directory (US ISSN 0516-8856) *616*
American Academy of Osteopathy Yearbook (US) *607*
American Academy of Pediatrics. Committee on Infectious Diseases. Report (US ISSN 0065-6909) *617*
American Academy of Political and Social Science. Monographs (US ISSN 0065-6917) *795*
American Academy of Religion Dissertation Series see A A R Dissertation Series *762*
American Academy of Religion Studies in Religion see A A R Studies in Religion *762*
American Academy of Religion Texts and Translations see A A R Texts and Translations *762*
American Accounting Association. Southeast Regional Group. Collected Papers of the Annual Meeting (US ISSN 0360-8840) *167*
American Agricultural Economics Association. Handbook (US) *26*
American Alpine Journal (US ISSN 0065-6925) *828*
American Animal Hospital Association. Annual Meeting Scientific Proceedings (US) *480, 894*
American Anthropological Association. Abstracts of Meetings (US) *47*
American Anthropological Association. Annual Report and Directory (US ISSN 0065-6933) *47*
American Anthropologist. Special Publication (US ISSN 0065-6941) *47*
American Art Directory (US ISSN 0065-6968) *71*
American Artist Art School Directory see American Artist Directory of Art Schools & Workshops *71*
American Artist Directory of Art Schools & Workshops (US ISSN 0146-9606) *71, 314*
American Artist Product Directory see Product Directory *913*
American Arts Pamphlet Series (UK) *71, 558, 656*
American Assembly of Collegiate Schools of Business. Accredited Schools, Officers, Committees see American Assembly of Collegiate Schools of Business. Membership Directory *141*

American Assembly of Collegiate Schools of Business. Membership Directory. (US) *141, 333*
American Association for Automotive Medicine. Proceedings (US ISSN 0401-6351) *592, 869*
American Association for Conservation Information. Yearbook (US ISSN 0065-6984) *903*
American Association for Textile Technology. Technical Review and Register (US ISSN 0065-7069) *854*
American Association for the Advancement of Science. Committee on Desert and Arid Zone Research. Contributions (US ISSN 0569-2393) *288*
American Association for the Advancement of Science. Handbook; Officers, Organization, Activities (US ISSN 0361-7874) *779*
American Association for the Advancement of Science. Meeting Program. (US ISSN 0361-1833) *779*
American Association for the Advancement of Science Selected Symposia Series see A A A S Selected Symposia Series *778*
American Association for the Advancement of Slavic Studies. Directory of Members (US ISSN 0516-9240) *448*
American Association of Cereal Chemists. Monograph Series (US ISSN 0065-7107) *403*
American Association of Colleges for Teacher Education. Bulletin (US ISSN 0002-7413) *333*
American Association of Colleges for Teacher Education. Directory (US ISSN 0516-9313) *330, 333*
American Association of Colleges for Teacher Education Yearbook see A C T E Yearbook *333*
American Association of Community and Junior Colleges. Governmental Affairs Special (US ISSN 0065-7239) *904*
American Association of Cost Engineers. Transactions of the Annual Meeting (US ISSN 0065-7158) *365*
American Association of Engineering Societies. Engineering Manpower Commission. Engineering and Technology Degrees (US ISSN 0071-0393) *365*
American Association of Engineering Societies. Engineering Manpower Commission. Engineering Enrollment Data. (US) *205, 365*
American Association of Engineering Societies. Engineering Manpower Commission. Engineers' Salaries: Special Industry Report. (US ISSN 0071-0415) *205, 365*
American Association of Engineering Societies. Engineering Manpower Commission. Placement of Engineering and Technology Graduates. (US) *205, 365*
American Association of Engineering Societies. Engineering Manpower Commission. Professional Income of Engineers. (US ISSN 0071-0423) *205, 365*
American Association of Engineering Societies. Engineering Manpower Commission. Salaries of Engineering Technicians and Technologists. (US) *205, 365*
American Association of Engineering Societies. Engineering Manpower Commission. Salaries of Engineers in Education. (US) *333, 365*
American Association of Equine Practitioners. Proceedings of the Annual Convention (US ISSN 0065-7182) *894*
American Association of Feed Microscopists Proceedings of Annual Meeting see A A F M Proceedings of Annual Meeting *626*
American Association of Foot Specialists. Program Journal (US ISSN 0065-7190) *624*

American Association of Genito-Urinary Surgeons. Transactions (US ISSN 0065-7204) *624, 625*
American Association of Instructors of the Blind. Biennial Conference Proceedings see Association for Education of the Visually Handicapped. Selected Papers from A E V H Biennial Conferences *345*
American Association of Medical Clinics. Directory see American Group Practice Association Directory *480*
American Association of Medical Milk Commissions. Methods and Standards for the Production of Certified Milk (US ISSN 0065-7263) *40*
American Association of Motor Vehicle Administrators. Annual Conference. Proceedings (US ISSN 0065-7271) *881*
American Association of Obstetricians and Gynecologists. Transactions (US ISSN 0065-728X) *614*
American Association of Pathologists and Bacteriologists. Symposium. Monographs (US ISSN 0065-7298) *100, 123, 592*
American Association of Petroleum Geologists. Memoir (US ISSN 0065-731X) *291, 677*
American Association of School Administrators. Annotated Bibliographies on Crucial Issues (US) *325*
American Association of State Colleges and Universities. Proceedings (US) *333*
American Association of State Colleges and Universities Studies see A A S C U Studies *333*
American Association of State Highway and Transportation Officals. Reference Book see Reference Book of Highway Personnel *863*
American Association of State Highway and Transportation Officials. Proceedings (US) *874*
American Association of State Highway and Transportation Officials. Sub-Committee on Computer Technology. Proceedings. National Conference (US ISSN 0091-5122) *270, 874*
American Association of Stratigraphic Palynologists. Abstracts of Papers Presented at the Annual Meetings. (US ISSN 0192-7272) *1, 290*
American Association of Stratigraphic Palynologists. Contributions Series (US ISSN 0160-8843) *291*
American Association of Suicidology. Proceedings of the Annual Meeting (US) *734*
American Association of Teachers of Italian. Directory (US) *314, 540*
American Association of Textile Chemists and Colorists. Buyer's Guide (US) *855*
American Association of Textile Chemists and Colorists. National Technical Conference. Book of Papers (US) *855*
American Association of Textile Chemists and Colorists. Products Buyer's Guide see American Association of Textile Chemists and Colorists. Buyer's Guide *855*
American Association of Theological Schools in the United States and Canada. Bulletin see Association of Theological Schools in the United States and Canada. Bulletin *763*
American Association of Theological Schools in the United States and Canada. Directory see Association of Theological Schools in the United States and Canada. Directory *763*
American Association of Variable Star Observers Bulletin see A A V S O Bulletin *80*
American Association of Veterinary Laboratory Diagnosticians. Proceedings of Annual Meeting (US ISSN 0098-3543) *894*
American Association of Workers for the Blind. Proceedings (US ISSN 0065-7395) *803*

American Association of Zoological Parks and Aquariums. Proceedings. Annual A A Z P A Conference (US ISSN 0090-4473) 127
American Astrology Digest (US ISSN 0516-9550) 80
American Authors and Critics Series (US ISSN 0516-9631) 558
American Automobile Association. Digest of Motor Laws (US ISSN 0093-4062) 508, 869
American Bankers Association. Committee on Uniform Security Identification Procedures. C U S I P Directory (US ISSN 0569-2954) 202
American Bankers Association. Committee on Uniform Security Identification Procedures. C U S I P Directory: Corporate Directory (US ISSN 0091-3804) 202
American Bankers Association. National Operations & Automation Conference. Proceedings (US ISSN 0095-5396) 168, 270
American Bankers Association. Operations and Automation Division. Results of the National Automation Survey see American Bankers Association. Operations and Automation Division. Results of the National Operations & Automation Survey 168
American Bankers Association. Operations and Automation Division. Results of the National Operations & Automation Survey (US ISSN 0363-2539) 168, 270
American Bankers Association Key to Routing Numbers (US) 168
American Bantam Association. Yearbook (US ISSN 0065-745X) 43
American Baptist Churches in the U.S.A. Directory (US ISSN 0091-9381) 771
American Baptist Churches in the U. S. A. Yearbook (US ISSN 0092-3478) 771
American Bar Association. Section of Administrative Law. Annual Reports of Committees (US ISSN 0090-3647) 508
American Bar Association. Section of Administrative Law. Annual Reports of Divisions and Committees see American Bar Association. Section of Administrative Law. Annual Reports of Committees 508
American Bar Association. Section of Labor Relations Law. Committee Reports. (US) 205, 508
American Bar Association. Section of Labor Relations Law. Proceedings (US) 205, 508
American Bar Association. Section of Labor-Relations Law. Report see American Bar Association. Section of Labor Relations Law. Committee Reports 205
American Bar Association. Section of Local Government Law. Committee Reports. (US ISSN 0587-2936) 508
American Bar Association. Standing Committee on Legal Assistance for Servicemen. Occasional Newsletter see L A M P Occasional Newsletter 639
American Bar Association Lawyers' Title Guaranty Funds Newsletter see A B A Lawyers' Title Guaranty Funds Newsletter 508
American Bar Foundation. Research Contributions (US ISSN 0065-7549) 508
American Bell Association. Directory (US ISSN 0093-1330) 656
American Bench-Judges of the Nation (US ISSN 0160-2578) 508
American Bibliography of Russian and East European Studies see American Bibliography of Slavic and East European Studies 437
American Bibliography of Slavic and East European Studies (US ISSN 0569-3497) 437
American Blue Book of Funeral Directors (US ISSN 0065-7565) 414

American Board of Professional Psychology. Policies and Procedures for the Creation of Diplomates in Professional Psychology (US) 734
American Book Prices Current (US ISSN 0091-9357) 760
American Book Prices Current. Five Year Index (US) 760
American Book Publishing Record/B P R (US ISSN 0002-7707) 760
American Book Trade Directory (US ISSN 0065-759X) 757
American Broncho-Esophagological Association. Transactions (US ISSN 0065-7603) 617
American Bureau of Metal Statistics. Year Book see Non-Ferrous Metal Data 629
American Bureau of Shipping. Record (US) 877
American Bus Association. Report (US) 861
American Business in Argentina (AG) 234
American Camellia Yearbook (US ISSN 0065-762X) 414
American Car Prices see Car Prices 870
American Catholic Philosophical Association. Proceedings (US ISSN 0065-7638) 687, 773
American Cement Directory (US ISSN 0065-7646) 134
American Ceramic Society. Special Publications (US ISSN 0065-7654) 244
American Chamber of Commerce for Brazil. Annual Directory (BL ISSN 0065-7662) 178
American Chamber of Commerce in France. Directory (FR ISSN 0065-7670) 178
American Chamber of Commerce in Italy. Directory (IT ISSN 0569-3667) 178
American Chamber of Commerce in Morocco. Annual Review see AMCHAM Morocco 178
American Chamber of Commerce in Thailand. Handbook Directory (TH) 178
American Chamber of Commerce of Venezuela. Yearbook and Membership Directory see Venezuelan-American Chamber of Commerce and Industry. Yearbook and Membership Directory 180
American Chemical Society. Abstracts of Papers (at the National Meeting) (US ISSN 0065-7727) 245
American Chemical Society. Abstracts of Papers (at the Regional Meetings) (US ISSN 0065-7735) 245
American Chemical Society. Directory of Graduate Research (US) 245, 330
American Chemical Society Laboratory Guide to Instruments, Equipment and Chemicals see Laboratory Guide to Instruments, Equipment and Chemicals 247
American Chemical Society Monographs see A C S Monographs 245
American Chemical Society Symposium on Analytical Calorimetry see Analytical Calorimetry 700
American Chemical Society Symposium Series see A C S Symposium Series 245
American Clinical and Climatological Association. Transactions (US ISSN 0065-7778) 592
American College of Cardiology. Symposia (US) 606
American College of Hospital Administrators. Directory (US ISSN 0065-7794) 480
American College of Physicians. Directory (US) 592
American College of Psychiatrists. Papers Presented at the Annual Meeting (US) 618

American College Public Relations Association. Directory see Council for Advancement and Support of Education. Membership Directory 335
American College Testing Program. Annual Report (US ISSN 0517-0680) 333
American College Testing Program. Handbook for Financial Aid Administrators (US ISSN 0094-2227) 343
American College Testing Program Monograph Series see A C T Monograph Series 333
American College Testing Program Research Report see A C T Research Report 333
American Concrete Institute. Compilation (US ISSN 0517-0745) 134
American Concrete Institute. Proceedings (US ISSN 0097-4145) 134
American Concrete Institute. Special Publication (US ISSN 0065-7891) 134
American Concrete Institute Bibliography see A C I Bibliography 87
American Concrete Institute Manual of Concrete Practice see A C I Manual of Concrete Practice 134
American Concrete Institute Monograph see A C I Monograph 134
American Conference of Academic Deans. Proceedings (US ISSN 0065-7905) 333
American Conference of Governmental Industrial Hygienists. Transactions of the Annual Meeting (US) 495
American Congress on Surveying and Mapping. Papers from the Annual Meetings see American Congress on Surveying and Mapping. Proceedings 419
American Congress on Surveying and Mapping. Proceedings (US ISSN 0161-0945) 419
American Constitutional and Legal History (US) 466, 508
American Cooperation Yearbook (US ISSN 0065-793X) 180
American Correctional Association. Annual Congress of Correction. Proceedings (US ISSN 0065-7948) 280
American Council of Independent Laboratories. Directory (US ISSN 0065-7964) 779, 850
American Council of Life Insurance. Economic and Investment Report (US ISSN 0459-3650) 202, 497
American Council on Consumer Interests. Proceedings of the Annual Conference (US ISSN 0275-1356) 279
American Council on Industrial Arts Teacher Education. Yearbook (US ISSN 0084-6333) 314
American Council on the Teaching of Foreign Languages Annual Review of Foreign Language Education see A C T F L Annual Review of Foreign Language Education 347
American Country Life Association. Proceedings of the Annual Conference (US ISSN 0065-7999) 314, 811
American Criminologist (US ISSN 0002-8126) 280
American Criminologist's Newsletter see American Criminologist 280
American Croat/Americki Hrvat (US) 391
American Crystallographic Association. Monographs (US ISSN 0514-8863) 250
American Crystallographic Association. Program & Abstracts (US ISSN 0569-4221) 250, 695
American Crystallographic Association. Transactions (US ISSN 0065-8006) 250
American Culture (US ISSN 0065-8014) 466

American Dental Association. Annual Reports and Resolutions (US ISSN 0090-3329) 609
American Dental Directory (US ISSN 0065-8073) 609
American Dexter Cattle Association. Herd Book (US ISSN 0065-8081) 43
American Dialect Society. Publication (US) 540
American Diamond and Jewelry Trade Directory (US) 503
American Dietetic Association. Annual Report and Proceedings (US) 665
American Diplomatic History Series (US) 466
American Dissertations on Foreign Education (US) 87, 325
American Doctoral Dissertations (US ISSN 0065-809X) 333
American Drop-Shippers Directory (US ISSN 0065-8103) 217, 234
American Drug Index (US ISSN 0065-8111) 683
American Druggist Blue Book (US ISSN 0364-7471) 683
American Educational Research Association. Annual Meeting Paper and Symposia Abstracts (US ISSN 0084-6341) 314
American Educational Theatre Association. Annual Directory of Members see American Theatre Association. Annual Directory of Members 858
American Electronics Association Directory (US) 351
American Engineering Model Society Seminar (Papers) see A E M S Seminar (Papers) 365
American Enterprise Institute for Public Policy Research. A E I Forums (US) 708
American Enterprise Institute for Public Policy Research. Debates, Meetings and Symposia see American Enterprise Institute for Public Policy Research. A E I Forums 708
American Enterprise Institute for Public Policy Research. Evaluative Studies Series see Contemporary Economic Problems 741
American Enterprise Institute for Public Policy Research. Legislative Analyses(US) 708
American Enterprise Institute for Public Policy Research. Legislative and Special Analyses see American Enterprise Institute for Public Policy Research. Legislative Analyses 708
American Enterprise Institute for Public Policy Research. Long-Range Studies see Contemporary Economic Problems 741
American Enterprise Institute for Public Policy Research. Reprints (US) 708
American Enterprise Institute for Public Policy Research. Review, Session of the Congress (US ISSN 0360-165X) 739
American Enterprise Institute for Public Policy Research Hoover Policy Studies see A E I Hoover Policy Studies 707
American Entomological Institute. Contributions (US ISSN 0569-4450) 120
American Entomological Institute. Memoirs (US ISSN 0065-8162) 120
American Entomological Society. Memoirs (US ISSN 0065-8170) 120
American Ephemeris and Nautical Almanac see Astronomical Almanac 81
American Ethnological Society. Monographs (US ISSN 0065-8197) 811
American Ethnological Society. Proceedings of Spring Meeting (US ISSN 0065-8200) 47
American Executive Travel Companion (US ISSN 0363-535X) 883
American Exploration and Travel (US ISSN 0065-8219) 466
American Export Register (US) 192
American Federation of Jews from Central Europe. Proceedings (US) 904

American Federation of Teachers. Convention Proceedings (Abridged) (US) 314, 506
American Federation of Teachers Issues Bulletin see A F T Issues Bulletin 506
American Fertilizer Handbook see Farm Chemicals Handbook 35
American Film Festival Guide (US) 648
American Film Review (US ISSN 0065-8308) 648
American Fisheries Directory and Reference Book (US) 395
American Fisheries Society. Special Publications (US ISSN 0097-0638) 395
American Folk Music Occasional (US ISSN 0065-8316) 656
American Forage and Grassland Council. Proceedings of the Research Industry Conference (US) 41
American Foreign Policy Library (US) 466
American Foreign Relations-a Documentary Record (US) 719
American Foundation for the Blind. Annual Report (US ISSN 0065-8359) 803
American Foundation for the Study of Man. Publications (US ISSN 0569-4833) 47
American Foundations and Their Fields see Foundation Directory 810
American Foundrymen's Society. Transactions (US ISSN 0065-8375) 626
American Friends Service Committee. Annual Report (US ISSN 0071-9617) 803
American Frozen Food Institute. Membership Directory (US ISSN 0084-635X) 403
American Fulbright Scholars (US) 342
American Gas Association. Operating Section. Proceedings (US ISSN 0362-4994) 677
American Gas Association. Research and Development (US ISSN 0091-2786) 677
American Gem Society. Member Suppliers (US ISSN 0065-8405) 503
American Geographical Society of New York. Occasional Publication (US ISSN 0065-8413) 419
American Geographical Society of New York. Research Series (US ISSN 0065-8421) 419
American Geographical Society of New York. Special Publication (US ISSN 0065-843X) 419
American Geophysical Union. Geophysical Monograph Series (US ISSN 0065-8448) 303
American Goat Society. Year Book (US ISSN 0065-8456) 43
American Government. Text see Annual Editions: Readings in American Government 708
American Group Practice Association Directory (US ISSN 0098-2377) 480
American Guild of Variety Artists Newsletter see A G V A Newsletter 506
American Gynecological Society. Transactions of the A G S (US ISSN 0065-8480) 614
American Heart Association. Monographs (US ISSN 0065-8499) 606
American Heart Association. Scientific Sessions. Abstracts (US ISSN 0065-8502) 606
American Helicopter Society. National Forum. Proceedings (US ISSN 0065-8510) 7
American-Hellenic Chamber of Commerce. Business Directory see American-Hellenic Chamber of Commerce. Business Directory. Special Issue 234
American-Hellenic Chamber of Commerce. Business Directory. Special Issue (GR ISSN 0065-8537) 234
American Heraldic Challenger-Informer(US) 416

American Heritage Index (US) 1, 437
American Historical Association. Annual Report (US ISSN 0065-8561) 466
American History Research Series (US) 466
American Home Economics Association. Textiles and Clothing Section. Textile Handbook (US ISSN 0065-8588) 855
American Hospital Association Guide to the Health Care Field see Guide to the Health Care Field 481
American Hospital Formulary Service (US) 683
American Hotel and Motel Association. Buyers Guide for Hotels & Motels. (US) 482
American Hotel and Motel Association. Product News. see American Hotel and Motel Association. Buyers Guide for Hotels & Motels 482
American Humane Association. National Humane Report see American Humane Association Annual Report 803
American Humane Association. National Symposium on Child Abuse. Interdisciplinary Papers (US) 803
American Humane Association Annual Report (US) 803
American Indian Law Review (US ISSN 0094-002X) 391, 508
American Indian Libraries Newsletter (US ISSN 0193-8207) 391, 525
American Industrial Arts Association. Addresses and Proceedings of the Annual Convention (US ISSN 0065-8618) 850
American Industrial Arts Association. Focus Series (US) 850
American Industrial Arts Association. Monograph Series (US ISSN 0517-2306) 850
American Industrial Arts Association. Yearbook see American Council on Industrial Arts Teacher Education. Yearbook 314
American Industrial Real Estate Association. Journal (US ISSN 0065-8642) 761
American Institute for Decision Sciences. National Conference Proceedings (US) 213
American Institute for Decision Sciences. Southeast Section. Proceedings (US ISSN 0360-7100) 214
American Institute for Exploration. Expedition Field Reports (US) 419
American Institute for Exploration. Occasional Contributions (US) 419
American Institute for Exploration. Occasional Papers see American Institute for Exploration. Occasional Contributions 419
American Institute for Exploration. Reprint Series (US) 419
American Institute for Marxist Studies. Bibliographic Series (US ISSN 0065-8650) 717
American Institute for Marxist Studies. Historical Series (US ISSN 0065-8669) 430
American Institute for Marxist Studies. Monograph Series (US ISSN 0065-8677) 708
American Institute for Marxist Studies. Occasional Papers (US ISSN 0084-6368) 708
American Institute of Aeronautics and Astronautics. A I A A Los Angeles Section. Monographs (US ISSN 0065-8685) 7
American Institute of Aeronautics and Astronautics. Paper (US ISSN 0065-8707) 7
American Institute of Aeronautics and Astronautics. Selected Reprint Series (US ISSN 0065-8715) 7
American Institute of Aeronautics and Astronautics Atmospheric Flight Mechanics Conference Proceedings see A I A A Atmospheric Flight Mechanics Conference Proceedings 6

American Institute of Aeronautics and Astronautics Communications Satellite Systems Conference. Technical Papers see A I A A Communications Satellite Systems Conference. Technical Papers 6
American Institute of Aeronautics and Astronautics Roster see A I A A Roster 6
American Institute of Architects Emerging Techniques see A I A Emerging Techniques 68
American Institute of Architects Energy Notebook see A I A Energy Notebook 68
American Institute of Certified Public Accountants. Division of Federal Taxation. Statements on Responsibilities in Tax Practice (US ISSN 0065-874X) 167, 226
American Institute of Certified Public Accountants. Management Advisory Services. Guideline Series (US ISSN 0065-8766) 167
American Institute of Certified Public Accountants Professional Standards see A I C P A Professional Standards 167
American Institute of Chemical Engineers Ch E Continuing Education Series see A I Ch E Continuing Education Series 372
American Institute of Chemical Engineers Ch E Equipment Testing Procedures see A I Ch E Equipment Testing Procedures 372
American Institute of Chemical Engineers Ch E Symposium Series see A I Ch E Symposium Series 372
American Institute of Chemists. Membership Directory (US ISSN 0084-6376) 245
American Institute of Indian Studies Annual Report see A I I S Annual Report 441
American Institute of Industrial Engineers. Computer and Information Systems Division. Monographs (US) 270
American Institute of Industrial Engineers. Engineering Economy Division. Monograph Series (US) 365
American Institute of Industrial Engineers. Facilities Planning and Design Division. Monographs (US) 365
American Institute of Industrial Engineers. Fall Industrial Engineering Conference. Proceedings(US ISSN 0163-1810) 365
American Institute of Industrial Engineers. Management Division. Monographs (US) 365
American Institute of Industrial Engineers. Manufacturing Systems Division. Monographs (US) 365
American Institute of Industrial Engineers. Material Handling Institute. Proceedings (US) 365
American Institute of Industrial Engineers. Operations Research Division. Monographs (US) 365
American Institute of Industrial Engineers. Proceedings of the Spring Annual Conference (US ISSN 0163-5573) 850
American Institute of Industrial Engineers. Production Planning and Control Division. Monographs (US) 365
American Institute of Industrial Engineers. Quality Control and Reliability Engineering Division. Monographs (US) 365
American Institute of Industrial Engineers. Systems Engineering Conference. Proceedings see American Institute of Industrial Engineers. Fall Industrial Engineering Conference. Proceedings 365
American Institute of Industrial Engineers. Work Measurement and Methods Engineering Division. Monographs (US) 365

American Institute of Industrial Engineers, Inc. Industrial and Labor Relations Monograph Series see A I I E. Industrial and Labor Relations Monograph Series 365
American Institute of Islamic Studies. Bibliographic Series (US ISSN 0065-8847) 769
American Institute of Mining, Metallurgical and Petroleum Engineers. Council of Economics. Proceedings of the Annual Meeting (US) 641
American Institute of Mining, Metallurgical and Petroleum Engineers. National Open Hearth and Basic Oxygen Steel Division. Proceedings of the Conference (US) 627, 641, 677
American Institute of Musicology. Miscellanea (GW ISSN 0065-8855) 656
American Institute of Physics. Symposium on Temperature. Proceedings see Temperature: Its Measurement and Control in Science and Industry 700
American Institute of Physics Conference Proceedings see A I P Conference Proceedings 695
American Institute of Ultrasound in Medicine. Annual Scientific Conference. Program (US ISSN 0065-8871) 592, 706
American Institute of Ultrasound in Medicine. Proceedings of Annual Meeting see Ultrasound in Medicine 600
American Insurance Association. Engineering and Safety Service. Special Interest Bulletin (US) 497
American Iron and Steel Institute. Annual Statistical Report (US) 140, 371
American Italian Historical Association. Proceedings (US) 391
American Jewish Committee. Domestic Affairs Department. Pertinent Papers(US) 708
American Jewish Committee. Institute of Human Relations. Pamphlet Series. see American Jewish Committee. Institute of Human Relations. Paperback Series 811
American Jewish Committee. Institute of Human Relations. Paperback Series (US) 811
American Jewish Communal History (US ISSN 0065-8936) 466
American Jewish Historical Society. News see American Jewish Historical Society. Report 770
American Jewish Historical Society. Report (US) 770
American Jewish Organizations Directory (US ISSN 0065-8979) 770
American Jewish Yearbook (US ISSN 0065-8987) 770
American Journal of Ancient History (US ISSN 0362-8914) 430
American Journal of Jurisprudence (US ISSN 0065-8995) 508
American Journal of Videology (US) 618
American Journal of Videotherapy see American Journal of Videology 618
American Junior Colleges (US ISSN 0065-9029) 330
American Laryngological, Rhinological and Otological Society. Transactions (US ISSN 0065-9037) 617
American Law Institute. Annual Meeting. Proceedings (US ISSN 0065-9045) 508
American Lectures in Allergy and Immunology (US) 603
American Lectures in Anatomy (US) 100, 592
American Lectures in Anesthesiology (US) 604
American Lectures in Behavioral Science and Law (US) 508, 734
American Lectures in Cerebral Palsy (US) 618
American Lectures in Clinical Microbiology (US) 123, 592
American Lectures in Clinical Psychiatry (US) 618

American Lectures in Dentistry (US) 609
American Lectures in Dermatology (US) 610
American Lectures in Environmental Studies (US) 384
American Lectures in Epidemiology (US) 750
American Lectures in Geriatrics (US) 428
American Lectures in Gynecology and Obstetrics (US) 615
American Lectures in Hematology (US) 613
American Lectures in Living Chemistry(US) 252
American Lectures in Medical Writing and Communication (US) 592
American Lectures in Nuclear Medicine(US) 622
American Lectures in Objective Psychiatry (US) 618
American Lectures in Orthopaedic Surgery (US) 616
American Lectures in Pharmacology (US) 683
American Lectures in Philosophy (US) 687
American Lectures in Psychology (US) 734
American Lectures in Public Protection (US) 750
American Lectures in Radiation Therapy (US) 622
American Lectures in Roentgen Diagnosis (US) 622
American Lectures in Social and Rehabilitation Psychology (US) 734, 811
American Lectures in Special Education(US) 345
American Lectures in Speech and Hearing (US) 286, 617
American Lectures in Sportsmedicine, Physical Education and Recreation (US) 624, 694
American Lectures in the History of Medicine and Science (US) 592, 779
American Library Association. Annual Conference Program (US) 525, 626
American Library Association Studies in Librarianship see A L A Studies in Librarianship 525
American Library Association Yearbook see A L A Yearbook 525
American Library Directory (US ISSN 0065-910X) 525
American Library Laws (US) 508, 525
American Life Insurance Association. Economic and Investment Report see American Council of Life Insurance. Economic and Investment Report 202
American Literary Scholarship (US ISSN 0065-9142) 558
American Littoral Society. Special Publications (US ISSN 0065-9150) 275
American Lutheran Church. Yearbook (US ISSN 0569-6348) 771
American Malacological Union. Bulletin(US ISSN 0065-9169) 127
American Management Association. Research Studies (US ISSN 0065-9185) 214
American Management Association. Seminar Program (US ISSN 0065-9193) 214
American Management Associations Management Briefings see A M A Management Briefings 213
American Management Associations Survey Reports see A M A Survey Reports 213
American Marine Register (US ISSN 0091-5491) 877
American Maritime Library (US ISSN 0065-9207) 877
American Marketing Association. Committee on Attitude Research. Papers Presented at the Annual Conference (US) 217
American Marketing Association. Directory of Marketing Services and Membership Roster (US ISSN 0093-1454) 217, 234

American Marketing Association. Proceedings (US ISSN 0065-9231) 217
American Mathematical Society. Colloquium Publications (US ISSN 0065-9258) 584
American Mathematical Society. Memoirs (US ISSN 0065-9266) 584
American Mathematical Society. Proceedings of Symposia in Applied Mathematics see S I A M - A M S Proceedings 589
American Mathematical Society. Translations. Series 2 (US ISSN 0065-9290) 584
American Meat Science Association. Reciprocal Meat Conference. Proceedings (US) 43, 403
American Medical Association. Directory of Accredited Residencies (US ISSN 0147-2291) 592
American Medical Association. Directory of Approved Residencies see American Medical Association. Directory of Accredited Residencies 592
American Medical Association. Directory of Officials and Staff (US ISSN 0569-6534) 592
American Medical Association Drug Evaluations see A M A Drug Evaluations 683
American Medical Directory (US ISSN 0065-9339) 592
American Men and Women of Science. Physical and Biological Sciences (US ISSN 0065-9347) 96, 779
American Merchant Marine Conference. Proceedings (US) 877
American Meteorological Society. Meteorological Monographs (US ISSN 0065-9401) 631
American Midland Naturalist Monograph Series (US ISSN 0065-9436) 100
American Montessori Society Proceedings of the National Seminar see A M S. Proceedings of the National Seminar 313
American Motor Carrier Directory: Illinois-Missouri Edition (US ISSN 0146-0781) 881
American Motor Carrier Directory: Middle Atlantic Edition (US ISSN 0146-0803) 881
American Motor Carrier Directory: National Edition see American Motor Carrier Directory: North American Edition 881
American Motor Carrier Directory: New England Edition (US ISSN 0146-0811) 881
American Motor Carrier Directory: New York-New Jersey Edition see American Motor Carrier Directory: Middle Atlantic Edition 881
American Motor Carrier Directory: North American Edition (US) 881
American Motor Carrier Directory: Southeastern Edition (US ISSN 0146-079X) 881
American Motor Carrier Directory: Specialized Services Edition (US ISSN 0569-6364) 881
American Museum Novitates (US ISSN 0003-0082) 779
American Museum of Natural History. Annual Report (US) 652, 779
American Museum of Natural History. Anthropological Papers (US ISSN 0065-9452) 47
American Musical Instrument Society. Journal (US) 656
American Musicological Society. Greater New York Chapter. Publications (US ISSN 0569-6666) 656
American Musicological Society. Studies and Documents (US) 656
American National Metric Council. Annual Report (US ISSN 0363-5260) 636
American National Red Cross. Annual Report see American Red Cross. Annual Report 803
American Neurological Association. Transactions (US ISSN 0065-9479) 618

American Newspaper Markets Circulation (US) 504
American Nuclear Society. Proceedings of the Executive Conference (US) 702
American Nuclear Society. Proceedings of the National Topical Meeting (US) 702
American Nuclear Society. Proceedings of the Pacific Basin Conference on Nuclear Power Development (US) 702
American Nuclear Society Nuclear Science Technology Monograph Series see Nuclear Science Technology Monograph Series 704
American Numismatic Society. Annual Report (US ISSN 0569-6720) 477
American Nurses' Association. Conference for Members and Professional Employees of State Boards of Nursing and A N A Advisory Council. Proceedings (US ISSN 0065-9509) 613
American Nurses' Association. House of Delegates. Reports (US ISSN 0065-9517) 613
American Nurses' Association. House of Delegates. Summary Proceedings (US ISSN 0361-0772) 613
American Nurses Association Clinical Sessions see A N A Clinical Sessions 903
American Ophthalmological Society. Transactions (US ISSN 0065-9533) 615
American Oriental Series (US ISSN 0065-9541) 442
American Ornithologists' Union. Publications (US) 124
American Orthopsychiatric Association. Papers Presented at the Annual Convention (US) 618
American Otological Society. Transactions (US) 617
American Pediatric Society and Society for Pediatric Research. Program and Abstracts (US) 617
American Personnel and Guidance Association. Convention Abstracts (US ISSN 0065-9622) 666
American Petroleum Institute. Central Abstracting and Indexing Service. Thesaurus (US ISSN 0193-5151) 525, 678
American Petroleum Institute. Committee on Medicine and Environmental Health. Medical Research Reports (US) 678, 750, 850
American Petroleum Institute. Division of Refining. Proceedings (US ISSN 0569-6909) 678
American Petroleum Institute. Information Retrieval System, Subject Authority List. see American Petroleum Institute. Central Abstracting and Indexing Service. Thesaurus 678
American Philatelic Congress. Congress Book (US) 478
American Philological Association. Directory of Members (US ISSN 0044-779X) 540
American Philological Association. Special Publications (US ISSN 0065-9703) 258, 540
American Philological Association. Transactions (US ISSN 0360-5949) 540
American Philological Association. Transactions and Proceedings see American Philological Association. Transactions 540
American Philosophical Society. Library Publications (US ISSN 0084-6430) 87
American Philosophical Society. Memoirs (US ISSN 0065-9738) 687
American Philosophical Society. Transactions (US ISSN 0065-9746) 687
American Philosophical Society. Yearbook (US ISSN 0065-9762) 687
American Phytopathological Society. Monographs (US ISSN 0569-6992) 113

American Podiatry Association. Desk Reference and Directory with Catalogue of Audio-Visual, Informational and Educational Materials and Standard Podiatric Nomenclature (US ISSN 0065-9770) 624
American Poetry Series (US) 578
American Political Science Association Departmental Services Program Survey of Departments see A P S A Departmental Services Program Survey of Departments 707
American Political Science Association Directory of Department Chairpersons see A.P.S.A. Directory of Department Chairpersons 707
American Popular Culture (US ISSN 0193-6859) 466
American Powder Metallurgy Institute. Membership Directory and Yearbook see Who's Who in P/M 630
American Power Boat Association. A P B A Rule Book (US ISSN 0065-9797) 826
American Power Conference. Proceedings. (US ISSN 0097-2126) 850
American Printing House for the Blind, Louisville, Kentucky. Department of Educational Research. Annual Report(US ISSN 0065-9800) 345
American Problems Studies (US) 430
American Production and Inventory Control Society. Annual Conference Proceedings (US ISSN 0191-1783) 214
American Psychiatric Association. Biographical Directory (US ISSN 0065-9827) 96, 618
American Psychiatric Association. Membership Directory (US ISSN 0090-4988) 618
American Psychiatric Association. Scientific Proceedings in Summary Form (US ISSN 0090-1881) 618
American Psychiatric Association. Task Force Reports (US) 618
American Psychoanalytic Association. Journal. Monograph (US ISSN 0065-9843) 734
American Psychoanalytic Association. Roster (US) 734
American Psychological Association. Biographical Directory see American Psychological Association. Directory 96
American Psychological Association. Directory (US ISSN 0196-6545) 96, 734
American Psychological Association. Membership Register (US ISSN 0569-714X) 96, 734
American Psychopathological Association. Proceedings of the Annual Meeting (US ISSN 0091-7389) 618
American Psychopathological Association. Publications (US ISSN 0065-9886) 618, 734
American Public Welfare Association. W-Memo (US ISSN 0163-8300) 803
American Public Works Association. Directory (US) 739, 850
American Public Works Association. Research Foundation. Special Reports (US ISSN 0065-9932) 374
American Radio (US) 265, 832
American Railway Bridge and Building Association. Proceedings (US ISSN 0065-9940) 134
American Railway Engineering Association. Proceedings (US) 872
American Red Cross. Annual Report (US) 803
American Reference Books Annual (US ISSN 0065-9959) 87, 538
American Register of Exporters and Importers see American Export Register 192
American Register of Inter-Corporate Ownership see Directory of Inter-Corporate Ownership 222
American Research Center in Egypt. Journal (US ISSN 0065-9991) 56, 71
American Review (JA) 719

American Review of World Health (US ISSN 0003-0813) *750*
American Rheumatism Association. Directory (US) *623*
American Road and Transportation Builders Association Officials and Engineers Directory, Transportation Agency Personnel *see* A R T B A Officials and Engineers Directory, Transportation Agency Personnel *874*
American Rose Annual (US ISSN 0066-0000) *414*
American School of Prehistoric Research. Bulletins (US ISSN 0066-0027) *56*
American Schools of Oriental Research. Annual (US ISSN 0066-0035) *56, 474*
American Series of Foreign Penal Codes (US ISSN 0066-0051) *280*
American Society for Abrasive Methods. Technical Conference. Proceedings *see* Abrasive Engineering Society. Abrasive Usage Conference. Proceedings *365*
American Society for Artificial Internal Organs. Transactions (US ISSN 0066-0078) *624*
American Society for Church Architecture. Journal (US ISSN 0363-5694) *68*
American Society for Conservation Archaeology. Proceedings (US) *56*
American Society for Engineering Education. Annual Conference Proceedings (US ISSN 0190-1052) *365*
American Society for Engineering Education. Review and Directory *see* A S E E Profile *365*
American Society for Engineering Education Profile *see* A S E E Profile *365*
American Society for Horticultural Science. Caribbean Region. Proceedings of the Annual Meeting *see* American Society for Horticultural Science. Tropical Region. Proceedings of the Annual Meeting *414*
American Society for Horticultural Science. Tropical Region. Proceedings of the Annual Meeting (MX ISSN 0066-0116) *414*
American Society for Information Science, Western Canada Chapter. Annual Meeting Proceedings (CN ISSN 0318-9937) *525*
American Society for Metals Bibliography Series *see* A S M. Bibliography Series *631*
American Society for Microbiology. Abstracts of the Annual Meeting (US ISSN 0067-2777) *123*
American Society for Microbiology. Eastern Pennsylvania Branch. Symposia (US) *123*
American Society for Neurochemistry. Transactions (US ISSN 0066-0132) *618*
American Society for Personnel Administration. Personnel and Industrial Relations Colleges (US ISSN 0095-2826) *219*
American Society for Public Administration. Section on International and Comparative Administration. Occasional Papers (US) *739*
American Society for Quality Control. Annual Technical Conference Transactions (US ISSN 0360-6929) *636*
American Society for Quality Control. Transactions of Annual Technical Conferences *see* American Society for Quality Control. Annual Technical Conference Transactions *636*
American Society for Reformation Research. Newsletter *see* Historians of Early Modern Europe. Newsletter *455*
American Society for Testing and Materials. Compilation of A S T M Standards in Building Codes (US ISSN 0066-0523) *134, 377*

American Society for Testing and Materials. Data Series Publications (US ISSN 0066-0531) *377*
American Society for Testing and Materials. Five-Year Index to A S T M Technical Papers and Reports (US ISSN 0066-054X) *377*
American Society for Testing and Materials. Special Technical Publications (US ISSN 0066-0558) *377*
American Society for Testing and Materials Annual Book of A S T M Standards. Part 1. Steel Piping, Tubing, and Fittings *see* Annual Book of A S T M Standards. Part 1. Steel Piping, Tubing, and Fittings *378*
American Society for Testing and Materials Proceedings *see* A S T M Proceedings *377*
American Society for Training and Development. Membership Directory *see* Who's Who in Training and Development *217*
American Society of Agronomy. A S A Special Publication (US ISSN 0066-0566) *12*
American Society of Anesthesiologists Refresher Courses in Anesthesiology *see* A S A Refresher Courses in Anesthesiology *604*
American Society of Animal Science. Western Section Proceedings (US ISSN 0569-7832) *894*
American Society of Appraisers. Appraisal and Valuation Manual (US ISSN 0569-7859) *71, 202, 761*
American Society of Appraisers Monograph *see* A S A Monograph *761*
American Society of Arms Collectors. Bulletin (US ISSN 0362-9457) *475*
American Society of Bakery Engineers. Proceedings of the Annual Meeting (US ISSN 0066-0582) *406*
American Society of Bookplate Collectors and Designers. Year Book (US) *71, 475, 757*
American Society of Chartered Life Underwriters Forum Report *see* C L U Forum Report *498*
American Society of Civil Engineers. Construction Division. Journal (US ISSN 0569-7948) *374*
American Society of Civil Engineers. Energy Division. Journal (US) *374*
American Society of Civil Engineers. Power Division. Journal *see* American Society of Civil Engineers. Energy Division. Journal *374*
American Society of Civil Engineers. Proceedings (US ISSN 0003-1119) *374*
American Society of Civil Engineers. Surveying and Mapping Division. Journal (US ISSN 0569-8073) *374*
American Society of Civil Engineers. Technical Councils. Journal (US) *374*
American Society of Civil Engineers. Transactions (US ISSN 0066-0604) *374*
American Society of Civil Engineers. Urban Planning and Development Division. Journal (US ISSN 0569-8081) *483*
American Society of Civil Engineers. Urban Water Resources Research Program. Technical Memorandum (US ISSN 0066-0612) *895*
American Society of Clinical Hypnosis. Directory (US ISSN 0517-5178) *613*
American Society of Composers, Authors and Publishers Biographical Dictionary *see* A S C A P Biographical Dictionary *656*
American Society of Heating, Refrigerating and Air-Conditioning Engineers Inc. Handbook & Product Directory *see* A S H R A E Handbook & Product Directory *429*
American Society of International Law. Occasional Papers *see* Studies in Transnational Legal Policy *519*
American Society of International Law. Proceedings (US ISSN 0066-0647) *522*

American Society of Mammalogists. Special Publications (US ISSN 0569-8219) *127*
American Society of Mechanical Engineers. Machine Design Division. Papers (US ISSN 0517-5356) *381*
American Society of Ocularists. Selected Papers and Discussions from the Annual Meeting (US) *904*
American Society of Ophthalmologic and Otolaryngologic Allergy. Transactions (US ISSN 0066-0655) *615, 617*
American Society of Pension Actuaries. Transcribings. Annual Conference (US ISSN 0094-422X) *205, 497*
American Society of Photogrammetry. Technical Papers from the Annual Meeting (US ISSN 0066-0663) *419*
American Society of Plant Physiologists. Proceedings of Annual Meeting *see* Plant Physiology. Supplement *117*
American Society of Plastic and Reconstructive Surgeons. Symposia (US) *624*
American Society of Safety Engineers. Proceedings. Professional Conference(US) *365*
American Society of Sanitary Engineering. Year Book (US ISSN 0066-068X) *750*
American Society of Sephardic Studies Series *see* Sephardic Scholar *393*
American Society of University Composers. Proceedings (US ISSN 0066-0701) *656*
American Sociological Association. Proceedings of Annual Meeting (US) *811*
American Speech-Language-Hearing Association Directory *see* A S H A Directory *617*
American Speech-Language-Hearing Association Reports *see* A S H A Reports *617*
American Stamp Catalog (US) *478*
American Statistical Association. Business and Economic Statistics Section. Proceedings (US ISSN 0066-0736) *151*
American Statistical Association. Social Statistics Section. Proceedings (US ISSN 0066-0752) *731*
American Statistical Association. Statistical Computing Section. Proceedings (of the Annual Meeting) (US ISSN 0149-9963) *832*
American Statistical Association. Survey Research Section. Proceedings (US) *832*
American Statistics Index (US ISSN 0091-1658) *832*
American Stock Exchange. AMEX Databook (US ISSN 0066-0760) *202*
American Stock Exchange. Annual Report (US ISSN 0066-0779) *202*
American Studies Research Centre. Newsletter (II ISSN 0066-0795) *466*
American Subsidiaries of German Firms(US) *178*
American Suffolk Sheep Society. Breeders List (US ISSN 0066-0825) *43*
American Surgical Association. Transactions (US ISSN 0066-0833) *624*
American Theatre Annual (US) *858*
American Theatre Association. Annual Directory of Members (US ISSN 0065-8138) *858*
American Theological Library Association. Conference. Summary of Proceedings (US ISSN 0066-0868) *525*
American Theological Library Association Bibliography Series *see* A T L A Bibliography Series *762*
American Theological Library Association Monograph Series *see* A T L A Monograph Series *762*
American Trail Series (US ISSN 0066-0884) *420, 883*
American Translators Association Professional Services Directory *see* A T A Professional Services Directory *539*

American Trucking Trends (US) *882*
American Trucking Trends. Statistical Report *see* American Trucking Trends *882*
American Type Culture Collection. Catalogue of Cells, Viruses, Rickettsiae, Chlamydiae (US) *123*
American Type Culture Collection. Catalogue of Strains Algae, Bacteria, Bacteriophages, Fungi and Protozoa (US ISSN 0363-2970) *123*
American Type Culture Collection. Catalogue of Viruses, Rickettsiae, Chlamydiae *see* American Type Culture Collection. Catalogue of Cells, Viruses, Rickettsiae, Chlamydiae *123*
American Universities and Colleges (US ISSN 0066-0922) *330*
American Universities Field Staff. Annual Report of the Executive Director (US ISSN 0066-1082) *333, 719*
American Universities Field Staff. List of Publications (US ISSN 0066-1104) *810*
American Universities Field Staff. Population: Perspective (US ISSN 0091-5610) *725*
American University. Energy Institute. Proceedings (US ISSN 0071-027X) *361*
American University in Cairo. Annual Report *see* American University in Cairo. President's Review *333*
American University in Cairo. President's Review (UA) *333*
American Veterinary Medical Association. Directory (US ISSN 0066-1147) *894*
American Vocational Association. Yearbook (US) *347*
American Water Resources Conferences. Annual Proceedings (US ISSN 0066-1171) *895*
American Water Works Association. Proceedings, A W W A Annual Conference (US ISSN 0360-814X) *895*
American Wildlife Region Series (US ISSN 0569-9096) *100, 275*
American Wine Society. Bulletin (US ISSN 0149-6778) *85, 475*
American Wine Society Manual (US ISSN 0149-676X) *85*
American Youth Hostels Guide and Handbook *see* A Y H Handbook *882*
American Youth Hostels, Inc. Handbook *see* A Y H Handbook *882*
Americans Before Columbus (US ISSN 0066-121X) *466*
Americans for Constitutional Action. Report (US ISSN 0066-1236) *708*
Americans for Constitutional Action Index *see* A C A Index *707*
Americki Hrvat *see* American Croat *391*
Amerindia (UY) *47*
Amerindia (FR) *47, 540*
Amino-Acids, Peptides and Proteins (UK ISSN 0306-0004) *110*
Amis de l'E.N.S.B.A.N.A. *see* Ecole Nationale Superieure de Biologie Appliquee a la Nutrition et a l'Alimentation. Cahiers *665*
Amis de l'Histoire de la Perade. Collection "Nos Vielles Familles" (CN) *416*
Amis de l'I.B.A.N.A.(Publication) *see* Ecole Nationale Superieure de Biologie Appliquee a la Nutrition et a l'Alimentation. Cahiers *665*
Amitie Henri Bosco. Cahiers (FR ISSN 0399-1121) *558*
AMLI Studies in Music Bibliography (IS ISSN 0066-1260) *656*
Ammonia Plant Safety and Related Facilities (US ISSN 0066-7011) *372*
Amnesty International (Toronto Group) Newsletter (CN ISSN 0382-6295) *708*
Amnesty International Annual Report *see* Amnesty International Report *719*
Amnesty International Report (UK) *719*

Amoeba (SA ISSN 0066-1279) 263, 592
Ampurias (SP) 56
Amsterdam. Gemeentelijke Archiefdienst. Jaarverslag (NE) 448
Amsterdam Hydrology Series (NE) 307
Amsterdam-Rotterdam Bank. Annual Report (NE ISSN 0066-1309) 168
Amsterdam Studies in the Theory and History of Linguistic Science. Series 1: Amsterdam Classics in Linguistics, 1800-1925 (NE ISSN 0304-0712) 540
Amsterdam Studies in the Theory and History of Linguistic Science. Series 3: Studies in the History of Linguistics (NE ISSN 0304-0720) 540
Amsterdam Studies in the Theory and History of Linguistic Science. Series 4: Current Issues in Linguistic Theory (NE ISSN 0304-0763) 540
Amsterdam Studies in Theology (NE) 763
Amsterdamer Beitraege zur Neueren Germanistik (NE) 448, 558
Amsterdamer Publikationen zur Sprache und Literatur (NE) 540, 558
Amusement Business's AudArena Stadium Guide see Audarena Stadium Guide and International Directory 4
Amusement Business's Cavalcade of Acts & Attractions see Cavalcade and Directory of Acts & Attractions 858
Amusement Business's Directory North American Fairs see Directory of North American Fairs and Expositions 5
Amusement Business's Funparks Directory see Funparks Directory 886
Amusement Equipment Buyers Guide see Buyers' Guide for the Mass Entertainment Industry 828
Anadolu Sanati Arastirmalari/ Researches on Anatolian Art (TU ISSN 0066-1333) 71
Anaesthesiologie und Intensivmedizin/ Anaesthesiology and Intensive Care Medicine (US) 604
Anaesthesiology and Intensive Care Medicine see Anaesthesiologie und Intensivmedizin 604
Anaesthesiology and Resuscitation see Anaesthesiologie und Intensivmedizin 604
Anais de Historia (BL) 430
Anais Hidrograficos (BL) 895
Aralecta Biblica. Investigationes Scientificae in Res Biblicas (VC ISSN 0066-135X) 763
Analecta Boerhaaviana (NE ISSN 0066-1368) 592
Analecta Cartusiana (AU) 448, 558, 763
Analecta Gregoriana (VC ISSN 0066-1376) 773
Analecta Husserliana (NE) 687
Analecta Musicologia (GW ISSN 0569-9827) 656
Analecta Orientalia (VC) 668
Analecta Praehistorica Leidensia (NE ISSN 0569-9843) 56
Analecta Romana Instituti Danici (DK ISSN 0066-1392) 448
Analecta Romana Instituti Danici. Supplementum (DK ISSN 0066-1406) 448
Analecta Romanica (GW ISSN 0569-986X) 540, 558
Analecta Vaticano-Belgica. Deuxieme Serie. Section A: Nonciature de Flandre (BE ISSN 0066-1414) 773
Analecta Vaticano-Belgica. Deuxieme Serie. Section B: Nonciature de Cologne (BE ISSN 0066-1422) 773
Analecta Vaticano-Belgica. Deuxieme Serie. Section C: Nonciature de Bruxelles (BE ISSN 0066-1430) 773
Analecta Vaticano-Belgica. Premiere Serie: Documents Relatifs aux Anciens Dioceses de Cambrai, Liege, Therouanne et Tournai (BE ISSN 0066-1449) 773

Anales de Arqueologia y Etnologia (AG) 47, 56
Anales de Cirugia (AG ISSN 0066-1465) 624
Anales de Geografia (MX) 420
Anales de la Comunidad Israelita de Buenos Aires (AG) 391
Anales de la Universidad Hispalense. Serie: Arquitectura (SP) 68
Anales de la Universidad Hispalense. Serie: Ciencias (SP) 779
Anales de la Universidad Hispalense. Serie: Ciencias Economicas y Empresariales see Anales de la Universidad Hispalense. Serie: Empresariales 141
Anales de la Universidad Hispalense. Serie: Derecho (SP) 508
Anales de la Universidad Hispalense. Serie: Empresariales (SP) 141
Anales de la Universidad Hispalense. Serie: Filosofia y Letras (SP) 489, 779
Anales de la Universidad Hispalense. Serie: Ingenieria (SP) 366
Anales de la Universidad Hispalense. Serie: Medicinas (SP) 592
Anales de la Universidad Hispalense. Serie: Veterinaria (SP) 894
Anales de Literatura Hispanoamericana (SP) 559
Anales de Medicina see Anales de Medicina. Especialidades 592
Anales de Medicina see Anales de Medicina. Medicina 592
Anales de Medicina. Especialidades (SP ISSN 0517-6832) 592
Anales de Medicina. Medicina (SP ISSN 0517-6824) 592
Anales de Moral Social y Economica (SP ISSN 0066-1473) 811
Anales del Instituto de Etnologia Americana see Anales de Arqueologia y Etnologia 56
Anales Galdosianos (US) 559
Anali za Sumarstvo see Annales Forestales 407
Analise (BL) 141
Analise Jurisprudencial (BL) 508
Analisis Tecnico del Seguro Privado en el Ecuador (EC) 497
Analizy i Proby Technik Badawczych w Socjologii (PL) 811
Analog Annual (US ISSN 0362-7403) 4
Analogo-Diskretnye Preobrazovaniya Signalov (UR) 270
Analysen (GW ISSN 0072-9426) 708
Analyses of Natural Gases of the United States (US ISSN 0066-149X) 678
Analysis (CN ISSN 0707-5723) 384
Analysis of Cyprus Foreign Trade (CY ISSN 0526-5053) 192
Analysis of Official Pesticide Samples see Louisiana. Department of Agriculture. Analysis of Official Pesticide Samples; Annual Report 37
Analysis of Oregon's Personal Income Tax Returns see Personal Income Tax Analysis 231
Analysis of Organic Materials: an International Series of Monographs (US) 252
Analysis of Public Utility Financing (US ISSN 0421-9910) 168
Analysis of School Finances, New York State School Districts (US ISSN 0077-9342) 343
Analysis of Workers' Compensation Laws (US ISSN 0191-118X) 497, 508, 803
Analysis of Workmen's Compensation Laws see Analysis of Workers' Compensation Laws 803
Analysis of World Tank Ship Fleet (US) 877
Analyst (US ISSN 0066-152X) 559
Analysts Handbook (US) 202
Analytical Calorimetry (US ISSN 0066-1538) 366, 700
Analytical Chemistry of the Elements Series (US) 249
Analytical Chemistry Symposia Series (NE) 249

Analytical Methods for Pesticides, Plant Growth Regulators and Food Additives (US) 12
Analytical Profiles of Drug Substances (US) 683
Analytical Sciences Monographs (UK ISSN 0583-8894) 249
Ananda Acharya Universal Series (II) 559, 687
Anarcho Surrealist Insurrectionary Feminists Collective see A S I F 47
Anasthesiologische Praxis see Intensivmedizinische Praxis 604
Anatolian Studies (UK ISSN 0066-1546) 56
Anatolica (NE ISSN 0066-1554) 56, 442
Anatomische Gesellschaft. Verhandlungen (GE ISSN 0066-1562) 100, 592
Anbar Management Publications Bibliography (UK ISSN 0261-0108) 151
Anbar Management Services Bibliography see Anbar Management Publications Bibliography 151
Anbar Yearbook (UK ISSN 0307-0409) 214
Anciens Eleves de l'Ecole Technique d'Aeronautique et de Construction Automobile. Annuaire (FR) 7, 869
Anciens Pay et Assemblees d'Etats (BE ISSN 0066-1589) 708
Ancient Ceylon (CE) 771
Ancient Coins in North American Collections (US) 477
Ancient Culture and Societies (US) 47, 430
Ancient Greek Cities Report (GR) 430, 483, 811
Ancient Interface (US ISSN 0097-8442) 877
Ancient Iranian Cultural Society. Publication/Ansoman-e Farhang-e Iran-e Bastan. Nashrijeh (IR ISSN 0517-8045) 771
Ancient Monuments Board for England. Annual Report (UK ISSN 0072-5625) 448
Ancient Monuments Society Transactions (UK) 56, 134, 448
Ancient Society (BE ISSN 0066-1619) 430
Anda (IO) 734
Andar per Ceramiche (IT ISSN 0003-2891) 244
Anderseniana (DK ISSN 0084-6465) 559
Anderson Hospital and Tumor Institute, Houston, Texas. General Report (US ISSN 0066-1627) 604
Anderson Hospital and Tumor Institute, Houston, Texas. Research Report (US ISSN 0066-1635) 604
Andhra Historical Research Society. Journal (II) 442
Andhra Pradesh, India. Department of Archaeology and Museums. Art and Architecture Series (II) 68, 71
Andhra Pradesh, India. Department of Archaeology and Museums. Epigraphy Series (II) 56, 442
Andhra Pradesh, India. Department of Archaeology and Museums. Museum Objects and Numismatics Series (II) 442, 477
Andhra Pradesh, India. Department of Archaeology. Epigraphy Series see Andhra Pradesh, India. Department of Archaeology and Museums. Epigraphy Series 56
Andhra Pradesh, India. Department of Archaeology. Museum Series see Andhra Pradesh, India. Department of Archaeology and Museums. Museum Objects and Numismatics Series 477
Andhra Pradesh Small Scale Industrial Development Corporation. Annual Report (II ISSN 0376-804X) 234
Andhra Pradesh State Financial Corporation. Report see Andhra Pradesh State Financial Corporation. Report and Accounts 226
Andhra Pradesh State Financial Corporation. Report and Accounts (II) 226

Andhra Pradesh State Trading Corporation Limited. Annual Report (II ISSN 0376-5512) 217
Andhra University Memoirs in Oceanography (II ISSN 0066-1686) 309
Andre Gide (FR) 559
Andrew H. Clark Series in the Historical Geography of North America (US) 420
Andrew W. Mellon Foundation. Report(US ISSN 0066-1694) 489
Andrews University. Monographs (US ISSN 0066-1708) 771
Anejos de Archivo Espanol de Arqueologia (SP ISSN 0561-3663) 56
Angewandte Ornithologie/Applied Ornithology (GW ISSN 0003-3154) 124
Anglers' Annual see Fishing Waters 829
Anglers Cooperative Association Review see A.C.A. Review 395
Anglesey Antiquarian Society Transactions (UK ISSN 0306-5790) 56
Anglica Germanica: Series 2 (UK) 540, 858
Anglican Church of Canada. General Synod. Journal of Proceedings (CN ISSN 0380-2469) 771
Anglican Crusader see Crusader (Toronto) 771
Anglican Year Book (CN ISSN 0317-8765) 771
Anglistica (DK ISSN 0066-1805) 559
Anglistische Forschungen (GW) 559
Anglo-American Aeronautical Conference. Proceedings (UK) 7
Anglo American Directory of Mexico (MX) 1, 731
Anglo-American Forum (SZ) 430, 540, 559
Anglo-Saxon England (UK) 489
Angol Filologiai Tanulmanyok/ Hungarian Studies in English (HU ISSN 0570-0973) 540, 559
Angola. Direccao dos Servicos de Estatistica. Anuario Estatistico (AO ISSN 0066-5193) 832
Angola. Direccao dos Servicos de Estatistica. Estatistica dos Veiculos Motorisados (AO) 864
Angola. Direccao dos Servicos de Estatistica. Estatisticas do Comercio Externo (AO ISSN 0066-1848) 151
Angola. Direccao dos Servicos de Estatistica. Informacoes Estatisticas (AO) 832
Angola. Direccao Provincial dos Servicos de Geologia e Minas. Boletim (AO ISSN 0003-3456) 291, 641
Angola. Secretaria Provincial de Saude, Trabalho. Previdencia e Assistencia. Sintese da Actividade dos Servicos e Organismos (AO) 694, 739
Animal Agriculture Series (US) 32
Animal Anti-Cruelty League. Chairman's Report (SA) 682
Animal Health see Animal Health Trust. Annual Report 894
Animal Health Trust. Annual Report (UK ISSN 0142-6591) 894
Animal Health Yearbook (UN ISSN 0066-1872) 894
Animal Quarantine (AT) 894
Animals for Research (US ISSN 0547-8626) 127
Anjoman-e Dabiran-e Zabanha-Ye Khareji. Nashriyeh see English Language Teachers Association. Review 348
Anleitung fuer die Chemische Laboratoriumspraxis (US ISSN 0066-1910) 245, 612
Annalen der Meteorologie. Neue Folge (GW ISSN 0072-4122) 631
Annalen der Mijnen van Belgie see Annales des Mines de Belgique 641
Annales Academiae Medicae Cracoviensis. Index Dissertationum Editarum (PL ISSN 0066-1937) 601
Annales Academiae Medicae Stetinensis(PL ISSN 0066-1945) 592

Annales Academiae Scientiarum Fennicae. Dissertationes Humanarum Litterarum (FI ISSN 0355-113X) 489
Annales Academiae Scientiarum Fennicae. Series A, 1: Mathematica (FI ISSN 0066-1953) 584
Annales Academiae Scientiarum Fennicae. Series A, 2: Chemica (FI ISSN 0066-1961) 245
Annales Academiae Scientiarum Fennicae. Series A, 3: Geologica-Geographica (FI ISSN 0066-197X) 291
Annales Academiae Scientiarum Fennicae. Series A, 5: Medica (FI ISSN 0066-1996) 592
Annales Academiae Scientiarum Fennicae. Series A, 6: Physica (FI ISSN 0066-2003) 695
Annales Academiae Scientiarum Fennicae. Series B (FI ISSN 0066-2011) 779
Annales Bogorienses (IO ISSN 0517-8452) 113
Annales d'Economie et de Sociologie Rurales (FR) 26, 811
Annales d'Esthetique/Chronika Aisthetikes (GR ISSN 0066-2119) 71, 687
Annales d'Etudes Internationales/Annals of International Studies (BE ISSN 0066-2135) 904
Annales de Demographie Historique (NE ISSN 0066-2062) 725
Annales de l'Institut Fourier see Universite Scientifique et Medicale de Grenoble. Institut Fourier. Annales 590
Annales des Antilles (MQ ISSN 0517-855X) 466
Annales des Mines de Belgique/Annalen der Mijnen van Belgie (BE ISSN 0003-4290) 641
Annales du Tabac (FR) 860
Annales Economiques de Clermont-Ferrand (FR) 141
Annales Forestales/Anali za Sumarstvo (YU) 407
Annales Hindemith see Hindemith-Jahrbuch 659
Annales Hydrographiques (FR ISSN 0373-3629) 307
Annales Medicinae Internae see Annals of Clinical Research. Supplementum 612
Annales Moreau de Tours (FR ISSN 0066-2186) 683
Annales Musei Archaeologici Posnaniensis see Fontes Archaeologici Posnanienses 60
Annales Musei Goulandris (GR) 652
Annales Odonto-Stomatologiques (FR ISSN 0066-2194) 609
Annales Paderewski (SZ) 656
Annales Paediatriae Fenniae. Supplementum see Annals of Clinical Research. Supplementum 612
Annales Polonici Mathematici (PL ISSN 0066-2216) 584
Annales Silesiae (PL ISSN 0066-2224) 448
Annales Societatis Mathematicae Polonae. Series 4: Fundamenta Informaticae (PL) 270, 584
Annales Universitatis Mariae Curie-Sklodowska. Sectio A. Mathematica (PL ISSN 0365-1029) 584
Annales Universitatis Mariae Curie-Sklodowska. Sectio B. Geographia, Geologia, Mineralogia et Petrographia (PL ISSN 0137-1983) 291, 420
Annales Universitatis Mariae Curie-Sklodowska. Sectio C. Biologia (PL ISSN 0066-2232) 100
Annales Universitatis Mariae Curie-Sklodowska. Sectio D. Medicina (PL ISSN 0066-2240) 592
Annales Universitatis Mariae Curie-Sklodowska. Sectio DD. Medicina Veterinaria (PL ISSN 0301-7737) 894
Annales Universitatis Mariae Curie-Sklodowska. Sectio E. Agricultura (PL ISSN 0365-1118) 12
Annales Universitatis Mariae Curie-Sklodowska. Sectio F. Humaniora (PL ISSN 0137-2033) 489

Annales Universitatis Mariae Curie-Sklodowska. Sectio G. Ius (PL ISSN 0458-4317) 508
Annales Universitatis Mariae Curie-Sklodowska. Sectio H. Oeconomia (PL ISSN 0459-9586) 141
Annales Universitatis Mariae Curie-Sklodowska. Sectio I. Philosophia-Sociologia (PL ISSN 0137-2025) 687, 811
Annales Universitatis Saraviensis. Rechtswissenschaftliche Abteilung. Schriftenreihe (GW) 508
Annales Universitatis Saraviensis. Reihe: Mathematisch-Naturwissenschaftliche Fakultaet (GW ISSN 0080-5165) 779
Annales Universitatis Saraviensis. Wirtschaftswissenschaftliche Abteilung. Schriftenreihe (GW) 141
Annales Universitatis Varsoviensis see Uniwersytet Warszawski. Roczniki 342
Annali di Laringologia, Otologia, Rinologia, Faringologia (IT ISSN 0066-2267) 617
Annali di Matematica (IT ISSN 0003-4622) 584
Annali di Sociologia (IT ISSN 0066-2275) 811
Annali di Storia Economica e Sociale see Quaderni Internazionali di Storia Economica e Sociale 459
Annali di Studi Giuridici e Socio-Economici sul Servizio Sanitari Nazionale e Regionale (IT) 750
Annali Lateranensi (1937-1962) see Pontifico Museo Missionario Etnologico. Annali 52
Annals of Air and Space Law/Annuaire de Droit Aerien et Spatial (CN ISSN 0701-158X) 7, 508
Annals of Clinical Research. Supplementum (FI ISSN 0066-2291) 592, 612
Annals of Glaciology (UK ISSN 0260-3055) 291
Annals of International Studies see Annales d'Etudes Internationales 904
Annals of Mathematics Studies (US) 584
Annals of Phenomenological Sociology (US ISSN 0363-647X) 811
Annals of the Carnegie Museum see Carnegie Museum of Natural History. Annals of (the) Carnegie Museum 780
Annals of the French Revolution (US) 448
Annee Automobile see Automobile Year 869
Annee Automobile (FR) 869
Annee Balzacienne (FR ISSN 0084-6473) 559
Annee Bateaux (FR) 826
Annee de l'Opera et de la Danse (FR) 285, 656
Annee du Cinema (FR) 648
Annee du Cyclisme (FR) 826
Annee du Football (FR) 823
Annee du Medecin (FR) 904
Annee du Rugby (FR) 823
Annee Epigraphique; Revue des Publications Epigraphiques Relatives a l'Antiquite Romaine (FR ISSN 0066-2348) 540
Annee Philologique (FR) 261
Annee Politique Africaine (SG ISSN 0066-2364) 708
Annee Politique Suisse/Schweizerische Politik in Jahre (SZ ISSN 0066-2372) 708
Annee Sociologique (FR ISSN 0066-2399) 812
Annee Sportive U.S.M.T. (Union Sportive Metropolitaine des Transports) (FR) 262, 819
Annee Therapeutique en Ophtalmologie see Annee Therapeutique et Clinique en Ophtalmologie 615
Annee Therapeutique et Clinique en Ophtalmologie (FR ISSN 0301-4495) 615
Annotated Accessions List of Studies and Reports in the Field of Science Statistics (UN) 87

Annotated Bibliography and Index of the Geology of Zambia (ZA ISSN 0066-2410) 291
Annotated Guide to Taiwan Periodical Literature (US ISSN 0066-2445) 87
Annotated Reference Tools in Music Series (US) 656
Annotated Secondary Bibliography Series on English Literature in Transition, 1880-1920 (US) 577
Annuaire Administratif de la Republique du Mali (ML ISSN 0066-2453) 739
Annuaire Administratif et Judiciaire de Belgique/Administratief en Gerechtelijk Jaarboek voor Belgie (BE ISSN 0066-2461) 739
Annuaire Agricole de la Tunisie (TI) 12
Annuaire Batiment et Travaux Publics (FR) 134, 374
Annuaire Bilingue de l'Industrie Nucleaire Francaise see Annuaire de l'Activite Nucleaire Francaise 702
Annuaire Biographique du Cinema et de la Television en France et en Belgique (FR ISSN 0066-247X) 266, 648
Annuaire Bleu/Blue Directory for International Trade (FR) 192
Annuaire Canadien de Droit International see Canadian Yearbook of International Law 522
Annuaire Catholique de France (FR ISSN 0066-2488) 773
Annuaire Chatfield European de Peintures et Produits Assimiles see Chatfield's European Directory of Paints and Allied Products 673
Annuaire d'Etudes en Education au Canada see Directory of Education Studies in Canada 316
Annuaire d'Exportation de l'Autriche see Herold Export-Adressbuch von Oesterreich 238
Annuaire de Droit Aerien et Spatial see Annals of Air and Space Law 7
Annuaire de l'Activite Nucleaire Francaise (FR ISSN 0066-2593) 366, 702
Annuaire de l'Administration et du Corps des Mines (FR ISSN 0071-822X) 641
Annuaire de l'Afrique du Nord (FR ISSN 0066-2607) 796
Annuaire de l'Agriculture (FR) 12
Annuaire de l'Ameublement see Annuaire de l'Ameublement et des Industries s'y Rattachant 503
Annuaire de l'Ameublement et des Industries s'y Rattachant (FR) 503
Annuaire de l'Armement a la Peche (FR ISSN 0066-2623) 395
Annuaire de l'Art International (FR) 71
Annuaire de l'Eclairage (FR ISSN 0066-264X) 351
Annuaire de l'Education Permanente (FR) 314
Annuaire de l'Eglise Catholique au Zaire (ZR) 773
Annuaire de l'Eglise du Quebec (CN ISSN 0706-8328) 773
Annuaire de l'Egyptologie (UA) 57, 668
Annuaire de l'Industrie du Caoutchouc et de ses Derives (FR ISSN 0066-2674) 777
Annuaire de l'U. R. S. S. see Annuaire de l'URSS et des Pays Socialistes Europeens 796
Annuaire de l'URSS et des Pays Socialistes Europeens (FR ISSN 0397-8249) 796
Annuaire de la Chapellerie et de la Mode (FR ISSN 0066-2518) 262
Annuaire de la Chaussure et des Cuirs (FR ISSN 0066-2526) 795
Annuaire de la Cooperation F.N.C.C. (Federation Nationale des Cooperatives de Consommation) (FR ISSN 0071-4356) 180
Annuaire de la France Rurale dans le Marche Commun (FR ISSN 0066-2534) 12
Annuaire de la Maree (FR ISSN 0066-2542) 395
Annuaire de la Marine Marchande (FR ISSN 0066-2550) 877

Annuaire de la Mecanique (FR) 582
Annuaire de la Mecanographie, Materiel de Bureau, Informatique (FR) 219
Annuaire de la Mercerie, Nouveautes, Bonneterie, Lingerie, Confections (FR) 261
Annuaire de la Noblesse de France et d'Europe (FR ISSN 0066-2569) 416
Annuaire de la Papeterie (FR) 675
Annuaire de la Papeterie Francaise see Annuaire de la Papeterie 675
Annuaire de la Photographie Professionnelle (FR ISSN 0084-6481) 692
Annuaire de la Presse et de la Publicite (FR ISSN 0066-2585) 504
Annuaire de la Presse Francaise et Etrangere see Annuaire de la Presse et de la Publicite 504
Annuaire de Legislation Francaise et Etrangere (FR ISSN 0066-2658) 508
Annuaire Defense d'Afrique et du Moyen Orient (FR) 638
Annuaire Dentaire (FR ISSN 0066-2712) 609
Annuaire der Societes Libanaises a Responsibilite Limitee see Year-Book of the Lebanese Limited Liability Companies 205
Annuaire des Agents Commerciaux Courtiers et Representants de Commerce-France et Marche Commun (FR) 192
Annuaire des Annuaires (FR ISSN 0066-2720) 87
Annuaire des Arachnologistes Mondiaux (FR ISSN 0066-2739) 127
Annuaire des Architectes (FR ISSN 0066-2747) 68
Annuaire des Assurances et l'Assureur-Conseil (FR) 497
Annuaire des Avocats (FR ISSN 0396-2318) 508
Annuaire des Boissons et des Liquides Alimentaires/Jahrbuch des Getraenke und Fluessigen Nahrmittel (FR ISSN 0066-2763) 85
Annuaire des Caisses d'Epargne; France et Outre-Mer (FR ISSN 0066-278X) 168
Annuaire des Centrales et Groupements d'Achats (FR) 234
Annuaire des Centres de Recherche Demographique/Directory of Demographic Research Centers (FR) 725
Annuaire des Chambres de Commerce et d'Industrie (FR ISSN 0066-2798) 178
Annuaire des Chercheurs Francais du Fonds de Bourses de Recherche Scientifique et Technique de l'Organisation du Traite de l'Atlantique Nord (FR ISSN 0066-2771) 333
Annuaire des Coiffeurs, des Estheticiens et des Parfumeurs (FR) 85
Annuaire des Communautes d'Enfants (FR ISSN 0069-7761) 256, 314
Annuaire des Departements de Sociologie et d'Anthropologie au Canada see Guide to Departments of Sociology and Anthropology in Canadian Universities 337
Annuaire des Docteurs (Lettres) de l'Universite de Paris et Autres Universites Francaises (FR ISSN 0066-281X) 333
Annuaire des Editeurs Belges (BE) 757
Annuaire des Employeurs des Nouveaux Diplomes de College see Employers of New University Graduates: Directory 667
Annuaire des Entreprises d'Outre-Mer, des Organismes Officiels et Professionels d'Outre-Mer, des Organismes de Cooperation Francais, Entrangers et Internationaux see Annuaire des Entreprises et Organismes d'Outre-Mer 192
Annuaire des Entreprises du Mali (ML ISSN 0080-0988) 178
Annuaire des Entreprises et Organismes d'Outre-Mer (FR) 192

Annuaire des Exportateurs Francais Commercant avec l'U.R.S.S. (FR) 234
Annuaire des Fournisseurs de Laboratoires de Recherches (FR) 779
Annuaire des Fournisseurs de Laboratoires Pharmaceutiques see Annuaire des Fournisseurs de Laboratoires Pharmaceutiques et Cosmetiques 683
Annuaire des Fournisseurs de Laboratoires Pharmaceutiques et Cosmetiques (FR ISSN 0396-0625) 683
Annuaire des Geographes de la France et de l'Afrique Francophone see Repertoire des Geographes de France 425
Annuaire des Hopitaux du Canada see Canadian Hospital Directory 480
Annuaire des Hypermarches (FR) 234
Annuaire des Institutions d'Enseignement Secondaire see Association des Institutions d'Enseignement Secondaire. Annuaire 314
Annuaire des Instituts de Religieuses en France (FR ISSN 0066-2860) 763
Annuaire des Laboratoires d'Analyses de Biologie Medicale de France (FR) 612
Annuaire des Laboratoires d'Analyses de France see Annuaire des Laboratoires d'Analyses de Biologie Medicale de France 612
Annuaire des Marees pour l'An... Tome 1. Ports de France (FR ISSN 0180-989X) 309
Annuaire des Marees pour l'An, Tome 2. Ports d'Outre Mer (FR ISSN 0180-9962) 877
Annuaire des Minerauex du Canada see Canadian Minerals Yearbook 642
Annuaire des Notables Regionaux (FR) 420
Annuaire des Orchestres et Orchestres des Jeunes Canadiens see Directory of Canadian Orchestras and Youth Orchestras 659
Annuaire des Organisations Internationales see Yearbook of International Organizations 725
Annuaire des Pays de l'Ocean Indien (FR) 447
Annuaire des Professeurs de Droit see Directory of Law Teachers 511
Annuaire des Professions au Liban see Lebanese Industrial and Commercial Directory 239
Annuaire des Recherches Africaines sur les Problemes de Developpement see African Development Research Annual 199
Annuaire des Societes Libanaises Par Action see Year-Book of the Lebanese Joint-Stock Companies 205
Annuaire des Stations Hydro-Minerales, Climatiques, et Balneaires de France et des Etablissements Medicaux see Annuaire des Stations Thermales et Climatiques et des Etablissements Medicaux Francais 592
Annuaire des Stations Thermales et Climatiques et des Etablissements Medicaux Francais (FR) 592
Annuaire des Statistiques du Commerce Exterieur du Togo (TG) 151, 832
Annuaire Desechaliers (FR) 234
Annuaire Desfosses (FR) 141
Annuaire Diplomatique et Consulaire de la Republique Francaise (FR ISSN 0066-295X) 719
Annuaire du Canada see Canada Yearbook 906
Annuaire du Cinema et Television (FR ISSN 0066-2968) 648
Annuaire du Commerce du Norvege see Norges Handels-Kalender 241
Annuaire du Commerce Exterieur d'Haiti: Importations, Exportations (HT) 192
Annuaire du Commerce Franco-Italien (IT ISSN 0069-6625) 178
Annuaire du Corps Interministeriel des Ingenieurs des Telecommunications (FR ISSN 0066-2976) 263

Annuaire du Diocese de Lyon (FR) 773
Annuaire du Marketing (FR ISSN 0066-300X) 217
Annuaire du Quebec (CN ISSN 0066-3018) 832
Annuaire du Spectacle (FR ISSN 0066-3026) 858
Annuaire du Tiers Monde (FR) 199
Annuaire Economique (FR) 141
Annuaire Economique d'Afrique et du Moyen-Orient (FR) 719
Annuaire Economique de la Tunisie (TI ISSN 0066-3042) 182
Annuaire et Statistique de l'Enseignement Catholique (BE ISSN 0068-2942) 314, 705
Annuaire Europeen des Directeurs Commerciaux et de Marketing (FR ISSN 0066-3077) 217
Annuaire Europeen du Petrole see European Petroleum Yearbook 679
Annuaire Francais d'Australie (AT) 234
Annuaire Francais de Droit International (FR ISSN 0066-3085) 522
Annuaire Franco-Italien (FR ISSN 0066-3115) 178
Annuaire Franco-Suisse (FR ISSN 0066-3123) 178
Annuaire Fructidor (FR ISSN 0066-3131) 32
Annuaire G D P F see Annuaire General des Publicitaires de France 4
Annuaire General Automobile see Annuaire National Automobile 869
Annuaire General de la Pharmacie Francaise (FR ISSN 0066-3158) 683
Annuaire General des Cooperatives Francaises et de Leurs Fournisseurs; France, Afrique et Marche Commun (FR ISSN 0066-3182) 181
Annuaire General des Publicitaires de France (FR) 4
Annuaire General des Publicitaires de France see Groupement des Directeurs Publicitaires de France. Annuaire 215
Annuaire-Guide du Chauffage et du Conditionnement d'Air. see Catalogue National du Genie Climatique-Chauffage et Conditionnement d'Air 429
Annuaire-Guide International de l'Energie Atomique et des Autres Energies see Guide International de l'Energie Nucleare 703
Annuaire H L M (Habitations a Loyer Modere) (FR) 483, 803
Annuaire Industriel. Repertoire Generale de la Production Francaise see Repertoire General de la Production Francaise 241
Annuaire International des Collectionneurs (FR) 475
Annuaire International des Dix-Huitiemistes (FR ISSN 0066-3247) 489
Annuaire International des Foires, Expositions et Salons Specialises (FR) 192
Annuaire International des Jus de Fruits(FR ISSN 0066-3255) 85
Annuaire International des Ventes (FR ISSN 0066-3263) 71
Annuaire International du Monde Sous-Marin see International Yearbook of the Underwater World 827
Annuaire Interprofessionnel de la Surgelation et de la Congelation (FR) 403
Annuaire Magnetique see Rocznik Magnetyczny 306
Annuaire Maritime (BE) 508, 877
Annuaire Medical de l'Hospitalisation Francaise. (FR ISSN 0066-3298) 480, 592
Annuaire Medical du Dr. Porcheron et Prof. G. Beltrami (FR) 592
Annuaire Mondial des Corses (FR) 96
Annuaire National Automobile (FR) 869
Annuaire National de l'Aviculture (FR ISSN 0066-3328) 43
Annuaire National de l'Industrie et du Commerce see L'Economie 237

Annuaire National de la Kinesitherapie (FR ISSN 0066-3301) 592
Annuaire National des Beaux-Arts (FR ISSN 0066-3352) 71
Annuaire National des Fournisseurs des Administrations Francaises (FR ISSN 0066-3379) 220
Annuaire National des Industries de la Conserve (FR ISSN 0084-652X) 403
Annuaire National des Lettres (FR ISSN 0066-3387) 559
Annuaire National des Masseurs Kinesitherapeutes (FR ISSN 0337-5935) 592
Annuaire National des Matieres Premieres de Recuperation et du Materiel d'Occasion (FR) 582
Annuaire National des Specialistes en Gynecologie-Obstetrique et des Competents Exlusifs en Gynecologie et Obstetrique (FR ISSN 0066-3395) 615
Annuaire National des Specialistes Qualifies en Chirurgie (FR ISSN 0066-3417) 624
Annuaire National des Specialistes Qualifies Exclusifs des Maladies de l'Appareil Digestif (FR ISSN 0066-3425) 613
Annuaire National des Specialistes Qualifies Exclusifs en Dermatologie et Venereologie (FR ISSN 0066-345X) 611
Annuaire National des Specialistes Qualifies Exclusifs en Electroradiologie (FR ISSN 0066-3468) 622
Annuaire National des Specialistes Qualifies Exclusifs en Neuropsychiatrie (FR ISSN 0066-3476) 618
Annuaire National des Specialistes Qualifies Exclusifs en Pediatrie (FR ISSN 0066-3514) 617
Annuaire National des Specialistes Qualifies Exclusifs en Rhumatologie (FR ISSN 0066-3522) 623
Annuaire National des Transports (FR ISSN 0066-3549) 861
Annuaire National du Lait (FR ISSN 0084-6538) 40
Annuaire National du Verre (FR ISSN 0066-3557) 244
Annuaire National M.K.D.E. France see Annuaire National des Masseurs Kinesitherapeutes 592
Annuaire National Officiel de la Republique Gabonaise (GO) 739
Annuaire Nautisme (FR) 826
Annuaire O. G. M. (Office General de la Musique) (FR ISSN 0066-3565) 266
Annuaire Paris: Bijoux (FR ISSN 0066-3581) 503
Annuaire Polonais de Droit International see Polish Yearbook of International Law 523
Annuaire Protestant; la France Protestante et les Eglises de Langue Francaise (FR ISSN 0066-362X) 771
Annuaire Repertoire de la Motoculture de Plaisance Jardinage (FR ISSN 0224-2478) 414, 582
Annuaire Statistique de Benin (DM) 832
Annuaire Statistique de l'Industrie Francaise du Jute (FR ISSN 0066-3697) 855
Annuaire Statistique de la Belgique (BE ISSN 0066-3646) 832
Annuaire Statistique de la Belgique et du Congo Belge see Annuaire Statistique de la Belgique 832
Annuaire Statistique de la France (FR ISSN 0066-3654) 832
Annuaire Statistique de la Sante Publique/Statistisch Jaarboek van Volksgezondheid (BE ISSN 0522-7690) 750
Annuaire Statistique de la Suisse see Statistisches Jahrbuch der Schweiz 847
Annuaire Statistique de la Tunisie (TI ISSN 0066-3689) 832

Annuaire Statistique des Telecommunications du Secteur Public see Yearbook of Common Carrier Telecommunication Statistics 265
Annuaire Statistique des Territoires d'Outre Mer (FR ISSN 0071-8793) 832
Annuaire Statistique du Dahomey see Annuaire Statistique de Benin 832
Annuaire Statistique du Maroc (MR ISSN 0066-3719) 832
Annuaire Statistique du Togo (TG) 832
Annuaire Statistique pour l'Asie et le Pacifique see Statistical Yearbook for Asia and the Pacific 847
Annuaire Sucrier (FR) 406
Annuaire Suisse de Science Politique/Schweizerisches Jahrbuch fur Politische Wissenschaft/Swiss Political Science Yearbook (SZ ISSN 0066-3727) 708
Annuaire Suisse du Monde et des Affaires/Wer ist Wer in der Schweiz und im Fuerstentum Liechtenstein/Swiss Biographical Index of Prominent Persons/Chi e Svizzera e nel Liechtenstein? (SZ) 96
Annuaire Technique de la Sous - Traitance Mecanique (FR) 582
Annuaires Chateaudun (FR) 739
Annuaires Francais et Listes d'Adresses Susceptibles d'Interesser le Commerce et l'Industrie (FR ISSN 0066-3743) 178
Annual Action Program - State Law Enforcement Agency see National State Law Enforcement and Juvenile Delinquency Planning Agency. Annual Action Program 281
Annual Aid Review, Memorandum of New Zealand (NZ) 199
Annual Allerton Conference on Circuit and System Theory (US) 351
Annual Art Sales Index: Oil Paintings, Drawings and Watercolours (US ISSN 0308-5910) 71
Annual Basic Hobby Industry Trade Directory see Craft, Model & Hobby Industry Annual Trade Directory 476
Annual Bibliography of English Language and Literature (UK ISSN 0066-3786) 577
Annual Bibliography of Indian Archaeology (NE ISSN 0066-3794) 67
Annual Bibliography of Scottish Literature (UK ISSN 0307-9864) 577
Annual Book of A S T M Standards. Part 1. Steel Piping, Tubing, and Fittings (American Society for Testing and Materials) (US ISSN 0066-0183) 377, 627
Annual Book of A S T M Standards. Part 2. Ferrous Castings, Ferro-Alloys (US ISSN 0066-0191) 377, 627
Annual Book of A S T M Standards. Part 3. Steel Plate, Sheet, Strip and Wire; Metallic Coated Products (US) 377, 627
Annual Book of A S T M Standards. Part 4. Structural Steel; Concrete Reinforcing Steel; Pressure Vessel Plate and Forgings; Steel Rails, Wheels, and Tires; Steel Fasteners (US) 378, 627
Annual Book of A S T M Standards. Part 5. Steel Bars, Chain, and Springs; Bearing Steel; Steel Forgings(US) 378, 627
Annual Book of A S T M Standards. Part 6. Copper and Copper Alloys (Including Electrical Conductors) (US ISSN 0066-0221) 378, 627
Annual Book of A S T M Standards. Part 7. Die-Cast Metals; Light Metals and Alloys (Including Electrical Conductors) (US ISSN 0066-023X) 378, 627
Annual Book of A S T M Standards. Part 8. Nonferrous Metals--Nickel, Lead, and Tin Alloys, Precious Metals, Primary Metals; Reactive Metals (US) 378, 627

Annual Book of A S T M Standards. Part 9. Electrodeposited Metallic Coatings; Metal Powders, Sintered P/M Structural Parts (US) *378,* 627
Annual Book of A S T M Standards. Part 10. Metals - Mechanical, Fracture, and Corrosion Testing; Fatigue; Erosion; Effect of Temperature (US) *378,* 627
Annual Book of A S T M Standards. Part 11. Metallography; Nondestructive Testing (US) *378,* 627
Annual Book of A S T M Standards. Part 12. Chemical Analysis of Metals; Sampling and Analysis of Metal Bearing Ores (US ISSN 0066-0485) 249, *378,* 627
Annual Book of A S T M Standards. Part 13. Cement; Lime; Ceilings and Walls (Including Manual of Cement Testing) (US) 134, *378*
Annual Book of A S T M Standards. Part 14. Concrete and Mineral Aggregates (Including Manual of Concrete Testing) (US ISSN 0066-0264) 134, *378*
Annual Book of A S T M Standards. Part 15. Road and Paving Materials; Bituminous Materials for Highway Construction, Waterproofing and Roofing, and Pipe; Skid Resistance (US) *378*
Annual Book of A S T M Standards. Part 16. Chemical-Resistant Nonmetallic Materials. Vitrified Clay and Concrete Pipe and Tile; Masonry Mortars and Units; Asbestos-Cement Products (US) 134, *378*
Annual Book of A S T M Standards. Part 17. Refractories, Glass and Other Ceramic Materials; Manufactured Carbon and Graphite Products (US ISSN 0066-0299) 244, *378*
Annual Book of A S T M Standards. Part 18. Thermal and Cryogenic Insulating Materials; Building Seals and Sealants; Fire Tests; Building Constructions; Environmental Acoustics (US ISSN 0066-0302) 134, *378*
Annual Book of A S T M Standards. Part 19. Natural Building Stones; Soil and Rock; Peats, Mosses, and Humus(US) 33, 134, *378*
Annual Book of A S T M Standards. Part 20. Paper; Packaging; Business Copy Products (US) *378,* 672, 675
Annual Book of A S T M Standards. Part 21. Cellulose; Leather; Flexible Barrier Materials (US) *378*
Annual Book of A S T M Standards. Part 22. Wood; Adhesives (US ISSN 0066-0329) *378,* 412, 706
Annual Book of A S T M Standards. Part 23. Petroleum Products and Lubricants (1) (US) *378,* 678
Annual Book of A S T M Standards. Part 24. Petroleum Products and Lubricants (2) (US) *378,* 678
Annual Book of A S T M Standards. Part 25. Petroleum Products and Lubricants (3); Aerospace Materials (US) 7, *378,* 678
Annual Book of A S T M Standards. Part 26. Gaseous Fuels; Coal and Coke; Atmospheric Analysis (US) *378,* 641, 678
Annual Book of A S T M Standards. Part 27. Paint - Tests for Formulated Products and Applied Coatings (US ISSN 0066-037X) *378,* 673
Annual Book of A S T M Standards. Part 28. Paint - Pigments, Resins and Polymers (US) *378,* 673
Annual Book of A S T M Standards. Part 29. Paint - Fatty Oils and Acids, Solvents, Miscellaneous; Aromatic Hydrocarbons; Naval Stores (US) 372, *378,* 673
Annual Book of A S T M Standards. Part 30. Soap; Engine Coolants; Polishes; Halogenated Organic Solvents; Activated Carbon; Industrial Chemicals (US ISSN 0066-0388) 372, *378*
Annual Book of A S T M Standards. Part 31. Water (US) *378,* 384

Annual Book of A S T M Standards. Part 32. Textiles--Yarn, Fabrics, and General Test Methods (US ISSN 0066-040X) *378,* 855
Annual Book of A S T M Standards. Part 33. Textiles--Fibers, Zippers; High Modulus Fibers (US ISSN 0066-0418) *378,* 855
Annual Book of A S T M Standards. Part 34. Plastic Pipe (US) 134, *379,* 706
Annual Book of A S T M Standards. Part 35. Plastics - General Test Methods; Nomenclature (US ISSN 0066-0434) *379,* 706
Annual Book of A S T M Standards. Part 36. Plastics--Materials, Film, Reinforced and Cellular Plastics; High Modulus Fibers and Their Composites (US) *379,* 706
Annual Book of A S T M Standards. Part 37. Rubber, Natural and Synthetic--General Test Methods; Carbon Black (US) *379,* 777
Annual Book of A S T M Standards. Part 38. Rubber Products, Industrial--Specifications and Related Test Methods; Gaskets; Tires (US) *379,* 777
Annual Book of A S T M Standards. Part 39. Electrical Insulation--Test Methods: Solids and Solidifying Fluids (US) 351, *379*
Annual Book of A S T M Standards. Part 40. Electrical Insulation--Specifications: Solids, Liquids, and Gases; Test Methods: Liquids and Gases (US) 351, *379*
Annual Book of A S T M Standards. Part 41. General Test Methods, Nonmetal; Statistical Methods; Space Simulation; Particle Size Measurement; General Laboratory Apparatus; Durability of Nonmetallic Materials; Metric Practice (US) *379*
Annual Book of A S T M Standards. Part 42. Emission, Molecular, and Mass Spectroscopy; Chromatography; Resinography; Microscopy (US) 249, *379*
Annual Book of A S T M Standards. Part 43. Electronics (US) 351, *379*
Annual Book of A S T M Standards. Part 44. Magnetic Properties and Magnetic Materials; Metallic Materials for Thermostats and for Electrical Resistance, Heating, and Contacts; Temperature Measurement; Illuminating Standards (US) *379*
Annual Book of A S T M Standards. Part 45. Nuclear Standards (US) 366, *379*
Annual Book of A S T M Standards. Part 46. End Use and Consumer Products (US) *379*
Annual Book of A S T M Standards. Part 47. Test Methods for Rating Motor, Diesel, and Aviation Fuels (US) *379*
Annual Book of A S T M Standards. Part 48. Index (US ISSN 0066-0493) *379*
Annual Bulletin of Coal Statistics for Europe (UN ISSN 0066-3808) *641*
Annual Bulletin of Electric Energy Statistics for Europe (UN ISSN 0066-3816) *359,* 364, 832
Annual Bulletin of Gas Statistics for Europe/Bulletin Annuel du Statistiques de Gaz pour l'Europe (UN ISSN 0066-3824) *678*
Annual Bulletin of General Energy Statistics for Europe (UN) *364*
Annual Bulletin of Historical Literature (UK ISSN 0066-3832) *430*
Annual Bulletin of Transport Statistics for Europe (UN ISSN 0066-3859) *861*
Annual Causes & Conditions of Poverty in South Dakota *see* Poverty in South Dakota *808*
Annual Conference of the British Columbia Provincial Judges' Association *see* British Columbia Provincial Judges' Association. Annual Conference *510*
Annual Conference on Applications of X-Ray Analysis. Proceedings *see* Advances in X-Ray Analysis *626*

Annual Conference on C A T V Reliability. (Proceedings) (US) *266*
Annual Conference on Labor at New York University. Proceedings (US) *205*
Annual Criminal Justice Plan for Illinois (US) *280*
Annual Descriptive Report of Program Activities for Vocational Education *see* Idaho. State Board for Vocational Education. Annual Descriptive Report of Program Activities for Vocational Education *329*
Annual Development Plan of Madhya Pradesh (II ISSN 0066-3891) *220*
Annual Directory of Booksellers in the British Isles Specialising in Antiquarian and Out-Of-Print Books (UK ISSN 0066-3913) *757*
Annual Directory of Press and Advertising *see* Stamm Leitfaden Durch Presse und Werbung *95*
Annual Dog Watch *see* Dog Watch *878*
Annual Drug Data Report (SP ISSN 0379-4121) *683*
Annual Economic Report, Nebraska *see* Nebraska. Department of Economic Development. Annual Economic Report *187*
Annual Editions: Educating Exceptional Children (US ISSN 0198-7518) *345*
Annual Editions: Readings in American Government (US ISSN 0090-547X) *708*
Annual Editions: Readings in American History (US ISSN 0090-4511) *466*
Annual Editions: Readings in Anthropology (US ISSN 0095-5582) *47*
Annual Editions: Readings in Biology (US ISSN 0090-4384) *100*
Annual Editions: Readings in Business (US ISSN 0090-4309) *142*
Annual Editions: Readings in Economics (US ISSN 0090-4430) *142*
Annual Editions: Readings in Education(US ISSN 0095-5787) *314*
Annual Editions: Readings in Environment (US ISSN 0196-4542) *384*
Annual Editions: Readings in Human Development (US ISSN 0090-5348) *125,* 592
Annual Editions: Readings in Human Sexuality (US ISSN 0163-836X) *100,* 734, 812
Annual Editions: Readings in Marketing(US) *217*
Annual Editions: Readings in Marriage and Family (US ISSN 0095-6155) *812*
Annual Editions: Readings in Personal Growth and Adjustment (US ISSN 0198-912X) *734*
Annual Editions: Readings in Personality and Adjustment *see* Annual Editions: Readings in Personal Growth and Adjustment *734*
Annual Editions: Readings in Psychology (US) *734*
Annual Editions: Readings in Social Problems (US ISSN 0094-9183) *804*
Annual Editions: Readings in Sociology(US ISSN 0090-4236) *812*
Annual Educational Summary, New York State (US ISSN 0085-4077) *314*
Annual Electric Power Survey (US ISSN 0190-5600) *351*
Annual Epidemiological and Vital Statistics *see* World Health Statistics Annual *757*
Annual Estimates of the Population of Scotland (UK ISSN 0066-3964) *725*
Annual Evaluation Report - North Dakota State Advisory Council for Vocational Education *see* North Dakota. State Advisory Council for Vocational Education. Annual Evaluation Report *350*

Annual Evaluation Report of the Tennessee State Advisory Council on Vocational Education *see* Tennessee. State Advisory Council on Vocational Education. Annual Evaluation Report *346*
Annual Evaluation Report Program Information *see* California. Department of Health. Annual Evaluation Report Program Information *315*
Annual Evaluation Report - State Advisory Council for Career and Vocational Education to Oregon's Citizens *see* Oregon. State Advisory Council for Career and Vocational Education. Annual Evaluation Report *321*
Annual Exhibition - National Sculpture Society *see* National Sculpture Society, New York. Annual Exhibition *77*
Annual Fertilizer Review (UN ISSN 0084-6546) *33*
Annual Financing Directory (US) *168*
Annual Foreign Trade Statistics of Bangladesh (BG ISSN 0071-7371) *151*
Annual General Meeting of the Asiatic Society of Bangladesh; Report of the General Secretary (BG) *669*
Annual Geomagnetic Bulletin of Pakistan (PK) *631*
Annual Guide to Careers for Young People *see* N U T Guide to Careers Work *667*
Annual Guide to Stewardess Career *see* Airline Guide to Stewardess & Stewards Career *666*
Annual Handbook for Group Facilitators (US ISSN 0094-601X) *812*
Annual Index of Rheumatology *see* Index of Rheumatology *602*
Annual Index to Motion Picture Credits(US ISSN 0163-5123) *648*
Annual Index to Popular Music Record Reviews (US ISSN 0092-3486) *818*
Annual Infectious Disease Symposia. Proceedings *see* Infectious Disease Reviews *608*
Annual Institute on Securities Law and Regulations. Proceedings (US ISSN 0161-4002) *202*
Annual International Congress Calendar(BE) *202*
Annual Investment File (UK) *202*
Annual Iowa Manpower Planning Report *see* Iowa. Department of Job Service. Research and Statistics Division. Annual Manpower Planning Report *208*
Annual Labor-Management Conference on Collective Bargaining and Labor Law (US) *904*
Annual Local Government Financial Report, State of Florida *see* Florida. Bureau of Local Government Finance. Annual Local Government Financial Report *229*
Annual Manpower Personnel Statistics (Washington) *see* U. S. Department of the Interior. Office of Personnel Management. Annual Manpower Personnel Statistics *915*
Annual Manpower Planning Report. Detroit Labor Market Area *see* Michigan. Employment Security Commission. Annual Planning Report *209*
Annual Medical Report (Pierre) *see* South Dakota. Department of Social Services. Annual Medical Report *811*
Annual Meeting - American Association for the Advancement of Science *see* American Association for the Advancement of Science. Meeting Program *779*
Annual Mosquito Review *see* New Jersey Mosquito Control Association. Proceedings *121*
Annual New Mexico Water Conference. Proceedings (US ISSN 0161-4924) *895*
Annual of Ad Production in Japan (JA) *4*

Annual of Advertising Art in Japan/ Nenkan Kokoku Bijutsu (JA ISSN 0548-1643) 4
Annual of Advertising, Editorial and Television Art and Design see Annual of Advertising, Editorial & Television Art & Design with the Annual Copy Awards 71
Annual of Advertising, Editorial & Television Art & Design with the Annual Copy Awards (US) 71
Annual of Czechoslovak Medical Literature (CS) 601
Annual of Indian Photography (II) 692
Annual of Jewish Studies see Gratz College Annual of Jewish Studies 392
Annual of Psychoanalysis (US ISSN 0092-5055) 734
Annual Performance Report and Continuation of the State Plan for Drug Abuse Prevention see Louisiana. Division of Mental Health. Annual Performance Report and Continuation of the State Plan for Drug Abuse Prevention 287
Annual Performance Report on Adult Education see Hawaii. Office of Instructional Services. Special Programs Branch. Annual Performance Report on Adult Education 329
Annual Plan of Work - Department of Human Resources see North Carolina. Department of Human Resources. Annual Plan of Work 808
Annual Potomac Report see Potomac Report 897
Annual Power and Conflict (UK) 719
Annual Practice see Supreme Court Practice 519
Annual Progress in Child Psychiatry and Child Development (US ISSN 0066-4030) 619
Annual Progress Report. State Migrant Plan for Public Health Services see Colorado. State Department of Public Health. Annual Progress Report. State Migrant Plan for Public Health Services 804
Annual Progress Report - U.S. Army Medical Research Institute of Infectious Diseases see U.S. Army Medical Research Institute of Infectious Diseases. Annual Progress Report 608
Annual Register of Grant Support (US ISSN 0066-4049) 343
Annual Register World Events (UK ISSN 0066-4057) 708
Annual Report see Zoologicka Zahrada v Praze. Vyrocni Zprava 131
Annual Report. Human Resources Agencies (Olympia) see Washington (State). Human Resources Agencies. Annual Report 810
Annual Report. Transportation Agencies. State of Washington see Washington (State). Transportation Agencies. Annual Report 864
Annual Report - Administration on Aging see U.S. Administration on Aging. Annual Report 428
Annual Report - Alaska Native Medical Center see Alaska Native Medical Center. Annual Report 803
Annual Report - American Institute of Indian Studies see A I I S Annual Report 441
Annual Report - American National Metric Council see American National Metric Council. Annual Report 636
Annual Report and Accounts-Cameroon Development Corporation see Cameroon Development Corporation. Annual Report and Accounts/ Rapport Annuel et Compte-Rendu Financier 221
Annual Report and Recommendations of the Maryland Council of Higher Education see Maryland. Council for Higher Education. Annual Report and Recommendations 911

Annual Report-Andhra Pradesh Small Scale Industrial Development Corporation see Andhra Pradesh Small Scale Industrial Development Corporation. Annual Report 234
Annual Report-Andhra Pradesh State Trading Corporation Limited see Andhra Pradesh State Trading Corporation Limited. Annual Report 217
Annual Report - Arizona. Department of Economic Security see Arizona. Department of Economic Security. Annual Report 739
Annual Report - Arkansas. Department of Mental Retardation see Arkansas. Department of Mental Retardation. Annual Report 619
Annual Report - Asia Society see Asia Society. Annual Report 442
Annual Report - Board of Public Accountancy see Massachusetts. Board of Public Accountancy. Annual Report 744
Annual Report - Central Sericultural Research and Training Institute see Central Sericultural Research and Training Institute. Annual Report 13
Annual Report - Citizens Advisory Council (Harrisburg) see Pennsylvania. Citizens Advisory Council to the Department of Environmental Resources. Annual Report 388
Annual Report - Commonwealth of Massachusetts, Department of Public Welfare, State Advisory Board see Massachusetts. Department of Public Welfare. State Advisory Board. Annual Report 807
Annual Report--Cotton Corporation of India see Cotton Corporation of India. Annual Report 27
Annual Report - Criminal Injuries Compensation Commission see Hawaii. Criminal Injuries Compensation Commission. Annual Report 281
Annual Report - Criminal Investigation Bureau see Alaska. Criminal Investigation Bureau. Annual Report 280
Annual Report - Damon Runyon-Walter Winchell Cancer Fund see Damon Runyon-Walter Winchell Cancer Fund. Annual Report 605
Annual Report - Department of Environmental Protection (Trenton) see New Jersey. Department of Environmental Protection. Annual Report 388
Annual Report - Department of Health and Social Services see Delaware. Department of Health and Social Service. Annual Report 751
Annual Report - Department of Management and Budget see Michigan. Department of Management and Budget. Annual Report 744
Annual Report - Department of Safety see Tennessee. Department of Safety. Annual Report 876
Annual Report - Division of Family and Children Services (Juneau) see Alaska. Division of Family and Children Services. Annual Report 803
Annual Report - Educational Testing Service see Educational Testing Service Annual Report 317
Annual Report - Engineering Experiment Station (Madison) see University of Wisconsin, Madison. Engineering Experiment Station. Annual Report 635
Annual Report - Family Planning Association of Kenya see Family Planning Association of Kenya. Annual Report 131
Annual Report - Federal Home Loan Bank of San Francisco see Federal Home Loan Bank of San Francisco. Annual Report 173
Annual Report for the Department of Industrial Relations see California. Department of Industrial Relations. Annual Report 206

Annual Report - Idaho State Department of Agriculture see Idaho. Department of Agriculture. Annual Report 15
Annual Report - Illinois. Department of Public Aid see Illinois. Department of Public Aid. Annual Report 806
Annual Report - Illinois Department of Transportation see Illinois. Department of Transportation. Annual Report 862
Annual Report - Illinois Fire Protection Personnel Standards and Education Commission see Illinois. Fire Protection Personnel Standards and Education Commission. Annual Report 395
Annual Report - Illinois Institute for Environmental Quality see Illinois Institute for Environmental Quality. Annual Report 386
Annual Report-Indian School of Mines see Indian School of Mines. Annual Report 644
Annual Report - Inspection Service Section see Virginia. Division of Product and Industry Regulation. Inspection Service Section. Annual Report 22
Annual Report-Institute of Secretariat Training and Management see Institute of Secretariat Training and Management. Annual Report 219
Annual Report - International Reading Association see International Reading Association. Annual Report 319
Annual Report-Jammu & Kashmir Minerals Limited see Jammu & Kashmir Minerals Limited. Annual Report 644
Annual Report - Kentucky Law Enforcement Council see Kentucky Law Enforcement Council. Annual Report 282
Annual Report-Madhya Pradesh State Agro-Industries Development Corporation Ltd. see Madhya Pradesh State Agro-Industries Development Corporation Ltd. Annual Report 29
Annual Report - Maine Department of Transportation see Maine. Department of Transportation. Annual Report 863
Annual Report - Maryland Commission on Intergovernmental Cooperation see Maryland. Commission on Intergovernmental Cooperation. Annual Report 744
Annual Report - Maryland Historical Trust see Maryland Historical Trust. Annual Report 69
Annual Report - Massachusetts Advocacy Center see Massachusetts Advocacy Center. Annual Report 515
Annual Report--Meghalaya Industrial Development Corporation see Meghalaya Industrial Development Corporation. Annual Report 146
Annual Report - Mississippi Marine Resources Council see Mississippi Marine Resources Council. Annual Report 311
Annual Report - Missouri River Basin Commission see Missouri River Basin Commission. Annual Report 897
Annual Report - Montana Advisory Council for Vocational Education see Montana Advisory Council for Vocational Education. Annual Report 349
Annual Report-National Advisory Council on Extension and Continuing Education see U.S. National Advisory Council on Extension and Continuing Education. Annual Report 330
Annual Report - National Arthritis Advisory Board see U.S. National Arthritis Advisory Board. Annual Report 624
Annual Report - National Association of Independent Schools see National Association of Independent Schools. Annual Report 320

Annual Report - National Paint & Coatings Association see National Paint and Coatings Association. Annual Report 673
Annual Report - Nebraska Library Commission see Nebraska Library Commission. Annual Report 534
Annual Report - Nebraska State Patrol see Nebraska. State Patrol. Annual Report 283
Annual Report - New Jersey State Legislature. Office of Fiscal Affairs see New Jersey. Legislature. Office of Fiscal Affairs. Annual Report 515
Annual Report-New York State Medical Care Facilities Finance Agency see New York State Medical Care Facilities Finance Agency. Annual Report 753
Annual Report of Births, Deaths, Marriages and Divorces as Reported to the Bureau of Vital Statistics (Little Rock) see Arkansas. Bureau of Vital Statistics. Annual Report of Births, Deaths, Marriages and Divorces as Reported to the Bureau of Vital Statistics i 725
Annual Report of Community Services Administration see U.S. Community Services Administration. Annual Report of Community Services Administration 809
Annual Report of Educational Psychology in Japan/Kyoiku Shinrigaku Nempo (JA ISSN 0452-9650) 314, 734
Annual Report of Life Insurance, Republic of China (CH) 497
Annual Report of Receipts and Disbursements. State of Nebraska see Nebraska. Accounting Division. Annual Report of Receipts and Disbursements State of Nebraska 744
Annual Report of Survey-Inventory Activities see Alaska. Division of Game. Annual Report of Survey-Inventory Activities 828
Annual Report of the Agricultural Opportunities Development Program see Virginia. Agricultural Opportunities Development Program. Annual Report 916
Annual Report of the Arizona Department of Health Services see Arizona. Department of Health Services. Annual Report 750
Annual Report of the Arts Activities in Alabama (US ISSN 0094-0402) 71
Annual Report of the Convenience Store Industry (US) 403
Annual Report of the Department of Business Regulation (Helena) see Montana. Department of Business Regulation. Annual Report 744
Annual Report of the Department of Environmental Quality see Wyoming. Department of Environmental Quality. Annual Report 390
Annual Report of the Department of Revenue and Taxation of the State of Wyoming see Wyoming. Department of Revenue and Taxation. Annual Report 233
Annual Report of the Department of Social and Rehabilitation Services to the Governor of Montana. see Montana. Department of Social and Rehabilitation Services. Annual Report 807
Annual Report of the Development of Agriculture in Japan/Nihon Nogaku Shimpo Nempo (JA ISSN 0546-109X) 26
Annual Report of the District of Columbia City Council see District of Columbia. City Council. Annual Report 749
Annual Report of the Division of Police (Cincinnati) see Cincinnati. Division of Police. Annual Report 281
Annual Report of the Division of Social Services of the Department of Health and Social Services see Delaware. Division of Social Services. Annual Report 804
Annual Report of the Federal Trade Commission see U. S. Federal Trade Commission. Annual Report 182

Annual Report of the Health and Social Services see Wyoming. Department of Health and Social Services. Annual Report 810
Annual Report of the Idaho Department of Labor and Industrial Services see Idaho. Department of Labor and Industrial Services. Annual Report 208
Annual Report of the Idaho Department of Water Resources see Idaho. Department of Water Resources. Annual Report 308
Annual Report of the Michigan State Advisory Council for Vocational Education see Michigan. Advisory Council for Vocational Education. Annual Report 346
Annual Report of the Mississippi Game and Fish Commission to the Regular Session of the Mississippi Legislature see Mississippi. State Game and Fish Commission. Annual Report to the Regular Session of the Mississippi Legislature 398
Annual Report of the Oklahoma Water Resources Research Institute see Oklahoma Water Resources Research Institute. Annual Report 897
Annual Report of the Population Studies Center, the University of Michigan see University of Michigan. Population Studies Center. Annual Report 730
Annual Report of the Register of Copyrights see U. S. Copyright Office. Annual Report of the Register of Copyrights 677
Annual Report of the State Geologist to the Geological Board see Iowa. Geological Survey. Annual Report of the State Geologist to the Geological Board 295
Annual Report of the State Superintendent of Public Instruction Utah Public School System see Utah. State Board of Education. Annual Report of the State Superintendent of Public Instruction 345
Annual Report of the Superintendent of Public Instruction see Arizona. Department of Education. Annual Report of the Superintendent of Public Instruction 314
Annual Report of the Treasurer, State of Connecticut see Connecticut. Treasury Department. Annual Report 228
Annual Report of the U.S. Department of Health, Education,and Welfare to the Congress of the United States on Services Provided to Handicapped Children in Project Head Start see U.S. Department of Health, Education and Welfare. Annual Report to the Congress of the United States on Services Provided to Handicapped Children in Project Head Start 347
Annual Report of the University of Kentucky Research Foundation see University of Kentucky Research Foundation. Annual Report 341
Annual Report of the Virginia State Water Control Board see Virginia. State Water Control Board. Annual Report 899
Annual Report of the Working and Affairs of Mysore Minerals Limited (II) 641
Annual Report of the Wyoming Governor's Office of Highway Safety see Wyoming. Governor's Office of Highway Safety. Annual Report 876
Annual Report of Welfare Programs see U.S. Social and Rehabilitation Service. Annual Report of Welfare Programs 809
Annual Report, Ohio Advisory Council for Vocational Education see Ohio. Advisory Council for Vocational Education. Annual Report 346
Annual Report - Ohio College Library Center see O C L C. Annual Report 534
Annual Report - Ohio Commission on Aging see Ohio. Commission on Aging. Annual Report 428

Annual Report-Oil Shale Environmental Adivsory Panel see U.S. Department of the Interior. Oil Shale Environmental Advisory Panel. Annual Report 389
Annual Report - Oklahoma Aeronautics Commission see Oklahoma. Aeronautics Commission. Annual Report 9
Annual Report - Ombudsman for Corrections (St. Paul) see Minnesota. Office of Ombudsman for Corrections. Annual Report 282
Annual Report on Advanced Dental Education (US) 347, 609
Annual Report on Dental Auxiliary Education (US ISSN 0084-6554) 325, 601
Annual Report on Dental Education (US ISSN 0065-8030) 325, 601
Annual Report on Ground Water in Arizona (US) 895
Annual Report on Highway Safety Improvement Programs see U. S. Department of Transportation. Annual Report on Highway Safety Improvement Programs 876
Annual Report on Results of Treatment in Gynecological Cancer (SW) 604
Annual Report on State and Area Occupational Requirements for Vocational Education (Aberdeen) see South Dakota. Department of Labor. Research and Statistics. Annual Report on State and Area Occupational Requirements for Vocational Education 164
Annual Report on the Comprehensive Water Resources Plan see West Virginia. Department of Natural Resources. Annual Report on the Comprehensive Water Resources Plan 899
Annual Report on the Quality of the Environment (St. Paul) see Minnesota. Governor. Annual Report on the Quality of the Environment 387
Annual Report on the Results of Treatment in Carcinoma of the Uterus, Vagina, and Ovary see Annual Report on Results of Treatment in Gynecological Cancer 604
Annual Report on the Working and Affairs of Mysore Sales International Limited (II) 181
Annual Report on Tourism Statistics, Republic of China (CH) 883
Annual Report on Work of Fabian Society see Fabian Society. Annual Report 710
Annual Report - Overseas Development Council see Overseas Development Council. Annual Report 200
Annual Report - Overseas Private Investment Corporation see Overseas Private Investment Corporation. Annual Report 204
Annual Report - Petroleum Division see Minnesota. Department of Revenue. Petroleum Division. Annual Report 680
Annual Report - Punjab National Bank see Punjab National Bank. Annual Report 176
Annual Report-Rajasthan State Tanneries Limited see Rajasthan State Tanneries Limited. Annual Report 524
Annual Report - Regional Institute of Social Welfare Research see Regional Institute of Social Welfare Research. Annual Report 808
Annual Report-Republic Forge Company see Republic Forge Company. Annual Report 225
Annual Report-Robert Wood Johnson Foundation see Robert Wood Johnson Foundation. Annual Report 808
Annual Report - San Francisco Bay Area Rapid Transit District see San Francisco Bay Area Rapid Transit District. Annual Report 863
Annual Report - Securities Investor Protection Corporation see Securities Investor Protection Corporation. Annual Report 204

Annual Report Soil Science Foundation see Agricultural Research Center. Annual Report 32
Annual Report - Southeast Michigan Council of Governments see Southeast Michigan Council of Governments. Annual Report 746
Annual Report - Southern California Rapid Transit District. see Southern California Rapid Transit District. Annual Report 863
Annual Report - State Consumer Protection Board see New York (State) Consumer Protection Board. Annual Report 280
Annual Report - State Economic Opportunity Office (Atlanta) see Georgia. State Economic Opportunity Office. Annual Report 742
Annual Report - State of Alaska. Violent Crimes Compensation Board see Alaska. Violent Crimes Compensation Board. Annual Report 280
Annual Report - State of Alaska, Legislative Budget and Audit Committee see Alaska. Legislature. Budget and Audit Committee. Annual Report 739
Annual Report - State of Connecticut, Council on Environmental Quality see Connecticut. Council on Environmental Quality. Annual Report 385
Annual Report - State of Florida, Department of Transportation see Florida. Department of Transportation. Annual Report 862
Annual Report - State of Hawaii. State Commission on the Status of Women see Hawaii. State Commission on the Status of Women. Annual Report 900
Annual Report: State of Idaho Johnson-O'Malley Program see Idaho. State Superintendent of Public Instruction. Annual Report. State of Idaho Johnson-O'Malley Program 318
Annual Report - State of New York, Division of Criminal Justice Services see New York (State). Division of Criminal Justice Service. Annual Report 283
Annual Report - State Planning Office. Executive Department. State of Maine see Maine. State Planning Office. Annual Report 744
Annual Report Summary - Michigan Department of Commerce see Michigan. Department of Commerce. Annual Report Summary 182
Annual Report - Susquehanna River Basin Commission see Susquehanna River Basin Commission. Annual Report 898
Annual Report, the Indian Economic Employment Assistance Program see Washington (State). Indian Assistance Division.Indian Economic Employment Assistance Program. Annual Report 394
Annual Reports to Congress by the Task Force on Environmental Cancer and Heart and Lung Disease see Task Force on Environmental Cancer and Heart and Lung Disease. Annual Report to Congress 389
Annual Report to the Congress by the Office of Technology Assessment see U.S. Office of Technology Assessment Annual Report to the Congress 746
Annual Report to the Congress of the United States from the National Council on Indian Education see U.S. National Advisory Council on Indian Education. Annual Report to the Congress of the United States 324
Annual Report to the Governor and General Assembly. Executive Summary see Connecticut. Energy Advisory Board. Annual Report to the Governor and General Assembly. Executive Summary 362

ANNUAL REVIEW 1287

Annual Report to the Governor and Legislature - Teacher's Retirement Board see California. Teachers Retirement Board. State Teacher's Retirement System. Annual Report to the Governor and the Legislature 343
Annual Report to the President and the Congress of the National Commission for Manpower Policy see U.S. National Commission for Manpower Policy. Annual Report to the President and the Congress 211
Annual Report to the President and the Congress on the State Energy Conservation Program see U.S. Department of Energy. Office of State and Local Programs. Annual Report to the President and the Congress on the State Energy Conservation Program 364
Annual Report to the Session of the General Assembly (Springfield) see Illinois. Cities and Villages Municipal Problems Commission. Annual Report to the Session of the General Assembly 749
Annual Report to the Supreme Court of Illinois see Illinois. Administrative Office of Illinois Courts. Annual Report to the Supreme Court of Illinois 513
Annual Report - University of Georgia, Institute of Ecology see University of Georgia. Institute of Ecology. Annual Report 389
Annual Report - Utah Juvenile Court see Utah. Juvenile Court. Annual Report 257
Annual Report - Vermont Industrial Development Authority see Vermont Industrial Development Authority. Annual Report 226
Annual Report - Western Society of Malacologists see Western Society of Malacologists. Annual Report 131
Annual Report - Woodrow Wilson International Center for Scholars see Woodrow Wilson International Center for Scholars. Annual Report 343
Annual Report - Youth Correctional Institution (Bordentown) see Youth Correctional Institution, Bordentown, N.J. Annual Report 257
Annual Reports in Inorganic and General Syntheses (US ISSN 0092-1335) 251, 254
Annual Reports in Medicinal Chemistry(US ISSN 0065-7743) 683
Annual Reports in Organic Synthesis (US ISSN 0066-409X) 254
Annual Reports of Committees see American Bar Association. Section of Administrative Law. Annual Reports of Committees 508
Annual Reports on Analytical Atomic Spectroscopy (UK ISSN 0306-1353) 705
Annual Reports on Competition Policy in O E C D Member Countries (FR ISSN 0300-1547) 220
Annual Reports on Fermentation Processes (US ISSN 0140-9115) 245
Annual Reports on N M R Spectroscopy (US ISSN 0066-4103) 705
Annual Review in Automatic Programming (US ISSN 0066-4138) 270
Annual Review of Agriculture, Kinkei District/Kinki Nogyo Josei Hokoku (JA) 12
Annual Review of Allergy (US ISSN 0090-1083) 603
Annual Review of Anthropology (US ISSN 0084-6570) 47
Annual Review of Astronomy and Astrophysics (US ISSN 0066-4146) 81, 695
Annual Review of Behavior Therapy Theory & Practice (US ISSN 0091-6595) 734
Annual Review of Biochemistry (US ISSN 0066-4154) 110

Annual Review of Biophysics and Bioengineering (US ISSN 0084-6589) 112, 366
Annual Review of California Oil & Gas Exploration (US) 678
Annual Review of Clinical Biochemistry(UK) 110
Annual Review of Earth and Planetary Sciences (US ISSN 0084-6597) 81, 288
Annual Review of Ecology and Systematics (US ISSN 0066-4162) 384
Annual Review of Energy (US ISSN 0362-1626) 362
Annual Review of English Books on Asia see Review of English Books on Asia 94
Annual Review of Entomology (US ISSN 0066-4170) 120
Annual Review of Fluid Mechanics (US ISSN 0066-4189) 701
Annual Review of Genetics (US ISSN 0066-4197) 122
Annual Review of Information Science and Technology (US ISSN 0066-4200) 525
Annual Review of Materials Science (US ISSN 0084-6600) 779
Annual Review of Medicine see Annual Review of Medicine: Selected Topics in the Clinical Sciences 592
Annual Review of Medicine: Selected Topics in the Clinical Sciences (US) 592
Annual Review of Microbiology (US ISSN 0066-4227) 123
Annual Review of N M R Spectroscopy(UK ISSN 0066-4235) 705
Annual Review of Neuroscience (US ISSN 0147-006X) 619
Annual Review of Nuclear and Particle Science (US ISSN 0163-8998) 702
Annual Review of Nuclear Science see Annual Review of Nuclear and Particle Science 702
Annual Review of Nutrition (US ISSN 0199-9885) 665
Annual Review of Pharmacology see Annual Review of Pharmacology and Toxicology 683
Annual Review of Pharmacology and Toxicology (US ISSN 0362-1642) 683
Annual Review of Physical Chemistry (US ISSN 0066-426X) 254
Annual Review of Physiology (US ISSN 0066-4278) 125
Annual Review of Phytopathology (US ISSN 0066-4286) 113
Annual Review of Plant Physiology (US ISSN 0066-4294) 113
Annual Review of Prehistoric and Ethnographical Art see I P E K 402
Annual Review of Psychology (US ISSN 0066-4308) 734
Annual Review of Research in Religious Education (US) 763
Annual Review of Sociology (US ISSN 0360-0572) 812
Annual Review of the Schizophrenic Syndrome (US ISSN 0090-287X) 619
Annual Review of United Nations Affairs (US ISSN 0066-4340) 719
Annual Roster - Texas State Board of Landscape Architects see Texas. State Board of Landscape Architects. Annual Roster 70
Annual Salaries of Hospital Nursing Personnel see Canada. Statistics Canada. Health Manpower Section. Annual Salaries of Hospital Nursing Personnel/Traitements Annuels du Personnel Infirmier des Hopitaux 905
Annual Simulation Symposium.(Proceedings) (US) 270
Annual Solar Heating and Cooling Research and Development Branch Contractors' Meeting. Proceedings (US) 362
Annual Statement of the Overseas Trade of the United Kingdom (UK ISSN 0072-5846) 193
Annual Statistical Bulletin Sarawak (MY ISSN 0080-6439) 832

Annual Statistical Report - Division of Family Services see Florida. Division of Family Services. Annual Statistical Report 810
Annual Statistical Report of the Colorado Judiciary (US ISSN 0094-7504) 521
Annual Statistical Review of Canadian Fisheries/Revue Statistique Annuelle des Peches Canadiennes (CN ISSN 0382-2249) 395
Annual Statistical Review: The Distilled Spirits Industry (US ISSN 0066-4367) 85
Annual Statistical Survey of the Electronics Industry (UK) 351
Annual Statistics of Actual Production of Railway Cars/Tetsudo Sharyoto Seisan Dotai Tokei Nenpo (JA) 864
Annual Statistics of Maritime Safety (JA ISSN 0448-3294) 877
Annual Summary of Australian Notices to Mariners (AT) 877
Annual Summary of Business Statistics, New York State (US ISSN 0066-4375) 151
Annual Summary of Information on Natural Disasters (UN ISSN 0066-4383) 303
Annual Summary of Merchant Ships Launched/Completed in the World (UK) 877
Annual Summary of Merchant Ships Launched in the World see Annual Summary of Merchant Ships Launched/Completed in the World 877
Annual Summary of Progress in Gravitation Sciences (US) 695
Annual Summary of Vital Statistics (Boise) see Idaho. Department of Health and Welfare. Annual Summary of Vital Statistics 841
Annual Summative Evaluation Report - National Education Association see National Education Association of the United States. Annual Summative Evaluation Report 320
Annual Survey of African Law (UK ISSN 0066-4405) 508
Annual Survey of American Law (US ISSN 0066-4413) 508
Annual Survey of Commonwealth Law (UK ISSN 0570-2665) 904
Annual Survey of Computer Users (JA) 270
Annual Survey of Illinois Law (US) 508
Annual Survey of Indian Law (II ISSN 0570-2666) 508
Annual Survey of Massachusetts Law (US ISSN 0570-2674) 508
Annual Symposium on Foundations of Computer Science. Proceedings (US) 270
Annual Symposium on Pulmonary Diseases (US ISSN 0361-5006) 623
Annual Symposium on Switching and Automata Theory. Proceedings see Annual Symposium on Foundations of Computer Science. Proceedings 270
Annual T N G Convention Officers' Report see Newspaper Guild. Annual T.N.G. Convention Officers' Report 505
Annual Textile Industry Technical Conference. (Publication) (US ISSN 0094-9884) 855
Annual Trade Report of Tanzania, Uganda and Kenya see Kenya. Commissioner of Customs and Excise. Annual Trade Report 196
Annual Water Quality Report to Congress see Wisconsin. Department of Natural Resources. Annual Water Quality Report to Congress 390
Annual Work Plan - North Cal-Neva Resource Conservation and Development Project see North Cal - Neva Resource Conservation and Development Project. Annual Work Plan 277
Annual Work Program - Southwest New Mexico Council of Governments see Southwest New Mexico Council of Governments. Annual Work Program 746
Annual World's Best S F (US) 559

Annuale Mediaevale (US ISSN 0066-4456) 559
Annuario Amministrativo Italiano (IT ISSN 0084-6619) 739
Annuario Cattolico d'Italia (IT ISSN 0066-4464) 773
Annuario Ceramica (IT ISSN 0066-4472) 244
Annuario dell' Industria Italiana della Gomma/Yearbook of the Italian Rubber Industry (IT ISSN 0066-4499) 777
Annuario dell'Industria Italiana della Maglieria e della Calzetteria (IT) 855
Annuario della Nautica (IT) 826
Annuario Delta-Larousse (BL) 360
Annuario di Diritto Comparato e di Studi Legislativi (IT ISSN 0003-5149) 508
Annuario di Elettronica (IT) 351
Annuario di Statistiche del Lavoro e dell'Emigrazione see Italy. Istituto Centrale di Statistica. Annuario di Statistiche del Lavoro 732
Annuario Diplomatico del Regno d'Italia see Annuario Diplomatico della Repubblica Italiana 719
Annuario Diplomatico della Repubblica Italiana (IT) 719
Annuario do Teatro Brasileiro (BL) 858
Annuario Generale delle Imprese di Viaggio e Turismo (IT) 883
Annuario Generale Italiano (IT ISSN 0084-6627) 181
Annuario Illustrato del Tennis (IT) 823
Annuario Italiano delle Imprese Assicuratrici (IT ISSN 0084-6635) 497
Annuario Musicale (IT) 656
Annuario Ottico Italiano (IT) 220
Annuario Politecnico Italiano (IT ISSN 0066-4510) 234
Annuario Sanitario (IT) 750
Annuario Statistico Italiano (IT ISSN 0066-4545) 832
Annuarium Statisticum Ecclesiae/Statistique de l'Eglise/Statistical Yearbook of the Church. (VC) 769, 832
Ano del Transporte (SP) 861
Ano Literario Espanol (SP) 559
Anon Nine (US) 559
Anorganische und Allgemeine Chemie in Einzeldarstellungen see Inorganic Chemistry Concepts 251
Anschriften Deutscher Verlage und Auslaendischer Verlage mit Deutschen Auslieferungen (GW ISSN 0066-4596) 757
Anschriften Deutschsprachiger Zeitschriften see Deutschsprachige Zeitschriften Deutschland - Oesterreich - Schweiz 90
Ansoman-e Farhang-e Iran-e Bastan. Nashrijeh see Ancient Iranian Cultural Society. Publication 559
Anson G. Phelps Lectureship on Early American History (US ISSN 0066-4618) 466
Antarctic Bibliography (US ISSN 0066-4626) 420
Antarctic Research Series (US ISSN 0066-4634) 420
Antartida (AG ISSN 0302-5691) 420
Antemurale (IT ISSN 0066-4642) 448
Antepasados (US ISSN 0044-8362) 466
Anthill (UK) 559, 578
Anthologia Medica Santoriana (IT) 592
Anthology Film Archives Series (US) 648
Anthology of Magazine Verse and Yearbook of American Poetry (US ISSN 0196-2221) 578
Anthony and Berryman's Magistrates' Court Guide (UK) 508
Anthropologia Hungarica (HU) 47
Anthropological Forum (AT ISSN 0066-4677) 47
Anthropological Handbook (US ISSN 0517-3868) 47
Anthropological Studies (US ISSN 0570-2976) 47
Anthropologie (GW ISSN 0066-4685) 47

Anthropologische Gesellschaft, Vienna. Mitteilungen (AU ISSN 0066-4693) 47
Anthropos (GW ISSN 0066-4723) 47, 673
Anthropos (GR) 47
Anthropos (IT ISSN 0391-3163) 47
Anti-Apartheid Movement. Annual Report of Activities and Developments (UK) 718
Anti-Quarium see A Q 71
Antibiotics (US) 123, 683
Antibiotics and Chemotherapy (SZ ISSN 0066-4758) 683
Antichita, Archeologia, Storia dell'Arte (IT) 57, 71
Antichita Classica e Cristiana (IT ISSN 0066-4766) 430, 540
Antichita Pisane (IT) 57
Antichthon (AT ISSN 0066-4774) 258
Anticipation (SZ) 763, 850
Antiekwereld (NE) 476
Antike Kunst. Beihefte (SZ ISSN 0066-4782) 57, 71
Antipode: A Radical Journal of Geography (US ISSN 0066-4812) 420
Antiquitas. Reihe 1. Abhandlungen zur Alten Geschichte (GW ISSN 0066-4839) 430
Antiquitas. Reihe 2. Abhandlungen aus dem Gebiete der Vor- und Fruehgeschichte (GW ISSN 0066-4847) 430
Antiquitas. Reihe 3. Abhandlungen zur Vor- und Fruehgeschichte, zur Klassischen und Provinzial-Roemischen Archaeologie und zur Geschichte des Altertums (GW ISSN 0066-4855) 57, 430
Antiquitas. Reihe 4. Beitraege zur Historia-Augusta-Forschung (GW ISSN 0066-4863) 430
Antiquites Africaines (FR ISSN 0066-4871) 57, 439
Antologia del Folklore Musical Chileno(CL ISSN 0066-4928) 904
Antologia Poetica del Partido de Esteban Echeverria (AG) 578
Antologias del Pensamiento Politico (VE ISSN 0066-4936) 708
Antropologia (PL) 47
Antropologia Andina (PE) 47
Antropologia Ecuatoriana (EC) 47
Antropologia Fisica (PE) 47
Antropologia Social (MX ISSN 0570-3697) 47
Anuario Antropologico (BL) 47
Anuario Baja California y sus Hombres (MX) 420
Anuario Bibliografico Colombiano (CK ISSN 0570-393X) 87
Anuario Bibliografico Costarricense (CR ISSN 0066-5010) 87
Anuario Bibliografico Ecuatoriano (EC) 87
Anuario Bibliografico Uruguayo (UY) 87
Anuario Brasileiro de Media (BL) 263
Anuario Brasileiro de Medicina Veterinaria (BL) 894
Anuario Brasileiro de Propaganda (BL ISSN 0570-3956) 4
Anuario Brasileiro de Supermercados (BL) 181, 217
Anuario Brasileiro de Transportes (BL) 861
Anuario Brasileiro do Frio (BL) 429
Anuario - C B A - Yearbook (UY) 87
Anuario Colombiano de Historia Social y de la Cultura (CK ISSN 0066-5045) 796
Anuario Comercial Iberoamericano (SP ISSN 0570-3980) 193
Anuario Cultural del Peru (PE ISSN 0570-4006) 555
Anuario da Industria Brasileira de Autopecas/Yearbook of the Brazilian Industry of Automotive Parts (BL) 869
Anuario da Provincia de Mocambique see Anuario do Estado de Mocambique 439
Anuario das Industrias do Estado do Rio Grande do Sul (BL) 220

Anuario de Bibliotecologia, Archivologia e Informatica see Centro de Bibliotecologia, Archivologia e Informacion. Anuario 528
Anuario de Cinema (BL ISSN 0066-5053) 648
Anuario de Comercio Exterior de Mexico (MX) 193
Anuario de Derecho Internacional (SP) 522
Anuario de Empresas Exportadoras (SP) 234
Anuario de Estudios Americanos (SP) 47
Anuario de Estudios Centroamericanos (CR ISSN 0377-7316) 708
Anuario de Estudios Medievales (SP ISSN 0066-5061) 448
Anuario de Eusko-Folklore (SP) 47, 401
Anuario de Exportacion de Austria see Herold Export-Adressbuch von Oesterreich 238
Anuario de Filologia (VE ISSN 0066-507X) 540
Anuario de Filologia (SP ISSN 0210-1343) 540
Anuario de Filosofia del Derecho (SP) 508
Anuario de Historia del Derecho Espanol (SP) 449, 522
Anuario de Historia Moderna y Contemporanea (SP ISSN 0210-9603) 430
Anuario de Jurisprudencia Argentina see Jurisprudencia Argentina 514
Anuario de la Arquitectura en Colombia (CK) 68
Anuario de la Biblioteca de la Cataluna y de las Populares y Especiales de Barcelona (SP) 525
Anuario de la Fotografia Artistica Argentina (AG) 692
Anuario de la Fotografia Espanola see Everfoto 693
Anuario de la Industria Nautica Espanola (SP) 904
Anuario de la Prensa Chilena (CL) 504
Anuario de la Relojeria en Espana see Anuario de Relojeria y Arte en Metal para Espana e Hispanoamerica 503
Anuario de las Relaciones Laborales en Espana (SP) 205
Anuario de Legislacion Argentina see Revista de Legislacion Argentina 517
Anuario de los Paises de A L A L C see Anuario del Comercio Exterior Latino-Americano 193
Anuario de Poetas Contemporaneos (AG) 904
Anuario de Poetas do Brasil (BL) 578
Anuario de Portos e Navios (BL) 877
Anuario de Psicologia (SP ISSN 0066-5126) 734
Anuario de Relojeria y Arte en Metal para Espana e Hispanoamerica (SP ISSN 0066-510X) 503
Anuario de Sociologia y Psicologia Juridicas (SP) 508, 734, 812
Anuario del Arte Espanol (SP ISSN 0302-6965) 71
Anuario del Comercio Exterior Latino-Americano (AG ISSN 0066-5118) 193
Anuario del Cuento Costarricense (CR ISSN 0587-5196) 559
Anuario del Desarrollo de la Educacion, la Ciencia y la Cultura en America Latina (US ISSN 0570-4200) 904
Anuario del Exportador (MX) 193
Anuario do Estado de Mocambique (MZ) 439
Anuario dos Criadores (BL ISSN 0518-0937) 12
Anuario Economico-Fiscal (BL) 191
Anuario Economico y Social de Espana(SP) 183
Anuario Ecuatoriano de Derecho Internacional (EC ISSN 0570-4251) 522
Anuario Empresarial de Colombia (CK) 234
Anuario Enfermedades de Notificacion Obligatoria (CL) 592

Anuario Espanol de Seguros (SP) 497
Anuario Estadistico Centroamericano de Comercio Exterior (GT ISSN 0570-426X) 151
Anuario Estadistico de Comercio Exterior de los Estados Unidos Mexicanos (MX) 151
Anuario Estadistico de Cuba (CU ISSN 0574-6132) 832
Anuario Estadistico de Espana (SP ISSN 0066-5177) 832
Anuario Estadistico de Los Andes; Venezuela (VE ISSN 0066-5185) 151
Anuario Estadistico del Paraguay (PY) 832
Anuario Estatistico da Guanabara see Anuario Estatistico do Estado do Rio de Janeiro 832
Anuario Estatistico do Brasil (BL) 832
Anuario Estatistico do Estado do Rio de Janeiro (BL) 832
Anuario Estatistico dos Transportes (BL) 861
Anuario F.H.I. Argentina: Frutas y Hortalizas Industriarizadas y Frescas/F. H. I. Annual: Fresh and Industrialized Fruits and Vegetables (AG ISSN 0066-5207) 33
Anuario Filosofico (SP ISSN 0066-5215) 687
Anuario Financiero y de Sociedades Anonimas de Espana (SP ISSN 0301-7443) 168, 220
Anuario Geografico del Peru (PE ISSN 0066-5223) 420, 466
Anuario Hidrologico del Istmo Centroamericano (UN) 307
Anuario Hortofruticola Espanol (SP) 27
Anuario Iberoamericano (SP ISSN 0570-4324) 796
Anuario Iberoamericano de Seguros (SP) 497
Anuario Indigenista/Indianist Yearbook(MX) 47
Anuario Industrial de Minas Gerais; Guia Economico e Industrial do Estado de Minas Gerais 643
Anuario Industrial do Espirito Santo (BL) 234
Anuario Interamericano de Derechos Humanos/Inter-American Yearbook on Human Rights (US) 522
Anuario Latinoamericano (US ISSN 0570-4359) 12
Anuario Martiano see Centro de Estudios Martianos. Anuario 467
Anuario Mineral Brasileiro (BL) 641
Anuario Politico de America Latina (MX) 708
Anuarios de Geomagnetismo - Ano... (SP) 291, 303
Anuarios del Servicio de Geomagnetismo y Aeronomia see Anuarios de Geomagnetismo - Ano 303
Anul Cinematografic (RM) 648
Anwaltsverzeichnis (GW ISSN 0402-6802) 509
Anzeiger fuer Slavische Philologie (AU ISSN 0066-5282) 559
Apartment Building Income-Expense Analysis see Income-Expense Analysis: Apartments 761
Apercu de la Statistique Federale Allemande see Survey of German Federal Statistics 848
Apocrypha Novi Testamenti (NE ISSN 0066-5320) 763
Apollonia (AT ISSN 0066-5339) 609
Apotheker-Jahrbuch (GW ISSN 0066-5347) 683
Appalachian Financial Review. see Financial Review 173
Appalachian Gas Measurement Short Course, West Virginia University. Proceedings (US ISSN 0066-5371) 678
Appalachian Regional Commission. Annual Report (US ISSN 0503-5422) 812
Appalachian Underground Corrosion Short Course, West Virginia University. Proceedings (US ISSN 0066-538X) 379
Appaloosa Horse; Stud Book and Registry (US) 827

Apparat Upravleniya Sotsialisticheskogo Gosudarstva. Izdanie V Dvukh Chastyakh (UR) 559
Apparel Buyers Guide Year Book (NZ) 234, 855
Apparel Plant Wages and Personnel Policies see Personnel Policies and Benefits for the Apparel Industry 220
Apparel Plant Wages and Personnel Policies see Apparel Plant Wages Survey 855
Apparel Plant Wages Survey (US) 261, 855
Appel Service; Repertoire d'Adresses Utiles pour le Commerce et l'Industrie (FR ISSN 0066-5398) 235
Appliance Technical Conference. Preprints (US ISSN 0066-5401) 351
Applications of Cryogenic Technology (US) 700
Applications of Library Science (US) 525
Applications of Management Science (US) 214
Applications of Mathematics (US) 584
Applied Chemistry Series (UK ISSN 0066-541X) 372
Applied Linguistics see Jezykoznawstwo Stosowane 546
Applied Mathematical Sciences (US ISSN 0066-5452) 584
Applied Mathematics and Mechanics (US ISSN 0066-5479) 584, 701
Applied Methods in Oncology (NE) 592
Applied Mineralogy. Technische Mineralogie (US ISSN 0066-5487) 641
Applied Optics. Supplement (US ISSN 0066-5495) 705
Applied Ornithology see Angewandte Ornithologie 124
Applied Physics and Engineering (US ISSN 0066-5509) 366, 695
Applied Polymer Symposia see Journal of Applied Polymer Science. Symposia 373
Applied Polymer Symposium. Papers (US ISSN 0066-5517) 372
Applied Solid State Science (US ISSN 0066-5533) 351
Applied Spectroscopy Reviews (US ISSN 0570-4928) 705
Applied Systems Science (US) 270
Appreciation of the Arts (US ISSN 0066-5568) 71
Approaches to Semiotics (NE ISSN 0066-5576) 541
Appropriation Accounts, Revenue Statements, Accounts of the Funds and Other Public Accounts of Tanzania (TZ ISSN 0496-8492) 226
Apricot, Peach and Pear Growers' Association Annual see A P G A Annual 414
Apulum (RM) 449
Apuntes de la Linea (AG) 555
Apuntes de Trabajo Social (AG) 804
Apuntes Oceanologicos (CL) 309
Aqua Fennica (FI ISSN 0356-7133) 895
Aquaculture Review (CN) 395
Aquarimantima (CK) 578
Aquario (AG) 578
Aquatics Guide see N A G W S Guide. Aquatics 820
Aqui (UY ISSN 0066-5606) 559
Aquiculture (CH) 395
Aquila (US) 578
Aquinas Law Journal (CE) 509
Aquinas Lecture Series (US ISSN 0066-5614) 687
Ar Gwyr see Cahiers Bretons 796
Arab and Afro-Asian Monograph Series see Institute for Arab Studies. Publications and Studies 475
Arab Bank for Economic Development in Africa. Annual Report (SJ) 168, 199
Arab Book Annual/Al-Kitab Al-Arabi Fi Aam (UA ISSN 0066-5630) 760
Arab Business Yearbook (UK ISSN 0140-1874) 193
Arab Countries (HK) 883
Arab Directory/Dalil el Arab (CN ISSN 0706-7917) 391

Arab Fund for Economic and Social Development. Annual Report (KU ISSN 0304-6729) 199
Arab Horse Stud Book (UK) 827
Arab Maritime Data (UK) 877
Arab Oil & Gas Directory (FR) 678
Arab Trade Directory (UK) 235
Arab Trade Guide (US) 235
Arab View (IS) 904
Arabia Past & Present Series (UK) 474
Arabian Government and Public Services Directory (UK) 739
Arabian Studies (UK ISSN 0305-036X) 474, 708
Arabian Transport Directory (US) 861
Arabian Yearbook (UK) 235
Al-Arabiyya (US) 541, 559
Araisa (VE) 555
Arbeidsongeschiktheidsfonds. Jaarverslag (NE) 497
Arbeiten aus dem Paul-Ehrlich-Institut, dem Georg-Speyer-Haus und dem Ferdinand-Blum-Institut (GW ISSN 0066-5665) 100, 592
Arbeiten zur Angewandten Statistik (GW ISSN 0066-5673) 832
Arbeiten zur Geschichte des Antiken Judentums und des Urchristentums (NE ISSN 0066-5681) 770
Arbeiten zur Literatur und Geschichte des Hellenistischen Judentums (NE) 770
Arbeiten zur Paedagogik (GW ISSN 0066-569X) 314
Arbeiten zur Rechtsvergleichung (GW ISSN 0066-5703) 509
Arbeiten zur Rheinischen Landeskunde (GW ISSN 0373-7187) 420
Arbeiten zur Theologie. Reihe 1 (GW ISSN 0066-5711) 763
Arbeiterbewegung- Theorie und Geschichte. Jahrbuecher (GW) 205
Arbeitsberichte zur Bibliothekstechnik Informationen see A B T Informationen 525
Das Arbeitsgebiet der Bundesstatistik (GW ISSN 0072-162X) 833
Arbeitsgemeinschaft der Parlaments- und Behoerdenbibliotheken. Arbeitshefte (GW ISSN 0518-2220) 525
Arbeitsgemeinschaft Erdoel-Gewinnung und-Verarbeitung Jahresbericht see M W V /A E V Jahresbericht 253
Arbeitsgemeinschaft fuer Forschung des Landes Nordrhein-Westfalen. Veroeffentlichungen see Rheinisch-Westfaelische Akademie der Wissenschaften. Veroeffentlichungen 789
Arbeitsgemeinschaft fuer Lebensniveauvergleiche. Schriftenreihe (AU) 796
Arbeitsgemeinschaft Katholisch-Theologischer Bibliotheken. Mitteilungsblatt (GW) 525
Arbeitsgruppe fuer Empirische Bildungsforschung. Uebersicht ueber die Bisherigen Arbeiten (GW) 314
Arbeitshefte zur Gemeinschaftskunde (GW ISSN 0066-5827) 796
Arbeitskosten in der Industrie Oesterreichs (AU) 206
Arbeitskreis der Deutschen Afrika-Forschungs- und Dokumentationsstellen. Rundbrief (GW) 439
Arbeitskreis fuer Jugendliteratur. Jahrbuch. (GW) 257
Arbeitsmarkt Politik (AU ISSN 0587-1689) 206
Arbeitsmedizin (GE ISSN 0066-5843) 495, 592
Arbeitsmedizinische Fragen in der Ophthalmologie/Problems of Industrial Medicine in Ophthalmology (SZ ISSN 0066-5851) 904
Arbeitsmethoden der Medizinischen und Naturwissenschaftlichen Kriminalistik (GW ISSN 0570-5886) 612
Arbeitsrecht der Gegenwart (GW ISSN 0066-586X) 206, 509
Arbeitsrecht und Arbeitslosenversicherung (SZ ISSN 0003-777X) 206
Arbok Visindafelags Islendinga (IC) 779

Arboretum Kornickie (PL ISSN 0066-5878) 113
Arch Reports see Franklin McLean Memorial Research Institute. Annual Report 111
Archaelogia Belgica (BE) 57
Archaeo-Physika (GW ISSN 0066-5886) 57
Archaeoastronomy (UK ISSN 0142-7253) 81
Archaeologia (UK) 57
Archaeologia Austriaca (AU ISSN 0003-8008) 47, 57
Archaeologia Cantiana (UK ISSN 0066-5894) 57
Archaeologia Geographica (GW ISSN 0066-5908) 57
Archaeologia Historica (CS) 57
Archaeologia Hungarica. Series Nova (HU ISSN 0066-5916) 57
Archaeologia Japonica (JA ISSN 0402-852X) 57
Archaeologia Polona (PL ISSN 0066-5924) 57
Archaeologica Slovaca. Catalogi (GW ISSN 0066-5932) 57
Archaeologica Slovaca. Fontes (GW ISSN 0066-5940) 57
Archaeological Bibliography for Great Britain and Ireland (UK ISSN 0066-5967) 57
Archaeological Completion Report Series (US) 57, 466
Archaeological Excavation Reports see Israel. Ministry of Education and Culture. Department of Antiquities and Museums. Atiqot (English Series) 62
Archaeological Excavations (UK) 57
Archaeological Exploration of Sardis. Monographs (US ISSN 0066-5975) 57
Archaeological Journal (UK ISSN 0066-5983) 57
Archaeological Society of Delaware. Bulletin (US ISSN 0003-8067) 57
Archaeological Society of Delaware. Monograph (US) 57
Archaeologicum Belgii Speculum (BE) 57
Archaeologische Bibliographie (GW) 67
Archaeologische Funde und Denkmaeler des Rheinlandes (GW ISSN 0066-6009) 57
Archaeologische Informationen. Mitteilungen zur Ur- und Fruehgeschichte (GW) 57
Archaeologische Kaarten van Belgie see Archeologische Kaarten van Belgie 57
Archaeologische Mitteilungen aus Iran. Neue Folge (GW ISSN 0066-6033) 57
Archaeologisches Korrespondenzblatt (GW) 57
Archaeology Abroad see Archaeology Abroad Service. Newsheet 57
Archaeology Abroad Service. Newsheet(UK) 57
Archaeology in Britain (Year) (UK ISSN 0308-8456) 57
Archaeology of Eastern North America(US ISSN 0360-1021) 57
Archaeonautica (FR) 57, 309
Archeion (PL ISSN 0066-6041) 449
Archenhold-Sternwarte. Vortraege und Schriften (GE) 81
Archeologia (PL ISSN 0066-605X) 57
Archeologia (PL) 57
Archeologia Classica (IT ISSN 0003-8172) 57, 258
Archeologie de la Moldavie see Arheologia Moldovei 449
Archeologie Mediterraneenne (FR ISSN 0066-6084) 57
Archeologische Kaarten van Belgie/ Archaeologische Kaarten van Belgie (BE ISSN 0066-6025) 57
Archery-Golf Guide see N A G W S Guide. Archery-Fencing 820
Archigram (UK ISSN 0066-6092) 68
Archimede. Quaderni (IT ISSN 0066-6106) 347
Architect and Contractors Yearbook (UK ISSN 0066-6114) 68
Architectes (FR ISSN 0066-6122) 68
Architectonika Themata see Architecture in Greece 68

Architects, Builders, and Contractors Blue-Book (SA ISSN 0084-6708) 904
Architects, Contractors & Engineers Guide to Construction Costs (US ISSN 0066-6157) 134
Architects' Guide to Glass, Metal & Glazing (US) 68, 244
Architect's Handbook of Professional Practice (US ISSN 0066-6173) 68
Architects Standard Catalogues (UK ISSN 0066-6181) 68
Architects' Year Book (UK ISSN 0066-619X) 68
Architectura (HU ISSN 0066-6270) 68
Architectural and Archaeological Society of Durham and Northumberland. Transactions. New Series (UK ISSN 0066-6203) 57, 449
Architectural Handbook (US) 68
Architectural History (UK ISSN 0066-622X) 68
Architectural Index (US ISSN 0570-6483) 68
Architectural Metalwork Association. Members Specialised Products (UK) 68
Architecture in Greece/Architectonika Themata (GR ISSN 0066-6262) 68
Architecture Schools in North America (US ISSN 0092-7856) 68
Architecture Series: Bibliography (US ISSN 0194-1356) 71, 87
Architettura Urbanistica: Metodi di Programmazione e Progetti (IT) 68
Archiv fuer Arzneitherapie (GW ISSN 0342-1694) 592
Archiv fuer Diplomatik, Schriftgeschichte, Siegel- und Wappenkunde (GW ISSN 0066-6297) 449
Archiv fuer Eisenbahntechnik (GW ISSN 0341-0463) 872
Archiv fuer Fischereiwissenschaft (GW ISSN 0003-9063) 395
Archiv fuer Geschichte von Oberfranken (GW ISSN 0066-6335) 449
Archiv fuer Hessische Geschichte und Altertumskunde (GW ISSN 0066-636X) 449
Archiv fuer Indische Philosophie see Wiener Zeitschrift fuer die Kunde Suedasiens und Archiv fuer Indische Philosphie 692
Archiv fuer Kinderheilkunde. Beihefte see Buecherei des Paediaters 617
Archiv fuer Liturgiewissenschaft (GW ISSN 0066-6386) 763
Archiv fuer Meteorologie, Geophysik und Bioklimatologie. Series A. Meteorology and Geophysics. Supplement (US ISSN 0066-6394) 303, 631
Archiv fuer Mittelrheinische Kirchengeschichte (GW ISSN 0066-6432) 763
Archiv fuer Musikorganologie (GW) 656
Archiv fuer Musikwissenschaft. Beihefte(GW ISSN 0570-6769) 657
Archiv fuer Orientforschung (AU ISSN 0066-6440) 474
Archiv fuer Papyrusforschung und Verwandte Gebiete (GE ISSN 0066-6459) 57, 430
Archiv fuer Rechts- und Sozialphilosophie. Beihefte. Neue Folge (GW ISSN 0341-079X) 509, 687
Archiv fuer Reformationsgeschichte see Archive for Reformation History 430
Archiv fuer Reformationsgeschichte. Literaturbericht see Archive for Reformation History. Literature Review 763
Archiv fuer Religionsgeschichte (GW ISSN 0084-6724) 734, 763
Archiv fuer Schlesische Kirchengeschichte (GW ISSN 0066-6491) 763
Archiv fuer Sozialgeschichte (GW ISSN 0066-6505) 449
Archiv fuer Vaterlaendische Geschichte und Topographie (AU ISSN 0003-9462) 449

Archiv fuer Vergleichende Kulturwissenschaft (GW ISSN 0570-6793) 48
Archiv fuer Voelkerkunde (AU ISSN 0066-6513) 48, 401
Archivalia Medica (MX ISSN 0066-6521) 592
Archivas de Farmacologia y Toxicologia(SP) 683
Archive for New Poetry Newsletter (US) 578
Archive for Reformation History/ Archiv fuer Reformationsgeschichte (US) 430
Archive for Reformation History. Literature Review/Archiv fuer Reformationsgeschichte. Literaturbericht (US) 559, 763
Archives and the User (UK ISSN 0066-653X) 525
Archives Bakounine/Bakunin-Archiv (NE ISSN 0066-6548) 449
Archives Claudeliennes (FR ISSN 0066-6556) 559
Archives d'Anthropologie see Musee Royal de l'Afrique Centrale. Archives d'Anthropologie 51
Archives d'Ethnographie see Musee Royal de l'Afrique Centrale. Archives d'Anthropologie 51
Archives d'Ethnologie Francaise (FR ISSN 0066-6580) 48
Archives d'Histoire Doctrinale et Litteraire du Moyen Age (FR) 687
Archives de Philosophie du Droit (FR ISSN 0066-6564) 509
Archives des Lettres Canadiennes (CN ISSN 0066-6572) 559
Archives des Lettres Modernes (FR ISSN 0003-9675) 559
Archives for Scandinavian Philology see Arkiv for Nordisk Filologi 541
Archives Internationales d'Histoire des Idees/International Archives of the History of Ideas (NE ISSN 0066-6610) 687
Archives News (US) 285
Archives of Asian Art (US ISSN 0066-6637) 71
Archives of Labor and Urban Affairs Newsletter (US) 206
Archives of Labor History and Urban Affairs Newsletter see Archives of Labor and Urban Affairs Newsletter 206
Archives of Podiatric Medicine and Foot Surgery (US ISSN 0092-7651) 904
Archives of Toxicology. Supplement (US) 683
Archiviniana (PH) 525
Archivio de Vecchi (IT ISSN 0004-0061) 592
Archivio del Teatro Italiano (IT ISSN 0066-6661) 858
Archivio di Oceanografia e Limnologia (IT ISSN 0066-667X) 307, 309
Archivio Italiano per la Storia della Pieta (IT ISSN 0066-6688) 763
Archivio Linguistico Veneto. Quaderni. (IT ISSN 0066-6696) 541
Archivio Putti di Chirurgia degli Organi di Movimento (IT ISSN 0066-670X) 624
Archivio Storico Italiano. Biblioteca (IT ISSN 0066-6718) 449
Archivio Storico Lodigiano (IT ISSN 0004-0347) 449
Archivo Epistolar Colombiano (CK ISSN 0066-6734) 559
Archivo General de la Nacion. Revista (AG ISSN 0325-2868) 525
Archivo General de la Nacion. Revista (PE) 904
Archivo Historico del Guayas. Coleccion Monografica (EC) 466
Archivos de Biologia y Medicina Experimentales (CL ISSN 0004-0533) 100, 612
Archivos de Botanica do Estado de Sao Paulo see Rickia 117
Archivos de Farmacologia y Toxicologia (SP) 683
Archivos Venezolanos de Folklore (VE ISSN 0570-7196) 401
Archivum (YU) 430
Archivum Bibliographicum Carmelitanum (VC ISSN 0570-7242) 769

Archivum Historiae Pontificae (VC ISSN 0066-6785) 773
Archivum Iuridicum Cracoviense (PL ISSN 0066-6882) 509
Archivum Musicum (IT) 657
Archivum Ottomanicum (US) 474
Archivum; Revue Internationale des Archives (GW ISSN 0066-6793) 526
Archivum Romanicum. Biblioteca. Serie 1: Storia Letteratura-Paleografia (IT ISSN 0066-6807) 449
Archivum Romanicum. Biblioteca. Serie 2: Linguistica (IT ISSN 0066-6815) 541
Archiwum Dziejow Oswiaty (PL ISSN 0066-6831) 314
Archiwum Etnograficzne (PL ISSN 0066-6858) 48, 812
Archiwum Filologiczne (PL ISSN 0066-6866) 258, 541
Archiwum Historii Filozofii i Mysli Spolecznej (PL ISSN 0066-6874) 687, 796
Archiwum Kryminologii (PL ISSN 0066-6890) 280
Archiwum Literackie (PL ISSN 0066-6904) 559
Archiwum Ochrony Srodowiska (PL ISSN 0324-8461) 384
Archiwum Slaskie Kultury Muzycznej see Prace Archiwum Slaskie Kultury Muzycznej 662
Archiwum Tlumaczen z Teorii Literatury i Metodologii Badan Literackich (PL) 541, 559
Arctic Institute of North America. Research Paper (CN ISSN 0066-6971) 420, 779
Arctic Institute of North America. Technical Paper (CN ISSN 0066-698X) 779
Arctinurus Newsletter (US) 779
Arctos; Acta Philologica Fennica (FI ISSN 0570-734X) 258, 541
Arctos; Acta Philologica Fennica. Supplementum (FI ISSN 0066-6998) 904
Ardis New Poets Series (US) 578
Area Metalurgia (CL) 627
Area Social Service Centers see North Dakota. Social Service Board. Area Social Service Centers 808
Arena, Auditorium, Stadium Guide see Audarena Stadium Guide and International Directory 4
Arenaturist (YU) 883
Areopag (GW ISSN 0570-751X) 263
Argamon (IS ISSN 0334-3261) 127
Argentina. Caja Federal de Ahorro y Prestamo para la Vivienda. Memoria y Balance (AG) 483
Argentina. Central de Estadisticas Nacionales. Informe (AG) 833
Argentina. Comision Nacional de Valores. Informacion Estadistica (AG) 833
Argentina. Departamento de Estadistica Educativa. Boletin Informativo. (AG ISSN 0066-7021) 314
Argentina. Departamento de Estudios Historicos Navales. Serie A: Cultura Nautica (AG ISSN 0066-703X) 638
Argentina. Departamento de Estudios Historicos Navales. Serie B: Historia Naval Argentina (AG ISSN 0066-7048) 638
Argentina. Departamento de Estudios Historicos Navales. Serie C: Biografias Navales Argentinas (AG ISSN 0066-7056) 96, 638
Argentina. Departamento de Estudios Historicos Navales. Serie E: Documentos (AG) 466, 638
Argentina. Departamento de Estudios Historicos Navales. Serie J: Libros y Impresos Raros (AG ISSN 0066-7080) 641
Argentina. Direccion de Investigaciones Forestales. Folleto Tecnico Forestal (AG) 407
Argentina. Direccion de Investigaciones Forestales. Notas Silvicolas (AG ISSN 0066-7102) 407

Argentina. Direccion de Investigaciones Forestales. Notas Tecnologicas Forestales see Argentina. Direccion de Investigaciones Forestales. Folleto Tecnico Forestal 407
Argentina. Direccion de Investigaciones Forrestales. Misceleneas Forestales (AG ISSN 0066-7099) 407
Argentina. Direccion General de Parques Nacionales. Anales de Parques Nacionales see Argentina. Servicio Nacional de Parques Nacional. Anales 739
Argentina. Direccion General de Planificacion y Control Energetico. Anuario Estadistico (AG) 364
Argentina. Direccion Nacional de Energia y Combustibles. Departamento de Estadistica. Anuario Estadistico Combustibles see Argentina. Direccion General de Planificacion y Control Energetico. Anuario Estadistico 364
Argentina. Division de Estadisticas Sociales. Conflictos del Trabajo (AG) 206
Argentina. Estacion Experimental Agropecuaria Manfredi. Serie Informacion Tecnica (AG ISSN 0066-7242) 12
Argentina. Instituto de Asuntos Tecnicos. Estadisticas (AG) 854
Argentina. Instituto Etnico Nacional. Anales (AG) 48, 466
Argentina. Instituto Forestal Nacional. Anuario de Estadistica Forestal (AG ISSN 0518-4142) 407
Argentina. Instituto Nacional de Derecho Aeronautico y Espacial (AG ISSN 0066-7188) 509, 867
Argentina. Instituto Nacional de Estadistica y Censos. Anuario Estadistico (AG) 833
Argentina. Instituto Nacional de Estadistica y Censos. Indicadores Industriales. Serie I (AG) 151
Argentina. Instituto Nacional de Estadistica y Censos. Informe Serie E: Edificacione (AG ISSN 0066-7196) 833
Argentina. Instituto Nacional de Estadistica y Censos. Navegacion Commercial Argentina (AG) 864
Argentina. Instituto Nacional de Estadistica y Censos. Serie Informacion Demografica (AG) 725
Argentina. Instituto Nacional de Geologia y Mineria. Revista see Argentina. Servicio Nacional Minero Geologico. Revista 291
Argentina. Instituto Nacional de Tecnologia Agropecuaria. Suelos (AG) 33
Argentina. Instituto Nacional de Tecnologia Industria. Boletin Tecnico(AG ISSN 0325-6278) 850
Argentina. Junta Nacional de Carnes. Sintesis Estadistica (AG ISSN 0066-7269) 23
Argentina. Mercado Nacional de Hacienda. Anuario (AG) 43
Argentina. Oficina Sectorial de Desarrollo de Energia. Anuarios Estadisticos: Combustible (AG ISSN 0066-7277) 351
Argentina. Oficina Sectorial de Desarrollo de Energia. Anuarios Estadisticos. Energia Electrica (AG ISSN 0066-7285) 351
Argentina. Secretaria de Estado de Agricultura y Ganaderia. Area de Trabajo de Lecheria. Resena Estadistica (AG) 23
Argentina. Secretaria de Estado de Agricultura y Ganaderia. Comunicado de Prensa (AG) 12
Argentina. Secretaria de Estado de Hacienda. Memoria (AG) 226
Argentina. Secretaria de Estado de Salud Publica. Programa Nacional de Estadisticas de Salud (AG) 756
Argentina. Secretaria de Guerra. Direccion de Estudios Historicos. Boletin Bibliografico (AG ISSN 0066-7293) 466, 638
Argentina. Servicio de Hidrografia Naval. Boletin (AG ISSN 0004-1076) 309

Argentina. Servicio de Inteligencia Naval. Bibliotecas de la Armada. Boletin Bibliografico. (AG ISSN 0066-7331) 641
Argentina. Servicio Nacional de Economia y Sociologia Rural. Publicacion E S R (AG) 12
Argentina. Servicio Nacional de Parques Nacional. Anales (AG ISSN 0302-5705) 739
Argentina. Servicio Nacional de Pesca. Monografias de Recursos Pesqueros (AG) 395
Argentina. Servicio Nacional Minero Geologico. Anales (AG ISSN 0066-7145) 291, 641
Argentina. Servicio Nacional Minero Geologico. Boletin (AG ISSN 0066-7153) 291, 641
Argentina. Servicio Nacional Minero Geologico. Estadistica Minera (AG ISSN 0066-7161) 641
Argentina. Servicio Nacional Minero Geologico. Informes Tecnicos (AG) 291
Argentina. Servicio Nacional Minero Geologico. Revista (AG ISSN 0066-717X) 291
Argentine Economic Development (AG) 183
Argentine Republic. Direccion Nacional de Geologia y Mineria. Anales see Argentina. Servicio Nacional Minero Geologico. Anales 291
Argentine Republic. Direccion Nacional de Geologia y Mineria. Boletin see Argentina. Servicio Nacional Minero Geologico. Boletin 291
Argentine Republic. Direccion Nacional de Geologia y Mineria. Estadistica Minera see Argentina. Servicio Nacional Minero Geologico. Estadistica Minera 641
Argentine Republic. Junta Nacional de Carnes. Resena see Argentina. Junta Nacional de Carnes. Sintesis Estadistica 23
Argentine Republic. Mercado Nacional de Hacienda. Memoria see Argentina. Mercado Nacional de Hacienda. Anuario 43
Argo see Probe (Santa Barbara) 719
Arguments et Documents see Collection "Arguments et Documents 796
Arguments of the Philosophers (UK) 687
Argus de la Poesie Francaise (FR ISSN 0066-734X) 578
Argus F. C. & S. Chart (Fire Casualty & Surety) (US ISSN 0360-8921) 497
Argus Insurance Chart see Argus F. C. & S. Chart 497
Arheologia Moldovei/Archeologie de la Moldavie (RM ISSN 0066-7358) 58, 449
Arhivski Vjesnik (YU) 449
Arid Zone Research (UN ISSN 0066-7366) 275, 288
Ariel (PK) 559
Aristo - Mitteilungen fuer Ingenieur- und Hochschulen (GW ISSN 0518-5378) 347, 584
Arizona. Advisory Commission on Arizona Environment. Annual Report see Arizona. Governor's Commission on Arizona Environment. Annual Report 384
Arizona. Department of Economic Security. Annual Report (US ISSN 0094-0712) 739
Arizona. Department of Economic Security. Report see Population Estimates of Arizona 729
Arizona. Department of Education. Annual Report of the Superintendent of Public Instruction (US ISSN 0095-5310) 314
Arizona. Department of Health Services. Annual Report (US ISSN 0362-1421) 750
Arizona. Department of Public Safety. Annual Report (US ISSN 0066-7382) 280
Arizona. Department of Public Safety. Statistical Reviews see Arizona. Department of Public Safety. Annual Report 280

Arizona. Governor's Commission on Arizona Environment. Annual Report (US) 384
Arizona. State Advisory Council for Vocational Education. Annual Report(US ISSN 0091-8792) 347
Arizona. State Dental Board. Report. (US ISSN 0098-6828) 609
Arizona. State Land Department. Water Resources Report see Arizona. Water Commission. Bulletin 895
Arizona. Water Commission. Bulletin. (US ISSN 0360-7461) 895
Arizona Commission on the Arts & Humanities. Report to the Governor.(US ISSN 0098-7387) 489
Arizona Directory of State Regulatory Agencies for Businesses and Occupations (US) 740
Arizona Forestry Notes (US ISSN 0066-7404) 407
Arizona Geological Society Digest (US ISSN 0066-7412) 291
Arizona Historical Society. Historical Monographs (US) 466
Arizona Historical Society. Museum Monograph Series (US) 466
Arizona Land Surveyors Conference. Proceedings (US ISSN 0066-7439) 374, 420
Arizona Landmarks (US) 12, 407, 641
Arizona Latin American Conference Papers (US) 904
Arizona Legislative Service (US ISSN 0094-4246) 509
Arizona Mining and Manufacturing (US ISSN 0146-2997) 220
Arizona Mobile Home & Recreational Vehicle Park Guide (US) 483
Arizona Model United Nations (US ISSN 0066-7447) 347, 522
Arizona, New Mexico Tour Book see Tourbook: Arizona, New Mexico 891
Arizona Political Almanac (US ISSN 0571-0111) 708
Arizona Reports (US) 509
Arizona-Sonora Desert Museum. Annual Report (US) 652
Arizona State Industrial Directory (US ISSN 0195-7082) 235
Arizona State Plan for the Education of Migratory Children (US) 314
Arizona State University. Bureau of Educational Research and Services. Educational Services Bulletin. (US ISSN 0066-7455) 314
Arizona State University. Bureau of Educational Research and Services. Research and Services Bulletin. (US ISSN 0066-7463) 314
Arizona State University. Center for Asian Studies. Occasional Papers (US) 442
Arizona State University. Center for Public Affairs. Monograph. (US) 708
Arizona State University. Faculty of Industrial Engineering. Industrial Engineering Research Bulletin (US ISSN 0570-9601) 366
Arizona State University. Governmental Finance Institute. Proceedings see Papers in Public Administration 745
Arizona State University Anthropological Research Papers (US ISSN 0271-0641) 48, 58
Arizona State University Directory of A S U Latin Americanists see Directory of A S U Latin Americanists 468
Arizona State University, Tempe. Institute of Public Administration. Monograph. see Arizona State University. Center for Public Affairs. Monograph 708
Arizona Statistical Review (US ISSN 0518-6242) 151, 833
Arizona Trailer Guide see Arizona Mobile Home & Recreational Vehicle Park Guide 483
Ark (AT ISSN 0311-2926) 559
Ark River Review (US ISSN 0044-8885) 559
Arkansas. Bureau of Vital Statistics. Annual Report of Births, Deaths, Marriages and Divorces as Reported to the Bureau of Vital Statistics (US ISSN 0094-3576) 725

Arkansas. Department of Mental Retardation. Annual Report (US ISSN 0093-7452) 619
Arkansas. Division of Rehabilitation Services. Annual Report (US) 592, 804
Arkansas. Geological Commission. Information Circulars (US) 291
Arkansas. Geological Commission. Miscellaneous Publications (US) 291
Arkansas. Geological Commission. Water Resources Circulars (US ISSN 0571-0278) 895
Arkansas Archaeological Survey. Publications on Archaeology. Research Reports (US) 58
Arkansas Archeological Survey. Publications on Archeology. Popular Series (US ISSN 0587-3533) 58
Arkansas Archeological Survey. Publications on Archeology. Research Series (US) 58
Arkansas Archeologist (US ISSN 0004-1718) 58
Arkansas Average Covered Employment and Earnings by County and Industry (US ISSN 0092-2889) 206
Arkansas, Kansas, Missouri, Oklahoma TourBook see Tourbook: Arkansas, Kansas, Missouri, Oklahoma 891
Arkansas State Directory (US) 708
Arkansas State Industrial Directory (US) 235
Arkansas Vital Statistics (US ISSN 0364-0728) 725
Arkansas Vital Statistics Report see Arkansas. Bureau of Vital Statistics. Annual Report of Births, Deaths, Marriages and Divorces as Reported to the Bureau of Vital Statistics 725
Arkeologisk Museum i Stavanger.Skrifter see A M S-Skrifter 56
Arkeologisk Museum i Stavanger Smaatrykk see A M S-Smaatrykk 56
Arkeologisk Museum i Stavanger Varia see A M S-Varia 56
Arkheologicheskie Raboty V Tadzhikistane (UR) 58
Arkheologiya i Etnografiya Udmurtii (UR) 58
Ha-Arkhiyon Ha-Merkazi le-Toldot Ha-Am Ha-Yehudi. Yediot see Central Archives for the History of the Jewish People Newsletter 474
Arkib Negara Malaysia. Penyata Tahunan see National Archives of Malaysia. Annual Report 444
Arkiv for Nordisk Filologi/Archives for Scandinavian Philology (SW ISSN 0066-7668) 541
Arkiv for Sjoerett/Scandinavian Journal of Maritime Law (NO ISSN 0004-2102) 509
Arkivinformation (SW ISSN 0571-0731) 214
Arlington Historical Magazine (US ISSN 0066-7684) 466
Armazenagem (BL) 33
Armidale and District Historical Society. Journal and Proceedings (AT ISSN 0084-6732) 447
Arms Study Series (CN) 476, 638
Armstrong Oil Directory: Central United States (US) 678
Armstrong Oil Directory: Louisiana, Mississippi, Arkansas, Texas Gulf Coast and East Texas (US) 678
Armstrong Oil Directory: Texas Including Southeast New Mexico (US) 678
Army Officer's Guide (US ISSN 0148-6799) 638
Arnamagnaean Institute. Bulletin see Arnamagnaean Institute and Dictionary. Bulletin 559
Arnamagnaean Institute and Dictionary. Bulletin (DK) 541, 559
Arnoldia Rhodesia (RH ISSN 0066-7781) 796
Aromatic and Heteroaromatic Chemistry (UK ISSN 0305-9715) 252
Arqueologicas (PE ISSN 0066-7803) 48, 466
Arquivo de Anatomia e Antropologia (PO ISSN 0066-7811) 125

Arquivos Brasileiros de Nutricao (BL ISSN 0084-6775) 665
Arquivos de Botanica do Estado de Sao Paulo see Hoehnea 115
Arquivos de Cirurgia Clinica e Experimental (BL ISSN 0066-7846) 624
Arquivos de Patologia Geral e Anatomia Patologica (PO ISSN 0066-7854) 592
Arquivos de Zoologia (BL ISSN 0066-7870) 127
Arrecadacao dos Tributos Federais (BL) 226
Ars Decorativa (HU ISSN 0133-6673) 652
Ars Islamica see Ars Orientalis 71
Ars Nova (SA ISSN 0379-6485) 657
Ars Orientalis (US ISSN 0571-1371) 71, 669
Ars Quatuor Coronatorum (UK ISSN 0066-7900) 262
Ars, Revista de Arte (AG) 71
Ars Suecica (SW ISSN 0066-7919) 71, 449
Art (UN ISSN 0004-5535) 71
Art/Kunst (SZ) 80
Art and Archaeology Research Papers Monographs see A A R P Monographs 71
Art and Architecture Bibliographies (US) 71, 80
Art and Architecture Book Guide see Bibliographic Guide to Art and Architecture 71
Art and Artists of the Monterey Peninsula (US ISSN 0066-7927) 71
Art & Crafts Market see Artist's Market(1979) 72
Art and Life (II ISSN 0004-3044) 72
Art and the Artist (II) 72
Art at Auction; the Year at Sotheby's and Parke-Bernet (US ISSN 0084-6782) 476
Art Bulletin of Victoria (AT ISSN 0066-7935) 652
Art Craft Teachers Association Magazine (AT ISSN 0311-0087) 72
Art Diary (IT) 72
Art Directors Club Milano (IT ISSN 0066-7943) 72
Art Dramatique Canadien see Canadian Drama 858
Art et les Grandes Civilisations (FR ISSN 0066-7951) 72
Art Gallery News (AT) 72
Art Gallery of Hamilton. Annual Exhibition see Art Gallery of Hamilton. Annual Winter Exhibition 652
Art Gallery of Hamilton. Annual Winter Exhibition (CN) 652
Art Gallery of Ontario. Annual Report (CN ISSN 0082-5018) 652
Art Gallery of South Australia. Special Exhibitions (AT ISSN 0066-796X) 652
Art History Series (US) 72
Art Institute of Chicago. Museum Studies (US ISSN 0069-3235) 652
Art-Language (UK ISSN 0587-3584) 541
Art Material Directory and Product Information Guide (US) 72
Art Material Trade News Directory of Art & Craft Materials see Art Material Directory and Product Information Guide 72
Art of the Orient see Kunst des Orients 76
Art of the World Library (US) 72
Art-Price Annual see Kunstpreis-Jahrbuch 76
Art Reference Collection (US ISSN 0193-6867) 72
Art Research in Scandinavia see A R I S 71
Art Romanic (SP) 58, 72
Art Workers Guild. Annual Report (UK) 72
ARTANES see Aids and Research Tools in Ancient Near Eastern Studies 474
De Arte (SA ISSN 0004-3389) 72
Arte Orientale in Italia (IT) 669
Arte y Arqueologia (BO ISSN 0587-5447) 58, 72
Arte y Vida (VE) 555

Arthika Vivaranaya see Central Bank of Ceylon. Review of the Economy 184
Arthritis Foundation. Conference Series(US ISSN 0518-794X) 623
Arthritis Foundation Annual Report (US ISSN 0191-2836) 623
Arthropods of Florida and Neighboring Land Areas (US ISSN 0066-8036) 120
Arthur Holmes Society. Journal (UK ISSN 0066-8044) 288
Arthur Machen Society Occasional see A M S Occasional 558
Arti Musices/Musicological Yearbook (YU ISSN 0587-5455) 657
Artibus Asiae Supplementa (SZ) 58, 72, 669
Articles on Neoplasia see Current Articles on Neoplasia 602
Articulos en Linguistica y Campos Afines (CK) 541
Artillery Journal (II ISSN 0004-3826) 638
Artistas Ecuatorianos (EC) 72
Artistes and Their Agents (UK ISSN 0143-8131) 858
Artist's & Photographer's Market see Artist's Market(1979) 72
Artists & Photographer's Market see Photographer's Market 693
Artists Associates Far East Businessman's Directory see A.A.'s Far East Businessman's Directory 234
Artists in Canada (CN) 72, 652
Artists in Perspective Series (US) 72
Artist's Market(1979) (US ISSN 0161-0546) 72
Artists - U S A: Guide to Contemporary American Art (US) 72
Arts (AT ISSN 0066-8095) 72
Arts Asiatiques (FR ISSN 0004-3958) 68, 72, 669
Arts Council of Australia. Annual Report (AT) 72
Arts Council of Great Britain. Annual Report and Accounts (UK ISSN 0066-8133) 72
Arts et Objets du Maroc (FR) 72
Arts in Alabama see Annual Report of the Arts Activities in Alabama 71
Arts of Himachal (II) 72
Arts Patronage Series (US ISSN 0066-8168) 72
Arts Review Yearbook (UK) 72
Arts Rhodesia see Arts Zimbabwe 72
Arts Support by Private Foundations see National Directory of Arts Support by Private Foundations 77
Arts Support by Private Foundations and Business Corporations see National Directory of Arts Support by Business Corporations 77
Arts Suppprt by Private Foundations and Business Corporations see National Directory of Arts Support by Private Foundations 77
Arts Zimbabwe (RH) 58, 72, 285
Artviews (AT ISSN 0311-0095) 72
Arussi Rural Development Unit Publication see A R D U Publication 11
Arv/Journal of Scandinavian Folklore (SW ISSN 0066-8176) 401
Arvernia Biologica: Botanique (FR ISSN 0066-8184) 113
Arzobispado de Santiago. Vicaria de la Solidaridad. Estudios (CL) 773
A's & B's of Academic Scholarships (US) 333
Asbestos Producer/Producteur d'Amiante (CN ISSN 0478-4049) 134, 641
Asclepio (SP ISSN 0210-4466) 48, 592
Asepelt Series (NE) 142
Asfar (NE) 769
Asia-Africa World Trade Register (II ISSN 0066-8230) 193
Asia & Pacific (UK) 183, 708
Asia and Pacific Annual Review see Asia & Pacific 183
Asia Electronics Conference. Proceedings (AT) 72
Asia Foundation. President's Review (US ISSN 0587-3606) 430

Asia in the Modern World Series (US ISSN 0084-6805) 904
Asia Monograph Series (II ISSN 0066-8265) 779, 850
Asia-Pacific Petroleum Directory (US) 678
Asia Pulse (US) 763
Asia Serials: Vietnam Report (US) 183, 708
Asia Society. Annual Report (US ISSN 0098-1214) 442
Asia Travel Trade Directory (HK) 883
Asia Yearbook (HK) 142
Asian American Trade Directory (US) 178, 235
Asian and African Studies (CS ISSN 0571-2742) 439, 442, 669
Asian and Pacific Archaeology Series (US ISSN 0066-829X) 58
Asian and Pacific Council. Cultural and Social Centre. Annual Report (KO ISSN 0066-8303) 442
Asian and Pacific Council. Museum Conference. Proceedings (KO) 652
Asian and Pacific Council Seminar on Audio-Visual Education. Proceedings see A S P A C Seminar on Audio-Visual Education. Proceedings 441
Asian Banking Guide see Banking Guides - Asia, Australia, New Zealand with Principal Hotels and Bank Holidays 170
Asian Book Trade Directory (II ISSN 0066-8362) 757
Asian Computer Yearbook (HK) 270
Asian Conference on Occupational Health. Proceedings (II ISSN 0518-8857) 495
Asian Cultural Centre for Unesco. Organization and Activities (JA) 669
Asian Cultural Studies (JA ISSN 0454-2150) 442, 669
Asian Development Bank. Annual Report (PH ISSN 0066-8370) 168, 199
Asian Development Bank. Board of Governors. Summary of Proceedings (of the) Annual Meeting (PH ISSN 0066-8389) 168, 199
Asian Development Bank. Occasional Papers (PH ISSN 0066-8397) 168, 199
Asian Information Center for Geotechnical Engineering Digest see A G E Digest 288
Asian Institute of Technology. Research Summary (TH ISSN 0572-4198) 850
Asian Institute Translations (US ISSN 0084-6813) 904
Asian Journal of Pharmacy (PH ISSN 0066-8419) 683
Asian Law Series (US) 509
Asian Living Costs (UK) 193
Asian Music Publications. Series A: Bibliographic and Research Aids (US ISSN 0081-1319) 657
Asian Music Publications. Series B. Translations (US ISSN 0081-1327) 657
Asian Music Publications. Series C: Reprints (US ISSN 0081-1335) 657
Asian Music Publications. Series D: Monographs (US ISSN 0081-1343) 657
Asian Pacific Congress of Cardiology. Symposia (IO ISSN 0587-5471) 606
Asian Pacific Dental Student Association Journal see A.P.D.S.A. Journal 608
Asian Parliamentarians' Union. Central Secretariat. Report on Meeting of APU Secretaries-General in Tokyo (JA) 719
Asian Peoples' Anti-Communist League. Charts About Chinese Communists on the Mainland (CH ISSN 0571-2939) 442
Asian Peoples' Anti-Communist League. China. Pamphlet (CH ISSN 0571-2920) 708
Asian Philosophical Studies (US ISSN 0066-8443) 904
Asian Population Programme News (UN ISSN 0084-6821) 725
Asian Population Studies Series (UN ISSN 0066-8451) 725

Asian Press (KO) 504
Asian Press and Media Directory (HK) 4
Asian Productivity Organization. Review of Activities of National Productivity (JA ISSN 0571-3005) 199, 220
Asian Productivity Organization Annual Report see A P O Annual Report 220
Asian Productivity Organization Profiles of the National Productivity Organizations in A P O Member Countries see Profiles of the National Productivity Organizations in A P O Member Countries 225
Asian Social Science Bibliography with Annotations and Abstracts (II ISSN 0066-8478) 802
Asian Studies (BG) 708
Asian Studies at Hawaii Monograph Series (US ISSN 0066-8486) 442
Asian Studies Monographs Series (CN) 442, 669
Asian Studies Series (SZ) 442, 669
Asian Theatre Reports (US ISSN 0161-4908) 669, 858
Asiatic Society, Bombay. Journal (II ISSN 0004-4709) 669
Asiatic Society, Calcutta. Journal (II ISSN 0571-3161) 669
Asiatic Society, Calcutta. Monograph Series (II) 669
Asiatic Society, Calcutta. Seminar Series (II) 669
Asiatische Forschungen (GW ISSN 0571-320X) 442
Asien - Afrika - Lateinamerika. Jahrbuch (GE) 439, 442, 466
Asilomar Conference on Circuits and Systems. Conference Record (US ISSN 0571-3218) 352
Asimptoticheskie Metody v Teorii Sistem (UR) 584
Aslib Membership List (UK ISSN 0066-8524) 526
Aslib Occasional Publications (UK ISSN 0066-8532) 526
Asociacion Argentina de Actores. Memoria y Balance (AG) 506, 858
Asociacion Costarricense de Bibliotecarios. Boletin (CR ISSN 0004-4784) 526
Asociacion Cultural Humboldt. Boletin (VE ISSN 0004-4792) 262
Asociacion de Academias de la Lengua Espanola. Comision Permanente. Boletin (SP) 541
Asociacion de Bibliotecarios de Instituciones de Ensenanza Superior e Investigacion. Archivos (MX) 526
Asociacion de Bibliotecarios de Instituciones de Ensenanza Superior e Investigaciones. Cuadernos (MX) 526
Asociacion de Bibliotecas Universitarias y Especializadas de Nicaragua. Boletin (NQ) 526
Asociacion de Economistas Argentinos. Coleccion Instituto Superior (AG) 142
Asociacion de Investigacion Textil Algodonera. Coleccion de Manuales Tecnicos (SP ISSN 0571-3609) 855
Asociacion de Investigacion Textil Algodonera. Estudios y Documentos (SP) 855
Asociacion de Tecnicos Azucareros de Venezuela Boletin Informativo see A T A V E Boletin Informativo 403
Asociacion Demografica Costarricense. Informe de Labores (CR) 725
Asociacion Espanola Contra el Cancer. Memoria de la Assemblea General see Asociacion Espanola Contra el Cancer. Memoria Tecnico-Administrativa 604
Asociacion Espanola Contra el Cancer. Memoria Tecnico-Administrativa (SP) 604
Asociacion Espanola de Orientalistas. Boletin (SP ISSN 0571-3692) 669
Asociacion Espanola de Tecnicos de Maquinaria para la Construccion y Obra Publicas Revista A T E M C O P. Especial Alquiladores see Revista A T E M C O P. Especial Alquiladores 376

Asociacion Interamericana de Bibliotecarios y Documentalistas Agricolas. Boletin Especial (CR ISSN 0074-0748) *12*, 526
Asociacion Interamericana de Bibliotecarios y Documentalistas Agricolas. Boletin Tecnico (CR ISSN 0074-0756) *904*
Asociacion Latinoamericana de Libre Comercio. Comercio Exterior. Argentina. Exportacion *see* Asociacion Latinoamericana de Libre Comercio. Estadisticas de Comercio Exterior--Serie A-Exportaciones *193*
Asociacion Latinoamericana de Libre Comercio. Comercio Exterior Argentina. Importacion *see* Asociacion Latinoamericana de Libre Comercio. Estadisticas de Comercio Exterior-Serie B-Importaciones *193*
Asociacion Latinoamericana de Libre Comercio. Comercio Exterior Brasil. Importacion *see* Asociacion Latinoamericana de Libre Comercio. Estadisticas de Comercio Exterior - Serie C - Importaciones Zonales *193*
Asociacion Latinoamericana de Libre Comercio. Estadisticas de Comercio Exterior--Serie A-Exportaciones (UY) *193*
Asociacion Latinoamericana de Libre Comercio. Estadisticas de Comercio Exterior-Serie B-Importaciones (UY) *193*
Asociacion Latinoamericana de Libre Comercio. Estadisticas de Comercio Exterior - Serie C - Importaciones Zonales (UY) *193*
Asociacion Latinoamericana de Libre Comercio. Lista Consolidada de Concesiones (UY ISSN 0571-3935) *193*
Asociacion Latinoamericana de Libre Comercio. Lista Nacional de Argentina (UY) *193*
Asociacion Latinoamericana de Libre Comercio. Lista Nacional de Bolivia (UY) *193*
Asociacion Latinoamericana de Libre Comercio. Lista Nacional de Brasil (UY ISSN 0571-396X) *193*
Asociacion Latinoamericana de Libre Comercio. Lista Nacional de Chile (UY ISSN 0571-3978) *193*
Asociacion Latinoamericana de Libre Comercio. Lista Nacional de Colombia (UY ISSN 0571-3986) *193*
Asociacion Latinoamericana de Libre Comercio. Lista Nacional de Ecuador(UY ISSN 0571-3994) *193*
Asociacion Latinoamericana de Libre Comercio. Lista Nacional de la Republica Argentina *see* Asociacion Latinoamericana de Libre Comercio. Lista Nacional de Argentina *193*
Asociacion Latinoamericana de Libre Comercio. Lista Nacional de Mexico (UY ISSN 0571-401X) *193*
Asociacion Latinoamericana de Libre Comercio. Lista Nacional de Paraguay (UY ISSN 0571-4028) *193*
Asociacion Latinoamericana de Libre Comercio. Lista Nacional de Peru (UY ISSN 0571-4036) *193*
Asociacion Latinoamericana de Libre Comercio. Lista Nacional de Uruguay (UY ISSN 0571-4044) *193*
Asociacion Latinoamericana de Libre Comercio. Lista Nacional de Venezuela (UY) *193*
Asociacion Latinoamericana de Libre Comercio. Serie Instrumentos (UY ISSN 0571-4087) *193*
Asociacion Latinoamericana de Produccion Animal. Memoria (MX) *43*
Asociacion Mexicana de Facultades y Escuelas de Medicina. Boletin (MX ISSN 0004-4857) *592*
Asociacion Nacional de Instituciones Financieras. Simposio sobre Mercado de Capitales (CK) *168*
Asociacion Nacional del Cafe. Departamento de Asuntos Agricolas. Informe Anual (GT ISSN 0066-8567) *85*

Asociacion Panamericana de Instituciones de Credito Educativo Revista A P I C E *see* Revista A P I C E *322*
Asociacion Venezolana de Archiveros. Coleccion Doctrina (VE ISSN 0066-8591) *526*
Asociacion Venezolana de Enfermeras Profesionales. Boletin (VE ISSN 0066-8613) *613*
Asociacion Venezolano Britanica de Comercio e Industria. Anuario *see* Camara Venezolano Britanica de Comercio e Industria. Anuario *178*
Aspectos Gerais e Principais Tendencias da Agropecuaria Paraibana (BL) *27*
Aspects of Education (UK ISSN 0066-8672) *314*
Aspects of Educational Technology (UK ISSN 0141-5956) *347*
Aspects of Greek and Roman Life (US) *430*, 796
Aspects of Homogeneous Catalysis: a Series of Advances (NE) *254*
Aspects of Plant Science *see* Current Trends in Life Sciences *102*
Aspen Chronicle (US) *796*
Aspen Institute Chronicle *see* Aspen Chronicle *796*
Asphalt Paving Technology *see* Association of Asphalt Paving Technologists. Proceedings *374*
Aspis (UK ISSN 0260-2474) *193, 235*
Assam Economic Journal (II) *191*
Assemblees de Dieu de France. Annuaire (FR ISSN 0083-6184) *776*
Assembling (US ISSN 0161-8318) *504, 757*
Assembly Directory and Handbook *see* Assembly Engineering Master Catalog *366*
Assembly Engineering Master Catalog (US ISSN 0066-8702) *366*
Assia (IS) *593*
Assises de Medecine (FR) *593*
Assistance Judiciaire Nouveau-Brunswick Rapport Annuel *see* Legal Aid New Brunswick Annual Report *514*
Associacao Brasileira da Industria Farmaceutica. Pesquisa (BL) *683*
Associacao Brasileira de Educao Agricola Superior. Anais de Reuniao Anual (BL) *13*, 333
Associacao de Educacao Catolica do Brasil. Boletim *see* Revista de Educacao A E C *322*
Associacao de Educacao Catolica do Brasil Revista de Educacao A E C *see* Revista de Educacao A E C *322*
Associate Committee on the National Building Code News *see* N B C /N F C News *137*
Associated Church Press. Directory (US ISSN 0066-8710) *769*
Associated Colleges of Illinois. Report (US ISSN 0066-8729) *333*
Associated Equipment Distributors. Rental Rates Compilation (US ISSN 0164-0593) *134*, 582
Associated Industries of New York State. Bulletin (US) *708*
Associated Industries of New York State, Inc. Recommends *see* A I Recommends *707*
Associated Public Schools Systems. Yearbook (US ISSN 0066-8753) *343*
Associated Western Universities. Annual Report *see* Associated Western Universities. Biennial Report *333*
Associated Western Universities. Biennial Report (US) *333*
Association Aeronautique et Astronautique de France. Annuaire (FR) *7*
Association Belge pour l'Etude, l'Essai et l'Emploi des Materiaux. Proces Verbal de l'Assemblee Generale Ordinaire (BE ISSN 0066-8818) *379*
Association Belge pour l'Etude, l'Essai et l'Emploi des Materiaux. Publication A.B.E.M (BE ISSN 0066-8796) *379*

Association Canadienne des Bibliothecaires de Langue Francaise. Rapport *see* Association pour l'Avancement des Sciences et des Techniques de la Documentation. Rapport *526*
Association Canadienne des Compagnies d'Assurance. Annuaire *see* Canadian Life Insurance Association. Directory *498*
Association Canadienne des Physiciens *see* Canadian Association of Physicists. Annual Report *696*
Association Canadienne-Francaise pour l'Avancement des Sciences. A C F A S; Resumes des Communications (CN) *779*
Association Canadienne-Francaise pour l'Avancement des Sciences. Annales (CN ISSN 0066-8842) *779*
Association Canadienne-Francaise pour l'Avancement des Sciences. Bulletin (CN ISSN 0066-8850) *779*
Association Canadienne pour la Sante Mentale. Rapport Annuel *see* Canadian Mental Health Association. Annual Report *735*
Association de l'Ecole Nationale Superieure des Bibliothecaires. Annuaire (FR ISSN 0066-8877) *526*
Association des Amis d'Alfred de Vigny. Bulletin (FR ISSN 0066-8893) *559*
Association des Amis de Pierre Teilhard de Chardin. Bulletin (FR ISSN 0066-8907) *763*
Association des Banques du Liban. Bilans des Banques (LE) *168*
Association des Banques du Liban. Rapport Annuel *see* Association des Banques du Liban. Rapport du Conseil *183*
Association des Banques du Liban. Rapport du Conseil (LE) *183*
Association des Bibliothecaires Francais. Annuaire (FR ISSN 0066-8931) *526*
Association des Bibliothecaires Francais Documents A B F *see* Documents A B F *529*
Association des Colleges du Quebec Annuaire (CN) *314*
Association des Ingenieurs et Anciens Eleves de l'Ecole Superieure d'Ingenieurs et Techniciens pour l'Agriculture. Annuaire (FR) *33*
Association des Ingenieurs et Techniciens Africains de Cote d'Ivoire. Annuaire (IV) *366*
Association des Institutions d'Enseignement Secondaire. Annuaire (CN ISSN 0066-8990) *314*
Association des Journalistes Agricoles. Annuaire (FR) *13*, 504
Association des Naturalistes du Mali. Bulletin (ML) *779*
Association des Societes et Fonds Francais d'Investissement. Annuaire (FR ISSN 0066-9008) *202*
Association des Traducteurs et Interpretes de l'Ontario. Annuaire (CN ISSN 0066-9016) *541*
Association des Traducteurs et Interpretes de l'Ontario. Informatio (CN ISSN 0381-5781) *541*
Association Euratom-Ital. Annual Report (NE ISSN 0066-9040) *13*, 404
Association Films. Free Loan Films (US) *648*
Association for Asian Studies. Enduring Scholarship. Reference Series (US) *442*
Association for Asian Studies. Monographs (US ISSN 0066-9059) *442*, 669
Association for Communication Administration Bulletin *see* A C A Bulletin *558*
Association for Computing Machinery. Proceedings of National Conference (US ISSN 0066-9091) *270*

Association for Computing Machinery Annual Workshop on Microprogramming. Conference Record *see* A C M Annual Workshop on Microprogramming. Conference Record *270*
Association for Computing Machinery, Inc. Administrative Directory of College and University Computer Science Data Processing Programs and Computer Facilities *see* A C M Administrative Directory of College and University Computer Science/ Data Processing Programs and Computer Facilities *330*
Association for Computing Machinery Monograph Series *see* A C M Monograph Series *270*
Association for Computing Machinery Symposium on the Theory of Computing *see* A C M Symposium on the Theory of Computing *270*
Association for Continuing Higher Education. Proceedings (US) *333*
Association for Education of the Visually Handicapped. Selected Papers from A E V H Biennial Conferences (US ISSN 0066-9105) *345*
Association for Educational Communications and Technology. Membership Directory & Data Book (US) *347*
Association for Educational Communications and Technology. Monographs (US) *263*, 314
Association for Educational Data Systems. Annual Convention Proceedings (US ISSN 0147-9296) *270*, 343
Association for Educational Data Systems. Handbook and Directory (US ISSN 0092-6280) *270*, 343
Association for Gravestone Studies. Newsletter (US ISSN 0146-5783) *48, 72, 416*
Association for Institutional Research. Annual Forum on Institutional Research. Proceedings (US ISSN 0587-1948) *333*
Association for Jewish Studies Review *see* A J S Review *390*
Association for Professional Education for Ministry. Report of the Biennial Meeting (US) *333*, 763
Association for Recorded Sound Collections Bulletin *see* A R S C Bulletin *656*
Association for Research in Nervous and Mental Disease. Research Publications (US ISSN 0091-7443) *619*
Association for School, College and University Staffing Annual-Teaching Opportunities for You *see* A S C U S Annual-Teaching Opportunities for You *343*
Association for Scottish Literary Studies Newsletter *see* A S L S Newsletter *558*
Association for Social Anthropology in Oceania. Monograph Series (US ISSN 0066-9172) *48*
Association for Systems Management Bookshelf Series *see* A S M Bookshelf Series *213*
Association for Teacher Education in Africa. Western Council. Report of the Annual Conference (NR ISSN 0331-0388) *333*
Association for the Advancement of Baltic Studies. Publications (US ISSN 0572-4287) *449*
Association for the Advancement of Polish Studies. Bulletin (US) *449*
Association Francaise d'Experts de la Cooperation Technique Internationale. Annuaire (FR ISSN 0066-9288) *850*
Association Francaise d'Informatique et de Recherche Operationnelle. Annuaire *see* Association Francaise pour la Cybernetique Economique et Technique. Annuaire *270*
Association Francaise de Calcul et de Traitement d'Information. Annuaire *see* Association Francaise pour la Cybernetique Economique et Technique. Annuaire *270*

Association Francaise des Documentalistes et des Bibliothecaires Specialises Annuaire see A D B S Annuaire 525
Association Francaise des Ingenieurs du Caoutchouc et des Plastiques. Annuaire (FR ISSN 0066-9229) 706, 777
Association Francaise des Ingenieurs et Techniciens de l'Aeronautique et de l'Espace. Annuaire see Association Aeronautique et Astronautique de France. Annuaire 7
Association Francaise des Relations Publiques. Annuaire (FR ISSN 0066-9253) 4
Association Francaise des Techniciens et Ingenieurs de Securite et des Medecins du Travail. Annuaire (FR ISSN 0066-927X) 495
Association Francaise pour la Cybernetique Economique et Technique. Annuaire (FR) 270
Association Francaise pour la Diffusion du Livre Scientifique, Technique et Medical (Bulletins Collectifs) (FR) 87, 601, 794, 854
Association France-Malte (FR ISSN 0339-705X) 262
Association France-Malte. Bulletin see Association France-Malte 262
Association Internationale du Droit Commercial et du Droit Affaires. Groupe Francais. Travaux (UK ISSN 0571-5873) 522
Association Internationale pour l'Histoire du Verre. Bulletin (BE ISSN 0447-9823) 244
Association Nationale d'Etude et de Lutte Contre les Fleaux Atmospheriques. Rapport de Campagne (FR ISSN 0373-7349) 631
Association Nationale de Lutte Contre les Fleaux Atmospheriques. Rapport de Campagne see Association Nationale d'Etude et de Lutte Contre les Fleaux Atmospheriques. Rapport de Campagne 631
Association Nationale des Entreprises Zairoises. Circulaire d'Information (ZR) 178
Association of Academies of Science. Directory and Proceedings see National Association of Academies of Science. Directory and Proceedings 786
Association of African Universities. Report of the General Conference (GH) 333
Association of American Battery Manufacturers. Yearbook see Storage Battery Manufacturing Industry Yearbook 359
Association of American Feed Control Officials. Official Publication (US) 41
Association of American Geographers. Handbook - Directory (US ISSN 0571-5962) 420
Association of American Geographers. Monograph Series (US ISSN 0066-9393) 420
Association of American Law Schools. Proceedings (US ISSN 0066-9407) 509
Association of American Law Schools Library Statistics see A A L S Library Statistics 525
Association of American Library Schools. Directory (US) 526
Association of American Medical Colleges Curriculum Directory see A. A. M. C. Curriculum Directory 591
Association of American Medical Colleges Directory of American Medical Education see A A M C Directory of American Medical Education 333
Association of American Pesticide Control Officials. Official Publication (US ISSN 0066-9431) 33
Association of American Physicians. Transactions (US ISSN 0066-9458) 593

Association of American Plant Food Control Officials. Official Publication (US ISSN 0094-8764) 404
Association of American Publishers. Exhibits Directory (US ISSN 0147-0310) 757
Association of American Railroads. Data Systems Division. Papers (US) 270, 872
Association of American University Presses Directory (US ISSN 0571-6098) 757
Association of Asphalt Paving Technologists. Proceedings (US ISSN 0066-9466) 374
Association of Attenders and Alumni of the Hague Academy of International Law. Yearbook (NE ISSN 0066-8923) 522
Association of Canadian Map Libraries. Annual Conference Proceedings see Association of Canadian Map Libraries. Bulletin 420
Association of Canadian Map Libraries. Bulletin (CN ISSN 0318-2851) 420
Association of Canadian Map Libraries. Newsletter see Association of Canadian Map Libraries. Bulletin 420
Association of Canadian Schools of Business. Proceedings of the Annual Conference see Canadian Association of Administrative Sciences. Proceedings, Annual Conference/Rapport, la Conference Annuelle 214
Association of College Admissions Counselors. Membership Directory see National Association of College Admissions Counselors. Membership Directory 338
Association of College and University Auditors. Proceedings: Annual Conference (US) 333
Association of College Honor Societies, Booklet of Information (US) 263
Association of College Unions-International. Directory (US) 334
Association of College Unions-International. Proceedings of the Annual Conference (US ISSN 0147-1120) 334
Association of Colleges for Further and Higher Education. Year Book (UK ISSN 0066-9539) 334
Association of Commonwealth Universities. Annual Report of the Council Together with the Accounts of the Association (UK ISSN 0307-2274) 334
Association of Commonwealth Universities. Report of the Council Together with the Accounts of the Association see Association of Commonwealth Universities. Annual Report of the Council Together with the Accounts of the Association 334
Association of Computer Programmers and Analysts. Proceedings of the Founders Conference (US) 270
Association of Consulting Engineers of Canada. Specialization Typical Projects see Consulting Engineers-Canada-Ingenieurs-Conseils 366
Association of Contemporary Historians. Bulletin (UK) 430
Association of Departments and Administrators in Speech Communication. Bulletin see A C A Bulletin 558
Association of Engineering Geologists. Special Publications (US) 374
Association of Exploration Geochemists. Special Publications (CN) 288
Association of Faculties of Pharmacy of Canada. Proceedings (CN ISSN 0066-9555) 683
Association of Graduate Schools in Association of American Universities. Journal of Proceedings and Addresses (US ISSN 0066-9563) 904
Association of Highway Officials of the North Atlantic States. Proceedings (US) 740, 874
Association of History Teachers in Nigeria (NR) 347, 431

Association of Independent Camps. Buyers Guide and Camp Directory (US) 828
Association of Indian Engineering Industry. Handbook of Statistics (II) 366
Association of Institutes for European Studies. Annuaire (SZ ISSN 0571-6322) 449
Association of Institutes for European Studies. Year-Book (SZ ISSN 0571-6330) 449
Association of International Libraries Doc see A I L/Doc 525
Association of Iron and Steel Engineers. A I S E Proceedings see A I S E Yearbook 626
Association of Iron and Steel Engineers Yearbook see A I S E Yearbook 626
Association of Island Marine Laboratories of the Caribbean. Proceedings (PR ISSN 0066-9571) 100
Association of Japanese Geographers. Special Publication (JA ISSN 0066-958X) 420
Association of Jewish Libraries. Proceedings of the Annual Convention (US) 526
Association of Life Insurance Medical Directors of America. Transactions (US ISSN 0066-9598) 497, 593
Association of Lunar and Planetary Observers. Journal (US ISSN 0039-2502) 81
Association of Marshall Scholars and Alumni. Newsletter see Marshall News 263
Association of Midwest Fish and Game Commissioners Proceedings see Association of Midwest Fish and Wildlife Commissioners. Proceedings 275
Association of Midwest Fish and Wildlife Commissioners. Proceedings (US) 275
Association of Military Dermatologists. Bulletin see Association of Military Dermatologists. Journal 611
Association of Military Dermatologists. Journal (US ISSN 0360-4020) 611
Association of New Brunswick Land Surveyors. Annual Report (CN ISSN 0318-2126) 761
Association of Official Analytical Chemists. Official Methods of Analysis (US ISSN 0066-961X) 249
Association of Official Seed Analysts Proceedings see Journal of Seed Technology 17
Association of Official Seed Certifying Agencies. Production Publication (US) 33
Association of Ontario Land Surveyors. Annual Report (CN ISSN 0700-5989) 374
Association of Overseas Educators, Inc. Directory see A.O.E. Directory 313
Association of Pacific Coast Geographers. Yearbook (US ISSN 0066-9628) 420
Association of Private Camps. Buyers Guide and Camp Directory see Association of Independent Camps. Buyers Guide and Camp Directory 828
Association of Professors of Missions. Biennial Meeting. Proceedings (US ISSN 0519-153X) 763
Association of Registered Professional Foresters of New Brunswick. Papers and Reports (CN ISSN 0066-9644) 407
Association of Research Libraries. University Library Management Studies Office. Management Supplement (US) 526
Association of Research Libraries. University Library Management Studies Office. Occasional Paper (US ISSN 0091-4479) 526
Association of Research Libraries Annual Salary Survey see A R L Annual Salary Survey 525
Association of Research Libraries Statistics see A R L Statistics 538

Association of Social Anthropologists of the Commonwealth. Studies (UK) 48
Association of Southeast Asian Institutions of Higher Learning. Handbook: Southeast Asian Institutions of Higher Learning (TH ISSN 0066-9687) 334
Association of Southeast Asian Institutions of Higher Learning. Newsletter (TH ISSN 0572-4325) 334
Association of Southeast Asian Institutions of Higher Learning Seminar Reports see A S A I H L. Seminar Reports 333
Association of Student International Law Societies International Law Journal see A S I L S International Law Journal 508
Association of Summer Session Deans and Directors. Summary of Reports see Association of University Summer Sessions. Summary Report 334
Association of Teachers of Management Occasional Papers see A T M Occasional Papers 213
Association of the Concrete Industry in Finland. Publication see Suomen Betoniteollisuuden Keskusjarjesto. Julkaisu 139
Association of the Russian-American Scholars in U.S.A. Zapiski Russkoi Akademicheskoi Gruppy v S. Sh. A. Transactions (US ISSN 0066-9717) 449
Association of Theological Schools in the United States and Canada. Bulletin (US ISSN 0362-1472) 763
Association of Theological Schools in the United States and Canada. Directory (US) 330, 763
Association of Trial Lawyers of America. Law Journal (US) 509
Association of Universities and Colleges of Canada. Annual Meeting. Proceedings (CN ISSN 0066-9725) 334
Association of University Evening Colleges. Proceedings see Association for Continuing Higher Education. Proceedings 333
Association of University Summer Sessions. Summary Report (US ISSN 0066-975X) 334
Association of Urban Authorities. Annual Bulletin (MF ISSN 0304-6451) 748
Association of Urban Universities. Proceedings (US) 334
Association of Veterinary Students of Great Britain and Ireland Journal see A. V. S. Journal 893
Association pour l'Avancement des Sciences et des Techniques de la Documentation. Rapport (CN ISSN 0316-0955) 526
Association pour l'Etude Taxonomique de la Flore d'Afrique Tropicale Index see A.E.T.F.A.T. Index 109
Association pour le Developpement International de l'Observatoire de Nice. Bulletin (FR) 81
Association pour le Developpement International de l'Observatoire de Nice. Bulletin d'Information see Association pour le Developpement International de l'Observatoire de Nice. Bulletin 81
Association Scientifique de la Precontrainte. Sessions d'Etudes (FR ISSN 0066-9792) 379
Association-Sterling Films. Free Loan Films see Association Films. Free Loan Films 648
Association Technique de Fonderie. Annuaire (FR) 627
Association Technique de l'Industrie du Gaz en France. Compte Rendu du Congres (FR ISSN 0066-9806) 678
Association Technique de l'Industrie Papetiere. Circulaire (FR) 904
Association Technique de l'Industrie Papetiere. Quelques Nouvelles (FR) 904
Association Technique Maritime et Aeronautique, Paris. Bulletin (FR ISSN 0066-9814) 7, 877

Associazione Elettrotecnica Ed
Elettronica Italiana. Rendiconti della
Riunione Annuale (IT ISSN 0066-
9822) *352*
Associazione Genetica Italiana. Atti (IT
ISSN 0066-9830) *122*
Associazione Italiana Biblioteche.
Quaderni del Bollettino
d'Informazioni (IT ISSN 0519-2048)
526
Associazione Italiana Laringectomizzati.
Atti (Del) Convegno Nazionale (IT
ISSN 0066-9865) *617*
Associazione Medica Chirurgica di
Tivoli e della Val d'Aniene. Atti e
Memorie (IT ISSN 0066-9873) *624*
Associazione Nazionale per la Tutela
del Patrimonio Storico Artistico e
Naturale della Nazione. Atti di
Convegni (IT) *449*
Associazione Nazionale per la Tutela
del Patrimonio Storico Artistico e
Naturale della Nazione. Documenti
(IT) *449*
Associazione Nazionale per la Tutela
del Patrimonio Storico Artistico e
Naturale della Nazione. Quaderni
(IT) *449*
Associazione Nazionale per la Tutela
del Patrimonio Storico Artistico e
Naturale della Nazione. Studi (IT)
449
Assur (US) *474*
Assurance-Chomage Canada. Rapport
Annuel *see* Unemployment Insurance
Canada. Annual Report *501*
Assurances Generales de France.
Informations (FR ISSN 0066-989X)
828
Assyriological Studies (US ISSN 0066-
9903) *541*
Asta-Press (GW ISSN 0076-1745) *343*
Asticou (FR ISSN 0066-992X) *466*
Astin Bulletin (NE ISSN 0515-0361)
497
Astrado (FR ISSN 0004-6116) *401*,
559
Astrofizicheskie Issledovaniia (BU) *81*
Astrology Annual Reference Book *see*
Astrology Reference Book *80*
Astrology Reference Book (US) *80*
Astronautical Research (US ISSN
0304-8705) *7*
Astronomia (PL) *81*
Astronomical Almanac (UK) *81*
Astronomical Ephemeris *see*
Astronomical Almanac *81*
Astronomical Ephemeris of Geocentric
Places of Planets (II ISSN 0066-
9970) *81*
Astronomical Phenomena (US ISSN
0083-2421) *81*
Astronomical Society of Australia.
Proceedings (AT ISSN 0066-9997)
81
Astronomical Society of Victoria.
Yearbook (AT ISSN 0067-0006) *81*
Astronomical Tables and Star Charts
for Hong Kong. (HK) *81*
Astronomicheski Kalendar na
Observatoriiata v Sofia (BU ISSN
0068-3639) *81*
Astronomische Grundlagen fuer den
Kalender (GW ISSN 0067-0014) *81*
Astronomy and Astrophysics Abstracts
(US ISSN 0067-0022) *1*, *85*, *700*
Astronomy Through Practical
Investigation (US) *81*
Astrophysica Norvegica/Norwegian
Journal of Theoretical Astrophysics
(NO ISSN 0067-0030) *81*, *695*
Astrophysics and Space Science
Library(NE ISSN 0067-0057) *81*,
695
Astrum (SP) *81*
Asturnatura (SP) *100*
Asunto (VE) *264*
At a Glance (CN ISSN 0708-0263)
526
At the Court of St. James's (UK ISSN
0067-0065) *719*
Atalanta (IT) *559*
Athanor (US ISSN 0044-9857) *559*
Atheist (US ISSN 0304-1409) *687*,
763
Athens Center of Ekistics. Research
Report (Athens Center of Ekistics)
(GR ISSN 0067-0073) *483*

Athens Center of Ekistics Athens
Center of Ekistics. Research Report
see Athens Center of Ekistics.
Research Report *483*
Atherosclerosis Reviews (US ISSN
0362-1650) *606*
Athletisme Francais (FR ISSN 0067-
012X) *819*
Atlanta Constitution: a Georgia Index
(US ISSN 0093-1179) *506*
Atlantic Canada Economics
Association. Annual Conference: A
C E A Papers (CN ISSN 0319-
003X) *142*
Atlantic Mail (FR ISSN 0519-3125)
522
Atlantic Oceanographic and
Meteorological Laboratories.
Collected Reprints *see* National
Ocean Survey. Collected Reprints
311
Atlantic Oceanographic Laboratory. A
O L Report *see* Bedford Institute of
Oceanography. Report *309*
Atlantic Provinces and Quebec; New
Brunswick Newfoundland, Nova
Scotia, Prince Edward Island, Quebec
TourBook *see* Tourbook: Atlantic
Provinces and Quebec *891*
Atlantic Provinces Checklist (CN
ISSN 0571-7817) *904*
Atlantic Provinces Economic Council.
Annual Report (CN ISSN 0067-
0162) *183*
Atlantic Provinces Inter-University
Committee on the Sciences. Annual
Report (CN ISSN 0067-0197) *779*
Atlantic Provinces Inter-University
Committee on the Sciences.
Newsletter (CN ISSN 0004-6825)
334, *779*
Atlantic Provinces Studies (CN ISSN
0067-0200) *122*
Atlantic Salmon Directory (CN ISSN
0707-5162) *395*
Atlantic Salmon References (CN) *109*
Atlantic States Marine Fisheries
Commission. Special Report (US)
395
Atlantico (BL) *555*
Atlantida (VE) *796*
Atlantide Report. Scientific Results of
the Danish Expedition to the Coasts
of Tropical West Africa (DK ISSN
0067-0227) *779*
Atlas Arqueologico de la Republica
Mexicana (MX ISSN 0067-0243)
58
Atlas d'Attraction Urbaine. (FR ISSN
0067-026X) *904*
Atlas Florae Europaeae (FI) *113*
Atlas Flory Polskiej i Ziem Osciennych
(PL ISSN 0067-0294) *113*
Atlas of External Diseases of the Eye
(US ISSN 0067-0308) *615*
Atlas of Molecular Structures in
Biology (US) *100*
Atlas of the Pacific Northwest (US)
420
Atlas Polskich Strojow Ludowych (PL
ISSN 0067-0316) *48*, *58*, *401*
Atlas Rozmieszczenia Drzew i
Krzewow w Polsce (PL ISSN 0067-
0324) *113*
Atma Jaya Research Centre. Annual
Report (IO) *347*
Atmospheric Optics (US) *705*
Atmospheric Pollution Technical
Bulletin *see* Atmospheric Quality
Improvement Technical Bulletin *384*
Atmospheric Quality Improvement
Technical Bulletin (US ISSN 0360-
8778) *384*
Atmospheric Science Paper *see*
Colorado State University.
Atmospheric Science Paper *632*
Atmospheric Science Research Report
see Colorado State University.
Atmospheric Science Paper *632*
Atmospheric Science Technical Paper
see Colorado State University.
Atmospheric Science Paper *632*
Atmospheric Technology (US ISSN
0091-2026) *8*
Atmospheric Turbidity and
Precipitation Chemistry Data for the
World (US ISSN 0094-4696) *631*
Atoll Research Bulletin (US ISSN
0077-5630) *779*

Atomedia (PH ISSN 0115-3757) *702*
Atomic and Nuclear Data Reprints
(US) *702*
Atomic Bomb Casualty Commission,
Hiroshima. Annual Report *see*
Radiation Effects Research
Foundation. Annual Report *622*
Atomic Energy Levels and Grotrian
Diagrams (NE) *695*
Atomic Energy of Canada. Annual
Report (CN ISSN 0067-0383) *362*,
702
Atomic Energy of Canada. List of
Publications (CN ISSN 0067-0405)
364, *700*
Atomic Energy of Canada Ltd.
Materials Research in A E C L *see*
Materials Research in A E C L *380*
Atomic Energy of Canada, Ltd. Report
Series *see* A E C L Report Series
701
Atomic Physics (US ISSN 0090-6360)
702
Attorneys and Agents Registered to
Practice Before the U.S. Patent and
Trademark Office (US ISSN 0361-
3844) *676*
Attorneys and Agents Registered to
Practice Before the U.S. Patent
Office *see* Attorneys and Agents
Registered to Practice Before the
U.S. Patent and Trademark Office
676
Attualita Cinematografiche (IT) *648*
Attualita di Laboratorio (IT ISSN
0004-7309) *496*
Attualita Mondiali *see* Informozioni e
Attualita Mondiali *596*
Au Grand Air (CN ISSN 0004-7384)
828
Auburn University. Project Themis
Research. Annual Report (US) *214*
Auburn University. Water Resources
Research Institute. Annual Report
(US ISSN 0067-043X) *895*
Auckland Institute and Museum.
Bulletin (NZ ISSN 0067-0456) *652*
Auckland Institute and Museum.
Records (NZ ISSN 0067-0464) *652*
Auckland University Law Review (NZ
ISSN 0067-0510) *509*
Audarena Stadium Guide and
International Directory (US ISSN
0067-0537) *4*
Audience and Programme Research
(SW ISSN 0044-9989) *266*
Audio Annual *see* Hi Fi News &
Record Review Annual *818*
Audio-Cassette Directory (US) *818*
Audio Critic (US ISSN 0146-4701)
818
Audio Digest (US) *904*
Audio-Technik (GW ISSN 0571-8678)
286
Audio Universal (AG) *818*
Audio-Visual Bulletin (AT) *347*
Audio-Visual Equipment Directory (US
ISSN 0571-8759) *347*
Audiotecnica News *see* Noise and
Smog News *388*
Audiovisual Market Place; A
Multimedia Guide (US ISSN 0067-
0553) *347*
Audiozine (US) *72*
Auditing Research Monograph (US)
167
Augsburger Schriften zum Staats- und
Voelkerrecht (SZ) *522*
August Derleth Society. Newsletter
(US) *559*
Augustana College Library Publications
see Augustana Library Publications
489
Augustana Historical Society, Rock
Island, Illinois. Publications (US
ISSN 0067-0588) *431*
Augustana Library Publications (US
ISSN 0067-057X) *489*
Augustinian Studies (US ISSN 0094-
5323) *773*
Aurora (GW ISSN 0341-1230) *72*,
559
Aurora AFX Road Racing Handbook
(US ISSN 0092-6256) *475*
Aurora-Buchreihe (GW ISSN 0171-
6530) *72*, *559*

Auroral Observatory. Magnetic
Observations (NO ISSN 0373-4854)
81, *695*
Aus dem Schweizerischen
Landesmuseum (SZ ISSN 0067-
0618) *652*
Aus der Schatzkammer der Buecher *see*
Buecher *760*
Aus Forschung und Kunst (GW ISSN
0067-0642) *72*
Aus Oesterreichs Wissenschaft (AU)
779
Auslaendische Aktiengesetze (GW
ISSN 0067-0669) *509*
Ausruestung in Luft- und Raumfahrt
(GW ISSN 0067-0685) *7*
Austin Healey Year Book (UK ISSN
0260-664X) *869*
Australasian and Pacific Society for
Eighteenth-Century Studies.
Newsletter (AT) *447*
Australasian Commercial Teachers'
Association. Journal (AT ISSN
0084-6961) *347*
Australasian Conference on Hydraulics
and Fluid Mechanics. Proceedings
(NZ ISSN 0571-9291) *380*
Australasian Institute of Metals.
Proceedings of the Annual
Conference (AT) *627*
Australasian Institute of Mining and
Metallurgy. Symposia Series (AT)
627, *641*
Australasian Insurance Journal Manual
of Australasian Life Assurance *see* A.
I. J. Manual of Australasian Life
Assurance *497*
Australasian Society of Engineers.
Engineers Handbook (AT ISSN
0084-6996) *366*
Australasian Stud and Stable *see* Stud
and Stable *828*
Australia. Advisory Committee on
Research and Development in
Education. Annual Report (AT) *314*
Australia. Air Transport Group.
Aerodromes and Ground Aids (AT)
7
Australia.Atomic Energy Commission.
Research Establishment. A A E C/
E(AT ISSN 0067-1657) *366*, *702*
Australia. Atomic Energy Commission.
Research Establishment. A A E C/
IP(AT) *702*
Australia.Atomic Energy Commission.
Research Establishment. A A E C/
M(AT ISSN 0067-1665) *366*, *702*
Australia. Atomic Energy Commission.
Research Establishment. List of
Report Publications (AT) *700*
Australia. Bureau of Agricultural
Economics. Coarse Grains and
Oilseeds Situation *see* Australia.
Bureau of Agricultural Economics.
Coarse Grains: Situation and Outlook
27
Australia. Bureau of Agricultural
Economics. Coarse Grains and
Oilseeds Situation *see* Australia.
Bureau of Agricultural Economics.
Oilseeds: Situation and Outlook *27*
Australia. Bureau of Agricultural
Economics. Coarse Grains: Situation
and Outlook (AT ISSN 0311-0788)
27, *41*
Australia. Bureau of Agricultural
Economics. Dairy Products: Situation
and Outlook (AT) *27*, *40*
Australia. Bureau of Agricultural
Economics. Dairy Situation *see*
Australia. Bureau of Agricultural
Economics. Dairy Products: Situation
and Outlook *27*
Australia. Bureau of Agricultural
Economics. Egg Situation *see*
Australia. Bureau of Agricultural
Economics. Eggs: Situation and
Outlook *27*
Australia. Bureau of Agricultural
Economics. Eggs: Situation and
Outlook (AT) *27*, *43*
Australia. Bureau of Agricultural
Economics. Fibre Review (AT ISSN
0311-2950) *27*
Australia. Bureau of Agricultural
Economics. Fibres Other Than Wool
see Australia. Bureau of Agricultural
Economics. Fibre Review *27*

Australia. Bureau of Agricultural Economics. Meat Situation *see* Australia. Bureau of Agricultural Economics. Meat: Situation and Outlook 27
Australia. Bureau of Agricultural Economics. Meat: Situation and Outlook (AT ISSN 0311-0885) 27, 43
Australia. Bureau of Agricultural Economics. Occasional Papers (AT) 27
Australia. Bureau of Agricultural Economics. Oilseeds: Situation and Outlook (AT) 27, 41
Australia. Bureau of Agricultural Economics. Wheat: Situation and Outlook (AT) 13, 42
Australia. Bureau of Census and Statistics. South Australian Office. Factories *see* Australia. Bureau of Statistics. South Australian Office. Manufacturing Establishments 152
Australia. Bureau of Meteorology. Bulletin (AT ISSN 0067-1312) 631
Australia. Bureau of Meteorology. Meteorological Study (AT ISSN 0067-1320) 631
Australia. Bureau of Mineral Resources, Geology and Geophysics. Bulletin (AT ISSN 0084-7089) 288
Australia. Bureau of Mineral Resources, Geology and Geophysics. Open File Circular (AT) 290, 648
Australia. Bureau of Mineral Resources, Geology, and Geophysics. Publications (AT) 87, 420
Australia. Bureau of Mineral Resources, Geology and Geophysics. Reports (AT ISSN 0084-7100) 288
Australia. Bureau of Mineral Resources, Geology, and Geophysics. 1: 250000 Geological Maps and Explanatory Notes Series (AT) 288, 291
Australia. Bureau of Statistics. Apparent Consumption of Foodstuffs and Nutrients (AT) 406
Australia. Bureau of Statistics. Apparent Consumption of Tea and Coffee (AT) 406
Australia. Bureau of Statistics. Australian Capital Territory. Statistical Summary (AT ISSN 0067-1754) 833
Australia. Bureau of Statistics. Australian Exports Bulletin *see* Australia. Bureau of Statistics. Australian Exports, Country by Commodity 151
Australia. Bureau of Statistics. Australian Exports, Country by Commodity (AT) 151
Australia. Bureau of Statistics. Australian Imports Bulletin *see* Australia. Bureau of Statistics. Australian Imports, Country by Commodity 151
Australia. Bureau of Statistics. Australian Imports, Country by Commodity (AT) 151
Australia. Bureau of Statistics. Australian National Accounts - National Income and Expenditure (AT ISSN 0312-6250) 151
Australia. Bureau of Statistics. Balance of Payments (AT ISSN 0045-0111) 151
Australia. Bureau of Statistics. Bee Farming. *see* Australia. Bureau of Statistics. Bee Keeping 23
Australia. Bureau of Statistics. Bee Keeping (AT) 23
Australia. Bureau of Statistics. Causes of Death (AT ISSN 0067-0766) 731
Australia. Bureau of Statistics. Census of Tourist Accomodation Establishments: Australia and Australian Capital Territory (AT) 833, 893
Australia. Bureau of Statistics. Child Care (AT) 257
Australia. Bureau of Statistics. Chronic Illnesses, Injuries and Impairments (AT) 756

Australia. Bureau of Statistics. Colleges of Advanced Education (AT) 325
Australia. Bureau of Statistics. Crop Statistics (AT) 33
Australia. Bureau of Statistics. Dairying and Dairy Products (AT) 23
Australia. Bureau of Statistics. Dairying Industry *see* Australia. Bureau of Statistics. Dairying and Dairy Products 23
Australia. Bureau of Statistics. Deaths (AT) 725
Australia. Bureau of Statistics. Divorces (AT) 818
Australia. Bureau of Statistics. Earnings and Hours of Employees (AT) 151
Australia. Bureau of Statistics. Economic Censuses: Electricity and Gas Establishments, Details of Operations (AT) 352, 362, 678
Australia. Bureau of Statistics. Estimates of Gross Product by Industry at Current and Constant Prices (AT) 151
Australia. Bureau of Statistics. Expenditure on Education (AT) 326
Australia. Bureau of Statistics. Imports Cleared for Home Consumption (AT ISSN 0067-0804) 151
Australia. Bureau of Statistics. Income Distribution (AT) 151
Australia. Bureau of Statistics. Indexes of Manufacturing Production (AT) 152
Australia. Bureau of Statistics. Labour Mobility (AT) 152
Australia. Bureau of Statistics. Labour Report *see* Australia. Bureau of Statistics. Labour Statistics 152
Australia. Bureau of Statistics. Labour Statistics (AT) 152
Australia. Bureau of Statistics. Leavers from Schools, Universities and Other Educational Institutions (AT) 326
Australia. Bureau of Statistics. Livestock Statistics (AT) 23
Australia. Bureau of Statistics. Manufacturing Commodities: Principal Articles Produced (AT) 833
Australia. Bureau of Statistics. Manufacturing Commodities: Principal Materials Used (AT) 833
Australia. Bureau of Statistics. Manufacturing Establishments: Summary of Operations by Industry Class (AT) 833
Australia. Bureau of Statistics. Marriages (AT) 725
Australia. Bureau of Statistics. Meat Industry *see* Australia. Bureau of Statistics. Meat Statistics (AT) 43
Australia. Bureau of Statistics. Meat Statistics (AT) 43
Australia. Bureau of Statistics. Mineral Exploration (AT) 648
Australia. Bureau of Statistics. Mineral Production (AT ISSN 0311-8975) 641
Australia. Bureau of Statistics. New South Wales Office. Education (AT) 326
Australia. Bureau of Statistics. New South Wales Office. Health and Welfare Services. (AT) 810
Australia. Bureau of Statistics. New South Wales Office. Trade, Transport and Communication *see* Australia. Bureau of Statistics. New South Wales Office. Transport and Communication 152
Australia. Bureau of Statistics. New South Wales Office. Transport and Communication (AT) 152, 265, 864
Australia. Bureau of Statistics. Northern Territory Statistical Summary (AT ISSN 0067-0855) 833
Australia. Bureau of Statistics. Outward Overseas Cargo (AT) 152
Australia. Bureau of Statistics. Overseas and Coastal Shipping (AT) 152, 864
Australia. Bureau of Statistics. Overseas Investments: Overseas Borrowings by Companies in Australia (AT) 904

Australia. Bureau of Statistics. Overseas Shipping Cargo *see* Australia. Bureau of Statistics. Overseas and Coastal Shipping 864
Australia. Bureau of Statistics. Overseas Trade Bulletin (AT ISSN 0067-0863) 152
Australia. Bureau of Statistics. Perinatal Deaths (AT) 615, 725
Australia. Bureau of Statistics. Pocket Compendium of Australian Statistics *see* Australia. Bureau of Statistics. Pocket Year Book of Australia 833
Australia. Bureau of Statistics. Pocket Year Book of Australia (AT) 833
Australia. Bureau of Statistics. Public Authority Finance: Authorities of the Australian Government *see* Australia. Bureau of Statistics. Public Authority Finance: Federal Authorities 740
Australia. Bureau of Statistics. Public Authority Finance: Federal Authorities (AT) 740
Australia. Bureau of Statistics. Public Authority Finance. Public Authority Estimates (AT) 833
Australia. Bureau of Statistics. Public Authority Finance. State and Local Authorities (AT) 152, 226, 833
Australia. Bureau of Statistics. Public Authority Finance. State Governments: Social Services (AT) 904
Australia. Bureau of Statistics. Queensland Office. Area and Estimated Population in Each Queensland Local Authority Area (AT) 833
Australia. Bureau of Statistics. Queensland Office. Government Finance (AT) 152
Australia. Bureau of Statistics. Queensland Office. Hospital Morbidity (AT) 481
Australia. Bureau of Statistics. Queensland Office. Law and Order (AT) 284
Australia. Bureau of Statistics. Queensland Office. Patients Treated in Hospitals *see* Australia. Bureau of Statistics. Queensland Office. Hospital Morbidity 481
Australia. Bureau of Statistics. Queensland Office. Private Finance (AT) 152
Australia. Bureau of Statistics. Queensland Office. Public Finance: Government Authorities *see* Australia. Bureau of Statistics. Queensland Office. Government Finance 152
Australia. Bureau of Statistics. Rail, Bus, and Air Transport (AT) 861, 872
Australia. Bureau of Statistics. Rural Land Use, Improvements, Agricultural Machinery and Labour *see* Australia. Bureau of Statistics. Rural Land Use, Improvements and Labour 23
Australia. Bureau of Statistics. Rural Land Use, Improvements and Labour (AT) 23
Australia. Bureau of Statistics. Sea and Air Cargo, Outward Overseas *see* Australia. Bureau of Statistics. Outward Overseas Cargo 152
Australia. Bureau of Statistics. Seasonally Adjusted Indicators (AT) 152
Australia. Bureau of Statistics. South Australian Office. Births (AT ISSN 0067-088X) 725
Australia. Bureau of Statistics. South Australian Office. Deaths (AT ISSN 0067-0898) 725
Australia. Bureau of Statistics. South Australian Office. Divisional Statistics (AT ISSN 0067-091X) 833
Australia. Bureau of Statistics. South Australian Office. Divorce (AT ISSN 0067-0901) 725
Australia. Bureau of Statistics. South Australian Office. Livestock. *see* Australia. Bureau of Statistics. South Australian Office. Livestock and Livestock Products 43

Australia. Bureau of Statistics. South Australian Office. Livestock and Livestock Products (AT) 43
Australia. Bureau of Statistics. South Australian Office. Manufacturing Establishments (AT ISSN 0310-0871) 152
Australia. Bureau of Statistics. South Australian Office. Marriages (AT ISSN 0067-0952) 725
Australia. Bureau of Statistics. South Australian Office. Rural Production (AT ISSN 0067-0987) 23, 152
Australia. Bureau of Statistics. Survey of Leavers from Schools, Universities or Other Educational Institutions *see* Australia. Bureau of Statistics. Leavers from Schools, Universities and Other Educational Institutions 326
Australia. Bureau of Statistics. Survey of Retail Establishments: Australian Capital Territory *see* Australia. Bureau of Statistics. Survey of Retail Establishments and Selected Service Establishments: Australian Capital Territory 152
Australia. Bureau of Statistics. Survey of Retail Establishments and Selected Service Establishments: Australian Capital Territory (AT) 152
Australia. Bureau of Statistics. Tasmanian Office. Agricultural Industry (AT ISSN 0314-1659) 27
Australia. Bureau of Statistics. Tasmanian Office. Building Industry (AT ISSN 0067-1010) 140
Australia. Bureau of Statistics. Tasmanian Office. Demography (AT ISSN 0067-1029) 725
Australia. Bureau of Statistics. Tasmanian Office. Education (AT ISSN 0314-1705) 812
Australia. Bureau of Statistics. Tasmanian Office. Finance *see* Australia. Bureau of Statistics. Tasmanian Office. Local Government Finance 152
Australia. Bureau of Statistics. Tasmanian Office. Fruit (AT) 23
Australia. Bureau of Statistics. Tasmanian Office. Fruit Production *see* Australia. Bureau of Statistics. Tasmanian Office. Fruit 23
Australia. Bureau of Statistics. Tasmanian Office. Industrial Accident Statistics (AT ISSN 0314-1721) 152, 496
Australia. Bureau of Statistics. Tasmanian Office. Labour, Wages and Prices (AT ISSN 0067-1045) 152
Australia. Bureau of Statistics. Tasmanian Office. Local Government Finance (AT ISSN 0312-7850) 152
Australia. Bureau of Statistics. Tasmanian Office. Meat Production (AT) 406
Australia. Bureau of Statistics. Tasmanian Office. Pocket Year Book of Tasmania (AT ISSN 0085-493X) 833
Australia. Bureau of Statistics. Tasmanian Office. Potato Production (AT) 23
Australia. Bureau of Statistics. Tasmanian Office. Potato Statistics *see* Australia. Bureau of Statistics. Tasmanian Office. Potato Production 23
Australia. Bureau of Statistics. Tasmanian Office. Primary Industries (Excluding Mining) *see* Australia. Bureau of Statistics. Tasmanian Office. Agricultural Industry 27
Australia. Bureau of Statistics. Tasmanian Office. Production of Meat in Tasmania *see* Australia. Bureau of Statistics. Tasmanian Office. Meat Production 406
Australia. Bureau of Statistics. Tasmanian Office. Public Justice (AT ISSN 0312-1356) 509
Australia. Bureau of Statistics. Tasmanian Office. Social *see* Australia. Bureau of Statistics. Tasmanian Office. Education 812

Australia. Bureau of Statistics. Tasmanian Office. Tasmanian Year Book (AT ISSN 0082-2116) *447*
Australia. Bureau of Statistics. Tasmanian Office. Trade and Shipping (AT ISSN 0067-107X) *152, 864*
Australia. Bureau of Statistics. Tasmanian Office. Wool Production and Disposal (AT) 43, *855*
Australia. Bureau of Statistics. Tasmanian Office. Wool Production Statistics see Australia. Bureau of Statistics. Tasmanian Office. Wool Production and Disposal *855*
Australia. Bureau of Statistics. Trade Union Statistics: Australia (AT ISSN 0312-1437) *152*
Australia. Bureau of Statistics. University Statistics (AT) *334*
Australia. Bureau of Statistics. Value of Agricultural Commodities Produced (AT) *23*
Australia. Bureau of Statistics. Value of Primary Production, Excluding Mining, and Indexes of Quantum and Unit Gross Value of Agricultural Production see Australia. Bureau of Statistics. Value of Agricultural Commodities Produced *23*
Australia. Bureau of Statistics. Victorian Office. Causes of Death (AT ISSN 0067-1088) *447, 726*
Australia. Bureau of Statistics. Victorian Office. Demography (AT ISSN 0067-1096) *726*
Australia. Bureau of Statistics. Victorian Office. Estimated Population and Dwellings by Local Government Areas see Australia. Bureau of Statistics. Victorian Office. Estimated Population in Local Government Areas *731*
Australia. Bureau of Statistics. Victorian Office. Estimated Population in Local Government Areas (AT) *731*
Australia. Bureau of Statistics. Victorian Office. General Statistics of Local Government Areas (AT ISSN 0067-1118) *437*
Australia. Bureau of Statistics. Victorian Office. Government Finance see Australia. Bureau of Statistics. Victorian Office. Local Government Finance *226*
Australia. Bureau of Statistics. Victorian Office. Industrial Accidents and Workers Compensation (AT) *904*
Australia. Bureau of Statistics. Victorian Office Industrial Accidents and Workers Compensation. Statistics see Australia. Bureau of Statistics. Victorian Office. Industrial Accidents and Workers Compensation *904*
Australia. Bureau of Statistics. Victorian Office. Land Utilisation and Crops (AT) *13, 33*
Australia. Bureau of Statistics. Victorian Office. Livestock (AT) *23*
Australia. Bureau of Statistics. Victorian Office. Local Government Finance (AT) *226*
Australia. Bureau of Statistics. Victorian Office. Manufacturing Establishments: Detail of Operations (AT) *152, 833*
Australia. Bureau of Statistics. Victorian Office. Manufacturing Establishments: Usage of Electricity and Fuels (AT) *364, 833*
Australia. Bureau of Statistics. Victorian Office. Mineral Production - Victoria(AT) *648, 833*
Australia. Bureau of Statistics. Victorian Office. Primary and Secondary Education (AT ISSN 0067-1150) *314, 447*
Australia. Bureau of Statistics. Victorian Office. Road Traffic Accidents Involving Casualties (AT ISSN 0067-1185) *447, 874*
Australia. Bureau of Statistics. Victorian Office. Value of Primary Commodities Produced (Excluding Mining) (AT) *23*

Australia. Bureau of Statistics. Victorian Office. Value of Primary Production see Australia. Bureau of Statistics. Victorian Office. Value of Primary Commodities Produced (Excluding Mining) *23*
Australia. Bureau of Statistics. Victorian Office. Victorian Pocket Yearbook (AT ISSN 0067-1207) *833*
Australia. Bureau of Statistics. Victorian Office. Victorian Statistical Publications (AT ISSN 0067-1215) *437*
Australia. Bureau of Statistics. Victorian Office. Victorian Yearbook (AT ISSN 0067-1223) *833*
Australia. Bureau of Statistics. Western Australian Office. Abstract of Statistics of Local Government Areas. see Australia. Bureau of Statistics. Western Australian Office. Statistics of Western Australia-Local Government *437*
Australia. Bureau of Statistics. Western Australian Office. Agricultural and Pastoral Statistics see Australia. Bureau of Statistics. Western Australian Office. Agricultural Statistics (General Summary) *23*
Australia. Bureau of Statistics. Western Australian Office. Agricultural Statistics (General Summary) (AT) *23*
Australia. Bureau of Statistics. Western Australian Office. Cattle and Pigs: Western Australia (AT) *23, 833*
Australia.Bureau of Statistics. Western Australian Office. Census of Manufacturing Establishments. Summary of Operations by Industry Class (AT) *152*
Australia. Bureau of Statistics. Western Australian Office. Economic Censuses: Manufacturing Establishments: Summary of Operations by Industry Class see Australia.Bureau of Statistics. Western Australian Office. Census of Manufacturing Establishments. Summary of Operations by Industry Class *152*
Australia. Bureau of Statistics. Western Australian Office. Fisheries (AT) *395*
Australia. Bureau of Statistics. Western Australian Office. Hospital in-Patient Statistics (AT ISSN 0312-7907) *480*
Australia. Bureau of Statistics. Western Australian Office. Industrial Accidents see Australia. Bureau of Statistics. Western Australian Office. Industrial Accidents. Series B: Absence from Work for One Week or More *152*
Australia. Bureau of Statistics. Western Australian Office. Industrial Accidents. Series A: Absence from Work for One Day or More (AT) *152, 496*
Australia. Bureau of Statistics. Western Australian Office. Industrial Accidents. Series B: Absence from Work for One Week or More (AT) *152, 496*
Australia. Bureau of Statistics. Western Australian Office. Population, Dwellings and Vital Statistics (AT ISSN 0067-1290) *731*
Australia. Bureau of Statistics. Western Australian Office. Rural Land Utilisation (AT) *23*
Australia. Bureau of Statistics. Western Australian Office. Sheep, Lambing and Wool Clip (AT ISSN 0312-844X) *833*
Australia. Bureau of Statistics. Western Australian Office. Statistics of Western Australia-Local Government(AT) *437*
Australia. Bureau of Statistics. Western Australian Office. Western Australia: Artificial Fertiliser Used on Rural Holdings (AT ISSN 0312-6269) *23*
Australia. Bureau of Statistics. Western Australian Office. Western Australian Cereal Crop Forecast (AT) *33, 42*
Australia. Bureau of Statistics. Wheat Industry see Australia. Bureau of Statistics. Wheat Statistics *33*

Australia. Bureau of Statistics. Wheat Statistics (AT) *33*
Australia. Bureau of Statistics. Year Book Australia (AT) *833*
Australia. Chamber of Industries, Northern Territory. Northern Territory Business Journal (AT ISSN 0310-3811) *178*
Australia. Department of Aboriginal Affairs. Report (AT) *391*
Australia. Department of Civil Aviation. Civil Aviation Report see Australian Transport *7*
Australia. Department of Customs and Excise. Review of Activities see Australia. Department of Police and Customs. Review of Activities *226*
Australia. Department of Foreign Affairs. Development Assistance Bureau. Annual Review (AT) *199*
Australia. Department of Foreign Affairs. International Treaties and Conventions (AT ISSN 0084-7135) *719*
Australia. Department of Foreign Affairs. Select Documents on International Affairs (AT ISSN 0519-5950) *719*
Australia. Department of Health. Annual Report (AT) *750*
Australia. Department of Industry and Commerce. Bulletin (AT) *220*
Australia. Department of Manufacturing Industry. Bulletin see Australia. Department of Industry and Commerce. Bulletin *220*
Australia. Department of Police and Customs. Review of Activities (AT) *226*
Australia. Department of Social Security. Annual Report of the Director-General (AT) *497*
Australia. Department of Territories. Territory of Norfolk Island; Report (AT ISSN 0572-0494) *447*
Australia. Department of the Environment and Conservation. Report (AT) 275, *384*
Australia. Department of the Treasury. Income Tax Statistics (AT ISSN 0067-1444) *152*
Australia. Department of the Treasury. Round-up of Economic Statistics (AT ISSN 0310-4230) *152*
Australia. Department of the Treasury. Taxation Branch. Taxation Statistics (AT ISSN 0519-6035) *152*
Australia. Department of the Treasury. Treasury Economic Paper (AT) *226*
Australia. Department of Veterans Affairs. Directory of Ex-Service Organisations (AT) *638*
Australia. Designs Office. Registered Owners of Designs and Articles in Respect of Which Designs Have Been Registered Under the Designs Act (AT) *676*
Australia. Fishing Industry Research Committee. Annual Report (AT) *395, 509*
Australia. Forestry and Timber Bureau. Bulletins see Commonwealth Scientific and Industrial Research Organization. Division of Forest Research. Bulletins *906*
Australia. Forestry and Timber Bureau. Leaflets see Commonwealth Scientific and Industrial Research Organization. Division of Forest Research. Leaflets *907*
Australia. Grants Commission. Grants Commission Report on Financial Assistance for Local Government (AT) *226*
Australia. Grants Commission. Grants Commission Report on Special Assistance for States see Australia. Grants Commission. Grants Commission Report on Financial Assistance for Local Government *226*
Australia. Industries Assistance Commission. Annual Report (AT) *220*
Australia. Insurance Commissioner. Annual Report (AT) *497*
Australia. Law Reform Commission. Annual Report (AT) *509*

Australia. Metric Conversion Board. Annual Report (AT) *636*
Australia. National Capital Development Commission. Annual Report (AT ISSN 0067-1517) *483*
Australia. National Capital Development Commission. Technical Papers (AT ISSN 0313-9948) *740*
Australia. National Drug Information Service. Technical Information Bulletin see Australia. National Information Service on Drug Abuse. Technical Information Bulletin *286*
Australia. National Information Service on Drug Abuse. Technical Information Bulletin (AT ISSN 0157-8200) *286*
Australia. National Library. Acquisitions Newsletter (AT ISSN 0312-259X) *526*
Australia. National Library. Annual Report of the Council (AT ISSN 0069-0082) *526*
Australia. Patent Office. Report (AT) *676*
Australia. Postmaster General's Department. Research Laboratories. Report (AT) *269*
Australia. Public Service Board. Annual Report (AT) *740*
Australia. Repatriation Department. Directory of Ex-Service Organisations see Australia. Department of Veterans Affairs. Directory of Ex-Service Organisations *638*
Australia Handbook (AT ISSN 0067-1495) *447*
Australia Indonesia Association of New South Wales. Bulletin see Kabar *722*
Australia Law Reform Commission Report Series see A L R C Report Series *508*
Australia Mineral Development Laboratories Bulletin see A M D E L Bulletin *290*
Australia Mineral Industry Review see Australian Mineral Industry. Annual Review *641*
Australian. Bureau of Statistics, Indexes of Factory Production see Australia. Bureau of Statistics. Indexes of Manufacturing Production *152*
Australian Academy of Science. National Committee for Antarctic Research. Australian Antarctic and Sub-Antarctic Research Programmes (AT) *303*
Australian Academy of Science. Records (AT ISSN 0067-155X) *779*
Australian Academy of Science. Reports (AT ISSN 0067-1568) *779*
Australian Academy of Science. Year Book (AT ISSN 0067-1584) *779*
Australian Academy of the Humanities. Proceedings (AT ISSN 0067-1592) *489*
Australian Accommodation Guide (AT) *482*
Australian Accounting Research Foundation. Research Studies (AT) *167*
Australian Advisory Council on Bibliographical Services. Library Services for Australia (AT ISSN 0310-8856) *526*
Australian Agriculture, Fisheries and Forestry Directory see Rural Industry Directory *19*
Australian-American News N.S.W. Annual Edition (AT) *719, 883*
Australian and New Zealand Hospitals and Health Services Yearbook see Australian Hospitals and Health Services Yearbook *480*
Australian and Pacific Book Prices Current (AT ISSN 0310-9879) *904*
Australian Anti-Metric Association. Newsletter (AT) *636*
Australian Association for the Teaching of English Guide to English Books see A. A. T. E. Guide to English Books *577*
Australian Association of Adult Education. Monograph (AT ISSN 0067-1630) *329*

Australian Association of Adult Education. Proceedings of the National Conference (AT ISSN 0067-1649) *329*
Australian Association of Neurologists Proceedings *see* Clinical and Experimental Neurology *619*
Australian Audio-Visual Reference Book (AT ISSN 0311-323X) *326*
Australian Aviation Yearbook (AT ISSN 0084-7232) *7*
Australian Banknote Catalogue (AT ISSN 0313-9611) *477*
Australian Biblical Review (AT ISSN 0045-0308) *763*
Australian Biochemical Society. Proceedings (AT ISSN 0067-1703) *110*
Australian Biochemical Society. Programme and Abstracts *see* Australian Biochemical Society. Proceedings *110*
Australian Books in Print (AT ISSN 0067-172X) *760*
Australian Books; Select List (AT ISSN 0067-1738) *87*
Australian Bureau of Statistics. Western Australian Office. Industrial Accidents *see* Australia. Bureau of Statistics. Western Australian Office. Industrial Accidents. Series A: Absence from Work for One Day or More *152*
Australian Capital Territory Soaring in the A.C.T. *see* Soaring in the A.C.T. *10*
Australian Careers Guide (AT) *666*
Australian Cat Federation, Inc. Year Book *see* A C I Year Book *682*
Australian Catholic Historical Society. Journal (AT ISSN 0084-7259) *447*
Australian Coal Industry Research Laboratories. Annual Report (AT ISSN 0067-1762) *641*
Australian Coin Catalogue (AT ISSN 0084-7267) *477*
Australian College of Education. Proceedings of the Annual Conference and Annual Report *see* Unicorn *323*
Australian Commonwealth Specialists' Catalogue (AT ISSN 0313-9603) *478*
Australian Composer (AT ISSN 0311-2764) *657*
Australian Computer Society. Conference Proceedings (AT ISSN 0313-3311) *270*
Australian Computer Society. Council. Report (AT ISSN 0067-1819) *270*
Australian Computer Society. Queensland Branch. Newsletter (AT) *270*
Australian Conference on Chemical Engineering. Proceedings (AT) *372, 678*
Australian Congress of Trade Unions. Decisions (AT) *506*
Australian Conservation Foundation. Annual Report (AT ISSN 0587-5846) *275*
Australian Conservation Foundation. Conservation Directory *see* Green Pages: Directory of Non-Government Environmental Groups in Australia *276*
Australian Copyright Council. Bulletin (AT ISSN 0311-2934) *676*
Australian Council for Educational Research. Annual Report (AT) *314*
Australian Council for Educational Research. Occasional Papers (AT ISSN 0067-1835) *314*
Australian Council for Educational Research. Research Series (AT) *314*
Australian Council on Awards in Advanced Education. Bulletin (AT ISSN 0311-3000) *334*
Australian Country Music Annual (AT) *657*
Australian Cricket Yearbook (AT ISSN 0084-7291) *823*
Australian Crime Prevention Council. National Conference. Proceedings. (AT) *280*
Australian Crime Prevention Council. National Newsletter (AT) *280*
Australian Defense Equipment Catalogue (AT) *638*

Australian Digest (AT ISSN 0067-1843) *509*
Australian Directory of Exports *see* Australian Exports *193*
Australian Economy; Business Forecast *see* Management Reports on the Australian Economy *187*
Australian Education Review (AT) *314*
Australian Energy Statistics (AT) *364, 833*
Australian Entomological Society. Miscellaneous Publications (AT) *120*
Australian Exports (AT) *193*
Australian Family Law Cases (AT) *509*
Australian Fisheries Paper (AT ISSN 0084-7356) *395*
Australian Forest Resources (AT) *407*
Australian Frontier Newsletter (AT) *812*
Australian Gas Industry Directory (AT) *381, 678*
Australian Geomechanics Journal (AT) *379, 641*
Australian Gliding Yearbook (AT ISSN 0084-7364) *7*
Australian Government Directory *see* Commonwealth Government Directory *741*
Australian Hi-Fi Annual (AT ISSN 0310-8902) *818*
Australian Honey Board. Annual Report (AT ISSN 0067-1894) *404*
Australian Horse Racing Annual (AT ISSN 0084-7402) *827*
Australian Hospital Association. Proceedings-National Congress (AT) *480*
Australian Hospital Association Health Services Monographs *see* A H A Health Services Monographs *480*
Australian Hospitals and Health Services Yearbook (AT ISSN 0312-5599) *480*
Australian Hotel, Motel, Club Catering Restaurant Handbook and Buyers Guide (AT) *482*
Australian Income Tax Assessment Act (AT) *226*
Australian Institute of Marine Science Monograph Series *see* A I M S Monograph Series *309*
Australian Institute of Metals. Proceedings of the Annual Conference *see* Australasian Institute of Metals. Proceedings of the Annual Conference *627*
Australian Institute of Petroleum. Annual Report (AT ISSN 0314-3171) *291, 678*
Australian Insurance Institute. Journal (AT ISSN 0084-7453) *497*
Australian Jaycees National Directory (AT) *262*
Australian Journal of American Studies *see* A J A S: Australian Journal of American Studies *465*
Australian Journal of Biblical Archaeology (AT ISSN 0084-747X) *58*
Australian Journal of Botany (AT ISSN 0067-1924) *113*
Australian Journal of Highter Education *see* Education Research and Perspectives *336*
Australian Key Business Directory (AT ISSN 0311-2667) *235*
Australian Labor Party. A. C. T. Branch. Newsletter (AT ISSN 0310-785X) *708*
Australian Labor Party (NSW Branch). Labor Year Book (AT ISSN 0310-5296) *506*
Australian Ladies Golf Union. Official Yearbook (AT) *828*
Australian Legal Aid Review Committee. Report (AT) *509*
Australian Lutheran Almanac *see* Lutheran Church of Australia. Yearbook *772*
Australian Mammalogy (AT ISSN 0310-0049) *127*
Australian Market Guide (US ISSN 0067-1959) *202, 235*
Australian Marxist Review (AT ISSN 0310-8252) *708*
Australian Master Tax Guide (AT) *226*
Australian Meat Research Committee. Annual Report. (AT) *43, 404*

Australian Metal Trades Export Group's Export Note Pad *see* M T I A N E G's Export Note Pad *628*
Australian Mineral Industries Research Association. Bulletin (AT) *641*
Australian Mineral Industries Research Association. Non-Confidential Research Information (AT) *641*
Australian Mineral Industry. Annual Review (AT ISSN 0084-7488) *641*
Australian Mining Yearbook (AT) *641*
Australian Mission to the United Nations. United Nations General Assembly. Australian Delegation. Report (AT) *719*
Australian Museum, Sydney. Memoirs (AT ISSN 0067-1967) *652*
Australian Museum, Sydney. Records (AT ISSN 0067-1975) *652*
Australian National Conference on Fire. Conference Papers (AT) *394*
Australian National Social Sciences Library Bibliography Series *see* A N S O L Bibliography Series *795*
Australian National University. Canberra. Department of Demography. Family and Fertility Change (AT) *726, 812*
Australian National University, Canberra. Centre of Oriental Studies. Occasional Papers *see* Australian National University, Canberra. Faculty of Asian Studies. Occasional Papers *442*
Australian National University, Canberra. Department of Demography. Studies in Migration and Urbanization (AT) *726*
Australian National University, Canberra. Department of Engineering Physics. Publication Ep-Rr (AT ISSN 0084-7496) *270, 366, 695*
Australian National University, Canberra. Department of Political Science. Occasional Paper. *see* Australian National University, Canberra. Research School of Social Sciences. Department of Political Science. Occasional Papers *708*
Australian National University, Canberra. Faculty of Asian Studies. Occasional Papers (AT ISSN 0067-2041) *442*
Australian National University, Canberra. Geology Department. Publication (AT ISSN 0084-750X) *291*
Australian National University, Canberra. Research School of Physical Sciences. Research Paper (AT ISSN 0084-7518) *695*
Australian National University, Canberra. Research School of Social Sciences. Department of Political Science. Occasional Papers (AT) *708*
Australian National University Historical Journal *see* A N U Historical Journal *447*
Australian Numismatic Journal (AT ISSN 0004-9875) *477*
Australian Packaging and Materials Handling Yearbook and Buyers Guide *see* Australian Packaging Buyers Guide *672*
Australian Packaging Buyers Guide (AT) *672*
Australian Parliamentary Handbook (AT) *708*
Australian Parliamentary Seminar. Summary Report of Proceedings (AT) *509*
Australian Petroleum Exploration Association Journal *see* A. P. E. A. Journal *677*
Australian Photography Directory (AT ISSN 0084-2076) *693*
Australian Plant Introduction Review (AT ISSN 0313-3192) *33*
Australian Renewable Energy Resources Index (AT ISSN 0155-9443) *1, 364*
Australian Research Grants Committee. Report (AT) *314*
Australian Road Research Board. Proceedings (AT ISSN 0572-1431) *374, 874*
Australian Road Research in Progress (AT ISSN 0705-9213) *374*

Australian Rose Annual (AT) *414*
Australian Sales Tax Guide (AT) *226*
Australian Science Education Research Association. Research in Science Education (AT ISSN 0157-244X) *347*
Australian Shipping and Shipbuilding (AT) *877*
Australian Ski Yearbook (AT ISSN 0084-7593) *828*
Australian Society for Education in Film and Television. President's Newsletter (AT) *347*
Australian Society for Historical Archaeology. (AT) *58*
Australian Society for Medical Research. Proceedings (UK ISSN 0067-2130) *593*
Australian Society for Music Education. Report of Proceedings of the National Conference (AT) *347, 657*
Australian Society of Accountants. Bulletin (AT ISSN 0005-0261) *167*
Australian Society of Animal Production. Proceedings (AT ISSN 0067-2149) *43*
Australian Society of Sugar Cane Technologists. Proceedings. (AT) *404*
Australian Speedway Yearbook *see* Peter Webster's International Speedway Review *826*
Australian Speleo Abstracts (AT) *291*
Australian Stamp Bulletin (AT) *478*
Australian Stud Pig Herd Book (AT) *43*
Australian Studies in Health Service Administration (AT ISSN 0067-2165) *750*
Australian Sugar Year Book (AT ISSN 0067-2173) *404*
Australian Superannuation and Employee Benefits Guide (AT) *497, 804*
Australian Superannuation and Employee Benefits Planning in Action *see* Australian Superannuation and Employee Benefits Guide *804*
Australian Tax Cases (AT) *227, 509*
Australian Taxpayer's Association. Annual Taxation Summary (AT) *227*
Australian Teacher *see* Teachers Guild of New South Wales. Proceedings *323*
Australian Teacher of the Deaf (AT ISSN 0005-0334) *286, 314*
Australian Teachers' Federation Annual Report *see* A T F Annual Report *313*
Australian Telecommunication Monographs (AT ISSN 0067-2181) *269*
Australian Tourist Commission. Annual Report (AT) *883*
Australian Transport (AT ISSN 0311-628X) *7*
Australian Treaty List *see* Australian Treaty Series *522*
Australian Treaty Series (AT) *522*
Australian Variety Directory (AT) *858*
Australian Water Resources Council. Hydrological Series (AT ISSN 0067-219X) *307*
Australian Water Resources Council Activities *see* A W R C Activities *903*
Australian Weed Control Handbook (AT) *33*
Australian Welding Research Association. Bulletin (AT ISSN 0084-7631) *631*
Australian Wool *see* Australian Wool Sale Statistics. Statistical Analysis. Part A & B *857*
Australian Wool Corporation. Statistical Analysis *see* Australian Wool Sale Statistics. Statistical Analysis. Part A & B *857*
Australian Wool Sale Statistics. Statistical Analysis. Part A & B (AT ISSN 0311-9882) *857*
Australian Workers' Union. Official Report of the Annual Convention (AT) *506*
Australian Yearbook of International Law (AT ISSN 0084-7658) *522*
Australian Zoologist (AT ISSN 0067-2238) *127*

Australiana Facsimile Editions (AT ISSN 0067-2246) *447*
Australia's External Aid *see* Australia's Overseas Development Assistance *719*
Australia's Overseas Development Assistance (AT ISSN 0312-9217) *719*
Austria. Bundesamt fuer Eich- und Vermessungswesen. Amtsblatt fuer das Eichwesen (AU) *636*
Austria. Bundeskammer fuer die Gewerbliche Wirtschaft (AU ISSN 0067-2254) *220*
Austria. Bundesministerium fuer Bauten und Technik. Abteilung Baukoordinierung. Vorschau (AU) *134*
Austria. Bundesministerium fuer Bauten und Technik. Wohnbauforschung (AU) *68, 502*
Austria. Bundesministerium fuer Land- und Forstwirtschaft. Taetigkeitsbericht (AU ISSN 0067-2262) *13*
Austria. Bundesministerium fuer Unterricht und Kunst. Erziehung, Wissenschaft, Forschung *see* Austria. Bundesministerium fuer Unterricht und Kunst. Schriftenreihe *314*
Austria. Bundesministerium fuer Unterricht und Kunst. Jahresbericht (AU ISSN 0067-2289) *314*
Austria. Bundesministerium fuer Unterricht und Kunst. Schriftenreihe (AU) *72, 347*
Austria. Bundesministerium fuer Unterricht und Kunst. Schriftenreihe (AU) *314*
Austria. Bundesministerium fuer Wissenschaft und Forschung. Bericht der Bundesregierung an den Nationalrat (AU ISSN 0300-2772) *779*
Austria. Bundesministerium fuer Wissenschaft und Forschung. Hochschulbericht (AU) *334*
Austria. Oberlandesgericht Wien im Leistungsstreitverfahren Zweiter Instanz der Sozialversicherung (SSV). Entscheidungen (AU ISSN 0567-1477) *509*
Austria. Statistisches Zentralamt. Die Natuerliche Bevoelkerungsbewegung (AU ISSN 0067-2335) *726*
Austria. Statistisches Zentralamt. Die Wohnbautaetigkeit (AU ISSN 0067-2300) *140*
Austria. Statistisches Zentralamt. Ergebnisse der Landwirtschaftlichen Maschinenzaehlung (AU) *23*
Austria. Statistisches Zentralamt. Ergebnisse der Landwirtschaftlichen Statistik (AU ISSN 0067-2327) *23*
Austria. Statistisches Zentralamt. Erhebung der Land-und Forstwirtschaftlichen Arbeitskraefte (AU) *152*
Austria. Statistisches Zentralamt. Gewerbestatistik (AU) *152*
Austria. Statistisches Zentralamt. Industrie Statistik (AU) *152, 833*
Austria. Statistisches Zentralamt. Jugendwohlfahrtspflege (AU) *804*
Austria. Statistisches Zentralamt. Mikrozensus; Jahresergebnisse (AU) *833*
Austria. Statistisches Zentralamt. Oeffentliche Fuersorge. (AU) *810*
Austria. Statistisches Zentralamt. Statistik der Aktiengesellschaften in Oesterreich (AU ISSN 0081-5233) *152*
Austria. Statistisches Zentralamt. Statistik der Rechtspflege (AU) *521*
Austria. Zentralanstalt fuer Meteorologie und Geodynamik. Jahrbuch (AU ISSN 0067-2351) *303, 631*
Austrian Export Directory *see* Herold Export-Adressbuch von Oesterreich *238*
Austrian Historical Bibliography/Oesterreichische Historische Bibliographie (US ISSN 0067-236X) *449*
Austrian History Newsletter *see* Austrian History Yearbook *449*

Austrian History Yearbook (US ISSN 0067-2378) *449*
Ausztraliai Magyar Ujsaf. Hungarian Weekly (AT) *391*
Auszuege aus der Literatur der Zellstoff- und Papier-Erzeugung und Celluloseverarbeitung (GW) *87, 371*
Author-Publisher News & Views (CN ISSN 0381-727X) *757*
Author's and Writer's Who *see* International Author's and Writer's Who's Who *97*
Authors in the News (US ISSN 0145-1499) *96, 559*
Auto Data Digest (SA) *869*
Auto-Jahr *see* Automobile Year *869*
Auto-Katalog (GW) *869*
Auto-Modelle *see* Auto-Katalog *869*
Auto Racing Guide (US ISSN 0067-2408) *819*
Auto-Universum (SZ ISSN 0067-2416) *869*
Auto-Writing *see* I I S T Bulletins *676*
Autocatalogue (FR ISSN 0067-2424) *869*
Autolla Ulkomaille (FI ISSN 0355-2896) *883*
Automatic Data Processing Information Bulletin (SZ ISSN 0379-0258) *270*
Automatic Support Systems Symposium for Advanced Maintainability. Proceedings *see* Autotestcon *352*
Automatic Taxfinder and Tax Preparer's Handbook (US ISSN 0092-6876) *227*
Automation Efforts at the Columbia University Libraries. Progress Report(US) *904*
Automobile Association. Budget Guide *see* Guesthouses, Farmhouses and Inns in Britain *886*
Automobile Association - Great Britain Road Atlas *see* A A/G B Road Atlas *882*
Automobile Association of East Africa Guide to Motoring in Kenya *see* A Guide to Motoring in Kenya *882*
Automobile Electronic Equipment (US ISSN 0587-5919) *352, 869*
Automobile Facts and Figures *see* M V M A Motor Vehicle Facts and Figures *871*
Automobile Legal Association. A L A Green Book *see* A L A Sights to See Book *882*
Automobile Legal Association Sights to See Book *see* A L A Sights to See Book *882*
Automobile News Annual (II ISSN 0067-2548) *869*
Automobile World *see* Auto-Universum *869*
Automobile Year/Annee Automobile/Auto-Jahr (SZ ISSN 0084-7674) *869*
Automotive and Ancillary Industry *see* Automotive Industry of India - Facts & Figures *869*
Automotive Encyclopedia (US) *869*
Automotive Industry of India - Facts & Figures (II) *869*
Automotive News Almanac *see* Automotive News Market Data Book *869*
Automotive News Market Data Book (US) *869*
Automotive Service Data Book (CN ISSN 0068-9629) *869*
Automotriz (MX) *870*
Autoridades e Executivos (BL) *235, 264*
Autotestcon (US) *352*
Available from Wales (UK) *178*
Avalon Dispatch (US) *578*
Avalon Foundation. Report *see* Andrew W. Mellon Foundation. Report *489*
Avances en Obstetricia y Ginecologia (SP) *615*
Avances en Terapeutica (SP) *683*
Avant-Siecle (FR ISSN 0067-2610) *559*
Avenir *see* Budeshte *391*
Avery Index to Architectural Periodicals. Supplement (US) *1, 71*
Aves del Arca (UY ISSN 0067-2637) *559*
Avian Chromosomes Newsletter (US) *127*
Aviation Annual (US) *7*

Aviation Cases in the Courts (US) *867*
Aviation Civile Suisse *see* Schweizerische Zivilluftfahrt *869*
Aviation Europe (UK ISSN 0143-1145) *7*
Aviation Medical Education Series (US ISSN 0067-2661) *7, 593*
Aviation/Space Writers Association Manual (US) *7*
Aviation Telephone Directory: Pacific and Western States (US) *867*
Aviation Week & Space Technology. Marketing Directory. (US ISSN 0067-267X) *7*
Avionics Data Sheets (UK) *7*
Avtokefalnaia Amerikanskaia Pravoslavnaia Tserkov. Ezhegodnik Pravoslavnoi Tserkvi V Amerike (US) *904*
Avtomatizirovannye Sistemy Upravleniya (UR) *270*
Avvenire Medico (IT) *593*
Awards for Commonwealth University Academic Staff (UK ISSN 0144-4611) *334*
Awards for Commonwealth University Staff *see* Awards for Commonwealth University Academic Staff *334*
Awards, Honors and Prizes (US) *360*
Awards to Academic Institutions by the Department of Transportation *see* U.S. Department of Transportation. Office of University Research. Awards to Academic Institutions by the Department of Transportation *864*
Ayer Directory of Newspapers, Magazines, and Trade Publications *see* Ayer Directory of Publications *87*
Ayer Directory of Publications (US ISSN 0145-1642) *87*
Azania (KE ISSN 0067-270X) *58, 439*
B A A *see* Uebersee-Museum, Bremen. Veroeffentlichungen. Reihe F: Bremer Afrika-Archiv *441*
B.A.C.A. Calendar of Cultural Events (Brooklyn Arts and Cultural Association) (US ISSN 0045-3242) *652*
B A H R E P International Hotel Directory (British Association of Hotel Representatives) (UK) *482, 883*
B. A. I. E. Membership Directory (British Association of Industrial Editors) (UK) *757*
B A I Index of Bank Performance (Bank Administration Institute) (US ISSN 0363-910X) *168*
B A Magazine (Brooklyn Academy of Music) (US) *657*
B A R-B R I Bar Review. Civil Procedure (US ISSN 0099-1244) *509*
B A R-B R I Bar Review. Community Property (US) *509*
B A R-B R I Bar Review. Constitutional Law (US ISSN 0098-7638) *509*
B A R-B R I Bar Review. Contracts (US ISSN 0098-762X) *509*
B A R-B R I Bar Review. Corporations (US ISSN 0099-1236) *509*
B A R-B R I Bar Review. Criminal Law(US ISSN 0098-8049) *280*
B A R-B R I Bar Review. Evidence (US) *509*
B A R-B R I Bar Review. Professional Responsibility (US) *509*
B A R-B R I Bar Review. Real Property (US) *509*
B A R-B R I Bar Review. Remedies (US ISSN 0098-7999) *509*
B A R-B R I Bar Review. Torts (US ISSN 0098-7611) *280*
B A R-B R I Bar Review. Trusts (US) *220*
B A R-B R I Bar Review. Wills (US) *509*
B A S A *see* Bangladesh Agricultural Sciences Abstracts *23*
B A S S Fishing Guide (Bass Anglers Sportsman Society) (US) *828*
B A S S Master Fishing Annual (Bass Anglers Sportsman Society) (US) *828*

B and C J Building Directory *see* B and C J Directory *134*
B and C J Directory (I P C Building and Contract Journals Ltd.) (UK ISSN 0068-3507) *134*
B and C J Public Works Directory *see* B and C J Directory *134*
B & T Year Book (AT) *4*
B B A Library (Biochemica & Biophysica Acta) (NE ISSN 0067-2734) *110*
B B C Music Guides (US ISSN 0084-8018) *657*
B. C. Association of Hospitals and Health Organizations. Proceedings of the Annual Conference *see* B. C. Health Association. Proceedings of the Annual Conference *480*
B. C. Association of Teachers of Classics. Newsletter *see* Vexillum *261*
B. C. Fresh Water Fishing Guide (CN ISSN 0709-7778) *828*
B. C. Health Association. Proceedings of the Annual Conference (CN) *480*
B C I T: The Career Campus (British Columbia Institute of Technology) (CN ISSN 0707-3291) *850*
B. C. Labour Directory (CN ISSN 0703-0878) *206*
B. C. Monthly (CN ISSN 0382-5272) *72, 559, 578*
B. C. Motor Transport Directory (CN) *861*
B. C. News *see* B. C. Peace News *719*
B. C. Peace News (CN ISSN 0708-0859) *719*
B. C. Planning Papers (CN) *483*
B. C. Research. Annual Report (CN) *779*
B C S T A Convention Reporter *see* A G M Reporter *343*
B. C. Salt Water Salmon Guide *see* B. C. Sea Angling Guide *828*
B. C. Sea Angling Guide (CN ISSN 0709-776X) *828*
B D I Alemania Suministra *see* B D I Deutschland Liefert *193*
B D I Deutschland Liefert/B D I Germany Supplies/B D I l'Allemagne Fournit/B D I Alemania Suministra (Bundesverband der Deutschen Industrie) (GW ISSN 0415-7508) *193*
B D I Germany Supplies *see* B D I Deutschland Liefert *193*
B D I l'Allemagne Fournit *see* B D I Deutschland Liefert *193*
B D I-Organisationsplan (Bundesverband der Deutschen Industrie) (GW) *220*
B E F A R. Publication (Bibliotheque des Ecoles Francaises d'Athenes et de Rome) (FR) *58*
B E M A Engineering Directory (Bristol and West of England Engineering Manufacturers Association Ltd.) (UK ISSN 0067-5709) *366*
B E N E L U X Economic Union. Conseil Central de l'Economie. Rapport du Secretaire sur l'Activite du Conseil (BE) *220*
B E P I (II) *87*
B G L *see* Bibliothek der Griechischen Literatur *259*
B. G. Rudolph Lectures in Judaic Studies (US ISSN 0067-2742) *770*
B H M Support (U.S. Bureau of Health Manpower) (US) *304*
B. H. R. A. Fluid Engineering Series (British Hydromechanics Research Association) (UK) *380*
B H R C A Guide to Hotels and Restaurants *see* Official Guide to Hotels & Restaurants in Great Britain, Ireland and Overseas *483*
B I A Certification Handbook (Boating Industry Association) (US ISSN 0067-9402) *826*
B I A S Journal (Bristol Industrial Archaeological Society) (UK ISSN 0306-1450) *366, 850*
B I C-Code (FR) *672, 861*
B I G Book *see* Big Book *134*
B.I.M. Boletin del Instituto de Maternidad "Alberto Peralta Ramos" (AG) *615*

B I N D E Annual Report see Revista do B I N D E 176
B I S Conference Report (Brain Information Service-Brain Research Institute) (US ISSN 0092-4334) 619
B L A C (Black Literature and Arts Congress) (SA) 72, 391, 559
B L V S see Literarischer Verein in Stuttgart. Bibliothek 567
B N A Noise Regulation Reporter see Noise Regulation Reporter 516
B N A's Law Reprints: Criminal Law Series (US) 509
B N A's Law Reprints: Labor Series (US) 509
B N A's Law Reprints: Patent, Trademark & Copyright Series (US) 509
B N A's Law Reprints: Securities Regulation Series (US) 509
B N A's Law Reprints: Tax Series (US) 509
B N A's Law Reprints: Trade Regulation (US) 193, 522
B N H Relatorio de Atividades (Banco Nacional da Habitacao) (BL) 168
B P C (Building Products Catalog) (US ISSN 0161-6293) 134
B P R see American Book Publishing Record 760
B R A D S (Bollettino del Repertorio e dell'Atlante Demologico Sardo) (IT ISSN 0067-9860) 401, 449
B R I C S Bracs (Black Resources Information Coordinating Services, Inc.) (US) 391
B R I Research Papers/Kenchiku Kenkyusho Chosa Shiken Kenkyu Gaiyo Hokoku (Building Research Institute) (JA) 134
B. R. P. T. Bulletin (Bureau of Research and Publications on Tripura) (II) 442
B S B I Abstracts (Botanical Society of the British Isles) (UK ISSN 0307-2657) 1, 109
B S J (Broad St. Journal) (US) 480
B S R I A Application Guides. Technical Notes (Building Services Research and Information Association) (UK) 429
B S R I A Technical Notes (Building Services Research and Information Association) (UK ISSN 0309-0248) 429
B T A Studycards (British Trades Alphabet Ltd.) (UK) 5
B T I Bibliographic Series (British Theatre Institute) (UK) 860
B T M A Directory (British Toy & Hobby Manufacturers Association) (UK ISSN 0068-2624) 429, 475
Baas Becking Geobiological Laboratory. Annual Report (AT ISSN 0572-5860) 123, 291
Babbler see Bird Behaviour 124
Babesch see Bulletin Antieke Beschaving 431
Baby John (US) 578
Baccalaureate Education in Nursing: Key to a Professional Career in Nursing (US ISSN 0069-5602) 334, 613
Bach-Jahrbuch (GE ISSN 0084-7682) 657
Back Roads (US) 72, 559
Backstage TV Film/Tape & Syndication Directory (US ISSN 0098-5481) 266, 649
Baconiana (UK) 555
Bacon's Publicity Checker (US ISSN 0162-3125) 6
Bacteriological Proceedings see American Society for Microbiology. Abstracts of the Annual Meeting 123
Bad Breath see So and So Magazine 581
Badania Fizjograficzne nad Polska Zachodnia. Seria A. Geografia Fizyczna (PL ISSN 0067-2807) 420
Badania Fizjograficzne nad Polska Zachodnia. Seria B. Biologia (PL ISSN 0067-2815) 113
Badania Fizjograficzne nad Polska Zachodnia. Seria C. Zoologia (PL) 127

Badania z Dziejow Spolecznych i Gospodarczych (PL ISSN 0067-2793) 449
Die Badeplaetze in Daenemark (GW) 883
Die Badeplaetze in Jugoslawien (GW) 883
Badischer Landesverein fuer Naturkunde und Naturschutz, Freiburg. Mitteilungen. Neue Folge (GW ISSN 0067-2858) 100, 291
Badlands Natural History Association. Bulletin (US ISSN 0067-2866) 779
Badminton (GW) 823
Badminton Association of England. Official Handbook (UK ISSN 0067-2882) 819
Badminton Ireland (IE) 819
Baha'i Studies (CN ISSN 0708-5052) 763
Baha'i World (IS ISSN 0045-1320) 763
Bahamas. Department of Statistics. External Trade (BF) 152
Bahamas. Department of Statistics. Household Income Report (BF) 152
Bahamas. Department of Statistics. Labour Force and Income Distribution see Bahamas. Department of Statistics. Household Income Report 152
Bahamas. Department of Statistics. Statistical Abstract (BF) 833
Bahamas. Ministry of Education and Culture Annual Report (BF) 314
Bahamas. Ministry of Works. Annual Report (BF) 374
Bahamas Handbook and Businessman's Annual (BF ISSN 0067-2912) 183
Bahia. Departamento de Geografia e Estatistica. Provoados do Estado da Bahia (BL) 833
Bahia, Brazil (State). Centro de Planejamento. Anuario Estatistico (BL) 833
Bahia's Foreign Trade Bulletin see Boletim do Comercio Exterior da Bahia 193
Bahrain. Monetary Agency. Annual Report (BA) 227
Bahrain Trade Directory (BA ISSN 0408-215X) 235
Bahubacana (BG) 858
Baileya (US ISSN 0005-4003) 113, 414
Baily's Hunting Directory (UK ISSN 0067-2947) 828
Baja California Travel Series (US ISSN 0067-2955) 466, 883
Baker Deer Hunting Annual (US) 828
Baker Series in Chemistry (US) 245
Baker Street Journal (US ISSN 0005-4070) 559
Baking Directory/Buyers Guide (US) 42, 235
Bakka Magazine (CN ISSN 0702-1437) 4
Bakunin-Archiv see Archives Bakounine 449
Balai Pendidikan Vdan Latihan Tenagh Social. Laporan (IO) 347, 804
Balai Penelitian Perkebunan, Bogor. Statistik Coklat see Research Institute for Estate Crops, Bogor. Cocoa Statistics 38
Balai Penelitian Perkebunan, Bogor. Statistik Karet see Research Institute for Estate Crops, Bogor. Rubber Statistics 38
Balai Penelitian Perkebunan, Bogor. Statistik Kopi see Research Institute for Estate Crops, Bogor. Coffee Statistics 38
Balance of Payments of Barbados (BB) 183
Balance of Payments of Jamaica (JM) 193
Balance of Payments of Sierra Leone (SL ISSN 0067-2998) 193, 227
Balance of Payments of Trinidad and Tobago (TR ISSN 0067-3005) 193, 227
Balance Suisse des Revenus see Ertragsbilanz der Schweiz 228
Balanco Energetico Nacional (BL) 362
Balanza de Pagos de Chile (CL ISSN 0067-3013) 904
Balanza de Pagos de Espana (SP ISSN 0067-3021) 193, 227

Balcanica (YU) 449
Baldwin Lectures in Teacher Education (US ISSN 0067-303X) 314
Baldwin's Ohio Legislative Service (US ISSN 0092-0959) 740
Bale Catalogue of Israel Stamps see Bale Catalogue of Palestine and Israel Postage Stamps 478
Bale Catalogue of Palestine and Israel Postage Stamps (UK ISSN 0305-4039) 478
Balkanistica (US ISSN 0360-2206) 449
Balkanskie Issledovaniya (UR) 449
Ball and Roller Bearing Engineering (GW ISSN 0522-0629) 381
Ball State Monographs (US ISSN 0073-6821) 489
Ballena Press Anthropological Papers (US) 48
Ballena Press Publications in Archaeology, Ethnology and History (US) 48, 58, 431
Ballena Press Publications on North American Rock Art (US) 58, 72
Ballena Press Studies in Mesoamerican Art, Archaeology and Ethnohistory (US) 48, 58
Ballon Kurier (GW ISSN 0005-4364) 478
Ballroom Dancing Year Book (UK ISSN 0404-6919) 285
Balskrishnan-Neustadt Series (US) 584, 850
Baltic Philology see Filologia Baltycka 543
Baltica (UR ISSN 0067-3064) 291
Baltische Studien (GW ISSN 0067-3099) 449
Bamladesa Arthanaitika Jaripa (BG) 142
Bampton Lectures in America (US ISSN 0067-3129) 72, 466, 763
Banbury Reports (US) 100
Banca d'Italia. Assemblea Generale Ordinaria dei Partecipanti. (IT ISSN 0067-3161) 168
Banca d'Italia. Contributi Alla Ricerca Economica (IT) 183
Banca d'Italia. Economic Papers see Banca d'Italia. Contributi Alla Ricerca Economica 183
Banca Romana de Comert Exterior. Annual Bulletin (RM) 168, 193
Banco Agrario del Peru. Memoria (PE) 27
Banco Agricola y Pecuario. Informe see Instituto de Credito Agricola y Pecuario. Informe Anual (VE) 27
Banco Central de Chile, Santiago. Memoria Anual (CL ISSN 0067-3196) 169, 183
Banco Central de Costa Rica. Balanza de Pagos (CR) 183
Banco Central de Costa Rica. Estadisticas Economicas (CR ISSN 0522-098X) 152
Banco Central de Costa Rica. Memoria Anual (CR ISSN 0067-320X) 169
Banco Central de Costa Rica. Serie "Comentarios sobre Asuntos Economicos" (CR) 183
Banco Central de Ecuador. Memoria Anual de Actividades see Banco Central del Ecuador. Boletin - Anuario 183
Banco Central de Honduras. Informe Economico (HO) 183
Banco Central de Honduras. Memoria (HO ISSN 0067-3218) 183
Banco Central de Honduras. Seccion de Seguros. Boletin de Estadisticas de Seguros (HO) 152, 501
Banco Central de la Republica Argentina. Centro de Estudios Monetarios y Bancarios. Discussion Paper (AG) 169
Banco Central de la Republica Argentina. Centro de Estudios Monetarios y Bancarios. Serie de Computacion (AG) 169
Banco Central de la Republica Argentina. Centro de Estudios Monetarios y Bancarios. Serie de Estudios Tecnicos (AG) 169
Banco Central de la Republica Argentina. Centro de Estudios Monetarios y Bancarios. Serie de Informacion Publica (AG) 169

Banco Central de Nicaragua. Boletin Anual (NQ) 169
Banco Central de Nicaragua. Boletin Semestral see Banco Central de Nicaragua. Boletin Anual 169
Banco Central de Nicaragua. Boletin Trimestral see Banco Central de Nicaragua. Boletin Anual 169
Banco Central de Nicaragua. Comercio Exterior de Nicaragua Por Productos y Paises (NQ) 193
Banco Central de Nicaragua. Departamento de Estudios Economicos. Indicadores Economicos(NQ) 183
Banco Central de Nicaragua. Informe Anual (NQ ISSN 0067-3226) 169
Banco Central de Reserva de el Salvador. Memoria (ES) 169
Banco Central de Reserva del Peru. Memoria (PE) 169
Banco Central de Venezuela. Informe Economico (VE ISSN 0067-3250) 183
Banco Central de Venezuela. Memoria (VE ISSN 0067-3269) 169
Banco Central de Venezuela. Seccion A.L.A.L.C. Algunas Estadisticas de los Paises de ALALC (Seccion Asociacion Latinoamericana de Libre Comercio) (VE ISSN 0522-1153) 152
Banco Central del Ecuador. Boletin - Anuario (EC) 183
Banco Central del Ecuador. Memoria del Gerente General (EC ISSN 0067-3277) 169
Banco Central del Paraguay. Memoria (PY ISSN 0067-3285) 169
Banco Central del Uruguay. Division Asesoria Economica y Estudios. Producto e Ingreso Nacionales. Actualizacion de las Principales Variables (UY) 212
Banco Central del Uruguay. Indicadores de la Actividad Economica-Financiera (UY) 183
Banco Central del Uruguay. Resena de la Actividad Economico-Financiera (UY) 183
Banco da Amazonia. Centro de Documentacao e Biblioteca. Contexto Boletim (BL) 219
Banco de Bilbao. Agenda Financiera (SP) 169
Banco de Bilbao. Economic Report (SP) 183
Banco de Bilbao. Informe Economico (SP ISSN 0522-1315) 169
Banco de Bilbao. Informe - Memoria (SP) 169
Banco de Bilbao. Memoria see Banco de Bilbao. Informe - Memoria 169
Banco de Desenvolvimento do Parana. Information on Parana see Information on Parana 186
Banco de Espana. Informe Anual (SP ISSN 0067-3315) 169
Banco de Financiacion Industrial. la Banca Privada (SP) 169
Banco de Guatemala. Estadisticas del Sector Externo (GT) 183
Banco de Guatemala. Estudio Economico y Memoria de Labores (GT) 169
Banco de la Republica. Bogota. Registros de Importaciones see Banco de la Republica. Registros de Exportacion e Importacion 193
Banco de la Republica. Financiamiento Externo (CK) 169
Banco de la Republica. Registros de Exportacion e Importacion (CK ISSN 0302-9611) 193
Banco de Mexico. Informe Anual (MX ISSN 0067-3374) 169, 183
Banco do Brasil. Annual Report (BL) 169
Banco do Estado de Pernambuco. BANDEPE Relatorio (BL) 169
Banco do Nordeste do Brasil. Serie Estudos Economicos e Sociais (BL) 183
Banco Nacional da Habitacao. Assessoria Tecnica de Documentacao. Boletim Bibliografico(BL) 488
Banco Nacional da Habitacao. Relatorio de Atividades (BL) 483

Banco Nacional da Habitacao Linhas de Financiamento do B N H *see* Linhas de Financiamento do B N H *174*
Banco Nacional da Habitacao Relatorio de Atividades *see* B N H Relatorio de Atividades *168*
Banco Nacional de Comercio Exterior, S.A., Mexico. Annual Report (MX) *169*
Banco Nacional de Fomento. Informe de Labores (EC) *183*
Banco Nacional de Fomento, Tegucigalpa. Memoria Anual (HO ISSN 0067-3390) *169*
Banco Nacional de Panama. Asesoria Economica. Memoria Anual (PN) *169*
Banco Nacional de Panama. Asesoria Economica y Planificacion. Carta Economica (PN) *183*
Banco Nacional de Panama. Informe del Gerente General (PN) *169*
Banco Nacional do Desenvolvimento Economico. Annual Report (BL) *169*
Banco Nacional do Desenvolvimento Economico. Annual Report *see* Banco Nacional do Desenvolvimento Economico. Relatorio das Atividades *183*
Banco Nacional do Desenvolvimento Economico. Plan of Action *see* Banco Nacional do Desenvolvimento Economico. Plano de Acao *220*
Banco Nacional do Desenvolvimento Economico. Plano de Acao/Banco Nacional do Desenvolvimento Economico. Plan of Action (BL) *220*
Banco Nacional do Desenvolvimento Economico. Relatorio Anual *see* Revista do B I N D E *176*
Banco Nacional do Desenvolvimento Economico. Relatorio das Atividades(BL) *183*
Banco Nacional do Desenvolvimento Economico Revista do B I N D E *see* Revista do B I N D E *176*
Banco Regional de Desenvolvimento do Extremo Sul. Relatorio da Directoria (BL ISSN 0522-2079) *183*
Banco Sindical. Memoria y Balance General (AG) *169*
Bancos Centrales de los Paises del Acuerdo de Cartagena. Boletin Estadistico (EC) *169*
Bancoseguros (UY) *497*
Bancroftiana (US ISSN 0067-3412) *526*
Band Music Guide (US ISSN 0084-7704) *657*
Bandersnatch (UK ISSN 0306-8404) *559*
Bangiya Sahityakosha (II) *87*
Bangkok, Thailand. College of Education. Thesis Abstract Series (TH ISSN 0067-3498) *326*
Bangladesh. Directorate of Agricultural Marketing. Agricultural Marketing Series (BG ISSN 0070-8143) *27*
Bangladesh. Directorate of Agriculture. Season and Crop Report (BG ISSN 0070-8151) *33*
Bangladesh. Education Directorate. Report on Pilot Project on Adult Education (BG ISSN 0070-8135) *329*
Bangladesh. Ministry of Foreign Affairs. List of the Diplomatic Corps and Other Foreign Representatives (BG) *740*
Bangladesh. Planning Commission. Annual Development Programme (BG) *183*
Bangladesh Agricultural Sciences Abstracts (BG) *1, 23*
Bangladesh Association for Voluntary Sterilization. Annual Report (BG) *131*
Bangladesh Bank. Annual Report (BG) *169*
Bangladesh Bank. Statistics Department. Annual Import Payments. (BG) *152*
Bangladesh Directory (BG) *87, 812*
Bangladesh Directory and Year Book (II) *235*
Bangladesh Economic Survey *see* Bamladesa Arthanaitika Jaripa *142*

Bangladesh Forest Industries Development Corporation. Annual Report (BG) *412*
Bangladesh Itihas Samiti. Journal/Itihasa Samiti Patrika (BG) *442*
Bangladesh Jatiya Ainjibi Samity. Annual Law Journal *see* Bangladesh Jatiya Ainjibi Samity Souvenir *509*
Bangladesh Jatiya Ainjibi Samity Souvenir (BG) *509*
Bangladesh Political Studies (BG) *708*
Bangladesh Research and Evaluation Centre. Report (BG ISSN 0070-8178) *812*
Bangladesh Rice Research Institute. Annual Report (BG) *33*
Bangladesh Shipping Directory (BG) *877*
Bangladesh Sugar Mills Corporation. Annual Report (BG) *404*
Bangladesh Tea Research Institute. Annual Report (BG) *13*
Bangladesh University of Engineering and Technology, Dacca. Technical Journal (BG ISSN 0070-8186) *366*
Bangor Occasional Papers in Economics(UK ISSN 0306-9338) *142*
Banicke Listy/Folia Montana (CS) *641*
Bank Administration Institute. Accounting Bulletins (US ISSN 0067-3501) *169*
Bank Administration Institute. Annual Report (US ISSN 0067-351X) *169*
Bank Administration Institute. Personnel Administration Commission. Biennial Survey of Bank Officer Salaries (US ISSN 0525-4620) *169, 219*
Bank Administration Institute. Personnel Policies and Practices *see* Biennial Survey of Bank Personnel Policies and Practices *220*
Bank Administration Institute. Security Bulletins (US ISSN 0067-3544) *169*
Bank Administration Institute Index of Bank Performance *see* B A I Index of Bank Performance *168*
Bank al-Inma al-Sinai. Annual Report and Balance Sheet *see* Industrial Development Bank. Annual Report and Balance Sheet *173*
Bank Al-Markazi Al-Urduni. Annual Report *see* Central Bank of Jordan. Annual Report *171*
Bank Directory of New England (US) *169*
Bank Ekspor Impor Indonesia. Annual Report/Laporan Tahunan (IO ISSN 0302-6795) *169*
Bank for International Settlements. Annual Report (SZ ISSN 0067-3560) *169*
Bank for International Settlements. Monetary and Economic Department. International Commodity Position. General Survey(SZ ISSN 0408-4284) *169*
Bank Guide (PK) *169*
Bank Ha-Sapanut le-Yisrael. Annual Report. *see* Maritime Bank of Israel. Annual Report *174*
Bank Holding Company Facts (US ISSN 0519-1572) *169*
Bank of Canada. Annual Report (CN ISSN 0067-3587) *169*
Bank of Canada. Staff Research Studies(CN ISSN 0067-3595) *169*
Bank of Ceylon. Annual Report *see* Bank of Ceylon. Annual Report and Accounts *170*
Bank of Ceylon. Annual Report and Accounts (CE) *170*
Bank of Ceylon. Report and Accounts *see* Bank of Ceylon. Annual Report and Accounts *170*
Bank of England. Report *see* Bank of England. Report and Accounts *170*
Bank of England. Report and Accounts (UK ISSN 0308-5279) *170*
Bank of Finland. Annual Statement (FI ISSN 0081-945X) *170*
Bank of Finland. Publications. Series A *see* Suomen Pankki. Julkaisuja. Serie A *148*
Bank of Finland. Publications. Series B *see* Suomen Pankki. Julkaisuja. Serie B *148*

Bank of Finland. Publications. Series C *see* Suomen Pankki. Julkaisuja. Serie C *149*
Bank of Finland. Publications. Series D *see* Suomen Pankki. Julkaisuja. Serie D *149*
Bank of Finland. Publications. Studies on Finland's Economic Growth *see* Suomen Pankki. Julkaisuja. Kasvututkimuksia *225*
Bank of Finland. Yearbook (FI ISSN 0081-9468) *170*
Bank of Israel. Annual Report (IS ISSN 0067-365X) *170*
Bank of Israel. Main Points of the Annual Report (IS ISSN 0067-3641) *170*
Bank of Jamaica. Report and Statement of Accounts (JM ISSN 0067-3668) *170*
Bank of Japan. Annual Report of the Policy Board (JA ISSN 0067-3676) *170*
Bank of Japan. Business Report (JA ISSN 0067-3684) *183*
Bank of Japan. Economic Research Department. B O J Special Paper (JA ISSN 0067-3692) *183*
Bank of Japan. Economic Statistics Annual (JA ISSN 0070-8666) *153*
Bank of Japan. Export and Import Price Indexes Annual *see* Bank of Japan. Price Indexes Annual *193*
Bank of Japan. Price Indexes Annual (JA) *193*
Bank of Korea. Annual Report (KO ISSN 0067-3706) *170*
Bank of Libya. Annual Report of the Board of Directors (LY ISSN 0067-3714) *183*
Bank of Libya. Balance of Payments (LY ISSN 0075-921X) *193, 227*
Bank of Mauritius. Annual Report (MF ISSN 0067-3722) *170*
Bank of Papua New Guinea. Report and Financial Statements (PP) *170*
Bank of Seoul and Trust Company. Economic Review (KO) *170*
Bank of Sierra Leone. Annual Report *see* Bank of Sierra Leone. Annual Report and Accounts *170*
Bank of Sierra Leone. Annual Report and Accounts (SL) *170*
Bank of Sudan. Foreign Trade Statistical Digest (SJ ISSN 0522-246X) *153*
Bank of Sudan. Report (SJ ISSN 0067-3749) *170*
Bank of Tanzania. Economic and Operations Report (TZ ISSN 0067-3757) *170, 183*
Bank of Tanzania. Economic Report *see* Bank of Tanzania. Economic and Operations Report *183*
Bank of Thailand. Annual Economic Report (TH ISSN 0067-3773) *183*
Bank of Thailand. Paper (TH) *183*
Bank of Thailand: Economic Highlights (TH) *183*
Bank Officer Salary Survey *see* Bank Administration Institute. Personnel Administration Commission. Biennial Survey of Bank Officer Salaries *219*
Bank Pembangunan Indonesia. Annual Report (IO ISSN 0408-4632) *170*
Bank Sorting Code Numbers (UK) *170*
Der Bankangestellte (GW ISSN 0067-3781) *170, 506*
Bankers Almanac and Year Book (UK ISSN 0067-379X) *170*
Bankers' Association for Foreign Trade. Proceedings (US) *170*
Bankers Diary and Guide (US) *170*
Bankers Handbook for Asia (HK) *170*
Bankers' Who's Who (II ISSN 0067-3803) *170*
Banking Buying Guide (US) *170*
Banking Guides - Asia, Australia, New Zealand with Principal Hotels and Bank Holidays (US) *170*
Banking Statistics of Pakistan (PK ISSN 0067-3811) *170*
Bankwirtschaftliche Forschungen (SZ ISSN 0067-382X) *170*
Bankwirtschaftliche Studien (GW ISSN 0067-3838) *170*

Banque Africaine de Developpement. Rapport Annuel *see* African Development Bank. Report by the Board of Directors *199*
Banque Africaine de Developpement. Rapport du Conseil d'Administration *see* African Development Bank. Report by the Board of Directors *199*
Banque Centrale de la Republique Malgache. Rapport d'Activite (MG) *170*
Banque Centrale de Tunisie. Bulletin (TI ISSN 0067-3854) *170*
Banque Centrale de Tunisie. Rapport d'Activite (TI ISSN 0067-3862) *170*
Banque Centrale des Etats de l'Afrique de l'Ouest. Rapport Annuel (SG ISSN 0067-3889) *170*
Banque Centrale des Etats de l'Afrique de l'Ouest. Rapport d'Activite. (SG ISSN 0067-3897) *170*
Banque Commerciale Zairoise. Reports and Balance Sheets (ZR) *170*
Banque de Bruxelles. Rapport Annuel (BE ISSN 0067-3919) *170*
Banque de Commerce Canadienne Imperiale. Lettre Commerciale (CN ISSN 0382-4756) *183*
Banque de France. Comite Monetaire de la Zone Franc. Secretariat. Rapport (FR) *183*
Banque de France. Compte- Rendu. (FR ISSN 0067-3927) *170*
Banque de France. Direction de la Conjoncture. Structure et Evolution Financiere des Regions de Province (FR ISSN 0522-3199) *183*
Banque de la Republique du Burundi. Rapport Annuel (BD ISSN 0067-3935) *170*
Banque des Etats de l'Afrique Centrale. Rapport d'Activite (FR ISSN 0067-3900) *170*
Banque des Mots (FR ISSN 0067-3951) *526*
Banque du Maroc Rapport Annuel (MR ISSN 0067-396X) *170*
Banque du Zaire. Rapport Annuel (ZR ISSN 0300-1172) *170*
Banque Internationale a Luxembourg. Cahiers Economiques (LU) *183*
Banque Internationale pour l'Afrique Occidentale. Conseil d'Administration. Rapport et Resolutions, Rapport des Commissaires aux Comptes (FR) *183*
Banque Marocaine du Commerce Exterieur. Annual Report (MR) *170*
Banque Nationale de Belgique. Rapport sur les Operations (BE ISSN 0067-3978) *170*
Banque Nationale de Rwanda. Rapport Annuel (RW) *170*
Banque Nationale du Congo. Rapport Annuel *see* Banque du Zaire. Rapport Annuel *170*
Banque Nationale Malagasy de Developpement. Rapport d'Activite (MG ISSN 0067-401X) *170*
Banque Nationale pour le Developpement Economique. Rapport Annuel (MR) *221*
Banque Populaire Suisse. Information (SZ ISSN 0067-4028) *170*
Banque Togolaise de Developpement. Rapport Annuel *see* Banque Togolaise de Developpement. Rapport d'Activites *171*
Banque Togolaise de Developpement. Rapport d'Activites (TG) *171*
Bantoe Beleggingskorporasie van Suid-Afrika. Jaarverslag *see* Bantu Investment Corporation of South Africa. Annual Report *221*
Bantu Investment Corporation of South Africa. Annual Report/Bantoe Beleggingskorporasie van Suid-Afrika. Jaarverslag (SA) *221*
Bantu Treasury (SA ISSN 0067-4044) *560*
Baptist Missionary Association of America. Directory and Handbook (US ISSN 0091-2743) *771*
Baptist Missionary Society, London. Annual Report (UK ISSN 0067-4060) *771*

Baptist Missionary Society, London. Official Report and Directory of Missionaries (UK ISSN 0067-4079) 771
Baptist Union Directory (UK ISSN 0302-3184) 771
Baptist Union of Western Canada. Year Book (CN ISSN 0067-4087) 771
Baptist World Alliance. Congress Reports (US ISSN 0067-4095) 771
Bar-Ilan: Annual of Bar-Ilan University (IS ISSN 0067-4109) 770, 796
Bar-Ilan University. Studies in Judaica and the Humanities see Bar-Ilan: Annual of Bar-Ilan University 770
Bar List of the United Kingdom (UK ISSN 0308-8219) 509
Barat Review (US ISSN 0005-5859) 555
Barataria (US ISSN 0149-0354) 555
Barataria Review see Barataria 555
Barbacane (FR) 72, 560
Barbados. Ministry of Agriculture and Fisheries. Bulletin (BB) 904
Barbados. Ministry of Health and National Insurance. Chief Medical Officer. Annual Report (BB) 750
Barbados. Ministry of Health and Welfare. Chief Medical Officer. Annual Report see Barbados. Ministry of Health and National Insurance. Chief Medical Officer. Annual Report 750
Barbados. Parks and Beaches Commission. Annual Report (BB) 883
Barbados. Registration Office. Report on Vital Statistics & Registrations (BB) 833
Barbados. Statistical Service. Digest of Tourism Statistics. (BB) 893
Barbados. Statistical Service. Financial Statistics (BB) 153
Barbados. Statistical Service. Overseas Trade Report (BB ISSN 0067-4125) 1, 153
Barbados Museum and Historical Society. Journal (BB ISSN 0005-5891) 72, 466
Barbados Nursing Journal (BB ISSN 0572-6042) 613
Barbados Society of Architects. Yearbook (BB) 68
Barbados Tourist Board. Annual Report(BB) 883
Barbey d'Aurevilly (FR) 560
Barcelona Port (SP) 877
Barclays Country Reports (UK ISSN 0307-4552) 183
Bargain Paradises of the World see Retirement Paradises of the World 890
Die Barke (AU ISSN 0067-4206) 257, 560
Barley Genetics Newsletter (US) 113
Baroda Reporter (II) 726
Baroque (FR ISSN 0067-4222) 560
Baroque Operatic Arias (US) 657
Barque's Pakistan Trade Directory and Who's Who (PK ISSN 0067-4230) 235
Barrister (NR) 509
Barron's Guide to Graduate Schools (US) 330, 796
Barron's Profiles of American Colleges. Vol. 1: Descriptions of the Colleges (US) 330
Barron's Profiles of American Colleges. Vol. 2: Index to Major Areas of Study (US ISSN 0533-1072) 330
Barshika Bibarani Bayaska Siksha Parikshya Prakalpa Bangladesh see Bangladesh. Education Directorate. Report on Pilot Project on Adult Education 329
Barshika Unnayana Karmasuci see Bangladesh. Planning Commission. Annual Development Programme 183
Bartlett Society. Transactions (UK ISSN 0459-7400) 384
Bartonia (US ISSN 0198-7356) 113
Baseball Annual (US ISSN 0067-4257) 823
Baseball Case Book (US) 823
Baseball Dope Book see Official Baseball Dope Book 825
Baseball Guide (US ISSN 0067-4273) 823

Baseball Register see Official Baseball Register 825
Baseball Rules (US) 823
Baseball Umpires Manual (US) 823
Basebook (US ISSN 0093-8025) 221
Basel Africa Bibliography. Communications see Basler Afrika Bibliographien. Mitteilungen 439
Basel Institute for Immunology. Annual Report (SZ ISSN 0301-3782) 603
Basic Anthropology Units (US) 48
Basic Auto Repair Manual (US ISSN 0067-4338) 870
Basic Bodywork and Painting (US ISSN 0067-4362) 870
Basic Cams, Valves and Exhaust Systems (US ISSN 0067-4370) 870
Basic Carburetion and Fuel Systems (US ISSN 0067-4389) 870
Basic Chassis, Suspension and Brakes (US ISSN 0067-4397) 870
Basic Clutches and Transmissions (US ISSN 0067-4400) 870
Basic Collection of Science and Technology Books see Science and Technology 535
Basic Concepts in Educational Psychology Series (US) 315, 734
Basic Concepts in Health Science Series(US) 750
Basic Concepts in Psychology Series (US) 315, 734
Basic Economic Data for Idaho (US ISSN 0094-1115) 183
Basic Facts about the United Nations (UN ISSN 0067-4575) 719
Basic Ignition and Electrical Systems (US ISSN 0067-4427) 870
Basic Life Sciences (US ISSN 0090-5542) 101
Basic Management Series (US) 214
Basic Port Statistics of India (II) 877
Basic Road Statistics of India (II ISSN 0067-6462) 864
Basic Software (SZ) 270
Basilian Historical Bulletins (CN ISSN 0702-634X) 466
Basis (GW ISSN 0067-446X) 560
Basketball Case Book (US ISSN 0525-4663) 823
Basketball Guide (US) 823
Basketball Guide, with Official Rules and Standards see N A G W S Guide. Basketball 824
Basketball Handbook (US) 823
Basketball Officials Manual (US) 823
Basketball Rules (US) 823
Basketball Rules - Simplified and Illustrated (US) 823
Basketball Statisticians' Manual (US) 823
Basler Afrika Bibliographien. Mitteilungen / Basel Africa Bibliography. Communications (SZ ISSN 0170-5091) 439
Basler Beitraege zur Geographie (SZ ISSN 0067-4486) 420
Basler Beitraege zur Geschichtswissenschaft (SZ) 431
Basler Drucke (SZ ISSN 0067-4494) 560
Basler Effektenboerse. Jahresbericht / Rapport Annuel / Annual Report (SZ) 202
Basler Geomethodisches Colloquium. Veroeffentlichungen / Basel Geomethodological Meeting. Proceedings see Geomethodica 289
Basler Statistik (SZ) 833
Basler Studien zur Deutschen Sprache und Literatur (SZ ISSN 0067-4508) 560
Basler Studien zur Rechtswissenschaft (SZ) 509
Basler Veroeffentlichungen zur Geschichte der Medizin und der Biologie (SZ ISSN 0067-4524) 101, 593
Basler Wirtschaftswissenschaftliche Vortraege (SZ ISSN 0067-4532) 796
Basler Zeitschrift fuer Geschichte und Altertumskunde (SZ ISSN 0067-4540) 740
Basrah Natural History Museum. Bulletin (IQ) 673
Basrah Natural History Museum. Publication (IQ) 779

Bass Anglers Sportsman Society Fishing Guide see B A S S Fishing Guide 828
Bass Anglers Sportsman Society Master Fishing Annual see B A S S Master Fishing Annual 828
Bass Fishing Guide see B A S S Fishing Guide 828
Bass World (US) 657
Bassmaster see B A S S Master Fishing Annual 828
Bath & West Show Catalogue see Royal Bath & West Show Catalogue 19
Bathrooms and Kitchens (UK) 502
Baton Twirling Rules and Regulations see A A U Baton Twirling Rules and Regulations 818
Battelle Institute Materials Science Colloquia (US) 379
Battelle Memorial Institute. Columbus Laboratories. Report on National Survey of Compensation Paid Scientists and Engineers Engaged in Research and Development Activities (US ISSN 0093-4267) 206
Battelle Memorial Institute. Published Papers and Articles (US ISSN 0084-7712) 794
Batter Performance Handbook (US) 823
Battery Council International. Convention Minutes (US) 861
Battery Replacement Data Book (US) 352
Bau und Baustoff Handbuch (GW ISSN 0067-4575) 904
Baubeschlag-Taschenbuch (GW ISSN 0067-4583) 141
Bauen mit Aluminium (GW) 134
Bauernhaeuser der Schweiz (GW ISSN 0067-4591) 401
Bauhinia (SZ ISSN 0067-4605) 113
Bauingenieur-Praxis (GW ISSN 0522-4950) 134
Baustatistisches Jahrbuch (GW ISSN 0084-7739) 140
Bausteine zur Geschichte des Neuhochdeutschen see Bausteine zur Sprachgeschichte des Neuhochdeutschen 541
Bausteine zur Sprachgeschichte des Neuhochdeutschen (GE) 541
Bauwelt Katalog (GW ISSN 0067-4664) 134
Baxter's Eurailpass Travel Guide (US ISSN 0146-8707) 883
Baxter's U.S.A. Bus Travel Guide (US) 883
Baxter's U.S.A. Train Travel Guide (US) 883
Bay Area Men's Resource Catalog (US) 419
Bay Area Review Course. Legal Ethics see B A R-B R I Bar Review. Professional Responsibility 509
Bay City Rollers Annual (UK) 657
Bayavaya Uskalos (CN ISSN 0005-6952) 391, 560
Bayer-Mitteilungen fuer die Gummi-Industrie (GW ISSN 0005-6987) 777
Bayer-Symposien (US ISSN 0067-4672) 593
Bayerische Akademie der Wissenschaften. Jahrbuch (GW ISSN 0084-6090) 779
Bayerische Akademie der Wissenschaften. Mathematisch-Naturwissenschaftliche Klasse. Sitzungsberichte (GW) 584, 779
Bayerische Akademie der Wissenschaften. Philosophisch-Historische Klasse. Sitzungsberichte (GW ISSN 0342-5991) 489, 780
Bayerische Botanische Gesellschaft. Berichte (GW ISSN 0373-7640) 113
Bayerische Staatsbibliothek, Munich. Jahresbericht (GW ISSN 0342-0221) 526
Bayerische Staatsgemaeldesammlungen. Jahresbericht (GW) 72
Bayerische Staatssammlung fuer Palaeontologie und Historische Geologie. Mitteilungen (GW ISSN 0077-2070) 291, 673
Bayerische Vorgeschichtsblaetter (GW ISSN 0341-3918) 449

Bayerisches Beamten-Jahrbuch (GW ISSN 0067-4702) 740
Bayerisches Forstdienst-Taschenbuch (GW ISSN 0067-4710) 407
Bayerisches Jahrbuch fuer Volkskunde (GW ISSN 0067-4729) 401
Bayerisches Staatsministerium fuer Unterricht und Kultus. Amtsblatt (GW ISSN 0005-7207) 315
Be-Ne-Lux Genealogist (US) 416
Be Safe at Home/Wees Veilig Tuis (SA) 750
Bean Improvement Cooperative. Annual Report (US ISSN 0084-7747) 33
Bears-Their Biology and Management (SZ) 127, 275
Beau Fleuve Series (US) 560
Beaufortia (NE ISSN 0067-4745) 127
Beaux-Arts (CN ISSN 0315-2359) 72
Bebop Drawing Club Book (US) 72, 391, 560
Bed and Breakfast in Britain (UK) 883
Bed and Breakfast in South and Southwest England see Bed and Breakfast in Britain 883
Bed and Breakfast in Wales, Northern England and Scotland see Bed and Breakfast in Britain 883
Bed & Breakfast Stops (UK) 883
Bed, Breakfast and Evening Meal (UK ISSN 0084-7755) 883
Bedford Institute of Oceanography. A O L Data Series see Bedford Institute of Oceanography. Data Report 309
Bedford Institute of Oceanography. Biennial Review see Bedford Institute of Oceanography Review 309
Bedford Institute of Oceanography. Computer Note (CN ISSN 0381-4831) 309
Bedford Institute of Oceanography. Data Report (CN) 309
Bedford Institute of Oceanography. Report 309
Bedford Institute of Oceanography Review (CN) 309
Bedfordshire Historical Record Society. Publications (UK ISSN 0067-4826) 449
Bedi Kartlisa (BE ISSN 0373-1537) 449
Bedrijfschap voor de Lederwarenindustrie. Jaarverslag (NE ISSN 0067-4834) 524
Beduin (II ISSN 0005-769X) 560
Beecham Society Bulletin (US ISSN 0084-7763) 657
Beecham Society Newsletter see Beecham Society Bulletin 657
Beef Roundup (US) 43
Beehive History (US) 466
Beer-Sheva. (IS) 474, 770
Beethoven-Jahrbuch (GW ISSN 0522-5949) 657
Behavioral Group Therapy (US ISSN 0191-5681) 734
Behaviormetrika (JA) 739
Behaviour (NE ISSN 0005-7959) 127
Behindertenhilfe Durch Erziehung, Unterricht und Therapie (GW ISSN 0171-9718) 345
Behoerden und Organisationen der Land- Forst- und Ernaehrungswirtschaft (GW ISSN 0522-604X) 13
Behring Institut. Mitteilungen (GW ISSN 0301-0457) 593
Behring-Werke. Mitteilungen see Behring Institut. Mitteilungen 593
Beiheft zu Leistlingssport (GW ISSN 0341-7492) 819
Beihefte der Bonner Jahrbuecher (GW ISSN 0067-4893) 72
Beihefte zur Theologischen Zeitschrift see Sonderbaende zur Theologischen Zeitschrift 767
Beilsteins Handbuch der Organischen Chemie. Fourth Supplement (US ISSN 0067-4915) 252
Beirat fuer Wirtschafts und Sozialfragen(AU) 142, 812
Beiruter Texte und Studien (GW ISSN 0067-4931) 474
Beitraege Zum Auslaendischen Oeffentlichen Recht und Voelkerrecht (US) 522

Beitraege zum Buch- und Bibliothekswesen (GW ISSN 0408-8107) *526*
Beitraege zum Buechereiwesen. Reihe B: Quellen und Texte (GW ISSN 0522-6201) *904*
Beitraege zum Rundfunkrecht (GW ISSN 0067-4966) *266, 509*
Beitraege zur Afrikakunde (SZ ISSN 0171-1660) *48, 439*
Beitraege zur Archaeologie see Technische Beitraege zur Archaeologie *66*
Beitraege zur Datenverarbeitung und Unternehmensforschung (GW) *214, 270*
Beitraege zur Empirischen Kriminologie(SZ) *280*
Beitraege zur Ernaehrungswissenschaft see Current Topics in Nutritional Sciences *665*
Beitraege zur Geographie (GE) *384, 420*
Beitraege zur Geologie von Thueringen (GW ISSN 0067-5008) *291*
Beitraege zur Gerichtlichen Medizin (AU ISSN 0067-5016) *612*
Beitraege zur Geschichte der Philosophie und Theologie des Mittelalters Neue Folge (GW ISSN 0067-5024) *687, 763*
Beitraege zur Geschichte der Reichskirche in der Neuzeit (GW ISSN 0408-8344) *449*
Beitraege zur Geschichte der Universitaet Erfurt (1392-1816) (GE ISSN 0522-6562) *449*
Beitraege zur Geschichte der Universitaet Mainz (GW ISSN 0408-8379) *449*
Beitraege zur Geschichte der Wissenschaft und der Technik (GW ISSN 0522-6570) *780*
Beitraege zur Geschichte des Alten Moenchtums und des Benediktinerordens (GW ISSN 0067-5032) *763*
Beitraege zur Geschichte des Parlementarismus und der Politischen Parteien (GW ISSN 0522-6643) *708*
Beitraege zur Geschichte des Religioesen und Wissenschaftlichen Denkens (GE ISSN 0067-5059) *687, 763*
Beitraege zur Geschichte Thueringens (GE) *796*
Beitraege zur Geschichte und Kultur der Stadt Nuernberg (GW ISSN 0078-2785) *450*
Beitraege zur Harmonikalen Grundlagenforschung (AU ISSN 0067-5067) *657*
Beitraege zur Heilpaedagogik und Heilpaedagogischen Psychologie (SZ ISSN 0067-5075) *735*
Beitraege zur Heimatkunde der Stadt Schwelm und ihrer Umgebung (GW) *450*
Beitraege zur Hygiene und Epidemiologie (GE ISSN 0067-5083) *750*
Beitraege zur Individualpsychologie (GW) *735*
Beitraege zur Informations- und Dokumentationswissenschaft (GW) *526*
Beitraege zur Inkunabelkunde. Dritte Folge (GE ISSN 0067-5091) *526, 757*
Beitraege zur Japanologie (AU ISSN 0522-6759) *442, 669*
Beitraege zur Jazzforschung/Studies in Jazz Research (AU) *657*
Beitraege zur Kardiologie und Angiologie (GW ISSN 0075-7101) *606*
Beitraege zur Kinderpsychotherapie (GW ISSN 0067-5105) *617*
Beitraege zur Klassischen Philologie (GW) *541*
Beitraege zur Kommunikationswissenschaft und Medienforschung (SZ) *264, 504*
Beitraege zur Kunst des Christlichen Ostens (GW ISSN 0067-5121) *72*
Beitraege zur Kunstgeschichte (GW) *72*

Beitraege zur Landesentwicklung (GW ISSN 0525-4736) *275*
Beitraege zur Literatur des 15-18. Jahrhunderts (GW ISSN 0170-3315) *560*
Beitraege zur Luxemburgischen Sprach- und Volkskunde (LU) *541*
Beitraege zur Meereskunde (GE ISSN 0067-5148) *309*
Beitraege zur Mittelamerikanischen Voelkerkunde (GW ISSN 0408-8514) *48*
Beitraege zur Mittelstandsforschung (GW) *812*
Beitraege zur Naturkunde in Osthessen (GW) *101, 291*
Beitraege zur Naturkundlichen Forschung in Suedwestdeutschland (GW ISSN 0005-8122) *113, 127, 291*
Beitraege zur Neurochirurgie (GE ISSN 0067-5156) *619, 624*
Beitraege zur Oberpfalzforschung (GW ISSN 0067-5164) *450*
Beitraege zur Oekumenischen Theologie(GW ISSN 0067-5172) *763*
Beitraege zur Oesterreichischen Statistik(AU ISSN 0067-2319) *833*
Beitraege zur Politischen Wissenschaft (GW ISSN 0582-0421) *708*
Beitraege zur Psychodiagnostik des Kindes (GW) *735*
Beitraege zur Psychologie und Soziologie des Kranken Menschen (GW) *593, 735, 812*
Beitraege zur Rheumatologie (GE ISSN 0067-5199) *623*
Beitraege zur Romanischen Philologie des Mittelalters (GW ISSN 0067-5202) *541*
Beitraege zur Sexualforschung (GW ISSN 0067-5210) *735*
Beitraege zur Sozial- und Wirtschaftsgeschichte (GW) *431*
Beitraege zur Strafvollzugswissenschaft (GW ISSN 0067-5237) *280*
Beitraege zur Suedasien Forschung (GW ISSN 0170-3137) *442*
Beitraege zur Umweltgestaltung. Reihe A (GW ISSN 0340-9716) *384*
Beitraege zur Umweltgestaltung. Reihe B. (GW ISSN 0340-949X) *384*
Beitraege zur Ur- und Fruehgeschichtlichen Archaeologie des Mittelmeerkulturraumes (GW ISSN 0067-5245) *58*
Beitraege zur Wehrforschung (GW ISSN 0067-5253) *638*
Beitraege zur Westfaelischen Familienforschung (GW ISSN 0067-5261) *416*
Beitraege zur Wirtschaftspolitik (SZ ISSN 0522-7216) *191*
Belaruski Instytut Navuki Mactatstva. Zapisy/Byelorussian Institute of Arts and Sciences. Annals (US ISSN 0510-3746) *391, 450*
Belastingdruk in Nederland/Burden of Taxes in the Netherlands (NE ISSN 0077-670X) *227*
Belfast and Northern Ireland Directory (UK ISSN 0067-5342) *883*
Belgica Estadisticas de Base see Belgium Basic Statistics *834*
Belgie Basis-Statistieken see Belgium Basic Statistics *834*
Belgien Statistische Grundzahlen see Belgium Basic Statistics *834*
Belgique Statistiques de Base see Belgium Basic Statistics *834*
Belgisch Centrum voor Landelijke Geschiedenis. Publikaties see Centre Belge Histoire Rurale. Publications *451*
Belgisch Instituut voor Voorlichting en Documentatie. Repertorium van de Voorlichting see Institut Belge d'Information et de Documentation. Repertoire de l'Information *759*
Belgische Cementnijverheid see Industrie Cimentiere Belge *136*
Belgische en Internationale Economie see Economie Belge et Internationale *144*
Belgium. Administration de la Marine et de la Navigation Interieure. Rapport Annuel sur l'Evolution de la Flotte de Peche (BE) *877*

Belgium. Administration de la Marine. Rapport Annuel sur l'Evolution de la Flotte de Peche see Belgium. Administration de la Marine et de la Navigation Interieure. Rapport Annuel sur l'Evolution de la Flotte de Peche *877*
Belgium. Administration des Eaux et Forets. Station de Recherches des Eaux et Forets. Travaux. Serie D. Hydrobiologie (BE ISSN 0067-5369) *101*
Belgium. Administration des Mines. Service: Statistiques. Siderurgie, Houille, Agglomeres, Cokes see Belgium. Administration des Mines. Statistiques: Houille, Cokes, Agglomeres Metallurgie, Carrieres/ Statistieken: Steenkolen, Cokes, Agglomeraten, Metallnijverheid, Groeven *641*
Belgium. Administration des Mines. Statistiques: Houille, Cokes, Agglomeres Metallurgie, Carrieres/ Statistieken: Steenkolen, Cokes, Agglomeraten, Metallnijverheid, Groeven (BE) *641*
Belgium. Commission Royale des Monuments et des Sites. Bulletin (BE ISSN 0522-7496) *58, 68*
Belgium. Conseil National du Travail. Rapport du Secretariat sur l'Activite du Conseil/Belgium. Nationale Arbeidsraad. Verslag van de Secretaris over de Activiteit van de Raad (BE ISSN 0067-5385) *206*
Belgium. Conseil Superieur des Classes Moyennes. Rapport Annuel du Secretaire General (BE ISSN 0067-5393) *234*
Belgium. Fonds National de la Recherche Scientifique. Liste Bibliographique des Travaux. Bibliografische Lijst van de Werken (BE) *794*
Belgium. Fonds National de la Recherche Scientifique. Liste des Beneficiaires d'Une Subvention (BE) *780*
Belgium. Fonds National de la Recherche Scientifique. Rapport Annuel (BE ISSN 0067-5407) *780*
Belgium. Hoge Raad voor de Middenstand. Jaarverslag van de Secretaris Generaal see Belgium. Conseil Superieur des Classes Moyennes. Rapport Annuel du Secretaire General *234*
Belgium. Institut National d'Assurances Sociales pour Travailleurs Independants. Rapport Annuel (BE) *497*
Belgium. Institut National d'Assurances Sociales pour Travailleurs Independants. Statistiques des Beneficiaires de Prestations de Retraite et de Survie/Belgium. Rijksinstituut voor de Social Verzekeringen der Zelfstandigen. Statistiek van de Personen die een Rust- en Overlevingsprestatie Genieten (BE) *497*
Belgium. Institut National d'Assurances Sociales pour Travailleurs Independants. Statistique des Enfants Beneficiaires d'Allocations Familiales/Belgium. Rijksinstituut voor de Sociale Verzekeringen der Zelfstandigen. Statistiek van de Kinderen die Recht Geven Op Kinderbijslag (BE) *501*
Belgium. Institut National d'Assurances Sociales pour Travailleurs Independants. Statistiques des Personnes Assujetties au Statut Social des Travailleurs Independants/ Belgium. Rijksinstituut voor de Sociale Verzekeringen der Zelfstandigen. Statistiek van de Personen die Onder de Toepassing Vallen van het Sociaal Statuut van de Zelfstandigen (BE) *497*
Belgium. Institut National de Statistique. Annuaire de Statistiques Regionales (BE) *833*
Belgium. Institut National de Statistique. Annuaire Statistique de Poche (BE ISSN 0067-5431) *834*

Belgium. Institut National de Statistique. Annuaire Statistique de l'Enseignement see Belgium. Ministere de l'Education Nationale et de la Culture Francaise. Annuaire Statistique de l'Enseignement *326*
Belgium. Institut National de Statistique. Batiments et Logements see Belgium. Institut National de Statistique. Statistiques de la Construction et du Logement *140*
Belgium. Institut National de Statistique. Bevolkingsstatistieken (BE) *731*
Belgium. Institut National de Statistique. Communique Hebdomadaire (BE) *834*
Belgium. Institut National de Statistique. Etudes Statistiques (BE) *834*
Belgium. Institut National de Statistique. Mouvement de la Population des Communes see Belgium. Institut National de Statistique. Statistiques Demographiques *731*
Belgium. Institut National de Statistique. Statistique de la Navigation du Rhin (BE ISSN 0067-5520) *833, 865*
Belgium. Institut National de Statistique. Statistique de la Navigation Interieure (BE ISSN 0067-5539) *833, 865*
Belgium. Institut National de Statistique. Statistique des Accidents de la Circulation sur la Voie Publique(BE ISSN 0067-5504) *756, 833*
Belgium. Institut National de Statistique. Statistique des Accidents de Roulage see Belgium. Institut National de Statistique. Statistique des Accidents de la Circulation sur la Voie Publique *756*
Belgium. Institut National de Statistique. Statistique des Vehicules a Moteur Neufs Mis en Circulation (BE ISSN 0067-5555) *833, 865*
Belgium. Institut National de Statistique. Statistique du Tourisme et de l'Hotellerie (BE ISSN 0067-5547) *833, 893*
Belgium. Institut National de Statistique. Statistiques de la Construction et du Logement (BE) *140, 833*
Belgium. Institut National de Statistique. Statistiques Demographiques (BE ISSN 0067-5490) *731, 833*
Belgium. Institut National de Statistique. Statistiques des Causes de Deces (BE) *731*
Belgium. Institut National de Statistique. Statistiques Financieres (BE) *153*
Belgium. Institut National de Statistique. Statistiques Judiciaires (BE) *521*
Belgium. Institut National de Statistique. Statistiques Sociales (BE ISSN 0067-5563) *803*
Belgium. Institut Royal Meteorologique. Annuaire: Magnetisme Terrestre/ Jaarboek: Aardmagnetisme (BE ISSN 0524-7764) *291*
Belgium. Institut Royal Meteorologique. Annuaire: Rayonnement Solaire/ Jaarboek: Zonnestraling (BE ISSN 0524-7780) *81*
Belgium. Institut Royal Meteorologique. Publications (BE ISSN 0020-255X) *303, 631*
Belgium. Ministere de l'Education Nationale et de la Culture Francaise. Annuaire Statistique de l'Enseignement (BE) *326, 834*
Belgium. Ministere de l'Education Nationale et de la Culture Francaise. Rapport Annuel (BE ISSN 0067-5598) *315*
Belgium. Ministere de la Prevoyance Sociale. Rapport General sur la Securite Sociale/Algemeen Verslag over de Sociale Zekerheid (BE ISSN 0067-558X) *497*

Belgium. Ministere de la Sante Publique et de la Famille. Centrum voor Bevolkings- en Gezinsstudien. Technisch Rapport (BE) 750, *804*
Belgium. Ministere de la Sante Publique et de la Famille. Rapport Annuel (BE) 750, *804*
Belgium. Ministerie des Affaires Etrangeres. Repertoire des Theses de Doctorat/Belgium. Ministerie van Buitenlandse Zaken. Repertorium van de Doctorale Proefschriften (BE) *334*
Belgium. Ministerie van Buitenlandse Zaken. Repertorium van de Doctorale Proefschriften *see* Belgium. Ministerie des Affaires Etrangeres. Repertoire des Theses de Doctorat *334*
Belgium. Nationale Arbeidsraad. Verslag van de Secretaris over de Activiteit van de Raad *see* Belgium. Conseil National du Travail. Rapport du Secretariat sur l'Activite du Conseil *206*
Belgium. Office Belge du Commerce Exterieur. Bijvoegsel B B H. Reeks B(BE ISSN 0067-561X) *193*
Belgium. Office National de l'Emploi. Liste des Informations Statistiques et des Publications de l'O N E M (BE) *153*
Belgium. Office National de l'Emploi. Rapport Annuel (BE ISSN 0067-5644) *206*
Belgium. Regie des Postes. Rapport d'Activite (BE) *266*
Belgium. Rijksinstituut voor de Social Verzekeringen der Zelfstandigen. Statistiek van de Personen die een Rust- en Overlevingsprestatie Genieten *see* Belgium. Institut National d'Assurances Sociales pour Travailleurs Independants. Statistiques des Beneficiaires de Prestations de Retraite et de Survie *497*
Belgium. Rijksinstituut voor de Sociale Verzekeringen der Zelfstandigen. Jaarverslag *see* Belgium. Institut National d'Assurances Sociales pour Travailleurs Independants. Rapport Annuel *497*
Belgium. Rijksinstituut voor de Sociale Verzekeringen der Zelfstandigen. Statistiek van de Kinderen die Recht Geven Op Kinderbijslag *see* Belgium. Institut National d'Assurances Sociales pour Travailleurs Independants. Statistique des Enfants Beneficiaires d'Allocations Familiales *501*
Belgium. Rijksinstituut voor de Sociale Verzekeringen der Zelfstandigen. Statistiek van de Personen die Onder de Toepassing Vallen van het Sociaal Statuut van de Zelfstandigen *see* Belgium. Institut National d'Assurances Sociales pour Travailleurs Independants. Statistiques des Personnes Assujetties au Statut Social des Travailleurs Independants *497*
Belgium. Rijksstation voor Landbouwtechniek. Mededelingen (BE ISSN 0303-9056) *13*
Belgium. Rijksstation voor Sierplantenteelt. Mededelingen (BE ISSN 0303-903X) *414*
Belgium. Rijksstation voor Zeevisserij. Mededelingen (BE ISSN 0303-9072) *395*
Belgium Basic Statistics (BE) *834*
Belgrade. Univerzitet. Elektrotehnicki Fakultet. Publikacije. Serija: Telekomunikacije i Elektronika *see* Beogradski Univerzitet. Elektrotehnicki Fakultet. Publikacije. Serija: Elektronika, Telekomunikacije, Automatika *352*
Belisane (FR ISSN 0339-8498) *687*
Bell Bryant News (AT ISSN 0310-1444) *372*
Bell Tower (US ISSN 0092-8666) *657*
Bellman Lecture (UK) *134*
Bellman Memorial Lecture *see* Bellman Lecture *134*
Belmontia (NE) *113*

Beloit Poetry Journal. Chapbook (US ISSN 0067-5695) *578*
Bemfam (BL) *804*
Ben-Gurion University of the Negev. Research and Development Authority. Scientific Activities. (IS) *780*
Benchmark Papers in Acoustics (US) *706*
Benchmark Papers in Analytical Chemistry (US ISSN 0145-5338) *249*
Benchmark Papers in Animal Behavior *see* Benchmark Papers in Behavior *127*
Benchmark Papers in Behavior (US) *127*, *739*
Benchmark Papers in Biological Concepts (US) *101*
Benchmark Papers in Ecology (US) *101*
Benchmark Papers in Electrical Engineering & Computer Science (US) 270, *352*
Benchmark Papers in Genetics (US) *122*
Benchmark Papers in Geology (US) *292*
Benchmark Papers in Human Physiology (US ISSN 0093-5557) *125*, *593*
Benchmark Papers in Inorganic Chemistry (US) *251*
Benchmark Papers in Microbiology (US) *123*
Benchmark Papers in Nuclear Physics (US) *702*
Benchmark Papers in Optics (US) *705*
Benchmark Papers in Organic Chemistry (US) *252*
Benchmark Papers in Physical Chemistry and Chemical Physics (US) *254*
Benchmark Papers in Polymer Chemistry (US) *245*, *706*
Benchmark Papers in Systematic and Evolutionary Biology (US) *101*, *122*
Benchmark Papers on Energy (US) *362*
Benco Report (US) *757*
Bendel State. Ministry of Home Affairs and Information. Mid-Western State Estimates *see* Bendel State. Ministry of Information, Social Development and Sports. Estimate *740*
Bendel State. Ministry of Information, Social Development and Sports. Estimate (NR) *740*
Benedictine Almanac *see* Benedictine Yearbook *773*
Benedictine Yearbook (UK ISSN 0522-8883) *773*
Benefits for Saskatchewan Industry from Resource Development (CN ISSN 0706-7852) *142*
Benelux Economic Union. Conseil Consultatif Economique et Social Rapport du Secretaire Concernant les Activites du Conseil *see* B E N E L U X Economic Union. Conseil Central de l'Economie. Rapport du Secretaire sur l'Activite du Conseil *220*
Benelux Publikatieblad/Bulletin Benelux(BE ISSN 0005-8777) *740*
Bengal Motion Picture Diary & General Information *see* Indian Motion Picture Almanac *650*
Benjamin F. Fairless Lectures (US ISSN 0067-5717) *708*
Benn's Hardware Directory (UK ISSN 0067-5725) *141*
Benn's International Hardware Exporter(UK) *141*
Benn's Press Directory (UK ISSN 0141-1772) *504*
Bent (CN ISSN 0067-5733) *560*
Bentley Library Annual (US ISSN 0362-6881) *526*
Benzene-Toluene-Xylenes and Derivatives *see* World Aromatics and Derivatives *248*
Beogradski Univerzitet. Elektrotehnicki Fakultet. Publikacije. Serija: Elektronika, Telekomunikacije, Automatika (YU) *352*
Berckers Katholischer Taschenkalender *see* Berckers Taschenkalender *763*
Berckers Taschenkalender (GW) *763*

Berg- und Huettenmaennische Monatshefte. Supplement (US ISSN 0067-5768) *627*, *641*
Bergakademie Freiberg. Wissenschaftliches Informationszentrum. Veroeffentlichungen (GE) *526*
Bergbau-Berufsgenossenschaft. Geschaeftsbericht (GW ISSN 0343-0510) *506*, *641*
Bergen County History (US ISSN 0094-7989) *466*
Bergey's Manual of Determinative Bacteriology (US) *123*
Bergischer Geschichtsverein. Zeitschrift (GW ISSN 0067-5792) *450*
Bericht der Bundesregierung an den Nationalrat *see* Austria. Bundesministerium fuer Wissenschaft und Forschung. Bericht der Bundesregierung an den Nationalrat *779*
Berichte des Vereins Natur und Heimat und des Naturhistorischen Museums zu Luebeck (GW ISSN 0067-5806) *780*
Berichte ueber Landwirtschaft. Sonderhefte (GW ISSN 0301-2689) *13*
Berichte zur Orts-, Regional- und Landesplanung (SZ) *483*
Berichten van de Afdeling Volkskredietwezen (NE ISSN 0005-9110) *171*
Berita Prasejarah *see* Bulletin of Prehistory *59*
Beri'ut Ha-Yeled Be-Yisrael *see* Child Health in Israel *617*
Berkeley Journal of Sociology (US ISSN 0067-5830) *812*
Berkeley Poets Cooperative (US) *578*
Berkeley Symposia on Mathematical Statistics and Probability (US) *584*
Berkshire Archaeological Committee. Publication (US) *58*
Berkshire Archaeological Journal (UK ISSN 0309-3093) *58*
Berkshire Studies in American History (US) *431*
Berkshire Studies in European History (US) *431*
Berlin. Freie Universitaet. Institut fuer Statistik und Versicherungsmathematik. Berichte *see* Arbeiten zur Angewandten Statistik *832*
Berlin in Zahlen *see* Statistisches Jahrbuch Berlin *847*
Berlin, Theater und Drama (GW ISSN 0067-6047) *858*
Berliner Byzantinistische Arbeiten (GE ISSN 0067-6055) 258, *450*
Berliner Handelsregister Verzeichnis (GW ISSN 0067-6063) *235*
Berliner Historische Kommission. Veroeffentlichungen (GW ISSN 0067-6071) *450*
Berliner Numismatische Zeitschrift (GW) *477*
Berliner Tierpark-Buch (GE ISSN 0067-6098) *127*
Berliner Wirtschaftsdaten (GW) *183*
Bermuda Historical Society. Occasional Publications (BM ISSN 0409-2163) *466*
Bernard Shaw Society Journal (UK) *560*, *858*
Bernard und Graefe Aktuell (GW) *638*
Bernards and Babani Press Radio & Electronics Books (UK) *266*
Berner Beitraege zur Nationaloekonomie (SZ ISSN 0067-6128) *142*
Berner Beitraege zur Soziologie (SZ ISSN 0067-6136) *812*
Berner Boersenverein. Jahresbericht (SZ) *202*
Berner Kriminologische Untersuchungen(SZ ISSN 0067-6144) *280*
Berner Studien zum Fremdenverkehr (SZ ISSN 0067-6152) *142*, *883*
Bernice P. Bishop Museum Bulletin (US ISSN 0005-9439) *780*
Bernice Pauahi Bishop Museum, Honolulu. Occasional Papers (US ISSN 0067-6160) *48*, *780*

Bernice Pauahi Bishop Museum, Honolulu. Special Publications (US ISSN 0067-6179) *48*, *780*
Bertine Koperberg Conference (Proceedings) (SW) *623*
Berytus: Archeological Studies (LE ISSN 0067-6195) *58*
Beschreibende Bibliographien (NE) *87*
Besonders Wertvoll. Kurzfilme (GW ISSN 0067-6209) *649*
Besonders Wertvoll. Langfilme (GW ISSN 0067-6217) *649*
Best American Plays *see* John Gassner's Best American Plays *566*
Best American Short Stories (US ISSN 0067-6233) *560*
Best Books for Children (US) *256*
Best Canadian Stories (CN ISSN 0703-9476) *560*
Best Detective Stories of the Year (US ISSN 0067-625X) *560*
Best Editorial Cartoons of the Year (US ISSN 0091-2220) 72, *555*
Best in Advertising (US) *5*
Best in Advertising Campaigns *see* Best in Advertising *5*
Best in Annual Reports (US ISSN 0360-8743) *214*
Best in Covers *see* Best in Covers and Posters *757*
Best in Covers and Posters (US) 72, *757*
Best in Environmental Graphics (US ISSN 0360-8271) *73*
Best in Packaging (US ISSN 0360-8689) *672*
Best in Posters *see* Best in Covers and Posters *757*
Best of E R I C (Educational Management) (US) *343*
Best of Micro (US ISSN 0271-8189) *270*
Best of National Lampoon (US ISSN 0092-5306) *556*
Best Plays of ... (Year) (US) *858*
Best Poems *see* Borestone Mountain Poetry Awards *905*
Best Science Fiction of the Year (US ISSN 0095-7119) *560*
Best Science Fiction Stories of the Year(US ISSN 0092-8119) *560*
Best Sellers & Best Choices (Year) (US ISSN 0275-0945) *757*
Best Short Plays (US ISSN 0067-6284) *560*
Best Sports Stories (US ISSN 0067-6292) *819*
Bestands-Statistik der Kraftfahrzeuge in Oesterreich (AU ISSN 0067-6306) *865*
Besterman World Bibliographies (US) *904*
Bestimmungsbuecher zur Bodenfauna Europas (GE ISSN 0067-6314) *127*
Best's Agents Guide to Life Insurance Companies (US ISSN 0094-9973) *497*
Best's Insurance Report: Life-Health (US) *498*
Best's Insurance Report: Property-Casualty (US ISSN 0148-3218) *498*
Best's Insurance Report: Property-Liability *see* Best's Insurance Report: Property-Casualty *498*
Best's Insurance Securities Research Service (US ISSN 0362-8701) *202*
Best's Recommended Independent Insurance Adjusters (US ISSN 0091-830X) *498*
Best's Recommended Insurance Adjusters *see* Best's Recommended Independent Insurance Adjusters *498*
Best's Recommended Insurance Attorneys (US) *498*
Best's Safety Directory (US ISSN 0090-7480) *495*
Bestsellers du Monde Entier (SZ ISSN 0067-6330) *904*
Bestuurlike Informasie/Managerial Information (SA ISSN 0067-6349) *167*
Beta Phi Mu Chapbook (US ISSN 0067-6357) *526*
Beton-Kalender (GW) *134*
Beton- und Fertigteil-Jahrbuch (GW ISSN 0067-6365) *374*
Betonstein-Jahrbuch *see* Beton- und Fertigteil-Jahrbuch *374*

Betontechnische Berichte (GW ISSN 0409-2740) *134*
Betriebs- und Arbeitswirtschaft in der Praxis (GW ISSN 0405-6485) *13*
Betriebs- und Marktwirtschaft im Gartenbau (GW ISSN 0303-1241) *414*
Betriebsstatistik Wissenschaftlicher Bibliotheken (GW) *526*
Betriebswirtschaftliche Mitteilungen (SZ ISSN 0067-639X) *214*
Better Brisbane (AT) *748*
Better Building Bulletin (CN ISSN 0067-642X) *134*
Better Homes and Gardens Bedroom and Bath Decorating Ideas (US ISSN 0164-0186) *502*
Better Homes and Gardens Brides Book(US) *262, 900*
Better Homes and Gardens Christmas Ideas (US ISSN 0405-6590) *475, 479*
Better Homes and Gardens Furnishings and Decorating Ideas (US ISSN 0092-7961) *502*
Better Homes and Gardens Garden Ideas and Outdoor Living (US) *414, 479*
Better Homes and Gardens Holiday Crafts (US) *476*
Better Homes and Gardens How to Buy a Home (US) *761*
Better Homes and Gardens Hundreds of Ideas (US ISSN 0090-6433) *414, 503*
Better Homes and Gardens Kitchen & Bath Ideas (US) *502*
Better Homes and Gardens Window Wall Ideas *see* Window & Wall Decorating Ideas *502*
Beverage Industry Annual Manual (US) *85*
Beverage Industry News California Goldbook (US) *85*
Bevoelkerungsstatistisches Jahrbuch der Deutschen Demokratischen Republik(GE) *726*
Bevoelkerungsstruktur und Wirtschaftskraft der Bundeslaender (GW ISSN 0072-1867) *726*
Beyond Baroque (1976) *see* Obras (Venice) *569*
Bhabha Atomic Research Centre. Nuclear Physics Division. Annual Report (II) *702*
Bhagyavati Panchanga (II) *81*
Bharat Krishak Samaj. Year Book (II ISSN 0067-6454) *13*
Bharatiya Purabhilekha Patrika *see* Studies in Indian Epigraphy *552*
Bhopal University Research Journal (II) *334*
Bhugola Samayiki (BG) *420*
Bialostockie Towarzystwo Naukowe. Prace (PL ISSN 0067-6470) *450*
Biannual of Electronics Research *see* Texas Annual of Electronics Research *359*
Bibb Eagle (US) *417*
Biblica et Orientalia (VC) *669*
Biblio-Cal Notes (US ISSN 0045-1851) *466*
Biblio-Mer (BE) *290*
Bibliografi Negara Malaysia *see* Malaysian National Bibliography *438*
Bibliografi over Danmarks Offentlige Publikationer (DK ISSN 0067-6543) *87*
Bibliografi over Dansk Kunst (DK) *80*
Bibliografi over Europaeiske Kunstneres Ex Libris/Europaeische Ex Libris/ European Book Plates/Ex Libris d'Europe (DK) *80*
Bibliografia Actual del Caribe *see* Current Caribbean Bibliography *437*
Bibliografia Agricola Chilena (CL) *23*
Bibliografia Analitica a Periodicelor Romanesti (RM ISSN 0067-6551) *87*
Bibliografia Argentina de Psicologia (AG ISSN 0523-1698) *739*
Bibliografia Bibliotecologica Argentina (AG ISSN 0067-656X) *538*
Bibliografia Boliviana *see* Bio-Bibliografia Boliviana *89*
Bibliografia Brasileira de Agricultura *see* Bibliografia Brasileira de Ciencias Agricolas *13*

Bibliografia Brasileira de Botanica (BL ISSN 0067-6586) *87, 109*
Bibliografia Brasileira de Ciencias Agricolas (BL ISSN 0067-6594) *13*
Bibliografia Brasileira de Ciencias Sociais (BL ISSN 0067-6608) *87, 810*
Bibliografia Brasileira de Direito (BL ISSN 0067-6616) *87, 521*
Bibliografia Brasileira de Documentacao(BL ISSN 0067-6624) *270, 526*
Bibliografia Brasileira de Engenharia (BL ISSN 0100-0705) *87, 371*
Bibliografia Brasileira de Fisica (BL ISSN 0067-6640) *87, 700*
Bibliografia Brasileira de Matematica (BL ISSN 0067-6667) *87, 591*
Bibliografia Brasileira de Matematica e Fisica *see* Bibliografia Brasileira de Matematica *591*
Bibliografia Brasileira de Matematica e Fisica *see* Bibliografia Brasileira de Fisica *700*
Bibliografia Brasileira de Medicina (BL ISSN 0067-6675) *87, 601*
Bibliografia Brasileira de Odontologia (BL ISSN 0100-6266) *87*
Bibliografia Brasileira de Quimica *see* Bibliografia Brasileira de Quimica e Quimica Tecnologica *153*
Bibliografia Brasileira de Quimica e Quimica Tecnologica (BL ISSN 0100-0756) *87, 153*
Bibliografia Brasileira de Quimica Tecnologia *see* Bibliografia Brasileira de Quimica e Quimica Tecnologica *153*
Bibliografia Brasileira de Zoologia (BL ISSN 0067-6691) *87, 109*
Bibliografia Cientifica da Junta de Investigacoes do Ultramar (PO) *717*
Bibliografia Cubana (CU ISSN 0067-6705) *87*
Bibliografia de la Literatura Hispanica (SP) *87, 577*
Bibliografia de Recursos Naturales (CL) *87, 279*
Bibliografia do Arroz (BL) *23, 88*
Bibliografia Dobrogei (RM) *88*
Bibliografia e Storia della Critica (IT) *577*
Bibliografia Economico-Social *see* Bibliografia Brasileira de Ciencias Sociais *810*
Bibliografia Historii Polskiej (PL ISSN 0067-6721) *437*
Bibliografia Internationala Cinema/ Bibliographie Internationale Cinema (RM ISSN 0084-7828) *651*
Bibliografia na Bulgarskata Bibliografiia/ Bibliography of Bulgarian Bibliographies (BU) *88*
Bibliografia Pomorza Zachodniego (PL ISSN 0409-3453) *437*
Bibliografia Portuguesa de Construcao Civil (PO ISSN 0067-6756) *371*
Bibliografia Sobre a Economia Portuguesa (PO ISSN 0067-6764) *153*
Bibliografia Teologica Comentada del Area Iberoamericana (AG) *88, 763*
Bibliografia Ticinese (SZ ISSN 0067-6772) *450*
Bibliografica Folclorica (BL) *48, 401*
Bibliograficky Zbornik (CS ISSN 0067-6780) *88*
Bibliografie van de Nederlandse Taal-en Literatuur Wetenschap (NE ISSN 0045-186X) *555*
Bibliografie van Nederlandse Proefschriften/Dutch Theses (NE ISSN 0166-9966) *48*
Bibliografija Medicinske Periodike Jugoslavije/Index Medicus Iugoslavicus (YU ISSN 0067-6799) *601*
Bibliographia Cartographica (GW ISSN 0340-0409) *88, 428*
Bibliographia Franciscana (IT) *99, 769*
Bibliographia Internationalis Spiritualitatis (VC ISSN 0084-7836) *692*
Bibliographia Medica Cechoslovaca (CS ISSN 0067-6802) *601*
Bibliographia Musicologica (NE ISSN 0084-7844) *88*
Bibliographia Phytosociologica Syntaxonomica (GW) *113*

Bibliographia Scientiae Naturalis Helvetica (SZ ISSN 0067-6829) *794*
Bibliographic Guide to Art and Architecture (US ISSN 0360-2699) *71, 88*
Bibliographic Guide to Black Studies (US ISSN 0360-2710) *88, 394*
Bibliographic Guide to Business and Economics (US ISSN 0360-2702) *153*
Bibliographic Guide to Conference Publications (US ISSN 0360-2729) *88*
Bibliographic Guide to Dance (US ISSN 0360-2737) *88, 286*
Bibliographic Guide to Government Publications (US ISSN 0360-2796) *88*
Bibliographic Guide to Government Publications-Foreign (US ISSN 0360-280X) *88*
Bibliographic Guide to Law (US ISSN 0360-2745) *88, 521*
Bibliographic Guide to Music (US ISSN 0360-2753) *88, 665*
Bibliographic Guide to North American History (US ISSN 0147-6491) *88, 437*
Bibliographic Guide to Psychology (US ISSN 0360-277X) *88, 739*
Bibliographic Guide to Soviet and European Studies (US) *450*
Bibliographic Guide to the Negro World *see* Guide Bibliographique du Monde Noir *91*
Bibliographic Guide to Theatre Arts (US ISSN 0360-2788) *858*
Bibliographia Judaica (US ISSN 0067-6853) *769*
Bibliographical Bulletin *see* Bibliographische Berichte *88*
Bibliographical Index of the Ukrainian Press Outside Ukraine *see* Bibliohrafichnyi Pokazhczu Ukrains'koi Presy Poza Mezhamy Ukrainy *88*
Bibliographical Selection of Museological Literature *see* Selected Bibliography of Museological Literature *656*
Bibliographical Series from the Yale University Library Collections (US) *538*
Bibliographical Series on Coconut (CE) *33*
Bibliographical Services Throughout the World (UN) *88*
Bibliographical Society of Australia and New Zealand. Bulletin (AT ISSN 0084-7852) *538*
Bibliographical Society of Canada. Facsimile Series (CN ISSN 0067-687X) *526*
Bibliographical Society of Canada. Monographs (CN ISSN 0067-6888) *526*
Bibliographical Society of Canada. Newsletter *see* Bibliographical Society of Canada. Papers *88*
Bibliographical Society of Canada. Papers (CN ISSN 0067-6896) *88*
Bibliographie Analytique de l'Afrique Antique (FR) *437*
Bibliographie Annuelle de l'Histoire de France (FR ISSN 0067-6918) *437*
Bibliographie Annuelle de Madagascar (MG ISSN 0067-6926) *88*
Bibliographie Bildende Kunst (GE) *80*
Bibliographie Cartographique Internationale (FR ISSN 0067-6934) *904*
Bibliographie Courante d'Articles de Periodiques Posterieurs a 1944 sur les Problemes Politiques, Economiques et Sociaux/Index to Post-1944 Periodical Articles on Political, Economic and Social Problems (US) *88, 803*
Bibliographie Courante de la Caraibe *see* Current Caribbean Bibliography *437*
Bibliographie d'Histoire Luxembourgeoise *see* Bibliographie zur Geschichte Luxemburgs *437*

Bibliographie de Jurisprudence Europeenne Concernant les Decisions Judiciares Relatives aux Traites Instituant les Communautes Europeennes (EI ISSN 0590-7233) *521*
Bibliographie de l'Histoire Bernoise *see* Bibliographie der Berner Geschichte *437*
Bibliographie de la Litterature Francaise du Moyen Age a Nos Jours (FR ISSN 0067-6942) *560*
Bibliographie der Antiquariats-, Auktions- und Kunstkataloge (GE) *80*
Bibliographie der Berner Geschichte/ Bibliographie de l'Histoire Bernoise (SZ) *88, 437*
Bibliographie der Chemisch-Archaeologischen Literatur (GE ISSN 0067-6950) *904*
Bibliographie der Deutschen Literaturwissenschaft *see* Bibliographie der Deutschen Sprach- und Literaturwissenschaft *577*
Bibliographie der Deutschen Sprach- und Literaturwissenschaft (GW ISSN 0523-2449) *577*
Bibliographie der Deutschsprachigen Psychologischen Literatur (GW) *739*
Bibliographie der Franzoesischen Literaturwissenschaft (GW ISSN 0523-2465) *577*
Bibliographie der Paedagogischen Veroeffentlichungen in der Deutschen Demokratischen Republik(GE ISSN 0067-6969) *326*
Bibliographie der Schweizerischen Amtsdruckschriften/Bibliographie des Publications Officielles Suisses (SZ) *88*
Bibliographie der Sozialethik (SZ ISSN 0067-6977) *692, 803*
Bibliographie des Auteurs Modernes de Langue Francaise (FR) *560*
Bibliographie des Publications Officielles Suisses *see* Bibliographie der Schweizerischen Amtsdruckschriften *88*
Bibliographie des Schweizerischen Recht (SZ) *521*
Bibliographie en la Langue Francaise d'Histoire du Droit de 987 a 1875 (FR ISSN 0067-6985) *521*
Bibliographie Ethnographique de l'Afrique Sud-Saharienne (BE) *55*
Bibliographie Ethnographique du Congo Belge et des Regions Avoisinantes *see* Bibliographie Ethnographique de l'Afrique Sud-Saharienne *55*
Bibliographie Internationala Cinema *see* Bibliografia Internationala Cinema *651*
Bibliographie Internationale de l'Humanisme et de la Renaissance (SZ ISSN 0067-7000) *756*
Bibliographie Internationale des Arts et Traditions Populaires *see* Internationale Volkskundliche Bibliographie *401*
Bibliographie Juridique *see* Rechtsbibliographie *521*
Bibliographie Linguistischer Literatur (GW) *555, 577*
Bibliographie Luxembourgeoise (LU) *88, 450*
Bibliographie Papyrologique sur Fiches (BE) *58, 541*
Bibliographie Relative aux Irrigations, au Drainage, a la Regularisation des Cours d'Eau et la Maitrise des Crues *see* Bibliography on Irrigation, Drainage, River Training and Flood Control *900*
Bibliographie Romane *see* Romanische Bibliographie *555*
Bibliographie Suisse de Statistique et d'Economie Politique *see* Schweizerische Bibliographie fuer Statistik und Volkswirtschaft *94*
Bibliographie Suisse de Statistique et d'Economie Politique (SZ) *142, 834*
Bibliographie Unselbstaendiger Literatur-Linguistik *see* Bibliographie Linguistischer Literatur *577*
Bibliographie zur Archaeo-Zoologie und Geschichte der Haustiere (GE) *58, 88*

1306 BIBLIOGRAPHIE ZUR

Bibliographie zur Geschichte Luxemburgs/Bibliographie d'Histoire Luxembourgeoise (LU ISSN 0067-7043) *437*
Bibliographie zur Symbolik, Ikonographie und Mythologie (GW ISSN 0067-706X) *55, 403*
Bibliographies Analytiques sur l'Afrique Centrale (BE) *88, 437*
Bibliographies in American Music (US) *665*
Bibliographies in Paint Technology (UK ISSN 0057-7094) *673*
Bibliographies on Educational Topics (US) *88, 326*
Bibliographische Berichte/Bibliographical Bulletin (GW ISSN 0006-1506) *88*
Bibliographisches Handbuch der Deutschen Litteraturwissenschaft 1945-1969 (GW) *904*
Bibliography and Subject Index of Current Computing Literature *see* A C M Guide to Computing Literature *274*
Bibliography and Subject Index of South African Geology (SA ISSN 0584-2360) *88, 290*
Bibliography, Corporate Responsibility for Social Problems *see* Bibliography of Corporate Social Responsibility *810*
Bibliography Newsletter (US ISSN 0145-3084) *538, 760*
Bibliography of Agricultural Bibliographies (US ISSN 0190-7077) *24, 88*
Bibliography of Appraisal Literature (US) *73, 202, 762*
Bibliography of Asian Studies (US ISSN 0067-7159) *437*
Bibliography of Bioethics (US ISSN 0363-0161) *601*
Bibliography of Books for Children (US) *760*
Bibliography of Bulgarian Bibliographies *see* Bibliografia na Bulgarskata Bibliografiia *88*
Bibliography of Canadian Bibliographies(CN ISSN 0067-7175) *88*
Bibliography of Corporate Social Responsibility (US) *810*
Bibliography of Developmental Medicine and Child Neurology. Books and Articles Received (UK ISSN 0067-7183) *601*
Bibliography of Doctoral Dissertations; Natural and Applied Sciences (II) *88, 794*
Bibliography of Economic and Statistical Publications on Tanzania (TZ) *88, 153, 834*
Bibliography of Electrical Recordings in the CNS and Related Literature (US ISSN 0084-7879) *88, 601*
Bibliography of Germfree Research (US) *109*
Bibliography of Higher Education Collective Bargaining Involving Other Than Faculty Personnel (US) *326, 507*
Bibliography of Historical Works Issued in the United Kingdom (UK ISSN 0067-7191) *431*
Bibliography of Interlingual Scientific and Technical Dictionaries (UN ISSN 0067-7205) *794, 854*
Bibliography of Noise (US ISSN 0092-5756) *88, 390*
Bibliography of Old Norse-Icelandic Studies (DK ISSN 0067-7213) *437*
Bibliography of Periodical Articles on Maritime and Naval History (US) *437, 865*
Bibliography of Periodical Articles Relating to the South Pacific (FJ) *88*
Bibliography of Psychology/Ketabname-Ye Ravanshenasi (IR) *739*
Bibliography of Publications from Economic Research Centres in India (II) *153*
Bibliography of Publications of University Bureaus of Business and Economic Research (US ISSN 0066-8761) *153*

Bibliography of Published Papers of the Atomic Bomb Casualty Commission *see* Bibliography of Published Papers of the Radiation Effects Research Foundation *601*
Bibliography of Published Papers of the Radiation Effects Research Foundation/Hoshasen Eikyo Kenkyusho Happyo Rombun Mokuroku (JA) *601*
Bibliography of Rubber Literature Including Patents (US) *778*
Bibliography of Society, Ethics and the Life Sciences (US ISSN 0094-4831) *110, 692*
Bibliography of South African Government Publications (SA ISSN 0067-7256) *88*
Bibliography of Surgery of the Hand (US ISSN 0067-7264) *601*
Bibliography of the Geology of Missouri (US ISSN 0067-7272) *290*
Bibliography of the History of Medicine(US ISSN 0067-7280) *601*
Bibliography of the Middle East (SY ISSN 0067-7302) *88*
Bibliography of Urban Studies in Australia (AT) *488*
Bibliography of Works by Polish Scholars and Scientists Published outside Poland in Languages Other Than Polish (UK ISSN 0067-7310) *88*
Bibliography on Cold Regions Science and Technology (US) *371*
Bibliography on Economics of Containerization *see* Containerization: A Bibliography *865*
Bibliography on Foreign and Comparative Law : Books and Articles in English. (US ISSN 0067-7329) *521*
Bibliography on Human Reproduction, Family Planning, and Population Dynamics (UN) *133*
Bibliography on Irrigation, Drainage, River Training and Flood Control/Bibliographie Relative aux Irrigations, au Drainage, a la Regularisation des Cours d'Eau et la Matrise des Crues (II ISSN 0523-302X) *900*
Bibliography on Population and Family Planning in Korea (KO) *88, 133*
Bibliography on Satellite Geodesy and Related Subjects *see* International Association of Geodesy. Central Bureau for Satellite Geodesy. Bibliography *428*
Bibliography on Smoking and Health (US ISSN 0067-7361) *695*
Bibliography on the Hypothalamic-Pituitary-Gonadal System (US ISSN 0084-7887) *601*
Bibliohrafichnyi Pokazhczyk Ukrains'koi Presy Poza Mezhamy Ukrainy/Bibliographical Index of the Ukrainian Press Outside Ukraine (US ISSN 0067-737X) *88*
Biblioteca Apostolica Vaticana. Cataloghi di Manoscritti (VC) *773*
Biblioteca Apostolica Vaticana. Cataloghi di Mostre (VC) *774*
Biblioteca Apostolica Vaticana. Illustrazioni di Codici. Codici Vaticani. Series Major (VC) *774*
Biblioteca Apostolica Vaticana. Illustrazioni di Codici. Codici Vaticani. Series Minor (VC) *774*
Biblioteca Apostolica Vaticana. Studi e Testi (VC) *774*
Biblioteca Clasica Gredos (FR) *258*
Biblioteca Clasicos Colorados (PY) *796*
Biblioteca Colombiana (CK) *560*
Biblioteca de Arheologie (RM ISSN 0067-7388) *58*
Biblioteca de Cultura Andina. Ediciones. (PE) *48*
Biblioteca de Cultura Vasca (AG ISSN 0067-7396) *401, 466*
Biblioteca de Economia (BL) *183*
Biblioteca de Filologia Hispanica Onomastica y Toponimia (SP) *541*
Biblioteca de Poesia (AG) *578*
Biblioteca de Secretos Politicos (AG) *708*
Biblioteca de Teologia (SP ISSN 0067-740X) *763*

Biblioteca degli Studi Classici e Orientali (IT) *258, 669*
Biblioteca di Bibliografia Italiana (IT ISSN 0067-7418) *88*
Biblioteca di Labeo (IT ISSN 0067-7434) *489*
Biblioteca di Letteratura e Arte (IT) *560*
Biblioteca di Storia Lombarda Moderna e Contemporanea. Studi e Ricerche (IT) *905*
Biblioteca di Storia Toscana Moderna e Contemporanea Studi e Documenti (IT ISSN 0067-7442) *450*
Biblioteca di Studi Etruschi (IT ISSN 0067-7450) *450*
Biblioteca do Educador Profissional (PO ISSN 0067-7469) *490*
Biblioteca Estudios Escelicer (SP) *526*
Biblioteca Filologica. Ensayos (SP) *541*
Biblioteca Filologica. Manuales (SP) *541*
Biblioteca Istorica (RM ISSN 0067-7493) *450*
Biblioteca Marsilio: Architettura e Urbanistica (IT) *68, 483*
Biblioteca N T (SP) *490*
Biblioteca Nacional. Boletin *see* Universidad Nacional Autonoma de Mexico. Instituto de Investigaciones Bibliograficas. Boletin *95*
Biblioteca Nacional de Angola. Novas (AO) *526*
Biblioteca Napoletana di Storia e Arte (IT) *73, 450*
Biblioteca Praehistorica Hispana (SP ISSN 0067-7507) *58*
Biblioteca Promocion del Pueblo (SP ISSN 0405-9212) *450*
Biblioteca Romanica Hispanica (SP) *560*
Biblioteca Romanica Hispanica. Estudios y Ensayos *see* Biblioteca Romanica Hispanica *560*
Biblioteca Statale e Libreria Civica di Cremona. Aannali (IT) *450*
Biblioteca Statale e Libreria Civica di Cremona. Mostre (IT) *450*
Biblioteca Storica Elbana (IT) *450*
Biblioteca Storica Toscana *see* Biblioteca Storica Toscana. Serie I *450*
Biblioteca Storica Toscana. Serie I (IT) *450*
Biblioteca Storica Toscana. Serie II (IT) *450*
Biblioteca Universitaria y Provincial, Barcelona. Boletin de Noticias (SP) *88*
Bibliotecas e Arquivos de Portugal (PO) *526*
Bibliotecas y Archivos (MX) *526*
Biblioteconomia (SP ISSN 0006-1778) *526*
Biblioteconomia e Bibliografia. Saggi e Studi (IT ISSN 0067-7531) *88*
Biblioteczka Ateisty (PL ISSN 0067-754X) *763*
Biblioteka Archeologiczna (PL ISSN 0067-7639) *58*
Biblioteka Etnografii Polskiej (PL ISSN 0067-7655) *812*
Biblioteka Klasykow Pedagogiki (PL ISSN 0067-7671) *315*
Biblioteka Kopernikanska (PL ISSN 0067-7558) *81*
Biblioteka Kornicka. Pamietnik (PL ISSN 0067-768X) *527*
Biblioteka Krakowska (PL ISSN 0067-7698) *73, 450*
Biblioteka Matematyczna (PL) *584*
Biblioteka Mechaniki Stosowanej (PL ISSN 0067-7701) *379*
Biblioteka Narodowa. Rocznik (PL ISSN 0083-7261) *527*
Biblioteka Nawigatora (PL ISSN 0067-7728) *877*
Biblioteka Pisarzow Polskich *see* Biblioteka Pisarzow Polskich. Seria A *560*
Biblioteka Pisarzow Polskich. Seria A (PL ISSN 0519-8631) *560*
Biblioteka Pisarzy Reformacyjnych (PL ISSN 0519-8658) *763*
Biblioteka Polska. Seria Tomistyczna (UK ISSN 0067-7752) *763*
Biblioteka Popularnonaukowa (PL ISSN 0067-7760) *48*

Biblioteka Samizdata (NE) *556*
Biblioteka Slaska. Biuletyn Informacyjny (PL) *527*
Biblioteka Sluchacza Koncertowego. Seria Wprowadzajaca (PL ISSN 0067-7779) *657*
Biblioteka Wiadomosci Statystycznych (PL ISSN 0067-7795) *731*
Bibliotekovedenie, Bibliografiya i Informatika (UR) *527*
Bibliotekoznanie, Bibliografiia, Knigoznanie, Nauchna Informatsiia (BU) *527*
Biblioteksaarbog (DK ISSN 0084-957X) *527*
Bibliotheca Aegyptiaca (BE ISSN 0067-7817) *58*
Bibliotheca Africana Droz (SZ ISSN 0067-7825) *439*
Bibliotheca Anatomica (SZ ISSN 0067-7833) *101, 593*
Bibliotheca Archaeologica (SP ISSN 0519-9603) *58*
Bibliotheca Arnamagnaeana (DK ISSN 0067-7841) *560*
Bibliotheca Arnamagnaeana. Supplementum (DK ISSN 0067-785X) *560*
Bibliotheca Athena (IT ISSN 0067-7868) *541*
Bibliotheca Australiana (NE ISSN 0067-7876) *447*
Bibliotheca Bibliographica Aureliana (GW ISSN 0067-7884) *88*
Bibliotheca Bibliographica Neerlandica (NE) *88*
Bibliotheca Botanica (GW ISSN 0067-7892) *113*
Bibliotheca Cardiologica (SZ ISSN 0067-7906) *606*
Bibliotheca Cartographica *see* Bibliographia Cartographica *428*
Bibliotheca Celtica (UK ISSN 0067-7914) *88*
Biblioteca del Planeamiento Educativo(AG ISSN 0067-7922) *343*
Bibliotheca Emblematica (NE ISSN 0067-7930) *73, 417*
Bibliotheca Ephemeridum Theologicarum Lovaniensium (BE) *763*
Bibliotheca Gastroenterologica *see* Frontiers of Gastrointestinal Research *613*
Bibliotheca Germanica. Handbuecher, Texte und Monographien aus dem Gebiete der Germanischen Philologie(SZ ISSN 0067-7477) *541*
Bibliotheca Haematologica (SZ ISSN 0067-7957) *613*
Bibliotheca Helvetica Romana (SZ ISSN 0067-7965) *258*
Bibliotheca Historica Romaniae. Monographies (RM ISSN 0067-799X) *450*
Bibliotheca Historica Romaniae. Studies(RM ISSN 0067-7981) *450*
Bibliotheca Historico Militaris (UK) *638*
Bibliotheca Hungarica Antiqua (HU ISSN 0067-8007) *733, 757*
Bibliotheca Ibero-Americana (GW ISSN 0067-8015) *717*
Bibliotheca Indonesica (NE ISSN 0067-8023) *48*
Bibliotheca Instituti Historici Societatis Iesu (IT) *774*
Bibliotheca Islamica (GW ISSN 0170-3102) *669, 769*
Bibliotheca Latina Medii et Recentiori Aevi (PL ISSN 0067-8031) *58, 450*
Bibliotheca Mesopotamica (US) *474*
Bibliotheca Microbiologia *see* Contributions to Microbiology and Immunology *603*
Bibliotheca Mycologica (GW ISSN 0067-8066) *113*
Bibliotheca Nutritio et Dieta (SZ ISSN 0067-8198) *665*
Bibliotheca Oecnomica (RM ISSN 0067-8082) *142*
Bibliotheca Ophthalmologica *see* Developments in Ophthalmology *615*
Bibliotheca Orientalis Hungarica (HU ISSN 0067-8104) *669*

Bibliotheca Paediatrica *see* Monographs in Paediatrics *617*
Bibliotheca Phonetica (SZ ISSN 0067-8120) *541*
Bibliotheca Phycologica (GW ISSN 0067-8112) *113*
Bibliotheca Primatologica *see* Contributions to Primatology *128*
Bibliotheca Psychiatrica (SZ ISSN 0067-8147) *619*
Bibliotheca Radiologica (SZ ISSN 0067-8155) *622*
Bibliotheca Rerum Historicarum (GW) *450*
Bibliotheca Romanica (SZ ISSN 0067-7515) *541*
Bibliotheca Russica (GW ISSN 0341-3217) *541*, *560*
Bibliotheca Seraphico-Capuccina (IT ISSN 0067-8163) *774*
Bibliotheca Vita Humana *see* Contributions to Human Development *594*
Bibliothek der Griechischen Literatur (GW ISSN 0340-7853) *259*
Bibliothek der Journalisten (CS) *504*
Bibliothek der Klassischen Altertumswissenschaften. Neue Folge(GW ISSN 0067-8201) *431*
Bibliothek des Buchwesens (B B) (GW ISSN 0340-8051) *527*
Bibliothek fuer das Gesamtgebiet der Lungenkrankheiten (GE ISSN 0067-8228) *623*
Bibliothek fuer Zeitgeschichte, Stuttgart. Jahresbibliographie (GW ISSN 0081-8992) *437*
Bibliothek fuer Zeitgeschichte, Stuttgart. Schriften (GW ISSN 0081-900X) *431*
Bibliothek und Wissenschaft (GW ISSN 0067-8236) *527*
Bibliothekar-Lehrinstitut des Landes Nordrhein-Westfalen. Arbeiten aus dem B L I (GW ISSN 0069-5858) *527*
Bibliothekar-Lehrinstitut des Landes Nordrhein-Westfalen. Bibliographische Hefte (GW ISSN 0069-5866) *89*
Bibliothekspraxis (GW ISSN 0300-287X) *527*
Bibliotheksstudien (GW) *527*
Bibliotheque Africaine. Catalogue des Acquisitions. Catologus van de Aanwinsten (BE ISSN 0067-5601) *89*, *437*
Bibliotheque d'Etudes Balkaniques (FR ISSN 0067-8325) *541*, *560*
Bibliotheque d'Histoire Antillaise (GP) *466*
Bibliotheque de la Mer (FR ISSN 0067-8260) *826*
Bibliotheque de la Revue d'Histoire Ecclesiastique (BE ISSN 0067-8279) *774*
Bibliotheque de la S E L A F (Societe d'Etudes Linguistiques et Anthropologiques de France) (FR ISSN 0081-1238) *541*
Bibliotheque de Museon *see* Institut Orientaliste de Louvain. Publications *670*
Bibliotheque des Cahiers Archeologiques (FR ISSN 0067-8309) *58*
Bibliotheque des Ecoles Francaises d'Athenes et de Rome Publication *see* B E F A R. Publication *58*
Bibliotheque des Lettres Quebecoises (CN) *490*
Bibliotheque du Museon *see* Universite Catholique de Louvain. Institut Orientaliste. Publications *446*
Bibliotheque Francaise et Romane. Serie A: Manuels et Etudes Linguistiques (FR ISSN 0067-8341) *541*
Bibliotheque Francaise et Romane. Serie B: Editions Critiques de Textes (FR ISSN 0067-835X) *560*
Bibliotheque Francaise et Romane. Serie C: Etudes Litteraires (FR ISSN 0067-8368) *560*
Bibliotheque Francaise et Romane. Serie D: Initiation, Textes et Documents (FR ISSN 0067-8376) *560*

Bibliotheque Francaise et Romane. Serie E: Langue et Litterature Francaises au Canada (FR ISSN 0067-8384) *541*, *560*
Bibliotheque Historique (FR) *431*
Bibliotheque Historique Vaudoise (SZ ISSN 0067-8406) *450*
Bibliotheque Internationale d'Etudes Maconniques (BE) *262*
Bibliotheque Introuvable (FR ISSN 0067-8422) *560*
Bibliotheque Iranienne (FR) *669*
Bibliotheque Publique et Universitaire de Geneve.Compte Rendu (SZ) *527*
Bibliotheque Rencontre des Lettres Anciennes et Modernes (SZ ISSN 0067-8457) *905*
Bibliotheque Royale Albert 1er. Acquisitions Majeures (BE ISSN 0524-7624) *527*
Bibliotheque Royale Albert 1er. Catalogue Collectif des Periodiques Etrangers/Koninklijke Bibliotheek Albert I. Centrale Catalogus van Buitenlandse Tidjschriften (BE ISSN 0068-2926) *89*
Bibliotheque Royale Albert 1er. Rapport Annuel (BE) *527*
Bibliotheque Royale de Belgique. Rapport Annuel *see* Bibliotheque Royale Albert 1er. Rapport Annuel *527*
Bibliotheque Universitaire, Grenoble. Publications (FR ISSN 0072-7520) *780*
Bibliotheques des Universites et des Colleges du Canada *see* University and College Libraries in Canada *915*
Bibliotheques Publiques du Canada. *see* Public Libraries in Canada *913*
Biblische Beitraege (SZ ISSN 0582-1673) *764*
Biblische Untersuchungen (GW ISSN 0523-5154) *764*
Biblisches Seminar (GW) *764*
Biblos (PO) *560*
Bicycle Bibliography *see* Bicycle Resource Guide *823*
Bicycle Resource Guide (US ISSN 0193-8584) *750*, *823*, *874*
Bidrag til H. C. Andersens Bibliografi (DK ISSN 0067-8473) *577*
Bidrag till Kaennedom av Finlands Natur och Folk (FI ISSN 0067-8481) *490*, *796*
Bielefelder Katalog - Jazz (GW) *657*
Biennale Internationale de la Tapisserie (SZ ISSN 0067-849X) *855*
Biennial Report-Educational Communications Board *see* Wisconsin. Educational Communications Board. Biennial Report *325*
Biennial Report - Minnesota. Department of Education *see* Minnesota. Department of Education. Biennial Report *911*
Biennial Report - Natural Areas Advisory Committee *see* Washington (State). Natural Areas Advisory Committee. Biennial Report *279*
Biennial Report of the Arts Activities in Alabama *see* Annual Report of the Arts Activities in Alabama *71*
Biennial Report of the Bureau of Property Taxation *see* Maine. Bureau of Property Taxation. Biennial Report *230*
Biennial Report - State of Minnesota, Department of Revenue *see* Minnesota. Department of Revenue. Biennial Report *230*
Biennial Report-State of Utah, Division of Wildlife Resources *see* Utah. Division of Wildlife Resources. Biennial Report *278*
Biennial Report - Texas Department of Health Resources *see* Texas. Department of Health Resources. Biennial Report *754*
Biennial Report to the Governor and the Legislature of the Alabama Commission on Higher Education *see* Alabama. Commission on Higher Education. Biennial Report to the Governor and the Legislature *333*
Biennial Survey of Advertising Expenditures Around the World *see* World Advertising Expenditures *6*

Biennial Survey of Bank Officer Salaries *see* Bank Administration Institute. Personnel Administration Commission. Biennial Survey of Bank Officer Salaries *219*
Biennial Survey of Bank Personnel Policies and Practices (US) *171*, *220*
Biennial Symposium on Cryogenic Instrumentation. Proceedings (US) *700*
Big Book (US) *134*
Big Book of Metalworking Machinery (US ISSN 0045-1983) *582*
Big Country Cariboo Magazine (CN ISSN 0703-1440) *812*
Big Eight (US) *823*
Big Enid Blyton Story Annual (UK) *257*
Biggest Greatest Cracked Annual (US) *556*
Bihar Research Society. Journal (II) *474*, *812*
Bijdragen en Mededelingen Betreffende de Geschiedenis der Nederlanden (NE ISSN 0165-0505) *450*
Bijdragen tot de Bibliotheckwetenschap/Contributions to Library Science (BE ISSN 0067-8538) *527*
Bijdragen tot de Geschiedenis van Arnhem (NE ISSN 0067-8554) *450*
Bikasa Eka Vihangam Drshti (NP) *183*
Bilateral Studies in Private International Law (US ISSN 0067-8562) *522*
Bildung im Geschichtsmuseum (GE) *450*, *652*
Bildung im Zahlenspiegel (GW) *326*, *834*
Bildungsplanung in Oesterreich/ Educational Policy and Planning. Austria/Politique et la Planification de l'Enseignement - Autriche (AU ISSN 0067-8589) *315*
Bilismen i Danmark (DK) *870*
Bilismen i Sverige *see* Motor Traffic in Sweden *871*
Billboard. International Buyer's Guide of the Music-Record Industry *see* Billboard's International Buyer's Guide of the Music-Record-Tape Industry *657*
Billboard Index (US ISSN 0360-2516) *905*
Billboard International Tape Directory *see* Billboard Tape/Audio/Video Sourcebook *818*
Billboard Tape/Audio/Video Sourcebook (US) *818*
Billboard's International Buyer's Guide of the Music-Record-Tape Industry (US ISSN 0067-8600) *657*
Billboard's International Club and Disco Equipment Sourcebook (US) *657*
Billboard's International Disco Sourcebook *see* Billboard's International Club and Disco Equipment Sourcebook *657*
Billboard's on Tour *see* International Talent and Touring Directory *660*
Billboard's Talent in Action (US) *657*
Bilten za Hematologiju i Transfuziju (YU ISSN 0523-6150) *613*
BiN *see* Bibliography Newsletter *760*
Bindery Data Index (UK ISSN 0306-4077) *905*
Die Binnengewaesser (GW ISSN 0067-8643) *101*, *307*
Binsted's Directory of Food Trade Marks and Brand Names (UK ISSN 0067-8651) *404*
Ha-Binui Be-Yisrael *see* Israel. Central Bureau of Statistics. Construction in Israel *137*
Bio-Bibliografia Boliviana (BO) *89*
Bio-Information (FR ISSN 0067-866X) *101*
Biochemica & Biophysica Acta Library *see* B B A Library *110*
Biochemical Actions of Hormones (US) *611*
Biochemical Pathology *see* Biochemistry of Disease *110*
Biochemical Preparations (US ISSN 0067-8686) *905*
Biochemical Reviews (II) *110*
Biochemical Society Symposia (UK ISSN 0067-8694) *110*

BIOMEDICAL SCIENCES 1307

Biochemistry of Disease (US ISSN 0067-8678) *110*, *593*
Bioengineering Series (US) *101*
Biofeedback Society of America. Proceedings of the Annual Meeting (US ISSN 0094-0895) *619*, *735*
Biofizika Zhivoi Kletki (UR ISSN 0301-2425) *119*
Biogenic Amines in the Central Nervous System (US) *110*
Biogeographica (NE) *288*, *384*, *420*
Biogeographical Society of Japan. Bulletin (JA ISSN 0067-8716) *101*
Biograficke Studie (CS ISSN 0067-8724) *97*
Biographical Dictionaries and Related Works (US) *89*, *97*
Biographical Dictionaries and Related Works. Supplement (US) *99*
Biographical Dictionaries Master Index (US) *1*, *99*
Biographical Directory of Americans and Canadians of Croatian Descent (CN) *97*, *391*
Biographical Encyclopedia and Who's Who of the American Theatre (US) *858*
Biographical Encyclopedia of Pakistan (PK ISSN 0067-8732) *97*
Biographies de Personnalites Francaises Vivantes (FR ISSN 0067-8740) *99*
Biologia (PL) *101*
Biologia Pesquera (CL ISSN 0067-8767) *395*
Biological Council. Coordinating Committee for Symposia on Drug Action. Symposium Proceedings (US ISSN 0520-1802) *286*
Biological Journal of Okayama University/Okayama Daigaku Rigakubu Seibutsugaku Kiyo (JA ISSN 0520-1810) *101*
Biological Macromolecules Series (US ISSN 0067-8775) *119*
Biological Monographs of the Canary Islands *see* Monographiae Biologicae Canarienses *105*
Biological Research Reports from the University of Jyvaskyla (FI ISSN 0356-1062) *101*
Biological Society of Nevada. Occasional Papers and Memoirs (US ISSN 0084-7895) *101*
Biological Society of Washington. Proceedings (US ISSN 0006-324X) *101*, *113*, *127*
Biological Structure and Function (UK ISSN 0308-5384) *125*
Biologicheskie Nauki (UR) *101*
Biologie du Sol *see* Pedofauna *38*
Biologisch Jaarboek (BE) *101*
Biologische Bundesanstalt fuer Land- und Forstwirtschaft, Berlin-Dahlem. Mitteilungen (Biologische Bundesanstalt fuer Land- und Forstwirtschaft in Berlin-Dahlem) (GW ISSN 0067-5849) *13*, *407*
Biologiya Laboratornykh Zhivotnykh (UR) *612*
Biology and Environment (US) *101*
Biology Series (Seattle) (US) *101*
Biomassa (BL) *254*
Biomaterials, Medical Devices and Artificial Organs (US ISSN 0090-5488) *612*
Biomathematics (US ISSN 0067-8821) *101*, *584*
Biomechanics *see* Biomekhanika *701*
Biomedical Computing Series (US) *593*
Biomedical Engineering and Health Systems: A Wiley-Interscience Series(US) *593*, *750*
Biomedical Engineering Series of Monographs *see* Biomedical Engineering and Health Systems: A Wiley-Interscience Series *593*
Biomedical Materials Research Symposia (US) *101*, *593*
Biomedical Sciences Instrumentation (US ISSN 0067-8856) *496*, *593*

Biomekhanika/Biomechanics (BU) 112, 701
Biomembranes (US ISSN 0067-8864) 119
Biometeorology; Proceedings (NE ISSN 0067-8902) 101, 631
Biophysical Society. Abstracts (US ISSN 0067-8910) 112
Biophysical Society. Symposium Proceedings see Biophysical Society. Abstracts 112
Biopsy Interpretation Series (US) 612
Biosis: List of Serials see Serial Sources for the Biosis Data Base 110
BIOSIS Search Guide (US) 1, 110
Biosphere Bulletin (SI) 101
Biosynthesis (UK ISSN 0301-0708) 110, 254
Biotechnology & Bioengineering Symposia (US ISSN 0572-6565) 101, 366
Bird Behaviour (AT ISSN 0156-1383) 124, 735
Bird Control Seminar. Proceedings (US ISSN 0067-8945) 124
Bird Research (UK) 124
Birdwatcher's Yearbook (UK ISSN 0144-364X) 124, 275
Birmingham & Warwickshire Archaeological Society. Transactions (UK ISSN 0140-4202) 58
Birth Defects Institute. Symposia (US) 593
Birth Defects Original Article Series (US ISSN 0547-6844) 593
Birth of Modern Britain Series (UK) 450
Birthstone (US) 73, 578
Bishops Mitre (CN) 315
Bit Information (YU) 267
Bithell Series of Dissertations see University of London. Institute of Germanic Studies. Bithell Series of Dissertations 576
Bittker and Eustice's Federal Income Taxation of Corporations and Shareholders (Supplement) (US) 227
Bittker Forms Book (Supplement) (US) 227
Bituminous Coal Data see Coal Data 642
Bituminous Coal Facts see Coal Facts 642
Biuletyn Fonograficzny/Bulletin Phonographique (PL ISSN 0067-8996) 541
Biuletyn Geologiczny (PL ISSN 0067-9003) 292
Biuletyn Peryglacjalny (PL ISSN 0067-9038) 303
Biuletyn Warzywniczy (PL) 414
Bixiana (US) 657
Black Book Vehicle Identification Guide (CN ISSN 0316-4896) 870
Black Communicators see Black Press Periodical Directory 394
Black Economic Research Center. Occasional Paper (US) 142, 391
Black Experience in Children's Books (US ISSN 0067-9070) 257
Black Forum (US) 391, 556
Black Jack (US) 391, 560
Black List (US) 1, 394
Black Literature and Arts Congress see B L A C 391
Black Pages Pamphlet Series (US) 391
Black Photographers Annual (US ISSN 0090-7197) 693
Black Press Information Handbook (US ISSN 0147-2828) 504
Black Press Periodical Directory (US) 394
Black Resources Information Coordinating Services, Inc. Bracs see B R I C S Bracs 391
Black Review (SA) 391
Black Studies Series (US) 391
Blackberry (US) 578
Blackface Sheep Breeders' Association Journal (UK) 43
Black's Guide to the Office Space Market (US) 761
Blacks in American Journalism Series (US) 391, 504
Blacks in the New World (US) 391
Blaetter fuer Wuerttembergische Kirchengeschichte (GW) 450, 764
Blakes Holidays Afloat (UK) 826, 883

Blakes International Holidays Afloat see Blakes Holidays Afloat 883
Blantyre Water Board. Annual Report and Statement of Accounts (MW ISSN 0084-7925) 895
Blick hinter die Fassade (GW ISSN 0067-9178) 804
Blindness (US ISSN 0067-9186) 804
Bliss Classification Bulletin (UK ISSN 0520-2795) 527
Bloodstock Breeders' Review (UK ISSN 0067-9224) 43
Blooming Grove Courier (US) 466
Bloomsbury Geographer (UK ISSN 0067-9232) 420
Blue Book: Leaders of the English-Speaking World (UK ISSN 0067-9240) 97
Blue Book of Canadian Business (CN ISSN 0381-7245) 184
Blue Book of College Athletics (US) 819
Blue Book of Food Store Operators & Wholesalers (CN ISSN 0316-9537) 406, 834
Blue Book of Fur Farming (US) 524
Blue Book of Junior College Athletics (US ISSN 0520-2973) 819
Blue Book of Major Home Builders (US ISSN 0195-8461) 134
Blue Book of Occupational Education see Occupational Education 339
Blue Book of Optometrists (US ISSN 0067-9283) 615
Blue-Book of S.A. Business (SA) 142
Blue Book, Official Inboard/Outdrive Boat Trade-in Guide (US ISSN 0520-2949) 827
Blue Chips (US) 823
Blue Directory for International Trade see Annuaire Bleu 192
Blue Guitar (IT) 560
Blue Mountain Press Chapbook (US) 578
Blue Print for Health (US) 751
Blue Sky (US) 267
Blues (BE) 657
Blues Research (US) 657
Bluewater Circle Drives (CN) 883
Bluewater Vacation Guide (CN) 883
Boat Equipment Buyers' Guide (UK ISSN 0306-3593) 235, 827
Boat Owners Buyers Guide see Yachting's Boat Buyers Guide 827
Boat World (UK ISSN 0067-933X) 827
Boatbuilders' & Chandlers' Directory of Suppliers see Boat Equipment Buyers' Guide 827
Boating Guide (US ISSN 0067-9399) 827
Boating Industry Association Certification Handbook see B I A Certification Handbook 826
Boating Industry Associations Engineering Manual of Recommended Practices see B I A Certification Handbook 826
Boating Industry Marine Buyers Guide (US) 827
Boating Registration Statistics (US ISSN 0163-7207) 823
Bob Zwirz' Fishing Annual (US ISSN 0363-5538) 828
Bobbs-Merrill Political Science Annual (US) 708
Bochumer Materialen zur Entwicklungsforschung und Entwicklungspolitik (GW ISSN 0170-1916) 199, 720
Bochumer Schriften zur Entwicklungsforschung und Entwicklungspolitik (GW ISSN 0572-6654) 199, 720
Bodendenkmalpflege in Mecklenburg (GE ISSN 0067-9461) 593
Bodleian Library Record (UK ISSN 0067-9488) 527
Body Fashions Directory and Source of Supply see Body Fashions-Intimate Apparel Directory 261
Body Fashions-Intimate Apparel Directory (US ISSN 0362-2452) 261
Boehlau Philosophica (GW) 687
Boerhaave Series for Postgraduate Medical Education (NE) 593
Boersen- und Wirtschaftshandbuch (GW ISSN 0067-9496) 142, 202

Boethius (GW ISSN 0523-8226) 780
Bogazici Universitesi Dergisi: Ey Oneticilik, Ekonomi, ve Sosyal Bilimler see Bogazici University Journal: Management, Economic and Social Sciences 796
Bogazici University Journal: Engineering (TU) 366
Bogazici University Journal: Management, Economic and Social Sciences/Bogazici Universitesi Dergisi: Ey Oneticilik, Ekonomi, ve Sosyal Bilimler (TU) 796
Bogazici University Journal: Sciences (TU) 780
Bogazici University Journal: Social Sciences see Bogazici University Journal: Management, Economic and Social Sciences 796
Bol og By (DK ISSN 0067-9550) 13, 450
Boletim Alagoano de Folclore (BL) 401
Boletim Climatologico (BL ISSN 0067-9585) 631
Boletim de Ciencias do Mar (BL ISSN 0067-9593) 101
Boletim de Engenharia de Producao (BL ISSN 0067-9607) 366
Boletim de Industria Animal (BL ISSN 0067-9615) 43
Boletim de Linguistica (BL) 541
Boletim de Zoologia (BL) 101
Boletim de Zoologia e Biologia Marinha. Nova Serie see Boletim de Zoologia 101
Boletim do Comercio Exterior da Bahia/Bahia's Foreign Trade Bulletin (BL) 193
Boletim Microssismico (PO) 303
Boletim Paranaense de Geociencias (BL ISSN 0067-964X) 292
Boletim Paranaense de Geografia see Boletim Paranaense de Geociencias 292
Boletim Paulista de Geografia (BL ISSN 0006-6079) 420
Boletim Sismico (PO ISSN 0006-6109) 303
Boletin de Estudios Medicos y Biologicos (MX ISSN 0067-9666) 101, 593
Boletin de Estudios Oaxaquenos/Bulletin of Oaxaca Studies (MX ISSN 0006-6257) 48
Boletin de Filologia (CL ISSN 0067-9674) 541
Boletin de Geologia (VE ISSN 0006-6281) 292
Boletin de Informacion Comercial (UY) 193
Boletin de Informacion Estadistica Sobre Cafe (CK ISSN 0084-7941) 85
Boletin de la S A D E (Sociedad Argentina de Escritores) (AG) 560
Boletin de la Sociedad Cientifica del Paraguay y del Museo Etnografico (PY ISSN 0560-4168) 48
Boletin de Patologia Vegetal y Entomologia Agricola see Spain. Instituto Nacional de Investigaciones Agrarias. Anales. Serie: Proteccion Vegetal 39
Boletin de Pequena Jurisprudencia (SP) 509
Boletin Epidemiologico Anual (MX) 751
Boletin Estadistico de Cuba see Anuario Estadistico de Cuba 832
Boletin Genetico (AG ISSN 0067-9720) 122
Boletin Hemerografico see Sintesis Bibliografica 164
Boletin Hidrologico (CR ISSN 0067-9747) 307
Boletin Informativo - CEdOclA (Centro Regional Latinoamericano de Estudios para la Conservacion y Restauracion de Bienes Culturales) (MX) 275
Boletin Ingenieria Comercial (CL) 366
Boletin Interamericano de Archivos (AG) 466, 527
Boletin de Contabilidad (AG) 167

Boletin para Bibliotecas Agricolas (CR) 905
Boletin Trimestral de Informacion Economica (EC) 142
Boletin Uruguayo de Sociologia (UY ISSN 0006-6508) 812
Bolivia. Instituto Nacional de Estadistica. Anuario de Comercio Exterior (BO) 194, 834
Bolivia. Instituto Nacional de Estadistica. Anuario de Estadisticas Industriales (BO) 221, 834
Bolivia. Instituto Nacional de Estadistica. Estadisticas Regionales Departamentales (BO) 740, 834
Bolivia. Servicio Geologico. Boletin (BO ISSN 0067-9828) 288
Bolivia. Servicio Geologico. Circulare (BO ISSN 0067-9836) 288
Bolivia. Servicio Geologico. Informe (BO ISSN 0067-9844) 288
Bolivia. Servicio Geologico. Serie Mineralogica. Contribucione (BO ISSN 0067-9852) 288, 641
Bolivia. Servicio Nacional de Caminos. Informe Anual (BO) 874
Bolivia. Superintendencia Nacional de Seguros y Reaseguros. Coleccion Estudios (BO) 498
Bolivia: Guia Eclesiastica (BO) 774
Bolivia Information Handbook (UK ISSN 0067-981X) 466
Bollettino del Repertorio e dell'Atlante Demologico Sardo see B R A D S 449
Bollettino Meteorologico Agrario see Osservazioni di Meteorologia Agraria della Puglia e Basilicata 634
Bolsa (AG) 178
Bolsa de Barcelona. Estadisticas see Bolsa de Barcelona. Memoria 202
Bolsa de Barcelona. Memoria (SP) 202
Bolsa de Cereales. Revista Institucional. Numero Estadistico (AG ISSN 0084-7968) 13
Bolsa de Comercio de Buenos Aires. Boletin see Bolsa 178
Bolsa de Comercio de Rosario. Boletin Informativo (AG) 905
Bolsa de Comercio de Rosario. Revista (AG ISSN 0006-6931) 178
Bolsa de Valores de Lima. Memoria (PE) 202
Bolsa de Valores de Montevideo. Estudios Estadisticos (UY) 171
Bolsa de Valores de Quito. Informes y Memoria Anual (EC) 202
Bolsa de Valores de Sao Paulo. Relatorio (BL) 202
Bolsa de Valores de Sao Paulo. Revista (BL ISSN 0034-7558) 202
Bolsa de Valores do Rio de Janeiro. Resumo Anual (BL ISSN 0557-0506) 202
Bolsilibros (UY ISSN 0067-9909) 466, 560
Bolton Landing Conference. Proceedings (US) 366
Bomb Summary see U.S. Federal Bureau of Investigation. Bomb Summary 284
Bombay Labour Journal (II ISSN 0067-9917) 206
Bombay Technologist (II ISSN 0067-9925) 245, 850
Bond Record (CN ISSN 0317-607X) 202
Bonner Akademische Reden (GW) 687
Bonner Arbeiten zur Deutschen Literatur (GW ISSN 0068-001X) 560
Bonner Beitraege zur Bibliotheks- und Buecherkunde (GW ISSN 0068-0028) 527
Bonner Beitraege zur Kunstwissenschaft (GW ISSN 0068-0036) 73
Bonner Beitraege zur Soziologie (GW ISSN 0068-0044) 812
Bonner Geographische Abhandlungen (GW ISSN 0373-0468) 420
Bonner Geschichtsblaetter (GW ISSN 0068-0052) 450
Bonner Meteorologische Abhandlungen (GW ISSN 0006-7156) 631
Bonner Orientalistische Studien (GW ISSN 0340-6377) 905
Bonner Zoologische Monographien (GW ISSN 0302-671X) 127

Bonny Moor Hen (UK ISSN 0142-7660) *124*
Book Auction Records (UK ISSN 0068-0095) *757*
Book Collectors' Handbook of Values (US) *757*
Book Dealers' and Collectors' Year-Book and Diary (UK ISSN 0142-9523) *757*
Book Dealers in North America (UK ISSN 0068-0109) *757*
Book Industry Study Group. Research Report *see* Book Industry Trends *757*
Book Industry Trends (US ISSN 0160-970X) *757*
Book of Bantams (US ISSN 0068-0117) *44*
Book of Canadian Prose (CN) *578*
Book of the States (US ISSN 0068-0125) *740*
Book on the World Series (US) *823*
Book Publishers in Canada *see* Book Trade in Canada *757*
Book Review Index: Annual Clothbound Cumulations (US ISSN 0524-0581) *1, 577*
Book Review Index to Social Science Periodicals (US) *1, 803*
Book Trade in Canada/Industrie du Livre au Canada (CN ISSN 0700-5296) *757*
Bookdealers in India, Pakistan and Sri Lanka (UK ISSN 0143-0270) *757*
Bookhunter's Guide to the Northeast (US) *905*
Bookhunter's Guide to the West and Southwest (US) *757*
Booklet (US) *478*
Bookman's Guide to Americana (US ISSN 0068-0133) *757*
Bookman's Price Index (US ISSN 0068-0141) *757*
Bookmark (US ISSN 0006-7393) *527*
Bookmark (US ISSN 0006-7407) *527*
Bookmark (AT ISSN 0310-0391) *527, 757*
Books About Malaysia *see* Books about Singapore *437*
Books About Negro Life for Children *see* Black Experience in Children's Books *257*
Books about Singapore (SI ISSN 0068-0176) *437*
Books and Libraries at the University of Kansas (US ISSN 0006-7458) *527, 757*
Books at Brown (US ISSN 0147-0787) *560*
Books Cataloged by Tehran Book Processing Centre (IR) *89*
Books for Kansas Schools (US ISSN 0363-6518) *315*
Books for Secondary School Libraries (US ISSN 0068-0184) *315, 527*
Books for the Teen Age (US ISSN 0068-0192) *527*
Books for Young Explorers Series (US) *257, 420*
Books from Israel (IS) *89, 760*
Books from Pakistan (PK ISSN 0068-0206) *89*
Books in Library and Information Science (US) *527*
Books in Print (US ISSN 0068-0214) *89*
Books in Series in the United States (US ISSN 0000-0515) *89*
Books in Soils and the Environment (US ISSN 0081-1890) *33*
Booksellers Association of Great Britain and Ireland. List of Members (UK ISSN 0068-0249) *757*
Booksellers Association of Great Britain and Ireland. Trade Reference Book (UK ISSN 0068-0257) *757*
Bor'ba s Gazom v Ugol'nykh Shakhtakh(UR) *641*
Bord Iascaigh Mhara. Tuarascail Agus Cuntaisi/Irish Sea Fisheries Board. Annual Report (IE ISSN 0068-0265) *395*
Border Leicester Flock Book (UK) *44*
Border States (US ISSN 0092-4571) *466*
Boreal Institute, Edmonton. Annual Report *see* Boreal Institute, Edmonton. Report of Activities *467*

Boreal Institute, Edmonton. Miscellaneous Publications (CN ISSN 0068-029X) *490*
Boreal Institute, Edmonton. Occasional Publications (CN ISSN 0068-0303) *467*
Boreal Institute, Edmonton. Report of Activities (CN ISSN 0316-7828) *467*
Borealis (CN ISSN 0706-9014) *560*
Borestone Mountain Poetry Awards (US ISSN 0067-6276) *905*
Bornholmske Samlinger (DK ISSN 0084-7976) *450*
Borough of Twickenham Local History Society. Papers (UK ISSN 0084-7984) *450*
Borzoi Books on Latin America (US ISSN 0520-6294) *467*
Borzoi Series in United States Constitutional History (US) *467*
Boston Bruins Official Yearbook (US ISSN 0361-6398) *819*
Boston Children's Medical Center. Publications for Parents (US) *256, 617*
Boston College International and Comparative Law Journal (US ISSN 0161-2832) *522*
Boston Marathon (US) *819*
Boston Museum Bulletin *see* M F A Bulletin *653*
Boston Museum of Fine Arts. Museum Year. Annual Reports (US) *73*
Boston Museum of Fine Arts Bulletin *see* M F A Bulletin *653*
Boston Studies in the Philosophy of Science (NE ISSN 0068-0346) *780*
Boston University Papers on Africa (US) *439*
Bostonian Society. Proceedings. (US) *467*
Bostwick Paper (US ISSN 0068-0354) *142*
Botanica Gothoburgensia (SW ISSN 0068-0370) *113*
Botanical Monographs (US) *113*
Botanical Museum Leaflets (US ISSN 0006-8098) *113*
Botanical Society of America. Directory(US) *113*
Botanical Society of America. Miscellaneous Publications *see* Careers in Botany *114*
Botanical Society of America. Yearbook *see* Botanical Society of America. Directory *113*
Botanical Society of Edinburgh. Transactions and Proceedings *see* Botanical Society of Edinburgh Transactions *113*
Botanical Society of Edinburgh Transactions (UK) *113*
Botanical Society of the British Isles Abstracts *see* B S B I Abstracts *109*
Botanical Survey of India. Occasional Publications (II) *113*
Botanical Survey of South Africa. Memoirs (SA) *113*
Botanisch Jaarboek *see* Biologisch Jaarboek *101*
Botaniste *see* Revue de Cytologie et de Biologie Vegetales-la Botaniste *117*
Botany as a Profession *see* Careers in Botany *114*
Botany Bay Project. Working Paper (AT) *384*
Both Sides Now (US ISSN 0006-8233) *556*
Bothalia (SA ISSN 0006-8241) *113*
Botschaft des Alten Testaments (GW ISSN 0068-0443) *764*
Botswana. Annual Statements of Accounts (BS ISSN 0068-0451) *227*
Botswana. Central Statistical Office. Statistical Newsletter *see* Botswana. Central Statistics Office. Statistical Bulletin *834*
Botswana. Central Statistical Office. Employment Survey (BS) *153*
Botswana. Central Statistics Office. Statistical Bulletin (BS) *834*
Botswana. Central Statistics Office. Tourist Statistics (BS) *893*
Botswana. Commissioner of the Police. Annual Report (BS ISSN 0068-046X) *280*

Botswana. Department of Health. Report *see* Botswana. Ministry of Health. Report *751*
Botswana. Department of Income Tax. Annual Report (BS) *227*
Botswana. Estimates of Revenue and Expenditure (BS ISSN 0524-1448) *227*
Botswana. Forest Department. Report (BS ISSN 0068-0486) *407*
Botswana. Geological Survey and Mines Department. Annual Reports (BS) *292*
Botswana. Ministry of Agriculture. Annual Report (BS ISSN 0068-0478) *13*
Botswana. Ministry of Agriculture. Division of Co-Operative Development. Annual Report (BS) *180*
Botswana. Ministry of Health. Report (BS) *751*
Botswana. National Archives. Report on the National Archives (BS) *527*
Botswana. National Library Service. Report (BS) *527*
Botswana Development Corporation. Annual Report (BS) *221*
Botswana Notes and Records (BS ISSN 0525-5090) *439*
Bottin Administratif (FR) *740*
Bottin Auto-Cycle-Moto (FR) *235, 826, 870*
Bottin de l'Auto et du Cycle *see* Bottin Auto-Cycle-Moto *870*
Bottin International (FR ISSN 0068-0494) *194*
Bottin Mondain (FR) *97*
Bottin Professions (FR) *235*
Bottlers Year Book (UK ISSN 0068-0508) *85*
Boundary Historical Society. Report (CN ISSN 0068-0524) *467*
Bourland Bulletin (US) *417*
Bourne Society Local History Records (UK ISSN 0520-6790) *450*
Bouscueil (CN ISSN 0382-5604) *905*
Boussole des Chiffres *see* Germany (Federal Republic, 1949-) Statistisches Bundesamt. Zahlenkompass *840*
Bouteille a la Mer (FR) *560*
Boutique (GE ISSN 0068-0532) *262*
Bouvier Disputanda (GW) *687*
Bowdoin College. Museum of Art. Occasional Papers (US ISSN 0084-7992) *652*
Bowker Annual (US ISSN 0068-0540) *527, 757*
Bowling and Billiard Buyers Guide (US ISSN 0068-0559) *823*
Bowling Buyers Guide *see* Bowling and Billiard Buyers Guide *823*
Bowling-Fencing Guide *see* N A G W S Guide. Bowling-Golf *824*
Bowling Guide (US ISSN 0068-0567) *823*
Boxing Guide (US) *819*
Boy Scouts World Bureau. Biennial Report *see* World Scout Bureau. Biennial Report *257*
Boyce Thompson Institute for Plant Research. Annual Report (US) *113*
Boys Baseball. Blue Book *see* Pony Baseball. Blue Book *825*
Boys' Brigade, London. Annual Report (UK ISSN 0068-0605) *257*
Boys Gymnastics Rules (US) *819*
Bracara Augusta (PO ISSN 0006-8640) *58, 450*
Braddock's Federal-State-Local Government Directory (US ISSN 0363-6275) *740*
Bradea (BL ISSN 0084-800X) *114*
Bradford's Directory of Marketing Research Agencies and Management Consultants in the United States and the World (US ISSN 0068-063X) *217*
Bradwell Abbey Field Centre for the Study of Archaeology, Natural History & Environmental Studies. Occasional Papers (UK ISSN 0306-8838) *58, 384, 780*
Brahmavidya (II ISSN 0001-902X) *669, 771*
Brahms-Gesellschaft Hamburg. Jahresgabe. (GW) *657*

BRAZIL. DEPARTAMENTO   1309

Braille Scores Catalog - Choral *see* Music & Musicians: Braille Scores Catalog - Choral *133*
Braille Scores Catalog - Organ *see* Music & Musicians: Braille Scores Catalog - Organ *133*
Braille Scores Catalog - Piano *see* Music & Musicians: Braille Scores Catalog - Piano *133*
Braille Scores Catalog - Voice *see* Music & Musicians: Braille Scores Catalog - Voice *133*
Brain Information Service-Brain Research Institute Conference Report *see* B I S Conference Report *619*
Brainchild (US) *578*
Brand Book (US) *827*
Brandeis University. Society of Bibliophiles. Publications (US ISSN 0068-0672) *757*
Brands and Alloys (UK ISSN 0308-7778) *627*
Brasier (CN ISSN 0381-596X) *262, 774*
Brasil(Year) (BL ISSN 0100-4271) *184*
Brasil Cinema (BL) *905*
Brasil Madeira (BL) *407, 412*
Brasilia. Departamento de Estradas de Rodagem do Distrito Federal. Diretoria Geral. Relatoria Anual (BL) *874*
Brasilia. Fundacao do Servico Social do Distrito Federal. Relatorio Anual das Atividades (BL) *804*
Brass Players' Guide (US) *657*
Brass Research Series (US ISSN 0363-454X) *657*
Brassey's Annual - the Armed Forces Year-Book *see* R. U. S. I. and Brassey's Defence Yearbook *640*
Bratislava-Studia (CS) *58*
Brauereien und Maelzereien in Europa (GW ISSN 0068-0710) *85*
Braunschweiger Geographische Studien (GW ISSN 0524-2444) *420*
Braunschweigische Wissenschaftliche Gesellschaft. Abhandlungen (GW) *780*
Braunschweigisches Jahrbuch (GW ISSN 0068-0745) *450*
Brazil. Arquivo Nacional. Serie de Publicacoes (BL) *467*
Brazil. Biblioteca Nacional. Anais (BL ISSN 0100-1922) *527*
Brazil. Centro de Informacoes Economico-Fiscais. Imposto sobre Produtos Industrializados; Arrecadacao Setorial *see* Brazil. Coordenacao do Sistema de Informacoes Economico-Fiscais. Imposto sobre Produtos Industrializados; Arrecadacao Setorial *227*
Brazil. Comissao de Financiamento da Producao. Anuario Estatistico (BL) *153, 834*
Brazil. Conselho Federal de Farmacia. Relatorio (BL) *683*
Brazil. Conselho Nacional de Desenvolvimento Cientifico e Tecnologico. Boletim (BL) *780, 850*
Brazil. Conselho Nacional de Desenvolvimento Cientifico e Tecnologico. Programa do Tropica Semi-Arido(Publicacion) (BL) *780*
Brazil. Conselho Nacional de Desenvolvimento Cientifico e Tecnologico. Relatorio de Atividades(BL) *780*
Brazil. Conselho Nacional de Desenvolvimento de Pecuaria. Mercado Atacadista de Gado e Carne: Analise da Variacao dos Precos (BL) *44*
Brazil. Coordenacao de Assistencia Medica e Hospitalar. Cadastro Hospitalar Brasileiro (BL) *480*
Brazil. Coordenacao do Sistema de Informacoes Economico-Fiscais. Imposto sobre Produtos Industrializados; Arrecadacao Setorial(BL) *227*
Brazil. Departamento de Assuntos Universitarios. Coordenacao de Avaliacao e Controle. Atividades das Instituicoes Federais de Ensino Superior (BL) *334*

Brazil. Departamento de Assuntos Universitarios. Coordenacao de Avaliiacao e Controle. Catalogo Geral das Instituicoes de Ensino Superior (BL) *334*
Brazil. Departamento Nacional da Producao Mineral. Avulso (BL) *642*
Brazil. Departamento Nacional da Producao Mineral. Boletim (BL) *642*
Brazil. Departamento Nacional de Obras Contras as Secas. Relatorio (BL) *740*
Brazil. Departamento Nacional de Pesquisa Agropecuaria. Divisao de Pesquisa Pedologica. Boletim Tecnico *see* Brazil. Servico Nacional de Levantamento e Conservacao de Solos. Boletim Tecnico *33*
Brazil. Diretoria do Patrimonio Historico e Artistico Nacional. Revista (BL ISSN 0068-0788) *73, 467*
Brazil. Escritorio de Estatistica. Pecuaria, Avicultura, Apicultura, Sericicultura (BL) *24*
Brazil. Fundacao Instituto Brasileiro de Geografia e Estatistica. Departamento de Estatisticas Industriais, Comerciais e de Servicos. Comercio Interestadual, Esportacao por Vias Internas (BL) *153*
Brazil. Fundacao Instituto Brasileiro de Geografia e Estatistica. Departamento de Estatisticas Industriais, Comerciais e de Servicos. Empresas de Transporte Rodoviario (BL) *834, 870*
Brazil. Inspetoria-Geral de Financas. Balancos Gerais da Uniao (BL) *740*
Brazil. Instituto Brasileiro de Desenvolvimento Florestal. Projeto de Desenvolvimento e Pesquisa Florestal. Comunicacao Tecnica (BL) *905*
Brazil. Instituto Brasileiro de Desenvolvimento Florestal.Projeto de Desenvolvimento e Pesquisa Florestal. Serie Divulgacao (BL) *905*
Brazil. Instituto Brasileiro de Geografia e Estatistica. Veiculos Licenciados (BL) *834*
Brazil. Instituto do Acucar e do Alcool. Conselho Deliberativo. Coletanea de Resolucoes *see* Brazil. Instituto do Acucar e do Alcool. Conselho Deliberativo. Coletanea de Resolucoes (e) Presidencia. Coletanea de Atos *33*
Brazil. Instituto do Acucar e do Alcool. Conselho Deliberativo. Coletanea de Resolucoes (e) Presidencia. Coletanea de Atos (BL) *33, 85, 509*
Brazil. Instituto do Acucar e do Alcool. Presidencia. Coletanea de Actas *see* Brazil. Instituto do Acucar e do Alcool. Conselho Deliberativo. Coletanea de Resolucoes (e) Presidencia. Coletanea de Atos *33*
Brazil. Instituto Nacional de Colonizacao e Reforma Agraria. Acao Associativista (BL) *13*
Brazil. Instituto Nacional de Previdencia Social. Balanco Geral (BL) *498*
Brazil. Instituto Nacional do Livro. Relatorio de Atividades (BL) *527*
Brazil. Ministerio da Agricultura Departamento de Assistencia ao Cooperativismo Serie Contabilidade (BL) *13*
Brazil. Ministerio da Agricultura Departamento de Assistenica ao Cooperativismo. Serie Integracao (BL) *13*
Brazil. Ministerio da Agricultura. Escritorio de Estatistica. Cadastro das Empresas Produtoras de Oleos, Gorduras Vegetais e Sabprodutos (BL) *24*
Brazil. Ministerio da Agricultura. Escritorio de Estatistica. Oleos e Gorduras Vegetais. (BL) *13*
Brazil. Ministerio da Agricultura. Subsecretaria de Planejamento e Orcamento. Producao e Abastecimento, Perspectivas e Proposicoes: Sintese (BL) *13*

Brazil. Ministerio da Educacao e Cultura. Servico de Estatistica da Educacao e Cultura (BL) *326*
Brazil. Ministerio da Educacao e Cultura. Servico de Estatistica da Educacao e Cultura. Sinopse Estatistica do Ensino Superior (BL) *326*
Brazil. Ministerio das Relacoes Exteriores. Biblioteca. Aquisicoes Bibliograficas (BL) *527*
Brazil. Ministerio das Relacoes Exteriores. Biblioteca. Bibliografia Anual *see* Brazil. Ministerio das Relacoes Exteriores. Biblioteca. Aquisicoes Bibliograficas *527*
Brazil. Ministerio do Interior. Relatorio de Atividades (BL) *740*
Brazil. Ministerio do Interior. Relatorio Sintetico, Andamento do Programa de Irrigacao do Nordeste (BL) *895*
Brazil. Ministerio do Trabalho e Previdencia Social. Centro de Documentacao e Informatica. Mercado de Trabalho: Flutuacao (BL) *206*
Brazil. Secretaria da Receita Federal. Centro de Informacoes Economico-Fiscais. Rendas Aduaneiras (BL) *227*
Brazil. Secretaria de Planejamento. Instituto de Planejamento Economico e Social. Serie Documentos (BL) *184*
Brazil. Servico de Estatistica da Educacao e Cultura. Sinopse Estatistica do Ensino Primario (BL) *326*
Brazil. Servico de Piscicultura. Publicacao (BL ISSN 0068-0850) *395*
Brazil. Servico Nacional de Levantamento e Conservacao de Solos. Boletim Tecnico (BL ISSN 0100-123X) *33*
Brazil. Servico Social do Comercio. Administracao Regional do Estado de Sao Paulo. Relatoria Annual (BL) *804*
Brazil. Servico Social do Comercio. Anuario Estatistico (BL) *834*
Brazil. Servico Social do Comercio. Colecao Bibliografica (BL) *89*
Brazil. Superintendencia da Borracha. Annuario Estatistico. Mercado Estrangeiro (BL ISSN 0572-5534) *778*
Brazil. Superintendencia do Desenvolvimento da Amazonia. S U D A M Documenta (BL ISSN 0045-2742) *221*
Brazil. Superintendencia do Desenvolvimento do Nordeste. Departamento de Agricultura e Abastecimento. Programa de Trabalho para a Agricultura Nordestina (BL) *27*
Brazil. Superintendencia do Desenvolvimento do Nordeste. Departamento de Recursos Naturais. Boletim de Recursos Naturais (BL) *275*
Brazil. Superintendencia do Desenvolvimento do Nordeste. Departamento de Servicos Basicos da Sudene. Estatistica de Trafego No Nordeste (BL) *865*
Brazil. Superintendencia do Desenvolvimento do Nordeste. Relatorio Anual (BL) *184*
Brazil. Superintendencia do Desenvolvimento do Nordeste. SUDENE Plano de Acao (BL) *483*
Brazil. Supremo Tribunal Federal. Indices da Legislacao Federal (BL) *510*
Brazil. Supremo Tribunal Federal. Jurisicvel do S.T.F. (BL) *510*
Brazil. Supremo Tribunal Federal. Relatorio dos Trabalhos Realizados (BL) *510*
Brazil Development Series/Series Desenvolvimento Brasileiro (BL) *221*
Brazil, Land of the Present (UK) *796*
Brazilian Economic Studies (BL) *142*
Brazilian Energy Statistics *see* Estatistica Brasileira de Energia *364*

Brazilian Index Yearbook *see* Indice do Brasil *186*
Braziller Series of Poetry (US) *578*
Breathing (CN ISSN 0707-7319) *556*
Brecht Heute *see* Brecht-Jahrbuch *556*
Brecht-Jahrbuch (GW) *556, 560*
Breifne (IE ISSN 0068-0877) *58, 450*
Bremer Afrika-Archiv *see* Uebersee-Museum, Bremen. Veroeffentlichungen. Reihe F: Bremer Afrika-Archiv *441*
Bremer Archaeologische Blaetter (GW ISSN 0068-0907) *58*
Bremer Schulblatt (GW ISSN 0006-9582) *343*
Bremer Suedpazifik-Archiv *see* Uebersee-Museum Bremen. Veroeffentlichungen. Reihe G: Bremer Suedpazifik-Archiv *447*
Bremisches Jahrbuch (GW ISSN 0341-9622) *450*
Brenesia (CR) *780*
Brennstoffstatistik der Waermekraftwerke fuer die Oeffentliche Elektrizitaetsversorgung in Oesterreich (AU ISSN 0520-9048) *352, 740*
Breviora (US ISSN 0006-9698) *127*
Brewers Digest Annual Buyers Guide and Brewery Directory (US) *85, 235*
Brewery Manual *see* Brewery Manual and Who's Who in British Brewing *86*
Brewery Manual and Who's Who in British Brewing (UK ISSN 0305-8123) *86*
Brewing and Malting Barley Research Institute. Annual Report (CN ISSN 0068-094X) *86*
Bricker's International Directory of University-Sponsored Executive Development Programs (US ISSN 0361-1108) *214, 330*
Bridge Bidding Guide (US) *819*
Bridge Digest *see* Canadian Bridge Digest *819*
Brigham Young University. Center for Thermochemical Studies. Contributions (US ISSN 0572-6921) *254*
Brigham Young University. College of Engineering Sciences and Technology. Annual Engineering Symposium. Abstracts (US ISSN 0068-1008) *366*
Bright Lights (US ISSN 0147-4049) *649*
Brightonian (UK ISSN 0007-0157) *263*
Bristol and Gloucestershire Archaeological Society, Bristol, England. Transactions (UK ISSN 0068-1032) *58, 450*
Bristol and West of England Engineering Manufacturers Association Ltd. Engineering Directory *see* B E M A Engineering Directory *366*
Bristol Folk News (UK) *285, 657*
Bristol Industrial Archaeological Society Journal *see* B I A S Journal *366*
Bristol Naturalists' Society. Proceedings(UK ISSN 0068-1040) *780*
Bristow's Book of Motor Cruisers *see* Bristow's Book of Yachts *827*
Bristow's Book of Sailing Cruisers *see* Bristow's Book of Yachts *827*
Bristow's Book of Yachts (UK ISSN 0309-1252) *827*
Britain: An Official Handbook (UK ISSN 0068-1075) *450*
Britain in the World Today (US ISSN 0068-1105) *451*
Britain Welcomes Coaches (UK) *883*
Britain's Heritage *see* Stately Homes, Museums, Castles and Gardens *891*
Britain's Top 1000 Private Companies (UK) *235*
Britannia (UK ISSN 0068-113X) *451*
Britannica Atlas (US ISSN 0068-1148) *420*
Britannica Book of the Year (US ISSN 0068-1156) *360*
Britannica Review of Foreign Language Education *see* A C T F L Annual Review of Foreign Language Education *347*

Britannica Yearbook of Science and the Future *see* Yearbook of Science and the Future *794*
Britischer Export *see* British Exports *194*
British Aid Statistics; Statistics of Economic Aid to Developing Countries (UK ISSN 0068-1210) *153*
British Alternative Theatre Directory (UK ISSN 0142-5218) *235, 858*
British Amateur Journalist (UK ISSN 0007-0238) *504*
British Antarctic Survey. Annual Report (UK) *780*
British Antarctic Survey. Scientific Reports (UK) *780*
British Archaeological Association. Conference Transactions (UK) *58, 68, 73*
British Archaeological Association. Journal (UK ISSN 0068-1288) *58*
British Art & Antiques Yearbook (UK) *476*
British Association of Hotel Representatives International Hotel Directory *see* B A H R E P International Hotel Directory *883*
British Association of Industrial Editors. B A I E Directory of Members *see* B. A. I. E. Membership Directory *757*
British Association of Industrial Editors Membership Directory *see* B. A. I. E. Membership Directory *757*
British Association of Orientalists. Bulletin (UK) *669*
British Association of Social Workers. Annual Report (UK) *804*
British Astronomical Association. Handbook (UK ISSN 0068-130X) *81*
British Astronomical Association. Observer's Handbook *see* British Astronomical Association. Handbook *81*
British Athletics (UK ISSN 0068-1326) *819*
British Authors Series (UK ISSN 0068-1334) *560*
British Baking Industries Research Association. Annual Report *see* Flour Milling and Baking Research Association. Annual Report and Accounts *404*
British Book Design & Production (UK ISSN 0302-2846) *758*
British Book Production *see* British Book Design & Production *758*
British Books in Print (UK ISSN 0068-1350) *89*
British Broadcasting Corporation. B B C Engineering (UK ISSN 0005-2817) *267*
British Broadcasting Corporation. B B C Handbook (UK ISSN 0068-1377) *267*
British Broadcasting Corporation. Engineering Division. Monograph *see* British Broadcasting Corporation. B B C Engineering *267*
British Building Products Catalogue (UK ISSN 0084-8026) *134*
British Carbonization Research Association. Annual Report (UK) *372*
British Catalogue of Music (UK ISSN 0068-1407) *657*
British Cave Research Association. Transactions (UK ISSN 0305-859X) *292*
British Ceramic Research Association. Special Publications (UK) *244*
British Ceramic Society. Proceedings (UK ISSN 0524-5141) *244*
British Chamber of Commerce in France. Year Book (FR ISSN 0068-1415) *178*
British Chemicals & Their Manufacturers *see* Chemicals *246*
British Club Year Book (UK ISSN 0524-5168) *262*
British Columbia. Alcohol and Drug Commission. Annual Report (CN) *286*
British Columbia. Cancer Foundation. Annual Report (CN ISSN 0068-1423) *604*

British Columbia. Department of Human Resources. Annual Report *see* Services for People 809

British Columbia. Department of Labour. Annual Report *see* British Columbia. Ministry of Labour. Annual Report 206

British Columbia. Department of Labour. Negotiated Working Conditions (CN) 206, 495

British Columbia. Department of Lands, Forests and Water Resources. Water Resources Service. Report (CN ISSN 0068-1873) 895

British Columbia. Department of Recreation and Conservation. Annual Report (CN ISSN 0068-1458) 275

British Columbia. Energy Commission. Annual Report (CN ISSN 0703-086X) 362

British Columbia. Forest Service. Annual Report *see* British Columbia. Ministry of Forests. Annual Report 408

British Columbia. Forest Service. Research Notes *see* British Columbia. Ministry of Forests. Research Notes 408

British Columbia. Forest Service. Research Review *see* British Columbia. Ministry of Forests. Research Review 408

British Columbia. Labour Relations Board. Annual Report (CN ISSN 0319-0404) 206

British Columbia. Library Development Commission. Public Libraries, Statistics *see* British Columbia Public Libraries, Statistics 538

British Columbia. Medical Services Plan. Physician's Newsletter (CN ISSN 0707-0462) 593, 751

British Columbia. Ministry of Agriculture D.A.T.E. Program Report (CN) 13

British Columbia. Ministry of Agriculture. Nursery Production Guide (CN ISSN 0705-5757) 33

British Columbia. Ministry of Energy, Mines and Petroleum Resources. Annual Report (CN ISSN 0365-9356) 642, 678

British Columbia. Ministry of Energy, Mines and Petroleum Resources. Bulletin (CN ISSN 0068-144X) 292, 678

British Columbia. Ministry of Forests. Annual Report (CN) 408

British Columbia. Ministry of Forests. Research Notes. (CN) 408

British Columbia. Ministry of Forests. Research Review (CN) 408

British Columbia. Ministry of Labour. Annual Report (CN ISSN 0705-9698) 206

British Columbia. Ministry of Labour. Research and Planning Branch. Negotiated Working Conditions (CN ISSN 0703-0665) 206

British Columbia. Ministry of the Environment. Annual Report (CN) 384

British Columbia. Ministry of the Environment. Northeast Coal Study Preliminary Environmental Report (CN ISSN 0707-3739) 384, 642

British Columbia. Provincial Educational Media Centre. Videotape Supplement *see* P. E. M. C. Catalogue: Supplement 350

British Columbia. Workers' Compensation Board. Workers' Compensation Reporter (CN) 498

British Columbia Art Teachers' Association. Journal (CN ISSN 0316-1544) 73, 347

British Columbia Art Teachers' Association. Newsletter *see* British Columbia Art Teachers' Association. Journal 347

British Columbia Association of Mathematics Teachers. Newsletter *see* Vector 591

British Columbia Counsellors' Association. Newsletter *see* British Columbia School Counsellors' Association. Newsletter 315

British Columbia Economic Activity (CN ISSN 0701-757X) 184

British Columbia Economic Outlook Survey *see* British Columbia Economic Activity 184

British Columbia Energy Board. Annual Report *see* British Columbia. Energy Commission. Annual Report 362

British Columbia Fruit Growers Association. Horticultural Conference Proceedings *see* British Columbia Fruit Growers Association. Horticultural Forum Proceedings 414

British Columbia Fruit Growers Association. Horticultural Forum Proceedings (CN ISSN 0701-757X) 414

British Columbia Fruit Growers Association. Minutes of the Proceedings of the Annual Convention (CN ISSN 0068-1563) 414

British Columbia Geographical Series: Occasional Papers in Geography (CN ISSN 0068-1571) 420

British Columbia Historical Documents Series (CN) 467

British Columbia Hospitals' Association. Proceedings of the Annual Conference *see* B. C. Health Association. Proceedings of the Annual Conference 480

British Columbia Institute for Economic Policy Analysis Series (CN) 142

British Columbia Institute of Technology. Annual Report *see* B C I T: The Career Campus 850

British Columbia Institute of Technology The Career Campus *see* B C I T: The Career Campus 850

British Columbia Insurance Directory. Insurance Companies, Agents and Adjusters (CN ISSN 0068-1598) 498

British Columbia Lumberman's Greenbook (CN ISSN 0068-1601) 412

British Columbia Monthly (CN ISSN 0382-5272) 579

British Columbia Motor Transport Directory (CN ISSN 0707-5014) 870

British Columbia Municipal Yearbook (CN ISSN 0068-161X) 202

British Columbia Music Educator (CN ISSN 0007-0564) 657

British Columbia Provincial Judges' Association. Annual Conference (CN ISSN 0317-297X) 510

British Columbia Public Libraries, Statistics (CN) 538

British Columbia Research Council. Annual Report *see* B. C. Research. Annual Report 779

British Columbia School Counsellors' Association. Newsletter (CN ISSN 0705-8802) 315

British Columbia School Trustees Association. Newsletter (CN ISSN 0381-5978) 343

British Columbia Water and Waste Association. Proceedings of the Annual Conference (CN) 895

British Commonwealth Stamp Catalogue (UK ISSN 0068-1903) 478

British Computer Society. Microform Specialist Group. Annual Proceedings(UK) 270

British Country Music Association. Yearbook (UK ISSN 0308-4698) 657

British Cycling Federation. Handbook (UK ISSN 0068-1938) 819

British Cycling Federation. Racing Handbook *see* British Cycling Federation. Handbook 819

British Decorators Association. Members Reference Handbook (UK) 673

British Directory of Little Magazines and Small Presses (UK ISSN 0307-434X) 733

British Exporters (UK ISSN 0140-5772) 194

British Exports/Exportations Britanniques/Britischer Export/Exportaciones Britanicas (UK) 194

British Exports. Export Services. *see* British Exports 194

British Federation of Master Printers. Master Printers Annual *see* Printing Industries Annual 733

British Fern Gazette *see* Fern Gazette 114

British Film Fund Agency. Annual Report (UK ISSN 0068-2004) 649

British Friesian Herd Book (UK ISSN 0068-2012) 44

British Frozen Food Federation. Year Book (UK) 404

British Gas Corporation. Report and Accounts (UK ISSN 0072-0216) 678

British Geomorphological Research Group. Technical Bulletin (UK ISSN 0306-3380) 292

British Glass Industry Research Association. Annual Report (UK ISSN 0068-2020) 244

British Goat Society. Herd Book (UK ISSN 0068-2039) 44

British Goat Society. Year Book (UK ISSN 0068-2047) 44

British Hospitals Contributory Schemes Association. Directory of Hospitals Contributory Scheme Benefits (UK ISSN 0068-2098) 480

British Hospitals Contributory Schemes Association. Report (UK ISSN 0068-2101) 480

British Hotels, Restaurants and Caterers Association Official Guide to Hotels & Restaurants in Great Britain, Ireland and Overseas *see* Official Guide to Hotels & Restaurants in Great Britain, Ireland and Overseas 483

British Hydromechanics Research Association. Proceedings of Hydrotransport (UK) 380

British Hydromechanics Research Association. Proceedings of Pneumotransport (UK) 380

British Hydromechanics Research Association Fluid Engineering Series *see* B. H. R. A. Fluid Engineering Series 380

British Imperial Calendar and Civil Service List *see* Civil Service Year Book 740

British Independent Steel Companies and Their Products (UK) 627

British Institute in Eastern Africa. Annual Report (KE ISSN 0068-2152) 439

British Institute in Eastern Africa. Memoirs (KE) 439

British Institute of History and Archaeology in East Africa. Report *see* British Institute in Eastern Africa. Annual Report 439

British Institute of International and Comparative Law. Comparative Law Series (UK ISSN 0068-2160) 510, 522

British Institute of International and Comparative Law. International Law Series (UK ISSN 0068-2179) 522

British International Law Cases (US ISSN 0068-2195) 522

British Isles and Ireland Travel Guide *see* Travel Guide to Europe 892

British Journal of Photography Annual (UK ISSN 0068-2217) 693

British Journal of Russian Philately (UK) 478

British Journal of Urology (UK ISSN 0007-1331) 625

British Labour Statistics. Year Book (UK) 153, 834

British Librarianship & Information Science (UK ISSN 0071-5662) 527

British Library. Board. Annual Report (UK ISSN 0305-7887) 527

British Library. Lending Division. Current Serials Received (UK ISSN 0309-0655) 89

British Middle Market Directory *see* Guide to Key British Enterprises I and II 238

BRITISH SOCIETY 1311

British Museum (Natural History) Bulletin. Botany (UK ISSN 0068-2292) 114

British Museum (Natural History). Bulletin. Entomology (UK ISSN 0007-1501) 120

British Museum (Natural History) Bulletin. Geology (UK ISSN 0007-1471) 292

British Museum (Natural History) Bulletin. Historical (UK ISSN 0068-2306) 101

British Museum (Natural History) Bulletin. Mineralogy *see* British Museum (Natural History) Bulletin. Geology 292

British Museum (Natural History) Bulletin. Zoology (UK ISSN 0007-1498) 127

British Music Yearbook (UK ISSN 0306-5928) 657

British National Association for Soviet and East European Studies. Information Bulletin (UK ISSN 0307-2061) 720

British National Committee on Large Dams. News and Views (UK ISSN 0525-4205) 374

British-North American Research Association. Committee Publications (UK) 221

British-North American Research Association. Occasional Papers (UK) 221

British Numismatic Journal (UK) 477

British Orthoptic Journal (UK ISSN 0068-2314) 615

British Paedodontic Society. Proceedings (UK ISSN 0308-4922) 609

British Paper and Board Industry Federation. Technical Division. Fundamental Research International Symposia (UK ISSN 0068-2322) 675

British Paper and Board Industry Federation. Technical Section. Technical Papers (UK ISSN 0068-2330) 675

British Paper and Board Industry Federation. Technical Section. Yearbook (UK ISSN 0068-2349) 675

British Pharmacological Society. Symposia (US) 683

British Political Sociology Yearbook (US) 708, 812

British Practice in International Law (UK ISSN 0007-1676) 522

British Printer Dataguide (UK) 733

British Printer Specification Manual *see* British Printer Dataguide 733

British Pteridological Society. Bulletin (UK ISSN 0301-9195) 114

British Pteridological Society. Newsletter *see* British Pteridological Society. Bulletin 114

British Pump Manufacturers Association. Technical Conference Proceedings (UK) 381

British Qualifications (UK ISSN 0141-5972) 315

British Railways Board. Report and Statement of Accounts (UK ISSN 0068-242X) 872

British Rate & Data Directories and Annuals (UK) 89

British Regional Geology (UK) 292

British Rowing Almanack (UK ISSN 0068-2446) 827

British Rubber Industry Directory (UK) 777

British School at Athens. Annual (UK ISSN 0068-2454) 58

British School at Rome. Papers. Archaeology (UK ISSN 0068-2462) 58

British Schools Exploring Society. Report (UK ISSN 0521-1573) 420

British Scientific Instrument Research Association. Annual Report *see* Sira Institute. Annual Report 497

British Ship Research Association. B. S. R. A. Bibliographies (UK) 865

British Shipping Review (UK ISSN 0142-2553) 877

British Society for the History of Pharmacy. Transactions (UK ISSN 0068-2519) 683

British Standards Year Book (UK ISSN 0068-2578) *636*
British Steel Corporation. Annual Report and Accounts (UK ISSN 0068-2586) *627*
British Theatre Directory (UK ISSN 0306-4107) *235, 858*
British Theatre Institute Bibliographic Series *see* B T I Bibliographic Series *860*
British Tourist Authority. Annual Report (UK ISSN 0068-2667) *883*
British Tourist Authority. Digest of Tourist Statistics (UK ISSN 0068-2616) *883*
British Toy & Hobby Manufacturers Association Directory *see* B T M A Directory *429*
British Trades Alphabet *see* B T A Studycards *5*
British Trades Alphabet Ltd. Studycards *see* B T A Studycards *5*
British Transport Docks Board. Annual Report and Accounts (UK ISSN 0068-2659) *877*
British Travel and Holidays Association. Annual Report *see* British Tourist Authority. Annual Report *883*
British Trust for Ornithology. Annual Report (UK ISSN 0068-2675) *124*
British Virgin Islands. Statistics Office. Balance of Payments (VB) *834*
British Virgin Islands. Statistics Office. National Income and Expenditure (VB) *834*
British Waterways Board. Annual Report and Accounts (UK ISSN 0068-2683) *877*
British Year Book of International Law (US ISSN 0068-2691) *522*
Brno Studies in English (CS) *541, 560*
Broad St. Journal *see* B S J *480*
Broadcast Monographs (US) *267*
Broadcast Yearbook and Diary (UK) *267*
Broadcasting and Television Year Book *see* B & T Year Book *4*
Broadcasting Cable Sourcebook *see* Broadcasting/Cable Yearbook *267*
Broadcasting/Cable Yearbook (US) *267*
Broadcasting Corporation of New Zealand. Report (NZ) *267*
Broadcasting Yearbook *see* Broadcasting/Cable Yearbook *267*
Broadman Comments; International Sunday School Lessons (US ISSN 0068-2721) *764*
Broads Book (UK ISSN 0068-273X) *420, 883*
Brome County Historical Society. Publication (CN ISSN 0381-6206) *467*
Bronneg:ds vir Musiek *see* Source Guide for Music *663*
Bronte Society Transactions (UK ISSN 0309-7765) *561*
Bronze Swagman Book of Bush Verse (AT ISSN 0310-2467) *579*
Brookfield Bandarlog (US ISSN 0068-2780) *127*
Brookhaven Highlights (US ISSN 0092-1548) *702*
Brookhaven Lecture Series (US) *702*
Brookhaven Symposia in Biology (US ISSN 0068-2799) *101*
Brookings Institution. Reprint *see* Brookings Pamphlet Series *796*
Brookings Pamphlet Series (US) *796*
Brooklyn Academy of Music Magazine *see* B A Magazine *657*
Brooklyn Arts and Cultural Association Calendar of Cultural Events *see* B.A.C.A. Calendar of Cultural Events *652*
Brookside Columns (US) *467*
Brookside Monographs (CN ISSN 0068-2853) *286*
Brots de Collcerola (SP) *262*
Brown and Haley Lecture Series (US ISSN 0068-2861) *796*
Brown Boveri Symposia. Proceedings (US) *352*
Brown Thumber's Handbook of House Plants (US) *414*
Browning Institute Studies (US ISSN 0092-4725) *561*

Brown's Directory of North American and International Gas Companies (US ISSN 0197-8098) *678*
Brown's Directory of North American Gas Companies *see* Brown's Directory of North American and International Gas Companies *678*
Browns Mills Review (US) *561*
Brown's Nautical Almanac (UK ISSN 0068-290X) *827*
Bruce County Historical Society. Year Book (CN ISSN 0084-8115) *467*
Brucellosis Surveillance; Annual Summary *see* U.S. Center for Disease Control. Brucellosis Surveillance: Annual Summary *754*
Bruecke-Archiv (GW ISSN 0572-7146) *73*
Bruges Quarterly *see* Cahiers de Bruges *708*
Brujula (AG) *498*
Brujula *see* Universidad de San Carlos. Facultad de Ingenieria. Escuela Regional de Ingenieria Sanitaria. Carta Periodica *755*
Brunei Annual Report (BX ISSN 0084-8123) *740*
Brunei Museum. Special Publication/Muzium Brunei. Penerbitan Khas (BX ISSN 0084-8131) *652*
Brunei Museum Journal (BX ISSN 0068-2918) *652*
Brussels. Nationaal Sekretariaat van Het Katholiek Onderwijs. Statisti Jaarboek van Het Katholiek Onderwijs *see* Annuaire et Statistique de l'Enseignement Catholique *314*
Bryn Mawr-Haverford Review (US ISSN 0068-3035) *561*
Bryn Mawr Review *see* Bryn Mawr-Haverford Review *561*
Das Buch der Jugend (GW ISSN 0068-3043) *89*
Buch und Buchhandel in Zahlen (GW ISSN 0068-3051) *758*
Buch und Zeitschrift in Geistesgeschichte und Wissenschaft (GW) *758*
Buchhandelsgeschichte. Zweite Folge (GW ISSN 0170-5105) *758*
Budapest Statisztikai Evkonyve (HU ISSN 0521-4882) *834*
Budapest Statisztikai Zsebkonyve (HU ISSN 0438-2242) *834*
Budapest Varostorteneti Monografiai (HU ISSN 0068-3337) *451*
Buddhist Studies (II) *771*
Budeshte/Avenir (FR) *391, 708*
Budget in Brief - Department of Transportation (Washington) *see* U.S. Department of Transportation. Fiscal Year Budget in Brief *864*
Budget in Brief - State of Florida *see* Florida. Department of Administration. Budget in Brief *742*
Budget of the Government of Liberia (LB) *740*
Budget of the Government of Pakistan. Demands for Grants and Appropriations (PK) *227*
Le Budget Tunisien (TI) *740*
Buecher (AU) *760*
Buecher fuer Alle *see* Buecher *760*
Buecherei des Augenarztes (GW ISSN 0068-3361) *615*
Buecherei des Frauenarztes (GW ISSN 0068-337X) *615*
Buecherei des Orthopaeden (GW ISSN 0068-3388) *616*
Buecherei des Paediaters (GW ISSN 0373-3165) *617*
Ein Buechertagebuch (GW ISSN 0068-3396) *577*
Buenos Aires. Centro de Investigacion de Biologia Marina. Contribucion Cientifica (AG ISSN 0068-340X) *101*
Buenos Aires. Instituto de Fitotecnia. Boletin Informativo (AG ISSN 0068-3418) *33*

Buenos Aires. Museo Argentino de Ciencias Naturales Bernardino Rivadavia. Instituto Nacional de Investigacion de las Ciencias Naturales. Revista. Ciencias Botanicas *see* Museo Argentino de Ciencias Naturales Bernardino Rivadavia. Instituto Nacional de Investigacion de las Ciencias Naturales. Revista. Botanica *116*
Buenos Aires. Museo Argentino de Ciencias Naturales Bernardino Rivadavia. Instituto Nacional de Investigacion de las Ciencias Naturales. Revista. Ciencias Geologicas *see* Museo Argentino de Ciencias Naturales Bernardino Rivadavia. Instituto Nacional de Investigacion de las Ciencias Naturales. Revista. Geologia *297*
Buenos Aires (Province). Archivo Historico. Publicaciones. Sexta Serie (AG ISSN 0524-9864) *467*
Buffalo (CN ISSN 0045-334X) *256, 262*
Build Kenya (KE) *68*
Builder of Progress (PH ISSN 0115-1843) *334*
Building Abstracts Service C I B (CS ISSN 0007-3326) *1, 140*
Building and Allied Industries Official Handbook (SA) *134*
Building and Allied Trades Official Handbook *see* Building and Allied Industries Official Handbook *134*
Building and Engineering Review (UK ISSN 0084-814X) *134*
Building and Estate Management Society. Proceedings of the Annual Seminar (SI) *134*
Building Board Directory (UK ISSN 0068-3523) *134*
Building Construction Cost Data (US ISSN 0068-3531) *134*
Building Cost File (US ISSN 0091-3499) *134*
Building National Security (US) *638*
Building Practice (II ISSN 0007-3571) *68, 135*
Building Products Catalog *see* B P C *134*
Building Research Establishment. Annual Report *see* Great Britain. Building Research Establishment. Annual Report *136*
Building Research Institute Research Papers *see* B R I Research Papers *134*
Building Services Research and Information Association Application Guides. Technical Notes *see* B S R I A Application Guides. Technical Notes *429*
Building Services Research and Information Association Technical Notes *see* B S R I A Technical Notes *429*
Building Societies. Year Book (UK ISSN 0068-3566) *171*
Buitenlandse Handel van de B.L.E.U. met de Industrielanden (Niet E.E.G.-en E.V.A.-Lidstaten Bruxelles) *see* Commerce Exterieur de l'U.E.B.L. avec les Pays Industrialises (Autre Que les Pays de la C.E.E. et l'A.E.L.E.) *194*
Buitenlandse Handel van de B.L.E.U. Met de Landen van Azie Bruxelles *see* Commerce Exterieur de l'U.E.B.L. Avec les Pays d'Asie *194*
Buitenlandse Handel van de B.L.E.U. Met de Landen van Latijns Amerika Bruxelles *see* Commerce Exterieur de l'U.E.B.L. Avec les Pays d'Amerique Latine *194*
Buitenlandse Handel van de B.L.E.U. Met de Oostlanden Bruxelles *see* Commerce Exterieur de l'U.E.B.L. Avec les Pays de l'Est *194*
Buitlandse Handel van de B.L.E.U. Met de E.E.G.-Lidstaten Bruxelles *see* Commerce Exterieur de l'U.E.B.L. Avec les Pays de la C.E.E *194*
Buku Saku Statistik Indonesia *see* Statistical Pocketbook of Indonesia *847*
Bulletin de Informare Pedagogica *see* Probleme de Pedagogie Contemporana *321*

Bulgaria in Foreign Literature *see* Bulgaria v Chuzhdata Literatura *89*
Bulgaria v Chuzhdata Literatura/Bulgaria in Foreign Literature (BU) *89*
Bulgarian Academic Books (BU) *89*
Bulgarian Periodicals *see* Bulgarski Periodichen Pechat *89*
Bulgarian Review (BL ISSN 0007-3946) *451*
Bulgarska Akademiia na Naukite. Arkheologicheski Institut Izvestiia (BU ISSN 0068-3620) *58*
Bulgarska Akademiia na Naukite. Botanicheski Institut. Izvestiia (BU ISSN 0068-3655) *114*
Bulgarska Akademiia na Naukite. Geofizichni Institut. Izvestiia (BU ISSN 0068-3736) *303*
Bulgarska Akademiia na Naukite. Geografski Institut. Izvestiia (BU ISSN 0068-3744) *420*
Bulgarska Akademiia na Naukite. Geologicheski Institut. Izvestiia. Seriia Neftena i Vuglishtna Geologiia *see* Neftena i Vuglishtna Geologiia *297*
Bulgarska Akademiia na Naukite. Institut po Filosofiia. Izvestiia (BU ISSN 0068-3973) *687*
Bulgarska Akademiia na Naukite. Institut po Khidrologiia i Meteorologiia. Izvestiia (BU ISSN 0068-3876) *631*
Bulgarska Akademiia na Naukite. Institut po Morfologiia. Izvestiia (BU ISSN 0068-3817) *101*
Bulgarska Akademiia na Naukite. Institut po Obshta i Sravnitelna Patalogiia. Izvestiia (BU ISSN 0068-3841) *127*
Bulgarska Akademiia na Naukite. Institut po Tekhnicheska Kibernetika. Izvestiia (BU ISSN 0068-385X) *270*
Bulgarska Akademiia na Naukite. Institut po Vodni Problemi. Izvestiia *see* Vodni Problemi *899*
Bulgarska Akademiia na Naukite. Institut za Bulgarski Ezik. Izvestiia (BU ISSN 0068-3787) *541*
Bulgarska Akademiia na Naukite. Institut za Istoriia. Izvestiia (BU ISSN 0068-3779) *451*
Bulgarska Akademiia na Naukite. Institut za Muzikoznanie. Izvestiia (BU ISSN 0068-3965) *657*
Bulgarska Akademiia na Naukite. Institut za Pravni Nauki. Izvestiia (BU ISSN 0068-3884) *510*
Bulgarska Akademiia na Naukite. Mikrobiologichni Institut. Izvestiia (BU ISSN 0068-3957) *123*
Bulgarska Akademiia na Naukite. Tsentralna Biblioteka. Izvestiia (BU ISSN 0068-3671) *527*
Bulgarska Akademiia na Naukite. Tsentralna Khelmintologichna Laboratoriia. Izvestiia (BU ISSN 0068-371X) *123, 593*
Bulgarska Akademiia na Naukite, Sofia. Tsentralnata Laboratoriia po Geodeziia. Izvestiia *see* Geodesy *289*
Bulgarska Akademiia na Naukite, Sofia. Zoologicheski Institut S Muzei. Izvestiia *see* Acta Zoologica Bulgarica *126*
Bulgarska Etnografiia (BU) *48*
Bulgarski Etimologichen Rechnik (BU) *541*
Bulgarski Folklor (BU) *401*
Bulgarski Gramofonni Plochi (BU) *665*
Bulgarski Periodichen Pechat/Bulgarski Periodicals (BU) *89*
Bulgarsko Istorichesko Druzhestvo. Izvestiia (BU ISSN 0081-1122) *451*
Bulk Wheat (AT) *42*
Bulletin - American Society of Arms Collectors *see* American Society of Arms Collectors. Bulletin *475*
Bulletin Annuel du Statistiques de Gaz pour l'Europe *see* Annual Bulletin of Gas Statistics for Europe *678*
Bulletin Antieke Beschaving (NE) *431*
Bulletin aux Consommateurs *see* Consumer Bulletin *475*
Bulletin Benelux *see* Benelux Publikatieblad *740*

Bulletin Bibliographique Thematique (FR ISSN 0076-0137) *89*
Bulletin d'Archeologie Marocaine (MR ISSN 0068-4015) *59*
Bulletin d'Archeologie Sud-Est Europeenne. (RM) *59*
Bulletin d'Histoire Economique et Sociale de la Revolution Francaise (FR ISSN 0068-4058) *451*
Bulletin d'Information *see* C I M M Y T Information Bulletin *42*
Bulletin d'Investigation *see* International Maize and Wheat Improvement Center. Research Bulletin *42*
Bulletin de Correspondance Hellenique (FR ISSN 0007-4217) *59, 259*
Bulletin de la Protection Civile de la Prefecture de Police *see* France. Service Interdepartemental de la Protection Civile. Bulletin *258*
Bulletin de Philosophie Medievale (BE ISSN 0068-4023) *687*
Bulletin de Societe Royale Belge de Geographie *see* Revue Belge de Geographie *425*
Bulletin des Consommateurs (FR ISSN 0220-5424) *279*
Bulletin des Jeunes Romanistes (FR ISSN 0068-4031) *541, 561*
Bulletin Economique et Social du Maroc (MR ISSN 0007-4586) *142, 796*
Bulletin for Psychologists (AT) *735*
Bulletin - Hudson Family Association, South *see* Hudson Family Association, South. Bulletin *417*
Bulletin International des Douanes *see* International Customs Journal *230*
Bulletin Linguistique et Ethnologique (LU ISSN 0068-4066) *541*
Bulletin - Museum of Natural History, University of Oregon *see* University of Oregon. Museum of Natural History. Bulletin *793*
Bulletin of Agri-Horticulture (SI) *13, 414*
Bulletin of Agricultural Statistics of the Sudan *see* Sudan Yearbook of Agricultural Statistics *30*
Bulletin of Brewing Science (JA ISSN 0521-7237) *86*
Bulletin of Chemical Thermodynamics (1977) (US ISSN 0149-2268) *1, 249*
Bulletin of Comparative Labour Relations (NE) *206*
Bulletin of Earth Sciences (II) *288*
Bulletin of Ethiopian Manuscripts (ET) *758*
Bulletin of Iranian Studies *see* University of Teheran. Faculty of Letters and Humanities. Bulletin of Iranian Studies *475*
Bulletin of Medieval Canon Law. New Series (US) *431, 510*
Bulletin of New Zealand Art History (NZ) *73*
Bulletin of Oaxaca Studies *see* Boletin de Estudios Oaxaquenos *48*
Bulletin of Prehistory/Berita Prasejarah (IO) *59*
Bulletin of Research in Music Education (US) *658*
Bulletin of Sugar Beet Research. Supplement/Tensai Kenkyu Hokoku Hokan (JA ISSN 0068-4090) *33*
Bulletin of Sung and Yuan Studies (US ISSN 0049-254X) *669*
Bulletin of the European Communities. Supplement (EI ISSN 0068-4120) *184*
Bulletin of the National Museums of Sri Lanka *see* Spolia Zeylanica *791*
Bulletin of the Seismological Laboratory (Reno) *see* University of Nevada. Seismological Laboratory. Bulletin *307*
Bulletin of the Slovak Seismographic Stations: Bratislava, Srobarova, Hurbanovo and Skalnate Pleso (CS) *303*
Bulletin of the Society of Vector Ecologists *see* Society of Vector Ecologists. Bulletin *895*
Bulletin of Thermodynamics and Thermochemistry *see* Bulletin of Chemical Thermodynamics (1977) *249*

Bulletin of Volcanic Eruptions (JA ISSN 0525-1524) *303*
Bulletin of Zoo Management (AT ISSN 0084-8182) *127*
Bulletin Officiel de la Marine Marchande (FR) *877*
Bulletin Officiel du Ministere de l'Environnement et du Cadre de Vie et du Ministere des Transports (FR ISSN 0154-0033) *740*
Bulletin: Open Court Newsletter *see* Educator: Open Court Newsletter *317*
Bulletin - Peabody Museum of Natural History *see* Peabody Museum of Natural History. Bulletin *788*
Bulletin Phonographique *see* Biuletyn Fonograficzny *541*
Bulletin - S V P *see* Environnement *386*
Bulletin Scientifique de Bourgogne (FR) *673, 780*
Bulletin Signaletique. Part 530: Repertoire d'Art et d'Archeologie. Nouvelle Serie (FR ISSN 0080-0953) *67, 80*
Bulletin Socialiste *see* Le Poing et la Rose *713*
Bulletin Thomiste *see* Rassegna di Letteratura Tomistica *690*
Bulletin - Utah Geological and Mineral Survey *see* Utah Geological and Mineral Survey. Bulletin *302*
Bulletin Volcanologique (IT) *303*
Bulletin - Washington Game Department, Enviromental Management Division, Applied Research Section *see* Washington (State) Game Department. Applied Research Section. Bulletin *822*
Bulletin - Yale University Art Gallery *see* Yale University Art Gallery. Bulletin *656*
Bullinger's Postal and Shippers Guide for the United States and Canada (US ISSN 0068-4201) *266, 877*
Bulwer Lytton Circle Chronicle (UK) *561*
Bunda College of Agriculture. Research Bulletin (MW) *13*
Bundesanstalt fuer Alpine Landwirtschaft. Versuchsergebnisse *see* Bundesversuchsanstalt fuer Alpenlaendische Landwirtschaft Gumpenstein. Versuchsergebnisse *13*
Bundesanstalt fuer Pflanzenbau und Samenpruefung, Vienna. Jahrbuch (AU ISSN 0068-421X) *114*
Bundesinstitut fuer Ostwissenschaftliche und Internationale Studien. Berichte (GW ISSN 0435-7183) *720*
Bundesinstitut fuer Sportwissenschaft. Berichte und Aspekte (GW) *819*
Bundesverband der Deutschen Industrie Deutschland Liefert *see* B D I Deutschland Liefert *193*
Bundesverband der Deutschen Industrie Organisationsplan *see* B D I-Organisationsplan *220*
Bundesversuchsanstalt fuer Alpenlaendische Landwirtschaft Gumpenstein. Versuchsergebnisse (AU) *13*
Bunka Kagaku Kiyo *see* Journal of Cultural Sciences *491*
Bunte Blaetter (GW) *556*
Burden of Taxes in the Netherlands *see* Belastingdruk in Nederland *227*
Bureau Euristop. Cahiers d'Information (EI) *702*
Bureau Euristop. Informations Technico-Economiques. (EI) *702*
Bureau International de l'Heure. Rapport Annuel (FR ISSN 0068-4236) *81*
Bureau International des Societes Gerant le Droits d'Enregistrement et de Reproduction Mecanique. Bulletin(FR ISSN 0572-7529) *733, 758*
Bureau of National Affairs, Inc. Noise Regulation Reporter *see* Noise Regulation Reporter *516*
Bureau of Research and Publications on Tripura Bulletin *see* B. R. P. T. Bulletin *442*
Bureau Universitaire de Recherche Operationnelle.Cahiers (FR ISSN 0078-950X) *214*

Bureaucrat (CE) *740*
Burgan Bank. Annual Report (KU) *171*
Burke's Family Index (UK) *417*
Burke's Irish Family Records (UK) *417*
Burns Beitraege fuer Klinische Chirurgie *see* Langenbecks Archiv fuer Chirurgie *624*
Burrelle's Maryland/Delaware and Local Washington, D.C., Media Directory (US) *5*
Burrelle's New Jersey Media Directory (US) *5*
Burrelle's New York State Media Directory (US) *5*
Burrelle's Pennsylvania Media Directory (US) *264*
Burrelle's Special Groups Media Directory (US) *5*
Burroughs Bulletin (US ISSN 0007-6333) *561*
Burt Franklin American Classics in History and Social Sciences (US ISSN 0068-4287) *467, 796*
Burt Franklin Art History and Art Reference Series (US ISSN 0068-4295) *73, 431*
Burt Franklin Bibliography and Reference Series (US ISSN 0068-4309) *89*
Burt Franklin Essays in History, Economics, and Social Sciences (US ISSN 0068-4317) *142, 431, 796*
Burt Franklin Essays in Literature and Criticism (US ISSN 0068-4325) *561*
Burt Franklin Ethnic Bibliographical Guides (US) *394*
Burt Franklin Philosophy Monograph Series *see* Monographs in Philosophy and Religious History *690*
Burt Franklin Research and Source Works Series (US ISSN 0068-4341) *431*
Burundi. Departement des Etudes et Statistiques. Bulletin Annuaire (BD) *834*
Bus Facts *see* American Bus Association. Report *861*
Bus Industry Directory *see* Bus Ride: Bus Industry Directory *861*
Bus Ride: Bus Industry Directory (US ISSN 0363-3764) *861*
Buses Annual (UK ISSN 0068-4376) *882*
Business Almanac Series (US ISSN 0068-4384) *214*
Business & Economics Book Guide *see* Bibliographic Guide to Business and Economics *153*
Business Archives Council. Broadsheet (UK) *191, 206*
Business Assistance Monograph Series (US ISSN 0146-4744) *142*
Business Blue-Book of Southern Africa *see* Blue-Book of S.A. Business *142*
Business Contacts in Finland (FI ISSN 0355-0346) *235*
Business Data Processing: a Wiley Series (US) *270*
Business Directory of Hong Kong (HK) *235*
Business Education Index (US ISSN 0068-4414) *326*
Business Graduates Association Address Book (UK ISSN 0308-0455) *214*
Business Guide Book to Jakarta (IO) *235*
Business Monitor Civil Aviation Series *see* Great Britain. Civil Aviation Authority. C A A Monthly Statistics *866*
Business Monitor: Miscellaneous Series. M2 Cinemas (UK ISSN 0068-4449) *649*
Business Monitor: Miscellaneous Series. M3 Company Finance (UK ISSN 0068-4457) *171*
Business Monitor: Miscellaneous Series. M4 Overseas Transactions (UK ISSN 0068-4465) *194*

Business Opportunities in Spain (SP) *184*
Business Outlook (US ISSN 0360-3938) *184*
Business People in the News (US ISSN 0145-7071) *142*
Business Prospects (PH) *221*
Business Prospects Conference. Proceedings *see* Business Prospects *221*
Business Radio Buyers Guide (US) *267*
Business Research Bulletin (US ISSN 0362-823X) *142*
Business Science Monographs (US ISSN 0068-449X) *142*
Business Studies Series (IE) *142*
Business Trends Asia Report (MY) *184*
Business Who's Who Australian Buying Reference (AT) *217*
Business Who's Who of Australia (AT ISSN 0068-4503) *235*
Business Who's Who of Australia and Australian Purchasing Yearbook *see* Business Who's Who of Australia *235*
Business Yearbook of Brazil, Mexico & Venezuela (UK) *194*
Businesscope (MY) *221*
Businessman's Directory of R.O.C. (CH) *235, 883*
Businessman's Directory, The Republic of China (CH) *235*
Buss Handbuch Europaeischer Produktenboersen (GW ISSN 0525-2989) *13*
Bust (CN ISSN 0045-3676) *758*
Butson Family Newsletter (US) *417*
Butsumon (US) *771*
Butterworths Budget Tax Tables (UK ISSN 0525-3063) *227*
Butterworths Current Law (NZ ISSN 0110-070X) *510*
Butterworths Orange Tax Handbook (UK) *227*
Butterworths Tax Handbook *see* Butterworths Yellow Tax Handbook *227*
Butterworths Yellow Tax Handbook (UK) *227*
Buy Books Where, Sell Books Where (US) *527, 758*
Buy from India (II) *235*
Buyer Study (US) *498*
Buyers' Guide for the Mass Entertainment Industry (US ISSN 0362-6180) *828*
Buyers' Guide of Chemicals *see* Chemistry and Industry Buyers' Guide *246*
Buyer's Guide to Microfilm Equipment, Products, and Services *see* Buyer's Guide to Micrographic Equipment, Products, and Services *693*
Buyer's Guide to Micrographic Equipment, Products, and Services (US ISSN 0362-0131) *693*
Buyers' Guide to Process Equipment, Controls & Instrumentation (CN) *270*
Buyers' Guide to the Motor Industry of Great Britain (UK) *870*
Buyer's Guide to the World of Tape *see* High Fidelity's Buying Guide to Tape Systems *818*
Buyers' Guide: Watch Industry, Jewellery and Allied Trades *see* Guide des Acheteurs: Horlogerie, Bijouterie et Branches Annexes *503*
Buying and Selling United States Coins (US ISSN 0068-4562) *477*
By og Bygd (NO ISSN 0084-8212) *48, 451*
Bydgoskie Towarzystwo Naukowe. Wydzial Nauk Humanistycznych. Prace. Seria B (Jezyk i Literatura) (PL ISSN 0068-4570) *542, 561*
Bydgoskie Towarzystwo Naukowe. Wydzial Nauk Humanistycznych. Prace. Seria C (Historia i Archeologia) (PL ISSN 0068-4589) *451*
Bydgoskie Towarzystwo Naukowe. Wydzial Nauk Humanistycznych. Prace. Seria D: (Sztuka) (PL ISSN 0067-947X) *73*
Bydgoskie Towarzystwo Naukowe. Wydzial Nauk Technicznych. Prace. Seria Z: (Prace Zbiorowe) (PL ISSN 0068-4597) *850*

Byelorussian Institute of Arts and Sciences. Annals see Belaruski Instytut Navuki Mactatstva. Zapisy *450*
Byggare och Byggnader i Gamla Mariehamn (FI) *68*
Bygge- og Boligpolitiske Udvikling (DK) *135*
Byggnormindex/Swedish Building Codes and Standards Index (SW ISSN 0348-9221) *1, 140*
Bygningsstatiske Meddelelser (DK ISSN 0106-3715) *135*
Byoin Yoran see Japanese Hospital Directory *481*
Byron Journal (UK ISSN 0301-7257) *579*
Byzantina Kai Metabyzantina (US) *474*
Byzantina Neerlandica (NE ISSN 0525-4507) *451*
Byzantine and Modern Greek Studies (UK ISSN 0307-0131) *542, 561*
C A A E Annual Report (Canadian Association for Adult Education) (CN ISSN 0068-8274) *329*
C.A.C. Document (Center for Advanced Computation) (US ISSN 0360-1617) *270*
C A D/G D V- Report (Computer Aided Design-Geometrische Daten Verarbeitung-EDV- Zeichnen) (GW) *271*
C A D U Publications see A R D U Publication *11*
C A I D Newsletter (Convention of American Instructors of the Deaf) (US ISSN 0045-8430) *286, 315*
C A L U S Research Reports (Centre for Advanced Land Use Studies) (UK) *135, 761*
C A M L Newsletter/A C B M Nouvelles (Canadian Association of Music Libraries) (CN ISSN 0383-1299) *527, 658*
C A N M E T Report (Canada Centre for Mineral and Energy Technology) (CN ISSN 0705-5196) *642*
C A N M E T Review see C A N M E T Report *642*
C A R A N E S see Computer Aided Research in Ancient Near Eastern Studies *474*
C.A.R. Scope (Canadian Arthritis and Rheumatism Society) (CN ISSN 0068-8258) *623*
C A T M O G (Concepts and Techniques in Modern Geography) (UK ISSN 0306-6142) *420*
C A T V and Station Coverage Atlas and 35-Mile Zone Maps see Cable and Station Coverage Atlas and 35-Mile Zone Maps *267*
C B D see Current Bibliographic Directory for the Arts & Sciences *781*
C B I Aarsberaettelse/Report of Activities (Cement- och Betonginstitutet) (SW) *135*
C B I Annual Report (Confederation of British Industry) (UK) *142*
C B I Forskning/Research (Cement-och Betonginstitutet) (SW ISSN 0346-6906) *135*
C B I Rapporter/Reports (Cement och Betonginstitutet) (SW ISSN 0346-8240) *135*
C B I Rekommendationer/ Recommendations (Cement- och Betonginstitutet) (SW ISSN 0348-2790) *135*
C B S News Almanac see Hammond Almanac *361*
C B S News Index (US ISSN 0362-3238) *504*
C. C. Furnas Memorial Conference Proceedings (US) *384*
C C I Journal (Canadian Conservation Institute) (CN ISSN 0380-9854) *275, 652*
C C I Technical Bulletins (Canadian Conservation Institute) (CN ISSN 0706-4152) *275*
C C I Year Book & Directory (Cape Chamber of Industries) (SA) *178*
C. C. Williamson Memorial Lecture (US ISSN 0045-4708) *527*
C D E (Conselho de Desenvolvimento Economico) (BL) *184*

C. D. Howe Research Institute Observations see Observations *147*
C. D. Howe Research Institute. Policy Review and Outlook (CN) *142*
C E A Handbook/Ki-es-Ki (Canadian Education Association) (CN ISSN 0068-8657) *315*
C E B V (Communaute Economique du Betail et de la Viande) (UV) *44*
C E Cost Guide see Engelsman's General Construction Cost Guide *136*
C.E.D.E. Documentos de Trabajo (Centro de Estudios sobre Desarrollo Economico) (CK) *142*
C.E.D.E. Monografias (Centro de Estudios sobre Desarrollo Economico) (CK) *184*
C E D Newsletter (Committee for Economic Development) (US ISSN 0069-682X) *199, 221*
C E M see Chilton's Control Equipment Master *366*
C E M A Bulletin (Connecticut Educational Media Association) (US) *315*
C E N I P E C Revista (Centro de Investigaciones Penales y Criminologicas) (VE) *280*
C E R N Annual Report (European Organization for Nuclear Research) (SZ ISSN 0304-2901) *695, 702*
C E R N-H E R A Reports (European Organization for Nuclear Research) (SZ ISSN 0366-5690) *695, 702*
C E R N Rapport Annuel see C E R N Annual Report *695*
C E R N Reports (European Organization for Nuclear Research) (SZ ISSN 0007-8328) *696, 702*
C E R N School of Computing. Proceedings (European Organization for Nuclear Research) (SZ ISSN 0304-2898) *271, 696, 702*
C E R N School of Physics. Proceedings (European Organization for Nuclear Research) (SZ ISSN 0531-4283) *696, 702*
C F A Monograph Series (Institute of Chartered Financial Analysts) (US ISSN 0073-9065) *905*
C F D C Annual Report (Canadian Film Development Corporation) (CN ISSN 0382-2273) *649*
C F F S Index of Feature Length Films (Canadian Federation of Film Societies) (CN ISSN 0316-5019) *649*
C F F S Index of 16 MM & 35 MM Feature Length Films Available in Canada see C F F S Index of Feature Length Films *649*
C F T C Databook (U.S. Commodity Futures Trading Commission) (US ISSN 0195-3591) *202*
C G O U Technical Report (U.S. Coast Guard, Oceanographic Unit) (US) *309*
C G R B Bulletin (Citizens' Governmental Research Bureau) (US) *315, 748*
C H C Publication (Collection for the History of Cartography) (US) *420*
C H I N O P E R L News see C H I N O P E R L Papers *561*
C H I N O P E R L Papers (Conference on Chinese Oral and Performing Literature) (US) *561*
C I A B Circular (Centro de Investigaciones Agricolas de el Bajio) (MX ISSN 0047-701X) *33*
C.I.A. Revue (Confederation Internationale des Accordeonistes) (UK ISSN 0574-9468) *658*
C I B Directory of Building Research Information and Development Organizations (International Council for Building Research, Studies and Documentation) (FR ISSN 0419-2281) *135*
C.I.C.A.E. Bulletin d'Information (Confederation Internationale des Cinemas d'Art et d'Essai) (FR ISSN 0526-6513) *649*
C I C A Handbook (Canadian Institute of Chartered Accountants) (CN ISSN 0068-8983) *167*

C I C R E D Bulletin (Committee for International Cooperation in National Research in Demography) (FR) *726*
C I C R I S Directory and Guide to Resources (Cooperative Industrial and Commercial Reference and Information Service) (UK ISSN 0069-9829) *527*
C I C's School Directories (Curriculum Information Center) (US ISSN 0162-9646) *330*
C I D A (Centro de Investigacion y Difusion Aeronautico Espacial) (UY) *7*
C I D A Annual Review (Canadian International Development Agency) (CN) *199*
C I E C Proceedings (College Industry Education Conference) (US) *334, 366*
C.I.E. Servicio Informativo (Centro de Investigaciones Energeticas) (AG) *642, 678*
C.I.I.A. Symposia (Commission Internationale des Industries Agricole et Alimentaires) (GW ISSN 0340-2002) *665*
C I I L Adult Literacy Series (Central Institute of Indian Languages) (II) *329*
C I I L Bilingual Hindi Series (Central Institute of Indian Languages) (II) *542*
C I I L Folklore Series (Central Institute of Indian Languages) (II) *401*
C I I L Grammar Series (Central Institute of Indian Languages) (II) *542*
C I I L Occasional Monograph Series (Central Institute of Indian Languages) (II) *542*
C I L T see Amsterdam Studies in the Theory and History of Linguistic Science. Series 4: Current Issues in Linguistic Theory *540*
C. I. M. Directory (Canadian Institute of Mining and Metallurgy) (CN ISSN 0068-9009) *627, 642*
C I M M Y T Annual Report on Maize and Wheat Improvement see C I M M Y T Report on Wheat Improvement *42*
C I M M Y T Annual Report on Maize and Wheat Improvement see C I M M Y T Report on Maize Improvement *42*
C I M M Y T hoy see C I M M Y T Today *42*
C I M M Y T Information Bulletin (Centro Internacional de Mejoramiento de Maiz y Trigo) (MX ISSN 0304-551X) *42*
C I M M Y T Report on Maize Improvement (Centro Internacional de Mejoramiento de Maiz y Trigo) (MX ISSN 0304-548X) *42*
C I M M Y T Report on Wheat Improvement (Centro Internacional de Mejoramiento de Maiz y Trigo) (MX ISSN 0304-5471) *42*
C I M M Y T Review (Centro Internacional de Mejoramiento de Maiz y Trigo) (MX ISSN 0304-5463) *42*
C I M M Y T Today (Centro Internacional de Mejoramiento de Maiz y Trigo) (MX ISSN 0304-5447) *42*
C I N A H L'S List of Subject Headings see Cumulative Index to Nursing & Allied Health Literature *602*
C I N D A (UN) *1, 700*
C I N D A S. Annual Report (Center for Information and Numerical Data Analysis and Synthesis) (US) *834*
C I N T E R F O R. Estudios y Monografias (Centro Interamericano de Investigacion y Documentacion Sobre Formacion Profesional) (UY ISSN 0577-2931) *315*
C I R I A. Bulletin see C I R I A Annual Report *374*
C I R I A Annual Report (Construction Industry Research and Information Association) (UK ISSN 0069-9209) *374*

C I R I A Report (Construction Industry Research and Information Association) (UK ISSN 0305-408X) *135*
C.I.R.M. (Centro Internazionale Radio-Medico) (IT) *622*
C I S (Chromosome Information Service) (JA ISSN 0574-9549) *122*
C I S Annual (Congressional Information Service) (US ISSN 0091-5319) *1, 748*
C L A Directory (Canadian Library Association) (CN) *527*
C L A I M Report to the British Library and Development Department (Centre for Library and Information Management) (UK) *780, 850*
C L A Organization Handbook and Membership List see C L A Directory *527*
C L C L see Computational Linguistics and Computer Languages *542*
C L R see Clinical Laboratory Reference *612*
C L R Recent Developments (Council on Library Resources, Inc.) (US ISSN 0034-1169) *527*
C L U Forum Report (American Society of Chartered Life Underwriters) (US ISSN 0066-0590) *498*
C M see Cobouw Magazine *135*
C M E A Data see R G W in Zahlen *201*
C M E A Statistical Yearbook (Council for Mutual Economic Assistance) (UK) *199*
C M I Year Book (BE) *877*
C M R E Monetary Tracts see C M R E Mongographs *171*
C M R E Monographs (Committee for Monetary Research and Education, Inc.) (US) *171*
C O F I E C. Informe Anual (Compania Financiera Ecuatoriana de Desarrollo) (EC) *171*
C O F Newsletter (Canadian Orienteering Federation) (CN ISSN 0382-8255) *829*
C O N S E R Microfiche (Conversion of Serials) (CN ISSN 0707-3747) *89*
C O R D Research Annual see Dance Research Annual *285*
C O R D Technical Note see Canada. Parks Canada. C O R D Study Technical Note *275*
C P T (Physicians' Current Procedural Terminology) (US ISSN 0590-4129) *593*
C Q (Contemporary Quarterly) (US) *73, 579*
C R C Handbook of Biochemistry and Molecular Biology (US) *905*
C R C Handbook of Marine Science (Chemical Rubber Company) (US) *309*
C R C Handbook of Mathematical Sciences (US) *584*
C R C Handbook of Tables for Mathematics see C R C Handbook of Mathematical Sciences *584*
C R C Report Series (Communication Research Center) (US) *264*
C R I C Rapport de Recherche (Centre National de Recherches Scientifiques et Techniques pour l'Industrie Cimentiere) (BE ISSN 0069-2026) *780, 850*
C S A Specs Buying Guide for Store Planners (Chain Store Age) (US ISSN 0098-3047) *217*
C S E Monograph Series in Evaluation (Center for the Study of Evaluation) (US) *347*
C S I R Annual Report (Council for Scientific and Industrial Research) (SA ISSN 0081-2382) *780, 850*
C S I R Annual Report (Council for Scientific and Industrial Research) (GH) *780*
C S I R Handbook (Council for Scientific and Industrial Research) (GH) *780*
C. S. I. R. O. Directory (AT) *780, 850*
C. S. I. R. O. Film Catalogue (AT ISSN 0069-7192) *780, 850*

C. S. I. R. O. Sheep and Wool Research (AT ISSN 0310-8163) *905*
C S I R Organization and Activities (Council for Scientific and Industrial Research) (SA ISSN 0081-2390) *780, 850*
C S I R Research Reports *see* National Institute for Transport and Road Research. Bulletins *875*
C S I R Special Reports *see* National Institute for Transport and Road Research. P A D Series *875*
C.S.O. Statistical Bulletins (Central Statistical Office) (TR) *834*
C S P Directory of Suppliers of Educational Foreign Language Materials (Cruzada Spanish Publications) (US ISSN 0162-5977) *347*
C S P Directory of Suppliers of Spanish Materials *see* C S P Directory of Suppliers of Educational Foreign Language Materials *347*
C S P G Memoirs (Canadian Society of Petroleum Geologists) (CN) *292, 678*
C S S E Yearbook (Canadian Society for the Study of Education) (CN ISSN 0315-727X) *315*
C T R C Newsletter *see* Caribbean Tourism Research Centre. Newsletter *884*
C.T.T.S. Annual (College of Textile Technology, Serampore) (II ISSN 0084-8859) *855*
C T V D: Cinema-TV-Digest (US ISSN 0007-9219) *267, 649*
C U B Communicator (Concerned United Birthparents, Inc.) (US) *812*
C U I S Credit Union Directory and Buyers' Guide *see* Credit Union Directory and Buyers' Guide *172*
C U S Bulletin (Centre for Urban Studies) (BG) *483*
C.U.S.I.P. Directory *see* American Bankers Association. Committee on Uniform Security Identification Procedures. C U S I P Directory *202*
C.U.S.I.P. Directory. Corporate Directory *see* American Bankers Association. Committee on Uniform Security Identification Procedures. C U S I P Directory: Corporate Directory *202*
C U Y B Directory of Software *see* International Directory of Software *272*
C V R Travel and Hotel Guide to Southern Africa (Chris van / Rensburg Publications (Pty) Ltd.) (SA) *482*
C W M Report (Council for World Mission (Congregational and Reformed)) (UK) *771*
C W/P S Special Studies (Center for War-Peace Studies) (US) *720*
C W/P S Study *see* C W/P S Special Studies *720*
Cabbages and Kings (AT ISSN 0310-1584) *447*
Cable and Station Coverage Atlas and 35-Mile Zone Maps (US) *267*
Cable/Broadband Communications Book (US) *264*
Cable File (US ISSN 0363-1915) *267*
Cable Handbook *see* Cable/Broadband Communications Book *264*
Cabo (SA) *439*
Cactus (CN ISSN 0409-7734) *676*
Cadastro Brasileiro de Materias-Primas Farmaceuticas, Por Produto, Por Fabricante (BL ISSN 0068-4775) *683*
Cadastro Industrial da Bahia (BL) *221*
Cadastro Industrial do Para (BL) *221*
Cadeau et l'Entreprise (FR) *5, 217*
Cadernos Condicao Feminina (PO) *900*
Cadernos de Debate (BL) *467*
Cadernos de Estudos Brasileiros. (BL) *490*
Cadernos de Estudos Linguisticos (BL) *542*
Cadernos de Estudos Rurais e Urbanos (BL) *812*
Cadernos de Lazer (BL) *812*

Cadernos Politicos de Educacao Popular (PO) *708*
Caesaraugusta (SP ISSN 0007-9502) *48, 59*
Cafeteria (US) *579*
Cahiers Africains *see* African News Sheet *497*
Cahiers Amitie Franco-Vietnamienne (FR ISSN 0084-8220) *720*
Cahiers Bretons/Ar Gwyr (FR ISSN 0068-4953) *401, 796*
Cahiers Canadiens Claudel (CN ISSN 0068-4961) *561*
Cahiers Cesairiens (US) *561, 858*
Cahiers Charles du Bos (FR ISSN 0575-0415) *561*
Cahiers Congolais de la Recherche et du Developpement *see* Cahiers Zairois de la Recherche et du Developpement *418*
Cahiers Culturels (CN) *431, 542, 561*
Cahiers d'Analyse Textuelle (FR ISSN 0575-0466) *561*
Cahiers d'Economie Politique (FR) *191*
Cahiers d'Etude de Sociologie Culturelle (BE) *812*
Cahiers d'Etudes Mongoles et Siberiennes (FR) *48, 542*
Cahiers d'Histoire et d'Archeologie *see* Cahiers Ligures de Prehistoire et d'Archeologie *59*
Cahiers de Bruges/Bruges Quarterly (BE ISSN 0575-0571) *708, 720*
Cahiers de Cite Libre (CN ISSN 0009-7489) *467*
Cahiers de Civilisation Medievale. Supplement (FR ISSN 0068-5011) *73, 451, 561*
Cahiers de l'A F S S A *see* French Studies in Southern Africa *564*
Cahiers de la Quatrieme Internationale (FR ISSN 0068-5038) *709*
Cahiers de la Renaissance Vaudoise (SZ ISSN 0007-9847) *561*
Cahiers de Linguistique Hispanique Medievale (FR) *542*
Cahiers de Linguistique Structurale *see* Cahiers de Psychomecanique de Langage *542*
Cahiers de Mariemont (BE) *652*
Cahiers de Medecine Veterinaire (FR ISSN 0007-9944) *894*
Cahiers de Micropaleontologie (FR ISSN 0068-5054) *673*
Cahiers de Philologie (FR ISSN 0153-5048) *542*
Cahiers de Psychomecanique de Langage (CN ISSN 0068-5070) *542*
Cahiers de Recherche Ethique (CN) *764*
Cahiers de Saint-Michel de Cuxa (FR ISSN 0068-5089) *561*
Cahiers de Sante Publique *see* Public Health Papers *754*
Cahiers de Sciences Sociales (CN ISSN 0068-5097) *796*
Cahiers Debussy (FR) *658*
Cahiers des Etudes Anciennes (CN ISSN 0317-5065) *59*
Cahiers des Explorateurs (FR ISSN 0526-8133) *48, 420*
Cahiers des Universites Francaises (FR ISSN 0068-5135) *315*
Cahiers du Tourisme (FR ISSN 0068-5151) *883*
Cahiers Ferdinand de Saussure (SZ ISSN 0068-516X) *542*
Cahiers Franco-Ecossais de Normandie (FR) *451*
Cahiers Geologiques (FR ISSN 0008-0241) *292*
Cahiers Internationaux d'Histoire Economique et Sociale *see* Quaderni Internazionali di Storia Economica e Sociale *459*
Cahiers Internationaux de Symbolisme (BE ISSN 0008-0284) *687*
Cahiers Ligures de Prehistoire et d'Archeologie (IT ISSN 0575-108X) *59*
Cahiers Naturalistes (FR ISSN 0008-0365) *561*
Cahiers Nepalais (FR ISSN 0068-5194) *709*
Cahiers O.R.S.T.O.M. Serie Geophysique *see* Geophysique *304*

Cahiers Philosophiques Africains/ African Philosophical Journal (ZR) *687*
Cahiers Rouge. Nouvelle Serie Internationale (FR ISSN 0068-5224) *720*
Cahiers Suisses Romain Rolland (SZ) *561*
Cahiers Syndicaux *see* Notes on Unions *507*
Cahiers Tristan l'Hermit (FR) *579*
Cahiers Zairois de la Recherche et du Developpement (ZR) *418*
Cain (VE ISSN 0068-5259) *467*
Cairngorm Club Journal (UK ISSN 0068-5267) *819*
Cairo Papers in Social Sciences (UA) *796*
Caisse Centrale de Cooperation Economique. Rapport Annuel (FR) *180*
Caisse Centrale de Cooperation Economique. Rapport d'Activite *see* Caisse Centrale de Cooperation Economique. Rapport Annuel *180*
Caisse d'Epargne de l'Etat du Grande-Duche de Luxembourg. Rapports et Bilans (LU) *171*
Caisse Nationale des Autoroutes. Rapport Annuel (FR) *874*
Caisses Centrales de Mutualite Sociale Agricole. Statistiques. (FR) *510, 812*
Caja de Ahorros y Monte de Piedad de las Baleares. Memoria (SP ISSN 0409-9192) *171*
Caja de Credito Agrario, Industrial y Minero. Financiamiento de la Pequena y Mediana Industria (CK) *234*
Cajal Club. Proceedings (US ISSN 0092-6930) *619*
Cal Job. Annual Report *see* California Job Creation Program Board. Annual Report *740*
Cal-Neva Wildlife *see* Cal-Neva Wildlife; Transactions *275*
Cal-Neva Wildlife; Transactions (US ISSN 0095-3601) *275, 395*
Calcutta Management Association. Annual Report (II ISSN 0068-5356) *214*
Calcutta Market *see* Thapar's Indian Industrial Directory and Import and Export Directory of the World *242*
Calendar of International and Regional Congresses of Medical Sciences (SZ ISSN 0301-2891) *593, 626*
Calendar of International Congresses of Medical Sciences *see* Calendar of International and Regional Congresses of Medical Sciences *626*
Calendar of Regional Congresses of Medical Sciences *see* Calendar of International and Regional Congresses of Medical Sciences *626*
Calendario Agricola (VE) *27*
Calendario Cultural do Brasil (BL) *883*
Calendars and Indexes to the Letters and Papers of the Archbishops of Canterbury in Lambeth Palace Library (UK) *771*
Calgary Archaeologist (CN ISSN 0384-191X) *48, 59*
Calgary Gastronomic (CN ISSN 0706-5310) *482*
Caliban (FR ISSN 0575-2124) *561*
California. Administrative Office of the California Courts. Annual Report (US ISSN 0068-5488) *510*
California. Air Resources Board. Annual Report (US ISSN 0068-5496) *384*
California. Air Resources Board. Fact Sheets (US) *384*
California. Bureau of Criminal Statistics. Crime and Delinquency *see* Crime and Delinquency in California *281*
California. Bureau of Entomology. Occasional Papers *see* Occasional Papers in Entomology *121*
California. Council on Criminal Justice. Comprehensive Plan for Criminal Justice (US ISSN 0093-8912) *280*
California. Department of Consumer Affairs. Annual Report (US) *217*

California. Department of Education. Office of Program Evaluation and Research. Innovative Programs for Child Care: Evaluation Report (US ISSN 0362-7063) *804*
California. Department of Fish and Game. Fish and Game Code (US) *275*
California. Department of Fish and Game. Fish and Game Code. Supplement (US) *275*
California. Department of Forestry. Range Improvement Studies (US ISSN 0068-5569) *408*
California. Department of Forestry. State Forest Notes (US ISSN 0068-5577) *408*
California. Department of Health. Annual Evaluation Report Program Information (US ISSN 0363-7484) *315*
California. Department of Industrial Relations. Annual Report (US ISSN 0362-4129) *206, 495*
California. Department of Parks and Recreation. Archaeological Report *see* California Archaeological Reports *59*
California. Department of Water Resources. Bulletin (US ISSN 0084-8263) *896*
California. Department of Water Resources. California State Water Project *see* California State Water Project *896*
California. Department of Water Resources. Inventory of Waste Water Production and Waste Water Reclamation Practices in California (US ISSN 0092-9158) *896*
California. Division of Mines and Geology. Bulletin (US ISSN 0008-1000) *292, 642*
California. Division of Oil and Gas. Annual Report of the State Oil and Gas Supervisor (US ISSN 0362-1243) *678*
California. Employment Data and Research Division. Taxable and Total Wages, Regular Benefits Paid, Employer Contributions Earned, and Average Covered Employment, by Industry (US ISSN 0098-8332) *206, 498*
California. Health and Welfare Agency. Proposed Comprehensive Annual Services Program Plan (US) *751*
California. Law Revision Commission. Reports, Recommendations and Studies (US) *510*
California. Livestock and Crop Reporting Service. Annual Report *see* Production and Marketing: California Eggs, Chicken and Turkeys *41*
California. State Board of Cosmetology. Rules and Regulations. (US ISSN 0094-4327) *85, 510*
California. State Board of Equalization. Annual Report (US ISSN 0068-5801) *227*
California. State College, San Francisco. Department of Anthropology. Occasional Papers in Anthropology *see* Adan E. Treganza Anthropology Museum. Papers *47*
California. State Energy Commission. Biennial Report (US) *362*
California. State Water Resources Control Board. Annual Program Guide *see* California. State Water Resources Control Board. Program Guide *896*
California. State Water Resources Control Board. Program Guide (US) *896*
California. Teachers Retirement Board. State Teacher's Retirement System; Annual Report to the Governor and the Legislature (US ISSN 0090-5593) *343*
California Academy of Sciences. Occasional Papers (US ISSN 0068-5461) *780*
California Academy of Sciences. Proceedings (US ISSN 0068-547X) *780*
California Air Basins (US) *384*

California Air Environment (US ISSN 0008-0861) 384
California Archaeological Reports (US) 59
California County Fact Book (US) 834
California County Law Library Basic List (US ISSN 0068-5879) 510
California Data Brief (US) 184
California Design (US ISSN 0068-5542) 73
California Environmental Directory (US ISSN 0148-0324) 384
California Environmental Yearbook & Directory see California Environmental Directory 384
California Fire Prevention Notes (US) 408
California Fish and Game Code see California. Department of Fish and Game. Fish and Game Code 275
California Forestry and Forest Products(US ISSN 0008-1094) 412
California Fruit and Nut Acreage (US ISSN 0527-2181) 24
California Government & Politics Annual (US ISSN 0084-8271) 709
California Handbook (US ISSN 0068-5615) 360, 796
California Industrial Relations Reports (US ISSN 0008-1191) 206
California Insect Survey. Bulletin (US ISSN 0068-5631) 120
California Institute of Technology. Division of Engineering and Applied Science. Annual Report (US) 366
California Institute of Technology. Division of Engineering and Applied Science. Report of Research and Other Activities see California Institute of Technology. Division of Engineering and Applied Science. Annual Report 366
California Institute of Technology. Division of Geological and Planetary Sciences. Report on Geological and Planetary Sciences for the Year (US ISSN 0045-3943) 81, 292
California International Trade Register (US) 194, 235
California Job Creation Program Board. Annual Report (US) 740
California Job Development Corporation Law Executive Board. Annual Report see California Job Creation Program Board. Annual Report 740
California Journal Almanac of State Government and Politics (US) 709
California Library Statistics and Directory (US) 528
California Livestock Statistics (US ISSN 0361-9095) 24
California Mosquito and Vector Control Association. Proceedings and Papers of the Annual Meeting (US) 751
California Mosquito Control Association. Proceedings and Papers of the Annual Meeting see California Mosquito and Vector Control Association. Proceedings and Papers of the Annual Meeting 751
California Natural History Guides (US ISSN 0068-5755) 101
California-Nevada Campbook (US) 829, 883
California-Nevada Camping see California-Nevada Campbook 883
California, Nevada TourBook see Tourbook: California, Nevada 891
California Newspaper Publishers' Association. Directory and Rate Book (US) 504
California Newspaper Publishers' Association. Newspaper Directory see California Newspaper Publishers' Association. Directory and Rate Book 504
California Periodicals Index (US) 1
California Periodicals on Microfilm (US) 89
California Personnel & Guidance Association. Monographs (US) 666
California Policy Seminar. Monograph (US) 740
California Private School Directory (US ISSN 0098-5147) 330
California Public School Directory (US ISSN 0068-5771) 330
California Publicity Outlets (US) 5

California Savings and Loan Data Book(US ISSN 0084-828X) 171
California Slavic Studies (US ISSN 0068-5798) 561
California State Health Plan (US) 480
California State Industrial Directory (US) 235
California State Plan for Hospitals and Related Health Facilities see California State Health Plan 480
California State University, Los Angeles. Center for the Study of Armament and Disarmament. Classroom Study Series see California State University, Los Angeles. Center for the Study of Armament and Disarmament. Political Issues Bibliography Series 717
California State University, Los Angeles. Center for the Study of Armament and Disarmament. Occasional Papers Series (US) 720
California State University, Los Angeles. Center for the Study of Armament and Disarmament. Political Issues Bibliography Series (US) 717
California State Water Project (US ISSN 0090-5968) 896
California Street and Highway Conference. Proceedings see California Transportation and Public Works Conference. Proceedings 874
California Studies in Classical Antiquity(US ISSN 0068-5895) 259
California Studies in the History of Art (US ISSN 0068-5909) 73
California Transportation and Public Works Conference. Proceedings (US ISSN 0068-5887) 374, 874
California University Center for Research and Development in Higher Education. Research Reporter (US ISSN 0034-5393) 334
Californians in Congress (US ISSN 0068-6530) 97, 709
Calling the World see World's Telephones 266
Calwer Theologische Monographien. Reihe A: Bibelwissenschaft (GW) 764
Calwer Theologische Monographien. Reihe B: Systematische Theologie und Kirchengeschichte (GW) 764
Calwer Theologische Monographien. Reihe C: Praktische Theologie und Missionswissenschaft (GW) 764
Camara Brasileira do Livro. Centro de Catalogaco na Fonte. Oficina de Livros: Novidades Catalogadas na Fonte (BL) 528
Camara de Comerciantes en Artefactos para el Hogar. Revista (AG) 181, 503
Camara de Comercio de la Guaira. Boletin Estadistico. (VE ISSN 0008-1876) 178
Camara Nacional de la Industria del Hierro y del Acero. Informe del Presidente (MX) 627
Camara Venezolano Britanica de Comercio e Industria. Anuario (VE) 178
Cambrian Law Review (UK ISSN 0084-8328) 510
Cambridge Air Surveys (UK ISSN 0068-659X) 59
Cambridge Authors' and Printers' Guides see Cambridge Authors' and Publishers' Guides 758
Cambridge Authors' and Publishers' Guides (UK) 733, 758
Cambridge Bibliographical Society. Transactions (UK ISSN 0068-6611) 89
Cambridge Bibliographical Society. Transactions. Monograph Supplements (UK ISSN 0068-662X) 89
Cambridge Chemistry Texts see Cambridge Texts in Chemistry and Biochemistry 245
Cambridge Classical Studies (UK) 259
Cambridge Classical Texts and Commentaries (UK ISSN 0068-6638) 259
Cambridge Commonwealth Series (UK) 431, 490, 796

Cambridge Computer Science Texts (UK) 271
Cambridge Earth Science Series (UK) 288
Cambridge Economic Handbooks. New Series (UK) 142
Cambridge Geographical Studies (UK ISSN 0068-6654) 420
Cambridge Greek and Latin Classics (UK) 561
Cambridge Latin American Studies (UK ISSN 0068-6689) 467
Cambridge Latin Texts (UK) 542, 561
Cambridge Monographs in Experimental Biology (UK ISSN 0068-6697) 101
Cambridge Monographs on Mathematical Physics (UK) 584, 696
Cambridge Monographs on Mechanics and Applied Mathematics (UK) 584, 701
Cambridge Monographs on Physics (UK) 696
Cambridge Papers in Social Anthropology (UK ISSN 0068-6719) 48
Cambridge Papers in Sociology (UK ISSN 0068-6727) 812
Cambridge Philological Society. Proceedings (UK ISSN 0068-6735) 259, 542
Cambridge Philological Society. Proceedings. Supplement (UK ISSN 0068-6743) 259, 542
Cambridge Quarterly (UK ISSN 0008-199X) 561
Cambridge Solid State Science Series (UK) 696
Cambridge South Asian Studies (UK ISSN 0575-6863) 442
Cambridge Studies in Chinese History, Literature and Institutions (UK) 442
Cambridge Studies in Cultural Systems (UK) 48
Cambridge Studies in Early Modern History (UK ISSN 0084-8336) 431
Cambridge Studies in Economic History(UK) 191
Cambridge Studies in English Legal History (UK) 510
Cambridge Studies in International and Comparative Law (UK ISSN 0068-6751) 510
Cambridge Studies in Linguistics (UK ISSN 0068-676X) 542
Cambridge Studies in Medieval Life and Thought. Third Series (UK ISSN 0068-6786) 451
Cambridge Studies in Social Anthropology (UK ISSN 0068-6794) 48
Cambridge Studies in Sociology (UK ISSN 0068-6808) 812
Cambridge Studies in the History and Theory of Politics (UK ISSN 0575-6871) 709
Cambridge Texts and Studies in the History of Education (UK ISSN 0068-6816) 315
Cambridge Texts in Chemistry and Biochemistry (UK) 245
Cambridge Town, Gown & County Series (UK) 418
Cambridge Tracts in Mathematics (UK) 584
Cambridge Tracts in Mathematics and Mathematical Physics see Cambridge Tracts in Mathematics 584
Cambridge University. Department of Applied Economics. Monographs (UK ISSN 0068-6832) 142
Cambridge University. Department of Applied Economics. Occasional Papers (UK ISSN 0068-6840) 142
Cambridge University. Department of Architecture. Autonomous Housing Study Working Papers (UK) 68
Cambridge University. Institute of Criminology. Bibliographical Series (UK ISSN 0068-6883) 284
Cambridge University. Institute of Criminology. Occasional Papers (UK) 281

Cambridge University. Library Management Research Unit. Report to the Office for Scientific and Technical Information see C L A I M Report to the British Library and Development Department 780
Cambridge University. Oriental Publications (UK ISSN 0068-6891) 442
Cambridge University Department of Applied Economics. Papers in Industrial Relations and Labour (UK) 206
Cambridge University Library. Genizah Series (UK) 89
Cambridge University Library. Historical Bibliography Series (UK) 89, 431
Cambridge University Library. Librarianship Series (UK) 528
Camden Fourth Series (UK ISSN 0068-6905) 451
Camden History Review (UK ISSN 0305-4756) 451
Camels Coming Newsletter (US) 561
Camera di Commercio Industria Artigianato e Agricultura di Milano. Scambi Commerciali Con l'Estero (IT) 178
Camera di Commercio, Industria, Artigianato e Agricultura di Padova. Notiziario Estero (IT) 178
CamerArt Photo Trade Directory (JA) 235, 693
Cameroon. Direction de la Statistique et de la Comptabilite Nationale. Comptes Nationaux du Cameroun see Comptes Nationaux du Cameroun 227
Cameroon. Direction de la Statistique et de la Comptabilite Nationale. Note Actuelle de Statistique (CM) 834
Cameroon. Provincial Statistical Service of the South West. Annual Statistical Report, South West Province (CM) 834
Cameroon. Regie Nationale des Chemins de Fer. Compte Rendu de Gestion (CM) 872
Cameroon. Regie Nationale des Chemins de Fer. Statistiques (CM) 872
Cameroon. Service d'Hydrometeorologie. Pluviometrie Mensuelle et Annuelle (CM) 631
Cameroon Development Corporation. Annual Report and Accounts/ Rapport Annuel et Compte-Rendu Financier (CM) 221
Cameroon Year Book (CM ISSN 0301-7753) 420
Cameroonian Culture see Culture Camerounaise 439
Cameroun Annuaire International see Republique Unie du Cameroun: Annuaire International 441
Camp Directors Purchasing Guide (US) 235, 829
Campaign Practices Reference Service (US) 709
Campaigner (US) 804
Campeggiare in Europa (IT) 829
Campeggio Annuario - Tuttocamping (IT) 829
Camper's Digest (US ISSN 0068-6913) 829
Camper's Guide to Area Campgrounds (US ISSN 0094-0054) 829, 883
Camping and Caravanning in Britain (UK) 829
Camping and Caravanning U. K. see Camping and Caravanning in Britain 829
Camping and Sports Equipment Trades Directory see Camping and Caravanning and Sports Equipment Trades Directory 235
Camping, Caravaning in France (FR ISSN 0076-7735) 883
Camping Caravanning and Sports Equipment Trades Directory (UK ISSN 0068-6948) 235, 829
Camping Club Handbook and Sites List(UK) 829
Camping Club of Great Britain and Ireland. Year Book with List of Camp Sites see Camping Club Handbook and Sites List 829

Camping-Guida (IT) *829*
Camping Guide (US ISSN 0068-6964) *829*
Camping Guide (US) 829, *883*
Camping Sites in Britain and France *see* Practical Camper's Sites Guide *831*
Camping Sites Yearbook *see* Camping Club Handbook and Sites List *829*
Campingboken (NO) *829,* 884
Campitur: Camping, Caravaning, Villaggi Turistici (IT) *829,* 884
Campus Attractions *see* International Talent and Touring Directory *660*
Can Manufacturers Institute. Annual Metal Cans Shipment Report (US ISSN 0068-7014) *672*
Canada. Advisory Council on the Status of Women. Annual Report (CN ISSN 0705-6028) *900*
Canada. Agence Canadienne de Developpement International. Reflexions sur le Developpement International *see* Canadian International Development Agency. Thoughts on International Development *199*
Canada. Agriculture Canada. Animal Research Institute. Research Report (CN ISSN 0066-1899) *44*
Canada. Agriculture Canada. Economics Branch. Trade in Agricultural Products (CN ISSN 0068-7286) *27*
Canada. Agriculture Canada. Food Research Institute, Ottawa. Research Report (CN ISSN 0068-7308) *404*
Canada. Agriculture Canada. Health of Animals Branch. Bovine Tuberculosis and Brucellosis (CN ISSN 0068-7316) *894*
Canada. Agriculture Canada. Livestock Market Review (CN ISSN 0068-7324) *44*
Canada. Agriculture Canada Publications (CN ISSN 0068-7340) *13*
Canada. Agriculture Canada. Research Branch. Annual Report (CN) *13*
Canada. Agriculture Canada. Research Institute. Research Branch Report (CN) *33*
Canada. Agriculture Canada. Research Station, Beaverlodge, Alberta. Research Report *see* Canada. Agriculture Canada. Research Branch. Annual Report *13*
Canada. Agriculture Canada. Research Station, Melfort, Saskatchewan. Research Highlights. Annual Publications (CN ISSN 0068-7472) *13*
Canada. Air Pollution Control Directorate. Annual Summary: National Air Pollution Surveillance (CN ISSN 0381-2995) *384*
Canada. Anti-Dumping Tribunal. Annual Report (CN) *384*
Canada. Atmospheric Environment Service. Ice Observations: Canadian Arctic (CN ISSN 0068-7723) *905*
Canada. Atmospheric Environment Service. Ice Observations: Canadian Inland Waterways (CN ISSN 0068-7731) *905*
Canada. Atmospheric Environment Service. Ice Observations: Eastern Canadian Seaboard (CN ISSN 0068-774X) *905*
Canada. Atmospheric Environment Service. Ice Summary and Analysis, Canadian Arctic (CN ISSN 0068-7758) *292*
Canada. Atmospheric Environment Service. Ice Summary and Analysis, Eastern Canadian Seaboard (CN ISSN 0068-7766) *292*
Canada. Atmospheric Environment Service. Ice Summary and Analysis, Hudson Bay and Approaches (CN ISSN 0068-7774) *292*
Canada. Atmospheric Environment Service. Meteorological Translations (CN ISSN 0068-7782) *632*
Canada. Atmospheric Environment Service. Snow Cover Data. Canada (CN ISSN 0068-7790) *632*
Canada. Atmospheric Environment Service. Technical Memoranda (CN ISSN 0068-7804) *632*

Canada. Board of Grain Commissioners. Canadian Grain Exports. *see* Canada. Grain Commission. Economics and Statistics Division. Canadian Grain Exports *42*
Canada. Canadian Radio-Television and Telecommunications Commission. Annual Report (CN) *267*
Canada. Commissioner of Official Languages. Annual Report (CN ISSN 0382-1161) *740*
Canada. Committee on Pesticide Use in Agriculture. Pesticide Research Report (CN ISSN 0068-7898) *33*
Canada. Correctional Investigator. Annual Report (CN ISSN 0383-4379) *281*
Canada. Department of Agriculture. Engineering & Statistical Research Institute, Ottawa. Research Report (CN) *33*
Canada. Department of Agriculture. Engineering Research Service, Ottawa. Research Report *see* Canada. Department of Agriculture. Engineering & Statistical Research Institute, Ottawa. Research Report *33*
Canada. Department of Agriculture. Library. Current Periodicals. Periodiques en Cours (CN ISSN 0084-8379) *89*
Canada. Department of Agriculture. Library. Periodicals Currently Received. Periodiques Couramment Recus *see* Canada. Department of Agriculture. Library. Current Periodicals. Periodiques en Cours *89*
Canada. Department of Consumer & Corporate Affairs. Annual Report (CN) *740*
Canada. Department of Consumer and Corporate Affairs. Directory of Investigations and Research Report (CN) *184*
Canada. Department of Energy, Mines and Resources. Solar Heating Catalogue (CN) *362*
Canada. Department of External Affairs. Reference Papers (CN) *720*
Canada. Department of External Affairs. Statements and Speeches (CN) *720*
Canada. Department of Finance. Economic Review (CN) *227*
Canada. Department of Indian Affairs and Northern Development. Mines and Minerals, Activities *see* Canada. Northern Natural Resources and Environment Branch. Mining Section. North of 60: Mines and Minerals, Activities *642*
Canada. Department of Indian and Northern Affairs. Indian and Inuit Graduate Register (CN) 334, *391*
Canada. Department of Indian and Northern Affairs. Oil and Gas Land and Exploration Section. Oil and Gas Activities. North of 60 (CN) *678*
Canada. Department of Indian and Northern Affairs. Schedule of Wells, Oil and Gas North of 60 (CN) *292*
Canada. Department of Industry, Trade and Commerce. Annual Report. (CN ISSN 0383-5154) *740*
Canada. Department of Industry, Trade and Commerce. Revue Annuelle-Industrie et Commerce (CN) *184*
Canada. Department of Insurance. Report. Co-Operative Credit Associations (CN ISSN 0068-7383) 171, *498*
Canada. Department of Insurance. Report of the Superintendent of Insurance (CN ISSN 0068-7405) *498*
Canada. Department of Insurance. Report. Small Loans Companies and Money-Lenders (CN ISSN 0068-7413) 171, *498*
Canada. Department of Insurance. Report. Trust and Loan Companies (CN ISSN 0068-7391) 171, *498*
Canada. Department of Labor. Labour and Industrial Relations Research in Canada. Progress Report *see* Industrial Relations Research in Canada *208*

Canada. Department of National Defence. Defence (CN ISSN 0383-4638) *638*
Canada. Department of National Defence. Directorate of History. Occasional Paper (CN) *638*
Canada. Department of National Health and Welfare. Annual Report (CN ISSN 0068-7456) *751,* 804
Canada. Department of National Health and Welfare. Library. Acquisitions (CN) *756,* 810
Canada. Department of National Revenue. Report: Customs, Excise and Taxation (CN) *227*
Canada. Department of Regional Economic Expansion. Annual Report on Prairie Farm Rehabilitation and Related Activities/Rapport Annuel: Retablissement Agricole des Prairies et Travaux Connexes (CN) *33*
Canada. Department of the Environment. Forest Insect and Disease Survey. Annual Report *see* Canada. Department of the Environment. Insect and Disease Conditions in Canada *408*
Canada. Department of the Environment. Forest Management Institute. Program Review (CN ISSN 0071-7495) *408*
Canada. Department of the Environment. Insect and Disease Conditions in Canada. (CN ISSN 0226-9759) *408*
Canada. Earth Physics Branch. Geodynamic Series (CN) *303*
Canada. Earth Physics Branch. Geomagnetic Series (CN) *303*
Canada. Earth Physics Branch. Geothermal Series (CN) *303*
Canada. Earth Physics Branch. Gravity Map Series (CN) *303*
Canada. Earth Physics Branch. Library. Library News (CN ISSN 0226-3343) *288,* 528
Canada. Earth Physics Branch. Seismological Series (CN ISSN 0084-8387) *303*
Canada. Environmental Protection Service. Canada-Ontario Agreement Research Report (CN ISSN 0381-2146) *384*
Canada. Epidemiology Division. Venereal Disease in Canada *see* Venereal Diseases in Canada *611*
Canada. Experimental Farm, St. John's West, Newfoundland. Annual Report (CN ISSN 0068-7480) *13*
Canada. Fisheries and Environment Canada. Annual Report (CN ISSN 0068-7375) *395*
Canada. Fisheries and Environment Canada. Occasional Paper (CN) *384*
Canada. Fisheries and Environment Canada. Report of Operations Under the Canada Water Act (CN) *275*
Canada. Fisheries & Marine Service Annual. *see* Canada. Fisheries Research Board Annual *396*
Canada. Fisheries and Marine Service. Biological Station, St. Andrews, New Brunswick. General Series Circular (CN ISSN 0068-7510) 101, *396*
Canada. Fisheries and Marine Service Bulletin Series. (CN ISSN 0068-7537) 101, *396*
Canada. Fisheries and Marine Service. Pacific Region. Annual Summary of British Columbia Catch Statistics (CN) *396*
Canada. Fisheries and Marine Service. Recreational Fisheries Branch. Statistics on Sales of Sport Fishing Licences in Canada (CN) *401*
Canada. Fisheries and Marine Service. Resource Management Branch-Central Region. Annual Report (CN) *396*
Canada. Fisheries and Marine Service. Technical Report Series (CN ISSN 0068-7553) 101, *396*
Canada. Fisheries Research Board Annual (CN) *396*
Canada. Fisheries Research Board. Miscellaneous Special Publication Series (CN) *396*
Canada. Foreign Investment Review Agency. Annual Report (CN) *202*

CANADA. LAW   1317

Canada. Forest Fire Research Institute. Bibliography. Supplement (CN ISSN 0068-7561) *412*
Canada. Forest Fire Research Institute. Information Report (FF-X) (CN ISSN 0068-757X) *408*
Canada. Geological Survey. Abstracts of Publications (CN) 1, *290*
Canada. Geological Survey. Bulletin (CN ISSN 0068-7626) *292*
Canada. Geological Survey. Economic Geology Report (CN) *292*
Canada. Geological Survey. Index of Publications of the Geological Survey of Canada (CN ISSN 0707-2996) 1, *290*
Canada. Geological Survey. Memoir (CN ISSN 0068-7634) *292*
Canada. Geological Survey. Miscellaneous Report (CN ISSN 0068-7642) *292*
Canada. Geological Survey. Paper (CN ISSN 0068-7650) *292*
Canada. Grain Commission. Economics and Statistics Division. Canadian Grain Exports (CN) *42,* 194
Canada. Grain Commission. Economics and Statistics Division. Visible Grain Supplies and Disposition (CN ISSN 0380-8718) 27, *42*
Canada. Grain Commission. Marketings, Distribution and Visible Carry-over of Canadian Grain in and Through Licensed Elevators *see* Canada. Grain Commission. Economics and Statistics Division. Visible Grain Supplies and Disposition *42*
Canada. Grains Council. Annual Report(CN ISSN 0700-2866) *42*
Canada. Grains Council. Statistical Handbook (CN) *42*
Canada. Hydrographic Service. Annual Report (CN ISSN 0704-3139) *896*
Canada. Hydrographic Service. Water Levels (CN ISSN 0068-7669) *307*
Canada. Inland Waters Directorate. Historical Streamflow Summary: Alberta (CN) *307*
Canada. Inland Waters Directorate. Historical Streamflow Summary: Atlantic Provinces (CN) *307*
Canada. Inland Waters Directorate. Historical Streamflow Summary: British Columbia (CN) *307*
Canada. Inland Waters Directorate. Historical Streamflow Summary: Manitoba (CN) *307*
Canada. Inland Waters Directorate. Historical Streamflow Summary: Ontario (CN) *307*
Canada. Inland Waters Directorate. Historical Streamflow Summary: Saskatchewan (CN) *307*
Canada. Inland Waters Directorate. Historical Streamflow Summary: Yukon Territory and Northwest Territories (CN) *307*
Canada.Inland Waters Directorate. Water Resources Research Support Program /Programme de Subvention a la Recherche sur les Resources en Eau (CN) *307*
Canada. Labour Canada. Annual Review (CN) *206*
Canada. Labour Canada. Wage Rates, Salaries and Hours of Labour (CN ISSN 0068-743X) *206*
Canada. Law Reform Commission. Administrative Law Series. Study Papers (CN) *510*
Canada. Law Reform Commission. Annual Report (CN ISSN 0382-1463) *510,* 740
Canada. Law Reform Commission. Criminal Law Series. Study Papers (CN) *510*
Canada. Law Reform Commission. Modernization of Statutes. Study Papers (CN) *510*
Canada. Law Reform Commission. Protection of Life Series. Study Papers (CN) *510*
Canada. Law Reform Commission. Report to Parliament (CN) *510*
Canada. Law Reform Commission. Working Paper (CN) *510*

Canada. Marine Environmental Data Service. Monthly and Yearly Mean Water Levels/Moyennes Mensuelles et Annuelles des Niveaux d'Eau (CN) *307*

Canada. Marine Sciences Directorate. Pacific Region. Pacific Marine Science Report (CN) *309*

Canada. Maritimes Forest Research Centre, Fredericton, New Brunswick. Information Report M-X (CN ISSN 0704-769X) *408*

Canada. Marketing and Trade Division. Animal and Animal Products; Outlook (CN) *27, 44*

Canada. Mineral Development Center. Mineral Survey *see* Canada. Mineral Policy Sector. Mineral Survey *642*

Canada. Mineral Development Sector. Mineral Information Bulletin. *see* Canada. Mineral Policy Sector. Mineral Information Bulletin *642*

Canada. Mineral Development Sector. Mineral Report *see* Canada. Mineral Policy Sector. Mineral Report *642*

Canada. Mineral Policy Sector. Mineral Information Bulletin (CN) *642*

Canada. Mineral Policy Sector. Mineral Report. (CN) *642*

Canada. Mineral Policy Sector. Mineral Survey (CN) *642*

Canada. Ministry of State for Science and Technology. Annual Report/Rapport Annuel (CN) *780, 850*

Canada. Ministry of State for Science and Technology. Federal Science Programs (CN ISSN 0701-7391) *780, 850*

Canada. Musee National de l'Homme. Collection Mercure. Centre Canadien d'Etudes sur la Culture Traditionnelle. Dossiers *see* Canada. National Museum of Man. Mercury Series. Canadian Centre for Folk Culture Studies. Papers *48*

Canada. Musee National de l'Homme. Collection Mercure. Commission Archaeologique du Canada. Dossiers. *see* Canada. National Museum of Man. Mercury Series. Archaeological Survey of Canada. Papers *59*

Canada. Musee National de l'Homme. Collection Mercure. Division de l'Histoire. Dossiers *see* Canada. National Museum of Man. Mercury Series. History Division. Papers *431*

Canada. Musee National de l'Homme. Collection Mercure. Division des Communications. Dossiers *see* Canada. National Museum of Man. Mercury Series. Communications Division. Papers *264*

Canada. Musee National de l'Homme. Collection Mercure. Musee Canadien de la Guerre. Dossiers *see* Canada. National Museum of Man. Mercury Series. Canadian War Museum. Papers *638*

Canada. Musee National de l'Homme. Collection Mercure. Service Canadien d'Ethnologie. Dossiers *see* Canada. National Museum of Man. Mercury Series. Canadian Ethnology Service. Papers *48*

Canada. Musees Nationaux. Publications d'Ethnologie *see* Canada. National Museums, Ottawa. Publications in Ethnology *905*

Canada. Musees Nationaux. Publications d'Histoire *see* Canada. National Museums, Ottawa. Publications in History *905*

Canada. Musees Nationaux. Publications d'Oceanographie Biologique *see* Canada. National Museums, Ottawa. Publications in Biological Oceanography *101*

Canada. Musees Nationaux. Publications de Botanique *see* Canada. National Museums, Ottawa. Publications in Botany *114*

Canada. Musees Nationaux. Publications de Zoologie *see* Canada. National Museums, Ottawa. Publications in Zoology *127*

Canada. National Energy Board. Annual Report (CN ISSN 0068-7901) *362*

Canada. National Energy Board. Reports to the Governor in Council (CN) *740*

Canada. National Energy Board. Staff Papers (CN ISSN 0068-791X) *740*

Canada. National Farm Products Marketing Council. Annual Report (CN ISSN 0383-414X) *27*

Canada. National Harbours Board. Annual Report *see* Canada. National Harbours Board. Port Directory *877*

Canada. National Harbours Board. Port Directory (CN) *877*

Canada. National Museum of Man. Mercury Series. Archaeological Survey of Canada. Papers/Canada. Musee National de l'Homme. Collection Mercure. Commission Archaeologique du Canada. Dossiers.(CN ISSN 0317-2244) *59*

Canada. National Museum of Man. Mercury Series. Canadian Centre for Folk Culture Studies. Papers/Canada. Musee National de l'Homme. Collection Mercure. Centre Canadien d'Etudes sur la Culture Traditionnelle. Dossiers (CN ISSN 0316-1897) *48*

Canada. National Museum of Man. Mercury Series. Canadian Ethnology Service. Papers/Canada. Musee National de l'Homme. Collection Mercure. Service Canadien d'Ethnologie. Dossiers (CN ISSN 0316-1862) *48*

Canada. National Museum of Man. Mercury Series. Canadian War Museum. Papers/Canada. Musee National de l'Homme. Collection Mercure. Musee Canadien de la Guerre. Dossiers (CN ISSN 0316-1919) *638*

Canada. National Museum of Man. Mercury Series. Communications Division. Papers/Canada. Musee National de l'Homme. Collection Mercure. Division des Communications. Dossiers (CN ISSN 0317-2716) *264*

Canada. National Museum of Man. Mercury Series. History Division. Papers/Canada. Musee National de l'Homme. Collection Mercure. Division de l'Histoire. Dossiers (CN ISSN 0316-1900) *431*

Canada. National Museums, Ottawa. Publications in Biological Oceanography (CN ISSN 0068-7995) *101*

Canada. National Museums, Ottawa. Publications in Botany/Canada. Musees Nationaux. Publications de Botanique (CN ISSN 0068-7987) *114*

Canada. National Museums, Ottawa. Publications in Ethnology/Canada. Musees Nationaux. Publications d'Ethnologie (CN ISSN 0068-8002) *905*

Canada. National Museums, Ottawa. Publications in Folk Culture/Canada, Musees Nationaux. Publications de Culture Traditionnelle (CN) *905*

Canada. National Museums, Ottawa. Publications in History/Canada. Musees Nationaux. Publications d'Histoire (CN ISSN 0068-8010) *905*

Canada. National Museums, Ottawa. Publications in Zoology/Canada. Musees Nationaux. Publications de Zoologie (CN ISSN 0068-8037) *127*

Canada. Northern Economic Development Branch. Oil and Gas Technical Reports- North of 60 *see* Canada. Northern Natural Resources and Environment Branch. Oil and Mineral Division. North of 60: Oil and Gas Technical Reports *678*

Canada. Northern Forest Research Centre. Forestry Report (CN) *408*

Canada. Northern Forest Research Centre. Information Report (CN ISSN 0704-7673) *408*

Canada. Northern Natural Resources and Environment Branch. Mining Section. North of 60: Mines and Minerals, Activities (CN ISSN 0590-580X) *642*

Canada. Northern Natural Resources and Environment Branch. Oil and Mineral Division. North of 60: Oil and Gas Technical Reports (CN ISSN 0317-4085) *678*

Canada. Pacific Forest Research Centre. Information Report (CN) *408*

Canada. Parks Canada. C O R D Study Technical Note (CN) *275*

Canada. Prairie Farm Rehabilitation Administration. Library. Newsletter/Nouvelles de la Bibliotheque (CN ISSN 0708-9325) *528*

Canada. Public Archives. Register of Post Graduate Dissertations in Progress in History and Related Subjects (CN ISSN 0068-8088) *431*

Canada. Radio-Television Commission. Annual Report *see* Canada. Canadian Radio-Television and Telecommunications Commission. Annual Report *267*

Canada. Research Institute, London, Ontario. Research Report *see* Canada. Agriculture Canada. Research Institute. Research Branch Report *33*

Canada. Statistics Canada. Aggregate Productivity Measures/Mesures Globales de Productivite (CN ISSN 0317-7882) *153, 834*

Canada. Statistics Canada. Aggregate Productivity Trends/Tendances de la Productivite des Agregats *see* Canada. Statistics Canada. Aggregate Productivity Measures/Mesures Globales de Productivite *153*

Canada. Statistics Canada. Air Passenger Origin and Destination. Canada-United States Report/Origine et Destination des Passagers Aeriens. Rapport sur le Trafic Canada-Etat Unis (CN ISSN 0705-4343) *834, 865*

Canada. Statistics Canada. Annual Report/Rapport Annuel (CN ISSN 0703-2633) *834*

Canada. Statistics Canada. Aviation Statistics Centre. Service Bulletin/Bulletin de Service du Centre des Statistiques de l'Aviation (CN ISSN 0068-7057) *834, 865*

Canada. Statistics Canada. Boatbuilding and Repair/Construction et Reparation d'Embarcations (CN ISSN 0527-4834) *834, 865*

Canada. Statistics Canada. Breweries/Brasseries (CN ISSN 0527-4869) *406, 834*

Canada. Statistics Canada. Building Permits. Annual Summary/Permis de Batir (CN ISSN 0575-7975) *140, 834*

Canada. Statistics Canada. Cable Television/Teledistribution (CN ISSN 0703-7244) *266, 834*

Canada. Statistics Canada. Canadian Statistical Review. Annual Supplement to Section 1/Revue Statistique du Canada. Supplement Annuel de la Section 1. (CN ISSN 0705-5765) *834*

Canada. Statistics Canada. Cane and Beet Sugar Processors/Traitement du Sucre de Canne et de Betteraves (CN ISSN 0384-2843) *406, 834*

Canada. Statistics Canada. Canned and Frozen Processed Foods/Aliments, Conditionnes en Boites et Congeles (CN) *905*

Canada. Statistics Canada. Canvas Products and Cotton and Jute Bag Industries/Industrie des Articles en Grosse Toile et des Sacs de Coton et de Jute (CN ISSN 0700-0278) *834, 857*

Canada. Statistics Canada. Carpet, Mat and Rug Industry/Industrie des Tapis, des Carpettes et de la Moquette (CN ISSN 0527-4893) *834, 857*

Canada. Statistics Canada. Causes of Death, Provinces by Sex and Canada by Sex and Age/Causes de Deces, Par Provinces Selon le Sexe et le Canada Selon le Sexe et l'Age (CN ISSN 0380-7533) *731, 834*

Canada. Statistics Canada. Coal Mines/Mines de Charbon (CN ISSN 0705-436X) *648, 834*

Canada. Statistics Canada. Coffin and Casket Industry/Industrie des Cercueils (CN ISSN 0527-4915) *414, 834*

Canada. Statistics Canada. Communications Equipment Manufacturers/Fabricants d'Equipement de Telecommunication(CN ISSN 0527-494X) *266, 834*

Canada. Statistics Canada. Community Antenna Television/Services de Television a Antenne Collective *see* Canada. Statistics Canada. Cable Television/Teledistribution *266*

Canada. Statistics Canada. Concrete Products Manufacturers/Fabricants de Produits en Beton (CN ISSN 0382-0971) *140, 834*

Canada. Statistics Canada. Consolidated Government Finance/Finances Publiques Consolidees (CN ISSN 0575-8254) *153, 835*

Canada. Statistics Canada. Continuing Education: Elementary-Secondary/Education Permanente: Niveau Elementaire-Secondaire (CN ISSN 0700-1444) *905*

Canada. Statistics Canada. Continuing Education. Part 1: Elementary-Secondary Institutions/Education Permanente. Partie 1: Etablissements de l'Elementaire-Secondaire *see* Canada. Statistics Canada. Continuing Education: Elementary-Secondary/Education Permanente: Niveau Elementaire-Secondaire *905*

Canada. Statistics Canada. Continuing Education. Part 2: Post-Secondary Level/Education Permanente. Partie 2: Niveau Postsecondaire *see* Canada. Statistics Canada. Continuing Education: Universities/Education Permanente: Universites *905*

Canada. Statistics Canada. Continuing Education: Universities/Education Permanente: Universites (CN ISSN 0700-141X) *905*

Canada. Statistics Canada. Contract Drilling for Petroleum and Other Contract Drilling/Forage de Puits de Petrole a Forfait et Autre Forage a Forfait (CN ISSN 0318-8841) *905*

Canada. Statistics Canada. Cordage and Twine Industry /Corderie et Ficellerie (Fabrication) (CN ISSN 0527-4990) *835, 857*

Canada. Statistics Canada. Corrugated Box Manufacturers/Fabricants de Boites en Carton Ondule (CN ISSN 0384-465X) *676, 835*

Canada. Statistics Canada. Cotton Yarn and Cloth Mills/Filature et Tissage du Coton (CN ISSN 0527-5016) *835, 857*

Canada. Statistics Canada. Crude Petroleum and Natural Gas Industry/Industrie du Petrole Brut et du Gaz Naturel (CN ISSN 0068-7103) *682, 835*

Canada. Statistics Canada. Dairy Statistics/Statistique Laitiere (CN ISSN 0068-7111) *905*

Canada. Statistics Canada. Direct Selling in Canada/Vente Directe au Canada (CN ISSN 0590-5702) *153, 835*

Canada. Statistics Canada. Distilleries (CN ISSN 0527-5024) *86, 835*

Canada. Statistics Canada. Educational Staff in Community Colleges/Personnel d'Enseignement des Colleges Communautaires (CN ISSN 0382-411X) *905*

Canada. Statistics Canada. Electric Lamp and Shade Manufacturers/Industrie des Lampes Electriques et des Abat-Jour (CN ISSN 0384-4161) *359, 835*

CANADA. STATISTICS 1319

Canada. Statistics Canada. Electric Power Statistics Volume 1: Annual Electric Power Survey of Capability and Load/Statistique de l'Energie Electrique. Volume 1: Enquete Annuelle sur la Puissance Maximale et sur la Charge des Reseaux (CN ISSN 0380-951X) *359, 364,* 835

Canada. Statistics Canada. Electrical Contracting Industry/Entrepreneurs d'Installations Electriques (CN ISSN 0702-8083) 140, *360,* 835

Canada. Statistics Canada. Elementary-Secondary School Enrolment/Effectifs des Ecoles Primaires et Secondaires (CN ISSN 0704-6596) *326,* 835

Canada. Statistics Canada. Employment, Earnings and Hours. Seasonally-Adjusted Series/Emploi, Remunerations et Heures; Series Desaisonnalisees (CN ISSN 0703-4873) *153,* 835

Canada. Statistics Canada. Enrollment in Community Colleges/Effectifs des Colleges Communautaires (CN ISSN 0382-0920) *326,* 835

Canada. Statistics Canada. Estimates of Population for Canada and the Provinces/Estimations de la Population du Canada et des Provinces (CN ISSN 0708-7012) *731,* 835

Canada. Statistics Canada. Estimates of Production and Disappearance of Meats/Estimation de la Production et de la Disparition des Viandes (CN ISSN 0575-8440) *905*

Canada. Statistics Canada. Estimation of Population by Marital Status, Age and Sex, Canada and Provinces/Estimations de la Population Suivant l'Etat Matrimonial, l'Age et le Sexe, Canada et Provinces (CN ISSN 0227-1796) *731,* 835

Canada. Statistics Canada. Exports-Merchandise Trade/Exportations-Commerce de Merchandises (CN ISSN 0317-5375) *153,* 835

Canada. Statistics Canada. Family Incomes(Census Families)/Revenus des Famille (Familles de Recensement) (CN ISSN 0703-7368) *153, 731,* 835

Canada. Statistics Canada. Farm Income and Prices Section. Farm Cash Receipts/Recettes Monetaires Agricoles (CN ISSN 0703-4857) *905*

Canada. Statistics Canada. Farm Net Income/Revenu Net Agricole (CN ISSN 0068-712X) *24,* 835

Canada. Statistics Canada. Federal Government Employment in Metropolitan Areas/Emploi dans l'Administration Federale Regions Metropolitaines (CN ISSN 0527-5148) 153, *748,* 835

Canada. Statistics Canada. Federal Government Finance/Finances Publiques Federales (CN ISSN 0575-8521) *153,* 835

Canada. Statistics Canada. Feldspar and Quartz Mines/Mines de Feldspath et de Quartz (CN ISSN 0319-4957) *905*

Canada. Statistics Canada. Felt and Fibre Processing Mills/Industrie du Feutre et du Traitement des Fibres (CN ISSN 0700-0731) 835, *857*

Canada. Statistics Canada. Financial Statistics of Education/Statistiques Financieres de l'Education (CN ISSN 0703-9328) *326,* 835

Canada. Statistics Canada. Fish Products Industry/Industrie de la Transformation du Poisson (CN ISSN 0527-5172) *401, 406,* 835

Canada. Statistics Canada. Flour and Breakfast Cereal Products Industry/Meunerie et Fabrication de Cereales de Table (CN ISSN 0700-0324) *406,* 835

Canada. Statistics Canada. for-Hire Trucking Survey/Enquete sur le Transport Routier de Marchandises pour Compte d'Autrui (CN ISSN 0382-0939) 835, *865*

Canada. Statistics Canada. Foundation Garment Industry/Industrie des Corsets et Soutiens-Gorge (CN ISSN 0384-2967) *262,* 835

Canada. Statistics Canada. Fruit and Vegetable Processing Industries/Preparation de Fruits et de Legumes (CN ISSN 0384-4420) *406,* 835

Canada. Statistics Canada. Fruit and Vegetable Production/Production de Fruits et de Legumes (CN ISSN 0383-008X) *24,* 835

Canada. Statistics Canada. Gas Utilities (Transport and Distribution Systems)/Services de Gaz (Reseaux de Transport et de Distribution) (CN ISSN 0527-5318) *682,* 835

Canada. Statistics Canada. General Review of the Mineral Industries/Revue Generale sur les Industries Minerales (CN ISSN 0575-8645) *648,* 835

Canada. Statistics Canada. Glass and Glass Products Manufacturers/Fabricants de Verre et d'Articles en Verre (CN ISSN 0575-8661) *245,* 835

Canada. Statistics Canada. Gold Quartz and Copper-Gold-Silver Mines/Mines de Quartz Aurifere et Mines de Cuivre-Or-Argent (CN ISSN 0380-4968) *905*

Canada. Statistics Canada. Health Manpower Section. Annual Salaries of Hospital Nursing Personnel/Traitements Annuels du Personnel Infirmier des Hopitaux (CN ISSN 0576-016X) *905*

Canada. Statistics Canada. Highway, Road, Street and Bridge Contracting Industry/Entrepreneurs de Grande Route, Chemin, rue et Pont (CN ISSN 0706-2451) *371,* 835

Canada. Statistics Canada. Historical Labour Force Statistics, Actual Data, Seasonal Factors, Seasonally Adjusted Data/Statistiques Chronologiques sur la Population Active, Chiffres Reels, Facteurs Saisonniers et Donnees Desaisonnalisees (CN ISSN 0703-2684) *153,* 835

Canada. Statistics Canada. Homicide Statistics/Statistique de l'Homicide (CN ISSN 0706-2788) *284,* 835

Canada. Statistics Canada. Hospital Statistics: Preliminary Annual Report/Statistique Hospitaliere: Rapport Annuel Preliminaire (CN ISSN 0381-8802) *481,* 835

Canada. Statistics Canada. Hospitals Section. List of Canadian Hospitals and Related Institutions and Facilities/Liste des Hopitaux Canadiens et des Etablissements et Installations Connexes *see* Canada. Statistics Canada. List of Canadian Hospitals and Special Care Facilities/Liste des Hopitaux Canadiens et des Etablissements de Soins Speciaux s *481*

Canada. Statistics Canada. Household Facilities and Equipment/L'Equipment Menager (CN ISSN 0318-5273) *480,* 835

Canada. Statistics Canada. Household Furniture Manufacturers/Industrie des Meubles de Maison (CN ISSN 0300-1199) *502,* 835

Canada. Statistics Canada. Imports-Merchandise Trade/Importations-Commerce de Marchandises (CN ISSN 0380-1349) *153,* 835

Canada. Statistics Canada. Index of Farm Production/Indice de la Production Agricole (CN ISSN 0068-7146) *24,* 835

Canada. Statistics Canada. Investment Statistics Service Bulletin/Bulletin de Service sur la Statistique des Investissements (CN ISSN 0380-7053) *153,* 835

Canada. Statistics Canada. Iron and Steel Mills/Siderurgie (CN ISSN 0575-884X) *631,* 835

Canada. Statistics Canada. Knitting Mills/Bonneterie (CN ISSN 0384-3343) *262,* 835

Canada. Statistics Canada. Labour Costs in Canada: Education, Libraries and Museums/Couts de la Main d'Oeuvre au Canada. Enseignement, Bibliotheques et Musees (CN ISSN 0380-2108) *153,* 835

Canada. Statistics Canada. Labour Costs in Canada: Finance, Insurance and Real Estate/Couts de la Main-d'Oeuvre au Canada: Finances, Assurances, et Immeuble (CN ISSN 0319-4930) *153,* 836

Canada. Statistics Canada. Leather Glove Factories/Fabriques de Gants en Cuir (CN ISSN 0384-3300) *905*

Canada. Statistics Canada. List of Canadian Hospitals and Special Care Facilities/Liste des Hopitaux Canadiens et des Etablissements de Soins Speciaux (CN ISSN 0225-5642) *481, 810,* 836

Canada. Statistics Canada. Livestock and Animal Products Statistics/Statistique du Betail et des Produits Animaux (CN ISSN 0068-7154) *24,* 836

Canada. Statistics Canada. Local Government Finance: Revenue and Expenditure, Assets and Liabilities, Actual/Finances Publiques Locales: Revenus et Depenses, Actif et Passif, Chiffres Reels (CN ISSN 0703-2749) *748,* 836

Canada. Statistics Canada. Manufacturers of Electric Wire and Cable/Fabricants de Fils et de Cables Electriques (CN ISSN 0527-5504) *352, 360, 627, 631,* 836

Canada. Statistics Canada. Manufacturers of Industrial Chemicals/Fabricants de Produits Chimiques Industriels (CN ISSN 0527-5539) *371,* 836

Canada. Statistics Canada. Manufacturers of Soap and Cleaning Compounds/Fabricants de Savon et de Produits de Nettoyage (CN ISSN 0384-3912) *261,* 836

Canada. Statistics Canada. Manufacturing Industries Division. Potash Mines/Mines de Potasse (CN ISSN 0382-4020) *905*

Canada. Statistics Canada. Manufacturing Industries of Canada: Type of Organization and Size of Establishment/Industries Manufacturieres du Canada: Forme d'Organisation et Taille des Etablissements (CN ISSN 0076-4248) *905*

Canada. Statistics Canada. Mechanical Contracting Industry/Les Entrepreneurs d'Installations Mecaniques (CN ISSN 0576-0097) 140, *371,* 836

Canada. Statistics Canada. Men's Clothing Industries/Industrie des Vetements pour Hommes (CN ISSN 0527-5679) *262,* 836

Canada. Statistics Canada. Miscellaneous Clothing Industries/Industries Diverses de l'Habillement (CN ISSN 0384-3769) *262,* 836

Canada. Statistics Canada. Miscellaneous Food Processors/Traitement des Produits Alimentaires Divers (CN ISSN 0384-3696) *406,* 836

Canada. Statistics Canada. Miscellaneous Leather Products Manufacturers/Fabricants d'Articles Divers en Cuir (CN ISSN 0384-4811) *525,* 836

Canada. Statistics Canada. Miscellaneous Manufacturing Industries/Industries Manufacturieres Diverses (CN ISSN 0575-9021) *153,* 836

Canada. Statistics Canada. Miscellaneous Metal Mines/Mines Metalliques Diverses. (CN ISSN 0575-9048) *905*

Canada. Statistics Canada. Miscellaneous Non-Metal Mines/Mines Non Metalliques Diverses (CN ISSN 0380-6952) *905*

Canada. Statistics Canada. Miscellaneous Non-Metallic Mineral Products Industries/Industries des Produits Mineraux Non-Metalliques Divers (CN ISSN 0381-9256) *648,* 836

Canada. Statistics Canada. Motion Picture Theatres and Film Distributors/Cinemas et Distributeurs de Films (CN ISSN 0380-6294) *651,* 836

Canada. Statistics Canada. Motor Vehicle. Part 2. Motive Fuel Sales/Vehicules a Moteur. Partie 2. Ventes des Carburants *see* Canada. Statistics Canada. Road Motor Vehicles-Fuel Sales/Vehicules Automobiles-Ventes de Carburants *865*

Canada. Statistics Canada. Murder Statistics/Statistique de l'Homicide *see* Canada. Statistics Canada. Homicide Statistics/Statistique de l'Homicide *284*

Canada. Statistics Canada. Non-Residential General Building Contracting Industry/Industrie des Entreprises Generales en Construction Non Domiciliaire (CN ISSN 0703-7295) *140,* 836

Canada. Statistics Canada. Office Furniture Manufacturers/Industrie des Meubles de Bureau (CN ISSN 0384-4080) *503,* 836

Canada. Statistics Canada. Ornamental and Architectural Metal Industry/Industrie des Produits Metalliques d'Architecture et d'Ornement (CN ISSN 0527-5997) *631,* 836

Canada. Statistics Canada. Passenger Bus and Urban Transit Statistics/Statistique du Transport des Voyageurs Par Autobus et du Transport Urbain (CN ISSN 0383-5766) 836, *865*

Canada. Statistics Canada. Petroleum Refineries/Raffineries de Petrole (CN ISSN 0068-7162) *682,* 836

Canada. Statistics Canada. Placer Gold Mines, Gold Quartz Mines and Copper-Gold-Silver Mines/Placers d'Or Mines de Quartz Aurifere et Mines de Cuivre-Or-Argent *see* Canada. Statistics Canada. Gold Quartz and Copper-Gold-Silver Mines/Mines de Quartz Aurifere et Mines de Cuivre-Or-Argent H *905C*

Canada. Statistics Canada. Police Administration Statistics/Statistique de l'Administration Policiere (CN ISSN 0575-9331) *906*

Canada. Statistics Canada. Private and Public Investment in Canada, Mid-Year Review/Investissements Prives et Publics au Canada. Revue de la Mi-Annee (CN ISSN 0707-9559) *154,* 836

Canada. Statistics Canada. Private and Public Investment in Canada. Outlook/Investissements Prives et Publics au Canada. Perspectives (CN ISSN 0318-2274) *154,* 836

Canada. Statistics Canada. Production and Value of Maple Products/Production et Valeur des Produits de l'Erable (CN ISSN 0317-9672) *24,* 836

Canada. Statistics Canada. Production of Poultry and Eggs/Production de Volaille et Oeufs (CN ISSN 0068-7189) *24,* 836

Canada. Statistics Canada. Products Shipped by Canadian Manufacturers/Produits Livres Par les Fabricants Canadiens (CN ISSN 0575-9455) *154,* 836

Canada. Statistics Canada. Provincial Government Enterprise Finance/Finances des Entreprises Publiques Provinciales (CN ISSN 0575-9463) *154,* 836

Canada. Statistics Canada. Provincial Government Finance, Assets, Liabilities, Sources and Uses of Funds/Finances Publiques Provinciales, Actif, Passif, Sources et Utilisations des Fonds (CN ISSN 0318-8876) *154,* 836

Canada. Statistics Canada. Provincial Government: Finance, Revenue and Expenditure (Estimates) / Finances Publiques Provinciales, Revenus et Defenses (Previsions) (CN ISSN 0575-9501) *154*, 836

Canada. Statistics Canada. Public Warehousing / Entreposage Public (CN ISSN 0704-5387) *906*

Canada. Statistics Canada. Pulp and Paper Mills / Usines de Pates et Papiers (CN ISSN 0384-4633) *412*, 836

Canada. Statistics Canada. Radio and Television Broadcasting / Radiodiffusion et Television (CN ISSN 0575-9560) *266*, 836

Canada. Statistics Canada. Railway Freight Traffic / Trafic Marchandises Ferroviaire (CN ISSN 0317-3445) 836, 865

Canada. Statistics Canada. Railway Transport / Transport Ferroviaire (CN) *872*

Canada. Statistics Canada. Report on Fur Farms / Rapport sur les Fermes a Fourrure (CN ISSN 0318-7888) *525*, 836

Canada. Statistics Canada. Retail Chain Stores / Magasins de Detail a Succursales (CN ISSN 0380-7878) *154*, 836

Canada. Statistics Canada. Road and Street Length and Financing / Voies Publiques, Longueur et Financement (CN ISSN 0706-3105) *906*

Canada. Statistics Canada. Road and Street Mileage and Expenditure / Voies Publiques: Longueur et Depenses *see* Canada. Statistics Canada. Road and Street Length and Financing / Voies Publiques, Longueur et Financement *906*

Canada. Statistics Canada. Road Motor Vehicles-Fuel Sales / Vehicules Automobiles-Ventes de Carburants (CN ISSN 0703-654X) 836, 865

Canada. Statistics Canada. Road Motor Vehicles-Registrations / Vehicules Automobiles-Immatriculations (CN ISSN 0706-067X) 836, 865

Canada. Statistics Canada. Salaries and Qualifications of Teachers in Public, Elementary and Secondary Schools / Traitements et Qualifications des Enseignants des Ecoles Publiques, Primaires et Secondaires (CN ISSN 0318-3874) *326*, 836

Canada. Statistics Canada. Sawmills and Planing Mills and Shingle Mills / Scieries et Ateliers de Rabotage et Usines de Bardeaux (CN ISSN 0318-7128) *412*, 836

Canada. Statistics Canada. Scientific and Professional Equipment Industries / Fabrication de Materiel Scientifique et Professionnel (CN ISSN 0384-4242) *497*, 836

Canada. Statistics Canada. Shipbuilding and Repair / Construction et Reparation de Navires (CN ISSN 0527-6144) 836, 865

Canada. Statistics Canada. Shipping Report. Part 1: International Seaborne Shipping (by Country) / Transport Maritime. Partie 1: Transport Maritime International (Par Pays) (CN ISSN 0318-8914) *906*

Canada. Statistics Canada. Shipping Report. Part 3: Coastwise Shipping / Transport Maritime. Partie 3: Navigation Nationale (CN ISSN 0318-3930) *906*

Canada. Statistics Canada. Shipping Report. Part 4: Origin and Destination for Selected Ports / Transport Maritime. Partie 4: Orgine et Destination pour Certains Ports (CN ISSN 0575-9757) *906*

Canada. Statistics Canada. Shipping Report. Part 5: Origin and Destination for Selected Commodities / Transport Maritime. Partie 5: Origine et Destination de Certaines Marchandises (CN ISSN 0318-8949) *906*

Canada. Statistics Canada. Shorn Wool Production / Production de Laine Tondue (CN ISSN 0527-6179) *24*, 836

Canada. Statistics Canada. Silver-Cobalt Mines and Silver-Lead-Zinc Mines / Mines d'Argent-Cobalt et Mines d'Argent-Plomb-Zinc (CN ISSN 0703-7406) *906*

Canada. Statistics Canada. Slaughtering and Meat Processors / Abattage et Conditionnement de la Viande (CN ISSN 0384-4951) *406*, 836

Canada. Statistics Canada. Smelting and Refining / Fonte et Affinage (CN ISSN 0527-5717) *627*

Canada. Statistics Canada. Sporting Goods and Toy Industries / Fabrication d'Articles de Sport et de Jouets (CN ISSN 0575-979X) *823*, 836

Canada. Statistics Canada. Statistical Profiles of Educational Staff in Community Colleges / Profiles Statistiques sur le Personnel d'Enseignement des Colleges Communautaires *see* Canada. Statistics Canada. Educational Staff in Community Colleges / Personnel d'Enseignement des Colleges Communautaires n *905*

Canada. Statistics Canada. Statistics of Criminal and Other Offences / Statistique de la Criminalite (CN ISSN 0319-8227) *906*

Canada. Statistics Canada. Stone Quarries / Carrieres (CN ISSN 0575-9846) *906*

Canada. Statistics Canada. Surgical Procedures and Treatments / Interventions Chirurgicales et Traitements (CN ISSN 0317-3720) *602*, 836

Canada. Statistics Canada. Survey of Canadian Nursery Trades Industry / Enquete sur l'Industrie des Pepinieres Canadiennes (CN ISSN 0318-5184) *416*, 837

Canada. Statistics Canada. Survey of Libraries. Part 1: Public Libraries / Releve des Bibliotheques. Partie 1: Bibliotheques Publiques *see* Public Libraries in Canada *913*

Canada. Statistics Canada. Survey of Libraries. Part 2: Academic Libraries / Releve des Bibliotheques. Partie 2: Bibliotheques Scolaires *see* University and College Libraries in Canada *915*

Canada. Statistics Canada. Survey of Production / Releve de la Production (CN ISSN 0068-7227) *154*, 837

Canada. Statistics Canada. Telecommunications Statistics / Statistique des Telecommunications (CN ISSN 0703-7252) *266*, 837

Canada. Statistics Canada. Therapeutic Abortions / Avortements Therapeutiques (CN ISSN 0700-138X) *133*, 837

Canada. Statistics Canada. Tobacco Products Industries / Industrie du Tabac (CN ISSN 0300-0249) 837, 861

Canada. Statistics Canada. Transportation and Communications Division. Communications Service Bulletin / Communications-Bulletin de Service (CN ISSN 0380-0334) *266*, 837

Canada. Statistics Canada. Travel, Tourism and Outdoor Recreation - a Statistical Digest / Voyages, Tourisme et Loisirs de Plein Air-Resume Statistique (CN) *906*

Canada. Statistics Canada. Trusteed Pension Plans-Financial Statistics / Regimes de Pensions en Fiducie Statistique Financiere (CN ISSN 0575-9978) *154*, 837

Canada. Statistics Canada. Tuberculosis Statistics. Volume 1: Tuberculosis Morbidity and Morality / La Statistique de la Tuberculose, Volume i: Morbidite et Mortalite (CN) *906*

Canada. Statistics Canada. Tuberculosis Statistics. Volume 2: Institutional Facilities, Services and Finances / La Statistique de la Tuberculose, Volume 2: Installations, Services et Finance des Etablissements (CN ISSN 0381-8845) *906*

Canada. Statistics Canada. University Financial Statistics / Universites Statistiques Financieres (CN ISSN 0700-2181) *906*

Canada. Statistics Canada. Vegetable Oil Mills / Moulins a Huile Vegetale (CN ISSN 0527-6403) *406*, 837

Canada. Statistics Canada. Vending Machine Operators / Exploitants de Distributeurs Automatiques (CN ISSN 0527-6411) *154*, 837

Canada. Statistics Canada. Warehousing-General Merchandise and Refrigerated Goods / Entreposage-Entrepots de Merchandises et Installations Frigorifiques *see* Canada. Statistics Canada. Public Warehousing / Entreposage Public *906*

Canada. Statistics Canada. Water Transportation / Transport Par Eau (CN ISSN 0380-0342) 837, 865

Canada. Statistics Canada. Women's and Children's Clothing Industries / Industries des Vetements pour Dames et pour Enfants (CN ISSN 0384-4498) *262*, 837

Canada. Statistics Canada. Wooden Box Factories / Fabriques de Boites en Bois (CN ISSN 0576-0070) *672*, 837

Canada. Statistics Canada. Wool Production and Supply / Production et Stocks de Laine (CN ISSN 0300-0265) 837, 857

Canada. Statistics Canada. Wool Yarn and Cloth Mills / Filature et Tissage de la Laine (CN ISSN 0300-1202) 837, 857

Canada. Tax Review Board. Annual Report / Rapport Annuel (CN) *227*

Canada. Transport Commission. Annual Report (CN ISSN 0068-9912) *861*

Canada. Treasury Board. Index of Federal Information Banks (CN) *171*

Canada. Treasury Board Secretariat. Estimates / Budget des Depenses (CN) *740*

Canada. Treasury Board Secretariat. Federal Expenditure Plan (CN ISSN 0706-6007) *740*

Canada. Water Survey. Surface Water Data: British Columbia. (CN) *307*

Canada. Western Forest Products Laboratory. Information Reports *see* Forintek Canada Corporation, Western Laboratory. Technical Reports *413*

Canada. Women's Bureau. Women in the Labour Force: Facts and Figures (CN ISSN 0068-7448) *206*

Canada Addictions Foundation. Directory / Fondation Canadienne des Toxicomanies. Repertoire (CN ISSN 0705-5587) *286*

Canada Business Corporations Act with Regulations (CN ISSN 0317-6649) *510*

Canada Centre for Mineral and Energy Technology Report *see* C A N M E T Report *642*

Canada Council. Touring Office. Bulletin (CN ISSN 0703-6078) *73*, 858

Canada Council Annual Report and Supplement (CN ISSN 0576-4300) *73*, 649, 858

Canada Department of Finance. Budget Papers *see* Canada. Department of Finance. Economic Review *227*

Canada Health Manpower Inventory (CN ISSN 0381-2561) *593*

Canada in the Atlantic Economy (CN ISSN 0068-7677) *142*, 194

Canada in World Affairs (CN ISSN 0068-7685) *720*

Canada Institute for Scientific and Technical Information. Annual Report / Institut Canadien de l'Information Scientifique et Technique. Rapport Annuel (CN ISSN 0703-0320) *780*

Canada-Japan, the Export-Import Picture (CN ISSN 0702-0333) *194*

Canada Land Inventory. Report (CN ISSN 0068-7693) *275*

Canada Mortgage and Housing Corporation. Annual Report (CN ISSN 0226-0336) *484*

Canada, Musees Nationaux. Publications de Culture Traditionnelle *see* Canada. National Museums, Ottawa. Publications in Folk Culture *905*

Canada North Almanac (CN ISSN 0319-583X) *467*

Canada: Official Handbook of Present Conditions and Recent Progress / Canada: Revue Officielle de la Situation Actuelle et des Progres Recents (CN ISSN 0705-5331) *906*

Canada on Stage: Canadian Theatre Review Yearbook (CN ISSN 0380-9455) *858*

Canada: Revue Officielle de la Situation Actuelle et des Progres Recents *see* Canada: Official Handbook of Present Conditions and Recent Progress *906*

Canada Supreme Court Reports / Recueil des Arrets de la Cour Supreme du Canada (CN ISSN 0045-4230) *510*

Canada-U.K. Year Book (UK ISSN 0309-0329) *178*

Canada-United States Law Journal (US) *522*

Canada Who's Who of the Poultry Industry (CN ISSN 0068-8134) *44*

Canada Yearbook (CN ISSN 0068-8142) *906*

Canada's International Investment Position / Bilan Canadien des Investissements Internationaux (CN ISSN 0318-8868) *154*, 837

Canada's Lost Plays (CN) *858*

Canada's Meat Industry (CN ISSN 0068-8150) *404*, 672

Canada's Mineral Production, Preliminary Estimate / Production Minerale du Canada, Calcul Preliminaire (CN ISSN 0380-7797) *648*, 837

Canada's Pulp and Paper Business Directory *see* Pulp & Paper Canada's Business Directory *675*

Canada's Wings *see* High Flight *8*

Canadian Agricultural Economics Society. Proceedings of the Workshop (CN ISSN 0707-4808) *27*

Canadian Agricultural Insect Pest Review (CN ISSN 0068-8185) *33*

Canadian Almanac and Directory (CN ISSN 0068-8193) *467*

Canadian Alpine Journal (CN ISSN 0068-8207) *829*

Canadian Amateur Advanced Study Guide (CN) *267*

Canadian Amateur Radio Regulations Handbook (CN) *267*

Canadian Amateur Softball Association. Facts & Figures (CN ISSN 0226-577X) *823*

Canadian and Provincial Golf Records (CN ISSN 0316-8131) *823*

Canadian Annual Review *see* Canadian Annual Review of Politics and Public Affairs *467*

Canadian Annual Review of Politics and Public Affairs (CN ISSN 0315-1433) *467*

Canadian Archaeological Association. Bulletin *see* Canadian Journal of Archaeology *59*

Canadian Architect Yearbook (CN) *68*

Canadian Architect's Yardsticks for Costing *see* Yardsticks for Costing *70*

Canadian Architecture Yearbook *see* Canadian Architect Yearbook *68*

Canadian Arthritis and Rheumatism Society Scope *see* C.A.R. Scope *623*

Canadian Artists Series / Collection: Artistes Canadiens (CN ISSN 0383-5405) *73*

Canadian Association for Adult Education Annual Report see C A A E Annual Report 329
Canadian Association of Administrative Sciences. Proceedings, Annual Conference/Rapport, la Conference Annuelle (CN ISSN 0318-5036) 214
Canadian Association of Geographers. Directory (CN) 420
Canadian Association of Geographers. Newsletter see Canadian Association of Geographers. Directory 420
Canadian Association of Management Consultants. Annual Report (CN ISSN 0068-8320) 214
Canadian Association of Music Libraries Newsletter see C A M L Newsletter 658
Canadian Association of Physicists. Annual Report/Association Canadienne des Physiciens (CN ISSN 0068-8339) 696
Canadian Automotive Aftermarket Directory/Marketing Guide (CN) 235, 870
Canadian Bankruptcy Reports (CN ISSN 0068-8347) 171
Canadian Bar Association. Annual Report of Proceedings (CN) 510
Canadian Bar Association. British Columbia Branch. Program Report (CN ISSN 0384-5753) 510
Canadian Biographical Studies/Etudes Biographiques Canadiennes (CN ISSN 0045-4486) 97
Canadian Book Prices Current (CN ISSN 0576-470X) 758
Canadian Book Review Annual (CN ISSN 0383-770X) 758
Canadian Books in Print (CN ISSN 0068-8398) 89
Canadian Bridge Digest (CN ISSN 0707-9524) 819
Canadian Building Abstracts (CN ISSN 0008-3089) 1, 140
Canadian Building Series (CN ISSN 0068-841X) 135
Canadian Campus see Canadian Campus Career Directory 263
Canadian Campus Career Directory (CN ISSN 0383-2406) 263
Canadian Cancer Society. B. C. and Yukon Division. Newsletter (CN ISSN 0708-0999) 604
Canadian Cancer Society. B.C. and Yukon Division. Provincial News see Canadian Cancer Society. B. C. and Yukon Division. Newsletter 604
Canadian Catholic Historical Association. Annual Report (CN) 774
Canadian Ceramic Society. Journal (CN ISSN 0068-8444) 244
Canadian Chemical Directory see Canadian Chemical, Pharmaceutical and Product Directory 684
Canadian Chemical, Pharmaceutical and Product Directory (CN ISSN 0068-8452) 684
Canadian Chemical Register (CN ISSN 0315-985X) 245, 372
Canadian Children's Annual (CN ISSN 0316-8484) 257
Canadian Church Historical Society Journal (CN ISSN 0008-3208) 431, 764
Canadian Commission for UNESCO. Annual Report (CN ISSN 0317-5693) 720
Canadian Community Law Journal/Revue Canadienne de Droit Communautaire (CN ISSN 0704-0857) 510
Canadian Composers Series (CN) 658
Canadian Conference of Pharmaceutical Faculties. Proceedings see Association of Faculties of Pharmacy of Canada. Proceedings 683
Canadian Conference of the Arts. Miscellaneous Reports (CN ISSN 0068-8487) 73
Canadian Conference on Information Science. Proceedings (CN ISSN 0703-3249) 528
Canadian Conference on Social Development. Proceedings/Compte Rendu (CN) 804

Canadian Conference on Social Welfare. Proceedings/Compte Rendu see Canadian Conference on Social Development. Proceedings/Compte Rendu 804
Canadian Conservation Directory (CN ISSN 0318-2789) 275
Canadian Conservation Institute Journal see C C I Journal 275
Canadian Conservation Institute Technical Bulletins see C C I Technical Bulletins 275
Canadian Controls & Instrumentation Control/Instrumentation Buyers' Guide see Canadian Controls & Instruments Control/Instruments Buyers' Guide 496
Canadian Controls & Instruments Control/Instruments Buyers' Guide (CN) 496
Canadian Corn (CN) 42
Canadian Correspondence Courses for University Credit (CN ISSN 0068-855X) 329
Canadian Council of Churches. Record of Proceedings (CN ISSN 0701-4309) 764
Canadian Council on International Law. Proceedings of the Annual Conference (CN ISSN 0317-9087) 522
Canadian Council on Social Development. Annual Report/Rapport Annuel (CN ISSN 0068-8584) 804
Canadian Critical Issues Series (CN) 709
Canadian Culture Series (CN) 421
Canadian Data Processing Directory (CN ISSN 0383-7319) 271
Canadian Dental Association. Directory(CN ISSN 0068-8622) 609
Canadian Dental Association. Transactions (CN ISSN 0068-8630) 609
Canadian Depreciation Guide (CN ISSN 0068-8649) 171
Canadian Directory of Railway Museums and Displays (CN ISSN 0384-6903) 652, 873
Canadian Directory of Shopping Centres (CN) 217
Canadian Drama/Art Dramatique Canadien (CN ISSN 0317-9044) 858
Canadian Education Association Handbook see C E A Handbook 315
Canadian Electrical Association. Engineering and Operating Division. Transactions (CN ISSN 0576-5161) 352
Canadian Electronics Engineering Annual Buyers' Guide and Catalog Directory see Canadian Electronics Engineering Components and Equipment Directory 352
Canadian Electronics Engineering Components and Equipment Directory (CN) 352
Canadian Engineering & Industrial Year Book (CN ISSN 0068-8665) 221, 366
Canadian Engineering & Machinery Year Book see Canadian Engineering & Industrial Year Book 366
Canadian Environmental Advisory Council. Annual Review (CN) 384
Canadian Environmental Advisory Council. Reports (CN) 384
Canadian Essay and Literature Index (CN ISSN 0316-0696) 1, 577
Canadian Federation and Municipalities. Annual Conference and Proceedings see Federation of Canadian Municipalities. Annual Conference Proceedings 741
Canadian Federation for the Humanities. Annual Report (CN) 490
Canadian Federation of Biological Societies. Canadian Federation News of the Annual Meeting (CN ISSN 0068-8681) 101

Canadian Federation of Biological Societies. Proceedings see Canadian Federation of Biological Societies. Programme and Proceedings of the Annual Meeting 102
Canadian Federation of Biological Societies. Programme and Proceedings of the Annual Meeting (CN) 102
Canadian Federation of Biological Societies. Programme of the Annual Meeting see Canadian Federation of Biological Societies. Programme and Proceedings of the Annual Meeting 102
Canadian Federation of Film Societies Index of Feature Length Films see C F F S Index of Feature Length Films 649
Canadian Film Development Corporation Annual Report see C F D C Annual Report 649
Canadian Film Digest Yearbook (CN ISSN 0316-5515) 649
Canadian Film Series (CN ISSN 0705-548X) 649
Canadian Filmography Series (CN ISSN 0068-872X) 906
Canadian Financial E-Z Directory (CN ISSN 0380-2221) 202
Canadian Florist, Keith's Directory & Horticultural Guide (CN) 416
Canadian Folk Music Journal (CN ISSN 0068-8746) 658
Canadian Food and Packaging Directory (CN ISSN 0068-8754) 404
Canadian Foreign Relations. (CN) 720
Canadian Forest Fire Weather Index (CN) 408
Canadian Forestry Service. Prairies Region. Forestry Report see Canada. Northern Forest Research Centre. Forestry Report 408
Canadian Forestry Service Dept. of Fisheries & Forestry Prairies Region. Information Report see Canada. Northern Forest Research Centre. Information Report 408
Canadian Frontier (CN ISSN 0315-0062) 467
Canadian Fruit Wholesalers' Association. Yearbook (CN ISSN 0068-8770) 404
Canadian Fur Trade Directory (CN) 262, 524
Canadian Gas Association. Membership Directory (CN ISSN 0315-8233) 362
Canadian Gas Association. Statistical Summary of the Canadian Gas Industry (CN ISSN 0068-8800) 678
Canadian Gas Facts (CN ISSN 0316-3547) 362, 678
Canadian Gas Utilities Directory (CN ISSN 0576-5269) 362, 678
Canadian Geophysical Bulletin (CN ISSN 0068-8819) 303
Canadian Gladiolus Society. Annual (CN ISSN 0319-1915) 414
Canadian Government Publications: Catalogue/Publications du Governement Canadien: Catalogue (CN ISSN 0318-675X) 89
Canadian Government Series (CN ISSN 0068-8835) 709
Canadian Grain Exports see Canada. Grain Commission. Economics and Statistics Division. Canadian Grain Exports 42
Canadian Grains for Beef Cattle (CN) 42, 44
Canadian Grains for Dairy Cattle (CN) 42, 44
Canadian Grains for Pigs (CN) 42, 44
Canadian Grains for Poultry (CN) 42, 44
Canadian Gunner (CN ISSN 0068-8843) 638
Canadian Hackney Stud Book (CN ISSN 0382-5795) 827
Canadian Hardware, Electrical & Building Supply Directory (CN ISSN 0456-3867) 135, 352
Canadian Heart Foundation. Annual Report (CN ISSN 0702-8733) 606
Canadian Highway Carriers Guide (CN ISSN 0702-8733) 874

Canadian Historic Sites; Occasional Papers in Archaeology and History (CN) 59, 467
Canadian Historical Association. Historical Booklets. Brochures Historiques (CN ISSN 0068-886X) 467
Canadian Historical Association. Historical Papers (CN ISSN 0068-8878) 431
Canadian Horticultural Council. Annual Meeting Reports (CN ISSN 0068-8908) 414
Canadian Horticultural Council. Committee on Horticultural Research. Annual Reports (CN ISSN 0068-8916) 414
Canadian Hospital Directory/Annuaire des Hopitaux du Canada (CN ISSN 0068-8932) 480
Canadian Hotel, Restaurant, Institution & Store Equipment Directory (CN ISSN 0381-5765) 482
Canadian Housing Statistics (CN ISSN 0068-8940) 488
Canadian Industry Shows and Exhibitions (CN ISSN 0068-8967) 626
Canadian Information Processing Society. Canadian Salary Survey (CN ISSN 0318-1944) 271
Canadian Information Processing Society. Computer Census (CN ISSN 0316-8956) 271
Canadian Information Processing Society. Software Survey (CN) 271
Canadian Insect Pest Review see Canadian Agricultural Insect Pest Review 33
Canadian Institute of Actuaries. Yearbook (CN ISSN 0068-8975) 498
Canadian Institute of Chartered Accountants. Intermediate and Final Examinations see Canadian Institute of Chartered Accountants. Uniform Final Examination Handbook 167
Canadian Institute of Chartered Accountants. Uniform Final Examination Handbook (CN) 167
Canadian Institute of Chartered Accountants Handbook see C I C A Handbook 167
Canadian Institute of Forestry. Annual Report (CN ISSN 0068-8991) 408
Canadian Institute of Mining and Metallurgy Directory see C. I. M. Directory 642
Canadian Insurance. Annual Statistical Issue (CN ISSN 0068-9025) 498
Canadian Insurance Law Bulletin Service (CN ISSN 0068-9033) 498
Canadian International Development Agency. Thoughts on International Development/Canada. Agence Canadienne de Developpement International. Reflexions sur le Developpement International (CN) 199
Canadian International Development Agency Annual Review see C I D A Annual Review 199
Canadian Jersey Cattle Club. Record see Canadian Jersey Herd Record 44
Canadian Jersey Herd Record (CN ISSN 0382-6406) 44
Canadian Jewish Archives (New Series) (CN ISSN 0576-5528) 391, 770
Canadian Journal of Archaeology (CN ISSN 0705-2006) 59
Canadian Journal of Information Science/Revue Canadienne des Sciences de Information (CN ISSN 0380-9218) 528
Canadian Journal of Political & Social Theory (CN ISSN 0380-9420) 709
Canadian Journal of Public and Cooperative Economy/Revue Canadienne d'Economie Publique et Cooperative (CN ISSN 0384-8744) 142
Canadian Key Business Directory (US ISSN 0315-0879) 235
Canadian L P & Tape Catalogue (CN ISSN 0381-9507) 1, 665
Canadian Labour Terms (CN ISSN 0068-905X) 206

Canadian Ladies' Golf Association. Year Book (CN ISSN 0084-8565) 823
Canadian Law List (CN ISSN 0084-8573) 510
Canadian Legal Manual Series (CN) 510
Canadian Legal Studies Series (CN ISSN 0576-5625) 510
Canadian Library Association. Occasional Papers (CN ISSN 0068-9092) 528
Canadian Library Association Directory see C L A Directory 527
Canadian Library Progress: a Selection of the Best Writings from Canadian Library Publications/Progres des Bibliotheques Canadiennes: Une Selection des Meilleures Oeuvres de Publications Canadiennes de Bibliotheconomie (CN ISSN 0315-2693) 528
Canadian Life Insurance Association. Directory/Association Canadienne des Compagnies d'Assurance. Annuaire (CN ISSN 0707-6150) 498
Canadian Life Insurance Facts (CN ISSN 0068-9157) 498
Canadian Livestock Feed Board. Annual Report (CN) 42
Canadian Local Histories to 1950. A Bibliography. Histoires Locales et Regionales Canadiennes des Origines A 1950 (CN ISSN 0068-9165) 467
Canadian Locations of Journals Indexed for Medline/Depots Canadiens des Revues Indexees pour Medline (CN) 2, 602
Canadian Locations of Journals Indexed in Index Medicus see Canadian Locations of Journals Indexed for Medline 602
Canadian Log House see Log House 69
Canadian Manhood (CN ISSN 0382-6031) 262
Canadian Mathematical Congress. Research Committee. Report (CN ISSN 0380-5921) 584
Canadian Medical Directory (CN ISSN 0068-9203) 593
Canadian Mental Health Association. Annual Report/Association Canadienne pour la Sante Mentale. Rapport Annuel (CN ISSN 0068-9211) 735, 751
Canadian Meteorological Memoirs (CN ISSN 0068-9246) 632
Canadian Meteorological Research Reports (CN) 632
Canadian Meteorological Society. Annual Congress (CN ISSN 0068-9254) 632
Canadian Minerals Yearbook/Annuaire des Mineraux du Canada (CN ISSN 0068-9270) 642
Canadian Mines Handbook (CN ISSN 0068-9289) 642
Canadian Mines Register of Dormant and Defunct Companies (CN ISSN 0068-9297) 642
Canadian Mines Register of Dormant and Defunct Companies. Supplement(CN ISSN 0068-9300) 642
Canadian Mining Journal's Reference Manual & Buyers' Guide (CN ISSN 0315-9140) 642
Canadian Mining Manual see Canadian Mining Journal's Reference Manual & Buyers' Guide 642
Canadian Music Directory (CN ISSN 0381-5730) 658
Canadian Music Industry Directory (CN ISSN 0068-9335) 658
Canadian Music Library Association. Newsletter see C A M L Newsletter 658
Canadian Muslim (CN ISSN 0707-2945) 391, 769
Canadian National Institute for the Blind. National Annual Report (CN ISSN 0068-9378) 133, 804
Canadian Nuclear Association. Annual International Conference Proceedings(CN ISSN 0706-1293) 702

Canadian Nuclear Association. Annual Meeting see Canadian Nuclear Association. Annual International Conference Proceedings 702
Canadian Nuclear Society. Annual Conference Proceedings (CN ISSN 0227-1907) 702
Canadian Nuclear Society. Transactions(CN ISSN 0226-7470) 702
Canadian Nurses Association. Biennial Meeting. Folio of Reports (CN ISSN 0068-9386) 613
Canadian Nurses Association. Library. Periodical Holdings (CN ISSN 0383-0101) 613
Canadian Office Redbook (CN ISSN 0319-2148) 219
Canadian Oil & Gas Handbook (CN) 642, 678
Canadian Oil Industry Directory (US) 678
Canadian Oil Register (CN ISSN 0068-9394) 678
Canadian Oral History Association. Journal (CN ISSN 0383-6894) 467
Canadian Orienteering Federation Newsletter see C O F Newsletter 829
Canadian Paraplegic Association. Annual Report (CN ISSN 0068-9424) 619, 804
Canadian Parliamentary Guide (CN ISSN 0315-6168) 709
Canadian Perspective (CN ISSN 0705-6680) 206, 804
Canadian Pest Management Society Proceedings (CN ISSN 0065-4485) 33
Canadian Phytopathological Society. Proceedings (CN ISSN 0068-9440) 114
Canadian Plastics Directory and Buyer's Guide (CN ISSN 0068-9459) 706
Canadian Play Series (CN) 561, 858
Canadian Political Science Association. Updating Theses in Canadian Political Studies, Completed and in Progress (CN) 709
Canadian Ports and Seaways Directory (CN ISSN 0068-9467) 861, 877
Canadian Public Health Association. Proceedings of the Annual Meeting (CN ISSN 0319-2644) 751
Canadian Pulp and Paper Association. Annual Newsprint Supplement (CN ISSN 0316-4241) 676
Canadian Pulp and Paper Association. Newsprint Data. (CN ISSN 0068-9491) 675
Canadian Pulp and Paper Association. Pulp and Paper Report (CN ISSN 0068-9505) 675
Canadian Pulp and Paper Association. Technical Section. Proceedings (CN ISSN 0316-3571) 675
Canadian Pulp and Paper Association. Woodlands Section. Publications (CN ISSN 0068-9548) 675
Canadian Real Estate Annual see Real Estate Development Annual 762
Canadian Red Cross Society. Annual Report (CN ISSN 0068-9572) 804
Canadian Rehabilitation Council for the Disabled. Annual Report (CN ISSN 0068-9580) 345, 593
Canadian Rock Mechanics Symposium. Proceedings (CN ISSN 0375-605X) 303, 642
Canadian Seed Growers Association. Annual Report (CN ISSN 0068-9610) 33
Canadian Serials Directory/Repertorie des Publications Seriees Canadiennes(CN ISSN 0000-0345) 538
Canadian Shipping Project Newsletter (CN ISSN 0708-0727) 877
Canadian Shoemaking Directory & Buyers' Guide see Footwear Shoemaking Directory 795
Canadian Society for Chemical Engineering Symposium Series (US) 372
Canadian Society for Education through Art. Annual Journal (CN ISSN 0068-9645) 73, 315

Canadian Society for Horticultural Science. Journal (CN ISSN 0315-6877) 414
Canadian Society for Immunology. Bulletin (CN ISSN 0068-9653) 603
Canadian Society for Immunology. International Symposium. Proceedings (SZ ISSN 0301-3146) 603
Canadian Society for the Study of Education Yearbook see C S S E Yearbook 315
Canadian Society of Agronomy. Annual Meeting. Proceedings (CN ISSN 0068-9688) 13
Canadian Society of Animal Production. Proceedings (CN ISSN 0068-9696) 44
Canadian Society of Biblical Studies. Bulletin/Societe Canadienne des Etudes Bibliques. Bulletin (CN ISSN 0068-970X) 764
Canadian Society of Petroleum Geologists Memoirs see C S P G Memoirs 678
Canadian Society of Rural Extension. Meeting and Convention. Proceedings (CN ISSN 0068-9718) 13
Canadian Special Truck Equipment Manual (CN ISSN 0068-9734) 882
Canadian Speech Communication Journal (CN) 264
Canadian Sporting Goods & Playthings. Directory (CN ISSN 0316-7771) 819
Canadian Standards Association. Annual Report (CN) 636
Canadian Standards Association. List of Publications see Canadian Standards Association. Standards Catalogue 636
Canadian Standards Association. Standards Catalogue (CN) 636
Canadian Structural Engineering Conference. Proceedings (CN ISSN 0318-0522) 374
Canadian Studies in Criminology (CN ISSN 0068-9777) 281
Canadian Studies in History and Government (CN ISSN 0068-9793) 467, 709
Canadian Symposium on Water Pollution Research. Water Pollution Research in Canada. Proceedings (CN ISSN 0576-6176) 384
Canadian Tax Foundation. Provincial and Municipal Finances (CN ISSN 0317-946X) 227
Canadian Tax Foundation. Provincial Finances see Canadian Tax Foundation. Provincial and Municipal Finances 227
Canadian Tax Foundation. Tax Conference. Report of Proceedings (CN ISSN 0316-3571) 227
Canadian Tax Papers (CN ISSN 0008-512X) 227
Canadian Teachers' Federation. Bibliographies in Education (CN) 326
Canadian Technical Asphalt Association. Proceedings of the Annual Conference (CN ISSN 0068-984X) 135
Canadian Textile Directory (CN ISSN 0068-9858) 855
Canadian Theatre Checklist (CN ISSN 0705-5064) 858
Canadian Theatre Review Yearbook (CN ISSN 0316-1323) 858
Canadian Theses/Theses Canadiennes (CN ISSN 0068-9874) 89
Canadian Theses on Microfiche (Supplement)/Theses Canadiennes sur Microfiche (Supplement) (CN ISSN 0316-0149) 334
Canadian Tide and Current Tables (CN ISSN 0068-9882) 309
Canadian Toy Fair. Trade Show Directory see Toy and Decoration Fair 429
Canadian Toy, Notion and Stationery Directory see Canadian Variety & Merchandise Directory 429
Canadian Transit Association. Proceedings see Canadian Urban Transit Association. Proceedings 861
Canadian Truck Marketing (CN) 882

Canadian Universities: Income and Expenditure/Universities Canadiennes: Recettes et Depenses see Canada. Statistics Canada. University Financial Statistics/Universites Statistiques Financieres 906
Canadian Urban Transit Association. Proceedings (CN ISSN 0316-7933) 861
Canadian Variety & Merchandise Directory (CN ISSN 0068-9955) 429
Canadian Volleyball Annual and Rule Book (CN) 824
Canadian War Museum. Historical Publications (CN) 431
Canadian War Museum. Historical Publications (CN) 467, 638
Canadian Who's Who (CN) 97
Canadian Wildlife Service. Monograph Series (CN ISSN 0069-0015) 125, 127, 275
Canadian Wildlife Service. Occasional Papers (CN) 275
Canadian Wildlife Service. Progress Notes/Service Canadien de la Faune. Cahiers de Biologie (CN ISSN 0069-0023) 275
Canadian Wildlife Service. Report Series (CN ISSN 0069-0031) 102, 275
Canadian Writers and Critics (CN) 504, 561
Canadian Yearbook of International Law/Annuaire Canadien de Droit International (CN ISSN 0069-0058) 522
Canals Book (UK ISSN 0069-0066) 877, 884
Canberra Mathematical Association. Newsletter (AT) 584
Canberra Papers in Continuing Education (AT ISSN 0310-1649) 329
Cancer Chemotherapy (NE) 604
Cancer Data: Deaths and Cases Reported (Wellington) (NZ ISSN 0548-9415) 602
Cancer Facts and Figures (US ISSN 0069-0147) 604
Cancer Immunology and Immunotherapy (US ISSN 0340-7004) 604
Cancer in Ontario (CN ISSN 0315-9884) 604
Cancer in Puerto Rico (PR) 604
Cancer in Slovenia. Tables see Rak v Sloveniji. Tabele 606
Cancer Incidence in Sweden (SW ISSN 0069-0155) 604
Cancer Institute Scientific Report (JA) 604
Cancer Research Campaign. Annual Report (UK ISSN 0365-9623) 604
Cancer Seminar Proceedings (US ISSN 0069-0171) 604
Cancer Treatment and Research Foundation. Annual Report (CN) 605
Candy & Snack Industry Buying Guide (US) 406
Candy Buyers Directory (US) 407
Candy Family History Newsletter (AT ISSN 0314-7894) 417
Canned Fishery Products (US) 396, 404
Canned Food Pack Statistics (US ISSN 0069-018X) 406
Canterbury Archaeological Society. Occasional Papers (UK ISSN 0069-0198) 59
Canterbury Botanical Society. Journal (NZ) 114
Canterbury Engineering Journal (NZ ISSN 0069-0201) 366
Canto Libre (US ISSN 0098-8340) 73, 391, 658
Canu Gwerin/Folk Song (UK) 401, 658
Cape Chamber of Industries Year Book & Directory see C C I Year Book & Directory 178
Cape of Good Hope. Department of Nature Conservation and Museum Services. Annual Report (SA) 275, 384

Cape of Good Hope. Department of Nature Conservation. Annual Report *see* Cape of Good Hope. Department of Nature Conservation and Museum Services. Annual Report 275
Capital Investments of the World Petroleum Industry (US ISSN 0577-571X) 202
Capital Punishment (US) 281
Capitalismo e Socialismo (IT ISSN 0391-1934) 191, 709
Capitulo Criminologico (VE) 281, 510
Car and Driver Buyers Guide (US) 870
Car and Driver Yearbook *see* Car and Driver Buyers Guide 870
Car and Locomotive Cyclopedia (US) 873
Car Care Handbook (US ISSN 0147-7684) 906
Car Prices (US) 870
Caraher Family History Society. Journal (UK ISSN 0260-8391) 417
CARANES *see* Computer Aided Research in Ancient Near Eastern Studies 474
Caravan & Chalet Sites Guide (UK ISSN 0069-0317) 884
Caravan and Touring Manual *see* Caravan Manual and Tourist Park Guide 884
Caravan Camping Directory (AT) 829
Caravan Factfinder (UK) 870, 884
Caravan Manual and Tourist Park Guide (AT ISSN 0069-0295) 884
Caravan Sites (UK) 884
Caravan Sites and Mobile Home Parks *see* Caravan Sites 884
Caravan Sites in Britain and Ireland *see* Caravan & Chalet Sites Guide 884
Caravan Yearbook *see* Caravan Factfinder 884
Carbohydrate Chemistry (UK ISSN 0576-7172) 252
Carbonization Research Report (UK ISSN 0305-9545) 372
Carcinogenesis (US ISSN 0147-4006) 605
Cardamom Statistics (II) 24
Cardinal (US) 125
Cardiology Update (US ISSN 0163-1675) 606
Cardiovascular Clinics (US ISSN 0069-0384) 606
Cardiovascular Diseases; Current Status and Advances *see* Clinical Cardiology Monographs 607
Cardiovascular Surgery (US ISSN 0069-0406) 606, 624
Career Education Program. Program Plan *see* National Institute of Education. Career Education Program: Program Plan 346
Career Index *see* Chronicle Career Index Annual 667
Careers (Saratoga) (US ISSN 0195-4156) 89, 668
Careers and Vocational Training (UK) 666
Careers for Graduates/Carrieres pour Diplomes (CN ISSN 0318-6229) 667
Careers for School Leavers (UK ISSN 0069-0422) 667
Careers in Botany (US) 114
Careers in Depth (US ISSN 0069-0449) 667
Careers Information Series (II) 667
Caribbean Bibliography (PR ISSN 0069-0465) 437
Caribbean Conference Series (US ISSN 0069-0457) 421, 467
Caribbean Development Bank. Board of Governors. Annual Meeting of the Board of Governors: Summary of Proceedings (BB) 171
Caribbean Documents (PR ISSN 0069-0473) 467
Caribbean Economic Almanac (TR ISSN 0069-0481) 184
Caribbean Free Trade Association. Directory (TR) 235, 884
Caribbean Islands Research Institute. Annual Report *see* Caribbean Research Institute. Report 467
Caribbean Monograph Series (PR ISSN 0069-0511) 467
Caribbean Newsletter (BB) 279
Caribbean Research Institute. Report (VI) 102, 275, 467

Caribbean Scholars' Conference. Proceedings (PR ISSN 0069-052X) 467
Caribbean Series (US ISSN 0069-0538) 467
Caribbean Tourism Research Centre. Newsletter (BB) 884
Caribbean Tourism Statistics (BB) 884
Caribbean Year Book (CN ISSN 0705-2731) 467, 884
Caribbean Yearbook of International Relations (NE) 720
Caritas Internationalis. International Yearbooks (IT ISSN 0069-0554) 764, 804
Caritas Internationalis. Reports of General Assemblies (IT ISSN 0069-0562) 764, 804
Caritas; Jahrbuch des Deutschen Caritasverbandes (GW ISSN 0069-0570) 804
Caritas-Kalender (GW) 360, 764
Carl Newell Jackson Lectures (US ISSN 0528-1458) 401, 764
Carl X Gustaf-Studier (SW ISSN 0069-0597) 906
Carleton Germanic Papers (CN ISSN 0317-7254) 561
Carleton Lecture Note Series (CN) 584
Carleton Mathematical Series (CN ISSN 0069-0600) 584
Carleton University, Ottawa. Department of Geology. Geological Papers (CN ISSN 0069-0619) 292
Carleton University, Ottawa. Norman Paterson School of International Affairs. Bibliography Series (CN ISSN 0383-2848) 720
Carlton Newsletter (AT) 484
Carmarthen County Museum. Publication (UK) 652
Carnahan Conference on Electronic Crime Countermeasures. Proceedings(US) 281
Carnegie Commission on Higher Education. Commission Reports (US) 334
Carnegie Commission on Higher Education. General Reports (US) 334
Carnegie Commission on Higher Education. Technical Reports (US) 334
Carnegie Corporation of New York. Annual Report (US ISSN 0069-0635) 490
Carnegie Council on Policy Studies in Higher Education. Carnegie Council Series (US) 334
Carnegie Endowment for International Peace. Financial Report (US ISSN 0094-3029) 720
Carnegie Endowment for International Peace in the 1970's (US ISSN 0069-0643) 720
Carnegie Endowment for International Peace Report *see* Carnegie Endowment for International Peace in the 1970's 720
Carnegie Foundation for the Advancement of Teaching. Report (US ISSN 0069-0651) 315
Carnegie Institution of Washington. Year Book (US ISSN 0069-066X) 780
Carnegie Museum of Natural History. Annals of (the) Carnegie Museum (US ISSN 0097-4463) 780
Carnegie Museum of Natural History. Bulletin (US ISSN 0145-9058) 48, 102
Carnegie Museum of Natural History. Special Publication (US ISSN 0145-9031) 780
Carnegie United Kingdom Trust. Annual Report (UK ISSN 0069-0686) 780
Carnival & Circus Booking Guide (US ISSN 0090-2985) 858
Carnival Glass Price Guide (US ISSN 0069-0708) 244
Carolina Geographical Symposium. Papers (US) 421
Carolina Population Center. Monograph(US ISSN 0069-0724) 726
Carolinas Companies (US ISSN 0162-6353) 142

Carotenoids Other Than Vitamin A (US ISSN 0069-0732) 110
Carpenter and Joiner (AT) 135
Carpet and Rug Institute. Directory (US) 855
Carpet and Rug Institute. Directory and Report *see* Carpet and Rug Institute. Directory 855
Carpet and Rug Institute. Industry Review (US) 503
Carpet and Rug Institute. Review--State of the Industry *see* Carpet and Rug Institute. Industry Review 503
Carpet Annual (UK ISSN 0069-0767) 855
Carpet Dyer International (UK) 855
Carpet Specifier's Handbook (US ISSN 0095-6457) 855
Carrell (US ISSN 0008-6894) 528
Carrieres pour Diplomes *see* Careers for Graduates 667
Carroll Studies (US) 89
Carson and Newman College, Jefferson City, Tennessee. Faculty Studies (US ISSN 0069-0783) 334
Carta Geologica de Chile (CL) 292
Carta Geologica do Brasil Ao Milionesimo (BL) 292
Cartes Synoptiques de la Chromosphere Solaire *see* Cartes Synoptiques de la Chromosphere Solaire et Catalogues des Filaments et des Centres d'Activite 81
Cartes Synoptiques de la Chromosphere Solaire et Catalogues des Filaments et des Centres d'Activite (FR) 81
Cartoonists' Market *see* Artist's Market(1979) 72
Carus Mathematical Monographs (US ISSN 0069-0813) 584
Casa de Velazquez, Madrid. Melanges/ Casa de Velasquez, Madrid. Miscellanies (FR ISSN 0076-230X) 73
Casa de Velasquez, Madrid. Miscellanies *see* Casa de Velazquez, Madrid. Melanges 73
Case Analysis in Social Science n Social Therapy (US ISSN 0149-6948) 735, 796, 812
Case Studies in Bilingual Education (US) 345
Case Studies in Cultural Anthropology (US) 48
Case Studies in Education and Culture (US) 315
Case Studies on Broadcasting Systems (UK) 267
Case Studies on Human Rights and Fundamental Freedoms (NE) 718
Cases and Materials on Constitutional Law (US) 510
Cases and Materials on Trade Regulation (US) 510
Cases Decided in the Court of Claims of the United States (US ISSN 0069-0872) 510
Cases in International Politics (US) 720
Cases in Practical Politics (US ISSN 0528-2187) 709
Cass Library of African Studies. Africana Modern Library (UK ISSN 0069-0880) 48
Cass Library of African Studies. General Studies (UK ISSN 0069-0899) 439
Cass Library of African Studies. Researches and Travels (UK ISSN 0069-0902) 439
Cass Library of African Studies. South African Studies (UK ISSN 0069-0910) 439
Cass Library of African Studies. Travels and Narratives (UK ISSN 0069-0929) 439
Cass Library of Industrial Classics (UK ISSN 0069-0937) 142
Cass Library of Science Classics (UK ISSN 0069-0945) 781
Cassal Bequest Lectures (UK ISSN 0069-0961) 561
Cassell and Publishers Association Directory of Publishing in Great Britain, the Commonwealth, Ireland, South Africa and Pakistan (UK) 758

Cassell's Directory of Publishing in Great Britain, The Commonwealth, Ireland, South Africa and Pakistan *see* Cassell and Publishers Association Directory of Publishing in Great Britain, the Commonwealth, Ireland, South Africa and Pakistan 758
Cassette Books (US ISSN 0363-9029) 133, 528
Castle's Guide to the Fruit, Flower, Vegetable and Allied Trades (UK ISSN 0069-0988) 404
Castle's Town and County Trades Directory (UK ISSN 0069-0996) 235
Casualty Return Statistical Summary (UK ISSN 0008-7572) 865
Cat Fanciers Association. Year Book (US ISSN 0069-1003) 682
Cat Fanciers' Magazine (AT) 682
Catalog of Books on Magnetic Tape (Lansing) *see* Michigan. State Library Services. Catalog of Books on Magnetic Tape 92
Catalog of Dealers' Prices for Marine Shells (US ISSN 0084-862X) 127
Catalog of Mailing Lists *see* United States & Canadian Mailing Lists 6
Catalog of Model Services and Supplies(US) 135, 366
Catalog of Modern World Coins (US ISSN 0069-102X) 477
Catalog of Museum Publications and Media (US) 2, 656
Catalog of Recorded Instruction for Television *see* Great Plains National Instructional Television Library. Recorded Visual Instruction 349
Catalog of Selected Films for Mental Health Education *see* Mental Health Media Center Film Catalog 736
Catalog of World Bank Publications (UN) 199
Catalogo Bolaffi d'Arte Moderna *see* Catalogo Nazionale Bolaffi d'Arte Moderna 73
Catalogo Bolaffi dei Vini d'Italia (IT) 86
Catalogo Bolaffi del Cacciatore e delle Armi (IT ISSN 0576-8888) 829
Catalogo Bolaffi del Cinema Italiano (IT) 649
Catalogo Bolaffi della Grafica Italiana *see* Catalogo Nazionale Bolaffi della Grafica 73
Catalogo Bolaffi della Pittura Italiana dell'Ottocento (IT) 73
Catalogo Colectivo de Publicaciones Periodicas (EC) 89, 506
Catalogo Colectivo de Publicaciones Periodicas Existentes en las Bibliotecas de la Universidad (MX) 89
Catalogo de Filmes Brasileiros *see* Brasil Cinema 905
Catalogo de la Fauna Cubana *see* Universidad de la Habana. Centro de Informacion Cientifica y Tecnica. Serie 4. Ciencias Biologicas 108
Catalogo de la Industria de Madrid *see* Guia del Comercio y de la Industria de Madrid 179
Catalogo de Pesquisas Concluidas e Em Desenvolvimento (BL) 334
Catalogo de Publicaciones Latinoamericanas Sobre Formacion Profesional (UY ISSN 0069-1046) 89, 315, 668
Catalogo dei Libri in Commercio/ Italian Books in Print (IT) 760
Catalogo dei Libri Italiani in Commercio *see* Catalogo dei Libri in Commercio 760
Catalogo dos Cursos de Pos-Graduacao No Brasil (BL) 334
Catalogo Ilustrado de las Plantas de Cundinamarca (CK) 114
Catalogo Internazionale delle Macchine per l' Imballaggio *see* International Encyclopedia on Packaging Machines 672
Catalogo Motoristico (IT) 870
Catalogo Nazionale Bolaffi d'Arte Moderna (IT) 73
Catalogo Nazionale Bolaffi della Grafica (IT) 73, 733
Catalogo Productos y Servicios del Estado de Mexico (MX) 235

Catalogue Collectif des Publications Scientifiques dans les Bibliotheques Canadiennes see Union List of Scientific Serials in Canadian Libraries 795
Catalogue de l'Edition Francaise see Livres Disponibles 92
Catalogue des Catalogues Automobile (FR ISSN 0069-1097) 870
Catalogue des Coleopteres de Belgique (BE) 120
Catalogue des Constructeurs Francais d'Equipements pour les Industries Alimentaires (FR) 582
Catalogue des Normes Francaises (FR) 636
Catalogue des Produits Agrees Par Qualite-France (FR ISSN 0069-1100) 181
Catalogue des Theses de Pharmacie Soutenues en France. Quinquennial Cumulation (FR ISSN 0069-4665) 684
Catalogue des Theses Francaises de Science Odontologiques et de Chirurgie Dentaire see Thesindex Dentaire 602
Catalogue General. Radio, Television, Electrophones, Magnetophones, Haute-Fidelite, Stereophonie, Audio-Visuel (FR ISSN 0069-1119) 267
Catalogue General de l'Industrie et du Commerce Automobile de Belgique (BE) 870
Catalogue International des Machines d'Emballage see International Encyclopedia on Packaging Machines 672
Catalogue National du Genie Climatique-Chauffage et Conditionnement d'Air/National Catalogue of Heating and Air Conditioning/Nazionaler Katalog der Heizung und Klimatisierung (FR ISSN 0153-999X) 429
Catalogue National du Traitement des Surfaces de l'Anticorrosion et des Traitements Thermiques (FR ISSN 0396-1214) 673
Catalogue Nationale du Chauffage et du Conditionnement d'Air see Catalogue National du Genie Climatique-Chauffage et Conditionnement d'Air 429
Catalogue of Arabic Manuscripts in Salar Jung Museum (II) 656
Catalogue of Books Recommended for Libraries/Sentei Tosho Somokuroku (JA) 89
Catalogue of Canadian Recreation and Leisure Research (CN) 829, 884
Catalogue of Indian Chemical Plants see Guide to Indian Chemical Plants and Equipment 373
Catalogue of Little Press Books in Print Published in the UK (UK ISSN 0591-0986) 89
Catalogue of N A L Technical Translations (National Aeronautical Laboratory) (II ISSN 0077-2968) 7
Catalogue of Persian Manuscripts in Salar Jung Museum (II) 656
Catalogue of Reproductions of Paintings Prior to 1860 (UN ISSN 0069-1135) 73
Catalogue of Reproductions of Paintings, 1860-1973 (UN ISSN 0069-1143) 73
Catalogue of Statistical Materials of Developing Countries (JA) 837
Catalogue of Technical and Specialised Periodicals - a Selected List see Technical and Specialised Periodicals Published in Britain 854
Catalogue of Urdu Manuscripts in Salar Jung Museum (II) 656
Catalogues of Short Films and Filmstrips see Selected List of Catalogues for Short Films and Filmstrips 651
Catalogus Musicus (GW ISSN 0069-116X) 658
Catalogus Translationem et Commentariorum (US ISSN 0528-2594) 578
Catalogus van Academische Geschriften in Nederland Verschenen see Bibliografie van Nederlandse Proefschriften 88

Catalogus van Nederlandse Zeekaarten en Andere Hydrografische Publikaties/Catalog of Charts and Other Hydrographic Publications (NE) 896
Cataluna Exporta (SP ISSN 0069-1178) 178
Catalysis by Metal Complexes (NE) 254
Catalysis: Science and Technology (US) 245
Catering & Hotel Management Year Book & Diary (UK ISSN 0069-1194) 482
Catholic Almanac (US ISSN 0069-1208) 774
Catholic Bible Quarterly Monograph Series (US) 774
Catholic Book Notes see Catholic Truth 774
Catholic Central Union of America. Proceedings (US ISSN 0069-1216) 774
Catholic Commission for Racial Justice. Notes & Reports (UK ISSN 0144-8285) 718
Catholic Directory (UK ISSN 0069-1224) 774
Catholic Directory for Scotland (UK ISSN 0306-5677) 774
Catholic Directory for the Clergy and Laity in Scotland see Catholic Directory for Scotland 774
Catholic Directory of Canada see Annuaire de l'Eglise du Quebec 773
Catholic Directory of Eastern Africa (TZ ISSN 0069-1240) 774
Catholic Health Association of Canada. Directory (CN) 593, 774
Catholic Hospital Association of Canada. Directory see Catholic Health Association of Canada. Directory 593
Catholic Periodical and Literature Index(US ISSN 0008-8285) 2, 769
Catholic Periodical Index see Catholic Periodical and Literature Index 769
Catholic Press Directory (US ISSN 0008-8307) 769
Catholic Schools in the United States see N C E A Ganley's Catholic Schools in America 332
Catholic Secondary Schools' Association of N.S.W. and A.C.T. Educational Media Committee. Bulletin see Audio-Visual Bulletin 347
Catholic Theological Society of America. Proceedings (US ISSN 0069-1267) 774
Catholic Truth (UK ISSN 0411-275X) 758, 774
Catholic University of America. School of Law. Center for National Policy Review. Annual Report (US) 709
Catholicisme Hier, Aujourd'hui, Demain (FR) 774
Cavalcade and Directory of Acts & Attractions (US ISSN 0090-2993) 858
Cavalcade and Directory of Fairs see Directory of North American Fairs and Expositions 5
Cave Research Group of Great Britain. Transactions. see British Cave Research Association. Transactions 292
Cave Studies (US ISSN 0069-1313) 292
Cayman Islands. Currency Board. Report (CJ) 227
Cayman Islands. Department of Finance and Development. Estimates of Gross Domestic Product and Related Aggregates (CJ) 212
Cayman Islands. Education Department. Report of the Chief Education Officer (CJ) 315
Cayman Islands. Legislative Assembly. Minutes (CJ ISSN 0300-4740) 740
Cayman Islands Handbook and Businessman's Guide (CJ) 235
Cayman Islands Holiday Guide (CJ) 884
Cecil H. Brite Lecture Series in Advertising and Publications Management (US) 5
Ceilings & Partitions (UK) 502
Celebrate (US ISSN 0361-0896) 479

Celebration (US) 579
Celebrity Service International Contact Book (US ISSN 0069-1372) 649, 858
Cell Biology (US) 119
Cell Biology Monographs (US) 119
Celtica (IE ISSN 0069-1399) 334
Cement Association of Japan. Review of the General Meeting (JA) 135
Cement Association of Japan. Review of the General Meeting. Technical Session (JA) 135
Cement Industry Technical Conference. Record (US ISSN 0069-1402) 135
Cement Market and Outlook see European Cement Association. Annual European Review 136
Cement- och Betonginstitutet Aarsberaettelse Report of Activities see C B I Aarsberaettelse/Report of Activities 135
Cement- och Betonginstitutet Forskning Research see C B I Forskning/Research 135
Cement och Betonginstitutet Rapporter Reports see C B I Rapporter/Reports 135
Cement- och Betonginstitutet Rekommendationer Recommendations see C B I Rekommendationer/Recommendations 135
Cement Research Institute of India. Annual Report (II) 135
Cemento Portland (AG ISSN 0008-8927) 135
Cenacolo (IT ISSN 0008-8935) 73, 561
Censo de Poblacion y Viviendas (CU) 837
Censored (US ISSN 0163-2280) 538
Census Bureau Methodological Research see U.S. Bureau of the Census. Census Bureau Methodological Research 803
Census of Industrial Production in Zambia (ZA ISSN 0069-1429) 154
Census of Inland Shipping in the Netherlands at Locks and Bridges see Statistiek van de Scheepvaartbeweging in Nederland 881
Census of Maine Manufactures (US ISSN 0090-7111) 221
Census of Manufacturing Industries of Puerto Rico (PR ISSN 0552-5276) 221
Census of Motor Traffic on Main International Traffic Arteries (UN) 874
Census of Private Non-Profit Making Institutions in Fiji. A Report (FJ) 154, 837
Census of Traffic on Main International Traffic Arteries see Census of Motor Traffic on Main International Traffic Arteries 874
Census of U.S. Civil Aircraft (US ISSN 0069-1437) 867
Centar za Proucavanje i Suzbijanje Alkoholizma i Drugih Ovisnosti. Radovi (YU ISSN 0033-8567) 286
Center Essay Series see University of Wisconsin, Milwaukee. Center for Latin America. Essay Series 473
Center for Adult Diseases, Osaka. Annual Report (JA ISSN 0078-6632) 593
Center for Agricultural Economic Research, Rehovot. Working Papers (IS) 27
Center for Agricultural Publishing and Documentation. Agricultural Research Reports (NE ISSN 0069-2212) 13
Center for Chinese Research Materials. Bibliographical Series (US ISSN 0084-6902) 539
Center for Consumer Education Services. Monographs (US ISSN 0084-8654) 279
Center for Creative Photography (US) 693
Center for Hermeneutical Studies in Hellenistic and Modern Culture. Protocol Series of the Colloquies (US ISSN 0098-0900) 490
Center for History of Physics. Newsletter (US) 696

Center for Holocaust Studies Newsletter (US) 391, 451
Center for Information and Numerical Data Analysis and Synthesis Annual Report see C I N D A S. Annual Report 834
Center for Libertarian Studies. Newsletter see In Pursuit of Liberty 711
Center for Pre-Columbian Studies. Conference Proceedings see Dumbarton Oaks Conference Proceedings 60
Center for Research Libraries. Handbook (US) 528
Center for Research on Learning and Teaching. Memo to the Faculty (US ISSN 0025-911X) 334
Center for the Study of the Presidency. Proceedings (US) 709
Center for War-Peace Studies Special Studies see C W/P S Special Studies 720
Center on Evaluation, Development, and Research. Occasional Paper Series (US) 315
Center on Human Policy. Notes from the Center (US) 315
Centering (US) 579
Centerpiece (UK ISSN 0307-4625) 429
Centers of Civilization Series (US ISSN 0069-1461) 431
Centraalbureau voor Schimmelcultures. List of Cultures (NE) 114
Central Africa Historical Association. Local Series Pamphlets see Historical Association of Zimbabwe. Local Series Pamphlets 440
Central African Power Corporation. Annual Report and Accounts (RH ISSN 0069-147X) 352
Central Archives for the History of the Jewish People Newsletter/Ha-Arkhiyon Ha-Merkazi le-Toldot Ha-Am Ha-Yehudi. Yediot (IS) 474
Central Atlantic States Manufacturers Directory see Directory of Central Atlantic States Manufacturers. Maryland, Delaware, Virginia, West Virginia, North Carolina, South Carolina 236
Central Bank of Barbados. Annual Report (BB) 184
Central Bank of Barbados. Annual Statistical Digest (BB) 171
Central Bank of Barbados. Balance of Payments (BB) 154
Central Bank of Ceylon. Annual Report(CE ISSN 0069-1496) 171
Central Bank of Ceylon. Review of the Economy/Arthika Vivaranaya (CE) 184
Central Bank of China, T'ai-Pei. Annual Report (CH ISSN 0069-150X) 171
Central Bank of Cyprus. Annual Report(CY ISSN 0069-1518) 171
Central Bank of Egypt. Annual Report (UA) 171
Central Bank of Egypt. Board of Directors. Report see Central Bank of Egypt. Annual Report 171
Central Bank of Iraq, Baghdad. Report (IQ ISSN 0069-1534) 171
Central Bank of Ireland. Report (IE ISSN 0069-1542) 171
Central Bank of Jordan. Annual Report/Bank Al-Markazi Al-Urduni. Annual Report (JO ISSN 0069-1550) 171
Central Bank of Kenya. Annual Report (KE ISSN 0069-1569) 171
Central Bank of Kuwait. Annual Report(KU) 171
Central Bank of Kuwait. Economic Report (KU) 184
Central Bank of Malta. Annual Report (MM ISSN 0577-0653) 171
Central Bank of Nigeria. Annual Report and Statement of Accounts (NR ISSN 0069-1577) 171
Central Bank of Nigeria. Economic and Financial Review (NR ISSN 0008-9281) 184
Central Bank of Somali. Annual Report and Statement of Accounts (SO) 171

Central Bank of Sweden. Annual Report *see* Sveriges Riksbank. Foervaltningsberaettelse *176*
Central Bank of Sweden. Statistical Yearbook *see* Sveriges Riksbank. Statistisk Aarsbok *176*
Central Bank of the Bahamas. Annual Report and Statement of Accounts. (BF) *171*
Central Bank of the Gambia. Annual Report (GM) *171*
Central Bank of the Philippines. Annual Report (PH ISSN 0069-1585) *171*
Central Bank of the Republic of Turkey. Annual Report (TU) *171*
Central Bank of Trinidad and Tobago. Report (TR ISSN 0069-1593) *171*
Central Bank of Yemen. Annual Report(YE ISSN 0301-6625) *171*
Central Building Research Institute. Building Digests (II ISSN 0557-319X) *135*
Central Building Research Institute. List of Publications (II ISSN 0557-322X) *135*
Central Conference of American Rabbis. Yearbook (US ISSN 0069-1607) *770*
Central Conference of Teamsters. Chairman's Report *see* Central Conference of Teamsters. Officers' Report *506*
Central Conference of Teamsters. Officers' Report (US ISSN 0069-1615) *506*
Central Electric Railfans' Association. Bulletin (US ISSN 0069-1623) *873*
Central Europe and Scandinavia Travel Guide *see* Travel Guide to Europe *892*
Central Inland Fisheries Research Institute. Bulletin (II ISSN 0008-9427) *396*
Central Institute of Indian Languages Adult Literacy Series *see* C I I L Adult Literacy Series *329*
Central Institute of Indian Languages Bilingual Hindi Series *see* C I I L Bilingual Hindi Series *542*
Central Institute of Indian Languages Folklore Series *see* C I I L Folklore Series *401*
Central Institute of Indian Languages Grammar Series *see* C I I L Grammar Series *542*
Central Institute of Indian Languages Occasional Monograph Series *see* C I I L Occasional Monograph Series *542*
Central Institute of Research and Training in Public Cooperation, New Delhi. Publications (II ISSN 0069-1631) *812*
Central Issues in Philosophy Series (US) *687*
Central Literary Magazine (UK ISSN 0069-164X) *561*
Central Marine Fisheries Research Institute. Bulletin (II ISSN 0577-084X) 309, *396*
Central Mine Planning & Design Institute. Manuals (II) *642*
Central Mining Research Station, Dhanbad. Progress Report (II ISSN 0070-4628) *642*
Central Mississippi Planning and Development District. Annual Report(US) *484*
Central Mortgage and Housing Corporation. Annual Report *see* Canada Mortgage and Housing Corporation. Annual Report *484*
Central Naugatuck Valley Regional Planning Agency. Annual Report (US ISSN 0069-1674) *221*
Central Nucleaire Ardennes (EI) 366, *702*
Central Ontario Construction Industry Directory and Purchasing Guide (CN) *135*
Central Road Research Institute, New Delhi. Road Research Paper (II ISSN 0069-1690) *862*
Central Sericultural Research and Training Institute. Annual Report (II ISSN 0304-6818) *13*
Central Statistical Office Statistical Bulletins *see* C.S.O. Statistical Bulletins *834*

Central Tobacco Research Institute. Annual Report *see* Central Tobacco Research Institute and its Regional Research Stations. Annual Report *861*
Central Tobacco Research Institute and its Regional Research Stations. Annual Report (II) *861*
Central Valley Project (California) Annual Report *see* U.S. Bureau of Reclamation. Mid-Pacific Region. Report *898*
Centrale Elletronucleare Latina. Relazione Annuale (EI ISSN 0591-1044) 362, 366, *702*
Centrale Nucleare Garigliano. Relazione Annuale (EI ISSN 0591-1036) 366, *702*
Centralite (PH) *263*
Centralny Osrodek Badan i Rozwoju Techniki Kolejnictwa. Prace COBiRTK (PL) *873*
Centre Belge Histoire Rurale. Publications/Belgisch Centrum voor Landelijke Geschiedenis. Publikaties (BE ISSN 0076-1192) *451*
Centre Canadien International de Recherches et d'Information sur l'Economie Publique et Cooperative. Revue du Canadien *see* Canadian Journal of Public and Cooperative Economy *142*
Centre Culturel Francais, Algiers. Rencontres Culturelles (AE ISSN 0069-1720) *561*
Centre d'Ecologie Forestiere. Notes Techniques *see* Centre d'Ecologie Forestiere et Rurale. Notes Techniques. B: Herbageres *408*
Centre d'Ecologie Forestiere. Notes Techniques *see* Centre d'Ecologie Forestiere et Rurale. Notes Techniques. A: Forestieres *408*
Centre d'Ecologie Forestiere et Rurale. Communications (BE) 102, *408*
Centre d'Ecologie Forestiere et Rurale. Notes Techniques. A: Forestieres (BE) *408*
Centre d'Ecologie Forestiere et Rurale. Notes Techniques. B: Herbageres (BE) *408*
Centre d'Enseignement Superieur de Brazzaville. Annales (CF) *334*
Centre d'Etude de la Delinquance Juvenile. Publication *see* Studiecentrum voor Jeugdmisdadigheid. Publikatie *284*
Centre d'Etudes et de Documentation Europeennes. Cahiers. Annals (CN ISSN 0069-1844) *796*
Centre d'Etudes et de Gestion Financieres. Notice Circulaire (FR) *214*
Centre d'Etudes et de Recherches de l'Industrie des Liants Hydrauliques, Paris. Rapport d'Activite (FR) *906*
Centre d'Etudes Ethnologiques. Publications. Serie 1: Rapports et Comptes Rendus (ZR ISSN 0577-1331) *48*
Centre d'Etudes Ethnologiques. Publications. Serie 2: Memoires et Monographies (ZR) *48*
Centre d'Etudes Ethnologiques. Publications. Serie 3: Travaux Linguistiques (ZR) *542*
Centre d'Etudes Pratiques d'Informatique et d'Automatique. Collection (FR ISSN 0069-1852) *906*
Centre d'Etudes Sociologiques. Travaux et Documents (FR ISSN 0071-8289) *812*
Centre d'Histoire et d'Art de la Thudinie. Publications (BE) 73, *451*
Centre d'Information des Services Medicaux d'Entreprises et Interentreprises. Annuaire (FR ISSN 0069-1879) *593*
Centre de Cartographie Phytosociologique. Communications *see* Centre d'Ecologie Forestiere et Rurale. Communications *408*
Centre de Documentation et de Recherche sur l'Asie. Etudes et Documents *see* Asian Studies Series *442*
Centre de Geomorphologie, Caen. Bulletin (FR ISSN 0068-4791) *292*

Centre de Recherche en Civilisation Canadienne-Francaise. Cahiers *see* French-Canadian Civilization Research Center. Cahiers *468*
Centre de Recherche en Litterature Canadienne-Francaise. Cahiers *see* French-Canadian Civilization Research Center. Cahiers *468*
Centre de Recherche Industrielles en Afrique Centrale. Bulletin d'Information *see* Sciences, Techniques, Informations C R I A C *225*
Centre de Recherches en Mathematiques Pures. Publications. Serie 1 (SZ) *584*
Centre de Recherches en Mathematiques Pures. Publications. Serie 2. Monographies (SZ) *585*
Centre de Recherches en Mathematiques Pures. Publications. Serie 3. Oeuvres (SZ) *585*
Centre de Recherches en Mathematiques Pures. Publications. Serie 4. Conferences Communications (SZ) *585*
Centre de Recherches Industrielles en Afrique Centrale Sciences, Techniques, Informations C R I A C *see* Sciences, Techniques, Informations C R I A C *225*
Centre de Recherches pour le Developpement International. Rapport Annuel *see* International Development Research Centre. Annual Report *145*
Centre Economie, Espace, Environnement. Cahiers (FR) 142, *384*
Centre Europeen d'Etudes Burgondo-Medianes. Publication (SZ ISSN 0069-1895) 421, *451*
Centre for Advanced Land Use Studies Research Reports *see* C A L U S Research Reports *761*
Centre for Environmental Studies, London. Conference Paper (UK ISSN 0069-1917) *384*
Centre for Environmental Studies, London. Information Paper (UK ISSN 0069-1925) *484*
Centre for Environmental Studies, London. Occasional Paper (UK) 384, *484*
Centre for Intergroup Studies. Annual Report (SA) *812*
Centre for Library and Information Management Report to the British Library and Development Department *see* C L A I M Report to the British Library and Development Department *780*
Centre for Urban Studies Bulletin *see* C U S Bulletin *483*
Centre Genealogique de Midi-Provence. Cahier Genealogique (FR) *417*
Centre Genealogique du Midi-Provence. Fiches Techniques (FR) *417*
Centre Geologique et Geophysique de Montpellier. Publications. Serie Geologie (FR) *292*
Centre International d'Etude des Problems Humains. Bulletins (MC ISSN 0577-1730) *796*
Centre International d'Information sur le Droit d'Auteur. Bulletin d'Information *see* International Copyright Information Centre. Information Bulletin *677*
Centre International de Documentation Arachnologiques. Liste des Travaux Arachnologiques (FR ISSN 0085-2783) *110*
Centre International de Documentation Economique et Sociale Africaine. Monographies Documentaires (BE ISSN 0069-1763) *439*
Centre International de Documentation et Sociale Africaine. Enquetes Bibliographiques (BE ISSN 0069-1755) *439*
Centre International de Documentation Occitane. Bibliotheque. Catalogue (FR) *542*
Centre International de Documentation Occitane. Serie Bibliographique (FR) 89, *451*

Centre International de Documentation Occitane. Serie Etudes (FR ISSN 0398-3765) *451*
Centre International de Liaison des Ecoles de Cinema et de Television. Bulletin d'Informations (BE ISSN 0528-4759) 267, *649*
Centre Medico-Social de Pro Familia (SZ) *315*
Centre National d'Archeologie et d'Histoire du Livre. Publication (BE ISSN 0069-1984) 59, *733*
Centre National d'Etudes Spatiales. Rapport d'Activite (FR ISSN 0069-2034) *7*
Centre National de Documentation Scientifique et Technique. Rapport d'Activite (BE ISSN 0069-1968) 781, *850*
Centre National de la Recherche Scientifique. Colloques Internationaux. Sciences Humaines (FR ISSN 0069-1976) *490*
Centre National de la Recherche Scientifique. Colloques Internationaux. Sciences Mathematiques, Physiques, Chimiques, Biologiques et Medicales (FR) *781*
Centre National de la Recherche Scientifique. Colloques Internationaux. Sciences Mathematiques, Physico-Chimiques, Biologiques et Naturelles *see* Centre National de la Recherche Scientifique. Colloques Internationaux. Sciences Mathematiques, Physiques, Chimiques, Biologiques et Medicales *781*
Centre National de la Recherche Scientifique. Rapport d'Activite (FR ISSN 0071-8327) *781*
Centre National de la Recherche Scientifique. Rapport National de Conjoncture Scientifique (FR ISSN 0071-8335) *781*
Centre National de la Recherche Scientifique. Seminaire d'Econometrie. Cahiers (FR ISSN 0071-8343) *142*
Centre National de la Recherche Scientifique. Seminaire d'Econometrie. Monographies (FR ISSN 0071-8270) *142*
Centre National de la Recherche Scientifique. Tableau de Classement des Chercheurs (FR ISSN 0071-8351) *781*
Centre National de Recherches Appliques au Developpement Rural. Departement de Recherches Agronomiques. Rapport Annuel (MG) *13*
Centre National de Recherches Appliques au Developpement Rural. Departement de Recherches Agronomiques. Rapport d'Activite (MG) *13*
Centre National de Recherches Archeologiques en Belgique. Repertoires Archeologiques. Serie A: Repertoires Bibliographiques/ Nationaal Centrum voor Oudheidkundige Navorsingen in Belgie. Oudheidkundige Repertoria. Reeks A: Bibliografische Repertoria (BE ISSN 0069-1992) *59*
Centre National de Recherches Archeologiques en Belgique. Repertoires Archeologiques. Serie B: Repertoires des Collections (BE ISSN 0069-200X) *59*
Centre National de Recherches Archeologiques en Belgique. Repertoires Archeologiques. Serie C: Repertoires Divers (BE ISSN 0069-2018) *59*
Centre National de Recherches Scientifiques et Techniques pour l'Industrie Cimentiere Rapport de Recherche *see* C R I C Rapport de Recherche *780*
Centre National du Commerce Exterieur. Annuaire (FR ISSN 0071-836X) *194*

Centre pour l'Etude des Problemes de Monde Musulman Contemporain. Initiations (BE ISSN 0077-0353) 442, 769
Centre pour l'Etude des Problemes du Monde Musulman Contemporain. Etude see Correspondance d'Orient 443
Centre pour l'Etude des Problemes du Monde Musulman Contemporain. Revue Annuelle see Correspondance d'Orient 443
Centre Regional de Documentation Pedagogique de Toulouse. Annales (FR ISSN 0069-2069) 315
Centre Regional de Recherche et de Documentation Pedagogiques de Lyon. Annales. (FR ISSN 0069-2050) 347
Centre Technique Forestiere Tropical du Cameroun. Rapport Annuel (CM) 408
Centre Universitaire de la Reunion. Cahier (RE ISSN 0337-6176) 348, 542
Centro Camuno di Studi Preistorici. Archivi (IT) 59
Centro Camuno di Studi Preistorici. Bollettino (IT ISSN 0577-2168) 48, 59
Centro Camuno di Studi Preistorici. Studi Camuni (IT) 59
Centro de Bibliotecologia, Archivologia e Informacion. Anuario (MX) 528
Centro de Desarrollo Industrial del Ecuador. Noticias Tecnicas (EC) 221
Centro de Estudios de Estado y Sociedad. Documentos de Trabajo (AG) 740
Centro de Estudios de la Realidad Puertorriquena. Cuadernos (PR) 709
Centro de Estudios Martianos. Anuario (CU) 467
Centro de Estudios Monetarios Latinoamericanos. Ensayos (MX ISSN 0577-2451) 171
Centro de Estudios Orientales. Anuario (MX ISSN 0066-8249) 442
Centro de Estudios Urbanos. Cuadernos (VE) 484
Centro de Estudos de Cabo Verde. Revista: Serie de Ciencias Humanas (CV) 796
Centro de Historia del Tachira. Boletin (VE ISSN 0411-5023) 467
Centro de Informaciones y Estudios del Uruguay. Cuadernos (UY) 796
Centro de Investigacion y Promocion del Campesinado. Cuadernos de Investigacion (BO) 184
Centro de Investigacion y Promocion del Campesinado Cuadernos C I P C A (Serie Popular) see Cuadernos C I P C A (Serie Popular) 329
Centro de Investigaciones Agricolas de el Bajio Circular see C I A B Circular 33
Centro de Investigaciones Agricolas de Tamaulipas. Circular CIAT (MX ISSN 0084-8689) 13
Centro de Investigaciones Agricolas de Tamaulipas. Informe Anual de Labores (MX ISSN 0084-8697) 13
Centro de Investigaciones en Administracion Publica. Documentos de Trabajo see Centro de Estudios de Estado y Sociedad. Documentos de Trabajo 740
Centro de Investigaciones en Ciencias de la Educacion. Seccion Lenguas Indigenas. Documento de Trabajo (AG) 348, 542
Centro de Investigaciones Energeticas Servicio Informativo see C.I.E. Servicio Informativo 678
Centro de Navegacion Transatlantica. C.N.T. Handbook. River Plate Handbook for Shipowners and Agents (AG) 877
Centro de Navegacion Transatlantica. C.N.T. Year Book; Ship Owners' and Agents' Handbook, River Plate Ports see Centro de Navegacion Transatlantica. C.N.T. Handbook. River Plate Handbook for Shipowners and Agents 877

Centro de Pesquisa Agropecuaria do Tropico Umido. Boletim Tecnico (BL) 14
Centro de Radio Astronomia e Astrofisica Mackenzie. Observatoria Nacional. Relatorio Anual (BL) 82, 267, 696
Centro de Salud "Max Arias Schreiber", Lima. Congreso Nacional de Tuberculosis y Enfermedades Respiratorias (PE ISSN 0069-2166) 623
Centro di Documentazione Sul Movimento dei Disciplinati. Quaderni (IT ISSN 0009-0026) 431
Centro Interamericano de Investigacion y Documentacion Sobre Formacion Profesional. Informes (UY) 329
Centro Interamericano de Investigacion y Documentacion Sobre Formacion Profesional. Serie Bibliografica (UY) 315
Centro Interamericano de Investigacion y Documentacion Sobre Formacion Profesional Colecciones Basicas C I N T E R F O R see Colecciones Basicas C I N T E R F O R 329
Centro Interamericano de Investigacion y Documentacion Sobre Formacion Profesional Estudios y Monografias see C I N T E R F O R. Estudios y Monografias 315
Centro Internacional de Informaciones sobre el Derecho de Autor. Bulletin de Informacion see International Copyright Information Centre. Information Bulletin 677
Centro Internacional de Mejoramiento de Maiz y Trigo Information Bulletin see C I M M Y T Information Bulletin 42
Centro Internacional de Mejoramiento de Maiz y Trigo Report on Maize Improvement see C I M M Y T Report on Maize Improvement 42
Centro Internacional de Mejoramiento de Maiz y Trigo Report on Wheat Improvement see C I M M Y T Report on Wheat Improvement 42
Centro Internacional de Mejoramiento de Maiz y Trigo Review see C I M M Y T Review 42
Centro Internacional de Mejoramiento de Maiz y Trigo Today see C I M M Y T Today 42
Centro Internazionale Radio-Medico see C.I.R.M 622
Centro Latinoamericano de Administracion Medica. Traducciones (AG) 593
Centro Latinoamericano de Demografia. Publicaciones P I S P A L (Programa de Investigaciones Sociales Sobre Problemas de Poblacion Relevantes para Politicas de Poblacion en America Latina) (UN) 726
Centro Latinoamericano de Demografia. Serie A: Informes sobre Investigaciones Realizadas see United Nations. Regional Centre for Demographic Training and Research in Latin America. Serie A 729
Centro Latinoamericano de Demografia. Serie C: Informes sobre Investigaciones Realizadas Por los Alumnos del Centro see United Nations. Regional Centre for Demographic Training and Research in Latin America. Serie C 730
Centro Latinoamericano de Demografia. Serie I: Recopilacion de Trabajos Sobres Paises see United Nations. Regional Centre for Demographic Training and Research in Latin America. Serie I 730
Centro Latinoamericano de Demografia. Textos de Divulgacion (UN) 726
Centro Latinoamericano de Trabajo Social. Serie CELATS (AG) 804
Centro Panamericano de Zoonosis. Boletin Informativo see Centro Panamericano de Zoonosis. Boletin Informativo. Tuberculosis en las Americas 608
Centro Panamericano de Zoonosis. Boletin Informativo see Centro Panamericano de Zoonosis. Boletin Informativo. Leptospirosis en las Americas 608

Centro Panamericano de Zoonosis. Boletin Informativo see Centro Panamericano de Zoonosis. Boletin Informativo. Hidatidosis en las Americas 608
Centro Panamericano de Zoonosis. Boletin Informativo see Centro Panamericano de Zoonosis. Boletin Informativo. Enfermedades Transmitidas por Alimentos en las Americas 608
Centro Panamericano de Zoonosis. Boletin Informativo. Enfermedades Transmitidas por Alimentos en las Americas (AG) 608
Centro Panamericano de Zoonosis. Boletin Informativo. Hidatidosis en las Americas (AG) 608
Centro Panamericano de Zoonosis. Boletin Informativo. Leptospirosis en las Americas (AG) 608
Centro Panamericano de Zoonosis. Boletin Informativo. Tuberculosis en las Americas (AG) 608
Centro Regional de Construcciones Escolares para America Latina. Documentos Asesoria see Centro Regional de Construcciones Escolares para America Latina y la Region del Caribe. Documentos Asesoria 343
Centro Regional de Construcciones Escolares para America Latina. Documentos Tecnicos see Centro Regional de Construcciones Escolares para America Latina y la Region del Caribe. Documentos Tecnicos 343
Centro Regional de Construcciones Escolares para America Latina y la Region del Caribe. Documentos Asesoria (MX) 343
Centro Regional de Construcciones Escolares para America Latina y la Region del Caribe. Documentos Tecnicos (MX) 343, 343
Centro Regional Latinoamericano de Estudios para la Conservacion y Restauracion de Bienes Culturales Boletin Informativo - CEdOclA see Boletin Informativo - CEdOclA 275
Centro Studi per la Magna Grecia, Naples. Pubblicazioni Proprie (IT ISSN 0069-2204) 59
Centro Superiore di Logica e Scienze Comparate. Quaderni (IT) 687
Centrul de Stiinte Sociale din Cluj. Seria Drept (RM) 510
Centur (UY) 870, 884
Ceol (IE ISSN 0009-0174) 658
Ceramic Data Book (US) 244
Ceramic Plants in Canada (CN ISSN 0069-2220) 244
Ceramica de Cultura Maya (US ISSN 0577-3334) 48, 59
Ceramics and Glass Series (US ISSN 0069-2239) 244
Cercetari de Muzicologie (RM) 658
Cercle Belge de la Librairie. Annuaire (BE) 528, 758
Cercle d'Etudes Numismatiques. Travaux (BE ISSN 0069-2247) 477
Cercle d'Histoire et d'Archeologie de Saint-Ghislain et de la Region. Anales (BE) 59, 451
Cercle d'Histoire et d'Archeologie de Saint-Ghislain et de la Region. Miettes d'Histoire see Cercle d'Histoire et d'Archeologie de Saint-Ghislain et de la Region. Anales 451
Cereal Rust Bulletin (US) 33
Cerebral Function Symposium. Proceedings (US) 619
Cerebral Vascular Diseases. Conference see Princeton Conference on Cerebrovascular Diseases 607
Cerebrovascular Diseases see Princeton Conference on Cerebrovascular Diseases 607
Ceredigion (UK ISSN 0069-2263) 431
Cerro Tololo Interamerican Observatory (La Serena, Chile). Contributions (US ISSN 0582-7094) 82
Certificats de Vaccination Exiges dans les Voyages Internationaux see Vaccination Certificate Requirements for International Travel 755

Certified Public Accountants, Public Accountants, Professional Corporations, and Accountants Authorized to Conduct Municipal Audits in Oregon see Oregon. State Board of Accountancy. Certified Public Accountants, Public Accountants, Professional Corporations, and Accountants Authorized to Conduct Municipal Audits in Oregon t 168h
Ceska Bibliografie (CS ISSN 0577-3490) 528
Ceskoslovenska Akademie Ved. Rozpravy. MPV: Rada Matematickych a Prirodnich Ved (CS ISSN 0069-228X) 781
Ceskoslovenska Akademie Ved. Rozpravy. SV: Rada Spolecenskych Ved (CS ISSN 0069-2298) 796
Ceskoslovenska Akademie Ved. Rozpravy. TV: Rada Technickych Ved (CS ISSN 0069-2301) 850
Ceskoslovensko (CS) 478
Ceskoslovensky Kolorista (CS ISSN 0009-0727) 261
Cespedesia (CK) 114
Ceux Qui Font l'Edition (FR) 758
Ceux Qui Font la Presse (FR) 504
Ceylon Chamber of Commerce. Annual Review of Business and Trade (CE) 178
Ceylon Coconut Planter's Review (CE ISSN 0009-0816) 14
Ceylon Economist (CE ISSN 0528-757X) 184
Ceylon Historical Journal (CE ISSN 0577-4691) 442
Ceylon Journal of Science. Biological Sciences (CE ISSN 0069-2379) 102
Ceylon Rationalist Ambassador (CE ISSN 0577-4772) 687
Ceylon Shipping Corporation. Annual Report & Statement of Accounts (CE) 877
Ceylon Yearbook see Sri Lanka Yearbook 846
Chain Shoe Stores and Leased Shoe Department Operators (US ISSN 0069-2387) 795
Chain Store Age Specs Buying Guide for Store Planners see C S A Specs Buying Guide for Store Planners 217
Chain Store Age Supermarket Sales Manual (US ISSN 0069-2395) 217
Chain Store Guide Directory: Food Service Distributors (US ISSN 0091-9152) 407
Chairman's Chat see Life Lines 694
Challenge see Cooperator 907
Challenges in the New Caribbean (BB) 419
Chalmers Tekniska Hogskola. Institutionen Foer Vattenfoersoerjnings och Avloppsteknik. Publikationsserie B (SW ISSN 0009-1111) 384, 896
Chamber of Commerce and Industry in West Java. Member List/Kamar Dagang dan Industri di Jawa Barat. Daftar Anggota (IO) 178
Chamber of Commerce and Industry of Malawi. Industrial and Trade Directory (MW) 235
Chamber of Commerce of Sierra Leone. Journal (SL ISSN 0080-9527) 178
Chamber of Commerce of the Phillippines. Trade Directory (PH) 178
Chamber's Trade Directory (PK) 235
Chambre de Commerce d'Agriculture et d'Industrie de Bamako, Mali. Annuaire Statistique see Mali. Service de la Statistique Generale, de la Comptabilite Nationale et de la Mecanographie. Annuaire Statistique 160
Chambre de Commerce, d'Industrie et des Mines du Cameroun. Compte-Rendu d'Activites (CM) 178
Chambre de Commerce, d'Industrie et des Mines du Cameroun. Rapport Annuel (CM ISSN 0069-2530) 642
Chambre de Commerce et d'Industrie de Paris. Contribution des Employeurs a l'Effort de Construction (FR) 484

Chambre de Commerce et d'Industrie du Mali. Precis Fiscal, Commercial, des Changes et des Echanges (ML ISSN 0067-3110) *178*

Chambre de Commerce Franco-Asiatique. Annuaire des Membres (FR ISSN 0069-2557) *178*

Chambre de Commerce Suedoise en France. Annuaire (FR ISSN 0069-2573) *178*

Chambre des Ingenieurs-Conseils de France. Annuaire (FR ISSN 0069-2611) *366*

Chambre Officielle Franco Allemande de Commerce et d'Industrie. Liste des Membres/Offizielle Deutsch-Franzoesische Industrie- und Handelskammer. Mitgliederliste (FR ISSN 0069-2581) *179*

Chambre Regionale de Commerce et d'Industrie d'Alsace. Rapport sur les Activites (FR) *179*

Chambre Syndicale de la Siderugie Francaise. Bulletin Statisque. Serie Bleue. Commerce Exterieur (FR) *627, 642*

Chambre Syndicale de la Siderugie Francaise. Bulletin Statisque. Serie Rouge. Production (FR) *627, 642*

Chambre Syndicale des Commissionaires pour le Commerce Exterieur. Annuaire Officiel (FR ISSN 0071-8378) *194*

Chambre Syndicale des Mines de Fer de France. Rapport d'Activite (FR ISSN 0069-259X) *642*

Chambre Syndicale Nationale des Electriciens et Specialistes de l'Automobile. Annuaire (FR) *352, 870*

Chambre Syndicale Nationale des Entreprises et Industries de l'Hygiene Publique. Annuaire (FR ISSN 0069-2603) *751*

Champlain Society, Toronto. Report (CN ISSN 0069-2646) *431*

Chanakya Defence Annual (II ISSN 0069-2654) *638*

Chancellor College. Department of Religious Studies. Staff Seminar Paper (MW) *764*

Chaney Chronical (US) *561*

Change and Continuity in Africa (NE) *439*

Changing Concept Series (US) *528*

Channel (New Paltz) (US ISSN 0009-1464) *329*

Channel Islands Specialised Catalogue (UK ISSN 0142-5625) *478*

Channels (AT) *315*

Chantiers de Pedagogie Mathematique (FR ISSN 0395-7837) *348, 585*

Chants des Peuples (FR ISSN 0395-7845) *561*

Chapel Hill Conference on Combinatorial Mathematics and Its Applications. Proceedings (US ISSN 0084-8719) *585*

Character Potential (US ISSN 0009-1669) *735*

Charbonnages de France. Rapport *see* Charbonnages de France. Rapport d'Activite *642*

Charbonnages de France. Rapport d'Activite (FR) *642*

Charge Fiscale en Suisse *see* Steuerbelastung in der Schweiz *232*

Charioteer (US ISSN 0577-5574) *73, 451, 561*

Charities Digest (UK ISSN 0590-9783) *804*

Charles C. Adams Center for Ecological Studies. Occasional Papers (US ISSN 0009-1766) *102*

Charles C. Moskowitz Lectures (US ISSN 0084-8727) *142*

Charles E. Merrill Monograph Series in the Humanities and Social Sciences (US ISSN 0069-2727) *490, 796*

Charles Eliot Norton Lectures (US) *490*

Charles F. Kettering Foundation. Annual Report (US ISSN 0069-2735) *804*

Charles Redd Monographs in Western History (US ISSN 0162-217X) *431*

Charles W. Hunt Lecture (US ISSN 0069-2751) *315*

Charlottes (CN ISSN 0316-6724) *467*

Chart Book of the Melbourne Share Price Index (AT ISSN 0311-3655) *202*

Charter (US ISSN 0069-2786) *490*

Charter Flight Directory *see* How to Fly for Less *868*

Chartered Builder (AT ISSN 0311-1903) *135*

Chartered Institute of Public Finance and Accountancy. Charges for Leisure Services (UK ISSN 0142-1484) *823, 837*

Chartered Institute of Public Finance and Accountancy. Crematoria Statistics. Actuals (UK ISSN 0534-2104) *751, 837*

Chartered Institute of Public Finance and Accountancy. Education Estimates Statistics (UK ISSN 0307-0514) *326, 837*

Chartered Institute of Public Finance and Accountancy. Education Statistics. Actuals (UK ISSN 0309-5614) *326, 837*

Chartered Institute of Public Finance and Accountancy. Education Statistics. Unit Costs (UK) *326, 819*

Chartered Institute of Public Finance and Accountancy. Financial General & Rating Statistics (UK ISSN 0141-5468) *154, 837*

Chartered Institute of Public Finance and Accountancy. Fire Service Statistics. Actuals (UK ISSN 0309-622X) *395, 837*

Chartered Institute of Public Finance and Accountancy. Fire Service Statistics. Estimates (UK ISSN 0307-0573) *395, 837*

Chartered Institute of Public Finance and Accountancy. Homelessness Statistics (UK) *488, 837*

Chartered Institute of Public Finance and Accountancy. Housing Estimate Statistics (UK ISSN 0260-4086) *484, 837*

Chartered Institute of Public Finance and Accountancy. Housing Maintenance & Management. Actuals Statistics (UK ISSN 0307-0468) *484, 837*

Chartered Institute of Public Finance and Accountancy. Housing Part 1: Rents. Actuals Statistics *see* Chartered Institute of Public Finance and Accountancy. Housing Rents. Statistics *488*

Chartered Institute of Public Finance and Accountancy. Housing Part 2: Revenue Accounts. Actuals Statistics *see* Chartered Institute of Public Finance and Accountancy. Housing Revenue Accounts. Actuals Statistics *488*

Chartered Institute of Public Finance and Accountancy. Housing Revenue Accounts. Actuals Statistics (UK ISSN 0260-4078) *488, 837*

Chartered Institute of Public Finance and Accountancy. Housing Rents. Statistics (UK ISSN 0260-406X) *488, 837*

Chartered Institute of Public Finance and Accountancy. Leisure Estimate Statistics (UK ISSN 0141-187X) *823, 837*

Chartered Institute of Public Finance and Accountancy. Local Authority Airports. Accounts and Statistics (UK ISSN 0143-540X) *837, 865*

Chartered Institute of Public Finance and Accountancy. Local Health & Social Services Statistics *see* Chartered Institute of Public Finance and Accountancy. Personal Social Services Statistics. Actuals *810*

Chartered Institute of Public Finance and Accountancy. Personal Social Services Estimate Statistics (UK ISSN 0144-610X) *810, 837*

Chartered Institute of Public Finance and Accountancy. Personal Social Services Statistics. Actuals (UK ISSN 0309-653X) *810, 837*

Chartered Institute of Public Finance and Accountancy. Planning and Development Statistics. Actuals (UK ISSN 0260-8642) *748, 837*

Chartered Institute of Public Finance and Accountancy. Planning Estimates Statistics. Actuals *see* Chartered Institute of Public Finance and Accountancy. Planning and Development Statistics. Actuals *748*

Chartered Institute of Public Finance and Accountancy. Police Estimates Statistics. Actuals *see* Chartered Institute of Public Finance and Accountancy. Police Statistics. Estimates *284*

Chartered Institute of Public Finance and Accountancy. Police Statistics. Actuals (UK) *284, 837*

Chartered Institute of Public Finance and Accountancy. Police Statistics. Estimates (UK ISSN 0144-9915) *284, 837*

Chartered Institute of Public Finance and Accountancy. Public Library Statistics. Actuals (UK ISSN 0309-6629) *539, 837*

Chartered Institute of Public Finance and Accountancy. Public Library Statistics. Estimates (UK ISSN 0307-0522) *539, 837*

Chartered Institute of Public Finance and Accountancy. Rate Collection Statistics. Actuals (UK ISSN 0260-5546) *154, 837*

Chartered Institute of Public Finance and Accountancy. Waste Collection Statistics. Actuals (UK ISSN 0260-7603) *748, 837*

Chartered Institute of Public Finance and Accountancy. Water and Sewage Treatment and Disposal Statistics. Actuals (UK ISSN 0142-1468) *756, 837*

Chartered Institute of Public Finance and Accountancy. Water Services Charges Statistics (UK ISSN 0141-7835) *837, 900*

Chartered Institute of Transport. Handbook (UK ISSN 0306-9559) *862*

Chartering Annual (US) *877*

Chartotheca Translationum Alphabetica (GW ISSN 0009-1944) *555*

Chase World Guide for Exporters (US) *194*

Chases' Calendar of Annual Events (US ISSN 0577-5728) *360*

Chasqui (CK) *256*

Chatfields Europaeisches Adressbuch fuer Anstrichmittel-und Verwandte Produkte *see* Chatfield's European Directory of Paints and Allied Products *673*

Chatfield's European Directory of Paints and Allied Products/Annuaire Chatfield European de Peintures et Produits Assimiles/Chatfields Europaeisches Adressbuch fuer Anstrichmittel-und Verwandte Produkte (UK) *673*

Chaukhambha Oriental Research Studies (II) *669*

Checklist of Available Vermont State Publications (US) *748*

Checklist of British Official Serial Publications (UK ISSN 0084-8085) *539*

Checklist of South Carolina State Publications (US) *89*

Checklists in the Humanities and Education (US ISSN 0069-2824) *495*

Chefs-d'Oeuvre de la Galerie Nationale du Canada *see* Masterpieces in the National Gallery of Canada *76*

Chefs-d'Oeuvre de la Science-Fiction (SZ ISSN 0069-2840) *906*

Chelates in Analytical Chemistry: A Collection of Monographs (US ISSN 0069-2867) *249*

Chelsea Speleological Society. Records (UK ISSN 0309-409X) *292*

Chelys (UK) *658*

Chem Sources - Europe (US ISSN 0094-3681) *235, 245*

Chem Sources - U.S.A. (US) *235, 245*

Chemagro Courier (US) *906*

Chemia (PL) *245*

Chemical Analysis (US ISSN 0069-2883) *249*

Chemical Engineering Catalog (US) *372*

Chemical Engineering Faculties of Canada and the United States (US) *334, 372*

Chemical Engineering Progress. Reprint Manuals (US ISSN 0069-2921) *372*

Chemical Engineering Progress. Safety in Air and Ammonia Plants *see* Ammonia Plant Safety and Related Facilities *372*

Chemical Engineering Progress. Technical Manuals (US ISSN 0069-2956) *372*

Chemical Engineering Progress Symposium Series *see* A I Ch E Symposium Series *372*

Chemical India Annual (II) *372*

Chemical Industries Yearbook and Buyers' Guide (SA) *245*

Chemical Industry Buyers' Guide for S.A. *see* Chemical Industries Yearbook and Buyers' Guide *245*

Chemical Industry Directory (UK ISSN 0069-2980) *372*

Chemical New Product Directory (US ISSN 0160-6360) *202, 217, 245*

Chemical Physics of Solids and Their Surfaces (UK) *254*

Chemical Processing Review *see* Chemical Technology Review *372*

Chemical Purchasing Chemicals Directory (US) *245*

Chemical Reference Manual (US ISSN 0094-6249) *245*

Chemical Rubber Company Handbook of Marine Science *see* C R C Handbook of Marine Science *309*

Chemical Society, London. Annual Reports on the Progress of Chemistry. Section A: General, Physical and Inorganic Chemistry *see* Chemical Society, London. Annual Reports on the Progress of Chemistry. Section A: Physical and Inorganic Chemistry *254*

Chemical Society, London. Annual Reports on the Progress of Chemistry. Section A: Physical and Inorganic Chemistry (UK ISSN 0308-6003) *251, 254*

Chemical Society, London. Annual Reports on the Progress of Chemistry. Section B: Organic Chemistry (UK ISSN 0069-3030) *252*

Chemical Society, London, Annual Report of Council and Accounts (UK ISSN 0306-4875) *245*

Chemical Society, London, Monographs for Teachers (UK ISSN 0080-4428) *246*

Chemical Technology Review (US) *372*

Chemical Thermodynamics (UK ISSN 0305-9731) *254*

Chemicals (UK) *246*

Chemicals and Allied Products Export Promotion Council. Exporters Directory (II ISSN 0531-5980) *194, 246*

Chemie der Pflanzenschutz- und Schaedlingsbekaempfungsmittel (US) *114*

Chemie, Physik und Technologie der Kunststoffe in Einzeldarstellungen *see* Polymers-Properties and Applications *707*

Chemische Analyse (GW ISSN 0340-8221) *249*

Chemist and Druggist Directory (UK) *684*

Chemist Catalogue (AT) *246*

Chemistry and Biochemistry of Amino Acids, Peptides, and Proteins (US ISSN 0069-3111) *110*

Chemistry and Industry Buyers' Guide (UK ISSN 0069-312X) *246*

Chemistry and Physics of Carbon: A Series of Advances (US ISSN 0069-3138) *252*

Chemistry of Functional Groups (US ISSN 0069-3146) *246*

Chemistry of Heterocyclic Compounds (US ISSN 0069-3154) *252*

Chemistry of Natural Products (US ISSN 0069-3162) *252*

Chemistry of Organometallic Compounds (US) *252*

Chesapeake Bay Journal (US) *384*
Cheshire Archaeological Bulletin (UK ISSN 0307-6628) *59*
Chess Express/Schach Express (SZ) *819*
Chess Informant *see* Sahovski Informator *822*
Chi e Dov e (IT) *658*
Chi e Svizzeria e nel Liechtenstein? *see* Annuaire Suisse du Monde et des Affaires *96*
Chiao T'ung Yin Hang. Annual Report (CH) *171*
Chiasma (AT ISSN 0084-8735) *14*
Chiba Daigaku Engeigakubu Gakujutsu Hokoku *see* Chiba University. Faculty of Horticulture. Technical Bulletin *415*
Chiba University. Faculty of Horticulture. Technical Bulletin/Chiba Daigaku Engeigakubu Gakujutsu Hokoku (JA ISSN 0069-3227) *415*
Chicago Academy of Sciences. Bulletin (US ISSN 0009-3491) *781*
Chicago Area Transportation Study. Annual Report (US) *862*
Chicago History of American Civilization (US ISSN 0069-3278) *467*
Chicago History of American Religion (US) *764*
Chicago History of Science and Medicine (US ISSN 0073-2745) *431, 593*
Chicago Lectures in Mathematics (US ISSN 0069-3286) *585*
Chicago Lectures in Physics (US ISSN 0069-3294) *696*
Chicago Linguistic Society. Papers from the Regional Meetings (US ISSN 0577-7240) *542*
Chicago M B A (US) *142*
Chicago Media Directory (US) *504*
Chicago Mercantile Exchange Yearbook(US ISSN 0577-7259) *194*
Chicago Renaissance (US) *561, 693*
Chicago Resource Directory for the Performing Arts (US) *858*
Chicano Law Review *see* La Raza Law Review *517*
Chicorel Index Series (US) *89*
Chien d'Or/Golden Dog (CN ISSN 0315-457X) *561*
Chigiana (IT ISSN 0069-3391) *658*
Chikusan Shikenjo, Chiba, Japan. Chikusan Shikenjo Kenkyu Hokoku *see* National Institute of Animal Industry, Chiba, Japan. Bulletin *45*
Child Behavior and Development (US) *617, 735*
Child Care (US) *256*
Child Care Handbook (US) *256*
Child Health in Israel/Beri'ut Ha-Yeled Be-Yisrael (IS ISSN 0069-3413) *617*
Child in His Family *see* International Association for Child Psychiatry and Allied Professions. Yearbook *619*
Child Welfare League of America. Directory of Member Agencies and Associates *see* Child Welfare League of America. Directory of Member Agencies and Associate Agencies Listing *804*
Child Welfare League of America. Directory of Member Agencies and Associate Agencies Listing (US) *804*
Childhood City Newsletter (US) *256, 384, 735*
Children in Custody (US) *256*
Children Welcome! (UK ISSN 0069-3456) *884*
Children's Book Review Index (US) *2, 257*
Children's Books; a List of Books for Preschool through Junior High School Age (US ISSN 0069-3464) *258*
Children's Books and Recordings: Suggested as Holiday Gifts *see* Children's Books: One Hundred Titles for Reading and Sharing *758*
Children's Books: Awards and Prizes (US ISSN 0069-3472) *758*
Children's Books for Schools and Libraries *see* Children's Books in Print *578*

Children's Books in Print (US ISSN 0069-3480) *578*
Children's Books of the Year (UK) *258, 758*
Children's Books: One Hundred Titles for Reading and Sharing (US) *758*
Children's Catalog (US) *257*
Children's Language (US ISSN 0163-2809) *542*
Children's Literary Almanac (US ISSN 0093-0431) *257, 760*
Children's Literature (New Haven) (US ISSN 0092-8208) *561*
Children's Literature Series (II) *258, 561*
Children's Media Market Place (US) *217*
Chile. Centro de Documentacion Pedagogica. Bibliografia de la Educacion Chilena (CL) *326*
Chile. Direccion de Agricultura y Pesquera. Departamento Estadistica. Anuario Estadistico de Pesca. *see* Chile. Servicio Nacional de Pesca. Anuario Estadistico de Pesca *396*
Chile. Direccion de Presupuestos. Calculo de Entradas de la Nacion (CL) *227*
Chile. Direccion de Presupuestos. Departamento de Estudios Financieros. Finanzas Publicas (CL) *227*
Chile. Direccion de Presupuestos. Exposicion sobre el Estado de la Hacienda Publica (CL) *227*
Chile. Direccion de Presupuestos. Instrucciones para la Ejecucion de la Ley de Presupuestos (CL) *227*
Chile. Direccion de Presupuestos. Ley de Presupuestos (CL) *227*
Chile. Instituto de Investigaciones Agropecuarias. Memoria Anual (CL) *14*
Chile. Instituto Nacional de Estadisticas. Anuario Estadistico (CL) *837*
Chile. Instituto Nacional de Estadisticas. Boletin de Edificacion *see* Chile. Instituto Nacional de Estadisticas. Sub-Departamento Construccion. Boletin de Edificacion *837*
Chile. Instituto Nacional de Estadisticas. Comercio Exterior (CL) *154*
Chile. Instituto Nacional de Estadisticas. Compendio Estadistico (CL) *837*
Chile. Instituto Nacional de Estadisticas. Estadisticas de Salud (CL) *756*
Chile. Instituto Nacional de Estadisticas. Indice de Precios al Consumidor (CL) *154*
Chile. Instituto Nacional de Estadisticas. Sub-Departamento Construccion. Boletin de Edificacion (CL) *837*
Chile. Oficina de Planificacion Nacional. Informe Economico Anual (CL) *184*
Chile. Servicio Agricola y Ganadero. Division Proteccion Pesquera. Anuario Estadistico *see* Chile. Servicio Nacional de Pesca. Anuario Estadistico de Pesca *396*
Chile. Servicio de Impuestos Internos. Memoria (CL ISSN 0577-8131) *227*
Chile. Servicio Nacional de Pesca. Anuario Estadistico de Pesca (CL) *396*
Chile. Superintendencia de Seguridad Social. Boletin de Estadisticas de Seguridad *see* Chile. Superintendencia de Seguridad Social. Seguridad Social: Estadistica *498*
Chile. Superintendencia de Seguridad Social. Seguridad Social: Estadistica (CL) *498*
Chilton's Auto Repair Manual (US ISSN 0069-3634) *870*
Chilton's Automotive Service Manual *see* Chilton's Motor-Age Professional Automotive Service Manual *870*

Chilton's Control Equipment Master (US ISSN 0163-0679) *366, 496*
Chilton's Import Automotive Repair Manual (US) *870*
Chilton's Motor Age Labor Guide and Parts Manual *see* Chilton's Motor-Age Professional Labor Guide and Parts Manual *870*
Chilton's Motor-Age Professional Automotive Service Manual (US ISSN 0363-2393) *870*
Chilton's Motor-Age Professional Labor Guide and Parts Manual (US ISSN 0361-9397) *870*
Chilton's Motorcycle Repair Manual (US) *826*
Chilton's Truck and Van Repair Manual(US) *870*
Chilton's Truck Repair Manual *see* Chilton's Truck and Van Repair Manual *870*
Chimaera (US) *556*
Chimes (US ISSN 0009-4285) *263, 561*
Chimes (HK ISSN 0069-3642) *561*
Chin-Tan Society. Chin-Tan Hak-po (KO) *796*
China (Republic). Department of Statistics. Yearbook of Tax Statistics (CH) *154*
China (Republic). Machinery and Electrical Apparatus Industry Yearbook/Chung-Hua Min Kuo Chi Chi Yu Tien Kung Chi Tsai Nien Chien (CH) *352, 583*
China Development Corporation. Annual Report (CH) *221*
China Directory (JA) *97, 740*
China Facts and Figures Annual (US) *442, 709*
China Facts & Figures Annual (US ISSN 0190-602X) *838*
China Glass and Tableware Red Book Directory (US ISSN 0069-3677) *244*
China, Republic. Directorate-General of Budget, Accounting and Statistics. Report on the Survey of Personal Income Distribution in Taiwan Area (CH) *212*
China, Republic. Export Processing Zone Administration. Exports of EPZ (CH) *194*
China, Republic. Mining Research and Service Organisation. M R S O Special Report (CH) *642*
China, Republic. Ministry of Economic Affairs. Main Statistics of Securities (CH) *202*
China, Republic. Telecommunication Laboratories. Quarterly Report *see* China, Republic. Telecommunication Laboratories. Technical Reports *352*
China, Republic. Telecommunication Laboratories. Technical Reports (CH) *352*
China Research Monographs (US ISSN 0069-3693) *442*
Chinese Art Society of America. Archives *see* Archives of Asian Art *71*
Chinese Culture Association, Magazine (US) *391*
Chinese Historical Society of America. Anniversary Bulletin (US) *391, 442*
Chinese Journal of Physiology (CH) *125, 593*
Chinese Science (US ISSN 0361-9001) *442, 669, 781*
Chinese University of Hong Kong. Chung Chi College. Music Department. Holdings of the Chinese Music Archives (HK) *658*
Chinese University of Hong Kong. Institute of Chinese Studies. Journal (HK) *669*
Chinese World Pulse (US) *764*
Chiron (GW ISSN 0069-3715) *59*
Chislennye Metody v Dinamike Razrezhennykh Gazov (UR) *701*
Chittagong Port Authority. Yearbook (BG) *877*
Chittagong Port Trust. Yearbook of Information *see* Chittagong Port Authority. Yearbook *877*
Chitty's Ontario Annual Practice *see* Ontario Annual Practice *516*
Choi Nenpo/Yearbook of Tidal Records(JA) *309*

Choice (Binghamton) (US) *73, 579*
Chonguk Kiopche Chongnam/Directory of Korean Business (KO) *235*
Chord *see* Tatzlil *664*
Chord and Discord (US ISSN 0069-3758) *658*
Der Chordirigent (GW ISSN 0009-5036) *658*
Chorherrenstift Klosterneuburg. Jahrbuch (AU) *451*
Chris van /Rensburg Publications (Pty) Ltd. Travel and Hotel Guide to Southern Africa *see* C V R Travel and Hotel Guide to Southern Africa *482*
Christian Camping International Directory *see* Guide to Christian Camps *765*
Christian Democratic Study and Documentation Center. Cahiers d'Etudes (IT) *709*
Christian Democratic World Union. Information Bulletin (IT) *709*
Christian Directory (TH) *776*
Christian Endeavour Topic Book (UK) *776*
Christian Endeavour Year Book *see* Christian Endeavour Topic Book *776*
Christian School Directory (US ISSN 0069-388X) *330, 764*
Christian Service Training Series (US ISSN 0069-3898) *776*
Christmas: An American Annual of Christmas Literature and Art (US ISSN 0069-3928) *561*
Christmas Annual *see* Good Old Days Christmas Annual *402*
Christmas Guide *see* Holiday Book *765*
Christmas Ideas for Children *see* Woman's Day Christmas Ideas for Children *258*
Chromatography Newsletter (US ISSN 0095-2214) *249*
Chromatography Symposia Series *see* Analytical Chemistry Symposia Series *249*
Chromosome Atlas: Fish, Amphibians, Reptiles and Birds (US ISSN 0084-876X) *122*
Chromosome Information Service *see* C I S *122*
Chronica Nova (SP) *451*
Chronicle (London) (UK ISSN 0144-7149) *720*
Chronicle Annual Vocational School Manual *see* Chronicle Vocational School Manual *330*
Chronicle Career Index Annual (US ISSN 0190-4663) *667*
Chronicle College Chart *see* Chronicle Four-Year College Databook *330*
Chronicle College Charts *see* Chronicle Two-Year College Databook *330*
Chronicle College Counseling for Transfers *see* Chronicle Guide for Transfers *330*
Chronicle Four-Year College Databook (US) *330*
Chronicle Guide for Transfers (US) *330*
Chronicle Guide to Two-Year College Majors and Careers *see* Chronicle Two-Year College Databook *330*
Chronicle of Parliamentary Elections *see* Chronicle of Parliamentary Elections and Developments *709*
Chronicle of Parliamentary Elections and Developments (SZ) *510, 709*
Chronicle Student Aid Annual (US ISSN 0190-339X) *334*
Chronicle Two-Year College Databook (US) *330*
Chronicle Vocational School Manual (US) *330*
Chronika Aisthetikes *see* Annales d'Esthetique *71*
Chroniko (GR) *556*
Chroniques de Port-Royal (FR ISSN 0529-4975) *561, 764*
Chronologie des Communautes Europeennes (BE ISSN 0069-3952) *143*
Chu Chen (CH) *14*
Chung Chi Bulletin (HK ISSN 0009-6261) *263*
Chung Chi College Bulletin *see* Chung Chi Bulletin *263*

Chung-Hua Min Kuo Chi Chi Yu Tien Kung Chi Tsai Nien Chien *see* China (Republic). Machinery and Electrical Apparatus Industry Yearbook *352*
Chung-Hua Min Kuo Tai-Wan Sheng She Hui Shih Yeh Tung Chi *see* Social Affairs Statistics of Taiwan *811*
Chung-Kuo Yin Hang. Annual Report *see* International Commercial Bank of China. Annual Report *174*
Chung Yang Yen Chiu Yuan. Chiu Tai Shih Yen Chiu So Chi K'an *see* Academia Sinica. Institute of Modern History. Bulletin *430*
Chuo Daigaku Rikogakubu Kiyo *see* Chuo University. Faculty of Science and Engineering. Bulletin *781*
Chuo University. Faculty of Science and Engineering. Bulletin/Chuo Daigaku Rikogakubu Kiyo (JA ISSN 0578-2228) *781, 850*
Church and School Handbook (UK) *764*
Church and Society Series (US ISSN 0069-3979) *776*
Church of England Yearbook (UK ISSN 0069-3987) *771*
Church of Scotland. Yearbook (UK ISSN 0069-3995) *771*
Church Pocket Book and Diary (UK) *764*
Church Pulpit Year Book (UK ISSN 0069-4002) *764*
Churchman's Pocket Book and Diary *see* Church Pocket Book and Diary *764*
CIBA Collection of Medical Illustrations (US ISSN 0084-8786) *593*
Ciencia (BL ISSN 0084-8794) *781*
Ciencia Agropecuaria (PN) *14*
Ciencia Biologica: Biologia Molecular e Celular (PO) *127*
Ciencias Biologicas (CU) *102*
Ciencias Economicas (BL) *143*
Ciencias Medicas Bolsillo (SP) *593*
Cifras de Cuentas Nacionales (CR) *838*
Cifras sobre Produccion Agropecuaria (CR) *27*
Cifras sobre Produccion Industrial (CR) *221*
Cimbebasia. Series A: Natural History (SX ISSN 0590-6342) *102*
Cimbebasia. Series B: Cultural History (SX) *796*
Cina (IT ISSN 0529-7451) *442*
Cincinnati. Division of Police. Annual Report (US ISSN 0091-8806) *281*
Cincinnati Art Museum. Bulletin (US ISSN 0069-4061) *652*
Cincinnati Classical Studies. New Series(NE) *259*
Cincinnati Dental Society Bulletin (US ISSN 0069-4096) *609*
Cine Club del Uruguay. Cuadernos (UY ISSN 0069-4118) *649*
Cineclube (PO ISSN 0704-061X) *649*
Cineclube do Porto. Boletim Circular *see* Cineclube *649*
CineFan (US) *649*
Cinegram (US ISSN 0145-3483) *649*
Cineguia (SP ISSN 0069-4134) *649*
Cinema and Society (UK) *649, 858*
Cinema e Societa (IT ISSN 0009-7152) *649*
Cinema Studies (US ISSN 0069-4150) *649*
Cinemonkey (US ISSN 0162-0126) *649*
Cinmay Smrti Pathagara (II) *73, 561*
Circe (FR ISSN 0069-4177) *561*
Circle (US) *579*
Circles of Friends: 200 New Ways to Make Friends in Washington DC (US) *262, 884*
Circlets (US) *579*
Circulation *see* American Newspaper Markets Circulation *504*
Circulation. Supplement (US ISSN 0069-4193) *607*
Circulation Auditing Around the World(UK) *167*
Circulation Research. Supplement (US ISSN 0069-4185) *607*
Circulo (US ISSN 0009-7349) *490*
Circulo Poetico (US) *579*

Circum-Spice (US ISSN 0069-4215) *528*
Cite Libre *see* Cahiers de Cite Libre *467*
Citizen's Business (US ISSN 0009-756X) *748*
Citizens Conference on State Legislatures. Information Bulletin (US) *906*
Citizens Conference on State Legislatures. Research Memorandum (US ISSN 0578-3364) *906*
Citizens' Governmental Research Bureau Bulletin *see* C G R B Bulletin *748*
Citizens Union Research Foundation. Occasional Paper Series (US) *748*
Citrus Engineering Conference. Transactions (US ISSN 0412-6300) *33*
City & Regional Magazine Directory (US) *5, 758*
City and Society (US) *812*
City College Papers (US ISSN 0077-894X) *334*
City Employment *see* Current Governments Reports: City Employment *154*
City Government Finances *see* Current Governments Reports: City Government Finances *228*
City Lights Anthology (US) *561*
City Manager Yearbook *see* Municipal Year Book *749*
City of Birmingham Symphony Orchestra. Annual Prospectus (UK) *658*
City of Birmingham Symphony Orchestra. Prom Prospectus (UK) *658*
City of London Directory & Livery Companies Guide (UK ISSN 0142-5072) *235*
City of Perth. Annual Report (AT) *748*
City Population Estimates *see* Georgia. State Data Center. City Population Estimates *839*
City Sparrows (UK) *256*
Cityguide-The San Francisco Bay Area and Northern California (US) *884*
Civetta (IT) *73*
Civic Municipal Reference Manual and Purchasing Guide *see* Civic Public Works Reference Manual and Buyer's Guide *740*
Civic Public Works Reference Manual and Buyer's Guide (US) *740*
Civica Stazione Idrobiologica di Milano. Quaderni (IT) *102*
Civil Engineering Report Series *see* Water Resources Report Series *899*
Civil Jet Transport. Avionic Equipment (SZ) *7, 867*
Civil Liberty (AT) *718*
Civil Procedure *see* B A R-B R I Bar Review. Civil Procedure *509*
Civil Rights in Michigan *see* Michigan. Civil Rights Commission. Annual Report *718*
Civil Service Digest *see* Public Employees Journal *745*
Civil Service News (US) *740*
Civil Service News Releases *see* Civil Service News *740*
Civil Service Poetry (UK) *579*
Civil Service Year Book (UK ISSN 0302-329X) *740*
Civil War Collectors' Dealer Directory (US ISSN 0094-1182) *476, 638*
Civilisation Malgache (FR ISSN 0578-3917) *48*
Civilisations et Societes (NE ISSN 0069-4290) *796*
Civilization and Society: Studies in Social, Economic and Cultural History (US) *431, 796*
Civilization of the American Indian (US ISSN 0069-4304) *467*
Civilta Asiatiche (IT ISSN 0069-4312) *442*
Civilta Veneziana. Dizionari Dialettali e Studi Linguistici (IT ISSN 0069-4339) *542*
Civilta Veneziana. Fonti e Testi. Serie Prima: Fonti e Testi per la Storia dell'Arte Veneta (IT ISSN 0069-4355) *73, 451*
Civilta Veneziana. Fonti e Testi. Serie Terza (IT ISSN 0069-4347) *451*

Civilta Veneziana. Saggi (IT ISSN 0069-4371) *451*
Civilta Veneziana. Studi (IT ISSN 0069-438X) *451*
Clan MacDonald Annual (CN) *335*
Clarence M. Hincks Memorial Lectures(CN) *619*
Clarendon Law Series (US) *510*
Clarendon Library of Logic and Philosophy (US) *687*
Claretianum (VC ISSN 0578-4182) *774*
Clark County History (US ISSN 0090-449X) *467*
Clark Guidebooks (US ISSN 0069-4401) *906*
Clark University (Worcester, Mass.) Dissertations and Theses (US ISSN 0578-4247) *326*
Clark's Directory of Southern Textile Mills (US) *855*
Clasicos Colombianos (CK ISSN 0069-4444) *561*
Classica et Mediaevalia (DK) *259*
Classical Association. Proceedings (UK ISSN 0069-4460) *259*
Classical Association of New England. Annual Bulletin (US) *259*
Classical Record Reference Book (US) *658*
Classici Greci e Latini (IT ISSN 0069-4479) *259*
Classici Italiani Minori (IT) *561*
Classics in Anthropology (US ISSN 0069-4487) *48*
Classics in Education (US ISSN 0069-4495) *906*
Classics of British Historical Literature (US ISSN 0069-4509) *451, 561*
Classification Management (US ISSN 0009-8434) *214*
Classification Society Bulletin (UK ISSN 0578-4565) *528*
Classified Directory of Wisconsin Manufacturers (US ISSN 0069-4525) *235*
Classified Fur Source Directory (US) *524*
Classiques de la Pensee Politique (SZ ISSN 0069-4533) *709*
Classroom Practices in Teaching English (US ISSN 0550-5755) *348*
Clay Resources Bulletin (US ISSN 0069-4592) *642*
Clean Air Conference (Gt. Brit.) (UK ISSN 0301-9039) *384*
Clegg's International Directory of the World'S Book Trade (UK ISSN 0069-4614) *758*
Clematis (AT) *781*
Clements' Encyclopedia of World Governments (US ISSN 0145-9686) *720*
Clemson University. Department of Forestry. Forest Research Series (US) *408*
Clemson University. Department of Forestry. Forestry Bulletin (US ISSN 0093-0083) *408*
Clemson University. Department of Forestry. Technical Paper (US) *408*
Clemson University. Water Resources Research Institute. Report (US ISSN 0069-4657) *896*
Clergy's Federal Income Tax Guide *see* Abingdon Clergy Income Tax Guide *226*
Cleveland Public Library Staff Association. News and Views (US ISSN 0009-885X) *528*
Climatological Data for Amundsen-Scott, Antarctica (US ISSN 0148-5628) *632*
Climatological Data for Jakarta Observatory (IO ISSN 0009-8957) *632*
Climatological Data for Selected U.S. Antarctic Stations *see* Climatological Data for Amundsen-Scott, Antarctica *632*
Clin-Alert (US ISSN 0069-4770) *2, 686*
Clincal Therapeutics (NE) *593*
Clinica Neuropsichiatrica (IT) *619*
Clinical and Biochemical Analysis (US ISSN 0095-4861) *110, 249, 593*

Clinical and Experimental Neurology (AT ISSN 0158-1597) *619*
Clinical Approaches to the Problems of Childhood: The Langley Porter Child Psychiatry Series (US ISSN 0069-4797) *906*
Clinical Biomechanics (US ISSN 0191-7870) *593*
Clinical Cardiology Monographs (US) *607*
Clinical Conference on Cancer. Papers (US ISSN 0069-4800) *906*
Clinical Engineering Series (US) *593*
Clinical Immunobiology (US) *102, 603*
Clinical Lab Products Annual Guide (US) *612*
Clinical Laboratory Reference (US ISSN 0093-8076) *496, 612*
Clinical Monographs in Hematology (US) *613*
Clinical Monographs in Obstetrics and Gynecology (US) *615*
Clinical Neuropharmacology (US ISSN 0362-5664) *684*
Clinical Neurosurgery; Proceedings (US ISSN 0069-4827) *619, 624*
Clinical Pharmacology and Drug Epidemiology (NE) *684*
Clinical Spinal Cord Injury Conference. Proceedings *see* U. S. Veteran's Administration. Spinal Cord Injury Conference. Conference Proceedings *621*
Clinical Studies (NE) *593*
Clinics in Developmental Medicine (UK ISSN 0069-4835) *617, 619*
Clinton Historical Society. Newsletter (US) *467*
Clio Bibliography Series (US) *803*
Clio: Devoted to Commercials (US ISSN 0009-9384) *264*
Clivages (FR) *579*
Clothing and Footwear Institute Year Book and Membership Register (UK) *261, 795*
Clothing and Textiles Educational Materials Directory *see* Educational Materials Directory *479*
Clothing Institute Year Book and Membership Register *see* Clothing and Footwear Institute Year Book and Membership Register *261*
Clover Leaflet (CN ISSN 0381-3932) *275, 408*
Club Book of the Knickerbocker Club *see* Knickerbocker Club. Club Book *262*
Coach Tours in Britain & Ireland (UK ISSN 0069-4886) *884*
Coaches & Parties Welcome (UK) *884*
Coal Data (US ISSN 0145-417X) *642*
Coal/Energy News (US) *362*
Coal Exploration Proceedings *see* International Coal Exploration Symposium. Proceedings *644*
Coal Facts (US) *642*
Coal in Canada, Supply and Demand (CN ISSN 0700-284X) *642*
Coal Mines in Canada (CN ISSN 0069-4894) *642*
Coal Monthly and Energy News *see* Coal/Energy News *362*
Coal Traffic Annual (US ISSN 0069-4916) *642*
Coast Marine and Transportation Directory (US) *877*
Coastal Engineering in Japan (JA ISSN 0578-5634) *374*
Coastal Notes (US) *384*
Coastal Pollution Research Highlights *see* Corvallis Environmental Research Laboratory. Research Highlights *385*
Coastline Magazine (US) *556*
Coates's Herd Book (Beef) (UK ISSN 0069-4924) *44*
Coates's Herd Book (Dairy) (UK ISSN 0069-4932) *40*
Cobouw Magazine (NE) *135*
Coburger Landesstiftung. Jahrbuch (GW ISSN 0084-8808) *451*
Cocoa Research Institute. Annual Report (GH ISSN 0300-1385) *404*
CODATA Bulletin (Committee on Data for Science and Technology) (FR ISSN 0366-757X) *781, 850*

CODATA Newsletter (Committee on Data for Science and Technology) (FR ISSN 0538-6918) *781*
Codes Larcier (BE ISSN 0010-0188) *510*
Codex Committee on Pesticide Residues. Report of the Meeting (UN ISSN 0587-5943) *751*
Codices Manuscripti, Bibliotheca Universitatis Leidensis (NE) *562*
COF Newsletter *see* C O F Newsletter *829*
Coffee Annual (US) *86*
Cognition and Language (US) *542, 735*
Cogwheel (US ISSN 0010-0293) *263, 366*
Coin World Almanac (US ISSN 0361-0845) *477*
Coin Yearbook (UK ISSN 0307-6571) *477*
Coins Annual *see* Coins Market Values *477*
Coins Market Values (UK ISSN 0069-4983) *477*
Coke Oven Managers' Association. Year Book (UK ISSN 0069-4991) *627, 642*
Coke Research Report *see* Carbonization Research Report *372*
Cold-Drill (US ISSN 0084-8816) *562*
Cold Spring Harbor Conferences on Cell Proliferation (US) *119*
Cold Spring Harbor Laboratory. Abstracts of Papers Presented at Meetings (US ISSN 0084-8824) *102*
Cold Spring Harbor Laboratory. Annual Report (US ISSN 0069-5009) *102*
Cold Spring Harbor Laboratory. Symposia on Quantitative Biology (US ISSN 0091-7451) *102*
Cold Spring Harbor Monograph Series (US) *102*
Coldspring Journal (US ISSN 0098-7093) *579*
Colecao Bernardo Pereira de Vasconcellos. Serie Estudos Historicos (BL) *467*
Colecao Caminhos Brasileiros (BL) *709*
Colecao de Estudos Bibliograficos (BL) *89*
Colecao de Estudos Filologicos (BL ISSN 0587-6435) *542*
Colecao de Estudos Historicos (BL) *467*
Colecao de Estudos Juridicos (BL ISSN 0530-0657) *510*
Colecao Documenta/Creso (BL) *217*
Colecao Economia (BL) *184*
Colecao Editora do Escritor Em Revista (BL) *562*
Colecao Fe e Realidade (BL) *774*
Colecao Jornalismo Catarinense (BL) *504*
Colecao Teatro (BL) *858*
Colecao Temas Brasileiros (BL) *467*
Colecao Testemunhos (BL) *556*
Coleccao N'gola (AO) *439, 556*
Coleccion Aberri ta Azkatasuna (AG ISSN 0069-5025) *709*
Coleccion Amanece (AG) *764*
Coleccion "Aniversarios Culturales" (VE ISSN 0069-5033) *97*
Coleccion Antropologia e Historia (ES) *49*
Coleccion Aragon (SP) *451*
Coleccion Arquitectura/Perspectivas (SP) *68*
Coleccion Arquitectura y Critica (SP) *68*
Coleccion "Bahia" (SP) *579*
Coleccion Canonica (SP ISSN 0069-505X) *764*
Coleccion Cien Temas Basicos (UY) *709*
Coleccion Ciencia Urbanistica (SP ISSN 0069-5068) *68, 484*
Coleccion Ciencias Biologicas (SP) *102*
Coleccion Ciencias, Humanidades e Ingenieria (SP) *781*
Coleccion Comunicacion (CK) *764*
Coleccion Comunicacion Visual (SP) *264*
Coleccion Conocimento de la Argentina(AG) *468*
Coleccion Cuadernos CEDAL (CR) *709*
Coleccion de Economia (SP) *191*

Coleccion Documentos (AG) *796*
Coleccion: Documentos e Historia de la Ciencia en Colombia (CK) *781*
Coleccion Ensayos (AG) *556*
Coleccion Estructuras y Formas (SP ISSN 0071-1632) *68*
Coleccion Fe e Historia (CL) *796*
Coleccion Filosofica (SP ISSN 0069-5076) *687*
Coleccion "Foros y Seminarios." Serie Foros (VE ISSN 0069-5084) *468*
Coleccion "Foros y Seminarios." Serie Seminarios (VE ISSN 0069-5092) *468*
Coleccion Fundacion FOESSA. Serie Estudios (Fundacion Fomento de Estudios Sociales y Sociologia Aplicada) (SP) *812*
Coleccion Historica (SP ISSN 0069-5106) *451*
Coleccion "Humanism y Ciencia" (VE ISSN 0069-5114) *490*
Coleccion Iberica (SP) *709*
Coleccion Illargi Amandrea (SP) *391*
Coleccion Juridica (SP ISSN 0069-5122) *510*
Coleccion Karpos (SP) *490*
Coleccion la Alquitrana (VE) *678*
Coleccion Medicina (SP) *593*
Coleccion Monografias Politicas (VE) *709*
Coleccion Oriente-Occidente (AG) *669*
Coleccion Pensamiento Argentino (AG ISSN 0069-5149) *688*
Coleccion Pentesilea (SP) *579*
Coleccion Poesia del Nuevo Tiempo (AG) *579*
Coleccion Primero de Mayo (SP) *506*
Coleccion Proyecto y Planificacion (MX) *484*
Coleccion Puyal (SP) *709*
Coleccion Senda Abierta. Serie II (Azul): Judaismo (SP) *770*
Coleccion Siurell. Serie de Cocina (SP) *404*
Coleccion Tecnologia y Sociedad (SP) *850*
Coleccion Temas Basicos de Ingenieria (SP) *366*
Coleccion Temas de Ahorro y Credito (SP) *181*
Coleccion Temas de Antropologia (AG) *49*
Coleccion Temas de Arquitectura Actual (SP ISSN 0082-2701) *69*
Coleccion Teologica (SP) *774*
Coleccion Testigo Directo (SP) *709*
Coleccion Textos Recuperados (SP) *451*
Colecciondina Mica y Siembra (VE) *97*
Colecciones Basicas C I N T E R F O R (Centro Interamericano de Investigacion y Documentacion Sobre Formacion Profesional) (UY) *329*
Colectanea de Jurisprudencia Canonica (SP) *764*
Colega Agropecuario (CK) *44*
COLEGAS (Colegio Antioqueno de Abogados) (CK) *510*
Colegio Antioqueno de Abogados COLEGAS *see* COLEGAS *510*
Colegio de Agentes de Cambio y Bolsa de Barcelona. Servicio de Estudios e Informacion. Evolucion de Capital y Renta en la Inversion en Acciones (SP) *906*
Colegio Mayor P. Felipe Scio. Publicaciones (SP) *774*
Colegio Militar do Rio de Janeiro. Revista Didactica (BL ISSN 0080-3103) *315*
Coleman Camping Annual *see* Coleman Outdoor Annual *829*
Coleman Outdoor Annual (US) *829*
Colfeian (UK ISSN 0010-0676) *263*
Collana del Teatro di Roma (IT) *858*
Collana di Cultura (IT ISSN 0069-5165) *562*
Collana di Poesia (IT) *579*
Collana di Storia Moderna e Contemporanea (IT ISSN 0391-3279) *451*
Collana di Studi e Documentazione (IT) *235*
Collana di Studi e Saggi (IT ISSN 0069-5203) *562*
Collana di Studi Paletnologici (IT) *49, 59*

Collana di Studi Su Problemi Urbanistici Fiorentino (IT) *484*
Collana di Testi e di Critica (IT) *562*
Collana di Testi Patristici (IT) *774*
Collana "Insegnare" (IT ISSN 0069-5246) *315, 348*
Collana Ricciana. Fonti (IT ISSN 0069-5254) *774*
Colleccio de Materials (SP) *73*
Collect Channel Islands Stamps (UK ISSN 0306-5103) *478*
Collect Isle of Man Stamps (UK ISSN 0307-7098) *478*
Collectable Old Advertising (US ISSN 0091-0473) *5*
Collectanea Botanica (SP ISSN 0010-0730) *114*
Collectanea Cartesiana (NE) *688*
Collectanea Historiae Musicae (IT ISSN 0069-5270) *658*
Collectanea Instituti Anthropos (SZ) *49*
Collected Papers of the Annual Meeting, Southeast Regional Group, American Accounting Association *see* American Accounting Association. Southeast Regional Group. Collected Papers of the Annual Meeting *167*
Collected Papers on Earth Sciences (JA) *288*
Collected Papers on Sciences of Atmosphere and Hydrosphere (JA ISSN 0547-1435) *288*
Collected Reprints-National Ocean Survey *see* National Ocean Survey. Collected Reprints *311*
Collected Studies in Criminological Research *see* Criminology, Criminal Law, Penology *281*
Collected Works of Erasmus (CN) *490, 688*
Collected Works on Cardio-Pulmonary Disease (US ISSN 0069-5319) *607*
Collected Works and Documents Illustrating the History of Paper *see* Monumenta Chartae Papyraceae Historiam Illustrantia *675*
Collection "Arguments et Documents" (BE) *796*
Collection: Artistes Canadiens *see* Canadian Artists Series *73*
Collection "Atlas" (CN) *421*
Collection Ca-Cinema (FR) *649*
Collection "Chants des Peuples" (FR) *562*
Collection d'Etudes Musicologiques *see* Sammlung Musikwissenschaftlicher Abhandlungen *69*
Collection d'Histoire Contemporaine (FR ISSN 0069-5343) *431*
Collection de Sociologie Generale et de Philosophie Sociale (BE ISSN 0069-5335) *812*
Collection E F G (Economie-Formation-Gestion) (FR) *214*
Collection Etudes et Travaux de la Revue "Mediterranee" (FR ISSN 0069-5378) *421*
Collection for the History of Cartography Publication *see* C H C Publication *420*
Collection Formation des Enseignants *see* Collection Formation des Enseignants et Formation Continue *585*
Collection Formation des Enseignants et Formation Continue (FR) *585*
Collection "Humor d'Aujourd'hui" (FR) *556*
Collection Knowledge & Technique: Youth (FR) *258*
Collection l'Etat et le Citoyen *see* Repertoire Administratif *714*
Collection les Rouges Gorges (CN) *562*
Collection Lignes Quebecioses (CN) *556*
Collection Lignes Quebecioses. Textuelles *see* Collection Lignes Quebecioses *556*
Collection Litterature du Jour (CN) *562*
Collection of Documents for the Study of International Non-Governmental Relations (BE ISSN 0503-2407) *522*
Collection Oralites-Documents (FR) *542*

Collection Panorama (CN ISSN 0530-8836) *73*
Collection Philosophica (CN) *688*
Collection Presence (CN) *562*
Collection PSI (FR ISSN 0069-5440) *688*
Collection Radiographie du Capital - les Liaisons Financieres (FR) *171*
Collection U. Serie Droit des Affaires et de l'Economie (FR ISSN 0069-5467) *510*
Collection U. Serie Droit des Communautes Europeennes (FR ISSN 0069-5475) *720*
Collection U. Serie Etudes Allemandes (FR ISSN 0069-5483) *709*
Collection U. Serie Histoire Ancienne (FR ISSN 0069-5491) *59, 431*
Collection U. Serie Relations et Institutions Internationales (FR ISSN 0069-5505) *720*
Collection Vietnamienne (BE) *442*
Collections: Les Idees du Jour (CN ISSN 0069-5513) *468*
Collectors' Auction (Baltimore) *see* Harris Auction Galleries. Collectors' Auction *652*
Collectors Club Handbooks (US ISSN 0069-5521) *478*
College Admissions Data *see* College Admissions Data Service *335*
College Admissions Data Service (US) *335*
College and Adult Reading *see* N C R A Yearbook *329*
College and Pro Football Guide *see* Football Guide *824*
College and University Admissions and Enrollment, New York State (US ISSN 0147-5894) *335*
College and University Degrees Conferred, New York State (US ISSN 0077-9172) *335*
College and University Employees, New York State (US ISSN 0093-3414) *335*
College and University Enrollment in New York State *see* College and University Admissions and Enrollment, New York State *335*
College Art Association Monographs (US) *73*
College Blue Book (US ISSN 0069-5572) *330*
College Board. Admissions Testing Program. National Report on College-Bound Seniors (US ISSN 0095-3377) *326*
College Bound Seniors *see* College Board. Admissions Testing Program. National Report on College-Bound Seniors *326*
College de France. Annuaire (FR ISSN 0069-5580) *335*
College de France. Institut des Hautes Etudes Chinoises. Memoirs (FR) *669*
College des Medecins et Chirurgiens de la Province de Quebec. Bulletin *see* Corporation Professionelle des Medecins du Quebec. Bulletin *594*
College Education: Key to a Professional Career in Nursing *see* Baccalaureate Education in Nursing: Key to a Professional Career in Nursing *613*
College Facts Chart (US ISSN 0069-5688) *335*
College Football Modern Record Book *see* N.C.A.A. Football Records *825*
College of Dairy Agriculture, Hokkaido. Journal *see* College of Dairying. Journal; Natural Science *41*
College of Dairy Agriculture, Hokkaido. Journal *see* College of Dairying. Journal; Cultural and Social Sciences *41*
College of Dairying. Journal; Cultural and Social Sciences/Rakuno Gakuen Daigaku Kiyo, Jinbun Shakaikagaku Hen (JA ISSN 0388-0028) *41, 796*
College of Dairying. Journal; Natural Science/Rakuno Gakuen Daigaku Kiyo, Shizen Kagaku Hen (JA ISSN 0388-001X) *41*
College of Engineering, Trivandrum. Magazine (II) *366*
College of Insurance. General Bulletin (US ISSN 0069-5718) *498*

College of Physicians and Surgeons of British Columbia. Annual Report (CN) *593*
College of Physicians and Surgeons of British Columbia. Medical Directory (CN ISSN 0069-5726) *593*
College of Textile Technology, Serampore Annual *see* C.T.T.S. Annual *855*
College Placement Annual (US ISSN 0069-5734) *667*
College Reading Association. Monographs (US) *539*
College Recruiting Report *see* Abbott, Langer & Associates. College Recruiting Report *666*
College Theology Society. Annual Publication (US) *764*
College Theology Society. Proceedings (US ISSN 0069-5750) *315, 774*
College Transfer Guide (US) *331*
Colleges and Universities Granting Degrees in Microbiology (US) *123, 331*
Colleges and Universities with Accredited Undergraduate Social Work Programs (US) *335, 804*
Colleges Classified (US ISSN 0588-2990) *906*
Collegiate Summer Employment Guide (US) *667*
Collegium Carolinum. Bohemia-Jahrbuch (GW) *451*
Collegium Carolinum. Veroeffentlichungen (GW) *451*
Collegium Philosophicum Jenense (GE) *688*
Collezione di Filosofia (IT ISSN 0069-5777) *688*
Collezione di Igiene e di Medicina del Lavro *see* Commission of the European Communities. Collection d'Hygiene et de Medecine du Travail *495*
Collier's Yearbook (US ISSN 0069-5793) *360*
Colloques Internationaux D'Astrophysique de Liege. Comptes Rendus *see* Societe Royale des Sciences de Liege. Memoires in 8 *913*
Colloid Science (UK ISSN 0305-9723) *254*
Colloque de Metallurgie (FR ISSN 0069-5807) *627*
Colloques A M P E R E (NE ISSN 0533-3180) *906*
Colloques Economiques (SZ) *143*
Colloques Europeens (BE) *720*
Colloques Internationaux d'Histoire Maritime. Travaux (FR ISSN 0069-5815) *877*
Colloques Internationaux de Droit Compare. Travaux *see* International Symposia on Comparative Law. Proceedings *513*
Colloques Phytosociologiques (GW) *114*
Colloquim Series on Transportation. Proceedings *see* University of Manitoba. Center for Transportation Studies. Seminar Series on Transportation. Proceedings *864*
Colloquium Geographicum (GW ISSN 0588-3253) *421*
Colloquium Mathematicum (PL ISSN 0010-1354) *585*
Colloquium on Hispanic Linguistics. Proceedings (US) *542*
Colloquium on Scottish Studies. Proceedings *see* Scottish Tradition *461*
Colloquium on the History of Landscape Architecture. Papers (US) *69*
Colloquium on the Law of Outer Space. Proceedings (US ISSN 0069-5831) *7, 522*
Colombia. Corporacion Nacional de Turismo. Boletin de Investigaciones e Informacinturistica (CK) *884*
Colombia. Departamento Administrativo Nacional de Estadistica. Anuario Demografico (CK) *726*
Colombia. Departamento Administrativo Nacional de Estadistica. Anuario de Estadisticas Fiscales y Financieras (CK) *154*

Colombia. Departamento Administrativo Nacional de Estadistica. Anuario de Estadisticas Industriales (CK) *221*
Colombia. Departamento Administrativo Nacional de Estadistica. Anuario de Justicia (CK) *838*
Colombia. Departamento Administrativo Nacional de Estadistica. Anuario General de Estadistica - Justicia *see* Colombia. Departamento Administrativo Nacional de Estadistica. Anuario de Justicia *838*
Colombia. Departamento Administrativo Nacional de Estadistica. Anuario General de Estadistica - Transportes y Comunicaciones (CK) *838*
Colombia. Departamento Administrativo Nacional de Estadistica. Division Politico-Administrativa (CK) *741*
Colombia. Departamento Administrativo Nacional de Estadistica. Estadisticas Historicas (CK) *838*
Colombia. Departamento Administrativo Nacional de Estadistica. Industria Manufacturera Nacional *see* Colombia. Departamento Administrativo Nacional de Estadistica. Anuario de Estadisticas Industriales *221*
Colombia. Direccion General del Presupuesto. Proyecto de Presupuesto(CK) *227*
Colombia. Direccion General del Presupuesto. Proyecto de Presupuesto *see* Colombia. Direccion General del Presupuesto. Proyecto de Presupuesto *227*
Colombia. Instituto Colombiano de Cultura. Archivo Nacional. Revista (CK) *468*
Colombia. Ministerio de Educacion Nacional. Educacion para Desarrollo (CK) *315*
Colombia. Ministerio de Minas y Energia. Boletin de Minas *see* Colombia. Ministerio de Minas y Energia. Boletin de Minas y Energia *642*
Colombia. Ministerio de Minas y Energia. Boletin de Minas y Energia (CK) *362, 642*
Colombia. Ministerio de Minas y Energia. Boletin de Petroleos *see* Colombia. Ministerio de Minas y Energia. Boletin de Minas y Energia *642*
Colombia. Ministerio de Minas y Energia. Memoria al Congreso de la Republica (CK) *292*
Colombia. Ministerio de Minas y Energia. Oficina de Planeacion. Indicadores de la Industria del Petroleo (CK) *678*
Colombia. Ministerio de Minas y Petroleos. Informe *see* Colombia. Ministerio de Minas y Energia. Memoria al Congreso de la Republica *292*
Colombia. Ministerio de Trabajo, Higiene y Prevision Social. Memoria *see* Colombia. Ministerio de Trabajo y Seguridad Social. Memoria *206*
Colombia. Ministerio de Trabajo y Seguridad Social. Memoria (CK) *206, 498*
Colombia. Observatorio Astronomico Nacional. Anuario (CK ISSN 0120-2758) *82*
Colombia. Observatorio Astronomico Nacional. Publicaciones (CK ISSN 0067-9518) *82*
Colombia. Superintendencia Bancaria. Informe de Labores (CK) *171*
Colombia. Superintendencia Bancaria. Seguros y Capitalizacion (CK) *143, 498*
Colombia. Universidad, Bogota. Facultad de Ingenieria Boletin Informative *see* Ingenieria. Boletin Informativo *367*
Colombia Economica (CK) *184*
Colombian Economy (CK) *212*
Colombo Law Review (CE ISSN 0069-5939) *510*

Colombo Observatory. Report (CE) *80, 632*
Colombo Plan Bureau. Technical Cooperation under the Colombo Plan. Report (CE ISSN 0069-5947) *199*
Colombo Plan for Co-operative Economic and Social Development in Asia and the Pacific. Consultative Committee. Report (CE) *199*
Colombo Plan for Co-Operative Economic Development in South and South-East Asia; Report of the Consultative Committee. *see* Colombo Plan for Co-operative Economic and Social Development in Asia and the Pacific. Consultative Committee. Report *199*
Colonial Society of Massachusetts. Publications (US) *468*
Colonial Williamsburg Archaeological Series (US ISSN 0069-5971) *59, 468*
Coloquio de Estudos Luso Brasileiros. Anais (JA ISSN 0069-598X) *542, 796*
Color Atlas Series (US) *594*
Color Photography (US ISSN 0069-5998) *693*
Color y Decoracion en el Hogar (SP) *502*
Colorado. Department of Highways. Traffic Volume Study (US ISSN 0069-6013) *874*
Colorado. Division of Wildlife. Game Research Review (US) *275*
Colorado. Division of Wildlife. Special Report (US ISSN 0084-8875) *275*
Colorado. Division of Wildlife. Technical Publication (US ISSN 0084-8883) *275*
Colorado. State Department of Public Health. Annual Progress Report. State Migrant Plan for Public Health Services (US ISSN 0588-4543) *751, 804*
Colorado. Water Conservation Board. Ground Water Series. Circular *see* Colorado Water Resources Circulars *896*
Colorado Cooperative Wildlife Research Unit. Special Scientific Reports. Technical Papers (US ISSN 0069-6005) *127, 275*
Colorado Farm and Home Research *see* Colorado State University Research *781*
Colorado Heritage (US) *468*
Colorado Magazine *see* Colorado Heritage *468*
Colorado Rail Annual (US ISSN 0069-6048) *873*
Colorado School of Mines. Professional Contributions (US ISSN 0069-6056) *642*
Colorado School of Mines. Research (US ISSN 0069-6064) *642*
Colorado Shakespeare Festival Annual *see* On-Stage Studies *859*
Colorado Ski and Winter Recreation Statistics (US ISSN 0084-8891) *819*
Colorado Springs Fine Arts Center. Report (US ISSN 0069-6072) *73*
Colorado State Industrial Directory (US) *235*
Colorado State Review *see* TransPacific *575*
Colorado State University. Atmospheric Science Paper (US ISSN 0067-0340) *632*
Colorado State University. Department of History. Germans from Russia in Colorado Study Project. Monographs, Papers and Reports Series (US) *468*
Colorado State University. Hydrology Papers (US ISSN 0069-6110) *307*
Colorado State University Libraries. Publication (US ISSN 0084-8905) *528*
Colorado State University Research (US) *781*
Colorado Traffic Volume Study *see* Colorado. Department of Highways. Traffic Volume Study *874*
Colorado, Utah TourBook *see* Tourbook: Colorado, Utah *891*
Colorado Water Resources Circulars (US ISSN 0092-2684) *896*

Colorado-Wyoming Academy of Sciences Journal (US ISSN 0096-2279) *781*
Colorado's Annual Highway Report (US ISSN 0413-7647) *874*
Colston Research Papers *see* Colston Research Society, Bristol, England. Proceedings of the Symposium. Colston Research Papers *781*
Colston Research Society, Bristol, England. Proceedings of the Symposium. Colston Research Papers(UK ISSN 0069-6277) *781*
Colstonian (UK ISSN 0010-1842) *315*
Colt American Handgunning Annual (US ISSN 0364-071X) *829*
Columbia (US ISSN 0161-486X) *562*
Columbia Biological Series (US ISSN 0069-6285) *102*
Columbia County History (Oregon) (US ISSN 0069-6293) *468*
Columbia Essays on the Great Economists (US ISSN 0069-6323) *191*
Columbia River Water Management Report (US ISSN 0360-6864) *896*
Columbia Series in Molecular Biology (US) *119*
Columbia Studies in Economics (US ISSN 0069-6331) *143*
Columbia University. American Language Program. Bulletin (US) *542*
Columbia University. Ancient Near Eastern Society. Journal (US ISSN 0010-2016) *669*
Columbia University. Center for Advanced Research in Urban and Environmental Affairs. Working Papers (US) *484, 812*
Columbia University. East Asian Institute. Studies (US) *442, 669*
Columbia University. Institute on East Central Europe. East Central European Studies (US) *451*
Columbia University. Russian Institute. Studies (US ISSN 0588-5477) *451*
Columbia University. Southern Asian Institute. Occasional Bibliographic Papers (US) *437*
Columbia University Graduate School of Business. Dissertations Series (US) *143*
Columbia University Oral History Collection Index Part 1 (US) *431*
Combat Culturel (FR) *709*
Combat Fleets of the World (US ISSN 0364-3263) *638*
Combined Cumulative Index to Pediatrics (US ISSN 0190-4981) *2, 602, 617*
Combined Jersey Herd Book, Directory & Elite Register of the U.K. *see* Jersey Herd Book and Members Directory *45*
Combined Rosters of Certified Public Accountants, Public Accountants and Accountants Authorized to Conduct Municipal Audits Registered to Practice in Oregon *see* Oregon. State Board of Accountancy. Certified Public Accountants, Public Accountants, Professional Corporations, and Accountants Authorized to Conduct Municipal Audits in Oregon *168*
Combustibles *see* Argentina. Direccion General de Planificacion y Control Energetico. Anuario Estadistico *364*
Come Cruising (UK) *884*
Comecon Merchant Ships Annual (UK) *877*
Comentario Sociologico (SP) *184*
Comentarios Bibliograficos Americanos. Anuario *see* Anuario - C B A - Yearbook *87*
Comercio Exterior do Brasil (BL) *194*
Comic Book Price Guide (US) *476*
Comision de Integracion Electrica Regional. Directorio del Sector Electrico (UY) *352*
Comision de Integracion Electrica Regional. Recursos Energeticos de los Paises de la C I E R (UY) *678, 896*

Comision Interamericana de Mujeres. Asamblea Extrarodinaria. Acta Final *see* Inter-American Commission of Women. Special Assembly. Final Act *718*

Comision Interamericana del Atun Tropical. Boletin *see* Inter-American Tropical Tuna Commission. Bulletin *398*

Comision Mixta de Coordinacion Estadistica de Barcelona. Estadisticas de Ensenanza de la Provincia de Barcelona (SP) *315*

Comissao de Integracao Eletrica Regional. Informe do Coordenador Tecnico (BL) *352*

Comitato Glaciologico Italiano. Bollettino (IT ISSN 0084-8948) *906*

Comitatus; a Journal of Medieval and Renaissance Studies (US ISSN 0069-6412) *73, 431, 562*

Comite d'Actor Cinematographique. Cahiers (CN) *649*

Comite de Accion Interamericana de Colombia. Boletin (CK) *709*

Comite de Controle de l'Electricite et du Gaz. Rapport Annuel (BE) *352, 678*

Comite de Investigaciones Tecnologicas de Chile (CL) *850*

Comite des Travaux Historiques et Scientifiques. Section de Geographie. Actes du Congres National des Societes Savantes (FR ISSN 0071-8424) *421*

Comite Euro-International du Beton. Bulletin d'Information (FR) *135*

Comite Europeen du Beton. Bulletin d'Information *see* Comite Euro-International du Beton. Bulletin d'Information *135*

Comite International de Cooperation dans les Recherches Nationales en Demographie. Actes des Seminaires (FR) *726*

Comite International de Dachau. Bulletin (BE ISSN 0572-9327) *451*

Comite International des Poids et Mesures. Comite Consultatif d'Electricite. (Rapport et Annexes) (FR) *352, 636*

Comite International des Poids et Mesures. Comite Consultatif de Photometrie et Radiometrie.(Rapport et Annexes) (FR ISSN 0588-621X) *636, 705*

Comite International des Poids et Mesures. Comite Consultatif de Thermometrie. Rapports et Annexes (FR) *636, 700*

Comite International des Poids et Mesures. Comite Consultatif des Unites (Rapport et Annexes) (FR) *636*

Comite International des Poids et Mesures. Comite Consultatif pour la Definition de la Seconde. (Rapport et Annexes) (FR ISSN 0588-6228) *636*

Comite International des Poids et Mesures. Comite Consultatif pour la Definition du Metre (Rapport et Annexes) (FR ISSN 0588-6236) *636*

Comite International des Poids et Mesures. Comite Consultatif pour les Etalons des Mesure des Radiations Ionisantes(Rapport et Annexes) *see* Comite International des Poids et Mesures. Comite Consultatif des Etalons des Mesure des Rayonnements Ionisants (Rapport et Annexes) A *636*

Comite International des Poids et Mesures. Comite Consultatif pour les Etalons des Mesure des Rayonnements Ionisants (Rapport et Annexes) (FR) *636*

Comite International des Poids et Mesures. Proces-Verbaux des Seances(FR) *636*

Comite National de l'Organisation Francaise. Annuaire (FR ISSN 0069-651X) *214*

Comite National Francais de Geodesie et Geophysique. Comptes-Rendus (FR ISSN 0069-6528) *303, 421*

Comite National Francais de Geodesie et Geophysique. Rapport National Francais a l'U G G I (FR ISSN 0069-6536) *304, 421*

Commanders' Conference Information Exchange Program. Report (US ISSN 0091-2905) *638*

Commentationes Humanarum Litterarum (FI ISSN 0069-6587) *490*

Commentationes Physico-Mathematicae(FI ISSN 0069-6609) *585, 696*

Commentationes Scientiarum Socialium(FI ISSN 0355-256X) *797*

Commerce. le Point (CN) *181*

Commerce Exterior de l'U.E.B.L. Avec les Pays d'Afrique (BE) *194*

Commerce Exterior de l'U.E.B.L. Avec les Pays d'Amerique Latine/Buitenlandse Handel van de B.L.E.U. Met de Landen van Latijns Amerika Bruxelles (BE) *194*

Commerce Exterior de l'U.E.B.L. Avec les Pays d'Asie/Buitenlandse Handel van de B.L.E.U. Met de Landen van Azie Bruxelles (BE) *194*

Commerce Exterior de l'U.E.B.L. Avec les Pays de l'Est/Buitenlandse Handel van de B.L.E.U. Met de Oostlanden Bruxelles (BE) *194*

Commerce Exterior de l'U.E.B.L. Avec les Pays de la C.E.E /Buitlandse Handel van de B.L.E.U. Met de E.E.G.-Lidstaten Bruxelles (BE) *194*

Commerce Exterior de l'U.E.B.L. avec les Pays Industrialises (Autre Que les Pays de la C.E.E. et l'A.E.L.E.)/Buitenlandse Handel van de B.L.E.U. met de Industrielanden (Niet E.E.G.-en E.V.A.-Lidstaten Bruxelles) (BE) *194*

Commerce Exterior de la Cote d'Ivoire: Resultats et Evolution (IV) *194*

Commerce Exterior de la Grece (GR) *154*

Commerce Exterior des Regions Provence, Cote d'Azur et Corse (FR) *179*

Commerce Exterior du Senegal (SG) *194*

Commerce Franco-Italien; Annuaire de Societes *see* Annuaire du Commerce Franco-Italien *178*

Commerce in Nigeria (NR ISSN 0069-6633) *179*

Commerce Journal (CN ISSN 0383-9737) *181*

Commerce Yearbook of Ports, Shipping and Shipbuilding (II) *877*

Commerce Yearbook of Public Sector (II ISSN 0591-1710) *181*

Commerce Yearbook of Road Transport(II) *874*

Commerce Yearbook of Shipping and Shipbuilding *see* Commerce Yearbook of Ports, Shipping and Shipbuilding *877*

Commercial Bank of Ethiopia. Annual Report (ET ISSN 0588-6694) *171*

Commercial Bank of Ethiopia. Trade Directory (ET) *236*

Commercial Bank of Greece. Report of the Chairman of the Board of Directors (GR ISSN 0424-9402) *171*

Commercial Bank of Kuwait. Annual Report of the Board of Directors and Accounts (KU) *171*

Commercial Transport Handbook and Buyer's Guide for S.A. *see* Transport Manager's Handbook *882*

Commercial West Bank Directory (US) *172*

Commission Belge de Bibliographie, Repertoire Annuel des Comptes-Rendus de Congres Scientifiques (BE ISSN 0080-0937) *90*

Commission d'Energie du Nord Canadien. Revue Annuelle *see* Northern Canada Power Commission. Annual Review *363*

Commission d'Energie du Nord Canadien. Revue de l'Exploitation *see* Northern Canada Power Commission. Annual Review *363*

Commission de Controle des Banques. Rapport Annuel (FR) *172*

Commission Departementale des Monuments Historiques du Pas-de-Calais. Bulletin (FR) *69, 451*

Commission des Communautes Europeennes. Rapports Annuels sur l'Etat des Travaux de Recherches Encouragees Par la CECA *see* Commission of the European Communities. Annual Reports on the Progress of Research Work Promoted by the ECSC *751*

Commission for the Geological Map of the World. Bulletin (CN ISSN 0074-9427) *288*

Commission Internationale des Industries Agricole et Alimentaires Symposia *see* C.I.I.A. Symposia *665*

Commission of the European Communities. Annual Reports on the Progress of Research Work Promoted by the ECSC (EI) *751*

Commission of the European Communities. Cahiers de Reconversion Industrielle (EI) *221*

Commission of the European Communities. Centre for Information and Documentation. Annual Report: Program Biology-Health Protection (EI) *102*

Commission of the European Communities. Collection d'Economie du Travail (EI ISSN 0531-3015) *221*

Commission of the European Communities. Collection d'Economie et Politique Regionale (EI ISSN 0531-3023) *143*

Commission of the European Communities. Collection d'Hygiene et de Medecine du Travail (EI ISSN 0530-749X) *495*

Commission of the European Communities. Collection du Droit du Travail (EI ISSN 0423-6955) *206, 511*

Commission of the European Communities. Collection Objectifs Generaux Acier (EI ISSN 0531-3198) *627, 643*

Commission of the European Communities. Collection Physiologie et Psychologie du Travail (EI ISSN 0425-4937) *206, 735*

Commission of the European Communities. Community Law (EI ISSN 0590-6563) *522*

Commission of the European Communities. Conjoncture Energetique dans la Communaute (EI ISSN 0531-304X) *362*

Commission of the European Communities. Directorate of Taxation. Inventory of Taxes (EI) *227*

Commission of the European Communities. Directory (EI ISSN 0591-1745) *522*

Commission of the European Communities. Etudes: Serie Aide au Developpement (EI ISSN 0069-6692) *199, 221*

Commission of the European Communities. Etudes: Serie Concurrence- Rapprochement des Legislations (EI ISSN 0069-6706) *221*

Commission of the European Communities. Etudes: Serie Energie (EI ISSN 0069-6714) *362*

Commission of the European Communities. Etudes: Serie Industrie(EI ISSN 0591-1737) *221*

Commission of the European Communities. Etudes: Serie Informations Internes sur l'Agriculture (EI ISSN 0069-6722) *27*

Commission of the European Communities. Etudes: Serie Politique Sociale (EI ISSN 0069-6730) *709*

Commission of the European Communities. Expose Annuel sur les Activites d'Orientation Professionelle dans la Communaute (EI ISSN 0588-6953) *335*

Commission of the European Communities. Expose Annuel sur les Activities des Services de Main-d'Oeuvre des Etats Membres de la Communaute (EI ISSN 0591-0110) *206*

Commission of the European Communities. Expose sur l'Evolution Sociale dans la Communaute (EI ISSN 0531-3724) *797*

Commission of the European Communities. Financial Report (EI ISSN 0590-6571) *227*

Commission of the European Communities. Fonte et Aciers *see* Fontes et Aciers *643*

Commission of the European Communities. Investments in the Community Coalmining and Iron and Steel Industries. Report on the Survey (EI ISSN 0069-6757) *643*

Commission of the European Communities. Marches Agricoles: Serie "Prix". Produits Animaux (EI) *27, 44*

Commission of the European Communities. Marches Agricoles: Serie "Prix". Produits Vegetaux (EI) *27, 33*

Commission of the European Communities. Recueils de Recherches Charbon (EI) *642*

Commission of the European Communities. Report on Competition Policy/Rapport sur la Politique de Concurrence (EI) *194, 221*

Commission of the European Communities. Studies: Agricultural Series (EI ISSN 0069-6765) *27*

Commission of the European Communities. Studies: Development Aid Series *see* Commission of the European Communities. Etudes: Serie Aide au Developpement *199*

Commission of the European Communities. Studies: Economic and Financial Series (EI ISSN 0069-6773) *143*

Commission of the European Communities. Studies: Transport Series (EI ISSN 0069-679X) *862*

Commission of the European Communities. Terminology Office. Terminology Bulletin/Bulletin de Terminologie (EI) *542*

Committee for Economic Development. Supplementary Paper (US ISSN 0084-8964) *906*

Committee for Economic Development Newsletter *see* C E D Newsletter *199*

Committee for Economic Development of Australia. C E D A Energy Project Position Papers (AT) *362*

Committee for Economic Development of Australia. C E D A Information Papers (IP Series) (AT) *221*

Committee for Economic Development of Australia. C E D A "M" Series (AT) *221*

Committee for Economic Development of Australia. C E D A Occasional Papers (AT ISSN 0591-0129) *906*

Committee for Economic Development of Australia. C E D A "P" Series (AT) *221*

Committee for Economic Development of Australia. C E D A Supplementary Papers (AT) *906*

Committee for International Cooperation in National Research in Demography Bulletin *see* C I C R E D Bulletin *726*

Committee for Monetary Research and Education, Inc. Mongographs *see* C M R E Mongographs *171*

Committee on Institutional Cooperation. Annual Report (US ISSN 0069-6854) *335*

Committee on Invisible Exports. Annual Report (UK ISSN 0308-4892) *194*

Committee on Space Research COSPAR Technique Manual *see* COSPAR Technique Manual *7*

Committee on Space Research COSPAR Transactions *see* COSPAR Transactions *7*

Committee Reports - Local Government Law Section of the American Bar Assocation. *see* American Bar Association. Section of Local Government Law. Committee Reports *508*
Committee to Combat Huntingtons Disease Newsletter (US) *619*
Commodities Magazine Reference Guide to Futures Markets (US) *202*
Commodity Classification for Foreign Trade Statistics: Japan (JA ISSN 0546-0786) *194*
Commodity Drain Report of Florida's Primary Forest Industries (US ISSN 0362-191X) *408*
Commodity Prices (US) *202*
Commodity Year Book (US ISSN 0069-6862) *202*
Common Market European and Comparative Law Series *see* British Institute of International and Comparative Law. Comparative Law Series *510*
Commons, Open Spaces and Footpaths Preservation Society. Annual Report (UK) *275, 829*
Commonwealth Economy Series (GW) *184*
Commonwealth Acoustic Laboratories, Sydney. Annual Report *see* National Acoustic Laboratories, Sydney. Annual Report *911*
Commonwealth Agricultural Bureaux. List of Research Workers (UK ISSN 0069-6897) *14*
Commonwealth Bibliographies (UK ISSN 0306-1124) *90*
Commonwealth Bureau of Agricultural Economics. Annotated Bibliographies Series A (UK ISSN 0305-1552) *24*
Commonwealth Bureau of Agricultural Economics. Annotated Bibliographies. Series B: Agricultural Policy and Rural Development in Africa (UK ISSN 0305-1552) *24*
Commonwealth Bureau of Animal Breeding and Genetics. Technical Communications (UK ISSN 0069-6919) *44*
Commonwealth Bureau of Animal Health. Review Series (UK ISSN 0069-6927) *894*
Commonwealth Bureau of Horticulture and Plantation Crops. Horticultural Review (UK ISSN 0069-6986) *415*
Commonwealth Bureau of Horticulture and Plantation Crops. Research Review (UK ISSN 0069-6994) *34, 415*
Commonwealth Bureau of Horticulture and Plantation Crops. Technical Communications (UK ISSN 0069-7001) *34, 415*
Commonwealth Bureau of Nutrition. Annotated Bibliographies (UK ISSN 0069-6935) *666*
Commonwealth Bureau of Nutrition. Technical Communications (UK ISSN 0069-6943) *665*
Commonwealth Bureau of Pastures and Field Crops. Bulletin (UK ISSN 0069-701X) *34*
Commonwealth Bureau of Soils. Annotated Bibliographies (UK ISSN 0305-2524) *24*
Commonwealth Bureau of Soils. Technical Communications (UK ISSN 0069-7036) *34*
Commonwealth Catalogue of Queen Elizabeth Stamps (UK ISSN 0142-7830) *478*
Commonwealth Entomological Conference. Report (UK ISSN 0069-7044) *120*
Commonwealth Forestry Bureau. Technical Communication (UK ISSN 0069-7060) *408*
Commonwealth Forestry Bureau Annotated Bibliographies (UK ISSN 0069-7052) *90, 412*
Commonwealth Geological Liaison Office. Liaison Report (UK ISSN 0588-7720) *292*
Commonwealth Geological Liaison Office. Special Publication (UK ISSN 0588-7763) *292*
Commonwealth Government Directory (AT) *741*

Commonwealth Grants to Tasmania *see* Tasmania. Department of the Treasury. Commonwealth Grants to Tasmania *232*
Commonwealth Institute, London. Annual Report (UK ISSN 0069-7109) *421, 720*
Commonwealth Institute of Biological Control. Technical Communications (UK ISSN 0069-7125) *102*
Commonwealth Law Reports (AT ISSN 0069-7133) *511*
Commonwealth Magistrates' Conference. Report (UK ISSN 0307-6539) *511*
Commonwealth Mycological Institute. Phytopathological Papers (UK ISSN 0069-7141) *114*
Commonwealth of Pennsylvania. Executive Budget *see* Pennsylvania. Office of the Budget. Program Budget *321*
Commonwealth Press Union. Record of Quadrennial Conference (UK) *504*
Commonwealth Scientific and Industrial Research Organization. Annual Report (AT ISSN 0069-7184) *850*
Commonwealth Scientific and Industrial Research Organization. CSIRO Textile News (AT) *855*
Commonwealth Scientific and Industrial Research Organization. Division of Applied Geomechanics. Geomechanics of Coal Mining Report (AT) *643*
Commonwealth Scientific and Industrial Research Organization. Division of Applied Geomechanics. Technical Paper (AT ISSN 0069-7257) *288, 374, 643*
Commonwealth Scientific and Industrial Research Organization. Division of Applied Geomechanics. Technical Report (AT ISSN 0069-7249) *288, 374, 643*
Commonwealth Scientific and Industrial Research Organization. Division of Animal Health. Annual Report (AT ISSN 0069-7273) *894*
Commonwealth Scientific and Industrial Research Organization. Division of Atmospheric Physics. Annual Report (AT ISSN 0310-1908) *632*
Commonwealth Scientific and Industrial Research Organization. Division of Applied Physics. Biennial Report (AT) *636*
Commonwealth Scientific and Industrial Research Organization. Division of Animal Production Report (AT ISSN 0155-7742) *125, 127*
Commonwealth Scientific and Industrial Research Organization. Division of Animal Physiology. Report. *see* Commonwealth Scientific and Industrial Research Organization. Division of Animal Production Report *125*
Commonwealth Scientific and Industrial Research Organization. Division of Animal Production Technical Report (AT) *44, 126*
Commonwealth Scientific and Industrial Research Organization. Division of Animal Physiology. Technical Report *see* Commonwealth Scientific and Industrial Research Organization. Division of Animal Production Technical Report *126*
Commonwealth Scientific and Industrial Research Organization. Division of Atmospheric Physics. Technical Paper (AT) *632*
Commonwealth Scientific and Industrial Research Organization. Division of Building Research. Technical Paper (AT) *135*
Commonwealth Scientific and Industrial Research Organization. Division of Chemical Technology. Research Review (AT ISSN 0312-9225) *372*
Commonwealth Scientific and Industrial Research Organization. Division of Entomology. Report (AT ISSN 0069-732X) *120*
Commonwealth Scientific and Industrial Research Organization. Division of Entomology. Technical Paper (AT ISSN 0069-7338) *120*

Commonwealth Scientific and Industrial Research Organization. Division of Fisheries and Oceanography. Annual Report (AT ISSN 0069-7397) *309, 396*
Commonwealth Scientific and Industrial Research Organization. Division of Fisheries and Oceanography. Circular (AT ISSN 0519-5659) *309, 396*
Commonwealth Scientific and Industrial Research Organization. Division of Fisheries and Oceanography. Fisheries Synopsis (AT ISSN 0069-7346) *127, 396*
Commonwealth Scientific and Industrial Research Organization. Division of Fisheries and Oceanography. Report (AT ISSN 0069-7370) *309, 396*
Commonwealth Scientific and Industrial Research Organization. Division of Forest Research. Bulletins (AT) *906*
Commonwealth Scientific and Industrial Research Organization. Division of Forest Research. Leaflets (AT) *907*
Commonwealth Scientific and Industrial Research Organization. Division of Food Research. Report of Research (AT ISSN 0069-7419) *404*
Commonwealth Scientific and Industrial Research Organization. Division of Food Research. Technical Paper (AT ISSN 0069-7427) *404*
Commonwealth Scientific and Industrial Research Organization. Division of Horticultural Research. Report (AT ISSN 0069-7435) *415*
Commonwealth Scientific and Industrial Research Organization. Division of Irrigation Research. Report (AT ISSN 0069-7443) *907*
Commonwealth Scientific and Industrial Research Organization. Division of Land Use Research. Technical Paper (AT ISSN 0069-746X) *27, 221*
Commonwealth Scientific and Industrial Research Organization. Division of Mechanical Engineering. Circular (AT ISSN 0069-7486) *381*
Commonwealth Scientific and Industrial Research Organization. Division of Mechanical Engineering. Engineering Development Reports *see* Commonwealth Scientific and Industrial Research Organization. Division of Mechanical Engineering. Technical Reports *381*
Commonwealth Scientific and Industrial Research Organization. Division of Mechanical Engineering. Report (AT ISSN 0069-7508) *381*
Commonwealth Scientific and Industrial Research Organization. Division of Mechanical Engineering. Technical Reports (AT) *381*
Commonwealth Scientific and Industrial Research Organization. Division of Mathematical Statistics. Technical Paper (AT ISSN 0069-7524) *838*
Commonwealth Scientific and Industrial Research Organization. Division of Plant Industry. Annual Report *see* Commonwealth Scientific and Industrial Research Organization. Division of Plant Industry. Report *34*
Commonwealth Scientific and Industrial Research Organization. Division of Plant Industry. Plant Introduction Review *see* Australian Plant Introduction Review *33*
Commonwealth Scientific and Industrial Research Organization. Division of Plant Industry. Report (AT) *34*
Commonwealth Scientific and Industrial Research Organization. Division of Plant Industry. Technical Paper (AT ISSN 0069-7567) *34*
Commonwealth Scientific and Industrial Research Organization. Division of Radiophysics. Report (AT ISSN 0069-7575) *82, 696*
Commonwealth Scientific and Industrial Research Organization. Division of Soils. Biennial Report (AT ISSN 0069-7583) *34*
Commonwealth Scientific and Industrial Research Organization. Division of Soils. Divisional Report (AT) *34*

Commonwealth Scientific and Industrial Research Organization. Division of Soil Mechanics. Technical Report *see* Commonwealth Scientific and Industrial Research Organization. Division of Applied Geomechanics. Technical Report *643*
Commonwealth Scientific and Industrial Research Organization. Division of Soils. Technical Papers (AT) *34*
Commonwealth Scientific and Industrial Research Organization. Division of Tropical Crops and Pastures. Technical Paper (AT) *34, 114*
Commonwealth Scientific and Industrial Research Organization. Division of Textile Physics. Annual Report (AT) *696, 855*
Commonwealth Scientific and Industrial Research Organization. Division of Tropical Pastures. Technical Paper *see* Commonwealth Scientific and Industrial Research Organization. Division of Tropical Crops and Pastures. Technical Paper *34*
Commonwealth Scientific and Industrial Research Organization. Division of Wildlife Research. Technical Memorandum (AT ISSN 0084-9073) *275*
Commonwealth Scientific and Industrial Research Organization. Division of Wildlife Research. Technical Paper (AT ISSN 0069-763X) *275*
Commonwealth Scientific and Industrial Research Organization. Forest Products Laboratory. Forest Products Newsletter (AT) *412*
Commonwealth Scientific and Industrial Research Organization. Institute of Earth Resources. Annual Report (AT) *288, 375, 643*
Commonwealth Scientific and Industrial Research Organization. Institute of Earth Resources. Investigation Report. (AT ISSN 0156-9953) *643*
Commonwealth Scientific and Industrial Research Organization. Institute of Earth Resources. Technical Communication. (AT ISSN 0156-9945) *643*
Commonwealth Scientific and Industrial Research Organization. Land Research Series (AT ISSN 0069-7648) *27, 221*
Commonwealth Scientific and Industrial Research Organization. Minerals Research Laboratories. Investigation Report *see* Commonwealth Scientific and Industrial Research Organization. Institute of Earth Resources. Investigation Report *643*
Commonwealth Scientific and Industrial Research Organization. Minerals Research Laboratories. Technical Communication. *see* Commonwealth Scientific and Industrial Research Organization. Institute of Earth Resources. Technical Communication *643*
Commonwealth Scientific and Industrial Research Organization. National Measurement Laboratory. Biennial Report *see* Commonwealth Scientific and Industrial Research Organization. Division of Applied Physics. Biennial Report *636*
Commonwealth Scientific and Industrial Research Organization. Wheat Research Unit. Report (AT ISSN 0069-7680) *42*
Commonwealth Scientific and Industrial Research Organization. Wool Research Laboratories. CSIRO Wool Textile News *see* Commonwealth Scientific and Industrial Research Organization. CSIRO Textile News *855*
Commonwealth Space-Flight Symposium. Proceedings (US ISSN 0573-0872) *7*
Commonwealth Teaching Service. Annual Report (AT) *315*
Commonwealth Universities Yearbook (UK ISSN 0069-7745) *335*
Communaute Economique du Betail et de la Viande *see* C E B V *44*

Communaute Europeene du Charbon et de l'Acier. Comite Consultatif. Annuaire see European Coal and Steel Community. Consultative Committee. Yearbook 199

Communaute Europeene du Charbon et de l'Acier. Commission des Communautes Europeennes. Comite Consultatif. Manuel see European Coal and Steel Community. Consultative Committee. Handbook 199

Communautes Mediterraneennes. Cahier (FR) 797

Communicatio Publica (SZ) 264

Communication and Cybernetics (US ISSN 0340-0034) 271

Communication Directory (US ISSN 0094-2588) 264

Communication Research and Broadcasting (GW) 267

Communication Research Center Report Series see C R C Report Series 264

Communication Research Notes (US) 264

Communication Theory in the Cause of Man (US ISSN 0162-8216) 264, 271

Communication Yearbook (US ISSN 0147-4642) 797

Communications (JA ISSN 0084-9081) 264

Communications de Demographie Historique see Historisch-Demographische Mitteilungen 727

Communications Directory & Yearbook see Ireland's Communication Directory 264

Communications Handbook (US ISSN 0069-777X) 264

Communications World (US ISSN 0095-4063) 264

Communicator (Radio Corporation of America) (US ISSN 0381-095X) 267, 352

Communicator (CN) 741

Communist China Problem Research Series (HK ISSN 0069-7788) 442

Communist China Yearbook Series (HK ISSN 0069-7796) 442

Communist Program (FR) 709

Communistes Francais et l'Europe (FR) 709

Community and Junior College Directory see Community, Junior, and Technical College Directory 331

Community-Clinical Psychology Series (US ISSN 0090-693X) 315, 735

Community Development Abstracts (US) 907

Community Development Focus (US) 749

Community Improvement Corporation. Annual Report/Societe d'Amenagement Regional. Rapport Annuel (CN ISSN 0069-7842) 184

Community, Junior, and Technical College Directory (US ISSN 0075-4552) 331

Community Leaders and Noteworthy Americans (US ISSN 0094-5587) 97

Community Mental Health Projects Summary Statistics see New Jersey. Department of Human Services. Community Mental Health Projects Summary Statistics 807

Community Psychology Series (US) 735, 812

Community Psychology Series see Community-Clinical Psychology Series 735

Community, Technical, and Junior College in the United States: a Guide for Foreign Students. (US) 331

Community Work (UK ISSN 0307-6067) 804

Compagnie Europeenne et d'Outre-Mer. Rapports see Compagnie Financiere Europeenne et d'Outre-Mer. Rapport Annuel 194

Compagnie Financiere Europeenne et d'Outre-Mer. Rapport Annuel (BE) 194

Companhia de Electricidade de Brasilia. Relatorio das Atividades (BL) 352

Companhia Estadual de Tecnologia de Saneamento Basico e de Defesa do Meio Ambiente. Directoria Relatoria Anual (BL) 751

Companhia Paranaense de Energia. Informe Estatistico Anual (BL) 838

Companhia Paulista de Forca e Luz. Acompanhamento de Mercado see Companhia Paulista de Forca e Luz. Assessoria de Planejamento e Gestao Empresarial. Relatorio Estatistico Anual 352

Companhia Paulista de Forca e Luz. Assessoria de Planejamento e Gestao Empresarial. Relatorio Estatistico Anual (BL) 352

Companhia Paulista de Forca e Luz. Boletim Estatistico (BL) 352

Compania Anonima de Administracion y Fomento Electrico. Informe Anual (VE) 352

Compania Argentina de Seguros. Memoria y Balance General see Brujula 498

Compania Financiera Ecuatoriana de Desarrollo Informe Anual see C O F I E C. Informe Anual 171

Company Approaches to Industrial Relations see Series on Company Approaches to Industrial Relations 210

Company of Master Mariners of Australia. Journal (AT ISSN 0084-909X) 877

Comparatist (US) 562

Comparative Animal Nutrition (SZ ISSN 0304-5374) 128, 894

Comparative Criticism (UK) 562

Comparative Digest of Credit Union Acts (US) 172

Comparative Education Society in Europe. Proceedings of the General Meeting (UK ISSN 0588-9049) 315

Comparative Juridical Review (US ISSN 0069-7893) 511

Comparative Political Economy and Public Policy Series (US) 191, 709

Comparative Studies in Behavioral Science: A Wiley Series (US) 735

Comparative Studies in Overseas History (NE) 451

Comparative Studies in Society and History (US ISSN 0069-7907) 431, 797

Comparative Studies in Sociology (US ISSN 0164-1247) 812

Comparazione dei Salari e del Costo del Lavoro in Europa (IT ISSN 0069-794X) 206

Compas d'Or see Gulden Passer 758

Compas de Cifras see Germany (Federal Republic, 1949-) Statistisches Bundesamt. Zahlenkompass 840

Compendio Estadistico Centroamericano (GT ISSN 0588-912X) 838

Compendio Estadistico de America see Statistical Compendium of the Americas 914

Compendio Statistico see Compendio Statistico Italiano 838

Compendio Statistico Italiano (IT ISSN 0069-7958) 838

Compendium Gezondheidsstatistiek Nederland/Compendium Health Statistics of the Netherlands (NE) 756

Compendium Health Statistics of the Netherlands see Compendium Gezondheidsstatistiek Nederland 756

Compendium of Pest Control Products Registered in Canada (CN) 34

Compendium of Pharmaceuticals and Specialties (CN ISSN 0069-7966) 684

Compendium of University Entrance Requirements for First Degree Courses in the United Kingdom (UK ISSN 0571-625X) 335

Compensation of Industrial Engineers (US) 366

Compensatory Education Report see California. Department of Health. Annual Evaluation Report Program Information 315

Compilation of State and Federal Privacy Laws (US) 511

Complete Catalogue of Contemporary Welsh Music (UK) 658

Complete Handbook of Pro Football (US ISSN 0361-2988) 824

Complete Handbook of Soccer (US ISSN 0363-6046) 824

Complete Internal Revenue Code see Internal Revenue Code 230

Complete Volkswagen Book (US ISSN 0069-8008) 870

Compliance and Legal Seminar. Proceedings (US ISSN 0093-7800) 202, 511

Composers of the Americas/Compositores de America (US ISSN 0069-8016) 97, 658

Composers of Wales Series (UK) 658

Composers' Voice (NE) 658

Composite Catalog of Oil Field Equipment & Services (US) 678

Compositores de America see Composers of the Americas 658

Composium Directory of New Music (US) 658

Comprehensive Annual Services Program Plan for Social Services Under Title 20 see Louisiana. Health and Human Resources Administration Comprehensive Annual Services Program Plan for Social Services Under Title 20 807

Comprehensive Annual Services Program Plan for the State of California (US ISSN 0363-5600) 804

Comprehensive Biochemistry (NE ISSN 0069-8032) 110

Comprehensive Chemical Kinetics (NE ISSN 0069-8040) 254

Comprehensive Dissertation Index. Supplement (US ISSN 0361-6657) 90

Comprehensive Endocrinology (US ISSN 0160-242X) 611

Comprehensive Health Plan for New Jersey (US ISSN 0094-1336) 594, 751

Comprehensive Law Enforcement and Criminal Justice Plan (Lansing) see Michigan. Office of Criminal Justice. Comprehensive Law Enforcement and Criminal Justice Plan 282

Comprehensive Law Enforcement Plan (Carson City) see Nevada. Commission on Crime, Delinquency and Corrections. Comprehensive Law Enforcement Plan 283

Comprehensive Listing of Recommended Periodicals for Catholic Secondary School Libraries (US) 315

Comprehensive Media Guide: Korea (KO ISSN 0069-8067) 5

Comprehensive Plan for Criminal Justice (Sacramento) see California. Council on Criminal Justice. Comprehensive Plan for Criminal Justice 280

Comptes Economiques de la Guadeloupe (GP) 154

Comptes Economiques de la Martinique(MQ) 154

Comptes Economiques du Territoire Francais des Afars et des Issas (FR) 154

Comptes Nationaux de la Belgique (BE ISSN 0069-8075) 154

Comptes Nationaux du Cameroun (CM) 227

Compton Yearbook (US ISSN 0069-8091) 360

Computational Linguistics and Computer Languages (NE) 271, 542

Computational Musicology Newsletter (US ISSN 0093-0253) 658

Computer Aided Design-Geometrische Daten Verarbeitung-EDV- Zeichnen Report see C A D/G D V- Report 271

Computer-Aided Design of Electronic Circuits (NE) 271, 352

Computer Aided Research in Ancient Near Eastern Studies (US) 474

Computer and Information Sciences Symposium. Proceedings (US) 271

Computer Design and Architecture Series (US) 271

Computer Directory and Buyer's Guide(US) 271

Computer Graphics and Art (US) 271

Computer Law Bibliography (US ISSN 0195-3567) 90, 274, 521

Computer Law Monograph Series (US ISSN 0194-4134) 271, 511

Computer Monographs (US) 271

Computer Networking Symposium. Proceedings (US) 271

Computer-Readable Data Bases: a Directory and Data Sourcebook (US) 271

Computer Science and Applied Mathematics (US) 271, 585

Computer und Recht (SZ) 271, 511

Computer Users' Year Book (UK) 271

Computer Yearbook (US ISSN 0069-8180) 271

Computer Yearbook and Directory see Computer Yearbook 271

Computers in Cardiology (US) 271, 607

Computers in Chemical and Biochemical Research (US) 110, 246, 271

Computers in Chemistry and Instrumentation (US) 246, 271

Comsearch: Geographic (US) 326

Comsearch Printouts see Comsearch Printouts: Subjects 326

Comsearch Printouts: Special Topics (US) 326

Comsearch Printouts: Subjects (US) 326

Comune di Roma. Ufficio di Statistica e Censimento. Bollettino Statistico (IT ISSN 0010-4957) 731

Comunicacion (VE) 264

Comunidad Latinoamericana de Escritores. Boletin see Comunidad Latinoamericana de Escritores. Revista 562

Comunidad Latinoamericana de Escritores. Revista (MX) 562

Comunidades y Culturas Peruanas (PE) 49, 401

Concentus Musicus (GW) 658

Concepts and Techniques in Modern Geography see C A T M O G 420

Concepts in Chemistry (US) 246

Concerned United Birthparents, Inc. Communicator see C U B Communicator 812

Concise Statistical Yearbook of Greece (GR ISSN 0069-8245) 838

Concrete Industries Yearbook (US ISSN 0069-827X) 135

Concrete Masonry Association of Australia. Project Review (AT ISSN 0311-1180) 135

Concrete Pipe Industry Statistics (US ISSN 0360-2877) 379

Concrete Society. Technical Report (UK) 135

Concrete Year Book (UK ISSN 0069-8288) 135

Condition of Education (US ISSN 0098-4752) 326

Condition of Farmworkers and Small Farmers (US) 14, 206

Conditions de Travail au Quebec des Activites Economiques Choisies (CN) 206

Conditions de Travail dans l'Industrie Canadienne. see Working Conditions in Canadian Industry 212

Condominium Development Guide (Supplement) (US) 484

Confederacao Brasileira de Desportos. Relatorio (BL) 819

Confederacao Nacional dos Trabalhadores Em Comunicacoes e Publicidade. Relatorio Anual (BL) 264, 506

Confederacion Colombiana de Camaras de Comercio. Asamblea General. Informe Final (CK) 179

Confederacion de la Industria. Memoria y Balance General see Confederacion General de la Industria. Memoria y Balance General 221

Confederacion Espanola de Cajas de Ahorros. Fondo para Investigacion Economica y Social. Coleccion Temas de Ahorro y Credito see Coleccion Temas de Ahorro y Credito 181

Confederacion General de la Industria. Comision Directiva. Informe de las Actuaciones Cumplidas (AG) *221*
Confederacion General de la Industria. Memoria y Balance General (AG ISSN 0301-9349) *221*
Confederacion Latinoamericana de Asociaciones Cristianas de Jovenes. Carta (UY) *764*
Confederation des Industries Ceramiques de France. Annuaire (FR ISSN 0069-830X) *244*
Confederation Europeene pour la Therapie Physique. Congress Reports(FR ISSN 0071-2817) *594*
Confederation Internationale des Accordeonistes Revue *see* C.I.A. Revue *658*
Confederation Internationale des Cinemas d'Art et d'Essai Bulletin d'Information *see* C.I.C.A.E. Bulletin d'Information *649*
Confederation Nationale de la Construction. Annuaire (BE ISSN 0045-8023) *135*
Confederation of British Industry Annual Report *see* C B I Annual Report *142*
Confederazione Italiana dei Servizi Pubblici degli Enti Locali. Annuario (IT) *749*
Conference Board. Annual Survey of Corporate Contributions (US) *143*
Conference Board. Cumulative Index (US ISSN 0069-8350) *143*
Conference Board. Report on Company Contributions *see* Conference Board. Annual Survey of Corporate Contributions *143*
Conference Board in Canada. Canadian Studies (CN ISSN 0069-8342) *214, 221*
Conference Board in Canada. Executive Bulletin (CN ISSN 0704-0601) *143, 214*
Conference Board in Canada. Occasional Papers (CN) *143*
Conference Board in Canada. Quarterly Provincial Forecast (CN ISSN 0381-0100) *184*
Conference Board in Canada. Technical Papers (CN ISSN 0384-9988) *143*
Conference Catholique Canadienne. Bulletin National de Liturgie (CN ISSN 0384-5087) *774*
Conference for College and University Leaders in Continuing Education. Proceedings (US ISSN 0084-9138) *329*
Conference Generale des Poids et Mesures. Comptes Rendus des Seances (FR) *637*
Conference in the Study of Twentieth-Century Literature, Michigan State University. Proceedings (US ISSN 0069-8407) *562*
Conference International de l'Education. Rapport Final *see* International Conference on Education. Final Report *319*
Conference of Executives of American Schools for the Deaf. Proceedings (US) *286*
Conference of Presidents of Major American Jewish Organizations. Report (US ISSN 0160-7057) *391, 770*
Conference of Southeast Asian Librarians. Proceedings (SI) *528*
Conference of State Employment Security Personnel Officers. Report (US ISSN 0093-1942) *220*
Conference of State Sanitary Engineers. Report of Proceedings (US ISSN 0069-8474) *751*
Conference of Vice-Chancellors. Report(II) *335*
Conference on Aerospace and Aeronautical Meteorology. Preprints *see* Conference on Atmospheric Environment of Aerospace Systems and Applied Meteorology. Preprints *632*
Conference on Artificial Insemination of Beef Cattle. Proceedings (US ISSN 0084-9146) *44*

Conference on Atmospheric Environment of Aerospace Systems and Applied Meteorology. Preprints (US) *632*
Conference on Bank Structure and Competition. Proceedings (US ISSN 0084-9154) *172*
Conference on Chinese Oral and Performing Literature Papers *see* C H I N O P E R L Papers *561*
Conference on Coastal Meteorology. (Preprints) (US) *632*
Conference on Computers in Radiology. Proceedings (US) *271, 622*
Conference on Coordination Chemistry Proceedings (CS) *246*
Conference on Data Systems Languages. Data Base Task Group. Report (US ISSN 0090-7383) *271*
Conference on Electric Process Heating in Industry. Conference Record *see* Electrical Process Heating in Industry. Technical Conference. Record *353*
Conference on Electrical Insulation and Dielectric Phenomena. Annual Report (US ISSN 0084-9162) *352*
Conference on Empirical Research in Black Psychology (US) *335, 391, 735*
Conference on Frontiers in Education. Digest (US ISSN 0069-8547) *316*
Conference on Great Lakes Research. Proceedings *see* Journal of Great Lakes Research *387*
Conference on Ground Water. Proceedings (US ISSN 0094-9671) *307*
Conference on Human Relations in Industry. Proceedings (II ISSN 0069-8555) *206*
Conference on Laser Engineering and Applications *see* I E E E/O S A Conference on Laser Engineering and Applications. Digest of Technical Papers *354*
Conference on Organization and Procedures of the United Nations. Report *see* Conference on United Nations Procedures. Report *720*
Conference on Planned and Inadvertent Weather Modification. Preprints (US) *632*
Conference on Prevention and Control of Oil Spills. Proceedings (US) *385*
Conference on Probability and Statistics in Atmospheric Sciences. Preprints (US) *585, 632*
Conference on Radar Meteorology. Preprints (US ISSN 0069-8636) *632*
Conference on Remote Systems Technology. Proceedings (US ISSN 0069-8644) *366, 702*
Conference on Research in Income and Wealth (US ISSN 0069-8652) *212*
Conference on Scottish Studies. Proceedings *see* Scotia *393*
Conference on Severe Local Storms. Preprints (US ISSN 0069-8679) *632*
Conference on Taxation. Proceedings *see* National Tax Association-Tax Institute of America. Proceedings of the Annual Conference *231*
Conference on Teacher Education in the Eastern Caribbean. Report *see* Eastern Caribbean Standing Conference on Teacher Education. Report *348*
Conference on the Caribbean, University of Florida. Papers *see* Caribbean Conference Series *467*
Conference on the Economics of Education. Proceedings (US ISSN 0084-9170) *316*
Conference on the United Nations of the Next Decade. Report *see* United Nations of the Next Decade Conference. Report *724*
Conference on Trace Substances in Environmental Health. Proceedings (US ISSN 0069-8741) *385, 751*
Conference on Underground Transmission and Distribution. Record. (US ISSN 0069-875X) *352*
Conference on United Nations Procedures. Report (US ISSN 0069-8601) *720*

Conference on Veterans Administration Cooperative Studies in Mental Health and Behavioral Sciences Highlights *see* Conference on Veterans Administration Studies in Mental Health and Behavioral Sciences. Highlights *735*
Conference on Veterans Administration Studies in Mental Health and Behavioral Sciences. Highlights (US ISSN 0069-8768) *735*
Conference on Weather Forecasting and Analysis. Preprints *see* Conference on Weather Forecasting and Analysis and Aviation Meteorology. Preprints *632*
Conference on Weather Forecasting and Analysis and Aviation Meteorology. Preprints (US) *632*
Conference on Weather Modification. Preprints *see* Conference on Planned and Inadvertent Weather Modification. Preprints *632*
Conference Papers Annual Index (US ISSN 0194-0546) *2, 626*
Conference Publications Guide *see* Bibliographic Guide to Conference Publications *88*
Conference Universitaire Suisse. Rapport Annuel (SZ) *335*
Conferences Meetings & Exhibitions Welcome (UK) *626, 884*
Conferencias de Bioquimica (CL ISSN 0069-8784) *102, 111*
Conferenze (PL ISSN 0079-3167) *490*
Confidential Beauty & Barber Buying Guide (US) *85*
Confins (BE ISSN 0010-5694) *562, 579*
Confluent Education Newsletter *see* M A C E Newsletter *319*
Confluents (FR) *431*
Congregational Council for World Mission. Annual Report *see* C W M Report *771*
Congres Archeologique de France (Publication.) (FR ISSN 0069-8881) *59*
Congres International d'Histoire des Sciences. Actes (UK ISSN 0074-9540) *504, 781*
Congres International de la Conserve. Textes des Communications *see* International Congress on Canned Foods. Texts of Papers Presented and Resolutions *405*
Congres International des Etudes Byzantines. Actes *see* International Congress for Byzantine Studies. Acts *433*
Congres National de Speleologie. Actes (SZ ISSN 0069-8911) *292*
Congres National des Peches et Industries Maritimes. Compte Rendu(FR ISSN 0069-889X) *396*
Congres Portuaire International. Compte-Rendu *see* International Harbour Congress. Proceedings *878*
Congreso Argentino de Saneamiento. Trabajos (AG) *751*
Congreso Internacional de Vivienda Popular (CK) *797*
Congreso Mexicano de Control de Calidad. Anual (MX) *637*
Congreso Nacional de Bibliotecas. Ponencias, Comunicaciones y Cronica (SP) *528*
Congreso Nacional de Profesionales en Ciencias Economicas. Memoria (ES) *143*
Congreso Regional Sobre Documentacao. Anais (BL) *528*
Congresos Indigenistas Interamericanos. Acta *see* Inter-American Conference on Indian Life. Acta *50*
Congress F A T I P E C (Federation d'Associations de Techniciens des Industries des Peintures, Vernis, Emaux et Encres d'Imprimerie de l'Europe Continentale) (FR ISSN 0430-2222) *372*
Congress for Recreation and Parks. Proceedings (US ISSN 0069-8903) *829*
Congress in Park and Recreation Administration. Programme (UK) *626*
Congress in Park and Recreation Administration. Reports (UK) *829*

Congress International Medical de Pays de Langue Francaise de l'Hemisphere Americain. Rapports et Communications (MQ ISSN 0414-4406) *594*
Congress Marches Ahead (II) *709*
Congress of International Congress Organizers and Technicians. Proceeding (BE ISSN 0573-5661) *626*
Congress of Micronesia. Joint Committee on Program and Budget Planning. Public Hearings on High Commissioner's Preliminary Budget (TT) *227, 741*
Congress of Micronesia. Senate. Journal(TT) *511, 741*
Congress on Research in Dance *see* Dance Research Annual *285*
Congressional Directory *see* U.S. Congress. Congressional Directory *716*
Congressional District Business Patterns(US ISSN 0275-746X) *181*
Congressional Information Service Annual *see* C I S Annual *748*
Congressional Staff Directory (US ISSN 0069-8938) *709*
Congresso Nacional de Anatomia Patologicas. Actas (MZ) *102, 594*
Congressus Numerantium (CN) *585*
Coniectanea Biblica. New Testament Series (SW ISSN 0069-8946) *764*
Coniectanea Biblica. Old Testament Series (SW ISSN 0069-8954) *764*
Coniectanea Neotestamentica *see* Coniectanea Biblica. New Testament Series *764*
Conimbriga (PO ISSN 0084-9189) *59*
Connaissance d'Israel (BE) *474*
Connaissance de l'Orient. Collection Unesco d'Oeuvres Representatives (FR ISSN 0589-3496) *562*
Connaissance de l'Ouest (FR ISSN 0396-2024) *221, 421*
Connaissance des Temps (FR ISSN 0181-3048) *82*
Connaitre la Wallonie/To Know Wallony (BE ISSN 0010-602X) *431*
Connecticut. Advisory Council on Vocational and Career Education. Vocational Education Evaluation Report (US ISSN 0363-650X) *316*
Connecticut. Auditors of Public Accounts. Report on Department of Transportation, Bureau of Rail and Motor Carrier Services (US ISSN 0362-9503) *862*
Connecticut. Commission on the Deaf and Hearing-Impaired. Annual Report (US) *286*
Connecticut. Commission to Study and Investigate the Problems of Deaf and Hearing-Impaired Persons. Annual Report *see* Connecticut. Commission on the Deaf and Hearing-Impaired. Annual Report *286*
Connecticut. Council on Environmental Quality. Annual Report (US ISSN 0095-4624) *385*
Connecticut. Department of Community Affairs. Division of Research and Program Evaluation. Construction Activity Authorized by Building Permits. Summary *see* Housing Units in Connecticut. Annual Summary *136*
Connecticut. Department of Correction. Publications (US ISSN 0090-2756) *281*
Connecticut. Department on Aging. Report to the Governor and General Assembly (US ISSN 0090-6077) *428*
Connecticut. Energy Advisory Board. Annual Report to the Governor and General Assembly. Executive Summary (US ISSN 0360-2257) *362*
Connecticut. Judicial Department. Report (US ISSN 0098-8138) *511*
Connecticut. Treasury Department. Annual Report (US ISSN 0099-0108) *228*
Connecticut Academy of Arts and Sciences. Memoirs (US ISSN 0069-8970) *490, 781*

Connecticut Academy of Arts and Sciences. Transactions (US ISSN 0069-8989) *490*, 781
Connecticut and Rhode Island Directory of Manufacturers (US) *236*
Connecticut Audiovisual Education Association. Bulletin *see* C E M A Bulletin *315*
Connecticut College Monograph (US ISSN 0069-9012) *335*
Connecticut Educational Media Association Bulletin *see* C E M A Bulletin *315*
Connecticut Health Services Research Series (US) *751*
Connecticut Highway Needs Report *see* Connecticut Master Transportation Plan *862*
Connecticut Library Association. Memo(US) *528*
Connecticut, Massachusetts, Rhode Island Tourbook *see* Tourbook: Connecticut, Massachusetts, Rhode Island *872*
Connecticut Master Transportation Plan(US ISSN 0069-9039) *862*
Connecticut Media Directory (US) *5*
Connecticut State Industrial Directory (US ISSN 0098-6186) *236*
Connecticut Urban Research Report (US ISSN 0069-9055) *812*
Connecticut Walk Book (US ISSN 0092-5764) *829*
Connecticut Water Resources Bulletin. (US ISSN 0589-400X) *307*
Connecticut West (US) *884*
Connections (US) *579*
Connections *see* Connections Two *709*
Connections Two (US) *709*
Connolly's Suppressed Writings (UK ISSN 0069-908X) *452*
Conscientia (GW) *688*
Consciousness and Self-Regulation: Advances in Research (US) *688*
Conseil de la Jeunesse Scientifique. Bottin (CN ISSN 0705-8292) *781*
Conseil International du Sport Militaire. Brochure Technique *see* International Military Sports Council. Technical Brochure *639*
Conseil National de la Recherche Scientifique. Rapport Annuel *see* National Council for Scientific Research. Annual Report *338*
Conseil National de Recherches, Canada, Comite Associe sur les Criteres Scientifiques. Rapport d'Activite *see* National Research Council, Canada. Associate Committee on Scientific Criteria for Environmental Quality. Status Report *387*
Conseil National de Recherches du Canada. Compte Rendu Annuel des Bourses et Subventions d'Aide a la Recherche *see* National Research Council, Canada. Annual Report on Scholarships and Grants in Aid of Research *320*
Conseil National du Patronat Francais. Annuaire (FR) *214*
Conseil Suisse de la Science. Rapport Annuel *see* Schweizerischer Wissenschaftsrat. Jahresbericht *790*
Conseil Superieur du Livre. Annuaire (CN ISSN 0084-9197) *528*
Consejo Central Ejecutivo del Partido Liberal de Honduras. Memoria (HO) *709*
Consejo Latinoamericano de Ciencias Sociales. Serie Poblacion. Informe de Investigacion (AG) *726*
Consejo Nacional de Investigaciones Cientificas y Tecnicas. Informe Sobre Un Ano de Labor (AG) *781*
Consejo Nacional de Investigaciones Cientificas y Tecnologicas. Departamento de Educacion. Directorio Nacional de Cursos de Postgrado (VE) *335*
Consejo Superior Universitario Centroamericano. Actas de la Reunion Ordinaria (ES ISSN 0589-4301) *335*
Consejo Superior Universitario Centroamericano. Publicaciones (NQ ISSN 0589-4360) *335*

Conselho de Desenvolvimento Economico *see* C D E *184*
Consenso: Revista de Literatura (US) *562*
Consequences (AT ISSN 0310-8228) *694*
Conservation Council of Ontario. Conference Proceedings (CN) *275*
Conservation Council of Ontario. Reports (CN) *275*
Conservation Directory (US ISSN 0069-911X) *275*
Conservation in Alberta (CN ISSN 0380-4496) *275*
Conservation in Kansas (US ISSN 0094-1670) *275*
Conservation Notes *see* Fish and Wildlife Facts *276*
Conservation of Cultural Property in India (II) *59*
Conservation of Library Materials (US ISSN 0069-9136) *528*
Conservation of Nature and Natural Resources *see* Nature and Environment Series *277*
Conservation Topics (CN ISSN 0573-715X) *276, 408*
Consolidated Annual Report of Licensees (Bismarck) *see* North Dakota. Consumer Credit Division. Consolidated Annual Report of Licensees *175*
Consolidated Report on Elementary and Secondary Education in Colorado (US ISSN 0095-5329) *316*
Consolidated Tax Return (Supplement) (US) *228*
Consommation de Denrees Alimentaires dans les Pays de l'O.C.D.E. *see* Food Consumption in the O. E. C. D. Countries *404*
Consort (UK) *658*
Consortium for Comparative Legislative Studies. Publications (US) *511*
Consortium for the Study of Nigerian Rural Development. C S N R D Working Paper (US ISSN 0069-9179) *27*
Consorzio Universitario. Pubblicazioni. Sezione Miscellanea (IT) *335*
Conspectus of History (US) *431*
Constitutional Law *see* B A R-B R I Bar Review. Constitutional Law *509*
Construction *see* American Society of Civil Engineers. Construction Division. Journal *374*
Construction au Canada *see* Construction in Canada *140*
Construction Directory (US) *874*
Construction Electrique *see* Industries Electriques et Electroniques *355*
Construction in Canada/Construction au Canada (CN ISSN 0527-4974) *140, 838*
Construction in Hawaii (US ISSN 0069-9187) *135*
Construction Industries and Trade Annual (II) *135*
Construction Industries and Trade Journal *see* Construction Industries and Trade Annual *135*
Construction Industry Europe (UK) *135, 484*
Construction Industry Research and Information Association Annual Report *see* C I R I A Annual Report *374*
Construction Industry Research and Information Association Report *see* C I R I A Report *135*
Construction Industry U.K. *see* House's Guide to the Construction Industry (1979) *136*
Construction Nautique Francaise/ French Boating Export (FR) *877*
Construction Navale (FR) *877*
Construction Writers Association. Newsletter (US ISSN 0069-9217) *135*
Constructioneer Directory (US) *135*
Consultants and Consulting Organizations Directory (US) *214, 236*
Consultation on Church Union. Digest (US ISSN 0589-4867) *764*
Consulting Engineer Who's Who and Year Book (UK ISSN 0069-9225) *366*

Consulting Engineers-Canada-Ingenieurs-Conseils (CN ISSN 0317-6525) *366*
Consumer Bulletin/Bulletin aux Consommateurs (CN ISSN 0708-3963) *279, 870*
Consumer Complaint Contact System, Annual Report (US ISSN 0193-9297) *279*
Consumer Credit Association of the United Kingdom. Membership Directory (UK) *172, 217*
Consumer Europe (UK ISSN 0308-4353) *217*
Consumer-Farmer Cooperator (US) *14, 479*
Consumer Finance Roster *see* N. C. F. A. Office Manual *175*
Consumer Guide: Best Buys & Discount Prices (US) *279*
Consumer Guide: Consumer Buying Guide *see* Consumer Guide: Best Buys & Discount Prices *279*
Consumer Guide Photo Annual (US) *693*
Consumer Guide Photographic Equipment Test Reports Quarterly *see* Consumer Guide Photo Annual *693*
Consumer Protection Directory (US) *279*
Consumer Sourcebook (US) *279*
Consumers Affairs Council of Tasmania. Annual Report (AT) *279, 804*
Consumers Digest Guide to Discount Buying (US) *279*
Consumers Directory (NE ISSN 0069-9284) *279*
Consumers Index to Product Evaluations and Information Sources (US ISSN 0094-0534) *2, 280*
Consumers Protection Council of Tasmania. Annual Report *see* Consumers Affairs Council of Tasmania. Annual Report *279*
Consumo Industrial de Energia Eletrica do Estado da Bahia (BL) *352*
Contabilidad Nacional de Espana (SP ISSN 0069-9292) *228*
Contact (US) *867*
Contact Lens Journal (US ISSN 0096-2716) *615*
Contact Lens Society of America Journal *see* Contact Lens Journal *615*
Contacts & Facilities (AT) *285, 658, 858*
Contacts in Consumerism (US) *279*
Container Contacts (GW) *236, 862*
Containerisation International Yearbook(UK) *862*
Containerization: A Bibliography (US ISSN 0069-9314) *865*
Containerization and Material Handling Annual (CN) *672, 862*
Containers (FR) *672, 862*
Contemporary African Monographs (KE ISSN 0069-9330) *439*
Contemporary American History Series (US ISSN 0069-9357) *468*
Contemporary Art Society of Australia. Broadsheet (AT) *73*
Contemporary Artists (US) *73*
Contemporary Authors (US ISSN 0010-7468) *97*
Contemporary Authors News *see* Authors in the News *559*
Contemporary Biology (UK) *102*
Contemporary Community Health Series (US) *751*
Contemporary Drama Series (US ISSN 0069-9381) *562*
Contemporary Economic Problems (US ISSN 0149-9130) *741*
Contemporary Educational Issues (US) *316*
Contemporary Evaluation Research (US) *797, 804*
Contemporary Government Series (US) *741*
Contemporary Hematology/Oncology (US) *613*
Contemporary Issues in International Accounting: Occasional Paper (US) *167, 194*
Contemporary Issues Series (UK ISSN 0069-942X) *431*

Contemporary Literary Criticism Series (US ISSN 0091-3421) *562*
Contemporary Literary Scene (US) *562*
Contemporary Metabolism (US) *611*
Contemporary Neurology Series (US ISSN 0069-9446) *619*
Contemporary Nursing Series (US) *613*
Contemporary Philosophy Series (US ISSN 0414-7790) *688*
Contemporary Poetry of British Columbia (CN ISSN 0384-0433) *579*
Contemporary Practice of the United Kingdom in the Field of International Law *see* British Practice in International Law *522*
Contemporary Problems in Cardiology (US ISSN 0093-5166) *607*
Contemporary Problems in Geography (US) *421*
Contemporary Problems of Childhood (US ISSN 0147-1082) *256*
Contemporary Quarterly *see* C Q *579*
Contemporary Religious Movements: A Wiley-Interscience Series (US) *688, 764*
Contemporary Studies in Economic and Financial Analysis (US) *143, 172*
Contemporary Topics in Immunobiology (US ISSN 0093-4054) *102*
Contemporary Topics in Molecular Immunology (US ISSN 0090-8800) *603*
Contempory Essay Series (US) *490, 562*
Contents of Recent Economics Journals(UK ISSN 0045-8368) *2, 154*
Continent (FR) *556*
Continental Camping & Caravan Sites (UK ISSN 0069-9527) *829, 884*
Continental Motoring Holidays (UK) *870, 884*
Continental Research Series (HK ISSN 0069-9535) *443*
Continuing Education for Health Care Providers (US ISSN 0160-6980) *907*
Continuing Education in Nursing Home Administration *see* Continuing Education for Health Care Providers *907*
Continuing Engineering Studies Series *see* C I E C Proceedings *366*
Continuing Series in Community Clinical Psychology *see* Community-Clinical Psychology Series *735*
Contraband (US) *562*
Contract Carpeting (UK ISSN 0069-9578) *502*
Contractors *see* E N R Directory of Contractors *136*
Contracts *see* B A R-B R I Bar Review. Contracts *509*
Contrast (IS ISSN 0010-7948) *562, 579*
Contrebis (UK ISSN 0307-5087) *59*
Contribuicoes em Ciencias Sociais (BL) *797*
Contribuicoes em Desenvolvimento Urbano (BL) *484*
Contribuicoes em Economia (BL) *143*
Contribuicoes em Psicologia, Psiquiatria e Psicanalise (BL) *619, 735*
Contribuicoes para o Estudo da Antropologia Portuguesa (PO) *49*
Contributi di Sociologia (IT ISSN 0391-1926) *812*
Contributi di Sociologia. Readings (IT ISSN 0391-3171) *812*
Contributii Botanice (RM ISSN 0069-9616) *114*
Contribution to Precambrian Geology (US) *292*
Contributions a la Connaissance des Elites Africaines (FR) *97, 439*
Contributions in Afro-American and African Studies (US ISSN 0069-9624) *439*
Contributions in American History (US ISSN 0084-9219) *468*
Contributions in American Studies (US ISSN 0084-9227) *468*
Contributions in Anthropology (US ISSN 0069-9632) *49*

Contributions in Comparative Colonial Studies (US ISSN 0163-3813) *468*
Contributions in Drama and Theatre Studies (US ISSN 0163-3821) *858*
Contributions in Economics and Economic History (US ISSN 0084-9235) *191*
Contributions in Family Studies (US ISSN 0147-1023) *813*
Contributions in Intercultural and Comparative Studies (US ISSN 0147-1031) *813*
Contributions in Labor History (US ISSN 0146-3608) *206*
Contributions in Legal Studies (US ISSN 0147-1074) *511*
Contributions in Librarianship and Information Science (US ISSN 0084-9243) *528*
Contributions in Marine Science (US) *102*
Contributions in Medical History (US ISSN 0147-1058) *594*
Contributions in Military History (US ISSN 0084-9251) *638*
Contributions in Oceanography *see* Texas A & M University. Department of Oceanography. Contributions in Oceanography *312*
Contributions in Philosophy (US ISSN 0084-926X) *688*
Contributions in Political Science (US ISSN 0147-1066) *709*
Contributions in Sociology (US ISSN 0084-9278) *813*
Contributions in Women's Studies (US ISSN 0147-104X) *900*
Contributions to Asian Studies (NE) *490, 797*
Contributions to Current Research in Geophysics (SZ) *304*
Contributions to Economic Analysis (NE ISSN 0573-8555) *191*
Contributions to Epidemiology and Biostatistics (SZ ISSN 0377-3574) *751*
Contributions to Gynecology and Obstetrics (SZ ISSN 0304-4246) *615*
Contributions to Human Development (SZ ISSN 0301-4193) *126, 594*
Contributions to Indian Sociology (II ISSN 0069-9659) *813*
Contributions to Information Science (IS) *528*
Contributions to Library Literature (US ISSN 0069-9683) *528*
Contributions to Library Science *see* Bijdragen tot de Bibliotheckwetenschap *527*
Contributions to Marine Science (UK ISSN 0069-9691) *309*
Contributions to Microbiology and Immunology (SZ ISSN 0301-3081) *123, 603*
Contributions to Music Education (US ISSN 0162-0088) *658*
Contributions to Primatology (SZ ISSN 0301-4231) *128*
Contributions to Sedimentology (GW ISSN 0343-4125) *292*
Contributions to Sensory Physiology (US ISSN 0069-9705) *126, 594*
Contributions to the Development of the Piano Sonata (SA) *658*
Contributions to the History of Science and Technology in Baltics/Iz Istorii Estestvoznaniya i Tekhniki Pribaltiki (UR ISSN 0069-9713) *781, 850*
Contributions to the Sociology of Language (NE) *542, 813*
Contributions to the Study of Music and Dance (US ISSN 0193-6891) *286, 658*
Contributions to the Study of Religion (US ISSN 0147-1066) *764*
Contributions to the Study of Science Fiction and Fantasy (US ISSN 0193-6875) *4, 562*
Contributions to Vertebrate Evolution (SZ ISSN 0376-4230) *122*
Controcampo (IT) *709*
Control and Dynamic Systems *see* Control and Dynamic Systems: Advances in Theory and Applications *7*

Control and Dynamic Systems: Advances in Theory and Applications (US ISSN 0090-5267) *7*
Control and Sale of Alcoholic Beverages in Canada/Controle et la Vente des Boissons Alcooliques au Canada (CN ISSN 0705-4319) *86, 838*
Control Magazine (UK ISSN 0069-973X) *73*
Control of Power Systems Conference. Conference Record (US) *362*
Control of Power Systems Conference and Exposition. Conference Record *see* Control of Power Systems Conference. Conference Record *362*
Controle et la Ventes des Boissons Alcooliques au Canada *see* Control and Sale of Alcoholic Beverages in Canada/Controle et la Vente des Boissons Alcooliques au Canada *86*
Controller Magazin (GW) *214*
Controversies in Nephrology (US ISSN 0270-2088) *625*
Convegno di Studi Sulla Magna Grecia. Atti (IT ISSN 0069-9748) *59*
Convegno Nazionale dei Commercianti de Mobili. Atti e Relazioni (IT ISSN 0069-9764) *503*
Convegno Nazionale per la Civilta del Lavoro. Atti. (IT ISSN 0069-9772) *206*
Convenience Store Industry Report (US ISSN 0084-9294) *407*
Convenience Store Study *see* Annual Report of the Convenience Store Industry *403*
Convenios Centroamericanos de Integration Economica. (GT ISSN 0553-6863) *199*
Convention of American Instructors of the Deaf. Proceedings *see* Convention of American Instructors of the Deaf. Proceedings and Selected Papers *286*
Convention of American Instructors of the Deaf. Proceedings and Selected Papers (US) *286, 345*
Convention of American Instructors of the Deaf Newsletter *see* C A I D Newsletter *286*
Convention of Electrical and Electronics Engineers in Israel. Proceedings (US) *352*
Conventions & Meetings-Canada (CN ISSN 0315-100X) *626*
Convergence: International Colloquium on Automotive Electronic Technology. Proceedings (US) *352, 870*
Conversations With (US) *419*
Conversion of Serials Microfiche *see* C O N S E R Microfiche *89*
Converter Directory (UK ISSN 0309-2143) *236*
Co-Op Directory (US) *407*
Cooper Monographs on English and American Language and Literature (SZ ISSN 0069-9780) *542*
Cooperador Dental (AG ISSN 0069-9799) *609*
Cooperation entre la France et les Etats Francophones d'Afrique Noire de l'Ocean Indien *see* France. Ministere de la Cooperation. Service des Etudes et Questions Internationales. Donnees Statistiques sur les Activites Economiques, Culturelles et Sociales *710*
Cooperative Bank of Taiwan. Annual Report/Tai-Wan Shena Ho Tso Chin Ku. Annual Report. (CH) *172*
Cooperative Education Association Membership Directory (US ISSN 0069-9810) *316*
Cooperative Education Association Newsletter (US ISSN 0010-843X) *316*
Cooperative Industrial and Commercial Reference and Information Service Directory and Guide to Resources *see* C I C R I S Directory and Guide to Resources *527*
Cooperative Press in South-East Asia (II) *504*
Co-Operative Statistics (UK) *180*

Cooperative Trade Directory for Southeast Asia (II ISSN 0069-9837) *180, 236*
Cooperatives & the Law (US) *180*
Cooperatives in Campus Areas of North America *see* N A S C O Campus Co-Op Directory *240*
Cooperator (US ISSN 0045-849X) *907*
Coordenacao do Sistema de Tributacao, Brazil. Pareceres Normativos (BL) *228*
Coordenadoria de Saude Mental, Sao Paulo. Arquivos (BL ISSN 0080-6404) *619*
Coordination Chemistry (US ISSN 0069-9845) *246*
Coordination Directory of State and Federal Agency Water and Land Resources Officials (US ISSN 0363-8170) *276, 896*
Coordinator (US ISSN 0077-3468) *861*
Copenhagen Handelsbank. Annual Report (DK) *172*
Copenhagen Stock Exchange. Annual Report *see* Koebenhavns Fondsboers. Aarsrapport *203*
Coping Catalog (US) *287*
Copper Survey (UK) *627*
Copperbelt Education (ZA) *316*
Copperbelt of Zambia Mining Industry Year Book *see* Zambia Mining Yearbook *648*
Copts (US ISSN 0360-649X) *474*
Copyright Law Symposium (US ISSN 0069-9950) *676*
Copyright Laws and Treaties of the World. Supplements (UN ISSN 0069-9969) *676*
Cor Serpentis (AT ISSN 0311-1245) *562*
Coral Gables Conference on Fundamental Interactions at High Energy. (Proceedings) (US ISSN 0069-9977) *702*
Cord Sportfacts Guns Guide (US ISSN 0590-6776) *476, 819*
Cord Sportfacts: Hunting (US ISSN 0092-8216) *829*
Cordell's Who's Who in Building: Housing (AT) *135*
Cordell's Who's Who in Building: Non-Housing (AT) *135*
Cordell's Who's Who in Design Specifying (AT) *69, 135*
Corn Annual (US ISSN 0069-9993) *34*
Cornell Agricultural Waste Management Conference. Proceedings (US ISSN 0065-4604) *385*
Cornell Biennial Electrical Engineering Conference (US ISSN 0070-0002) *352*
Cornell International Agricultural Development Mimeographs *see* Cornell International Agriculture Mimeographs *14*
Cornell International Agricultural Development Series. Bulletins Reporting Research on the Economics of Asian Agriculture (US) *27*
Cornell International Agriculture Mimeographs (US) *14*
Cornell International Industrial and Labor Relations Reports (US ISSN 0070-0029) *207*
Cornell Linguistic Contributions (NE) *542*
Cornell Recommendations for Commercial Tree-Fruit Production (US) *415*
Cornell Recommendations for Commercial Vegetable Production (US) *34*
Cornell Studies in Industrial and Labor Relations (US ISSN 0070-0053) *207*
Cornell University. Department of Agricultural Economics. Prices, Employment and Income Distribution Research Project. Occasional Papers (US) *27*
Cornell University. Libraries. Guide Series (US) *90*

Cornell University. Modern Indonesia Project. Monographs (US ISSN 0589-7300) *669*
Cornell University. New York State College of Agriculture and Life Sciences. Biometrics Unit. Annual Report (US) *110*
Cornell University. Program in Urban and Regional Studies. Occasional Papers (US) *484*
Cornell University. Program in Urban and Regional Studies. Research Reports (US) *484*
Cornell University. Southeast Asia Program. Data Papers (US ISSN 0070-0215) *443*
Cornell University. Thailand Project. Interim Reports Series (US ISSN 0070-0223) *443*
Cornell University Conference on Agricultural Waste Management *see* Cornell Agricultural Waste Management Conference. Proceedings *385*
Cornell University East Asia Papers (US) *443*
Cornfield Review (US ISSN 0363-4574) *73*
Cornish Archaeology (UK ISSN 0070-024X) *59*
Cornish Biological Records (UK) *102, 391*
Cornish Play Series (UK) *858*
Cornwall Archaeological Society. Field Guide (UK ISSN 0070-0258) *59*
Corona (US) *562, 688*
Corporacion Boliviana de Fomento. Marcha de la Economia Nacional. Resumen Estadistico (BO) *154*
Corporacion Costarricense de Financiamiento Industrial. Memoria Anual (CR) *221*
Corporacion de Investigaciones Economicas para Latinoamerica Estudios CIEPLAN *see* Estudios CIEPLAN *185*
Corporacion Financiera Colombiana. Ejercicio (CK) *143*
Corporacion Nacional de Fertilizantes. Memoria Anual (PE ISSN 0589-7742) *34*
Corporate Buyers of Design Services/U S A (US ISSN 0145-3017) *69, 135*
Corporate Diagrams and Administrative Personnel of the Chemical Industry (US ISSN 0574-1181) *236*
Corporate Fund Raising Directory (US) *172*
Corporate Insurance in Canada (CN ISSN 0315-8098) *498*
Corporate Management Tax Conference(CN ISSN 0070-0282) *228*
Corporate Pension Fund Seminar. Proceedings (US ISSN 0070-0290) *207, 498*
Corporate Planner's Yearbook (US ISSN 0307-3025) *214*
Corporate Profiles for Executives & Investors (US ISSN 0145-692X) *143, 202*
Corporate Report Fact Book (US ISSN 0589-7920) *236*
Corporation des Ingenieurs Forestiers du Quebec. Congres Annuel. Texte des Conferences *see* Ordre des Ingenieurs Forestiers du Quebec. Congres Annuel. Texte des Conferences *410*
Corporation Professionnelle des Medecins du Quebec. Annuaire Medical (CN ISSN 0315-226X) *594*
Corporation Professionnelle des Medecins du Quebec. Bulletin (CN ISSN 0315-2979) *594*
Corporations *see* B A R-B R I Bar Review. Corporations *509*
Corpus Almanac of Canada (CN ISSN 0315-7083) *360*
Corpus Antiquatum Americanensium (MX ISSN 0070-0312) *59, 468*
Corpus Catholicorum (GW ISSN 0070-0320) *774*
Corpus Christianorum. Series Graeca (BE) *774*
Corpus Commentariorum in Aristotelem. Versio Anglica (US) *907*

Corpus Commentariorum in Aristotolem. Versio Arabica (US) *907*
Corpus Commentariorum in Aristotolem. Versio Hebraica (US) *907*
Corpus Commentariorum in Aristotolem. Versio Latina (US) *907*
Corpus der Byzantinischen Miniaturenhandschriften (C B M) (GW) *259*
Corpus Hispanorum de Pace (SP ISSN 0589-8056) *511*
Corpus Medicorum Graecorum (GE ISSN 0070-0347) *594*
Corpus Mensurabilis Musicae (GW ISSN 0070-0363) *658*
Corpus Musicae Popularis Hungaricae *see* Regi Magyar Dallamok Tara *663*
Corpus Palladianum (US ISSN 0070-038X) *69*
Corpus Sacrae Scripturae Neerlandicae Medii Aevii *see* Verzameling van Middelnecerlandse Bijbelteksten *576*
Corpus Scriptorum Christianorum Orientalium: Aethiopica (BE ISSN 0070-0398) *776*
Corpus Scriptorum Christianorum Orientalium: Arabica (BE ISSN 0070-0401) *776*
Corpus Scriptorum Christianorum Orientalium: Armeniaca (BE ISSN 0070-041X) *776*
Corpus Scriptorum Christianorum Orientalium: Coptica (BE ISSN 0070-0428) *776*
Corpus Scriptorum Christianorum Orientalium: Iberica (BE ISSN 0070-0436) *776*
Corpus Scriptorum Christianorum Orientalium: Subsidia (BE ISSN 0070-0444) *776*
Corpus Scriptorum Christianorum Orientalium: Syriaca (BE ISSN 0070-0452) *776*
Corpus Scriptorum de Musica (GW ISSN 0370-0460) *658*
Corpus Vasorum Antiquorum. Italia (IT ISSN 0070-0479) *652*
Correctional Literature Published in Canada/Ouvrages de Criminologie Publies au Canada (CN ISSN 0070-0509) *907*
Correio Agricola (Brazil) (BL) *34*
Correio Agricola (Portugal) (PO) *34*
Correios e Telecomunicacoes de Portugal. Anuario Estatistico (PO) *264, 266*
Correo Fitosanitario (International) (GW) *34*
Correspondance d'Orient (BE ISSN 0070-0517) *443, 769*
Correspondence Educational Directory (US) *316*
Corriedale (NZ) *44*
Corrosion Monograph Series (US) *627*
Corsi Internazionali di Cultura sull'Arte Ravennate e Bizantina. Atti (IT) 59, *73*
Corvallis Environmental Research Laboratory. Research Highlights (US) *385*
Corvette, Sportscar of America (US) *870*
Corvette, the Sensuous American *see* Corvette, Sportscar of America *870*
Coscienza del Tempo (IT) *490*
Cosmetic Formulary (US ISSN 0070-0533) *907*
Cosmetics Handbook/Guide des Cosmetiques (CN ISSN 0084-9324) *85*
Cosmic Circus (US) *562*
Cosmos Newsletter (UK ISSN 0143-2028) *82*
COSPAR Technique Manual (Committee on Space Research) (FR ISSN 0084-9332) *7*
COSPAR Transactions (Committee on Space Research) (FR ISSN 0084-9340) *7*
Cost of Health Care in the Netherlands *see* Kosten en Financiering van de Gezondheidzorg in Nederland *752*
Cost of Personal Borrowing in the United States. (US ISSN 0091-3855) *172*

Cost of Storing and Handling Cotton at Public Storage Facilities *see* U.S. Department of Agriculture. Economics, Statistics and Cooperatives Service. Cost of Storing and Handling Cotton at Public Storage Facilities *31*
Costa Rica. Archivo Nacional. Revista (CR ISSN 0034-9003) *421, 431*
Costa Rica. Direccion General de Estadistica y Censos. Accidentes de Transito *see* Accidentes de Transito en Costa Rica *874*
Costa Rica. Direccion General de Estadistica y Censos. Encuesta de Hogares, Empleo y Desempleo: Area Metropolitana de San Jose (CR) *154*
Costa Rica. Direccion General de Estadistica y Censos. Inventario de las Estadisticas Nacionales (CR ISSN 0589-8544) *838*
Costa Rica. Direccion General de la Tributacion Directa. Estadistica Demografia Fiscal del Impuesto Sobre la Renta. Periodos (CR) *228*
Costa Rica. Ministerio de Hacienda Oficina del Presupuesto. Informe (CR ISSN 0070-0576) *228*
Costa Rica. Ministerio de Obras Publicas y Transportes. Memorias (CR) *874*
Costa Rica. Ministerio de Transportes. Memoria *see* Costa Rica. Ministerio de Obras Publicas y Transportes. Memorias *874*
Costa Rica. Revista de Estudios y Estadisticas. Serie Demografica (CR) *726*
Costume (UK ISSN 0590-8876) *262, 452*
Costume Society of Ontario. Newsletter (CN ISSN 0383-4239) *262, 401*
Cote d'Ivoire en Chiffres (SG) *439*
Cotton and Allied Textile Industries *see* International Textile Manufacturing *856*
Cotton Corporation of India. Annual Report (II ISSN 0304-6907) *27*
Cotton Ginnings in the United States (US ISSN 0070-0681) *24*
Cotton International (US ISSN 0070-0673) *855*
Cotton Production in the United States *see* Cotton Ginnings in the United States *24*
Cotton Trade Journal International *see* Cotton International *855*
Council for Advancement and Support of Education. Directory *see* Council for Advancement and Support of Education. Membership Directory *335*
Council for Advancement and Support of Education. Membership Directory (US) *335*
Council for Agricultural and Chemurgic Research. Proceedings of Annual Conferences (US) *14*
Council for Basic Education. Occasional Papers (US ISSN 0070-069X) *316*
Council for British Archaeology. Current Offprints and Reports (UK ISSN 0305-5280) *59*
Council for Financial Aid to Education. C.F.A.E. Corporation Support of Higher Education (US ISSN 0589-9087) *344*
Council for High Blood Pressure Research. Proceedings *see* Hypertension Series *607*
Council for Mutual Economic Assistance Statistical Yearbook *see* C M E A Statistical Yearbook *199*
Council for Mutual Economic Assistance Zahlen *see* R G W in Zahlen *201*
Council for Old World Archaeology: C O W A Surveys and Bibliographies. Area 1: British Isle (US ISSN 0070-072X) *907*
Council for Old World Archaeology: C O W A Surveys and Bibliographies. Area 2: Scandinavia (US ISSN 0070-0738) *907*
Council for Old World Archaeology: C O W A Surveys and Bibliographies. Area 3: Western Europe: Part 1 (US ISSN 0070-0746) *907*

Council for Old World Archaeology: C O W A Surveys and Bibliographies. Area 3: Western Europe: Part 2 (US ISSN 0070-0754) *907*
Council for Old World Archaeology: C O W A Surveys and Bibliographies. Area 4: Western Mediterranean (US ISSN 0070-0762) *907*
Council for Old World Archaeology: C O W A Surveys and Bibliographies. Area 7: Eastern Mediterranean (US ISSN 0070-0797) *907*
Council for Old World Archaeology: C O W A Surveys and Bibliographies. Area 8: European Russia (US ISSN 0070-0800) *907*
Council for Old World Archaeology: C O W A Surveys and Bibliographies. Area 9: Northeast Africa (US ISSN 0070-0819) *907*
Council for Old World Archaeology: C O W A Surveys and Bibliographies. Area 10: Northwest Africa (US ISSN 0070-0827) *907*
Council for Old World Archaeology: C O W A Surveys and Bibliographies. Area 11. West Africa (US ISSN 0070-0835) *907*
Council for Old World Archaeology: C O W A Surveys and Bibliographies. Area 12. Equatorial Africa (US ISSN 0070-0843) *907*
Council for Old World Archaeology: C O W A Surveys and Bibliographies. Area 13. South Africa (US ISSN 0070-0851) *907*
Council for Old World Archaeology: C O W A Surveys and Bibliographies. Area 14. East Africa (US ISSN 0070-086X) *907*
Council for Old World Archaeology: C O W A Surveys and Bibliographies. Area 15. Western Asia (US ISSN 0070-0878) *907*
Council for Old World Archaeology: C O W A Surveys and Bibliographies. Area 16. Southern Asia (US ISSN 0070-0886) *907*
Council for Old World Archaeology: C O W A Surveys and Bibliographies. Area 17. Far East (US ISSN 0070-0894) *907*
Council for Old World Archaeology: C O W A Surveys and Bibliographies. Area 18. Northern Asia (US ISSN 0070-0916) *907*
Council for Old World Archaeology: C O W A Surveys and Bibliographies. Area 19. Southeast Asia (US ISSN 0070-0924) *907*
Council for Old World Archaeology: C O W A Surveys and Bibliographies. Area 20. Indonesia (US ISSN 0070-0932) *907*
Council for Old World Archaeology: C O W A Surveys and Bibliographies. Area 21. Pacific Islands (US ISSN 0070-0940) *907*
Council for Old World Archaeology: C O W A Surveys and Bibliographies. Area 22. Australia (US ISSN 0070-0959) *907*
Council for Scientific and Industrial Research Annual Report *see* C S I R Annual Report *780*
Council for Scientific and Industrial Research Annual Report *see* C S I R Annual Report *780*
Council for Scientific and Industrial Research, Ghana. Forest Products Research Institute. Annual Report (GH ISSN 0586-8440) *412*
Council for Scientific and Industrial Research Handbook *see* C S I R Handbook *780*
Council for Scientific and Industrial Research Organization and Activities *see* C S I R Organization and Activities *780*
Council for the Social Sciences in East Africa. Social Science Conference. Proceedings (TZ) *797*
Council for Tobacco Research--U.S.A. Report (US ISSN 0361-1612) *287, 861*
Council for World Mission (Congregational and Reformed) Report *see* C W M Report *771*

Council of Better Business Bureaus. Annual Report (US ISSN 0094-8853) *279*
Council of Europe. Committee of Independent Experts on the European Social Charter. Conclusions. (FR) *720, 804*
Council of Europe. Committee on Cooperation in Municipal and Regional Matters. Study Series: Local and Regional Authorities in Europe *see* Council of Europe. Steering Committee on Regional and Municipal Matters. Study Series: Local and Regional Authorities in Europe *749*
Council of Europe. Concise Handbook (FR ISSN 0589-9508) *522*
Council of Europe. Consultative Assembly. Documents; Working Papers/Documents de Seance *see* Council of Europe. Parliamentary Assembly. Documents; Working Papers/Documents de Seance *522*
Council of Europe. Consultative Assembly. Orders of the Day, Minutes of Proceedings/Ordres du Jour, Proces Verbaux *see* Council of Europe. Parliamentary Assembly. Orders of the Day, Minutes of Proceedings/Ordres du Jour, Proces Verbaux *522*
Council of Europe. Consultative Assembly. Texts Adopted by the Assembly/Textes Adoptes Par l'Assemblee *see* Council of Europe. Parliamentary Assembly. Texts Adopted by the Assembly/Textes Adoptes Par l'Assemblee *522*
Council of Europe. Council for Cultural Cooperation. Annual Report (FR ISSN 0589-9478) *720*
Council of Europe. European Committee on Crime Problems. International Exchange of Information Bills and Draft Regulations on Penal Matters. *see* European Committee on Crime Problems. Bulletin on Legislative Activities *281*
Council of Europe. European Information Centre for Nature Conservation. Documentation Series (FR) *276*
Council of Europe. European Treaty Series (FR ISSN 0070-105X) *522*
Council of Europe. Exchange of Information Between the Member States on Their Legislative Activity and Regulations (New Series) (FR ISSN 0589-9362) *522*
Council of Europe. Parliamentary Assembly. Documents; Working Papers/Documents de Seance (FR) *522*
Council of Europe. Parliamentary Assembly. Orders of the Day, Minutes of Proceedings/Ordres du Jour, Proces Verbaux (FR) *522*
Council of Europe. Parliamentary Assembly. Texts Adopted by the Assembly/Textes Adoptes Par l'Assemblee (FR) *522*
Council of Europe. Standing Committee on the European Convention on Establishment (Individuals). Periodical Report. (FR) *718*
Council of Europe. Steering Committee on Regional and Municipal Matters. Study Series: Local and Regional Authorities in Europe (FR) *749*
Council of Europe Film Weeks (FR ISSN 0589-9591) *649*
Council of Graduate Schools in the United States. Proceedings of the Annual Meeting (US ISSN 0070-1076) *335*
Council of Legal Education. Calendar (UK ISSN 0305-411X) *511, 626*
Council of Ontario Universities. Research Division. Application Statistics (CN ISSN 0382-912X) *326*
Council of Ontario Universities Biennial Review *see* Council of Ontario Universities Triennial Review *335*
Council of Ontario Universities Triennial Review (CN ISSN 0315-9590) *335*

Council of Planning Librarians. Exchange Bibliography see Public Administration Series: Bibliography 748
Council of State Governments. Southern Legislative Conference. Summary, Annual Meeting (US ISSN 0099-006X) 741
Council of State Governments. Suggested State Legislation see Suggested State Legislation 746
Council of the European Communities. Review of the Council's Work (EI) 184
Council on Foreign Relations. Annual Report (US) 720
Council on Foreign Relations. Council Papers on International Affairs (US) 720
Council on Foreign Relations. President's Report see Council on Foreign Relations. Annual Report 720
Council on International Educational Exchange. Summer Study, Travel and Work Programs see Whole World Handbook: a Student Guide to Work, Study and Travel Abroad 343
Council on International Nontheatrical Events. Yearbook (US) 649
Council on Library Resources Annual Report (US) 528
Council on Library Resources, Inc. Recent Developments see C L R Recent Developments 527
Council on Library Resources Report see Council on Library Resources Annual Report 528
Council on Municipal Performance. Annual Report (US) 749
Council on the Teaching of Hebrew. Bulletin (US ISSN 0070-1203) 542
Councils, Committees and Boards (UK ISSN 0070-1211) 741
Counselor Education Directory: Personnel and Programs (US) 316
Countries of the World (US) 709
Country Dance and Song (US ISSN 0070-1262) 401, 658
Country Music Sourcebook (US) 658
Country Shows Annual see Agricultural Shows Annual 12
Country Studies (SZ) 184
Country Vacations U.S.A. (US ISSN 0147-3867) 884
Countryside Planning Yearbook (UK ISSN 0143-8190) 484
Countrywide Annual Year Book (US ISSN 0092-5454) 658
Countway Library Associates Historical Publications (US) 528, 594
County Agents Directory (US) 14
County and Municipal Year Book for Scotland see Scotlands Regions 746
County Court Practice (UK) 511
County Kildare Archaeological Society. Journal (IE) 59
County Louth Archaeological and Historical Journal (IE ISSN 0070-1327) 59
County Louth Archaeological Journal see County Louth Archaeological and Historical Journal 59
Cour Europeenne des Droits de l'Homme. Publications. Serie A: Arrets et Decisions see European Court of Human Rights. Publications. Series A: Judgments and Decisions 718
Cour Europeenne des Droits de l'Homme. Publications. Serie B: Memoires, Plaidoiries et Documents see European Court of Human Rights. Publications. Series B: Pleadings, Oral Arguments and Documents 718
Courrier du Transporteur (FR) 862
Courrier Technique Arts Graphiques (FR) 733
Cours et Documents de Biologie (US ISSN 0590-7225) 102
Cours et Documents de Chimie (US) 246
Cours et Documents de Mathematiques et de Physique (US) 585, 696
Course Guide for High School Theatre see Course Guide in the Theatre Arts at the Secondary School Level 858

Course Guide in the Theatre Arts at the Secondary School Level (US) 348, 858
Courses Offered by California Schools see Directory of Private Postsecondary Institutions in California 348
Court of Justice of the European Communities. Bibliographie de Jurisprudence Europeenne. Supplement see Bibliographie de Jurisprudence Europeenne Concernant les Decisions Judiciares Relatives aux Traites Instituant les Communautes Europeennes 521
Court of Justice of the European Communities. Publications Juridiques Concernant l'Integration Europeene; Bibliographie Juridique. Supplement see Publications Juridiques Concernant l'Integration Europeenne; Bibliographie Juridique. Supplement 521
Court of Justice of the European Communities. Recueil de la Jurisprudence (EI ISSN 0070-1386) 522
Courtenay Facsimiles see Courtenay Reformation Facsimiles 452
Courtenay Library of Reformation Classics (UK ISSN 0070-1394) 452, 764
Courtenay Reformation Facsimiles (UK) 452, 764
Courtenay Studies in Reformation Theology (UK ISSN 0070-1408) 452, 764
Coventry Chamber of Commerce & Industry Directory (UK ISSN 0140-8186) 179
Coventry Evening Telegraph Year Book & Who's Who (UK) 452
Covered Wagon (US ISSN 0574-3680) 468
Cowles Foundation for Research in Economics at Yale University. Monographs see Cowles Foundation Monographs 143
Cowles Foundation Monographs (US) 143
Coyote (US ISSN 0084-9421) 391
Coyote's Journal (US ISSN 0011-0736) 579
Craft and Hobby Trade Directory (UK ISSN 0142-0097) 476
Craft, Model & Hobby Industry Annual Trade Directory (US) 476
Crafts Annual (US) 476
Cranbrook Institute of Science, Bloomfield Hills, Michigan. Bulletin (US ISSN 0070-1416) 781
Crane-Crane Bulletin (US) 417
Cranfield Fluidics Conference. Proceedings (UK ISSN 0070-1424) 701
Crazy Horse (US ISSN 0011-0841) 579
Creation and Detection of the Excited State (US) 252
Creative Black Book (US) 5
Creative Camera Collection (UK) 693
Creative Camera International Year Book see Creative Camera Collection 693
Creative Canada (CN ISSN 0315-3290) 97, 858
Creative Drama (UK ISSN 0011-0892) 316, 858
Creative Guitar International (US ISSN 0092-8887) 907
Creativity (US ISSN 0097-6075) 5, 73
Credit Agricole Annual Report see France. Caisse Nationale de Credit Agricole. Rapport sur le Credit Agricole Mutuel 173
Credit and Capital Markets (US) 203
Credit Communal de Belgique. Actes des Colloques Internationaux. Collection Histoire. Series in 8 (BE) 452
Credit Manual of Commercial Laws (US ISSN 0070-1467) 172, 217
Credit Union Directory and Buyers' Guide (US ISSN 0092-4954) 172, 180
Credit Union Yearbook (US ISSN 0074-4468) 172, 180

Creditanstalt-Bankverein. Annual Report (AU) 172
Creditanstalt-Bankverein. Report see Creditanstalt-Bankverein. Annual Report 172
Cremation Society Handbook and Directory of Crematoria (UK ISSN 0305-9537) 414
Cremation Society of Great Britain. Conference Report (UK ISSN 0070-1475) 414
Cricket Annual (PK) 824
Cricket Quadrant (AT ISSN 0310-9356) 824
Crime and Delinquency in California (US) 281
Crime and Delinquency Issues, Monographic Series see Crime and Delinquency Topics, Monograph Series 281
Crime and Delinquency Topics, Monograph Series (US) 281
Crime and Justice (US) 281
Crime in Nebraska see State of Nebraska Uniform Crime Report 284
Crime in the United States see Uniform Crime Reports for the United States 284
Crime in Virginia (US ISSN 0146-5759) 281
Crimean Astrophysical Observatory, North Caucasus. Bulletin (US) 82
Criminal Appeal Reports (UK ISSN 0070-1521) 281
Criminal Justice Comprehensive Plan see Nebraska. Commission on Law Enforcement and Criminal Justice. Criminal Justice Comprehensive Plan 912
Criminal Justice Plan (Richmond) (US ISSN 0362-8353) 281
Criminal Justice Plan for New Jersey (US ISSN 0092-4652) 281
Criminal Law see B A R-B R I Bar Review. Criminal Law 280
Criminal Law Outline (US ISSN 0145-7322) 511
Criminal Legislation Manual see Maine Prosecutor, Criminal Legislation Manual 282
Criminal Procedure see Gilbert Law Summaries. Criminal Procedure 512
Criminal Victimization in the United States (US ISSN 0095-5833) 281
Criminalidad (1963-1973) see Estadistica de Criminalidad 285
Criminology, Criminal Law, Penology (FR) 281
Criminology Review Yearbook (US) 281
Criss-Cross Art Communications (US) 73
Critica Andina (PE) 797
Critica Social (BL) 804
Critical Bibliography of French Literature (US) 562
Critical Essays in Modern Literature (US ISSN 0070-153X) 562
Critical Heritage Series (UK) 562
Critical Issues in Education (US) 316
Critical Periods of History Series (US) 431
Critical Review (AT) 562
Critical Review Melbourne see Critical Review 562
Criticism and Interpretation (IS ISSN 0084-9456) 490, 562
Criticism Monographs (US) 562
Critiques (US ISSN 0090-4112) 73
Critiques (New York) see Critiques 73
Critiques de Notre Temps Et... (FR ISSN 0070-1556) 562
Croatian Information Series (US) 710
Crocodiles (SZ) 128, 276
Croissance Urbaine et Progres des Nations (FR ISSN 0070-1572) 191
Cromwelliana (UK ISSN 0307-5583) 452
Cronache Ercolanesi (IT ISSN 0391-1535) 542
Cronache Pompeiane (IT ISSN 0391-1527) 60
Crop Production see U.S. Crop Reporting Board. Crop Production 39
Crop Protection Courier (International) (GW ISSN 0590-1243) 34

CUADERNOS DE 1339

Crop Protection Courier (South Africa) (GW) 34
Crops Guide (CN) 34
Cropwood Round-Table Conference Papers (UK) 281
Cross Cultural Research and Methodology Series (US) 49, 735
Cross River State. Ministry of Economic Development and Reconstruction. State Development Plan (NR) 228
Crover Family History and Genealogy (US) 417
Crown Court (US) 511
Croydon Chamber of Commerce and Industry Directory (UK) 179
Croydon Natural History & Scientific Society. Proceedings and Transactions (UK ISSN 0309-8656) 781
Crude-Oil and Products Pipelines (US) 362, 678
Crude-Oil and Refined-Products Pipeline Mileage in the United States see Crude-Oil and Products Pipelines 362
Crusader (Toronto) (CN ISSN 0382-4314) 771
Crustal and Upper Mantle Structure in Europe. Monographs (US) 304
Cruzada Spanish Publications Directory of Suppliers of Educational Foreign Language Materials see C S P Directory of Suppliers of Educational Foreign Language Materials 347
Cryogenic Engineering Conference Proceedings see Advances in Cryogenic Engineering 700
Crystal Mirror (US ISSN 0097-7209) 771
Crystal Structures (US ISSN 0070-167X) 907
Crystals: Growth, Properties and Applications (US) 250
Cuadernas Simancas de Investigaciones Historicas. Monografias see Investigaciones Historicas 456
Cuadernos C I P C A (Serie Popular) (Centro de Investigacion y Promocion del Campesinado) (BO) 329, 813
Cuadernos de Alhambra (SP) 74
Cuadernos de Capacitacion (PE) 329
Cuadernos de Derecho Internacional Privado (UY) 523
Cuadernos de Educacion (CL) 316
Cuadernos de Estudio (PE) 774
Cuadernos de Estudios Judios (AG) 391
Cuadernos de Estudios Latinoamericanos (AG) 710
Cuadernos de Estudios Medievales (SP) 431
Cuadernos de Farmacologia (SP) 684
Cuadernos de Filosofia (AG) 688
Cuadernos de Filosofia (CK) 688
Cuadernos de Geologia Iberica (SP) 293
Cuadernos de Historia de la Farmacia (SP) 684
Cuadernos de Historia del Arte (AG ISSN 0070-1688) 74
Cuadernos de Historia del Arte (MX) 74
Cuadernos de Historia del Islam (SP) 769
Cuadernos de Historia del Islam. Serie Monografica Islamica Occidentalia see Cuadernos de Historia del Islam 769
Cuadernos de la Gaya Ciencia (SP) 562
Cuadernos de Linguistica (MX) 542
Cuadernos de los Institutos (AG) 511
Cuadernos de Orientacion (VE ISSN 0070-170X) 335
Cuadernos de Pedagogia (VE ISSN 0070-1718) 316
Cuadernos de Prehistoria (SP) 60
Cuadernos de Psicologia (CL) 735
Cuadernos de Psicologia (CK) 735
Cuadernos de Realidades Sociales (SP ISSN 0302-7724) 813
Cuadernos de Salud Publica see Public Health Papers 754
Cuadernos de Semiotica (UY) 542
Cuadernos de Sociedad y Politica (PE) 797

Cuadernos de Sociologia (AG ISSN 0070-1734) 813
Cuadernos de Teologia Actual, Ciencias Sociales y Realidad Nacional (PE) 764
Cuadernos de Teologia y Pastoral (CK) 774
Cuadernos de Trabajo de Historia (SP) 452
Cuadernos de Trabajo Social (SP) 804
Cuadernos del Mexico Prehispanico (MX ISSN 0070-1750) 468
Cuadernos del Taller de Folklore (PE) 401
Cuadernos Geograficos (SP ISSN 0210-5462) 421
Cuadernos Geograficos del Sur (CL) 421
Cuadernos Obreros (MX) 207
Cuadernos para el Estudio de la Estetica y la Literatura (AG) 562
Cuadernos para Estudiantes: Los Poetas(VE ISSN 0070-1785) 579
Cuadernos Populares (PE) 329
Cuadernos Salmantinos de Filosofia (SP) 688
Cuadernos Universitarios de Planificacion Empresarial y Marketing (SP) 214, 217
Cuadernos Uruguayos de Filosofia (UY ISSN 0590-2568) 688
Cuba. Centro de Informacion y Documentacion Agropecuario. Boletin de Resenas. Serie: Arroz (CU) 14
Cuba. Centro de Informacion y Documentacion Agropecuario. Boletin de Resenas. Serie: Avicultura(CU) 44
Cuba. Centro de Informacion y Documentacion Agropecuario. Boletin de Resenas Serie: Citricos (CU) 34
Cuba. Centro de Informacion y Documentacion Agropecuario. Boletin de Resenas. Serie: Ganaderia see Cuba. Centro de Informacion y Documentacion Agropecuario. Boletin de Resenas. Serie: Rumiantes 44
Cuba. Centro de Informacion y Documentacion Agropecuario. Boletin de Resenas. Serie: Ganado Porcino (CU) 44
Cuba. Centro de Informacion y Documentacion Agropecuario. Boletin de Resenas. Serie: Genetica y Reproduccion (CU) 14, 128
Cuba. Centro de Informacion y Documentacion Agropecuario. Boletin de Resenas. Serie: Mecanizacion (CU) 32
Cuba. Centro de Informacion y Documentacion Agropecuario. Boletin de Resenas. Serie: Pastos (CU) 42
Cuba. Centro de Informacion y Documentacion Agropecuario. Boletin de Resenas. Serie: Proteccion de Plantas (CU) 34
Cuba. Centro de Informacion y Documentacion Agropecuario. Boletin de Resenas. Serie: Rumiantes(CU) 44
Cuba. Centro de Informacion y Documentacion Agropecuario. Boletin de Resenas. Serie: Riego y Drenaje (CU) 34
Cuba. Centro de Informacion y Documentacion Agropecuario. Boletin de Resena. Serie: Suelos y Agroquimica (CU) 34
Cuba. Centro de Informacion y Documentacion Agropecuario. Boletin de Resenas. Serie: Veterinaria(CU) 894
Cuba. Centro de Informacion y Documentacion Agropecuario. Boletin de Resenas. Serie: Viandas, Hortalizas y Granos (CU) 42
Cuban Economy see Economia Cubana 184
Cuenta de la Hacienda Publica Federal (MX) 228
Cuisine Chez Sol (FR ISSN 0339-7963) 479
Cultura (IT) 490
Cultura Sarda (IT) 452
Cultura Universitaria (VE) 490

Cultural Activist (US) 907
Culture & Tradition (CN ISSN 0701-0184) 401
Culture Camerounaise/Cameroonian Culture (CM) 439
Cumann Leabharlannaithe Scoile. C L S Bulletin (IE ISSN 0007-8565) 528
Cumulated Abridged Index Medicus (US ISSN 0090-1377) 2, 602
Cumulated Index Medicus (US ISSN 0590-3408) 2, 602
Cumulative Annual Statistics: Alberta Coal Industry. (CN) 643
Cumulative Bibliography of Literature Examined by the Radiation Shielding Information Center (US) 90, 700, 702
Cumulative Index to Nursing & Allied Health Literature (US ISSN 0146-5554) 2, 602
Cumulative Index to Nursing Literature see Cumulative Index to Nursing & Allied Health Literature 602
Cumulative Index to Nursing Literature, Nursing Subject Headings see Cumulative Index to Nursing & Allied Health Literature 602
Curiospress International (FR) 90
Current African Directories (UK ISSN 0309-5460) 154
Current & Forthcoming Offprints on Archaeology in Great Britain & Ireland see Council for British Archaeology. Current Offprints and Reports 59
Current Articles on Neoplasia (US) 2, 602
Current Asian & Australasian Directories (UK) 154
Current Audiovisuals for Mental Health Education (US) 348, 735
Current Australian Serials (AT ISSN 0070-184X) 90
Current Aviation Statistics (US ISSN 0096-3364) 7, 867
Current Bibliographic Directory for the Arts & Sciences (US) 781
Current Biographies of Leading Archaeologists (US ISSN 0361-4735) 97
Current Biography Yearbook (US ISSN 0084-9499) 97
Current British Directories (UK ISSN 0070-1858) 154
Current Business Reports (US) 184
Current Cardiology (US) 607
Current Cardiovascular Topics (US) 607
Current Career and Occupational Literature (US ISSN 0161-0562) 2, 668
Current Caribbean Bibliography/ Bibliografia Actual del Caribe/ Bibliographie Courante de la Caraibe (PR ISSN 0070-1866) 437
Current Chemical Concepts (US) 246
Current Christian Books (US) 90, 769
Current Christian Books. Authors and Titles see Current Christian Books 769
Current Christian Books. Titles, Authors, and Publishers see Current Christian Books 769
Current Coins of the World (US ISSN 0070-1882) 477
Current Comment (CN) 720
Current Concepts in Biology (US) 102
Current Concepts in Clinical Nursing (US ISSN 0070-1890) 614
Current Concepts in Emergency Medicine (US ISSN 0145-4498) 594
Current Concepts in Nutrition (US ISSN 0090-0443) 665
Current Concepts in Ophthalmology (US ISSN 0097-8353) 615
Current Concepts in Radiology (US ISSN 0149-2454) 622
Current Construction Costs (US ISSN 0161-7257) 135
Current Construction Reports: Housing Units Authorized for Demolition in Permit-Issuing Places (US) 135, 484
Current Contents of Academic Journals in Japan (JA) 90
Current Diagnostic Pediatrics (US) 617
Current Education Law (US) 316, 511
Current Esperanto Book List (US) 555

Current European Directories (UK ISSN 0070-1955) 154
Current Geological and Geophysical Studies in Montana (US ISSN 0092-9565) 293, 304
Current Government Reports: State Tax Collections (US) 228
Current Governments Reports (US) 741
Current Governments Reports: Chart Book on Government Data. Organization, Finances and Employment (US ISSN 0360-2508) 228
Current Governments Reports: City Employment (US ISSN 0091-9209) 154
Current Governments Reports: City Government Finances (US ISSN 0082-9439) 228
Current Governments Reports: County Employment (US) 207, 741
Current Governments Reports: County Government Finances (US ISSN 0098-678X) 228
Current Governments Reports: Finances of Employee Retirement Systems of State and Local Governments (US) 207, 228, 741
Current Governments Reports, GE-Government Employment (US) 207, 741
Current Governments Reports, GF - Government Finance (US ISSN 0090-5259) 228
Current Governments Reports: Governmental Finances (US ISSN 0095-3741) 228
Current Governments Reports, GR Finances of Selected Public Employee Retirement Systems (US) 207, 228, 741
Current Governments Reports, GSS State and Local Government Special Studies (US) 228
Current Governments Reports, GT Quarterly Summary of State and Local Tax Revenue (US ISSN 0501-7718) 228
Current Governments Reports: Local Government Employment in Selected Metropolitan Areas and Large Counties (US ISSN 0098-3497) 154, 748
Current Governments Reports: Local Government Finances in Selected Metropolitan Areas and Large Counties (US) 228
Current Governments Reports: Public Employment (US) 207
Current Governments Reports: State Government Finances (US ISSN 0090-5895) 154
Current Housing Reports (US) 484
Current Housing Reports: Housing Characteristics (US ISSN 0498-8450) 484
Current Housing Reports: Housing Vacancies (US ISSN 0498-8469) 484
Current Index to Statistics (US ISSN 0364-1228) 2, 838
Current Industrial Relations Scene in Canada (CN ISSN 0318-952X) 207
Current Industrial Reports (US ISSN 0498-8477) 222
Current Inquiry into Language and Linguistics (CN) 542
Current Issues (US) 720
Current Issues and Research in Advertising (US ISSN 0163-3392) 5
Current Issues in Higher Education (US ISSN 0070-1971) 335
Current Issues in Music Education (US ISSN 0070-198X) 348, 658
Current Issues in Psychiatry (US ISSN 0590-3955) 619
Current Labour Force Statistics for Nova Scotia (CN ISSN 0382-1102) 838
Current Legal Problems (UK ISSN 0070-1998) 511
Current Medical Information and Terminology (US ISSN 0070-2005) 594
Current Medical Research and Opinion (UK ISSN 0300-7995) 594

Current Medical Terminology see Current Medical Information and Terminology 594
Current Municipal Problems (US ISSN 0011-3727) 511, 749
Current Nephrology (US ISSN 0148-4265) 625
Current Neurology (US ISSN 0161-780X) 619
Current Population Reports (US ISSN 0082-9471) 726
Current Population Reports: Consumer Buying Indicators (US) 212, 726
Current Population Reports: Consumer Income (US) 212, 726
Current Population Reports: Consumer Income. Income in (Year) of Families and Persons in the United States (US) 212
Current Population Reports: Consumer Income. Money Income (in Year) of Families and Persons in the United States (US) 213
Current Population Reports: Farm Population (US) 726
Current Population Reports: Federal-State Cooperative Program for Population Estimates (US ISSN 0565-0917) 726
Current Population Reports: International Population Reports (US ISSN 0082-9498) 726
Current Population Reports, P-20: Population Characteristics. Marital Status and Family Status see Current Population Reports: Populaion Characteristics. Marital Status and Living Arrangements 726
Current Population Reports, P-20: Population Characteristics. Mobility of the Population of the United States see Current Population Reports: Population Characteristics. Geographic Mobility 726
Current Population Reports, P-25: Population Estimates and Projections. Estimates of the Population of the United States by Age, Color, and Sex see Current Population Reports: Population Estimates and Projections. Estimates of the Population of the United States by Age, Sex and Race 726
Current Population Reports: Population Characteristics (US ISSN 0363-6836) 726
Current Population Reports: Population Characteristics. Geographic Mobility (US) 726
Current Population Reports: Population Characteristics. Household and Family Characteristics (US ISSN 0082-948X) 726
Current Population Reports: Population Characteristics. Marital Status and Living Arrangements (US) 726
Current Population Reports: Population Characteristics. School Enrollment: Social and Economic Characteristics of Students (US) 726
Current Population Reports: Population Characteristics. Social and Economic Characteristics of the Black Population (US) 726
Current Population Reports: Population Estimates and Projections (US) 726
Current Population Reports; Population Estimates and Projections. Estimates of the Population of the United States and Components of Population Change (US ISSN 0071-1616) 726
Current Population Reports: Population Estimates and Projections. Estimates of the Population of the United States by Age, Sex and Race (US) 726
Current Population Reports: Special Censuses (US) 726
Current Population Reports: Special Studies (US ISSN 0498-8485) 727
Current Practice in Family Centered Community Nursing (US) 614, 813
Current Practice in Obstetric and Gynecological Nursing (US ISSN 0361-9249) 614, 615
Current Practice in Oncologic Nursing (US) 605, 614
Current Practice in Orthopaedic Surgery (US ISSN 0070-203X) 616

Current Practice in Pediatric Nursing (US ISSN 0361-9257) *614*, 617
Current Problems in Clinical Biochemistry (SZ ISSN 0300-1725) *111*, 594
Current Problems in Dermatology (SZ ISSN 0070-2064) *611*
Current Procedural Terminology *see* C P T *593*
Current Programs Annual Index *see* Conference Papers Annual Index *2*
Current Psychiatric Therapies (US ISSN 0070-2080) *619*
Current Radiology (US ISSN 0161-7818) *622*
Current Research and Development Projects in Israel: Natural Sciences and Technology (IS ISSN 0301-4657) *781*
Current Research in British Studies by American and Canadian Scholars (US ISSN 0590-417X) *490*, 797
Current Research in the Netherlands: Humanities (NE) *490*
Current Sweden (SW) *452*
Current Swedish Periodicals *see* Svensk Tidskriftsfoerteckning *95*
Current Therapy in Dentistry (US ISSN 0070-2110) *609*
Current Tissue Culture Literature *see* Index of Tissue Culture *910*
Current Topics in Anaesthesia (UK ISSN 0144-8684) *604*
Current Topics in Bioenergetics (US ISSN 0070-2129) *112*, 694
Current Topics in Cellular Regulation (US ISSN 0070-2137) *102*
Current Topics in Classroom Instruction Series (US ISSN 0095-2885) *348*
Current Topics in Clinical and Community Psychology (US ISSN 0070-2145) *735*
Current Topics in Comparative Pathobiology (US ISSN 0090-8584) *102*, 594
Current Topics in Critical Care Medicine (SZ ISSN 0376-4249) *594*, 624
Current Topics in Developmental Biology (US ISSN 0070-2153) *102*
Current Topics in Environmental and Toxicological Chemistry (US) *246*, 385, 684
Current Topics in Experimental Endocrinology (US ISSN 0091-7397) *611*
Current Topics in Eye Research (US ISSN 0190-2970) *615*
Current Topics in Hematology (US) *613*
Current Topics in Immunology (UK ISSN 0141-3368) *603*
Current Topics in Infection (UK) *594*
Current Topics in Intensive Care Medicine *see* Aktuelle Probleme der Intensivmedizin *591*
Current Topics in Materials Science (NE) *696*
Current Topics in Membranes and Transport (US ISSN 0070-2161) *102*, *128*
Current Topics in Microbiology and Immunology (US ISSN 0070-217X) *123*
Current Topics in Molecular Endocrinology (US ISSN 0094-6761) *611*
Current Topics in Nutrition and Disease (US) *665*
Current Topics in Nutritional Sciences/Beitraege zur Ernaehrungswissenschaft (GW ISSN 0067-4982) *665*
Current Topics in Pathology (US ISSN 0070-2188) *102*, 594
Current Topics in Physical Chemistry *see* Fortschritte der Physikalischen Chemie *254*
Current Topics in Science. Reihe 1. Basic Research. Abt. A. Chemistry and Physics *see* Wissenschaftliche Forschungsberichte. Reihe 1. Grundlagenforschung und Grundlegende Methodik. Abt. A. Chemie und Physik *248*

Current Topics in Science. Reihe 1. Basic Research. Abt. B. Biology and Medicine *see* Wissenschaftliche Forschungsberichte. Reihe 1. Grundlagenforschung und Grundlegende Methodik. Abt. B. Biologie und Medizin *109*
Current Topics in Science. Reihe 1. Basic Research Abt. C. Psychology *see* Wissenschaftliche Forschungsberichte. Reihe 1. Grundlagenforschung und Grundlegende Methodik. Abt. C. Psychologie *739*
Current Topics in Science. Reihe 2. Engineering *see* Wissenschaftliche Forschungsberichte. Reihe 2. Anwendungstechnik und Angewandte Wissenschaft *371*
Current Topics in Surgical Research (US ISSN 0070-2196) *624*
Current Topics of Contemporary Thought (US) *781*
Current Trends in Life Sciences (II) *102*
Current Trends in Programming Methodology (US) *271*
Currents (US) *896*
Curricula in the Atmospheric and Oceanographic Sciences. (US) 335, *632*
Curricula in the Atmospheric Sciences *see* Curricula in the Atmospheric and Oceanographic Sciences *632*
Curriculum Improvement (US ISSN 0094-1050) *316*
Curriculum Information Center School Directories *see* C I C's School Directories *330*
Curriculum Materials Clearinghouse. Index and Curriculum Briefs (US ISSN 0095-4977) *348*
Curriculum Plans *see* United Methodist Church. Curriculum Plans *773*
Currituck County Historical Society. Journal (US ISSN 0091-9640) *468*
Curtain, Drapery and Bedspread National Buyers Guide (US ISSN 0084-9502) *855*
Curtis Casewit's Guide to Ski Areas and Resorts (US) *829*
Curtis Casewit's Guide to Tennis Resorts (US) *824*
Curwood Collector (US ISSN 0147-0965) *97*
Cusanus-Gesellschaft. Buchreihe (GW ISSN 0070-2234) *764*
Cushman Foundation for Foraminiferal Research. Special Publication (US ISSN 0070-2242) *673*
Custom House Guide (US ISSN 0070-2250) *194*
Customs and Practices of Notaries Public and Digest of Notary Laws in the U.S. *see* Journal of Notarial Acts and Recordkeeping Practices *514*
Customs and Practices of Notaries Public and Digest of Notary Laws in the U.S. *see* Notary Public Practices & Glossary *514*
Customs Officer's Association of Australia. Fourth Division. Fourth Division Customs Officer (AT) *194*
Cybernetics: Documents de Travail *see* Cybernetics: Works in Progress *271*
Cybernetics: Works in Progress/Cybernetics: Documents de Travail (BE) *271*
Cycle Buyers Guide (US ISSN 0070-2277) *870*
Cycle Guide Road Test Annual (US ISSN 0590-4641) *826*
Cycle World Road Test Annual (US) *826*
Cyclo-Flame (US ISSN 0011-4359) *579*
Cyclopedia (CN) *316*
Cyclotron *see* Cyclo-Flame *579*
Cyfres Barddoniaeth Pwllgor Cyfieithiadau Yr Academi (UK) *579*
Cyfres Clasuron Yr Academi (UK) *562*
Cyfres Llygad y Ffynnon (UK) *431*
Cypher (UK) *562*
Cypriot Students Abroad (CY) *342*
Cyprus. Agricultural Research Institute. Annual Report (CY ISSN 0070-2307) *14*
Cyprus. Agricultural Research Institute. Progress Report (CY) *907*

Cyprus. Agricultural Research Institute. Technical Bulletin (CY ISSN 0070-2315) *14*
Cyprus. Agricultural Research Institute. Technical Paper (CY ISSN 0379-0932) *14*
Cyprus. Budget: Estimates of Revenue and Expenditure (CY ISSN 0070-2323) *228*
Cyprus. Chief Veterinary Officer. Annual Report (CY) *894*
Cyprus. Department of Agriculture. Soils and Plant Nutrition Section. Report (CY ISSN 0070-234X) *34*
Cyprus. Department of Antiquities. Annual Report (CY ISSN 0070-2374) *60*
Cyprus. Department of Antiquities. Monographs (CY ISSN 0070-2366) *60*
Cyprus. Department of Antiquities. Report (CY) *60*
Cyprus. Department of Fisheries. Annual Report of the Cyprus Fisheries *see* Cyprus. Department of Fisheries. Annual Report on the Department of Fisheries and the Cyprus Fisheries *396*
Cyprus. Department of Fisheries. Annual Report on the Department of Fisheries and the Cyprus Fisheries (CY) *396*
Cyprus. Department of Social Welfare Services. Annual Report (CY ISSN 0070-2404) *804*
Cyprus. Department of Statistics and Research. Agricultural Survey (CY) *14*
Cyprus. Department of Statistics and Research. Analysis of Wholesale and Retail Trade (CY) *155*
Cyprus. Department of Statistics and Research. Annual Industrial Production Survey (CY ISSN 0590-4854) *222*
Cyprus. Department of Statistics and Research. Annual Report of Vacancies (CY) *155*, 838
Cyprus. Department of Statistics and Research. Annual Report on Unemployment (CY) *155*, 838
Cyprus. Department of Statistics and Research. Construction and Housing Report (CY) *135*
Cyprus. Department of Statistics and Research. Criminal Statistics (CY) *285*, 838
Cyprus. Department of Statistics and Research. Demographic Report (CY ISSN 0590-4846) *731*
Cyprus. Department of Statistics and Research. Economic Report (CY ISSN 0070-2412) *155*
Cyprus. Department of Statistics and Research. Index Numbers of Industrial Production (CY) *222*
Cyprus. Department of Statistics and Research. Manpower Survey (CY) *155*, 838
Cyprus. Department of Statistics and Research. Motor Vehicles and Road Accidents (CY ISSN 0574-8399) *865*
Cyprus. Department of Statistics and Research. Road Motor Transport Sample Survey (CY) *862*
Cyprus. Department of Statistics and Research. Services Survey (CY) *222*
Cyprus. Department of Statistics and Research. Shipping and Aviation Statistics *see* Cyprus. Department of Statistics and Research. Shipping Statistics *877*
Cyprus. Department of Statistics and Research. Shipping Statistics (CY ISSN 0070-2439) *877*
Cyprus. Department of Statistics and Research. Statistical Abstract (CY ISSN 0590-4862) *838*
Cyprus. Department of Statistics and Research. Statistical Pocket Book (CY) *838*
Cyprus. Department of Statistics and Research. Statistics of Imports and Exports (CY ISSN 0070-2420) *194*
Cyprus. Department of Statistics and Research. Tourism, Migration and Travel Statistics (CY) *731*, 893

Cyprus. Department of Statistics and Research. Wages, Salaries and Hours of Work (CY) *155*
Cyprus. Development Estimates (CY ISSN 0084-9510) *228*
Cyprus. Geological Survey Department. Annual Report (CY ISSN 0574-8267) *288*
Cyprus. Geological Survey Department. Bulletin (CY) *288*
Cyprus. Geological Survey Department. Memoirs (CY ISSN 0574-8259) *288*
Cyprus. Loan Commissioners. Accounts and Statistics for the Year (CY ISSN 0574-8305) *228*
Cyprus. Ministry of Labour and Social Insurance. Annual Report (CY ISSN 0070-2390) *207*, 498
Cyprus. Ministry of Labour and Social Insurance. Labour Research and Statistics Section. Report on the Island-Wide Manpower Survey (CY) *207*
Cyprus. Tourism Organisation. Annual Report (CY) *194*, 884
Cyprus Chamber of Commerce and Industry Directory (CY ISSN 0070-2331) *236*
Cyprus Development Bank. Annual Report (CY) *172*
Cyprus Research Center. Annual *see* Kentron Epistemonikon Ereunion. Epeteris *546*
Cystic Fibrosis G A P Conference Reports (US) *623*
Czasopismo Prawno-Historyczne (PL ISSN 0070-2471) *452*
Czechoslovak Cooperative Movement in Figures (CS) *180*
Czechoslovak Economic Papers (CS ISSN 0590-5001) *143*
Czechoslovak Symposium on Graph Theory (CS) *585*
Czechoslovakia. Federalni Statisticky Urad. Statisticka Rocenka (CS ISSN 0070-248X) *838*
C4 Hydrocarbons and Derivatives *see* World C4 Hydrocarbons and Derivatives *248*
D.A.T.A. Book of Discontinued Integrated Circuits *see* Discontinued Integrated Circuit D.A.T.A. Book *271*
D A T A Book of Discontinued Semiconductor Diodes (US ISSN 0148-7604) *352*
D.A.T.A. Book of Discontinued Thyristors (US ISSN 0092-508X) *352*
D A T A Book of Discontinued Transistors (US ISSN 0070-2498) *353*
D'Art (SP) *74*
D B Report (Deutsche Bundesbahn) (GW ISSN 0072-1549) *873*
D C C-Camping Fuehrer Europa (Deutscher Camping-Club e.V.) (GW ISSN 0078-3943) *884*
D C C-Caravan Modellfuehrer (Deutscher Camping Club e.V.) (GW) 829, *870*
D C C-Caravanfuehrer (Deutscher Camping Club e.V.) (GW) 829, *884*
D C C-Touristik Service (Deutscher Camping Club e.V.) (GW) 829, *884*
D D R Film Information (GE) *649*
D D R-Publikationen zur Imperialismusforschung, Auswahlbibliographie (GE) *2*, *717*, 803
D F V L R-Forschungsberichte und D F V L R-Mitteilungen (Deutsche Forschungs- und Versuchsanstalt fuer Luft- und Raumfahrt e.V.) (GW) *7*
D F V L R Jahresbericht (Deutsche Forschungs- und Versuchsanstalt fuer Luft- und Raumfahrt e.V.) (GW ISSN 0070-3966) *7*
D G D Schriftenreihe (Deutsche Gesellschaft fuer Dokumentation e.V.) (GW) *528*
D. G. L. R. Jahrbuecher (Deutsche Gesellschaft fuer Luft und Raumfahrt e.V.) (GW ISSN 0070-4083) *8*
D.H.E. Data Briefs *see* D.H.E. Research Note *335*
D.H.E. Research Note (Department of Higher Education) (US) *335*

D.H. Hill Library Focus (US) *528*
D I A Yearbook - Design Action (UK ISSN 0306-6185) *385*
D I S A Information. Measurement and Analysis (US ISSN 0070-6639) *353, 637*
D I S C U S Facts Book (Distilled Spirits Council of the United States, Inc.) (US ISSN 0160-1504) *86*
D M G Occasional Papers (US) *69, 484*
D M M A in Depth (Direct Mail-Marketing Association) (US) *217*
D N O C S-Fins e Atividades (Departamento Nacional de Obras Contra as Secas) (BL) *34, 381*
D N P A (Departamento Nacional de Producao Animal) (BL) *44*
D P E D Newsletter (Department of Planning and Economic Development) (US) *484*
D.P.I. Yellow Pages (Department of Public Institutions) (US ISSN 0360-4357) *741, 804*
D P Index (AT) *236, 271*
D P International (UK ISSN 0143-1102) *271*
D R C Book & Monograph Series (Disaster Research Center) (US ISSN 0164-1875) *813*
D R C Historical and Comparative Disasters Series (Disaster Research Center) (US ISSN 0164-1867) *813*
D R I European Review (Data Resources, Inc.) (US ISSN 0362-4730) *184*
D T. I (Diagnostische und Therapeutische Informationen) (GW ISSN 0300-8096) *594*
D.V.R.P.C. Annual Report *see* Delaware Valley Regional Planning Commission. Annual Report *222*
D W *see* Dialectes de Wallonie *543*
Da Biyurokrat *see* Bureaucrat *740*
Dacca Visva Vidyalaya Patrika *see* Dhaka Bisvabidyalaya Patrika *418*
Dacia; Revue d'Archeologie et d'Histoire Ancienne (RM ISSN 0070-251X) *60*
Dacoromania (GW) *542, 562*
Dacotah Territory (US ISSN 0084-9529) *579*
Dada/Surrealism (US ISSN 0084-9537) *562*
Dadazine (US) *74*
Dados Estatisticos da Movimentacao de Carga e Passageiros (BL) *878*
Dados Estatisticos da Navegacao *see* Dados Estatisticos da Movimentacao de Carga e Passageiros *878*
Daedalus (SW ISSN 0070-2528) *652, 781, 850*
Daedalus Library (US ISSN 0070-2536) *490*
Daffodil and Tulip Year Book *see* Daffodils *415*
Daffodil Society. Journal (UK) *415*
Daffodils (UK ISSN 0070-2544) *415*
Daftar Pengadaan Bahan Indonesia *see* Indonesian Acquisitions List *91*
Dagestanskii Etnograficheskii Sbornik (UR) *49, 813*
Daily Bread (US ISSN 0092-7147) *776*
Daily Mail Motor Show Review (UK) *870*
Daily Mail Skier's Holiday Guide (UK ISSN 0309-5134) *829*
Daily Mail Year Book (UK ISSN 0301-7761) *360*
Daily Planet Almanac (US) *80, 415*
Daily Planetary Guide (US) *80*
Daily Watchwords (UK) *776*
Dairy Herd Improvement *see* Dairy Herd Improvement Letter *41*
Dairy Herd Improvement Letter (US) *41*
Dairy Industries Catalog (US ISSN 0070-2587) *41, 404*
Dairy Industry Research Report (CN ISSN 0707-7904) *41*
Dairy Producer Highlights (US) *41*
Dairy Roundup (US) *41*
Dairyman's Yearbook (UK ISSN 0144-5251) *41*
Daito Hogaku *see* Journal of Law and Politics *514*
Daiwa Fishing Annual (US ISSN 0145-613X) *829*

Daiwa Sportfishing Annual *see* Daiwa Fishing Annual *829*
Daiyamondo Kabushiki-Toshi-Ban *see* Diamond, Stock Investment Edition *203*
Dalhousie Dental Journal (CN) *609*
Dalhousie Labour Institute for the Atlantic Provinces. Proceedings (CN ISSN 0316-0688) *506*
Dalhousie University. Computer Centre. Newsletter (CN ISSN 0384-8116) *271*
Dalhousie University. Institute of Public Affairs. Occasional Papers (CN ISSN 0381-7024) *184*
Dalhousie University. School of Library Service. Occasional Papers (CN ISSN 0318-7403) *271, 528*
Dalhousie University. School of Library Service. Y-A Hotline (CN ISSN 0701-8894) *528*
Dalil el Arab *see* Arab Directory *391*
Dallas Cowboys Outlook (US) *824*
Dalyaglyady Litaraturny Zbornik (UR) *562*
Damascus Road (US) *562*
Damilica (II) *259*
Damon Runyon Memorial Fund for Cancer Research. Report *see* Damon Runyon-Walter Winchell Cancer Fund. Annual Report *605*
Damon Runyon-Walter Winchell Cancer Fund. Annual Report (US ISSN 0095-6775) *605*
Dana-Report (DK ISSN 0070-2668) *102, 309*
Dance Directory (US ISSN 0070-2676) *285*
Dance Gazette (UK ISSN 0306-0128) *285*
Dance Heritage-Focus on Dance *see* Focus on Dance *285*
Dance Life (US) *285*
Dance Life in New York *see* Dance Life *285*
Dance Magazine Annual (US ISSN 0070-2684) *285*
Dance Magazine Directory of College and University Dance (US) *285, 331*
Dance Research Annual (Congress on Research in Dance) (US) *49, 285*
Dance World (US ISSN 0070-2692) *285*
Dane Digest (AT ISSN 0311-0761) *682*
Daneshgah-e Tehran. Daneshkade-Ye Adabiyat va 'olum-e Ensani. Majalle-Ye Iranshenasi *see* University of Teheran. Faculty of Letters and Humanities. Bulletin of Iranian Studies *475*
Daneshgah-e Tehran. Ketabkhane-Ye Markazi. Nashriye-Ye Ketabkhaneh *see* University of Teheran. Central Library. Library Bulletin *538*
Danforth Foundation. Annual Report (US) *335*
Dangerous Cargo Contacts *see* Gefahrgut Kontakte *878*
Dania Polyglotta (DK ISSN 0070-2714) *90, 578*
Danish Book Auctions with an Outline of the Book Prices *see* Danske Bogauktioner med en Oversigt over Bogpriserne *758*
Danish Films (DK ISSN 0418-3304) *649*
Danish Medical Bulletin (DK ISSN 0011-6092) *594*
Danish National Bibliography. Serials. Supplement *see* Dansk Periodicafortegnelse. Supplement *90*
Danish Ophthalmological Society. Transactions (DK) *615*
Danish Review of Game Biology (DK ISSN 0070-2730) *128*
Danish Ships and Shipping *see* Danmarks Skibe og Skibsfart *865*
Danish Yearbook of Philosophy (DK ISSN 0070-2749) *688*
Danmarks Adels Aarbog (DK ISSN 0084-9561) *417*
Danmarks Biblioteksforening. Biblioteksvejviser/Guide to Danish Libraries (DK) *528*
Danmarks Biblioteksskole. Skrifter (DK ISSN 0069-9861) *528*

Danmarks Biblioteksskole. Studier (DK) *528*
Danmarks Eksportmarkeder (DK) *194*
Danmarks Folkeminder (DK ISSN 0070-2765) *401*
Danmarks Geologiske Undersoegelse. Serie A/Geological Survey of Denmark. Series A (DK) *293*
Danmarks Handels-Kalender *see* Kongeriget Danmarks Handels-Kalender *239*
Danmarks Riges Breve *see* Diplomatarium Danicum *452*
Danmarks Skibe og Skibsfart/Danish Ships and Shipping (DK ISSN 0070-3486) *865*
Danmarks Vareindfoersel og-Udfoersel/Foreign Trade of Denmark(DK ISSN 0070-2781) *155*
Danmarks 1000 Stoerste Virkomheder *see* Danmarks 2000 Stoerste Virksomheder *222*
Danmarks 2000 Stoerste Virksomheder/2000 Largest Companies in Denmark(DK) *222*
Dans le Fantastique (FR ISSN 0070-279X) *562, 688*
Dansk Botanisk Arkiv (DK ISSN 0011-6211) *114*
Dansk Elforsyning (DK) *353*
Dansk Elvaerksstatistik *see* Dansk Elforsyning *353*
Dansk Forsikrings Aarbog (DK) *498*
Dansk Geologisk Forening. Aarsskrift (DK) *293*
Dansk Historisk Aarsbibliografi (DK) *437*
Dansk Kulturhistorisk Museumsforening. Museumsregister (DK) *652*
Dansk Maskinhandlerforening. Handbog (DK ISSN 0302-5349) *32*
Dansk Medicinhistorisk Aarbog/Yearbook of Danish Medical History(DK ISSN 0084-9588) *594*
Dansk Ornithologisk Forenings Tidsskrift (DK ISSN 0011-6394) *125*
Dansk Periodicafortegnelse. Supplement/Danish National Bibliography. Serials. Supplement (DK ISSN 0084-9596) *90*
Danske Bank af 1871. Annual Report (DK) *172*
Danske Bogauktioner med en Oversigt over Bogpriserne/Danish Book Auctions with an Outline of the Book Prices (DK ISSN 0070-2811) *758*
Danske Landmandsbank. Annual Report *see* Danske Bank af 1871. Annual Report *172*
Danske Magazin (DK ISSN 0070-2846) *452*
Danske Reklamebureauers Brancheforening. Oplagstal og Markedstal (DK ISSN 0070-2854) *5*
Danske Skolehaandbog (DK) *316*
Dante Society of America. Report, with Accompanying Papers *see* Dante Studies *562*
Dante Studies (US ISSN 0070-2862) *562*
Dar es Salaam University Law Journal (TZ ISSN 0418-3770) *511*
Darmstaedter Archivschriften (GW) *452*
Dartmouth College. Dept. of Geography. Geography Publications at Dartmouth *see* Geography Publications at Dartmouth *422*
Dat Was de Toestand in de Wereld (NE) *431*
Data and Documents About Environment Protection *see* Daten und Dokumente Zum Umweltschutz *385*
Data Base Monograph Series (US) *271*
Data Book of Social Studies Materials and Resources (US) *348, 797*
Data Book on Illinois Higher Education(US ISSN 0098-5279) *335*
Data Communications Buyers' Guide (US) *271*
Data-Data Iklim di Indonesia (IO) *632*

Data on Iowa's Area Schools (US ISSN 0092-3761) *335*
Data on Iowa's Area Schools and Public Junior College *see* Data on Iowa's Area Schools *335*
Data Processing in Medicine/Datenverarbeitung in der Medizin (SZ ISSN 0070-2889) *907*
Data Processing Yearbook *see* Computer Yearbook *271*
Data Resources, Inc. European Review *see* D R I European Review *184*
Data Use and Access Laboratories. Annual Report (US) *271*
Date of Music in Western Japan *see* Music Cultures *661*
Daten und Dokumente Zum Umweltschutz/Data and Documents About Environment Protection (GW) *385*
Datenverarbeitung in der Medizin *see* Data Processing in Medicine *907*
Dati Meteorologico della Puglia e Luciania *see* Osservazioni di Meteorologia Agraria della Puglia e Basilicata *634*
Datos Etno-Linguisticos (PE) *49, 401, 542*
Datos Socio-Economicos de Costa Rica(CR) *184*
Datos y Cifras de la Ensenanza en Espana (SP ISSN 0070-2897) *316*
David Davies Memorial Institute of International Studies, London. Annual Memorial Lecture (UK ISSN 0070-2900) *720*
David Dunlap Observatory Publications(CN) *82*
Davis Medieval Texts and Studies (NE) *452*
Davison's Knit Goods Trade (US ISSN 0070-2943) *855*
Davison's Salesman's Book (US ISSN 0363-5252) *855*
Davison's Textile Blue Book (US ISSN 0070-2951) *855*
Davison's Textile Buyer's Guide (US) *855*
Davison's Textile Catalog and Buyer's Guide *see* Davison's Textile Buyer's Guide *855*
Davison's Textile Directory for Executives and Salesmen *see* Davison's Salesman's Book *855*
Davy's Devon Herd Book (UK ISSN 0070-2986) *44*
Dawn Song *see* Dawn Song and All Day *276*
Dawn Song and All Day (UK ISSN 0070-3001) *276*
Dawsons Guide to Australian & Worldwide Hotels (AT) *482, 884*
Ha-Dayig Be-Yisrael Be-Misparim *see* Israel. Ministry of Agriculture. Department of Fisheries. Israel Fisheries in Figures *398*
Day's Register of Registrars (UK ISSN 0482-1319) *172*
Dayton Art Institute. Annual Report (US ISSN 0070-3028) *652*
De Proprietatibus Litterarum. Series Didactica (NE) *563*
De Proprietatibus Litterarum. Series Major (NE ISSN 0070-3060) *563*
De Proprietatibus Litterarum. Series Minor (NE ISSN 0070-3079) *563*
De Proprietatibus Litterarum. Series Practica (NE ISSN 0070-3087) *563*
Dead Sea Works, Beersheba, Israel. Report of the Directors (IS ISSN 0070-3095) *309*
Death Education and Thanatology (US ISSN 0275-3510) *735*
Debate Socialista (PE) *710*
Debates en Antropologia (PE) *49*
Debates of the European Parliament (EI ISSN 0071-3015) *523*
Debreceni Orvostudomanyi Egyetem. Evkonyv (HU) *594*
Debunker *see* Scientists Forum *791*
Deccan College. Postgraduate & Research Institute. Bulletin (II ISSN 0045-9801) *443, 542, 797*
December (US ISSN 0070-3141) *563*
Dechema Monographien (US ISSN 0070-315X) *249, 612*
Decision (II) *214*

Decisions of the United States Courts Involving Copyrights (US ISSN 0070-3176) *676*
Deck Plan Guide *see* Ford's Deck Plan Guide *886*
Decorating Contractor Annual Directory (UK ISSN 0070-3192) *502*
Decorating Made Easy (US) *502*
Decorative Art and Modern Interiors (UK ISSN 0070-3206) *502*
Deems Lectureship (US ISSN 0070-3222) *907*
Defects in Cristalline Solids *see* Defects in Solids *696*
Defects in Solids (NE) *250, 696*
Defence Market Profiles (SZ) *638*
Defense Foreign Affairs Handbook (US) *638, 720*
DeGarmo Lectures (US) *335*
Degree Programs Offered by West Virginia Institutions of Higher Education (US) *335*
Degrees Conferred by West Virginia Institutions of Higher Education (US ISSN 0092-606X) *335*
Dejiny Vyrobnich Sil (CS) *854*
Delaware. Court of Chancery. Delaware Chancery Reports *see* Delaware Reporter *511*
Delaware. Courts. Delaware Reports *see* Delaware Reporter *511*
Delaware. Department of Health and Social Service. Annual Report (US ISSN 0095-6422) *751, 804*
Delaware. Department of Highways and Transportation. Traffic Summary (US ISSN 0070-329X) *874*
Delaware. Department of Natural Resources and Environmental Control. Annual Report (US ISSN 0084-9642) *276, 385*
Delaware. Department of Public Instruction. Educational Personnel Directory (US ISSN 0091-6188) *316*
Delaware. Department of Public Instruction. Teacher Supply and Demand *see* Supply and Demand: Educational Personnel in Delaware *323*
Delaware. Division of Social Services. Annual Report (US ISSN 0090-3051) *804*
Delaware. State Board of Education. Report of Educational Statistics (US ISSN 0362-8787) *316*
Delaware. State Highway Department. Traffic Summary *see* Delaware. Department of Highways and Transportation. Traffic Summary *874*
Delaware. State Treasurer. Annual Report (US ISSN 0084-9685) *228*
Delaware Art Museum. Annual Report (US) *74*
Delaware Basin Bulletin (US ISSN 0045-9844) *896*
Delaware Bay Microcomputer Conference. Proceedings *see* Micro-DelCon Delaware Bay Microcomputer Conference. Proceedings *273*
Delaware Geological Survey Bulletins (US ISSN 0070-3273) *293*
Delaware Geological Survey Reports of Investigations (US ISSN 0011-7749) *293*
Delaware Museum of Natural History. Monograph Series (US ISSN 0084-9650) *781*
Delaware Museum of Natural History. Reproduction Series (US ISSN 0084-9669) *781*
Delaware Museum of Natural History. Special Publications (US ISSN 0084-9677) *781*
Delaware Reporter (US ISSN 0091-5564) *511*
Delaware River Basin Water Resources Conference. Proceedings (US) *896*
Delaware State Industrial Directory (US ISSN 0148-5652) *236*
Delaware State Minority Business Directory (US ISSN 0098-6755) *236*
Delaware State Planning Office. School Facilities Planning Study (US) *344*

Delaware Statistical Abstract (US ISSN 0094-7911) *741*
Delaware Valley Regional Planning Commission. Annual Report (US) *222*
Delaware Valley Regional Planning Commission. Biennial Report *see* Delaware Valley Regional Planning Commission. Annual Report *222*
Delegation Archeologique Francaise en Iran. Cahiers (FR) *60*
Delegations to the United Nations (UN ISSN 0070-3303) *720*
Delek. Annual Report (IS) *678*
Delphica (FR ISSN 0070-3338) *543*
Delphinium Society Yearbook (UK) *415*
Delpinoa (IT ISSN 0416-928X) *102*
Delta Onderzoek Hydrobiologisch Instituut. Communication (NE) *128*
Delta Pi Epsilon. Research Bulletin (US ISSN 0416-9336) *348*
Demografie (BE) *731*
Demografska Statistika (YU ISSN 0084-4357) *727*
Demographic Monographs (US) *727*
Demographic Training and Research Centre. Annual Report. *see* International Institute for Population Studies. Director's Report *727*
Demographic Yearbook (UN ISSN 0082-8041) *727*
Demographie Africaine: Bulletin de Liaison (FR) *727*
Demographie en Afrique d'Expression Francaise; Bulletin de Liaison *see* Demographie Africaine: Bulletin de Liaison *727*
Demographie et Sciences Humaines (FR ISSN 0070-3354) *727*
Demographie et Societes (FR ISSN 0070-3362) *727*
Demokratische Existenz Heute (GW ISSN 0070-3389) *710*
Denken, Schauen, Sinnen (GW ISSN 0070-3419) *688*
Denki Seirigaku *see* Electrophysiology *112*
Denki Tsushin Daigaku Denki Tsushin Kenkyu Shisetsu Nenpo *see* University of Telecommunications. Research Laboratory of Communication Sciences. Annual Report *265*
Denkmaeler der Buchkunst (GW ISSN 0341-2474) *74*
Denmark. Atomenergikommissionens Forsoegsanslaeg, Risoe. (Annual Report) (DK) *702*
Denmark. Atomenergikommissionens Forsoegsanslaeg, Risoe. Risoe Report(DK ISSN 0418-6443) *362, 366, 702*
Denmark. Danmarks Fiskeri- og Havundersoegelser. Dana (DK ISSN 0106-553X) *396*
Denmark. Danmarks Fiskeri- og Havundersoegelser. Meddeleser *see* Denmark. Danmarks Fiskeri- og Havundersoegelser. Dana *396*
Denmark. Danmarks Fiskeri og Havundersoegelser. Skrifter *see* Fisk og Hav *397*
Denmark. Danmarks Statistik. Arbejdsloesheden/Unemployment (DK ISSN 0070-346X) *155*
Denmark. Danmarks Statistik. Befolkningens Bevaegelser (DK ISSN 0070-3478) *727*
Denmark. Danmarks Statistik. Ejendoms- og Personbeskatingen i Skattearet *see* Denmark. Danmarks Statistik. Ejendoms- og Selskabsbeskatningen i Skatteaaret *155*
Denmark. Danmarks Statistik. Ejendoms- og Selskabsbeskatningen i Skatteaaret (DK) *155*
Denmark. Danmarks Statistik. Ejendomssalg/Sales of Real Property (DK ISSN 0070-3508) *762*
Denmark. Danmarks Statistik. Faerdselsuheld (DK ISSN 0070-3516) *727, 751*
Denmark. Danmarks Statistik. Indkomstansaettelser Til Staten *see* Denmark. Danmarks Statistik. Indkomster og Formver Ved Slutligningen *155*

Denmark. Danmarks Statistik. Indkomster og Formver Ved Slutligningen (DK) *155*
Denmark. Danmarks Statistik. Industristatistik/Industrial Statistics (DK ISSN 0070-3532) *155*
Denmark. Danmarks Statistik. Konjunkturo. Versigt/Economic Trends (DK) *155*
Denmark. Danmarks Statistik. Kriminalstatistik (DK ISSN 0070-3540) *285*
Denmark. Danmarks Statistik. Landbrugsstatistik Herunder Gartneri og Skovbrug/Statistics on Agriculture, Gardening and Forestry (DK ISSN 0070-3559) *24*
Denmark. Danmarks Statistik. Statistisk Aarbog/Statistical Yearbook (DK ISSN 0070-3567) *838*
Denmark. Danmarks Statistik. Statistisk Tabelvaerk/Statistical Tables (DK ISSN 0039-0658) *838*
Denmark. Danmarks Statistik. Statistisk Tiars-Oversigt (DK ISSN 0070-3583) *838*
Denmark. Danmarks Statistik. Statistiske Efterretninger (DK ISSN 0039-0674) *838*
Denmark. Danmarks Statistik. Statistiske Meddelelser (DK) *838*
Denmark. Danmarks Statistik. Statistiske Undersogelser (DK ISSN 0039-0682) *838*
Denmark. Direktoratet for Kriminalforsorgen. Kriminalforsorgen(DK) *281*
Denmark. Direktoratet for Patent- og Varemaerkevaesenet. Aarsberetning (DK) *676*
Denmark. Direktoratet for Toldvaesenet. Toldvaesenet *see* Denmark. Direktoratet for Toldvaesenet. Toldvaesenets Aktiviteter *228*
Denmark. Direktoratet for Toldvaesenet. Toldvaesenets Aktiviteter (DK) *228*
Denmark. Fiskeriministeriet. Forsoegslaboratorium. Aarsberetning/Annual Report (DK ISSN 0070-3605) *102, 396*
Denmark. Folketinget. Folketingsaarbog(DK ISSN 0084-9707) *710*
Denmark. Forsoegslaboratoriet. Beretning *see* Denmark. Statens Husdyrbrugsudvalg. Beretning *44*
Denmark. Jordbrugsoekonomisk Institut. Aarsberetning (DK ISSN 0106-4967) *143*
Denmark. Jordbrugsoekonomisk Institut. Landbrugets Oekonomi (DK ISSN 0106-1291) *143*
Denmark. Jordbrugsoekonomisk Institut. Meddelelse (DK ISSN 0106-2689) *143*
Denmark. Jordbrugsoekonomisk Institut. Memorandum (DK ISSN 0106-3642) *143*
Denmark. Jordbrugsoekonomisk Institut. Undersoegelse (DK ISSN 0106-0864) *143*
Denmark. Jordfordelingssekretariatet. Aarsberetning (DK) *761*
Denmark. Justervaesenet. Aarsberetning(DK) *637*
Denmark. Kongelige Bibliotek. Fund og Forskning (DK ISSN 0069-9896) *528*
Denmark. Landoekonomiske Driftsbureau. Meddelelse *see* Denmark. Jordbrugsoekonomisk Institut. Meddelelse *143*
Denmark. Landoekonomiske Driftsbureau. Memorandum *see* Denmark. Jordbrugsoekonomisk Institut. Memorandum *143*
Denmark. Landoekonomiske Driftsbureau. Undersoegelse *see* Denmark. Jordbrugsoekonomisk Institut. Undersoegelse *143*
Denmark. Ministeriet for Groenland. Oekonomisk-Statiske Kontor. Meddelelser *see* Denmark. Ministeriet for Groenland. Statistisk Kontor. Meddelelser *184*

Denmark. Ministeriet for Groenland. Statistisk Kontor. Meddelelser (DK ISSN 0106-2891) *184*
Denmark. Nationalmuseet. Arbejdsmarkt (DK ISSN 0084-9308) *652*
Denmark. Nationalmuseet. Publications: Archaeological Historical Series (DK) *60*
Denmark. Nationalmuseet. Publications: Ethnographical Series (DK) *49*
Denmark. Nationalmuseet. Working Papers (DK) *652*
Denmark. Planlaegningsraadet for Forskningen. Beretning (DK) *781*
Denmark. Rigsbibliotekarembedet. Accessionskatalog (DK ISSN 0084-9715) *90*
Denmark. Socialforskningsinstituttet. Beretning om Socialforskningsinstituttes Virksomhed (DK ISSN 0081-0584) *805*
Denmark. Socialforskningsinstituttet. Meddelelse (DK) *805, 813*
Denmark. Socialforskningsinstituttet. Pjece (DK) *805, 813*
Denmark. Socialforskningsinstituttet. Publikation (DK) *805, 813*
Denmark. Socialforskningsinstituttet. Smaatryk (DK) *805, 813*
Denmark. Socialforskningsinstituttet. Socialforskningsinstituttets Virksomhed *see* Denmark. Socialforskningsinstituttet. Beretning om Socialforskningsinstituttes Virksomhed *805*
Denmark. Socialforskningsinstituttet. Studie (DK) *805, 813*
Denmark. Socialforskningsinstituttet. Ungdomsforloebsundersoegelsen. Rapport (DK) *805*
Denmark. Statens Bygningsfredningsfond. Beretning (DK) *69*
Denmark. Statens Filmcentral. S F C Film (DK ISSN 0070-3621) *649*
Denmark. Statens Husdyrbrugsudvalg. Beretning (DK) *44, 123, 126*
Denmark. Undervisningsministeriet. Oekonomisk-Statistiske Konsulent. Statistik de Videregaende Uddannelser (DK) *326*
Denmarks Deltagelse i det Internationale Udviklingssamarbejde (DK) *199*
Denmark's Development Assistance. Annual Report (DK) *199*
Denning Law Society. Journal *see* Dar es Salaam University Law Journal *511*
Denominations in America (US ISSN 0193-6883) *764*
Dental Admission Testing Program (US) *609*
Dental Anaesthesia and Sedation (AT ISSN 0311-0699) *604, 609*
Dental Guide (CN ISSN 0070-3656) *609*
Dental Practitioner Handbook (UK ISSN 0070-3699) *609*
Dental Products Annual Report (US ISSN 0070-3702) *609*
Dental Register of Ireland (IE ISSN 0084-9685) *609*
Dental Research in the United States and Other Countries (US ISSN 0147-264X) *609*
Dental Research in the United States, Canada, and Great Britain *see* Dental Research in the United States and Other Countries *609*
Dental Students' Register *see* Annual Report on Dental Education *601*
Dental Technician Yearbook (UK) *609*
Dentistry in Japan/Nihon no Shika Iryo(JA ISSN 0070-3737) *609*
Dentist's Desk Reference (US) *609*
Departamento Nacional de Obras Contra as Secas Fins e Atividades *see* D N O C S-Fins e Atividades *34*
Department of Fish and Game Technical Data Report *see* A. D. F. &. G. Technical Data Report *395*
Department of Higher Education Research Note *see* D.H.E. Research Note *335*

Department of Planning and Economic Development Newsletter *see* D P E D Newsletter 484
Department of Public Institutions Yellow Pages *see* D.P.I. Yellow Pages 741
Department Store Suppliers *see* I.R.D.S 218
Deposit Insurance Corporation. Annual Report: Directors' Report, Balance Sheet and Accounts (II ISSN 0304-6966) 498
Depots Canadiens des Revues Indexees pour Medline *see* Canadian Locations of Journals Indexed for Medline 602
Deputazione di Storia Patria per l'Umbria. Bollettino (IT ISSN 0300-4422) 452
Derbyshire Archaeological Journal (UK ISSN 0070-3788) 60
Derecho Financiero (CK) 511
Derechos Sociales (PE) 511
Dermatology Update (US ISSN 0163-1691) 611
Desarrollo (MX ISSN 0011-9199) 813
Desarrollo Industrial y Mercantil en la Provincia de Zaragoza *see* Provincia de Zaragoza. Informe Economico 180
Description and Analysis of Contemporary Standard Russian (NE ISSN 0070-3826) 543
Descriptions of Plant Viruses (UK ISSN 0305-2680) 34
Descriptive Report of Program Activities for Vocational Education *see* Montana. Department of Public Instruction. Descriptive Report of Program Activities for Vocational Education 911
Desenvolvimento Brasileiro *see* Brazil Development Series 221
Deseret News Church Almanac (US ISSN 0093-786X) 776
Desert Bighorn Council. Transactions (US ISSN 0418-7598) 276
Desert First Works (US) 579
Desert Locust Control Organization for Eastern Africa. Annual Report (ET ISSN 0418-761X) 34
Desert Research Institute Publications in the Social Sciences (US ISSN 0077-7951) 49
Desert Speaks (US) 907
Desert Tortoise Council. Proceedings of Symposium (US ISSN 0191-3875) 102, 288
Design and Industries Association. Year Book and Membership List *see* D I A Yearbook - Design Action 385
Design Automation Conference.(Proceedings) (US) 271
Design Automation Workshop. Proceedings *see* Design Automation Conference.(Proceedings) 271
Design Directory (US ISSN 0195-4326) 236, 502
Design Firms *see* E N R Directory of Design Firms 366
Design from Denmark *see* Design from Scandinavia 503
Design from Scandinavia (DK ISSN 0011-9369) 502, 503, 855
Design in Greece/Themata Chorou & Technon (GR ISSN 0074-1191) 69, 74
Design News. Fastening (US ISSN 0190-2296) 366
Design News. Fluid Power (US ISSN 0164-2871) 850
Design News. Materials (US ISSN 0164-2839) 850
Design News Annual. Fastening Edition *see* Design News. Fastening 366
Design News Annual. Fluid Power Edition *see* Design News. Fluid Power 850
Design News Annual. Materials Edition *see* Design News. Materials 850
Design News Electrical/Electronic Reference Edition (US) 583
Design News Fastening Reference Edition (US) 583
Design News Fluid Power Reference Edition (US) 583
Design News Materials Reference Edition (US) 583
Design News Power Transmission Reference Edition (US) 583
Design Research Interactions (US) 69, 484
Designed in Finland (FI ISSN 0418-7717) 502
Designer (CN) 502
Designers in Britain (UK ISSN 0084-974X) 74
Designers West Resource Directory (US ISSN 0420-011X) 502
Desitter Regional Geology Series (US) 293
Deskbook of Kentucky Economic Statistics *see* Kentucky Deskbook of Economic Statistics 159
Desperado (US) 563
Dessinateurs, Peintres et Sculpteurs de Belgique *see* Jaarboek der Schone Kunsten 75
Destabanda (UY) 556
Destaques (BL) 643
Detroit Dental Spectrum *see* Detroit Mirror and Explorer 609
Detroit Mirror and Explorer (US) 609
Detroit Monographs in Musicology (US) 658
Detroit Studies in Music Bibliography (US ISSN 0070-3885) 665
Deutsch-Auslaendische Beziehungen. Schriftenreihe (GW ISSN 0080-7125) 720
Deutsch-Slawische Forschungen zur Namenkunde und Siedlungsgeschichte (GE ISSN 0070-3893) 452, 543
Deutsche Akademie fuer Sprache und Dichtung. Jahrbuch (GW ISSN 0070-3923) 543
Deutsche Akademie fuer Sprache und Dichtung. Schriftenreihe (GW ISSN) 563
Deutsche Annalen (GW) 452
Deutsche Bibliographie. Fuenfjahres-Verzeichnis (GW ISSN 0070-3885) 760
Deutsche Bibliographie. Verzeichnis Amtlicher Druckschriften (GW) 748
Deutsche Bibliographie. Zeitschriften-Verzeichnis (GW) 506
Deutsche Buecherei. Jahrbuch (GE ISSN 0459-004X) 758
Deutsche Bundesbahn Report *see* D B Report 873
Deutsche Bundesbank. Geschaeftsbericht (GW ISSN 0070-394X) 172
Das Deutsche Firmen-Alphabet (GW ISSN 0418-8381) 236
Deutsche Forschungs- und Versuchsanstalt fuer Luft- und Raumfahrt e.V. Forschungsberichte und D F V L R-Mitteilungen *see* D F V L R-Forschungsberichte und D F V L R-Mitteilungen 7
Deutsche Forschungs- und Versuchsanstalt fuer Luft- und Raumfahrt e.V. Jahresbericht *see* D F V L R Jahresbericht 7
Deutsche Forschungsgemeinschaft. Denkschriften zur Lage der Deutschen Wissenschaft (GW ISSN 0070-3974) 781
Deutsche Forschungsgemeinschaft. Forschungsberichte (GW ISSN 0070-3982) 781
Deutsche Forschungsgemeinschaft. Kommissionen. Mitteilungen (GW ISSN 0070-3990) 782
Deutsche Forschungsgemeinschaft. Mexiko-Projekt (GW ISSN 0418-842X) 782
Deutsche Genossenschaftsbank. Annual Report *see* Deutsche Genossenschaftsbank. Bericht 172
Deutsche Genossenschaftsbank. Bericht (GW) 172
Deutsche Geodaetische Kommission. Veroeffentlichungen: Reihe A. Theoretische Geodaesie (GW ISSN 0065-5309) 421
Deutsche Geodaetische Kommission. Veroeffentlichungen: Reihe B. Angewandte Geodaesie (GW ISSN 0065-5317) 421
Deutsche Geodaetische Kommission. Veroeffentlichungen: Reihe C. Dissertationen (GW ISSN 0065-5325) 421
Deutsche Geodaetische Kommission. Veroeffentlichungen: Reihe D. Tafelwerke (GW ISSN 0065-5333) 421
Deutsche Geodaetische Kommission. Veroeffentlichungen: Reihe E. Geschichte und Entwicklung der Geodaesie (GW ISSN 0065-5341) 421
Deutsche Geographische Blaetter (GW) 421
Deutsche Geschichte. Jahresberichte (GE ISSN 0075-286X) 452
Deutsche Gesellschaft fuer Amerikastudien. Mitteilungsblatt (GW) 468
Deutsche Gesellschaft fuer Chronometrie. Jahrbuch (GW ISSN 0070-4040) 503
Deutsche Gesellschaft fuer Dokumentation e.V. Schriftenreihe *see* D G D Schriftenreihe 528
Deutsche Gesellschaft fuer Hygiene und Mikrobiologie. Berichte ueber Tagungen (GW ISSN 0084-9758) 908
Deutsche Gesellschaft fuer Innere Medizin. Verhandlungen (US) 594
Deutsche Gesellschaft fuer Kreislaufforschung. Verhandlungen (GW ISSN 0070-4075) 607
Deutsche Gesellschaft fuer Luft und Raumfahrt e.V. Jahrbuecher *see* D. G. L. R. Jahrbuecher 8
Deutsche Gesellschaft fuer Musik des Orients. Mitteilungen (GW ISSN 0417-2051) 658
Deutsche Gesellschaft fuer Ostasienkunde. Koordinierungsstelle fuer Gegenwartsbezogene Ost- und Suedostasienforschung. Mitteilungen (GW) 669
Deutsche Gesellschaft fuer Ostasienkunde. Koordinierungsstelle fuer Gegenwartsbezogene Ostasienforschung Mitteilungen *see* Deutsche Gesellschaft fuer Ostasienkunde fuer Gegenwartsbezogene Ost- und Suedostasienforschung. Mitteilungen 669
Deutsche Gesellschaft fuer Pathologie. Verhandlungen (GW ISSN 0070-4113) 102, 594
Deutsche Gesellschaft fuer Rheumatologie. Verhandlungen. (GW ISSN 0070-4121) 623
Deutsche Gesellschaft fuer Urologie. Verhandlungsbericht (US ISSN 0070-413X) 625
Deutsche Gesellschaft fuer Volkskunde. D G V Informationen (GW) 401
Deutsche Handelsakten des Mittelalters und der Neuzeit (GW ISSN 0170-3080) 452
Die Deutsche Handelsflotte (GW ISSN 0070-4148) 878
Deutsche Hydrographische Zeitschrift. Ergaenzungsheft. Reihe A (GW ISSN 0070-4164) 309
Deutsche Hydrographische Zeitschrift. Ergaenzungsheft. Reihe B (GW ISSN 0070-4172) 309
Deutsche Keramische Gesellschaft. Fachausschussberichte (GW ISSN 0070-4199) 244
Deutsche Kraftfahrtforschung und Strassenverkehrstechnik (GW ISSN 0070-4210) 862
Deutsche Krankenhausgesellschaft. Jahresbericht (GW) 480
Die Deutsche Lebensversicherung (GW ISSN 0070-4237) 498
Deutsche Messen und Ausstellungen - Ein Zahlenspiegel (GW ISSN 0084-9766) 217
Deutsche Morgenlaendische Gesellschaft. Zeitschrift. Supplementa (GW ISSN 0341-0803) 669
Deutsche Ophthalmologische Gesellschaft. Zusammenkunft. Bericht (US ISSN 0070-427X) 615
Deutsche Rheologische Gesellschaft. Berichte *see* Dokumentation Rheologie 700
Deutsche Schiller-Gesellschaft. Jahrbuch (GW ISSN 0070-4318) 563
Deutsche Shakespeare-Gesellschaft West. Jahrbuch (GW ISSN 0070-4326) 563
Deutsche Sprache in Europa und Uebersee (GW ISSN 0170-3153) 543
Deutsche Studien (GW ISSN 0418-9140) 563
Deutsche Texte des Mittelalters (GE ISSN 0070-4334) 563
Deutsche UNESCO-Kommission. Seminarbericht (GW) 490
Deutsche Verkehrswissenschaftliche Gesellschaft. Schriftenreihe. Reihe A. Dokumentation (GW) 862
Deutsche Zoologische Gesellschaft. Verhandlungen (GW ISSN 0070-4342) 128
Deutscher Arbeitsamtskalender (GW ISSN 0415-6552) 207
Deutscher Arbeitskreis Wasser. Schriftenreihe *see* Dokumentationszentrale Wasser Schriftenreihe 896
Deutscher Camping-Club e.V. Camping Fuehrer Europa *see* D C C-Camping Fuehrer Europa 884
Deutscher Camping Club e.V. Caravan Modellfuehrer *see* D C C-Caravan Modellfuehrer 870
Deutscher Camping Club e.V. Caravanfuehrer *see* D C C-Caravanfuehrer 884
Deutscher Camping Club e.V. Touristik Service *see* D C C-Touristik Service 884
Deutscher Fachhochschulfuehrer (GW) 329
Deutscher Fischerei-Almanach *see* Deutscher Kuesten-Almanach 878
Deutscher Forstverein. Jahresbericht (GW) 408
Deutscher Gartenbau (GW ISSN 0341-2091) 415
Deutscher Glaserkalender (GW) 244
Deutscher Hochschulfuehrer (GW) 331
Deutscher Hugenotten-Verein E.V. Geschichtsblaetter (GW ISSN 0344-2934) 452, 771
Deutscher Justiz-Kalender (GW) 511
Deutscher Kuesten-Almanach (GW ISSN 0070-4377) 878
Deutscher Schiffbau (GW) 878
Deutscher Sozialversicherungs-Kalender (GW ISSN 0417-3228) 498
Deutscher Turner-Bund. Jahrbuch der Turnkunst (GW ISSN 0075-2401) 819
Deutscher Werbekalender (GW) 5
Deutscher Wetterdienst. Berichte (GW ISSN 0072-4130) 632
Deutscher Wetterdienst. Bibliographien (GW ISSN 0072-4149) 90, 636
Deutscher Wetterdienst. Seewetteramt. Einzelveroeffentlichungen (GW ISSN 0072-1603) 632
Deutscher Zahnaerztekalender (GW) 609
Deutsches Beamten-Jahrbuch; Bundesausgabe (GW ISSN 0070-4423) 741
Deutsches Buecherverzeichnis (GE ISSN 0323-374X) 528, 758
Deutsches Buehnen-Jahrbuch (GW ISSN 0070-4431) 858
Deutsches Bundes-Adressbuch der Firmen aus Industrie, Handel und Verkehr *see* Deutsches Bundes-Adressbuch: Industrie, Gross- und Aussenhandel, Dienstleistungen, Organisationen 236
Deutsches Bundes-Adressbuch: Industrie, Gross- und Aussenhandel, Dienstleistungen, Organisationen (GW) 236
Deutsches Gewaesserkundliches Jahrbuch. Donaugebiet (GW ISSN 0340-5176) 307, 896
Deutsches Gewaesserkundliches Jahrbuch. Kuestengebiet der Nort- und Ostsee (GW ISSN 0340-5184) 307, 896

Deutsches Gewaesserkundliches Jahrbuch. Rheingebiet: Abschnitt Main (GW) 307, 896
Deutsches Hydrographisches Institut. Jahresbericht (GW ISSN 0070-4458) 309
Deutsches Industrieinstitut. Berichte zu Gewerkschaftsfragen see Institut der Deutschen Wirtschaft. Gewerkschaftsreport 506
Deutsches Institut fuer Normung e.V. DIN-Taschenbuecher see DIN-Taschenbuecher 637
Deutsches Institut fuer Puppenspiel. Forschung und Lehre (GW ISSN 0070-4490) 858
Deutsches Jahrbuch der Musikwissenschaft see Jahrbuch Peters 660
Deutsches Krebsforschungszentrum. Veroeffentlichungen (GW ISSN 0070-4229) 605
Deutsches Mittelalter, Kritische Studientexte der Monumenta Germaniae Historica (GW ISSN 0340-8396) 452
Deutsches Soldatenjahrbuch (GW ISSN 0417-3635) 638
Deutsches Wollforschungsinstitut. Vortraege (GW) 855
Deutschkanadisches Jahrbuch see German-Canadian Yearbook 392
Deutschkurse/German Language Courses (AU ISSN 0012-1398) 348
Deutschland Liefert see B D I
Deutschland Liefert 193
Deutschlandfunk. Jahrbuch (GW ISSN 0084-9790) 267
Deutschsprachige Zeitschriften Deutschland - Oesterreich - Schweiz (GW ISSN 0419-005X) 90
Developing Nations Monograph Series One (US) 797
Developing Railways (UK ISSN 0309-1465) 873
Development (MY) 90, 797
Development Academy of the Philippines. Annual Report (PH) 222
Development in Mammals (NE) 128
Development Journal (CN ISSN 0315-9248) 335, 344
Development of Education in Pakistan (PK ISSN 0080-1321) 316
Development of Education in the Netherlands see Ontwikkeling van het Onderwijs in Nederland 321
Development of Western Samoa see Western Samoa. Department of Economic Development. Development of Western Samoa 226
Developmental and Cell Biology Series (UK) 102
Developments in Agricultural and Managed Forest Ecology (NE) 14, 408
Developments in Atmospheric Science (NE) 632
Developments in Biochemistry (NE) 111
Developments in Bioenergetics and Biomembranes (NE) 102
Developments in Biological Standardization (SZ ISSN 0301-5149) 603
Developments in Cell Biology (NE) 102
Developments in Economic Geology (NE) 293
Developments in Endocrinology (NE) 611
Developments in Food Science (NE) 252
Developments in Geochemistry (NE) 293
Developments in Geomathematics (NE) 304, 585
Developments in Geotechnical Engineering (NE) 375
Developments in Geotectonics (NE ISSN 0419-0254) 293
Developments in Human Services Series(US ISSN 0092-5470) 805, 813
Developments in Immunology (NE) 102

Developments in Industrial Microbiology (US ISSN 0070-4563) 123
Developments in Landscape Management and Urban Planning (NE) 484
Developments in Neuroscience (NE) 619
Developments in Ophthalmology (SZ ISSN 0250-3751) 615
Developments in Palaeontology and Stratigraphy (NE) 673
Developments in Petroleum Science (NE) 679
Developments in Petrology (NE) 293
Developments in Precambrian Geology (NE) 293
Developments in Sedimentology (NE ISSN 0070-4571) 293
Developments in Soil Science (NE) 34
Developments in Solar System and Space Science (NE) 8, 82
Developments in Solid Earth Geophysics (NE ISSN 0070-458X) 304
Developments in Statistics (US ISSN 0163-3384) 838
Developments in Toxicology and Environmental Science (NE) 102
Developments in Transport Studies (NE) 862
Developments in Water Science (NE) 307
Developpement Social see Social Development 800
Devenir. Cuadernos del Seminario de Historia (MX) 468
Devindex (CN) 2, 155
Devindex Canada see Devindex 155
Devon and Cornwall Holidays in the Sun see Holidays in the Sun, Devon, Cornwall, Somerset and Dorset 886
Devon Archaeological Society. Proceedings (UK ISSN 0305-5795) 60
Devon Country Chronicle (US) 563
Dewey Decimal Classification Additions, Notes and Decisions (US ISSN 0083-1573) 529
Dhaka Bisvabidyalaya Patrika (BG) 418
Dhaniram Bhalla Granthamala (II) 443, 669
Diabetes-Related Literature Index by Authors and Key Words in the Title (US ISSN 0070-4652) 2, 602
Diagnosticos APEC (BL) 184
Diagnostische Informationen fuer die aerztliche Praxis see D T. I 594
Diagnostische und Therapeutische Informationen see D T. I 594
Dial Industry see Telekompass 242
Dialectes de Wallonie (BE) 543
Dialectic (AT ISSN 0084-9804) 688
Dialettica (IT) 688
Dialog der Gesellschaft (GW ISSN 0419-0637) 5
Dialogue (SA) 563
Dialogues d'Histoire Ancienne (FR) 431
Diamond, Stock Investment Edition/Daiyamondo Kabushiki-Toshi-Ban (JA) 203
Diamond's Japan Business Directory (JA) 236
Dianoia (MX ISSN 0419-0890) 688
Diario de Centro Americo (GT) 741
Diario de Congresos Medicos (SP ISSN 0210-5578) 594, 626
Diatomeenschalen im Elektronenmikroskopschen Bild (GW ISSN 0070-4687) 124
Dibrugarh University. Centre for Sociological Study of the Frontier Region. North Eastern Research Bulletin (II) 813
Dic-Agri see Dictionnaire-Annuaire de l'Agriculture 14
Diccionario de Especialidades Farmaceuticas (MX) 684
Diccionario de la Produccion y de la Industria (UY) 236
Dichter und Zeichner (GW ISSN 0070-4695) 74, 579
Dicionario de Especialidades Farmaceuticas (BL) 684
Dickson Mounds Museum Anthropological Studies (US ISSN 0095-2907) 908

Dictionaries, Encyclopedias, and Other Word-Related Books (US) 555
Dictionary, Encyclopedia & Handbook Review (US ISSN 0270-3750) 543
Dictionary of Canadian Biography (CN ISSN 0070-4717) 97
Dictionary of Contemporary Quotations(US ISSN 0360-215X) 543, 563
Dictionary of International Biography (UK ISSN 0419-1137) 97
Dictionary of Latin American and Caribbean Biography (UK ISSN 0070-4733) 97
Dictionary of Scandinavian Biography (UK) 97
Dictionary of Social Services (UK) 805
Dictionnaire-Annuaire de l'Agriculture (FR) 14
Dictionnaire de Specialites Pharmaceutiques see Dictionnaire Vidal 684
Dictionnaire des Communes (Lavauzelle et Cie) (FR) 360, 741
Dictionnaire des Communes (Michelin) (FR) 884
Dictionnaire des Parfums de France et des Lignes pour Hommes (FR ISSN 0070-475X) 85
Dictionnaire des Produits de Beaute et de Cosmetologie see Dictionnaire des Produits de Soins de Beaute 85
Dictionnaire des Produits de Soins de Beaute (FR) 85
Dictionnaire des Valeurs des Meubles et Objets d'Art (FR ISSN 0070-4776) 74
Dictionnaire Vidal (FR ISSN 0419-1153) 684
Dictionnaires du Savoir Moderne (FR ISSN 0073-4640) 360
Didactica Classica Gandensia (BE ISSN 0070-4792) 259
Diderot Studies (SZ ISSN 0070-4806) 688
Diebeners Goldschmiede- und Uhrmacher-Jahrbuch (GW ISSN 0070-4814) 503
Dielectric and Related Molecular Processes (UK ISSN 0305-974X) 254
Dielheimer Blaetter zum Alten Testament (GW) 764
Diesel and Gas Turbine World Wide Catalog (US ISSN 0070-4822) 382
Diesel Electric Locomotive Examination Book see Diesel Locomotive Question & Answer Manual 873
Diesel Locomotive Question & Answer Manual (US ISSN 0070-4830) 873
Diet & Exercise (US) 694
A Different Drummer (US ISSN 0162-8739) 579
Diffusion and Defect Monograph Series(SZ) 627, 696
Diffusion Monograph Series see Diffusion and Defect Monograph Series 627
Digest of Commercial Laws of the World (US ISSN 0419-1285) 194, 511
Digest of Health Statistics for England and Wales see Health and Personal Social Services Statistics 752
Digest of Legal Activities of International Organizations and Other Institutions (IT ISSN 0070-4857) 511
Digest of Literature on Dielectrics (US ISSN 0070-4865) 2, 360
Digest of Motor Laws see American Automobile Association. Digest of Motor Laws 869
Digest of Scottish Statistics see Scottish Abstract of Statistics 845
Digest of Technical Papers see S I D International Symposium. Digest of Technical Papers 370
Digest of the Decisions of the International Court (NE) 523
Digest of the United States Practice in International Law (US ISSN 0095-3369) 523
Digest of United Kingdom Energy Statistics (UK ISSN 0307-0603) 362
Digest of World Events (PK ISSN 0070-4873) 431, 720

Digester see Illinois. Environmental Protection Agency. Operator Certification Section. Digester 386
Dime Bag: Fiction Issue (CN ISSN 0702-8520) 563
Dimension: Languages (US ISSN 0070-4881) 348, 543
Dimensions (US) 281
Dimensions of Nations (US) 720
Dimensions of Philippine Exports (PH) 194
DIN-Taschenbuecher (Deutsches Institut fuer Normung e.V.) (GW ISSN 0070-4261) 637
Dinamika Izluchayuschego Gaza (UR) 679
Dine Israel (IS ISSN 0070-4903) 511
Diotima (GR) 688
Dipavali (II) 579
Diplomaciai Iratok Magyarorszag Kulpolitikajahoz (HU ISSN 0070-492X) 452, 720
Diplomatarium Danicum (DK ISSN 0070-4938) 452
Diplomatic Corps and Consular and Other Representatives in Canada. Corps Diplomatique et Representants Consulaires et Autres au Canada (CN ISSN 0486-4514) 720
Diplomatic Corps of Belgrade (YU ISSN 0070-4946) 721
Diplomatic List and List of Representatives of United Nations and Its Specialized Agencies and Other Missions (NP) 721
Al-Dirasat al-Islamiyah (PK ISSN 0002-399X) 769
Direccion de Empresas y Organizaciones (SP) 214
Direct Levies on Gaming in Nevada (US ISSN 0093-8823) 228
Direct Mail-Marketing Association Depth see D M M A in Depth 217
Direct Selling (US ISSN 0070-4970) 217
Directie Kinderbescherming (NE) 256
Direction (Regina) (CN ISSN 0706-7860) 805
Directions (US ISSN 0012-3234) 421
Directorio Agropecuario de Colombia (CK) 14
Directorio Colombiano de Unidades de Informacion (CK) 529
Directorio da E M B R A P A see Guia da E M B R A P A e de Instituicoes Brasileiras de Pesquisa Agropecuaria 15
Directorio de Instituciones Financieras (CK) 172
Directorio de la Industria y Comercio de Centroamerica y Panama (CR) 236
Directorio de Servicios para Familias Migrantes see Directory of Services for Migrant Families 805
Directorio Industrial Azucarero (VE) 34
Directorio Industrial, Centroamerica-Panama (GT) 236
Directorio Nacional de Entidades Cooperativos (CK) 180
Directorio Nacional de Instituciones Privadas Filantropicas y de Desarrollo Social (CK) 805
Directorio Nacional de Profesionales (CK) 667
Directors Encyclopedia of Newspapers (US ISSN 0270-7543) 414
Directors Guild of America. Directory of Members (US ISSN 0419-2052) 214
Directory. Diocesan Agencies of Catholic Charities. United States, Puerto Rico and Canada (US ISSN 0091-1003) 805
Directory: a Guide to Colleges, Vocational-Technical and Diploma Schools of Nursing (US) 331
Directory - American Bell Association see American Bell Association. Directory 656
Directory - American Nuclear Society see Directory: Who's Who in Nuclear Energy 702
Directory and Handbook - Baptist Missionary Association of America see Baptist Missionary Association of America. Directory and Handbook 771

Directory and Statistics of Oregon Libraries (US ISSN 0162-0290) 529
Directory and Who's Who in Liberia (LB) 236
Directory: Community Development Education and Training Programs Throughout the World (US ISSN 0362-4366) 484
Directory, Federal, State and Local Government Consumer Offices see U. S. Office of Consumer Affairs. Directory: Federal, State, and Local Government Consumer Offices 280
Directory for a New World (US) 721
Directory for Exceptional Children (US ISSN 0070-5012) 345, 735
Directory for the Eastern Association of Student Financial Aid Administrators see Eastern Association of Student Financial Aid Administrators. Directory 344
Directory for the Nonwoven Fabrics and Disposable Soft Goods Industries see International Directory of the Nonwoven Fabrics Industry 856
Directory - International Mimes & Pantomimists see I M P Directory 910
Directory Iron and Steel Plants (US ISSN 0070-5039) 627
Directory - Juvenile and Adult Correctional Departments, Institutions, Agencies, and Paroling Authorities of the United States and Canada (US ISSN 0362-9287) 281
Directory Listing Curriculums Offered in the Community Colleges of Pennsylvania (US ISSN 0092-8526) 331
Directory: North Dakota City Officials (US ISSN 0090-1989) 749
Directory of A S U Latin Americanists (Arizona State University) (US ISSN 0091-3235) 468
Directory of Accredited Camps for Boys and Girls see Parents' Guide to Accredited Camps. Midwest Edition 830
Directory of Accredited Home Study Schools (US) 331
Directory of Accredited Institutions (US) 143, 331
Directory of Accredited Private Home Study Schools see Directory of Accredited Home Study Schools 331
Directory of Administrative and Supervisory Personnel of California Public Schools see California Public School Directory 330
Directory of Administrative Officials in Public Education - Canada see C E A Handbook 315
Directory of Aerospace Education (US) 8, 331
Directory of African and Afro-American Studies in the United States (US ISSN 0147-9466) 391
Directory of African Studies in the United States see Directory of African and Afro-American Studies in the United States 391
Directory of Agricultural Co-Operatives in the United Kingdom (UK ISSN 0307-689X) 27
Directory of Alcohol and Drug Treatment Sources in Ontario (CN ISSN 0228-863X) 287
Directory of American Business in Argentina see American Business in Argentina 234
Directory of American College Theatre (US ISSN 0070-5063) 858
Directory of American Fiction Writers see Directory of American Poets and Fiction Writers 579
Directory of American Firms Operating in Foreign Countries (US ISSN 0070-5071) 194, 236
Directory of American Horticulture (US ISSN 0417-5522) 415
Directory of American Jewish Institutions see Who's Who in American Jewry 98
Directory of American Medical Education see A A M C Directory of American Medical Education 333
Directory of American Philosophers (US ISSN 0070-508X) 688

Directory of American Poets see Directory of American Poets and Fiction Writers 579
Directory of American Poets and Fiction Writers (US) 579
Directory of American Savings and Loan Associations (US ISSN 0070-5098) 172
Directory of American Scholars (US ISSN 0070-5101) 97
Directory of Approved Counseling Agencies see Directory of Counseling Services 316
Directory of Architects, Engineers and Land Surveyors (Juneau) see Alaska. State Board of Registration for Architects, Engineers and Land Surveyors. Directory of Architects, Engineers and Land Surveyors 68
Directory of Asian Book Trade see Asian Book Trade Directory 757
Directory of Asian Forest Products see White Paper on Japan's Forest Industries 413
Directory of Associations in Canada (CN ISSN 0316-0734) 360
Directory of Australian Associations (AT ISSN 0110-666X) 2, 90
Directory of Automated Criminal Justice Information Systems (US) 271, 281
Directory of Bankers Schools (US ISSN 0084-9855) 172, 331
Directory of Blood Establishments Registered Under Section 510 of the Food, Drug, and Cosmetic Act (US ISSN 0163-6065) 607
Directory of Bond Agents see Standard and Poor's Directory of Bond Agents 204
Directory of British Associations (UK ISSN 0070-5152) 360
Directory of British Brass Bands (UK) 658
Directory of British Publishers and Their Terms (UK) 758
Directory of Brush and Allied Trades (UK ISSN 0070-5179) 503
Directory of Business Schools see Directory of Accredited Institutions 143
Directory of Buying Offices and Accounts (US ISSN 0070-5195) 261
Directory of California Justice Agencies Serving Juveniles and Adults (US ISSN 0361-7327) 281
Directory of California Services for Juvenile and Adult Offenders see Directory of California Justice Agencies Serving Juveniles and Adults 281
Directory of Canadian Chartered Accountants (CN ISSN 0527-9275) 167
Directory of Canadian Community Funds and Councils see United Way of Canada. Directory of Members 809
Directory of Canadian Map Collections(CN ISSN 0070-5217) 421, 529
Directory of Canadian Orchestras and Youth Orchestras/Annuaire des Orchestres et Orchestres des Jeunes Canadiens (CN ISSN 0705-6249) 659
Directory of Canadian Plays and Playwrights (CN ISSN 0707-5456) 90, 578, 860
Directory of Canadian Trust Companies(CN ISSN 0070-5225) 172
Directory of Canadian Universities/ Repertoire des Universites Canadiennes (CN ISSN 0706-2338) 335
Directory of Canadian Universities and Colleges see Directory of Canadian Universities 335
Directory of Canadian Welfare Services/Repertoire des Services Sociaux Canadiens (CN ISSN 0084-9871) 805
Directory of Candy Brokers see Candy Buyers Directory 407
Directory of Cardamom Planters (II) 34, 236

Directory of Career Planning and Placement Offices (US) 667
Directory of Catholic Schools and Colleges (UK ISSN 0070-5233) 331
Directory of Central Atlantic States Manufacturers. Maryland, Delaware, Virginia, West Virginia, North Carolina, South Carolina (US ISSN 0070-5241) 236
Directory of Chemical Engineering Research in Canadian Universities (CN ISSN 0070-525X) 372
Directory of Chemical Producers-U.S.A.(US ISSN 0012-3277) 246
Directory of Chemical Producers-Western Europe (US) 246
Directory of Chinese American Librarians (US) 529
Directory of Church of England Moral and Social Welfare Work see Directory of Church of England Social Services 805
Directory of Church of England Social Services (UK ISSN 0070-5268) 805
Directory of College and University Libraries in New York State (US ISSN 0070-5276) 529
Directory of College Placement Offices see Directory of Career Planning and Placement Offices 667
Directory of College Recruiting Personnel (US ISSN 0272-2135) 667
Directory of College Stores (US ISSN 0084-988X) 335
Directory of Colorado Libraries (US ISSN 0094-8403) 529
Directory of Colorado Manufacturers (US ISSN 0084-9898) 236
Directory of Communication Organizations see Communication Directory 264
Directory of Communicators in Agriculture (US ISSN 0419-2400) 14
Directory of Community-Based Mental Retardation Services see Nebraska. Office of Mental Retardation. Directory of Community-Based Mental Retardation Services 346
Directory of Community Services for Drug Abuse in California (US) 287
Directory of Community Services in Maryland (US ISSN 0070-5306) 805
Directory of Community Services of Greater Montreal (CN ISSN 0319-258X) 805
Directory of Companies and Their Subsidiaries in the Wine, Spirit and Brewing Trades see Off Licence News Directory 86
Directory of Companies Filing Annual Reports with the Securities and Exchange Commission Under the Securities Exchange Act of 1934 see Directory of Companies Required to File Annual Reports with the Securities and Exchange Commission Under the Securities Exchange Act of 1934 n 203
Directory of Companies Required to File Annual Reports with the Securities and Exchange Commission Under the Securities Exchange Act of 1934 (US ISSN 0149-6581) 203
Directory of Company Secretaries (II ISSN 0070-5322) 214
Directory of Computerized Information in Science and Technology (US ISSN 0070-5330) 782, 850
Directory of Conservative and Libertarian Serials, Publishers, and Freelance Markets (US ISSN 0149-7847) 90, 717, 760
Directory of Consumer Protection and Environmental Agencies see Consumer Protection Directory 279
Directory of Consumer Protection and Environmental Agencies see Environmental Protection Directory 385
Directory of Continuing Education Opportunities in New York City (US ISSN 0094-095X) 329
Directory of Convenience Store Companies (US) 404
Directory of Conventions (US ISSN 0417-5751) 626

Directory of Cooperative Education (US ISSN 0070-5357) 316
Directory of Cooperative Education Activities in Florida (US) 335
Directory of Corporate Affiliations (US ISSN 0070-5365) 5
Directory of Correctional Services in Canada /Repertoire des Services de Correction du Canada see Justice-Directory of Services 806
Directory of Counseling Services (US ISSN 0094-7512) 316, 335
Directory of Courses. Tourism-Hospitality-Recreation (CN ISSN 0705-8160) 335, 667
Directory of Crematoria in the British Isles & Overseas Cremation Societies see Cremation Society Handbook and Directory of Crematoria 414
Directory of Cultural Relations Services and the Index of Cultural Agreements see Unesco Handbook of International Exchanges 343
Directory of Current Research in Israel: Physical and Life Sciences see Current Research and Development Projects in Israel: Natural Sciences and Technology 781
Directory of Dealers in Secondhand and Antiquarian Books in the British Isles (UK ISSN 0070-5411) 758
Directory of Defense Electronic Products and Services: United States Suppliers (US) 353
Directory of Delaware Schools (US ISSN 0362-5710) 335
Directory of Demographic Research Centers see Annuaire des Centres de Recherche Demographique 725
Directory of Dental Educators (US ISSN 0090-0141) 335, 609
Directory of Dental Educators in the United States and Canada see Directory of Dental Educators 609
Directory of Department Stores (US) 236
Directory of Departments and Programs of Religious Studies in North America (CN) 765
Directory of Directories (US) 539
Directory of Directors (II ISSN 0070-542X) 97, 214
Directory of Directors (UK ISSN 0070-5438) 214
Directory of Drug Store Chains (US) 236
Directory of East Asian Collections in North American Libraries (US ISSN 0148-0065) 443, 529
Directory of Economic Research Centres in India (II) 143
Directory of Education Associations (US ISSN 0160-0508) 316
Directory of Education Studies in Canada/Annuaire d'Etudes en Education au Canada (CN ISSN 0070-5454) 316
Directory of Educational Consultants (US) 316
Directory of Educational Facilities for the Learning Disabled (US ISSN 0093-7703) 331, 345
Directory of Educational Institutions in New Mexico (US ISSN 0084-991X) 316
Directory of Educational Opportunities in Georgia see Directory: a Guide to Colleges, Vocational-Technical and Diploma Schools of Nursing 331
Directory of Electric Light and Power Companies (US ISSN 0092-4970) 236, 353, 679
Directory of Electronic Representatives (US) 353
Directory of Electronics & Instrumentation (NZ) 353
Directory of Employers Offering Employment to New University Graduates see Employers of New University Graduates: Directory 667
Directory of Engineering Capacity (UK) 236
Directory of Engineering College Research and Graduate Study see Engineering College Research and Graduate Study 367
Directory of Engineering Societies and Related Organizations (US ISSN 0070-5470) 366

Directory of Engineers *see* Institution of Engineers of Ireland. Register of Chartered Engineers and Members *368*
Directory of Environmental Education Facilities. *see* Directory of Nature Centers and Related Environmental Education Facilities *276*
Directory of Ethnic Publishers and Resource Organizations (US) *90, 394*
Directory of European Associations. Part 1: National Industrial Trade & Professional Associations (UK ISSN 0070-5500) *236*
Directory of European Associations. Part 2: National Learned, Scientific & Technical Societies (UK ISSN 0309-5339) *782*
Directory of Executive Recruiters (US ISSN 0090-6484) *214*
Directory of Exhibit Opportunities *see* Association of American Publishers. Exhibits Directory *757*
Directory of Export Buyers in the U.K. (UK ISSN 0142-4769) *194, 236*
Directory of Exporters (CE) *179*
Directory of Exporters and Manufacturers (PK) *194*
Directory of Facilities for the Learning Disabled *see* Directory of Educational Facilities for the Learning Disabled *345*
Directory of Farmer Cooperatives (US) *14*
Directory of Farmers' Organizations and Marketing Boards in Canada (CN ISSN 0070-5527) *28*
Directory of Federally Supported Research in Universities/Repertoire de la Recherche dans les Universites Subventionnee Par le Gouvernement Federal (CN ISSN 0316-0297) *782*
Directory of Fee-Based Information Services (US ISSN 0147-1678) *529*
Directory of Financial Directories (UI) *172*
Directory of Fire Research (US) *394*
Directory of Fire Research in the United States *see* Directory of Fire Research *394*
Directory of Foreign Firms Operating in the United States (US ISSN 0070-5543) *236*
Directory of Franchising Organizations (US ISSN 0070-556X) *217*
Directory of Fulbright Alumni (II ISSN 0084-9936) *335*
Directory of Further Education (UK) *336*
Directory of Gas Utilities *see* Canadian Gas Utilities Directory *362*
Directory of Gas Utility Companies (US) *236, 679*
Directory of Genealogical Societies in the USA & Canada (US) *417*
Directory of General Merchandise, Mail Order Firms and Family Centers (US) *236*
Directory of Geophysical and Oil Companies Who Use Geophysical Service (US ISSN 0417-5905) *236, 679*
Directory of Geoscience Libraries, U.S. and Canada (US) *288, 529*
Directory of Governmental Air Pollution Agencies (US) *385*
Directory of Governments in Metropolitan Toronto (CN ISSN 0084-9944) *90*
Directory of Graduate Programs in the Speech Communication Arts and Sciences (US ISSN 0070-5616) *316*
Directory of Grant-Making Trusts (UK ISSN 0070-5624) *805*
Directory of Grants, Awards, and Loans; B H M Support *see* B H M Support *334*
Directory of Health Sciences Libraries (US) *529, 594*
Directory of Health, Welfare and Recreation Services of Greater Montreal *see* Directory of Community Services of Greater Montreal *805*
Directory of Higher Education *see* Illinois. Board of Higher Education. Directory of Higher Education *337*

Directory of Historical Societies and Agencies in the United States and Canada (US ISSN 0070-5659) *468*
Directory of Home Care Services in New York *see* Home Care Services in New York State *806*
Directory of Homosexual Organizations and Publications (US) *480*
Directory of Hong Kong Industries (HK) *236*
Directory of Hotel and Motel Systems (US) *482*
Directory of Housing Cooperatives in the United States (US) *484*
Directory of Incorporated (Registered) Companies in Nigeria (NR ISSN 0084-9952) *236*
Directory of Indian Engineering Exporters (II ISSN 0417-5964) *236, 366*
Directory of Indian Exporters (II) *195*
Directory of Indonesian Importers (US) *236*
Directory of Industrial Establishments in Punjab (PK) *236*
Directory of Information on Medical Practitioners in Malaysia (MY) *594*
Directory of Institutions of Higher Education in Missouri (US ISSN 0070-5675) *331*
Directory of Institutions of Oriental Studies in Overseas Countries (II) *669*
Directory of Institutions Offering or Planning Programs for the Training of Library Technical Assistants (US) *529*
Directory of Instruments, Electronics, Automation (UK) *271*
Directory of Insurance Companies Licensed in New York State (US ISSN 0070-5691) *498*
Directory of Inter-Corporate Ownership(US) *222*
Directory of Investor-Owned Hospitals and Hospital Management Companies (US ISSN 0095-5191) *480*
Directory of Iranian Periodicals (IR ISSN 0084-9960) *90*
Directory of Iron and Steel Works of the United States and Canada (US) *627*
Directory of Israel (IS) *236*
Directory of Israeli Merchants and Manufacturers *see* Directory of Israel *236*
Directory of Japanese Firms, Offices and Other Organizations in the United States (US) *143*
Directory of Japanese Firms, Offices and Subsidiaries in the United States *see* Directory of Japanese Firms, Offices and Other Organizations in the United States *143*
Directory of Japanese Scientific Periodicals (JA) *794*
Directory of Jewellery and Precious Metals (SA) *503*
Directory of Jewish Federations, Welfare Funds and Community Councils (US ISSN 0161-2638) *805*
Directory of Jewish Health and Welfare Agencies (US ISSN 0419-2818) *751, 805*
Directory of Key Bulgarian Government and Party Officials (BU) *710*
Directory of Korean Business *see* Chonguk Kiopche Chongnam *235*
Directory of Labor Education *see* Directory of Workers Education *316*
Directory of Labour Organizations in Canada/Repertoire des Organisations de Travailleurs au Canada (CN ISSN 0075-7578) *506*
Directory of Labour Unions in Nova Scotia *see* Labour Organizations in Nova Scotia *507*
Directory of Land Drilling and Oilwell Servicing Contractors (US) *366, 679*
Directory of Latin Americanists *see* Directory of A S U Latin Americanists *468*
Directory of Law Libraries (US) *511, 529*
Directory of Law Teachers (US ISSN 0070-573X) *511*

Directory of Law Teachers/Annuaire des Professeurs de Droit (CN ISSN 0383-8358) *511*
Directory of Libraries and Library Resources in the South Central Research Library Council Region (US) *529*
Directory of Libraries in Manitoba (CN ISSN 0317-8536) *529*
Directory of Libraries in Southeast Saskatchewan *see* Southeast Regional Library (Sask.) Library Directory *535*
Directory of Library Reprographic Services (US ISSN 0160-6077) *529, 693*
Directory of Library Resources for the Blind and Physically Handicapped *see* Library Resources for the Blind and Physically Handicapped *533*
Directory of Library Science Collections (US) *529*
Directory of Library Science Libraries *see* Directory of Library Science Collections *529*
Directory of Lifestyle Change Services (CN ISSN 0707-0047) *694*
Directory of Little Magazines, Small Presses and Underground Newspapers *see* International Directory of Little Magazines and Small Presses *760*
Directory of Louisiana Cities, Towns and Villages (US ISSN 0092-0614) *749*
Directory of Machine Tools and Related Products (US ISSN 0070-5772) *382*
Directory of Magistrates Courts *see* Shaw's Directory of Courts in England and Wales *518*
Directory of Mail Drops in the United States and Canada (US) *266*
Directory of Mailing List Houses (US ISSN 0419-2923) *5, 236*
Directory of Maine Labor Organizations (US) *506*
Directory of Maine Manufacturers *see* Maine Marketing Directory *240*
Directory of Management Consultants (US) *214*
Directory of Manufacturers-Minnesota (US) *236*
Directory of Manufacturers, State of Hawaii (US ISSN 0190-3047) *179*
Directory of Marine Scientists in the United States *309*
Directory of Maryland Exporters-Importers (US ISSN 0070-5799) *195, 236*
Directory of Massachusetts Manufacturers (US) *236*
Directory of Medical Libraries in New York State (US ISSN 0070-5810) *529*
Directory of Medical Practitioners Malaysia *see* Directory of Information on Medical Practitioners in Malaysia *594*
Directory of Medical Specialists (US ISSN 0070-5829) *97, 594*
Directory of Michigan Institutions of Higher Education (US) *336*
Directory of Michigan Manufacturers (US ISSN 0070-5845) *236*
Directory of Michigan Mineral Operators *see* Michigan Mineral Producers Annual Directory *644*
Directory of Middle East Imports (US) *195*
Directory of Minnesota's Area Mental Health, Mental Retardation, Inebriety Programs (US ISSN 0095-4888) *619*
Directory of Minnesota's Area Mental Health - Mental Retardation Programs *see* Directory of Minnesota's Area Mental Health, Mental Retardation, Inebriety Programs *619*
Directory of Missouri Libraries (US ISSN 0092-4067) *529*
Directory of Missouri's Regional Planning Commissions (US) *222*
Directory of Missouri's Regional Planning System *see* Directory of Missouri's Regional Planning Commissions *222*

DIRECTORY OF   1347

Directory of Municipal Natural Gas Systems (US) *679*
Directory of Municipal Officials of New Mexico (US ISSN 0070-5888) *741*
Directory of Music Faculties in American Colleges and Universities *see* Directory of Music Faculties in Colleges & Universities U.S. and Canada *659*
Directory of Music Faculties in Colleges & Universities U.S. and Canada (US) *316, 659*
Directory of National Organizations Concerned with Land Pollution Control (US ISSN 0084-9987) *385*
Directory of National Organizations Concerned with School Health (US) *344, 751*
Directory of Nature Centers and Related Environmental Education Facilities (US ISSN 0070-5497) *276*
Directory of New England College, University and Institute Libraries (US) *529*
Directory of New York State Public Library Systems (US ISSN 0070-5950) *529*
Directory of Nonpublic Schools and Administrators, New York State (US) *344*
Directory of North American Computer Companies *see* Worldwide Directory of Computer Companies *274*
Directory of North American Fairs and Expositions (US ISSN 0361-4255) *5*
Directory of North Carolina Municipal Officials (US) *749*
Directory of North Dakota Lawyers (US) *511*
Directory of Nursing Homes in the United States, U.S. Possessions and Canada *see* Modern Nursing Home Directory of Nursing Homes in the United States, U.S. Possessions and Canada *807*
Directory of Obsolete Securities *see* Financial Stock Guide Service. Directory of Obsolete Securities *203*
Directory of Occupational Education Programs in New York State (US ISSN 0098-096X) *331*
Directory of Oceanographers in the United States *see* Directory of Marine Scientists in the United States *309*
Directory of Official Architects and Planners *see* Directory of Official Architecture and Planning *69*
Directory of Official Architecture and Planning (UK) *69, 385*
Directory of Oil Marketing and Wholesale Distributors (US ISSN 0070-5993) *679*
Directory of Oil Well Drilling Contractors (US ISSN 0415-9764) *236, 679*
Directory of Oil Well Supply Companies (US ISSN 0415-9772) *237, 679*
Directory of Oklahoma Airports (US ISSN 0094-5390) *867*
Directory of On-Going Research in Smoking and Health (US ISSN 0070-6000) *695*
Directory of Opportunities for Graduates (UK ISSN 0070-6019) *667*
Directory of Opportunities for School Leavers *see* Careers for School Leavers *667*
Directory of Oregon Libraries *see* Directory and Statistics of Oregon Libraries *529*
Directory of Organizations and Personnel in Educational Administration *see* Directory of Organizations and Personnel in Educational Management *344*
Directory of Organizations and Personnel in Educational Management (US ISSN 0070-6035) *344*
Directory of Organizations Concerned with Scientific Research and Technical Services in Rhodesia (RH) *782*
Directory of Overseas Summer Jobs (UK ISSN 0070-6051) *667*

Directory of Pakistan Exporters *see* Directory of Exporters and Manufacturers *194*
Directory of Pakistani Scholars Abroad (PK ISSN 0070-606X) *342*
Directory of Pathology Training Programs (US ISSN 0070-6086) *102, 594*
Directory of Periodicals Publishing Articles on English and American Literature and Language (US ISSN 0070-6094) *543, 563*
Directory of Philippine Exporters and Importers (PH) *237*
Directory of Philippine Manufacturers and Producers (PH) *237*
Directory of Physics and Astronomy Faculties in North American Colleges & Universities *see* Directory of Physics & Astronomy Staff Members *336*
Directory of Physics & Astronomy Staff Members (US ISSN 0361-2228) *82, 336, 696*
Directory of Polish Officials (US ISSN 0090-9955) *97*
Directory of Post Offices *see* National Zip Code & Post Office Directory *266*
Directory of Premium and Incentive Buyers *see* Directory of Premium, Incentive and Travel Buyers *218*
Directory of Premium, Incentive and Travel Buyers (US) *218, 237*
Directory of Private Elementary Schools and High Schools in California *see* California Private School Directory *330*
Directory of Private Postsecondary Institutions in California (US) *348*
Directory of Professional Electrologists (US ISSN 0417-6383) *85*
Directory of Professional Genealogists and Related Services (US) *417*
Directory of Professional Personnel: State Higher Education Agencies and Boards (US) *336*
Directory of Professional Photography (US ISSN 0070-6140) *693*
Directory of Property Investors and Developers (AT) *203, 761*
Directory of Public Enterprises in India(II) *222*
Directory of Public Refrigerated Warehouses (US ISSN 0070-6167) *429*
Directory of Public Schools and Administrators, New York State (US) *344*
Directory of Public Schools in the U.S. (US) *331*
Directory of Public Service Internships (US) *667*
Directory of Publishing Opportunities *see* Directory of Publishing Opportunities in Journals and Periodicals *758*
Directory of Publishing Opportunities in Journals and Periodicals (US) *758*
Directory of Reference and Research Library Resources Systems in New York State (US ISSN 0070-6183) *529*
Directory of Regional Councils *see* National Association of Regional Councils. Directory *744*
Directory of Registered Dentists and Registered Dental Hygienists in Connecticut (US ISSN 0085-0004) *908*
Directory of Registered Federal and State Lobbyists *see* Directory of Registered Lobbyists and Lobbyist Legislation *710*
Directory of Registered Lobbyists and Lobbyist Legislation (US ISSN 0146-0323) *710*
Directory of Research and Special Libraries in Ghana (GH) *529*
Directory of Research Grants (US ISSN 0146-7336) *336*
Directory of Research Institutes and Industrial Laboratories in Israel (IS) *782*
Directory of Research Institutes and Industrial Research Units in Israel *see* Directory of Research Institutes and Industrial Laboratories in Israel *782*

Directory of Research Institutions in Thailand (TH) *797*
Directory of Research Reports Relating to Produce Packaging and Marketing(US ISSN 0070-6213) *404, 672*
Directory of Resources for Alcoholics *see* Coping Catalog *287*
Directory of San Francisco Attorneys (US ISSN 0092-9174) *511*
Directory of Science Resources for Maryland (US ISSN 0070-6256) *782*
Directory of Scientific and Technical Associations and Institutes in Israel *see* Directory of Scientific and Technical Associations in Israel *782*
Directory of Scientific and Technical Associations in Israel (IS ISSN 0334-2824) *782, 850*
Directory of Scientific Directories (UK ISSN 0070-6272) *782*
Directory of Scientific Periodicals of Pakistan (PK) *2, 794*
Directory of Scientific Research in Indian Universities (II) *794*
Directory of Scientific Research in Nigeria (NR ISSN 0070-6280) *782*
Directory of Scientific Research Projects in Sri Lanka(Ceylon) (CE) *782*
Directory of Secondary Schools with Occupational Curriculums, Public and Nonpublic *see* Occupational Education: Enrollments and Programs in Noncollegiate Post Secondary Schools *332*
Directory of Securities Research (US) *203*
Directory of Selected Illinois State Agencies (US ISSN 0094-6346) *741*
Directory of Self-Assessment Programs for Physicians (US) *594*
Directory of Services for Migrant Families/Directorio de Servicios para Familias Migrantes (US ISSN 0362-7179) *805*
Directory of Shipowners, Shipbuilders and Marine Engineers (UK ISSN 0070-6310) *878*
Directory of Shop-by-Mail Bargain Sources (US) *218*
Directory of Shopping Centers (US ISSN 0419-3512) *237*
Directory of Singapore Manufacturers (SI ISSN 0070-6337) *237*
Directory of Small Magazine/Press Editors and Publishers (US) *90, 760*
Directory of Social Agencies in the A.C.T. (AT) *805*
Directory of Social and Health Agencies of New York City (US ISSN 0085-0012) *751, 805*
Directory of Social Science Research Institutions in India (II) *797*
Directory of Special Education and Guidance Services in New Zealand (NZ) *345*
Directory of Special Libraries and Information Centers in the U.S. & Canada (US ISSN 0070-6361) *529*
Directory of Special Libraries in Ghana *see* Directory of Research and Special Libraries in Ghana *529*
Directory of Special Libraries in Indonesia (IO ISSN 0376-8600) *529*
Directory of Special Libraries in Israel (IS ISSN 0070-637X) *529*
Directory of Special Libraries in Montreal (CN ISSN 0070-6396) *529*
Directory of Special Programs for Minority Group Members; Career Information Services, Employment Skills, Banks, Financial Aid Sources (US ISSN 0093-9501) *331, 391, 667*
Directory of Spoken-Voice Audio-Cassettes *see* Audio-Cassette Directory *818*
Directory of Sports, Recreation and Physical Education (CN ISSN 0708-6113) *348, 819*
Directory of State Agencies Concerned with Land Pollution Control (US) *385*

Directory of State and Federal Funds Available for Business Development (US ISSN 0070-640X) *143*
Directory of State Corporations (CE) *237*
Directory of State, County , and Federal Officials (US ISSN 0440-4947) *741*
Directory of State, Regional and Commercial Organizations *see* Pennsylvania Chamber of Commerce. Directory of State, Regional and Commercial Organizations *180*
Directory of Statisticians (US) *838*
Directory of Steel Foundries in the United States, Canada and Mexico (US ISSN 0070-6426) *237, 627*
Directory of Summer Jobs in Britain (UK) *667*
Directory of Technical and Further Education (UK ISSN 0309-5290) *667*
Directory of Texas Manufacturers (US ISSN 0070-6450) *237*
Directory of the American Left (US) *710*
Directory of the American Right (US) *710*
Directory of the Australian Gas Industry *see* Australian Gas Industry Directory *678*
Directory of the Canning, Freezing, Preserving Industires (US) *237, 404*
Directory of the College Student Press in America (US ISSN 0085-0020) *90*
Directory of the Cultural Organizations of the Republic of China (CH ISSN 0419-3733) *2, 326*
Directory of the Mutual Savings Banks of the United States (US ISSN 0092-6132) *172*
Directory of the Public Aquaria of the World (US ISSN 0085-0039) *128*
Directory of the Research Establishments in Pakistan (PK) *782*
Directory of the Scientists, Technologists, and Engineers of the P C S I R (Pakistan Council of Scientific and Industrial Research) (PK) *366, 782, 850*
Directory of the Solar Industry (US) *237, 696*
Directory of the Stainless Steel Industry *see* Stainless Steel Directory *630*
Directory of the Turf (UK ISSN 0419-3806) *827*
Directory of Travel Agencies (FR ISSN 0070-6515) *884*
Directory of Trust Institutions (US ISSN 0093-951X) *172*
Directory of Trust Institutions of United States and Canada *see* Directory of Trust Institutions *172*
Directory of U.S. and Canadian Marketing Surveys and Services (US ISSN 0364-8966) *218, 237*
Directory of U. S. Government Audiovisual Personnel (US ISSN 0098-1109) *264, 348*
Directory of U.S. Institutions of Higher Education *see* Education Directory. (School Year): Colleges and Universities *331*
Directory of Unit Trusts *see* Unit Trust Yearbook *177*
Directory of United States Electronic Mail Drops (US) *269*
Directory of United States Importers (US ISSN 0070-6531) *195, 237*
Directory of United States Standardization Activities (US ISSN 0070-6558) *637*
Directory of University Correspondence Courses (CN ISSN 0708-2193) *336*
Directory of Unpublished Experimental Mental Measures (US) *735, 813*
Directory of Visiting Fulbright Scholars in the United States (US ISSN 0098-1508) *342*
Directory of Visiting Lecturers and Research Scholars in the United States Under the Mutual Educational Exchange Program (the Fulbright-Hays Act) *see* Directory of Visiting Fulbright Scholars in the United States *342*

Directory of Visiting Scholars in the United States Awarded Grants Under the Mutual Educational and Cultural Exchange Act (the Fulbright-Hays Act) *see* Directory of Visiting Fulbright Scholars in the United States *342*
Directory of Washington Representatives of American Associations & Industry *see* Washington Representatives *717*
Directory of Water Pollution Research Laboratories (FR ISSN 0419-3865) *276, 385*
Directory of Western New York Business and Civic Organizations (US) *179*
Directory of Women Physicians in the U.S. (US ISSN 0094-5471) *594*
Directory of Wool, Hosiery & Fabrics (II) *237, 855*
Directory of Workers Education (US) *316, 506*
Directory of World Chemical Producers(US ISSN 0196-0555) *237, 246*
Directory of Zambian Industry (ZA) *908*
Directory: Research in Housing - Australia and New Zealand (AT) *484*
Directory - Technical Association of the Pulp and Paper Industry *see* Technical Association of the Pulp and Paper Industry. Directory *675*
Directory to Co-Operative Naturalists' Projects in Ontario. (CN ISSN 0707-0942) *125, 276*
Directory to the Furnishing Trade (UK ISSN 0070-6604) *503*
Directory: Who's Who in Nuclear Energy (US ISSN 0092-8518) *702*
Diretorio Brasileiro de Industria Farmaceutica (BL ISSN 0070-6612) *684*
Dirigo: ME (US) *556*
Diritto e Societa (Naples) (IT ISSN 0390-8542) *511*
Dirt Bike Buyer's Guide (US ISSN 0090-8185) *908*
Disaster Medicine (US) *594*
Disc Collector *see* Disc Collector Newsletter *659*
Disc Collector Newsletter (US ISSN 0360-8700) *659*
Disclosure (US) *279*
Discographies (US ISSN 0192-334X) *818*
Discography Series (US ISSN 0095-8115) *659*
Discontinued Integrated Circuit D.A.T.A. Book (US ISSN 0271-0129) *271*
Discontinued Semiconductor Diode D A T A Book *see* D A T A Book of Discontinued Semiconductor Diodes *352*
Discount Buying Guide. *see* Consumers Digest Guide to Discount Buying *279*
Discourse Analysis Monographs (UK ISSN 0307-1006) *543*
Discourse Units in Human Communication for Librarians (US ISSN 0070-6663) *529*
Discoveries in the Judaean Desert of Jordan (US ISSN 0070-668X) *60*
Discovery (New Haven) Supplement (US) *782*
Discovery Reports (UK ISSN 0070-6698) *309*
Discussions in Environmental Health Planning (US) *385, 484*
Discussions on Teaching (US) *316*
Dislocations in Solids (NE) *696*
Disoo (SG) *267*
Disorders of Human Communication (US) *264*
Disquisitiones Mathematicae Hungariae(HU ISSN 0070-671X) *585*
Dissertationes Archaeologicae Gandenses (BE ISSN 0419-4241) *60*
Dissertationes Botanicae (GW ISSN 0070-6728) *114*
Dissertationes Mathematicae/Rozprawy Matematyczne (PL ISSN 0012-3862) *585*

Dissertationes Orientales (CS) *669*
Distilled Spirits Council of the United States. Facts Book. *see* D I S C U S Facts Book *86*
Distilled Spirits Council of the United States, Inc. Facts Book *see* D I S C U S Facts Book *86*
Distillers Feed Conference. Proceedings(US) *42*
Distribution of High School Graduates and College Going Rate, New York State (US ISSN 0077-9210) *316*
Distribution of Physicians *see* Physician Distribution & Medical Licensure in the U. S *598*
District of Columbia. Air Monitoring Division. Annual Report on the Quality of the Air in Washington, D. C. (US) *385*
District of Columbia. City Council. Annual Report (US ISSN 0092-8364) *749*
Divine Path (SA) *688*, *771*
Diving Rules *see* Official A A U Diving Rules *821*
Divulgacao (AO) *222*
Dix-Huitieme Siecle (FR ISSN 0070-6760) *490*
Dixie Gun Works Muzzleloaders' Annual (US ISSN 0146-6143) *829*
Dizionario Bibliografico delle Riviste Giuridiche Italiane (IT ISSN 0419-4632) *521*
Dizionario Enciclopedico d'Informazioni (IT) *360*
Djakarta Business Guide Book *see* Business Guide Book to Jakarta *235*
Do It This Way *see* National Council for Geographic Education. Do It This Way *349*
Do-It-Yourself. Annual (UK ISSN 0070-6779) *479*
Do-It-Yourself Gardening Annual (UK ISSN 0070-6787) *415*
Doblinger's News Letter (AU) *908*
Doblingers Verlagsnachrichten (AU ISSN 0070-6795) *908*
Doboku Kenkyusho Hokoku *see* Japan. Public Works Research Institute. Journal of Research *376*
Doc; Documentazione (IT ISSN 0391-5018) *336*
Doctoral Dissertations on Transportation (US ISSN 0070-6809) *90*, *865*
Doctoral Scientists and Engineers in the United States. Profile *see* Science, Engineering, and Humanities Doctorates in the United States: Profile *668*
Doctor's Coop Newsletter (MY) *594*
Documenta (SW ISSN 0347-5719) *782*
Documenta Missionalia (VC ISSN 0080-3995) *774*
Documenta Musicae Novae (BE) *659*
Documenta Ophthalmologica Proceedings Series (NE) *616*
Documenta Romaniae Historica. Serie A: La Moldavie (RM ISSN 0070-6825) *452*
Documenta Romaniae Historica. Serie B: La Valachie (RM ISSN 0070-6833) *452*
Documentacao Amazonica (BL) *90*
Documentacao Bibliotecologica (AG ISSN 0070-6841) *529*
Documentaria (IT) *710*
Documentatio Didactica Classica (BE ISSN 0070-685X) *259*
Documentation du Batiment (SZ ISSN 0070-6868) *136*
Documentation Europeenne - Serie Agricole (EI ISSN 0537-6297) *14*
Documentation Europeenne - Serie Syndicale et Ouvriere (EI) *207*
Documentation, Libraries and Archives: Bibliographies and Reference Works (UN) *539*
Documentation, Libraries and Archives: Studies and Research (UN) *529*
Documentation on Asia (II) *717*
Documentation Rheology *see* Dokumentation Rheologie *700*
Documentation Theatrale (FR) *859*
Documentation Tribology *see* Dokumentation Tribologie *371*

Documentazione Europea - Serie Agricola *see* Documentation Europeenne - Serie Agricole *14*
Documente Istorice (RM ISSN 0070-6884) *452*
Documente si Manuscrise Literare (RM ISSN 0070-6892) *563*
Documenti e Testimonianze di Storia Contemporanea (IT) *432*
Documenti Sulle Arti del Libro (IT ISSN 0070-6906) *90*
Documento Abril (BL) *908*
Documentologie (FR ISSN 0070-6817) *908*
Documentos Institucionales Oficiales (BO) *813*
Documentos Oficiales de la Organizacion de los Estados Americanos: Lista General Indice Analitico *see* Organization of American States. Official Records. Indice y Lista General *471*
Documentos Taller Multidisciplinario del Medio Ambiente (CL) *385*
Documents A B F (Association des Bibliothecaires Francais) (FR ISSN 0066-894X) *529*
Documents d'Etudes (FR) *511*
Documents d'Histoire de l'Art Canadien *see* Documents in the History of Canadian Art *74*
Documents d'Histoire Maghrebine (FR) *669*
Documents de Cartographie Ecologique(FR ISSN 0335-5330) *103*, *421*
Documents de Linguistique Quantitative(FR ISSN 0085-4786) *543*
Documents et Recherches sur l'Economie des Pays Byzantins, Islamiques et Slaves et Leurs Relations Commerciales au Moyen Age (FR ISSN 0070-6957) *908*
Documents for New Poetry (US) *579*
Documents in Biology (US) *103*
Documents in Chemistry (US) *246*
Documents in Socialist History (UK) *710*
Documents in the History of Canadian Art/Documents d'Histoire de l'Art Canadien (CN ISSN 0383-4514) *74*
Documents in the History of Education(US) *316*
Documents of Medieval History *see* Reign of Charlemagne-Documents of Medieval History *459*
Documents of Modern Art (US) *74*
Documents of Modern History (US) *432*
Documents of Revolution (US) *432*, *710*
Documents of the National and International Policy of the G D R *see* Documents on the Policy of the German Democratic Repubic *721*
Documents of 20th Century Art (US) *74*
Documents on American Foreign Relations *see* American Foreign Relations-a Documentary Record *719*
Documents on Modern Physics (US) *696*
Documents on the Policy of the German Democratic Repubic (GE) *721*
Documents Pedozoologiques (FR ISSN 0180-9555) *34*
Documents Phytosociologiques. Nouvelle Serie (GW) *114*
Documents pour la Carte de la Vegetation des Alpes *see* Documents de Cartographie Ecologique *103*
Documents sur l'Esperanto. Nouvelle Serie *see* Esperanto Documents. New Series *543*
Dod's Parliamentary Companion (UK ISSN 0070-7007) *710*
Dog Watch (AT) *878*
Dog World Annual (UK ISSN 0070-7015) *682*
Dogs in Canada Annual (CN) *682*
Dokkyo Journal of Medical Sciences (JA ISSN 0385-5023) *594*
Dokumentation Deutschsprachiger Verlage (GW) *758*

Dokumentation Impfschaeden-Impferfolge (GW ISSN 0340-5559) *2*, *602*, *756*
Dokumentation Rheologie/ Documentation Rheology (GW ISSN 0340-8388) *2*, *700*
Dokumentation Tribologie/ Documentation Tribology (GW ISSN 0340-3475) *2*, *371*
Dokumentation Verschleiss, Reibung und Schmierung *see* Dokumentation Tribologie *371*
Dokumentationszentrale Wasser Schriftenreihe (GW ISSN 0012-0030) *896*
Dokumente zum Hochschulsport (GW ISSN 0173-0843) *336*, *819*
Dokumente zur Deutschlandpolitik (GW ISSN 0070-7031) *452*, *710*
Dokumente zur Deutschlandpolitik. Beihefte (GW ISSN 0341-3276) *452*, *710*
Dollars and Cents of Shopping Centers (US ISSN 0070-704X) *218*
Domestic and International Commercial Loan Charge-Offs *see* Report on Domestic and International Commercial Loan Charge-Offs *176*
Domestic Oceanborne and Great Lakes Commerce of the United States *see* Domestic Waterborne Trade of the United States *878*
Domestic Waterborne Trade of the United States (US) *181*, *878*
Dominica. Ministry of Finance and Development. Annual Overseas Trade Report (DQ ISSN 0417-9382) *195*
Dominica. Ministry of Finance and Development. Statistical Digest (DQ) *184*
Dominica. Ministry of Finance and Development. Vital Statistics Report (DQ) *184*
Dominica. Registrar of Co-Operative Societies. Report (DQ) *14*
Dominica Agricultural and Industrial Development Bank. Annual Report and Financial Statements *see* National Commercial & Development Bank. Annual Report and Financial Statements *175*
Dominican Republic. Centro Nacional de Investigaciones Agropecuarias. Laboratorio. de Sanidad Vegetal. Sanidad Vegetal (DR) *103*
Dominican Republic. Direccion General de Bellas Artes. Catalogo de la Bienal de Artes Plasticas (DR) *74*
Dominican Republic. Oficina Nacional de Presupuesto. Ejecucion del Presupuesto *see* Dominican Republic. Oficina Nacional de Presupuesto. Ejecucion Presupuestaria. Informe *741*
Dominican Republic. Oficina Nacional de Presupuesto. Ejecucion Presupuestaria. Informe (DR) *741*
Dominican Republic. Secretaria de Obras Publicas y Comunicaciones. Estadistica *see* Dominican Republic Secretaria de Estado de Obras Publicas y Comunicaciones. OPC *741*
Dominican Republic. Secretaria de Sanidad y Asistencia Publica. Cuadros Estadisticos (DR) *810*
Dominican Republic. Superintendencia de Bancos. Anuario Estadistico (DR) *172*
Dominican Republic Secretaria de Estado de Obras Publicas y Comunicaciones. OPC (DR) *741*
Domova Pokladnica (CS) *563*, *626*, *710*, *884*
Donauschwaebisches Schrifttum (GW ISSN 0070-7074) *452*
Donizetti Society. Journal (UK ISSN 0307-1448) *659*
Donnelley-Directory Record (US) *758*
Don't Miss Out (US) *336*
Donum Dei (CN ISSN 0318-0123) *765*
Doors & Windows (UK) *136*, *502*
Dorset Down Flock Book (UK) *44*
Dorset Natural History and Archaeological Society. Proceedings (UK ISSN 0070-7112) *60*, *782*

Dorset Worthies (UK ISSN 0070-7120) *97*
Dortmunder Beitraege zur Zeitungsforschung (GW ISSN 0417-9994) *504*
Doshisha Studies in Foreign Literature (JA) *563*
Dossiers Beaux-Jeux (CN) *813*
Dossiers d'Education Familiale (FR ISSN 0070-7139) *316*
Dossiers de Demographie de la Belgique (BE) *727*
Dossiers du Cinema (FR ISSN 0070-7155) *649*
Dow Jones Commodities Handbook (US ISSN 0362-0689) *203*
Dow Jones-Irwin Business Almanac (US ISSN 0146-6534) *143*
Downdraft (US ISSN 0070-7171) *316*, *468*
Downhill Only Journal (UK ISSN 0070-718X) *829*
Downtown Mall Annual & Urban Design Report (US ISSN 0364-586X) *908*
Downtown Malls *see* Downtown Mall Annual & Urban Design Report *908*
Downtown Planning & Development Annual (US ISSN 0145-1715) *908*
Dozenal Review (UK ISSN 0309-8648) *585*
Dragon (UK ISSN 0012-589X) *74*, *563*, *649*, *659*
Drake Law Review (US ISSN 0012-5938) *511*
Dramasripts Series (UK ISSN 0070-7198) *563*
Dramau'r Byd (UK ISSN 0141-1179) *859*
Dredging Seminar. Proceedings (US) *896*
Drehpunkt. Sondernummer (SZ) *563*
Dress (US ISSN 0361-2112) *262*
Drexel Research Conference. Summary Report (US ISSN 0085-0071) *782*
Drexel University Research Review (US ISSN 0085-008X) *782*
Drivers License Guide (US) *870*
Drop Ship Buyers Guide (US) *218*, *237*
Drop Shipping Source Directory of Major Consumer Product Lines (US) *218*, *237*
Drosophila Information Service (US ISSN 0070-7333) *120*
Drover's Post (US) *468*
Drug Abuse (US ISSN 0364-0671) *287*
Drug Abuse Bibliography (US ISSN 0093-2515) *90*, *288*
Drug Abuse Council. Handbook (US) *908*
Drug Abuse Council. Public Policy (US ISSN 0091-2662) *908*
Drug Abuse Council. Special Studies (US) *908*
Drug Abuse: Directory of Community Services in California *see* Directory of Community Services for Drug Abuse in California *287*
Drug Abuse Papers (US ISSN 0070-735X) *287*
Drug Abuse Training Resource Directory *see* Drug Abuse *287*
Drug Approval and Licensing Procedures in Japan (JA) *684*
Drug-Induced Diseases (NE ISSN 0586-2779) *594*
Drug Interactions (US ISSN 0095-599X) *684*
Drug Store Market Guide (US) *218*, *684*
Drug Topics Health & Beauty Aids Directory (US ISSN 0419-764X) *684*
Drug Topics Marketing Guide *see* Marketing Guide *218*
Drug Topics Redbook (US ISSN 0070-7376) *684*
Drugs in Current Use and New Drugs (US ISSN 0070-7392) *684*
Drugs of Choice (US ISSN 0070-7406) *684*
Drumlin (UK) *421*
Drustveni Proizvod i Narodni Dohodak(YU ISSN 0300-2527) *155*

Dublin. National Library of Ireland. Council of Trustees Report (IE ISSN 0332-0006) 529
Dublin Institute for Advanced Studies. Communications. Series A (IE ISSN 0070-7414) 696
Dublin Institute for Advanced Studies. Communications. Series D see Dublin Institute for Advanced Studies. School of Cosmic Physics. Geophysical Bulletin 304
Dublin Institute for Advanced Studies. School of Cosmic Physics. Geophysical Bulletin (IE ISSN 0070-7422) 304
Dublin Seminar for New England Folklife. Annual Proceedings (US) 813
Ductile Iron Pipe News (US) 627
Dudley, England (West Midlands) Public Libraries. Archives Department. Transcripts (UK ISSN 0070-7430) 452
Duengungsratschlaege fuer den Bauernhof (GW) 34
Duesseldorf in Zahlen (GW) 838
Duetsche Luft- und Raumfahrt. Forschungsberichte see D F V L R- Forschungsberichte und D F V L R- Mitteilungen 7
Duke Endowment. Annual Report (US ISSN 0419-8050) 490
Duke University. Commonwealth- Studies Center. Publications (US ISSN 0070-7473) 721
Duke University. Cooperative Oceanographic Program. Progress Report (US ISSN 0070-7481) 309
Duke University. Council on Aging and Human Development. Proceedings of Seminars (US ISSN 0419-8093) 428
Duke University Library Newsletter (US ISSN 0012-7108) 529
Dumbarton Oaks Bibliographies (UK) 90
Dumbarton Oaks Conference Proceedings (US) 60, 74
Dumbarton Oaks Papers (US ISSN 0070-7546) 60
Dumbarton Oaks Studies (US ISSN 0070-7554) 60
Dumbarton Oaks Texts (US ISSN 0070-7562) 432
Dumortiera (BE) 114
Dun & Bradstreet Exporters' Encyclopaedia-World Marketing Guide (US ISSN 0149-8118) 195
Dun and Bradstreet Metalworking Directory (US ISSN 0070-7597) 237, 527
Dun & Bradstreet Middle Market Directory see Dun and Bradstreet Million Dollar Directory. Vol. 2 218
Dun and Bradstreet Million Dollar Directory. Vol. 1 (US ISSN 0070-7619) 218
Dun and Bradstreet Million Dollar Directory. Vol. 2 (US) 218
Dun and Bradstreet Reference Book of Corporate Managements (US ISSN 0070-7627) 214
Dun & Bradstreet Reference Book of Transportation (US ISSN 0093-9528) 203
Dun & Bradstreet Register see Dun & Bradstreet Standard Register 237
Dun & Bradstreet/Seyd's Register see Dun & Bradstreet Standard Register 237
Dun & Bradstreet Standard Register (US) 237
Dun & Bradstreet's Guide to Your Investments (US ISSN 0098-2466) 203
Dun's Reference Book of Transportation, Inc. see Dun & Bradstreet Reference Book of Transportation 203
Dundee and Tayside Chamber of Commerce and Industry. Buyer's Guide & Trade Directory (UK) 179, 237
Dundee Chamber of Commerce. Buyer's Gudie & Trade Directory see Dundee and Tayside Chamber of Commerce and Industry. Buyer's Guide & Trade Directory 179

Dunsink Observatory. Publications (IE ISSN 0070-7643) 82
Duodecimal Review see Dozenal Review 585
Duquesne Studies. Language and Literature (US) 543
Duquesne Studies. Philological Series see Duquesne Studies. Language and Literature 543
Duquesne Studies. Philosophical Series (US ISSN 0070-7708) 688
Duquesne Studies. Psychological Series (US ISSN 0070-7716) 735
Duquesne Studies. Theological Series (US ISSN 0070-7732) 765
Duquesne Studies in Phenomenological Psychology (US) 735
Durban Municipal Library. Annual Report (SA) 529
Durch Stipendien Studieren (GW ISSN 0070-7767) 316
Durham University Geological Society. Journal see Arthur Holmes Society. Journal 288
Dutch Studies (NE) 452
Dutch Theses see Bibliografie van Nederlandse Proefschriften 88
Dwarf Iris Society Portfolio (US ISSN 0418-2057) 415
Dwight's Special Truck Equipment Manual (US) 862
Dychova Hudba (CS) 659
Dyn (UK) 49
Dynamic Economics Series (NE) 143
Dynamica (SA) 143
Dzieje Lublina (PL ISSN 0419-8816) 452
Dzieje Polskiej Granicy Zachodniej (PL ISSN 0070-7791) 452
E A A A Newsletter (European Association of Advertising Agencies) (BE ISSN 0531-2701) 5
E A A Review (Edinburgh Architectural Association) (UK ISSN 0307-1634) 69
E A G Publicaciones (Secretaria de Estado de Agricultura y Ganaderia) (AG) 14
E A M Accents (European American Music Distributors Corporation) (US) 659
E A P R Abstracts of Conference Papers (European Association for Potato Research) (NE) 34
E. A. R. (Edinburgh Architectural Research) (UK ISSN 0140-5039) 69
E.A.S.C.O.N. Convention Record see Electronics and Aerospace Systems Convention. E A S C O N Record 354
E & N R Library Journals see Energy and Natural Resources Library Journals 362
E B G (Electronics Buyers Guide) (JA) 237, 353
E B U Monographs, Legal and Administrative Series (European Broadcasting Union) (SZ) 267
E B U Seminars for Producers and Directors of Educational Television for Schools and Adults (European Broadcasting Union) (SZ) 267
E B U Workshops for Producers and Directors of Television Programmes for Children and Young People (European Broadcasting Union) (SZ) 267
E C A Year Book Desk Diary (Electrical Contractors' Association) (UK) 237, 353
E C & M's Electrical Products Yearbook (Electrical Construction and Maintenance) (US ISSN 0093-3236) 353
E D A Research Review (U.S. Economic Development Administration) (US ISSN 0163-3457) 143
E E G Vademecum/Selected Agri-Figures of the E.E.C (NE) 24
E E M (Electronic Engineers Master) (US ISSN 0423-9938) 353
E E O C Compliance Manual (US) 207
E E R C Reports (Earthquake Engineering Research Center) (US) 375

E F I L Documentation (European Federation for Intercultural Learning) (BE) 342
E F I News see E F I Nytt 155
E F I Nytt/E F I News (Ekonomiska Forskningsinstitutet) (SW) 2, 155
E F T A Trade (European Free Trade Association) (SZ ISSN 0531-4119) 195
E I A Guide (US ISSN 0070-7821) 218
E I B-Information (European Investment Bank) (EI) 203
E I S Annual Review (Environmental Impact Statement) (US) 908
E I S Cumulative (Environmental Impact Statement) (US) 390
E I U World Outlook see Economist Intelligence Unit. E I U World Outlook 185
E M C Directory of Summer Session Courses on Educational Media (Educational Media Council) (US) 336
E M Complaint Directory for Consumers (US ISSN 0363-2083) 279
E M I Ssary (Evangelical Missions Information Service) (US) 765
E/M J International Directory of Mining and Mineral Processing Operations (US) 627, 643
E N I Annual Report (Ente Nazionale Idrocarburi) (IT) 362, 366, 643, 855
E N R Directory of Contractors (Engineering News-Record) (US ISSN 0098-6453) 136
E N R Directory of Design Firms (Engineering News-Record) (US ISSN 0098-6305) 366
E N S B A N A Cahiers see Ecole Nationale Superieure de Biologie Appliquee a la Nutrition et a l'Alimentation. Cahiers 665
E P A Activities Under the Resource Conservation and Recovery Act of 1976 (U.S. Environmental Protection Agency) (US ISSN 0161-8490) 385
E P A C: Electronic Production Aids Catalog see Electronic Packaging and Production Vendor Selection Issue 367
E P A Research Review (U.S. Environmental Protection Agency) (US) 385
E R B Occasional Paper Series see University of Dar es Salaam. Economic Research Bureau. Occasional Paper 150
E R B Papers see University of Dar es Salaam. Economic Research Bureau. Papers 150
E-R-C Directory (Employee Relocation Council) (US) 761
E R D A (Engineering Research and Development in Agriculture) (CN ISSN 0012-7892) 34
E R E A C Directory see E-R-C Directory 761
E R I C Clearinghouse for Junior Colleges. Topical Paper Series (US ISSN 0531-9315) 336
E R I C Clearinghouse on Teacher Education. Special Current Issues Publications (US) 316
E R I C Clearinghouse on Tests, Measurement, and Evaluation. T M Report Series (US) 316, 735
E S A Scientific-Technical Reports, Notes and Memoranda (European Space Agency) (FR) 8
E S C A P Country Monograph Series (UN) 727
E S R O Scientific-Technical Reports, Notes and Memoranda see E S A Scientific-Technical Reports, Notes and Memoranda 8
E.S. Woodward Lectures in Economics (CN) 143
E.T.A. Hoffmann-Gesellschaft. Mitteilungen (GW ISSN 0073-2885) 563
E T B A Investment Guide see Hellenic Industrial Development Bank. Investment Guide 203
E U M E N Action (Entr'aide Universitaire Mondiale) (US ISSN 0424-0227) 336

E U R O N O R M (EI) 637
Ealing Occasional Papers in the History of Libraries (UK) 452, 529
Ear Research Institute. Progress Report(US ISSN 0197-3657) 617
Early Childhood Development in Texas(US ISSN 0092-7368) 256, 617
Early China (US ISSN 0362-5028) 443
Early Diagnosis Papers (UK) 594
Early English Text Society. Publications. Extra Series (US ISSN 0070-7864) 563
Early English Text Society. Publications. Original Series (US ISSN 0070-7872) 563
Early English Text Society. Publications. Supplementary Texts (US ISSN 0070-7880) 563
Early Music Laboratory. Bulletins and Tapes (US) 659
Earth and You (CN ISSN 0085-011X) 385, 556
Earth Sciences Series (UN ISSN 0070-7910) 288
Earthmind Newsletter (US) 362
Earthquake History of the United States(US) 304
East Africa High Commissions Desert Locust Survey. Report see Desert Locust Control Organization for Eastern Africa. Annual Report 34
East African Academy. Foundation Lectures see Kenya National Academy for Advancement of Arts and Sciences. Foundation Lectures 491
East African Academy. Proceedings see Kenya National Academy for Advancement of Arts and Sciences. Proceedings 491
East African Freshwater Fisheries Research Organization. Annual Report (UG ISSN 0070-7953) 396
East African Geographical Review (UG ISSN 0070-7961) 421
East African Research Information Centre. E A R I C Information Circular see Kenya National Academy for Advancement of Arts and Sciences. Research Information Circulars 440
East African Studies (KE ISSN 0424-0928) 797
East Anglia Guide (UK) 884
East Asia Travel Association. Proceedings of the General Meeting (JA ISSN 0424-0944) 884
East Asian Genealogist (US) 417
East Carolina College Publications in History see East Carolina University Publications in History 468
East Carolina University Publications in History (US ISSN 0070-8089) 468
East Central Europe/Europe du Centre Est (US ISSN 0094-3037) 452
East Europe in German Books (US ISSN 0070-8097) 437
East Europe Monographs (US ISSN 0070-8100) 721
East Lakes Geographer (US ISSN 0070-8127) 421
East Midland Archaeological Bulletin (UK ISSN 0424-1088) 60
East of England Show Catalogue (UK) 14
East Pakistan. Education Directorate. Adult Education Branch. Report on Pilot Project on Adult Education see Bangladesh. Education Directorate. Report on Pilot Project on Adult Education 329
East Riding Archaeologist (UK ISSN 0012-852X) 60
East Tennessee Historical Society's Publications (US ISSN 0361-6193) 468
East Tennessee State University. Research Development Committee. Publications (US ISSN 0082-2744) 805
East West European Economic Interaction (US) 143
East-West Perspectives (NE) 721
East-West Trade Yearbook (BE) 195
East Yorkshire Local History Series (UK ISSN 0070-8208) 452

Eastbournian (UK ISSN 0012-8643) *263*
Eastern Africa (HK) *884*
Eastern Association of Student Financial Aid Administrators. Directory (US ISSN 0091-7168) *344*
Eastern Canada Campbook (US ISSN 0363-2091) *829*, *884*
Eastern Canada Camping *see* Eastern Canada Campbook *884*
Eastern Caribbean Standing Conference on Teacher Education. Report (BB) *348*
Eastern Europe Report: Economic and Industrial Affairs (US) *184*, 191
Eastern Europe Report: Political, Sociological and Military Affairs (US) *638*, *710*, 813
Eastern Europe Report: Scientific Affairs (US) *782*
Eastern Europe Travel Guide *see* Travel Guide to Europe *892*
Eastern European Genealogist (US) *417*, 452
Eastern Finance Association. Proceedings of the Annual Meeting (US ISSN 0163-6855) *172*
Eastern Hemisphere Petroleum Directory *see* Africa-Middle East Petroleum Directory *677*
Eastern Hemisphere Petroleum Directory *see* Asia-Pacific Petroleum Directory *678*
Eastern Hemisphere Petroleum Directory *see* European Petroleum Directory *679*
Eastern New Mexico University. Contributions in Anthropology (US ISSN 0070-8232) *49*
Eastern Pennsylvania, Southern Delaware and Eastern Maryland Blue Book (US) *353*
Eat Well-Live Well (US) *665*
Eaton Electronics Research Laboratories. Technical Report (CN ISSN 0070-8275) *353*
Echange d'Informations sur les Recherches en Droit Europeen *see* Exchange of Information on Research in European Law *521*
Echo of Iran *see* Iran Almanac and Book of Facts *440*
Echo of the Forest *see* Girios Aidas *409*
Ecole d'Ete de Physique Theorique. Les Houches *see* Les Houches Summer School Proceedings *696*
Ecole de Medecine Veterinaire, Saint-Hyacinthe, Quebec. Annuaire *see* Universite de Montreal. Ecole de Medecine Veterinaire. Annuaire *895*
Ecole des Hautes Etudes en Sciences Sociales. Dossiers Africains (FR) *49*, *439*
Ecole Francaise d'Extreme-Orient.Bulletin (FR) *669*
Ecole Francaise de Rome. Collection (FR) *60*
Ecole Francaise de Rome. Melanges: Antiquite (FR) *60*
Ecole Francaise de Rome. Melanges: Moyen Ages, Temps Moderne (FR) *60*
Ecole Francaise de Rome. Melanges: Supplement *see* Ecole Francaise de Rome. Collection *60*
Ecole Francaise des Attaches de Presse. Association des Anciens Eleves. Annuaire (FR ISSN 0070-8321) *504*
Ecole Nationale Superieure de Biologie Appliquee a la Nutrition et a l'Alimentation. Cahiers (FR) *665*
Ecole Nationale Superieure de Techniques Avancees Centre d'Edition et de Documentation. Rapport d'Activite sur les Recherches (FR) *850*
Ecole Polytechnique Federale de Lausanne. Publication (SZ) *782*
Ecole Pratique des Hautes Etudes. Quatrieme Section. Historiques et Philologiques. Annuaire (SZ ISSN 0078-964X) *432*
Ecoles Francaises d'Athenes et de Rome. Bibliotheque. Publications (FR) *60*

Ecological Society of Australia. Memoirs (AT) *103*
Ecological Society of Australia. Proceedings (AT ISSN 0070-8348) *103*
Ecological Studies; Analysis and Synthesis (US ISSN 0070-8356) *103*
Ecology *see* University of Georgia. Institute of Ecology. Annual Report *389*
Ecology and Conservation Series (UN ISSN 0070-8372) *103*
Econometrics and Operations Research *see* Oekonometrie und Unternehmensforschung *147*
Economia (CK) *143*
Economia (PE) *143*
Economia *see* Revista de Economia *148*
Economia Alavesa (SP) *179*
Economia Brasileira e suas Perspectivas-APECAO (BL) *184*
Economia Colombiana (CK ISSN 0422-2733) *184*
Economia Cubana (CU) *184*
Economia de Puglia (IT) *179*
Economia e Financas (PO) *143*
Economia e Storia (IT ISSN 0070-8402) *191*
Economia Gran Colombiana (1959-1963) *see* Economia *143*
Economia Marche (IT) *185*
Economia Politica (HO ISSN 0424-2483) *143*
Economia Salvadorena *see* El Salvador, Informe Economico y Social *185*
Economic Analysis of North American Ski Areas (US ISSN 0147-4243) *143*, *829*
Economic and Investment Report *see* American Council of Life Insurance. Economic and Investment Report *202*
Economic and Scientific Research Foundation, New Delhi. Annual Report (II ISSN 0070-8437) *143*
Economic and Social Committee of the European Communities. Annuaire (EI) *797*
Economic and Social Progress in Latin America *see* Economic and Social Progress in Latin America; Annual Report *185*
Economic and Social Progress in Latin America; Annual Report (US ISSN 0095-2850) *185*
Economic and Social Research Institute. Policy Series (IE) *143*
Economic and Social Research Institute. Publications Series. Paper (IE ISSN 0070-8755) *144*
Economic and Social Survey of Asia and the Pacific (UN) *185*
Economic Assumptions *see* Virginia. Employment Commission. Manpower Research Division. Economic Assumptions *190*
Economic Conditions in/And Outlook for Thailand (TH) *185*
Economic Council of Canada. Annual Report (CN ISSN 0070-847X) *185*
Economic Council of Canada. Annual Review (CN ISSN 0070-8488) *185*
Economic Council of Canada. Discussion Paper (CN ISSN 0225-8013) *144*
Economic Development of Malawi Since Independence (MW) *185*
Economic Development Programme for the Republic of South Africa (SA ISSN 0070-8518) *222*
Economic Development Series (US) *144*
Economic Education Experiences of Enterprising Teachers (US ISSN 0070-8534) *348*
Economic Fact Book on Metropolitan Milwaukee *see* Metropolitan Milwaukee Economic Fact Book *187*
Economic Handbook of the Machine Tool Industry (US ISSN 0070-8550) *583*
Economic Indicators of Turkey (TU) *213*
Economic Outlook for New Jersey (US) *144*

Economic Questions for Illinois Agriculture (US ISSN 0070-8615) *28*
Economic Reflections (TZ) *144*
Economic Research Reports. Series A (SW) *144*
Economic Review (BG ISSN 0070-8631) *144*
Economic Review of New Zealand Agriculture (NZ) *28*
Economic Review of World Tourism (SP ISSN 0070-864X) *884*
Economic Statistics of Japan *see* Bank of Japan. Economic Statistics Annual *153*
Economic Studies Quarterly (JA) *144*
Economic Survey of Asia and the Far East *see* Economic and Social Survey of Asia and the Pacific *185*
Economic Survey of Europe (UN ISSN 0070-8712) *185*
Economic Survey of India (II) *185*
Economic Survey of Indian Agriculture (II ISSN 0085-0160) *28*
Economic Survey of Japan (English edition of: Annual Economic White Paper of Economic Planning Agency, Japan) (JA ISSN 0021-4833) *185*
Economic Survey of Latin America (UN ISSN 0070-8720) *185*
Economic Survey of Liberia (LB) *185*
Economic Survey of Rhodesia (RH ISSN 0070-8739) *185*
Economic Survey of Singapore (SI) *185*
Economic Topics Series (US ISSN 0013-0397) *144*
Economic Trends and Their Implications for the United States *see* Foreign Economic Trends and Their Implications for the United States *186*
Economic Yearbook of Tunisia *see* Annuaire Economique de la Tunisie *182*
Economic Yearbook of Tunisia (TI ISSN 0070-8747) *185*
Economics. Text *see* Annual Editions: Readings in Economics *142*
Economics: Encyclopedia (US ISSN 0090-4422) *144*, 360
Economics of Fruit Farming (UK ISSN 0070-8763) *28*, 34
Economicus (BG) *191*
L'Economie (MG) *237*
Economie Africaine (SG) *199*
Economie Belge et Internationale/Belgische en Internationale Economie(BE ISSN 0070-8771) *144*
Economie de la Tunisie en Chiffres (TI ISSN 0070-878X) *185*
Economie et Sante (FR) *751*
Economie et Societe (FR ISSN 0070-8801) *144*
Economie-Formation-Gestion Collection E F G *see* Collection E F G *214*
Economie Francaise en Donnes d'Encadrement (FR) *185*
Economie Francaise en Perspectives Sectorielles: Filiere Batiment, Genie Civil, Materiaux de Construction (FR) *136*, 144, 185, 375
Economie Francaise en Perspectives Sectorielles: Industries de Biens d'Equipement (FR) *185*, 222
Economie Francaise en Perspectives Sectorielles: Industries de Biens de Consommation (FR) *185*, 222
Economie Francaise en Perspectives Sectorielles: Industries de Biens Intermediaires (FR) *185*, 222
Economie Ivoirienne (FR) *185*
Economie Malgache *see* L'Economie *237*
Economie Sucriere *see* Zuckerwirtschaftliches Taschenbuch *406*
Economies et Societes. Serie AB. Economie du Travail (FR ISSN 0068-4821) *144*, 207
Economies et Societes. Serie AF. Histoire Quantitative de l'Economie Francaise (FR ISSN 0068-4864) *191*
Economies et Societes. Serie AG. Progres et Agriculture (FR ISSN 0068-4899) *28*

Economies et Societes. Serie F. Developpement, Croissance, Progres des Pays en Voie de Developpement (FR ISSN 0068-4813) *199*
Economies et Societes. Serie G. Economie Planifiee (FR ISSN 0068-483X) *144*
Economies et Societes. Serie GS. Science de Gestion (FR) *214*
Economies et Societes. Serie M. Philosophie - Sciences Sociales Economie (FR ISSN 0068-4880) *144*
Economies et Societes. Serie Mo. Economie Monetaire (FR) *172*
Economies et Societes. Serie P. Relations Economiques Internationales (FR ISSN 0068-4902) *805*
Economies et Societes. Serie S. Etudes de Marxologie (FR ISSN 0068-4856) *191*
Economies et Societes. Serie T. Information - Recherche Innovation (FR ISSN 0068-4872) *144*
Economies of the World (US) *185*
Economisch- en Sociaal-Historisch Jaarboek (NE) *191*, 452
Economisch-Historisch Jaarboek *see* Economisch- en Sociaal-Historisch Jaarboek *191*
Economisch Instituut voor Het Midden-en Kleinbedrijf. Bedrijfsgegevens voor de Detailhandel in Koffers en Lederwaren (NE) *524*
Economisch Instituut voor Het Midden-en Kleinbedrijf. Verslag (NE ISSN 0070-8836) *234*
Economist Intelligence Unit. E I U World Outlook (UK ISSN 0424-3331) *185*
Economy of Hawaii *see* Hawaii Annual Economic Review *186*
Ecrits Libres (FR ISSN 0070-8860) *765*
Ecriture (SZ ISSN 0070-8879) *563*
Ecuador. Centro de Desarrollo Industrial. Informe de Labores (EC ISSN 0070-8887) *222*
Ecuador. Comision de Valores. Corporacion Financiera Nacional. Memoria *see* Ecuador. Corporacion Financiera Nacional. Memoria *228*
Ecuador. Corporacion Financiera Nacional. Boletin Estadistico (EC) *185*
Ecuador. Corporacion Financiera Nacional. Memoria (EC) *228*
Ecuador. Direccion General de Recaudaciones. Boletin (EC) *228*
Ecuador. Instituto Nacional de Estadistica y Censos. Encuesta Anual de Manufactura y Mineria (EC ISSN 0302-5233) *155*
Ecuador. Instituto Nacional de Estadistica y Censos. Estadistica del Trabajo (EC ISSN 0070-8917) *155*
Ecuador. Instituto Nacional de Investigaciones Agropecuarias. Informe Tecnico (EC) *34*
Ecuador.Instituto Nacional de Meteorologia e Hidrologia. Anuario Hidrologico (EC) *307*
Ecuador. Instituto Nacional de Meteorologia e Hidrologia. Anuario Meteorologico (EC) *632*
Ecuador. Ministerio de Industrias, Comercio e Integracion. Boletin de Informacion de las Empresas Acogidas a la Ley de Fomento Industrial (EC) *222*
Ecuador. Ministerio de Industrias, Comercio e Integracion.Documento (EC) *181*
Ecuador. Ministerio de Industrias, Comercio e Integracion. Empresas Acogidas a la Ley de Fomento Industrial. Directorio Industrial (EC) *237*
Ecuador. Ministerio de Industrias, Comercio e Integracion. Informe a la Nacion (EC) *181*
Ecuador. Ministerio de Recursos Naturales y Energeticos. Informe de Labores (EC) *276*

Ecuador. Servicio Nacional de Meteorologia e Hidrologia. Anuario Hidrologico see Ecuador.Instituto Nacional de Meteorologia e Hidrologia. Anuario Hidrologico 307
Ecuador. Servicio Nacional de Meteorologia e Hidrologia. Anuario Meteorologico see Ecuador. Instituto Nacional de Meteorologia e Hidrologia. Anuario Meteorologico 632
Ecuador. Superintendencia de Bancos. Conferencia Bancaria Nacional. Memoria (EC) 172
Ecuador. Superintendencia de Bancos. Documentos (EC) 172
Ecuador. Superintendencia de Bancos. Inversiones Extranjeras en el Ecuador (EC) 172
Ecuador. Superintendencia de Bancos. Memoria (EC) 172
Ecuador Economico (EC ISSN 0070-8925) 144
Ecumene (US ISSN 0531-786X) 421
Edgar Brookes Academic and Human Freedom Lecture (SA ISSN 0070-8976) 336, 416
Ediciones Peninsula. Serie Universitaria. Historia, Ciencia, Sociedad (SP) 797
Ediciones Rikchay Peru (PE) 710
Edicoes Cadernos Culturais (BL) 556
Edinburgh Architectural Association E A A Yearbook see E A A Review 69
Edinburgh Architectural Association Review see E A A Review 69
Edinburgh Architectural Research see E. A. R 69
Edinburgh Studies in Sociology (UK) 813
Edisi Chusus Bulletin Koperasi (IO) 185
Edison Electric Institute. Statistical Yearbook of the Electric Utility Industry. (US) 353
Editiones Arnamagnaeanae. Series A (DK ISSN 0070-9069) 543, 563
Editiones Arnamagnaeanae. Series B (DK ISSN 0070-9077) 543, 563
Editiones Arnamagnaeanae. Supplementum (DK ISSN 0070-9085) 563
Editions Organisation. Fiches E O-Formation Permanente see Fiches E O-Formation Permanente 215
Editor & Publisher International Year Book (US ISSN 0424-4923) 264, 504
Editor and Publisher Market Guide (US) 218
Editorial Eye (US ISSN 0193-7383) 504, 758
Editorial Offices in the West (US ISSN 0070-9107) 908
Edmonton Revival Centre. News see End-Time News 772
Edmund's Auto-Pedia (US) 870
Edmund's Car Prices (US) 870
Edmund's Van, Pickup, Off Road Vehicles (US) 870
Edubba (AT ISSN 0085-0187) 432
Educacao e Realidade (BL) 317
Educacion y Planeamiento (GT) 317
Educare (SA) 317
Educating Exceptional Children see Annual Editions: Educating Exceptional Children 345
Educating the Disadvantaged (US ISSN 0531-8327) 345
Education Advisory (CN) 317
Education & Careers in South Africa (SA) 317, 667
Education & Culture/Opvoeding en Kultuur (SA) 317
Education and Science (UK ISSN 0070-9115) 317
Education au Canada see Education in Canada 326
Education Authorities' Directory and Annual (UK ISSN 0070-9131) 317
Education Commission of the States. National Assessment of Educational Progress. Assessment Reports (US) 348
Education Committees Year Book see Education Year Book 317
Education des Adultes see I. C. E. A. Cahiers 329

Education Development Center. Annual Report (US ISSN 0424-5407) 317
Education Directory. Local Education Agencies (US) 317
Education Directory. Public Schools see Education Directory. Local Education Agencies 317
Education Directory. (School Year): Colleges and Universities (US) 331
Education Directory: Education Associations see Directory of Education Associations 316
Education Environment (IE) 317
Education Exchange see Educational International 342
Education for a Journalism Career see Accredited Journalism Education 504
Education for Migrant Children; Arizona State Plan see Arizona State Plan for the Education of Migratory Children 314
Education for Nursing: The Diploma Way (US ISSN 0070-9166) 336, 614
Education in Asia and Oceania: Reviews, Reports and Notes (UN) 317
Education in Asia: Reviews, Reports and Notes see Education in Asia and Oceania: Reviews, Reports and Notes 317
Education in Canada/Education au Canada (CN ISSN 0706-3679) 326, 838
Education in Europe. Section 1: Higher Education and Research (FR ISSN 0070-9182) 336
Education in Europe. Section 2: General and Technical Education (FR ISSN 0070-9190) 317
Education in Europe. Section 3: Out-Of-School Education (FR ISSN 0070-9204) 317
Education in Europe. Section 4 (General) (FR ISSN 0070-9212) 317
Education in India (II) 317
Education in Japan; A Graphic Presentation (JA ISSN 0070-9220) 317
Education in the North (UK ISSN 0424-5512) 317
Education Law Bulletin (US) 317, 511
Education News from Metrologic (US ISSN 0046-144X) 317, 496
Education Research and Perspectives (AT) 336
Education Social Worker (UK) 317, 805
Education Statistics for the United Kingdom (UK) 317
Education Statistics, New York State (US) 326, 838
Education Studies in Progress in Canadian Universities see Directory of Education Studies in Canada 316
Education Welfare Officer see Education Social Worker 805
Education Year Book (UK) 317
Educational ABC of Canadian Industry (CN ISSN 0319-034X) 144
Educational Administration and History Monographs (UK) 344, 432
Educational and Psychological Interactions (SW ISSN 0070-9263) 317, 735
Educational Assessment Program State Report see New Jersey. Department of Education. Educational Assessment Program State Report 320
Educational Commission for Foreign Medical Graduates. Annual Report (US ISSN 0145-2037) 594
Educational Council for Foreign Medical Graduates. Annual Report see Educational Commission for Foreign Medical Graduates. Annual Report 594
Educational Directory of Mississippi Schools (US ISSN 0363-874X) 331
Educational Films (US) 326, 651
Educational International (UK) 342
Educational Law Review see Nihon Kyoikuho Gakkai Nempo 516
Educational Materials Directory (US) 348, 479

Educational Media Catalogs on Microfiche (US) 348
Educational Media Council Directory of Summer Session Courses on Educational Media see E M C Directory of Summer Session Courses on Educational Media 336
Educational Media Yearbook (US ISSN 0000-037X) 348
Educational Opportunities of Greater Boston (US) 329
Educational Personnel in Delaware see Supply and Demand: Educational Personnel in Delaware 323
Educational Policy and Planning. Austria see Bildungsplanung in Oesterreich 315
Educational Reports Umeaa (SW) 317
Educational Research and Practice (UN) 908
Educational Research and Studies (IR) 317
Educational Series - North Dakota Geological Survey see North Dakota. Geological Survey. Educational Series 298
Educational Standards in Japan (JA) 317
Educational Statistics of Punjab (PK) 317
Educational Statistics Yearbook (FR) 317
Educational Studies and Documents (UN ISSN 0070-9344) 317
Educational Technology Bibliography Series (US ISSN 0070-9352) 327
Educational Testing Service Annual Report (US ISSN 0091-8989) 317
Educational Therapy (US ISSN 0070-9379) 345
Educator: Open Court Newsletter (US) 317
Educators Grade Guide to Free Teaching Aids (US ISSN 0070-9387) 348
Educators Guide to Free Audio and Video Materials (US ISSN 0160-1296) 348
Educators Guide to Free Films (US ISSN 0070-9395) 348
Educators Guide to Free Filmstrips (US ISSN 0070-9409) 348
Educators Guide to Free Guidance Materials (US ISSN 0070-9417) 348
Educators Guide to Free Health, Physical Education & Recreation Materials (US ISSN 0424-6241) 348
Educators Guide to Free Science Materials (US ISSN 0070-9425) 348
Educators Guide to Free Social Studies Materials (US ISSN 0070-9433) 348
Educators Guide to Free Tapes, Scripts, and Transcriptions see Educators Guide to Free Audio and Video Materials 348
Educators Index of Free Materials (US) 348
Edward H. Tarr Series (US ISSN 0363-4558) 659
Edward Sapir Monograph Series in Language, Culture, and Cognition (US ISSN 0163-3848) 543
Edwardian Studies (UK) 563, 859
Effects of Pollution Abatement on International Trade see U.S. Department of Commerce. Effects of Pollution Abatement on International Trade 915
Efrydiau Athronyddol (UK ISSN 0142-3371) 688
Egeszsegneveles Szakkonyvtara (HU ISSN 0073-4012) 751
Egg Production Tests: United States and Canada (US) 44
Ego (US) 579
Egon Ronay's Dunlop Guide to Hotels and Restaurants in the British Isles see Egon Ronay's Lucas Guide to Hotels, Restaurants and Inns in Great Britain and Ireland 482
Egon Ronay's Lucas Guide to Hotels, Restaurants and Inns in Great Britain and Ireland (UK) 482

Egypt. Central Agency for Public Mobilisation and Statistics. Statistical Yearbook (UA) 838
Egypt. Meteorological Authority. Annual Meteorological Report (UA) 632
Egypt. Service des Antiquites. Annales (UA ISSN 0082-7835) 60
Egyptian Journal of Phytopathology (UA) 114
Egyptian National Museum. Library. Catalogue (UA ISSN 0068-5275) 67, 90
Egyptian Review of International Law/Revue Egyptienne de Droit International (UA ISSN 0080-259X) 523
Egyptian Society of Endocrinology and Metabolism. Journal (UA ISSN 0070-9506) 611
Ehe- und Familienrechtliche Entscheidungen (AU ISSN 0531-674X) 511
Eidgenoessische Sternwarte, Zurich. Astronomische Mitteilungen (SZ ISSN 0085-8420) 82
Eidgenoessische Sternwarte, Zurich. Taetigkeitsbericht (SZ) 82
Eidgenoessische Technische Hochschule Zuerich. Bibliothek. Schriftenreihe (SZ ISSN 0514-0668) 529
Eidgenoessische Technische Hochschule Zuerich. Institut fuer Baustatik und Konstruktion. Allgemeine Berichte (SZ) 379
Eidgenoessische Technische Hochschule Zuerich. Institut fuer Baustatik und Konstruktion. Versuchsberichte (SZ) 379
Eidgenoessische Technische Hochschule Zuerich. Institut fuer Geophysik.Schweizerische Erdbebendienst. Jahresbericht (SZ ISSN 0084-5779) 304
Eidgenoessische Technische Hochschule Zuerich. Mitteilungen. Aerodynamik (SZ ISSN 0084-5744) 701
Eidgenoessische Technische Hochschule Zuerich. Mitteilungen. Photoelastizitaet (SZ ISSN 0084-5752) 705
Eidgenoessische Technische Hochschule Zuerich. Mitteilungen. Textilmaschinenbau und Textilindustrie (SZ ISSN 0084-5760) 855
Eidgenoessische Technische Hochschule Zuerich. Versuchsanstalt fuer Wasserbau, Hydrologie und Glaziologie. Jahresbericht (SZ) 307, 381
Eidgenoessische Technische Hochschule Zuerich. Versuchsanstalt fuer Wasserbau, Hydrologie und Glaziologie. Mitteilungen (SZ) 307, 381
Eidgenoessische Zukunft: Bausteine fuer Die Kommende Schweiz (SZ ISSN 0070-9514) 213
Eight Peak Index of Mass Spectra (UK) 2, 249, 700
Eighteen Nineties Society.Journal (UK) 563
Eigo Kyoiku Jaanaru see Modern English Journal 547
Einfuehrung in die Information und Dokumentation (GE ISSN 0070-9522) 529
Einkaufs 1x1 der Deutschen Industrie (GW) 237
Einkaufsfuehrer durch die Pelz- und Ledermode (GW ISSN 0070-9530) 524
Eisei Shikenjo Hokoku see National Institute of Hygienic Sciences. Bulletin 753
Eisenbahngeschichte der Vereinigten Staaten von Amerika (SZ) 873
Ek Bacharer Srestha Kabita (II) 579
Ekologiia (BU) 103
Ekologiya Ptits Litovskoi S.S.R. (UR) 103
Ekonomika i Organizatsiya Promyshlennogo Proizvodstva (UR) 222
Ekonomika Promyslovosti (UR) 222
Ekonomika Ugol'noi Promyshlennosti (UR) 648

Ekonomiko-Matematicheskie Metody Planirovaniya i Upravleniya (UR) *214*
Ekonomiko-Matematicheskie Metody v Planirovanii Narodnogo Khozyaistva (UR) *191*
Eksperimental'naya i Prikladnaya Psikhologiya (UR) *735*
Eksperimental'noe Issledovanie Lichnosti i Temperamenta (UR) *735*
El Hi Textbooks in Print (US ISSN 0070-9565) *327*
El Paso Archaeological Society. Special Reports (US ISSN 0070-9573) *60*
El Salvador. Direccion General de Economia Agropcuaria. Anuario de Estadisticas Agropcuarias (ES) *14*
El Salvador. Direccion General de Economia Agropecuaria. Prognostico de Zafra (ES) *24*
El Salvador. Direccion General de Estadistica y Censos. Anuario Estadistico (ES ISSN 0080-5661) *838*
El Salvador. Ministerio de Agricultura y Ganaderia. Direccion General de Recursos Naturales Renovables. Plan Anual Operativo (ES) *276*
El Salvador. Ministerio de Planificacion y Coordinacion del Desarrollo Economico y Social. Indicadores Economicos y Sociales (ES ISSN 0581-4111) *838*
El Salvador. Ministerio de Planificacion y Coordinacion del Desarrollo Economico y Social. Memoria de Labores (ES) *185*
El Salvador. Superintendencia de Bancos y Otras Instituciones Financieras. Estadisticas: Seguros, Fianzas, Bancos (ES) *172, 498*
El Salvador. Superintendencia de Bancos y Otras Instituciones Financieras. Estadisticas: Seguros, Finanzas, Capitalizacion *see* El Salvador. Superintendencia de Bancos y Otras Instituciones Financieras. Estadisticas: Seguros, Fianzas, Bancos *498*
El Salvador en Cifras (ES) *838*
El Salvador, Informe Economico y Social (ES) *185*
Elder Brewster Press (US) *417*
Eldridge Reeves Johnson Foundation for Medical Physics. Colloquium. Proceedings (US ISSN 0070-959X) *595*
Election Index (US ISSN 0095-7186) *710*
Election Laws of Hawaii (US ISSN 0091-9101) *511*
Electric Power Industry in Japan/Nihon no Denki Jigyo (JA ISSN 0420-9397) *353*
Electric Power Survey *see* Annual Electric Power Survey *351*
Electric Utility Generation Planbook (US) *353*
Electrical and Electronic Trader Year Book (UK ISSN 0070-9638) *353*
Electrical and Electronics Trades Directory (UK ISSN 0070-9646) *353*
Electrical Blue Book (CN) *353*
Electrical Blue Book-Directory of New York & Northern New Jersey's Electrical Market (US) *353*
Electrical Buyer's Guide (US) *237, 353*
Electrical Construction and Maintenance Electrical Products Yearbook *see* E C & M's Electrical Products Yearbook *353*
Electrical Contacts (US) *353*
Electrical Contractors' Association Year Book Desk Diary *see* E C A Year Book Desk Diary *353*
Electrical Contractors' Year Book *see* E C A Year Book Desk Diary *353*
Electrical Electronics Insulation Conference. Record (US ISSN 0070-9697) *353*
Electrical Engineering and Electronics (US) *353*
Electrical Engineering Research Abstracts. Canadian Universities (CN ISSN 0070-9662) *2, 360*
Electrical Guide *see* Electrical Installation & Repair Projects *908*

Electrical Installation & Repair Projects (US ISSN 0095-084X) *908*
Electrical Insulation Technical Conference. Record *see* Electrical Electronics Insulation Conference. Record *353*
Electrical Process Heating in Industry. Technical Conference. Record (US ISSN 0070-9719) *353*
Electrical Products Yearbook *see* E C & M's Electrical Products Yearbook *353*
Electrical Trades Directory *see* Electrical and Electronics Trades Directory *353*
Electrical World Directory of Electric Utilities (US) *353*
Electricite de France. Rapport d'Activite (FR ISSN 0070-9735) *353*
Electricite de France. Statistiques de la Production et de la Consommation (FR ISSN 0070-9751) *353*
Electricity Supply Handbook (UK ISSN 0070-976X) *353, 379*
Electrification and Mechanization in Mining and Metallurgy *see* Elektryfikacja i Mechanizacja Gornictwa i Hutnictwa *643*
Electrification Council *see* T E C Report *359*
Electro (SI) *353*
Electro. Annuaire (FR) *353*
Electro Medical Trade Association. Products Directory (UK) *595*
Electroanalytical Chemistry: A Series of Advances (US ISSN 0070-9778) *249*
Electrochemical Society Series (US) *251*
Electrochemistry (UK ISSN 0305-9979) *251*
Electrodeposition and Surface Treatment *see* Surface Technology *250*
Electromechanical Bench Reference (US) *353*
Electron, Ion and Laser Beam Technology Conference. Record *see* I E E E/O S A Conference on Laser Engineering and Applications. Digest of Technical Papers *354*
Electron Microscopy Society of America. Proceedings (US ISSN 0424-8201) *124*
Electron Spectroscopy: Theory, Techniques and Applications (US) *353*
Electron Spin Resonance (UK ISSN 0305-9758) *254*
Electronic Components Conference. Proceedings (US ISSN 0569-5503) *353*
Electronic Connector Study Group. Annual Connector Symposium. Proceedings (US ISSN 0145-0085) *353*
Electronic Design's Gold Book (US) *237, 353*
Electronic Engineers Master *see* E E M *353*
Electronic Experimenter's Handbook (US) *353*
Electronic Industries Yearbook *see* Electronic Market Data Book *353*
Electronic Industry Telephone Directory (US ISSN 0422-9053) *237, 353*
Electronic Market Data Book (US ISSN 0070-9867) *353*
Electronic News Financial Fact Book and Directory (US ISSN 0070-9875) *353*
Electronic Packaging and Production Buyers Guide *see* Electronic Packaging and Production Vendor Selection Issue *367*
Electronic Packaging and Production Vendor Selection Issue (US) *367, 672*
Electronic Procurement Index for Canada (CN) *353*
Electronic Representatives Directory (US) *237, 353*
Electronic Structure & Magnetism of Inorganic Compounds (UK ISSN 0305-9766) *254*
Electronic Warfare (SZ) *638*

Electronics and Aerospace Systems Convention. E A S C O N Record (US ISSN 0531-6863) *8, 354*
Electronics Buyers Guide *see* E B G *353*
Electronics Buyers' Guide (US ISSN 0090-5291) *354*
Electronics Components Conference. Record *see* Electronic Components Conference. Proceedings *353*
Electronics Hobbyist (US ISSN 0424-8384) *354, 476*
Electronics in Japan (JA ISSN 0070-9913) *354*
Electronics New Product Directory (US) *203, 218, 354*
Electronics Theory Handbook (US) *354*
Electronique Francaise (FR) *354*
Electrophysiology/Denki Seirigaku (JA) *112*
Elektro-Industrie (GW) *354*
Elektro-Jahr (GW ISSN 0070-9956) *354*
Elektroenergetika i Avtomatizatsiya Energoustanovok (UR) *367*
Elektronik Nyt Buyers Guide (DK) *908*
Elektronikindustriens Indkoebsbog (DK) *237, 908*
Elektrotechnika ir Mechanika (UR) *354, 382*
Elektrovymiriuvalna Tekhnika (UR) *354*
Elektryfikacja i Mechanizacja Gornictwa i Hutnictwa/ Electrification and Mechanization in Mining and Metallurgy (PL ISSN 0070-9964) *627, 643*
Elementa Ad Fontium Editiones (IT ISSN 0070-9972) *452*
Elementary Teachers Guide to Free Curriculum Materials (US ISSN 0070-9980) *348*
Elements de Mathematique (FR ISSN 0070-9999) *908*
Elements du Bilan Economique (ML ISSN 0071-0008) *179*
Elements Fondamentaux de l'Impot *see* Tax Principles to Remember *233*
Elenchus Bibliographicus Biblicus (VC) *765*
Elettronica *see* Annuario di Elettronica *351*
Elevator Manager, Farm Chemical & Fertilizer Dealer (CN) *35*
Eliot Janeway Lectures on Historical Economics (US) *144*
Elizabethan and Renaissance Studies (AU) *563*
Elizabethan Club Series (US ISSN 0085-0225) *452*
Elizabethan Stamp Catalogue (UK ISSN 0071-0024) *478*
Elizabethan Theatre (US ISSN 0071-0032) *859*
Elkab (BE) *60*
Elsevier Oceanography Series (NE ISSN 0078-3226) *309*
Elsner; Handbuch fuer Strassenbau und Strassenverkehrstechnik *see* Elsners Handbuch fuer Strassenwesen *375*
Elsners Handbuch fuer Staedtischen Ingenieurbau *see* Elsners Handbuch fuer Staedtisches Ingenieurwesen *367*
Elsners Handbuch fuer Staedtisches Ingenieurwesen (GW) *367*
Elsners Handbuch fuer Strassenwesen (GW) *375*
Elsners Taschenbuch der Eisenbahntechnik (GW ISSN 0071-0075) *873*
Embroidery Directory (US ISSN 0080-6811) *237, 855*
Eme Eme (DR) *774*
Emeriti for Employment (US) *667*
Emissary (US) *688*
EMISsary *see* E M I Ssary *765*
Emmenager a Ottawa/Hull *see* Moving to Ottawa/Hull *761*
Empire State Historical Publications (US ISSN 0071-0091) *468*
Empirica (GW) *185*
Empirical Research in Accounting; Selected Studies *see* Journal of Accounting Research. Supplement *167*

Empirical Research in Theatre (US ISSN 0361-2767) *859*
Empleo y Desempleo en Puerto Rico/ Employment and Unemployment in Puerto Rico: Calendar Years (PR ISSN 0555-6635) *207*
Employee Benefit Costs in Canada (CN ISSN 0701-1539) *207*
Employee Compensaton in the Private Nonfarm Economy *see* U.S. Bureau of Labor Statistics. Employee Compensation in the Private Nonfarm Economy *166*
Employee Relocation Council Directory *see* E-R-C Directory *761*
Employees in Colleges and Universities, New York State *see* College and University Employees, New York State *335*
Employers of New Community College Graduates: Directory (CN ISSN 0381-3711) *667*
Employers of New University Graduates: Directory (CN ISSN 0381-372X) *667*
Employment and Earnings Statistics for the United States *see* Employment and Earnings: United States *155*
Employment and Earnings: United States (US) *155*
Employment and Unemployment in Puerto Rico: Calendar Years *see* Empleo y Desempleo en Puerto Rico *207*
Employment Opportunities for Advanced Post-Graduate Scientists and Engineers (UK ISSN 0071-0148) *667*
Employment Relations Abstracts: Subject Heading List *see* Work Related Abstracts Subject Heading List *538*
Empresa Brasileira de Pesquisa Agropecuaria Guia da E M B R A P A e de Instituicoes Brasileiras de Pesquisa Agropecuaria *see* Guia da E M B R A P A e de Instituicoes Brasileiras de Pesquisa Agropecuaria *15*
Empresa Brasileira de Telecommunicacoes. Relatorio (BL) *264*
Empresa Brasileira de Turismo. Anuario Estatistico (BL) *884*
Empresa Brasileira de Turismo. Calendario Turistico (BL) *884*
Empresa Brasileira de Turismo. Calendrier Touristique *see* Empresa Brasileira de Turismo. Calendario Turistico *884*
Empresa Brasileira de Turismo. Tourist Calendar *see* Empresa Brasileira de Turismo. Calendario Turistico *884*
Empresa de Navegacao da Amazonia. Estatistica da Navegacao (BL) *878*
Empresa Nacional de Energia Electrica. Datos Estadisticos (HO) *354*
Empresa Nacional de Telecomunicaciones del Peru. Memoria Anual (PE) *267*
Empresa y Su Entorno. Serie AC (SP) *214*
Empresa y Su Entorno. Serie L (SP) *215*
En Direct Avec l'Histoire (FR ISSN 0071-0156) *452*
En el Nuevo Uruguay/In the New Uruguay (UY) *556*
Enchoria (GW ISSN 0340-627X) *543*
Enciclopedia Nacional del Petroleo Petrolquimica y Gas (SP) *679*
Encomia (US ISSN 0363-4841) *563*
Encore (US ISSN 0071-0164) *563, 859*
Encounterer (US) *619, 735*
Encuesta Agropecuaria (VE) *28*
Encuesta Avicola (ES) *44*
Encuesta Industrial *see* Guatemala. Direccion General de Estadistica. Departamento de Estudios Especiales y Estadisticas Continuas. Produccion, Venta y Otros Ingresos de la Encuesta Anual de la Industria Manufacturera Fabril *841*
Encuesta Industrial: Resultados Nacionales (VE) *155*
Encyclia (US) *74, 782*

Encyclopaedia Africana. Information Report (GH ISSN 0013-712X) 432, 797
Encyclopaedia Judaica Year Book (IS) 770
Encyclopedia Buying Guide (US ISSN 0361-1094) 360
Encyclopedia of Associations (US ISSN 0071-0202) 360
Encyclopedia of Business Information Sources (US ISSN 0071-0210) 215
Encyclopedia of Geographic Information Sources (US) 421
Encyclopedia of Governmental Advisory Organizations (US ISSN 0092-8380) 741
Encyclopedia of Information Systems and Services (US) 237, 271
Encyclopedia of Physics see Handbuch der Physik 909
Encyclopedia of Plant Physiology. New Series (US) 114
Encyclopedia of Social Work (US ISSN 0071-0237) 805
Encyclopedia Year Book (US) 360
End-Time News (CN ISSN 0702-844X) 772
Endeudamiento Externo del Uruguay (UY) 195
Endocrine Society of Australia. Proceedings (AT) 611
Energie Electrique de la Cote d'Ivoire. Compte Rendu de Gestion see Energie Electrique de la Cote d'Ivoire. Rapport Annuel 354
Energie Electrique de la Cote d'Ivoire. Rapport Annuel (IV) 354
Energiebesparing (NE) 362
Energy see American Society of Civil Engineers. Energy Division. Journal 374
Energy and Natural Resources Library Journals (CN ISSN 0707-1000) 362, 529
Energy Balances of O E C D Countries (Organization for Economic Cooperation and Development) (FR) 362
Energy Developments (GW ISSN 0342-5665) 362
Energy Guidebook (US ISSN 0163-5662) 362
Energy Index (US ISSN 0094-6281) 2, 364, 390
Energy Information Locator (US) 362
Energy Magazine's Annual International Conference on Energy. Proceedings (US) 362
Energy, Power, and Environment (US) 362, 385
Energy Report to the Illinois General Assembly (US) 362
Energy Resources Conservation Board. Cumulative Annual Statistics: Alberta Electric Industry. (CN) 354, 362
Energy Sources (US) 362
Energy Technology Review (US) 362, 850
Enfant du Premier Age (FR) 256
Enfo (US) 385
Engelsman's General Construction Cost Guide (US) 136
Engenharia see Engenharia Civil 375
Engenharia Civil (BL) 375
Engineer Buyers Guide (UK ISSN 0071-0288) 237, 367
Engineering and Society Series (US ISSN 0094-7288) 367, 813
Engineering and Technology Enrollments see American Association of Engineering Societies. Engineering Manpower Commission. Engineering Enrollment Data 365
Engineering College Research and Graduate Study. (US) 336, 367
Engineering Committee on Oceanic Resources. Proceedings of the General Assembly (US) 367, 896
Engineering Design Guides (US) 367
Engineering Foundation Annual Report(US) 367
Engineering Geology and Soils Engineering Symposium. Proceedings(US ISSN 0071-0318) 375
Engineering Geology Case Histories (US ISSN 0071-0326) 375

Engineering Geology Symposium. Proceedings see Engineering Geology and Soils Engineering Symposium. Proceedings 375
Engineering in Medicine (US ISSN 0360-7577) 595
Engineering in Medicine and Biology Conference. Record (US ISSN 0071-0334) 595
Engineering Index. Notes & Comment (US ISSN 0145-207X) 2, 371
Engineering Index Annual (US ISSN 0360-8557) 371
Engineering Industries Association. Classified Directory and Buyers Guide (UK ISSN 0071-0342) 237, 367
Engineering Industries in O E C D Member Countries: New Basic Statistics (FR) 222
Engineering Industries in OECD Member Countries see Engineering Industries in O E C D Member Countries: New Basic Statistics 222
Engineering Journal of Singapore (SI) 367
Engineering Know-How in Engine Design (US ISSN 0489-5606) 870
Engineering Laboratories Series (UN ISSN 0071-0350) 367
Engineering Manpower Bulletin (US) 367
Engineering Manpower News/Main d'Oeuvre en Genie Bulletin (CN) 367
Engineering News-Record Directory of Contractors see E N R Directory of Contractors 136
Engineering News-Record Directory of Design Firms see E N R Directory of Design Firms 366
Engineering Research and Development in Agriculture see E R D A 34
Engineering Research Highlights (US ISSN 0149-0605) 367
Engineering Science Library see Ingenieurwissenschaftliche Bibliothek 367
Engineering Sciences Data Index see Engineering Sciences Data Unit Index 371
Engineering Sciences Data Unit Index (UK) 2, 371
Engineering, Scientific and Technical Salary Survey (US ISSN 0093-5735) 207
Engineering Times Annual Directory (II) 367
Engineers of Distinction see Who's Who in Engineering 371
England's Best Holidays (UK) 884
English and American Studies in German (GW ISSN 0071-0490) 543
English and Germanic Studies see English Philological Studies 543
English Ceramic Circle. Transactions (UK ISSN 0071-0547) 244
English Church Music see World of Church Music 664
English Guernsey Herd Book (UK ISSN 0071-0571) 44
English Historical Documents (US ISSN 0071-058X) 452
English Institute. Selected Essays (US ISSN 0071-0598) 563
English Language and Orientation Programs in the United States (US ISSN 0071-0601) 348
English Language Publications from Pakistan see Books from Pakistan 89
English Language Teachers Association. Review/Anjoman-e Dabiran-e Zabanha-Ye Khareji. Nashriyeh (IR) 348
English Legal Manuscripts (SZ) 511
English Literary Renaissance Monographs see English Literary Renaissance Supplements 563
English Literary Renaissance Supplements (US) 563
English Little Magazines (UK ISSN 0071-061X) 563
English Miscellany (IT ISSN 0425-0575) 563
English Monarch Series (US ISSN 0071-0628) 452
English Philological Studies (UK ISSN 0308-0129) 543

English Place-Name Society (UK ISSN 0071-0636) 543
English Studies Series (US ISSN 0071-0644) 348, 543
English Teacher see Alberta English 540
English-Teaching Information Centre, London. Information Guides (UK) 348, 543
English Translations of German Standards (GW ISSN 0071-0660) 637
Enjoy Scotland (UK) 884
Enjoying the Arts (US) 285, 659, 859
Enlace (CK) 372
Enquete Economique des Societes de Service et Conseil en Informatique (FR) 271
Enquete sur les Enterprises Industrielles et Commerciales du Togo (TG) 181, 222
Enquetes et Documents d'Histoire Africaine (BE) 440
Enrico Fermi International Summer School of Physics (NE) 696
Enrollment in Institutions of Higher Education in Illinois (US) 336
Enrollment in Institutions of Higher Learning in Illinois see Enrollment in Institutions of Higher Education in Illinois 336
Ensaios Linguisticos (BL) 543
Ensayo y Testimonio (UY ISSN 0071-0679) 563
Ensayos E C I E L (Programa de Estudios Conjuntos sobre Integracion Economica Latinoamericano) (BL) 185
Enseignement Superieur en Cote-d'Ivoire (IV) 317
Ensemble (GW) 563
Ente Nazionale Idrocarburi. Report and Statement of Accounts (IT ISSN 0071-0687) 679
Ente Nazionale Idrocarburi Annual Report see E N I Annual Report 362
Enterprise (AT ISSN 0085-0268) 181
Enterprise Magazine see Enterprise Newsletter 179
Enterprise Newsletter (CE) 179
Entertainment Industry Directory (US ISSN 0271-8014) 237, 267, 649
Entertainment Industry Series (US ISSN 0071-0695) 218
Entomologia Generalis (GW ISSN 0171-8177) 120
Entomologia Germanica see Entomologia Generalis 120
Entomologica Scandinavica. Supplementum (SW ISSN 0105-3574) 120
Entomological Society of Alberta. Proceedings (CN ISSN 0071-0709) 120
Entomological Society of America. Miscellaneous Publications (US ISSN 0071-0717) 120
Entomological Society of Australia (N.S.W.) Journal see General and Applied Entomology 120
Entomological Society of Canada. Memoirs (CN ISSN 0071-075X) 120
Entomological Society of Egypt. Bulletin see Societe Entomologique d'Egypte. Bulletin 121
Entomological Society of Manitoba. Proceedings (CN ISSN 0315-2146) 120
Entomological Society of Ontario. Proceedings (CN ISSN 0071-0768) 120
Entomological Society of Southern Africa. Proceedings of the Congress (SA) 120
Entomologicke Problemy (CS ISSN 0071-0792) 120
Entomology Memoirs see South Africa. Department of Agricultural Technical Services. Entomology Memoirs 121
Entr'aide Universitaire Mondiale Action see E U M E N Action 336
L'Entreprise Ivoirienne (IV) 179
Entretiens sur l'Antiquite Classique (SZ ISSN 0071-0822) 259

Entscheidungen des Bundesoberseeamtes und der Seeamter der Bundesrepublik Deutschland (GW) 511, 878
Envase y Embalaje (MX) 672
Envirofacts (AT) 385, 672
Environ (TR) 385
Environment Film Review (US ISSN 0090-0486) 385
Environment Index (US) 390
Environment Information Center. State Laws and Regulations see State Laws and Regulations 518
Environment Law Review see Land Use and Environment Law Review 387
Environment Planning and Conservation in Sweden see Current Sweden 452
Environment Probe (CN ISSN 0381-646X) 385
Environmental Assessment of the Alaskan Continental Shelf. Annual Reports Summary (US) 385, 421
Environmental Chemistry (UK ISSN 0305-7712) 246, 385
Environmental Defense Fund. Annual Report (US ISSN 0091-9837) 385
Environmental Design Perspectives (US) 69, 385
Environmental Design Research Association. International Conference. Proceedings see Design Research Interactions 69
Environmental Geology (US ISSN 0071-0857) 293
Environmental Health Engineering Series (US ISSN 0071-0873) 751
Environmental Health Series: Air Pollution (US ISSN 0071-089X) 385, 751
Environmental Health Series: Radiological Health (US ISSN 0071-0911) 622, 751
Environmental Hotline (US) 276, 385
Environmental Hygiene for the Public Health Inspector see Environmental Management for the Public Health Inspector 385
Environmental Impact Statement Annual Review see E I S Annual Review 908
Environmental Impact Statement Cumulative see E I S Cumulative 390
Environmental Information Systems Directory (US ISSN 0094-3231) 385, 529
Environmental Investigations Special Report see Oregon. Department of Fish and Wildlife. Environmental Management Section. Special Report 388
Environmental Law Papers see Environmental Policy and Law Papers 385
Environmental Law Reform Group. Publication (AT) 385
Environmental Leaders Forum. Proceedings (US) 908
Environmental Legislative Bulletin (US) 276, 385
Environmental Management for the Public Health Inspector (CN ISSN 0316-0661) 385, 751
Environmental Policy and Law Papers (SZ) 385
Environmental Programmes of Intergovernmental Organizations (NE) 721
Environmental Protection Directory (US) 385
Environmental Protection Survey (UK) 385
Environmental Radiation Surveillance in Washington State; Annual Report (US ISSN 0509-769X) 385, 751
Environmental Research (SW) 386
Environmental Science and Technology: a Wiley-Interscience Series of Texts and Monographs (US) 386, 850
Environmental Science Series (US) 386
Environmental Sciences and Applications (US) 386
Environmental Wastes Control Manual see Public Works Manual 750
Environnement (CN) 386
Envol/Flight (CN ISSN 0707-7165) 125
Enzymology Series (US) 111

EOS (SP ISSN 0013-9440) *120*
Ephemerides *see* France. Bureau des Longitudes. Annuaire: Ephemerides *82*
Ephemerides Astronomiques *see* France. Bureau des Longitudes. Annuaire: Ephemerides *82*
Ephemeris of the Sun, Polaris and Other Selected Stars with Companion Data and Tables (US ISSN 0071-0962) *82*
Epidecides Lunaires/Lunar Epidecis (FR ISSN 0240-8376) *82*
Epigraphia Indica (II ISSN 0013-9564) *60*
Epigraphic Society. Occasional Publications (US) *60, 543*
Epigraphische Studien (GW ISSN 0071-0989) *432*
Epilepsy (Year) (UK) *619*
Epimenides/Epimenis (FR ISSN 0240-8368) *82, 309*
Epimenis *see* Epimenides *82*
Episteme (NE) *782*
Equal Credit Opportunity Manual (Supplement) (US) *172*
Equal Employment Opportunity Report *see* U.S. Equal Employment Opportunity Commission. Annual Report *211*
Equality (US) *556*
Equipo (MX) *583*
Equity Investment (NZ) *908*
Erasmus in English (CN ISSN 0071-1063) *490*
Erasmus Universiteit, Rotterdam. Centrum voor Maatschappijgeschiedenis. Mededelingen/Information Bulletin (NE) *813*
Erdbau (AU ISSN 0013-998X) *136, 583*
Erdkundliches Wissen (GW ISSN 0425-1741) *421*
Erdstall (GW) *304*
Erdwissenschaftliche Forschung (GW ISSN 0170-3188) *288*
Eretz-Israel. Archaeological, Historical and Geographical Studies (IS ISSN 0071-108X) *60, 421, 443*
Ergebnisse der Allgemeinen Pathologie und Pathologischen Anatomie *see* Current Topics in Pathology *594*
Ergebnisse der Angewandten Mathematik *see* Springer Tracts in Natural Philosophy *791*
Ergebnisse der Exacten Naturwissenschaften *see* Springer Tracts in Modern Physics *699*
Ergebnisse der Inneren Medizin und Kinderheilkunde. New Series/ Advances in Internal Medicine and Pediatrics (US ISSN 0071-111X) *595, 617*
Ergebnisse der Limnologie (GW ISSN 0071-1128) *307*
Ergebnisse der Mathematik und Ihrer Grenzgebiete (US ISSN 0071-1136) *585*
Ergebnisse der Mikrobiologie und Immunitaetsforschung *see* Current Topics in Microbiology and Immunology *123*
Ergebnisse der Physiologie, Biologischen Chemie und Experimentellen Pharmakologie *see* Reviews of Physiology, Biochemistry and Experimental Pharmacology *126*
Ergebnisse und Fortschritte der Zoologie *see* Fortschritte der Zoologie *128*
Erlanger Geologische Abhandlungen (GW ISSN 0071-1160) *293*
Ernest Bloch Lectures (US ISSN 0071-1187) *336*
Ernest Bloch Society. Bulletin (US ISSN 0071-1195) *659*
Ernst-Mach-Institut, Freiburg. Bericht (GW ISSN 0340-8833) *782*
Ernst-Mach-Institut, Freiburg. Wissenschaftlicher Bericht *see* Ernst-Mach-Institut, Freiburg. Bericht *782*
Erotic Folklore Newsletter (US) *401*
Ertekezesek a Torteneti Tudomanyok Korebol. Uj Sorozat (HU ISSN 0071-1233) *432*
Ertragsbilanz der Schweiz (SZ) *228*
Erwerbsgaertner *see* Deutscher Gartenbau *415*

Erziehung und Unterricht (SZ ISSN 0071-125X) *317*
Erziehungs- und Schulgeschichte Jahrbuch (GE ISSN 0075-2622) *317*
Esakia (JA ISSN 0071-1268) *120*
Escribano (US ISSN 0014-0376) *432*
Escritos (CK ISSN 0120-1263) *563*
Escuela de Gerentes de Cooperativas. Cartillas de Cooperacion (SP ISSN 0084-5132) *222*
Escuela de Gerentes de Cooperativas. Coleccion Textos (SP ISSN 0084-5159) *222*
Escuela de Gerentes de Cooperativas. Cuadernos de Practicas (SP ISSN 0084-5167) *222*
Escuela de Gerentes de Cooperativas. Serie Especial (SP ISSN 0084-5175) *222*
Escuela Diplomatica. Cuadernos (SP ISSN 0464-3755) *710*
Escuela Interamericana de Bibliotecologia. Estadisticas (CK ISSN 0071-1314) *529*
Espana al Dia (SP) *185*
Espana - sus Monumentos y Artes; Su Naturaleza e Historia (SP) *453*
Esperanto-Actualites (FR) *543*
Esperanto Documents. New Series (NE ISSN 0165-2575) *543*
Esperanto-Dokumentoj. Nova Serio *see* Esperanto Documents. New Series *543*
Esprit et Liberte (FR ISSN 0071-1330) *772*
Essais de Dialectologie Interlinguale (NE) *543*
Essays and Studies (US ISSN 0071-1357) *563*
Essays in Biochemistry (UK ISSN 0071-1365) *111*
Essays in Chemistry (US ISSN 0071-1373) *246*
Essays in Economics (US ISSN 0014-0864) *144*
Essays in Foreign Languages and Literatures/Gaikokugo Gaikoku Bungaku Kenkyu (JA) *543, 563*
Essays in French Literature (AT ISSN 0071-139X) *564*
Essays in Fundamental Immunology (UK ISSN 0301-4703) *603*
Essays in History (US ISSN 0071-1411) *432*
Essays in International Finance (US ISSN 0071-142X) *172*
Essays in Physics (US ISSN 0071-1438) *696*
Essays in Public Works History (US) *432, 741*
Essays in Toxicology (US ISSN 0071-1446) *684*
Essays on Asian Theater, Music and Dance (US) *285, 859*
Essays on the Economy and Society of the Sudan (SJ) *185, 797*
Essener Bibliographie (GW ISSN 0071-1462) *90*
Essential Articles (US ISSN 0071-1470) *564*
Essex Family Historian (UK ISSN 0140-7503) *417*
Essex Naturalist (UK ISSN 0071-1489) *103*
Establecimientos Manufactureras en Puerto Rico (PR) *838*
Estadistica Basica del Sistema Educativo Nacional (MX) *327*
Estadistica de Criminalidad (CK) *285*
Estadistica Educativa *see* Estadisticas de la Educacion *327*
Estadistica Panamena. Estadistica Electoral (PN ISSN 0078-897X) *710*
Estadistica Panamena. Inversiones Directas Extranjeras en Panama (PN) *155*
Estadistica Panamena. Seccion 221. Movimento de Proablacion *see* Estadistica Panamena. Seccion 221. Demografica. Seccion 221. Estadisticas Vitales - Cifras Preliminares *727*
Estadistica Panamena. Situacion Cultural. Seccion 511. Educacion (PN ISSN 0378-4967) *317*

Estadistica Panamena. Situacion Demografica. Seccion 221. Estadisticas Vitales (PN) *838*
Estadistica Panamena. Situacion Demografica. Seccion 221. Estadisticas Vitales - Cifras Preliminares (PN ISSN 0378-6749) *727*
Estadistica Panamena. Situacion Demografica. Seccion 231. Migracion Internacional (PN ISSN 0378-4975) *731*
Estadistica Panamena. Situacion Economica. Seccion 312. Produccion Pecuaria (PN ISSN 0378-2581) *838*
Estadistica Panamena. Situacion Economica. Seccion 312. Superficie Sembrada y Cosecha de Arroz y Maiz (PN) *28*
Estadistica Panamena. Situacion Economica. Seccion 312. Superficie Sembrada y Cosecha de Cafe, Tabaco y Cana de Azucar (PN ISSN 0378-2573) *838*
Estadistica Panamena. Situacion Economica. Seccion 321 y 325. Industria Encuesta (PN) *155*
Estadistica Panamena. Situacion Economica. Seccion 331-Comercio. Comercio Exterior (PN ISSN 0553-0660) *839*
Estadistica Panamena. Situacion Economica. Seccion 341. Balanza de Pagos (PN ISSN 0378-7397) *195, 228*
Estadistica Panamena. Situacion Economica. Seccion 342. Cuentas Nacionales (PN ISSN 0378-2603) *741*
Estadistica Panamena. Situacion Economica. Seccion 343-344. Hacienda Publica y Finanzas (PN ISSN 0378-6730) *839*
Estadistica Panamena. Situacion Economica. Seccion 351. Precios Pagados por el Productor Agropecuario (PN ISSN 0378-2530) *839*
Estadistica Panamena. Situacion Economica. Seccion 352. Hoja de Balance de Alimentos (PN ISSN 0378-4991) *839*
Estadistica Panamena. Situacion Economica. Secciones 333 y 334. Transportes y Comunicaciones (PN ISSN 0378-7389) *264, 862*
Estadistica Panamena. Situacion Fisica. Seccion 121-Clima. Meteorologia (PN ISSN 0378-6757) *632*
Estadistica Panamena. Situacion Politica, Administrativa y Justicia. Seccion 631. Justicia (PN ISSN 0378-259X) *839*
Estadistica Panamena. Situacion Social. Seccion 431. Asistencia Social (PN ISSN 0378-262X) *839*
Estadistica Panamena. Situacion Social. Seccion 441-Trabajo y Salarios. Estadisticas del Trabajo (PN) *155*
Estadistica Panamena. Situacion Social. Seccion 451. Accidentes de Transito (PN ISSN 0378-6765) *839*
Estadistica Venezolana (VE) *839*
Estadisticas de la Aviacion Civil en Espana (SP ISSN 0421-4986) *867*
Estadisticas de la Educacion (AG) *327*
Estadisticas de Produccion Industrial (SP) *155*
Estadisticas de Vehiculos en Circulacion en Guatemala (GT) *839*
Estadisticas del Comercio Exterior de Venezuela. Boletin (VE) *155*
Estadisticas del Turismo Mundial *see* World Travel Statistics *893*
Estadisticas Minera y Metalurgica de Espana (SP ISSN 0071-156X) *643*
Estadisticas, Seguros, Fianzas, Bancos *see* El Salvador. Superintendencia de Bancos y Otras Instituciones Financieras. Estadisticas: Seguros, Fianzas, Bancos *498*
Estado de Sao Paulo; Amalise e Acompanhemento do Mercado de Energia Electrica dos Autoprodutores (BL) *354, 870*
Estampage, Forge, Extrusion et Techniques Connexes (FR) *627*

Estates Gazette Digest of Land and Property Cases (UK ISSN 0071-1586) *511*
Estatistica Brasileira de Energia/ Brazilian Energy Statistics (BL ISSN 0512-350X) *364*
Estatisticas da Energia: Continente e Ilhas Adjacentes (PO) *362*
Estimated World Requirements of Narcotic Drugs (UN ISSN 0082-8335) *684*
Estimated World Requirements of Narcotic Drugs, Supplement (UN ISSN 0082-8327) *684*
Estimates of Area and Production of Principal Crops in India. Summary Tables (II ISSN 0085-0314) *35*
Estimates of the Population of the United States and Components of Population Change *see* Current Population Reports; Population Estimates and Projections. Estimates of the Population of the United States and Components of Population Change *726*
Estimates of the Population of the United States by Age, Sex, and Race *see* Current Population Reports: Population Estimates and Projections. Estimates of the Population of the United States by Age, Sex and Race *726*
Estimates of the Revenue and Expenditure of the Kingdom of Lesotho (LO) *228*
Esto es Venezuela (VE) *419*
Estructuras y Formas *see* Coleccion Estructuras y Formas *68*
Estudio Atacamenos (CL) *60*
Estudios Agrarios (MX ISSN 0425-3442) *14*
Estudios CIEPLAN (Corporacion de Investigaciones Economicas para Latinoamerica) (CL) *185*
Estudios Criticos (UY) *564*
Estudios de Arqueologia (AG) *60*
Estudios de Arte y Estetica (MX ISSN 0071-1659) *74*
Estudios de Cultura Maya (MX ISSN 0071-1667) *468*
Estudios de Folklore (MX ISSN 0071-1683) *401*
Estudios de Historia Moderna y Contemporanea de Mexico (MX ISSN 0014-147X) *468*
Estudios de Historia Novohispana (MX) *468*
Estudios de Linguistica y Literatura (MX) *543, 564*
Estudios de Literatura (MX ISSN 0071-1691) *564*
Estudios de Literatura Contemporanea (SP ISSN 0071-1705) *564*
Estudios de Poblacion y Desarrollo (BO) *813*
Estudios de Promocion Femenina (BO) *900*
Estudios de Recursos Humanos (BO) *813*
Estudios de Sociologia Familiar (BO) *813*
Estudios Economicos (SP) *185*
Estudios en el Extranjero *see* Study Abroad *343*
Estudios Etnohistoricos del Ecuador (EC) *49, 468*
Estudios Filologicos (CL ISSN 0071-1713) *543*
Estudios Filologicos. Anejo (CL ISSN 0071-1721) *543*
Estudios Filosoficos (VE) *688*
Estudios Folkloricos Paraguayos (PY) *401*
Estudios Historicos y Documentos de los Archivos de Protocolos (SP) *453*
Estudios Latinoamericanos (PL ISSN 0137-3080) *468*
Estudios Monetarios (CL) *172*
Estudios Pedagogicos (CL) *336*
Estudios Romanicos (SP) *543, 564*
Estudios Urbanos (BO) *813*
Estudios y Fuentes del Arte en Mexico (MX ISSN 0071-1748) *74*
Estudo de Deflatores para a Economia do Rio Grande do Sul (BL) *144*
Estudos Baianos (BL) *228*
Estudos de Psicanalise (BL ISSN 0014-1593) *735*
Estudos Historicos (BL) *468*

Estudos Italianos em Portugal (PO) 74, 432, 564
Estudos sobre o Nordeste (BL) 185
Estudos Universitarios (BL) 490
Etat de la Noblesse Francaise Subsistante (FR) 417
Ethiope Law Series (NR) 511
Ethiopia. Customs Head Office. External Trade Statistics (ET ISSN 0425-4309) 155
Ethiopian Chamber of Commerce. Statistical Digest (ET) 179
Ethiopian Monograph Series (US) 391, 440
Ethiopian Publications: Books, Pamphlets, Annuals and Periodical Articles (ET ISSN 0071-1772) 90
Ethnic Chronology Series (US ISSN 0071-1780) 468
Ethnic Directory of Canada (CN) 391
Ethnic Press in the United States (US) 908
Ethnic Review (US) 391
Ethnike Trapeza tes Hellados. Apologismos see National Bank of Greece. Annual Report 175
Ethnocultural Directory of Ontario (CN ISSN 0226-1928) 797
Ethnodisc Journal of Recorded Sound (US ISSN 0364-9210) 659
Ethnodisc Recordings see Ethnodisc Journal of Recorded Sound 659
Ethnographic Review see Neprajzi Ertesito 52
Ethnographica (GW ISSN 0071-1837) 49
Ethnographical Museum of Sweden. Monograph Series (SW ISSN 0081-5632) 49
Ethnologia (GW ISSN 0071-1845) 49, 401
Ethnologia Europaea (GW ISSN 0425-4597) 49
Ethnologica Scandinavia (SW) 49
Ethnomedizin (GW ISSN 0071-1853) 595
Ethos (AG ISSN 0325-5387) 688
Ethylene and Derivatives see World Ethylene and Derivatives 248
Etienne Gilson Series (CN ISSN 0708-319X) 688
Etnografia (PL) 401
Etnografski Muzej na Cetinju. Glasnik (YU) 49
Etnografski Muzej u Beogradu. Glasnik (YU) 49
Etnologia (IT) 49
Etnologia-Antropologia Culturale (IT) 49
Etnologiska Studier (SW) 49
Etnoloski Pregled/Revue d'Ethnologie (YU ISSN 0423-5509) 49
Ettela'at Va Tazeha-Ye Fanni see Informations et Nouveautes Techniques 784
Etude des Ouvrages en Acier et Construction Metallique see Forschung und Konstruktion im Stahlbau 379
Etude du Marche Automobile Belge (BE) 870
Etude sur la Situation Financiere des Regions (BE) 185
Etudes a l'Etranger see Study Abroad 343
Etudes Africaines (BE ISSN 0071-187X) 440
Etudes Baudelairiennes (SZ ISSN 0531-9455) 564, 579
Etudes Bernanosiennes (FR ISSN 0425-4791) 564
Etudes Biographiques Canadiennes see Canadian Biographical Studies 97
Etudes Celtiques (FR) 543
Etudes Cinematographiques (FR ISSN 0014-1992) 649, 859
Etudes d'Histoire Africaine/Studies in African History (ZR ISSN 0071-1993) 440
Etudes d'Histoire de l'Art (BE ISSN 0071-1969) 74
Etudes d'Histoire Economique et Sociale (BE ISSN 0071-1977) 191
Etudes de Cas de Conflits Internationaux (BE ISSN 0071-1896) 721
Etudes de Logique Juridique (BE) 511

Etudes de Philologie, d'Archeologie et d'Histoire Ancienne (BE ISSN 0071-1926) 60, 688
Etudes de Philologie et d'Histoire (SZ ISSN 0071-1934) 453, 564
Etudes de Physiologie et Psychologie du Travail see Commission of the European Communities. Collection Physiologie et Psychologie du Travail 206
Etudes de Pollution Atmospherique a Paris et dans les Departments Peripheriques (FR ISSN 0071-1942) 386
Etudes Eburneennes (IV ISSN 0423-5673) 49
Etudes et Documentation de la R.T.A. (FR) 870
Etudes et Documents Missionnaires see Missionswissenschaftliche Abhandlungen und Texte 766
Etudes et Travaux d'Archeologie Marocaine (MR ISSN 0071-2027) 60
Etudes Ethnologiques (BE ISSN 0071-2035) 49
Etudes Europeennes (FR ISSN 0071-2043) 908
Etudes Finno-Ougriennes (FR ISSN 0071-2051) 543, 564
Etudes Foreziennes (FR ISSN 0071-206X) 453
Etudes Gobiniennes (FR ISSN 0071-2078) 564
Etudes Gregoriennes (FR ISSN 0071-2086) 659, 765
Etudes Historiques (HU ISSN 0071-2108) 432
Etudes Irlandaises (FR) 453
Etudes Linguistiques (FR ISSN 0071-2124) 543
Etudes Mathematiques en Vue des Applications: Formulaire de Mathematiques a l'Usage des Physiciens et des Ingenieurs (FR ISSN 0071-7614) 585
Etudes Mauritaniennes (SG) 49, 440
Etudes Militaires (FR) 432, 638
Etudes Mongoles see Cahiers d'Etudes Mongoles et Siberiennes 48
Etudes Nigeriennes (NG) 49
Etudes Orientales (BE ISSN 0531-1926) 669
Etudes Picardes (FR ISSN 0071-2140) 453
Etudes Prehistoriques (FR) 60
Etudes Savoisiennes (FR) 453
Etudes Senegalaises (SG) 440, 813
Etudes Slaves et Est-Europeennes see Cahiers Culturels 542
Etudes sur l'Egypte et le Soudan Anciens (FR ISSN 0153-5021) 440
Etudes sur la Culture Medievale see Sredniowiecze.Studia o Kulturze 573
Etudes Teilhardiennes/Teilhardian Studies (FR ISSN 0082-2612) 765
Etudes Universitaires sur l'Integration Europeenne/University Studies on European Integration (EI ISSN 0071-2213) 721
Etudes Voltaiques (UV) 49, 543
Etudos Anglo-Hispanico see Mimesis 568
Etyka (PL ISSN 0014-2263) 688
Eucarpia (NE ISSN 0071-2221) 114
Eugenics Society Symposia (UK ISSN 0071-223X) 122
Eurail Guide (US ISSN 0085-0330) 873, 884
Eureka; the Archimedean's Journal (UK ISSN 0071-2248) 585
EURFIMA Annual Report see European Company for the Financing of Railway Rolling Stock. Annual Report 873
Euro Cooperation; Economic Studies on Europe (FR ISSN 0302-0622) 144
Euro Property see Villa Guide 483
Euroasiatica (IT) 543
Eurocontrol (BE ISSN 0531-2248) 8
Eurofinas. Annual Report see European Federation of Finance House Associations. Annual Report 172
Eurofinas. Conference Proceedings see European Federation of Finance House Associations. Conference Proceedings 172
Europa. Revue de Presse Europeenne (FR ISSN 0071-2299) 504

Europa Camping und Caravaning. Internationaler Fuehrer (GW ISSN 0071-2272) 829, 884
Europa Facile (IT) 884
Europa Handbuch der Werbegesellschaften (GW ISSN 0085-0349) 5
Europa Year Book (UK ISSN 0071-2302) 360
Europaeische Dokumentation - Schriftenreihe Landwirtschaft see Documentation Europeenne - Serie Agricole 14
Europaeische Ex Libris see Bibliografi over Europaeiske Kunstneres Ex Libris 80
Europaeische Gemeinschaft fuer Kohle und Stahl. Beratender Ausschuss. Jahrbuch see European Coal and Steel Community. Consultative Committee. Yearbook 199
Europaeische Schriften (GW ISSN 0071-2329) 721
Europaeische Volksmusikinstrumente. Handbuch (GE ISSN 0073-0025) 401, 659
Europaeischer Fernwanderweg (GW) 884
Europautomation (FR) 271
Europe du Centre Est see East Central Europe 452
Europe in the Middle Ages (NE) 453
Europe Laitiere (FR) 41
Europe Pulse (US) 765
European American Music Distributors Corporation Accents see E A M Accents 659
European and Mediterranean Plant Protection Organization. E P P O Bulletin/Bulletin O E P P (FR ISSN 0071-2388) 35
European and Mediterranean Plant Protection Organization. Publications. Series A; Reports of Technical Meetings see European and Mediterranean Plant Protection Organization. E P P O Bulletin/Bulletin O E P P 35
European and Mediterranean Plant Protection Organization. Publications. Series B: Plant Health Newsletter (FR ISSN 0071-2396) 35
European and Mediterranean Plant Protection Organization. Publications. Series C: Reports of Working Parties see European and Mediterranean Plant Protection Organization. E P P O Bulletin/Bulletin O E P P 35
European Applied Research Reports (US ISSN 0272-4626) 386
European Art Exhibitions. Catalog (FR ISSN 0071-2426) 74
European Aspects, Law Series (FR ISSN 0531-2671) 511
European Aspects, Social Studies Series (FR ISSN 0531-2663) 813
European Association for Animal Production. Publications (IT ISSN 0071-2477) 44
European Association for Animal Production. Symposia on Energy Metabolism (IT ISSN 0071-2485) 44
European Association for Personnel Management. Congress Reports (FR ISSN 0071-2493) 220
European Association for Potato Research. Proceedings of the Triennial Conference see E A P R Abstracts of Conference Papers 34
European Association for Potato Research Abstracts of Conference Papers see E A P R Abstracts of Conference Papers 34
European Association for Research on Plant Breeding. Report of the Congress see Eucarpia 114
European Association of Advertising Agencies Newsletter see E A A A Newsletter 5
European Association of Exploration Geophysicists. Constitution and By-Laws, Membership List. (NE ISSN 0531-2728) 304
European Atomic Energy Community. Contamination Radioactive des Denrees Alimentaires dans les Pays de la Communaute (EI) 751

European Atomic Energy Community. Resultats des Mesures de la Radioactivite Ambiante dans les Pays de la Communaute: Air-Retombee-Eaux (EI) 751
European Book Plates see Bibliografi over Europaeiske Kunstneres Ex Libris 80
European Bookdealers (UK ISSN 0071-2523) 758
European Brewery Convention. Proceedings of the International Congress (NE ISSN 0071-2531) 86
European Broadcasting Union Monographs, Legal and Administrative Series see E B U Monographs, Legal and Administrative Series 267
European Broadcasting Union Seminars for Producers and Directors of Educational Television for Schools and Adults see E B U Seminars for Producers and Directors of Educational Television for Schools and Adults 267
European Broadcasting Union Workshops for Producers and Directors of Television Programmes for Children and Young People see E B U Workshops for Producers and Directors of Television Programmes for Children and Young People 267
European Cement Association. Annual European Review (FR) 136
European Cement Association. World Statistical Review (FR) 140
European Cement Association, Statistical Review see European Cement Association. World Statistical Review 140
European Chemical Buyer's Guide (UK) 246
European Civil Aviation Conference (Report of Session) (UN ISSN 0071-2558) 867
European Co-Operation (FR ISSN 0589-9575) 523
European Coal and Steel Community. Consultative Committee. Handbook (EI) 199
European Coal and Steel Community. Consultative Committee. Yearbook (EI ISSN 0423-6831) 199
European Coal and Steel Community. High Authority. Rapport sur la Situation Energetique de la Communaute et Perspective d'Approvisionnement dans la Communaute en 1962 see Commission of the European Communities. Conjoncture Energetique dans la Communaute 362
European Coal and Steel Community. Organe Permanent pour la Securite dans les Mines de Houille. Rapport see Mines Safety and Health Commission. Report 644
European Colloquium on Renal Physiology (Proceedings) (SW) 625
European Commission of Human Rights. Annual Review/Compte Rendu Annual (FR) 511
European Commission of Human Rights. Report (FR) 718
European Committee on Crime Problems. Bulletin on Legislative Activities (FR) 281
European Companies (UK ISSN 0071-2582) 155
European Company for the Financing of Railway Rolling Stock. Annual Report (SZ ISSN 0071-2264) 873
European Conference of Local and Regional Authorities. Documents (FR) 741
European Conference of Local and Regional Authorities. Official Reports of Debates (FR) 741
European Conference of Local and Regional Authorities. Texts Adopted (FR) 741
European Conference of Local Authorities. Documents see European Conference of Local and Regional Authorities. Documents 741

European Conference of Local Authorities. Official Reports of Debates see European Conference of Local and Regional Authorities. Official Reports of Debates 741
European Conference of Local Authorities. Texts Adopted see European Conference of Local and Regional Authorities. Texts Adopted 741
European Conference on Microcirculation. Proceedings (SZ ISSN 0071-2655) 607
European Conference on Mixing and Centrifugal Separation. Proceedings (UK) 382
European Congress of Anaesthesiology. Proceedings (SP ISSN 0071-2671) 604
European Congress of Cardiology. Abstracts of Papers (BE ISSN 0421-7527) 607
European Congress of Cardiology. (Proceedings) (BE ISSN 0423-7242) 607
European Congress of Perinatal Medicine. Proceedings (AU ISSN 0071-2698) 615
European Congress on Ballistocardiography and Cardiovascular Dynamics. Proceedings (SZ ISSN 0302-511X) 607
European Congress on Electron Microscopy (IS ISSN 0071-2647) 124
European Congress on Molecular Spectroscopy. Proceedings (US) 249
European Congress on Sleep Research. Proceedings see Sleep 599
European Convention on Human Rights. Yearbook see Yearbook of Human Rights 719
European Coordination Centre for Research and Documentation in Social Sciences. Publications (NE ISSN 0071-271X) 797
European Cotton Industry Statistics (IT ISSN 0423-7269) 857
European Court of Human Rights. Publications. Series A: Judgments and Decisions/Cour Europeenne des Droits de l'Homme. Publications. Serie a: Arrets et Decisions (GW ISSN 0073-3903) 718
European Court of Human Rights. Publications. Series B: Pleadings, Oral Arguments and Documents/Cour Europeenne des Droits de l'Homme. Publications. Serie B: Memoires, Plaidoiries et Documents (GW ISSN 0073-3911) 718
European Curriculum Studies (FR ISSN 0071-2728) 348
European Directory of Paints and Allied Products see Chatfield's European Directory of Paints and Allied Products 673
European Distributor Directory see European Electronic Component Distributor Directory 354
European Economic Community Savings Bank Group. Report (EI) 172
European Electro-Optics Markets and Technology Conference. Proceedings (UK) 851
European Electronic Component Distributor Directory (UK) 237, 354
European Federation for Intercultural Learning Documentation see E F I L Documentation 342
European Federation of Chemical Engineering. Annual Report (GW) 372
European Federation of Finance House Associations. Annual Report (BE ISSN 0071-2787) 172
European Federation of Finance House Associations. Conference Proceedings(BE ISSN 0071-2795) 172
European Free Trade Association. Annual Report (SZ ISSN 0531-4127) 195

European Free Trade Association. Jahresbericht see European Free Trade Association. Annual Report 195
European Free Trade Association Trade see E F T A Trade 195
European Glass Directory and Buyer's Guide (UK ISSN 0306-204X) 627
European Grassland Federation. Proceedings of the General Meeting (BE ISSN 0071-2825) 35
European Institute on the Prevention and Treatment of Alcoholism. Selected Papers see International Institute on the Prevention and Treatment of Alcoholism. Selected Papers 287
European Investment Bank. Annual Report (EI ISSN 0071-2868) 172
European Investment Bank Information see E I B-Information 203
European Journal of Nuclear Medicine (US ISSN 0340-6997) 622
European Journal of Respiratory Diseases. Supplementum (DK) 623
European League for Economic Cooperation. Publications (BE ISSN 0071-2884) 199
European League for Economic Cooperation. Report of the Secretary General on the Activities of E. L. E. C. (BE ISSN 0531-7436) 199
European League for Economic Cooperation. Reports of the International Congress (BE ISSN 0071-2892) 199
European Leather Guide see Leather Guide 524
European Literary Market Place see International Literary Market Place 759
European Marketing Data and Statistics(UK ISSN 0071-2930) 218
European Monographs in Social Psychology (US) 735
European Offshore Oil and Gas Yearbook see Offshore Oil & Gas Yearbook 680
European Ophthalmological Society. Congress. Abstracts (NE ISSN 0071-2965) 616
European Ophthalmological Society. Congress Acta (NE ISSN 0301-326X) 616
European Organisation for Civil Aviation Electronics. General Assembly. Annual Report (FR ISSN 0531-7444) 8, 354
European Organization for Nuclear Research. Liste des Publications Scientifiques/List of Scientific Publications (SZ ISSN 0304-2871) 90, 700
European Organization for Nuclear Research. Repertoire des Communications Scientifiques. Index of Scientific Publications see European Organization for Nuclear Research. Liste des Publications Scientifiques/List of Scientific Publications 700
European Organization for Nuclear Research Annual Report see C E R N Annual Report 695
European Organization for Nuclear Research Reports see C E R N-H E R A Reports 695
European Organization for Nuclear Research Reports see C E R N Reports 696
European Organization for Nuclear Research School of Computing. Proceedings see C E R N School of Computing. Proceedings 696
European Organization for Nuclear Research School of Physics. Proceedings see C E R N School of Physics. Proceedings 696
European Organization for Quality Control. Conference Proceedings (SZ ISSN 0071-2981) 637
European Organization for Research on Treatment of Cancer. Monograph Series (US) 605
European Parliament. Documents de Seance (EI ISSN 0071-3023) 523
European Parliament. Informations (EI ISSN 0531-4321) 523

European Parliament. Selected Documents (EI) 626
European Parliament Digest (US ISSN 0095-7607) 908
European Passenger Timetable Conference Minutes (SZ ISSN 0071-3120) 862
European Petroleum Directory (US) 679
European Petroleum Yearbook/Jahrbuch der Europaeischen Erdoelindustrie/Annuaire Europeen du Petrole (GW ISSN 0342-6947) 679
European Plastics Buyers Guide (UK ISSN 0306-5502) 706
European Purchasing Conference. (Proceedings) (BE ISSN 0423-8044) 218
European Racing Manual (IT) 827
European Rig- and Supply Ship Owners(NO) 237, 878
European Rubber Directory (UK ISSN 0306-414X) 777
European Scrap Directory (UK ISSN 0308-7786) 627
European Social Fund. Annual Report on the Activities of the New European Social Fund (EI) 345
European Society for Surgical Research. Congress Proceedings (SZ) 624
European Society for the Study of Drug Toxicity. Proceedings see European Society of Toxicity. Proceedings 684
European Society of Toxicity. Proceedings (NE) 684
European Southern Observatory. Annual Report (GW ISSN 0531-4496) 82
European Southern Observatory. Rapport Annuel see European Southern Observatory. Annual Report 82
European Space Agency Scientific-Technical Reports, Notes and Memoranda see E S A Scientific-Technical Reports, Notes and Memoranda 8
European Studies in Law (NE) 511
European Symposium on Chemical Reaction Engineering. Proceedings (GW ISSN 0071-3112) 372
European Symposium on Concrete Pavements. Reports (FR) 375
European Travel Guide for Jews see Guide Touristique Europeen pour Israelites 392
European University Institute Series (NE) 512
European Yearbook (NE ISSN 0071-3139) 90
European Yearbook in Law and Sociology (NE) 512, 813
Europe's 5000 Largest Companies (NO) 222
Europhysics Conference Abstracts (SZ) 696
Europinion (FR ISSN 0071-3155) 453
Europlastics Year Book see European Plastics Buyers Guide 706
Eurovet Bulletin (UK ISSN 0260-0498) 894
Euthanasia Conference. Excerpts from Papers and Discussions (US) 908
Evaluation see Evaluation and Change 805
Evaluation and Change (US ISSN 0090-4449) 805
Evaluation Methods Series see U.S. Civil Service Commission. Bureau of Personnel Management Evaluation. Evaluation Methods Series 220
Evaluation Studies Review Annual (US ISSN 0364-7390) 797
Evaluations of Drug Interactions (US ISSN 0090-6654) 684
Evaluations of Drug Interactions. Supplement (US ISSN 0094-8640) 684
Evangel Refugee see Rock Magazine 767
Evangelical Baptist Churches in Canada. Fellowship Yearbook (CN ISSN 0317-266X) 772
Evangelical Missions Information Service Ssary see E M I Ssary 765
Evangelische Mission Jahrbuch (GW ISSN 0531-4798) 765

EXPERIMENT 1357

Evening Times Wee Red Book (UK) 824
Evensongs/Yeh Ko (CH) 556
Evento Teatrale. Sezione: Autori Italiani del Novecento (IT) 859
Everfoto (SP) 693
Everyman (US ISSN 0094-2367) 564, 579
Everymans Own Lawyer (UK) 512
Everyman's United Nations (UN ISSN 0071-3244) 721
Evolution de l'Economie des Pays Sud-Americains (FR ISSN 0071-3252) 185
Evolutionary Biology (US ISSN 0071-3260) 122
Evolutionary Theory (US ISSN 0093-4755) 122
Ex (BL) 710
Ex Libris d'Europe see Bibliografi over Europaeiske Kunstneres Ex Libris 80
Exact Scale Quarterly see Mini-Auto International 476
Excavaciones Arqueologicas en Espana (SP ISSN 0071-3279) 60
Excavations at Dura-Europos (US ISSN 0071-3287) 60
Excellent Paperbacks for Children see Bibliography of Books for Children 760
Exceptional Infant (US ISSN 0071-3295) 735
Excerpta Botanica. Sectio A: Taxonomica et Chorologica (GW ISSN 0014-4037) 114
Excerpta Historica Nordica (DK ISSN 0085-0365) 453
Exchange of Information on Research in European Law/Echange d'Informations sur les Recherches en Droit Europeen (FR) 521
Excited States (US ISSN 0093-1713) 246
Executive (PK) 215
Executive Compensation (US) 215
Executive Compensation Service. Professional, Scientific, Technical Remuneration, Canada (CN ISSN 0709-5597) 207
Executive Compensation Service. Reports on International Compensation. Argentina (US ISSN 0095-4144) 215
Executive Compensation Service. Reports on International Compensation. Brazil (US) 207, 215
Executive Compensation Service. Reports on International Compensation. Puerto Rico (US ISSN 0090-9971) 215
Executive Compensation Service. Technician Report (US ISSN 0093-8750) 207, 215
Executive Directory of the U.S. Pharmaceutical Industry (US ISSN 0071-3309) 237, 684
Executive Pensions and Benefits (UK) 498
Executives Guide to Information Sources see Encyclopedia of Business Information Sources 215
Exercise and Sport Sciences Reviews (US ISSN 0091-6331) 694
Exhibit Newsletter (US) 529
Exhibitor's Handbook (UK ISSN 0260-1508) 144
Exile (US ISSN 0421-9090) 564
Existing Home Sales see National Association of Realtors. Existing Home Sales 761
Exlibriskunst und Gebrauchsgraphik. Jahrbuch (GW ISSN 0075-2630) 74
Expectations (US) 133, 258
Expenditure and Employment Data for the Criminal Justice System (US) 281
Expenditures Report of the Massachusetts Rehabilitation Commission see Massachusetts. Rehabilitation Commission. Expenditures Report 346
Expense Analysis: Condominiums, Cooperatives and Planned Unit Developments (US) 761
Experientia. Supplementum (SZ ISSN 0071-335X) 782, 851
Experiment (US ISSN 0014-4770) 579

Experiment in International Living. Annual Report (US) *342*
Experiment in International Living. President's Report *see* Experiment in International Living. Annual Report *342*
Experiment Theatre (US) *859*
Experimental Biology and Medicine (SZ ISSN 0071-3384) *103, 595*
Experimental Botany; An International Series of Monographs (US ISSN 0071-3392) *114*
Experimental Mechanics; Proceedings (US ISSN 0071-3422) *379*
Exploration Geophysics (US ISSN 0071-3473) *304*
Exploration in British Columbia (CN) *293, 643*
Explorations (US ISSN 0014-4967) *688, 735*
Explorations in Education (US ISSN 0071-3481) *317*
Explorations in Language Study (UK) *543*
Explorations in Urban Analysis (UK) *797, 813*
Explore Canada *see* Guide to Canada *886*
Export-Adressbuch von Oesterreich *see* Herold Export-Adressbuch von Oesterreich *238*
Export Canada (CN ISSN 0708-1332) *195*
Export Data (UK ISSN 0071-3554) *195*
Export Data Exporters Year Book *see* Export Data *195*
Export Directory of Brazil/Guia Brasileiro de Exportacao (BL) *237*
Export Directory of Denmark (DK) *195*
Export Directory/U.S. Buying Guide (US) *195*
Export Graficas U S A (US) *195*
Export Grafics U S A (US ISSN 0147-409X) *195*
Export-Import Bank of Japan. Annual Report (JA ISSN 0071-3503) *173, 195*
Export-Import Bank of Korea. Annual Report (KO) *195*
Export-Import Bank of the United States. Annual Report *see* Export-Import Bank of the United States. Summary of Operations *173*
Export-Import Bank of the United States. Summary of Operations (US ISSN 0071-3511) *173*
Export-Import Markets (PR) *195*
Export Profile of South Africa (SA) *195*
Export Statistics of Afghanistan/ Ihsa'iyah-i Amual-i Sadirati-i Afghanistan (AF) *155, 839*
Exportaciones Britanicas *see* British Exports *194*
Exportaciones Mineras del Peru (PE) *908*
Exportations Britanniques *see* British Exports *194*
Exporter Guide - Caribbean and Latin America *see* Export-Import Markets *195*
Exporters' Encyclopaedia-World Marketing Guide *see* Dun & Bradstreet Exporters' Encyclopaedia-World Marketing Guide *195*
Exports by Pennsylvania Manufacturers(US ISSN 0556-3585) *195*
Exports of the Republic of China (CH ISSN 0301-9217) *195*
Expression (AT ISSN 0085-039X) *564*
Extensions and Corrections to the U D C (NE ISSN 0014-5424) *529*
Extent of Growth of Private Health Insurance in the United States *see* Health Insurance Association of America. Consumer and Professional Relations Division. Extent of Growth--Private Health Insurance Coverage in the United States *909*

Extent of Voluntary Health Insurance in the United States *see* Health Insurance Association of America. Consumer and Professional Relations Division. Extent of Growth--Private Health Insurance Coverage in the United States *909*
External Trade of Liberia: Import and Export (LB) *195*
External Trade Statistics of Gambia (GM) *155, 839*
External Walls (UK ISSN 0307-0107) *136*
Extra Special Cracked (US) *556*
Exxon Background Series (US) *362*
F A O African Regional Meeting on Animal Production and Health. Report of the Meeting. (UN ISSN 0532-0623) *44*
F A O Agricultural Development Papers (UN ISSN 0071-6960) *14*
F A O Agricultural Studies (UN ISSN 0071-6987) *14*
F A O Atomic Energy Series (UN ISSN 0071-6979) *908*
F A O Commodity Review and Outlook (UN ISSN 0071-7002) *28*
F A O Fisheries Circulars (UN ISSN 0429-9329) *396*
F A O Fisheries Reports (UN ISSN 0429-9337) *396*
F A O Fisheries Studies (UN ISSN 0071-7037) *396*
F A O Fisheries Technical Paper (UN ISSN 0429-9345) *396*
F A O Food Additive Control Series (UN ISSN 0071-7010) *404*
F A O Forestry and Forest Products Studies (UN ISSN 0532-0283) *408, 412*
F A O Forestry Development Papers (UN ISSN 0071-7029) *408*
F A O Legislative Series (UN ISSN 0071-7045) *14*
F A O Library List of Recent Accessions (UN ISSN 0532-0291) *24*
F A O Manuals in Fisheries Science (UN ISSN 0071-7061) *396*
F A O Nutrition Meeting for Europe. Report. (UN ISSN 0425-5089) *908*
F A O Nutrition Meetings Report Series (UN ISSN 0071-707X) *666*
F A O Nutrition Special Reports (UN ISSN 0532-0305) *908*
F A O Nutritional Study (UN ISSN 0071-7088) *666*
F A O Papers on Demand Analysis (UN ISSN 0428-9625) *908*
F A O Regional Conference for Africa (UN ISSN 0429-9353) *14*
F A O Regional Conference for Asia and the Far East. Report (UN ISSN 0427-8070) *14*
F A O Regional Conference for Europe. Report of the Conference (UN) *14*
F A O Regional Conference for Latin America. Report (UN) *14*
F A O Regional Conference for the Near East. Report (UN ISSN 0427-8089) *14*
F A O Terminology Bulletin (UN ISSN 0532-0313) *15*
F A O/W H O Expert Panel on Veterinary Education. Report of the Meeting (UN ISSN 0429-9388) *908*
F & O S. Executive and Ownership Report (Financial and Operating Statistics) (US) *882*
F & S Index Europe. Annual (US) *2, 155*
F & S Index International Annual (US) *2, 155*
F & S Index of Corporations and Industries. Annual *see* Predicasts F & S Index United States *163*
F B W-Information (Filmbewertungsstelle Wiesbaden) (GW ISSN 0427-8186) *649*
F D A Clinical Experience Abstracts (U. S. Food and Drug Administration) (US ISSN 0429-9442) *404, 684*
F D A Compliance Policy Guide (US) *404, 684*
F D A Drug Bulletin (US ISSN 0361-4334) *287*
F E & Z N. (UK ISSN 0014-5785) *627*

F F Communications (Folklore Fellows) (FI ISSN 0014-5815) *402*
F. F. M. Annuaire Officiel (Federation Francaise de Motocyclisme) (FR ISSN 0071-4186) *819*
F.H.A. Homes *see* U.S. Federal Housing Administration. F H A Homes *488*
F. H. I. Annual: Fresh and Industrialized Fruits and Vegetables *see* Anuario F.H.I. Argentina: Frutas y Hortalizas Industriarizadas y Frescas *33*
F I D Annual Report (International Federation for Documentation) (NE ISSN 0074-5820) *908*
F.I.D./C.R. Report Series (International Federation for Documentation) (NE ISSN 0074-5804) *271, 530*
F I D Directory (International Federation for Documentation) (NE ISSN 0379-3680) *530*
F I D/E T Occasional Papers (International Federation for Documentation, Committee on Education and Training) (NE) *908*
F I D/R I Meetings Reports (International Federation for Documentation, Committee on Research on the Theoretical Basis of Information) (UR) *530*
F I D /R I Series of Collected Articles *see* F I D/R I Series on Problems of Information Science *530*
F I D/R I Series on Problems of Information Science (International Federation for Documentation, Committee on Research on the Theoretical Basis of Information) (NE) *530*
F I D Yearbook *see* F I D Directory *530*
F I S Frettabref (Felag Islenzkra Storkaupmanna) (IC) *237*
F I V Meddelanden (Foereningen foer Inre Vattenvaegar) (SW ISSN 0015-5268) *878*
F I W - Schriftenreihe (Forschunginstitut fuer Wirtschaftsverfassung und Wettbewerb e.V.) (GW ISSN 0071-769X) *144*
F L C Newsletter (Federal Library Committee) (US ISSN 0014-5939) *530*
F M Compilation of the Statutes of Canada (CN ISSN 0380-2639) *512*
F. M. O. Q. Nouvelles (Federation des Medecins Omnipraticiens du Quebec) (CN) *595*
F M U Occasional Lectures (Financial Management Unit) (II ISSN 0085-1795) *741*
F.N.P.P. Annuaire *see* Federation Nationale de la Photographie Profesionelle. Annuaire *693*
F. O. S. Year Book & Annual Report (Fisheries Organization Society Ltd.) (UK) *396*
F P A P Biennial Report (Family Planning Association of Pakistan) (PK) *131*
F S U Faculty Publications *see* Florida State University. Publications of the Faculty *336*
Fabian Society. Annual Report (UK ISSN 0071-3570) *710*
Fabrics, Wallcoverings & Furniture (UK) *503*
Fabulous Mexico (US ISSN 0429-9639) *884*
Face the Nation (Annual) (US ISSN 0160-063X) *504*
Facets (US ISSN 0046-3051) *74*
Facetten (AU) *564*
Fachberichte Messen-Steuern-Regeln (US) *851*
Fachliteratur zum Buch- und Bibliothekswesen/International Bibliography of the Book Trade and Librarianship (GW ISSN 0071-3627) *530, 758*
Fachschwester - Fachpfleger (US) *614*
Fachwoerterbuecher und Lexika. Ein Internationales Verzeichnis/ International Bibliography of Dictionaries (GW) *90, 555*
Facilities Directory/Repertoire des Salles de Spectacle (CN) *859*

Facilities for Atmospheric Research *see* Atmospheric Technology *631*
Facility Manager's Buyer's Guide *see* Buyers' Guide for the Mass Entertainment Industry *828*
Faconnage de l'Imprime (FR) *733*
Fact Book. Alabama Institutions of Higher Education, Universities and Colleges (US ISSN 0095-0637) *336*
Fact Book and Report of the West Virginia State System of Higher Education (US ISSN 0093-8831) *336*
Fact Book for Academic Administration *see* Fact Book for Academic Administrators *336*
Fact Book for Academic Administrators(US) *336*
Fact Book on Higher Education in the South (US ISSN 0191-1643) *336*
Fact Book on Theological Education (US) *765*
Fact Paper on Southern Africa (US) *710*
Fact Sheet on the Netherlands (NE) *805*
Factbook: Chartered Banks of Canada. (CN) *173*
Factfile (US) *649*
Factory Outlet Shopping Guide for Eastern Pennsylvania *see* Factory Outlet Shopping Guide for Pennsylvania *280*
Factory Outlet Shopping Guide for New England (US) *279*
Factory Outlet Shopping Guide for New Jersey and Rockland County (US ISSN 0146-1125) *280*
Factory Outlet Shopping Guide for New York, Long Island, Westchester(US ISSN 0146-2865) *280*
Factory Outlet Shopping Guide for North and South Carolina (US ISSN 0146-2881) *280*
Factory Outlet Shopping Guide for Pennsylvania (US ISSN 0146-2903) *280*
Factory Outlet Shopping Guide for Washington D.C., Maryland, Delaware, Virginia (US ISSN 0146-2873) *280*
Facts About Alaska *see* Alaska Almanac: Facts About Alaska *883*
Facts About Australia (AT) *360*
Facts About Doing Business in Guam U.S.A. (GU) *185*
Facts About Haryana (II) *839*
Facts About Israel (IS ISSN 0071-3635) *474*
Facts About Maryland Public Education (US ISSN 0092-461X) *317*
Facts About Maryland Schools *see* Facts About Maryland Public Education *317*
Facts about New England Colleges, Universities and Institutes (US ISSN 0071-3643) *331*
Facts About New Super Markets (US ISSN 0081-9522) *407*
Facts about Nursing (US ISSN 0071-3651) *614*
Facts About States for the Dentist Seeking a Location (US ISSN 0517-1024) *609*
Facts and Figures in Israel *see* Facts About Israel *474*
Facts & Figures on Footwear *see* Footwear Manual *795*
Facts and Figures on Government Finance (US ISSN 0071-3678) *228*
Facts on File. Yearbook (US) *437, 710*
Factuelles (FR) *735*
Faculdade de Filosofia, Ciencias e Letras de Araraquara. Cadeira de Sociologia e Fundamentos Sociologicos da Educao. Boletim (BL) *813*
Faculte de Droit de Namur. Travaux (BE) *512*
Faculty Characteristics: Public Colleges and Universities in West Virginia (US) *336*
Faculty of Actuaries in Scotland. Transactions (UK ISSN 0071-3686) *498*
Faculty of Building. Register of Members. (UK) *136*

Fair Credit Reporting Manual (US) 173
Fairchild's Financial Manual of Retail Stores (US ISSN 0071-3716) 218
Fairchild's Textile & Apparel Financial Directory (US) 261, 855
Fairplay World Shipping Year Book (UK) 878
Faith and Order Papers (SZ ISSN 0512-2589) 765
Faits et les Decisions de la Communaute Economique Europeenne (BE) 185
Falkland Islands Journal (FK) 884
Familienverband Avenarius. Familienzeitschrift (GW ISSN 0014-7176) 417
Family Album (US ISSN 0094-5862) 564
Family Circle's Home Decorating Guide see Decorating Made Easy 502
Family Holiday Guide (UK ISSN 0071-3740) 885
Family Notes see Family Notes: a Journal of the Hueck Families 417
Family Notes: a Journal of the Hueck Families (US) 417
Family Planning Association of India. Report (II) 131
Family Planning Association of Kenya. Annual Report (KE) 131
Family Planning Association of Pakistan. Annual Report see F P A P Biennial Report 131
Family Planning Association of Pakistan Biennial Report see F P A P Biennial Report 131
Family Planning in Five Continents (UK ISSN 0538-9089) 131
Family Planning Programs in Oklahoma(US ISSN 0095-3121) 131
Family Planning Services; Annual Survey see U.S. Center for Disease Control. Family Planning Services: Annual Summary 133
Fanatic (UK) 556
FAO Irrigation and Drainage Papers (Food and Agriculture Organization of the United Nations) (UN) 896
Far East and Australasia (UK ISSN 0071-3791) 185, 421, 447
Far East Businessman's Directory see A.A.'s Far East Businessman's Directory 234
Far Eastern Economic Review. Yearbook see Asia Yearbook 142
Far East Series see U. S. Department of State. East Asian and Pacific Series 724
Faraday Symposia (UK ISSN 0301-5696) 254
Farm and Garden Equipment Guide (UK ISSN 0071-3880) 32
Farm and Garden Periodicals on Microfilm (US) 90, 416
Farm Business Review (UK ISSN 0306-719X) 28
Farm Business Statistics for South East England (UK) 24, 839
Farm Chemicals Handbook (US ISSN 0430-0750) 35
Farm Classification in England and Wales (UK ISSN 0071-3848) 28
Farm Credit Corporation. Annual Report (CN ISSN 0071-3864) 173
Farm Credit Corporation. Federal Farm Credit Statistics/Statistiques du Credit Agricole Federal (CN ISSN 0071-3872) 173
Farm Economist see Oxford Agrarian Studies 29
Farm Equipment Buyers Guide see Farm and Garden Equipment Guide 32
Farm Equipment Directory see Farm and Garden Equipment Guide 32
Farm Facts see Kansas. State Board of Agriculture. Annual Report with Farm Facts 17
Farm Holiday Guide (UK) 482
Farm Holidays in Ireland (IE) 885
Farm Implement Buyers Guide see Farm and Garden Equipment Guide 32
Farm Incomes in England and Wales (UK ISSN 0071-3910) 15

Farm Labor Report (Casper) see Wyoming. Employment Security Commission. Research and Analysis Section. Farm Labor Report 212
Farm Machinery Yearbook/Nogyo Kikai Nenkan (JA ISSN 0071-3937) 32
Farm Management Notes see Farming in the East Midlands 35
Farm Management Notes for Asia and the Far East (UN ISSN 0430-084X) 28
Farm Management Pocketbook (UK) 28
Farm Production and Practice see AgLink 11
Farm, Ranch and Country Vacations see Country Vacations U.S.A 884
Farm Real Estate Taxes see U. S. Department of Agriculture, Economics, Statistics, and Cooperatives Service. Farm Real Estate Taxes, Recent Trends and Developments 31
Farmer Forums (CN) 15
Farmers' Market (CN ISSN 0381-2421) 15
Farming in the East Midlands (UK ISSN 0071-3961) 35
Farming in the East Midlands. Financial Results (UK) 28
Farming Statistics (NZ ISSN 0110-084X) 24
Farnborough Air Show (Public Programme) (UK ISSN 0071-402X) 8
Fasciculi Historici (PL ISSN 0071-4038) 453
Fastener Standards (US ISSN 0071-4046) 379
Fasteners and Adhesives (SA) 672
Fastes Hippiques Belges (BE) 827
Fastfacts U.S.A. Hotel Motel Locator (US ISSN 0197-9477) 885
Fatal Accident Reporting System; Annual Report (US ISSN 0147-6939) 874
Fate of Drugs in the Organism see Fate of Drugs in the Organism; a Bibliographic Survey 686
Fate of Drugs in the Organism; a Bibliographic Survey (US ISSN 0098-2806) 686
Fathar (US) 564
Fathers of the Church (US ISSN 0014-8814) 774
Fault (US) 564
Fauna & Flora (SA ISSN 0046-3388) 114, 128, 275
Fauna Entomologica Scandinavica (DK) 103, 120
Fauna Fennica (FI ISSN 0071-4054) 128
Fauna Hungariae see Magyarorszag Allatvilaga 129
Fauna Japonica (JA ISSN 0428-061X) 128
Fauna of Russia and Adjacent Countries (IS) 128
Fauna of the U.S.S.R. (IS) 128
Fauna Slodkowodna Polski (PL ISSN 0071-4089) 128
Fawley Foundation Lectures (UK ISSN 0071-4097) 851
Faxon Librarians' Guide (US ISSN 0146-2660) 90
Faxon Librarians' Guide to Periodicals see Faxon Librarians' Guide 90
Fe de Un Pueblo (CL) 765
Fearnleys Review (NO) 878
Fearnly & Egers Chartering Co. Review see Fearnleys Review 878
Feature Editor's Directory (US) 504
Feature Films on 8mm and 16mm see Feature Films on 8mm, 16mm and Videotape 348
Feature Films on 8mm, 16mm and Videotape (US) 348
Federacao dos Trabalhadores na Agricultura do Estado do Parana. Relatorio (BL) 506
Federacion Argentina de Periodistas. Gaceta (AG) 758
Federacion Espanola de Natacion. Anuario. (SP) 829
Federacion Espanola Galguera. Anuario y Memoria Deportiva (SP ISSN 0071-4119) 819

Federacion Nacional de Cafeteros de Colombia. Informe de Labores de los Comites Departamentales de Cafeteros (CK) 35
Federacion Sudamericana de Asociaciones Cristianas de Jovenes. Noticias see Confederacion Latinoamericana de Asociaciones Cristianas de Jovenes. Carta 764
Federal Aid Reference Manual (US) 344
Federal Art Patronage Notes (US) 74, 741
Federal Aviation Administration. National Aviation System Policy Summary see U.S. Federal Aviation Administration. National Aviation System: Challenges of the Decade Ahead 869
Federal Aviation Regulations for Pilots (US ISSN 0533-0963) 8
Federal Budget: Focus and Perspectives.(US ISSN 0363-5422) 741
Federal Business Development Bank. Annual Report (CN) 173
Federal Civilian Work Force Statistics. Annual Report of Employment by Geographic Area (US) 741
Federal Civilian Work Force Statistics. Equal Employment Opportunity Statistics (US) 207
Federal Civilian Work Force Statistics. Occupations of Federal Blue-Collar Workers (US) 155
Federal Civilian Work Force Statistics. Occupations of Federal White-Collar Workers (US) 207
Federal Civilian Work Force Statistics. Pay Structure of the Federal Civil Service (US) 207
Federal Civilian Work Force Statistics. Work Years and Personnel Costs. Executive Branch, United States Government (US) 155
Federal Civilian Workforce Statistics. Minority Group Employment in the Federal Government see Federal Civilian Work Force Statistics. Equal Employment Opportunity Statistics 207
Federal Coal Management Report (US) 679
Federal Controls (US ISSN 0163-5514) 908
Federal Employees Almanac (US ISSN 0071-4127) 741
Federal Employment Directory (US) 667
Federal Estate and Gift Taxes Explained see Federal Estate and Gift Taxes Explained, Including Estate Planning 228
Federal Estate and Gift Taxes Explained, Including Estate Planning (US ISSN 0092-6531) 228
Federal Funding Guide for Elementary and Secondary Education (US ISSN 0095-3342) 228, 344
Federal Funding Guide for Local Governments (US ISSN 0362-4285) 228
Federal Government (US ISSN 0364-1678) 362
Federal Government & Cooperative Education (US) 336
Federal Government Legal Career Opportunities see Washington Want Ads 668
Federal Graduated Withholding Tax Tables (US ISSN 0071-4135) 228
Federal Grant-in-Aid Activity in Florida: a Summary Report (US ISSN 0361-1582) 228
Federal Home Loan Bank of Atlanta. Annual Report (US) 173
Federal Home Loan Bank of San Francisco. Annual Report. (US ISSN 0098-2830) 173
Federal Home Loan Bank of San Francisco. Proceedings of the Annual Conference (US) 173
Federal Home Loan Mortgage Corporation. Report (US ISSN 0094-7156) 173
Federal Income Taxation of Banks and Financial Institutions (Supplement) (US) 173, 228
Federal Index. Annual (US) 2, 748

FEDERATION DES 1359

Federal Law Reports (AT ISSN 0085-0462) 512
Federal Maritime Commission Service (US) 512, 878
Federal Opportunity Research see Federal Reporter 8
Federal Outlays in Summary see U. S. Community Services Administration. Federal Outlays in Summary 233
Federal Programs, State of Arizona (US ISSN 0363-7166) 228
Federal Reclamation Projects: Water and Land Resource Accomplishments see U.S. Water and Power Resources Service. Annual Report 278
Federal Register: What It Is and How to Use It see U.S. Office of the Federal Register. Federal Register: What It Is and How to Use It 519
Federal Reporter (US ISSN 0198-6503) 8, 741
Federal Reserve Bank of Atlanta. Research Paper Series (US) 186
Federal Reserve Bank of Atlanta. Working Paper Series (US) 144
Federal Reserve Bank of Minneapolis. Annual Report (US ISSN 0361-8013) 173
Federal Reserve Bank of Minneapolis. Annual Statistical Review (US) 908
Federal Savings and Loan Insurance Corporation. List of Member Institutions (US ISSN 0428-1365) 498
Federal-State Market News Service. California Egg and Poultry Summary see Production and Marketing: California Eggs, Chicken and Turkeys 41
Federal Tax Return Manual (US ISSN 0071-4143) 228
Federally Coordinated Program of Highway Research and Development see U.S. Federal Highway Administration. Federally Coordinated Program of Highway Research and Development 876
Federalni Ministerstvo Financi. Vestnik see Financni Zpravodaj 173
Federated Taxpayer's Association of Australia. Annual Taxation Summary see Australian Taxpayer's Association. Annual Taxation Summary 227
Federatie van Bedrijfsverenigingen. Jaarverslag (NE ISSN 0071-4151) 498
Federation Canadienne des Archers. Livret des Reglements see Federation of Canadian Archers. Rules Book 820
Federation d'Associations de Techniciens des Industries des Peintures, Vernis, Emaux et Encres d'Imprimerie de l'Europe Continentale. Congress Proceedings see Congress F A T I P E C 372
Federation d'Associations de Techniciens des Industries des Peintures, Vernis, Emaux et Encres d'Imprimerie de l'Europe Continentale Congress F A T I P E C see Congress F A T I P E C 372
Federation d'Associations de Techniciens des Industries des Peintures, Vernis, Emaux et Encres d'Imprimerie de l'Europe Continentale. Annuaire Officiel. Official Yearbook. Amtliches Jahrbuch (FR ISSN 0071-416X) 673
Federation des Associations de Parents et Instituteurs Langues Francaise de l'Ontario. Liaison (CN ISSN 0705-1026) 543
Federation des Debitants de Tabac de l'Ile-de-France. Annuaire Officiel (FR) 861
Federation des Entrepreneurs de Nettoyage de France. Annuaire Officiel (FR) 261
Federation des Entreprises de Belgique. Rapport Annuel (BE) 222

Federation des Entreprises de l'Industrie des Fabrications Metalliques, Mecaniques, Electriques et de la Transformation des Matieres Plastiques. Centre de Recherches Scientifiques et Techniques. Section: Fonderie (FD). Research Reports (BE) *628*

Federation des Industries Belges. Rapport Annuel *see* Federation des Entreprises de Belgique. Rapport Annuel *222*

Federation des Industries Chimiques de Belgique. Annuaire (BE ISSN 0425-9076) *372*

Federation des Industries Chimiques de Belgique. Rapport (BE ISSN 0085-0489) *372*

Federation des Medecins Omnipraticiens du Quebec Nouvelles *see* F. M. O. Q. Nouvelles *595*

Federation Francaise de Motocyclisme Annuaire Officiel *see* F. F. M. Annuaire Officiel *819*

Federation Francaise de Natation. Annuaire (FR ISSN 0071-4194) *827*

Federation Francaise de Sports pour Handicaps Physiques. Informations *see* Federation Francaise Handisport. Informations *820*

Federation Francaise des Sports Equestres. Annuaire Officiel (FR ISSN 0071-4232) *819*

Federation Francaise et Europeenne du Commerce, de l'Industrie et de l'Epargne. Revue (FR ISSN 0071-4240) *144, 195*

Federation Francaise Handisport. Informations (FR) *805, 820*

Federation Horlogere Suisse. Annual Report (SZ ISSN 0071-4259) *503*

Federation Internationale de Laiterie. Bulletin Annuel *see* International Dairy Federation. Annual Bulletin *41*

Federation Internationale de Laiterie. Memento Annuel *see* International Dairy Federation. Annual Memento *41*

Federation Internationale de Laiterie. Norme Internationale *see* International Dairy Federation. International Standard *41*

Federation Internationale de Rugby Amateur. Annuaire (FR ISSN 0071-4267) *824*

Federation Internationale des Syndicats Chretiens d'Ouvriers Agricoles. Travailleur de la Terre (BE ISSN 0430-2419) *908*

Federation Internationale Motocycliste. Annuaire (SZ ISSN 0071-4283) *826*

Federation Interprofessionnelle de la Congelation Ultra-Rapide. Rapport Statistique Annuel (FR) *404*

Federation Nationale de l'Industrie de la Chaussure de France. Annuaire (FR ISSN 0071-4291) *795*

Federation Nationale de la Photographie Profesionelle. Annuaire(BE) *693*

Federation Nationale des Agences de Presse. Annuaire (FR ISSN 0071-4305) *504*

Federation Nationale des Chambres de Commerce, d'Industrie et d'Agriculture de la Republique du Zaire. Circulaire d'Information *see* Association Nationale des Entreprises Zairoises. Circulaire d'Information *178*

Federation Nationale des Conseils Juridiques et Fiscaux. Cahiers (FR ISSN 0071-4348) *228*

Federation Nationale des Cooperatives de Consommation Annuaire de la Cooperation F.N.C.C. *see* Annuaire de la Cooperation F.N.C.C *180*

Federation Nationale des Societes d'Economie Mixte de Construction, d'Amenagement et de Renovation. Annuaire (FR ISSN 0081-1262) *484*

Federation of Canadian Archers. Rules Book (CN ISSN 0226-773X) *820*

Federation of Canadian Municipalities. Annual Conference Proceedings (CN ISSN 0708-9511) *741*

Federation of Children's Book Groups. Yearbook *see* About Books for Children *257*

Federation of Egyptian Industries. Yearbook *see* Ittihad al-Sinaat al-Misriyah. Yearbook *238*

Federation of European Biochemical Societies. (Proceedings of Meeting) (US ISSN 0071-4402) *111*

Federation of Finnish Industries. List of Members *see* Suomen Teollisuusliitto. Jasenluettelo *242*

Federation of Genealogical Societies. Monograph (US) *417*

Federation of Migros Cooperatives. Abridged Report (SZ ISSN 0071-4410) *180*

Federation of Migros Cooperatives. Annual Report *see* Federation of Migros Cooperatives. Abridged Report *180*

Federation of Pakistan Chambers of Commerce and Industry. Directory of Exporters (PK) *237*

Federation of Pakistan Chambers of Commerce Industry. Brief Report of Activities (PK ISSN 0071-4429) *179*

Federation of Societies for Coatings Technology. Yearbook and Annual Membership Directory (US) *673*

Federation of Societies for Paint Technology. Yearbook *see* Federation of Societies for Coatings Technology. Yearbook and Annual Membership Directory *673*

Federation of Swedish Co-Operative Banks. Annual Report (SW) *173, 180*

Fed's Fiscale Brochures (NE) *228*

Feed Additive Compendium (US ISSN 0071-450X) *42*

Feed Bag Red Book *see* Feed Industry Red Book *42*

Feed Industry Red Book (US ISSN 0071-4518) *42, 237*

Feinkost-Revue (GW ISSN 0014-9691) *404*

Felag Islenzkra Storkaupmanna Frettabref *see* F I S Frettabref *237*

Felix Ravenna; Rivista di Antichita Ravennati, Cristiane e Bizantine (IT ISSN 0085-0500) *74*

Fellowship of Australian Composers. Newsletter *see* Australian Composer *657*

Fellowship Yearbook *see* Evangelical Baptist Churches in Canada. Fellowship Yearbook *772*

Felsmechanik und Ingenieurgeologie. Rock Mechanics and Engineering Geology. Supplement *see* Rock Mechanics/Felsmechanik/Mechanique des Roches. Supplement *646*

Felt and Damaging Earthquakes (UK) *304*

Female Studies (US) *900*

Feminist Press. News/Notes (US ISSN 0145-8299) *900*

Femmes en Litterature (FR) *564, 900*

Fencing Rules for Competitions (US) *820*

Fenix (PE ISSN 0015-0002) *530*

Fenno-Ugrica (GW ISSN 0341-311X) *543*

Fer-Blanc en France et dans le Monde (FR ISSN 0085-0519) *628*

Ferber's Freshwater Fisherman *see* Freshwater Fisherman *829*

Ferguson-Florissant Schools (US ISSN 0015-0037) *317*

Ferguson's Ceylon Directory (CE) *237*

Fern Gazette (UK ISSN 0308-0838) *114*

Ferro-Alloys Survey (UK ISSN 0141-4690) *628*

Ferroelectricity and Related Phenomena(US) *354*

Der Fertighaus-Katalog (GW ISSN 0071-4585) *136*

Fertigung und Betrieb (US) *222*

Fertiliser Association of India. Fertiliser Statistics (II ISSN 0430-327X) *24, 839*

Fertilizer Industry Round Table. Proceedings (US) *15*

Fertilizer Industry Series (UN ISSN 0071-4615) *35*

Fertilizer Science and Technology Series (US ISSN 0071-4623) *35*

Fertilizer Trends (US ISSN 0071-4631) *35*

Fertilizers: an Annual Review of World Production, Consumption and Trade *see* Annual Fertilizer Review *33*

Festival Film Guide *see* American Film Festival Guide *648*

Festivals Sourcebook (US) *885*

Festschrift Series (US) *659*

Fettesian (UK ISSN 0046-3701) *263*

Feuerwehr-Jahrbuch (GW ISSN 0071-4674) *394*

Fiber Science Series (US ISSN 0071-4682) *855*

Fiches Analytiques de la Presse Technique Francaise (FR ISSN 0071-4704) *195*

Fiches E O-Formation Permanente (FR) *215*

Fiches Techniques R.T.A. (FR) *871*

Fiches Techniques R.T.C. (FR) *871*

Fiches Techniques R.T.D. (FR) *871*

Fiches Techniques R.T.D. Applications Agricoles (FR) *32*

Fiches Typologiques Africaines (AE ISSN 0071-4712) *49*

Fichiers Industriels du Sud Ouest (FR) *237*

Fiction Catalog (US ISSN 0160-4880) *578*

Field & Stream Bass Fishing Annual (US ISSN 0163-5468) *829*

Field and Stream Deer Hunting Annual(US) *829*

Field & Stream Fishing Annual (US ISSN 0362-6385) *829*

Field & Stream Hunting Annual (US ISSN 0361-3011) *829*

Field Hockey-Lacrosse Guide *see* N A G W S Guide. Field Hockey *824*

Field Studies (UK ISSN 0428-304X) *386*

Fieldiana: Anthropology (US ISSN 0071-4739) *49*

Fieldiana: Geology (US ISSN 0096-2651) *293*

Fielding's Caribbean (US) *885*

Fielding's Caribbean, Including Cuba *see* Fielding's Caribbean *885*

Fielding's Europe (US ISSN 0192-5326) *885*

Fielding's Favorites: Hotels & Inns, Europe (US ISSN 0191-0329) *885*

Fielding's Low-Cost Europe (US ISSN 0095-6406) *885*

Fielding's Selected Favorites: Hotels and Inns, Europe *see* Fielding's Favorites: Hotels & Inns, Europe *885*

Fielding's Selective Shopping Guide to Europe (US ISSN 0071-478X) *885*

Fielding's Super Economy Europe *see* Fielding's Low-Cost Europe *885*

Fielding's Travel Guide to Europe *see* Fielding's Europe *885*

Fifth Sun (US) *564*

Figura. Nova Series (SW ISSN 0071-481X) *74, 453*

Figures de Wallonie (BE ISSN 0069-5386) *97, 453*

Fiji. Bureau of Statistics. Annual Statistical Abstract (FJ ISSN 0071-4828) *839*

Fiji. Bureau of Statistics. Fiji Household Income and Expenditure Survey (FJ) *155*

Fiji. Bureau of Statistics. Statistical News (FJ) *839*

Fiji. Central Monetary Authority. Annual Report (FJ) *229*

Fiji. Department of Agriculture. Annual Report *see* Fiji. Ministry of Agriculture & Fisheries. Annual Report *15*

Fiji. Department of Agriculture. Annual Research Report *see* Fiji. Ministry of Agriculture & Fisheries. Annual Research Report *15*

Fiji. Department of Agriculture. Bulletin *see* Fiji. Ministry of Agriculture & Fisheries. Bulletin *15*

Fiji. Housing Authority. Report (FJ) *484*

Fiji. Mineral Resources Division. Memoir (FJ) *293*

Fiji. Ministry of Agriculture & Fisheries. Annual Report (FJ ISSN 0071-4844) *15*

Fiji. Ministry of Agriculture & Fisheries. Annual Research Report (FJ) *15*

Fiji. Ministry of Agriculture & Fisheries. Bulletin (FJ) *15*

Fiji. Ministry of Education. Report (FJ) *317*

Fiji. Ministry of Education, Youth and Sport. Report *see* Fiji. Ministry of Education. Report *317*

Fiji. Office of the Ombudsman. Annual Report of the Ombudsman (FJ) *512*

Fiji. Printing Department Report (FJ) *504*

Fiji Information (FJ) *741*

Fiji Library Directory (FJ) *530*

Fiji Sugar Year Book (FJ) *35, 404*

Fiji Timbers and Their Uses (FJ) *412*

Filipiniana Book Guild. Publications (US ISSN 0071-4852) *564*

Film and TV Festival Directory (US ISSN 0085-0535) *908*

Film & TV Graphics (SZ) *649*

Film Angels (US) *203, 649*

Film Canadiana: The Canadian Film Institute Yearbook of Canadian Cinema (CN ISSN 0015-1173) *649*

Film Catalog. Florida State University *see* Florida State University. Instructional Support Center. Film *651*

Film de Recherche *see* Research Film *913*

Film-Echo Filmwoche. Verleih-Katalog (GW ISSN 0071-4879) *649*

Film Edmonton (CN ISSN 0704-9536) *649*

Film-English/Humanities Association. Journal (US ISSN 0071-4887) *348*

Film Music Buyer's Guide (US) *649, 659*

Film News Omnibus (US) *649*

Film Reader (US ISSN 0361-722X) *649*

Film Review (UK ISSN 0071-4917) *649*

Filmaarsboken/Swedish Film Annual (SW ISSN 0071-4925) *649*

Filmbewertungsstelle Wiesbaden Information *see* F B W-Information *649*

Filmliste *see* Spielfilmliste *651*

Filmmakers and Film Production Services of Israel (IS) *649*

Filmmaking in Israel (IS) *650*

Filmo-Bibliografischer Jahresbericht (GE ISSN 0015-1750) *90*

Filmoteca Ultramarina Portuguesa. Boletim (PO ISSN 0430-4497) *432, 721*

Films: the Visualization of Anthropology (US) *56, 651*

Filmstatistisches Taschenbuch (GW ISSN 0071-4941) *650*

Filmvidenskabeligt Arbog (DK) *650*

Filologia (AG ISSN 0071-495X) *543*

Filologia Angielska (PL) *543*

Filologia Baltycka/Baltic Philology (PL) *543, 564*

Filologia e Critica (IT ISSN 0071-4968) *543*

Filologia Klasyczna (PL) *259, 543*

Filologos Colombianos (CK ISSN 0071-4976) *544*

Filosofia della Religione. Testi e Studi (IT) *765*

Filosofskie Nauki (UR) *688*

Filozofia-Logika (PL) *688*

Filozofiai Irok Tara (HU ISSN 0071-4984) *688*

Filozofiai Tanulmanyok (HU ISSN 0071-4992) *688*

Filter: a Paper for Science Teachers (AT ISSN 0310-6020) *348*

Filtration Engineering Catalog (US) *372*

Finafrica Bulletin (IT) *199*

Finances Publiques en Suisse *see* Offentliche Finanzen der Schweiz *231*

Financial Accounting Problems with Detailed Solutions (CN ISSN 0226-6822) *167*

Financial Aid News (US ISSN 0430-4748) *317*

Financial Aids to Illinois Students (US ISSN 0085-0543) *336*

Financial Analysis of a Group of Petroleum Companies (US) *203*
Financial Analysis of the For-Hire Tank Truck Industry (US) *882*
Financial Analysis of the Motor Carrier Industry (US ISSN 0099-2445) *882*
Financial Analysts Research Foundation. Occasional Paper (US) *173*
Financial and Monetary Studies (NE) *173*
Financial and Operating Results of Department and Specialty Stores (US ISSN 0547-8804) *181*
Financial and Operating Statistics Executive and Ownership Report *see* F & O S. Executive and Ownership Report *882*
Financial Assistance for Library Education (US ISSN 0569-6275) *336,* 530
Financial Corporate Bond Transfer Service (US ISSN 0360-5825) *203*
Financial Industry Number Standard Directory (US ISSN 0362-1405) *173*
Financial Post Canadian Markets (CN) *218*
Financial Post Directory of Directors (CN ISSN 0071-5042) *215*
Financial Post Report on Conventions, Conferences and Business Meetings *see* Meetings, Conferences & Conventions: a Financial Post Guide *146*
Financial Post Survey of Energy Resources *see* Financial Post Survey of Mines and Energy Resources *643*
Financial Post Survey of Industrials (CN ISSN 0071-5050) *203*
Financial Post Survey of Markets *see* Financial Post Canadian Markets *218*
Financial Post Survey of Mines *see* Financial Post Survey of Mines and Energy Resources *643*
Financial Post Survey of Mines and Energy Resources (CN ISSN 0227-1656) *362, 643*
Financial Post Survey of Predecessor and Defunct Companies (CN) *144*
Financial Report - Carnegie Endowment for International Peace *see* Carnegie Endowment for International Peace. Financial Report *720*
Financial Report of the Division of Corrections to the Department of Health and Rehabilitative Services *see* Florida. Division of Corrections. Financial Report *805*
Financial Reporting in Canada (CN ISSN 0071-5115) *167*
Financial Reporting Trends: Fire and Casualty Insurance *see* Financial Reporting Trends: Property/Casualty Insurance *498*
Financial Reporting Trends: Life Insurance (US ISSN 0148-8880) *167, 498*
Financial Reporting Trends: Property/Casualty Insurance (US) *167, 498*
Financial Reporting Trends: Savings and Loan (US ISSN 0160-8827) *167, 173*
Financial Review (US ISSN 0066-5363) *173*
Financial Statistics of Education in Cyprus (CY ISSN 0301-7559) *327*
Financial Stock Guide Service. Directory of Active Stocks (US ISSN 0364-0752) *203*
Financial Stock Guide Service. Directory of Obsolete Securities (US ISSN 0085-0551) *203*
Financial Studies of the Small Business (US ISSN 0363-8987) *173*
Financial Times Mining International Year Book (UK ISSN 0141-3244) *643*
Financial Times Oil and Gas International Year Book (UK ISSN 0141-3228) *679*
Financial Times Who's Who in World Oil and Gas(UK ISSN 0141-3236) *679*
Financial Times World Hotel Directory (UK ISSN 0308-8464) *482, 885*

Financial Times World Insurance Year Book (UK ISSN 0309-751X) *498*
Financial Times World Shipping Yearbook (UK) *878*
Financing Higher Education (US) *336*
Financni Zpravodaj (CS ISSN 0322-9653) *173*
Finanzwissenschaftliche Schriften (SZ) *191*
Findex (US) *218*
Finding Aids to the Microfilmed Manuscript Collection of the Genealogical Society of Utah (US) 90, *418,* 539
Fine Arts Work Center in Provincetown. Newsletter (US) *74*
Finger Lakes Travel Guide *see* I Love New York: The Finger Lakes Travel Guide *877*
Finishing Diary (UK) *673*
Finishing Handbook and Directory (UK ISSN 0071-5182) *628*
Finland (FI ISSN 0356-827X) *453,* 710
Finland. Central Statistical Office. Banks *see* Finland. Tilastokeskus. Pankit *156*
Finland. Central Statistical Office. Causes of Death in Finland *see* Finland. Tilastokeskus. Kuolemansyyt *155*
Finland. Central Statistical Office. Communal Finances *see* Finland. Tilastokeskus. Kuntien Finanssitilasto *155*
Finland. Central Statistical Office. Function of Courts *see* Finland. Tilastokeskus. Tuomioistuinten Toiminta *285*
Finland. Central Statistical Office. General Education *see* Finland. Tilastokeskus. Yleissivistavat Oppilaitokset *327*
Finland. Central Statistical Office. Handbooks *see* Finland. Tilastokeskus. Kasikirjoja *839*
Finland. Central Statistical Office. Higher Education *see* Finland. Tilastokeskus. Korkeakoulut *327*
Finland. Central Statistical Office. House Construction Statistics *see* Finland. Tilastokeskus. Talonrakennustilasto *682*
Finland. Central Statistical Office. Industrial Statistics *see* Finland. Tilastokeskus. Teollisuustilasto *156*
Finland. Central Statistical Office. Life Tables *see* Finland. Tilastokeskus. Kuolleisuus- Ja Eloonjaamistauluja *731*
Finland. Central Statistical Office. Municipal Elections *see* Finland. Tilastokeskus. Kunnallisvaalit *748*
Finland. Central Statistical Office. Parliamentary Elections *see* Finland. Tilastokeskus. Kansanedustajain Vaalit *717*
Finland. Central Statistical Office. Population *see* Finland. Tilastokeskus. Vaesto *731*
Finland. Central Statistical Office. Population Census *see* Finland. Tilastokeskus. Vaestolaskenta *731*
Finland. Central Statistical Office. Production of Dwellings *see* Finland. Tilastokeskus. Asuntotuotanto *489*
Finland. Central Statistical Office. Research Activity *see* Finland. Tilastokeskus. Tutkimustoiminta *794*
Finland. Central Statistical Office. Statistical Surveys *see* Finland. Tilastokeskus. Tilastollisia Tiedonantoja *839*
Finland. Central Statistical Office. Statistics of Income and Property *see* Finland. Tilastokeskus. Tulo- Ja Omaisuustilasto *156*
Finland. Central Statistical Office. Studies *see* Finland. Tilastokeskus. Tutkimuksia *156*
Finland. Central Statistical Office. Yearbook of Transport Statistics *see* Finland. Tilastokeskus. Liikennetilastollinen Vuosikirja *865*
Finland. Folkpensionsanstalt. Beraettelse *see* Finland Kansanelakelaitos. Toiminta Kertomus *499*

Finland. Folkpensionsanstalt. Statistik Aarsbok *see* Finland. Kansanelakelaitos. Tilastollinen Vuosikirja *501*
Finland. Ilmatieteen Laitos. Ilmasahkohavaintoja/Finnish Meteorological Institute. Observations of Atmospheric Electricity (FI ISSN 0358-2671) *632*
Finland. Ilmatieteen Laitos. Tiedonantoja (FI ISSN 0071-5204) *632*
Finland. Ilmatieteen Laitos. Tutkimusseloste (FI ISSN 0355-1717) *632*
Finland. Kansanelakelaitos. Julkaisuja. Sarja A (FI ISSN 0430-5205) *499*
Finland. Kansanelakelaitos. Julkaisuja. Sarja AL (FI ISSN 0355-4813) *595*
Finland. Kansanelakelaitos. Julkaisuja. Sarja E (FI ISSN 0355-4848) *498, 595*
Finland. Kansanelakelaitos. Julkaisuja. Sarja EL (FI ISSN 0355-4856) *595,* 666
Finland. Kansanelakelaitos. Julkaisuja. Sarja M (FI ISSN 0355-4821) *499, 595*
Finland. Kansanelakelaitos. Julkaisuja. Sarja ML (FI ISSN 0355-483X) *595,* 666
Finland. Kansanelakelaitos. Tilastollinen Vuosikirja/Finland. Folkpensionsanstalt. Statistik Aarsbok/Finlan. Social Insurance Institution. Statistical Yearbook (FI ISSN 0071-5247) *501*
Finland. Kansantalousosasto. Kansantalouden Kehitysarvio. Summary: National Budget for Finland (FI ISSN 0071-5255) *229*
Finland. Kansantalousosasto. Taloudellinen Katsaus. Economic Survey (FI ISSN 0071-5271) *186*
Finland. Laakintohallitus. Laakarit, Hammaslaakarit/Lakare, Tandlaekare(FI) *595,* 609
Finland. Laakintohallitus. Laakarit, Hammaslaakarit, Sairaalat *see* Finland. Laakintohallitus. Laakarit, Hammaslaakarit/Lakare, Tandlaekare *595*
Finland. Merentutkimuslaitos. Julkaisu *see* Finnish Marine Research *310*
Finland. Ministry of Labour. Labour Reports *see* Finland. Tyoviomaministerio. Tyovoimakatsaus *207*
Finland. Ministry of Social Affairs and Health. Special Social Studies *see* Finland. Sosiaali- ja Terveysministerio. Sosiaalisia Erikoistutkimuksia *805*
Finland. National Board of Social Welfare. Yearbook of Social Welfare Statistics *see* Finland. Sosiaalihallitus. Sosiaalihuoltotilaston Vuosikirja *805*
Finland. Posti- ja Lennatinlaitos. Kotimaisten Sanomalehtien Hinnasto. Inhemsk Tidningstaxa (FI ISSN 0071-5298) *90*
Finland. Posti-ja Lennatinlaitos. Ulkomaisten Sanomalehtien Hinnasto. Utlandsk Tidningstaxa (FI ISSN 0071-5301) *504*
Finland. Rakennushallitus. Tiedotuksia *see* Finland. Rakennushallitus. Tutkimus-ja Kehitystoiminnan. Tiedote *136*
Finland. Rakennushallitus. Tutkimus-ja Kehitystoiminnan. Tiedote (FI ISSN 0071-531X) *136*
Finland. Social Insurance Institution. Annual Report *see* Finland Kansanelakaitos. Toiminta Kertomus *499*
Finland. Social Insurance Institution. Statistical Yearbook *see* Finland. Kansanelakelaitos. Tilastollinen Vuosikirja *501*
Finland. Socialstyrelsen. Socialvaardsstatistisk Aarsbok *see* Finland. Sosiaalihallitus. Sosiaalihuoltotilaston Vuosikirja *805*

FINLAND. TILASTOKESKUS. 1361

Finland. Sosiaali- ja Terveysministerio. Sosiaalisia Erikoistutkimuksia/Finland. Ministry of Social Affairs and Health. Special Social Studies (FI ISSN 0071-5336) *805*
Finland. Sosiaalihallitus. Sosiaalihuoltotilaston Vuosikirja/Finland. National Board of Social Welfare. Yearbook of Social Welfare Statistics/Finland. Socialstyrelsen. Socialvaardsstatistisk Aarsbok (FI ISSN 0071-5328) *805*
Finland. Statistikcentralen. Allmaenbildande Laeroanstalter *see* Finland. Tilastokeskus. Yleissivistavat Oppilaitokset *327*
Finland. Statistikcentralen. Bankerna *see* Finland. Tilastokeskus. Pankit *156*
Finland. Statistikcentralen. Befolkning *see* Finland. Tilastokeskus. Vaeso *731*
Finland. Statistikcentralen. Bostadsproduktionen *see* Finland. Tilastokeskus. Asuntotuotanto *489*
Finland. Statistikcentralen. Doedlighets- och Livslaengdstabeller *see* Finland. Tilastokeskus. Kuolleisuus- Ja Eloonjaamistauluja *731*
Finland. Statistikcentralen. Doedsorsaker *see* Finland. Tilastokeskus. Kuolemansyyt *155*
Finland. Statistikcentralen. Domstolarnas Verksamhet *see* Finland. Tilastokeskus. Tuomioistuinten Toiminta *285*
Finland. Statistikcentralen. Folkraekningen *see* Finland. Tilastokeskus. Vaestolaskenta *731*
Finland. Statistikcentralen. Forskningsverksamheten *see* Finland. Tilastokeskus. Tutkimustoiminta *794*
Finland. Statistikcentralen. Handboecker *see* Finland. Tilastokeskus. Kasikirjoja *839*
Finland. Statistikcentralen. Hoegskolora *see* Finland. Tilastokeskus. Korkeakoulut *327*
Finland. Statistikcentralen. Husbyggnadsstatistik *see* Finland. Tilastokeskus. Talonrakennustilasto *682*
Finland. Statistikcentralen. Inkomst- och Foermoegenhetstatistik *see* Finland. Tilastokeskus. Tulo- Ja Omaisuustilasto *156*
Finland. Statistikcentralen. Kommunal Finansstatistik *see* Finland. Tilastokeskus. Kuntien Finanssitilasto *155*
Finland. Statistikcentralen. Kommunalvalen *see* Finland. Tilastokeskus. Kunnallisvaalit *748*
Finland. Statistikcentralen. Ridsdagsmannavalen *see* Finland. Tilastokeskus. Kansanedustajain Vaalit *717*
Finland. Statistikcentralen. Samfaerdselstatistiskaarsbok *see* Finland. Tilastokeskus. Liikennetilastollinen Vuosikirja *865*
Finland. Statistikcentralen. Statistiska Meddelanden *see* Finland. Tilastokeskus. Tilastollisia Tiedonantoja *839*
Finland. Statistikcentralen. Undersoekningar *see* Finland. Tilastokeskus. Tutkimuksia *156*
Finland. Statistiska Centralbyraan *see* Finland. Tilastokeskus. Teollisuustilasto *156*
Finland. Tilastokeskus. Asuntotuotanto/Finland. Statistikcentralen. Bostadsproduktionen/Finland. Central Statistical Office. Production of Dwellings (FI ISSN 0355-2152) *489,* 682
Finland. Tilastokeskus. Kansanedustajain Vaalit/Finland. Statistikcentralen. Ridsdagsmannavalen/Finland. Central Statistical Office. Parliamentary Elections (FI ISSN 0355-2209) *717*
Finland. Tilastokeskus. Kansanopetus *see* Finland. Tilastokeskus. Yleissivistavat Oppilaitokset *327*

Finland. Tilastokeskus. Kasikirjoja/ Finland. Statistikcentralen. Handboecker/Finland. Central Statistical Office. Handbooks (FI ISSN 0355-2063) *839*
Finland. Tilastokeskus. Korkeakoulut/ Finland. Statistikcentralen. Hoegskolora/Finland. Central Statistical Office. Higher Education (FI ISSN 0355-2225) *327*
Finland. Tilastokeskus. Kunnallisvaalit/ Finland. Statistikcentralen. Kommunalvalen/Finland. Central Statistical Office. Municipal Elections(FI ISSN 0355-2217) *748*
Finland. Tilastokeskus. Kuntien Finanssitilasto/Finland. Statistikcentralen. Kommunal Finansstatistik/Finland. Central Statistical Office. Communal Finances (FI ISSN 0430-5566) *155*
Finland. Tilastokeskus. Kuolemansyyt/ Finland. Statistikcentralen. Doedsorsaker/Finland. Central Statistical Office. Causes of Death in Finland (FI ISSN 0355-2144) *155*
Finland. Tilastokeskus. Kuolleisuus- Ja Eloonjaamistauluja/Finland. Statistikcentralen. Doedlighets- och Livslaengdstabeller/Finland. Central Statistical Office. Life Tables (FI ISSN 0355-2128) *731*
Finland. Tilastokeskus. Liikennetilastollinen Vuosikirja/ Finland. Statistikcentralen. Samfaerdselstatistiskaarsbok/Finland. Central Statistical Office. Yearbook of Transport Statistics (FI ISSN 0430-5272) *865*
Finland. Tilastokeskus. Liikepankit Ja Kiinnitys Luottolaitokset *see* Finland. Tilastokeskus. Pankit *156*
Finland. Tilastokeskus. Oppikoulut *see* Finland. Tilastokeskus. Yleissivistavat Oppilaitokset *327*
Finland. Tilastokeskus. Osuuspankkitilasto *see* Finland. Tilastokeskus. Pankit *156*
Finland. Tilastokeskus. Pankit/Finland. Statistikcentralen. Bankerna/Finland. Central Statistical Office. Banks (FI ISSN 0355-2454) *156*
Finland. Tilastokeskus. Saastopankkitilasto *see* Finland. Tilastokeskus. Pankit *156*
Finland. Tilastokeskus. Talonrakennustilasto/Finland. Statistikcentralen. Husbyggnadsstatistik/Finland. Central Statistical Office. House Construction Statistics (FI ISSN 0430-5604) *682*
Finland. Tilastokeskus. Teollisuustilasto/Finland. Statistiska Centralbyraan/Finland. Central Statistical Office. Industrial Statistics (FI ISSN 0071-5344) *156*
Finland. Tilastokeskus. Tilastollisia Tiedonantoja/Finland. Statistikcentralen. Statistiska Meddelanden/Finland. Central Statistical Office. Statistical Surveys (FI ISSN 0355-208X) *839*
Finland. Tilastokeskus. Tulo- Ja Omaisuustilasto/Finland. Statistikcentralen. Inkomst- och Foermoegenhetstatistik/Finland. Central Statistical Office. Statistics of Income and Property (FI ISSN 0355-211X) *156*
Finland. Tilastokeskus. Tuomioistuinten Toiminta/Finland. Statistikcentralen. Domstolarnas Verksamhet/Finland. Central Statistical Office. Function of Courts (FI ISSN 0355-2187) *285*
Finland. Tilastokeskus. Tutkimuksia/ Finland. Statistikcentralen. Undersoekningar/Finland. Central Statistical Office. Studies (FI ISSN 0355-2071) *156*
Finland. Tilastokeskus. Tutkimustoiminta/Finland. Statistikcentralen. Forskningsverksamheten/Finland. Central Statistical Office. Research Activity (FI ISSN 0355-2233) *794*

Finland. Tilastokeskus. Vaesto/Finland. Statistikcentralen. Befolkning/ Finland. Central Statistical Office. Population (FI) *731*
Finland. Tilastokeskus. Vaestolaskenta/ Finland. Statistikcentralen. Folkraekningen/Finland. Central Statistical Office. Population Census (FI ISSN 0355-2136) *731*
Finland. Tilastokeskus. Vaestonmuutokset *see* Finland. Tilastokeskus. Vaesto *731*
Finland. Tilastokeskus. Yleissivistavat Oppilaitokset/Finland. Statistikcentralen. Allmaenbildande Laeroanstalter/Finland. Central Statistical Office. General Education (FI ISSN 0355-2446) *327*
Finland. Tyoviomaministerio. Tyovoimakatsaus/Finland. Ministry of Labour. Labour Reports (FI ISSN 0430-5280) *207*
Finland. Valtakunnansuunnittelutoimisto. Julkaisuja. Sarja A *see* Finland. Valtioneuvoston Kanslian. Julkaisuja *222*
Finland. Valtioneuvoston Kanslian. Julkaisuja (FI ISSN 0355-8878) *222*
Finland. Vestientutkimuslaitos. Julkasuja/Finland. Water Research Institute. Publications (FI ISSN 0355-0982) *896*
Finland. Water Research Institute. Publications *see* Finland. Vestientutkimuslaitos. Julkasuja *896*
Finland Kansanelakelaitos. Toiminta Kertomus (FI ISSN 0355-5003) *499*
Finlands Bank. Aarsbok *see* Bank of Finland. Yearbook *170*
Finlands Bank. Institut foer Ekonomisk Forskning. Publikationer *see* Suomen Pankki. Julkaisuja. Serie B *148*
Finlands Bank. Publikationer. Serie A *see* Suomen Pankki. Julkaisuja. Serie A *148*
Finlands Bank. Publikationer. Serie B *see* Suomen Pankki. Julkaisuja. Serie B *148*
Finlands Bank. Publikationer. Serie C *see* Suomen Pankki. Julkaisuja. Serie C *149*
Finlands Bank. Publikationer. Serie D *see* Suomen Pankki. Julkaisuja. Serie D *149*
Finlands Industrifoerbund. Medlemsfoerteckning *see* Suomen Teollisuusliitto. Jasenluettelo *242*
Finlands Litteratur Aarskatalog *see* Suomen Kirjallisuus Vuosiluettelo *95*
Finnische Geodaetische Institut. Veroeffentlichungen *see* Suomen Geodeettisen Laitoksen. Julkaisuja *306*
Finnische Handelsrundschau *see* Technik und Form aus Finnland *198*
Finnish Boatbuilding Industry (FI ISSN 0356-7753) *827*
Finnish Bond Issues *see* Suomen Obligaatiokirja *205*
Finnish Broadcasting Company. Section for Long-Range Planning. Research Reports (FI ISSN 0084-4225) *267*
Finnish Dental Society. Proceedings. Supplement *see* Suomen Hammaslaakariseura. Toimituksia. Supplementa *610*
Finnish Fisheries Research (FI ISSN 0301-908X) *396*
Finnish Game Research/ Riistateiteellisia Julkaisuja (FI ISSN 0015-2447) *276*
Finnish Geodetic Institute. Publications *see* Suomen Geodeettisen Laitoksen. Julkaisuja *306*
Finnish Insurance Yearbook *see* Suomen Vakuutusvuosikirja *501*
Finnish Marine Research (FI ISSN 0357-1076) *310*
Finnish Meteorological Institute. Contributions (FI ISSN 0071-5190) *632*
Finnish Meteorological Institute. Observations of Atmospheric Electricity *see* Finland. Ilmatieteen Laitos. Ilmasahkohavaintoja *632*
Finnish Meteorological Institute. Observations of Radioactivity (FI ISSN 0071-5220) *632*

Finnish Meteorological Institute. Observations of Satellites. Visual Observations of Artificial Earth Satellites in Finland (FI ISSN 0355-2004) & *632*
Finnish Meteorological Institute. Soil Temperature Measurements (FI ISSN 0071-5239) *632*
Finnish Meteorological Institute. Studies on Earth Magnetism (FI ISSN 0081-783X) *304*
Finnish Meterological Institute. Technical Report (FI ISSN 0355-1733) *632*
Finnish National Bibliography Annual Volume *see* Suomen Kirjallisuus Vuosiluettelo *95*
Finnish Photographic Yearbook *see* Valokuvauksen Vuosikirja *694*
Finnish Psychiatry *see* Psychiatria Fennica *621*
Finnish State Railways (FI ISSN 0506-3876) *873*
Finsk Fotografisk Arsbok *see* Valokuvauksen Vuosikirja *694*
Fire Casualty & Surety Argus F. C. & S. Chart *see* Argus F. C. & S. Chart *497*
Fire Control Notes (CN ISSN 0428-4666) *394*
Fire Exit (US) *564*
Fire Marshals Association of North America. Year Book (US ISSN 0090-5313) *394*
Fire Prevention News (CN ISSN 0071-5395) *394*
Fire Protection Directory (UK ISSN 0071-5409) *394*
Fire Protection Handbook (US ISSN 0071-5417) *394*
Fire Protection Handbook Study Guide (US ISSN 0071-5425) *394*
Fire Protection Reference Directory (US ISSN 0361-8382) *394*
Fire Safety Aspects of Polymeric Materials (US) *394*
Fire Yearbook (US ISSN 0071-5468) *394*
Firelands Arts Review *see* Firelands Review *564*
Firelands Review (US) *564*
First Canadian Conference on Earthquake Engineering. Proceedings(CN) *375*
First Hand Information (GE) *453, 721*
First National City Bank, Liberia. Annual Report (LB) *173*
First to Final (US ISSN 0015-2803) *733*
Fish and Wildlife Facts (US ISSN 0069-9128) *276*
Fish and Wildlife Gazette (AT) *396*
Fish Disease Leaflets (US ISSN 0071-5492) *396*
Fish Farming Review *see* Aquaculture Review *395*
Fishdex (NZ) *396*
Fisheries and Wildlife Paper. Victoria (AT ISSN 0071-5522) *276, 396*
Fisheries Bulletin *see* Malawi. Fisheries Department. Fisheries Bulletin *398*
Fisheries Fact Sheet. (CN ISSN 0317-1817) *396*
Fisheries of Scotland Report (UK ISSN 0080-1283) *396*
Fisheries of the United States (US) *396*
Fisheries Organization Society Ltd. Year Book & Annual Report *see* F. O. S. Year Book & Annual Report *396*
Fisheries Research Bulletin of Zambia (ZA ISSN 0084-4713) *396*
Fisheries Statistics of Japan (JA ISSN 0071-5581) *397*
Fisherman Union of Indonesia. Central Governing Board. Annual Report/ Himpunan Nelayan Seluruh Indonesia. Dewan Pimpnan Pusat. Laporan Kegiatan (IO) *397*
Fishermen's Digest (US ISSN 0430-6090) *829*
Fishery Statistics of the United States *see* Fisheries of the United States *396*
Fishes of the Western North Atlantic (US) *128*
Fishing Annual *see* Bob Zwirz' Fishing Annual *828*

Fishing Prospects (UK ISSN 0308-0935) *397*
Fishing Waters (UK) *829*
Fisk og Hav (DK ISSN 0105-9211) *397*
Fiske (SW) *397, 820*
Fisken og Havet (NO ISSN 0071-5638) *397*
FItech (UK ISSN 0307-2118) *394*
Fitzgerald/Hemingway Annual (US ISSN 0071-5654) *564*
Five Year Economic Forecast/Gokanen Keizai Yosoku (JA) *186*
Five Years Work in Librarianship *see* British Librarianship & Information Science *527*
Fix Your Chevrolet (US ISSN 0071-5670) *871*
Fix Your Ford (US ISSN 0071-5689) *871*
Fix Your Volkswagen (US ISSN 0071-5697) *871*
Fizicheskaya Mekhanika (UR) *701*
Fizika Aerodispersnykh Sistem (UR) *633*
Fizika Nizhnei Atmosfery (UR) *633*
Fiziko-Khimicheska Mekhanika/ Physico-Chemical Mechanics (BU) *254, 701*
Fizyka (PL) *696*
Flakt Review *see* Flakten *429*
Flakten (SW ISSN 0015-3400) *429*
Flannery O'Connor Bulletin (US ISSN 0091-4924) *97, 564*
Flea Market Almanac (US) *476*
Flea Market Quarterly *see* Flea Market Almanac *476*
Flea Market Trader (US ISSN 0364-023X) *476*
Flight *see* Envol *125*
Flight Safety (NZ) *8*
Flinders Asian Studies Lecture (AT ISSN 0085-0586) *669*
Flinders Institute for Atmospheric and Marine Sciences. Computing Reports(AT) *310, 633*
Flinders Institute for Atmospheric and Marine Sciences. Cruise Reports (AT) *310*
Flinders Institute for Atmospheric and Marine Sciences. Research Reports (AT) *310, 633*
Flinders Institute for Atmospheric and Marine Sciences. Technical Reports (AT) *310, 633*
Flinders Journal of History and Politics (AT) *447, 710*
Flinders University of South Australia. School of Social Sciences. Occasional Monograph (AT) *797*
Flintshire Historical Society. Publications, Journal and Record Series (UK ISSN 0140-8429) *453*
Floating Island (US ISSN 0147-1686) *564*
Flood Damage Prevention; an Indexed Bibliography (US ISSN 0071-5735) *371*
Floodlight (UK) *329*
Flooring (UK) *136*
Flora (EC ISSN 0015-380X) *114*
Flora Ecologica de Restingas do Sudeste do Brasil (BL ISSN 0071-5751) *114*
Flora et Vegetatio Mundi (GW ISSN 0071-576X) *114*
Flora Malesiana. Series 2: Pteridophyta (NE ISSN 0071-5786) *114*
Flora Neotropica. Monographs (US ISSN 0071-5794) *114*
Flora of Ecuador (SW) *114*
Flora of New South Wales. (AT ISSN 0077-8761) *114*
Flora of the U.S.S.R. (IS) *114*
Flora Polska; Rosliny Naczyniowe Polski i Ziem Osciennych (PL ISSN 0071-5816) *114*
Flora Polska: Rosliny Zarodnikowe Polski i Ziem Osciennych (PL ISSN 0071-5824) *115*
Flora Slodkowodna Polski (PL ISSN 0071-5840) *115*
Flore d'Afrique Centrale (Zaire-Rwanda-Burundi) (BE) *115*

Flore de la Nouvelle Caledonie et Dependances (FR ISSN 0430-666X) *115*
Flore de Madagascar et des Comores (FR) *115*
Flore du Cambodge, du Laos et du Vietnam (FR ISSN 0071-5867) *115*
Flore du Cameroun (FR ISSN 0071-5875) *115*
Flore du Congo, du Rwanda et du Burundi *see* Flore d'Afrique Centrale (Zaire-Rwanda-Burundi) *115*
Flore du Gabon (FR ISSN 0071-5883) *115*
Florida. Bureau of Geology. Geological Bulletins (US ISSN 0085-0608) *293*
Florida. Bureau of Geology. Information Circulars (US ISSN 0085-0616) *293*
Florida. Bureau of Geology. Map Series(US ISSN 0085-0624) *293*
Florida. Bureau of Geology. Report of Investigations (US ISSN 0085-0632) *293*
Florida. Bureau of Geology. Special Publications (US ISSN 0085-0640) *293*
Florida. Bureau of Historic Sites and Properties. Bulletin (US ISSN 0085-0659) *468*
Florida. Bureau of Local Government Finance. Annual Local Government Financial Report (US ISSN 0094-8551) *229*
Florida. Department of Administration. Budget in Brief (US ISSN 0095-5175) *742*
Florida. Department of Commerce. Annual Report (US) *839*
Florida. Department of Education. Florida Statewide Assessment Program: Capsule Report (US ISSN 0094-1468) *327*
Florida. Department of Education. Professional Practices Council. Report (US) *317*
Florida. Department of Transportation. Annual Report (US ISSN 0095-2060) *862*
Florida. Division of Corrections. Financial Report (US ISSN 0094-6435) *805*
Florida. Division of Family Services. Annual Statistical Report (US ISSN 0093-6715) *810*
Florida. Division of Local Resource Management. Community Program Development and Management Series (US) *484*
Florida. Division of Local Resource Management. Miscellaneous Series (US) *749*
Florida. Division of Local Resource Management. Personnel Assistance Series (US) *749*
Florida. Division of Local Resource Management. Technical Paper Series (US) *484*
Florida. Division of Motor Vehicles. Tags and Revenue (US ISSN 0092-0177) *862*
Florida. Division of Plant Industry. Biennial Report (US ISSN 0071-5948) *15, 115*
Florida. Division of State Planning. Annual Report on State and Regional Planning (US) *484*
Florida. Governor. Annual Report on State Housing Goals (US ISSN 0091-9942) *484*
Florida. Legislature. Joint Legislative Management Committee. Summary of General Legislation (US ISSN 0090-1520) *512*
Florida. Mental Health Program Office. Statistical Report of Community Mental Health Programs (US) *735, 751*
Florida. Mental Health Program Office. Statistical Report of Hospitals (US ISSN 0094-2294) *482*
Florida. State Board of Independent Colleges and Universities. Report (US ISSN 0093-1071) *331, 336*
Florida Anthropological Society Publications (US) *49*
Florida Bank Monitor (US ISSN 0094-8535) *173*
Florida Education Directory (US) *331*

Florida Festival Arts Directory (US) *74, 659*
Florida Folk Arts Directory *see* Florida Festival Arts Directory *74*
Florida Housing and Community Development Series (US) *484*
Florida Housing Assistance Series *see* Florida Housing and Community Development Series *484*
Florida Housing Rehabilitation Series *see* Florida Housing and Community Development Series *484*
Florida Marine Research Publications (US ISSN 0095-0157) *310*
Florida Requirements for Teacher Certification (US ISSN 0071-5999) *336*
Florida Senate (US ISSN 0093-4089) *512*
Florida Speleological Society. Special Papers (US ISSN 0071-6006) *293*
Florida State Industrial Directory (US ISSN 0163-4712) *237*
Florida State Museum. Bulletin. Biological Sciences (US) *103*
Florida State Museum. Bulletin. Biological Series *see* Florida State Museum. Bulletin. Biological Sciences *103*
Florida State Museum. Contributions. Anthropology and History (US) *49*
Florida State Museum. Contributions. Social Sciences *see* Florida State Museum. Contributions. Anthropology and History *49*
Florida State University. Center for Yugoslav-American Studies, Research, and Exchanges. Proceedings and Reports of Seminars and Research (US) *453, 797*
Florida State University. Instructional Support Center. Film (US) *651*
Florida State University. Media Services. Motion Pictures *see* Florida State University. Instructional Support Center. Film *651*
Florida State University. Publications of the Faculty. (US ISSN 0428-6766) *336*
Florida State University. Publications of the Faculty and Theses Archival *see* Florida State University. Publications of the Faculty *336*
Florida State University. Slavic Papers *see* Florida State University. Center for Yugoslav-American Studies, Research, and Exchanges. Proceedings and Reports of Seminars and Research *453*
Florida Statewide Assessment Program *see* Florida. Department of Education. Florida Statewide Assessment Program: Capsule Report *327*
Florida Statistical Abstract (US ISSN 0071-6022) *839*
Florida Tour Book *see* Tourbook: Florida *891*
Florida's Local Retirement Systems: a Survey (US) *428, 742*
Floristisch-Soziologische Arbeitsgemeinschaft. Mitteilungen (GW ISSN 0373-7632) *839*
Flotation Index (US ISSN 0071-6235) *648*
Flour Milling and Baking Research Association. Annual Report and Accounts (UK ISSN 0071-6243) *404*
Flow of Funds in Taiwan District, Republic of China (CH) *173*
Flowering Plants of Africa (SA ISSN 0015-4504) *115*
Flowering Plants of South Africa *see* Flowering Plants of Africa *115*
Fluid Dynamics Transactions (PL) *701*
Fluid Meters: Their Theory and Application (US) *382*
Fluid Power Handbook & Directory (US ISSN 0428-7738) *379*
Fluid Power Symposium. Proceedings (UK ISSN 0071-6278) *381*
Fluoridation Census (US) *609*
Fluorocarbon and Related Chemistry (UK ISSN 0301-8938) *252*
Flygtekniska Foersoeksanstalten. Meddelande/Report (SW ISSN 0081-5640) *8*

Flying Annual & Buyers' Guide (US ISSN 0163-1144) *8*
Flying Annual and Pilots' Buying Guide *see* Flying Annual & Buyers' Guide *8*
Focus *see* Public Continuing and Adult Education Almanac *329*
Focus (Moscow) (US) *276*
Focus (Waterloo) (CN ISSN 0430-8247) *367*
Focus, an Economic Profile of the Apparel Industry (US) *261*
Focus: Biology *see* Annual Editions: Readings in Biology *100*
Focus: Human Sexuality *see* Annual Editions: Readings in Human Sexuality *100*
Focus on Dance (US ISSN 0071-6294) *285*
Focus on Nebraska Highways *see* Nebraska. Department of Roads. Challenge of the 80's *376*
Focus on Politics (SA) *432, 710*
Focus on Vancouver (CN ISSN 0383-2708) *468*
Focus Series (Washington) *see* American Industrial Arts Association. Focus Series *850*
Focus: Unexplored Deviance (US ISSN 0160-9807) *735*
Focus: Urban Society (US ISSN 0160-9815) *813*
Fodor's Australia, New Zealand and the South Pacific (US ISSN 0191-2321) *885*
Fodor's Austria (US ISSN 0071-6340) *885*
Fodor's Belgium and Luxembourg (US ISSN 0071-6359) *885*
Fodor's Budget France (US) *885*
Fodor's Budget Italy (US ISSN 0270-787X) *885*
Fodor's California (US ISSN 0192-9925) *885*
Fodor's Caribbean, Bahamas and Bermuda (US ISSN 0098-2547) *885*
Fodor's Central America (US ISSN 0270-8183) *885*
Fodor's Cruises Everywhere (US ISSN 0160-3914) *885*
Fodor's Czechoslovakia (US ISSN 0071-6367) *885*
Fodor's Egypt (US ISSN 0147-8176) *885*
Fodor's Europe Talking (US) *885*
Fodor's Far West (US ISSN 0192-3730) *885*
Fodor's Florida (US) *885*
Fodor's France (US ISSN 0071-6383) *885*
Fodor's Germany *see* Fodor's Germany: West and East *885*
Fodor's Germany: West and East (US ISSN 0192-0952) *885*
Fodor's Great Britain (US ISSN 0071-6405) *885*
Fodor's Greece (US ISSN 0071-6413) *885*
Fodor's Guide to Europe (US ISSN 0071-6375) *885*
Fodor's Guide to the Caribbean, Bahamas, and Bermuda *see* Fodor's Caribbean, Bahamas and Bermuda *885*
Fodor's Hawaii (US ISSN 0071-6421) *885*
Fodor's Holland (US ISSN 0071-643X) *885*
Fodor's India *see* Fodor's India & Nepal *885*
Fodor's India & Nepal (US) *885*
Fodor's Ireland (US ISSN 0071-6464) *885*
Fodor's Israel (US ISSN 0071-6588) *885*
Fodor's Italy (US ISSN 0071-6472) *885*
Fodor's Japan and East Asia *see* Fodor's Japan and Korea *885*
Fodor's Japan and East Asia *see* Fodor's Southeast Asia *885*
Fodor's Japan and Korea (US ISSN 0098-1613) *885*
Fodor's London (US ISSN 0071-6596) *885*

Fodor's Mexico (US ISSN 0071-6499) *885*
Fodor's Midwest (US ISSN 0192-5571) *885*
Fodor's New England (US ISSN 0192-3412) *885*
Fodor's New York (US) *885*
Fodor's Paris (US ISSN 0149-1288) *885*
Fodor's Portugal (US ISSN 0071-6510) *885*
Fodor's Scandinavia (US ISSN 0071-6529) *885*
Fodor's South (US ISSN 0147-8680) *885*
Fodor's South America (US ISSN 0071-6537) *885*
Fodor's Southeast Asia (US ISSN 0160-8991) *885*
Fodor's Southwest (US ISSN 0147-8656) *885*
Fodor's Soviet Union (US ISSN 0095-1358) *885*
Fodor's Spain (US ISSN 0071-6545) *885*
Fodor's Switzerland (US ISSN 0071-6553) *885*
Fodor's Turkey (US ISSN 0071-6618) *885*
Fodor's U.S.A. (US ISSN 0147-8745) *885*
Fodor's Yugoslavia (US ISSN 0071-657X) *885*
Foederalismus-Studien (AU) *710*
Foerdermittelkatalog (SZ) *583*
Foeredrag vid Pyrotekknikdagen (SW ISSN 0348-6613) *372*
Foereningen Armemusei Vaenner. Meddelanden: Armemuseum *see* Foereningen Armemusei Vaenner. Meddelanden: Kungliga Armemuseum *652*
Foereningen Armemusei Vaenner. Meddelanden: Kungliga Armemuseum (SW) *638, 652*
Foereningen foer Inre Vattenvaegar Meddelanden *see* F I V Meddelanden *878*
Foersaekringsaarsbok foer Finland *see* Suomen Vakuutusvuosikirja *501*
Foerteckning Oever Advokater och Advokatbyraaer (SW) *512*
Fogra-Literatur-Profil (GW) *733*
Foi Aujourd'hui (FR) *765*
Foldrajzi Monografiak (HU ISSN 0071-6642) *421*
Foldrajzi Tanulmanyok (HU ISSN 0071-6650) *421*
Folger Shakespeare Library Annual Report (US ISSN 0428-8211) *530, 564*
Folia Anatomica Iugoslavica (YU ISSN 0350-0233) *595*
Folia Antropologica (VE ISSN 0428-8254) *49*
Folia Dendrologica (CS) *103, 408, 415*
Folia Entomologica Mexicana (MX ISSN 0430-8603) *120*
Folia Facultatis Scientiarum Naturalium Universitatis Purkynianae Brunensis: Biologia (CS) *103*
Folia Facultatis Scientiarum Naturalium Universitatis Purkynianae Brunensis: Chemia (CS) *246*
Folia Facultatis Scientiarum Naturalium Universitatis Purkynianae Brunensis: Geologia (CS) *293*
Folia Facultatis Scientiarum Naturalium Universitatis Purkynianae Brunensis: Geographia (CS) *782*
Folia Facultatis Scientiarum Naturalium Universitatis Purkynianae Brunensis: Physica (CS) *696*
Folia Forestalia Polonica. Series A. Lesnictwo (PL ISSN 0071-6677) *408*
Folia Forestalia Polonica. Series B. Drzewnictwo (PL ISSN 0071-6685) *412*
Folia Geographica. Geographica-Oeconomica (PL ISSN 0071-6707) *421*
Folia Geographica. Geographica-Physica (PL ISSN 0071-6715) *293, 421*
Folia Geographica Danica (DK ISSN 0071-6693) *421*

Folia Historiae Artium (PL ISSN 0071-6723) *74*
Folia Historica (HU ISSN 0133-6622) *453*
Folia Historica del Nordeste (AG ISSN 0325-8238) *468*
Folia Linguistica (GW ISSN 0430-862X) *544*
Folia Mendeliana *see* Acta Musei Moraviae. Scientia Naturales 3: Folia Mendeliana *122*
Folia Montana *see* Banicke Listy *641*
Folia Oeconomica Cracoviensia (PL ISSN 0071-674X) *144*
Folia Orientalia (PL ISSN 0015-5675) *669*
Folia Quaternaria (PL ISSN 0015-573X) *673*
Folia Slavica (US ISSN 0160-9394) *544*
Folio: Annual (US) *504*
Folio Limnologica Scandinavica (DK) *307*
Folk and Kinfolk of Harris County (US ISSN 0190-8189) *417*
Folk Dance Directory (US ISSN 0163-528X) *285*
Folk; Dansk Etnografisk Tidsskrift (DK ISSN 0085-0756) *49*
Folk Directory (UK) *285*
Folk Life (UK ISSN 0430-8778) *49*
Folk Literature of the Sephardic Jews (US) *591, 564, 770*
Folk Music Journal (UK ISSN 0531-9684) *285, 659*
Folk News *see* Bristol Folk News *657*
Folk og Kultur (DK ISSN 0105-1024) *402*
Folk Song *see* Canu Gwerin *658*
Folkl-Liv (SW) *49*
Folklivsskildringar och Bygdesstudier (SW ISSN 0071-6766) *402*
Folklivsstudier (FI ISSN 0085-0764) *49*
Fol'klor Urala (UR) *402*
Folklore and Mythology Studies (US ISSN 0162-6280) *402*
Folklore Annual (US ISSN 0071-6782) *402*
Folklore Bibliography for (Year) (US ISSN 0272-8494) *403*
Folklore du Monde (BE) *402*
Folklore Fellows Communications *see* F F Communications *402*
Folkskolans Aarsbok *see* Aarsbok foer Skolan *313*
Folktales of the World (US ISSN 0071-6804) *402*
Folleto de Informacion *see* C I M M Y T Information Bulletin *42*
Folleto de Investigacion *see* International Maize and Wheat Improvement Center. Research Bulletin *42*
Fomento de las Artes Decorativas, Barcelona. Agrupacion de Diseno Industrial. Guia de Asociados (SP) *74*
Fondation Canadienne des Toxicomanies. Repertoire *see* Canada Addictions Foundation. Directory *286*
Fondation pour la Recherche et le Developpement dans l'Ocean Indien. Documents et Recherches (RE) *440*
Fondazione Giangiacomo Feltrinelli. Annali (IT ISSN 0544-1374) *797*
Fondazione Giovanni Agnelli. Progetto Politica Industriale. Quaderno di Ricerca (IT) *144*
Fondo de Cultura. Serie de Lecturas (MX) *144*
Fondo de Promocion de Exportaciones. Directorio de Exportadores/Export Directory (CK) *195*
Fonds Africain de Developpement. Rapport Annuel *see* African Development Fund. Annual Report *199*
Fonds de Developpment Economique et Social. Conseil de Direction. Rapport(FR ISSN 0071-6847) *222*
Fonetica si Dialectologie (RM ISSN 0071-6855) *544*
Fonoweek (NE) *908*
Fontes (CS) *60*

Fontes Archaeologici Posnanienses/ Annales Musei Archaeologici Posnaniensis (PL ISSN 0071-6863) *60, 453*
Fontes Archaeologici Pragenses (CS ISSN 0015-6183) *60*
Fontes et Aciers/Ghise ed Acciai/ Roheisen und Stahlerzeugnisse/ Ruwijer en Stallprodukten (EI ISSN 0531-3120) *628, 643*
Fontes et Commentationes (GW ISSN 0077-1953) *908*
Fontes Iuris Gentium (US ISSN 0428-903X) *523*
Fontes Praehistorici *see* Fontes Archaeologici Posnanienses *60*
Fontes Rerum Austriacarum. Reihe 1. Scriptores (AU ISSN 0071-6871) *453*
Fontes Rerum Austriacarum. Reihe 2. Diplomataria et Acta (AU ISSN 0071-688X) *453*
Fontes Rerum Austriacarum. Reihe 3. Fontes Juris (AU ISSN 0071-6898) *453, 512*
Fonti e Studi per la Storia del Santo a Padova (IT) *774*
Fonti e Studi per la Storia di Bologna e delle Province Emiliane e Romagnole(IT) *74, 453*
Fonti Sui Comuni Rurali Toscani (IT ISSN 0071-6901) *453*
Food and Agriculture Organization of the United Nations. Agricultural Planning Studies (UN ISSN 0532-0194) *28*
Food and Agriculture Organization of the United Nations. Animal Health Branch. Animal Health Monograph (UN ISSN 0428-9552) *908*
Food and Agriculture Organization of the United Nations. Asia and the Far East Commission on Agricultural Statistics. Periodic Report (UN) *24*
Food and Agriculture Organization of the United Nations. Basic Texts (UN ISSN 0532-0208) *15*
Food and Agriculture Organization of the United Nations. Committee for Inland Fisheries of Africa. CIFA Reports (UN) *397*
Food and Agriculture Organization of the United Nations. Committee for Inland Fisheries of Africa. CIFA Technical Papers (UN) *397*
Food and Agriculture Organization of the United Nations. Commodity Policy Studies (UN ISSN 0071-6928) *28*
Food and Agriculture Organization of the United Nations. Commodity Reference Series (UN ISSN 0071-6952) *908*
Food and Agriculture Organization of the United Nations. European Inland and Fisheries Advisory Commission. E I F A C Newsletter (UN ISSN 0532-9396) *397*
Food and Agriculture Organization of the United Nations. Fishery Committee for the Eastern Central Atlantic. Report of the Session (UN) *908*
Food and Agriculture Organization of the United Nations. Forest Tree Seed Directory (UN ISSN 0532-0666) *408*
Food and Agriculture Organization of the United Nations. Forestry and Forest Products Division. World Forest Products Statistics (UN ISSN 0532-0690) *908*
Food and Agriculture Organization of the United Nations. Forestry Occasional Paper (UN ISSN 0428-9374) *909*
Food and Agriculture Organization of the United Nations. Index of Agricultural Institutions in Europe (UN ISSN 0428-9390) *909*
Food and Agriculture Organization of the United Nations. Interamerican Meeting on Animal Production and Health. Report (UN ISSN 0532-0348) *909*
Food and Agriculture Organization of the United Nations. National Grain Policies (UN ISSN 0071-710X) *42*

Food and Agriculture Organization of the United Nations. Plant Protection Committee for Southeast Asia and Pacific Region. Information Letter (UN) *35*
Food and Agriculture Organization of the United Nations. Plant Protection Committee for Southeast Asia and Pacific Region. Technical Document (UN ISSN 0428-9765) *35*
Food and Agriculture Organization of the United Nations. Production Yearbook (UN ISSN 0071-7118) *28*
Food and Agriculture Organization of the United Nations.Review of FAO Field Programmes (UN) *909*
Food and Agriculture Organization of the United Nations. Soils Bulletins (UN ISSN 0532-0437) *35*
Food and Agriculture Organization of the United Nations. Trade Yearbook (UN ISSN 0071-7126) *28, 195*
Food and Agriculture Organization of the United Nations. World Soil Resources Reports (UN ISSN 0532-0488) *35*
Food and Agriculture Organization of the United Nations Conference. Report (UN ISSN 0071-6944) *15*
Food and Agriculture Organization of the United Nations FAO Irrigation and Drainage Papers *see* FAO Irrigation and Drainage Papers *896*
Food and Nutrition Programs *see* U.S. Food and Nutrition Service. Food and Nutrition Programs *811*
Food Co-Op Directory *see* Co-Op Directory *407*
Food Consumption in the O. E. C. D. Countries/Consommation de Denrees Alimentaires dans les Pays de l'O.C.D.E. (FR ISSN 0474-537X) *404*
Food Economics Yearbook/Shokuryo Keizai Nenkan (JA) *237*
Food Fish Market Review and Outlook (US ISSN 0091-8105) *397*
Food Fish Situation and Outlook *see* Food Fish Market Review and Outlook *397*
Food Industries Yearbook and Buyers' Directory *see* Food Industries Yearbook and Buyers' Guide *404*
Food Industries Yearbook and Buyers' Guide (SA) *404*
Food Industry Studies (UN ISSN 0071-7193) *404*
Food Marketing Industry Speaks (US ISSN 0190-3349) *407*
Food Processing and Packaging Directory *see* Food Processing Industry Directory *404*
Food Processing Industry Directory (UK) *404*
Food Processing Review *see* Food Technology Review *404*
Food Publications Round-up (US ISSN 0146-3780) *406*
Food Science Series (US ISSN 0071-7223) *404*
Food Service Directory and Buyers Guide for Fresh Produce (US) *407*
Food Service Research Abstracts (US) *404*
Food Technology Review (US ISSN 0093-0075) *404*
Food Trades Directory, Food Buyer's Yearbook (UK ISSN 0071-7231) *404*
Foodborne & Waterborne Disease Outbreaks. Annual Summary *see* U.S. Center for Disease Control. Foodborne & Waterborne Disease Outbreaks. Annual Summary *754*
Foodnews Dairy Products Review (UK) *41*
Football Association Year Book (UK ISSN 0071-724X) *824*
Football Case Book (US ISSN 0163-6200) *824*
Football Champions (UK) *824*
Football Guide (US ISSN 0069-5548) *824*
Football Handbook (US) *824*
Football Officials Handbook (US) *824*
Football Register (US ISSN 0071-7258) *824*
Football Roundup (US) *824*

Football Rules (US) *824*
Football Rules - Simplified and Illustrated (US) *824*
Football Statistician's Manual (US) *824*
Footwear Industry Statistical Review (UK ISSN 0308-9398) *795*
Footwear Manual (US ISSN 0095-1048) *795*
Footwear News Fact Book (US ISSN 0429-0208) *795*
Footwear Shoemaking Directory (CN) *795*
For Now (US) *564*
For Younger Readers, Braille and Talking Books (US ISSN 0071-7266) *90, 133, 327*
Forces Nouvelles Info (FR) *710*
Ford Almanac (US) *15, 360*
Ford Foundation Annual Report (US ISSN 0071-7274) *360, 490*
Ford's Deck Plan Guide (US ISSN 0096-1353) *878, 886*
Forecast (US ISSN 0071-7282) *186*
Foreign Aero-Space Literature/Gaikoku Koku Uchu Bunken Mokuroku (JA ISSN 0454-191X) *11*
Foreign Affairs Studies *see* Contemporary Economic Problems *741*
Foreign Buyers of Philippine Cottage Industry Products (PH) *237*
Foreign Compound Metabolism in Mammals (UK ISSN 0300-3493) *252*
Foreign Consular Offices in the United States (US ISSN 0071-7320) *721*
Foreign Economic Trends and Their Implications for the United States (US ISSN 0090-9467) *186*
Foreign Exchange Rates and Restrictions (US ISSN 0363-5430) *909*
Foreign Investment Opportunities in the Philippines (PH ISSN 0085-0802) *222*
Foreign Investments in Brazil (BL) *195*
Foreign Market Airgrams (US) *195*
Foreign Markets Reports (US) *195*
Foreign Medical School Catalogue (US ISSN 0085-0829) *331, 595*
Foreign Policy Research Institute. Monograph Series (US) *721*
Foreign Policy Research Institute. Research Monograph Series *see* Foreign Policy Research Institute. Monograph Series *721*
Foreign Radio Amateur Callbook Magazine (US ISSN 0015-7260) *267*
Foreign Relations of the United States (US ISSN 0071-7355) *721*
Foreign Trade Marketplace (US) *195*
Foreign Trade of Brazil (BL) *195*
Foreign Trade of Denmark *see* Danmarks Vareindfoersel og-Udfoersel *155*
Foreign Trade of Greece *see* Commerce Exterieur de la Grece *154*
Foreign Trade Reports. Bunker Fuels (US ISSN 0363-6798) *195, 679*
Foreign Trade Reports. Summary of U.S. Export and Import Merchandise Trade (US ISSN 0361-0047) *195*
Foreign Trade Reports. U.S. Airborne Exports and General Imports (US ISSN 0095-7771) *195*
Foreign Trade Reports. U.S. Waterborne Exports and General Imports (US ISSN 0095-0890) *195*
Foreign Trade Reports. Vessel Entrances and Clearances (US) *195*
Foreign Trade Statistics of Africa. Series A: Direction of Trade (UN ISSN 0071-7398) *156*
Foreign Trade Statistics of Africa. Series B: Trade by Commodity (UN ISSN 0071-7401) *156*
Foreign Trade Statistics of Iran. Yearbook (IR ISSN 0075-0492) *156*
Foreign Trade Statistics of the Philippines (PH) *156*
Foreign Trade Statistics of Yemen Arab Republic (YE) *156*
Foreningen til Norske Fortidsminnesmerkers Bevaring. Aarbok (NO ISSN 0071-7436) *453*

Forensic Sciences. Official Publication of the American Academy of Forensic Sciences *see* What's New in Forensic Sciences *613*
Forest Engineering Symposium. Proceedings (US ISSN 0071-7444) *408*
Forest Farmer. Manual Edition (US ISSN 0071-7452) *408*
Forest Insect and Disease Conditions in the United States *see* Forest Insect Conditions in the United States *409*
Forest Insect and Disease Leaflets (US) *408*
Forest Insect Conditions in the United States (US ISSN 0071-7487) *409*
Forest Pest Leaflets *see* Forest Insect and Disease Leaflets *408*
Forest Products Trade Statistics of Indonesia *see* Indonesian Statistics on Trade of Forest Products *409*
Forest Research in India (II ISSN 0071-7533) *409*
Forest Research News for the South *see* U.S. Forest Service. Southern Forest Experiment Station. Research Accomplished *411*
Forest Resources *see* Australian Forest Resources *407*
Forest Resources Reports *see* U.S. Forest Service. Forest Service Research Accomplishments *411*
Forest Science Monographs (US ISSN 0071-7568) *409*
Forest Tax Report *see* Washington (State). Department of Revenue. Forest Tax Report *233*
Forest Tree Nurseries in the United States (US ISSN 0071-7576) *409*
Forestry Abstracts. Leading Article Reprint Series (UK ISSN 0071-7584) *2, 412*
Forestry Log (AT) *409*
Forestry Newsletter of the Asia-Pacific Region (UN ISSN 0532-0747) *409*
Forestry Occasional Paper *see* Food and Agriculture Organization of the United Nations. Forestry Occasional Paper *909*
Forges (SP) *556*
Forintek Canada Corporation, Western Laboratory. Review Reports (CN ISSN 0226-0786) *412*
Forintek Canada Corporation, Western Laboratory. Special Publications (CN ISSN 0226-1170) *412*
Forintek Canada Corporation, Western Laboratory. Technical Reports (CN ISSN 0708-6172) *413*
Forma Abierta (SP) *556*
Formal Linguistics (US ISSN 0361-0977) *271, 585*
Formal Linguistics Series (NE ISSN 0071-7592) *544*
Format (UK ISSN 0015-7740) *579*
Formator Symposium on Mathematical Methods for the Analysis of Large-Scale Systems (CS) *585*
Forme del Significato (IT ISSN 0390-2153) *564*
Formulaire Thera (FR ISSN 0071-7622) *684*
Foro Hondureno (HO) *512*
Forretnings- og Bedriftslederen (NO ISSN 0071-7630) *215*
Forschung im Strassenwesen (GW ISSN 0340-3998) *375*
Forschung Stadtverkehr (GW ISSN 0341-0951) *862*
Forschung Stadtverkehr: Sonderreihe/ Urban Transport Research: Special Series (GW ISSN 0171-1547) *874*
Forschung und Konstruktion im Stahlbau/Research and Construction on Steel-Engineering/Etude des Ouvrages en Acier et Construction Metallique (SZ ISSN 0071-7649) *375, 379*
Forschungen aus Staat und Recht (US ISSN 0071-7657) *512*

Forschungen und Beitraege zur Wiener Stadtgeschichte (AU) *432*
Forschungen zur Aelteren Musikgeschichte (AU) *659*
Forschungen zur Antiken Sklaverei (GW ISSN 0071-7665) *432*
Forschungen zur Europaeischen und Vergleichenden Rechtsgeschichte (AU) *512*
Forschungen zur Innsbrucker Universitaetsgeschichte (AU ISSN 0429-1573) *336*
Forschungen zur Kunstgeschichte und Christlichen Archaeologie (GW ISSN 0532-2189) *60, 74*
Forschungen zur Mittelalterlichen Geschichte (GE ISSN 0071-7673) *453*
Forschungen zur Raumentwicklung (GW ISSN 0341-244X) *484*
Forschungen zur Rechtsarchaeologie und Rechtlichen Volkskunde (SZ) *60, 402, 512*
Forschungen zur Romanischen Philologie (GW ISSN 0071-7681) *544*
Forschungen zur Volkskunde (GW) *49*
Forschunginstitut fuer Wirtschaftsverfassung und Wettbewerb e.V. Schriftenreihe *see* F I W - Schriftenreihe *144*
Forschungsberichte zur D D R-Literatur (NE) *564*
Forschungsfilm *see* Research Film *913*
Forschungsgesellschaft fuer das Strassenwesen. Arbeitsgruppe Asphalt- und Teerstrassen. Schriftenreihe (GW ISSN 0426-9918) *375*
Forschungsgesellschaft fuer das Strassenwesen. Arbeitsgruppe Betonstrassen. Schriftenreihe (GW ISSN 0429-1816) *375*
Forschungsinstitut der Eidgenoessischen Turn- und Sportschule Magglingen. Wissenschaftliche Schriftenreihe (SZ) *694*
Forschungsprobleme der Vergleichenden Literaturgeschichte (GW ISSN 0071-7703) *564*
Forschungsstelle fuer Jagdkunde und Wildschadenverhuetung. Schriftenreihe (GW ISSN 0071-7711) *409, 829*
Forschungstelle fuer Voelkerrecht und Auslaendisches Oeffentliches Recht. Werkhefte *see* Universitaet Hamburg. Institut fuer Internationale Angelegenheiten. Werkhefte *524*
Forstatistisches Jahrbuch (GW ISSN 0084-7690) *412*
Forstlige Forsoegsvaesen i Danmark (DK ISSN 0085-0837) *409*
Forstwissenschaftliche Forschungen (GW ISSN 0071-772X) *409*
Fort Belknap Genealogical Association. Bulletin (US ISSN 0071-7738) *417*
Fort Burgwin Research Center. Publications (US ISSN 0071-7754) *468*
Fort Concho Report (US ISSN 0046-4651) *468*
Fort Hare Papers (SA ISSN 0015-8054) *263*
Fortbildung und Praxis (GW ISSN 0071-7835) *805*
Fortbildungskurse fuer Praktische Gastroenterologie *see* Gastroenterologische Fortbildungskurse fuer die Praxis *909*
Fortbildungskurse fuer Rheumatologie (SZ ISSN 0071-7851) *623*
Fortschritte der Arzneimittelforschung/ Progress in Drug Research/Progres des Recherches Pharmaceutiques (SZ ISSN 0071-786X) *684*
Fortschritte der Botanik *see* Progress in Botany *117*
Fortschritte der Chemie Organischer Naturstoffe/Progress in the Chemistry of Organic Natural Products (US ISSN 0071-7886) *252*
Fortschritte der Chemischen Forschung *see* Topics in Current Chemistry *248*
Fortschritte der Haematologie (GE) *595*

Fortschritte der Hochpolymeren-Forschung *see* Advances in Polymer Science *252*
Fortschritte der Immunitaetsforschung *see* Immunology Reports and Reviews *603*
Fortschritte der Kiefer- und Gesichts-Chirurgie (GW ISSN 0071-7916) *624*
Fortschritte der Krebsforschung *see* Recent Results in Cancer Research *606*
Fortschritte der Pflanzenzuechtung/ Advances in Plant Breeding (GW ISSN 0301-2727) *35*
Fortschritte der Physikalischen Chemie/Current Topics in Physical Chemistry (GW ISSN 0071-7924) *254*
Fortschritte der Praktischen Dermatologie und Venerologie (US ISSN 0071-7932) *611*
Fortschritte der Psychoanalyse (GW ISSN 0071-7940) *736*
Fortschritte der Urologie und Nephrologie (GW ISSN 0071-7975) *625*
Fortschritte der Verhaltensforschung/ Advances in Ethology (GW ISSN 0301-2808) *128*
Fortschritte der Veterinaermedizin/ Advances in Veterinary Medicine (GW ISSN 0301-2794) *894*
Fortschritte der Zoologie/Progress in Zoology (GW ISSN 0071-7991) *128*
Fortschritte im Acker- und Pflanzenbau/Advances in Agronomy and Crop Science (GW ISSN 0301-2735) *35*
Fortschritte in der Geologie von Rheinland und Westfalen (GW ISSN 0071-8009) *293*
Fortschritte in der Tierphysiologie und Tierernaehrung/Advances in Animal Physiology and Animal Nutrition (GW ISSN 0301-2743) *44, 128*
Fortschrittsberichte ueber Kolloide und Polymere *see* Progress in Colloid and Polymer Science *255*
Fortune Double 500 Directory (US) *222*
Fortune World Business Directory (US) *237*
Forum (Baltimore) *see* Forum Law Journal *512*
Forum der Psychiatrie (GW ISSN 0071-8025) *619*
Forum for Development Studies *see* Forum for Utviklingsstudier *721*
Forum for Utviklingsstudier/Forum for Development Studies (NO ISSN 0332-8244) *721*
Forum Law Journal (US ISSN 0360-2044) *512*
Forum Linguisticum (SZ) *544*
Forum on Fundamental Surgical Problems (US ISSN 0071-8041) *624*
Forum Phoneticum (GW ISSN 0341-3144) *544*
Forward and Back (US) *285*
Fossil Energy Research and Development Program of the U.S. Department of Energy *see* U.S. Department of Energy. Fossil Energy Research and Development Program *364*
Fossils and Strata (NO) *673*
Foto Cine Guia (AG) *650*
Foto Galaxis (SP) *693*
Fotogrametria, Fotointerpretacion y Geodesia (MX) *693*
Fotogrammetriska Meddelanden/ Photogrammetric Information (SW ISSN 0071-8068) *421*
Fotointerpretacja w Geografii (PL ISSN 0071-8076) *421, 693*
Fouilles de Delphes: Collection (FR) *60*
Foulsham's Original Old Moore's Almanack (UK ISSN 0071-8084) *360*
Foundation Center. Annual Report (US ISSN 0190-3357) *805*
Foundation Center. Report *see* Foundation Center. Annual Report *805*

Foundation Center National Data Book(US) *336, 805*
Foundation Directory (US ISSN 0071-8092) *810*
Foundation for Business Responsibilities. Dialogues (UK) *144*
Foundation for Business Responsibilities. Discussion Paper (UK ISSN 0073-7410) *144*
Foundation for Business Responsibilities. Occasional Papers (UK ISSN 0073-7429) *144*
Foundation for Business Responsibilities. Research Paper (UK ISSN 0073-7437) *144*
Foundation for Reformation Research. Bulletin of the Library *see* Sixteenth Century Bibliography *438*
Foundation for the Study of Cycles. Research Bulletin (US ISSN 0071-8106) *191*
Foundation Grants Index (US) *336*
Foundation Grants Index; Subjects on Microfiche *see* Comsearch Printouts: Subjects *326*
Foundation Grants to Individuals (US) *336, 805*
Foundation 500 (US) *839*
Foundations of Medieval History (UK) *453, 474*
Foundry Catalog File (US ISSN 0533-005X) *136*
Foundry Directory and Register of Forges (UK ISSN 0071-8130) *628*
Foundry Yearbook (UK ISSN 0306-4212) *628*
Four Things Every Woman Should Know *see* Homemaker's Handbook *479*
Fourth Quadrant (US) *271*
Fra Als og Sundeved (DK ISSN 0085-0845) *453*
Fra Holback Amt: Historiske Aarboeger(DK) *453*
Fra Viborg Amt. Aarbog (DK ISSN 0085-0853) *453*
Fracht-Schiffahrts-Konferenzen (GW) *878*
Fraenkische Geographische Gesellschaft. Mitteilungen (GW ISSN 0071-8173) *421*
Fraenkische Studien *see* Wuerzburger Geographische Arbeiten *428*
Fragmenta Entomologica (IT ISSN 0429-288X) *120*
Fragments (US ISSN 0015-9344) *564*
France. Archives Nationales. Centre d'Information de la Recherche Historique en France. Bulletin (FR ISSN 0071-819X) *453*
France. Bureau Central de Statistique Industrielle. Annuaire de Statistique Industrielle *see* France. Service du Traitement de l'Information et des Statistiques Industrielles. Annuaire de Statistique Industrielle *156*
France. Bureau de Recherches Geologiques et Minieres. Memoires (FR ISSN 0071-8246) *293, 643*
France. Bureau de Recherches Geologiques et Minieres. Resume des Principaux Resultats Scientifiques et Techniques (FR) *293*
France. Bureau des Longitudes. Annuaire: Ephemerides (FR) *82*
France. Caisse Nationale de Credit Agricole. Rapport sur le Credit Agricole Mutuel (FR ISSN 0071-8254) *28, 173*
France. Caisse Nationale de l'Assurance Maladie des Travailleurs Salaries. Statistiques de l'Annee (FR) *501*
France. Caisse Nationale des Allocations Familiales. Action Sociale (FR) *810*
France. Caisse Nationale des Allocations Familiales. Prestations Familiales. Resultats Generaux: Recettes, Depenses, Beneficiaires (FR) *810*
France. Centre de Recherches sur les Zones Arides. Publications. Serie Geologie *see* Centre Geologique et Geophysique de Montpellier. Publications. Serie Geologie *292*

France. Centre National de Coordination des Etudes et Recherches sur la Nutrition et l'Alimentation. Cahiers Techniques (FR ISSN 0071-8297) *666*
France. Centre National de la Recherche Scientifique. Colloques Nationaux (FR ISSN 0071-8319) *782*
France. Centre National de Recherche Zoologique. Departement de Genetique Animale. Bulletin Technique *see* France. Centre National de Recherche Zootechnique. Departement de Genetique Animale. Bulletin Technique *894*
France. Centre National de Recherche Zootechnique. Departement de Genetique Animale. Bulletin Technique (FR) *894*
France. Centre National pour l'Exploitation des Oceans. Centre Oceanologique de Bretagne. Recueil des Travaux (FR ISSN 0336-3112) *310*
France. Centre National pour l'Exploitation des Oceans. Colloques. Actes (FR ISSN 0335-8259) *310*
France. Centre National pour l'Exploitation des Oceans. Publications. Serie: Rapports Economiques et Juridiques (FR ISSN 0339-2910) *310, 512*
France. Centre National pour l'Exploitation des Oceans. Publications. Serie: Rapports Scientifiques et Techniques (FR ISSN 0339-2899) *310*
France. Centre National pour l'Exploitation des Oceans. Publications. Serie: Resultats des Campagnes a la Mer (FR ISSN 0339-2902) *310*
France. Comite des Travaux Historiques et Scientifiques. Bulletin Archeologique. (FR ISSN 0071-8394) *60*
France. Comite des Travaux Historiques et Scientifiques. Bulletin Philologique et Historique (Jusqu'a 1610) (FR ISSN 0071-8408) *453, 544*
France. Comite des Travaux Historiques et Scientifiques. Bulletin Philologique (Jusqu'a 1715) *see* France. Comite des Travaux Historiques et Scientifiques. Bulletin Philologique et Historique (Jusqu'a 1610) *453*
France. Comite des Travaux Historiques et Scientifiques. Section d'Archeologie. Actes du Congres National des Societes Savantes (FR ISSN 0071-8416) *60*
France. Comite des Travaux Historiques et Scientifiques. Section de Geographie. Bulletin (FR ISSN 0071-8432) *421*
France. Comite des Travaux Historiques et Scientifiques. Section d'Histoire Moderne et Contemporaine. Actes du Congres National des Societes Savantes (FR ISSN 0071-8440) *453*
France. Comite des Travaux Historiques et Scientifiques. Section d'Histoire Moderne et Contemporaine. Bulletin (FR ISSN 0071-8459) *453*
France. Comite des Travaux Historiques et Scientifiques. Section d'Histoire Moderne et Contemporaine (Depuis 1610). Bulletin *see* France. Comite des Travaux Historiques et Scientifiques. Section d'Histoire Moderne et Contemporaine. Bulletin *453*
France. Comite des Travaux Historiques et Scientifiques. Section d'Histoire Moderne et Contemporaine. Notices, Inventaires et Documents (FR) *432*
France. Comite Monetaire de la Zone Franc. Rapport *see* La Zone Franc *178*
France. Commissariat a l'Energie Atomique. Annual Report (FR ISSN 0071-8467) *363, 367, 702*

France. Commission Centrale des Marches. Guide du Fournisseur de l'Etat *see* France. Commission Centrale des Marches. Guide du Fournisseur de l'Etat et des Collectivites Locales *181*
France. Commission Centrale des Marches. Guide du Fournisseur de l'Etat et des Collectivites Locales (FR ISSN 0071-8483) *181*
France. Commission Centrale pour la Navigation du Rhin. Rapport Annuel(FR) *878*
France. Commission Departementale des Monuments Historiques du Pas de Calais. Bulletin (FR) *453*
France. Commission Departementale des Monuments Historiques du Pas de Calais. Memoires (FR) *453*
France. Commission des Operations de Bourse. Rapport au President de la Republique (FR) *203*
France. Commission Nationale de l'Amenagement du Territoire. Rapport (FR ISSN 0071-8491) *742*
France. Commission Technique des Ententes. Economiques Rapports (FR ISSN 0071-8505) *186*
France. Conseil des Impots. Rapport au President de la Republique (FR) *229*
France. Conseil National de la Comptabilite. Rapport d'Activite (FR ISSN 0071-8513) *742*
France. Conseil National du Credit. Rapport Annuel (FR) *173*
France. Delegation Generale a la Recherche Scientifique et Technique. Recherche dans le Domaine de l'Eau: Repertoire des Laboratoires (FR ISSN 0071-853X) *896*
France. Delegation Generale a la Recherche Scientifique et Technique. Repertoire des Scientifiques Francais. Tome 3: Biologie (FR ISSN 0080-1038) *103*
France. Delegation Generale a la Recherche Scientifique et Technique. Repertoire des Scientifiques Francais. Tome 4: Chimie (FR ISSN 0080-1046) *246*
France. Delegation Generale a la Recherche Scientifique et Technique. Repertoire des Scientifiques Francais. Tome 5: Physique (FR ISSN 0080-1062) *696*
France. Delegation Generale a la Recherche Scientifique et Technique. Repertoire National des Chercheurs: Sciences Sociales et Humaines. Tome 1: Ethnologie, Linguistique, Psychologie, Psychologie Sociale, Sociologie (FR ISSN 0080-116X) *544, 813*
France. Delegation Generale a la Recherche Scientifique et Technique. Repertoire National des Laboratoires; la Recherche Universitaire; Sciences Exactes et Naturelles. Tome 2: Biologie (FR ISSN 0071-8548) *103*
France. Delegation Generale a la Recherche Scientifique et Technique. Repertoire National des Laboratoires; la Recherche Universitaire; Sciences Exactes et Naturelles. Tome 3: Chimie (FR ISSN 0071-8556) *246*
France. Delegation Generale a la Recherche Scientifique et Technique. Repertoire National des Laboratoires; la Recherche Universitaire; Sciences Exactes et Naturelles. Tome 4: Mathematiques, Sciences de l'Espace et de la Terre (FR ISSN 0071-8564) *585*
France. Delegation Generale a la Recherche Scientifique et Technique. Repertoire National des Laboratoires; la Recherche Universitaire; Sciences Exactes et Naturelles. Tome 1: Physique (FR ISSN 0071-8572) *696*
France. Delegation Generale a la Recherche Scientifique et Technique. Repertoire Permanent de l'Administration Francaise (FR ISSN 0080-1186) *742*
France. Departement d'Economie et de Sociologie Rurales. Bulletin d'Information (FR ISSN 0339-2945) *186*

France. Departement des Statistiques de Transport. Annuaire Statistique des Transports (FR) *865*
France. Departement des Statistiques de Transport. Memento de Statistiques des Transports (FR) *865*
France. Direction des Affaires Exterieures et de la Cooperation. Rapport d'Activite-Electricite de France (FR) *354*
France. Direction des Forets. Production de la Branche Exploitation Forestiere et Production des Branches Science et Carbonisation en Foret (FR) *409*
France. Direction des Forets. Rapport sur le Fonds Forestier National (FR) *409*
France. Direction du Gaz et de l'Electricite. Statistiques Officielles de l'Industrie Gaziere en France *see* Statistiques de l'Industrie Gaziere en France *681*
France. Direction Generale de la Concurrence et des Prix. Bulletin Officiel des Services des Prix (FR ISSN 0071-870X) *222*
France. Direction Generale des Douanes et Droits Indirects. Annuaire Abrege de Statistiques (FR ISSN 0071-8637) *229*
France. Direction Generale des Douanes et Droits Indirects. Commentaires Annuels des Statistiques du Commerce Exterieur (FR ISSN 0071-8645) *195*
France. Direction Generale des Douanes et Droits Indirects. Statistiques du Commerce Exterieur: Importations- Exportations. Nomenclature: N.G.P. (Nomenclature Generale des Produits) (FR ISSN 0071-8688) *156*
France. Direction Nationale des Douanes et Droits Indirects. Tableau General des Transports (FR ISSN 0071-8726) *195*
France. Direction Nationale des Douanes et Droits Indirects. Transport du Commerce Exterieur (FR ISSN 0071-8718) *195*
France. Imprimerie Nationale. Annuaire. (FR ISSN 0078-9666) *758*
France. Inspection Generale des Finances. Annuaire (FR ISSN 0071-8742) *229*
France. Institut National d'Etudes Demographiques. Cahiers de Travaux et Documents (FR ISSN 0071-8823) *727*
France. Institut National d'Etudes Demographiques. Centre d'Etudes de l'Emploi. Cahiers (FR) *207*
France. Institut National de la Sante et de la Recherche Medicale. Colloques(FR) *595, 626*
France. Institut National de la Statistique et des Etudes Economiques. Collections. Serie C, Comptes et Planification (FR) *156*
France. Institut National de la Statistique et des Etudes Economiques. Collections. Serie D, Demographie et Emploi (FR) *207, 727*
France. Institut National de la Statistique et des Etudes Economiques. Collections. Serie E, Enterprises (FR) *156*
France. Institut National de la Statistique et des Etudes Economiques. Collections. Serie M, Menages (FR) *156*
France. Institut National de la Statistique et des Etudes Economiques. Collections. Serie R, Regions (FR) *839*
France. Institut National de la Statistique et des Etudes Economiques. Documents Divers (FR ISSN 0336-6979) *156*
France. Institut National de la Statistique et des Etudes Economiques. Enquete sur l'Emploi (FR) *727*

France. Institut National de la Statistique et des Etudes Economiques. l'Enseignement dans les Departments d'Outre-Mer (FR) *327*
France. Institut National de Recherche et de Documentation Pedagogiques. Cahiers de Documentation (FR) *344*
France. Institut National de Recherche et de Documentation Pedagogiques. Repertoire d'Etablissements Publics d'Enseignement et de Services (FR ISSN 0071-8963) *331*
France. Laboratoires des Ponts et Chaussees. Rapport de Recherche (FR ISSN 0085-2643) *375*
France. Mediateur. Rapport Annuel du Mediateur (FR) *721*
France. Ministere de l'Agriculture. Collections de Statistique Agricole, Serie Etudes (FR) *28*
France. Ministere de l'Agriculture. Enquete Communautaire sur la Structure des Exploitations Agricoles(FR) *15*
France. Ministere de l'Agriculture et du Developpement Rural. Service Central des Enquetes et Etudes Statistiques. Statistique Agricole Annuelle *see* France. Ministere de l'Agriculture. Enquete Communautaire sur la Structure des Exploitations Agricoles e *15*
France. Ministere de l'Agriculture. Information Rapides Statistiques des Entreprises *28*
France. Ministere de l'Agriculture. Informations Rapides Agro-Alimentaires *see* France. Ministere de l'Agriculture. Information Rapides Statistiques des Entreprises *28*
France. Ministere de l'Economie et des Finances. Balance des Paiements Entre la France et l'Exterieur (FR ISSN 0071-8890) *195, 229*
France. Ministere de l'Economie et des Finances. Budget *see* France. Ministere du Budget. Budget *229*
France. Ministere de l'Economie et des Finances. Caisses d'Epargne Ordinaire (FR) *173*
France. Ministere de l'Economie et des Finances. Rapport du Conseil de Direction du Fonds de Developpement Economique et Social *see* France. Ministere de l'Economie. Rapport du Conseil de Direction du Fonds de Developpement Economique et Social *222*
France. Ministere de l'Economie. Rapport du Conseil de Direction du Fonds de Developpement Economique et Social (FR ISSN 0071-8920) *222*
France. Ministere de la Cooperation. Service des Etudes et Questions Internationales. Donnees Statistiques sur les Activites Economiques, Culturelles et Sociales (FR) *710*
France. Ministere de la Cooperation. Service des Etudes et Questions Internationales. Etudes et Documents(FR) *721*
France. Ministere de la Culture et de l'Environnement. Bilan d'Activite des Agences Financieres de Bassin (FR) *386*
France. Ministere de la Qualite de la Vie. Bulletin de Documentation (FR) *90, 390*
France. Ministere de la Sante et de la Securite Sociale. Notes d'Information(FR) *751*
France. Ministere de la Sante et de la Securite Sociale. Tableaux Statistiques "Sante et Securite Sociale" (FR) *751*
France. Ministere de la Sante. Note d'Information *see* France. Ministere de la Sante et de la Securite Sociale. Notes d'Information *751*
France. Ministere de la Sante Publique et de la Securite Sociale. Annuaire Statistique de la Sante et de l'Action Sociale *see* France. Ministere de la Sante et de la Securite Sociale. Tableaux Statistiques "Sante et Securite Sociale *751*

France. Ministere de la Sante. Tableaux Sante et Securite Sociale *see* France. Ministere de la Sante et de la Securite Sociale. Tableaux Statistiques "Sante et Securite Sociale *751*
France. Ministere des Affaires Etrangeres. Recueil des Traites et Accords de la France (FR ISSN 0071-8971) *523*
France. Ministere des Affaires Sociales. Information Actualites *see* France. Ministere de la Sante et de la Securite Sociale. Notes d'Information *751*
France. Ministere du Budget. Budget (FR ISSN 0071-8904) *229*
France. Office National d'Etudes et de Recherches Aerospatiales. Activities (FR ISSN 0078-3773) *8*
France. Office National d'Etudes et de Recherches Aerospatiales. Notes Techniques (FR ISSN 0078-3781) *8*
France. Office National d'Etudes et de Recherches Aerospatiales. Publications (FR ISSN 0078-379X) *8*
France. Office National d'Etudes et de Recherches Aerospatiales. Recueil de Notes sur l'Activite de ONERA *see* France. Office National d'Etudes et de Recherches Aerospatiales. Activities *8*
France. Office National d'Immigration. Statistiques de l'Immigration (FR ISSN 0071-903X) *732*
France. Secretariat d'Etat aux Affaires Etrangeres Charge de la Cooperation. Direction de l'Aide au Developpement. Mali. Dossier d'Information Economique (FR) *200*
France. Secretariat d'Etat aux Affaires Etrangeres Charge de la Cooperation. Direction de l'Aide au Developpement. Niger. Dossier d'Information Economique (FR) *200*
France. Service de Documentation et de Cartographie Geographiques. Memoires et Documents. (FR ISSN 0071-8262) *422*
France. Service du Traitement de l'Information et des Statistiques Industrielles. Annuaire de Statistique Industrielle (FR ISSN 0071-8211) *156*
France. Service du Traitement de l'Information et des Statistiques Industrielles. Recueil Statistiques (FR) *156*
France. Service Interdepartemental de la Protection Civile. Bulletin (FR) *258*
France-Allemagne (FR ISSN 0071-8181) *721*
France-Collectivites: Guide National des Chefs des Services d'Achats et des Fournisseurs de Collectivites (FR ISSN 0071-8386) *181*
France des Points Chauds (FR) *710*
France en Poche. Total Guide (FR ISSN 0071-8734) *886*
France-Iberie Recherche. Etudes et Documents (FR ISSN 0082-5409) *710*
France-Iberie Recherche. Theses et Documents (FR ISSN 0082-5417) *453*
France-Peinture (FR ISSN 0071-9048) *673*
France Plastiques (FR ISSN 0071-9056) *706*
France Protestante (FR ISSN 0071-9064) *772*
France, Secretariat d'Etat aux Affaires Etrangeres Charge de la Cooperation. Direction de l'Aide au Developpement. Cote d'Ivoire. Dossier d'Information Economique (FR) *200*
France-Sports (FR ISSN 0071-9102) *820, 829*
Franchise Annual (US ISSN 0318-8752) *237*
Francis Thompson Society. Journal *see* Eighteen Nineties Society.Journal *563*
Franciscan Studies (US ISSN 0080-5459) *774*

Franco British Trade Directory (UK ISSN 0071-917X) *179, 196*
Frankfurt am Main. Statistisches Amt und Wahlamt. Statistisches Jahrbuch (GW ISSN 0071-9218) *839*
Frankfurt Am Main. Universitaet. Institut fuer Wissenschaftliche Irenik. Schriften *see* Studia Irenica *767*
Frankfurter Abhandlungen zur Slavistik (GW ISSN 0473-5277) *544*
Frankfurter Althistorische Studien (GW) *453*
Frankfurter Beitraege zur Germanistik (GW ISSN 0071-9226) *544, 564*
Frankfurter Geographische Hefte (GW ISSN 0071-9234) *422*
Frankfurter Turkologische Arbeitsmittel(GW ISSN 0342-1082) *474, 669*
Franklin McLean Memorial Research Institute. Annual Report (US) *111, 595*
Franklin Mint. Limited Editions (US) *477*
Franklin Mint. Numismatic Issues *see* Franklin Mint. Limited Editions *477*
De Franse Nederlanden/Pays-Bas Francais (BE) *391, 782*
Fraser's Canadian Trade Directory (CN ISSN 0071-9277) *218, 237*
Fraser's Construction & Building Directory (CN ISSN 0318-0344) *136*
Fraternal Actuarial Association. Proceedings (US ISSN 0071-9293) *499*
Frau mit Herz (GW) *900*
Die Frauenfrage in Deutschland. Bibliographie (GW ISSN 0344-1415) *90, 901, 901*
Free Albanian/Shqiptari i Lire (US ISSN 0488-728X) *710*
Free and Inexpensive Learning Materials (US ISSN 0071-9307) *348*
Free China *see* Free China Today *909*
Free China Today (CH ISSN 0304-1204) *909*
Free Loan Films *see* Association Films. Free Loan Films *648*
Free Loan 16 mm. Sound Motion Pictures *see* Association Films. Free Loan Films *648*
Free Stock Photography Directory (US ISSN 0190-1567) *693*
Free-World Trends in Passenger-Car Production and Engines *see* World Trends in Passenger-Car Production and Engines *872*
Freedom from Hunger Campaign. Basic Studies (UN ISSN 0071-934X) *15, 404*
Freedom from Hunger Campaign. F F H C Report (UN ISSN 0532-6370) *28, 200*
Freedom from Hunger Campaign/ Action for Development (UN) *909*
Freedom from Hunger Campaign/ Campaign Development Bulletin *see* Freedom from Hunger Campaign/ Action for Development *909*
Freedom from Hunger Campaign/Ideas and Action Bulletin *see* Freedom from Hunger Campaign/Action for Development *909*
Freedom of Speech Yearbook *see* S C A Free Speech Yearbook *74*
Freedom of Vision (UK ISSN 0016-0571) *74*
Freeman and Freeman's Tax Practice Deskbook (Supplement) (US) *229*
Freemen (UK) *454*
Freer Gallery of Art, Washington, D.C. Occasional Papers (US ISSN 0071-9382) *74*
Freiberger Forschungshefte. Montanwissenschaften: Reihe A. Bergbau und Geotechnik, Arbeitsschutz und Sicherheitstechnik, Grundstoff-Verfahrenstechnik, Maschinen- und Energietechnik (GE ISSN 0071-9390) *293, 643*
Freiberger Forschungshefte. Montanwissenschaften: Reihe B. Metallurgie *see* Freiberger Forschungshefte. Montanwissenschaften: Reihe B. Metallurgie und Werbstofftechnik *628*

Freiberger Forschungshefte. Montanwissenschaften: Reihe B. Metallurgie und Werbstofftechnik (GE) *628*
Freiberger Forschungshefte. Montanwissenschaften: Reihe C. Geowissenschaften (GE ISSN 0071-9404) *288, 673*
Freiburger Altorientalische Studien (GW ISSN 0170-3307) *669*
Freiburger Beitraege zur Indologie (GW ISSN 0340-6261) *443, 544*
Freiburger Geographische Arbeiten (GW ISSN 0071-9439) *909*
Freiburger Geographische Hefte (GW ISSN 0071-9447) *422*
Freiburger Islamstudien (GW ISSN 0170-3285) *670, 769*
Freie Universitaet Berlin. John F. Kennedy-Institut fuer Nordamerika Studien. Materialien (GW) *468*
Freie Universitaet Berlin. Osteuropa-Institut. Berichte (GW ISSN 0067-5873) *454, 490, 710*
Freie Universitaet Berlin. Osteuropa-Institut. Bibliographische Mitteilungen (GW ISSN 0067-5881) *437*
Freie Universitaet Berlin. Osteuropa-Institut. Erziehungswissenschaftliche Veroeffentlichungen (GW ISSN 0067-589X) *318, 710*
Freie Universitaet Berlin. Osteuropa-Institut. Historische Veroeffentlichungen (GW ISSN 0067-5903) *454*
Freie Universitaet Berlin. Osteuropa-Institut. Philosophische und Soziologische Veroeffentlichungen (GW ISSN 0067-5911) *688, 710, 813*
Freie Universitaet Berlin. Osteuropa-Institut. Rechtswissenschaftliche Veroeffentlichungen (GW) *512*
Freie Universitaet Berlin. Osteuropa-Institut. Slavistische Veroeffentlichungen (GW ISSN 0067-592X) *544, 564*
Freie Universitaet Berlin. Osteuropa-Institut. Wirtschaftswissenschaftliche Veroeffentlichungen (GW ISSN 0067-5938) *144*
Freies Deutsches Hochstift, Frankfurt am Main. Jahrbuch (GW ISSN 0071-9463) *454*
Freight Industry Yearbook (UK ISSN 0071-9471) *862*
Freighthoppers' Manual for North America (UK) *886*
Freiwilliger Feuerwehren *see* Feuerwehr-Jahrbuch *394*
Fremdenverkehr in Oesterreich (AU ISSN 0071-948X) *886*
French Boating Export *see* Construction Nautique Francaise *877*
French-Canadian Civilization Research Center. Cahiers/Centre de Recherche en Civilisation Canadienne-Francaise. Cahiers (CN ISSN 0069-1771) *468*
French Colonial Historical Society. Proceedings of the Meeting (US) *454*
French Farm and Village Holiday Guide (UK) *886*
French Genealogist (US) *417*
French III *see* French *74*
French Periodical Index/Repertoriex (US ISSN 0362-5044) *90*
French Studies in Southern Africa (SA) *564*
French VII Bibliography, Critical and Biographical References for the Study of Contemporary French Literature *see* French XX Bibliography; Critical and Biographical References for the Study of French Literature since 1885 *91*
French XX Bibliography; Critical and Biographical References for the Study of French Literature since 1885 (US ISSN 0085-0888) *91*
French (US) *91, 437*
Frente Nacional pro-Defensa del Petroleo Venezolano. Actuaciones (VE) *679*
Fresh Water Fishing Guide (US ISSN 0071-5611) *829*

Freshwater Fisherman (US) *829*
Fresno County Medical Society. Bulletin (US ISSN 0016-1160) *595*
Freude mit Buechern (GW) *760*
Friends Historical Society. Journal (UK ISSN 0071-9587) *776*
Friends of the National Libraries. Annual Report (UK) *530, 758*
Friends Service Council. Annual Report *see* Quaker Peace and Service. Annual Report *808*
Fringe Benefit Costs in Canada *see* Employee Benefit Costs in Canada *207*
Frodskaparrit; Annales Societatis Scientiarum Faeroensis (FA ISSN 0085-0896) *782*
Frodskaparrit; Annales Societatis Scientiarum Faeronsis. Supplementa (FA ISSN 0429-7539) *782*
La Fronde (SZ) *900*
Frontera Oberta (FR ISSN 0071-9633) *556*
Frontier Military Series (US ISSN 0071-9641) *468, 638*
Frontier News (AT ISSN 0016-2108) *772*
Frontiers (US ISSN 0016-2159) *782*
Frontiers in Education Conference. Proceedings (US ISSN 0190-5848) *272*
Frontiers in Education Conference. Publication *see* Conference on Frontiers in Education. Digest *316*
Frontiers in Neuroendocrinology (US ISSN 0532-7466) *611*
Frontiers in Physics (US ISSN 0429-7725) *696*
Frontiers of Biology (NE ISSN 0071-965X) *909*
Frontiers of Economics (US ISSN 0362-6911) *909*
Frontiers of Gastrointestinal Research (SZ ISSN 0302-0665) *613*
Frontiers of Hormone Research (SZ ISSN 0301-3073) *611*
Frontiers of Matrix Biology (SZ ISSN 0301-0155) *103*
Frontiers of Oral Physiology (SZ ISSN 0301-536X) *609*
Frontiers of Power Technology Conference. Proceedings (US ISSN 0161-5319) *851*
Frontiers of Radiation Therapy and Oncology (SZ ISSN 0071-9676) *605, 622*
Frozen Fishery Products. Annual Summary (US ISSN 0162-6108) *401, 839*
Frozen Food Factbook and Directory (US ISSN 0071-9684) *404*
Frozen Foods in Denmark (DK) *404*
Frozen Foods Year Book (UK ISSN 0071-9692) *404*
Fructidor International (FR) *35*
Fruehmittelalterliche Studien (GW ISSN 0071-9706) *454*
Fruit World Annual and Orchardists Guide (AT ISSN 0085-090X) *415*
Fryske Namen (NE) *417*
Fuchsia Annual (UK ISSN 0071-9730) *415*
Fuehrer durch die Technische Literatur (GW ISSN 0071-9749) *851*
Fuehrer zu Vor- und Fruegeschichtlichen Denkmaelern (GW ISSN 0071-9757) *60, 74*
Fuehrung und Organisation der Unternehmung (SZ ISSN 0071-9765) *215*
Fuel and Energy Science Series (US) *363, 372*
Fuel Oil Sales (US) *363, 679*
Fuentes Cartograficas Espanolas (SP) *422*
Fuentes Indigenas de la Cultura Nahuatl (MX ISSN 0071-9773) *469*
Fuer die Sicherheit im Bergland (AU) *829*
Fujikura Technical Review (JA) *354*
Fukui University. Faculty of Education. Memoirs. Series 2: Natural Science (JA ISSN 0071-9781) *782*
Fukui University. Faculty of Education. Memoirs. Series 5: Applied Science and Agricultural Science (JA) *15*

Fukui University. Faculty of Education. Memoirs. Series 5: Applied Science and Home Economics (JA) 479
Fukui University. Faculty of Education. Memoirs. Series 5: Applied Science and Technology (JA) 851
Fukui University. Faculty of Education. Memoirs. Series 6: Physical Education (JA) 348
Fulbright Awards Abroad (US) 342
Fulcrum (SA ISSN 0071-979X) 367
Functiones et Approximatio Commentarii Mathematici (PL) 585
Fundacao Calouste Gulbenkian. Centro de Investigacao Pedagogica. Estudos (PO) 318
Fundacao Carlos Chagas. Departamento de Pesquisas Educacionais. Profissoes(BL) 909
Fundacao Carlos Chagas. Departamento de Pesquisas Educacionais. Simposios(BL) 909
Fundacao Centro de Pesquisas Economicas e Sociais do Piaui. Atividades C E P R O see Fundacao Centro de Pesquisas Economicas e Sociais do Piaui. Relatorio de Atividades 813
Fundacao Centro de Pesquisas Economicas e Sociais do Piaui. Relatorio de Atividades (BL) 144, 813
Fundacao Cultural de Curitiba. Relatorio (BL) 469
Fundacao de Assistencia Aos Municipios do Estado do Parana. Boletim dos Municipios (BL) 805
Fundacao de Assistencia Aos Municipios do Estado do Parana. Boletim Informativo (BL) 749
Fundacion Bariloche. Boletin see Universitaet Zuerich. Soziologisches Institut. Bulletin 817
Fundacion Bariloche. Departamento de Recursos Naturales y Energia. Publicaciones see Fundacion Bariloche. Instituto de Economia de la Energia. Publicaciones 363
Fundacion Bariloche. Departamento de Recursos Naturales y Energia. Publicaciones see Fundacion Bariloche. Grupo de Analisis de Sistemas Ecologicos. Publicaciones 386
Fundacion Bariloche. Departamento de Sociologia. Documentos de Trabajo see Fundacion Bariloche. Desarrollos Sinergicos. Publicaciones 813
Fundacion Bariloche. Departamento de Sociologia. Publicaciones see Fundacion Bariloche. Desarrollos Sinergicos. Publicaciones 813
Fundacion Bariloche. Desarrollos Sinergicos. Publicaciones (AG) 813
Fundacion Bariloche. Grupo de Analisis de Sistemas Ecologicos. Publicaciones (AG) 386
Fundacion Bariloche. Instituto de Economia de la Energia. Publicaciones (AG) 363, 643
Fundacion Bariloche. Memoria Anual (AG) 782
Fundacion Bariloche. Programa de Recursos Naturales y Energia. Publicaciones see Fundacion Bariloche. Instituto de Economia de la Energia. Publicaciones 363
Fundacion Dominicana de Desarrollo. Informe Anual (DR) 186
Fundacion Fomento de Estudios Sociales y Sociologia Aplicada Coleccion Fundacion FOESSA. Serie Estudios see Coleccion Fundacion FOESSA. Serie Estudios 812
Fundacion Miguel Lillo. Miscelanea (AG ISSN 0074-025X) 115, 120, 293
Fundacion Roux-Ocefa. Archivos (AG ISSN 0016-271X) 619
Fundamenta Informaticae see Annales Societatis Mathematicae Polonae. Series 4: Fundamenta Informaticae 584
Fundamental Concepts of Estate Administration (US ISSN 0164-1255) 512
Fundamental Studies in Computer Science (NE) 272

Fundamental Studies in Engineering (NE) 367
Fundamentals of Aerospace Instrumentation (US ISSN 0094-3975) 8
Fundamentals of Botany Series (US) 115
Fundamentals of Educational Planning (UN ISSN 0071-9862) 342
Fundamentals of Educational Planning. Lecture-Discussion Series (UN ISSN 0071-9870) 342
Fundberichte aus Baden-Wuerttemberg (GW) 61
Fundberichte aus Hessen (GW ISSN 0071-9889) 61
Fundberichte aus Oesterreich (AU) 69
Fundberichte aus Schwaben, Neue Folge see Fundberichte aus Baden-Wuerttemberg 61
Fundheft fuer Arbeitsrecht (GW ISSN 0071-9900) 207, 512
Fundheft fuer Oeffentliches Recht (GW ISSN 0071-9919) 512
Fundheft fuer Zivilrecht (GW ISSN 0071-9927) 512
Fungicide and Nematicide Tests (US) 35
Fungus see Kavaka 116
Funktionsanalyse Biologischer Systeme (GW ISSN 0340-0840) 103, 126
Funparks Directory (US) 886
Funspots Directory see Funparks Directory 886
Furdek (US) 392
Furnished Holiday Homes & Caravans (UK ISSN 0071-996X) 886
Furnished Holidays in Britain see Self-Catering and Furnished Holidays 890
Furnishing and Decorating Ideas see Better Homes and Gardens Furnishings and Decorating Ideas 502
Fusion-Fission Energy Systems Review Meeting. Proceedings (US) 363
Future Gas Consumption of the United States (US) 679
Futurist Library (US) 782
Fynske Aarboeger (DK ISSN 0085-0918) 454
G A/Global Architecture (JA) 69
G.A.I.U. Handbook of Wages, Hours and Fringe Benefits (Graphic Arts International Union) (US ISSN 0094-4211) 207, 733
G.A.P.E (Guyana Association of Professional Engineers) (GY) 367
G A T F Technical Services Report (Graphic Arts Technical Foundation) (US) 851
G A T T Studies in International Trade (General Agreement on Tariffs and Trade) (UN) 196
G B E: Export Directory of Brazil see Export Directory of Brazil/Guia Brasileiro de Exportacao 237
G C S A A Membership Directory see Golf Course Superintendents Association of America. Membership Directory 824
G; Documentation Technique et Commerciale des Vendeurs de Gaz (FR ISSN 0072-0046) 144
G E C-A E I Telecommunications see G E C Telecommunications Journal 264
G E C Telecommunications Journal (General Electric Co. Ltd. of England) (UK ISSN 0046-5593) 264
G R I Newsletter (Gravure Research Institute) (US ISSN 0534-0489) 733
GA Houses (JA) 69, 484
Gaba Pastoral Papers see Spearhead 767
Gabinetto Disegni e Stampe degli Uffizi. Cataloghi. (IT ISSN 0072-0070) 652
Gabon. Direction Generale des Finances et du Budget. Projet du Budget General (GO) 229
Gaceta (CK) 556
Gaceta Agricola (MX) 15

Gaceta Bibliotecaria del Peru (PE ISSN 0433-0730) 530
Gadney's Guide to 1800 International Contests, Festivals & Grants in Film & Video, Photography, TV-Radio Broadcasting, Writing, Poetry, Playwriting & Journalism (US) 267, 504, 650, 693
Gaertnerische Berufspraxis (GW ISSN 0301-2719) 415
Gaikoku Koku Uchu Bunken Mokuroku see Foreign Aero-Space Literature 11
Gaikokugo Gaikoku Bungaku Kenkyu see Essays in Foreign Languages and Literatures 543
Gal-ed (IS) 392
Galerie Nationale du Canada. Bulletin Annuelle see National Gallery of Canada. Annual Bulletin 654
Galerie Nationale du Canada. Journal see National Gallery of Canada. Journal 77
Galerie Nierendorf, Berlin. Kunstblaetter (GW ISSN 0072-0089) 652
Galerie Sanct Lucas. Gemaelde Alter Meister (AU) 652
Galicia y Rio de la Plata. Compania de Seguros. Memoria y Balance General(AG) 499
Gallagher Presidents' Report (US) 5, 218
Galleria del Cavallino. Mostre (IT) 652
Gallia. Supplement (FR ISSN 0072-0119) 61
Gallia Prehistoire. Supplement (FR ISSN 0072-0100) 61, 422
Galloway Herd Book (UK) 44
Galloway Journal (UK ISSN 0430-9928) 44
Galpin Society Journal (UK ISSN 0072-0127) 659
Gambia. Central Statistics Department. Annual Report of External Trade Statistics see External Trade Statistics of Gambia 155
Gambia. Central Statistics Department. Directory of Establishments (GM) 238
Gambia. Central Statistics Department. Education Statistics (GM) 327, 839
Gambia. Central Statistics Department. Statistical Working Paper (GM) 909
Gambia. Central Statistics Department. Tourist Statistics (GM) 839, 893
Gambia. Education Department. Education Statistics see Gambia. Central Statistics Department. Education Statistics 327
Gambia. Oilseeds Marketing Board. Report see Gambia. Produce Marketing Board. Annual Report 28
Gambia. Produce Marketing Board. Annual Report (GM ISSN 0301-8423) 28
Gambit (US ISSN 0016-4275) 564
Gamma Field Symposia (JA ISSN 0435-1096) 15, 122
Gandhi Memorial Lectures (KE ISSN 0072-0143) 443, 512
Gandhi Peace Foundation Lectures (II) 721
Ganglia see Gronk 556
Gann Monographs (US ISSN 0072-0151) 605
Garcia Lorca Review (US ISSN 0162-0029) 556
Garden Fax (CN) 415
Garden Supply Retailer Green Book (US) 415
Garden Writers Bulletin (US ISSN 0016-4631) 415
Gardening and Outdoor Ideas see Woman's Day 101 Gardening & Outdoor Ideas 416
Gardens' Bulletin, Singapore (SI ISSN 0072-0178) 115
Gardens of England and Wales Open to the Public see Gardens Open to the Public in England and Wales 415
Gardens Open to the Public in England and Wales (UK ISSN 0141-2361) 415
Gardens to Visit (UK) 415
Garment Manufacturer's Index (US) 261
Garuda (US ISSN 0046-5445) 771

Gas and Fuel Corporation of Victoria. Annual Report (AT ISSN 0072-0208) 679
Gas Council (Great Britain) Report and Accounts see British Gas Corporation. Report and Accounts 678
Gas Directory and Undertakings of the World see Gas Directory and Who's Who 679
Gas Directory and Who's Who (UK ISSN 0307-3084) 679
Gas Facts (US) 679
Gas Industry Directory see Gas Directory and Who's Who 679
Gas Journal Directory see Gas Directory and Who's Who 679
Gas Kinetics and Energy Transfer (UK ISSN 0309-6890) 255
Gas Marketing Pocket Book and Diary (UK ISSN 0072-0259) 679
Gas Processors Association. Annual Convention. Proceedings (US ISSN 0096-8870) 679
Gas Resource Studies (US) 363, 679
Gas Services Pocket Book see Gas Marketing Pocket Book and Diary 679
Gas Turbine Catalog see Turbomachinery Catalog and Workbook 383
Gas Utility and Pipeline Industry Projections (US ISSN 0065-8391) 909
Gasolin 23 (GW) 564
Gaster; l'Annuaire de Gastro-Enterologie (FR ISSN 0072-0291) 613
Gastroenterologische Fortbildungskurse fuer die Praxis (SZ ISSN 0071-7843) 909
GATT-Fly (CN) 721
Gauhati University. Department of Anthropology. Bulletin. (II) 49
Gauldalsminne (NO) 454
Gayana: Botanica (CL ISSN 0016-5301) 115
Gayana: Zoologica (CL ISSN 0016-531X) 128
Gaz de France. Secretariat General. Schema d'Organisation Profor (FR ISSN 0072-0321) 0
Gaz et L'Industrie see G; Documentation Technique et Commerciale des Vendeurs de Gaz 144
Gazdasagtorteneti Ertekezesek (HU ISSN 0072-033X) 191
Gazeteer of India (II ISSN 0072-0348) 443
Gazeto (FR ISSN 0072-0356) 544
Gazetteer of Canada (CN ISSN 0576-1999) 422
Gdanski Rocznik Kulturalny see Rocznik Kulturalny Ziemi Gdanskiej 460
Gdanskie Towarzystwo Naukowe. Wydzial I. Nauk Spolecznych i Humanistycznych. Komisja Archeologiczna. Prace (PL ISSN 0072-0410) 61, 454
Gdanskie Towarzystwo Naukowe. Wydzial I. Nauk Spolecznych i Humanistycznych. Seria Monografii (PL ISSN 0433-230X) 454
Gdanskie Towarzystwo Naukowe. Wydzial I. Nauk Spolecznych i Humanistycznych. Seria Popularnonaukowa "Pomorze Gdanskie" (PL ISSN 0072-0429) 454
Gdanskie Towarzystwo Naukowe. Wydzial I. Nauk Spolecznych i Humanistycznych. Seria Zrodel (PL ISSN 0072-0437) 454
Gdanskie Towarzystwo Naukowe. Wydzial III. Nauk Matematyczno-Przyrodniczych. Rozprawy (PL ISSN 0072-0445) 585, 782
Gebbie House Magazine Directory see Internal Publications Directory 759
Gebbie Press All-in-One Directory (US ISSN 0097-8175) 264
GECAMINES Annual Report/GECAMINES Rapport Annuel (Generale des Carrieres et des Mines) (ZR) 643
GECAMINES Rapport Annuel see GECAMINES Annual Report 643

Geesaman Cousins (US) *417*
Gefahrgut Kontakte/Dangerous Cargo Contacts (GW) 238, *878*
Gegenschein (AT ISSN 0310-9968) *556*
Gegenwartsfragen der Ost-Wirtschaft (GW ISSN 0072-0534) *144*
Geijutsu Shunju (JA ISSN 0385-5694) *74*
Geiriadur Prifysgol Cymru (UK ISSN 0072-0542) *544*
Geirui Kenkyusho Eibun Hokoku see Whales Research Institute, Tokyo, Japan. Scientific Reports *131*
Geistige Begegnung (GW ISSN 0072-0550) *564*
Geltende Seekriegsrecht in Einzeldarstellungen see Das Geltende Seevoelkerrecht in Einzeldarstellungen *523*
Das Geltende Seevoelkerrecht in Einzeldarstellungen (GW) *523,* 639
Gem & Jewellery Yearbook (II) *503*
Gemeinsames Amtsblatt des Landes Baden-Wuerttemberg (GW ISSN 0016-6200) *749*
Gemeinschaft der Selbst-Verwirklichung. Jahresheft (US ISSN 0072-0577) *688*
Genava (SZ ISSN 0072-0585) *61,* 74
Genealogical Society of Greater Miami. Newsletter (US) *417*
Genealogisches Handbuch des Bayerischen Adels (GW ISSN 0085-0934) *417*
Geneeskundig Adresboek (NE) *595*
Geneeskundig Adresboek voor Nederland see Geneeskundig Adresboek *595*
Geneeskundig Jaarboek see Geneeskundig Jaarboek Medicijnen *595*
Geneeskundig Jaarboek Medicijnen (NE) *595*
Geneeskundig Jaarboekje see Geneeskundig Adresboek *595*
Geneeskundig Jaarboekje see Geneeskundig Jaarboek Medicijnen *595*
General Agreement on Tariffs and Trade. Basic Instruments and Selected Documents Series. Supplement (UN ISSN 0072-0623) *196*
General Agreement on Tariffs and Trade. G A T T Activities in (Year) (UN ISSN 0072-0615) *196*
General Agreement on Tariffs and Trade. International Trade (UN ISSN 0072-064X) *196*
General Agreement on Tariffs and Trade Studies in International Trade see G A T T Studies in International Trade *196*
General and Applied Entomology (AT ISSN 0158-0760) *120*
General and Synthetic Methods (UK) *252*
General Atomic Company. Library. Journal of Holdings of the Library (US ISSN 0072-0712) *702*
General Catalogue of Unesco and Unesco-Sponsored Publications (UN ISSN 0072-0658) *717*
General Commission on Safety and Health in the Iron and Steel Industry. Report (EI) *495,* 628
General Conference of the New Church. Yearbook (UK ISSN 0072-0666) *776*
General Convention of the New Jerusalem. Journal (US) *765*
General Council of British Shipping. Annual Report (UK) *878*
General Dental Council. Dentists Register (UK ISSN 0072-0674) *609*
General Dental Council. Minutes of the Proceedings (UK ISSN 0072-0682) *609*
General Directory of the Press and Periodicals in Jordan and Kuwait (SY ISSN 0072-0690) 504, *758*
General Directory of the Press and Periodicals in Syria (SY ISSN 0072-0704) 504, *758*

General Dynamic Corporation. General Atomic Division. Library. Journal of Holdings see General Atomic Company. Library. Journal of Holdings of the Library *702*
General Education Reading Material Series (II ISSN 0072-0720) *318*
General Electric Co. Ltd. of England Telecommunications Journal see G E C Telecommunications Journal *264*
General Encyclopedias in Print see Encyclopedia Buying Guide *360*
General Fisheries Council for the Mediterranean. Proceedings and Technical Papers. Debats et Documents Techniques (UN ISSN 0072-0747) *397*
General Fisheries Council for the Mediterranean. Reports of the Sessions (UN ISSN 0072-0755) *397*
General Fisheries Council for the Mediterranean. Studies and Reviews (UN ISSN 0433-3519) *397*
General Information Concerning Trademarks (US ISSN 0083-3029) *676*
General Medical Council, London. Medical Register (UK ISSN 0072-0763) *595*
General Mills American Family Report (US) *813*
General Minutes of the Annual Conferences of the United Methodist Church see United Methodist Church. General Minutes of the Annual Conferences *773*
General Motors Public Interest Report (US) 222, *871*
General Motors Symposia Series (US) *871*
General Report on the Activities of the European Communities (EI ISSN 0069-6749) *186*
General Semantics Bulletin (US ISSN 0072-0771) *544*
General Systems Yearbook (US ISSN 0072-0798) *782*
General Treaty for Central American Economic Integration. Permanent Secretariat. Newsletter (GT ISSN 0553-6898) *200*
Generale des Carrieres et des Mines. Monographie (ZR) *643*
Generale des Carrieres et des Mines GECAMINES Annual Report see GECAMINES Annual Report *643*
Generale des Carrieres et Mines du Zaire. Monographie see Generale des Carrieres et des Mines. Monographie *643*
Geneseo Studies in Library and Information Science (US ISSN 0072-0801) *530*
Genetik.Grundlagen und Perspektiven (GW ISSN 0170-0561) *122*
Genie Industriel; Catalogue de l'Ingeinerie (FR ISSN 0072-0844) *367*
Genootschap Amstelodamum. Jaarboek (NE) *454*
Die Genossenschaften in der Bundesrepublik Deutschland (GW) *181*
Genshiryoku Nenpo see Japan Atomic Energy Commission. Annual Report *703*
Gentes Herbarum (US ISSN 0072-0879) *115*
Gentle Folk and Other Creatures (AT ISSN 0310-639X) *579*
Genuine Irish Old Moore's Almanac (IE ISSN 0072-0887) *360*
Geo Abstracts. Annual Index (UK) *422*
Geochemical Society of India. Journal (II ISSN 0368-2323) *293*
GeoChile (CL ISSN 0431-1930) *886*
Geodesy (BU) *289*
Geodynamics Highlights see Geodynamics International *304*
Geodynamics International (US) *304*
Geoecological Research (GW ISSN 0170-3250) *289,* 386
Geofizicheskii Byulleten/Geophysical Bulletin (UR ISSN 0072-1182) *304*
Geofizikai Kozlemenyek/Geophysical Transactions (HU ISSN 0016-7657) *304*
Geografia (PL) *422*

Geografia (BL ISSN 0100-7912) *422*
Geografica (AG) *422*
Geografija ir Geologija (UR ISSN 0072-0976) 293, *422*
Geografinis Metrastis/Geographical Annual (UR ISSN 0072-0917) *422*
Geographers (UK ISSN 0308-6992) *422*
Geographia Medica (HU ISSN 0435-3730) *422,* 595
Geographia Medica Hungarica see Geographia Medica *422*
Geographica (MY) *422*
Geographical Abstracts: Annual Index see Geo Abstracts. Annual Index *422*
Geographical Annual see Geografinis Metrastis *422*
Geographical Distribution of Financial Flows to Less Developed Countries. (Disbursements) (FR ISSN 0474-5434) *200*
Geographical Education (AT ISSN 0085-0969) *348,* 422
Geographical Field Group (Nottingham). Regional Studies (UK ISSN 0078-2084) *422*
Geographical Journal of Nepal (NP) *422*
Geographical Observer (II ISSN 0072-0925) *422*
Geographische Gesellschaft, Munich. Mitteilungen (GW ISSN 0072-0941) *422*
Geographisches Jahrbuch (GE ISSN 0072-095X) *422*
Geographisches Taschenbuch (GW ISSN 0072-0968) *422*
Geography of the British Isles Series (UK) *422*
Geography of World Agriculture (HU) *422*
Geography Publications at Dartmouth (US ISSN 0418-3975) *422*
Geography Teachers Association of Queensland. Journal see Queensland Geographer *350*
GeoJournal (GW ISSN 0343-2521) *289*
Geokhimiya Translations (US ISSN 0094-7091) *289*
Geologia Colombiana (CK ISSN 0072-0992) *293*
Geologia Sudetica (PL ISSN 0072-100X) *293*
Geologic Field Trip Guidebooks of North America; a Union List Incorporating Monographic Titles (US ISSN 0533-7356) *293*
Geologica Bavarica (GW ISSN 0016-755X) *293*
Geologica et Palaeontologica (GW ISSN 0072-1018) *293,* 673
Geologica Ultraiectina (NE ISSN 0072-1026) *293*
Geological Association of Canada. Special Paper (CN ISSN 0072-1042) *293*
Geological Society of America. Memoirs (US ISSN 0072-1069) *293*
Geological Society of America. Memorials (US ISSN 0091-5041) *293*
Geological Society of America. Special Papers (US ISSN 0072-1077) *294*
Geological Society of America. Yearbook (US ISSN 0095-3547) *294*
Geological Society of Australia. Special Publication (AT ISSN 0072-1085) *294*
Geological Society of China. Memoirs (CH) *294*
Geological Society of Egypt. Annual Meeting. Abstracts of Papers (UA ISSN 0446-4648) *294*
Geological Society of Iraq. Journal (IQ ISSN 0533-8301) *294*
Geological Society of Jamaica Journal (JM ISSN 0435-401X) *294*
Geological Society of Malaysia. Bulletin(MY ISSN 0072-1093) *294*
Geological Society of South Africa. Special Publication (SA) *294*
Geological Society of Denmark. Series A see Danmarks Geologiske Undersoegelse. Serie A *293*

Geological Survey of Fiji Memoir see Fiji. Mineral Resources Division. Memoir *293*
Geological Survey of Greenland. Bulletin see Groenlands Geologiske Undersoegelse. Bulletin *294*
Geological Survey of Greenland. Report see Groenlands Geologiske Undersoegelse. Rapport *294*
Geological Survey of Ireland. Bulletin (IE ISSN 0085-0985) *294*
Geological Survey of Ireland. Information Circulars (IE ISSN 0085-0993) *294*
Geological Survey of Ireland. Memoirs (IE ISSN 0085-1000) *294*
Geological Survey of Ireland. Special Papers (IE ISSN 0085-1019) *294*
Geological Survey of Queensland. Report (AT ISSN 0079-8819) *294*
Geologische Bundesanstalt, Vienna. Abhandlungen (AU) *294*
Geologisches Jahrbuch. Reihe F: Bodenkunde (GW ISSN 0341-6445) *294*
Geologists' Year Book (UK) *294*
Geology and Mineral Resources of Japan/Nihon Chishitsu Kosanshi (JA) *294*
Geology, Exploration, and Mining in British Columbia see Exploration in British Columbia *293*
Geomethodica (SZ ISSN 0171-1687) *289*
Geonews (PK ISSN 0435-4311) *294*
Geophysica Norvegica/Norwegian Journal of Geophysics (NO ISSN 0072-1174) *304*
Geophysical Bulletin see Geofizicheskii Byulleten *304*
Geophysical Directory (US) *304*
Geophysical Transactions see Geofizikai Kozlemenyek *304*
Geophysics and Astrophysics Monographs (NE) *82,* 304
Geophysik und Geologie (GE) *304*
Geophysique (FR ISSN 0398-3218) *304*
Georg Brandes Aarbog (DK) *490*
George Ernest Morrison Lectures in Ethnology (AT ISSN 0072-1190) *50*
George Washington University. Population Information Program. Population Report. Series A. Oral Contraceptives see Johns Hopkins University. Population Information Program. Population Report. Series A. Oral Contraceptives *132*
George Washington University. Population Information Program. Population Report. Series B. Intrauterine Devices see Johns Hopkins University. Population Information Program. Population Report. Series B. Intrauterine Devices *132*
George Washington University. Population Information Program. Population Report. Series C. Sterilization (Female) see Johns Hopkins University. Population Information Program. Population Report. Series C. Sterilization (Female) *132*
George Washington University. Population Information Program. Population Report. Series D. Sterilization (Male) see Johns Hopkins University. Population Information Program. Population Report. Series D. Sterilization (Male) *132*
George Washington University. Population Information Program. Populaton Report. Series E. Law and Policy see Johns Hopkins University. Population Information Program. Population Report. Series E. Law and Policy *132*
George Washington University. Population Information Program. Population Report. Series F. Pregnancy Termination see Johns Hopkins University. Population Information Program. Population Report. Series F. Pregnancy Termination *132*

George Washington University. Population Information Program. Population Report. Series G. Prostaglandins see Johns Hopkins University. Population Information Program. Population Report. Series G. Prostaglandins *132*

George Washington University. Population Information Program. Population Report. Series H. Barrier Methods see Johns Hopkins University. Population Information Program. Population Reports. Series H. Barrier Methods *132*

George Washington University. Population Information Program. Population Report. Series I. Periodic Abstinence see Johns Hopkins University. Population Information Program. Population Report. Series I. Periodic Abstinence *132*

George Washington University. Population Information Program. Population Report. Series J. Family Planning Programs see Johns Hopkins University. Population Information Program. Population Report. Series J. Family Planning Programs *132*

George Washington University. Population Information Program. Population Report. Series K. Injectables and Implants see Johns Hopkins University. Population Information Program. Population Report. Series K. Injectables and Implants *132*

George Washington University. Social Research Group. Annual Report (US) *813*

Georgetown University Center for Strategic and International Studies. Significant Issues Series (US) *710*

Georgetown University Round Table on Languages and Linguistics (US ISSN 0196-7207) *544*

Georgia. Department of Education. Statistical Report (US ISSN 0094-1557) *327*

Georgia. Geological Survey. Bulletin (US) *294*

Georgia. Geological Survey. Circular 2. Mining Directory of Georgia (US) *643*

Georgia. Geological Survey. Information Circular (US ISSN 0433-5473) *643*

Georgia. State Data Center. City Population Estimates (US ISSN 0362-3904) *839*

Georgia. State Economic Opportunity Office. Annual Report (US ISSN 0091-3448) *742*

Georgia. Water Resources Survey. Hydrologic Report (US ISSN 0149-2462) *896*

Georgia Congress of Parents and Teachers. Annual Leadership Training Conference. Workshop for P T A Leaders (US) *344*

Georgia Congress of Parents and Teachers. Annual Summer Institute. Handbook for P T A Leaders see Georgia Congress of Parents and Teachers. Annual Leadership Training Conference. Workshop for P T A Leaders *344*

Georgia Legislative Review (US ISSN 0362-5931) *512*

Georgia Manufacturing Directory (US ISSN 0435-5482) *238*

Georgia Museum of Art Bulletin (US ISSN 0147-1902) *74*

Georgia, North Carolina, South Carolina TourBook see Tourbook: Georgia, North Carolina, South Carolina *891*

Georgia State Industrial Directory (US ISSN 0161-8571) *238*

Georgia State University. College of Business Administration. Report of Publications and Research (US) *909*

Georgia State University. Hospital Administration Program. Occasional Publication see Georgia State University. Institute of Health Administration. Occasional Publication *480*

Georgia State University. Institute of Health Administration. Occasional Publication (US ISSN 0093-8041) *480*

Georgia State University. School of Business Administration. Report of Publications by the Faculty see Georgia State University. College of Business Administration. Report of Publications and Research *909*

Georgia Statistical Abstract (US ISSN 0085-1043) *839*

Georgia Vital and Health Statistics (US ISSN 0362-0662) *727*

Georgia Vital and Morbidity Statistics see Georgia Vital and Health Statistics *727*

Georgia Welcome Center. Research Report (US ISSN 0533-8387) *886*

Georgian Bay Regional Library System. Directory-Member Libraries (CN ISSN 0380-8068) *530*

Geoscience and Man see Palynology *298*

Geoscience Information Society. Proceedings (US ISSN 0072-1409) *289*

Geoscience Wisconsin (US) *294*

Geoserials see Geosources *289*

Geosources (UK) *289*

Geostandards Newsletter (FR) *294*

Geotehnika (YU) *294*

Geoteknisk Institut, Copenhagen. Bulletin (DK ISSN 0069-987X) *304*

Geothermal World Directory (US ISSN 0094-9779) *294*

German-American Studies see Journal of German-American Studies *566*

German Arab Trade (UA ISSN 0072-1433) *179*

German Books in Print see Verzeichnis Lieferbarer Buecher *96*

German-Canadian Yearbook / Deutschkanadisches Jahrbuch (CN ISSN 0316-8603) *392, 469*

German Language Courses see Deutschkurse *348*

German Motor Tribune (GW ISSN 0072-145X) *871*

German Political Studies (US) *710*

German-Thai Chamber of Commerce Handbook (TH) *179*

German Yearbook of International Law (GW) *523*

Germanistische Linguistik (GW ISSN 0072-1492) *544*

Germany (Democratic Republic, 1949-) Meteorologischer Dienst. Abhandlungen (GE ISSN 0072-1506) *633*

Germany (Democratic Republic, 1949-). Ministerium fuer Hoch- und Fachschulwesen. Verfuegungen und Mitteilungen (GE) *336*

Germany (Democratic Republic, 1949-). Staatliche Zentralverwaltung fuer Statistik. Abteilung Bevoelkerung und Kulturell-Soziale Bereiche der Volkswirtschaft see Bevoelkerungsstatistisches Jahrbuch der Deutschen Demokratischen Republik *726*

Germany (Federal Republic). Bundesministerium fuer das Post- und Fernmeldewesen. Jahresnachweisung ueber die Einnahmen und Ausgaben der Deutschen Bundespost see Germany (Federal Republic, 1949-) Bundesministerium fuer das Post- und Fernmeldewesen. Jahresrechnung, Nachweisung ueber die Einnahmen und Ausgaben der Deutschen Bundespost e *266*

Germany (Federal Republic), Bundesministerium fuer Verkehr. Strassenbaubericht (GW) *874*

Germany (Federal Republic, 1949-) Bundesanstalt fuer Arbeit. Berufsberatung. Ergebnisse der Berufsberatungsstatistik (GW) *156, 839*

Germany (Federal Republic, 1949-) Bundesanstalt fuer Arbeit. Foerderung der Beruflichen Bildung; Ergebnisse der Teilnehmerstatistik (GW) *349*

Germany (Federal Republic, 1949-). Bundesanstalt fuer Gewaesserkunde. Hydrologische Bibliographie (GW ISSN 0340-4242) *91, 290, 900*

Germany (Federal Republic, 1949-). Bundesanstalt fuer Gewaesserkunde. Jahresbericht (GW) *896*

Germany (Federal Republic, 1949-) Bundesanstalt fuer Materialpruefung. Jahresbericht (GW ISSN 0341-0528) *379*

Germany (Federal Republic, 1949-) Bundesanstalt fuer Strassenwesen, Erfahrungsaustauch ueber Erdarbeiten im Strassenbau (GW) *375*

Germany (Federal Republic, 1949-) Bundesaufsichtsamt fuer das Versicherungswesen. Geschaeftsbericht (GW ISSN 0525-1737) *499*

Germany (Federal Republic,1949-) Bundesministerium fuer Arbeit und Sozialordnung. Hauptergebnisse der Arbeits-und Sozialstatistik (GW ISSN 0072-1557) *156*

Germany (Federal Republic, 1949-). Bundesministerium fuer Bildung and Wissenschaft. Forschungsbericht der Bundesregierung (GW) *742*

Germany (Federal Republic, 1949-) Bundesministerium fuer das Post-und Fernmeldewesen. Jahresrechnung, Nachweisung ueber die Einnahmen und Ausgaben der Deutschen Bundespost (GW ISSN 0435-7329) *266*

Germany (Federal Republic,1949-) Bundesministerium fuer Ernaehrung, Landwirtschaft und Forsten. Agrarbericht der Bundesregierung (GW ISSN 0072-1565) *15*

Germany (Federal Republic, 1949-) Bundesministerium fuer Ernaehrung, Landwirtschaft und Forsten. Jahresbericht. Forschung im Bereich des Bundesministers. see Germany (Federal Republic, 1949-) Bundesministerium fuer Ernaehrung, Landwirtschaft und Forsten. Jahresbericht. Forschung im Geschaeftsbereich des Bundesministers fuer Ernaehrung, la Wirtschaft und Forsten *15*

Germany(Federal Republic, 1949-) Bundesministerium fuer Ernaehrung, Landwirtschaft und Forsten. Jahresbericht. Forschung im Geschaeftsbereich des Bundesministerium fuer Ernaehrung, la Wirtschaft und Forsten (GW ISSN 0343-7477) *15*

Germany (Federal Republic,1949-) Bundesministerium fuer Forschung und Technologie. BMFT Foerderungskatalog (GW) *782, 851*

Germany (Federal Republic, 1949-). Bundesversicherungsamt. Taetigkeitsbericht (GW) *909*

Germany (Federal Republic, 1949-) Deutscher Bundestag. Wissenschaftliche Dienste. Bibliographien (GW ISSN 0433-762X) *91*

Germany (Federal Republic, 1949-) Deutscher Bundestag. Wissenschaftliche Dienste. Materialien (GW ISSN 0435-7590) *91*

Germany (Federal Republic, 1949-) Presse- und Informationsamt Bulletin Archive Supplement (GW) *742*

Germany (Federal Republic, 1949-) Sachverstaendigenrat zur Begutachtung der Gesamtwirtschaftlichen Entwicklung. Jahresgutachten (GW ISSN 0072-159X) *222*

Germany (Federal Republic, 1949-) Statistiches Bundesamt Arbeiten see Survey of German Federal Statistics *848*

Germany(Federal Republic, 1949-) Statistiches Bundesamt. Fachserie 4, Reihe 5: Beschaeftigung, Umsatz, Investitionen und Kosten Struktur in Baugewerbe see Germany(Federal Republic, 1949-) Statistisches Bundesamt. Fachserie 4, Reihe 5 *140*

Germany(Federal Republic, 1949-) Statistiches Bundesamt. Fachserie 15, Reihe 1: Wirtschaftsrechnungen see Germany (Federal Republic, 1949-) Statistisches Bundesamt. Fachserie 15, Reihe 1: Einnahmen und Ausgaben Ausgewaehlter Privater Haushalte *157*

Germany (Federal Republic, 1949-) Statistisches Bundesamt. Alphabetisches Laenderverzeichnis fuer die Aussenhandelsstatistik (GW ISSN 0072-1638) *156*

Germany (Federal Republic, 1949-) Statistisches Bundesamt. Ausgewaehlte Zahlen fuer die Bauwirtschaft (GW ISSN 0072-1719) *140, 839*

Germany(Federal Republic, 1949-) Statistisches Bundesamt. Auslandsstatistik Nr. 6370010: Foreign Trade According to the Standard International Trade Classification (SITC) - Special Trade (GW) *156*

Germany (Federal Republic, 1949-) Statistisches Bundesamt. Aussenhandel. Reihe 7: Sonderbeitraege (GW ISSN 0072-1700) *156, 839*

Germany (Federal Republic, 1949-) Statistisches Bundesamt. Fachserie Auslandsstatistik, Reihe 2: Produzierende Gewerbe im Ausland (GW) *156, 839*

Germany (Federal Republic, 1949-) Statistisches Bundesamt. Fachserie Auslandsstatistik, Reihe 4: Loehne und Gehaelter im Ausland (GW) *156, 839*

Germany (Federal Republic, 1949-) Statistisches Bundesamt. Fachserie Auslandsstatistik, Reihe 5: Preise und Preisindizes im Ausland (GW ISSN 0072-3940) *156, 839*

Germany (Federal Republic, 1949-) Statistisches Bundesamt. Fachserie 1, Reihe 1: Gebiet und Bevoelkerung (GW ISSN 0072-1786) *732, 839*

Germany (Federal Republic, 1949-) Statistisches Bundesamt. Fachserie 1, Reihe 2: Bevoelkerungsbewegung (GW ISSN 0072-1794) *732*

Germany (Federal Republic, 1949-) Statistisches Bundesamt. Fachserie 1, Reihe 2.3: Wanderungen (GW ISSN 0072-1808) *732*

Germany (Federal Republic, 1949-) Statistisches Bundesamt. Fachserie 1, Reihe 3: Haushaelte und Familien (GW) *732*

Germany (Federal Republic, 1949-) Statistisches Bundesamt. Fachserie 1, Reihe 4: Erwerbetaetigkeit (GW ISSN 0072-1832) *156*

Germany (Federal Republic, 1949-) Statistisches Bundesamt. Fachserie 2, Reihe 2.1: Abschluesse der Kapitalgesellschaften (GW) *156*

Germany (Federal Republic, 1949-) Statistisches Bundesamt. Fachserie 2, Reihe 3: Abschluesse der Oeffentlichen Versorgungs- und Verkehrunternehmen (GW) *156*

Germany (Federal Republic, 1949-) Statistisches Bundesamt. Fachserie 2, 4: Zahlungsschwierigkeiten (GW ISSN 0072-2030) *156, 839*

Germany (Federal Republic, 1949-) Statistisches Bundesamt. Fachserie 3, Reihe 2: Betriebs-, Arbeits- und Einkommensverhaeltnisse (GW ISSN 0072-3681) *24, 839*

Germany(Federal Republic, 1949-) Statistisches Bundesamt. Fachserie 3, Reihe 3: Gartenbau und Weinwirtschaft see Germany (Federal Republic, 1949-) Statistisches Bundesamt. Fachserie 3, Reihe 3: Pflanzliche Erzeugung *24*

Germany (Federal Republic, 1949-) Statistisches Bundesamt. Fachserie 3, Reihe 3: Pflanzliche Erzeugung (GW) *24*, 416
Germany (Federal Republic, 1949-) Statistisches Bundesamt. Fachserie 3, Reihe 4: Tierische Erzeugung (GW) *24*
Germany (Federal Republic, 1949-) Statistisches Bundesamt. Fachserie 3, Reihe 4.5: Fischerei (GW ISSN 0072-3673) *401*
Germany (Federal Republic, 1949-) Statistisches Bundesamt. Fachserie 4, Reihe S: Sonderbeitraege (GW ISSN 0072-2073) *157*
Germany (Federal Republic, 1949-) Statistisches Bundesamt. Fachserie 4, Reihe 1: Zusammenfassende Daten fuer das Produzierende Gewerbe (GW) *157*
Germany (Federal Republic, 1949-) Statistisches Bundesamt. Fachserie 4, Reihe 2: Indices des Auftragseingangs in Ausgewaehlten Industriezweigen und im Bauhauptgewerbe see Germany (Federal Republic, 1949-) Statistisches Bundesamt. Fachserie 4, Reihe 2.2: Indices des Auftragseingangs, des Umsatzes und des Auftragsbestands fuer das Verarbeitende Gewerbe und fuer das Bauhaupt Gewerbe *157*
Germany (Federal Republic, 1949-) Statistisches Bundesamt. Fachserie 4, Reihe 2: Indizes fuer das Produzierende Gewerbe (GW) *157*
Germany (Federal Republic, 1949-) Statistisches Bundesamt. Fachserie 4, Reihe 2.2: Indices des Auftragseingangs, des Umsatzes und des Auftragsbestands fuer das Verarbeitende Gewerbe und fuer das Bauhaupt Gewerbe (GW) *157*
Germany (Federal Republic, 1949-) Statistisches Bundesamt. Fachserie 4, Reihe 3.1: Produktion im Produzierenden Gewerbe (GW) *157*, 839
Germany(Federal Republic, 1949-) Statistisches Bundesamt. Fachserie 4, Reihe 5. (GW) *140*
Germany (Federal Republic, 1949-) Statistisches Bundesamt. Fachserie 4, Reihe 7: Handwerk (GW ISSN 0072-2103) *157*
Germany (Federal Republic, 1949-) Statistisches Bundesamt. Fachserie 5, Reihe 1: Bautaetigkeit (GW ISSN 0072-1735) *140*, 839
Germany (Federal Republic, 1949-) Statistisches Bundesamt. Fachserie 5, Reihe 2: Bewilligungen im Sozialen Wohnungsbau (GW ISSN 0072-1743) *140*, 839
Germany (Federal Republic, 1949-) Statistisches Bundesamt. Fachserie 5, Reihe 3: Bestand an Wohnungen (GW ISSN 0072-1751) *140*
Germany (Federal Republic, 1949-) Statistisches Bundesamt. Fachserie 6, Reihe 1: Grosshandel (GW ISSN 0072-1964) *157*
Germany (Federal Republic, 1949-) Statistisches Bundesamt. Fachserie 6, Reihe 3: Einzelhandel (GW ISSN 0072-1972) *157*, 839
Germany (Federal Republic, 1949-) Statistisches Bundesamt. Fachserie 6, Reihe 5: Wahrenverkehr mit Berlin (West) (GW) *157*, 839
Germany (Federal Republic, 1949-) Statistisches Bundesamt. Fachserie 6, Reihe 6: Wahrenverkehr mit der Deutschen Demokratischen Republik und Berlin (Ost) (GW ISSN 0072-1980) *157*, 840
Germany (Federal Republic, 1949-) Statistisches Bundesamt. Fachserie 6, Reihe 7: Reiseverkehr (GW ISSN 0072-1999) *893*
Germany (Federal Republic, 1949-) Statistisches Bundesamt. Fachserie 7, Reihe 1: Zusammenfassende Uebersichten fuer den Aussenhandel (GW ISSN 0072-1646) *157*, 840

Germany (Federal Republic, 1949-) Statistisches Bundesamt. Fachserie 7, Reihe 2: Aussenhandel nach Waren und Laendern (Spezialhandel) (GW ISSN 0072-1654) *157*, 840
Germany (Federal Republic, 1949-) Statistisches Bundesamt. Fachserie 7, Reihe 3: Aussenhandel Nach Laendern und Warengruppen (Spezialhandel) (GW ISSN 0072-1662) *157*, 840
Germany (Federal Republic, 1949-) Statistisches Bundesamt. Fachserie 7, Reihe 4. Aussenhandel mit Ausgewaehlten Waren (GW) *157*
Germany (Federal Republic, 1949-) Statistisches Bundesamt. Fachserie 7, Reihe 6: Durchfuhr im Seeverkehr und Seeumschlag (GW ISSN 0072-1697) *157*
Germany (Federal Republic, 1949-) Statistisches Bundesamt. Fachserie 8, Reihe 3: Strassenverkehr (GW ISSN 0072-405X) *865*
Germany (Federal Republic, 1949-) Statistisches Bundesamt. Fachserie 8, Reihe 3.3: Strassenverkehrsunfaelle (GW ISSN 0072-4068) *840*, *865*
Germany (Federal Republic, 1949-) Statistisches Bundesamt. Fachserie 8, Reihe 5: Seeschiffahrt (GW ISSN 0072-4025) *840*, *866*
Germany (Federal Republic, 1949-) Statistisches Bundesamt. Fachserie 8, Reihe 6: Luftverkehr (GW ISSN 0072-4033) *840*, *866*
Germany (Federal Republic, 1949-) Statistisches Bundesamt. Fachserie 9, Reihe 1: Boden- und Kommunalkreditinstitute (GW ISSN 0072-2014) *909*
Germany (Federal Republic, 1949-) Statistisches Bundesamt. Fachserie 9, Reihe 2: Aktienmaerkte (GW) *157*, 840
Germany (Federal Republic, 1949-) Statistisches Bundesamt. Fachserie 10. Rechtspflege (GW ISSN 0072-1859) *521*, 840
Germany (Federal Republic, 1949-) Statistisches Bundesamt. Fachserie 11: Bildung und Kultur (GW ISSN 0072-1778) *327*, 840
Germany (Federal Republic, 1949-) Statistisches Bundesamt. Fachserie 12, Reihe 1: Ausgewaehlte Zahlen fuer das Gesundheitswesen (GW ISSN 0072-1840) *756*, 840
Germany (Federal Republic, 1949-) Statistisches Bundesamt. Fachserie 13, Reihe 2,3: Sozialhilfe; Kriegsopferfuersorge (GW ISSN 0072-3754) *811*
Germany (Federal Republic, 1949-) Statistisches Bundesamt. Fachserie 13, Reihe 5: Oeffentliche Jugendhilfe(ISSN 0072-3762) *257*, *811*
Germany (Federal Republic, 1949-) Statistisches Bundesamt. Fachserie 14: Finanzen und Steuern (GW) *157*
Germany (Federal Republic, 1949-) Statistisches Bundesamt. Fachserie 15, Reihe 1: Einnahmen und Ausgaben Ausgewaehlter Privater Haushalte (GW) *157*
Germany (Federal Republic, 1949-) Statistisches Bundesamt. Fachserie 16, Reihe 1: Arbeiterverdienste in der Landwirtschaft (GW) *24*, *157*
Germany (Federal Republic, 1949-) Statistisches Bundesamt. Fachserie 16, Reihe 2: Arbeitnehmerverdienste in Industrie und Handel (GW ISSN 0072-3789) *157*

Germany (Federal Republic, 1949-) Statistisches Bundesamt. Fachserie 16, Reihe 3: Arbeiterverdienste im Handwerk (GW ISSN 0072-3797) *157*, 840
Germany (Federal Republic, 1949-) Statistisches Bundesamt. Fachserie 16, Reihe 4: Tarifloehne und Tarifgehaelter (GW ISSN 0072-3843) *157*
Germany (Federal Republic, 1949-) Statistisches Bundesamt. Fachserie 17, Reihe 1: Preise und Preisindizes fuer die Land- und Forstwirtschaft (GW ISSN 0072-3894) *24*, 840
Germany (Federal Republic, 1949-) Statistisches Bundesamt. Fachserie 17, Reihe 2: Preise und Preisindizes fuer Gewerbliche Produkte. Erzeugerpreise (GW) *157*, 840
Germany (Federal Republic, 1949-) Statistisches Bundesamt. Fachserie 17, Reihe 2: Preise und Preisindizes fuer Industrielle Produkte. Erzeugerpreise see Germany (Federal Republic, 1949-) Statistisches Bundesamt. Fachserie 17, Reihe 2: Preise und Preisindizes fuer Gewerbliche Produkte. Erzeugerpreise d *157*
Germany (Federal Republic, 1949-) Statistisches Bundesamt. Fachserie 17, Reihe 3: Index der Grundstoffpreise (GW ISSN 0072-3878) *157*, 840
Germany (Federal Republic, 1949-) Statistisches Bundesamt. Fachserie 17, Reihe 4: Messzahlen fuer Bauleistungspreise und Preisindizes fuer Bauwerke (GW) *157*, 840
Germany (Federal Republic, 1949-) Statistisches Bundesamt. Fachserie 17, Reihe 5: Kaufwerte fuer Bauland (GW) *140*
Germany (Federal Republic, 1949-) Statistisches Bundesamt. Fachserie 17, Reihe 7: Preise und Preisindizes der Lebenshaltung (GW ISSN 0072-3916) *158*
Germany (Federal Republic, 1949-) Statistisches Bundesamt. Fachserie 17, Reihe 8: Preise und Preisindizes fuer den Ein- und Ausfuhr (GW) *158*, 840
Germany (Federal Republic, 1949-) Statistisches Bundesamt. Fachserie 17, Reihe 9: Preise fuer Verkehrsleistungen (GW ISSN 0072-3924) *840*, *866*
Germany (Federal Republic, 1949-) Statistisches Bundesamt. Fachserie 17, Reihe 10: Internationaler Vergleich der Preise fuer die Lebenshaltung (GW ISSN 0072-3827) *158*, 840
Germany (Federal Republic, 1949-) Statistisches Bundesamt. Fachserie 18, Reihe 1: Konten und Standardtabellen (GW ISSN 0072-4009) *158*
Germany (Federal Republic, 1949-) Statistisches Bundesamt Fachserie 19, Reihe 2: Wasserversorgung und Abwasserbeseitigung (GW) *364*, 900
Germany (Federal Republic, 1949-) Statistisches Bundesamt. Geld und Kredit. Reihe 2: Aktienkurse see Germany (Federal Republic, 1949-) Statistisches Bundesamt. Fachserie 9, Reihe 2: Aktienmaerkte *157*
Germany (Federal Republic, 1949-) Statistisches Bundesamt. Laenderberichte (GW) *840*
Germany (Federal Republic, 1949-) Statistisches Bundesamt. Laenderkurzberichte (GW) *840*
Germany(Federal Republic, 1949-) Statistisches Bundesamt. Preise, Loehne, Wirtschaftsrechnungen. Reihe 5: Preise und Preisindizes fuer Bauwerke und Bauland see Germany (Federal Republic, 1949--) Statistisches Bundesamt. Fachserie 17, Reihe 5: Kaufwerte fuer Bauland w *140*

Germany(Federal Republic, 1949-) Statistisches Bundesamt. Preise, Loehne, Wirtschaftsrechnungen. Reihe 14: Arbeiterverdinste in der Landwirtschaft see Germany (Federal Republic, 1949-) Statistisches Bundesamt. Fachserie 16, Reihe 1: Arbeiterverdienste in der Landwirtschaft *157*
Germany (Federal Republic, 1949-) Statistisches Bundesamt. Warenverzeichnis fuer die Aussenhandelsstatistik (GW ISSN 0072-4106) *158*, 840
Germany (Federal Republic, 1949-) Statistisches Bundesamt. Zahlenkompass/Statistical Compass/ Boussole des Chiffres/Compas de Cifras (GW ISSN 0072-4114) *840*
Germany, Federal Republic. Bundesstelle fuer Aussenhandelsinformation. Publikations-Spiegel (GW) *158*
Germinal Ideas (US) *595*
Geron (FI ISSN 0072-4157) *428*
Gesamthochschule Wuppertal. Schriftenreihe Literaturwissenschaft (GW) *564*
Gesamtregister mit den Rechtssaetzen und Fundstellen der Entscheidungen der Zeitschrift fuer Verkehrsrecht (AU) *512*
Gesamtstatistik der Kraftfahrtversicherung (GW ISSN 0435-7442) *501*
Gesamtverzeichnis der Zeitschriften und Serien in Bibliotheken der Bundesrepublik Deutschland Einschliesslich Berlin (West)/Union List of Serials in Libraries of the Federal Republic of Germany Including Berlin (West) (GW ISSN 0302-0657) *91*
Gesamtverzeichnis Oesterreichischer Dissertationen (AU ISSN 0072-4165) *91*
Geschichte der Naturwissenschaften, Technik und Medizin. Schriftenreihe (GE ISSN 0036-6978) *783*
Geschichte des Buchwesens. Beitraege (GE ISSN 0067-5040) *758*
Geschichtliche Landeskunde (GW ISSN 0072-4203) *454*
Geselecteerde Agrarische Cijfers van de E E C see E E G Vademecum *24*
Gesellschaft fuer Biologische Chemie, Mosbach. Colloquium (US) *111*
Gesellschaft fuer die Geschichte und Bibliographie des Brauwesens. Jahrbuch (GW ISSN 0072-422X) *86*
Gesellschaft fuer Griechische und Hellenistische Rechtsgeschichte. Akten (AU) *512*
Gesellschaft fuer Kernforschung. Bericht ueber Forschungs- und Entwicklungsarbeiten see Kernforschungszentrum Karlsruhe. Ergebnisbericht ueber Forschung und Entwicklung *703*
Gesellschaft fuer Naturkunde in Wuerttemberg. Jahreshefte (GW ISSN 0368-2307) *103*
Gesellschaft fuer Physiologische Chemie, Mosbach. Colloquium see Gesellschaft fuer Biologische Chemie, Mosbach. Colloquium *111*
Gesellschaft fuer Regionalforschung. Seminarberichte (GW) *484*
Gesellschaft pro Vindonissa. Jahresbericht (SZ ISSN 0072-4270) *61*
Gesellschaft pro Vindonissa. Veroeffentlichungen (SZ ISSN 0072-4289) *61*
Gesellschaft, Recht, Wirtschaft (GW) *797*
Gesellschaftspolitische Bildungsmaterialien (GW) *797*
Gesetz und Verordnungsblatt fuer das Land Hessen (GW ISSN 0342-3557) *749*
Gesher (US ISSN 0016-9145) *556*, 688, *770*
Gestalt und Gedanke; Jahrbuch see Ensemble *563*
Gestione Informata (IT) *215*
Getting Your Poetry Published (UK) *579*

Gewestelijke Economische Raad voor Vlaanderen. Activiteitsverslag (BE ISSN 0304-5978) *223*
Geyer's Who Makes It Directory (US ISSN 0072-4327) *219*
Gezeitentafeln (GW ISSN 0084-9774) *310*
Gezinssociologische Documentatie (BE) 2, *732*
Al-Ghad (YE) 181, *556*
Ghana (GH) *186*
Ghana. Central Bureau of Statistics. Economic Survey (GH ISSN 0072-4335) 158, *840*
Ghana. Meteorological Department. Climatological Notes (GH) *633*
Ghana. Meteorological Department. Professional Notes (GH) *633*
Ghana. Meteorological Department. Sun and Moon Tables for Ghana (GH) *633*
Ghana. Ministry of Education. Educational Statistics (GH) *318*
Ghana. National Council for Higher Education. Annual Report (GH) *336*
Ghana. National Council on Women and Development. Annual Report (GH) *900*
Ghana. Railway and Ports Administration. Report (GH ISSN 0072-4408) *862*
Ghana. Supreme Military Council. Budget Proposals (GH) *229*
Ghana Commercial Bank. Annual Report (GH ISSN 0435-9348) *186*
Ghana Economic Review (GH) *144*
Ghana Geographical Association. Bulletin (GH ISSN 0016-9536) *422*
Ghana Journal of Sociology (GH ISSN 0435-9380) *813*
Ghana National Bibliography (GH ISSN 0072-4378) *91*
Ghana Population Studies (GH) *727*
Ghana Year Book (GH ISSN 0433-969X) *440*
Ghise ed Acciai *see* Fontes et Aciers *643*
Giannini Foundation of Agricultural Economics. Information Series (US) *28*
Giannini Foundation of Agricultural Economics. Monograph (US ISSN 0575-4208) *28*
Giannini Foundation of Agricultural Economics. Paper (US) *28*
Giannini Foundation of Agricultural Economics. Research Report (US ISSN 0072-4459) *28*
Giappone (IT) *443*
Gids bij de Prijscourant (NE ISSN 0072-4467) *203*
Giessener Schriftenreihe Tierzucht und Haustiergenetik (GW ISSN 0434-0035) *44*
Gift and Decorative Accessories Buyers Directory (US ISSN 0072-4505) 244, *429*
Gift and Tableware Reporter. Gift Guide (US ISSN 0148-9437) *429*
Gifted Pupil (US ISSN 0016-9870) *318*
Gifts Annual Buyers' Guide *see* Gifts International Buyers' Guide *429*
Gifts International Buyers' Guide (UK) *429*
Giftware News Management/Merchandising Guide and Tableware Directory (US) *218*
Gifu Daigaku Nogakubu Kenkyu Hokoku *see* Gifu University. Faculty of Agriculture. Research Bulletin *15*
Gifu University. Faculty of Agriculture. Research Bulletin/Gifu Daigaku Nogakubu Kenkyu Hokoku (JA ISSN 0072-4513) *15*
Gilbert Law Summaries. Criminal Procedure (US ISSN 0193-922X) *512*
Gilberto Amado Memorial Lecture (UN) *523*
Giorgio Levi della Vida Conferences (GW ISSN 0340-6369) *474*
Giornale di Fisica. Quaderni (IT) *696*
Giornale di Geologia (IT ISSN 0017-0291) *294*
Giornale Italiano di Psicologia. Quaderni (IT) *736*
Giovanni Lorenzi Foundation. Symposia (NE) *103*

Gioventu Passionista/Passionist Youth (IT ISSN 0072-4548) *765*
Girios Aidas/Echo of the Forest (US ISSN 0072-4556) *409*
Girls & Boys Together. (US ISSN 0361-9729) *258*
Girls Gymnastics Manual (US) *820*
Girls Gymnastics Rules (US ISSN 0270-2029) *820*
Girls School Year Book (UK ISSN 0072-4564) *344*
Giunta Centrale per gli Studi Storici, Rome. Bibliografia Storica Nazionale (IT ISSN 0085-2317) *91*
Giurisprudenza Annotata di Diritto Industriale (IT) *512*
Giustizia Civile. Repertorio Generale Annuale (IT) *512*
Giving U.S.A. Annual Report (US) *806*
Gizeh (US ISSN 0270-3580) 579, *688*
Glaciological Data (US ISSN 0149-1776) *294*
Glaciological Notes *see* Glaciological Data *294*
Glaciology *see* Glyatsiologiya *304*
Gladius (SP ISSN 0436-029X) 476, *639*
Glamorgan County History Series (UK) *454*
Glanures (MF) *840*
Glasenapp-Stiftung (GW ISSN 0170-3455) *670*
Glasgow Archaeological Journal (UK ISSN 0305-8986) *61*
Glasgow Chamber of Commerce. Industrial Index to Glasgow & West of Scotland *see* Glasgow Chamber of Commerce. Regional Directory *179*
Glasgow Chamber of Commerce. Regional Directory (UK) *179*
Glasnik Arhiva i Drustava Arhivskih Radnika Bosne i Hercegovine (YU) *454*
Glasnik Hemicara i Tehnologa Bosne i Hercegovine (YU ISSN 0367-4444) 246, *372*
Glasnik Zemaljskog Muzeja u Sarajevu *see* Zemaljski Muzej Bosne i Hercegovine. Glasnik. Arheologija *67*
Glasnik Zemaljskog Muzeja u Sarajevu *see* Zemaljski Muzej Bosne i Hercegovine. Glasnik. Prirodne Nauke *794*
GLASRA (IE ISSN 0332-0235) *115*
Glass Containers (US ISSN 0072-4637) *672*
Glass Directory and Buyer's Guide *see* European Glass Directory and Buyer's Guide *627*
Glass/Metal Catalog *see* International Glass/Metal Catalog *244*
Glass, Potteries and Ceramic Annual (IT) *244*
Glass, Potteries and Ceramic Journal *see* Glass, Potteries and Ceramic Annual *244*
Glass's Car Check Book (UK) *871*
Glass's Commercial Vehicle Check Book (UK) *862*
Glass's Motor Cycle Check Book (UK) *826*
Glenbow-Alberta Institute. Occasional Paper (CN ISSN 0072-467X) 392, *469*
Glenbow Foundation. Archives Series *see* Glenbow Museum. Archives Series *469*
Glenbow Foundation. Occasional Paper *see* Glenbow-Alberta Institute. Occasional Paper *469*
Glenbow Museum. Archives Series (CN) *469*
Glimpse of London with American Express (UK) *886*
Glitch (US) *579*
Global Atmospheric Research Programme. G A R P Special Reports (UN ISSN 0084-1986) *633*
Global Atmospheric Research Programme. Publication Series (UN ISSN 0084-1978) *633*
Global Focus Series (US ISSN 0072-4742) *721*
Globetrotter *see* Der Trotter *892*

Globusfreund (AU ISSN 0436-0664) *422*
Glossary of Health Care Terminology (UN) 595, *751*
Glottodidactica; an International Journal of Applied Linguistics (PL ISSN 0072-4769) *544*
Gloucester County Newsletter (US) *749*
Glove News (US ISSN 0072-4777) *261*
Glyatsiologicheskie Issledovaniya *see* Glyatsiologiya *304*
Glyatsiologiya/Glaciology (UR ISSN 0568-6245) *304*
Glyndebourne Festival Programme Book (UK ISSN 0434-1066) *659*
Goa, Daman, and Diu. Bureau of Economics, Statistics, and Evaluation. Evaluation Report (II) *186*
Godisen Zbornik na Medicinskiot Fakultet vo Skopje/Acta Facultatis Medicinae Skopiensis (YU ISSN 0065-1214) *595*
Goeteborg Studies in Educational Sciences (SW ISSN 0436-1121) *318*
Goeteborg Studies in Politics (SW) *710*
Goeteborger Germanistische Forschungen (SW ISSN 0072-4793) 544, *564*
Goeteborgs Kungliga Vetenskaps- och Vitterhets-Samhaelle. Handlingar *see* Acta Regiae Societatis Scientiarum et Litterarum Gothoburgensis. Botanica *112*
Goeteborgs Kungliga Vetenskaps- och Vitterhets-Samhaelle. Handlingar *see* Acta Regiae Societatis Scientiarum et Litterarum Gothoburgensis. Zoologica *126*
Goeteborgs Kungliga Vetenskaps- och Vitterhets-Samhaelle. Handlingar *see* Acta Regiae Societatis Scientiarum et Litterarum Gothoburgensis. Geophysica *303*
Goeteborgs Kungliga Vetenskaps- och Vitterhets-Samhaelle. Handlingar *see* Acta Regiae Societatis Scientiarum et Litterarum Gothoburgensis. Humaniora *489*
Goeteborgs Kungliga Vetenskaps- och Vitterhets-Samhaelles Handligar. Bihang *see* Goeteborgs Kungliga Vetenskaps- och Vitterhets-Samhaellet *490*
Goeteborgs Kungliga Vetenskaps- och Vitterhets-Samhaellet (SW ISSN 0436-113X) *490*
Goeteborgs Tandlaekare Saellskap. Aarsbok (SW ISSN 0072-4831) *609*
Goeteborgs Universitet. Demographic Research Institute. Reports (SW) *727*
Goeteborgs Universitet. Ekonomisk-Historiska Institutionen. Meddelanden (SW ISSN 0072-5080) *191*
Goeteborgs Universitet. Institutionen foer Praktisk Pedagogik. Rapport (SW ISSN 0348-2219) *349*
Goeteborgs Universitet. Nationalekonomiska Institutionen. Ekonomiska Studier (SW) *191*
Goeteborgs Universitet. Oceanografiska Institutionen. Reports (SW) *310*
Goeteborgs Universitet. Sociologiska Institutionen. Forsknings-Rapport (SW ISSN 0072-5099) *797*
Goeteborgs Universitet. Sociologiska Institutionen. Monografier (SW ISSN 0072-5102) *813*
Goeteborgs Universitet. Statistiska Institutionen. Skriftserie. Publications (SW ISSN 0072-5110) *840*
Goeteborgs Universitet. Universitetsbibliotek. Aarsberaettelse (SW ISSN 0347-884X) *530*
Goethe-Gesellschaft. Jahrbuch *see* Goethe-Jahrbuch *564*
Goethe-Institut zur Pflege Deutscher Sprache und Kultur im Ausland. Jahrbuch (GW ISSN 0072-4858) *544*
Goethe-Jahrbuch (GE) *564*
Goettinger Abhandlungen zur Soziologie (GW ISSN 0072-4874) *813*

Goettinger Jahrbuch (GW ISSN 0072-4882) *454*
Goettinger Orientforschungen. Reihe: Grundlagen und Ergebnisse (GW ISSN 0171-4910) *670*
Goettinger Orientforschungen. Reihe I: Syriaca (GW ISSN 0340-6326) 443, *670*
Goettinger Orientforschungen. Reihe III: Iranica (GW ISSN 0340-6334) 443, *670*
Goettinger Orientforschungen. Reihe IV: Aegypten (GW ISSN 0340-6342) 443, *670*
Goettinger Orientforschungen. Reihe VI: Hellenistica (GW ISSN 0340-6350) *670*
Goettinger Quellenhefte (GW) *710*
Goettinger Studien zur Rechtsgeschichte (GW) *512*
Goettinger Universitaetsreden (GW ISSN 0085-1108) *336*
Goff's Guide to Cater Yourself Holidays (UK) *886*
Goff's Guide to Motels and Motorways in Great Britain and Ireland (UK) *482*
Goff's Guide to Motels in Great Britain and Europe *see* Goff's Guide to Motels and Motorways in Great Britain and Ireland *482*
Going-To-College Handbook (US ISSN 0072-4904) *336*
Gokanen Keizai Yosoku *see* Five Year Economic Forecast *186*
Gokhale Institute Mimeograph Series (II ISSN 0436-1326) 144, *710*
Gokhale Institute of Politics and Economics. Studies (II ISSN 0072-4912) 144, *710*
Gokuldas Sanskrit Series (II) *688*
Gold Book (US) *871*
Gold Book of Multi Housing (US ISSN 0195-847X) 136, *484*
Gold Circle Numismatics (UK) *477*
Gold Star Family Album *see* Family Album *724*
Golden Blade (UK) 688, *813*
Golden Dog *see* Chien d'Or *561*
Golden Guide to South and East Asia *see* All-Asia Guide *419*
Golden Legacy (US ISSN 0046-6077) *392*
Golden List of Beaches (UK) 386, *830*
Golf & Country Club Guest Policy Directory *see* Private Country Club Guest Policy Directory *825*
Golf Course Superintendents Association of America. Membership Directory (US ISSN 0436-1474) *824*
Golf Course Superintendents Association of America. Proceedings of the International Conference and Show (US ISSN 0072-4947) *824*
Golf en France (FR) *824*
Golf Guide (US ISSN 0072-4955) *820*
Golf Informacion *see* Golfinformacion *820*
Golf Rules Illustrated (UK ISSN 0072-4963) *824*
Golfer's Digest (US ISSN 0072-4971) *824*
Golfer's Handbook (UK ISSN 0072-498X) *824*
Golfinformacion (SP) *820*
Golfing Year (UK) *824*
Gondwana Newsletter (BL ISSN 0072-4998) *289*
Gonzalez Lecture Series *see* Richard J. Gonzalez Lecture *148*
Good Camps Guide (UK ISSN 0142-5978) 830, *886*
Good Food Guide (UK ISSN 0072-5005) *482*
Good Health (AT ISSN 0085-1124) *909*
Good Hotel Guide (UK) *482*
Good Old Days Christmas Annual (US) *402*
Good Sam Club's Recreational Vehicle Owners Directory *see* Trailer Life's Recreational Vehicle Campground and Services Directory *831*
Good Vehicle Year Book *see* Freight Industry Yearbook *862*
Good Wine Guide (UK) *86*
Goodfellow Catalog of Wonderful Things (US) *476*

Goodwin Series (SA) 61
Gornoslaskie Studia Socjologiczne (PL ISSN 0072-5013) 813
Gorog es Latin Irok Tara/Scriptores Graeci et Latini (HU ISSN 0072-5021) 259, 544
Gorsac Koerier (BE) 35
Goryo Daehakgyo Nonmunjip Science see Science and Technology 790
Gospel Music Association. Annual Directory (US) 659
Gospel Music Association. Annual Directory and Yearbook see Gospel Music Association. Annual Directory 659
Gosudarstvennyi Muzei Izobrazitel'nykh Iskusstv im. Pushkina. Soobshcheniya (UR ISSN 0077-1562) 652
Gothenburg Monographs in Linguistics (SW) 544
Gothenburg Studies in Art and Architecture (SW ISSN 0348-4114) 69, 74
Gothenburg Studies in English (SW ISSN 0072-503X) 544, 564
Gothenburg Studies in Social Anthropology (SW ISSN 0348-4076) 50
Gothenburg Studies in the History of Science and Ideas (SW ISSN 0348-6788) 783
GOURS (SP) 294
Governance of Metropolitan Regions. Series (US) 749
Government and Municipal Contractors(UK ISSN 0140-5764) 742
Government and Public Administration Society. Journal (SI) 742
Government Businesss Worldwide Reports (US) 639
Government Contracts Guide (US ISSN 0072-5145) 909
Government Contracts Monographs (US ISSN 0072-5153) 742
Government Finance Brief. New Series (US ISSN 0072-5161) 229
Government in Hawaii (US ISSN 0072-517X) 742
Government of Andhra Pradesh. Audit Report see Government of Andhra Pradesh. Report 742
Government of Andhra Pradesh. Report(II) 742
Government Oriental Manuscripts Library. Bulletin. (II) 530, 670
Government Publications Guide see Bibliographic Guide to Government Publications 88
Government Reference Books (US ISSN 0072-5188) 91
Governmental Finances (Washington) see Current Governments Reports: Governmental Finances 228
Governmental Research Association Directory (US ISSN 0072-520X) 783, 851
Gradjevinski Fakultet. Institut za Materijale i Konstrukcije. Zbornik Istrazivackih Radova (YU ISSN 0350-1701) 136
Graduate (US ISSN 0098-3284) 263
Graduate Assistant Directory in Computer Sciences (US) 272
Graduate Fellowship Awards Announced by National Science Foundation (US ISSN 0072-5250) 336
Graduate Professional Schools of Social Work in Canada and the U.S.A. see Schools of Social Work with Accredited Master's Degree Programs 339
Graduate Programs: Physics, Astronomy, and Related Fields (US ISSN 0147-1821) 82, 336, 696
Graduate School Programs in Public Affairs and Public Administration (US ISSN 0094-6648) 742
Graduate Science Education Student Support and Postdoctorals see U.S. National Science Foundation. Graduate Science Education Student Support and Postdoctorals 340
Graduate Study in Management see Guide to Graduate Management Education 331

Graduate Study in Psychology (US ISSN 0072-5277) 736
Graduate Texts in Mathematics (US ISSN 0072-5285) 585
Graham's Town Series (SA) 97
Grain Directory/Buyers Guide (US) 42, 238
Grammatica (FR) 544
Grand Manan Historian (CN ISSN 0316-2702) 469
Grandes Figures de la Charite (FR ISSN 0072-5404) 454
Grandes Todos (UY ISSN 0072-5439) 564
Grandes Vultos da Engenharia Brasileira (BL) 367
Grands Naturalistes Francais (FR ISSN 0434-3581) 783
Grant Data Quarterly see Annual Register of Grant Support 343
Grants and Aid to Individuals in the Arts see National Directory of Grants and Aid to Individuals in the Arts, International 77
Grants and Awards Available to American Writers (US ISSN 0092-5268) 564
Grants for Study Visits by University Administrators and Librarians (UK ISSN 0144-462X) 336
Grants Register (US ISSN 0072-5471) 342
Grants Register (UK) 336
Grapevine (Saratoga) (US ISSN 0092-0592) 659
Graphic Arts Green Book. (US ISSN 0147-1651) 733
Graphic Arts International Union Handbook of Wages, Hours and Fringe Benefits see G.A.I.U. Handbook of Wages, Hours and Fringe Benefits 733
Graphic Arts Japan (JA ISSN 0072-548X) 74
Graphic Arts Technical Foundation. Research Progress Report see Graphic Arts Technical Foundation. Research Project Report 733
Graphic Arts Technical Foundation. Research Project Report (US ISSN 0096-1159) 733
Graphic Arts Technical Foundation Technical Services Report see G A T F Technical Services Report 851
Graphic Arts Trade Directory and Register see Graphic Arts Green Book 733
Graphic Communications Marketplace (US ISSN 0160-0303) 733
Graphic Guide to Consumer Markets see Guide to Consumer Markets 909
Graphic Pictorial Shoe and Leather Industry (AT) 909
Graphical Survey of the Economy of Taiwan District, Republic of China (CH) 186
Graphiq'emballage see J'emballe 672
Graphis Annual (SZ ISSN 0072-5528) 5, 74, 733
Graphis Packaging (SZ ISSN 0072-5536) 672
Graphis Posters (SZ) 74, 693
Graphische Unternehmungen Oesterreichs. Jahrbuch (AU ISSN 0075-2266) 733
Graphoscope's Historical Performance Review (CN) 203
Grass Roots Guides (US) 710
Grass Roots Perspectives on American History (US ISSN 0148-771X) 469
Grassland Research Institute, Hurley, England (Berkshire) Technical Reports (UK ISSN 0072-5552) 35
Grassland Soceity of Southern Africa. Proceedings of the Annual Congresses (SA ISSN 0072-5560) 35
Grassland Society of Victoria. Newsletter (AT) 35
Gratz College Annual of Jewish Studies(US ISSN 0149-8487) 392, 770
Gravure Environmental and O S H A Newsletter (US ISSN 0091-5203) 733
Gravure Research Institute Newsletter see G R I Newsletter 733
Gray Herbarium. Contributions (US) 115

Gray Panther News (US) 428, 718
Great Britain. Advisory Council for Adult and Continuing Education. Annual Report (UK ISSN 0260-3306) 329
Great Britain. Aeronautical Research Council. Current Paper Series (UK ISSN 0072-5595) 8
Great Britain. Aeronautical Research Council. Reports and Memoranda Series (UK ISSN 0072-5609) 8
Great Britain. Air Transport Licensing Board. Report see Great Britain. Civil Aviation Authority. Annual Report and Accounts 867
Great Britain. Board of Inland Revenue. the Survey of Personal Incomes (UK) 213, 229
Great Britain. Board of Trade. Insurance Business: Annual Report see Great Britain. Department of Trade. Insurance Business: Annual Report 499
Great Britain. British Airports Authority. Annual Report and Accounts (UK ISSN 0068-1229) 867
Great Britain. Building Research Establishment. Annual Report (UK ISSN 0068-354X) 136
Great Britain. Building Research Establishment. Reports (UK) 136, 395, 413
Great Britain. Central Health Services Council. Report (UK ISSN 0072-5714) 752
Great Britain. Central Office of Information. Reference Division. Reference Pamphlets (UK ISSN 0072-5722) 454
Great Britain. Central Statistical Office. Annual Abstract of Statistics (UK ISSN 0072-5730) 840
Great Britain. Central Statistical Office. Guide to Official Statistics (UK ISSN 0261-1791) 840
Great Britain. Central Statistical Office. Regional Statistics see Great Britain. Central Statistical Office. Regional Trends 840
Great Britain. Central Statistical Office. Regional Trends (UK ISSN 0261-1783) 840
Great Britain. Central Statistical Office. Research Series (UK ISSN 0072-5757) 840
Great Britain. Central Statistical Office. Social Trends (UK ISSN 0072-5765) 814
Great Britain. Central Statistical Office. Studies in Official Statistics (UK ISSN 0081-8313) 840
Great Britain. Centre for Overseas Pest Research. Report (UK ISSN 0307-9082) 35
Great Britain. Cinematograph Films Council. Annual Report (UK ISSN 0072-5773) 650
Great Britain. Civil Aviation Authority. Air Transport Users Committee Annual Report (UK) 867
Great Britain. Civil Aviation Authority. Annual Report and Accounts (UK ISSN 0306-3569) 867
Great Britain. Civil Aviation Authority. Annual Statistics (UK) 867
Great Britain. Civil Aviation Authority. C A A Monthly Statistics (UK ISSN 0306-3577) 866
Great Britain. Civil Aviation Authority. Civil Aviation Publications (UK ISSN 0072-5641) 867
Great Britain. Civil Aviation Authority. General Aviation Safety Information (UK) 867
Great Britain. Civil Aviation Authority. International Register of Civil Aircraft (UK) 867
Great Britain. Civil Service Department. Central Computer Agency. Guide (UK) 272
Great Britain. Civil Service Department. Report (UK ISSN 0307-9589) 742
Great Britain. Commission on Industrial Relations. Annual Report (UK ISSN 0306-5413) 207
Great Britain. Committee on Safety of Medicines. Report (UK) 752

GREAT BRITAIN. 1373

Great Britain. Commonwealth Office. Yearbook see Yearbook of the Commonwealth 465
Great Britain. Department of Education and Science. Architects and Building Branch. Broadsheet (UK ISSN 0260-0471) 344
Great Britain. Department of Education and Science. Building Bulletins (UK ISSN 0072-5870) 344
Great Britain. Department of Education and Science. Computer Board for Universities and Research Councils. Report (UK ISSN 0072-582X) 272
Great Britain. Department of Education and Science. Education Surveys (UK ISSN 0072-5897) 318
Great Britain. Department of Education and Science. Science Policy Studies (UK ISSN 0072-5919) 783
Great Britain. Department of Education and Science. Statistics of Education (UK ISSN 0072-5900) 318
Great Britain. Department of Employment. Family Expenditure Survey (UK ISSN 0072-5927) 213
Great Britain. Department of Employment. New Earnings Survey (UK ISSN 0308-1419) 207
Great Britain. Department of Employment. Research (UK) 207
Great Britain. Department of Employment. Statistics Division. Time Rates of Wages and Hours of Work (UK) 158
Great Britain. Department of Employment. Training Information Papers (UK ISSN 0072-5943) 909
Great Britain. Department of Energy. Electricity: Annual Report (UK) 354, 363
Great Britain. Department of Energy. Electricity: Report of the Secretary of State for Energy (UK) 354
Great Britain. Department of Energy. Report on Research and Development (UK ISSN 0307-6547) 363
Great Britain. Department of Health and Social Security. Annual Report (UK ISSN 0072-596X) 752
Great Britain. Department of Health and Social Security. Capricode Capital Projects Code. Hospital Building Procedure Notes (UK ISSN 0072-5978) 480
Great Britain. Department of Health and Social Security. Health Building Notes (UK) 480, 806
Great Britain. Department of Health and Social Security. Health Equipment Notes (UK ISSN 0141-1403) 480, 806
Great Britain. Department of Health and Social Security. Hospital Building Notes see Great Britain. Department of Health and Social Security. Health Building Notes 480
Great Britain. Department of Health and Social Security. Hospital Equipment Notes see Great Britain. Department of Health and Social Security. Health Equipment Notes 480
Great Britain. Department of Health and Social Security. Hospital In-Patient Inquiry (UK ISSN 0072-6036) 752, 806
Great Britain. Department of Health and Social Security. Notes on Good Practices (UK) 480
Great Britain. Department of Health and Social Security. On the State of the Public Health (UK ISSN 0072-6087) 752
Great Britain. Department of Health and Social Security. Social Security Statistics (UK) 806
Great Britain. Department of Health and Social Security. Statistical and Research Report Series (UK) 481, 806
Great Britain. Department of Health and Social Security. Statistical Report Series see Great Britain. Department of Health and Social Security. Statistical and Research Report Series 481

GREAT BRITAIN.

Great Britain. Department of Industry. Business Statistics Office Report on the Census of Production (UK) *158*

Great Britain. Department of the Environment. Archaeological Reports(UK ISSN 0072-6842) *61, 454*

Great Britain. Department of the Environment. Committee on Synthetic Detergents. Progress Report (UK ISSN 0072-5803) *386*

Great Britain. Department of the Environment. Engineering Specifications (UK ISSN 0072-6850) *375*

Great Britain. Department of the Environment. Fire Research Station. Fire Notes *see* Great Britain. Building Research Establishment. Reports *395*

Great Britain. Department of the Environment. Fire Research Station. Technical Papers *see* Great Britain. Building Research Establishment. Reports *395*

Great Britain. Department of the Environment. Highway Statistics *see* Transport Statistics Great Britain *876*

Great Britain. Department of the Environment. Housing and Construction. Design Bulletin (UK) *485*

Great Britain. Department of the Environment. Housing and Construction. Planning Bulletin (UK) *485*

Great Britain. Department of the Environment. Library Services. D. O. E. Annual List of Publications *see* Great Britain. Departments of the Environment and Transport. Library Services. Annual List of Publications *390*

Great Britain. Department of the Environment. Local Government Financial Statistics: England and Wales (UK ISSN 0308-1745) *229, 749*

Great Britain. Department of the Environment. Metrication in the Construction Industry (UK ISSN 0072-6869) *136, 637*

Great Britain. Department of the Environment. Rate Rebates in England and Wales (UK) *229*

Great Britain. Department of the Environment. Rates and Rateable Values in England and Wales (UK) *229*

Great Britain. Department of the Environment. Report on Research and Development (UK) *386, 814*

Great Britain. Department of the Environment. Sand and Gravel Production. *see* Production of Aggregates in Great Britain *138*

Great Britain. Department of the Environment. Statistics for Town and Country Planning. Series 1 (UK ISSN 0072-6818) *485, 742*

Great Britain. Department of the Environment. Statistics for Town and Country Planning. Series 2 (UK ISSN 0072-6826) *485, 742*

Great Britain. Department of Trade and Industry. Business Statistics Office. Report on the Census of Production *see* Great Britain. Department of Industry. Business Statistics Office Report on the Census of Production *158*

Great Britain. Department of Trade and Industry. Digest of Energy Statistics *see* Digest of United Kingdom Energy Statistics *362*

Great Britain. Department of Trade and Industry. Report on Research and Development *see* Great Britain. Department of Energy. Report on Research and Development *363*

Great Britain. Department of Trade. Bankruptcy: General Annual Report (UK ISSN 0072-5633) *173*

Great Britain. Department of Trade. Companies: General Annual Report (UK ISSN 0072-565X) *223*

Great Britain. Department of Trade. Export of Works of Art (UK ISSN 0072-5668) *74, 196*

Great Britain. Department of Trade. Import Duties Act 1958. Annual Report (UK ISSN 0072-5676) *196*

Great Britain. Department of Trade. Insurance Business: Annual Report (UK ISSN 0308-499X) *499*

Great Britain. Department of Trade. Particulars of Dealers in Securities and of Trust Units (UK ISSN 0072-5692) *203*

Great Britain. Department of Trade. Patents, Design and Trade Marks(Annual Report) (UK ISSN 0072-5706) *676*

Great Britain. Department of Transport. Highway Statistics (UK ISSN 0072-6893) *866*

Great Britain. Department of Transport. Roads in England (UK) *875*

Great Britain. Departments of the Environment and Transport. Library Services. Annual List of Publications (UK ISSN 0141-2604) *390*

Great Britain. Domestic Coal Consumers' Council. Annual Report (UK) *223, 643*

Great Britain. Electricity Council. Report and Accounts (UK ISSN 0307-1146) *354*

Great Britain. Foreign and Commonwealth Office. Treaty Series (UK ISSN 0072-6397) *721*

Great Britain. General Register Office. Studies on Medical and Population Subjects (UK ISSN 0072-6400) *595, 727*

Great Britain. Geological Survey. Summary of Progress *see* Great Britain. Institute of Geological Sciences. Annual Report *294*

Great Britain. Government Actuary. Occupational Pension Board. Annual Report (UK) *797*

Great Britain. H.M.S.O. Government Publications Sectional Lists (UK) *136*

Great Britain. Home Office. Research Studies (UK ISSN 0072-6435) *281*

Great Britain. Home Office. Studies in the Causes of Delinquency and the Treatment of Offenders (UK ISSN 0072-6443) *256, 281*

Great Britain. Hydraulics Research Station. Reports (UK ISSN 0073-4187) *381, 701*

Great Britain. Industrial Coal Consumers' Council. Report *see* Great Britain. Domestic Coal Consumers' Council. Annual Report *643*

Great Britain. Institute of Animal Physiology. Report (UK ISSN 0065-4507) *128*

Great Britain. Institute of Geological Sciences. Annual Report (UK ISSN 0073-9308) *294*

Great Britain. Institute of Geological Sciences. Bulletin of the Geological Survey of Great Britain (UK ISSN 0366-4198) *909*

Great Britain. Institute of Geological Sciences. Classical Areas of British Geology (UK) *294*

Great Britain.Institute of Geological Sciences. Geomagnetic Bulletins (UK ISSN 0073-9316) *304*

Great Britain. Institute of Geological Sciences. Memoirs of the Geological Survey of Great Britain (UK ISSN 0072-6494) *294*

Great Britain. Institute of Geological Sciences. Metric Well Inventory (UK) *289*

Great Britain. Institute of Geological Sciences. Mineral Assessment Report(UK ISSN 0308-5333) *294, 643*

Great Britain.Institute of Geological Sciences. Mineral Monographs (UK) *909*

Great Britain. Institute of Geological Sciences. Overseas Geology and Mineral Resources (UK ISSN 0073-9332) *294, 643*

Great Britain. Institute of Geological Sciences. Overseas Memoirs (UK ISSN 0308-5325) *294*

Great Britain.Institute of Geological Sciences. Report (UK ISSN 0073-9359) *294*

Great Britain. Institute of Geological Sciences. Seismological Bulletins (UK ISSN 0308-5082) *304*

Great Britain. Institute of Geological Sciences. Well Inventory Series. Metric Units *see* Great Britain. Institute of Geological Sciences. Metric Well Inventory *289*

Great Britain. Institute of Terrestrial Ecology. Report (UK) *103*

Great Britain. Institute of Terrestrial Ecology. Symposia (UK) *276*

Great Britain. Keeper of Public Records. Annual Report of the Keeper of Public Records on the Work of the Public Record Office and the Report of the Advisory Council on Public Records (UK ISSN 0072-6516) *454, 530*

Great Britain. Laboratory of the Government Chemist. Annual Report of the Government Chemist (UK ISSN 0072-6524) *246*

Great Britain. Manpower Research Unit. Manpower Studies (UK ISSN 0072-6532) *207*

Great Britain. Medical Research Council. Annual Report (UK) *595*

Great Britain. Medical Research Council. Handbook (UK ISSN 0309-0132) *595*

Great Britain. Medical Research Council. Report *see* Great Britain. Medical Research Council. Annual Report *595*

Great Britain. Mercantile Navy List (UK ISSN 0072-6591) *878*

Great Britain. Meteorological Office. Annual Report (UK ISSN 0072-6605) *633*

Great Britain. Meteorological Office. Geophysical Memoirs (UK ISSN 0072-6613) *304*

Great Britain. Meteorological Office. Scientific Paper (UK ISSN 0072-6621) *633*

Great Britain. Ministry of Agriculture. Fisheries and Food. Fatstock Guarantee Scheme (UK ISSN 0072-6672) *28, 44*

Great Britain. Ministry of Agriculture, Fisheries and Food. Fisheries Research Technical Report (UK ISSN 0308-5589) *397*

Great Britain. Ministry of Agriculture, Fisheries and Food. Laboratory Leaflet (UK ISSN 0072-6699) *397*

Great Britain. Ministry of Agriculture, Fisheries and Food. Report of the Director of Fisheries Research (UK) *397*

Great Britain. Ministry of Agriculture, Fisheries and Food. Technical Bulletin (UK ISSN 0072-6729) *15*

Great Britain. Ministry of Housing and Local Government. Design Bulletin *see* Great Britain. Department of the Environment. Housing and Construction. Design Bulletin *485*

Great Britain. Ministry of Housing and Local Government. Planning Bulletin *see* Great Britain. Department of the Environment. Housing and Construction. Planning Bulletin *485*

Great Britain. Ministry of Power. Annual Report on Electricity *see* Great Britain. Department of Energy. Electricity: Annual Report *363*

Great Britain. Monks Wood Experimental Station. Symposia *see* Great Britain. Institute of Terrestrial Ecology. Symposia *276*

Great Britain. National Economic Development Office. Monographs (UK ISSN 0072-694X) *223*

Great Britain. National Film Finance Corporation. Annual Report (UK ISSN 0072-6958) *650*

Great Britain. National Health Service. Health Service Costing Returns (UK) *481*

Great Britain. National Health Service. Hospital Costing Returns *see* Great Britain. National Health Service. Health Service Costing Returns *481*

Great Britain. Natural Environment Research Council. Report (UK ISSN 0072-7008) *814*

Great Britain. Office of Fair Trading. Report (UK) *512*

Great Britain. Pest Infestation Control Laboratory. Report (UK ISSN 0072-6486) *35*

Great Britain. Public Record Office. Handbooks (UK ISSN 0072-7016) *530*

Great Britain. Public Works Loan Board. Report (UK ISSN 0072-7032) *742*

Great Britain. Regional Agricultural Service. Annual Report (UK) *15*

Great Britain. Royal Commission on Historical Manuscripts. Accessions to Repositories and Reports Added to the National Register of Archives (UK) *91, 437*

Great Britain. Royal Commission on Historical Manuscripts. Commissioners' Reports to the Crown (UK ISSN 0072-7083) *91, 437*

Great Britain. Royal Commission on Historical Manuscripts. Joint Publication (UK ISSN 0072-7091) *91, 437*

Great Britain. Royal Commission on Historical Manuscripts.Secretary's Report to the Commissioners (UK ISSN 0533-9685) *432*

Great Britain. Royal Commission on the Ancient and Historical Monuments and Constructions of England. Interim Report (UK ISSN 0072-7067) *61, 454*

Great Britain. Royal Commission on the Ancient and Historical Monuments and Constructions of Wales and Monmouthshire. Interim Report (UK ISSN 0072-7075) *61, 454*

Great Britain. Royal Greenwich Observatory. Annals (UK ISSN 0080-4371) *82*

Great Britain. Royal Mint. Annual Report (UK ISSN 0072-7105) *173*

Great Britain. Schools Council Publications. Curriculum Bulletins (UK ISSN 0072-7113) *349*

Great Britain. Schools Council Publications. Examinations Bulletins (UK ISSN 0072-7121) *318*

Great Britain. Schools Council Publications. Working Papers (UK ISSN 0072-713X) *318*

Great Britain. Science Research Council. Report (UK ISSN 0072-7148) *783, 851*

Great Britain. Scottish Law Commission. Annual Report (UK ISSN 0080-7915) *512*

Great Britain. Social Science Research Council. Bursary Scheme (UK) *337, 797*

Great Britain. Social Science Research Council. Fellowships (UK) *909*

Great Britain. Social Science Research Council. Report (UK ISSN 0081-0444) *797*

Great Britain. Social Science Research Council. Research Supported by the Social Science Research Council (UK ISSN 0583-6948) *797*

Great Britain. Social Science Research Council. Studentship Handbook (UK) *337, 797*

Great Britain. Soil Survey of England and Wales. Records (UK ISSN 0072-7180) *35*

Great Britain. Soil Survey of England and Wales. Report (UK ISSN 0072-7199) *35*

Great Britain. Soil Survey of England and Wales. Special Surveys (UK ISSN 0072-7202) *35*

Great Britain. Soil Survey of England and Wales. Technical Monographs (UK ISSN 0072-7210) *35*

Great Britain. Treasury. Supply Estimates (UK) *229*

GUIDA DI   1375

Great Britain. University Grants Committee. Annual Survey (UK ISSN 0072-7237) *337*
Great Britain. Victoria and Albert Museum. Illustrated Booklets (UK ISSN 0083-5900) *652*
Great Britain. Victoria and Albert Museum. Monographs (UK ISSN 0083-5919) *652*
Great Britain. Warren Spring Laboratory. Annual Review (UK ISSN 0141-3279) *386*
Great Britain. Warren Spring Laboratory. Investigation of Air Pollution: National Survey, Smoke and Sulphur Dioxide (UK ISSN 0585-2730) *386*
Great Britain. Water Resources Board. Publication (UK ISSN 0072-7245) *896*
Great Britain. Water Resources Board. Report (UK ISSN 0072-7253) *896*
Great Britain. White Fish Authority. Annual Report and Accounts (UK ISSN 0072-7261) *397*
Great Centers of Art *see* Weltstaedte der Kunst. Edition Leipzig *80*
Great Ideas Today (US ISSN 0072-7288) *622*
Great Lakes Basin Commission. Annual Report (US) *896*
Great Lakes Campbook (US) *830*
Great Lakes Camping *see* Great Lakes Campbook *830*
Great Lakes Commission. Report to the States (US ISSN 0533-196X) *909*
Great Lakes Fishery Commission (United States and Canada) Annual Report (US ISSN 0072-7296) *397*
Great Lakes Fishery Commission (United States and Canada) Technical Report (US ISSN 0072-730X) *397*
Great Lakes Navigation (CN) *878*
Great Lakes Red Book (US ISSN 0072-7318) *878*
Great Lakes Research Checklist (US ISSN 0072-7326) *896*
Great Plains Journal (US ISSN 0017-3673) *419*
Great Plains National Instructional Television Library. Recorded Visual Instruction (US) *349*
Great Wall (AT) *478*
Great West and Indian Series (US ISSN 0072-7342) *469*
Greater Boston Media Directory (US) *5, 267, 504*
Greater London Arts Association. Annual Report (UK ISSN 0309-1945) *75*
Greater London Arts Association. Annual Report and Yearbook *see* Greater London Arts Association. Annual Report *75*
Greater London Papers (UK ISSN 0072-7350) *742*
Greater Richmond Chamber of Commerce. Research Bulletin (US ISSN 0035-5100) *179*
Greece (GR ISSN 0432-6105) *886*
Greece. National Statistical Service. Annuaire Statistique de l'Enseignement *see* Greece. National Statistical Service. Education Statistics *327*
Greece. National Statistical Service. Annual Industrial Survey (GR ISSN 0072-7393) *158*
Greece. National Statistical Service. Annual Statistical Survey of Mines, Quarries and Salterns (GR ISSN 0072-7415) *648, 840*
Greece. National Statistical Service. Education Statistics (GR) *327, 840*
Greece. National Statistical Service. Employment Survey Conducted in Urban and Semi-Urban Areas (GR) *158, 840*
Greece. National Statistical Service. Public Finance Statistics (GR) *158*
Greece. National Statistical Service. Results of Sea Fishery Survey by Motor Vessels (GR) *401, 840*

Greece. National Statistical Service. Results of the Annual Industrial Survey *see* Greece. National Statistical Service. Annual Industrial Survey *158*
Greece. National Statistical Service. Shipping Statistics (GR ISSN 0072-7423) *840, 866*
Greece. National Statistical Service. Social Welfare and Health Statistics (GR) *756, 811, 840*
Greece. National Statistical Service. Statistical Yearbook of Public Finance *see* Greece. National Statistical Service. Public Finance Statistics *158*
Greece. National Statistical Service. Statistics on Civil, Criminal and Reformatory Justice (GR) *285, 840*
Greece. National Statistical Service. Statistics on the Declared Income of Legal Entities and Its Taxation (GR) *158, 841*
Greece. National Statistical Service. Statistics on the Declared Income of Physical Persons and Its Taxation (GR) *158, 841*
Greece. National Statistical Service. Transport and Communication Statistics (GR) *266, 841, 866*
Greece as Link Between Arab Countries and the West (HK) *203, 886*
Greek Agricultural Directory (GR) *15*
Greek and Latin Studies Series (UK) *259*
Greek Coins in North American Collections *see* Ancient Coins in North American Collections *477*
Greek Mathematical Society. Bulletin/Hellenike Mathematike Hetaireia. Deltion (GR ISSN 0072-7466) *585*
Greek National Committee for Astronomy. Annual Reports of the Astronomical Institutes of Greece (GR ISSN 0072-7385) *82*
Greek, Roman and Byzantine Monographs (US ISSN 0072-7474) *259*
Greek, Roman and Byzantine Studies. Scholarly Aids (US ISSN 0072-7482) *259*
Green Book (UK ISSN 0017-3932) *32*
Green Book of Home Improvement Contractors (US ISSN 0194-083X) *136*
Green Pages: Directory of Non-Government Environmental Groups in Australia (AT) *276, 386*
Green Sheet (US ISSN 0046-6409) *263, 337*
Greenfield Review Chapbook (US) *579*
Greenland Biosciences (DK) *103, 386*
Greenland Geoscience (DK) *294*
Greenland, Man and Society (DK) *50*
Greensward (UK ISSN 0017-4092) *15*
Greenwood'S Guide to Great Lakes Shipping (US ISSN 0072-7490) *878*
Greifswald-Stralsunder Jahrbuch. (GE) *454*
Greinar (IC) *783*
Grenzfragen (GW) *783*
Greves et Lock-out au Canada *see* Strikes and Lockouts in Canada *210*
Grey Bibliographies (SA) *539*
Grey Matter (AT) *5*
Greyfriar/Siena Studies in Literature (US ISSN 0533-2869) *556*
Grist (US) *579*
Grocer Directory *see* Grocer Marketing Directory *407*
Grocer Marketing Directory (UK) *407*
Grocers Bags and Grocers Sacks (US ISSN 0553-1454) *672*
Groenlands Geologiske Undersoegelse. Bulletin/Geological Survey of Greenland. Bulletin (DK ISSN 0105-3507) *294*
Groenlands Geologiske Undersoegelse. Rapport/Geological Survey of Greenland. Report (DK ISSN 0418-6559) *294*
Gronk (CN ISSN 0017-453X) *556*
Der Grosse Gartenkatalog (GW ISSN 0072-7717) *415*
Grosse Heimatbuecher (SZ ISSN 0072-7725) *454*
Grosse Naturforscher (GW ISSN 0072-7741) *97*

Grosse Pointe Public Library. Newsletter (US ISSN 0017-4610) *530*
Ground Zero (US) *579*
Groundwater Bulletin (US ISSN 0468-5067) *307*
Group for the Advancement of Psychiatry. Publication (US) *619*
Group for the Advancement of Psychiatry. Report *see* Group for the Advancement of Psychiatry. Publication *619*
Group for the Advancement of Psychiatry. Symposium *see* Group for the Advancement of Psychiatry. Publication *619*
Group Therapy - an Overview (US) *736*
Groupe International d'Etude de la Ceramique Egyptienne. Bulletin de Liaison (UA) *244*
Groupe Linguistique d'Etudes Chamito-Semitiques. Comptes Rendus (FR) *544*
Groupe, Union, Defense Vaincre *see* Vaincre *1*
Groupement des Directeurs Publicitaires de France. Annuaire (FR ISSN 0072-7792) *5, 215*
Groupement des Entreprises Francaises dans la Lutte Contre le Cancer. Bulletin National de Liaison (FR ISSN 0072-7806) *605*
Groupement des Societes Immobilieres d'Investissement. Annuaire (FR ISSN 0066-2933) *173*
Groups: a Journal of Group Dynamics and Psychotherapy (US ISSN 0093-4763) *736*
Growing Native Plants (AT) *115*
Growth (AT ISSN 0085-1280) *223*
Growth of Crystals (US ISSN 0072-7814) *250*
Grundbegriffe der Modernen Biologie. (GW ISSN 0085-1299) *103*
Grundlagen und Fortschritte der Lebensmitteluntersuchung *see* Grundlagen und Fortschritte der Lebensmitteltechnologie *405*
Grundlagen und Fortschritte der Lebensmitteluntersuchung und Lebensmitteltechnologie (GW ISSN 0341-0498) *405*
Grundlagen und Praxis des Bank- und Boersenwesens (GW) *173, 203*
Grundlehren der Mathematischen Wissenschaften in Einzeldarstellungen (US ISSN 0072-7830) *585*
Gruppenpsychotherapie und Gruppendynamik (GW ISSN 0017-4947) *619*
Gruppenpsychotherapie und Gruppendynamik. Beihefte (GW ISSN 0085-1302) *736*
Guam. Department of Commerce. Annual Economic Report (GU) *181*
Guam. Department of Commerce. Occasional Paper (GU) *182*
Guam. Department of Commerce. Personal Income Study (GU) *213*
Guam. Department of Commerce. Proceedings from Economic Conference (GU) *182*
Guam. Department of Commerce. Quarterly Review of Business Conditions *see* Guam Economic Annual Review *186*
Guam. Department of Commerce. Statistical Abstract (GU) *158*
Guam. Department of Revenue and Taxation. Report (GU ISSN 0072-7873) *219*
Guam Business Directory (GU ISSN 0072-7865) *238*
Guam Economic Annual Review (GU) *186*
Guam Statistical Abstract *see* Guam. Department of Commerce. Statistical Abstract *158*
Guam Statistical Annual Report (GU ISSN 0085-1310) *841*
Guanabara: O Balanco Economico (BL) *186*
Guardia Nacional (NQ ISSN 0017-5005) *639*

Guatemala. Banco Nacional de Desarrollo Agricola. Memoria (GT) *28, 186*
Guatemala. Direccion General de Estadistica. Anuario Estadistico (GT) *841*
Guatemala. Direccion General de Estadistica. Boletin Estadistico (GT ISSN 0017-5048) *841*
Guatemala. Direccion General de Estadistica. Departamento de Estudios Especiales y Estadisticas Continuas. Produccion, Venta y Otros Ingresos de la Encuesta Anual de la Industria Manufacturera Fabril (GT) *841*
Guatemala. Direccion General de Estadistica. Directoria Nacional de Establecimientos Industriales (GT) *158*
Guatemala Filatelica (GT ISSN 0046-6549) *478*
Guatemalteco *see* Diario de Centro Americo *741*
Guest Author (US ISSN 0160-6565) *564*
Guesthouses, Farmhouses and Inns in Britain (UK) *871, 886*
Guia Bolivia (BO) *186*
Guia da E M B R A P A e de Instituicoes Brasileiras de Pesquisa Agropecuaria (Empresa Brasileira de Pesquisa Agropecuaria) (BL) *15*
Guia das Editoras Brasileiras (BL) *238, 758*
Guia das Livrarias e Pontos de Venda de Livros No Brasil (BL) *758*
Guia de Audio (AG) *818*
Guia de Centros Docentes de la Iglesia *see* Guia de Centros Educativos Catolicos *331*
Guia de Centros Educativos Catolicos (SP) *331*
Guia de Comunicacao a Distancia (BL) *264*
Guia de Editores y de Libreros de Espana (SP ISSN 0072-7903) *758*
Guia de Hoteles: Espana (SP) *886*
Guia de Investigaciones en Curso de la Universidad de Buenos Aires (AG) *783*
Guia de la Iglesia *see* Bolivia: Guia Eclesiastica *774*
Guia de la Industria del Caucho (AG ISSN 0533-4500) *777*
Guia de Latinoamerica (UY) *331, 652*
Guia de los Caballos Verificadas en Espana (SP ISSN 0085-1337) *827*
Guia de Productores y Exportadores Latinoamericanos GUIPREX *see* GUIPREX *238*
Guia de Reuniones Cientificas y Tecnicas en la Argentina (AG ISSN 0301-7567) *626*
Guia de Turismo (AG) *886*
Guia de Valencia: Turistica, Urbana, Comercial (SP) *886*
Guia del Comercio y de la Industria de Madrid (SP) *179*
Guia del Tercer Mundo (MX) *360, 710*
Guia Eclesiastica Latinoamericana (CK) *772*
Guia Economico e Industrial do Estado de Minas Gerais (BL) *643*
Guia Filcar Mar del Plata *see* Guia Turistica y de Calles de la Ciudad de Mar del Plata *886*
Guia Oficial de Centro-America (HO) *886*
Guia para Inversiones en el Uruguay (UY) *186*
Guia Peuser de Turismo Argentina y Sudamericana (AG) *886*
Guia Turistica de Rosario y Sante Fe (AG) *886*
Guia Turistica y de Calles de la Ciudad de Mar del Plata (AG) *886*
Guia Turistica y Hoteles de Venezuela y el Caribe (VE) *886*
Guida All'abbigliamento Italiano (IT) *261*
Guida Camping d'Italia (IT ISSN 0072-792X) *830*
Guida della Stampa Periodica Italiana (IT) *91*
Guida Dello Sciatore (IT) *820, 886*
Guida di Veterinaria e Zootecnia (IT) *894*

Guida Nazionale del Commercio Con l'Estero (IT ISSN 0432-9120) *238*
Guida Sardegna d'Oggi (IT ISSN 0487-3750) *886*
Guidance Control and Flight Mechanics Conference. Proceedings *see* American Institute of Aeronautics and Astronautics. Paper *7*
Guide a i Musei e Agli Scavi Archeologici della Calabria (IT) *61*
Guide a l'Usage des Amateurs de Livres(FR) *758*
Guide Analytique du Pharmacien d'Officine (FR ISSN 0072-7954) *684*
Guide-Annuaire de l'Equipement Agricole (FR) *32*
Guide Annuaire des H.L.M. *see* Annuaire H L M *483*
Guide Annuaire du Commerce Franco-Allemand/Jahrbuch fuer den Deutsch-Franzoesischen Handel (FR ISSN 0072-7962) *179*
Guide-Annuaire Officiel de l'Artisanat et des Metiers (FR) *851*
Guide Annuaire Officiel du Complexe de Rungis GUIDOR *see* GUIDOR *407*
Guide Astrologique (FR) *80*
Guide Bibliographique du Monde Noir/Bibliographic Guide to the Negro World (CM) *91*
Guide Camping *see* Guide du Camping *830*
Guide d'Achat de la Photographie: 160 Objectifs pour Appareils Reflex 24 x 36 (FR) *693*
Guide d'Achat de la Photographie: 50 Appareils Reflex 24 x 36 (FR) *693*
Guide d'Une Carriere a Succes *see* Guide de Reussite dans le Carriere d'Assureur-Vie *499*
Guide de l'Acheteur NF (FR ISSN 0335-394X) *637*
Guide de l'Artisan (FR) *851*
Guide de l'Habitat et de l'Amenagement Rural (FR) *485*
Guide de l'Habitat Rural *see* Guide de l'Habitat et de l'Amenagement Rural *485*
Guide de l'Homme d'Affaires Voltaique(UV) *196*
Guide de l'Investisseur Industriel au Senegal (SG) *223*
Guide de l'Organisation de l'Informatique et de la Formation (FR) *909*
Guide de l'Organisation et de la Modernisation des Industries et Collectives *see* Guide de l'Organisation de l'Informatique et de la Formation *909*
Guide de la Chimie International (FR) *246*
Guide de la Jeune Maman (FR) *256*
Guide de la Parfumerie (FR ISSN 0072-7989) *85, 238*
Guide de Reussite dans la Carriere d'Assureur-Vie *see* Guide to a Successful Life Insurance Career *499*
Guide de Reussite dans le Carriere d'Assureur-Vie (CN ISSN 0317-2678) *499*
Guide des Acheteurs: Horlogerie, Bijouterie et Branches Annexes/Buyers' Guide: Watch Industry, Jewellery and Allied Trades (SZ) *503*
Guide des Acheteurs pour l'Horlogerie et les Branches Annexes *see* Guide des Acheteurs: Horlogerie, Bijouterie et Branches Annexes *503*
Guide des Cosmetiques *see* Cosmetics Handbook *85*
Guide des Prix Litteraires (FR ISSN 0072-8020) *565*
Guide des Relais Routiers (FR) *482, 886*
Guide du Camping (CN ISSN 0705-8314) *830*
Guide du Directeur de Tournees de Spectacles *see* Tour Organizers' Handbook *860*
Guide du Feu (FR ISSN 0337-5781) *395*
Guide du Feu et de la Protection Civile *see* Guide du Feu *395*

Guide du Livre Ancien et du Livre d'Occasion *see* Guide a l'Usage des Amateurs de Livres *758*
Guide du Petrole, Gaz, Chimie *see* Guide du Petrole, Gaz, Petrochimie *679*
Guide du Petrole, Gaz, Petrochimie (FR) *679*
Guide du Show-Business; Guide Professionnel du Spectacle (FR ISSN 0072-8063) *859*
Guide du Slaviste (FR ISSN 0072-8071) *909*
Guide du Tourisme Nigerien *see* Nigeria Tourist Guide *889*
Guide Economique de la Tunisie (TI) *238*
Guide Emer *see* Guide Europeen de l'Amateur d'Art, de l'Antiquaire et du Bibliophile *75*
Guide Europeen de l'Amateur d'Art, de l'Antiquaire et du Bibliophile (FR ISSN 0066-3069) *75*
Guide for Laboratory Animal Facilities and Care *see* Guide for the Care and Use of Laboratory Animals *612*
Guide for Planning Educational Facilities (US ISSN 0072-8101) *344*
Guide for Planning School Plants *see* Guide for Planning Educational Facilities *344*
Guide for the Care and Use of Laboratory Animals (US) *612*
Guide International de l'Energie Atomique et des Etudes Spatiales *see* Guide International de l'Energie Nucleare *703*
Guide International de l'Energie Nucleare (FR ISSN 0337-2219) *703*
Guide International des Machines, Appareils, Outils (SZ ISSN 0072-8136) *909*
Guide Kleber France (FR) *482, 886*
Guide Medical et Hospitalier (FR ISSN 0072-8144) *481, 595*
Guide National de l'Education Permanente *see* Annuaire de l'Education Permanente *314*
Guide National des Douanes et Droits Indirects (FR ISSN 0072-8187) *229*
Guide Naturiste Internationale *see* International Naturist Guide *830*
Guide Officiel Camping-Caravaning (FR) *830*
Guide Offshore (FR) *679*
Guide Pharma (PK) *595*
Guide Pratique de l'Usager des Prefectures (FR) *749*
Guide Pratique des Aeroports et de l'Aviation Commerciale (FR) *867*
Guide Rosenwald: Annuaire Medical et Pharmaceutique (FR ISSN 0072-8209) *595*
Guide Routier et Touristique: Madagascar, Reunion, Maurice, Comores et Seychelles (MG) *871*
Guide to a Successful Life Insurance Career (CN ISSN 0381-6532) *499*
Guide to a Successful Life Insurance Career *see* Guide de Reussite dans le Carriere d'Assureur-Vie *499*
Guide to Afro-American Resources (US) *392*
Guide to Alternative Periodicals (US) *91*
Guide to American Directories (US ISSN 0533-5248) *91*
Guide to American Educational Directories (US ISSN 0072-8225) *91, 327*
Guide to American Scientific and Technical Directories (US ISSN 0094-4505) *91, 794, 854*
Guide to Biomedical Standards (US ISSN 0085-1353) *103, 595*
Guide to Britain's Best Holidays (UK) *886*
Guide to British Offshore Suppliers (UK ISSN 0306-9192) *679*
Guide to Broadcasting (UK ISSN 0508-850X) *267*
Guide to Business & Investment Books *see* S I E Guide to Business and Investment Books *163*
Guide to Canada (US) *91*
Guide to Caravan and Camping Holidays (UK) *830, 886*

Guide to Chinese Periodicals (CH) *2, 760*
Guide to Christian Camps (US) *765*
Guide to Collections of Manuscripts Relating to Australia (AT) *91, 437*
Guide to College Courses in Film and Television (US ISSN 0072-8284) *329, 650*
Guide to Consumer Markets (US ISSN 0072-8314) *909*
Guide to Correspondence Studies in Colleges and Universities *see* Guide to Independent Study Through Correspondence Instruction *331*
Guide to Cross Country Skiing in Minnesota *see* Guide to Skiing in Minnesota *886*
Guide to Danish Libraries *see* Danmarks Biblioteksforening. Bibliotekvejviser *528*
Guide to Dental Materials and Devices *see* Dentist's Desk Reference *609*
Guide to Departments of Sociology and Anthropology in Canadian Universities/Annuaire des Departementes de Sociologie et d'Anthropologie au Canada (CN ISSN 0315-0895) *337*
Guide to Discount Buying *see* Consumers Digest Guide to Discount Buying *279*
Guide to Downhill Skiing in Minnesota *see* Guide to Skiing in Minnesota *886*
Guide to Electronics Industry in India (II) *354*
Guide to Employment Abroad (US ISSN 0434-8850) *667*
Guide to External and Continuing Education (US ISSN 0363-0927) *909*
Guide to Film and Television Courses in Canada (CN ISSN 0383-0187) *650*
Guide to Fluorescence Literature (US ISSN 0072-8403) *246, 696*
Guide to Foreign Government-Loan Film (16 MM) *see* Guide to Free Loan Films About Foreign Lands *651*
Guide to Foreign Legal Materials Series(US ISSN 0072-842X) *512*
Guide to Four-Year College Databook *see* Chronicle Four-Year College Databook *330*
Guide to Free Loan Films About Foreign Lands (US) *651*
Guide to Free-Loan Training Films (16 MM) (US ISSN 0072-8438) *318, 650*
Guide to Gas Chromatography Literature (US ISSN 0072-8446) *249*
Guide to Government in Hawaii (US ISSN 0072-8454) *742*
Guide to Government-Loan Films (US) *639, 650*
Guide to Government-Loan Films Volume 1: the Civilian Agencies (US ISSN 0072-8462) *651*
Guide to Graduate and Professional Study (US ISSN 0145-8035) *909*
Guide to Graduate Departments of Geography in the United States and Canada (US ISSN 0072-8497) *331, 422*
Guide to Graduate Departments of Sociology (US ISSN 0091-7052) *814*
Guide to Graduate Management Education (US ISSN 0162-2463) *215, 331*
Guide to Graduate Study in Botany for the United States and Canada (US ISSN 0072-8500) *115, 331*
Guide to Graduate Study in Political Science. (US ISSN 0091-9632) *711*
Guide to Holiday Houses, Cottages and Chalets *see* Self Catering in Britain *890*
Guide to Hotels in South Africa *see* C V R Travel and Hotel Guide to Southern Africa *482*
Guide to Independent Study Through Correspondence Instruction (US ISSN 0149-1083) *331*
Guide to Independent Television and Independent Local Radio *see* Television & Radio *268*

Guide to Indian Chemical Plants and Equipment (II) *373*
Guide to Japanese Taxes (JA ISSN 0072-8551) *229*
Guide to Key British Enterprises I and II (US) *238*
Guide to Manufactured Homes (US ISSN 0160-7340) *136*
Guide to Manuscripts Relating to Australia *see* Guide to Collections of Manuscripts Relating to Australia *437*
Guide to Microforms in Print *see* Guide to Microforms in Print. Author, Title *91*
Guide to Microforms in Print. Author, Title (US ISSN 0164-0747) *91*
Guide to Micrographic Equipment (US ISSN 0360-8654) *693*
Guide to Microreproduction Equipment *see* Guide to Micrapic Equipment *693*
Guide to Military-Loan Films *see* Guide to Government-Loan Films *650*
Guide to Minority Resources *see* Guide to Afro-American Resources *392*
Guide to National Bibliographical Information Centres (UN ISSN 0072-8608) *530*
Guide to Nebraska State Agencies (US ISSN 0091-0716) *742*
Guide to New Zealand Income Tax Practice (NZ ISSN 0072-8616) *229*
Guide to Periodicals and Newspapers in the Public Libraries of Metropolitan Toronto (CN ISSN 0315-7288) *91*
Guide to Professional Bodies in Malawi(MW) *360*
Guide to Professional Development Opportunities for College and University Administrators: Seminars, Workshops, Conferences, and Internships (US ISSN 0098-9835) *337*
Guide to Programs in Linguistics (US) *544*
Guide to Publishers and Related Industries in Japan (JA) *5, 758*
Guide to Quality Construction Products(US) *136*
Guide to Radio Electronics & Components Trade and Industry in India *see* Guide to Electronics Industry in India *354*
Guide to Reference Books (US ISSN 0072-8624) *91*
Guide to Reference Material (UK ISSN 0072-8640) *91*
Guide to Reprints (US ISSN 0072-8667) *91*
Guide to Science and Technology in Eastern Europe (UK) *783, 851*
Guide to Science and Technology in the Asia/Pacific Area (UK) *783, 851*
Guide to Scientific Instruments *see* Science Guide to Scientific Instruments *9*
Guide to Skiing in Minnesota (US) *830, 886*
Guide to Summer Camps and Summer Schools (US ISSN 0072-8705) *331*
Guide to Texas State Agencies (US) *742*
Guide to Thailand (TH) *886*
Guide to the American Left *see* Directory of the American Left *710*
Guide to the Antique Shops of Britain (UK) *476*
Guide to the Coalfields (UK ISSN 0072-8713) *643*
Guide to the Evaluation of Educational Experiences in the Armed Services (US) *344*
Guide to the Health Care Field (US ISSN 0094-8969) *481, 752*
Guide to the National Merit Scholarship Program (US ISSN 0072-8721) *337*
Guide to the Port of Yokohama (JA) *878*
Guide to the Press of the World (UK ISSN 0072-8748) *504*

Guide to the Recommended Country Inns of New England (US ISSN 0093-4585) *482*
Guide to the Social Services (UK ISSN 0072-8756) *806*
Guide to the Sources of the History of the Nations. B: Africa (SZ) *438*
Guide to the Use of Insecticides and Fungicides in South Africa (SA) *35*
Guide to Traffic Safety Literature (US ISSN 0533-5485) *91, 866*
Guide to Traveling Around the World by Passenger-Carrying Freighters *see* Travel Routes Around the World: Guide to Traveling Around the World by Passenger-Carrying Freighters *915*
Guide to Traveling on Business in 50 States *see* American Executive Travel Companion *883*
Guide Touristique Europeen pour Israelites/European Travel Guide for Jews (BE) *392*
Guidebook of Catholic Hospitals (US ISSN 0090-2535) *481*
Guidebook of English Coins, Nineteenth and Twentieth Centuries (US ISSN 0072-8802) *477*
Guidebook of Modern United States Currency (US ISSN 0072-8810) *477*
Guidebook of U.S. & Canadian Postdoctoral Dental Programs (US ISSN 0361-9273) *337, 609*
Guidebook of United States Coins (US ISSN 0072-8829) *477*
Guidebook - State of Ohio, Department of Natural Resources, Division of Geological Survey *see* Ohio. Division of Geological Survey. Guidebook *298*
Guidebook to California Taxes (US ISSN 0072-8837) *229*
Guidebook to Florida Taxes (US ISSN 0093-8637) *229*
Guidebook to Illinois Taxes (US ISSN 0072-8845) *229*
Guidebook to Labor Relations (US ISSN 0072-8853) *207, 512*
Guidebook to Massachusetts Taxes (US ISSN 0072-8861) *229*
Guidebook to Michigan Taxes (US ISSN 0072-887X) *229*
Guidebook to New Jersey Taxes (US ISSN 0072-8888) *229*
Guidebook to New York Taxes (US ISSN 0072-8896) *229*
Guidebook to North Carolina Taxes (US ISSN 0091-1186) *229*
Guidebook to Ohio Taxes (US ISSN 0091-4010) *229*
Guidebook to Pennsylvania Taxes (US ISSN 0072-890X) *229*
Guidebook to Wisconsin Taxes (US ISSN 0093-8645) *229*
Guidelines for Industrial Investors in Kenya (KE) *186*
Guidelines for Teachers (UK ISSN 0072-8918) *349*
Guidelines for the Use of Insecticides to Control Insects Affecting Crops, Livestock, Households, Stored Products, Forest & Forest Products (US) *36*
Guides to Historical Resources (US) *469*
Guides to Information Sources *see* United Nations Industrial Development Organization. Guides to Information Sources *165*
Guides to Information Sources in Science and Technology (US ISSN 0072-8934) *909*
Guides to Jewish Subjects in Social and Humanistic Research (US ISSN 0533-5620) *392*
GUIDOR (Guide Annuaire Officiel du Complexe de Rungis) (FR) *238, 407*
Guild of Prescription Opticians of America. Reference List (US ISSN 0072-8977) *616*
Guildhall Poets (UK) *579*
Guillaume Apollinaire (FR ISSN 0072-8993) *565*
Guimaraes. Arquivo Municipal "Alfredo Pimento." Boletim de Trabalhos Historicos (PO) *469*

Guinness Book of Records *see* Guinness Book of World Records *361*
Guinness Book of World Records (US) *361*
GUIPREX (Guia de Productores y Exportadores Latinoamericanos) (AG) *238*
Gujarat Industrial Development Corporation. Annual Report (II) *223*
Gujarat State Financial Corporation. Annual Report (II ISSN 0533-649X) *229*
Gulden Passer/Compas d'Or (BE) *758*
Gulf and Caribbean Fisheries Institute. Annual Proceedings (US ISSN 0072-9019) *397*
Gulf Coast Conference Proceedings (US) *469*
Gulf Coast Molecular Biology Conference. Transactions (US) *103*
Gulf Coast Research Laboratory. Publications of the Museum (US) *103*
Gulf Handbook (US) *474*
Gulf Research Reports (US ISSN 0072-9027) *310*
Gumma Journal of Liberal Arts and Sciences (JA ISSN 0367-4061) *490*
Gumma Symposia on Endocrinology (JA ISSN 0533-6724) *611*
Gumma University. Faculty of Education. Annual Report: Art and Technology Series (JA ISSN 0072-9051) *75, 851*
Gumma University. Faculty of Education. Annual Report: Cultural Science Series (JA ISSN 0386-4294) *490*
Gun Digest (US ISSN 0072-9043) *830*
Gun World Annual (US) *830*
Gun World Hunting Guide *see* Gun World Annual *830*
Gunneria (NO) *61, 103, 115*
Guns and Ammo Annual (US ISSN 0072-906X) *830*
Guns Guide *see* Cord Sportfacts Guns Guide *476*
Guns Illustrated (US ISSN 0072-9078) *830*
Gustav Stern Symposia on Perspectives in Virology *see* Perspectives in Virology *608*
Gutenberg (FR) *733*
Gutenberg-Jahrbuch (GW ISSN 0072-9094) *733*
Guyana. Geological Survey Department.Annual Reports *see* Guyana. Geology & Mines Commission. Annual Report *295*
Guyana. Geological Survey Department. Mineral Resources Pamphlet *see* Guyana. Geology & Mines Commission. Mineral Resources Pamphlet *295*
Guyana. Geology & Mines Commission. Annual Report (GY) *295*
Guyana. Geology & Mines Commission. Mineral Resources Pamphlet (GY) *295*
Guyana. Hydrometeorological Service. Annual Climatological Data Summary (GY) *633*
Guyana. National Insurance Board. Annual Report (GY) *499*
Guyana. Ombudsman. Report (GY) *512*
Guyana. Statistical Bureau. Annual Account Relating to External Trade (GY ISSN 0533-991X) *196*
Guyana Association of Professional Engineers *see* G.A.P.E *367*
Guyana Sugar Corporation. Annual Reports and Accounts (GY) *36*
Gwechall (FR) *61, 454*
Gwynedd Archives Service. Bulletin (UK ISSN 0306-3151) *454*
Gymnasieingenjoeren *see* T L I-Ingenjoeren *370*
Gymnastics Guide *see* N A G W S Guide. Gymnastics *821*
H I S Brief (Hochschul-Informations-System GmbH) (GW) *337*
H I S S Yearbook of Herpetology *see* Yearbook of Herpetology *131*
H M T: the Science and Application of Heat Mass Transfer (US) *429, 700*

H P A C Info-Dex (Heating/Piping/Air Conditioning Mechanical Systems Information Index) (US) *429*
H R I Observations *see* Observations *147*
H. R. Macmillan Lectureship in Forestry (CN ISSN 0072-9140) *409*
H R W Newsletter (Human Rights for Women, Inc.) (US ISSN 0046-8207) *718*
H.S.M.A. Hotel Facilities Digest (Hotel Sales Management Association) (US) *482*
H.S.M.A. Hotel-Motel Directory and Facilities Guide *see* H.S.M.A. Hotel Facilities Digest *482*
H S S Quarterly *see* Alaska. Department of Health and Social Services. Quarterly *903*
H U D Statistical Yearbook *see* U.S. Department of Housing and Urban Development. Statistical Yearbook *489*
H V A C Red Book of Heating, Ventilating and Air Conditioning Equipment (UK) *429*
Habelts Dissertationsdrucke. Reihe Aegyptologie (GW) *474*
Habelts Dissertationsdrucke. Reihe Alte Geschichte (GW ISSN 0072-9175) *432*
Habelts Dissertationsdrucke. Reihe Germanistik (GW) *565*
Habelts Dissertationsdrucke. Reihe Klassische Archaeologie (GW ISSN 0072-9183) *61*
Habelts Dissertationsdrucke. Reihe Klassische Philologie (GW ISSN 0072-9191) *544*
Habelts Dissertationsdrucke. Reihe Kunstgeschichte (GW ISSN 0072-9205) *75*
Habelts Dissertationsdrucke. Reihe Mittelalterliche Geschichte (GW ISSN 0072-9213) *432*
Habis (SP) *259*
Habitation Space (IT) *69*
Habitations a Loyer Modere Annuaire H L M *see* Annuaire H L M *483*
Hacettepe Fen ve Muhendislik Bilimleri Dergisi (TU ISSN 0072-9221) *367, 783*
Hackney Horse Society Year Book (UK) *828*
Hackney Stud Book (UK) *828*
Hadassah Medical Organization. Report(IS ISSN 0072-923X) *595*
Hadassah Vocational Guidance Institute. Report (IS ISSN 0072-9248) *667*
Haematologie und Bluttransfusion (US ISSN 0440-0607) *613*
Hafenbautechnische Gesellschaft. Jahrbuch (US ISSN 0072-9264) *375*
Hafnia; Copenhagen Papers in the History of Art (DK ISSN 0085-1361) *75*
Hague Conference on Private International Law. Actes et Documents (NE ISSN 0072-9272) *523*
Hahn-Meitner-Institut fuer Kernforschung Berlin. Bericht *see* Hahn-Meitner-Institut fuer Kernforschung Berlin. Jahresbericht *703*
Hahn-Meitner-Institut fuer Kernforschung Berlin. Jahresbericht (GW) *703*
Haiku (US) *579*
Haiteny, Haisorata, Hairaha (MG) *556*
Haiti. Conseil National de Developpement et de Planification. Plan Annuel et Budget de Developpement (HT) *191*
Haiti. Institut Haitien de Statistique. Bulletin Trimestriel de Statistique (HT ISSN 0017-6788) *841*
Haiti-Culture (HT) *361*
Hakko Kenkyusho Hokoku *see* Institute for Fermentation, Osaka. Research Communications *123*
Hakodate Kogyo Koto Senmon Gakko Kiyo *see* Hakodate Technical College. Research Reports *851*
Hakodate Technical College. Research Reports/Hakodate Kogyo Koto Senmon Gakko Kiyo (JA) *851*
Halle Prospectus (UK) *659*

HANDBOOK OF 1377

Halloween (CN) *859*
Hals-, Nasen- und Ohrenheilkunde (GE ISSN 0072-9418) *617*
Halsbury's Laws of England Annual Abridgment (UK ISSN 0308-4388) *512*
Hambone (US) *392, 859*
Hambro Euromoney Directory (UK ISSN 0306-3933) *173*
Hamburg. Unesco Institute for Education. Educational Research and Practice *see* Educational Research and Practice *908*
Hamburg the Quick Port (GW) *878*
Hamburger Abhandlungen (GW ISSN 0072-9507) *512*
Hamburger Beitraege fuer Russischlehrer (GW ISSN 0072-9515) *544*
Hamburger Beitraege zur Afrika-Kunde (GW) *440*
Hamburger Beitraege zur Archaeologie (GW ISSN 0341-3152) *61*
Hamburger Beitraege zur Numismatik (GW ISSN 0072-9523) *477*
Hamburger Historische Studien (GW ISSN 0072-9558) *432*
Hamburger Jahrbuch fuer Musikwissenschaft (GW) *659*
Hamburger Jahrbuch fuer Wirtschafts- und Gesellschaftspolitik (GW ISSN 0072-9566) *145*
Hamburger Juristische Studien (GW ISSN 0341-3179) *512*
Hamburger Oeffentlich-Rechtliche Nebenstunden (GW ISSN 0072-9574) *512, 523*
Hamburger Philologische Studien (GW ISSN 0072-9582) *544*
Hamburger Phonetische Beitraege (GW ISSN 0341-3187) *544*
Hamburger Studien zur Philosophie (GW ISSN 0072-9604) *689*
Hamburgisches Museum fuer Voelkerkunde. Mitteilungen (GW ISSN 0072-9469) *50*
Hamburgisches Zoologisches Museum und Institut. Mitteilungen (GW ISSN 0072-9612) *128*
Hammond Almanac (US) *361*
Hampshire Field. Proceedings *see* Hampshire Field Club and Archaeological Society Proceedings *61*
Hampshire Field Club and Archaeological Society Proceedings (UK ISSN 0142-8950) *61, 454*
Hand Book (US) *75, 565*
Handakten fuer die Standesamtliche Arbeit (GW ISSN 0438-5004) *512, 742*
Handball und Faustball in Oesterreich (AU ISSN 0072-9698) *820*
Handbook and Directory - Association for Educational Data Systems *see* Association for Educational Data Systems. Handbook and Directory *270*
Handbook for Christian Writers *see* Successful Writers and Editors Guidebook *768*
Handbook for Metric Usage (US) *637*
Handbook for Recruiting at the Historically Black Colleges (US ISSN 0146-5104) *337*
Handbook of Adult Education in Scotland (UK) *329*
Handbook of Adult Education in the United States (US) *329*
Handbook of Advertising and Marketing Services (US) *5, 218*
Handbook of American College Financial Aid (US) *331*
Handbook of Basic Statistics of Maharashtra State (II ISSN 0072-9728) *841*
Handbook of Biochemistry *see* C R C Handbook of Biochemistry and Molecular Biology *905*
Handbook of Denominations in the U.S. (US ISSN 0072-9787) *765*
Handbook of Electronic Materials (US ISSN 0072-9795) *354, 379*
Handbook of Elemental Abundances in Meteorites Series: Extraterrestrial Chemistry (US) *7*
Handbook of Experimental Pharmacology *see* Handbuch der Experimentellen Pharmakologie *684*

Handbook of Fiji (AT ISSN 0072-9809) 886
Handbook of Food Preparation (US) 405, 479
Handbook of Geochemistry (US ISSN 0072-9817) 909
Handbook of Illinois Government (US ISSN 0095-2842) 711
Handbook of Labor Force Data for Selected Areas of Oklahoma (US) 207
Handbook of Latin American Studies. Humanities (US) 490
Handbook of Latin American Studies. Social Sciences (US) 797
Handbook of Latin American Studies: A Selected and Annotated Guide to Recent Publications (US ISSN 0072-9833) 469
Handbook of Non Prescription Drugs (US) 684
Handbook of Ocular Therapeutics and Pharmacology see Ocular Therapeutics and Pharmacology 616
Handbook of Oklahoma Employment Statistics (US) 158
Handbook of Papua and New Guinea see Papua New Guinea Handbook 890
Handbook of Physiology (US ISSN 0072-9875) 126
Handbook of Private Schools (US ISSN 0072-9884) 331
Handbook of Science and Technology see Kwahak Kisul Yoram 852
Handbook of Securities of the United States Government and Federal Agencies and Related Money Market Instruments (US ISSN 0072-9892) 203
Handbook of Self-Employed Pensions see Self-Employed Pensions 500
Handbook of Sensory Physiology (US ISSN 0072-9906) 126
Handbook of Service Members' and Veterans' Benefits (US) 639
Handbook of Servicemen's and Veterans' Benefits see Handbook of Service Members' and Veterans' Benefits 639
Handbook of the Indian Cotton Textile Industry (II) 855
Handbook of the Japan Drug Industry see Japan Drug Industry Review 685
Handbook of the Northern Wood Industries (SW ISSN 0072-9922) 413
Handbook of Trade and Technical Careers and Training (US) 329, 331
Handbook of United States Coins (US ISSN 0072-9949) 477
Handbook on International Study see Handbook on U.S. Study for Foreign Nationals 909
Handbook on International Study: for Foreign Nationals see Handbook on U.S. Study for Foreign Nationals 909
Handbook on International Study for U.S. Nationals. Vol. 2: Study in the American Republics Area (US ISSN 0440-1948) 342
Handbook on the U.S.-German Tax Convention (NE) 229
Handbook on U. S. Luminescent Stamps (US ISSN 0072-9981) 478
Handbook on U.S. Study for Foreign Nationals (US) 909
Handbook on Women Workers (US ISSN 0083-3622) 207
Handbuch der Allgemeinbildenden Hoeheren Schulen Oesterreichs (AU) 337
Handbuch der Experimentellen Pharmakologie/Handbook of Experimental Pharmacology (US ISSN 0073-0033) 684
Handbuch der Grossunternehmen (GW ISSN 0073-0068) 223
Handbuch der Internationalen Dokumentation und Information (GW ISSN 0340-1332) 530
Handbuch der Internationalen Kautschukindustrie/International Rubber Directory/Manuel International de Caoutchouc (SZ ISSN 0073-0076) 777

Handbuch der Internationalen Kunstoffindustrie/International Plastics Directory/Manuel International des Plastiques (SZ ISSN 0073-0084) 706
Handbuch der Justiz (GW ISSN 0073-0092) 512
Handbuch der Klassifikation (GW ISSN 0073-0106) 530
Handbuch der Mikroskopischen Anatomie des Menschen (US ISSN 0073-0114) 119
Handbuch der Oeffentlichen Bibliotheken (GW ISSN 0301-9225) 530
Handbuch der Oesterreichischen Sozialversicherung (AU) 502, 841
Handbuch der Physik/Encyclopedia of Physics (US ISSN 0085-140X) 909
Handbuch der Rationalisierung (GW ISSN 0073-0122) 215
Handbuch der Steuerveranlagungen: Einkommensteuer, Koerperschaftsteuer, Gewerbesteuer, Umsatzsteuer (GW) 229
Handbuch der Stratigraphischen Geologie (GW ISSN 0073-0130) 295
Handbuch der Sudetendeutschen Kulturgeschichte (GW ISSN 0073-0149) 432
Handbuch der Technischen Dokumentation und Bibliographie see Handbuch der Internationalen Dokumentation und Information 530
Handbuch der Virusforschung see Virology Monographs 124
Handbuch des Oeffentlichen Lebens in Oesterreich (AU ISSN 0440-2103) 361
Handbuch fuer Berufskraftfahrer (GW ISSN 0073-0157) 871
Handbuch fuer den Werbenden Buch- und Zeitschriftenhandel (GW ISSN 0073-0165) 758
Handbuch fuer die Druckindustrie Berlin (GW ISSN 0073-0173) 733
Handbuch fuer die Sanitaetsberufe Oesterreich (AU ISSN 0073-0181) 614
Handbuch Holz (GW ISSN 0518-0147) 413
Handbuch Oeffentlicher Verkehrsbetriebe (GW ISSN 0073-019X) 862
Handbuch zur Deutschen Militaergeschichte (GW) 639
Handels- og Soefartsmuseet paa Kronborg. Aarbog (DK ISSN 0085-1418) 878
Handelshoegskolan vid Aabo Akademi. Ekonomisk-Geografiska Institutionen. Memoranda see Aabo Akademi. Ekonomisk-Geografiska Institutionen. Memoranda 141
Handelshoegskolan vid Aabo Akademi. Ekonomisk-Geografiska Institutionen. Meddelanden see Aabo Akademi. Ekonomisk-Geografiska Institutionen. Meddelanden 141
Handelshoejskolen i Koebenhavn. Instituttet for Udenrigshandel. Smaaskrifter (DK ISSN 0069-9888) 196
Handelsrechtliche Entscheidungen (AU ISSN 0567-1469) 512
Handelsregister Oesterreich (AU) 238
Handicapped Requirements Handbook (US) 207
Handling & Shipping. Presidential Issue (US) 862
Handloader's Digest (US ISSN 0073-0211) 830
Handsatzletter (GW) 733, 758
Haney Foundation Series (US ISSN 0073-022X) 491
Hanguk Tonggye Yongam see Korea Statistical Yearbook 438
Hank Seale Oil Directory: Central United States see Armstrong Oil Directory: Central United States 678
Hank Seale Oil Directory: Louisiana, Mississippi, Arkansas, Texas Gulf Coast and East Texas see Armstrong Oil Directory: Louisiana, Mississippi, Arkansas, Texas Gulf Coast and East Texas 678

Hank Seale Oil Directory: Texas Including Southeast New Mexico see Armstrong Oil Directory: Texas Including Southeast New Mexico 678
Hankuk Baksa Mit Seuksa Hak Wee Lonmun Chong Mokrok see List of Theses for the Doctor's and Master's Degree in Korea 327
Han'quk Ch'ulp; an Yon'gam. see Korean Publications Yearbook 759
Hans Kelsen-Institut. Schriftenreihe (AU) 512
Hanseniasis Letter (BL) 608, 611
Hansische Geschichtsblaetter (GW ISSN 0073-0327) 435
Hap Jones Motorcycle and Scooter Blue Book see Motorcycle Blue Book 826
Hapdong Yongam see Korea Annual 239
Happy Day Diary (UK) 765
Hard Cheese (UK ISSN 0305-9839) 318, 814
Hard Core News (US ISSN 0085-1434) 719
Hardsyssels Aarbog (DK ISSN 0046-6840) 454
Hardware Merchandising's Canadian Hardware Handbook (CN) 136
Hardware Merchandising's Hardware Handbook see Hardware Merchandising's Canadian Hardware Handbook 136
Hardwood Purchasing Directory see Hardwood Purchasing Handbook 413
Hardwood Purchasing Handbook (US) 413
Hardy's Encyclopaedia Guide to Agra, Jaipur, Delhi, Varanasi (II ISSN 0073-0378) 886
Hardy's Encyclopaedia Hotels of India and Nepal (II ISSN 0073-0386) 482
Harmon Memorial Lectures in Military History (US ISSN 0073-0394) 639
Harold C. Mack Symposium. Proceedings (US) 126, 615
Harpers Directory and Manual of the Wine and Spirit Trade see Harpers Directory of the Wine and Spirit Trade 86
Harpers Directory of the Wine and Spirit Trade (UK) 86
Harpers Guide to Sports Trade (UK ISSN 0073-0416) 238, 820
Harris Auction Galleries. Collectors' Auction (US ISSN 0093-1047) 652
Harris Survey Yearbook of Public Opinion (US ISSN 0085-1442) 909
Harrison Street Review (US) 556, 565
Harry Frank Guggenheim Foundation. Report (US) 806
Harry S. Truman Research Institute, Jerusalem. Occasional Papers (IS) 91
Harry Steenbock Symposia (US) 111
Harsunan Nijeriya (NR) 544
Hartford Studies in Linguistics (US ISSN 0073-0432) 544
Harvard Architecture Review (US ISSN 0194-3650) 69
Harvard Armenian Texts and Studies (US ISSN 0073-0459) 454
Harvard Books in Biology (US ISSN 0073-0467) 103
Harvard Books in Biophysics (US ISSN 0073-0475) 112
Harvard East Asian Monographs (US ISSN 0073-0483) 443
Harvard East Asian Series (US ISSN 0073-0491) 443
Harvard Economic Studies (US ISSN 0073-0505) 145
Harvard English Studies (US ISSN 0073-0513) 544, 565
Harvard Environmental Law Review (US) 512
Harvard Historical Monographs (US ISSN 0073-0521) 432
Harvard Historical Studies (US ISSN 0073-053X) 432
Harvard Iranian Series (US) 474
Harvard Journal of Asiatic Studies (US ISSN 0073-0548) 670
Harvard Judaic Monographs (US) 392, 770
Harvard Middle Eastern Monographs (US ISSN 0073-0572) 443

Harvard Middle Eastern Studies (US ISSN 0073-0580) 474
Harvard Monographs in Applied Science (US ISSN 0440-3452) 851
Harvard Monographs in the History of Science (US) 783
Harvard Oriental Series (US ISSN 0073-0599) 443
Harvard Paperbacks (US ISSN 0073-0602) 491, 797
Harvard Papers in Theoretical Geography (US ISSN 0073-0610) 422
Harvard Political Classics (US) 711
Harvard Political Studies (US) 711
Harvard Publications in Music (US ISSN 0073-0629) 659
Harvard Semitic Monographs (US ISSN 0073-0637) 544, 765
Harvard Semitic Series (US ISSN 0073-0645) 474
Harvard Slavic Monographs (US) 454, 544, 565
Harvard Studies in American-East Asian Relations (US) 443
Harvard Studies in Business History (US ISSN 0073-067X) 191
Harvard Studies in Classical Philology (US ISSN 0073-0688) 259, 544
Harvard Studies in Comparative Literature (US ISSN 0073-0696) 565
Harvard Studies in International Affairs (US) 721
Harvard Studies in Romance Languages (US ISSN 0073-0718) 544
Harvard Studies in Urban History (US) 485
Harvard Studies in World Religions (US ISSN 0440-3509) 765
Harvard Theological Studies (US ISSN 0073-0726) 765
Harvard Ukrainian Research Institute. Minutes of the Seminar in Ukrainian Studies (US) 392
Harvard University. Center for International Affairs. Annual Report (US ISSN 0073-0734) 721
Harvard University. Computation Laboratory. Mathematical Linguistics and Automatic Translation; Report to National Science Foundation (US ISSN 0073-0769) 530
Harvard University. Graduate School of Business Administration. Baker Library. Core Collection, an Author and Subject Guide (US) 158
Harvard University. Graduate School of Business Administration. Baker Library. Current Periodical Publications in Baker Library (US) 158
Harvard University. Graduate School of Business Administration. Baker Library. Kress Library of Business and Economics. Publications (US ISSN 0073-0777) 145
Harvard University. Graduate School of Business Administration. Program for Management Development. Publication (US ISSN 0073-0785) 215
Harvard University. Law School. Library. Annual Legal Bibliography (US ISSN 0073-0793) 512
Harvard University. Museum of Comparative Zoology. Bulletin (US ISSN 0027-4100) 128
Harvard University. Museum of Comparative Zoology. Department of Mollusks. Occasional Papers on Mollusks (US ISSN 0073-0807) 128
Harvard University. Program on Information Technologies and Public Policy. Working Paper (US) 742
Harvard University. Russian Research Center. Russian Research Center Studies (US ISSN 0073-0831) 454
Harvard-Yenching Institute. Monograph Series (US ISSN 0073-084X) 443, 544, 565
Harvard-Yenching Institute. Studies (US ISSN 0073-0858) 443
Harvard-Yenching Library Bibliographical Series (US) 91
Harvest (US ISSN 0073-0866) 565
Harvest (US ISSN 0362-7888) 565

Harvey Lectures (US ISSN 0073-0874) 595
Harz-Zeitschrift (GW ISSN 0073-0882) 454
Haskins & Sells. Selected Papers (US ISSN 0440-4122) 167
Hat Life Year Book see Hat Life Year Book & Directory 261
Hat Life Year Book & Directory (US) 261
Hatcheries and Dealers Participating in the National Poultry Improvement Plan (US ISSN 0082-9722) 45
Hattori Botanical Laboratory. Journal/ Hattori Shokubutsu Kenkyusho Hokoku (JA ISSN 0073-0912) 115
Hattori Shokubutsu Kenkyusho Hokoku see Hattori Botanical Laboratory. Journal 115
Haulage Manual (UK) 882
Hauptverband der Oesterreichischen Sparkassen. Jahresbericht (AU) 173
Hautes Etudes du Monde Greco-Romain (SZ ISSN 0073-0939) 259, 544
Hautes Etudes Islamiques et Orientales d'Histoire Comparee (SZ ISSN 0073-0947) 475
Hautes Etudes Medievales et Modernes(SZ ISSN 0073-0955) 454
Hautes Etudes Numismatiques (SZ ISSN 0073-0963) 432
Hautes Etudes Orientales (SZ ISSN 0073-0971) 670
Hawaii. Children's Health Services Division. Crippled Children Branch Report see Hawaii. Family Health Services Division. Crippled Children Services Branch. Report 806
Hawaii. Commission on Aging. Report of Achievements of Programs for the Aging (US ISSN 0090-2233) 428, 806
Hawaii. Criminal Injuries Compensation Commission. Annual Report. (US ISSN 0098-5708) 281
Hawaii. Department of Education. Educational Directory: State & District Office (US ISSN 0092-1777) 318
Hawaii. Department of Education. Office of Business Services. Report on Federally Connected Pupils: Hawaii Public Schools (US ISSN 0090-9440) 318
Hawaii. Department of Education. Office of Business Services. Student Information & Records Administration Branch. Public and Private School Enrollment (US) 318
Hawaii. Department of Education. Office of Library Services. Report (US ISSN 0073-103X) 530
Hawaii. Department of Education. Office of Research and Planning. Information Systems Branch. Public and Private School Enrollment see Hawaii. Department of Education. Office of Business Services. Student Information & Records Administration Branch. Public and Private School Enrollment 318
Hawaii. Department of Health. Division of Mental Health. Children's Health Services see Hawaii. Department of Health. Waimano Training School and Hospital Division (Report) 481
Hawaii. Department of Health. Mental Health Services for Children and Youth (US ISSN 0362-6296) 256, 752, 806
Hawaii. Department of Health. Mental Health Statistical Section. Psychiatric Outpatient, Inpatient and Community Programs (US) 619, 806
Hawaii. Department of Health. Mental Health Statistical Section Psychiatric Outpatient Program see Hawaii. Department of Health. Mental Health Statistical Section. Psychiatric Outpatient, Inpatient and Community Programs 806
Hawaii. Department of Health. Research and Statistics Office. R & S Report (US ISSN 0093-3481) 694, 727

Hawaii. Department of Health. Waimano Training School and Hospital Division (Report) (US) 481, 806
Hawaii. Department of Labor and Industrial Relations. Labor Force Statistics (US) 158
Hawaii. Department of Labor and Industrial Relations. Sub-Area Review (US) 207
Hawaii. Department of Planning and Economic Development. Annual Report (US ISSN 0073-1072) 223
Hawaii. Family Health Services Division. Crippled Children Services Branch. Report (US) 617, 806
Hawaii. Insurance Division. Report of the Insurance Commissioner of Hawaii (US ISSN 0073-1110) 499
Hawaii. Judiciary Department. Annual Report (US) 512
Hawaii. Legislative Auditor. Special Reports (US) 229, 742
Hawaii. Legislative Reference Bureau. Digest and Index of Laws Enacted (US ISSN 0095-6619) 513
Hawaii. Legislative Reference Bureau. Report (US ISSN 0073-1277) 742
Hawaii. Office of Instructional Services. Special Programs Branch. Annual Performance Report on Adult Education (US ISSN 0362-2940) 329
Hawaii. Office of the Ombudsman. Report (US ISSN 0073-1137) 718
Hawaii. State Commission on the Status of Women. Annual Report (US ISSN 0092-9190) 513, 900
Hawaii. State Law Enforcement and Juvenile Delinquency Planning Agency. Annual Action Program (US ISSN 0095-4209) 281
Hawaii Agricultural Experiment Station, Honolulu. Research Bulletin (US ISSN 0073-098X) 15
Hawaii Agricultural Experiment Station, Honolulu. Research Report (US ISSN 0073-0998) 15
Hawaii Agricultural Experiment Station, Honolulu. Technical Bulletin (US ISSN 0073-1005) 15
Hawaii Annual Economic Review (US ISSN 0067-3633) 186
Hawaii Dental Association. Transactions (US ISSN 0073-1021) 609
Hawaii Institute of Geophysics. Biennial Report (US) 304
Hawaii Institute of Geophysics. Contributions (US) 304
Hawaii Institute of Geophysics. Technical Reports (US) 304
Hawaii Institute of Marine Biology. Technical Reports (US ISSN 0073-1331) 103
Hawaii International Conference on System Sciences. Proceedings (US ISSN 0073-1129) 272
Hawaii Labor Trends see Hawaii. Department of Labor and Industrial Relations. Sub-Area Review 207
Hawaii Library Association Journal (US ISSN 0017-8586) 530
Hawaii on 20 Dollars a Day see Hawaii on 25 Dollars a Day 886
Hawaii on 25 Dollars a Day (US ISSN 0197-8527) 886
Hawaii Series (US ISSN 0073-1145) 469
Hawaii State Industrial Directory (US) 238
Hawaii Topical Conference in Particle Physics. Proceedings (US ISSN 0073-1153) 703
Hawaii TourBook see TourBook: Hawaii 891
Hawaii Vistors Bureau. Annual Research Report (US ISSN 0066-412X) 886
Hawaiian Historical Society. Annual Report (US) 447
Hawaiian Journal of History (US ISSN 0440-5145) 447
Hawaiian Planters' Record (US ISSN 0073-1358) 36
Hawaiian Sugar Planters' Association Experiment Station. Annual Report (US ISSN 0073-1366) 36

Haydn-Studien (GW ISSN 0440-5323) 97, 659
Haydn Yearbook. Haydn Jahrbuch (US ISSN 0073-1390) 659
Hayes & Becker Information Sciences Series see Information Sciences Series 531
Hayes Directory of Dental Supply Houses (US ISSN 0073-1404) 609
Hayes Directory of Physician and Hospital Supply Houses (US ISSN 0073-1412) 481
Hayes Druggist Directory (US ISSN 0073-1420) 684
Head Start Services to Handicapped Children see U.S. Department of Health, Education and Welfare. Annual Report to the Congress of the United States on Services Provided to Handicapped Children in Project Head Start 347
Health and Personal Social Services Statistics (UK) 752
Health and Physical Education Bulletin for Teachers in Secondary Schools see Physical Education and Health 350
Health and Welfare of Andhra Pradesh Series see Social Sciences Research Series 800
Health Consequences of Smoking (US ISSN 0098-311X) 287, 595
Health Education Index (UK ISSN 0140-3273) 2, 695
Health in New South Wales (AT ISSN 0046-7073) 752
Health in North Dakota see North Dakota. State Department of Health. Report 753
Health Insurance Association of America. Consumer and Professional Relations Division. Extent of Growth--Private Health Insurance Coverage in the United States (US) 909
Health Insurance Viewpoints (US ISSN 0017-9027) 499
Health Law Bulletin (US) 513, 595, 752
Health Media Buyer's Guide (US) 5, 694
Health Physics Research Abstracts (UN ISSN 0085-1450) 2, 756
Health Physics Society. Newsletter (US ISSN 0073-1498) 595, 622
Health Sciences Audiovisual Resource List (US ISSN 0190-2989) 595
Health Service Buyers Guide (UK ISSN 0140-5748) 481
Health Systems Management (US ISSN 0361-0195) 752
Health, United States (US) 806
Heather Society. Yearbook (UK ISSN 0440-5757) 415
Heating and Ventilating Research Association. Laboratory Reports see B S R I A Application Guides. Technical Notes 429
Heating and Ventilating Research Association. Technical Notes see B S R I A Technical Notes 429
Heating and Ventilating Year Book see Heating, Ventilating and Air Conditioning Year Book 429
Heating/Piping/Air Conditioning Mechanical Systems Information Index Info-Dex see H P A C Info-Dex 429
Heating, Plumbing, Air Conditioning Buyers' Guide (CN ISSN 0382-6996) 429
Heating, Ventilating and Air Conditioning Year Book (UK ISSN 0306-3585) 429
Heavy Construction Cost File (US) 136
Hebbel-Jahrbuecher (GW ISSN 0073-1560) 565
Hebert's Catalogue of Plate Number Singles (US) 478
Hebert's Catalogue of Used Plate Number Singles see Hebert's Catalogue of Plate Number Singles 478
Hebrew Annual Review (US) 491
Hebrew Computational Linguistics (IS) 544
Hebrew Union College Annual (US ISSN 0360-9049) 392, 770

Hebrew Union College Annual Supplements (US) 392, 770
Hebrew University of Jerusalem. Authority for Research and Development. Current Research (IS) 797
Hebrew University of Jerusalem. Authority for Research and Development. Research Report: Humanities, Social Sciences, Law, Education, Social Work, Library see Hebrew University of Jerusalem. Authority for Research and Development. Current Research 797
Hebrew University of Jerusalem. Authority for Research and Development. Research Report. Science and Agriculture see Hebrew University of Jerusalem. Authority for Research and Development. Current Research 797
Hebrew University of Jerusalem. Authority for Research and Development. Research Report. Medicine, Pharmacy, Dental Medicine see Hebrew University of Jerusalem. Authority for Research and Development. Current Research 797
Hebrew University of Jerusalem. Department of Atmospheric Sciences. List of Contributions (IS) 633
Hebrew University of Jerusalem. Folklore Research Center. Studies (IS ISSN 0075-3661) 402
Hebrew University of Jerusalem. Lionel Cohen Lectures (IS ISSN 0075-9740) 513
Hefte zur Unfallheilkunde (US ISSN 0085-1469) 616
Hegel-Jahrbuch (GW ISSN 0073-1579) 689
Hegel Society of America. Proceedings (US) 689
Hegel-Studien (GW ISSN 0073-1587) 689
Heidelberg Science Library (US ISSN 0073-1595) 783
Heidelberger Akademie der Wissenschaften. Mathematisch-Naturwissenschaftliche Klasse. Sitzungsberichte (US ISSN 0073-1625) 783
Heidelberger Arbeitsbuecher (US ISSN 0073-1633) 783, 851
Heidelberger Jahrbuecher (US ISSN 0073-1641) 783, 851
Heidelberger Politische Schriften (GW) 711
Heidelberger Rechtsvergleichende und Wirtschaftsrechliche Studien (GW) 513
Heidelberger Rechtswissenschaftliche Abhandlungen. Neue Folge (GW ISSN 0073-165X) 513
Heidelberger Sociologica (GW ISSN 0073-1676) 814
Heidelberger Taschenbuecher (US ISSN 0073-1684) 783, 851
Heilige in Bild und Legende (GW ISSN 0440-6087) 75
Heimatgruss (GW ISSN 0440-6230) 454
Heimatkundliches Jahrbuch fuer den Kreis Segeberg (GW) 454
Heine-Jahrbuch (GW ISSN 0073-1692) 565
Heirs (US ISSN 0017-9884) 75, 565, 693
Helikon (IT ISSN 0017-9981) 259
Hellenic Industrial Development Bank. Investment Guide (GR) 203
Hellenika (GW ISSN 0018-0084) 491, 565
Hellenike Mathematike Hetaireia. Deltion see Greek Mathematical Society. Bulletin 585
Help (Washington) (US ISSN 0363-9185) 280
Helps for Students of History (UK ISSN 0073-1714) 349
Helsingen Kauppakorkeakoulu. Julkaisusarja D (FI) 158
Helsingen Kauppakorkeakoulu. Kirjasto. Julkaisusarja see Helsingen Kauppakorkeakoulu. Julkaisusarja D 158

Helsingfors Universitet. Bibliotek. Skrifter see Helsingin Yliopisto. Kirjasto. Julkaisuja 530
Helsingin Yliopisto. Kirjasto. Julkaisuja / Helsingfors Universitet. Bibliotek. Skrifter / University of Helsinki. Library. Publication (FI ISSN 0355-1350) 530
Helsingin Yliopisto Keskussairaala. Psykiatria Klinika. Julkaisusarja see Psychiatria Fennica. Julkaisusarja 621
Helvetia Politica (SZ ISSN 0073-182X) 711
Helvetica Paediatrica Acta. Supplementum (SZ ISSN 0073-1811) 617
Hempstead County Historical Society. (Publication) (US) 469
Her World Annual (SI) 900
Herald Caravanning Guide (AT ISSN 0085-1477) 830, 886
Herald Motel Guide (AT ISSN 0085-1485) 432
Heraldisch-Genealogische Gesellschaft Adler. Jahrbuch (AU ISSN 0073-1897) 417
Heraldo Dental (CK ISSN 0073-1900) 609
Herb Collector's Manual & Marketing Guide (US) 415
Herbarist (US) 415
Herbert Read Series (UK ISSN 0073-1927) 565
Herd Book of Hereford Cattle (UK ISSN 0073-1943) 45
Here and Now (CN ISSN 0085-1493) 736
Here Is Your Indiana Government (US) 179
Hereford Breed Journal (UK ISSN 0073-1951) 45
Herforder Jahrbuch; Beitraege zur Geschichte der Stadt und des Stiftes Herford (GW ISSN 0073-196X) 454
Heriot-Watt University Lectures (UK) 491
Heritage of Sociology (US ISSN 0073-1986) 814
Hermeneutics: Studies in the History of Religion (US) 765
Hermes-Einzelschriften (GW ISSN 0341-0064) 259, 544
Herold Export-Adressbuch von Oesterreich / Austrian Export Directory / Annuaire d'Exportation de l'Autriche / Anuario de Exportacion de Austria (AU ISSN 0531-5824) 238
Heron (JA ISSN 0387-9348) 544, 565
Herpetological Information Search Systems Yearbook of Herpetology see Yearbook of Herpetology 131
Hesse. Ministerium fuer Landwirtschaft und Umwelt. Ernten, Maerkte, Preise. Jahresbericht (GW) 407
Hessische Beitraege zur Geschichte der Arbeiterbewegung (GW) 454, 506
Hessischer Kultusminister. Bildungspolitische Informationen (GW) 344
Hessisches Jahrbuch fuer Landesgeschichte (GW ISSN 0073-2001) 455
Hestia (GW) 689
Heutiges Deutsch. Reihe I: Linguistische Grundlagen (GW ISSN 0073-201X) 545
Hewitt-Donlon Catalog of United States Small Size Paper Money (US ISSN 0070-7082) 173
Heybob (AT) 830
Hi Fi Aarbogen (DK ISSN 0441-5833) 659
Hi Fi News & Record Review Annual (UK) 659, 818
Hi-Fi Report (GW) 659, 818
Hi-Fi Sound Annual see Hi-Fi Test Annual 818
Hi-Fi Test Annual (UK) 818
Hi-Fi Year Book (UK ISSN 0073-2060) 818
Hierro (VE) 648
Hiersemanns Bibliographische Handbuecher (GW ISSN 0170-2408) 91

High Energy Particle Physics see Physics and Applications 698
High Fidelity's Buying Guide to Speaker Systems (US ISSN 0147-7676) 818
High Fidelity's Buying Guide to Tape Systems (US ISSN 0161-4371) 659, 818
High Fidelity's Test Reports (US ISSN 0090-3981) 818
High Flight (CN ISSN 0708-4331) 8, 639
High Polymers (US ISSN 0073-2109) 252, 373
High Schools Statistics in Punjab (PK) 318
Higher Education Exchange see Educational International 342
Higher Education in New England (US ISSN 0440-7881) 337
Highlands Field Station Report (KE) 485
Highlights of V A Medical Research see Medical Research in the V.A 597
Highway Planning Notes (US ISSN 0073-2176) 375
Highway Research Board Special Publication see Transportation Research Board Special Report 876
Highway Research Record (II) 375, 875
Highway Research Record see Transportation Research Record 876
Highway Safety Program, Annual Report see Utah. Department of Transportation. Highway Safety Program, Annual Report 876
Highway Safety Report to the Legislature see Wisconsin. Division of Highway Safety Coordination. Highway Safety Report to the Legislature 876
Highway Transportation Research and Development Studies see U.S. Federal Highway Administration. Highway Transportation Research and Development Studies 377
Hilgardia (US ISSN 0073-2230) 15
Himalaya see Journal of Himalayan Studies and Regional Development 51
Himalayan Geology (II) 295
Himalayan Journal (II) 830
Himalayan Review (NP) 422
Himpunan Nelayan Selurah Indonesia. Dewan Pimpanan Pusat. Laporan Kegiatan see Fisherman Union of Indonesia. Central Governing Board. Annual Report 397
Hind Mazdoor Sabha. Report of the Annual Convention (II ISSN 0073-2273) 506
Hindemith-Jahrbuch / Annales Hindemith (GW) 659
Hindu Astronomical and Mathematical Text Series (II ISSN 0073-2281) 585
Hindustan Latex. Annual Reports see Hindustan Latex. Varshika Riporta 706
Hindustan Latex. Varshika Riporta / Hindustan Latex. Annual Reports (II) 246, 706
Hine's Insurance Counsel (US) 499, 513
Hinnat ja Kilpailu / Priser och Konkurrens (FI ISSN 0356-5092) 182
Hints to Potato Growers (US ISSN 0018-1986) 36
Hip (US ISSN 0095-7216) 616
Hippocrene (US ISSN 0085-1531) 579
Hirosaki Daigaku Nogakubu Gakujutsu Hokoku see Hirosaki University. Faculty of Agriculture. Bulletin 15
Hirosaki University. Faculty of Agriculture. Bulletin / Hirosaki Daigaku Nogakubu Gakujutsu Hokoku (JA ISSN 0073-229X) 15
Hiroshima Daigaku Genbaku Hoshano Igaku Kenkyusho Nenpo see Hiroshima University. Research Institute for Nuclear Medicine and Biology. Proceedings 622
Hiroshima Daigaku Rika Kiyo, Dobutsugaku see Hiroshima University. Journal of Science. Series B. Division 1: Zoology 128

Hiroshima Daigaku Rika Kiyo, Shokubutsu see Hiroshima University. Journal of Science. Series B. Division 2. Botany 115
Hiroshima University. Department of Geology. Geological Report (JA ISSN 0073-2303) 295
Hiroshima University. Faculty of Engineering. Memoirs (JA ISSN 0073-2311) 367
Hiroshima University. Faculty of General Education. Memoirs: Studies in Humanities and Social Sciences (JA) 491, 798
Hiroshima University. Faculty of General Education. Memoirs: Studies in Natural Sciences (JA) 783
Hiroshima University. Journal of Science. Series B. Division 1: Zoology / Hiroshima Daigaku Rika Kiyo, Dobutsugaku (JA) 128
Hiroshima University. Journal of Science. Series B. Division 2. Botany / Hiroshima Daigaku Rika Kiyo, Shokubutsu (JA ISSN 0075-4366) 115
Hiroshima University. Journal of Science. Series C. Geology and Mineralogy (JA ISSN 0075-4374) 295, 643
Hiroshima University. Laboratory for Amphibian Biology. Scientific Report(JA) 103, 128
Hiroshima University. Research Institute for Nuclear Medicine and Biology. Proceedings / Hiroshima Daigaku Genbaku Hoshano Igaku Kenkyusho Nenpo (JA ISSN 0073-232X) 622
Hispania Antiqua Epigraphica (SP ISSN 0437-5602) 61, 545
Hispanic American Periodical Index (US ISSN 0361-5502) 438
Hispano-Italic Studies (US ISSN 0160-3493) 545, 565
Histoire de la Pensee (FR ISSN 0073-2362) 783
Histoire des Idees et Critique Litteraire (SZ ISSN 0073-2397) 565
Histoire et Civilisation Arabe (FR ISSN 0073-2400) 440, 443
Histoire et Civilisation du Livre (SZ ISSN 0073-2419) 432
Histoire et Theorie (FR) 455
Historia (CL ISSN 0073-2435) 469
Historia. Einzelschriften (GW ISSN 0341-0056) 432
Historia Archaeologica (YU) 61, 455
Historia, Cadernos de Pesquisa (BL) 469
Historia de la Iglesia (SP) 774
Historia Grafica de Catalunya Dia a Dia (SP) 455
Historia Moderna e Contemporanea see Universidade do Parana. Departamento de Historia. Boletim 436
Historia Sztuki (PL ISSN 0083-4270) 75
Historia Universal (SP) 432
Historia Uruguaya. Segunda Serie: los Hombres (UY) 469
Historia y Cultura (PE ISSN 0073-2486) 469
Historia y Filosofia de la Ciencia. Serie Mayor. Encuadernada (SP ISSN 0073-2494) 783
Historia y Filosofia de la Ciencia. Serie Menor. Rustica (SP ISSN 0073-2508) 783
Historiae Musicae Cultores Biblioteca (IT ISSN 0073-2516) 659
Historiae Naturalis Classica (GW ISSN 0073-2524) 103
Historiae Scientiarum Elementa (GW ISSN 0073-2532) 783
Historiallinen Arkisto (FI ISSN 0073-2540) 455
Historiallisia Tutkimuksia (FI ISSN 0073-2559) 455
Historian Aitta (FI ISSN 0439-2183) 432
Historians of Early Modern Europe. Newsletter (US) 455, 765
Historic Bethlehem. Newsletter (US) 469
Historic Documents (US) 469, 711

Historic Houses, Castles and Gardens see Historic Houses, Castles and Gardens in Great Britain and Ireland 455
Historic Houses, Castles and Gardens in Great Britain and Ireland (UK) 455
Historic Madison. Journal (US ISSN 0361-574X) 469
Historic Society of Lancashire and Cheshire. Transactions (UK ISSN 0140-332X) 455
Historic Textiles of India (II) 855
Historica Carpatica (CS ISSN 0441-8026) 455, 711, 814
Historical Archaeology (US ISSN 0440-9213) 61
Historical Arms Series (CN ISSN 0440-9221) 476, 639
Historical Association, London. Aids for Teachers (UK ISSN 0073-2591) 349, 455
Historical Association of Kenya. Pamphlet (KE) 440
Historical Association of Tanzania. Papers (KE ISSN 0440-9264) 440
Historical Association of Zimbabwe. Local Series Pamphlets (RH) 440
Historical Aviation Album (US ISSN 0018-2443) 8
Historical Blue Book of New Mexico see New Mexico Blue Book 470
Historical Breechloading Smallarms Association. Journal (UK ISSN 0305-0440) 639
Historical Chart Book (US) 173
Historical Conservation Society. Publications (PH ISSN 0073-2613) 432
Historical Geography Research Series (UK ISSN 0143-683X) 422
Historical Journal (AT ISSN 0311-8924) 447
Historical Miscellany (SI) 432
Historical Musings (US ISSN 0046-7553) 432
Historical Problems: Studies and Documents (UK ISSN 0073-2621) 432
Historical Research for University Degrees in the United Kingdom. Part 1: Theses Completed (UK ISSN 0308-7417) 432
Historical Research for University Degrees in the United Kingdom. Part 2: Theses in Progress (UK ISSN 0308-7425) 432
Historical Society of Princeton, New Jersey. News & Notes (US) 276, 469
Historical Society of the Church in Wales. Journal (UK) 455, 772
Historical Society of the Presbyterian Church of Wales. Journal (UK) 455, 772
Historical Southeastern Statistics see Southeastern Historical Statistics 846
Historical Statistics of the Gas Industry(US ISSN 0073-2656) 679
Historical Statistics of the United States(US ISSN 0073-2664) 841
Historical Studies (Pakistan) Series (PK) 443
Historical Studies in the Life Sciences (US) 595, 783
Historical Studies in the Physical Sciences (US) 783
Historicke Studie (CS ISSN 0440-9515) 455
Histories of the Ruling Communist Parties Series (US) 721
Historisch-Demographische Mitteilungen / Communications de Demographie Historique (HU) 727
Historisch Jaarboek Vlaardingen (NE) 455
Historische Forschungen (GW ISSN 0440-9558) 432
Historische Kommission zu Berlin. Einzelverdeffentlichungen (GW ISSN 0067-5857) 432
Historische Studien (GW) 455
Historische Vereniging Vlaardingen. Tijdschrift see Historisch Jaarboek Vlaardingen 455
Historischer Verein der Pfalz. Mitteilungen (GW ISSN 0073-2680) 455

Historischer Verein des Kantons Bern. Archiv (SZ) 417, 455
Historischer Verein des Kantons St. Gallen. Neujahrsblaett (SZ) 455
Historischer Verein Dillingen an der Donau. Jahrbuch (GW ISSN 0073-2699) 455
Historisches Jahrbuch der Stadt Linz (AU ISSN 0440-9736) 455
Historisk Aarbog for Skive og Omegn (DK ISSN 0046-7588) 455
Historiska och Litteraturhistoriska Studier (FI ISSN 0073-2702) 491
Historiske Meddelelser om Koebenhavn(DK) 455
Historiske Studier fra Fyn (NO ISSN 0105-7154) 455
History. Annual Supplement see U. S. Army Infantry Center. History; Annual Supplement 640
History and Philosophy of Logic (UK) 689
History and Structure of Languages (US ISSN 0073-2710) 545
History in Africa (US ISSN 0361-5413) 440
History in Africa (US) 440
History in Newspaper Front Pages (US ISSN 0098-163X) 432
History in Zambia (ZA) 438
History of Civilization (UK) 432
History of Technology (UK ISSN 0307-5451) 851
History of Technology Series (UK) 851
History of Universities (UK ISSN 0144-5138) 337, 455
History of World Architecture (US) 69
History Teachers Association of New South Wales. Newsletter (AT ISSN 0085-1558) 349, 432
Historyka; Studia Metodologiczne (PL ISSN 0073-277X) 455
Hito to Kokudo. see People and National Land Policy 224
Hitotsubashi Journal of Arts and Sciences (JA ISSN 0073-2788) 491, 783
Hitotsubashi Journal of Commerce and Management (JA ISSN 0018-2796) 215
Hitotsubashi Journal of Law and Politics (JA ISSN 0073-2796) 513, 711
Hitotsubashi Journal of Social Studies (JA ISSN 0073-280X) 798
Hob-Nob Annual (US) 476, 565
Hob-Nob Quarterly see Hob-Nob Annual 565
Hobart Paperbacks (UK ISSN 0309-1783) 191
Hobart Papers (UK ISSN 0073-2818) 145
Hochschul-Informations-System GmbH Brief see H I S Brief 337
Hochschulbuecher fuer Mathematik (GE ISSN 0073-2842) 585
Hochschulbuecher fuer Physik (GE ISSN 0073-2850) 696
Hochschule fuer Bodenkultur in Wien. Dissertationen see Universitaet fuer Bodenkultur in Wien. Dissertationen 21
Hochschule fuer Maschinenbau Karl-Marx-Stadt. Wissenschaftliche Zeitschrift see Technische Hochschule Karl-Marx-Stadt. Wissenschaftliche Zeitschrift 370
Hochschule fuer Welthandel in Wien. Dissertationen see Wirtschaftsuniversitaet Wien. Dissertationen 151
Hochschule fuer Welthandel, Wien. Institut fuer Organisation und Revisionswesen. Verhandlungen (AU) 167
Hochschule St. Gallen fuer Wirtschafts- und Sozialwissenschaften. Forschungsinstitut fuer Absatz und Handel. Schriftenreihe (SZ ISSN 0080-603X) 182
Hochschule St. Gallen fuer Wirtschafts- und Sozialwissenschaften. Veroeffentlichungen. Schriftenreihe Betriebswirtschaft (SZ) 215
Hochschulplanung see H I S Brief 337
Hocken Lecture (NZ) 50, 447

Hockey Association. Official Handbook(UK ISSN 0085-1566) 824
Hockey Register (US ISSN 0090-2292) 824
Hoehnea (BL ISSN 0073-2877) 115
Hoerbiger Institut. Mitteilungen (AU) 82, 633
Hoerbuchverzeichnis (GE) 133
Hofstra University Yearbook of Business (US ISSN 0073-2907) 145
Hohenheimer Arbeiten (GW ISSN 0340-9783) 15
Hojas de Poesia (AG) 579
Hojin Kigyo No Jittai see Zeimu Tokei Kara Mita Hojin Kigyo No Jittai 233
Hokkaido Daigaku Rigakubu Kaiso Kenkyusho Obun Hokoku see Hokkaido University. Institute of Algological Research. Scientific Papers 115
Hokkaido Dental Association. Journal/ Hokkaido Shika Ishikaishi, Doshikai Tsushin (JA ISSN 0073-2915) 609
Hokkaido Economic Papers (JA) 145
Hokkaido Kogai Boshi Kenkyujo Ho. see Hokkaido Research Institute for Environmental Pollution. Report 386
Hokkaido Kogyo Kaihatsu Shikenjo Gijutsu see Japan. Government Industrial Development Laboratory, Hokkaido. Technical Data 851
Hokkaido Kogyo Kaihatsu Shikenjo Hokoku see Japan. Government Industrial Development Laboratory, Hokkaido. Reports 851
Hokkaido Kogyo Kaihatsu Shikenjo Nempo see Japan. Government Industrial Development Laboratory, Hokkaido. Annual Report 223
Hokkaido Librarians Study Circle. Bulletin/Hokkaido Toshokan Kenkyukai. Kaiho (JA ISSN 0018-3431) 530
Hokkaido National Agricultural Experiment Station. Soil Survey Report/Hokkaido Nogyo Shikenjo Dosei Chosa Hokoku (JA ISSN 0073-2923) 36
Hokkaido Nogyo Shikenjo Dosei Chosa Hokoku see Hokkaido National Agricultural Experiment Station. Soil Survey Report 36
Hokkaido Rehabilitation/Hokkaido Rihabirteshon Gakkai Zasshi (JA) 595
Hokkaido Research Institute for Environmental Pollution. Report/ Hokkaido Kogai Boshi Kenkyujo Ho.(JA) 386
Hokkaido Rihabirteshon Gakkai Zasshi see Hokkaido Rehabilitation 595
Hokkaido Shika Ishikaishi, Doshikai Tsushin see Hokkaido Dental Association. Journal 609
Hokkaido Toshokan Kenkyukai. Kaiho see Hokkaido Librarians Study Circle. Bulletin 530
Hokkaido University. Faculty of Engineering. Memoirs (JA) 367
Hokkaido University. Faculty of Fisheries. Data Record of Oceanographic Observations and Exploratory Fishing/Kaiyo Chosa Gyogyo Shiken Yoho (JA ISSN 0439-3511) 310, 397
Hokkaido University. Faculty of Science. Journal. Series 5: Botany (JA) 115
Hokkaido University. Faculty of Science. Journal. Series 6: Zoology (JA ISSN 0368-2188) 128
Hokkaido University. Faculty of Science. Journal. Series 7: Geophysics (JA ISSN 0441-067X) 304
Hokkaido University. Institute of Algological Research. Scientific Papers/Hokkaido Daigaku Rigakubu Kaiso Kenkyusho Obun Hokoku (JA) 115
Hokkaido University. Institute of Immunological Science. Bulletin (JA) 603, 623

Hokkaido University. Institute of Low Temperature Science. Series A. Physical Science (JA ISSN 0073-2931) 700
Hokkaido University. Institute of Low Temperature Science. Series B. Biological Science (JA ISSN 0073-294X) 103
Hokkaido University. Research Institute of Applied Electricity. Monograph Series (JA ISSN 0439-3465) 354
Hokke Bunka Kenkyu see Institute for the Comprehensive Study of Lotus Sutra. Journal 771
Holbrooks Guide to the Antique Trade in Scotland (UK) 476
Holiday Book (US) 432, 765
Holiday Book (UK ISSN 0073-2958) 909
Holiday Camps and Centres Directory (UK) 886
Holiday Camps Directory and Magazine see Holiday Camps and Centres Directory 886
Holiday Chalets and Caravans Directory Magazine (UK ISSN 0073-2982) 482
Holidays in Britain (UK ISSN 0073-3024) 886
Holidays in the Sun, Devon, Cornwall, Somerset and Dorset (UK) 886
Holidays in Wales (UK) 886
Holland Exports (NE ISSN 0073-3032) 196
Hollinger Mines Limited. Annual Report (CN ISSN 0382-0734) 643
Hollis Press and Public Relations Annual (UK ISSN 0073-3059) 5
Holm Seminar on Electrical Contacts. Proceedings see Electrical Contacts 353
Holy Beggars' Gazette (US) 392, 770
Holy Places of Palestine (IS) 475, 765, 886
Home & Garden Supply Merchandiser Green Book see Garden Supply Retailer Green Book 415
Home Appliance Blue Book see Home Appliance Trade-in Blue Book 479
Home Appliance Trade-in Blue Book (US) 479
Home Care Services in New York State(US) 614, 806
Home Decorating Ideas see Woman's Day Home Decorating Ideas 502
Home Economics in Institutions Granting Bachelors or Higher Degrees (US ISSN 0073-3105) 337, 479
Home Economics Research Abstracts (US ISSN 0018-4020) 2, 480
Home Gunsmithing Digest (US ISSN 0073-3121) 830
Home Science for Teachers in Secondary Schools (AT) 479
Home University Library (US ISSN 0073-3148) 909
Homebook (US) 502
Homemaker's Guide see Homemaker's Handbook 479
Homemaker's Handbook (US) 479
Homesewing Resource Directory of Branded Line Merchandise in the Homesewing Industry (US) 262
Homicide in California (US ISSN 0098-8537) 281
Homine (IT ISSN 0018-4292) 689
Homing World Stud Book (UK ISSN 0073-3164) 820
Homme Face a la Nature (FR ISSN 0073-3180) 783
Hommes et Eglise; Annuaire du Cerdic (FR) 765
Hommes et la Terre (FR ISSN 0073-3202) 422, 432
Hommes et les Lettres (FR) 565
Homo (FR ISSN 0563-9743) 814
Homogeneous Catalysis in Organic and Inorganic Chemistry see Catalysis by Metal Complexes 254
Homosexual Information Center. Newsletter (US) 480, 718
Honduras. Direccion General de Estadistica y Censos. Investigacion Industrial (HO) 158
Honduras. Secretaria de Trabajo y Prevision Social. Boletin de Estadisticas Laborales (HO) 806
Honduras al Dia (HO) 418

Honduras en Cifras (HO) 841
Hong Kong. Annual Digest of Statistics(HK) 841
Hong Kong. Census and Statistics Department. The Budget: Economic Background (HK) 229
Hong Kong. Estimates of Gross Domestic Product (HK) 158, 841
Hong Kong. Fisheries Research Station. Bulletin (HK ISSN 0065-0269) 397
Hong Kong. Royal Observatory. Climatological Note (HK) 633
Hong Kong. Royal Observatory. Occasional Paper (HK) 633
Hong Kong Annual Report (HK) 186
Hong Kong Builder Directory (HK) 136
Hong Kong Catholic Directory and Year Book/Hsiang-Kang T'ien Chu Chiao Shou T'se (HK ISSN 0073-3210) 774
Hong Kong Economic Papers (HK ISSN 0018-4578) 145
Hong Kong Export Credit Insurance Corporation. Annual Report (HK) 173
Hong Kong Geographical Association. Bulletin (HK) 422
Hong Kong Industrial Products Directory/Hsiang-Kang Kung Yeh Chih Pin Nien Chien (HK) 851
Hong Kong Junior Chamber. Annual Review (HK) 179
Hong Kong Library Association. Journal (HK ISSN 0073-3237) 530
Hong Kong Manager (HK ISSN 0018-4594) 215
Hong Kong Manufacturers and Exporters Register (HK ISSN 0073-3245) 238
Hong Kong Medical Association. Bulletin. (HK) 595
Hong Kong Review of Overseas Trade (HK) 196
Hong Kong Social and Economic Trends (HK) 186, 814
Hong Kong Streets and Places (HK) 886
Hong Kong Tourist Association. Digest of Annual Statistics see Statistical Review of Tourism in Hong Kong 891
Hong Kong Toys (HK) 429
Hong Kong Trade Directory (UK ISSN 0073-3261) 238
Hong Kong Training Council. Report (HK) 667
Honky Tonkin': A Travel Guide to American Music (UK) 659, 886
Honolulu. Mayor's Committee on the Status of Women. Annual Report (US ISSN 0091-8121) 900
Honpo Kogyo No Susei see Mining Yearbook of Japan 645
Hontanar (AG ISSN 0073-327X) 91
Hooker's Icones Planetarium (UK) 115
Hoover Institution Bibliographies Series(US ISSN 0085-1582) 97, 711
Hoover Institution on War, Revolution and Peace. Archival Documentary (US) 721
Hoover Institution on War, Revolution and Peace. Foreign Language Publications Series (US) 711
Hoover Institution on War, Revolution and Peace. International Studies Series (US) 721
Hoover Institution on War, Revolution and Peace. Lecture Series (US) 721
Hoover Institution on War, Revolution and Peace. Library Surveys (US ISSN 0085-1590) 711
Hoover Institution on War, Revolution, and Peace. Publications Series (US ISSN 0073-3296) 711
Hoover Institution on War, Revolution, and Peace. Report (US ISSN 0091-6293) 721
Hoover Institution Studies Series (US ISSN 0073-330X) 711
Hoppenstedt Vademecum der Investmentfonds (GW ISSN 0073-3342) 203
Hoppenstedt Versicherungs-Jahrbuch (GW ISSN 0073-3350) 499
Hor Yezh (FR) 556

Horace M. Albright Conservation Lectureship (US ISSN 0073-3369) 276, 409
Horbly Gnome (US) 580
Horizon (NR ISSN 0073-3385) 440
Horizons in Biochemistry and Biophysics (US ISSN 0096-2708) 111, 112
Hormonal Proteins and Peptides (US) 111, 611
Hormones and Cell Regulation (NE) 103
Hornero/Oven Bird (AG ISSN 0073-3407) 125
Hornsey Historical Society. Occasional Papers (UK) 455
Horse Action (US) 828
Horse & Rider All-Western Yearbook (US) 828
Horse Care (US ISSN 0162-8127) 828
Horse Industry Directory (US) 828
Horse Racing Guide (US) 828
Horse Women (US) 828
Horseshit: the Offensive Review (US ISSN 0439-5794) 556
Horticultural Produce and Practice see AgLink 11
Horticultural Research International (NE ISSN 0441-7461) 415
Horticultural Reviews (US ISSN 0163-7851) 415
Hoseasons Holidays Boats and Bungalows Hire (UK ISSN 0073-3431) 886
Hoshasen Eikyo Kenkyusho Happyo Rombun Mokuroku see Bibliography of Published Papers of the Radiation Effects Research Foundation 601
Hoshasen Eikyo Kenkyusho Nenpo see Radiation Effects Research Foundation. Annual Report 622
Hoshasen Ikushujo Kenkyu Hokoku see Acta Radiobotanika et Genetika 100
Hosiery Statistics (US) 261
Hospital and Nursing Year Book of South Africa see Hospital and Nursing Yearbook of Southern Africa 481
Hospital and Nursing Yearbook of Southern Africa (SA ISSN 0441-2613) 481, 614
Hospital and Selected Morbidity Data (NZ ISSN 0548-9938) 482
Hospital-Escola Sao Camilo e Sao Luis. Boletim (BL) 481
Hospital for Sick Children, Toronto. Research Institute. Annual Report (CN ISSN 0082-5034) 595, 617
Hospital Statistics see Hospital Statistics; Data from American Hospital Association Annual Survey 841
Hospital Statistics; Data from American Hospital Association Annual Survey (US ISSN 0090-6662) 841
Hospital Statistics of New Zealand see New Zealand. Department of Health. Hospital Management Data 482
Hospitalite (CN ISSN 0704-6359) 482
Hospitality Buyers Guide (AT) 482
Hospitality Buyers Guide & Diary see Hospitality Buyers Guide 482
Hospitals & Health Services Year Book and Directory of Hospital Suppliers (UK ISSN 0073-3474) 481
Hospitals Year Book and Directory of Hospital Suppliers see Hospitals & Health Services Year Book and Directory of Hospital Suppliers 481
Hosteling Holidays (US) 830, 886
Hot Rod Magazine Yearbook see Hot Rod Yearbook 910
Hot Rod Yearbook (US ISSN 0073-3482) 910
Hot Water Review (US) 580
Hotel and Catering Executives Year Book and Diary see Catering & Hotel Management Year Book & Diary 482
Hotel and Motel Directory see Hotel, Motel and Travel Directory 482
Hotel and Motel Red Book (US ISSN 0073-3490) 482
Hotel and Restaurant Guide see Hotels and Restaurants in Britain 482
Hotel Guide to Turkey see Turkey: Hotels-Camping 483
Hotel, Motel and Travel Directory (AT) 482

Hotel, Restaurant and Catering Supplies(UK ISSN 0142-1824) 405
Hotel Sales Management Association Hotel Facilities Digest see H.S.M.A. Hotel Facilities Digest 482
Hoteles de Spana; Guia Oficial Abreviada. see Guia de Hoteles: Espana 886
Hotelfuehrer Deutschland (GW) 482, 887
Hotels and Restaurants in Britain (UK ISSN 0073-3512) 482
Hotels de la France (FR) 482
Hotels de la France et d'Outre-Mer see Hotels de la France 482
Hotelsko-Turisticki Adresar see Yugoslavia; Hotel and Tourist Directory 483
Les Houches Summer School Proceedings (NE) 696
House & Garden Gardening Guide (US ISSN 0147-8591) 415
House & Garden Kitchen & Bath Guide(US ISSN 0147-832X) 502
House & Garden Plans Guide (US ISSN 0161-2336) 69
House Beautiful's Gardening and Outdoor Living (US ISSN 0073-3563) 415
House Beautiful's Houses and Plans (US ISSN 0073-3571) 69
Households with Television Sets in the United States (US ISSN 0073-3601) 267
House's Guide to the Construction Industry (1979) (UK) 136
Housing (US) 485, 814
Housing Activity in Hawaii see Construction in Hawaii 135
Housing and Urban Development Legislation in New York State (US ISSN 0073-3652) 485
Housing Finance Company of Kenya. Annual Report and Accounts (KE) 173, 485
Housing in Florida see Florida. Governor. Annual Report on State Housing Goals 484
Housing Legislation in New York State see Housing and Urban Development Legislation in New York State 485
Housing Units in Connecticut. Annual Summary (US) 136
Housing Units in the United States see Current Housing Reports: Housing Vacancies 484
Housman Society Journal (UK ISSN 0305-926X) 565
Houston, Texas. Museum of Fine Arts Bulletin (US ISSN 0018-6708) 652
How to Avoid Financial Tangles: Section A. Elementary Property Problems and Financial Relationships(US ISSN 0085-1620) 173
How to Avoid Financial Tangles: Section B. Wills and Trusts, Taxes, and Help for the Widow (US ISSN 0085-1639) 173
How to Become a Citizen of the United States (US) 513
How to Fly for Less (US ISSN 0147-4030) 868
How to Invest in Brazil (BL) 203
How to Score (US) 824
Howard-Tilton Memorial Library. Report (US ISSN 0082-6790) 530
Howard University. African Studies Department. Seminar Papers on African Studies (US) 440
Hsiang-Kang Kung Yeh Chih Pin Nien Chien see Hong Kong Industrial Products Directory 851
Hsiang-Kang T'ien Chu Chiao Shou T'se see Hong Kong Catholic Directory and Year Book 774
Hsin-Ya Hsueh Pao/New Asia Journal (HK ISSN 0073-375X) 491
Huber Law Survey (US ISSN 0094-0763) 281, 806
Hudobny Archiv (CS) 659
Hudson Family Association, South. Bulletin (US ISSN 0363-8847) 417
Hudson Institute. Report to the Members (US ISSN 0073-3776) 721
Hudson River Anthology (US) 580

Hudson's Washington News Media Contacts Directory (US ISSN 0441-389X) 505
Hueber Hochschulreihe (GW ISSN 0073-3792) 318, 545
Huebner Foundation Monograph (US) 499
Huerta see Huerta Chapbook Series 565
Huerta Chapbook Series (US) 565
Huguenot Historian (US ISSN 0199-9583) 417, 469
Huguenot Society of London. Proceedings (UK ISSN 0309-8346) 417, 433
Huguenot Society of London, Quarto Series (UK ISSN 0309-8354) 417, 433
Hukerikar Memorial Lecture Series (II ISSN 0419-0432) 145
Hull Monographs on South-East Asia (SZ) 443
Human Basics Library (US ISSN 0073-3822) 736
Human Factors Society. Proceedings of the Annual Meeting see Human Factors Society Annual Meeting. Proceedings 814
Human Factors Society Annual Meeting. Proceedings (US ISSN 0163-5182) 736, 814
Human Gene Mapping (SZ ISSN 0378-9861) 122, 612
Human Genetics. Supplement (US ISSN 0340-6717) 122
Human Industrial Design (AU ISSN 0018-7224) 851
Human-Oekologie see Uebersee-Museum, Bremen. Veroeffentlichungen. Reihe E: Human-Oekologie 817
Human Relations (CN ISSN 0441-4128) 718
Human Reproductive Medicine (NE) 595
Human Resources Research Organization. Bibliography of Publications (US ISSN 0073-3865) 742
Human Resources Research Organization. Professional Papers (US ISSN 0073-3873) 742
Human Resources Research Organization. Technical Report (US ISSN 0073-389X) 742
Human Rights Action Guide (US) 721
Human Rights and the U.S. Foreign Assistance Program (US ISSN 0161-6684) 200
Human Rights for Women, Inc. Newsletter see H R W Newsletter 718
Human Rights Organizations & Periodicals Directory (US ISSN 0098-0579) 718
Human Sciences Research Council. Annual Report (SA) 491, 798
Human Sciences Research Council. General Information (SA) 491, 798
Human Sciences Research Council. Institute for Manpower Research. Project Talent Survey: Findings of Research (SA) 318
Humana Civilitas (US) 433
Humanidad (PR ISSN 0441-4144) 806
Humanidades (MX) 491
Humaniora (DK ISSN 0105-5216) 491
Humanistic Studies in the Communications Arts (US) 264, 491
Humanistica Lovaniensia (BE) 259
Humanistica Lovaniensia. Supplementa (BE) 259
Humanities, Christianity and Culture (JA ISSN 0073-3938) 765
Humanities Research Council of Canada. Report see Canadian Federation for the Humanities. Annual Report 490
Humboldt-Universitaet zu Berlin. Universitaetsbibliothek. Schriftenreihe(GE) 530
Hundreds of Ideas see Better Homes and Gardens Hundreds of Ideas 503

Hungarian Academy of Sciences. Central Research Institute for Physics. Yearbook/Magyar Tudomanyos Akademia.Kozponti Fizikai Kutato Intezet. Evkonyv (HU ISSN 0133-5502) 246, 696
Hungarian Academy of Sciences. Research Institute for Agricultural Economics. Bulletin see Research Institute for Agricultural Economics. Bulletin 30
Hungarian Academy of Sciences. Research Institute for Microbiology. Proceedings see Magyar Tudomanyos Akademia. Mikrobiologiai Kutato Intezet. Proceedings 124
Hungarian Economic Literature see Magyar Kozgazdasagi Irodalom 160
Hungarian Musical Guide (HU ISSN 0441-4446) 659
Hungarian P.E.N/P.E.N. Hongrois (HU ISSN 0439-9080) 565
Hungarian Studies in English see Angol Filologiai Tanulmanyok 540
Hungary. Kozponti Statisztikai Hivatal. Belkereskedelmi Evkonyv (HU ISSN 0134-1138) 158
Hungary. Kozponti Statisztikai Hivatal. Beruhazasi, Epitoipari, Lakasepitesi Zsebkonyv-/-Pocketbook of Investments, Building Industry and Home-Building (HU) 140
Hungary. Kozponti Statisztikai Hivatal. Demografiai Evkonyv (HU ISSN 0073-4020) 727
Hungary. Kozponti Statisztikai Hivatal. Epitoipari Arak Alakulasa (HU) 140
Hungary. Kozponti Statisztikai Hivatal. Ipari Zsebkonyv (HU ISSN 0133-8684) 158
Hungary. Kozponti Statisztikai Hivatal. Kepzettseg-Kereset (HU) 158
Hungary. Kozponti Statisztikai Hivatal. Kozlekedesi es Hirkozlesi Evkonyv (HU) 266
Hungary. Kozponti Statisztikai Hivatal. Kulkereskedelmi Statisztikai Evkonyv(HU ISSN 0133-9133) 158
Hungary. Kozponti Statisztikai Hivatal. Mezogazdasagi Statisztikai Zsebkonyu (HU ISSN 0441-4683) 24
Hungary. Kozponti Statisztikai Hivatal. Nepgazdasagi Merlegek (HU) 229
Hungary. Kozponti Statisztikai Hivatal. Teruleti Statisztikai Evkonyv (HU ISSN 0303-5344) 841
Hungary. Kozponti Statisztikai Hivatal. Torteneti Statisztikai Tanulmanyok (HU) 841
Hungary. Kozponti Statisztikai Hivatal. Tudomanyos Kutatas/Scientific Research (HU) 794
Hunter Valley Poets (AT) 580
Hunter Valley Research Foundation. Monographs (AT ISSN 0085-1663) 276
Hunting Annual see Field & Stream Hunting Annual 829
Huntsville Association of Folk Musicians. Newsletter (US ISSN 0091-9764) 659
Hvalraadets Skrifter/Scientific Results of Marine Biological Research (NO ISSN 0073-4128) 103
Hybrid Microelectronics Symposium. (Papers) (UK ISSN 0073-4136) 354
Hydraulic Research in the United States see Hydraulic Research in the United States and Canada 381
Hydraulic Research in the United States and Canada (US ISSN 0094-1832) 381
Hydrobiology (BU) 103
Hydrocarbon Processing Catalog (US) 679
Hydrological Yearbook of Israel/ Shenaton Hidrologi Le-Yisrael (IS ISSN 0073-4217) 307
Hydrologische Bibliographie see Germany(Federal Republic, 1949-). Bundesanstalt fuer Gewaesserkunde. Hydrologische Bibliographie 290
Hydrometeorologicky Ustav. Bratislava. Zbornik Prac (CS) 633
Hydrometeorologicky Ustav. Sbornik Predpisu (CS) 633
Hydrometeorologicky Ustav. Vyrocni Zprava (CS) 633

Hydronymia Germaniae (GW ISSN 0441-5302) *422*
Hyman Blumberg Symposium Series (US) *318, 736*
Hyn Anthology (US) *580*
Hyogo Cancer Hospital. Bulletin/ Hyogo-kenritsu Byoin Gan Senta Kiyo (JA) *605*
Hyogo-ken Gan Senta Nenpo see Hyogo Cancer Hospital. Bulletin *605*
Hyogo-kenritsu Byoin Gan Senta Kiyo see Hyogo Cancer Hospital. Bulletin *605*
Hype (US ISSN 0097-6539) *659*
Hyperguide des Hypermarches see Annuaire des Hypermarches *234*
Hypertension Series (US ISSN 0073-425X) *607*
Hypomnemata (GW ISSN 0085-1671) *259, 689*
I A (Industrial Archeology) (US) *61*
I A A E E Monographs (International Association for the Advancement of Ethnology and Eugenics) (US ISSN 0074-1523) *50*
I A A E E Reprint (International Association for the Advancement of Ethnology and Eugenics) (US ISSN 0074-1515) *50*
I A E A Film Catalog see I A E A Library Film Catalog *700*
I A E A Library Film Catalog (International Atomic Energy Agency) (UN ISSN 0534-7319) *700*
I A E S T E Annual Report see International Association for the Exchange of Students for Technical Experience. Annual Report *342*
I A G A News (International Association of Geomagnetism and Aeronomy) (JA ISSN 0536-1095) *304*
I A M P News Bulletin (International Association of Meteorology and Atmospheric Physics) (US) *633*
I.A.M.R. Reports (Institute of Applied Manpower Research) (II ISSN 0418-5633) *208*
I A R C Monographs on the Evaluation of Carcinogenic Risk of Chemicals to Man see I A R C Monographs on the Evaluation of the Carcinogenic Risk of Chemicals to Humans *605*
I A R C Monographs on the Evaluation of the Carcinogenic Risk of Chemicals to Humans (International Agency for Research on Cancer) (UN) *605*
I A R C Scientific Publications (International Agency for Research on Cancer) (UN ISSN 0300-5038) *605*
I A S Bulletin (Iowa Academy of Science) (US ISSN 0075-0344) *783*
I A S L Conference Proceedings (International Association of School Librarianship) (US) *318, 530*
I A S L I C Special Publication (Indian Association of Special Libraries and Information Centres) (II ISSN 0073-6279) *530*
I A S L I C Technical Pamphlets (Indian Association of Special Libraries and Information Centres) (II ISSN 0073-6260) *530*
I A S S W Directory see I A S S W Directory; Member Schools and Associations *806*
I A S S W Directory; Member Schools and Associations (International Association of Schools of Social Work) (US ISSN 0098-8278) *806*
I A T A News Review see I A T A Review *868*
I A T A Review (International Air Transport Association.) (CN ISSN 0376-6427) *868*
I A T A Travel Agents Directory of Europe (UK) *482, 887*
I A T S S Research (International Association of Traffic and Safety Sciences) (JA ISSN 0386-1112) *871*
I A T U L Newsletter see I A T U L Proceedings *530*

I A T U L Proceedings (International Association of Technological Universities Libraries) (SW ISSN 0018-8476) *367, 530, 783*
I B A Occasional Paper (US ISSN 0075-0255) *203*
I B A Technical Review (Independent Broadcasting Authority) (UK ISSN 0308-423X) *267*
I B E R Special Publications (Institute of Business and Economic Research) (US ISSN 0068-6069) *145*
I B M Agribusiness Symposium. Proceedings (International Business Machines Corp.) (US) *28*
I B M Medical Symposium. Proceedings (International Business Machines Corp.) (US ISSN 0536-1184) *596*
I B M Research Symposia Series (US ISSN 0085-2082) *585, 696*
I C A A C Program and Abstracts see Interscience Conference on Antimicrobial Agents and Chemotherapy. Program and Abstracts *123*
I C A M Annuaire (Institut Catholique d'Arts et Metiers de Lille) (FR ISSN 0066-8982) *367*
I C A O Circulars (International Civil Aviation Organization) (UN ISSN 0074-2481) *868*
I C A P Lista de Nuevas Adquisiciones (Instituto Centroamericano de Administracion Publica) (CR ISSN 0487-1596) *539*
I C B O Plumbing Code (International Conference of Building Officials) (US) *429*
I. C. E. A. Cahiers (Institut Canadien d'Education des Adultes) (CN ISSN 0018-8891) *329*
I C E I(Year) see Industrial and Control Applications of Microprocessors. Proceedings *496*
I C E L References (International Council on Environmental Law) (GW) *390, 521*
I C E S Oceanographic Data Lists see I C E S Oceanographic Data Lists and Inventories *310*
I C E S Oceanographic Data Lists and Inventories (DK) *310*
I C E Supplement. Serie C (BE ISSN 0067-5628) *196*
I C E Yearbook (Institution of Civil Engineers) (UK ISSN 0308-4159) *375*
I C H P E R Congress Proceedings (International Council on Health, Physical Education and Recreation) (US) *596, 694*
I C H P E R Congress Reports see I C H P E R Congress Proceedings *596*
I C I A Information Bulletin (International Center of Information on Antibiotics) (BE ISSN 0018-8948) *686*
I C N -U C L A Symposium on Molecular Biology Proceedings (International Chemical and Nuclear Corp) (US) *119*
I. C. Nachrichten (Institutum Canarium) (AU) *50, 61*
I C R Studies (Institute for Cross-Cultural Research) (US ISSN 0073-8646) *814*
I C S A Bulletin (International Committee against Apartheid, Racism and Colonialism in Southern Africa) (UK ISSN 0260-7522) *718*
I C S S R Union Catalogue of Social Science Periodicals/Serials (Indian Council of Social Science Research) (II) *91, 803*
I C T A Directory (Institute of Certified Travel Agents) (US) *887*
I C T A Roster see I C T A Directory *887*
I/D/E/A Monographs (Institute for Development of Educational Activities, Inc.) (US ISSN 0073-8697) *318*
I/D/E/A Occasional Papers (Institute for Development of Educational Activities, Inc.) (US ISSN 0073-8700) *318*
I D E Special Papers (Institute for Developing Economies) (JA) *196*

I D S Research Report (Institute of Development Studies) (UK ISSN 0141-1314) *200, 814*
I. E. A. (Australia) Report (AT ISSN 0310-558X) *349*
I E C Catalogue of Publications (International Electrotechnical Commission) (SZ) *360*
I. E. (Chicago) (US ISSN 0422-4108) *765*
I E E Conference Publication Series (Institution of Electrical Engineers) (UK) *354*
I E E Control Engineering Series (Institution of Electrical Engineers) (UK) *354*
I E E E Annual Pulp and Paper Industry Technical Conference. Conference Record (US ISSN 0190-2172) *675*
I E E E Computer Society Conference on Pattern Recognition and Image Processing. Proceedings (Institute of Electrical and Electronics Engineers, Inc.) (US) *272*
I E E E Intercon Digest see I E E E International Convention Digest *354*
I E E E International Conference on Acoustics, Speech and Signal Processing. Conference Record (Institute of Electrical and Electronics Engineers, Inc.) (US) *354*
I E E E International Conference on Communications. Conference Record(US ISSN 0536-1486) *264*
I E E E International Convention and Exhibition. Record (US ISSN 0073-9138) *354*
I E E E International Convention Digest (US ISSN 0090-7294) *354*
I E E E International Pulsed Power Conference. Digest of Technical Papers (US) *367*
I E E E International Symposium on Circuit Theory. Symposium Digest. Summaries of Papers see I E E E International Symposium on Circuits and Systems. Proceedings *354*
I E E E International Symposium on Circuits and Systems. Proceedings (US) *354*
I E E E International Symposium on Electrical Insulation. Conference Record (Institute of Electrical and Electronics Engineers, Inc.) (US) *354*
I E E E International Symposium on Information Theory. Abstracts of Papers (US) *272*
I E E E Membership Directory (US ISSN 0073-9146) *354*
I E E E/O S A Conference on Laser Engineering and Applications. Digest of Technical Papers (US ISSN 0099-121X) *354*
I E E E Power Electronics Specialists Conference. Record (US) *8*
I E E E Power Engineering Society. Winter Meeting. Preprints (US ISSN 0073-9154) *354*
I E E E Power Processing and Electronics Specialists Conference. Record see I E E E Power Electronics Specialists Conference. Record *8*
I E E E Region 3 Conference. Record (US ISSN 0073-9170) *354*
I E E E Region 5 Conference. Record (US ISSN 0073-9197) *354*
I E E E Region 6. Conference. Proceedings (US) *355*
I E E E Region 6. Technical Conference. Record see I E E E Region 6. Conference. Proceedings *355*
I E E E Rural Electric Power Conference. Papers Presented (Institute of Electrical and Electronics Engineers, Inc.) (US) *355*
I E E E Standards (US ISSN 0073-9162) *355*
I E E E Student Papers (Institute of Electrical and Electronics Engineers, Inc.) (US ISSN 0362-4536) *355*

I E E E Symposium on Computer Software Reliability. Record see International Conference on Reliable Software.(Proceedings) *272*
I E E E Vehicular Technology Conference. Record (Institute of Electrical and Electronics Engineers, Inc.) (US ISSN 0098-3551) *871*
I E E E Vehicular Technology Group. Proceedings of the Annual Conference (US) *355*
I E E Electromagnetic Waves Series (Institution of Electrical Engineers) (UK) *355*
I E E Medical Electronics Monographs (Institution of Electrical Engineers) (UK ISSN 0305-9596) *596*
I E E Monograph Series (Institution of Electrical Engineers) (UK ISSN 0073-9766) *355*
I. E. E. Reprint Series (Institution of Electrical Engineers) (UK) *355*
I E E Reviews (Institution of Electrical Engineers) (UK) *910*
I E E Telecommunications Series (UK) *264*
I. E. N. S. Press Handbook see Indian & Eastern Newspaper Society Press Handbook *505*
I E S Lighting Handbook (Illuminating Engineering Society) (US ISSN 0073-5469) *355*
I F A C Symposium on Multivariable Technical Control Systems. Proceedings (International Federation of Automatic Control) (NE) *382*
I F C A T I Directory see I T M F Directory *856*
I F C A T I Newsletter see Textile Country Reporter *857*
I F F Bulletin (Institut fuer Festkoerperforschung) (GW) *703*
I.F.H.P.M. News see I.F.P.S.M. News *752*
I F I D A Film Directory (International Film Importers and Distributors of America) (US) *650*
I F I P Information Bulletin (International Federation for Information Processing) (SZ) *530*
I F I P Summary (International Federation for Information Processing) (SZ) *530*
I F L A Annual (International Federation of Library Associations and Institutions) (GW ISSN 0074-5987) *531*
I F L A Directory (International Federation of Library Associations and Institutions) (NE ISSN 0074-6002) *531*
I F L A Publications (International Federation of Library Associations and Institutions) (GW) *531*
I F M R Publications (Institute for Financial Management and Research, Madras) (II) *215*
I F O Institut fuer Wirtschaftsforschung. Studien zu Handels- und Dienstleistungsfragen (GW ISSN 0170-5695) *145*
I F O Institut fuer Wirtschaftsforschung. Studien zu Handelsfragen see I F O Institut fuer Wirtschaftsforschung. Studien zu Handels- und Dienstleistungsfragen *145*
I.F.P.S.M. News (International Federation for Preventive and Social Medicine) (IT) *752*
I F T World Directory and Guide (Institute of Food Technologists) (US ISSN 0073-9286) *405*
I F U (Institut fuer Umformtechnik) (US) *851*
I. G. I. see Indian Geological Index *290*
I H B Reporter (Industrial Home for the Blind) (US ISSN 0018-9812) *133*
I I A S A Annual Report (International Institute for Applied Systems Analysis) (AU) *272*
I I A S Occasional Papers (Indian Institute of Advanced Study) (II) *337, 491*
I I M P see Information Industry Market Place *264*

I I R B Winter Congress Proceedings see International Institute for Sugar Beet Research. Reports of the Winter Congress 37
I I R S Occasional Report Series (Institute for Industrial Research and Standards) (IE) 851
I I S E Publications see Michigan State University. Institute for International Studies in Education. Publications 320
I I S T Bulletins (Indian Institute of Soul Technology) (II) 676, 689, 776
I I T C Directory (Indian International Trade Center) (II ISSN 0073-6546) 196
I J A L Native American Texts Series (International Journal of American Linguistics) (US ISSN 0361-3399) 545
I K O Newsletter (NE) 696
I L R Paperbacks (New York State School of Industrial and Labor Relations) (US ISSN 0070-0177) 208
I L T A M Technical Reports (IS) 272
I L Z R O Annual Research Report (International Lead Zinc Research Organization, Inc.) (US) 628
I L Z R O Lead Research Digest (International Lead Zinc Research Organization, Inc.) (US ISSN 0146-7980) 628
I L Z R O Zinc Research Digest (International Lead Zinc Research Organization, Inc.) (US ISSN 0146-7999) 628
I Love New York: The Finger Lakes Travel Guide (US) 887
I M B I S (GW ISSN 0303-4577) 110, 602
I M E Directory: Mines, Minerals, Equipment (Indian Mining and Engineering) (II ISSN 0073-6597) 643
I M F Studies (International Metalworkers Federation) (SZ) 506, 628
I M P Directory (International Mimes & Pantomimists) (US ISSN 0095-2087) 910
I M P H O S Congress Proceedings/World Phosphate Rock Institute. Proceedings (Institut Mondial du Phosphate) (FR) 373
I M U Canberra Circular (International Mathematical Union) (AT ISSN 0311-0621) 585
I N D A Association of the Nonwoven Fabrics Industry. Technical Symposium Papers (US) 855
I N E S Informations (FR ISSN 0339-4212) 491
I N F A Press and Advertisers Year Book (India News and Feature Alliance) (II ISSN 0073-4284) 361
I N I R E B Informa (Instituto Nacional de Investigaciones sobre Recursos Bioticos) (MX) 103
I N I S Reference Series (UN) 531, 703
I N S D O C Union Catalogue Series (Indian National Scientific Documentation Centre) (II ISSN 0073-6627) 91
I N S E A D Address Book see INSEAD Address Book 215
I N U F A: Internationaler Nutzfahrzeug-Katalog/International Catalogue for Commercial Vehicles (SZ ISSN 0073-4292) 882
I O I Occasional Papers see University of Malta. International Ocean Institute. Occasional Papers 313
I P A C Newsletter see I P A C Petroleum News 679
I P A C Petroleum News (Independent Petroleum Association of Canada) (CN ISSN 0073-5760) 679
I P C Building and Contract Journals Ltd. Directory see B and C J Directory 134
I P C Monographs (Institute of Philippine Culture) (PH ISSN 0073-9537) 814
I P C Papers (Institute of Philippine Culture) (PH ISSN 0073-9545) 814

I P C Poverty Research Series (Institute of Philippine Culture) (PH) 814
I P C R Cyclotron Progress Report (Institute of Physical and Chemical Research) (JA) 703
I P C R Cyclotron Report (Institute of Physical and Chemical Research) (JA) 703
I P C R Cyclotron Technical Report (Institute of Physical and Chemical Research) (JA) 703
I P E A Serie Monografica (Instituto de Planejamento Economico e Social) (BL) 223
I P E K/Annual Review of Prehistoric and Ethnographical Art (Jahrbuch fuer Praehistorische und Ethnographische Kunst) (GW ISSN 0075-0468) 402, 433
I P I Bulletin (International Potash Institute) (SZ) 36
I P I Research Topics (International Potash Institute) (SZ) 36
I P P F in Action (International Planned Parenthood Federation) (UK) 131
I P R A Studies in Peace Research (International Peace Research Association) (FI ISSN 0074-7289) 721
I. P. T. C. Newsletter (International Press Telecommunications Council) (UK ISSN 0579-6903) 269
I P Z Information. Reihe S: Subversion (Institut fuer Politologische Zeitfragen) (SZ) 711
I.Q.S. (Instituto Quimico de Sarria) (SP) 246
I.R.C.A. Foreign Log (International Radio Club of America) (US ISSN 0093-1926) 267
I R C S Medical Science: Key Reports in Cell and Molecular Biology (International Research Communications System (IRCS)) (UK ISSN 0142-484X) 103
I R C Special Publication (Indian Roads Congress) (II) 875
I.R.D.S. (International Register of Department Stores) (IT) 218
I R R I Annual Report (International Rice Research Institute) (PH ISSN 0074-7793) 42
I R R I Research Paper Series (International Rice Research Institute) (PH ISSN 0115-3862) 42
I R T S Gold Medal Annual (International Radio and Television Society, Inc.) (US ISSN 0074-7564) 267
I S A Mining and Metallurgy Instrumentation Symposium. Proceedings (Instrument Society of America) (US) 628
I S A Transducer Compendium (Instrument Society of America) (US ISSN 0074-0500) 496
I S B N Review (International Standard Book Number) (GW ISSN 0342-4634) 531, 759
I S E C Monograph (Institute for Social and Economic Change) (II) 186
I S E G R Occasional Papers see I S E R Occasional Papers 798
I S E G R Research Notes see I S E R Research Notes 145
I S E R Occasional Papers (Institute of Social and Economic Research) (US) 798
I S E R Research Notes (Institute of Social and Economic Research) (US) 145
I S H I Occasional Papers in Social Change (Institute for the Study of Human Issues, Inc.) (US) 814
I S I Journal Citation Reports (Institute for Scientific Information) (US) 783
I S I R I Yearbook (Institute of Standards and Industrial Research of Iran) (IR) 637
I S I's Who Is Publishing in Science see Current Bibliographic Directory for the Arts & Sciences 781
I S M A Occasional Papers (Institute for the Study of Man in Africa) (SA ISSN 0073-893X) 50
I S M A Papers (Institute for the Study of Man in Africa) (SA ISSN 0073-8921) 50

I S M A Technical Conference. Proceedings (International Superphosphate Manufactures Association, Ltd.) (FR) 36
I S M E Yearbook (International Society for Music Education) (GW) 659
I S O Annual Review (International Organization for Standardization) (SZ ISSN 0303-3317) 637
I S O Catalogue (International Organization for Standardization) (SZ ISSN 0303-3309) 637
I S O Information see Organ Building Periodical 662
I S O International Standards (International Organization for Standardization) (SZ) 637
I S O Memento (International Organization for Standardization) (SZ ISSN 0536-2067) 637
I S U Constitution (International Skating Union) (SZ) 820
I S U Regulations (International Skating Union) (SZ) 820
I T C Information Booklets (NE ISSN 0536-2113) 422
I T C - Publications. Series A (Photogrammetry) (International Training Centre for Aerial Survey) (NE ISSN 0074-915X) 422
I T C Publications. Series B. Photo-Interpretation (International Institute for Aerial Survey and Earth Sciences) (NE ISSN 0539-0893) 422
I T C-U N E S C O International Seminar. Proceedings (International Institute for Aerial Survey and Earth Sciences) (NE) 386
I T E M (Interference Technology Engineers Master) (US ISSN 0190-0943) 355
I T F Panorama (International Transport Worker's Federation) (UK) 506, 862
I T G Journal see International Trumpet Guild. Journal 660
I T M F Directory (International Textile Manufacturers Federation) (SZ) 856
I U C N Annual Report (International Union for Conservation of Nature and Natural Resources) (SZ) 276
I U C N Yearbook see I U C N Annual Report 276
I U L A (Publication) (International Union of Local Authorities) (NE ISSN 0539-1083) 485, 742
I U S S P Papers (BE) 131, 727
I U S Y Bulletin (International Union of Socialist Youth) (AU) 711
I U S Y Survey see I U S Y Bulletin 711
I W G I A Documents (International Work Group for Indigenous Affairs) (DK ISSN 0105-4503) 50, 392, 718
I W G I A Newsletter (International Work Group for Indigenous Affairs) (DK) 50, 392, 718
I'anson Times (UK) 417
Ibadan Social Sciences Series (NR) 798
Ibadan University Library Bibliographic Series see University of Ibadan. Library. Bibliographical Series 96
Ibaraki University. Faculty of Science. Bulletin. Series A: Mathematics (JA) 585
Ibero-American Bureau of Education. Information and Publications Department Series V: Technical Seminars and Meetings (SP ISSN 0536-2512) 318
Ibero-Americana (US ISSN 0073-4349) 469
Iberoamericana Pragensia (CS) 469
Ibro Neuroscience Calendar (US ISSN 0271-521X) 469
Ibsen Aarboken/Ibsen Yearbook (NO ISSN 0073-4365) 455, 565
Ibsen Yearbook see Ibsen Aarboken 565
Icarus (IE ISSN 0019-1027) 565
Icefield Ranges Research Project Scientific Results (US ISSN 0073-4373) 103, 289, 633

Iceland. Landsbokasafn Islands. Arbok see Iceland. Landsbokasafn Islands. Arbok. Nyr Flokkur 531
Iceland. Landsbokasafn Islands. Arbok see Islenzk Bokaskra 539
Iceland. Landsbokasafn Islands. Arbok. Nyr Flokkur (IC) 531
Icelandic National Bibliography see Islenzk Bokaskra 539
Icon. Cahier (BE) 565
Icon-Werkgroep Jean Ray. Cahier see Icon. Cahier 565
Icones Plantarum Africanarum (SG ISSN 0073-4403) 115
Iconographia Ecclesiae Orientalis (GW ISSN 0341-8448) 75
Iconographia Mycologia (NE ISSN 0073-4411) 115
Idaho. Bureau of Mines and Geology. Bulletin (US ISSN 0073-442X) 295, 643
Idaho. Bureau of Mines and Geology. Information Circular (US ISSN 0073-4446) 295, 643
Idaho. Bureau of Mines and Geology. Pamphlet (US ISSN 0073-4462) 910
Idaho. Department of Agriculture. Annual Report (US ISSN 0098-5716) 15
Idaho. Department of Employment. Annual Rural Employment Report (US) 15
Idaho. Department of Employment. Annual Rural Manpower Report see Idaho. Department of Employment. Annual Rural Employment Report 15
Idaho. Department of Fish and Game. Federal Aid Investigation Projects. Progress Reports and Publications (US ISSN 0073-4527) 276, 397
Idaho. Department of Health and Welfare. Annual Summary of Vital Statistics (US ISSN 0362-9279) 841
Idaho. Department of Labor and Industrial Services. Annual Report (US ISSN 0362-3912) 208
Idaho. Department of Water Resources. Annual Report (US ISSN 0362-3289) 308
Idaho. Law Enforcement Planning Commission. Comprehensive Plan for Law Enforcement and Criminal Justice see Idaho's Comprehensive Plan for Criminal Justice 281
Idaho. State Board for Vocational Education. Annual Descriptive Report of Program Activities for Vocational Education (US ISSN 0091-5882) 329
Idaho. State Superintendent of Public Instruction. Annual Report. State of Idaho Johnson-O'Malley Program (US ISSN 0093-7223) 318, 392
Idaho Agricultural Statistics. (US ISSN 0094-1271) 24
Idaho Education Association. Proceedings (US ISSN 0073-4497) 318
Idaho Environmental Overview (US) 386
Idaho, Montana, Wyoming TourBook see Tourbook: Idaho, Montana, Wyoming 891
Idaho Museum of Natural History. Occasional Papers (US) 653
Idaho Pea and Lentil Commission. Annual Report (US ISSN 0085-1701) 36
Idaho State Industrial Directory (US) 238
Idaho State University Museum. Occasional Papers see Idaho Museum of Natural History. Occasional Papers 653
Idaho Statistical Abstract (US ISSN 0073-456X) 841
Idaho's Comprehensive Plan for Criminal Justice (US ISSN 0093-7134) 281
Ideal Men see Canadian Manhood 262
Idealeda (PO) 556
Ideas (VE) 75
Ideas (II ISSN 0301-9101) 469
Ideas for Management (US ISSN 0073-4624) 215
Ideas y Valores (CK ISSN 0019-140X) 689

INDEKS MAJALAH 1385

Identified Sources of Supply (US) 637
Idesia (CL ISSN 0073-4675) 15
Idryma Meleton Chersonesou Aimou. Ekthoseis see Institute for Balkan Studies. Publications 455
IG-TNO Research Institute for Environmental Hygiene. Annual Report see IMG-TNO Research Institute for Environmental Hygiene. Annual Report 386
Igbo Philosophy (NR) 50
Iheringia. Serie Antropologia (BL ISSN 0073-4691) 50
Iheringia. Serie Botanica (BL ISSN 0073-4705) 115
Iheringia. Serie Geologia (BL ISSN 0073-4713) 295
Iheringia. Serie Zoologia (BL ISSN 0073-4721) 128
Ihsa'iyah-i Amual-i Sadirati-i Afghanistan see Export Statistics of Afghanistan 155
Ihsa'iyah-i Amual-i Varidati-i Afghanistan see Imports Statistics of Afghanistan 158
Ikonenkalender (GW) 75
Ilkeston and District Local History Society. Occasional Paper (UK ISSN 0306-977X) 433
Illinois. Administrative Office of Illinois Courts. Annual Report to the Supreme Court of Illinois (US ISSN 0536-3713) 513
Illinois. Board of Higher Education. Directory of Higher Education (US ISSN 0094-8322) 337
Illinois. Board of Higher Education. Report (US ISSN 0073-4756) 337
Illinois. Board of Higher Education. Statewide Space Survey (US ISSN 0362-5524) 337
Illinois. Cities and Villages Municipal Problems Commission. Annual Report to the Session of the General Assembly (US ISSN 0094-5978) 749
Illinois. Department of Mental Health. Administrator's Data Manual for Mental Health Statistics for Illinois 807
Illinois. Department of Mental Health and Developmental Disabilities. Annual Report (US ISSN 0361-3534) 619, 806
Illinois. Department of Mental Health. Annual Report see Illinois. Department of Mental Health and Developmental Disabiliities. Annual Report 806
Illinois. Department of Mental Health. Drug Abuse Program. Progress Report (US ISSN 0093-7819) 287, 752
Illinois. Department of Public Aid. Annual Report (US ISSN 0091-6099) 806
Illinois. Department of Public Health. Digester see Illinois. Environmental Protection Agency. Operator Certification Section. Digester 386
Illinois. Department of Public Health. Division of Health Facilities. Directory of Health Care Facilities (US) 752
Illinois. Department of Public Health. Poison Control Program Report (US ISSN 0094-6494) 756
Illinois. Department of Public Instruction. Annual State of Education Message see Illinois. State Board of Education. Annual Report 318
Illinois. Department of Transportation. Annual Report (US ISSN 0095-5019) 862
Illinois. Department of Transportation. Physical Research Report (US ISSN 0095-6686) 375
Illinois. Division of Air Pollution Control. Annual Air Quality Report (US) 386
Illinois. Division of Fire Prevention. Annual Report (US) 409
Illinois. Energy Resources Commission. Report to the General Assembly of the State of Illinois see Energy Report to the Illinois General Assembly 362

Illinois. Environmental Protection Agency. Operator Certification Section. Digester (US ISSN 0362-8795) 386
Illinois. Environmental Protection Agency. Water Pollution Control Plan (US ISSN 0091-4541) 386
Illinois. Fire Protection Personnel Standards and Education Commission. Annual Report (US ISSN 0095-8247) 395
Illinois. Housing Development Authority. Annual Report (US ISSN 0090-3248) 485
Illinois. Judicial Inquiry Board. Report (US ISSN 0093-8939) 718
Illinois. Junior College Board. Annual Report see Illinois Community College Board. Biennial Report 337
Illinois. Legislative Investigating Commission. Annual Report (US ISSN 0094-9795) 513
Illinois. Natural History Survey. Biological Notes (US ISSN 0073-490X) 104
Illinois. Natural History Survey. Bulletin (US ISSN 0073-4918) 783
Illinois. Natural History Survey. Circular (US ISSN 0073-4926) 783
Illinois. State Board of Education. Annual Report (US) 318
Illinois. State Board of Investment. Investment Transactions (US ISSN 0095-3148) 203
Illinois. State Fire Marshal. Annual Report. see Illinois. Division of Fire Prevention. Annual Report 409
Illinois. State Geological Survey. Bulletins (US ISSN 0073-5051) 295
Illinois. State Geological Survey. Circulars (US ISSN 0073-506X) 295
Illinois. State Geological Survey. Educational Series (US ISSN 0073-5078) 295
Illinois. State Geological Survey. Environmental Geology Notes (US ISSN 0073-5086) 295
Illinois. State Geological Survey. Guidebook Series (US ISSN 0073-5094) 295
Illinois. State Geological Survey. Industrial Mineral Notes see Illinois Minerals Notes 643
Illinois. State Geological Survey. Mineral Economic Briefs see Illinois Minerals Notes 643
Illinois. State Museum. Guidebooklet Series (US ISSN 0162-1939) 783
Illinois. State Museum. Handbook of Collections (US ISSN 0445-3387) 75
Illinois. State Museum. Inventory of the Collections (US ISSN 0095-2893) 783
Illinois. State Museum. Popular Science Series (US ISSN 0360-0297) 783
Illinois. State Museum. Reports of Investigations (US ISSN 0360-0270) 61
Illinois. State Museum. Research Series. Papers in Anthropology (US ISSN 0095-2915) 50
Illinois. State Museum. Scientific Papers Series (US ISSN 0445-3395) 61, 104, 295, 469
Illinois. State Museum. Story of Illinois Series (US ISSN 0360-0289) 783
Illinois Air Quality Report see Illinois. Division of Air Pollution Control. Annual Air Quality Report 386
Illinois Air Sampling Network Report see Illinois. Division of Air Pollution Control. Annual Air Quality Report 386
Illinois Biological Monographs (US ISSN 0073-4748) 104
Illinois Classical Studies (US ISSN 0363-1923) 259
Illinois Community College Board. Biennial Report (US ISSN 0092-7783) 337
Illinois Dealer Directory and Buyer's Guide (US) 136
Illinois Directory and Suppliers Listing see Illinois Dealer Directory and Buyer's Guide 136
Illinois Education Review (US) 318

Illinois Government. see Illinois Government Research 742
Illinois Government Research (US ISSN 0195-7783) 711, 742
Illinois Handcrafts Directory (US ISSN 0095-5337) 476
Illinois Health Sciences Libraries Serials Holdings List (US ISSN 0148-0650) 91, 539, 602
Illinois, Indiana, Ohio, TourBook see Tourbook: Illinois, Indiana, Ohio 891
Illinois Institute for Environmental Quality. Annual Report (US ISSN 0090-8967) 386
Illinois Issues Annual (US ISSN 0149-3752) 742
Illinois Labor History Society Reporter (US ISSN 0085-1728) 208
Illinois Law Enforcement Commission. Annual Report (US ISSN 0073-487X) 281
Illinois Minerals Notes (US ISSN 0094-9442) 295, 643
Illinois Mining Institute. Proceedings (US) 644
Illinois Petroleum (US) 295, 679
Illinois State and Regional Economic Data Book (US ISSN 0093-9552) 186
Illinois State Bar Association. Antitrust Law Newsletter (US ISSN 0073-5000) 513
Illinois State Bar Association. Federal Tax Section Newsletter (US ISSN 0073-5027) 229
Illinois State Bar Association. Local Government Law Newsletter (US ISSN 0073-5035) 513
Illinois State Bar Association. Patent, Trademark, and Copyright Newsletter (US ISSN 0073-5043) 676
Illinois State Industrial Directory (US) 238
Illinois Studies in Anthropology (US ISSN 0073-5167) 50
Illinois Studies in Language and Literature (US ISSN 0073-5175) 545, 565
Illinois Studies in the Social Sciences (US ISSN 0073-5183) 798
Illinois Water Quality Network. Summary of Data (US ISSN 0073-5450) 386
Illuminating Engineering Society Lighting Handbook see I E S Lighting Handbook 355
Illumination Annual see Divine Path 688
Illustration in Japan (JA) 75
Illustrators; The Annual of American Illustration (US ISSN 0073-5477) 75
Ilmatieteen Laitos. Tiedonantoja see Finland. Ilmatieteen Laitos. Tiedonantoja 632
Ilmatieteen Laitos. Tutkimusseloste see Finland. Ilmatieteen Laitos. Tutkimusseloste 632
Ilmi A'ino (PK) 760
Ilmu Alam (MY) 422
Image of Woman (US) 900
Imagen U.C.V. (Universidad Catolica de Valparaiso) (CL) 263
Images de la Chimie (FR) 246
Imago Mvndi (UK ISSN 0308-5694) 422
IMG-TNO Research Institute for Environmental Hygiene. Annual Report (NE) 386
Immunological Reviews (DK ISSN 0105-2896) 603
Immunology: an International Series of Monographs and Treatises (US ISSN 0092-6019) 603
Immunology Reports and Reviews/ Fortschritte der Immunitaetsforschung (GW ISSN 0071-7908) 603
Immunopathology (US ISSN 0073-5531) 603
Impact (Syracuse) (US ISSN 0163-8262) 132, 694
Impact: American Distilled Spirits Market Review and Forecast (US ISSN 0163-9536) 86
Impact Films Catalog (US) 650

Impact of Travel on State Economies (US) 887
Impact: the American Wine Market Review and Forecast (US ISSN 0163-9544) 86
Imperial Cancer Research Fund. Scientific Report (UK) 605
Implement & Tractor Product File (US ISSN 0073-5566) 32
Implement & Tractor Red Book (US ISSN 0073-5574) 32
Import Car Buyer's Guide (US ISSN 0073-5582) 910
Import/Export Wood Purchasing Guide(US) 196, 413
Import Trade Control: Handbook of Rules and Procedures (II ISSN 0536-9983) 196
Import Trade Control Policy (II ISSN 0536-9061) 196
Importations-Commerce de Marchandises see Canada. Statistics Canada. Imports-Merchandise Trade 153
Importers and Exporters Trade Promotion Guide (US ISSN 0073-5604) 196
Imports of the Republic of China (CH) 196
Imports Statistics of Afghanistan/ Ihsa'iyah-i Amual-i Varidati-i Afghanistan (AF) 158, 841
Imprimatur; Jahrbuch fuer Buecherfreunde. Neue Folge (GW ISSN 0073-5620) 733
Impulse (SA) 783
Impulstechniken (GW) 703
In a Nutshell (CN ISSN 0380-2892) 619, 806
In Care (US) 481
In Common (US ISSN 0363-5058) 765
In Gang Fun Arbet: Yidish Un Mizrakh Eyropeishe Yidishe Shtudies see Working Papers in Yiddish and East European Jewish Studies 394
In Print (AT ISSN 0310-3048) 565
In Pursuit of Liberty (US) 711
In Terris (PE ISSN 0300-4031) 580
In the Light (US) 580
In the New Uruguay see En el Nuevo Uruguay 556
Incentives for Better Books in Pakistan see Literary Prizes in Pakistan 567
Inchieste di Urbanistica e Architettura (IT ISSN 0019-3399) 69, 485
Incite (AT ISSN 0158-0876) 531
Income, Estate and Gift Tax Provisions: Internal Revenue Code (US ISSN 0073-5671) 229
Income-Expense Analysis: Apartments (US) 136, 761
Income-Expense Analysis Apartments, Condominiums and Cooperatives see Income-Expense Analysis: Apartments 761
Income-Expense Analysis Apartments, Condominiums and Cooperatives see Expense Analysis: Condominiums, Cooperatives and Planned Unit Developments 761
Income-Expense Analysis: Suburban Office Buildings (US) 761
Income in (Year) of Families and Persons in the United States see Current Population Reports: Consumer Income. Income in (Year) of Families and Persons in the United States 212
Income Tax Guide for Military Personnel (US ISSN 0098-1729) 229, 639
Inconscio e Cultura (IT) 736
Incontri Linguistici (IT) 545
Incorporated Law Society of Sri Lanka. Annual Report (CE ISSN 0073-5728) 513
Incorporated Law Society of Sri Lanka. Journal (CE ISSN 0073-5736) 513
Incorporated Society of Musicians Handbook & Register of Members (UK) 659
Incunabula Graeca (IT ISSN 0073-5752) 259
Indeks Madjalah Ilmiah see Index of Indonesian Learned Periodicals 91
Indeks Majalah Malaysia see Malaysian Periodicals Index 3

Independent Broadcasting Authority. Annual Report and Accounts (UK ISSN 0309-0175) *267*
Independent Broadcasting Authority Technical Review *see* I B A Technical Review *267*
Independent Petroleum Association of Canada Petroleum News *see* I P A C Petroleum News *679*
Independent Phonefacts (US) *269*
Independent Schools Association of the Southwest. Membership List (US ISSN 0073-5779) *331*
Independent Telephone Statistics *see* United States Independent Telephone Association. Annual Statistical Volume *269*
Index Alphabetique Annuel des Sujets Traites dans les Theses de Medecine *see* Thesindex Medical *603*
Index Asia Series in Humanities (II) *2, 495*
Index Bio-Bibliographicus Notorium Hominum (GW) *99*
Index de References: Inventaire des Stations Hydrometriques (CN) *308, 896*
Index der Rechtsmittelentscheidungen und des Schrifttums (AU) *513*
Index des Projects en Development sur l'Ecologie des Zones Arides *see* Indice de Proyectos en Desarrollo en Ecologia de Zonas Aridas *104*
Index/Directory of Women's Media (US) *900*
Index Hepaticarum (GW ISSN 0073-5787) *115*
Index Islamicus (UK ISSN 0306-9524) *91*
Index Medicus Iugoslavicus *see* Bibliografija Medicinske Periodike Jugoslavije *601*
Index Nominum (SZ) *684*
Index of American Periodical Verse (US ISSN 0090-9130) *2, 578*
Index of Art in the Pacific Northwest (US ISSN 0085-1760) *75*
Index of Articles on Jewish Studies/ Reshimat Ma'amarim Be-Mada'e Ha-Yahadut (IS ISSN 0073-5817) *2, 769*
Index of Biochemical Reviews (NE) *2, 110*
Index of Current Equine Research (US ISSN 0070-1947) *45*
Index of Current Government and Governmental-Supported Research in Environmental Pollution in Great Britain (UK) *386*
Index of Current Research in Arid Zones Ecology *see* Indice de Proyectos en Desarrollo en Ecologia de Zonas Aridas *104*
Index of Current Research on Pigs (UK) *2, 45*
Index of Current Tropical Ecology Research *see* Indice de Proyectos en Desarrollo en Ecologia Tropical *3*
Index of Economic Articles in Journals and Collective Volumes (US) *2, 158*
Index of Graduate Theses in Baptist Theological Seminaries (US ISSN 0073-5825) *772*
Index of Indonesian Learned Periodicals/Indeks Madjalah Ilmiah (IO ISSN 0019-3607) *91*
Index of N L M Serial Titles (National Library of Medicine) (US ISSN 0162-6639) *602*
Index of Patents Issued from the United States Patent and Trademark Office (US ISSN 0362-0719) *676*
Index of Pig Research *see* Meat and Livestock Commission, Bucks, England. Index of Research *45*
Index of Psychoanalytic Writings (US ISSN 0073-5884) *739*
Index of Publications of the Geological Survey of Canada *see* Canada. Geological Survey. Index of Publications of the Geological Survey of Canada *290*
Index of Reviews in Organic Chemistry (UK ISSN 0536-6518) *2, 249*
Index of Rheumatology (US ISSN 0019-3933) *2, 602*
Index of Tissue Culture (US ISSN 0090-0753) *910*

Index of Trademarks Issued from the U.S. Patent and Trademark Office (US ISSN 0099-0809) *676*
Index of Trademarks Issued from the United States Patent Office *see* Index of Trademarks Issued from the U.S. Patent and Trademark Office *676*
Index to Book Reviews in Historical Periodicals (US ISSN 0362-8671) *438*
Index to Book Reviews in the Humanities (US ISSN 0073-5892) *495*
Index to Chinese Legal Periodicals (CH) *2, 521*
Index to Early American Periodical Literature, 1728-1870 (US ISSN 0073-5914) *578*
Index to Ecology *see* N I C E M Index to Environmental Studies-Multimedia *390*
Index to Finnish Periodicals *see* Suomen Aikakauslehti-Indeksi *4*
Index to How to Do It Information (US ISSN 0073-5930) *2, 476*
Index to Indian Periodical Literature (II) *2, 803*
Index to International Public Opinion (US ISSN 0193-905X) *721, 798*
Index to Literature on the American Indian (US ISSN 0091-7346) *2, 394*
Index to Little Magazines (US ISSN 0073-5949) *910*
Index to Model Making & Miniatures (US) *2, 476*
Index to Mormonism in Periodical Literature (US ISSN 0148-6586) *2, 776*
Index to New Zealand Periodicals (NZ ISSN 0073-5957) *2*
Index to Periodical Articles by and About Blacks (US ISSN 0161-8245) *2, 394*
Index to Periodical Articles by and About Negroes *see* Index to Periodical Articles by and About Blacks *394*
Index to Periodicals of the Church of Jesus Christ of Latter-Day Saints. Cumulative Edition (US ISSN 0073-5981) *769*
Index to Post-1944 Periodical Articles on Political, Economic and Social Problems *see* Bibliographie Courante d'Articles de Periodiques Posterieurs a 1944 sur les Problemes Politiques, Economiques et Sociaux *803*
Index to Reviews of Bibliographical Publications (US) *91*
Index to Selected Periodicals *see* Index to Periodical Articles by and About Blacks *394*
Index to South African Periodicals/ Repertorium van Suid-Afrikaanse Tydskrifartikels (SA) *2, 760*
Index to Textile Auxiliaries (UK ISSN 0073-604X) *856*
Index to Thai Newspapers (TH) *2, 506*
Index to Thai Periodical Literature (TH ISSN 0125-5827) *2, 803*
Index to the National Assembly Records/Kuk Hoe Hoe Eu Rok Saegin (KO) *2, 539*
Index to the Science Fiction Magazines *see* N.E.S.F.A. Index: Science Fiction Magazines and Anthologies *4*
Index to Titles of English News Releases of Hsinhua News Agency (HK ISSN 0082-7789) *505*
Index Translationum (UN ISSN 0073-6074) *531*
India. Cardamom Board. Annual Report (II) *36, 742*
India. Central Board of Revenue. Central Excise Manual (II ISSN 0073-6120) *229*
India. Central Statistical Organization. Annual Survey of Industries/ Udyogen Ka Varshika Sarvekshana (II ISSN 0073-6139) *158*
India. Central Statistical Organization. Estimates of National Income *see* India. Central Statistical Organization. National Accounts Statistics *213*

India. Central Statistical Organization. National Accounts Statistics (II) *213*
India. Central Statistical Organization. Sample Surveys of Current Interest in India; Report (II ISSN 0073-6163) *841*
India. Central Statistical Organization. Statistical Abstract (II ISSN 0073-6155) *841*
India. Central Vigilance Commission. Report (II ISSN 0073-6171) *742*
India. Committee on Science and Technology. Annual Report (II ISSN 0085-1779) *783, 851*
India. Department of Atomic Energy. Annual Report (II ISSN 0073-618X) *703*
India. Department of Culture. Demands for Grants/Samskriti Vibhaga Ki Anudanom Ki Mangem (II) *344*
India. Department of Economic Affairs. Budget Division. Key to the Budget Documents (II) *742*
India. Department of Labour and Employment. Annual Report *see* India. Ministry of Labour. Annual Report *208*
India. Department of Power. Report (II) *363, 742*
India. Department of Science and Technology. Report. (II) *851*
India. Department of Space. Annual Report (II) *8*
India. Finance Department. Budget of the Central Government (II) *229*
India. Labour Bureau. Pocket Book of Labour Statistics (II) *158*
India. Ministry of Education and Social Welfare. Department of Education. Report (II) *318*
India. Ministry of Education and Social Welfare. Department of Social Welfare. Documentation Service Bulletin (II) *2, 803*
India. Ministry of Education and Social Welfare. Provisional Statistics of Education in the States (II ISSN 0579-6105) *318*
India. Ministry of Finance. Budget *see* India. Finance Department. Budget of the Central Government *229*
India. Ministry of Heavy Industry. Report (II) *145*
India. Ministry of Home Affairs. Vital Statistics Division. Causes of Death; a Survey (II) *727*
India. Ministry of Labour. Annual Report (II) *208*
India. Office of the Comptroller and Auditor-General. Report: Union Government (Posts and Telegraphs) (II ISSN 0536-7506) *264*
India. Parliament. Public Accounts Committee. Report on the Accounts (II ISSN 0445-6831) *742*
India (Republic). Meteorological Department Report on Seismology *see* National Report for India: Seismology and Physics of the Earth's Interior *634*
India (Republic). Ministry of Shipping and Transport. Statistics of Water Transport Industries *see* Water Transport Statistics of India *881*
India. Rural Electrification Corporation. Annual Report and Statement of Accounts (II) *355*
India. Union Public Service Commission Report (II ISSN 0073-6236) *742*
India. Zoological Survey. Annual Report (II ISSN 0537-0744) *128*
India. Zoological Survey. Newsletter (II) *128*
India. A Reference Annual (II ISSN 0073-6090) *91*
India & Pakistan Wool, Hosiery & Fabrics *see* Directory of Wool, Hosiery & Fabrics *855*
India and World Affairs: an Annual Bibliography (II) *438, 717*
India at a Glance. (II) *887*
India Forum (US) *443*

India News and Feature Alliance Press and Advertisers Year Book *see* I N F A Press and Advertisers Year Book *361*
India Transport Statistics *see* Pocket Book of Transport Statistics of India *863*
India Who's Who (II ISSN 0073-6244) *97*
Indian Academy of Geoscience. Journal (II) *289*
Indian Agriculture in Brief (II ISSN 0084-781X) *15*
Indian & Eastern Newspaper Society Press Handbook (II) *505, 733*
Indian Association of American Studies. Papers (II) *433*
Indian Association of Physiotherapists. Journal (II) *596*
Indian Association of Special Libraries and Information Centres Special Publication *see* I A S L I C Special Publication *530*
Indian Association of Special Libraries and Information Centres Technical Pamphlets *see* I A S L I C Technical Pamphlets *530*
Indian Astronomical Ephemeris (II) *82*
Indian Biophysical Society. Proceedings (II) *112*
Indian Book Review Digest (CN) *392, 759*
Indian Book Review Index (II) *91, 760*
Indian Books; Bibliography of Indian Books Published or Reprinted in the English Language *see* B E P I *87*
Indian Chemical Directory (II ISSN 0073-6295) *246, 373*
Indian Chemicals and Pharmaceuticals Statistics (II) *686*
Indian Congress of American History. Papers *see* Indian Association of American Studies. Papers *433*
Indian Cotton Textile Industry; Annual Statistical Bulletin (II) *857*
Indian Council for Child Welfare. Annual Report (II) *258, 806*
Indian Council of Social Science Research Union Catalogue of Social Science Periodicals Serials *see* I C S S R Union Catalogue of Social Science Periodicals/Serials *803*
Indian Education Annual Report *see* Idaho. State Superintendent of Public Instruction. Annual Report. State of Idaho Johnson-O'Malley Program *318*
Indian Education Newsletter (CN ISSN 0318-000X) *318, 392*
Indian Electronics Directory (II ISSN 0377-7340) *355*
Indian Engineering & Industries Register *see* Engineering Times Annual Directory *367*
Indian Engineering Association. Handbook of Statistics *see* Association of Indian Engineering Industry. Handbook of Statistics *366*
Indian Ephemeris and Nautical Almanac *see* Indian Astronomical Ephemeris *82*
Indian Export Directory *see* Directory of Indian Exporters *195*
Indian Fertilizer Statistics (II) *24*
Indian Films (II) *650*
Indian Forest Bulletin (New Series) (II ISSN 0073-635X) *409*
Indian Forest Leaflets (New Series) (II ISSN 0073-6368) *409*
Indian Forest Records (New Series) Botany (II ISSN 0073-6376) *115*
Indian Forest Records (New Series) Composite Wood (II ISSN 0073-6384) *413*
Indian Forest Records (New Series) Entomology (II ISSN 0073-6392) *121*
Indian Forest Records (New Series) Forest Pathology (II ISSN 0073-6406) *409*
Indian Forest Records (New Series) Logging (II ISSN 0073-6414) *413*
Indian Forest Records (New Series) Mycology *see* Indian Forest Records (New Series) Forest Pathology *409*
Indian Forest Records (New Series) Silviculture (II ISSN 0073-6422) *409*

Indian Forest Records (New Series) Statistical (II ISSN 0073-6430) *409*
Indian Forest Records (New Series) Timber Mechanics (II ISSN 0073-6449) *413*
Indian Geological Index (II) 3, *290*
Indian Geophysical Union Bulletin (II) *304*
Indian Geoscience Association. Journal *see* Indian Academy of Geoscience. Journal *289*
Indian Health Trends and Services (US) 727, *752*
Indian Hosiery Directory (II) 238, *261*
Indian Institute of Advanced Study. Transactions and Monographs (II ISSN 0073-6465) *491*
Indian Institute of Advanced Study Occasional Papers *see* I A S Occasional Papers *337*
Indian Institute of Foreign Trade. Report (II ISSN 0073-6473) *196*
Indian Institute of Mass Communication. Annual Report (II) *264*
Indian Institute of Metals. Proceedings (II) *628*
Indian Institute of Soul Technology Bulletins *see* I I S T Bulletins *676*
Indian Institute of Sugarcane Research, Lucknow. Annual Report (II ISSN 0073-649X) *36*
Indian Institute of Technology, Bombay. Series (II ISSN 0073-6503) *851*
Indian Institute of Technology, Madras. Annual Report (II ISSN 0073-6511) *851*
Indian Institute of Technology, Madras. M.S., Ph.D. Dissertation Abstracts (II) 3, *854*
Indian Institute of Technology, Madras. Ph.D. Dissertation Abstracts *see* Indian Institute of Technology, Madras. M.S., Ph.D. Dissertation Abstracts *854*
Indian Institute of Tropical Meteorology. Annual Report (II ISSN 0250-6017) *633*
Indian Institute of Tropical Meteorology. Research Report (II ISSN 0250-6009) *633*
Indian Institute of World Culture. Annual Report (II) *491*
Indian International Trade Center Directory *see* I I T C Directory *196*
Indian Journal of Engineers. Annual Foundry Number (II ISSN 0073-6554) *367*
Indian Journal of Fisheries (II ISSN 0537-2003) 128, *397*
Indian Journal of Medical Research, Supplement (II ISSN 0367-9012) *596*
Indian Journal of Psychiatric Social Work (II ISSN 0302-1610) *619*, 806
Indian Journal of Sericulture (II) *856*
Indian Jute Mills Association. Annual Summary of Jute and Gunny Statistics (II ISSN 0073-6562) *856*
Indian Jute Mills Association. Loom and Spindle Statistics (II ISSN 0073-6570) *856*
Indian Linguistics Monograph Series (II ISSN 0073-6589) *545*
Indian Literature in Environmental Engineering (II) 372, *390*
Indian Mathematical Society. Journal (II ISSN 0019-5839) *585*
Indian Minerals Year Book (II ISSN 0445-7897) *644*
Indian Mining and Engineering Directory: Mines, Minerals, Equipment *see* I M E Directory: Mines, Minerals, Equipment *643*
Indian Motion Picture Almanac (II) *650*
Indian National Science Academy. Biographical Memoirs of Fellows (II) 97, *783*
Indian National Science Academy. Bulletin (II) *783*
Indian National Science Academy. Mathematical Tables (II) *585*
Indian National Science Academy. Monographs (II) *783*

Indian National Science Academy. Proceedings (II ISSN 0073-6600) *784*
Indian National Science Academy. Transactions (II) *784*
Indian National Science Academy. Year Book (II ISSN 0073-6619) *784*
Indian National Scientific Documentation Centre Union Catalogue Series *see* I N S D O C Union Catalogue Series *91*
Indian Ocean Fishery Commission. Report of the Session (UN) *397*
Indian Petroleum and Chemicals Statistics *see* Indian Petroleum and Petrochemicals Statistics *682*
Indian Petroleum and Petrochemicals Statistics (II) *682*, 841
Indian Pharmaceutical Guide (II ISSN 0073-6635) *684*
Indian Philosophical Annual. (II) *689*
Indian Phytopathological Society. Bulletin (II ISSN 0537-2410) *115*
Indian Poultry Industry Yearbook (II) 45, *894*
Indian Railways Yearbook (II) *866*
Indian Records (II ISSN 0302-6744) 659, *818*
Indian Review of Life Sciences (II) *15*, 50
Indian Roads Congress. Highway Research Board Bulletin (II ISSN 0376-4788) *875*
Indian Roads Congress. Road Research Bulletin *see* Indian Roads Congress. Highway Research Board Bulletin *875*
Indian Roads Congress Special Publication *see* I R C Special Publication *875*
Indian Rubber Statistics (II ISSN 0073-6651) *777*
Indian School of Mines. Annual Report(II ISSN 0304-1158) *644*
Indian Science Congress Association. Proceedings (II ISSN 0085-1817) *784*
Indian Science Index (II) 3, *794*
Indian Society of Gastroenterology. Proceedings of the Annual Conference (II) *613*
Indian Society of International Law. Publications (II ISSN 0073-6678) *523*
Indian Statistical Institute. Annual Report (II ISSN 0073-6686) *841*
Indian Statistical Institute. Documentation Research and Training Centre. Annual Seminar (II ISSN 0067-3439) *531*
Indian Statistical Institute. Econometric and Social Sciences Series. Research Monographs (II ISSN 0073-6694) *798*
Indian Statistical Institute. Lecture Notes (II) *841*
Indian Statistical Institute. Library. Bibliographic Series (II ISSN 0073-6708) *91*
Indian Statistical Institute. Research and Training School. Publications *see* Indian Statistical Institute. Lecture Notes *841*
Indian Statistical Institute. Statistics and Probability Series. Research Monographs (II ISSN 0073-6716) *841*
Indian Statistical Series (II ISSN 0073-6724) *841*
Indian Stratigraphy (II) *295*
Indian Textile Annual & Directory (II) *856*
Indian Tobacco *see* Tobacco News *861*
Indian Veterinary Research Institute. Annual Report (II ISSN 0304-7067) *894*
Indian Yearbook of International Affairs (II ISSN 0537-2704) 443, *721*
Indiana (GW ISSN 0341-8642) *50*, 61, 469
Indiana. Aeronautics Commission. Annual Report (US ISSN 0073-6775) *8*

Indiana. Agricultural Experiment Station. Inspection Report (US ISSN 0073-6783) *15*
Indiana. Agricultural Experiment Station. Research Bulletin (US ISSN 0073-6791) *15*
Indiana. Civil Rights Commission. Annual Report *see* Indiana. Civil Rights Commission. Triennial Report *718*
Indiana. Civil Rights Commission. Triennial Report (US) *718*
Indiana. Division of Fish and Wildlife. Annual Report (US ISSN 0073-6872) *276*
Indiana. Division of Fish and Wildlife. Management Series (US ISSN 0095-1676) *276*
Indiana. Environmental Management Board. Annual Report (US ISSN 0094-5749) *386*
Indiana. Geological Survey. Annual Report of the State Geologist (US ISSN 0362-3513) *295*
Indiana. Office of Community Services Administration. Annual Report (US ISSN 0148-9232) *742*
Indiana. State Advisory Council for Vocational Technical Education. Annual Report (US ISSN 0091-8970) *349*
Indiana Academy of Science. Monograph (US ISSN 0073-6759) *784*
Indiana Academy of Science. Proceedings (US ISSN 0073-6767) *784*
Indiana Ball State Teachers College *see* Ball State Monographs *489*
Indiana Directory of Music Teachers (US) 318, *659*
Indiana Historical Collections (US ISSN 0073-6880) *469*
Indiana Historical Society. Prehistory Research Series (US ISSN 0073-6899) *50*
Indiana Historical Society. Publications (US ISSN 0073-6902) *469*
Indiana History Resource Series (US) *469*
Indiana International Trade Directory (US) *196*
Indiana Library Association Membership Directory (US) *531*
Indiana State Industrial Directory (US ISSN 0190-1362) *238*
Indiana State Medical Association. Journal: Roster and Yearbook Issue (US) *910*
Indiana State Plan for Vocational Education. Annual Program Plan (US) *345*
Indiana State University. Department of Geography and Geology. Professional Papers (US ISSN 0073-6937) *422*
Indiana Studies in Higher Education (US) *349*
Indiana Studies in Prediction *see* Indiana Studies in Higher Education *349*
Indiana University. Department of Geography. Geographic Monograph Series (US ISSN 0073-6953) *423*
Indiana University. Folklore Institute. Monograph Series (US ISSN 0073-6996) *402*
Indiana University. Research Center for Language and Semiotic Studies. African Series (US ISSN 0073-7062) *545*
Indiana University. Research Center for Language and Semiotic Studies. Uralic and Altaic Series (US ISSN 0073-7097) *545*
Indiana University. Research Center for the Language Sciences. African Studies *see* Indiana University. Research Center for Language and Semiotic Studies. African Series *545*
Indiana University. School of Public and Environmental Affairs. Occasional Papers (US) 276, *386*, 742
Indiana University. Sesquicentennial Series on Insurance (US ISSN 0073-7127) *499*
Indiana University Art Museum. Publications (US ISSN 0073-7038) *653*

Indiana University Bookman (US ISSN 0019-6800) *759*
Indiana University Monograph Series in Adult Education (US ISSN 0073-702X) *329*
Indiana University Publications. African Series (US) *440*
Indianist Yearbook *see* Anuario Indigenista *47*
India's Exports and Internal Consumption of Coir and Coir Goods *see* India's Production, Exports, and Internal Consumption of Coir *196*
India's Production, Exports, and Internal Consumption of Coir (II) *196*
Indicadores Socio-Economicos del Campo Espanol (SP) *28*
Indicadores Socioeconomicos y de Coyuntura (VE) 158, *818*
Indice Agricola Colombiano (CK ISSN 0073-7151) *24*
Indice-Catalogo Medico Brasileiro *see* Bibliografia Brasileira de Medicina *601*
Indice de Actualidad Farmacologica (SP) *684*
Indice de Articulos de Publicaciones Periodicas en el Area de Ciencias Sociales y Humanidades (CK) 3, *803*
Indice de Precios al Consumidor, Ciudad de la Paz (Anual) (BO) *158*
Indice de Proyectos en Desarrollo en Ecologia de Zonas Aridas/Index of Current Research in Arid Zones Ecology/Index des Projects en Developpment sur l'Ecologie des Zones Arides (MX) *104*
Indice de Proyectos en Desarrollo en Ecologia Tropical/Index of Current Tropical Ecology Research (MX) *3*, 104
Indice do Brasil/Brazilian Index Yearbook (BL) *186*, 841
Indice Economico Colombiano (CK ISSN 0019-7033) *158*
Indice General de Publicaciones Periodicas Cubanas (CU) *3*
Indice Medico Colombiano (CK ISSN 0019-705X) 3, *602*
Indices Naturwissenschaftlich-Medizinischer Periodica bis 1850 (GW ISSN 0340-8094) *602*
Indices of Urban Land Prices and Construction Cost of Wooden Houses in Japan (JA ISSN 0073-7186) *761*
Indices Verborum Linguae Mongoliae Monumentis Traditorum (HU ISSN 0073-7194) *545*, 670
Indices Zum Altdeutschen Schrifttum (NE) *565*
Indices zur Deutschen Literatur (GW ISSN 0073-7208) *578*
Indigena (US) *392*
Individual Onsite Wastewater Systems *see* National Conference on Individual Onsite Wastewater Systems. Proceedings *387*
Indo-Burma Petroleum Company. Annual Report (II) *679*
Indo-Pacific Fisheries Council. Regional Studies (UN ISSN 0537-3654) *397*
Indo-Pacific Mollusca (US ISSN 0073-7240) *128*
Indogermanische Forschungen (GW ISSN 0019-7262) *545*
Indologica Taurinensia (IT) *670*
Indonesia. Departemen Pekerjaan Umum dan Tenaga Listrik. Biro Umum. Laporan Tahunan *see* Indonesia. Department of Public Works and Electric Power. Administration Bureau. Annual Report *355*
Indonesia. Departemen Penerangan. Siaran Umum (IO) *742*
Indonesia. Department of Public Works and Electric Power. Administration Bureau. Annual Report/Indonesia. Departemen Pekerjaan Umum dan Tenaga Listrik. Biro Umum. Laporan Tahunan (IO) *355*

Indonesia. Directorate General of Higher Education. Annual Report/ Indonesia. Direktorat Jenderal Pendidikan Tinggi. Laporan Tahunan.(IO) 337
Indonesia. Directorate General of Protestant Affairs. Annual Report/ Indonesia. Direktorat Jenderal Bimbingan Masyarakat Kristen/ Protestan Laporan Tahunan (IO) 772
Indonesia. Direktorat Jenderal Bimbingan Masyarakat Kristen/ Protestan Laporan Tahunan *see* Indonesia. Directorate General of Protestant Affairs. Annual Report 772
Indonesia. Direktorat Jenderal Pendidikan Tinggi. Laporan Tahunan *see* Indonesia. Directorate General of Higher Education. Annual Report 337
Indonesia. Direktorat Perumahan Rakjat. Laporan Kerdja (IO) 485
Indonesia. National Scientific Documentation Centre. Annual Report/Indonesia. Pusat Dokumentasi Ilmiah Nasional. Laporan Tahunan (IO) 784
Indonesia. Pusat Dokumentasi Ilmiah Nasional. Laporan Tahunan *see* Indonesia. National Scientific Documentation Centre. Annual Report 784
Indonesia do-It-Yourself (AT) 887
Indonesia Statistics (IO ISSN 0376-9984) 158, 841
Indonesia Tourist Statistics (IO) 841, 893
Indonesian Acquisitions List/Daftar Pengadaan Bahan Indonesia (AT ISSN 0310-6659) 91
Indonesian Shipping Directory (IO) 238, 878
Indonesian Statistics on Trade of Forest Products (IO) 409
Indonesian Women's Congress. Bulletin/Kongres Wanita Indonesia. Berita (IO) 900
Industria del Petrolio in Italia (IT ISSN 0073-7275) 679
Industria Italiana del Ciclo e del Motociclo. Annuario (IT ISSN 0073-7291) 871
Industrial Accident Prevention Association. Annual Report (CN ISSN 0073-7305) 495
Industrial Accident Prevention Association. Guide to Safety (CN ISSN 0073-7313) 208
Industrial Alabama *see* Alabama Directory of Mining and Manufacturing 178
Industrial and Commercial Power Systems and Electrical Space Heating and Air Conditioning Joint Technical Conference. Record (US ISSN 0073-733X) 355
Industrial and Control Applications of Microprocessors. Proceedings (US) 496
Industrial and Labor Relations Bibliography Series (US ISSN 0070-0142) 159
Industrial and Labor Relations Forum (US ISSN 0019-7912) 208
Industrial Arbitration Reports, New South Wales (AT ISSN 0155-2589) 208
Industrial Arbitration Service (AT ISSN 0312-4029) 513
Industrial Archeology *see* I A 61
Industrial Bank of Kuwait. Annual Report (KU) 173
Industrial Bank of Sudan. Board of Directors. Annual Report (SJ ISSN 0073-7356) 173
Industrial Catering (UK ISSN 0073-7364) 482
Industrial Cities News Service (US ISSN 0085-1833) 469
Industrial Contact List for North Carolina Communities (US ISSN 0095-1870) 223
Industrial Development and the Social Fabric (US) 145

Industrial Development Bank. Annual Report and Balance Sheet/Bank al-Inma al-Sinai. Annual Report and Balance Sheet (JO) 173
Industrial Development Bank Limited. Annual Report and Accounts (KE) 173
Industrial Development Bank of India. Annual Report (II ISSN 0073-7372) 174
Industrial Development Bank of Israel Limited. Report (IS ISSN 0073-7380) 174
Industrial Development Bank of Pakistan. Report (PK ISSN 0073-7399) 174
Industrial Development Bank of Turkey. Annual Statement (TU ISSN 0073-7402) 174
Industrial Development in the T.V.A. Area (Tennessee Valley Authority) (US ISSN 0495-145X) 223
Industrial Directory and Brand Names Index of Malawi *see* Chamber of Commerce and Industry of Malawi. Industrial and Trade Directory 235
Industrial Directory of the Commonwealth of Pennsylvania (US) 238
Industrial Directory of Wales (UK) 238
Industrial Educational and Research Foundation. Dialogues *see* Foundation for Business Responsibilities. Dialogues 144
Industrial Engineering Conference. Proceedings (US ISSN 0073-7445) 367
Industrial Enterprises Incorporated. Annual Report (CN) 223
Industrial Fishery Products (US ISSN 0093-8726) 397
Industrial Group Newsletter (UK) 531
Industrial Growth in Tennessee, Annual Report (US ISSN 0099-1872) 223
Industrial Health Foundation. Chemical-Toxicological Series. Bulletin (US ISSN 0073-7488) 495
Industrial Health Foundation. Engineering Series. Bulletin (US ISSN 0073-7496) 495
Industrial Health Foundation. Legal Series Bulletin. (US ISSN 0073-750X) 495, 513
Industrial Health Foundation. Medical Series. Bulletin (US ISSN 0073-7518) 495, 596
Industrial Health Foundation. Nursing Series. Bulletins (US) 495, 614
Industrial Health Foundation. Technical Bulletin. Management Series (US) 495
Industrial Home for the Blind Reporter *see* I H B Reporter 133
Industrial Hygiene Foundation. Chemical-Toxicological Series. Bulletin *see* Industrial Health Foundation. Chemical-Toxicological Series. Bulletin 495
Industrial Hygiene Foundation. Nursing Series. Bulletins *see* Industrial Health Foundation. Nursing Series. Bulletins 495
Industrial Hygiene Foundation of America. Legal Series Bulletin. *see* Industrial Health Foundation. Legal Series Bulletin 495
Industrial Institute for Economic and Social Research. Current Research Projects (SW) 191
Industrial Investment Hong Kong (HK) 203
Industrial Location Handbook/Kogyo Ritchi Handobukku (JA) 223
Industrial Locations in Canada (CN ISSN 0073-7569) 223
Industrial Machinery and Equipment Pricing Guide (US ISSN 0091-8370) 583
Industrial Marketing. *see* Marketing Industriel 218
Industrial Minerals Directory (UK ISSN 0141-5263) 644
Industrial Pharmacology (US ISSN 0093-3589) 684
Industrial Planning and Programming Series (UN ISSN 0073-7577) 200
Industrial Policy Group. Papers (UK) 223

Industrial Pollution Control Yearbook (UK ISSN 0306-8285) 910
Industrial Production: Historical Statistics (FR) 223
Industrial Property Law. Annual (UK) 513, 676
Industrial Relations Chronologies (US) 208
Industrial Relations Research Association. Proceedings of the Annual Spring Meeting (US) 208
Industrial Relations Research Association. Proceedings of the Annual Winter Meeting (US) 208
Industrial Relations Research in Canada(CN ISSN 0073-7593) 208
Industrial Relations Service Bureau's Wisconsin Employment Relations Commission, Reporter *see* Wisconsin. Employment Relations Commission. Reporter 212
Industrial Research in United Kingdom (UK ISSN 0073-7615) 223
Industrial Research Laboratories of the U. S (US ISSN 0073-7623) 851
Industrial Review of Japan (JA ISSN 0537-5452) 186, 223
Industrial Society. Handbook and Diary(UK) 223
Industrial South Africa (SA ISSN 0073-7658) 223
Industrial Structure of Rajasthan (II ISSN 0073-7666) 223
Industrial Ventilation; a Manual of Recommended Practice (US ISSN 0569-4043) 429, 495
Industrial Waste Conference, Purdue University, Lafayette, Indiana. Proceedings (US ISSN 0073-7682) 386
Industrie Adresboek van Noord-Holland (NE) 223
Industrie-Adresboek voor Zuid-Holland *see* Adreslijst van de Zuid-Hollandse Industrie 220
Industrie Camerounaise (CM) 223
Industrie Cimentiere Belge/Belgische Cementnijverheid (BE) 136
Industrie Compass Oesterreich (AU ISSN 0073-7712) 238
Industrie de la Manutention dans les Ports Francais (FR ISSN 0073-7720) 878
Industrie des Pates et Papiers dans les Pays Membres de l'OCDE et la Finlande *see* Pulp and Paper Industry in the O E C D Member Countries and Finland 675
Industrie du Livre au Canada *see* Book Trade in Canada 757
Industrie Electronique Francaise (FR) 355
Industrie et Artisanat (NE ISSN 0073-7739) 851
Industrie Francaise des Moteurs a Combustion Interne (FR ISSN 0073-7747) 871
Industrie- und Handelskammer Hannover-Hildesheim. Information - Kommentare (GW) 179
Industrieabwaesser (GW ISSN 0073-7755) 381
Industriegesellschaft und Recht (GW) 513
Industriegewerkschaft Druck und Papier. Schriftenreihe fuer Betriebsrate (GW ISSN 0170-3463) 675, 733
Industries Directory, Capitals (II ISSN 0073-7763) 238
Industries Directory, Delhi (II ISSN 0073-7771) 238
Industries Directory, Northern India (II ISSN 0073-7798) 238
Industries Electriques et Electroniques (FR) 355
Industries Manufacturieres du Canada: Niveau Infraprovincial *see* Manufacturing Industries of Canada: Sub-Provincial Areas 160
Industries of Japan (JA ISSN 0446-1266) 223
Industrijski Proizvodi (YU) 159
Industry-Engineering Education Series *see* C I E C Proceedings 366
Industry in East Africa (KE ISSN 0073-781X) 223
Inedita (PE) 469

Inedits Russes (FR ISSN 0073-7828) 361, 531
Inequality in Education (US) 910
Infectious Disease Reviews. (US ISSN 0090-6549) 608
Info-Nature (RE) 276
Informacao Cultural (PO) 556
Informacije Rade Koncar (YU ISSN 0033-7536) 355
Informacion Comercial Espanol. Cuadernos Economicos (SP) 186
Informacion Juridica (CU) 513
Informaciones Bayer para la Industria del Caucho (GW) 355
Informaciones Tecnicas para la Construccion (MX) 136
Informacoes sobre a Industria Cinematografica Brasileira. Anuario (BL) 650
Informatie Nederlandse Lexikologie (NE) 545
Informatik (GW) 272
Informatik-Fachberichte (US) 272
Information for Foreign Students Intending to Study at Austrian Universities (AU ISSN 0020-0077) 337
Information about Investment in Tasmania (AT ISSN 0082-1985) 186, 203
Information and Investigation Report/ Joho Chosa Report (JA) 234
Information and Systems Theory (US ISSN 0537-6149) 272
Information Circular - State of Washington, Department of Natural Resources, Division of Geology and Earth Resources *see* Washington (State) Division of Geology and Earth Resources. Information Circular 647
Information, Computer and Communications Policy (FR) 200
Information for Foreign Students Intending to Study at Austrian Universities *see* Information 337
Information Heute (GW) 910
Information Industry Market Place (US ISSN 0000-0450) 264
Information Malaysia (MY) 443
Information Market Place *see* Information Industry Market Place 264
Information on Parana (BL) 186
Information Please Almanac (US ISSN 0073-7860) 361
Information Processing Association of Israel. National Conference on Data Processing. Proceedings (IS ISSN 0073-7879) 272, 531
Information Sciences Series (US) 531
Information Series in Agricultural Economics (US ISSN 0073-7887) 28
Information Series on Agricultural Economics *see* Giannini Foundation of Agricultural Economics. Information Series 28
Information Series - Tennessee State Board of Vocational Education *see* Tennessee. State Board for Vocational Education. Information Series 346
Information Service of the European Communities. Documentation Europeenne - Serie Agricole *see* Documentation Europeenne - Serie Agricole 14
Information Service of the European Communities. Documentation Europeenne - Serie Syndical et Ouvriere *see* Documentation Europeenne - Serie Syndicale et Ouvriere 207
Information Service of the European Communities. Newsletter on the Common Agricultural Policy (EI ISSN 0073-7895) 28
Information Service of the European Communities. Trade Union News (EI ISSN 0073-7909) 506
Information Sources (US) 238
Information Trade Directory *see* Information Industry Market Place 264
Information Veterinaire (CN ISSN 0581-3263) 894

Informational Report- United States Department of the Interior, Mining Enforcement and Safety Administration see U.S. Mining Enforcement and Safety Administration. Informational Report 647

Informationen aus dem Philosophischen Leben in der DDR see Informationsbulletin. aus dem Philosophischem Leben der DDR 689

Informationen ueber Verstaerkte Kunststoffe (GW) 706

Informationen zu Aktuellen Fragen der Sozial- und Wirtschaftpolitik (AU ISSN 0083-6125) 711

Informations Annuelles de Caryosystematique et Cytogenetique (FR ISSN 0073-7917) 115

Informations Bayer pour l'Industrie du Caoutchouc (GW) 777

Informations et Etudes Socialistes (FR ISSN 0073-7925) 711

Informations et Nouveautes Techniques/Ettela'at Va Tazeha-Ye Fanni (IR) 784

Informations Topografiques see Vermessungs-Informationen 377

Informationsaufnahme und Informationsverarbeitung im Lebenden Organismus (GW ISSN 0344-4430) 104

Informationsblaetter zu Nachbarwissenschaften der Ur- und Fruehgeschichte (GW) 61

Informationsbulletin. aus dem Philosophischem Leben der DDR (GE) 689

Informationsdienst Uebersetzungen (GE) 531

Informationsdienst Verpackung (AU) 672

Informatique dans les Administrations Francaises (FR) 272, 742

Informatique dans les Entreprises Publiques (FR) 531

Informator Archeologiczny (PL ISSN 0085-1876) 61

Informator dla Kandydaton na Studia Podyplomowe i Doktoranckie (PL) 337

Informator Nauki Polskiej (PL ISSN 0537-667X) 784

Informator Robotniczy (PL) 361

Informatore Farmaceutico (IT ISSN 0073-7984) 684

Informe Anual de las Actividades de las Unidades Operativas de Salud en el Programa de Planificacion Familiar del Ministerio de Salud (EC) 132

Informe de Operacion de las Principales Empresas Productoras y Distribuidoras de Energia Electrica de Costa Rica (CR ISSN 0074-0047) 355

Informe del C I M M Y T Sobre Mejoramiento de Maiz see C I M M Y T Report on Maize Improvement 42

Informe del C I M M Y T Sobre Mejoramiento de Trigo see C I M M Y T Report on Wheat Improvement 42

Informes J. E. N. (Junta de Energia Nuclear) (SP ISSN 0081-3397) 703

Informozioni e Attualita Mondiali (IT) 596

Infoterm Series (International Information Centre for Terminology, Vienna) (GW) 545

Infrared Information Exchange. Proceedings (US) 355

Ingenieria. Boletin Informativo (CK ISSN 0073-7992) 367

Ingenieurbauten (US) 375

Ingenieurwissenschaftliche Bibliothek/ Engineering Science Library (US) 367

Ingenioeren Indkoebsbog (DK ISSN 0446-2491) 223, 238

Ingenioersvetenskapsakademien. Transportforskningskommission. Rapporter (SW) 862

Inglis Lecture (US ISSN 0073-800X) 318

Ingresos y Egresos de la Familias en la Republica Mexicana (MX) 186

Ingresos y Egresos de la Poblacion de Mexico see Ingresos y Egresos de la Familias en la Republica Mexicana 186

Ingrid (GW) 900

Initiation. Serie Textes, Bibliographies (FR ISSN 0073-8034) 91

Initiation a la Linguistique. Serie A. Lectures (FR ISSN 0073-8018) 545

Initiation a la Linguistique. Serie B. Problemes et Methodes (FR ISSN 0073-8026) 545

Initiations et Etudes Africaines see Institut Fondamental d'Afrique Noire. Initiations et Etudes Africaines 440

Initiative (AU) 258

Inklings (US ISSN 0190-0234) 565

Inland River Guide (US) 878

Inland River Record (US) 878

Inlet (US ISSN 0085-1884) 580

Inmersion y Ciencia (SP) 310

Innovative Graduate Programs Directory (US ISSN 0363-2601) 337

Innovative Programs for Child Care, Evaluation Report see California. Department of Education. Office of Program Evaluation and Research. Innovative Programs for Child Care: Evaluation Report 804

Innsbrucker Beitraege zur Musikwissenschaft (AU) 659

Innsbrucker Universitaetsreden (AU) 337

Inorganic Chemistry Concepts (US) 251

Inorganic Chemistry of the Main Group Elements (UK ISSN 0305-697X) 251

Inorganic Chemistry of the Transition Elements (UK ISSN 0305-9774) 251

Inorganic Reaction Mechanisms (UK ISSN 0305-8255) 251, 255

Inorganic Syntheses Series (US ISSN 0073-8077) 255

Inquiry into the Future (KO) 443

Ins and Outs (NE ISSN 0167-3696) 556

Inscape (US ISSN 0020-1774) 580

Inscape (US ISSN 0094-2715) 580

Inscape (Pasadena) see Inscape 580

Inschriften Griechischer Staedte aus Kleinasien (GW) 61

Inscriptions (US) 469

INSEAD Address Book/I N S E A D Address Book (UK ISSN 0304-4270) 215

Insecta Matsumurana (JA ISSN 0020-1804) 121

Insecticide and Acaricide Tests (US) 121

Insects of Micronesia (US ISSN 0073-8115) 121

Insects of Virginia (US ISSN 0098-1222) 121

Insel-Almanach (GW ISSN 0443-2460) 565

Inseminacao Artificial (BL) 45

Inside (CN ISSN 0380-2957) 565

Inside Outside Bankstreet (US) 349

Insiders Baseball Compendium (US) 910

Insiders Baseball Fact Book (US) 824

Insiders' Guide to the Colleges (US ISSN 0093-5220) 263

Insight (AT) 711

Insights (US ISSN 0073-8123) 318

Insite (Year) (US) 405

INSPEC Reports (UK ISSN 0308-8111) 272, 531

INSPEC Thesaurus (UK) 355

Inspiration Three (US ISSN 0092-9018) 765

Institucion Principe de Viana. Coleccion Historia (SP) 455

Institut Africain de Developpement Economique et de Planification. Collection d'Etudes sur le Developpement Economique et Social see African Institute for Economic Development and Planning. Series in Economic and Social Development 199

Institut Agricole du Canada. Liste des Membres see Agricultural Institute of Canada. Membership Directory 11

Institut Archeologique du Luxembourg. Annales (BE) 61

Institut Armoricain de Recherches Historiques, Rennes. (Publication) see Universite de Rennes. Institut Armoricain de Recherches Economiques et Humaines. (Publication) 464

Institut Belge d'Information et de Documentation. Repertoire de l'Information (BE ISSN 0073-8166) 759

Institut Belge de Science Politique. Bibliotheque. Nouvelle Serie (BE ISSN 0073-8131) 711

Institut Belge de Science Politique. Bibliotheque. Serie Documents (BE ISSN 0073-814X) 711

Institut Belge de Science Politique. Documents (BE ISSN 0073-8158) 711

Institut Canadien d'Education des Adultes Cahiers see I. C. E. A. Cahiers 329

Institut Canadien de l'Information Scientifique et Technique. Rapport Annuel see Canada Institute for Scientific and Technical Information. Annual Report 780

Institut Catholique d'Arts et Metiers de Lille Annuaire see I C A M Annuaire 367

Institut Catholique de Paris. Annuaire (FR) 774

Institut Collegial Europeen. Bulletin (FR ISSN 0073-8174) 318

Institut d'Astronomie et de Geophysique Georges Lemaitre. Publications (BE) 82, 304

Institut d'Economie Regionale Bourgogne-Franche-Comte. Cahiers (FR) 186

Institut d'Emission d'Outre Mer, Paris. Rapport d'Activite (FR ISSN 0073-8247) 200

Institut d'Emission Malgache. Rapport d'Activite see Banque Centrale de la Republique Malgache. Rapport d'Activite 170

Institut d'Etudes du Developpement. Cahiers (FR) 200

Institut d'Etudes Politiques de Paris. Livret (FR ISSN 0078-995X) 711

Institut d'Etudes Slaves. Lexiques (FR ISSN 0154-0157) 545

Institut d'Etudes Slaves, Paris. Annuaire(FR ISSN 0078-9968) 910

Institut d'Etudes Slaves, Paris. Bibliotheque Russe (FR ISSN 0078-9976) 565

Institut d'Etudes Slaves, Paris. Collection de Grammaires (FR ISSN 0078-9984) 545

Institut d'Etudes Slaves, Paris. Collection de Manuels (FR ISSN 0078-9992) 545

Institut d'Etudes Slaves, Paris. Collection Historique (FR ISSN 0079-0001) 455

Institut d'Etudes Slaves, Paris. Documents Pedagogiques (FR ISSN 0300-2594) 545

Institut d'Etudes Slaves, Paris. Textes (FR ISSN 0079-001X) 565

Institut d'Etudes Slaves, Paris. Travaux (FR ISSN 0079-0028) 455, 545, 565

Institut d'Hessarek. Archives see Institute Razi. Archives 894

Institut de Droit International. Annuaire (SZ ISSN 0073-8182) 523

Institut de France. Annuaire (FR ISSN 0073-8190) 491, 784

Institut de la Communaute Europeenne pour les Etudes Universitaires. Recherche. Research (EI) 337

Institut de Linguistique de Louvain. Bibliotheque de la C I L L (BE) 545

Institut de Linguistique de Louvain. Cahiers. Cours et Documents (BE) 545

Institut de Medecine Legale et de Medecine Sociale. Archives (FR ISSN 0075-9473) 612

Institut de Recherche et d'Histoire des Textes, Paris. Documents, Etudes et Repertoires (FR ISSN 0073-8212) 565

Institut der Deutschen Wirtschaft. Gewerkschaftsreport (GW ISSN 0084-9782) 506

Institut des Banquiers Canadiens. Programmes d'Education see Institute of Canadian Bankers. Educational Programs 174

Institut des Etudes Occitanes. Publications (FR ISSN 0073-8263) 565

Institut des Hautes Etudes de l'Amerique Latine. Centre d'Etudes Politiques, Economiques et Sociales. Publications Multigraphiees. (FR ISSN 0073-828X) 469, 711, 798

Institut des Hautes Etudes de l'Amerique Latine. Travaux et Memoires (FR ISSN 0073-8298) 469, 711

Institut des Peches Maritimes. Bulletin (MR ISSN 0069-0821) 397

Institut Eksperimental'noi Meteorologii. Trudy (UR) 633

Institut "Finanzen und Steuern." Gruene Briefe (GW ISSN 0067-9941) 174, 230

Institut "Finanzen und Steuern." Schriftenreihe (GW ISSN 0067-995X) 174, 230

Institut Fondamental d'Afrique Noire. Catalogues et Documents (SG ISSN 0070-2617) 440

Institut Fondamental d'Afrique Noire. Initiations et Etudes Africaines (SG ISSN 0070-2625) 440

Institut Fondamental d'Afrique Noire. Memoires (SG ISSN 0070-2633) 440

Institut Fondamental d'Afrique Noire. Rapport Annuel (SG) 806

Institut Francais d'Archeologie d'Istanbul. Bibliotheque Archeologique et Historique (FR ISSN 0537-779X) 61, 670

Institut Francais d'Etudes Andines. Travaux (PE) 50

Institut Francais d'Indologie. Publications (II ISSN 0073-8352) 443, 565

Institut Francais de Pondichery. Section Scientifique et Technique. Travaux (II ISSN 0073-8336) 784

Institut Francais de Pondichery. Section Scientifique et Technique. Travaux. Hors Serie (II ISSN 0073-8344) 784

Institut Francais des Experts Comptables. Cahiers (FR) 167

Institut Francais des Sciences Administratives. (Publications) (FR) 215

Institut Francais du Petrole. Collection Colloques et Seminaires (FR ISSN 0073-8360) 679

Institut Francais du Petrole. Rapport Annuel (FR ISSN 0073-8379) 679

Institut fuer Allgemeine Botanik und Botanischer Garten. Mitteilungen (GW) 115

Institut fuer Angewandte Geodaesie. Mitteilungen (GW ISSN 0071-9196) 423

Institut fuer Asienkunde. Schriften (GW ISSN 0073-8387) 443, 711

Institut fuer den Wissenschaftlichen Film. Publikationen zu Wissenschaftlichen Filmen. Sektion Biologie (GW ISSN 0073-8417) 104, 650

Institut fuer den Wissenschaftlichen Film. Publikationen zu Wissenschaftlichen Filmen. Sektion Ethnologie (GW ISSN 0341-5910) 50, 650

Institut fuer den Wissenschaftlichen Film. Publikationen zu Wissenschaftlichen Filmen. Sektion Geschichte, Publizistik (GW ISSN 0341-5937) 318, 433, 650

Institut fuer den Wissenschaftlichen Film. Publikationen zu Wissenschaftlichen Filmen. Sektion Medizin (GW ISSN 0341-5929) 596, 650

Institut fuer den Wissenschaftlichen Film. Publikationen zu Wissenschaftlichen Filmen. Sektion Technische Wissenschaften, Naturwissenschaften (GW ISSN 0073-8433) 650, 851
Institut fuer den Wissenschaftlichen Film. Publikationen zu Wissenschaftlichen Filmen. Sektion Voelkerkunde see Institut fuer den Wissenschaftlichen Film. Publikationen zu Wissenschaftlichen Filmen. Sektion Ethnologie 650
Institut fuer Europaeische Geschichte, Mainz. Veroeffentlichungen. Abteilung Universalgeschichte. Beihefte (GW ISSN 0170-365X) 433
Institut fuer Europaeische Geschichte, Mainz. Veroeffentlichungen. Abteilung Universitaetsgeschichte und Abteilung fuer Abendlaendische Religionsphilosophie see Institut fuer Europaeische Gesichte, Mainz. Veroeffentlichungen. Abteilung Universalgeschichte und Abteilung Religionsgeschichte 433
Institut fuer Europaeische Geschichte, Mainz. Veroeffentlichungen. Abteilung Universalgeschichte und Abteilung Religionsgeschichte (GW) 433, 765
Institut fuer Europaeische Geschichte, Mainz. Vortraege. Abteilung Universalgesschichte und Abteilung fuer Abendlaendische Religionsphilosophie see Institut fuer Europaeische Geschichte, Mainz. Vortraege. Abteilung Universalgesschichte und Abteilung Religionsgeschichte 433
Institut fuer Europaeische Geschichte, Mainz. Vortraege. Abteilung Universalgesschichte und Abteilung Religionsgeschichte (GW) 433, 765
Institut fuer Festkoerperforschung Bulletin see I F F Bulletin 703
Institut fuer Gegenwartsvolkskunde. Mitteilungen (AU) 402
Institut fuer Gewerbeforschung, Vienna. Taetigkeitsbericht (AU ISSN 0073-8468) 223
Institut fuer Iberoamerika-Kunde. Schriftenreihe (GW ISSN 0073-8948) 200, 721
Institut fuer Internationales Recht und Internationale Beziehungen. Schriftenreihe (SZ) 523
Institut fuer Konfliktforschung. Schriftenreihe (SZ ISSN 0344-1849) 513, 736, 814
Institut fuer Meeresforschung, Bremerhaven. Veroeffentlichungen (GW ISSN 0068-0915) 104, 310
Institut fuer Ostrecht. Studien (GW ISSN 0073-8492) 513
Institut fuer Politologische Zeitfragen Information. Reihe S: Subversion see I P Z Information. Reihe S: Subversion 711
Institut fuer Raumordnung. Mitteilungen. see Forschungen zur Raumentwicklung 484
Institut fuer Reaktorsicherheit der Technischen Ueberwachungs-Vereine. Taetigkeitsbericht (GW) 367
Institut Geographique du Congo. Rapport see Institut Geographique du Zaire. Rapport Annuel 423
Institut Geographique du Zaire. Rapport Annuel (ZR ISSN 0443-3173) 423
Institut Henri Poincare. Groupe d'Etude d'Analyse Ultrametrique. Exposes (FR) 586
Institut Henri Poincare. Seminaire Paul Kree. Exposes (FR) 586
Institut Historique Belge de Rome. Bibliotheque (BE ISSN 0073-8522) 455
Institut Historique Belge de Rome. Bulletin (BE ISSN 0073-8530) 455
Institut Historique et Archeologique Neerlandais de Stamboull. Publications (NE ISSN 0073-8549) 61, 443

Institut Jules Destree. Collection: Connaitre la Wallonie see Connaitre la Wallonie 431
Institut Jules Destree. Collection: Etudes et Documents see Institut Jules Destree. Etudes et Documents 455
Institut Jules Destree. Etudes et Documents (BE ISSN 0073-8557) 455
Institut Michel Pacha. Annales (FR ISSN 0073-8565) 126
Institut Mondial du Phosphate Congress Proceedings see I M P H O S Congress Proceedings 373
Institut Napoleon. Revue (FR ISSN 0020-2371) 433
Institut National de la Recherche Agronomique de Tunisie. Documents Techniques (TI ISSN 0020-238X) 16
Institut National de Preparation Professionnelle. Cahier (ZR) 208
Institut National des Industries Extractives. Rapport Annuel (BE) 644
Institut National des Langues et Civilisations Orientales. Livret de l'Etudiant (FR) 443
Institut National Genevois. Acts (SZ) 491
Institut National pour l'Etude et la Recherche Agronomique. Rapport Annuel (ZR) 16
Institut Oceanographique. Memoires (MC ISSN 0304-5714) 310
Institut Orientaliste de Louvain. Publications (BE) 670
Institut Panafricain pour le Developpement. Centre d'Etudes et de Recherches Appliquees. Evaluation du Seminaire sur la Methodologie du Management des Projets (CM) 200, 215
Institut Panafricain pour le Developpement. Centre de Formation au Management des Projets. Bilan des Activities (CM) 200, 215
Institut Panafricain pour le Developpement. Travaux Manuscrits (CM) 28, 200
Institut Pasteur d'Algerie. Archives (AE ISSN 0020-2460) 123, 608
Institut Pasteur de Lille. Annales (FR ISSN 0073-8573) 123
Institut Pasteur Hellenique. Archives (GR ISSN 0004-6620) 123, 608
Institut Royal de Patrimoine Artistique. Bulletin / Koninklijk Instituut voor het Kunstpatrimonium. Bulletin (BE ISSN 0085-1892) 75
Institut Teknologi Mara. Laporan Tahunan see Mara Institute of Technology. Annual Report 338
Institut Vodnogo Transporta, Leningrad. Gidrotekhnicheskaya Laboratoriya. Materialy (IT) 381
Institut za Arhitekturu i Urbanizam Srbije. Zbornik Radova (YU) 69, 485
Institut za Kriminoloska i Sociloska Istrazivanja. Zbornik (YU) 281, 814
Instituta et Monumenta. Series I: Monumenta (IT ISSN 0073-8611) 660
Instituta et Monumenta. Series II. Instituta (IT) 660
Institute for Arab Studies. Publications and Studies (IS) 475
Institute for Balkan Studies. Publications / Idryma Meleton Chersonesou Aimou. Ekthoseis (GR ISSN 0073-862X) 455
Institute for Clinical Science. Proficiency Test Service. Report (US ISSN 0073-8638) 596
Institute for Cross-Cultural Research Studies see I C R Studies 814
Institute for Defense Analyses. Papers (US ISSN 0073-8654) 639
Institute for Defense Analyses. Reports (US ISSN 0073-8662) 639
Institute for Defense Analyses. Studies (US ISSN 0073-8670) 639
Institute for Developing Economics Special Papers see I D E Special Papers 196

Institute for Development of Educational Activities, Inc. Monographs see I/D/E/A Monographs 318
Institute for Development of Educational Activities, Inc. Occasional Papers see I/D/E/A Occasional Papers 318
Institute for Fermentation, Osaka. Annual Report see Institute for Fermentation, Osaka. Research Communications 123
Institute for Fermentation, Osaka. Research Communications / Hakko Kenkyusho Hokoku (JA ISSN 0073-8751) 123
Institute for Financial Management and Research, Madras Publications see I F M R Publications 215
Institute for Industrial Research and Standards Occasional Report Series see I I R S Occasional Report Series 851
Institute for Land and Water Management Research. Miscellaneous Reprints see Instituut voor Cultuurtechniek en Waterhuishouding. Verspreide Overdrukken 36
Institute for Land and Water Management Research. Technical Bulletin see Instituut voor Cultuurtechniek en Waterhuishouding. Technical Bulletin 36
Institute for Management Education and Development. Report (IO) 215
Institute for Migration, Turku. Migration Studies see Migration Institute. Migration Studies 728
Institute for Monetary Research. Monographs (US ISSN 0073-8778) 174
Institute for Palestine Studies. Arabic Annual Documentary Series (US) 443
Institute for Palestine Studies. Basic Documents Series (US ISSN 0073-8794) 443
Institute for Palestine Studies. International Annual Documentary Series (US ISSN 0073-8808) 443
Institute for Palestine Studies. Monograph Series (US ISSN 0073-8816) 443
Institute for Palestine Studies. Yearbook Series (US) 443
Institute for Petroleum Research and Geophysics, Holon, Israel. Report (IS ISSN 0073-8832) 304, 679
Institute for Psychoanalysis. Newsletter (US) 736
Institute for Psychoanalysis. Report see Institute for Psychoanalysis. Newsletter 736
Institute for Research on Public Policy. Occasional Papers (CN) 742
Institute for Rewriting Indian History. Annual Report and General Meeting Invitation (II) 433
Institute for Scientific Information Journal Citation Reports see I S I Journal Citation Reports 783
Institute for Sea Training. Journal (JA) 310
Institute for Social and Economic Change Monograph see I S E C Monograph 186
Institute for Studies in American Music. Monographs (US) 660
Institute for the Comprehensive Study of Lotus Sutra. Journal / Hokke Bunka Kenkyu (JA) 771
Institute for the Study of Earth and Man Newsletter (US) 61, 289
Institute for the Study of Human Issues, Inc. Occasional Papers in Social Change see S H I Occasional Papers in Social Change 814
Institute for the Study of Man in Africa Occasional Papers see I S M A Occasional Papers 50
Institute for the Study of Man in Africa Papers see I S M A Papers 50
Institute Jules Destree. Collection: Figures de Wallonie see Figures de Wallonie 453
Institute of Actuaries. Year Book (UK ISSN 0073-8980) 499
Institute of Actuaries of Australia. Transactions (AT) 499

Institute of Actuaries of Australia and New Zealand. Transactions see Institute of Actuaries of Australia. Transactions 499
Institute of Actuaries Students' Society. Journal (UK ISSN 0020-269X) 499
Institute of Agricultural Engineering, Bet Dagan. Scientific Activities (IS) 32
Institute of Applied Manpower Research Reports see I.A.M.R. Reports 208
Institute of Bankers in Pakistan. Council. Report and Accounts (PK ISSN 0073-8999) 174
Institute of British Geographers. Special Publication (UK ISSN 0073-9006) 423
Institute of Building. Year Book and Directory of Members (UK ISSN 0073-9014) 136
Institute of Canadian Bankers. Educational Programs (CN ISSN 0318-4315) 174
Institute of Certified Travel Agents Directory see I C T A Directory 887
Institute of Chartered Accountants in Australia. Annual Report and Accounts (AT) 167
Institute of Chartered Accountants in England and Wales. Management Information Series (UK ISSN 0073-9030) 167
Institute of Chartered Accountants in England and Wales. Practice Administration Series, Exposure Drafts and Statements of Standard Accounting Practice (UK ISSN 0073-9049) 167
Institute of Chartered Accountants of Guyana. Newsletter (GY ISSN 0380-4011) 167
Institute of Chartered Accountants of Scotland. Official Directory (UK ISSN 0073-9057) 167
Institute of Chartered Financial Analysts Monograph Series see C F A Monograph Series 905
Institute of Clerk of Works' of Great Britain Incorporated. Year Book (UK ISSN 0073-9073) 136
Institute of Cornish Studies. Special Bibliography (UK) 392
Institute of Developing Economies. Annual Report (JA) 200
Institute of Development Management. Report of the Activities of the Institute (TZ) 215
Institute of Development Studies. Annual Report (UK) 200, 223
Institute of Economic Affairs. Occasional Papers (UK ISSN 0073-909X) 145
Institute of Economic Affairs. Research Monographs (UK ISSN 0073-9103) 145
Institute of Economic Growth, Delhi. Census Studies (II ISSN 0070-3311) 727
Institute of Economic Research. Publications on Demography (II) 727
Institute of Economic Research. Publications on Economics (II) 145
Institute of Economic Research. Publications on Family Planning (II) 132
Institute of Electrical and Electronics Engineers. Southwestern I E E E Conference and Exhibition. Record see I E E E Region 5 Conference. Record 354
Institute of Electrical and Electronics Engineers, Inc. Computer Society Conference on Pattern Recognition and Image Processing. Proceedings see I E E E Computer Society Conference on Pattern Recognition and Image Processing. Proceedings 272
Institute of Electrical and Electronics Engineers, Inc. International Conference on Acoustics, Speech and Signal Processing. Conference Record see I E E E International Conference on Acoustics, Speech and Signal Processing. Conference Record 354

Institute of Electrical and Electronics Engineers, Inc. International Symposium on Electrical Insulation. Conference Record *see* I E E E International Symposium on Electrical Insulation. Conference Record *354*

Institute of Electrical and Electronics Engineers, Inc. Rural Electric Power Conference. Papers Presented *see* I E E E Rural Electric Power Conference. Papers Presented *355*

Institute of Electrical and Electronics Engineers, Inc. Student Papers *see* I E E E Student Papers *355*

Institute of Electrical and Electronics Engineers, Inc. Vehicular Technology Conference. Record *see* I E E E Vehicular Technology Conference. Record *871*

Institute of Electrolysis. List of Qualified Operators (UK) *85*

Institute of Energy. Northern Ireland Section. Year Book (UK) *679*

Institute of Energy. Papers of the National Convention (UK) *679*

Institute of Energy. Symposium Series. (UK) *373*

Institute of Environmental Sciences. Annual Meeting. Proceedings (US ISSN 0073-9227) *104, 367, 386*

Institute of Environmental Sciences. Tutorial Series (US ISSN 0073-9251) *104, 367, 386*

Institute of European Studies. Announcements (US ISSN 0073-926X) *342*

Institute of European Studies. Papers and Addresses of the Annual Conference and Academic Council (US ISSN 0073-9278) *342*

Institute of Field and Garden Crops. Scientific Activities (IS) *36*

Institute of Food Technologists World Directory and Guide *see* I F T World Directory and Guide *405*

Institute of Forest Genetics, Suwon, Korea. Research Report (KO ISSN 0073-9294) *409*

Institute of Freshwater Research, Drottningholm. Report (SW ISSN 0082-0032) *308*

Institute of Fuel. Northern Ireland Section. Year Book *see* Institute of Energy. Northern Ireland Section. Year Book *679*

Institute of Fuel. Papers of the National Convention *see* Institute of Energy. Papers of the National Convention *679*

Institute of Fuel. Symposium Series *see* Institute of Energy. Symposium Series *373*

Institute of Gas Technology. Annual Report (US) *679*

Institute of Gas Technology. Director's Report *see* Institute of Gas Technology. Annual Report *679*

Institute of Geological Sciences, London. Statistical Summary of the Mineral Industry *see* World Mineral Statistics *648*

Institute of Geoscience. Annual Report (JA) *304*

Institute of Human Biology, Papua New Guinea. Monograph Series *see* Papua New Guinea Institute of Medical Research. Monograph Series *598*

Institute of International Politics and Economics. Documentation Bulletin (YU) *159, 717*

Institute of Jamaica, Kingston. West India Reference Library. Jamaican Accessions *see* Jamaican National Bibliography *92*

Institute of Judicial Administration. Juvenile Justice Standards Project. Juvenile Law Litigation Directory *see* Juvenile Law Litigation Directory *514*

Institute of Labor and Industrial Relations. Policy Papers in Human Resources and Industrial Relations (US ISSN 0073-9421) *208*

Institute of Labor and Industrial Relations. Reprint Series (US ISSN 0073-943X) *208*

Institute of Management Sciences. Symposium on Planning. Proceedings(US ISSN 0082-0911) *215*

Institute of Market Officers. List of Members and Proceedings of the Annual General Meetings (UK) *749*

Institute of Mathematical Sciences, Madras, India. Proceedings of Symposia and Summer Schools *see* Symposia on Theoretical Physics and Mathematics *589*

Institute of Mathematics and Its Applications. Proceedings (UK) *586*

Institute of Medical Laboratory Sciences. London, Annual Report (UK) *612*

Institute of Medical Laboratory Technology. London. Annual Report *see* Institute of Medical Laboratory Sciences. London, Annual Report *612*

Institute of Mennonite Studies Series (US ISSN 0073-9456) *776*

Institute of Mining and Metallurgy. Transactions: Metallurgical Series *see* Vysoka Skola Banska. Sbornik Vedeckych Praci: Rada Hutnicka *630*

Institute of Nuclear Agriculture. Annual Report (BG) *16*

Institute of Nuclear Materials Management. Proceedings of Annual Meeting (US ISSN 0073-9472) *367, 703*

Institute of Oceanographic Sciences. Annual Report (UK ISSN 0309-4472) *310*

Institute of Oceanographic Sciences. Collected Reprints (UK ISSN 0309-7463) *310*

Institute of Paper Chemistry. Bibliographic Series (US ISSN 0073-9480) *676*

Institute of Pastoral Psychology. Proceedings *see* Pastoral Psychology Series *737*

Institute of Patent Attorneys of Australia. Annual Proceedings (AT) *513, 676*

Institute of Physical and Chemical Research Cyclotron Progress Report *see* I P C R Cyclotron Progress Report *703*

Institute of Physical and Chemical Research Cyclotron Report *see* I P C R Cyclotron Report *703*

Institute of Physical and Chemical Research Cyclotron Technical Report *see* I P C R Cyclotron Technical Report *703*

Institute of Physics, London. Conference Series. Proceedings (UK ISSN 0305-2346) *696*

Institute of Phytopathological Research. Annual Report *see* Instituut voor Plantenziektenkundig Onderzoek. Jaarverslag *36*

Institute of Phytopathological Research. Communications *see* Instituut voor Plantenziektenkundig Onderzoek. Mededeling *36*

Institute of Psychophysical Research. Proceedings (UK ISSN 0073-9561) *736*

Institute of Public Administration, Dublin. Administration Yearbook and Diary (IE ISSN 0073-9596) *743*

Institute of Public Administration, Dublin. Annual Report (IE ISSN 0073-9588) *743*

Institute of Public Administration, Khartoum. Occasional Papers (SJ ISSN 0073-9618) *743*

Institute of Public Administration, Khartoum. Proceedings of the Annual Round Table Conference (SJ ISSN 0073-9626) *743*

Institute of Public Administration of Canada. Bulletin (CN ISSN 0380-3988) *743*

Institute of Public Health. Annual Report/Kokuritsu Koshu Eisei-in Nenpo (JA) *752*

Institute of Purchasing and Supply. Yearbook (UK ISSN 0073-9650) *218*

Institute of Quantity Surveyors. Year Book (UK ISSN 0073-9669) *136*

Institute of Race Relations. Annual Report (UK) *814*

Institute of Refrigeration, London. Proceedings (UK ISSN 0073-9677) *429*

Institute of Secretariat Training and Management. Annual Report (II ISSN 0304-7083) *219*

Institute of Social and Economic Research. Reports (US) *145*

Institute of Social, Economic and Government Research. Reports *see* Institute of Social and Economic Research. Reports *145*

Institute of Southeast Asian Studies. Annual Report (SI) *443*

Institute of Southeast Asian Studies. Annual Review (SI) *443*

Institute of Southeast Asian Studies. Current Issues Seminar Series (SI) *443*

Institute of Southeast Asian Studies. Field Reports Series (SI) *443*

Institute of Southeast Asian Studies. Library Bulletin (SI ISSN 0073-9723) *531*

Institute of Southeast Asian Studies. Monographs Series (SI) *444*

Institute of Southeast Asian Studies. Occasional Paper (SI ISSN 0073-9731) *444*

Institute of Southeast Asian Studies. Oral History Programmes (SI) *444*

Institute of Southeast Asian Studies. Proceedings and International Conferences (SI) *444*

Institute of Southeast Asian Studies. Research Notes and Discussion Series (SI) *444*

Institute of Standards and Industrial Research of Iran Yearbook *see* I S I R I Yearbook *637*

Institute of Statistical Mathematics. Annual Report/Tokei Suri Kenkyusho Nenpo (JA) *586*

Institute of the Black World. Black Paper (US) *392*

Institute of the Black World. Occasional Paper Series (US) *392*

Institute of United States Studies Monographs (UK ISSN 0306-5499) *469*

Institute on Coal Mine Health and Safety. (Proceedings) (US) *644*

Institute on Pluralism and Group Identity. Working Paper Series (US) *392, 814*

Institute Orientaliste de Louvain. Publications *see* Universite Catholique de Louvain. Institut Orientaliste. Publications *446*

Institute Razi. Archives (IR) *894*

Institutet foer Metallforskning. Forskningsverksamheten (SW ISSN 0015-7953) *628*

Institution of Civil Engineers Yearbook *see* I C E Yearbook *375*

Institution of Electrical Engineers Conference Publication Series *see* I E E Conference Publication Series *354*

Institution of Electrical Engineers Control Engineering Series *see* I E E Control Engineering Series *354*

Institution of Electrical Engineers Electromagnetic Waves Series *see* I E E Electromagnetic Waves Series *355*

Institution of Electrical Engineers Medical Electronics Monographs *see* I E E Medical Electronics Monographs *596*

Institution of Electrical Engineers Monograph Series *see* I E E Monograph Series *355*

Institution of Electrical Engineers Reprint Series *see* I. E. E. Reprint Series *355*

Institution of Electrical Engineers Reviews *see* I E E Reviews *910*

Institution of Engineers (India). Directory (II ISSN 0073-9782) *367*

Institution of Engineers (India). Yearbook *see* Institution of Engineers (India). Directory *367*

Institution of Engineers. Year Book (BG ISSN 0073-9219) *367*

Institution of Engineers, Australia. General Engineering Transactions (AT) *367*

Institution of Engineers, Australia. National Conference Publications (AT) *367*

Institution of Engineers of Ireland. Register of Chartered Engineers and Members (IE) *368*

Institution of Engineers of Ireland. Transactions (IE ISSN 0073-9790) *368*

Institution of Engineers, Singapore. Journal (SI) *368*

Institution of Engineers, Sri Lanka. Year Book (CE) *368*

Institution of Mechanical Engineers. Proceedings (UK ISSN 0020-3483) *382*

Institution of Railway Signal Engineers. Proceedings (UK ISSN 0073-9839) *873*

Institution of Structural Engineers. Yearbook (UK ISSN 0073-9847) *375*

Institutiones Mathematicae (IT) *586*

Instituto Antartico Chileno. Boletin (CL ISSN 0073-9863) *447*

Instituto Antartico Chileno. Contribution. Serie Cientifica (CL ISSN 0073-9871) *447*

Instituto Antartico Chileno. Publicacion *see* Instituto Antartico Chileno. Contribution. Serie Cientifica *447*

Instituto Antituberculoso Francisco Moragas. Publicaciones (SP ISSN 0302-7406) *623*

Instituto Bahiano do Fumo. Boletim Informativo: Comercio Exterior - Esportacao de Fumo Em Folhas (BL) *861*

Instituto Biologico da Bahia. Boletim (BL ISSN 0020-3661) *104*

Instituto Brasileiro de Economia. Centro de Estudos Agricolas. Agropecuaria (BL) *16*

Instituto Brasileiro do Cafe. Departamento Economico. Anuario Estatistico do Cafe (BL) *86*

Instituto Brasileiro do Cafe. Departamento Economico. Anuario Estatistico do Cafe. *see* Instituto Brasileiro do Cafe. Departamento Economico. Anuario Estatistico do Cafe *86*

Instituto Brasileiro do Cafe. Grupo Executivo de Racionalizacao de Cafeicultura. Relatorio (BL) *86*

Instituto Brasileiro do Couro, Calcados e Afins. Sistema de Informacao Estatistica para e Industria Nacional de Couros: Boletim de Informacoes (BL) *524*

Instituto Butantan. Coletanea de Trabalhos (BL) *596*

Instituto Butantan. Memorias (BL ISSN 0073-9901) *128*

Instituto Caro y Cuervo. Publicaciones (CK) *491*

Instituto Caro y Cuervo. Seminario Andres Bello. Cuadernos (CK) *545*

Instituto Caro y Cuervo. Serie Bibliografica (CK ISSN 0073-991X) *91*

Instituto Caro y Cuervo. Serie Granada Entreabierta (CK) *565*

Instituto Caro y Cuervo. Serie Minor (CK ISSN 0073-9928) *545, 565*

Instituto Centro Americano de Investigacion y Tecnologia Industrial. Publicaciones Geologicas (GT ISSN 0073-9936) *295*

Instituto Centroamericano de Administracion Publica. Administracion, Desarrollo, Integracion *see* Administracion, Desarrollo, Integracion *739*

Instituto Centroamericano de Administracion Publica. Serie 100. Aspectos Humanos de la Administracion (CR ISSN 0073-9944) *743*

Instituto Centroamericano de Administracion Publica. Serie 200. Ciencia de la Administracion (CR ISSN 0073-9952) *743*

1392 INSTITUTO CENTROAMERICANO

Instituto Centroamericano de Administracion Publica. Serie 300: Investigacion (CR ISSN 0073-9960) 743

Instituto Centroamericano de Administracion Publica. Serie 400: Economia y Finanzas (CR ISSN 0073-9979) 743

Instituto Centroamericano de Administracion Publica. Serie 600: Informes de Seminarios (CR ISSN 0073-9995) 743

Instituto Centroamericano de Administracion Publica. Serie 700: Materiales de Informacion (CR ISSN 0074-0004) 743

Instituto Centroamericano de Administracion Publica. Serie 800: Metodologia de la Administracion (CR ISSN 0074-0012) 743

Instituto Centroamericano de Administracion Publica. Serie 900: Miscelaneas (CR ISSN 0074-0020) 743

Instituto Centroamericano de Administracion Publica Lista de Nuevas Adquisiciones see I C A P Lista de Nuevas Adquisiciones 539

Instituto Colombiano Agropecuario. Boletin Tecnico (CK ISSN 0538-0391) 16

Instituto Colombiano Agropecuario. Catalogo de Publicaciones Periodicas (CK) 24

Instituto Colombiano de Pedagogia. Boletin Informativo y de Documentacion (CK) 337

Instituto Colombiano para el Fomento de la Educacion Superior. Boletin Bibliografico (CK) 91, 337

Instituto Costarricense de Cultura Hispanica. Publicacion (CR ISSN 0074-0039) 469

Instituto Costarricense de Turismo.. Memoria Anual (CR) 887

Instituto Cultural Italo-Brasileiro. Caderno (BL) 721

Instituto de Anthropologia e Historia del Estado Carabobo. Boletin (CK) 50, 61

Instituto de Antropologia e Historia. Anuario (VE) 50, 469

Instituto de Biologia Marinha e Oceanografia. Trabalhos see Universidade Federal de Pernambuco. Departamento de Oceanografia. Centro de Tecnologia. Trabalhos Oceanograficas 108

Instituto de Botanica "Dr. Goncalo Sampaio". Publicacoes. 3 Serie (PO ISSN 0473-0658) 115

Instituto de Ciencia Politica Rafael Bielsa. Anuario (AG ISSN 0074-0063) 711

Instituto de Credito Agricola y Pecuario. Informe Annual (VE) 186

Instituto de Desarrollo de los Recursos Naturales Renovables. Oficina de Planeacion. Estadisticas Pesqueras (CK) 401

Instituto de Desarrollo Urbano Noticiero I.D.U.N. see Noticiero I.D.U.N 486

Instituto de Estudios Andinos. Cuadernos (PE) 814

Instituto de Estudios Andinos. Trabajo de Campo (PE) 50

Instituto de Estudios de Administracion Local. Secretariado Iberoamericano de Municipios. Boletin de Informacion (SP ISSN 0210-0975) 749

Instituto de Estudios de Administracion Local. Seminarios y Simposios de Investigacion, Conclusiones (SP) 749

Instituto de Estudios Gerundenses. Anales (SP) 392

Instituto de Estudios Gerundenses. Serie Monografica (SP) 392

Instituto de Estudios Madrilenos. Anales (SP ISSN 0584-6374) 491

Instituto de Estudios Peruanos. Analisis Economico (PE) 186

Instituto de Estudios Peruanos. Coleccion Minima (PE) 814

Instituto de Estudios Peruanos. Estudios de la Sociedad Rural (PE) 814

Instituto de Estudios Peruanos. Historia Andina (PE) 469

Instituto de Estudios Peruanos. Proyecto de Estudios Etnologicos del Valle de Chancay. Monografia (PE) 50

Instituto de Estudios Tarraconenses Ramon Berenguer IV. Publicacion (SP ISSN 0534-3364) 455

Instituto de Estudios Tarraconenses Ramon Berenguer IV. Seccion de Estudios Juridicos. Publicacion (SP) 513

Instituto de Fomento Pesquero. Boletin Cientifico see Serie Investigacion Pesquera 400

Instituto de Fomento Pesquero. Informes Pesquero (CL) 397

Instituto de Higiene e Medicina Tropical. Anais (PO ISSN 0075-9767) 608, 752

Instituto de Investigacao Agronomica de Angola. Divisao de Meteorologia Agricola. Anuario (AO) 16, 633

Instituto de Investigacao Agronomica de Angola. Relatorio (AO ISSN 0078-2254) 16

Instituto de Investigacao Agronomica de Angola. Serie Cientifica (AO ISSN 0078-2262) 16

Instituto de Investigacao Agronomica de Angola. Serie Tecnica (AO ISSN 0078-2270) 16

Instituto de Investigacao Agronomica de Mocambique. Comunicacoes see Agronomia Mocambicana 12

Instituto de Investigacao Cientifica de Angola. Bibliograficas Tematicas (AO ISSN 0074-008X) 794

Instituto de Investigacao Cientifica de Angola. Memorias e Trabalhos (AO ISSN 0074-0098) 784

Instituto de Investigacao Cientifica de Angola. Relatorios e Communicacoes (AO ISSN 0003-343X) 784

Instituto de Investigacion de Recursos Naturales. Publicacion (CL ISSN 0538-0898) 276

Instituto de Investigaciones Geologicas. Boletin (CL ISSN 0020-3939) 295

Instituto de Investigaciones sobre Recursos Bioticos. Serie: Estudio Botanico y Ecologico de la Region del Rio Uxpanapa (MX) 115

Instituto de Investigaciones Veterinarias. Boletin see Veterinaria Tropical 895

Instituto de la Patagonia. Anales (CL ISSN 0085-1922) 104, 469

Instituto de Nutricion de Centro America y Panama. Informe Anual (UN ISSN 0533-4179) 666

Instituto de Pesca, Sao Paulo. Boletim (BL ISSN 0046-9939) 397

Instituto de Pesca, Sao Paulo. Boletim. Serie de Divulgacao (BL) 397

Instituto de Planejamento Economico e Social. Estudos para O Planejamento (BL) 223

Instituto de Planejamento Economico e Social. Relatorios de Pesquisa (BL) 814

Instituto de Planejamento Economico e Social Serie Monografica see I P E A Serie Monografica 223

Instituto de Tecnologia de Alimentos. Coletanea (BL ISSN 0100-350X) 405, 666

Instituto de Tecnologia de Alimentos. Instrucoes Praticas (BL ISSN 0074-0144) 666

Instituto de Tecnologia de Alimentos. Instrucoes Tecnicas (BL ISSN 0074-0152) 666

Instituto de Tonantzintla. Boletin (MX ISSN 0303-7584) 82

Instituto de Vivienda y Urbanismo. Memoria Presentada por el Director General see Panama. Ministerio de Vivienda. Memoria 486

Instituto de Zoologia "Dr. Augusto Nobre". Publicacoes (PO ISSN 0020-4021) 45

Instituto de Zootecnia. Facultad de Veterinaria. Catalogo de Publicaciones (SP) 45

Instituto del Mar del Peru. Boletin (PE ISSN 0458-7766) 397

Instituto del Mar del Peru. Informe. (PE ISSN 0458-7774) 397

Instituto di Biologia Marina. Serie Contribuciones see Instituto Nacional de Investigacion y Desarrollo Pesquero. Serie Contribuciones 310

Instituto do Azeite e Produtos Oleaginosos. Boletim (PO) 36

Instituto do Patrimonio Historico e Artistico Nacional. Publicacoes (BL) 491

Instituto Espanol de Oceanografia. Boletin (SP ISSN 0074-0195) 310

Instituto Espanol de Oceanografia. Trabajos (SP ISSN 0074-0209) 310

Instituto Femenino de Investigaciones Historicas. Anuario (PY) 469, 900

Instituto Florestal. Boletim Tecnico (BL ISSN 0100-3151) 409

Instituto Forestal. Boletin Estadistico (CL) 412

Instituto Geografico Agustin Codazzi. Informe de Labores (CK) 423

Instituto Hondureno de Seguridad Social. Departamento de Estadistica y Procesamiento de Datos. Anuario Estadistico (HO ISSN 0074-0233) 499

Instituto Indigenista Interamericano Serie de Ediciones Especiales (MX) 50

Instituto Interamericano de Ciencias Agricola de la OEA. Hemispheric and Humanistic Projection: I I C A Report (CR) 910

Instituto Interamericano de Ciencios Agricolas de la OEA. Documentos Oficiales (CR ISSN 0301-4355) 16

Instituto Interamericano del Nino. Publicaciones Sobre Servicio Social (UY) 806

Instituto Internacional de Historia del Derecho Indiano. Actas y Estudios (SP) 521

Instituto Joaquim Nabuco de Pesquisas Sociais. Serie Cursos e Conferencias (BL) 814

Instituto Joaquim Nabuco de Pesquisas Sociais. Serie Estudos e Pesquisas (BL) 814

Instituto Joaquim Nabuco de Pesquisas Sociais. Serie Monografias (BL) 798

Instituto Linguistico de Verano. Documentos de Trabajo (PE) 545

Instituto Linguistico de Verano. Serie Sintactica (CK) 545

Instituto Linguistico de Verano en Colombia. Bibliografia (CK) 555

Instituto Maternal, Lisbon. Revista Clinica see Maternidade Dr. Alfredo da Costa, Lisbon. Arquivo Clinico 615

Instituto Nacional de Antropologia e Historia. Anales (MX ISSN 0076-7557) 50, 469

Instituto Nacional de Antropologia e Historia. Coleccion Breve (MX ISSN 0076-7565) 75

Instituto Nacional de Antropologia e Historia. Departamento de Monumentos Coloniales. (Publicaciones) (MX ISSN 0076-7506) 75

Instituto Nacional de Antropologia e Historia. Investigaciones (MX ISSN 0076-7573) 50

Instituto Nacional de Antropologia e Historia. Obras Varias (MX ISSN 0076-7603) 50, 469

Instituto Nacional de Antropologia e Historia. Serie Cientifica (MX ISSN 0076-7611) 50

Instituto Nacional de Antropologia e Historia. Serie Culturas del Mundo (MX ISSN 0076-762X) 433

Instituto Nacional de Antropologia e Historia. Sociedad de Alumnos. (Publicaciones) (MX ISSN 0076-7549) 50

Instituto Nacional de Cancerologia, Mexico. Revista (MX ISSN 0076-7131) 605

Instituto Nacional de Colonizacao e Reforma Agraria. Coordenadoria Regional do Parana. Sinopse do Cooperativismo No Parana (BL) 181

Instituto Nacional de Energia Nuclear. Publication (MX ISSN 0076-7476) 703

Instituto Nacional de Enfermedades Neoplasicas. Trabajos de Investigacion Clinica y Experimental (PE ISSN 0079-1083) 605

Instituto Nacional de Industria Resumen de Actividades I N I (Year) see Resumen de Actividades I N I (Year) 225

Instituto Nacional de Investigacion y Desarrollo Pesquero. Memoria (AG ISSN 0325-6987) 397

Instituto Nacional de Investigacion y Desarrollo Pesquero. Serie Contribuciones (AG ISSN 0325-6790) 310

Instituto Nacional de Investigaciones Agronomicas. Anales see Spain. Instituto Nacional de Investigaciones Agrarias. Anales. Serie: Produccion Animal 46

Instituto Nacional de Investigaciones Folkloricas. Cuadernos (AG) 402

Instituto Nacional de Investigaciones Geologico Mineras. Publicaciones Geologicas Especiales del Ingeominas (CK) 295

Instituto Nacional de Investigaciones sobre Recursos Bioticos Informa see I N I R E B Informa 103

Instituto Nacional de Medicina Legal de Colombia. Revista (CK) 613

Instituto Nacional de Seguros. Informe Anual see Instituto Nacional de Seguros Memoria Anual 499

Instituto Nacional de Seguros. Memoria Anual I.N.S. see Instituto Nacional de Seguros Memoria Anual 499

Instituto Nacional de Seguros Memoria Anual (CR) 499

Instituto para el Desarrollo de Ejecutivos en la Argentina. Noticias (AG) 215

Instituto Peruano de Derecho Agrario. Cuadernos Agrarios (PE) 16, 513

Instituto Politecnico Nacional. Escuela National de Ciencias Biologicas. Revista Anales (MX ISSN 0026-1777) 128

Instituto Provincial de Investigaciones y Estudios Toledanos. Publicaciones (SP) 455

Instituto Quimico de Sarria see I.Q.S 246

Instituto Sperimentale Talassografico, Trieste. Pubblicazione (IT ISSN 0082-6456) 310

Instituto Superior de Estudios Eclesiasticos. Libro Anual (MX) 765

Instituto Tecnologico y de Estudios Superiores. Publicaciones. Serie: Catalogos de Biblioteca (MX ISSN 0074-0306) 92

Instituto Tecnologico y de Estudios Superiores. Publicaciones. Serie Historia (MX ISSN 0077-1228) 469

Instituto Tecnologico y de Estudios Superiores. Publicaciones. Serie Letras (MX ISSN 0077-1236) 565

Instituto Teologico del Uruguay. Cuadernos (UY) 765

Instituto Torcuato di Tella. Centro de Estudios Urbanos Regionales. Documentos de Trabajo (AG ISSN 0074-0330) 485

Instituto Torcuato di Tella. Centro de Investigaciones Economicas. Documentos de Trabajo (AG ISSN 0074-0349) 145

Instituto Torcuato di Tella. Centro de Investigaciones Economicas. Informes de Investigacion (AG) 186

Instituto Torcuato di Tella. Centro de Investigaciones Sociales. Documentos de Trabajo (AG ISSN 0074-0357) 814

Instituto y Observatorio de Marina. Efemerides Astronomicas (SP ISSN 0080-5971) 82

Instituto y Observatorio de Marina. Observaciones Meteorologicas, Magneticas y Sismicas. Anales (SP ISSN 0080-5955) 304

Institutul Agronomic "Dr. Petru Groza". Buletinul (RM) 16

Institutul Agronomic "Ion Ionescu de la Brad". Lucrari Stiintifice. I. Agronomie - Horticultura (RM ISSN 0075-3505) 16

Institutul Agronomic "Ion Ionescu de la Brad" Lucrari Stiintifice II Zootehnie - Medicina Veterinara (RM ISSN 0075-3513) 45, 894
Institutul de Cercetari Pentru Cultura Cartofului si Sfeclei de Zahar, Brasov. Anale. Cartoful (RM ISSN 0074-0373) 36
Institutul de Cercetari Pentru Cultura Cartofului si Sfeclei de Zahar, Brasov. Anale. Sfecla de Zahar (RM ISSN 0074-0381) 36
Institutul de Fizica Atomica. Sesiunea Stiintifica Anuala de Comunicari; Program si Rezumate (RM) 703
Institutul de Geologie si Geofizica. Anuarul (RM) 295
Institutul de Geologie si Geofizica. Dari de Seama ale Sedintelor (RM ISSN 0068-306X) 304
Institutul de Geologie si Geofizica. Studii Tehnice si Economice (RM) 295
Institutul de Istorie si Arheologie "A. D. Xenopol". Anuarul (RM ISSN 0074-039X) 61, 455
Institutul de Meteorologie si Hidrologie. Studii de Climatologie (RM) 633
Institutul de Mine Petrosani. Lucrari Stiintifice (RM) 295
Institutul de Speologie Emil Racovitza. Travaux (RM ISSN 0065-0498) 304
Institutul de Studii, Cercetari si Proiectari Pentru Gospodarirea Apelor. Studii de Economia Apelor. (RM) 896
Institutul Pedagogic Oradea. Lucrari Stiintifice Seria Biologic (RM) 104
Institutul Pedagogic Oradea. Lucrari Stiintifice Seria Chimie (RM) 246
Institutul Pedagogic Oradea. Lucrari Stiintifice Seria Educatie Fizica si Sport (RM) 820
Institutul Pedagogic Oradea. Lucrari Stiintifice: Seria Fizica (RM) 696
Institutul Pedagogic Oradea. Lucrari Stiintifice: Seria Geografie (RM) 423
Institutul Pedagogic Oradea. Lucrari Stiintifice: Seria Istorie (RM) 433
Institutul Pedagogic Oradea. Lucrari Stiintifice: Seria Lingvistica (RM) 545
Institutul Pedagogic Oradea. Lucrari Stiintifice: Seria Literatura (RM) 565
Institutul Pedagogic Oradea. Lucrari Stiintifice: Seria Matematica (RM) 586
Institutul Pedagogic Oradea. Lucrari Stiintifice: Seria Pedagogie, Psihologie, Metodica (RM) 318, 736
Institutul Pedagogic Oradea. Lucrari Stiintifice: Seria Stiinte Sociale (RM) 798
Institutum Canarium Nachrichten see I. C. Nachrichten 50
Instituut voor Cultuurtechniek en Waterhuishouding. Jaarverslag (NE ISSN 0511-0688) 36
Instituut voor Cultuurtechniek en Waterhuishouding. Mededeling (NE ISSN 0074-0411) 36
Instituut voor Cultuurtechniek en Waterhuishouding. Technical Bulletin/Institute for Land and Water Management Research. Technical Bulletin (NE ISSN 0074-042X) 36
Instituut voor Cultuurtechniek en Waterhuishouding. Verspreide Overdrukken/Institute for Land and Water Management Research. Miscellaneous Reprints (NE ISSN 0074-0438) 36
Instituut voor Kernphysisch Onderzoek. Annual Report (NE) 696
Instituut voor Kernphysisch Onderzoek. Progress Report (NE) 910
Instituut voor Plantenziektenkundig Onderzoek. Jaarverslag (NE ISSN 0074-0446) 36
Instituut voor Plantenziektenkundig Onderzoek. Mededeling/Institute of Phytopathological Research. Communications (NE ISSN 0019-0349) 36

Instituut voor Rassenonderzoek van Landbouwgewassen. Jaarverslag see Rijksinstituut voor het Rassenonderzoek van Cultuurgewassen. Jaarverslag 39
Instituut voor Rassenonderzoek van Landbouwgewassen. Mededelingen see Rijksinstituut voor het Rassenonderzoek van Cultuurgewassen. Mededelingen 39
Instituut voor Veevoedingsonderzoek. Report (NE) 45
Instituut voor Veevoedingsonderzoek "Hoorn." Report see Instituut voor Veevoedingsonderzoek. Report 45
Instituut voor Veevoedingsonderzoek "Hoorn" Jaarverslag see Instituut voor Veevoedingsonderzoek Jaarverslag 45
Instituut voor Veevoedingsonderzoek Jaarverslag (NE) 45
Instructional Cassette Recordings Catalog see Music & Musicians: Instructional Cassette Recordings Catalog 133
Instrument and Control Systems Buyers Guide (US ISSN 0074-0497) 496
Instrument Maintenance Management (US) 496
Instrument Society of America. I S A Final Control Elements Symposium. Final Control Elements; Proceedings (US ISSN 0091-7699) 496
Instrument Society of America. International I S A Aerospace Instrumentation Symposium. Tutorial Proceedings see Fundamentals of Aerospace Instrumentation 8
Instrument Society of America. Standards and Practices for Instrumentation (US ISSN 0074-0527) 496
Instrument Society of America Mining and Metallurgy Instrumentation Symposium. Proceedings see I S A Mining and Metallurgy Instrumentation Symposium. Proceedings 628
Instrument Society of America Transducer Compendium see I S A Transducer Compendium 496
Instrumentation in Nuclear Medicine (US ISSN 0074-0543) 622
Instrumentation in the Chemical and Petroleum Industry (US ISSN 0074-0551) 373, 496
Instrumentation in the Cryogenic Industry (US) 496
Instrumentation in the Mining and Metallurgy Industries (US) 644
Instrumentation in the Power Industry (US ISSN 0074-056X) 496
Instrumentation in the Pulp and Paper Industry (US) 675
Instruments and Experimental Techniques (English translation of: Pribory i Teknika Eksperimenta) (US ISSN 0020-4412) 496
Instruments, Electronics and Automation Purchasing Directory see Directory of Instruments, Electronics, Automation 271
Instytut Automatyki Systemow Energetycznych. Prace (PL ISSN 0084-2788) 368
Instytut Badan Jadrowych. Zaklad Radiobiologii i Ochrony Zdrowia. Prace Doswiadczaine (PL ISSN 0074-0640) 112, 622, 752
Instytut Elektrotechniki. Prace (PL ISSN 0032-6216) 355
Instytut Gospodarki Wodnej. Prace (PL ISSN 0074-0586) 896
Instytut Lacznosci. Prace (PL ISSN 0020-451X) 264
Instytut Meteorologii i Gospodarki Wodnej. Prace (PL) 308, 633
Instytut Slaski. Kommunikaty. Seria Niemcoznawcza (PL ISSN 0074-0616) 455
Instytut Slaski. Wydawnictwa (PL ISSN 0074-0632) 455
Instytut Transportu Samochodowego. Zeszyty Naukowe (PL) 862
Insulation/Circuits Desk Manual (US) 355
Insulation /Circuits Directory / Encyclopedia see Insulation/Circuits Desk Manual 355

Insulation Directory/Encyclopedia see Insulation/Circuits Desk Manual 355
Insulation Handbook (UK) 136, 395
Insurance Almanac; Who, What, When and Where in Insurance (US ISSN 0074-0675) 499
Insurance Casebook (US ISSN 0074-0683) 499
Insurance Directory and Year Book (UK ISSN 0074-0691) 499
Insurance Directory of New Zealand (NZ) 499
Insurance Facts (US ISSN 0074-0713) 499
Insurance in Australia and New Zealand (AT) 499
Insurance Institute of Canada. Report (CN ISSN 0074-0721) 499
Insurance Law Symposium see Drake Law Review 511
Insurance Life/Non-Life Annual Statistics (JA ISSN 0085-1930) 499
Insurance Market Place (US ISSN 0538-2629) 499
Insurance Marketer (CN ISSN 0317-1272) 499
Insurance Periodicals Index (US ISSN 0074-073X) 3, 502
Insurance Statistics of Fiji (FJ) 502
Insurance Statistics Yearbook (KO) 502
Intellectual Property Law Review (US) 677
Intelligence Digest Special Briefs (UK) 711
Intensivmedizinische Praxis (GW ISSN 0303-6200) 604
Inter-Acao (BL) 337
Inter-African Phyto-Sanitary Commission. Publication (CM ISSN 0534-4859) 36
Inter-American Bar Association. Conference Proceedings (US) 513
Inter-American Bar Association. Letter to Members (US) 513
Inter-American Centre for Agricultural Documentation and Information. Documentacion e Informacion Agricola (CR ISSN 0301-438X) 25
Interamerican Children's Institute. Report of the General Director (UY) 258, 806
Inter-American Commission of Women. News Bulletin (US ISSN 0538-2912) 900
Inter-American Commission of Women. Noticiero (US ISSN 0538-2920) 900
Inter-American Commission of Women. Special Assembly. Final Act/ Comision Interamericana de Mujeres. Asamblea Extraordinaria. Acta Final (US ISSN 0074-0764) 718
Inter-American Conference on Indian Life. Acta/Congresos Indigenistas Interamericanos. Acta (MX ISSN 0074-0810) 50
Inter-American Council for Education, Science, and Culture. Final Report (US ISSN 0074-0829) 318, 784
Inter-American Council of Commerce and Production. Uruguayan Section. Publicaciones (UY ISSN 0538-3048) 200
Inter-American Development Bank. Annual Report (US ISSN 0074-087X) 174, 200
Inter-American Development Bank. Board of Governors. Anales (de la) Reunion see Inter-American Development Bank. Board of Governors. Proceedings of the Meeting 174
Inter-American Development Bank. Board of Governors. Proceedings of the Meeting (US ISSN 0074-0861) 174, 200
Inter-American Development Bank. Informe Anual see Inter-American Development Bank. Annual Report 174
Inter-American Development Bank. Institute for Latin American Integration. Annual Report (AG ISSN 0538-3110) 200

Inter-American Development Bank. Statement of Loans see Inter-American Development Bank. Annual Report 174
Inter-American Economic and Social Council. Final Report of the Annual Meeting at the Ministerial Level (US ISSN 0074-0918) 469, 798
Inter-American Institute of Agricultural Sciences. Bibliografias see Inter-American Centre for Agricultural Documentation and Information. Documentacion e Informacion Agricola 25
Inter-American Institute of Agricultural Sciences. Center for Training and Research. Bibliotecologia y Documentacion see Inter-American Centre for Agricultural Documentation and Information. Documentacion e Informacion Agricola 25
Inter-American Institute of Agricultural Sciences. Informe Anual (CR ISSN 0538-3277) 16
Inter-American Institute of Agricultural Sciences. Technical Advisory Council. Junta Directiva. Reunion Anual. Resoluciones y Documentos (CR) 16
Inter-American Institute of Agricultural Sciences. Technical Advisory Council. Report of the Meeting see Inter-American Institute of Agricultural Sciences. Technical Advisory Council. Junta Directiva. Reunion Anual. Resoluciones y Documentos 16
Inter-American Nuclear Energy Commission. Final Report (US ISSN 0074-0942) 363, 368, 703
Inter-American Press Association. Committee on Freedom of the Press. Report (US ISSN 0579-6695) 505, 711
Inter-American Press Association. Minutes of the Annual Meeting (US) 505
Inter-American Statistical Institute. Committee on Improvement of National Statistics. Report (US ISSN 0538-3579) 841
Inter-American Tropical Tuna Commission. Bulletin/Comision Interamericana del Atun Tropical. Boletin (US ISSN 0074-0993) 398
Inter-American Tropical Tuna Commission. Data Report (US ISSN 0538-3609) 397
Inter-American Tropical Tuna Commission. Informe Anual. Annual Report (US ISSN 0074-1000) 398
Inter-American Yearbook on Human Rights see Anuario Interamericano de Derechos Humanos 522
Interauteurs (FR ISSN 0020-515X) 565, 677
Interavia A B C (SZ ISSN 0074-1116) 8
Inter-Church Committee on Human Rights in Latin America. Newsletter (CN ISSN 0226-661X) 718
Intercity Truck Tonnage see Motor Carrier Statistical Summary 882
Intercollege Research (US) 910
Intercollegiate Bibliography. New Cases in Administration (US ISSN 0095-490X) 159
Intercom (CN ISSN 0383-6061) 772
Intercom; the Newsletter for California Community College Librarians (US) 531
Intercommunity - International Community Education see Youth International 343
Intercultural Research Institute Translation Series (II) 491
Interdisciplinary Topics in Gerontology (SZ ISSN 0074-1132) 428
Inter-Documentation Company. Newsletter (SZ ISSN 0074-1019) 539
Interest-Adjusted Index (US ISSN 0095-5221) 499
Interface N.Z. (NZ) 910
Interference Technology Engineers Master see I T E M 355
Interferences, Arts, Lettres (FR ISSN 0074-1140) 75, 565

Intergovernmental Committee for European Migration. Review of Achievements (SZ) 727
Intergovernmental Council for Automatic Data Processing. Proceedings of Conference (SP ISSN 0085-1981) 272
Intergovernmental Council of Copper Exporting Countries. Statistical Bulletin (FR) 648
Intergovernmental Oceanographic Commission. Technical Series (UN ISSN 0074-1175) 310
Inter-Guiana Geological Conference. Proceedings (GY ISSN 0074-1027) 295
Interior Design Catalogues (UK) 502, 503
Intermediate Teacher (CN ISSN 0020-563X) 318
Internal Publications Directory (US) 759
Internal Revenue Code (US) 230
Internal Revenue Guide to Your Federal Income Tax (US ISSN 0074-1205) 230
Internal Trade of Iran (IR ISSN 0074-1213) 182
Internationaal Havenkongres. Verslagboek see International Harbour Congress. Proceedings 878
International Academy of Indian Culture. Report (II ISSN 0074-123X) 444
International Academy of Legal Medicine and of Social Medicine. (Congress Reports) (IT ISSN 0074-1248) 613
International Academy of Oral Pathology. Proceedings (US ISSN 0074-1256) 609
International Actuarial Congress. Transactions (SZ ISSN 0074-1264) 499
International Advances in Surgical Oncology (US ISSN 0190-1575) 605
International Advertising Association. United Kingdom Chapter. Concise Guide to International Markets (UK ISSN 0538-4168) 5
International Advertising Association. World Advertising Expenditures see World Advertising Expenditures 6
International Aeronautic Federation. Annual Information Bulletin (FR) 8
International Aeronautic Federation. General Conference Minutes (of the) Business Meetings see International Aeronautic Federation. Annual Information Bulletin 8
International Aeronautic Federation. Latest World Records see World Aeronautical Records 11
International African Seminar. Studies Presented and Discussed (US ISSN 0534-655X) 440
International Agency for Research on Cancer. I A R C Technical Publications see I A R C Scientific Publications 605
International Agency for Research on Cancer Monographs on the Evaluation of the Carcinogenic Risk of Chemicals to Humans see I A R C Monographs on the Evaluation of the Carcinogenic Risk of Chemicals to Humans 605
International Agency for Research on Cancer Scientific Publications see I A R C Scientific Publications 605
International Air Transport Association. Annual Report (CN) 868
International Air Transport Association. Bulletin see International Air Transport Association. Annual Report 868
International Air Transport Association. Review see I A T A Review 868
International Alban Berg Society. Newsletter (US ISSN 0538-4257) 660
International Amateur Basketball Federation. Official Report of the World Congress (GW ISSN 0534-6622) 824
International Anatomical Congress. Proceedings (UR ISSN 0074-1353) 104, 596

International and Comparative Broadcasting (US) 267
International and Intercultural Communication Annual (US) 318
International Animated Film Association. Bulletin (RM ISSN 0538-4281) 650
International Antenna and Propagation Symposium Program and Digest (US) 355
International Antonio Vivaldi Society. Informations see Vivaldi Informations 664
International Archery Federation. Bulletin Officiel (UK ISSN 0074-137X) 820
International Archives of the History of Ideas see Archives Internationales d'Histoire des Idees 687
International Arthurian Society. Bibliographical Bulletin (US ISSN 0074-1388) 403, 578
International Arthurian Society. Report of Congress/Societe Internationale Arthurienne. Rapports du Congres (UK ISSN 0074-1396) 565
International Association for Bridge and Structural Engineering. Final Report (of Congress) (SZ ISSN 0074-1418) 375
International Association for Bridge and Structural Engineering. Preliminary Report (of Congress) (SZ ISSN 0074-1434) 375
International Association for Bridge and Structural Engineering. Reports of the Working Commissions (SZ ISSN 0074-1442) 375
International Association for Byzantine Studies. Bulletin d'Information et de Coordination (GR ISSN 0571-5857) 455, 475
International Association for Cereal Chemistry. Working and Discussion Meetings Reports (AU ISSN 0074-1450) 405
International Association for Child Psychiatry and Allied Professions. Yearbook (US ISSN 0074-963X) 619
International Association for Classical Archaeology. Proceedings of Congress (IT ISSN 0074-1469) 61, 259
International Association for Cross-Cultural Psychology. International Conference. Selected Papers (NE) 736
International Association for Hydraulic Research. Congress Proceedings (NE ISSN 0074-1477) 381
International Association for Mass Communication Research. Letter from the President (UK ISSN 0579-3742) 264
International Association for Mass Communications Research. Monographs (UK) 264
International Association for Scientific Study of Mental Deficiency. Proceedings of International Congress (UK ISSN 0085-2007) 619
International Association for Shell and Spatial Structures. Bulletin (SP ISSN 0538-4400) 375
International Association for the Advancement of Educational Research. Congress Reports see World Association for Educational Research. Congress Reports 325
International Association for the Advancement of Ethnology and Eugenics Monographs see I A A E E Monographs 50
International Association for the Advancement of Ethnology and Eugenics Reprint see I A A E E Reprint 50
International Association for the Evaluation of Educational Achievement (Australia). Newsletter (AT ISSN 0310-5571) 342
International Association for the Exchange of Students for Technical Experience. Annual Report (GR ISSN 0538-4427) 342

International Association for the Physical Science of Oceanography. Proces-Verbaux (FR) 310
International Association of Applied Psychology. Proceedings of Congress (BE ISSN 0074-1574) 736
International Association of Biological Standardization. (Symposium Proceedings) (SZ) 603
International Association of Chain Stores. Report of Plenary Session (FR ISSN 0074-1582) 218
International Association of Coroners and Medical Examiners. Proceedings (US) 626, 743
International Association of Democratic Lawyers. Congress Report (BE ISSN 0074-1604) 513
International Association of Fish and Wildlife Agencies. Proceedings of the Convention (US ISSN 0161-3332) 276
International Association of French Studies. Cahiers (FR ISSN 0571-5865) 565
International Association of Geodesy. Central Bureau for Satellite Geodesy. Bibliography (GR) 428
International Association of Geodesy. Central Bureau for Satellite Geodesy. Information Bulletin (GR ISSN 0081-0312) 423
International Association of Geodesy. Commission Permanente des Marees Terrestres. Marees Terrestres Bulletin d'Information (BE ISSN 0542-6766) 423
International Association of Geomagnetism and Aeronomy News see I A G A News 304
International Association of Hydrogeologists. Memoires (FR ISSN 0579-6733) 308
International Association of Law Libraries. Directory (US) 531
International Association of Liberal Religious Women. Newsletter (GW) 765
International Association of Logopedics and Phoniatrics. Reports of Congress (SZ ISSN 0074-1655) 619
International Association of Meteorology and Atmospheric Physics News Bulletin see I A M P News Bulletin 633
International Association of Milk Control Agencies. Proceedings of Annual Meetings (US ISSN 0074-1671) 41
International Association of Museums of Arms and Military History. Congress Reports (UK ISSN 0074-168X) 639, 653
International Association of Philatelic Journalists. Bulletin (FR ISSN 0074-1701) 478
International Association of Philatelic Journalists. Minutes of Annual Congresses (FR ISSN 0074-171X) 479
International Association of Philatelic Journalists Yearbook see A. I. J. P. Yearbook 478
International Association of Physical Education and Sports for Girls and Women. Proceedings of the International Congress (JA ISSN 0074-1728) 820
International Association of Plant Breeders for the Protection of Plant Varieties. Congress Reports (NE ISSN 0074-7408) 115
International Association of School Librarianship Conference Proceedings see I A S L Conference Proceedings 530
International Association of Schools of Social Work. Directory of Members and Constitution see I A S S W Directory; Member Schools and Associations 806
International Association of Schools of Social Work Directory; Member Schools and Associations see I A S S W Directory; Member Schools and Associations 806
International Association of Seed Crushers. Proceedings of the Annual Congress (UK ISSN 0074-1736) 16

International Association of State Lotteries. (Reports of Congress) (SZ ISSN 0074-1744) 230
International Association of Technological Universities Libraries Proceedings see I A T U L Proceedings 530
International Association of Thalassotherapy. Congress Reports (FR ISSN 0074-1760) 596
International Association of Theoretical and Applied Limnology. Communications (GW ISSN 0538-4680) 308
International Association of Theoretical and Applied Limnology. Proceedings/Internationale Vereinigung fuer Theoretische und Angewandte Limnologie. Verhandlungen (GW ISSN 0368-0770) 308, 310
International Association of Traffic and Safety Sciences Research see I A T S S Research 871
International Association of Universities. Papers & Reports (UK) 337
International Association of University Professors & Lecturers. Communication (UK ISSN 0018-8492) 337
International Association of Volcanology and Chemistry of the Earth's Interior. Newsletter (IT ISSN 0579-5362) 289, 305
International Association of Workers for Maladjusted Children. Congress Reports (FR ISSN 0074-1787) 345
International Associations of Science and Technology for Development. Proceedings see Simulation 273
International Astronautical Congress. Proceedings see Astronautical Research 7
International Astronautical Federation. Proceedings of the Congress see Astronautical Research 7
International Astronomical Union. General Assembly. Proceedings (NE) 82
International Astronomical Union. Proceedings of Symposia (NE ISSN 0074-1809) 82
International Astronomical Union. Transactions and Highlights (NE ISSN 0080-1372) 82
International Atlantic Salmon Foundation. Special Publication Series (CN) 276, 398
International Atomic Energy Agency. Annual Report (UN ISSN 0085-2023) 368, 703
International Atomic Energy Agency. Law Library. Books and Articles in the I A E A Law Library. List (UN ISSN 0538-4893) 910
International Atomic Energy Agency. Legal Series (UN ISSN 0074-1868) 513, 703
International Atomic Energy Agency. Panel Proceedings Series (UN ISSN 0074-1876) 368, 703
International Atomic Energy Agency. Power Reactors in Member States (UN) 368, 703
International Atomic Energy Agency. Proceedings Series (UN ISSN 0074-1884) 368, 703
International Atomic Energy Agency. Radiation Data for Medical Use; Catalogue see Radiation Dosimetry Data; Catalogue 622
International Atomic Energy Agency. Safety Series (UN ISSN 0074-1892) 752
International Atomic Energy Agency. Technical Directories (UN ISSN 0074-1906) 368, 703
International Atomic Energy Agency. Technical Report Series (UN ISSN 0074-1914) 368, 703
International Atomic Energy Agency Library Film Catalog see I A E A Library Film Catalog 700
International Auction Records (US ISSN 0074-1922) 75
International Author's and Writer's Who's Who (UK ISSN 0143-8263) 97

International Authors and Writers Who's Who (US) *97, 566*
International Baccalaureate Office. Annual Bulletin (SZ ISSN 0074-1973) *319*
International Baccalaureate Office. Semi-Annual Bulletin *see* International Baccalaureate Office. Annual Bulletin *319*
International Badminton Federation. Annual Handbook *see* International Badminton Federation. Annual Statute Book *820*
International Badminton Federation. Annual Statute Book (UK) *820*
International Banff Conference on Man and His Environment. Proceedings (US) *386, 752*
International Beekeeping Congress. Reports (RM ISSN 0074-2007) *16*
International Beilinson Symposium (Proceedings) (SZ) *611*
International Bibliographical and Library Series (US) *531*
International Bibliography of Cropping Systems (PH) *25*
International Bibliography of Dictionaries *see* Fachwoerterbuecher und Lexika. Ein Internationales Verzeichnis *555*
International Bibliography of Directories *see* Internationale Bibliographie der Fachadressbuecher *92*
International Bibliography of Economics *see* International Bibliography of the Social Sciences. Economics *159*
International Bibliography of Historical Sciences (FR ISSN 0074-2015) *438*
International Bibliography of Political Science *see* International Bibliography of the Social Sciences. Political Science *717*
International Bibliography of Research in Marriage and the Family *see* Inventory of Marriage and Family Literature *818*
International Bibliography of Rice Research (PH ISSN 0074-2031) *25*
International Bibliography of Selected Police Literature (UK) *285*
International Bibliography of Social and Cultural Anthropology *see* International Bibliography of the Social Sciences. Social and Cultural Anthropology *56*
International Bibliography of Sociology *see* International Bibliography of the Social Sciences. Sociology *818*
International Bibliography of Studies on Alcohol (US ISSN 0074-204X) *288*
International Bibliography of the Book Trade and Librarianship *see* Fachliteratur zum Buch- und Bibliothekswesen *530*
International Bibliography of the Forensic Sciences (US) *602*
International Bibliography of the Social Sciences. Economics (UK ISSN 0085-204X) *159*
International Bibliography of the Social Sciences. Political Science (UK ISSN 0085-2058) *717*
International Bibliography of the Social Sciences. Social and Cultural Anthropology (UK ISSN 0085-2074) *56*
International Bibliography of the Social Sciences. Sociology (UK ISSN 0085-2066) *818*
International Bibliography on Burns (US ISSN 0090-0575) *602*
International Biennial Exhibition of Prints in Tokyo (JA ISSN 0074-2066) *75*
International Bio-Sciences Monographs (II) *104*
International Biodeterioration Symposium. Proceedings. Biodeterioration of Materials (US) *123*
International Biometeorological Congress. Proceedings *see* Biometeorology; Proceedings *101*
International Biometeorological Congress. Summaries and Reports Presented to the Congress (NE ISSN 0074-2082) *104*

International Biophysics Congress. Abstracts (US) *3, 110*
International Book Design & Production(UK) *759*
International Book Trade Directory (UK) *759*
International Books in Print (GW) *92, 760*
International Botanical Congress. Abstracts of Papers (AT ISSN 0074-2090) *115*
International Botanical Congress. Proceedings (AT) *115*
International Brain Research Organization Monograph Series (US ISSN 0361-0462) *619*
International Brewers' Directory and Soft Drink Guide/Registre International des Brasseurs, Eaux et Limonades (SZ) *86*
International Bureau of Fiscal Documentation. Annual Report (NE ISSN 0074-2104) *230*
International Bureau of Fiscal Documentation. Publication (NE ISSN 0074-2112) *230*
International Business Machines Corp. Agribusiness Symposium. Proceedings *see* I B M Agribusiness Symposium. Proceedings *28*
International Business Machines Corp. Medical Symposium. Proceedings *see* I B M Medical Symposium. Proceedings *596*
International Buyer's Guide of Mobile Air Conditioning (US) *430*
International Buyers Guide of the Music, Record and Tape Industry *see* Billboard's International Buyer's Guide of the Music-Record-Tape Industry *657*
International Cadmium Conference. Proceedings (UK) *628*
International Cargo Handling Coordination Association. Rapports des Comites Nationaux (UK ISSN 0534-7793) *196, 878*
International Catalogue of Films, Filmstrips and Slides on Public Education About Cancer (SZ) *605*
International Catalogue of Films for Public Education About Cancer *see* International Catalogue of Films, Filmstrips and Slides on Public Education About Cancer *605*
International Catalogue of Occupational Safety and Health Films (UN ISSN 0074-2147) *496*
International Catecholamine Symposium. Proceedings (US) *252*
International Catholic Movement for Intellectual Cultural Affairs. Proceedings of the Plenary Assembly *see* Pax Romana *775*
International Cemetery Directory (US ISSN 0074-2155) *414*
International Center of Information on Antibiotics Information Bulletin *see* I C I A Information Bulletin *686*
International Center of Tropical Agriculture. Annual Report (CK) *16*
International Center of Tropical Agriculture. Information Bulletin (CK) *16*
International Center of Tropical Agriculture. Reference Bulletins (CK) *16*
International Center of Tropical Agriculture. Technical Bulletin (CK) *16*
International Centre for Heat and Mass Transfer. Proceedings (US ISSN 0272-880X) *368*
International Centre for Mechanical Sciences (CISM). Courses and Lectures (US) *382*
International Centre for Settlement of Investment Disputes. Annual Report (US ISSN 0074-2163) *203, 523*
International Centre for Theoretical Physics. Annual Report (UN ISSN 0304-7091) *696*
International Centre for Theoretical Physics. Report *see* International Centre for Theoretical Physics. Annual Report *696*
International Centre of Fertilizers. World Congress. Acts (SZ ISSN 0074-2171) *36*

International Centre of Insect Physiology and Ecology. Annual Report (KE) *122, 276*
International Ceramic Congress. Proceedings (FR ISSN 0074-218X) *244*
International Chamber of Commerce. Handbook (FR) *179*
International Chamber of Commerce. Iranian Committee. Publication/Komite-Ye Irani-Ye Otaq-e Bazargani-Ye Beynolmelali. Nashriyeh (IR) *179*
International Chamber of Commerce. United States Council. Report (US ISSN 0538-5466) *179*
International Chemical and Nuclear Corp Symposium on Molecular Biology Proceedings *see* I C N -U C L A Symposium on Molecular Biology Proceedings *119*
International Children's Centre. Paris. Report of the Director-General to the Executive Board (FR ISSN 0538-5490) *256, 814*
International Children's Centre. Paris. Travaux et Documents (FR ISSN 0534-8021) *256, 814*
International Christian Democratic Study and Documentation Center. Bulletin International *see* Christian Democratic World Union. Information Bulletin *709*
International Christian Democratic Study and Documentation Center. Cahiers d'Etudes *see* Christian Democratic Study and Documentation Center. Cahiers d'Etudes *709*
International Christian Democratic Study and Documentation Center. Informations *see* Panorama Democrate Chretien *713*
International Christian University. Institute for Educational Research and Service. Educational Studies/Kokusai Kirisutokyo Daigaku, Kyoiku Kenkyu (JA) *319*
International Christian University. Publications IV-B. Christianity and Culture *see* Humanities, Christianity and Culture *765*
International Chromatography Guide *see* Journal of Chromatographic Science *249*
International Civil Aviation Association. Aeronautical Agreements and Arrangements. Annual Supplement (UN ISSN 0074-221X) *868*
International Civil Aviation Organization. Air Navigation Plan. Africa-Indian Ocean Region (UN ISSN 0074-2287) *868*
International Civil Aviation Organization. Air Navigation Plan. Caribbean and South American Regions. *see* International Civil Aviation Organization. Air Navigation Plan. Caribbean Region *868*
International Civil Aviation Organization. Air Navigation Plan. Caribbean Region (UN) *868*
International Civil Aviation Organization. Air Navigation Plan. European Region (UN ISSN 0074-2309) *868*
International Civil Aviation Organization. Air Navigation Plan. Middle East and South East Asia Regions (UN ISSN 0074-2317) *868*
International Civil Aviation Organization. Air Navigation Plan. North Atlantic, North American and Pacific Regions (UN ISSN 0074-2325) *868*
International Civil Aviation Organization. Airworthiness Committee. Report of Meeting (UN ISSN 0074-2244) *8*
International Civil Aviation Organization. All-Weather Operations Panel. Report of Meeting (UN ISSN 0074-2333) *8*
International Civil Aviation Organization. Assembly. Report and Minutes of the Legal Commission (UN ISSN 0074-2368) *868*

International Civil Aviation Organization. Assembly. Report of the Economic Commission (UN ISSN 0074-2376) *868*
International Civil Aviation Organization. Assembly. Report of the Technical Commission (UN ISSN 0074-2384) *8*
International Civil Aviation Organization. Assembly. Resolutions (UN ISSN 0074-235X) *868*
International Civil Aviation Organization. Automated Data Interchange Systems Panel. Report of Meeting (UN ISSN 0074-2252) *8*
International Civil Aviation Organization. Council. Annual Report (UN) *868*
International Civil Aviation Organization. Digests of Statistics. Series AT. Airport Traffic (UN ISSN 0074-2422) *868*
International Civil Aviation Organization. Digests of Statistics. Series F. Financial Data (UN ISSN 0074-2430) *868*
International Civil Aviation Organization. Digests of Statistics. Series FP. Fleet, Personnel (UN ISSN 0074-2449) *868*
International Civil Aviation Organization. Digests of Statistics. Series R. Civil Aircraft on Register (UN ISSN 0074-2457) *868*
International Civil Aviation Organization. Digests of Statistics. Series T. Traffic (UN ISSN 0074-2465) *868*
International Civil Aviation Organization. Indexes to I C A O Publications. Annual Cumulation (UN ISSN 0074-249X) *11, 866*
International Civil Aviation Organization. Legal Committee. Minutes and Documents (of Sessions) (UN ISSN 0074-2503) *868*
International Civil Aviation Organization. Obstacle Clearance Panel. Report of Meeting (UN ISSN 0074-252X) *8*
International Civil Aviation Organization. (Panel On) Application of Space Techniques Relating to Aviation. Report of Meeting (UN ISSN 0074-2228) *8*
International Civil Aviation Organization. Report of the Air Navigation Conference (UN ISSN 0074-2546) *8*
International Civil Aviation Organization. Sonic Boom Panel. Report of the Meeting (UN ISSN 0074-2562) *9*
International Civil Aviation Organization. Technical Panel on Supersonic Transport. Report of Meeting (UN ISSN 0074-2570) *9*
International Civil Aviation Organization. Visual Aids Panel. Report of Meeting (UN ISSN 0074-2589) *9*
International Civil Aviation Organization Circulars *see* I C A O Circulars *868*
International Claim Association Proceedings (US) *499*
International Clay Conference. Proceedings (IS ISSN 0074-2597) *244*
International Clean Air Congress. Proceedings (US ISSN 0085-2090) *386*
International Coal (US) *196, 644*
International Coal Exploration Symposium. Proceedings (US) *644*
International College of Dentists. European Section. Newsletter (UK) *609*
International College of Dentists. India Section. Newsletter (II ISSN 0074-2600) *609*
International College of Psychosomatic Medicine. Proceedings of the Congress (SZ ISSN 0302-5136) *620*

1396   INTERNATIONAL COLLOQUIUM

International Colloquium on Plant Analysis and Fertilizer Problems. Proceedings (US) 36, 116
International Colloquium on Prospective Biology (Proceedings) (SZ) 612
International Colloquium on Rapid Mixing and Sampling Techniques Applicable to the Study of Biochemical Reactions. Proceedings (US ISSN 0538-5644) 111, 255
International Colloquy About the European Convention on Human Rights. Proceedings (FR) 814
International Commercial Bank of China. Annual Report (CH) 174
International Commercial Law of Nations (US) 513
International Commission for the Conservation of Atlantic Tunas. Report (SP) 128, 276
International Commission for the Northwest Atlantic Fisheries. Annual Report see N A F O Annual Report 398
International Commission for the Northwest Atlantic Fisheries. List of Fishing Vessels see N A F O List of Fishing Vessels 399
International Commission for the Northwest Atlantic Fisheries. Meetings Proceedings see N A F O Meeting Proceedings 399
International Commission for the Northwest Atlantic Fisheries. Redbook see N A F O Scientific Council Meeting Reports 399
International Commission for the Northwest Atlantic Fisheries. Sampling Yearbook see N A F O Sampling Yearbook 399
International Commission for the Northwest Atlantic Fisheries. Selected Papers see N A F O Scientific Council Studies 399
International Commission for the Northwest Atlantic Fisheries. Statistical Bulletin see N A F O Statistical Bulletin 399
International Commission for Uniform Methods of Sugar Analysis. Report of the Proceedings of the Session (UK) 405
International Commission of Agricultural Engineering. Reports of Congress (FR ISSN 0074-2694) 36
International Commission of Maritime History. Colloques. Actes (FR) 878
International Commission of Sugar Technology. Proceedings of the General Assembly (BE ISSN 0074-2708) 405
International Commission on Illumination. Proceedings (FR ISSN 0074-2724) 355
International Commission on Irrigation and Drainage. Congress Reports (II ISSN 0074-2732) 381
International Commission on Irrigation and Drainage. Report (II ISSN 0538-5768) 16, 896
International Commission on Large Dams. Bulletin (FR ISSN 0534-8293) 375
International Commission on Large Dams. Transactions (US ISSN 0074-4115) 375
International Commission on Radiological Protection. Report (US ISSN 0074-2759) 622
International Commission on Trichinellosis. Proceedings (PL ISSN 0074-3356) 608
International Committee against Apartheid, Racism and Colonialism in Southern Africa Bulletin see I C S A Bulletin 718
International Committee for Historical Science. Bulletin d'Information (FR ISSN 0074-2783) 433
International Committee for Standardization in Hematology. Symposia (GW) 613
International Committee of Onomastic Sciences. Congress Proceedings (BE ISSN 0074-2791) 545

International Committee of the Red Cross. Annual Report/Rapport d'Activite/Informe de Actividad/Taetigkeitsbericht (SZ) 806
International Committee on Laboratory Animals. Proceedings of Symposium see International Council for Laboratory Animal Science. Proceedings of the Symposium 596
International Committee on Urgent Anthropological and Ethnological Research. Bulletin (AU ISSN 0538-5865) 50
International Communist (UK ISSN 0140-0649) 711
International Comparative Literature Association. Proceedings of the Congress (GW ISSN 0074-2813) 566
International Computer Bibliography (NE ISSN 0074-283X) 274
International Confederation for Agricultural Credit. Assembly and Congress Reports (SZ ISSN 0074-2856) 28
International Confederation of Free Trade Unions. Features (BE ISSN 0538-5946) 506
International Confederation of Free Trade Unions. World Congress Reports (BE ISSN 0074-2872) 506
International Confederation of Societies of Authors and Composers (FR ISSN 0074-2899) 677
International Conference in Particle Technology. Proceedings (US) 703
International Conference of Agricultural Economists. Proceedings (US ISSN 0074-2902) 28
International Conference of Building Officials. Accumulative Supplements to the Codes (US) 136
International Conference of Building Officials. Analysis of Revisions to the Uniform Building Code (US) 136
International Conference of Building Officials. Building Department Administration (US) 136
International Conference of Building Officials. Dwelling Construction Under the Uniform Building Code (US) 136
International Conference of Building Officials. One and Two Family Dwelling Code (US) 136
International Conference of Building Officials. Plan Review Manual (US) 136
International Conference of Building Officials. Uniform Code for the Abatement of Dangerous Buildings (US) 137
International Conference of Building Officials. Uniform Fire Code (US) 137
International Conference of Building Officials. Uniform Housing Code (US ISSN 0501-1213) 137
International Conference of Building Officials. Uniform Mechanical Code (US) 137
International Conference of Building Officials Plumbing Code see I C B O Plumbing Code 429
International Conference of Social Work. Conference Proceedings (US ISSN 0074-2961) 806
International Conference of Social Work. Japanese National Committee. Progress Report see Japanese Report to the International Council on Social Welfare 806
International Conference of Sociology of Religion (FR ISSN 0074-297X) 765, 814
International Conference on Acoustics. Reports (CN ISSN 0074-400X) 706
International Conference on Advances in Welding Processes. Proceedings (UK) 631
International Conference on Atomic Physics. Proceedings see Atomic Physics 702
International Conference on Bear Research and Management. Papers see Bears-Their Biology and Management 127

International Conference on Calorimetry and Thermodynamics. Proceedings (PL) 700
International Conference on Cloud Physics. Proceedings (CN ISSN 0074-3011) 633
International Conference on Computer Communications.(Proceedings) (US) 272
International Conference on Computers in Cardiology. Proceedings see Computers in Cardiology 271
International Conference on Computing Fixed Points with Applications. Proceedings (US) 586
International Conference on Congenital Malformations. Proceedings (NE ISSN 0074-3038) 596
International Conference on Cybernetics and Society. Proceedings(US ISSN 0360-8913) 272
International Conference on Digital Satellite Communications. Proceedings (US) 264
International Conference on Education. Final Report/Conference International de l'Education. Rapport Final (UN) 319
International Conference on Education. Proceedings see International Conference on Education. Final Report 319
International Conference on Elizabethan Theatre, University of Waterloo. Proceedings see Elizabethan Theatre 859
International Conference on Endodontics. Transactions (US ISSN 0074-3054) 610
International Conference on Engineering in the Ocean Environment. Digest (US ISSN 0074-3062) 368
International Conference on Experimental Meson Spectroscopy. Proceedings (US) 703, 705
International Conference on Fibrous Proteins. Proceedings (UK) 111, 112
International Conference on Finite Elements in Flow Problems. Proceedings (CN) 696
International Conference on Fluid Sealing. Proceedings (UK ISSN 0074-3089) 382
International Conference on Global Impacts of Applied Microbiology. Proceedings (US ISSN 0074-3097) 123
International Conference on Health and Health Education. Proceedings (SZ ISSN 0074-3100) 694
International Conference on High Energy Physics and Nuclear Structure. Proceedings (CN) 703
International Conference on High Pressure. Proceedings (JA) 255
International Conference on Intra-Uterine Contraception. Proceedings (NE ISSN 0074-3135) 615
International Conference on Ion Implantation in Semiconductors. Proceedings (US) 355
International Conference on Large High Tension Electric Systems. Proceedings see International Conference on Large High Voltage Electric Systems. Proceedings 355
International Conference on Large High Voltage Electric Systems. Proceedings (FR ISSN 0074-3151) 355
International Conference on Lasers. Proceedings (US ISSN 0190-4132) 705
International Conference on Lead. Proceedings (UK ISSN 0074-316X) 628
International Conference on Lighthouses and Other Aids to Navigation. (Reports) (FR ISSN 0538-6128) 878
International Conference on Liquefied Natural Gas. Papers (US) 679
International Conference on Liquefied Natural Gas. Proceedings see International Conference on Liquefied Natural Gas. Papers 679

International Conference on Oral Biology. Proceedings (US ISSN 0074-3216) 610
International Conference on Parallel Processing. Proceedings (US) 272
International Conference on Phenomena in Ionized Gases. Proceedings (UK ISSN 0074-3143) 697
International Conference on Physics of Semiconductors. Proceedings (FR ISSN 0074-3240) 355
International Conference on Piagetian Theory and the Helping Professions. Proceedings (US) 319, 345
International Conference on Planned Parenthood. Proceedings (UK ISSN 0074-3259) 910
International Conference on Plutonium and Other Actinides. Proceedings (US) 251
International Conference on Pressure Surges. Proceedings (UK) 382
International Conference on Pressure Vessel Technology. Papers (US) 379, 851
International Conference on Production Disease in Farm Animals. Proceedings (NE) 45
International Conference on Reliable Software.(Proceedings) (US) 272
International Conference on Shielding Around High Energy Accelerators. Papers (FR ISSN 0534-8811) 368, 703
International Conference on Social Welfare. Proceedings (US ISSN 0074-3305) 806
International Conference on Software Engineering. Proceedings (US) 272
International Conference on Soil Mechanics and Foundation Engineering. Proceedings (MX ISSN 0074-3313) 375
International Conference on Synthetic Fibronolytic--Thrombolytic Agents. Proceedings see Progress in Chemical Fibrinolysis and Thrombolysis 607
International Conference on Systems, Man and Cybernetics. Record see International Conference on Cybernetics and Society. Proceedings 272
International Conference on the Environmental Impact of Aerospace Operations in the High Atmosphere. (Proceedings) (US) 9, 386
International Conference on the Physics of Electronic and Atomic Collisions. Papers (JA ISSN 0074-333X) 703
International Conference on the Protection of Pipes. Proceedings (UK) 628
International Conference on the Theory and Applications of Differential Games. Proceedings (US) 355, 586
International Conference on Thermoelectric Energy Conversion. Proceedings (US) 355
International Conference on Trends in Industrial and Labour Relations (CN) 208
International Conference on Vehicle Structural Mechanics. Proceedings (US) 871
International Conference on Very Large Data Bases. Proceedings (US) 272
International Conference on Water Law and Administration. Background Paper. (IT) 896
International Conference on Water Pollution Research. International Congress Proceedings see Advances in Water Pollution Research 383
International Conference on Water Pollution Research. Proceedings (US) 387
International Congress for Byzantine Studies. Acts/Congres International des Etudes Byzantines. Actes (GR ISSN 0074-3542) 433
International Congress for Child Psychiatry. Proceedings (NE ISSN 0074-3372) 620
International Congress for Cybernetics. Proceedings. Actes (BE ISSN 0074-3380) 272

International Congress for Logic, Methodology and Philosophy of Science. Proceedings (NE ISSN 0074-3402) 784
International Congress for Papyrology. Proceedings (UK ISSN 0074-3429) 61
International Congress for Stereology. Proceedings (US ISSN 0074-3437) 379
International Congress for the Study of Pre-Columbian Cultures of the Lesser Antilles. Proceedings (CN ISSN 0538-6381) 50
International Congress of Acarology. Proceedings (CS ISSN 0074-3445) 128
International Congress of Accountants. Proceedings (US) 167
International Congress of Allergology. Abstracts of Reports of Discussion and of Communications (NE ISSN 0443-8604) 603
International Congress of Allergology. Proceedings (US ISSN 0074-3453) 603
International Congress of Angiology. Proceedings (IT ISSN 0074-347X) 607
International Congress of Anthropological and Ethnological Sciences. Proceedings (UK ISSN 0074-3496) 50
International Congress of Archives. Proceedings (FR ISSN 0074-3518) 531
International Congress of Automatic Control. Proceedings (GW ISSN 0074-3526) 272
International Congress of Automotive Safety. Proceedings (US) 871
International Congress of Biochemistry. Proceedings (JA ISSN 0074-3534) 111
International Congress of Cell Biology. Summaries of Reports and Communications (NE ISSN 0074-3550) 119
International Congress of Chemotherapy. Proceedings (GW ISSN 0074-3577) 684
International Congress of Cybernetic Medicine. Proceedings (IT ISSN 0074-3615) 272, 596
International Congress of Electroencephalography and Clinical Neurophysiology (Proceedings) (IE ISSN 0074-3631) 620
International Congress of Endocrinology. Proceedings (NE ISSN 0538-6462) 611
International Congress of Entomology (UK ISSN 0074-364X) 121
International Congress of Food Science and Technology. Proceedings (US ISSN 0074-3666) 405
International Congress of Graphoanalysts. Proceedings (US ISSN 0534-9044) 736
International Congress of Hematology. Proceedings (US ISSN 0074-3682) 613
International Congress of Histochemistry and Cytochemistry. Proceedings (NE ISSN 0074-3690) 111, 119
International Congress of Historical Sciences. Proceedings see Etudes Historiques 432
International Congress of Home Economics. Report (FR ISSN 0074-3712) 479
International Congress of Human Genetics. Abstracts (NE) 122
International Congress of Life Assurance Medicine. Proceedings (SZ ISSN 0074-3747) 499, 596
International Congress of Linguists. Proceedings (NE ISSN 0074-3755) 545
International Congress of Microbiology. Proceedings (GW) 123
International Congress of Nephrology. Proceedings (SZ ISSN 0074-378X) 625
International Congress of Neurological Sciences. Abstracts and Descriptions of Contributions of the Scientific Program (NE ISSN 0534-9109) 620

International Congress of Neurological Surgery. Abstracts of Papers (NE ISSN 0074-3801) 620, 624
International Congress of Occupational Therapy. Proceedings (SA ISSN 0074-3828) 596
International Congress of Ophthalmology see Acta Concilium Ophthalmologicum 615
International Congress of Parasitology. Proceedings (GW ISSN 0074-3860) 128
International Congress of Physical Medicine. Abstracts of Papers Presented (NE ISSN 0074-3887) 596
International Congress of Plastic and Reconstructive Surgery. Transactions (NE ISSN 0579-3785) 624
International Congress of Primatology. Proceedings (US ISSN 0074-3895) 50, 129
International Congress of Psychology. Proceedings (US ISSN 0085-2112) 736
International Congress of Psychopathological Art. Program. Programme (FR ISSN 0534-9168) 676
International Congress of Psychosomatic Medicine in Obstetrics and Gynaecology. Proceedings (SZ ISSN 0302-5152) 615
International Congress of Psychosurgery. Proceeding (US) 620, 624
International Congress of Psychotherapy. Proceedings/Verhandlungen/Comptes Rendus (SZ ISSN 0074-3917) 620
International Congress of Pure and Applied Chemistry. (Lectures) (US ISSN 0074-3925) 246, 373
International Congress of Radiation Research. Proceedings (US ISSN 0538-6586) 703
International Congress of Radiology. (Reports) (SZ ISSN 0074-3933) 622
International Congress of Sugarcane Technologists. Proceedings (US ISSN 0074-3968) 405
International Congress of the Transplantation Society. Proceedings see Transplantation Today 625
International Congress of Verdi Studies. Proceedings. (IT) 660
International Congress of Zoology. Proceedings (US) 129
International Congress on Alcoholism and Drug Dependence. Proceedings (SZ) 287
International Congress on Animal Reproduction and Artificial Insemination. Proceedings (UK ISSN 0074-4026) 894
International Congress on Canned Foods. Report (FR ISSN 0074-4034) 405
International Congress on Canned Foods. Texts of Papers Presented and Resolutions/Congres International de la Conserve. Textes des Communications (FR ISSN 0534-9257) 405
International Congress on Catalysis. Proceedings (US ISSN 0538-6640) 255
International Congress on Clinical Chemistry. Abstracts (UK ISSN 0074-4042) 111, 684
International Congress on Clinical Chemistry. Papers (UK ISSN 0074-4069) 111, 684
International Congress on Clinical Chemistry. Proceedings (UK ISSN 0074-4050) 111, 684
International Congress on Combustion Engines. Proceedings (FR ISSN 0074-4077) 382
International Congress on Experimental Mechanics. Proceedings see Experimental Mechanics; Proceedings 379

International Congress on Hormonal Steroids. Abstracts of Papers Presented (NE ISSN 0074-4107) 611
International Congress on Hygiene and Preventive Medicine. Proceedings (IT) 694, 752
International Congress on Medical Librarianship. Proceedings (NE) 531, 596
International Congress on Metallic Corrosion. (Proceedings) (GW ISSN 0074-4123) 628
International Congress on Muscle Diseases. Abstracts (NE) 596
International Congress on Mushroom Science. Proceedings see Mushroom Science 116
International Congress on Occupational Health. Proceedings (JA ISSN 0074-4131) 495
International Congress on Photobiology. Proceedings (US) 104
International Congress on the History of Art. Proceedings (FR ISSN 0074-4190) 75
International Congress Science Series (BE ISSN 0538-6772) 626
International Congress Series (NE ISSN 0531-5131) 626
International Congresses on Tropical Medicine and Malaria. (Proceedings) (GR ISSN 0074-4212) 608
International Convention Facilities Directory (US) 626
International Convocation on Immunology. Papers (SZ ISSN 0074-4220) 603
International Cooperation Council. Directory see Directory for a New World 721
International Cooperative Alliance. Congress Report (UK ISSN 0074-4247) 181
International Cooperative Alliance. Cooperative Series (II ISSN 0074-4255) 181
International Copyright Information Centre. Information Bulletin (UN ISSN 0336-3686) 677
International Cotton Advisory Committee. Country Statements Presented in Connection with the Plenary Meetings (US) 36
International Cotton Industry Statistics (SZ ISSN 0538-6829) 841, 857
International Cotton Industry Statistics. Supplement see International Textile Machinery Shipment Statistics 857
International Council for Bird Preservation. British Section. Report (UK ISSN 0074-4263) 125
International Council for Bird Preservation. Proceedings of Conferences (UK ISSN 0074-4271) 125
International Council for Building Research, Studies and Documentation. Congress Reports (FR ISSN 0074-428X) 137
International Council for Building Research, Studies and Documentation Directory of Building Research Information and Development Organizations see C I B Directory of Building Research Information and Development Organizations 135
International Council for Laboratory Animal Science. Proceedings of the Symposium (NO) 596, 612
International Council for Philosophy and Humanistic Studies. Bulletin (UN) 689
International Council for Philosophy and Humanistic Studies. General Assembly. Compte Rendu see International Council for Philosophy and Humanistic Studies. Bulletin 689
International Council for Scientific Management. Proceedings of World Congress (JA ISSN 0085-2120) 215
International Council for the Exploration of the Sea. Annales Biologiques (DK ISSN 0106-1003) 104

International Council for the Exploration of the Sea. Bulletin Hydrographique / C E S Oceanographic Data Lists and Inventories 310
International Council for the Exploration of the Sea. Bulletin Statistique (DK ISSN 0373-2045) 310
International Council for the Exploration of the Sea. Cooperative Research Reports (DK ISSN 0074-431X) 311
International Council for the Exploration of the Sea. Journal du Conseil (DK ISSN 0020-6466) 311
International Council for the Exploration of the Sea. Rapports et Proces-Verbaux des Reunions (DK ISSN 0074-4336) 311
International Council of Homehelp Services. Reports of Congress (NE ISSN 0074-4360) 479
International Council of Scientific Unions. Year Book (FR ISSN 0074-4387) 784
International Council of Voluntary Agencies. Documents Series (SZ ISSN 0074-4395) 806
International Council of Voluntary Agencies. General Conference. Record of Proceedings (SZ ISSN 0074-4409) 806
International Council on Archives. East and Central Africa Regional Branch. General Conference Proceedings (KE) 531
International Council on Archives. Microfilm Committee. Bulletin (SP) 531
International Council on Environmental Law References see I C E L References 390
International Council on Health, Physical Education and Recreation Congress Proceedings see I C H P E R Congress Proceedings 596
International Council on Social Welfare. European Symposium. Proceedings (FR ISSN 0074-4425) 806
International Countermeasures Handbook (US ISSN 0145-2584) 639
International Court of Justice. Yearbook (UN ISSN 0074-445X) 523
International Craft Swap (US) 75
International Credit Union Yearbook see Credit Union Yearbook 172
International Crop Improvement Association. Production Publication see Association of Official Seed Certifying Agencies. Production Publication 33
International Cryogenics Monograph Series (US ISSN 0538-7051) 700
International Customs Journal/Bulletin International des Douanes (BE ISSN 0074-4476) 196, 230
International Cyclotron Conference. Proceedings (US) 703
International Dairy Federation. Annual Bulletin/Federation Internationale de Laiterie. Bulletin Annuel (BE ISSN 0074-4484) 41
International Dairy Federation. Annual Memento/Federation Internationale de Laiterie. Memento Annuel (BE ISSN 0538-7078) 41
International Dairy Federation. Catalogue of I D F Publications. Catalogue des Publications de la F I L (BE ISSN 0538-7086) 25
International Dairy Federation. International Standard/Federation Internationale de Laiterie. Norme Internationale (BE ISSN 0538-7094) 41
International Dairy Products Review see Foodnews Dairy Products Review 41
International Data Processing Conference. Proceedings (US) 272
International Decade of Ocean Exploration. Progress Report (US ISSN 0092-0002) 910

International Development Research Centre. Annual Report/Centre de Recherches pour le Developpement International. Rapport Annuel (CN ISSN 0704-7584) *145*

International Diabetes Federation. Proceedings of Congress (NE ISSN 0074-4522) *611*

International Directory of Antiquarian Booksellers/Repertoire International de la Librairie Ancienne (DK ISSN 0538-7159) *759*

International Directory of Arts (GW ISSN 0074-4565) *75*

International Directory of Behavior and Design Research (US ISSN 0094-4084) *69, 736*

International Directory of Conchologists (US) *476*

International Directory of Executive Recruiters (US ISSN 0092-4989) *220*

International Directory of Investigators in Psychopharmacology (US) *685*

International Directory of Little Magazines and Small Presses (US ISSN 0092-3974) *92, 760*

International Directory of Occupational Safety and Health Services and Institutions (UN ISSN 0579-8140) *495*

International Directory of Oceanographers *see* Directory of Marine Scientists in the United States *309*

International Directory of Philosophy and Philosophers (US ISSN 0074-4603) *689*

International Directory of Prisoners' Aid Agencies (US ISSN 0538-7191) *281, 806*

International Directory of Programs in Business and Commerce (US ISSN 0074-4611) *145, 331*

International Directory of Published Market Research (UK) *218*

International Directory of Software (US) *272*

International Directory of Specialized Cancer Research and Treatment Establishments (SZ) *605*

International Directory of the Nonwoven Fabrics Industry (US ISSN 0095-683X) *856*

International Directory of 16MM Film Collectors (US ISSN 0074-462X) *650*

International Disco Sourcebook *see* Billboard's International Club and Disco Equipment Sourcebook *657*

International District Heating Association. Proceedings (US ISSN 0074-4638) *430*

International Documents on Palestine *see* Institute for Palestine Studies. International Annual Documentary Series *443*

International Dostoevsky Society Bulletin (US ISSN 0047-0686) *556, 565*

International Economic Association. Proceedings of the Conferences and Congresses (UK ISSN 0074-4646) *145*

International Economic Report of the President *see* U.S. Executive Office of the President. International Economic Report of the President *198*

International Economic Studies Institute. Contemporary Issues (US) *145*

International Economics *see* Surrey Papers in Economics *149*

International Electron Devices Meeting. Abstracts (US ISSN 0074-4670) *355*

International Electrotechnical Commission. Annuaire/International Electrotechnical Commission. Handbook (SZ) *355*

International Electrotechnical Commission. Central Office Report *see* International Electrotechnical Commission. Report on Activities *355*

International Electrotechnical Commission. Handbook *see* International Electrotechnical Commission. Annuaire *355*

International Electrotechnical Commission. Report on Activities (SZ ISSN 0074-4697) *355*

International Electrotechnical Commission Catalogue of Publications *see* I E C Catalogue of Publications *360*

International Encyclopedia on Packaging Machines/Catalogue International des Machines d' Emballage/Catalogo Internazionale delle Macchine per l' Imballaggio/ Internationaler Verpackungsmaschinen- Katalog fuer Die Abpackende Industrie (GW ISSN 0074-5766) *672*

International Engineering Directory (US ISSN 0074-5774) *368*

International Falcon Movement. Conference Reports (AU ISSN 0074-5790) *258*

International Federation for Documentation. Committee for Developing Countries. Occasional Publications (HU) *910*

International Federation for Documentation. P-Notes (NE ISSN 0378-7656) *531*

International Federation for Documentation. Proceedings of Congress (NE ISSN 0074-5812) *531*

International Federation for Documentation. Secretary General. Report *see* F I D Annual Report *908*

International Federation for Documentation Annual Report *see* F I D Annual Report *908*

International Federation for Documentation Directory *see* F I D Directory *530*

International Federation for Documentation Meetings Reports *see* F I D/R I Meetings Reports *530*

International Federation for Documentation Occasional Papers *see* F I D/E T Occasional Papers *908*

International Federation for Documentation Report Series *see* F.I.D./C.R. Report Series *530*

International Federation for Documentation Series on Problems of Information Science *see* F I D/R I Series on Problems of Information Science *530*

International Federation for Housing and Planning. Directory (NE) *485*

International Federation for Housing and Planning. Yearbook *see* International Federation for Housing and Planning. Directory *485*

International Federation for Information Processing Information Bulletin *see* I F I P Information Bulletin *530*

International Federation for Information Processing Summary *see* I F I P Summary *530*

International Federation for Medical Psychotherapy. Congress Reports (SZ ISSN 0074-5847) *620*

International Federation for Modern Languages and Literature. Congress Reports (FR ISSN 0074-5855) *545, 566*

International Federation for Preventive and Social Medicine News *see* I.F.P.S.M. News *752*

International Federation of Agricultural Producers. General Conference Proceedings (FR ISSN 0074-5863) *16*

International Federation of Asian and Western Pacific Contractors' Associations. Proceedings of the Annual Convention (PH ISSN 0074-588X) *137*

International Federation of Associations of Textile Chemists and Colorists. Reports of Congress (SZ ISSN 0074-5898) *261, 856*

International Federation of Automatic Control Symposium on Multivariable Technical Control Systems. Proceedings *see* I F A C Symposium on Multivariable Technical Control Systems. Proceedings *382*

International Federation of Catholic Universities. General Assembly. (Report) (FR ISSN 0579-3866) *337*

International Federation of Fruit Juice Producers. Proceedings. Berichte. Rapports (FR ISSN 0535-0182) *405*

International Federation of Fruit Juice Producers. Proceedings of Congress. Compte-Rendu du Congres (FR ISSN 0074-5952) *86*

International Federation of Journalists and Travel Writers. Official List/ Repertoire Officiel (BE ISSN 0074-5979) *505, 887*

International Federation of Library Associations and Institutions Annual *see* I F L A Annual *531*

International Federation of Library Associations and Institutions Directory *see* I F L A Directory *531*

International Federation of Library Associations and Institutions Publications *see* I F L A Publications *531*

International Federation of Medical Students' Associations. Reports of General Assembly (FI ISSN 0074-6037) *596*

International Federation of Operational Research Societies. Airline Group (A G I F O R S) Proceedings (US ISSN 0538-7442) *868*

International Federation of Plantation, Agricultural and Allied Workers. Report of the Secretariat to the I F P A A W World Congress (SZ ISSN 0074-7477) *29, 506*

International Federation of Prestressing. Congress Proceedings (UK ISSN 0074-6045) *379*

International File of Micrographics Equipment & Accessories (US ISSN 0148-5121) *238, 693*

International Film and T.V. Yearbook *see* Screen International Film and T.V. Yearbook *651*

International Film Guide (UK ISSN 0074-6053) *650*

International Film Importers and Distributors of America Film Directory *see* I F I D A Film Directory *650*

International Finance Corporation. Report (UN ISSN 0074-6061) *174*

International Finishing Industries Manual *see* Finishing Diary *673*

International Fiscal Association. Yearbook (NE) *523*

International Fiscal Harmonization Series (NE) *230*

International Flight Information Manual(US) *9*

International Foamed Plastic Markets and Directory *see* United States Foamed Plastic Markets and Directory *707*

International Folk Music Council. Internationale Arbeitstagung der Study Group on Folk Musical Instruments (SW) *660*

International Folk Music Council. Yearbook (CN ISSN 0074-6096) *402, 660*

International Folk Music Council Journal *see* International Folk Music Council. Yearbook *660*

International Folklore Bibliography *see* Internationale Volkskundliche Bibliographie *401*

International Football Book (UK ISSN 0074-610X) *824*

International Forum of Light Music in Radio (SZ) *267*

International Foundation Directory (US) *342*

International Gas Bearing Symposium. Proceedings (UK) *382, 679*

International Gas Union. Proceedings of Conferences (UK ISSN 0074-6126) *680*

International Geographical Union. Report of Congress (UR ISSN 0074-6134) *423*

International Geophysics Series (US ISSN 0074-6142) *305*

International Geoscience Electronics Symposium Digest (US) *355*

International Glass/Metal Catalog (US ISSN 0147-300X) *244*

International Gondwana Symposium. Papers (AT) *295*

International Graphical Federation. Report of Activities (SZ ISSN 0074-6177) *507*

International Grassland Congress. Proceedings (UR ISSN 0074-6185) *36*

International Gravimetric Bureau. Bulletin d'Information (FR) *305*

International Green Book (US ISSN 0074-6193) *238*

International Handbook of Resources for the Educators of Adults *see* Resources for Educators of Adults *329*

International Handbook of Universities *see* International Handbook of Universities and Other Institutions of Higher Education *337*

International Handbook of Universities and Other Institutions of Higher Education (UK ISSN 0074-6215) *337*

International Harbour Congress. Proceedings/Internationaal Havenkongres. Verslagboek/Congres Portuaire International. Compte-Rendu/Internationale Hafentagung. Berichte (BE) *878*

International Higher Education (UK) *337, 342*

International Histological Classification of Tumours (UN ISSN 0538-7736) *605*

International Hop Growers Convention. Report of Congress (YU ISSN 0074-6223) *42*

International Horticultural Congress. Proceedings (NE ISSN 0074-6231) *415*

International Hotel Guide (FR ISSN 0074-624X) *482*

International Humanist and Ethical Union. Proceedings of the Congress (NE ISSN 0074-6258) *689*

International Hydrographic Bureau. Yearbook *see* International Hydrographic Organization. Yearbook *311*

International Hydrographic Conference. Reports of Proceedings (MC ISSN 0074-6274) *308, 311*

International Hydrographic Organization. Yearbook (MC) *308, 311*

International Hydrological Decade: Yearbook of the Federal Republic of Germany *see* Internationale Hydrologische Dekade: Jahrbuch der Bundesrepublik Deutschland *308*

International I S A Pulp and Paper Instrumentation Symposium Proceedings *see* Instrumentation in the Pulp and Paper Industry *675*

International I U P A C Congress of Pesticide Chemistry. Proceedings (US) *36*

International Index to Film Periodicals (US ISSN 0000-0388) *3, 651*

International Indian Ocean Expedition. Collected Reprints (UN ISSN 0074-6320) *311*

International Information Centre for Terminology, Vienna Infoterm Series *see* Infoterm Series *545*

International Institute for Aerial Survey and Earth Sciences International Seminar. Proceedings *see* I T C-U N E S C O International Seminar. Proceedings *386*

International Institute for Aerial Survey and Earth Sciences Publications. Series B. Photo-Interpretation *see* I T C Publications. Series B. Photo-Interpretation *422*

International Institute for Applied Systems Analysis Annual Report *see* I I A S A Annual Report *272*

INTERNATIONAL ORGANISATIONS

International Institute for Educational Planning. Occasional Papers (UN ISSN 0074-6401) *342*
International Institute for Labour Studies. International Educational Materials Exchange. List of Available Materials (UN ISSN 0074-641X) *159*
International Institute for Labour Studies. Public Lecture Series (UN) *208*
International Institute for Labour Studies. Publications (UK ISSN 0074-6509) *208*
International Institute for Labour Studies. Research Series (UN) *208*
International Institute for Land Reclamation and Improvement. Annual Report (NE ISSN 0074-6428) *36*
International Institute for Land Reclamation and Improvement. Bibliography (NE ISSN 0074-6436) *25*
International Institute for Land Reclamation and Improvement. Bulletin (NE ISSN 0074-6444) *36*
International Institute for Land Reclamation and Improvement. Publication (NE ISSN 0074-6452) *36*
International Institute for Population Studies. Annual Report *see* International Institute for Population Studies. Director's Report *727*
International Institute for Population Studies. Director's Report (II) *727*
International Institute for Social History. Annual Report (NE) *814*
International Institute for Sugar Beet Research. Reports of the Winter Congress (BE ISSN 0074-6460) *37*
International Institute of Administrative Sciences. Reports of the International Congress (BE ISSN 0074-6479) *743*
International Institute of Differing Civilizations. (Session Papers) (BE ISSN 0074-6487) *721*
International Institute of Ibero-American Literature. Congress Proceedings. Memoria (US ISSN 0074-6495) *566*
International Institute of Philosophy. Actes (FR ISSN 0074-6525) *689*
International Institute of Public Finance. Papers and Proceedings (GW ISSN 0074-6533) *230*
International Institute of Refrigeration. Proceedings of Commission Meetings(FR ISSN 0074-6541) *430*
International Institute of Seismology and Earthquake Engineering. Bulletin(JA ISSN 0074-655X) *305, 375*
International Institute of Seismology and Earthquake Engineering. Earthquake Report (JA ISSN 0074-6568) *305, 375*
International Institute of Seismology and Earthquake Engineering. Lecture Note (JA ISSN 0074-6584) *305, 375*
International Institute of Seismology and Earthquake Engineering. Progress Report (JA ISSN 0074-6592) *305, 375*
International Institute of Seismology and Earthquake Engineering. Report of Individual Study by Participants to I I S E E (JA ISSN 0074-6606) *305, 375*
International Institute of Seismology and Earthquake Engineering. Year Book (JA ISSN 0074-6614) *305, 375*
International Institute on the Prevention and Treatment of Alcoholism. Selected Papers (SZ ISSN 0074-6622) *287*
International Institute on the Prevention and Treatment of Drug Dependence. Selected Papers (SZ) *287*
International Interdisciplinary Seminar on Piagetian Theory and Its Implications for the Helping Professions. Proceedings (US) *345*

International Joint Conference on Artificial Intelligence. Advance Papers of the Conference (US) *272*
International Joint Conference on Pattern Recognition. Conference Record (US) *272*
International Journal of American Linguistics Native American Texts Series *see* I J A L Native American Texts Series *545*
International Journal of Chemical Kinetics. Symposium (US) *255*
International Journal of Economic and Social History *see* Quaderni Internazionali di Storia Economica e Sociale *459*
International Journal of Psychiatry *see* International Journal of Psychoanalytic Psychotherapy *620*
International Journal of Psychoanalytic Psychotherapy (US ISSN 0091-0600) *620, 736*
International Journal of Quantum Chemistry. Symposium *see* International Symposium on Atomic, Molecular and Solid-State Theory, Collision Phenomena and Computational Methods. Proceedings *246*
International Journal of Slavic Linguistics and Poetics (NE ISSN 0020-7632) *545, 566*
International Labor Press Association. Directory of Member Publications (US) *505, 507*
International Labour Conference. Reports to the Conference and Record of Proceedings (UN ISSN 0074-6673) *208*
International Labour Law Reports (NE) *208, 513*
International Labour Office. P R E A L C. Investigaciones sobre Empleo (UN) *186, 191*
International Labour Office. Special Report of the Director-General on the Application of the Declaration Concerning the Policy of Apartheid of the Republic of South Africa (UN ISSN 0538-8333) *718*
International Law Association. American Branch. Proceedings (US) *523*
International Law Association. Reports of Conferences (UK ISSN 0074-6738) *523*
International Lead Zinc Research Organization, Inc. Annual Research Report *see* I L Z R O Annual Research Report *628*
International Lead Zinc Research Organization, Inc. Lead Research Digest *see* I L Z R O Lead Research Digest *628*
International Lead Zinc Research Organization, Inc. Zinc Research Digest *see* I L Z R O Zinc Research Digest *628*
International League for Human Rights. Annual Report (US ISSN 0363-9347) *718*
International League for the Rights of Man. Annual Report *see* International League for Human Rights. Annual Report *718*
International League of Societies for the Mentally Handicapped. World Congress Proceedings. (BE ISSN 0074-6754) *620, 736*
International Leprosy Congress. Abstracts and Papers *see* International Leprosy Congress. Transactions *608*
International Leprosy Congress. Transactions (US) *608*
International Lesson Annual (US ISSN 0074-6770) *765*
International Linguistic Association. Monograph (US ISSN 0074-6797) *545*
International Linguistic Association. Special Publications (US ISSN 0074-6800) *545*
International Literary and Artistic Association. Proceedings and Reports of Congress (FR ISSN 0074-6819) *491*
International Literary Market Place (US ISSN 0074-6827) *759*

International Livestock Centre for Africa. Programme and Budget (ET) *45*
International Livestock Centre for Africa. Report on Activities *see* International Livestock Centre for Africa. Programme and Budget *45*
International Machine Tool Design and Research Conference. Proceedings (UK ISSN 0074-6835) *583*
International Magnetics Conference. Digest (US ISSN 0074-6843) *697*
International Maize and Wheat Improvement Center. Research Bulletin (MX ISSN 0074-6878) *42*
International Maritime Committee. Documentation *see* C M I Year Book *877*
International Market Guide - Continental Europe (US ISSN 0074-6908) *203, 238*
International Marketing Data and Statistics (UK ISSN 0308-2938) *159*
International Mathematical Union Canberra Circular *see* I M U Canberra Circular *585*
International Measurement Conference. Proceedings. Acta IMEKO *see* Acts IMEKO *636*
International Medical Congress. Year Book (US ISSN 0074-6932) *596*
International Medical Directory (FR) *596*
International Medical Who's Who (UK) *97, 596*
International Meeting of Animal Nutrition Experts. Proceedings (SP ISSN 0074-6959) *45*
International Meeting on Cattle Diseases. Reports (GW ISSN 0074-6975) *45, 894*
International Metalworkers' Congress. Reports (SZ ISSN 0074-6983) *628*
International Metalworkers Federation Studies *see* I M F Studies *628*
International Meteorological Institute in Stockholm. Annual Report (SW) *633*
International Microfilm Source Book *see* International Micrographics Source Book *539*
International Microforms in Print *see* Subject Guide to Microforms in Print *95*
International Micrographics Source Book (US) *539*
International Microstructural Analysis Society. Proceedings: Annual Technical Meeting *see* Microstructural Science *629*
International Microwave Power Institute. Transactions (US) *355*
International Microwave Symposium Digest (US ISSN 0074-7009) *355*
International Migration Newsletter *see* International Newsletter on Migration *727*
International Military Sports Council. Technical Brochure/Conseil International du Sport Militaire. Brochure Technique (BE) *639, 820*
International Military Sports Council Academy. Technical Brochure *see* International Military Sports Council. Technical Brochure *639*
International Mimes & Pantomimists Directory *see* I M P Directory *910*
International Mineralogical Association. Proceedings of Meetings (US ISSN 0074-7017) *644*
International Monetary Fund. Annual Report of the Executive Board (UN) *174*
International Monetary Fund. Annual Report of the Executive Directors *see* International Monetary Fund. Annual Report of the Executive Board *174*
International Monetary Fund. Annual Report on Exchange Arrangements and Exchange Restrictions (UN) *174*
International Monetary Fund. Annual Report on Exchange Restrictions *see* International Monetary Fund. Annual Report on Exchange Arrangements and Exchange Restrictions *174*

International Monetary Fund. Balance of Payments Yearbook (UN) *196, 213*
International Monetary Fund. Government Finance Statistics Yearbook (UN) *159, 841*
International Monetary Fund. Pamphlet Series (UN ISSN 0538-8759) *174*
International Monetary Fund. Selected Decisions of the Executive Directors and Selected Documents *see* International Monetary Fund. Selected Decisions of the International Monetary Fund and Selected Documents *174*
International Monetary Fund. Selected Decisions of the International Monetary Fund and Selected Documents (UN ISSN 0094-1735) *174*
International Monetary Fund. Summary Proceedings of the Annual Meeting of the Board of Governors (UN ISSN 0074-7025) *174*
International Monetary Market Yearbook (US) *174*
International Monograph Series on Early Child Care (US) *256*
International Monographs on Advanced Biology and Biophysics (II ISSN 0074-7033) *104, 112*
International Monographs on Advanced Chemistry (II ISSN 0074-7041) *246*
International Monographs on Advanced Mathematics and Physics (II ISSN 0074-705X) *586, 697*
International Monographs on Studies in Indian Economics (II ISSN 0074-7068) *145*
International Motion Picture Almanac (US ISSN 0074-7084) *650*
International Music Guide (UK) *660*
International Narcotic Conference. Report: Proceedings of Annual Conference (US ISSN 0074-7114) *287*
International Narcotics Control Board. Comparative Statement of Estimates and Statistics on Narcotic Drugs Furnished by Governments in Accordance with the International Treaties (UN) *287*
International Naturist Guide/Internationaler FKK-Reisefuehrer/Guide Naturiste Internationale (GW ISSN 0074-7122) *830*
International Navigation Congress. Papers: Inland Navigation (BE) *878*
International Navigation Congress. Papers: Ocean Navigation (BE) *878*
International Navigation Congress. Proceedings (BE) *878*
International Newsletter (FR ISSN 0308-762X) *721*
International Newsletter on Migration (CN ISSN 0383-2767) *727*
International North Pacific Fisheries Commission. Annual Report (CN ISSN 0074-7165) *398*
International North Pacific Fisheries Commission. Bulletin (CN ISSN 0074-7157) *398*
International North Pacific Fisheries Commission. Statistical Yearbook (CN ISSN 0535-1588) *398*
International Oceanographic Tables (UN ISSN 0538-8880) *311*
International Offshore Craft Conference. Proceedings (UK) *878*
International Oil and Gas Development(US) *680*
International Olive Growers Federation. Congress Reports (SP ISSN 0074-7173) *37*
International Olympic Academy. Report of the Sessions (GR ISSN 0074-7181) *820*
International Online Information Meeting (Proceedings) (GW) *272*
International Optical Computing Conference. Digest of Papers (US) *272, 356*
International Optical Year Book (UK) *616*
International Organisations in World Politics Yearbook (US ISSN 0363-7123) *711*

International Organization for Cooperation in Health Care. General Assembly. Report (GW) 596
International Organization for Medical Cooperation. General Assembly. Report see International Organization for Cooperation in Health Care. General Assembly. Report 596
International Organization for Standardization Annual Review see I S O Annual Review 637
International Organization for Standardization Catalogue see I S O Catalogue 637
International Organization for Standardization International Standards see I S O International Standards 637
International Organization for Standardization Memento see I S O Memento 637
International Organization for the Study of the Old Testament. Proceedings of the International Congress (NE ISSN 0074-719X) 765
International Organization of Citrus Virologists. Proceedings of the Conference (US ISSN 0074-7203) 415
International Organization of Consumers Unions. Proceedings (NE ISSN 0538-8988) 280
International Organizing Committee of World Mining Congresses. Report see World Mining Congress. Report 647
International Ozone Institute. Workshop Series (US) 373
International P. E. N. Congress. Report (UK ISSN 0074-722X) 566
International Pacific Halibut Commission. Report see International Pacific Halibut Commission (U.S. and Canada). Technical Reports 398
International Pacific Halibut Commission (U.S. and Canada). Annual Report (US ISSN 0074-7233) 398
International Pacific Halibut Commission (U.S. and Canada). Scientific Reports (US ISSN 0074-7246) 398
International Pacific Halibut Commission (U.S. and Canada). Technical Reports (US ISSN 0579-3920) 398
International Pacific Salmon Fisheries Commission. Annual Report (CN ISSN 0074-7254) 398
International Pacific Salmon Fisheries Commission. Bulletin (CN ISSN 0074-7262) 398
International Pacific Salmon Fisheries Commission. Progress Report (CN ISSN 0074-7270) 398
International Peace Research Association. Proceedings of the Conference (FI ISSN 0074-7297) 722
International Peace Research Association Studies in Peace Research see I P R A Studies in Peace Research 721
International Peace Research Institute. Basic Social Science Monographs (NO ISSN 0522-4497) 798
International Peat Society. Bulletin/ Internationale Moor- und Torf-Gesellschaft. Mitteilungen (FI ISSN 0355-1008) 37
International Percussion Reference Library. Catalog (US ISSN 0085-218X) 660
International Petroleum Encyclopedia (US ISSN 0148-0375) 680
International Pharmacopoeia see Pharmacopoeia Internationalis 685
International Philatelic Federation. General Assembly. Proces-Verbal (LU ISSN 0074-7343) 479
International Photobiological Congress. Proceedings (SW ISSN 0074-7351) 111
International Planned Parenthood Federation. Annual Report see I P P F in Action 131

International Planned Parenthood Federation. Proceedings of the Conference of the Europe and near East Region (UK ISSN 0074-7386) 910
International Planned Parenthood Federation. Report to Donors, Programme Development & Financial Statements (UK ISSN 0308-213X) 132
International Planned Parenthood Federation. Working Papers (UK ISSN 0074-7394) 910
International Planned Parenthood Federation Action see I P P F in Action 131
International Plastics Directory see Handbuch der Internationalen Kunstoffindustrie 706
International Playground Association. Conference Report (UK ISSN 0074-7416) 258
International Polar Motion Service. Annual Report/Kokusai Kyoku-Undo Kansoku Jigyo Nenpo (JA ISSN 0074-7432) 82
International Police Association. Meeting of the International Executive Council (UK ISSN 0579-5567) 282
International Police Association. Travel Scholarships (UK ISSN 0579-6881) 282
International Policy Report (US) 722
International Political Science Association. Circular see Participation 713
International Political Science Association. World Conference. Proceedings see International Political Science Association. World Congress 711
International Political Science Association. World Congress (CN) 711
International Poplar Commission. Session Reports (UN ISSN 0074-7475) 409
International Population Conference. Proceedings (BE ISSN 0074-9338) 132, 727
International Population Reports see Current Population Reports: International Population Reports 726
International Potash Institute. Colloquium. Compte Rendu (SZ ISSN 0074-7491) 37
International Potash Institute. Congress Report (SZ ISSN 0074-7505) 37
International Potash Institute Bulletin see I P I Bulletin 36
International Potash Institute Research Topics see I P I Research Topics 36
International Powder Metallurgy Conference. Proceedings-Modern Developments in Powder Metallurgy (US ISSN 0074-7513) 628
International Press Institute. Survey (UK ISSN 0085-2198) 505
International Press Telecommunications Council Newsletter see I. P. T. C. Newsletter 269
International Pressure Die Casting Conferences. Proceedings (UK) 583
International Pressure Die Casting Conferences. Report see International Pressure Die Casting Conferences. Proceedings 583
International Program of Laboratories for Population Statistics. Occasional Publications (US) 727, 752
International Program of Laboratories for Population Statistics. Scientific Report Series (US) 727, 752
International Progress in Urethanes (US) 706
International Psychic Register (US ISSN 0147-782X) 676
International Psycho-Analytical Library (UK ISSN 0074-7548) 736
International Publications (US) 92
International Publishers Association. Proceedings of Congress (SZ ISSN 0074-7556) 759
International Pulp & Paper Directory (US ISSN 0097-2509) 238, 675

International Quantum Electronics Conference. Digest of Technical Papers (US ISSN 0538-9275) 356
International Radio and Television Society, Inc. Gold Medal Annual see I R T S Gold Medal Annual 267
International Radio Club of America Foreign Log see I.R.C.A. Foreign Log 267
International Railway Progress see Developing Railways 873
International Railway Statistics. Statistics of Individual Railways (FR ISSN 0074-7580) 873
International Rayon and Synthetic Fibres Committee. Statistical Yearbook (FR ISSN 0074-7599) 3, 857
International Rayon and Synthetic Fibres Committee. Technical Conference. Reports (FR ISSN 0074-7602) 856
International Rayon and Synthetic Fibres Committee. World Congress. Report (FR ISSN 0074-7610) 856
International Reading Association. Annual Report (US ISSN 0538-933X) 319
International Real Estate Federation. Reports of Congress (FR ISSN 0074-7637) 761
International Recording Equipment and Studio Directory (US) 818
International Recording Studio and Equipment Directory see International Recording Equipment and Studio Directory 818
International Reference Annual for Building and Equipment of Sports, Tourism, Recreation Installations (FR ISSN 0074-7645) 820
International Reference Handbook of Marketing, Management and Advertising Organizations. (US) 910
International Reference Handbook of Services, Organizations, Diplomatic Representation, Marketing and Advertising Channels see International Reference Handbook of Marketing, Management and Advertising Organizations 910
International Refractories Handbook & Directory (UK) 238, 244
International Register of Department Stores see I.R.D.S 218
International Reinforced Plastics Conference. Papers and Proceedings. see Reinforced Plastics Congress 707
International Relations Association. Journal see Journal of International Relations 722
International Rescue Committee Annual Report (US ISSN 0538-9461) 806
International Research Communications System (IRCS) Medical Science: Key Reports in Cell and Molecular Biology see I R C S Medical Science: Key Reports in Cell and Molecular Biology 103
International Review of Biochemistry (US ISSN 0147-7366) 111
International Review of Connective Tissue Research (US ISSN 0074-767X) 119
International Review of Criminal Policy (UN ISSN 0074-7688) 282
International Review of Cytology (US ISSN 0074-7696) 119
International Review of Cytology. Supplement (US ISSN 0074-770X) 119
International Review of Experimental Pathology (US ISSN 0074-7718) 596
International Review of General and Experimental Zoology (US ISSN 0074-7734) 129
International Review of Neurobiology (US ISSN 0074-7742) 620
International Review of Physiology see Physiology, Series One 126
International Review of Physiology (US ISSN 0363-3918) 126
International Review of Research in Mental Retardation (US ISSN 0074-7750) 346, 620

International Review of Tropical Medicine (US ISSN 0074-7777) 608
International Reviews in Aerosol Physics and Chemistry (US ISSN 0074-7785) 910
International Rice Research Institute. Research Highlights (PH ISSN 0115-1142) 42
International Rice Research Institute Annual Report see I R R I Annual Report 42
International Rice Research Institute Research Paper Series see I R R I Research Paper Series 42
International Road Congresses. Proceedings (FR ISSN 0074-7815) 375, 875
International Rubber Directory see Handbuch der Internationalen Kautschukindustrie 777
International Rubber Study Group. Summary of Proceedings of the Group Meetings and Assemblies (UK ISSN 0074-7823) 777
International Rural Housing Journal see Revista Internacional de Vivienda Rural 487
International Safety Conference. Proceedings (UK) 375
International Savings Banks Institute. Report (SZ) 174
International Scholars Directory (US) 319
International School of Physics "Enrico Fermi." Proceedings (US ISSN 0074-784X) 697
International School of Physics "Ettore Majorana," Erice, Italy. Proceedings (US ISSN 0074-7858) 703
International Science Review Series (US ISSN 0074-7866) 784
International Scientific Radio Union. Proceedings of General Assemblies see International Union of Radio Science. Proceedings of General Assemblies 267
International Seaweed Symposium. Proceedings (NO ISSN 0074-7874) 116
International Secretariat of Entertainment Trade Unions. Newsletter (BE ISSN 0538-9755) 507
International Security Directory (UK ISSN 0074-7890) 743, 752
International Sedimentary Petrographical Series (NE ISSN 0538-9771) 305
International Sedimentological Congress. Guidebook (GW ISSN 0074-7904) 295
International Seminar on Integrated Surveys. Proceedings see I T C-U N E S C O International Seminar. Proceedings 386
International Seminar on Reproductive Physiology and Sexual Endocrinology. Proceedings (SZ ISSN 0074-7920) 126
International Seminar on Special Education. Proceedings (US ISSN 0074-7939) 346
International Series in Aeronautics and Astronautics. Division 1. Solid and Structural Mechanics (US) 9
International Series in Aeronautics and Astronautics. Division 2. Aerodynamics and Astronautics (US) 9
International Series in Aeronautics and Astronautics. Division 3. Propulsion Systems Including Fuels (US) 9
International Series in Aeronautics and Astronautics. Division 7. Astronautics (US) 9
International Series in Aeronautics and Astronautics. Division 9. Symposia (US) 9
International Series in Library and Information Sciences (US ISSN 0074-820X) 531
International Series in Natural Philosophy (US ISSN 0074-8064) 689
International Series in Nonlinear Mathematics (US) 586

International Series in Pure and Applied Mathematics (US ISSN 0539-0125) *586*
International Series in Solid State Physics (US ISSN 0539-0133) *697*
International Series of Monographs in Aeronautics and Astronautics. Division 1. Solid and Structural Mechanics *see* International Series in Aeronautics and Astronautics. Division 1. Solid and Structural Mechanics *9*
International Series of Monographs in Aeronautics and Astronautics. Division 2. Aerodynamics *see* International Series in Aeronautics and Astronautics. Division 2. Aerodynamics and Astronautics *9*
International Series of Monographs in Aeronautics and Astronautics. Division 3. Propulsion Systems Including Fuels *see* International Series in Aeronautics and Astronautics. Division 3. Propulsion Systems Including Fuels *9*
International Series of Monographs in Aeronautics and Astronautics. Division 7. Astronautics *see* International Series in Aeronautics and Astronautics. Division 7. Astronautics *9*
International Series of Monographs in Aeronautics and Astronautics. Division 9. Symposia *see* International Series in Aeronautics and Astronautics. Division 9. Symposia *9*
International Series of Monographs in Cerebrovisceral and Behavioral Psychology and Conditioned Reflexes *see* International Series on Cerebrovisceral and Behavioral Psychology and Conditioned Reflexes *736*
International Series of Monographs in Chemical Engineering *see* International Series on Chemical Engineering *373*
International Series of Monographs in Electrical Engineering (US ISSN 0074-803X) *356*
International Series of Monographs in Natural Philosophy *see* International Series in Natural Philosophy *689*
International Series of Monographs in Pure and Applied Mathematics *see* International Series in Pure and Applied Mathematics *586*
International Series of Monographs on Analytical Chemistry *see* International Series on Analytical Chemistry *249*
International Series of Monographs on Automation and Automatic Control *see* International Series on Automation and Automatic Control *272*
International Series of Monographs on Chemistry (US) *246*
International Series of Monographs on Civil Engineering *see* International Series on Civil Engineering *376*
International Series of Monographs on Earth Sciences *see* International Series on Earth Sciences *289*
International Series of Monographs on Electro- Magnetic Waves *see* International Series on Electromagnetic Waves *356*
International Series of Monographs on Electronics and Instrumentation *see* International Series on Electronics and Instrumentation *697*
International Series of Monographs on Experimental Psychology (US ISSN 0074-8137) *736*
International Series of Monographs on Heating, Ventilation and Refrigeration *see* International Series on Heating, Ventilation and Refrigeration *430*
International Series of Monographs on Library and Information Sciences *see* International Series in Library and Information Sciences *531*
International Series of Monographs on Oral Biology *see* International Series on Oral Biology *104*
International Series of Monographs on Organic Chemistry *see* International Series on Organic Chemistry *252*
International Series of Monographs on Physics (US) *697*
International Series of Monographs on Pure and Applied Biology. Division: Biochemistry *see* International Series on Pure and Applied Biology. Biochemistry Division *111*
International Series of Monographs on Pure and Applied Biology. Division: Botany *see* International Series on Pure and Applied Biology. Botany Division *116*
International Series of Monographs on Pure and Applied Biology. Division: Modern Trends in Physiological Sciences *see* International Series on Pure and Applied Biology. Modern Trends in Physiological Science Division *126*
International Series of Monographs on Pure and Applied Biology. Division: Plant Physiology *see* International Series on Pure and Applied Biology. Plant Physiology Division *116*
International Series of Monographs on Pure and Applied Biology. Division: Zoology *see* International Series on Pure and Applied Biology. Zoology Division *129*
International Series of Monographs on Semiconductors *see* International Series on Semiconductors *356*
International Series of Monographs on Solid State Physics *see* International Series in Solid State Physics *697*
International Series on Analytical Chemistry (US ISSN 0074-8099) *249*
International Series on Automation and Automatic Control (US ISSN 0074-8030) *272*
International Series on Biomechanics (US ISSN 0146-8197) *596*
International Series on Cerebrovisceral and Behavioral Psychology and Conditioned Reflexes (US ISSN 0538-9968) *736*
International Series on Chemical Engineering (US ISSN 0074-8021) *373*
International Series on Civil Engineering (US ISSN 0538-9887) *376*
International Series on Earth Sciences (US ISSN 0538-9984) *289*
International Series on Electromagnetic Waves (US ISSN 0538-9992) *356*
International Series on Electronics and Instrumentation (US ISSN 0074-8129) *356, 697*
International Series on Experimental Psychology (US) *736*
International Series on Heating, Ventilation and Refrigeration (US ISSN 0538-9895) *430*
International Series on Oral Biology (US ISSN 0074-8234) *104*
International Series on Organic Chemistry (US ISSN 0074-8242) *252*
International Series on Pure and Applied Biology. Biochemistry Division (US) *111*
International Series on Pure and Applied Biology. Botany Division (US) *116*
International Series on Pure and Applied Biology. Modern Trends in Physiological Science Division (US) *126*
International Series on Pure and Applied Biology. Plant Physiology Division (US) *116*
International Series on Pure and Applied Biology. Zoology Division (US) *129*
International Series on Semiconductors (US ISSN 0074-8315) *356*
International Series on Sports Sciences (US) *820*
International Shipping and Shipbuilding Directory (UK ISSN 0074-8358) *878*
International Sivananda Yoga Life and Yoga Vacations (CN ISSN 0708-076X) *689, 694*
International Skating Union. Bestimmungen ueber das Eistanzen (SZ ISSN 0539-0168) *820*
International Skating Union. Minutes of Congress (SZ ISSN 0535-2479) *820*
International Skating Union Constitution *see* I S U Constitution *820*
International Skating Union Regulations *see* I S U Regulations *820*
International Social Science Council. Publications (NE ISSN 0074-8404) *798*
International Social Security Association. Etudes et Recherches/ Studies and Research (SZ) *499*
International Social Security Association. Technical Reports of Assemblies (SZ ISSN 0074-8439) *499*
International Society for Music Education Yearbook *see* I S M E Yearbook *659*
International Society for Performing Arts. Libraries and Museums. Congress Proceedings (FR ISSN 0074-7882) *75, 531*
International Society for Research on the Moors. Report of Congress (AU ISSN 0074-8471) *423*
International Society for Rock Mechanics. Congress. Proceedings (PO ISSN 0074-848X) *376*
International Society for Terrain-Vehicle Systems. Proceedings of International Conference (US ISSN 0074-8498) *376*
International Society for the Study of Time. Conference. Proceedings. *see* Study of Time *84*
International Society of Blood Transfusion. Proceedings of the Congress (FR ISSN 0074-8528) *607*
International Society of Criminology. Bulletin (FR ISSN 0539-032X) *282*
International Society of Geographical Pathology. Proceedings of the Conference (SZ ISSN 0074-8536) *596*
International Society of Internal Medicine. Congress Proceedings (SZ ISSN 0074-8544) *596*
International Society of Organbuilders Organ Building Periodical *see* Organ Building Periodical *662*
International Society of Orthopaedic Surgery and Traumatology. Proceedings of Congresses (BE ISSN 0074-8552) *616*
International Society of Plant Morphologists. Yearbook (II ISSN 0539-0346) *116*
International Society of Urology. Reports of Congress (FR ISSN 0074-8579) *625*
International Softball Congress(Year) Official Yearbook and Guide (US) *824*
International Solar Energy Society. American Section. Annual Meeting. Proceedings (US ISSN 0146-4566) *363*
International Solid State Circuits Conference. Digest (US ISSN 0074-8587) *356*
International Specialty Conference on Cold-Formed Steel Structures. (Proceedings) (US) *628*
International Sporting Press Association. Bulletin. N.S. (UK ISSN 0539-0370) *505, 820*
International Standard Book Number Review *see* I S B N Review *759*
International Statistical Handbook of Urban Public Transport/Recueil International de Statistiques des Transports Publics Urbains/ Internationales Statistik-Handbuch fuer den Oeffentlichen Stadtverkehr (BE ISSN 0378-1968) *862*
International Statistical Institute. Bulletin. Proceedings of the Biennial Sessions (NE ISSN 0074-8609) *841*
International Statistical Institute. Proceedings of Specialized Meetings (NE) *841*
International Steel Statistics - World Tables (UK) *631*
International Straits of the World (NE) *423, 722*
International Studies in Economics and Econometrics (NE) *145*
International Studies in Education (UN) *319*
International Studies in Planning (US) *485*
International Studies in Sociology and Social Anthropology (NE ISSN 0074-8684) *798, 814*
International Sugar Organization. Annual Report (UK ISSN 0074-8706) *37, 405*
International Superphosphate and Compound Manufacturers Association Limited. Technical Meeting. Proceedings (UK ISSN 0074-8714) *37*
International Superphosphate Manufacturers Association. Technical Meeting. Proceedings *see* International Superphosphate and Compound Manufacturers Association Limited. Technical Meeting. Proceedings *37*
International Superphosphate Manufactures Association, Ltd. Technical Conference. Proceedings *see* I S M A Technical Conference. Proceedings *36*
International Survey of Roman Law. Index *see* Quaderni Camerti di Studi Romanistici. Index *517*
International Symposia on Comparative Law. Proceedings/Colloques Internationaux de Droit Compare. Travaux (CN ISSN 0074-8722) *513*
International Symposium on Acoustical Holography. Proceedings *see* Acoustical Imaging: Recent Advances in Visualization and Characterization *706*
International Symposium on Adsorption-Desorption Phenomena. Proceedings (US) *255*
International Symposium on Aerobiology. Proceedings (UK ISSN 0074-8757) *752*
International Symposium on Animal and Plant Toxins. Proceedings (US) *111*
International Symposium on Atherosclerosis. Proceedings (SZ ISSN 0074-8765) *607*
International Symposium on Atomic, Molecular and Solid-State Theory and Quantum Statistics. Proceedings *see* International Symposium on Atomic, Molecular and Solid-State Theory, Collision Phenomena and Computational Methods. Proceedings *246*
International Symposium on Atomic, Molecular and Solid-State Theory, Collision Phenomena and Computational Methods. Proceedings(US) *246*
International Symposium on Brain-Endocrine Interaction. Proceedings (SZ ISSN 0301-309X) *611, 620*
International Symposium on Canine Heartworm Disease. Proceedings (US) *894*
International Symposium on Captopril (GW) *685*
International Symposium on Cell Biology and Cytopharmacology. Proceedings *see* Advances in Cytopharmacology *119*
International Symposium on Combustion. Proceedings *see* Symposium (International) on Combustion *256*
International Symposium on Comparative Endocrinology. Proceedings (US ISSN 0539-0559) *611*
International Symposium on Crop Protection. Communications *see* International Symposium on Crop Protection. Proceedings *37*
International Symposium on Crop Protection. Proceedings (BE) *37*
International Symposium on Dredging Technology. Proceedings (UK) *381*
International Symposium on Electromagnetic Compatibility. Record (US ISSN 0074-8811) *356*

International Symposium on Environmental Biogeochemistry. Proceedings (US) 111
International Symposium on Fault-Tolerant Computing. Digest see International Symposium on Fault-Tolerant Computing. Proceedings 272
International Symposium on Fault-Tolerant Computing. Proceedings (US ISSN 0363-8928) 272
International Symposium on Growth Hormone. Abstracts (NE) 126, 596
International Symposium on Immunopathology see Immunopathology 603
International Symposium on Jet Cutting Technology. Proceedings (UK) 382
International Symposium on Laboratory Animals see International Council for Laboratory Animal Science. Proceedings of the Symposium 596
International Symposium on Mini and Microcomputers. Proceedings (US) 272
International Symposium on Molecular Biology. Proceedings (US) 119
International Symposium on Molecular Biology Publications. see Miles International Symposium 119
International Symposium on Nitrite in Meat Products. Proceedings (NE) 405
International Symposium on Nitrogen Fixation. Proceedings (US) 246
International Symposium on Nonlinear Acoustics. Abstracts of Papers (US) 706
International Symposium on Pharmacological Treatment in Burns. Proceedings (NE) 616, 685
International Symposium on Plastic and Reconstructive Surgery of the Face and Neck. Proceedings (US) 624
International Symposium on Quantum Biology and Quantum Pharmacology. Proceedings (US) 104, 685
International Symposium on Regional Development. Papers and Proceedings (JA ISSN 0074-8897) 485
International Symposium on Residual Gases in Electron Tubes. Proceedings(UK) 356
International Symposium on Subscriber Loop and Services. Proceedings (US) 356
International Symposium on Switching Arc Phenomena. Proceedings (PL) 368
International Symposium on the Aerodynamics and Ventilation of Vehicle Tunnels. Proceedings (UK) 375, 862
International Symposium on the Continuous Cultivation of Microorganisms. Proceedings (CS ISSN 0074-8927) 123
International Symposium on the Pharmacology of Thermoregulation (SZ) 596
International Symposium on Transport and Handling of Minerals. Minerals Transportation; Proceedings (US ISSN 0094-7466) 862
International Symposium on Urban Hydrology, Hydraulics and Sediment Control. Proceedings (US) 308, 381
International Symposium on Urban Storm Water Management. Proceedings see International Symposium on Urban Hydrology, Hydraulics and Sediment Control. Proceedings 308
International Symposium on Wave and Tidal Energy. Proceedings (UK) 363, 897
International Symposium on Wind Energy Systems. Proceedings (UK) 356, 363
International Symposium on Wound Ballistics. Proceedings (SW) 282
International T N O Conference. (Proceedings) (NE ISSN 0074-8951) 851
International Talent and Touring Directory (US) 660

International Talent Directory see International Talent and Touring Directory 660
International Telecommunication Union. Central Library. Liste des Periodiques. List of Periodicals. Lista de Revistas (UN) 266
International Telecommunication Union. Central Library. Listes des Publications Annuelles. List of Annuals. Lista de Publicaciones Anuales (UN) 266
International Telecommunication Union. List of Telegraph Offices Open for International Service (UN ISSN 0074-9044) 269
International Telecommunication Union. Report on the Activities (UN ISSN 0085-2201) 269
International Telephone Directory of the Deaf (US ISSN 0160-7472) 269, 286
International Television Almanac (US ISSN 0539-0761) 267
International Television Symposium and Technical Exhibit, Montreux. (Papers) (SZ ISSN 0082-0776) 267
International Telex Directory. International Service (AT ISSN 0310-8031) 269
International Textile Machinery (UK ISSN 0074-9087) 583, 856
International Textile Machinery Shipment Statistics (SZ) 841, 857
International Textile Manufacturers Federation Directory see I T M F Directory 856
International Textile Manufacturing (SZ) 856
International Textile Review (US) 856
International Thermal Spraying Conference. Preprint of Papers (US) 631
International Thyroid Conference. Proceedings (US ISSN 0074-9095) 611
International Tin Council. Statistical Yearbook see Tin Statistics 630
International Tin Research Council. Annual Report (UK ISSN 0074-9125) 628
International Touring Alliance. Minutes of the General Assembly (SZ ISSN 0074-9133) 887
International Tourism Policy in OECD Member Countries see Organization for Economic Cooperation and Development. Tourism Committee. Tourism Policy and International Tourism in O E C D Member Countries 889
International Towing Tank Conference. Proceedings (CN) 368
International Tracts in Computer Studies (UI) 272
International Trade and Singapore (SI) 196
International Trade Conference of Workers of the Building, Wood and Building Materials Industries. (Brochure) (FI) 137
International Trade Union Committee of Solidarity with the Workers and People of Chile. Bulletin (CS) 507, 722
International Trade Union Conference for Action Against Apartheid. Resolution (CS) 507, 718
International Training Centre for Aerial Survey Publications. Series A (Photogrammetry) see I T C -Publications. Series A (Photogrammetry) 422
International Transplutonium Element Symposium. Proceedings (US) 251
International Transport Worker's Federation Panorama see I T F Panorama 506
International Transport Workers' Federation Report on Activities (UK ISSN 0539-0915) 507, 862
International Travel Guide to Florida (US) 887
International Travel Statistics see World Travel Statistics 893
International Trombone Association Series (US ISSN 0363-5708) 660

International Trumpet Guild. Journal (International Trumpet Guild) (US ISSN 0363-2849) 660
International Trumpet Guild International Trumpet Guild. Journal see International Trumpet Guild. Journal 660
International Tuberculosis Yearbook see International Union against Tuberculosis. Bulletin 623
International Turquoise Annual (US) 503
International Union against Cancer. Manual/Union Internationale Contre le Cancer. Manuele (SZ ISSN 0074-9192) 605
International Union against Cancer. Proceedings of Congress (SZ ISSN 0074-9206) 605
International Union Against Cancer Technical Report Series see U I C C Technical Report Series 606
International Union against Tuberculosis. Bulletin (FR ISSN 0074-9249) 623
International Union against Tuberculosis. Conference Proceedings(NE) 623
International Union for Conservation of Nature and Natural Resources. Proceedings and Papers of the Technical Meeting (SZ ISSN 0074-9281) 276
International Union for Conservation of Nature and Natural Resources. Proceedings of the General Assembly(SZ ISSN 0074-929X) 276
International Union for Conservation of Nature and Natural Resources Annual Report see I U C N Annual Report 276
International Union for Inland Navigation. Annual Report (BE ISSN 0074-9311) 862
International Union for Quaternary Research. Congress Proceedings (NZ ISSN 0074-932X) 295
International Union for the Scientific Study of Population. Documents du l'Union see I U S S P Papers 727
International Union for the Scientific Study of Population. Newsletter (BE) 132, 727
International Union of Biological Sciences. General Assemblies. Proceedings (FR) 104
International Union of Biological Sciences. Reports of General Assemblies see International Union of Biological Sciences. General Assemblies. Proceedings 104
International Union of Building Societies and Savings Associations. Congress Proceedings (US ISSN 0074-9370) 174
International Union of Crystallography. Abstracts of the Triennial Congress (DK ISSN 0074-9389) 251
International Union of Crystallography. Structure Reports (NE ISSN 0074-9397) 251
International Union of Food and Allied Workers' Associations. Meeting of the Executive Committee. I. Documents of the Secretariat. II. Summary Report (SZ ISSN 0579-8299) 405, 507
International Union of Food and Allied Workers' Associations. Tobacco Workers' Trade Group Board. Meeting (SZ ISSN 0579-8302) 861
International Union of Forest Research Organizations. Congress Proceedings/Rapports du Congres/ Kongressberichte (GW ISSN 0074-9400) 409
International Union of Geodesy and Geophysics. Monograph (CN ISSN 0539-1016) 305, 423
International Union of Geodesy and Geophysics. Proceedings of the General Assembly (FR ISSN 0074-9419) 305, 423
International Union of Liberal Christian Women. Newsletter see International Association of Liberal Religious Women. Newsletter 765

International Union of Local Authorities. Reports of Congress (NE ISSN 0074-9443) 749
International Union of Local Authorities Publication) see I U L A (Publication) 742
International Union of Official Travel Organizations. Technical Bulletin see World Tourism Organization. Collection of Technical Bulletins 893
International Union of Physiological Sciences. Newsletter (HU ISSN 0539-1113) 126
International Union of Physiological Sciences. Proceedings of Congress (FR ISSN 0074-946X) 126
International Union of Prehistoric and Protohistoric Sciences. Proceedings of Congress (YU ISSN 0074-9478) 50, 61
International Union of Producers and Distributors of Electrical Energy. (Congress Proceedings) (FR ISSN 0074-9486) 356
International Union of Public Transport. Proceedings of the International Congress (BE) 862
International Union of Public Transport. Reports and Proceedings of the International Congress see International Union of Public Transport. Proceedings of the International Congress 862
International Union of Public Transport. Technical Reports of the Congresses (BE ISSN 0378-1976) 862
International Union of Public Transport. Transports Publics dans les Principales Villes du Monde see International Statistical Handbook of Urban Public Transport 862
International Union of Pure and Applied Chemistry. Chemical Data Series (US) 246
International Union of Pure and Applied Chemistry. Comptes Rendus of IUPAC Conference (US ISSN 0074-9508) 910
International Union of Radio Science. Proceedings of General Assemblies (BE ISSN 0074-9516) 267
International Union of Railways. Talbeaux et Graphiques (FR) 866
International Union of School and University Health and Medicine. Congress Reports (SZ ISSN 0074-9524) 319, 596, 752
International Union of Socialist Youth Bulletin see I U S Y Bulletin 711
International Union of Students. Congress Resolutions (CS ISSN 0074-9532) 337
International Vegetarian Health Food Handbook (UK) 666
International Vending Buyer's Guide and Directory (US) 218
International Water Conference. Proceedings (US ISSN 0074-9575) 381, 897
International Water Supply Congress. Proceedings (UK ISSN 0074-9583) 897
International Whaling Commission. Report (UK ISSN 0074-9591) 398
International Wheat Council. Annual Report (UK) 16
International Wheat Council. Record of Operations of Member Countries (UK ISSN 0539-130X) 16
International Wheat Council. Report for Crop Year see International Wheat Council. Annual Report 16
International Wheat Council. Review of the World Grains Situation see Review of the World Wheat Situation 19
International Wheat Council. Secretariat Papers (UK ISSN 0539-1326) 16
International Who's Who (UK ISSN 0074-9613) 97
International Who's Who in Art and Antiques (UK) 75, 97, 476
International Who's Who in Education (UK) 97, 319
International Who's Who in Music and Musicians' Directory (UK ISSN 0307-2894) 660

International Who's Who in Poetry (UK ISSN 0539-1342) *97*
International Women's News (UK ISSN 0020-9120) *722*
International Work Group for Indigenous Affairs Documents *see* I W G I A Documents *50*
International Work Group for Indigenous Affairs Newsletter *see* I W G I A Newsletter *50*
International Workshop on Nude Mice. Proceedings (NO) *612*
International Year Book and Statesmen's Who's Who (UK ISSN 0074-9621) *711, 798*
International Yearbook for Child Psychiatry and Allied Disciplines *see* International Association for Child Psychiatry and Allied Professions. Yearbook *619*
International Yearbook of Educational & Instructional Technology (UK ISSN 0307-9732) *349*
International Yearbook of Organization Studies (UK) *798*
International Yearbook of Organizational Democracy (US) *507, 711*
International Yearbook of the Underwater World/Annuaire International du Monde Sous-Marin (FR ISSN 0074-9648) *827*
International Yoga Life and Yoga Vacations *see* International Sivananda Yoga Life and Yoga Vacations *694*
International Zinc & Galvanizing Directory (UK ISSN 0141-5271) *628*
International Zoo Yearbook (UK ISSN 0074-9664) *129*
International Zurich Seminar on Digital Communications.(Proceedings) (US) *272*
Internationale Beitraege zur Markt-, Meinungs- und Zukunftsforschung (GW) *218*
Internationale Bibliographie der Fachadressbuecher/International Bibliography of Directories (GW ISSN 0074-9672) *92*
Internationale Bibliographie der Fachwoerterbuecher *see* Fachwoerterbuecher und Lexika. Ein Internationales Verzeichnis *555*
Internationale Gesellschaft fuer Geschichte der Pharmazie. Veroeffentlichungen. Neue Folge (GW ISSN 0074-9729) *685*
Internationale Gesellschaft fuer Urheberrecht. Schriftenreihe (AU) *513*
Internationale Gesellschaft fuer Urheberrecht. Yearbook (GW ISSN 0539-1512) *677*
Internationale Hafentagung. Berichte *see* International Harbour Congress. Proceedings *878*
Internationale Hydrologische Dekade: Jahrbuch der Bundesrepublik Deutschland/International Hydrological Decade: Yearbook of the Federal Republic of Germany (GW ISSN 0538-7779) *308*
Internationale Moor- und Torf-Gesellschaft. Mitteilungen *see* International Peat Society. Bulletin *37*
Internationale Politik und Wirtschaft (GW) *722*
Die Internationale Unternehmung (GW) *910*
Internationale Vereinigung fuer Theoretische und Angewandte Limnologie. Verhandlungen *see* International Association of Theoretical and Applied Limnology. Proceedings *308*
Internationale Vereinigung zur Foerderung des Studiums der Hegelschen Philosophie. Veroeffentlichung (GW) *689*
Internationale Volkskundliche Bibliographie/International Folklore Bibliography/Bibliographie Internationale des Arts et Traditions Populaires (GW ISSN 0074-9737) *401*

Internationaler Campingfuehrer *see* ADAC-Campingfuehrer. Band 1: Suedeuropa *828*
Internationaler FKK-Reisefuehrer *see* International Naturist Guide *830*
Internationaler Kongress fuer Reprographie und Information. Fachreferate und Plenarvortraege (GW) *693*
Internationaler Spitalbedarf (SZ ISSN 0074-977X) *481*
Internationaler Verband fuer Oeffentliches Verkehrswesen. Technische Berichte zu den Internationalen Kongressen *see* International Union of Public Transport. Technical Reports of the Congresses *862*
Internationaler Verpackungsmaschinen-Katalog fuer Die Abpackende Industrie *see* International Encyclopedia on Packaging Machines *672*
Internationales Archiv fuer Sozialgeschichte der Deutschen Literatur (GW ISSN 0340-4528) *566*
Internationales Bibliotheks-Handbuch/World Guide to Libraries (GW ISSN 0000-0221) *531*
Internationales Firmenregister der Brauindustrie, Malzerien, Mineralwasser und Erfrischungsgetranke *see* International Brewers' Directory and Soft Drink Guide *86*
Internationales Forschungszentrum fuer Grundfragen der Wissenschaften, Salzburg. Forschungsgespraeche (AU ISSN 0074-980X) *784*
Internationales Handbuch fuer Rundfunk und Fernsehen (GW ISSN 0535-4358) *268*
Internationales Institut fuer den Frieden. Cultural Anniversaries Series (AU ISSN 0574-6817) *491*
Internationales Jahrbuch fuer Geschichts und Geographieunterricht(GW ISSN 0074-9834) *349*
Internationales Jahrbuch fuer Geschichtsunterricht *see* Internationales Jahrbuch fuer Geschichts und Geographieunterricht *349*
Internationales Jahrbuch fuer Kartographie (GW ISSN 0341-0986) *423*
Internationales Jahrbuch fuer Religionssoziologie (GW ISSN 0074-9850) *765, 814*
Internationales Recht und Diplomatie (GW ISSN 0020-9503) *523, 722*
Internationales Statistik-Handbuch fuer den Oeffentlichen Stadtverkehr *see* International Statistical Handbook of Urban Public Transport *862*
Internationales Verlagsadressbuch/Publishers' International Directory (GW ISSN 0074-9877) *760*
Internationales Verzeichnis der Wirtschaftsverbaende/World Guide to Trade Associations (GW ISSN 0094-1611) *238*
Internationes *see* Transfines *801*
Inter-Nord; Revue Internationale d'Etudes Arctiques et Nordiques (NE ISSN 0074-1035) *423*
Inter-Parliamentary Union. Conference Proceedings/Union Interparlementaire. Comptes Rendus des Conferences (SZ ISSN 0074-1051) *722*
Inter-Parliamentary Union. Series: "Reports and Documents" (SZ ISSN 0579-8337) *711*
Interpretations (US) *566*
Interprete (IT) *545*
Interscience Conference on Antimicrobial Agents and Chemotherapy. Program and Abstracts (US) *123*
Interscience Monographs and Texts in Physics and Astronomy (US ISSN 0074-9931) *82, 697*

Interscience Tracts in Pure and Applied Mathematics *see* Pure and Applied Mathematics: A Wiley Interscience Series of Texts, Monographs and Tracts *588*
Interscience Tracts on Physics and Astronomy (US ISSN 0074-9958) *82, 697*
Intersociety Energy Conversion Conference. Proceedings (US ISSN 0579-5664) *363, 703*
Interstate Commission on the Potomac River Basin. Proceedings (US ISSN 0535-4676) *387, 897*
Interstate Commission on the Potomac River Basin. Technical Bulletin *see* Interstate Commission on the Potomac River Basin. Technical Reports *387*
Interstate Commission on the Potomac River Basin. Technical Reports (US) *387*
Interstate Conference on Labor Statistics. Proceedings *see* North American Conference on Labor Statistics. Selected Papers *161*
Interstate Oil Compact Commission Annual Report (US) *680*
Inter-Union Commission on Geodynamics Report *see* Geodynamics International *304*
Inter-University Case Program. Case Study (US ISSN 0074-106X) *743*
Interuniversity Centre for European Studies. International Colloquium Proceedings (CN) *455*
Inter-university Consortium for Political and Social Research. Annual Report (US ISSN 0074-1078) *711*
Inter-University Consortium for Political and Social Research. Guide to Resources and Services. (US ISSN 0362-8736) *798*
Intervention (AT ISSN 0311-1989) *711*
Intisari (MY) *814*
Inventaire des Archives Historiques/Inventaris van het Historisch Archief(BE) *456*
Inventaire General des Monuments et des Richesses Artistiques de la France (FR ISSN 0075-0018) *69, 75, 653*
Inventaires Economiques et Industriels Regionaux (FR) *145*
Inventare Nichtstaatlicher Archive (GW ISSN 0535-5079) *92*
Inventari dei Manoscritti delle Biblioteche d'Italia (IT ISSN 0075-0026) *539*
Inventaria Archaeologica Belgique (GW ISSN 0075-0034) *61*
Inventaria Archaeologica Ceskoslovensko (GW ISSN 0075-0042) *61*
Inventaria Archaeologica Denmark (GW ISSN 0075-0050) *61*
Inventaria Archaeologica Deutschland (GW ISSN 0075-0069) *61*
Inventaria Archaeologica Espana (GW ISSN 0075-0077) *62*
Inventaria Archaeologica France (GW ISSN 0075-0085) *62*
Inventaria Archaeologica Great Britain (GW ISSN 0075-0093) *62*
Inventaria Archaeologica Italia (GW ISSN 0075-0107) *62*
Inventaria Archaeologica Jugoslavija (GW ISSN 0075-0115) *62*
Inventaria Archaeologica Norway (GW ISSN 0075-0123) *62*
Inventaria Archaeologica Oesterreich (GW ISSN 0075-0131) *62*
Inventaria Archaeologica Pologne (GW ISSN 0075-014X) *62*
Inventaria Archaeologica The Netherlands (GW) *62*
Inventaria Archaeologica Ungarn (GW ISSN 0075-0158) *62*
Inventaris van Het Historisch Archief *see* Inventaire des Archives Historiques *456*
Inventaris van Het Kunstpatrimonium van Oost-Vlaanderen (BE ISSN 0075-0166) *456*
Inventory of Agricultural Research (US ISSN 0360-5841) *25*

IOWA. COLLEGE 1403

Inventory of Continuing Education Activities in Pennsylvania Secondary School Districts *see* Inventory of Continuing Education Activities in the Public School Districts of Pennsylvania *319*
Inventory of Continuing Education Activities in the Public School Districts of Pennsylvania (US) *319*
Inventory of Industrial Parks in Quebec(CN) *145*
Inventory of Marriage and Family Literature (US ISSN 0094-7814) *818*
Inventory of Programs in Maryland's Private and Public Universities and Colleges (US ISSN 0075-0174) *910*
Inventory of Research into Higher Education in Canada (CN ISSN 0318-8329) *337*
Inventory of Waste Water Production and Waste Water Reclamation Practices in California *see* California. Department of Water Resources. Inventory of Waste Water Production and Waste Water Reclamation Practices in California *896*
Invest in Panama (PN) *203*
Invest Yourself (US ISSN 0148-6802) *806*
Investicije (YU) *159*
Investigacion y Progreso Agricola (CL ISSN 0539-239X) *910*
Investigaciones Antropologicas (MX ISSN 0075-0204) *50*
Investigaciones de Campo (PE) *50*
Investigaciones Historicas (SP) *456*
Investigations in Fish Control *see* U. S. Fish and Wildlife Service. Investigations in Fish Control *400*
Investissements Etrangers en Belgique (BE ISSN 0075-0247) *203*
Investment Bankers Association. State Pension Fund *see* Securities Industry Association. State and Local Pension Funds *204*
Investment Bankers Association of America. State and Local Pension Funds *see* Securities Industry Association. State and Local Pension Funds *204*
Investment Dealers' Association of Canada. Canada and Canadian Provinces: Funded Debts Outstanding *see* Bond Record *202*
Investment Outlook *see* Credit and Capital Markets *203*
Investment Sources and Ideas *see* S I E Sophisticated Investor *204*
Investment Transactions *see* Illinois. State Board of Investment. Investment Transactions *203*
Investment Trust Year Book (UK) *203*
Investments and Credit Corporation of Oyo State. Industrial Directory (NR) *238*
Investments in Tomorrow *see* Leading Edge *785*
Investor Responsibility Research Center. Annual Report (US) *203*
Investors Guide of Japan (JA) *203, 238*
Investors' Guide to Nepal (NP) *203*
Invisible City (US ISSN 0147-4936) *556, 580*
Invited Lectures on the Middle East at the University of Texas at Austin (US) *475*
Ion Exchange; a Series of Advances *see* Ion Exchange and Solvent Extraction *255*
Ion Exchange and Solvent Extraction (US ISSN 0092-0193) *255*
Ionenaustauscher in Einzeldarstellungen(GE ISSN 0075-0336) *373*
Iowa. Bureau of Labor. Occupational Injuries and Illnesses Survey (US ISSN 0092-6299) *495*
Iowa. Bureau of Labor. Research and Statistics Division. Biennial Report (US) *159*
Iowa. College Aid Commission. Biennium Report (US) *344*

1404   IOWA. CROP

Iowa. Crop and Livestock Reporting Service. Planting to Harvest. Weather and Field Crops see Iowa Crop and Livestock Reporting Service. Planting to Harvest. Weather and Field Crops 37
Iowa. Department of Job Service. Annual Report (US ISSN 0149-449X) 208
Iowa. Department of Job Service. Research and Statistics Division. Annual Manpower Planning Report (US ISSN 0091-262X) 208
Iowa. Department of Public Instruction. Summary of Federal Programs (US ISSN 0091-8962) 319
Iowa. Employment Security Commission. Annual Report see Iowa. Department of Job Service. Annual Report 208
Iowa. Geological Survey. Annual Report of the State Geologist to the Geological Board (US ISSN 0361-7629) 295
Iowa. Higher Education Facilities Commission. Biennium Report see Iowa. College Aid Commission. Biennium Report 344
Iowa Academy of Science Bulletin see I A S Bulletin 783
Iowa Advocate (US ISSN 0578-6533) 513
Iowa Agriculture and Home Economics Experiment Station. Special Report see Iowa State University. Iowa Agriculture and Home Economics Experiment Station. Special Report 16
Iowa Civil Rights Commission. Annual Report (US) 718
Iowa Comprehensive State Plan for Drug Abuse Prevention: Annual Performance Report (US ISSN 0363-4507) 287
Iowa Crop and Livestock Reporting Service. Planting to Harvest. Weather and Field Crops (US) 37
Iowa Detailed Report of Vital Statistics see Vital Statistics of Iowa 849
Iowa Genealogical Society. Surname Index (US ISSN 0090-905X) 417
Iowa Geological Survey. Reports of Investigations (US) 295
Iowa International Directory (US) 238
Iowa Manufacturer's Export Directory see Iowa International Directory 238
Iowa Nurses' Association. Bulletin (US ISSN 0075-0387) 614
Iowa Publications in Philosophy (NE ISSN 0075-0395) 689
Iowa State Archaeologist. Report (US ISSN 0085-2252) 62
Iowa State Engineering Research see Engineering Research Highlights 367
Iowa State Industrial Directory (US) 238
Iowa State Nurses' Association. Bulletin see Iowa Nurses' Association. Bulletin 614
Iowa State University. Engineering Research Institute. Engineering Research Report (US ISSN 0075-0433) 368
Iowa State University. Iowa Agriculture and Home Economics Experiment Station. Research Bulletin Series (US ISSN 0021-0692) 16, 479, 697
Iowa State University. Iowa Agriculture and Home Economics Experiment Station. Special Report (US ISSN 0578-6258) 16
Iowa State University. Library. Annual Report (US ISSN 0075-0425) 531
Iowa State University. Library. Series in Bibliography (US) 539
Iowa Wildlife Research Bulletin (US ISSN 0090-4856) 276
Iparmuveszeti Muzeum. Evkonyv see Ars Decorativa 652
Ipse (UK) 556
Iran. Geological Survey. Report (IR ISSN 0075-0484) 295
Iran. Ministry of Economy. Bureau of Statistics. Series (IR) 159

Iran. Ministry of Economy. Internal Wholesale Trade Statistics (IR) 159
Iran. Ministry of Economy. International Trade Statistics (IR) 159
Iran Almanac and Book of Facts (IR ISSN 0075-0476) 440
Iran Banking Almanac (IR) 174
Iran Chamber of Commerce, Industries and Mines. Directory (IR) 179
Iran Yearbook (IR) 475, 841
Iranian Industrial Statistics (IR ISSN 0075-0506) 159
Iranian Mineral Statistics (IR ISSN 0075-0514) 644
Iranica Antiqua (NE ISSN 0021-0870) 62, 650
Iraq. Central Statistical Organization. Annual Abstract of Statistics (IQ) 841
Iraq. Central Statistical Organization. Results of the Industrial Survey of Large Establishments in Iraq (IQ) 159
Iraq. Central Statistical Organization. Statistical Pocket Book (IQ) 841
Iraq. Central Statistical Organization. Summary of Foreign Trade Statistics (IQ ISSN 0021-0900) 159
Iraq. Ministry of Information. Information Series (IQ) 743
Iraq Natural History Research Center and Museum. Bulletin (IQ) 784
Iraq Natural History Research Centre. Bulletin see Iraq Natural History Research Center and Museum. Bulletin 784
Iraq Natural History Research Centre. Publication see Iraq Natural History Research Centre and Museum. Publication 784
Iraq Natural History Research Centre and Museum. Publication (IQ) 104, 784
Iraqi Journal of Agricultural Science (IQ ISSN 0075-0530) 16
Ireland. Central Statistics Office. Distribution of Cattle and Pigs by Size of Herd (IE) 25
Ireland. Central Statistics Office. Pig Enumeration (IE) 25
Ireland (Eire) Central Statistics Office. Crops and Livestock Numbers. see Ireland (Eire) Central Statistics Office. Crops and Pasture and Numbers of Livestock 37
Ireland (Eire) Central Statistics Office. Crops and Pasture and Numbers of Livestock (IE) 37, 45
Ireland (Eire) Central Statistics Office. Estimated Gross and Net Agricultural Output (IE) 16
Ireland (Eire) Central Statistics Office. Estimates of the Quantity and Value of Agricultural Output see Ireland (Eire) Central Statistics Office. Estimated Gross and Net Agricultural Output 16
Ireland (Eire) Central Statistics Office. Hire-Purchase and Credit Sales (IE ISSN 0075-0573) 174, 218
Ireland (Eire) Central Statistics Office. Inquiry into Advertising Agencies Activities (IE ISSN 0075-0581) 6
Ireland (Eire) Central Statistics Office. Livestock Numbers (IE ISSN 0075-059X) 45
Ireland (Eire) Central Statistics Office. National Income and Expenditure (IE ISSN 0075-0603) 213, 230
Ireland (Eire) Central Statistics Office. Trend of Employment and Unemployment (IE ISSN 0075-0638) 159
Ireland (Eire) Central Statistics Office. Tuarascail Ar Staidreamh Beatha. Report on Vital Statistics (IE ISSN 0075-062X) 841
Ireland (Eire) Department of Agriculture and Fisheries. Annual Report (IE ISSN 0075-0646) 16
Ireland (Eire) Department of Agriculture and Fisheries. Journal (IE ISSN 0075-0654) 16, 398
Ireland (Eire) Department of Education. Liosta de Iar-Bhunscoileanna Aitheanta. List of Recognised Post-Primary Schools (IE ISSN 0075-0662) 331

Ireland (Eire) Department of Finance. Financial Statement of the Minister for Finance (IE ISSN 0075-0670) 230
Ireland. Public Service Advisory Council. Report (IE) 743
Ireland Socialist Review (UK) 711
Ireland's Communication Directory (IE) 264
Iris Year Book (UK ISSN 0075-0700) 415
Irish Agricultural Organization Society. Annual Report see Irish Cooperative Organization Society. Annual Report 16
Irish Archives Bulletin (IE) 531
Irish Badminton Handbook see Badminton Ireland 819
Irish Baptist Historical Society. Journal (UK ISSN 0075-0727) 772
Irish Bird Report see Irish Birds 125
Irish Birds (IE) 125
Irish Catholic Directory (UK ISSN 0075-0735) 774
Irish Concrete Review see Irish Construction Materials Review Series 137
Irish Construction Materials Review Series (IE) 137
Irish Construction Metals Review see Irish Construction Materials Review Series 137
Irish Cooperative Organization Society. Annual Report (IE) 16
Irish Countrywomen's Association. an Grianan Programme (IE) 319
Irish Creamery Managers' Association. Creamery Directory and Diary (IE) 41
Irish Creamery Managers' Association. Creamery Yearbook and Diary see Irish Creamery Managers' Association. Creamery Directory and Diary 41
Irish Drama Selections (UK ISSN 0260-7964) 566, 859
Irish Economic and Social History (UK) 456, 798
Irish Folk Music Studies (IE) 660
Irish Geography (IE ISSN 0075-0778) 423
Irish Literary Studies (UK ISSN 0140-895X) 566
Irish Play Series (US ISSN 0075-0816) 566
Irish Renaissance Annual (US ISSN 0193-9777) 566
Irish Roofing and Cladding Review see Irish Construction Materials Review Series 137
Irish Sea Fisheries Board. Annual Report see Bord Iascaigh Mhara. Tuarascail Agus Cuntaisi 395
Irish Statistical Survey see Ireland (Eire) Central Statistics Office. National Income and Expenditure 230
Irish Timber Review see Irish Construction Materials Review Series 137
Irodalom - Szocializmus (HU ISSN 0075-0824) 566, 711
Irodalomelmelet Klasszikusai (HU ISSN 0075-0832) 566
Irodalomtorteneti Fuzetek (HU ISSN 0075-0840) 566
Irodalomtorteneti Konyvtar (HU ISSN 0075-0859) 566
Iron & Manganese Ores Survey (UK ISSN 0140-8402) 628
Iron and Steel. Annual Statistics for the United Kingdom (UK ISSN 0075-0867) 628
Iron and Steel Works of the World (UK ISSN 0075-0875) 628
Irregular Serials and Annuals (US ISSN 0000-0043) 92
Irrigation Research Institute, Lahore. Report (PK) 897
Is see Transient 575
ISIS Cumulative Bibliography (UK) 92
Isizwe (SA) 423
Iske Ha-Bituah Be-Yisrael see Israel. Central Bureau of Statistics. Insurance in Israel 502
Islam in Paperback (US ISSN 0075-0921) 769
Islamic Development Bank. Annual Report (SU) 174

Islamic Studies (US ISSN 0362-1480) 769
Islamic Surveys (UK ISSN 0075-093X) 444
Isle of Man Natural History and Antiquarian Society. Proceedings (UI) 433, 784
Islenzk Bokaskra/Icelandic National Bibliography (IC) 539
Isotope and Radiation Research (UA ISSN 0021-1907) 622
Isotopes in Organic Chemistry (NE) 252
Isotype Titles see Zidis 166
Isozymes: Current Topics in Biological and Medicine Research (US) 104
Ispata (BG) 628
Israel. Atomic Energy Commission. IA-Reports (IS ISSN 0075-0980) 703
Israel. Atomic Energy Commission. Technical Information Department. Literature Surveys (IS) 700
Israel. Central Bureau of Statistics. Annual Foreign Trade Statistics (IS) 159
Israel. Central Bureau of Statistics. Causes of Death (IS ISSN 0075-0999) 727
Israel. Central Bureau of Statistics. Construction in Israel/Ha-Binui Be-Yisrael (IS ISSN 0069-9195) 137
Israel. Central Bureau of Statistics. Criminal Statistics (IS ISSN 0075-1006) 282
Israel. Central Bureau of Statistics. Diagnostic Statistics of Hospitalized Patients (IS ISSN 0075-1014) 481, 806
Israel. Central Bureau of Statistics. Foreign Trade Statistics Quarterly see Israel. Central Bureau of Statistics. Annual Foreign Trade Statistics 159
Israel. Central Bureau of Statistics. Inputs in Research and Development in Academic Institutions (IS) 327
Israel. Central Bureau of Statistics. Insurance in Israel/Iske Ha-Bituah Be-Yisrael (IS ISSN 0074-0705) 502
Israel. Central Bureau of Statistics. Israel's Foreign Trade/Sehar Huts Shel Yisrael (IS ISSN 0075-1421) 159
Israel. Central Bureau of Statistics. Judicial Statistics (IS ISSN 0075-1030) 513
Israel. Central Bureau of Statistics. Juvenile Delinquency (IS ISSN 0075-1022) 256
Israel. Central Bureau of Statistics. Kupot Gemel Be-Yisrael (IS) 502
Israel. Central Bureau of Statistics. Labour Force Surveys (IS ISSN 0075-1049) 159
Israel. Central Bureau of Statistics. Motor Vehicles (IS ISSN 0075-1057) 882
Israel. Central Bureau of Statistics. Road Accidents with Casualties (IS) 866
Israel. Central Bureau of Statistics. Schools and Kindergartens (IS ISSN 0075-1065) 327
Israel. Central Bureau of Statistics. Statistical Abstract of Israel/Shenaton Statisti le-Yisrael (IS ISSN 0081-4679) 841
Israel. Central Bureau of Statistics. Strikes and Lock-Outs (IS ISSN 0075-1073) 159
Israel. Central Bureau of Statistics. Students in Academic Institutions (IS ISSN 0075-1081) 319
Israel. Central Bureau of Statistics. Suicides and Attempted Suicides (IS) 727
Israel. Central Bureau of Statistics. Survey of Housing Conditions (IS ISSN 0075-109X) 485
Israel. Central Bureau of Statistics. Trade Survey (IS ISSN 0075-1103) 159
Israel. Central Bureau of Statistics. Traveling Habits Survey (IS) 893
Israel. Central Bureau of Statistics. Vital Statistics (IS ISSN 0075-1111) 841

Israel. Commissioner for Complaints from the Public (Ombudsman) Annual Report (IS) *743*
Israel. Department of Surveys. Cartographic Papers (IS) *423*
Israel. Department of Surveys. Geodetic Papers (IS ISSN 0075-1138) *423*
Israel. Department of Surveys. Photogrammetric Papers (IS) *423*
Israel. Environmental Protection Agency. Ekhut Ha-Sevivah Be-Yisrael. Duakh Shnati (IS ISSN 0334-3162) *387*
Israel. Geological Survey. Bulletin (IS ISSN 0075-1200) *295*
Israel. Goverment Press Office. Newspapers and Periodicals Appearing in Israel (IS ISSN 0078-0448) *531*
Israel. Knesset. Finance Committee. Data on Activities *see* Israel. Knesset. Va'adat Ha-Kesafim Misparim al Va'adat Ha-Kesafim *230*
Israel. Knesset. Hava'ada Leinyanei Bikoret Hamedina. Sikumeha ve-Hatsa 'oteha Shel Hava'ada Leinyanei Bikoret Hamedina le-Din ve-Hesbon Shel Mevaker Ha-Medina(IS) *749*
Israel. Knesset. Va'adat Ha-Kesafim Misparim al Va'adat Ha-Kesafim/ Israel. Knesset. Finance Committee. Data on Activities (IS) *230*
Israel. Meteorological Service. Annual Rainfall Summary. Series B (Observational Data) (IS ISSN 0075-126X) *633*
Israel. Meteorological Service. Annual Weather Report. Series B (Observational Data) (IS ISSN 0075-1286) *633*
Israel. Meteorological Service. Series A (Meteorological Notes) (IS ISSN 0075-1278) *633*
Israel. Meteorological Service. Series C (Miscellaneous Papers) (IS ISSN 0444-6801) *633*
Israel. Meteorological Service. Solar Radiation and Radiation Balance at Bet Dagan, Israel. Series B (Observational Data) (IS) *633*
Israel. Ministry of Agriculture. Department of Fisheries. Israel Fisheries in Figures/Ha-Dayig Be-Yisrael Be-Misparim (IS ISSN 0075-1189) *398*
Israel. Ministry of Commerce and Industry. Surveys and Development Plans of Industry in Israel/Ha-Ta'Asiyah Ha-Yisre'Elit (IS ISSN 0081-9743) *223*
Israel. Ministry of Communications. Statistics/Israel. Misrad Ha-Tikshoret. Statistikah (IS ISSN 0075-1308) *266*
Israel. Ministry of Education and Culture. Department of Antiquities and Museums. Atiqot (English Series) (IS ISSN 0066-488X) *62*
Israel. Ministry of Education and Culture. Department of Antiquities and Museums. Atiqot (Hebrew Series) (IS ISSN 0067-0138) *62*
Israel. Ministry of Education and Culture. Department of Educational Technology. Bulletin/Alon le-Technologyah Be-Khinukh (IS) *349*
Israel. Ministry of Labour. Registrar of Cooperative Societies. Report on the Cooperative Movement in Israel (IS ISSN 0080-1313) *181*
Israel. Misrad Ha-Tikshoret. Statistikah *see* Israel. Ministry of Communications. Statistics *266*
Israel. National Council for Research and Development. Scientific Research in Israel (IS ISSN 0080-7753) *784*
Israel. Rural Planning and Development Authority. Agricultural and Rural Development Report *see* Israel. Rural Planning and Development Authority. Agricultural and Rural Economic Report *16*
Israel. Rural Planning and Development Authority. Agricultural and Rural Economic Report (IS) *16*

Israel Annual Conference on Aviation and Astronautics. Proceedings (IS ISSN 0075-0972) *9*
Israel Book Trade Directory (IS) *733, 759*
Israel Book Trades Directory: a Select List *see* Israel Book Trade Directory *759*
Israel C P A (IS) *167*
Israel Discount Bank. Report (IS ISSN 0075-1146) *174*
Israel Export and Trade Journal (IS) *186*
Israel Export Annual *see* Israel Export and Trade Journal *186*
Israel Film-Making Plus *see* Filmmaking in Israel *650*
Israel Institute for Biological Research. OHOLO Biological Conference. Proceedings (IS) *104*
Israel Institute of Applied Social Research. Research Report (IS ISSN 0075-1227) *814*
Israel Institute of Technology. President's Report and Reports of Other Officers *see* Technion-Israel Institute of Technology. President's Report *853*
Israel Journal of Entomology (IS ISSN 0075-1243) *121*
Israel Medical Bibliography (IS ISSN 0075-1251) *602*
Israel Oceanographic and Limnological Research. Annual Report (IS ISSN 0304-7423) *311*
Israel Oriental Studies (IS) *670*
Israel Petroleum and Energy Year Book(IS ISSN 0075-1367) *680*
Israel Physical Society. Annals (IS) *697*
Israel Society for Rehabilitation of the Disabled. Annual (IS ISSN 0075-1383) *346, 806*
Israel Studies in Criminology (IS ISSN 0075-1391) *282*
Israel Studies in Musicology (IS) *660*
Israel Tourist Statistics/Ha-Tayarut Be-Yisrael (IS ISSN 0075-1405) *887*
Israel Yearbook (IS ISSN 0075-1413) *444*
Israel Yearbook on Human Rights (IS) *513, 718*
Israeli Life Table (IS ISSN 0077-5037) *499*
Issledovania po Teorii Algorifmov i Matematicheskoi Logike (UR ISSN 0302-9085) *586, 689*
Issledovanie, Proektirovanie i Raschet Rezbovykh Soedinenii (UR) *368*
Issledovaniya v Oblasti Khimii Redkozemel'nykh Elementov (UR) *251, 289*
Issue (CN) *776*
Issues in Contemporary Politics (NE) *711*
Issues in Higher Education (US) *337*
Issues in Media Management (US ISSN 0098-7239) *349*
Issues in the Library and Information Sciences (US) *531*
Issues in the New Caribbean *see* Challenges in the New Caribbean *419*
Istituto Centrale per la Patologia del Libro "Alfonso Gallo." Bollettino (IT) *92, 760*
Istituto Comeliana di Lugano. Collectio Monographica Minor (IT) *784*
Istituto della Enciclopedia Italiana. Annuario (IT) *361*
Istituto della Enciclopedia Italiana. Bibliotheca Biographica (IT) *361*
Istituto di Diritto Internazionale-D. Anzilotti. Pubblicazioni (IT) *523*
Istituto di Diritto Romano. Bullettino (IT) *513*
Istituto di Fisica dell'Atmosfera, Rome. Bibliografia Generale. (IT ISSN 0075-1901) *636*
Istituto di Fisica dell'Atmosfera, Rome. Contributi Scientifici: Pubblicazioni di Fisica dell'Atmosfera e di Metteorologia. (IT ISSN 0075-191X) *634*
Istituto di Fisica dell' Atmosfera, Rome. Pubblicazioni Didattiche (IT ISSN 0075-1928) *634*

Istituto di Fisica dell'Atmosfera, Rome. Pubblicazioni Scientifiche (IT ISSN 0075-1936) *634*
Istituto di Fisica dell'Atmosfera, Rome. Pubblicazioni Varie. (IT ISSN 0075-1944) *634*
Istituto di Fisica dell'Atmosfera, Rome. Rapporti Interni Provvisori Adiffusione Limitata (IT ISSN 0075-1952) *633*
Istituto di Fisica dell'Atmosfera, Rome. Rapporti Scientifici (IT ISSN 0075-1960) *633*
Istituto di Fisica dell'Atmosfera, Rome. Rapporti Tecnici (IT ISSN 0075-1979) *633*
Istituto di Patologia del Libro "Alfonso Gallo." Bollettino *see* Istituto Centrale per la Patologia del Libro "Alfonso Gallo." Bollettino *760*
Istituto di Studi e Documentazioni sull'Est Europeo. Serie Giuridica (IT) *523*
Istituto di Studi Pirandelliani e Sul Teatro Contemporaneo (IT ISSN 0075-1480) *859*
Istituto e Museo di Storia della Scienza. Biblioteca (IT ISSN 0075-1499) *784*
Istituto Ellenico di Studi Bizantini e Postbizantini, Venice. Biblioteca (IT ISSN 0075-1502) *433*
Istituto Giapponese di Cultura, Rome. Annuario. (IT ISSN 0080-391X) *444*
Istituto Giapponese di Cultura, Rome. Notiziario. (IT ISSN 0080-3928) *444*
Istituto Gramsci Piemontese. Materiali (IT) *711*
Istituto Internazionale di Studi Liguri. Collezione di Monografie Preistoriche Ed Archeologiche (IT ISSN 0530-9867) *62*
Istituto Italiano di Idrobiologia. Memorie (IT ISSN 0075-1510) *104*
Istituto Italiano di Preistoria e Protostoria. Atti della Riunione Scientifica (IT) *433*
Istituto Italiano per gli Studi Filosofici. Serie Studi (IT) *689*
Istituto Lombardo Accademia di Scienze e Lettere. Rendiconti. A (IT ISSN 0021-2504) *784*
Istituto Mobiliare Italiano. Annual Report (IT ISSN 0075-1529) *145*
Istituto Nazionale di Geofisica. Anali di Geofisica (IT) *305*
Istituto Nazionale per l'Assicurazione Contro le Malattie, Rome. Bilancio Consuntivo (IT ISSN 0075-1537) *910*
Istituto per la Storia del Movimento Liberale. Quaderno (IT) *711*
Istituto Siciliano di Studi Bizantini e Neoellenici. Quaderni (IT ISSN 0075-1545) *456*
Istituto Siciliano di Studi Bizantini e Neoellenici. Testi e Monumenti. Testi (IT ISSN 0075-1553) *456*
Istituto Sperimentale per l'Enologia Asti. Annali (IT ISSN 0374-5791) *86*
Istituto Sperimentale Talassografico, Trieste. Annuario. (IT ISSN 0082-6448) *634*
Istituto Storico Artistico Orvietano. Bollettino (IT ISSN 0085-2287) *456*
Istituto Storico della Resistenza in Modena e Provincia. Quaderni (IT ISSN 0075-1561) *456*
Istituto Superiore Europeo di Studi Politici. Collana di Studi (IT) *722*
Istituto Universitario Navale, Naples. Annali (IT ISSN 0075-1588) *639*
Istituto Universitario Orientale di Napoli. Annali. Sezione Germanica (IT ISSN 0077-2763) *566*
Istituto Universitario Orientale di Napoli. Annali. Sezione Slava (IT ISSN 0077-2771) *545*
Istituto Universitario Orientale di Napoli. Seminario di Studi del Mondo Classico. Annali. Sezione Linguistica (IT ISSN *259, 670*
Istituzioni Culturali (IT ISSN 0391-321X) *798*

Istituzioni Culturali Piemontesi. Pubblicazioni (IT) *859*
Istituzioni e Monumenti dell' Arte Musicale Italiana Nuova Serie (IT ISSN 0075-1596) *660*
Istochnikovedenie Otechestvennoi Istorii (UR) *456*
Istoria Limbii Romane (RM ISSN 0075-160X) *545*
Istoricheskie Zapiski (UR) *433*
Istorie si Civilizatie (RM ISSN 0075-1626) *433*
Istoriia na Bulgarskoto Izobrazitelno Izkustvo (BU) *75*
Istoriko-Matematicheskie Issledovaniya (UR) *586*
It (AT) *830*
Italia (IS) *392*
Italia Dialettale (IT ISSN 0085-2295) *545*
Italia Nella Politica Internazionale (IT) *711*
Italian Books in Print *see* Catalogo dei Libri in Commercio *760*
Italian Culture (US) *566*
Italian Genealogist (US) *417, 456*
Italian Journal of Zoology. Monographs *see* Monitore Zoologico Italiano. Monografie *129*
Italian Journal of Zoology. Supplement *see* Monitore Zoologico Italiano. Supplemento *129*
Italian Studies (UK ISSN 0075-1634) *566*
Italy. Direzione Generale delle Fonti di Energia e delle Industrie di Base. Bilanci Energetici (IT ISSN 0075-1650) *363*
Italy. Ente Nazionale Idrocarburi. Chimica. Sommario Statistico (IT) *373*
Italy. Ente Nazionale Idrocarburi. Energia ed Idrocarburi. Sommario Statistico (IT) *644*
Italy. Istituto Centrale di Statistica. Annuari di Statistiche Giudiziarie (IT ISSN 0075-1715) *513*
Italy. Istituto Centrale di Statistica. Annuario delle Statistiche Culturali (IT ISSN 0075-1677) *759*
Italy. Istituto Centrale di Statistica. Annuario di Statistica Agraria (IT ISSN 0021-2504) *16*
Italy. Istituto Centrale di Statistica. Annuario di Statistica Forestale (IT ISSN 0075-1707) *409*
Italy. Istituto Centrale di Statistica. Annuario di Statistiche del Lavoro (IT ISSN 0390-6450) *732*
Italy. Istituto Centrale di Statistica. Annuario di Statistiche Demografiche(IT ISSN 0075-1685) *727*
ltaly. Istituto Centrale di Statistica. Annuario di Statistiche Industriali (IT ISSN 0075-1723) *159, 841*
Italy. Istituto Centrale di Statistica. Annuario di Statistiche Meteorologiche (IT ISSN 0075-1731) *634*
Italy. Istituto Centrale di Statistica. Annuario di Statistiche Sanitarie (IT ISSN 0075-1758) *752*
Italy. Istituto Centrale di Statistica. Annuario Statistiche Zootecniche *see* Italy. Istituto Centrale di Statistica. Annuario Statistico della Zootecnia, della Pesca e della Caccia *25*
Italy. Istituto Centrale di Statistica. Annuario Statistico del Commercio Interno (IT ISSN 0075-1782) *159, 196, 842*
Italy. Istituto Centrale di Statistica. Annuario Statistico dell'Assistenza e della Previdenza Sociale (IT ISSN 0075-1790) *502*
Italy. Istituto Centrale di Statistica. Annuario Statistico della Navigazione Marittima (IT ISSN 0075-1898) *842, 866, 878*
Italy. Istituto Centrale di Statistica. Annuario Statistico della Zootecnia, della Pesca e della Caccia (IT ISSN 0390-6426) *25*
Italy. Istituto Centrale di Statistica. Bolletino Mensile di Statistica (IT ISSN 0390-6434) *842*

Italy. Istituto Centrale di Statistica. Popolazione e Movimento Anagrafico dei Comuni (IT ISSN 0075-1863) *728*
Italy. Istituto Centrale di Statistica. Statistica Annuale del Commercio con l'Estero *see* Italy. Istituto Centrale di Statistica. Statistica Annuale del Commercio con l'Estero. Tomo I *159*
Italy. Istituto Centrale di Statistica. Statistica Annuale del Commercio con l'Estero *see* Italy. Istituto Centrale di Statistica. Statistica Annuale del Commercio con l'Estero. Tomo II *159*
Italy. Istituto Centrale di Statistica. Statistica Annuale del Commercio con l'Estero. Tomo I (IT ISSN 0390-6558) *159, 196, 842*
Italy. Istituto Centrale di Statistica. Statistica Annuale del Commercio con l'Estero. Tomo II (IT ISSN 0390-6566) *159, 196, 842*
Italy. Istituto di Studi sulla Ricerca e Documentazione Scientifica. Note Bibliografia e Documentazione Scientifica (IT) *531*
Italy. Istituto Nazionale per Lo Studio della Congiuntura. Quaderni Analitici(IT ISSN 0075-1987) *223*
Italy. Laboratorio di Studi sulla Ricerca e sulla Documentazione. Note di Bibliografia e Documentazione Scientifica *see* Italy. Istituto di Studi sulla Ricerca e Documentazione Scientifica. Note Bibliografia e Documentazione Scientifica *531*
Italy. Ministero del Bilancio e della Programmazione Economica. Relazione Generale Sulla Situazione Economica del Paese (IT ISSN 0075-1995) *186*
Italy: An Economic Profile (US ISSN 0075-1642) *186*
Itihasa Samiti Patrika *see* Bangladesh Itihas Samiti. Journal *442*
Itinera Romana (SZ ISSN 0075-2002) *423*
Itogi Nauki i Tekhniki: Genetika Cheloveka (UR) *122*
Itogi Nauki i Tekhniki: Geomagnetizm i Vysokie Sloi Atmosfery (UR) *305*
Itogi Nauki i Tekhniki: Stratigrafiya, Paleontologiya (UR) *673*
Itogi Nauki i Tekhniki: Tekhnologiia Organicheskikh Veshchestv (UR ISSN 0303-2361) *252*
Itogi Nauki: Stratigrafiya, Paleontologiya *see* Itogi Nauki i Tekhniki: Stratigrafiya, Paleontologiya *673*
Itogi Nauki i Tekhniki: Tekhnologiia Organicheskikh Veshchestv *see* Itogi Nauki i Tekhniki: Tekhnologiia Organicheskikh Veshchestv *252*
It's Happening (US) *346*
Itsuu Kenkyusho Nenpo *see* Itsuu Laboratory, Tokyo. Annual Report *252*
Itsuu Laboratory, Tokyo. Annual Report/Itsuu Kenkyusho Nenpo (JA ISSN 0075-2010) *252*
Ittihad al-Sinaat al-Misriyah. Yearbook (UA) *238*
Ittihad al-Sinaat Bi-al-Jumhuriyah al-Arabiyah al-Muttahidah. Yearbook *see* Ittihad al-Sinaat al-Misriyah. Yearbook *238*
Iura (IT ISSN 0021-3241) *513*
Ius Commune (GW ISSN 0579-2428) *513*
Ius Commune. Sonderhefte (GW) *513*
Ius Romanum Medii Aevi (IT ISSN 0075-2037) *513*
Ivory Coast. Annuaire International/International Directory (IV) *440*
Ivory Coast. Bureau de Developpement Industriel. Couts des Facteurs en Cote d'Ivoire (IV) *223*
Ivory Coast. Bureau de Developpement Industriel. Programme d'Activite (IV) *223*
Ivory Coast. Bureau de Developpement Industriel. Programme Triennial des Activites (IV) *223*
Ivory Coast. Bureau de Developpement Industriel. Rapport d'Activites (IV) *223*

Ivory Coast. Bureau du Developpement Industriel. Situation de l'Industrie Ivoirienne (IV) *223*
Ivory Coast. Direction des Mines et de la Geologie. Rapport Provisoire sur les Activities du Secteur (IV) *295, 644*
Ivory Coast. Direction du Budget Special d'Investissement et d'Equipment. Rapport de Presentation du Budget Special d'Investissement et d'Equipment (IV) *743*
Ivory Coast. Ministere de l'Agriculture. Statistiques Agricoles (IV) *25*
Ivory Coast. Ministere de l'Economie, es Finances et du Plan. Comptes de la Nation (IV) *230*
Ivory Coast. Ministere du Plan. Comptes de la Nation *see* Ivory Coast. Ministere de l'Economie, es Finances et du Plan. Comptes de la Nation *230*
L'Ivre de Pierres (FR) *69, 75*
Iwate Daigaku Kogakubu Kenkyu Hokoku *see* Iwate University. Faculty of Engineering. Technology Reports *368*
Iwate University. Faculty of Engineering. Technology Reports/Iwate Daigaku Kogakubu Kenkyu Hokoku (JA ISSN 0085-2325) *368*
Iwate University. Mountains Land Use Research Laboratory. Bulletin (JA) *29*
Iyo Kizai Kenkyusho Hokoku *see* Tokyo Medical and Dental University. Institute for Medical and Dental Engineering. Reports *600*
Iz Istorii Estestvoznaniya i Tekhniki Pribaltiki *see* Contributions to the History of Science and Technology in Baltics *781*
Izsledovaniia po Bulgarska Istoriia (BU) *456*
Izvori Srpskog Prava/Sources de Droit Serbe/Serbische Rechtsquellen (YU) *513*
J A B A Monograph Series (Journal of Applied Behavior Analysis) (US) *736*
J A G Journal (U.S. Department of the Navy) (US ISSN 0021-3519) *513, 639*
J A P T A List: Japanese Drug Directory (Japan Pharmaceutical Traders' Association) (JA) *685*
J. Anderson Fitzgerald Lecture (US ISSN 0075-2045) *145*
J. B. Speed Art Museum Bulletin (US ISSN 0021-356X) *653*
J E B-Points (BE) *256, 319*
J E B Theatre (BE) *859*
J I L A Information Center. Report (Joint Institute for Laboratory Astrophysics) (US ISSN 0449-1343) *82*
J. K. Lasser's Your Income Tax (US ISSN 0084-4314) *230*
J. K. Lasser's Your Income Tax, Professional Ed (US ISSN 0075-2061) *230*
J. L. B. Smith Institute of Ichthyology. Ichthyological Bulletin (SA ISSN 0073-4381) *129*
J. L. B. Smith Institute of Ichthyology. Occasional Paper (SA ISSN 0075-207X) *910*
J. L. B. Smith Institute of Ichthyology. Special Publication (SA ISSN 0075-2088) *129*
J. Paul Getty Museum Journal (US ISSN 0362-1979) *75*
J. T. Stewart Lecture in Planning (NZ ISSN 0075-210X) *423*
Jaarbericht "Ex Oriente Lux" (NE ISSN 0075-2118) *62, 444*
Jaarboek der Schone Kunsten/Algemeen Jaarboek der Schone Kunsten (BE ISSN 0066-3174) *75*
Jaarboek Eindhoven (NE) *842*
Jaarboek/Vademecum voor het Verzekeringswezen (NE) *499*
Jaarboek van de Openbare Gasvoorziening (NE) *363, 680*
Jaarstatistiek van de in-en Uitvoer per Goederensoort van de Nederlandse Antillen (NA ISSN 0077-6653) *159*

Jaarstatistiek van de in-en Uitvoer per Land van de Nederlandse Antillen (NA ISSN 0077-6645) *159*
Jackson Laboratory Annual Report (US) *122, 596*
Jacksonville Port Handbook (US ISSN 0160-2241) *878*
Jacob Blaustein Lectures in International Affairs (US ISSN 0075-2142) *722*
Jacob Marschak Interdisciplinary Colloquium on Mathematics in the Behavioral Sciences (US ISSN 0160-7146) *215*
Jacobean Drama Studies (AU) *566, 859*
Jadavpur Journal of Comparative Literature (II ISSN 0448-1143) *566*
Jaeger and Waldmann International Telex Directory (GW) *269*
Jaeger and Waldmann World Telex Directory *see* Jaeger and Waldmann International Telex Directory *269*
Jaeger's Intertravel (GW ISSN 0075-2150) *887*
Jaguar Journal of Australia (AT ISSN 0310-3137) *826*
Jahangirnagar University. Department of English. Bulletin (BG) *566*
Jahrbuch Deutsch Als Fremdsprache (GW ISSN 0342-6300) *337, 545*
Jahrbuch der Auktionspreise (GW ISSN 0075-2193) *531, 653, 759*
Jahrbuch der Berliner Museen (GW ISSN 0075-2207) *653*
Jahrbuch der Bibliotheken, Archive und Informationsstellen der Deutschen Demokratischen Republik (GE ISSN 0075-2215) *531*
Jahrbuch der Bibliotheken, Informationsstellen und Archive der D D R *see* Jahrbuch der Bibliotheken, Archive und Informationsstellen der Deutschen Demokratischen Republik *531*
Jahrbuch der Deutschen Bibliotheken (GW ISSN 0075-2223) *531*
Jahrbuch der Europaeischen Erdoelindustrie *see* European Petroleum Yearbook *679*
Jahrbuch der Export- und Versandtleiter (GW ISSN 0075-224X) *196*
Jahrbuch der Hamburger Kunstsammlungen (GW ISSN 0075-2274) *653*
Jahrbuch der Leichtathletik (GW) *820*
Jahrbuch der Luftfahrt und Raumfahrt *see* Reuss Jahrbuch der Luft- und Raumfahrt *10*
Jahrbuch der Luftwaffe (GW ISSN 0075-2320) *639*
Jahrbuch der Oeffentlichen Meinung *see* Allensbacher Jahrbuch der Demoskopie *811*
Jahrbuch der Oesterreichischen Sozialversicherung *see* Handbuch der Oesterreichischen Sozialversicherung *502*
Jahrbuch der Oesterreichischen Wirtschaft (AU) *186*
Jahrbuch der Psychoanalyse (SZ ISSN 0075-2363) *736*
Jahrbuch der Schleiff-, Hon-, Laepp- und Poliertechnik *see* Jahrbuch Schleiffen, Honen, Laeppen und Polieren, Verfahren und Maschinen *382*
Jahrbuch der Wehrmedizin (GW ISSN 0075-241X) *596*
Jahrbuch der Wehrtechnik (GW ISSN 0075-2428) *639*
Jahrbuch der Werbung (GW) *653*
Jahrbuch der Wirtschaft Osteuropas/Yearbook of East-European Economics (GW ISSN 0449-5225) *186*
Jahrbuch der Wittheit zu Bremen (GW ISSN 0447-2624) *784*
Jahrbuch des Baltischen Deutschtums (GW ISSN 0075-2436) *456*
Jahrbuch des Deutschen Bergbaus *see* Jahrbuch fuer Bergbau, Energie, Mineraloel und Chemie *644*
Jahrbuch des Eisenbahnwesens (GW ISSN 0075-2479) *873*
Jahrbuch des Getraenke und Fluessigen Nahrmittel *see* Annuaire des Boissons et des Liquides Alimentaires *85*

Jahrbuch des Heeres (GW ISSN 0075-2282) *639*
Jahrbuch des Instituts fuer Christliche Sozialwissenschaften *see* Jahrbuch fuer Christliche Sozialwissenschaften *814*
Jahrbuch des Kameramanns (GW ISSN 0075-2509) *650*
Jahrbuch des Oeffentlichen Rechts der Gegenwart (GW ISSN 0075-2517) *514*
Jahrbuch fuer Antike und Christentum (GW ISSN 0075-2541) *765*
Jahrbuch fuer Bergbau, Energie, Mineraloel und Chemie (GW ISSN 0075-255X) *644*
Jahrbuch fuer Berlin-Brandenburgische Kirchengeschichte (GW ISSN 0075-2568) *765*
Jahrbuch fuer Brandenburgische Kirchengeschichte *see* Jahrbuch fuer Berlin-Brandenburgische Kirchengeschichte *765*
Jahrbuch fuer Bundesbahnbeamte (GW ISSN 0075-2576) *873*
Jahrbuch fuer Christliche Sozialwissenschaften (GW ISSN 0075-2584) *765, 814*
Jahrbuch fuer den Deutsch-Franzoesischen Handel *see* Guide Annuaire du Commerce Franco-Allemand *179*
Jahrbuch fuer den Kreis Pinneberg (GW ISSN 0448-150X) *456*
Jahrbuch fuer den Oesterreichischen Tierarzt (AU ISSN 0075-2606) *894*
Jahrbuch fuer die Gefluegelwirtschaft (GW ISSN 0447-2713) *45*
Jahrbuch fuer Fremdenverkehr (GW ISSN 0075-2649) *887*
Jahrbuch fuer Geologie (GE) *295*
Jahrbuch fuer Geschichte des Feudalismus (GE) *456*
Jahrbuch fuer Geschichte von Staat, Wirtschaft und Gesellschaft Lateinamerikas. (GW ISSN 0075-2673) *456*
Jahrbuch fuer Internationales Recht *see* German Yearbook of International Law *523*
Jahrbuch fuer Liturgik und Hymnologie(GW ISSN 0075-2681) *660, 766*
Jahrbuch fuer Musikalische Volks- und Voelkerkunde (GW ISSN 0075-2703) *402, 660*
Jahrbuch fuer Numismatik und Geldgeschichte (GW ISSN 0075-2711) *477*
Jahrbuch fuer Optik und Feinmechanik (GW ISSN 0075-272X) *705*
Jahrbuch fuer Ostdeutsche Volkskunde (GW ISSN 0075-2738) *50, 402*
Jahrbuch fuer Ostrecht (GW ISSN 0075-2746) *514*
Jahrbuch fuer Praehistorische und Ethnographische Kunst *see* I P E K *402*
Jahrbuch fuer Praktiker des Rechnungswesens (GW) *167*
Jahrbuch fuer Regionalgeschichte (GE ISSN 0085-2341) *456*
Jahrbuch fuer Salesianische Studien (GW ISSN 0075-2754) *456*
Jahrbuch fuer Schlesische Kirchengeschichte (GW ISSN 0075-2762) *766*
Jahrbuch fuer Volksliedforschung (GW ISSN 0075-2789) *660*
Jahrbuch fuer Westdeutsche Landesgeschichte (GW ISSN 0170-2025) *456*
Jahrbuch fuer Wirtschaftsgeschichte (GE ISSN 0075-2800) *191*
Jahrbuch Krankenhaus (AU ISSN 0075-7063) *481*
Jahrbuch Oberflaechentechnik (GW ISSN 0075-2819) *628*
Jahrbuch Peters (GW) *660*
Jahrbuch Schleiffen, Honen, Laeppen und Polieren, Verfahren und Maschinen (GW) *382*
Jahrbuch Ueberblicke Mathematik (GW) *586*
Jahrbuch zur Alkohol- und Tabakfrage *see* Jahrbuch zur Frage der Suchtgefahren *287*
Jahrbuch zur Frage der Suchtgefahren (GW) *287*

Jahrbuch zur Geschichte Dresdens (GE) *456*
Jahresbericht der Bayerischen Bodendenkmalpflege (GW ISSN 0075-2835) *433*
Jahresbericht ueber die Deutsche Fischwirtschaft (GW ISSN 0075-2851) *398*
Jahresbibliographie Massenkommunikation (GW) *92, 266*
Jahresfachkatalog Recht-Wirtschaft-Steuern (GW ISSN 0075-2886) *145,* 230, 514
Jahreshefte fuer Karst- und Hoehlenkunde (GW ISSN 0075-2894) *295*
Jahreskatalog Kybernetik, Automation, Informatik *see* Kybernetik Jahreskatalog *273*
Jahreskatalog Philosophie (GW ISSN 0075-2916) *689*
Jahreskatalog Psychologie (GW ISSN 0075-2924) *736*
Jahresverzeichnis der Deutschen Hochschulschriften *see* Jahresverzeichnis der Hochschulschriften der DDR, der BRD und Westberlins *327*
Jahresverzeichnis der Hochschulschriften der DDR, der BRD und Westberlins (GE) *3, 327*
Jahresverzeichnis der Musikalien und Musikschriften (GE ISSN 0075-2959) *665*
Jahresverzeichnis der Musikalien und Musikschriften *see* Jahresverzeichnis der Musikalien und Musikschriften *665*
Jahresverzeichnis der Verlagsschriften und Einer Auswahl der ausserhalb des Buchhandels Erschienenen Veroeffentlichungen der DDR, der BRD und Westberlins sowie der Deutschsprachigen Werke Anderer Laender (GE ISSN 0300-8436) *92*
Jahresverzeichnis des Deutschen Schrifttums *see* Jahresverzeichnis der Verlagsschriften und Einer Auswahl der ausserhalb des Buchhandels Erschienenen Veroeffentlichungen der DDR, der BRD und Westberlins sowie der Deutschsprachigen Werke Anderer Laender *92*
Jahrhunderte der Volkskunst *see* Nepmuveszet Evszazadai *402*
J'aime Lire (FR) *258, 766*
Jakarta Business Directory (IO) *238*
Jakarta Buyer's Guide (IO) *238*
Jakarta Metropolitan Buyers' Guide (IO) *238*
Jam to-Day (US ISSN 0362-8302) *566*
Jamaica. Department of Statistics. Abstract of Building and Construction Statistics (JM) *137, 842*
Jamaica. Department of Statistics. Annual Abstract of Statistics *see* Jamaica. Department of Statistics. Statistical Abstract *842*
Jamaica. Department of Statistics. Demographic Statistics (JM) *842*
Jamaica. Department of Statistics. External Trade Annual Review (JM) *159*
Jamaica. Department of Statistics. Monetary Statistics Report (JM ISSN 0026-9638) *842*
Jamaica. Department of Statistics. National Income and Product (JM) *842*
Jamaica. Department of Statistics. Pocketbook of Statistics (JM) *842*
Jamaica. Department of Statistics. Statistical Abstract (JM) *842*
Jamaica. Ministry of Pensions and Social Security. Report *see* Jamaica. Ministry of Social Security. Report *499*
Jamaica. Ministry of Social Security. Report (JM) *499*
Jamaica. National Insurance Scheme. Annual Reports *see* Jamaica. Ministry of Social Security. Report *499*
Jamaica Annual (UK ISSN 0447-3280) *887*

Jamaica Children's Service Society. Annual Report (JM) 256, *806*
Jamaica Dental Association. Newsletter(JM) *610*
Jamaica Library Association. Annual Bulletin *see* Jamaica Library Association. Bulletin *532*
Jamaica Library Association. Bulletin (JM) *532*
Jamaican Association of Sugar Technologists. Proceedings (JM) *37*
Jamaican Bar Association. Annual Report (JM) *514*
Jamaican Historical Review (JM) *470*
Jamaican National Bibliography (JM ISSN 0075-2991) *92*
James Cook University of North Queensland. Department of Geography. Monograph Series (AT) *423*
James Cook University of North Queensland. Research and Publications Report (0312-9012) (AT) *92, 794*
James K. Whittemore Lectures in Mathematics Given at Yale University (US) *586*
James Terry Duce Memorial Series (US ISSN 0075-3009) *475, 711*
Jaminraitu (II) *580*
Jammu and Kashmir. Legislative Council. Committee on Privileges. Report (II ISSN 0448-2433) *711*
Jammu & Kashmir Minerals Limited. Annual Report (II ISSN 0304-7164) *644*
JAMS Guide de la Demeure et des Jeunes Maries (FR) *479,* 503
Jane's All the World Aircraft (UK ISSN 0075-3017) *9*
Jane's Armour and Artillery (UK) *639*
Jane's Combat Support Equipment (UK) *639*
Jane's Fighting Ships (UK ISSN 0075-3025) *639,* 879
Jane's Freight Containers (UK ISSN 0075-3033) *873*
Jane's Infantry Weapons (UK ISSN 0306-3410) *639*
Jane's Military Communications (UK) *639*
Jane's Surface Skimmers (UK ISSN 0075-305X) *879*
Jane's Weapon Systems (UK ISSN 0075-3068) *639*
Jane's World Railways (UK ISSN 0075-3084) *873*
Janua Linguarum. Series Anastatica (NE) *545*
Janua Linguarum. Series Critica (NE ISSN 0075-3092) *545*
Janua Linguarum. Series Didactica (NE ISSN 0075-3106) *546*
Janua Linguarum. Series Major (NE ISSN 0075-3114) *546*
Janua Linguarum. Series Minor (NE ISSN 0075-3122) *546*
Janua Linguarum. Series Practica (NE ISSN 0075-3130) *546*
January Bulletin (UK) *415*
Japan. Bureau of Statistics. Annual Report on Family Income and Expenditures (JA ISSN 0075-3173) *842*
Japan. Bureau of Statistics. Employment Status Survey/Japan. Sorifu. Tokeikyoku. Shugyokozo Kihon Chosa (JA ISSN 0075-3181) *159, 842*
Japan. Forestry and Forest Products Research Institute. Annual Report/ Norinsho Ringyo Shikenjo Nenpo (JA) *409*
Japan. Forestry and Forest Products Research Institute. Bulletin (JA) *409*
Japan. Geological Survey. Cruise Report (JA) *295*
Japan. Government Forest Experiment Station. Kyushu Branch. Annual Report/Ringyo Shikenjo Kyushu Shijo Nenpo (JA ISSN 0557-0395) *409*
Japan. Government Forest Experiment Station, Tokyo. Annual Report *see* Japan. Forestry and Forest Products Research Institute. Annual Report *409*

Japan. Government Industrial Development Laboratory, Hokkaido. Annual Report/Hokkaido Kogyo Kaihatsu Shikenjo Nempo (JA) *223*
Japan. Government Industrial Development Laboratory, Hokkaido. Reports/Hokkaido Kogyo Kaihatsu Shikenjo Hokoku (JA ISSN 0441-0734) *851*
Japan. Government Industrial Development Laboratory, Hokkaido. Technical Data/Hokkaido Kogyo Kaihatsu Shikenjo Gijutsu (JA) *851*
Japan. Government Industrial Research Institute, Kyushu Annual Report/ Kyushu Kogyo Gijutsu Shikenjo Nempo (JA) *223*
Japan. Maritime Safety Agency. Hydrographic Department. Report of Hydrographic Research (JA) *308*
Japan. Meteorological Agency. Annual Report/Kisho-cho Nenpo Zenkoku Kishohyo (JA ISSN 0448-3758) *634*
Japan. Ministry of Agriculture and Forestry. Annual Report/Norin-sho Nenpo (JA ISSN 0446-5458) *17,* 409
Japan. Ministry of Health and Welfare. Statistics and Information Department. Vital Statistics (JA ISSN 0075-3270) *842*
Japan. Ministry of Labour. Yearbook of Labour Statistics (JA) *159*
Japan. National Diet Library. Annual Report/Kokuritsu Kokkai Toshokan Nenpo (JA ISSN 0385-325X) *532*
Japan. National Institute of Animal Health. Annual Report/Norin-sho Kachiku Eisei Shikenjo Nempo (JA ISSN 0453-0535) *894*
Japan. Public Works Research Institute. Journal of Research/Doboku Kenkyusho Hokoku (JA) *376*
Japan. Ship Research Institute. Papers/ Senpaku Gijutsu Kenkyusho Obun Hokoku (JA) *879*
Japan. Sorifu. Tokeikyoku. Shugyokozo Kihon Chosa *see* Japan. Bureau of Statistics. Employment Status Survey *159*
Japan Almanach (JA) *361*
Japan-America Society of Washington. Bulletin (US ISSN 0021-4299) *392, 670, 722*
Japan Annual of Law and Politics (JA ISSN 0075-3157) *514, 711*
Japan Anti-Tuberculosis Association. Reports on Medical Research Problems/Kekkaku Yobokai Kenkyu Gyoseki (JA ISSN 0075-3165) *623*
Japan Association for Philosophy of Science. Annals (JA ISSN 0453-0691) *689, 784*
Japan Atomic Energy Commission. Annual Report/Genshiryoku Nenpo (JA ISSN 0449-4830) *368, 703*
Japan Audio-Visual Education Association Japan *see* A V E in Japan *347*
Japan Census of Manufactures: Report by Commodities (JA ISSN 0075-3289) *223*
Japan Chemical Annual (JA ISSN 0075-319X) *373*
Japan Chemical Directory (JA ISSN 0075-3203) *373*
Japan Chemical Review (JA ISSN 0448-858X) *373*
Japan Congress on Materials Research. Proceedings/Zairyo Kenkyu Rengo Koenkai Ronbunshu (JA ISSN 0514-5171) *380*
Japan Cotton Statistics and Related Data (JA ISSN 0447-5321) *857*
Japan Directory (JA ISSN 0075-322X) *238*
Japan Drug Industry Review (JA) *685*
Japan Economic Research Center. Center Paper Series (JA ISSN 0075-3238) *186*
Japan Economic Year Book (JA ISSN 0075-3246) *187*
Japan English Books in Print (JA) *92*
Japan English Magazine Directory (JA ISSN 0387-3935) *759*
Japan Fact Book (US) *356*
Japan Federation of Composers. Catalogue of Publications (JA) *665*

Japan Foundation Annual Report (JA) *491*
Japan Hotel Guide (JA ISSN 0446-6217) *482*
Japan Institute of Labour. Proceedings (JA) *208*
Japan Oceanology Directory/Kaiyo Sangyo Jimmeiroku (JA) *311*
Japan Petroleum and Energy Yearbook (JA) *363, 680*
Japan Pharmaceutical Traders' Association List: Japanese Drug Directory *see* J A P T A List: Japanese Drug Directory *685*
Japan Port Information (JA) *879*
Japan Printing Art Annual/Nihon Insatsu Nenkan (JA ISSN 0546-0719) *733*
Japan Register of Merchants, Manufacturers and Shippers *see* Standard Trade Index of Japan *180*
Japan Report (US) *187, 711*
Japan Road Association. Annual Report of Roads (JA ISSN 0075-3319) *875*
Japan Science Review: Economic Sciences (JA ISSN 0448-8709) *159*
Japan Society for Cancer Therapy. Proceedings of the Congress (JA ISSN 0075-3327) *605*
Japan Society of Civil Engineers. Transactions (JA ISSN 0047-1798) *376*
Japan Statistical Yearbook (JA ISSN 0075-3335) *842*
Japan Steel Works Technical News (JA) *628*
Japan Sugar Yearbook. (JA) *405*
Japan: the Official Guide *see* New Official Guide: Japan *889*
Japan Times Directory (JA) *238*
Japan Typography Annual/Nihon Taipogurafi Nenkan (JA) *733*
Japanese Annual Bibliography of Economics (JA) *159*
Japanese Antarctic Research Expedition Data Reports. (JA ISSN 0075-3343) *289*
Japanese Antarctic Research Expedition, 1956-1962. Scientific Reports. Series A: Aeronomy *see* National Institute of Polar Research. Memoirs. Series A: Aeronomy *297*
Japanese Antarctic Research Expedition, 1956-1962. Scientific Reports. Series B: Meteorology *see* National Institute of Polar Research. Memoirs. Series B: Meteorology *634*
Japanese Antarctic Research Expedition, 1956-1962. Scientific Reports. Series C: Earth Sciences. *see* National Institute of Polar Research. Memoirs. Series C: Earth Sciences *289*
Japanese Antarctic Research Expedition, 1956-1962. Scientific Reports. Series D: Oceanography *see* National Institute of Polar Research . Memoirs. Series D: Oceanography *311*
Japanese Antarctic Research Expedition, 1956-1962. Scientific Reports. Series E. Biology *see* National Institute of Polar Research. Memoirs. Series E. Biology and Medical Science *105*
Japanese Antarctic Research Expedition, 1956-1962. Scientific Reports. Series F: Logistic *see* National Institute of Polar Research. Memoirs. Series F: Logistics *786*
Japanese Books in Print (Year) (JA) *92*
Japanese Bulletin of Art Therapy (JA) *75,* 736
Japanese Communist Party. Central Committee. Bulletin: Information for Abroad (JA ISSN 0007-4683) *712*
Japanese Drug Directory *see* J A P T A List: Japanese Drug Directory *685*
Japanese Economic Statistics *see* Economic Survey of Japan *185*
Japanese General Trading Companies Yearbook/Sogo-Shosha (JA) *182*
Japanese Hospital Directory/Byoin Yoran (JA ISSN 0408-0904) *481*
Japanese National Bibliography/Zen Nihon Shuppanbutsu Somokuroku (JA ISSN 0385-3284) *92*
Japanese National Railways. Facts and Figures (JA ISSN 0546-093X) *873*

Japanese Neurochemical Society. Bulletin/Shinkei Kagaku (JA) 620
Japanese Phonograph Records of Folk Songs, Classical and Popular Music (JA ISSN 0075-3459) 660
Japanese Political Science Association. Yearbook/Nihon Seiji Gakkai Nenpo: Seijigaku (JA ISSN 0549-4192) 712
Japanese Progress in Climatology/Nippon no Kikogaku no Shinpo (JA ISSN 0075-3467) 634
Japanese Report to the International Council on Social Welfare (JA) 806
Japanese Society for Public Administration. Annals/Nippon Gyosei Kenkyu Nenpo (JA) 743
Japanese Studies in the History of Science (JA ISSN 0090-0176) 784
Japanese Sword Society of the U.S. Bulletin (US) 75
Japan's Bicycle Guide (JA ISSN 0446-6667) 826
Japan's Economy and Trade (US) 196
Japan's Iron and Steel Industry (JA ISSN 0075-3475) 628
Jardin Botanique de Montreal. Annuelle see Jardin Botanique de Montreal. Annuelles et Legumes: Resultats des Cultures d'Essai 415
Jardin Botanique de Montreal. Annuelles et Legumes: Resultats des Cultures d'Essai (CN ISSN 0319-3098) 415
Jardin Botanique de Montreal. Memoire(CN ISSN 0077-1325) 116, 415
Jarlibro (NE ISSN 0075-3491) 546
Jazykovedne Studie (CS ISSN 0448-9241) 546
Jazz Publicity II (US) 910
Jazz Research see Jazzforschung 660
Jazzforschung/Jazz Research (AU ISSN 0075-3572) 660
Jazzologist (US) 660
Jean Giono (FR) 566
Jean-Paul-Gesellschaft. Jahrbuch (GW ISSN 0075-3580) 566
Jebat (MY) 444
Jednota Kalendar (US) 774
Jefferson Memorial Lecture Series (US ISSN 0075-3599) 470
Jehovah's Witnesses Yearbook (US ISSN 0075-3602) 776
J'emballe (FR) 672
Jernal Antropoloji dan Sosiologi (MY) 50, 814
Jernal Sains Malaysia see Malaysian Journal of Science 785
Jernal Sejarah (MY) 444
Jerome Lectures (US ISSN 0075-3610) 433
Jersey Herd Book and Members Directory (UK) 45
Jerusalem Conference on Accountancy (IS) 167
Jerusalem Historical Medical Publications (IS ISSN 0449-4881) 602
Jerusalem Studies on Asia (IS) 444
Jerusalem Symposia on Quantum Chemistry and Biochemistry (NE ISSN 0075-3696) 111, 246
Jerusalem Urban Studies (IS) 485, 814
Jeune Science see Science Nouvelle 790
Jewelry Fashion Guide (US) 503
Jewish Agency for Israel. Office for Economic and Social Research. Annual (IS) 145, 798
Jewish Book Annual (US ISSN 0075-3726) 770
Jewish Boston (US ISSN 0085-2368) 392
Jewish Boston and New England Jewry see Jewish Boston 392
Jewish Federations, Welfare Funds and Community Councils Directory see Directory of Jewish Federations, Welfare Funds and Community Councils 805
Jewish Historical Society of Delaware. Newsletter (US) 770
Jewish Historical Society of England. Annual Report and Accounts for the Session (UK ISSN 0306-7998) 770

Jewish Historical Society of England. Report and Balance Sheet see Jewish Historical Society of England. Annual Report and Accounts for the Session 770
Jewish Historical Society of New York. Publications (US) 392
Jewish Historical Society of Western Canada. Annual Publication (CN ISSN 0317-1655) 392
Jewish Law Annual (NE) 514, 770
Jewish Pickle (US) 392
Jewish Press in America (US) 5, 505
Jewish Social Service Yearbook (US ISSN 0075-3742) 806
Jewish Social Work Forum (US ISSN 0021-6712) 806
Jewish Travel Guide (UK ISSN 0075-3750) 887
Jewish Year Book (UK ISSN 0075-3769) 770
Jezykoznawstwo Stosowane/Applied Linguistics (PL) 546
Jiddah Chamber of Commerce & Industry Annual Trade Directory (US) 238
Jimbun (JA ISSN 0084-5515) 491
Jisunu (BO) 51
Jiwaji University. Journal: Science, Technology & Medicine. (II) 596, 784, 851
Joanneum. Museum fuer Bergbau, Geologie und Technik. Mitteilungen see Landesmuseum Joanneum. Abteilung fuer Geologie, Palaeontologie und Bergbau. Mitteilungen 673
Job Catalog (US) 667
Jobson's Mining Year Book (AT ISSN 0075-3777) 644
Jobson's Year Book of Public Companies of Australia and New Zealand (AT ISSN 0075-3785) 203
Jodhpur Management Journal (II) 215
Joensuun Korkeakoulu. Julkaisuja. Sarja B see Joensuun Korkeakoulu. Julkaisuja. Sarja B2 337
Joensuun Korkeakoulu. Julkaisuja. Sarja B2/University of Joensuu. Publications. Series B2 (FI ISSN 0355-6832) 337
Johannes-Kepler-Hochschule Linz. Dissertationen see Johannes-Kepler-Universitaet Linz. Dissertationen 784
Johannes-Kepler-Universitaet Linz. Dissertationen (AU) 784
Johannesburg Public Library. Annual Report (SA) 532
Johari za Kiswahili (KE ISSN 0449-0738) 587
John Alexander Monograph Series on Various Phases of Thoracic Surgery (US ISSN 0075-3815) 624
John Creasy's Mystery Bedside Book (UK) 566
John Gassner's Best American Plays (US) 566
John Jay College of Criminal Justice. Criminal Justice Center. Monograph (US) 282
John Lister Queen Elizabeth II Stamp Catalogue (UK) 667
Johns Hopkins Oceanographic Studies (US ISSN 0075-3858) 311
Johns Hopkins Series in Integration and Community Building in Eastern Europe (US ISSN 0075-3866) 814
Johns Hopkins Studies in Atlantic History and Culture (US) 470
Johns Hopkins Studies in the History of Technology (US) 851
Johns Hopkins Symposia in Comparative History (US ISSN 0075-3874) 433
Johns Hopkins University. Population Information Program. Population Report. Series A. Oral Contraceptives (US ISSN 0097-9074) 132
Johns Hopkins University. Population Information Program. Population Report. Series B. Intrauterine Devices (US ISSN 0092-9344) 132
Johns Hopkins University. Population Information Program. Population Report. Series C. Sterilization (Female) (US ISSN 0091-9268) 132

Johns Hopkins University. Population Information Program. Population Report. Series D. Sterilization (Male) (US ISSN 0093-4488) 132
Johns Hopkins University. Population Information Program. Population Report. Series E. Law and Policy (US ISSN 0097-9082) 132
Johns Hopkins University. Population Information Program. Population Report. Series F. Pregnancy Termination (US ISSN 0091-9284) 132
Johns Hopkins University. Population Information Program. Population Report. Series G. Prostaglandins (US ISSN 0091-9276) 132
Johns Hopkins University. Population Information Program. Population Reports. Series H. Barrier Methods (US ISSN 0093-4496) 132
Johns Hopkins University. Population Information Program. Population Report. Series I. Periodic Abstinence (US ISSN 0097-9090) 132
Johns Hopkins University. Population Information Program. Population Report. Series J. Family Planning Programs (US) 132
Johns Hopkins University. Population Information Program. Population Report. Series K. Injectables and Implants (US ISSN 0097-9104) 132
Johns Hopkins University. Population Information Program. Population Report. Series L. Issues in World Health (US) 728
Johns Hopkins University Studies in Geology (US ISSN 0075-3890) 295
Johns Hopkins University Studies in Historical and Political Science (US ISSN 0075-3904) 433, 712
Johnsonia (US ISSN 0075-3920) 129
Johnson's Investment Company Charts (US) 203
Joho Chosa Report see Information and Investigation Report 234
Joint Automatic Control Conference. Record (US ISSN 0075-3939) 356
Joint Center for Urban Studies. Publications (US ISSN 0075-3947) 485
Joint Center for Urban Studies. Research Report from M I T-Harvard (US ISSN 0098-5244) 485
Joint College Curricula Workshop in Computer Science, Engineering and Data Processing.(Papers) (US) 273
Joint Engineering Management Conference. Conference Record (US) 368
Joint Engineering Societies Management Conference. Proceedings see Joint Engineering Management Conference. Conference Record 368
Joint F A O/W H O Codex Alimentarius Commission. Report of the Session (UN ISSN 0449-122X) 405, 752
Joint F A O/W H O Expert Committee on Food Additives Report (UN ISSN 0075-3963) 405
Joint F A O/W H O Expert Committee on Nutrition. Report (UN ISSN 0075-3971) 666
Joint Federal-State Land Use Planning Commission for Alaska. Annual Report see Alaska's Land 383
Joint Governmental Salary Survey : Arizona (US) 208
Joint Institute for Laboratory Astrophysics Information Center. Report see J I L A Information Center. Report 82
Joint Meeting of the Members of the Consultative Assembly of the Council of Europe and of the Members of the European Parliamentary Assembly. Official Report of Debates (EI ISSN 0447-8452) 722
Joint Nuclear Research Center, Ispra, Italy. Annual Report (EI) 703
Joint Power Generation Conference. Conference Record (US) 356

Joint Power Generation Technical Conference. Preprint see Joint Power Generation Conference. Conference Record 356
Joint Railroad Conference. Conference Record (US) 873
Joint Railroad Technical Conference. Preprint see Joint Railroad Conference. Conference Record 873
Joint Services Staff College Gazette see National Defence College Gazette 639
Jokull (IC ISSN 0449-0576) 295
Jordan. Department of Statistics. Agricultural Statistical Yearbook and Agricultural Sample Survey (JO) 17
Jordan. Department of Statistics. Annual Statistical Yearbook (JO ISSN 0075-4013) 842
Jordan. Department of Statistics. External Trade Statistics (JO ISSN 0075-4021) 159
Jordan. Department of Statistics. Hotel Statistics (JO) 483
Jordan. Department of Statistics. Morbidity Statistics (JO) 842
Jordan. Department of Statistics. Multi-Purpose Household Survey (JO) 842
Jordan. Department of Statistics. National Accounts (JO ISSN 0449-1513) 213
Jordan. Ministry of Tourism and Antiquities. Tourism Annual Report (JO) 887
Jordan. Ministry of Tourism and Antiquities. Tourist Arrivals in Numbers (JO) 887
Jordan. Ministry of Tourism and Antiquities. Travel Statistics see Jordan. Ministry of Tourism and Antiquities. Tourist Arrivals in Numbers 887
Jordan Lectures in Comparative Religion (UK ISSN 0449-1602) 766
Jornadas Nacionales de Derecho Aeronautico y Espacial. Trabajos (AG) 9, 514, 868
Joseph Haas Gesellschaft. Mitteilungsblatt (GW ISSN 0446-9577) 660
Jouets et Jeux (FR ISSN 0075-4056) 429
Journal de l'Annee (FR ISSN 0449-4733) 361
Journal de la Majorite (CN ISSN 0705-0852) 712
Journal des Employes Publics see Public Employees Journal 745
Journal des Oiseaux du Monde (FR ISSN 0075-4080) 125
Journal for Studies in Economics and Econometrics/Tydskryf vir Studies in Ekonomie en Ekonometrie (SA ISSN 0379-6205) 191
Journal for the Protection of All Beings(US ISSN 0075-4099) 566
Journal for the Study of the New Testament. Supplement Series (UK ISSN 0143-5108) 766
Journal for the Study of the Old Testament. Supplement Series (UK ISSN 0309-0787) 766
Journal fuer die Reine und Angewandte Mathematik (GW ISSN 0075-4102) 586
Journal Holdings in the Washington-Baltimore Area (US ISSN 0362-4544) 532
Journal of Accounting Research. Supplement (US) 167
Journal of African Studies/Afurika Kenkyu (JA ISSN 0065-4140) 440
Journal of Agricultural Labour Science (UK) 17
Journal of Agronomic Education (US ISSN 0094-2391) 37, 349
Journal of Ancient Indian History (II ISSN 0075-4110) 444
Journal of Animal Breeding and Genetics see Zeitschrift fuer Tierzuechtung und Zuechtungsbiologie 46
Journal of Animal Science. Supplement (US ISSN 0075-4129) 45, 894
Journal of Applied Behavior Analysis Monograph Series see J A B A Monograph Series 736

Journal of Applied Polymer Science. Symposia (US ISSN 0570-4898) *373*
Journal of Applied Systems Analysis (UK ISSN 0308-9541) *273*
Journal of Arabic Literature (NE ISSN 0085-2376) *566, 670*
Journal of Asian Art (SI) *75, 653*
Journal of Astrological Studies (US ISSN 0085-2384) *80*
Journal of Biodynamic Psychology (UK ISSN 0143-1218) *736*
Journal of Biomedical Materials Research. Symposia (US) *104, 596*
Journal of Black Poetry *see* Kitabu Cha Jua *580*
Journal of Byelorussian Studies (UK ISSN 0075-4161) *456*
Journal of Cardiovascular Surgery. Congress Proceedings (IT) *624*
Journal of Child Psychotherapy (UK ISSN 0075-417X) *736*
Journal of Chinese Art History *see* Soochow University Journal of Chinese Art History *78*
Journal of Chromatographic Science (US ISSN 0021-9665) *249*
Journal of Chromatography Library (NE) *249*
Journal of Civil Procedure/Minji Sosho Zasshi (JA ISSN 0075-4188) *514*
Journal of Classical Studies/Seiyo Kotengaku Kenkyu (JA ISSN 0582-4524) *259*
Journal of Commerce Transportation Telephone Tickler *see* Transportation Telephone Tickler *864*
Journal of Croatian Studies (US ISSN 0075-4218) *456, 556*
Journal of Cultural Sciences/Bunka Kagaku Kiyo (JA ISSN 0521-7903) *491*
Journal of Cytology and Genetics (II) *122, 596*
Journal of Development Planning (UN ISSN 0085-2392) *200*
Journal of Drug Research *see* Journal of Drug Research of Egypt *685*
Journal of Drug Research of Egypt (UA ISSN 0085-2406) *685*
Journal of Earth Sciences (JA ISSN 0022-0442) *289*
Journal of Economics (US ISSN 0361-6576) *145*
Journal of Educational Research/Jurnal Pendidikan (MY) *319*
Journal of Egyptian Archaeology (UK ISSN 0307-5133) *62*
Journal of English Linguistics (US ISSN 0075-4242) *546*
Journal of Financial Education (US ISSN 0093-3961) *174, 337*
Journal of Freshwater (US) *387, 897*
Journal of Gas Chromatography *see* Journal of Chromatographic Science *249*
Journal of Geological Sciences: Anthropozoic *see* Sbornik Geologickych Ved: Antropozoikum *299*
Journal of Geological Sciences: Applied Geophysics *see* Sbornik Geologickych Ved: Uzita Geofyzika *306*
Journal of Geological Sciences: Economic Geology, Mineralogy *see* Sbornik Geologickych Ved: Loziskova Geologie, Mineralogie *299*
Journal of Geological Sciences: Geology *see* Sbornik Geologickych Ved: Geologie *299*
Journal of Geological Sciences: Hydrogeology, Engineering Geology *see* Sbornik Geologickych Ved: Hydrogeologie, Inzenyrska Geologie *308*
Journal of Geological Sciences: Paleontology *see* Sbornik Geologickych Ved: Paleontologie *674*
Journal of Geological Sciences: Technology, Geochemistry *see* Sbornik Geologickych Ved: Technologie, Geochemie *299*
Journal of Geosciences/Osaka-shiritsu Daigaku Rigakubu Chigaku Kiyo (JA ISSN 0449-2560) *289*

Journal of German-American Studies (US) *566*
Journal of Glass Studies (US ISSN 0075-4250) *75, 244*
Journal of Great Lakes Research (US ISSN 0380-1330) *308, 387*
Journal of Hellenic Studies (UK ISSN 0075-4269) *259, 546*
Journal of Himalayan Studies and Regional Development (II) *51*
Journal of Historic Madison, Inc. of Wisconsin *see* Historic Madison. Journal *469*
Journal of History and Political Science(PK) *444, 712*
Journal of Holistic Health (US ISSN 0161-5491) *596*
Journal of Indian Museums (II) *653*
Journal of Indo-European Studies Monograph Series (US) *798*
Journal of Industry and Management/Sangyo Keiei Kenkyushoho (JA) *215*
Journal of Intercultural Studies (JA) *798*
Journal of International Relations (TZ) *722*
Journal of Jewish Art (US ISSN 0160-208X) *75, 770*
Journal of Jewish Music and Liturgy (US) *660, 770*
Journal of Juristic Papyrology (PL ISSN 0075-4277) *62, 514*
Journal of Juvenile Law (US ISSN 0160-2098) *514*
Journal of Karyopathology/Saibokaku Byorigaku Zasshi (JA ISSN 0022-2119) *605*
Journal of Law and Politics/Daito Hogaku (JA) *514*
Journal of Library History. State Library History Bibliography Series (US) *470, 532*
Journal of Maltese Studies (MM ISSN 0075-4285) *456*
Journal of Mathematics (JA ISSN 0075-4293) *586*
Journal of Medical Entomology. Supplement (US) *121*
Journal of Mexican American History (US ISSN 0047-2581) *470*
Journal of Mormon History (US ISSN 0094-7342) *776*
Journal of Muscle Shoals History (US ISSN 0094-8039) *470*
Journal of Natural Resource Management and Interdisciplinary Studies (CN ISSN 0381-0984) *387*
Journal of Natural Science (JA ISSN 0075-4307) *784*
Journal of Necromantic Numismatics (US ISSN 0022-2976) *477*
Journal of Neural Transmission. Supplement (US ISSN 0303-6995) *620*
Journal of Neuro-Visceral Relations. Supplement *see* Journal of Neural Transmission. Supplement *620*
Journal of New World Archaeology (US ISSN 0147-9024) *62*
Journal of Notarial Acts and Recordkeeping Practices (US) *514*
Journal of Oriental Research (II ISSN 0022-3301) *670*
Journal of Our Time (CN ISSN 0381-6524) *566, 580*
Journal of Periodontal Research. Supplementum (DK ISSN 0075-4331) *610*
Journal of Philosophy of Sport (US ISSN 0094-8705) *689, 820*
Journal of Polymer Science. Part C: Polymer Symposia *see* Journal of Polymer Science. Polymer Symposia Edition *252*
Journal of Polymer Science. Polymer Symposia Edition (US ISSN 0360-8905) *252*
Journal of Population Studies (KO) *132, 615*
Journal of Psychoanalysis in Groups *see* Groups: a Journal of Group Dynamics and Psychotherapy *736*
Journal of Roman Studies (UK ISSN 0075-4358) *259*
Journal of Scandinavian Folklore *see* Arv *401*
Journal of Seed Technology (US ISSN 0146-3071) *17*

Journal of Social and Political Studies Monograph Series (US) *712*
Journal of Social Science (MW ISSN 0302-3060) *798*
Journal of Social Science Review (TH) *798*
Journal of Social Sciences (JA) *798*
Journal of Social Studies (BG) *798*
Journal of Soil and Water Conservation in India (II ISSN 0022-457X) *17, 276, 897*
Journal of Studies on Alcohol. Supplement (US ISSN 0363-468X) *287*
Journal of Supervision and Training in Ministry (US ISSN 0160-7774) *766*
Journal of Systems Engineering *see* Journal of Applied Systems Analysis *273*
Journal of the Graduate Music Students at the Ohio State University (US ISSN 0364-2216) *660*
Journal of the Legal Profession (US) *514*
Journal of the Midwest History of Education Society *see* Midwest History of Education Society. Journal *320*
Journal of the New Alchemists (US ISSN 0162-833X) *363, 387, 851*
Journal of the Philadelphia Association for Psychoanalysis *see* Philadelphia Association for Psychoanalysis. Journal *737*
Journal of the Philosophy of Sport (US ISSN 0094-8705) *689, 820*
Journal of the St. Clair County Historical Society *see* St. Clair County Historical Society. Journal *471*
Journal of the Warburg and Courtauld Institutes (UK ISSN 0075-4390) *491*
Journal of Ultrastructure Research. Supplement (US ISSN 0075-4404) *104*
Journal of Weather Modification (US) *634*
Journal - Oswego County Historical Society *see* Oswego County Historical Society. Journal *471*
Journalism Abstracts (US ISSN 0075-4412) *505*
Journalism Career and Scholarship Guide (US) *319, 505*
Journalism Scholarship Guide *see* Journalism Career and Scholarship Guide *505*
Journalist (NE ISSN 0022-555X) *505*
Journalisten-Handbuch (GW) *505*
Journals of Dissent and Social Change (US) *717, 818*
Journee de Reeducation (FR ISSN 0075-4420) *346*
Journee Scientifique de Mars. Conferences et Communications (BE) *685*
Journees Annuelles de Diabetologie de l'Hotel Dieu (FR ISSN 0075-4439) *611*
Journees de Physiologie Appliquee au Travail Humain (FR ISSN 0075-4455) *126*
Journees Internationales d'Etude du Baroque. Actes *see* Baroque *560*
Journees Internationales d'Etudes du Baroque *see* Baroque *560*
Journees Parisiennes de Pediatrie (FR ISSN 0075-4471) *617*
Joyous Struggle: a Women's Newsletter *see* University of New Mexico. Women's Center Newsletter *725*
Judean Desert Studies (IS ISSN 0075-4501) *62*
Judicial Function Outline (US ISSN 0148-4982) *514*
Judicial Function Outline for Administrative Law Judges (US) *514*
Judicial Statistics *see* Michigan. Office of the Court Administrator. Judicial Statistics *521*
Jugendherbergs-Verzeichnis (GW ISSN 0075-4528) *423*
Jugopetrol, Trgovinsko Preduzece za Promet Nafte i Naftinih Derivata. Bilten (YU) *680*

K I 1409

Jugoslavenska Akademija Znanosti i Umjetnosti. Historijski Institut, Dubrovnik. Anali. (YU ISSN 0449-3648) *456*
Jugoslovenska Investiciona Banka. Annual Report (YU ISSN 0075-4536) *174*
Juifs Celebres *see* Sir Moses Montefiore Collections des Juifs Celebres *767*
Jules Verne Voyages (UK) *566*
Julius C. Stevens Annual Lectures in Education (LB) *319*
Jumbo Guide to Rhodesia (RH) *887*
Junction (US) *580*
Junior Age Year Book and Diary (UK) *258, 261*
Junior Eagle (US ISSN 0193-6131) *423, 798*
Junior High School Association of Illinois. Study (US ISSN 0075-4560) *319*
Junior High School Library Catalog (US) *532*
Junta de Energia Nuclear Informes J. E. N. *see* Informes J. E. N *703*
Junta de Estudios Historicos de Mendoza. Revista (AG ISSN 0076-6380) *470*
Juntendo University, Tokyo. Medical Ultrasonics Research Center. Annual Report (JA ISSN 0075-4579) *596*
Juridica (MX) *514*
Juris-Classeurs. Droit Civil *see* Recueil Periodique des Juris-Classeurs: Droit Civil *517*
Jurisprudencia Aragonesa. (SP) *514*
Jurisprudencia Argentina (AG) *514*
Jurisprudencia y Textos Legales (SP) *514*
Juristische Abhandlungen (GW ISSN 0449-4342) *514*
Jurnal Pendidikan *see* Journal of Educational Research *319*
Just a Bite (UK) *483*
Just B'twx Us: an Interlibrary Loan Newsletter (US) *532*
Just B'twx Us: An Interlibrary Loan Service Newsletter *see* Just B'twx Us: an Interlibrary Loan Newsletter *532*
Justice Department Watch (US) *514, 718*
Justice-Directory of Services/Justice-Repertoire des Services (CN ISSN 0225-4115) *806*
Justice in America Series (US) *282, 514*
Justice in Urban America Series *see* Justice in America Series *514*
Justice-Repertoire des Services *see* Justice-Directory of Services *806*
Jutaku Sangyo Handobukku (JA) *485*
Juvenile Law Litigation Directory (US) *282, 514*
Juvenile Probation Admissions *see* Wisconsin. Division of Corrections. Office of Informatiom Management. Juvenile Probation Admissions *284*
Jyvaskyla Studies in Computer Science, Economics and Statistics (FI ISSN 0357-9921) *145, 273, 842*
Jyvaskyla Studies in Education, Psychology and Social Research (FI ISSN 0075-4625) *319, 736*
Jyvaskyla Studies in the Arts (FI ISSN 0075-4633) *75, 566*
Jyvaskylan Yliopisto. Department of Physics. Research Report (FI ISSN 0075-465X) *697*
Jyvaskylan Yliopisto. Matematiikan Laitos. Report (FI ISSN 0075-4641) *586*
K B S-Rapporter (SW ISSN 0022-7293) *137, 376, 485*
K G I Preprint *see* Kiruna Geophysical Institute. Preprint *305*
K G I Report *see* Kiruna Geophysical Institute. Report *305*
K G I Software Report *see* Kiruna Geophysical Institute. Software Report *305*
K G I Technical Report *see* Kiruna Geophysical Institute. Technical Report *305*
K G I Teknisk Rapport *see* Kiruna Geophysical Institute. Technical Report *305*
K I A Occasional Papers (Kenya Institute of Administration) (KE ISSN 0075-5761) *743*

K J E S *see* Kakatiya Journal of English Studies 556
K N A A S News *see* Kenya National Academy for Advancement of Arts and Sciences. Newsletter 785
K R *see* Kjeller Report 704
K T B L-Schriften (Kuratorium fuer Technik und Bauwesen in der Landwirtschaft e.V.) (GW) 17
Kabar (AT ISSN 0311-0419) 722
Kaduna State. Ministry of Works. Report (NR) 743
Kaduna State Statistical Yearbook (NR) 842
Kaerntner Heimatleben (AU ISSN 0022-7560) 402
Kaerntner Museumsschriften (AU ISSN 0022-7587) 75, 653
Kagai Keizai Kyoryoku Kikin Nenpo *see* Overseas Economic Cooperation Fund. Annual Report 201
Kagaja (BG) 580
Kagaku Keisatsu Kenkyusho Nenpo *see* National Research Institute of Police Science. Annual Report 283
Kagaku Keisatsu Kenkyusho Shiryo *see* National Research Institute of Police Science. Data 744
Kagoshima University. Historical Science Reports (JA) 444
Kaigai Kogyo Jijo Chosa Hokokusho: Indo, Pakisutan, Banguradisshu *see* Report of Overseas Mining Investigation: India, Pakistan, Bangladesh 646
Kaigai Kogyo Jijo Chosa Hokokusho: Madagasukaru, Suwajirando *see* Report of Overseas Mining Investigation: Madagascar, Swaziland 646
Kaigaki Kagaku Gijutsu Joho Shiryo *see* Scientific and Technical Information in Foreign Countries 791
Kairi (TR) 556
Kaiser Foundation Medical Care Program. Annual Report (US ISSN 0075-4668) 752
Kaiyo Chosa Gyogyo Shiken Yoho *see* Hokkaido University. Faculty of Fisheries. Data Record of Oceanographic Observations and Exploratory Fishing 310
Kaiyo Sangyo Jimmeiroku *see* Japan Oceanology Directory 311
Kakatiya Journal of English Studies (II) 566
Kakteen. Gesamtdarstellung (Monographie) der Eingefuehrten Arten nebst Anzucht- und Pflege (GW ISSN 0075-4676) 116
Kalamanakaranaya (CE) 215
Kalastuspaikkaopas (FI ISSN 0075-4684) 820
Kalava Ha Sahityaya (CE) 75, 566
Kale Memorial Lectures *see* R.B.R.R. Kale Memorial Lectures 714
Kalendar Odborara (CS) 507, 626
Kalendarz Robotniczy *see* Informator Robotniczy 361
Kalender van Internationale Jaar- en Vakbeurzen (NE) 218
Al-Kalima (YE) 556
Kalininskii Nauchno-issledovatel'skii Institut Tekstil'noi Promyshlennosti. Nauchno-issledovatel'skie Trudy (UR) 856
Kalulu (MW) 51, 566
Kamar Dagang dan Industri di Jawa Barat. Daftar Anggota *see* Chamber of Commerce and Industry in West Java. Member List 178
Kami Parupu Tokei Nenpo *see* Yearbook of Pulp and Paper Statistics 675
Kanagawa University. Institute of Humanities. Bulletin (JA) 491
Kanan (PE) 566
Kanazawa Daigaku Kyoikugakubu Kiyo, Shizenkagaku- Hen *see* Kanazawa University. Faculty of Education. Bulletin: Natural Science 784
Kanazawa Daigaku Kyoyobu Ronshu, Shizenkagaku- Hen *see* Kanazawa University. College of Liberal Arts. Annals of Science 784

Kanazawa University. College of Liberal Arts. Annals of Science/Kanazawa Daigaku Kyoyobu Ronshu, Shizenkagaku- Hen (JA ISSN 0302-0479) 784
Kanazawa University. Faculty of Education. Bulletin: Humanities, Social and Educational Sciences (JA) 319
Kanazawa University. Faculty of Education. Bulletin: Natural Science/ Kanazawa Daigaku Kyoikugakubu Kiyo, Shizenkagaku- Hen (JA) 784
Kanazawa University. Faculty of Law and Literature. Studies and Essays (JA ISSN 0453-1981) 514, 566
Kano State of Nigeria Gazette (NR) 514, 743
Kano State Statistical Year Book (NR) 842
Kano Studies (NR) 814
Kansai Daigaku Kogaku Kenkyu Hokoku *see* Kansai University Technology Reports 851
Kansai Ongaku Bunka Shiryo *see* Music Cultures 661
Kansai University Technology Reports/ Kansai Daigaku Kogaku Kenkyu Hokoku (JA ISSN 0453-2198) 851
Kansainvalinen Automatkailu *see* Autolla Ulkomaille 883
Kansas. Advisory Council on Ecology. Annual Report (US) 387
Kansas. Department of Health and Environment. Annual Summary of Vital Statistics (US) 728
Kansas. Legislative Research Department. Report on Kansas Legislative Interim Studies (US ISSN 0270-4331) 712
Kansas. State Board of Agriculture. Annual Report with Farm Facts (US) 17
Kansas. State Board of Agriculture. Report *see* Kansas. State Board of Agriculture. Annual Report with Farm Facts 17
Kansas. State Department of Education. Administration and Finance Division. Annual Statistical Report (US ISSN 0091-9802) 344
Kansas. State Department of Education. Bulletin (US) 319
Kansas. State Department of Public Instruction. Bulletin *see* Kansas. State Department of Education. Bulletin 319
Kansas. State Soil Conservation Committee. Soil Conservation in Kansas *see* Conservation in Kansas 276
Kansas Agriculture Report *see* Kansas. State Board of Agriculture. Annual Report with Farm Facts 17
Kansas Corn Performance Tests (US) 42
Kansas Educational Directory (US ISSN 0099-0728) 319
Kansas Geographer (US) 423
Kansas Geological Survey. Basic Data Series. Ground-Water Releases (US) 308
Kansas Geological Survey. Bulletin (US) 295
Kansas Geological Survey. Chemical Quality Series (US) 295
Kansas Geological Survey. Computer Contribution (US ISSN 0075-4927) 295
Kansas Geological Survey. Educational Series (US) 296
Kansas Geological Survey. Energy Resources Series (US) 289, 363
Kansas Geological Survey. Geology Series (US) 296
Kansas Geological Survey. Ground Water Series (US) 308
Kansas Geological Survey. Short Papers in Research (US ISSN 0075-4935) 296
Kansas Geological Survey. Subsurface Geology Series (US) 296
Kansas Grain Sorghum Performance Tests *see* Kansas Sorghum Performance Tests. Grain & Forage 42
Kansas Linguistics Conference. Papers *see* Mid-America Linguistics Conference. Papers 547

Kansas Oil Lifting Short Course Selected Papers (US) 680
Kansas Sorghum Performance Tests. Grain & Forage (US) 42
Kansas State Industrial Directory (US) 238
Kansas State University. Center for Energy Studies. Report (US ISSN 0145-0093) 363
Kansas State University. Food and Feed Grain Institute. Technical Assistance in Food Grain Drying, Storage, Handling and Transportation *see* Kansas State University. Food and Feed Grain Institute. Technical Assistance in Grain Storage, Processing and Marketing, and Agribusiness Development 42
Kansas State University. Food and Feed Grain Institute. Technical Assistance in Grain Storage, Processing and Marketing, and Agribusiness Development (US) 42
Kansas State University. Library Bibliography Series (US ISSN 0075-4951) 92
Kansas Water Resources Research Institute. Annual Report (US ISSN 0160-2659) 897
Kapitalistate (US) 145, 712
Kappa Pi International Honorary Art Fraternity. Sketch Book *see* Sketch Book 78
Kappa Tau Alpha Yearbook (US ISSN 0075-5060) 505
Karachi. Chamber of Commerce and Industry. Report (PK ISSN 0075-5079) 179
Karachi Law Journal (PK ISSN 0075-5095) 514
Karachi Port Trust. Year Book of Information, Port of Karachi, Pakistan (PK ISSN 0075-5109) 862
Karamu (US ISSN 0022-8990) 556
Karate International Annual (MY ISSN 0085-2481) 820
Karger Highlights: Cardiology (SZ ISSN 0378-9853) 607
Karger Highlights: Gerontology (SZ ISSN 0379-1068) 622
Karger Highlights: Medical Imaging (SZ ISSN 0379-4474) 622
Karger Highlights: Nephrology (SZ ISSN 0378-8490) 625
Karger Highlights: Oncology (SZ ISSN 0379-1998) 605
Karger Highlights: Oral Science (SZ ISSN 0379-2005) 610
Kariba Studies (RH ISSN 0085-249X) 51, 129
Karl-August-Forster-Lectures (GW ISSN 0340-5419) 104
Karl-May-Gesellschaft. Jahrbuch (GW) 566
Karnatak University, Dharwad, India. Journal. Humanities (II ISSN 515X) 491
Karnatak University, Dharwad, India. Journal. Science (II ISSN 0075-5168) 785
Karnatak University, Dharwad, India. Journal. Social Sciences (II ISSN 0075-5176) 798
Karnataka. Department of Tourism. Annual Report (II) 433, 887
Karnataka. Finance Department. Annual Report (II) 230
Karthago (FR ISSN 0453-3429) 62
Karthago. Collection Epigraphique (FR ISSN 0075-5184) 62
Kartofel *see* Ziemniak 40
Kasetsart Journal (TH ISSN 0075-5192) 17
Kasetsart University, Bangkok, Thailand. Faculty of Fisheries. Notes (TH ISSN 0075-5206) 398
Kasmera (VE ISSN 0075-5222) 596
Kastlemusick Directory for Collectors of Recordings (US) 660
Kataliticheskaya Konversiya Uglevodorodov (UR) 680
Katallagete (US ISSN 0022-9288) 718, 766
Katalog Ceskoslovenskych Znamek *see* Ceskoslovensko 478
Katalog Fauny Pasozytniczej Polski (PL ISSN 0075-5230) 129
Katalog Fauny Polski (PL ISSN 0075-5249) 129

Katalog Sefarim Kelali (IS) 759
Katalog Slovenskych Plagatov (CS) 75
Katalog Zabytkow Sztuki w Polsce (PL ISSN 0075-5257) 75
Katherine Asher Engel Lectures (US ISSN 0075-5265) 491
Katholiek Documentatie Centrum. Archieven (NE) 774
Katholiek Documentatie Centrum. Bibliografieen (NE) 769
Katholiek Documentatie Centrum. Jaarboek (NE) 774
Katholiek Documentatie Centrum. Publicaties (NE) 775
Katholisches Leben und Kirchenreform im Zeitalter der Glaubensspaltung (GW ISSN 0075-5273) 775
Katolicki Uniwersytet Lubelski. Wydzial Filozoficzny. Rozprawy (PL) 689
Katolicki Uniwersytet Lubelski. Wydzial Nauk Spolecznych. Rozprawy (PL) 798
Katolicki Uniwersytet Lubelski. Wydzial Teologiczno-Kanoniczny. Rozprawy (PL) 775
Katolicki Uniwersytet Lubelski Wydzial Historyczno-Filologiczny. Rozprawy (PL) 433, 546
Kauperts Deutschland Staedte-, Hotel- und Reisefuehrer (GW) 887
Kavaka/Fungus (II) 116
Kawa to Hakimono *see* Leather & Footwears 524
Kazakhskii Nauchno-issledovatel'skii Institut Onkologii i Radiologii. Trudy (UR ISSN 0075-529X) 605, 622
Kazanskii Gosudarstvennyi Pedagogicheskii Institut. Voprosy Istorii, Teorii Muzyki i Muzykal'nogo Vospytaniya. Sbornik (UR) 660
Kazanskii Universitet. Sbornik Aspirantskikh Rabot: Teoriya Plastin i Obolochek (UR) 368
Keadaan Angkatan Kerja di Indonesia: Angka Sementara *see* Labour Force Situation in Indonesia: Preliminary Figures 160
Keats-Shelley Journal (US ISSN 0453-4387) 580
Keeping Track, Current News from the Department of Agricultural Economics at Purdue (US ISSN 0075-5303) 29
Keepsake (US ISSN 0075-5311) 532
Keepsake Poems (UK) 580
Keidanren Keizai Shiryo (JA) 187
Keidanren Pamphlet (JA) 187
Keidanren Pocket Series (JA) 187
Keiei Romu No Shishin (JA) 220
Keikinzoku Kogyo Tokei Nenpo *see* Light Metal Statistics in Japan 631
Keilschrifttexte aus Boghazkoi (GW ISSN 0075-5338) 62, 546, 670
Keilschrifturkunden aus Boghazkoei (GE ISSN 0075-532X) 62, 444
Keio Business Review (JA ISSN 0453-4557) 145
Keio Engineering Reports. (JA) 368
Keio Monographs of Business and Commerce (JA ISSN 0075-5346) 145
Keio University. Fujihara Memorial Faculty of Engineering. Proceedings. *see* Keio Engineering Reports 368
Keith Callard Lecture Series (CN ISSN 0541-623X) 910
Kekkaku No Kenkyu. *see* Hokkaido University. Institute of Immunological Science. Bulletin 623
Kekkaku Yobokai Kenkyu Gyoseki *see* Japan Anti-Tuberculosis Association. Reports on Medical Research Problems 623
Keleti Tanulmanyok *see* Oriental Studies 670
Kelly's British Industry and Services in the Common Market (UK) 238
Kelly's Manufacturers and Merchants Directory (UK ISSN 0075-5370) 239
Kelly's Post Office London Directory (UK ISSN 0075-5389) 239
Kemia Ujabb Eredmenyei (HU ISSN 0075-5397) 247
Kemiai Kozlemenyek (HU) 247
Kemistin Kalenteri (FI ISSN 0356-7818) 247

Kempe's Engineers Year Book (UK ISSN 0075-5400) *368*
Kemps Directory (UK ISSN 0075-5419) *239*
Kemps Estate Agents Yearbook and Directory *see* Kemps Property Industry Yearbook *761*
Kemps Film and Television Year Book (International) *see* Kemps International Film and Television Year Book *650*
Kemps International Film and Television Year Book (UK) *650*
Kemps International Music and Record Yearbook (UK) *660*
Kemps Music and Record Industry Year Book International *see* Kemps International Music and Record Yearbook *660*
Kemps Property Industry Yearbook (UK) *239, 761*
Kenchiku Kenkyusho Chosa Shiken Kenkyu Gaiyo Hokoku *see* B R I Research Papers *134*
Kennel Review (US ISSN 0164-4289) *682*
Kent Family History Society. Record Publication (UK ISSN 0308-9037) *417*
Kent State University. Center for Business and Economic Research. Comparative Administration Research Institute Series (US ISSN 0078-4184) *145, 215*
Kent State University. Center for Business and Economic Research. Labor and Industrial Relations Series(US ISSN 0078-4192) *208*
Kent State University. Center for Business and Economic Research. Printed Series (US ISSN 0078-4206) *145*
Kent State University. Center for Business and Economic Research. Research Papers (US ISSN 0078-4214) *145*
Kent State University. Libraries. Occasional Paper (US ISSN 0078-4222) *491*
Kentron Epistemonikon Ereunion. Epeteris/Cyprus Research Center. Annual (CY ISSN 0071-0954) *475, 546*
Kentucky. Adjutant-General's Office. Report (US) *470, 639*
Kentucky. Council of Economic Advisors. Policy Papers Series (US) *187*
Kentucky. Council of Economic Advisors. Studies in Applied Economics (US) *191*
Kentucky. Council on Public Higher Education. Origin of Enrollments, Accredited Colleges and Universities (US ISSN 0098-9770) *327*
Kentucky. Department for Human Resources. Selected Vital Statistics and Planning Data (US ISSN 0145-5990) *756, 842*
Kentucky. Department of Child Welfare. Annual Report *see* Kentucky. Department of Human Resources. Annual Report *807*
Kentucky. Department of Human Resources. Annual Report (US) *807*
Kentucky Agricultural Statistics (US) *25*
Kentucky Deskbook of Economic Statistics (US ISSN 0361-591X) *159*
Kentucky Folklore Series (US ISSN 0075-5508) *402*
Kentucky Law Enforcement Council. Annual Report (US ISSN 0095-6384) *282*
Kentucky Local Debt Report (US ISSN 0095-1498) *230*
Kentucky Manufacturing Developments(US) *851*
Kentucky Nature Studies (US ISSN 0075-5524) *159*
Kentucky Oil and Gas Association. Technical Session. Proceedings *see* University of Kentucky. Geological Survey. Series XI. Special Publication *301*
Kentucky Personal Income *see* Kentucky Personal Income Report *213*

Kentucky Personal Income Report (US) *213*
Kentucky School Directory (US ISSN 0091-0775) *331*
Kentucky State Industrial Directory (US ISSN 0190-1354) *239*
Kentucky, Tennessee TourBook *see* Tourbook: Kentucky, Tennessee *891*
Kentucky Vital Statistics *see* Kentucky. Department for Human Resources. Selected Vital Statistics and Planning Data *756*
Kenya. Central Bureau of Statistics. Agricultural Census (Large Farm Areas) (KE ISSN 0300-2373) *842*
Kenya. Central Bureau of Statistics. Development Estimates (KE) *223*
Kenya. Central Bureau of Statistics. Directory of Industries (KE) *239*
Kenya. Central Bureau of Statistics. Economic Survey (KE) *187*
Kenya. Central Bureau of Statistics. Employment and Earnings in the Modern Sector (KE) *842*
Kenya. Central Bureau of Statistics. Estimates of Recurrent Expenditures (KE) *224*
Kenya. Central Bureau of Statistics. Estimates of Revenue Expenditures (KE) *224*
Kenya. Central Bureau of Statistics. Migration and Tourism Statistics (KE) *887*
Kenya. Central Bureau of Statistics. Register of Manufacturing Firms (KE) *159*
Kenya. Central Bureau of Statistics. Social Perspectives *see* Social Perspectives *816*
Kenya. Central Bureau of Statistics. Statistical Abstract (KE) *159*
Kenya. Commissioner of Customs and Excise. Annual Trade Report (KE) *196*
Kenya. Dairy Board. Annual Report (KE ISSN 0453-5944) *41*
Kenya. Government Printing and Stationery Department. Catalogue of Government Publications (KE) *92*
Kenya. Mines and Geological Department. Annual Report (KE ISSN 0075-580X) *296, 644*
Kenya. Ministry of Commerce and Industry. Industrial Investment Guidelines *see* Guidelines for Industrial Investors in Kenya *186*
Kenya. Ministry of Economic Planning and Development. Economic Survey *see* Kenya. Central Bureau of Statistics. Economic Survey *187*
Kenya. Ministry of Economic Planning and Development. Estimates of Revenue Expenditures *see* Kenya. Central Bureau of Statistics. Estimates of Revenue Expenditures *224*
Kenya. Ministry of Economic Planning and Development. Statistics Division. Development Estimates *see* Kenya. Central Bureau of Statistics. Development Estimates *223*
Kenya. Ministry of Economic Planning and Development. Statistics Division. Estimates of Recurrent Expenditures *see* Kenya. Central Bureau of Statistics. Estimates of Recurrent Expenditures *224*
Kenya. Ministry of Economic Planning and Development. Statistics Division. Statistical Abstract *see* Kenya. Central Bureau of Statistics. Statistical Abstract *159*
Kenya. Ministry of Education. Annual Report (KE ISSN 0075-5869) *319*
Kenya. Ministry of Finance and Economic Planning. Budget Speech *see* Kenya. Ministry of Finance and Planning. Budget Speech by Minister for Finance and Planning *743*
Kenya. Ministry of Finance and Economic Planning. Statistics Division. Register of Manufacturing Firms *see* Kenya. Central Bureau of Statistics. Register of Manufacturing Firms *159*

Kenya. Ministry of Finance and Economic Planning. Statistics Division. Register of Manufacturing Firms *see* Kenya. Central Bureau of Statistics. Directory of Industries *239*
Kenya. Ministry of Finance and Planning. Budget Speech by Minister for Finance and Planning (KE) *743*
Kenya. Ministry of Finance and Planning. Plan Implementation Report (KE) *743*
Kenya. Ministry of Health and Housing. Annual Report *see* Kenya. Ministry of Housing. Annual Report *485*
Kenya. Ministry of Housing. Annual Report (KE) *485*
Kenya. Ministry of Information and Broadcasting. Annual Report (KE) *440*
Kenya. Ministry of Information, Broadcasting and Tourism. Annual Report *see* Kenya. Ministry of Information and Broadcasting. Annual Report *440*
Kenya. National Housing Corporation. Annual Report (KE) *485*
Kenya. National Irrigation Board. Reports and Accounts (KE ISSN 0075-5915) *37*
Kenya. National Library Service Board. Annual and Audit Report (KE ISSN 0075-5923) *532*
Kenya. Public Accounts Committee. Annual Report (KE ISSN 0075-5931) *743*
Kenya. Public Service Commission. Annual Report (KE ISSN 0075-594X) *807*
Kenya Commercial Bank. Director's Report and Accounts and Executive Chairman's Statement (KE) *174*
Kenya Enterprise (KE) *145, 239*
Kenya Fisheries Reports (KE) *398*
Kenya Institute of Administration. Journal (KE ISSN 0065-1966) *743*
Kenya Institute of Administration Occasional Papers *see* K I A Occasional Papers *743*
Kenya Library Association Chairman's Annual Report (KE) *532*
Kenya Media Advertising Review (KE) *5*
Kenya National Academy for Advancement of Arts and Sciences. Foundation Lectures (KE) *491*
Kenya National Academy for Advancement of Arts and Sciences. Newsletter (KE) *785, 851*
Kenya National Academy for Advancement of Arts and Sciences. Proceedings (KE) *491*
Kenya National Academy for Advancement of Arts and Sciences. Research Information Circulars (KE) *440*
Kenya National Chamber of Commerce and Industry. Annual Report (KE) *179*
Kenya Past and Present (KE) *440, 785*
Kenya Regional Studies (KE) *440*
Kenya, Uganda, Tanzania, East African Community Directory; Trade Commerce Index (KE) *239*
Kenya, Uganda, Tanzania, Zambia, Malawi and Ethiopia Directory; Trade and Commercial Index *see* Kenya, Uganda, Tanzania, East African Community Directory; Trade Commerce Index *239*
Kenya Uhuru Yearbook (KE ISSN 0378-2158) *440*
Kenya Yearbook (UK) *187*
Kenyatta University College. Directory of Research (NR) *337*
Kerala (India). Board for Prevention and Control of Water Pollution. Annual Report (II) *387*
Kerala; an Economic Review (II ISSN 0453-7440) *187*
Kernenergiecentrale van 50 MWE; Doodeward. Jaarverslag (EI) *363, 368*
Kernforschungszentrum Karlsruhe. Ergebnisbericht ueber Forschung und Entwicklung (GW) *368, 703*
Kernkraft Lingen. Jahresbericht (EI) *363, 368, 703*

Kernkraft Zentrale, Gundremmingen. Jahresberichte (EI ISSN 0453-767X) *363, 368, 703*
Kernkraftwerk Obrigheim. Jahresbericht(EI) *363, 368, 704*
Kerry Archaeological and Historical Society. Journal (IE ISSN 0085-2503) *62*
Kerrygold International (IE ISSN 0303-7002) *41*
Kesatuan Bulletin (SI ISSN 0047-3383) *338*
Ketabname-Ye Ravanshenasi *see* Bibliography of Psychology *739*
Kew Bulletin (UK ISSN 0075-5974) *116*
Kew Bulletin. Additional Series (UK ISSN 0075-5982) *116*
Key Word Index of Wildlife Research (SZ) *3, 794*
Keystone (CN) *263*
Khar'kovskii Gosudarstvennyi Iniversitet. Matematika i Mekhanika (UR) *586*
Kharkovskii Gosudarstvennyi Universitet. Filolohiya (UR) *546*
Kharkovskii Gosudarstvennyi Universitet. Radiofizyka i Elektronika(UR) *356*
Khatru (US) *566*
Ki-es-Ki *see* C E A Handbook *315*
Kianja (MG) *418*
The Kibbutz (IS) *814*
Kidney International. Supplement (US) *625*
Kieler Studien (GW) *196*
Kierkegaard's Writings (US) *689*
Kihara Institute for Biological Research. Report/Kihara Seibutsugaku Kenkyusho. Seiken Ziho (JA ISSN 0080-8539) *122*
Kihara Institute for Biological Research. Wheat Information Service (JA) *116*
Kihara Seibutsugaku Kenkyusho. Seiken Ziho *see* Kihara Institute for Biological Research. Report *122*
Kijkboekjes (NE) *660*
Killaly Chapbooks (CN) *580*
Kilpailunvapauslehti *see* Hinnat ja Kilpailu *182*
Kime's International Law Directory (UK ISSN 0075-6040) *523*
Kimia (MY) *247*
Kinaadman/Wisdom (PH) *402, 444*
Kinematografija u Srbiji *see* Kinematografija u Srbiji - Uporedo SFRJ *650*
Kinematografija u Srbiji - Uporedo SFRJ (YU) *650*
Kinetics and Mechanisms of Polymerization (US ISSN 0075-6067) *910*
King Sized Cracked (US) *556*
King's Gazette (UK ISSN 0085-2546) *481, 597*
Kings of Tomorrow Series (UK ISSN 0075-6083) *97*
Kingston History Society. Annual Papers *see* Kingston History Society. Papers *456*
Kingston History Society. Papers (UK ISSN 0260-583X) *456*
Kinki Nogyo Josei Hokoku *see* Annual Review of Agriculture, Kinkei District *12*
Kirchenmusikalisches Jahrbuch (GW ISSN 0075-6199) *660*
Kirchliches Jahrbuch fuer die Evangelische Kirche in Deutschland (GW ISSN 0075-6210) *772*
Kirin Biru K. K. Sogo Kenkyusho Kenkyu Hokoku *see* Kirin Brewery Company, Tokyo. Research Laboratory. Report *86*
Kirin Brewery Company, Tokyo. Research Laboratory. Report/Kirin Biru K. K. Sogo Kenkyusho Kenkyu Hokoku (JA ISSN 0075-6229) *86*
Kirkia (RH ISSN 0451-9930) *116*
Kirkon Nuoriso-Pistis *see* Pistis *766*
Kirtlandia (US ISSN 0075-6245) *785*
Kiruna Geophysical Institute. Preprint (SW) *305*
Kiruna Geophysical Institute. Report (SW) *305*
Kiruna Geophysical Institute. Software Report (SW) *305*
Kiruna Geophysical Institute. Technical Report (SW) *305*

Kisho-cho Nenpo Zenkoku Kishohyo see Japan. Meteorological Agency. Annual Report *634*
Al-Kitab Al-Arabi Fi Aam see Arab Book Annual *760*
Kitabu Cha Jua (US) *580*
Kitanihon Byogaichu Kenkyukai Kaiho see Society of Plant Protection of North Japan. Annual Report *39*
Kitchen & Bath Improvements (US) *503*
Kitchin's Road Transport Law (UK ISSN 0308-8987) *514*
Kjelberg-e SAB-Schriften; Erfahrungsberichte ueber Lichtbogen-Schweisstechnik see Svetsaren *630*
Kjeller Report (NO ISSN 0534-4050) *368, 704*
Klasings Bootsmarkt International; Yachten und Boote Zubehoer, Ausruestung, Motoren (GW ISSN 0075-627X) *827*
Klaus-Groth-Gesellschaft. Jahresgaben (GW) *546, 566*
Kleine Deutsche Prosadenkmaeler des Mittelalters (GW ISSN 0075-6318) *566*
Kleine Ikonenbuecherei (GW ISSN 0445-2577) *75*
Kleine Museumshefte (GW ISSN 0075-6326) *653*
Kleio (SA ISSN 0023-2084) *433, 759*
Klimat i Gidrografiya Zabaikal'ya (UR) *634*
Kline Guide to the Chemical Industry (US) *373*
Kline Guide to the Packaging Industry (US) *672*
Kline Guide to the Paint Industry (US) *673*
Kline Guide to the Paper and Pulp Industry (US) *675*
Kline Guide to the Plastics Industry (US) *239, 706*
Klinische Anaesthesiologie und Intensivtherapie (US) *604*
Klio (GE ISSN 0075-6334) *433*
Klucze do Oznaczania Owadow Polski (PL ISSN 0075-6350) *121*
Knickerbocker Club. Club Book (US ISSN 0362-5168) *262*
Kniha (CS) *532*
KnitOrations see Woolknit Annual *857*
Knitting Times Yearbook (US ISSN 0085-2562) *856*
Knizna Kultura see Kniha *532*
Kniznicny Zbornik/Library Studies (CS ISSN 0075-6369) *532*
Knotty Problems of Baseball (US ISSN 0075-6385) *824*
Know Your Congress (US) *712, 743*
Know Your Training Films (UK) *220*
Knowing Children (AT) *256*
Kobe Daigaku Igakubu Kiyo see Kobe University Medical Journal *597*
Kobe Economic and Business Research Series (JA ISSN 0075-6415) *146*
Kobe Economic and Business Review (JA ISSN 0075-6407) *146*
Kobe University. School of Business Administration. Annals (JA ISSN 0085-2570) *215*
Kobe University Economic Review (JA ISSN 0454-1111) *146*
Kobe University Law Review. International Edition (JA ISSN 0075-6423) *514*
Kobe University Medical Journal/Kobe Daigaku Igakubu Kiyo (JA ISSN 0075-6431) *597*
Kobe University of Mercantile Marine. Review. Part 1. Studies in Humanities and Social Science (JA) *491, 798*
Kobe University of Mercantile Marine. Review. Part 2. Navigation, Marine Engineering, Nuclear Engineering and Scientific Section (JA) *368, 785*
Kobenhavns Statistiske Aarbog (DK) *842*
KOBIE (SP) *296*
Kodaly Institute of Canada. Monograph(CN) *92, 349, 665*
Koebenhavns Fondsboers. Aarsrapport/Copenhagen Stock Exchange. Annual Report (DK) *203*

Koebenhavns Universitet. Geologisk Centralinstitut. Aarsberetning (DK) *296*
Koebenhavns Universitet. Historiske Institut. Skrifter (DK ISSN 0525-6844) *456*
Koebenhavns Universitet. Institut for Anvendt og Matematisk Lingvistik. Skrifter (DK) *546, 586*
Koebenhavns Universitet. Institut for Filmvidenskab. Skrifter see Filmvidenskabeligt Arbog *650*
Koebenhavns Universitet, Institut for Filmvidenskab Skrifter see Saerrakke *651*
Koedoe (SA ISSN 0075-6458) *276*
Koedoe. Monographs (SA ISSN 0075-6466) *276*
Koehlers Flottenkalender. Jahrbuch fuer Schiffahrt und Haefen (GW ISSN 0075-6474) *639, 879*
Koelner Beitraege zur Musikforschung (GW) *660*
Koelner Beitraege zur Sozialen Forschung und Angewandten Soziologie (GW) *910*
Koelner Ethnologische Mitteilungen (GW ISSN 0075-6490) *51*
Koelner Jahrbuch fuer Vor- und Fruehgeschichte (GW ISSN 0075-6512) *62*
Koelner Roemer-Illustrierte (GW) *62, 456, 653*
Koelner Romanistische Arbeiten (SZ ISSN 0075-6520) *491*
Koelner Vortraege zur Sozial- und Wirtschaftsgeschichte (GW) *456*
Kogai Shigen Kenkyusho Hokoku see National Research Institute for Pollution and Resources. Science Report *388*
Kogai Shigen Kenkyusho Nenpo see National Research Institute for Pollution and Resources. Annual Report *387*
Kogyo Ritchi Handobukku see Industrial Location Handbook *223*
Kokuritsu Eiyo Kenkyusho Hokoku see National Institute of Nutrition. Annual Report *666*
Kokuritsu Gan Senta Nenpo see National Cancer Center. Annual Report *605*
Kokuritsu Gan Senta, Tokyo. Collected Papers see National Cancer Center. Collected Papers *605*
Kokuritsu Idengaku Kenkyusho, Mishima, Japan. Nenpo see National Institute of Genetics, Mishima, Japan. Annual Report *122*
Kokuritsu Kokkai Toshokan Nenpo see Japan. National Diet Library. Annual Report *532*
Kokuritsu Kokugo Kenkyusho Nenpo see National Language Research Institute. Annual Report *547*
Kokuritsu Koshu Eisei-in Nenpo see Institute of Public Health. Annual Report *752*
Kokusai Kirisutokyo Daigaku, Kyoiku Kenkyu see International Christian University. Institute for Educational Research and Service. Educational Studies *319*
Kokusai Kyoku-Undo Kansoku Jigyo Nenpo see International Polar Motion Service. Annual Report *82*
Koleopterologische Rundschau (AU ISSN 0075-6547) *104*
Kolloid-Gesellschaft. Verhandlungsberichte (GW ISSN 0075-6555) *255*
Kolloquium ueber Spaetantike und Fruehmittelalterliche Skulptur (GW ISSN 0075-6563) *75*
Koltsa; Bibliografiya (UR) *591*
Komite-Ye Irani-Ye Otaq-e Bazargani-Ye Beynolmelali. Nashriyeh see International Chamber of Commerce. Iranian Committee. Publication *179*
Kommission fuer Geschichtliche Landeskunde in Baden-Wuerttemberg. Veroeffentlichungen. Reihe A. Quellen (GW ISSN 0067-2831) *456*

Kommission fuer Geschichtliche Landeskunde in Baden-Wuerttemberg. Veroeffentlichungen. Reihe B: Forschungen (GW ISSN 0521-9884) *456*
Kommission fuer Neuere Geschichte Oesterreichs. Veroeffentlichungen (AU) *456*
Kommunikation und Kybernetik in Einzeldarstellungen see Communication and Cybernetics *271*
Kommunikation und Politik (GW) *505*
Kommunisticheskaya Partiya Sovetskogo Soyuza. Vysshaya Partiinaya Shkola. Uchenye Zapiski (UR) *712*
Kompas Danmark (DK ISSN 0075-661X) *239*
Kompass Alimentation (FR) *239, 405*
Kompass Australia (AT ISSN 0075-6628) *239*
Kompass Belgium/Luxembourg (BE ISSN 0075-6636) *239*
Kompass Deutschland (GW) *239*
Kompass Espana (SP ISSN 0075-6644) *239*
Kompass France see Repertoire General de la Production Francaise *241*
Kompass Holland (NE ISSN 0075-6660) *239*
Kompass Hong Kong (HK ISSN 0075-6679) *239*
Kompass Italia (IT ISSN 0075-6687) *239*
Kompass Maroc (MR ISSN 0075-6695) *239*
Kompass Norge (NO ISSN 0075-6709) *239*
Kompass Schweiz/Liechtenstein (SZ ISSN 0075-6717) *239*
Kompass Special Services (FR) *239*
Kompass Sverige (SW ISSN 0075-6725) *239*
Kompass Textile et Habillement (FR) *239, 261*
Kompass United Kingdom (UK) *239*
Kompass United Kingdom/CBI see Kompass United Kingdom *239*
Kongelig Dansk Hof- og Statskalender; Statshaandbog for Kongeriget Danmark (DK ISSN 0085-2589) *743*
Kongelige Danske Videnskabernes Selskab. Biologiske Skrifter (DK ISSN 0006-3320) *104*
Kongelige Danske Videnskabernes Selskab. Historisk-Filosofiske Meddelelser (DK ISSN 0106-0481) *491*
Kongelige Danske Videnskabernes Selskab. Historisk-Filosofiske Skrifter (DK ISSN 0023-3307) *491*
Kongelige Danske Videnskabernes Selskab. Matematisk-Fysiske Meddelelser (DK ISSN 0023-3323) *586, 697*
Kongelige Danske Videnskabernes Selskab. Oversigt over Selskabets Virksomhed (DK ISSN 0023-3315) *491*
Kongelige Norske Videnskabers Selskab. Forhandlinger (NO) *491, 785*
Kongelige Norske Videnskabers Selskab. Museet. Miscellanea see Gunneria *61*
Kongelige Norske Videnskabers Selskab. Skrifter/Royal Norwegian Society of Sciences. Publications (NO) *491, 785*
Kongelige Veterinaer- og Landbohoejskole. Aarskrift (DK ISSN 0368-7171) *17, 894*
Kongeriget Danmarks Handels-Kalender (DK ISSN 0302-5403) *239*
Konglomerati (US ISSN 0146-2377) *580*
Kongres Wanita Indonesia. Berita see Indonesian Women's Congress. Bulletin *900*
Kongresa Libro (NE ISSN 0083-3851) *546*
Koninklijk Instituut voor de Tropen. Afdeling Agrarisch Onderzoek. Annual Report (NE) *17*
Koninklijk Instituut voor de Tropen. Afdeling Agrarisch Onderzoek. Communication (NE) *17*

Koninklijk Instituut voor de Tropen. Department of Tropical Hygiene. Annual Report (NE) *752*
Koninklijk Instituut voor het Kunstpatrimonium. Bulletin see Institut Royal de Patrimoine Artistique. Bulletin *75*
Koninklijk Instituut voor Taal-, Land- en Volkenkunde. Bibliographical Series (NE ISSN 0074-0462) *56*
Koninklijk Instituut voor Taal-, Land- en Volkenkunde. Translation Series (NE ISSN 0074-0470) *51*
Koninklijk Museum voor Midden-Afrika. Annalen. Reeks in 8. Economische Wetenschappen see Musee Royal de l'Afrique Centrale. Annales. Serie in 8. Sciences Economiques *192*
Koninklijk Museum voor Midden-Afrika. Annalen. Reeks in 8. Geologische Wetenschappen see Musee Royal de l'Afrique Centrale. Annales. Serie in 8. Sciences Geologiques *297*
Koninklijk Museum voor Midden-Afrika. Annalen. Reeks in 8. Historische Wetenschappen see Musee Royal de l'Afrique Centrale. Annales. Serie in 8. Sciences Historiques *434*
Koninklijk Museum voor Midden-Afrika. Annalen. Reeks in 8. Menselijke Wetenschappen see Musee Royal de l'Afrique Centrale. Annales. Serie in 8. Sciences Humaines *492*
Koninklijk Museum voor Midden-Afrika. Annalen. Reeks in 8. Zoologische Wetenschappen see Musee Royal de l'Afrique Centrale. Annales. Serie in 8. Sciences Zoologiques *129*
Koninklijk Museum voor Midden-Afrika. Economische Documentatie see Musee Royal de l'Afrique Centrale. Documentation Economique *146*
Koninklijk Museum voor Midden-Afrika. Zoologische Documentatie see Musee Royal de l'Afrique Centrale. Documentation Zoologique *129*
Koninklijk Nederlands Geologisch Mijnbouwkundig Genootschap. Verhandelingen (NE ISSN 0075-6741) *296, 644*
Koninklijke Academie voor Nederlandse Taal- en Letterkunde. Jaarboek (BE) *546, 566*
Koninklijke Academie voor Overzeese Wetenschappen. Bibliografisch Overzicht see Academie Royale des Sciences d'Outre Mer. Revue Bibliographique *903*
Koninklijke Bibliotheek Albert I. Centrale Catalogus van Buitenlandse Tidjschriften see Bibliotheque Royale Albert 1er. Catalogue Collectif des Periodiques Etrangers *89*
Koninklijke Bibliotheek Albert I. Jaarverslag see Bibliotheque Royale Albert 1er. Rapport Annuel *527*
Koninklijke Bibliotheek Albert I. Voorname Aanwinsten see Bibliotheque Royale Albert 1er. Acquisitions Majeures *527*
Koninklijke Nederlandse Akademie van Wetenschapen. Afdeling Natuurkunde, Verhandelingen. Eerste Reeks (NE ISSN 0065-5503) *785*
Koninklijke Nederlandse Akademie van Wetenschappen. Afdeling Letterkunde. Verhandelingen. Nieuwe Reeks (NE ISSN 0065-5511) *492*
Koninklijke Nederlandse Akademie van Wetenschappen. Afdeling Natuurkunde. Verhandelingen. Tweede Reeks (NE ISSN 0065-552X) *785*
Koninklijke Nederlandse Chemische Vereniging. Chemisch Jaarboek (NE) *910*
Die Konjunktur im Handwerk (GW ISSN 0341-0978) *224*
Konjunkturberichte ueber das Handwerk see Die Konjunktur im Handwerk *224*

Konstitutsiya i Svoista Mineralov (UR ISSN 0454-3343) *296*
Konstruktionsbuecher (US ISSN 0075-6768) *137*
Konstruktorsko-Tekhnologicheskii Institut Avtomatizatsii Avtomobilstroeniya. Sbornik Trudov (UR) *871*
Kontaks (PH) *239*
Kontakte (GW) *356*
Kontrollraadet foer Betongvaror. Meddelande (SW ISSN 0075-6776) *137*
Konyvtartudomanyi Tanulmanyok (HU ISSN 0075-6784) *532*
Koodal Historical Series (II) *433*
Koolewong (AT) *129*
Kopenhagener Beitraege zur Germanistischen Linguistik (DK ISSN 0105-0257) *546*
Koranyi Sandor Tarsasag. Tudomanyos Ulesek (HU ISSN 0075-6792) *597*
Korea (Republic) Bureau of Statistics. Annual Report of the Price Survey/ Mulga Yonbo (KO ISSN 0075-6830) *159*
Korea (Republic) Bureau of Statistics. Annual Report on the Family Income and Expenditure Survey/Tosi Gagye Yonbo (KO ISSN 0075-6822) *160*
Korea (Republic) Bureau of Statistics. Report on Mining and Manufacturing Survey/Kwanggongup Tonggye Zo Sa Bogo Seo (KO ISSN 0075-6849) *3, 160, 648*
Korea (Republic) Bureau of Statistics. Wholesale and Retail Trade Census Report/Tosomaeup Census Bogo Seo(KO ISSN 0075-6857) *160*
Korea (Republic). Central Meteorological Office. Annual Report (KO) *634*
Korea (Republic) Economic Planning Board. Annual Report on Current Industrial Production Survey (KO) *224*
Korea (Republic) Economic Planning Board. Annual Report on the Economically Active Population (KO ISSN 0454-7543) *208*
Korea (Republic) Economic Planning Board. Yearbook of Migration Statistics (KO) *728*
Korea (Republic). Ministry of Education. Basic Statistics of Education (KO) *327*
Korea (Republic). Ministry of Education. Educational Development in Korea: (KO) *327*
Korea (Republic) Nongch'on Chinhungch'ong. Nongsa Sihom Yon'gu Pogo *see* Korea (Republic) Office of Rural Development. Agricultural Research Report *17*
Korea (Republic) Office of Rural Development. Agricultural Research Report/Korea (Republic) Nongch'on Chinhungch'ong. Nongsa Sihom Yon'gu Pogo (KO ISSN 0075-6865) *17*
Korea(Republic). Population & Housing Census Report (KO) *842*
Korea (Republic). Tongil Chuche Kungmin Hoeui. Kungmin Hoeui Bo/ National Conference Review (KO) *712*
Korea Annual (KO) *239*
Korea Development Bank; Its Functions and Activities (KO ISSN 0075-6806) *174*
Korea Directory (KO ISSN 0075-6814) *239*
Korea Film Catalog (KO) *650*
Korea Policy Series (KO) *187, 712*
Korea Research Monographs (US) *444*
Korea Social Work College. Research Institute for Special Education. Journal/Kwang-Eung Yeo (KO) *346*
Korea Statistical Yearbook/Hanguk Tonggye Yongam (KO ISSN 0075-6873) *438*
Korean Affairs Report (US) *187, 712*
Korean Astronomical Society. Journal (KO) *82*
Korean Institute for Family Planning. Annual Report (KO) *132*
Korean Journal of International Relations (KO) *722*

Korean Journal of Sociology. (KO) *814*
Korean Population and Family Planning. Bibliography Series *see* Bibliography on Population and Family Planning in Korea *133*
Korean Publications Yearbook/Han'quk Ch'ulp; an Yon'gam. (KO ISSN 0075-6881) *759*
Korean Studies (US ISSN 0145-840X) *444*
Kornik, Poland. Zaklad Dendrologii i Pomologii. Prace *see* Arboretum Kornickie *113*
Korosi Csoma Kiskonyvtar (HU ISSN 0075-6911) *444, 546*
Korrespondens /Utbildningskontakt (SW ISSN 0023-4125) *329*
Korrosionsverhalten von Zink (GW) *628*
Korunk Tudomanya (HU ISSN 0075-6946) *785, 851*
Kosmos (US) *580*
Kosmosophie (GW ISSN 0454-448X) *689*
Kosten en Financiering van de Gezondheidzorg in Nederland/Cost of Health Care in the Netherlands (NE ISSN 0075-6954) *752, 807*
Koszen es Koolaj Anyagismereti Monografiak (HU ISSN 0075-6962) *680*
Kothari's Economic and Industrial Guide of India (II) *204, 224*
Kothari's Economic Guide and Investor's Handbook of India *see* Kothari's Economic and Industrial Guide of India *204*
Kothari's World of Reference Works (II ISSN 0075-6970) *92*
Kovel's Complete Antiques Price List (US) *476*
Kovel's Official Bottle Price List (US) *476*
Kowan Gijutsu Kenkyusho. Guide *see* Port and Harbour Technical Research Institute. Guide *880*
Kozgazdasagi Ertekezesek (HU ISSN 0075-6989) *146*
Kraevye Zadachi dlya Differentsial'nykh Uravnenii (UR) *586*
Kraftfahrt-Bundesamt. Statistische Mitteilungen (GW ISSN 0341-468X) *871*
Krak (DK) *239*
Krakow Dawnej i Dzis (PL ISSN 0075-7020) *456*
Krakowskie Studia Prawnicze (PL ISSN 0023-4478) *514*
Krankenhaus-Probleme der Gegenwart (SZ ISSN 0075-708X) *807*
Krasoslovni Zbornik *see* Acta Carsologica *288*
Krebsforschung. Beitraege (GE ISSN 0067-5113) *910*
Kreislauf Buecherei *see* Beitraege zur Kardiologie und Angiologie *606*
Kresge Foundation. Annual Report (US ISSN 0075-711X) *807*
Kriminalbiologische Gegenwartsfragen *see* Kriminologische Gegenwartsfragen *282*
Kriminalitaet und ihre Verwalter (GW) *282*
Kriminalwissenschaftliche Abhandlungen (GW ISSN 0454-5265) *282*
Kriminologie. Abhandlungen ueber abweiges Sozialverhalten (GW ISSN 0075-7144) *282*
Kriminologische Abhandlungen (US ISSN 0075-7152) *282*
Kriminologische Cahiers (NE) *282*
Kriminologische Gegenwartsfragen (GW ISSN 0075-7136) *282*
Kriminologische Schriftenreihe (GW) *282*
Kristofer Lehmkuhl Forelesning (NO ISSN 0452-7208) *146*
Kritische Studien zur Geschichtswissenschaft (GW) *433*
Kroeber Anthropological Society. Papers (US ISSN 0023-4869) *51*
Kryptadia: Journal of Erotic Folklore (FR ISSN 0075-7160) *402*
Krystalinikum (CS) *296*
Ksiazka w Dawnej Kulturze Polskiej (PL ISSN 0075-7179) *492*
Ktema (FR) *259, 444*

Ktemata (BE) *785*
Kuala Lumpur Stock Exchange. Companies Handbook (MY ISSN 0126-7558) *204*
Die Kueste (GW ISSN 0452-7739) *311, 368, 387*
Kuk Hoe Hoe Eu Rok Saegin *see* Index to the National Assembly Records *539*
Kuka Kukin On/Who's Who in Finland(FI) *97*
Kuksu (US) *580*
Kultur und Gesellschaft (GW) *433, 798*
Kultureller Wandel (GW) *910*
Kulturen (SW) *259*
Kulturnopoliticky Kalendar (CS) *626, 887*
Kulturpflanze (GE ISSN 0075-7209) *116, 122*
Kumamoto Daigaku Kogakubu Kiyo *see* Kumamoto University. Faculty of Engineering. Memoirs *368*
Kumamoto University. Department of Geology. Journal (JA) *296*
Kumamoto University. Department of Physics. Physics Reports (JA) *697*
Kumamoto University. Faculty of Engineering. Memoirs/Kumamoto Daigaku Kogakubu Kiyo (JA ISSN 0023-5334) *368*
Kumamoto University. Institute of Constitutional Medicine. Bulletin. Supplement (JA ISSN 0075-7217) *597*
Kumasitech *see* University of Science and Technology. Journal *793*
Kungliga Skogshoegskolan. Institutionen foer Virkeslaera. Rapporter *see* Sveriges Lantbruksuniversitet. Institutionen foer Virkeslaera. Rapporter *410*
Kungliga Skogshoegskolan. Institutionen foer Virkeslaera. Uppsatser *see* Sveriges Lantbruksuniversitet. Institution foer Virkeslaera. Uppsatser *410*
Kungliga Svenska Vetenskapsakademien. Bidrag till Kungliga Vetenskapsakademiens Historia (SW ISSN 0081-9956) *785*
Kungliga Tekniska Hoegskolan. Flygtekniska Institutionen. K T H Aero Memo F I (SW) *9*
Kungliga Vitterhets-, Historie- och Antikvitets Akademien. Aarsbok (SW ISSN 0083-6796) *456*
Kungliga Vitterhets-, Historie- och Antikvitets Akademien. Antikvarisk Arkiv (SW ISSN 0083-6737) *456*
Kungliga Vitterhets-, Historie- och Antikvitets Akademien. Filologiskt Arkiv (SW ISSN 0083-6745) *456*
Kungliga Vitterhets-, Historie- och Antikvitets Akademien. Handlingar. Antikvariska Serien/Royal Academy of Letters, History and Antiquities. Proceedings. Antiquarian Series (SW ISSN 0083-6761) *456*
Kungliga Vitterhets-, Historie- och Antikvitets Akademien. Handlingar. Filologisk-Filosofiska Serien/Royal Academy of Letters, History and Antiquities. Proceedings. Philological-Philosophical Series (SW ISSN 0083-677X) *546, 689*
Kungliga Vitterhets-, Historie- och Antikvitets Akademien. Handlingar. Historiska Serien/Royal Academy of Letters, History and Antiquities. Proceedings. Historical Series (SW ISSN 0083-6788) *456*
Kungliga Vitterhets-, Historie- och Antikvitets Akademien. Historiskt Arkiv (SW ISSN 0083-6753) *456*
Kunitachi College of Music. Memoirs/ Kunitachi Ongaku Daigaku Kenkyu Kiyo (JA) *660*
Kunitachi Ongaku Daigaku Kenkyu Kiyo *see* Kunitachi College of Music. Memoirs *660*
Kunst *see* Art *80*
Kunst des Orients/Art of the Orient (GW ISSN 0023-5393) *76, 670*
Kunst-Katalog: Auktionen (AU ISSN 0075-7241) *76*
Kunst und Altertum am Rhein (GW ISSN 0075-725X) *62*
Kunst und Gesellschaft (GW) *76*

Kunsthistorische Musea, Antwerp. Schone Kunsten (BE ISSN 0066-4979) *653*
Kunsthistorische Sammlungen in Wien. Jahrbuch (AU ISSN 0075-2312) *76*
Kunsthistorisches Institut in Florenz. Mitteilungen (IT) *76, 433*
Kunstindustrimuseet i Oslo. Aarbok (NO) *851*
Das Kunstjahrbuch (GW) *76*
Kunstjahrbuch der Stadt Linz (AU) *76*
Kunstpreis-Jahrbuch (GW ISSN 0174-3511) *76, 476*
Kunststoff-Industrie und ihre Helfer (GW ISSN 0075-7276) *706*
Kunststoffe im Lebensmittelverkehr (GW ISSN 0075-7292) *706*
Kunststoffe in Oesterreich (AU) *706*
Kupat-Holim Yearbook (IS ISSN 0301-4843) *752*
Kuratorium fuer Technik und Bauwesen in der Landwirtschaft e.V. Schriften *see* K T B L-Schriften *17*
Kuratorium fuer Verkehrssicherheit. Kleine Fachbuchreihe (AU ISSN 0075-7306) *875*
Kurukshetra Law Journal (II) *514*
Kush (UK ISSN 0075-7349) *51*
Kuwait. Central Statistical Office. Annual Statistical Abstract (KU) *842*
Kuwait. Central Statistical Office. Monthly Statistical Bulletin *see* Kuwait. Central Statistical Office. Annual Statistical Abstract *842*
Kuwait. Central Statistical Office. Yearly Bulletin of Price Index Numbers (KU) *213*
Kuwait Investment Company. (Report) (KU) *174*
Kvinnebulletin (SW) *900*
Kwahak Kisul Yoram/Handbook of Science and Technology (KO) *852*
Kwang-Eung Yeo *see* Korea Social Work College. Research Institute for Special Education. Journal *346*
Kwanggongup Tonggye Zo Sa Bogo Seo *see* Korea (Republic) Bureau of Statistics. Report on Mining and Manufacturing Survey *648*
Kybernetik - Datenverarbeitung - Recht(GW ISSN 0340-5982) *514*
Kybernetik Jahreskatalog (GW) *273*
Kyoi *see* Kuksu *580*
Kyoiku Shinrigaku Nempo *see* Annual Report of Educational Psychology in Japan *734*
Kyoka Kyoiku Kenkyu (JA) *349*
Kyoto Daigaku Genshi Energui Kenkyusho Kenkyu Hokoku *see* Kyoto University. Institute of Atomic Energy. Technical Reports *704*
Kyoto Daigaku Ogata Keisanki Senta Eibun Repoto *see* Kyoto University. Data Processing Center. Report *273*
Kyoto Daigaku Uirusu Kenkyusho Nenkan Kiyo *see* Kyoto University. Institute for Virus Research. Annual Report *123*
Kyoto-furitsu Daigaku Gakujutsu Hokoku Jimbun *see* Kyoto Prefectural University. Scientific Reports: Humanities *492*
Kyoto-furitsu Daigaku Gakujutsu Hokoku Nagaku *see* Kyoto Prefectural University. Scientific Reports: Agriculture *17*
Kyoto-furitsu Daigaku Gakujutsu Hokoku Rigaku Seikatsukagaku *see* Kyoto Prefectural University. Scientific Reports: Natural Science and Living Science *785*
Kyoto Kogei Sen'i Daigaku Kogeigakubu Kiyo Riko-hen *see* Kyoto Technical University. Faculty of Industrial Arts. Memoirs: Science and Technology *785*
Kyoto Prefectural University. Scientific Reports: Agriculture/Kyoto-furitsu Daigaku Gakujutsu Hokoku Nagaku (JA ISSN 0075-7373) *17*
Kyoto Prefectural University. Scientific Reports: Humanities/Kyoto-furitsu Daigaku Gakujutsu Hokoku Jimbun (JA ISSN 0075-7381) *492*

Kyoto Prefectural University. Scientific Reports: Natural Science and Living Science/Kyoto-furitsu Daigaku Gakujutsu Hokoku Rigaku Seikatsukagaku (JA) 785
Kyoto Prefectural University. Scientific Reports: Natural Science, Domestic Science and Social Welfare see Kyoto Prefectural University. Scientific Reports: Natural Science and Living Science 785
Kyoto Technical University. Faculty of Industrial Arts. Memoirs: Science and Technology/Kyoto Kogei Sen'i Daigaku Kogeigakubu Kiyo Rikohen(JA ISSN 0453-0047) 785, 852
Kyoto University. Data Processing Center. Report/Kyoto Daigaku Ogata Keisanki Senta Eibun Repoto (JA) 273
Kyoto University. Faculty of Science. Memoirs. Series of Biology (JA ISSN 0454-7802) 104
Kyoto University. Institute for Virus Research. Annual Report/Kyoto Daigaku Uirusu Kenkyusho Nenkan Kiyo (JA ISSN 0075-7357) 123
Kyoto University. Institute of Atomic Energy. Research Activities (JA ISSN 0386-0752) 704
Kyoto University. Institute of Atomic Energy. Technical Reports/Kyoto Daigaku Genshi Enerugi Kenkyusho Kenkyu Hokoku (JA) 704
Kyoto University. Research Activities in Civil Engineering and Related Fields (JA ISSN 0075-7365) 376
Kyoto University. Research Institute for Food Science. Memoirs/Shokuryo Kagaku Kenkyusho Kiyo (JA ISSN 0452-9995) 405
Kyoyo Ronshu see Review on Liberal Arts 492
Kypriakai Spoudai see Society of Cypriot Studies. Bulletin 461
Kyrkohistorisk Aarsskrift (SW ISSN 0085-2619) 766
Kyushu American Literature Studies (JA ISSN 0454-8132) 566
Kyushu Daigaku Nogakubu Suisangakka Gyosekishu see Kyushu University. Contributions from the Department of Fisheries and the Fishery Research Laboratory 398
Kyushu Daigaku Rigakubu Kiyo, B, Butsurigaku see Kyushu University. Faculty of Science. Memoirs Series B: Physics 697
Kyushu Daigaku Rigakubu Kiyo, C. Kagaku see Kyushu University. Faculty of Science. Memoirs. Series C: Chemistry 247
Kyushu Daigaku Rigakubu Kiyo, D, Chishitsugaku see Kyushu University. Faculty of Science. Memoirs. Series D: Geology 296
Kyushu Institute of Technology. Bulletin: Humanities, Social Sciences/Kyushu Kogyo Daigaku Kenkyu Hokoku, Jinbun-Shakai-Kagaku (JA ISSN 0453-0349) 492, 798
Kyushu Institute of Technology. Bulletin: Mathematics, Natural Science/Kyushu Kogyo Daigaku Kenkyu Hokoku, Shizenkagaku (JA ISSN 0454-8221) 586, 785
Kyushu Institute of Technology. Memoirs: Engineering (JA ISSN 0369-0512) 368
Kyushu Kogyo Daigaku Kenkyu Hokoku, Jinbun-Shakai-Kagaku see Kyushu Institute of Technology. Bulletin: Humanities, Social Sciences 492
Kyushu Kogyo Daigaku Kenkyu Hokoku, Shizenkagaku see Kyushu Institute of Technology. Bulletin: Mathematics, Natural Science 586
Kyushu Kogyo Gijutsu Shikenjo Nempo see Japan. Government Industrial Research Institute, Kyushu Annual Report 223
Kyushu University. Contributions from the Department of Fisheries and the Fishery Research Laboratory/Kyushu Daigaku Nogakubu Suisangakka Gyosekishu (JA ISSN 0453-0314) 398

Kyushu University. Faculty of Science. Memoirs Series B: Physics/Kyushu Daigaku Rigakubu Kiyo, B, Butsurigaku (JA ISSN 0085-2627) 697
Kyushu University. Faculty of Science. Memoirs. Series C: Chemistry/Kyushu Daigaku Rigakubu Kiyo, C. Kagaku (JA ISSN 0085-2635) 247
Kyushu University. Faculty of Science. Memoirs. Series D: Geology/Kyushu Daigaku Rigakubu Kiyo, D, Chishitsugaku (JA ISSN 0023-6179) 296
Kyushu University. Institute of Tropical Agriculture. Bulletin (JA) 17
Kyushu University. Research Institute for Applied Mechanics. Abstracts of Papers (JA) 380
L A C U N Y Occasional Papers (Library Association of the City University of New York) (US ISSN 0094-615X) 532
L A C U S Forum (Linguistic Association of Canada and the United States) (US) 546
L A M P Occasional Newsletter (Standing Committee on Legal Assistance for Military Personnel) (US ISSN 0163-1373) 639
L B A Handbook (London Boroughs Association) (UK ISSN 0305-1137) 749
L C Science Tracer Bullet (US ISSN 0090-5232) 795
L D V Bogen (Landsforeningen Danske Vognmaend) (DK) 862
L E A Yearbook (Lutheran Education Association) (US ISSN 0076-1532) 772
L I R I Research Bulletin (Leather Industries Research Institute) (SA ISSN 0085-2724) 524
L I R I Technical Bulletin (Leather Industries Research Institute) (SA) 524
L J Special Reports (US ISSN 0362-448X) 532
L L S E E see Linguistic & Literary Studies in Eastern Europe 546
L P-Gas Market Facts (US ISSN 0075-9759) 680
L R I Guides to Management. Monographs (US) 215
L.S.C.A. Annual Program, Hawaii State Library System (Library Services and Construction Act) (US ISSN 0095-4721) 532
L S E Research Monographs (London School of Economics and Political Science) (UK ISSN 0076-0668) 146
L.S.I. (FR ISSN 0335-9190) 567
L S U Wood Utilization Notes (US ISSN 0076-1109) 413
L T C Newsletter see Land Tenure Center. Newsletter 29
L T C Paper see Land Tenure Center. Paper 29
L T P Publications (Library Technology Program) (US ISSN 0065-9088) 910
L U A C Monitor (Life Underwriters Association of Canada) (CN ISSN 0318-8116) 49
L'Universite de Sofia. Faculte de Philosophie. Annuaire see Sofiiski Universitet. Filosofski Fakultet. Godishnik 461
L'Universite de Sofia. Faculte des Lettres. Annuaire see Sofiiski Universitet. Fakultet po Zapadni Filologii. Godishnik 551
L'Universite de Sofia. Faculte des Mathematiques et de Mecanique. Annuaire see Sofiiski Universitet. Fakultet po Matematika i Mekhanika. Godishnik 589
La Punta, Peru (Lima) Instituto del Mar del Peru. Boletin see Instituto del Mar del Peru. Boletin 397
La Punta, Peru (Lima) Instituto del Mar del Peru. Informe see Instituto del Mar del Peru. Informe 397
La Trobe Historical Studies (AT) 447
La Trobe Sociology Papers (AT) 814
La Zona Norte. Informa (GT) 17
Labor Force in Idaho (US) 208
Labor Force Status of Indiana Residents (US ISSN 0362-3793) 208

Labor Rates for the Construction Industry (US ISSN 0098-3608) 137, 208
Labor Relations Yearbook (US ISSN 0075-7489) 209
Labor Research Report see New York (State) Department of Labor. Division of Research and Statistics. Labor Research Report 209
Labor Research Report (Albany) see New York (State) Department of Labor. Division of Research and Statistics. Labor Research Report 209
Laboratoire de Recherche des Musees de France. Annales (FR) 653
Laboratorio di Tecnologia della Pesca. Quaderni (IT) 311, 398
Laboratorios de Especialidades y Control (MX) 612
Laboratory and Research Methods in Biology and Medicine (US) 612
Laboratory Animal Handbooks (UK ISSN 0458-5933) 612
Laboratory Equipment Directory (UK) 496
Laboratory Equipment Directory & Buyers Guide see Laboratory Equipment Directory 496
Laboratory Guide to Instruments, Equipment and Chemicals (American Chemical Society) (US ISSN 0458-595X) 247
Laboratory Techniques in Biochemistry and Molecular Biology (NE ISSN 0075-7535) 104, 111, 612
Labour/Travailleur (CN ISSN 0700-3862) 208
Labour Force Situation in Indonesia: Preliminary Figures/Keadaan Angkatan Kerja di Indonesia: Angka Sementara (IO) 160, 842
Labour History (CN ISSN 0706-8441) 208
Labour in the Public Sector Undertakings: Basic Information (II) 208
Labour Law Cases (PK) 208, 514
Labour Literature: A Bibliography (II ISSN 0075-756X) 160
Labour Organizations in Nova Scotia (CN ISSN 0383-3437) 507
Labour Standards in Canada. Normes du Travail au Canada (CN ISSN 0075-7586) 208
Lady-Unique-Inclination-of-the-Night (US) 900
Laendermonographien (GW) 423, 433
Laerarhoegskolan i Moelndal. Pedagogiska Institutionen. Rapport see Goeteborgs Universitet. Institutionen foer Praktisk Pedagogik. Rapport 349
Lafayette Clinic Handbooks in Psychiatry (US ISSN 0075-7608) 620
Lafayette Clinic Monographs in Psychiatry (US ISSN 0075-7616) 620
Lagertechnik (GW) 218
Lagos Librarian (NR ISSN 0047-3901) 532
Lagos Notes and Records (NR ISSN 0075-7640) 440
Lake Carriers' Association. Annual Report (US ISSN 0075-7748) 879
Lake Chelan History Notes (US) 470
Lake Michigan Shore and Open Water Report (US ISSN 0094-6311) 387
Lake Michigan Water Quality Report (US ISSN 0361-8188) 308, 387
Lakeland Dialect Society. Bulletin (UK ISSN 0307-9341) 546
Lakeland Rambler (UK) 887
Lalbhai Dalpatbhai Institute of Indology. Publications (II) 670
Lalit Kala (II ISSN 0458-6506) 76
Lamar Lecture Series (US ISSN 0075-7772) 433, 567
Lamiss see Informozioni e Attualita Mondiali 596
Lammergeyer (SA ISSN 0075-7780) 276
Lancashire Dialect Society. Journal (UK ISSN 0075-7799) 546
Land Bank of the Philippines. Annual Report (PH) 174

Land Drilling and Oilwell Servicing Contractors Directory see Directory of Land Drilling and Oilwell Servicing Contractors 679
Land Economics Monographs (US ISSN 0075-7837) 29
Land Laws Service (AT ISSN 0085-266X) 514, 761
Land Resource Bibliography (UK ISSN 0460-1408) 92, 279
Land Tenure Center. Newsletter (US ISSN 0084-0785) 29
Land Tenure Center. Paper (US ISSN 0084-0793) 29
Land Tenure Center. Research Paper (US ISSN 0084-0815) 29
Land Use and Environment Law Review (US) 387
Land Use and Transportation (US ISSN 0149-4007) 863
Landarbeit und Technik (GW ISSN 0455-2342) 17
Landbouw-Economisch Instituut. Bedrijfsuitkomsten in de Landbouw (NE) 29
Landbouw-Economisch Instituut. Stafafdeling. Landbouw-Economisch Bericht (NE) 29
Landbouw-Economisch Instituut. Tuinbouwcijfers (NE) 416
Landbouwhogeschool, Wageningen. Miscellaneous Papers (NE ISSN 0083-6990) 17
Landbouwproefstation Suriname. Jaarverslag/Agricultural Experiment Station Surinam. Annual Report (SR) 17
Landbrukets Aarbok. Jordbruk, Hagebruk, Skogbruk (NO ISSN 0075-7853) 17, 409
Landbrukets Aarbok. Skogbruk see Landbrukets Aarbok. Jordbruk, Hagebruk, Skogbruk 409
Landeskonservator Rheinland. Arbeitsheft (GW) 69
Landeskundliche Luftbildauswertung im Mitteleuropaeischen Raum (GW ISSN 0457-0715) 423
Landesmuseum fuer Kaernten. Buchreihe. (AU ISSN 0007-280X) 76
Landesmuseum fuer Vorgeschichte, Dresden. Veroeffentlichungen (GE ISSN 0070-7201) 456, 653
Landesmuseum fuer Vorgeschichte, Halle. Veroeffentlichungen (GE ISSN 0072-940X) 456, 653
Landesmuseum Joanneum. Abteilung fuer Botanik. Mitteilungen (AU) 116
Landesmuseum Joanneum. Abteilung fuer Geologie, Palaeontologie und Bergbau. Mitteilungen (AU) 296, 644, 673
Landesmuseum Joanneum. Abteilung fuer Zoologie. Mitteilungen (AU) 129
Landis & Gyr Review see Landis und Gyr Mitteilungen 356
Landis und Gyr Mitteilungen/Revue Landis et Gyr/Landis & Gyr Review (SZ ISSN 0023-7949) 356
Landolt-Boernstein Numerical Data and Functional Relationships in Science and Technology. New Series see Landolt-Boernstein, Zahlenwerte und Funktionen aus Naturwissenschaften und Technik. Neue Serie. Group 1: Nuclear Physics 704
Landolt-Boernstein, Zahlenwerte und Funktionen aus Naturwissenschaften und Technik. Neue Serie. Group 1: Nuclear Physics/Landolt-Boernstein Numerical Data and Functional Relationships in Science and Technology. New Series (US ISSN 0075-7888) 704
Landolt-Boernstein, Zahlenwerte und Funktionen aus Naturwissenschaften und Technik. Neue Serie. Group 2: Atomic Physics (US ISSN 0075-7918) 704
Landolt-Boernstein, Zahlenwerte und Funktionen aus Naturwissenschaften und Technik. Neue Serie. Group 3: Crystal Physics (US ISSN 0075-787X) 251, 697

Landolt-Boernstein, Zahlenwerte und Funktionen aus Naturwissenschaften und Technik. Neue Serie. Group 4: Macroscopic and Technical Properties of Matter (US ISSN 0075-7926) *852*

Landolt-Boernstein, Zahlenwerte und Funktionen aus Naturwissenschaften und Technik. Neue Serie. Group 5: Geophysics (US ISSN 0075-790X) *305*

Landolt-Boernstein, Zahlenwerte und Funktionen aus Naturwissenschaften und Technik. Neue Serie. Group 6: Astronomy (US ISSN 0075-7896) *82*

Landscape Architects Reference Manual (Illustrated for Desk & Field Use) (US) *69*

Landscape History (UK ISSN 0143-3768) *17, 69, 456*

Landscape Research (UK) *69*

Landscape Research News *see* Landscape Research *69*

Landschaftsverband Westfalen-Lippe. Volkskundliche Kommission. Schriften (GW ISSN 0075-7942) *402*

Landsforeningen Danske Vognmaend Bogen *see* L D V Bogen *862*

Landsorganisationen i Sverige. Yttranden till Offentlig Myndighet (SW) *507*

Lane Studies in Regional Government (US) *743*

Langenbecks Archiv fuer Chirurgie (US ISSN 0023-8236) *624*

Language (SI) *546*

Language and Thought Series (UK) *546*

Language Forum Monograph Series (II) *546*

Language in Education. Theory and Practice (US) *319, 546*

Language Science Monographs (NE ISSN 0075-7969) *546*

Langue et Civilisation a Tradition Orale(FR) *51, 546*

Langue et Cultures (SZ ISSN 0085-2678) *546*

Langue Internationale (FR ISSN 0085-2686) *523*

Langues du Cameroun (CM) *546*

Langues et Styles (FR ISSN 0075-7985) *546, 567*

Lansky: Bibliotheksrechtliche Vorschriften (GW) *514, 532*

Lantbrukshoegskolan Institutionen foer Vaextodling. Rapporter och Arhandlingar *see* Sveriges Lantbruksuniversitet. Institutionen foer Vaextodling. Rapporter och Arhandlingar *20*

Lares. Biblioteca (IT ISSN 0075-8019) *402*

Large-Print Scores and Books Catalog *see* Music & Musicians: Large-Print Scores and Books Catalog *133*

Larvae du Golden Gate (US ISSN 0023-8511) *580*

Laser (UK) *785, 852*

Laser Applications (US) *356*

Laser Focus Buyers' Guide (US ISSN 0075-8027) *255, 705*

Laser Marketers' and Buyers' Guide *see* Laser Focus Buyers' Guide *705*

Lasers: A Series of Advances (US ISSN 0075-8035) *705*

Last Month's Newsletter (US) *262, 492*

Lateinamerika: Wirtschaftliche Daten (GW) *187*

Lathrop Report on Newspaper Indexes (US) *3*

Latin America & Caribbean (UK) *187, 712*

Latin America Annual Review & the Caribbean *see* Latin America & Caribbean *187*

Latin America Pulse (US) *766*

Latin America Report (US) *187, 712*

Latin America Review (UK) *92*

Latin America Review of Books *see* Latin America Review *92*

Latin American Anthropology Group. Contributions (US) *51*

Latin American Food Production Conference Summary Report (US) *405*

Latin American Historical Dictionaries Series (US) *470*

Latin American Histories (US) *470*

Latin American International Affairs (US) *470, 722*

Latin American Monographs (US ISSN 0075-8108) *470*

Latin American Petroleum Directory (US ISSN 0075-8116) *680*

Latin American Studies in the Universities of the United Kingdom (UK ISSN 0085-2694) *92, 438*

Latin American Studies in the Universities of the United Kingdom. Staff Research in Progress or Recently Completed in the Humanities and the Social Sciences (UK ISSN 0085-2708) *92, 438*

Latin American Studies Working Papers(US) *470*

Latin American Travel Guide *see* Latin American Travel Guide & Pan American Highway Guide (Mexico-Central-South America) *887*

Latin American Travel Guide & Pan American Highway Guide (Mexico-Central-South America) (US) *887*

Latin Language Mathematicians Group. Actes et Travaux du Congres (RM ISSN 0075-8175) *586*

Latinoamericana (SW) *92, 470*

Latomistica (IT) *137*

Latvija Sodien (US ISSN 0093-8920) *392*

Latvju Maksla (US ISSN 0362-7047) *76*

Laughing Bear (US ISSN 0363-2164) *580*

Lauriston S. Taylor Lecture Series (US) *752*

Lava (II) *580*

Law (NZ) *514*

Law and Accounting Practice Management Manual (AT) *167*

Law and Ethics Series (US) *514*

Law and Political Review (KO) *514, 712*

Law and Psychology Review (US ISSN 0098-5961) *514, 736, 798*

Law & Women Series (US) *514, 900*

Law Bibliography *see* Rechtsbibliographie *521*

Law Books in Print (US ISSN 0075-8221) *514*

Law Enforcement and Criminal Justice Education Directory (US) *282*

Law in Eastern Europe (NE ISSN 0075-823X) *523*

Law in Society (NR ISSN 0458-8592) *514*

Law List *see* Bar List of the United Kingdom *509*

Law Practice for the Senior Lawyer (PH) *910*

Law Reprints. Securities Regulation Series *see* B N A's Law Reprints: Securities Regulation Series *509*

Law Reprints. Tax Series *see* B N A's Law Reprints: Tax Series *509*

Law Reprints. Trade Regulation Series *see* B N A's Law Reprints: Trade Regulation *193*

Law Reprints: Criminal Law Series *see* B N A's Law Reprints: Criminal Law Series *509*

Law Reprints: Labor Series *see* B N A's Law Reprints: Labor Series *509*

Law Reprints, Patent, Trademark and Copyright Series *see* B N A's Law Reprints: Patent, Trademark & Copyright Series *509*

Law Society of Upper Canada. Special Lectures (CN ISSN 0316-5310) *514*

Law Study and Practice in the United States: Pre-Law Handbook *see* Pre-Law Handbook. Official Law School Guide *516*

Lawrence Berkeley Laboratory. Inorganic Materials Research Division. Annual Report *see* Lawrence Berkeley Laboratory. Materials and Molecular Research Division. Annual Report *380*

Lawrence Berkeley Laboratory. Materials and Molecular Research Division. Annual Report (US) *380*

Lawrence Berkeley Laboratory. Research Highlights (US ISSN 0091-9489) *697*

Laws of England Annual Abridgment *see* Halsbury's Laws of England Annual Abridgment *512*

Lawyer-to-Lawyer Consultation Panel (US ISSN 0091-0430) *514*

Lawyers in the United States. Distribution and Income (US) *514*

Lawyer's Remembrance (UK) *514*

Laxton's Building Price Book (UK ISSN 0305-6589) *137*

Lazy Man's Guide to Holidays Afloat (UK ISSN 0075-8272) *827*

Lazy Way to Book Your Car Ferries (UK) *879, 887*

Lea (CK) *92, 567*

Lead Battery Power (AT) *356*

Leader (AT ISSN 0023-9585) *349*

Leader (MY) *505*

Leading Edge (US) *785, 852*

League of Red Cross Societies. Annual Report *see* League of Red Cross Societies. Biennial Report *807*

League of Red Cross Societies. Biennial Report (SZ) *807*

Learning and Society (US ISSN 0191-8850) *319*

Learning Disorders (US ISSN 0075-8337) *346*

Learning Resources Corporation. Selected Reading Services (US ISSN 0077-5908) *736*

Learning Traveler. U.S. College-Sponsored Programs Abroad: Academic Year (US) *342*

Learning Traveler. Vacation Study Abroad (US) *342*

Leather & Footwears/Kawa to Hakimono (JA) *524, 795*

Leather Buyers Guide and Leather Trade Marks (US ISSN 0075-8345) *524*

Leather Guide (UK) *524*

Lebanese Industrial and Commercial Directory/Annuaire des Professions au Liban (LE ISSN 0075-8353) *239*

Lebanon. Direction Centrale de la Statistique. Comptes Economiques (LE ISSN 0075-837X) *160*

Lebanon. Direction Centrale de la Statistique. Recueil de Statistiques Libanaises (LE ISSN 0075-8388) *842*

LeBaron Russell Briggs Prize Honors Essays in English (US ISSN 0075-8396) *567*

Lebensbilder aus Schwaben und Franken (GW) *97*

Lebensdarstellungen Deutscher Naturforscher (GE ISSN 0075-8418) *98, 104*

Leccio - Press Agency (IT) *418*

Lecciones de Historia Juridica (AG) *433, 514*

Lecciones y Ensayos (AG) *514, 523*

Lectura Dantis Romana (IT ISSN 0075-8426) *567*

Lecture Notes in Biomathematics (US ISSN 0341-633X) *104, 586*

Lecture Notes in Chemistry (US) *247*

Lecture Notes in Computer Science (US) *273*

Lecture Notes in Control and Information Sciences (US) *532*

Lecture Notes in Economics and Mathematical Systems (US ISSN 0075-8442) *146, 586*

Lecture Notes in Mathematics (US ISSN 0075-8434) *586*

Lecture Notes in Medical Informatics (US) *597*

Lecture Notes in Operations Research and Mathematical Systems *see* Lecture Notes in Economics and Mathematical Systems *586*

Lecture Notes in Physics (US ISSN 0075-8450) *697*

Lecture Notes in Pure and Applied Mathematics (US ISSN 0075-8469) *586*

Lecture Notes in Statistics (US) *842*

Lecture Notes on Coastal and Estuarine Studies (US) *311*

Lectures Bar Extension *see* W. C. J. Meredith Memorial Lectures *747*

Lectures in Applied Mathematics (US ISSN 0075-8485) *586*

Lectures in Commercial Diplomacy (UK ISSN 0309-1961) *196*

Lectures in Heterocyclic Chemistry (US ISSN 0090-2268) *253*

Lectures on Mathematics in the Life Sciences (US ISSN 0075-8523) *104, 586*

Lectures on the History of Religions. New Series (US ISSN 0075-8531) *766*

Lee County Historical Society. Historical Yearbook (US) *470*

Leeds Medieval Studies (UK ISSN 0140-8089) *456, 567, 859*

Leeds Philosophical and Literary Society. Proceedings. Scientific (UK) *785*

Leeds Studies in English (UK ISSN 0075-8566) *567*

Leeds Studies in English and Kindred Languages *see* Leeds Studies in English *567*

Leeds Texts and Monographs (UK ISSN 0075-8574) *546*

Left Curve (US) *556*

Legal Aid New Brunswick Annual Report/Assistance Judiciaire Nouveau-Brunswick Rapport Annuel (CN ISSN 0381-2049) *514*

Legal Almanac Series (US ISSN 0075-8582) *514*

Legal Connection: Corporations and Law Firms (US ISSN 0270-3424) *146, 515*

Legal Medicine Annual (US ISSN 0075-8590) *613*

Legal Report of Oil and Gas Conservation Activities (US ISSN 0539-2063) *680*

Legal Services Monthly *see* Legal Services Occasional *515*

Legal Services Occasional (US) *485, 515*

Legon Family Research Papers (GH) *51, 814*

Leica Manual (US ISSN 0093-9374) *693*

Leica Photography (US ISSN 0024-063X) *693*

Leicestershire Archaeological and Historical Society. Transactions (UK) *62, 456*

Leicestershire Family History Circle. Newsletter (UK ISSN 0140-9301) *417*

Leicestershire Historian (UK ISSN 0024-0664) *433*

Leiden Botanical Series (NE) *116*

Leidse Geologische Medelingen (NE ISSN 0075-8639) *296*

Leidse Germanistische en Anglistische Reeks (NE ISSN 0458-9971) *567*

Leidse Historische Reeks (NE ISSN 0458-998X) *433*

Leidse Juridische Reeks (NE ISSN 0458-9998) *515*

Leidse Kunsthistorische Reeks (NE ISSN 0460-2048) *76*

Leidse Romanistische Reeks (NE ISSN 0075-8647) *546, 567*

Leidse Voordrachten (NE) *492*

Leidse Wijsgerige Reeks (NE ISSN 0459-0007) *689*

Leipzig. Universitaet. Geophysikalisches Institut. Veroeffentlichungen. Zweite Serie *see* Geophysik und Geologie *304*

Leipziger Messejournal (GE) *5*

Leisure Study Canada/Loisirs au Canada (CN) *187*

Leisureguide - Boston (US) *887*

Leisureguide - Chicago (US) *887*

Leisureguide - Grand Strand (Myrtle Beach, S.C.) (US) *887*

Leisureguide - Houston (US) *887*

Leisureguide - Louisville (US) *887*

Leisureguide - Orlando (US) *887*

Leisureguide - Puerto Rico (US) *887*

Leisureguide - Tampa Bay (US) *887*

Leisureguide - the Florida Gold Coast (US) *887*

Leisurewheels Campground Directory (CN) *830*

Leitende Maenner der Wirtschaft (GW ISSN 0075-871X) *98, 216*

Leitfaden der Schweizer Presse *see* Repertoire de la Presse Suisse *505*

Lejeunia (BE ISSN 0457-4184) *116*

Lekarske Prace (CS ISSN 0075-8736) 597
Leket (IS) 567
Lembaga Keluarga Berentjana Nasional (IO) 728
Leningrad University. Vestnik. Mathematics (US ISSN 0146-9231) 586
Leningradskii Universitet. Uchenye Zapiski. Seriya Geologicheskikh Nauk (UR ISSN 0459-0805) 296
Leo Baeck Institute. Year Book (UK ISSN 0075-8744) 457, 770
Leo M. Franklin Memorial Lectures in Human Relations (US) 814
Leonardo (IT ISSN 0075-8760) 319
Leopoldina (GE) 785
Lepidopterists' Society. Memoirs (US ISSN 0075-8795) 121
Leprosy Mission, London. Annual Report (UK ISSN 0075-8809) 766
Lesotho. Ministry of Education and Culture. Annual Report of the Permanent Secretary (LO) 319
Lesotho. Ministry of Foreign Affairs. Diplomatic and Consular List (LO ISSN 0460-2099) 722
Lesotho. Treasury. Report on the Finances and Accounts (LO ISSN 0075-8817) 230
Lesotho Bank. Annual Report see Lesotho Bank. Report and Accounts 174
Lesotho Bank. Report and Accounts (LO) 174
Lesotho National Development Corporation. Newsletter (LO) 187
Lessico Intellettuale Europeo (IT ISSN 0075-8825) 546
Lessing Yearbook (GW ISSN 0075-8833) 567
Letopis Pamatnika Slovenskej Literatury see Literarno-Muzejny Letopis 567
Let's Go Spinning see Spinning Around the World 476
Let's Go: the Budget Guide to Italy (US ISSN 0192-2920) 887
Let's Go: the Student Guide to Europe.(US ISSN 0075-8868) 887
Let's Go: the Student Guide to the United States and Canada (US ISSN 0090-788X) 887
Let's Halt Awhile in Great Britain (UK ISSN 0075-8876) 483
Letteratura Italiana. Studi e Testi (IT) 567
Lettere Italiane. Biblioteca (IT ISSN 0075-8892) 567
Letterheads (US) 76
La Lettre (FR ISSN 0075-8906) 910
Levant (UK ISSN 0075-8914) 62
Lexport (II) 524
Liaison (CN ISSN 0318-1340) 137
Liaisons Financieres en France see Collection Radiographique du Capital - les Liaisons Financieres 171
Liberal Focus (UK) 712
Liberal Party Organisation. Study Paper see Liberal Publication Department. Study Paper 712
Liberal Publication Department. Study Paper (UK) 712
Liberia. Bureau of Economic Research and Statistics. Annual Report to the President on the Operation and Activities see Liberia. Office of National Planning. Annual Report to the President on the Operation and Activities 743
Liberia. Department of Planning and Economic Affairs. Annual Report see Liberia. Ministry of Planning and Economic Affairs. Annual Report to the Session of the Legislature of the Republic of Liberia 224
Liberia. General Auditing Office. Annual Report on the Operation of the General Auditing Office (LB) 230
Liberia. General Services Agency. Annual Report (LB) 807
Liberia. Institute of Public Administration. Annual Report (LB) 743
Liberia. Ministry of Action for Development and Progress Annual Report (LB) 743

Liberia. Ministry of Agriculture. National Rice Production Estimates see Liberia. Ministry of Agriculture. Production Estimates of Major Crops 25
Liberia. Ministry of Agriculture. Production Estimates of Major Crops(LB) 25
Liberia. Ministry of Agriculture. Statistical Handbook (LB) 29
Liberia. Ministry of Commerce, Industry and Transportation. Annual Report (LB) 224, 863
Liberia. Ministry of Finance. Annual Report (LB ISSN 0304-727X) 230
Liberia. Ministry of Foreign Affairs. Annual Report (LB) 722
Liberia. Ministry of Health and Social Welfare. Annual Report (LB) 752
Liberia. Ministry of Information, Cultural Affairs & Tourism. Annual Report to the Session of the Legislature (LB) 887
Liberia. Ministry of Justice. Annual Report to the Legislature (LB) 515
Liberia. Ministry of Labour, Youth & Sports. Annual Report (LB) 257, 807
Liberia. Ministry of Lands and Mines. Annual Report (LB ISSN 0304-7296) 376, 644
Liberia. Ministry of Local Government, Rural Development & Urban Reconstruction. Annual Report (LB ISSN 0304-730X) 749
Liberia. Ministry of National Defense. Annual Report (LB) 639
Liberia. Ministry of Planning and Economic Affairs. Activity Report (LB) 224
Liberia. Ministry of Planning and Economic Affairs. Annual Report to the Session of the Legislature of the Republic of Liberia (LB ISSN 0459-2182) 224
Liberia. Ministry of Public Works. Annual Report (LB ISSN 0304-7326) 743
Liberia. Office of National Planning. Annual Report to the President on the Operation and Activities (LB) 743
Liberia Baptist Missionary and Educational Convention. Yearbook (LB) 772
Liberia Ministry of Posts and Telecommunications. Annual Report (LB) 264
Liberian Studies Monograph Series (US) 798
Liberian Studies Research Working Papers (US) 798
Liberian Trade Directory (LB) 239
Libra (SA ISSN 0024-2101) 910
Librarians, Censorship and Intellectual Freedom (US ISSN 0075-8973) 539
Librarians' Guide to Back Issues of International Periodicals (US) 92, 506
Libraries in the United Kingdom & the Republic of Ireland (UK) 532
Libraries, Museums and Art Galleries Year Book (UK ISSN 0075-899X) 532, 653
Libraries of Maine; Directory and Statistics (US ISSN 0092-833X) 532
Library and Information Science (JA) 532
Library Association. Proceedings, Papers and Summaries of Discussions at the ... Conference (UK) 532
Library Association. Reference, Special and Information Section. North Western Group. Occasional Papers (UK ISSN 0075-9058) 910
Library Association. Students Handbook (UK) 910
Library Association (Valletta). Ghaqda Bibljotekarji/Library Association Yearbook (MM) 532
Library Association (Valletta). Ghaqda Bibljotekarji/Library Association Newsletter (MM) 532
Library Association. Year Book (UK ISSN 0075-9066) 532
Library Association: a Librarian's Handbook (UK) 532

Library Association of Alberta. Occasional Papers (CN ISSN 0075-904X) 532
Library Association of Australia. Handbook (AT) 532
Library Association of Barbados. Bulletin (BB) 532
Library Association of Barbados. Occasional Newsletter (BB) 532
Library Association of China. Bulletin (CH) 532
Library Association of the City University of New York Occasional Papers see L A C U N Y Occasional Papers 532
Library Association of Trinidad and Tobago. Bulletin (TR ISSN 0521-9590) 532
Library Bibliographies and Indexes (US) 532
Library Buildings see New Library Buildings 534
Library Development in Alaska: Long Range Program (US ISSN 0094-8829) 532
Library, Documentation and Archives Serials (NE) 539
Library Industry (MY) 532
Library Innovator (CN) 532, 759
Library Journal Book Review (US ISSN 0075-9082) 532
Library Lectures see Louisiana State University. Library. Library Lectures 533
Library Lectures(Knoxville) see University of Tennessee. Library Lectures 538
Library Lit (US ISSN 0085-2767) 3, 539
Library Literature in India Series (II) 532
Library Log (US) 532
Library Networks (US) 532
Library Notes (US ISSN 0024-2438) 532
Library of Analytical Psychology (UK) 736
Library of Anthropology (US) 51
Library of Congress (US ISSN 0162-6426) 533
Library of Congress Classification Schedules: a Cumulation of Additions and Changes (US) 539
Library of Congress Publications in Print see U. S. Library of Congress. Library of Congress Publications in Print 539
Library of Exact Philosophy (US ISSN 0075-9104) 785
Library of Great Painters (US) 76
Library of Jewish Law and Ethics (US) 770
Library of Law and Contemporary Problems (US ISSN 0075-9120) 515, 798
Library of Peasant Studies (UK) 392
Library of Philosophy and Religion (UK) 689, 766
Library of Protestant Thought (US) 772
Library of Scandinavian Literature (US ISSN 0075-9155) 567
Library Resources for the Blind and Physically Handicapped (US ISSN 0364-1236) 133, 533
Library Resources in Scotland (UK) 533
Library Resources Notes (US ISSN 0095-4098) 533
Library School Review (US ISSN 0453-2406) 533
Library Services and Construction Act Annual Program, Hawaii State Library System see L.S.C.A. Annual Program, Hawaii State Library System 532
Library Studies see Kniznicny Zbornik 532
Library Telecommunications Directory: Canada - United States (US) 265, 533
Library Trustee (US) 533
Libro del Ano (AG) 361
Libro di Casa (IT) 502
Librorama Internacional (SP) 92
Libros al Dia (VE) 92
Libros de Enfermeria (SP) 614
Libros Espanoles I S B N (SP ISSN 0377-0974) 92

Libros y Material de Ensenanza (SP ISSN 0075-9201) 319
Libya. Census and Statistical Office. General Population Census (LY ISSN 0075-9236) 728
Libya. Census and Statistical Office. Industrial Census (LY ISSN 0075-9244) 160
Libya. Census and Statistical Office. Report of the Annual Survey of Large Manufacturing Establishments (LY ISSN 0075-9252) 160
Libya. Census and Statistical Office. Report of the Annual Survey of Petroleum Mining Industry (LY ISSN 0075-9260) 682
Libya. Census and Statistical Office. Report of the Survey of Licensed Construction Units (LY ISSN 0075-9279) 140
Libya. Census and Statistical Office. Statistical Abstract (LY ISSN 0075-9287) 842
Libya Past and Present Series (UK) 887
Libyan Journal of Sciences (LY) 785
Libyan Travel Series see Libya Past and Present Series 887
Libyca (FR ISSN 0459-3030) 51, 62
Lichtwark-Stiftung. Veroeffentlichung (GW) 567
Lick Observatory. Publications (US ISSN 0075-9325) 83
Licni Dohoci (YU ISSN 0300-2535) 160
Liechtenstein. Botanisch-Zoologische Gesellschaft Sargans-Werdenberg. Bericht (LH) 104
Liechtenstein. Politische Schriften (LH) 712
Liechtenstein. Press and Information Office. Press Folder (LH) 187
Liechtenstein Economy (LH) 187
Lietuviu Tautos Praeitis/Lithuanian Historical Review (US ISSN 0091-4347) 457
Lieux et les Dieux (FR ISSN 0075-9376) 457
Life Agency Management Program Brochure (US ISSN 0072-0607) 500
Life Insurance Agency Management Association. Proceedings of the Annual Meeting see Life Insurance Marketing and Research Association. Proceedings of the Annual Meeting 500
Life Insurance Fact Book (US ISSN 0075-9406) 500
Life Insurance Institute of Canada. Annual Report (CN) 500
Life Insurance Marketing and Research Association. Proceedings of the Annual Meeting (US) 500
Life Insurers Conference. Annual Proceedings (US ISSN 0075-9414) 500
Life Lines (US ISSN 0163-0253) 694
Life Office Management Association. Annual Conference. Highlights see Life Office Management Association. Annual Conference. Proceedings of Concurrent Sessions 500
Life Office Management Association. Annual Conference. Proceedings of Concurrent Sessions (US) 500
Life Rates & Data (US) 500
Life Sciences (US ISSN 0459-3774) 104
Life Underwriters Association of Canada Monitor see L U A C Monitor 499
Light (US ISSN 0147-121X) 580
Light Metal Statistics in Japan/ Keikinzoku Kogyo Tokei Nenpo (JA ISSN 0451-6001) 631
Lightworks (US ISSN 0161-4223) 76, 693
Ligne Creatrice (FR) 557
Ligue Antituberculeuse de Quebec. Rapport (CN ISSN 0075-9465) 623
Ligue Suisse pour la Litterature de la Jeunesse. Rapport Annuel see Schweizerischer Bund fuer Jugendliteratur. Jahresbericht 258
Liguria Territorio e Civilta (IT) 423
Liikearkistoyhdistys. Julkaisuja (FI) 146
Liikenneturva. Reports (FI) 752

Liikuntakasvatus (FI ISSN 0355-7073) 349, 694
Lijstenboek (BE) 759
LiLi. Beihefte (Zeitschrift fuer Literaturwissenschaft und Linguistik) (GW) 546, 567
Lilies and Other Liliaceae (UK ISSN 0075-949X) 415
Lilloa (AG ISSN 0075-9481) 116
Lillooet District Historical Society. Bulletin (CN ISSN 0383-9133) 470
Lily Year Book see Lilies and Other Liliaceae 415
Limba si Literatura (RM ISSN 0583-8045) 546
Limi (SA ISSN 0024-3558) 546, 567
Limnologica (GE ISSN 0075-9511) 308
Lincoln College. Agricultural Economics Research Unit. Discussion Paper (NZ ISSN 0110-7720) 29
Lincoln College. Agricultural Economics Research Unit. Research Report (NZ ISSN 0069-3790) 29
Lincoln College. Department of Horticulture. Bulletin (NZ ISSN 0069-3820) 415
Lincoln College. Farmers' Conference. Proceedings (NZ ISSN 0069-3839) 17
Lincolnshire History and Archaeology (UK ISSN 0459-4487) 62, 457
Lindes - Cuadernos de Poesia (SP) 580
Lindley Lecture (US ISSN 0075-9554) 689
Linens, Domestics & Bath Products Annual Directory (US) 503
Lingua e Literatura (BL ISSN 0047-4711) 546, 567
Lingua Posnaniensis (PL ISSN 0079-4740) 546
Linguarum Minorum Documenta Historiographica (GW ISSN 0341-3225) 433, 546
Lingue e Iscrizioni dell'Italia Antica (IT) 546
Linguistic & Literary Studies in Eastern Europe (NE ISSN 0165-7712) 546, 567
Linguistic Association of Canada and the United States Forum see L A C U S Forum 546
Linguistic Bibliography (NE) 555
Linguistic Circle of Manitoba and North Dakota. Proceedings (CN ISSN 0075-9597) 547
Linguistic Communications (AT) 911
Linguistic Society of India. Bulletin (II ISSN 0075-9627) 547
Linguistica (YU ISSN 0024-3922) 547
Linguistica Silesiana (PL) 547
Linguistik Aktuell (NE ISSN 0166-0829) 547
Linguistische Reihe (GW ISSN 0075-9686) 547
Lingvisticae Investigaciones: Supplementa (NE) 547
Lingvisticae Investigationes (NE ISSN 0378-4169) 547
Lingvisticheskie Issledovaniya (UR ISSN 0301-6900) 547
Lingvisticke Citanky/Readings in Linguistics (CS) 547
Lingvologia Revuo (AT ISSN 0024-3965) 547
Linhas de Financiamento do B N H (Banco Nacional da Habitacao) (BL) 174
Link-Up (SA ISSN 0024-4015) 338
Linnaean Society of New York. Proceedings (US ISSN 0075-9694) 125
Linnaean Society of New York. Transactions (US ISSN 0075-9708) 125
Linn's World Stamp Almanac (US) 477
Linschoten-Vereeniging. Werken (NE) 457
Linzer Hochschulschriften see Linzer Universitaetsschriften 338
Linzer Jahrbuch fuer Kunstgeschichte see Kunstjahrbuch der Stadt Linz 76
Linzer Universitaetsschriften (US) 338
Lipunan Journal (PH ISSN 0459-4835) 444
Liquified Petroleum Gas Sales (US) 363, 680

Lisbon. Escola Nacional de Saude Publica de Medicina Tropical. Anais see Instituto de Higiene e Medicina Tropical. Anais 752
List Bio-Med; Biomedical Serials in Scandinavian Libraries (SW ISSN 0075-9813) 602
List of Accredited Schools of Architecture see Accredited Programs in Architecture 68
List of American Firms in France (FR) 179
List of Cables Forming the World Submarine Network (UN ISSN 0074-9001) 269
List of Current Serial Publications Being Received at the University of Puerto Rico Medical Sciences Campus Library (PR) 602
List of Destination Indicators and Telex Identification Codes (UN ISSN 0074-901X) 269
List of Grants and Awards Available to American Writers see Grants and Awards Available to American Writers 564
List of International Telephone Routes (UN ISSN 0074-9028) 269
List of Journals Indexed in Index Medicus (US ISSN 0093-3821) 602
List of Legal Investments for Savings Banks in Connecticut (US ISSN 0098-0005) 204
List of Member Institutions - Federal Saving and Loan Insurance Corporation see Federal Savings and Loan Insurance Corporation. List of Member Institutions 498
List of Scientific and Technical Literature Relating to Thailand (TH ISSN 0125-4537) 795
List of Serials and Monographs Indexed for Online Users (US ISSN 0196-755X) 602
List of Shipowners (UK ISSN 0260-7387) 879
List of Theses for the Doctor's and Master's Degree in Korea/Hankuk Baksa Mit Seuksa Hak Wee Lonmun Chong Mokrok (KO) 327
List of United States Air Carriers (US) 868
Liste d'Identification des Entomophages (FR) 911
Liste des Societes Savantes et Litteraires (FR ISSN 0457-9976) 338
Liste Officielle des Navires de Mer Belges et de la Flotte de la Force Navale (BE) 879
Listening Library of LP Recordings (US ISSN 0075-9864) 660
Lists of P A N S Doc Bibliographies see Lists of P A S T I C Bibliographies 854
Lists of P A S T I C Bibliographies (PK) 854
Liszt Information-Communication (AU) 660
Liszt Society. Journal (UK ISSN 0141-0792) 660
Liszt Society, London. Newsletter see Liszt Society. Journal 660
Liteinoe Proizvodstvo, Metallovedenie i Obrabotka Metallov Davleniem (UR ISSN 0302-9069) 628
Literacy in Development (IR) 329
Literarische Hefte (GW) 567
Literarischer Verein in Stuttgart. Bibliothek (GW ISSN 0340-7888) 567
Literarno-Muzejny Letopis (CS) 567, 660
Literarny Archiv (CS ISSN 0075-9872) 567
Literarria (CS) 567
Literary and Library Prizes (US ISSN 0075-9880) 539, 578
Literary Magazine of Fantasy and Terror see Windhaven 576
Literary Market Place (US ISSN 0075-9899) 759
Literary Monographs (US ISSN 0075-9902) 567
Literary Onomastics Studies (US ISSN 0160-8703) 567
Literary Prizes in Pakistan (PK ISSN 0075-9929) 567

Literatur fuer Leser (GW ISSN 0343-1657) 567
Literatur und Wirklichkeit (GW ISSN 0075-9937) 567
Literatura Drevnei Rusi (UR) 567
Literatura o Sakhalinskoi Oblasti (UR) 92
Literatura o Vologodskoi Oblasti, Vologada, Biblioteka im Babushkina (UR) 567
Literatura Ob Arkhangel'skoi Oblasti (UR) 567
Literatura Piekna. Adnotowany Rocznik Bibliograficzny (PL ISSN 0075-9945) 92
Literaturberichte ueber Wasser, Abwasser, Luft und Feste Abfallstoffe (GW ISSN 0340-4900) 387
Literaturdokumentation zur Arbeitsmarkt- und Berufsforschung (GW) 160
Literature About the Book and Librarianship see Fachliteratur zum Buch- und Bibliothekswesen 530
Literature and Ideology see New Literature and Ideology 557
Literaturwissenschaftliches Jahrbuch. Neue Folge (GW ISSN 0075-997X) 567
Litfass (GW) 567
Lithuanian Historical Review see Lietuviu Tautos Praeitis 457
Litologiya i Paleogeografiya (UR) 289
Litomericko (CS ISSN 0075-9988) 457
Litteraria (PL ISSN 0084-3008) 567
Litterature. Science. Ideologie. see L.S.I 567
Litteratures (FR ISSN 0563-9751) 567
Litteratures Anciennes (FR ISSN 0069-5459) 567
Little Black Book (US) 239, 244
Little Red Book, Classified to All Public Transport Fleet Owners and Operators and Vehicle Manufacturers (UK ISSN 0076-0013) 863
Little Word Machine (UK) 580
Lituanistika V. S.S.S.R. Istoriya (UR) 457
Liturgiewissenschaftliche Quellen und Forschungen (GW ISSN 0076-0048) 766
Live Wire (US) 268
Livestock and Poultry in Latin America. Annual Conference (US ISSN 0085-2805) 45
Living Bird (US ISSN 0459-6137) 125
Living Conditions Yearbook see Sweden. Statistiska Centralbyraan. Levnadsfoerhaallanden Aarsbok 848
Living in Malawi (MW) 187, 887
Livraria Figueirinhas Catalogo (PO) 759
Livre d'Art Information (FR) 80
Livre de Langue Francaise-Repertoire des Editeurs see Repertoire International des Editeurs et Diffuseurs de Langue Francaise 759
Livre et Societes (FR ISSN 0076-0129) 911
Livres Belges see Livres Belges de Langue Francaise 92
Livres Belges de Langue Francaise (BE) 92
Livres d'Aujourd'hui see Bulletin Bibliographique Thematique 89
Livres Disponibles (FR) 92
Livres et Auteurs Canadiens see Livres et Auteurs Quebecois 567
Livres et Auteurs Quebecois (CN ISSN 0076-0153) 567
Llafur (UK ISSN 0306-0837) 208
Llen Cymru (UK ISSN 0076-0188) 567
Llewellyn's Astrological Calendar (US ISSN 0145-8868) 80
Llewellyn's Moon Sign Book (US) 80, 415
Lloyd's Calendar & Nautical Book see Lloyd's Nautical Yearbook & Calendar 879
Lloyd'S Maritime Atlas, Including a Comprehensive List of Ports and Shipping Places of the World (UK ISSN 0076-020X) 879
Lloyd's Nautical Yearbook & Calendar (UK) 879

Lloyd's Register of American Yachts see North American Yacht Register 827
Lloyd'S Register of Shipping. Statistical Tables (UK ISSN 0076-0234) 879
Lloyd's Register of Ships (UK) 879
Local and Regional Authorities in Europe see Council of Europe. Steering Committee on Regional and Municipal Matters. Study Series: Local and Regional Authorities in Europe 749
Local Government Companion (UK) 749
Local Government Employment in Selected Metropolitan Areas and Large Counties see Current Governments Reports: Local Government Employment in Selected Metropolitan Areas and Large Counties 748
Local Government Finances in Maryland (US ISSN 0085-2821) 230
Local Government in Mauritius see Association of Urban Authorities. Annual Bulletin 748
Local Government Law Bulletin (US ISSN 0362-5729) 515, 749
Local Government Reports of Australia (AT ISSN 0076-0242) 743
Local Government Review (JA ISSN 0449-0193) 749
Local Government Trends (UK ISSN 0307-0441) 743
Local Health Services Annual Summary (Portland) see Oregon. Office of Community Health Services. Local Health Services Annual Summary 753
Locations of Industries in Gujarat State (II ISSN 0076-0269) 224
Locations Vacances (FR ISSN 0024-5674) 761
Locke Newsletter (UK ISSN 0307-2606) 689
Lockert Library of Poetry in Translation (US) 580
Lockheed Orion Service Digest (US ISSN 0024-5704) 9
Locksmith Ledger/Security Guide & Directory (US) 141
Lockwood's Directory of the Paper and Allied Trades (US ISSN 0076-0277) 675
Locomotive Maintenance Officers Association. Annual Proceedings (US ISSN 0076-0285) 873
Locomotive Maintenance Officers Association. Preconvention Report (US ISSN 0076-0293) 873
Locus Select (US) 76, 653
Lodging Industry see U. S. Lodging Industry 483
Lodzkie Studia Etnograficzne (PL ISSN 0076-0382) 51, 402
Lodzkie Towarzystwo Naukowe. Komisji Jezykowej. Rozprawy (PL ISSN 0076-0390) 547
Lodzkie Towarzystwo Naukowe. Wydzial I. Prace (PL ISSN 0076-0404) 567
Lodzkie Towarzystwo Naukowe. Wydzial III. Nauk Matematyczno-Przyrodniczych. Prace (PL ISSN 0076-0412) 586
Lodzkie Towarzystwo Naukowe. Wydzial IV. Nauk Lekarskich. Prace (PL ISSN 0076-0420) 597
Lodzkie Towarzystwo Naukowe. Wydzial V. Nauk Technicznych. Prace (PL ISSN 0076-0439) 852
Loeb Classical Library (US) 567
Loewdin Symposia; Proceedings of the International Symposium on Atomic, Molecular, and Solid-State Theory and Quantum Biology (US ISSN 0076-1370) 247
Log House (CN ISSN 0315-8756) 69, 137
Log of the Star Class (US ISSN 0076-0455) 827
Logos (PH ISSN 0076-0471) 766
Loi de l'Impot sur le Revenu, Canadienne (CN ISSN 0076-048X) 230
Loisires au Canada see Leisure Study Canada 887
Loka (US ISSN 0364-068X) 567, 689

Loma Linda University Dentist see S D A Dentist 610
London. University. University College. Bartlett Society. Transactions see Bartlett Society. Transactions 384
London and Middlesex Archaeological Society. Transactions (UK ISSN 0076-0501) 62
London Bibliography of the Social Sciences (UK ISSN 0076-051X) 803
London Bird Report (UK ISSN 0141-4348) 125
London Boroughs Association Handbook see L B A Handbook 749
London Chamber of Commerce & Industry. Annual Report & Annual Directory see London Chamber of Commerce & Industry. Directory 179
London Chamber of Commerce & Industry. Directory (UK) 179
London Community Services Directory (CN ISSN 0700-4982) 807
London Directory see London Directory of Industry and Commerce 240
London Directory of Industry & Commerce (UK) 240
London Divinity Series. New Testament (UK ISSN 0076-0536) 766
London Facts and Figures (UK ISSN 0308-0900) 842
London German Studies (UK) 567
London History Studies (UK ISSN 0076-0544) 433
London Hospital League of Nurses Review (UK) 614
London Mathematical Society. Lecture Note Series (UK ISSN 0076-0552) 586
London Mathematical Society. Monographs (US ISSN 0076-0560) 586
London Naturalist (UK ISSN 0076-0579) 104
London, Ont. University of Western Ontario Series in Philosophy of Science see University of Western Ontario Series in Philosophy of Science 692
London Papers in Regional Science (LK ISSN 0076-0633) 485
London Police Court Mission. Annual Report see Rainer Foundation. Annual Report 283
London Record Society. Occasional Publications (UK ISSN 0085-283X) 457
London Record Society. Publications (UK ISSN 0085-2848) 457
London Red Guide (UK ISSN 0076-0498) 423, 887
London School of Business. Centre for Economic Forecasting. Economic Outlook (UK) 146
London School of Economics and Political Science. Department of Geography. Geographical Papers (UK ISSN 0076-0641) 423
London School of Economics and Political Science Research Monographs see L S E Research Monographs 146
London School of Economics Monographs on Social Anthropology (UK ISSN 0077-1074) 51
London School of Economics Papers in Soviet and East European Law, Economics and Politics (UK ISSN 0078-9224) 798
London Shipping Contacts (UK) 240, 879
London Society. Journal (UK ISSN 0024-6158) 485
London Stage Information Bank. Newsletter (US) 859
London Studies on South Asia (UK ISSN 0142-601X) 670
London: Your Sightseeing Guide (UK) 887
Long Island Water Resources Bulletin (US) 308
Longitude (SW ISSN 0024-6328) 433, 879
Longwood Program Seminars (US) 116, 415

Look Quick (US) 580
Looking for Employment in Foreign Countries Reference Handbook (US) 667
Looking into Leadership Series (US ISSN 0076-0889) 220
Lorand Eotvos Hungarian Geophysical Institute. Annual Report see Magyar Allami Eotvos Lorand Geofizikai Intezet. Evi Jelentes 305
Lorentzia (AG ISSN 0076-0897) 289
Lormatic (CS) 273
Los Alamos Symposium on Mathematics in the Natural Sciences. Proceedings (US) 586
Los Angeles Council of Engineers & Scientists. Proceedings Series (US) 368, 785
Los Angeles County Museum of Art. Bulletin (US ISSN 0024-6557) 76, 653
Los Angeles County Museum Quarterly see Los Angeles County Museum of Art. Bulletin 76
Los Angeles Foundation of Otology. Progress Report see Ear Research Institute. Progress Report 617
Los Angeles Geographical Society. Publication (US ISSN 0076-096X) 423
Lost and Found Times (US) 557
Lost Play Series (US ISSN 0076-1001) 567
Loto-Quebec. Rapport Annuel (CN) 230
Lotus; a Review of Contemporary Architecture (IT ISSN 0076-101X) 69
Loughborough Occasional Papers in Economics (UK) 146
Louisburg College Journal of Arts and Sciences (US) 76, 785
Louisiana. Department of Agriculture. Analysis of Official Pesticide Samples; Annual Report (US ISSN 0099-1929) 37
Louisiana. Division of Mental Health. Annual Performance Report and Continuation of the State Plan for Drug Abuse Prevention (US ISSN 0362-7098) 287
Louisiana. Geological Survey. Water Resources Bulletin (US ISSN 0459-8474) 296
Louisiana. Health and Human Resources Administration Comprehensive Annual Services Program Plan for Social Services Under Title 20 (US ISSN 0362-8868) 807
Louisiana. Polytechnic Institute, Ruston. School of Agriculture and Forestry. Research Bulletin see Louisiana Tech University. Division of Life Science Research. Research Bulletin 104
Louisiana. State Board of Nurse Examiners. Report (US ISSN 0095-5884) 614
Louisiana Academy of Sciences. Proceedings (US) 785
Louisiana Fairs and Festivals (US ISSN 0093-0687) 17
Louisiana Folklore Miscellany (US ISSN 0459-8962) 402
Louisiana Philosophy of Education Journal (US) 319
Louisiana State Industrial Directory (US ISSN 0190-129X) 240
Louisiana State of the State (US) 798
Louisiana State University. Animal Science Department. Livestock Producers' Day Report (US ISSN 0076-1052) 45
Louisiana State University. Division of Engineering Research. Engineering Research Bulletin (US ISSN 0076-1060) 368
Louisiana State University. Law School. Institute on Mineral Law. Proceedings (US ISSN 0076-1087) 515, 644
Louisiana State University. Library. Library Lectures (US ISSN 0085-2759) 533
Louisiana State University. Library. Report of the Director (US) 533
Louisiana State University. Museum of Geoscience. Melanges (US) 289

Louisiana State University. School of Forestry and Wildlife Management. Annual Forestry Symposium. Proceedings (US ISSN 0076-1095) 409
Louisiana State University. School of Geoscience. Miscellaneous Publications (US) 51, 289
Louisiana Tech University. Division of Life Sciences Research. Research Bulletin. (US ISSN 0076-1044) 104
Louisiana Tech University. Research Monograph Series (US) 146
Louisiana Water Resources Research Institute. Annual Report (US) 308, 897
Lovejoy's Career and Vocational School Guide (US ISSN 0076-1346) 331
Lovejoy's College Guide (US ISSN 0076-132X) 331
Lovejoy's Prep School Guide (US ISSN 0459-925X) 331
Lovoe Geomagnetic Observatory Yearbook (SW ISSN 0076-1354) 296
Lowdin Symposia see International Symposium on Atomic, Molecular and Solid-State Theory, Collision Phenomena and Computational Methods. Proceedings 246
Lower Palaeozic Rocks of the New World (US ISSN 0076-1389) 673
Loyola University. Center for Urban Policy. Studies (US ISSN 0076-1397) 743
Lozania (CK ISSN 0085-2899) 129
Lubelskie Towarzystwo Naukowe. Wydzial Humanistyczny. Prace. Monografie (PL) 492
Lubrication and Wear Convention. Proceedings see Tribology Convention. Proceedings 383
Luckiamute (US) 580
Lucrari de Muzicologie (RM) 660
Lud (PL ISSN 0076-1435) 51, 815
Ludas Matyi Evkonyve (HU) 361
Ludwig Boltzmann-Institut fuer Umweltwissenschaften und Naturschutz. Mitteilungen (AU) 276, 387
Luftverunreinigung (GW ISSN 0460-2374) 387
Luksave (PP ISSN 0085-2902) 798
Lumen/Avenue A (US) 557
Lunar Epidecis see Epidecides Lunaires 82
Lund Studies in English (SW ISSN 0076-1451) 547
Lund Studies in Geography. Series A. Physical Geography (SW ISSN 0076-146X) 423
Lund Studies in Geography. Series B. Human Geography (SW ISSN 0076-1478) 104, 423
Lund Studies in Geography. Series C. General and Mathematical Geography (SW ISSN 0076-1486) 423
Lund Studies in International History (SW ISSN 0076-1494) 433
Lundastudier i Nordisk Spraakvetenskap. Serie D: Meddelanden (SW) 547
Lusaka. Medical Officer of Health. Annual Report (ZA) 752
Lusaka City Library. Annual Report (ZA) 533
Lusitania Sacra (PO ISSN 0076-1508) 766
Lustracje Dobr Krolewskich XVI-XVIII Wieku (PL ISSN 0076-1516) 457
Lustrum (GW ISSN 0024-7421) 259
Lute Society Journal (UK ISSN 0460-007X) 660
Lute Society of America. Journal (US ISSN 0076-1524) 660
Lutheran Almanac see Lutheran Church of Australia. Yearbook 772
Lutheran Annual (US) 772
Lutheran Church in America. Western Canada Synod. Minutes of the Annual Convention (CN ISSN 0460-024X) 772
Lutheran Church of Australia. Yearbook (AT) 772
Lutheran Churches in Canada. Directory (CN ISSN 0316-800X) 772

Lutheran Education Association Yearbook see L E A Yearbook 772
Lutheran World Federation. Proceedings of the Assembly (US ISSN 0076-1540) 772
Lutra (NE ISSN 0024-7634) 129
Luttes Sociales (FR) 712
Luxembourg. Administration de l'Emploi. Rapport Annuel (LU) 208
Luxembourg. Inspection Generale de la Securite Sociale. Rapport General sur la Securite Sociale au Grand-Duche de Luxembourg (LU) 500
Luxembourg. Ministere des Finances. Budget de l'Etat (LU ISSN 0076-1559) 230
Luxembourg. Ministere des Finances. Projet de Loi Concernant le Budget des Recettes et des Depenses de l'Etat (LU) 230
Luxembourg. Office de la Statistique Generale. Annuaire Statistique see Luxembourg. Service Central de la Statistique et des Etudes Economiques. Annuaire Statistique 842
Luxembourg. Office National du Travail. Rapport Annuel see Luxembourg. Administration de l'Emploi. Rapport Annuel 208
Luxembourg. Service Central de la Statistique et des Etudes Economiques. Annuaire Statistique (LU ISSN 0076-1575) 842
Luxembourg. Service Central de la Statistique et des Etudes Economiques. Annuaire Statistique Retrospectif (LU) 842
Luxembourg. Service Central de la Statistique et des Etudes Economiques. Bulletin du STATEC (LU ISSN 0076-1583) 160
Luxembourg. Service Central de la Statistique et des Etudes Economiques. Collection D et M: Definitions et Methodes (LU ISSN 0076-1591) 842
Luxembourg. Service Central de la Statistique et des Etudes Economiques. Cahiers Economiques. Serie A: Economie Luxembourgeoise (LU ISSN 0070-881X) 160
Luxembourg. Service Central de la Statistique et des Etudes Economiques. Cahiers Economiques. Serie B: Comptes Nationaux (LU) 160
Luxembourg. Service Central de la Statistique et des Etudes Economiques. Cahiers Economiques. Serie C: Apercus sur l'Industrie (LU) 160
Luxembourg. Service Central de la Statistique et des Etudes Economiques. Cahiers Economiques. Serie D: Etudes Diverses (LU) 160
Luxembourg. Service Central de la Statistique et des Etudes Economiques. Collection RP: Recensements de la Population (LU ISSN 0076-1613) 732
Luz (VE) 17, 174
Lychnos-Bibliotek. Studies och Kaellskrifter Udgivna av Laerdomshistoriska Samfundet. Studies and Sources Published by the Swedish History of Science Society (SW ISSN 0076-163X) 785
Lychnos-Laerdomshistoriska Samfundets Aarsbok. Annual of the Swedish History of Science Society (SW ISSN 0076-1648) 785
Lyle Official Antiques Review (US) 476
Lyles Official Arms & Armour Review (US) 417
Lyles Official Arts Review (US) 76
Lynx (CS ISSN 0024-7774) 129
Lyrical Iowa (US ISSN 0076-1699) 580
M A C E Newsletter (Manitoba Association of Confluent Educators) (CN) 319
M.A.N. Forschen, Planen, Bauen (Maschinenfabrik Augsburg-Nuernberg AG) (GW) 368
M.A.N. Research, Engineering, Manufacturing see M.A.N. Forschen, Planen, Bauen 368

M A P A Annual Report (Omaha-Council Bluffs Metropolitan Area Planning Agency) (US) *743*
M A P A Annual Transportation Report (Omaha-Council Bluffs Metropolitan Area Planning Agency) (US) *863*
M A R D I Research Bulletin (Malaysian Agricultural Research and Development Institute) (MY) *17*
M B I's Indian Industries Annual (II ISSN 0541-5357) *224*
M B L Lectures in Biology (Marine Biological Laboratory) (US) *104*
M. C. B. News (Metric Conversion Board) (AT) *637*
M. C. B. Newsletter *see* M. C. B. News *637*
M C D S Occasional Paper Series (Malaysian Centre for Development Studies) (MY) *798*
M D Anderson Clinical Conferences on Cancer (US ISSN 0160-2454) *605*
M D Anderson Symposia in Fundamental Cancer Research (US) *605*
M D Anderson Symposia on the Diagnosis and Management of Cancer (US) *605*
M D C Business Journal (Management Development Centre) (JM) *146*
M E I Marketing Economics Guide (Marketing Economics Institute, Ltd.) (US ISSN 0092-4857) *218*
M E O Bulletin (Middle East Observer) (UA) *187*
M E R C Directory (Media Equipment Resource Center) (US) *650*
M F A Bulletin (Boston Museum of Fine Arts) (US) *653*
M G International (US) *871*
M G S News (Manitoba Genealogical Society) (CN) *417*
M G World *see* M G International *871*
M.H.S. Miscellany (Massachusetts Historical Society) (US ISSN 0024-8185) *470*
M.I.I. Series (Muslim Intellectuals' International) (PK ISSN 0541-5462) *769*
M I L U S *see* University of Stockholm. Institute of Linguistics. Monographs *554*
M I M C Microforms Annual (Microforms International Marketing Corporation) (US ISSN 0362-4552) *92, 160*
M I M P *see* Magazine Industry Market Place *759*
M I M S Desk Reference (SA ISSN 0076-8847) *685*
M I M S Reference Manual *see* M I M S Desk Reference *685*
M I V: Museerne i Viborg Amt (DK) *457*
M L A Directory of Periodicals (Modern Language Association of America) (US) *403, 555, 578*
M L A International Bibliography of Books and Articles on the Modern Languages and Literatures (Modern Language Association of America) (US ISSN 0024-8215) *3, 92, 547, 567*
M.L. Seidman Memorial Town Hall Lecture Series (US ISSN 0076-1729) *712*
M. L. T. A. News (Modern Language Teachers' Association of New South Wales) (AT ISSN 0310-9674) *547*
M M P *see* Microform Market Place *533*
M O T A (Museum of Temporary Art) (US ISSN 0149-4902) *557*
M. Oliver Newsletter (US ISSN 0085-2929) *29*
M P (Ministerio Publico) (BL) *515*
M P A News *see* In a Nutshell *619*
M P R C Report on Finance, Commerce, Industry: Indonesia (MY) *187*
M P R C Report on Finance, Commerce, Industry: Indonesia. Supplement (MY) *187*
M P R C Report on Finance, Commerce, Industry: Singapore (MY) *187*

M P R C Report on Finance, Commerce, Industry: South East Asia (MY) *187*
M P R C Report on Finance, Commerce, Industry: Thailand (MY) *187*
M P, the Microprocessor (US ISSN 0361-5421) *273*
M R A Research Service Directory (Marketing Research Association, Inc.) (US) *218*
M R I Compensation in Mass Retailing, Salaries and Incentives *see* N M R I Compensation in Mass Retailing, Salaries and Incentives *209*
M R I Quarterly (Midwest Research Institute) (US ISSN 0024-8347) *785*
M R I Report *see* M R I Quarterly *785*
M. R. U *see* Modelle fuer den Religionsunterricht *766*
M S H A (Michigan Speech and Hearing Association) (US ISSN 0024-8398) *286, 547, 617*
M S H D A Review (State Housing Development Authority) (US) *485*
M S Ontario (Multiple Sclerosis Society of Canada) (CN ISSN 0707-0934) *597*
M S U U Newsletter (Ministerial Sisterhood Unitarian Universalist) (US ISSN 0360-7046) *772*
M S Z: Muenchener Studentenzeitung *see* Asta-Press *343*
M T A C Journal *see* Management Journal *216*
M T A S Technical Report *see* University of Tennessee. Institute for Public Service. MTAS Municipal Technical Report *747*
M. T. I. A. Annual Report (Metal Trades Industry Association of Australia) (AT ISSN 0085-3321) *208, 628*
M T I A N E G's Export Note Pad (Metal Trades Industry Association National Export Group) (AT) *196, 628*
M T L A, the Micropublishers' Trade List Annual *see* Micropublishers' Trade List Annual *93*
M T P International Review of Science. Inorganic Chemistry, Series 1 (US ISSN 0076-1753) *251*
M T P International Review of Science. Organic Chemistry (US ISSN 0076-1761) *253*
M T P International Review of Science. Physical Chemistry (US ISSN 0076-177X) *255*
M V C Bulletin (Mississippi Valley Collection) (US ISSN 0076-9525) *470*
M V M A Motor Vehicle Facts and Figures (US ISSN 0146-9932) *871*
M W V /A E V Jahresbericht (Arbeitsgemeinschaft Erdoel-Gewinnung und-Verarbeitung) (Mineraloelwirtschafts Verband e.V.) (GW ISSN 0076-891X) *253*
Macabre (US ISSN 0024-8886) *4*
Macau Industry (MH) *146*
McCall's Beauty Guide (US) *85*
McCall's Cooking School (US ISSN 0094-0305) *479*
McCall's Creative Clothes (US) *262*
McCall's Holiday Bake-It Book (US) *479*
Macedonian Review (YU ISSN 0350-3089) *76, 567*
McGill Dental Review (CN ISSN 0024-9025) *610*
McGill Medical Journal (CN ISSN 0024-905X) *597*
McGill Sub-Arctic Research Papers (CN ISSN 0076-1982) *423*
McGill University, Montreal. Axel Heiberg Island Research Reports (CN ISSN 0076-1850) *289*
McGill University, Montreal. Brace Research Institute. Annual Report (CN ISSN 0076-1877) *634*
McGill University, Montreal. Centre for Developing-Area Studies. Annual Report (CN ISSN 0076-1893) *798*

McGill University, Montreal. Centre for Developing-Area Studies. Bibliography Series (CN ISSN 0316-6570) *92, 440*
McGill University, Montreal. Centre for Developing-Area Studies. Occasional Monograph Series (CN ISSN 0702-8431) *798*
McGill University, Montreal. Centre for Developing-Area Studies. Occasional Paper Series *see* McGill University, Montreal. Centre for Developing-Area Studies. Occasional Monograph Series *798*
McGill University, Montreal. Centre for Developing-Area Studies. Reprint Series (CN ISSN 0076-1915) *911*
McGill University, Montreal. Centre for Developing-Area Studies. Working Papers (CN ISSN 0384-059X) *799*
McGill University, Montreal. Department of Geography. Climatological Research Series (CN ISSN 0076-1931) *634*
McGill University, Montreal. Department of Meteorology. Publication in Meteorology (CN ISSN 0076-1842) *634*
McGill University, Montreal. Industrial Relations Centre. Annual Conference Proceedings (CN ISSN 0076-194X) *209*
McGill University, Montreal. Marine Sciences Centre. Annual Report (CN ISSN 0541-6299) *289*
McGill University, Montreal. Marine Sciences Centre. Manuscript Report (CN) *311*
McGill University, Montreal. Mechanical Engineering Research Laboratories. Report (CN ISSN 0076-1966) *382*
McGill University, Montreal. Mechanical Engineering Research Laboratories. Technical Note (CN ISSN 0076-1974) *382*
McGoldrick's Handbook of Canadian Customs Tariff and Excise Duties (CN ISSN 0076-1990) *196, 230*
McGraw-Hill Advanced Physics Monograph Series (US) *697*
McGraw-Hill Series in Missile and Space Technology (US ISSN 0460-3400) *9, 639*
McGraw-Hill Yearbook of Science and Technology (US ISSN 0076-2016) *785, 852*
Machine Design Reference Issues (US) *382*
Machine Intelligence Workshop (US ISSN 0076-2032) *273*
Machinepark (NE) *137*
Machinery and Equipment Pricing Guide *see* Industrial Machinery and Equipment Pricing Guide *583*
Machinery's Annual Buyer's Guide *see* Machinery's Buyers' Guide *382*
Machinery's Buyers' Guide (UK ISSN 0305-3121) *382*
Machines Outils Suedoises *see* Swedish Machine Tools *583*
Machines Utiles Suedoises *see* Swedish Machine Tools *583*
Mackinac History (US ISSN 0541-6507) *470*
Mackintosh Yearbook of West European Electronics Data (UK ISSN 0306-5774) *360*
McMaster Old English Studies and Texts (CN) *567*
McMaster University, Hamilton, Ontario. Institute for Materials Research. Annual Report (CN ISSN 0076-2059) *380*
McMaster University Library Research News (CN ISSN 0024-9270) *533*
Macmillan New Studies in Ethics Series(US) *911*
Macromolecular Chemistry (US ISSN 0076-2075) *253*
Macromolecular Reviews (US ISSN 0076-2083) *253*
Macromolecular Syntheses (US ISSN 0076-2091) *253, 255*
Made in Austria (AU ISSN 0076-2105) *240*
Made in Brazil (BL) *196*
Made in Europe Buyers' Guide (GW ISSN 0085-2937) *196*

Made in Tunisia (TI) *240*
Madhya Pradesh. Directorate of Agriculture. Agricultural Statistics (II ISSN 0304-6184) *25*
Madhya Pradesh Itihasa Parishad. Journal (II) *670*
Madhya Pradesh State Agro-Industries Development Corporation Ltd. Annual Report (II ISSN 0304-7245) *29*
Madhya Pradesh Varshiki *see* Madhya Pradesh Yearbook *418*
Madhya Pradesh Yearbook (II) *418*
Madison Avenue Handbook (US ISSN 0076-2148) *5*
Madoqua (SX) *785*
Madoqua. Series I *see* Madoqua *785*
Madoqua. Series II *see* Madoqua *785*
Madras. Government Museum. Bulletin. New Series (II ISSN 0085-2945) *785*
Maerchen der Europaeischen Voelker (GW ISSN 0076-2326) *402, 568*
Mafogra (FR) *240*
Mag *see* Magazine *580*
Magallat Aden *see* Aden Magazine *441*
Magazin Polovnika (CS ISSN 0541-8836) *479, 568, 830*
Magazin Vier und Zwanzig *see* Initiative *258*
Magazine (US ISSN 0076-2334) *580*
Magazine Industry Market Place (US ISSN 0000-0434) *240, 759*
Magazine of Albemarle County History(US ISSN 0076-2342) *470*
Magenta Frog (CN ISSN 0076-2350) *568*
Magill's Literary Annual (US ISSN 0163-3058) *759*
Magnetic Results from Nurmijarvi Geophysical Observatory (FI ISSN 0071-5212) *305*
Magnitnoimpulsnaya Obrabotka Metallov (UR) *356*
Magnito-Poluprovodnikovye i Elektromashinnye Elementy Avtomatiki (UR) *356*
Magon. Serie Scientifique (LE ISSN 0076-2369) *17*
Magon. Serie Technique (LE ISSN 0076-2377) *17*
Magyar Allami Eotvos Lorand Geofizikai Intezet. Evi Jelentese/Lorand Eotvos Hungarian Geophysical Institute. Annual Report(HU ISSN 0524-8655) *305*
Magyar Irodalomtortenetiras Forrasai; Fontes Ad Historiam Litterariam Hungariae Spectantes (HU ISSN 0076-2385) *568*
Magyar Konyv (HU ISSN 0076-2393) *760*
Magyar Korhazak es Klinikak Evkonyve (HU) *481*
Magyar Kozgazdasagi Irodalom/ Hungarian Economic Literature (HU ISSN 0133-0152) *160*
Magyar Kozlony (HU ISSN 0076-2407) *457*
Magyar Kulpolitikai Evkonyv (HU ISSN 0541-9220) *722*
Magyar Munkasmozgalmi Muzeum. Evkonyv (HU ISSN 0076-2415) *507, 712*
Magyar Naptar (New York) (US ISSN 0094-1484) *361*
Magyar Olajipari Muzeum. Evkonyv (HU) *680*
Magyar Statisztikai Zsebkonyv *see* Statistical Pocket Book of Hungary *847*
Magyar Szo Naptara (YU ISSN 0541-9344) *361*
Magyar Testnevelesi Foiskola. Tudomanyos Kozlemenyek (HU) *820*
Magyar Tudomanyos Akademia. Agrartudomanyok Osztalya. Monografiasorozat (HU ISSN 0076-2423) *17*
Magyar Tudomanyos Akademia. Konyvtar. Kezirattar Katalogusai (HU) *92*

Magyar Tudomanyos Akademia.Kozponti Fizikai Kutato Intezet. Evkonyv see Hungarian Academy of Sciences. Central Research Institute for Physics. Yearbook 696
Magyar Tudomanyos Akademia. Mikrobiologiai Kutato Intezet. Proceedings/Hungarian Academy of Sciences Research Institute for Microbiology. Proceedings (HU ISSN 0076-2431) 124
Magyar Tudomanyok Akademia. Tudomanyok Osztalya. Kozlemenyek see Kemiai Kozlemenyek 247
Magyarorszag Allatvilaga/Fauna Hungariae (HU ISSN 0076-2474) 129
Magyarorszag Kulturfloraja (HU ISSN 0076-2482) 116
Magyarorszag Muemleki Topografiaja (HU ISSN 0076-2490) 76, 457
Magyarorszag Regeszeti Topografiaja (HU ISSN 0076-2504) 62
Magyarorszag Tajfoldrajza (HU ISSN 0076-2512) 423
Maharaja Sawai Man Singh II Memorial Series (II) 653
Maharaja Sayajirao University of Baroda. Department of Archaeology and Ancient History. Archaeology Series (II ISSN 0076-2520) 62
Maharaja Sayajirao University of Baroda. Department of History Series(II ISSN 0464-5030) 434
Maharashtra: an Economic Review see Economic Survey of India 185
Maharashtra Archives Bulletin (II ISSN 0076-2547) 444
Maharashtra State Budget in Brief (II ISSN 0076-2555) 230
Maharashtra State Financial Corporation. Annual Report (II ISSN 0076-2563) 174
Mahratta (II ISSN 0076-2571) 444
Mail Order Business Directory (US ISSN 0085-2953) 218
Main Currents in Indian Sociology (US) 815
Main d'Oeuvre en Genie Bulletin see Engineering Manpower News 367
Main Deck (CN ISSN 0383-7769) 507, 879
Main Hurdman & Cranstoun News Summary (US) 167, 230
Main Hurdman & Cranstoun Tax Newsletter (US) 230
Main Trends of Technical and Economic Development see Muszaki es Gazdasagi Fejlodes Fo Iranyai 852
Maine. Bureau of Labor and Industry. Occupational Wage Survey (US ISSN 0093-7886) 209
Maine. Bureau of Property Taxation. Biennial Report (US ISSN 0361-3550) 230
Maine. Criminal Justice Planning & Assistance Agency. Criminal Justice Internship Program. Report and Evaluation (US ISSN 0090-9386) 282
Maine. Criminal Justice Planning & Assistance Agency. Progress Report (US) 282
Maine. Department of Marine Resources. Fisheries Circulars (US) 398
Maine. Department of Marine Resources. Fishery Bulletin (US) 398
Maine. Department of Marine Resources. Research Bulletin (US) 398
Maine. Department of Sea and Shore Fisheries. General Bulletin see Maine. Department of Marine Resources. Fisheries Circulars 398
Maine. Department of Transportation. Annual Report (US ISSN 0094-5048) 863
Maine. Law Enforcement Planning & Assistance Agency. Maine Criminal Justice Internship Program; Report and Evaluation see Maine. Criminal Justice Planning & Assistance Agency. Criminal Justice Internship Program. Report and Evaluation 282

Maine. Law Enforcement Planning & Assistance Agency. Progress Report see Maine. Criminal Justice Planning & Assistance Agency. Progress Report 282
Maine. State Library. Special Subject Resources in Maine (US ISSN 0091-0759) 533
Maine. State Planning Office. Annual Report (US ISSN 0091-0678) 744
Maine Facts see State O'Maine Facts 891
Maine Farm Research see Research in the Life Sciences 19
Maine Geological Survey. Bulletins (US) 296
Maine Heritage Series (US ISSN 0076-2652) 470
Maine Historical Society. Research Series (US) 470
Maine Marketing Directory (US ISSN 0145-9007) 240
Maine Media Directory (US) 5
Maine, New Hampshire, Vermont Tour Book see Tourbook: Maine, New Hampshire, Vermont 872
Maine Prosecutor, Criminal Legislation Manual (US ISSN 0098-079X) 282
Maine State Grocers Bulletin (US) 407
Maine State Industrial Directory (US ISSN 0098-6194) 240
Maine, Vermont and New Hampshire Directory of Manufacturers (US) 240
Maine Writers' Conference Chapbook (US ISSN 0076-2717) 568
Mainfraenkisches Jahrbuch fuer Geschichte und Kunst (GW ISSN 0076-2725) 76, 457
Maintenance Buyers Guide (UK) 137
Maintoba Conference on Numerical Mathematics and Computing. Proceedings see Congressus Numerantium 585
Mainzer Philosophische Forschungen (GW ISSN 0076-2776) 689
Mainzer Reihe (GW ISSN 0076-2784) 568
Mainzer Romanistische Arbeiten (GW ISSN 0542-1551) 547
Mainzer Studien zur Sprach- und Volksforschung (GW ISSN 0170-3560) 547
Mainzer Zeitschrift (GW ISSN 0076-2792) 62, 76, 457
Maison Franco-Japonaise. Bulletin (FR ISSN 0495-7725) 670
Maisons d'Enfants et d'Adolescents de France. Album-Annuaire National (FR ISSN 0076-2814) 257, 752
Maize Virus Information Service see Ohio Agricultural Research and Development Center, Wooster. Library. List of References: Maize Virus Diseases and Corn Stunt 25
Majalah Universitas Sumatera Utara see University of North Sumatra. Bulletin 341
Majallah Pantai see University of Malaya. Chinese Language Society. Journal 554
Majallah Perpustakaan Malaysia (MY ISSN 0126-7809) 533
Majallah Syarikat Kerjasama Serbaguna Malaysia see Malaysian Multi-Purpose Cooperative Society. Review 17
Maji Review (TZ) 363, 897
Majlis Pengeluar-Pengeluar Getah Tanah Melayu. Lapuran Tahunan see Rubber Producers' Council of Malaysia. Annual Report 777
Major Companies of Brazil, Mexico and Venezuela (UK) 240
Major Companies of Nigeria (UK) 240
Major Companies of the Arab World (UK) 240
Major European Author Series (UK) 568
Major League Baseball (US ISSN 0076-2849) 824
Major Mass Market Merchandisers (US) 261
Major Problems in Ophthalmology (US) 616
Makedonika (GR ISSN 0076-289X) 259, 402, 457

Makerere Library Publications see Makerere University. Library. Makerere Library Publications 533
Makerere Medical Journal (UG ISSN 0025-1119) 597
Makerere Political Review (UG) 712
Makerere University. Albert Cook Library. Library Bulletin and Accession List (UG) 533, 597
Makerere University. Department of Geography. Occasional Paper (UG ISSN 0075-4722) 423
Makerere University. Faculty of Agriculture. Handbook (UG ISSN 0075-4730) 17
Makerere University. Faculty of Agriculture. Technical Bulletin (UG ISSN 0075-4773) 17
Makerere University. Faculty of Education. Handbook (UG) 338
Makerere University. Faculty of Law. Handbook (UG ISSN 0075-4781) 515
Makerere University. Library. Makerere Library Publications (UG ISSN 0075-4854) 533
Makerere University. Science Faculty. Handbook (UG) 785
Making It: A Guide to Student Finances (US) 338
Making of the Twentieth Century (US) 434
Makromolekulare Chemie. Rapid Communications (SZ) 253
Makromolekulare Chemie. Short Communications see Makromolekulare Chemie. Rapid Communications 253
Maksvadaya (CE) 712
Mala Biblioteka Baletowa (PL ISSN 0076-2989) 285
Malacologia (US ISSN 0076-2997) 129
Malacological Review (US ISSN 0076-3004) 129
Maladies Veneriennes au Canada see Venereal Diseases in Canada 611
Malagasy Republic. Institut National de la Statistique et de la Recherche Economique. Recensement Industriel(MG) 842
Malawi. Accountant General. Report (MW ISSN 0076-3020) 230
Malawi. Department of Agricultural Research. Annual Report (MW) 17
Malawi. Department of Agricultural Research. Research Bulletin (MW) 17
Malawi. Department of Agriculture. Annual Report see Malawi. Department of Agricultural Research. Annual Report 17
Malawi. Department of Civil Aviation. Annual Report (MW ISSN 0076-3055) 868
Malawi. Department of Forestry and Game. Report (MW ISSN 0076-3071) 277, 409
Malawi. Department of Information. Parliamentary Biographies (MW) 712
Malawi. Department of Information. Year in Review (MW) 440
Malawi. Department of Veterinary Services and Animal Industry. Annual Report (MW ISSN 0076-3365) 894
Malawi. Fisheries Department. Fisheries Bulletin (MW) 398
Malawi. Geological Survey. Annual Report (MW ISSN 0076-311X) 296
Malawi. Geological Survey. Bulletin (MW ISSN 0076-3128) 296
Malawi. Geological Survey. Memoir (MW ISSN 0076-3136) 296
Malawi. Geological Survey. Records (MW ISSN 0076-3144) 296
Malawi. Meteorological Services. Totals of Monthly and Annual Rainfall (MW) 634
Malawi. Ministry of Finance. Budget Statement (MW ISSN 0076-3195) 230
Malawi. Ministry of Finance. Financial Statement (MW) 230
Malawi. Ministry of Justice. Annual Report (MW ISSN 0076-3160) 515

Malawi. Ministry of Local Government. Annual Report (MW ISSN 0076-3225) 712
Malawi. National Library. Annual Report see Malawi. National Library Service. Annual Report 533
Malawi. National Library Service. Annual Report (MW) 533
Malawi. National Statistical Office. Annual Statement of External Trade (MW ISSN 0076-325X) 160
Malawi. National Statistical Office. Annual Survey of Economic Activities (MW ISSN 0076-3241) 160
Malawi. National Statistical Office. Balance of Payments (MW ISSN 0085-3003) 196, 230
Malawi. National Statistical Office. Compendium of Agricultural Statistics (MW ISSN 0085-3011) 17
Malawi. National Statistical Office. Compendium of Statistics see Malawi Statistical Yearbook 843
Malawi. National Statistical Office. Household Income and Expenditure Survey (MW ISSN 0076-3276) 842
Malawi. National Statistical Office. National Accounts Report (MW ISSN 0076-3284) 842
Malawi. National Statistical Office. National Sample Survey of Agriculture (MW ISSN 0076-3292) 17
Malawi. National Statistical Office. Population Census Final Report (MW ISSN 0076-3306) 732
Malawi. National Statistical Office. Reported Employment and Earnings: Annual Report (MW) 160
Malawi. National Statistical Office. Tourist Report see Malawi Tourism Report 887
Malawi. Office of the Auditor General. Report (MW ISSN 0076-3314) 230
Malawi. Police Force. Annual Report (MW ISSN 0076-308X) 282
Malawi. Post Office Savings Bank. Annual Report (MW ISSN 0076-3322) 174
Malawi. Registrar of Insurance. Report (MW ISSN 0076-3349) 500
Malawi Economic Report (MW ISSN 0076-3101) 187
Malawi Housing Corporation. Annual Report and Accounts (MW ISSN 0581-0892) 485
Malawi Journal of Science (MW) 785
Malawi Railways. Annual Reports and Accounts (MW ISSN 0076-3330) 873
Malawi Railways. Directors' Reports and Accounts see Malawi Railways. Annual Reports and Accounts 873
Malawi Statistical Yearbook (MW) 843
Malawi Tourism Report (MW) 887
Malawi Treaty Series (MW ISSN 0076-3357) 523
Malawi Year Book see Malawi. Department of Information. Year in Review 440
Malaya (Federation) Public Records Office and National Archives. Report see National Archives of Malaysia. Annual Report 444
Malaysia. Department of Inland Revenue. Annual Report/Malaysia. Jabatan Hasil Dalam Negeri. Lapuran Tahunan (MY) 182
Malaysia. Department of Statistics. Annual Bulletin of Statistics (MY ISSN 0542-3570) 843
Malaysia. Department of Statistics. Survey of Construction Industries: Peninsular Malaysia (MY ISSN 0085-3046) 140
Malaysia. Department of Statistics. Vital Statistics: Peninsular Malaysia (MY) 732, 843
Malaysia. Geological Survey. Annual Report (MY ISSN 0126-5628) 296
Malaysia. Jabatan Hasil Dalam Negeri. Lapuran Tahunan see Malaysia. Department of Inland Revenue. Annual Report 182

Malaysia. Kementerian Pertanian. Bahagian Perikanan. Perangkaan Tahunan Perikanan see Malaysia. Ministry of Agriculture. Fisheries Division. Annual Fisheries Statistics 398
Malaysia. Meteorological Service. Summary of Observations for Malaysia (MY ISSN 0126-8864) 634
Malaysia. Meterological Service. Summary of Observations for Malaya, Sabah and Sarawak see Malaysia. Meteorological Service. Summary of Observations for Malaysia 634
Malaysia. Ministry of Agriculture. Fisheries Division. Annual Fisheries Statistics/Malaysia. Kementerian Pertanian. Bahagian Perikanan. Perangkaan Tahunan Perikanan (MY) 398
Malaysia. Ministry of Agriculture. Technical and General Bulletins (MY) 17, 398
Malaysia. Ministry of Agriculture. Technical Bulletins see Malaysia. Ministry of Agriculture. Technical and General Bulletins 17
Malaysia. Perbendaharaan. Anggaran Belanjawan (MY) 168, 230
Malaysia. Treasury. Economic Report (MY) 187
Malaysia in Brief (MY ISSN 0301-7095) 444
Malaysia Official Year Book (MY ISSN 0076-3373) 444
Malaysia Year Book see Information Malaysia 443
Malaysian Agricultural Research and Development Institute Research Bulletin see M A R D I Research Bulletin 17
Malaysian Centre for Development Studies Occasional Paper Series see M C D S Occasional Paper Series 798
Malaysian Chinese Association. Annual Report (MY ISSN 0542-397X) 444
Malaysian Journal of Science/Jernal Sains Malaysia (MY ISSN 0301-0554) 785
Malaysian Multi-Purpose Cooperative Society. Review (MY) 17
Malaysian National Bibliography/Bibliografi Negara Malaysia (MY ISSN 0126-5210) 438
Malaysian Periodicals Index/Indeks Majalah Malaysia (MY ISSN 0126-5040) 3
Malaysian Pineapple (MY) 17
Malaysian Veterinary Journal (MY ISSN 0460-8518) 894
Maledicta Press Publications (US ISSN 0363-9037) 547
Mali. Service de la Statistique Generale, de la Comptabilite Nationale et de la Mecanographie. Annuaire Statistique (ML ISSN 0076-3411) 160
Mali. Service de la Statistique Generale, de la Comptabilite Nationale et de la Mecanographie. Statistiques Douanieres du Commerce Exterior (ML) 160
Malignant Intrigue (US ISSN 0076-342X) 605
Malta. Central Office of Statistics. Annual Abstract of Statistics (MM ISSN 0081-4733) 843
Malta. Central Office of Statistics. Census of Agriculture and Fisheries (MM) 17
Malta. Central Office of Statistics. Census of Production Report (MM ISSN 0076-3462) 160
Malta. Central Office of Statistics. Demographic Review (MM ISSN 0076-3470) 728
Malta. Central Office of Statistics. Economic Survey (MM) 187
Malta. Central Office of Statistics. Education Statistics (MM ISSN 0076-3489) 319
Malta. Office of Statistics. Census of Agriculture see Malta. Central Office of Statistics. Census of Agriculture and Fisheries 17
Malta Chamber of Commerce. Trade Directory (MM) 240

Malta Library Association Newsletter see Library Association (Valletta). Ghaqda Biblotekarji/Library Association Newsletter 532
Malta Library Association Yearbook see Library Association (Valletta). Ghaqda Bibljotekarji/Library Association Yearbook 532
Malta Trade Directory see Malta Chamber of Commerce. Trade Directory 240
Malta Yearbook (UK) 712, 887
Maltese Directory: Canada, United States (CN ISSN 0317-6983) 392, 470
Ma'lumat-i Ihsa'ivi-i Afghanistan see Statistical Information of Afghanistan 847
Mamashee (CN ISSN 0702-7575) 568
Mambo Occasional Papers. Socio-Economic Series (RH) 815
Mammalia Depicta (GW ISSN 0301-2778) 129
Mammalian Species (US ISSN 0076-3519) 129
Man & Environment (II) 51, 62, 673
Man and His Environment see International Banff Conference on Man and His Environment. Proceedings 386
Man and Society/Manusia dan Masyarakat (MY ISSN 0303-3171) 51, 815
Man-Environment System in the Late Twentieth Century (US) 799
Man-Environment Systems/Focus Series (US) 387, 485, 815
Man, His Community and Natural Resources Series (US) 277
Man in Southeast Asia (AT) 51, 799
Man in the North Project. Technical Reports (CN) 51
Man-Made Fibers of Japan (JA) 856
Mana (FJ ISSN 0379-5268) 568
Mana Annual of Creative Writing see Mana 568
Managed and Property Bonds (UK) 204
Management see Management Journal 216
Management (Baltimore) (US ISSN 0565-7199) 9, 216
Management Aids for Small Business Annual (US ISSN 0190-3225) 234
Management Aids for Small Manufacturers see Management Aids for Small Business Annual 234
Management Development Centre Business Journal see M D C Business Journal 146
Management Guide to N C (US ISSN 0076-3624) 216
Management in Papua New Guinea (PP) 216
Management Journal (UG ISSN 0300-2144) 216
Management Monographs see L R I Guides to Management. Monographs 215
Management Monographs (New York) (US ISSN 0085-3054) 216
Management of Malignant Disease Series (UK) 605
Management Report - General Services Administration see U.S. General Services Administration. Management Report 809
Management Reports on the Australian Economy (AT) 187
Management Series (Indianapolis) see Indiana. Division of Fish and Wildlife. Management Series 276
Management Wissen Jahrbuch (GW) 216
Manager and Entrepreneur (ET ISSN 0580-8898) 216
Managerial Information see Bestuurlike Informasie 167
Manassas Review (US) 568
Manchester Association of Engineers. Transactions (UK ISSN 0076-3705) 368
Manchester Chamber of Commerce and Industry. Regional Directory (UK) 179
Manchester Chamber of Commerce and Industry. Yearbook (UK ISSN 0306-5758) 179
Manchester Folk Directory (UK) 661

Manchester Guardian Society for the Protection of Trade. Annual Report (UK ISSN 0076-3713) 196
Manchester Literary and Philosophical Society. Memoirs and Proceedings (UK ISSN 0076-3721) 689
Manchester United Football Book (UK ISSN 0308-8405) 824
La Mandragore Qui Chante (SZ ISSN 0076-3748) 580
Maneggiare (BG) 216
Manifesto. Quaderno (IT) 712
Manipur State Museum. Bulletin (II) 653
Manitoba. Co-Operative Loans and Loans Guarantee Board. Annual Report (CN) 174
Manitoba. Department of Co-Operative Development. Report. Rapport (CN) 174, 181
Manitoba. Environmental Council. Annual Report (CN ISSN 0380-9803) 387
Manitoba. Environmental Council. Studies (CN ISSN 0380-979X) 387
Manitoba. Health Services Commission. Annual Report (CN ISSN 0383-3925) 752
Manitoba. Health Services Commission. Statistical Supplement to the Annual Report (CN ISSN 0383-3933) 752
Manitoba. Horse Racing Commission. Annual Report (CN ISSN 0317-7262) 828
Manitoba. Human Rights Commission. Annual Report (CN ISSN 0383-5588) 718
Manitoba. Lotteries Commission. Annual Report (CN ISSN 0703-0827) 820
Manitoba. Mineral Resources Division. Geological Paper (CN) 296, 644
Manitoba. Mineral Resources Division. Publication (CN) 296, 644
Manitoba. Mineral Resources Division. Report of Field Activities (CN) 296
Manitoba. Mining Engineering Division. Geological Paper see Manitoba. Mineral Resources Division. Geological Paper 644
Manitoba. Mining Engineering Division. Publication see Manitoba. Mineral Resources Division. Publication 296
Manitoba. Mining Engineering Division. Report of Field Activities see Manitoba. Mineral Resources Division. Report of Field Activities 296
Manitoba. Municipal Employees Benefits Board. Annual Report (CN ISSN 0706-3792) 209
Manitoba. Pension Commission. Annual Report (CN ISSN 0381-3215) 500
Manitoba. Public Library Services. Newsletter (CN ISSN 0706-7798) 533
Manitoba. Social Services Advisory Committee. Annual Report (CN) 807
Manitoba. Water Services Board. Annual Report (CN ISSN 0318-3912) 897
Manitoba. Welfare Advisory Committee. Annual Report see Manitoba. Social Services Advisory Committee. Annual Report 807
Manitoba Association of Confluent Educators Newsletter see M A C E Newsletter 319
Manitoba Cancer Treatment and Research Foundation. Report (CN ISSN 0076-3802) 605
Manitoba Community Reports (CN ISSN 0318-6415) 187
Manitoba Construction Industry Directory. Purchasing Guide (CN) 137, 368
Manitoba Credit Unions: Annual Report see Manitoba. Department of Co-Operative Development. Report. Rapport 174
Manitoba Crop Insurance Corporation. Annual Report (CN ISSN 0542-5395) 37, 500
Manitoba Decisions, Civil and Criminal Cases (CN ISSN 0380-0008) 515
Manitoba Educational Research Council. Policy Study (CN) 319

Manitoba Entomologist (CN ISSN 0076-3810) 121
Manitoba Genealogical Society News see M G S News 417
Manitoba Grassland Projects (CN ISSN 0382-2028) 42
Manitoba Labour-Management Review Committee. Annual Report (CN ISSN 0076-3853) 209
Manitoba Museum of Man and Nature. Annual Report see Manitoba Museum of Man and Nature. Biennial Report 653
Manitoba Museum of Man and Nature. Biennial Report (CN ISSN 0076-3888) 653
Manitoba Record Society. Publications (CN ISSN 0076-3896) 470
Manitoba Vacation Guide, Canada (CN) 887
Manitoba Vacation Handbook see Manitoba Vacation Guide, Canada 887
Mankind Monographs (US ISSN 0076-4116) 51
Manned Undersea Science and Technology Program see U. S. National Oceanic and Atmospheric Administration. Manned Undersea Science and Technology Program; Report 370
Mannheimer Sozialwissenschaftliche Studien (GW) 799
Manomet Bird Observatory Research Report (US) 125
Manpower Research Projects see U.S. Department of Labor. Employment and Training Administration. Manpower Research and Development Projects 211
Manual Azucarero Mexicano (MX ISSN 0464-882X) 37
Manual de Impuestos (CK) 515
Manual do Interno e Residente (BL) 597
Manual of Building Maintenance see Maintenance Buyers Guide 137
Manual of Death Education and Simple Burial (US) 414
Manual of Foreign Exchange Control in Japan (JA) 204
Manual of Foreign Investment in Japan (JA) 204
Manual of Materials Handling and Ancillary Equipment see Materials Handling Buyers Guide 218
Manual of Mutual Funds see Mutual Funds Almanac 204
Manual of Simple Burial see Manual of Death Education and Simple Burial 414
Manual of the Textile Industry of Canada (CN ISSN 0381-551X) 856
Manual-State of Maryland see Maryland Manual 744
Manuali di Politica Internazionale (IT) 722
Manuel de l' O T A N see N A T O Handbook 722
Manuel International de Caoutchouc see Handbuch der Internationalen Kautschukindustrie 777
Manuel International des Plastiques see Handbuch der Internationalen Kunstoffindustrie 706
Manuels Pratiques d'Economie (FR ISSN 0076-4205) 911
Manufacturers' Agents' Guide (US ISSN 0076-4213) 240
Manufacturing Developments in Kentucky see Kentucky Manufacturing Developments 851
Manufacturing Directory of Idaho (US) 240
Manufacturing Engineering Transactions (US ISSN 0363-700X) 368
Manufacturing Industries of Canada see Canada. Statistics Canada. Manufacturing Industries of Canada: Type of Organization and Size of Establishment/Industries Manufacturieres du Canada: Forme d'Organisation et Taille des Etablissements 905

Manufacturing Industries of Canada: Sub-Provincial Areas/Industries Manufacturieres du Canada: Niveau Infraprovincial (CN ISSN 0382-4012) 160, 843
Manusia dan Masyarakat see Man and Society 51
Manx Museum, Douglas, Isle of Man. Journal (UK ISSN 0076-4264) 457
Manxman (UK ISSN 0306-8536) 392
Maori Education Foundation. Annual Report (NZ ISSN 0076-4280) 319
MAR Year Book see Centro de Navegacion Transatlantica. C.N.T. Handbook. River Plate Handbook for Shipowners and Agents 877
Mara Institute of Technology. Annual Report/Institut Teknologi Mara. Laporan Tahunan (MY) 338
Marburger Abhandlungen zur Politischen Wissenschaft (GW ISSN 0542-6480) 712
Marconi's International Register (US ISSN 0076-4418) 240, 269
Mare Balticum (GW ISSN 0542-6758) 879
Marga Institute. Progress Report (CE) 799
Marginal Notes (US) 533
Marian Library Studies. New Series (US ISSN 0076-4434) 533, 766
Marihuana and Health; Annual Report to the U.S. Congress from the Secretary of Health, Education and Welfare (US) 287
Marine Academie. Mededelingen see Academie de Marine. Communications 876
Marine Affairs Journal (US) 712
Marine Biological Laboratory Lectures in Biology see M B L Lectures in Biology 104
Marine Biology; Proceedings of the Interdisciplinary Conference (US ISSN 0076-4442) 105
Marine Board of Hobart. Annual Report (AT) 879
Marine Catalog (US ISSN 0076-4450) 879
Marine Catalog Buyers Guide (US) 879
Marine Ecology (US) 105
Marine Engineering/Log Annual Maritime Review and Yearbook Issue(US ISSN 0076-4469) 879
Marine Equipment Directory (CN) 879
Marine Geology and Geophysics see Morskaya Geologiya i Geofizika 311
Marine Mammal Protection Act of 1972 Annual Report (US ISSN 0196-4690) 277
Marine Marchand: Etudes et Statistiques see Transport Maritime: Etudes et Statistiques 881
Marine Marchande (FR ISSN 0076-4485) 879
Marine Products Export Review (II) 196
Marine Recreational Fisheries (US ISSN 0161-522X) 398
Marine Research (UK ISSN 0076-4493) 129
Marine Research in Indonesia (IO ISSN 0079-0435) 311
Marine Resources of the Atlantic Coast(US ISSN 0542-7029) 398
Marine Science Affairs see Reports on Marine Science Affairs 312
Marine Sciences Instrumentation (US) 368
Marine Standardization see Marine Standardization in Japan 879
Marine Standardization in Japan (JA) 637, 879
Marine Surface Observations see U. S. National Weather Service. Data Acquisition Division. Marine Surface Observations 635
Marine Technology Society. Annual Conference Proceedings (US) 879
Mariner's Catalog (US ISSN 0198-9618) 311, 879
Mario Negri Institute for Pharmacological Research. Monographs (US ISSN 0085-3100) 685

Maritime Bank of Israel. Annual Report/Bank Ha-Sapanut le-Yisrael. Annual Report. (IS ISSN 0076-4515) 174
Maritime Monographs and Reports (UK ISSN 0307-8590) 879
Marken-Handbuch der Werbung und Etatbetreuung (GW ISSN 0085-3119) 5
Market Information Series (II) 218
Market Research Handbook (CN ISSN 0590-9325) 160, 843
Market Research Society. Yearbook (UK ISSN 0076-4523) 218
Market Scope (US ISSN 0146-9223) 405
Market Share Reports (US) 160
Market Statistics Key Plant Directory see Marketing Economics Key Plants 218
Marketing Boards in Canada/Offices de Commercialisation au Canada (CN ISSN 0527-6624) 29
Marketing California Dried Fruits see Marketing California Dried Fruits: Prunes, Raisins, Dried Apricots & Peaches 29
Marketing California Dried Fruits: Prunes, Raisins, Dried Apricots & Peaches (US ISSN 0094-2510) 29, 182
Marketing California Pears for Fresh Market (US ISSN 0098-8928) 29
Marketing Economics Guide see M E I Marketing Economics Guide 218
Marketing Economics Institute, Ltd. Marketing Economics Guide see M E I Marketing Economics Guide 218
Marketing Economics Key Plants (US ISSN 0098-1397) 218
Marketing et Developpement Industriel see Marketing Industriel 218
Marketing Guide (US ISSN 0093-125X) 218, 685
Marketing Guide to the Chemical Industry see Kline Guide to the Chemical Industry 373
Marketing Guide to the Packaging Industries see Kline Guide to the Packaging Industry 672
Marketing Guide to the Paint Industry see Kline Guide to the Paint Industry 673
Marketing Guide to the Paper and Pulp Industry see Kline Guide to the Paper and Pulp Industry 675
Marketing Industriel (FR) 218
Marketing Research Association, Inc. Research Service Directory see M R A Research Service Directory 218
Markets Year Book (UK ISSN 0076-4647) 218
Maroc see Arts et Objets du Maroc 72
Maroc en Chiffre (MR ISSN 0076-4655) 196
Marquette Slavic Studies (US ISSN 0076-4671) 457
Marshall News (US) 263
Marsyas (US ISSN 0076-4701) 76
Martin Classical Lectures (US ISSN 0076-471X) 259
Martin-Luther-Universitaet Halle-Wittenberg. Wissenschaftliche Beitraege (GE) 597
Martindale-Hubbell Law Directory (US) 515
Martindale: the Extra Pharmacopoeia (UK) 685
Marx Karoly Kozgazdasagtudomanyi Egyetem: Doktori Ertekezesek (HU ISSN 0521-4211) 160
Marx Karoly Kozgazdasagtudomanyi Egyetem Oktatoinak Szakirodalmi Munkassaga (HU) 92, 160
Marxism and the Mass Media (US ISSN 0098-9509) 712
Marxist Anthropology (SZ) 911
Marxista Europea (IT) 712
Marxisticka Filozofia see Univerzita Komenskeho. Ustav Marxizmu-Leninizmu. Zbornik: Marxisticka Filozofia 911
Mary C. Richardson Lecture (US ISSN 0076-4728) 911
Maryland. Bureau of Air Quality and Noise Control. Data Report see Maryland Air Quality Programs. Data Report 387

Maryland. Commission on Intergovernmental Cooperation. Annual Report (US ISSN 0098-8766) 744
Maryland. Correctional Training Commission. Annual Report see Maryland. Police and Correctional Training Commissions. Report to the Governor, the Secretary of Public Safety and Correctional Services, and Members of the General Assembly 282
Maryland. Council for Higher Education. Annual Report see Maryland. Council for Higher Education. Annual Report and Recommendations 911
Maryland. Council for Higher Education. Annual Report and Recommendations (US ISSN 0361-140X) 911
Maryland. Department of Juvenile Services. Annual Statistical Report see Maryland. Juvenile Services Administration. Annual Statistical Report 257
Maryland. Department of Natural Resources. Annual Activities Report (US) 277
Maryland. Department of State Planning. Activities Report (US ISSN 0076-4752) 744
Maryland. Division of Correction. Report (US ISSN 0362-9198) 282
Maryland. Geological Survey. Archeological Studies (US) 62
Maryland. Geological Survey. Bulletin (US ISSN 0076-4779) 296
Maryland. Geological Survey. Educational Series (US ISSN 0076-4787) 296
Maryland. Geological Survey. Information Circular (US ISSN 0076-4795) 296
Maryland. Geological Survey. Report of Investigations (US ISSN 0076-4809) 296
Maryland. Geological Survey. Water Resources Basic Data Report (US ISSN 0076-4817) 897
Maryland. Governor's Commission on Law Enforcement and the Administration of Justice. Comprehensive Plan (US) 282
Maryland. Juvenile Services Administration. Annual Statistical Report (US) 257
Maryland. Police and Correctional Training Commissions. Report to the Governor, the Secretary of Public Safety and Correctional Services, and Members of the General Assembly (US) 282
Maryland. Police Training Commission. Annual Report see Maryland. Police and Correctional Training Commissions. Report to the Governor, the Secretary of Public Safety and Correctional Services, and Members of the General Assembly 282
Maryland. State Department of Legislative Reference. Snynopsis of Laws Enacted by the State of Maryland (US ISSN 0093-0520) 515
Maryland. State Highway Administration. Traffic Trends (US ISSN 0094-6265) 875
Maryland Air Quality Data Report see Maryland Air Quality Programs. Data Report 387
Maryland Air Quality Programs. Data Report (US) 387
Maryland Historical Trust. Annual Report (US ISSN 0098-3403) 69
Maryland Lawyer's Manual (US ISSN 0542-836X) 515
Maryland Manual (US ISSN 0094-4491) 744
Maryland State Industrial Directory (US ISSN 0148-5660) 240
Maschinenfabrik Augsburg-Nuernberg AG Forschen, Planen, Bauen see M.A.N. Forschen, Planen, Bauen 368
Maschinenwelt-Elektrotechnik (AU ISSN 0025-4533) 356, 583

Maschinenwelt und Elektrotechnik see Maschinenwelt-Elektrotechnik 583
Mash Family Bulletin (US) 417
Mask see Masque 568
Al-Maskukat (IQ ISSN 0002-4058) 477
Masque (UK ISSN 0025-4711) 568, 661
Mass Communication Review Yearbook(US ISSN 0196-8017) 265
Mass Line (CN ISSN 0047-6110) 712
Mass Media in India (II) 268
Mass Media Review (AT) 265
Mass Spectrometry (UK ISSN 0305-9987) 247, 697
Massachusetts. Advisory Committee on Correction. Annual Report (US ISSN 0076-4884) 282
Massachusetts. Board of Public Accountancy. Annual Report (US ISSN 0362-1898) 744
Massachusetts. Department of Correction. Commissioner of Correction. Statistical Reports (US) 282
Massachusetts. Department of Public Health. Annual Report (US) 752
Massachusetts. Department of Public Welfare. State Advisory Board. Annual Report (US ISSN 0095-4020) 807
Massachusetts. Division of Employment Security. Annual Planning Report (US ISSN 0076-4930) 209
Massachusetts. Division of Employment Security. Employment and Wages in Establishments Subject to the Massachusetts Employment Security Law. State Summary (US ISSN 0076-4922) 209
Massachusetts. Division of Employment Security. Statistical Digest (US ISSN 0076-4949) 209
Massachusetts. Division of Employment Security. Survey of Unfilled Job Openings - Boston (US) 209, 667
Massachusetts. Division of Fisheries and Game. Annual Report (US ISSN 0076-4957) 277
Massachusetts. Rehabilitation Commission. Expenditures Report (US ISSN 0095-8050) 346
Massachusetts Advocacy Center. Annual Report (US ISSN 0362-1383) 319, 515
Massachusetts Agricultural Statistics (US ISSN 0092-9794) 17
Massachusetts Correctional Institution, Norfolk, Norfolk Colony School. Report (US ISSN 0085-3143) 282
Massachusetts Directory of Manufacturers (US) 240
Massachusetts Historical Society. Proceedings (US ISSN 0076-4981) 434
Massachusetts Historical Society Miscellany see M.H.S. Miscellany 470
Massachusetts Housing Finance Agency. Annual Report (US ISSN 0076-499X) 485
Massachusetts Institute of Technology. Flight Transportation Laboratory. F T L Report (US) 9
Massachusetts Institute of Technology. Research Laboratory of Electronics. Quarterly Progress Report see Massachusetts Institute of Technology. Research Laboratory of Electronics. R L E Progress Report 356
Massachusetts Institute of Technology. Research Laboratory of Electronics. R L E Progress Report (US) 265, 356
Massachusetts State Industrial Directory (US ISSN 0148-7558) 240
Massachusetts State Scholarship Programs see Report: Massachusetts State Scholarship Programs 339
Masson Cancer Management Series (US) 605
Masson Monographs in Dentistry (US) 610
Masson Monographs in Dermatopathology (US) 611
Masson Monographs in Diagnostic Pathology (US) 597

Masson Monographs in Pediatric Hematology/Oncology (US) 605, *617*
Masssstaebe (GW) 76, *492*
Master Federal Tax Manual (US) *230*
Master Plan for Higher Education in Illinois *see* Master Plan for Postsecondary Education in Illinois *338*
Master Plan for Postsecondary Education in Illinois (US) *338*
Master Saddlers Yearbook (UK) *524*
Masterpieces in the National Gallery of Canada/Chefs-d'Oeuvre de la Galerie Nationale du Canada (CN ISSN 0383-5391) *76*
Masterplots Annual *see* Magill's Literary Annual *759*
Masters Education: Route to Opportunities in Contemporary Nursing (US) 338, *614*
Masters Education; Route to Opportunities in Modern Nursing *see* Masters Education: Route to Opportunities in Contemporary Nursing *614*
Master's Theses in Education (US ISSN 0076-5112) *319*
Masterskaya (UR) *568*
Match (GW ISSN 0340-6253) *247, 586*
Matematicheskaya Fizika i Funktsionalnyi Analiz (UR) *586, 697*
Matematicheskie Metody V Ekonomike(UR) *69*
Matematicheskie Problemy Geofiziki (UR ISSN 0301-6897) *273, 305*
Matematyka (PL) *587*
Material Culture Monographs (American Indian) (US ISSN 0076-5139) *51*
Material for Thought (US) *689*
Material Handling and Industrial Engineer *see* American Institute of Industrial Engineers. Material Handling Institute. Proceedings *365*
Material Handling Engineering Handbook and Directory (US) *583, 672*
Materiale si Cercetari Arheologice (RM ISSN 0076-5147) *62, 457*
Materiales de la Ciudad (SP) *485*
Materiali di Storia Urbana (IT) *434*
Materialia Turcica (GW ISSN 0344-449X) *457*
Materialien zur Hochschulpolitik (GW) *338*
Materialien zur Roemisch-Germanischen Keramik (GW ISSN 0076-5171) *62, 244*
Materialien zur Sozial- und Wirtschaftspolitik (AU ISSN 0506-9122) *744, 815*
Materialien zur Wirtschafts- und Sozialgeschichte (AU) *457*
Materialimarsilio (IT) *712*
Materialkundlich-Technische Reihe (GW) *911*
Materialoznanie i Teknhologiia (BU) *380*
Materials and Studies for Kassite History (US ISSN 0146-6798) *444*
Materials Handling Buyers Guide (UK ISSN 0076-4167) *218*
Materials Performance Buyer's Guide (US ISSN 0095-7976) *628*
Materials Processing: Theory and Practices (NE) *697*
Materials Research and Engineering/Werkstoff- Forschung und -Technik (US) 368, *628*
Materials Research in A E C L (Atomic Energy of Canada Ltd.) (CN) *380*
Materials Research in Science and Engineering at Purdue University. Annual Report *see* Materials Research in Science and Engineering at Purdue University. Progress Report *380*
Materials Research in Science and Engineering at Purdue University. Progress Report (US ISSN 0079-8126) *380*
Materials Science Monographs (NE) *368*
Materials Science Research (US ISSN 0076-5201) *380*

Materials Selector (US ISSN 0465-2886) *380*
Materialy Historyczno-Metodyczne (PL) *434*
Materialy i Prace Antropologiczne (PL ISSN 0076-521X) *51*
Materialy Zachodnio-Pomorskie (PL ISSN 0076-5236) *62, 457*
Materialy Zrodlowe do Dziejow Kosciola W Polsce (PL ISSN 0076-5244) *775*
Matériaux pour l'Etude de l'Asie Orientale Moderne et Contemporaine. Etudes Linguistiques(FR) *547*
Materiel Graphique (FR) *733*
Maternidade Dr. Alfredo da Costa, Lisbon. Arquivo Clinico (PO ISSN 0302-4326) *615*
Mathematicae Notae (AG ISSN 0025-553X) *587*
Mathematical Chronicle (NZ ISSN 0581-1155) *587*
Mathematical Expositions (CN ISSN 0076-5333) *587*
Mathematical Linguistics and Automatic Translation *see* Formal Linguistics *585*
Mathematical Notes *see* Notas Matematicas *587*
Mathematical Notes (Princeton) (US) *587*
Mathematical Physics and Applied Mathematics (NE) *587, 697*
Mathematical Society of Japan. Publications (JA ISSN 0549-4540) *587*
Mathematical Surveys (US ISSN 0076-5376) *587*
Mathematical Systems in Economics (GW) *191, 587*
Mathematical Table Series (US ISSN 0076-5384) *587*
Mathematics Annual *see* Alberta Teachers Association. Mathematics Monograph *584*
Mathematics in School (UK ISSN 0305-7259) *349, 587*
Mathematics in Science and Engineering (US ISSN 0076-5392) *368, 587*
Mathematics International (US ISSN 0091-7214) *587*
Mathematiques et Sciences de l'Homme(FR ISSN 0076-5406) *587*
Mathematische Lehrbuecher und Monographien. Abteilung: Mathematische Monographien. (GE ISSN 0076-5430) *587*
Mathematische Schuelerbuecherei (GE ISSN 0076-5449) *587*
Mathilda and Terence Kennedy Institute of Rheumatology. Annual Report (UK) *623*
Matter of Degree (UK ISSN 0140-7961) *423*
Mauri Ora (NZ ISSN 0302-086X) *105*
Maurice Falk Institute for Economic Research in Israel. Report (IS ISSN 0076-5473) *146*
Mauritius. Archives Department. Annual Report (MF ISSN 0076-5481) *533*
Mauritius. Central Electricity Board. Annual Report (MF) *356*
Mauritius. Customs and Excise Department. Annual Report (MF ISSN 0076-549X) *230*
Mauritius. Legislative Assembly. Sessional Paper (MF ISSN 0076-5503) *744*
Mauritius. Meteorological Services. Report (MF ISSN 0076-5511) *634*
Mauritius. Ministry of Housing, Lands and Town and Country Planning. Annual Reports (MF ISSN 0076-552X) *485*
Mauritius. Ministry of Social Security. Annual Report (MF ISSN 0076-5538) *807*
Mauritius. Ministry of Works and Internal Communications. Report (MF ISSN 0076-5554) *744, 863*
Mauritius. Public Accounts Committee. Report (MF ISSN 0076-5562) *230*
Mauritius. Registrar of Insurance. Annual Report (MF) *500*
Mauritius. Tobacco Board. Annual Report (MF) *861*

Mauritius Directory of the Diplomatic Corps (MF ISSN 0085-3194) *722*
Mawdsley Memoirs (CN) *423, 470*
Max C. Fleischmann College of Agriculture. Publications. B (Series) (US ISSN 0076-5589) *17*
Max C. Fleischmann College of Agriculture. Publications. C (Series) (US ISSN 0076-5597) *18*
Max C. Fleischmann College of Agriculture. Publications. R (Series) (US ISSN 0076-5600) *18*
Max C. Fleischmann College of Agriculture. Publications. T (Series) (US ISSN 0076-5619) *18*
Max Freiherr von Oppenheim-Stiftung. Schriften (GW ISSN 0543-1719) *475*
Max-Planck-Gesellschaft zur Foerderung der Wissenschaften. Jahrbuch (GW ISSN 0076-5635) *785*
Max-Planck-Gesellschaft zur Foerderung der Wissenschaften Berichte und Mitteilungen (GW) *785*
Max-Planck-Gesellschaft zur Foerderung der Wissenschaften Mitteilungen *see* Max-Planck-Gesellschaft zur Foerderung der Wissenschaften Berichte und Mitteilungen *785*
Max-Planck-Institut fuer Aeronomie. Mitteilungen (US ISSN 0076-5643) *634*
Max-Planck-Institut fuer Auslaendisches Oeffentliches Recht und Voelkerrecht. Fontes *see* Max-Planck-Institut fuer Auslaendisches Oeffentliches Recht und Voelkerrecht. Fontes Iuris Gentium *515*
Max-Planck-Institut fuer Auslaendisches Oeffentliches Recht und Voelkerrecht. Fontes Iuris Gentium (GW) *515*
Max-Planck-Institut fuer Bildungsforschung, Berlin. Studien und Berichte (GW ISSN 0076-5627) *319*
Ma'yanot (IS ISSN 0543-1786) *392*
ME *see* Dirigo: ME *556*
Me Judice *see* Singapore Law Review *518*
Measuring Mormonism (US ISSN 0094-5633) *776*
Meat and Livestock Commission, Bucks, England. Index of Research (UK ISSN 0076-5716) *45*
Meat Research Institute. Biennial Report (UK) *405*
Meat Science Institute. Proceedings (US ISSN 0090-5641) *405*
Meat Trade Yearbook (UK ISSN 0082-7967) *45, 405*
Meatworker (AT ISSN 0310-6721) *405, 507*
Mechanical & Electrical Cost Data (US) *137, 356*
Mechanics and Building Engineering *see* Mechanika i Budownictwo Ladowe *382*
Mechanics: Dynamical Systems (NE) *701*
Mechanika *see* Elektrotekhnika ir Mechanika *354*
Mechanika i Budownictwo Ladowe/Mechanics and Building Engineering (PL ISSN 0324-9182) *137, 382*
Mechanine Technologija *see* Mekhanicheskaya Tekhnologiya *382*
Mechanisms of Molecular Migrations (US ISSN 0076-5791) *911*
Mecman-Technique (SW ISSN 0025-6609) *369*
Mecman-Teknik *see* Mecman-Technique *369*
Med Bil i Europa (NO) *887*
Meddelelser om Groenland *see* Greenland, Man and Society *50*
Meddelelser om Groenland *see* Greenland Biosciences *103*
Meddelelser om Groenland *see* Greenland Geoscience *294*
Mededelingen "Ex Oriente Lux" *see* Vooraziatisch-Egyptisch Genootschap "Ex Oriente Lux". Mededelingen en Verhandelingen *446*
Media Encyclopedia (US) *5, 268, 505*

MEDICAL RESEARCH 1423

Media Equipment Resource Center Directory *see* M E R C Directory *650*
Media Guide International. Airline Inflight Magazines Edition *see* Media Guide International. Airline Inflight/Travel Magazines Edition *866*
Media Guide International. Airline Inflight/Travel Magazines Edition (US) *6, 866*
Media Guide International. Business/Professional Publications Edition (US ISSN 0164-1743) *6*
Media Guide International. Edition Newspapers-Newsmagazines *see* Media Guide International. Newspapers/Newsmagazines Edition *6*
Media Guide International. Newspapers/Newsmagazines Edition (US ISSN 0093-9447) *6*
Media Personnel Directory (US) *505, 759*
Media Review Digest (US ISSN 0363-7778) *3, 651, 665*
Media Scandinavia (DK ISSN 0076-5821) *5*
Mediaeval and Modern Breton Series (IE) *434, 547*
Mediaeval Philosophical Texts in Translation (US ISSN 0076-5856) *689*
Mediaeval Scandinavia (DK ISSN 0076-5864) *457*
Mediaeval Sources in Translation (CN ISSN 0316-0874) *457, 568*
Mediaeval Studies (CN ISSN 0076-5872) *457*
Mediaevalia (US ISSN 0361-946X) *76, 434, 568*
Mediaevalia Lovaniensia. Series I (BE) *457*
Mediaevalia Philosophica Polonorum (PL ISSN 0076-5880) *689*
Mediaevistic Studies *see* Studia Mediewistyczne *691*
Medicaid (Washington) *see* Medicaid Statistics *807*
Medicaid Recipient Characteristics and Units of Selected Medical Services (US ISSN 0098-3616) *597, 807*
Medicaid Statistics (US ISSN 0091-8164) *597, 807*
Medical and Health Annual (US ISSN 0363-0366) *694*
Medical & Health Information Directory (US) *694*
Medical Annual (UK ISSN 0076-5899) *597*
Medical Books and Serials in Print (US ISSN 0000-0574) *602*
Medical Books in Print *see* Medical Books and Serials in Print *602*
Medical Council of Iran. Publication/Nezam Pezeshki-Ye Iran. Nashriyeh (IR) *597*
Medical Education Sources (US) *597*
Medical Electronics and Equipment News Buyers' Guide (US) *597*
Medical Electronics and Equipment News Dictionary and Buyers' Guide *see* Medical Electronics and Equipment News Buyers' Guide *597*
Medical Group Management Association. International Directory (US ISSN 0094-9604) *216, 597*
Medical Physics Series (US ISSN 0076-5953) *597, 697*
Medical Product of Japan (JA) *240, 597*
Medical Protection Society. Annual Report (UK ISSN 0076-5961) *597*
Medical Research Bulletin (AT ISSN 0025-7494) *597*
Medical Research Centre, Nairobi. Annual Report (KE ISSN 0076-5988) *597*
Medical Research Centres in Ghana: Current Research Projects (GH) *597*
Medical Research Council (Ireland). Report (IE ISSN 0076-5996) *597*
Medical Research Council of Canada. Grants and Awards Guide/Guide de Subventions et Bourses (CN) *597*
Medical Research Council of Canada. Report of the President (CN) *597*
Medical Research in the V.A. (US) *597*

Medical Research Index (UK ISSN 0076-6003) 3, 602
Medical School Admission Requirements, U. S. A. and Canada (US ISSN 0066-9423) 597
Medical Society of London. Transactions (UK ISSN 0076-6011) 597
Medical Society of the State of North Carolina Transactions see North Carolina Medical Society. Transactions 598
Medical Subject Headings (US ISSN 0565-811X) 597
Medicinal Chemistry (US ISSN 0076-6054) 585
Medicinal Research: A Series of Monographs (US ISSN 0076-6062) 597
Medicine (New York) (US) 597
Medicine and Sport (SZ ISSN 0076-6070) 624
Medicinhistorisk Aarsbok see Nordisk Medicinhistorisk Aarsbok 598
Medico-Legal Society of New South Wales. Proceedings (AT ISSN 0047-6587) 515
Medico-Legal Society of Sri Lanka. Proceedings (CE) 613
Medieval Academy Books (US) 76, 457, 568
Medieval Academy of America. Publications see Medieval Academy Books 457
Medieval Academy Reprints for Teaching (US) 76, 457, 568
Medieval and Renaissance Studies (US) 911
Medieval Archaeology (UK ISSN 0076-6097) 62, 457
Medieval Iberian Penninsula (NE ISSN 0076-6100) 457
Medieval India; a Miscellany (US ISSN 0076-6119) 444
Medio Ambiente (CL) 387
Medio Ambiente en Espana (SP) 387
Medioevo (IT) 689
Medioevo: Saggi e Rassegne (IT) 434
Mediquiz Annual (US) 597
Medium Industry Bank, Seoul. Report see Small and Medium Industry Bank, Seoul. Annual Report 176
Medizinhistorisches Journal (GW ISSN 0025-8431) 597
Medizinische Akademie "Carl Gustav Carus" Dresden. Schriften (GE ISSN 0070-721X) 597
Medizinische Informatik und Statistik (US) 597
Medizinische Laenderkunde. Geomedical Monograph Series (US ISSN 0076-6151) 598
Medizinische Praxis (GW ISSN 0076-616X) 598
Medizinische und Paedagogische Jugendkunde see Sozialmedizinische und Paedagogische Jugendkunde 600
Meeting Ground (US) 392, 470
Meeting of International Organizations for the Joint Study of Programs and Activities in the Field of Agriculture in Europe. Report. (UN ISSN 0532-0402) 18
Meeting on Soil Correlation for North America. (Report) (UN ISSN 0543-3770) 37
Meeting on Soil Survey Correlation and Interpretation for Latin America. Report (UN ISSN 0543-3789) 37
Meetings, Conferences & Conventions: a Financial Post Guide (CN) 146, 626
Megadrilogica (CN ISSN 0380-9633) 37, 629
Meghalaya Industrial Development Corporation. Annual Report (II ISSN 0376-5423) 146
Meharry Medical College. School of Dentistry. Proceedings of an Oral Research Seminar (US) 610
Mehkarim Be-Ge'ografyah Shel Erets-Yisrael see Studies in the Geography of Israel 426
Meier-Dudy/Meier's Directory of Exporters and Importers (GW ISSN 0076-6208) 197
Meier's Directory of Exporters and Importers see Meier-Dudy 197

Meister des Puppenspiels (GW ISSN 0076-6216) 859
Mekevot see Sources of Contemporary Jewish Thought 557
Mekhanicheskaya Tekhnologiya/Mechanine Technologija (UR) 382
Melanderia (US ISSN 0076-6224) 121
Melanges GRAPEL see Universite de Nancy II. Centre de Recherches et d'Applications Pedagogiques en Langues. Melanges 351
Melbourne Historical Journal (AT ISSN 0076-6232) 447
Melbourne International Philosophy Series (NE) 689
Melbourne Journal of Politics (AT ISSN 0085-3224) 712
Melbourne Notes on Agricultural Extension (AT ISSN 0085-3232) 18
Melbourne Politics Monographs (AT) 712
Melbourne Slavonic Studies (AT ISSN 0076-6267) 547, 568
Melbourne Studies in Education (AT ISSN 0076-6275) 319
Melbourne University Magazine (AT ISSN 0085-3283) 338, 568
Melbourne Walker (AT) 830
Melibea (PE) 568
Melita Theologica (MM) 766
Melland Schill Lectures on International Law (UK ISSN 0076-6313) 523
Melodie pre Vas (CS) 661
Melsheimer Entomological Series (US ISSN 0076-6321) 121
Members of the Stock Exchange see Stock Exchange, London. Members and Firms of the Stock Exchange 204
Membership Directory - National Association of College Admissions Counselors see National Association of College Admissions Counselors. Membership Directory 338
Membership Directory of the Golf Course Superintendents Association of America see Golf Course Superintendents Association of America. Membership Directory 824
Membership Directory of the Photographic Historical Society of N.Y. see Photographic Historical Society of New York. Membership Directory 693
Membrane Structure and Function (UK) 119
Membrane Transport Processes (US ISSN 0160-2462) 112, 598
Membranes: A Series of Advances (US ISSN 0076-6356) 105, 598
Memento de l'O.I.V. (Office International de la Vigne et du Vin) (FR ISSN 0085-221X) 86
Memento des Mines et Carrieres. (FR) 644
Memento General de la Quincaillerie see Memento General Tequi Quincaillerie 141
Memento General Tequi Quincaillerie (FR ISSN 0025-9055) 141
Memento Pratique des Societes Commerciales (FR) 515
Memento Therapeutique de Tunisie (MR) 240
Memento Therapeutique du Maroc (MR) 240
Memento Therapeutique pour l'Afrique Noire Francophone (MR) 240
Memo from Belgium (BE ISSN 0025-908X) 187, 712
Memoire des Femmes (FR) 98, 900
Memoires C.E.R.E.S. (Centre d'Etudes de Recherches, d'Essais Scientifiques de Genie Civil) (BE ISSN 0025-9195) 376
Memoires de Photo-Interpretation (FR ISSN 0076-6364) 693
Memoires O.R.S.T.O.M. (FR ISSN 0071-9005) 852
Memoires pour Servir a l'Explication des Cartes Geologiques et Minieres de la Belgique (BE) 296, 644
Memoires Suisse de Paleontologie see Schweizerische Palaeontologische Abhandlungen 674
Memoirs of the Hourglass Cruises (US ISSN 0085-0683) 311

Memorabilia Zoologica (PL ISSN 0076-6372) 129
Memoria Deportiva see Federacion Espanola Galguera. Anuario y Memoria Deportiva 819
Memorial Sloan-Kettering Cancer Center. New York. Report see Sloan-Kettering Institute for Cancer Research. Progress Report 606
Memorial University of Newfoundland. Library. Serials Holdings in the Libraries of Memorial University of Newfoundland and St. John's Public Library see Serials Holdings in the Libraries of Memorial University of Newfoundland, St. John's Public Library and College of Trades and Technology 94Æ
Memorial University, St. John's Newfoundland. Library Bulletin see Memorial University, St. John's, Newfoundland. Marine Sciences Research Laboratory. M.S.R.L. Bulletin 311
Memorial University, St. John's, Newfoundland. Marine Sciences Research Laboratory. M.S.R.L. Bulletin (CN) 105, 311
Memorials - Geological Society of America see Geological Society of America. Memorials 293
Memorie Domenicane (IT) 766
Memphis State University. Anthropological Research Center. Occasional Papers (US ISSN 0564-8602) 51
Men and Women of Distinction (UK) 98
Men and Women of Hawaii (US ISSN 0461-7398) 98
Men of Achievement (UK ISSN 0306-3666) 98
Menarini Series on Immunopathology (US) 604
Mendelssohn Studien (GW ISSN 0340-8140) 434
Mennonite History Series (US ISSN 0076-6429) 776
Mennonite Yearbook and Directory (US) 776
Mens en Milieu (NE) 387
Men's Wear Year Book and Diary (UK ISSN 0076-6437) 262
Mental Health Data (NZ ISSN 0548-992X) 602
Mental Health Directory (US) 752
Mental Health in Deafness (US) 286
Mental Health Media Center Film Catalog (US) 736, 752
Mental Health, Retardation and Hospitals (Cranston) see Rhode Island. Department of Mental Health, Retardation and Hospitals. Mental Health, Retardation and Hospitals 754
Mental Health Services for Children and Youth see Hawaii. Department of Health. Mental Health Services for Children and Youth 806
Mental Health Statistics for Illinois (US ISSN 0076-6453) 752, 807
Mental Measurements Yearbook (US ISSN 0076-6461) 349, 736
Mental Retardation see Mental Retardation and Developmental Disabilities 620
Mental Retardation and Developmental Disabilities (US ISSN 0091-6315) 620
Mentalis (US ISSN 0360-7232) 610
Mentor see Ark 559
Mercado Comum Brasileiro (BL) 182
Merchandise & Operating Results of Department and Speciality Stores (US) 218
Merchant Explorer (US ISSN 0543-5056) 457
Merchant Ships Totally Lost, Broken up Etc see Casualty Return Statistical Summary 865
Merchant Vessels of the United States (US ISSN 0076-650X) 879
Merck Index; an Encyclopedia of Chemicals and Drugs (US ISSN 0076-6518) 629
Merck Manual; a Handbook of Diagnosis and Therapy (US ISSN 0076-6526) 598

Merck Veterinary Manual; a Handbook of Diagnosis and Therapy for the Veterinarian (US ISSN 0076-6542) 895
Mergers & Acquisitions. a Comprehensive World Bibliography (US) 160
Merhavim (IS) 424
Merida, Venezuela (City) Universidad de Los Andes. Facultad de Derecho. Revista see Universidad de los Andes. Facultad de Derecho. Anuario 519
Meridiano Deportivo (CK) 820
Merite du Defricheur. Rapport de l'Ordre du Merite Agricole (CN) 37
Merite du Defricheur. Rapport de l'Ordre du Merite du Defricheur see Merite du Defricheur. Rapport de l'Ordre du Merite Agricole 37
Merkels' Builders' Pricing and Management Manual (SA) 137
Merkel's Electrician's Manual (SA) 137, 356
Merkel's S.A. Plumber's Costing Manual (SA) 430
Merlewood Research Station. Report see Great Britain. Institute of Terrestrial Ecology. Report 103
Merseyside Chamber of Commerce and Industry. Directory (UK ISSN 0302-4148) 179
Ha-Mesivta (US ISSN 0094-9701) 515, 770
Mesopotamia (IT ISSN 0076-6615) 63
Message (GO) 319
Message d'Extreme-Orient (BE) 444
Metal (CK) 644
Metal & Engineering Industry Year Book (AT ISSN 0314-1586) 240, 369
Metal Bulletin Handbook (UK ISSN 0076-664X) 628
Metal Distribution (US ISSN 0098-2210) 628
Metal Finishing Guidebook & Directory(US) 629
Metal Ions in Biological Systems (US) 251
Metal Stamping Buyer's Guide (US) 629
Metal Statistics (US ISSN 0076-6658) 629
Metal Traders of the World (UK ISSN 0143-7607) 629
Metal Trades Industry Association National Export Group Export Note Pad see M T I A N E G's Export Note Pad 628
Metal Trades Industry Association of Australia Annual Report see M. T. I. A. Annual Report 208
Metal Working Blue Book see National Metalworking Blue Book 629
Metallgesellschaft Aktiengesellschaft. Review of the Activities (GW ISSN 0026-0770) 629
Metalli Non Ferrosi in Italia: Statistiche(IT) 644
Metallurgical Engineer (II) 629
Metallurgical Plantmakers of the World(UK ISSN 0308-7794) 629
Metallurgical Works in Canada, Nonferrous and Precious Metals (CN ISSN 0076-6704) 644
Metallurgical Works in Canada, Primary Iron and Steel (CN ISSN 0076-6712) 644
Metallurgy and Material Science (UK) 629
Metallurgy-Materials Education Yearbook (US ISSN 0094-5447) 629
Metalmecanica (MX) 356, 629
Metalurgia (PE) 51, 629
Metalurgia see Area Metalurgia 627
Metaphysische Rundschau (AU ISSN 0076-6720) 689
"Meteor" Forschungsergebnisse. Reihe A. Allgemeines, Physik und Chemie des Meeres (GW ISSN 0543-5900) 311
"Meteor" Forschungsergebnisse. Reihe B. Meteorologie und Aeronomie (GW ISSN 0543-5919) 305, 634
"Meteor" Forschungsergebnisse. Reihe C. Geologie und Geophysik (GW ISSN 0543-5919) 305, 311

"Meteor" Forschungsergebnisse. Reihe D. Biologie (GW ISSN 0543-5935) 105, 311
Meteorological Yearbook of Finland. Part 1A: Climatological Data (FI ISSN 0076-6747) 634
Meteorological Yearbook of Finland. Part 1B: Climatological Data from Jokioinen and Sodankyla Observatories (FI ISSN 0076-6739) 634
Meteorological Yearbook of Finland. Part 2: Precipitation and Snow Cover Data (FI ISSN 0076-6755) 634
Meteorological Yearbook of Finland. Part 4: Measurements of Radiation and Bright Sunshine (FI ISSN 0076-6763) 634
Meteorologiske Annaler (NO) 634
Methoden und Verfahren der Mathemathischen Physik (GW) 587, 697
Methodensammlung der Elektronenmikroskopie (GW ISSN 0076-6771) 124
Methodes de la Cartographie Thematique (SZ) 424
Methods and Achievements in Experimental Pathology (SZ ISSN 0076-681X) 598
Methods and Models in the Social Sciences (NE ISSN 0076-6828) 799
Methods and Techniques in Geophysics(US ISSN 0076-6836) 911
Methods in Cancer Research (US ISSN 0076-6852) 605
Methods in Cell Biology (US ISSN 0091-679X) 119
Methods in Cell Physiology see Methods in Cell Biology 119
Methods in Computational Physics: Advances in Research and Applications (US ISSN 0076-6860) 697
Methods in Enzymology (US ISSN 0076-6879) 111
Methods in Geochemistry and Geophysics (NE ISSN 0076-6895) 289, 305
Methods in Geomathematics (NE) 587
Methods in Hydroscience see Advances in Hydroscience 307
Methods in Immunology and Immunochemistry (US ISSN 0076-6917) 124, 604
Methods in Membrane Biology (US ISSN 0093-4771) 105
Methods in Virology (US ISSN 0076-6933) 124, 608
Methods of Biochemical Analysis (US ISSN 0076-6941) 111, 249
Methods of Experimental Botany see Metodicke Prirucky Experimentalni Botaniky 116
Methods of Experimental Physics (US ISSN 0076-695X) 697
Methods of Information and Documentation see Modszertani Kiadvanyok 852
Methods of Operations Research see Operations Research-Verfahren 216
Metodicke Prirucky Experimentalni Botaniky/Methods of Experimental Botany (CS ISSN 0076-6984) 116
Metodicky Zpravodaj Cs. Soustavy Vedeckych, Technickych a Ekonomickych Informaci (CS ISSN 0322-7243) 533, 785, 852
Metodistkyrkans i Sverige. Aarsbok (SW ISSN 0543-6206) 772
Metodologicheski i Istoriografski Problemi na Istoricheskata Nauka (BU) 434
Metric Conversion Board News see M. C. B. News 637
Metric Fact Sheets (CN ISSN 0383-9184) 637
Metric Fastener Standards (US) 380
Metric Yearbook (US) 637
Metro: a Bibliography (BE ISSN 0378-195X) 866
Metro Building Industry Directory (US ISSN 0076-700X) 137
METRO C.A.P. Catalog (US ISSN 0363-1257) 533
Metro California Media (US) 5

METRO; New York Metropolitan Reference and Research Library Agency. METRO Miscellaneous Publications Series (US ISSN 0076-7018) 533
Metron (IT ISSN 0026-1424) 843
Metropolitan College of Technology, Tokyo. Memoirs/Tokyo-toritsu Koka Tanki Daigaku Kenkyu Hokoku (JA) 852
Metropolitan Library Service Agency. Annual Report (US ISSN 0076-7050) 533
Metropolitan Milwaukee Association of Commerce. Economic Studies see Metropolitan Milwaukee Economic Fact Book 187
Metropolitan Milwaukee Economic Fact Book (US) 187
Metropolitan Museum Journal (US ISSN 0077-8958) 653
Metropolitan Toronto (CN ISSN 0076-7093) 749
Metropolitan Washington Council of Governments. Annual Report (US ISSN 0076-7107) 744
Metropolitan Washington Council of Governments. Regional Directory (US ISSN 0076-7115) 744
Metsatilastollinen Vuosikirja/Yearbook of Forest Statistics (FI ISSN 0356-343X) 409
Mexican American Monograph Series (US) 392
Mexican Society for Soil Mechanics Meeting. Proceedings (MX) 37
Mexico (MX ISSN 0543-7741) 187
Mexico. Archivo General de la Nacion. Archivo Historico de Hacienda. Coleccion Documental (MX) 533
Mexico. Centro de Informacion Tecnica y Documentacion. Indice de Peliculas(MX) 651
Mexico (City). Universidad Nacional. Observatorio Astronomico, Tacubaya. Boletin de los Observatorios Tonantzintla y Tacubaya see Instituto de Tonantzintla. Boletin 82
Mexico. Comision Nacional Bancaria y de Seguros. Anuario Estadistico de Seguros (MX) 500
Mexico. Comison Nacional de los Salarios Minimos. Informe de Labores (MX ISSN 0302-4822) 209
Mexico. Direccion de Estadistica. Estadistica Industrial Mensual (MX) 160
Mexico. Direccion General de Estadistica. Estadistica Industrial Anual (MX ISSN 0071-1543) 160, 843
Mexico. Direccion General de Estadistica. Estadistica Minerometalurgica: Produccion y Exportacion (MX) 644
Mexico. Direccion General de Oceanografia. Calendario Grafico de Mareas (MX) 311
Mexico. Direccion General de Prensa, Memorias, Bibliotecas y Publicaciones. Coleccion: Documentos Economicos de la Administracion Publica (MX ISSN 0076-7530) 744
Mexico. Secretaria de Agricultura y Recursos Hidraulicos. Informe Estadistico (MX) 29, 897
Mexico. Secretaria de Educacion Publica. Informe de Labores (MX) 319
Mexico. Secretaria de Programacion y Presupuesto (MX ISSN 0076-7492) 160
Mexico; Hechos, Cifras, Tendencias see Mexico 187
Meyers Grosses Jahreslexikon (GW ISSN 0076-7670) 92
Meyniana (GW ISSN 0076-7689) 296
Miam (US) 568
Michael (IS) 392
Michel-Briefmarken-Kataloge (GW ISSN 0076-7727) 479
Michelin Annual Camping Guide for France see Camping, Caravaning in France 883
Michelin Green Guide Series: Alpes (FR) 887
Michelin Green Guide Series: Austria (FR) 888

Michelin Green Guide Series: Auvergne(FR) 888
Michelin Green Guide Series: Belgique (FR) 888
Michelin Green Guide Series: Belgium-Luxemburg (FR) 888
Michelin Green Guide Series: Bourgogne (FR) 888
Michelin Green Guide Series: Brittany (FR) 888
Michelin Green Guide Series: Causses Cevennes (FR) 888
Michelin Green Guide Series: Chateaux of the Loire (FR) 888
Michelin Green Guide Series: Corse (FR) 888
Michelin Green Guide Series: Cote Atlantique (FR) 888
Michelin Green Guide Series: Dordogne (FR) 888
Michelin Green Guide Series: Environs de Paris (FR) 888
Michelin Green Guide Series: French Riviera (FR) 888
Michelin Green Guide Series: Germany(FR) 888
Michelin Green Guide Series: Italy (FR) 888
Michelin Green Guide Series: Jura (FR) 888
Michelin Green Guide Series: Londres (FR) 888
Michelin Green Guide Series: Maroc (FR) 888
Michelin Green Guide Series: New York (City) (FR) 888
Michelin Green Guide Series: Nord de la France (FR) 888
Michelin Green Guide Series: Normandy (FR) 888
Michelin Green Guide Series: Paris (FR) 888
Michelin Green Guide Series: Pays Bas (FR) 888
Michelin Green Guide Series: Perigord see Michelin Green Guide Series: Dordogne 888
Michelin Green Guide Series: Portugal (FR) 888
Michelin Green Guide Series: Provence(FR) 888
Michelin Green Guide Series: Pyrenees (FR) 888
Michelin Green Guide Series: Rome (FR) 888
Michelin Green Guide Series: Spain (FR) 888
Michelin Green Guide Series: Switzerland (FR) 888
Michelin Green Guide Series: Vallee du Rhone (FR) 888
Michelin Green Guide Series: Vosges (FR) 888
Michelin Red Guide Series: Benelux (FR ISSN 0076-7743) 888
Michelin Red Guide Series: France (FR ISSN 0076-7778) 888
Michelin Red Guide Series: Germany (FR ISSN 0076-7751) 888
Michelin Red Guide Series: Great Britain and Ireland (FR) 888
Michelin Red Guide Series: Greater London (FR) 483, 888
Michelin Red Guide Series: Italy (FR ISSN 0076-7786) 888
Michelin Red Guide Series: Paris (FR ISSN 0076-7794) 888
Michelin Red Guide Series: Spain & Portugal (FR ISSN 0076-776X) 888
Michelin Spain (UK) 889
Michigan. Advisory Council for Vocational Education. Annual Report(US ISSN 0093-9137) 346
Michigan. Civil Rights Commission. Annual Report (US) 718
Michigan. Department of Education. College Admissions & Financial Assistance Handbook see Michigan Postsecondary Admissions & Financial Assistance Handbook 331
Michigan. Department of Administration. Report see Michigan. Department of Management and Budget. Annual Report 744
Michigan. Department of Commerce. Annual Report Summary (US ISSN 0094-3479) 182

Michigan. Department of Corrections. Criminal Statistics see Dimensions 281
Michigan. Department of Management and Budget. Annual Report (US ISSN 0095-733X) 744
Michigan. Department of Natural Resources. Institute for Fisheries Research. Miscellaneous Publication (US ISSN 0076-7905) 398
Michigan. Department of Social Services. Program Statistics (US ISSN 0093-7835) 811
Michigan. Department of Social Services. Public Assistance Statistics (US ISSN 0093-6774) 811
Michigan. Department of State Police. Annual Report (US) 282
Michigan. Division of Vocational Education. Report (US ISSN 0076-7913) 338
Michigan. Employment Security Commission. Annual Planning Report (US ISSN 0090-8401) 209
Michigan. Employment Security Commission. Labor Market Analysis Section. Annual Manpower Planning Report: Detroit Labor Market Area see Michigan. Employment Security Commission. Annual Planning Report 209
Michigan. Geological Survey Division. Bulletin (US ISSN 0543-8497) 296
Michigan. Geological Survey Division. Report of Investigation (US) 296
Michigan. Office of Criminal Justice. Comprehensive Law Enforcement and Criminal Justice Plan (US ISSN 0093-9390) 282
Michigan. Office of Highway Safety Planning. Annual Highway Safety Work Plan. see State of Michigan's Annual Highway Safety Plan 876
Michigan. Office of the Court Administrator. Judicial Statistics (US ISSN 0098-7875) 521
Michigan. State Board of Control for Vocational Education. Annual Descriptive Report see Michigan. Division of Vocational Education. Report 338
Michigan. State Library Services. Catalog of Books on Magnetic Tape (US ISSN 0092-5349) 92
Michigan. State Police. Annual Report see Michigan. Department of State Police. Annual Report 282
Michigan. Technological University Houghton. Library. Journal and Serial Holdings see Michigan Technological University. Library. Serial Holdings List 93
Michigan Abstracts of Chinese and Japanese Works on Chinese History (US ISSN 0076-7808) 438
Michigan Beef Cattle Day Report (US ISSN 0076-7824) 45
Michigan Business and Economic Research Bibliography (US ISSN 0091-9047) 160
Michigan Business Cases (US ISSN 0076-7832) 146
Michigan Business Papers (US ISSN 0076-7840) 146
Michigan Business Reports (US ISSN 0076-7859) 146
Michigan Business Studies (US ISSN 0076-7867) 146
Michigan Geographical Publications (US ISSN 0076-7948) 424
Michigan Governmental Studies (US ISSN 0076-7956) 744
Michigan Health Statistics (US ISSN 0539-7413) 756
Michigan Housing Market Information System Monograph Series (US) 485
Michigan in Books (US ISSN 0026-2218) 760
Michigan International Business Studies(US ISSN 0076-7972) 146
Michigan International Labor Studies (US ISSN 0076-7999) 209
Michigan Law Enforcement Officials Report on Crime see Uniform Crime Report for the State of Michigan 285
Michigan Library Directory & Statistics (US ISSN 0076-8081) 533

MICHIGAN LIBRARY

Michigan Library News *see* Michigan Library Directory & Statistics *533*
Michigan Linguistic Society. Annual Report *see* Michigan Linguistic Society. Papers *547*
Michigan Linguistic Society. Papers (US) *547*
Michigan Mineral Producers Annual Directory: (US ISSN 0085-3372) *644*
Michigan Municipal League. Municipal Legal Briefs (US ISSN 0076-8014) *749*
Michigan Municipal League. Salaries, Wages and Fringe Benefits for Michigan Villages and Cities 1000-4000 Population (US ISSN 0077-216X) *749*
Michigan Municipal League. Salaries, Wages, and Fringe Benefits in Michigan Municipalities over 4,000 Population (US ISSN 0080-5548) *749*
Michigan Natural Resources Council. Scientific Advisory Committee. Annual Report (US ISSN 0076-8057) *277*
Michigan Occasional Papers in Women's Studies (US) *900*
Michigan Papers in Chinese Studies (US ISSN 0076-8065) *444*
Michigan Papers on South and Southeast Asia (US) *444*
Michigan Police Journal (US ISSN 0085-3380) *282*
Michigan Postsecondary Admissions & Financial Assistance Handbook (US) *331*
Michigan Public Health Statistics *see* Michigan Health Statistics *756*
Michigan Series in South and Southeast Asian Languages and Linguistics (US) *547*
Michigan Slavic Contributions (US ISSN 0076-8103) *568*
Michigan Slavic Materials (US ISSN 0543-9930) *547, 568*
Michigan Slavic Translations (US) *568*
Michigan Speech and Hearing Association *see* M S H A *286*
Michigan State Employees' Retirement System *see* Michigan State Employees' Retirement System Financial and Statistical Report *209*
Michigan State Employees' Retirement System Financial and Statistical Report (US ISSN 0092-9212) *209, 744*
Michigan State Housing Development Authority. Annual Report (US) *485*
Michigan State Industrial Directory (US ISSN 0190-1338) *240*
Michigan State Plan for Vocational Education (US ISSN 0094-1506) *329*
Michigan State University. Agricultural Economics Report (US ISSN 0065-4442) *29*
Michigan State University. Asian Studies Center. Occasional Papers: East Asian Series (US ISSN 0076-812X) *444*
Michigan State University. Asian Studies Center. Occasional Papers: South Asian Series (US ISSN 0076-8138) *444*
Michigan State University. Center for International Programs. International Report (US ISSN 0047-7141) *911*
Michigan State University. Center for Rural Manpower & Public Affairs. Report (US) *29, 209*
Michigan State University. Cooperative Extension Service. Annual Report (US) *329*
Michigan State University. Department of Physics. Cyclotron Project (US ISSN 0076-8146) *704*
Michigan State University. Institute for International Studies in Education. Publications (US) *320*
Michigan State University. Institute of Water Research. Annual Report (US) *897*
Michigan State University. Institute of Water Research. Technical Report (US ISSN 0580-9746) *897*

Michigan State University. Latin American Studies Center. Monograph Series (US ISSN 0076-8189) *470*
Michigan State University. Latin American Studies Center. Research Reports (US ISSN 0076-8200) *470*
Michigan State University. Library. Africana: Select Recent Acquisitions (US ISSN 0147-0604) *93*
Michigan State University. Museum Publications. Anthropological Series. (US) *51*
Michigan State University. Museum Publications. Biological Series (US ISSN 0076-8227) *105*
Michigan State University. Museum Publications. Cultural Series (US ISSN 0076-8235) *653*
Michigan State University. Museum Publications. Folk Art Series (US) *76*
Michigan State University. Museum Publications. Paleontological Series (US) *673*
Michigan State University. Public Administration Program. Research Report (US ISSN 0076-8243) *744*
Michigan State University. Rural Manpower Center. R M C Report *see* Michigan State University. Center for Rural Manpower & Public Affairs. Report *29*
Michigan Statistical Abstract (US ISSN 0076-8308) *843*
Michigan Technological University. Library. Library Publication (US ISSN 0076-8324) *533*
Michigan Technological University. Library. Serial Holdings List (US ISSN 0076-8316) *93*
Michigan, Wisconsin TourBook *see* Tourbook: Michigan, Wisconsin *891*
Michigan's Mineral Industries *see* Mineral Industry of Michigan Annual Statistical Summary *644*
Michigan's Oil and Gas Fields: Annual Statistical Summary (US ISSN 0085-3429) *680*
Mickle Street Review (US) *580*
Micro-Bibliotheca Anthropos (SZ) *51*
Micro-DelCon Delaware Bay Microcomputer Conference. Proceedings (US) *273*
Micro Proceedings *see* A C M Annual Workshop on Microprogramming. Conference Record *270*
Microbiologia Espanola (SP ISSN 0026-2595) *124*
Microbiology (Washington) (US ISSN 0098-1540) *124*
Microbiology Series (US) *124*
Microform Market Place (US ISSN 0362-0999) *533*
Microform Review (US ISSN 0002-6530) *533, 759*
Microforms in Print. Supplement (US ISSN 0164-0739) *93*
Microforms International Marketing Corporation Microforms Annual *see* M I M C Microforms Annual *160*
Micrographics Equipment Review (US ISSN 0362-1006) *533*
Microlist *see* Microforms in Print. Supplement *93*
Micropaleontology Special Publications (US ISSN 0160-2071) *673*
Micropublishers' Trade List Annual (US ISSN 0361-2635) *93*
Microscopica Acta. Supplementa (GW ISSN 0342-958X) *124*
Microstructural Science (US ISSN 0361-1213) *629*
Microtables Imports-Exports of O E C D Countries (FR) *197*
Microwave Power Symposium. Proceedings (US) *356*
Microwaves Product Data Directory (US) *356*
Mid-America Linguistics Conference. Papers (US) *547*
Mid-Atlantic-Delaware, District of Columbia, Maryland, Virginia, West Virginia TourBook *see* Tourbook: Mid-Atlantic *891*
Mid-Atlantic Industrial Waste Conference Proceedings (US ISSN 0544-0327) *387*

Mid-Hudson Language Studies (US) *568*
MidAmerica (East Lansing) (US ISSN 0190-2911) *557, 568*
Middle Ages (US) *457*
Middle Ages Studies in Culture *see* Sredniowiecze.Studia o Kulturze *573*
Middle East and North Africa (UK ISSN 0076-8502) *424, 475*
Middle East Annual Review *see* Middle East Review *187*
Middle East Contemporary Survey (US ISSN 0163-5476) *475*
Middle East Institute Newsletter (US) *712*
Middle East Living Costs (UK ISSN 0140-7953) *197*
Middle East Observer Bulletin *see* M E O Bulletin *187*
Middle East Record (IS ISSN 0076-8529) *475*
Middle East Review (UK ISSN 0305-3210) *187*
Middle East Series (US) *475*
Middle East Trader & Company Directory (JA) *240*
Middle East Yearbook (UK) *146, 712*
Middle Eastern Monographs (US ISSN 0076-8537) *444*
Middle Schools Statistics in Punjab (PK) *320*
Middle States Council for the Social Studies. Journal (US) *799*
Middle States Council for the Social Studies. Proceedings *see* Middle States Council for the Social Studies. Journal *799*
Middletown Historical Society. Newsletter (US) *470*
Mideast Business Guide (US) *224*
Mideastern Campbook (US) *830, 889*
Mideastern Camping *see* Mideastern Campbook *889*
Midia (BL) *5*
Midland History (UK ISSN 0047-729X) *457*
Midland Macromolecular Monographs (US) *697*
Midwest Auto Racing Guide *see* National Speedway Directory *821*
Midwest Conference on Graduate Study and Research. Proceedings *see* Midwestern Association of Graduate Schools. Proceedings of the Annual Meeting *338*
Midwest History of Education Society. Journal (US ISSN 0092-2986) *320*
Midwest Media (US) *265*
Midwest Monographs. Series 1 (Drama) (US ISSN 0076-8596) *568*
Midwest Monographs. Series 2 (Poetry) (US ISSN 0076-860X) *580*
Midwest Monographs. Series 3 (Graphic Works) (US ISSN 0076-8618) *568*
Midwest Monographs. Series 4 (Translation) (US ISSN 0076-8626) *568, 580*
Midwest Monographs. Series 5 (Culture and Criticism) (US ISSN 0076-8634) *568*
Midwest Research Institute Quarterly *see* M R I Quarterly *785*
Midwest Studies in Philosophy (US ISSN 0363-6550) *689*
Midwest Symposium on Circuit Theory. Proceedings *see* Midwest Symposium on Circuits and Systems. Proceedings *356*
Midwest Symposium on Circuits and Systems. Proceedings (US) *356*
Midwestern Annual *see* MidAmerica (East Lansing) *568*
Midwestern Association of Graduate Schools. Proceedings of the Annual Meeting (US) *338*
Midwestern Miscellany (US) *568*
Mie-Ken Kogai Senta Nempo *see* Mie Prefecture. Environmental Science Institute. Annual Report *387*
Mie-kenritsu Daigaku Suisan Gakubu Kiyo *see* Mie Prefectural University. Faculty of Fisheries. Bulletin *398*
Mie Prefectural University. Faculty of Fisheries. Bulletin/Mie-kenritsu Daigaku Suisan Gakubu Kiyo (JA ISSN 0539-998X) *398*

Mie Prefecture. Environmental Science Institute. Annual Report/Mie-Ken Kogai Senta Nempo (JA) *387*
Mieterechtliche Entscheidungen (AU) *515*
MietSlg *see* Mieterechtliche Entscheidungen *515*
Migration Institute. Migration Studies (FI) *728*
Migration Today (SZ ISSN 0544-1188) *728*
Mikrobielle Umwelt und Antimikrobielle Massnahmen (GE) *598*
Mikrochimica Acta. Supplement (US ISSN 0076-8642) *249*
Mikrofauna des Meeresbodens (GW ISSN 0342-3247) *105*
Milepost: All-the-North Travel Guide (US ISSN 0361-1361) *889*
Miles International Symposium (US) *119*
Milestones of History (US) *434*
Milford Series (US ISSN 0163-2469) *568*
Militaerhistorisk Tidskrift (SW) *457, 639*
Militaerpsykologiske Meddelelser (NO ISSN 0026-3842) *639*
Militant Pamphlets (UK) *712*
Military Balance (UK ISSN 0459-7222) *639*
Military Communications (SZ) *639*
Military Intelligence Critical Attributes (UK) *639*
Military Journal (US ISSN 0160-0311) *639*
Military Museum, Belgrade. Bulletin *see* Vojni Muzej, Belgrade. Vesnik *640*
Military Year Book (II ISSN 0076-8782) *639*
Miljoe-Projekter (DK ISSN 0105-3094) *387*
Milk Facts (US) *41*
Milk Quarterly (US) *580*
Mill (US) *568*
Mill Report (US) *856*
Milla Wa-Milla (AT ISSN 0076-8790) *766*
Millesime (FR ISSN 0076-8812) *216*
Milling and Grain Directory *see* Milling Directory/Buyers Guide *240*
Milling Directory/Buyers Guide (US) *42, 240*
Milton Society of America. Proceedings(US ISSN 0540-0961) *580*
Milton Studies (US ISSN 0076-8820) *568*
Milu; Wissenschaftliche und Kulturelle Mitteilungen aus dem Tierpark Berlin(GE ISSN 0076-8839) *129*
Mimesis (BL) *568*
MIMI *see* International Symposium on Mini and Microcomputers. Proceedings *272*
Minas Gerais, Brazil. Departamento de Estradas de Rodagem. Servico de Transito. Estatistica de Trafego (BL) *843*
Mindolo News Letter (ZA ISSN 0076-8901) *766*
Mine and Quarry Mechanisation (AT ISSN 0085-3453) *644*
Mineral Industries Newsletter (US ISSN 0026-4547) *296, 629*
Mineral Industry of Michigan Annual Statistical Summary: (US ISSN 0085-3445) *644*
Mineraloelwirtschafts Verband e.V. Jahresbericht *see* M W V /A E V Jahresbericht *253*
Mineralogie und Petrographie in Einzel Darstellungen *see* Minerals and Rocks *296*
Minerals and Rocks (US) *296, 644*
Minerals Transportation *see* International Symposium on Transport and Handling of Minerals. Minerals Transportation; Proceedings *862*
Minerva; Internationales Verzeichnis Wissenschaftlicher Institutionen (GW) *492*
Mines au Canada-Renseignements et Statistiques *see* Mining in Canada - Facts & Figures *644*
Mines Directory (US) *644*

Mines Safety and Health Commission. Report/Organe Permanent pour la Securite dans les Mines e Houille. Rapport (EI ISSN 0588-702X) 495, 644
Mini-Auto International (US) 476
Mini-Images (US) 6, 650
Miniatura e Arti Minori in Campania (IT) 76
Miniature and Subminiature Relay D.A.T.A. Book see Relay D.A.T.A.Book 358
Miniatures Catalog (US) 476
Mining and Allied Machinery Corporation. Annual Report (II) 583, 644
Mining & Construction Methods and Equipment (AT) 644
Mining Annual Review (UK ISSN 0076-8995) 644
Mining in Canada - Facts & Figures (CN ISSN 0316-2281) 644
Mining in Rhodesia see Mining in Zimbabwe 644
Mining in Zimbabwe (RH) 644
Mining Industry & Trade Annual (II) 644
Mining Industry & Trade Journal see Mining Industry & Trade Annual 644
Mining Industry of Idaho. Annual Report (US) 645
Mining-What Mining Means to Canada (CN ISSN 0317-9508) 645
Mining Year Book see Financial Times Mining International Year Book 643
Mining Yearbook (US) 645
Mining Yearbook of Japan/Honpo Kogyo No Susei (JA) 645
Ministerial Sisterhood Unitarian Universalist Newsletter see M S U U Newsletter 772
Ministerio Publico see M P 515
Minji Sosho Zasshi see Journal of Civil Procedure 514
Minkus New American Stamp Catalog (US ISSN 0076-9061) 479
Minkus New World Wide Stamp Catalog (US ISSN 0076-907X) 479
Minneapolis Institute of Arts. Annual Report (US ISSN 0076-9096) 76
Minneapolis Institute of Arts. Bulletin (US ISSN 0076-910X) 76
Minnesota. Crime Control Planning Board. Comprehensive Plan (US) 282
Minnesota. Department. of Corrections. Characteristics on Institutional Populations (US) 282
Minnesota. Department of Corrections. Research, Information and Data Systems Unit. Characteristics of Populations Under Supervision of the Institutions and Field Services. see Minnesota. Department. of Corrections. Characteristics on Institutional Populations 1 282
Minnesota. Department of Economic Security. Annual Report (US) 209
Minnesota. Department of Education. Biennial Report (US ISSN 0093-870X) 911
Minnesota. Department of Employment Services. Annual Report see Minnesota. Department of Economic Security. Annual Report 209
Minnesota. Department of Human Rights. Biennial Report (US ISSN 0076-9118) 718
Minnesota. Department of Natural Resources. Biennial Report (US ISSN 0090-8177) 277
Minnesota. Department of Natural Resources. Proposed Program Budget, Detailed Estimates (US) 277
Minnesota. Department of Revenue. Biennial Report (US ISSN 0095-0645) 230
Minnesota. Department of Revenue. Petroleum Division. Annual Report (US ISSN 0095-3024) 680
Minnesota. Department of Taxation. Biennial Report see Minnesota. Department of Revenue. Biennial Report 230
Minnesota. Division of Fish and Wildlife, Environment Section. Special Publication (US ISSN 0363-5341) 277

Minnesota. Division of Fish & Wildlife. Technical Bulletin (US) 277
Minnesota. Division of Game and Fish. Technical Bulletin see Minnesota. Division of Fish & Wildlife. Technical Bulletin 277
Minnesota. Geological Survey. Bulletin (US ISSN 0076-9169) 911
Minnesota. Geological Survey. Information Circulars (US ISSN 0544-3105) 296
Minnesota. Geological Survey. Report of Investigations (US ISSN 0076-9177) 296
Minnesota. Governor. Annual Report on the Quality of the Environment (US ISSN 0094-1697) 387
Minnesota. Governor's Commission on Crime Prevention and Control. Comprehensive Plan see Minnesota. Crime Control Planning Board. Comprehensive Plan 282
Minnesota. Office of Ombudsman for Corrections. Annual Report (US ISSN 0094-1409) 282
Minnesota. State Board of Health. Biennial Report (US ISSN 0090-6425) 752
Minnesota. State Planning Agency. Environmental Planning Division. Land Use Planning Report (US) 277
Minnesota Alcohol Programs for Highway Safety (US ISSN 0093-2558) 911
Minnesota Dairy Plants (US) 41
Minnesota Drama Editions (US ISSN 0076-9142) 568, 859
Minnesota Export Survey Summary (US) 197
Minnesota Exporter's Assistance Guide (US) 197
Minnesota Fish and Game Investigations. Fish Series see Minnesota Fisheries Investigations 398
Minnesota Fisheries Investigations (US ISSN 0076-9150) 398
Minnesota Health Statistics (US ISSN 0094-5641) 756
Minnesota Medical Assistance Biennial Report see People. Biennial Report 808
Minnesota Monographs in the Humanities (US ISSN 0076-9215) 492
Minnesota New & Expanding Industry (US) 224
Minnesota Periodicals on Microfilm (US) 93
Minnesota Private College Fund. Report (US ISSN 0076-9223) 338
Minnesota Profile (US) 187
Minnesota State Industrial Directory (US ISSN 0195-7112) 240
Minnesota Statutes (US ISSN 0191-1562) 515
Minnesota Statutes. Supplement (US ISSN 0094-1727) 515
Minnesota Studies in the Philosophy of Science (US ISSN 0076-9258) 689, 785
Minnesota Symposia on Child Psychology (US ISSN 0076-9266) 736
Minnesota's Role in International Trade(US) 197
Minor Metals Survey (UK ISSN 0140-8399) 629
Minority/Ethnic Media Guide (US) 6, 394
Minority Group Media Guide see Minority/Ethnic Media Guide 394
Minority Information Trade Annual (US) 394
Minority Organizations: a National Directory (US) 392
Minority Rights Group. Reports (UK ISSN 0305-6252) 718, 815
Minority Students Opportunities in United States Medical Schools (US ISSN 0085-3488) 338, 598
Minority Supplies Report & Directory (US) 240
Minus One (UK ISSN 0026-5721) 712
Mirabel Airport Directory (CN) 868
Mirador (AG) 146
Mirror and Probe (CE) 610

Mirror Class Association of Australia. Yearbook (AT) 827
Mirror Northwest (US) 568
Mirrored Spectrum (CN) 785, 852
Miscelanea de Textos Medievales (SP) 457
Miscellanea Byzantina Monacensia (GW ISSN 0076-9347) 457, 568
Miscellanea Mediaevalia (GW ISSN 0076-9355) 661
Miscellanea Musicologica (CS ISSN 0544-4136) 661
Miscellanea Musicologica (AT ISSN 0076-9355) 661
Miscellanea Zoologica (SP) 129
Miscellaneous Publications - University of Kansas, Museum of Natural History see University of Kansas. Museum of Natural History. Miscellaneous Publications 793
Miscellaneous Report - State of Ohio, Department of Natural Resources, Division of Geological Survey see Ohio. Division of Geological Survey. Miscellaneous Report 298
Mise-en-Scene (US) 911
Mision Arqueologica Espanola en Nubia. Memorias (SP ISSN 0076-9371) 63
Mision Cientifica Espanola en Hispanoamerica. Memorias (SP) 799
Mission Handbook: North American Protestant Ministries Overseas (US ISSN 0093-8130) 772
Mission Studies and Documents see Missionswissenschaftliche Abhandlungen und Texte 766
Mission to Lepers, London. Annual Report see Leprosy Mission, London. Annual Report 766
Missions Digest and Year Book see Evangelical Baptist Churches in Canada. Fellowship Yearbook 772
Missions to Seamen Annual Report (UK) 766
Missions to Seamen Handbook see Missions to Seamen Annual Report 766
Missionswissenschaftliche Abhandlungen und Texte/Etudes et Documents Missionnaires/Mission Studies and Documents (GW ISSN 0076-941X) 766
Missionswissenschaftliche Forschungen (GW ISSN 0076-9428) 766
Mississippi. Board of Trustees of State Institutions of Higher Learning. Annual Report (US) 263
Mississippi. State Board of Architecture. Annual Report (US) 69
Mississippi. State Game and Fish Commission. Annual Report to the Regular Session of the Mississippi Legislature (US ISSN 0098-7840) 277, 398
Mississippi Congress of Parents and Teachers. Proceedings (US ISSN 0076-9460) 344
Mississippi Congress of Parents and Teachers. Yearbook (US ISSN 0076-9479) 344
Mississippi Educational Directory see Educational Directory of Mississippi Schools 331
Mississippi Geographer (US) 424
Mississippi Manufacturing Atlas (US) 911
Mississippi Marine Resources Council. Annual Report (US ISSN 0095-6783) 311
Mississippi State Industrial Directory (US ISSN 0190-1346) 240
Mississippi State University. Christian Student Center. Annual Lectureship (US ISSN 0076-9517) 766
Mississippi State University. College of Arts and Sciences. Department of Anthropology. Occasional Papers in Anthropology (US) 51
Mississippi State University. College of Arts and Sciences. Department of Sociology and Anthropology. Sociology-Anthropology Reports see Mississippi State University. College of Arts and Sciences. Department of Anthropology. Occasional Papers in Anthropology 51

Mississippi State University. Forest Products Utilization Laboratory. Information Series (US ISSN 0076-9509) 413
Mississippi State University. Forest Products Utilization Laboratory. Research Report (US ISSN 0026-640X) 413
Mississippi State University Abstracts of Theses see Mississippi State University Abstracts of Theses and Dissertations 327
Mississippi State University Abstracts of Theses and Dissertations (US ISSN 0540-3847) 3, 327
Mississippi Valley Collection Bulletin see M V C Bulletin 470
Mississippi Water Resources Conference. Proceedings (US ISSN 0076-9533) 897
Missouri. Department of Conservation. Annual Report (US ISSN 0085-3496) 277
Missouri. Department of Mental Health. Annual Report (US) 753
Missouri. Department of Revenue. Annual Combined Financial Report (US) 230
Missouri. Division of Geological Survey and Water Resources. Engineering Geology Series (US ISSN 0076-9606) 376
Missouri. Division of Geological Survey and Water Resources. Water Resources Report (US ISSN 0076-9614) 308, 897
Missouri. Division of Highway Safety. Highway Safety Plan (US) 753, 875
Missouri. Division of Insurance. Annual Report and Statistical Data (US) 500
Missouri. Division of Mental Health. Annual Report see Missouri. Department of Mental Health. Annual Report 753
Missouri. Division of Youth Services. Annual Report (US) 807
Missouri. State Division of Youth Services. Annual Report see Missouri. Division of Youth Services. Annual Report 807
Missouri Archaeological Society. Memoir Series (US ISSN 0076-9541) 63
Missouri Archaeological Society. Research Series (US ISSN 0544-5094) 63
Missouri Archaeologist (US ISSN 0076-9576) 63
Missouri Economic Indicators (US) 187
Missouri Handbook Series (US ISSN 0076-9630) 470
Missouri Journal of Research in Music Education (US ISSN 0085-350X) 349, 661
Missouri Literary Frontiers Series (US ISSN 0076-9649) 568
Missouri Political Science Association. Proceedings of the Annual Meeting (US) 712
Missouri River Basin Commission. Annual Report (US ISSN 0092-7945) 897
Missouri Speech Journal (US) 265, 859
Missouri State Industrial Directory (US) 240
Missouri Vital Statistics (US ISSN 0098-1974) 756
Missouri's Annual Highway Safety Program see Missouri. Division of Highway Safety. Highway Safety Plan 875
Missouri's New and Expanding Industries (US ISSN 0540-4193) 224
Mitchell Business Review (AT ISSN 0311-2780) 146
Mitre see New Mitre 557
Mitsubishi Technical Bulletin (JA ISSN 0540-469X) 852
Mitsui News (AT ISSN 0311-0273) 197
Mitteilungen aus dem Max-Planck-Institut fuer Stroemungsforschung (GW ISSN 0374-1257) 701

Mitteilungen aus dem Max-Planck-Institut fuer Stroenmungsforschung und der Aerodynamischen Versuchsanstalt *see* Mitteilungen aus dem Max-Planck-Institut fuer Stroemungsforschung *701*
Mitteldeutsche Vorgeschichte. Jahresschrift (GE ISSN 0075-2932) *457*
Mittellateinische Studien und Texte (NE ISSN 0076-9754) *457*
Mittellateinisches Jahrbuch (GW ISSN 0076-9762) *547*
Mitzion Tetzeh Torah. M.T.T. (IS ISSN 0541-5632) *690, 770*
Miyazaki Daigaku Kogakubu Kiyo *see* Miyazaki University. Faculty of Engineering. Memoirs *369*
Miyazaki University. Faculty of Engineering. Memoirs/Miyazaki Daigaku Kogakubu Kiyo (JA ISSN 0540-4924) *369*
Mobile Air Conditioning *see* International Buyer's Guide of Mobile Air Conditioning *430*
Mobile Radio Handbook (US) *268*
Mobili per Ufficio (IT) *219*
Model Railway Constructor Annual (UK) *476, 873*
Modeling and Simulation (US) *273*
Modelle fuer den Religionsunterricht (GW) *766*
Models Mart Directory of Modeling Schools and Agencies USA and Canada (US) *262*
Modern Accounting and Auditing Checklists (Supplement) (US) *168*
Modern America (US ISSN 0076-9894) *470*
Modern Analytic and Computational Methods in Science and Mathematics(US ISSN 0076-9908) *587*
Modern Approaches to the Diagnosis and Instruction of Multi-Handicapped Children (NE ISSN 0076-9916) *346*
Modern Artists (US) *76*
Modern Aspects of Electrochemistry (US ISSN 0076-9924) *251*
Modern Biology Series (US) *105*
Modern Brewery Age Blue Book (US ISSN 0076-9932) *86*
Modern China Studies. International Bulletin (US ISSN 0305-7429) *670*
Modern Comparative Politics Series (US) *712*
Modern Concepts in Medical Physiology (US) *598*
Modern Concepts of Allergy (US) *911*
Modern Concepts of Cardiology (US) *911*
Modern Concepts of Dermatology (US) *911*
Modern Concepts of Education (US) *911*
Modern Concepts of Industrial Medicine (US) *911*
Modern Concepts of Medical Virology, Oncology and Cytology (US ISSN 0544-6511) *911*
Modern Concepts of Neurology (US) *911*
Modern Concepts of Orthopedic Surgery (US) *911*
Modern Concepts of Pathology (US) *911*
Modern Concepts of Philosophy (US) *911*
Modern Concepts of Pulmonary Disease (US) *911*
Modern Concepts of Radiology, Nuclear Medicine and Ultrasound (US) *911*
Modern Concepts of Surgery (US) *911*
Modern Construction Forms (Supplement) (US) *485*
Modern Developments in Powder Metallurgy *see* International Powder Metallurgy Conference. Proceedings-Modern Developments in Powder Metallurgy *628*
Modern Drug Encyclopedia and Therapeutic Index (US ISSN 0076-9959) *685*
Modern English Journal/Eigo Kyoiku Jaanaru (JA) *349, 547*
Modern Film Scripts (US) *650*

Modern Filologiai Fuzetek (HU ISSN 0076-9967) *547*
Modern German Studies (GW) *690*
Modern Health Care Forms (Supplement) (US) *753*
Modern Humanities Research Association. Monograph *see* Modern Humanities Research Association. Publications *492*
Modern Humanities Research Association. Publications (UK) *492*
Modern Inshore Fishing (UK) *830*
Modern Jazz (IT) *661*
Modern Language Association of America Directory of Periodicals *see* M L A Directory of Periodicals *578*
Modern Language Association of America International Bibliography of Books and Articles on the Modern Languages and Literatures *see* M L A International Bibliography of Books and Articles on the Modern Languages and Literatures *92*
Modern Language Teachers' Association of New South Wales News *see* M. L. T. A. News *547*
Modern Locomotive Handbook (US) *873*
Modern Machine Shop N C Guidebook and Directory *see* Modern Machine Shop NC/CAM Guidebook *382*
Modern Machine Shop NC/CAM Guidebook (US) *382*
Modern Materials. Advances in Development and Applications (US ISSN 0077-0000) *380*
Modern Middle East Series (US ISSN 0077-0027) *444, 670*
Modern Nursing Home Directory of Nursing Homes in the United States, U.S. Possessions and Canada (US) *481, 807*
Modern Orthodox Saints (US) *776*
Modern Packaging Encyclopedia (US ISSN 0077-0035) *672*
Modern Personnel Forms (Supplement) (US) *220*
Modern Perspectives in Biology Series (US) *105*
Modern Perspectives in Psychiatry (US ISSN 0077-0051) *620*
Modern Pharmacology *see* Modern Pharmacology-Toxicology *685*
Modern Pharmacology-Toxicology (US ISSN 0098-6925) *685*
Modern Photography Annual (US ISSN 0580-8162) *693*
Modern Photography's Guide to the World's Best Cameras (US ISSN 0197-5986) *693*
Modern Photography's Photo Buying Guide (US) *693*
Modern Physics in Chemistry (UK) *255*
Modern Plastics Encyclopedia (US ISSN 0085-3518) *707*
Modern Plywood Techniques (US ISSN 0361-7238) *141*
Modern Problems in Ophthalmology *see* Developments in Ophthalmology *615*
Modern Problems in Paediatrics (SZ ISSN 0077-0086) *617*
Modern Problems of Pharmacopsychiatry (SZ ISSN 0077-0094) *620, 685*
Modern Publicity (UK ISSN 0077-0108) *6*
Modern Quaternary Research in Southeast Asia (NE) *673*
Modern Recording's Buyer's Guide (US) *661, 818*
Modern Sawmill Techniques (US ISSN 0094-9329) *413*
Modern Scholarship on European History (US) *457*
Modern Styles and How-To's (US) *85*
Modern Surgical Monographs (US ISSN 0540-5556) *624*
Modern Teaching (AT ISSN 0085-3526) *349*
Modern Technics in Surgery. Abdominal Surgery (US ISSN 0196-1918) *624*
Modern Technics in Surgery. Cardiac/Thoracic Surgery (US ISSN 0163-7029) *624*

Modern Technics in Surgery. Head and Neck Surgery (US ISSN 0271-8219) *624*
Modern Technics in Surgery. Neurosurgery (US ISSN 0163-7037) *624*
Modern Technics in Surgery. Urologic Surgery (US) *625, 625*
Modern Tire Dealer Products Catalog (US) *777, 863*
Modern Trends in Orthopaedics (UK ISSN 0077-0159) *616*
Modern Wood *see* Treated Wood Perspectives *413*
Modernist Studies: Literature and Culture, 1920-1940 (CN ISSN 0316-5973) *568*
Modern's How-to Book *see* Modern Styles and How-To's *85*
Modern's Market Guide (US ISSN 0544-7178) *85*
Modszertani Kiadvanyok/Methods of Information and Documentation (HU ISSN 0324-7341) *533, 852*
Modulator Symposium (Record) *see* Pulsed Power Modulator Conference (Record) *358*
Moebel-Industrie und Ihre Helfer (GW ISSN 0077-0205) *503*
Mokuzai Kenkyu *see* Wood Research *413*
Molecular Biology, Biochemistry and Biophysics (US ISSN 0077-0221) *111, 112, 119*
Molecular Biology; Proceedings of the International Conference (US ISSN 0077-023X) *119*
Molecular Spectroscopy (UK ISSN 0305-9782) *249*
Molecular Structure by Diffraction Methods (UK ISSN 0305-9790) *249*
Molekulyarnaya Fizika i Biofizika Vodnykh Sistem (UR) *111, 112*
Molysulfide Newsletter (US) *629*
Mon-Khmer Studies (US ISSN 0147-5207) *547*
Monarchist Book Review (UK ISSN 0077-0280) *438*
Monarchist Press Association. Historical Series (UK ISSN 0077-0299) *457*
Monash Papers on Southeast Asia (AT) *444, 712*
Monash University. Higher Education Advisory and Research Unit. Notes on Higher Education (AT ISSN 0310-5695) *349*
Monash University. Publications in Geography (AT) *424*
Monatsblaetter fuer Freiheitliche Wirtschaftspolitik (GW ISSN 0026-9239) *712*
Monatshefte fuer die Unterrichtspraxis - die Scholle (GW) *349*
Monde des Loisirs (CN ISSN 0702-858X) *820*
Money and Ships (UK) *879*
Money Business: Grants and Awards for Creative Artists (US ISSN 0161-5866) *76*
Money Income (in Year) of Families and Persons in the United States *see* Current Population Reports: Consumer Income. Money Income (in Year) of Families and Persons in the United States *213*
Money Income (in Year) of Families, Unrelated Individuals and Persons in the United States *see* Current Population Reports: Consumer Income. Money Income (in Year) of Families and Persons in the United States *213*
Money Masters Annual (US) *174*
Moneywise Guide to North America (UK) *889*
Mongol Nyelvemlektar *see* Monumenta Linguae Mongolicae Collecta *670*
Mongolia Report (US) *187, 712*
Mongolia Society. Occasional Papers (US ISSN 0077-0396) *444*
Mongolia Society Bulletin *see* Mongolian Studies *670*
Mongolia Society Newsletter *see* Mongolian Studies *670*
Mongolian Studies (US) *670*

Mongrafie della Scuola Archeologica di Atene e delle Missioni Italiane in Oriente (IT ISSN 0067-009X) *63*
Monitor (US ISSN 0077-040X) *224*
Monitore Zoologico Italiano. Monografie/Italian Journal of Zoology. Monographs (IT ISSN 0391-1632) *129*
Monitore Zoologico Italiano. Supplemento/Italian Journal of Zoology. Supplement (IT ISSN 0374-9444) *129*
Monitoring the Future (US ISSN 0190-9185) *320*
Monmouth Reviews; Journal of the Literary Arts (US ISSN 0085-3534) *568*
La Monnaie en (Year) (FR) *175*
Monnaies, Prix, Conjoncture (FR ISSN 0077-0434) *175, 434*
Monografias de Filosofia Juridica y Social/Monographs of Social and Legal Philosophy (SP ISSN 0077-0442) *515*
Monografias de Matematica (BL) *587*
Monografias de Poblacion y Desarrollo (BO) *815*
Monografias de Psicologia, Normal y Patologica (SP ISSN 0077-0469) *736*
Monografias de Recursos Humanos (BO) *815*
Monografias de Sociologia Familiar (BO) *815*
Monografias sobre Numismatica Antigua (SP) *477*
Monografias Urbanas (BO) *485*
Monografie Biochemiczne (PL ISSN 0077-0485) *111*
Monografie di Archeologia Libica (IT ISSN 0077-0493) *63*
Monografie Fauny Polski (PL) *129*
Monografie Matematyczne (PL ISSN 0077-0507) *587*
Monografie Psychologiczne (PL ISSN 0077-0515) *736*
Monografie Slaskie Ossolineum (PL ISSN 0077-0523) *457*
Monografie Slawistyczne (PL ISSN 0077-0531) *457, 568*
Monografie z Dziejow Nauki i Techniki(PL ISSN 0077-054X) *786, 852*
Monografie z Dziejow Oswiaty (PL ISSN 0077-0558) *349*
Monografieen over Kleipijpen (NE) *861*
Monografii Matematice (RM) *587*
Monograph Series in World Affairs (US ISSN 0077-0582) *722*
Monograph Series on Malaysian Economic Affairs (MY) *146*
Monograph Series on Metallurgy in Nuclear Technology (US) *369, 380, 629*
Monograph Series on Schizophrenia (US ISSN 0077-0620) *620*
Monographiae Biologicae (NE ISSN 0077-0639) *105*
Monographiae Biologicae Canarienses/Biological Monographs of the Canary Islands (SP ISSN 0077-0647) *105*
Monographiae Botanicae (PL ISSN 0077-0655) *116*
Monographie der Flaumeichen-Buschwaelder (HU ISSN 0077-0663) *116*
Monographien aus dem Gesamtgebiete der Psychiatrie - Psychiatry Series (US ISSN 0077-0671) *620*
Monographien zur Angewandten Entomologie (GW ISSN 0077-0698) *121*
Monographien zur Philosophischen Forschung (GW) *690*
Monographien zur Rheinisch-Westfaelischen Kunst der Gegenwart (GW ISSN 0463-1935) *76*
Monographien zur Terrestrischen, Solaren und Kosmischen Physik (GE) *697*
Monographies de l'Industrie et du Commerce en France (FR ISSN 0077-0701) *182, 224*
Monographies Francaises de Psychologie (FR ISSN 0077-071X) *736*
Monographies Juridiques (CN ISSN 0077-0728) *515*

Monographies Reine Elisabeth (BE) *63*
Monographs and Studies in Mathematics (UK) *587*
Monographs and Textbooks in Material Science (US ISSN 0077-0744) *380*
Monographs and Texts in the Behavioral Sciences (US ISSN 0077-0752) *799*
Monographs for Students of Medicine (US) *598*
Monographs in Allergy (SZ ISSN 0077-0760) *604*
Monographs in Anaesthesiology (NE ISSN 0303-254X) *604*
Monographs in Asian Law (NE) *515*
Monographs in Basic Neurology *see* Monographs in Neural Sciences *620*
Monographs in Chemistry in Non-Aqueous Ionizing Solvents (US ISSN 0077-0795) *255*
Monographs in Clinical Cytology (SZ ISSN 0077-0809) *120, 598*
Monographs in Computer Science and Computer Applications (BL ISSN 0077-0817) *273*
Monographs in Developmental Biology (SZ ISSN 0077-0825) *111*
Monographs in Developmental Pediatrics (US ISSN 0162-6906) *617*
Monographs in Electrical and Electronic Engineering (US) *356*
Monographs in Electroanalytical Chemistry and Electrochemistry (US ISSN 0077-0833) *249, 251*
Monographs in Fetal Physiology (NE) *105*
Monographs in Geology and Paleontology (US ISSN 0077-085X) *296, 674*
Monographs in Geoscience (US) *289*
Monographs in Hormone Research *see* Frontiers of Hormone Research *611*
Monographs in Human Genetics (SZ ISSN 0077-0876) *122*
Monographs in Inorganic Chemistry (US) *251*
Monographs in Lipid Research (US ISSN 0094-8950) *111*
Monographs in Low Temperature Physics (US) *700*
Monographs in Macromolecular Chemistry (US ISSN 0077-0884) *253*
Monographs in Modern Concepts of Philosophy (US ISSN 0085-3542) *911*
Monographs in Modern Neurobiology (US) *105, 620*
Monographs in Neural Sciences (SZ ISSN 0300-5186) *620*
Monographs in Oral Science (SZ ISSN 0077-0892) *610*
Monographs in Organic Functional Group Analysis *see* Analysis of Organic Materials: an International Series of Monographs *252*
Monographs in Paediatrics (SZ ISSN 0077-0914) *617*
Monographs in Pathology (US ISSN 0077-0922) *598*
Monographs in Pharmacology and Physiology (US ISSN 0364-2569) *126, 685*
Monographs in Philosophy and Religious History (US ISSN 0068-4333) *690*
Monographs in Physical Measurement (UK) *369, 697*
Monographs in Population Biology (US ISSN 0077-0930) *728*
Monographs in Psychology: an International Series (US) *737*
Monographs in Quantitative Biophysics (US) *112*
Monographs in Semiconductor Physics (US ISSN 0544-8417) *356*
Monographs in the Economics of Development (PK ISSN 0544-8433) *200*
Monographs in Virology (SZ ISSN 0077-0922) *124*
Monographs of Marine Mollusca (US ISSN 0162-8321) *129*
Monographs of Social and Legal Philosophy *see* Monografias de Filosofia Juridica y Social *515*

Monographs on American Art (US ISSN 0544-845X) *76*
Monographs on Astronomical Subjects (US) *83*
Monographs on Atherosclerosis (SZ ISSN 0077-099X) *607*
Monographs on Drugs (SZ ISSN 0301-3057) *911*
Monographs on Education (UN ISSN 0077-1007) *320*
Monographs on Endocrinology (US ISSN 0077-1015) *611*
Monographs on Immunology (US ISSN 0077-1023) *124*
Monographs on Industrial Hygiene (US) *495*
Monographs on Industrial Property and Copyright Law (NE) *515, 677*
Monographs on Linguistic Analysis (NE ISSN 0077-1031) *547*
Monographs on Music, Dance and Theater in Asia (US) *285, 661, 859*
Monographs on Numerical Analysis (US) *587*
Monographs on Oceanographic Methodology (UN ISSN 0077-104X) *311*
Monographs on Physical Biochemistry (US) *111, 255*
Monographs on Plastic Surgery (US) *625*
Monographs on Plastics (US) *707*
Monographs on Rockets and Missiles (US) *9*
Monographs on Soil Survey (US) *296*
Monographs on Standardization of Cardioangiological Methods (SZ ISSN 0302-2293) *607*
Monographs on the Ancient Near East (US) *434*
Monographs on the Physics and Chemistry of Materials (US) *247, 697*
Monographs on Theoretical and Applied Genetics (US) *122*
Montalban (VE) *51, 492*
Montana. Bureau of Mines and Geology. Bulletin (US ISSN 0077-1090) *296, 645*
Montana. Bureau of Mines and Geology. Directory of Mining Enterprises (US ISSN 0077-1104) *645*
Montana. Bureau of Mines and Geology. Ground Water Reports *see* Montana. Bureau of Mines and Geology. Bulletin *296*
Montana. Bureau of Mines and Geology. Memoir (US ISSN 0077-1120) *297, 645*
Montana. Bureau of Mines and Geology. Special Publications (US ISSN 0077-1139) *297, 645*
Montana. Department of Business Regulation. Annual Report (US ISSN 0093-8246) *744*
Montana. Department of Public Instruction. Descriptive Report of Program Activities for Vocational Education (US ISSN 0090-6743) *911*
Montana. Department of Social and Rehabilitation Services. Annual Report (US ISSN 0091-0996) *807*
Montana. Environmental Quality Council. Annual Report (US ISSN 0091-0457) *387*
Montana. Governor's Annual Report (US ISSN 0085-3550) *230, 744*
Montana. Office of the Legislative Auditor. Department of Institutions Reimbursements Program; Report on Audit (US ISSN 0090-4325) *744*
Montana. Office of the Legislative Auditor. State of Montana Board of Investments. Report on Examination of Financial Statements (US ISSN 0090-9912) *204, 744*
Montana. State Department of Health. Annual Statistical Supplement *see* Montana Vital Statistics *756*
Montana. State Department of Public Welfare. Report *see* Montana. Department of Social and Rehabilitation Services. Annual Report *807*

Montana. Water Resources Board. Inventory Series (US ISSN 0077-1201) *897*
Montana. Water Resources Division Progress Report of the Montana State Water Plan (US) *911*
Montana Advisory Council for Vocational Education. Annual Report(US ISSN 0093-6472) *349*
Montana Environmental Indicators *see* Montana. Environmental Quality Council. Annual Report *387*
Montana Journalism Review (US ISSN 0077-1147) *505*
Montana Library Directory, with Statistics of Montana Public Libraries(US ISSN 0094-873X) *533*
Montana Newsletter (US) *533*
Montana State Industrial Directory (US ISSN 0195-7120) *240*
Montana State Plan for Alcohol Abuse and Alcoholism Prevention, Treatment and Rehabilitation (US ISSN 0090-3809) *287*
Montana University Joint Water Resources Research Center. Annual Report (US) *897*
Montana Vital Statistics (US ISSN 0077-1198) *756*
Montana's Water Planning Program Progress Report *see* Montana. Water Resources Division Progress Report of the Montana State Water Plan *911*
Montevideo. Museo de Historia Natural. Anales *see* Museo Nacional de Historia Natural. Anales *786*
Monthly Extract (US) *615, 900*
Montre Suisse. Annuaire/Watch Review. Curriculum (SZ ISSN 0077-1309) *503*
Montreal Port Guide & Directory (CN) *879*
Montserrat. Statistical Office. Statistical Digest (VB) *843*
Monument in Cantos and Essays (US ISSN 0027-0733) *568, 580*
Monumenta Aegyptiaca (BE ISSN 0077-1376) *63*
Monumenta Americana (GW ISSN 0077-1384) *63, 470*
Monumenta Antiquitatis Extra Fines Hungariae Reperta Quae in Museo Artium Hungarico Aliisque Museis et Collectionibus Hungaricis Conservantur (HU ISSN 0077-1392) *63*
Monumenta Archaeologica (Los Angeles) (US ISSN 0363-7565) *63*
Monumenta Artis Romanae (GW ISSN 0077-1406) *63, 76*
Monumenta Chartae Papyraceae Historiam Illustrantia/Collection of Works and Documents Illustrating the History of Paper (NE ISSN 0077-1414) *675*
Monumenta Germaniae Historica. Schriften (GW ISSN 0080-6951) *457*
Monumenta Germaniae Historica. Staatsschriften des Spaeteren Mittelalters (GW ISSN 0340-8035) *457*
Monumenta Historica Budapestinensia (HU ISSN 0077-1430) *63, 457*
Monumenta Historica Ordinis Minorum Capuccinorum (IT ISSN 0077-1449) *775*
Monumenta Historica Societatis Iesu (IT) *775*
Monumenta Iuris Canonici (VC ISSN 0077-1457) *775*
Monumenta Lexicographica Neerlandia. Reek 3: Studies (NE) *547*
Monumenta Linguae Mongolicae Collecta (HU) *670*
Monumenta Literaria Neerlandica (NE) *568*
Monumenta Musicae in Polonia (PL ISSN 0077-1465) *661*
Monumenta Musicae Suecicae (SW ISSN 0077-1473) *661*
Monumenta Paedagogica (GE ISSN 0077-1481) *320*
Monumenta Serica (SZ ISSN 0077-149X) *670*
Monuments de la Catalunya Romanica (SP) *76*

Monuments of Culture. New Discoveries *see* Pamyatniki Kul'tury. Novye Otkrytiya *77*
Monuments of Renaissance Music (US ISSN 0077-1503) *661*
Moody's Bank & Finance Manual (US ISSN 0027-0814) *204*
Moody's Handbook of Corporate Managements *see* Dun and Bradstreet Reference Book of Corporate Managements *214*
Moody's Industrial Manual (US ISSN 0545-0217) *204*
Moody's Investors Fact Sheets (US) *204*
Moody's Municipal & Government Manual (US ISSN 0545-0233) *204*
Moody's O T C Industrial Manual (US) *204*
Moody's Public Utility Manual (US ISSN 0545-0241) *204*
Moody's Transportation Manual (US) *204*
Mool Sarak Ankrey *see* Basic Road Statistics of India *864*
Moonaboola Quill (AT) *568*
Moravske Numismaticke Zpravy (CS ISSN 0077-152X) *477*
Morbilidad (UY) *753*
Morgannwg (UK ISSN 0545-0373) *457*
Morgonbris (SW ISSN 0027-1101) *718, 900*
Morocco. Direction de la Statistique. Comptes de la Nation (MR) *744*
Morocco. Direction de la Statistique. Statistiques Retrospectives (MR) *843*
Morocco. Direction des Mines et de la Geologie. Activite du Secteur Petrolier (MR) *680*
Morris Arboretum Bulletin (US ISSN 0027-1187) *911*
Morskaya Geologiya i Geofizika/Marine Geology and Geophysics (UR ISSN 0076-4477) *311*
Morski Instytut Rybacki, Gdynia. Prace. Seria A: Oceanograficzno - Ichtiologiczna (PL ISSN 0072-0496) *311, 398*
Morski Instytut Rybacki, Gdynia. Prace. Seria B: Technika Rybacka i Technologia Ryb (PL ISSN 0072-050X) *398*
Morski Instytut Rybacki, Gdynia. Prace. Seria C: Ekonomika Rybacka (PL ISSN 0072-0518) *398*
Mortality and Demographic Data (NZ ISSN 0548-9911) *843*
Mortgage Banking: Financial Statements and Operating Ratios (US ISSN 0077-1546) *175*
Mortgage Banking: Loans Closed and Servicing Volume (US) *175*
Mortgage Banking: Survey of Single-Family Loan Operations (Cost Study) (US) *175*
Mortgage Banking: Trends, Financial Statements and Operating Ratios *see* Mortgage Banking: Financial Statements and Operating Ratios *175*
Morton Arboretum Quarterly (US ISSN 0027-125X) *116, 415*
Mort's Guide to Low-Cost Vacations & Lodgings on College Campuses (US ISSN 0095-0386) *483*
Moscow Mathematical Society. Transactions (English edition of: Moskovskoe Matematicheskoe Obshchestvo. Trudy) (US ISSN 0077-1554) *587*
Moskovskii Institut Stali i Splavov. Nauchnye Trudy. (UR) *629*
Moskovskii Universitet. Biblioteka. Rukopisnaya i Pechatnaya Kniga v Fondakh (UR) *93*
Moskovskoe Matematicheskoe Obshchestvo. Trudy (UR) *587*
Mostre e Musei (IT) *76*
Motelfuehrer International (GW) *483*
Moteurs Diesel (FR) *871*
Motocyclo Catalogue (FR ISSN 0077-1570) *820*
Motoneigiste Canadien (CN) *820*
Motor Auto Repair Manual (US) *871*
Motor Carrier Statistical Summary (US) *882*

Motor Cycle and Cycle Trader Year Book (UK ISSN 0306-4867) *826*
Motor Cycle Diary (UK ISSN 0077-1589) 820, *871*
Motor Handbook (US ISSN 0094-1514) *871*
Motor Industry of Great Britain (UK ISSN 0077-1597) *871*
Motor Industry of Japan (JA) *871*
Motor Industry Year Book (NZ) *863*
Motor Manual (UK ISSN 0077-1600) 871, *882*
Motor Parts and Time Guide (US ISSN 0077-1716) *871*
Motor Racing Year. (US ISSN 0090-2144) *820*
Motor Sport Yearbook (US ISSN 0091-8822) *911*
Motor Trader Directory (UK) *240*
Motor Traffic in Sweden (SW ISSN 0077-1619) *871*
Motor Truck & Diesel Repair Manual *see* Motor Truck Repair Manual *871*
Motor Truck Facts *see* M V M A Motor Vehicle Facts and Figures *871*
Motor Truck Repair Manual (US ISSN 0098-3624) *871*
Motor Vehicle Engineering Specifications-Japan (JA) *871*
Motor Vehicle Facts & Figures *see* M V M A Motor Vehicle Facts and Figures *871*
Motor Vehicle Registrations by Standard Metropolitan Statistical Areas *see* U. S. Federal Highway Administration. Motor Vehicle Registrations by Standard Metropolitan Statistical Areas *872*
Motor Vehicle Safety (US) *753*
Motor Vehicle Statistics of Japan (JA ISSN 0463-6635) *866*
Motorboat & Equipment Directory (US ISSN 0148-8740) *827*
Motorcoach Tour Mart (US) *889*
Motorcycle Blue Book (US ISSN 0091-3774) *826*
Motorcycle Buyer's Guide (US ISSN 0077-1678) 820, *871, 882*
Motorcycle Facts (US ISSN 0091-5793) *871*
Motoring in Malaya (MY ISSN 0077-1694) *882, 889*
Motor's Flat Rate and Parts Manual *see* Motor Parts and Time Guide *871*
Motor's Handbook *see* Motor Handbook *871*
Mount Desert Island Biological Laboratory. Bulletin (US) *105*
Mountain State Geology (US ISSN 0163-2825) *297*
Mountain Summer (US) *580*
Mountaineer (US ISSN 0027-2620) 277, *830*
Mouvement Naturel de la Population de la Grece (GR ISSN 0077-6114) *728*
Movement of California Fruits and Vegetables by Rail, Truck, and Air (US ISSN 0094-2790) 405, *863*
Movie Life Yearbook (US) *650*
Movie/TV Marketing Global Motion Picture Year Book (JA ISSN 0085-3577) 268, *650*
Movimiento Natural de la Poblacion de Espana (SP ISSN 0077-1767) *728*
Moving Finger (US) *580*
Moving Out (US ISSN 0047-830X) *900*
Moving to Ottawa/Hull (CN ISSN 0226-7837) *761, 889*
Moving to Saskatchewan (CN ISSN 0225-5383) *761, 889*
Moving to Toronto *see* Moving to Toronto & Area *761*
Moving to Toronto & Area (CN ISSN 0226-7829) *761, 889*
Moving to Vancouver & B.C. (CN ISSN 0226-7276) *761, 889*
Moving to Vancouver/Victoria *see* Moving to Vancouver & B C *761*
Moyens de la Recherche Scientifique et Technique en Haute-Normandie. (FR ISSN 0077-1775) *911*
Mozambique. Servico Meteorologico. Anuario de Observacoes. Parte I: Observacoes de Superficie (MZ) *305*

Mozambique. Servico Meteorologico. Anuario de Observacoes. Parte II: Observacoes de Altitude (MZ) *305*
Mozambique. Servico Meteorologico. Informacoes de Caracter Astronomico (MZ) 83, *305*
Mozart-Jahrbuch (GW ISSN 0077-1805) *661*
Muelleria (AT ISSN 0077-1813) *116*
Muenchener Geographische Abhandlungen (GW) *424*
Muenchener Indologische Studien (GW ISSN 0077-1880) *444*
Muenchener Ostasiatische Studien (GW ISSN 0170-3668) *670*
Muenchener Ostasiatische Studien. Sonderreihe (GW ISSN 0077-3676) *670*
Muenchener Studien zur Sprachwissenschaft (GW ISSN 0077-1910) *547*
Muenchner Entomologische Gesellschaft. Mitteilungen (GW ISSN 0077-1864) *121*
Muenchner Germanistische Beitraege (GW ISSN 0077-1872) 547, *568*
Muenchner Jahrbuch der Bildenden Kunst (GW ISSN 0077-1899) *76*
Muenchner Studien zur Sozial- und Wirtschaftsgeographie (GW ISSN 0077-1902) *424*
Muenchner Zeitschrift fuer Balkanologie (GW ISSN 0170-8929) 457, *475*
Muenstersche Beitraege zur Deutschen Literaturwissenschaft (GW ISSN 0077-1996) *568*
Muenstersche Beitraege zur Vor- und Fruehgeschichte (GW ISSN 0077-2003) *434*
Muenstersche Beitraege zur Vorgeschichtsforschung *see* Muenstersche Beitraege zur Vor- und Fruehgeschichte *434*
Muenstersche Studien zur Kunstgeschichte (GW ISSN 0580-1583) *76*
Muenstersschwarzacher Studien (GW ISSN 0077-2011) *775*
Mugwumps' Instrument Herald. Catalog Reprint Series (US) *661*
Al-Mujtama *see* Sudan Society *54*
Muktesar, India. Imperial Veterinary Research Institute. Report *see* Indian Veterinary Research Institute. Annual Report *894*
Mule Deer Aerial Survey Report *see* Saskatchewan. Department of Tourism and Renewable Resources. Game Surveys Unit. Winter Mule Deer Survey in Southwestern Saskatchewan *278*
Mulga Yonbo *see* Korea (Republic) Bureau of Statistics. Annual Report of the Price Survey *159*
Multi Media Reviews Index *see* Media Review Digest *651*
Multilingual Forestry Terminology Series (US ISSN 0077-2046) *409*
Multinational Corporation: Studies on U.S. Foreign Investment (US) *197*
Multinational Corporations Operating Overseas *see* Multinational Marketing & Employment Directory *240*
Multinational Executive Travel Companion (US ISSN 0093-7487) 197, *889*
Multinational Marketing & Employment Directory (US ISSN 0363-4426) *240*
Multiphase Science and Technology (US ISSN 0276-1459) *369*
Multiple Sclerosis Society of Canada Ontario *see* M S Ontario *597*
Mundo Antiguo (SP ISSN 0077-2054) *434*
Munger Africana Library Notes (US ISSN 0047-8350) 392, *440*
Munich Round up (GW) 568, *786*
Municipal Association of Tasmania. Session. Minutes of Proceedings (AT ISSN 0085-3585) *749*
Municipal Association of Victoria. Minutes of Proceedings of Annual Session (AT ISSN 0077-2143) *712*
Municipal Index (US ISSN 0077-2151) *749*

Municipal Research and Services Center of Washington. Information Bulletins (US ISSN 0090-1768) 515, *749*
Municipal Waste Facilities in the U. S (US ISSN 0077-2178) *387*
Municipal Year Book (US ISSN 0077-2186) *749*
Munyeyungam *see* Yearbook of Cultural & Artistic Activities *80*
Musashino Art University. Bulletin (JA) *76*
Muse (US ISSN 0077-2194) *63*
Muse (NR ISSN 0331-3468) *568*
Musee d'Ethnographie de la Ville de Geneve. Bulletin Annuel (SZ ISSN 0072-0828) *51*
Musee de l'Homme, Paris. Catalogues. Serie B: Afrique Blanche et Levant (FR ISSN 0553-2507) *653*
Musee de l'Homme, Paris. Catalogues. Serie C: Afrique Noire (FR) *653*
Musee de l'Homme, Paris. Catalogues. Serie E: Oceanie (FR) *653*
Musee de l'Homme, Paris. Catalogues. Serie E: Polynesie *see* Musee de l'Homme, Paris. Catalogues. Serie E: Oceanie *653*
Musee de l'Homme, Paris. Catalogues. Serie F: Madagascar (FR) *653*
Musee de l'Homme, Paris. Catalogues. Serie G: Arctiques (FR ISSN 0553-2515) *653*
Musee de l'Homme, Paris. Catalogues. Serie H: Amerique (FR) *653*
Musee de l'Homme, Paris. Catalogues. Serie K: Asie (FR) *653*
Musee Guimet, Paris. Bibliotheque d'Etudes (FR ISSN 0078-9704) 63, *76*
Musee Guimet, Paris. Etude des Collections du Musee (FR ISSN 0078-9712) 63, *76*
Musee Royal de l'Afrique Centrale. Annales. Serie in 8. Sciences Economiques/Koninklijk Museum voor Midden-Afrika. Annalen. Reeks in 8. Economische Wetenschappen (BE) *192*
Musee Royal de l'Afrique Centrale. Annales. Serie in 8. Sciences Geologiques/Koninklijk Museum voor Midden-Afrika. Annalen. Reeks in 8. Geologische Wetenschappen (BE) *297*
Musee Royal de l'Afrique Centrale. Annales. Serie in 8. Sciences Historiques/Koninklijk Museum voor Midden-Afrika. Annalen. Reeks in 8. Historische Wetenschappen (BE) *434*
Musee Royal de l'Afrique Centrale. Annales. Serie in 8. Sciences Humaines/Koninklijk Museum voor Midden-Afrika. Annalen. Reeks in 8. Menselijke Wetenschappen (BE) 492, *799*
Musee Royal de l'Afrique Centrale. Annales. Serie in 8. Sciences Zoologiques/Koninklijk Museum voor Midden-Afrika. Annalen. Reeks in 8. Zoologische Wetenschappen (BE) *129*
Musee Royal de l'Afrique Centrale. Archives d'Anthropologie (BE) *51*
Musee Royal de l'Afrique Centrale. Departement de Geologie et de Mineralogie. Rapport Annuel (BE) *297*
Musee Royal de l'Afrique Centrale. Documentation Economique/Koninklijk Museum voor Midden-Afrika. Economische Documentatie (BE) *146*
Musee Royal de l'Afrique Centrale. Documentation Zoologique/Koninklijk Museum voor Midden-Afrika. Zoologische Documentatie (BE) *129*
Museen der Welt *see* Museums of the World *654*
Museerne i Viborg Amt *see* M I V: Museerne i Viborg Amt *457*
Museion (AU ISSN 0077-2208) *533*

Museo Argentina de Ciencias Naturales "Bernardino Rivadavia." Instituto Nacional de Investigacion de las Ciencias Naturales. Revista. Entomologia (AG ISSN 0524-949X) *121*
Museo Argentino de Ciencias Naturales Bernardino Rivadavia. Instituto Nacional de Investigacion de las Ciencias Naturales. Revista. Botanica. (AG ISSN 0376-2793) *116*
Museo Argentino de Ciencias Naturales "Bernardino Rivadavia." Instituto Nacional de Investigacion de las Ciencias Naturales. Revista. Ecologia (AG ISSN 0524-9481) *105*
Museo Argentino de Ciencias Naturales Bernardino Rivadavia. Instituto Nacional de Investigacion de las Ciencias Naturales. Revista. Geologia (AG) *297*
Museo Argentino de Ciencias Naturales "Bernardino Rivadavia." Instituto Nacional de Investigacion de las Ciencias Naturales. Revista. Hidrobiologia (AG ISSN 0524-9503) *105*
Museo Argentino de Ciencias Naturales "Bernardino Rivadavia." Instituto Nacional de Investigacion de las Ciencias Naturales. Revista. Paleontologia (AG ISSN 0524-9511) *674*
Museo Argentino de Ciencias Naturales "Bernardino Rivadavia." Instituto Nacional de Investigacion de las Ciencias Naturales. Revista. Parasitologia (AG ISSN 0524-952X) *608*
Museo Argentino de Ciencias Naturales "Bernardino Rivadavia" e Instituto Nacional de Investigaciones de la Ciencias Naturales. Revista y Communicaciones (AG ISSN 0027-3880) *786*
Museo Arqueologico de Valladolid. Monografias (SP) *63*
Museo Arqueologico Nacional. Monografias Arqueologicas (SP) *63*
Museo Bodoniano. Bolletino (IT) *653*
Museo Canario (SP) *458*
Museo Civico di Storia Naturale di Verona. Memorie *see* Museo Civico di Storia Naturale, Verona. Bolletino *786*
Museo Civico di Storia Naturale "Giacomo Doria," Genoa. Annali (IT) *786*
Museo Civico di Storia Naturale, Verona. Bolletino (IT) *786*
Museo Civico di Storia Naturale, Verona. Memorie (IT ISSN 0085-767X) *786*
Museo de Historia Natural de San Rafael. Instituto de Ciencias Naturales. Notas (AG) *297*
Museo de Historia Natural de San Rafael. Revista (AG) *786*
Museo de Historia Natural de San Rafael. Revista Cientifica de Investigaciones *see* Museo de Historia Natural de San Rafael. Revista *786*
Museo de Hombre Dominicano. Papeles Ocasionales (DR) *51*
Museo del Hombre Dominicano. Serie Catalogos y Memorias (DR) 51, *653*
Museo del Hombre Dominicano. Serie Conferencias (DR) *51*
Museo del Hombre Dominicano. Serie Estudio y Arte (DR) *51*
Museo del Hombre Dominicano. Serie Investigaciones Antropologicas (DR) *51*
Museo del Hombre Dominicano. Serie Mesas Redondas (DR) 51, *653*
Museo dell'Impero Romano. Studi e Materiali. (IT ISSN 0080-3936) *653*
Museo Egizio, Turin. Catalogo. Serie Prima: Monumenti e Testi. (IT ISSN 0082-6863) *434*
Museo Nacional de Antropologia y Arqueologia. Serie: Antropologia Fisica (PE) *51*
Museo Nacional de Antropologia y Arqueologia. Serie: Investigaciones de Campo (PE) 51, *63*

Museo Nacional de Antropologia y Arqueologia. Serie: Metalurgia (PE) 51, *63*
Museo Nacional de Costa Rica. Informe Rendido al Minsterio de Educacion Publica. (CR) *653*
Museo Nacional de Historia Natural. Anales (UY) 653, *786*
Museo Nacional de Historia Natural. Communicaciones Antropologicas (UY ISSN 0077-1244) *51*
Museo Nacional de Historia Natural. Communicaciones Paleontologicas (UY) *674*
Museo Nacional de la Cultural Peruana. Revista (PE) *653*
Museo Nazionale d'Arte Orientale. Schede (IT) 653, *670*
Museo Nazionale di Castel San Angelo. Quaderni (IT) *653*
Museologia (IT) *654*
Museon (BE) *670*
Museu do Indio. Documentacao (BL) *470,* 654
Museu Nacional de Antropologia. Cuadernos (MX ISSN 0076-7158) *51*
Museu Nacional, Rio de Janeiro. Arquivos (BL ISSN 0080-3111) *654*
Museu Nacional, Rio de Janeiro. Boletim. Nova Serie. Antropologia (BL ISSN 0080-3189) *51*
Museu Nacional, Rio de Janeiro. Boletim. Nova Serie. Botanica (BL ISSN 0080-3197) *116*
Museu Nacional, Rio de Janeiro. Boletim. Nova Serie. Geologie (BL ISSN 0080-3200) *297*
Museu Nacional, Rio de Janeiro. Boletim. Nova Serie. Zoologia (BL ISSN 0080-312X) *129*
Museu Paraense Emilio Goeldi. Boletim Antropologia. Nova Serie (BL ISSN 0522-7291) *51*
Museu Paraense Emilio Goeldi. Boletim Botanica. Nova Serie (BL ISSN 0077-2216) *116*
Museu Paraense Emilio Goeldi. Boletim Zoologia. Nova Serie (BL ISSN 0077-2224) *129*
Museu Paraense Emilio Goeldi. Publicacoes Avulsas (BL ISSN 0077-2240) *786*
Museu Paulista. Colecao *see* Universidade de Sao Paulo. Museu Paulista. Colecao. Serie de Etnologia *54*
Museu Paulista. Colecao *see* Universidade de Sao Paulo. Museu Paulista. Colecao. Serie de Arqueologia *66*
Museu Paulista. Colecao *see* Universidade de Sao Paulo. Museu Paulista Colecao. Serie de Geografia *426*
Museu Paulista. Colecao *see* Universidade de Sao Paulo. Museu Paulista. Colecao. Serie de Historia *473*
Museu Paulista. Colecao *see* Universidade de Sao Paulo. Museu Paulista. Colecao. Serie de Numismatica *478*
Museu Paulista. Colecao *see* Universidade de Sao Paulo. Museu Paulista. Colecao. Serie de Mobiliario *655*
Museum Africum (NR) *259*
Museum Boymans-van Beuningen. Agenda-Diary (NE ISSN 0077-2275) *654*
Museum Briefs *see* University of Missouri, Columbia. Museum of Anthropology. Museum Briefs *55*
Museum Catalog of Publications and Media *see* Catalog of Museum Publications and Media *656*
Museum Criticum (IT) *569*
Museum fuer Ur- und Fruehgeschichte des Bezirkes Potsdam, Frankfurt/Oder and Cottbus. Veroeffentlichungen (GE ISSN 0079-4376) *434,* 654
Museum fuer Ur- und Fruehgeschichte Thueringens. Jahrbuch *see* Alt-Thueringen *448*

Museum fuer Ur- und Fruehgeschichte Thueringens. Veroeffentlichungen (GE ISSN 0077-2291) *51*
Museum fuer Voelkerkunde, Berlin. Veroeffentlichungen. Neue Folge. Abteilung: Afrika (GW ISSN 0067-5962) *52,* 440
Museum fuer Voelkerkunde, Berlin. Veroeffentlichungen. Neue Folge. Abteilung: Amerikanische Naturvoelker (GW) *52,* 76
Museum fuer Voelkerkunde, Berlin. Veroeffentlichungen. Neue Folge. Abteilung: Suedsee (GW ISSN 0067-5989) *52,* 447
Museum fuer Voelkerkunde in Hamburg. Mitteilungen (GW) *402,* 654
Museum fuer Voelkerkunde, Leipzig. Jahrbuch (GE ISSN 0075-8663) *654*
Museum fuer Voelkerkunde, Leipzig. Veroeffentlichungen (GE ISSN 0075-8671) *654*
Museum Memoir (RH ISSN 0304-5323) 52, 63, *130*
Museum National d'Histoire Naturelle, Paris. Annuaire (FR ISSN 0078-9720) *786*
Museum National d'Histoire Naturelle, Paris. Archives (FR ISSN 0078-9739) *786*
Museum National d'Histoire Naturelle, Paris. Bibliotheque Centrale. Liste des Periodiques Francais et Etrangers.Supplement (FR ISSN 0085-476X) *93*
Museum National d'Histoire Naturelle, Paris. les Grands Naturalistes Francais (FR) *786*
Museum National d'Histoire Naturelle, Paris. Memoires. Nouvelle Serie. Serie A. Zoologie (FR ISSN 0078-9747) *130*
Museum National d'Histoire Naturelle, Paris. Memoires. Nouvelle Serie. Serie B. Botanique (FR ISSN 0078-9755) *116*
Museum National d'Histoire Naturelle, Paris. Memoires. Nouvelle Serie. Serie C. Sciences de la Terre (FR ISSN 0078-9763) *289*
Museum National d'Histoire Naturelle, Paris. Memoires. Nouvelle Serie. Serie D. Sciences Physico-Chimiques(FR ISSN 0078-9771) 247, *697*
Museum National d'Histoire Naturelle, Paris. Notes et Memoires de la Section d'Etudes Geologiques de Haut-Commissariat Francais en Syrie et au Liban *see* Museum National d'Histoire Naturelle, Paris. Notes et Memoires sur le Moyen-Orient *297*
Museum National d'Histoire Naturelle, Paris. Notes et Memoires sur le Moyen-Orient (FR) *297,* 424
Museum Notes (US ISSN 0027-4097) *654*
Museum Notes (New York) (US ISSN 0145-1413) *477*
Museum of Antiquities of Tel-Aviv-Yafo. Publications (IS ISSN 0082-2620) *63,* 424
Museum of Far Eastern Antiquities. Bulletin (SW ISSN 0081-5691) 76, *654,* 670
Museum of Northern Arizona Ceramic Series (US ISSN 0430-635X) *654*
Museum of Northern Arizona Technical Series (US ISSN 0428-5395) *786*
Museum of Temporary Art *see* M O T A *557*
Museum Philologum Londiniense (NE) *547*
Museums and Galleries *see* Museums and Galleries in Great Britain and Ireland *654*
Museums and Galleries in Great Britain and Ireland (UK ISSN 0141-6723) *654*
Museums and Monuments Series (UN ISSN 0077-233X) *654*
Museums Association Information Sheets (UK ISSN 0306-5332) *654*
Museums Calendar *see* Museums Yearbook
Museums Journal of Pakistan (PK ISSN 0077-2348) *654*

Museums Newsletter (II) *654*
Museums of the World/Museen der Welt (GW) *654*
Museums Yearbook (UK ISSN 0307-7675) *654*
Mushroom Science (UK ISSN 0077-2364) *116*
Music Academy. Conference Souvenir (II) *661*
Music Academy. Journal (II) *661*
Music and Life (UK ISSN 0085-3607) *661*
Music & Musicians: Braille Scores Catalog - Choral (US ISSN 0145-3173) 93, *133,* 665
Music & Musicians: Braille Scores Catalog - Organ (US ISSN 0145-3149) 93, *133,* 665
Music & Musicians: Braille Scores Catalog - Piano (US ISSN 0145-3130) 93, *133,* 665
Music & Musicians: Braille Scores Catalog - Voice (US ISSN 0145-3157) 93, *133,* 665
Music & Musicians: Instructional Cassette Recordings Catalog (US ISSN 0145-2525) 93, *133,* 665
Music & Musicians: Instructional Disc Recordings Catalog (US ISSN 0145-2517) 93, *133,* 665
Music & Musicians: Large-Print Scores and Books Catalog (US ISSN 0363-8472) 93, *133,* 665
Music & Video Week Yearbook (UK) *661*
Music Association of Ireland. Annual Report (IE) *661*
Music Book Guide *see* Bibliographic Guide to Music *665*
Music Cultures/Kansai Ongaku Bunka Shiryo (JA) *661*
Music Educators National Conference. Selective Music List: Vocal Solos and Ensembles (US ISSN 0077-2402) *661*
Music Educators National Conference. Selective Music Lists: Band, Orchestra, and String Orchestra *see* Music Educators National Conference. Selective Music Lists: Full Orchestra, String Orchestra *661*
Music Educators National Conference. Selective Music Lists: Full Orchestra, String Orchestra (US) *661*
Music Educators National Conference. Selective Music Lists: Instrumental Solos and Ensembles (US) *661*
Music Forum (US) *661*
Music Handbook (US ISSN 0077-2372) *661*
Music in American Life (US) *661*
Music in Danish Libraries *see* Musikalier i Danske Biblioteker *665*
Music in Higher Education (US ISSN 0077-2410) 349, *661*
Music-in-Print Annual Supplement (US) *665*
Music Indexes and Bibliographies (US ISSN 0077-2429) *665*
Music Library Association. Index and Bibliography Series (US ISSN 0094-6478) *665*
Music Library Association. Index Series *see* Music Library Association. Index and Bibliography Series *665*
Music Library Association. Technical Reports (US ISSN 0094-5099) *533,* 661
Music Master (UK ISSN 0308-9347) *661*
Music Notes (US) *661*
Music O C L C Users Group. Newsletter (US ISSN 0161-1704) *533,* 661
Music of the Environment Series (CN) 387, *706*
Music Theory Spectrum (US) *661*
Music Therapy Index (US) 327, *665*
Music Trades Directory (UK ISSN 0307-8523) *661*
Music Trades International Directory *see* Music Trades Directory *661*
Music Week Industry Year Book *see* Music & Video Week Yearbook *661*
Music Yearbook *see* British Music Yearbook *657*
Musica Asiatica (US ISSN 0140-6078) *661,* 670

Musica Britannica (UK ISSN 0580-2954) *661*
Musica Disciplina (GW ISSN 0077-2461) *661*
Musica Judaica (US) *661,* 770
Musica Medii Aevi (PL ISSN 0077-247X) *661*
Musical America Annual Directory Issue *see* Musical America International Directory of the Performing Arts *661*
Musical America International Directory of the Performing Arts (US) *661*
Musical Instruments of East Africa (KE) *661*
Musicologia Espanola (SP) *661*
Musicologica Hungarica. Neue Folge (HU ISSN 0077-2488) *661*
Musicologica Slovaca (CS ISSN 0581-0558) *661*
Musicological Annual *see* Muzikoloski Zbornik *662*
Musicological Studies and Documents (GW ISSN 0077-2496) *661*
Musicological Yearbook *see* Arti Musices *657*
Musicology (AT ISSN 0077-250X) *662*
Musik aus der Steiermark (GW) *662*
Musik i Sverige (SW ISSN 0077-2518) *662*
Musik og Forskning (DK) *662*
Musikalier i Danske Biblioteker/Music in Danish Libraries (DK ISSN 0085-3623) *665*
Musikalische Denkmaeler (GW ISSN 0077-2526) *662*
Musikhistoriska Museet, Stockholm. Skrifter (SW ISSN 0081-5675) *662*
Musikpaedagogische Bibliothek (GW) *662*
Musique Liturgique (CN ISSN 0384-5133) *911*
Muskeg Research Conference. Proceedings (CN ISSN 0541-4393) *305*
Muskeg Review (CN) *557*
Muslim Intellectuals' International Series *see* M.I.I. Series *769*
Musteranlagen der Energiewirtschaft (GW ISSN 0580-3403) *363*
Muszaki es Gazdasagi Fejlodes Fo Iranyai/Main Trends of Technical and Economic Development (HU ISSN 0133-5707) 146, *852*
Mutisia (CK ISSN 0027-5123) *116*
Muttersprache (GW ISSN 0027-514X) *547*
Mutual Funds Almanac (US ISSN 0076-4175) *204*
Muzea Walki (PL ISSN 0077-2577) *458*
Muzeul de Istorie Naturala "Gr. Antipa." Travaux (RM ISSN 0068-3078) *105*
Muzeul National (RM) *654*
Muzeum Archeologiczne i Etnograficzne, Lodz. Prace i Materialy. Seria Archeologiczna (PL ISSN 0458-1520) *63*
Muzeum Archeologiczne i Etnograficzne, Lodz. Prace i Materialy. Seria Etnograficzna (PL ISSN 0076-0315) *52*
Muzeum Archeologiczne, Krakow. Materialy Archeologiczne (PL ISSN 0075-7039) *63*
Muzeum Etnograficzne, Wroclaw. Zeszyty Etnograficzne (PL ISSN 0084-2796) *52*
Muzeum Gornoslaskie w Bytomiu. Rocznik. Seria Archeologia (PL ISSN 0068-4635) *63*
Muzeum Gornoslaskie w Bytomiu. Rocznik. Seria Etnografia (PL ISSN 0068-4643) *52*
Muzeum Gornoslaskie w Bytomiu. Rocznik. Seria Historia (PL ISSN 0068-4651) *458*
Muzeum Gornoslaskie w Bytomiu. Rocznik. Seria Przyroda (PL ISSN 0068-466X) *105*
Muzeum Gornoslaskie w Bytomiu. Rocznik. Seria Sztuka (PL ISSN 0068-4678) *76*
Muzikoloski Zbornik/Musicological Annual (YU ISSN 0580-373X) *662*

Muzium Brunei. Penerbitan Khas see Brunei Museum. Special Publication 652
Muzykal'naya Folkloristika (UR) 402, 662
Muzykal'noe Vospitanie v Shkole (UR ISSN 0302-847X) 349, 662
Mycological Papers (UK ISSN 0027-5522) 116
Mycotaxon (US ISSN 0093-4666) 116
Mykenische Studien (AU) 260
Mynule i Suchasne Pivnichnoi Bukovyny/Proshloe i Nastoyaschchee Severnoi Bukoviny (UR) 458
Myrin Institute for Adult Education Proceedings (US) 329
Mysore. Finance Department. Annual Report see Karnataka. Finance Department. Annual Report 230
Mysore Orientalist (II ISSN 0580-4396) 670
Mystery & Detection Annual. (US ISSN 0000-0302) 569
Mystic Seaport Manuscripts Inventory (US ISSN 0077-2615) 879
Mythril (US) 569
N A A (Nordic Archaeological Abstracts) (DK ISSN 0105-6492) 3, 67
N A A C P Annual Report (National Association for the Advancement of Colored People) (US ISSN 0077-3212) 815
N A A F I Reports (Navy, Army and Air Force Institutes) (UK) 639
N A A Where to Stay Book (National Automobile Association) (US ISSN 0099-0205) 483
N A B T E Review (National Association for Business Teacher Education) (US) 146, 338
N. A. C. D. S. Lilly Digest (National Association of Chain Drug Stores) (US ISSN 0092-8410) 218, 685
N A F A Annual Reference Book (National Association of Fleet Administrators, Inc.) (US) 871
N A F A Conference Brochure & Reference Book see N A F A Annual Reference Book 871
N A F O Annual Report (CN ISSN 0704-4798) 398
N A F O List of Fishing Vessels (Northwest Atlantic Fisheries Organization) (CN ISSN 0250-7811) 399
N A F O Meeting Proceedings (Northwest Atlantic Fisheries Organization) (CN ISSN 0704-4771) 399
N A F O Sampling Yearbook (Northwest Atlantic Fisheries Organization) (CN ISSN 0250-6424) 399
N A F O Scientific Council Meeting Reports (Northwest Atlantic Fisheries Organization) (CN ISSN 0250-6416) 399
N A F O Scientific Council Studies (Northwest Atlantic Fisheries Organization) (CN ISSN 0250-6432) 399
N A F O Statistical Bulletin (CN ISSN 0250-6394) 399
N A F S A Directory (National Association for Foreign Student Affairs) (US ISSN 0077-3190) 343
N A G W S Guide. Aquatics (National Association for Girls and Women in Sport) (US ISSN 0361-719X) 820
N A G W S Guide. Archery-Fencing (National Association for Girls and Women in Sport) (US) 820
N A G W S Guide. Badminton-Squash-Racquetball (National Association for Girls and Women in Sport) (US) 820
N A G W S Guide. Basketball (National Association for Girls and Women in Sport) (US ISSN 0362-3254) 824
N A G W S Guide. Basketball, Volleyball (National Association for Girls and Women in Sport) (US) 824
N A G W S Guide. Bowling-Golf (National Association for Girls and Women in Sport) (US) 820, 824

N A G W S Guide. Competitive Swimming and Diving (National Association for Girls and Women in Sport) (US) 821
N A G W S Guide. Field Hockey (National Association for Girls and Women in Sport) (US) 824
N A G W S Guide. Flag Football, Speedball, Speed-a-Way (National Association for Girls and Women in Sport) (US) 824
N A G W S Guide. Gymnastics (National Association for Girls & Women in Sport) (US ISSN 0363-9282) 821
N A G W S Guide. Lacrosse (National Association for Girls and Women in Sport) (US) 824
N A G W S Guide. Soccer (National Association for Girls and Women in Sport) (US ISSN 0163-4747) 824
N A G W S Guide. Softball (National Association for Girls and Women in Sport) (US ISSN 0363-2504) 825
N A G W S Guide. Synchronized Swimming (National Association for Girls and Women in Sport) (US ISSN 0163-4267) 821
N A G W S Guide. Team Handball, Orienteering (National Association for Girls and Women in Sport) (US) 821
N A G W S Guide. Team Handball, Racquetball, Orienteering see N A G W S Guide. Team Handball, Orienteering 821
N A G W S Guide. Tennis (National Association for Girls and Women in Sport) (US) 821
N A G W S Guide. Track and Field (National Association for Girls and Women in Sport) (US ISSN 0362-9481) 830
N A G W S Guide. Volleyball (National Association for Girls and Women in Sport) (US) 825
N A G W S Rules. Skiing (National Association for Girls and Women in Sport) (US ISSN 0148-1150) 830
N A I A Handbook (National Association of Intercollegiate Athletics) (US ISSN 0077-3336) 821
N A I A Official Record Book (National Association of Intercollegiate Athletics) (US ISSN 0077-3344) 821
N A L G O Annual Report (UK ISSN 0077-4456) 744
N A M F Accounting Manual (National Association of Metal Finishers) (US ISSN 0077-3360) 168
N A M F Management Manual (National Association of Metal Finishers) (US ISSN 0077-3379) 629
N A P E Journal see Communicator 741
N A R D Almanac (National Association of Retail Druggists) (US) 361, 685
N A S A Factbook see National Aeronautics and Space Administration. N A S A Factbook 9
N A S A Facts (National Aeronautics and Space Administration) (US ISSN 0077-3093) 9
N A S A Technical Memorandum see National Aeronautics and Space Administration. Technical Memorandums 9
N A S A-University Conference on Manual Control (Papers) (National Aeronautics and Space Administration) (US ISSN 0077-2623) 9
N A S C O Campus Co-Op Directory (North American Students of Cooperation) (US) 240
N A S O Journal (National Astrological Society) (US) 80
N A S P A A Roster see Graduate School Programs in Public Affairs and Public Administration 742
N. A. T. A. Directory (National Association of Testing Authorities) (AT) 380

N. A. T. A. Index see N. A. T. A. Directory 380
N A T I S-News (UN) 533
N A T I S Noticias see N A T I S-News 533
N A T I S-Nouvelles see N A T I S-News 533
N A T O Advanced Study Institute Series. C: Mathematical and Physical Sciences (NE) 587, 786
N A T O Advanced Study Institute Series E: Applied Science (North Atlantic Treaty Organization) (NE) 852
N A T O Handbook (North Atlantic Treaty Organization) (BE ISSN 0549-7175) 722
N A V A Membership Directory (National Audio-Visual Association, Inc.) (US) 349
N B C / N F C News (National Building Code / National Fire Code) (Associate Committee on the National Building Code) (CN ISSN 0380-8599) 137
N B C News see N B C / N F C News 137
N B C Official Yearbook (National Baseball Congress) (US) 825
N C A A Baseball Annual Guide (National Collegiate Athletic Association) (US) 825
N C A A Basketball Records (National Collegiate Athletic Association) (US) 825
N C A A Basketball Rules and Interpretations (US) 825
N C A A Directory (National Collegiate Athletic Association) (US) 821
N.C.A.A. Football Records (National Collegiate Athletic Association) (US) 825
N C A A Gymnastics Rules (National Collegiate Athletic Association) (US) 821
N C A A Illustrated Basketball Rules (National Collegiate Athletic Association) (US) 825
N C A A Lacrosse Guide (National Collegiate Athletic Association) (US) 825
N C A A Manual see National Collegiate Athletic Association. Manual 821
N C A A Official Football Rules & Interpretations see Official National Collegiate Athletic Association Football Rules & Interpretations 825
N C A A Television Committee Report (National Collegiate Athletic Association) (US) 821
N C E A Ganley's Catholic Schools in America (National Catholic Educational Association) (US ISSN 0147-8044) 332
N. C. F. A. Office Manual (National Consumer Finance Association) (US ISSN 0094-1522) 175
N C P Documenta (Noticias de Cosmetica y de Perfumeria) (SP) 85
N C P E A M Proceedings (National College Physical Education Association for Men) (US) 349
N C R A Yearbook (North Central Reading Association) (US) 329
N C R P Report (National Council on Radiation Protection and Measurements) (US ISSN 0083-209X) 753
N C R P Statements (National Council on Radiation Protection and Measurements) (US) 622
N C S R Bibliography see Zambia. National Council for Scientific Research. N C S R Bibliography 795
N. C. S. Yearbook (National Chrysanthemum Society) (UK) 415
N E D A Statistical Yearbook of the Philippines (National Economic and Development Authority) (PH) 160
N E I W P C C Report (New England Interstate Water Pollution Control Commission) (US) 387
N E R C News Journal (UK ISSN 0305-8336) 387

N.E.S.F.A. Index: Science Fiction Magazines and Anthologies (New England Science Fiction Association Inc.) (US ISSN 0361-3038) 3, 4
N E U R B see Nucleo de Estudos Sociais para Habitacao e Urbanismo 486
N F P A Technical Committee. Report (National Fire Protection Association) (US ISSN 0077-4553) 395
N F R C Yearbook (National Federation of Roofing Contractors) (UK) 137
N F T A Annual Report (Niagara Frontier Transportation Authority) (US) 863
N F T A Port of Buffalo Handbook (Niagara Frontier Transportation Authority) (US) 863
N G T F Action Report (National Gay Task Force) (US) 480, 718
N G U Bulletin (Norges Geologiske Undersoekelse) (NO) 297
N G U Skrifter (Norges Geologiske Undersoekelse) (NO) 297
N H K Gijutsu Kenkyojo see N H K Technical Monograph 268
N H K Technical Monograph / N H K Gijutsu Kenkyojo (Nippon Hoso Kyokai) (JA ISSN 0077-2631) 268
N.H.L. Pro Hockey (CN ISSN 0079-5569) 821
N.I.A.A.A.-R.U.C.A.S. Alcoholism Treatment Monographs see N.I.A.A.A.-R.U.C.A.S. Alcoholism Treatment Series 287
N.I.A.A.A.-R.U.C.A.S. Alcoholism Treatment Series (US ISSN 0147-0515) 287
N I B Annual Report see National Investment Bank, Ghana. Annual Report 175
N I B R Occasional Paper (Norsk Institutt for By- og Regionforskning) (NO) 911
N I B R Rapport (Norsk Institutt for By- og Regionforskning) (NO ISSN 0085-4263) 485
N I C E M Index to Educational Audio Tapes (National Information Center for Educational Media) (US) 3, 327
N I C E M Index to Educational Overhead Transparencies (National Information Center for Educational Media) (US) 3, 327
N I C E M Index to Educational Records (National Information Center for Educational Media) (US) 3, 327
N I C E M Index to Educational Slides (National Information Center for Educational Media) (US) 3, 327
N I C E M Index to Educational Video Tapes (US) 3, 327
N I C E M Index to Environmental Studies-Multimedia (National Information Center for Educational Media) (US) 3, 390
N I C E M Index to Health and Safety Education-Multimedia (National Information Center for Educational Media) (US) 3, 695
N I C E M Index to Producers and Distributors (National Information Center for Educational Media) (US) 3, 327, 651
N I C E M Index to Psychology-Multimedia (National Information Center for Educational Media) (US) 349, 737
N I C E M Index to Vocational and Technical Education-Multimedia (National Information Center for Educational Media) (US) 3, 349
N I C E M Index to 8mm Motion Cartridges (National Information Center for Educational Media) (US) 3, 327
N I C E M Index to 16mm Educational Films (National Information Center for Educational Media) (US) 3, 327
N I C E M Index to 35mm Educational Filmstrips (National Information Center for Educational Media) (US) 3, 327
N I D A Research Monograph see U. S. National Institute on Drug Abuse. Research Monograph Series 287

N I D A Supported Drug Treatment Programs (U.S. National Institute on Drug Abuse) (US ISSN 0360-9642) 287
N I D I Publikaties (Nederlands Interuniversitair Demografish Instituut) (NE) 728
N I F P General Series (National Institute of Family Planning) (II ISSN 0077-4944) 132
N I F P Manual Series (National Institute of Family Planning) (II ISSN 0077-4952) 132
N I F P Monograph Series (National Institute of Family Planning) (II ISSN 0077-4960) 132
N I F P Report Series (National Institute of Family Planning) (II ISSN 0077-4979) 132
N I F P Technical Paper Series (National Institute of Family Planning) (II ISSN 0077-4987) 132
N I H A E Technical Report (National Institute of Health Administration and Education) (II) 694
N I H Factbook (U.S. National Institutes of Health) (US) 753
N I M Reports (National Institute for Metallurgy) (SA) 629
N I W R Information Sheet (National Institute for Water Research) (SA) 897
N K B Publication Series see N K B Skriftserie 137
N K B Skriftserie/N K B Publication Series (Nordiske Komite for Bygningsbestemmelsei) (FI ISSN 0078-1126) 137
N L N Nursing Data Book: Statistical Information on Nursing Education & Newly Licensed Nurses (US) 614
N M R (Nuclear Magnetic Resonance) (US ISSN 0078-088X) 704
N M R I Compensation in Mass Retailing, Salaries and Incentives (National Mass Retailing Institute) (US ISSN 0092-5950) 209
N N A National Directory of Weekly Newspapers (National Newspaper Association) (US) 505
N P N Factbook (National Petroleum News) (US) 680
N R C - Nouvelle Revue Canadienne (CN ISSN 0547-0749) 557
N R C P Research Bulletin (National Research Council of the Philippines) (PH) 786
N. R. I. Special Report see University of Maryland. Natural Resources Institute. N. R. I. Special Report 109
N R L/Neue Russische Literatur (AU) 569
N R M C A Publication (National Ready Mixed Concrete Association) (US ISSN 0077-5355) 137
N. S. C. A. Reference Book (National Society for Clean Air) (UK ISSN 0140-6795) 387
N. S. C. A. Yearbook see N. S. C. A. Reference Book 387
N S C Review (National Science Council of the Republic of China) (CH) 786
N S C Special Publication (National Science Council of the Republic of China) (CH) 786
N S C Symposium Series (National Science Council of the Republic of China) (CH) 786
N S F Factbook see U. S. National Science Foundation. N S F Factbook 792
N S G A Circular (National Sand and Gravel Association) (US ISSN 0077-5673) 297
N S R A Memo (Nuclear Safety Research Association) (JA) 704
N S T Directory of Malaysia (New Straits Times Press (Malaysia) Berhad) (MY) 240
N T A Journal (CN ISSN 0027-7037) 320
N U M U S Numismatica, Medalhistica, Argueologia (PO ISSN 0085-364X) 476
N U P I Notat (Norsk Utenrikspolitisk Instituut) (NO) 722

N U P I Rapport (Norsk Utenrikspolitisk Instituut) (NO) 722
N U S Yearbook (National Union of Students) (UK ISSN 0077-5932) 320
N U T Guide to Careers Work (National Union of Teachers) (UK ISSN 0066-3972) 667
N. Z. A. R. T. Amateur Radio Callbook (New Zealand Association of Radio Transmitters, Inc.) (NZ) 268
N Z O I Records (New Zealand Oceanographic Institute) (NZ ISSN 0110-618X) 311
Nachrichten aus dem Karten- und Vermessungswesen see Nachrichten aus dem Karten- und Vermessungswesen. Reihe 1: Originalbeitraege 424
Nachrichten aus dem Karten- und Vermessungswesen. Reihe 1: Originalbeitraege (GW ISSN 0469-4236) 424
Nachrichtentechnik (US) 505
NADA (RH ISSN 0085-3658) 392, 440
NAECON see National Aerospace and Electronics Conference. Record 9
Nagaland Education Bulletin (II) 320
Nagoya. Environmental Pollution Research Institute. Annual Report (JA) 387
Nagoya Daigaku Kankyo Igaku Kenkyusho Nenpo see Nagoya University. Research Institute of Environmental Medicine. Annual Report 598
Nagoya Daigaku Kogakubu Jido Seigyo see Nagoya University. Faculty of Engineering. Automatic Control Laboratory. Research Reports 273
Nagoya Daigaku Kuden Kenkyusho Hokoku see Nagoya University. Research Institute of Atmospherics. Proceedings 634
Nagoya Daigaku Purazuma Kenkyusho Nenpo see Nagoya University. Institute of Plasma Physics. Annual Review 697
Nagoya Port Statistics Annual/Nagoyako Tokei Nenpo (JA ISSN 0469-4783) 866
Nagoya University. Faculty of Engineering. Automatic Control Laboratory. Research Reports/Nagoya Daigaku Kogakubu Jido Seigyo (JA) 273
Nagoya University. Institute of Plasma Physics. Annual Review/Nagoya Daigaku Purazuma Kenkyusho Nenpo (JA ISSN 0547-1567) 697
Nagoya University. Institute of Plasma Physics. Technical Reports (JA) 697
Nagoya University. Research Institute of Atmospherics. Proceedings/Nagoya Daigaku Kuden Kenkyusho Hokoku (JA ISSN 0077-264X) 634
Nagoya University. Research Institute of Environmental Medicine. Annual Report/Nagoya Daigaku Kankyo Igaku Kenkyusho Nenpo (JA ISSN 0469-4759) 387, 598
Nagoya University. Water Research Institute. Annual Report/Suiken Kagaku Kenkyujo Nenpo (JA) 897
Nagoyako Tokei Nenpo see Nagoya Port Statistics Annual 866
Nagyuzemi Gazdalkodas Kerdesei (HU ISSN 0077-2658) 18
Nairobi Airport. Annual Report (KE ISSN 0077-2666) 869
Names in South Carolina (US ISSN 0077-2690) 547
Namib Desert Research Station. Scientific Papers see Madoqua 785
Namn och Bygd (SW ISSN 0077-2704) 424
Nanta Mathematica (SI ISSN 0077-2739) 587
Nantucket Maria Mitchell Association. Annual Report (US) 786
Nanyang Orchid (SI) 416
Napao: A Saskatchewan Anthropology Journal (CN ISSN 0077-2755) 52
Naprstkovo Muzeum Asijskych, Africkych a Amerikcych Kultur. Annals (CS ISSN 0554-9256) 52, 402

Naprstkovo Muzeum Asijskych, Africkych a Amerikcych Kultur. Anthropological Papers (CS) 52, 402
Narcotics Progress Report see Action Committee Against Narcotics. Annual Report 286
Narcotics Report, Hong Kong (HK) 287
Nargun (AT) 297
Narodna in Univerzitetna Knjiznica, Ljubljana. Zbornik (YU ISSN 0350-3569) 533
Narodni Technicke Muzeum. Bibliografie. Prameny (CS) 854
Narodni Technicke Muzeum. Catalogues of Collections (CS) 654, 852
Narodni Technicke Muzeum. Rozpravy (CS ISSN 0035-9378) 434, 852
Naropa Institute Journal of Psychology (US) 737
Narradores de Arca (UY ISSN 0077-2801) 569
Narragansett Marine Laboratory. Technical Reports see University of Rhode Island. Graduate School of Oceanography. Marine Technical Reports 313
Narrativa Latinoamericana (UY ISSN 0077-2844) 470, 569
Al-Nashra see Al-Arabiyya 541
Nashrat al-Abhath Assyiahiyah see Tourism Research Bulletin 892
Nasionale Instituut vir Vervoer- en Padnavorsing. Gebruikershandboeke vir Rekenaarprogramme see National Institute for Transport and Road Research. User Manuals for Computer Programs 875
Nasionale Instituut vir Vervoer- en Padnavorsing. Jaarverslag see National Institute for Transport and Road Research. Annual Report 376
Nasionale Instituut vir Vervoer- en Padnavorsing. Tegniese Metodes vir Hootwee see National Institute for Transport and Road Research. Technical Methods for Highways 875
Nasionale Instituut vir Vervoer- en Padnavorsing. Tegniese Riglyne vir Hoofwee see National Institute for Transport and Road Research. Technical Recommendations for Highways 875
Nasionale Instituut vir Vervoer- en Padnavorsing. Tegniese Verslag see National Institute for Transport and Road Research. Technical Report 875
Nasionale Konferensie van Suid-Afrikaanse Opmeters. Verrigtinge see National Conference of South African Surveyors. Proceedings 376
Nassau Review (US ISSN 0077-2879) 569
Nassauische Annalen (GW ISSN 0077-2887) 458
Natal Museum. Occasional Publicatons (SA) 654
Natalia (SA ISSN 0085-3674) 440
Nathaniel Hawthorne Journal (US ISSN 0073-1382) 569
Nation Armee (FR) 639
Nationaal Centrum voor Oudheidkundige Navorsingen in Belgie. Oudheidkundige Repertoria. Reeks A: Biblibgrafische Repertoria see Centre National de Recherches Archeologiques en Belgique. Repertoires Archeologiques. Serie A: Repertoires Bibliographiques 59
Nationaal Instituut voor de Extractiebedrijven. Jaarbericht see Institut National des Industries Extractives. Rapport Annuel 644
National Academy of Sciences. Annual Report (US ISSN 0077-2925) 786
National Academy of Sciences. Biographical Memoirs (US ISSN 0077-2933) 98, 786
National Accounts and Balance of Payments of Rhodesia see National Accounts of Rhodesia 230
National Accounts of Botswana (BS ISSN 0302-2056) 213
National Accounts of Rhodesia (RH) 197, 230

National Accounts of the Maltese Islands (MM ISSN 0077-295X) 230
National Acoustic Laboratories, Sydney. Annual Report (AT ISSN 0311-8983) 911
National Advisory Council on Women's Educational Programs. Annual Report (US) 320, 900
National Aeronautical Laboratory. Annual Report (II ISSN 0077-2976) 9
National Aeronautical Laboratory. Technical Note (II ISSN 0077-300X) 9
National Aeronautical Laboratory Catalogue of N A L Technical Translations see Catalogue of N A L Technical Translations 7
National Aeronautics and Space Administration. N A S A Factbook (US ISSN 0077-3085) 9
National Aeronautics and Space Administration. Technical Memorandums (US ISSN 0499-9320) 9
National Aeronautics and Space Administration. Technical Notes (US ISSN 0077-3131) 9
National Aeronautics and Space Administration. Technical Reports (US ISSN 0077-314X) 9
National Aeronautics and Space Administration. Technical Translations (US ISSN 0077-3158) 9
National Aeronautics and Space Administration Facts see N A S A Facts 9
National Aeronautics and Space Administration University Conference on Manual Control (Papers) see N A S A-University Conference on Manual Control (Papers) 9
National Aerospace and Electronics Conference. Record (US ISSN 0065-373X) 9
National Aerospace Meeting. (Proceedings) (US) 9
National Agricultural Society of Ceylon. Journal (CE ISSN 0547-3616) 18
National Air Monitoring Program Air Quality and Emissions Trends. Report see National Air Quality Emissions Trends. Report 387
National Air Quality Emissions Trends. Report 387
National & International Employment Handbook for Specialized Personnel see Multinational Marketing & Employment Directory 240
National Apparel Suppliers and Contractors Directory (US) 240, 261
National Archives of Malaysia. Annual Report/Arkib Negara Malaysia. Penyata Tahunan (MY ISSN 0076-3381) 444
National Archives of Zambia. Annual Report (ZA ISSN 0084-4942) 440, 533
National Archives of Zambia. National Archives Occasional Paper (ZA) 440
National Art Education Association. Research Monograph (US ISSN 0077-3174) 76, 349
National Association for Business Teacher Education Review see N A B T E Review 338
National Association for Deaf/Blind and Rubella Children. Newsletter see National Association for Deaf/Blind and Rubella Handicapped. Newsletter 807
National Association for Deaf/Blind and Rubella Handicapped. Newsletter(UK) 257, 807
National Association for Foreign Student Affairs Directory see N A F S A Directory 343
National Association for the Advancement of Colored People Annual Report see N A A C P Annual Report 815
National Association for the Blind. Annual Report. (II) 133

National Association of Academies of Science. Directory and Proceedings (US) 786
National Association of Almshouses. Yearbook and Statement of Accounts(UK) 807
National Association of Animal Breeders Annual Proceedings (US ISSN 0077-3255) 45
National Association of Australian State Road Authorities. Guide to the Activities, Publications and Standards of N A A S R A (AT) 875
National Association of Australian State Road Authorities. Guide to the Publications and Policies of N A A S R A see National Association of Australian State Road Authorities. Guide to the Activities, Publications and Standards of N A A S R A 875
National Association of Boards of Pharmacy. Proceedings (US ISSN 0077-3263) 685
National Association of Chain Drug Stores Lilly Digest see N. A. C. D. S. Lilly Digest 218
National Association of College Admissions Counselors. Membership Directory (US ISSN 0090-3965) 338
National Association of College Admissions Counselors. Newsletter (US ISSN 0027-8416) 338
National Association of College Deans and Registrars. Proceedings (US ISSN 0077-328X) 338
National Association of Fleet Administrators, Inc. Annual Reference Book see N A F A Annual Reference Book 871
National Association of Independent Schools. Annual Report (US ISSN 0550-7421) 320
National Association of Intercollegiate Athletics Handbook see N A I A Handbook 821
National Association of Intercollegiate Athletics Official Record Book see N A I A Official Record Book 821
National Association of Jewish Center Workers. Conference Papers (US ISSN 0077-3352) 807
National Association of Manufacturers. Fiscal & Economic Policy Department. Taxation Report (US) 230
National Association of Metal Finishers Accounting Manual see N A M F Accounting Manual 168
National Association of Metal Finishers Management Manual see N A M F Management Manual 629
National Association of Railroad and Utilities Commissioners. Proceedings see National Association of Regulatory Utility Commissioners. Proceedings 873
National Association of Real Estate Investment Trusts Fact Book see R.E.I.T. Fact Book 762
National Association of Realtors. Department of Economics and Research. Existing Home Sales Series, Annual Report. see National Association of Realtors. Existing Home Sales 761
National Association of Realtors. Existing Home Sales (US ISSN 0161-5882) 761
National Association of Regional Councils. Directory (US ISSN 0095-1455) 744
National Association of Regulatory Utility Commissioners. Annual Report on Utility and Carrier Regulation (US) 744
National Association of Regulatory Utility Commissioners. Proceedings (US ISSN 0077-3387) 873
National Association of Retail Druggists Almanac see N A R D Almanac 361
National Association of Schools of Art. Directory (US) 77, 332
National Association of Schools of Music. Directory (US ISSN 0547-4175) 349, 662

National Association of Schools of Music. Proceeding of the Annual Meeting (US ISSN 0077-3409) 662
National Association of Social Workers. Directory of Agencies: U.S. Voluntary, International, Voluntary Intergovernmental (US) 807
National Association of State Universities and Land-Grant Colleges. Appropriations of State Tax Funds for Higher Education (US ISSN 0077-3425) 338
National Association of State Universities and Land-Grant Colleges. Proceedings (US ISSN 0077-3433) 338
National Association of Suggestion Systems. Statistical Report (US ISSN 0077-3441) 220
National Association of Teachers' Agencies. List of the Accredited Members (US ISSN 0077-345X) 344
National Association of Testing Authorities Directory see N. A. T. A. Directory 380
National Association of Training Schools and Juvenile Agencies. Proceedings (US ISSN 0077-3476) 282, 346
National Association of Waste Disposal Contractors. Trade Directory (UK) 240, 753
National Association of Women Artists. Annual Exhibition Catalog (US) 77
National Astrological Society Journal see N A S O Journal 80
National Audio-Visual Association, Inc. Membership Directory see N A V A Membership Directory 349
National Automobile Association Where to Stay Book see N A A Where to Stay Book 483
National Awami Party of Bangla Desh (in Great Britain). Bulletin (UK) 712
National Bank of Ethiopia. Local Prices(ET ISSN 0077-3506) 187
National Bank of Greece. Annual Report/Ethnike Trapeza tes Hellados. Apologismos (GR ISSN 0077-3514) 175
National Bank of Kuwait S.A.K. Annual Report of the Board of Directors and Accounts (KU) 175
National Bank of Liberia. Annual Report (LB) 175
National Bank of Pakistan. Annual Report (PK) 175
National Bank of Pakistan. Report and Statement of Accounts (PK ISSN 0077-3522) 175
National Bank of Yugoslavia. Annual Report (YU ISSN 0077-2798) 175, 187
National Bar Examination Digest (US ISSN 0098-2857) 515
National Baseball Congress. Official Baseball Annual see N B C Official Yearbook 825
National Baseball Congress Official Yearbook see N B C Official Yearbook 825
National Bible Society of Scotland. Annual Report (UK ISSN 0077-3557) 772
National Bibliography of Zambia (ZA) 93
National Board Examiner (US ISSN 0027-8785) 598
National Botanic Gardens. Contributions see GLASRA 115
National Botanic Gardens, Lucknow. Annual Report see National Botanic Gardens, Lucknow. Progress Report 116
National Botanic Gardens, Lucknow. Bulletin (II ISSN 0076-1419) 116
National Botanic Gardens, Lucknow. Progress Report (II) 116
National Budget of Norway (NO ISSN 0077-3573) 231
National Building Code / National Fire Code News see N B C / N F C News 137
National Building Research Institute. Complete List of N B R I Publications (SA ISSN 0077-3581) 140

National Bureau of Economic Research. Annual Report (US ISSN 0077-3611) 146
National Bureau of Economic Research. Fiscal Studies (US ISSN 0071-5484) 213, 231
National Bureau of Economic Research. General Series (US ISSN 0077-3638) 146
National Bureau of Economic Research. Urban and Regional Studies (US) 146
National Bureau of Economic Research. Working Paper (US) 146
National Business Education Yearbook (US ISSN 0547-4728) 219, 349
National Cancer Center. Annual Report/Kokuritsu Gan Senta Nenpo (JA) 605
National Cancer Center. Collected Papers/Kokuritsu Gan Senta, Tokyo. Collected Papers (JA ISSN 0077-3662) 605
National Cancer Conference. Proceedings (US ISSN 0077-3670) 605
National Cancer Institute of Canada. Report (CN ISSN 0077-3689) 606
National Cancer Program; Report of the National Cancer Advisory Board Submitted to the President of the United States for Transmittal to the Congress of the United States. see U. S. National Cancer Program. Report of the National Cancer Advisory Board Submitted to the President of the United States for Transmittal to the Congress of the United States 606
National Carousel Association Carousel Census (US) 77, 476
National Catalogue of Heating and Air Conditioning see Catalogue National du Genie Climatique-Chauffage et Conditionnement d'Air 429
National Catholic Almanac see Catholic Almanac 774
National Catholic Educational Association. Occasional Papers (US) 320, 775
National Catholic Educational Association Ganley's Catholic Schools in America see N C E A Ganley's Catholic Schools in America 332
National Catholic Women's Union. Proceedings (US) 775
National Cellular Plastics Conference. Proceedings (US) 911
National Center for Audio Tapes. Catalog (US ISSN 0077-3719) 265, 349
National Center for State Courts. Publications (US) 515
National Center for the Study of Collective Bargaining in Higher Education. Annual Conference Proceedings (US ISSN 0095-9294) 338, 507
National Children's Bureau. Annual Review (UK ISSN 0302-1998) 257
National Chrysanthemum Society Yearbook see N. C. S. Yearbook 415
National Civic Council. Facts (AT ISSN 0085-3682) 713
National Coal Board (Great Britain). Annual Report and Accounts. Vol. 2, Accounts and Statistical Tables see National Coal Board Statistical Tables 645
National Coal Board. Report and Accounts (UK ISSN 0077-3786) 645
National Coal Board Statistical Tables (UK ISSN 0307-7691) 645
National College of the State Judiciary (US ISSN 0095-2028) 515
National College Physical Education Association for Men Proceedings see N C P E A M Proceedings 349
National Collegiate Athletic Association. Annual Reports. (US ISSN 0077-3794) 821
National Collegiate Athletic Association. Convention Proceedings(US ISSN 0077-3808) 821

National Collegiate Athletic Association. Manual (US ISSN 0077-3816) 821
National Collegiate Athletic Association. Proceedings of the Special Convention (US ISSN 0094-4459) 821
National Collegiate Athletic Association Baseball Annual Guide see N C A A Baseball Annual Guide 825
National Collegiate Athletic Association Basketball Records see N C A A Basketball Records 825
National Collegiate Athletic Association Directory see N C A A Directory 821
National Collegiate Athletic Association Football Records see N.C.A.A. Football Records 825
National Collegiate Athletic Association Gymnastics Rules see N C A A Gymnastics Rules 821
National Collegiate Athletic Association Illustrated Basketball Rules see N C A A Illustrated Basketball Rules 825
National Collegiate Athletic Association Lacrosse Guide see N C A A Lacrosse Guide 825
National Collegiate Athletic Association Television Committee Report see N C A A Television Committee Report 821
National Collegiate Championships (US ISSN 0077-3824) 821
National Colloquium on Oral History. Proceedings see Oral History Review 434
National Commercial & Development Bank. Annual Report and Financial Statements (DQ) 175
National Committee on Science and Technology. Research and Development Statistics (II) 795, 854
National Computer Conference and Exposition see National Computer Conference and Exposition. (Proceedings) 273
National Computer Conference and Exposition. (Proceedings) (US ISSN 0095-6880) 273
National Conference of Commissioners on Uniform State Laws. Handbook and Proceedings (US) 515
National Conference of South African Surveyors. Proceedings/Nasionale Konferensie van Suid-Afrikaanse Opmeters. Verrigtinge (SA) 376, 424
National Conference of Standards Laboratories. Proceedings (US ISSN 0081-4318) 637
National Conference of State Social Security Administrators. Proceedings (US) 807
National Conference on Complete Water Use. Proceedings (US) 897
National Conference on Energy and the Environment. Proceedings (US) 363, 387
National Conference on Fluid Power. Proceedings (US) 381, 626
National Conference on Individual Onsite Wastewater Systems. Proceedings (US ISSN 0160-6662) 387
National Conference on Industrial Hydraulics. Proceedings see National Conference on Fluid Power. Proceedings 626
National Conference on Power Transmission. Proceedings (US ISSN 0095-6481) 356
National Conference on Safety. Proceedings (II) 753
National Conference on Weights and Measures. Report (US ISSN 0077-3964) 637
National Consumer Finance Association Office Manual see N. C. F. A. Office Manual 175
National Cooperative Highway Research Program Reports (US ISSN 0077-5614) 376, 875
National Cooperative Highway Research Program Synthesis of Highway Practice (US ISSN 0547-5570) 376, 875

National Cottonseed Products Association. Trading Rules (US ISSN 0077-4022) *373, 856*
National Council for Geographic Education. Do It This Way (US ISSN 0469-9130) *349, 424*
National Council for Geographic Education. Instructional Activities Series (US) *349, 424*
National Council for Geographic Education. Pacesetter Series (US) *424*
National Council for Geographic Education. Special Publications (US ISSN 0547-5643) *349, 424*
National Council for Geographic Education. Topics in Geography (US) *349, 424*
National Council for Geographic Education. Yearbook *see* National Council for Geographic Education. Pacesetter Series *424*
National Council for Scientific Research. Annual Report (LE) *338*
National Council for Voluntary Organizations. Annual Report (UK) *807*
National Council of Churches, Bangladesh. Annual Report (BG) *776*
National Council of Engineering Examiners. Proceedings (US ISSN 0077-4081) *369*
National Council of Physical Distribution Management. Annual Meeting. Proceedings (US) *218*
National Council of Social Service. Annual Report *see* National Council for Voluntary Organizations. Annual Report *807*
National Council of Teachers of Mathematics. Yearbook (US ISSN 0077-4103) *320, 587*
National Council of the Churches of Christ in the U.S.A. Triennial Report(US) *772*
National Council of the Churches of Christ in the United States of America. Church World Service. Annual Report *see* National Council of the Churches of Christ in the U.S.A. Triennial Report *772*
National Council of the Churches of Christ in the United States of America. Division of Overseas Ministries. Overseas Ministries (US ISSN 0077-412X) *772*
National Council of the Paper Industry for Air and Stream Improvement. Report to Members (US ISSN 0077-4146) *753*
National Council of the Paper Industry for Air and Stream Improvement. Technical Bulletin *see* Stream Improvement Technical Bulletin *389*
National Council on Family Relations. Annual Meeting Proceedings (US ISSN 0077-4162) *911*
National Council on Radiation Protection and Measurements. Proceedings of the Annual Meeting (US ISSN 0195-7740) *753*
National Council on Radiation Protection and Measurements Report *see* N C R P Report *753*
National Council on Radiation Protection and Measurements Statements *see* N C R P Statements *622*
National Cutting Horse Association. Rule Book (US) *828*
National Dahlia Society Annual (UK ISSN 0077-4189) *415*
National Dean's List (US) *338*
National Defence College Gazette (UK ISSN 0021-7336) *639*
National Development Bank. Annual Report and Accounts (SL) *175*
National Die Casting Congress. Transactions *see* S D C E International Die Casting Congress. Transactions *583*
National Directory of Arts Support by Business Corporations (US) *77*
National Directory of Arts Support by Private Foundations (US) *77*
National Directory of Budget Motels (US) *483*

National Directory of College Athletics (Men's Edition) (US ISSN 0547-616X) *821*
National Directory of College Athletics (Women) (US ISSN 0092-5489) *821*
National Directory of Free Tourist Attractions (US) *889*
National Directory of Free Vacation & Travel Information (US) *889*
National Directory of Grants and Aid to Individuals in the Arts, International (US) *77*
National Directory of Law Enforcement Administrators and Correctional Agencies (US) *282*
National Directory of Low-Cost Tourist Attractions (US) *889*
National Directory of Newsletters and Reporting Services (US) *759*
National Directory of Providers of Psychiatric Services to Religious Institutions (US ISSN 0090-4074) *620, 766*
National Directory of State Agencies (US ISSN 0095-3113) *240, 713*
National Directory of Summer Interships for Undergraduate Students (US ISSN 0098-1451) *332*
National Directory of Theme Parks and Amusement Areas (US) *889*
National Directory of Women's Athletics *see* National Directory of College Athletics (Women) *821*
National Distribution Directory of Local Cartage-Short Haul Carriers Warehousing *see* Warehousing/Distribution Directory *882*
National Documentation Center for Sport, Physical Education and Recreation. List of Periodical Holdings *see* Sports Documentation Centre. List of Periodical Holdings *695*
National Documentation Centre for Sport, Physical Education and Recreation. Abstract Journal Holdings *see* Sports Documentation Centre. Abstract Journal Holdings *328*
National Economic and Development Authority Statistical Yearbook of the Philippines *see* N E D A Statistical Yearbook of the Philippines *160*
National Education Association of the United States. Addresses and Proceedings *see* National Education Association of the United States. Proceedings of the Annual Meeting *320*
National Education Association of the United States. Annual Summative Evaluation Report (US ISSN 0092-5691) *320*
National Education Association of the United States. Proceedings of the Annual Meeting (US ISSN 0190-7662) *320*
National Education Society of Sri Lanka. Journal (CE ISSN 0085-3747) *320*
National Electronics Conference. Proceedings *see* National Electronics Conference-National Communications Forum. Proceedings *356*
National Electronics Conference. Record (US ISSN 0077-4421) *356*
National Electronics Conference-National Communications Forum. Proceedings (US) *356*
National Electronics Council. Review *see* National Electronics Review *356*
National Electronics Review (UK ISSN 0305-2257) *356*
National Employment Listing Service for the Criminal Justice System. Federal Employment Information Directory (US ISSN 0194-1704) *282, 667*
National Employment Listing Service for the Criminal Justice System. Police Employment Guide (US ISSN 0194-0813) *283, 667*
National Employment Listing Service for the Criminal Justice System. Special Edition: Education Opportunities (US ISSN 0194-0805) *283, 667*

National Endowment for the Arts. Guide to Programs (US ISSN 0547-6658) *77*
National Endowment for the Humanities. Annual Report (US ISSN 0083-2111) *492*
National Endowment for the Humanities. Program Announcement(US ISSN 0361-1221) *338*
National Energy Studies *see* Contemporary Economic Problems *741*
National Equine (and Smaller Animals) Defence League. Annual Report (UK ISSN 0077-4448) *682*
National Faculty Directory (US ISSN 0077-4472) *344*
National Federation of Plastering Contractors. Year Book (UK ISSN 0077-4480) *137*
National Federation of Roofing Contractors Yearbook *see* N F R C Yearbook *137*
National Fertilizer Development Center. Annual Report (US ISSN 0077-4510) *37*
National Finances; an Analysis of the Revenues and Expenditures of the Government of Canada (CN ISSN 0077-4529) *231*
National Fire Codes *see* National Fire Protection Association. National Fire Codes *395*
National Fire Prevention Gazette (UK ISSN 0077-4537) *395*
National Fire Protection Association. National Fire Codes (US ISSN 0077-4545) *395*
National Fire Protection Association Technical Committee. Report *see* N F P A Technical Committee. Report *395*
National Fisherman. Yearbook Issue (US ISSN 0077-457X) *399*
National Football Guide *see* Sporting News' National Football Guide *826*
National Football League. Record Manual (US ISSN 0077-4588) *825*
National Formulary *see* United States Pharmacopeia-National Formulary *686*
National Free Library of Rhodesia. Annual Report *see* National Free Library Service. Annual Report *533*
National Free Library Service. Annual Report (RH) *533*
National Fresh Produce Market, Johannesburg. Annual Report of the Director (SA) *182*
National Fresh Produce Market, Johannesburg. Annual Trading Results/Jaarliske Handelsyfers (SA) *29*
National Gallery, London. Technical Bulletin (UK) *77, 654*
National Gallery of Art. Annual Report(US ISSN 0091-7222) *77*
National Gallery of Canada. Annual Bulletin/Galerie Nationale du Canada. Bulletin Annuelle (CN) *654*
National Gallery of Canada. Annual Review *see* National Gallery of Canada. Annual Bulletin *654*
National Gallery of Canada. Bulletin *see* National Gallery of Canada. Annual Bulletin *654*
National Gallery of Canada. Journal/Galerie Nationale du Canada. Journal (CN ISSN 0319-5864) *77, 654*
National Gallery of Canada. Library. Canadiana in the Library of the National Gallery of Canada: Supplement (CN ISSN 0078-6985) *77, 654*
National Gallery of Canada. Library. Checklist of Canadian Artists' Files *see* Artists in Canada *72*
National Gallery of Rhodesia. Annual Report and Balance Sheet and Income and Expenditure Account *see* National Gallery of Zimbabwe-Rhodesia. Annual Report and Balance Sheet and Income and Expenditure Account *654*

National Gallery of Zimbabwe-Rhodesia. Annual Report and Balance Sheet and Income and Expenditure Account (RH) *654*
National Gay Task Force Action Report *see* N G T F Action Report *480*
National Geographer (II ISSN 0470-0929) *424*
National Geographic Books (Series) (US ISSN 0077-4618) *424*
National Geographic Society. Special Publications Series *see* National Geographic Books (Series) *424*
National Geographic Society Research Reports (US ISSN 0077-4626) *424, 786*
National Geophysical Research Institute. Publications (II ISSN 0073-4144) *305*
National Governors' Association. Annual Meeting. Proceedings (US ISSN 0191-3441) *744*
National Governors' Conference. Proceedings of the Annual Meeting *see* National Governors' Association. Annual Meeting. Proceedings *744*
National Guard Almanac (US ISSN 0363-8618) *639*
National Guide to Credit Recommendations for Noncollegiate Courses *see* National Guide to Educational Credit for Training Programs *344*
National Guide to Educational Credit for Training Programs (US) *344*
National Guild of Catholic Psychiatrists. Bulletin (US ISSN 0547-7115) *620, 737, 766*
National Hardware Wholesalers' Guide (US) *141*
National Health Council. Annual Report (US ISSN 0085-3755) *753*
National Heart Foundation of Australia. Research-In-Progress (AT ISSN 0077-4685) *607*
National Hockey League. Guide (CN ISSN 0316-8174) *825*
National Hockey League. Official Rule Book (CN) *821*
National Hurricane Operations Plan *see* U. S. Office of Federal Coordinator for Meteorological Services and Supporting Research. National Hurricane Operations Plan *635*
National Hydro Electric Power Corporation. Annual Report (II) *356*
National Ice Cream Retailers Association. Yearbook (US) *219*
National Incinerator Conference. Proceedings *see* National Waste Processing Conference. Proceedings *753*
National Income and Product Accounts of the United States: Statistical Tables (US ISSN 0361-3895) *160*
National Income of Iran (IR ISSN 0572-5941) *187*
National Income Statistics of Thailand (TH ISSN 0077-4723) *160*
National Indian Law Library. Catalogue(US) *394*
National Industrial Conference Board. Business Outlook: an Evening with the Economic Forum *see* Business Outlook *184*
National Information Center for Educational Media Index to Educational Audio Tapes *see* N I C E M Index to Educational Audio Tapes *327*
National Information Center for Educational Media Index to Educational Overhead Transparencies *see* N I C E M Index to Educational Overhead Transparencies *327*
National Information Center for Educational Media Index to Educational Records *see* N I C E M Index to Educational Records *327*
National Information Center for Educational Media Index to Educational Slides *see* N I C E M Index to Educational Slides *327*

National Information Center for Educational Media Index to Environmental Studies-Multimedia *see* N I C E M Index to Environmental Studies-Multimedia *390*

National Information Center for Educational Media Index to Health and Safety Education-Multimedia *see* N I C E M Index to Health and Safety Education-Multimedia *695*

National Information Center for Educational Media Index to Producers and Distributors *see* N I C E M Index to Producers and Distributors *651*

National Information Center for Educational Media Index to Psychology-Multimedia *see* N I C E M Index to Psychology-Multimedia *737*

National Information Center for Educational Media Index to Vocational and Technical Education-Multimedia *see* N I C E M Index to Vocational and Technical Education-Multimedia *3*

National Information Center for Educational Media Index to 8mm Motion Cartridges *see* N I C E M Index to 8mm Motion Cartridges *327*

National Information Center for Educational Media Index to 16mm Educational Films *see* N I C E M Index to 16mm Educational Films *327*

National Information Center for Educational Media Index to 35mm Educational Filmstrips *see* N I C E M Index to 35mm Educational Filmstrips *327*

National Institute for Architectural Education. Bulletin *see* National Institute for Architectural Education. Yearbook *69*

National Institute for Architectural Education. Yearbook (US ISSN 0077-474X) *69*

National Institute for Educational Research. Research Bulletin (JA ISSN 0085-378X) *320*

National Institute for Medical Research. Report (UK ISSN 0072-6567) *598*

National Institute for Medical Research. Scientific Report *see* National Institute for Medical Research. Report *598*

National Institute for Metallurgy Reports *see* N I M Reports *629*

National Institute for Personnel Research. Annual Report (SA ISSN 0077-4758) *220, 737*

National Institute for Personnel Research. List of N I P R Publications (SA ISSN 0077-4766) *93, 161*

National Institute for Research in Dairying. Biennial Report *see* National Institute for Research in Dairying. Report *41*

National Institute for Research in Dairying. Report (UK ISSN 0302-0851) *41*

National Institute for Road Research. Annual Report *see* National Institute for Transport and Road Research. Annual Report *376*

National Institute for Social Work Training Series *see* National Institute Social Services Library *807*

National Institute for Transport and Road Research. Annual Report/ Nasionale Instituut vir Vervoer- en Padnavorsing. Jaarverslag (SA ISSN 0379-6124) *376, 863*

National Institute for Transport and Road Research. Bulletins (SA) *875*

National Institute for Transport and Road Research. P A D Series (SA) *875*

National Institute for Transport and Road Research. Technical Methods for Highways/Nasionale Instituut vir Vervoer- en Padnavorsing. Tegniese Metodes vir Hootwee (SA) *875*

National Institute for Transport and Road Research. Technical Recommendations for Highways/ Nasionale Instituut vir Vervoer- en Padnavorsing. Tegniese Riglyne vir Hoofwee (SA) *875*

National Institute for Transport and Road Research. Technical Report/ Nasionale Instituut vir Vervoer- en Padnavorsing. Tegniese Verslag (SA) *875*

National Institute for Transport and Road Research. User Manuals for Computer Programs/Nasionale Instituut vir Vervoer- en Padnavorsing. Gebruikershandboeke vir Rekenaarprogramme (SA) *273, 376, 875*

National Institute for Water Research Information Sheet *see* N I W R Information Sheet *897*

National Institute of Agricultural Botany, Cambridge, England. Annual Report of the Council and Accounts (UK ISSN 0077-4782) *37*

National Institute of Agricultural Botany, Cambridge, England. Farmers Leaflets (UK) *37*

National Institute of Agricultural Botany, Cambridge, England. Journal (UK ISSN 0077-4790) *37*

National Institute of Agricultural Botany, Cambridge, England. Technical Leaflets (UK) *37*

National Institute of Agricultural Botany, Cambridge, England. Vegetable Growers Leaflets (UK) *37*

National Institute of Agricultural Engineering, Silsoe, England. Translations (UK ISSN 0077-4812) *37*

National Institute of Agricultural Sciences, Tokyo. Bulletin. Series A (Physics and Statistics) (JA ISSN 0077-4820) *18*

National Institute of Agricultural Sciences, Tokyo. Bulletin. Series B (Soils and Fertilizers) (JA ISSN 0077-4839) *37*

National Institute of Agricultural Sciences, Tokyo. Bulletin. Series C (Plant Pathology and Entomology) (JA ISSN 0077-4847) *117, 121*

National Institute of Agricultural Sciences, Tokyo. Bulletin. Series D (Physiology and Genetics) (JA ISSN 0077-4855) *117*

National Institute of Agricultural Sciences, Tokyo. Bulletin. Series H (Farm Management, Land Utilization, Rural Life) (JA ISSN 0077-4863) *18*

National Institute of Agricultural Sciences, Tokyo. Miscellaneous Publication (JA ISSN 0077-4871) *18*

National Institute of Animal Industry, Chiba, Japan. Annual Report (JA) *45*

National Institute of Animal Industry, Chiba, Japan. Bulletin/Chikusan Shikenjo, Chiba, Japan. Chikusan Shikenjo Kenkyu Hokoku (JA ISSN 0077-488X) *45*

National Institute of Animal Industry, Chiba, Japan. Bulletin Summaries (JA ISSN 0077-4898) *45*

National Institute of Economic and Social Research. Annual Report (UK ISSN 0077-491X) *799*

National Institute of Economic and Social Research, London. Economic and Social Studies (UK ISSN 0070-8453) *146, 799*

National Institute of Economic and Social Research, London. Occasional Papers (UK ISSN 0077-4928) *146*

National Institute of Economic and Social Research, London. Regional Papers (UK) *146*

National Institute of Economic and Social Research, London. Regional Studies *see* National Institute of Economic and Social Research, London. Regional Papers *146*

National Institute of Education. Career Education Program: Program Plan (US ISSN 0361-1507) *346*

National Institute of Family Planning General Series *see* N I F P General Series *132*

National Institute of Family Planning Manual Series *see* N I F P Manual Series *132*

National Institute of Family Planning Monograph Series *see* N I F P Monograph Series *132*

National Institute of Family Planning Report Series *see* N I F P Report Series *132*

National Institute of Family Planning Technical Paper Series *see* N I F P Technical Paper Series *132*

National Institute of Genetics, Mishima, Japan. Annual Report/Kokuritsu Idengaku Kenkyusho, Mishima, Japan. Nenpo (JA ISSN 0077-4995) *122*

National Institute of Health Administration and Education Technical Report *see* N I H A E Technical Report *694*

National Institute of Hygienic Sciences. Bulletin/Eisei Shikenjo Hokoku (JA ISSN 0077-5002) *753*

National Institute of Nutrition. Annual Report/Kokuritsu Eiyo Kenkyusho Hokoku (JA) *666*

National Institute of Nutrition. Report (II) *666*

National Institute of Polar Research. Memoirs. Series A: Aeronomy (JA ISSN 0386-5517) *297*

National Institute of Polar Research. Memoirs. Series B: Meteorology (JA ISSN 0386-5525) *634*

National Institute of Polar Research. Memoirs. Series C: Earth Sciences (JA ISSN 0386-5533) *289*

National Institute of Polar Research . Memoirs. Series D: Oceanography (JA) *311*

National Institute of Polar Research. Memoirs. Series E. Biology and Medical Science (JA ISSN 0386-5541) *105, 598*

National Institute of Polar Research. Memoirs. Series F: Logistics (JA ISSN 0386-555X) *786*

National Institute of Sciences of India. Biographical Memoirs of Fellows *see* Indian National Science Academy. Biographical Memoirs of Fellows *97*

National Institute of Sciences of India. Bulletin *see* Indian National Science Academy. Bulletin *783*

National Institute of Sciences of India. Mathematical Tables *see* Indian National Science Academy. Mathematical Tables *585*

National Institute of Sciences of India. N I S I Monographs *see* Indian National Science Academy. Monographs *783*

National Institute of Sciences of India. Proceedings *see* Indian National Science Academy. Proceedings *784*

National Institute of Sciences of India. Yearbook *see* Indian National Science Academy. Year Book *784*

National Institute of Sciences of India, Calcutta. Year Book *see* Indian National Science Academy. Year Book *784*

National Institute Social Services Library (UK ISSN 0077-4774) *807*

National Insurance Institute, Jerusalem. Full Actuarial Report (IS ISSN 0075-1324) *500*

National/International Sculpture Conference. Proceedings (US ISSN 0363-5937) *77*

National Investment Bank, Ghana. Annual Report (National Investment Bank) (GH) *175*

National Investment Bank, Ghana. Report of the Directors *see* National Investment Bank, Ghana. Annual Report *175*

National Investment Bank National Investment Bank, Ghana. Annual Report *see* National Investment Bank, Ghana. Annual Report *175*

National Investor Relations Institute. Executive Summary of the Annual National Conference (US) *204*

National Investor Relations Institute. Proceedings of the Annual National Conference *see* National Investor Relations Institute. Executive Summary of the Annual National Conference *204*

National Jail and Adult Detention Directory (US) *283*

National Jeweler Annual Fashion Guide (US) *504*

National Jewish Welfare Board. Yearbook (US ISSN 0077-507X) *807*

National Junior Horticultural Association. Newsletter (US ISSN 0077-5088) *416*

National Kidney Foundation. Annual Report (US ISSN 0077-5096) *625*

National Language Research Institute. Annual Report/Kokuritsu Kokugo Kenkyusho Nenpo (JA) *547*

National League for Nursing. Associate Degree Education for Nursing (US ISSN 0077-5118) *338, 614*

National League for Nursing. Baccalaureate Programs Accredited for Public Health Nursing Preparation (US) *614*

National League for Nursing. Directory of Career Mobility Programs in Nursing Education (US) *614*

National League for Nursing. League Exchange (US ISSN 0077-5134) *614*

National League of Cities. National Municipal Policy *see* National Municipal Policy *749*

National Library of Canada. Annual Report (CN ISSN 0078-7000) *533*

National Library of Canada. National Conference on the State of Canadian Bibliography. Proceedings (CN) *93*

National Library of Canada: A Bibliography (CN) *93*

National Library of Medicine. Literature Search Series (US ISSN 0083-2251) *602*

National Library of Medicine. Programs and Services (US ISSN 0093-0393) *533*

National Library of Medicine Index of N L M Serial Titles *see* Index of N L M Serial Titles *602*

National List of Advertisers (CN ISSN 0077-5177) *6*

National Maritime Board. (Great Britain) Year Book (UK ISSN 0077-5185) *879*

National Maritime Museum. Occasional Lecture Series (UK ISSN 0141-1268) *654, 879*

National Mass Retailing Institute Compensation in Mass Retailing, Salaries and Incentives *see* N M R I Compensation in Mass Retailing, Salaries and Incentives *209*

National Medico-Legal Symposium (US) *613*

National Metalworking Blue Book (US ISSN 0363-1737) *240, 629*

National Microfilm Association. Proceedings of the Annual Convention *see* National Micrographics Association. Proceedings of the Annual Conference *693*

National Micrographics Association. Proceedings of the Annual Conference (US) *693*

National Minority Business Directory *see* Try Us *149*

National Motor Museum Pictorial Guide (UK) *871*

National Multiple Sclerosis Society. Annual Report (US) *620*

National Municipal Policy (US) *749*

National Museum, Bloemfontein. Memoirs (SA ISSN 0067-9194) *786*

National Museum, Bloemfontein. Navorsinge/Researches (SA ISSN 0067-9208) *786*

National Museum of Natural Sciences. Natural History Notebook Series (CN ISSN 0703-4660) *786*

National Museum of Natural Sciences. Syllogeus (CN ISSN 0704-576X) *786*

National Museum of Tanzania. Annual Report (TZ ISSN 0082-1675) *654*

National Museum of the Philippines. Annual Report (PH ISSN 0076-3756) *654*
National Museum of the Philippines. Monograph Series (PH ISSN 0076-3772) *52*
National Museum of the Philippines. Museum Publications (Pamphlet Series) (PH ISSN 0076-3764) *117*
National Museum of Wales. Annual Report (UK) *654*
National Museums and Monuments Administration. Occasional Papers. Series A: Human Sciences (RH) *799*
National Museums and Monuments of Rhodesia. Occasional Papers. Series A: Human Sciences. see National Museums and Monuments Administration. Occasional Papers. Series A: Human Sciences *799*
National Newspaper Association National Directory of Weekly Newspapers see N N A National Directory of Weekly Newspapers *505*
National Observer Index (US ISSN 0077-524X) *911*
National Ocean Survey. Collected Reprints (US ISSN 0361-2805) *311*
National Opera Association. Membership Directory (US ISSN 0085-381X) *662*
National Opinion Research Center. Newsletter (US ISSN 0077-5266) *815*
National Opinion Research Center. Report (US ISSN 0077-5274) *799*
National Outdoor Living Directory (US) *277, 476, 830*
National P C President (Progressive Conservative Party of Canada) (CN ISSN 0707-0349) *713*
National Paint and Coatings Association. Annual Report (US ISSN 0095-2729) *673*
National Panorama of American Youth (US ISSN 0360-0815) *320*
National Party Platforms. Supplement (US ISSN 0077-5282) *713*
National Patterns of R. & D. Resources; Funds & Manpower in the United States (US ISSN 0093-8572) *786*
National Peach Council. Proceedings (US ISSN 0092-2633) *37*
National Petroleum News Factbook see N P N Factbook *680*
National Pig Breeders' Association Herd Book (UK ISSN 0077-5312) *45*
National Planning Association Reports (US) *213*
National Press Council of the Republic of China Bulletin see P C O T Bulletin *505*
National pro-Life Journal (US) *807*
National Productivity Centre, Malaysia. Annual Report/Pusat Daya Pengeluaran Negara. Lapuran Tahunan (MY) *216*
National Psychological Association for Psychoanalysis. Bulletin (US ISSN 0077-5339) *737*
National Publishing Directory (CN ISSN 0077-5347) *759*
National Radio Publicity Directory (US) *268*
National Ready Mixed Concrete Association Publication see N R M C A Publication *137*
National Real Estate Directory (US) *761*
National Recreational, Sporting and Hobby Organizations of the United States (US) *821*
National Register of Microform Masters(US ISSN 0547-8448) *533*
National Register of Prominent Americans and International Notables (US ISSN 0077-5371) *98*
National Register of Research Projects: Natural and Human Sciences (SA) *786*
National Register of Research Projects: Natural Sciences see National Register of Research Projects: Natural and Human Sciences *786*
National Relay Conference. Proceedings(US ISSN 0077-5401) *356*

National Report for India: Meteorology and Atmospheric Analysis (II) *634*
National Report for India: Seismology and Physics of the Earth's Interior (II) *634*
National Reporter (CN) *515*
National Research Center for Disaster Prevention. Seismological Bulletin (JA) *305*
National Research Council. Committee on Polar Research. Report on United States Antarctic Research Activities (US ISSN 0361-2279) *424*
National Research Council. Transportation Research Board. Bibliography (US ISSN 0148-849X) *863*
National Research Council. Transportation Research Board. Record (US ISSN 0361-1981) *863*
National Research Council, Canada. Annual Report on Scholarships and Grants in Aid of Research/Conseil National de Recherches du Canada. Compte Rendu Annuel des Bourses et Subventions d'Aide a la Recherche(CN ISSN 0316-4047) *320, 786*
National Research Council, Canada. Annual Report on Support of University Research see National Research Council, Canada. Annual Report on Scholarships and Grants in Aid of Research *320*
National Research Council, Canada. Associate Committee on Geotechnical Research. Technical Memorandum (CN ISSN 0077-5428) *289, 369*
National Research Council, Canada. Associate Committee on Scientific Criteria for Environmental Quality. Status Report/Conseil National de Recherches, Canada, Comite Associe sur les Criteres Scientifiques. Rapport d'Activite (CN ISSN 0316-0114) *387*
National Research Council, Canada. Division of Building Research. Bibliography (CN ISSN 0085-3828) *140*
National Research Council, Canada. Division of Building Research. Building Practice Note (CN ISSN 0701-5216) *137*
National Research Council, Canada. Division of Building Research. Building Research Note (CN ISSN 0077-5460) *137*
National Research Council, Canada. Division of Building Research. Computer Program (CN ISSN 0077-5479) *137*
National Research Council, Canada. Division of Building Research. D B R Paper (CN ISSN 0381-4319) *137*
National Research Council, Canada. Division of Building Research. Proceedings (CN) *137*
National Research Council, Canada. Division of Building Research. Research Program (CN ISSN 0077-5517) *137*
National Research Council, Canada. Division of Building Research. Special Technical Publication (CN ISSN 0701-5208) *137*
National Research Council, Canada. Man-Computer Communications Conference. Proceedings (CN) *273*
National Research Council, Canada. National Aeronautical Establishment. Aeronautical Report (L R Series) (CN ISSN 0077-5541) *9*
National Research Council, Canada. National Aeronautical Establishment. Mechanical Engineering Reports (CN ISSN 0077-555X) *9, 382*
National Research Council, Canada. National Aeronautical Establishment. Publications List and Supplements (CN ISSN 0077-5568) *11*
National Research Council, Canada. Publications (CN ISSN 0077-5584) *786, 852*
National Research Council, Canada. Space Research Facilities Branch. Report. (SRFB Series) (CN ISSN 0077-5592) *9*

National Research Council, Canada. Technical Translation (CN ISSN 0077-5606) *786, 852*
National Research Council of Canada. Report of the President/Rapport du President (CN) *786*
National Research Council of the Philippines Research Bulletin see N R C P Research Bulletin *786*
National Research Institute for Pollution and Resources. Annual Report/Kogai Shigen Kenkyusho Nenpo (JA) *387, 645*
National Research Institute for Pollution and Resources. Science Report/Kogai Shigen Kenkyusho Hokoku (JA) *388, 645*
National Research Institute of Agriculture. Annual Report/Nogyo Sogo Kenkyusho Nenpo (JA) *18*
National Research Institute of Police Science. Annual Report/Kagaku Keisatsu Kenkyusho Nenpo (JA ISSN 0453-0667) *283*
National Research Institute of Police Science. Data/Kagaku Keisatsu Kenkyusho Shiryo (JA ISSN 0453-0675) *283, 744*
National Roster of Black Elected Officials (US ISSN 0092-2935) *392, 713*
National Roster of Realtors (US ISSN 0090-1741) *761*
National Rural Electric Cooperative Association. Government Relations Department. Research Division. Research Papers and Circulars. (US ISSN 0077-5657) *356*
National Rural Electric Cooperative Association. Legislation and Communications Department. Research Division. Research Papers and Circulars. see National Rural Electric Cooperative Association. Government Relations Department. Research Division. Research Papers and Circulars *356*
National Rural Electric Cooperative Association. Legislative Research Staff. Research Paper see National Rural Electric Cooperative Association. Government Relations Department. Research Division. Research Papers and Circulars *356*
National S A M P E Technical Conference Series. N S T C Preprint Series (Society for the Advancement of Material and Process Engineering) (US ISSN 0081-1556) *380*
National Sand and Gravel Association Circular see N S G A Circular *297*
National School Boards Association. Yearbook (US ISSN 0077-569X) *344*
National Science Council (Ireland). Progress Report (IE) *786*
National Science Council (Ireland). Register of Scientific Research Personnel (IE ISSN 0085-3836) *786*
National Science Council of the Republic of China Review see N S C Review *786*
National Science Council of the Republic of China Special Publication see N S C Special Publication *786*
National Science Council of the Republic of China Symposium Series see N S C Symposium Series *786*
National Science Council, Republic of China. Annual Report (CH) *786*
National Science Library of Canada. Annual Report see Canada Institute for Scientific and Technical Information. Annual Report *780*
National Science Museum. Memoirs (JA ISSN 0082-4755) *786*
National Sculpture Society, New York. Annual Exhibition (US ISSN 0098-4817) *77*
National Securities and Research Corporation. Annual Forecast (US ISSN 0077-5703) *204*
National Security Traders Association. Traders' Annual (US ISSN 0092-4679) *204*
National Service Data; Domestic (US) *871*

National Shellfisheries Association. Proceedings (US ISSN 0077-5711) *130*
National Shipping Corporation. Report and Accounts (PK) *879*
National Skeet Shooting Association. Records Annual (US ISSN 0077-5738) *830*
National Society for Clean Air Reference Book see N. S. C. A. Reference Book *387*
National Society for Prevention of Cruelty to Children. Annual Report (UK ISSN 0077-5754) *807*
National Society for the Prevention of Blindness. Report see National Society to Prevent Blindness. Report *133*
National Society for the Study of Education. Yearbook (US ISSN 0077-5762) *320*
National Society of College Teachers of Education. Monographs see S P E Monographs *322*
National Society of Public Accountants. Proceedings of the Annual Professional Institute (US ISSN 0077-5770) *168*
National Society to Prevent Blindness. Report (US ISSN 0270-4234) *133*
National Soybean Processors Association. Yearbook (US ISSN 0077-5789) *43*
National Speedway Directory (US) *821*
National Strategy Information Center. Strategy Papers (US) *639*
National Stripper Well Survey (US ISSN 0470-3219) *363, 680*
National Survey, Smoke and Sulphur Dioxide see Great Britain. Warren Spring Laboratory. Investigation of Air Pollution: National Survey, Smoke and Sulphur Dioxide *386*
National Symposium on the State of the Black Economy. Selected Proceedings (US) *911*
National Taiwan Normal University. Graduate Institute of Education. Bulletin (CH) *320*
National Taiwan University. College of Agriculture. Memoirs (CH ISSN 0077-5819) *18*
National Taiwan University. College of Engineering. Bulletin (CH) *369*
National Taiwan University. College of Law. Journal of Social Science (CH ISSN 0077-5835) *799*
National Taiwan University. Department of Geography. Science Reports (CH) *424*
National Taiwan University. Institute of Fishery Biology. Report (CH) *399*
National Taiwan University Journal of Sociology/Tai-Wan ta Hsueh She Hui Hsueh K'an (CH ISSN 0077-5851) *815*
National Tank Truck Carrier Directory (US ISSN 0077-586X) *882*
National Tape Recording Catalog see National Center for Audio Tapes. Catalog *349*
National Tax Association-Tax Institute of America. Proceedings of the Annual Conference (US ISSN 0069-8687) *231*
National Telecommunication Conference. Record see National Telecommunication Forum. Conference Record *265*
National Telecommunication Forum. Conference Record (US) *265*
National Telemetering Conference. Record see National Telecommunication Forum. Conference Record *265*
National Tool, Die and Precision Machining Association. Buyers Guide (US) *583*
National Tourist Guide of Nigeria see Nigeria Tourist Guide *889*
National Trade-Index of Southern Africa (SA ISSN 0077-5894) *182*
National Training Laboratories. Institute of Applied Behavioural Science. Selected Readings Series see Learning Resources Corporation. Selected Reading Services *736*
National Transportation Safety Board Service (US) *869*

National Travel Expenditure Study: Summary Report (US) 889
National Trust for Scotland Yearbook (UK ISSN 0077-5916) 277
National Trust of Australia (Western Australia) Annual Report (AT) 447
National Union Catalog of Manuscript Collections (US ISSN 0090-0044) 93
National Union of Insurance Workers. Prudential Section. Gazette (UK) 500
National Union of Students Yearbook see N U S Yearbook 320
National Union of Teachers. Annual Report (UK ISSN 0077-5940) 349
National Union of Teachers Guide to Careers Work see N U T Guide to Careers Work 667
National University Continuing Education Association. Handbook and Directory (US) 332, 338
National University Extension Association. Handbook and Directory see National University Continuing Education Association. Handbook and Directory 338
National Urban League Annual Report (US) 485
National Urban League Progress Report see National Urban League Annual Report 485
National Waste Processing Conference. Proceedings (US) 369, 753
National Waterways Conference Newsletter (US ISSN 0028-0380) 879, 897
National Wheelchair Basketball Association. Directory (US) 825
National Writers Club. Bulletin for Professional Members see Professional Freelance Writers Directory 505
National Yellow Book of Funeral Directors & Suppliers see Yellow Book of Funeral Directors & Services 414
National Zip Code & Post Office Directory (US ISSN 0191-6971) 266
National Zip Code Directory see National Zip Code & Post Office Directory 266
Nationale Maatschappij voor de Huisvesting. Jaarverslag see Societe National du Logement. Rapport Annuel 487
Nationale-Nederlanden. Annual Report (NE ISSN 0077-5975) 500
National's Forecast For...(Year) see National Securities and Research Corporation. Annual Forecast 204
Nationwide Directory of Gift and Housewares Buyers (US) 429, 479
Nationwide Directory of Men's and Boys Wear Buyers (Exclusive of New York Metropolitan Area) (US ISSN 0077-5983) 261
Nationwide Directory of Sporting Goods Buyers (US) 261
Nationwide Directory of Women's and Children's Wear Buyers (Exclusive of New York Metropolitan Area) (US ISSN 0077-5991) 261
Nationwide Major Mass Market Merchandisers (Exclusive of New York Metropolitan Area) (US ISSN 0077-6009) 261
Native American Rights Fund. Catalogue see National Indian Law Library. Catalogue 394
Native American Texts Series see I J A L Native American Texts Series 545
Natur Historisches Museum der Stadt Bern. Jahrbuch (SZ) 787
Natur und Land (AU ISSN 0028-0607) 787
Natur und Mensch; Jahresmitteilungen der Naturhistorischen Gesellschaft Nuernberg (GW ISSN 0077-6025) 63, 105, 297
Natura Jutlandica (DK ISSN 0077-6033) 105
Natural Gas (Annual) (US) 363, 680
Natural Gas Manual (UK) 911
Natural Gas Processing Plants in Canada (CN ISSN 0077-6041) 680

Natural Gas Processors Association. Annual Convention. Proceedings see Gas Processors Association. Annual Convention. Proceedings 679
Natural Hazard Research Working Papers (US ISSN 0082-5166) 424
Natural History Miscellanea (US) 105
Natural History Museum of Los Angeles County. Contributions in History (US ISSN 0076-0927) 105
Natural History Museum of Los Angeles County. Contributions in Science (US ISSN 0076-0900) 787
Natural History Museum of Los Angeles County. Science Series (US ISSN 0076-0943) 787
Natural Law Forum see American Journal of Jurisprudence 508
Natural Resources Research (UN ISSN 0077-6092) 277, 289
Natural Science News (US) 787
Naturalia Hispanica (SP) 388
Nature and Environment Series (FR) 277
Nature Centers and Outdoor Education Facilities see Directory of Nature Centers and Related Environmental Education Facilities 276
Nature Conservation Council of N. S. W. Bulletin (Nature Conservation Council of New South Wales) (AT ISSN 0311-0745) 277, 388
Nature Conservation Council of New South Wales Nature Conservation Council of N. S. W. Bulletin see Nature Conservation Council of N. S. W. Bulletin 277
Nature in Cambridgeshire (UK ISSN 0466-6046) 277
Nature/Science Annual (US ISSN 0085-3860) 911
Naturforschende Gesellschaft in Basel. Verhandlungen/Society for Natural Sciences, Basel. Proceedings (SZ ISSN 0077-6122) 787
Naturforschende Gesellschaft in Bern. Mitteilungen (SZ ISSN 0077-6130) 787
Naturhistorische Gesellschaft Nuernberg. Abhandlungen (GW ISSN 0077-6149) 105
Naturhistorische Gesellschaft Nuernberg. Mitteilungen und Jahresbericht see Natur und Mensch; Jahresmitteilungen der Naturhistorischen Gesellschaft Nuernberg 105
Naturhistorisches Museum in Wien. Annalen (AU ISSN 0083-6133) 787
Naturhistorisches Museum in Wien. Flugblatt (AU ISSN 0083-6141) 911
Naturhistorisches Museum in Wien. Neue Denkschriften (AU) 787
Naturhistorisches Museum in Wien. Veroeffentlichungen. Neue Folge (AU ISSN 0505-5164) 787
Naturkundliches Jahrbuch der Stadt Linz (AU ISSN 0470-3901) 787
Naturkundliches Museum "Mauritianum" Altenburg. Abhandlungen und Berichte (GE ISSN 0065-6631) 654, 787
Naturwissenschaftliche Rundschau. Buecher der Zeitschrift (GW ISSN 0077-6157) 787
Naturwissenschaftlicher Verein fuer Schleswig-Holstein. Schriften (GW ISSN 0077-6165) 787
Naturwissenschaftlicher Verein fuer Steiermark. Mitteilungen (AU) 787
Naturwissenschaftlicher Verein in Hamburg. Abhandlungen und Verhandlungen (GW ISSN 0301-2697) 105
Nauchno-Issledovatel'skii Institut Kul'tury. Trudy see Sotsiologiya Kul'tury 816
Nauchno-Issledovatel'skii Institut Prikladnoi Geodezii. Trudy (UR) 297
Naucni Sastanak Slavista u Vukove Dane. Referati i Saopstenja (YU) 547
Nauheimer Fortbildungs-Lehrgaenge (GW ISSN 0077-6173) 598
Nauka dla Wszystkich (PL ISSN 0077-6181) 787

Nauka o Zemi. Seria Geograficna (CS) 289, 424
Nauka Segodnya (UR) 787
Nauki Polityczne (PL) 713
Nautical Almanac (UK ISSN 0077-619X) 83
Nautisches Jahrbuch (GE) 83
Nautisches Jahrbuch, oder Ephemeriden und Tafeln (GW ISSN 0077-6211) 83
Navajo Historical Publications. Biographical Series (US ISSN 0091-6684) 98, 392
Navajo Historical Publications. Cultural Series (US) 393
Navajo Historical Publications. Documentary Series (US) 393
Navajo Historical Publications. Historical Series (US) 393
Navigation (AT ISSN 0077-6262) 863
Navis (FR ISSN 0077-6270) 879
Navy, Army and Air Force Institutes Reports see N A A F I Reports 639
Nawpa Pacha (US ISSN 0077-6297) 63
Nazionaler Katalog der Heizung und Klimatisierung see Catalogue National du Genie Climatique-Chauffage et Conditionnement d'Air 429
Nea Paphos (PL) 63
Near and Middle East Monographs (NE) 475
Near and Middle East Series (CN ISSN 0077-6300) 569
Near East and North Africa Report (US ISSN 0145-9317) 187, 713
Near East Foundation. Annual Report (US ISSN 0077-6319) 200, 722
Nebraska. Accounting Division. Annual Report of Receipts and Disbursements State of Nebraska (US ISSN 0090-628X) 744
Nebraska. Agricultural Experiment Station, North Platte. Fall Crops and Irrigation Field Day (US ISSN 0085-3879) 37
Nebraska. Commission on Law Enforcement and Criminal Justice. Criminal Justice Action Plan (US ISSN 0091-9195) 912
Nebraska. Commission on Law Enforcement and Criminal Justice. Criminal Justice Comprehensive Plan (US ISSN 0091-9128) 912
Nebraska. Department of Economic Development. Annual Economic Report (US ISSN 0362-1138) 187
Nebraska. Department of Public Institutions. Mental Health and Mental Retardation Services Annual Statistical Report (US) 756
Nebraska. Department of Roads. Challenge of the 80's (US) 376
Nebraska. Department of Roads. Highway Statistics: State and Local Road and Street Data for (Year) (US) 875
Nebraska. Department of Roads. Traffic Analysis Unit. Continuous Traffic Count Data and Traffic Characteristics on Nebraska Streets and Highways (US ISSN 0091-844X) 875
Nebraska. Fisheries Production Division. Annual Report (US ISSN 0092-1696) 399
Nebraska. Indian Commission. Report (US ISSN 0360-683X) 393
Nebraska. Natural Resources Commission. State Water Plan Publication (Lincoln) (US ISSN 0092-6442) 897
Nebraska. Office of Athletic Commissioner. Report (US ISSN 0091-942X) 821
Nebraska. Office of Mental Retardation. Directory of Community-Based Mental Retardation Services (US ISSN 0096-3054) 346
Nebraska. State Patrol. Annual Report (US ISSN 0094-1247) 283
Nebraska Academy of Sciences. Proceedings (US ISSN 0077-6343) 787
Nebraska Academy of Sciences. Transactions (US ISSN 0077-6351) 787

Nebraska Community Improvement Program (US) 187
Nebraska Highway Statistics: State and Local Construction Mileage see Nebraska. Department of Roads. Highway Statistics: State and Local Road and Street Data for (Year) 875
Nebraska Law Enforcement Training Center. Annual Report (US) 283
Nebraska Library Commission. Annual Report (US ISSN 0099-0299) 534
Nebraska State Industrial Directory (US) 240
Nebraska Statistical Handbook (US ISSN 0097-9325) 843
Nebraska Statistical Report of Abortions (US ISSN 0095-3105) 133
Nebraska Symposium on Motivation (Publication) (US ISSN 0070-2099) 737
Nebraska Transcript (US) 515
Nebraska Water Resources Research Institute, University of Nebraska. Annual Report of Activities (US ISSN 0077-6394) 897
Nebula Award Stories see Nebula Winners 569
Nebula Winners (US ISSN 0162-3818) 569
NebulouSFan (US) 4
Neckwear Industry Directory (US) 261, 262, 856
Nederlands Bibliotheek en Lektuur Centrum. Index (NE) 912
Nederlands Interuniversitair Demografisch Instituut. Publications (NE) 728
Nederlands Interuniversitair Demografisch Instituut. Working Papers (NE) 728
Nederlands Interuniversitair Demografish Instituut Publikaties see N I D I Publikaties 728
Nederlands Theater- en Televisie Jaarboek (NE) 268, 859
Nederlands-Zuidafrikaanse Vereniging. Jaarverslag (NE ISSN 0077-6416) 440
Nederlandsche Entomologische Vereniging. Monographs (NE ISSN 0548-1163) 121
Nederlandse Bosstatistiek (NE) 843
Nederlandse Centrale Organisatie voor Toegepast-Natuurwetenschappelijk Onderzoek. Technisch-Physische Dienst. Annual Report (NE) 697
Nederlandse Houtbond. Jaarverslag (NE) 141
Nederlandse Jeugd en Haar Onderwijs/Netherlands Youth and Its Education (NE ISSN 0077-6750) 320
Nederlandse Schadeverzekeringsmaatschappijen/Netherlands Non-Life Insurance Companies (NE ISSN 0077-6874) 500
Nederlandse Vereniging voor Internationaal Recht. Mededelingen (NE ISSN 0077-6440) 523
Need a Lift? (US ISSN 0548-1384) 320
Neftegazonosnye i Perspektivnye Kompleksy Tsentralnykh i Vostochnykh Oblastei Russkoi Platformy (UR) 680
Neftena i Vuglishtna Geologiia/Petroleum and Coal Geology (BU) 297, 680
Negev Institute for Arid Zone Research, Beer-Sheva, Israel. Report for Year see Ben-Gurion University of the Negev. Research and Development Authority. Scientific Activities 780
Negritud (CK) 393
Negro American Biographies and Autobiographies (US ISSN 0077-6475) 98
Negro in the Congressional Record (US ISSN 0077-6483) 815
Nehezipari Muszaki Egyetem, Miskolc. Publications. Series A: Mining (HU ISSN 0324-4628) 645
Nehezipari Muszaki Egyetem, Miskolc. Publications. Series B: Metallurgy (HU ISSN 0324-4679) 629

Nehezipari Muszaki Egyetem, Miskolc. Publications. Series C: Machinery (HU ISSN 0133-297X) *583*
Nehezipari Muszaki Egyetem, Miskolc. Publications. Series D: Natural Sciences (HU ISSN 0133-2929) *787*
Neki Pokazatelji Tehnickog Razvoja Privrede Jugoslavije (YU ISSN 0300-2497) *161*
Nekotorye Filosofskie Voprosy Sovremennogo Estestvoznaniya (UR) *690, 787*
Nelson Gallery and Atkins Museum. Bulletin (US ISSN 0077-6513) *654*
Nemity (PY) *492*
Nemouria; Occasional Papers of the Delaware Museum of Natural History (US ISSN 0085-3887) *787*
Nempo Nihon no Roshi Kankei see Nihon no Roshi Kankei *209*
Nenkan Kokoku Bijutsu see Annual of Advertising Art in Japan *4*
Neo-Hellenika (US ISSN 0077-6521) *260*
Neodidagmata (PL ISSN 0077-653X) *350*
Neologie en Marche. Serie A. Langue Generale (CN ISSN 0380-9366) *548*
Neologie en Marche. Serie B. Langues de Specialities (CN ISSN 0701-7995) *548*
Neotestamentica (SA) *766*
Nepal. Central Bureau of Statistics. Statistical Pocket Book (NP) *843*
Nepal. Department of Agricultural Education and Research. Annual Report (NP) *18, 320*
Nepal. Department of Medicinal Plants. Annual Report (NP) *117, 685*
Nepal. Rashtriya Pancayata. Arthika Samiti (NP) *187*
Nepal-Antiquary. Bibliographical Series (NP) *670*
Nepal Bank Limited. Annual Report and Balance Sheet (NP) *175*
Nepal Documentation (NP) *3, 161*
Nepal Family Planning and Maternal Child Health Board. Annual Report (NP) *132, 807*
Nepal Gazette Translation Service see Nepal Recorder *515*
Nepal Industrial Development Corporation. Annual Report (NP ISSN 0077-6548) *224*
Nepal Industrial Development Corporation. Industrial Digest (NP ISSN 0077-6556) *224*
Nepal Industrial Development Corporation. Statistical Abstracts (NP ISSN 0077-6564) *161*
Nepal Law Translation Series see Nepal Miscellaneous Series *515*
Nepal Miscellaneous Series (NP) *515*
Nepal Rastra Bank. Annual Report (NP) *175*
Nepal Rastra Bank. Report of the Board of Directors see Nepal Rastra Bank. Annual Report *175*
Nepal Recorder (NP) *515*
Nepi Kultura-Nepi Tarsadalom (HU) *815*
Nepmuveszet Evszazadai/Jahrhunderte der Volkskunst (HU) *402*
Neprajzi Ertesito/Ethnographic Review (HU ISSN 0077-6599) *52*
Neprajzi Kozlemenyek (HU ISSN 0028-2774) *52, 402*
Neprajzi Tanulmanyok (HU ISSN 0077-6602) *52*
Neptune's Kingdom (IE) *580*
Neraca (MY) *515*
Nerve Chemistry see Japanese Neurochemical Society. Bulletin *620*
Nes og Helg Ya (NO) *458*
Netherlands. Centraal Bureau voor de Statistiek. Beleggingen van Institutionele Beleggers. Investments of Institutional Investors (NE ISSN 0077-6718) *204*
Netherlands. Centraal Bureau voor de Statistiek. Bezoek aan Vermakelijkheidsinstellingen. Attendance at Public Entertainments (NE ISSN 0077-6688) *859*

Netherlands. Centraal Bureau voor de Statistiek. Bibliografie van Regionale Onderzoekingen Op Sociaalwetenschappelijk Terrein. Bibliography of Regional Studies in the Social Sciences (NE ISSN 0077-6726) *803*
Netherlands. Centraal Bureau voor de Statistiek. Criminele Statistiek. Criminal Statistics (NE ISSN 0077-6734) *283*
Netherlands. Centraal Bureau voor de Statistiek. Diagnosestatistiek Bedrijfsverenigingen (Omslagleden). Social Insurance Sickness Statistics (NE ISSN 0077-6742) *500, 807*
Netherlands. Centraal Bureau voor de Statistiek. Faillissementsstatistiek. Bankruptcies (NE ISSN 0077-6793) *161*
Netherlands. Centraal Bureau voor de Statistiek. Gevangenisstatistiek. Statistics of Prisons (NE ISSN 0077-6815) *283*
Netherlands. Centraal Bureau voor de Statistiek. Hypotheken en Hypotheekbanken. Statistics of Mortgages see Netherlands. Centraal Bureau voor de Statistiek. Hypotheken. Statistics of Mortgages *161*
Netherlands. Centraal Bureau voor de Statistiek. Hypotheken. Statistics of Mortgages (NE) *161*
Netherlands. Centraal Bureau voor de Statistiek. Jaaroverzicht Bevolking en Volksgezondheid. Population and Health Statistics (NE) *728, 753*
Netherlands. Centraal Bureau voor de Statistiek. Justiciele Kinderbescherming (NE) *257*
Netherlands. Centraal Bureau voor de Statistiek. Justitiele Statistiek. Judicial Statistics (NE ISSN 0077-684X) *515*
Netherlands. Centraal Bureau voor de Statistiek. Muziek en Theater (NE) *859*
Netherlands. Centraal Bureau voor de Statistiek. Naamlijsten voor de Statistiek van de Buitenlandse Handel. List of Goods for the Statistics of Foreign Trade (NE ISSN 0077-6882) *161*
Netherlands. Centraal Bureau voor de Statistiek. Naamlijsten voor de Statistiek van de Buitenlandse Handel. Supplement. List of Goods for the Statistics of Foreign Trade. Supplement (NE ISSN 0077-6890) *161*
Netherlands. Centraal Bureau voor de Statistiek. Nationale Rekeningen. National Accounts (NE ISSN 0077-6866) *231*
Netherlands. Centraal Bureau voor de Statistiek. Per Leerling Beschikbaar Gestelde Bedragen voor het Lager Onderwijs. Amounts per Pupil Provided for Primary Education (NE) *327, 843*
Netherlands. Centraal Bureau voor de Statistiek. Productie Statistiek van de Zuivelindustrie. Production Statistics of the Dairy Industry (NE) *41*
Netherlands. Centraal Bureau voor de Statistiek. Produktiestatistieken: Bierbrouwerijen en Mouterijen, Alcoholfabrieken, Distileerderijen en Frisdrankenindustrie (NE) *161*
Netherlands. Centraal Bureau voor de Statistiek. Produktiestatistieken: Bierbrouwerijen en Mouterijen, Distileerderijen en Likeurstokerijen, Frisdrankenindustrie see Netherlands. Centraal Bureau voor de Statistiek. Produktiestatistieken: Bierbrouwerijen en Mouterijen, Alcoholfabrieken, Distileerderijen en Frisdrankenindustrie *161*
Netherlands. Centraal Bureau voor de Statistiek. Produktiestatistieken: Papier- en Kartonindustrie (NE) *676*
Netherlands. Centraal Bureau voor de Statistiek. Produktiestatistieken: Rijwiel- en Motorrijwielindustrie (NE) *826*

Netherlands. Centraal Bureau voor de Statistiek. Produktiestatistieken: Suikerfabrieken (NE) *406*
Netherlands. Centraal Bureau voor de Statistiek. Produktiestatistiek Strokartonindustrie see Netherlands. Centraal Bureau voor de Statistiek. Produktiestatistieken: Papier- en Kartonindustrie *676*
Netherlands. Centraal Bureau voor de Statistiek. Produktiestatistieken: Veevoederindustrie (NE) *43*
Netherlands. Centraal Bureau voor de Statistiek. Produktiestatistiek van de Papierindustries see Netherlands. Centraal Bureau voor de Statistiek. Produktiestatistieken: Papier- en Kartonindustrie *676*
Netherlands. Centraal Bureau voor de Statistiek. Regionaal Statistisch Zakboek (NE) *843*
Netherlands. Centraal Bureau voor de Statistiek. Regional Statistical Studies (NE ISSN 0077-7064) *843*
Netherlands. Centraal Bureau voor de Statistiek. Statistiek der Branden. Fire Statistics (NE ISSN 0077-6955) *395*
Netherlands. Centraal Bureau voor de Statistiek. Statistiek der Lonen in de Landbouw. Statistics of Wages in Agriculture (NE ISSN 0077-6963) *25, 161*
Netherlands. Centraal Bureau voor de Statistiek. Statistiek der Motorrijtuigen see Netherlands. Centraal Bureau voor de Statistiek. Statistiek der Motorvoertuigen. Statistics of Motor Vehicles *882*
Netherlands. Centraal Bureau voor de Statistiek. Statistiek der Motorvoertuigen. Statistics of Motor Vehicles (NE) *882*
Netherlands. Centraal Bureau voor de Statistiek. Statistiek der Verkiezingen. Gemeenteraden. Election Statistics. Municipal Councils (NE ISSN 0077-7013) *717*
Netherlands. Centraal Bureau voor de Statistiek. Statistiek der Verkiezingen. Provinciale Staten. Election Statistics. Provincial Councils (NE ISSN 0077-7021) *748*
Netherlands. Centraal Bureau voor de Statistiek. Statistiek der Verkiezingen. Tweede Kamer der Staten-Generaal. Election Statistics. Second Chamber of the States-General (NE ISSN 0077-703X) *718*
Netherlands. Centraal Bureau voor de Statistiek. Statistiek van de Algemene Bijstand. Statistics of Public Assistance (NE ISSN 0077-7072) *807*
Netherlands. Centraal Bureau voor de Statistiek. Statistiek van de Bejaardenoorden. Homes for the Aged (NE ISSN 0077-7099) *807*
Netherlands. Centraal Bureau voor de Statistiek. Statistiek van de Gemeentewege per Leerling Beschikbaar Gestelde Bedragenter Bestrijding van de Materiele Exploitatiekosten der Lagere Scholen. Statistics of the Amounts per Pupil Provided by the Municipality to Meet the Material Cost of Elementary Education see Netherlands. Centraal Bureau voor de Statistiek. Per Leerling Beschikbaar Gestelde Bedragen voor het Lager Onderwijs. Amounts per Pupil Provided for Primary Education *327*
Netherlands. Centraal Bureau voor de Statistiek. Statistiek van de Internationale Binnenvaart. Statistics of the International Inland Shipping (NE ISSN 0077-7102) *879*
Netherlands. Centraal Bureau voor de Statistiek. Statistiek van de Inkomsten en Uitgaven der Overheid voor Cultuur en Recreatie. Statistics of Government Expenditure on Culture and Recreation (NE) *823*

Netherlands. Centraal Bureau voor de Statistiek. Statistiek van de Investeringen in Vaste Activa in de Industrie see Netherlands. Centraal Bureau voor de Statistiek. Statistiek van de Investeringen in Vaste Activa in de Nijverheid. Statistics on Fixed Capital Formation in Industry *161*
Netherlands. Centraal Bureau voor de Statistiek. Statistiek van de Investeringen in Vaste Activa in de Nijverheid. Statistics on Fixed Capital Formation in Industry (NE) *161, 843*
Netherlands. Centraal Bureau voor de Statistiek. Statistiek van de Koopvaardijvloot. Statistics of the Merchant Marine (NE ISSN 0077-7129) *879*
Netherlands. Centraal Bureau voor de Statistiek. Statistiek van de Luchtvaart. Civil Aviation Statistics (NE ISSN 0077-7137) *869*
Netherlands. Centraal Bureau voor de Statistiek. Statistiek van de Land- en Tuinbouw. Statistics of Agriculture (NE ISSN 0077-7145) *25*
Netherlands. Centraal Bureau voor de Statistiek. Statistiek van de Openbare Bibliotheken (NE) *534*
Netherlands. Centraal Bureau voor de Statistiek. Statistiek van de Spaargelden. Statistics of Savings (NE) *161*
Netherlands.Centraal Bureau voor de Statistiek. Statistiek van de Uitgaven der Overheid voor Cultuur en Recreatie see Netherlands. Centraal Bureau voor de Statistiek. Statistiek van de Inkomsten en Uitgaven der Overheid voor Cultuur en Recreatie. Statistics of Government Expenditure on Culture and Recreation *823*
Netherlands. Centraal Bureau voor de Statistiek. Statistiek van de Uitgaven der Overheid voor Onderwijs. Statistics of the Expenditure of the State, the Provinces and the Municipalities on Education (NE ISSN 0077-7188) *344*
Netherlands. Centraal Bureau voor de Statistiek. Statistiek van de Voorlichting Bij Beroepskeuze. Statistics of Vocational Guidance and Selection of Personnel see Netherlands. Centraal Bureau voor de Statistiek. Statistiek van de Voorlichting Bij Scholen en Beroepskeuze. Statistics of Vocational Guidance *327*
Netherlands. Centraal Bureau voor de Statistiek. Statistiek van de Voorlichting Bij Scholen en Beroepskeuze. Statistics of Vocational Guidance (NE) *327, 668*
Netherlands. Centraal Bureau voor de Statistiek. Statistiek van de Verkeersongevallen op de Openbare Weg. Statistics of Road-Traffic Accidents (NE ISSN 0077-7234) *866*
Netherlands. Centraal Bureau voor de Statistiek. Statistiek van de Visserij. Statistics of Fisheries (NE ISSN 0077-7242) *399*
Netherlands. Centraal Bureau voor de Statistiek. Statistiek van de Zeevaart. Statistics of Seaborne Shipping (NE ISSN 0077-7250) *879*
Netherlands. Centraal Bureau voor de Statistiek. Statistiek van het Beroepsonderwijs see Netherlands. Centraal Bureau voor de Statistiek. Statistiek van het Beroepsonderwijs: Technisch en Nautisch Onderwijs. Statistics on Vocational Training *328*
Netherlands. Centraal Bureau voor de Statistiek. Statistiek van het Beroepsonderwijs: Agrarisch Onderwijs (NE) *328, 668*
Netherlands. Centraal Bureau voor de Statistiek. Statistiek van Het Beroepsonderwijs: Beroepsbegeleidend Onderwijs Leerlingwezen (NE) *320*

Netherlands. Centraal Bureau voor de Statistiek. Statistiek van het Beroepsonderwijs: Huishoud- en Nijverheidsonderwijs (NE) *350*
Netherlands. Centraal Bureau voor de Statistiek. Statistiek van het Beroepsonderwijs: Kunstonderwijs. Art Colleges (NE) *332, 338*
Netherlands. Centraal Bureau voor de Statistiek. Statistiek van het Beroepsonderwijs: Landbouwonderwijs *see* Netherlands. Centraal Bureau voor de Statistiek. Statistiek van het Beroepsonderwijs: Agrarisch Onderwijs *328*
Netherlands. Centraal Bureau voor de Statistiek. Statistiek van het Beroepsonderwijs: Opleidingsscholen Kleuterleidsters en Pedagogische Academies (NE) *328*
Netherlands. Centraal Bureau voor de Statistiek. Statistiek van Het Binnenlands Goederenvervoer. Statistics of Internal Goods Transport in the Netherlands (NE ISSN 0077-7269) *879*
Netherlands. Centraal Bureau voor de Statistiek. Statistiek van het Buitengewoon Onderwijs. Statistics of Special Education (NE) *346*
Netherlands. Centraal Bureau voor de Statistiek. Statistiek van het Beroepsonderwijs: Sociaal-Pedagogisch Onderwijs (NE) *320*
Netherlands. Centraal Bureau voor de Statistiek. Statistiek van het Beroepsonderwijs: Technisch en Nautisch Onderwijs. Statistics on Vocational Training (NE) *328, 668*
Netherlands. Centraal Bureau voor de Statistiek. Statistiek van het Erkende Schriftelijk Onderwijs. Statistics on Correspondence Courses (NE) *350*
Netherlands. Centraal Bureau voor de Statistiek. Statistiek van het Gesubsidieerde Toneel *see* Netherlands. Centraal Bureau voor de Statistiek. Muziek en Theater *859*
Netherlands. Centraal Bureau voor de Statistiek. Statistiek van Het Internationaal Goederenvervoer. Statistics of the International Goods Traffic (NE ISSN 0077-7293) *161*
Netherlands. Centraal Bureau voor de Statistiek. Statistiek van het Kunstonderwijs. Statistics on Art Colleges *see* Netherlands. Centraal Bureau voor de Statistiek. Statistiek van het Beroepsonderwijs: Kunstonderwijs. Art Colleges *338*
Netherlands. Centraal Bureau voor de Statistiek. Statistiek. van het Kweekschoolonderwijs. Statistics on Teacher Training Colleges *see* Netherlands. Centraal Bureau voor de Statistiek. Statistiek van het Beroepsonderwijs: Opleidingsscholen Kleuterleidsters en Pedagogische Academies *328*
Netherlands. Centraal Bureau voor de Statistiek. Statistiek van het Land- en Tuinbouwonderwijs. Statistics Concerning Agricultural and Horticultural Education *see* Netherlands. Centraal Bureau voor de Statistiek. Statistiek van het Beroepsonderwijs: Agrarisch Onderwijs *328*
Netherlands. Centraal Bureau voor de Statistiek. Statistiek van het Nijverheidsonderwijs *see* Netherlands. Centraal Bureau voor de Statistiek. Statistiek van het Beroepsonderwijs: Huishoud- en Nijverheidsonderwijs *350*
Netherlands. Centraal Bureau voor de Statistiek. Statistiek van Het Personenvervoer. Statistics of Passenger Transport (NE ISSN 0077-7358) *863*

Netherlands. Centraal Bureau voor de Statistiek. Statistiek van het Schriftelijk Onderwijs. Statistics on Correspondence Courses *see* Netherlands. Centraal Bureau voor de Statistiek. Statistiek van het Erkende Schriftelijk Onderwijs. Statistics on Correspondence Courses *350*
Netherlands. Centraal Bureau voor de Statistiek. Statistiek van het Sociaal-Pedagogisch Onderwijs. Statistics on Socio-Pedagogic Training *see* Netherlands. Centraal Bureau voor de Statistiek. Statistiek van het Beroepsonderwijs: Sociaal-Pedagogisch Onderwijs *320*
Netherlands. Centraal Bureau voor de Statistiek. Statistiek van het Voorbereidend Hoger en Middelbaar Onderwijs: Leraren. Statistics of Secondary Education: Teachers *see* Netherlands. Centraal Bureau voor de Statistiek. Statistiek van het W V O, H A V O en M A V O; Instroom, Doorstroom en Uitstroom van Leerlingen *344*
Netherlands. Centraal Bureau voor de Statistiek. Statistiek van Het Wetenschappelijk Onderwijs. Statistics of University Education (NE ISSN 0077-7439) *338*
Netherlands. Centraal Bureau voor de Statistiek. Statistiek van het W V O, H A V O en M A V O; Instroom, Doorstroom en Uitstroom van Leerlingen (NE) *344*
Netherlands. Centraal Bureau voor de Statistiek. Statistiek Vreemdelingenverkeer. Tourism Statistics (NE ISSN 0077-7447) *889*
Netherlands. Centraal Bureau voor de Statistiek. Statistiek Werkzame Personen (NE) *161*
Netherlands. Centraal Bureau voor de Statistiek. Statistisch Bulletin (NE ISSN 0077-6947) *843*
Netherlands. Centraal Bureau voor de Statistiek. Statistisch Zakboek. Pocket Yearbook (NE ISSN 0077-7463) *843*
Netherlands. Centraal Bureau voor de Statistiek. Statistische en Econometrische Onderzoekingen. Statistical and Econometric Studies *see* Netherlands. Centraal Bureau voor de Statistiek. Statistische Onderzoekingen *161*
Netherlands. Centraal Bureau voor de Statistiek. Statistische Onderzoekingen (NE) *161, 843*
Netherlands. Centraal Bureau voor de Statistiek. Toepassing der Kinderwetten. Application of Juvenile Law *see* Netherlands. Centraal Bureau voor de Statistiek. Justiciele Kinderbescherming *257*
Netherlands. Centraal Bureau voor de Statistiek. Toepassing der Wegenverkeerswet. Statistics of the Application of the Road Traffic Act (NE ISSN 0077-748X) *875*
Netherlands. Centraal Bureau voor de Statistiek. Vakantieonderzoek (NE) *889*
Netherlands. Centraal Bureau voor de Statistiek. Vermogensverdeling. Regionale Gegevens. Distribution of Personal Wealth. Regional Data (NE ISSN 0077-7498) *161*
Netherlands. Centraal Bureau voor de Statistiek. Voortgezet Onderwijs Regionaal Bezien (NE) *328*
Netherlands. Centraal Bureau voor de Statistiek. Voorziening in de Behoefte aan Onderwijzers Bij het Lager Onderwijs. Supplying the Need for Teachers in Elementary Education (NE ISSN 0077-6785) *344*
Netherlands. Centraal Bureau voor de Statistiek. Winststatistiek der Grotere Naamloze Vennootschappen. Profit-Statistics of the Limited Liability Companies (NE ISSN 0077-751X) *161*

Netherlands. Centraal Bureau voor de Statistiek. Zuivelstatistiek. Dairy Statistics *see* Netherlands. Centraal Bureau voor de Statistiek. Productie Statistiek van de Zuivelindustrie. Production Statistics of the Dairy Industry *41*
Netherlands. Centraal Planbureau. Central Economic Plan (NE ISSN 0077-7536) *224*
Netherlands. Centrale Commissie voor de Statistiek. Jaarverslag (NE) *843*
Netherlands. Commissie Zeehavenoverleg. Jaarverslag (NE ISSN 0077-7552) *879*
Netherlands. Departement van Marine. Catalogus van Nederlandse Zeekaarten en Boekwerken *see* Catalogus van Nederlandse Zeekaarten en Andere Hydrografische Publikaties/Catalog of Charts and Other Hydrographic Publications *896*
Netherlands. Ministerie van Buitenlandse Zaken. Voorlichtingsdienst Ontwikkelingssamenwerking/Implementation and Vindication of Policy (NE) *200*
Netherlands. Ministerie van Cultuur, Recreatie en Maatschappelijk Werk. Openluchtrecreatie (NE) *830*
Netherlands. Ministerie van Onderwijs en Wetenschappen. Onderwijsverslag (NE) *320*
Netherlands. Ministerie van Volksgezondheid en Milieuhygiene. Verslag Levensmiddelen en Keuring van Waren (NE) *405*
Netherlands. Ministerie van Volkshuisvesting en Ruimtelijke Ordening. Afdeling Voorlichting. Current Trends and Policies in Housing and Building (NE) *486*
Netherlands. Raad voor de Beroepskeuzevoorlichting. Verslag van de Werkzaamheden (NE) *667*
Netherlands. Rijks Geologische Dienst. Jaarverslag/Netherlands Geological Survey. Annual Report (NE ISSN 0077-7617) *297*
Netherlands. Rijkscommissie voor Geodesie. Publications on Geodesy. New Series (NE ISSN 0077-7625) *424*
Netherlands. Rijksinstituut voor Oorlogsdocumentatie. Progress Report (NE) *458*
Netherlands. Rijksvoorlichtingsdienst. Hoofpunten van het Regeringsbeleid (NE) *713*
Netherlands. Sociale Verzekeringsraad. Verslag van de Stand der Ziekengeldverzekering (NE ISSN 0489-2992) *500*
Netherlands-American Trade Directory (NE) *179*
Netherlands Antilles. Bureau voor de Statistiek. Statistiek van de Meteorologische Waarnemingen in de Nederlandse Antillen (NA ISSN 0077-667X) *634*
Netherlands Antilles. Bureau voor de Statistiek. Statistisch Jaarboek (NA ISSN 0077-6661) *843*
Netherlands Banking Digest (NE) *175*
Netherlands-British Trade Directory (UK ISSN 0308-1273) *180*
Netherlands - Current Trends and Policies in Housing and Building *see* Netherlands. Ministerie van Volkshuisvesting en Ruimtelijke Ordening. Afdeling Voorlichting. Current Trends and Policies in Housing and Building *486*
Netherlands Geological Survey. Annual Report *see* Netherlands. Rijks Geologische Dienst. Jaarverslag *297*
Netherlands Institute of Archaeology and Arabic Studies in Cairo. Publications (NE) *63, 475*
Netherlands Institute of Bankers and Stock Brokers. Publications (NE) *175, 204*
Netherlands Investment Bank for Developing Countries. Annual Report (NE ISSN 0077-7560) *175, 200*

Netherlands Nitrogen Technical Bulletin (NE ISSN 0077-7595) *37*
Netherlands Non-Life Insurance Companies *see* Nederlandse Schadeverzekeringsmaatschappijen *500*
Netherlands Yearbook of International Law (NE) *523*
Netherlands Youth and Its Education *see* Nederlandse Jeugd en Haar Onderwijs *320*
Network Planning Paper (US ISSN 0160-9742) *273, 534*
Neudrucke Deutscher Literaturwerke des XVIII und XIX Jahrhunderts *see* Neudrucke Deutscher Literaturwerke *569*
Neudrucke Deutscher Literaturwerke (GW ISSN 0077-7668) *569*
Neudrucke Deutscher Literaturwerke. Sonderreihe (GW ISSN 0077-7676) *569*
Neudrucke Deutscher Literaturwerke des XVI und XVII Jahrhunderts *see* Neudrucke Deutscher Literaturwerke *569*
Neue Beitraege zur Englischen Philologie (GW ISSN 0077-7684) *548*
Neue Columbus (SZ) *821*
Neue Hefte fuer Philosophie (GW ISSN 0085-3917) *690*
Neue Muenchner Beitraege zur Geschichte der Medizin und Naturwissenschaften. Medizinhistorische Serie (GW ISSN 0300-8371) *598*
Neue Muenchner Beitraege zur Geschichte der Medizin und Naturwissenschaften. Naturwissenschaftshistorische Reihe (GW) *787*
Neue Muenstersche Beitraege zur Geschichtsforschung (GW ISSN 0077-7706) *458*
Neue Musikgeschichtliche Forschungen (GW ISSN 0077-7714) *662*
Neue Russische Literatur *see* N R L *569*
Neues Jahrbuch fuer Geologie und Palaeontologie. Abhandlungen (GW ISSN 0077-7749) *297, 674*
Neues Jahrbuch fuer Mineralogie, Geologie und Palaeontologie. Abhandlungen *see* Neues Jahrbuch fuer Geologie und Palaeontologie. Abhandlungen *297*
Neues Trierisches Jahrbuch *see* Neues Trierisches Jahrbuch fuer Heimatpflege und Heimatgeschichte *458*
Neues Trierisches Jahrbuch fuer Heimatpflege und Heimatgeschichte (GW) *458*
Neuindische Studien (GW ISSN 0340-6385) *444, 548*
Neumanns Jahrbuch der Deutschen Versicherungswirtschaft. Teil 1: Personenversicherung (Lebens- und Krankenversicherung) (GW ISSN 0077-7773) *500*
Neumanns Jahrbuch der Deutschen Versicherungswirtschaft. Teil 2: Schaden- und Rueckversicherung (GW ISSN 0077-7781) *500*
Neumanns Jahrbuch der Deutschen Versicherungswirtschaft. Teil 3: Institutionen, Uebersichten und Anschriften (GW ISSN 0077-779X) *500*
Neuro-Ophthalmology (US ISSN 0077-7803) *616*
Neuro-Ophthalmology (NE) *616*
Neurolinguistics (NE ISSN 0301-6412) *548, 620*
Neurologia Medico-Chirurgica (JA ISSN 0470-8105) *620, 625*
Neuropaediatrie *see* Neuropediatrics *618*
Neuropediatrics (GW ISSN 0174-304X) *618, 625*
Neuroradiology Workshop (US ISSN 0077-7838) *620, 622*
Neuroscience Research (US ISSN 0077-7846) *620*
Neuroscience Symposia (US) *620*
Neurospora Newsletter (US ISSN 0028-3975) *620*

Neurotoxicology (US ISSN 0160-2748) 620
Neusser Jahrbuch fuer Kunst, Kulturgeschichte und Heimatkunde (GW ISSN 0077-7862) 458
Neuzeit im Aufbau (GW) 434
Nevada. Advisory Council for Manpower Training and Career Education. Annual Evaluation Report see Nevada. Advisory Council for Vocational-Technical Education. Annual Evaluation Report 346
Nevada. Advisory Council for Vocational-Technical Education. Annual Evaluation Report (US) 346
Nevada. Bureau of Mines and Geology. Bulletin (US) 297, 645
Nevada. Bureau of Mines and Geology. Report (US ISSN 0095-5264) 297, 645
Nevada. Bureau of Mines. Report see Nevada. Bureau of Mines and Geology. Report 297
Nevada. Commission on Crime, Delinquency and Corrections. Comprehensive Law Enforcement Plan (US ISSN 0092-1084) 283
Nevada. Department of Highways. Planning Survey Division. Status of Road Systems see Nevada. Department of Transportation. Planning Division. Status of Road Systems 875
Nevada. Department of Transportation. Planning Division. Status of Road Systems (US) 875
Nevada. Division of Personnel. Biennial Report (US ISSN 0077-7889) 220
Nevada. Office of Fiscal Analyst. Annual Report see Nevada. Office of Legislative Auditor. Biennial Report 744
Nevada. Office of Legislative Auditor. Biennial Report (US ISSN 0092-6841) 744
Nevada. State Board for Vocational Education. Annual Program Plan for Vocational Education (US) 329
Nevada. State Museum, Carson City. Anthropological Papers (US ISSN 0077-7897) 52, 63
Nevada. State Museum, Carson City. Natural History Publications (US ISSN 0077-7900) 787
Nevada. State Museum, Carson City. Occasional Papers (US ISSN 0077-7919) 654
Nevada. State Museum, Carson City. Popular Series (US ISSN 0077-7927) 654
Nevada Law Enforcement Plan see Nevada. Commission on Crime, Delinquency and Corrections. Comprehensive Law Enforcement Plan 283
Nevada Library Directory and Statistics(US) 534
Nevada State Industrial Directory (US ISSN 0195-7139) 240
Nevada State Plan for Career Education see Nevada. State Board for Vocational Education. Annual Program Plan for Vocational Education 329
Nevada State Plan for Vocational Education see Nevada. State Board for Vocational Education. Annual Program Plan for Vocational Education 329
Nevada Statewide Wage Survey see Nevada Wage Survey 209
Nevada Studies in History and Political Science (US ISSN 0077-7935) 470
Nevada Wage Survey (US) 209
New Acronyms and Initialisms see New Acronyms, Initialisms and Abbreviations 548
New Acronyms, Initialisms and Abbreviations (US) 548
New African Literature and the Arts (US ISSN 0077-7994) 569
New African Yearbook (UK) 146, 713
New and Expanding Industries Report for Alabama (US) 224
New Art Review (US) 77, 569, 662
New Asia Journal see Hsin-Ya Hsueh Pao 491
New Aspects of Breast Cancer (UK ISSN 0307-6695) 606

New Baby (UK) 257
New Babylon: Studies in the Social Sciences (NE ISSN 0077-801X) 737, 815
New Book of Knowledge Annual (US ISSN 0196-0148) 361
New Books on Film/TV see Nye Boeger om Film/TV 651
New Brunswick. Beach Resources-Eastern New Brunswick (CN) 645
New Brunswick. Department of Health. Annual Report (CN) 753
New Brunswick. Department of Labour and Manpower. Annual Report (CN ISSN 0077-8052) 209
New Brunswick. Department of Labour. Annual Report see New Brunswick. Department of Labour and Manpower. Annual Report 209
New Brunswick. Department of Municipal Affairs. Report (CN ISSN 0077-8060) 750
New Brunswick. Department of Tourism. Annual Report (CN ISSN 0703-6566) 889
New Brunswick. Department of Youth and Welfare. Report see New Brunswick. Department of Youth. Report 258
New Brunswick. Department of Youth. Report (CN ISSN 0077-8079) 257, 258
New Brunswick. Field Services Branch. Provincial Park Statistics (CN) 277
New Brunswick. Forest Products Commission. Progress Report (CN ISSN 0704-0970) 413
New Brunswick. Health Services Advisory Council. Annual Report/Rapport Annuel (CN) 753
New Brunswick. Liquor Control Commission. Report (CN ISSN 0077-8087) 86
New Brunswick. Mineral Resources Branch. Report of Investigations (CN ISSN 0077-8109) 645
New Brunswick. Research and Productivity Council. Report (CN ISSN 0077-8117) 224
New Brunswick. Wetlands-Peatlands Resources (CN) 645
New Brunswick Chapbooks (CN) 569, 580
New Brunswick Construction Products Directory (CN ISSN 0708-1375) 137, 240
New Brunswick Department of Fisheries. Annual Report (CN ISSN 0077-8036) 399
New Brunswick Home Economics Association. Newsletter (CN ISSN 0548-4081) 479
New Brunswick Museum. Journal (CN ISSN 0703-0606) 654
New Brunswick Museum. Memo see New Brunswick Museum. Journal 654
New Brunswick Public Employees Association. News Letter (CN ISSN 0381-7970) 750
New Caducean (US ISSN 0467-1872) 569
New Caledonia. Service des Mines et de la Geologia. Rapport Annuel (NL) 297, 645
New Campus (US ISSN 0077-8168) 338
New Canadian Film (CN ISSN 0548-4162) 650
New Canadian Stories see Best Canadian Stories 560
New Ceylon Writing (AT) 548, 569
New City Songster (UK) 662
New Collector's Directory (US ISSN 0363-3284) 262, 476
New Departures (UK) 77, 569
New Detroit Incorporated see New Detroit Progress Report 6
New Detroit Progress Report (US) 6
New Dimensions (Garden City) see New Dimensions Science Fiction 569
New Dimensions Science Fiction (US ISSN 0099-0906) 569
New Directions in Librarianship (US ISSN 0147-1090) 534
New Electronics' Distributor Product Finder and Guide (UK) 357

New England Accounting Practice Report (AT) 168
New England Board of Higher Education. New England Regional Student Program: Enrollment Report (US) 338
New England Board of Higher Education. New England Regional Student Program: Graduate Level (US) 338
New England Board of Higher Education. New England Regional Student Program: Undergraduate Level (US) 338
New England Crop and Livestock Reporting Service. Massachusetts Agricultural Statistics see Massachusetts Agricultural Statistics 17
New England Electrical Blue Book (US ISSN 0548-4456) 357
New England Guide (US ISSN 0077-8222) 889
New England Interstate Water Pollution Control Commission Annual Report see N E I W P C C Annual Report 387
New England Media Directory (US) 6
New England Papers on Education (AT ISSN 0077-8230) 912
New England Road Builders Association. N E R B A Annual Directory see Construction Directory 874
New England Science Fiction Association Inc. Index: Science Fiction Magazines and Anthologies see N.E.S.F.A. Index: Science Fiction Magazines and Anthologies 4
New England War Tax Resistance Newsletter (US) 231
New Fishing (US ISSN 0092-1734) 830
New Guinea Bibliography (PP) 93
New Guinea Periodical Index (PP ISSN 0028-5161) 3, 418
New Hampshire. Agricultural Experiment Station, Durham. Research Reports (US ISSN 0077-832X) 18
New Hampshire. Agricultural Experiment Station, Durham. Station Bulletins (US ISSN 0077-8338) 18
New Hampshire. Fish and Game Department. Biennial Report (US ISSN 0077-8362) 277
New Hampshire. Fish and Game Department. Management and Research. Biological Survey Bulletin (US ISSN 0077-8397) 105, 399
New Hampshire. Fish and Game Department. Management and Research. Biological Survey Series (US ISSN 0077-8370) 105
New Hampshire. Fish and Game Department. Management and Research. Technical Circular Series (US ISSN 0077-8389) 105, 399
New Hampshire Annual Rural Manpower Report (US ISSN 0094-7687) 209
New Hampshire Archeologist (US ISSN 0077-8346) 63
New Hampshire Audubon Annual (US) 125
New Hampshire Audubon Quarterly see New Hampshire Audubon Annual 125
New Hampshire Camping Guide (US ISSN 0077-8354) 830
New Hampshire Comprehensive Criminal Justice Plan (US) 283
New Hampshire Comprehensive Law Enforcement Plan see New Hampshire Comprehensive Criminal Justice Plan 283
New Hampshire Media Directory (US) 6
New Hampshire Occupational Outlook (US ISSN 0095-1102) 209
New Hampshire State Industrial Directory (US ISSN 0098-6216) 240
New Hampshire Vital Statistics (US ISSN 0095-5523) 843

New Hebrides. Anglo-French Condominium Geological Survey. Annual Reports. see New Herbrides. Condominium Geological Survey. Annual Reports 297
New Hebrides. Bureau of Statistics. Business Licenses. Patents Deliverees(NN) 843
New Hebrides. Bureau of Statistics. Census of Population and Housing, Vila and Santo, Final Results: Part 1: Housing Data/Recensement de la Population et de l'Habitation, Vila et Luganville, Resultats Definitifs: 1ere Partie: Donnes sur l'Habitat (NN) 728
New Hebrides. Bureau of Statistics. Census of Population and Housing, Vila and Santo, Final Results: Part 2: Population Data/Recensement de la Population et de l'Habitat, Vila et Luganville, Resultats Definitifs: 2eme Parti: Donnes sur la Population (NN) 728
New Hebrides. Bureau of Statistics. Manpower and Employment Survey. Final Results/Enquete sur l'Emploi et la Main d'Oeuvre. Definitifs (NN) 667
New Hebrides. Bureau of Statistics. Manpower and Employment Survey. Preliminary Results/Enquete sur l'Emploi et la Main d'Oeuvre (NN) 667
New Hebrides. Bureau of Statistics. New Motor Vehicle Registrations and Motor Vehicles on the Register/Nouvelles Immatriculations et Vehicules Automobiles Immatricules (NN) 871
New Hebrides. Bureau of Statistics. Overseas Shipping and Aircraft Statistics/Statistiques de Navigation Maritime et Aerienne Internationales(NN) 843
New Hebrides. Bureau of Statistics. Overseas Trade/Commerce Exterieur(NN) 197
New Hebrides. Condominium Bureau of Statistics Census of Population and Housing, Vila and Santo, Preliminary Results/Recensement de la Population et de l'Habitat, Port Vila et Luganville, Resultats Preliminaires(NN) 728
New Hebrides. Condominium Geological Survey. Annual Reports (NN) 297
New Hebrides. Condominium Geological Survey. Reports (NN ISSN 0077-8443) 297
New Horizons and Cardiovascular Diseases. Basic Science and Diagnosis (US) 607
New Image of Man in Medicine (US) 598
New Jersey. Administrative Office of the Courts. Annual Report of the Administrative Director of the Courts (US) 515
New Jersey. Bureau of Geology and Topography. Bulletin (US) 297
New Jersey. Bureau of Geology and Topography. Geologic Report Series (US) 297
New Jersey. Bureau of Statistical Analysis and Social Research. Schools for the Mentally Retarded (US ISSN 0548-5150) 328
New Jersey. Department of Agriculture. Highlights of the Annual Report (US ISSN 0077-846X) 18
New Jersey. Department of Banking. Annual Report (US) 175
New Jersey. Department of Education. Educational Assessment Program State Report (US ISSN 0362-5958) 320
New Jersey. Department of Environmental Protection. Annual Report (US ISSN 0092-3311) 388
New Jersey. Department of Higher Education. Research Report (US) 338
New Jersey. Department of Human Services. Community Mental Health Projects Summary Statistics (US ISSN 0098-6399) 753, 807

New Jersey. Department of Transportation. Annual Report (US) 863
New Jersey. Department of Transportation. Highlight of Activities see New Jersey. Department of Transportation. Annual Report 863
New Jersey. Developmental Disabilities Council. Annual Report (US ISSN 0090-077X) 807
New Jersey. Division of Banking. Annual Report see New Jersey. Department of Banking. Annual Report 175
New Jersey. Division of Savings and Loan Associations. Annual Report see New Jersey. Department of Banking. Annual Report 175
New Jersey Division of Water Resources. Special Report (US ISSN 0092-1602) 308
New Jersey. Division of Water Resources. Water Resources Circulars (US ISSN 0545-2252) 308
New Jersey. Economic Policy Council. Annual Report of Economic Policy Council and Office of Economic Policy (US ISSN 0077-8478) 224
New Jersey. Legislature. Office of Fiscal Affairs. Annual Report (US ISSN 0093-9986) 515
New Jersey. Office of Demographic and Economic Analysis. Population Estimates for New Jersey (US ISSN 0091-9187) 732
New Jersey. State Agency for Social Security. Annual Report (US) 500
New Jersey Airport Directory (US ISSN 0091-6978) 869
New Jersey Area Library Directory (US ISSN 0362-2967) 534
New Jersey Clean Air Council. Report (US ISSN 0077-8451) 388
New Jersey Covered Employment Trends by Geographical Areas of the State (US ISSN 0092-1459) 209
New Jersey Directory of Manufacturers(US) 240
New Jersey Media Directory see Burrelle's New Jersey Media Directory 5
New Jersey Mental Retardation Planning Board. Annual Report see New Jersey. Developmental Disabilities Council. Annual Report 807
New Jersey Mosquito Control Association. Proceedings (US) 121
New Jersey Mosquito Extermination Association. Proceedings see New Jersey Mosquito Control Association. Proceedings 121
New Jersey Orchard and Vineyard Survey (US ISSN 0098-9541) 37
New Jersey, Pennsylvania TourBook see Tourbook: New Jersey, Pennsylvania 891
New Jersey Plan for Criminal Justice. see Criminal Justice Plan for New Jersey 281
New Jersey Public Employer-Employee Relations (US ISSN 0077-8508) 209
New Jersey Public Libraries. Statistics (US ISSN 0093-1098) 539
New Jersey Speech and Hearing Association. Newsletter (US ISSN 0077-8516) 617
New Jersey State Industrial Directory (US ISSN 0098-6224) 240
New Jersey State Plan for Vocational Education (US) 346
New Legislation of the Australian Parliament (AT) 515
New Library Buildings (UK ISSN 0307-9767) 534
New Literature and Ideology (CN ISSN 0702-7532) 557, 580
New Local Government Series (UK) 750
New Magic Lantern Journal (UK ISSN 0143-036X) 693
New Mexico. Agricultural Experiment Station. Research Report (US ISSN 0548-5967) 18
New Mexico. Bureau of Mines and Mineral Resources. Bulletin (US) 645

New Mexico. Bureau of Mines and Mineral Resources. Circular (US) 645
New Mexico. Bureau of Mines and Mineral Resources. Hydrologic Report (US) 308
New Mexico. Bureau of Mines and Mineral Resources. Memoir (US ISSN 0548-5975) 645
New Mexico. Bureau of Mines and Mineral Resources. Progress Report (US ISSN 0098-7077) 645
New Mexico. Employment Security Commission. Annual Rural Manpower Service Report see New Mexico. Employment Services Department. Annual Rural Manpower Service Report 912
New Mexico. Employment Services Department. Annual Rural Manpower Service Report (US) 912
New Mexico. Governor's Council on Criminal Justice Planning. Comprehensive Criminal Justice Plan(US) 283
New Mexico. State Records Center & Archives. Publications and Rules Filed (US) 438
New Mexico. Veterans' Service Commission. Report (US ISSN 0094-7326) 640, 807
New Mexico Agricultural Statistics (US ISSN 0077-8540) 18
New Mexico Almanac see New Mexico Digest 361
New Mexico; an Annotated Directory of Information Sources (US) 93
New Mexico Blue Book (US ISSN 0196-3929) 470
New Mexico Digest (US) 361
New Mexico Forest Products Directory (US ISSN 0094-2782) 413
New Mexico Geological Society. Guidebook, Field Conference (US ISSN 0077-8567) 297
New Mexico Reports see Report of Cases Determined in the Supreme Court and Court of Appeals of the State of New Mexico 517
New Mexico State Industrial Directory (US) 240
New Mexico State Records Center and Archives. Publications Filed see New Mexico. State Records Center & Archives. Publications and Rules Filed 438
New Mexico Statistical Abstract (US ISSN 0077-8575) 843
New Mitre (CN) 557
New Nigeria Development Company Limited. Annual Report and Accounts (NR) 224
New Nippon Electric Technical Review/Shin Nippon Denki Giho (JA ISSN 0037-3745) 265, 357
New Official Guide: Japan (JA ISSN 0077-8591) 889
New Orleans Academy of Ophthalmology. Transactions (US ISSN 0077-8605) 616
New Oxford History of Music (US) 662
New Pages Guide to Alternative Periodicals (US) 558, 803
New Periodicals Index (US ISSN 0146-5716) 3, 558, 818
New Perspectives in History (US) 434
New Perspectives in Powder Metallurgy(US) 629
New Poems see Poetry Supplement 581
New Poetry (UK ISSN 0077-8621) 580
New Poets (UK) 580
New Poets Series (US) 580
New Priorities Library (US) 787
New Product Directory of N.Y.S.E. Listed Companies see Chemical New Product Directory 217
New Rambler (UK ISSN 0028-6540) 569
New Renaissance (US ISSN 0028-6575) 77, 569
New Review see New Review of East-European History 458
New Review of East-European History (CN ISSN 0381-9140) 458
New Schools Exchange. Directory and Resource Guide (US) 320

New Settler's Guide for Washington, D.C. and Communities in Nearby Maryland and Virginia (US ISSN 0097-8213) 889
New South Wales. Attorney-General. Bureau of Crime Statistics and Research. Statistical Report (AT ISSN 0310-3684) 283
New South Wales. Board of Architects. Architects Roll (AT ISSN 0077-8656) 69
New South Wales. Commonwealth Housing Commission. Annual Report(AT) 486
New South Wales. Department of Education. Home Economics Bulletin for Teachers in Secondary Schools see Home Science for Teachers in Secondary Schools 479
New South Wales. Department of Education. School Management Bulletin (AT ISSN 0085-3976) 344
New South Wales. Department of Mineral Resources and Development. Annual Report (AT) 645
New South Wales. Department of Mineral Resources and Development. Annual Report. Statistical Supplement. (AT) 645
New South Wales. Department of Mines. Annual Report see New South Wales. Department of Mineral Resources and Development. Annual Report 645
New South Wales. Department of Mines. Annual Report. Statistical Supplement see New South Wales. Department of Mineral Resources and Development. Annual Report. Statistical Supplement 645
New South Wales. Department of Mines. Chemical Laboratory. Report (AT ISSN 0077-8672) 373, 645
New South Wales. Department of Mines. Coalfields Branch. Reports (AT ISSN 0077-8680) 645
New South Wales. Department of Mines. Memoirs: Palaeontology see New South Wales. Geological Survey. Memoirs: Palaeontology 674
New South Wales. Forestry Commission. Research Notes (AT ISSN 0085-3984) 409
New South Wales. Geological Survey. Bulletin (AT ISSN 0155-5561) 297
New South Wales. Geological Survey. Memoirs: Geology (AT ISSN 0077-8710) 297
New South Wales. Geological Survey. Memoirs: Palaeontology (AT ISSN 0077-8699) 674
New South Wales. Geological Survey. Mineral Industry Series (AT ISSN 0077-8729) 297, 645
New South Wales. Geological Survey. Mineral Resources Series (AT ISSN 0077-8737) 297, 645
New South Wales. Geological Survey. Records (AT ISSN 0155-3372) 297
New South Wales. Higher Education Board. Annual Report (AT) 338
New South Wales. Higher Education Board. Higher Education Handbook (AT ISSN 0310-0103) 912
New South Wales. Law Reform Commission. Report (AT ISSN 0085-400X) 515
New South Wales. National Herbarium. Contributions see Flora of New South Wales 114
New South Wales. National Parks and Wildlife Service. National Parks and Wildlife-a Review (AT) 105
New South Wales. National Parks and Wildlife Service. Parks and Wildlife (AT ISSN 0310-6756) 277
New South Wales. State Fisheries. Research Bulletin (AT ISSN 0077-8788) 912
New South Wales Bar Association. Annual Report (AT) 515
New South Wales District Court Reports (AT ISSN 0548-6793) 515
New South Wales National Herbarium. Contributions see Telopea 118
New South Wales Veterinary Proceedings (AT ISSN 0085-4026) 895
New Stories (UK) 569

New Straits Times Press (Malaysia) Berhad Directory of Malaysia see N S T Directory of Malaysia 240
New Studies in Archaeology (UK) 63
New Studies in Practical Philosophy (US) 690
New Surveys in the Classics (UK) 260
New Swedish Books (SW) 557
New Teacher (PK ISSN 0077-8826) 320, 350
New Techniques in Biophysics and Cell Biology (US ISSN 0301-374X) 112, 120
New Testament Tools and Studies (NE ISSN 0077-8842) 766
New Trade Names (US) 677
New Trade Names in the Rubber and Plastics Industries (UK ISSN 0077-8869) 707, 777
New Trends in Biology Teaching (UN ISSN 0077-8877) 105
New Trends in Chemistry Teaching (UN ISSN 0077-8885) 247
New Trends in Integrated Science Teaching (UN) 350
New Trends in Mathematics Teaching (UN ISSN 0077-8893) 587
New Trends in Physics Teaching (UN ISSN 0077-8907) 697
New Voices (US) 569
New Worlds Newsletter (US) 799
New Yeats Papers (IE) 569
New York (City). Comprehensive Plan for Drug Abuse Prevention and Treatment. (US) 287
New York (City) Mayor. Schedules Supporting the Executive Budget (US ISSN 0094-7547) 750
New York (City). Office of Labor Relations. Interpretive Memorandum (US) 209
New York (State) Consumer Protection Board. Annual Report (US ISSN 0095-5590) 280
New York (State) Crime Victims Compensation Board. Report (US ISSN 0077-9148) 283
New York (State) Department of Commerce. Exports of New York Manufactures (US) 197
New York (State). Department of Environmental Conservation. Annual Report (US) 277
New York(State). Department of Health. Monograph (US) 753
New York (State) Department of Labor. Division of Research and Statistics. Employment Statistics (US ISSN 0091-0767) 161
New York (State) Department of Labor. Division of Research and Statistics. Labor Research Report (US ISSN 0093-5034) 209
New York (State). Department of Labor. Statistics on Operations (US ISSN 0550-6638) 161
New York (State) Department of Social Services. Bureau of Data Management and Analysis. Program Analysis Report (US ISSN 0090-4716) 807
New York(State) Department of Social Services. Bureau of Data Management and Analysis. Program Brief (US ISSN 0162-6302) 808
New York (State) Department of Social Services. Bureau of Research. Program Analysis Report see New York (State) Department of Social Services. Bureau of Data Management and Analysis. Program Analysis Report 807
New York (State) Department of Social Services. Bureau of Research. Program Brief. see New York(State) Department of Social Services. Bureau of Data Management and Analysis. Program Brief 808
New York (State) Department of State. Manual for the Use of the Legislature of the State of New York(US) 744
New York (State). Division of Criminal Justice Service. Annual Report (US ISSN 0095-4047) 283

New York (State) Division of Employment. Research and Statistics Office. Research Bulletin. *see* New York (State) Department of Labor. Division of Research and Statistics. Labor Research Report *209*
New York (State). Division of Human Rights. Annual Report (US) *719*
New York (State) Division of the Budget. New York State Statistical Yearbook (US ISSN 0077-9334) *843*
New York (State) Education Department. Public School Professional Personnel Report *see* Public School Enrollment and Staff, New York State *345*
New York (State). Environmental Quality Research and Development Unit. Technical Paper (US ISSN 0362-6210) *388*
New York (State). Health Planning Commission, Administrative Program for Health Planning and Development (US) *753*
New York (State) Insurance Department. Annual Report of the Superintendent of Insurance to the New York Legislature (US) *500*
New York (State) Insurance Department. Directory of Insurance Brokers Licensed in New York State *see* New York Insurance Brokers Directory *500*
New York (State) Insurance Department. Fees and Taxes Charged Insurance Companies Under the Laws of New York Together with Abstracts of Fees, Taxes and Other Requirements of Other States (US) *500*
New York (State) Insurance Department. Loss and Expense Ratios (US) *500*
New York (State) Insurance Department. Statistical Tables from Annual Statements (US) *502*
New York. State Library, Albany. Checklist of Official Publications of the State of New York (US ISSN 0077-9296) *744*
New York. State Library, Albany. Division of Library Development. Excerpts from New York State Education Law, Rules of the Board of Regents, and Regulations of the Commissioner of Education Pertaining to Public and Free Association Libraries, Library Systems, Trustees and Librarians (US ISSN 0077-930X) *534*
New York. State Library, Albany. Division of Library Development. Institution Libraries Statistics (US ISSN 0077-9318) *534*
New York. State Library, Albany. Division of Library Development. Public and Association Libraries Statistics (US ISSN 0077-9326) *534*
New York (State) Opinions of the Attorney General (US) *516*
New York (State). University. Information Center on Education. Education Statistics New York State *see* Education Statistics, New York State *326*
New York (State) Workmen's Compensation Board. Summary of Activities (US) *500*
New York Academy of Sciences. Annals (US) *787*
New York Academy of Sciences. Transactions (US ISSN 0028-7113) *787*
New York Agricultural Statistics (US ISSN 0077-8966) *37*
New York Botanical Garden. Memoirs (US ISSN 0077-8931) *117*
New York City Trade Union Handbook(US ISSN 0545-6061) *507*
New York Crop Reporting Service. Statistics Relative to the Dairy Industry in New York State *see* New York Dairy Statistics *41*
New York Dairy Statistics (US) *41*
New York Index (US) *912*
New York Insurance Brokers Directory(US) *500*
New York Jets Official Yearbook (US) *825*
New York Knicks Yearbook (US) *825*
New York L P N (US ISSN 0028-730X) *614*
New York Metropolitan Reference & Research Library Agency. Directory of Members (US ISSN 0362-8744) *534*
New York Paleontological Society. Notes (US) *674*
New York Pro Musica Instrumental Series (US ISSN 0085-4042) *662*
New York Production Manual (US ISSN 0163-1276) 240, *650*
New York Psychoanalytic Institute. Kris Study Group. Monograph (US ISSN 0077-9008) *737*
New York Public Library. Films (US ISSN 0077-9016) *534*
New York Publicity Outlets (US ISSN 0077-9024) *6*
New York Quarterly (US ISSN 0028-7482) *580*
New York Rangers Blue Book *see* New York Rangers Yearbook *821*
New York Rangers Yearbook (US) *821*
New York Red Book (US) *744*
New York Sea Grant Institute. Annual Report (US) *744*
New York State Archeological Association. Occasional Papers (US ISSN 0077-9059) *63*
New York State Archeological Association. Researches and Transactions (US ISSN 0077-9067) *63*
New York State Association for Retarded Children. Annual Report of Executive Director (US) *346*
New York State Association for the Mentally Retarded. Annual Report of Executive Director *see* New York State Association for Retarded Children. Annual Report of Executive Director *346*
New York State Business Fact Book. Part 1: Business and Manufacturing (US ISSN 0077-9083) *188*, 240
New York State Business Fact Book. Part 2: Population and Housing (US ISSN 0077-9091) *188*, 486, 728
New York State Business Fact Book. Supplement (US ISSN 0077-9105) *188*, 240
New York State English Council. Monograph Series (US ISSN 0548-9040) 350, *569*
New York State Horticultural Society. Proceedings (US) *416*
New York State Industrial Directory (US ISSN 0548-9067) *241*
New York State Library, Albany. Miscellaneous Publication (US) *534*
New York State Media Directory *see* Burrelle's New York State Media Directory *5*
New York State Medical Care Facilities Finance Agency. Annual Report (US ISSN 0361-4018) *753*
New York State School of Industrial and Labor Relations. Bulletin (US ISSN 0070-0134) *209*
New York State School of Industrial and Labor Relations. Institute of Public Employment. Monograph (US) *209*
New York State School of Industrial and Labor Relations. Institute of Public Employment. Occasional Papers (US) *209*
New York State School of Industrial and Labor Relations. Key Issues Series (US ISSN 0070-0185) *209*
New York State School of Industrial and Labor Relations Paperbacks *see* I L R Paperbacks *208*
New York State Sea Grant Program. Annual Report *see* New York Sea Grant Institute. Annual Report *744*
New York State Statistical Yearbook *see* New York (State) Division of the Budget. New York State Statistical Yearbook *843*
New York State Urban Development Corporation. Annual Report (US ISSN 0077-9423) *744*
New York Theatre Annual *see* American Theatre Annual *858*
New York Times Film Reviews (US ISSN 0362-3688) *650*
New York Times School Microfilm Collection Index (US) *434*
New York Times School Microfilm Collection Index by Reels *see* New York Times School Microfilm Collection Index *434*
New York TourBook *see* Tourbook: New York *891*
New York University. Comparative Criminal Law Project. Publications (US ISSN 0077-944X) *283*
New York University. Criminal Law Education and Research Center. Monograph Series (US ISSN 0077-9458) *283*
New York University. Institute of Finance. Bulletin *see* New York University. Center for the Study of Financial Institutions. Bulletin; Monograph Series in Finance and Economics *175*
New York University. Institute of Labor Relations. Annual Conference on Labor at New York University *see* Annual Conference on Labor at New York University. Proceedings *205*
New York University. Libraries. Bulletin of the Tamiment Library (US ISSN 0077-9490) *534*
New York University. Salomon Brothers Center for the Study of Financial Institutions. Monograph Series in Finance and Economics (US) *175*
New York University Post-Graduate Medical School. Inter-Clinic Information Bulletin (US ISSN 0028-7911) *598*
New York University Studies in Comparative Literature (US ISSN 0077-9504) *569*
New Zealand. Broadcasting Council. Report *see* Broadcasting Corporation of New Zealand. Report *267*
New Zealand. Central Advisory Committee on the Appointments and Promotion of Primary Teachers. Report to the Minister of Education (NZ ISSN 0077-958X) *320*
New Zealand. Council for Recreation and Sport. Report (NZ) *821*
New Zealand. Dairy Board. Annual Report and Statement of Accounts (NZ) *41*
New Zealand. Dairy Production and Marketing Board. Annual Report and Statement of Accounts *see* New Zealand. Dairy Board. Annual Report and Statement of Accounts *41*
New Zealand. Department of External Affairs. Publicatiion *see* New Zealand. Ministry of Foreign Affairs. Publication *722*
New Zealand. Department of External Affiars. United Nations and Specialised Agencies Handbook *see* New Zealand. Ministry of Foreign Affairs. United Nations Handbook *722*
New Zealand. Department of Health. Hospital Management Data (NZ ISSN 0110-1900) *482*
New Zealand. Department of Internal Affairs. Report (NZ) *713*
New Zealand. Department of Maori Affairs. Report (NZ) *744*
New Zealand. Department of Scientific and Industrial Research. Annual Report (NZ ISSN 0077-9601) *852*
New Zealand. Department of Scientific and Industrial Research. Bulletin (NZ ISSN 0077-961X) *852*
New Zealand. Department of Scientific and Industrial Research. Geophysics Division. Report (NZ ISSN 0110-6112) *305*
New Zealand. Department of Scientific and Industrial Research. Geophysics Division. Technical Note (NZ ISSN 0110-7089) *305*
New Zealand. Department of Scientific and Industrial Research. Geological Survey. Bulletin (NZ ISSN 0077-9628) *297*
New Zealand. Department of Scientific and Industrial Research. Information Series (NZ ISSN 0077-9636) *852*
New Zealand. Department of Social Welfare. Report (NZ) *808*
New Zealand. Department of Statistics. Agricultural Statistics (NZ ISSN 0110-4624) *18*
New Zealand. Department of Statistics. Annual Report of the Government Statistician (NZ ISSN 0077-9652) *843*
New Zealand. Department of Statistics. Balance of Payments (NZ ISSN 0110-4616) *161*
New Zealand. Department of Statistics. Building Statistics (NZ) *140*
New Zealand. Department of Statistics. Census of Building and Construction (NZ) *140*
New Zealand. Department of Statistics. Census of Libraries (NZ) *539*
New Zealand. Department of Statistics. Exports (NZ ISSN 0077-9660) *161*
New Zealand. Department of Statistics. Household Sample Survey *see* New Zealand Household Survey *161*
New Zealand. Department of Statistics. Imports (NZ ISSN 0077-9679) *161*
New Zealand. Department of Statistics. Incomes and Income Tax Statistics (NZ ISSN 0110-3776) *161*
New Zealand. Department of Statistics. Industrial Production (NZ ISSN 0077-9865) *912*
New Zealand. Department of Statistics. Insurance Statistics (NZ ISSN 0110-3474) *502*
New Zealand. Department of Statistics. Justice Statistics. (NZ ISSN 0110-3482) *516*
New Zealand. Department of Statistics. Life Annuity Tables (NZ) *502*
New Zealand. Department of Statistics. Local Authority Statistics (NZ ISSN 0110-3466) *744*
New Zealand. Department of Statistics. National Income and Expenditure *see* New Zealand. Department of Statistics. System of National Accounts *161*
New Zealand. Department of Statistics. Part A: Prices. (NZ ISSN 0110-5019) *161*
New Zealand. Department of Statistics. Part B: Wages and Labour (NZ ISSN 0110-5027) *209*, 843
New Zealand. Department of Statistics. Population and Migration *see* New Zealand. Department of Statistics. Population and Migration Part A: Population *728*
New Zealand. Department of Statistics. Population and Migration *see* New Zealand. Department of Statistics. Population and Migration. Part B: External Migration *728*
New Zealand. Department of Statistics. Population and Migration Part A: Population (NZ ISSN 0110-375X) 137, *728*
New Zealand. Department of Statistics. Population and Migration. Part B: External Migration (NZ ISSN 0110-3768) 137, *728*
New Zealand. Department of Statistics. Population Census: Ages and Marital Status (NZ ISSN 0077-9687) *728*
New Zealand. Department of Statistics. Population Census: Birthplaces and Ethnic Origin (NZ) *728*
New Zealand. Department of Statistics. Population Census: Dwellings (NZ ISSN 0077-9695) *728*
New Zealand. Department of Statistics. Population Census: Education (NZ ISSN 0077-9709) *728*
New Zealand. Department of Statistics. Population Census: General Report (NZ ISSN 0077-9717) *728*
New Zealand. Department of Statistics. Population Census: Households, Families & Fertility (NZ) *728*
New Zealand. Department of Statistics. Population Census: Households *see* New Zealand. Department of Statistics. Population Census: Households, Families & Fertility *728*

New Zealand. Department of Statistics. Population Census: Incomes (NZ ISSN 0077-9733) 728

New Zealand. Department of Statistics. Population Census: Increase and Location of Population see New Zealand. Department of Statistics. Population Census. Location and Increase of Population. Part A: Population Size and Distribution 732

New Zealand. Department of Statistics. Population Census: Increase and Location of Populaion see New Zealand. Department of Statistics. Population Census. Location and Increase of Population. Part B: Population Density 732

New Zealand. Department of Statistics. Population Census: Industries and Occupations (NZ ISSN 0077-9741) 728

New Zealand. Department of Statistics. Population Census: Internal Migration (NZ) 843

New Zealand. Department of Statistics. Population Census. Location and Increase of Population. Part A: Population Size and Distribution (NZ) 732, 843

New Zealand. Department of Statistics. Population Census. Location and Increase of Population. Part B: Population Density (NZ) 732, 843

New Zealand. Department of Statistics. Population Census: Maori Population and Dwellings (NZ ISSN 0077-975X) 728

New Zealand. Department of Statistics. Population Census: Provisional Population and Dwelling Statistics (NZ) 729

New Zealand. Department of Statistics. Population Census: Provisional Report on Population and Dwellings see New Zealand. Department of Statistics. Population Census: Provisional Population and Dwelling Statistics 729

New Zealand. Department of Statistics. Population Census: Race see New Zealand. Department of Statistics. Population Census: Birthplaces and Ethnic Origin 728

New Zealand. Department of Statistics. Population Census: Religious Professions (NZ ISSN 0077-9784) 729

New Zealand. Department of Statistics. Price, Wages and Labour see New Zealand. Department of Statistics. Part A: Prices 161

New Zealand. Department of Statistics. Prices, Wages and Labour see New Zealand. Department of Statistics. Part B: Wages and Labour 209

New Zealand. Department of Statistics. Report and Analysis of External Trade (NZ ISSN 0077-9806) 161

New Zealand. Department of Statistics. Statistical Report of Farm Production see New Zealand. Department of Statistics. Agricultural Statistics 18

New Zealand. Department of Statistics. System of National Accounts (NZ ISSN 0110-344X) 161

New Zealand. Department of Statistics. Transport Statistics (NZ ISSN 0110-3458) 863

New Zealand. Department of Statistics. Vital Statistics (NZ ISSN 0110-4586) 843

New Zealand. Department of Trade and Industry. Import Licensing Schedule (NZ) 197

New Zealand. Department of Trade & Industry. Report (NZ) 224

New Zealand. Forest Research Institute. Report (NZ ISSN 0077-9997) 409

New Zealand. Forest Research Institute. Technical Paper (NZ ISSN 0078-0006) 409

New Zealand. Forest Service. Report of the Director General of Forests (NZ ISSN 0078-0014) 409

New Zealand. Industrial Research and Development Grants Advisory Committee. Report (NZ) 224

New Zealand. Inland Revenue Department. Report (NZ) 231

New Zealand. Law Revision Commission. Report (NZ) 516

New Zealand. Lottery Board of Control. Report see New Zealand Lottery Board. Report 231

New Zealand. Marine Department. Annual Report on Fisheries (NZ ISSN 0078-0111) 912

New Zealand. Meat and Wool Boards' Economic Service. Annual Review of the Sheep Industry (NZ ISSN 0078-0138) 45

New Zealand. Mines Department. Annual Returns of Production from Quarries and Mineral Production Statistics see New Zealand. Ministry of Energy. Mines Division. Annual Returns of Production from Quarries and Mineral Production Statistics 648

New Zealand. Mines Department. Mines Statement see New Zealand. Ministry of Energy. Mines Division. Annual Report 645

New Zealand. Ministry of Agriculture and Fisheries. Fisheries Research Division. Bulletin. (NZ ISSN 0110-1749) 399

New Zealand. Ministry of Agriculture and Fisheries. Fisheries Research Division: Information Leaflet (NZ ISSN 0110-4519) 399

New Zealand. Ministry of Agriculture and Fisheries. Fisheries Technical Report (NZ) 399

New Zealand. Ministry of Defence. Report (NZ) 640

New Zealand. Ministry of Defence. Review of Defence Policy (NZ) 640

New Zealand. Ministry of Energy. Mines Division. Annual Report (NZ) 645

New Zealand. Ministry of Energy. Mines Division. Annual Returns of Production from Quarries and Mineral Production Statistics (NZ) 648, 843

New Zealand. Ministry of Energy. Report (NZ) 277, 363

New Zealand. Ministry of Energy Resources. Report see New Zealand. Ministry of Energy. Report 363

New Zealand. Ministry of Foreign Affairs. Publication. (NZ) 722

New Zealand. Ministry of Foreign Affairs. Report (NZ) 722

New Zealand. Ministry of Foreign Affairs. United Nations Handbook (NZ) 722

New Zealand. Ministry of Transport. Annual Report (NZ ISSN 0085-4123) 863

New Zealand. National Research Advisory Council. Report (NZ ISSN 0078-0162) 852

New Zealand. National Research Advisory Council. Senior and Post Doctoral Research Fellowship Awards for Research in New Zealand Government Departments (NZ ISSN 0078-0154) 787, 852

New Zealand. Railways Department. Annual Report (NZ) 873

New Zealand. Road Research Unit. Bulletin (NZ ISSN 0549-0030) 875

New Zealand. Soil Bureau. Bibliographic Report (NZ) 25

New Zealand. Soil Bureau. Bulletin (NZ ISSN 0077-9644) 37

New Zealand. Soil Bureau Scientific Report (NZ) 37

New Zealand. Soil Bureau. Soil Survey Reports (NZ) 277

New Zealand. Urban Public Passenger Transport Council. Report (NZ) 863

New Zealand Agricultural Engineering Institute. Annual Report (NZ ISSN 0077-9520) 37, 897

New Zealand Agricultural Engineering Institute. Current Publications (NZ ISSN 0111-0829) 25, 900

New Zealand Agriculture see AgLink 11

New Zealand Annual (NZ ISSN 0110-0831) 889

New Zealand Association of Radio Transmitters, Inc. Amateur Radio Callbook see N. Z. A. R. T. Amateur Radio Callbook 268

New Zealand Books in Print (AT) 760

New Zealand Business Who's Who (NZ ISSN 0077-9571) 98, 241

New Zealand Civil Aviation Statistics (NZ) 11

New Zealand Economic Papers (NZ ISSN 0077-9954) 146

New Zealand Economic Statistics (NZ) 912

New Zealand Electronics Review (NZ) 357

New Zealand Entomologist (NZ ISSN 0077-9962) 121

New Zealand Export-Import Corporation. Report (NZ) 197

New Zealand Federation of Labour. Official Trade Union Directory (NZ) 507

New Zealand Geographical Society. Miscellaneous Series (NZ ISSN 0078-0022) 424

New Zealand Geography Conference Proceedings Series (NZ ISSN 0078-0030) 424

New Zealand Health Statistics Report (NZ) 753

New Zealand Household Survey (NZ ISSN 0110-392X) 161

New Zealand Income Tax Law and Practice (AT) 231

New Zealand Institute of Economic Research. Discussion Paper (NZ ISSN 0078-0049) 146

New Zealand Institute of Economic Research. Report (NZ ISSN 0078-0057) 146

New Zealand Institute of Economic Research. Research Paper (NZ ISSN 0078-0065) 146

New Zealand Institute of Economic Research. Technical Memorandum (NZ ISSN 0078-0073) 146

New Zealand Journal of Archaeology (NZ) 63

New Zealand Law Register (NZ ISSN 0078-0081) 516

New Zealand Lottery Board. Report (NZ) 231

New Zealand Master Tax Guide (AT) 231

New Zealand Numismatic Journal (NZ ISSN 0028-8527) 477

New Zealand Oceanographic Institute. Collected Reprints (NZ ISSN 0083-789X) 311

New Zealand Oceanographic Institute. Memoir (NZ ISSN 0083-7903) 311

New Zealand Oceanographic Institute Records see N Z O I Records 311

New Zealand Official Year-Book (NZ ISSN 0078-0170) 447

New Zealand Planning Council. Planning Paper (NZ ISSN 0111-0470) 744

New Zealand Pottery and Ceramics Research Association. Technical Report (NZ ISSN 0078-0189) 244

New Zealand Poultry Board. Report and New Zealand Marketing Authority Report and Statement of Accounts (NZ ISSN 0078-0197) 29, 45

New Zealand Red Cross Society. Report (NZ ISSN 0080-0392) 808

New Zealand Register of Specialists (NZ) 598

New Zealand Shipping Directory (NZ ISSN 0545-7866) 879

New Zealand Society of Accountants. Cost and Management Accounting Division. C M A Bulletin (NZ) 168

New Zealand Trade Union Directory (NZ) 507

New Zealand Visitor Statistics (NZ) 889

New Zealand Wheat Review (NZ ISSN 0078-0219) 43

New Zealand Whole Earth Catalogue (NZ) 241, 388

Newberry Library Bulletin (US) 534

Newcastle History Monographs (AT ISSN 0078-0243) 447

Newcomen Society for the Study of the History of Engineering and Technology. Transactions (UK ISSN 0372-0187) 369, 852

Newes (US) 476, 505

Newfoundland. Department of Fisheries. Annual Report (CN) 399

Newfoundland. Department of Social Services. Annual Report (CN ISSN 0078-0294) 808

Newfoundland. Mineral Development Division. Geological Survey. Bulletin (CN ISSN 0078-0308) 297

Newfoundland. Mineral Development Division. Information (CN ISSN 0078-0340) 645

Newfoundland. Mineral Development Division. Information Circular. (CN ISSN 0078-0359) 645

Newfoundland. Mines Branch. Annual Report Series (CN ISSN 0078-0367) 645

Newfoundland. Mines Branch. Geological Survey of Newfoundland. Bulletin Series (CN ISSN 0078-0375) 297

Newfoundland. Mines Branch. Geological Survey of Newfoundland. Report Series (CN ISSN 0078-0383) 297

Newfoundland and Labrador. Bulletin (CN) 645

Newfoundland and Labrador. Geological Report (CN) 297

Newfoundland and Labrador. Mineral Resources Report (CN) 645

Newfoundland & Labrador Business Directory (CN) 241

Newfoundland and Labrador Engineer (CN ISSN 0384-1898) 369

Newfoundland and Labrador Who's Who (CN ISSN 0078-0286) 98

Newfoundland Medical Directory (CN ISSN 0078-0316) 598

Newfoundland Who's Who see Newfoundland and Labrador Who's Who 98

Newman (UK ISSN 0048-0207) 775

News Dictionary (US) 438, 713

News from the Rare Book Room (CN ISSN 0085-4166) 93

News Letter - New Brunswick Public Employees Association see New Brunswick Public Employees Association. News Letter 750

News Novel (US) 676

Newsletter - Huntsville Association of Folk Musicians see Huntsville Association of Folk Musicians. Newsletter 659

Newsletter - New Brunswick Home Economics Association see New Brunswick Home Economics Association. Newsletter 479

Newsletter - Nova Scotia Bird Society see Nova Scotia Bird Society. Newsletter 125

Newsletter of Research on Japanese Politics (US) 713

Newsletter on Contemporary Japanese Prints (US ISSN 0085-4174) 77

Newsletter - Processing Department (Washington) see U.S. Library of Congress. Processing Department. Newsletter 536

Newsletter-Society for the Preservation of Long Island Antiquities. see Society for the Preservation of Long Island Antiquities. Newsletter 78

Newsletter-State Bar of Arizona see State Bar of Arizona. Newsletter 518

Newsletter Yearbook Directory (US) 505

Newsletters on Stratigraphy (GW ISSN 0078-0421) 298

Newsmedia Guide International see Media Guide International. Newspapers/Newsmagazines Edition 6

Newsnovel (US) 569

Newspaper Guild. Annual T.N.G. Convention Officers' Report (US ISSN 0090-2209) 505

Newspaper Guild. Proceedings of the Annual Convention (US) 505

Newspaper Press Directory see Benn's Press Directory 504

Newspaper Requirements (US) 912

Newspapers Currently Received and Permanently Retained in the Library of Congress (US ISSN 0083-1646) 505
Newspapers in Microform (US ISSN 0097-9627) 93
Newsprint Association of Canada. Newsprint Data see Canadian Pulp and Paper Association. Newsprint Data 675
Newsseeker (NE ISSN 0028-9582) 912
Next Year, Next Decade, Next Century see Metropolitan Washington Council of Governments. Annual Report 744
Neydhartinger Moorpost (AU ISSN 0028-9620) 694
Nezam Pezeshki-Ye Iran. Nashriyeh see Medical Council of Iran. Publication 597
Nhu Jah (NP) 569
Niagara Frontier Transportation Authority Annual Report see N F T A Annual Report 863
Niagara Frontier Transportation Authority Port of Buffalo Handbook see N F T A Port of Buffalo Handbook 863
Niagara Parks Commission. Annual Report (CN ISSN 0078-0502) 277
Nicaragua. Corte Suprema de Justicia. Boletin Judicial (NQ) 516
Nicaragua. Direccion General de Aduanas. Memoria (NQ ISSN 0078-0510) 182
Nicaragua. Oficina Ejectiva de Encuestos y Censos. Boletin Demografico (NQ) 729
Nicaragua. Oficina Ejecutiva de Encuestos y Censos. Compendio Estadistico (NQ) 428
Nickelodeon see Trumpet 4
Niederdeutsche Beitraege zur Kunstgeschichte (GW ISSN 0078-0537) 77
Niederdeutsches Wort (GW ISSN 0078-0545) 548
Niederoesterreichische Sozialhilfe und Jugendwohlfahrtspflege (AU) 808
Niedersaechsische Staats- und Universitaetsbibliothek, Goettingen. Arbeiten (GW ISSN 0072-4866) 534
Niedersaechsisches Jahrbuch fuer Landesgeschichte (GW ISSN 0078-0561) 458
Niet Zo Benauwd (NE) 417
Nietzsche-Studien (GW) 690
Niger. Office des Postes et Telecommunications. Annuaire Officiel des Telephones (NG) 269
Nigeria. Anti-Inflation Task Force. Report (NR) 224
Nigeria. Federal Department of Fisheries. Federal Fisheries Occasional Paper (NR) 399
Nigeria. Federal Department of Forest Research. Research Paper (NR ISSN 0300-2403) 410
Nigeria. Federal Office of Statistics. Annual Abstract of Statistics (NR ISSN 0078-0626) 843
Nigeria. Federal Office of Statistics. Review of External Trade (NR ISSN 0078-0634) 161
Nigeria. Federal Office of Statistics. Trade Report (NR ISSN 0078-0642) 161
Nigeria. National Electric Power Authority. Annual Report and Accounts (NR) 357
Nigeria. National Manpower Board. Manpower Studies (NR) 209
Nigeria. National Universities Commission. Annual Report (NR) 338
Nigeria and the Classics see Museum Africum 259
Nigeria Annual and Trading Directory (NR ISSN 0078-057X) 241
Nigeria Business Directory (NR ISSN 0078-0596) 241
Nigeria Tourist Guide/Guide du Tourisme Nigerien (NR) 483, 889
Nigeria Year Book (NR ISSN 0078-0685) 722
Nigerian Chamber of Mines. Annual Review (NR ISSN 0078-0707) 645

Nigerian Economic Society. Proceedings of the Annual Conference (NR ISSN 0331-0361) 146
Nigerian Field Monographs (UK) 787
Nigerian Industrial Development Bank. Annual Report and Accounts (NR ISSN 0549-2734) 175
Nigerian Institute for Oil Palm Research. Journal (NR ISSN 0078-0715) 117
Nigerian Institute of International Affairs. Lecture Series (NR ISSN 0078-0731) 722
Nigerian Institute of International Affairs. Monograph Series (NR ISSN 0331-6254) 722
Nigerian Institute of International Affairs. Seminar Series (NR) 722
Nigerian Institute of Social and Economic Research. Annual Report (NR ISSN 0078-074X) 147, 799
Nigerian Journal of International Affairs(NR ISSN 0331-3646) 722
Nigerian Law Journal (UK ISSN 0078-0774) 516
Nigerian Medical Directory (NR ISSN 0078-0782) 598
Nigerian Names (NR) 417
Nigerian National Advisory Council for the Blind. Annual Report (NR ISSN 0078-0804) 808
Nigerian Office and Quarters Directory see Nigerian Office and Residential Directory 219
Nigerian Office and Residential Directory (NR) 219
Nigerian Tobacco Company. Annual Report and Accounts (NR) 861
Nigerian Tobacco Company. Report see Nigerian Tobacco Company. Annual Report and Accounts 861
Nihon Chishitsu Kosanshi see Geology and Mineral Resources of Japan 294
Nihon Hakushiroku (JA) 93
Nihon Insatsu Nenkan see Japan Printing Art Annual 733
Nihon Kaihatsu Ginko. Chosabu. Chosa Geppo (JA) 131
Nihon Kyoikuho Gakkai Nempo (JA) 320, 516
Nihon no Denki Jigyo see Electric Power Industry in Japan 353
Nihon no Roshi Kankei (JA) 209
Nihon no Shika Iryo see Dentistry in Japan 609
Nihon Nogaku Shimpo Nempo see Annual Report of the Development of Agriculture in Japan 26
Nihon Ongaku Bunken Yoshi Mokuroku see Ongaku Bunken Yoshi Mokuroku 665
Nihon Retaringu Nenkan see Japan Typography Annual 733
Nihon Seiji Gakkai Nenpo: Seijigaku see Japanese Political Science Association. Yearbook 712
Nihon Shosen Sempuku Tokei (JA) 879
Nihon Soshiki Baiyo Kenkyu Nenpo see Tissue Culture Studies in Japan: The Annual Bibliography 603
Nihon Taipogurafi Nenkan see Japan Typography Annual 733
Nihon University. Atomic Energy Research Institute. Annual Report (JA) 363, 369, 704
Niigata Airglow Observatory. Bulletin (JA) 697
Niigata Daigaku Nogakubu Kiyo see Niigata University. Faculty of Agriculture. Memoirs 18
Niigata Daigaku Rigakubu Fuzoku Sado Rinkai Jikkenjo Kenkyu Nenpo see Sado Marine Biological Station. Annual Report 107
Niigata University. Faculty of Agriculture. Memoirs/Niigata Daigaku Nogakubu Kiyo (JA ISSN 0549-4826) 18
Niigata University. Faculty of Science. Science Reports. Series A: Mathematics (JA) 587
Niigata University. Faculty of Science. Science Reports. Series B: Physics (JA) 697
Niigata University. Faculty of Science. Science Reports. Series C: Chemistry(JA) 247

Niigata University. Faculty of Science. Science Reports. Series D: Biology (JA) 105
Niigata University. Faculty of Science. Science Reports. Series E: Geology and Mineralogy (JA) 298, 645
Nijenrode Studies in Business (NE) 147
Nikon World (US ISSN 0029-0513) 693
Nimrod (AT ISSN 0085-4204) 569
Nippon Gyosei Kenkyu Nenpo see Japanese Society for Public Administration. Annals 743
Nippon Hoso Kyokai Technical Monograph see N H K Technical Monograph 268
Nippon no Kikogaku no Shinpo see Japanese Progress in Climatology 634
Nippon Steel Report (JA) 629
Nippon Tungsten Review (JA) 251
Niti Vimamsa (CE) 516
Nityanand Universal Series (II ISSN 0078-0855) 445
Niv Hamidrashia (IS ISSN 0048-0460) 770
Nivadaka Ekankika (II) 569, 859
Niveaux de Contamination Radioactive du Milieu Ambiant et de la Chaine Alimentaire (EI) 753
Nivel de la Economia Argentina (AG ISSN 0078-0863) 188
Nivim (US) 393
No Deadline (US) 6
No More Fun and Games (US ISSN 0029-0815) 719, 900
Nobel Prize Lectures - Chemistry (NE) 247
Nobel Prize Lectures - Peace (NE) 722
Nobel Prize Lectures - Physics (NE) 697
Nobel Prize Lectures-Physiology of Medicine (NE) 126, 598
Noble Official Catalog of Canada Precancels (US ISSN 0078-091X) 479
Noble Official Catalog of United States Bureau Precancels (US ISSN 0078-0928) 479
Noctes Romanae (SZ ISSN 0078-0936) 260
Noda Institute for Scientific Research. Report/Noda Sangyo Kagaku Kenkyusho Kenkyu Hokoku (JA ISSN 0078-0944) 787
Noda Sangyo Kagaku Kenkyusho Kenkyu Hokoku see Noda Institute for Scientific Research. Report 787
Nogaku Kenkyu see Okayama University. Ohara Institute fuer Landwirtschaftliche Biologie. Berichte 29
Nogyo Kikai Nenkan see Farm Machinery Yearbook 32
Nogyo Sogo Kenkyusho Nenpo see National Research Institute of Agriculture. Annual Report 18
Noise and Smog News (IT ISSN 0546-2347) 388
Noise Regulation Reporter (Bureau of National Affairs, Inc.) (US ISSN 0148-7957) 388, 516
Nomad (US) 889
Nomenclator Zoologicus (UK ISSN 0078-0952) 130
Nomenclature des Entreprises Nationales a Caractere Industriel ou Commercial et des Societies d'Economie Mixte d'Interet National(FR ISSN 0078-0960) 224
Nomina (UK ISSN 0141-6340) 63, 417, 458
Nomismatika Chronica (GR) 477
Nomos (US ISSN 0078-0979) 713
Non-European Societies see Studies of Developing Countries 817
Non-Ferrous Metal Data (US ISSN 0360-9553) 629
Non-Ferrous Metal Works of the World(UK ISSN 0078-0987) 629
Non-Ionizing Radiation (UK ISSN 0550-8398) 112, 622
Non-Metallic Solids (US ISSN 0078-0995) 697
Non Solus (US ISSN 0094-8977) 534
Nonaligned Third World Annual (US ISSN 0078-1002) 722

Nonpublic School Enrollment and Staff, New York State (US ISSN 0077-9253) 320
Nord-Norge Naeringsliv og Oekonomi (NO ISSN 0078-1029) 147
Nord Nytt (DK ISSN 0008-1345) 402
Nordelbingen (GW ISSN 0078-1037) 458
Nordens Jaernvaegar (SW) 873
Nordfriesisches Jahrbuch (GW ISSN 0078-1045) 458
Nordfriesland (GW) 182
Nordic Archaeological Abstracts see N A A 67
Nordicana (CN ISSN 0078-1053) 470
Nordisk Arkivkunskab (DK) 434, 534
Nordisk Ekumenisk Aarsbok (SW ISSN 0085-4212) 766
Nordisk Flaggskrift (DK) 417
Nordisk Institut for Teoretisk Atomfysik. Virksomhedsberetning/Nordita Report (DK) 704
Nordisk Medicinhistorisk Aarsbok (SW ISSN 0078-1061) 598
Nordisk Numismatisk Aarsskrift/Scandinavian Numismatic Journal (NO ISSN 0078-107X) 477
Nordisk Statistisk Aarsbok/Yearbook of Nordic Statistics (SW ISSN 0078-1088) 843
Nordisk Statistisk Skriftserie/Statistical Reports of the Nordic Countries (DK ISSN 0332-6527) 843
Nordisk Statutsamling (SW ISSN 0300-3094) 516
Nordiska Samarbetskommitten foer Namnforskning NORNA - Rapporter see NORNA - Rapporter 548
Nordiska Samarbetsorgan (DK) 507
Nordiske Domme i Sjofartsanliggender (NO ISSN 0085-4220) 516
Nordiske Komite for Bygningsbestemmelsei Skriftserie see N K B Skriftserie 137
Nordistica Gothoburgensia (SW ISSN 0078-1134) 548, 569
Nordita Report see Nordisk Institut for Teoretisk Atomfysik. Virksomhedsberetning 704
Norfolk Broads Holidays Afloat see Blakes Holidays Afloat 883
Norfolk Holiday Handbook (UK ISSN 0078-1150) 889
Norfolk Holiday Hints Handbook see Norfolk Holiday Handbook 889
Norfolk Record Society. Publications (UK ISSN 0078-1169) 458
Norge-Amerika Foreningen. Report see Norge-Amerika Foreningen. Yearbook 722
Norge-Amerika Foreningen. Yearbook (NO) 722
Norges Bank. Annual Report see Norges Bank. Report and Accounts 175
Norges Bank. Report and Accounts (NO ISSN 0078-1185) 175
Norges Bank. Skriftserie (NO) 188
Norges Geologiske Undersoekelse. Armelding (NO) 298
Norges Geologiske Undersoekelse Bulletin see N G U Bulletin 297
Norges Geologiske Undersoekelse Skrifter see N G U Skrifter 297
Norges Geotekniske Institutt. Publikasjon/Norwegian Geotechnical Institute. Publications (NO ISSN 0078-1193) 305
Norges Handels-Kalender/Norwegian Directory of Commerce/Annuaire du Commerce du Norvege/Norwegische Handels-Adressbuch (NO ISSN 0078-1215) 241
Norges Landbrukshoegskole. Institutt for Bygningsteknikk. Aarsmelding/Annual Report (NO ISSN 0065-0226) 138
Norges Landbrukshoegskole. Institutt for Bygningsteknikk. Byggekostnadsindeks for Driftsbygninger i Jordbruket. Prisutviklingen (NO ISSN 0065-0218) 18, 138
Norges Landbrukshoegskole. Institutt for Bygningsteknikk. Melding (NO ISSN 0065-0234) 138
Norges Landbrukshoegskole. Institutt for Jordskifte og Eiendomsutforming. Melding (NO ISSN 0065-0242) 29

Norges Landbruksoekonomiske
 Institutt. Driftsgranskinger i Jord- og
 Skogbruk (NO) 29
Norges Landbruksoekonomiske
 Institutt. Driftsgranskinger i
 Jordbruker see Norges
 Landbruksoekonomiske Institutt.
 Driftsgranskinger i Jord- og Skogbruk
 29
Norges Samarbeid Med
 Utviklingslandene (NO) 200
Norges Teknisk-Naturvitenskapelige
 Forskningsraad. Aarsberetning (NO
 ISSN 0078-1231) 787, 852
Norges Teknisk-Naturvitenskapelige
 Forskningsraad.
 Transportoekonomisk Institutt.
 Aarsberetning see
 Transportoekonomisk Institutt.
 Aarsberetning 874
Norges Veterinaerhoegskole.
 Aarsberetning/Veterinary College of
 Norway. Annual Report (NO ISSN
 0078-6713) 895
Norin-sho Kachiku Eisei Shikenjo
 Nenpo see Japan. National Institute
 of Animal Health. Annual Report
 894
Norin-sho Nenpo see Japan. Ministry of
 Agriculture and Forestry. Annual
 Report 17
Norin Suisan Nenkan see Japan.
 Ministry of Agriculture and Forestry.
 Annual Report 17
Norinsho Ringyo Shikenjo Nenpo see
 Japan. Forestry and Forest Products
 Research Institute. Annual Report
 409
Norman Ford's Florida (US ISSN
 0546-3432) 889
NORNA - Rapporter (Nordiska
 Samarbetskommitten foer
 Namnforskning) (SW ISSN 0346-
 6728) 548
Norsk Etnologisk Gransking.
 Smaaskrifter (NO ISSN 0489-2089)
 52
Norsk Fiskaralmanakk (NO) 399, 830
Norsk Institutt for By- og
 Regionforskning Occasional Paper
 see N I B R Occasional Paper 911
Norsk Institutt for By- og
 Regionforskning Rapport see N I B
 R Rapport 485
Norsk Institutt for Vannforskning.
 Aarbok (NO) 308
Norsk Institutt for Vannforskning.
 Temarapport (NO) 308
Norsk Litteraer Aarbok (NO ISSN
 0078-1266) 569
Norsk Polarinstitutt. Aarbok (NO
 ISSN 0085-4271) 298, 424
Norsk Polarinstitutt. Meddelelser (NO)
 298, 424
Norsk Polarinstitutt. Polarhaandbok
 (NO ISSN 0474-8042) 298, 424
Norsk Polarinstitutt. Skrifter (NO)
 298, 424
Norsk Sjoefartsmuseum. Aarsberetning
 (NO) 63, 458
Norsk Teknisk Museum. Yearbook see
 Volund 655
Norsk Utenrikspolitisk Aarbok (NO
 ISSN 0332-7299) 722
Norsk Utenrikspolitisk Institutt Notat
 see N U P I Notat 722
Norsk Utenrikspolitisk Institutt Rapport
 see N U P I Rapport 722
Norske Arkitektkonkurranser (NO
 ISSN 0332-6578) 69
Norske Creditbank (NO) 175
Norske Creditbank. Annual Report see
 Norske Creditbank 175
Norske Creditbank. Report of the
 Board of Directors see Norske
 Creditbank 175
Norske Institutt for Kosmisk Fysikk.
 Magnetic Observations see Auroral
 Observatory. Magnetic Observations
 81
Norske Veritas Classification and
 Registry of Shipping. Publication
 (NO ISSN 0549-7000) 380, 879
Norske Videnskaps-Akademi. Historisk-
 Filosofisk Klasse. Avhandlinger Two
 (NO ISSN 0029-2311) 434, 690

Norske Videnskaps-Akademi.
 Matematisk-Naturvidenkapelig
 Klasse. Skrifter see Norske
 Videnskaps-Akademi.
 Naturvidenskapelig Klasse. Skrifter
 787
Norske Videnskaps-Akademi.
 Naturvidenskapelig Klasse. Skrifter
 (NO) 787
Norte (AG) 470
North American Association of
 Alcoholism Programs. Meeting.
 Selected Papers see A D P A
 Selected Papers of Annual Meetings
 286
North American Conference on Labor
 Statistics. Selected Papers (US ISSN
 0074-9974) 161
North American Fauna (US ISSN
 0078-1304) 130
North American Flora (US ISSN
 0078-1312) 117
North American Forest Soils
 Conference. Proceedings (US ISSN
 0078-1320) 38
North American Human Rights
 Directory (US ISSN 0270-2282)
 719
North American Manufacturers &
 Suppliers Directory (US) 241
North American Protestant Ministries
 Overseas see Mission Handbook:
 North American Protestant
 Ministries Overseas 772
North American Radio-T V Guide (US
 ISSN 0078-1347) 268
North American Society for Sport
 History. Proceedings (US) 470, 821
North American Students of
 Cooperation Campus Co-Op
 Directory see N A S C O Campus
 Co-Op Directory 240
North American Wildlife and Natural
 Resources Conference. Transactions
 (US ISSN 0078-1355) 277
North American Yacht Register (US
 ISSN 0163-285X) 827
North Atlantic Treaty Organization.
 Directorate of Economic Affairs.
 Colloquium. Series (BE) 197
North Atlantic Treaty Organization.
 Expert Panel on Air Pollution
 Modeling. Proceedings (BE ISSN
 0377-7669) 388
North Atlantic Treaty Organization
 Advanced Study Institute Series E:
 Applied Science see N A T O
 Advanced Study Institute Series E:
 Applied Science 852
North Atlantic Treaty Organization
 Handbook see N A T O Handbook
 722
North Cal - Neva Resource
 Conservation and Development
 Project. Annual Work Plan (US
 ISSN 0097-7268) 277
North Carolina. Council on State Goals
 and Policy. Annual Report see North
 Carolina. State Goals and Policy
 Board. Annual Report 744
North Carolina. Department of Human
 Resources. Annual Plan of Work (US
 ISSN 0095-4942) 808
North Carolina. Department of Human
 Resources. Annual Report (US) 224
North Carolina. Department of
 Revenue. Franchise Tax and
 Corporate Income Tax Bulletins for
 Taxable Years (US ISSN 0078-
 138X) 231
North Carolina. Department of
 Transportation. Office of Highway
 Safety. Summary of Activities (US)
 875
North Carolina. Division of Ground
 Water. Ground Water Bulletin see
 Groundwater Bulletin 307
North Carolina. Division of Health
 Services. Public Health Statistics
 Branch. North Carolina Vital
 Statistics (US ISSN 0078-1371)
 732, 756
North Carolina. Division of Mineral
 Resources. Bulletin see North
 Carolina. Geological Survey Section.
 Bulletin 645

North Carolina. Division of Mineral
 Resources. Economic Paper see
 North Carolina. Geological Survey
 Section. Economic Paper 645
North Carolina. Division of Mineral
 Resources. Information Circular see
 North Carolina. Geological Survey
 Section. Information Circular 645
North Carolina . Division of Mineral
 Resources. Special Publication see
 North Carolina. Geological Survey
 Section. Special Publication 645
North Carolina. Geological Survey
 Section. Bulletin (US) 645
North Carolina. Geological Survey
 Section. Economic Paper (US) 645
North Carolina. Geological Survey
 Section. Information Circular (US)
 645
North Carolina. Geological Survey
 Section. Special Publication (US)
 645
North Carolina. Laws, Statutes, Etc.
 Planning Legislation in North
 Carolina (US ISSN 0550-7006) 486
North Carolina. Secretary of State.
 North Carolina Elections (US ISSN
 0092-1726) 744
North Carolina. State Goals and Policy
 Board. Annual Report (US) 744
North Carolina Agricultural Chemicals
 Manual (US ISSN 0065-4418) 38
North Carolina Communicable Disease
 Morbidity Statistics (US ISSN 0085-
 428X) 756
North Carolina Companies see
 Carolinas Companies 142
North Carolina Elections see North
 Carolina. Secretary of State. North
 Carolina Elections 744
North Carolina Governor's Highway
 Safety Program. Summary of
 Activities see North Carolina.
 Department of Transportation. Office
 of Highway Safety. Summary of
 Activities 875
North Carolina Industrial Contact List
 see Industrial Contact List for North
 Carolina Communities 223
North Carolina Manual (US) 713
North Carolina Medical Society.
 Transactions (US ISSN 0361-5537)
 598
North Carolina Metalworking
 Directory(US) 241, 583, 629
North Carolina Museum of Art.
 Bulletin (US ISSN 0029-2567) 654
North Carolina Reported Abortions
 (US) 132
North Carolina Seed Law (US) 18
North Carolina State Industrial
 Directory (US ISSN 0161-4738)
 241
North Carolina State University.
 Department of Crop Science.
 Research Report (US ISSN 0078-
 1517) 38
North Carolina State University.
 Development Council. Report (US
 ISSN 0078-1428) 338
North Carolina State University. School
 of Design. (Student Publication) (US
 ISSN 0078-1444) 77
North Carolina State University. School
 of Forest Resources. Technical
 Report. (US ISSN 0090-0664) 410
North Carolina State University. Water
 Resources Research Insitute. Report
 (US ISSN 0078-1525) 897
North Carolina Studies in the Romance
 Languages and Literatures. (US) 569
North Carolina, University. State
 College of Agriculture and
 Engineering, Raleigh. Development
 Council. Report see North Carolina
 State University. Development
 Council. Report 338
North Central Campbook (US) 830,
 889
North Central Camping see North
 Central Campbook 889
North Central-Iowa, Minnesota,
 Nebraska, North Dakota, South
 Dakota TourBook see Tourbook:
 North Central 891
North Central Reading Association
 Yearbook see N C R A Yearbook
 329

North Central Regional Center for
 Rural Development. Research
 Report(US) 486
North-Central State. Ministry of Works.
 Report see Kaduna State. Ministry of
 Works. Report 743
North Central State Statistical
 Yearbook see Kaduna State
 Statistical Yearbook 842
North Country Reference & Research
 Resources Council. Newsletter (US
 ISSN 0029-2699) 534
North Dakota. Consumer Credit
 Division. Consolidated Annual
 Report of Licensees (US ISSN 0091-
 2093) 175
North Dakota. Department of
 Agriculture. Annual Report see
 North Dakota. Department of
 Agriculture. Biennial Report 18
North Dakota. Department of
 Agriculture. Biennial Report (US) 18
North Dakota. Department of Public
 Instruction. Biennial Report of the
 Superintendent of Public Instruction
 (US) 328
North Dakota. Employment Security
 Bureau. Annual Report (US ISSN
 0078-155X) 209
North Dakota. Employment Security
 Bureau. Biennial Report to the
 Governor (US ISSN 0078-1568)
 209
North Dakota. Geological Survey.
 Bulletin (US) 298
North Dakota. Geological Survey.
 Educational Series (US ISSN 0091-
 9004) 298
North Dakota. Geological Survey.
 Miscellaneous Series (US ISSN
 0078-1576) 298
North Dakota. Geological Survey.
 Report of Investigations (US) 298
North Dakota. Judicial Council. Annual
 Report (US) 516, 843
North Dakota. Judicial Council.
 Statistical Compilation and Report
 see North Dakota. Judicial Council.
 Annual Report 516
North Dakota. Milk Stabilization Board.
 Annual Report of Administrative
 Activities (US ISSN 0091-9446) 41
North Dakota. Public Welfare Board.
 Report see North Dakota. Social
 Service Board. Report 808
North Dakota. Social Service Board.
 Area Social Service Centers (US
 ISSN 0095-6333) 808
North Dakota. Social Service Board.
 Juvenile Court and State Youth
 Authority. Delinquency, Dependency
 and Neglect. Special Proceedings
 (US) 257, 285
North Dakota. Social Service Board.
 Report (US ISSN 0095-6325) 808
North Dakota. Social Service Board.
 Statistics (US ISSN 0095-1633) 811
North Dakota. Social Service Board
 Statistics, Juvenile Court and State
 Youth Authority see North Dakota.
 Social Service Board. Juvenile Court
 and State Youth Authority.
 Delinquency, Dependency and
 Neglect. Special Proceedings 257
North Dakota. State Advisory Council
 for Vocational Education. Annual
 Evaluation Report (US ISSN 0094-
 8306) 350
North Dakota. State Department of
 Health. Report (US ISSN 0094-
 1816) 753
North Dakota. State Wheat
 Commission. Biennial Report (US)
 43
North Dakota Academic Library
 Statistics. see North Dakota Library
 Statistics 539
North Dakota Academy of Science.
 Proceedings (US) 787
North Dakota Crop and Livestock
 Statistics (US ISSN 0078-1541) 25
North Dakota Growth Indicators (US
 ISSN 0549-8368) 188
North Dakota Library Statistics (US)
 539
North Dakota State Industrial Directory
 (US) 241

North Dakota State Plan for Rehabilitation Facilities and Workshops (US ISSN 0093-7843) 346
North Dakota's Highway Safety Work Program (US) 875
North-Holland Linguistic Series (NE ISSN 0078-1592) 548
North-Holland Mathematical Library (NE) 587
North-Holland Mathematics Studies (NE) 587
North-Holland Series in Applied Mathematics and Mechanics (NE ISSN 0066-5460) 587
North-Holland Series in Crystal Growth(NE) 697
North-Holland Series in Low Temperature Physics (NE) 912
North of Scotland College of Agriculture, Aberdeen. Annual Report see School of Agriculture, Aberdeen. Annual Report 19
North of Scotland College of Agriculture, Aberdeen. Bulletin (UK) 18
North Pacific Fur Seal Commission. Proceedings of the Annual Meeting (US ISSN 0078-1622) 130
North Queensland Naturalist (AT ISSN 0078-1630) 105
North-South (CN) 393, 424
North Staffordshire Journal of Field Studies (UK ISSN 0078-1649) 424, 458
Northamptonshire Archaeology (UK ISSN 0305-4659) 63
Northamptonshire Federation of Archaeological Societies. Bulletin see Northamptonshire Archaeology 63
Northamptonshire Natural History Society and Field Club Journal (UK) 787
Northamptonshire Past and Present (UK ISSN 0140-9131) 458
Northeast Coal Study. Preliminary Environmental Report see British Columbia. Ministry of the Environment. Northeast Coal Study Preliminary Environmental Report 642
Northeast Conference on the Teaching of Foreign Languages. Reports of the Working Committees (US ISSN 0078-1665) 350, 548
Northeast Electronics Research and Engineering Meeting. Record (US ISSN 0078-1673) 357
Northeast Folklore (US ISSN 0078-1681) 402
North East India Geographical Society. Journal see North Eastern Geographer 424
Northeast Pacific Pink and Chum Salmon Workshop. Proceedings (US ISSN 0094-128X) 399
Northeastern Campbook (US) 830
Northeastern Camping see Northeastern Campbook 830
North Eastern Geographer (II) 424
Northeastern Oklahoma State University. Faculty Research, Publications, In-Service Activities (US) 338
Northeastern Regional Antipollution Conference. Proceedings (US ISSN 0048-0746) 388, 753
Northeastern Tour Book see Tourbook: Connecticut, Massachusetts, Rhode Island 872
Northeastern Tour Book see Tourbook: Maine, New Hampshire, Vermont 872
Northeastern University Studies in Rehabilitation (US ISSN 0078-169X) 209
Northeastern Weed Control Conference see Northeastern Weed Science Society. Proceedings 38
Northeastern Weed Science Society. Proceedings (US ISSN 0078-1703) 38
Northern Arizona Scene (US) 424
Northern California Golf Association. Blue Book (US) 821

Northern Canada Power Commission. Annual Review/Commission d'Energie du Nord Canadien. Revue Annuelle (CN ISSN 0704-1551) 363
Northern History (UK ISSN 0078-172X) 458
Northern Illinois University. Center for Southeast Asian Studies. Occasional Papers Series (US) 445, 492
Northern Illinois University. Center for Southeast Asian Studies. Special Report Series (US ISSN 0073-4934) 445, 492
Northern Ireland. Commissioner for Complaints. Annual Report (UK) 744
Northern Ireland. Department of Agriculture. Annual Report on Research and Technical Work (UK ISSN 0078-1746) 18
Northern Ireland. Department of Agriculture. Record of Agricultural Research (UK ISSN 0078-1754) 18
Northern Libraries Bulletin (US ISSN 0048-0789) 534
Northern New England Review (US ISSN 0190-3012) 569
Northern Nigeria. Ministry of Economic Planning. Statistical Year Book see Kano State Statistical Year Book 842
Northern Nigeria Development Corporation. Report see New Nigeria Development Company Limited. Annual Report and Accounts 224
Northern Nigeria Gazette see Kano State of Nigeria Gazette 743
Northern Nut Growers Association. Annual Report (US) 117
Northwest Association of Schools and Colleges. Proceedings. (US) 320, 339
Northwest Association of Secondary and Higher Schools see Northwest Association of Schools and Colleges. Proceedings 339
Northwest Atlantic Fisheries Organization List of Fishing Vessels see N A F O List of Fishing Vessels 399
Northwest Atlantic Fisheries Organization Meeting Proceedings see N A F O Meeting Proceedings 399
Northwest Atlantic Fisheries Organization Sampling Yearbook see N A F O Sampling Yearbook 399
Northwest Atlantic Fisheries Organization Scientific Council Meeting Reports see N A F O Scientific Council Meeting Reports 399
Northwest Atlantic Fisheries Organization Scientific Council Studies see N A F O Scientific Council Studies 399
North West England Industrial Classified Directory (UK) 180
Northwest Geology (US) 298
Northwest Historical Series (US ISSN 0078-1789) 470
North West Industrial Development Association. Annual Report (UK) 224
Northwest Wood Products Clinic. Proceedings (US ISSN 0078-1797) 413
Northwestern Campbook (US) 830, 889
Northwestern Camping see Northwestern Campbook 889
Northwestern-Iowa Dealer Reference Manual (US ISSN 0078-1800) 138
Northwestern Ontario Construction Industry Directory. Purchasing Guide(CN) 138, 369
Northwestern States see Tourbook: Idaho, Montana, Wyoming 891
Northwestern Tour Book see Tourbook: Idaho, Montana, Wyoming 891
Northwestern University. Dental School Library. Current Subscriptions List (US) 602
Northwestern University. Materials Research Center. Annual Technical Report (US) 380
Norveg (NO ISSN 0029-3601) 52
Norway (NO ISSN 0029-3628) 197

Norway. Arbeidsdirektoratet. Aarsmelding (NO ISSN 0078-1835) 209
Norway. Direktoratet for Arbeidstilsynet. Forskrifter/Regulations (NO) 339
Norway. Fiskeridirektoratet. Fiskeflaaten (NO) 399
Norway. Fiskeridirektoratet. Skrifter. Serie Ernaering (NO) 666
Norway. Fiskeridirektoratet. Skrifter. Serie Fiskeri (NO ISSN 0078-1843) 912
Norway. Fiskeridirektoratet. Skrifter. Serie Havundersoekelser (NO ISSN 0015-3117) 399
Norway. Forsvarets Forskningsinstitutt. N D R E Report (NO ISSN 0085-4301) 787
Norway. Komite for Romforskning. N.S.R.C. Report see Space Activity in Norway 10
Norway. Ministry of Industry and Handicraft. Reports to the Storting (NO) 339
Norway. Riksbibliotektjenesten. Aarsmelding (NO) 534
Norway. Sprengstoffinspeksjonen. Aarsberetning see Norway. Statens Sprengstoffinspeksjon. Aarsberetning 373
Norway. Statens Arbeidstilsyn Direktoratet. Verneregler see Norway. Direktoratet for Arbeidstilsynet. Forskrifter/Regulations 339
Norway. Statens Institutt for Alkoholforskning. Skrifter (NO ISSN 0078-673X) 287
Norway. Statens Sprengstoffinspeksjon. Aarsberetning (NO) 373
Norway. Statistisk Sentralbyraa. Alkohol og Andre Rusmidler/Alcohol and Drugs (NO) 288, 843
Norway. Statistisk Sentralbyraa. Arbeidsmarkedstatistikk/Labour Market Statistics (NO ISSN 0078-1878) 162, 844
Norway. Statistisk Sentralbyraa. Artikler/Articles (NO ISSN 0085-431X) 192, 815
Norway. Statistisk Sentralbyraa. Electrisitesstatistikk/Electricity Statistics (NO) 364, 844
Norway. Statistisk Sentralbyraa. Familie Statistikk/Family Statistics (NO) 732, 844
Norway. Statistisk Sentralbyraa. Folkemengd Etter Alder og Ekteskapelig Status/Population by Age and Marital Status (NO ISSN 0550-7170) 732, 844
Norway. Statistisk Sentralbyraa. Forretnings- og Sparebanker/Commercial and Savings Banks (NO) 162, 844
Norway. Statistisk Sentralbyraa. Framskriving Av Folkemengden: Regionale Tall/Population Projections: Regional Figures (NO) 732, 844
Norway. Statistisk Sentralbyraa. Helsepersonellstatistikk (NO) 602, 844
Norway. Statistisk Sentralbyraa. Helsestatistikk/Health Statistics (NO) 756, 844
Norway. Statistisk Sentralbyraa. Industristatistikk/Industrial Statistics (NO ISSN 0078-1886) 162, 844
Norway. Statistisk Sentralbyraa. Jordbruksstatistikk/Agricultural Statistics (NO ISSN 0078-1894) 25, 844
Norway. Statistisk Sentralbyraa. Kommune og Fylkestings Valget/Municipal and County Elections (NO) 748, 844
Norway. Statistisk Sentralbyraa. Kommunevalget/Municipal Elections see Norway. Statistisk Sentralbyraa. Kommune og Fylkestings Valget/Municipal and County Elections 748
Norway. Statistisk Sentralbyraa. Kredittmarked Statistikk/Credit Market Statistics (NO ISSN 0078-1908) 162, 844

Norway. Statistisk Sentralbyraa. Kriminalstatistikk/Criminal Statistics: Prisoners (NO) 285, 844
Norway. Statistisk Sentralbyraa. Legestatistikk see Norway. Statistisk Sentralbyraa. Helsepersonellstatistikk 602
Norway. Statistisk Sentralbyraa. Loennsstatistikk/Wage Statistics (NO ISSN 0078-1916) 162, 844
Norway. Statistisk Sentralbyraa. Nasjonalregnskap/National Accounts(NO) 162, 844
Norway. Statistisk Sentralbyraa. Oekonomisk Utsyn/Economic Survey(NO ISSN 0078-1924) 162, 844
Norway. Statistisk Sentralbyraa. Reiselivstatiskk/Statistics on Travel (NO) 844, 893
Norway. Statistisk Sentralbyraa. Samferdselsstatistikk/Transport and Communication Statistics (NO) 266, 844, 866
Norway. Statistisk Sentralbyraa. Samfunnsoekonomiske Studier/Social Economic Studies (NO ISSN 0085-4344) 815
Norway. Statistisk Sentralbyraa. Sivilrettsstatistikk/Civil Judicial Statistics (NO) 285, 844
Norway. Statistisk Sentralbyraa. Skugstatstikk/Forestry Statistics (NO) 412, 844
Norway. Statistisk Sentralbyraa. Statistisk Aarbok/Statistical Yearbook (NO ISSN 0078-1932) 844
Norway. Statistisk Sentralbyraa. Stortingsvalg/Parliamentary Elections(NO) 748, 844
Norway. Statistisk Sentralbyraa. Utdanningsstatistikk: Educational Statistics (NO) 328, 844
Norway. Statistisk Sentralbyraa. Utenrikshandel/External Trade (NO ISSN 0078-1940) 162, 844
Norway. Statistisk Sentralbyraa. Varehandelsstatistikk/Wholesale and Retail Trade Statistics (NO ISSN 0078-1959) 162, 844
Norway. Televerket. Statistikk (NO) 266
Norway. Televerket. Statistisk Arbok see Norway. Televerket. Statistikk 266
Norwegian-American Historical Association. Newsletter (US ISSN 0078-1967) 470
Norwegian-American Historical Association. Topical Studies (US ISSN 0085-4352) 470
Norwegian American Historical Association. Travel and Description Series (US ISSN 0078-1975) 470
Norwegian-American Studies (US ISSN 0078-1983) 470
Norwegian-American Studies and Records see Norwegian-American Studies 470
Norwegian Chamber of Commerce. Year Book and Directory of Members (UK ISSN 0305-0998) 180
Norwegian Directory of Commerce see Norges Handels-Kalender 241
Norwegian Foreign Policy Studies see Utenrikspolitiske Skrifter 725
Norwegian Geotechnical Institute. Publications see Norges Geotekniske Institutt. Publikasjon 305
Norwegian Geotechnical Institute. Technical Report (NO ISSN 0078-1207) 305
Norwegian Journal of Geophysics see Geophysica Norvegica 304
Norwegian Journal of Social Research see Tidsskrift for Samfunnsforskning 801
Norwegian Journal of Theoretical Astrophysics see Astrophysica Norvegica 81
Norwegian Offshore Index (NO) 680
Norwegian Research Council for Science and the Humanities. Annual Report (NO) 492, 787
Norwegian Studies in English (NO ISSN 0078-1991) 548, 569

Norwegian Yearbook of Maritime History *see* Sjoefartshistorisk Aarbok *461*
Norwegische Handels-Adressbuch *see* Norges Handels-Kalender *241*
Notable Books (US) *93*
Notary Public Practices & Glossary (US) *516*
Notas de Algebra y Analisis (AG ISSN 0078-2009) *587*
Notas de Logica Matematica (AG ISSN 0078-2017) *587*
Notas e Communicacoes de Matematica(BL ISSN 0085-5413) *587*
Notas Matematicas (CL) *587*
Notatki z Mistetstba *see* Ukrainian Art Digest *79*
Notes (New York) (US) *729*
Notes de Conjoncture Regionale (FR) *188*
Notes for Medical Catalogers (US ISSN 0078-2025) *534*
Notes from the Royal Botanic Garden, Edinburgh (UK ISSN 0080-4274) *117*
Notes in Anthropology (US ISSN 0078-2041) *52*
Notes in Pure Mathematics (AT) *587*
Notes on Mathematics and Its Applications (US) *587*
Notes on Unions (CN ISSN 0316-0386) *587*
Noticiario Arqueologico Hispanico: Arqueologia (SP) *63*
Noticias de Cosmetica y de Perfumeria Documenta *see* N C P Documenta *85*
Noticias del Trabajo (PR ISSN 0029-4195) *209, 516*
Noticiero I.D.U.N. (Instituto de Desarrollo Urbano) (CK) *486*
Noticiero Tuberosas (VE ISSN 0085-4387) *117*
Notre Dame Studies in American Catholicism (US) *775*
Nottingham Medieval Studies (UK ISSN 0078-2122) *458*
Notulae Naturae (US ISSN 0029-4608) *788*
Notulae Vertebratologicae *see* Vertebratologicke Zpravy *131*
Nouveau Cinema Canadien *see* New Canadian Film *650*
Nouveau Pouvoir (CN) *320*
Nouveautes Techniques Maritimes (FR ISSN 0078-2157) *880*
Nouvelle Bibliotheque Nervalienne (FR ISSN 0305-9804) *98, 569*
Nouvelle Litterature et Ideologie *see* New Literature and Ideology *557*
Nouvelle Revue Canadienne *see* N R C - Nouvelle Revue Canadienne *557*
Nova Acta Leopoldina (GE) *788*
Nova Acta Regiae Societatis Scientiarum Upsaliensis (SW ISSN 0029-5000) *788*
Nova Dumka (YU) *393*
Nova Hedwiga, Beihefte (GW ISSN 0078-2238) *434*
Nova Kepleriana. Neue Folge (GW ISSN 0078-2246) *83*
Nova Scotia. Commission on Drug Dependency. Annual Report (CN ISSN 0707-9834) *287*
Nova Scotia. Department of Bacteriology. Annual Report (CN ISSN 0078-2319) *912*
Nova Scotia. Department of Development. Annual Report (CN) *745*
Nova Scotia. Department of Labour. Annual Report (CN ISSN 0380-5689) *209*
Nova Scotia. Department of Labour. Economics and Research Division. Wage Rates, Salaries and Hours of Labour in Nova Scotia (CN ISSN 0550-1741) *209*
Nova Scotia. Department of Pathology. Annual Report (CN ISSN 0078-2351) *912*
Nova Scotia. Department of Public Health. Nutrition Division. Annual Report (CN ISSN 0078-236X) *666, 753*
Nova Scotia. Department of Recreation. Annual Report (CN) *821*

Nova Scotia. Emergency Measures Organization. Report (CN ISSN 0078-2378) *258, 753*
Nova Scotia. Environmental Control Council. Annual Report (CN ISSN 0317-3526) *388*
Nova Scotia. Fire Marshal. Annual Report (CN ISSN 0085-4395) *395*
Nova Scotia. Office of the Ombudsman. Annual Report (CN) *745*
Nova Scotia Bird Society. Newsletter (CN ISSN 0383-9567) *125*
Nova Scotia Community Planning Conference Proceedings (CN ISSN 0078-2300) *745*
Nova Scotia Dental Association. Newsletter (CN) *610*
Nova Scotia Fisherman (CN ISSN 0708-3629) *399*
Nova Scotia Fruit Growers Association. Annual Report and Proceedings (CN ISSN 0078-2386) *38*
Nova Scotia Labour-Management Study Conference. Proceedings (CN ISSN 0550-9955) *210*
Nova Scotia Power Corporation. Annual Report (CN ISSN 0078-2459) *357*
Nova Scotia Research Foundation. Bulletin (CN ISSN 0078-2483) *912*
Nova Scotia Research Foundation Corporation. Annual Report (CN) *788, 852*
Nova Scotia Technical College. School of Architecture. Report Series *see* Technical University of Nova Scotia. School of Architecture. Report Series *70*
Nova Scotian Institute of Science. Proceedings (CN ISSN 0078-2521) *788*
Novantiqua (IT) *548*
Novarien (IT ISSN 0078-253X) *775*
Novaya Literatura po Tsenoobrazovaniyu, Opublikovannaya v S.S.S.R. (IO ISSN 0078) *93, 162*
Novedades (SP) *93*
Novye Issledovaniya v Gornoi Elektromekhanike (UR) *357*
Novye Issledovaniya v Khimii, Metallurgii i Obogashchenii (UR) *373, 629*
Now in Japan (JA) *197*
Nuclear Canada. Yearbook (CN) *704*
Nuclear Engineering (US ISSN 0078-2599) *369, 704*
Nuclear Fuel Cycle Requirements (FR) *363, 704*
Nuclear Magnetic Resonance (UK ISSN 0305-9804) *255*
Nuclear Magnetic Resonance *see* N M R *704*
Nuclear Medicine Annual (US) *622*
Nuclear Methods Monographs (NE) *247*
Nuclear News Buyers Guide (US ISSN 0078-2610) *704*
Nuclear News Industry Report *see* Nuclear News Buyers Guide *704*
Nuclear Physics (US ISSN 0550-3205) *704*
Nuclear Physics Monographs (US) *704*
Nuclear Safety Research Association Memo *see* N S R A Memo *704*
Nuclear Science and Applications (US ISSN 0078-2637) *704*
Nuclear Science Applications-Section B-in Depth Reviews (US) *704*
Nuclear Science Technology Monograph Series (American Nuclear Society) (US) *369, 704*
Nucleo de Estudos Sociais para Habitacao e Urbanismo (BL) *486*
Nucleus (AT ISSN 0085-4409) *697*
Nudist Park Guide (US) *889*
Nuernberger Forschungen (GW ISSN 0078-2653) *458*
Nuernberger Wirtschafts-und Sozialgeographische Arbeiten (GW) *424*
Nueruolog (US) *676*
Nuestromundo (SP) *713*
Nueva Ciencia (VE) *188*
Nukada Institute for Medical and Biological Research. Reports (JA ISSN 0469-6271) *105, 598*
Numerus Clausus - Alternativen *see* Numerus Clausus - Finessen *320*
Numerus Clausus - Finessen (GW) *320*

Numis-Notas (CK) *477*
Numismatic Books in Print (US) *477*
Numismatic Chronicle and Journal (UK ISSN 0078-2696) *477*
Numismatic Communications *see* Numismatiska Meddelanden *478*
Numismatic Notes and Monographs (US ISSN 0078-2718) *477*
Numismatic Studies (US ISSN 0517-404X) *477*
Numismatica Moravica (CS ISSN 0078-2726) *477*
Numismatiska Meddelanden/ Numismatic Communications (SW ISSN 0078-2734) *478*
Nuntiaturberichte aus Deutschland Nebst Ergaenzenden Aktenstuecken (GW ISSN 0078-2742) *434*
Nuova Dirigenza (IT ISSN 0078-2750) *745*
Nuova Universale Studium (IT) *434, 569, 690*
Nuovi Saggi (IT ISSN 0078-2769) *492*
Nuovo Medioevo (IT ISSN 0391-6049) *458*
Nuovo 75 (IT) *557*
Nursing(Year) Career Directory (US) *614*
Nursing and Allied Health Literature Index (US ISSN 0146-5554) *3, 602, 614*
Nursing Education Monographs (US ISSN 0078-2831) *912*
Nursing Job Guide to over 7000 Hospitals *see* Nursing Job News: Nursing Job Guide to over 7000 Hospitals *614*
Nursing Job News: Nursing Job Guide to over 7000 Hospitals (US ISSN 0162-9069) *614*
Nursing Journal (CE) *614*
Nursing Literature Index *see* Nursing and Allied Health Literature Index *602*
Nursing Opportunities (US) *614*
Nusa (IO ISSN 0126-2874) *548*
Nutrition and the Brain (US) *105, 666*
Nutrition in Health and Disease (US ISSN 0160-2470) *666*
Nutrition News in Zambia (ZA ISSN 0078-284X) *405, 666*
Nutrition Research Laboratories. Annual Report *see* National Institute of Nutrition. Report *666*
Nutshell (US) *263*
Nuttall Ornithological Club. Publications (US ISSN 0550-4082) *125*
Nuytsia (AT ISSN 0085-4417) *117*
Ny Carlsberg Glyptotek. Meddelelser (DK ISSN 0085-3208) *63, 77*
Ny Mponin'i Madagasikara (MG) *729*
Nyam News (JM) *690*
Nye Boeger om Film *see* Nye Boeger om Film/TV *651*
Nye Boeger om Film/TV/New Books on Film/TV (DK) *651*
Nye Family Newsletter (US) *417*
Nyelveszeti Tanulmanyok (HU ISSN 0078-2858) *548*
Nyelvtudomanyi Ertekezesek (HU ISSN 0078-2866) *548*
O A S. General Secretariat. Annual Report (Organization of American States) (US ISSN 0078-6403) *470*
O A T U U Information Tips (Organization of African Trade Union Unity) (GH) *912*
O C L C. Annual Report (US ISSN 0090-8673) *534*
O D C Planning Reports (Oahu Development Conference) (US) *486*
O E C D Financial Statistics/ Statistiques Financieres de l'OCDE (Organization for Economic Cooperation and Development) (FR ISSN 0304-3371) *162*
O E C D Foreign Trade Statistics. Serie C *see* Organization for Economic Cooperation and Development. Statistics of Foreign Trade. Series C: Tables by Commodities. Imports and Exports/Statistiques du Commerce Exterieur. Serie C: Tableaux Par Produits *162*
O E C D Halden Reactor Project (Organization for Economic Cooperation and Development) (FR ISSN 0078-6284) *369, 704*

O E C D Informatics Studies Series *see* Information, Computer and Communications Policy *200*
O E C D Studies in Resource Allocation (FR) *231, 745*
O H O L O Biological Conferences (Proceedings) (SZ ISSN 0379-220X) *105*
O Literature Dlya Detei (UR) *569*
O.O.B.A. Guidebook of Theatres (Off Off Broadway Alliance) (US ISSN 0361-6606) *859*
O. P. Market (US ISSN 0078-2882) *759*
O.R.S.T.O.M. Annales Hydrologiques (FR ISSN 0071-8998) *308*
O.R.S.T.O.M. Memoires *see* Memoires O.R.S.T.O.M *852*
O. R. S. T. O. M. Recueil de Travaux. Oceanographie (Office de la Recherche Scientifique et Technique Outre-Mer) (NL ISSN 0078-2130) *298, 311*
O R T E S O L Journal (Oregon Teachers of English to Speakers of Other Languages) (US ISSN 0192-401X) *350, 548*
O R T Yearbook (Organization for Rehabilitation Through Training) (SZ) *346*
O S G N Wetenschappelijke Publikatie (Organisatie van Studenten in de Geschiedenis van Nederland) (NE) *458*
O.S.S.C. Bulletin (US ISSN 0095-6694) *320*
O.T.S. *see* O.T.S.: off-the-Shelf Catalog of Electro Products *357*
O.T.S.: off-the-Shelf Catalog of Electro Products (US ISSN 0095-7143) *357*
O y M (Servicio Central de Organizacion y Metodos) (SP) *745*
Oahu Development Conference. Annual Report (US) *486*
Oahu Development Conference Planning Reports *see* O D C Planning Reports *486*
Oak Ridge Associated Universities. Medical Division. Research Report (US ISSN 0078-2890) *598*
Oak Ridge Associated Universities. Report (US ISSN 0078-2904) *339*
Obelisk (JA) *569*
Oberhessische Gesellschaft fuer Natur-und Heilkunde, Giessen. Berichte (GW ISSN 0078-2920) *788*
Oberrheinische Geologische Abhandlungen (GW ISSN 0078-2939) *298*
Oberrheinischer Geologischer Verein. Jahresberichte und Mitteilungen (GW ISSN 0078-2947) *298*
Objectivist Calendar (US) *569*
Obligationsbok foer Finland *see* Suomen Obligaatiokirja *205*
Obrabotka Simvol'noi Informatsii (UR) *273*
Obras (Venice) (US) *569*
Obraz Literatury Polskiej (PL ISSN 0078-2963) *569*
Observacoes Magneticas (Acores) (PO) *306*
Observation (US ISSN 0078-2971) *693*
Observations (C. D. Howe Research Institute) (CN) *147*
Observatoire Astronomique d'Alger. Annales (AE ISSN 0065-6232) *83*
Observatoire de Geneve. Publications. Serie A (SZ ISSN 0085-0942) *83*
Observatoire de Geneve. Publications. Serie B (SZ ISSN 0435-2939) *83*
Observatoire de Strasbourg. Publication (FR ISSN 0081-590X) *83*
Observatorio Astronomico de Madrid. Anuario (SP) *83*
Observatorio Astronomico Municipal de Rosario. Boletin (AG ISSN 0302-2277) *83*
Observatorio Nacional Rio de Janeiro. Anuario *see* Observatorio Nacional Rio de Janeiro. Efemerides Astronomicas *83*
Observatorio Nacional Rio de Janeiro. Contribuicoes Cientificas (BL) *306*
Observatorio Nacional Rio de Janeiro. Efemerides Astronomicas (BL) *83*
Observatorio Nacional Rio de Janeiro. Publicacoes (BL) *83, 306*

Observatorul Astronomic din Bucuresti. Anuarul (RM ISSN 0068-3086) 83
Observatorul Astronomic din Bucuresti. Observations Solaires (RM ISSN 0068-3094) 83
Obserwatorium Krakowski. Rocznik Astronomiczny. Dodatek Miedzynarodowy (PL ISSN 0075-7047) 83
Obvestila Republiske Matisne Knjiznice(YU ISSN 0350-3577) 93
Obwaldner Geschichtsblaetter (SZ) 458
Occasional Paper - Stanley Foundation see Stanley Foundation. Occasional Paper 723
Occasional Papers in Anthropology (US ISSN 0078-3005) 52
Occasional Papers in Anthropology (AT) 52
Occasional Papers in Economic and Social History (UK ISSN 0078-3013) 192, 799
Occasional Papers in English Local History (UK ISSN 0078-303X) 458
Occasional Papers in Entomology (US ISSN 0362-2622) 121
Occasional Papers in Estate Management (UK ISSN 0078-3048) 761
Occasional Papers in Geography (UK ISSN 0078-3056) 424
Occasional Papers in German Studies (UK ISSN 0307-7497) 458, 548, 569
Occasional Papers in Industrial Relations (NZ ISSN 0078-3064) 210
Occasional Papers in International Affairs see Harvard Studies in International Affairs 721
Occasional Papers in Librarianship (AT ISSN 0078-3080) 534
Occasional Papers in Linguistics (US) 548
Occasional Papers in Linguistics and Language Learning (UK ISSN 0308-2075) 548
Occasional Papers in Metropolitan Business and Finance (US) 175
Occasional Papers in Modern Dutch Studies (UK ISSN 0144-3070) 458, 713
Occasional Papers in Modern Languages (UK ISSN 0078-3099) 569
Occasional Papers of the Museum of Zoology, University of Michigan see University of Michigan. Museum of Zoology. Occasional Papers 131
Occasional Papers - Office of University Library Management Studies see Association of Research Libraries. University Library Management Studies Office. Occasional Paper 526
Occasional Publications in Northeastern Anthropology (US) 52
Occuaptions of Federal White-Collar Workers see Federal Civilian Work Force Statistics. Occupations of Federal White-Collar Workers 207
Occultism Update (US) 676
Occupational Education (US ISSN 0360-5434) 339
Occupational Education: Enrollments and Programs in Noncollegiate Post Secondary Schools (US) 332
Occupational Hygiene Monographs (UK ISSN 0141-7568) 496
Occupational Injuries and Illnesses by Industry see Virginia. Department of Labor and Industry. Division of Research and Statistics. Occupational Injuries and Illnesses by Industry 496
Occupational Safety and Health Decisions (US ISSN 0092-3435) 496
Occupational Safety and Health Series (UN ISSN 0078-3129) 496
Occupations of Federal Blue-Collar Workers see Federal Civilian Work Force Statistics. Occupations of Federal Blue-Collar Workers 155
Ocean see International Conference on Engineering in the Ocean Environment. Digest 368
Ocean Dumping Report (CN ISSN 0704-2701) 388

Ocean Engineering: a Wiley Series (US) 311, 369
Ocean Engineering Information Series (US ISSN 0078-3137) 311, 369
Ocean Freedom see Ocean Living 827
Ocean Living (US ISSN 0029-8034) 827
Ocean Series (US) 311
Ocean Thermal Energy Conversion Workshop. Workshop Proceedings (US) 363
Ocean Yearbook (US) 311
Oceana Docket Classics (US ISSN 0078-3161) 912
Oceanic Linguistics. Special Publications (US ISSN 0078-3188) 548
Oceanografiska Institutet, Goeteborg. Meddelanden see Goeteborgs Universitet. Oceanografiska Institutionen. Reports 310
Oceanographic Research Institute, Durban. Investigational Report (SA ISSN 0078-320X) 311
Oceanography and Marine Biology see Oceanography and Marine Biology: an Annual Review 312
Oceanography and Marine Biology: an Annual Review (UK) 105, 312
Oceanologia (PL ISSN 0078-3234) 312
Oceanology International. Conference Papers (UK) 312
Oceans (Year) see Marine Technology Society. Annual Conference Proceedings 879
Ochistka Vodnogo i Vozdushnogo Basseinov na Predpriyatiyakh Chernoi Metallurgii (RU) 629
Ochrona Przyrody (PL ISSN 0078-3250) 277
Ocular Therapeutics and Pharmacology (US) 616, 685
Ocultaciones de Estrellas Por la Luna (SP) 83
Odawuru in Series (GH) 52
Odense Universitet. Universitetsbibliotek. Musikklitteratur og Musikalier. Nyanskaffelser (DK) 665
Odense University Classical Studies (DK) 63, 260
Odense University Slavic Studies (DK ISSN 0078-3277) 548
Odense University Studies in Art History (DK ISSN 0078-3285) 77
Odense University Studies in English (DK ISSN 0078-3293) 548
Odense University Studies in History and Social Sciences (DK ISSN 0078-3307) 458
Odense University Studies in Linguistics (DK ISSN 0078-3315) 548
Odense University Studies in Literature(DK ISSN 0078-3323) 569
Odense University Studies in Philosophy (DK) 690
Odense University Studies in Psychiatry and Medical Psychology (DK) 620, 737
Odense University Studies in Scandinavian Languages and Literatures (DK ISSN 0078-3331) 548, 569
Odontologiska Samfundet i Finland. Aarsbok (FI ISSN 0078-3358) 610
Odrodzenie i Reformacja w Polsce (PL ISSN 0029-8514) 458
O'Dwyer's Directory of Corporate Communications (US ISSN 0149-1091) 147
O'Dwyer's Directory of Public Relations Executives (US) 6, 98
O'Dwyer's Directory of Public Relations Firms (US ISSN 0078-3374) 6, 241
Oecumene (FR) 769
Oeffentliche Baumappe der Ostschweiz (SZ) 69, 138
Der Oeffentliche Haushalt (GW) 231, 745
Oeffentliche Kunstsammlung. Jahresbericht (SZ ISSN 0067-4311) 654
Oeffentliche Schiffahrt auf den Schweizer Seen (SZ) 827

Oekonometrie und Unternehmensforschung/ Econometrics and Operations Research (US ISSN 0078-3390) 147, 216
Oekonomische Studientexte (GE ISSN 0078-3404) 147
Oenologie Pratique (FR ISSN 0078-3412) 912
Oerlikon Schweissmitteilungen (GW ISSN 0078-3420) 629
Oesterreich Archiv (AU) 458
Oesterreichische Akademie der Wissenschaften. Almanach (AU ISSN 0078-3447) 492, 788
Oesterreichische Akademie der Wissenschaften. Archiv fuer Oesterreichische Geschichte (AU ISSN 0003-9322) 458
Oesterreichische Akademie der Wissenschaften. Iranische Kommission. Veroeffentlichungen (AU) 492
Oesterreichische Akademie der Wissenschaften. Kommission fuer die Tabula Imperii Byzantini. Veroeffentlichungen (AU) 458
Oesterreichische Akademie der Wissenschaften. Kommission fuer Linguistik und Kommunikationsforschung. Veroeffentlichungen (AU) 548
Oesterreichische Akademie der Wissenschaften. Kommission fuer Literaturwissenschaft. Veroeffentlichungen (AU) 570
Oesterreichische Akademie der Wissenschaften. Kommission fuer Sozial-und Wirtschaftswissenschaften. Veroeffentlichungen (AU) 799
Oesterreichische Akademie der Wissenschaften. Kommission zur Herausgabe der Corpus der Lateinischen Kirchenvaeter. Veroeffentlichungen (AU) 775
Oesterreichische Akademie der Wissenschaften. Numismatische Kommission. Veroeffentlichungen (AU) 478
Oesterreichische Akademie der Wissenschaften. Philosophisch-Historische Klasse. Anzeiger (AU ISSN 0065-5368) 458, 690
Oesterreichische Akademie der Wissenschaften. Praehistorische Kommission. Mitteilungen (AU ISSN 0065-5376) 458
Oesterreichische Bankwissenschaftliche Gesellschaft. Schriftenreihe (AU) 175
Das Oesterreichische Buch (AU ISSN 0078-3455) 759
Oesterreichische Byzantinische Gesellschaft Jahrbuch see Oesterreichische Byzantinistik. Jahrbuch 458
Oesterreichische Byzantinistik. Jahrbuch(AU ISSN 0075-2355) 458
Oesterreichische Galerie. Mitteilungen (AU ISSN 0029-909X) 654
Oesterreichische Gesellschaft fuer Musik. Beitraege (GW ISSN 0078-3471) 662
Oesterreichische Gesellschaft fuer Musikwissenschaft. Mitteilungen (AU) 662
Oesterreichische Historische Bibliographie see Austrian Historical Bibliography 449
Oesterreichische Hochschulstatistik (AU ISSN 0067-2343) 328
Oesterreichische Komponisten des XX. Jahrhunderts (AU ISSN 0078-3501) 98, 662
Oesterreichische Moorforschung (AU ISSN 0078-351X) 289
Oesterreichische Nationalbank. Bericht ueber das Geschaeftsjahr mit Rechnungsabschluss (AU ISSN 0078-3528) 175

OEFFENTLICHE FINANZEN 1449

Oesterreichische Schriften zur Entwicklungshilfe (AU ISSN 0078-3536) 200
Oesterreichische Volkskundliche Bibliographie (AU) 52, 77, 402
Oesterreichische Zeitschrift fuer Oeffentliches Recht. Supplement (US ISSN 0078-3552) 516
Oesterreichischer Alpenverein. Akademische Sektion Graz. Mitteilungen (AU ISSN 0029-8840) 830
Oesterreichischer Auslandsstudentendienst. Rechenschaftsbericht (AU) 343
Oesterreichischer Buchklub der Jugend. Jahrbuch (AU ISSN 0078-3560) 258
Oesterreichischer Krankenpflegerverband. Fortbildungsprogramm (AU) 339, 614
Oesterreichischer Schwesternkalender (AU) 614
Oesterreichisches Archaeologisches Institut. Jahreshefte (AU) 63
Oesterreichisches Archaeologisches Institut. Jahreshefte: Grabungen see Oesterreichisches Archaeologisches Institut. Jahreshefte 63
Oesterreichisches Institut fuer Mittelstandspolitik. Schriftenreihe see Oesterreichisches Wirtschaftsinstitut fuer Strukturforschung und Strukturpolitik. Schriftenreihe 147
Oesterreichisches Institut fuer Raumplanung. Taetigkeitsbericht (AU ISSN 0078-3617) 486
Oesterreichisches Institut fuer Raumplanung. Veroeffentlichungen (AU ISSN 0078-3625) 486
Oesterreichisches Institut fuer Verpackung. Mitteilungen see Informationsdienst Verpackung 672
Oesterreichisches Jahrbuch fuer Exlibris und Gebrauchsgraphik (AU ISSN 0078-3633) 77
Oesterreichisches Jahrbuch fuer Politik (AU ISSN 0170-0847) 713
Oesterreichisches Kulturinstitut, Rom. Abteilung fuer Historische Studien. Publikationen I. Abteilung: Abhandlungen (AU ISSN 0078-3641) 458
Oesterreichisches Kulturinstitut, Rom. Abteilung fuer Historische Studien. Publikationen II. Abteilung: Quellen (AU ISSN 0078-365X) 458
Oesterreichisches Museum fuer Volkskunde. Kataloge (AU) 656
Oesterreichisches Museum fuer Volkskunde: Veroeffentlichungen (AU) 52, 77, 402
Oesterreichisches Ost- und Suedosteuropa Institut. Schriftenreihe(AU ISSN 0078-3439) 458
Oesterreichisches Staatsarchiv. Mitteilungen (AU ISSN 0067-2297) 458
Oesterreichisches Staatsarchiv. Publikationen (AU) 534
Oesterreichisches Volksliedwerk. Jahrbuch (AU ISSN 0473-8624) 662
Oesterreichisches Wirtschaftsinstitut fuer Strukturforschung und Strukturpolitik. Schriftenreihe (AU ISSN 0078-3595) 147
Oesterreichs Presse, Werbung, Graphik (AU ISSN 0030-0004) 505, 759
Oesterreichs Volkseinkommen (AU ISSN 0085-4433) 162
Oesteuropa Frimaerkekatalog see A F A Oesteuropa Frimaerkekatalog 478
Off Duty - Pacific (GW) 640
Off Duty - West (GW) 640
Off Licence News Directory (UK) 86
Off Off Broadway Alliance Guidebook of Theatres see O.O.B.A. Guidebook of Theatres 859
Off-Shore Technology Conference. Record (US ISSN 0078-3706) 357
Offa-Jahrbuch; Vor- und Fruehgeschichte (GW ISSN 0078-3714) 458
Offtliche Finanzen der Schweiz/Finances Publiques en Suisse (SZ) 231

Office de la Recherche Scientifique et Technique Outre-Mer. Initiations Documentations Techniques (FR ISSN 0071-9021) *852*
Office de la Recherche Scientifique et Technique Outre-Mer. Rapport d'Activite (FR ISSN 0071-9013) *788, 852*
Office de la Recherche Scientifique et Technique Outre-Mer Recueil de Travaux. Oceanographie see O. R. S. T. O. M. Recueil de Travaux. Oceanographie *311*
Office des Communications Sociales, Montreal. Cahiers d'Etudes et de Recherches (CN ISSN 0078-3722) *265, 268*
Office des Communications Sociales, Montreal. Selection de Films in 16 MM (CN) *650*
Office des Communications Sociales, Montreal. Selection de Films pour Cine Clubs. see Office des Communications Sociales, Montreal. Selection de Films in 16 MM *650*
Office Equipment Exporter (US ISSN 0471-1424) *197, 219*
Office General de la Musique Annuaire O. G. M. see Annuaire O. G. M *266*
Office International de la Vigne et du Vin Memento de l'O.I.V. see Memento de l'O.I.V *86*
Office of Emergency Services Annual Report see W.V.O.E.S. Annual Report *747*
Officer's Guide see Army Officer's Guide *638*
Offices de Commercialisation au Canada see Marketing Boards in Canada *29*
Official A A U Diving Rules (Amateur Athletic Union of the United States) (US) *821*
Official A A U Judo Rules. (Amateur Athletic Union of the United States.) (US) *821*
Official A A U Synchronized Swimming Handbook (Amateur Athletic Union of the United States) (US) *821*
Official A A U Trampoline and Tumbling Handbook (Amateur Athletic Union of the United States) (US ISSN 0361-2899) *821*
Official A A U Wrestling Handbook (Amateur Athletic Union of the United States) (US) *821*
Official American and National League Baseball Schedules and Records (US) *825*
Official Baseball Dope Book (US ISSN 0162-5411) *825*
Official Baseball Guide (US ISSN 0078-3838) *825*
Official Baseball Record Book (US ISSN 0078-4605) *825*
Official Baseball Register (US ISSN 0162-542X) *825*
Official Baseball Rules (US ISSN 0078-3846) *825*
Official Catholic Directory (US ISSN 0078-3854) *775*
Official Field Hockey Rules for School Girls (US ISSN 0362-3270) *821*
Official Guide to Airline Careers (US) *567*
Official Guide to Hotels & Restaurants in Great Britain, Ireland and Overseas (British Hotels, Restaurants and Caterers Association) (UK ISSN 0307-062X) *483*
Official Handbook of Ghana (GH ISSN 0072-9825) *440*
Official Handbook of the A.A.U. Code see Amateur Athletic Union of the United States. Official Handbook of the A A U Code *819*
Official Meeting Facilities Guide (US ISSN 0094-5242) *626*
Official Motor Home Trade-in Guide (US ISSN 0093-1195) *882*
Official Museum Directory (US ISSN 0090-6700) *654*
Official N B A and College Basketball Schedules (US) *912*
Official N F L and Collegiate Football Schedules and Records (US) *825*

Official National Basketball Association Guide (US ISSN 0078-3862) *825*
Official National Collegiate Athletic Association Baseball Guide (US) *825*
Official National Collegiate Athletic Association Baseball Guide see N C A A Baseball Annual Guide *825*
Official National Collegiate Athletic Association Basketball Guide (US) *825*
Official National Collegiate Athletic Association Basketball Rules and Interpretations see N C A A Basketball Rules and Interpretations *825*
Official National Collegiate Athletic Association Basketball Scores see N C A A Basketball Records *825*
Official National Collegiate Athletic Association Football Guide (US) *825*
Official National Collegiate Athletic Association Football Rules & Interpretations (US ISSN 0094-5226) *825*
Official National Collegiate Athletic Association Ice Hockey Guide (US) *821*
Official National Collegiate Athletic Association Skiing Rules (US) *830*
Official National Collegiate Athletic Association Soccer Guide (US) *825*
Official National Collegiate Athletic Association Swimming Guide (US) *821*
Official National Collegiate Athletic Association Track and Field Guide (US) *830*
Official National Collegiate Athletic Association Water Polo Rules (US) *821*
Official National Collegiate Athletic Association Wrestling Guide (US) *821*
Official Port of Detroit World Handbook (US ISSN 0093-1799) *880*
Official Read-Easy Basketball Rules (US) *825*
Official Read-Easy Football Rules (US) *825*
Official Registry of C B Operators (US) *268*
Official Rules for Competitive Swimming see Amateur Athletic Union of the United States. Athletic Library. Official Rules for Competitive Swimming *819*
Official Rules for Water Polo see Amateur Athletic Union of the United States. Official Rules for Water Polo *819*
Official Rules of Sports and Games (US) *821*
Official Southern California Ports Maritime Directory and Guide (US ISSN 0094-8454) *880*
Official Talent & Booking Directory (US ISSN 0078-3889) *662*
Official Touring Guide to East Africa see A A Guide to Motoring in Kenya *870*
Official Truck Camper Trade-in Guide (US ISSN 0094-1131) *882*
Official Wisconsin Pastoral Handbook (US) *775*
Official World Series Records (US ISSN 0078-3900) *825*
Official Year Book of Australia see Australia. Bureau of Statistics. Year Book Australia *833*
Official Year Book of New South Wales(AT US ISSN 0085-4441) *844*
Official Year Book of Western Australia see Western Australian Yearbook. New Series *448*
Offizielle Deutsch-Franzoesische Industrie- und Handelskammer. Mitgliederliste see Chambre Officielle Franco Allemande de Commerce et d'Industrie. Liste des Membres *179*
Offset Data Index (UK ISSN 0308-4485) *912*
Offshore Contractors and Equipment Directory (US ISSN 0475-1310) *680*
Offshore Europe (UK ISSN 0078-3692) *912*

Offshore Oil & Gas Yearbook (UK ISSN 0260-6437) *680*
Oficina; Revista de Equipos para Oficinas (US ISSN 0085-445X) *219*
Ohio. Advisory Council for Vocational Education. Annual Report (US ISSN 0098-5139) *346*
Ohio. Attorney General's Office. Report (US ISSN 0098-8820) *516*
Ohio. Commission on Aging. Annual Report (US ISSN 0363-9207) *428*
Ohio. Department of Mental Health and Mental Retardation. Annual Financial and Statistical Report (US ISSN 0094-6508) *753, 808*
Ohio. Division of Geological Survey. Bulletin (US) *298*
Ohio. Division of Geological Survey. Educational Leaflet (US ISSN 0472-6685) *298*
Ohio. Division of Geological Survey. Geological Note (US) *298*
Ohio. Division of Geological Survey. Guidebook (US ISSN 0097-9473) *298*
Ohio. Division of Geological Survey. Information Circular (US) *298*
Ohio. Division of Geological Survey. Miscellaneous Report (US ISSN 0361-0519) *298*
Ohio. Division of Geological Survey. Report of Investigations (US) *298*
Ohio. Division of Mines. Annual Report with Coal and Industrial Mineral Directories of Reporting Firms see Ohio. Division of Mines. Report *645*
Ohio. Division of Mines. Report (US ISSN 0078-401X) *645*
Ohio. Division of State Personnel. Annual Report (US ISSN 0078-4001) *220*
Ohio. State Library. State Library Review (US) *534*
Ohio Agricultural Research and Development Center, Wooster. Library. List of References: Maize Virus Diseases and Corn Stunt (US) *25*
Ohio Agricultural Research and Development Center, Wooster. Research Bulletin (US ISSN 0078-3951) *18*
Ohio Agricultural Research and Development Center, Wooster. Research Circular (US ISSN 0078-396X) *18*
Ohio Arts Council. Annual Report (US) *77*
Ohio Biological Survey. Biological Notes (US ISSN 0078-3986) *105*
Ohio Biological Survey. Bulletin. New Series (US ISSN 0078-3994) *106*
Ohio Biological Survey. Informative Circular (US) *106*
Ohio Fish and Wildlife Report (US ISSN 0085-4468) *130, 277*
Ohio Fish Monographs see Ohio Fish and Wildlife Report *277*
Ohio Game Monographs see Ohio Fish and Wildlife Report *277*
Ohio Geographers: Recent Research Themes (US ISSN 0094-9043) *424*
Ohio Inventory of Business and Industrial Change (US ISSN 0362-9716) *188*
Ohio Juvenile Court Statistics (US ISSN 0094-2677) *257*
Ohio Legislative Service see Baldwin's Ohio Legislative Service *740*
Ohio Speech Journal (US ISSN 0078-4052) *548*
Ohio State Industrial Directory (US) *241*
Ohio State University. College of Administrative Science. Monograph (US ISSN 0078-4087) *912*
Ohio State University. College of Law. Law Forum Series (US ISSN 0078-4095) *516*
Ohio State University. Disaster Research Center. D R C - T R see D R C Book & Monograph Series *813*
Ohio State University. Disaster Research Center. Report Series (US ISSN 0078-4133) *753, 808*
Ohio State University. Institute of Polar Studies. Contribution Series (US ISSN 0472-6979) *424*

Ohio State University. Institute of Polar Studies. Miscellaneous Series (US) *424*
Ohio State University. Institute of Polar Studies. Report Series (US ISSN 0078-415X) *424*
Ohio State University. School of Public Administration. Working Paper Series (US) *745*
Ohio State University Annual Biosciences Colloquia (US) *106*
Ohio University. Center for Educational Research and Service. Pupil Services Series (US ISSN 0078-4230) *320*
Ohio's Comprehensive Criminal Justice Plan (US ISSN 0094-0984) *283*
Oil and Arab Cooperation. Annual Review (KU) *363, 680*
Oil and Australia (AT ISSN 0472-7584) *844*
Oil & Gas Directory (US ISSN 0471-380X) *680*
Oil and Natural Gas Commission. Bulletin (II) *680*
Oil and Petroleum Year Book see Financial Times Oil and Gas International Year Book *679*
Oil Directories of Foreign Companies Outside the U.S.A. and Canada see Oil Directory of Companies Outside the U.S. and Canada *680*
Oil Directory of Alaska (US ISSN 0471-3850) *241, 680*
Oil Directory of Canada (US ISSN 0474-0114) *241, 680*
Oil Directory of Companies Outside the U.S. and Canada (US ISSN 0472-7711) *241, 680*
Oil Directory of Houston, Texas (US ISSN 0471-3877) *241, 680*
Oil Marketing and Wholesale Distributors see Directory of Oil Marketing and Wholesale Distributors *679*
Oil Palm News (UK ISSN 0048-1580) *18*
Oil Price Databook (US) *680*
Oil Producing Industry in Your State (US) *680*
Oil Shale Symposium Proceedings (US) *645*
Oil Spill Conference(Prevention, Behavior, Control, Cleanup) see Conference on Prevention and Control of Oil Spills. Proceedings *385*
Oita University. Research Institute of Economics. Bulletin (JA) *147*
Ojito (US) *557*
Okayama Daigaku Rigakubu Seibutsugaku Kiyo see Biological Journal of Okayama University *101*
Okayama University. Ohara Institute fuer Landwirtschaftliche Biologie. Berichte (JA) *29, 106*
Okayama University. Research Laboratory for Surface Science. Reports (JA ISSN 0078-429X) *255*
Okeanologiia (BU) *9*
Oklahoma. Ad Valorem Tax Division. Progress Report to the Legislature on Property Revaluation (US) *231*
Oklahoma. Aeronautics Commission. Annual Report (US ISSN 0092-9980) *9*
Oklahoma. Attorney General's Office. Opinions of the Attorney General (US ISSN 0475-0926) *516*
Oklahoma. Conservation Commission. Biennial Report (US ISSN 0095-442X) *277*
Oklahoma. Crime Commission. Annual Report (US) *283*
Oklahoma. Department of Highways. Sufficiency Rating Report and Needs Study: Oklahoma State Highways see Oklahoma. Department of Transportation. Sufficiency Rating Report and Needs Study: Oklahoma State Transportation *875*
Oklahoma. Department of Institutions, Social and Rehabilitative Services. Annual Report (US) *808*
Oklahoma. Department of Institutions, Social and Rehabilitative Services. Chart Book (US) *808*

Oklahoma. Department of Libraries. Annual Report and Directory of Libraries in Oklahoma (US ISSN 0066-4065) *534*
Oklahoma. Department of Public Welfare. Annual Report *see* Oklahoma. Department of Institutions, Social and Rehabilitative Services. Annual Report *808*
Oklahoma. Department of Transportation. Sufficiency Rating Report and Needs Study: Oklahoma State Transportation (US) *875*
Oklahoma. Drug Abuse Division. Annual Report (US) *287*
Oklahoma. Employment Security Commission. Actuarial Division. Handbook of Employment Security Program Statistics (US) *162*
Oklahoma. Employment Security Commission. Research and Planning Division. Annual Report to the Governor (US) *210*
Oklahoma. Employment Security Commission. Research and Planning Division. County Employment and Wage Data (US) *162*
Oklahoma. Fishery Research Laboratory, Norman. Bulletin (US ISSN 0078-4370) *399*
Oklahoma. Geological Survey. Bulletin (US ISSN 0078-4389) *298*
Oklahoma. Geological Survey. Circular (US ISSN 0078-4397) *298*
Oklahoma. Geological Survey. Educational Publication (US) *298*
Oklahoma. Geological Survey. Guidebook (US ISSN 0078-4400) *298*
Oklahoma. Office of Drug Abuse. Annual Performance Report, Drug Abuse Treatment Programs and Continuation Plan *see* Oklahoma. Drug Abuse Division. Annual Report *287*
Oklahoma Academy of Science. Proceedings (US ISSN 0078-4303) *788*
Oklahoma Airport Directory *see* Directory of Oklahoma Airports *867*
Oklahoma Anthropological Society. Bulletin (US ISSN 0078-432X) *52*
Oklahoma Anthropological Society. Memoir (US ISSN 0474-0696) *52*
Oklahoma Art Center. Annual Eight State Art Exhibition *see* Oklahoma Art Center. Annual Eight State Exhibition of Painting and Sculpture Catalog *77*
Oklahoma Art Center. Annual Eight State Exhibition of Painting and Sculpture Catalog (US ISSN 0085-4484) *77*
Oklahoma Council on Economic Education Newsletter (US) *147, 350*
Oklahoma Directory of Manufacturers *see* Oklahoma Directory of Manufacturers and Products *241*
Oklahoma Directory of Manufacturers and Products (US) *241*
Oklahoma Health Statistics (US ISSN 0098-5651) *756*
Oklahoma Journal of Forensic Medicine(US ISSN 0363-2679) *613*
Oklahoma Lake Living (US) *424*
Oklahoma Population Estimates (US) *732*
Oklahoma Series (US) *470*
Oklahoma State Industrial Directory (US) *241*
Oklahoma State University. College of Business Administration. Extension Service. Business Papers *see* Oklahoma State University. College of Business Administration. Working Papers *147*
Oklahoma State University. College of Business Administration. Working Papers (US) *147*
Oklahoma Turnpike Authority. Annual Report to the Governor (US) *875*
Oklahoma Water Resources Research Institute. Annual Report (US ISSN 0092-2528) *897*
Oklahoma's Grand River Dam Authority. Annual Report (US ISSN 0078-4508) *381*

Okyeame (GH ISSN 0048-1629) *393, 570*
Old Age: a Register of Social Research (UK) *428, 808*
Old Athlone Society Journal (IE ISSN 0475-1388) *459*
Old Car Value Guide (US ISSN 0475-1876) *871*
Old Car Value Guide Annual *see* Old Car Value Guide *871*
Old Dominion Foundation. Report *see* Andrew W. Mellon Foundation. Report *489*
Old Farmer's Almanac (US ISSN 0078-4516) *361*
Old Glory (US) *470*
Old House Catalog (US) *69, 503*
Old-House Journal Buyers' Guide *see* Old-House Journal Catalog *138*
Old-House Journal Catalog (US) *69, 138, 277, 761*
Old Red Kimono (US) *570*
Old Salem Gleaner (US ISSN 0078-4540) *470*
Old Salem Newsletter *see* Old Salem Gleaner *470*
Old Sturbridge Village Booklet Series (US ISSN 0078-4559) *471*
Oleander Games and Pastimes Series (UK) *821*
Oleo (SP) *253*
Oliver's Guide to the City of London (UK) *889*
Oljyposti (FI ISSN 0472-8874) *680*
Omaha-Council Bluffs Metropolitan Area Planning Agency Annual Report *see* M A P A Annual Report *743*
Omaha-Council Bluffs Metropolitan Area Planning Agency Annual Transportation Report *see* M A P A Annual Transportation Report *863*
Ombres de l'Histoire (FR ISSN 0078-4591) *459*
Ombudsman and Other Complaint-Handling Systems Survey (US) *516, 713, 745*
Ombudsman Survey *see* Ombudsman and Other Complaint-Handling Systems Survey *516*
Omvang der Vakbeweging in Nederland/Statistics of the Trade Unions in the Netherlands (NE ISSN 0077-6904) *507*
On Books and Readers *see* Al Safarim ve-Korim *525*
On S I T E (Sculpture in the Environment) (US) *77, 745*
On-Stage Studies (US) *859*
On-Your-Own Guide to Asia (US ISSN 0162-5950) *889*
One for the Book *see* Official Baseball Record Book *825*
One Hundred and One Electronics Projects (US) *357*
One Parent Family (US) *912*
One Shot (US) *570*
Ongaku Bunken Yoshi Mokuroku (JA) *665*
Onomastica (PL ISSN 0078-4648) *548*
Onsei Kagaku Kenkyu *see* Studia Phonologica *552*
Ontario. Advisory Council on the Physically Handicapped. Annual Report (CN ISSN 0700-3730) *808*
Ontario. Agricultural Research Institute. Report (CN ISSN 0078-4664) *18*
Ontario. Division of Forests. Research Library. Research Report *see* Ontario. Ministry of Natural Resources. Forest Research Report *277*
Ontario. Division of Mines. Geochemical Reports *see* Ontario. Geological Survey. Report *646*
Ontario. Division of Mines. Geological Reports *see* Ontario. Geological Survey. Report *646*
Ontario. Division of Mines. Guide Books *see* Ontario. Geological Survey. Guide Books *298*
Ontario. Division of Mines. Mineral Resource Circulars *see* Ontario. Geological Survey. Mineral Deposit Circulars *646*

Ontario. Division of Mines. Miscellaneous Papers *see* Ontario. Geological Survey. Miscellaneous Papers *646*
Ontario. Geological Survey. Annual Report of the Regional and Resident Geologist (CN ISSN 0704-2752) *298, 646*
Ontario. Geological Survey. Guide Books (CN) *298, 646*
Ontario. Geological Survey. Mineral Deposit Circulars (CN) *646*
Ontario. Geological Survey. Miscellaneous Papers (CN) *646*
Ontario. Geological Survey. Report (CN) *298, 646*
Ontario. Ministry of Community and Social Services. Social Assistance Review Board. Annual Report of the Chairman (CN) *808*
Ontario. Ministry of Consumer and Commercial Relations. Statistical Review (CN ISSN 0317-8161) *162*
Ontario. Ministry of Housing. Annual Report (CN ISSN 0078-4885) *486*
Ontario. Ministry of Natural Resources. Forest Research Report (CN ISSN 0381-3924) *277*
Ontario. Ministry of Natural Resources. Petroleum Resources Branch. Drilling and Production Report, Oil and Natural Gas (CN ISSN 0078-5059) *680*
Ontario. Ministry of Natural Resources. Statistics (CN) *390*
Ontario. Ministry of the Environment. Annual Report. (CN) *277, 388*
Ontario. Ministry of the Environment. Ground Water Bulletin (CN ISSN 0078-5156) *897*
Ontario. Ministry of the Environment. Industrial Waste Conference. Proceedings (CN ISSN 0078-4893) *388*
Ontario. Ministry of the Environment. Pollution Control Branch. Research Publication (CN ISSN 0078-5148) *388*
Ontario. Ministry of Transportation and Communications. Highway Traffic Collisions *see* Ontario. Ministry of Transportation and Communications. Motor Vehicle Accident Facts *871*
Ontario. Ministry of Transportation and Communications. Motor Vehicle Accident Facts (CN) *871*
Ontario. Status of Women Council. Annual Report (CN) *900*
Ontario Annual Practice (CN) *516*
Ontario Arts Council. Annual Report (CN) *77*
Ontario Association for Curriculum Development. Annual Conference (Report) (CN ISSN 0078-4680) *350*
Ontario Cancer Treatment and Research Foundation. Annual Report *see* Cancer in Ontario *604*
Ontario Catholic Directory (CN ISSN 0078-4702) *775*
Ontario Digest (CN) *369*
Ontario Directory of Education (CN ISSN 0316-8549) *321*
Ontario Economic Council. Research Studies (CN) *147*
Ontario Energy Board. Annual Report (CN) *363*
Ontario Federation of Labour. Report of Proceedings (CN ISSN 0078-4826) *507*
Ontario Geography (CN ISSN 0078-4850) *424*
Ontario Geological Survey Study (CN ISSN 0704-2590) *298*
Ontario Golden Horseshoe Construction Industry Directory. Purchasing Guide (CN) *138, 369*
Ontario Hydro. Statistical Yearbook (CN ISSN 0382-2834) *357*
Ontario Institute of Pedology. Department of Land Resource Science. Progress Report (CN) *38, 298*
Ontario Petroleum Institute. Annual Conference Proceedings (CN ISSN 0078-5040) *680*
Ontario Research Foundation. Annual Report (CN ISSN 0078-5083) *147*

Ontario Ringette Association. Official Rules (CN) *821*
Ontario Series (CN ISSN 0078-5091) *471*
Ontario Statistical Review *see* Ontario Statistics *844*
Ontario Statistics (CN) *844*
Ontario TourBook *see* Tourbook: Ontario *891*
Ontological Thought *see* Emissary *688*
Ontwikkeling van het Onderwijs in Nederland/Development of Education in the Netherlands (NE ISSN 0077-6769) *321*
Oondoona (AT ISSN 0085-4506) *424*
Opema Em Ritmo de Brasil Jovem (BL) *852*
Open Book (AT) *321*
Open Door International for the Emancipation of the Woman Worker. Report of Congress (BE ISSN 0078-5164) *210, 900*
Open Doors (US ISSN 0078-5172) *343*
Opening Fall Enrollment in Higher Education *see* U.S. National Center for Education Statistics. Fall Enrollment in Higher Education *340*
Openspaces (US) *580*
Opera Botanica (DK ISSN 0078-5237) *117*
Opera Botanica. Series B. Flora of Ecuador *see* Flora of Ecuador *114*
Opera Lilloana (AG ISSN 0078-5245) *117, 121, 130, 298*
Operatie Veiligheid (NE) *753*
Operating Section Proceedings *see* American Gas Association. Operating Section. Proceedings *677*
Operation Liberte (CN) *719*
Operational Hydrology Reports (UN) *308*
Operations and Policy Research. Institute for the Comparative Study of Political Systems. Election Analysis Series (US ISSN 0078-530X) *713*
Operations and Policy Research. Institute for the Comparative Study of Political Systems. Political Study Series (US ISSN 0078-5288) *713*
Operations Research-Verfahren/Methods of Operations Research (GW ISSN 0078-5318) *216*
Operculum (AT) *106, 277*
Ophthalmological Societies of the United Kingdom. Transactions (UK ISSN 0078-5334) *616*
Ophthalmological Society of Egypt. Bulletin (UA ISSN 0078-5342) *616*
Ophthalmological Society of the Republic of China. Transactions (CH) *616*
Opinions of the Utah State Superintendent of Public Instruction *see* Utah. State Board of Education. Opinions of the Utah State Superintendent of Public Instruction *345*
Opolskie Roczniki Ekonomiczne (PL ISSN 0474-2893) *147*
Opportunities Abroad for Teachers *see* U.S. Office of Education. Opportunities for Teachers Abroad *343*
Opportunities for Graduates in Southern Africa (SA) *667*
Opportunities in Iowa's Area Schools (US ISSN 0093-3465) *321*
Opportunities Unlimited (CN) *871*
Opportunity in Northern Canada (CN) *188*
Optical Computing Symposium. Digest of Papers *see* International Optical Computing Conference. Digest of Papers *272*
Optical Industry and Systems Directory(US ISSN 0078-5474) *705*
Optical Information Processing (US) *705*
Optical Physics and Engineering (US ISSN 0078-5482) *369, 705*
Optics and Spectroscopy. Supplement (US ISSN 0078-5504) *705*
Optimizatsiya (UR) *587*
Optioneer (US) *204*
Opus (UK) *440*
Opus (CN ISSN 0700-5318) *662*

Opuscula Atheniensia (GR ISSN 0078-5520) 63, 260
Opuscula - aus Wissenschaft und Dichtung (GW ISSN 0078-5539) 492
Opvoeding en Kultuur see Education & Culture 317
Or du Rhine (FR) 459
Oral History Review (US ISSN 0094-0798) 434
Orange Free State. Director of Hospital Services. Report/Orange Free State. Direkteur van Hospitaldienste. Verslag (SA ISSN 0078-5547) 481
Orange Free State. Direkteur van Hospitaldienste. Verslag see Orange Free State. Director of Hospital Services. Report 481
Orange Free State. Nature Conservation Division. Annual Report (SA) 277
Orange Free State. Nature Conservation Division. Miscellaneous Publications Series (SA) 106, 277
Orbis Antiquus (GW ISSN 0078-5555) 260
Orbis Artium (NE ISSN 0078-5563) 77
Orbis Geographicus (GW ISSN 0030-4395) 425
Orbit (New York) (US ISSN 0474-3326) 570
Orcrist (US ISSN 0474-3369) 570
Ordinary Lives (UK) 570
Ordo (GW ISSN 0048-2129) 216
Ordo et Annuaire de l'Archdiocese de Lyon see Annuaire du Diocese de Lyon 773
Ordre des Architectes. Conseil Regional de Paris. Bulletin see Architectes 68
Ordre des Geometres-Experts. Annuaire(FR ISSN 0078-5601) 788
Ordre des Ingenieurs Forestiers du Quebec. Congres Annuel. Texte des Conferences (CN) 410
Ore (UK ISSN 0030-459X) 580
Oregon. Department of Education. Racial and Ethnic Survey (US ISSN 0090-1059) 393
Oregon. Department of Fish and Wildlife. Environmental Management Section. Special Report (US) 388
Oregon. Department of Revenue. Sales Ratio Study see Oregon Ratio and Assessment Data Roll 231
Oregon. Department of Revenue. Summary of Levies and Statistics see Oregon Property Tax Statistics 231
Oregon. Educational Coordinating Council. Annual Program Amendment for Title I, Higher Education Act of 1965 (US) 339
Oregon. Mass Transit Division. Annual Report see Public Transportation in Oregon 863
Oregon. Motor Vehicles Division. Oregon Motorcycle Accidents (US ISSN 0092-9913) 863
Oregon. Office of Community Health Services. Local Health Services Annual Summary (US ISSN 0092-3060) 753, 808
Oregon. Public Utility Commissioner. Statistics of Electric, Gas, Steam Heat, Telephone, Telegraph and Water Companies (US ISSN 0091-0546) 748
Oregon. State Advisory Council for Career and Vocational Education. Annual Evaluation Report (US ISSN 0364-0027) 321
Oregon. State Board of Accountancy. Certified Public Accountants, Public Accountants, Professional Corporations, and Accountants Authorized to Conduct Municipal Audits in Oregon (US ISSN 0090-6735) 168
Oregon. State Board of Accountancy. Roster of Accountants Authorized to Conduct Municipal Audits see Oregon. State Board of Accountancy. Certified Public Accountants, Public Accountants, Professional Corporations, and Accountants Authorized to Conduct Municipal Audits in Oregon 168

Oregon. State Department of Geology and Mineral Industries. Bulletin (US ISSN 0078-5709) 298, 646
Oregon. State Department of Geology and Mineral Industries. G M I Short Papers (US ISSN 0078-5717) 298, 646
Oregon. State Department of Geology and Mineral Industries. Miscellaneous Papers (US ISSN 0078-5725) 298, 646
Oregon. State Department of Geology and Mineral Industries. Miscellaneous Publications (US ISSN 0078-5733) 298, 646
Oregon. State Department of Geology and Mineral Industries. Oil and Gas Investigations (US ISSN 0078-5741) 298, 680
Oregon, an Economic Profile (US) 188
Oregon Blue Book (US) 745
Oregon Motorcycle Accidents see Oregon. Motor Vehicles Division. Oregon Motorcycle Accidents 863
Oregon Property Tax Statistics (US) 231
Oregon Public Health Statistics Report (US) 844
Oregon Ratio and Assessment Data Roll (US) 231
Oregon School-Community College Directory see Oregon School Directory 332
Oregon School Directory (US ISSN 0078-5679) 332
Oregon School Study Council. Bulletin see O.S.S.C. Bulletin 320
Oregon State Health Division, Vital Statistics Annual Report see Oregon Public Health Statistics Report 844
Oregon State Industrial Directory (US ISSN 0195-7147) 241
Oregon State Monographs. Bibliographic Series (US ISSN 0078-5768) 93
Oregon State Monographs. Studies in Botany (US ISSN 0078-5776) 117
Oregon State Monographs. Studies in Economics (US ISSN 0078-5784) 147
Oregon State Monographs. Studies in Education and Guidance (US ISSN 0078-5792) 321
Oregon State Monographs. Studies in Entomology (US ISSN 0078-5806) 121
Oregon State Monographs. Studies in Geology (US ISSN 0078-5814) 298
Oregon State Monographs. Studies in History (US ISSN 0078-5822) 434
Oregon State Monographs. Studies in Literature and Language (US) 548, 570
Oregon State Monographs. Studies in Political Science (US) 713
Oregon State Monographs. Studies in Zoology (US ISSN 0078-5830) 130
Oregon State University. Annual Biology Colloquium. Proceedings (US ISSN 0078-5857) 106
Oregon State University. Forest Research Laboratory. Annual Report (US ISSN 0078-5865) 410
Oregon State University. Forest Research Laboratory. Research Bulletin (US ISSN 0078-5903) 410
Oregon State University. Forest Research Laboratory. Research Note (US ISSN 0078-5911) 410
Oregon State University. Forest Research Laboratory. Research Paper(US ISSN 0078-592X) 410
Oregon State University. School of Engineering. Graduate Research and Education (US ISSN 0078-5938) 339, 369
Oregon State University. School of Engineering. Research Activities (US ISSN 0078-5946) 369
Oregon State University. Water Resources Research Institute. Water Research Summary (US ISSN 0078-5849) 897
Oregon Teachers of English to Speakers of Other Languages Journal see O R T E S O L Journal 548
Oregon Truck Accidents (US) 875
Oregon Unemployment Insurance Tax Rates (US) 500

Orestes Brownson Series on Contemporary Thought and Affairs (US ISSN 0078-608X) 434, 690
Organ Building Periodical/Zeitschrift fuer Orgelbau (International Society of Organbuilders) (GW) 662
Organ Historical Society. National Convention (Proceedings) (US) 662
Organ Yearbook (NE ISSN 0078-6098) 662
Organe Permanent pour la Securite dans les Mines e Houille. Rapport see Mines Safety and Health Commission. Report 644
Organic Chemistry (US ISSN 0078-611X) 253
Organic Chemistry. Series Two (UK) 253
Organic Compounds of Sulphur, Selenium and Tellurium (UK ISSN 0305-9812) 253
Organic Directory (US ISSN 0078-6128) 38
Organic Electronic Spectral Data (US ISSN 0078-6136) 249, 253
Organic Photochemical Syntheses (US ISSN 0078-6144) 253, 255
Organic Photochemistry: A Series of Advances (US ISSN 0078-6152) 253, 255
Organic Reaction Mechanisms. Annual Survey (US ISSN 0078-6160) 253, 255
Organic Reactions (US ISSN 0078-6179) 253, 255
Organic Substances of Natural Origin (US ISSN 0078-6187) 253
Organic Syntheses (US ISSN 0078-6209) 253, 255
Organic Syntheses Collective Volumes (US ISSN 0078-6217) 253, 255
Organisatie van Studenten in de Geschiedenis van Nederland Wetenschappelijke Publikatie see O S G N Wetenschappelijke Publikatie 458
Organisation de l'Enseignement en France (FR) 344
Organisation Internationale et Relations Internationales (BE) 723
Organisation of European Aluminum Smelters. Economic Situation of the Aluminum Smelters in Europe see Aluminum Smelters 641
Organisations, People, Society/O P S (NE) 912
Organische Chemie in Einzeldarstellungen (US ISSN 0078-6225) 253
Organizaciones Voluntarias de Accion Social. Catalogo (DR) 808
Organization for Economic Cooperation and Development. Activities of O E C D: Report by the Secretary General (FR) 200
Organization for Economic Cooperation and Development. Annual Reports on Consumer Policy in O E C D Member Countries (FR) 182
Organization for Economic Cooperation and Development. Catalogue of Publications (FR ISSN 0474-5086) 93, 419
Organization for Economic Cooperation and Development. Cement Industry. Industrie du Ciment (FR ISSN 0474-5493) 138
Organization for Economic Cooperation and Development. Council. Code de la Liberation des Mouvements de Capitaux. Code of Liberalisation of Capital Movements (FR ISSN 0474-5655) 175, 197, 200
Organization for Economic Cooperation and Development. Development Assistance Committee. Report by the Chairman on the Annual Review (FR ISSN 0474-5663) 200
Organization for Economic Cooperation and Development. Development Cooperation (FR) 200
Organization for Economic Cooperation and Development. Development Centre. Employment Series (FR) 210

Organization for Economic Cooperation and Development. Economic Conditions in Austria and Switzerland see Organization for Economic Cooperation and Development. Economic Surveys: Austria 188
Organization for Economic Cooperation and Development. Economic Surveys: Australia (FR) 188
Organization for Economic Cooperation and Development. Economic Surveys: Austria (FR ISSN 0474-5124) 188
Organization for Economic Cooperation and Development. Economic Surveys: Belgium-Luxembourg Economic Union (FR ISSN 0474-5132) 188
Organization for Economic Cooperation and Development. Economic Surveys: Canada (FR ISSN 0474-5140) 188
Organization for Economic Cooperation and Development. Economic Surveys: Denmark (FR ISSN 0474-5159) 188
Organization for Economic Cooperation and Development. Economic Surveys: Finland (FR) 188
Organization for Economic Cooperation and Development. Economic Surveys: France (FR ISSN 0474-5167) 188
Organization for Economic Cooperation and Development. Economic Surveys: Germany (FR ISSN 0474-5175) 188
Organization for Economic Cooperation and Development. Economic Surveys: Greece (FR ISSN 0474-5183) 188
Organization for Economic Cooperation and Development. Economic Surveys: Iceland (FR ISSN 0474-5191) 188
Organization for Economic Cooperation and Development. Economic Surveys: Ireland (FR ISSN 0474-5205) 188
Organization for Economic Cooperation and Development. Economic Surveys: Italy (FR ISSN 0474-5213) 188
Organization for Economic Cooperation and Development. Economic Surveys: Japan (FR ISSN 0474-5221) 188
Organization for Economic Cooperation and Development. Economic Surveys: Netherlands. (FR ISSN 0474-523X) 188
Organization for Economic Cooperation and Development. Economic Surveys: New Zealand (FR ISSN 0376-6438) 188
Organization for Economic Cooperation and Development. Economic Surveys: Norway (FR ISSN 0474-5248) 188
Organization for Economic Cooperation and Development. Economic Surveys: Portugal (FR ISSN 0474-5256) 188
Organization for Economic Cooperation and Development. Economic Surveys: Socialist Federal Republic of Yugoslavia (FR ISSN 0474-5264) 189
Organization for Economic Cooperation and Development. Economic Surveys: Spain (FR ISSN 0474-5272) 188
Organization for Economic Cooperation and Development. Economic Surveys: Sweden (FR ISSN 0474-5280) 188
Organization for Economic Cooperation and Development. Economic Surveys. Switzerland. (FR ISSN 0474-5299) 188
Organization for Economic Cooperation and Development. Economic Surveys: Turkey (FR ISSN 0474-5302) 189
Organization for Economic Cooperation and Development. Economic Surveys: United Kingdom (FR ISSN 0474-5310) 189

Organization for Economic Cooperation and Development. Economic Surveys: United States (FR ISSN 0474-5329) *189*

Organization for Economic Cooperation and Development. Electricity Supply Industry. l'Industrie de l'Electricite (FR ISSN 0474-5477) *357*

Organization for Economic Cooperation and Development. Employment of Special Groups (FR ISSN 0474-5337) *210*

Organization for Economic Cooperation and Development. Energy Statistics (FR) *364*

Organization for Economic Cooperation and Development. Flow of Financial Resources to Less Developed Countries *see* Geographical Distribution of Financial Flows to Less Developed Countries. (Disbursements) *200*

Organization for Economic Cooperation and Development. Guide to Legislation on Restrictive Business Practices. Supplements (FR ISSN 0304-3282) *197*

Organization for Economic Cooperation and Development. Historical Statistics. Statistiques Retrospectives (FR ISSN 0474-5442) *162*

Organization for Economic Cooperation and Development. Industrial Production. Production Industrielle (FR ISSN 0474-5450) *224*

Organization for Economic Cooperation and Development. Industrial Statistics. Statistiques Industrielles (FR ISSN 0474-5469) *162*

Organization for Economic Cooperation and Development. Inter-Regional Dry Cargo Movements/Mouvements Interregionaux de Cargaisons Seches (FR) *162, 844*

Organization for Economic Cooperation and Development. International Energy Agency. Annual Report on Energy Research, Development and Demonstration (FR) *363*

Organization for Economic Cooperation and Development. Labour Force Statistics (Yearbook) /Statistiques de la Population Active (FR ISSN 0474-5515) *162*

Organization for Economic Cooperation and Development. Liaison Bulletin Between Development Research and Training Institutes (FR) *200*

Organization for Economic Cooperation and Development. Liaison Bulletin Between Research and Training Institutes (FR ISSN 0029-7038) *224*

Organization for Economic Cooperation and Development. Library. Catalogue of Periodicals/Catalogue des Periodiques (FR) *93*

Organization for Economic Cooperation and Development. Library. Special Annotated Bibliography; Automation. Bibliographie Speciale Analytique (FR ISSN 0474-5868) *274*

Organization for Economic Cooperation and Development. Maritime Transport Committee. Maritime Transport (FR ISSN 0474-5884) *880*

Organization for Economic Cooperation and Development. Nuclear Energy Agency. Activity Report (FR ISSN 0078-625X) *363, 369, 704*

Organization for Economic Cooperation and Development. Oil Statistics/Statistiques Petrolieres (FR) *682*

Organization for Economic Cooperation and Development. Provisional Oil Statistics/Statistiques Petrolieres Provisoires *see* Organization for Economic Cooperation and Development. Oil Statistics/Statistiques Petrolieres *682*

Organization for Economic Cooperation and Development. Revenue Statistics of OECD Member Countries (FR) *162*

Organization for Economic Cooperation and Development. Reviews of Manpower and Social Policies (FR ISSN 0473-6788) *210*

Organization for Economic Cooperation and Development. Social Affairs Division. Developing Job Opportunities (FR ISSN 0474-5892) *210, 667*

Organization for Economic Cooperation and Development. Social Affairs Division. Employment of Special Groups (FR ISSN 0474-5922) *210*

Organization for Economic Cooperation and Development. Special Committee for Iron and Steel. Iron and Steel Industry (FR ISSN 0474-5973) *629*

Organization for Economic Cooperation and Development. Speaial Committee for Oil. Oil Statistics. Supply and Disposal (FR ISSN 0474-6007) *680*

Organization for Economic Cooperation and Development. Statistics of Energy *see* Organization for Economic Cooperation and Development. Energy Statistics *364*

Organization for Economic Cooperation and Development. Statistics of Foreign Trade. Series C: Tables by Commodities. Imports and Exports/Statistiques du Commerce Exterieur. Serie C: Tableaux Par Produits (FR) *162*

Organization for Economic Cooperation and Development. Statistics of Foreign Trade. Series C: Trade by Commodities. Market Summaries. Imports and Exports/Statistiques du Commerce Exterieur. Serie C: Exchange Par Produits. Resume Par Marches. Importations et Exportations *see* Organization for Economic Cooperation and Development. Statistics of Foreign Trade. Series C: Tables by Commodities. Imports and Exports/Statistiques du Commerce Exterieur. Serie C: Tableaux Par Produits *162*

Organization for Economic Cooperation and Development. Survey of Electric Power Equipment. Enquete sur l'Equipment Electrique (FR ISSN 0474-5353) *382*

Organization for Economic Cooperation and Development. Tourism Committee. Tourism Policy and International Tourism in O E C D Member Countries (FR) *889*

Organization for Economic Cooperation and Development Energy Balances of O E C D Countries *see* Energy Balances of O E C D Countries *362*

Organization for Economic Cooperation and Development Financial Statistics *see* O E C D Financial Statistics *162*

Organization for Economic Cooperation and Development Halden Reactor Project *see* O E C D Halden Reactor Project *704*

Organization for Rehabilitation Through Training World O R T Union. Congress Report *see* World O R T Union. Congress Report *325*

Organization for Rehabilitation Through Training Yearbook *see* O R T Yearbook *346*

Organization of African Trade Union Unity Information Tips *see* O A T U U Information Tips *912*

Organization of African Unity. Health, Sanitation and Nutrition Commission. Proceedings and Report (ET ISSN 0473-3657) *753*

Organization of African Unity. Inter-African Bureau for Soils. Bibliographie (CX ISSN 0538-2769) *25*

Organization of African Unity. Scientific Technical and Research Commission. Publication (NG ISSN 0474-6171) *788, 852*

Organization of American States. Department of Cultural Affairs. Estudios Bibliotecarios (US ISSN 0078-6373) *534*

Organization of American States. Department of Cultural Affairs Manuales del Bibliotecario (US ISSN 0078-6381) *534*

Organization of American States. Department of Scientific Affairs. Report of Activities (US) *788*

Organization of American States. Department of Scientific Affairs. Serie de Biologia: Monografias (US ISSN 0553-0342) *106*

Organization of American States. Department of Scientific Affairs. Serie de Fisica: Monografias (US ISSN 0078-6322) *697*

Organization of American States. Department of Scientific Affairs. Serie de Matematica: Monografias (US ISSN 0078-6330) *588*

Organization of American States. Department of Scientific Affairs. Serie de Quimica: Monografias (US ISSN 0553-0377) *247*

Organization of American States. General Assembly. Actas y Documentos (US) *723*

Organization of American States. Official Records. Indice y Lista General (US ISSN 0078-642X) *471*

Organization of American States. Permanent Council. Decisions Taken at Meetings (Cumulated Edition) (US ISSN 0078-6438) *471, 523*

Organization of American States. Regional Scientific and Technological Program. Newsletter (US ISSN 0250-7536) *788, 852*

Organization of American States General Secretariat. Annual Report *see* O A S. General Secretariat. Annual Report *470*

Organization of Arab Petroleum Exporting Countries. Annual Energy Report (KU) *363, 680*

Organization of Arab Petroleum Exporting Countries. Annual Statistical Report (KU) *680*

Organization of Arab Petroleum Exporting Countries. Secretary General's Annual Report (KU) *681*

Organization of the Government of Canada/Administration Federale du Canada (CN) *745*

Organization of the Petroleum Exporting Countries. Annual Review and Record (AU ISSN 0474-6317) *681*

Organization of the Petroleum Exporting Countries. Annual Statistical Bulletin (AU ISSN 0475-0608) *681*

Organizational Communications Abstracts (US) *216*

Organizational Directory of the Government of Thailand (TH ISSN 0475-2015) *745*

Organizatsiya Upravleniya (UR) *216*

Organometallic Chemistry (UK ISSN 0301-0074) *253*

Organometallic Compounds of the Group IV Elements (US ISSN 0078-6489) *253*

Organometallic Reactions and Syntheses (US) *253, 255*

Organometallic Reactions Series *see* Organometallic Reactions and Syntheses *253*

Organon (PL ISSN 0078-6500) *788*

Organophosphorus Chemistry (UK ISSN 0475-1582) *253*

Oriens (NE ISSN 0078-6527) *670*

Oriens Christianus (GW ISSN 0340-6407) *766*

Orientacion Familiar (SP) *808*

Oriental Insects Monograph Series (II) *121*

Oriental Insects Supplements Series (II ISSN 0300-2713) *121*

Oriental Institute Communications (US ISSN 0146-678X) *445*

Oriental Library. Research Department. Memoirs/Zaidan Hojin Toyo Bunko (JA ISSN 0082-562X) *445*

Oriental Notes and Studies (IS ISSN 0078-6543) *445*

Oriental Society of Australia. Journal (AT ISSN 0030-5340) *670*

Oriental Studies (US ISSN 0078-6551) *77*

Oriental Studies/Toho Gakuho (JA) *670*

Oriental Studies/Keleti Tanulmanyok (HU) *670*

Orientalia Christiana Analecta (VC) *670, 775*

Orientalia Gothoburgensia (SW ISSN 0078-656X) *670*

Orientalia Lovaniensia Periodica (BE ISSN 0085-4522) *671*

Orientalia Rheno-Traiectina (NE) *671*

Orientalia Suecana (SW ISSN 0078-6578) *671*

Orientamenti Linguistici (IT) *548*

Orienteering *see* C O F Newsletter *829*

Origin of Enrollments, Accredited Colleges and Universities *see* Kentucky. Council on Public Higher Education. Origin of Enrollments, Accredited Colleges and Universities *327*

Original Manuscript Music for Wind and Percussion Instruments (US ISSN 0078-6586) *662*

Origins of Behavior Series (US ISSN 0094-6206) *737*

Orissa, India. Finance Department. White Paper on Departmental Activities, Government of Orissa *see* Orissa, India. Finance Department. White Paper on the Economic Conditions and the Developmental Activities in Orissa *189*

Orissa, India. Finance Department. White Paper on the Economic Conditions and the Developmental Activities in Orissa (II) *189*

Orissa State Road Transportation Corporation. Annual Administration Report (II) *875*

Ornithological Monographs (US ISSN 0078-6594) *125*

Orquidea (Mexico) (MX ISSN 0300-3701) *117*

Orszagos Muemleki Felugyeloseg. Kiadvanyok (HU ISSN 0073-4063) *69*

Orszagos Szechenyi Konyvtar. Evkonyv (HU ISSN 0524-8868) *534*

Orthodontie Francaise (FR ISSN 0078-6608) *610*

Orthodox Church in America. Yearbook and Church Directory (US ISSN 0145-7950) *776*

Orthopaedic Practitioner (GW) *616*

Orthophoto Workshop. Papers (US) *425*

Orton Society. Bulletin (US ISSN 0078-6624) *346*

Orton Society. Monograph. *see* Orton Society. Bulletin *346*

Osaka (Prefecture). Radiation Center, Annual Report/Osaka-furitsu Hoshasen Chuo Kenkyusho Nenpo (JA) *255*

Osaka City University. Faculty of Engineering. Memoirs/Osaka-shiritsu Daigaku Kogakubu Obun Kiyo (JA ISSN 0078-6659) *369*

Osaka City University Economic Review (JA ISSN 0078-6640) *147*

Osaka Daigaku Sangyo Kagaku Kenkyusho Kiyo *see* Osaka University. Institute of Scientific and Industrial Research. Memoirs *852*

Osaka Daigaku Yakugakubu Kiyo *see* Osaka University. Faculty of Pharmaceutical Sciences. Memoirs *685*

Osaka-furitsu Daigaku Kiyo, B Nogaku, Seibutsugaku *see* University of Osaka Prefecture. Bulletin. Series B: Agriculture and Biology *22*

Osaka-furitsu Hoshasen Chuo Kenkyusho Nenpo *see* Osaka (Prefecture). Radiation Center, Annual Report *255*

Osaka Museum of Natural History. Bulletin/Osaka-shiritsu Shizenshi Hakubutsukan Kenkyu Hokoku (JA ISSN 0078-6675) *788*

Osaka Museum of Natural History. Occasional Papers/Shizenshi Kenkyu (JA ISSN 0078-6683) *788*

Osaka-shiritsu Daigaku Kogakubu Obun Kiyo *see* Osaka City University. Faculty of Engineering. Memoirs *369*

Osaka-shiritsu Daigaku Rigakubu Chigaku Kiyo see Journal of Geosciences 289
Osaka-shiritsu Shizenshi Hakubutsukan Kenkyu Hokoku see Osaka Museum of Natural History. Bulletin 788
Osaka University. Faculty of Pharmaceutical Sciences. Memoirs/Osaka Daigaku Yakugakubu Kiyo (JA ISSN 0387-480X) 685
Osaka University. Institute for Cancer Research. Annual Report (JA) 606
Osaka University. Institute for Protein Research. Memoirs (JA ISSN 0078-6705) 111, 253
Osaka University. Institute of Scientific and Industrial Research. Memoirs/Osaka Daigaku Sangyo Kagaku Kenkyusho Kiyo (JA) 852
Osaka University. Laboratory of Nuclear Studies. Report (JA ISSN 0473-4580) 704
Osakako see Port of Osaka 880
Osawatomie (US) 912
Oscar Annual see Academy Awards Oscar Annual 648
Oslo Boers. Beretning (NO ISSN 0085-4565) 204
Oslo Studies in English see Norwegian Studies in English 569
Osmania University. Department of Psychology. Research Bulletin (II) 737
Osnabruecker Naturwissenschaftliche Mitteilungen (GW ISSN 0340-4781) 788
Osram-Gesellschaft. Technisch-Wissenschaftliche Abhandlungen (US ISSN 0078-6799) 852
Osservatorio Regionale per le Malattie della Vite. Osservazioni di Meteorologia, Fenologia e Patologia della Vite (IT ISSN 0552-9506) 38, 117
Osservazioni di Meteorologia Agraria della Puglia e Basilicata (IT) 18, 634
Ostbairische Grenzmarken (GW ISSN 0078-6845) 459
Osteuropa Institut, Munich. Veroeffentlichungen. Reihe Geschichte (GW ISSN 0078-687X) 459
Osteuropastudien der Hochschulen des Landes Hessen. Reihe 1. Giessener Abhandlungen zur Agrar- und Wirtschaftsforschung des Europaeischen Ostens (GW ISSN 0078-6888) 29, 147
Ostinformation (GW) 189
Ostpanorama (AU ISSN 0078-6896) 459
Ostracodologist (IS ISSN 0085-4573) 130, 674
Ostseejahrbuch (GW) 180
Oswego County Historical Society. Journal (US ISSN 0092-9549) 471
Otago Geographer (NZ ISSN 0078-690X) 425
Otago Law Review (NZ ISSN 0078-6918) 516
Otago Museum. Records. Anthropology (NZ ISSN 0474-8603) 52
Otago Museum. Records. Zoology (NZ ISSN 0474-8611) 130
Otago Museum Bulletin: Zoology (NZ) 130
Other Scenes (UK ISSN 0030-6568) 557
Other Side (Washington) (US) 729
Otia (BE ISSN 0030-6584) 260
Oto-Laryngological Society of Australia. Journal (AT ISSN 0030-6614) 617
Ottawa. Dominion Observatory. Seismological Series see Canada. Earth Physics Branch. Seismological Series 303
Ottawa Ethnic Groups Directory (CN ISSN 0315-0771) 393
Ottawa Hispanica (CN) 548
Otterbein Miscellany (US) 557
Ottokarforschungen (AU) 459
Ou Monter a Cheval (FR ISSN 0078-7035) 821
Our Stake in the Urban Condition see American Jewish Committee. Domestic Affairs Department. Pertinent Papers 708

Out of School Scientific and Technical Education (BE) 258, 788
Out There (US) 570
Outboard Boating Handbook (US ISSN 0094-8101) 912
Outdoor Crest (CN ISSN 0700-9909) 830
Outdoor Crest Newsletter see Outdoor Crest 830
Outdoor Life's Guide to Fishing the Midwest (US) 830
Outdoor Life's Guide to Fishing the South (US) 830
Outline of Japanese Tax (JA ISSN 0078-7094) 231
Outlook (CN) 43, 45
Outlook see In Care 481
Outwest Magazine (CN ISSN 0707-803X) 889
Ouvrages de Criminologie Publies au Canada see Correctional Literature Published in Canada 907
Oven Bird see Hornero 125
Over the Hills (UK ISSN 0030-7378) 889
Overseas Development Council. Annual Report (US ISSN 0092-7643) 200
Overseas Development Council. Communique (US) 201
Overseas Development Council. Development Papers (US) 201
Overseas Development Council. Monograph Series (US ISSN 0078-7108) 201
Overseas Development Council. Occasional Papers (US) 201
Overseas Directories, Who's Who, Press Guides, Year Books and Overseas Periodical Subscriptions (UK ISSN 0078-7124) 93
Overseas Economic Cooperation Fund. Annual Report/Kaigai Keizai Kyoryoku Kikin Nenpo (JA) 201
Overseas Media Guide (UK ISSN 0078-7132) 6, 505
Overseas Newspapers and Periodicals (UK ISSN 0078-7159) 759
Overseas Private Investment Corporation. Annual Report (US ISSN 0196-1276) 204
Overseas Trade Directories (UK) 241
Overview of Blood (US ISSN 0093-9404) 613
Overview of the F A A Engineering & Development Programs (U. S. Federal Aviation Administration) (US ISSN 0092-3591) 10
Owen's Commerce and Travel and International Register (UK ISSN 0078-7167) 197, 889
Owners, Masters, Brokers and Agents Handbook on S. American Caribbean and Pacific Ports in Venezuela, Colombia, Panama, Ecuador, Peru, Bolivia and Chile see South American Ports Handbook 881
Ox Head (US ISSN 0030-7629) 581
Oxbridge Directory of Ethnic Periodicals (US ISSN 0195-4202) 93, 393
Oxbridge Directory of Newsletters (US ISSN 0163-7010) 93
Oxbridge Directory of Religious Periodicals (US ISSN 0191-4502) 93, 766
Oxford Agrarian Studies (UK) 29
Oxford Applied Mathematics and Computing Science Series (US) 588
Oxford Bibliographical Society. Occasional Publications (UK ISSN 0078-7175) 93
Oxford Bibliographical Society. Publications. New Series (UK ISSN 0078-7183) 93
Oxford Chemistry Series (US ISSN 0302-4199) 247
Oxford Early Christian Texts (US) 766
Oxford Engineering Science Series (US) 369
Oxford English Memoirs and Travels (US) 98, 459
Oxford English Monographs (US) 492, 570
Oxford Forestry Memoirs (US) 410
Oxford German Studies (UK ISSN 0078-7191) 548, 570

Oxford Historical Monographs (US) 459
Oxford Historical Series (US ISSN 0078-7205) 434
Oxford History of England (US) 459
Oxford History of English Art (US) 77
Oxford History of English Literature (US ISSN 0078-7221) 570
Oxford History of Modern Europe (US) 459
Oxford in Asia; Current Affairs (US) 445
Oxford in Asia; Historical Reprints (US) 445
Oxford in Asia; Modern Authors (US) 570
Oxford Library of African Literature (US) 570
Oxford Library of the Physical Sciences (US ISSN 0472-3325) 698
Oxford Logic Guides (US) 588
Oxford Mathematical Handbooks (US) 588
Oxford Mathematical Monographs (US) 588
Oxford Medical Engineering Series (US) 496, 598
Oxford Modern Language and Literature Monographs (US) 570
Oxford Monographs on Classical Archaeology (US) 63, 260
Oxford Monographs on Medical Genetics (US) 122, 598
Oxford Monographs on Meteorology (US) 634
Oxford Monographs on Social Anthropology (US) 52
Oxford Neurological Monographs (US) 620
Oxford Paleographical Handbooks (US) 548
Oxford Paperbacks University Series (US ISSN 0078-723X) 492
Oxford Physics Series (US) 698
Oxford Readings in Philosophy (US) 690
Oxford Readings in Social Studies (US) 799
Oxford Research Studies in Geography (US) 425
Oxford Science Research Papers (US ISSN 0078-7248) 788
Oxford Studies in African Affairs (US) 440
Oxford Studies in Nuclear Physics (US) 704
Oxford Studies in Physics (US) 698
Oxford Studies in the History of Art and Architecture (US) 69, 77
Oxford Studies of Composers (US ISSN 0078-7264) 662
Oxford Theatre Texts (UK ISSN 0141-1152) 570, 859
Oxford Theological Monographs (US ISSN 0078-7272) 766
Oxford Tropical Handbooks (US) 18, 45
Oxford University Almanack (US) 339
Oxford University Calendar (US) 339
Oxford University Handbook (US) 339
Oxoniensia (UK ISSN 0308-5562) 64, 69, 459
Oyez (CN ISSN 0475-1671) 516
Oyo State. Estimates Including Budget Speech and Memorandum (NR) 745
Oyo State. Ministry of Economic Planning and Community Development. Annual Report (NR) 224
Oyo State of Nigeria Estimates see Oyo State. Estimates Including Budget Speech and Memorandum 745
Oyo State of Nigeria Gazette (NR) 745
Oziana (US) 262, 570
P A A B S Symposium Series (Pan-American Association of Biochemical Societies) (US ISSN 0364-2801) 111
P A D S see American Dialect Society. Publication 540
P A - Kontakte (AU) 321
P A N S D O C Translations see P A S T I C Translations 852
P A S T I C Translations (Pakistan Scientific and Technological Information Centre) (PK) 852

P C E A Annual Engineering & Operating Conference (Pacific Coast Electrical Association, Inc.) (US) 357
P C O T Bulletin (National Press Council of the Republic of China) (CH) 505
P C R see Psychological Cinema Register 739
P C R Information (World Council of Churches, Programme to Combat Racism) (SZ) 766
P D B (Professional Development Bulletin) (CN ISSN 0384-0972) 339
P E. M. C. Catalogue: Supplement (Provincial Educational Media Centre) (CN ISSN 0707-7777) 350
P. E. I. Community Studies (Prince Edward Island) (CN) 52, 815
P. E. L. State Bulletin (Pennsylvania Economy League) (US ISSN 0079-0486) 189
P.E.N. Hongrois see Hungarian P.E.N 565
P E P see P S I: Broadsheet Series and Major Reports 713
P F R A Annual Report see Canada. Department of Regional Economic Expansion. Annual Report on Prairie Farm Rehabilitation and Related Activities/Rapport Annuel: Retablissement Agricole des Prairies et Travaux Connexes 33
P F R A Library Newsletter see Canada. Prairie Farm Rehabilitation Administration. Library. Newsletter/Nouvelles de la Bibliotheque 528
P I E (Publications Indexed for Engineering) (US ISSN 0085-4581) 372
P I /L T; Occasional Papers on Programmed Instruction and Language Teaching (US ISSN 0078-7388) 350, 548
P I N (Physicians Information Network) (US) 598
P.I.O.L. see Universite Catholique de Louvain. Institut Orientaliste. Publications 446
P K L Kemikalier (Plast- och Kemikalieleverantoerers Foerening) (SW) 247
P K L Plaster (Plast- och Kemikalieleverantoerers Foerening) (SW) 707
P L A Report (Post Library Association) (US ISSN 0146-2237) 534
P L D Reporter see Public Library Reporter 535
P L S see Publications in Language Sciences 550
P.M.B.R. Physician's Medical Book Reference (US ISSN 0093-2248) 602
P M E A see Bulletin of Research in Music Education 658
P N A H F Journal (Pacific Northwest Aviation Historical Foundation) (US) 10
P R B Report (Population Reference Bureau, Inc.) (US ISSN 0146-7646) 912
P R B Selection see P R B Report 912
P R D see Publizistik Wissenschaftlicher Referatedienst 506
P R E P. Reports (Putting Research into Educational Practice) (US) 912
P S A Library Bibliographies (Property Services Agency) (UK) 539
P S C P Times (Philadelphia Society of Clinical Psychologists) (US) 737
P S I: Broadsheet Series and Major Reports (Policy Studies Institute) (UK) 713, 799
P S I Discussion Papers (Policy Studies Institute) (UK) 713, 799
P y S (MX) 500
Paasikivi-Society. Mimeograph Series (FI ISSN 0355-1849) 723
Pacem in Terris (US) 912
Pacific Anthropological Records (US ISSN 0078-740X) 52
Pacific Area Destination Handbook see Pacific Destinations Handbook 889

Pacific Aviation Yearbook (AT ISSN 0156-3726) 1Q, 869
Pacific Boating Almanac. Northern California & Nevada (US ISSN 0193-3515) 827, 889
Pacific Boating Almanac. Pacific Northwest & Alaska (US ISSN 0148-1177) 827, 889
Pacific Boating Almanac. Southern California, Arizona, Baja (US ISSN 0193-3507) 827, 889
Pacific Chemical Engineering Congress. Proceedings (US) 373
Pacific Coast Aviation Directory see Aviation Telephone Directory: Pacific and Western States 867
Pacific Coast Avifauna see Studies in Avian Biology 125
Pacific Coast Council on Latin American Studies. Proceedings (US ISSN 0190-2229) 197, 471, 570
Pacific Coast Electrical Association, Inc. Annual Engineering & Operating Conference see P C E A Annual Engineering & Operating Conference 357
Pacific Coast Obstetrical and Gynecological Society. Transactions (US ISSN 0078-7442) 615
Pacific Coast Philology (US ISSN 0078-7469) 548
Pacific Coast Society of Obstetrics and Gynecology. Transactions see Pacific Coast Obstetrical and Gynecological Society. Transactions 615
Pacific Destinations Handbook (US) 889
Pacific Forest Research Centre. Pest Leaflet (CN) 410
Pacific Forest Research Centre. Pest Report (CN) 410
Pacific Insects Monographs (US ISSN 0078-7515) 121
Pacific Islands Studies and Notes (US ISSN 0085-459X) 93, 438
Pacific Islands Year Book (AT ISSN 0078-7523) 447
Pacific Islands Year Book and Who's Who see Pacific Islands Year Book 447
Pacific Linguistics. Series A: Occasional Papers (AT ISSN 0078-7531) 548
Pacific Linguistics. Series B: Monographs (AT ISSN 0078-754X) 548
Pacific Linguistics. Series C: Books (AT ISSN 0078-7558) 548
Pacific Linguistics. Series D: Special Publications (AT ISSN 0078-7566) 548
Pacific Marine Fisheries Commission. Annual Report (US ISSN 0078-7574) 399
Pacific Marine Fisheries Commission. Bulletin (US ISSN 0078-7582) 399
Pacific Marine Fisheries Commission. Newsletter (US ISSN 0078-7590) 399
Pacific Marine Station, Dillon Beach, California. Research Report (US ISSN 0078-7604) 312
Pacific Maritime Studies Series (CN) 471
Pacific Northwest Aviation Historical Foundation Journal see P N A H F Journal 10
Pacific Northwest Conference on Foreign Languages. Proceedings see Pacific Northwest Council on Foreign Languages. Proceedings 548
Pacific Northwest Conference on Higher Education. Proceedings (US ISSN 0078-7620) 339
Pacific Northwest Council on Foreign Languages. Proceedings (US ISSN 0363-8391) 548
Pacific Northwest Metals and Minerals Conference. Proceedings of Gold and Money Session and Gold Technical Session (US) 147, 646
Pacific Rim Research Series (US) 312
Pacific Science Association. Congress and Inter-Congress Proceedings (US) 788
Pacific Science Association. Congress Proceedings see Pacific Science Association. Congress and Inter-Congress Proceedings 788

Pacific Stock Exchange. Annual Report (US) 204
Pacific Travel Directory (AT ISSN 0311-0826) 889
Packaging Council of Australia. Environment Newsletter see Envirofacts 672
Packaging Directory (UK ISSN 0078-768X) 672
Packaging Machinery Directory see Packaging Machinery Manufacturers Institute. Official Packaging Machinery Directory 672
Packaging Machinery Manufacturers Institute. Official Packaging Machinery Directory (US ISSN 0078-7698) 672
Packaging Marketplace (US) 672
Packaging Update (II) 672
Paco (GE) 549
Pact (BE) 64
Paedagogica Belgica Academica (BE ISSN 0079-0370) 321
Paediatrie und Paedologie. Supplement (US) 618
Paediatrie: Weiter- und Fortbildung (US) 618
Pages Juridiques de la Vie Ouvriere (FR) 507
Paideia (US) 321
Paideia (PL ISSN 0137-3943) 321
Paideuma (GW ISSN 0078-7809) 52
Paint, Oil Colour Year Book see Polymers Paint and Colour Year Book 673
Paint Red Book (US ISSN 0090-5402) 673
Painting and Decorating Craftsman Manual and Textbook (US) 673
Painting Holidays (UK ISSN 0078-7833) 889
Pakha Sanjam (II) 549
Pakistan. Building Research Station. Biennial Report (PK) 486
Pakistan. Central Bureau of Education. Educational Statistics Bulletin Series (PK ISSN 0078-7914) 321
Pakistan. Central Bureau of Education. Yearbook see Pakistan. Ministry of Education. Yearbook 321
Pakistan. Central Statistical Office. Statistical Yearbook see Pakistan. Statistics Division. Statistical Yearbook 844
Pakistan. Directorate of Livestock Farms. Report (PK ISSN 0083-8292) 45
Pakistan. Directorate of Rural Works Programme. Evaluation Report (PK ISSN 0083-8306) 815
Pakistan. Export Promotion Bureau. Export Guide Series (PK ISSN 0078-8104) 197
Pakistan. Export Promotion Bureau. Fresh Fruits (PK ISSN 0078-8112) 29, 197
Pakistan. Finance Division. Annual Budget Statement (Final) (PK) 231
Pakistan. Finance Division. Budget in Brief (PK) 231
Pakistan. Finance Division. Economic Analysis of the Budget (PK) 231
Pakistan. Finance Division. Estimates of Foreign Assistance (PK) 231
Pakistan. Finance Division. Public Finance Statistics (PK) 162
Pakistan. Finance Division. Supplementary Demands for Grants and Appropriations (PK) 231
Pakistan. Food and Agriculture Division. Yearbook of Agricultural Statistics (PK ISSN 0078-8139) 18
Pakistan. Geological Survey. Memoirs; Paleontologia Pakistanica (PK ISSN 0078-8155) 674
Pakistan. Geological Survey. Records (PK ISSN 0078-8163) 298
Pakistan. Ministry of Education. Yearbook (PK ISSN 0078-8287) 321
Pakistan. Ministry of Finance. Basic Facts About the Budget see Pakistan Basic Facts 231
Pakistan. Ministry of Finance. Budget in Brief see Pakistan. Finance Division. Budget in Brief 231

Pakistan. Ministry of Finance. Budget of the Central Government see Budget of the Government of Pakistan. Demands for Grants and Appropriations 227
Pakistan. Ministry of Finance. Economic Analysis of the Central Government see Pakistan. Finance Division. Economic Analysis of the Budget 231
Pakistan. Ministry of Finance Estimates of Foreign Assistance see Pakistan. Finance Division. Estimates of Foreign Assistance 231
Pakistan. National Assembly. Debates. Official Report (PK ISSN 0078-8333) 516, 713, 745
Pakistan. Office of the Economic Adviser. Government Sponsored Corporations and Other Institutions (PK ISSN 0078-8392) 224
Pakistan. Planning and Development Division. Development Programme (PK ISSN 0078-8414) 224
Pakistan. Statistical Division. Statistical Yearbook see Pakistan. Statistics Division. Statistical Yearbook 844
Pakistan. Statistics Division. Consumer Price Index: Scope and Limitations (PK ISSN 0078-7981) 162
Pakistan. Statistics Division. Household Income & Expenditure Survey (PK) 162
Pakistan. Statistics Division. Key to Official Statistics (PK ISSN 0078-799X) 844
Pakistan. Statistics Division. N S S Series (PK ISSN 0078-8007) 844
Pakistan. Statistics Division. Statistical Yearbook (PK) 844
Pakistan. Survey of Pakistan. General Report (PK ISSN 0078-8481) 445
Pakistan. Water and Power Development Authority. Report (PK ISSN 0083-8349) 381
Pakistan Annual Law Digest (PK ISSN 0078-785X) 516
Pakistan Archaeology (PK ISSN 0078-7868) 64
Pakistan Association for the Advancement of Science. Annual Report (PK) 788
Pakistan Banking Directory (PK ISSN 0078-7884) 175
Pakistan Basic Facts (PK ISSN 0078-7892) 231
Pakistan Book of Cricket (PK) 825
Pakistan Business and Shopping Guide (PK) 241
Pakistan Central Cotton Committee. Agricultural Survey Report (PK ISSN 0078-7930) 38, 856
Pakistan Central Cotton Committee. Technological Bulletin. Series A (PK ISSN 0078-7949) 38, 856
Pakistan Central Cotton Committee. Technological Bulletin. Series B (PK ISSN 0078-7957) 38, 856
Pakistan Council of Scientific and Industrial Research. Report (PK ISSN 0078-804X) 788, 852
Pakistan Council of Scientific and Industrial Research Directory of the Scientists, Technologists, and Engineers of the P C S I R see Directory of the Scientists, Technologists, and Engineers of the P C S I R 782
Pakistan Customs Tariff (PK ISSN 0078-8058) 197, 231
Pakistan Directory of Trade and Industry (PK) 180
Pakistan Economic Survey (PK ISSN 0078-8082) 189
Pakistan Export Directory (PK ISSN 0078-8090) 197
Pakistan Forest Institute, Peshawar. Annual Progress Report (PK ISSN 0078-8147) 410
Pakistan Historical Society. Memoir (PK ISSN 0078-8171) 445
Pakistan Historical Society. Proceedings of the Pakistan History Conference (PK ISSN 0078-818X) 445
Pakistan Hotel and Restaurant Guide (PK) 483
Pakistan Hotel Guide (PK ISSN 0552-8968) 889
Pakistan Hotels & Tourism (PK) 889

Pakistan Industrial Credit and Investment Corporation. Report (PK ISSN 0078-8198) 204
Pakistan Industrial Development Corporation. Report (PK ISSN 0078-8201) 224
Pakistan Institute of Development Economics. Report (PK ISSN 0078-821X) 147, 201
Pakistan Institute of Development Economics. Research Report (PK ISSN 0078-8228) 147, 201
Pakistan Institute of Development Economics. Statistical Papers (PK) 162, 844
Pakistan Insurance Year Book (PK ISSN 0078-8236) 500
Pakistan National Scientific and Technical Documentation Centre. PASTIC Translations see P A S T I C Translations 852
Pakistan Petroleum Limited. Annual Report (PK ISSN 0552-9115) 681
Pakistan Philosophical Congress. Proceedings (PK ISSN 0078-8406) 690
Pakistan Postage Stamp Catalogue see Pakstampage Catalogue 479
Pakistan Postage Stamps (PK ISSN 0078-8422) 479
Pakistan Railways. Yearbook of Information (PK) 873
Pakistan Science Conference. Proceedings (PK ISSN 0078-8430) 788
Pakistan Scientific and Technological Information Center. Lists of PASTIC Bibliographies see Lists of P A S T I C Bibliographies 854
Pakistan Scientific and Technological Information Centre Translations see P A S T I C Translations 852
Pakistan Society Bulletin (UK) 723
Pakistan Standards Institution. Report (PK ISSN 0078-8457) 637
Pakistan Statistical Association. Proceedings (PK ISSN 0078-8473) 844
Pakistan Western Railway. Yearbook of Information see Pakistan Railways. Yearbook of Information 873
Pakistan's Balance of Payments (PK ISSN 0078-852X) 197, 231
Pakstampage Catalogue (PK) 479
Palaeoecology of Africa and the Surrounding Islands and Antarctica (NE ISSN 0078-8538) 674
Palaeontographica. Supplementbaende (GW ISSN 0085-4611) 674
Palaeontographica Americana (US ISSN 0078-8546) 674
Palaeontologia Africana (SA ISSN 0078-8554) 674
Palaeontologia Polonica (PL ISSN 0078-8562) 674
Palavra Poetica (BL) 581
Paleobiologia (PE) 52, 106
Paleontological Bulletins (NZ ISSN 0078-8589) 674
Paleontological Society. Memoir (US ISSN 0078-8597) 674
Paleontology and Geology of the Badwater Creek Area, Central Wyoming (US) 298, 674
Palestine! (US) 475, 713
Palestine Documents see Institute for Palestine Studies. Arabic Annual Documentary Series 443
Palestine-Jordanian Bibliography (JO) 93, 475
Palestine Yearbook see Institute for Palestine Studies. Yearbook Series 443
Palingenesia (GW ISSN 0552-9638) 260
Pallas (BE) 640
Palynology (US ISSN 0191-6122) 298
Pamatky Archeologicke. Bibliographical Register (CS) 64
Pamietnik Slowianski (PL ISSN 0078-866X) 549
Pamyatniki Kul'tury. Novye Otkrytiya/Monuments of Culture. New Discoveries (UR) 64, 77
Pan-American Association of Biochemical Societies Symposium Series see P A A B S Symposium Series 111

Pan American Associations in the United States; A Directory with Supplementary Lists of Other Associations. Inter-American and General (US ISSN 0553-0326) *523*
Pan American Development Foundation. Annual Report (US ISSN 0552-9913) *201*
Pan American Institute of Geography and History. Commission on Geophysics. Boletin (BO) *306*
Pan American Institute of Geography and History. Commission on History. Bibliografias (MX ISSN 0078-8813) *64, 471*
Pan American Institute of Geography and History. Commission on History. Guias (MX ISSN 0078-8821) *471*
Pan American Institute of Geography and History. Commission on History. Historiografias Americanas (MX ISSN 0078-883X) *471*
Pan American Institute of Geography and History. Commission on History. Historiadores de America (MX ISSN 0078-8848) *471*
Pan American Institute of Geography and History. Commission on History. Monumentos Historicos y Arqueologicos (MX ISSN 0078-8856) *471*
Pan American Medical Women's Alliance. Newsletter (US ISSN 0078-8864) *598*
Pan American Union. Department of Scientific Affairs. Report of Activities. *see* Organization of American States. Department of Scientific Affairs. Report of Activities *788*
Pan American Union. Department of Social Affairs. Studies and Monographs (US ISSN 0553-0407) *912*
Pan Am's World Guide (US ISSN 0553-0601) *889*
Pan T'ai Hsueh Pao *see* University of Malaya. Chinese Language Society. Journal *554*
Panama. Direccion de Estadistica y Censo. Estadistica Panamena Serie M: Empleo *see* Estadistica Panamena. Situacion Social. Seccion 441-Trabajo y Salarios. Estadisticas del Trabajo *155*
Panama. Direccion General de Recursos Naturales Renovables. Memoria (PN) *277*
Panama. Direccion Nacional de Planeamiento y Reforma Educativa. Departamento de Estadistica. Serie: Analisis Estadistico (PN) *328*
Panama. Instituto de Investigacion Agropecuaria. Carta Informativa Agricola (PN) *18*
Panama. Instituto de Investigacion Agropecuaria. Carta Informativa Pecuaria (PN) *45*
Panama. Instituto de Investigacion Agropecuaria. Informe Anual (PN) *18*
Panama. Instituto de Investigacion Agropecuaria. Publicacion Tecnica (PN) *18*
Panama. Ministerio de Agricultura y Ganaderia. Boletin Tecnico (PN ISSN 0085-4654) *19*
Panama. Ministerio de Planificacion y Politica Economica. Informe Economico (PN) *189*
Panama. Ministerio de Vivienda. Memoria (PN) *486*
Panama. Tribunal Electoral. Memoria (PN) *745*
Panama Canal Company. Meteorological and Hydrographic Branch. Climatological Data: Canal Zone and Panama (PN ISSN 0078-8899) *634*
Panama en Cifras (PN ISSN 0078-8996) *844*
Panamin Foundation Research Series (PH) *52, 117, 549*
Pangnirtung (CN ISSN 0319-1214) *77, 393*
Panguna (AT) *646*
Panhandler (US) *570*
Panjab University Indological Series (II) *445, 671*

Panorama (UK) *417, 459*
Panorama Aujourd'hui (FR) *766*
Panorama de Agricultura en (Year) (SP) *19*
Panorama de la Teologia Latinoamericana (SP) *775*
Panorama Democrate Chretien (IT) *713*
Panoramas Bibliograficos de Espana (SP) *93*
Panoramica sugli Artisti Italiani (IT) *77*
Panta-Rhei (IO) *516*
Papeis Avulsos de Zoologia (BL ISSN 0031-1049) *130*
Paper Air (US) *549, 581*
Paper Bag (UK ISSN 0144-4379) *280*
Paper, Paperboard, Woodpulp Capacity (US) *675*
Paper Pudding *see* Back Roads *559*
Paper Review of the Year (UK ISSN 0302-4180) *675*
Paper Year Book (US) *675*
Paperbacks in Print (UK ISSN 0031-1219) *760*
Papermakers' and Merchants' Directory of All Nations *see* Phillips' Paper Trade Directory- Europe-Mills of the World *675*
Papers and Reports on Child Language Development (US) *257, 549*
Papers and Studies in Contrastive Linguistics (PL) *549*
Papers in Anthropology (US ISSN 0078-9054) *52*
Papers in Anthropology (Springfield) *see* Illinois. State Museum. Research Series. Papers in Anthropology *50*
Papers in Australian Linguistics (AT ISSN 0078-9062) *549*
Papers in Borneo Linguistics (AT ISSN 0078-9070) *549*
Papers in Japanese Linguistics (US) *350, 549*
Papers in Linguistics of Melanesia (AT ISSN 0078-9127) *549*
Papers in New Guinea Linguistics (AT ISSN 0078-9135) *549*
Papers in Philippine Linguistics (AT ISSN 0078-9143) *549*
Papers in Public Administration (US ISSN 0078-9151) *745*
Papers in Public Administration (US ISSN 0078-916X) *745*
Papers in Sociology (IS) *815*
Papers in South East Asian Linguistics (AT ISSN 0078-9178) *549*
Papers in Textlinguistics *see* Papiere zur Textlinguistik *549*
Papers on Formal Linguistics (NE ISSN 0078-9194) *549*
Papers on Game Research *see* Finnish Game Research *276*
Papers on Islamic History (US ISSN 0085-4662) *475*
Papers on the History of Bourke (AT ISSN 0085-4670) *447*
Papers - Peace Science Society International *see* Peace Science Society (International). Papers *713*
Papers - Southeast Louisiana Historical Association *see* Southeast Louisiana Historical Association. Papers *472*
Papiere zur Textlinguistik/Papers in Textlinguistics (GW ISSN 0341-3195) *549*
Papiri Greci e Latini (IT ISSN 0078-9240) *434*
Papua and New Guinea Law Reports (AT ISSN 0085-4689) *516*
Papua and New Guinea Scientific Society. Annual Report and Proceedings (PP ISSN 0085-4697) *788*
Papua and New Guinea Scientific Society. Transactions (PP ISSN 0085-4700) *788*
Papua New Guinea. Bureau of Statistics. Household Expenditure Survey. Preliminary Bulletin. (PP) *844*
Papua New Guinea. Bureau of Statistics. Industrial Accidents *see* Papua New Guinea. Bureau of Statistics. Workers' Compensation Claims *502*
Papua New Guinea. Bureau of Statistics. International Trade Statistics. (PP) *162*

Papua New Guinea. Bureau of Statistics. Overseas Trade Statistics *see* Papua New Guinea. Bureau of Statistics. International Trade Statistics *162*
Papua New Guinea. Bureau of Statistics. Private Overseas Investment (PP ISSN 0078-9283) *197*
Papua New Guinea. Bureau of Statistics. Rural Industries (PP ISSN 0078-7701) *162*
Papua New Guinea. Bureau of Statistics. Rural Industries. Preliminary Statement (PP ISSN 0078-9321) *162*
Papua New Guinea. Bureau of Statistics. Secondary Industries (PP ISSN 0078-933X) *162*
Papua New Guinea. Bureau of Statistics. Secondary Industries (Factories and Works). Preliminary Statement (PP ISSN 0078-9313) *163*
Papua New Guinea. Bureau of Statistics. Statistical Bulletin: Capital Expenditure by Private Businesses (PP ISSN 0078-9259) *162*
Papua New Guinea. Bureau of Statistics. Statistical Bulletin: Registered Motor Vehicles (PP) *866*
Papua New Guinea. Bureau of Statistics. Statistical Bulletin: Survey of Retail Sales and Selected Services (PP) *162*
Papua New Guinea. Bureau of Statistics. Statistics of Religious Organisations (PP ISSN 0078-9356) *766*
Papua New Guinea. Bureau of Statistics. Summary of Statistics (PP) *844*
Papua New Guinea. Bureau of Statistics. Taxation Statistics. Preliminary Bulletin (PP ISSN 0078-9372) *163*
Papua New Guinea. Bureau of Statistics. Workers' Compensation Claims (PP) *502, 844*
Papua New Guinea. Department of Labour. Industrial Review. (PP ISSN 0085-4719) *912*
Papua New Guinea. Public Service Board. Report. (PP ISSN 0078-9399) *745*
Papua New Guinea Handbook (AT) *890*
Papua New Guinea Income Tax Legislation (AT) *231*
Papua New Guinea Institute of Medical Research. Monograph Series (PP) *598*
Papyrologica Bruxellensia (BE ISSN 0078-9402) *64*
Papyrologica Coloniensia (GW ISSN 0078-9410) *459*
Papyrologica Florentina (IT) *434*
Papyrologische Texte und Abhandlungen (GW) *434*
Paraguay. Ministerio de Industria y Comercio. Division de Registro y Estadistica Industrial. Encuesta Industrial (PY ISSN 0085-4743) *163*
Paralogue (FR ISSN 0078-9429) *570*
Paramagnitnyi Rezonans (UR) *698*
Parameters (US) *557*
Parana, Brazil. Secretaria de Estado da Agricultura. Plano de Acao. (BL) *19*
Parana, Brazil. Secretaria de Estado para os Negocios da Fazenda (BL) *163*
Parana em Tres Dimensoes (BL) *557*
Parana Informacoes *see* Information on Parana *186*
Parapharmex (FR) *611, 685*
Parapsychological Association. Proceedings *see* Research in Parapsychology *676*
Parapsychological Monographs (US ISSN 0078-9437) *676*
Parapsychology Foundation. Proceedings of International Conferences (US) *676*
Parazyty, Parazytozy ta Shliakhyikh Likvidatsii (UR) *121*
Parc Automobile du Maroc (MR) *871*
Parc National de la Vanoise. Travaux Scientifiques (FR) *788*

Parchemin. Recueil Genealogique et Heraldique (BE) *417*
Pardon Me, But (US ISSN 0085-4751) *713*
Parent Cooperative Preschools International. Directory (CN) *321*
Parents' Guide to Accredited Camps. Midwest Edition (US) *830*
Parents' Guide to Accredited Camps. Northeast Edition (US) *830*
Parents' Guide to Accredited Camps. South Edition (US) *830*
Parents' Guide to Accredited Camps. West Edition (US) *830*
Parfums-Beaute (FR) *85*
Paris-Bijoux Exportation (FR ISSN 0078-9496) *504*
Parker Directory of Attorneys *see* Parker Directory of California Attorneys *516*
Parker Directory of California Attorneys (US) *516*
Parkes Library Pamphlets (UK ISSN 0079-0052) *770*
Parkinson's Disease and Related Disorders. Cumulative Bibliography (US ISSN 0079-0060) *602*
Parklands Poets Series (UK ISSN 0079-0087) *581*
Parliament House Book (UK ISSN 0079-0095) *516*
Parliamentary Handbook of the Commonwealth of Australia *see* Australian Parliamentary Handbook *708*
Parma Eldalamberon (US) *570*
Parole in the United States (US) *283*
Participation (FR) *210*
Participation (CN) *713*
Particles and Nuclei Series (US) *704*
Partido Comunista de Colombia. Documentos (CK) *713*
Partido Socialista Popular. Congreso. (Actas) (SP) *713*
Partido Socialista Revolucionario . Informes (PE) *713*
Partners in Learning (UK ISSN 0079-0117) *772*
Partnership in Priorities *see* Minnesota. Department of Education. Biennial Report *911*
Parto (BL) *650, 713*
Pass-Age: a Futures Journal (US) *557*
Passaic County Dental Society. Bulletin(US ISSN 0079-0125) *610*
Passeggiate nel Lazio (IT) *890*
Passenger Train Annual (US) *873*
Passenger Transport in Great Britain *see* Transport Statistics Great Britain *876*
Passenger Transport Year Book *see* Little Red Book, Classified to All Public Transport Fleet Owners and Operators and Vehicle Manufacturers *863*
Passionist Youth *see* Gioventu Passionista *765*
Past & Present (CN) *713*
Pastoral Care and Counseling Abstracts(US) *3, 769*
Pastoral Psychology Series (US ISSN 0079-0141) *737*
Patent and Trademark Institute of Canada. Annual Proceedings (CN ISSN 0079-015X) *677*
Patent Law Annual-Southwestern Legal Foundation (US ISSN 0553-3864) *677*
Patent Law Review *see* Intellectual Property Law Review *677*
Patent Office Technical Society. Journal(II) *677*
Paterson's Licensing Acts (UK) *516*
Pathology and Practice *see* Pathology, Research and Practice *598*
Pathology Annual (US ISSN 0079-0184) *106, 598*
Pathology, Research and Practice (GW ISSN 0344-0338) *598*
Patronato Municipal de la Vivienda de Barcelona. Memoria (SP ISSN 0067-4168) *486*
Patterns of American Prejudice Series (US ISSN 0079-0192) *815*

Patterson Smith Reprint Series in Criminology. Law Enforcement and Social Problems *see* Patterson Smith Series in Criminology, Law Enforcement and Social Problems *283*
Patterson Smith Series in Criminology, Law Enforcement and Social Problems (US ISSN 0079-0222) *283*
Patterson's American Education (US ISSN 0079-0230) *332*
Patterson's American Educational Directory *see* Patterson's American Education *332*
Patterson's Schools Classified (US ISSN 0553-4054) *332*
Paul Anthony Brick Lectures (US ISSN 0079-0249) *690*
Paul Carus Lectures (US ISSN 0079-0257) *690*
Paul Valery (FR) *570*
Paul's Record Magazine (US ISSN 0360-2109) *662, 818*
Paving Conference. Proceedings (US ISSN 0079-0273) *376*
Pax Romana (SZ ISSN 0079-0281) *775*
Pays-Bas Francais *see* De Franse Nederlanden *782*
PdR Press Publications in Literary Systems (NE) *570*
PdR Press Publications on Dutch (NE) *549*
PdR Press Publications on William Butler Yeats (NE) *557*
Peabody Museum Bulletins (US) *64*
Peabody Museum of Archaeology and Ethnology. Memoirs (US ISSN 0079-029X) *64*
Peabody Museum of Archaeology and Ethnology. Monographs (US) *64*
Peabody Museum of Archaeology and Ethnology. Papers (US ISSN 0079-0303) *64*
Peabody Museum of Natural History. Bulletin (US ISSN 0079-032X) *788*
Peabody Museum of Natural History. Special Publication (US ISSN 0079-0338) *788*
Peace Plans (AT ISSN 0031-3564) *723*
Peace Research Laboratory. Annual Report (US ISSN 0085-4808) *723*
Peace Research Reviews (CN ISSN 0553-4283) *713*
Peace Research Society (International). Papers *see* Peace Science Society (International). Papers *713*
Peace Science Society (International). Papers (US ISSN 0094-8055) *713*
Peaceful Settlement Series *see* U N I T A R-P S Series *723*
Pearce-Sellards Series (US ISSN 0079-0354) *654*
Pears Cyclopaedia (UK ISSN 0079-0362) *361*
Peche Hauturiere au Quebec (CN) *401*
Pedagogicka Fakulta v Ostrave. Matematika, Fyzika (CS) *588, 698*
Pedagogicka Fakulta v Usti nad Labem. Sbornik: Rada Bohemisticka (CS) *549*
Pedagogicka Fakulta v Usti nad Labem. Sbornik: Rada Chemicka (CS) *247*
Pedagogisk Debatt Umeaa (SW) *321*
Pedagogiska Monografier Umeaa (SW) *912*
Pedagogiska Rapporter Umeaa (SW) *321*
Pedestal (CN ISSN 0319-1001) *900*
Pediatric and Adolescent Endocrinology(SZ ISSN 0304-4254) *611*
Pediatric Nephrology (US ISSN 0097-5257) *912*
Pedofauna (FR ISSN 0378-181X) *38*
Pegg/Professional Engineer, Geologist, Geophysicist (CN ISSN 0030-7912) *298, 369*
Pembroke Magazine (US) *557*
Pembrokeshire Historian (UK ISSN 0479-8244) *459*
Pen (AT ISSN 0311-1490) *321*
Penguin Modern Poets (US ISSN 0553-4917) *912*
Penn State Studies (US ISSN 0079-0451) *321*

Pennsylvania. Administration on Aging. State Plan on Aging (US) *428, 808*
Pennsylvania. Anthracite, Bituminous Coal and Oil and Gas Divisions. Annual Report. *see* Pennsylvania. Office of Mines and Land Protection. Annual Report *646*
Pennsylvania. Bureau of Aviation. Aviation Newsletter (US) *869*
Pennsylvania. Citizens Advisory Council to the Department of Environmental Resources. Annual Report (US ISSN 0092-7937) *388*
Pennsylvania. Crime Commission. Report (US ISSN 0091-4118) *283*
Pennsylvania. Department of Commerce. Bureau of Statistics, Research and Planning. Statistics for Manufacturing Industries (US ISSN 0556-3615) *163*
Pennsylvania. Department of Commerce. Bureau of Statistics. Statistics by Industry and Size of Establishment (US ISSN 0556-3593) *844*
Pennsylvania. Department of Education. Our Colleges and Universities Today (US ISSN 0085-4816) *339*
Pennsylvania. Department of Education. Special Education Programs-Services (US ISSN 0099-0302) *346*
Pennsylvania. Department of Environmental Resources. Annual Report on Mining, Oil and Gas and Land Reclamation and Conservaion Activities *see* Pennsylvania. Office of Mines and Land Protection. Annual Report *646*
Pennsylvania. Department of Public Welfare. Public Welfare Annual Statistics (US ISSN 0098-8510) *808*
Pennsylvania. Department of Public Welfare. Public Welfare Report *see* Pennsylvania. Department of Public Welfare. Public Welfare Annual Statistics *808*
Pennsylvania. Developmental Disabilities Planning Council. Pennsylvania State Plan (US) *808*
Pennsylvania. Historical and Museum Commission. Anthropological Series (US) *52, 471*
Pennsylvania. Labor Relations Board. Report. (US) *210*
Pennsylvania. Office of Mines and Land Protection. Annual Report (US) *646*
Pennsylvania. Office of the Budget. Program Budget (US ISSN 0085-4824) *321*
Pennsylvania. State Tax Equalization Board. Annual Certification (US) *231*
Pennsylvania Aircraft Accident and Violation Analysis (US) *10*
Pennsylvania Chamber of Commerce. Directory of State, Regional and Commercial Organizations (US ISSN 0098-5368) *180*
Pennsylvania Conference of Economists. Proceedings of the Annual Meeting (US) *147*
Pennsylvania Crop and Livestock Annual Summary (US ISSN 0079-046X) *38*
Pennsylvania Crop Reporting Service. C.R.S. *see* Pennsylvania Crop and Livestock Annual Summary *38*
Pennsylvania Directory of Manufacturers (US) *241*
Pennsylvania Economy League State Bulletin *see* P. E. L. State Bulletin *189*
Pennsylvania Exporters *see* Pennsylvania Exporters Directory *241*
Pennsylvania Exporters Directory (US ISSN 0360-8859) *241*
Pennsylvania Journal of Urban Economic Development (US) *189, 486*
Pennsylvania Manufacturing Exporters *see* Pennsylvania Exporters Directory *241*
Pennsylvania School Study Council. Reports (US ISSN 0079-0508) *321*
Pennsylvania State Industrial Directory (US ISSN 0553-6065) *241*

Pennsylvania State Plan for the Administration of Vocational-Technical Education Programs (US ISSN 0091-5114) *329*
Pennsylvania State University. College of Business Administration. Center for Research. Occasional Papers (US ISSN 0079-0540) *147*
Pennsylvania State University. Council on Research. Research Publications and Other Contributions *see* Pennsylvania State University. Research Publications and Professional Activities *321*
Pennsylvania State University. Earth and Mineral Sciences Experiment Station. Bulletin (US ISSN 0079-0591) *646*
Pennsylvania State University. Earth and Mineral Sciences Experiment Station. Bulletin. Mineral Conservation Series. Paper (US ISSN 0079-0605) *646*
Pennsylvania State University. Earth and Mineral Sciences Experiment Station. Circular (US ISSN 0079-0613) *646*
Pennsylvania State University. Institute for Research on Land and Water Resources. Information Reports (US ISSN 0079-0621) *277*
Pennsylvania State University. Institute for Research on Land and Water Resources. Research Publication (US ISSN 0079-063X) *277*
Pennsylvania State University. Libraries. Bibliographic Series (US ISSN 0079-0656) *534*
Pennsylvania State University. Research in the College of Agriculture (US) *912*
Pennsylvania State University. Research in the College of Earth and Mineral Sciences (US) *912*
Pennsylvania State University. Research in the College of Engineering (US) *912*
Pennsylvania State University. Research in the College of Health, Physical Education, and Recreation (US) *912*
Pennsylvania State University. Research in the College of Human Development (US) *912*
Pennsylvania State University. Research in the College of Medicine (US) *912*
Pennsylvania State University. Research in the College of Science *see* Pennsylvania State University. Research in the College of Health, Physical Education, and Recreation *912*
Pennsylvania State University. Research in the College of the Liberal Arts (US) *912*
Pennsylvania State University. Research Publications and Professional Activities (US ISSN 0093-7568) *321*
Pennsylvania Statistical Abstract (US ISSN 0476-1103) *844*
Pennsylvania's Machinery Custom Rates *see* Pennsylvania Crop and Livestock Annual Summary *38*
Penrose Annual (UK ISSN 0079-0710) *733*
Pensamiento Costarricense (CR) *418*
Pensamiento Literario Espanol (SP) *570*
Pension Boards *see* United Church of Christ. Pension Boards (Annual Report) *777*
Pension Plans in Canada/Regimes de Pensions au Canada (CN ISSN 0701-5488) *502, 844*
People. Biennial Report (US) *808*
People and Communication (US) *265*
People and National Land Policy/Hito to Kokudo (JA) *224*
People and Projects (RH) *815*
People and the Pursuit of Truth (US) *557, 713*
People from the Past Series. (UK ISSN 0079-0729) *98*
People like That (UK) *570*
Peoples of East Africa (KE) *52, 440*
Peoria Academy of Science. Proceedings (US ISSN 0079-0745) *788*

Per Jacobsson Foundation. Proceedings (US ISSN 0079-0761) *175*
Per Jacobsson Memorial Lecture *see* Per Jacobsson Foundation. Proceedings *175*
Perbadanan Perpustakaan Awam Selangor. Lapuran Tahunan *see* Selangor Public Library. Annual Report *535*
Percy Thrower's Guide to Modern Gardening *see* Amateur Gardening Guide *903*
Pere Marquette Theology Lecture Series (US) *766*
Perekrestki (US ISSN 0160-5534) *581*
Perfiles Contemporaneos (AG) *98*
Perfis Parlamentares (BL) *98, 745*
Performance Data on Architectural Acoustical Materials *see* Acoustical and Board Products. Bulletin *68*
Performance Report of the Alaska Economy (US) *189*
Performing Arts Resources (US ISSN 0360-3814) *859*
Performing Arts Year Book of Australia(AT) *859*
Performing Right *see* Performing Right News *662*
Performing Right News (UK ISSN 0309-0019) *662*
Performing Right Year Book (UK ISSN 0309-0884) *662*
Performing Woman (US ISSN 0191-1554) *662, 900*
Pergamino. Estacion Experimental Agropecuaria. Informe Tecnico *see* Pergamino, Argentina. Estacion Experimental Regional Agropecuaria. Informe Tecnico *19*
Pergamino, Argentina. Estacion Experimental Regional Agropecuaria. Informe Tecnico (AG ISSN 0325-1799) *19*
Pergamon Biological Sciences Series (US) *106*
Pergamon Frontiers in Anthropology Series (US) *52*
Pergamon General Psychology Series (US ISSN 0079-0818) *737*
Pergamon Management and Business Series (US) *147, 216*
Pergamon Mathematical Tables Series (US ISSN 0079-0826) *588*
Pergamon Studies in the Life Sciences (US) *106*
Pergamon Unified Engineering Series (US ISSN 0079-0869) *369*
Perinatal Medicine: Review and Comments (US) *615*
Periodical Literature on Social Sciences and Area Studies (II) *803*
Periodical Periodical (US) *534, 759*
Periodical Title Abbreviations (US) *759*
Periodicals in East African Libraries: a Union List *see* Periodicals in Eastern African Libraries: a Union List *93*
Periodicals in Eastern African Libraries: a Union List (KE) *93*
Periodicals That Progressive Scientists Should Know About (US) *93, 788, 852*
Periodicos Brasileiros de Ciencias e Tecnologia (BL ISSN 0100-2767) *93, 852*
Periodicos Brasileiros de Cultura *see* Periodicos Brasileiros de Ciencias e Tecnologia *93*
Permail Hospital Book (AT) *481*
Permanent International Altaistic Conference (PIAC). Newsletter (US ISSN 0031-5508) *671*
Pernambuco, Brazil. Secretaria da Agricultura. Plano Anual de Trabalho(BL) *570*
Persea (US) *570*
Persica (NE ISSN 0079-0893) *64, 445*
Persona y Derecho (SP) *516*
Personal Income in Counties of New York State (US ISSN 0079-0907) *213*
Personal Income Tax Analysis (US ISSN 0092-6655) *231*
Personal Injury Magazine (US) *570, 581*
Personality and Psychopathology (US ISSN 0079-0931) *737*

Personnel and Industrial Relations Colleges, an A.S.P.A. Directory *see* American Society for Personnel Administration. Personnel and Industrial Relations Colleges *219*
Personnel and Training Management Yearbook (UK ISSN 0306-6673) *220*
Personnel Policies and Benefits for the Apparel Industry (US) *220*
Perspecta; The Yale Architectural Journal (US ISSN 0079-0958) *69*
Perspective (NZ ISSN 0553-738X) *425*
Perspectives (US) *570*
Perspectives de l'Economique. Serie 1. les Fondateurs de l'Economie (FR ISSN 0079-0982) *192*
Perspectives de l'Economique. Serie 2. Economie Contemporaine (FR) *147*
Perspectives de l'Economique. Serie 3. Critique (FR) *147*
Perspectives des Bois Traites *see* Treated Wood Perspectives *413*
Perspectives in American History (US ISSN 0079-0990) *471*
Perspectives in Audiology (US) *598*
Perspectives in Cardiovascular Research (US ISSN 0361-0527) *607*
Perspectives in Criticism (US ISSN 0079-1008) *570*
Perspectives in Geography (US) *425*
Perspectives in Immunology (US) *604*
Perspectives in Jewish Learning *see* Solomon Goldman Lectures *770*
Perspectives in Law and Psychology (US) *516, 737*
Perspectives in Mathematical Logic (US) *588*
Perspectives in Medicine (SZ ISSN 0301-3014) *598*
Perspectives in Nephrology and Hypertension (US ISSN 0092-2900) *607, 625*
Perspectives in Powder Metallurgy *see* New Perspectives in Powder Metallurgy *629*
Perspectives in Quantum Chemistry and Biochemistry (US) *111, 247*
Perspectives in Social Work (US ISSN 0079-1040) *808*
Perspectives in Toxicology (US) *685*
Perspectives in Virology (US ISSN 0072-9086) *124, 608*
Perspectives on Academic Gaming & Simulation (UK ISSN 0141-5964) *350*
Perspectives on Marketing Series (US) *219*
Perspectives on Southern Africa (US) *440, 713*
Perspectives on the Energy Crisis (US) *353*
Perspektiven der Philosophie. Neues Jahrbuch (GW) *690*
Perth Observatory. Communications (AT ISSN 0079-1067) *83*
Peru. Biblioteca Nacional. Boletin (PE ISSN 0031-6067) *93, 534*
Peru. Biblioteca Nacional. Boletin (PE ISSN 0031-6067) *534*
Peru. Consejo Nacional de Justicia. Memoria (PE) *516*
Peru. Ministerio de Educacion Publica. Oficina Sectorial de Planificacion.Plan Bienal (PE) *321*
Peru. Oficina Regional de Desarrollo del Norte. Analisis General de Situacion de la Region Norte (PE ISSN 0085-4840) *189*
Peru Indigena (PE) *52*
Peru - Problema (PE ISSN 0079-1075) *815*
Perugia Quadrennial International Conferences on Cancer. Proceedings (IT ISSN 0069-8520) *606*
Pesquisas Educacionais (BL) *912*
Pesquisas: Publicacoes de Antropologia (BL ISSN 0553-8467) *52*
Pesquisas: Publicacoes de Botanica (BL ISSN 0553-8475) *117*
Pesquisas: Publicacoes de Historia (BL ISSN 0553-8491) *434*
Pesquisas: Publicacoes de Zoologia (BL ISSN 0553-8505) *130*
Pesticide Dictionary (US) *38*
Pesticide Handbook-Entoma (US) *38*
Pesticide Index (US) *3, 25*

Pesticide Review (US ISSN 0079-1148) *38*
Pesticide Situation *see* Pesticide Review *38*
Pesticides Annual (II) *38*
Peter W. Rodino Institute of Criminal Justice. Annual Journal (US) *283*
Peter Webster's International Speedway Review (AT) *826*
Petersen's Mini-Cars (US) *913*
Petersen's Pro Basketball (US ISSN 0192-2238) *825*
Petersen's Pro Football Annual *see* Pro Football *825*
Petersen's Pro Hockey (US ISSN 0271-2636) *821*
Peterson's Annual Guide to Undergraduate Study (US ISSN 0147-8451) *332*
Peterson's Guides. Annual Guides to Graduate Study. Book 1: Accredited Institutions Offering Graduate Work - An Overview (US) *332*
Peterson's Guides. Annual Guides to Graduate Study. Book 2: Humanities and Social Sciences (US) *332*
Peterson's Guides. Annual Guides to Graduate Study. Book 3: Biological, Agricultural and Health Sciences (US) *106, 332*
Peterson's Guides. Annual Guides to Graduate Study. Book 4: Physical Sciences (US) *332, 788*
Peterson's Guides. Annual Guides to Graduate Study. Book 5: Engineering and Applied Sciences (US) *332, 369*
Petro Quimica (MX) *646, 681*
Petrobras. Consolidated Report (BL) *681*
Petrochemical Units in the OPEC and OAPEC Countries *see* Unites Petrochimiques dans les Pays de l'OPEP et de l'OPAEP *681*
Petrochemical Units in Western Europe *see* Unites Petrochimiques en Europe de l'Ouest *682*
Petrole(Year) (FR ISSN 0069-6552) *681*
Petroleo e Gas (BL) *681*
Petroleum and Arab Economic Development *see* Oil and Arab Cooperation. Annual Review *680*
Petroleum and Chemical Industry Technical Conference. Record (US ISSN 0079-1288) *373, 681*
Petroleum and Coal Geology *see* Neftena i Vuglishtna Geologiia *297*
Petroleum Equipment Directory (US) *681*
Petroleum Geology of Taiwan/T'aiwan Shih Yu Ti Chih (CH) *299, 681*
Petroleum Industry in Japan (JA) *681*
Petroleum Marketer's Handbook (US) *681*
Petroleum Refineries in Canada (CN ISSN 0079-1296) *681*
Petroleum Statement (Annual) (US) *363, 681*
Pets Welcome (UK ISSN 0079-130X) *682, 890*
Pettaquamscutt Reporter (US) *471*
Pflanzenschutz-Kurier *see* Agro Chemie-Koerier *32*
Pflanzenschutz-Kurier *see* Correio Agricola (Portugal) *34*
Pflanzenschutz-Kurier *see* Gorsac Koerier *35*
Pflanzenschutz-Kurier (GW ISSN 0405-0738) *38*
Pflanzenschutz-Kurier *see* Vaextskydds-Kuriren *40*
Pflanzenschutz-Kurier *see* Chemagro Courier *906*
Pflanzenschutz-Nachrichten Bayer (GW ISSN 0079-1342) *38*
Pflanzenschutzberichte (AU ISSN 0031-675X) *117*
Die Pforte (GW ISSN 0031-6784) *557, 690*
Phaenomenologica (NE ISSN 0079-1350) *690*
Phanerogamarum Monographiae (GW ISSN 0079-1369) *117*
Pharmaceutical Directory (US ISSN 0569-6917) *685*
Pharmaceutical Historian (UK ISSN 0079-1393) *685*

Pharmaceutical Medicine (UK ISSN 0142-1581) *598, 685*
Pharmacology of Anaesthetic Drugs (US) *685*
Pharmacopeia of the United States of America *see* United States Pharmacopeia-National Formulary *686*
Pharmacopoeia Internationalis/International Pharmacopoeia (UN ISSN 0553-9382) *685*
Pharmatherapeutica (UK) *685*
Pharmindex (US ISSN 0031-7152) *3, 686*
Pharos (CN) *263*
Pharos (US ISSN 0031-7160) *654*
Phase Transition Phenomena (NE) *247*
Phenomenology Information Bulletin (US) *690*
Philadelphia Association for Psychoanalysis. Bulletin *see* Philadelphia Association for Psychoanalysis. Journal *737*
Philadelphia Association for Psychoanalysis. Journal (US ISSN 0094-1476) *737*
Philadelphia Society of Clinical Psychologists Times *see* P S C P Times *737*
Philatelic Directory (US) *479*
Philippine Agricultural Meteorology Bulletin (PH) *19, 634*
Philippine Astronomical Handbook (PH ISSN 0115-1207) *83*
Philippine Atomic Energy Commission. Annual Report (PH ISSN 0553-9978) *704*
Philippine Coconut Authority. Agricultural Research Department. Annual Report (PH) *38*
Philippine Development Report (PH) *189*
Philippine Export Directory (PH) *197, 241*
Philippine Library Association. Bulletin (PH) *534*
Philippine Mining and Engineering Journal. Mining Annual and Directory (PH ISSN 0085-4875) *646*
Philippine Normal College. Language Study Center. Occasional Paper (PH ISSN 0076-3780) *321, 549*
Philippine Normal College Research Series (PH) *339*
Philippine Scientist (PH ISSN 0079-1466) *788*
Philippine Standard Community Classification (PH) *204*
Philippine Yearbook *see* Philippines. National Census and Statistics Office. Yearbook *732*
Philippine Yearbook of International Law (PH) *523*
Philippines. Atmosphere, Geophysical and Astronomical Services Administration. Table of Sunrise, Sunset, Twilight, Moonrise and Moonset (PH ISSN 0115-3307) *83*
Philippines. Board of Investments. Annual Report (PH ISSN 0079-1504) *204*
Philippines. Bureau of Agricultural Economics. Crop and Livestock Statistics (PH) *29*
Philippines. Bureau of Agricultural Economics. Crop, Livestock and Natural Resources Statistics *see* Philippines. Bureau of Agricultural Economics. Crop and Livestock Statistics *29*
Philippines. Bureau of Agricultural Economics. Report (PH ISSN 0079-1520) *29*
Philippines. Bureau of Mines. Annual Report (PH) *277, 646*
Philippines. Bureau of Vocational Education. Agricultural Education Program; Information and Statistical Guide (PH) *19*
Philippines. Department of Agrarian Reform. Planning Service. Annual Report (PH) *29*
Philippines. Department of Commerce and Industry. Annual Report *see* Philippines. Ministry of Trade. Annual Report *197*

Philippines. Department of Natural Resources. Annual Report (PH) *277, 388*
Philippines. Department of Natural Resources. Plans and Programs (PH) *277, 388*
Philippines. Department of Public Information. Policy Statements (PH) *745*
Philippines. Food and Nutrition Center. Annual Report *see* Philippines. Food and Nutrition Research Institute. Annual Report *666*
Philippines. Food and Nutrition Research Institute. Annual Report (PH) *666*
Philippines. Government Printing Office. Itemization of Personal Services and Organizational Charts (PH) *534, 745*
Philippines. Insurance Commission. Annual Report (PH) *500*
Philippines. Labor Statistics Service. Year Book of Labor Statistics (PH) *163*
Philippines. Ministry of Trade. Annual Report (PH) *182, 197*
Philippines. Ministry of Trade. Trend Analysis of the Twenty Leading Exports and Prospects in the Year Ahead (PH) *197*
Philippines. Ministry of Trade. Twenty Leading Imports (PH) *197*
Philippines. National Census and Statistics Office. Annual Survey of Establishments (PH) *163*
Philippines. National Census and Statistics Office. Annual Survey of Wholesale and Retail Establishments (PH) *163*
Philippines. National Census and Statistics Office. Coastwise Trade Report (PH) *163*
Philippines. National Census and Statistics Office. Directory of Large Establishments (PH) *163*
Philippines. National Census and Statistics Office. Listing of Cities, Municipalities and Municipal Districts by Province (PH) *489*
Philippines. National Census and Statistics Office. Social Indicator (PH) *729*
Philippines. National Census and Statistics Office. Special Report (PH) *844*
Philippines. National Census and Statistics Office. Vital Statistical Report (PH ISSN 0554-0186) *844*
Philippines. National Census and Statistics Office. Yearbook (PH) *732*
Philippines. National Economic and Development Authority. Food Balance Series (PH) *29*
Philippines. National Economic and Development Authority. National Income Series (PH) *213*
Philippines. National Economic and Development Authority. Report on the Economy *see* Philippine Development Report *189*
Philippines. National Library. T N L Research Guide Series (PH) *94*
Philippines. National Tax Research Center. Report (PH ISSN 0079-1547) *231*
Philippines Business Directory (PH) *241*
Philippines Chinese Historical Association. Annals (PH) *445, 723*
Philippines Nuclear Journal (PH ISSN 0079-1490) *704*
Philips Reporter (AT) *357*
Phillips' Paper Trade Directory-Europe-Mills of the World (UK ISSN 0079-158X) *675*
Philologen-Jahrbuch (GW ISSN 0079-1598) *549*
Philological Monographs (US ISSN 0079-1628) *549*
Philological Society Transactions (UK ISSN 0079-1636) *549*
Philologische Beitraege zur Suedost- und Osteuropaforschung (AU ISSN 0079-1644) *549, 570*
Philosopher's Annual (US ISSN 0162-234X) *690*
Philosophia (GR) *690*

Philosophia Antiqua (NE ISSN 0079-1687) 260, *690*
Philosophia Mathematica (US ISSN 0031-8019) *588,* 690
Philosophica (CL) *690*
Philosophical Memoirs of Sciences & Maths. (CN) *588, 788*
Philosophical Society of the Sudan. Proceedings of the Annual Conference (SJ ISSN 0079-1695) *690*
Philosophical Studies Series in Philosophy (NE) *690*
Philosophical Texts and Studies *see* Wijsgerige Teksten en Studies *692*
Philosophie (FR) *690*
Philosophische Abhandlungen (GW) *690*
Philosophische Studientexte (GE ISSN 0079-1717) *690*
Philosophisches Jahrbuch (GW ISSN 0031-8183) *690*
Philosophy and Medicine (NE) *598, 690*
Philosophy of Education *see* Curriculum Improvement *316*
Philosophy of Education Society. Proceedings of the Annual Meetings (US ISSN 0079-1733) *321*
Philosophy Research Archives (US ISSN 0164-0771) *690*
Phoebus (US) *77*
Phoenix (US ISSN 0079-1776) *799*
Phoenix (UK ISSN 0031-8337) *913*
Phoenix. Supplementary Volumes (CN ISSN 0079-1784) *570*
Photo Information Almanac (US ISSN 0093-1365) *693*
Photo-Lab Index (US) *693*
Photobiology Bulletin (UK) *112*
Photochemistry (UK ISSN 0556-3860) *247*
Photochemistry (US ISSN 0079-1806) *255*
Photoelectric Spectrometry Group Bulletin *see* U.V. Spectrometry Group. Bulletin *706*
Photofact Annual Index (US ISSN 0556-5006) *268*
Photogrammetric Information *see* Fotogrammetriska Meddelanden *421*
Photographer's Market (US ISSN 0147-247X) *693*
Photographic Historical Society of New York. Membership Directory (US ISSN 0093-254X) *693*
Photographic Techniques in Scientific Research (US ISSN 0302-4210) *693*
Photographic Trade News Master Buying Guide (US) *693*
Photographic World Annual (AT) *693*
Photographic World Buyer's Guide. Cameras (AT) *693*
Photographic World Buyer's Guide. Cine (AT) *694*
Photographic World Buyer's Guide. Darkrooms (AT) *694*
Photographic World Buyer's Guide. Index (AT) *694*
Photographic World Buyer's Guide. Lenses (AT) *694*
Photographic World Buyer's Guide. Projectors (AT) *694*
Photographis (SZ ISSN 0079-1830) *694*
Photography Annual (US ISSN 0079-1849) *694*
Photography Directory and Buying Guide (US ISSN 0079-1857) *694*
Photography Index (US ISSN 0193-2810) *3, 694*
Photography/Politics (UK ISSN 0142-7865) *694*
Photography Year (US ISSN 0090-4406) *694*
Photography Year Book (UK ISSN 0079-1865) *694*
Photon (US ISSN 0031-8833) *650*
Photosynthesis Bibliography (NE) *110*
Physica Mathematica Universitatis Osloensis (NO ISSN 0078-6780) *588, 698*
Physical Acoustics: Principles and Methods (US ISSN 0079-1873) *706*
Physical Chemistry (US ISSN 0079-1881) *255*
Physical Chemistry. Series Two (UK) *255*

Physical Communications (NE) *698*
Physical Education and Health (AT) *350*
Physical Education around the World. Monograph (US ISSN 0079-189X) *350*
Physical Education Association of Great Britain and Northern Ireland. Report (UK ISSN 0079-1903) *350*
Physical Facilities at Institutions of Higher Education in West Virginia (US ISSN 0093-884X) *339*
Physical Inorganic Chemistry (NE) *255*
Physical Research Laboratory, Ahmedabad: Annual Report. (II) *698*
Physical Research Report *see* Illinois. Department of Transportation. Physical Research Report *375*
Physical Review Index (US ISSN 0094-0003) *3, 700*
Physical Sciences Data (NE) *255*
Physician Distribution & Medical Licensure in the U. S. (US) *598*
Physicians' Current Procedural Terminology *see* C P T *593*
Physicians' Desk Reference (US ISSN 0093-4461) *599*
Physicians' Desk Reference for Nonprescription Drugs (US) *599*
Physician's Medical Book Reference *see* P.M.B.R. Physician's Medical Book Reference *602*
Physico-Chemical Mechanics *see* Fiziko-Khimicheska Mekhanika *254*
Physics (US ISSN 0092-8437) *698*
Physics and Applications (CS) *698*
Physics and Biology (US) *106, 698*
Physics and Chemistry in Space (US ISSN 0079-1938) *83, 247, 698*
Physics and Chemistry of Materials with Layered Structures (NE) *247, 701*
Physics and Chemistry of the Organic Solid State (US ISSN 0079-1954) *255, 698*
Physics and Contemporary Needs (US) *698*
Physics Manpower - Education and Employment Statistics (US ISSN 0569-5716) *339, 698*
Physics of Quantum Electronics (US) *357*
Physics of Thin Films; Advances in Research and Development (US ISSN 0079-1970) *698*
Physikalisch-Chemische Trenn- und Messmethoden (GE ISSN 0079-1997) *698*
Physiological Society. Monographs (UK ISSN 0079-2020) *126*
Physiological Society of Philadelphia. Monographs (US) *126*
Physiology, Series One (UK) *126*
Physioquebec (CN ISSN 0708-1006) *599*
Phytochemical Society Symposia Series. Proceedings (UK) *117*
Phytologia (US ISSN 0031-9430) *117*
Phyton. Annales Rei Botanicae (AU ISSN 0079-2047) *117*
Phytopathological Papers *see* Commonwealth Mycological Institute. Phytopathological Papers *114*
Pianeta Fresco (IT ISSN 0079-2055) *77*
Picenum Seraphicum (IT) *775*
Pick's Currency Yearbook (US ISSN 0079-2063) *175*
Pictorial Directory - Washington State Legislature *see* Washington (State) Legislature. Pictorial Directory *747*
Pigment Cell (SZ ISSN 0301-0139) *122*
Pikestaff Forum (US ISSN 0192-8716) *570*
Pikestaff Review (US ISSN 0192-8724) *570*
Pilgrim's Guide to Planet Earth (US) *890*
Pilot Studies Approved for State Aid in Public School Systems in Virginia (US ISSN 0079-2071) *344*
Pinery (US) *471*
Pink Book *see* Drug Topics Health & Beauty Aids Directory *684*

Pinkes Fun der Kehile in Buenos Ayres *see* Anales de la Comunidad Israelita de Buenos Aires *391*
Pion Applied Physics Series (UK ISSN 0079-208X) *369, 698*
Pioneer *see* Pioneer Quarterly *19*
Pioneer Days (CN) *471*
Pioneer Quarterly (US) *19*
Pipe Line & Pipe Line Contractors (US) *681*
Pipe Line Annual Directory of Pipelines(US) *681*
Pipes of Pan *see* Inscape *580*
Pisarze Slascy XIX i XX Wieku (PL ISSN 0079-211X) *570*
Pistis (FI ISSN 0356-794X) *258, 766*
Pistolier *see* Point de Mire *418*
Pit & Quarry Handbook and Buyers Guide (US) *646*
Pit and Quarry Handbook and Purchasing Guide *see* Pit & Quarry Handbook and Buyers Guide *646*
Pitcher Performance Handbook (US) *825*
Pittsburgh Regional Library Center. Newsletter (US) *534*
Plain Turkey (AT ISSN 0311-0753) *570*
Plainsong & Mediaeval Music Society. Journal (UK) *662*
Plan *see* Build Kenya *68*
Plan *see* Plan Canada *486*
Plan Canada (CN) *486*
Plan Data (NO) *486*
Planeacion Regional (CK) *486*
Planet Drum (SI) *570*
Planews (SI) *486*
Planificacion (MX) *486*
Planning, Programming, Budgeting for City, State, County Objectives. P P B Note Series (US ISSN 0079-2217) *231, 750*
Planning Research Index (NZ) *486*
Plano da Safra Acucar e Alcool (BL) *38, 86, 516*
Plano Nacional de Educacao Especial (BL) *346, 745*
Plans for the Implementation of the Post-Vietnam Era Veterans' Educational Assistance Act of 1977 (US ISSN 0190-4930) *640*
Plant Breeding Institute, Cambridge. Annual Report (UK ISSN 0079-2225) *38*
Plant Engineering Directory & Specifications Catalog (US ISSN 0554-2693) *369*
Plant Engineering Extension Industrial Construction and Renovation File *see* Sweet's System for the Industrial Construction & Renovation Market *370*
Plant Food Dictionary (US) *38*
Plant Genetic Resources Newsletter (UN ISSN 0048-4334) *117, 278*
Plant Introduction Newsletter *see* Plant Genetic Resources Newsletter *278*
Plant Life (US ISSN 0032-0846) *117*
Plant Location (US ISSN 0554-2731) *224*
Plant Monograph: Reprints (GW ISSN 0079-2233) *117*
Plant Physiology. Supplement (US ISSN 0079-2241) *117*
Plant Protection Abstracts. Supplement (IS ISSN 0079-225X) *3, 110*
Plant Protection Center. Annual Report(CH) *38, 416*
Planter (MY ISSN 0032-0951) *19*
Planung und Kontrolle in der Unternehmung (SZ ISSN 0079-2276) *216*
Planungsstudien (GW ISSN 0079-2284) *224*
Plasma Physics (US) *698*
Plast- och Kemikalieleverantoerers Foerening Kemikalier *see* P K L Kemikalier *247*
Plast- och Kemikalieleverantoerers Foerening Plaster *see* P K L Plaster *707*
Plastichem (SI) *255, 373, 707*
Plasticos y Resinas (Annual) (MX) *707*
Plastics and Rubber Yearbook and Buyers' Guide of S.A. (SA) *707, 777*
Plastics Manufacturing Capabilities in Mississippi (US ISSN 0099-0450) *707*

Plastics, Rubber and Paint Buyers' Guide and Yearbook for Southern Africa *see* Plastics and Rubber Yearbook and Buyers' Guide of S.A *707*
Plastics Technology. Plastics Manufacturing Handbook and Buyers Guide (US) *707*
Platou Report (NO) *880*
Platt Saco Lowell Bulletin (UK) *856*
Platt Saco Lowell Replacement Parts News (US) *856*
Platte Valley Review (US ISSN 0092-4318) *263*
Play Index (US ISSN 0554-3037) *3, 578*
Playfair Cricket Annual (UK ISSN 0079-2314) *825*
Playfair Football Annual (UK ISSN 0079-2322) *825*
Playgirl Health and Beauty Guide (US) *85, 694*
Playing Rules *see* Women's International Bowling Congress. Playing Rules *822*
Plays. A Classified Guide to Play Selection (UK ISSN 0554-3045) *859*
Plays of the Year (UK) *859*
Playthings Directory (US ISSN 0079-2349) *429*
Pleiadi (IT) *570*
Pluma y Pincel (AG) *557*
Plunkett Development Series (UK ISSN 0143-8484) *29, 201*
Plunkett Foundation for Co-Operative Studies. Occasional Papers (UK ISSN 0551-0910) *29*
Plunkett Foundation for Co-Operative Studies. Study Series (UK ISSN 0142-5005) *29, 168, 216*
Plus-Profit Publicity (US ISSN 0300-7731) *6*
Poche-Couleurs Larousse (FR ISSN 0079-2373) *788*
Pocket Book of Transport Statistics of India (II ISSN 0079-2381) *863*
Pocket Data Book, USA (US ISSN 0079-2403) *732*
Pocket Digest of New Zealand Statistics(NZ ISSN 0079-2411) *438*
Pocket Library of Studies of Art (IT ISSN 0079-242X) *77*
Pocket Mathematical Library (US) *588*
Pocket Poets Series (US ISSN 0079-2438) *581*
Pocket Watch Price Indicator (US) *504*
Pocket Year Book of South Australia (AT ISSN 0079-2446) *845*
Pocket Yearbook of New South Wales (AT ISSN 0085-4921) *845*
Podiatric Medicine and Surgery (US) *913*
Poe Messenger (US) *570*
Poem Pamphlet (UK) *581*
Poema Convidado (US) *581*
Poesia (UY ISSN 0079-2462) *581*
Poesia (SP) *581*
Poet (US) *581*
Poetas (PY) *581*
Poetes et Prosateurs du Portugal (FR ISSN 0079-2470) *570, 581*
Poeti e Prosatori Tedeschi (IT ISSN 0079-2500) *570*
Poetic Drama and Poetic Theory (AU) *570, 581*
Poetry Bag (US ISSN 0032-2067) *581*
Poetry Clearinghouse (US) *581*
Poetry Market (UK ISSN 0032-2083) *581*
Poetry Miscellany (US ISSN 0048-4601) *581*
Poetry New Zealand (NZ) *581*
Poetry: People (US) *570*
Poetry Supplement (UK) *581*
Poetry Venture (US ISSN 0032-2199) *913*
Poets of Australia (AT ISSN 0311-2810) *581*
Poet's Yearbook (UK) *581*
Poetyka. Zarys Encyklopedyczny (PL ISSN 0079-2527) *581*
Poeyana (CU) *130*
Poeziya(Moscow) (UR) *581*
Pohjois-Suomen Bibliografia (FI) *94*
Pohjoismaiden Yhdyspankki. Report *see* Union Bank of Finland. Annual Report *177*
Le Poing et la Rose (FR) *713*

Point *see* Commerce. le Point *181*
Point de Mire (CN ISSN 0707-8021) *418*
Point of Reference (US ISSN 0094-4998) *434*
Point Theologique (FR) *775*
Points *see* J E B-Points *256*
Points. Films (FR ISSN 0079-2535) *650*
Points Chauds *see* France des Points Chauds *710*
Points for Emphasis; International Sunday School Lessons in Pocket Size (US ISSN 0079-2543) *767*
Points Northwest (US) *534*
Poison Control Program Report *see* Illinois. Department of Public Health. Poison Control Program Report *756*
Poland. Glowny Urzad Statystyczny. Atlas Statystyczny. Statistical Atlas (PL ISSN 0079-2586) *845*
Poland. Glowny Urzad Statystyczny. Budzet Panstwa. State Budget (PL ISSN 0079-2594) *231*
Poland. Glowny Urzad Statystyczny. Kultura *see* Poland. Glowny Urzad Statystyczny. Rocznik Statystyczny Kultury. Statistical Yearbook of Culture *495*
Poland. Glowny Urzad Statystyczny. Maly Rocznik Statystyczny. Concise Statistical Yearbook (PL ISSN 0079-2608) *845*
Poland. Glowny Urzad Statystyczny. Maly Rocznik Statystyki Miedzynarodowej (PL) *845*
Poland. Glowny Urzad Statystyczny. Rocznik Demograficzny (PL ISSN 0079-2616) *732*
Poland. Glowny Urzad Statystyczny. Rocznik Statystyczny Budownictwa. Yearbook of Construction Statistics (PL ISSN 0079-2632) *140*
Poland. Glowny Urzad Statystyczny. Rocznik Statystyczny Finansow. Yearbook of Finance Statistics (PL ISSN 0079-2640) *163*
Poland. Glowny Urzad Statystyczny. Rocznik Statystyczny Gornictwa. Yearbook of Mining Statistics (PL ISSN 0079-2675) *648*
Poland. Glowny Urzad Statystyczny. Rocznik Statystyczny Gospodarki Morskiej. Yearbook of Sea Economy Statistics (PL ISSN 0079-2667) *866*
Poland. Glowny Urzad Statystyczny. Rocznik Statystyczny Gospodarski Mieszkaniowej i Komunalnej (PL ISSN 0079-2659) *489*
Poland. Glowny Urzad Statystyczny. Rocznik Statystyczny Handlu Wewnetrznego/Yearbook of International Trade Statistics (PL ISSN 0079-2683) *163*
Poland. Glowny Urzad Statystyczny. Rocznik Statystyczny Inwestycji i Srodkow Trwalych. Yearbook of Investment and Fixed Assets Statistics (PL ISSN 0079-2705) *163*
Poland. Glowny Urzad Statystyczny. Rocznik Statystyczny Kultury. Statistical Yearbook of Culture (PL) *495*
Poland. Glowny Urzad Statystyczny. Rocznik Statystyczny Lesnictwa. Yearbook of Forestry Statistics (PL ISSN 0079-2721) *412*
Poland. Glowny Urzad Statystyczny. Rocznik Statystyczny Ochrony Zdrowia. Yearbook of Public Health Statistics (PL ISSN 0079-2748) *756*
Poland. Glowny Urzad Statystyczny. Rocznik Statystyczny Powiatow. Statistical Yearbook of Counties (PL ISSN 0079-2756) *845*
Poland. Glowny Urzad Statystyczny. Rocznik Statystyczny Pracy. Yearbook of Labour Statistics (PL ISSN 0079-2772) *163*
Poland. Glowny Urzad Statystyczny. Rocznik Statystyczny Przemyslu. Yearbook of Industry Statistics (PL ISSN 0079-2764) *163*
Poland. Glowny Urzad Statystyczny. Rocznik Statystyczny Rolnictwai Gospodarki Zywnosciowej. Yearbook of Agricultural Statistics (PL) *25*

Poland. Glowny Urzad Statystyczny. Rocznik Statystyczny. Statistical Yearbook (PL ISSN 0079-2780) *845*
Poland. Glowny Urzad Statystyczny. Rocznik Statystyczny Szkolnictwa. Yearbook of Education Statistics (PL ISSN 0079-2799) *328*
Poland. Glowny Urzad Statystyczny. Rocznik Statystyczny Transportu. Yearbook of Transport Statistics (PL ISSN 0079-2802) *866*
Poland. Glowny Urzad Statystyczny. Rocznik Statystyczny Handlu Zagranicznego (PL ISSN 0079-2691) *163*
Poland. Glowny Urzad Statystyczny. Rocznik Statystyki Miedzynarodowej. Yearbook of International Statistics (PL ISSN 0079-273X) *845*
Poland. Glowny Urzad Statystyczny. Rolniczy Rocznik Statystyczny. Yearbook of Agricultural Statistics *see* Poland. Glowny Urzad Statystyczny. Rocznik Statystyczny Rolnictwai Gospodarczej. Yearbook of Agricultural Statistics *25*
Poland. Glowny Urzad Statystyczny. Statystyka Zegluci Srodladowej i Drog Wodnych Srodladowych (PL ISSN 0079-2837) *866*
Poland. Glowny Urzad Statystyczny. Studia i Prace Statystyczne (PL ISSN 0079-2845) *845*
Poland. Glowny Urzad Statystyczny. Turystyka (PL) *893*
Poland. Glowny Urzad Statystyczny. Ubezpieczenia Majatkowe i Osobowe. Property and Personal Insurance (PL ISSN 0079-2853) *502*
Poland. Glowny Urzad Statystyczny. Uzytkowanie Gruntow i Powierzchnia Zasiewow Oraz Zwierzeta Gospodarskie (PL ISSN 0079-2861) *25*
Poland. Glowny Urzad Statystyczny. Wypadki Drogowe (PL ISSN 0079-287X) *756*
Poland. Glowny Urzad Statystyczny. Wypadki Przy Pracy. Accidents at Work (PL ISSN 0079-2888) *756*
Poland. Glowny Urzad Statystyczny. Zatrudnienie w Gospodarce Narodowej (PL ISSN 0079-2896) *163*
Poland. Glowny Urzad Statystyczny,. Zeszyty Metodyczne (PL ISSN 0079-2829) *845*
Polar Bears (SZ) *130, 278*
Polar Research *see* National Research Council. Committee on Polar Research. Report on United States Antarctic Research Activities *424*
Polarhaandbok *see* Norsk Polarinstitutt. Polarhaandbok *298*
Polemologische Studien (NE ISSN 0079-2926) *713*
Police and Law Enforcement (US ISSN 0092-8933) *283*
Police Chief (US) *283*
Police Statistics of Cincinnati *see* Cincinnati. Division of Police. Annual Report *281*
Police Yearbook (US ISSN 0079-2950) *283*
Policies and Procedures for the Creation of Diplomates in Professional Psychology *see* American Board of Professional Psychology. Policies and Procedures for the Creation of Diplomates in Professional Psychology *734*
Policy Analysis and Education Series (US) *913*
Policy Grants Directory (US ISSN 0160-2675) *713*
Policy Publishers and Associations Directory (US) *713, 759*
Policy Research Centers Directory (US) *713*
Policy Studies Directory (US ISSN 0362-6016) *713*
Policy Studies in Employment and Welfare (US) *808*

Policy Studies Institute Broadsheet Series and Major Reports *see* P S I: Broadsheet Series and Major Reports *713*
Policy Studies Institute Discussion Papers *see* P S I Discussion Papers *713*
Policy Studies Personnel Directory (US) *713*
Policy Studies Review Annual (US) *745*
Polimery v Melioratsii i Vodnom Khozyaistve (UR) *381, 897*
Polish Academy of Sciences. Institute of Computer Science. Reports (PL) *273, 588*
Polish Academy of Sciences. Institute of Fundamental Technological Research. Scientific Activities (PL ISSN 0079-323X) *369*
Polish Academy of Sciences. Mathematical Institute. Banach Center Publications (PL) *588*
Polish Archaeological Abstracts (PL ISSN 0137-4885) *3, 68*
Polish Journal of Soil Science (PL ISSN 0079-2985) *38*
Polish Round Table (PL ISSN 0079-3000) *713*
Polish Sociological Bulletin (PL) *815*
Polish Sociology *see* Polish Sociological Bulletin *815*
Polish Yearbook of International Law/Annuaire Polonais de Droit International (PL ISSN 0554-498X) *523*
Politechnika Czestochowska. Zeszyty Naukowe. Nauki Podstawowe (PL ISSN 0574-9069) *369*
Politechnika Czestochowska. Zeszyty Naukowe. Nauki Spoleczno-Ekonomiczne (PL ISSN 0574-9077) *799*
Politechnika Czestochowska. Zeszyty Naukowe. Nauki Techniczne. Elektrotechnika (PL ISSN 0137-6977) *357*
Politechnika Czestochowska. Zeszyty Naukowe. Nauki Techniczne. Hutnictwo (PL ISSN 0372-9699) *629*
Politechnika Czestochowska. Zeszyty Naukowe. Nauki Techniczne. Mechanika (PL ISSN 0137-6969) *382*
Politechnika Gdanska. Zeszyty Naukowe. Architektura (PL) *70*
Politechnika Gdanska. Zeszyty Naukowe. Budownictwo Ladowe (PL) *138, 376*
Politechnika Gdanska. Zeszyty Naukowe. Budownictwo Okretowe (PL ISSN 0416-7287) *880*
Politechnika Gdanska. Zeszyty Naukowe. Budownictwo Wodne (PL ISSN 0416-7295) *381*
Politechnika Gdanska. Zeszyty Naukowe. Chemia (PL ISSN 0416-7309) *247*
Politechnika Gdanska. Zeszyty Naukowe. Ekonomia (PL) *147*
Politechnika Gdanska. Zeszyty Naukowe. Elektronika (PL ISSN 0418-3614) *357*
Politechnika Gdanska. Zeszyty Naukowe. Elektryka (PL) *357*
Politechnika Gdanska. Zeszyty Naukowe. Fizyka (PL ISSN 0072-0364) *698*
Politechnika Gdanska. Zeszyty Naukowe. Matematyka (PL ISSN 0072-0372) *588*
Politechnika Gdanska. Zeszyty Naukowe. Mechanika (PL ISSN 0072-0380) *382*
Politechnika Krakowska. Zeszyty Naukowe. Chemia (PL ISSN 0075-7055) *247*
Politechnika Lodzka. Zeszyty Naukowe. Budownictwo (PL ISSN 0076-0323) *138, 376*
Politechnika Lodzka. Zeszyty Naukowe. Chemia (PL ISSN 0458-1555) *247*
Politechnika Lodzka. Zeszyty Naukowe. Chemia Spozywcza (PL ISSN 0528-9254) *405*
Politechnika Lodzka. Zeszyty Naukowe. Cieplne Maszyny Przeplywowe (PL) *382*

Politechnika Lodzka. Zeszyty Naukowe. Elektryka (PL ISSN 0459-682X) *357*
Politechnika Lodzka. Zeszyty Naukowe. Fizyka (PL) *698*
Politechnika Lodzka. Zeszyty Naukowe. Inzynieria Chemiczna (PL) *373*
Politechnika Lodzka. Zeszyty Naukowe. Matematyka (PL) *588*
Politechnika Lodzka. Zeszyty Naukowe. Mechanika (PL ISSN 0458-1563) *382*
Politechnika Lodzka. Zeszyty Naukowe. Nauki Spoleczno-Ekonomiczne (PL) *799*
Politechnika Lodzka. Zeszyty Naukowe. Wlokiennictwo (PL ISSN 0076-0331) *856*
Politechnika Lodzka. Zeszyty Naukowe. Zeszyt Specjalny (PL ISSN 0458-1547) *339*
Politechnika Poznanska. Materialy Historyczno-Metodyczne. Studia Filozoficzne *see* Materialy Historyczno-Metodyczne *434*
Politechnika Poznanska. Zeszyty Naukowe. Bibliografia (PL ISSN 0551-651X) *94*
Politechnika Poznanska. Zeszyty Naukowe. Budownictwo (PL) *376*
Politechnika Poznanska. Zeszyty Naukowe. Budownictwo Ladowe *see* Politechnika Poznanska. Zeszyty Naukowe. Budownictwo *376*
Politechnika Poznanska. Zeszyty Naukowe. Chemia Techniki Zastosowan (PL ISSN 0137-6896) *247*
Politechnika Poznanska. Zeszyty Naukowe. Chemia Techniki Zastosowan *see* Politechnika Poznanska. Zeszyty Naukowe. Chemia Techniki Zastosowan *247*
Politechnika Poznanska. Zeszyty Naukowe. Ekonomika i Organizacja Przemyslu (PL ISSN 0137-690X) *224*
Politechnika Poznanska. Zeszyty Naukowe. Elektryka (PL ISSN 0079-4503) *357*
Politechnika Poznanska. Zeszyty Naukowe. Fizyka (PL ISSN 0079-4511) *698*
Politechnika Poznanska. Zeszyty Naukowe. Maszyny Robocze i Pojazdy (PL ISSN 0137-6918) *32*
Politechnika Poznanska. Zeszyty Naukowe. Mechanika (PL ISSN 0079-4538) *701*
Politechnika Poznanska. Zeszyty Naukowe. Mechanizacja i Elektryfikacja Rolnictwa *see* Politechnika Poznanska. Zeszyty Naukowe. Maszyny Robocze i Pojazdy *32*
Politechnika Slaska. Zeszyty Naukowe. Automatyka (PL ISSN 0434-0760) *273*
Politechnika Slaska. Zeszyty Naukowe. Budownictwo (PL ISSN 0434-0779) *376*
Politechnika Slaska. Zeszyty Naukowe. Chemia (PL ISSN 0372-9494) *247*
Politechnika Slaska. Zeszyty Naukowe. Elektryka (PL ISSN 0072-4688) *357*
Politechnika Slaska. Zeszyty Naukowe. Energetyka (PL ISSN 0372-9796) *363*
Politechnika Slaska. Zeszyty Naukowe. Gornictwo (PL ISSN 0372-9508) *646*
Politechnika Slaska. Zeszyty Naukowe. Hutnictwo (PL ISSN 0324-802X) *629*
Politechnika Slaska. Zeszyty Naukowe. Inzynieria Sanitarna (PL ISSN 0072-4696) *753*
Politechnika Slaska. Zeszyty Naukowe. Matematyka-Fizyka (PL ISSN 0072-470X) *588, 698*
Politechnika Slaska. Zeszyty Naukowe. Mechanika (PL ISSN 0434-0817) *382*
Politechnika Slaska. Zeszyty Naukowe. Nauki Spoleczne (PL ISSN 0072-4718) *799*
Politechnika Warszawska. Instytut Fizyki. Prace (PL) *698*

Politechnika Warszawska. Instytut Technologii i Organizacji Produkcji Budowlanej. Prace (PL) *138*
Politechnika Wroclawska. Biblioteka Glowna i Osrodek Informacji Naukowo-Technicznej. Prace Naukowe. Konferencje (PL ISSN 0137-6217) *788*
Politechnika Wroclawska. Biblioteka Glowna i Osrodek Informacji Naukowo-Technicznej. Prace Naukowe. Prace Bibliograficzne (PL) *795*
Politechnika Wroclawska. Biblioteka Glowna i Osrodek Informacji Naukowo-Technicznej. Prace Naukowe. Studia i Materialy (PL ISSN 0137-6225) *788*
Politechnika Wroclawska. Instytut Architektury i Urbanistyki. Prace Naukowe. Monografie (PL ISSN 0324-9905) *70, 77*
Politechnika Wroclawska. instytut Architektury i Urbanistyki. Prace Naukowe. Studia i Materialy (PL ISSN 0324-9891) *70, 77*
Politechnika Wroclawska. Instytut Budownictwa. Prace Naukowe. Konferencje (PL ISSN 0324-9883) *138*
Politechnika Wroclawska. Instytut Budownictwa. Prace Naukowe. Monografie (PL ISSN 0324-9875) *138*
Politechnika Wroclawska. Instytut Budownictwa. Prace Naukowe. Studia i Materialy (PL ISSN 0137-6241) *138*
Politechnika Wroclawska. Instytut Chemii i Technologii Nafty i Wegla. Prace Naukowe. Konferencje (PL ISSN 0324-9867) *373*
Politechnika Wroclawska. Instytut Chemii i Technologii Nafty i Wegla. Prace Naukowe. Monografie (PL ISSN 0324-9859) *373*
Politechnika Wroclawska. Instytut Chemii i Technologii Nafty i Wegla. Prace Naukowe. Studia i Materialy (PL ISSN 0084-2818) *373*
Politechnika Wroclawska. Instytut Chemii Nieorganicznej i Metalurgii Pierwiastkow Rzadkich. Prace Naukowe. Konferencje (PL ISSN 0324-9832) *251*
Politechnika Wroclawska. Instytut Chemii Nieorganicznej i Metalurgii Pierwiastkow Rzadkich. Prace Naukowe. Monografie (PL ISSN 0324-9840) *251*
Politechnika Wroclawska. Instytut Chemii Nieorganicznej i Metalurgii Pierwiastkow Rzadkich. Prace Naukowe. Studia i Materialy (PL ISSN 0370-0755) *251*
Politechnika Wroclawska. Instytut Chemii Organicznej i Fizycznej. Prace Naukowe. Konferencje (PL ISSN 0324-9824) *253, 255*
Politechnika Wroclawska. Instytut Chemii Organicznej i Fizycznej. Prace Naukowe. Monografie (PL ISSN 0324-9816) *253, 255*
Politechnika Wroclawska. Instytut Chemii Organicznej i Fizycznej. Prace Naukowe. Studia i Materialy (PL ISSN 0370-081X) *253, 255*
Politechnika Wroclawska. Instytut Cybernetyki Technicznej. Prace Naukowe. Konferencje (PL ISSN 0324-9794) *273*
Politechnika Wroclawska. Instytut Cybernetyki Technicznej. Prace Naukowe. Monografie (PL ISSN 0324-9786) *273*
Politechnika Wroclawska. Instytut Cybernetyki Technicznej. Prace Naukowe. Studia i Materialy (PL ISSN 0324-9808) *273*
Politechnika Wroclawska. Instytut Energoelektryki. Prace Naukowe. Konferencje (PL ISSN 0324-9778) *357*
Politechnika Wroclawska. Instytut Energoelektryki. Prace Naukowe. Monografie (PL ISSN 0324-976X) *357*

Politechnika Wroclawska. Instytut Energoelektryki. Prace Naukowe. Studia i Materialy (PL ISSN 0084-2826) *357*
Politechnika Wroclawska. Instytut Fizyki. Prace Naukowe. Monografie (PL ISSN 0370-0828) *698*
Politechnika Wroclawska. Instytut Fizyki. Prace Naukowe. Studia i Materialy (PL ISSN 0324-9697) *698*
Politechnika Wroclawska. Instytut Geotechniki. Prace Naukowe. Konferencje (PL ISSN 0370-0836) *289*
Politechnika Wroclawska. Instytut Geotechniki. Prace Naukowe. Monografie (PL ISSN 0084-2834) *289*
Politechnika Wroclawska. Instytut Geotechniki. Prace Naukowe. Studia i Materialy (PL ISSN 0084-2842) *289*
Politechnika Wroclawska. Instytut Gornictwa. Prace Naukowe. Konferencje (PL ISSN 0324-9670) *646*
Politechnika Wroclawska. Instytut Gornictwa. Prace Naukowe. Monografie (PL ISSN 0324-9689) *646*
Politechnika Wroclawska. Instytut Gornictwa. Prace Naukowe. Studia i Materialy (PL) *646*
Politechnika Wroclawska. Instytut Historii Architektury, Sztuki i Techniki. Prace Naukowe. Monografie (PL) *70, 77*
Politechnika Wroclawska. Instytut Historii Architektury, Sztuki i Techniki. Prace Naukowe. Studia i Materialy (PL ISSN 0324-9654) *70, 77*
Politechnika Wroclawska. Instytut Inzynieri Ochrony Srodowska. Prace Naukowe. Monografie (PL ISSN 0084-2869) *753*
Politechnika Wroclawska. Instytut Inzynierii Chemicznej i Urzadzen Cieplnych. Prace Naukowe. Konferencje (PL) *373*
Politechnika Wroclawska. Instytut Inzynierii Chemicznej i Urzadzen Cieplnych. Prace Naukowe. Monografie (PL ISSN 0084-2850) *373*
Politechnika Wroclawska. Instytut Inzynierii Chemicznej i Urzadzen Cieplnych. Prace Naukowe. Studia i Materialy (PL ISSN 0324-9751) *138, 373*
Politechnika Wroclawska. Instytut Inzynierii Ladowej. Prace Naukowe. Konferencje (PL ISSN 0324-9743) *376*
Politechnika Wroclawska. Instytut Inzynierii Ladowej. Prace Naukowe. Monografie (PL ISSN 0324-9727) *376*
Politechnika Wroclawska. Instytut Inzynierii Ladowej. Prace Naukowe. Studia i Materialy (PL ISSN 0370-0844) *376*
Politechnika Wroclawska. Instytut Inzynierii Ochrony Srodowiska. Prace Naukowe. Konferencje (PL ISSN 0324-9719) *369*
Politechnika Wroclawska. Instytut Inzynierii Ochrony Srodowiska. Prace Naukowe. Studia i Materialy (PL ISSN 0084-2877) *369*
Politechnika Wroclawska. Instytut Konstrukcji i Eksploatacji Maszyn. Prace Naukowe. Konferencje (PL ISSN 0324-9646) *583*
Politechnika Wroclawska. Instytut Konstrukcji i Eksploatacji Maszyn. Prace Naukowe. Monografie (PL ISSN 0324-962X) *583*
Politechnika Wroclawska. Instytut Konstrukcji i Eksploatacji Maszyn. Prace Naukowe. Studia i Materialy (PL ISSN 0324-9638) *583*
Politechnika Wroclawska. Instytut Matematyki. Prace Naukowe. Monografie (PL ISSN 0324-9603) *588*

Politechnika Wroclawska. Instytut Matematyki. Prace Naukowe. Studia i Materialy (PL ISSN 0324-9611) *588, 698*
Politechnika Wroclawska. Instytut Materialoznawstwa i Mechaniki Technicznej. Prace Naukowe. Konferencje (PL ISSN 0324-9573) *382, 701*
Politechnika Wroclawska. Instytut Materialoznawstwa i Mechaniki Technicznej. Prace Naukowe. Monografie (PL ISSN 0324-9565) *701*
Politechnika Wroclawska. Instytut Materialoznawstwa i Mechaniki Technicznej. Prace Naukowe. Studia i Materialy (PL ISSN 0370-0917) *701*
Politechnika Wroclawska. Instytut Metrologii Elektrycznej. Prace Naukowe. Konferencje (PL ISSN 0324-9557) *357, 637*
Politechnika Wroclawska. Instytut Metrologii Elektrycznej. Prace Naukowe. Monografie (PL ISSN 0324-9549) *357, 637*
Politechnika Wroclawska. Instytut Metrologii Elektrycznej. Prace Naukowe. Przemysl (PL ISSN 0324-9530) *357, 637*
Politechnika Wroclawska. Instytut Metrologii Elektrycznej. Prace Naukowe. Studia i Materialy (PL ISSN 0084-2958) *357, 637*
Politechnika Wroclawska. Instytut Nauk Spolecznych. Prace Naukowe. Monografie (PL ISSN 0324-9506) *799*
Politechnika Wroclawska. Instytut Nauk Spolecznych. Prace Naukowe. Studia i Materialy (PL ISSN 0324-9514) *799*
Politechnika Wroclawska. Instytut Organizacji i Zarzadzania. Prace Naukowe. Konferencje (PL ISSN 0324-9484) *216*
Politechnika Wroclawska. Instytut Organizacji i Zarzadzania. Prace Naukowe. Monografie. (PL ISSN 0324-9492) *216*
Politechnika Wroclawska. Instytut Organizacji i Zarzadzania. Prace Naukowe. Studia i Materialy (PL ISSN 0324-9468) *216*
Politechnika Wroclawska. Instytut Podstaw Elektrotechniki i Elektrotechnologii. Prace Naukowe. Konferencje (PL ISSN 0324-9441) *357*
Politechnika Wroclawska. Instytut Podstaw Elektrotechniki i Elektrotechnologii. Prace Naukowe. Monografie (PL ISSN 0324-945X) *357*
Politechnika Wroclawska. Instytut Podstaw Elektrotechniki i Elektrotechnologii. Prace Naukowe. Studia i Materialy (PL ISSN 0370-0852) *357*
Politechnika Wroclawska. Instytut Podstaw Elektrotechniki i Elektrotechnologii. Prace Naukowe. Wspolpraca (PL) *357*
Politechnika Wroclawska. Instytut Techniki Cieplnej i Mechaniki Plynow. Prace Naukowe. Konferencje(PL ISSN 0324-9395) *701*
Politechnika Wroclawska. Instytut Techniki Cieplnej i Mechaniki Plynow. Prace Naukowe. Monografie(PL ISSN 0324-9387) *701*
Politechnika Wroclawska. Instytut Techniki Cieplnej i Mechaniki Plynow. Prace Naukowe. Studia i Materialy (PL ISSN 0324-9409) *701*
Politechnika Wroclawska. Instytut Technologii Budowy Maszyn. Prace Naukowe. Konferencje (PL ISSN 0324-9379) *382*
Politechnika Wroclawska. Instytut Technologii Budowy Maszyn. Prace Naukowe. Monografie (PL) *382*

POLITICAL HANDBOOK 1461

Politechnika Wroclawska. Instytut Technologii Budowy Maszyn. Prace Naukowe. Studia i Materialy (PL ISSN 0324-9360) *383*
Politechnika Wroclawska. Instytut Technologii Elektronowej. Prace Naukowe. Konferencje (PL ISSN 0370-0887) *357*
Politechnika Wroclawska. Instytut Technologii Elektronowej. Prace Naukowe. Monografie (PL ISSN 0084-280X) *358*
Politechnika Wroclawska. Instytut Technologii Elektronowej. Prace Naukowe. Studia i Materialy (PL ISSN 0084-2885) *358*
Politechnika Wroclawska. Instytut Technologii Nieorganicznej i Nawozow Mineralnych. Prace Naukowe. Konferencje (PL ISSN 0084-2893) *373*
Politechnika Wroclawska. Instytut Technologii Nieorganicznej i Nawozow Mineralnych. Prace Naukowe. Monografie (PL ISSN 0084-2907) *373*
Politechnika Wroclawska. Instytut Technologii Nierorganicznej i Nawozow Mineralnych. Prace Naukowe. Studia i Materialy (PL ISSN 0084-2915) *373*
Politechnika Wroclawska. Instytut Technologii Organicznej i Tworzyw Sztucznych. Prace Naukowe. Konferencje (PL ISSN 0137-1398) *373*
Politechnika Wroclawska. Instytut Technologii Organicznej i Tworzyw Sztucznych. Prace Naukowe. Monografie (PL ISSN 0370-0879) *373*
Politechnika Wroclawska. Instytut Technologiii Organicznej i Tworzyw Sztucznych. Prace Naukowe. Studia i Materialy (PL ISSN 0370-0879) *707*
Politechnika Wroclawska. Instytut Telekomunikacji i Akustyki. Prace Naukowe. Konferencje (PL ISSN 0324-9344) *269, 358*
Politechnika Wroclawska. Instytut Telekomunikacji i Akustyki. Prace Naukowe. Monografie (PL ISSN 0324-9328) *269, 358*
Politechnika Wroclawska. Instytut Telekomunikacji i Akustyki. Prace Naukowe. Studia i Materialy (PL ISSN 0324-9336) *269, 358*
Politechnika Wroclawska. Instytut Ukladow Elektromaszynowich. Prace Naukowe. Konferencje (PL ISSN 0324-931X) *358*
Politechnika Wroclawska. Instytut Ukladow Elektromaszynowych. Prace Naukowe. Monografie (PL ISSN 0137-6284) *358*
Politechnika Wroclawska. Instytut Ukladow Elektromaszynowych. Prace Naukowe. Przemysl (PL ISSN 0137-6292) *358*
Politechnika Wroclawska. Instytut Ukladow Elektromaszynowych. Prace Naukowe. Studia i Materialy (PL ISSN 0084-294X) *358*
Politechnika Wroclawska. Osrodek Badan Prognostycznych. Prace Naukowe. Konferencje (PL ISSN 0137-6306) *147*
Politechnika Wroclawska. Studium Praktycznej Nauki Jezykow Obcych. Prace Naukowe. Studia i Materialy (PL ISSN 0137-6349) *549*
Politecnica (EC ISSN 0032-3055) *369, 788*
Politeia (VE) *714*
Politekhnichnyi Instytut Kiev. Vestnik. Seriya Mashinostroeniya (UR) *583*
Politica (UY ISSN 0079-3027) *714*
Political Documents of the German Democratic Republic (GE) *714*
Political Economy of World-Systems Annuals (US) *192, 714*
Political Economy Series (CN ISSN 0381-1603) *147*
Political Events Annual (II) *714*
Political Handbook and Atlas of the World *see* Political Handbook of the World *714*

Political Handbook of the World (US) 425, 714
Political Issues Bibliography Series *see* California State University, Los Angeles. Center for the Study of Armament and Disarmament. Political Issues Bibliography Series 717
Political Parties of the World (UK) 714
Political Power and Social Theory (US) 714, 815
Political Science Reviewer (US ISSN 0091-3715) 714
Political Science Utilization Directory (US ISSN 0362-4765) 745
Political Studies Association of the United Kingdom. Newsletter (UK ISSN 0144-7440) 714
Political Terrorism (US) 714
Politiek Aktueel (NE) 714
Politik und Waehler (GW) 714
Politikwissenschaftliche Forschung (GW ISSN 0340-9244) 714
Politique de la Science (SZ ISSN 0085-4980) 714
Politique des Sciences, la Recherches et le Developpement au Canada *see* Scientific Policy, Research and Development in Canada 791
Politique et la Planification de l'Enseignement - Autriche *see* Bildungsplanung in Oesterreich 315
Politische Bildung (AU) 350, 714
Polk's World Bank Directory. International Edition (US ISSN 0085-4999) 175
Polling (US) 599, 808
Pollution Control Conference. Proceedings (US) 388
Pollution Control Review *see* Pollution Technology Review 753
Pollution Research Index (UK) 388, 788
Pollution Technology Review (US ISSN 0079-3116) 753
Polonia Typographica Saeculi Sedecimi (PL ISSN 0079-3132) 77, 733
Polonica (PL) 549
Polska Adakemia Nauk. Centrum Badan Naukowych w Wojewodztwie Katowickim. Prace i Studia (PL ISSN 0079-3582) 369, 492
Polska Akademia Nauk. Biblioteka, Krakow. Rocznik (PL ISSN 0079-3140) 534
Polska Akademia Nauk. Centrum Obliczeniowe. Prace *see* Polish Academy of Sciences. Institute of Computer Science. Reports 273
Polska Akademia Nauk. Instytut Geofizyki. Materialy i Prace (PL ISSN 0079-3574) 306
Polska Akademia Nauk. Instytut Geografii i Przestrzennego Zagospodarowania. Prace Geograficzne (PL ISSN 0373-6547) 425
Polska Akademia Nauk. Instytut Geografii. Prace Geograficzne *see* Polska Akademia Nauk. Instytut Geografii i Przestrzennego Zagospodarowania. Prace Geograficzne 425
Polska Akademia Nauk. Instytut Maszyn Przeplywowych. Prace (PL ISSN 0079-3205) 383
Polska Akademia Nauk. Instytut Podstaw Inzynierii Srodowiska. Prace i Studia (PL) 369, 388
Polska Akademia Nauk. Komisja Metalurjaodlewnia. Metalurgia *see* Polska Akademia Nauk. Oddzial w Krakowie. Komisja Metalurgiczno-Odlewnicza. Prace: Metalurgia 629
Polska Akademia Nauk Nauk Technicznych. Prace *see* Polska Akademia Nauk. Oddzial w Krakowie. Komisja Mechaniki Stosowanej. Prace: Mechanika 701
Polska Akademia Nauk. Komitet Gospodarki Wodnej. Prace i Studia (PL ISSN 0079-3477) 753
Polska Akademia Nauk. Komitet Przestrzennego Zagospodarowania Kraju. Biuletyn (PL ISSN 0079-3493) 486

Polska Akademia Nauk. Komitet Przestrzennego Zagospodarowania Kraju. Studia (PL ISSN 0079-3507) 486
Polska Akademia Nauk. Oddzial w Krakowie Komisja Archeologiczna. Prace (PL ISSN 0079-3256) 64
Polska Akademia Nauk. Oddzial w Krakowie. Komisja Ceramiczna. Prace: Ceramika (PL ISSN 0079-3264) 244
Polska Akademia Nauk. Oddzial w Krakowie. Komisja Filologii Klasycznej. Prace (PL ISSN 0079-3272) 549
Polska Akademia Nauk. Oddzial w Krakowie. Komisja Gorniczo-Geodezyjna. Prace: Geodezja (PL ISSN 0079-3299) 425
Polska Akademia Nauk. Oddzial w Krakowie. Komisja Gorniczo-Geodezyjna. Prace: Gornictwo (PL ISSN 0079-3280) 646
Polska Akademia Nauk. Oddzial w Krakowie. Komisja Historycznoliteracka. Prace (PL ISSN 0554-579X) 570
Polska Akademia Nauk. Oddzial w Krakowie. Komisja Historycznoliteracka. Rocznik (PL ISSN 0079-3302) 434, 570
Polska Akademia Nauk. Oddzial w Krakowie. Komisja Jezykoznawstwa. Prace (PL ISSN 0079-3310) 549
Polska Akademia Nauk. Oddzial w Krakowie. Komisja Jezykoznawstwa. Wydawnictwa Zrodlowe (PL ISSN 0079-3329) 549
Polska Akademia Nauk. Oddzial w Krakowie. Komisja Mechaniki Stosowanej. Prace: Mechanika (PL ISSN 0079-3337) 701
Polska Akademia Nauk. Oddzial w Krakowie. Komisja Metalurgiczno-Odlewnicza. Prace: Metalurgia (PL ISSN 0079-3345) 629
Polska Akademia Nauk. Oddzial w Krakowie. Komisja Nauk Ekonomicznych. Prace (PL ISSN 0079-3353) 147
Polska Akademia Nauk. Oddzial w Krakowie. Komisja Nauk Historycznych. Prace (PL ISSN 0079-3388) 459
Polska Akademia Nauk. Oddzial w Krakowie. Komisja Nauk Historycznych. Materialy (PL ISSN 0079-337X) 434
Polska Akademia Nauk. Oddzial w Krakowie. Komisja Nauk Mineralogicznych. Prace Mineralogiczne (PL ISSN 0079-3396) 299
Polska Akademia Nauk. Oddzial w Krakowie. Komisja Nauk Pedagogicznych. Prace (PL ISSN 0079-340X) 321
Polska Akademia Nauk. Oddzial w Krakowie. Komisja Nauk Pedagogicznych. Rocznik (PL ISSN 0079-3418) 321
Polska Akademia Nauk. Oddzial w Krakowie. Komisja Naukowych. Sprawozdania z Posiedzen (PL ISSN 0079-354X) 789, 799
Polska Akademia Nauk. Oddzial w Krakowie. Komisja Orientalistyczna. Prace (PL ISSN 0079-3426) 671
Polska Akademia Nauk. Oddzial w Krakowie. Komisja Slowianoznawstwa. Prace (PL ISSN 0079-3434) 570
Polska Akademia Nauk. Oddzial w Krakowie. Komisja Socjologiczna. Prace (PL ISSN 0079-3442) 815
Polska Akademia Nauk. Oddzial w Krakowie. Komisja Urbanistyki i Architektury. Teka (PL ISSN 0079-3450) 70, 486
Polska Akademia Nauk. Oddzial w Krakowie. Osrodek Dokumentacji Fizjograficznej. Studia (PL ISSN 0137-2939) 425
Polska Akademia Nauk. Oddzial w Krakowie. Rocznik (PL ISSN 0079-3531) 492
Polska Akademia Nauk. Wydzial Nauk Medycznych. Rozprawy (PL ISSN 0079-3558) 599

Polska Akademia Nauk. Zaklad Archeologii Srodziemnomorskiej. Etudes et Travaux (PL ISSN 0079-3566) 64
Polska Akademia Nauk. Zaklad Archeologii Srodziemnomorskiej. Prace *see* Polska Akademia Nauk. Zaklad Archeologii Srodziemnomorskiej. Etudes et Travaux 64
Polska Akademia Nauk. Zaklad Badan Naukowych Gornoslaskiego Okregu Przemyslowego. Prace i Studia *see* Polska Adakemia Nauk. Centrum Badan Naukowych w Wojewodztwie Katowickim. Prace i Studia 492
Polska Bibliografia Literacka (PL ISSN 0079-3590) 578
Polska Klasa Robotnicza. Studia Historyczna (PL) 459
Polska Piesn i Muzyka Ludowa. Zrodla i Materialy (PL ISSN 0079-3612) 662
Polska w Europie (FR) 913
Polska 2000 (PL ISSN 0079-3620) 459, 815
Polski Zwiazek Krotkofalowcow. Biuletyn (PL) 268
Polskie Archiwum Weterynaryjne (PL ISSN 0079-3647) 895
Polskie Towarzystwo Botaniczne. Sekcja Dendrologiczna. Rocznik (PL ISSN 0080-357X) 117
Polskie Towarzystwo Cybernetyczne. Biuletyn *see* Postepy Cybernetyki 273
Polskie Towarzystwo Geologiczne. Rocznik/Societe Geologique de Pologne. Annales (PL ISSN 0079-3663) 299
Polskie Towarzystwo Jezykoznawcze. Biuletyn (PL ISSN 0032-3802) 549
Polskie Towarzystwo Matematyczne. Roczniki. Seria I: Commentationes Mathematicae. Prace Matematyczne (PL ISSN 0079-368X) 588
Polskie Towarzystwo Naukowe na Obczyznie. Rocznik (UK ISSN 0079-371X) 492, 789
Polutehniline Instituut Tallinn. Matematika i Teoreticheskaya Mekhanika (UR) 588, 701
Polymer Engineering and Technology Series (US ISSN 0079-3728) 373
Polymer Journal *see* Plastichem 373
Polymer Monographs (US) 253
Polymer Physics (US) 698
Polymer Reviews (US ISSN 0079-3736) 253
Polymer Science Library (NE) 247
Polymers Paint and Colour Year Book (UK ISSN 0078-7817) 77, 673
Polymers-Properties and Applications (US) 707
Polytekniske Laereanstalt, Danmarks Tekniske Hoejskole. Afdelingen for Baerende Konstruktioner. Rapport R (DK ISSN 0105-922X) 380
Polytekniske Laereanstalt, Danmarks Tekniske Hoejskole. Laboratoriet for Elektronik. Beretning (DK) 358
Pomarania Antiqua (PL ISSN 0556-0691) 459
Pomorskie Monografie Toponomastyczne (PL) 425
Pondicherry Industrial Promotion, Development and Investment Corporation. Annual Reports and Accounts (II) 182, 204
Pontifical Institute of Mediaeval Studies. Studies and Texts (CN ISSN 0082-5328) 459
Pontificia Universidad Catolica. Revista(PE) 799
Pontificia Universidad Catolica. Taller de Estudios Urbano Industriales. Serie: Estudios Sindicales (PE) 507
Pontificia Universidad Catolica del Ecuador. Revista (EC) 263
Pontificia Universidad Catolica del Peru. Departamento de Ciencias Sociales. Serie: Ediciones Previas (PE) 799
Pontificia Universita Gregoriana. Documenta Missionalia (VC) 775
Pontificia Universita Gregoriana. Istituto di Scienze Sociali Studia Socialia. (VC ISSN 0080-3960) 799

Pontificia Universita Gregoriana. Miscellanea Historiae Pontificiae (VC ISSN 0080-3979) 775
Pontificia Universita Gregoriana. Studia Missionalia (VC ISSN 0080-3987) 775
Pontifico Museo Missionario Etnologico. Annali (VC) 52
Pony Baseball. Blue Book (US) 825
Pool & Spa News Directory (US) 241
Pool News Directory *see* Pool & Spa News Directory 241
Poompuhar Shipping Corporation. Annual Report (II) 880
Poor Joe's Pennsylvania Almanac (US ISSN 0362-8523) 361
Poor Richard's Record (US ISSN 0361-9419) 339
Poor's Register of Corporations, Directors and Executives (US ISSN 0079-3825) 216, 224
Popes through History (US ISSN 0079-3833) 913
Populacni Zpravy (CS) 570
Populaire Literatuur (NE) 570
Popular Culture Bio-Bibliographies (US ISSN 0193-6891) 471
Popular Lectures in Mathematics Series(US ISSN 0079-3841) 588
Popular Mechanics Do-It-Yourself Yearbook (US ISSN 0360-2273) 701
Popular Music Periodicals Index (US ISSN 0095-4101) 662
Popular Music Record Reviews *see* Annual Index to Popular Music Record Reviews 818
Popular Science Series *see* Illinois. State Museum. Popular Science Series 783
Population. Perspective *see* American Universities Field Staff. Population: Perspective 725
Population: an International Directory of Organizations and Information Resources (US) 729
Population and Family Planning Programs (US) 132, 729
Population and Occupied Dwelling Units in Southeast Michigan (US ISSN 0362-5079) 486
Population and the Population Explosion: a Bibliography (US ISSN 0091-2263) 913
Population Census of Papua New Guinea. Population Characteristics Bulletin Series (PP ISSN 0079-3868) 729
Population Education in Asia Newsletter (UN) 321
Population Estimates by Marital Status, Age & Sex, Canada and Provinces/Estimations de la Population Suivant l'Etat Matrimonial, l'Age et le Sexe, Canada et Provinces *see* Canada. Statistics Canada. Estimation of Population by Marital Status, Age and Sex, Canada and Provinces/Estimations de la Population Suivant l'Etat Matrimonial, l'Age et le Sexe, Canada et Provinces b 73lo
Population Estimates of Arizona (US ISSN 0079-3906) 729
Population Growth in Seychelles (SE) 732, 845
Population Growth of Iran (IR) 729, 845
Population Mobility in Hawaii (US ISSN 0094-0348) 729
Population Newsletter (TH) 729
Population of the Municipalities of the Netherlands (NE ISSN 0079-3930) 729
Population Profile *see* P R B Report 912
Population Profiles (US) 729
Population Reference Bureau, Inc. Report *see* P R B Report 912
Population Studies (UN ISSN 0082-805X) 729
Pork Roundup (US) 45
Port(Year) *see* Barcelona Port 877
Port and Harbour Technical Research Institute. Guide/Kowan Gijutsu Kenkyusho. Guide (JA) 376, 880
Port Authority of New York & New Jersey. Aviation Department. Airport Statistics (US) 869
Port Bustamante Handbook (JM) 880

Port of Baltimore Handbook (US ISSN 0079-3981) *880*
Port of Bristol. Handbook (UK) *880*
Port of Kingston Handbook *see* Port Bustamante Handbook *880*
Port of New Orleans Annual Directory (US ISSN 0085-5030) *863*
Port of Osaka/Osakako (JA) *880*
Port of Piraeus Authority. Annual Report (GR) *880*
Port of Piraeus Authority. Statistical Bulletin *see* Port of Piraeus Authority. Statistical Report *880*
Port of Piraeus Authority. Statistical Report (GR) *880*
Port of Tokyo (JA) *880*
Port of Yokohama. Annual Report (JA) *880*
Port Transport Statistics of India *see* Basic Port Statistics of India *877*
Portefeuille (ZR) *189*
Portico (IT) *570*
Portland and the Pacific Northwest (US) *890*
Ports Annual (CN) *880*
Ports of New South Wales Journal (AT) *880*
Ports of South Africa (SA) *880*
Ports of the World (UK ISSN 0079-4066) *880*
Portsmouth Papers (UK ISSN 0554-7598) *459*
Portugal. Comissao da Condicao Feminina. Coleccao Informar as Mulheres (PO) *900*
Portugal. Estatisticas Industriais: Continente e Ilhas Adjacentes (PO) *163*
Portugal. Instituto Nacional de Estatistica. Anuario Demografico. *see* Portugal. Instituto Nacional de Estatistica. Estatisticas Demograficas *729*
Portugal. Instituto Nacional de Estatistica. Anuario Estatistico (PO ISSN 0079-4112) *845*
Portugal. Instituto Nacional de Estatistica. Centro de Estudos Demograficos. Caderno (PO) *729*
Portugal. Instituto Nacional de Estatistica. Centro de Estudos Demograficos. Revista (PO ISSN 0079-4082) *729*
Portugal. Instituto Nacional de Estatistica. Estatistica Industrial *see* Portugal. Estatisticas Industriais: Continente e Ilhas Adjacentes *163*
Portugal. Instituto Nacional de Estatistica. Estatisticas Agricolas (PO ISSN 0079-4139) *19*
Portugal. Instituto Nacional de Estatistica. Estatisticas da Pesca/Statistiques de la Peche (PO) *399*
Portugal. Instituto Nacional de Estatistica. Estatisticas das Financas Publicas (PO ISSN 0079-4171) *163*
Portugal. Instituto Nacional de Estatistica. Estatisticas das Organizacoes Sindicais (PO ISSN 0079-4163) *815*
Portugal. Instituto Nacional de Estatistica. Estatisticas de Educacao (PO ISSN 0079-4155) *321*
Portugal. Instituto Nacional de Estatistica. Estatisticas Demograficas (PO) *729*
Portugal. Instituto Nacional de Estatistica. Estatisticas do Comercio Externo (PO ISSN 0079-4147) *163*
Portugal. Instituto Nacional de Estatistica. Estatisticas do Turismo (PO) *890*
Portugal. Instituto Nacional de Estatistica. Estatisticas das Contribucoes e Impostos (PO ISSN 0079-4120) *163*
Portugal. Instituto Nacional de Estatistica. Indicadores Economics-Sociais/Social-Economic Indicators (PO) *815*
Portugal. Instituto Nacional de Estatistica. Serie Estatisticas Regionais (PO) *845*
Portugal. Instituto Nacional de Estatistica. Servicos Centrais. Estatisticas dos Sociedades: Continente e Ilhas Adjacentes (PO) *225, 845*

Portugal. Instituto Nacional de Estatistica. Servicos Centrais. Estatisticas dos Transportes e Communicacoes: Continente, Acores e Madeira (PO) *265, 845, 863*
Portugal. Instituto Nacional de Estatistica. Servicos Centrais. Recenseamento da Habitacao: Continente e Ilhas Adjacentes (PO) *486*
Portugal. Instituto Nacional de Estatistica. Servicos Centrais. Sinopse de Dados Estatisticos: Continente e Ilhas Adjacentes *see* Portugal (Year) *845*
Portugal. Instituto Nacional de Meteorologia e Geofisica. Revista (PO) 306, *634*
Portugal. Ministerio da Habitacao e Obras Publicas. Comissao Nacional do Ambiente. Relatorio de Actividades (PO) *388*
Portugal. Ministerio da Justicia. Boletin (PO) *516*
Portugal. Ministerio das Corporacoes e Previdencia Social. Gabinete de Planeamento. Inguerito Emprego (PO) *220*
Portugal. Ministerio das Financas. Relatorio do Orcamento Geral do Estado (PO ISSN 0079-4201) *231*
Portugal. Ministerio do Equipamento Social e do Ambiente. Comissao Nacional do Ambiente. Relatorio de Actividades *see* Portugal. Ministerio da Habitacao e Obras Publicas. Comissao Nacional do Ambiente. Relatorio de Actividades *388*
Portugal. Ministerio do Plano e da Coordenacao Economica. Departamento Central de Planeamento. Plano (PO) *189*
Portugal. Ministerio do Trabalho. Servico de Estatisticas. Estatisticas do Trabalho (PO) *163*
Portugal. Ministerio do Trabalho. Servico de Informacao Cientifica e Tecnica. Boletim do Trabalho e Emprego (PO) *210*
Portugal. Ministerio do Ultramar. Relatorio das Actividades (PO) *745*
Portugal (Year) (PO) *845*
Portugaliae Acta Biologica (PO ISSN 0032-5147) *106*
Portugiesische Forschungen der Goerresgesellschaft. Reihe 1: Aufsaetze zur Portugiesischen Kulturgeschichte (GW ISSN 0079-421X) *459*
Portugiesische Forschungen der Goerresgesellschaft. Reihe 2: Monographien (GW ISSN 0079-4228) *459*
Portuguese-American Business Review/Directory (US) *241*
Portuguese Economic Situation from an External Relationship Point of View (PO) *189*
Post Library Association Report *see* P L A Report *534*
Post Magazine Almanack. Insurance Directory *see* Insurance Directory and Year Book *499*
Post-Medieval Archaeology (UK ISSN 0079-4236) *64*
Postage Stamps of the United States (US ISSN 0079-4244) *479*
Postbuechl (AU) 231, *266*
Postepy Cybernetyki (PL ISSN 0137-3595) 273, *588*
Postepy Napedu Elektrycznego (PL ISSN 0079-4260) *358*
Postepy Pediatrii (PL ISSN 0079-4279) *618*
Postgraduate Radiology (US ISSN 0273-0278) *622*
Postilla (US ISSN 0079-4295) *789*
Postsecondary Education in California: Information Digest (US) *339*
Potato *see* Ziemniak *40*
Potato Marketing Board, London. Annual Report and Accounts (UK ISSN 0079-4309) 30, *38*
Potchefstroom University for Christian Higher Education. Wetenskaplike Bydraes. Reeks A: Geesteswetenskappe (SA ISSN 0079-4333) *492*

Potchefstroom University for Christian Higher Education. Wetenskaplike Bydraes. Reeks B: Natuurwetenskappe. Series (SA ISSN 0079-4341) *789*
Potchefstroom University for Christian Higher Education. Wetenskaplike Bydraes. Reeks H: Inougurele Redes (SA) *339*
Potentially Reactive Carbonate Rocks *see* Potentially Reactive Carbonate Rocks; Progress Report *376*
Potentially Reactive Carbonate Rocks; Progress Report (US ISSN 0091-0813) *376*
Potentials in Marketing (US ISSN 0032-5619) *219*
Potomac Issues (US) *897*
Potomac Report (US) *897*
Potomac River Basin Water Quality Reports (US) 388, *897*
Potomac River Water Quality Network *see* Potomac River Basin Water Quality Reports *897*
Pottery Quarterly (UK ISSN 0032-5678) *244*
Poultry Health and Management Short Course. Proceedings (US ISSN 0069-4630) *45*
Poultry Market Review (CN ISSN 0032-5775) *46*
Poultry Market Statistics (US ISSN 0565-1980) 25, 46, 845
Poultry Roundup (US) *46*
Poultry Science Symposium. Proceedings (UK) *46*
Poverty in South Dakota (US ISSN 0091-0724) *808*
Powder Coating Conference (US ISSN 0092-0479) *369*
Powder Diffraction File Search Manual. Alphabetical Listing. Inorganic (US ISSN 0092-0509) 249, *251*
Powder Diffraction File Search Manual. Fink Method. Inorganic (US ISSN 0092-1300) 249, *251*
Powder Diffraction File Search Manual. Hanawalt Method. Inorganic (US ISSN 0092-1319) 249, *251*
Powder Diffraction File Search Manual. Organic (US ISSN 0092-0576) *253*
Power Conditioning Specialists Conference. Record *see* I E E E Power Electronics Specialists Conference. Record *8*
Power Farming Technical Annual (AT ISSN 0079-4422) *32*
Power Industry Computer Applications Conference. Record (US ISSN 0079-4430) 273, *358*
Power Sources Symposium. Proceedings (US ISSN 0079-4457) *358*
Power Statistics Journal of Nepal (NP) *358*
Power Systems Computation Conference. P S C C Proceedings (SW) *369*
Power Transmission & Bearing Handbook *see* Power Transmission Design Handbook *358*
Power Transmission Design Handbook (US) *358*
Power's Electric Utility Generation Planbook *see* Electric Utility Generation Planbook *353*
Power's Energy Management Guidebook (US) *363*
Powstanie Styczniowe. Materialy i Dokumenty (PL ISSN 0079-4465) *459*
Powys Newsletter (US) *570*
Poznanskie Towarzystwo Przyjaciol Nauk. Komisja Archeologiczna. Prace (PL) *64*
Poznanskie Towarzystwo Przyjaciol Nauk. Komisja Automatyki. Prace *see* Studia z Automatyki *274*
Poznanskie Towarzystwo Przyjaciol Nauk. Komisja Biologiczna. Prace (PL ISSN 0079-4619) *106*
Poznanskie Towarzystwo Przyjaciol Nauk. Komisja Budownictwa i Architektury. Prace (PL ISSN 0079-4597) 70, *138*
Poznanskie Towarzystwo Przyjaciol Nauk. Komisja Elektrotechniki. Prace (PL ISSN 0079-4627) *358*

Poznanskie Towarzystwo Przyjaciol Nauk. Komisja Filozoficzna. Prace (PL ISSN 0079-4635) *690*
Poznanskie Towarzystwo Przyjaciol Nauk. Komisja Geograficzno-Geologiczna. Prace (PL ISSN 0079-4643) 299, *425*
Poznanskie Towarzystwo Przyjaciol Nauk. Komisja Historii Sztuki. Prace (PL ISSN 0079-466X) *77*
Poznanskie Towarzystwo Przyjaciol Nauk. Komisja Historyczna. Prace (PL ISSN 0079-4651) *459*
Poznanskie Towarzystwo Przyjaciol Nauk. Komisja Jezykoznawcza. Prace (PL ISSN 0079-4678) *549*
Poznanskie Towarzystwo Przyjaciol Nauk. Komisja Matematyczno-Przyrodnicza. Prace (PL ISSN 0079-4686) *588*
Poznanskie Towarzystwo Przyjaciol Nauk. Komisja Nauk Rolniczych i Komisja Nauk Lesnych. Prace (PL ISSN 0079-4708) 19, *410*
Poznanskie Towarzystwo Przyjaciol Nauk. Komisja Nauk Spolecznych. Prace (PL ISSN 0079-4716) *799*
Poznanskie Towarzystwo Przyjaciol Nauk. Komisja Technologii Drewna. Prace (PL ISSN 0079-4724) *413*
Prace Archiwum Slaskie Kultury Muzycznej (PL) *662*
Prace Astronomickeho Observatoria na Skalnatom Plese/Activities of the Astronomical Observatory on Skalnate Pleso (CS) *83*
Prace Etnologiczne (PL) *52*
Prace Geologiczne (PL ISSN 0079-3361) *299*
Prace i Materialy Etnograficzne (PL ISSN 0079-4759) *52*
Prace Jezykoznawcze (PL ISSN 0079-3485) *549*
Prace Literackie (PL ISSN 0079-4767) *570*
Prace Onomastyczne (PL ISSN 0079-4775) *549*
Prace Orientalistyczne (PL ISSN 0079-4783) *671*
Prace Polonistyczne (PL ISSN 0079-4791) *571*
Prace Popularnonaukowe (PL ISSN 0079-4805) *789*
Practical Camper's Sites Guide (UK) *831*
Practical Forms and Precedents (New South Wales) (AT ISSN 0048-508X) *516*
Practical Guide to Individual Income Tax Return Preparation *see* 1040 Preparation *234*
Practical Guide to the Use of the European Communities' Scheme of Generalized Tariff Preferences (EI) *197*
Practical Information Science *see* Vade-Mecum for Information Scientists *538*
Practical Methods in Electron Microscopy (NE) *124*
Practical Nursing Career (US) *614*
Practical Table Series (US ISSN 0079-4821) *588*
Practical Welder (AT ISSN 0085-5065) *631*
Practices of the Wind (US ISSN 0196-822X) *581*
Praehistorische Forschungen (AU ISSN 0032-6534) *52*
Praehistorische Zeitschrift (GW ISSN 0079-4848) *64*
Prairie Provinces Water Board Annual Report (CN) *897*
Prairie Scout (US ISSN 0092-8313) *471*
Prajnan (II ISSN 0032-6690) 321, 789, *852*
Prakit Jain Institute Research Publication Series (II ISSN 0554-9906) *771*
Prakrit Text Society. Publications (II) 549, *571*
Prakshepana (BG) *650*
Praktische Betriebswirtschaft (SZ ISSN 0079-4880) *216*
Praktische Chirurgie (GW ISSN 0079-4899) *625*
Pram and Nursery Trader Year Book *see* Toy Trader Year Book *429*

Prameny Ceske a Slovenske Lingvistiky. Rada Ceska (CS ISSN 0079-4902) 549
Pravnehistoricke Studie (CS ISSN 0079-4929) 516
Pravoslavny Theologicky Sbornik (CS ISSN 0079-4937) 767
Prawo (PL) 516
Praxis der Kinderpsychologie und Kinderpsychiatrie. Beihefte (GW ISSN 0085-5073) 620, 737
Praxis der Klinischen Psychologie (GW ISSN 0079-4945) 737
Praxis der Sozialpsychologie (GW ISSN 0340-2150) 737
Pre-Law Handbook. Official Law School Guide (US ISSN 0075-8264) 516
Precinct Returns for Major Elections in South Dakota (US ISSN 0085-5081) 714
Precos Pagos Pelos Agricultores (BL ISSN 0302-5195) 30
Precos Recebidos Pelos Agricultores (BL ISSN 0100-5219) 30
Predicasts. Source Directory (US ISSN 0092-7767) 163
Predicasts Basebook see Basebook 221
Predicasts F & S Index United States (US) 3, 163
Prediction Annual (UK ISSN 0079-4953) 676
Pregled Sudske Prakse (YU) 516
Prehistoric Archaeology and Ecology (US) 64, 106
Prehistoric Society, London. Proceedings (UK ISSN 0079-497X) 64
Prent 190 (NE ISSN 0032-7476) 78, 733
Preparation and Properties of Solid State Materials (US ISSN 0081-1939) 255
Prepared Papers - University of Florida Growth Conference see University of Florida. Growth Conference. Prepared Papers 488
Presbyterian Church in Canada. General Assembly. Acts and Proceedings (CN ISSN 0079-4996) 767
Prescription Drug Industry Fact Book (US) 685
Presenca Filosofica (BL) 690
Presence de Gabriel Marcel. Cahier (FR) 690
Presencia Universitaria (HO) 339
President's National Urban Policy Report (US ISSN 0163-8602) 486
Presidio (US) 283, 571
Press Braille, Adult (US ISSN 0079-502X) 94, 133, 328
Press Directory of Australia and New Zealand see Press Radio and T.V. Guide 505
Press in India (II ISSN 0445-6653) 94
Press Radio and T.V. Guide (AT ISSN 0079-5046) 268, 505
Pressure Gauge (US ISSN 0079-5054) 373
Preventive Law Newsletter (US ISSN 0555-0963) 516
Preview/Engineering (US) 219, 369
Previews Guide to the World's Fine Real Estate (US) 762
Prevision a Un An de l'Economie see Economie Francaise en Perspectives Sectorielles: Industries de Biens Intermediaires 185
Prevision a Un An de l'Economie Francaise. see Economie Francaise en Donnes d'Encadrement 185
Prevision a Un An de l'Economie Francaise see Economie Francaise en Perspectives Sectorielles: Filiere Batiment, Genie Civil, Materiaux de Construction 136
Prevision a Un An de l'Economie Francaise see Economie Francaise en Perspectives Sectorielles: Industries de Biens de Consommation 185
Prevision a Un An de la Filiere Construction see Economie Francaise en Perspectives Sectorielles: Filiere Batiment, Genie Civil, Materiaux de Construction 136

Prevision a Un de l'Economie Francaise see Economie Francaise en Perspectives Sectorielles: Industries de Biens d'Equipement 185
Prevision Glissante a Cinq Ans see Previsions Glissantes Detaillees 1979-1984 147
Previsions Glissantes Detaillees 1979-1984 (FR) 147
Previson a Moyen Terme de l'Economie Francaise. see Previsions Glissantes Detaillees 1979-1984 147
Priamur'e Moe (UR) 571
Prices and Earnings Around the Globe (SZ) 213
Priesterjahrheft (GW) 775
Prikladnaya Geofizika (UR) 306
Prikladnaya Mekhanika i Priborostroenie (UR) 701
Primate Report (GW ISSN 0343-3528) 53
Primates (US ISSN 0079-5100) 130
Primates in Medicine (SZ ISSN 0079-5119) 612
Primatologia (SZ ISSN 0079-5127) 612
Primavera (US ISSN 0364-7609) 571, 901
Primer for Herb Growing (US) 416
Primo (NE) 258
Prince Edward. Department of Community Services. Annual Report see Prince Edward Island. Department of Municipal Affairs. Annual Report 748
Prince Edward Island. Civil Service Commission. Annual Report (CN) 714
Prince Edward Island. Department of Development. Annual Report (CN) 745
Prince Edward Island. Department of Fisheries. Annual Report (CN ISSN 0079-5143) 399
Prince Edward Island. Department of Health. Annual Report (CN ISSN 0317-4530) 753
Prince Edward Island. Department of Industry and Commerce. Annual Report (CN) 745
Prince Edward Island. Department of Labour. Annual Report (CN ISSN 0085-512X) 210
Prince Edward Island. Department of Municipal Affairs. Annual Report (CN ISSN 0706-4403) 748
Prince Edward Island. Department of the Environment and Tourism. Annual Report see Prince Edward Island. Department of Tourism, Parks and Conservation. Annual Report 890
Prince Edward Island. Department of the Environment. Annual Report (CN ISSN 0085-5138) 388, 745
Prince Edward Island. Department of Tourism, Parks and Conservation. Annual Report (CN) 890
Prince Edward Island. Economics, Marketing & Statistics Branch. Agricultural Statistics (CN) 19
Prince Edward Island. Land Development Corporation. Annual Report (CN) 762
Prince Edward Island. Public Utilities Commission. Annual Report (CN ISSN 0079-5151) 745
Prince Edward Island Community Studies see P. E. I. Community Studies 815
Prince Edward Island Water Authority. Annual Report see Prince Edward Island. Department of the Environment. Annual Report 388
Princess Takamatsu Cancer Research Symposia (US) 606
Princeton-Cambridge Series in Chinese Linguistics (UK) 549
Princeton-Cambridge Studies in Chinese Linguistics see Princeton-Cambridge Series in Chinese Linguistics 549
Princeton Conference on Cerebrovascular Diseases (US ISSN 0146-6917) 607
Princeton Essays in Literature. (US ISSN 0079-5186) 571
Princeton Essays on the Arts (US) 78, 492

Princeton Mathematical Series (US ISSN 0079-5194) 588
Princeton Monographs in Art and Archaeology (US ISSN 0079-5208) 64, 78
Princeton Series in Physics (US ISSN 0079-5216) 698
Princeton Series of Contemporary Poets(US) 581
Princeton Studies in Mathematical Economics (US ISSN 0079-5240) 147, 588
Princeton Studies in Music (US ISSN 0079-5259) 662
Princeton University. Center of International Studies Policy Memorandum (US ISSN 0079-5267) 524, 723
Princeton University. Center of International Studies. Research Monograph Series (US ISSN 0555-1501) 523, 723
Princeton University. Center of International Studies. World Order Studies Program: Occasional Paper (US) 723
Princeton University. Computer Sciences Laboratory. Technical Report (US ISSN 0079-5283) 273
Princeton University. Econometric Research Program. Research Memorandum (US ISSN 0079-5291) 147
Princeton University. Industrial Relations Section. Research Report (US ISSN 0079-5305) 210
Principal International Businesses (US) 197, 219
Principales Industries Installees en Cote d'Ivoire (IV) 225
Principales Industries Ivoiriennes see Principales Industries Installees en Cote d'Ivoire 225
Principality of Liechtenstein: a Documentary Handbook (LH ISSN 0048-5306) 459
Principaux Mecanismes de Distribution de Credit (FR) 175
Principles and Techniques of Human Research and Therapeutics (US ISSN 0094-9264) 913
Prindle, Weber and Schmidt Complementary Series in Mathematics (US ISSN 0079-5313) 588
Printed in Tanzania see Tanzania National Bibliography 95
Printing Historical Society. Journal (UK ISSN 0079-5321) 733
Printing Industries Annual (UK ISSN 0308-1443) 733
Printing Magazine Purchasing Guide (US ISSN 0079-533X) 913
Printing Trades Blue Book. Delaware Valley-Ohio Edition (US ISSN 0193-3949) 733
Printing Trades Blue Book. New York Edition (US ISSN 0079-5348) 733
Printing Trades Blue Book. Northeastern Edition (US ISSN 0079-5356) 733
Printing Trades Blue Book. Southeastern Edition (US ISSN 0079-5364) 733
Printing Trades Directory (UK ISSN 0079-5372) 733
Printout see Young Women's Christian Association of the United States of America. The Printout 768
Prirodnjacki Muzej u Beogradu. Glasnik. Serija A: Mineralogija, Geologija, Paleontologija (YU ISSN 0367-4983) 299, 674
Prirodnjacki Muzej u Beogradu. Glasnik. Serija B: Bioloske Nauke (YU ISSN 0373-2134) 106
Prirodnjacki Muzej u Beogradu. Glasnik. Serija C: Sumarstvo i Lov (YU) 410, 831
Prirodnyi Gaz Sibiri (UR) 681
Priser och Konkurrens see Hinnat ja Kilpailu 182
Prisoners Yellow Pages (US) 283
Prisons see South Africa. Prisons Department. Report of the Commissioner of Prisons/Verslag van die Kommissaris van Gevangenisse 284

Private Campgrounds & RV Parks Buying Guide (US) 831
Private Country Club Guest Policy Directory (US) 825
Private Higher Education (US ISSN 0364-3735) 339
Private Independent Schools (US ISSN 0079-5399) 332
Private Investors Abroad (US ISSN 0090-9742) 204, 524
Private Island "Inventory" (US) 762
Private Post (UK ISSN 0140-8003) 479
Private Press Books (UK ISSN 0079-5402) 94
Privates Bausparwesen (GW ISSN 0085-5154) 138
Prix de la Revue Etudes Francaises (CN) 571
Prix Nobel. Nobel Prizes (NE) 492
Prize Stories; The O. Henry Awards (US ISSN 0079-5453) 571
Pro and Amateur Hockey Guide (US ISSN 0079-550X) 821
Pro Basketball Guide see Basketball Guide 823
Pro Football (US ISSN 0079-5526) 825
Pro Football (US ISSN 0079-5534) 825
Pro Football see Street and Smith's Official Yearbook: Pro Football 826
Pro Hockey Guide (US ISSN 0079-5577) 822
Pro Senior Hockey Guide see Pro and Amateur Hockey Guide 821
Pro Soccer Guide (US) 825
Probability and Mathematical Statistics (US ISSN 0079-5607) 588
Probable Levels of R & D Expenditures: Forecast and Analysis (US) 789, 852
Probas see Bass World 657
Probation and Parole (US ISSN 0079-5615) 283
Probe see Environment Probe 385
Probe (AT ISSN 0079-5631) 610
Probe (Santa Barbara) (US ISSN 0032-9177) 719
Probitas (II) 571
Problem Books in Mathematics (US) 588
Problemas del Mundo Contemporaneo see Problems of the Contemporary World 799
Problemata (GW) 492, 690
Probleme de Pedagogie Contemporana (RM) 321
Probleme der Festkoerperelektronik (GE ISSN 0079-564X) 358
Probleme Grenznaher Raeume (AU) 486
Problemes Actuels d'Endocrinologie et de Nutrition (FR ISSN 0079-5666) 611, 666
Problemes d'Histoire du Christianism (BE) 775
Problemes du Monde Contemporain see Problems of the Contemporary World 799
Problemi e Ricerche di Storia Antica (IT ISSN 0079-5682) 459
Problemi na Tekhnicheskata Kibernetika (BU) 273
Problems and Progress in Development (US) 201
Problems in a Business Society (US) 147, 815
Problems in American Civilization (US) 471, 492
Problems in Ancient History (US) 434
Problems in European Civilization (US) 459, 492
Problems in European History (US) 459
Problems in Mathematical Analysis Report (US ISSN 0079-5739) 588
Problems in Private International Law (NE) 524
Problems of American Society (US) 799
Problems of Diffraction and Spreading of Waves see Problemy Difraktsii i Rasprostraneniia Voln 706
Problems of Human Reproduction: A Wiley Biomedical Series (US) 126

Problems of Industrial Medicine in Ophthalmology *see* Arbeitsmedizinische Fragen in der Ophthalmologie *904*
Problems of Journalism (US) *505*
Problems of National Liberation (II) *714*
Problems of the Baltic (SW ISSN 0552-2005) *714*
Problems of the Contemporary World/ Problemes du Monde Contemporain/ Problemas del Mundo Contemporaneo (UR ISSN 0079-5763) *434, 799*
Problems of the Far East *see* U S S R Report: Problems of the Far East *724*
Problems of the Modern Economy Series (US) *147*
Problems of the North (CN ISSN 0079-5771) *425*
Problems of Transportation in Japan (JA) *863*
Problemy Arkheologii i Etnografii (UR) *64*

Problemy Biologie Krajiny/Questiones Geobiologicae (CS) *106*

Problemy Bioniki (UR) *106*

Problemy Difraktsii i Rasprostraneniia Voln/Problems of Diffraction and Spreading of Waves (UR) *706*
Problemy Fiziki Atmosfery (UR) *634, 698*
Problemy Handlu Zagranicznego (PL) *197*
Problemy Istorii Matematiki i Mekhaniki (UR) *588, 701*
Problemy Mashinostroeniya (UR) *583*
Problemy Poles'ya (UR) *897*
Problemy Polonii Zagranicznej (PL ISSN 0079-5798) *434, 714*
Problemy Rad Narodowych. Studia i Materialy (PL ISSN 0079-5801) *745*
Problemy Rejonow Uprzemyslawianych (PL ISSN 0079-581X) *225*
Procedures in Computer Sciences (US ISSN 0095-1951) *273*
Proceedings. Annual A.A.Z.P.A. Conference *see* American Association of Zoological Parks and Aquariums. Proceedings. Annual A A Z P A Conference *127*
Proceedings. Annual Meeting - Transportation Research Forum *see* Transportation Research Forum. Proceedings: Annual Meeting *864*
Proceedings. Annual Symposium. Incremental Motion Control Systems and Devices *see* Symposium on Incremental Motion Control Systems and Devices. Proceedings *583*
Proceedings, A W W A Annual Conference *see* American Water Works Association. Proceedings, A W W A Annual Conference *895*
Proceedings - Committee on Computer Technology *see* American Association of State Highway and Transportation Officials. Sub-Committee on Computer Technology. Proceedings. National Conference *270*
Proceedings - Compliance and Legal Seminar *see* Compliance and Legal Seminar. Proceedings *202*
Proceedings - Conference on Ground Water *see* Conference on Ground Water. Proceedings *307*
Proceedings - International Symposium on Fault-Tolerant Computing *see* International Symposium on Fault-Tolerant Computing. Proceedings *272*
Proceedings of Annual Meeting - American Association of Veterinary Laboratory Diagnosticians *see* American Association of Veterinary Laboratory Diagnosticians. Proceedings of Annual Meeting *894*
Proceedings of Pacem in Maribus (MM) *312*
Proceedings of Sugar Beet Research *see* Bulletin of Sugar Beet Research. Supplement *33*

Proceedings of the Annual Meeting of the Western Society for French History *see* Western Society for French History. Proceedings of the Annual Meeting *465*
Proceedings of the Annual Southeastern Symposium on System Theory *see* Southeastern Symposium on System Theory. Proceedings *273*
Proceedings of the Cajal Club *see* Cajal Club. Proceedings *619*
Proceedings of the National Conference on Power Transmission *see* National Conference on Power Transmission. Proceedings *356*
Proceedings of the National/ International Sculpture Conference *see* National/International Sculpture Conference. Proceedings *77*
Proceedings of the Northeast Pacific Pink Salmon Workshop *see* Northeast Pacific Pink and Chum Salmon Workshop. Proceedings *399*
Proceedings of the San Diego Biomedical Symposium *see* San Diego Biomedical Symposium. Proceedings *599*
Proceedings of the South Carolina Historical Association *see* South Carolina Historical Association. Proceedings *472*
Proceedings of the Southwest Regional Conference for Astronomy and Astrophysics *see* Southwest Regional Conference for Astronomy and Astrophysics. Proceedings *84*
Proceedings of the Special Convention of the National Collegiate Athletic Association *see* National Collegiate Athletic Association. Proceedings of the Special Convention *821*
Proceedings - Southern Weed Science Society *see* Southern Weed Science Society. Proceedings *39*
Proceedings - Ultrasonics Symposium *see* Ultrasonics Symposium. Proceedings *706*
Proceso Politico (VE) *714*
Process Engineering Directory (UK) *241, 374*
Process Equipment Series (US) *247*
Process Metallurgy (NE) *629*
Processes and Materials in Electronics (US) *358*
Processing & Manufacturing Guide (CN ISSN 0708-3017) *30*
Processo Legislativo nel Parlamento Italiano (IT) *516*
Prodei (SP ISSN 0079-5836) *241*
Produccion Agricola - Periodo de Invierno (VE) *25*
Produccion Agricola - Periodo de Verano (VE) *845*
Produccion Quimica Mexicana (MX) *374*
Produce Marketing Almanac (US) *405, 672*
Produce Marketing Association. Yearbook *see* Produce Marketing Almanac *405*
Produce Marketing Association Almanac *see* Produce Marketing Almanac *405*
Product Directory (US) *913*
Product File for Agricultural Machinery and Related Material (JA) *32*
Producteur d'Amiante *see* Asbestos Producer *134*
Production and Marketing: California Eggs, Chicken and Turkeys (US) *41, 46*
Production and Marketing California Grapes, Raisins and Wine *see* California Fruit and Nut Acreage *24*
Production Minerale du Canada, Calcul Preliminaire *see* Canada's Mineral Production, Preliminary Estimate *648*
Production of Aggregates in Great Britain (UK) *138*
Production's Manufacturing Planbook (US) *225*
Productividad (PE ISSN 0032-9908) *225*
Producto Neto de la Agricultura Espanola (SP ISSN 0079-5895) *19*
Productos Quimicos (MX) *374*

Produktschap voor Siergewassen. Jaarverslag *see* Produktschap voor Siergewassen. Jaarverslag/Statistiek *416*
Produktschap voor Siergewassen. Jaarverslag/Statistiek (NE) *416*
Produktschap voor Siergewassen. Statistiek *see* Produktschap voor Siergewassen. Jaarverslag/Statistiek *416*
Professional and Trade Organisations in India (II ISSN 0079-5925) *241*
Professional Development Bulletin *see* P D B *339*
Professional Farm Management Guidebook (AT) *30*
Professional Freelance Writers Directory (US) *505*
Professional Guide to Public Relations Services (US) *6*
Professional Photographic Equipment Directory and Buying Guide (US) *694*
Professional School Psychology (US ISSN 0079-5933) *737*
Professional Women and Minorities (US) *667, 901*
ProFile (US) *70*
Profiles of the National Productivity Organizations in A P O Member Countries (Asian Productivity Organization) (JA) *201, 225*
Profitability of Citrus Growing in Israel/Ha-Rivhiyut Shel Gidul Hadavim (IS) *38*
Profitability of Cotton Growing in Israel/Ha-Rivhiyut Shel Gidul Ha-Kutnah (IS ISSN 0079-595X) *38*
Profitability of Dairy in Israel/Ha-Rivhiyut Shel Anaf Ha-Refet (IS) *41*
Profitability of Poultry Farming in Israel/Ha-Rivhiyut Shel 'anaf Ha-Lul(IS ISSN 0079-5968) *46*
Profitability of Sugarbeet Growing in Israel/Ha-Rivhiyut Shel Gidul Selek Ha-Sukar (IS ISSN 0079-5976) *38*
Profits (FR ISSN 0079-5984) *147*
Prognostico (BL ISSN 0100-526X) *38*
Prognostico da Agricultura Paulista *see* Prognostico *38*
Prognostico Regiao Centro-Sul (BL ISSN 0100-5316) *38*
Prognozirovanie Razvitiya Bibliotechnogo Dela v S.S.S.R. (UR) *534*
Program Statistics - Michigan Department of Social Services *see* Michigan. Department of Social Services. Program Statistics *811*
Programa de Estudios Conjuntos sobre Integracion Economica Latinoamericano Ensayos E C I E L *see* Ensayos E C I E L *185*
Programme for Growth Series (US) *147*
Programs in Public Affairs and Administration *see* Graduate School Programs in Public Affairs and Public Administration *742*
Progres des Recherches Pharmaceutiques *see* Fortschritte der Arzneimittelforschung *684*
Progreso Economico y Social en America Latina. Informe *see* Economic and Social Progress in Latin America; Annual Report *185*
Progress des Bibliotheques Canadiennes: Une Selection des Meilleures Oeuvres de Publications Canadiennes de Bibliotheconomie *see* Canadian Library Progress: a Selection of the Best Writings from Canadian Library Publications *528*
Progress in Aeronautical Sciences *see* Progress in Aerospace Sciences *10*
Progress in Aerospace Sciences (US ISSN 0376-0421) *10*
Progress in Allergy (SZ ISSN 0079-6034) *604*
Progress in Analytical Chemistry (US ISSN 0079-6042) *249*
Progress in Anesthesiology (US ISSN 0099-1546) *604*
Progress in Astronautics and Aeronautics Series (US ISSN 0079-6050) *10*
Progress in Behavior Modification (US ISSN 0099-037X) *737*

Progress in Bio-Organic Chemistry (US ISSN 0079-6077) *111, 253*
Progress in Biochemical Pharmacology (SZ ISSN 0079-6085) *685*
Progress in Biometeorology (NE) *634*
Progress in Biophysics and Molecular Biology (US ISSN 0079-6107) *112*
Progress in Botany (US ISSN 0340-4773) *117*
Progress in Brain Research (NE ISSN 0079-6123) *620*
Progress in Cancer Research and Therapy (US ISSN 0145-3726) *606*
Progress in Cardiac Rehabilitation (US) *607*
Progress in Cardiology (US ISSN 0097-109X) *607*
Progress in Chemical Fibrinolysis and Thrombolysis (US ISSN 0361-0233) *607*
Progress in Chemical Toxicology (US ISSN 0079-6158) *685*
Progress in Clinical and Biological Research (US ISSN 0361-7742) *106, 599*
Progress in Clinical Cancer (US ISSN 0079-6166) *606*
Progress in Clinical Neurophysiology (SZ ISSN 0378-4045) *126, 621*
Progress in Clinical Pathology (US ISSN 0079-6174) *607*
Progress in Clinical Psychology (US ISSN 0079-6182) *737*
Progress in Colloid and Polymer Science/Fortschrittsberichte ueber Kolloide und Polymere (GW ISSN 0071-8017) *253, 255*
Progress in Communication Sciences (US ISSN 0163-5689) *265, 534*
Progress in Community Mental Health (US) *913*
Progress in Cybernetics and Systems Research (US ISSN 0275-8717) *273*
Progress in Drug Research *see* Fortschritte der Arzneimittelforschung *684*
Progress in Elementary Particle and Cosmic Ray Physics (NE ISSN 0079-6247) *913*
Progress in Experimental Personality Research (US ISSN 0079-6255) *737*
Progress in Experimental Tumor Research (SZ ISSN 0079-6263) *606*
Progress in Extractive Metallurgy (US ISSN 0091-6145) *629*
Progress in Filtration and Separation (NE) *247*
Progress in Fire Retardancy (US ISSN 0048-5497) *395*
Progress in Gastroenterology (US ISSN 0079-6271) *613*
Progress in Geophysics (II ISSN 0079-628X) *306*
Progress in Gynecology (US ISSN 0079-6298) *615*
Progress in Haematology (US ISSN 0079-6301) *613*
Progress in Hemostasis *see* Progress in Hemostasis and Thrombosis *607*
Progress in Hemostasis and Thrombosis(US) *607*
Progress in Histochemistry and Cytochemistry (GW ISSN 0079-6336) *111, 120*
Progress in Human Nutrition (US) *666*
Progress in Immunobiological Standardization *see* Developments in Biological Standardization *603*
Progress in Industrial Microbiology (NE ISSN 0555-3989) *124*
Progress in Inorganic Chemistry (US ISSN 0079-6379) *251*
Progress in Land Reform (UN ISSN 0085-5197) *19*
Progress in Learning Disabilities (US ISSN 0079-6387) *344, 346*
Progress in Lipid Research (US ISSN 0163-7827) *253*
Progress in Liver Diseases (US ISSN 0079-6409) *613*
Progress in Low Temperature Physics (NE ISSN 0079-6417) *700*
Progress in Materials Science (US ISSN 0079-6425) *380*
Progress in Mathematical Social Sciences (NE) *913*

Progress in Medical Ultrasound (NE) 599
Progress in Medical Virology (SZ ISSN 0079-645X) 124, 608
Progress in Medicinal Chemistry (NE ISSN 0079-6468) 247, 599
Progress in Molecular and Subcellular Biology (US ISSN 0079-6484) 120
Progress in Neurobiology (US ISSN 0301-0082) 106
Progress in Neurological Surgery (SZ ISSN 0079-6492) 621, 625
Progress in Neuropathology (US) 621
Progress in Nuclear Energy(New Series) (US ISSN 0149-1970) 247, 698
Progress in Nuclear Energy. Series 3- Process Chemistry see Progress in Nuclear Energy(New Series) 247
Progress in Nuclear Energy. Series 9- Analytical Chemistry see Progress in Nuclear Energy(New Series) 247
Progress in Nuclear Magnetic Resonance Spectroscopy (US ISSN 0079-6565) 249, 704, 705
Progress in Nuclear Magnetic Resonance Spectrosopy of Cyclopentadienyl Compounds see Progress in Nuclear Magnetic Resonance Spectroscopy 704
Progress in Nuclear Medicine see Recent Advances in Nuclear Medicine 622
Progress in Nuclear Medicine (SZ ISSN 0079-6573) 622
Progress in Nucleic Acid Research and Molecular Biology (US ISSN 0079-6603) 106
Progress in Oceanography (US ISSN 0079-6611) 312
Progress in Optics (NE ISSN 0079-6638) 706
Progress in Orthopaedic Surgery (US) 616
Progress in Pediatric Radiology (SZ ISSN 0079-6646) 618, 622
Progress in Pediatric Surgery (GW ISSN 0079-6654) 618, 625
Progress in Physical Organic Chemistry(US ISSN 0079-6662) 253, 255
Progress in Physiological Psychology see Psychobiology and Physiological Psychology 737
Progress in Phytochemistry (US ISSN 0079-6689) 117
Progress in Planning (US ISSN 0305-9006) 486
Progress in Polymer Science (US ISSN 0079-6700) 253, 374
Progress in Powder Metallurgy (US ISSN 0079-6719) 629
Progress in Psychiatric Drug Treatment(US) 913
Progress in Psychobiology and Physiological Psychology (US) 737
Progress in Quantum Electronics (US ISSN 0079-6727) 358
Progress in Radiation Protection (US ISSN 0094-8470) 753
Progress in Radiation Therapy (US ISSN 0079-6735) 622
Progress in Reaction Kinetics (US ISSN 0079-6743) 255
Progress in Reproductive Biology (SZ ISSN 0304-4262) 126
Progress in Respiration Research (SZ ISSN 0079-6751) 623
Progress in Sensory Physiology (US) 599
Progress in Solid Mechanics (NE ISSN 0555-4276) 913
Progress in Solid State Chemistry (US ISSN 0079-6786) 255
Progress in Surface and Membrane Science (US) 255
Progress in Surface Science (US ISSN 0079-6816) 698
Progress in Surgery (SZ ISSN 0079-6824) 625
Progress in the Chemistry of Fats and Other Lipids see Progress in Lipid Research 253
Progress in the Chemistry of Organic Natural Products see Fortschritte der Chemie Organischer Naturstoffe 252

Progress in Theoretical Biology (US ISSN 0079-6859) 106
Progress in Underwater Science (UK) 308
Progress in Zoology see Fortschritte der Zoologie 128
Progress of Education in the United States of America (US) 321
Progress of Medical Parasitology in Japan (JA ISSN 0555-4349) 608
Progress of Public Education in the United States see Progress of Education in the United States of America 321
Progress of Science in India (II ISSN 0556-1906) 789
Progress Polimernoi Khimii (UR ISSN 0079-6883) 253
Progress Report. The Minority Business Enterprise Program see U.S. Office of Minority Business Enterprise. Minority Enterprise Progress Report 393
Progress Report - Ear Research Institute see Ear Research Institute. Progress Report 617
Progress Report - New Mexico Bureau of Mines & Mineral Resources see New Mexico. Bureau of Mines and Mineral Resources. Progress Report 645
Progress Report - State of Illinois. Department of Mental Health. Drug Abuse Program see Illinois. Department of Mental Health. Drug Abuse Program. Progress Report 287
Progressive Conservative Party of Canada. Leader's Report (CN ISSN 0702-7222) 714
Progressive Conservative Party of Canada National P C President see National P C President 713
Progressive Grocer's Annual Report of the Grocery Industry (US) 407
Progressive Grocer's Annual Report of the Grocery Trade see Progressive Grocer's Annual Report of the Grocery Industry 407
Progressive Grocer's Market Scope see Market Scope 405
Progressive Grocer's Marketing Guidebook (US ISSN 0079-6921) 405
Project (Elmsford) (US ISSN 0191-5630) 789
Project Skywater. Annual Report (US ISSN 0079-6956) 381, 897
Projects Recommended for Deauthorization, Annual Report see U.S. Department of the Army. Projects Recommended for Deauthorization, Annual Report 898
Projekty-Problemy. Budownictwo Weglowe (PL) 646
Projeto (BL) 913
Proletarian Internationalism (US) 714
Promotrans (FR ISSN 0079-6972) 863
Propagation & Distribution of Fishes from National Fish Hatcheries (US) 399
Property and Managed Bonds see Managed and Property Bonds 204
Property Services Agency Library Bibliographies see P S A Library Bibliographies 539
Property Studies in the U.K. and Overseas (UK ISSN 0305-5752) 762
Property Tax Bulletin (US) 231
Proprietary Association. Committee on Scientific Development. Annual Research and Scientific Development Conference. Proceedings (US ISSN 0079-7006) 753
Propylene and Derivatives see World Propylene and Derivatives 248
Propylene Annual. (US ISSN 0095-4128) 682
Prosa Galega (SP) 571
Proshloe i Nastoyaschchee Severnoi Bukoviny see Mynule i Suchasne Pivnichnoi Bukovyny 458
Prospects (US ISSN 0361-2333) 393, 471
Prospects for America (US ISSN 0079-7014) 471

Prospects of Engineering and Technology Graduates see American Association of Engineering Societies. Engineering Manpower Commission. Placement of Engineering and Technology Graduates 365
Prospettive dell'Industria Italiana (IT ISSN 0555-4810) 225
Prostaglandins in Fertility Control (UN) 106, 132
Protection Directory of Industrial & Environmental Personnel (UK) 496
Protein Synthesis: a Series of Advances (US ISSN 0079-7049) 111, 255
Prothese (SZ) 571
Protides of the Biological Fluids (US ISSN 0079-7065) 106
Protokolle zur Fischereitechnik (GW ISSN 0438-4555) 399
Protoplasmologia; Handbuch der Protoplasmaforschung see Cell Biology Monographs 119
Proud Black Images (US ISSN 0048-5640) 393, 571
Province of Saskatchewan Motor Vehicle Traffic Accidents see Saskatchewan. Government Insurance Office. Province of Saskatchewan Motor Vehicle Traffic Accidents. Annual Report 876
Provincia (SP) 581
Provincia (AG) 581
Provincia de Zaragoza. Informe Economico (SP) 180
Provincia di Forli in Cifre (IT ISSN 0033-1902) 189
Provincial Educational Media Centre Catalogue: Supplement see P. E. M. C. Catalogue: Supplement 350
Provincial Results in Canada of Fire & Casualty Companies see Provincial Results in Canada of General Insurance Companies 500
Provincial Results in Canada of General Insurance Companies (CN) 500
Provinzialinstitut fuer Westfaelische Landes- und Volksforschung. Veroeffentlichungen (GW ISSN 0079-709X) 459
Prudential Insurance Company of America. Economic Forecast (US) 189
Prudential Staff Gazette see National Union of Insurance Workers. Prudential Section. Gazette 500
Pruefen und Entscheiden (SZ ISSN 0079-7111) 216
Przeglad Archeologiczny (PL ISSN 0079-7138) 64
Przeglad Naukowej Literatury Rolniczej i Lesnej. Gleboznawstwo. Chemia Rolna. Ogolna Uprawa Roli i Roslin i Siedliska Lesne (PL ISSN 0079-7154) 38
Przeglad Naukowej Literatury Zootechnicznej (PL ISSN 0079-7162) 46
Przestepczosc na Swiecie (PL) 283
Przeszlosc Demograficzna Polski. Materialy i Studia (PL ISSN 0079-7189) 729
Pseudepigrapha Veteris Testamenti Graece (NE ISSN 0079-7197) 767
Psikhologicheskie Issledovaniya (UR) 737
Psychiatria Fennica/Finnish Psychiatry (FI ISSN 0079-7227) 621
Psychiatria Fennica. Julkisuserja/ Psychiatria Fennica. Reports (FI ISSN 0355-7693) 621
Psychiatria Fennica. Monografiasarja/ Psychiatria Fennica. Monographs (FI ISSN 0355-7707) 621
Psychiatria Fennica. Monographs see Psychiatria Fennica. Monografiasarja 621
Psychiatria Fennica. Reports see Psychiatria Fennica. Julkaisuserja 621
Psychiatrie de l'Enfant (FR ISSN 0079-726X) 618
Psychiatry and Art (SZ ISSN 0079-7286) 621
Psychiatry and the Humanities (US ISSN 0363-8952) 492, 621
Psychic Studies (US) 676
Psychoanalytic Study of Society (US ISSN 0079-7294) 737

Psychoanalytic Study of the Child (US ISSN 0079-7308) 737
Psychobiology and Physiological Psychology (US) 737
Psychologen Adresboek (NE ISSN 0079-7324) 737
Psychologia a Skola (CS) 321, 737
Psychologia Africana (SA ISSN 0079-7332) 220, 737
Psychologia-Pedagogika (PL) 737
Psychologia Universalis Forschungsergebnisse aus dem Gesamtgebiet der Psychologie (GW) 737
Psychological Cinema Register (US ISSN 0272-0582) 651, 739
Psychological Institute of the Republic of South Africa. Proceedings/ Sielkundige Instituut van die Republiek van Suid-Afrika. Verrigtings (SA) 737
Psychological Issues. Monograph (US ISSN 0079-7359) 737
Psychological Research Bulletin (SW ISSN 0555-5620) 737
Psychological Studies (NE) 737
Psychological Studies. Major Series see Psychological Studies 737
Psychologie und Gesellschaft (GW ISSN 0341-938X) 737
Psychologie und Person (GW ISSN 0079-7405) 737
Psychologische Praxis (SZ ISSN 0079-7413) 738
Psychology Book Guide see Bibliographic Guide to Psychology 739
Psychology Information Guide Series (US) 94, 739
Psychology of Learning and Motivation: Advances in Research and Theory (US ISSN 0079-7421) 738
Psychotheque (FR ISSN 0079-7448) 799
Pszichologia a Gyakorlatban (HU ISSN 0079-7456) 738
Pszichologiai Tanulmanyok (HU ISSN 0079-7464) 738
Ptolemy (US) 581
Pubblicazioni di Verifiche (IT) 459, 690
Pubblicita e Organizzazione Oggi (IT) 6
Pubblicita in Italia (IT ISSN 0079-7472) 6
Pubblico (IT) 557
Public Administration see Public Administration and Finance Newsletter 745
Public Administration and Democracy (US) 714, 745
Public Administration and Finance Newsletter (UN) 745
Public Administration in Israel and Abroad (IS ISSN 0079-7499) 913
Public Administration Series: Bibliography (US ISSN 0193-970X) 94, 748
Public Affairs Bulletin (US) 750
Public and Preparatory Schools. Yearbook (UK ISSN 0079-7537) 344
Public Assistance Statistics (Lansing) see Michigan. Department of Social Services. Public Assistance Statistics 811
Public Citizen (US) 714
Public Citizen Platform (US) 280
Public Cleansing Service in Tokyo/ Seiso Jigyo Gaiyo (JA) 753
Public Continuing and Adult Education Almanac (US ISSN 0079-7545) 329
Public Education Directory (US ISSN 0160-8126) 332
Public Employees Journal/Journal des Employes Publics (CN ISSN 0381-7962) 745
Public Health and Hygiene (UG) 753
Public Health Conference on Records and Statistics. Proceedings (US ISSN 0079-7588) 756
Public Health Monograph (US ISSN 0079-7596) 754
Public Health Papers (UN ISSN 0555-6015) 754
Public Health Technical Monograph see Public Health Monograph 754
Public Housing in Singapore: a Multi-Disciplinary Study (SI) 486

Public International Law (US ISSN 0340-7349) 516, 524
Public Land Statistics see U. S. Bureau of Land Management. Public Land Statistics 746
Public Libraries in Canada/Bibliotheques Publiques du Canada. (CN ISSN 0317-4921) 913
Public Library Catalog (US) 539
Public Library Reporter (US ISSN 0555-6031) 535
Public Occurrence (US) 557
Public Papers of the Presidents of the United States (US ISSN 0079-7626) 745
Public Policy Issues in Resource Management (US ISSN 0079-7634) 225
Public Policy Studies (US) 745
Public Policy Studies in the South (US) 799
Public Revenues from Alcohol Beverages (US) 86, 231
Public School Enrollment and Staff, New York State (US) 345
Public School Professional Personnel Report, New York State (US ISSN 0077-9229) 321
Public Transportation in Oregon (US) 863
Public Use of the National Park System (Washington) see U. S. National Park Service. Public Use of the National Park System; Fiscal Year Report 278
Public Utilities Law Anthology (US) 516, 745
Public Water Supply Engineers Conference (Proceedings) (US) 388
Public Welfare Annual Statistics see Pennsylvania. Department of Public Welfare. Public Welfare Annual Statistics 808
Public Welfare Directory (US ISSN 0163-8297) 808
Public Welfare in California (US ISSN 0362-742X) 808
Public Works Manual (US ISSN 0163-9730) 750
Publicacoes Culturais da Companhia (AO) 789, 799
Publication - Brome County Historical Society see Brome County Historical Society. Publication 467
Publication de Scriptorium (BE) 759
Publications-Bureau of Business Research, the University of Texas at Austin see University of Texas, Austin. Bureau of Business Research. Publications 150
Publications de Recherche Scientifique en France/Scholarly Books in France(FR) 94
Publications du Governement Canadien: Catalogue see Canadian Government Publications: Catalogue 89
Publications in Archaelogy (US) 278
Publications in Climatology (US) 635
Publications in Language Sciences (NE) 550
Publications in Medieval Science (US ISSN 0079-7685) 789
Publications in Near and Middle East Studies. Series A (NE ISSN 0079-7707) 445
Publications in Near and Middle East Studies. Series B (NE ISSN 0079-7715) 445, 550
Publications in Psychology (NZ ISSN 0079-7731) 738
Publications in Seismology (FI ISSN 0079-774X) 306
Publications in the American West (US ISSN 0085-5227) 471
Publications in Tropical Geography Savanna Research Series (CN ISSN 0079-7758) 425
Publications in Water Research at Oregon State University (US ISSN 0079-7766) 897
Publications Indexed for Engineering see P I E 372
Publications Juridiques Concernant l'Integration Europeenne; Bibliographie Juridique. Supplement (EI) 521

Publications of the Faculty - Research Council, Florida State University see Florida State University. Publications of the Faculty 336
Publications on Asia (US ISSN 0079-7782) 445
Publications on Political Science in Japan (JA) 718
Publications on Russia and Eastern Europe (US ISSN 0079-7790) 714
Publications on Social History (NE ISSN 0079-7804) 815
Publications Romanes et Francaises (SZ ISSN 0079-7812) 550, 571
Publications Yearbook, Republic of China (CH) 759
Publicatons Gramma (US) 789
Publicus (SZ ISSN 0080-7249) 745
Publikationen zu Wissenschaftlichen Filmen. Sektion Geschichte, Paedagogik see Institut fuer den Wissenschaftlichen Film. Publikationen zu Wissenschaftlichen Filmen. Sektion Geschichte, Publizistik 650
Publishers and Distributors of the United States see Publishers, Distributors and Wholesalers of the United States 241
Publishers, Distributors and Wholesalers of the United States (US ISSN 0000-0671) 241, 759
Publishers in the United Kingdom and Their Addresses (UK ISSN 0079-7839) 759
Publishers' International Directory see Internationales Verlagsadressbuch 760
Publishers' Trade List Annual (US ISSN 0079-7855) 94
Publizistik-Historische Beitraege (GW) 505
Publizistik Wissenschaftlicher Referatedienst (GW ISSN 0552-6981) 3, 506
Puente: Lectura para Todos (AG) 571
Puerto del Sol (US) 571
Puerto Rico. Bureau of Labor Statistics. Census of Manufacturing Industries of Puerto Rico see Census of Manufacturing Industries of Puerto Rico 221
Puerto Rico. Comision de Derechos Civiles. Estudios y Monografias (PR) 516
Puerto Rico. Comision de Derechos Civiles. Informe Anual (PR) 517
Puerto Rico. Departamento de Agricultura. Contribuciones Agropecuarias y Pesqueras see Puerto Rico. Department of Agriculture. Agricultural and Fisheries Contributions 399
Puerto Rico. Departamento de la Vivienda. Secretaria Auxiliar de Planificacion y Programacion. Informe Anual (PR) 486
Puerto Rico. Department of Agriculture. Agricultural and Fisheries Contributions/Puerto Rico. Departamento de Agricultura. Contribuciones Agropecuarias y Pesqueras (PR) 399
Puerto Rico. Department of Labor. Directorio de Organizaciones del Trabajo (PR) 507
Puerto Rico. Department of the Treasury. Economy & Finances (PR ISSN 0079-7871) 189
Puerto Rico. Division of Demographic Registry and Vital Statistics. Annual Vital Statistics Report (PR ISSN 0555-6511) 845
Puerto Rico. Division of Health Facilities. Plan for Hospital and Medical Facilites (PR) 481
Puerto Rico. Government Development Bank. Annual Report (PR) 175
Puerto Rico. Government Development Bank. Report of Activities see Puerto Rico. Government Development Bank. Annual Report 175
Puerto Rico. Negociado del Presupuesto. Boletin de Gerencia Administrativa (PR) 745

Puerto Rico. Negociado del Presupuesto. Resoluciones Conjuntas del Presupuesto General y de Presupuestos Especiales (PR ISSN 0079-7863) 231
Puerto Rico Highway Improvement Program (US ISSN 0092-8941) 875
Puerto Rico Living (PR ISSN 0033-4049) 419
Puerto Rico Official Industrial Directory (PR ISSN 0090-3612) 241
Puku (ZA ISSN 0079-7901) 106
Pulp & Paper Buyers Guide (US) 241, 675
Pulp & Paper Canada's Business Directory (CN ISSN 0317-3550) 675
Pulp and Paper, Canada's Reference Manual & Buyers' Guide (CN) 675
Pulp and Paper Industry in the O E C D Member Countries and Finland/Industrie des Pates et Papiers dans les Pays Membres de l'OCDE et la Finlande (FR ISSN 0474-5485) 675
Pulp and Paper Industry Technical Conference. Record see I E E E Annual Pulp and Paper Industry Technical Conference. Conference Record 675
Pulp & Paper Magazine of Canada's Reference Manual & Buyers' Guide see Pulp and Paper, Canada's Reference Manual & Buyers' Guide 675
Pulp and Paper Research Institute of Canada. Annual Report (CN ISSN 0079-7960) 675
Pulse (SA ISSN 0555-6945) 369
Pulsed Power Modulator Conference (Record) (US) 358
PUMRL see Purdue University Monographs in Romance Language 550
Punjab National Bank. Annual Report (II ISSN 0304-8101) 176
Punjab State Industrial Development Corporation. Annual Report (II) 225
Pupila: Libros de Nuestro Tiempo (UY ISSN 0079-8061) 434
Purchaser's Guide to the Music Industries (US) 662
Purdue Air Quality Conference. Proceedings (US) 388
Purdue University. Civil Engineering Reprints (US ISSN 0079-8096) 376
Purdue University. Engineering Experiment Station. Joint Highway Research Project. Research Reports (US ISSN 0079-810X) 376
Purdue University. Office of Manpower Studies. Manpower Report (US ISSN 0079-8134) 210
Purdue University. Road School. Proceedings of Annual Road School (US ISSN 0079-8142) 875
Purdue University Monographs in Romance Language (NE ISSN 0165-8743) 550, 571
Pure and Applied Mathematics (US ISSN 0079-8169) 588
Pure and Applied Mathematics; a Series of Texts and Monographs see Pure and Applied Mathematics: A Wiley Interscience Series of Texts, Monographs and Tracts 588
Pure and Applied Mathematics: A Wiley Interscience Series of Texts, Monographs and Tracts (US) 588
Pure and Applied Mathematics Series (US ISSN 0079-8177) 588
Pure and Applied Physics (US ISSN 0079-8193) 369, 698
Purificacion (UY) 71
Pusat Daya Pengeluaran Negara. Lapuran Tahunan see National Productivity Centre, Malaysia. Annual Report 216
Pushcart Prize: Best of the Small Presses (US ISSN 0149-7863) 571
Puteoli (IT) 459
Putting Research into Educational Practice Reports see P R E P. Reports 912
Pyramid Film and Video Catalog (US) 651
Pyrenae: Cronica Arqueologica (SP ISSN 0079-8215) 64

Pyttersen's Nederlandse Almanak (NE ISSN 0079-8223) 361
Q L A Bulletin (Quebec Library Association) (CN ISSN 0380-7150) 535
Qantas Airways. Report (AT) 869
Qatar National Bank (S.A.Q.). Report of the Directors and Balance Sheet (QA) 176
Qatar Yearbook (QA) 475, 845
Qedem (IS) 64
Quad (CN) 263
Quaderni (AT) 492
Quaderni Camerti di Studi Romanistici. Index/International Survey of Roman Law. Index (IT) 517
Quaderni de "la Terra Santa" (IS) 475, 767, 890
Quaderni dei Padri Benedettini di San Giorgio Maggiore (IT ISSN 0079-824X) 775
Quaderni del Salvemini (IT) 714
Quaderni del Vittoriale (IT ISSN 0391-3104) 581
Quaderni di Analisi Matematica (IT ISSN 0391-3236) 588
Quaderni di Archeologia della Libia (IT ISSN 0079-8258) 64
Quaderni di Chimica Applicata (IT) 247
Quaderni di Cultura Materiale (IT) 459
Quaderni di Fabbrica e Stato (IT) 225
Quaderni di Letterature Americane (IT) 571
Quaderni di Poesia Neogreca (IT ISSN 0079-8274) 581
Quaderni di Rinnovamento Veneto (IT) 486
Quaderni di Scacchi: i Grandi Giocatori(IT) 822
Quaderni di Scienza (IT) 789
Quaderni di Sessualita (IT) 106, 350
Quaderni di Studi Storici Toscani (IT) 459
Quaderni di Verifiche (IT) 690
Quaderni Internazionali di Storia Economica e Sociale/International Journal of Economic and Social History/Cahiers Internationaux d'Histoire Economique et Sociale (IT ISSN 0066-2283) 459
Quaderni Siciliani (IT) 714
Quaestiones Geographicae (PL) 425
Quaker Encounters (UK) 690, 776
Quaker Peace and Service. Annual Report (UK ISSN 0260-9584) 776, 808
Quaker Religious Thought (US ISSN 0033-5088) 776
Qualita della Vita (IT) 815
Quality Control in the Pharmaceutical Industry (US) 685
Quality Control: States' Corrective Action Activities see U.S. Social and Rehabilitation Service. Office of Management. Quality Control, States' Corrective Action Activities 809
Quality of Life in Iowa (US ISSN 0091-5696) 189
Quantibuild (SI) 138
Quantitative Applications in the Social Sciences (US) 799
Quantitative Methoden der Unternehmungsplanung (GW) 216
Quantitative Methods for Biologists and Medical Scientists (US) 106, 599
Quantum Chemistry see Theoretical Chemistry 248
Quantum Physics and Its Applications (US ISSN 0481-1275) 698
Quarry (SA) 571
Quartaer (GW ISSN 0375-7471) 64
Quarterbacks (CN) 263
Quarterly Index Islamicus (UK ISSN 0308-7395) 438
Quarterly Journal of Studies on Alcohol. Supplement see Journal of Studies on Alcohol. Supplement 287
Quarterly Review of Australian Education. see Australian Education Review 314
Quarterly Review of Literature see Quarterly Review of Literature Contemporary Poetry Series 571
Quarterly Review of Literature Contemporary Poetry Series (US) 571, 581

Quaternaria (IT ISSN 0085-5235) 299, 674
Quatre Mille Imprimeries see Quatre Mille Imprimeries Francaises 734
Quatre Mille Imprimeries Francaises (FR ISSN 0066-3638) 734
Quebec (City) Universite Laval. Centre d'Etudes Nordiques. Travaux Divers see Nordicana 470
Quebec (Province) Bureau of Statistics Statistiques (CN) 845
Quebec (Province) Commission des Services Juridiques. Rapport Annuel (CN) 517
Quebec (Province) Department of Lands and Forests. Research Service. Memoire see Quebec (Province) Ministere de l'Energie et des Ressources. Service de la Recherche. Memoire 410
Quebec (Province) Department of Natural Resources. Geological Reports (CN ISSN 0079-8738) 299
Quebec (Province) Department of Natural Resources. Geological Services. Field Work see Quebec (Province) Ministere des Richesses Naturelles. Travaux sur le Terrain 299
Quebec (Province). Department of Natural Resources. Report see Quebec (Province) Ministere des Richesses Naturelles. Rapport 278
Quebec (Province) Department of Tourism, Fish and Game. Annual Report (CN ISSN 0481-2786) 890
Quebec (Province) Direction Generale des Peches Maritimes Cahiers d'Information (CN) 106
Quebec (Province) Direction Generale des Peches Maritimes. Direction de la Recherche. Rapport Annuel (CN ISSN 0318-8779) 106
Quebec (Province) Health Insurance Board. Annual Statistics/Regie de l'Assurance Malade. Statistiques Annuelles (CN) 502
Quebec (Province). Liquor Board. Rapport Annuel see Societe des Alcools du Quebec. Rapport Annuel 287
Quebec (Province) Marine Biological Station, Grande-Riviere. Cahiers d'Information see Quebec (Province) Direction Generale des Peches Maritimes Cahiers d'Information 106
Quebec (Province) Marine Biological Station, Grande-Riviere. Rapport see Quebec (Province) Direction Generale des Peches Maritimes. Direction de la Recherche. Rapport Annuel 106
Quebec (Province) Ministere de l'Energie et des Ressources. Service de la Recherche Forestiere. Guide (CN) 410
Quebec(Province) Ministere de l'Energie et des Ressources. Service de la Recherche Forestiere. Note (CN) 410
Quebec (Province) Ministere de l'Energie et des Ressources. Service de la Recherche. Memoire/Quebec (Province) Department of Lands and Forests. Research Service. Memoire (CN) 410
Quebec (Province) Ministere des Communications. Rapport Annuel (CN) 265
Quebec (Province) Ministere des Richesses Naturelles. Rapport (CN) 278, 388
Quebec (Province) Ministere des Richesses Naturelles. Repertoire des Publications (CN) 279
Quebec (Province) Ministere des Richesses Naturelles. Travaux sur le Terrain (CN ISSN 0079-8746) 299
Quebec (Province) Ministere des Terres et Forets. Conseil Consultatif des Reserves Ecologiques. Rapport Annuel (CN ISSN 0700-3749) 278, 410
Quebec (Province) Office de la Langue Francaise. Cahiers (CN ISSN 0079-8770) 550

Quebec (Province) Office de la Protection du Consommateur. Rapport d'Activites (CN) 280
Quebec at a Glance (CN ISSN 0702-6943) 890
Quebec Library Association. Newsletter(CN ISSN 0079-8428) 535
Quebec Library Association Bulletin see Q L A Bulletin 535
Quebec Port Guide & Directory (CN) 880
Queen Alexandra Hospital for Children. Annual Report (CN) 481
Queen Alexandra Solarium for Crippled Children Annual Report see Queen Alexandra Hospital for Children. Annual Report 481
Queen Mary College. Department of Geography. Occasional Papers (UK ISSN 0306-2740) 425
Queen Victoria Museum and Art Gallery. Launceston, Tasmania. Records (AT ISSN 0085-5278) 789
Queens College Publications in Anthropology (US) 53
Queens College Studies in Librarianship(US ISSN 0146-8677) 535
Queen's Medical Review (CN ISSN 0079-8789) 599
Queen's Papers on Pure and Applied Mathematics (CN ISSN 0079-8797) 588
Queen's University. Industrial Relations Centre. Research and Current Issues Series (CN ISSN 0317-2546) 210
Queen's University. Industrial Relations Centre. Research Series see Queen's University. Industrial Relations Centre. Research and Current Issues Series 210
Queen's University. Institute for Economic Research. Discussion Paper (CN ISSN 0316-5078) 147
Queen's University at Kingston. Annual Report on the Libraries (CN) 535
Queen's University at Kingston. Department of Electrical Engineering. Research Report (CN ISSN 0075-6091) 358
Queen's University at Kingston. Department of Mathematics. Research Report see Queen's Papers on Pure and Applied Mathematics 588
Queen's University at Kingston. Douglas Library. Occasional Papers (CN ISSN 0075-6113) 539
Queen's University at Kingston. Industrial Relations Centre. Bibliography Series (CN ISSN 0075-613X) 163
Queen's University at Kingston. Industrial Relations Centre. Report of Activities (CN ISSN 0075-6148) 210
Queen's University at Kingston. Industrial Relations Centre. Reprint Series (CN ISSN 0075-6156) 210
Queensland. Air Pollution Council. Annual Report (AT) 388
Queensland. Department of Commercial and Industrial Development. Annual Report (AT) 225
Queensland. Department of Education. Information and Publications Branch. Document (AT) 345
Queensland. Department of Education. Information and Publications Branch. Information Statement (AT) 350
Queensland. Department of Education. Research and Curriculum Branch. Curriculum Paper (AT ISSN 0310-4079) 321
Queensland. Department of Education. Research and Curriculum Branch. Document see Queensland. Department of Education. Information and Publications Branch. Document 345
Queensland. Department of Education. Research and Curriculum Branch. Information Statement see Queensland. Department of Education. Information and Publications Branch. Information Statement 350

Queensland. Department of Education. Research and Curriculum Branch. Reporting Research see Queensland. Department of Education. Research Branch. Reporting Research 350
Queensland. Department of Education. Research Branch. Reporting Research(AT) 350
Queensland. Department of Education. Research Branch, Research Series (AT) 321
Queensland. Department of Forestry. Research Paper (AT ISSN 0157-809X) 410
Queensland. Department of Local Government. Conference of Local Authority Engineers. Proceedings (AT ISSN 0311-9491) 376
Queensland. Geological Survey. Publications (AT ISSN 0079-8800) 299
Queensland. Land Administration Commission. Annual Report (AT) 19, 745
Queensland. Registrar of Co-Operative and Other Societies. Report (AT ISSN 0481-3375) 181
Queensland Education Digest (AT ISSN 0313-8143) 321
Queensland Geographer (AT ISSN 0314-3457) 350, 425
Queensland Geographical Journal (AT) 425
Queensland Law Almanac see Queensland Legal Directory 517
Queensland Legal Directory (AT) 517
Queensland Littoral Society. Newsletter see Operculum 106
Queensland Museum, Brisbane. Memoirs (AT ISSN 0079-8835) 654
Queensland Naturalist (AT ISSN 0079-8843) 106
Queensland Pocket Yearbook (AT ISSN 0085-5316) 845
Queensland Primary Producers' Co-Operative Association. Primary Producers' Guide (AT ISSN 0085-5332) 19
Queensland Society of Sugar Cane Technologists. Proceedings see Australian Society of Sugar Cane Technologists. Proceedings 404
Queensland Yearbook (AT ISSN 0085-5359) 845
Quellen und Forschungen aus Italienischen Archiven und Bibliotheken (GW ISSN 0079-9068) 535
Quellen und Forschungen zur Basler Geschichte (SZ ISSN 0079-9076) 459
Quellen und Forschungen zur Wuerttembergischen Kirchengeschichte (GW ISSN 0079-9084) 767
Quellen und Studien see Schriften zur Kooperationsforschung. Studien 181
Quellen und Studien zur Geschichte der Pharmazie (GW ISSN 0085-5367) 685
Quellen und Studien zur Geschichte des Oestlichen Europa (GW ISSN 0170-3595) 459
Quellen und Studien zur Geschichte Osteuropas (GE ISSN 0079-9114) 459
Quellen und Studien zur Geschichte des Islamischen Aegyptens (GW ISSN 0481-0023) 440
Quellenkataloge zur Musikgeschichte (GW ISSN 0079-905X) 662
Quellenschriften zur Westdeutschen Vor- und Fruehgeschichte (GW ISSN 0079-9149) 64
Quellenwerke zur Alten Geschichte Amerikas (GW ISSN 0079-9157) 402, 471
Quelques Donnees Statistiques sur l'Industrie Francaise des Pates, Papiers, Cartons see Statistiques de l'Industrie Francaise des Pates, Papiers et Cartons 676
Quest for a Common Denominator see Mamashee 106
Question (UK ISSN 0079-919X) 492
Questiones Geobiologicae see Problemy Biologie Krajiny 106

Quetico-Superior Wilderness Research Center, Ely, Minnesota. Annual Report (US ISSN 0079-9211) 106, 278
Quetico-Superior Wilderness Research Center, Ely, Minnesota. Technical Notes (US ISSN 0079-922X) 278
Qufo (SW) 299
Qui Est Qui en France see Who's Who in France 99
Qui Fabrique et Fournit Quoi (FR) 673
Qui Represente Qui (FR ISSN 0079-9262) 197, 216
Qui Vend et Achete Quoi? (FR ISSN 0079-9270) 241
Quick Frozen Foods Directory of Frozen Food Processors (US ISSN 0079-9289) 405
Quick Frozen Foods Directory of Wholesale Distributors (US) 405
Quick Help from the Governor: A Directory of State Financial Aid Agencies (US) 339
Quien Vende en Espana los Productos Extranjeros/Who Sells Foreign Products in Spain (SP) 241
Quin's Metal Handbook see Metal Bulletin Handbook 628
Quirindi and District Historical Notes (AT ISSN 0085-5375) 447
Quitumbe (EC) 471
R A I A News (Royal Australian Institute of Architects) (AT) 70
R A-Nytt (SW ISSN 0347-4585) 438
R A P R A Recent Literature on Hazardous Environments in Industry (Rubber and Plastics Research Association of Great Britain) (UK ISSN 0140-4156) 707, 777
R & D Economic Comment (US) 147
R & D in Higher Education (SW ISSN 0347-4976) 339
R & D Review (Schenectady) (US ISSN 0361-4689) 852
R & S Report (Honolulu) see Hawaii. Department of Health. Research and Statistics Office. R & S Report 727
R.B.R.R. Kale Memorial Lectures (II) 147, 714
R C A Plain Talk and Technical Tips see Communicator 352
R C Buyers Guide see Radio Control Buyers Guide 241
R E C S A M Annual Report (Regional Centre for Education in Science and Mathematics) (MY) 321, 350
R E C S A M News (Regional Centre for Education in Science and Mathematics) (MY ISSN 0126-7612) 350, 588, 789
R E C S A M Newsletter see R E C S A M News 350
R.E.I.T. Fact Book (National Association of Real Estate Investment Trusts) (US ISSN 0095-1374) 204, 762
R E L C Annual Report (Regional Language Centre) (SI) 550
R E M E Journal (Royal Electrical & Mechanical Engineers) (UK ISSN 0432-2924) 358, 383
R E S World Diaconal Bulletin (Reformed Ecumenical Synod) (US) 772
R G W in Zahlen/C M E A Data (Council for Mutual Economic Assistance) (AU) 201
R. H. S. Gardener's Diary (Royal Horticultural Society) (UK ISSN 0080-441X) 416
R I A S-Funkuniversitaet, Berlin. Forschung und Information (GW ISSN 0067-5997) 339
R I: Revista dos Recursos Humanos na Empresa (BL) 220
R L A (CL ISSN 0033-698X) 550
R. L. C.'s Museum Gazette (CN ISSN 0035-7154) 654
R L; Revista Literaria see Universidade Federal de Minas Gerais. Corpo Discente. Revista Literaria 575
R L S: Regional Language Studies... Newfoundland (CN ISSN 0079-9335) 550
R M A Annual Statement Studies (Robert /Morris Associates) (US ISSN 0080-3340) 176

R. M. Bucke Memorial Society for the Study of Religious Experience. Newsletter-Review (CN ISSN 0079-9343) 767
R. M. Bucke Memorial Society for the Study of Religious Experience. Proceedings of the Conference (CN ISSN 0079-9351) 767
R. M. C. Historical Journal (Royal Military College of Australia) (AT ISSN 0310-4141) 447, 640
R P A Bulletin see R P A News 486
R P A News (Regional Plan Association, Inc.) (US) 486
R P P see Religionspaedagogische Praxis 767
R. S. A. Postage Stamp Catalogue (SA) 479
R S em Numeros (BL) 845
R S G B Amateur Radio Call Book (Radio Society of Great Britain) (UK ISSN 0079-9475) 268
R S P B Annual Report and Accounts (Royal Society for the Protection of Birds) (UK ISSN 0080-4509) 130, 278
R T ; a Journal of Radical Therapy see State and Mind 738
R. U. S. I. and Brassey's Defence Yearbook (Royal United Services Institute) (US ISSN 0305-6155) 640
R V and Tent Sites in Alabama, Florida, Georgia, Kentucky, Louisiana, Mississippi, North Carolina, South Carolina, Tennessee see Southeastern Campbook 890
R V and Tent Sites in Alberta, British Columbia, Manitoba, Northwest Territories, Saskatchewan, Yukon Territory and Alaska see Western Canada Alaska Campbook 893
R V and Tent Sites in Arizona, Colorado, New Mexico, Utah see Southwestern Campbook 891
R V and Tent Sites in Arkansas, Kansas, Missouri, Oklahoma, Texas see South Central Campbook 890
R V and Tent Sites in California, Nevada see California-Nevada Campbook 883
R V and Tent Sites in Connecticut, Maine, Massachusetts, New Hampshire, New York, Rhode Island, Vermont see Northeastern Campbook 830
R V and Tent Sites in Delaware, District of Columbia, Maryland, New Jersey, Pennsylvania, Virginia, West Virginia see Mideastern Campbook 889
R V and Tent Sites in Idaho, Montana, Oregon, Washington, Wyoming see Northwestern Campbook 889
R V and Tent Sites in Iowa, Minnesota, Nebraska, North Dakota, South Dakota see North Central Campbook 889
R V and Tent Sites in New Brunswick, Newfoundland, Nova Scotia, Ontario, Prince Edward Island, Quebec see Eastern Canada Campbook 884
R V Campground & Services Guide see Trailer Life's Recreational Vehicle Campground and Services Directory 831
R W P Steuerrecht. Ausgabe A (Rechts- und Wirtschafts-Praxis.) (GW) 231, 517
R W P Steuerrecht. Ausgabe B (Rechts- und Wirtschafts-Praxis) (GW) 231, 517
Raabe- Gesellschaft. Jahrbuch (GW ISSN 0075-2371) 571
Raabser Maerchen-Reihe (AU) 402
Rabbinical Assembly, New York. Proceedings (US ISSN 0079-936X) 770
Rabibasara (II) 571
Rabindra Bharati Journal (II) 418
Raccolta di Tavole Statistiche see Annuarium Statisticum Ecclesiae 769
Race and Nations Series (US) 719
Race Question in Modern Science (UN ISSN 0501-3615) 53
Raceform up-to-Date Form Book Annual (UK ISSN 0081-377X) 822
Racehorses (UK ISSN 0079-9408) 828

Racial and Ethnic Survey see Oregon. Department of Education. Racial and Ethnic Survey 393
Racial/Ethnic Distribution of Public School Students and Staff, New York State (US ISSN 0085-4093) 321
Racing and Football Outlook: Racing Annual (UK ISSN 0079-9424) 822, 826
Racing and Football Racing Annual see Racing and Football Outlook: Racing Annual 822
Rackham Literary Studies (US ISSN 0360-7887) 571
Radiation Dosimetry Data; Catalogue (UN) 622
Radiation Effects Research Foundation. Annual Report/Hoshasen Eikyo Kenkyusho Nenpo (JA) 622
Radiation Observations in Bergen (NO) 635
Radiation Protection Activities see U.S. Environmental Protection Agency. Radiation Protection Activities 389
Radical Science Journal (UK ISSN 0305-0963) 714, 789
Radio Amateur Callbook Magazine (US ISSN 0033-7706) 268
Radio Amateur's Handbook (US ISSN 0079-9440) 268
Radio Amateur's License Manual (US) 268
Radio Control Buyers Guide (US ISSN 0098-9215) 241
Radio Corporation of America Communicator see Communicator 352
Radio Facts and Figures (AT) 268
Radio Handbook (US ISSN 0079-9467) 268
Radio Society of Great Britain Amateur Radio Call Book see R S G B Amateur Radio Call Book 268
Radio Technical Commission for Aeronautics. Proceedings of the Annual Assembly Meeting (US) 10, 268
Radioactivity Survey Data in Japan (JA ISSN 0441-2516) 255
Radiochemistry (UK ISSN 0301-0716) 255
Radiological Quality of the Environment see U.S. Environmental Protection Agency. Radiological Quality of the Environment in the United States 389
Radiological Quality of the Environment in the United States see U.S. Environmental Protection Agency. Radiological Quality of the Environment in the United States 389
Radiology Today (US) 622
Radionavigation Journal (US) 312, 369
Radiotekhnika (UR) 706
Radner Lectures (US ISSN 0079-9491) 714, 723
Radnorshire Society. Transactions (UK ISSN 0306-848X) 459
Radovi Poljoprivrednog Fakuteta Univerziteta u Sarajevu (YU ISSN 0033-8583) 19
Rail Transportation Proceedings (US) 873
Railroad Station Historical Society. Railroad Station Monograph (US) 873
Railway Accounting Rules (US) 168, 873
Railway Directory and Yearbook (UK ISSN 0079-9513) 873
Railway Fuel and Operating Officers Association. Proceedings (US ISSN 0079-9521) 873
Railway Line Clearances (US) 873
Railway Passenger Car Annual (US ISSN 0094-2278) 873
Railway Statistical Manual (US) 866
Railway Technical Review (GW ISSN 0079-9548) 873
Railway World Annual (UK ISSN 0082-5891) 873
Railways of Sweden see Sveriges Jaernvaegar 874
Raincoast Chronicles (CN ISSN 0315-2804) 471
Rainer Foundation. Annual Report (UK) 283

Raionnye Biblioteki Belorussii (UR) 535
Rajasthan Forest Statistics (II) 410
Rajasthan, India. Directorate of Economics and Statistics. Basic Statistics (II ISSN 0079-9564) 845
Rajasthan, India. Directorate of Economics and Statistics. Budget Study (II ISSN 0079-9556) 231
Rajasthan State Tanneries Limited. Annual Report (II ISSN 0302-4881) 524
Rajasthan State Warehousing Corporation. Annual Report and Accounts (II) 225
Rajasthan University Studies in English (II ISSN 0448-1690) 550, 571
Rajasthan University Studies in Sociology see Studies in Sociology 817
Rajasthan Year Book and Who's Who (II ISSN 0079-9572) 445
Rajshahi University Studies (BG ISSN 0483-9218) 492
Rak v Sloveniji. Tabele/Cancer in Slovenia. Tables (YU ISSN 0079-9580) 606
Rakennusalan Julkaisuhakemisto (FI) 94, 140
Rakentajain Kalenteri (FI ISSN 0355-550X) 138
Rakuno Gakuen Daigaku Kiyo, Jinbun Shakaikagaku Hen see College of Dairying. Journal; Cultural and Social Sciences 41
Rakuno Gakuen Daigaku Kiyo, Shizen Kagaku Hen see College of Dairying. Journal; Natural Science 41
Ralph H. Blanchard Memorial Endowment Series (US) 500, 808
Ramsay Society of Chemical Engineers. Journal (UK ISSN 0456-4804) 374
Ranchi University Mathematical Journal (II ISSN 0079-9602) 588
Rand Corporation. Paper see Rand Report Series 789
Rand McNally Campground and Trailer Park Guide (US ISSN 0079-9610) 831
Rand McNally Commercial Atlas and Marketing Guide (US) 219, 425
Rand McNally Discover Historic America (US ISSN 0079-9637) 890
Rand McNally Guidebook to Campgrounds see Rand McNally Campground and Trailer Park Guide 831
Rand McNally List of Bank-Recommended Attorneys (US) 176, 517
Rand McNally National Park Guide (US ISSN 0079-9629) 831
Rand McNally Travel Trailer Guide see Rand McNally Campground and Trailer Park Guide 831
Rand McNally Vacation Guide see Rand McNally Discover Historic America 890
Rand Paper Series see Rand Report Series 789
Rand Report Series (US ISSN 0092-2803) 789, 852
Randax Education Guide (US) 332
Randgebieden (NE) 273, 550
Random Lengths Yearbook (US ISSN 0485-9960) 413
Randse Afrikaanse Universiteit. Jaarboek (SA) 322
Randse Afrikaanse Universiteit. Op en Om die Kampus (SA) 322
Randse Afrikaanse Universiteit. Opsommings van Proefskrifte en Verhandelinge/Abstracts of Dissertations and Theses (SA) 339
Randse Afrikaanse Universiteit. Prospektus (SA) 322
Rapport Annuel sur l'Economie Arabe (SY ISSN 0079-9688) 189
Rapport Annuel sur l'Economie Syrienne (SY ISSN 0079-9696) 189
Rapport General sur la Securite Sociale au Grande-Duche du Luxembourg see Luxembourg. Inspection Generale de la Securite Sociale. Rapport General sur la Securite Sociale au Grand-Duche de Luxembourg 500
Rapport National de Conjoncture Scientifique. Rapport de Synthese (FR) 789

Rapport sur la Situation Demographique de la France (FR) 729
Rapporto sulla Industria Cotoniera Italiana (IT) 856
Rasmi Jaridah see Afghanistan. Ministry of Justice. Official Gazette 508
Rassegna di Letteratura Tomistica (IT) 690
Rassegna Internazionale del Film Scientifico - Didattico (IT ISSN 0079-9726) 913
Rastitel'nye Resursy Sibiri i Dal'nego Vostoka see Rastitel'nyi Mir Sibiri i Dal'nego Vostoka 110
Rastitel'nyi Mir Sibiri i Dal'nego Vostoka (UR) 110
Ratcliffian (UK ISSN 0048-6809) 263
Rationalist Annual see Question 492
Raumplanung und Umweltschutz im Kanton Zurich (SZ) 486, 754
Raven Press Series in Experimental Physiology (US) 126, 612
Ravi (PK) 571
Rayford W. Logan Lecture Series (US) 471
Raymond Dart Lecture (SA ISSN 0079-9815) 53
La Raza Law Review (US) 393, 517
Razon Mestiza (US) 393, 719, 901
Reaching the Manitoba Market (CN ISSN 0706-8085) 6
Reaction Kinetics see Gas Kinetics and Energy Transfer 255
Reaction Mechanisms in Organic Chemistry (NE ISSN 0079-9823) 253, 255
Reactive Intermediates in Organic Chemistry (US ISSN 0486-0748) 253, 255
Reactivity and Structure: Concepts of Organic Chemistry (US) 254
Reader's Digest Almanac and Yearbook (US ISSN 0079-9831) 361
Reader's Guide Series (US) 94
Readers in Social Problems (US) 799
Readex Microprint Publications (US ISSN 0079-984X) 94
Reading Geographer (UK ISSN 0309-3263) 425
Reading in Political Economy (UK ISSN 0305-814X) 147
Reading Journal (II) 350
Reading/Legon Joint Research Project in Village Development, South East Ghana. Report (UK) 30
Reading University Studies on Contemporary Europe (UK ISSN 0079-9866) 459
Readings for Introduction to Teaching (US) 322
Readings in Anthropology see Annual Editions: Readings in Anthropology 47
Readings in Development Economics (PK ISSN 0557-8280) 201
Readings in Economic History and Theory (UK) 192
Readings in Education see Annual Editions: Readings in Education 314
Readings in Educational Psychology: Contemporary Perspectives (US ISSN 0363-5953) 322
Readings in Environment see Annual Editions: Readings in Environment 384
Readings in Human Sexuality. Annual Editions see Annual Editions: Readings in Human Sexuality 100
Readings in Linguistics see Lingvisticke Citanky 547
Readings in Marketing see Annual Editions: Readings in Marketing 217
Readings in Marriage and Family see Annual Editions: Readings in Marriage and Family 812
Readings in Personal Growth and Adjustment see Annual Editions: Readings in Personal Growth and Adjustment 734
Readings in Political Economy see Reading in Political Economy 147
Readings in Social Problems see Annual Editions: Readings in Social Problems 804
Readings in Spanish-English Contrastive Linguistics (PR) 550
Reagent Chemicals (US) 249

Real Academia de Cordoba de Ciencias, Bellas Letras y Nobles Artes. Boletin(SP ISSN 0034-060X) *571*
Real Conservatorio Superior de Musica. Anuario (SP ISSN 0076-2318) *662*
Real Estate Development Annual (CN) *762*
Real Estate Directory of Manhattan (US ISSN 0098-8936) *762*
Real Estate Directory of the Borough of Manhattan *see* Real Estate Directory of Manhattan *762*
Real Estate for Professional Practitioners: a Wiley Series (US) *762*
Real Estate Law Digest (Supplement) (US) *517, 762*
Real Estate Reports (US ISSN 0079-9890) *762*
Real Estate Trends in Metropolitan Vancouver (CN ISSN 0085-5405) *762*
Real Estate Valuation Cost File (US ISSN 0098-9568) *138*
Real Sociedad Espanola de Historia Natural. Boletin de Geologia y Biologia (SP) *106, 299*
Realidad Peruana (PE) *189*
Realty Bluebook (US ISSN 0090-399X) *762*
Rebecca (UK) *557*
Rebis Chapbook Series (US ISSN 0147-0396) *581*
Recap of Milk Utilization in Montana *see* Report of Milk Utilization in Montana *41*
Recent Advances in Nuclear Medicine (US ISSN 0163-6170) *622*
Recent Advances in Obesity Research (US) *599, 695*
Recent Advances in Plasma Diagnostics(US ISSN 0079-9939) *599*
Recent Advances in Studies on Cardiac Structure and Metabolism *see* Advances in Myocardiology *606*
Recent Articles and Research in Progress (US) *789*
Recent Developments in the Chemistry of Natural Carbon Compounds (HU ISSN 0079-9947) *254*
Recent Developments of Neurobiology in Hungary (HU ISSN 0079-9955) *106*
Recent Key Publications for Retrieving Essential Sources of Information Covering All Fields of Human Endeavour *see* Vade-Mecum for Information Scientists *538*
Recent Progress in Hormone Research. Proceedings of the Laurentian Hormone Conference (US ISSN 0079-9963) *612*
Recent Progress in Surface Science (US ISSN 0079-9971) *256*
Recent Progress of Natural Science in Japan (JA) *789*
Recent Researches in Geology (II) *299*
Recent Results in Cancer Research/ Fortschritte der Krebsforschung (US ISSN 0080-0015) *606*
Recent Sociology (US ISSN 0080-0023) *815*
Recent Trends in Social Sciences (II) *799*
Recherche Urbaine (NE) *486*
Recherches Agronomiques Sommaire des Resultats (CN) *19*
Recherches Anglaises et Americaines (FR ISSN 0557-6989) *800*
Recherches d'Economie et de Sociologie Rurales *see* Annales d'Economie et de Sociologie Rurales *811*
Recherches d'Histoire et de Sciences Sociales/Studies in History and Social Sciences (FR ISSN 0249-5619) *434, 800*
Recherches de Psychologie Experimentale et Comparee (BE ISSN 0080-0058) *913*
Recherches en Linguistique Etrangere (FR) *550*
Recherches et Documents d'Art et d'Archeologie (FR ISSN 0080-0074) *64, 78*
Recherches Germaniques (FR ISSN 0399-1989) *550, 571*

Recherches Institutionnelles (FR) *94, 767*
Recherches Linguistiques (FR) *550*
Recherches sur la Musique Francaise Classique (FR ISSN 0080-0139) *662*
Recherches Voltaiques (UV ISSN 0486-1426) *53, 440*
Recht und Geschichte (GW ISSN 0486-1493) *434*
Rechts- und Staatswissenschaften (US ISSN 0080-0163) *517, 714*
Rechts- und Wirtschafts-Praxis. Steuerrecht. Ausgabe A *see* R W P Steuerrecht. Ausgabe A *517*
Rechts- und Wirtschafts-Praxis Steuerrecht. Ausgabe B *see* R W P Steuerrecht. Ausgabe B *517*
Rechtsbibliographie/Bibliographie Juridique/Law Bibliography (SZ) *94, 521*
Rechtshistorische Studien (NE) *517*
Rechtspflege Jahrbuch (GW ISSN 0080-018X) *517*
Rechtsrheinisches Koeln (GW) *459*
Rechtsstaat in der Bewaehrung (GW) *517, 524*
Rechtswissenschaft und Sozialpolitik (AU ISSN 0486-1558) *517, 714*
Recife, Brazil. Secretaria de Assuntos Juridicos. Revista (BL) *517*
Recife, Brazil. Secretaria de Educacao e Culturo. Arquivos (BL) *471*
Reciprocal Meat Conference. Proceedings *see* American Meat Science Association. Reciprocal Meat Conference. Proceedings *403*
Recommended Country Hotels of Britain (UK) *890*
Recommended Wayside Inns of Britain (UK ISSN 0080-0252) *890*
Reconstruction of Society Series (US) *815*
Reconstruction Surgery and Traumatology (SZ ISSN 0080-0260) *616, 625*
Reconstructionist Rabbinical College. Publications (US) *770*
Recopilacion de Doctrina Legal (SP) *517*
Record Prices *see* Music Master *661*
Record - Vehicular Technology Conference *see* I E E E Vehicular Technology Conference. Record *871*
Recording for the Blind. Catalog of Recorded Books (US ISSN 0484-1506) *133*
Recording in Great Britain (UK) *662, 818*
Records in Review (US) *663*
Records of Civilization. Sources and Studies (US ISSN 0080-0287) *435, 671*
Records of Early English Drama (CN) *571*
Records of the Ancient Near East (GW ISSN 0340-8450) *475*
Recreation and Outdoor Life Directory (US) *831*
Recreation Management Handbook (UK ISSN 0144-624X) *822*
Recreation Management Yearbook *see* Recreation Management Handbook *822*
Recreational Vehicle Campground and Services Directory *see* Trailer Life's Recreational Vehicle Campground and Services Directory *831*
Recruitment and Training Services Handbook (UK) *210*
Recueil Annuel de Jurisprudence Belge (BE) *517*
Recueil Complet des Budgets de la Syrie (SY ISSN 0080-0309) *231*
Recueil des Arrets de la Cour Supreme du Canada *see* Canada Supreme Court Reports *510*
Recueil des Corrections de Cartes (Year) (FR ISSN 0180-9970) *425*
Recueil des Films (CN ISSN 0085-543X) *651*
Recueil des Instructions Donnees aux Ambassadeurs et Ministres de France(FR ISSN 0080-0333) *723*
Recueil des Travaux de l'Histoire de la Litterature *see* Zbornik Istorije Knjizevnosti *577*

Recueil des Travaux sur la Protection des Monuments Historiques *see* Zbornik Zastite Spomenika Kulture *80*
Recueil International de Statistiques des Transports Publics Urbains *see* International Statistical Handbook of Urban Public Transport *862*
Recueil Periodique des Juris-Classeurs: Droit Civil (FR) *517*
Recurring Bibliography, Education in the Allied Health Professions (US ISSN 0080-0341) *756*
Red Book of Eye, Ear, Nose and Throat Specialists *see* Red Book of Ophthalmology *616*
Red Book of Housing Manufacturers (US ISSN 0149-7642) *138*
Red Book of Ophthalmology (US ISSN 0146-4582) *616*
Red Contable Agraria Nacional (SP) *30*
Red Deer College. Learning Resources Centre. What's the Use...? (CN ISSN 0380-5727) *339, 350*
Red Dust (US) *571*
Red Hill Press *see* Invisible City *580*
Red Letters (UK) *714*
Red Menace (CN) *714, 901*
Redbook's Young Mother (US) *257*
Rede Ferroviaria Federal, S.A. Sistema Ferroviario R F F S A *see* Sistema Ferroviario R F F S A *873*
Reden zur Wirtschaftspolitik (GW) *147*
Reducing Your Income Tax (AT ISSN 0080-0414) *231*
Reed's Nautical Almanac (UK ISSN 0080-0422) *863*
Reeks Arbeidshygiene en Arbeidsgeneeskunds *see* Commission of the European Communities. Collection d'Hygiene et de Medecine du Travail *495*
Reference and Subscription Books Reviews (US ISSN 0080-0430) *535*
Reference Book - Argentina (US ISSN 0080-0449) *189*
Reference Book of Highway Personnel (US ISSN 0516-9445) *863*
Reference Book of Transportation *see* Dun & Bradstreet Reference Book of Transportation *203*
Reference Book - Republic of South Africa (US ISSN 0080-0457) *189*
Reference Book Review Index (US) *3, 761*
Reference Catalogue of Indian Books in Print (II) *94*
Reference Data for Radio Engineers (US) *268*
Reference Data on Profile of Medical Practice (US) *599*
Reference Data on Socioeconomic Issues of Health (US ISSN 0092-8836) *599, 806*
Reference Encyclopedia of the American Indian (US) *361, 393*
Reference Guide & Comprehensive Catalog of International Serials *see* Librarians' Guide to Back Issues of International Periodicals *506*
Reference Sources (US) *94*
References to Scientific Literature on Fire (UK ISSN 0306-5766) *395*
Refining, Construction, Petrochemical & Natural Gas Processing Plants of the World (US) *681*
Reflection (Spokane) (US ISSN 0484-2650) *571*
Reform in Northern Ireland (UK) *517*
Reformationsgeschichtliche Studien und Texte (GW ISSN 0080-0473) *772*
Reformed Church of America. Historical Series (US ISSN 0080-0481) *772*
Reformed Ecumenical Synod World Diaconal Bulletin *see* R E S World Diaconal Bulletin *772*
Refractory Materials (US ISSN 0080-049X) *244*
Refrigeration and Air Conditioning Directory *see* Refrigeration and Air Conditioning Year Book *430*
Refrigeration and Air Conditioning Year Book (UK ISSN 0305-0777) *430*
Refrigeration Annual (AT ISSN 0080-0511) *430*

Regency International Directory (UK ISSN 0080-0538) *176, 283*
Reger-Studien (GW) *663*
Regesta Regum Scottorum (UK ISSN 0080-0554) *435*
Regi Magyar Dallamok Tara/Corpus Musicae Popularis Hungaricae (HU ISSN 0080-0562) *663*
Regi Magyar Prozai Emlekek (HU ISSN 0080-0570) *571*
Regie de l'Assurance Malade. Statistiques Annuelles *see* Quebec (Province) Health Insurance Board. Annual Statistics *502*
Regimen Legal Tributario (CK) *517*
Regimes de Pensions au Canada *see* Pension Plans in Canada *502*
Regina Geographical Studies (CN) *425*
Regional Advisory Council for Technological Education. Science Education in the Region *see* Science Education in the Region *790*
Regional Breakdown of World Travel Statistics (SP) *845, 890*
Regional Conference on Water Resources Development in Asia and the Far East. Proceedings (UN ISSN 0080-0589) *897*
Regional Council Directory *see* National Association of Regional Councils. Directory *744*
Regional Institute of Social Welfare Research. Annual Report (US ISSN 0091-2859) *808*
Regional Plan Association, Inc. News *see* R P A News *486*
Regional Planning (NE) *808*
Regional Science Dissertation and Monograph Series (US) *486*
Regional Science Research Institute, Philadelphia. Bibliography Series (US ISSN 0080-0619) *795*
Regional Science Research Institute, Philadelphia. Monograph Series (US ISSN 0080-0627) *148*
Regional'naya Nauka o Razmeshchenii Proizvoditel'nykh Sil (UR) *225*
Regionalplanung in Kanton Zurich *see* Raumplanung und Umweltschutz im Kanton Zurich *486*
Region's Agenda (US ISSN 0034-3420) *486*
Register of Companies in New South Wales (AT ISSN 0085-5456) *913*
Register of Defunct & Other Companies(UK) *241*
Register of Early Music (UK) *663*
Register of Manufacturing Industries in New South Wales *see* Register of Companies in New South Wales *913*
Register of Medical Practitioners, Interns and Dentists for the Republic of South Africa (SA) *799*
Register of On-Going Labour Research (CN ISSN 0708-1065) *800*
Register of Patent Agents (UK) *677*
Register of Research and Investigation in Adult Education (US ISSN 0080-147X) *328*
Register of Thoroughbred Stallions (UK ISSN 0305-5892) *828*
Register over Gaellande SFS-Foerfattningar (SW) *517, 535*
Registre Aeronautique International (FR ISSN 0080-066X) *880*
Registre International de Classification de Navires et d'Aeronefs *see* Registre Maritime *880*
Registre International des Brasseurs, Eaux et Limonades *see* International Brewers' Directory and Soft Drink Guide *86*
Registre Maritime (FR) *880*
Registro de Organismos de Salud (CK) *754*
Registry of Accredited Facilities and Certified Individuals in Orthotics and Prosthetics (US ISSN 0080-0686) *616*
Registry of Certified Prosthetic and Orthopedic Appliance Facilities *see* Registry of Accredited Facilities and Certified Individuals in Orthotics and Prosthetics *616*
Registry of Toxic Effects of Chemical Substances (US) *496*

Regulae Benedicti Studia. Annuarium Internationale (GW) 767
Regular Savings Plans see Unit-Linked Savings Plans 501
Regulations for the Electrical Equipment of Buildings (UK) 358
Reha-Rundbrief (GW) 133, 346
Rehabilitation/Ryoiku (JA ISSN 0036-0538) 599
Rehabilitation der Entwicklungsgehemmten (GW ISSN 0080-0708) 346, 599
Rehabilitation Gazette (US ISSN 0361-4166) 133, 286, 346
Rehabilitation Industries Corporation. Annual Report (II ISSN 0080-0724) 225, 346
Rehabilitation und Praevention (US) 599
Rehovot (IS ISSN 0034-3609) 350, 789
Reichenbachia (GE ISSN 0070-7279) 121
Reign of Charlemagne-Documents of Medieval History (UK) 459
Reihe Strafrecht (SZ) 517
Reilly-Lake Shore Graphics. R O P Color Requirements Report see Newspaper Requirements 912
Reimpressions G & B (US) 789
Reine und Angewandte Metallkunde in Einzeldarstellungen see Materials Research and Engineering 628
Reinforced Concrete Research Council. Bulletins (US ISSN 0569-8057) 138
Reinforced Plastics Congress (UK ISSN 0306-3607) 707
Reinwardtia (IO ISSN 0034-365X) 117
Reisen in Deutschland; Deutsches Handbuch fuer Fremdenverkehr (GW) 890
Relacion de Ingenieros de Caminos, Canales y Puertos (SP) 376
Relations Etrangeres du Canada see Canadian Foreign Relations 720
Relatoria D N O C S see Brazil. Departamento Nacional de Obras Contras as Secas. Relatorio 740
Relatos Ineditos Argentinos (AG) 571
Relay D.A.T.A.Book (US) 358
Reliability and Maintainability Conference. Record (US) 358
Reliability Physics Symposium Abstracts (US ISSN 0080-0821) 700
Religioese Graphik (AU ISSN 0034-3935) 78, 767
Religion and Reason; Method and Theory in the Study and Interpretation of Religion (NE ISSN 0080-0848) 767
Religion et Sciences de l'Homme (FR ISSN 0080-0864) 767
Religion Index Two: Multi-Author Works (US ISSN 0149-8436) 769
Religion, Wissenschaft, Kultur. Jahrbuch (AU ISSN 0080-0872) 767
Religione e Societa (IT) 767, 815
Religionspaedagogische Praxis (GW) 767
Religious & Theological Abstracts (US ISSN 0034-4044) 3, 769
Religious Books and Serials in Print (US ISSN 0000-0612) 94, 767
Remains, Historical and Literary, Connected with the Palatine Counties of Lancaster and Chester (UK ISSN 0080-0880) 460
Remedia Hoechst (GW ISSN 0080-0899) 685
Remedies see B A R-B R I Bar Review. Remedies 509
Remember Our Fires see Shameless Hussy Review 901
Remington Hunting & Shooting Guide (US) 831
Remote Systems Technology Proceedings see Conference on Remote Systems Technology. Proceedings 702
Renaissance and Modern Studies (UK ISSN 0486-3720) 492
Renaissance Drama (US ISSN 0486-3739) 571, 859
Renaissance Manuscript Studies (GW) 663

Renaissance Papers (US ISSN 0584-4207) 571
Renaissance Two; Journal of Afro-American Studies (US ISSN 0360-7410) 393
Renaissance 2 see Renaissance Two; Journal of Afro-American Studies 393
Rencontres Internationales de Geneve (SZ) 690, 800
Renderers' Yearbook see Spectrum 406
Renegade (US) 393
Renewal of Town and Village (NE ISSN 0486-3887) 913
Renovatie en Onderhoud (NE) 138
Renta Nacional de Espana (SP) 745
Repertoire Administratif (CN) 714, 808
Repertoire Bibliographique des Livres Imprimes en France (GW ISSN 0085-5499) 94
Repertoire Complementaire Alphabetique des Valeurs Mobilieres Francaises et Etrangeres Non Cotees en France (FR ISSN 0080-0945) 231
Repertoire de l'Edition au Quebec (CN ISSN 0315-5943) 94, 761
Repertoire de la Presse Suisse/Leitfaden der Schweizer Presse (SZ) 505
Repertoire de la Recherche dans les Universites Subventionnee Par le Gouvernement Federal see Directory of Federally Supported Research in Universities 782
Repertoire de Materiaux et Elements Controles du Batiment (FR ISSN 0335-3559) 138, 637
Repertoire des Associations (CN) 180
Repertoire des Centres de Recherche Alimentaire (FR) 405
Repertoire des Cooperatives du Quebec(CN ISSN 0080-097X) 181
Repertoire des Cours d'Ete (CN ISSN 0382-5914) 350
Repertoire des Entreprises Financieres, Commerciales Industrielles Exercant en Republique du Mali see Annuaire des Entreprises du Mali 178
Repertoire des Geographes de France (FR) 425
Repertoire des Livres de Langue Francaise Disponibles see Livres Disponibles 92
Repertoire des Organisations de Travailleurs au Canada see Directory of Labour Organizations in Canada 506
Repertoire des Principaux Textes Legislatifs et Reglementaires Promulgues en Republique du Mali (ML ISSN 0080-1011) 180
Repertoire des Productions de l'Industrie Cotonniere Francaise (FR ISSN 0080-102X) 856
Repertoire des Produits Electroniques (CN) 358
Repertoire des Produits Fabriques au Quebec (CN ISSN 0704-7940) 856
Repertoire des Salles de Spectacle see Facilities Directory 859
Repertoire des Services Sociaux Canadiens see Directory of Canadian Welfare Services 805
Repertoire des Societes de Commerce Exterieur Francaises (FR ISSN 0080-1070) 197
Repertoire des Universites Canadiennes see Directory of Canadian Universities 335
Repertoire Dictionnaire Industriel (FR ISSN 0080-1089) 225
Repertoire General Alphabetique des Valeurs Cotees en France et des Valeurs Non Cotees (FR ISSN 0080-1127) 231
Repertoire General de la Production Francaise (FR ISSN 0337-5714) 241, 677
Repertoire General des Clubs Sportifs de France (FR ISSN 0080-1135) 822
Repertoire International de la Librairie Ancienne see International Directory of Antiquarian Booksellers 759
Repertoire International des Editeurs et Diffuseurs de Langue Francaise (FR) 759

Repertoire International des Medievistes (FR ISSN 0080-1151) 460, 492
Repertoire Mondial des Ecoles de Medecine see World Directory of Medical Schools 332
Repertoire Pratique de la Publicite (FR ISSN 0080-1194) 6
Repertoire Technique de la Sous-Traitance des Industries Plastiques (FR) 707
Repertoire Tequi Quincaillerie see Memento General Tequi Quincaillerie 141
Repertoriex see French Periodical Index 90
Repertorio Chimico Italiano (IT) 374
Repertorio del Foro Italiano (IT) 517
Repertorio delle Decisioni della Corte Costituzionale (IT) 517
Repertorio delle Industrie Siderurgiche Italiane (IT ISSN 0080-1216) 629
Repertorio di Giurisprudenza del Lavoro (IT) 517
Repertorio Tecniche Ambientali (IT) 388, 754
Repertorio Terapeutico (IT) 685
Repertorium Plantarum Succulentarum (AU ISSN 0486-4271) 117
Repertorium van Suid-Afrikaanse Tydskrifartikels see Index to South African Periodicals 760
Repertorium van Werken, in Vlaanderen Uitgegeven, of Door Monopoliehouders Ingevoerd (BE ISSN 0080-1224) 94
Report and Studies in the History of Art see Studies in the History of Art 79
Report - Arizona State Dental Board. see Arizona. State Dental Board. Report 609
Report by the Auditor General on the Accounts of Lesotho (LO ISSN 0085-2740) 232
Report - C.O.D.A.S.Y.L. Data Base Task Group see Conference on Data Systems Languages. Data Base Task Group. Report 271
Report for the Half Year of the Imperial Bank of India see State Bank of India. Report of the Central Board of Directors 176
Report - Hoover Institution on War, Revolution and Peace see Hoover Institution on War, Revolution, and Peace. Report 721
Report - Judicial Inquiry Board (Chicago) see Illinois. Judicial Inquiry Board. Report 718
Report - Louisiana State Board of Nurse Examiners see Louisiana. State Board of Nurse Examiners. Report 614
Report - Maryland Division of Correction see Maryland. Division of Correction. Report 282
Report: Massachusetts State Scholarship Programs (US) 339
Report - Nevada Bureau of Mines and Geology see Nevada. Bureau of Mines and Geology. Report 297
Report - North Dakota State Department of Health see North Dakota. State Department of Health. Report 753
Report of Achievements of Programs for the Aging see Hawaii. Commission on Aging. Report of Achievements of Programs for the Aging 806
Report of Cases Argued and Determined in the Supreme Court of the State of Arizona see Arizona Reports 509
Report of Cases Determined in the Supreme Court and Court of Appeals of the State of New Mexico (US ISSN 0094-7148) 517
Report of Educational Statistics see Delaware. State Board of Education. Report of Educational Statistics 316
Report of Forest and Windbarrier Planting in the United States see Report of Forest Planting, Seeding and Silvical Treatments in the United States 410

REPORT ON   1471

Report of Forest Planting, Seeding and Silvical Treatments in the United States (US) 410
Report of Ionosphere and Space Research in Japan see Solar Terrestrial Environmental Research in Japan 306
Report of Milk Utilization in Montana (US ISSN 0080-1267) 41
Report of National Survey on Family Planning in Singapore (SI) 132
Report of Overseas Mining Investigation: India, Pakistan, Bangladesh/Kaigai Kogyo Jijo Chosa Hokokusho: Indo, Pakisutan, Banguradisshu (JA) 646
Report of Overseas Mining Investigation: Madagascar, Swaziland/Kaigai Kogyo Jijo Chosa Hokokusho: Madagasukaru, Suwajirando (JA) 646
Report of Probation Supervision Workload (US ISSN 0362-7489) 283
Report of Secretary of Defense to the Congress see U. S. Department of Defense. Report of Secretary of Defense to the Congress 640
Report of the Annual Conference of State Employment Security Personnel Officers see Conference of State Employment Security Personnel Officers. Report 220
Report of the Auditor General on the Accounts of Trinidad and Tobago (TR) 232
Report of the Carcinogenesis Program see U.S. National Cancer Institute. Report of the Carcinogenesis Program 606
Report of the Council for Tobacco Research-U.S.A., Inc. see Council for Tobacco Research--U.S.A. Report 287
Report of the Federal Home Loan Mortgage Corporation see Federal Home Loan Mortgage Corporation. Report 173
Report of the General Assembly of the Members of the International Office of Cocoa and Chocolate and the International Sugar Confectionary Manufacturers' Association (BE ISSN 0535-1626) 407
Report of the Judicial Department, State of Connecticut see Connecticut. Judicial Department. Report 511
Report of the Legislative Transportation Committee see Washington (State) Legislature. Transportation Committee. Report 864
Report of the Nebraska Indian Commission see Nebraska. Indian Commission. Report 393
Report of the New Mexico Veteran's Service Commission see New Mexico. Veterans' Service Commission. Report 640
Report of the Ombudsman (Juneau) see Alaska. Office of Ombudsman. Report of the Ombudsman 739
Report of the State Board of Indenpendent Colleges and Universities (Tallahassee) see Florida. State Board of Independent Colleges and Universities. Report 336
Report - Office of Alcoholism, Department of Health and Social Services, State of Alaska see Alaska. Office of Alcoholism. Report 286
Report on Annual Commanders' Conference Information Exchange Program see Commanders' Conference Information Exchange Program. Report 638
Report on Applications for Orders Authorizing or Approving the Interception of Wire or Oral Communications see U.S. Administrative Office of the United States Courts. Report on Applications for Orders Authorizing or Approving the Interception of Wire or Oral Communications s 519
Report on Australian Universities (AT ISSN 0085-5510) 339
Report on Czechoslovak Jewry (UK ISSN 0306-9567) 393

Report on Department of
Transportation, Bureau of Rail and
Motor Carrier Services. see
Connecticut. Auditors of Public
Accounts. Report on Department of
Transportation, Bureau of Rail and
Motor Carrier Services 862
Report on Domestic and International
Commercial Loan Charge-Offs (US)
176
Report on Federal Funds Received in
Iowa (US ISSN 0091-8695) 232
Report on Federally Connected Pupils.
Hawaii Public Schools see Hawaii.
Department of Education. Office of
Business Services. Report on
Federally Connected Pupils: Hawaii
Public Schools 318
Report on Foreign Currencies Held by
the U. S. Government see U. S.
Treasury Department. Bureau of
Government Financial Operations.
Report on Foreign Currencies Held
by the U. S. Government 177
Report on National Survey of
Compensation Paid Scientists and
Engineers Engaged in Research and
Development Activities see Battelle
Memorial Institute. Columbus
Laboratories. Report on National
Survey of Compensation Paid
Scientists and Engineers Engaged in
Research and Development Activities
206
Report on Passenger Road Transport in
Zambia (ZA) 845, 866
Report on Research and Publications
(Knoxville) see University of
Tennessee. Report on Research and
Publications 328
Report on the Availability of
Postsecondary and Adult Vocational
Education to Oregon's Citizens see
Oregon. State Advisory Council for
Career and Vocational Education.
Annual Evaluation Report 321
Report on the Background, Current
Programmes and Planned
Development of the Bangladesh
Institute of Development Studies
(BG) 189
Report on the Credit Given by
Educational Institutions see Transfer
Credit Practices by Selected
Education Institutions 323
Report on the Progress of Education in
Pakistan see Development of
Education in Pakistan 316
Report on the World Health Situation
(UN ISSN 0085-5529) 754
Report on Tourism Statistics in
Tanzania (TZ ISSN 0564-836X)
390
Report on United States Antarctic
Research Activities see National
Research Council. Committee on
Polar Research. Report on United
States Antarctic Research Activities
424
Report on Urban Research/Toshi
Kenkyu Hokoku (JA) 487
Report - Social Service Board of North
Dakota see North Dakota. Social
Service Board. Report 808
Report to S C A R on South African
Antarctic Research Activities
(Scientific Committee for Antarctic
Research) (SA ISSN 0081-2412)
789, 852
Report to the Congress on Ocean
Pollution, Overfishing, and Offshore
Development see U.S. National
Oceanic and Atmospheric
Administration. Report to the
Congress on Ocean Pollution,
Overfishing, and Offshore
Development 389
Report to the Governor - Arizona
Commission on the Arts &
Humanities see Arizona Commission
on the Arts & Humanities. Report to
the Governor 489
Report - Workshop for Child Care Staff
of Florida's Child Caring Facilities
see Workshop for Child Care Staff of
Florida's Child Caring Facilities.
Report 257
Reportages Fantastiques (FR ISSN
0080-133X) 460

Reports and Papers in the Social
Sciences (UN ISSN 0080-1348)
800
Reports and Papers on Mass
Communications (UN ISSN 0080-
1356) 265
Reports in Mackinac History and
Archaeology (US) 64, 471
Reports of Investigations - Illinois State
Museum see Illinois. State Museum.
Reports of Investigations 61
Reports of Patent, Design, Trade Mark
and Other Cases (UK ISSN 0080-
1364) 677
Reports of Research Supported by the
Petroleum Research Fund (US) 681
Reports on Astronomy see International
Astronomical Union. Transactions
and Highlights 82
Reports on Education (UK) 322
Reports on International Compensation.
Argentina see Executive
Compensation Service. Reports on
International Compensation.
Argentina 215
Reports on International Compensation.
Puerto Rico see Executive
Compensation Service. Reports on
International Compensation. Puerto
Rico 215
Reports on Marine Science Affairs
(UN) 312
Reprints in International Finance (US
ISSN 0080-1380) 176
Reproductions (PH) 106, 729
Repsol Pamphlets (IE) 714
Republic Forge Company. Annual
Report (II) 225
Republican Almanac (US ISSN 0363-
9290) 714
Republique Unie du Cameroun:
Annuaire International/United
Republic of Cameroon International
Year Book (CM) 441
Requirements for Certification of
Teachers, Counsellors, Librarians,
Administrators for Elementary
Schools, Secondary Schools, Junior
Colleges (US ISSN 0080-1429) 345
Research Activities 1973 see
Commonwealth Scientific and
Industrial Research Organization.
Division of Radiophysics. Report 82
Research Advances in Alcohol & Drug
Problems (US ISSN 0093-9714)
287
Research and Clinical Forums (UK
ISSN 0143-3083) 599
Research and Clinical Studies in
Headache (SZ ISSN 0080-1453)
621
Research and Construction on Steel-
Engineering see Forschung und
Konstruktion im Stahlbau 379
Research and Developement Program
see U.S. Federal Highway
Administration Research and
Development Program 377
Research and Development Activities in
the Netherlands see Speur- en
Ontwikkelingswerk in Nederland
853
Research and Development - American
Gas Association see American Gas
Association. Research and
Development 677
Research and Development in Ireland
(IE ISSN 0085-5545) 789
Research and Publications in New York
State History (US ISSN 0080-1488)
438
Research and Statistics Annual Report
see South Dakota. State Department
of Public Welfare. Research and
Statistics Annual Report 811
Research Centers Directory (US ISSN
0080-1518) 789
Research Council of Alberta. Report
see Alberta Research Council.
Reports 850
Research Division Report - Virginia
Polytechnic Institute and State
University see Virginia Polytechnic
Institute and State University.
Research Division. Report 22
Research Fields in Physics at United
Kingdom Universities and
Polytechnics (UK ISSN 0308-9290)
339, 698

Research Film/Film de Recherche/
Forschungsfilm (GW ISSN 0034-
5202) 913
Research Group for European
Migration Problems. Publications
(NE ISSN 0080-1623) 729
Research in Community and Mental
Health (US ISSN 0192-0812) 738,
754
Research in Contemporary and Applied
Geography (US) 425
Research in Corporate Social
Performance and Policy (US) 148
Research in Economic Anthropology
(US ISSN 0190-1281) 53
Research in Economic History (US
ISSN 0363-3268) 192
Research in Economics/Business
Administration (US ISSN 0080-
1631) 148, 216
Research in Experimental Economics
(US) 192
Research in Finance (US ISSN 0196-
3821) 176
Research in Fisheries (US ISSN 0083-
7555) 399
Research in Health Economics see
Advances in Health Economics and
Health Services Research 694
Research in Human Capital and
Development (US ISSN 0194-3960)
213
Research in International Business and
Finance (US) 197
Research in Labor Economics (US)
210
Research in Law and Economics (US
ISSN 0193-5895) 148, 517
Research in Law and Sociology see
Research in Law, Deviance and
Social Control 517
Research in Law, Deviance and Social
Control (US) 517, 815
Research in Marketing (US ISSN
0191-3026) 219
Research in Molecular Biology (GW
ISSN 0340-5400) 120
Research in Norway (NO) 789
Research in Organizational Behavior
(US ISSN 0191-3085) 738
Research in Parapsychology (US ISSN
0094-7172) 676
Research in Phenomenology (US ISSN
0085-5553) 690
Research in Philosophy and
Technology(US ISSN 0161-7249)
690, 852
Research in Political Economy (US
ISSN 0161-7230) 192, 714
Research in Population Economics (US
ISSN 0163-7878) 729
Research in Protozoology (US ISSN
0080-1658) 130
Research in Public Policy and
Management (US) 216, 745
Research in Race and Ethnic Relations
(US) 815
Research in Social Movements,
Conflicts and Change (US ISSN
0163-786X) 815
Research in Social Problems and Public
Policy (US ISSN 0196-1152) 714,
815
Research in Sociology of Education and
Socialization (US ISSN 0197-5080)
322
Research in Surface Forces (US ISSN
0080-1666) 256, 698
Research in the History of Education:
A List of Theses for Higher Degrees
in the Universities of England and
Wales (UK ISSN 0080-1674) 328
Research in the Interweave of Social
Roles: Women and Men (US ISSN
0272-2801) 815
Research in the Life Sciences (US
ISSN 0034-5261) 19, 106
Research in Water Quality and Water
Technology see Vizminosegi es
Viztechnologiai Kutatasi Eredmenyek
899
Research Institute for Agricultural
Economics. Bulletin (HU) 30
Research Institute for Estate Crops,
Bogor. Cocoa Statistics/Balai
Penelitian Perkebunan, Bogor.
Statistik Coklat (IO) 38

Research Institute for Estate Crops,
Bogor. Coffee Statistics/Balai
Penelitian Perkebunan, Bogor.
Statistik Kopi (IO) 38
Research Institute for Estate Crops,
Bogor. Communications (IO) 38
Research Institute for Estate Crops,
Bogor. Rubber Statistics/Balai
Penelitian Perkebunan, Bogor.
Statistik Karet (IO) 38
Research Institute Master Federal Tax
Manual see Master Federal Tax
Manual 230
Research Institute on International
Change. Studies (US) 714
Research into Disease (TH ISSN 0557-
7330) 599
Research Journal: Humanities and
Social Sciences (II) 492, 800
Research Methods in Neurochemistry
(US) 111, 621
Research Monographs on Human
Population (US) 729
Research Opportunities in Renaissance
Drama (US ISSN 0098-647X) 859
Research Papers in Geography (AT)
425
Research Problems in Biology (US
ISSN 0569-5376) 106
Research Program Reports see U.S.
National Institute of Neurological
Diseases and Stroke. Research
Program Reports 621
Research Report - Department of
Motor Vehicles Research and
Technology Division (Olympia) see
Washington (State). Department of
Motor Vehicles. Research and
Technology. Research Report 872
Research Report from M I T-Harvard
Joint Center for Urban Studies see
Joint Center for Urban Studies.
Research Report from M I T-
Harvard 485
Research Report - Texas Department of
Corrections; Treatment Directorate,
Research and Development Division
see Texas. Department of
Corrections. Research and
Development Division. Research
Report 284
Research Reports in Public Policy see
University of California, Santa
Barbara. Urban Economics Program.
Research Reports in Public Policy
747
Research Strengths of Universities in
the Developing Countries of the
Commonwealth (UK) 339
Research Studies in Library Science
(US ISSN 0080-1739) 535
Researcher's Guide to Washington (US)
789, 852
Researches on Anatolian Art see
Anadolu Sanati Arastirmalari 71
Reserve Bank of Australia. Annual
Report (AT ISSN 0080-1771) 176
Reserve Bank of Australia. Occasional
Papers (AT ISSN 0080-178X) 176,
189
Reserve Bank of Australia. Statistical
Bulletin. Supplement (AT ISSN
0080-1798) 163
Reserve Bank of India. Annual Report
(II ISSN 0080-1801) 176
Reserve Bank of Malawi. Report and
Accounts (MW ISSN 0486-5383)
176
Reserve Bank of New Zealand.
Research Papers (NZ) 189
Reserve Forces Almanac (US ISSN
0363-860X) 640
Reserves of Coal, Province of Alberta
(CN ISSN 0380-4275) 363, 646
Reshimat Ma'amarim Be-Mada'e Ha-
Yahadut see Index of Articles on
Jewish Studies 769
Residential Cost Manual (US) 138
Residue Reviews (US ISSN 0080-
181X) 247
Resolutions of the General Assembly of
the United Nations (UN ISSN
0082-8211) 723

Resolutions of the Seminar on the Acquisition of Latin American Library Materials and List of Committees *see* Seminar on the Acquisition of Latin American Library Materials. Resolutions and Lists of Commitees 913
Resorts & Parks Purchasing Guide (US) 483
Resorts & R V Parks Purchasing Guide *see* Resorts & Parks Purchasing Guide 483
Resource and Environmental Science Series (UK) 106, 388
Resource Directory of Branded Line Merchandise in the Homesewing Industry *see* Homesewing Resource Directory of Branded Line Merchandise in the Homesewing Industry 262
Resources(Cambridge) (US) 419
Resources en Eau de Tunisie (TI) 897
Resources Exploitation Institute. Bulletin/Shigen Sogo Kaihatsu Kenkyusho Obun Hokoku (JA) 370
Resources for Educators of Adults (US) 329
Resources for the Study of Anthropology (US) 53
Resources for Tourism/Hospitality/Recreation (CN) 339, 667
Resources of Music (UK ISSN 0080-1828) 663
Responsa Meridiana (SA ISSN 0486-5588) 517
Restatement in the Courts. Pocket Parts(US) 517
Restatement in the Courts. Supplements *see* Restatement in the Courts. Pocket Parts 517
Restaurant Operations *see* Table Service Restaurant Operations 483
Reston Series in Construction Technology (US) 138
Results and Problems in Cell Differentiation (US ISSN 0080-1844) 120
Results of the National Operations & Automation Survey *see* American Bankers Association. Operations and Automation Division. Results of the National Operations & Automation Survey 168
Resume Annuel d'Informations sur les Catastrophes Naturelles *see* Annual Summary of Information on Natural Disasters 303
Resumen Cinematografico (SP) 651
Resumen de Actividades I N I (Year) (Instituto Nacional de Industria) (SP) 225
Resumo Meteorologico (PO) 913
Retail Credit Federation Membership Directory *see* Consumer Credit Association of the United Kingdom. Membership Directory 172
Retail Trade Europe *see* Retail Trade International 219
Retail Trade International (UK) 219
Retail Wages and Salaries in Canada (CN ISSN 0080-1860) 210
Retailing in Tennessee (US ISSN 0361-0020) 163
Retired Military Almanac (US ISSN 0149-7197) 640
Retirement Paradises of the World (US) 890
Return of Outstanding Debt (UK ISSN 0143-103X) 845
Reumatismo (IT ISSN 0048-7449) 623
Reuniao Geral de Cultura do Arroz. Anais (BL) 43
Reunion. Secretariat General pour les Affaires Economiques. Statistiques et Indicateurs Economiques (RE) 213
Reunion Annuelle des Sciences de la Terre (FR) 289
Reunion Nacional Sobre Problemas de Contaminacion Ambiental. Memoria (MX) 388
Reuniones Bibliotecologicas *see* Seminar on the Acquisition of Latin American Library Materials. Final Report and Working Papers 535

Reunions Jointes des Membres de l'Assemblee Consultative du Conseil de l'Europe et des Membres du Parlement Europeen. Compte Rendu in Extenso des Debats *see* Joint Meeting of the Members of the Consultative Assembly of the Council of Europe and of the Members of the European Parliamentary Assembly. Official Report of Debates 722
Reuss Jahrbuch der Luft- und Raumfahrt (GW) 10
Revenue and Cost Analysis-Support Group (Washington) *see* U. S. Postal Service. Support Group. Revenue and Cost Analysis 266
Reverse Acronyms and Initialisms Dictionary *see* Reverse Acronyms, Initialisms and Abbreviations Dictionary 550
Reverse Acronyms, Initialisms and Abbreviations Dictionary (US) 550
Review (Charlottesville) (US ISSN 0190-3233) 550, 1072
Review Journal of Philosophy and Social Science (II) 690, 800
Review of Accidents on Indian Government Railways (II ISSN 0080-1933) 873
Review of Agricultural Economics Malaysia (MY ISSN 0034-6403) 30
Review of Architecture and Landscape Architecture (CN ISSN 0705-1913) 70
Review of Child Development Research(US ISSN 0091-3065) 257, 322
Review of Commerce Studies (II) 148
Review of Economic Situation of Air Transport (UN ISSN 0085-5596) 869
Review of Economics and Business (JA ISSN 0302-6574) 148
Review of Education in India (II) 322
Review of English Books on Asia (US) 94
Review of Fisheries in OECD Member Countries (FR ISSN 0078-6241) 399
Review of Maritime Transport (UN ISSN 0085-560X) 880
Review of National Literatures (US ISSN 0034-6640) 571
Review of Plant Protection Research (JA ISSN 0557-7527) 38
Review of Progress in Coloration and Related Topics (UK) 852
Review of Public and Co-Operative Economy in Israel. (IS) 181
Review of Research in Education (US ISSN 0091-732X) 350
Review of Special Education (US ISSN 0091-5580) 346
Review of the Economy of Rhodesia *see* Economic Survey of Rhodesia 185
Review of the Mineral Industry in Tanzania (TZ ISSN 0082-1659) 646
Review of the New Zealand Aid Programme *see* Annual Aid Review, Memorandum of New Zealand 199
Review of the World Wheat Situation (UK) 19
Review on Liberal Arts/Kyoyo Ronshu (JA) 492
Review on the Working of the Trade Unions Act, 1926 *see* Trade Unions in India 507
Reviews in Biochemical Toxicology (US ISSN 0163-7673) 112
Reviews in Engineering Geology (US ISSN 0080-2018) 376
Reviews in Perinatal Medicine (US ISSN 0362-5699) 615
Reviews of Modern Physics Monographs (US) 698
Reviews of Neuroscience (US) 621
Reviews of Physiology, Biochemistry and Experimental Pharmacology (US ISSN 0080-2042) 112, 126, 685
Reviews of Plasma Physics (US ISSN 0080-2050) 698
Revision de Programas *see* C I M M Y T Review 42
Revista A P I C E/A P I C E Journal (Asociacion Panamericana de Instituciones de Credito Educativo) (CK) 176, 322

Revista A T E M C O P. Especial Alquiladores (Asociacion Espanola de Tecnicos de Maquinaria para la Construccion y Obra Publicas) (SP) 376
Revista Agronomica del Noroeste Argentino (AG ISSN 0080-2069) 19
Revista Argentina de Politica (AG) 714
Revista Brasileira de Entomologia (BL ISSN 0085-5626) 121
Revista Brasileira de Teleducacao (BL) 268, 322
Revista C I A F *see* Revista Centro Interamericano de Fotointerpretacion 425
Revista Centro Interamericano de Fotointerpretacion (CK ISSN 0120-2499) 425
Revista Chilena de Entomologia (CL ISSN 0034-740X) 121
Revista Chilena de Historia Y Geografia (CL ISSN 0080-2093) 471
Revista Chilena en Venta (CL) 94
Revista Ciencias Farmaceuticas (CR) 685
Revista Ciencias Sociales (EC) 800
Revista Colombiana de Antropologia (CK) 53
Revista de Agricultura de Puerto Rico (PR) 19
Revista de Antropologia (BL ISSN 0034-7701) 53
Revista de Biologia del Uruguay (UY ISSN 0304-971X) 106
Revista de Biologia Marina (CL ISSN 0080-2115) 106
Revista de Ciencia Urbana (SP) 750
Revista de Ciencias Economicas; Economia, Finanzas, Administracao, Estatistica *see* Ciencias Economicas 143
Revista de Ciencias Juridicas Sociales (AG ISSN 0325-0601) 517
Revista de Derecho (HO) 517
Revista de Derecho Publico (AG) 517
Revista de Derecho Social Ecuatoriano (EC ISSN 0484-6923) 517
Revista de Derecho y Reforma Agraria (VE) 19, 517
Revista de Direito do Trabalho (BL) 517
Revista de Economia (VE) 148
Revista de Educacao A E C (Associacao de Educacao Catolica do Brasil) (BL) 322
Revista de Educacao e Cultura (BL ISSN 0482-5527) 322
Revista de Estudios Hispanicos (PR ISSN 0378-7974) 492
Revista de Filosofia Latinoamericana (AG) 691
Revista de Historia (CK) 435
Revista de Historia (CR) 471
Revista de Historia de Derecho (AG) 517
Revista de Historia de las Ideas (EC ISSN 0556-5987) 471
Revista de Historia de Rosario (AG ISSN 0556-5995) 471
Revista de Historia del Derecho (SP) 517
Revista de Industria Animal *see* Boletim de Industria Animal 43
Revista de la Integracion Centroamericana *see* Revista de la Integracion y el Desarrollo de Centroamerica 201
Revista de la Integracion y el Desarrollo de Centroamerica (HO) 201
Revista de la Universidad Catolica *see* Pontificia Universidad Catolica del Ecuador. Revista 263
Revista de Legislacion Argentina (AG ISSN 0034-8481) 517
Revista de Letras (BL ISSN 0080-2352) 571
Revista de Linguistica Aplicada *see* R L A 550
Revista de Matematica y Fisica Teorica. Serie A (AG ISSN 0080-2360) 698
Revista de Planeacion y Desarrollo (CK ISSN 0034-8686) 225
Revista de Poesia e Critica (BL) 581

Revista de Problemas Argentinos y Americanos (AG) 815
Revista de Psicologia Normal e Patologica (BL ISSN 0048-7740) 738
Revista de Servicio Social (PR ISSN 0034-8937) 808
Revista de Sociologia (CK) 815
Revista de Studios Historico Juridico (CL) 517
Revista del Folklore Ecuatoriano (EC ISSN 0556-6436) 402
Revista del Museo Americanista (AG) 53
Revista di Archeologia (IT) 64
Revista do B I N D E (Banco Nacional do Desenvolvimento Economico) (BL) 176
Revista Economica y Financiera *see* Universidad Nacional Mayor de San Marcos. Facultad de Ciencias Economicas y Comerciales. Revista 149
Revista Geografica de Valparaiso (CL ISSN 0034-9577) 425
Revista Geologica de Chile (CL) 299
Revista Hiperion (SP) 571
Revista Historica (UY) 471
Revista Humanidades (AG ISSN 0080-2387) 492
Revista I N I D E F *see* Revista Instituto Interamericano de Etnomusicologia y Folklore 663
Revista Iberica (US ISSN 0482-6558) 550, 571
Revista Instituto Interamericano de Etnomusicologia y Folklore (VE) 402, 663
Revista Internacional de Vivienda Rural/International Rural Housing Journal (VE) 487
Revista Juridica Panamena (PN ISSN 0302-6655) 517
Revista Latinoamericana de Ciencias Agricolas (VE) 19
Revista Latinoamericana de Microbiologia (MX ISSN 0034-9771) 124
Revista Mexicana de Seguridad Social (MX ISSN 0482-6876) 500
Revista Nacional de Cultura (VE) 492
Revista Pacifica Sur (PE) 106
Revista Paraguaya de Microbiologia (PY ISSN 0556-6908) 124, 130
Revista Paranaense de Desenvolvimento(BL ISSN 0556-6916) 176
Revista Peruana de Entomologia (PE ISSN 0080-2425) 121
Revista Portuguesa de Filologia (PO ISSN 0080-2433) 550
Revista Scriitorilor Romani (IT ISSN 0080-2441) 571
Revista Signos *see* Revista Signos de Valparaiso 571
Revista Signos de Valparaiso (CL ISSN 0035-0451) 550, 571
Revista Telebras (BL) 268
Revista UNIMAR (Universidade Estadual de Maringa) (BL) 339
Revista Universidad La Gran Colombia (CK) 418
Revistas Espanolas en Curso de Publicacion (SP ISSN 0210-0002) 94
Revistero (UY ISSN 0085-5642) 94
Revolutionary Virginia: the Road to Independence (US) 471
Revolutionary World (NE ISSN 0303-3856) 691
Revue Annuelle d'Histoire du Quatorzieme Arrondissement de Paris (FR ISSN 0556-7335) 460
Revue Archeologique de Narbonnaise (FR ISSN 0557-7705) 64
Revue Belge d'Archeologie et d'Histoire de l'Art (BE ISSN 0035-077X) 64, 78
Revue Belge de Geographie (BE ISSN 0035-0796) 425
Revue Belge de Numismatique et de Sigillographie (BE) 64, 460, 478
Revue Bibliographique de Sinologie (NE ISSN 0080-2484) 94, 438
Revue Canadienne d'Economie Publique et Cooperative *see* Canadian Journal of Public and Cooperative Economy 142

Revue Canadienne de Droit
 Communautaire *see* Canadian
 Community Law Journal *510*
Revue Canadienne des Sciences de
 Information *see* Canadian Journal of
 Information Science *528*
Revue Clivages *see* Clivages *579*
Revue d'Egyptologie (FR ISSN 0035-
 1849) *64, 435, 671*
Revue d'Ethnologie *see* Etnoloski
 Pregled *49*
Revue d'Histoire et de Civilisation du
 Maghreb (AE ISSN 0556-7343)
 441
Revue de Cytologie et de Biologie
 Vegetales *see* Revue de Cytologie et
 de Biologie Vegetales-la Botaniste
 117
Revue de Cytologie et de Biologie
 Vegetales-la Botaniste (FR ISSN
 0181-7582) *117*
Revue de Droit Compare (CN ISSN
 0080-2514) *517*
Revue de Droit Suisse *see* Zeitschrift
 fuer Schweizerisches Recht *521*
Revue de Geologie et de Geographie
 see Revue Roumaine de Geologie,
 Geophysique et Geographie.
 Geologie *299*
Revue de Geologie et de Geographie
 see Revue Roumaine de Geologie,
 Geophysique et Geographie.
 Geophysique *306*
Revue de la Mercerie, Nouveautes,
 Bonneterie, Lingerie; Confections
 (FR) *261*
Revue de La Saintonge et de l'Aunis
 (FR) *460*
Revue de Pau et du Bearn (FR) *493*
Revue de Theologie et de Philosophie.
 Cahiers (SZ) *691, 767*
Revue des Archaeologues et Historiens
 d'Art de Louvain (BE ISSN 0080-
 2530) *64, 78*
Revue des Etudes Anciennes (FR
 ISSN 0035-2004) *260*
Revue des Etudes Grecques (FR ISSN
 0035-2039) *64, 260*
Revue des Etudes Latines (FR) *260,
 550*
Revue des Etudes Slaves (FR ISSN
 0080-2557) *550, 571*
Revue des Lettres Modernes (FR ISSN
 0035-2136) *571*
Revue des Sciences Sociales de la
 France de l'Est (FR ISSN 0336-
 1573) *800*
Revue du Travail (HT ISSN 0482-
 8062) *210, 808*
Revue du Vieux Geneve (SZ) *460*
Revue Economique France-Israel *see*
 Revue Francaise de Cooperation
 Economique Avec Israel *180*
Revue Egyptienne de Droit
 International *see* Egyptian Review of
 International Law *523*
Revue Francaise de Cooperation
 Economique Avec Israel (FR ISSN
 0080-2506) *180*
Revue Francaise des Fournisseurs de
 Laboratoires *see* Revue Francaise des
 Laboratoires *496*
Revue Francaise des Laboratoires (FR)
 496
Revue Historique de Bordeaux et du
 Departement de la Gironde (FR)
 460
Revue Historique et Archeologique du
 Maine (FR) *64, 460*
Revue Historique Vaudoise (SZ) *64,
 460*
Revue Hittite et Asiatique (FR ISSN
 0080-2603) *550*
Revue Internationale d'Histoire de la
 Banque (SZ ISSN 0080-2611) *176*
Revue Internationale des Cadres (FR)
 216
Revue Landis et Gyr *see* Landis und
 Gyr Mitteilungen *356*
Revue Metapsychique (FR ISSN 0484-
 8934) *676*
Revue Numismatique (FR ISSN 0484-
 8942) *478*
Revue Odonto-Stomatologique du
 Nord-Est *see* Societe Odonto-
 Stomatologique du Nord-Est. Revue
 Annuelle *610*

Revue Ouest Africaine des Langues
 Vivantes *see* West African Journal of
 Modern Languages *554*
Revue Roumaine d'Histoire de l'Art.
 Serie Beaux-Arts (RM ISSN 0080-
 262X) *78*
Revue Roumaine d'Histoire de l'Art.
 Serie Theatre, Musique,
 Cinematographie (RM ISSN 0080-
 2638) *78*
Revue Roumaine de Geologie,
 Geophysique et Geographie.
 Geologie (RM ISSN 0556-8102)
 299
Revue Roumaine de Geologie,
 Geophysique et Geographie.
 Geophysique (RM ISSN 0556-8110)
 306
Revue Roumaine de l'Histoire de l'Art.
 Serie Arts Plastiques *see* Revue
 Roumaine d'Histoire de l'Art. Serie
 Beaux-Arts *78*
Revue Roumaine des Sciences Sociales.
 Serie de Sociologie (RM ISSN 0080-
 2646) *815*
Revue Statistique Annuelle des Peches
 Canadiennes *see* Annual Statistical
 Review of Canadian Fisheries *395*
Revue Statistique du Quebec *see*
 Quebec (Province) Bureau of
 Statistics Statistiques *845*
Revue Suisse d'Histoire. Supplement *see*
 Schweizerische Zeitschrift fuer
 Geschichte. Beihefte *461*
Revue Suisse de Numismatique/
 Schweizerische Numismatische
 Rundschau (SZ ISSN 0035-4163)
 478
Reynard (UK ISSN 0484-9035) *571*
Rhein-Mainische Forschungen (GW
 ISSN 0080-2662) *425*
Rheinisch-Westfaelische Akademie der
 Wissenschaften. Veroeffentlichungen
 (GW ISSN 0066-5754) *789, 852*
Rheinische Ausgrabungen (GW ISSN
 0557-7853) *64*
Rheinische Lebensbilder (GW ISSN
 0080-2670) *98*
Rheinische Schriften (GW ISSN 0080-
 2689) *289*
Rheinisches Jahrbuch fuer Volkskunde
 (GW ISSN 0080-2697) *402*
Rheinisches Landesmuseum, Bonn.
 Schriften (GW ISSN 0067-9968) *64*
Rheinisches Landesmuseum in Bonn.
 Bonner Jahrbuecher (GW ISSN
 0067-9976) *460*
Rheology Bulletin (US ISSN 0035-
 4538) *701*
Rheumatism Review (US ISSN 0080-
 2700) *623*
Rheumatismus (GW ISSN 0080-2719)
 624
Rheumatology (SZ ISSN 0080-2727)
 624
Rhode Island. Department of
 Education. Statistical Table (US)
 845
Rhode Island. Department of Health.
 Vital Statistics (US) *729*
Rhode Island. Department of Mental
 Health, Retardation and Hospitals.
 Mental Health, Retardation and
 Hospitals (US ISSN 0094-291X)
 481, 754
Rhode Island. State Library. Check-List
 of Publications of State Agencies
 (US) *539, 748*
Rhode Island Education Association.
 Journal (US ISSN 0080-2751) *322*
Rhode Island Jewish Historical Notes
 (US ISSN 0556-8609) *393, 435*
Rhode Island Media Directory (US) *6,
 268, 505*
Rhode Island School of Design.
 Museum of Art. Bulletin *see* Museum
 Notes *654*
Rhode Island State Industrial
 Directory(US ISSN 0148-5679) *241*
Rhodes Directory of Black Dentists
 Registered in the United States (US
 ISSN 0090-7995) *393, 610*
Rhodes Directory of Black Physicians
 in the United States (US) *599*
Rhodes-Livingstone Papers *see* Zambian
 Papers *474*
Rhodes Newsletter *see* Rhodes Review
 263

Rhodes Review (SA) *263*
Rhodesia. Central Statistical Office.
 Agricultural Production in African
 Purchase Lands. Part 1: National and
 Provincial Totals *see* Zimbabwe.
 Central Statistical Office.
 Agricultural Production in Purchase
 Lands: National and Provincial
 Totals *40*
Rhodesia. Central Statistical Office.
 Agricultural Production in European
 Areas. Part 1. Livestock. National
 and Provincial Totals *see* Zimbabwe.
 Central Statistical Office.
 Agricultural Production in European
 Areas: Livestock. National and
 Provincial Totals *46*
Rhodesia. Central Statistical Office.
 Agricultural Production in Tribal
 Trust Land Irrigation Schemes *see*
 Zimbabwe. Central Statistical Office.
 Agricultural Production in Tribal
 Trust Land Irrigation Schemes and
 Tilcor Estates *23*
Rhodesia. Central Statistical Office.
 Insurance Statistics *see* Zimbabwe.
 Registrar of Insurance. Report *501*
Rhodesia. Ministry of Finance. Budget
 Statement *see* Zimbabwe. Ministry of
 Finance. Financial Statement *234*
Rhodesia. Ministry of Mines and Lands.
 Report of the Secretary for Mines
 and Lands *see* Zimbabwe. Ministry
 of Lands and Natural Resources.
 Report of the Secretary for Lands
 and Natural Resources *279*
Rhodesia, a Field for Investment (RH)
 189
Rhodesia National Bibliography *see*
 Zimbabwe National Bibliography *96*
Rhodesia Research Index (RH) *3, 795*
Rhodesia Scientific Association.
 Transaction (RH) *789*
Rhodesia Stamp Catalogue (RH) *479*
Rhododendron and Camellia Yearbook
 see Rhododendrons, with Magnolias
 and Camellias *416*
Rhododendrons, with Magnolias and
 Camellias (UK ISSN 0080-2891)
 416
Rhombus (AT) *350, 589*
Rice University. Program of
 Development Studies. Discussion
 Papers (US) *225*
Ricerche di Biologia della Selvaggina
 (IT) *130*
Ricerche di Sociologia dell'Educazione
 e Pedagogia Comparata (IT) *322*
Ricerche di Storia della Lingua Latina
 (IT ISSN 0080-293X) *550*
Ricerche di Zoologia Applicata alla
 Caccia *see* Ricerche di Biologia della
 Selvaggina *130*
Ricerche Sulle Dimore Rurali in Italia
 (IT ISSN 0080-2964) *70*
Richard J. Gonzalez Lecture (US ISSN
 0080-2972) *148*
Richerche di Storia Moderna (IT) *460*
Richmond Chamber of Commerce.
 Research Bulletin *see* Greater
 Richmond Chamber of Commerce.
 Research Bulletin *179*
Rickia (BL ISSN 0080-3014) *117*
Rickia. Suplemento (BL ISSN 0080-
 3022) *117*
Riddell's Australian Purchasing
 Yearbook *see* Business Who's Who
 Australian Buying Reference *217*
Riista- ja Kalatalouden Tutkimuslaitos.
 Kalantutkimusosasto. Tiedonantoja
 (FI ISSN 0355-0648) *399*
Riistatieteellisia Julkaisuja *see* Finnish
 Game Research *276*
Rijks Geschiedkundige Publicatien.
 Grote Serie (NE) *460*
Rijks Geschiedkundige Publicatien.
 Kleine Serie (NE) *460*
Rijksinstituut voor het Rassenonderzoek
 van Cultuurgewassen. Jaarverslag
 (NE) *39*
Rijksinstituut voor het Rassenonderzoek
 van Cultuurgewassen. Mededelingen
 (NE) *39*
Rijksinstituut voor
 Oorlogsdocumentatie. Documenten
 (NE ISSN 0066-1287) *460*
Rijksinstituut voor
 Oorlogsdocumentatie. Monografieen
 (NE ISSN 0066-1295) *460*

Rijksmuseum van Natuurlijke Historie.
 Zoologische Bijdragen (NE) *130*
Rijksmuseum van Natuurlijke Historie.
 Zoologische Mededelingen (NE
 ISSN 0024-0672) *130*
Rijksuniversiteit te Gent. Faculteit van
 de Economische Wetenschappen.
 Werken (BE) *148*
Rijksuniversiteit te Gent. Laboratorium
 voor Experimentele, Differentiele en
 Genetische Psychologie.
 Mededlingen en Werkdocumenten
 (BE ISSN 0085-1078) *738*
Rijksuniversiteit te Gent. Sterrenkundig
 Observatorium. Mededelingen:
 Astronomie (BE ISSN 0072-4432)
 83
Rijksuniversiteit te Gent. Sterrenkundig
 Observatorium. Mededelingen:
 Meteorologie en Geofysica (BE
 ISSN 0072-4440) *306, 635*
Rijksuniversiteit te Leiden. Instituut
 voor Culturele Antropologie en
 Sociologie der Niet-Westerse Volken.
 Publicatie (NE) *53, 815*
Rijksuniversiteit te Utrecht. Geografisch
 Instituut. Bulletin. Serie 1: Sociale
 Geografie *see* Utrechtse Geografische
 Studies *427*
Rikkyo University. Institute for Atomic
 Energy. Report (JA) *370, 704*
Rinascimento (IT ISSN 0080-3073)
 460, 493
Rinascita *see* Rinascimento *493*
Rinderproduktion. Zucht,
 Leistungspruefungen, Besamung in
 der Bundesrepublik Deutschland
 (GW) *46*
Rinehart Press Series in Electronic
 Technology (US) *358*
Ring Index: A List of Ring Systems
 Used in Organic Chemistry.
 Supplement (US ISSN 0080-309X)
 254
Ringing and Migration (UK ISSN
 0307-8698) *125*
Ringyo Shiken Kenkyu Hokoku *see*
 Tokyo Metropolitan Agricultural
 Experiment Station, Itsukaichi Office.
 Forestry Experimental Bulletin *411*
Ringyo Shikenjo Kyushu Shijo Nenpo
 see Japan. Government Forest
 Experiment Station. Kyushu Branch.
 Annual Report *409*
Rio de Janeiro, Brazil (State). Instituto
 Estadual do Livro. Divisao de
 Bibliotecas. Boletim Bibliografico
 (BL) *94*
Rio Grande do Sul, Brazil. Fundacao de
 Economia e Estatistica. Indicadores
 Sociais (BL ISSN 0301-8156) *808*
Rio Grande Valley Horticultural
 Society. Journal (US ISSN 0485-
 2044) *416*
Rio Negro, Argentina. Direccion
 Provincial de Cultura. Monografias
 (AG) *571*
Ripartizone Cultura e Spettacolo.
 Rassegna di Studi e di Notizie (IT)
 78
Ripley P. Bullen Monographs in
 Anthropology and History (US
 ISSN 0271-6925) *53, 471*
Rit Occasional Papers (IC) *789*
River Behaviour and Control (II) *897*
River Bend Library System. Report of
 the Director (US ISSN 0080-3227)
 535
Ha-Rivhiyut Shel 'anaf Ha-Lul *see*
 Profitability of Poultry Farming in
 Israel *46*
Ha-Rivhiyut Shel Anaf Ha-Refet *see*
 Profitability of Dairy in Israel *46*
Ha-Rivhiyut Shel Gidul Ha-Kutnah *see*
 Profitability of Cotton Growing in
 Israel *38*
Ha-Rivhiyut Shel Gidul Hadavim *see*
 Profitability of Citrus Growing in
 Israel *38*
Ha-Rivhiyut Shel Gidul Selek Ha-Sukar
 see Profitability of Sugarbeet
 Growing in Israel *38*
Rivista Archeologica dell'Antica
 Provincia e Diocesi di Como (IT
 ISSN 0080-3235) *64*
Rivista Archeologica della Provincia di
 Como *see* Rivista Archeologica
 dell'Antica Provincia e Diocesi di
 Como *64*

Rivista di Antropologia (IT ISSN 0085-5723) 53
Rivista di Cultura Classica e Medioevale. Quaderni (IT ISSN 0080-3251) 260
Rivista di Etnografia see Etnologia 49
Rivista di Etnografia (IT ISSN 0085-5731) 816
Rivista di Farmacologia e Terapia (IT) 685
Road Accidents in Great Britain (UK ISSN 0307-6822) 875
Road Builder's Clinic. Proceedings (US ISSN 0080-3278) 376
Road Notes (UK ISSN 0080-3294) 376, 875
Road Research see Transport and Road Research 876
Roadmasters and Maintenance of Way Association of America. Proceedings (US ISSN 0080-3316) 873
Roadwise (US) 882
Roanoke Historical Society. Journal see Roanoke Valley Historical Society Journal 471
Roanoke Valley Historical Society Journal (US) 471
Robert Burns Chronicle (UK) 571
Robert /Morris Associates Annual Statement Studies see R M A Annual Statement Studies 176
Robert Wood Johnson Foundation. Annual Report (US ISSN 0091-3472) 599, 808
Robinson Newsletter (US) 418
Robot (SA ISSN 0035-7391) 754, 876
Robotron Technische Mitteilungen (GE) 265, 358
Rocenka Odborara (CS ISSN 0557-1693) 507
Rocenka Povetrnostnich Pozorovani Observatore Karlov (CS ISSN 0554-9221) 635
Rocenka Znecisteni Ovzdusi na Uzemi C S R (CS) 388, 635, 754
Rochester Conference on Programmed Instruction in Medical Education. Proceedings (US ISSN 0080-3359) 339, 599
Rock Magazine (US ISSN 0080-3367) 767
Rock Magnetism and Paleogeophysics (JA) 306
Rock Mechanics/Felsmechanik/ Mechanique des Roches. Supplement(US ISSN 0080-3375) 646
Rockbridge Historical Society, Lexington, Virginia. Proceedings (US ISSN 0080-3383) 471
Rockefeller Foundation. Annual Report (US ISSN 0080-3391) 808
Rockefeller Foundation. Working Papers (US) 30, 800
Rockefeller University, New York. Annual Report see Rockefeller University, New York. Scientific and Educational Programs 599
Rockefeller University, New York. Scientific and Educational Programs (US) 599
Rocket and Space Science Series (US ISSN 0080-3413) 10
Rocket News (JA ISSN 0485-2877) 10
Rocky Mountain Symposium on Microcomputers: Systems, Software, Architecture (US) 273
Rocznik Bialostocki (PL ISSN 0080-3421) 460
Rocznik Dolnoslaski (PL) 493
Rocznik Ekonomiczny (PL ISSN 0080-343X) 148
Rocznik Elektrycznosci Atmosferycznej i Meteorologii (PL ISSN 0080-3448) 635
Rocznik Gdanski (PL ISSN 0080-3456) 460
Rocznik Grudziadzki (PL ISSN 0080-3464) 460
Rocznik Historii Sztuki (PL ISSN 0080-3472) 78
Rocznik Jeleniogorski (PL ISSN 0080-3480) 460
Rocznik Kaliski (PL ISSN 0137-3501) 460
Rocznik Krakowski (PL ISSN 0080-3499) 460

Rocznik Kulturalny Ziemi Gdanskiej (PL) 460
Rocznik Lodzki (PL ISSN 0080-3502) 460
Rocznik Lubelski (PL ISSN 0080-3510) 460
Rocznik Magnetyczny/Annuaire Magnetique (PL ISSN 0082-0458) 306
Rocznik Olsztynski (PL ISSN 0080-3537) 460
Rocznik Orientalistyczny (PL ISSN 0080-3545) 671
Rocznik Pedagogiczny (PL ISSN 0137-9585) 322
Rocznik Sadecki (PL ISSN 0080-3561) 402, 460
Rocznik Slawistyczny (PL ISSN 0080-3588) 550
Rocznik Wroclawski (PL ISSN 0080-3618) 460
Rocznik Ziemi Klodzkiej (PL) 460
Roczniki Dziejow Spolecznych i Gospodarczych (PL ISSN 0080-3634) 460
Roczniki Gleboznawcze (PL ISSN 0080-3642) 39
Roczniki Nauk Rolniczych. Seria A. Produkcja Roslinna (PL ISSN 0080-3650) 39
Roczniki Nauk Rolniczych. Seria B. Zootechniczna (PL ISSN 0080-3669) 46
Roczniki Nauk Rolniczych. Seria C.Technika Rolnicza (PL ISSN 0080-3677) 32
Roczniki Nauk Rolniczych. Seria D. Monografie (PL ISSN 0080-3685) 19
Roczniki Nauk Rolniczych. Seria E. Ochrona Roslin (PL ISSN 0080-3693) 39
Roczniki Nauk Rolniczych. Seria F. Melioracji i Vzytkow Zielonych (PL ISSN 0080-3707) 39
Roczniki Nauk Rolniczych. Seria G. Ekonomika Rolnictwa (PL ISSN 0080-3715) 30
Roczniki Nauk Rolniczych. Seria H. Rybactwo (PL ISSN 0080-3723) 19, 399
Roczniki Nauk Spolecznych (PL) 800
Roczniki Socjologii Wsi. Studia i Materialy (PL ISSN 0080-3731) 816
Rodd's Chemistry of Carbon Compounds (NE ISSN 0080-3758) 254
Rodino Institute Journal see Peter W. Rodino Institute of Criminal Justice. Annual Journal 283
Roemer-Illustrierte see Koelner Roemer-Illustrierte 653
Roemisch-Germanisches Zentralmuseum, Mainz. Ausstellungskataloge (GW ISSN 0076-2733) 64
Roemisch-Germanisches Zentralmuseum, Mainz. Jahrbuch (GW ISSN 0076-2741) 460
Roemisch-Germanisches Zentralmuseum, Mainz. Kataloge Vor- und Fruehgeschichtlicher Alterteumer (GW ISSN 0076-275X) 435
Roemische Bronzen aus Deutschland (GW ISSN 0080-3782) 64, 78
Roemische Historische Mitteilungen (AU ISSN 0080-3790) 260, 460, 767
Roessleria (BL) 278
Roheisen und Stahlerzeugnisse see Fontes et Aciers 643
Role of State Legislatures in the Freedom Struggle (II) 714, 745
Roll of Arms (US) 418
Rollcall (CN ISSN 0707-3542) 599
Rolls-Royce Owners' Club, Directory and Register (US ISSN 0485-3695) 872
Roma e Provincia Attraverso la Statistica (IT ISSN 0035-7960) 845
Romance Bibliography see Romanische Bibliographie 555
Romanfuehrer (GW ISSN 0557-2614) 571
Romanica Gandensia (BE ISSN 0080-3855) 550

Romanica Gothoburgensia (SW ISSN 0080-3863) 550, 571
Romanica Helvetica (SZ ISSN 0080-3871) 550, 571
Romanische Bibliographie/Bibliographie Romane/Romance Bibliography (GW ISSN 0080-388X) 555
Romanistik in Geschichte und Gegenwart (GW ISSN 0341-3209) 260
Romanistisches Jahrbuch (GW ISSN 0080-3898) 550
Romanobarbarica (IT) 260
Romantic Reassessment (AU) 571
Romantist (US ISSN 0161-682X) 572
Romantizm v Russkoi i Sovetskoi Literature (UR) 460, 572
Romford Record (UK ISSN 0306-1140) 460
Roofing (UK ISSN 0080-4037) 138
Room (US) 581, 901
Roots News (JM) 663
Rose Annual (UK ISSN 0483-3686) 416
Rosenberg Library Bulletin (US ISSN 0035-8312) 435, 535
Roster of Black Elected Officials in the South (US ISSN 0093-9951) 393
Roster of Women in Political Science (US) 714, 901
Rotacion de la Tierra (SP) 83
Rothmans Football Yearbook (UK ISSN 0080-4088) 826
Routes (UK) 241, 863
Routledge History of English Poetry (UK) 581
Roving Commissions (UK ISSN 0485-5175) 827
Rowland's Tax Guide (UK ISSN 0143-280X) 232
Royal Academy of Letters, History and Antiquities. Proceedings. Antiquarian Series see Kungliga Vitterhets-, Historie- och Antikvitets Akademien. Handlingar. Antikvariska Serien 456
Royal Academy of Letters, History and Antiquities. Proceedings. Historical Series see Kungliga Vitterhets-, Historie- och Antikvitets Akademien. Handlingar. Historiska Serien 456
Royal Academy of Letters, History and Antiquities. Proceedings. Philological-Philosophical Series see Kungliga Vitterhets-, Historie- och Antikvitets Akademien. Handlingar. Filologisk-Filosofiska Serien 546
Royal Agricultural Society of England. Journal (UK ISSN 0080-4134) 19
Royal Asiatic Society. Hong Kong Branch. Journal (HK ISSN 0085-5774) 671
Royal Asiatic Society. Sri Lanka Branch. Journal (CE) 800
Royal Asiatic Society, Ceylon Branch. Journal (CE) 800
Royal Astronomical Society of Canada. Observer's Handbook (CN ISSN 0080-4193) 83
Royal Australasian College of Dental Surgeons. Annals (AT) 610
Royal Australian College of Dental Surgeons. Annals see Royal Australasian College of Dental Surgeons. Annals 610
Royal Australian Institute of Architects News see R A I A News 70
Royal Automobile Association of South Australia. Accommodation Guide see Australian Accommodation Guide 482
Royal Bath & West Show Catalogue (UK) 19
Royal Botanical Gardens, Hamilton, Ont. Special Bulletin (CN ISSN 0072-9647) 117, 416
Royal Botanical Gardens, Hamilton, Ont. Technical Bulletin (CN ISSN 0072-9655) 117, 416
Royal Caledonian Curling Club. Annual(UK ISSN 0080-4282) 822
Royal Canadian Academy of Arts. Annual Exhibition. Catalogue (CN ISSN 0080-4290) 78
Royal Canadian Golf Association. National Tournament Records see Canadian and Provincian Golf Records 823
Royal Canadian Institute. Proceedings (CN ISSN 0080-4304) 789

Royal Canadian Institute. Transactions (CN ISSN 0080-4312) 789
Royal College of General Practitioners. Occasional Papers (UK) 599
Royal College of Organists. Year Book (UK ISSN 0080-4320) 663
Royal College of Pathologists of Australia. Broadsheets (AT) 107, 599
Royal College of Physicians of Edinburgh. Directory (UK) 599
Royal College of Physicians of Edinburgh. Yearbook and Calendar see Royal College of Physicians of Edinburgh. Directory 599
Royal College of Surgeons of England. Faculty of Anaesthetists. Newsletter (UK) 604
Royal College of Surgeons of England. Handbook (UK) 625
Royal Dublin Society. Scientific Proceedings Series A (IE ISSN 0080-4339) 789
Royal Dublin Society. Scientific Proceedings. Series B (IE ISSN 0080-4347) 789
Royal Electrical & Mechanical Engineers Journal see R E M E Journal 358
Royal Entomological Society of London. Symposia (UK ISSN 0080-4363) 121
Royal Geographical Society of Australasia. South Australian Branch. Proceedings (AT ISSN 0085-5790) 425
Royal Greenwich Observatory Bulletins(UK ISSN 0308-5074) 83
Royal Highland and Agricultural Society of Scotland. Show Guide and Review (UK) 19
Royal Historical Society. Annual Bibliography of British and Irish History (UK ISSN 0308-4558) 438
Royal Historical Society. Guides and Handbooks (UK ISSN 0080-4398) 460
Royal Historical Society. Transactions. Fifth Series (UK ISSN 0080-4401) 460
Royal Historical Society of Queensland. Journal (AT ISSN 0085-5804) 435
Royal Horticultural Society Gardener's Diary see R. H. S. Gardener's Diary 416
Royal Humane Society. Annual Report.(UK) 808
Royal Institue of Chemistry. Monographs for Teachers see Chemical Society, London, Monographs for Teachers 246
Royal Institute of Philosophy. Lectures (UK ISSN 0080-4436) 691
Royal Institute of the Architects of Ireland. Yearbook (IE ISSN 0080-4444) 70
Royal Institution of Chartered Surveyors Year Book (UK ISSN 0308-1451) 762
Royal Institution of Great Britain. Annual Report see Royal Institution of Great Britain. Record 789
Royal Institution of Great Britain. Record (UK) 789
Royal Institution of Naval Architects. Supplementary Papers (UK ISSN 0373-529X) 880
Royal Institution of Naval Architects. Transactions (UK ISSN 0035-8967) 880
Royal Irish Academy. Conference on Numerical Analysis. Proceedings (UK) 589
Royal Irish Academy. Proceedings. Section B: Biological, Geological and Chemical Sciences (IE ISSN 0035-8983) 107, 247, 299
Royal Irish Academy. Proceedings. Section C: Archaeology, Celtic Studies, History, Linguistics and Literature (IE ISSN 0035-8991) 65, 460, 572
Royal Irish Academy of Music. Prospectus (IE) 663
Royal Military College of Australia Historical Journal see R. M. C. Historical Journal 447

Royal Musical Association, London. Proceedings (UK ISSN 0080-4452) *663*

Royal Musical Association, London. R. M. A. Research Chronicle (UK ISSN 0080-4460) *663*

Royal National Institute for the Blind. Information Leaflets (UK ISSN 0080-4479) *133*

Royal New Zealand Institute of Horticulture. Annual Journal (NZ ISSN 0110-5760) *416*

Royal New Zealand Institute of Horticulture. Journal *see* Royal New Zealand Institute of Horticulture. Annual Journal *416*

Royal Norwegian Society of Sciences. Publications *see* Kongelige Norske Videnskabers Selskab. Skrifter *785*

Royal Observatory, Edinburgh. Annual Report (UK ISSN 0309-0108) *83*

Royal Observatory, Edinburgh. Communications (UK ISSN 0142-8977) *83*

Royal Observatory, Edinburgh. Occasional Reports (UK ISSN 0309-099X) *83*

Royal Observatory, Edinburgh. Publications (UK ISSN 0305-2001) *83*

Royal Ontario Museum. Annual Report(CN ISSN 0082-5115) *654*

Royal Ontario Museum. Archaeology Monographs (CN ISSN 0316-1285) *65, 654*

Royal Ontario Museum. Art and Archaeology. Occasional Papers (CN ISSN 0082-5077) *65, 78*

Royal Ontario Museum. Ethnography Monograph (CN ISSN 0316-1277) *53, 393*

Royal Ontario Museum. History, Technology and Art Monographs (CN ISSN 0316-1269) *78, 435*

Royal Ontario Museum. Life Sciences. Contributions (CN ISSN 0384-8159) *107, 130*

Royal Ontario Museum. Life Sciences. Miscellaneous Publications (CN ISSN 0082-5093) *107*

Royal Ontario Museum. Life Sciences. Occasional Papers (CN ISSN 0082-5107) *107*

Royal School of Mines, London. Journal (UK ISSN 0080-4495) *646*

Royal Society for the Protection of Birds Annual Report and Accounts *see* R S P B Annual Report and Accounts *278*

Royal Society of Canada. Proceedings (CN ISSN 0080-4517) *789*

Royal Society of Canada. Proceedings and Transactions (CN ISSN 0316-4616) *789*

Royal Society of Canada. Transactions (CN ISSN 0035-9122) *789*

Royal Society of Edinburgh. Communications, Physical Sciences (UK ISSN 0308-129X) *789*

Royal Society of Edinburgh. Proceedings. (Biological Sciences) (UK) *107*

Royal Society of Edinburgh. Proceedings. (Natural Environment) *see* Royal Society of Edinburgh. Proceedings. (Biological Sciences) *107*

Royal Society of Edinburgh. Year Book(UK ISSN 0080-4576) *789*

Royal Society of Health. Papers (UK) *695*

Royal Society of London. Biographical Memoirs of Fellows of the Royal Society (UK ISSN 0080-4606) *98*

Royal Society of London. Philosophical Transactions. Series A. Mathematical and Physical Sciences (UK ISSN 0080-4614) *589, 789*

Royal Society of London. Philosophical Transactions. Series B. Biological Sciences (UK ISSN 0080-4622) *107*

Royal Society of London. Proceedings. Series A. Mathematical and Physical Sciences (UK ISSN 0080-4630) *589, 789*

Royal Society of London. Proceedings. Series B. Biological Sciences (UK ISSN 0080-4649) *107*

Royal Society of London. Year Book (UK ISSN 0080-4673) *789*

Royal Society of Medicine. Annual Report of the Council (UK ISSN 0144-8676) *599*

Royal Society of Queensland, St. Lucia. Proceedings (AT ISSN 0080-469X) *790*

Royal Society of South Africa. Transactions (SA ISSN 0035-919X) *790*

Royal Society of South Australia. Transactions (AT ISSN 0085-5812) *790*

Royal Society of Tasmania, Hobart. Papers and Proceedings (AT ISSN 0080-4703) *435, 790*

Royal Society of Tropical Medicine and Hygiene, London. Yearbook (UK ISSN 0080-4711) *608*

Royal Society of Ulster Architects. Year Book (IE ISSN 0080-472X) *70*

Royal Society of Victoria. Proceedings (AT ISSN 0035-9211) *790*

Royal United Services Institute Brassey's Defence Yearbook *see* R. U. S. I. and Brassey's Defence Yearbook *640*

Royal Western Australian Historical Society. Journal and Proceedings (AT ISSN 0080-4738) *447*

Royal Zoological Society of New South Wales. Proceedings *see* Koolewong *129*

Royal Zoological Society of Scotland. Zoo Guide (UK) *130*

Rozprawy Hydrotechniczne (PL ISSN 0035-9394) *370, 897*

Rozprawy Matematyczne *see* Dissertationes Mathematicae *585*

Rozprawy z Dziejow Oswiaty (PL ISSN 0080-4754) *322*

Rubber and Plastics Industry Technical Conference. Record (US ISSN 0080-4762) *707, 777*

Rubber and Plastics Research Association of Great Britain Recent Literature on Hazardous Environments in Industry *see* R A P R A Recent Literature on Hazardous Environments in Industry *777*

Rubber Directory of Great Britain *see* European Rubber Directory *777*

Rubber Producers' Council of Malaysia. Annual Report/Majlis Pengeluar-Pengeluar Getah Tanah Melayu. Lapuran Tahunan (MY) *777*

Rubber Red Book (US ISSN 0361-0640) *777*

Rubber Research Institute of Ceylon. Annual Review *see* Rubber Research Institute of Sri Lanka. Annual Review *777*

Rubber Research Institute of Malaysia. Planters Conference Proceedings (MY ISSN 0126-5849) *777*

Rubber Research Institute of Sri Lanka. Annual Review (CE) *777*

Rubber Research Institute of Sri Lanka. Journal (CE) *707, 777*

Rubber Research Institute of Sri Lanka. Quarterly Journal *see* Rubber Research Institute of Sri Lanka. Journal *777*

Rubber World Blue Book (US) *777*

Rudolf Steiner Publications (FR ISSN 0080-4789) *94, 692*

Rudolf Virchow Medical Society in the City of New York. Proceedings (AU ISSN 0080-4797) *599*

Ruestungsbeschraenkung und Sicherheit(GW ISSN 0080-4800) *913*

Ruff's Guide to the Turf and The Sporting Life Annual (UK ISSN 0080-4819) *822*

Rugby Football League Official Guide (UK ISSN 0080-4827) *826*

Ruhr-Universitaet Bochum. Ostasien Institut. Veroeffentlichungen (GW ISSN 0340-6687) *445*

Rules and Regulations - Board of Cosmetology (Sacramento) *see* California. State Board of Cosmetology. Rules and Regulations *85*

Rumanian Studies (NE) *460*

Runa (PE) *557*

Rundschreiben (GW) *535*

Rural Advance (US ISSN 0557-8183) *808*

Rural Development Bibliography Series (US) *25*

Rural Development Research Paper (UG ISSN 0080-4851) *30*

Rural Development Series *see* Scandinavian Institute of African Studies. Rural Development *53*

Rural Industry Directory (AT ISSN 0067-2106) *19, 399, 410*

Rural Real Estate Values in Alberta *see* Agricultural Real Estate Values in Alberta *761*

Rural Reconstruction Authority of Western Australia. Annual Report (AT ISSN 0310-4923) *487*

Rural Roundup (US ISSN 0036-0104) *46*

Rural Technology Guide (UK ISSN 0141-898X) *19*

Rusky Jazyk a Literatura *see* Universita Palackeho. Pedagogicka Fakulta. Sbornik Praci: Rusky Jazyk a Literatura *553*

Russian and East European Studies (US ISSN 0080-4886) *460*

Russian Monographs and Texts on the Physical Sciences (US) *790*

Russian Orthodox Greek Catholic Church of America. Yearbook and Church Directory *see* Orthodox Church in America. Yearbook and Church Directory *776*

Russian Series on Social History (NE ISSN 0080-4916) *445, 800*

Russian Tracts on the Physical Sciences(US) *790*

Russica Olomucensia (CS) *550, 572*

Russischer Samisdat *see* Samisdat *460*

Rutas de Cataluna (SP) *429*

Rutgers Byzantine Series (US) *460*

Rutgers University.Bureau of Engineering Research. Annual Report (US ISSN 0080-4975) *370*

Rutgers University. Center of Alcohol Studies. Monograph (US ISSN 0080-4983) *287*

Rutherglen, Australia. Research Station. Digest of Recent Research (AT ISSN 0080-5009) *19*

Ruwijer en Stallprodukten *see* Fontes et Aciers *643*

Ruygh-Bewerp (NE) *550, 572*

Rwanda. Direction Generale de la Documentation et de la Statistique Generale. Situation Economique de la Republique Rwandaise au 31 Decembre *see* Rwanda. Direction Generale de la Statistique. Situation Economique de la Republique Rwandaise au 31 Decembre *189*

Rwanda. Direction Generale de la Documentation et de la Statistique. Rapport Annuel *see* Rwanda. Direction Generale de la Statistique. Rapport Annuel *745*

Rwanda. Direction Generale de la Statistique. Rapport Annuel (RW) *745*

Rwanda. Direction Generale de la Statistique. Situation Economique de la Republique Rwandaise au 31 Decembre (RW) *189*

Rydge's CCEM Industry Report and Buyers Guide (AT ISSN 0310-4257) *138*

Rydge's Office Equipment Buyers Guide (AT ISSN 0078-3749) *219*

Ryland'S Directory (UK ISSN 0080-505X) *629*

Ryoiku *see* Rehabilitation *599*

Ryukyu Daigaku Nogakubu Gakujutsu Hokoku *see* University of the Ryukyus. College of Agriculture. Science Bulletin *22*

S.A. Computer Guide (SA) *273*

S A E Handbook (Society of Automotive Engineers) (US ISSN 0362-8205) *872*

S A E Technical Papers (Society of Automotive Engineers) (US) *872*

S A E Transactions (Society of Automotive Engineers) (US ISSN 0096-736X) *872*

S A F R A *see* Soviet Armed Forces Review Annual *640*

S A F T O Annual Report/Suid-Afrikaanse Buitelandse Handelsorgonisasie Jaarverslag (South African Foreign Trade Organization) (SA ISSN 0081-2552) *197*

S.A. Fishing Industry Handbook and Buyer's Guide *see* South African Fishing Industry Handbook and Buyer's Guide *400*

S.A. Guernsey *see* Suid-Afrikaanse Guernsey *46*

S.A. Mining and Engineering Yearbook *see* South African Mining and Engineering Yearbook *647*

S A N B (South African National Bibiography) (SA ISSN 0036-0864) *94*

S A N T A Annual Report/S A N T A Jaarlikse Verslag (South African National Tuberculosis Association) (SA ISSN 0081-2501) *623*

S A N T A Jaarlikse Verslag *see* S A N T A Annual Report *623*

S A R Statistics (Search and Rescue) (US ISSN 0163-2833) *880*

S.A.W.E. Journal (Society of Allied Weight Engineers) (US ISSN 0583-9270) *10*

S A W T R I Technical Report (South African Wool and Textile Research Institute) (SA ISSN 0081-2560) *856*

S B A R M O. Bulletin (Scientific Ballooning and Radiations Monitoring Organization) (FR) *635*

S B C Booklet (Schweizerischer Bankverein) (SZ) *176*

S B I C Directory and Handbook of Small Business Finance (US) *176, 234*

S B I C Industry Review *see* U.S. Small Business Administration. SBIC Digest *234*

S C A Free Speech Yearbook (Speech Communication Association) (US) *714*

S C A G: a Record of Accomplishment *see* S C A G Annual Report *487*

S C A G Annual Report (Southern California Association of Governments) (US ISSN 0094-050X) *487*

S C E A Emphasis (South Carolina Education Association) (US) *322*

S C I S Newsletter (Science Curriculum Improvement Study) (US) *350, 790*

S D A Dentist (School of Dentistry Alumni Association) (US ISSN 0024-5968) *610*

S D A I (Syndicat National de la Distribution pour l'Automobile et l'Industrie) (FR) *872*

S D C E International Die Casting Congress. Transactions (Society of Die Casting Engineers, Inc.) (US ISSN 0074-4557) *583*

S E A G Boletin del Algodon *see* E A G Publicaciones *14*

S E A G Boletin del Maiz *see* E A G Publicaciones *14*

S E A G Boletin del Trigo *see* E A G Publicaciones *14*

S E C O L A S Annals (Southeastern Conference on Latin American Studies) (US ISSN 0081-2951) *471*

S E E *see* Journal for Studies in Economics and Econometrics *191*

S E T: Research Information for Teachers (NZ ISSN 0110-6376) *322*

S F S Catalogue (Suomen Standardisoimisliitto) (FI ISSN 0357-0312) *370, 637*

S F W Scientific Films-Holland (NE) *651, 672*

S H A R E (Sisters Have Resources Everywhere) (US) *535, 901*

S H E (Subject Headings for Engineering) (US) *370, 535*

S I A M - A M S Proceedings (Society for Industrial and Applied Mathematics) (US ISSN 0080-5084) *589*

S I A Yearbook (Singapore Institute of Architects) (SI) *70*

S I C 20 Buyer's Guide (US) *405*

S I D A Development Studies (SW) *723*

S I D International Symposium. Digest of Technical Papers (Society for Information Display) (US ISSN 0097-966X) 370
S I E Guide to Business and Investment Books (Select Information Exchange) (US ISSN 0361-3917) 163
S I E Sophisticated Investor (Select Information Exchange) (US) 204
S I H O L see Amsterdam Studies in the Theory and History of Linguistic Science. Series 3: Studies in the History of Linguistics 540
S I K Annual Report see Swedish Food Institute. Annual Report 406
S I K Information (Svenska Livsmedelsinstitutet) (SW) 405
S. I. L. Museum of Anthropology Publication (Summer Institute of Linguistics) (US) 53, 550
S I L Publications in Linguistics and Related Fields (Summer Institute of Linguistics) (US ISSN 0079-7669) 550
S I L Series see S I L Publications in Linguistics and Related Fields 550
S I N Information see SIN-Staedtebauinstitut. Information 487
S I N Jahresberichte see SIN-Staedtebauinstitut. Jahresberichte 487
S.I.O. see S I O: a Report on the Work and Programs of Scripps Institution of Oceanography 312
S I O: a Report on the Work and Programs of Scripps Institution of Oceanography (US ISSN 0091-1518) 312
S.I.S.F. Documenti (Societa Italiana di Scienze Farmaceutiche) (IT ISSN 0081-0703) 686
S. J. Hall Lectureship in Industrial Forestry (UK ISSN 0080-5092) 410
S L A Newsletter (Southern Comparative Literature Association) (US) 572
S L A State-of-the-Art Review Series (Special Libraries Association) (US) 535
S. M. B. A. Collected Reprints (Scottish Marine Biological Association) (UK ISSN 0080-8121) 107
S N G A N S see Sylloge Nummorum Graecorum 478
S N I C Bulletin (Singapore National Institute of Chemistry) (SI) 248
S.O.S. Directory (Save on Shopping, Shop Outlet Stores) (US ISSN 0092-8003) 280
S. P. A. N. (State Planning Authority News) (AT) 487
S P E Monographs (Society of Professors of Education) (US) 322
S P E R Annuaire (Syndicat des Industries de Materiel Professionel Electronique et Radioelectrique) (FR) 358
S P I E Seminar Proceedings see Society of Photo-Optical Instrumentation Engineers. Proceedings 706
S P R I Informerar see Sweden. Sjukvaardens och Socialvaardens Planerings- och Rationaliseringsinstitut. S P R I Informerar 754
S P R I Raad see Sweden. Sjukvaardens och Socialvaardens Planerings- och Rationaliseringsinstitut. S P R I Raad 754
S P R I Rapport see Sweden. Sjukvaardens och Socialvaardens Planerings- och Rationaliseringsinstitut. S P R I Rapport 754
S P R I Specifikationer see Sweden. Sjukvaardens och Socialvaardens Planerings- och Rationaliseringsinstitut. S P R I Specifikationer 754
S R E B Educational Board. Annual Report (Southern Regional Education Board) (US ISSN 0081-3060) 322
S S R C Studentship Handbook (Social Science Research Council) (UK) 800
S S R C Survey Archive Bulletin (UK ISSN 0307-1391) 816

S S S A Special Publication Series (Soil Science Society of America) (US ISSN 0081-1904) 39
S.S.S.L. see Society for the Study of Southern Literature. Newsletter 572
S T A Digest see S T A Educator 913
S T A Educator (Stockton Teachers Association) (US ISSN 0036-1941) 913
S T C Matrikel (Sveriges Trae- och Byggvaruhandlares Centralfoerbund) (SW) 241
S T Directory of Singapore see Straits Times Directory of Singapore 242
S T P Notes (Inter-Union Commission of Solar Terrestrial Physics) (US ISSN 0085-1965) 83, 698
S T U Investigation (Styrelsen foer Teknisk Utveckling) (SW) 853
S U N Y L A Newsletter (State University of New York Librarians Association) (US) 535
S.W.A. Scientific Society. Journal (SX) 800
S W A T H (UK ISSN 0080-5122) 572
S. Y. A. Internal Bulletin (Socialist Youth Alliance) (AT) 714
SAAB-SCANIA Technical Notes see SAAB Technical Notes 10
SAAB Technical Notes (SW ISSN 0080-5149) 10
Saalburg-Jahrbuch (GW ISSN 0080-5157) 65, 655
Saarbruecker Beitraege zur Altertumskunde (GW ISSN 0080-5181) 435
Saarbruecker Studien zur Musikwissenschaft (GW ISSN 0080-519X) 663
Sabah. Department of Statistics. Annual Bulletin of Statistics/Sabah. Jabatan Perangkaan. Siaran Perangkaan Tahunan (MY ISSN 0080-5203) 845
Sabah. Forest Department. Annual Report (MY ISSN 0080-5211) 410
Sabah. Jabatan Perangkaan. Siaran Perangkaan Tahunan see Sabah. Department of Statistics. Annual Bulletin of Statistics 845
Sabah. Marine Department. Annual Report (MY ISSN 0080-522X) 880
Sabah Society. Journal (MY ISSN 0036-2131) 790
Saco-Lowell Bulletin see Platt Saco Lowell Bulletin 856
Sado Marine Biological Station. Annual Report/Niigata Daigaku Rigakubu Fuzoku Sado Rinkai Jikkenjo Kenkyu Nenpo (JA) 107
Saechsische Akademie der Wissenschaften, Leipzig. Jahrbuch (GE ISSN 0080-5262) 790
Saechsische Akademie der Wissenschaften, Leipzig. Mathematisch-Naturwissenschaftliche Klasse. Abhandlungen (GE ISSN 0080-5289) 589, 790
Saechsische Akademie der Wissenschaften, Leipzig. Mathematisch-Naturwissenschaftliche Klasse. Sitzungsberichte (GE ISSN 0080-5270) 589, 790
Saechsische Akademie der Wissenschaften, Leipzig. Philologisch-Historische Klasse. Abhandlungen (GE ISSN 0080-5297) 435, 550
Saechsische Akademie der Wissenschaften, Leipzig. Philologisch-Historische Klasse. Sitzungsberichte (GE ISSN 0080-5300) 435, 550
Saecula Spiritalia (GW ISSN 0343-2009) 435, 493
Saeculum (GW ISSN 0080-5319) 435
Saenger-Taschenkalender (GW) 663
Saerrakke (DK) 651
Safaho-Monographien see Safaho-Monographs 535
Safaho-Monographs (NE ISSN 0581-2674) 535
Saga och Sed (SW) 402
Saga of the Sanpitch (US) 402, 471
Sage Annual Review of Social and Educational Change (US) 322, 816
Sage Annual Reviews of Communication Research (US) 265

Sage Annual Reviews of Drug and Alcohol Abuse (US) 287
Sage Annual Reviews of Studies in Deviance (US) 816
Sage Contemporary Social Science Anthologies. (US) 800
Sage Contemporary Social Science Issues (US) 800
Sage Electoral Studies Yearbook (US) 714
Sage International Yearbook of Foreign Policy Studies (US ISSN 0094-0658) 723
Sage Library of Social Research (US) 800
Sage Research Progress Series in Criminology (US) 283
Sage Research Progress Series on War, Revolution and Peacekeeping (US ISSN 0080-536X) 640, 723
Sage Series on African Modernization and Development (US) 201, 441, 715
Sage Series on Armed Forces and Society (US ISSN 0080-5378) 640, 715
Sage Studies in International Sociology (US) 816
Sage Yearbooks in Politics and Public Policy (US) 715
Sageret; Annuaire General du Batiment et des Travaux Publics (FR) 138
Saggi e Memorie di Storia dell'Arte (IT ISSN 0080-5394) 78
Saggi Filosofici (IT) 691
Sagittarius see Schuetz-Jahrbuch 663
Sagrada Biblia (SP) 767
Sahitya Akademi, New Delhi. Report (II ISSN 0080-5416) 493
Sahmatnyj Informator see Sahovski Informator 822
Sahovski Informator/Chess Informant/Sahmatnyj Informator (YU ISSN 0045-6586) 822
Sahyog (II) 181
Saibokaku Byorigaku Zasshi see Journal of Karyopathology 605
Sailboat & Sailboat Equipment Directory (US) 827
Sailing the Road Clear (US) 581
Saint Bonaventure University. Franciscan Institute. Philosophy Series (US ISSN 0080-5432) 775
Saint Bonaventure University. Franciscan Institute. Text Series (US ISSN 0080-5440) 775
Saint Bonaventure University. Science Studies (US ISSN 0080-5467) 107
St. Clair County Historical Society. Journal (US ISSN 0095-3911) 471
St. David's Day Bilingual Series (UK) 98
St. Dunstan's Annual Report (UK) 133
Saint George's Hospital Gazette (UK ISSN 0036-2840) 481, 599
St. James Press Car Ferry Guide (UK) 880
St. Lawrence University. Conference on the Adirondack Park (Proceedings) (US ISSN 0094-8845) 278, 831
Saint Louis Police Journal (US) 283
St. Louis Statistical Abstract (US) 845
St. Louis University. Pius XII Library. Publications (US ISSN 0080-5483) 913
St. Paul, Minnesota. Metropolitan Transit Commission. Annual Report see St. Paul, Minnesota. Twin Cities Area Metropolitan Transit Commission. Annual Report 882
St. Paul, Minnesota. Twin Cities Area Metropolitan Transit Commission. Annual Report (US) 882
St. Paul Urban League Annual Report (US) 808
St. Thomas More Lectures (US ISSN 0082-4208) 767
St. Thomas More Society. Journal (AT ISSN 0310-6861) 517
Saitama University. Science Reports. Series A: Mathematics (JA ISSN 0558-2431) 248, 589, 698
Saitama University. Science Reports. Series A: Mathematics, Physics and Chemistry see Saitama University. Science Reports. Series A: Mathematics 589
Salar Jung Museum. Annual Report (II) 655

Salaries of Engineering Technicians see American Association of Engineering Societies. Engineering Manpower Commission. Salaries of Engineering Technicians and Technologists 365
Salaries of Scientists, Engineers and Technicians (US ISSN 0146-5015) 668
Sales & Marketing Management Survey of Buying Power (Part I) (US) 163
Sales & Marketing Management Survey of Buying Power (Part II) (US) 163
Sales & Marketing Management Survey of Industrial Puchasing Power (US) 163
Sales & Marketing Management Survey of Selling Costs (US) 163
Sales Management Survey of Buying Power (Part I) see Sales & Marketing Management Survey of Buying Power (Part I) 163
Sales Management Survey of Buying Power (Part II) see Sales & Marketing Management Survey of Buying Power (Part II) 163
Sales Management Survey of Industrial Purchasing Power see Sales & Marketing Management Survey of Industrial Puchasing Power 163
Sales Management Survey of Selling Costs see Sales & Marketing Management Survey of Selling Costs 163
Sales of Fuel Oil and Kerosene see Fuel Oil Sales 363
Sales of Vine Products Manufactured in Cyprus (CY) 30
Sales Results Holland (NE) 78
Sales/Slants (US ISSN 0036-3464) 500
Saling Aktienfuehrer (GW ISSN 0080-5572) 204
Salon Nacional de Artes Plasticas y Visuales (UY) 78
Salt Lake City Messenger (US ISSN 0586-7282) 776
Salt Lick (US ISSN 0036-360X) 581
Salted in the Shell (US) 581
Saltzman's Eurail Guide Annual see Eurail Guide 884
Salvation Army Year Book (UK ISSN 0080-567X) 776
Salzburger Beitraege zur Paracelsusforschung (AU ISSN 0558-3489) 435, 691
Salzburger Jahrbuch fuer Philosophie (AU ISSN 0080-5696) 691
Salzburger Romanistische Schriften (GW) 550
Salzburger Studien zur Anglistik und Amerikanistik (AU ISSN 0080-5718) 913
Salzburger Studien zur Philosophie (AU ISSN 0080-5726) 691
Salzburger Universitaetsreden (AU ISSN 0080-5734) 339
Sam Houston State University. Institute of Contemporary Corrections and the Behavioral Sciences. Proceedings Interagency Workshop (US) 283
Samaru Miscellaneous Paper (NR ISSN 0080-5769) 19
Samaru Research Bulletin (NR ISSN 0080-5777) 19
Sambalpur University. Post-Graduate Department of Oriya. Journal (II) 572
Sambalpur University Journal: Humanities (II) 493
Sambalpur University Journal: Science and Technology (II) 790, 853
Samenspel (NE) 94
Samisdat (SZ) 460, 715
Samiske Samlinger (NO ISSN 0581-4480) 53, 816
Sammlung Dalp (SZ ISSN 0080-5807) 493
Sammlung Dialog (GW ISSN 0080-5815) 913
Sammlung Geltender Staatsangehoerigkeitsgesetze (GW ISSN 0080-5823) 517
Sammlung Groos (GW ISSN 0344-0591) 339, 550
Sammlung Lebensmittelrechtlicher Entscheidungen (GW ISSN 0080-5831) 405, 517
Sammlung Meusser (GE ISSN 0080-584X) 610

Sammlung Musikwissenschaftlicher Abhandlungen/Collection d'Etudes Musicologiques (GW ISSN 0085-588X) 663
Samos (GW ISSN 0080-5866) 65
Sample Surveys in the ESCAP Region (UN) 153
Samskriti Vibhaga Ki Anudanom Ki Mangem see India. Department of Culture. Demands for Grants 344
Samvadadhvam (II ISSN 0581-4790) 845
Samvardhana (CE) 189
San Diego. Museum of Man. Ethnic Technology Notes (US ISSN 0080-5890) 53
San Diego. Museum of Man. Papers (US ISSN 0080-5904) 53
San Diego Biomedical Symposium. Proceedings (US ISSN 0095-5876) 599
San Diego Business Survey (US ISSN 0080-5882) 180
San Diego County Planning and Land Use Department. County Data Base (US) 489
San Diego County Planning Department. Planning Data see San Diego County Planning and Land Use Department. County Data Base 489
San Diego Society of Natural History. Memoirs (US ISSN 0080-5920) 790
San Diego Society of Natural History. Occasional Papers (US ISSN 0080-5939) 790
San Diego Society of Natural History. Transactions (US ISSN 0080-5947) 790
San Diego State University. Bureau of Business and Economic Research. Monographs (US ISSN 0068-5836) 148
San Diego State University. Bureau of Business and Economic Research. Research Studies and Position Papers(US ISSN 0068-5844) 148
San Diego Symposium for Biomedical Engineering. Proceedings see San Diego Biomedical Symposium. Proceedings 599
San Francisco Bay Area Rapid Transit District. Annual Report (US ISSN 0362-2300) 863
San Francisco Bay Conservation and Development Commission. Annual Report (US ISSN 0085-5898) 278
San Francisco Cancer Symposium. Proceedings see West Coast Cancer Symposium. Proceedings 622
San Francisco Gallery (US) 581
San Francisco State University. Audio-Visual Center. Media Catalog (US ISSN 0068-5860) 350
San Joaquin Valley Business Perspectives (US) 189
San Mateo County Dental Society. Bulletin (US ISSN 0080-598X) 610
Sanavik Cooperative. Baker Lake Prints(CN ISSN 0319-5465) 479
Sand see Sands 572
Sands (US) 572
Sangyo Keiei Kenkyushoho see Journal of Industry and Management 215
Sanitary Services in Tennessee (US ISSN 0162-6256) 756, 845
Sanitation Industry Yearbook (US ISSN 0080-6021) 754
Sankt Galler Beitraege Zum Fremdenverkehr und zur Verkehrswirtschaft: Reihe Verkehrswirtschaft (SZ ISSN 0080-6048) 873
St. Galler Studien Zum Wettbewerbs und Immaterialgueterrecht (SZ) 518
St. Galler Studien zur Politikwissenschaft (SZ) 715
Sankt Gallische Naturwissenschaftliche Gesellschaft. Bericht ueber Die Taetigkeit (SZ ISSN 0080-6056) 790
Sankyo Research Laboratories. Annual Report (JA ISSN 0080-6064) 107
Sannivedana (CE) 265
Santa Ana Mountain Series (US) 471
Santa Fe. Centro de Documentacion e Informacion Educativa. Boletin de Informacion Educativa (AG ISSN 0080-6099) 322

Santa Gertrudes Cattle Journal (SA) 46
Santakuti Vedic Research Series (II ISSN 0080-6137) 445
Santiago de Chile. Instituto de Fomento Pesquero Publicacion see Instituto de Fomento Pesquero. Informes Pesquero 397
Santiago del Estero. Direccion General de Investigaciones Estadistica y Censos. Estadistica Agricola-Ganadera (AG) 25
Santiago del Estero. Direccion General de Investigaciones Estadistica y Censos. Estadisticas Sociales (AG) 845
Sao Paulo, Brazil (State). Departamento de Edificios e Obras Publicas. Relatorio de Atividades (BL) 376, 746
Sao Paulo, Brazil (State) Departamento de Estatistica. Transcricao de Transmissoes de Imoveis Por Comarca, Segundo a Naturez das Escrituras (BL) 762
Sao Paulo, Brazil (State) Observatorio. Anuario Astronomico see Universidade de Sao Paulo. Instituto Astronomico e Geofisico. Anuario Astronomico 84
Sao Paulo, Brazil (State). Secretaria da Educacao. Atividades Desenvolvidas (BL) 322, 518
Sao Paulo, Brazil (State). Superintendencia de Saneamento Ambiental. Relatorio Anual de Atividades (BL) 388
Sao Paulo Yearbook (BL) 180
Sarah Lawrence Literary Review see Sarah Lawrence Review 557
Sarah Lawrence Review (US) 557
Sarang Magazine (PK) 418
Sarawak. Department of Agriculture. Research Branch. Annual Report (MY ISSN 0080-6420) 19
Sarawak. Department of Statistics. Annual Statistical Bulletin see Annual Statistical Bulletin Sarawak 832
Sarawak Annual Bulletin of Statistics see Annual Statistical Bulletin Sarawak 832
Sarawak Economic Development Corporation. Annual Report and Statement of Accounts (MY) 225
Sarawak Electricity Supply Corporation. Annual Report (MY) 358
Sarawak External Trade Statistics (MY ISSN 0080-6455) 163
Sarawak Statistical Handbook see Statistical Handbook of Sarawak 847
Sarawak Vital Statistics (MY ISSN 0080-6447) 845
Sardegna d'Oggi; Guida Practica see Guida Sardegna d'Oggi 886
Sarkiyat Mecmuasi (TU ISSN 0578-9761) 475
Sarojini Naidu Memorial Lecture Series(US) 445
Sarsia (NO ISSN 0036-4827) 107
Sarvadanand Universal Series (II ISSN 0080-6471) 445
Sarvotkrushta Marathi Katha (II) 572
Saskatchewan. Advisory Council on the Status of Women. Publication (CN ISSN 0380-8297) 901
Saskatchewan. Alcoholism Commission. Annual Report (CN ISSN 0381-2278) 287
Saskatchewan. Department of Agriculture. Family Farm Improvement Branch. Technical Bulletin (CN ISSN 0080-648X) 19
Saskatchewan. Department of Culture and Youth. Annual Report (CN ISSN 0317-4344) 257
Saskatchewan. Department of Industry and Commerce. Report for the Fiscal Year (CN ISSN 0080-6498) 746
Saskatchewan. Department of Labour. Wages and Working Conditions by Occupation (CN ISSN 0706-4926) 210
Saskatchewan. Department of Mineral Resources. Annual Report (CN ISSN 0581-8109) 646
Saskatchewan. Department of Mineral Resources. Petroleum and Natural Gas Reservoir Annual (CN) 681

Saskatchewan. Department of Mineral Resources. Statistical Yearbook (CN ISSN 0707-2570) 646
Saskatchewan. Department of Natural Resources. Forestry Branch. Technical Bulletins see Saskatchewan. Department of Tourism and Renewable Resources. Technical Bulletins 410
Saskatchewan. Department of Social Services. Child Care Statistics (CN) 808
Saskatchewan. Department of Social Statistics. Annual Report (CN ISSN 0708-3882) 808
Saskatchewan. Department of the Environment. Annual Report (CN ISSN 0317-4611) 388
Saskatchewan. Department of Tourism and Renewable Resources. Annual Report (CN ISSN 0318-4684) 278
Saskatchewan. Department of Tourism and Renewable Resources. Game Surveys Unit. Aerial Antelope Survey Report (CN) 107
Saskatchewan. Department of Tourism and Renewable Resources. Game Surveys Unit. Sex and Age Ratios of Sharp-Tailed Grouse and Gray (Hungarian) Partridge (CN) 125
Saskatchewan. Department of Tourism and Renewable Resources. Game Surveys Unit. Spring Survey of Sharp-Tailed Grouse and Cock Pheasant (CN) 130, 278
Saskatchewan. Department of Tourism and Renewable Resources. Game Surveys Unit. Winter Mule Deer Survey in Southwestern Saskatchewan (CN) 278
Saskatchewan. Department of Tourism and Renewable Resources. Technical Bulletins (CN) 410
Saskatchewan. Government Insurance Office. Province of Saskatchewan Motor Vehicle Traffic Accidents. Annual Report (CN) 876
Saskatchewan. Medical Care Insurance Commission. Annual Report (CN ISSN 0080-6544) 500
Saskatchewan. Prescription Drug Plan. Annual Report (CN ISSN 0707-0152) 500, 686
Saskatchewan. Water Supply Board. Annual Report (CN ISSN 0586-5522) 898
Saskatchewan Centre of the Arts. Annual Report (CN) 78
Saskatchewan Construction Industry Directory. Purchasing Guide (CN) 138, 370
Saskatchewan Decisions, Civil and Criminal Cases (CN ISSN 0319-7999) 518
Saskatchewan Economic Review (CN ISSN 0558-6976) 189
Saskatchewan Farm Science see Agricultural Science Bulletin 11
Saskatchewan Farmers' Markets Annual Report (CN ISSN 0381-3223) 30
Saskatchewan FarmStart Corporation. Annual Report (CN) 30
Saskatchewan Fur Marketing Service. Annual Report (CN ISSN 0581-8389) 524
Saskatchewan Housing Corporation. Annual Report (CN) 487
Saskatchewan Labour Report (CN ISSN 0317-7335) 210
Saskatchewan Motor Transport Guide (CN ISSN 0707-0365) 882
Saskatchewan Natural History Society. Special Publications (CN ISSN 0080-6552) 790
Saskatchewan Oil and Gas Corporation. Annual Report (CN) 681
Saskatchewan Poetry Book (CN ISSN 0080-6560) 581
Saskatchewan Research Council. Annual Report (CN ISSN 0080-6587) 790, 853
Saskatchewan Research Council. Physics Division. Annual Climatic Summary (CN ISSN 0706-9391) 635
Saskatchewan Telecommunications. Annual Report (CN ISSN 0080-6633) 269

Saskatchewan Trading Corporation. Annual Report (CN ISSN 0383-4352) 182
Saskatchewan Universities Commission. Annual Report (CN ISSN 0382-1838) 339
Saskatchewan's Financial and Economic Position (CN ISSN 0080-6676) 189
Sat Nam Series (US) 776
Satapitaka. Indo-Asian Literatures (II ISSN 0581-8532) 572
Sather Classical Lectures (US ISSN 0080-6684) 260
Saturated Heterocyclic Chemistry (UK ISSN 0305-6198) 254
Saturday Morning (UK) 557
Saudi Arabia. Central Department of Statistics. Foreign Trade Statistics (SU) 163
Saudi Arabia. Central Department of Statistics. Statistical Indicator (SU) 164
Saudi Arabia. Central Department of Statistics. Statistical Yearbook (SU) 845
Saudi Arabia. Ministry of Education. Educational Statistics (SU) 328, 845
Saudi Arabia Trade Directory (US) 241
Saudi Arabian Monetary Agency. Annual Report (SU ISSN 0558-7220) 232
Saudi Arabian Monetary Agency. Statistical Summary (SU ISSN 0581-8672) 176
Saussurea (SZ ISSN 0373-2525) 118
Sav-on-Hotels (US ISSN 0098-4507) 483
Sav-on-Hotels Across Europe see Sav-on-Hotels 483
Savacou (JM ISSN 0036-5068) 78, 572
Savanna Forestry Research Station, Nigeria. Annual Report (NR) 410
Savannah Port Handbook (US) 880
Savannah State College Bulletin (US ISSN 0036-5076) 263
Save on Shopping, Shop Outlet Stores Directory see S.O.S. Directory 280
Savez Geodetskih Inzenjera i Geometara Hrvatske. Geodet (YU) 306
Savez Geodetskih Inzenjera i Geometara Hrvatske. Obavijesti see Savez Geodetskih Inzenjera i Geometara Hrvatske. Geodet 306
Savigny-Stiftung fuer Rechtsgeschichte. Zeitschrift. Germanistische, Romanistische und Kanonistische Abteilung (GE ISSN 0084-5264) 518
Savings and Loan Fact Book (US ISSN 0581-8761) 176
Savings and Loan Market Study (US ISSN 0163-6782) 176
Savings Association Annals see United States League of Savings Associations. Annals 177
Savonia (FI ISSN 0356-3189) 107, 278
Sawyer's Gas Turbine Catalog see Turbomachinery Catalog and Workbook 383
Sbornik Geologickych Ved: Antropozoikum/Journal of Geological Sciences: Anthropozoic (CS ISSN 0036-5270) 299
Sbornik Geologickych Ved: Geologie/Journal of Geological Sciences: Geology (CS ISSN 0581-9172) 299
Sbornik Geologickych Ved: Hydrogeologie, Inzenyrska Geologie/Journal of Geological Sciences: Hydrogeology, Engineering Geology (CS ISSN 0036-5289) 308
Sbornik Geologickych Ved: Loziskova Geologie, Mineralogie/Journal of Geological Sciences: Economic Geology, Mineralogy (CS ISSN 0581-9180) 299
Sbornik Geologickych Ved: Paleontologie/Journal of Geological Sciences: Paleontology (CS ISSN 0036-5297) 674

Sbornik Geologickych Ved: Technologie, Geochemie/Journal of Geological Sciences: Technology, Geochemistry (CS ISSN 0036-5300) *299*
Sbornik Geologickych Ved: Uzita Geofyzika/Journal of Geological Sciences: Applied Geophysics (CS ISSN 0036-5319) *306*
Sbornik Statei po Frantsuzskoi Lingvistike i Metodike Prepodavaniya Inostrannogo Yazika v VUZE (UR) *572*
Scandal Sheet (US) *476*
Scandinavian Africana (SW) *56, 94*
Scandinavian Building Research (DK ISSN 0581-9423) *138*
Scandinavian Corrosion Congress. Proceedings (DK ISSN 0581-9431) *629*
Scandinavian Institute of African Studies. Annual Seminar Proceedings(SW ISSN 0080-6706) *441*
Scandinavian Institute of African Studies. Research Report (SW ISSN 0080-6714) *441*
Scandinavian Institute of African Studies. Rural Development (SW) *30, 53*
Scandinavian Institute of Asian Studies. Annual Newsletter (DK ISSN 0069-1704) *671*
Scandinavian Institute of Asian Studies. Monograph Series (DK ISSN 0069-1712) *671*
Scandinavian Journal of Clinical and Laboratory Investigation. Supplement(UK ISSN 0085-591X) *599, 612*
Scandinavian Journal of Gastroenterology. Supplement (NO ISSN 0085-5928) *613*
Scandinavian Journal of Haematology. Supplementum (DK ISSN 0080-6722) *613*
Scandinavian Journal of Maritime Law *see* Arkiv for Sjoerett *509*
Scandinavian Journal of Respiratory Diseases. Supplementum *see* European Journal of Respiratory Diseases. Supplementum *623*
Scandinavian Numismatic Journal *see* Nordisk Numismatisk Aarsskrift *477*
Scandinavian Studies in Criminology (NO ISSN 0085-5936) *283*
Scandinavian Studies in Law (SW ISSN 0085-5944) *518*
Scando-Slavica (DK ISSN 0080-6765) *550, 572*
Scando-Slavica. Supplementum (DK) *550, 572*
Scanning Electron Microscope Symposium. Proceedings *see* Scanning Electron Microscopy *124*
Scanning Electron Microscopy (US) *124, 706*
Scarecrow Author Bibliographies (US) *94*
Scena Svizzera *see* Szene Schweiz *860*
Scenarium (NE) *859*
Scene Suisse *see* Szene Schweiz *860*
Schach Express *see* Chess Express *819*
Schatzkammer (US) *460, 471, 550*
Schauspielfuehrer (GW ISSN 0342-4553) *859*
Schedule of Postgraduate Courses in United Kingdom Universities (UK ISSN 0306-1728) *332*
Schedule of Wells Drilled for Oil and Gas, Province of Alberta (CN ISSN 0380-4305) *363, 681*
Schedule of Wells Drilled for Oil and Natural Gas in British Columbia (CN ISSN 0524-5508) *363, 681*
Schedules Supporting the Executive Budget *see* New York (City) Mayor. Schedules Supporting the Executive Budget *750*
Schiff und Zeit (GW) *880*
Schiffahrtmedizinisches Institut der Marine, Kiel. Veroeffentlichungen (GW ISSN 0080-679X) *599*
Schiffbau-Normung (GW ISSN 0036-6048) *637, 880*
Schiffbautechnische Gesellschaft. Jahrbuch (GW ISSN 0080-6803) *880*
Schiffli Digest and Directory *see* Embroidery Directory *855*

Schleswig-Holsteinischer Heimatkalender (GW) *572*
Schmankerl (GW ISSN 0085-5952) *572*
Schmerzensgeld-Betraege (GW) *524*
Schnittmuster Modeblatt (GW) *262*
Schoenste Schweizer Buecher (SZ ISSN 0080-6838) *759*
Die Schoensten Buecher der Deutschen Demokratischen Republik (GE) *759*
Scholae Adriani de Buck Memoriae Dicatae (NE ISSN 0080-6854) *65*
Scholarly Books in France *see* Publications de Recherche Scientifique en France *94*
Scholarships at Boys' Public Schools *see* Scholarships at Independent Schools *322*
Scholarships at Girls' Schools *see* Scholarships at Independent Schools *322*
Scholarships at Independent Schools (UK ISSN 0140-878X) *322*
Scholarships for Foreign Students and University Graduates at Austrian Institutions of Higher Learning/ Stipendien fuer Auslaendische Studierende und Akademiker an Oesterreichischen Hochschulen (AU ISSN 0036-6374) *339*
Scholarships Guide for Commonwealth Postgraduate Students (UK ISSN 0306-1736) *322*
School Guide (US) *332*
School Nursing Monographs (US ISSN 0569-230X) *614*
School of Agriculture, Aberdeen. Annual Report (UK ISSN 0143-8654) *19*
School Universe Data Book *see* C I C's School Directories *330*
Schools (UK ISSN 0080-6897) *332*
Schools Abroad (US ISSN 0080-6900) *343*
Schools Abroad of Interest to Americans *see* Schools Abroad *343*
Schools and Colleges Welcome (UK) *890*
Schools for the Mentally Retarded (Trenton) *see* New Jersey. Bureau of Statistical Analysis and Social Research. Schools for the Mentally Retarded *328*
Schools in the United States and Canada Offering Graduate Education in Pharmacology (US) *332, 686*
Schools of England, Wales, Scotland and Ireland (UK ISSN 0080-6919) *332*
Schools of English in Great Britain *see* Where to Learn English in Great Britain *332*
Schools of Social Work with Accredited Master's Degree Programs (US) *339, 809*
Schopenhauer-Jahrbuch (GW ISSN 0080-6935) *691*
Schott Aktuell (GW) *663*
Schott-Kurier *see* Schott Aktuell *663*
Schouler Lectures in History and Political Science (US) *435, 715*
Showalter Memorial Lecture Series (US ISSN 0080-6943) *776*
Schriften des Werksarchivs (GW) *225*
Schriften und Quellen der Alten Welt (GE ISSN 0080-696X) *65, 435*
Schriften zur Geistesgeschichte des Oestlichen Europa (GW ISSN 0340-6490) *460*
Schriften zur Geschichte und Kultur des Alten Orient (GE ISSN 0080-6994) *445, 671*
Schriften zur Handelsforschung (GW ISSN 0080-7001) *182*
Schriften zur Jugendlektuere (AU ISSN 0080-701X) *258, 572*
Schriften zur Kooperationsforschung. Berichte (GW ISSN 0080-7028) *181*
Schriften zur Kooperationsforschung. Studien (GW ISSN 0080-7036) *181*
Schriften zur Kooperationsforschung. Vortraege (GW ISSN 0080-7044) *181*
Schriften zur Mittelstandsforschung (GW) *816*
Schriften zur Oeffentlichen Verwaltung und Oeffentlichen Wirtschaft (GW) *746*

Schriften zur Politischen Wissenschaft (GW) *715*
Schriften zur Rechtslehre und Politik (GW ISSN 0080-7060) *518*
Schriften zur Sozialpsychologie (SZ ISSN 0080-7079) *738*
Schriften zur Ur- und Fruehgeschichte (GE) *435*
Schriften zur Wirtschaftswissenschaftlichen Forschung (GW) *148*
Schriftenreihe Aktuelle Fragen der Energiewirtschaft (GW) *363*
Schriftenreihe aus den Naturschutzgebieten Bayerns (GW) *278, 388*
Schriftenreihe Betriebswirtschaftliche Beitraege zur Organisation und Automation (GW ISSN 0067-6381) *216*
Schriftenriehe Chemische Analytik und Umwelttechnologie (GW) *388*
Schriftenreihe des Buchklubs der Jugend (AU ISSN 0080-7117) *258, 572*
Schriftenreihe Finanzwirtschaft und Finanzrecht (SZ) *176, 518*
Schriftenreihe fuer Agrarwirtschaft (AU) *19, 518*
Schriftenreihe fuer Laendliche Sozialfragen (GW ISSN 0080-7133) *809*
Schriftenreihe fuer Raumforschung und Raumplanung. (AU ISSN 0558-9746) *487*
Schriftenreihe fuer Sportwissenschaft und Sportpraxis *see* Sportwissenschaft und Sportpraxis *822*
Schriftenreihe fuer Vegetationskunde (GW ISSN 0085-5960) *118*
Schriftenreihe: Gesellschaft und Betrieb (AU) *518*
Schriftenreihe Kernenergie (GW) *364*
Schriftenreihe Luftreinhaltung (GW) *388*
Schriftenreihe Naturschutz und Landschaftspflege (GW) *278, 388*
Schriftenreihe Neurologie/Neurology Series (US ISSN 0080-715X) *621*
Schriftenreihe Unternehmensfuehrung und Marketing (GW) *219*
Schriftenreihe zur Geschichte und Politischen Bildung (GW ISSN 0080-7168) *435*
Schriftenreihe zur Orts-, Regional- und Landesplanung (SZ) *487*
Schriftenreihe zur Theoretischen und Angewandten Betriebswirtschaftslehre (GW ISSN 0080-7087) *216*
Schriftenriehe Risikopolitik (SZ) *715*
Schrifttum zur Deutschen Kunst (GW ISSN 0080-7176) *78*
Schrijvers Prentenboek (NE ISSN 0080-7192) *572*
Schuetz-Jahrbuch (GW) *663*
Schuylerite (US) *472*
Schwann Artist Catalog (US ISSN 0582-1487) *665*
Schwann Children's & Christmas Record & Tape Guide (US) *258, 663*
Schweich Lectures (UK ISSN 0080-7206) *767*
Schweizer Anglistische Arbeiten/Swiss Studies in English (SZ ISSN 0080-7214) *550*
Schweizer Beitraege zur Kulturgeschichte und Archaeologie des Mittelalters (SZ) *65*
Schweizer Buchhandels-Adressbuch (SZ ISSN 0080-7230) *759*
Schweizer Verpackungskatalog (SZ) *672*
Schweizerische Amerikanisten-Gesellschaft. Bulletin *see* Societe Suisse des Americanistes.Bulletin *472*
Schweizerische Bankwesen (SZ) *176*
Schweizerische Beitraege zur Altertumswissenschaft (SZ ISSN 0080-7273) *461*
Schweizerische Bibliographie fuer Statistik und Volkswirtschaft/ Bibliographie Suisse de Statistique et d'Economie Politique (SZ) *94, 845*

SCIENCE AND 1479

Schweizerische Geisteswissenschaftliche Gesellschaft. Schriften (SZ ISSN 0080-729X) *493*
Schweizerische Gesellschaft fuer Aussenpolitik. Schriftenreihe (SZ) *723*
Schweizerische Gesellschaft fuer Marktforschung. Geschaeftsbericht (SZ ISSN 0302-2048) *219*
Schweizerische Gesellschaft fuer Theaterkultur. Jahrbuecher (SZ) *859*
Schweizerische Gesellschaft fuer Theaterkultur. Schriften (SZ) *859*
Schweizerische Gesellschaft fuer Ur- und Fruehgeschichte. Institut fuer Ur- und Fruehgeschichte der Schweiz. Jahrbuch (SZ ISSN 0080-7311) *461*
Schweizerische Gesellschaft fuer Volkskunde. Schriften (GW ISSN 0080-732X) *402*
Schweizerische Hochschulkonferenz. Jahresbericht *see* Conference Universitaire Suisse. Rapport Annuel *335*
Schweizerische Konjunktur und ihre Aussichten (SZ) *189*
Schweizerische Luftverkehrsstatistik/ Statistique du Trafic Aerien Suisse *see* Schweizerische Zivilluftfahrt *869*
Schweizerische Meteorologische Zentralanstalt. Annalen (SZ ISSN 0080-7338) *635*
Schweizerische Meteorologische Zentralanstalt. Veroeffentlichungen (SZ ISSN 0080-7346) *635*
Schweizerische Musikforschende Gesellschaft. Publikationen. Serie II (SZ ISSN 0080-7354) *663*
Schweizerische Naturforschende Gesellschaft. Jahrbuch/Societe Helvetique des Sciences Naturelles. Annuaire (SZ) *790*
Schweizerische Naturforschende Gesellschaft. Verhandlungen *see* Schweizerische Naturforschende Gesellschaft. Jahrbuch *790*
Schweizerische Numismatische Rundschau *see* Revue Suisse de Numismatique *478*
Schweizerische Palaeontologische Abhandlungen/Memoires Suisse de Paleontologie (SZ ISSN 0080-7389) *674*
Schweizerische Politik in Jahre *see* Annee Politique Suisse *708*
Schweizerische Zeitschrift fuer Geschichte. Beihefte/Revue Suisse d'Histoire. Supplement (SZ ISSN 0080-7397) *461*
Schweizerische Zivilluftfahrt/Aviation Civile Suisse (SZ) *869*
Schweizerischer Bankverein Booklet *see* S B C Booklet *176*
Schweizerischer Bund fuer Jugendliteratur. Jahresbericht/Ligue Suisse pour la Litterature de la Jeunesse. Rapport Annuel (SZ) *258*
Schweizerischer Ernaehrungsbericht (SZ) *406*
Schweizerischer Forstverein. Zeitschrift. Beihefte (SZ) *410*
Schweizerischer Medizinalkalender (SZ) *599*
Schweizerischer Wissenschaftsrat. Jahresbericht/Conseil Suisse de la Science. Rapport Annuel (SZ) *790*
Schweizerisches Bundesarchiv. Studien und Quellen/Etudes et Sources/Studi e Fonti (SZ) *913*
Schweizerisches Institut fuer Nuklearforschung. Jahresbericht (SZ) *704*
Schweizerisches Jahrbuch fuer Politische Wissenschaft *see* Annuaire Suisse de Science Politique *708*
Schweizerisches Medizinisches Jahrbuch(SZ ISSN 0080-7400) *599*
Schweizerisches Sozialarchiv (SZ ISSN 0080-7419) *809*
Science & Engineering Careers - a Bibliography (US) *668*
Science and Engineering Policy Series (US) *790, 853*
Science & Mechanics' Electrical Guide *see* Electrical Installation & Repair Projects *908*
Science and Society Series (US) *790, 816*

Science and Technology (US ISSN 0080-746X) *535*, 790
Science and Technology (KO) *790, 853*
Science and Technology Education Newsletter (UN) *790*
Science Chelsea (UK ISSN 0300-3361) *790*
Science Council of Japan. Annual Report (JA) *790*
Science Curriculum Improvement Study Newsletter *see* S C I S Newsletter *350*
Science Education in the Region (UK) *790*
Science Education in Zambia (ZA) *322*, 790
Science, Engineering, and Humanities Doctorates in the United States: Profile (US) *668*
Science, Engineering and Related Career Hints (SEARCH) - Bibliography of Career Information *see* Science & Engineering Careers - a Bibliography *668*
Science et Technologie Annuaire/ Wetenschap en Technologie Jaarboek(BE) *790, 853*
Science Fiction Book Review Index (US ISSN 0085-5979) *3, 578*
Science for the Modern Mind (US) *790*
Science Guide to Scientific Instruments (US) *497*
Science in Alaska *see* Alaska Science Conference. Proceedings *778*
Science in Geography (US) *425*
Science in Iceland *see* Scientia Islandica *913*
Science Information Sources *see* Vade-Mecum for Information Scientists *538*
Science Museum of Minnesota. Monograph (US) *790*
Science Museum of Minnesota. Scientific Bulletin *see* Science Museum of Minnesota. Scientific Publications, New Series *790*
Science Museum of Minnesota. Scientific Publications *see* Science Museum of Minnesota. Scientific Publications, New Series *790*
Science Museum of Minnesota. Scientific Publications, New Series (US ISSN 0161-4452) *790*
Science Museum of Victoria. Monographs (AT) *790*
Science Museum of Victoria. Report of Activities (AT ISSN 0076-6240) *655*
Science Notes and News (JM) *350, 790*
Science Nouvelle (FR ISSN 0080-7540) *790*
Science of Advanced Material and Process Engineering Series (US ISSN 0080-7559) *380*
Science of Ceramics (UK ISSN 0080-7575) *244*
Science Policy Studies and Documents (UN ISSN 0080-7591) *790*
Science Student Explores (US) *790*
Science Teachers Association of Queensland. Newsletter (AT) *790*
Science Year (US ISSN 0080-7621) *361*, 790
Sciences (FR ISSN 0080-763X) *790*
Sciences de l'Education (FR ISSN 0080-7648) *913*
Sciences de la Terre: Informatique Geologique *see* Sciences de la Terre: Serie Informatique Geologique *299*
Sciences de la Terre: Serie Informatique Geologique (FR) *299*
Sciences Geologiques - Memoires (FR ISSN 0302-2684) *299*
Sciences Secretes (FR ISSN 0080-7672) *676*
Sciences, Techniques, Informations C R I A C (Centre de Recherches Industrielles en Afrique Centrale) (ZR ISSN 0377-5135) *225*
Scientia Islandica/Science in Iceland (IC) *913*
Scientific and Technical Books and Serials in Print (US ISSN 0000-054X) *795, 854*
Scientific and Technical Books in Print *see* Scientific and Technical Books and Serials in Print *795*
Scientific and Technical Information in Foreign Countries/Kaigaki Kagaku Gijutsu Joho Shiryo (JA) *791, 853*
Scientific and Technical Periodicals Published in South Africa/ Wetenskaplike en Tegniese Tydskrifte in Suid-Afrika Uitgegee (SA ISSN 0080-7702) *791, 853*
Scientific and Technical Societies in South Africa/Wetenskaplike en Tegniese Vereinigings in Suid-Afrika (SA ISSN 0080-7710) *791, 853*
Scientific and Technical Societies of Canada/Societes Scientifiques et Techniques du Canada (CN ISSN 0586-7746) *791, 853*
Scientific Ballooning and Radiations Monitoring Organization Bulletin *see* S B A R M O. Bulletin *635*
Scientific Committee for Antarctic Research Report to S C A R on South African Antarctic Research Activities *see* Report to S C A R on South African Antarctic Research Activities *789*
Scientific Directory of Hong Kong (HK ISSN 0586-5751) *791*
Scientific Exploration Society. Newsletter (UK) *425*
Scientific Horticulture (UK ISSN 0080-7737) *416*
Scientific Policy, Research and Development in Canada/Politique des Sciences, la Recherches et le Developpement au Canada (CN ISSN 0791, 853*
Scientific Publications of the Science Museum of Minnesota *see* Science Museum of Minnesota. Scientific Publications, New Series *790*
Scientific Report (La Jolla) *see* Scripps Clinic and Research Foundation. Scientific Report *599*
Scientific Research Organizations in South Africa/Wetenskaplike Navorsingsorganisasies in Suid-Afrika(SA ISSN 0080-7761) *791, 853*
Scientific Results of Marine Biological Research *see* Hvalraadets Skrifter *103*
Scientific Serials in Thai Libraries (TH ISSN 0125-4529) *94, 795, 854*
Scientific Symposium on the Cultivated Mushroom. Proceedings *see* Mushroom Science *116*
Scientific, Technical and Related Societies of the United States (US ISSN 0085-5995) *791, 853*
Scientists Forum (US ISSN 0080-777X) *791*
Scienze della Materia (IT ISSN 0391-3244) *248, 698*
Scienze Geografiche (IT) *425*
Scienze Pedagogiche (IT) *322*
Scintilation *see* Cinemonkey *649*
Scope (AT) *278*
Scope /Wheelers Canadian Campground Guide (CN ISSN 0380-8343) *831*
Scope/Woodall's Canadian Campgrounds Directory *see* Scope / Wheelers Canadian Campground Guide *831*
Scotch Game Call Hunting Annual (US) *831*
Scotia (US) *393*
Scotland. Department of Agriculture and Fisheries. Freshwater Fisheries Triennial (UK ISSN 0140-5004) *399*
Scotland. Department of Agriculture and Fisheries. Red Deer Commission. Annual Report (UK ISSN 0080-7850) *278*
Scotland. Department of Agriculture and Fisheries. Triennial Review of Research (UK ISSN 0140-5012) *400*
Scotland. Directorate of Fisheries Research. Annual Report *see* Scotland. Department of Agriculture and Fisheries. Triennial Review of Research *400*
Scotland. Registrar General. Annual Report (UK ISSN 0080-7869) *732, 845*
Scotland. Scottish Home and Health Department. Hospital Design in Use (UK ISSN 0080-7885) *913*
Scotland: a World of a Difference *see* Enjoy Scotland *884*
Scotland: Camping and Caravan Sites (UK) *890*
Scotland: Conferences, Meetings, Seminars (UK) *626*
Scotland for Fishing (UK ISSN 0080-7834) *831, 890*
Scotland for Hillwalking (UK) *890*
Scotland for Sea Angling (UK) *831, 890*
Scotland for the Motorist (UK) *890*
Scotland for Touring Caravans *see* Scotland: Camping and Caravan Sites *890*
Scotland-Home of Golf (UK ISSN 0080-7842) *826*, 890
Scotland: in Famous Footsteps (UK) *890*
Scotland: Self Catering Accommodation(UK) *890*
Scotland Tomorrow *see* Scotlink *180*
Scotland: Travel Trade Guide (UK) *890*
Scotland: Where to Stay, Bed and Breakfast (UK) *890*
Scotland: Where to Stay, Hotels and Guest Houses (UK) *890*
Scotland: 1001 Things to See (UK) *890*
Scotland: 600 Things to See *see* Scotland: 1001 Things to See *890*
Scotland's Architectural Heritage (UK) *70*
Scotland's Best Holidays (UK) *890*
Scotlands Regions (UK ISSN 0305-6562) *746*
Scotlink (UK) *180*
Scottish Abstract of Statistics (UK) *845*
Scottish Agricultural Economics; Some Studies of Current Economic Conditions in Scottish Farming (UK ISSN 0080-7966) *30*
Scottish Art Review (UK ISSN 0036-911X) *78*
Scottish Bakers' Year Book (UK ISSN 0080-7974) *407*
Scottish Building & Civil Engineering Year Book (UK ISSN 0085-6002) *138, 376*
Scottish Council for Research in Education. Publications (UK ISSN 0080-8008) *322*
Scottish Decorators' Review *see* Scottish Decorators' Year Book and Review *502*
Scottish Decorators' Year Book and Review (UK) *502*
Scottish Episcopal Church Yearbook (UK ISSN 0080-8016) *772*
Scottish Fisheries Bulletin (UK ISSN 0559-1791) *400*
Scottish Fisheries Information Pamphlets (UK ISSN 0309-9105) *400*
Scottish Fisheries Research Reports (UK) *400*
Scottish Folk Directory (UK) *663*
Scottish Georgian Society. Annual Report (UK) *70*
Scottish Georgian Society. Bulletin *see* Scottish Georgian Society. Annual Report *70*
Scottish Government Yearbook (UK) *715*
Scottish Graduate (UK ISSN 0080-8032) *339, 668*
Scottish Hardware and Drysalters Association. Yearbook (UK ISSN 0080-8059) *138*, 141
Scottish Health Services (UK) *754*
Scottish Journal of Science (UK ISSN 0080-8075) *791*
Scottish Law Directory (UK ISSN 0080-8083) *518*
Scottish Libraries (UK ISSN 0080-8091) *535*
Scottish Marine Biological Association Collected Reprints *see* S. M. B. A. Collected Reprints *107*
Scottish Mountaineering Club. Journal (UK ISSN 0080-813X) *831*
Scottish National Register of Classified Trades (UK ISSN 0080-8148) *241*
Scottish Postmark Group. Handbook (UK ISSN 0080-8164) *266, 479*
Scottish Sea Fisheries Statistical Tables (UK ISSN 0080-8202) *400*
Scottish Small Presses (UK ISSN 0306-0861) *759*
Scottish Social Work Statistics (UK ISSN 0307-9971) *913*
Scottish Society for Prevention of Vivisection. Annual Pictorial Review (UK ISSN 0080-8210) *682*
Scottish Studies (UK ISSN 0036-9411) *53, 402, 461*
Scottish Tradition (CN) *461*
Scottish Universities' Summer School in Physics. Proceedings (UK ISSN 0080-8253) *668*
Scottish Women's Liberation Journal (UK ISSN 0140-5810) *901*
Scott's Trade Directory of Metropolitan Toronto (CN) *241*
Scout Association of Australia. Review of Progress (AT ISSN 0310-818X) *262*
Scouting 'round the World/Scoutisme a Travers le Monde (SZ) *257*
Scoutisme a Travers le Monde *see* Scouting 'round the World *257*
Screen Achievement Records Bulletin *see* Annual Index to Motion Picture Credits *648*
Screen International Film and T.V. Yearbook (UK) *268, 651*
Screen World (US ISSN 0080-8288) *651*
Scribe (AT) *505, 507*
Scripps Clinic and Research Foundation. Annual Report (US ISSN 0080-830X) *853*
Scripps Clinic and Research Foundation. Scientific Report (US ISSN 0361-3054) *599*
Scripps Institution of Oceanography. Bulletin (US ISSN 0080-8318) *312*
Scripps Institution of Oceanography. Contributions (US ISSN 0080-8326) *312*
Scripps Institution of Oceanography. Deep Sea Drilling Project. Initial Reports. (US ISSN 0080-8334) *312*
Scripta Artis Monographia (NE ISSN 0080-8350) *78*
Scripta Classica Israelica (IS) *260*
Scripta Geobotanica (GW ISSN 0341-3772) *118*
Scripta Geologica (NE ISSN 0375-7587) *299*
Scripta Hierosolymitana (IS ISSN 0080-8369) *493, 800*
Scripta Mongolica (US ISSN 0080-8377) *445, 572*
Scriptores Byzantini (RM ISSN 0080-8385) *435, 572*
Scriptores Graeci et Latini *see* Gorog es Latin Irok Tara *259*
Scriptores Latini; Collana di Scrittori Latini ad Uso Accademico (IT ISSN 0080-8393) *260*
Scrittura e Civilta (IT) *260*
Sculpture in the Environment On S I T E *see* On S I T E *77*
Sea Boating Almanac. Northern California and Nevada *see* Pacific Boating Almanac. Northern California & Nevada *827*
Sea Boating Almanac. Pacific Northwest and Alaska *see* Pacific Boating Almanac. Pacific Northwest & Alaska *827*
Sea Boating Almanac. Southern California, Arizona, Baja *see* Pacific Boating Almanac. Southern California, Arizona, Baja *827*
Sea Grant Publications Index (US) *3, 290, 400*
Sea Technology Buyers Guide/ Directory (US) *312, 370*
Sea Technology Handbook and Directory *see* Sea Technology Buyers Guide/Directory *370*
Seabird Bulletin *see* Seabird Report *125*
Seabird Report (UK ISSN 0080-8415) *125*
Seaby's Standard Catalogue of British Coins (UK) *478*
Seahorn Lore (US) *418*

Seahorse (US ISSN 0037-0118) *312*
Seaports and the Shipping World. Annual Issue (CN ISSN 0080-8423) *880*
Search and Rescue Statistics *see* S A R Statistics *880*
Sears Foundation for Marine Research. Memoirs (US) *107, 312*
Seatrade Guide to Arab Shipping (UK ISSN 0141-4151) *880*
Seatrade Guide to EEC Shipping (UK ISSN 0141-4585) *880*
Seatrade Guide to Latin American Shipping (UK ISSN 0142-5064) *880*
Seatrade U.S. Yearbook (UK ISSN 0142-5056) *880*
Seawater and Desalting (US) *898*
SEAX Series of Teaching Portfolios (UK) *435*
Second 1,500 Companies (US ISSN 0275-7443) *148*
Secretaria de Estado de Agricultura y Ganaderia Publicaciones *see* E A G Publicaciones *14*
Secretariat Permanent des Organisations Non Gouvernementales. Rapport d'Activities (UV) *361*
Securite Industrielle (CN) *496*
Securitech (UK ISSN 0307-7780) *283*
Securities Exchange of Thailand. Handbook (TH) *204*
Securities Industry Association. State and Local Pension Funds (US ISSN 0075-0263) *204*
Securities Investor Protection Corporation. Annual Report (US ISSN 0094-467X) *204*
Securities Law Review (US ISSN 0080-8474) *176, 518*
Securities Market in Japan (JA) *204*
Security and Protection Manual (SA) *283, 395, 496*
Security Industry Yearbook (US) *204*
Security Products and Services Index (SA) *241, 284*
Sedar (SI ISSN 0559-2674) *769*
Sediment Data for Selected Canadian Rivers (CN ISSN 0080-8482) *299*
See Australia (AT) *425, 890*
Seed Savers Exchange (US) *416, 476*
Seed Trade Buyer's Guide (US ISSN 0080-8504) *39*
Seeing Eye Annual Report (US) *133*
Seeker's Guide (US ISSN 0080-8512) *361*
Seeley Genealogical Society (Newsletter) (US) *418*
Sefunim (IS ISSN 0077-5193) *65, 655, 880*
Sehar Huts Shel Yisrael *see* Israel. Central Bureau of Statistics. Israel's Foreign Trade *159*
Seijigaku *see* Japanese Political Science Association. Yearbook *712*
Seishin-Igaku Institute of Psychiatry, Tokyo. Bulletin/Seishin-Igaku Kenkyusho, Tokyo. Gyoseki Shu (JA ISSN 0080-8547) *621*
Seishin Igaku Kenkyusho, Tokyo. Gyoseki Shu *see* Seishin-Igaku Institute of Psychiatry, Tokyo. Bulletin *621*
Seiso Jigyo Gaiyo *see* Public Cleansing Service in Tokyo *753*
Seiyo Kotengaku Kenkyu *see* Journal of Classical Studies *259*
Sejahtera (MY) *572*
Selangor Public Library. Annual Report/Perbadanan Perpustakaan Awam Selangor. Lapuran Tahunan (MY) *535*
Selbstbedienung--Dynamik im Handel (GW ISSN 0343-3226) *216, 407*
Selbstbedienung und Supermarkt *see* Selbstbedienung--Dynamik im Handel *407*
Selbyana (US ISSN 0361-185X) *118*
Selden Society, London. Handbook: Publications, List of Members and Rules (UK) *435, 518*
Selden Society, London. Lectures (UK) *435, 518*
Selden Society, London. Main (Annual) Series (UK) *435, 518*
Selden Society, London. Supplementary Series (UK ISSN 0582-4788) *435, 518*
Select Bibliographical Guides (US) *558*

Select Data on Students, Alabama Institutions of Higher Learning (US ISSN 0091-5246) *339*
Select Information Exchange Guide to Business and Investment Books *see* S I E Guide to Business and Investment Books *163*
Select Information Exchange Sophisticated Investor *see* S I E Sophisticated Investor *204*
Selected Agri-Figures of the E.E.C *see* E E G Vademecum *24*
Selected Alaska Hunting & Fishing Tales (US ISSN 0361-137X) *913*
Selected and Annotated Bibliography of Reference Materials in Consumer Credit (US ISSN 0077-4014) *164*
Selected Annotated Bibliography of Population Studies in the Netherlands (NE ISSN 0167-4757) *732*
Selected Annual Reviews of the Analytical Sciences (UK ISSN 0300-9963) *249*
Selected Bibliography of Homosexuality(US) *480*
Selected Bibliography of Museological Literature (CS) *656*
Selected Bibliography of Recent Economic Development Publications (US) *164*
Selected Documents of the International Petroleum Industry (AU ISSN 0080-858X) *681*
Selected Irrigation Return Flow Quality Abstacts *see* U.S. Environmental Protection Agency. Office of Research and Development. Selected Irrigation Return Flow Quality Abstracts *390*
Selected Labour Statistics for Nova Scotia (CN ISSN 0702-9888) *210*
Selected List of Catalogues for Short Films and Filmstrips (UN ISSN 0503-440X) *322, 651*
Selected List of Federal Laws and Treaties Relating to Sport Fish and Wildlife *see* U.S. Fish and Wildlife Service. Selected List of Federal Laws and Treaties Relating to Sport Fish and Wildlife *519*
Selected Monographs on Taxation (NE) *232*
Selected Papers - Haskins & Sells *see* Haskins & Sells. Selected Papers *167*
Selected Papers in Biochemistry (US) *112*
Selected Reports in Ethnomusicology (US ISSN 0361-6622) *663*
Selected Statistics of the Tourism Industry in Puerto Rico (PR) *890*
Selected Streamflow Data for Ontario (CN) *308*
Selected Tables in Mathematical Statistics. (US ISSN 0094-8837) *589*
Selected Topics in Solid State Physics (NE ISSN 0080-8636) *698*
Selected Trade and Professional Associations in Texas *see* Texas Trade and Professional Associations and Other Selected Organizations *242*
Selected Translations in Mathematical Statistics and Probability (US ISSN 0065-9274) *589*
Selected Vital Statistics and Planning Data *see* Kentucky. Department for Human Resources. Selected Vital Statistics and Planning Data *756*
Selection *see* Selection Sketsmasa *418*
Selection Guide Series (US) *94*
Selection Sketsmasa (IO) *418*
Selections from Educational Records of the Government of India (II) *322*
Selective Guide to Audiovisuals for Mental Health and Family Life Education (US) *350, 695, 738*
Selective Guide to Materials for Mental Health and Family Life Education *see* Selective Guide to Publications for Mental Health and Family Life Education *739*
Selective Guide to Publications for Mental Health and Family Life Education (US) *350, 695, 738, 739*
Self-Catering and Furnished Holidays (UK) *890*

Self Catering Holidays (UK ISSN 0080-8679) *890*
Self Catering in Britain (UK) *890*
Self-Employed Pensions (UK) *500*
Sell's British Aviation *see* Aviation Europe *7*
Sell's British Exporters *see* British Exporters *194*
Sell's Building Index (UK ISSN 0080-8717) *138*
Sell's Directory (UK) *241*
Sell's Directory of Products & Services *see* Sell's Directory *241*
Sell's Government and Municipal Contractors Register *see* Government and Municipal Contractors *742*
Sell's Health Service Buyers Guide *see* Health Service Buyers Guide *481*
Sell's Hotel, Restaurant and Canteen Supplies *see* Hotel, Restaurant and Catering Supplies *405*
Sell's Marine Market (UK ISSN 0143-1153) *827*
Semaine des Hopitaux (FR) *599*
Semainier Beaux Pays de France (FR ISSN 0080-8768) *890*
Semainier de Paris *see* Semainier Beaux Pays de France *890*
Semana Internacional de Antropologia Vasca. Actas (SP) *53, 393*
Semiconductor Heat Sink, Socket & Associated Hardware D.A.T.A. Book(US ISSN 0092-6302) *358*
Semiconductor Test Symposium. Digest of Papers (US) *273, 358*
Semiconductors and Semimetals (US ISSN 0080-8784) *358*
Seminaire Belge de Perfectionnement aux Affaires. Exposes (BE ISSN 0080-8792) *180*
Seminar Arghriiade (RM) *589*
Seminar de Fizica Teoretica (RM ISSN 0080-8806) *698*
Seminar for Arabian Studies. Proceedings (UK) *475*
Seminar on Canadian-American Relations (Papers) (CN ISSN 0080-8814) *723*
Seminar on Dravidian Linguistics. Proceedings (II) *550*
Seminar on Integrated Surveys of Environment. Proceedings *see* I T C- U N E S C O International Seminar Proceedings *386*
Seminar on Leadership in Continuing Education *see* Conference for College and University Leaders in Continuing Education. Proceedings *329*
Seminar on the Acquisition of Latin American Library Materials. Final Report and Working Papers (US ISSN 0080-8849) *472, 535*
Seminar on the Acquisition of Latin American Library Materials. Microfilming Projects Newsletter (US ISSN 0080-8857) *535*
Seminar on the Acquisition of Latin American Library Materials. Resolutions and Lists of Committees (US ISSN 0361-9966) *913*
Seminario Brasileiro sobre Tecnicas Exploratorias em Geologia. Anais (BL) *299*
Seminario de Estudos Brasileiros. Anais(BL) *913*
Seminario de Filologia Vasca Julio de Urquijo. Anuario (SP) *550*
Seminario di Studi e Ricerche Sul Linguaggio Musicale. Atti (IT) *663*
Seminario Matematico Garcia de Galdeano. Publicaciones (SP ISSN 0085-6029) *589*
Seminario Nacional de Controle de Qualidade. Anais (BL) *225*
Seminars in Infectious Disease (US ISSN 0162-5454) *608*
Seminars in Neurological Surgery (US ISSN 0160-2489) *621, 625*
Semiotica & Psicanalisi (IT) *738*
Semitic Study Series (NE) *671, 770*
Semitic Texts with Translations (NE ISSN 0080-8881) *770*
Semitica (FR ISSN 0085-6037) *493*

SERIES IN 1481

Senckenbergiana Maritima. Zeitschrift fuer Meeresgeologie und Meeresbiologie (GW ISSN 0080-889X) *107, 312*
Senckenbergische Naturforschende Gesellschaft. Abhandlungen (GW ISSN 0365-7000) *107, 299*
Senegal. Archives. Rapport Annuel (SG) *535*
Senegal. Liste du Corps Diplomatique (SG) *723*
Senegal. Service du Protocole. Liste Diplomatique et Consulaire *see* Senegal. Liste du Corps Diplomatique *723*
Senegal en Chiffres (SG) *441*
Senior High School Library Catalog (US) *535*
Sennacieca Revuo (FR ISSN 0080-8903) *723*
Senpaku Gijutsu Kenkyusho Obun Hokoku *see* Japan. Ship Research Institute. Papers *879*
Sentei Tosho Somokuroku *see* Catalogue of Books Recommended for Libraries *89*
Sentiers Poesie (FR) *581*
Seoul National University. Economic Review (KO) *148*
Seoul National University. Faculty Papers. (KO) *599*
Seoul National University. Faculty Papers. Biology and Agriculture Series. (KO) *19, 107*
Seoul National University. Population and Development Studies Center. Bulletin (KO) *729*
Sephardic Scholar (US) *393*
Sequel (CN) *480, 719*
Serbische Rechtsquellen *see* Izvori Srpskog Prava *513*
Serbska Pratyja (GE) *393*
Serengeti Research Institute. Annual Report (TZ) *278*
Serial Handbook of Modern Psychiatry (US ISSN 0094-6184) *621*
Serial Sources for the Biosis Data Base (US) *3, 110*
Serials Holdings in the Libraries of Memorial University of Newfoundland, St. John's Public Library and College of Trades and Technology (CN ISSN 0316-6597) *94*
Serials in Education in Australian Libraries: a Union List (AT ISSN 0311-2373) *322, 535*
Serials in Transition (US ISSN 0148-4451) *535*
Serials Updating Service Annual (US ISSN 0095-2702) *94, 535*
Serie Afrique Noire (FR ISSN 0080-8938) *715*
Serie Cadernos de Historia (BL) *472*
Serie Cana de Azucar (CU) *39*
Serie de Ciencias Humanas *see* Centro de Estudos de Cabo Verde. Revista: Serie de Ciencias Humanas *796*
Serie di Matematica e Fisica (IT ISSN 0391-3252) *589, 698*
Serie di Matematica e Fisica. Problemi Risolti (IT) *589, 698*
Serie Economia Colombiana (CK) *148*
Serie EO/International (FR) *189*
Serie Estudios Literarios (CR) *572*
Serie Estudos Penitenciaros (BL) *284*
Serie Investigacion Pesquera (CL) *400*
Serie Legislacion Educativa Argentina (AG) *322, 518*
Serie Linguistica Peruana (PE) *550*
Serie Literatura Hoy (PR) *572*
Serie Pensamento Economico Brasileiro(BL) *148*
Serie Poeyana *see* Poeyana *130*
Serie Praxis (PE) *210, 225*
Serie Thesaurus-Folclore (BL) *402*
Serie Vie Locale (FR ISSN 0586-9889) *715*
Serie Welstandstoezicht (NE) *816*
Series Barbey d'Aurevilly *see* Barbey d'Aurevilly *560*
Series Desenvolvimento Brasileiro *see* Brazil Development Series *221*
Series Entomologica (NE ISSN 0080-8954) *121*
Series Georges Bernanos *see* Etudes Bernanosiennes *564*
Series in Administration (US) *216*

Series in Clinical and Community Psychology (US ISSN 0146-0846) 346, 738, 809
Series in Clinical Psychology see Series in Clinical and Community Psychology 738
Series in Computational Methods in Mechanics and Thermal Sciences (US ISSN 0272-4804) 383
Series in Decision and Control (US ISSN 0080-8962) 589
Series in English Language and Literature (II) 550
Series in Geotechnical Engineering (US) 39
Series in Indian Languages and Linguistics (II) 550
Series in Philosophy of Science see University of Western Ontario Series in Philosophy of Science 692
Series in Sikh History and Culture (II) 445, 572
Series in the Philosophy of Science (US ISSN 0080-8970) 691, 791
Series in Thermal and Fluids Engineering (US ISSN 0146-0854) 381
Series Jean Giono see Jean Giono 566
Series on Bulk Materials Engineering see Series on Bulk Materials Handling 370
Series on Bulk Materials Handling (US) 370
Series on Company Approaches to Industrial Relations (US ISSN 0080-8997) 210
Series on Contemporary Javanese Life (US ISSN 0582-8155) 53, 403, 800
Series on Extraterrestrial Chemistry (US) 83, 248
Series on Rock and Soil Mechanics (US ISSN 0080-9004) 290, 377
Series Paedopsychiatrica (SZ ISSN 0080-9012) 621
Series, Serials, and Packages (US) 268
Service Canadien de la Faune. Cahiers de Biologie see Canadian Wildlife Service. Progress Notes 275
Service de la Carte Geologique d'Alsace et de Lorraine. Memoires see Sciences Geologiques - Memoires 299
Service Employees International Union. International Convention. Official Proceedings (US) 507
Services for People (CN ISSN 0317-4670) 809
Servicio Central de Organizacion y Metodos see O y M 745
Seto Marine Biological Laboratory. Special Publications (JA ISSN 0080-9098) 107
Setting up in Denmark (DK) 189
Seven (US) 581
Seventies (US ISSN 0037-5969) 557, 581
Sewage Facilities Construction (US ISSN 0083-050X) 388
Seychelles. Office of the President. Budget Address (SE) 232, 746
Seychelles. President's Office. Statistics Division. Census (SE) 845
Seychelles. President's Office. Statistics Division. Statistical Abstract (SE) 846
Seychelles. President's Office. Statistics Division. Tourism and Migration Report (SE) 846, 893
Seychelles Trade Report (SE) 197
Seyd's Commercial Lists see Dun & Bradstreet Standard Register 237
Seznam Platnych Ceskoslovenskych Statnich a Oborovych Norem (CS) 537
Shakai Fukushi No Doko (JA) 809
Shakai-jinruigaku Nenpo (JA) 53
Shakespeare-Jahrbuch (GE ISSN 0080-9128) 572
Shakespeare Research and Opportunities; Report of the Modern Language Association of America Conference (US ISSN 0080-9144) 339, 572
Shakespeare Studies (JA ISSN 0582-9402) 572
Shakespeare Studies (US ISSN 0582-9399) 572

Shakespeare Survey (UK ISSN 0080-9152) 572
Shalshelet: the Chain (US) 663
Shameless Hussy Review (US) 901
Shankpainter (US) 572
Shantih (US ISSN 0037-329X) 581
Share see S H A R E 535
Shareholder (AT ISSN 0037-3311) 204
Sharing of Total Public School Expenditures see Understanding Financial Support of Public Schools 345
Shavings from the Chronicle of the Early American Industries Association (US) 225
Shaw Annual (US ISSN 0080-9179) 572, 691
Shaw Review see Shaw Annual 572
Shaw's Directory of Courts in England and Wales (UK ISSN 0085-6061) 518
Shaw's Directory of Magistrates' Courts & Crown Courts see Shaw's Directory of Courts in England and Wales 518
Sheet Metal Industries International (UK ISSN 0143-7844) 629, 631
Sheet Metal Industries Year Book (UK ISSN 0305-7798) 629, 631
Shell Tourist Guide to South Africa (SA) 890
Shellac Export Promotion Council. Annual Report (II) 673
Sheller's Directory of Clubs, Books, Periodicals and Dealers (US ISSN 0085-607X) 130
Shenaton Hidrologi Le-Yisrael see Hydrological Yearbook of Israel 307
Shenaton Statisti: Le Nemlei Israel see Yearbook of Israel Ports Statistics 198
Shenaton Statisti le-Yisrael see Israel. Central Bureau of Statistics. Statistical Abstract of Israel 841
Shepard's Acts and Cases by Popular Names, Federal and State (US ISSN 0080-9233) 518
Sherborn Fund Facsimiles (UK ISSN 0080-9241) 791
Shevchenko Scientific Society. Proceedings of the Section of Chemistry, Biology and Medicine (US) 107, 248, 599
Shevchenko Scientific Society. Proceedings of the Section of Mathematics and Physics (US) 791
Shiborudia see Sieboldia Acta Biologica 107
Shigen Gijutsu Shikenjo Nempo see National Research Institute for Pollution and Resources. Annual Report 387
Shigen Kagaku Kenkyusho see Tokyo Institute of Technology. Research Laboratory of Resources Utilization. Report 853
Shigen Sogo Kaihatsu Kenkyusho Obun Hokoku see Resources Exploitation Institute. Bulletin 179
Shih Tzu Bulletin (US) 682
Shiloach Center for Middle Eastern & African Studies. Monograph Series (US) 441, 475, 572
Shimane University. Faculty of Law and Literature. Memoirs (JA) 800
Shimane University. Faculty of Science. Memoirs (JA) 791
Shin Nippon Denki Giho see New Nippon Electric Technical Review 357
Shinkei Kagaku see Japanese Neurochemical Society. Bulletin 620
Shinshu University. Faculty of Textile Science and Technology. Journal. Series A: Biology (JA ISSN 0583-0648) 19, 107, 856
Shinshu University. Faculty of Textile Science and Technology. Journal. Series B: Engineering (JA) 370
Shinshu University. Faculty of Textile Science and Technology. Journal. Series C: Chemistry (JA ISSN 0559-8621) 374, 856
Shinshu University. Faculty of Textile Science and Technology. Journal. Series D: Arts (JA ISSN 0583-0664) 78, 856

Shinshu University. Faculty of Textile Science and Technology. Journal. Series E: Agriculture and Sericulture (JA) 19
Shinshu University. Faculty of Textile Science and Technology. Journal. Series F: Physics and Mathematics (JA) 589, 791
Shipping and Aviation Statistics of the Maltese Islands (MM ISSN 0080-9268) 880
Shipping Marks on Timber (UK ISSN 0080-9284) 413
Shipping Statistics Yearbook (GW) 880
Ships and Aircraft of the United States Fleet (US ISSN 0080-9292) 640
Shirley Institute Publications. S: Series (UK ISSN 0306-5154) 856
Shivaji University, Kolhapur, India. Journal. Humanities and Sciences (PK ISSN 0080-9314) 493, 791
Shizenshi Kenkyu see Osaka Museum of Natural History. Occasional Papers 788
Shizuoka Daigaku Rigakubu Kenkyu Hokoku see Shizuoka University. Faculty of Science. Reports 791
Shizuoka University. Faculty of Science. Reports/Shizuoka Daigaku Rigakubu Kenkyu Hokoku (JA ISSN 0583-0923) 791
Shoe Retailers Manual (UK ISSN 0140-5578) 795
Shoe Trades Directory (UK ISSN 0080-9349) 795
Shoes and Leather Trades Directory of Southern Africa (SA) 795
Shokuryo Kagaku Kenkyusho Kiyo see Kyoto University. Research Institute for Food Science. Memoirs 405
Shokuryo Keizai Nenkan see Food Economics Yearbook 237
Shop Equipment & Materials Guide (UK) 141
Shop Equipment & Shopfitting Directory see Shop Equipment & Materials Guide 141
Shopping Center Directory see Directory of Shopping Centers 237
Shopping: Opcoes de Compra para a Grande Sao Paulo (BL) 219
Shoreline/Coastal Zone Management (US) 388
Short Oxford History of the Modern World (US ISSN 0080-939X) 435
Short Play Series (US ISSN 0080-9403) 572
Short Story Index (US) 3, 578
Shorter Studies in East-European History (CN) 461
Show Business Who's Where see Who's Where 269
Showcall (UK) 663, 859
Showcast Directory (AT) 859
Showcast General Directory see Showcast Directory 859
Showtime (US) 913
Shqiptari i Lire see Free Albanian 710
Shrew (US) 913
Shri Chhatrapati Shivaji University. Report (II ISSN 0080-9322) 340
Shrimp Culture Research Centre. Bulletin (IO) 400
Shvut (IS) 393, 715, 770
SI see A C M Annual Workshop on Microprogramming. Conference Record 270
Sickle Cell Hemoglobinopathies: a Comprehensive Bibliography (US) 913
Siddha Vani (II) 771
Side Effects of Drugs (NE ISSN 0583-1881) 599, 686
Siderurgia Brasileira S.A. Relatorio de Diretoria (BL) 629
Sieboldia Acta Biologica/Shiborudia (JA ISSN 0559-9822) 107
Siecle Eclate: Dada, Surrealisme et les Avant-Gardes (FR) 572
Sielkundige Instituut van die Republiek van Suid-Afrika. Verrigtings see Psychological Institute of the Republic of South Africa. Proceedings 737
Siemens-News (GW) 853
Sierra Club Exhibit Format Series (US ISSN 0080-9519) 278
Sierra Leone. Library Board. Report (SL ISSN 0583-2268) 535

Sierra Leone. Ministry of Education. Report (SL ISSN 0080-9551) 322
Sierra Leone. Ministry of Finance. Budget Speech (SL) 232
Sierra Leone Chamber of Commerce. Journal see Chamber of Commerce of Sierra Leone. Journal 178
Sierra Leone Geographical Association. Bulletin see Sierra Leone Geographical Journal 425
Sierra Leone Geographical Journal (SL ISSN 0583-239X) 425
Sierra Leone in Figures (SL ISSN 0080-9535) 846
Sierra Leone Publications (SL) 539
Sigma (CE ISSN 0080-956X) 589
Sigma Zetan (US ISSN 0080-9578) 791
Sign Makers and Suppliers Year Book and Directory (UK) 242
Significant Issues Facing Directors (US ISSN 0193-4201) 216
Significant State Appellate Decisions Outline (US) 518
Signos (PY) 557
Signpost (UK) 332
Sikh Religious Studies Information (US ISSN 0193-1466) 769
Silesia Antiqua (PL ISSN 0080-9594) 65
Silicon Gulch Gazette (US) 273
Silk in India (II) 858
Sillages (FR) 551, 572
Silo (US ISSN 0037-5306) 78, 572, 663
Silumine Fizika/Teplofizika (UR ISSN 0082-4089) 700
Silver Lining (US) 258
Silver Market (US ISSN 0066-4332) 629
Silvicultura Em Sao Paulo (BL ISSN 0583-3132) 410
Simulation (US) 273
SIN-Staedtebauinstitut. Information (GW) 487
SIN-Staedtebauinstitut. Jahresberichte (GW) 487
SIN-Staedtebauinstitut. Schriftenreihe (GW ISSN 0078-2807) 487
SIN-Staedtebauinstitut. Studienhefte (GW ISSN 0078-2815) 487
SIN-Staedtebauinstitut. Werkberichte (GW ISSN 0078-2823) 487
Sinal (BL) 677
Sind University Journal of Education (PK ISSN 0560-0871) 322
Sindicato Nacional del Metal, Madrid. Informe-Economico y Social (SP ISSN 0085-6096) 630
Singapore. Board of Commissioners of Currency, Annual Report (SI) 176
Singapore. Catalogue of Government Publications see Singapore National Printers. Publications Catalogue 718
Singapore. Department of Statistics. Report on the Census of Industrial Production (SI ISSN 0080-9675) 164
Singapore. Department of Statistics. Report on the Household Expenditure Survey (SI) 480
Singapore. Economic Development Board. Annual Report (SI ISSN 0080-9683) 225
Singapore. Housing and Development Board. Annual Report (SI) 487
Singapore. Metrication Board. Annual Report (SI) 487
Singapore. Metrication Board. Metric Guide for Consumers (SI) 637
Singapore. Ministry of Labour. Annual Report (SI) 210
Singapore. Ministry of National Development. Annual Report (SI) 487
Singapore. Ministry of Science and Technology. National Survey of Scientific Manpower (SI) 210, 791
Singapore. Ministry of the Environment. Annual Report (SI) 754
Singapore. National Library. Annual Report (SI ISSN 0080-9721) 535
Singapore. National Statistical Commission. Singapore Standard Crime Classification (SI) 285
Singapore. National Statistical Commission. Singapore Standard Industrial Classification (SI) 164

Singapore. Science Council. Annual Reports (SI) *791*
Singapore Accountant (SI ISSN 0080-9640) *168*
Singapore Banking, Finance & Insurance(SI) *176, 500*
Singapore Book World (SI ISSN 0080-9659) *759*
Singapore Business Yearbook (SI) *242*
Singapore Computer Society. Journal (SI) *273*
Singapore Facts and Pictures (SI ISSN 0080-9691) *445*
Singapore Indian Chamber of Commerce. Directory (SI) *242*
Singapore Institute of Architects Yearbook *see* S I A Yearbook *70*
Singapore Institute of Planners. Newsletter *see* Planews *486*
Singapore International Chamber of Commerce. Investor's Guide (SI) *180*
Singapore International Chamber of Commerce. Report (SI ISSN 0583-3736) *180*
Singapore Journal of Education (SI) *322*
Singapore Journal of Social Work (SI) *809*
Singapore Law Review (SI ISSN 0080-9705) *518*
Singapore Libraries (SI ISSN 0085-6118) *535*
Singapore Motoring Guide (SI) *872*
Singapore National Institute of Chemistry. Bulletin *see* S N I C Bulletin *248*
Singapore National Institute of Chemistry Bulletin *see* S N I C Bulletin *248*
Singapore National Printers. Publications Catalogue (SI) *718*
Singapore Periodicals Index (SI ISSN 0377-7928) *3*
Singapore Polytechnic Engineering Society. Journal (SI) *370*
Singapore Public Health Bulletin (SI) *754*
Singapore Telephone Board Annual Report *see* Telecommunication Authority of Singapore. Telecoms Annual Report *269*
Singapore Tourist Promotion Board. Annual Statistical Report on Visitor Arrivals (SI) *890*
Singapore Trade & Industry Yearbook *see* Singapore Business Yearbook *242*
Singapore Trade Classification & Customs Duties (SI) *232*
Singles Master *see* Music Master *661*
Sino-United States Trade Statistics (US) *197*
Sinologica Coloniensia (GW ISSN 0170-3706) *445, 671*
Sinopse Estatistica do Brasil (BL) *846*
Sinopsis Dun - Brazil (US ISSN 0080-9756) *189*
Sintesis Bibliografica (AG ISSN 0080-9772) *164*
Sir Frederic Hooper Award Essay (UK) *148, 216*
Sir George Earle Memorial Lecture on Industry and Government (UK ISSN 0080-9780) *148, 715*
Sir Moses Montefiore Collections des Juifs Celebres (FR ISSN 0075-4544) *767*
Sir Thomas Browne Instituut. Publications. General Series *see* Sir Thomas Browne Instituut. Publications. General Series and Special Series *461*
Sir Thomas Browne Instituut. Publications. General Series and Special Series (NE) *461*
Sira Institute. Annual Report (UK) *497*
Sires and Dams *see* U S T A Sires and Dams *828*
Siskiyou Pioneer and Yearbook (US ISSN 0583-4449) *472*
Sistema Ferroviario R F F S A (Rede Ferroviaria Federal, S.A.) (BL) *873*
Sisters Have Resources Everywhere *see* S H A R E *535*
Situation Economique de Cote d'Ivoire (IV ISSN 0080-9829) *189*

Situation Economique de la Republique Rwandaise au 31 Decembre *see* Rwanda. Direction Generale de la Statistique. Situation Economique de la Republique Rwandaise au 31 Decembre *189*
Situation Economique du Maroc (MR ISSN 0080-9845) *190*
Situation Economique du Senegal (SG ISSN 0080-9853) *190*
Situation Economique et Perspectives d'Avenir (FR) *190*
Situation Economique Suisse et ses Perspectives *see* Schweizerische Konjunktur und ihre Aussichten *189*
Sivananda School of Yoga. News Bulletin *see* Divine Path *688*
Sixteen Mm Films Available in the Public Libraries of Metropolitan Toronto (CN ISSN 0315-7326) *651*
Sixteenth Century Bibliography (US) *438*
Sixties *see* Seventies *557*
Sjoefartshistorisk Aarbok/Norwegian Yearbook of Maritime History (NO ISSN 0080-9888) *461*
Skandinavisk Tidskrift for Faerg och Lack. Aarsbok (DK ISSN 0085-6126) *673*
Skandinaviske Skipsrederier/Yearbook of Scandinavian Shipowners (NO) *242, 880*
Skeletal Radiology (US ISSN 0364-2348) *622*
Skenectada (US ISSN 0270-2614) *107, 388*
Sketch Book (US) *78*
Ski Francais (FR) *822*
Ski Magazine's Guide to Cross Country Skiing (US) *831*
Ski X-C (US) *831*
Skiers' Almanac (US) *831*
Skier's Guide (US ISSN 0080-9918) *822*
Skinner's Record Tufting Yearbook *see* Tufting Year Book *857*
Skipsfartens Innkjoepsbok (NO) *880*
Skogbrukets og Skogindustriennes Forsknings-Forening. Arbok *see* Skogbrukets og Skogindustriennes Forskningsraad. Aarbok *413*
Skogbrukets og Skogindustriennes Forskningsraad. Aarbok (NO) *413*
Skolan (SW) *332*
Skolens Aarbok (NO ISSN 0080-9950) *322*
Skolvaerldens Aarsbok *see* Skolan *332*
Skywriting (US) *572*
Slade Magazine (UK ISSN 0144-6428) *78, 572*
SLAM: Trade Year Book of Africa (SP ISSN 0080-9985) *198*
Slapstick (US) *572*
Slaskie Studia Historyczne (PL) *461*
Slavia Antiqua (PL ISSN 0080-9993) *65*
Slavia Occidentalis (PL ISSN 0081-0002) *551*
Slavica Gothoburgensia (SW ISSN 0081-0010) *551*
Slavica Lundensia (SW) *551, 572*
Slavistic Printing and Reprintings (NE ISSN 0081-0029) *445, 572*
Slavyanskaya Filologiya (UR) *551*
SLCS *see* Studies in Language Companion Series *552*
Sleep (SZ ISSN 0302-5128) *599*
Sleep Research (US ISSN 0093-0407) *621*
Slit Wrist Magazine (US) *572*
Sloan-Kettering Institute for Cancer Research. Progress Report (US ISSN 0081-0045) *606*
Slough (US) *572*
Slovaci v Zahranici (CS ISSN 0081-0061) *53, 461, 551*
Slovak Press Digest (US ISSN 0037-6914) *393, 715*
Slovakia (US ISSN 0583-5623) *393*
Slovakia *see* Slowakei *557*
Slovanske Historicke Studie (CS ISSN 0081-007X) *461*
Slovanske Studie (CS ISSN 0583-564X) *393, 461, 715, 816*
Slovenska Akademia Vied. Geofyzikalny Ustav. Contributions (CS ISSN 0586-4607) *306*

Slovenska Akademia Vied. Geologicky Ustav D. Stura. Geologicke Prace *see* Slovenska Akademia Vied. Geologicky Ustav D. Stura: Zbornik: Zapadne Karpaty *299*
Slovenska Akademia Vied. Geologicky Ustav D. Stura: Zbornik: Zapadne Karpaty (CS ISSN 0036-1372) *299*
Slovenska Bibliografija (YU ISSN 0350-3585) *94*
Slovenska Numizmatika (CS ISSN 0081-0088) *478*
Slovenske Ludove Piesne pre Akordeon(CS) *663*
Slovenske Narodne Muzeum. Muzeologicky Kabinet. Vyrocne Spravy o Cinnosti Slovenskych Muzei *see* Ustredna Sprava Muzei a Galerii. Vyrocne Spravy o Cinnosti Slovenskych Muzei *655*
Slovenski Etnograf (YU) *53*
Slovenski Jezuiti V Kanade. Year Book (CN ISSN 0085-6134) *775*
Slowakei/Slovakia (GW ISSN 0037-7058) *557*
Sluzben Vesnik na Socijalisticka Republika Makedonija (YU ISSN 0037-7147) *746*
Sluzbene Novine Opcine Karlovac (YU ISSN 0037-7104) *750*
Sluzbeni Glasnik Opcine Rovinj (YU ISSN 0037-7120) *750*
Small and Medium Industry Bank, Seoul. Annual Report (KO) *176*
Small Business Management Series (US ISSN 0081-0118) *234*
Small Business News (CN ISSN 0708-3041) *234*
Small Business Reporter (US) *234*
Small Industries Guide (II) *234*
Small Moon (US) *581*
Small Press Record of Books in Print (US) *94, 761*
Small-Scale Industries: South Eastern and Benue Plateau States of Nigeria (NR) *234*
Smallholder Tea Authority. Annual Report (MW) *39*
Smar's Industrial Directory of Pakistan (PK) *242*
Smith College Studies in History (US ISSN 0081-0193) *435*
Smithsonian Contributions to Anthropology (US ISSN 0081-0223) *53*
Smithsonian Contributions to Astrophysics (US ISSN 0081-0231) *83, 699*
Smithsonian Contributions to Botany (US ISSN 0081-024X) *118*
Smithsonian Contributions to Paleobiology (US ISSN 0081-0266) *674*
Smithsonian Contributions to the Earth Sciences (US ISSN 0081-0274) *290*
Smithsonian Contributions to Zoology (US ISSN 0081-0282) *130*
Smithsonian Institution. Astrophysical Observatory. Central Bureau for Astronomical Telegrams. Circular (US ISSN 0081-0304) *83*
Smithsonian Institution. Astrophysical Observatory. S A O Special Report (US ISSN 0081-0320) *83, 699*
Smithsonian Institution. Center for Short Lived Phenomena. Annual Report (US ISSN 0085-6142) *290*
Smithsonian Institution Opportunities for Research and Advanced Study *see* Smithsonian Opportunities for Research and Study in History Art Science *791*
Smithsonian Opportunities for Research and Study in History Art Science (US ISSN 0081-0339) *791*
Smithsonian Research Opportunities *see* Smithsonian Opportunities for Research and Study in History Art Science *791*
Smithsonian Studies in Air and Space (US) *10*
Smithsonian Studies in History and Technology (US ISSN 0081-0258) *435*
Smoker's Handbook (UK ISSN 0081-0355) *861*
Smoking and Health Bibliographical Bulletin *see* Smoking and Health Bulletin *695*

Smoking and Health Bulletin (US ISSN 0081-0363) *695*
Snoeck's Almanach (BE ISSN 0085-6169) *493*
Snoeck's; Literatuur Kunst Film Toneel Mode Reizen (BE ISSN 0085-6177) *493, 557*
Snow Brand Milk Products Co., Ltd. Research Laboratory. Reports/ Yukijirushi Nyugyo Gijutsu Kenkyusho Hokoku (JA ISSN 0082-4763) *41*
Snowmobile Accidents, Manitoba (CN ISSN 0707-9184) *863*
Snowmobile Sports Annual (CN) *831*
Snowy Mountains Engineering Corporation. Annual Report (AT) *312, 370*
So and So Magazine (US) *581, 859*
Soaring in the A.C.T. (Australian Capital Territory) (AT ISSN 0310-9399) *10, 822*
Soccer Rules (US ISSN 0163-4763) *826*
Soccer-Speedball-Flag Football Guide *see* N A G W S Guide. Flag Football, Speedball, Speed-a-Way *824*
Soccer Year Book for Northern Ireland (UK ISSN 0081-038X) *826*
Sociaal-Economische Raad. Verslag (NE ISSN 0560-3641) *148, 816*
Sociaal-Geografische Studien (NE ISSN 0081-0398) *53, 425, 800*
Sociaal-Historische Studien (NE ISSN 0081-0401) *441, 800*
Social Affairs Statistics of Taiwan/ Chung-Hua Min Kuo Tai-Wan Sheng She Hui Shih Yeh Tung Chi (CH) *811*
Social and Human Forecasting Documentation (IT) *800*
Social Change (US) *816*
Social Development (CN ISSN 0316-313X) *800*
Social Development Research Institute. Organization and Activities (JA ISSN 0559-698X) *800*
Social, Economic and Political Studies of the Middle East (NE ISSN 0085-6193) *475*
Social Education Yearly (CH) *322*
Social History of Canada (CN ISSN 0085-6207) *472*
Social Impact Assessment Series (US) *816*
Social Indicators Newsletter (US ISSN 0363-3195) *816*
Social Indicators of the Philippines *see* Philippines. National Census and Statistics Office. Social Indicator *729*
Social Insurance Funds in Israel *see* Israel. Central Bureau of Statistics. Kupot Gemel Be-Yisrael *502*
Social Perspectives (KE) *816*
Social Psychiatry (US ISSN 0095-0858) *621*
Social Psychiatry (New York. 1974) *see* Social Psychiatry *621*
Social Science Abstracts *see* University of Tokyo. Institute of Social Science. Annals *802*
Social Science Federation of Canada. Annual Report (CN) *800*
Social Science Journal (KO) *800*
Social Science Reports (US) *800*
Social Science Research Council (Gt. Brit.) Postgraduate Studentships in the Social Sciences *see* S S R C Studentship Handbook *800*
Social Science Research Council of Canada. Report *see* Social Science Federation of Canada. Annual Report *800*
Social Science Research Council Studentship Handbook *see* S S R C Studentship Handbook *800*
Social Science Studies (CN ISSN 0081-0460) *800*
Social Sciences Research Series (II) *800*
Social Scientist (NR ISSN 0081-0487) *800*
Social Security Documentation: African Series (SZ ISSN 0379-704X) *501*
Social Security Documentation: Asian Series (SZ) *501*

Social Security Documentation: European Series (SZ) *501*
Social Security Handbook (US ISSN 0081-0495) *501*, *809*
Social Service Delivery Systems (US) *809*
Social Services in North Dakota (US ISSN 0094-1220) *809*
Social Services in Nova Scotia (CN ISSN 0317-4336) *809*
Social Services Yearbook (UK ISSN 0307-093X) *322*
Social Strategies (SZ) *816*
Social Structure and Social Change (UK) *800*, *816*
Social Studies Materials and Resources Data Book. Annual *see* Data Book of Social Studies Materials and Resources *348*
Social Studies Student Investigates (US) *800*
Social Trends in New Zealand (NZ) *846*
Social Welfare Services in Japan (JA) *809*
Social Work and Social Issues (US ISSN 0081-055X) *809*
Social Work Year Book *see* Encyclopedia of Social Work *805*
Socialismo Oggi (IT) *715*
Socialist Register (UK ISSN 0081-0606) *715*
Socialist Shipping Contacts (GW) *242*, *880*
Socialist Youth Alliance Internal Bulletin *see* S. Y. A. Internal Bulletin *714*
Sociedad Argentina de Biologia. Revista (AG ISSN 0037-8380) *107*
Sociedad Argentina de Escritores Boletin de la S A D E *see* Boletin de la S A D E *560*
Sociedad Argentina de Estudios Geograficos Boletin (AG) *425*
Sociedad Boliviana de Historia Natural. Revista (BO) *107*
Sociedad Botanica de Mexico. Boletin (MX) *118*
Sociedad Cientifica Argentina. Ciclo de Conferencias (AG) *791*
Sociedad Colombiana de Endocrinologia. Revista (CK ISSN 0037-8445) *612*
Sociedad Colombiana de Planificacion. Cuadernos (CK) *225*
Sociedad de Historia Natural de Baleares. Boletin (SP ISSN 0583-7405) *107*, *299*
Sociedad de Ingenieros. Informaciones y Memorias (PE) *370*
Sociedad Espanola de Automoviles de Turismo. Memoria y Balance (SP) *872*, *890*
Sociedad Espanola de Historia de la Medicina. Boletin (SP ISSN 0583-7480) *600*
Sociedad Espanola de Literatura General y Comparada. Anuario (SP) *572*
Sociedad Folklorica de Mexico. Anuario (MX) *403*
Sociedad Geologica del Peru. Boletin (PE ISSN 0079-1091) *299*, *472*
Sociedad Interamericana de Planificacion. Ediciones SIAP (AG) *487*
Sociedad Mexicana de Historia de la Ciencia y de la Tecnologia. Anales (MX) *791*
Sociedad Mexicana de Micologia. Boletin (MX ISSN 0085-6223) *118*
Sociedad Mexicana de Micologia. Boletin Informativo *see* Sociedad Mexicana de Micologia. Boletin *118*
Sociedad Rural Argentina. Memoria (AG ISSN 0081-0630) *46*
Sociedad Uruguaya (UY ISSN 0081-0649) *816*
Sociedad Venezolana de Planificacion. Cuadernos (VE ISSN 0583-7774) *487*
Sociedade Brasileira (BL) *98*
Sociedade Brasileira de Economistas Rurais. Anais da Reuniao (BL) *30*
Sociedade Broteriana. Anuario (PO) *118*
Sociedade Broteriana. Boletim (PO ISSN 0081-0657) *118*

Sociedade Broteriana. Memorias (PO ISSN 0081-0665) *107*
Sociedades por Acoes (BL) *148*, *518*
Societa di Studi Romagnoli. Guide (IT ISSN 0081-0681) *461*
Societa e Dello Stato Veneziano. Istituto di Storia. Bollettino *see* Studi Veneziani *462*
Societa e Diritto di Roma (IT ISSN 0391-3260) *518*
Societa e la Scienza (IT ISSN 0391-609X) *791*
Societa Italiana di Fisica. Bollettino (IT ISSN 0037-8801) *699*
Societa Italiana di Scienze Farmaceutiche Documenti *see* S.I.S.F. Documenti *686*
Societa Storica Valtellinese. Bollettino (IT ISSN 0085-6231) *435*
Societas Uralo-Altaica. Veroeffentlichungen (GW ISSN 0340-6423) *551*
Societatea de Stiinte Istorice si Filologice Din R. P. R. Limba si Literatura. *see* Limba si Literatura *546*
Societatea de Stiinte Istorice si Filologice Din R.P.R. Studii si Articole de Istorie *see* Studii si Articole de Istorie *463*
Societatis Scientiarum Lodziensis. Acta Chimica (PL ISSN 0081-0711) *248*
Societe Archeologique de Tarn et Garonne. Bulletin Archeologique, Historique et Artistique (FR) *65*
Societe Archeologique de Touraine. Bulletin (FR) *65*
Societe Archeologique de Touraine. Memoires (FR) *65*, *461*
Societe Astronomique de Bordeaux. Bulletin (FR ISSN 0081-0738) *83*
Societe Belge d'Ophtalmologie. Bulletin (BE ISSN 0081-0746) *616*
Societe Botanique de Geneve. Travaux *see* Saussurea *118*
Societe Canadienne des Etudes Bibliques. Bulletin *see* Canadian Society of Biblical Studies. Bulletin *764*
Societe Chateaubriand. Bulletin. Nouvelle Series (FR ISSN 0081-0754) *572*
Societe Chimique de France. Annuaire (FR) *248*
Societe d'Amenagement Regional. Rapport Annuel *see* Community Improvement Corporation. Annual Report *184*
Societe d'Archeologie Copte. Bibliotheque de Manuscrits (UA ISSN 0068-5283) *65*
Societe d'Archeologie Copte. Bulletin (UA ISSN 0068-5291) *65*
Societe d'Archeologie Copte. Textes et Documents (UA ISSN 0068-5305) *65*
Societe d'Archeologie, d'Histoire et de Folklore de Nivelles et du Brabant Wallon. Annales (BE) *65*, *461*
Societe d'Archeologie et d'Histoire de la Charente Maritime. Bulletin de Liaison (FR) *65*
Societe d'Emulation de Montbeliard. Memoires (FR) *461*
Societe d'Emulation Historique et Litteraire d'Abbeville. Bulletin (FR ISSN 0081-0819) *461*
Societe d'Ergonomie de Langue Francaise. Actes du Congres (FR ISSN 0081-0835) *701*
Societe d'Etude du Vingtieme Siecle. Bulletin (FR ISSN 0085-624X) *572*
Societe d'Etudes Dantesques. Bulletin (FR) *572*
Societe d'Etudes Linguistiques et Anthropologiques de France. Numero Special (FR) *53*, *551*
Societe d'Etudes Linguistiques et Anthropologiques de France. Bibliotheque de la S E L A F *see* Bibliotheque de la S E L A F *541*
Societe d'Histoire de France. Annuaire (FR ISSN 0081-0940) *461*
Societe d'Histoire et d'Archeologie de Geneve. Bulletin (SZ ISSN 0081-0959) *65*
Societe d'Histoire et d'Archeologie de la Goele. Bulletin d'Information (FR ISSN 0081-0967) *65*, *461*

Societe d'Histoire et d'Archeologie de la Lorraine. Annuaire (FR) *65*, *461*
Societe d'Histoire Moderne. Annuaire (FR ISSN 0081-0975) *435*
Societe d'Ophtalmologie de France. Bulletin (FR ISSN 0081-1270) *616*
Societe de Geographie de Marseille. Bulletin (FR ISSN 0081-0789) *425*
Societe de l'Ecole des Chartes. Memoires et Documents (SZ ISSN 0078-9518) *435*
Societe de l'Industrie Minerale. Annuaire (FR ISSN 0081-0797) *646*
Societe des Alcools du Quebec. Rapport Annuel (CN) *287*
Societe des Amis de Montaigne. Bulletin (FR ISSN 0037-9182) *572*
Societe des Amis des Sciences et des Lettres de Poznan. Bulletin. Serie D: Sciences Biologiques (PL ISSN 0079-4570) *107*
Societe des Antiquaires de l'Ouest. Memoires (FR) *461*
Societe des Antiquaires de Picardie. Memoires (FR) *461*
Societe des Auteurs, Compositeurs, Editeurs pour la Gerance des Droits de Reproduction Mecanique. (Bulletin) (FR ISSN 0081-0843) *518*
Societe des Explorateurs et des Voyageurs Francais. Annuaire General (FR ISSN 0081-086X) *53*, *425*
Societe des Francs-Bibliophiles. Annuaire (FR ISSN 0081-0878) *759*
Societe des Ingenieurs Civils de France. Annuaire (FR ISSN 0081-0886) *377*
Societe des Oceanistes. Publications (FR ISSN 0081-0894) *800*
Societe des Poetes Francais. Annuaire (FR ISSN 0081-0908) *581*
Societe des Professeurs Francais en Amerique. Bulletin Annuel (US ISSN 0081-0916) *322*
Societe des Sciences Medicales du Grand-Duche de Luxembourg. Bulletin (LU ISSN 0037-9247) *600*
Societe des Sciences Physiques et Naturelles de Bordeaux. Memoires (FR) *791*
Societe Entomologique d'Egypte. Bulletin/Entomological Society of Egypt. Bulletin (UA ISSN 0081-0983) *121*
Societe Entomologique d'Egypte. Bulletin. Economic Series (UA ISSN 0081-0991) *121*
Societe Entomologique du Quebec. Memoires (CN ISSN 0071-0784) *121*
Societe Finno-Ougrienne. Journal *see* Suomalais-Ugrilaisen Seura. Aikakauskirja *552*
Societe Francaise de Chirurgie Orthopedique et Traumatologique. Conferences d'Enseignement (FR ISSN 0081-1033) *616*
Societe Francaise de Microbiologie. Annuaire (FR ISSN 0081-1068) *124*
Societe Francaise de Physique. Annuaire (FR ISSN 0081-1076) *699*
Societe Francaise de Recherche Operationelle. Annuaire *see* Association Francaise pour la Cybernetique Economique et Technique. Annuaire *270*
Societe Francaise du Vide. Comptes Rendus des Travaux des Congres et Colloques (FR) *699*
Societe Generale de Banque. Rapport (BE) *176*
Societe Generale de Belgique. Rapport/Report (BE ISSN 0081-1114) *176*
Societe Generale pour Favoriser le Developpement du Commerce et de l'Industrie en France. Bulletin (FR ISSN 0151-8720) *190*
Societe Geographique de Liege. Bulletin (BE ISSN 0583-8622) *425*
Societe Geologique de France. Memoires (FR) *299*

Societe Geologique de Pologne. Annales *see* Polskie Towarzystwo Geologiczne. Rocznik *299*
Societe Guernesiaise. Report and Transactions (UI) *461*
Societe Helvetique des Sciences Naturelles. Annuaire *see* Schweizerische Naturforschende Gesellschaft. Jahrbuch *790*
Societe Historique de Quebec. Textes (CN ISSN 0081-1130) *435*
Societe Historique de Villiers sur Marne et de la Brie Francaise. Revue (FR) *461*
Societe Historique et Archeologique dans le Limbourg. Publications (NE ISSN 0085-6266) *461*
Societe Historique et Archeologique de Pontoise, du Val d'Oise et du Vexin. Memoires (FR) *461*
Societe Internationale Arthurienne. Rapports du Congres *see* International Arthurian Society. Report of Congress *565*
Societe Internationale pour l'Etude de la Philosophie Medievale. Bulletin *see* Bulletin de Philosophie Medievale *687*
Societe J.K. Huysmans. Bulletin (FR) *557*
Societe National du Logement. Rapport Annuel (BE ISSN 0067-5652) *487*
Societe Nationale des Antiquaires de France. Bulletin (FR ISSN 0081-1181) *65*
Societe Nationale des Chemins de Fer Belges. Rapport Annuel (BE ISSN 0081-119X) *874*
Societe Nationale Elf Aquitaine. Rapport Annuel (FR) *681*
Societe Nucleaire Canadienne. Sommaire des Communications *see* Canadian Nuclear Society. Transactions *702*
Societe Odonto-Stomatologique du Nord-Est. Revue Annuelle (FR ISSN 0081-1203) *610*
Societe Philomatique Vosgienne. Bulletin (FR) *461*
Societe pour l'Etude des Langues Africaines. Bulletin *see* Bibliotheque de la S E L A F *541*
Societe pour le Developpement Minier de la Cote d'Ivoire. Rapport Annuel (IV ISSN 0250-3697) *646*
Societe pour Vaincre la Pollution. Bulletin de Liaison *see* Environnement *386*
Societe Royale Belge d'Anthropologie et de Prehistoire. Bulletin (BE) *53*
Societe Royale Belge d'Entomologie. Memoires (BE) *121*
Societe Royale des Sciences de Liege. Memoires in 8 (BE ISSN 0085-6282) *913*
Societe Saint-Jean-Baptiste de Montreal. Information Nationale (CN ISSN 0537-6211) *767*
Societe Saint-Jean-Baptiste de Montreal Bulletin *see* Societe Saint-Jean-Baptiste de Montreal. Information Nationale *767*
Societe Speleologique et Prehistorique de Bordeaux. Memoire (FR) *435*
Societe Suisse des Americanistes. Bulletin/Schweizerische Amerikanisten-Gesellschaft. Bulletin (SZ ISSN 0582-1592) *53*, *65*, *472*
Societe Vaudoise des Sciences Naturelles. Memoires (SZ ISSN 0037-9611) *791*
Societes et Fournisseurs d'Afrique Noire et de Madagascar. Guide Economique Noire (FR ISSN 0081-1289) *198*
Societes Scientifiques et Techniques du Canada *see* Scientific and Technical Societies of Canada *791*
Society for African Church History. Bulletin (UK ISSN 0081-1297) *767*
Society for American Archaeology. Memoirs (US ISSN 0081-1300) *65*
Society for Analytical Chemistry. Annual Reports on Analytical Atomic Spectroscopy (UK ISSN 0306-1353) *249*

Society for Applied Anthropology. Monographs (US ISSN 0583-8916) *53*
Society for Asian Music. Publication Series. Series A: Bibliographic and Research Aids *see* Asian Music Publications. Series A: Bibliographic and Research Aids *657*
Society for Asian Music. Publication Series. Series B: Translations *see* Asian Music Publications. Series B. Translations *657*
Society for Asian Music. Publication Series. Series C: Reprints *see* Asian Music Publications. Series C: Reprints *657*
Society for Asian Music. Publications Series. Series D: Monographs *see* Asian Music Publications. Series D: Monographs *657*
Society for Developmental Biology. Symposium (US ISSN 0583-9009) *107*
Society for Endocrinology (Great Britain) Memoirs (UK ISSN 0081-136X) *612*
Society for Experimental Biology. Seminar Series (UK) *107*
Society for Experimental Biology. Symposia (US ISSN 0081-1386) *107*
Society for General Microbiology. Symposium (UK ISSN 0081-1394) *124*
Society for General Systems Research. Annual Meeting Proceedings (US) *791*
Society for Historical Archaeology. Special Publication Series (US) *65*
Society for Industrial and Applied Mathematics Proceedings *see* S I A M - A M S Proceedings *589*
Society for Industrial Microbiology. Proceedings of the Annual Meeting *see* Developments in Industrial Microbiology *123*
Society for Information Display International Symposium. Digest of Technical Papers *see* S I D International Symposium. Digest of Technical Papers *370*
Society for International Development. World Conference Proceedings (IT ISSN 0081-1416) *201, 723*
Society for Italian Historical Studies. Newsletter (US ISSN 0081-1424) *461*
Society for Latin America Studies. Bulletin (UK ISSN 0308-1540) *472*
Society for Lincolnshire History and Archaeology. Annual Report and Statement of Accounts (UK ISSN 0306-4859) *65, 461*
Society for Louisiana Irises. Special Publications (US) *416*
Society for Natural Sciences, Basel. Proceedings *see* Naturforschende Gesellschaft in Basel. Verhandlungen *787*
Society for Neuroscience. Annual Meeting. Conference Report (US ISSN 0091-6528) *621*
Society for New Testament Studies. Monograph Series (UK ISSN 0081-1432) *767*
Society for Old Testament Study. Book List (UK ISSN 0081-1440) *769*
Society for Pediatric Research. Program and Abstracts *see* American Pediatric Society and Society for Pediatric Research. Program and Abstracts *617*
Society for Psychical Research. Proceedings (UK ISSN 0081-1475) *676*
Society for Renaissance Studies. Occasional Papers (UK) *78, 572, 691*
Society for Research in Child Development. Monographs (US ISSN 0037-976X) *257*
Society for Slovene Studies. Documentation Series (US) *461, 551*
Society for the Advancement of Food Service Research. Proceedings (US ISSN 0081-1483) *406*

Society for the Advancement of Material and Process Engineering National S A M P E Technical Conference Series. N S T C Preprint Series *see* National SA M P E Technical Conference Series. N S T C Preprint Series *380*
Society for the History of Discoveries. Annual Report (US) *791*
Society for the History of Technology. Monograph Series (US ISSN 0081-1491) *853*
Society for the Preservation of Long Island Antiquities. Newsletter (US ISSN 0583-9181) *78*
Society for the Promotion of Nature Conservation. Technical Publications (UK) *278*
Society for the Promotion of Nature Reserves. Technical Publications *see* Society for the Promotion of Nature Conservation. Technical Publications *278*
Society for the Protection of Unborn Children. Bulletin (UK) *615*
Society for the Study of Human Biology. Symposia (UK ISSN 0081-153X) *126*
Society for the Study of Inborn Errors of Metabolism. Symposia (US) *126*
Society for the Study of Pre-Han China. Newsletter *see* Early China *443*
Society for the Study of Southern Literature. Newsletter (US) *572*
Society of Actuaries. Transactions (US ISSN 0037-9794) *501*
Society of Aerospace Material and Process Engineers. National S A M P E Technical Conference. N S T C Preprint Series *see* National SA M P E Technical Conference Series. N S T C Preprint Series *380*
Society of Allied Weight Engineers Journal *see* S.A.W.E. Journal *10*
Society of Antiquaries of Scotland. Proceedings (UK ISSN 0081-1564) *461*
Society of Archer-Antiquaries. Journal (UK ISSN 0560-6152) *822*
Society of Automotive Engineers Handbook *see* S A E Handbook *872*
Society of Automotive Engineers of Japan. Transactions (JA) *872*
Society of Automotive Engineers Technical Papers *see* S A E Technical Papers *872*
Society of Automotive Engineers Transactions *see* S A E Transactions *872*
Society of Biblical Literature. Texts and Translations (US) *767*
Society of Biological Chemists. Proceedings (II ISSN 0300-0486) *112*
Society of Catholic College Teachers of Sacred Doctrine. Proceedings *see* College Theology Society. Proceedings *774*
Society of Colonial Wars. Bulletin (US) *472, 640*
Society of Cypriot Studies. Bulletin/Kypriakai Spoudai (CY ISSN 0081-1580) *461*
Society of Die Casting Engineers, Inc. International Die Casting Congress. Transactions *see* S D C E International Die Casting Congress. Transactions *583*
Society of Exploration Geophysicists. Special Publications (Symposia) Series (US) *306*
Society of Federal Linguists. Newsletter(US) *551*
Society of Flight Test Engineers. Annual Symposium Proceedings (US) *10*
Society of General Physiologists. Distinguished Lecture Series (US) *126*
Society of General Physiologists Series (US ISSN 0094-7733) *126*
Society of Glass Decorators. Papers Presented at Annual Seminar (US ISSN 0081-1602) *244*
Society of Manufacturing Engineers. Collected Papers and Technical Papers Presented at Western Metal and Tool Exposition and Conference (US ISSN 0081-1645) *380*

Society of Manufacturing Engineers. S M E Transactions *see* Manufacturing Engineering Transactions *368*
Society of Medalists. News Bulletin (US ISSN 0037-9948) *478*
Society of Naval Architects and Marine Engineers. Transactions (US ISSN 0081-1661) *881*
Society of Nippon Dental College. Annual Publications (JA) *610*
Society of Petroleum Engineers of American Institute of Mining, Metallurgical and Petroleum Engineers. Petroleum Transactions Reprint Series (US ISSN 0081-1688) *681*
Society of Petroleum Engineers of American Institute of Mining, Metallurgical and Petroleum Engineers. Transactions (US ISSN 0081-1696) *681*
Society of Photo-Optical Instrumentation Engineers. Proceedings (US ISSN 0361-0748) *497, 706*
Society of Plant Protection of North Japan. Annual Report/Kitanihon Byogaichu Kenkyukai Kaiho (JA ISSN 0081-170X) *39*
Society of Plastics Engineers Monographs (US) *707*
Society of Professional Well Logging Analysts. S P W L A Annual Logging Symposium Transactions (US ISSN 0081-1718) *681*
Society of Professors of Education. Occasional Papers (US) *340*
Society of Professors of Education Monographs *see* S P E Monographs *322*
Society of Public Teachers of Law. Journal (UK ISSN 0038-0016) *518*
Society of Radiographers. Newsletter (JM) *913*
Society of the Plastics Industry. Cellular Plastics Division. Conference Proceedings (US) *707*
Society of the Plastics Industry. Urethane Division. Conference Proceedings (US) *707*
Society of Vector Ecologists. Bulletin (US ISSN 0146-6429) *895*
Society of Wireless Pioneers. Yearbook (US ISSN 0098-5910) *269*
Socio-Economic Progress in Latin America; Annual Report *see* Economic and Social Progress in Latin America; Annual Report *185*
Socio-Economic Review of Punjab (II) *190, 816*
Sociobiology (US ISSN 0361-6525) *107*
Socioeconomic Issues of Health *see* Reference Data on Socioeconomic Issues of Health *599*
Sociologia (IT) *816*
Sociologia II (BL ISSN 0081-1742) *816*
Sociological Journal (UG) *816*
Sociological Methodology (US ISSN 0081-1750) *816*
Sociological Microjournal (DK) *816*
Sociological Observations (US ISSN 0149-4872) *53, 816*
Sociological Review. Monograph (UK ISSN 0081-1769) *816*
Sociologie Permanente (FR) *816*
Sociologische Verkenningen (BE) *816*
Sociologist (NR ISSN 0081-1807) *816*
Sociology of the Sciences (NE) *791, 816*
Sociomedical Sciences Series (US) *600, 800*
Socker Handlingar (SW ISSN 0038-0466) *913*
Soelleroedbogen (DK ISSN 0085-6339) *461*
Soermlandsbygden (SW) *461*
Soester Beitraege (GW) *461*
Soester Zeitschrift (GW) *461*
Sofiiski Universitet. Biologicheski Fakultet. Godishnik (BU ISSN 0081-1823) *107*
Sofiiski Universitet. Fakultet po Matematika i Mekhanika. Godishnik/L'Universite de Sofia. Faculte des Mathematiques et de Mecanique. Annuaire (BU ISSN 0081-1858) *589*

Sofiiski Universitet. Fakultet po Slavianska Filologiia. Godishnik (BU ISSN 0081-1831) *551*
Sofiiski Universitet. Fakultet po Zapadni Filologii. Godishnik/L'Universite de Sofia. Faculte des Lettres. Annuaire (BU ISSN 0584-0252) *551*
Sofiiski Universitet. Filosofski Fakultet. Godishnik/L'Universite de Sofia. Faculte de Philosophie. Annuaire (BU ISSN 0081-184X) *461*
Sofiiski Universitet. Filosofski-Istoricheski Fakultet. Godishnik *see* Sofiiski Universitet. Filosofski Fakultet. Godishnik *461*
Sofiiski Universitet. Geologo-Geografski Fakultet. Geografiia. Godishnik. (BU) *425*
Sofiiski Universitet. Geologo-Geografski Fakultet. Geologiia. Godishnik. (BU) *299*
Sofiiski Universitet. Iuridicheski Fakultet. Godishnik (BU ISSN 0081-1866) *518*
Soft Stone (US) *78, 573*
Sogo Keizai Nenkan *see* Food Economics Yearbook *237*
Sogo-Shosha *see* Japanese General Trading Companies Yearbook *182*
Soil Engineering Series *see* Series in Geotechnical Engineering *39*
Soil Science Library *see* Books in Soils and the Environment *33*
Soil Science Society of America Special Publication Series *see* S S S A Special Publication Series *39*
Soil Science Society of Ceylon. Journal (CE) *39*
Soils and Land Use Series (AT ISSN 0081-1912) *39*
Soils News (AT) *39*
Solar Energy Handbook (US) *913*
Solar Energy Progress in Australia and New Zealand (AT ISSN 0584-0651) *913*
Solar Energy Research and Development Reports (US) *364*
Solar Terrestrial Environmental Research in Japan (JA) *306, 699*
Soldier Shop Annual (US) *476, 640*
Soldier Shop Quarterly *see* Soldier Shop Annual *476*
Solent Yearbook (UK) *827*
Solicitor's Review *see* U.S. Solicitor for the Department of the Interior. Solicitor's Review *915*
Solid State Physics; Advances in Research and Applications (US ISSN 0081-1947) *699*
Solid State Physics; Advances in Research and Applications. Supplement (US ISSN 0081-1955) *699*
Solid State Physics Literature Guides (US ISSN 0081-1963) *700*
Solid State Surface Science (US ISSN 0081-1971) *699*
Solid Waste Management: Abstracts from the Literature (US ISSN 0092-0541) *754*
Solid Waste Management; Available Information Materials (US) *748, 756*
Solinet. Annual Report (Southeastern Library Network) (US) *535*
Solnechnaya Radiatsiya i Radiatsionnyi Balans Mirovaya Set' (UR) *306*
Solomon Goldman Lectures (US) *770*
Solomon Islands Museum Association. Journal (BP) *53, 655*
Solomon Islands Research Register (BP) *447*
Solubility Data Series (US ISSN 0191-5622) *112*
Solvent Extraction Reviews *see* Ion Exchange and Solvent Extraction *255*
Som (BL) *818*
Somali National Bank. Annual Report and Statement of Accounts *see* Central Bank of Somali. Annual Report and Statement of Accounts *171*
Somalia in Figures (SO) *846*
Some Current Research in East Africa (KE) *803*
Some Friends (US) *573*

Some Hard-to-Locate Sources of Information on Current Affairs see Censored 538
Some Statistics on Baccalaureate and Higher Degree Programs in Nursing see N L N Nursing Data Book: Statistical Information on Nursing Education & Newly Licensed Nurses 614
Somerset Archaeology and Natural History (UK ISSN 0081-2056) 65, 791
Somerset Birds (UK ISSN 0081-2048) 125
Somersetshire Archaeological and Natural History Society. Proceedings see Somerset Archaeology and Natural History 65
Something on Paper (AT ISSN 0310-4389) 675
Sonderbaende zur Theologischen Zeitschrift (SZ ISSN 0067-4907) 767
Sonderinformation Philosophie see Thematische Information Philosophie 691
Sonderschuldienst (GW) 323
Songsmith's Journal (US ISSN 0145-210X) 663
Songwriter's Annual Directory (US ISSN 0560-8325) 663
Songwriter's Market (US ISSN 0161-5971) 663
Sonic Exchange (US) 600
Sons and Daughters of the Soddies. Reports (US) 418, 472
Soochow Journal of Humanities (CH) 493
Soochow Journal of Mathematical & Natural Sciences (CH) 589, 791
Soochow Journal of Social & Political Sciences (CH) 715, 800
Soochow Law Review (CH) 518
Soochow University Journal of Chinese Art History (CH) 78
Sophisticated Investor see S I E Sophisticated Investor 204
Sorgo - Uma Alternativa Economica (BL) 30, 43
Sort des Medicaments dans l'Organisme see Fate of Drugs in the Organism; a Bibliographic Survey 686
Sotsiologiya Kul'tury (UR) 816
Soul in Review (US ISSN 0098-0730) 653
Sound Approach to the Railroad Market (US ISSN 0362-8213) 874
Soundings (Santa Barbara) (US ISSN 0038-1853) 535, 573
Soundings: A Music Journal (UK ISSN 0081-2080) 663
Source (Ann Arbor) (US ISSN 0085-6347) 535
Source (Washington) see Identified Sources of Supply 637
Source Books on Curricula and Methods see Unesco Source Books on Curricula and Methods 351
Source Directory of Predicasts, Inc. see Predicasts. Source Directory 163
Source Guide for Music/Bronnegids vir Musiek (SA) 663
Source Material of Finnish History see Suomen Historian Laehteitae 463
Source Materials on the History of Science in India (II) 791
Source of Supply Directory see Sources of Supply/Buyers Guide 675
Source References for Facts and Figures on Government Finance (US ISSN 0494-8203) 232
Sourcebook of Criminal Justice Statistics (US) 284
Sourcebook of Equal Educational Opportunity (US ISSN 0149-8924) 323
Sourcebook on Aging (US) 809
Sourcebook on Food and Nutrition (US) 666
Sources de Droit Serbe see Izvori Srpskog Prava 513
Sources from the Ancient Near East (US) 475
Sources in Ancient History (AT ISSN 0081-2110) 435
Sources in the History of Mathematics and Physical Sciences (US) 589, 699

Sources in Western Political Thought (US ISSN 0560-8996) 715
Sources of Contemporary Jewish Thought/Mekevot (IS ISSN 0082-4585) 557, 770
Sources of Serials (US ISSN 0000-0523) 94
Sources of Supply/Buyers Guide (US ISSN 0081-2129) 675
South Africa. Bureau of Standards. S A B S Yearbook (SA ISSN 0081-2137) 637
South Africa. Dairy Control Board. Annual Report (SA) 41
South Africa. Department of Agricultural Economics and Marketing. Division of Agricultural Marketing Research. Abstract of Agricultural Statistics (SA) 25, 846
South Africa. Department of Agricultural Technical Services. Agricultural Bulletins (SA ISSN 0002-1393) 20
South Africa. Department of Agricultural Technical Services. Agricultural Research (SA ISSN 0081-2145) 20
South Africa. Department of Agricultural Technical Services. Entomology Memoirs (SA ISSN 0013-8940) 121
South Africa. Department of Agricultural Technical Services. List of Research Workers and Lecturing Staff in the Agricultural Field see South Africa. Department of Agricultural Technical Services. Official List of Professional Research Workers, Lecturing Staff and Extension Workers in the Agricultural Field 20
South Africa. Department of Agricultural Technical Services. Official List of Professional Research Workers, Lecturing Staff and Extension Workers in the Agricultural Field (SA) 20
South Africa. Department of Agricultural Technical Services. Report of the Secretary for Agricultural Technical Services (SA ISSN 0081-2153) 20
South Africa. Department of Agricultural Technical Services. Science Bulletins (SA ISSN 0038-1934) 20
South Africa. Department of Agricultural Technical Services. Special Publication (SA ISSN 0081-2161) 20
South Africa. Department of Agricultural Technical Services. Technical Communication (SA ISSN 0081-217X) 20
South Africa. Department of Bantu Education. Annual Report (SA ISSN 0081-2188) 323
South Africa. Department of Coloured Relations and Rehoboth Affairs. Annual Report (SA ISSN 0584-2166) 719
South Africa. Department of Customs and Excise. Foreign Trade Statistics (SA ISSN 0081-2196) 164
South Africa. Department of Defense. White Paper on Defense and Armament Production (SA) 640
South Africa. Department of Higher Education. Annual Report (SA ISSN 0081-220X) 340
South Africa. Department of Mines. Annual Report (SA) 299, 646
South Africa. Department of National Education. Jaarverslag/Annual Report (SA) 323
South Africa. Department of Statistics. Annual Report of the Statistics Advisory Council and of the Secretary of Statistics (SA) 846
South Africa. Department of Statistics. Building Plans Passed and Buildings Completed (SA) 140, 846
South Africa. Department of Statistics. Census of Electricity, Gas and Steam(SA ISSN 0301-8105) 846
South Africa. Department of Statistics. Census of Manufacturing (SA) 846, 854

South Africa. Department of Statistics. Education: Coloureds and Asians (SA) 328, 846
South Africa. Department of Statistics. Education: Whites (SA) 328, 846
South Africa. Department of Statistics. Labour Statistics: Wage Rates, Earnings and Average Hours Worked in the Printing and Newspaper Industry, Engineering Industry, Building Industry and Commerce (SA) 164, 846
South Africa. Department of Statistics. Local Government Statistics (SA) 748, 846
South Africa. Department of Statistics. Mining: Financial Statistics (SA) 648, 846
South Africa. Department of Statistics. Report on Agricultural and Pastoral Production (SA) 25, 846
South Africa. Department of Statistics. Report on Births see South Africa. Department of Statistics. Report on Births: White, Coloured and Asians 732
South Africa. Department of Statistics. Report on Births: White, Coloured and Asians (SA) 732, 846
South Africa. Department of Statistics. Report on Marriages and Divorces: South Africa (SA) 732, 846
South Africa. Department of Statistics. Report on Prices (SA) 164, 846
South Africa. Department of Statistics. Road Traffic Accidents (SA ISSN 0584-195X) 846, 866
South Africa. Department of Statistics. Statistical Year Book see South African Statistics 846
South Africa. Department of Statistics. Statistics of Administration Boards (SA) 748, 846
South Africa. Department of Statistics. Statistics of Bantu Affairs Administration Boards see South Africa. Department of Statistics. Statistics of Administration Boards 748
South Africa. Department of Statistics. Statistics of Houses and Domestic Servants and of Flats (SA) 489, 846
South Africa. Department of Statistics. Statistics of Motor and Other Vehicles (SA) 846, 866
South Africa. Department of Statistics. Statistics of New Vehicles Licensed see South Africa. Department of Statistics. Statistics of New Vehicles Registered 866
South Africa. Department of Statistics. Statistics of New Vehicles Registered(SA) 846, 866
South Africa. Department of Statistics. Survey of the Accounts of Companies in Secondary and Tertiary Industries (SA) 164, 846
South Africa. Department of Statistics. Survey of the Accounts of Mining Companies (SA) 648, 846
South Africa. Department of Statistics. Tourism and Migration (SA) 732, 846, 893
South Africa. Department of Statistics. Transfers of Rural Immovable Property (SA) 762, 846
South Africa. Division of Sea Fisheries. Fisheries Bulletin see South Africa. Sea Fisheries Branch. Fisheries Bulletin 400
South Africa. Division of Surveys. Report of the Director-General of Surveys (SA) 30
South Africa. Geological Survey. Annals (SA ISSN 0584-2352) 299
South Africa. Geological Survey. Bulletin (SA) 299
South Africa. Geological Survey. Handbook (SA ISSN 0560-9208) 299
South Africa. Geological Survey. Memoirs (SA) 299
South Africa. Geological Survey. Report of the Director of the Geological Survey see South Africa. Department of Mines. Annual Report 646
South Africa. Geological Survey. Seismologic Series (SA) 300

South Africa. Geological Survey. Special Publications (SA) 300
South Africa. Kantoor van die Direkteur van Argiewe. Jaarverslag van die Direkeur van Argiewe see South Africa. Office of the Director of Archives. Annual Report of the Director of Archives 438
South Africa. Law Commission. Jaarverslag van die Suid-Afrikaanse Regskommissie/Annual Report of the South African Law Commission (SA) 518
South Africa. Maize Board. Report on Grain Sorghum and Buckwheat for the Financial Year (SA ISSN 0300-5747) 43
South Africa. Maize Board. Report on Maize for the Financial Year (SA) 43
South Africa. Maize Board. Review of the Maize Position see South Africa. Maize Board. Report on Maize for the Financial Year 43
South Africa. Milk Board. Annual Report see South Africa. Dairy Control Board. Annual Report 41
South Africa. Office of the Director of Archives. Annual Report of the Director of Archives/South Africa. Kantoor van die Direkteur van Argiewe. Jaarverslag van die Direkeur van Argiewe (SA) 438
South Africa. Official Yearbook of the Republic of South Africa (SA ISSN 0302-0681) 438, 846
South Africa. Prisons Department. Annual Statistics by the Commissioner of Prisons/Jaarlikse Statistieke Deur die Kommissaris van Gevangenisse (SA) 284
South Africa. Prisons Department. Report of the Commissioner of Prisons/Verslag van die Kommissaris van Gevangenisse (SA ISSN 0300-1555) 284
South Africa. Sea Fisheries Branch. Annual Report (SA) 400
South Africa. Sea Fisheries Branch. Fisheries Bulletin (SA) 400
South Africa. Sea Fisheries Branch. Investigational Report see South Africa. Sea Fisheries Institute. Investigational Report 400
South Africa. Sea Fisheries Institute. Investigational Report (SA) 400
South Africa. State Library Council. Report/Verslag (SA) 535
South Africa. Tobacco Board. Annual Report/Jaarverslag (SA) 861
South Africa. Tobacco Industry Control Board. Report see South Africa. Tobacco Board. Annual Report/Jaarverslag 861
South Africa. Unemployment Insurance Fund. Report/South Africa. Werkloosheidversekeringsfonds. Verslag (SA) 210, 501
South Africa. Water Research Commission. Annual Report (SA) 898
South Africa. Weather Bureau. Annual Radiation Bulletin/Jaarlikse Stralingsbulletin (SA) 635
South Africa. Weather Bureau. Radiosonde Rawin Data (SA ISSN 0081-2315) 635
South Africa. Weather Bureau. Report on Meteorological Data of the Year/Verslag Oor Weerkundige Data van die Jaar (SA ISSN 0081-2323) 635
South Africa. Weather Bureau. Technical Paper/Tegniese Verhandelinge (SA) 635
South Africa. Weather Bureau. W.B. Series (SA ISSN 0081-2331) 635
South Africa. Werkloosheidversekeringsfonds. Verslag see South Africa. Unemployment Insurance Fund. Report 501
South Africa. Wheat Board. Annual Report (SA) 43
South Africa: a Guide to Foreign Investors (SA) 204
South Africa, National Parks Board (SA) 278
South African Archives Journal see Suid-Afrikaanse Argiefblad 536

South African Association for Marine Biological Research. Bulletin (SA ISSN 0081-234X) *107*
South African Association of Consulting Engineers. Directory of Members' Firms/Gids van Lede Se Firmas *see* South African Association of Consulting Engineers. Directory of Registered Firms *370*
South African Association of Consulting Engineers. Directory of Registered Firms/Suid-Africaanse Vereniging van Raadgewende Ingenieurs. Gids van Geregistreede Firmas (SA) *370*
South African Biographical and Historical Studies (SA ISSN 0085-6363) *98, 441*
South African Careers Guide (SA) *668*
South African Fishing Industry Handbook and Buyer's Guide (SA ISSN 0080-5076) *400*
South African Foreign Trade Organization Annual Report *see* S A F T O Annual Report *197*
South African Historical Journal (SA) *441*
South African Institute of International Affairs. Annual Report (SA) *723*
South African Institute of International Affairs. Bibliographical Series/Suid-Afrikaanse Instituut van Internasionale Aangeleenthede. Bibliografiese Reeks (SA) *94, 718*
South African Institute of International Affairs. Occasional Papers (SA) *723*
South African Institute of Mining and Metallurgy. Monograph Series (SA) *630, 646*
South African Institute of Race Relations. (Publication) RR (SA) *816*
South African Jewry and Who's Who (SA) *98, 393*
South African Journal of Antarctic Research (SA ISSN 0081-2455) *791, 853*
South African Journal of Communication Disorders/Suid-Afrikaanse Tydskrif vir Kommunikasieafwykings (SA) *617*
South African Journal of Photogrammetry (SA ISSN 0085-6398) *426*
South African Labour Bulletin (SA) *210*
South African Library Association. Annual Report/Suid-Afrikaanse Biblioteekvereniging. Jaarverslag (SA) *535*
South African Medical and Dental Council. Register of Supplementary Health Service Professions (SA) *600, 809*
South African Medical Research Council. Annual Report/Suid-Afrikaanse Mediese Navorsingsraad. Jaarverslag (SA ISSN 0081-248X) *600*
South African Metal Industries Directory & Handbook (SA) *630*
South African Mining and Engineering Yearbook (SA ISSN 0081-2498) *370, 647*
South African National Bibiography *see* S A N B *94*
South African National Council for the Deaf. Annual Diary (SA) *286*
South African National Council of the Blind. Biennial Report (SA) *133*
South African National Tuberculosis Association Annual Report *see* S A N T A Annual Report *623*
South African Pollen Grains and Spores(SA ISSN 0081-251X) *118*
South African Reserve Bank. Annual Economic Report/Suid-Afrikoanse Reserwebank. Jaarlikse Ekonomiese Verslag (SA ISSN 0081-2528) *190*
South African Reserve Bank. Report of the Ordinary General Meeting (SA) *176*
South African Speech and Hearing Association. Journal *see* South African Journal of Communication Disorders *617*
South African Statistics (SA ISSN 0081-2544) *846*
South African Sugar Year Book (SA) *39, 406*

South African Wool and Textile Research Institute. Annual Report (SA ISSN 0560-9941) *856*
South African Wool and Textile Research Institute Technical Report *see* S A W T R I Technical Report *856*
South African Yearbook of International Law/Suid-Afrikaanse Jaarboek vir Volkereg (SA) *524*
South American Handbook (US ISSN 0081-2579) *890*
South American Ports Handbook (AG) *881*
South and East Asia Report (US) *190, 715*
South Asia Church Aid Association. Annual (UK) *767*
South Asia Church Aid Newsletter *see* South Asia Church Aid Association. Annual *767*
South Asia; Journal of South Asian Studies (AT ISSN 0085-6401) *445*
South Asian Studies (GW ISSN 0584-3170) *445, 671*
South Atlantic Urban Studies (US) *487*
South Australia. Department of Agriculture and Fisheries. Focus on Extension *see* South Australia. Department of Agriculture. Focus on Extension *20*
South Australia. Department of Agriculture. Focus on Extension (AT) *20*
South Australia. Department of Labour and Industry. Guide to Legislation (AT ISSN 0311-0702) *210*
South Australia. Department of Woods and Forests. Bulletin (AT) *410*
South Australia. Geological Survey. Bulletin (AT ISSN 0016-7673) *300*
South Australia. Geological Survey. Report of Investigations (AT ISSN 0016-7681) *300*
South Australia. Libraries Board. Annual Report (AT ISSN 0081-2633) *535*
South Australia. Libraries Board. Books for Young People (AT ISSN 0081-2641) *257*
South Australia. State Library. Reference Services Branch. Reference Services Bibliographies (AT ISSN 0311-3078) *94*
South Australian Baker and Pastrycook (AT) *407*
South Australian Museum, Adelaide. Records (AT ISSN 0081-2676) *130*
South Australian Racehorse (AT) *828*
South Australian Yearbook (AT ISSN 0085-6428) *846*
South Carolina. Department of Archives and History. Annual Report(US) *472*
South Carolina. Department of Labor. Annual Report (US) *210*
South Carolina Arts Commission. Annual Report (US ISSN 0081-2684) *78*
South Carolina Education Association Emphasis *see* S C E A Emphasis *322*
South Carolina Education News Emphasis *see* S C E A Emphasis *322*
South Carolina Historical Association. Proceedings (US ISSN 0361-6207) *472*
South Carolina Metalworking Directory(US ISSN 0363-5090) *630*
South Carolina School Directory (US ISSN 0363-9495) *332*
South Carolina State Industrial Directory (US ISSN 0162-0878) *242*
South Carolina State Library. Annual Report (US) *535*
South Carolina State Plan for Construction and Modernization of Hospital and Medical Facilities *see* South Carolina State Plan for Franchising, Construction and Modernization of Hospital and Related Medical Facilities *481*
South Carolina State Plan for Franchising, Construction and Modernization of Hospital and Related Medical Facilities (US ISSN 0081-2692) *481, 809*

South Carolina Statistical Abstract (US) *846*
South Carolina Vital and Morbidity Statistics (US ISSN 0094-6338) *729*
South Carolina's Manpower in Industry(US ISSN 0095-4799) *210*
South Central Campbook (US) *831, 890*
South Central Camping *see* South Central Campbook *890*
South Central Ontario Construction Industry Directory. Purchasing Guide(CN ISSN 0704-6790) *138, 370*
South Central Research Library Council. Library Directory *see* Directory of Libraries and Library Resources in the South Central Research Library Council Region *529*
South Dakota. Department of History. Historical Collections *see* South Dakota State Historical Society. Collections *472*
South Dakota. Department of Labor. Annual Planning Report South Dakota (US) *210*
South Dakota. Department of Labor. Office of Administrative Services. Annual Report Vocational Education Report (US) *210*
South Dakota. Department of Labor. Research and Statistics. Annual Report on State and Area Occupational Requirements for Vocational Education (US ISSN 0094-2200) *164*
South Dakota. Department of Revenue. Annual Report *see* South Dakota. Department of Revenue. Annual Statistical Report *164*
South Dakota. Department of Revenue. Annual Statistical Report (US ISSN 0085-6460) *164*
South Dakota. Department of Social Services. Annual Medical Report (US ISSN 0148-8325) *602, 811, 846*
South Dakota. Geological Survey. Biennial Reports of the State Geologist (US) *300*
South Dakota. State Department of Public Welfare. Research and Statistics Annual Report (US ISSN 0099-2305) *811, 846*
South Dakota Academy of Science. Proceedings (US) *791*
South Dakota Geological Survey. Bulletin (US ISSN 0085-6479) *300*
South Dakota Geological Survey. Circular (US ISSN 0085-6487) *300*
South Dakota Geological Survey. Reports of Investigation (US ISSN 0085-6495) *300*
South Dakota Highway Safety Work Program (US ISSN 0361-3461) *876*
South Dakota Indian Recipients of Social Welfare (US ISSN 0094-372X) *393, 809*
South Dakota State Historical Society. Collections (US ISSN 0081-2773) *472*
South Dakota State Industrial Directory(US) *242*
South Dakota Vital Statistics Annual Report (US ISSN 0095-4802) *846*
South Florida Ports Handbook (US ISSN 0160-2233) *881*
South Indian Art and Archaeological Series (II) *65, 70, 78*
South of Tuk *see* Sequel *480*
South Pacific Commission. Annual Report (NL) *723*
South Pacific Commission. Handbook (NL ISSN 0081-2811) *715*
South Pacific Commission. Information Circular (NL ISSN 0081-282X) *715*
South Pacific Commission. Information Document (NL ISSN 0081-2838) *715*
South Pacific Commission. Occasional Paper (NL) *715*
South Pacific Commission. Report of S P C Technical Meetings (NL ISSN 0081-2846) *715*
South Pacific Commission. South Pacific Report *see* South Pacific Commission. Annual Report *723*

South Pacific Commission. Statistical Bulletin (NL) *846*
South Pacific Commission. Technical Paper (NL ISSN 0081-2862) *715*
South Seas Society. Journal (SI ISSN 0081-2889) *445*
South Seas Society. Monograph (SI ISSN 0081-2897) *445*
South Shore (US) *78*
South Staffordshire Archaeological and Historical Society. Transactions (UK ISSN 0457-7817) *65, 435*
South Wales Institute of Engineers. Proceedings (UK ISSN 0038-3570) *370*
South Wood County Historical Corporation. Newsletter (US) *472*
Southampton Chamber of Commerce Regional Directory (UK) *180*
Southeast Asia Development Corporation Berhad. Reports and Accounts (MY) *201*
South East Asia Library Group Newsletter (UK ISSN 0308-4035) *535, 671*
Southeast Asian Affairs (SI) *445*
Southeast Asian Archives (MY ISSN 0085-6509) *445*
Southeast Asian Fisheries Development Center. Report of the Meeting (PH) *400*
Southeast Asian Fisheries Development Center Marine Fisheries Research Department. Annual Report (SI) *400*
Southeast Asian Institutions of Higher Learning *see* Association of Southeast Asian Institutions of Higher Learning. Handbook: Southeast Asian Institutions of Higher Learning *334*
South-East Asian Journal of Social Sciences (SI) *816*
South-East Asian Journal of Sociology *see* South-East Asian Journal of Social Sciences *816*
Southeast Asian-Ministers of Education Organisation. Regional Centre for Education in Science and Mathematics. Governing Board Meeting. Final Report (MY ISSN 0126-8155) *350*
Southeast Asian Perspective Series (SI) *445*
Southeast Asian Research Materials Group. Newsletter (AT ISSN 0311-290X) *493*
Southeast Louisiana Historical Association. Papers (US ISSN 0098-9193) *472*
Southeast Michigan Council of Governments. Annual Report (US ISSN 0362-3475) *746*
Southeast Michigan Council of Governments. Planning Division. Planning Data. Series C: Population and Occupied Dwelling Units in the Detroit Region. Report *see* Population and Occupied Dwelling Units in Southeast Michigan *486*
Southeast Regional Library (Sask.) Library Directory (CN ISSN 0707-6894) *535*
Southeastcon. Record *see* I E E E Region 3 Conference. Record *354*
Southeastern Association of Fish and Wildlife Agencies. Proceedings (US) *831*
Southeastern Association of Game and Fish Commissioners. Proceedings of the Annual Conference *see* Southeastern Association of Fish and Wildlife Agencies. Proceedings *831*

Southeastern Campbook (US) *831, 890*

Southeastern Camping *see* Southeastern Campbook *890*

Southeastern Conference on Combinatorics, Graph Theory and Computing Proceedings *see* Congressus Numerantium *585*

Southeastern Conference on Latin American Studies Annals *see* S E C O L A S Annals *471*

Southeastern Historical Statistics (US) *846*

Southeastern Library Network Solinet. Annual Report *see* Solinet. Annual Report 535

South-Eastern State. Ministry of Economic Development and Reconstruction. State Development Plan *see* Cross River State. Ministry of Economic Development and Reconstruction. State Development Plan 228

Southeastern Symposium on System Theory. Proceedings (US ISSN 0094-2898) 273

Southern Africa and the Indian Ocean Islands Travel Trade Directory (SA) 890

Southern African and Indian Ocean Islands Travel Industry's Yearbook, Directory and Who's Who (SA) 98, 891

Southern Africa's Travel Industry *see* Southern African and Indian Ocean Islands Travel Industry's Yearbook, Directory and Who's Who 891

Southern Angler's and Hunter's Guide (US ISSN 0081-2986) 831

Southern Anthropological Society. Proceedings (US ISSN 0081-2994) 53

Southern Asia Social Science Bibliography *see* Asian Social Science Bibliography with Annotations and Abstracts 802

Southern Baptist Convention. Annual (US ISSN 0081-3001) 772

Southern Baptist Convention. Historical Commission. Microfilm Catalogue (US ISSN 0081-301X) 772

Southern Baptist Periodical Index (US ISSN 0081-3028) 3, 769

Southern California Association of Governments Annual Report *see* S C A G Annual Report 487

Southern California Rapid Transit District. Annual Report (US ISSN 0362-2843) 863

Southern Comparative Literature Association Newsletter *see* S L A Newsletter 572

Southern Conference on Gerontology Report (US ISSN 0071-6111) 914

Southern Europe Travel Guide *see* Travel Guide to Europe 892

Southern Historical Publications (US ISSN 0081-3036) 754

Southern History (UK ISSN 0142-4688) 461

Southern Illinois University. University Museum Studies (US ISSN 0073-4985) 655

Southern Illinois University, Carbondale. Business Research Bureau. Regional Studies in Business and Economics. Monographs (US ISSN 0073-4942) 148

Southern Illinois University, Carbondale. Department of Geography. Discussion Paper (US ISSN 0073-4950) 426

Southern Illinois University, Carbondale. Occasional Paper Series in Geography (US ISSN 0073-4969) 426

Southern Illinois University, Carbondale. University Libraries. Bibliographic Contributions (US ISSN 0073-4977) 94

Southern Illinois University, Edwardsville. Asian Studies. Occasional Paper Series (US) 671, 723

Southern Illinois University, Edwardsville. Center for Urban and Environmental Research and Services. C U E R S. Report (US ISSN 0073-4993) 487

Southern Indian Studies (US ISSN 0085-6525) 65

Southern Methodist University. Industrial Information Services. Newsletter (US ISSN 0038-4364) 370

Southern Methodist University Contributions in Anthropology *see* Contributions in Anthropology 49

Southern Progressive Periodicals Directory Update (US) 94

Southern Regional Education Board. State and Local Revenue Potential (US ISSN 0090-8649) 232, 323

Southern Regional Education Board. State Legislation Affecting Higher Education in the South (US ISSN 0081-3087) 340

Southern Regional Education Board Educational Board. Annual Report *see* S R E B Educational Board. Annual Report 322

Southern Rhodesia. National Archives. Occasional Papers *see* Zimbabwe. National Archives. Occasional Papers 441

Southern Surgical Association. Transactions (US) 625

Southern Universities Nuclear Institute. Annual Research Report (SA) 704

Southern Weed Science Society. Proceedings (US ISSN 0362-4463) 39

Southern Wholesalers' Guide *see* National Hardware Wholesalers' Guide 141

Southsubkin (US) 418, 472

South West Africa Administration: White Paper on the Activities of the Different Branches (SX) 746

South West Africa Scientific Society Journal *see* S.W.A. Scientific Society. Journal 800

South West Africa Series. Memoirs (SA) 300

South West Africa Survey (SA) 746

Southwest New Mexico Council of Governments. Annual Work Program(US ISSN 0095-4810) 746

Southwest Regional Conference for Astronomy and Astrophysics. Proceedings (US ISSN 0147-2003) 84

Southwestern Campbook (US) 831, 891

Southwestern Camping *see* Southwestern Campbook 891

Southwestern Ontario Construction Industry Directory. Purchasing Guide(CN) 138, 370

Sovetskaya Arkhitektura *see* Zodchestvo 70

Sovetskaya Literatura, Traditsii i Novatorstvo (UR) 573

Sovetskaya Skul'ptura (UR) 78

Sovetskie Ljudi Segodnja/Vie Quotidienne en U.R.S.S. Prise sur le Vif (FR ISSN 0303-111X) 573

Soviet Affairs Symposium (US ISSN 0085-6533) 461

Soviet Armed Forces Review Annual (US) 640, 846

Soviet Merchant Ships (UK) 881

Soviet Progress in Polyurethanes (US ISSN 0049-1764) 707

Soviet Research Reports (US) 621

Soviet Seismological Research (US) 306

Soviet Union/Union Sovietique (US ISSN 0094-2863) 426

Soviet Union (US ISSN 0163-6057) 723

Soviet Union (Pittsburgh) *see* Soviet Union 426

Soviet Union and Eastern Europe *see* World Today Series: Soviet Union and Eastern Europe 465

Sovietica. Monographs *see* Sovietica. Publications and Monographs 461

Sovietica. Publication *see* Sovietica. Publications and Monographs 461

Sovietica. Publications and Monographs(NE) 461

Soya Bluebook (US) 39

Soybean Digest Blue Book *see* Soya Bluebook 39

Sozial- und Wirtschaftshistorische Studien (AU) 192, 800

Soziale Forschung und Praxis (GW ISSN 0340-7217) 816

Soziale Sicherheit (SZ ISSN 0081-3249) 809

Sozialforschung. Beitraege (AU) 816

Sozialforschung und Gesellschaftspolitik(GW ISSN 0340-8248) 816

Sozialisation und Kommunikation (GW ISSN 0340-9201) 816

Sozialmedizinische und Paedagogische Jugendkunde (SZ ISSN 0076-6186) 600, 695

Sozialversicherungsrechtliche Entscheidungen (AU) 518

Sozialwissenschaftliches Jahrbuch fuer Politik (GW) 715, 800

Soziologische Gegenwartsfragen. Neue Folge (GW ISSN 0081-3265) 816

Soziooekonomische Forschungen (SZ) 800

Space Activity in Norway (NO) 10

Space Biology and Aerospace Medicine *see* U S S R Report: Space Biology and Aerospace Medicine 600

Space Flight Technology (US) 10

Space in Japan (JA) 10

Space Science and Technology Today (US) 10

Space Science Text Series (US) 10

Spain. Consejo Superior de Investigaciones Cientificas. Instituto de Farmacologia Experimental. Archivos *see* Archivas de Farmacologia y Toxicologia 683

Spain. Direccion General de Bellas Artes. Semana de Musica en la Navidad (SP) 663

Spain. Direccion General de Capacitacion y Extension Agrarias. Resumen de Actividades (SP ISSN 0085-6541) 20

Spain. Direccion General de la Produccion Agraria. Campana Algodonera (SP) 39

Spain. Direccion General de Pesca Maritima. Anuario de Pesca Maritima. (SP) 401

Spain. Direccion General de Pesca Maritima. Estadistica de Pesca *see* Spain. Direccion General de Pesca Maritima. Anuario de Pesca Maritima 401

Spain. Direccion General de Pesca Maritima. Flota Pesquera Espanola *see* Spain. Direccion General de Pesca Maritima. Anuario de Pesca Maritima 401

Spain. Direccion General de Pesca Maritima. Publicaciones Tecnicas (SP) 400

Spain. Direccion General de Sanidad. Resumen Cronologico de la Legislacion del Estado Que Afecta a Servicos de Sanidad (SP) 767

Spain. Direccion General de Trafico. Anuario Estadistico de Accidentes. Boletin Informativo (SP ISSN 0085-655X) 866

Spain. Direccion General de Trafico. Anuario Estadistico General. (SP ISSN 0085-6568) 866

Spain. Instituto de Credito Oficial. Memoria del Credito Oficial (SP ISSN 0081-3451) 232

Spain. Instituto Geologico y Minero. Catalogo de Ediciones (SP) 3, 290

Spain. Instituto Geologico y Minero. Colleccion Memorias (SP) 647

Spain. Instituto Geologico y Minero. Informes (SP) 300

Spain. Instituto Nacional de Estadistica. Estadistica Industrial (SP ISSN 0081-3354) 164

Spain. Instituto Nacional de Estadistica. Indice del Coste de la Vida (SP) 846

Spain. Instituto Nacional de Estadistica. Industrias Derivadas de la Pesca (SP ISSN 0081-3362) 400

Spain. Instituto Nacional de Estadistica. Informe Sobre la Distribucion de las Rentas (SP ISSN 0081-3370) 762

Spain. Instituto Nacional de Estadistica. Poblacion Activa (SP ISSN 0081-3389) 164

Spain. Instituto Nacional de Industria. Memoria I N I (Year) (SP) 148

Spain. Instituto Nacional de Industria. Programa de Investigaciones Economicas: Serie E (SP) 148

Spain. Instituto Nacional de Industria. Resumen de Actividades *see* Resumen de Actividades I N I (Year) 225

Spain. Instituto Nacional de Investigaciones Agrarias. Anales. Serie: General (SP) 20

Spain. Instituto Nacional de Investigaciones Agrarias. Anales. Serie: Higiene y Sanidad Animal (SP) 46

Spain. Instituto Nacional de Investigaciones Agrarias. Anales. Serie: Produccion Animal (SP) 46

Spain. Instituto Nacional de Investigaciones Agrarias. Anales. Serie: Produccion Vegetal (SP) 39

Spain. Instituto Nacional de Investigaciones Agrarias. Anales. Serie: Proteccion Vegetal (SP) 39

Spain. Instituto Nacional de Investigaciones Agrarias. Anales. Serie: Recursos Naturales (SP ISSN 0210-3338) 20

Spain. Instituto Nacional de Investigaciones Agrarias. Anales. Serie: Technologia (SP) 20

Spain. Instituto Nacional de Investigaciones Agrarias. Comunicaciones. Serie: General (SP) 20, 118

Spain. Instituto Nacional de Investigaciones Agrarias. Comunicaciones. Serie: Produccion Animal (SP ISSN 0210-3303) 46

Spain. Instituto Nacional de Investigaciones Agrarias. Comunicaciones. Serie: Produccion Vegetal (SP ISSN 0210-329X) 20

Spain. Instituto Nacional de Investigaciones Agronomicas. Anales *see* Spain. Instituto Nacional de Investigaciones Agrarias. Anales. Serie: General 20

Spain. Instituto Nacional de Investigaciones Agronomicas. Anales *see* Spain. Instituto Nacional de Investigaciones Agrarias. Anales. Serie: Economia y Sociologica Agrarias 30

Spain. Instituto Nacional de Investigaciones Agronomicas. Anales *see* Spain. Instituto Nacional de Investigaciones Agrarias. Anales. Serie: Proteccion Vegetal 39

Spain. Instituto Nacional para la Conservacion de la Naturaleza. Monografias (SP) 389

Spain. Instituto Nacional de Investigaciones Agrarias. Anales. Serie: Economia y Sociologica Agrarias (SP) 30, 819

Spain. Ministerio de Agricultura. Secretaria General Tecnica. Anuario de Estadistica Agraria (SP) 25

Spain. Ministerio de Agricultura. Secretaria General Tecnica. Cuentas del Sector Agrario (SP) 25

Spain. Ministerio de Comercio y Turismo. Estadisticas de Turismo (SP) 891

Spain. Ministerio de Educacion y Ciencia. Guia (SP) 323

Spain. Ministerio de Educacion y Ciencia. Junta Nacional Contra el Analfabetismo. Boletin (SP ISSN 0561-4619) 323

Spain. Ministerio de Hacienda. Delegacion del Gobierno en Campsa. Memoria (SP) 681

Spain. Ministerio de Hacienda. Direccion General de Seguros. Balances y Cuentas (SP) 232

Spain. Ministerio de Hacienda. Informacion Estadistica (SP ISSN 0081-3435) 164

Spain. Ministerio de Hacienda. Memoria *see* Spain. Ministerio de Hacienda. Direccion General de Seguros. Balances y Cuentas 232

Spain. Ministerio de Hacienda. Subdireccion General de Organizacion e Informacion. Estadistica de la Informacion al Publico (SP) 746

Spain. Ministerio de Industria. Resultados de la Encuesta de Coyuntura Industrial: Sector Industrial (SP) 225

Spain. Ministerio de Informacion y Turismo. Estadisticas de Turismo *see* Spain. Ministerio de Comercio y Turismo. Estadisticas de Turismo 891

Spain. Ministerio de la Vivienda. Estadistica de la Industria de la Construccion (SP ISSN 0561-4902) *141*
Spain. Ministerio de la Vivienda. Serie 3: Vivienda (SP) *746*
Spain. Servicio Central de Publicaciones de la Presidencia del Gobierno. Coleccion Informe (SP) *746*
Spain. Servicio de Extension Agraria. Serie Tecnica (SP ISSN 0081-3478) *30*
Spanische Forschungen der Goerresgesellschaft. Reihe 1: Gesammelte Aufsaetze zur Kulturgeschichte Spaniens (GW ISSN 0081-3486) *461*
Spanische Forschungen der Goerresgesellschaft. Reihe 2: Monographien (GW ISSN 0081-3494) *461*
Spanish Institute. Annual Report (US ISSN 0081-3516) *723*
Spanish, Lusitanian, American Trade Directory *see* SLAM: Trade Year Book of Africa *198*
Spark (LO) *557*
Sparks (US) *268*
Speak (AT) *278, 816*
Spearhead (KE) *767*
Special Analysis: Budget of the United States Government *see* U.S. Office of Management and Budget. Special Analysis: Budget of the United States Government *233*
Special Education and Rehabilitation Monograph Series *see* Syracuse Special Education and Rehabilitation Monograph Series *346*
Special Education Directory (US ISSN 0364-0035) *346*
Special Education Programs-Services *see* Pennsylvania. Department of Education. Special Education Programs-Services *346*
Special Issues (UK ISSN 0435-3951) *300*
Special Libraries Association State-of-the-Art Review Series *see* S L A State-of-the-Art Review Series *535*
Special Libraries Directory of Greater New York (US ISSN 0093-9587) *535*
Special Papers in International Economics (US ISSN 0081-3559) *148, 176*
Special Project Grants and Contracts Awarded for Improvement in Nurse Training *see* U.S. Bureau of Health Resources Development. Division of Nursing. Special Project Grants and Contracts Awarded for Improvement in Nurse Training *614*
Special Publication - Minnesota Department of Natural Resources, Division of Fish and Wildlife, Environment Section *see* Minnesota. Division of Fish and Wildlife, Environment Section. Special Publication *277*
Special Subject Resources in Maine *see* Maine. State Library. Special Subject Resources in Maine *533*
Special Topics in Endocrinology and Metabolism (US ISSN 0193-0982) *612*
Specification (UK ISSN 0081-3567) *70*
Specimen (NE) *78*
Specola Astronomica Vaticana, Castel Gandolfo, Italy. Annual Report (VC ISSN 0081-3575) *84*
Specola Astronomica Vaticana, Castel Gandolfo, Italy. Miscellanea Astronomica (VC ISSN 0081-3583) *84*
Specola Astronomica Vaticana, Castel Gandolfo, Italy. Ricerche Astronomiche (VC ISSN 0081-3591) *84*
Specola Astronomica Vaticana, Castel Gandolfo, Italy. Ricerche Spettroscopiche (VC ISSN 0081-3605) *84*
Spectacular Diseases (UK) *600*
Spectator (US) *419*
Spectra of Anthropological Progress (II) *53*

Spectroscopic Properties of Inorganic & Organometallic Compounds (UK ISSN 0584-8555) *248, 706*
Spectrum (US) *406*
Spectrum (St. Paul) (US) *472, 729*
Specula (GW) *691*
Speculum Anniversary Monographs (US) *78, 462, 573*
Speculum Artium (IT) *573*
Speculum Juris (SA ISSN 0584-8652) *518*
Speech Communication Association Free Speech Yearbook *see* S C A Free Speech Yearbook *714*
Speech Communication Directory (US) *346, 551*
Speech Communication Directory of S C A and the Regional Speech Communication Organizations *see* Speech Communication Directory *346*
Speech Index (US ISSN 0081-3656) *4, 555*
Spektrum (UK) *557, 719*
Spektrum des Geistes (GW ISSN 0085-6584) *573*
Spenser Studies (US) *573*
Speur- en Ontwikkelingswerk in Nederland/Research and Development Activities in the Netherlands (NE ISSN 0077-7056) *853*
Spezial (GE ISSN 0081-3672) *262*
Spezialbibliographien zu Fragen des Staates und des Rechts (GE ISSN 0081-3680) *521*
Spezielle Anorganische Chemie (GW ISSN 0340-2509) *251*
Spezielle Pathologische Anatomie (US ISSN 0081-3699) *107, 600*
Spicae (FR) *551*
Spiegel Deutscher Buchkunst *see* Die Schoensten Buecher der Deutschen Demokratischen Republik *759*
Spielfilmliste (GW ISSN 0071-4933) *651*
Spinning Around the World (US) *476*
Spinoff (US) *853*
Spiritual Community Guide (US ISSN 0160-0354) *776, 891*
Spirituosen-Jahrbuch (GW ISSN 0081-3729) *86*
Spolia Zeylanica/Bulletin of the National Museums of Sri Lanka (CE ISSN 0081-3745) *791*
Spon's Architects' & Builders' Price Book (UK ISSN 0306-3046) *70, 138*
Spon's Landscape Handbook *see* Spon's Landscape Pricebook *138*
Spon's Landscape Pricebook (UK ISSN 0144-8404) *138*
Spon's Mechanical & Electrical Services Price Book (UK ISSN 0305-4543) *358*
Sponsors' Handbook for Touring Attractions (CN) *860*
Spore Research (US ISSN 0306-2074) *118*
Spores (US ISSN 0584-9144) *118*
Sport Fishery and Wildlife Research *see* U. S. Fish and Wildlife Service. Sport Fishery and Wildlife Research *831*
Sport International Yearbook (BE) *822*
Sportaccommodatie in Nederland/Sports: Public Accommodation (NE ISSN 0077-6777) *822*
Sportfishing (CN) *831, 891*
Sporting Chronicle "Horses in Training"(UK ISSN 0081-3761) *822*
Sporting News' National Football Guide (US ISSN 0081-3788) *826*
Sporting News Official Baseball Record Book *see* Official Baseball Record Book *825*
Sportmedizinische Schriftenreihe (GE ISSN 0075-8655) *625*
Sports Afield Almanac *see* Sports Afield Outdoor Almanac *831*
Sports Afield Fishing Annual (US) *831*
Sports Afield Gun Annual (US ISSN 0490-5326) *831*
Sports Afield Outdoor Almanac (US ISSN 0190-1249) *831*
Sports All Stars Baseball (US) *826*
Sports and Recreational Programs of the Nation's Universities and Colleges (US) *822*

Sports Collectors Directory (US ISSN 0198-6597) *476, 822*
Sports Documentation Centre. Abstract Journal Holdings (UK) *4, 328*
Sports Documentation Centre. List of Periodical Holdings (UK) *94, 695*
Sports Management Review (US) *219, 822*
Sports: Public Accommodation *see* Sportaccommodatie in Nederland *822*
Sports Quarterly-Football Pros (US) *826*
Sportsguide for Individual Sports (US) *242, 822*
Sportsguide for Team Sports (US ISSN 0198-8190) *242, 822*
Sportwetenschappelijke Onderzoekingen(NE) *822*
Sportwissenschaft und Sportpraxis (GW ISSN 0342-457X) *822*
Sportwissenschaftliche Dissertationen (GW ISSN 0340-0956) *822*
Spotlight (BF) *323*
Sprache und Datenverarbeitung (GW ISSN 0343-5202) *274, 551*
Sprache und Dichtung. Neue Folge (SZ ISSN 0081-3826) *551*
Sprache und Gesellschaft (GE) *551*
Sprachfuehrer fuer die Krankenpflege (GW) *614*
Sprawozdania Archeologiczne (PL ISSN 0081-3834) *65*
Sprenger Instituut. Communications (NE) *39, 406*
Sprenger Instituut. Jaarverslag/Annual Report (NE ISSN 0081-3850) *39, 406*
Sprenger Instituut. Rapporten (NE) *406*
Spring (US) *738*
Spring (Syracuse) (US) *581*
Spring Rain (US) *581*
Springer Advanced Texts in Life Sciences (US) *108*
Springer Series in Chemical Physics (US) *248, 699*
Springer Series in Computational Physics (US) *699*
Springer Series in Electrophysics (US) *358, 699*
Springer Series in Experimental Entomology (US) *121*
Springer Series in Information Sciences (US) *535*
Springer Series in Language and Communication (US) *551*
Springer Series in Microbiology (US) *124*
Springer Series in Optical Sciences (US) *706*
Springer Series in Solid State Sciences (US) *791*
Springer Series in Statistics (US) *846*
Springer Series on Environmental Management (US) *389*
Springer Tracts in Modern Physics (US ISSN 0081-3869) *699*
Springer Tracts in Natural Philosophy (US ISSN 0081-3877) *791*
Sprocket (AT) *651*
Sprog og Kultur (DK ISSN 0038-8645) *403, 551*
Sputnik Sel'skoi Molodezhi (UR) *258*
Squash Rackets Association. Handbook (UK ISSN 0081-3885) *826*
Squires Companion *see* Martindale: the Extra Pharmacopoeia *685*
Sredniowiecze.Studia o Kulturze/Etudes sur la Culture Medievale/Middle Ages Studies in Culture (PL ISSN 0079-3183) *573*
Sri Aurobindo Centenary Annual (CE) *691*
Sri Lanka. Irrigation Department. Hydrology Division. Hydrological Annual (CE) *308*
Sri Lanka. Ministry of Planning and Economic Affairs. Division of External Resources. Economic Indicators (CE) *190*
Sri Lanka Association for the Advancement of Science. Proceedings (CE) *551*
Sri Lanka Export Directory (CE ISSN 0069-2360) *198*
Sri Lanka Film Annual (CE) *651*
Sri Lanka Foundation Institute. News (CE) *330*

Sri Lanka in Brief (CE) *180*
Sri Lanka Institute of Architects. Journal (CE) *70*
Sri Lanka Yearbook (CE) *846*
Sri Venkateswara University. Department of Sanskrit. Symposium (II ISSN 0081-3915) *551*
Sri Venkateswara University. Oriental Journal (II ISSN 0081-3907) *445, 551*
Srpska Akademija Nauka i Umetnosti. Etnografski Institut. Glasnik (YU) *53*
Srpska Akademija Nauka i Umetnosti. Etnografski Institut. Zbornik Radova (YU) *53*
Srpska Akademija Nauka i Umetnosti. Odeljenje Drustvenih Nauka. Glas (YU ISSN 0081-394X) *800*
Srpska Akademija Nauka i Umetnosti. Odeljenje Drustvenih Nauka. Posebna Izdanja (YU ISSN 0081-3982) *800*
Srpska Akademija Nauka i Umetnosti. Odeljenje Drustvenih Nauka. Spomenik (YU ISSN 0081-4059) *65, 70, 800*
Srpska Akademija Nauka i Umetnosti. Odeljenje Jezika i Knjizevnosti. Posebna Izdanja (YU ISSN 0081-3990) *551, 573*
Srpska Akademija Nauka i Umetnosti. Odeljenje Jezika i Knjizevnosti. Glas (YU ISSN 0081-3958) *551*
Srpska Akademija Nauka i Umetnosti. Odeljenje Likovne i Muzicke Umetnosti. Muzicka Izdanja (YU ISSN 0490-6659) *663*
Srpska Akademija Nauka i Umetnosti. Odeljenje Likovne i Muzicke Umetnosti. Posebna Izdanja (YU ISSN 0081-4008) *78, 663*
Srpska Akademija Nauka i Umetnosti. Odeljenje Medicinskih Nauka. Glas (YU ISSN 0081-3966) *600*
Srpska Akademija Nauka i Umetnosti. Odeljenje Medicinskih Nauka. Posebna Izdanja (YU ISSN 0081-4016) *600*
Srpska Akademija Nauka i Umetnosti. Odeljenje Prirodno-Matematickih Nauka. Posebna Izdanja (YU ISSN 0081-4024) *791*
Srpska Akademija Nauka i Umetnosti. Odeljenje Tehnickih Nauka. Glas (YU ISSN 0081-3974) *853*
Srpska Akademija Nauka i Umetnosti. Odeljenje Tehnickih Nauka. Posebna Izdanja (YU ISSN 0081-4040) *853*
Srpska Akademija Nauka i Umetnosti. Povremena Izdanja (YU) *791*
Srpska Akademija Nauka i Umetnosti. Predavanja (YU ISSN 0561-7383) *792*
Srpska Akademija Nauka i Umetnosti Spomenica (YU ISSN 0081-4032) *493, 792, 800*
Srpski Etnografski Zbornik. Naselja i Poreklo Stanovnistva (YU ISSN 0081-4067) *53, 462*
Srpski Etnografski Zbornik. Rasprave i Gradja (YU ISSN 0081-4075) *53, 462*
Srpski Etnografski Zbornik. Srpske Narodne Umotvorine (YU ISSN 0081-4083) *53, 462*
Srpski Etnografski Zbornik. Zivot i Obicaji Narodni (YU ISSN 0081-4091) *53, 462*
Staat und Politik (SZ ISSN 0081-4105) *715*
Staatliche Kunsthalle Karlsruhe. Bildhefte (GW ISSN 0075-5133) *655*
Staatliche Kunsthalle Karlsruhe. Graphik-Schriftenreihe (GW ISSN 0075-5141) *655*
Staatliche Kunstsammlungen in Baden-Wuerttemberg. Jahrbuch (GW ISSN 0067-284X) *655*
Staatliche Museen zu Berlin. Jahrbuch. Forschungen und Berichte (GE ISSN 0067-6004) *78, 655*
Staatlicher Mathematisch-Physikalischer Salon, Dresden. Veroeffentlichungen (GE ISSN 0081-4113) *589, 699*

Staatliches Museum fuer Mineralogie und Geologie, Dresden. Abhandlungen (GE ISSN 0070-7228) *914*
Staatliches Museum fuer Mineralogie und Geologie, Dresden. Jahrbuch *see* Staatliches Museum fuer Mineralogie und Geologie, Dresden. Abhandlungen *914*
Staatliches Museum fuer Tierkunde in Dresden. Entomologische Abhandlungen (GE ISSN 0070-7244) *122*
Staatliches Museum fuer Tierkunde in Dresden. Faunistische Abhandlungen(GE ISSN 0070-7252) *130*
Staatliches Museum fuer Tierkunde in Dresden. Malakologische Abhandlungen (GE ISSN 0070-7260) *130*
Staatliches Museum fuer Tierkunde in Dresden. Zoologische Abhandlungen (GE ISSN 0070-7287) *130*
Staatliches Museum fuer Voelkerkunde Dresden. Abhandlungen und Berichte(GE ISSN 0070-7295) *53, 655*
Staatliches Museum fuer Voelkerkunde und Tierkunde. Abhandlungen und Berichte *see* Staatliches Museum fuer Voelkerkunde Dresden. Abhandlungen und Berichte *655*
Staatsbibliothek Preussischer Kulturbesitz. Ausstellungskataloge (GW ISSN 0340-0700) *536*
Stadler Genetics Symposium. Proceedings (US ISSN 0081-4148) *123*
Die Stadt (GW) *487*
Stadtbibliothek Nuernberg. Ausstellungskatalog (GW ISSN 0078-2777) *655*
Stage (ZA) *860*
Stagecast-Irish Stage and Screen Directory (IE) *651, 860*
Stahl und Form (GW ISSN 0081-4172) *630*
Stahleisen Kalender (GW ISSN 0081-4180) *630*
Stainless Steel Directory (UK) *630*
Stainless Steel World Guide (UK ISSN 0141-5298) *630*
Stallion Review (UK) *828*
Stamm Leitfaden Durch Presse und Werbung/Annual Directory of Press and Advertising (GW ISSN 0075-8728) *95*
Stamp Preview *see* Australian Stamp Bulletin *478*
Stamps of the World (UK ISSN 0081-4210) *479*
Standard and Poor's Directory of Bond Agents (US) *204*
Standard Australian Coin Catalogue (AT ISSN 0085-6606) *478*
Standard Catalog for Public Libraries *see* Public Library Catalog (US)
Standard Directory of Advertisers (US ISSN 0081-4229) *6, 242*
Standard Education Almanac (US ISSN 0081-4237) *323*
Standard Lesson Commentary (US ISSN 0081-4245) *767*
Standard Nomenclature of Athletic Injuries (US ISSN 0081-427X) *625*
Standard Periodical Directory (US ISSN 0085-6630) *95*
Standard Specifications for Highway Bridges (US) *377*
Standard Trade Index of Japan (JA ISSN 0585-0444) *180*
Standardization of Cardioangiological Methods *see* Monographs on Standardization of Cardioangiological Methods *607*
Standards and Recommendations for Hospital Care of Newborn Infants (US) *481, 618*
Standards Engineers Society. Proceedings of Annual Meeting (US ISSN 0081-430X) *380*
Standards for Australian Aluminium Mill Products (AT ISSN 0085-6657) *630, 637*
Stanford Center for Research and Development in Teaching. Occasional Papers. (US) *350*

Stanford Center for Research and Development in Teaching. Research and Development Memoranda (US) *350*
Stanford French & Italian Studies (US) *573*
Stanford Journal of International Studies (US ISSN 0081-4326) *524*
Stanford Museum (US ISSN 0085-6665) *655*
Stanford Occasional Papers in Linguistics (US ISSN 0085-6673) *551*
Stanford Series on Methods and Techniques in the Clinical Laboratory (US) *612*
Stanford University. Hoover Institution on War, Revolution and Peace. Report *see* Hoover Institution on War, Revolution, and Peace. Report *721*
Stanford University. Libraries. Annual Report (US) *536*
Stanford University. Publications. Geological Sciences (US ISSN 0081-4350) *300*
Stanley and Kilcullen's Federal Income Tax Law (Supplement) (US) *232*
Stanley Foundation. Occasional Paper (US ISSN 0145-8841) *723*
Stanstead County Historical Society. Journal (CN ISSN 0081-4369) *472*
Stapp Car Crash Conference Proceedings (US ISSN 0585-086X) *872*
Star Almanac for Land Surveyors (UK ISSN 0081-4377) *84*
Stardance (UK) *582*
Starfish Book of Farm and Country Holidays (UK ISSN 0081-4385) *891*
Starwhispering (US) *582*
Stat a Pravo (CS) *210, 518, 715*
State Administrative Officials (Classified by Functions) (US ISSN 0561-8630) *746*
State Agencies Cooperating with the U.S. Department of Agriculture Forest Service in Administration of Various Forestry Programs (US ISSN 0490-8287) *410*
State and Economic Life Series (CN) *435*
State and Mind (US ISSN 0161-1089) *738*
State-Approved Schools of Nursing - L. P. N./L. V. N. (US ISSN 0081-4423) *332, 614*
State-Approved Schools of Nursing - R. N (US ISSN 0081-4431) *332, 614*
State Bank of India. Report of the Central Board of Directors (II ISSN 0585-0991) *176*
State Bank of Pakistan. Index Numbers of Stock Exchange Securities (PK ISSN 0081-4466) *204*
State Bar of Arizona. Newsletter (US ISSN 0099-1058) *518*
State Charities Aid Association Annual Report *see* State Communities Aid Association Annual Report *809*
State Communities Aid Association Annual Report (US ISSN 0585-1149) *809*
State Consumer Action (US ISSN 0190-2210) *280*
State Court Caseload Statistics (US) *284*
State Court Systems (US ISSN 0081-4482) *914*
State Directory of Higher Education Institutions and Agencies in Maryland (US ISSN 0098-4132) *914*
State Domestic Product of Himachal Pradesh (II) *164*
State Elective Officials and the Legislatures (US) *746*
State Electricity Profiles (US) *358*
State Geologists Journal (US ISSN 0039-0089) *300*
State Government Finances *see* Current Governments Reports: State Government Finances *154*
State Government Undertakings in Gujarat (II ISSN 0081-4504) *746*
State Health Benefits Program of New Jersey. Annual Report (US ISSN 0099-2100) *501*

State Housing Development Authority Review *see* M S H D A Review *485*
State Income of Himachal Pradesh *see* State Domestic Product of Himachal Pradesh *164*
State Industrial Directories. Chicago Geographic Edition (US) *242*
State Information Book (US) *746*
State Institute of Education, Rajasthan. Annual Report (II) *323*
State Investment Portfolio. (Juneau) *see* Alaska. Department of Revenue. State Investment Portfolio *202*
State Laws and Regulations (US ISSN 0163-2914) *518*
State Legislative Leadership, Committees and Staff (US) *746*
State Municipal League Directory (US) *750*
State of Black America (US) *719*
State of Florida Comprehensive Manpower Plan (US ISSN 0095-6430) *210*
State of Florida Land Development Guide (US) *487, 762*
State of Food and Agriculture (UN ISSN 0081-4539) *20*
State of Greek Industry in (Year) (GR ISSN 0072-7458) *225*
State of Hawaii Data Book (US ISSN 0073-1080) *190*
State of Michigan's Annual Highway Safety Plan. (US) *876*
State of Montana Investment Program. Report on Audit *see* Montana. Office of the Legislative Auditor. State of Montana Board of Investments. Report on Examination of Financial Statements *204*
State of Nebraska Annual Fiscal Report *see* Nebraska. Accounting Division. Annual Report of Receipts and Disbursements State of Nebraska *744*
State of Nebraska Uniform Crime Report (US ISSN 0090-3221) *284*
State of Nevada Comprehensive Criminal Justice Plan (US) *284*
State of Nevada Wage Report *see* Nevada Wage Survey *209*
State of New York's Environment *see* New York (State). Department of Environmental Conservation. Annual Report *277*
State of South Africa (SA ISSN 0585-1289) *846*
State of the Air Transport Industry (CN ISSN 0081-4571) *869*
State of Virginia's Environment: Annual Report (US) *389*
State of Washington Comprehensive Plan for Crime Control and the Administration of Justice. (US ISSN 0363-5643) *284*
State O'Maine Facts (US ISSN 0097-1189) *891*
State Planning Authority News *see* S. P. A. N *487*
State Planning in Maryland *see* Maryland. Department of State Planning. Activities Report *744*
State Planning Issues (US ISSN 0092-8488) *746*
State Planning Issues (Lexington) *see* State Planning Issues *746*
State Tax Handbook (US ISSN 0081-4598) *232*
State University of New York at Albany. Faculty Senate. Annual Faculty Assembly Proceedings (US ISSN 0077-9350) *340*
State University of New York at Albany. School of Library and Information Science. Bulletin (US) *536*
State University of New York Librarians Association Newsletter *see* S U N Y L A Newsletter *535*
Stately Homes, Museums, Castles and Gardens (UK) *891*
Statement of Secretary of Defense Before the House Armed Services Committee on the Defense Budget and Program *see* U. S. Department of Defense. Defense Department Report *746*
Statens Geotekniska Institut. Proceedings *see* Statens Geotekniska Institut. Rapports *306*

Statens Geotekniska Institut. Rapports/ Swedish Geotechnical Institute. Reports (SW) *306*
Statens Goetekniska Institut. Meddelander *see* Statens Geotekniska Institut. Rapports *306*
Statens Goetekniska Institut. Saertryck och Preliminaera Rapporter *see* Statens Geotekniska Institut. Rapports *306*
States of Malaya Chamber of Mines. Council Report (MY ISSN 0302-6620) *647*
States of Malaya Chamber of Mines. Yearbook (MY) *647*
Statesman (NR) *715*
Statesman's Year Book (UK ISSN 0081-4601) *715*
Statewide Space Survey *see* Illinois. Board of Higher Education. Statewide Space Survey *337*
Station Biologique de Bonnevaux (Doubs). Section de Biologie et d'Ecologie Animales. Publications (FR ISSN 0068-0087) *108*
Stationery Trade Reference Book and Buyer Guide (UK ISSN 0081-461X) *219*
Statistical Abstract for Bangladesh (BG ISSN 0081-4628) *846*
Statistical Abstract of Higher Education in North Carolina (US ISSN 0081-4644) *340*
Statistical Abstract of Iceland (IC ISSN 0081-4652) *846*
Statistical Abstract of Ireland (IE ISSN 0081-4660) *846*
Statistical Abstract of Latin America (US ISSN 0081-4687) *438*
Statistical Abstract of Louisiana (US ISSN 0081-4695) *164*
Statistical Abstract of Maharashtra State (II ISSN 0081-4709) *846*
Statistical Abstract of Oklahoma (US ISSN 0191-0310) *164*
Statistical Abstract of Rajasthan (II ISSN 0081-4717) *846*
Statistical Abstract of Sri Lanka (CE ISSN 0081-4636) *847*
Statistical Abstract of the Government of the Cayman Islands (CJ) *847*
Statistical Abstract of the Maltese Islands *see* Malta. Central Office of Statistics. Annual Abstract of Statistics *843*
Statistical Abstract of the United States(US ISSN 0081-4741) *847*
Statistical Abstract of Virginia (US ISSN 0081-475X) *914*
Statistical Analysis of New Zealand Wool Production and Disposal (NZ) *856*
Statistical Analysis of World's Merchant Fleets Showing Age, Size, Speed and Draft by Frequency Groupings (US ISSN 0081-4768) *881*
Statistical and Social Inquiry Society of Ireland. Journal (IE ISSN 0081-4776) *847*
Statistical Compass *see* Germany (Federal Republic, 1949-) Statistisches Bundesamt. Zahlenkompass *840*
Statistical Compendium of the Americas (US ISSN 0585-1432) *914*
Statistical Data on Commercial Banks in Thailand (TH) *164*
Statistical Data on Libraries in Bulgaria *see* Statisticeski Danni za Bibliotekite v Bulgaria *536*
Statistical Digest of Bangladesh *see* Statistical Yearbook of Bangladesh *847*
Statistical Guides in Educational Research (UK ISSN 0081-4784) *914*
Statistical Handbook of Egypt *see* Egypt. Central Agency for Public Mobilisation and Statistics. Statistical Yearbook *838*
Statistical Handbook of Japan (JA ISSN 0081-4792) *847*
Statistical Handbook of Korea/Tonggye Suchup (KO ISSN 0081-4806) *847*
Statistical Handbook of Sarawak (MY ISSN 0081-4814) *847*

Statistical Handbook of Tamil Nadu (II) 847
Statistical Handbook of Thailand (TH ISSN 0081-4822) 847
Statistical Handbook of the Republic of Ghana (GH) 847
Statistical Information of Afghanistan/ Ma'lumat-i Ihsa'ivi-i Afghanistan (AF) 847
Statistical Mechanics (UK ISSN 0305-9960) 699
Statistical Meteorological Conference. Proceedings see Conference on Probability and Statistics in Atmospheric Sciences. Preprints 632
Statistical Notes of Japan (JA ISSN 0561-922X) 847
Statistical Office of the European Communities. Associes Statistique du Commerce Exterieur. Annuaire (EI ISSN 0081-4857) 164
Statistical Office of the European Communities. Aussenhandel: Analitische Ubersichten. Foreign Trade: Analytical Tables (EI ISSN 0586-4925) 164
Statistical Office of the European Communities. Balances of Payments Yearbook (EI ISSN 0081-4865) 213, 232
Statistical Office of the European Communities. Basic Statistics (EI ISSN 0081-4873) 164
Statistical Office of the European Communities. Commerce Exterieur: Nomenclature des Pays (EI) 198
Statistical Office of the European Communities. Commerce Exterieur: Products C E C A (EI ISSN 0081-4881) 164
Statistical Office of the European Communities. Energy Statistics. Yearbook (EI ISSN 0081-489X) 364
Statistical Office of the European Communities. Foreign Trade: Standard Country Classification (EI ISSN 0081-4903) 164
Statistical Office of the European Communities. National Accounts. Yearbook (EI ISSN 0081-4911) 164
Statistical Office of the European Communities. Overseas Associates. Annuaire Statistiques des Etats Africains et Malgache (EI ISSN 0081-492X) 164
Statistical Office of the European Communities. Recettes Fiscales. Annuaire (EI ISSN 0081-4938) 164
Statistical Office of the European Communities. Siderurgie Annuaire (EI ISSN 0081-4954) 630
Statistical Office of the European Communities. Statistique Agricole (EI ISSN 0081-4946) 20
Statistical Office of the European Communities. Statistiques des Transports. Annuaire (EI ISSN 0081-4962) 863
Statistical Office of the European Communities. Statistiques Industrielles Annuaire (EI ISSN 0081-4970) 164
Statistical Office of the European Communities. Statistiques Sociales. Annuaire (EI ISSN 0081-4989) 816
Statistical Office of the European Communities. Yearbook Regional Statistics (EI ISSN 0081-4997) 164
Statistical Pocket Book: India (II ISSN 0081-5012) 847
Statistical Pocket-Book of Afghanistan (AF) 847
Statistical Pocket Book of Hungary/ Magyar Statisztikai Zsebkonyv (HU) 847
Statistical Pocket-Book of Pakistan (PK ISSN 0081-5004) 847
Statistical Pocket Book of Sri Lanka see Statistical Pocket Book of the Democratic Socialist Republic of Sri Lanka 847
Statistical Pocket Book of the Democratic Socialist Republic of Sri Lanka (CE) 847
Statistical Pocket Book of the Indian Union see Statistical Pocket Book: India 847

Statistical Pocket Book of Turkey/ Turkiye Istatistik Cep Yilligi (TU) 847
Statistical Pocketbook of Indonesia/ Buku Saku Statistik Indonesia (IO ISSN 0537-3808) 847
Statistical Profile of Iowa (US) 847
Statistical Profile of the Soft Drink Industry (US) 86
Statistical Profile of the U.S. Exchange Program (US ISSN 0091-8075) 328
Statistical Report - Georgia Department of Education see Georgia. Department of Education. Statistical Report 327
Statistical Report of Hospitals (Tallahassee) see Florida. Mental Health Program Office. Statistical Report of Hospitals 482
Statistical Report Series (Cheyenne) see Wyoming. Division of Planning, Evaluation and Information Services. Statistical Report Series 849
Statistical Reports of the Nordic Countries see Nordisk Statistisk Skriftserie 843
Statistical Research Monographs (US ISSN 0081-5020) 847
Statistical Review of Arizona see Arizona Statistical Review 151
Statistical Review of Government in Utah (US) 847
Statistical Review of the World Oil Industry (UK ISSN 0081-5039) 681
Statistical Review of Tourism in Hong Kong (HK) 891
Statistical Survey of Economy of Japan (JA ISSN 0081-5047) 164
Statistical Survey of the East African Community Institutions (KE) 164
Statistical Tables - Department of Employment Security see Vermont. Department of Employment Security. Statistical Tables 166
Statistical Yearbook see Statisztikai Evkonyv 848
Statistical Yearbook for Asia and the Far East see Statistical Yearbook for Asia and the Pacific 847
Statistical Yearbook for Asia and the Pacific/Annuaire Statistique pour l'Asie et le Pacifique (UN) 847
Statistical Yearbook of Bangladesh (BG ISSN 0302-2374) 847
Statistical Yearbook of Finland see Suomen Tilastollinen Vuosikirja 848
Statistical Yearbook of Greece (GR ISSN 0081-5071) 847
Statistical Yearbook of Iran (IR) 847
Statistical Yearbook of Jamaica (JM) 847
Statistical Yearbook of the Church. see Annuarium Statisticum Ecclesiae 769
Statistical Yearbook of the Netherlands (NE ISSN 0077-6858) 361
Statistical Yearbook of the Republic of China (CH) 164, 847
Statistical Yearbook of the U.S. Department of Housing and Urban Development see U.S. Department of Housing and Urban Development. Statistical Yearbook 489
Statistical Yearbook of Turkey see Turkiye Istatistik Yilligi 849
Statisticeski Danni za Bibliotekite v Bulgaria/Statistical Data on Libraries in Bulgaria (BU) 536
Statistiches Handbuch der Oesterreichischen Sozialversicherung see Handbuch der Oesterreichischen Sozialversicherung 502
Statistisches Taschenbuch der DDR (GE ISSN 0433-6844) 847
Statisticheski Godishnik na Narodna Republika Bulgaria (BU) 847
Statisticheski Spravochnik (BU) 847
Statisticians and Others in Allied Professions see Directory of Statisticians 838
Statistics - Africa (UK ISSN 0081-5098) 164
Statistics - America (UK ISSN 0309-5452) 164
Statistics & Facts About Nebraska Schools (US ISSN 0561-9440) 323
Statistics - Asia & Australasia: Sources for Market Research (UK ISSN 0309-5371) 95, 847

Statistics by Industry and Size of Establishment (Harrisburg) see Pennsylvania. Department of Commerce. Bureau of Statistics. Statistics by Industry and Size of Establishment 844
Statistics - Europe (UK ISSN 0081-5101) 164
Statistics for Electric Utilities in Pennsylvania (US) 360
Statistics for Gas Utilities in Pennsylvania (US) 682
Statistics for Iron and Steel Industry in India (II ISSN 0081-511X) 630
Statistics for Manufacturing Industries. (Harrisburg) see Pennsylvania. Department of Commerce. Bureau of Statistics, Research and Planning. Statistics for Manufacturing Industries 163
Statistics for Water Utilities Including Water Authorities in Pennsylvania (US ISSN 0094-4335) 900
Statistics of Education in Cyprus (CY) 328
Statistics of Education in Somalia (SO) 323
Statistics of Foreign Trade of Syria (SY ISSN 0081-5136) 164
Statistics of Indiana Libraries (US ISSN 0081-5152) 536
Statistics of Privately Owned Electric Utilities in the United States (US ISSN 0161-9004) 360, 364, 847
Statistics of Road Traffic Accidents in Europe (UN ISSN 0081-5160) 866
Statistics of the Communications Industry in the United States (US ISSN 0081-5179) 265
Statistics of the State Finances of the Netherlands see Statistiek der Rijksfinancien 232
Statistics of the Trade Unions in the Netherlands see Omvang der Vakbeweging in Nederland 507
Statistics of Virginia Public Libraries see Statistics of Virginia Public Libraries and Institutional Libraries 536
Statistics of Virginia Public Libraries and Institutional Libraries (US) 536
Statistics of World Trade in Steel (UN ISSN 0081-5195) 630
Statistics on Japanese Industries (JA ISSN 0081-5209) 165
Statistics on Narcotic Drugs see United Nations. International Narcotics Control Board. Statistics on Narcotic Drugs Furnished by Governments in Accordance with the International Treaties and Maximum Levels of Opium Stocks 754
Statistics on Social Work Education see Statistics on Social Work Education in the United States 809
Statistics on Social Work Education in the United States (US ISSN 0091-7192) 809
Statistics on the Developing South see Southeastern Historical Statistics 846
Statistics on the Hotel Industry in Fiji see Statistics on Tourism and Hotel Industry in Fiji 483
Statistics on the Mexican Economy (MX) 165
Statistics on Tourism and Hotel Industry in Fiji (FJ) 483, 891
Statistics on Visitor and Other Arrivals see Statistics on Tourism and Hotel Industry in Fiji 483
Statistics on Work Stoppages, New York State (US) 210
Statistics - Social Service Board, North Dakota see North Dakota. Social Service Board. Statistics 811
Statistics Sources (US ISSN 0585-198X) 847
Statistiek der Rijksfinancien/Statistics of the State Finances of the Netherlands (NE ISSN 0077-6998) 232
Statistiek van de Gasvoorziening in Nederland (NE ISSN 0081-5225) 681
Statistiek van de Scheepvaartbeweging in Nederland/Census of Inland Shipping in the Netherlands at Locks and Bridges (NE ISSN 0077-7161) 881

Statistik der Kommunalen Oeffentlichen Bibliotheken der Bundesrepublik (GW ISSN 0081-5241) 914
Statistik der Oeffentlichen Buechereien der Bundesrepublik see Statistik der Kommunalen Oeffentlichen Bibliotheken der Bundesrepublik 914
Statistik des Hamburgischen Staates (GW ISSN 0073-0203) 881
Statistik Indonesia see Statistical Pocketbook of Indonesia 847
Statistika Spoljne Trgovine SFR Jugoslavije (YU ISSN 0084-4373) 165
Statistique Criminelle de la Belgique (BE ISSN 0081-5268) 285, 847
Statistique de l'Eglise see Annuarium Statisticum Ecclesiae 769
Statistique Judiciare de la Belgique see Statistique Criminelle de la Belgique 285
Statistiques de l'Enseignement au Gabon (GO) 328
Statistiques de l'Industrie Francaise des Pates. Papiers et Cartons (FR) 676
Statistiques de l'Industrie Gaziere en France (FR) 681
Statistiques du Commerce Exterieur de Cote d'Ivoire (IV ISSN 0081-5276) 165
Statistiques du Commerce Exterieur de l'Algerie (AE) 165
Statistiques du Commerce Exterieur de la Tunisie (TI ISSN 0081-5292) 165
Statistiques du Commerce Exterieur de Madagascar (MG ISSN 0081-5306) 165, 847
Statistiques du Tourisme Mondial see World Travel Statistics 893
Statistiques Financieres de l'OCDE see O E C D Financial Statistics 162
Statistiques Mondiales de Transport see World Transport Data 867
Statistisch Jaarboek van Volksgezondheid see Annuaire Statistique de la Sante Publique 750
Statistische Mitteilungen der Bergbehoerden der Bundesrepublik (GW) 648
Statistische Nachrichten ueber Bildungs- und Sozialeinrichtungen fuer Hoergeschaedigte im Deutschprachigen Raum (GW) 286
Statistische Studien (GW ISSN 0531-9323) 148, 847
Statistisches Handbuch fuer die Republik Oesterreich (AU ISSN 0081-5314) 847
Statistisches Jahrbuch Berlin (GW ISSN 0081-5322) 847
Statistisches Jahrbuch der DDR (GE) 847
Statistisches Jahrbuch der Eisen- und Stahlindustrie (GW ISSN 0081-5365) 630
Statistisches Jahrbuch der Schweiz/ Annuaire Statistique de la Suisse (SZ ISSN 0081-5330) 847
Statistisches Jahrbuch der Stadt Augsburg (GW) 848
Statistisches Jahrbuch fuer die Bundesrepublik Deutschland (GW ISSN 0081-5357) 848
Statistisches Jahrbuch Muenchen (GW ISSN 0077-2062) 848
Statistisches Jahrbuch ueber Ernaehrung, Landwirtschaft und Forsten der Bundesrepublik Deutschland (GW ISSN 0072-1581) 20
Statisk Aarsbok Foer Finland see Suomen Tilastollinen Vuosikirja 848
Statisk Aarsbok foer Sverige (SW ISSN 0081-5381) 848
Statisztikai Evkonyv/Statistical Yearbook (HU ISSN 0073-4039) 848
Statni Banka Ceskoslovenska. Bulletin (CS ISSN 0081-539X) 176
Statsforetag. Aarsredovisning/Swedish State Company. Annual Report (SW) 225
Status of the Market Nuclear Fuel Fabrication (US ISSN 0094-7482) 704
Stavanger Museum. Aarbok (NO ISSN 0333-0656) 655

Stavanger Museum. Skrifter (NO ISSN 0333-0664) *655*
Steam & Organ Year Book & Preserved Transport Guide (UK) *863*
Steam Electric Fuels *see* Steam-Electric Plant Factors (1978) *647*
Steam-Electric Plant Construction Cost and Annual Production Expenses (US ISSN 0083-0852) *139*
Steam-Electric Plant Factors (1978) (US) *647, 681*
Steam Passenger Service Directory (US ISSN 0081-542X) *874*
Steel Fabrications (SA) *139, 630*
Steel Structures Painting Bulletin (US) *673*
Steel Times Annual Review of the Steel Industry (UK) *630*
Steel Traders of the World (UK ISSN 0308-8006) *630*
Steelmaking Proceedings *see* American Institute of Mining, Metallurgical and Petroleum Engineers. National Open Hearth and Basic Oxygen Steel Division. Proceedings of the Conference *641*
Steinbeck Monograph Series (US ISSN 0085-6746) *573*
Steirische Beitraege zur Hydrogeologie (US ISSN 0376-4826) *308*
Stelle Filanti (IT) *98, 651*
Stephen F. Austin State University. School of Forestry. Bulletin (US ISSN 0082-318X) *410*
Stephen Wilson Annual Pharmacy Seminar. Report (US ISSN 0585-2471) *686*
Stephens, Maxfield and Lind's Federal Estate and Gift Taxation (Supplement) (US) *232*
Stereo Buyer's Guide. Amplifiers (AT) *818*
Stereo Buyer's Guide. Cassettes (AT) *818*
Stereo Buyer's Guide. Directory (AT) *818*
Stereo Buyer's Guide. FM Radio (AT) *818*
Stereo Buyer's Guide. Manual (AT) *818*
Stereo Buyer's Guide. Speakers (AT) *818*
Stereo Buyer's Guide. Turntables (AT) *818*
Stereo Directory & Buying Guide (US ISSN 0090-6786) *818*
Stereo/Hi-Fi Directory *see* Stereo Directory & Buying Guide *818*
Stereo Review's Tape Recording & Buying Guide (US) *818*
Steuer-Gewerkschafts-Handbuch (GW) *232, 507*
Steuerbelastung in der Schweiz/Charge Fiscale en Suisse (SZ) *232*
Steuerberater-Jahrbuch (GW ISSN 0081-5519) *232*
Stewart Nursing Conference Series (US) *914*
Stichting Film en Wetenschap. Catalogue 16mm Films (NE) *651*
Stichting Stedelijke Raad voor Maatschappelijk Welzijn. Informatie-Bulletin (NE ISSN 0039-1395) *809*
Stichwoerter zur Entwicklungspolitik (GW) *715*
Der Stickstoff (GW ISSN 0081-5535) *39*
Stifterverband fuer die Deutsche Wissenschaft. Jahrbuch *see* Stifterverband fuer die Deutsche Wissenschaft. Taetigkeitsbericht *792*
Stifterverband fuer die Deutsche Wissenschaft. Taetigkeitsbericht (GW) *792*
Stiftung Preussische Kulturbesitz. Jahrbuch (GW ISSN 0081-5578) *462*
Stikhi (UR) *582*
Still: Yale Photography Annual (US ISSN 0081-5586) *694*
Stille Schar (AU ISSN 0081-5594) *462, 775*
Stimmen Indianischer Voelker (GW ISSN 0081-5608) *403, 472*

Stipendien fuer Auslaendische Studierende und Akademiker an Oesterreichischen Hochschulen *see* Scholarships for Foreign Students and University Graduates at Austrian Institutions of Higher Learning *339*
Stock Exchange, London. Members and Firms of the Stock Exchange (UK ISSN 0305-1129) *204*
Stock Exchange, London. Stock Exchange Official Year Book (UK ISSN 0076-0684) *204*
Stock Exchange of Singapore. Handbook (SI ISSN 0583-3981) *205*
Stock Trader's Almanac (US) *205*
Stock Values and Dividends for Tax Purposes (US ISSN 0081-5624) *205, 232*
Stockholm International Peace Research Institute World Armaments and Disarmament: S I P R I Yearbook *see* World Armaments and Disarmament: S I P R I Yearbook *725*
Stockholm Stock Exchange. Report *see* Stockholms Fondboers. Beraettelse *205*
Stockholm Studies in English (SW) *551*
Stockholm Studies in Finnish Language and Literature (SW) *551, 573*
Stockholm Studies in History of Literature (SW ISSN 0491-0869) *573*
Stockholm Studies in Philosophy (SW ISSN 0491-0877) *691*
Stockholm Studies in Politics (SW ISSN 0085-6762) *715*
Stockholm Studies in Russian Literature(SW) *573*
Stockholms Fondboers. Beraettelse/Stockholm Stock Exchange. Report (SW) *205*
Stockholms Universitet. Psykologiska Institutionen. Report Series (SW ISSN 0081-5756) *738*
Stockholms Universitet. Psykologiska Institutionen. Reports. Supplement Series (SW ISSN 0345-021X) *738*
Stockton Teachers Association Educator *see* S T A Educator *913*
Stone (US ISSN 0039-176X) *582*
Stone and Cox General Insurance Register (CN) *501*
Stone and Cox General Insurance Year Book *see* Stone and Cox General Insurance Register *501*
Stone and Cox Life Insurance Tables (CN ISSN 0081-5780) *501*
Stone's Justices' Manual (UK) *518*
Stones of Pittsburgh (US ISSN 0081-5799) *70*
Stony Thursday Book (IE) *573, 582*
Stopout: Working Ways to Learn (US) *323*
Storage Battery Manufacturing Industry Yearbook (US ISSN 0081-5802) *359*
Stores and Shops Retail Directory (UK ISSN 0081-5810) *219, 242*
Stores of the World Directory (UK ISSN 0081-5829) *219, 242*
Storia, Costumi e Tradizioni (IT ISSN 0081-5837) *403*
Storia della Miniatura. Studi e Documenti (IT ISSN 0081-5845) *78*
Storia e Societa (IT) *462*
Storia, Letteratura e Arte nel Mezzogiorno (IT) *462*
Stories: a List of Stories to Tell and to Read Aloud (US) *95, 257*
Stories from the Hills (US ISSN 0081-5861) *472, 573*
Storm Warning (CN) *582*
Storrs Agricultural Experiment Station. Bulletin (US) *20*
Storrs Agricultural Experiment Station. Research Report (US ISSN 0069-8997) *20*
Story of Illinois Series *see* Illinois. State Museum. Story of Illinois Series *783*
Story Quarterly *see* StoryQuarterly *573*
Story So Far (CN) *573*
StoryQuarterly (US) *573*
Stowage and Segregation to I M D G Code (GW) *242, 881*

Strahovska Knihovna (CS ISSN 0081-5896) *573*
Straits Times Annual (SI ISSN 0585-3923) *419*
Straits Times Directory of Malaysia *see* N S T Directory of Malaysia *240*
Straits Times Directory of Malaysia and Singapore *see* N S T Directory of Malaysia *240*
Straits Times Directory of Malaysia and Singapore *see* Straits Times Directory of Singapore *242*
Straits Times Directory of Singapore (SI) *242*
Strand Europa (GW) *891*
Strategic Survey (UK ISSN 0459-7230) *723*
Strategy for Peace Conference. Report *see* Strategy for Peace U.S. Foreign Policy Conference. Report *723*
Strategy for Peace U.S. Foreign Policy Conference. Report (US) *723*
Stratford Festival (CN ISSN 0085-6770) *860*
Stratford Festival Story (CN ISSN 0085-6789) *860*
Stratificazione e Classi Sociali in Italia. Quaderni di Ricerca (IT) *816*
Stream Improvement Technical Bulletin(US ISSN 0360-8751) *389*
Street and Highway Manual *see* Public Works Manual *750*
Street and Smith's Baseball Yearbook *see* Street & Smith's Official Yearbook: Baseball *826*
Street and Smith's College & pro Official Basketball Yearbook *see* Street & Smith's Official Yearbook: Basketball *826*
Street & Smith's Official Yearbook: Baseball (US ISSN 0161-2018) *826*
Street & Smith's Official Yearbook: Basketball (US ISSN 0149-7103) *826*
Street and Smith's Official Yearbook: College Football (US ISSN 0091-9977) *826*
Street and Smith's Official Yearbook: Pro Football (US ISSN 0092-3214) *826*
Stress and Anxiety (US ISSN 0364-1112) *738*
Streudaten der Schweizer Presse (SZ) *6, 760*
Striae (SW ISSN 0345-0074) *300*
Strick und Haekelmode (GW) *262*
Strikes and Lockouts in Canada/Greves et Lock-out au Canada (CN ISSN 0081-5985) *210*
Striolae (SW ISSN 0348-4386) *300*
Stroiizdat: The Best-Designed Books (UR) *95*
Strolling Astronomer *see* Association of Lunar and Planetary Observers. Journal *81*
Structural Foam Conference. Proceedings (US) *707*
Structural Mechanics Software Series (US ISSN 0146-2059) *383*
Structure and Bonding (US ISSN 0081-5993) *248*
Structure of Glass (US ISSN 0081-6000) *244*
Structure of the Cotton and Allied Textile Industries (SZ) *856*
Structurist (CN ISSN 0081-6027) *78*
Struktura i Rol' Vody v Zhivom Organizme *see* Molekulyarnaya Fizika i Biofizika Vodnykh Sistem *111*
Strumenti Linguistici (IT ISSN 0391-1942) *551*
Stubbs Buyers Guide *see* Stubbs Directory *242*
Stubbs Directory (UK) *242, 881*
Stubs (Metro N.Y.) (US ISSN 0081-6051) *860*
Stud and Stable (AT ISSN 0311-8215) *828*
Student Aid Annual *see* Chronicle Student Aid Annual *334*
Student Enrollment in New England Institutions of Higher Education (US) *340*

Student Enrollment Report; West Virginia Institutions of Higher Education (US ISSN 0091-8938) *340*
Student Journalist Guide Series (US ISSN 0081-6078) *350*
Student Mathematics (CN ISSN 0085-6800) *589*
Studi Albanesi. Studi e Testi (IT ISSN 0081-6116) *551, 573*
Studi Americani (IT ISSN 0085-6819) *472, 573*
Studi Classici e Orientali (IT ISSN 0081-6124) *435, 445*
Studi d'Architettura Antica (IT ISSN 0081-6140) *70*
Studi d'Economia (IT ISSN 0391-6103) *190*
Studi Danteschi (IT) *573*
Studi di Letteratura Francese (IT ISSN 0585-4768) *573*
Studi di Metrica Classica (IT ISSN 0081-6159) *260*
Studi e Documenti (IT) *462*
Studi e Saggi Linguistici (IT ISSN 0085-6827) *551*
Studi e Testi dell'Antichita (IT) *573*
Studi e Testi di Letteratura Italiana (IT) *573*
Studi e Testi di Lingua e Letteratura Italiana (IT) *551, 573*
Studi e Testi di Papirologia (IT ISSN 0081-6183) *760*
Studi e Testi di Storia e Critica dell'Arte (IT) *78*
Studi Etruschi (IT) *462*
Studi Genuensi (IT ISSN 0585-4911) *65, 435*
Studi Ispanici (IT ISSN 0585-492X) *573*
Studi Linguistici Salentini (IT) *551*
Studi Romagnoli (IT ISSN 0081-6205) *462*
Studi Romagnoli. Estratti di Sezione (IT ISSN 0081-6213) *462*
Studi Romagnoli. Quaderni (IT ISSN 0081-6221) *462*
Studi Secenteschi (IT ISSN 0081-6248) *462*
Studi Tassiani (IT ISSN 0081-6256) *573*
Studi Veneziani (IT ISSN 0081-6264) *462*
Studia Ad Corpus Hellenisticum Novi Testamenti (NE) *767*
Studia Algoligica Lovaniensia (BE) *792*
Studia Anglica Posnaniensia; an International Review of English Studies (PL ISSN 0081-6272) *551*
Studia Anglistica Upsaliensas (SW ISSN 0562-2719) *551*
Studia Archaeologica (HU ISSN 0081-6280) *65*
Studia Archaeologica (IT ISSN 0081-6299) *65*
Studia Archaeologica (GW) *65*
Studia Archeologiczne (PL ISSN 0081-6302) *65*
Studia Aristotelica (IT ISSN 0081-6310) *691*
Studia Balcanica (BU ISSN 0081-6329) *462*
Studia Bibliogica (US) *573*
Studia Biologica Academiae Scientiarum Hungaricae (HU ISSN 0076-244X) *108*
Studia Biophysica (GE ISSN 0081-6337) *112*
Studia Cartesiana (NE) *691*
Studia Caucasica (NE ISSN 0081-6345) *462, 551*
Studia Celtica (UK ISSN 0081-6353) *551*
Studia Comitatensia (HU ISSN 0133-3046) *655*
Studia Copernicana (PL ISSN 0081-6701) *84*
Studia Ephemeridis Augustinianum (IT) *767*
Studia Estetyczne (PL ISSN 0081-637X) *691*
Studia et Documenta Historiae et Iuris (VC) *435*
Studia et Documenta Historiae Musicae: Bibliotheca (IT ISSN 0081-6388) *663*

Studia Ethnographica Upsaliensia (SW ISSN 0491-2705) *53*
Studia Ethnologica (GW) *53*
Studia Ethnologica Upsaliensia (SW) *53*
Studia Fennica: Revue de Linguistique et d'Ethnologie Finnoises (FI ISSN 0085-6835) *54, 551*
Studia Forestalia Suecica (SW ISSN 0039-3150) *410*
Studia Francisci Scholten Memoriae Dicata (NE ISSN 0081-6396) *65*
Studia Geograficzne (PL ISSN 0081-640X) *426*
Studia Geograficzno-Fizyczne z Obszaru Opolszczyzny (PL ISSN 0081-6418) *300, 426*
Studia Geologica Polonica (PL ISSN 0081-6426) *300*
Studia Geomorphologica Carpatho-Balcanica (PL ISSN 0081-6434) *306*
Studia Germanica Gandensia (BE ISSN 0081-6442) *551*
Studia Germanica Posnaniensia (PL) *573*
Studia Graeca et Latina Gothoburgensia(SW ISSN 0081-6450) *260*
Studia Grammatica (GE ISSN 0081-6469) *551*
Studia Hellenistica (BE) *260*
Studia Hibernica (IE ISSN 0081-6477) *462, 573*
Studia Historiae Oeconomica (PL ISSN 0081-6485) *192*
Studia Historica (FI ISSN 0081-6493) *462*
Studia Historica (IT ISSN 0081-6507) *462*
Studia Historica Academiae Scientiarum Hungaricae (HU ISSN 0076-2458) *435*
Studia Historica et Philoga: Sectio Romanica (IT) *551*
Studia Historica et Philogica: Sectio Slavica (IT) *551*
Studia Historica et Philogica: Sectio Slavo-Romanica (IT) *551*
Studia Historica Gothoburgensia (SW ISSN 0081-6515) *462*
Studia Historica Jyvaskylaensia (FI ISSN 0081-6523) *462*
Studia Historica Slavo-Germanica (PL) *462*
Studia Historica Upsaliensia (SW ISSN 0081-6531) *462*
Studia i Materialy do Dziejow Teatru Polskiego (PL) *860*
Studia i Materialy do Dziejow Wielkopolski i Pomorza (PL ISSN 0081-654X) *462*
Studia i Materialy do Teorii i Historii Architektury i Urbanistyki (PL ISSN 0081-6566) *70, 487*
Studia i Materialy z Dziejow Nauki Polskiej. Seria A. Historia Nauk Spolecznych (PL ISSN 0081-6574) *462, 800*
Studia i Materialy z Dziejow Nauki Polskiej. Seria B. Historia Nauk Biologicznych i Medycznych (PL ISSN 0081-6582) *108, 600*
Studia i Materialy z Dziejow Nauki Polskiej. Seria C. Historia Nauk Matematycznych, Fizyko-Chemicznych i Geologiczno-Geograficznych (PL ISSN 0081-6590) *792*
Studia i Materialy z Dziejow Nauki Polskiej. Seria D. Historia Techniki i Nauk Technicznych (PL ISSN 0081-6604) *853*
Studia i Materialy z Dziejow Nauki Polskiej. Seria E. Zagadnienia Ogolne(PL ISSN 0081-6612) *792, 853*
Studia i Materialy z Dziejow Polski w Okresie Oswiecenia (PL ISSN 0081-6620) *462*
Studia i Materialy z Dziejow Teatru Polskiego see Studia i Materialy do Dziejow Teatru Polskiego *860*
Studia Instituti Anthropos (SZ) *54*
Studia Irenica (GW ISSN 0081-6663) *767*
Studia Iuridica (PL ISSN 0081-6671) *518*

Studia Iuridica Auctoriatate Universitatis Pecs Publicata (HU) *518*
Studia Juridica (IT ISSN 0081-6698) *518*
Studia Leibnitiana. Sonderhefte (GW ISSN 0341-0765) *691*
Studia Leibnitiana. Supplementa (GW ISSN 0303-5980) *691*
Studia Linguistica et Philologica (US) *551*
Studia Lituanica (US) *462*
Studia Mathematica (PL ISSN 0039-3223) *589*
Studia Mediewistyczne/Mediaevistic Studies (PL ISSN 0039-3231) *691*
Studia Missionalia (VC) *775*
Studia Missionalia Upsaliensia (NO ISSN 0585-3273) *914*
Studia Musicologica Norvegica (NO ISSN 0332-5024) *663*
Studia Musicologica Upsaliensia. Nova Series (SW ISSN 0081-6744) *663*
Studia nad Zagadnieniami Gospodarczymi i Spolecznymi Ziem Zachodnich (PL ISSN 0081-6752) *462*
Studia Naturae. Seria A. Wydawnictwa Naukowe (PL) *278*
Studia Naturae. Seria B. Wydawnictwa Popularno-Naukowe (PL) *278*
Studia Norvegica see Studia Norvegica Ethnologica et Folkloristica *403*
Studia Norvegica Ethnologica et Folkloristica (NO) *403*
Studia Numismatica et Medailistica (CS ISSN 0081-6779) *478*
Studia Orientalia (FI ISSN 0039-3282) *671*
Studia Palmyrenskie (PL ISSN 0081-6787) *65*
Studia Pedagogiczne (PL ISSN 0081-6795) *323*
Studia Philologiae Scandinavicae Upsaliensia (SW ISSN 0081-6809) *552*
Studia Philologica Jyvaskylaensia (FI ISSN 0585-5462) *552*
Studia Philosophica (SZ ISSN 0081-6825) *914*
Studia Philosophica Academiae Scientiarum Hungaricae (HU ISSN 0076-2466) *691*
Studia Phonologica/Onsei Kagaku Kenkyu (JA ISSN 0300-1067) *552*
Studia Pohl (VC) *671*
Studia Pohl: Series Maior (VC) *671*
Studia Polonijne (PL) *729*
Studia Polonistyczne (PL) *552*
Studia Polono-Slavica Orientalia. Acta Litteraria (PL ISSN 0137-4389) *573*
Studia Prawno - Ekonomiczne (PL ISSN 0081-6841) *518*
Studia Rossica Posnaniensia (PL ISSN 0081-6884) *573*
Studia Scientiae Paedagogicae Upsaliensia see Uppsala Studies in Education *324*
Studia Semiotyczne (PL ISSN 0137-6608) *552*
Studia Semitica Neerlandica (NE ISSN 0081-6914) *770*
Studia Silesiana (SP) *767*
Studia Slovenica (US ISSN 0585-5543) *462*
Studia Slovenica. Special Series (US ISSN 0081-6922) *462*
Studia Societatis Scientiarum Torunensis. Sectio B (Chemia) (PL ISSN 0082-5530) *248*
Studia Societatis Scientiarum Torunensis. Sectio C (Geografia et Geologia) (PL ISSN 0082-5549) *300, 426*
Studia Societatis Scientiarum Torunensis. Sectio D (Botanika) (PL ISSN 0082-5557) *118*
Studia Societatis Scientiarum Torunensis. Sectio E (Zoologia) (PL ISSN 0082-5565) *130*
Studia Societatis Scientiarum Torunensis. Sectio F. (Astronomia) (PL ISSN 0082-5573) *84*
Studia Societatis Scientiarum Torunensis. Sectio G (Physiologia) (PL ISSN 0082-5581) *126*
Studia Spoleczno-Ekonomiczne (PL ISSN 0081-6930) *148*

Studia Staropolskie (PL ISSN 0081-6949) *573*
Studia Sumiro-Hungarica (US ISSN 0585-5578) *54*
Studia Theodisca (NE ISSN 0081-6957) *552*
Studia Ubezpieczeniowe (PL) *501*
Studia Universitatis "Babes-Bolyai". Biologia (RM ISSN 0039-3398) *108*
Studia Universitatis "Babes-Bolyai". Chemia (RM ISSN 0039-3401) *248*
Studia Universitatis "Babes-Bolyai". Geologia. Geographia (RM ISSN 0039-341X) *300, 426*
Studia Universitatis "Babes-Bolyai". Historia (RM ISSN 0039-3428) *435*
Studia Universitatis "Babes-Bolyai". Iurisprudentia (RM ISSN 0578-5464) *518*
Studia Universitatis "Babes-Bolyai." Oeconomica. (RM ISSN 0578-5472) *148*
Studia Universitatis "Babes-Bolyai". Philologia (RM ISSN 0039-3444) *552*
Studia Universitatis "Babes-Bolyai". Philosophia (RM ISSN 0578-5480) *691*
Studia Universitatis "Babes-Bolyai". Physica. (RM) *699*
Studia Universitatis Babes-Bolyai. Psychologia-Pedagogia see Studia Universitatis "Babes-Bolyai". Philosophia *691*
Studia Universitatis Babes-Bolyai. Sociologia see Studia Universitatis "Babes-Bolyai". Philosophia *691*
Studia Uralica (AU) *552*
Studia Uralica et Altaica Upsaliensia (SW ISSN 0081-7015) *552*
Studia Warszawskie (PL ISSN 0081-7023) *462*
Studia z Automatyki (PL) *274*
Studia z Dziejow Gornictwa i Hutnictwa (PL ISSN 0081-704X) *914*
Studia z Dziejow Osadnictwa (PL ISSN 0081-7058) *462*
Studia z Dziejow ZSRR i Europy Srodkowej (PL ISSN 0081-7082) *462*
Studia z Filologii Polskiej i Slowianskiej(PL ISSN 0081-7090) *552*
Studia z Historii Sztuki (PL ISSN 0081-7104) *78*
Studia z Okresu Oswiecenia (PL ISSN 0081-7112) *573*
Studia z Zakresu Budownictwa see Studia z Zakresu Inzynierii *377*
Studia z Zakresu Inzynierii (PL) *377*
Studia Zrodloznawcze (PL ISSN 0081-7147) *462*
Studiecentrum voor Jeugdmisdadigheid. Publikatie/Centre d'Etude de la Delinquance Juvenile. Publication (BE ISSN 0585-5721) *257, 284, 809*
Studiecentrum voor Kernenergie. Annual Scientific Report (BE ISSN 0081-7155) *370, 704*
Studien ueber Asien, Afrika und Lateinamerika (GE) *435*
Studien ueber Wirtschaft-und Systemvergleiche (US) *192*
Studien und Dokumentationen zur Deutschen Bildungsgeschichte (GW) *323*
Studien und Quellen zur Oesterreichischen Zeitgeschichte (AU) *462*
Studien und Texte zur Geistesgeschichte des Mittelalters (NE ISSN 0585-5837) *462*
Studien und Texte zur Kirchengeschichte und Geschichte (AU) *772*
Studien zu den Bogazkoy-Texten (GW ISSN 0585-5853) *552*
Studien zum Politischen System der Bundesrepublik Deutschland (GW) *715*
Studien zur Agrarwirtschaft (GW ISSN 0081-7198) *30*
Studien zur Altaegyptischen Kultur (GW ISSN 0340-2215) *260*
Studien zur Antiken Philosophie (NE) *691*

STUDIES AND 1493

Studien zur Bibliotheksgeschichte (AU) *536*
Studien zur Deutschen Kunstgeschichte(GW ISSN 0081-7228) *78*
Studien zur Deutschen Literatur (GW ISSN 0081-7236) *573*
Studien zur Englischen Literatur (GW) *573*
Studien zur Englischen Philologie, Neue Folge (GW ISSN 0081-7244) *552*
Studien zur Europaeischen Geschichte (GW ISSN 0081-7252) *462*
Studien zur Finanzpolitik (GW ISSN 0081-7279) *176*
Studien zur Franzoesischen Philosophie des Zwanzigsten Jahrhunderts (GW ISSN 0340-5958) *691*
Studien zur Germanistik, Anglistik und Komparatistik (GW) *573*
Studien zur Geschichte Asiens, Afrikas und Lateinamerikas. see Studien ueber Asien, Afrika und Lateinamerika *435*
Studien zur Geschichte der Katholischen Moraltheologie (GW ISSN 0081-7295) *775*
Studien zur Geschichte des Neunzehnten Jahrhunderts (GW ISSN 0081-7309) *435*
Studien zur Geschichte Osteuropas/Studies in East European History (NE ISSN 0081-7317) *462*
Studien zur Indologie und Iranistik (GW ISSN 0341-4191) *445, 552*
Studien zur Japanologie (GW ISSN 0585-6094) *445*
Studien zur Kulturkunde (GW ISSN 0170-3544) *54*
Studien zur Kunst des Neunzehnten Jahrhunderts (GW ISSN 0081-7325) *78*
Studien zur Literatur der Moderne (GW) *573*
Studien zur Literatur- und Sozialgeschichte Spaniens und Lateinamerikas (GW) *573, 816*
Studien zur Medizingeschichte des Neunzehnten Jahrunderts (GW ISSN 0081-7333) *600*
Studien zur modernen Geschichte (GW) *435*
Studien zur Musikgeschichte des Neunzehnten Jahrhunderts (GW ISSN 0081-7341) *663*
Studien zur Ostasiatischen Schriftkunst (GW ISSN 0170-3684) *78, 671*
Studien zur Philosophie des 18. Jahrhunderts (SZ) *691*
Studien zur Philosophie und Literatur des Neunzehnten Jahrhunderts (GW ISSN 0081-735X) *573, 691*
Studien zur Publizistik. Bremer Reihe (GW ISSN 0585-6175) *505*
Studien zur Rechts-, Wirtschafts- und Kulturgeschichte (AU) *192, 518*
Studien zur Wissenschaftstheorie im Neunzehnten Jahrhundert (GW ISSN 0081-7376) *792*
Der Studienbeginn (GW) *323*
Studienbuecherei (GE ISSN 0081-7384) *792*
Studienhefte der Paedagogischen Hochschule see Studienhefte Psychologie in Erziehung und Unterricht *340*
Studienhefte Psychologie in Erziehung und Unterricht (GW ISSN 0081-7392) *340, 738*
Studienreihe Paedagogische Psychologie(GW) *323, 738*
Studienstiftung. Jahresbericht (GW) *340, 809*
Studientage fuer Die Pfarrer (SZ ISSN 0081-7406) *772*
Studienunterlagen zur Orts-, Regional- und Landesplanung (SZ) *487*
Studier i Arbetarroerelsens Historia (SW) *507*
Studier i Nordisk Arkeologi/Studies in North European Archaeology (SW ISSN 0081-7414) *66*
Studier i Politik/Studies in Politics see Goeteborg Studies in Politics *710*
Studierenden an den Schweizerischen Hochschulen/Les Etudiants dans les Hautes Ecoles Suisses (SZ) *340*
Studies and Documents on Cultural Policies (UN ISSN 0586-6898) *493*

Studies and Reports in Hydrology Series (UN ISSN 0081-7449) *308*
Studies in Accounting Research (US ISSN 0586-5050) *168*
Studies in Adult Education (TZ) *330*
Studies in African History *see* Etudes d'Histoire Africaine *440*
Studies in American History (NE ISSN 0081-7503) *472*
Studies in American Humor (US) *557*
Studies in American Jewish History (US ISSN 0081-7511) *770*
Studies in American Jewish Literature (US) *393, 573*
Studies in American Literature (NE ISSN 0081-752X) *574*
Studies in American Negro Life (US) *393*
Studies in Anabaptist and Mennonite History (US ISSN 0081-7538) *777*
Studies in Ancient Art and Archaeology (US) *66, 79*
Studies in Ancient History (NE ISSN 0081-7546) *435*
Studies in Ancient Oriental Civilization (US ISSN 0081-7554) *445*
Studies in Anglesey History (UK ISSN 0585-6515) *462*
Studies in Anthropological Method (US ISSN 0585-6523) *54*
Studies in Anthropology (US ISSN 0085-6843) *54*
Studies in Anthropology (NE) *54*
Studies in Anthropology (US) *54*
Studies in Applied Mechanics (NE) *701*
Studies in Applied Psycholinguistics (US) *552, 738*
Studies in Automation and Control (NE) *274*
Studies in Avian Biology (US) *125*
Studies in Bantoetale (SA) *552*
Studies in Bayesian Econometrics (NE) *148*
Studies in Behavioral Political Science (US) *715*
Studies in Bibliography (US ISSN 0081-7600) *539*
Studies in Bibliography and Booklore (US ISSN 0039-3568) *761, 769*
Studies in Bilingual Education *see* Case Studies in Bilingual Education *345*
Studies in Biology (US) *108*
Studies in Biology (UK ISSN 0537-9024) *108*
Studies in British Art (US) *79*
Studies in British History and Culture (US ISSN 0081-7619) *462*
Studies in Business and Society (US ISSN 0081-7635) *148*
Studies in Business Cycles (US ISSN 0081-7643) *192*
Studies in Capital Formation and Financing (US ISSN 0081-766X) *176*
Studies in Chinese Communist Terminology *see* Studies in Chinese Terminology *552*
Studies in Chinese Terminology. (US) *552*
Studies in Christian Antiquity (US) *435*
Studies in Classical Literature (NE ISSN 0081-7724) *260, 574*
Studies in Comparative Literature (US ISSN 0081-7767) *574*
Studies in Comparative Literature (US ISSN 0081-7775) *574*
Studies in Comparative Politics Series *see* Studies in International and Comparative Politics *715*
Studies in Compulsory Education (UN ISSN 0081-7783) *323*
Studies in Construction Economy (UK) *139, 762*
Studies in Consumer Instalment Financing (US ISSN 0081-7791) *176*
Studies in Contemporary Philosophy (US) *914*
Studies in Contemporary Politics (US) *715*
Studies in Contemporary Satire (US ISSN 0163-4143) *557*
Studies in Corporate Bond Financing (US ISSN 0081-7805) *176*
Studies in Crime and Justice (US) *284*

Studies in Curriculum Development (TZ) *350*
Studies in Defense Policy (US) *640, 715*
Studies in Descriptive Linguistics (GW) *552*
Studies in Development and Planning (US) *148, 201*
Studies in East African Society and History (US) *441, 800*
Studies in East European and Soviet Planning, Development and Trade (US) *225, 715*
Studies in East European History *see* Studien zur Geschichte Osteuropas *462*
Studies in East European Social History(NE) *462*
Studies in Ecology (US) *108*
Studies in Economic History (US) *192*
Studies in Economics (UK ISSN 0081-7856) *148*
Studies in Economics (US ISSN 0148-6535) *148*
Studies in Education (US) *323*
Studies in Education and Teaching Techniques (II) *323, 350*
Studies in Eighteenth Century Culture (US) *435, 493*
Studies in Electoral Politics in the Indian States (II) *715*
Studies in Electrical and Electronic Engineering (NE) *359*
Studies in English *see* U C T Studies in English *553*
Studies in English Literature (NE ISSN 0081-7899) *574*
Studies in Environmental Science (NE) *389*
Studies in Ethnomusicology (US ISSN 0081-7902) *663*
Studies in European History (NE ISSN 0081-7910) *462*
Studies in European Politics (UK) *715, 800*
Studies in European Society (NE) *54*
Studies in Export Promotion (US ISSN 0553-0237) *198*
Studies in Federal Taxation. Tax Study (US ISSN 0081-7929) *232*
Studies in Financial Economics (NE) *914*
Studies in Folklore (NE) *54*
Studies in French Literature (NE ISSN 0081-7937) *574*
Studies in General and Comparative Literature (NE ISSN 0081-7945) *574*
Studies in General Anthropology (NE ISSN 0081-7953) *54*
Studies in Generative Grammar (NE) *552*
Studies in Geography (US) *426*
Studies in Geography in Hungary (HU ISSN 0081-7961) *426*
Studies in German Literature (NE ISSN 0081-797X) *574*
Studies in Greek and Latin Linguistics (NE) *552*
Studies in Higher Education in Canada (CN ISSN 0081-7988) *340*
Studies in Hispanic Literatures (US) *574*
Studies in Historical and Political Science. Extra Volumes (US ISSN 0081-7996) *715*
Studies in Historical Archaeology *see* Australian Society for Historical Archaeology *58*
Studies in History and Philosophy. Pamphlet Series (US ISSN 0148-6543) *435, 691*
Studies in History and Social Sciences *see* Recherches d'Histoire et de Sciences Sociales *434*
Studies in History of Biology (US ISSN 0149-6700) *108*
Studies in Human Resources Development (US) *210*
Studies in Human Rights (US ISSN 0146-3586) *719, 723*
Studies in Imperialism (US) *715*
Studies in Indian Epigraphy/Bharatiya Purabhilekha Patrika (II) *552*
Studies in Inorganic Chemistry (NE) *251*
Studies in Inter-American Laws (US ISSN 0585-6795) *524*

Studies in International Affairs (US ISSN 0081-8046) *524, 723*
Studies in International Affairs (US ISSN 0081-802X) *715*
Studies in International and Comparative Politics (US) *715*
Studies in International Communism (US ISSN 0081-8054) *715*
Studies in International Economic Relations (US ISSN 0081-8062) *148, 198, 201*
Studies in International Economics (NE) *148*
Studies in International Finance (US ISSN 0081-8070) *176*
Studies in International Relations (BE) *723*
Studies in Irish History (CN ISSN 0081-8097) *463*
Studies in Italian Literature (NE ISSN 0081-8119) *574*
Studies in Japanese Culture (US ISSN 0081-8127) *445*
Studies in Jazz Research *see* Beitraege zur Jazzforschung *657*
Studies in Jewish Jurisprudence (US ISSN 0085-686X) *518*
Studies in Joint Disease (UK ISSN 0260-9320) *616*
Studies in Judaica (US ISSN 0585-6833) *771*
Studies in Labor and Social Law (UK) *211*
Studies in Labour History (UK) *211*
Studies in Land Use History and Landscape Change (CN ISSN 0225-4123) *389*
Studies in Language (US) *552*
Studies in Language and Linguistics (US ISSN 0586-6928) *552*
Studies in Language Companion Series (NE ISSN 0165-7763) *552, 574*
Studies in Language Disability and Remediation (UK ISSN 0144-3127) *323, 552*
Studies in Latin Literature and Its Influence *see* Greek and Latin Studies Series *259*
Studies in Law (US ISSN 0148-6551) *518*
Studies in Legal History (US) *518*
Studies in Librarianship (US ISSN 0081-8151) *536*
Studies in Library Management (US) *536*
Studies in Library Management (UK ISSN 0307-0808) *536*
Studies in Literature and Criticism (US) *574*
Studies in Logic and the Foundations of Mathematics (NE ISSN 0049-237X) *589*
Studies in Management Science and Systems (NE) *216*
Studies in Manuscript Illumination (US ISSN 0081-8178) *79*
Studies in Mathematical and Managerial Economics (NE ISSN 0081-8194) *216*
Studies in Mathematics (US ISSN 0081-8208) *589*
Studies in Mathematics (US ISSN 0081-8216) *589*
Studies in Mathematics and Its Applications (NE) *589*
Studies in Media Management (US) *216, 505*
Studies in Medieval and Reformation Thought (NE ISSN 0585-6914) *767*
Studies in Medieval and Renaissance History (CN ISSN 0081-8224) *463*
Studies in Medieval Culture (US ISSN 0085-6878) *436, 574*
Studies in Mediterranean Archaeology. Monograph Series (SW ISSN 0081-8232) *66, 260*
Studies in Mediterranean Archaeology. Pocket-Book Series (SW) *66, 260*
Studies in Middle Eastern History (US) *475*
Studies in Middle Eastern Literatures (US) *574*
Studies in Modern European History and Culture (US ISSN 0098-275X) *463*
Studies in Modern Hebrew Literature (US) *574*
Studies in Modern Thermodynamics (NE) *256*

Studies in Museology (II ISSN 0081-8259) *655*
Studies in Music (AT ISSN 0081-8267) *663*
Studies in Mycenaean Inscriptions and Dialect (UK ISSN 0081-8275) *260, 552*
Studies in Mycology (NE ISSN 0166-0616) *118*
Studies in Near Eastern Civilization (US ISSN 0081-8291) *816*
Studies in North European Archaeology *see* Studier i Nordisk Arkeologi *66*
Studies in Operations Research (US ISSN 0141-1004) *274*
Studies in Organic Chemistry (US) *254*
Studies in Oriental Culture (US ISSN 0081-8321) *445, 800*
Studies in Oriental Religions (GW ISSN 0340-6792) *771*
Studies in Philosophical Psychology (US) *738*
Studies in Philosophy (JA ISSN 0081-8380) *691*
Studies in Philosophy (NE ISSN 0081-8399) *691*
Studies in Philosophy & the History of Philosophy (US ISSN 0585-6965) *691*
Studies in Physical and Theoretical Chemistry (NE) *256*
Studies in Population (US) *729*
Studies in Population and Urban Demography (US ISSN 0147-1104) *729*
Studies in Pre-Columbian Art and Archaeology (US ISSN 0585-7023) *66, 79*
Studies in Public Communication (US ISSN 0585-7031) *265*
Studies in Public Economics (NE) *148*
Studies in Radiation Effects in Solids (US) *704*
Studies in Rajput History and Culture Series (II) *445*
Studies in Regional Science and Urban Economics (NE) *190*
Studies in Romance Languages (US ISSN 0085-6894) *574*
Studies in Rural Land Use (UK ISSN 0081-8453) *30*
Studies in Russian and East European History (UK) *463*
Studies in Scottish Literature (US ISSN 0039-3770) *574*
Studies in Semiotics and Literature (II) *552, 574*
Studies in Semitic Languages and Linguistics (NE ISSN 0081-8461) *552*
Studies in Social and Economic Demography (US) *729*
Studies in Social Anthropology (NE ISSN 0081-8496) *54*
Studies in Social Discontinuity (US) *816*
Studies in Social Economics (US) *148, 816*
Studies in Social Experimentation (US) *801, 817*
Studies in Social History (CN ISSN 0081-850X) *436*
Studies in Social History (NE) *801*
Studies in Social Life (NE ISSN 0081-8518) *817*
Studies in Social Policy and Welfare (UK) *809*
Studies in Social Theory (US ISSN 0148-656X) *817*
Studies in Society (AT ISSN 0156-4420) *817*
Studies in Sociology (II) *817*
Studies in Sociology and Social Anthropology (II) *817*
Studies in Spanish Literature (NE ISSN 0081-8534) *574*
Studies in Speleology (UK ISSN 0585-718X) *300*
Studies in Sport, Physical Education and Health (FI) *695, 822*
Studies in Statistical Mechanics (NE ISSN 0081-8542) *699*
Studies in Symbolic Interaction (US ISSN 0163-2396) *817*
Studies in the American Renaissance (US ISSN 0149-015X) *574*
Studies in the Development of African Resources (KE) *441*

Studies in the Economics of Poultry Farming in Punjab (II) *30,* 46
Studies in the Foundations, Methodology and Philosophy of Science (US ISSN 0081-8577) *792*
Studies in the Geography of Israel/ Mehkarim Be-Ge'ografyah Shel Erets-Yisrael (IS ISSN 0081-8585) *426*
Studies in the Germanic Languages and Literatures (US ISSN 0081-8593) *574*
Studies in the History of Art (US ISSN 0091-7338) *79*
Studies in the History of Christian Thought (NE ISSN 0081-8607) *767*
Studies in the History of Discoveries (US ISSN 0081-8615) *792, 853*
Studies in the History of Mathematics and Physical Sciences (US) *589, 699*
Studies in the History of Modern Science (NE) *792*
Studies in the History of Science (US) *801*
Studies in the Learning Sciences (FR) *323,* 738
Studies in the Logic of Science (US) 691, *792*
Studies in the Modern Russian Language (UK ISSN 0081-8631) *552*
Studies in the National Income and Expenditure of the United Kingdom (UK ISSN 0081-864X) *213*
Studies in the Natural Sciences (US) *792*
Studies in the Reformation (US) *436*
Studies in the Romance Languages and Literatures *see* North Carolina Studies in the Romance Languages and Literatures *569*
Studies in the Social Sciences (NE ISSN 0081-8674) *801*
Studies in the Social Sciences *see* West Georgia College Studies in the Social Sciences *802*
Studies in the Structure of Power: Decision Making in Canada (CN ISSN 0081-8690) *715*
Studies in the Theory of Science (SW ISSN 0081-8704) *792*
Studies in Transnational Legal Policy (US) *519*
Studies in Tropical Oceanography (US ISSN 0081-8720) *312*
Studies in Tudor and Stuart Literature (US) *574*
Studies in U.S. National Security (NE) *640*
Studies in Urban Geography (US ISSN 0586-5107) *426, 487*
Studies in Vermont Geology (US ISSN 0081-8747) *300*
Studies in Virgin Islands Librarianship (VI) *536*
Studies in Wage-Price Policy (US) *148,* 213
Studies in Welsh History (UK ISSN 0141-030X) *463*
Studies in World Civilization (US) *493*
Studies in Zambian Society (ZA) 441, *817*
Studies of Brain Function (US) *621*
Studies of Broadcasting (JA) *268*
Studies of Developing Countries (NE ISSN 0081-8771) *817*
Studies of Government Finance: Second Series (US) *232*
Studies of Law in Social Change and Development (SW ISSN 0348-1964) *519*
Studies of Nationalities in the USSR (US) *914*
Studies of Negro Employment (US ISSN 0081-878X) *211*
Studies of Urban Society (US ISSN 0081-8801) *487, 817*
Studies on Asia *see* Publications on Asia *445*
Studies on Asian Topics (UK ISSN 0142-6028) *671*
Studies on Current Health Problems (UK ISSN 0473-8837) *600, 754*
Studies on East Asia (US) *671*
Studies on Education (NE) *914*
Studies on Finland's Economic Growth *see* Suomen Pankki. Julkaisuja. Kasvututkimuksia *225*

Studies on Selected Development Problems in Various Countries in the Middle East (UN ISSN 0085-6908) *201*
Studies on Statistics (GW ISSN 0072-3967) *848*
Studies on Tax Administration Series (PN) *232*
Studies on Taxation and Economic Development (NE ISSN 0071-2191) 225, *232*
Studies on the Development of Behavior and the Nervous System (US ISSN 0093-3317) *621*
Studies on the Fauna of Suriname and Other Guyanas (NE ISSN 0300-5488) *130*
Studies on the Morphology and Systematics of Scale Insects (US) 95, *122,* 148
Studies on the Radioactive Contamination of the Sea. Annual Report (EI) *754*
Studies on the Soviet Union (GW) *715*
Studies over Internationaal Economisch Recht (NE) *914*
Studii Clasice (RM ISSN 0081-8844) *260*
Studii de Filozofie si Socialism Stiintific(RM) *691,* 715
Studii de Hidraulica (RM) *308*
Studii de Irigatii Si Desecari (RM) *898*
Studii de Literatura Universala si Comparata (RM ISSN 0081-8852) *574*
Studii de Slavistica (RM ISSN 0081-8860) *552*
Studii Istorice Sud-Est Europene (RM) *463*
Studii si Articole de Istorie (RM) *463*
Studii si Cercetari de Bibliologie. Serie Noua (RM ISSN 0081-8879) *95*
Studii si Cercetari de Istoria Artei. Seria Teatru-Muzica-Cinematografie (RM ISSN 0039-3991) 651, 663, *860*
Studii si Cercetari de Numismatica (RM ISSN 0081-8887) *478*
Studii si Materiale de Istorie Medie (RM) *463*
Studii si Materiale de Istorie Moderna (RM) *463*
Studium (AT ISSN 0311-2233) *260*
Studium Biblicum Franciscanum. Analecta (IS ISSN 0081-8909) *767*
Studium Biblicum Franciscanum. Collectio Major (IS ISSN 0081-8917) *767*
Studium Biblicum Franciscanum. Collectio Minor (IS ISSN 0081-8925) *767*
Studium Biblicum Franciscanum. Liber Annuus (IS ISSN 0081-8933) *767*
Studium Niemcoznawcze (PL ISSN 0081-8941) *463*
Study Abroad/Etudes a l'Etranger/ Estudios en el Extranjero (UN ISSN 0081-895X) *343*
Study Centre for Yugoslav Affairs. Review (UK ISSN 0585-7694) *715*
Study Group on Eighteenth-Century Russia. Newsletter (UK) *463*
Study in Denmark (US) *343*
Study in Denmark: Courses for Foreigners *see* Study in Denmark *343*
Study of Federal Tax Law. Income Tax Volume *see* Study of Federal Tax Law. Income Tax Volume: Business Enterprises *519*
Study of Federal Tax Law. Income Tax Volume *see* Study of Federal Tax Law. Income Tax Volume: Individuals *519*
Study of Federal Tax Law. Income Tax Volume: Business Enterprises (US ISSN 0362-2983) *519*
Study of Federal Tax Law. Income Tax Volume: Individuals (US ISSN 0362-5230) *519*
Study of Nursing Care: Research Project Series (UK ISSN 0302-1440) *614*
Study of Time (US) *84*
Stuttgarter Geographische Studien (GW) *426*
Style Auto (IT ISSN 0039-4254) *872*

Styrelsen foer Teknisk Utveckling Investigation *see* S T U Investigation *853*
Sub-Cellular Biochemistry (US) *112*
Subject Collections (US ISSN 0000-0140) *539*
Subject Directory of Special Libraries and Information Centers (US) *536*
Subject Guide to Books in Print (US ISSN 0000-0159) *95*
Subject Guide to Canadian Books in Print. (CN) *761*
Subject Guide to Children's Books in Print (US ISSN 0000-0167) *95*
Subject Guide to Microforms in Print (US ISSN 0090-290X) *95*
Subject Guide to Reprints (US ISSN 0149-810X) *95*
Subject Headings for Engineering *see* S H E *535*
Subject Index to Children's Magazines (US ISSN 0039-4351) 4, *257*
Subsaharan Africa Report (US) *190,* 715
Subscription Books Bulletin Reviews *see* Reference and Subscription Books Reviews *535*
Subsida Hagiographica (BE) *767*
Subsidia Mediaevalia (CN ISSN 0316-0769) *463*
Subsidia Scientifica Franciscalia (IT ISSN 0562-4649) *775*
Substance Abuse Book Review Index (CN ISSN 0228-8648) *287*
Successful Ventures in Contemporary Education in Oklahoma (US ISSN 0090-4023) *350*
Successful Writers and Editors Guidebook (US) *768*
Suction (US) *574*
Sudan. Department of Statistics. Internal Trade and Other Statistics (SJ) *182*
Sudan. Department of Statistics. National Income Accounts and Supporting Tables (SJ) *213*
Sudan. Department of Statistics. Statistical Yearbook (SJ) *848*
Sudan. Economic and Social Research Council. Bulletin (SJ) 190, *801*
Sudan. Economic and Social Research Council. Research Report (SJ) 190, *801*
Sudan. Ministry of Finance and National Economy. Annual Budget Speech, Proposals for the General Budget and the Development Budget(SJ) *746*
Sudan. Ministry of Finance and National Economy. Economic and Financial Research Section. Economic Survey (SJ) *190*
Sudan. Ministry of Finance and National Economy. General Budget: Review, Presentation and Analysis (SJ) *746*
Sudan. National Council for Research. Science Policy and Annual Report (SJ) *792*
Sudan. National Planning Commission. Economic Survey *see* Sudan. Ministry of Finance and National Economy. Economic and Financial Research Section. Economic Survey *190*
Sudan Commercial Bank. Report of the Board of Directors (SJ) *176*
Sudan Cotton Review (SJ ISSN 0562-5068) *39*
Sudan Economic and Social Research Council. Occasional Paper (SJ) 190, *801*
Sudan Law Journal and Reports (SJ ISSN 0585-8631) *519*
Sudan Notes and Records (SJ) *475*
Sudan Research Information Bulletin (SJ ISSN 0453-8129) *493, 792, 801*
Sudan Society/Al-Mujtama (SJ ISSN 0562-5130) *54*
Sudan Yearbook of Agricultural Statistics (SJ) *30*
SUDENE Plano de Acao *see* Brazil. Superintendencia do Desenvolvimento do Nordeste. SUDENE Plano de Acao *483*
Sudhoffs Archiv. Beihefte (GW ISSN 0341-0773) *600,* 792

SULPHUR INSTITUTE 1495

Suedost-Forschungen (GW ISSN 0081-9077) *463*
Suedostdeutsche Historische Kommission. Buchreihe (GW) *463*
Suedostdeutsches Archiv (GW ISSN 0081-9085) *403, 463*
Suedostdeutsches Kulturwerk, Munich. Kleine Suedostreihe (GW ISSN 0081-9093) *463*
Suedostdeutsches Kulturwerk, Munich. Schriftenreihen. Reihe A. Kultur und Dichtung (GW ISSN 0081-9107) *463,* 574
Suedostdeutsches Kulturwerk, Munich. Schriftenreihen. Reihe B. Wissenschaftliche Arbeiten (GW ISSN 0081-9115) *463*
Suedostdeutsches Kulturwerk, Munich. Schriftenreihen. Reihe C. Erinnerungen und Quellen (GW ISSN 0081-9123) *463*
Suedosteuropa-Bibliographie (GW ISSN 0081-9131) *95*
Suedosteuropa-Jahrbuch (GW ISSN 0081-914X) *463*
Suedosteuropa-Schriften (GW ISSN 0081-9158) *463*
Suedosteuropa-Studien (GW ISSN 0081-9166) *463*
Suedosteuropaeische Arbeiten (GW) *463*
Suelos *see* Argentina. Instituto Nacional de Tecnologia Agropecuaria. Suelos *33*
Suesswaren Jahrbuch (GW ISSN 0081-9174) *406*
Sugar Economy *see* Zuckerwirtschaftliches Taschenbuch *406*
Sugar Industry's Who's Who and Directory (II) 20, *98*
Sugar Technologists' Association of Trinidad and Tobago. Proceedings. (TR ISSN 0302-4555) *406*
Sugar y Azucar Yearbook (US ISSN 0081-9212) *406*
Suggested State Legislation (US ISSN 0070-1157) *746*
Sui Yuan Wen Hsien (CH) 445, *671*
Suid-Africaanse Vereniging van Raadgewende Ingenieurs. Gids van Geregistreede Firmas *see* South African Association of Consulting Engineers. Directory of Registered Firms *370*
Suid-Afrikaanse Argiefblad/South African Archives Journal (SA) *536*
Suid-Afrikaanse Biblioteekvereniging. Jaarverslag *see* South African Library Association. Annual Report *535*
Suid-Afrikaanse Buitelandse Handelsorgonisasie Jaarverslag *see* S A F T O Annual Report *197*
Suid-Afrikaanse Guernsey (SA ISSN 0081-9220) *46*
Suid-Afrikaanse Instituut van Internasionale Aangeleenthede. Bibliografiese Reeks *see* South African Institute of International Affairs. Bibliographical Series *718*
Suid-Afrikaanse Jaarboek vir Volkereg *see* South African Yearbook of International Law *524*
Suid-Afrikaanse Mediese Navorsingsraad. Jaarverslag *see* South African Medical Research Council. Annual Report *600*
Suid-Afrikaanse Tydskrif vir Kommunikasieafwykings *see* South African Journal of Communication Disorders *617*
Suid-Afrikaanse Reserwebank. Jaarlikse Ekonomiese Verslag *see* South African Reserve Bank. Annual Economic Report *190*
Suido Sangyo Shimbun *see* Water Japan *899*
Suiken Kagaku Kenkyujo Nenpo *see* Nagoya University. Water Research Institute. Annual Report *897*
Sul Filo del Tempo (IT) *715*
Sulfur Reports (US ISSN 0196-1772) *248, 254*
Sulphur in Agriculture (US ISSN 0160-0680) *20*
Sulphur Institute. Technical Bulletin (US ISSN 0081-9255) *39*
Sulphur Institute Journal *see* Sulphur in Agriculture *20*

Sulphur River (US) *582*
Sulu Studies (PH) *34, 403*
Sumer (IQ ISSN 0081-9271) *66*
Sumitomo Bulletin of Industrial Health/ Sumitomo Sangyo Eisei (JA ISSN 0081-928X) *496, 695*
Sumitomo Sangyo Eisei *see* Sumitomo Bulletin of Industrial Health *496*
Summaries in Important Labour Judgements (II) *519*
Summary, Annual Meeting of the Southern Legislative Conference of the Council of State Governments *see* Council of State Governments. Southern Legislative Conference. Summary, Annual Meeting *741*
Summary Information on Master of Social Work Programs (US) *340, 809*
Summary of Awards *see* U.S. National Science Foundation. Division of Environmental Systems and Resources. Summary of Awards *915*
Summary of Congress (US ISSN 0146-2156) *716*
Summary of Expenditure Data for Michigan Public Schools (US ISSN 0094-8268) *323*
Summary of Ground Water Data for Tennessee (US ISSN 0093-0539) *898*
Summary of Kentucky Education *see* Summary of Kentucky Education Statistics *323*
Summary of Kentucky Education Statistics (US ISSN 0362-6679) *323*
Summary of Marine Activities of the Coastal Plains Region (US) *914*
Summary of Mineral Industry Activities in Colorado (US) *647*
Summary of Postgraduate Diplomas and Courses in Medicine (UK ISSN 0302-3494) *340*
Summary of State Laws and Regulations Relating to Distilled Spirits (US ISSN 0081-931X) *86*
Summary of U.S. Export and Import Merchandise Trade *see* Foreign Trade Reports. Summary of U.S. Export and Import Merchandise Trade *195*
Summary Proceedings, A N A House of Delegates *see* American Nurses' Association. House of Delegates. Summary Proceedings *613*
Summary Report - Food Protection and Toxicology Center, University of California, Davis *see* University of California, Davis. Food Protection and Toxicology Center. Summary Report *686*
Summer Breezes (CN ISSN 0226-7004) *258, 822*
Summer Computer Simulation Conference. Proceedings (US ISSN 0094-7474) *274*
Summer Employment Directory of the United States (US ISSN 0081-9352) *668*
Summer Institute in Linguistics. Descriptive and Applied Linguistics (JA) *552*
Summer Institute in Linguistics. Studies in Descriptive and Applied Linguistics *see* Summer Institute in Linguistics. Descriptive and Applied Linguistics *552*
Summer Institute of Linguistics. Language Data. African Series (US) *552*
Summer Institute of Linguistics. Language Data. Amerindian Series (US) *552*
Summer Institute of Linguistics. Language Data. Asian-Pacific Series (US) *552*
Summer Institute of Linguistics. Publications Catalog (US) *555*
Summer Institute of Linguistics. Serie Linguistica (BL) *552*
Summer Institute of Linguistics. Work Papers (US) *552*
Summer Institute of Linguistics Museum of Anthropology Publication *see* S. I. L. Museum of Anthropology Publication *550*

Summer Institute of Linguistics Publications in Linguistics and Related Fields *see* S I L Publications in Linguistics and Related Fields *550*
Summer Study Abroad *see* Learning Traveler. Vacation Study Abroad *342*
Summer Theatre Directory (US ISSN 0081-9387) *860*
Sun and Moon Tables for Ghana *see* Ghana. Meteorological Department. Sun and Moon Tables for Ghana *633*
Sun Tracks (US) *393*
Sunbury Poetry Series by Women (US) *582*
Sung Studies Newsletter *see* Bulletin of Sung and Yuan Studies *669*
Sunset Christmas Ideas and Answers (US ISSN 0090-2578) *476*
Sunset Garden Ideas and Answers (US) *416*
Sunset Joy of Gardening *see* Sunset Garden Ideas and Answers *416*
Sunset Western Travel Adventures (US ISSN 0191-3468) *891*
Sunspark *see* Guide to Alternative Periodicals *91*
Suomalainen Tiedeakatemia. Vuosikirja *see* Academia Scientiarum Fennica. Yearbook *778*
Suomalais-Ugrilaisen Seura. Aikakauskirja/Societe Finno-Ougrienne. Journal (FI ISSN 0355-0214) *54, 552*
Suomen Aikakauslehti-Indeksi/Index to Finnish Periodicals (FI ISSN 0081-9395) *4*
Suomen Betoniteollisuuden Keskusjarjesto. Julkaisu/Association of the Concrete Industry in Finland. Publication (FI) *139*
Suomen Geodeettisen Laitoksen. Julkaisuja/Finnish Geodetic Institute. Publications/Finnische Geodaetische Institut. Veroeffentlichungen (FI ISSN 0085-6932) *306*
Suomen Hammaslaakariseura. Toimituksia. Supplementa/Finnish Dental Society. Proceedings. Supplement (FI ISSN 0355-4651) *610*
Suomen Historiallinen Seura. Kasikirjoja (FI ISSN 0081-9417) *438*
Suomen Historian Laehteitae/Source Material of Finnish History (FI ISSN 0081-9425) *463*
Suomen Kalatalous (FI ISSN 0085-6940) *400*
Suomen Kirjallisuus Vuosiluettelo/Finnish National Bibliography Annual Volume/Finlands Litteratur Aarskatalog (FI ISSN 0355-0001) *95*
Suomen Naishammaslaakarit Ryhma. Julkaisu (FI ISSN 0081-9433) *610*
Suomen Obligaatiokirja/Finnish Bond Issues/Obligationsbok foer Finland (FI ISSN 0585-9581) *205*
Suomen Osallistuminen Yhdistyneiden Kansakuntien Toimintaan (FI ISSN 0081-9441) *723*
Suomen Pankki. Julkaisuja. Kasvututkimuksia/Bank of Finland. Publications. Studies on Finland's Economic Growth (FI ISSN 0355-6050) *225*
Suomen Pankki. Julkaisuja. Serie A/Bank of Finland. Publications. Series A/Finlands Bank. Publikationer. Serie A (FI ISSN 0355-6034) *148*
Suomen Pankki. Julkaisuja. Serie B/Bank of Finland. Publications. Series B/Finlands Bank. Publikationer. Serie B (FI ISSN 0357-4776) *148*
Suomen Pankki. Julkaisuja. Serie C/Bank of Finland. Publications. Series C/Finlands Bank. Publikationer. Serie C (FI ISSN 0081-9492) *149*
Suomen Pankki. Julkaisuja. Serie D/Bank of Finland. Publications. Series D/Finlands Bank. Publikationer. Serie D (FI ISSN 0081-6042) *149*

Suomen Pankki. Taloustieteellinen Tutkimuslaitos. Julkaisuja. Series Kasvututkimuksia *see* Suomen Pankki. Julkaisuja. Kasvututkimuksia *225*
Suomen Pankki. Vuosikirja *see* Bank of Finland. Yearbook *170*
Suomen Pankki Series D. Mimeographed Series *see* Suomen Pankki. Julkaisuja. Serie D *149*
Suomen Pankki Taloustieteellinen Tutkimuslaitos. Julkaisuja. Series A: Taloudellisia Selvityksia *see* Suomen Pankki. Julkaisuja. Serie A *148*
Suomen Standardisoimisliitto Catalogue *see* S F S Catalogue *637*
Suomen Teollisuusliitto. Jasenluettelo/Finlands Industrifoerbund. Medlemsfoerteckning/Federation of Finnish Industries. List of Members (FI) *242*
Suomen Tilastollinen Vuosikirja/Statistisk Aarsbok Foer Finland/Statistical Yearbook of Finland (FI ISSN 0081-5063) *848*
Suomen Vakuutusvuosikirja/Finnish Insurance Yearbook (FI ISSN 0356-7826) *501*
Suomi Merella (FI ISSN 0039-5633) *640*
Super-8 Journal *see* Amateurfilm Journal *648*
Supermarket Industry Speaks *see* Food Marketing Industry Speaks *407*
Supermarket Trends (US ISSN 0163-4488) *407*
Supplements to Electroencephalography and Clinical Neurophysiology (NE) *621*
Supplementum Epigraphicum Graecum (NE) *260*
Supply and Demand: Educational Personnel in Delaware (US ISSN 0094-2308) *323*
Supreme Court Gazette (AT) *519*
Supreme Court Historical Society. Yearbook (US ISSN 0362-5249) *284, 519*
Supreme Court Law Review (CN ISSN 0228-0108) *519*
Supreme Court Practice (UK ISSN 0039-5978) *519*
Supreme Court Review (US ISSN 0081-9557) *519*
Surface and Colloid Science (US ISSN 0081-9573) *914*
Surface and Defect Properties of Solids *see* Chemical Physics of Solids and Their Surfaces *254*
Surface Technology (SZ) *250*
Surface Water Year Book of Great Britain (UK ISSN 0081-959X) *898*
Surfaces (Paris, 1978) (FR) *691*
Surfactant Science Series (US ISSN 0081-9603) *108, 248*
Surfboard Builders' Yearbook (US ISSN 0081-9611) *822*
Surgery Annual (US ISSN 0081-9638) *625*
Surgery Yearbook (MX) *625*
Surgical Forum *see* Forum on Fundamental Surgical Problems *624*
Surgical Pathology (US ISSN 0081-9646) *625*
Surgical Trade Buyers Guide (US ISSN 0081-9654) *625*
Surinam. Algemeen Bureau voor de Statistiek. Kwartaal Statistiek van de Industriele Produktie (SR) *165*
Surinam. Algemeen Bureau voor de Statistiek. Nationale Rekeningen (SR) *848*
Surinam. Centraal Bureau Luchtkartering. Jaarverslag (SR) *10, 426*
Surmach (UK ISSN 0491-6204) *436, 640, 716*
Surplus Dealers Directory (US ISSN 0081-9662) *219, 242*

Surrealist Transformaction (UK ISSN 0039-6168) *79, 493, 574*
Surrey Archaeological Collections (UK ISSN 0309-7803) *66*
Surrey Archaeological Society. Research Volumes (UK ISSN 0308-342X) *66*
Surrey Papers in Economics (UK ISSN 0081-9670) *149*
Survey of Biological Progress (US ISSN 0081-9697) *108*
Survey of Buying Power (US) *213, 219*
Survey of Consumer Finances *see* Surveys of Consumers *213*
Survey of Current Jewish Research (US) *340, 393, 771*
Survey of German Federal Statistics/Apercu de la Statistique Federale Allemande (GW) *848*
Survey of Grant-Making Foundations (US) *493*
Survey of Hospital Charges *see* Hospital Statistics; Data from American Hospital Association Annual Survey *841*
Survey of India's Exports (II ISSN 0537-1120) *180*
Survey of Industry in Israel *see* Israel. Ministry of Commerce and Industry. Surveys and Development Plans of Industry in Israel *223*
Survey of International Affairs (US) *723*
Survey of Living Costs in Major Cities Worldwide (SZ) *165*
Survey of Local Chambers of Commerce (US ISSN 0069-2441) *180*
Survey of London (UK ISSN 0081-9751) *79*
Survey of Migration in Bangkok Metropolis (TH) *732*
Survey of New Products Introduced by N.Y.S.E. Listed Companies *see* Chemical New Product Directory *217*
Survey of New Products Introduced by N.Y.S.E. Listed Companies *see* Electronics New Product Directory *218*
Survey of Progress in Chemistry (US ISSN 0081-976X) *248*
Survey of Race Relations in South Africa (SA ISSN 0081-9778) *719*
Survey of Retirement, Thrift and Profit Sharing Plans Covering Salaried Employees of the 50 Largest U. S. Industrial Companies (US ISSN 0190-1133) *211, 501*
Survey of Salaries and Employee Benefits of Private and Public Employers in Arizona. *see* Joint Governmental Salary Survey : Arizona *208*
Survey of Sources Newsletter (US ISSN 0362-3246) *108, 472*
Survey of State Travel Offices (US) *891*
Survey of the Activities of Scientific Unions; Special and Scientific Committees of I C S U in the Field of Information (FR) *536, 792*
Survey of the Emerging Solar Energy Industry (US) *364, 699*
Surveying and Mapping *see* American Society of Civil Engineers. Surveying and Mapping Division. Journal *374*
Surveying News *see* Vermessungs-Informationen *377*
Surveyor (US) *108*
Surveys of Applied Economics (US) *149*
Surveys of Consumers (US ISSN 0085-3410) *213*
Surveys of the Position of Various Pests and Diseases in Europe and the Mediterranean Area *see* European and Mediterranean Plant Protection Organization. Publications. Series B: Plant Health Newsletter *35*
Surviving in America (US) *574*
Susquehanna River Basin Commission. Annual Report (US ISSN 0094-6427) *898*
Susquehanna River Basin Commission. Publication (US) *898*
Susquehannock Hiker (US) *831*
Sussex Essays in Anthropology (UK) *54*

Svensk Bergs- och Brukstidning (SW ISSN 0039-6435) 647
Svensk Exegetisk Aarsbok (SW) 768
Svensk Foersaekrings-Aarsbok/Swedish Insurance Year-Book (SW ISSN 0081-9794) 501
Svensk Obligationsbok (SW) 176
Svensk Tidskrift foer Musikforskning/Swedish Journal of Musicology (SW ISSN 0081-9816) 663
Svensk Tidskriftsfoerteckning/Current Swedish Periodicals (SW ISSN 0586-0431) 95
Svenska Arkivsamfundet. Skriftserie (SW ISSN 0562-7451) 436, 536
Svenska Barnboksinstitutet. Skrifter/Swedish Institute for Children's Books. Studies (SW) 258, 536
Svenska Bokfoerlaeggarefoereningen. Matrikel (SW ISSN 0081-9859) 760
Svenska Filminstitutet. Dokumentationsavdelningen. Skrifter (SW ISSN 0081-9867) 651
Svenska Handelsbanken. Annual Report(SW ISSN 0081-9913) 176
Svenska Handelsbanken. Annual Report and Auditors' Report see Svenska Handelsbanken. Annual Report 176
Svenska Historiska Foereningen. Skrifter (SW) 463
Svenska Institutet i Athen. Skrifter (GR ISSN 0081-9921) 66, 260
Svenska Institutet i Rom. Skrifter. Acta Series Prima (IT ISSN 0081-993X) 66, 260
Svenska Kraftverksfoereningens Publikationer (SW ISSN 0039-6931) 359
Svenska Litteratursaellskapet i Finland. Skrifter (FI ISSN 0039-6842) 436, 552
Svenska Livsmedelsinstitutet Information see S I K Information 405
Svenska Mejiernas Riksfoerening. Meddelande (SW ISSN 0039-6869) 41
Svenska Riksbyggen. Byggteknisk Information (SW ISSN 0068-0613) 139
Svenska Traeforskningsinstitutet. Meddelande. Series A (SW ISSN 0085-6983) 410
Svenska Traeskyddinstitutet. Meddelanden/Swedish Wood Preservation Institute. Reports (SW ISSN 0346-7090) 413
Svenska Vattenkraftfoereningens Publikationer see Svenska Kraftverksfoereningens Publikationer 359
Svenskt Musikhistoriskt Arkiv. Bulletin (SW ISSN 0586-0709) 663
Svenskt Varumaerkesarkiv/Swedish Trademark Archive (SW) 677
Sverige-EG (SW) 723
Sverige-Europeiska Gemenskaperna see Sverige-EG 723
Sveriges Foerfattarfoerbund. Medlemsfoerteckning (SW) 98, 574
Sveriges Jaernvaegar/Railways of Sweden (SW ISSN 0081-9964) 874
Sveriges Lantbruksuniversitet. Institutionen foer Vaextodling. Rapporter och Arhandlingar (SW) 20
Sveriges Lantbruksuniversitet. Institutionen foer Virkeslaera. Rapporter (SW ISSN 0348-4599) 410
Sveriges Lantbruksuniversitet. Institutionen foer Virkeslaera. Uppsatser (SW) 410
Sveriges Riksbank. Aarsbok see Sveriges Riksbank. Statistisk Aarsbok 176
Sveriges Riksbank. Foervaltningsberaettelse (SW) 176
Sveriges Riksbank. Statistisk Aarsbok/Central Bank of Sweden. Statistical Yearbook (SW ISSN 0348-7342) 176
Sveriges Trae- och Byggvaruhandlares Centralfoerbund Matrikel see S T C Matrikel 241
Sveriges 1000 Stoersta Foeretag/1000 Largest Companies in Sweden (SW) 225

Svetovy Kongres Slovakov. Bulletin. (CN ISSN 0317-4018) 393, 626
Svetsaren (GW) 630
Sveuciliste u Zagrebu. Fakultet Strojarstva i Brodogradnje. Zbornik Radova (YU ISSN 0350-3097) 383, 881
Swamp Gas Journal (CN ISSN 0707-7106) 10
Swansea Geographer (UK ISSN 0081-9980) 426
Swarbica Journal (II) 445, 536
Swaziland. Central Statistical Office. Annual Statistical Bulletin (SQ ISSN 0586-1357) 848
Swaziland. Central Statistical Office. Annual Survey of Swazi Nation Land(SQ) 848
Swaziland. Central Statistical Office. Capital Fund Estimates (SQ) 176
Swaziland. Central Statistical Office. Census of Individual Tenure Farms (SQ) 20
Swaziland. Central Statistical Office. Commercial Timber Plantation and Wood Products Statistics (SQ) 412, 848
Swaziland. Central Statistical Office. Employment and Wages (SQ) 211
Swaziland. Central Statistical Office. Recurrent Estimates of Public Expenditure (SQ) 746
Swaziland. Economic Planning Office. Economic Review (SQ) 190
Swaziland. Geological Survey and Mines Department. Annual Report (SQ ISSN 0081-9999) 300
Swaziland. Geological Survey and Mines Department. Bulletin (SQ ISSN 0082-0008) 300
Swaziland. Ministry of Agriculture. Annual Report (SQ) 20
Swaziland. Monetary Authority. Annual Report (SQ) 232
Swaziland National Bibliography (SQ) 95, 761
Swaziland National Centre. Yearbook see Swaziland National Museum. Yearbook 441
Swaziland National Museum. Yearbook (SQ) 441
Sweden. Finansdepartmentet. Regeringens Budgetfoerslag (SW) 232
Sweden. Fisheries Board. Series Hydrography. Reports see Sweden. Fishery Board. Institute of Marine Research. Report 108
Sweden. Fishery Board. Institute of Marine Research. Report (SW ISSN 0346-8666) 108
Sweden. Konjunkturinstitutet. Occasional Paper (SW ISSN 0082-0067) 149
Sweden. Luftfartsverket. Aarsbok (SW ISSN 0348-2251) 848, 866
Sweden. Medicinalvaesendet. Foerfattningssamling see Sweden. Socialstyrelsen. Foerfattningssamling: Medical 600
Sweden. Medicinalvaesendet. Foerfattningssamling see Sweden. Socialstyrelsen. Foerfattningssamling: Social 809
Sweden. National Road and Traffic Research Institute. Annual Report see Sweden. Statens Vaeg- och Trafikinstitut. Verksamhetsberaettelse 876
Sweden. Nationalmuseum. Skriftserie (SW ISSN 0081-5683) 655
Sweden. Patent- och Registereringsverket. Aarsberaettelse/Sweden. Royal Patent and Registration Office. Annual Report (SW) 677
Sweden. Riksarkivet. Meddelanden (SW ISSN 0039-6893) 463, 536
Sweden. Riksdagen. Foerteckning Oever Riksdagens Ledamoeter (SW) 716
Sweden. Riksdagen. Riksdag see Sweden. Riksdagen. Riksdagen Aarsbok 716
Sweden. Riksdagen. Riksdagen Aarsbok(SW) 716
Sweden. Riksfoersaekringsverket. Allmaen Foersaekring (SW ISSN 0082-0075) 501

Sweden. Riksfoersaekringsverket. Yrkesskador (SW ISSN 0562-861X) 501
Sweden. Riksgaeldskontoret. Aarsbok (SW ISSN 0082-0091) 176
Sweden. Riksrevisionsverket. Statens Finanser (SW ISSN 0079-7561) 232
Sweden. Royal Patent and Registration Office. Annual Report see Sweden. Patent- och Registereringsverket. Aarsberaettelse 677
Sweden. Sjukvaardens och Socialvaardens Planerings- och Rationaliseringsinstitut. S P R I Informerar (SW ISSN 0346-8445) 754
Sweden. Sjukvaardens och Socialvaardens Planerings- och Rationaliseringsinstitut. S P R I Raad(SW ISSN 0082-0113) 754
Sweden. Sjukvaardens och Socialvaardens Planerings- och Rationaliseringsinstitut. S P R I Rapport (SW ISSN 0586-1691) 754
Sweden. Sjukvaardens och Socialvaardens Planerings- och Rationaliseringsinstitut. S P R I Specifikationer (SW ISSN 0082-0105) 754
Sweden. Socialstyrelsen. Foerfattningssamling: Medical (SW ISSN 0346-6000) 600
Sweden. Socialstyrelsen. Foerfattningssamling: Social (SW ISSN 0346-6019) 809
Sweden. Socialstyrelsen. Legitimerade Laekare/Authorized Physicians (SW) 600
Sweden. Socialstyrelsen. Redoviser (SW) 809
Sweden. Statens Arbetsgivarverk. Arbetsgivarverket Informerar (SW) 211
Sweden. Statens Arbetsgivarverk. Foereskrifter om Statlight Tjaenstepensionering; F S P (SW) 501
Sweden. Statens Arbetsgivarverk. Foerfattningar om Statlight Regleradtjaenster; F S T (SW) 507
Sweden. Statens Avtalsverk. Foereskrifter om Statlight Tjaenstepensionering; F S P see Sweden. Statens Arbetsgivarverk. Foereskrifter om Statlight Tjaenstepensionering; F S P 501
Sweden. Statens Avtalsverk. Foerfattningar om Statlight Regleradtjaenster; F S T see Sweden. Statens Arbetsgivarverk. Foerfattningar om Statlight Regleradtjaenster; F S T 507
Sweden. Statens Avtalsverk. Information Fraan S A V see Sweden. Statens Arbetsgivarverk. Arbetsgivarverket Informerar 211
Sweden. Statens Institut foer Konsumentfraagor. Meddelar (SW ISSN 0082-0121) 280
Sweden. Statens Jaernvaegars Centralfoervaltning. Geoteknik och Ingenjoergeologi. Meddelanden (SW) 853
Sweden. Statens Jaernvaegars Centralfoervaltning. Geotekniska Kontoret. Meddelanden see Sweden. Statens Jaernvaegars Centralfoervaltning. Geoteknik och Ingenjoergeologi. Meddelanden 853
Sweden. Statens Konsumentraad. Verksamhetsberaettelse (SW) 219
Sweden. Statens Naturvaardsverk. Naturvaardsverkets Aarsbok (SW ISSN 0347-8173) 278
Sweden. Statens Raad Foer Byggnadsforskning. Current Projects (SW) 139
Sweden. Statens Raad foer Byggnadsforskning. Document (SW ISSN 0586-6766) 139, 377, 487
Sweden. Statens Raad foer Byggnadsforskning. Informationsblad (SW ISSN 0585-3400) 139, 377, 487
Sweden. Statens Raad foer Byggnadsforskning. Rapport (SW) 139, 377, 487

Sweden. Statens Raad Foer Byggnadsforskning. Synopses (SW) 139
Sweden. Statens Raad foer Byggnadsforskning. Verksamhetsplan (SW) 139, 377, 487
Sweden. Statens Vaeg- och Trafikinstitut. Rapport (SW ISSN 0347-6030) 876
Sweden. Statens Vaeg- och Trafikinstitut. Verksamhetsberaettelse(SW ISSN 0347-6057) 876
Sweden. Statistiska Centralbyraan. Allmaan Fastighetstaxering (SW) 489
Sweden. Statistiska Centralbyraan. Arbetskraftunderoekningen. Arsmedeltal (SW) 165
Sweden. Statistiska Centralbyraan. Befolkningsfoeraendringar (SW ISSN 0082-0156) 729
Sweden. Statistiska Centralbyraan. Folkmaengd (SW ISSN 0082-0164) 729
Sweden. Statistiska Centralbyraan. Industri (SW ISSN 0082-0172) 165
Sweden. Statistiska Centralbyraan. Information i Prognosfragor/Forecasting Information (SW ISSN 0082-0180) 165
Sweden. Statistiska Centralbyraan. Jordbruksstatistisk Aarsbok (SW ISSN 0082-0199) 25
Sweden. Statistiska Centralbyraan. Kommunal Personal (SW ISSN 0082-0202) 165
Sweden. Statistiska Centralbyraan. Levnadsfoerhaallanden Aarsbok/Living Conditions Yearbook (SW) 848
Sweden. Statistiska Centralbyraan. Loener (SW ISSN 0082-0210) 165
Sweden. Statistiska Centralbyraan. Meddelanden i Samordningsfraagor (SW ISSN 0082-0229) 848
Sweden. Statistiska Centralbyraan. Statistiska Meddelanden. Subgroup Am (Labor Market) (SW ISSN 0082-0237) 165
Sweden. Statistiska Centralbyraan. Statistiska Meddelanden. Subgroup Be (Population) (SW ISSN 0082-0245) 438, 732
Sweden. Statistiska Centralbyraan. Statistiska Meddelanden. Subgroup Bo (Housing and Construction) (SW ISSN 0085-6991) 141, 848
Sweden. Statistiska Centralbyraan. Statistiska Meddelanden. Subgroup H (Trade) (SW ISSN 0082-0261) 165
Sweden. Statistiska Centralbyraan. Statistiska Meddelanden. Subgroup I (Manufacturing) (SW ISSN 0082-027X) 165
Sweden. Statistiska Centralbyraan. Statistiska Meddelanden. Subgroup J (Agriculture) (SW ISSN 0082-0288) 25
Sweden. Statistiska Centralbyraan. Statistiska Meddelanden. Subgroup N (National Accounts and Finance) (SW ISSN 0082-0296) 165
Sweden. Statistiska Centralbyraan. Statistiska Meddelanden. Subgroup P (Prices and Price Indices) (SW ISSN 0082-030X) 165
Sweden. Statistiska Centralbyraan. Statistiska Meddelanden. Subgroup R (Judicial Statistics. Law and Social Welfare) (SW ISSN 0082-0318) 521
Sweden. Statistiska Centralbyraan. Statistiska Meddelanden. Subgroup S (Social Welfare Statistics) (SW ISSN 0082-0326) 811
Sweden. Statistiska Centralbyraan. Statistiska Meddelanden. Subgroup T (Transport and Other Forms of Communication) (SW ISSN 0082-0334) 266, 866
Sweden. Statistiska Centralbyraan. Statistiska Meddelanden. Subgroup U (Education and Culture) (SW ISSN 0082-0342) 328
Sweden. Statistiska Centralbyraan. Urval Skriftseries/Selection Series (SW ISSN 0082-0350) 848

Sweden. Statistiska Centralbyraan. Utbildningsstatistisk/Swedish Educational Statistics (SW) *323*
Sweden. Statistiska Centralbyraan. Utrikeshandel/Foreign Trade (SW ISSN 0082-0369) *165*
Sweden. Sveriges Geologiska Undersoekning. Jordmagnetiska Publikationer/Geomagnetic Publications (SW ISSN 0075-403X) *300*
Sweden. Sveriges Geologiska Undersoekning. Serie C. Avhandlingar och Uppsatser/ Memoirs and Notices (SW ISSN 0082-0024) *300*
Sweden. Sveriges Geologiska Undersoekning.Serie Ca. Avhandlingar och Uppsatser i Kvarto/Notices in Quarto and Folio (SW ISSN 0082-0016) *300*
Sweden. Universitetskanslersaembetet. Educational Development *see* R & D in Higher Education *339*
Sweden. Universitetskanslersaembetet. Hoegre Utbildning och Forskning (SW) *340*
Sweden Institute of Marine Research. Series Biology. Reports *see* Sweden. Fishery Board. Institute of Marine Research. Report *108*
Swedish Archaeological Bibliography (SW ISSN 0586-2000) *68*
Swedish Budget (SW ISSN 0082-0393) *232*
Swedish Building Codes and Standards Index *see* Byggnormindex *140*
Swedish Building Research News (SW) *139*
Swedish Educational Statistics *see* Sweden. Statistiska Centralbyraan. Utbildningsstatistisk/Swedish Educational Statistics *323*
Swedish Film Annual *see* Filmaarsboken *649*
Swedish Food Institute. Annual Report (SW) *406*
Swedish Geotechnical Institute. Reports *see* Statens Geotekniska Institut. Rapports *306*
Swedish Institute for Children's Books. Studies *see* Svenska Barnboksinstitutet. Skrifter *258*
Swedish Insurance Year-Book *see* Svensk Foersaekrings-Aarsbok *501*
Swedish Journal of Musicology *see* Svensk Tidskrift foer Musikforskning *663*
Swedish Machine Tools/Machines Outils Suedoises/Machines Utiles Suedoises (US) *583*
Swedish Natural Science Research Council. Ecological Bulletins (SW ISSN 0587-1433) *389*
Swedish Natural Science Research Council. Swedish Committee on Research Economics. FEK Reports (SW) *149*
Swedish Nutrition Foundation. Symposia (SW ISSN 0082-0415) *666*
Swedish Social Security Scheme (SW ISSN 0082-0083) *501*
Swedish State Company. Annual Report *see* Statsfoeretag. Aarsredovisning *225*
Swedish Steel Manual (SW) *630*
Swedish Theological Institute, Jerusalem. Annual (SW ISSN 0082-0423) *768*
Swedish Trademark Archive *see* Svenskt Varumaerkesarkiv *677*
Swedish Wood Preservation Institute. Reports *see* Svenska Traeskyddinstitutet. Meddelanden *413*
Sweet's Canadian Construction Catalogue File (CN ISSN 0082-0431) *139*
Sweet's Engineering Catalog File. Summary Edition: Mechanical, Sanitary and Related Products (US ISSN 0361-1388) *139*
Sweet's Industrial Construction & Renovation File with Plant Engineering Extension Market List (US ISSN 0094-825X) *139*

Sweet's Plant Engineering Extension Industrial Construction and Renovation File *see* Sweet's System for the Industrial Construction & Renovation Market *370*
Sweet's System for the Engineering Market (US) *370*
Sweet's System for the Industrial Construction & Renovation Market (US ISSN 0092-8763) *370*
Swiatowit (PL ISSN 0082-044X) *66*
Swimming & Diving Case Book *see* Swimming and Diving Rules *822*
Swimming and Diving Rules (US ISSN 0163-2884) *822*
Swimming Pool Weekly/Age - Data and Reference Annual (US ISSN 0082-0466) *822*
Swimming Rules *see* Swimming and Diving Rules *822*
Swiss Bank Corporation. Report of the Board of Directors to the Annual General Meeting of Shareholders (SZ) *177*
Swiss Biographical Index of Prominent Persons *see* Annuaire Suisse du Monde et des Affaires *96*
Swiss Federal Observatory, Zurich. Publications (SZ) *84*
Swiss Financial Year Book (SZ) *190*
Swiss Political Science Yearbook *see* Annuaire Suisse de Science Politique *708*
Swiss Society of Plastic and Reconstructive Surgeons. Proceedings (of) Annual Meeting (NE ISSN 0082-0482) *625*
Swiss Studies in English *see* Schweizer Anglistische Arbeiten *550*
Switching and Automata Theory Conference. Record (US ISSN 0082-0490) *359*
Switzerland. Commission de Recherches Economiques. Etudes Occasionnelles *see* Switzerland. Kommission fuer Konjunkturfragen. Allfaellige Studien *149*
Switzerland. Directorate General of Customs. Annual Report (SZ) *165, 848*
Switzerland. Eidgenoessische Anstalt fuer das Forstliche Versuchswesen. Berichte (SZ) *410*
Switzerland. Eidgenoessische Anstalt fuer das Forstliche Versuchswesen. Mitteilungen (SZ) *411*
Switzerland. Kommission fuer Konjunkturfragen. Allfaellige Studien(SZ) *149*
Switzerland. Schweizerische Anstalt fuer das Forstliche Versuchswesen. Mitteilungen *see* Switzerland. Eidgenoessische Anstalt fuer das Forstliche Versuchswesen. Mitteilungen *411*
Switzerland. Statistisches Amt. Eingefuehrte Motorfahrzeuge: In Verkehr Gesetzte Neue Motorfahrzeuge *see* Switzerland. Statistisches Amt. In Verkehr Gesetzte Neue Motorfahrzeuge/ Vehicules a Moteur Neufs Mis en Circulation *866*
Switzerland. Statistisches Amt. Eingefuehrte Motorfahrzeuge; in Verkehr Gesetzte Neue Motorfahrzeuge *see* Switzerland. Statistisches Amt. Eingefuehrte Motorfahrzeuge/Vehicules a Moteur Importes *866*
Switzerland. Statistisches Amt. Eingefuehrte Motorfahrzeuge/ Vehicules a Moteur Importes (SZ) *866*
Switzerland. Statistisches Amt. Heiraten, Lebendgeborene und Gestorbene in den Gemeinden/ Mariages, Naissances et Deces dans les Communes (SZ) *848*
Switzerland. Statistisches Amt. In Verkehr Gesetzte Neue Motorfahrzeuge/Vehicules a Moteur Neufs Mis en Circulation (SZ) *866*
Switzerland. Statistisches Amt. Schuelerstatistik/Statistique des Eleves (SZ) *328, 848*

Switzerland. Statistisches Amt. Strassenverkehrsunfaelle/Accidents de la Circulation Routiere en Suisse (SZ) *872*
Switzerland: Directorate General of Customs. Annual Statistics (SZ ISSN 0081-525X) *165, 848*
Sword of Light *see* Ais-Eiri *391*
Sydney Law Review (AT ISSN 0082-0512) *519*
Sydney Observatory Papers (AT ISSN 0085-7009) *84*
Sydney Speleological Society. Communications *see* Sydney Speleological Society. Occasional Paper *300*
Sydney Speleological Society. Occasional Paper (AT) *300*
Sydney Stock Exchange. Research and Statistical Department. Company Review Service *see* Sydney Stock Exchange. Research Department, Company Review Service *205*
Sydney Stock Exchange. Research Department, Company Review Service. (AT) *205*
Sydney Studies in Literature (AT ISSN 0082-0520) *574*
Sydowia: Annales Mycologici (AU ISSN 0082-0598) *118*
Sylloge Nummorum Graecorum (US ISSN 0271-3993) *478*
Sylloge Nummorum Graecorum Deutschland (GW ISSN 0082-061X) *66, 478*
Sylloge of Coins of the British Isles (US ISSN 0082-0628) *478*
Symbolae. Series A (BE) *260*
Symbolae Botanicae Upsalienses (SW ISSN 0082-0644) *118*
Symbolae Osloenses (NO ISSN 0039-7679) *260*
Symbolae Philologorum Posnaniensium (PL) *260*
Symbolon (GW ISSN 0082-0660) *691*
Symposia Biologica Hungarica (HU ISSN 0082-0695) *108*
Symposia Mathematica (IT ISSN 0082-0725) *589*
Symposia of the Faraday Society *see* Faraday Symposia *254*
Symposia on Fundamental Cancer Research. Papers (US ISSN 0082-0733) *256*
Symposia on the Pharmacology of Thermoregulation (SZ) *256, 686*
Symposia on Theoretical Physics and Mathematics (II ISSN 0082-075X) *589, 699*
Symposia Series in Immunobiological Standardization *see* Developments in Biological Standardization *603*
Symposium (International) on Combustion (US ISSN 0082-0784) *256*
Symposium Anaesthesiologiae Internationale. Berichte (GE) *604*
Symposium on Advanced Propulsion Concepts. Proceedings (US ISSN 0082-0806) *10*
Symposium on Applications of Walsh Functions. Record (US ISSN 0082-0814) *359*
Symposium on Atmospheric Turbulence, Diffusion and Air Quality. Preprints *see* Symposium on Turbulence, Diffusion and Air Pollution. Preprints *635*
Symposium on Care of the Professional Voice. Transcripts (US) *664*
Symposium on Coal Mine Drainage Research. Papers (US ISSN 0085-7068) *647*
Symposium on Computer Applications in Medical Care (US) *274, 600*
Symposium on Computer Architecture. Conference Proceedings (US) *274*
Symposium on Drug-Induced Diseases. Proceedings *see* Drug-Induced Diseases *594*
Symposium on Ethical Issues in Human Experimentation. Proceedings (US) *600, 626*
Symposium on Flames and Industry. Proceedings (UK) *374*
Symposium on Hybrid Microelectronics *see* Hybrid Microelectronics Symposium. (Papers) *354*

Symposium on Incremental Motion Control Systems and Devices. Proceedings (US ISSN 0092-1661) *583*
Symposium on Information Display. Digest of Technical Papers *see* S I D International Symposium. Digest of Technical Papers *370*
Symposium on Jet Pumps & Ejectors and Gas Lift Techniques. Proceedings (UK) *381*
Symposium on Machine Processing of Remotely Sensed Data.(Papers) (US) *274*
Symposium on Meteorological Observation and Instrumentation. Preprints (US) *635*
Symposium on Naval Hydrodynamics. Proceedings (US ISSN 0082-0849) *701*
Symposium on Nondestructive Evaluation. Proceedings (US) *380*
Symposium on Nondestructive Evaluation of Components and Materials in Aerospace, Weapons Systems and Nuclear Applications (US ISSN 0082-0857) *10*
Symposium on Nondestructive Testing of Aircraft and Missile Components *see* Symposium on Nondestructive Evaluation of Components and Materials in Aerospace, Weapons Systems and Nuclear Applications *10*
Symposium on Nonlinear Estimation Theory and Its Applications. Proceedings (US) *589*
Symposium on Particleboard. Proceedings (US ISSN 0082-089X) *413*
Symposium on Photographic Gelatin. Proceedings (UK) *694*
Symposium on Physics and Nondestructive Testing, San Antonio. Proceedings *see* Symposium on Nondestructive Evaluation. Proceedings *380*
Symposium on Reliability. Proceedings (US ISSN 0082-092X) *359*
Symposium on Special Ceramics, Stoke-On-Trent, England. Special Ceramics, Proceedings (US ISSN 0082-0954) *245*
Symposium on Surface Mining and Reclamation (US) *647*
Symposium on Textile Flammability. Proceedings (US) *856*
Symposium on the Art of Glassblowing Proceedings. (US ISSN 0569-7468) *245*
Symposium on the Physiology and Pathology of Human Reproduction *see* Harold C. Mack Symposium. Proceedings *126*
Symposium on the Use of Cybernetics on the Railway (JA) *274, 874*
Symposium on Thermophysical Properties. Proceedings (US ISSN 0082-0989) *256*
Symposium on Turbulence, Diffusion and Air Pollution. Preprints (US) *635*
Symposium on Urban Renewal. Papers (UK) *487*
Symposium on Water Resources Research. Proceedings (US ISSN 0082-1012) *898*
Synchronized Swimming Rules *see* Official A A U Synchronized Swimming Handbook *821*
Syndicat des Industries de Material Professionnel Electronique et Radioelectrique. Annuaire *see* S P E R Annuaire *358*
Syndicat General de l'Industrie Cotonniere Francaise. Annuaire (FR ISSN 0082-1047) *856*
Syndicat General de la Construction Electrique. Annuaire (FR) *359, 507*
Syndicat General des Commerces et Industries du Caoutchouc et des Plastiques. Guide (FR ISSN 0224-2435) *242, 707, 777*
Syndicat General des Impots. Guide Fonciers (FR) *232*

Syndicat General des Impots. Guide National de l'Enregistrement et des Domaines *see* Syndicat General des Impots. Guide Fonciers *232*
Syndicat des Industries Medico - Chirurgicales et Dentaires. Annuaire (FR ISSN 0396-0382) *610, 625*
Syndicat National de la Distribution pour l'Automobile et l'Industrie *see* S D A I *872*
Syndicat National de la Librairie Ancienne et Moderne. Repertoire *see* Guide a l'Usage des Amateurs de Livres *758*
Syndicated Columnists (US) *505*
Syndrome Identification (US ISSN 0091-1747) *914*
Synopses of the British Fauna (US ISSN 0082-1101) *130*
Synopsis of Family Therapy Practice (US ISSN 0162-7171) *738*
Synopsis of Laws Enacted by the State of Maryland *see* Maryland. State Department of Legislative Reference. Snynopsis of Laws Enacted by the State of Maryland *515*
Syntax and Semantics (US ISSN 0092-4563) *552*
Synthese Historical Library (NE ISSN 0082-111X) *691*
Synthese Library (NE ISSN 0082-1128) *691, 801*
Synthesis (RM) *574*
Synthetic Methods of Organic Chemistry (SZ ISSN 0082-1136) *254, 256*
Synthetic Organic Chemicals, United States Production and Sales (US ISSN 0082-1144) *374*
Synthetic Pipeline Gas Symposium. Proceedings (US) *681*
Synthetic Procedures in Nucleic Acid Chemistry (US ISSN 0082-1152) *914*
Syracuse Geographical Series (US ISSN 0082-1160) *426*
Syracuse Special Education and Rehabilitation Monograph Series (US) *346*
Syracuse University. Foreign and Comparative Studies. African Series (US) *803*
Syracuse University. Foreign and Comparative Studies. Latin American Series (US) *803*
Syracuse University. Foreign and Comparative Studies. South Asian Series (US) *803*
Syracuse University. Foreign and Comparative Studies. South Asian Special Publications (US) *803*
Syracuse University. Libraries. Annual Report (US ISSN 0094-5900) *914*
Syracuse University. Maxwell School of Citizenship and Public Affairs. Foreign and Comparative Studies: African Series (US) *441, 801*
Syracuse University. Program of East African Studies. East African Bibliographic Series (US ISSN 0586-3414) *914*
Syracuse University. Program of East African Studies. Eastern African Studies *see* Syracuse University. Maxwell School of Citizenship and Public Affairs. Foreign and Comparative Studies: African Series *801*
Syracuse University. Program of East African Studies. Occasional Bibliographies (US ISSN 0586-3422) *914*
Syracuse University. Program of East African Studies. Occasional Papers (US ISSN 0586-3430) *914*
Syracuse University. Program of East African Studies. Special Publications (US) *914*
Syracuse University Publications in Continuing Education. Landmark and New Horizons Series (US) *330*
Syracuse University Publications in Continuing Education. Notes and Essays (US) *330*
Syracuse University Publications in Continuing Education. Occasional Papers (US ISSN 0082-1179) *330*

Syracuse Wood Science Series (US) *413*
Syria. Central Bureau of Statistics. Statistical Abstract (SY ISSN 0081-4725) *848*
Syro-Mesopotamian Studies (US) *475*
System of Ophthalmology (UK ISSN 0082-1195) *616*
Systematische Politikwissenschaft (GW) *716*
Systeme d'Information sur les Transports de Marchandises: Resultats Generaux, Trafic International *see* Systeme d'Information sur les Transports de Marchandises: Resultats Generaux, Trafic Interieur et International *198*
Systeme d'Information sur les Transports de Marchandises: Resultats Generaux, Trafic Interieur et International (FR) *198*
Systemes-Decisions. Section II. Gestion Financiere et Comptabilite (FR ISSN 0082-1209) *232*
Systems Engineering of Education Series (US ISSN 0082-1217) *323*
Szczecinskie Towarzystwo Naukowe. Sprawozdania (PL ISSN 0082-1241) *792*
Szczecinskie Towarzystwo Naukowe. Wydzial Nauk Lekarskich. Prace (PL ISSN 0082-125X) *600*
Szczecinskie Towarzystwo Naukowe. Wydzial Nauk Matematyczno Technicznych. Prace (PL ISSN 0082-1268) *589*
Szczecinskie Towarzystwo Naukowe. Wydzial Nauk Przyrodniczo-Rolniczych. Prace (PL ISSN 0082-1276) *39*
Szczecinskie Towarzystwo Naukowe. Wydzial Nauk Spolecznych. Prace (PL ISSN 0082-1284) *801*
Szczecinskie Towarzystwo Naukowe. Wydzial Nauk Spolecznych. Wydawnictwa (PL ISSN 0082-1292) *801*
Szene Schweiz/Scene Suisse/Scena Svizzera (SZ) *860*
Szep Versek (HU ISSN 0586-3783) *582*
Szilikatkemiai Monografiak (HU ISSN 0082-1306) *251*
Szkice Legnickie (PL ISSN 0137-5326) *792*
Szkice o Kulturze Muzycznej XIX Wieku. Studia i Materialy (PL) *664*
Szkolna Glowna Gospodarstwa Wiejskiego. Zeszyty Naukowe. Zootechnika *see* Akademia Rolnicza, Warsaw. Zeszyty Naukowe. Zootechnika *127*
Szociologiai Tanulmanyok (HU ISSN 0082-1322) *817*

T.A. Documents (FR ISSN 0066-9776) *552*
T. A. E. Report (IS ISSN 0072-9302) *10*
T A G A Proceedings (Technical Association of the Graphic Arts) (US ISSN 0082-2299) *734*
T A I C H Country Reports: Development Assistance Programs of U.S. Non-Profit Organizations Abroad (Technical Assistance Information Clearing House) (US) *201*
T A I U S (Texas A & I University Studies) (US ISSN 0564-7169) *493*
T A P P I Directory *see* Technical Association of the Pulp and Paper Industry. Directory *675*
T A P P I Standards and Provisional Methods *see* T A P P I Test Methods *675*
T A P P I Test Methods (Technical Association of the Pulp and Paper Industry) (US) *675*
T & A M Report (Department of Theoretical and Applied Mechanics) (US ISSN 0073-5264) *380, 701*
T & C (Theorie et Critique) (AG) *79*
T. B. Davie Memorial Lecture (SA ISSN 0082-1330) *493*

T C G National Working Conference. Proceedings (Theatre Communications Group) (US) *860*
T C U G Notes *see* Theater Computer Users Group Notes *860*
T E C Report (The Electrification Council) (US ISSN 0039-8314) *359*
T L I-Ingenjoeren (SW) *370*
T.M. (Tatsachen und Meinungen) (SZ ISSN 0080-7427) *801*
T M R Travel Marketing Report (US ISSN 0197-6753) *139*
T N L Research Guide Series *see* Philippines. National Library. T N L Research Guide Series *94*
T R I U M F, Vancouver, British Columbia. Report (Tri-University Meson Facility) (CN ISSN 0082-6367) *704*
T R U K-P A C T (Transvaalse Raad vir die Uitvoerende Kunste-Performing Arts Council Transvaal) (SA ISSN 0085-7416) *664, 860*
T R W Series of Software Technology (NE) *29*
T S E: Tulane Studies in English (US) *552*
T.U.B.A. Series (Tubists Universal Brotherhood Association) (US) *664*
T U G *see* Urban Guerilla *717*
T V Basics (US) *268*
T V Color (IT) *268*
T V Feature Film Source Book (US ISSN 0082-1357) *268*
T V-Film Filebook (CN ISSN 0082-1365) *268*
T V Film Source Book. Series, Serials and Packages *see* Series, Serials, and Packages *268*
T V "Free" Film Source Book (US ISSN 0082-1381) *914*
T V Season (US ISSN 0363-9487) *914*
Ha-Ta'Asiyah Ha-Yisre'Elit *see* Israel. Ministry of Commerce and Industry. Surveys and Development Plans of Industry in Israel *223*
Tabard (UK) *418*
Tablas de Mareas: Costas de Cuba *see* Academia de Ciencias de Cuba. Instituto de Oceanologia. Tablas de Mareas *309*
Table of International Telex Relations and Traffic (UN ISSN 0074-9052) *269*
Table Ronde Francaise. Annuaire (FR ISSN 0082-1403) *463*
Table Service Restaurant Operations (US) *483*
Tableaux Fiscaux Europeens (FR) *232*
Tableaux Numeriques des Analyses Physico-Chimiques des Eaux du Rhin Ainsi Que de la Moselle. *see* Zahlestafeln der Physikalisch-Chemischen Untersuchungen des Rheins sowie der Mosel *390*
Tables on Hatchery and Flock Participation in the National Poultry Improvement Plan (US ISSN 0082-8661) *46*
Tableservice Restaurant Operations Report (US) *483*
Tableware and Pottery Gazette Reference Book *see* Tableware Reference Book *245*
Tableware Reference Book (UK) *245, 503*
Taccuino dell'Azionista (IT ISSN 0082-1446) *205*
Tack 'n Togs Book (US) *828*
Taeglicher Hafenbericht. Jahresausgabe (GW) *881*
Taehan Cheykhoe. Cheyuk Chongso (KO) *822*
Taft Corporate Foundation Directory (US) *809*
Tagore Studies (II ISSN 0082-1454) *574*
Tai-Wan Shena Ho Tso Chin Ku. Annual Report. *see* Cooperative Bank of Taiwan. Annual Report *172*
Tai-Wan Sheng Chiao Tung Tung Chi Nien Pao *see* Taiwan Annual Statistical Report of Transportation *866*
Tai-Wan ta Hsueh She Hui Hsueh K'an *see* National Taiwan University Journal of Sociology *815*
Tailing Disposal Today (US) *647*
Tailspinner (CN ISSN 0316-2494) *10*

Taiwan. Fisheries Research Institute, Keelung. Bulletin (CH ISSN 0082-1489) *400*
Taiwan. Fisheries Research Institute, Keelung. Laboratory of Fishery Biology. Report (CH ISSN 0082-1497) *400*
Taiwan Agricultural Research Institute. Annual Report (CH) *20*
Taiwan Agricultural Research Institute. Bulletin (CH) *20, 118*
Taiwan Agricultural Research Institute. Research Summary (CH) *20, 118*
Taiwan Annual Statistical Report of Transportation/Tai-Wan Sheng Chiao Tung Tung Chi Nien Pao (CH) *866*
Taiwan Buyers' Guide (CH ISSN 0082-1470) *242*
Taiwan Exporters Guide (CH) *242*
Taiwan Exports (CH ISSN 0494-5336) *198*
Taiwan Railway (CH) *874*
T'aiwan Shih Yu Ti Chih *see* Petroleum Geology of Taiwan *681*
Taiwan Sugar (CH ISSN 0492-1712) *406*
Taiwan Sugar Research Institute. Annual Report (CH) *39*
Taiwan Trade Directory (CH) *242*
Taiwania (CH ISSN 0065-1125) *118*
Talent in Action *see* Billboard's Talent in Action *657*
Talespinner *see* Tailspinner *10*
Talking Books, Adult (US ISSN 0082-1519) *95, 133, 328*
Talking Books in the Public Library Systems of Metropolitan Toronto (CN ISSN 0380-2973) *133, 536*
Tall Timbers Conference on Ecological Animal Control by Habitat Management. Proceedings (US ISSN 0070-833X) *278*
Tall Timbers Fire Ecology Conference. Proceedings (US ISSN 0082-1527) *411*
Talladegan (US) *263, 393*
Taller de Letras (CL) *574*
Tallinskii Politekhnicheskii Institut. Trudy (UR) *792, 853*
Taloha (MG) *66, 79, 655*
Tam-Tam *see* Message *319*
Tamagawa University. Faculty of Agriculture. Bulletin (JA ISSN 0082-156X) *20*
Tamil Icaic Cankam Maturai. Antu Vila Malar (II) *664*
Tamil Nadu. Department of Statistics. Annual Statistical Abstract (II ISSN 0082-1578) *848*
Tamil Nadu. Department of Statistics. Season and Crop Report (II ISSN 0082-1586) *39*
Tamil Nadu. Legislative Council. Quinquennial Review (II ISSN 0082-1594) *746*
Tamil Nadu Industrial Development Corporation. Annual Report (II) *225*
Tamil Nadu Tourism Development Corporation. Annual Report (II) *225, 891*
Tamkang College. Institute of Area Studies. Area Studies (CH) *446, 671*
Tampa Port Handbook (US) *881*
Tamworth Annual (US ISSN 0082-1608) *46*
Tane (NZ ISSN 0496-8026) *792*
Tangente (AU) *716*
Tantara (MG) *441*
Tanulmanyok a Nevelestudomany Korebol (HU ISSN 0082-1632) *323*
Tanzania (HK) *891*
Tanzania. Bureau of Standards. Director's Annual Report (TZ) *637*
Tanzania. Bureau of Statistics. Directory of Industries (TZ) *242*
Tanzania. Bureau of Statistics. Migration Statistics (TZ) *848*
Tanzania. Bureau of Statistics. Survey of Industrial Production (TZ) *165, 848*
Tanzania. Capital Development Authority. Report and Accounts (TZ) *487*
Tanzania.Central Statistical Bureau. Survey of Industrial Production *see* Tanzania. Bureau of Statistics. Survey of Industrial Production *165*

Tanzania. Geology and Mines Division. Review of the Mineral Industry see Review of the Mineral Industry in Tanzania 646
Tanzania. Ministry of Economic Affairs and Development Planning. Annual Economic Survey see Tanzania. Ministry of Economic Affairs and Development Planning. Hali Ya Uchumi Wa Taifa 225
Tanzania. Ministry of Economic Affairs and Development Planning. Hali Ya Uchumi Wa Taifa (TZ) 225
Tanzania. Ministry of Lands, Housing and Urban Development. Urban Planning Division. Annual Report (TZ) 487
Tanzania Directory of Trades (TZ ISSN 0564-724X) 242
Tanzania Import and Export Directory (TZ) 198
Tanzania Industrial Studies and Consulting Organisation. Annual Report and Accounts (TZ) 149
Tanzania National Bibliography (TZ) 95, 536
Tanzanian Studies (TZ) 441
Tape Recording and Buying Guide see Stereo Review's Tape Recording & Buying Guide 818
Tape Teacher (UK ISSN 0306-7858) 351
Tar River Poetry (US) 582
Tar River Poets see Tar River Poetry 582
Tarbell's Teacher's Guide (US ISSN 0082-1713) 768
Target Organ Toxicity (US) 686
Tariff Schedules of the United States Annotated (US ISSN 0082-173X) 232
Tarsadalomtudomanyi Kismonografiak (HU ISSN 0082-1748) 801
Taschenbuch der Fernmelde-Praxis (GW ISSN 0082-1764) 265
Taschenbuch der Giesserei-Praxis (GW ISSN 0082-1772) 630
Taschenbuch der Pflanzenarztes (GW ISSN 0082-1799) 39
Taschenbuch der Post- und Fernmelde-Verwaltung (GW ISSN 0082-190X) 269
Taschenbuch der Textilen Raumausstattung (GW) 856
Taschenbuch der Werbung see Deutscher Werbekalender 5
Taschenbuch der Werkzeugmaschinen und Werkzeuge (GW ISSN 0082-1810) 383
Taschenbuch des Oeffentlichen Lebens (GW ISSN 0082-1829) 463
Taschenbuch des Textileinzelhandels (GW ISSN 0082-1837) 856
Taschenbuch fuer Agrarjournalisten (GW ISSN 0082-1845) 20, 505
Taschenbuch fuer den Buchhalter see Jahrbuch fuer den Praktiker des Rechnungswesens 167
Taschenbuch fuer den Fernmeldedienst (GW ISSN 0082-1861) 269, 640
Taschenbuch fuer den Kirchenmusiker see Taschenbuch fuer Liturgie und Kirchenmusik 664
Taschenbuch fuer den Oeffentlichen Dienst (GW ISSN 0082-1888) 746
Taschenbuch fuer die Bekleidungs-Industrie (GW) 261
Taschenbuch fuer die Textil-Industrie (GW ISSN 0082-1896) 856
Taschenbuch fuer Fernmelde-Verwaltung see Taschenbuch der Post- und Fernmelde-Verwaltung 269
Taschenbuch fuer Ingenieure und Techniker im Oeffentlichen Dienst (GW ISSN 0082-1926) 370
Taschenbuch fuer Ingenieure und Techniker in Industrie und Wirtschaft (GW ISSN 0082-1918) 370
Taschenbuch fuer Kriminalisten (GW ISSN 0082-1934) 284
Taschenbuch fuer Liturgie und Kirchenmusik (GW ISSN 0082-187X) 664, 768
Taschenbuch fuer Logistik (GW ISSN 0082-1942) 640
Taschenbuchreihe Geschichte (GE ISSN 0082-1950) 436

Taschenbuecher zur Musikwissenschaft (GW ISSN 0082-1969) 664
Taschenfachbuch der Kraftfahrzeugbetriebe (GW) 872
Task Force on Environmental Cancer and Heart and Lung Disease. Annual Report to Congress (US ISSN 0164-0968) 389, 606, 607, 623
Tasmania. Department of Agriculture. Annual Report (AT ISSN 0082-1993) 20
Tasmania. Department of Mines. Geological Survey Bulletins (AT ISSN 0082-2043) 300
Tasmania. Department of Mines. Technical Reports (AT ISSN 0082-2078) 300, 647
Tasmania. Department of the Treasury. Commonwealth Grants to Tasmania (AT) 198, 232
Tasmania. Department of the Treasury. Consolidated Revenue Fund (AT) 232
Tasmania. Metropolitan Water Board. Report (AT ISSN 0082-2094) 389
Tasmania; a Businessman's Handbook see Information about Investment in Tasmania 203
Tasmanian Almanac (AT ISSN 0083-7016) 447
Tasmanian Manufacturers Directory (AT) 242
Tasmanian Meat Industry Journal (AT) 46, 406
Tasmanian State Reports (AT ISSN 0085-7106) 519
Tasmanian Tramp (AT) 831
Tasmanian University Law Review see University of Tasmania Law Review 520
Taste of Scotland (UK) 891
Tata Institute Lecture Notes (US) 589
Tata Institute of Fundamental Research. Lectures on Mathematics and Physics. Mathematics see Tata Institute Lecture Notes 589
Tata Institute of Fundemental Research. Lectures on Mathematics and Physics. Physics see Tata Institute Lecture Notes 589
Tata Institute of Social Sciences. Case Records (II) 809
Tata Institute Studies in Mathematics (US) 589
Tatsachen und Meinungen see T.M 801
Tatsachen und Zahlen aus der Kraftverkehrswirtschaft (GW ISSN 0083-548X) 872
Tatura, Australia. Horticultural Research Station. Annual Research Report (AT ISSN 0082-2124) 416
Tatzlil/Chord (IS ISSN 0082-2132) 664
Tavkozlesi Kutato Intezet. Annual (HU) 269
Tax Burden on Tobacco (US ISSN 0563-6191) 232, 848, 861
Tax Court Practice (Supplement) (US) 232
Tax Foundation, New York. Research Publications. New Series (US ISSN 0082-2159) 232
Tax Foundation's Research Bibliography (US ISSN 0496-974X) 95, 165
Tax Fraud and Evasion (Supplement) (US) 232
Tax Memo (CN) 232
Tax Planning Review (UK) 232
Tax Practitioner's Diary (UK) 232
Tax Principles to Remember (CN ISSN 0227-1265) 233
Tax Year in Review (US) 233
Taxable Sales in California (Sales and Use Tax) (US ISSN 0068-581X) 233
Taxation in Middle East, Africa & Asia (UK) 233
Taxation in Western Europe (UK ISSN 0082-2167) 233
Taxation of Closely Held Corporations (Supplement) (US) 233
Taxation of Patents, Trademarks, Copyrights and Know-How (Supplement) (US) 233, 677
Taxation Structure of Pakistan (PK) 233
Taxation Tables (NZ ISSN 0082-2175) 233

Ha-Tayarut Be-Yisrael see Israel Tourist Statistics 887
Taylor's Encyclopedia of Government Officials. Federal and State (US ISSN 0082-2183) 746
Tbilisi Universitet. Institut Prikladnoi Matematiki. Seminar. Annotatsii Dokladov (UR ISSN 0082-2191) 589
Tchebec (CN) 125
Te Reo (NZ) 552
Tea Directory (II) 86
Tea Research Association. Advisory Bulletin (II) 86
Tea Research Association. Memorandum (II) 39, 86
Tea Research Association. Occasional Scientific Papers (II) 39, 86
Tea Research Association. Scientific Annual Report (II ISSN 0564-6723) 39, 86
Tea Trading Corporation of India. Annual Report (II) 219
Teacher Education (CN ISSN 0082-2205) 340
Teacher Education in Uganda see Makerere University. Faculty of Education. Handbook 338
Teachers' Associations. Associations d'Enseignants. Asociaciones de Personal Docente (UN ISSN 0082-2213) 345
Teachers Guild of New South Wales. Proceedings (AT) 323
Teachers of History in the Universities of the United Kingdom (UK ISSN 0085-7114) 323
Teaching (US ISSN 0082-223X) 351
Teaching Abroad (US) 343
Teaching of Adults Series (CN ISSN 0707-9087) 330
Teaching of History (UK ISSN 0073-2605) 351, 436
Teaching Opportunities Overseas (US) 323
Teamwork (US ISSN 1661-2434) 536, 768
Teatro Italiano (IT) 860
Tebiwa see Tebiwa Miscellaneous Papers 792
Tebiwa Miscellaneous Papers (US) 54, 66, 792
Tech-Embal (FR) 672
Tech Notes (US) 914
Technical and Specialised Periodicals Published in Britain (UK) 854
Technical Assistance Information Clearing House Country Reports: Development Assistance Programs of U.S. Non-Profit Organizations Abroad see T A I C H Country Reports: Development Assistance Programs of U.S. Non-Profit Organizations Abroad 201
Technical Association of the Graphic Arts Proceedings see T A G A Proceedings 734
Technical Association of the Pulp and Paper Industry. Directory (US ISSN 0091-7737) 675
Technical Association of the Pulp and Paper Industry. Proceedings (US) 675
Technical Association of the Pulp and Paper Industry Test Methods see T A P P I Test Methods 675
Technical Bulletin - Department of Natural Resources (Madison) see Wisconsin. Department of Natural Resources. Technical Bulletin 279
Technical Conference on Artifical Insemination and Reproduction (US) 46
Technical Highlights of the National Bureau of Standards see U.S. National Bureau of Standards. Annual Report 637
Technical Notes for the Rubber Industry (GW) 777
Technical Paper-New York State, Department of Environmental Conservation, Environmental Quality Research and Development Unit see New York (State). Environmental Quality Research and Development Unit. Technical Paper 388

Technical Paper - U.S. Department of Commerce, Social and Economics Statistics Administration, Bureau of the Census see U. S. Bureau of the Census. Technical Paper 849
Technical Papers in Hydrology Series (UN ISSN 0082-2310) 308
Technical Papers on New Zealand Wool (NZ) 856
Technical Research Centre of Finland. Biomedical Engineering Laboratory. Report see Valtion Teknillinen Tutkimuskeskus. Sairaalatekniikan Laboratorio. Tiedonanto 612
Technical Research Centre of Finland. Biotechnical Laboratory. Report see Valtion Teknillinen Tutkimuskeskus. Biotekniikan Labboratorio. Tiedonanto 109
Technical Research Centre of Finland. Chemical Laboratory. Report see Valtion Teknillinen Tutkimuskeskus. Kemian Laboratorio. Tiedonanto 374
Technical Research Centre of Finland. Computing Service. Report see Valtion Teknillinen Tutkimuskeskus. A T K-Palvelutoimisto. Tiedonanto 274
Technical Research Centre of Finland. Concrete Laboratory. Report see Valtion Teknillinen Tutkimuskeskus. Betoni- ja Silikaattitekniikan Laboratorio. Tiedonanto 139
Technical Research Centre of Finland. Electrical Engineering Laboratory. Report see Valtion Teknillinen Tutkimuskeskus. Sahkotekniikan Laboratorio. Tiedonanto 359
Technical Research Centre of Finland. Fire Technology Laboratory. Report see Valtion Teknillinen Tutkimuskeskus. Palotekniikan Laboratorio. Tiedonanto 395
Technical Research Centre of Finland. Food Research Laboratory. Report see Valtion Teknillinen Tutkimuskeskus. Elintarvikelaboratorio. Tiedonanto 406
Technical Research Centre of Finland. Fuel and Lubricant Research Laboratory. Report see Valtion Teknillinen Tutkimuskeskus. Polttl- ja Voiteluainelaboratorio. Tiedonanto 682
Technical Research Centre of Finland. Geotechnical Laboratory. Report see Valtion Teknillinen Tutkimuskeskus. Geotekniikan Laboratorio. Tiedonanto 302
Technical Research Centre of Finland. Graphic Arts Laboratory. Report see Valtion Teknillinen Tutkimuskeskus. Graafinen Labboratorio. Tiedonanto 734
Technical Research Centre of Finland. Instrument Laboratory. Report see Valtion Teknillinen Tutkimuskeskus. Kojetekniikan Laboratorio. Tiedonanto 497
Technical Research Centre of Finland. Laboratory of Land Use. Report see Valtion Teknillinen Tutkimuskeskus. Maankayton Laboratorio. Tiedonanto 488
Technical Research Centre of Finland. Laboratory of Metallurgy and Mineral Engineering. Report see Valtion Teknillinen Tutkimuskeskus. Metallurgian ja Mineraalitekniikan Laboratorio. Tiedonanto 630
Technical Research Centre of Finland. Laboratory of Structural Engineering. Report see Valtion Teknillinen Tutkimuskeskus. Rakennetekniikan Laboratorio. Tiedonanto 371
Technical Research Centre of Finland. Metals Laboratory. Report see Valtion Teknillinen Tutkimuskeskus. Metallilaboratorio. Tiedonanto 631
Technical Research Centre of Finland. Nuclear Engineering Laboratory. Report see Valtion Teknillinen Tutkimuskeskus. Ydinvoimatekniikan Laboratorio. Tiedonanto 705

Technical Research Centre of Finland. Publication. Building Technology and Community Development (FI ISSN 0355-337X) *914*

Technical Research Centre of Finland. Publication. Electrical and Nuclear Technology (FI ISSN 0355-3396) *914*

Technical Research Centre of Finland. Publication. Materials and Processing Technology (FI ISSN 0355-3388) *914*

Technical Research Centre of Finland. Reactor Laboratory. Report *see* Valtion Teknillinen Tutkimuskeskus. Reaktorilaboratorio. Tiedonanto *705*

Technical Research Centre of Finland. Technical Information Service. Report *see* Valtion Teknillinen Tutkimuskeskus. Teknillinen Informaatiopalvelulaitos. Tiedonanto *538*

Technical Research Centre of Finland. Telecommunications Laboratory. Report *see* Valtion Teknillinen Tutkimuskeskus. Teletekniikan Laboratorio. Tiedonanto *265*

Technical Research Centre of Finland. Textile Laboratory. Report *see* Valtion Teknillinen Tutkimuskeskus. Tekstiililaboratorio. Tiedonanto *857*

Technical Research Centre of Finland. Tiedonanto (FI) *914*

Technical Service Data (Automotive) (UK ISSN 0082-2329) *853*

Technical Study - U.S. Civil Service Commission. Personnel Research and Development Center *see* U. S. Civil Service Commission. Personnel Research and Development Center. Technical Study *220*

Technical University of Denmark. Institute of Roads, Transport and Town Planning. Report (DK) *487, 876*

Technical University of Nova Scotia. School of Architecture. Report Series(CN) *70*

Technician Education Yearbook (US ISSN 0082-2353) *340*

Technik und Form aus Finnland (FI) *198*

Technikgeschichte in Einzeldarstellungen (GW ISSN 0082-2361) *853*

Technine Kibernetika/Tekhnicheskaya Kibernetika (UR) *274*

Technion-Israel Institute of Technology. Braverman Memorial Lecture (IS ISSN 0068-0761) *406*

Technion-Israel Institute of Technology. Faculty of Agricultural Engineering. Publications (IS ISSN 0333-5879) *20*

Technion-Israel Institute of Technology. President's Report (IS) *853*

La Technique du Roulement (GW ISSN 0170-303X) *383*

Technique of Inorganic Chemistry *see* Techniques of Chemistry *248*

Technique of Organic Chemistry *see* Techniques of Chemistry *248*

Techniques and Applications in Organic Synthesis (US ISSN 0082-2418) *254, 256*

Techniques and Instrumentation in Analytical Chemistry (NE) *250*

Techniques and Methods of Polymer Evaluation (US ISSN 0082-2434) *254*

Techniques Artisanales Modernes (FR ISSN 0082-2442) *668*

Techniques d'Aujourd'Hui (FR ISSN 0082-2469) *853*

Techniques Economiques Modernes. Analyse Economique (FR ISSN 0082-2477) *192*

Techniques Economiques Modernes. Espace Economique (FR ISSN 0082-2485) *914*

Techniques Economiques Modernes. Histoire et Pensee Economique (FR ISSN 0082-2493) *914*

Techniques Economiques Modernes. Production et Marches (FR ISSN 0082-2507) *914*

Techniques in Pure and Applied Microbiology (US ISSN 0082-2515) *124*

Techniques Industrielles du Japon (JA) *853*

Techniques of Biochemical and Biophysical Morphology (US ISSN 0082-2523) 108, *112,* 112

Techniques of Chemistry (US ISSN 0082-2531) *248,* 612

Techniques of Electrochemistry (US ISSN 0082-254X) *251*

Techniques of Marriage and Family Counseling (US ISSN 0091-8385) *914*

Techniques of Metals Research (US ISSN 0082-2558) *914*

Technisch Fysische Dienst TNO-TH. Jaarverslag (NE) *699*

Technische Akademie Wuppertal. Berichte (GW ISSN 0084-3091) *853*

Technische Beitraege zur Archaeologie (GW ISSN 0067-4974) *66*

Technische Fortschrittsberichte (GE ISSN 0082-2566) *914*

Technische Hochschule Karl-Marx-Stadt. Wissenschaftliche Schriftenreihe (GE) *359*

Technische Hochschule Karl-Marx-Stadt. Wissenschaftliche Zeitschrift (GE ISSN 0040-1528) *370*

Technische Hogeschool te Delft. Bibliotheek. Lijst van Lopende Tijdschriftabonnementen (NE) *370*

Technische Physik in Einzeldarstellungen (US ISSN 0082-2590) *699*

Technische Sehenswuerdigkeiten in Deutschland. Band 1: Schleswig-Holstein, Niedersachsen, Hamburg, Bremen (GW) *891*

Technische Sehenswuerdigkeiten in Deutschland. Band 2: Nordrhein-Westfalen (GW) *891*

Technische Sehenswuerdigkeiten in Deutschland. Band 3: Hessen, Rheinland-Pfalz, Saarland, Baden-Wuerttemberg (GW) *891*

Technische Sehenswuerdigkeiten in Deutschland. Band 4: Bayern, Berlin (GW) *891*

Technische Universitaet Berlin. Institut fuer Sozialoekonomie der Agrarentwicklung. Annual Report (Abridged Version) (GW) *30*

Technische Universitaet Berlin. Institut fuer Sozialoekonomie der Agrarentwicklung. Jahresbericht (GW) *30*

Technische Universitaet Berlin. Institut fuer Sozialoekonomie der Agrarentwicklung. Taetigkeitsbericht *see* Technische Universitaet Berlin. Institut fuer Sozialoekonomie der Agrarentwicklung. Jahresbericht *30*

Technische Universitaet Braunschweig. Berichtsband. Forschung (GW) *340*

Technische Universitaet Braunschweig. Pharmaziegeschichtlichen Seminar. Veroeffentlichungen (GW ISSN 0068-0729) *686*

Technische Universitaet Hannover. Astronomische Station. (Veroeffentlichungen) (GW) *84*

Technische Universitaet Hannover. Institut fuer Siedlungswasserwirtschaft. Veroeffentlichungen (GW ISSN 0073-0319) *898*

Technische Universitaet Hannover. Institut fuer Statistik. Mitteilungen *see* Universitaet Hannover. Institut fuer Statistik. Mitteilungen *380*

Technische Universitaet Hannover. Lehrstuhl fuer Stahlbau. Schriftenreihe *see* Universitaet Hannover. Lehrstuhl fuer Stahlbau. Schriftenreihe *380*

Technische Universitaet Muenchen. Institut fuer Wirtschaftslehre des Gartenbaues. Forschungsberichte zur Oekonomie in Gartenbau (GW) *416*

Technischer Fortschritt (Berlin) (GW) *213*

Techniscne Universitaet Wien. Institut fuer Eisenbahnwesen, Spezialbahnen und Verkehrswirtschaft. Arbeiten (AU) *874*

Techno-Loisirs (FR) *822*

Techno-Tip (GW ISSN 0341-5570) 225, *853*

Technocracy. Information Briefs (US) *792*

Technographics (SI) *70,* 139

Technological Monographs (GT) *853*

Technology and Democratic Society *see* Organisations, People, Society/O P S *912*

La Tecnica de los Rodamientos (GW ISSN 0170-3056) *383*

Tecniche Ambientali *see* Repertorio Tecniche Ambientali *388*

Teilhardian Studies *see* Etudes Teilhardiennes *765*

Tekhnicheskaya Kibernetika *see* Technine Kibernetika *274*

Teki Historyczne (UK ISSN 0085-4956) *463*

Tekisutairu Japan *see* Textile Japan *857*

Teknisk Nyt Buyers Guide (DK) *914*

Tekniska Nomenklaturcentralen Publikationer (SW ISSN 0081-573X) *553,* 853

Teknologi (MY) 359, *853*

Tekstiiliteollisuuden Vuosikirja/Textilindustrins Aarsbok/Textile Industry Yearbook (FI) *857*

Tektonika i Stratigrafiya (UR) *300*

Tel-Aviv University. David Horowitz Institute for the Research of Developing Countries. Research Reports and Papers (IS) *723*

Tel Aviv University. Institut fuer Deutsche Geschichte. Jahrbuch (IS) *463*

Tel-Aviv University. Ph.D. Degrees and Abstracts (IS) *340*

Tel-Aviv-Yafo. Aamerkas le-Mechkar Kalkali ve-Hevrati. Mehkarim ve-Sekarim *see* Tel Aviv-Yafo. Center for Economic and Social Research. Research and Surveys Series *848*

Tel Aviv-Yafo. Center for Economic and Social Research. Research and Surveys Series/Tel-Aviv-Yafo. Aamerkas le-Mechkar Kalkali ve-Hevrati. Mehkarim ve-Sekarim (IS) *848*

Tel Aviv-Yafo. Center for Economic and Social Research. Yearbook (IS) *817*

Tel Aviv-Yafo. Department of Research and Statistics. Yearbook. *see* Tel Aviv-Yafo. Center for Economic and Social Research. Yearbook *817*

Tel Aviv-Yafo. Research and Statistical Department. Special Surveys *see* Tel Aviv-Yafo. Center for Economic and Social Research. Research and Surveys Series *848*

Telecommunication Authority of Singapore. T A S Annual Report *see* Telecommunication Authority of Singapore. Telecoms Annual Report *269*

Telecommunication Authority of Singapore. Telecoms Annual Report (SI) *269*

Telecommunication Statistics *see* Yearbook of Common Carrier Telecommunication Statistics *265*

Telecommunications Policy. Research and Development *see* Worldwide Report: Telecommunications Policy. Research and Development *265*

Telekompass (UK) *242*

Telephone Engineer and Management Directory (US ISSN 0082-2655) *269*

Telephone Tickler for Insurance Men *see* Telephone Tickler for Insurance Men and Women *501*

Telephone Tickler for Insurance Men and Women (US) *501*

Telephony's Directory & Buyer's Guide for the Telephone Industry (US) *269*

Telephony's Directory of the Telephone Industry *see* Telephony's Directory & Buyer's Guide for the Telephone Industry *269*

Telepulestudomanyi Kozlemenyek (HU ISSN 0040-2680) *487*

Television & Radio (UK) *268*

Television Blue Book *see* Television Trade-in Blue Book *268*

Television Contacts (US) *268*

Television Factbook (US ISSN 0082-268X) *268*

Television Network Movies (US) *268, 651*

Television Trade-in Blue Book (US) *268*

Telopea (AT ISSN 0312-9764) *118*

Telugu Akademi Language Monograph Series (II) *553*

Temadokumentacios Kiadvanyok/Thematical Reviews (HU ISSN 0133-3267) 149, *853*

Temas de Historia y Politica Contemporaneas (SP) *463*

Temas N T *see* Biblioteca N T *490*

Temas Nacionales (MX) *716*

Tempera (UK) *79*

Temperature: Its Measurement and Control in Science and Industry (US) *700*

Temple University. Center for the Study of Federalism. Center Report (US) *716*

Temporary Military Lodging Around the World (US) 640, *891*

Temporary Occupations and Employment (UK) *668*

Tennessee. Department of Safety. Annual Report (US ISSN 0095-1994) *876*

Tennessee. Division of Water Quality Control. Annual Report (US) *898*

Tennessee. Division of Water Resources. Summary of Ground Water Data for Tennessee *see* Summary of Ground Water Data for Tennessee *898*

Tennessee. Higher Education Commission. Biennial Report (US) *340*

Tennessee. State Advisory Council on Vocational Education. Annual Evaluation Report (US ISSN 0093-0903) *346*

Tennessee. State Board for Vocational Education. Information Series (US ISSN 0093-9889) *346*

Tennessee. State Planning Office. State Planning Office Publication (US ISSN 0082-2752) *746*

Tennessee Annual Average Labor Force Estimates (US) *211*

Tennessee Annual Average Work Force Estimates *see* Tennessee Annual Average Labor Force Estimates *211*

Tennessee Anthropological Association. Miscellaneous Paper (US) *54*

Tennessee Civilian Work Force Estimates *see* Tennessee Annual Average Labor Force Estimates *211*

Tennessee Cooperative Economic Insect Survey Report: Annual Summary (US) *118*

Tennessee Labor Market Information Directory (US) *211*

Tennessee Plumbing, Heating & Mechnical Contractor *see* Tennessee Plumbing, Heating, Cooling Contractor *430*

Tennessee Plumbing, Heating, Cooling Contractor (US) *430*

Tennessee Public Library Statistics (US ISSN 0363-7158) *536*

Tennessee Research Coordinating Unit for Vocational Education. Research Series (US) *323*

Tennessee State Industrial Directory (US ISSN 0190-1311) *242*

Tennessee Statistical Abstract (US ISSN 0082-2760) *848*

Tennessee Studies in Literature (US ISSN 0497-2384) *574*

Tennessee Tech Journal (US ISSN 0082-2779) *493*

Tennessee Valley Authority. Agricultural and Chemical Development Annual Report *see* National Fertilizer Development Center. Annual Report *37*

Tennessee Valley Authority. Annual Report (US ISSN 0082-2787) *278*

Tennessee Valley Authority. Division of Land and Forest Resources. Technical Note (US ISSN 0096-1248) *278*

Tennessee Valley Authority. Engineering Laboratory. Research in the Fields of Civil Engineering, Mechanical Engineering, Instrumentation (US ISSN 0071-0369) *914*

Tennessee Valley Authority.
  Operations: Municipal and
  Cooperative Distributors of T.V.A.
  Power see Tennessee Valley
  Authority. Power Program Summary
  359
Tennessee Valley Authority. Power
  Annual Report see Tennessee Valley
  Authority. Power Program Summary
  359
Tennessee Valley Authority. Power
  Program Summary (US) 359
Tennessee Valley Authority. Technical
  Monographs (US ISSN 0082-2809)
  359
Tennessee Valley Authority. Technical
  Reports (US ISSN 0082-2817) 359
Tennessee Valley Authority Industrial
  Development in the T.V.A. Area see
  Industrial Development in the T.V.A.
  Area 223
Tennis-Badminton-Squash Guide see N
  A G W S Guide. Tennis 825
Tennis for Travelers (US ISSN 0082-
  2825) 914
Tennis Guide (US ISSN 0082-2833)
  826
Tennyson Research Bulletin (UK ISSN
  0082-2841) 574
Tennyson Society, Lincoln, England.
  Monographs (UK ISSN 0082-285X)
  574
Tennyson Society, Lincoln, England.
  Occasional Papers (UK ISSN 0307-
  3572) 574
Tennyson Society, Lincoln, England.
  Report (UK ISSN 0082-2868) 574
Tensai Kenkyu Hokoku Hokan see
  Bulletin of Sugar Beet Research.
  Supplement 33
Teorie e Oggetti (IT) 716
Teorie Economiche (IT ISSN 0391-
  3295) 192
Teoriya Funktsii, Funktsional'nyi Analiz
  i Ikh Prilozheniya (UR) 589
Teoriya Funktsii Kompleksnogo
  Peremennogo i Kraevye Zadachi
  (UR) 589
Teoriya Sluchainykh Protsessov (UR)
  590
Teplofizika see Silumine Fizika 700
Teploprovodnost' i Diffuziya (UR) 700
Tequesta (US) 472
Tequi Electricite Electronique (FR
  ISSN 0154-0009) 359
Teramo (IT ISSN 0040-3652) 891
Terapia (EC ISSN 0040-3679) 915
Terem (US) 393
Terezinske Listy (CS) 463
Terpenoids and Steroids (UK ISSN
  0300-5992) 254
Terrae Incognitae (US ISSN 0082-
  2884) 436
Tertiary Research Group. Special
  Papers (NE ISSN 0308-7506) 300,
  674
Tesis Presentadas a la Universidad de
  Buenos Aires (AG ISSN 0325-0245)
  340
Testi Medievali di Interesse Dantesco
  (IT) 463
Testigos de Espana (SP) 817
Testimonios (en Historieta) (PE) 472
Tests in Print (US ISSN 0361-025X)
  738, 738
Tetanus Surveillance; Report see U.S.
  Center for Disease Control. Tetanus
  Surveillance; Report 754
Teton (US ISSN 0049-3481) 831
Tetradi Obshchestvennogo
  Zdravookhranenia see Public Health
  Papers 754
Tetsudo Sharyoto Seisan Dotai Tokei
  Nenpo see Annual Statistics of
  Actual Production of Railway Cars
  864
Texas. Coordinating Board. Texas
  College and University System. C B
  Annual Report (US ISSN 0082-
  2981) 340
Texas. Coordinating Board. Texas
  College and University System. C B
  Policy Paper (US ISSN 0082-299X)
  340
Texas. Coordinating Board. Texas
  College and University System. C B
  Study Paper (US ISSN 0082-3007)
  340

Texas. Department of Corrections.
  Research and Development Division.
  Research Report (US ISSN 0095-
  1900) 284
Texas. Department of Health
  Resources. Biennial Report (US
  ISSN 0163-1667) 754
Texas. Department of Water Resources.
  Report (US) 898
Texas. Forest Service. Cooperative
  Forest Tree Improvement Program.
  Progress Report (US ISSN 0082-
  3031) 411
Texas. Governor's Committee on
  Aging. Biennial Report (US ISSN
  0082-3058) 809
Texas. Industrial Commission. Annual
  Report (US ISSN 0361-2597) 225
Texas. Legislative Reference Library.
  Chief Elected and Administrative
  Officials. (US) 746
Texas. Railroad Commission. Oil and
  Gas Division. Annual Report (US)
  681
Texas. State Board of Landscape
  Architects. Annual Roster (US ISSN
  0092-3745) 70
Texas. Water Development Board.
  Report see Texas. Department of
  Water Resources. Report 898
Texas. Water Quality Board. Agency
  Publication (US ISSN 0091-0848)
  915
Texas. Water Quality Board. Biennial
  Report (US ISSN 0082-3570) 915
Texas A & I University Studies see T A
  I U S 493
Texas A & M Oceanographic Studies
  (US ISSN 0082-2922) 312
Texas A & M University. Department
  of Oceanography. Contributions in
  Oceanography. (US ISSN 0069-
  9640) 312
Texas Almanac and State Industrial
  Guide (US ISSN 0082-2914) 472
Texas Annual of Electronics Research
  (US) 359
Texas Archeological Society. Bulletin
  (US ISSN 0082-2930) 66
Texas Archeological Society. Special
  Publication (US ISSN 0495-2944)
  66
Texas Archeology (US ISSN 0082-
  2949) 66
Texas Banking Red Book (US) 177
Texas Biannual of Electronics Research
  see Texas Annual of Electronics
  Research 359
Texas Blue Book of Life Insurance
  Statistics (US) 501, 848
Texas Child Migrant Program. Annual
  Report (US) 323
Texas Christian University Monographs
  in History and Culture (US ISSN
  0082-2973) 436
Texas Conference on Computing
  Systems. Proceedings (US) 274
Texas Cotton Review (US ISSN 0082-
  3392) 30, 39
Texas Fact Book (US) 165
Texas Family Physician (US ISSN
  0098-1052) 600
Texas Field Crop Statistics (US ISSN
  0092-153X) 39
Texas Folklore Society. Publications
  (US ISSN 0082-3023) 403
Texas Forestry Papers (US ISSN 0082-
  304X) 411
Texas Industry Series (US ISSN 0082-
  3066) 149
Texas Legislative Issues: Report of the
  Texas Legislature Pre-Session
  Conference (US) 716, 746
Texas Legislature Pre-Session
  Conference. Proceedings and Report
  see Texas Legislative Issues: Report
  of the Texas Legislature Pre-Session
  Conference 716
Texas List of Scientific and Technical
  Serial Publications (US) 536
Texas Livestock Statistics (US ISSN
  0091-1550) 25
Texas Memorial Museum. Bulletin (US
  ISSN 0082-3074) 655
Texas Memorial Museum.
  Miscellaneous Papers (US ISSN
  0082-3082) 655
Texas Memorial Museum. Museum
  Notes (US) 655

Texas Migrant Program. Annual Report
  see Texas Child Migrant Program.
  Annual Report 323
Texas Ornithological Society. Bulletin
  (US ISSN 0040-4543) 125
Texas Public Library Statistics (US
  ISSN 0082-3120) 536
Texas Public School Law Bulletin (US
  ISSN 0362-6334) 323
Texas Reports on Biology and
  Medicine(US ISSN 0040-4675)
  108, 600
Texas Research Foundation, Renner.
  Contributions (US ISSN 0082-3139)
  118
Texas School Directory (US ISSN
  0363-4566) 332
Texas Slough see Slough 572
Texas Small Grains Statistics (US
  ISSN 0091-4673) 25
Texas Special Libraries Directory (US
  ISSN 0082-3163) 536
Texas Speech Communication Journal
  (US ISSN 0363-8782) 553
Texas State Industrial Directory (US)
  242
Texas Tech University. Graduate
  Studies (US ISSN 0082-3198) 340
Texas Tech University.
  Interdepartmental Committee on
  Comparative Literature. Proceedings
  of the Comparative Literature
  Symposium (US ISSN 0084-9103)
  574
Texas TourBook see Tourbook: Texas
  892
Texas Trade and Professional
  Associations and Other Selected
  Organizations (US) 242
Texas Vital Statistics (US ISSN 0495-
  257X) 729
Texas Water Resources Institute.
  Technical Report (US) 898
Texas Yearbook (US ISSN 0092-7996)
  681
Texscope. European Textile Distribution
  (US) 857
Texscope (New York) see Texscope; U
  S A Textile Industry Overview 857
Texscope: European Overview (US)
  857
Texscope: Open End Spinning (US)
  857
Texscope: Textile Technological
  Investment Climate (US) 857
Texscope; U S A Textile Industry
  Overview (US ISSN 0092-3540)
  857
Text (SW ISSN 0345-0112) 578
Textausgaben zur Fruehen
  Sozialistischen Literatur in
  Deutschland (GE ISSN 0081-3257)
  574
Textbooks in Print see El Hi Textbooks
  in Print 327
Texte und Untersuchungen zur
  Geschichte der Altchristlichen
  Literatur (GE ISSN 0082-3589)
  768
Texte zur Kirchen- und
  Theologiegeschichte (GW ISSN
  0082-3597) 768
Textes d'Interet General (FR) 519
Textes Klanken Beeld (NE) 860
Textes Litteraires Francais (SZ) 574
Textil-Industrie und ihre Helfer (GW
  ISSN 0082-3627) 857
Textile & Engineering Directory for
  India & Pakistan see Worrall's Textile
  & Engineering Directory 243
Textile Buyer's Guide and Directory of
  Southern Africa (SA) 242, 857
Textile Council of Australia. Textile
  Information Service (AT) 915
Textile Country Reporter (SZ) 857
Textile Handbook see American Home
  Economics Association. Textiles and
  Clothing Section. Textile Handbook
  855
Textile History (UK ISSN 0040-4969)
  857
Textile Industries Buyers Guide (US)
  857
Textile Industry in O E C D Countries
  (FR ISSN 0474-6023) 857
Textile Industry Technical Conference.
  Record see Annual Textile Industry
  Technical Conference. (Publication)
  855

Textile Industry Yearbook see
  Tekstiiliteollisuuden Vuosikirja 857
Textile Institute. Annual Conference
  (UK) 857
Textile Institute. Annual Report (UK)
  857
Textile Japan/Tekisutairu Japan (JA
  ISSN 0082-366X) 857
Textile Museum Journal (US ISSN
  0083-7407) 857
Textile Recorder Annual and
  Machinery Review see International
  Textile Machinery 856
Textile World Buyer's Guide/Fact File
  (US ISSN 0495-369X) 857
Textilindustrins Aarsbok see
  Tekstiiliteollisuuden Vuosikirja 857
Texts and Monographs in Computer
  Science (US) 274
Texts and Monographs in Physics (US)
  699
Texts and Studies in the History of
  Mediaeval Education (US ISSN
  0082-3732) 323, 463
Texts from Cuneiform Sources (US
  ISSN 0082-3759) 436
Textus (IS ISSN 0082-3767) 768
Textus Patristici et Liturgici (GW
  ISSN 0082-3775) 768
Thacker's Calcutta Directory (II) 242
Thai Chamber of Commerce. Business
  Directory (TH ISSN 0563-3400)
  242
Thailand. Division of Agricultural
  Chemistry. Report on Fertilizer
  Experiments and Soil Fertility
  Research (TH ISSN 0085-7246) 39
Thailand. Ministry of Foreign Affairs.
  News Bulletin (TH) 723
Thailand. National Statistical Office,
  Report of Industrial Survey in
  Northeast Region/Thailand.
  Samnakngan Sathiti Haeng Chat
  (TH) 165
Thailand. National Statistical Office.
  Research Paper (TH) 848
Thailand. National Statistical Office.
  Statistical Bibliography (TH ISSN
  0082-3791) 95, 848
Thailand. Samnakngan Sathiti Haeng
  Chat see Thailand. National
  Statistical Office, Report of Industrial
  Survey in Northeast Region 165
Thailand Standard Industrial
  Classification (TH) 211
Thailand Trade Index (TH) 198
Thailand Year Book (TH ISSN 0563-
  3737) 446
Thailand's Budget in Brief (TH) 233
Thailand's Foreign Trade Statistics (TH)
  165
Thames Book (UK ISSN 0082-3805)
  426, 891
Thapar's Indian Industrial Directory
  and Import and Export Directory of
  the World (II) 242
The Electrification Council Report see
  T E C Report 359
Theata (US) 54, 393, 403
Theater Computer Users Group Notes
  (US) 274, 860
Theater Klanken Beeld (NE) 860
Theatre Angels (US) 205, 860
Theatre Annual (US ISSN 0082-3821)
  860
Theatre Canada. Special Bulletin (CN
  ISSN 0703-5640) 860
Theatre Communications Group
  National Working Conference.
  Proceedings see T C G National
  Working Conference. Proceedings
  860
Theatre d'Aujourd'hui (FR) 860
Theatre Directory (UK) 860
Theatre Ouvert (FR ISSN 0082-383X)
  860
Theatre Perspectives (US) 860
Theatre Profiles (US ISSN 0361-7947)
  860
Theatre Student Series (US ISSN
  0082-3848) 860
Theatre Studies (US) 860
Theatre World (US ISSN 0082-3856)
  860
Themata Chorou & Technon see Design
  in Greece 69
Thematic Catalogue Series (US) 664

Thematical Reviews *see* Temadokumentacios Kiadvanyok *853*
Thematische Information Philosophie (GE) *691*
Themen der Zeit (GW) *915*
Theodor-Storm-Gesellschaft. Schriften (GW ISSN 0082-3880) *574*
Theokratia; Jahrbuch des Institutum Judaicum Delitzschianum (NE ISSN 0082-3899) *771*
Theologica *see* Claretianum *774*
Theological and Religious Index (UK ISSN 0306-087X) *4, 769*
Theological Markings (US ISSN 0362-0603) *768*
Theologie und Dienst (GW) *768*
Theologische Dissertationen (SZ ISSN 0082-3902) *768*
Theoretical and Experimental Biology (US ISSN 0082-3945) *108*
Theoretical Chemistry (UK ISSN 0305-9995) *248*
Theoretical Chemistry (US ISSN 0082-3961) *248*
Theoretical Chemistry: Advances and Perspectives (US ISSN 0361-0551) *248*
Theoretische und Experimentelle Methoden der Regelunstechnik (GW) *274*
Theorie de la Production (FR ISSN 0082-3988) *149*
Theorie des Systemes (US ISSN 0563-4407) *274*
Theorie et Critique *see* T & C *79*
Theorie und Organisation (GW) *716*
Theory and Decision Library (NE) *801*
Theory and Practice of Scientific Information *see* Tudomanyos Tajekoztatas Elmelete es Gyakorlata *536*
Theory and Research in Teaching Series(US) *915*
Theriaca (DK ISSN 0082-4003) *686*
Thermodynamics Research Center. A P I 44. Hydrocarbon Project. Selected Values of Properties of Hydrocarbons and Related Compounds. Category A: Tables of Selected Values of Physical and Thermodynamic Properties of Hydrocarbons *see* Thermodynamics Research Center. Hydrocarbon Project. Selected Values of Properties of Hydrocarbons and Related Compounds. Category A: Tables of Selected Values of Physical and Thermodynamic Properties of Hydrocarbons *256*
Thermodynamics Research Center. A P I 44. Hydrocarbon Project. Selected Values of Properties of Hydrocarbons and Related Compounds. Category B: Selected Infrared Spectral Data *see* Thermodynamics Research Center. Hydrocarbon Project. Selected Values of Properties of Hydrocarbons and Related Compounds. Category B: Selected Infrared Spectral Data *250*
Thermodynamics Research Center. A P I 44. Hydrocarbon Project. Selected Values of Properties of Hydrocarbons and Related Compounds. Category C: Selected Ultraviolet Spectral Data *see* Thermodynamics Research Center. Hydrocarbon Project. Selected Values of Properties of Hydrocarbons and Related Compounds. Category C: Selected Ultraviolet Spectral Data *250*
Thermodynamics Research Center. A P I 44. Hydrocarbon Project. Selected Values of Properties of Hydrocarbons and Related Compounds. Category D: Selected Raman Spectral Data *see*

Thermodynamics Research Center. A P I 44. Hydrocarbon Project. Selected Values of Properties of Hydrocarbons and Related Compounds. Category E: Selected Mass Spectral Data *see* Thermodynamics Research Center. Hydrocarbon Project. Selected Values of Properties of Hydrocarbons and Related Compounds. Category E: Selected Mass Spectral Data *250*
Thermodynamics Research Center. A P I 44. Hydrocarbon Project. Selected Values of Properties of Hydrocarbons and Related Compounds. Category F: Selected Nuclear Magnetic Resonance Data *see* Thermodynamics Research Center. Hydrocarbon Project. Selected Values of Properties of Hydrocarbons and Related Compounds. Category F: Selected Nuclear Magnetic Resonance Data *250*
Thermodynamics Research Center. Hydrocarbon Project. Selected Values of Properties of Hydrocarbons and Related Compounds. Category A: Tables of Selected Values of Physical and Thermodynamic Properties of Hydrocarbons (US) *256*
Thermodynamics Research Center. Hydrocarbon Project. Selected Values of Properties of Hydrocarbons and Related Compounds. Category B: Selected Infrared Spectral Data (US) *250*
Thermodynamics Research Center. Hydrocarbon Project. Selected Values of Properties of Hydrocarbons and Related Compounds. Category C: Selected Ultraviolet Spectral Data (US) *250*
Thermodynamics Research Center. Hydrocarbon Project. Selected Values of Properties of Hydrocarbons and Related Compounds. Category D: Selected Raman Spectral Data (US) *250*
Thermodynamics Research Center. Hydrocarbon Project. Selected Values of Properties of Hydrocarbons and Related Compounds. Category E: Selected Mass Spectral Data (US) *250*
Thermodynamics Research Center. Hydrocarbon Project. Selected Values of Properties of Hydrocarbons and Related Compounds. Category F: Selected Nuclear Magnetic Resonance Data (US) *250*
Thermodynamics Research Center. Hydrocarbon Project. Selected Values of Properties of Hydrocarbons and Related Compounds. Category G: Selected 130 Nuclear Magnetic Resonance Spectral Data *see* Thermodynamics Research Center Hydrocarbon Project. Selected Values of Properties of Hydrocarbons and Related Compounds. Category G: Selected C-13 Nuclear Magnetic Resonance Spectral Data *250*
Thermodynamics Research Center. International Data Series. Selected Data on Mixtures. Series A. Thermodynamic Properties of Non-reacting Binary Systems of Organic Substances (US ISSN 0147-1503) *254, 256*
Thermodynamics Research Center Data Project. Selected Values of Properties of Chemical Compounds. Category A. Tables of Selected Values of Physical and Thermodynamic Properties of Chemical Compounds (US ISSN 0082-4046) *250, 256*
Thermodynamics Research Center Data Project. Selected Values of Properties of Chemical Compounds. Category B. Selected Infrared Spectral Data (US ISSN 0082-402X) *250*

Thermodynamics Research Center Data Project. Selected Values of Properties of Chemical Compounds. Category C. Selected Ultraviolet Spectral Data *see* Thermodynamics Research Center. Hydrocarbon Project. Selected Values of Properties of Hydrocarbons and Related Compounds. Category C: Selected Ultraviolet Spectral Data *250*
Thermodynamics Research Center Data Project. Selected Values of Properties of Chemical Compounds. Category D. Selected Raman Spectral Data *see* Thermodynamics Research Center. Hydrocarbon Project. Selected Values of Properties of Hydrocarbons and Related Compounds. Category D: Selected Raman Spectral Data *250*
Thermodynamics Research Center Data Project. Selected Values of Properties of Chemical Compounds. Category E. Selected Mass Spectral Data *see* Thermodynamics Research Center. Hydrocarbon Project. Selected Values of Properties of Hydrocarbons and Related Compounds. Category E: Selected Mass Spectral Data *250*
Thermodynamics Research Center Data Project. Selected Values of Properties of Chemical Compounds. Category F. Selected Nuclear Magnetic Resonance Spectral Data (US ISSN 0082-4070) *250*
Thermodynamics Research Center Hydrocarbon Project. Selected Values of Properties of Hydrocarbons and Related Compounds. Category G: Selected C-13 Nuclear Magnetic Resonance Spectral Data (US) *250*
Thesaurismata (IT ISSN 0082-4097) *436*
Thesaurus - American Petroleum Institute *see* American Petroleum Institute. Central Abstracting and Indexing Service. Thesaurus *678*
Theses and Dissertations Accepted in Partial Fulfillment of the Requirements for Degrees Granted by the Michigan Technological University (US) *95, 854*
Theses and Other Publications of the University of Copenhagen (DK) *95*
Theses Canadiennes *see* Canadian Theses *89*
Theses Canadiennes sur Microfiche (Supplement) *see* Canadian Theses on Microfiche (Supplement) *334*
Theses in Germanic Studies (UK ISSN 0082-4119) *574*
Theses in Latin American Studies at British Universities in Progress and Completed (UK ISSN 0307-109X) *95, 472*
Thesindex Dentaire (FR ISSN 0399-0656) *602*
Thesindex Medical (FR ISSN 0399-0648) *603*
Thirteenth District Dental Society. Bulletin *see* Thirtieth District Dental Society, Fresno, California. Bulletin *610*
Thirtieth District Dental Society, Fresno, California. Bulletin (US) *610*
This Is Rhode Island (US) *891*
Thomas Grocery Register (US ISSN 0082-4151) *407*
Thomas Hardy Society. Review (UK ISSN 0307-1642) *574*
Thomas Hardy Year Book (UI ISSN 0082-416X) *574*
Thomas Jefferson Center for Political Economy. Research Monographs. (US ISSN 0082-4178) *915*
Thomas Mann Gesellschaft. Blaetter (SZ ISSN 0082-4186) *574*
Thomas Register of American Manufacturers *see* Thomas Register of American Manufacturers and Thomas Register Catalog File *219*
Thomas Register of American Manufacturers and Thomas Register Catalog File (US) *219, 242*
Thom's Commercial Directory (IE ISSN 0082-4224) *242*
Thom's Dublin & County Street Directory (IE) *377, 426*
Thorbecke-Colleges (NE) *463*
Thoreau Society Booklets (US) *557*

Thoresby Society, Leeds, England. Publications (UK ISSN 0082-4232) *436*
Thorndike Encyclopedia of Banking and Financial Tables (Supplement) (US) *177*
Thoroton Society of Nottinghamshire. Transactions (UK ISSN 0309-9210) *66, 463*
Thoroughbred Racing Associations. Directory and Record Book (US ISSN 0082-4240) *828*
Thorvaldsen Museum. Meddelelser (DK ISSN 0085-7262) *79, 655*
Thoughts on International Development(CN) *201*
Thousand Eyes (US) *651*
Threads in Action Monograph (US) *857*
Three Minutes a Day (US) *768*
Three Thousand Books for Secondary School Libraries *see* Books for Secondary School Libraries *527*
Threshold (UK ISSN 0040-6562) *575*
Through Casa Guidi Windows (US) *582*
Through Europe by Train (FR ISSN 0579-8256) *874*
Thrum's All About Hawaii (US) *891*
Thruway-Interstate Highway Guide (US ISSN 0082-4267) *891*
Thunder Bay Camping Guide (CN ISSN 0380-6197) *831, 891*
Thunder Bay Historical Museum Society. Papers and Records (CN ISSN 0082-4283) *472*
Thunderer (UK) *263*
Thurgauische Museum. Mitteilungen (SZ) *655*
Thyssen Technische Berichte (GW ISSN 0340-5060) *630*
Thyssenforschung *see* Thyssen Technische Berichte *630*
Tibet Society Newsletter (US ISSN 0363-311X) *393*
Tibiscus. Seria Arta (RM) *79*
Tibiscus. Seria Etnografie (RM) *54*
Tibiscus. Seria Istorie (RM) *463*
Tibiscus. Seria Stiintele Naturii (RM) *792*
Tidbits (CN) *428*
Tide of Time (AT) *447*
Tidevandstabeller for Groenland (DK) *312*
Tidings (IS) *346*
Tidsskrift for Samfunnsforskning/ Norwegian Journal of Social Research (NO ISSN 0040-716X) *801*
Tierra y Sociedad (PE) *20*
Tierreich (GW ISSN 0040-7305) *130*
Tiers-Monde en Marche (FR) *201*
Tierwelt Deutschlands (GE ISSN 0082-4305) *130*
Tijdschrift voor Entomologie (NE ISSN 0040-7496) *122*
Tilburg Studies in Econometrics (NE) *190*
Tilburg Studies in Economics (NE ISSN 0564-6278) *190*
Timber and Plywood. Board News Annual (UK ISSN 0082-433X) *413*
Timber Tax Journal (US ISSN 0563-5446) *233, 411*
Timber Trades Directory (UK ISSN 0082-4372) *242, 413*
Timber Trades Journal. Annual Special Issue (UK ISSN 0082-4364) *413*
Time Service (IT) *84*
Timeless Fellowship (II ISSN 0563-5489) *536*
Times Guide to the House of Commons(UK ISSN 0082-4399) *716*
Times Literary Supplement. T.L.S; Essays and Reviews (US ISSN 0082-4410) *575*
Times of India Annual (II ISSN 0082-4437) *446*
Times of India Directory and Yearbook Including Who's Who (II ISSN 0082-4445) *446*
Times Trade and Industrial Directory (NR) *242*
Times 1000 (UK ISSN 0082-4429) *225*
Tin Statistics (UK) *630*
Tinplate World Survey (UK ISSN 0141-5301) *630*

Tio Sam y Usted (US) *915*
Tire and Rim Association. Standards Year Book (US ISSN 0082-4496) *777*
Tiroler Landesmuseum Ferdinandeum, Innsbruck. Veroeffentlichungen (AU) *655*
Tiroler Ortschroniken (AU) *463*
Tiroler Verkehrswirtschaftliche Zahlen (AU ISSN 0300-1997) *876*
Tiroler Geschichtsquellen (AU) *463*
Tiryns (GW ISSN 0082-450X) *66, 260*
Tissue Culture Studies in Japan: The Annual Bibliography/Nihon Soshiki Baiyo Kenkyu Nenpo (JA ISSN 0082-4518) *603*
Titles in Series (US ISSN 0082-4526) *95*
Titles of Dissertations and Theses Completed in Home Economics (US ISSN 0082-4534) *479*
Titmouse Annual (CN) *582*
Titmouse Review *see* Titmouse Annual *582*
Tjaenstemaennens Centralorganisation. Aaret (SW ISSN 0082-4542) *211*
Tlaloc (US) *575*
To Know Wallony *see* Connaitre la Wallonie *431*
To the Source/El Ha'ayin *see* Sources of Contemporary Jewish Thought *557*
Tobacco Associates. Annual Report (US ISSN 0082-4593) *861*
Tobacco Export Promotion Council. Annual Report and Accounts (II) *39*
Tobacco Merchants Association of the United States. National Bulletin (US) *861*
Tobacco News (II) *861*
Tobacco Reprint Series (US) *861*
Tobacco Research Council. Research Papers (UK ISSN 0082-4607) *915*
Tobacco Research Council. Review of Activities (UK ISSN 0082-4615) *915*
Tobacco Science Yearbook (US ISSN 0082-4623) *861*
Tobacco Trade Year Book and Diary (UK ISSN 0082-4631) *861*
Todaa (IS) *393, 901*
Todo (BL) *182*
Toern *see* Wudd *770*
Toestand in de Wereld *see* Dat Was de Toestand in de Wereld *431*
Togo. Direction de la Meteorologie Nationale. Resume Annuel du Temps(TG) *635*
Toho Gakuho *see* Oriental Studies *670*
Tohoku Daigaku Rigakubu Chishitsugaku Koseibutsugaku Kyoshitsu Kenkyu Hobun Hokoku *see* Tohoku University. Institute of Geology and Paleontology. Contributions *300*
Tohoku Psychologica Folia (JA ISSN 0040-8743) *738*
Tohoku University. Institute for Agricultural Research. Reports (JA) *26*
Tohoku University. Institute of Geology and Paleontology. Contributions/ Tohoku Daigaku Rigakubu Chishitsugaku Koseibutsugaku Kyoshitsu Kenkyu Hobun Hokoku (JA ISSN 0082-4658) *300, 674*
Tohoku University. Institute of Geology and Paleontology. Science Reports. Second Series (JA ISSN 0082-464X) *300, 674*
Tohoku University. Research Institute of Electrical Communication. Technical Report (JA) *265*
Tohoku University. Research Institutes. Science Reports. Series D: Agriculture *see* Tohoku University. Institute for Agricultural Research. Reports *20*
Tokei Suri Kenkyusho Nenpo *see* Institute of Statistical Mathematics. Annual Report *586*
Tokushima University. Faculty of Engineering. Bulletin (JA ISSN 0040-8883) *370*
Tokyo Astronomical Bulletin. Second Series (JA ISSN 0082-4690) *84*

Tokyo Astronomical Observatory. Annals. Second Series (JA ISSN 0082-4704) *84*
Tokyo Astronomical Observatory. Report (JA) *84*
Tokyo Astronomical Observatory. Reprints (JA ISSN 0082-4712) *84*
Tokyo College of Domestic Science. Bulletin/Tokyo Kasei Daigaku Kenkyu Kiyo (JA) *479*
Tokyo Daigaku Chirigaku Kyoshitsu Kaiho *see* University of Tokyo. Department of Geography. Bulletin *427*
Tokyo Daigaku Kaiyo Kenkyusho *see* University of Tokyo. Ocean Research Institute. Bulletin *313*
Tokyo Daigaku Rigakubu Kiyo, Dai-2-rui, Chishitsugaku, Kobutsugaku, Chirigaku, Chiyu Butsurigaku *see* University of Tokyo. Faculty of Science. Journal. Section 2: Geology, Mineralogy, Geography, Geophysics *290*
Tokyo Daigaku Rigakubu Kiyo, Dai-3-rui, Shokubutsugaku *see* University of Tokyo. Faculty of Science. Journal. Section 3: Botany *119*
Tokyo Daigaku Rigakubu Kiyo Dai-4-rui, Dobutsugaku *see* University of Tokyo. Faculty of Science. Journal. Section 4: Zoology *131*
Tokyo Daigaku Rigakubu Kiyo, Dai-5-rui, Jinruigaku *see* University of Tokyo. Faculty of Science. Journal. Section 5: Anthropology *55*
Tokyo Institute of Technology. Bulletin (JA ISSN 0495-8020) *853*
Tokyo Institute of Technology. Research Laboratory of Resources Utilization. Report/Shigen Kagaku Kenkyusho (JA ISSN 0495-8055) *853*
Tokyo Kasei Daigaku Kenkyu Kiyo *see* Tokyo College of Domestic Science. Bulletin *479*
Tokyo Kyoiku Daigaku Rika Kiyo B, Dobutsugaku to Shokubutsugu *see* Tokyo University of Education. Faculty of Science. Science Reports. Section B: Zoology and Botany *130*
Tokyo Kyoiku Daigaku Rigakubu Kiyo A *see* Tokyo University of Education. Faculty of Science. Science Reports. Section A: Mathematics and Physics *590*
Tokyo Lincoln Book Center. Report *see* Tokyo Lincoln Center. Report *438*
Tokyo Lincoln Center. Report (JA) *438*
Tokyo Medical and Dental University. Institute for Medical and Dental Engineering. Reports/Iyo Kizai Kenkyusho Hokoku (JA ISSN 0082-4739) *600, 610*
Tokyo Metropolitan Agricultural Experiment Station, Itsukaichi Office. Forestry Experimental Bulletin/ Ringyo Shiken Kenkyu Hokoku (JA ISSN 0082-4720) *411*
Tokyo Metropolitan Institute of Neurosciences. Annual Report/ Tokyo-to Shinkei Kagaku Sogo Kenkyujo Nempo (JA) *621*
Tokyo Metropolitan Research Laboratory of Public Health, Annual Report/Tokyo-toritsu Eisei Kenkyusho Kenyu Nenpo (JA ISSN 0082-4771) *600, 754*
Tokyo Metropolitan University. Department of Geography. Geographical Reports/Tokyo-toritsu Daigaku Chirigaku Hokoku (JA ISSN 0386-8710) *426*
Tokyo Metropolitan University. Faculty of Technology. Memoirs/Tokyo-toritsu Daigaku Kogakubu Hokoku (JA ISSN 0082-4747) *853*
Tokyo No Ikebana (JA) *416*
Tokyo Suisan Daigaku Ronshu *see* Tokyo University of Fisheries. Report *400*
Tokyo-to Shinkei Kagaku Sogo Kenkyujo Nempo *see* Tokyo Metropolitan Institute of Neurosciences. Annual Report *621*

Tokyo-toritsu Daigaku Chirigaku Hokoku *see* Tokyo Metropolitan University. Department of Geography. Geographical Reports *426*
Tokyo-toritsu Daigaku Kogakubu Hokoku *see* Tokyo Metropolitan University. Faculty of Technology. Memoirs *853*
Tokyo-toritsu Eisei Kenkyusho Kenkyu Nenpo *see* Tokyo Metropolitan Research Laboratory of Public Health, Annual Report *600*
Tokyo-toritsu Koka Tanki Daigaku Kenkyu Hokoku *see* Metropolitan College of Technology, Tokyo. Memoirs *852*
Tokyo University of Education. Faculty of Science. Science Reports. Section A: Mathematics and Physics/Tokyo Kyokai Daigaku Rigakubu Kiyo A (JA) *590, 699*
Tokyo University of Education. Faculty of Science. Science Reports. Section B: Zoology and Botany/Tokyo Kyoiku Daigaku Rika Kiyo B, Dobutsugaku to Shokubutsugu (JA) *118, 130*
Tokyo University of Education. Faculty of Science. Science Reports. Section C: Geography, Geology and Mineralogy (JA) *300, 426, 647*
Tokyo University of Fisheries. Journal. Special Edition *see* Tokyo University of Fisheries. Transactions *400*
Tokyo University of Fisheries. Report/ Tokyo Suisan Daigaku Ronshu (JA ISSN 0563-8372) *400*
Tokyo University of Fisheries. Transactions (JA) *400*
Tokyo University of Foreign Studies. Summary (JA ISSN 0082-4844) *340*
Toledo Area Artists Exhibition (US ISSN 0082-4852) *79*
Toll Free Business (US ISSN 0146-6801) *149, 269*
Toll Free Digest (US ISSN 0363-2962) *269*
Tolley's Corporation Tax (UK) *233*
Tolley's Income Tax (UK ISSN 0305-8921) *233*
Tolley's Tax Tables (UK ISSN 0307-6687) *233*
Tonga. Minister of Health. Report (TO ISSN 0082-4895) *754*
Tonggye Suchup *see* Statistical Handbook of Korea *847*
Tools and Tillage (DK ISSN 0563-8887) *21, 436*
Toomey J Gazette *see* Rehabilitation Gazette *346*
Tooth of Time Review (US) *575*
Toothpick, Lisbon & the Orcas Islands (US) *79, 575, 664*
Top Companies (SA ISSN 0563-8895) *225*
Top Executive Compensation (US) *211, 216*
Top Symbols & Trademarks of the World *see* Top Trademarks Annual *677*
Top Tens and Trivia of Rock and Roll and Rhythm and Blues. Annual Supplement (US) *664*
Top Trademarks Annual (IT) *677*
Top 1,000 Directories Used in British Libraries (UK) *536*
Top 1,500 Companies (US ISSN 0275-7435) *149*
Top 1,500 Private Companies (US ISSN 0275-7427) *149*
Topic (US ISSN 0049-4127) *493, 792, 801*
Topical New Issues (US ISSN 0090-7286) *479*
Topical Reviews in Rheumatic Disorders (UK) *624*
Topical Stamp Handbooks (US ISSN 0049-4135) *479*
Topicator (US ISSN 0040-9340) *4, 6, 165*
Topics in Applied Physics (US) *370, 699*
Topics in Astrophysics and Space Physics (US ISSN 0564-6294) *10, 84, 699*
Topics in Bioelectrochemistry and Bioenergetics (US) *112*

Topics in Cognitive Development (US) *738*
Topics in Current Chemistry (US) *248*
Topics in Current Physics (US) *699*
Topics in Environmental Health (NE) *108, 389*
Topics in Infectious Diseases (US ISSN 0360-4977) *608*
Topics in Inorganic and General Chemistry (NE ISSN 0082-495X) *248, 251*
Topics in Ocean Engineering (US ISSN 0085-7297) *312, 370*
Topics in Philosophy (US) *691*
Topics in Phosphorous Chemistry (US ISSN 0082-4992) *251*
Topics in Photosynthesis (NE) *108*
Topics in Stereochemistry (US ISSN 0082-500X) *248*
Toposcope (SA) *441*
Torch (LB) *441*
Torchlighter *see* Campaigner *804*
Toronto. Public Libraries. Guide to Serials Currently Received in the Public Libraries of Metropolitan Toronto *see* Guide to Periodicals and Newspapers in the Public Libraries of Metropolitan Toronto *91*
Toronto & Area Construction Industry Directory. Purchasing Guide (CN) *139, 370*
Toronto Historical Board. Year Book (CN ISSN 0226-7209) *472*
Toronto Mediaeval Latin Texts (CN ISSN 0082-5050) *463, 575*
Toronto Medieval Bibliographies (CN ISSN 0082-5042) *438*
Toronto Semitic Texts and Studies (CN ISSN 0082-5123) *446*
Torquay Natural History Society. Transactions and Proceedings (UK ISSN 0082-5344) *792*
Torre Davidica (IT ISSN 0040-960X) *768*
Torry Research Station, Aberdeen, Scotland. Annual Report (UK ISSN 0082-5352) *400*
Torteneti Statisztikai Evkonyv *see* Hungary. Kozponti Statisztikai Hivatal. Torteneti Statisztikai Tanulmanyok *841*
Torts *see* B A R-B R I Bar Review. Torts *280*
Tosan (US) *393*
Toshi Kenkyu Hokoku *see* Report on Urban Research *487*
Tosi Gagye Yonbo *see* Korea (Republic) Bureau of Statistics. Annual Report on the Family Income and Expenditure Survey *160*
Tosoguian Hak (KO) *536*
Tosomaeup Census Bogo Seo *see* Korea (Republic) Bureau of Statistics. Wholesale and Retail Trade Census Report *160*
Totalisator Agency Board. Annual Report (NZ) *746*
Totok: Handbuch der Geschichte der Philosophie (GW) *691*
Tottori Daigaku Nogakubu Fuzoku Enshurin Hokoku *see* Tottori University Forests. Bulletin *411*
Tottori University. Faculty of Agriculture. Journal (JA ISSN 0082-5360) *21*
Tottori University Forests. Bulletin/ Tottori Daigaku Nogakubu Fuzoku Enshurin Hokoku (JA ISSN 0082-5379) *411*
Tour Organizers' Handbook/Guide du Directeur de Tournees de Spectacles (CN) *860*
Tourbook: Alabama, Louisiana, Mississippi (US ISSN 0361-4948) *891*
Tourbook: Arizona, New Mexico (US ISSN 0362-3599) *891*
Tourbook: Arkansas, Kansas, Missouri, Oklahoma (US) *891*
Tourbook: Atlantic Provinces and Quebec (US ISSN 0363-1788) *891*
Tourbook: California, Nevada (US) *891*
Tourbook: Colorado, Utah (US ISSN 0362-9821) *891*
Tourbook: Connecticut, Massachusetts, Rhode Island (US) *872*
Tourbook: Florida (US ISSN 0516-9674) *891*

Tourbook: Georgia, North Carolina, South Carolina (US ISSN 0361-4956) *891*
TourBook: Hawaii (US) *891*
Tourbook: Idaho, Montana, Wyoming (US ISSN 0363-2695) *891*
Tourbook: Illinois, Indiana, Ohio (US) *891*
Tourbook: Kentucky, Tennessee (US ISSN 0361-4964) *891*
Tourbook: Maine, New Hampshire, Vermont (US) *872*
Tourbook: Michigan, Wisconsin (US) *891*
Tourbook: Mid-Atlantic (US ISSN 0364-0086) *891*
Tourbook: New Jersey, Pennsylvania (US) *891*
Tourbook: New York (US) *891*
Tourbook: North Central (US) *891*
Tourbook: Ontario (US) *891*
Tourbook: Texas (US) *892*
Tourbook: Western Canada and Alaska (US ISSN 0362-3602) *892*
Touring Artists Directory (CN) *860*
Touring Club Italiano. Servizio Informazioni Turistiche. Fascicoli di Documentazione per i Viaggi in Europa *see* Europa Facile *884*
Touring Directory of the Performing Arts in Canada *see* Touring Artists Directory *860*
Touring Guide to England (UK) *892*
Touring Guide to Ireland (UK) *892*
Touring Guide to Scotland (UK) *892*
Touring Guide to Wales (UK) *892*
Touring with Towser (US ISSN 0082-5441) *682*
Tourism (UK ISSN 0144-8099) *892*
Tourism and Migration Statistics (FJ) *848*, *893*
Tourism Compendium (SP) *95*, *893*
Tourism in Africa. Annual Bulletin (UN) *892*
Tourism in Arkansas; Activity Report (US) *892*
Tourism in Greece (GR ISSN 0082-545X) *892*
Tourism in the British Virgin Islands (VB) *892*
Tourism Industry Association of Canada. Convention Report (CN) *892*
Tourism Research Bulletin/Nashrat al-Abhath Assyiahiyah (JO) *892*
Tourist Bibliography *see* Tourism Compendium *893*
Tourist Guide/Touristique (CN) *892*
Tournees de Spectacles (CN ISSN 0317-5979) *860*
Tout le Tricot - Tricot d'Art (FR ISSN 0183-3928) *477*
Toute la Boisson. International (FR ISSN 0082-5484) *86*
Towards a Shipping Policy for the EEC(UK) *198*, *881*
Towarzystwo Literackie im. A. Mickiewicza. Biblioteka (PL ISSN 0067-7787) *575*
Towarzystwo Naukowe w Toruniu. Fontes (PL ISSN 0082-5506) *436*, *463*
Towarzystwo Naukowe w Toruniu. Komisja Historii Sztuki. Teka (PL ISSN 0082-5514) *79*
Towarzystwo Naukowe w Toruniu. Prace Archeologiczne (PL) *66*
Towarzystwo Naukowe w Toruniu. Roczniki (PL ISSN 0082-5522) *792*
Tower Bibliography Series *see* University of Texas. Humanities Research Center. Tower Bibliographical Series *96*
Town and Country Planning Association. Annual Report (UK ISSN 0308-082X) *487*
Town and Country Planning Summer School; Report of Proceedings (UK ISSN 0078-2114) *487*
Townsend Society of America. Newsletter (US) *418*
Toxicology Annual (US ISSN 0361-3410) *686*
Toy and Decoration Fair (CN ISSN 0317-9443) *429*
Toy Trader Year Book (UK ISSN 0082-5611) *429*

Toyama-ken Eisei Tokei Nenpo *see* Toyama Prefecture. Annual Report of Public Health *754*
Toyama Mercantile Marine College. Journal/Toyama Shosen Koto Senmon Gakko Kenkyu Shuroku (JA) *881*
Toyama Prefecture. Annual Report of Public Health/Toyama-ken Eisei Tokei Nenpo (JA) *754*
Toyama Shosen Koto Senmon Gakko Kenkyu Shuroku *see* Toyama Mercantile Marine College. Journal *881*
Toyo Tsushinki Giho *see* Toyo's Technical Bulletin *265*
Toyo's Technical Bulletin/Toyo Tsushinki Giho (JA) *265*
Toyota in Brief (JA) *872*
Toys Directory *see* Toys, Hobbies & Crafts Directory Issue *429*
Toys, Hobbies & Crafts Directory Issue (US) *429*
Trabajo (CK) *211*
Trabajos de Prehistoria. Nueva Serie (SP ISSN 0082-5638) *66*
Trabajos Monograficos sobre la Independencia de Norteamerica (SP) *472*
Trabrennen (AU ISSN 0082-5646) *828*
Track and Field Guide *see* N A G W S Guide. Track and Field *830*
Track and Field Rules and Records (US) *831*
Tractocatalogue (FR ISSN 0082-5662) *32*
Tractor Performance Pocket Book (US) *32*
Trade and Industrial Directory of Nepal(NP) *242*
Trade Associations and Professional Bodies of the United Kingdom (US ISSN 0082-5689) *242*
Trade Directory and Guide Book to Ethiopia (ET ISSN 0564-0490) *892*
Trade Directory of Guyana (UK) *242*
Trade Directory of Malta (UK ISSN 0082-5697) *242*
Trade Directory of Papua New Guinea (UK) *242*
Trade Directory of Seychelles (SE) *242*
Trade Directory of Spanish-Lusitanian and Latin American Countries and the U.S.A. *see* Anuario Comercial Iberoamericano *193*
Trade Directory of the Republic of the Sudan (UK ISSN 0082-5735) *242*
Trade Directory of Western Sweden (SW) *180*
Trade Directory Wine and Spirit *see* Off Licence News Directory *86*
Trade Index of Iran (IR ISSN 0082-5751) *198*
Trade-Mark Register of the United States (US ISSN 0082-5786) *677*
Trade Names Dictionary (US) *677*
Trade of China (CH ISSN 0082-5778) *198*
Trade Outlets and Taxable Retail Sales in California *see* Taxable Sales in California (Sales and Use Tax) *233*
Trade Union Register (UK ISSN 0307-7543) *507*
Trade Unions in India (II ISSN 0445-6289) *507*
Trade Unions International of Chemical, Oil and Allied Workers. International Trade Conference. Documents (HU ISSN 0084-1544) *507*
Trader Handbook *see* Motor Trader Directory *240*
Trades Union Directory (AT) *507*
Tradeshow/Convention Guide (US) *149*
Tradisjon (NO ISSN 0332-5997) *54*
Traditio (US ISSN 0362-1529) *463*, *493*
Traditional Home Ideas (US) *502*
Traditiones (YU) *403*
Trado; Asian-African Directory of Exporters, Importers and Manufacturers (II ISSN 0082-5824) *242*
Trae Nyt Buyers Guide (DK) *915*
Traffic Laws Commentary (US ISSN 0082-5859) *876*

Traffic Report of the St. Lawrence Seaway (US ISSN 0082-5867) *881*
Traffic Safety (US) *876*
Traffic Trends *see* Maryland. State Highway Administration. Traffic Trends *875*
Trail Blazer's Almanac (US) *831*
Trail Guide (US) *472*
Trailer Life's Recreational Vehicle Campground and Services Directory (US) *831*, *892*
Trails and Tales (US ISSN 0091-6455) *418*
Training and Development Organizations Directory (US) *216*
Training Directory of the Rehabilitation Research and Training Centers (US ISSN 0099-1554) *346*
Training for Agriculture *see* Training for Agriculture and Rural Development *330*
Training for Agriculture and Rural Development (UN) *21*, *330*
Training Resources (US ISSN 0098-5619) *211*, *220*
Trains Annual *see* Railway World Annual *873*
Trains Illustrated Annual *see* Railway World Annual *873*
Transactions - North Carolina Medical Society *see* North Carolina Medical Society. Transactions *598*
Transafrica Historical Papers (KE) *441*
Transatlantic Perspectives (US) *723*
Transcribings. Annual Conference - American Society of Pension Actuaries *see* American Society of Pension Actuaries. Transcribings. Annual Conference *497*
Transfer Credit Practices by Selected Education Institutions (US) *323*
Transfines (GW) *801*
Transient (US) *575*
Transit Fact Book *see* Transit Fact Book & Membership Directory *863*
Transit Fact Book & Membership Directory (CN ISSN 0706-7658) *863*
Transition Metal Chemistry: A Series of Advances (US ISSN 0082-5921) *252*
Translation News (NE ISSN 0046-2837) *553*
Translations and Reprints from the Original Sources of European History *see* Middle Ages *457*
Translations from "Kommunist" *see* U S S R Report: Translations from "Kommunist *716*
Translations of Mathematical Monographs (US ISSN 0065-9282) *590*
Translations on Eastern Europe. Economic and Industrial Affairs *see* Eastern Europe Report: Economic and Industrial Affairs *184*
Translations on Eastern Europe. Political, Sociological and Military Affairs *see* Eastern Europe Report: Political, Sociological and Military Affairs *710*
Translations on Eastern Europe. Scientific Affairs *see* Eastern Europe Report: Scientific Affairs *782*
Translations on Environmental Quality *see* Worldwide Report: Environmental Quality *390*
Translations on Japan *see* Japan Report *187*
Translations on Latin America *see* Latin America Report *187*
Translations on Law of the Sea *see* Worldwide Report: Law of the Sea *524*
Translations on Mongolia *see* Mongolia Report *187*
Translations on Near East and North Africa *see* Near East and North Africa Report *187*
Translations on North Korea *see* Korean Affairs Report *187*
Translations on South and East Asia *see* South and East Asia Report *190*
Translations on Subsaharan Africa *see* Subsaharan Africa Report *190*
Translations on U S S R Agriculture *see* U S S R Report: Agriculture *21*

Translations on U S S R Economic Affairs *see* U S S R Report: Economic Affairs *149*
Translations on U S S R Industrial Affairs *see* U S S R Report: Industrial Affairs *226*
Translations on U S S R Military Affairs *see* U S S R Report: Military Affairs *640*
Translations on U S S R Political and Sociological Affairs *see* U S S R Report: Political and Sociological Affairs *716*
Translations on U S S R Resources *see* U S S R Report: Resources *364*
Translations on U S S R Trade and Services *see* U S S R Report: Trade and Services *226*
Translations on Vietnam *see* Asia Serials: Vietnam Report *183*
Translations on Western Europe *see* Western Europe Report *190*
TransPacific (US ISSN 0041-1299) *575*, *582*
Transplantation Reviews *see* Immunological Reviews *603*
Transplantation Today (US ISSN 0074-3984) *625*
Transporanonces *see* Courrier du Transporteur *862*
Transport & Communications Bulletin for Asia & the Far East (UN ISSN 0041-1396) *265*, *863*
Transport and Handling in the Pulp and Paper Industry (US) *675*
Transport and Road Digest/Vervoer- en Padoorsigte (SA ISSN 0379-4792) *876*
Transport and Road Research (UK) *377*, *876*
Transport Industry and Trade Annual (II) *863*
Transport Industry and Trade Journal *see* Transport Industry and Trade Annual *863*
Transport Manager's Handbook (UK ISSN 0306-9435) *863*
Transport Manager's Handbook (SA) *882*
Transport Maritime: Etudes et Statistiques (FR) *881*
Transport Museums (PL ISSN 0137-4435) *864*
Transport Services Directory (AT) *864*
Transport Statistics Great Britain (UK) *876*
Transport Studies Group. Annual Seminar on Rural Public Transport. Papers and Proceedings (UK) *864*
Transport Workers Union. Triennial Report (MY) *864*
Transportation and Products Legal Directory (US ISSN 0092-6175) *519*
Transportation Law Seminar. Papers and Proceedings (US ISSN 0164-1689) *519*, *864*
Transportation R & D in Canada (CN) *864*
Transportation Research Board Special Report (US ISSN 0360-859X) *377*, *876*
Transportation Research Forum. Proceedings: Annual Meeting (US ISSN 0091-2468) *864*
Transportation Research in Canada *see* Transportation R & D in Canada *864*
Transportation Research Record (US ISSN 0361-1981) *377*, *876*
Transportation Statistics in the United States (US ISSN 0082-5956) *182*, *864*
Transportation Telephone Tickler (US ISSN 0447-9181) *864*
Transportieren Umschlagen Lagern (GW ISSN 0082-5964) *864*
Transportoekonomisk Institutt. Aarsberetning (NO) *874*
Transtelel; Transmissions, Telecommunications, Electronique en France (FR ISSN 0082-5980) *269*
Transvaal Museum. Annals/Transvaal Museum Annale (SA ISSN 0041-1752) *792*
Transvaal Museum. Bulletin (SA ISSN 0496-1102) *655*
Transvaal Museum. Memoirs (SA) *655*

Transvaal Museum Annale *see* Transvaal Museum. Annals 792
Transvaalse Raad vir die Uitvoerende Kunste-Performing Arts Council Transvaal *see* T R U K-P A C T 860
Trattati di Architettura (IT ISSN 0082-6006) 70
Travailleur *see* Labour 208
Travaux d'Histoire Ethico-Politique (SZ ISSN 0082-6073) 436
Travaux d'Humanisme et Renaissance (SZ ISSN 0082-6081) 79, 463
Travaux de Droit, d'Economie de Sociologie et de Sciences Politiques (SZ ISSN 0082-6022) 801
Travaux de Linguistique (BE ISSN 0082-6049) 553
Travaux de Linguistique et de Litterature (FR ISSN 0082-6057) 553, 575
Travaux de Linguistique Japonaise (FR) 553
Travaux et Documents de Geographie Tropicale (FR ISSN 0336-5522) 426
Travaux sur les Pecheries du Quebec (CN ISSN 0082-609X) 400
Travel Abroad: Frontier Formalities (SP ISSN 0082-6103) 892
Travel Alberta-Annual Review (CN) 892
Travel Between Canada and Other Countries/Voyages Entre le Canada et les Autres Pays (CN ISSN 0317-6738) 848, 893
Travel Data Locator Index (US) 892
Travel Executives of New Zealand (NZ) 892
Travel Guide, S.A. (SA) 892
Travel Guide to Europe (US) 892
Travel in America (US) 892
Travel in Greece (GR) 892
Travel Industry Association of Canada. Convention Report *see* Tourism Industry Association of Canada. Convention Report 892
Travel Industry Personnel Directory (US ISSN 0082-6146) 892
Travel Market Yearbook (1980) (US) 892
Travel Marketing *see* Travel Market Yearbook (1980) 892
Travel on Saskatchewan Highways (CN ISSN 0581-8079) 876
Travel Outlook Forum. Proceedings (US) 892
Travel Routes Around the World: Guide to Traveling Around the World by Passenger-Carrying Freighters (US ISSN 0072-8772) 915
Travel Trade Directory, U K and Ireland (UK ISSN 0082-7932) 892
Travel Trade Yearbook (AT) 892
Travel Trends in the United States and Canada (US) 892
Travel Trends in the United States and Canadian Provinces *see* Travel Trends in the United States and Canada 892
Travel Weekly's World Travel Directory (US) 892
Travel World Year Book and Diary (UK ISSN 0082-6219) 892
Travelaid Guide to Egypt (UK) 892
Travelaid Guide to Greece (UK) 892
Traveler's Directory of Fast-Food Restaurants (US) 483, 892
Travelers Guide to Mexico (MX) 892
Traveling with Your Pet (US) 915
Traveller's Guide to Africa (UK ISSN 0140-1300) 892
Traveller's Guide to the Middle East (UK ISSN 0140-1319) 892
Travelog (US) 892
Traza y Baza (SP) 553, 575
Treasury Alaska (US) 848
Treated Wood Perspectives/Perspectives des Bois Traites (CN) 139, 413
Treatise on Analytical Chemistry. Part 1: Theory and Practice of Analytical Chemistry (US ISSN 0082-6243) 250

Treatise on Analytical Chemistry. Part 2: Analytical Chemistry of the Elements; Analytical Chemistry of Organic and Inorganic Compounds (US ISSN 0082-6251) 250
Treatise on Analytical Chemistry. Part 3: Analytical Chemistry in Industry (US ISSN 0082-626X) 250
Treatise on Coatings (US ISSN 0082-6278) 915
Treatise on Materials Science & Technology (US) 380, 853
Tree (US ISSN 0041-2171) 575, 768
Tree Fruit Production Recommendations *see* Cornell Recommendations for Commercial Tree-Fruit Production 415
Tree-Ring Bulletin (US ISSN 0041-2198) 118
Treewell (US ISSN 0085-7378) 582
Trellis (US) 582
Trends in Analytical Chemistry (NE ISSN 0167-2940) 250
Trends in Collective Bargaining Settlements in Nova Scotia (CN ISSN 0381-3258) 211
Trends in Developing Asia (PH) 201
Trends in Expenditure and Employment Data for the Criminal Justice System(US) 284
Trends in Health and Health Services (NZ ISSN 0550-824X) 756
Trends in Southeast Asia (SI ISSN 0082-6316) 446
Trends in the International Petroleum-Refining Industry (US ISSN 0082-6324) 681
Trends in World Economy (HU ISSN 0133-7769) 149
Treubia (IO ISSN 0082-6340) 108
Trevithick Society. Occasional Publication (UK) 853
Tri-State Regional Planning Commission. Annual Regional Report (US) 487
Tri-State Regional Planning Commission. Regional Profile (US) 487
Tri-State Transportation Commission. Public Transport Services to Non C/B/D Employment Concentrations; Progress Report (US ISSN 0082-6359) 876
Tri-University Meson Facility Vancouver, British Columbia. Report *see* T R I U M F, Vancouver, British Columbia. Report 704
Triangle Papers (US) 723
Tribhuvan University. Natural History Museum. Journal (NP) 118
Tribolium Information Bulletin (US ISSN 0082-6391) 122
Tribology Convention. Proceedings (UK ISSN 0082-6405) 383
Tribunal de Commerce, Paris. Annuaire(FR ISSN 0071-9129) 519
Tribus (GW ISSN 0082-6413) 54
Trierer Grabungen und Forschungen (GW ISSN 0082-643X) 66
Trilobite News (NO ISSN 0085-7386) 674
Trinc's Blue Book of the Trucking Industry (US ISSN 0082-6499) 882
Trinidad and Tobago. Central Statistical Office. Annual Statistical Digest (TR ISSN 0082-6502) 848
Trinidad and Tobago. Central Statistical Office. Business Surveys (TR) 190, 848
Trinidad and Tobago. Central Statistical Office. Continuous Sample Survey of Population (TR ISSN 0564-2612) 729
Trinidad and Tobago. Central Statistical Office. Digest of Statistics on Education (TR ISSN 0082-6510) 323
Trinidad and Tobago. Central Statistical Office. Financial Statistics (TR ISSN 0082-6529) 165
Trinidad and Tobago. Central Statistical Office. International Travel Report (TR ISSN 0082-6537) 892

Trinidad and Tobago. Central Statistical Office. Labour Force by Sex (TR) 165
Trinidad and Tobago. Central Statistical Office. Overseas Trade. Annual Report (TR ISSN 0082-6545) 165
Trinidad and Tobago. Central Statistical Office. Pocket Digest (TR) 848
Trinidad and Tobago. Central Statistical Office. Population and Vital Statistics; Report (TR ISSN 0082-6553) 848
Trinidad and Tobago. Central Statistical Office. Staff Papers (TR) 848
Trinidad and Tobago. Ministry of Energy and Energy-Based Industries. Annual Report (TR) 681
Trinidad and Tobago. Ministry of Petroleum and Mines. Annual Report *see* Trinidad and Tobago. Ministry of Energy and Energy-Based Industries. Annual Report 681
Trinidad and Tobago Directory of Commerce, Industry & Tourism (TR) 242
Trinidad and Tobago Today (TR ISSN 0082-6561) 848
Trinidad and Tobago Trade Directory (UK ISSN 0082-657X) 243
Trinitarian Bible Society. Annual Report (UK ISSN 0082-6588) 777
Trinity University Monograph Series in Religion (US) 768
Trinity University Studies in Religion (US ISSN 0082-6596) 768
Triological Society. Transactions *see* American Laryngological, Rhinological and Otological Society. Transactions 617
Triomphe *see* Triomphe Saint-Cyr 640
Triomphe Saint-Cyr (FR ISSN 0036-2794) 640
Tromsoe Museum. Skrifter (NO ISSN 0085-7394) 655
Tropical Diseases Research Series (SZ) 608
Tropical Grain Legume Bulletin (NR ISSN 0304-5765) 43
Tropical Pesticides Research Institute. Annual Report (TZ ISSN 0082-6642) 39
Tropical Science Center, Costa Rica. Occasional Paper (CR ISSN 0069-2107) 792
Tropische und Subtropische Pflanzenwelt (GW ISSN 0302-9417) 118
Der Trotter (GW) 892
Trotting and Pacing Guide (US ISSN 0083-3509) 822
Truck (US) 915
Truck & Bus Tests & Specs (AT) 864, 882
Truck & Van Buyer's Guide (US ISSN 0190-3101) 882
Truck Beat *see* Motor Carrier Statistical Summary 882
Truck Broker Directory (US ISSN 0362-5737) 882
Truck Data Book (CN ISSN 0564-3392) 882
Truck Taxes by States (US ISSN 0517-5666) 233, 882
True Seed Exchange *see* Seed Savers Exchange 476
True to Life (US ISSN 0085-7408) 133, 809
Trufax Directory & Consumer Guide (CN) 280
Trumpet (US) 4
Trust (CN ISSN 0381-9612) 346
Trust Territory of the Pacific Islands. Territorial Housing Commission. Annual Report (TT) 487
Trustees of Wealth (US) 809
Try Us (US) 149, 243, 393
Tsentral'nyi Nauchno-Issledovatel'skii Institut Geodezii, Aeros"Emki i Kartografii. Trudy (UR) 426
Ha-Tsiyonut *see* Zionism; Studies in the History of the Zionist Movement and of the Jews in Palestine 771
Tsuda Review (JA ISSN 0496-3547) 575
Tsushin (US) 716
Tube (AT ISSN 0310-6217) 557

Tuberkulose-Bibliothek *see* Bibliothek fuer das Gesamtgebiet der Lungenkrankheiten 623
Tubists Universal Brotherhood Association Series *see* T.U.B.A. Series 664
Tubular Structures (UK ISSN 0041-3909) 139
Tudomanyos Tajekoztatas Elmelete es Gyakorlata/Theory and Practice of Scientific Information (HU ISSN 0373-5354) 536
Tudomanyszervezesi Fuzetek (HU ISSN 0082-6707) 792
Tudomanytorteneti Tanulmanyok (HU ISSN 0082-6715) 792, 853
Tuduv-Studien. Reihe Sozialwissenschaften (GW) 801
Tuebinger Aegyptologische Beitraege (GW) 475
Tuebinger Geographische Studien (GW ISSN 0564-4232) 426
Tuebinger Rechtswissenschaftliche Abhandlungen (GW ISSN 0082-6731) 519
Tufting Year Book (UK ISSN 0082-674X) 857
Tulane Studies in English *see* T S E: Tulane Studies in English 552
Tulane Studies in Philosophy (NE ISSN 0082-6766) 691
Tulane Studies in Political Science (US ISSN 0082-6774) 716
Tulane Tax Institute (US ISSN 0564-4402) 233
Tulane University of Louisiana. Library. Report *see* Howard-Tilton Memorial Library. Report 530
Tune up (US ISSN 0161-3081) 664
Tunisia. Institut National de la Statistique. Recensement des Activites Industrielles (TI) 165, 848
Tunisia. Institut National de la Statistique. Statistiques Industrielles *see* Tunisia. Institut National de la Statistique. Recensement des Activites Industrielles 165
Tunisia. Institut National Scientifique et Technique d'Oceanographie et de Peche. Bulletin (TI ISSN 0579-7926) 312, 400
Tunisia. Ministere du Plan. Budget Economique (TI ISSN 0082-6820) 233
Tunisia. Office des Ports Nationaux. Bulletin Annuel des Statistiques (TI) 881
Tunisia. Office des Ports Nationaux. Trafic Maritime *see* Tunisia. Office des Ports Nationaux. Bulletin Annuel des Statistiques 881
Turbomachinery Catalog and Workbook(US) 383
Turbomachinery Symposium. Proceedings (US) 583
Turcica; Revue d'Etudes Turques (BE ISSN 0082-6847) 553
Turism *see* Turizum 893
Turismo, Guia Peuser *see* Guia Peuser de Turismo Argentina y Sudamericana 886
Turizum/Turism (BU) 893
Turk Etnografya Dergisi *see* Turkish Review of Ethnography 817
Turk Tarih-Arkeologya ve Etnografya Dergisi *see* Turkish Review of Ethnography 817
Turk Ticaret Rehberi ve Teleks Indeks *see* Turkish Trade Directory & Telex Index 243
Turkey. Devlet Istatistik Enstitusu. Dis Ticaret Yillik Istatistigi/Statistique Annuelle du Commerce Exterieur/Annual Foreign Trade Statistics (TU ISSN 0082-6901) 165
Turkey. Devlet Istatistik Enstitusu. Milli Egitim Istatistikleri: Ogretim Yili Basi (TU) 323
Turkey. Devlet Istatistik Enstitusu. Tarim Istatistikleri Ozeti/Summary of Agricultural Statistics (TU ISSN 0082-6928) 21
Turkey. Devlet Istatistik Enstitusu. Tarimsal Yapi ve Uretim/Agricultural Structure and Production (TU ISSN 0082-6936) 21

Turkey. Devlet Planama Teskilati. Yili Programi Ucuncu Bes Yil/Annual Program of the Five Year Development Plan (TU ISSN 0082-6944) *225*
Turkey: Hotels-Camping (TU) *483*
Turkish Dissertation Index (TU) *4, 795*
Turkish Electricity Authority. Annual Report (TU) *359*
Turkish Review of Ethnography/Turk Etnografya Dergisi (TU ISSN 0082-6898) *817*
Turkish Trade Directory & Telex Index/Turk Ticaret Rehberi ve Teleks Indeks (TU ISSN 0082-6952) *243*
Turkiyat Mecmuasi (TU ISSN 0085-7432) *475, 493*
Turkiye Istatistik Cep Yilligi see Statistical Pocket Book of Turkey *847*
Turkiye Istatistik Yilligi/Statistical Yearbook of Turkey (TU ISSN 0082-691X) *849*
Turkiye Ozetli Nufus Bibliyografyasi (TU) *732*
Turquoise Annual see International Turquoise Annual *503*
Turun Historiallinen Arkisto (FI ISSN 0085-7440) *463*
Turun Historiallisen Yhdistyksen Julkaisuja see Turun Historiallinen Arkisto *463*
Turun Yliopisto. Julkaisuja. Sarja A. I. Astronomica-Chemica-Physica-Mathematica (FI ISSN 0082-7002) *792*
Turun Yliopisto. Julkaisuja. Sarja A. II. Biologica- Geographica- Geologica (FI ISSN 0082-6979) *108, 300, 426*
Turun Yliopisto. Julkaisuja. Sarja B. Humaniora (FI ISSN 0082-6987) *493*
Turun Yliopisto. Julkaisuja. Sarja C. Scripta Lingua Fennica Edita (FI ISSN 0082-6995) *493, 792*
Turun Yliopisto. Julkaisuja. Sarja D. Medica-Odontologica (FI ISSN 0355-9483) *600*
Turun Yliopisto. Kirjasto. Julkaisuja (FI ISSN 0082-7010) *536*
Turun Yliopisto. Klassillisen Filologian Laitos. Opera Ex Instituto Philologiae Classicae Universitatis Turkuensis Edita (FI ISSN 0082-7029) *260, 553*
Turun Yliopisto. Psykologian Laitos. Reports see University of Turku Psychological Reports *738*
Turun Yliopisto. Psykologian Laitos. Reports see Turun Yliopisto Psykologian Tutkimuksia *738*
Turun Yliopisto Psykologian Tutkimuksia (FI) *738*
Tutor & Textbook - Elementary Piping & Drumming (UK) *664*
Tutora. Memoria y Balance General (AG) *501*
TV Film/Tape & Syndication Directory see Backstage TV Film/Tape & Syndication Directory *649*
Tweetalige Losbladige Wetboeken (BE) *519*
Twentieth Century Legal Philosophy Series (US ISSN 0082-7088) *519*
Twentieth-Century Literary Criticism (US) *575*
Twentieth Century Petroleum Statistics (US) *682*
Two Feet of Poetry (US) *582*
Two-Year College in the United States see Community, Technical, and Junior College in the United States: a Guide for Foreign Students *331*
Tydskryf vir Studies in Ekonomie en Ekonometrie see Journal for Studies in Economics and Econometrics *191*
Tyndale Bulletin (UK ISSN 0082-7118) *768*
Typewriter (US) *575*
Tzaddikim (US) *394, 769*
Tzaddikim Review (US) *393, 771*
U A S Extension Series (University of Agricultural Sciences, Bangalore) (II ISSN 0067-3471) *21*

U A S Miscellaneous Series (University of Agricultural Sciences, Bangalore) (II ISSN 0067-348X) *21*
U B S Publications on Business, Banking and Monetary Problems (Union de Banques Suisses) (SZ) *177*
U. C. C. Record (University College, Cork) (IE) *263*
U C E A Case Series in Educational Administration (University Council for Educational Administration) (US ISSN 0083-3967) *345*
U C E A Case Series in Higher Education (US) *345*
U C I S Series in Russian & East European Studies (University Center for International Studies) (US) *464*
U C L A Business Forecast for the Nation and California (University of California, Los Angeles) (US ISSN 0082-7126) *149*
U C L A Forum in Medical Sciences (University of California, Los Angeles) (US ISSN 0082-7134) *600*
U C L A Music Library Bibliography Series (University of California, Los Angeles) (US) *95, 665*
U C L A Music Library Discography Series (US) *664*
U. C. Review (CN ISSN 0226-3440) *575, 582*
U C T Studies in English (University of Cape Town) (SA) *553, 575*
U - das Technische Umweltmagazin see Umweltmagazin *389*
U.E.E.S. Report (Utah Engineering Experiment Station) (US) *370*
U F O Annual (Unidentified Flying Objects) (US ISSN 0162-8046) *10*
U F O Insight (UK) *10*
U I C C Technical Report Series (International Union Against Cancer) (SZ ISSN 0074-9222) *606*
U I E Monographs (Unesco Institute for Education) (UN) *323*
U K Chemical Industry Statistics Handbook (UK ISSN 0309-2356) *248*
U. K. I. R. T. Newsletter (United Kingdom Infrared Telescope) (UK ISSN 0143-0599) *84*
U. K. I. R. T. Report (United Kingdom Infrared Telescope) (UK ISSN 0260-9983) *84*
U K R F Annual Report see University of Kentucky Research Foundation. Annual Report *341*
U K S T U Newsletter (United Kingdom Schmidt Telescope Unit) (UK ISSN 0143-053X) *84*
U K Trade Names (UK ISSN 0082-7142) *243*
U N A M Directorio de Bibliotecas (Universidad National Autonoma de Mexico) (MX) *536*
U N C T A D Guide to Publications (United Nations Conference on Trade and Development) (UN ISSN 0041-5227) *165*
U N E Bulletin see U N E Convocation Bulletin & Alumni News *340*
U N E Convocation Bulletin & Alumni News (University of New England) (AT ISSN 0156-1006) *340*
U N H C R Report (United Nations High Commissioner for Refugees) (UN ISSN 0041-5308) *723, 817*
U.N.I.C.E.M. Annuaire Officiel (Union Nationale des Industries de Carrieres et Materiaux de Construction) (FR) *139*
U N I S A Psychologia (SA) *738*
U N I T A R Conference Reports (United Nations Institute for Training and Research) (UN) *524*
U N I T A R News (United Nations Institute for Training and Research) (UN ISSN 0049-5395) *211, 668*
U N I T A R-P S Series (Peaceful Settlement) (United Nations Institute for Training and Research) (UN) *723*
U N I T A R Regional Studies (United Nations Institute for Training and Research) (UN) *724*
U N Resolutions on Palestine see Institute for Palestine Studies. Basic Documents Series *443*

U P E C (Union de Periodistas de Cuba) (CU) *760*
U. P. Irrigation Research Institute. General Annual Report (II ISSN 0080-4045) *381*
U.P. Irrigation Research Institute. Technical Memorandum (II ISSN 0080-4053) *381*
U S A-Japan Computer Conference. Proceedings (US) *274*
U S A N and the U S P Dictionary of Drug Names (US ISSN 0090-6816) *686*
U S A Oil Industry Directory (US ISSN 0082-8599) *681*
U S A Textile Industry Overview see Texscope; U S A Textile Industry Overview *857*
U S and the Developing World: Agenda for Action see U S and World Development: Agenda *201*
U S and World Development: Agenda (US) *201*
U S C Annual Distinguished Lecture Series Monographs in Special Education and Rehabilitation (University of Southern California) (US ISSN 0070-6736) *347*
U S-Canadian Range Management (US) *21, 95, 278*
U S College-Sponsored Programs Abroad. Academic Year see Learning Traveler. U.S. College-Sponsored Programs Abroad: Academic Year *342*
U S M A Library Bulletin (US) *536, 640*
U S Medical Directory (US ISSN 0091-8393) *600*
U S O Annual Report (United Service Organizations, Inc.) (US ISSN 0082-8556) *809*
U S P Guide to Select Drugs. (US ISSN 0091-3839) *686*
U S S R and Eastern Europe Scientific Abstracts: Biomedical and Behavioral Sciences see U S S R Report: Biomedical and Behavioral Sciences *600*
U S S R and Eastern Europe Scientific Abstracts: Chemistry see U S S R Reports: Chemistry *249*
U S S R and Eastern Europe Scientific Abstracts: Cybernetics, Computers, and Automation Technology see U S S R Report: Cybernetics, Computers, and Automation Technology *274*
U S S R and Eastern Europe Scientific Abstracts: Electronics and Electrical Engineering see U S S R Report: Electronics and Electrical Engineering *360*
U S S R and Eastern Europe Scientific Abstracts: Engineering and Equipment see U S S R Report: Engineering and Equipment *372*
U S S R and Eastern Europe Scientific Abstracts: Geophysics, Astronomy, and Space see U S S R Report: Geophysics, Astronomy, and Space *290*
U S S R and Eastern Europe Scientific Abstracts: Materials Science and Metallurgy see U S S R Report: Materials Science and Metallurgy *372*
U S S R and Eastern Europe Scientific Abstracts: Physics and Mathematics see U S S R Report: Physics and Mathematics *591*
U.S.S.R. Facts & Figures Annual (US) *849*
U S S R Report: Agriculture (US) *21*
U S S R Report: Biomedical and Behavioral Sciences (US) *600, 738, 817*
U S S R Report: Cybernetics, Computers, and Automation Technology (US) *4, 274*
U S S R Report: Economic Affairs (US) *149, 190*
U S S R Report: Electronics and Electrical Engineering (US) *4, 360*
U S S R Report: Engineering and Equipment (US) *4, 372*
U S S R Report: Geophysics, Astronomy, and Space (US) *4, 85, 290*

U S S R Report: Industrial Affairs (US) *190, 226*
U S S R Report: Materials Science and Metallurgy (US) *4, 372, 631*
U S S R Report: Military Affairs (US) *640*
U S S R Report: Physics and Mathematics (US) *4, 591*
U S S R Report: Political and Sociological Affairs (US) *716, 817*
U S S R Report: Problems of the Far East (US) *190, 716, 724*
U S S R Report: Resources (US) *364*
U S S R Report: Space Biology and Aerospace Medicine (English translation of: Kosmicheskaia Biologiia i Aviakosmicheskaia Meditsina) (US) *10, 600*
U S S R Report: Trade and Services (US) *190, 226*
U S S R Report: Translations from "Kommunist" (US) *716*
U S S R Reports: Chemistry (US) *4, 249*
U.S.S.R. Special Astrophysical Observatory Bulletin (US) *84*
U S Statistical Atlas (US) *428*
U S Symposium on Rock Mechanics. Proceedings (US ISSN 0586-3031) *647*
U S T A Sires and Dams (United States Trotting Association) (US) *828*
U S T A Year Book (US ISSN 0083-3517) *828*
U S 1 Worksheets (US) *557*
U V Curing Buyer's Guide (US ISSN 0146-5031) *248*
U.V. Spectrometry Group. Bulletin (UK) *706*
U Vejviser (DK ISSN 0106-3014) *536*
U W I Students' Law Review (University of the West Indies) (BB) *519*
U W O/D S S Journal (University of Western Ontario, Dental Students Society) (CN) *610*
Udayana State University Bulletin (IO) *340*
Uddannelse og Erhverv Katalog (DK) *651*
Udyogen Ka Varshika Sarvekshana see India. Central Statistical Organization. Annual Survey of Industries *158*
Uebersee-Museum, Bremen. Veroeffentlichungen. Reihe A: Naturwissenschaften (GW ISSN 0068-0885) *792*
Uebersee-Museum, Bremen. Veroeffentlichungen. Reihe B: Voelkerkunde (GW ISSN 0068-0893) *54, 403*
Uebersee-Museum, Bremen. Veroeffentlichungen. Reihe C: Geographie see Deutsche Geographische Blaetter *421*
Uebersee-Museum, Bremen. Veroeffentlichungen. Reihe D: Voelkerkundliche Monographien (GW ISSN 0341-9274) *54*
Uebersee-Museum, Bremen. Veroeffentlichungen. Reihe E: Human-Oekologie (GW ISSN 0170-2416) *817*
Uebersee-Museum, Bremen. Veroeffentlichungen. Reihe F: Bremer Afrika-Archiv (GW ISSN 0344-4317) *441*
Uebersee-Museum Bremen. Veroeffentlichungen. Reihe G: Bremer Suedpazifik-Archiv (GW ISSN 0342-6610) *447*
Der Uebersetzer (GW) *553*
Uebersetzungen Auslaendischer Arbeiten zur Antiken Sklaverei (GW ISSN 0170-348X) *436*
Uganda. Forestry Department. Annual Report (UG ISSN 0082-7177) *411*
Uganda. Forestry Department. Technical Notes (UG ISSN 0082-7193) *411*
Uganda. Game Department Annual Report (UG) *278*
Uganda. Geological Survey and Mines Department. Annual Report (UG ISSN 0082-7215) *300*

Uganda. Ministry of Planning and Economic Development. Statistics Division. Background to the Budget (UG ISSN 0082-7231) *233*

Uganda. Ministry of Planning and Economic Development. Statistics Division. Enumeration of Employees (UG ISSN 0082-724X) *211*

Uganda. Public Libraries Board. Proceedings (UG) *536*

Uganda Estimates of Development Expenditures (UG) *226*

Uganda Journal (UG ISSN 0041-574X) *441, 557*

Uhrmacher-Jahrbuch fuer Handwerk und Handel (GW ISSN 0082-7290) *504*

Uitkomsten van de Belgische Zeevisserij(BE) *400*

Uj Magyar Nepkoltesi Gyujtemeny (HU ISSN 0082-7312) *403, 582*

Ukrainian Archives (US) *393*

Ukrainian Art Digest/Notatki z Mistetstba (US ISSN 0550-0850) *79, 393*

Ukrainian Literary Library (US) *575*

Ukrainian Studies (US) *792*

Ukulele Yes! (CN) *664*

Ulrich's International Periodicals Directory (US ISSN 0000-0175) *95*

Ulster Folklife (UK ISSN 0082-7347) *403*

Ulster Genie (US) *418*

Ulster Journal of Archaeology (UK ISSN 0082-7355) *66*

Ulster-Scot Historical Series (UK ISSN 0082-7363) *464*

Ulster Year Book (UK ISSN 0082-7371) *464*

Ultrasonics Symposium. Proceedings (US ISSN 0090-5607) *370, 706*

Ultrasound in Biomedicine (US) *600*

Ultrasound in Medicine (US ISSN 0098-0382) *600, 706*

Ultrasound Patents & Papers (UK ISSN 0260-4043) *622*

Umbra (US) *575*

Umeaa Studies in the Humanities (SW) *493*

Umweltmagazin (GW ISSN 0341-1206) *389*

Underground Transmission and Distribution Conference. Record *see* Conference on Underground Transmission and Distribution. Record *352*

Understanding Conflict and War (US) *724, 738*

Understanding Financial Support of Public Schools (US ISSN 0362-3610) *345*

Underwriting Results in Canada (CN ISSN 0082-7452) *501*

Unemployment Insurance Canada. Annual Report/Assurance-Chomage Canada. Rapport Annuel (CN ISSN 0576-4157) *501*

Unesco. Records of the General Conference. Proceedings (UN ISSN 0082-7509) *724*

Unesco. Records of the General Conference. Resolutions (UN ISSN 0082-7517) *343, 724*

Unesco. Regional Office for Education in Asia and Oceana. Bulletin (UN) *323*

Unesco. Regional Office for Education in Asia.Bulletin. *see* Unesco. Regional Office for Education in Asia and Oceana. Bulletin *323*

Unesco. Report of the Director-General on the Activities of the Organization (UN ISSN 0082-7525) *343, 724*

Unesco. Scientific Maps and Atlases and Other Related Publications (UN) *95*

Unesco Asian Fiction Series (UN ISSN 0566-6201) *575*

Unesco Bibliographical Handbooks *see* Documentation, Libraries and Archives: Bibliographies and Reference Works *539*

Unesco Earthquake Study Missions (UN ISSN 0082-7479) *306*

Unesco Handbook of International Exchanges (UN ISSN 0082-7487) *343*

Unesco Institute for Education Monographs *see* U I E Monographs *323*

Unesco Manuals for Libraries *see* Documentation, Libraries and Archives: Studies and Research *529*

Unesco Regional Office for Education in Asia. Regional Conference Reports *see* Population Education in Asia Newsletter *321*

Unesco Source Books on Curricula and Methods (UN ISSN 0502-9554) *351*

Unesco Statistical Reports and Studies (UN ISSN 0082-7533) *849*

Unesco Statistical Yearbook (UN ISSN 0082-7541) *849*

Unesco Technical Papers in Marine Science (UN ISSN 0503-4299) *108, 312*

Unga Diktara (SW) *575*

Ungarische Akademie der Wissenschaften. Archaelogisches Institut. Mitteilungen (HU) *66*

Ungarn-Jahrbuch (GW ISSN 0082-755X) *464*

Unican (CN ISSN 0706-9820) *915*

Unicorn (AT ISSN 0311-4775) *323, 340*

Unicorn German Series (US) *464, 575*

Unidentified Flying Objects Annual *see* U F O Annual *10*

Uniform Building Code (US ISSN 0082-7584) *139*

Uniform Crime Report for the State of Michigan (US ISSN 0360-9146) *285*

Uniform Crime Reports for the United States (US ISSN 0082-7592) *284*

Uniformed Services Almanac. Special Reserve Forces Edition *see* Reserve Forces Almanac *640*

Union (Cranford) (US ISSN 0098-9525) *263*

Union Academique Internationale. Compte Rendu de la Session Annuelle du Comite (BE ISSN 0074-9346) *493*

Union Bancaria Hispano Marroqui. Assemblee Generale Ordinaire des Actionnaires. Rapport (MR) *177*

Union Bank of Finland. Annual Report (FI ISSN 0355-0133) *177*

Union Catalog of Scientific and Technical Periodicals in the Libraries of Pakistan (PK) *95*

Union Catalogue of Theses and Dissertations of the South African Universities (SA ISSN 0079-4325) *95*

Union College. Character Research Project. Newsletter (US) *738, 768*

Union de Banques Suisses Publications on Business, Banking and Monetary Problems *see* U B S Publications on Business, Banking and Monetary Problems *177*

Union de Periodistas de Cuba *see* U P E C *760*

Union Democracy in Action *see* Union Democracy Review *507*

Union Democracy Review (US) *507, 716*

Union des Superieures Majeurs de France. Annuaire (FR ISSN 0396-2393) *790*

Union Internationale Contre le Cancer. Manuele *see* International Union against Cancer. Manual *605*

Union Internationale des Transports Publics. Rapports Techniques des Congres Internationaux *see* International Union of Public Transport. Technical Reports of the Congresses *862*

Union Interparlementaire. Comptes Rendus des Conferences *see* Inter-Parliamentary Union. Conference Proceedings *722*

Union List of Library and Information Science Periodicals in the Libraries of Iran (IR) *95*

Union List of Scientific Serials in Canadian Libraries/Catalogue Collectif des Publications Scientifiques dans les Bibliotheques Canadiennes (CN ISSN 0082-7657) *795*

Union List of Serials in Libraries of the Federal Republic of Germany Including Berlin (West) *see* Gesamtverzeichnis der Zeitschriften und Serien in Bibliotheken der Bundesrepublik Deutschland Einschliesslich Berlin (West) *91*

Union Mondiale des Organisations Syndicales sur Bases Economique et Sociale Liberales. Conferences: Rapport (SZ ISSN 0503-2334) *507*

Union Nationale de l'Enseignement Agricole Prive. Annuaire (FR ISSN 0082-7711) *21, 323*

Union Nationale des Industries de Carrieres et Materiaux de Construction Annuaire Officiel *see* U.N.I.C.E.M. Annuaire Officiel *139*

Union of American Hebrew Congregations. State of Our Union (US ISSN 0363-3810) *771*

Union of British Columbia Municipalities. Minutes of Annual Convention (CN ISSN 0082-7746) *746*

Union of European Football Associations. Handbook of U E F A (SZ ISSN 0570-2070) *826*

Union of European Pedopsychiatrists. Proceedings (SW) *621*

Union of International Associations. Documents *see* Collection of Documents for the Study of International Non-Governmental Relations *522*

Union of Nova Scotia Municipalities. Proceedings of the Annual Convention (CN ISSN 0082-7762) *746*

Union Postale Universelle (UN ISSN 0083-3878) *266*

Union Postale Universelle. Statistique des Services Postaux (UN ISSN 0085-7602) *266*

Union Professionnelle Feminine. Annuaire (FR ISSN 0082-7770) *719*

Union Sovietique *see* Soviet Union *426*

Union Sportive Metropolitaine des Transports Annee Sportive U.S.M.T. *see* Annee Sportive U.S.M.T *819*

Unispiegel (GW) *340*

Unispiegel Aktuell *see* Unispiegel *340*

Unit-Linked Savings Plans (UK) *501*

Unit Trust Yearbook (UK ISSN 0503-2628) *177*

Unitarian and Free Christian Churches. Handbook and Directory of the General Assembly (UK) *772*

Unitarian and Free Christian Churches. Yearbook of the General Assembly *see* Unitarian and Free Christian Churches. Handbook and Directory of the General Assembly *772*

Unitarian Historical Society. Proceedings (US ISSN 0082-7819) *772*

Unitarian Historical Society, London. Transactions (UK ISSN 0082-7800) *773*

Unitarian Universalist Directory (US ISSN 0082-7827) *773*

United Arab Emirates. Currency Board. Annual Report (TS) *233*

United Arab Emirates. Currency Board. Bulletin (TS) *233*

United Arab Emirates. Ministry of Petroleum and Industry. Akhbar al-Petrol Wall Sinaa (TS) *681*

United Baptist Convention of the Atlantic Provinces. Yearbook (CN ISSN 0082-7843) *773*

United Church of Canada. Committee on Archives. Bulletin. Records and Proceedings (CN ISSN 0082-786X) *773*

United Church of Canada. General Council. Record of Proceedings (CN ISSN 0082-7878) *773*

United Church of Canada. Year Book (CN ISSN 0082-7886) *773*

United Church of Christ. Pension Boards (Annual Report) (US ISSN 0360-9782) *501, 777*

United Free Church of Scotland. Handbook (UK ISSN 0082-7908) *773*

United Graphic Guide (US ISSN 0082-7916) *205*

United Kingdom Atomic Energy Authority. Annual Report (UK ISSN 0082-7940) *370, 704*

United Kingdom Fire and Loss Statistics *see* United Kingdom Fire Statistics *603*

United Kingdom Fire Statistics (UK) *603*

United Kingdom Geodesy Report (UK) *426*

United Kingdom Infrared Telescope Newsletter *see* U. K. I. R. T. Newsletter *84*

United Kingdom Infrared Telescope Report *see* U. K. I. R. T. Report *84*

United Kingdom Meat Trade Annual *see* Meat Trade Yearbook *405*

United Kingdom Mineral Statistics (UK ISSN 0308-5090) *647*

United Kingdom Schmidt Telescope Unit Newsletter *see* U K S T U Newsletter *84*

United Malays National Organisation. Penvata (MY) *716*

United Methodist Church. Curriculum Plans (US ISSN 0160-0885) *773*

United Methodist Church. General Minutes of the Annual Conferences (US ISSN 0503-3551) *773*

United Methodist Church (United States) Division of Education. Adult Planbook. (US ISSN 0082-7983) *773*

United Methodist Directory (US ISSN 0503-356X) *773*

U. N. Annual Bulletin of Housing and Building Statistics for Europe (UN) *139*

United Nations. Centro Latino-americano de Demografia. Serie A. *see* United Nations. Regional Centre for Demographic Training and Research in Latin America. Serie A *729*

United Nations. Centro Latinoamericano de Demografia. Serie C *see* United Nations. Regional Centre for Demographic Training and Research in Latin America. Serie C *730*

United Nations. Centro Latinoamericano de Demografia. Serie D *see* United Nations. Regional Centre for Demographic Training and Research in Latin America. Serie D *730*

United Nations. Commission on International Trade Law. Report on the Work of Its Session (UN) *524*

United Nations. Commission on International Trade Law. Yearbook (UN) *198, 524*

United Nations. Disarmament Commission. Official Records (UN ISSN 0082-8076) *640*

United Nations. Economic and Social Council. Index to Proceedings (UN ISSN 0082-8084) *724*

United Nations. Economic and Social Council. Official Records (UN ISSN 0082-8092) *190, 724*

United Nations. Economic Commission for Africa. Tourism in Africa; Annual Bulletin *see* Tourism in Africa. Annual Bulletin *892*

United Nations. Economic Commission for Asia and the Far East. Sample Surveys in the ECAFE Region. *see* Sample Surveys in the ESCAP Region *163*

United Nations. Economic Commission for Europe. Annual Bulletin of General Energy Statistics for Europe *see* Annual Bulletin of General Energy Statistics for Europe *364*

United Nations. General Assembly. Index to Proceedings (UN ISSN 0082-8157) *724*

United Nations. International Law Commission. Yearbook (UN ISSN 0082-8289) *524*

United Nations. International Narcotics Control Board. Statistics on Narcotic Drugs Furnished by Governments in Accordance with the International Treaties and Maximum Levels of Opium Stocks (UN ISSN 0566-7658) *754*

United Nations. Multilateral Treaties in Respect of Which the Secretary-General Performs Depositary Functions (UN ISSN 0082-8319) 524

United Nations. Permanent Central Narcotics Board. Report to the Economic and Social Council on the Work of the Permanent Central Narcotics (Opium) Board see United Nations. Permanent Central Narcotics (Opium) Board. Report of the International Narcotics Control Board on Its Work t 754

United Nations. Permanent Central Narcotics (Opium) Board. Report of the International Narcotics Control Board on Its Work (UN) 754

U. N. Quarterly Housing Construction Summary for Europe see U. N. Annual Bulletin of Housing and Building Statistics for Europe 139

United Nations. Regional Centre for Demographic Training and Research in Latin America. Serie A/Centro Latinoamericano de Demografia. Serie A: Informes sobre Investigaciones Realizadas (UN ISSN 0503-3934) 729

United Nations. Regional Centre for Demographic Training and Research in Latin America. Serie C/Centro Latinoamericano de Demografia. Serie C: Informes sobre Investigaciones Realizadas Por los Alumnos del Centro (UN ISSN 0503-3942) 730

United Nations. Regional Centre for Demographic Training and Research in Latin America. Serie D (UN ISSN 0503-3950) 730

United Nations. Regional Centre for Demographic Training and Research in Latin America. Serie I/Centro Latinoamericano de Demografia. Serie I: Recopilacion de Trabajos Sobres Paises (UN) 730

United Nations. Security Council. Index to Proceedings (UN ISSN 0082-8408) 724

United Nations. Security Council. Official Records (UN ISSN 0082-8416) 724

United Nations. Statistical Yearbook (UN ISSN 0082-8459) 849

United Nations. Trade and Development Board. Official Records(UN ISSN 0082-8475) 201

United Nations. Trade and Development Board. Official Records. Supplements (UN ISSN 0082-8483) 724

United Nations. Trusteeship Council. Index to Proceedings (UN ISSN 0082-8491) 724

United Nations. Trusteeship Council. Official Records (UN ISSN 0082-8505) 724

United Nations. Trusteeship Council. Official Records. Supplements (UN ISSN 0082-8513) 724

United Nations. Yearbook (UN ISSN 0082-8521) 724

United Nations and What You Should Know about It (UN ISSN 0082-8009) 724

United Nations Annual Documentary Series see Institute for Palestine Studies. International Annual Documentary Series 443

United Nations Association of Australia. United Nations Reporter (AT ISSN 0085-7475) 724

United Nations Conference on Trade and Development Guide to Publications see U N C T A D Guide to Publications 165

United Nations Congress on the Prevention of Crime and the Treatment of Offenders. Report (UN ISSN 0082-8025) 284

United Nations Economic and Social Commission for Asia and the Pacific. Development Programming Techniques Series (UN ISSN 0082-8106) 201

United Nations Economic and Social Commission for Asia and the Pacific. Mineral Resources Development Series (UN ISSN 0082-8114) 647

United Nations Economic and Social Commission for Asia and the Pacific. Regional Economic Cooperation Series (UN ISSN 0082-8122) 201

United Nations Educational, Scientific and Cultural Organization (US ISSN 0250-779X) 724

United Nations High Commissioner for Refugees Report see U N H C R Report 723

United Nations Industrial Development Organization. Guides to Information Sources (UN) 165

United Nations Institute for Training and Research. Report of the Executive Director (UN) 724

United Nations Institute for Training and Research Conference Reports see U N I T A R Conference Reports 524

United Nations Institute for Training and Research News see U N I T A R News 211

United Nations Institute for Training and Research Regional Studies see U N I T A R Regional Studies 724

United Nations Institute for Training and Research Series see U N I T A R-P S Series 723

United Nations Juridical Yearbook (UN ISSN 0082-8297) 524

United Nations Legislative Series (UN ISSN 0082-8300) 524

United Nations of the Next Decade Conference. Report (US) 724

United Nations Regional Cartographic Conference for Asia and the Far East. Proceedings of the Conference and Technical Papers (UN ISSN 0082-836X) 426

United Nations Research Institute for Social Development. Regional Planning see Regional Planning 808

United Nations Research Institute for Social Development. Report (UN) 809

United Nations Research Institute for Social Development. Research Notes(UN) 801

United Nations Social Defense Research Institute. Publication (UN) 724

United Planting Association of Malaysia. Annual Report (MY) 30

United Presbyterian Church in the United States of America. Minutes of the General Assembly (US ISSN 0082-8548) 773

United Reformed Church in England and Wales. United Reformed Church Year Book (UK ISSN 0069-8849) 773

United Republic of Cameroon International Year Book see Republique Unie du Cameroun: Annuaire International 441

United Schools Organisation of India. Annual Report (II) 324

United Service Organizations, Inc. Annual Report see U S O Annual Report 809

United Society for the Propagation of the Gospel. Annual Report/Review (UK ISSN 0144-9508) 768

U.S. A I P see U.S. Aeronautical Information Publication 10

U.S. Administration on Aging. Annual Report (US ISSN 0098-8405) 428

U.S. Administration on Aging. Elderly Population: Estimates by County (US ISSN 0190-3896) 811, 849

U. S. Administration on Aging. Facts and Figures on Older Americans see U.S. Administration on Aging. Statistical Reports on Older Americans 428

U.S. Administration on Aging. Statistical Memos see U.S. Administration on Aging. Statistical Reports on Older Americans 428

U.S. Administration on Aging. Statistical Reports on Older Americans (US) 428

U.S. Administrative Office of the United States Courts. Report on Applications for Orders Authorizing or Approving the Interception of Wire or Oral Communications (US ISSN 0097-7977) 265, 519

U.S. Aeronautical Information Publication (US) 10

U. S. Agency for International Development. Proposed Foreign Aid Program, Summary Presentation to Congress (US ISSN 0082-8637) 915

U.S. Agricultural Marketing Service. Annual Report on Tobacco Statistics (US) 861

U. S. Agricultural Research Service. A R S-N C (US ISSN 0092-1785) 21

U. S. Agricultural Research Service. A R S-S (US ISSN 0092-1939) 21

U. S. Agricultural Research Service. Animal Science Research Division. Tables on Hatchery and Flock Participation in the National Turkey Improvement Plan see Tables on Hatchery and Flock Participation in the National Poultry Improvement Plan 46

U.S. Air Force Academy Assembly. Proceedings (US ISSN 0082-8688) 724

U. S. Air Force Academy Library. Special Bibliography Series (US ISSN 0082-8696) 95

U.S. Air Force Cambridge Research Laboratories. AFCRL (Series) see U.S. Air Force Geophysics Laboratory. AFGL (Series) 640

U.S. Air Force Geophysics Laboratory. AFGL (Series) (US) 306, 640

U.S. Airborne Exports and General Imports see Foreign Trade Reports. U.S. Airborne Exports and General Imports 195

U. S. Arms Control and Disarmament Agency. Annual Report to Congress (US ISSN 0082-8769) 519

U.S. Army. Corps of Engineers. Port Series (US ISSN 0083-0305) 881

U.S. Army. Corps of Engineers. Technical Reports, T R (Series) (US ISSN 0083-0313) 370

U. S. Army Infantry Center. History; Annual Supplement (US ISSN 0091-2271) 640

U.S. Army Medical Research Institute of Infectious Diseases. Annual Progress Report. (US) 608

U. S. Brookhaven National Laboratory, Upton, N.Y. Brookhaven Highlights see Brookhaven Highlights 702

U. S. Bureau of Alcohol, Tobacco and Firearms. Annual Report (US) 86, 519, 861

U. S. Bureau of Commercial Fisheries. United States Fisheries see Fisheries of the United States 396

U.S. Bureau of Domestic and International Business Administration. Overseas Business Reports (US ISSN 0082-9846) 198

U.S. Bureau of East-West Trade. Export Administration Regulations (US ISSN 0094-8411) 198

U.S. Bureau of Health Manpower Support see B H M Support 334

U.S. Bureau of Health Resources Development. Division of Nursing. Special Project Grants and Contracts Awarded for Improvement in Nurse Training (US ISSN 0095-2141) 614

U. S. Bureau of International Commerce. Annual Reports (US ISSN 0082-8939) 198

U. S. Bureau of International Commerce. Trade Lists (US ISSN 0082-8963) 198

U.S. Bureau of International Labor Affairs. Monograph (US) 211

U. S. Bureau of Labor Statistics. Analysis of Work Stoppages (US ISSN 0082-9013) 211

U.S. Bureau of Labor Statistics. Area Wage Surveys (US) 165

U. S. Bureau of Labor Statistics. B L S Staff Paper (US ISSN 0082-903X) 211

U. S. 1509

U. S. Bureau of Labor Statistics. Bulletins (US ISSN 0082-9021) 211

U.S. Bureau of Labor Statistics. Digest of Selected Pension Plans (US) 166

U. S. Bureau of Labor Statistics. Employee Compensation in the Private Nonfarm Economy (US ISSN 0091-8261) 166

U. S. Bureau of Labor Statistics. Employment and Earnings: States and Areas (US) 211

U.S. Bureau of Labor Statistics. Employment and Earnings Statistics for States and Areas see U. S. Bureau of Labor Statistics. Employment and Earnings: States and Areas 211

U. S. Bureau of Labor Statistics. Handbook of Labor Statistics (US ISSN 0082-9056) 166

U.S. Bureau of Labor Statistics. Indexes of Output per Man-Hour; Selected Industries see U.S. Bureau of Labor Statistics. Productivity Indexes for Selected Industries 166

U. S. Bureau of Labor Statistics. Industry Wage Surveys (US ISSN 0082-9064) 211

U. S. Bureau of Labor Statistics. Major Programs (US) 166

U.S. Bureau of Labor Statistics. National Survey of Professional, Administrative, Technical and Clerical Pay (US ISSN 0501-7041) 166

U.S. Bureau of Labor Statistics. Occupational Outlook Handbook (US) 668

U.S. Bureau of Labor Statistics. Productivity Indexes for Selected Industries (US) 166

U. S. Bureau of Labor Statistics. Union Wages and Hours Surveys (US ISSN 0082-9099) 211

U.S. Bureau of Labor Statistics. Wage Chronologies (US ISSN 0082-9102) 211

U. S. Bureau of Land Management. Public Land Statistics (US ISSN 0082-9110) 746

U. S. Bureau of Mines. Bulletin (US ISSN 0082-9129) 647

U. S. Bureau of Mines. Commodity Data Summaries (US ISSN 0082-9137) 647

U.S. Bureau of Mines. Mineral Industry Surveys (US ISSN 0498-7845) 647

U.S. Bureau of Mines. Minerals Yearbook (US ISSN 0076-8952) 647

U. S. Bureau of Mines. Technical Progress Report (US) 647

U.S. Bureau of Outdoor Recreation. Recreation Grants-in-Aid Manual (US) 831

U.S. Bureau of Reclamation. Engineering and Research Center. Research Reports see U.S. Water and Power Resources Service. Engineering and Research Center. Research Reports 898

U.S. Bureau of Reclamation. Engineering and Research Center. Technical Records of Design and Construction see U.S. Water and Power Resources Service. Engineering and Research Center. Technical Records of Design and Construction 377

U.S. Bureau of Reclamation. Engineering Monograph see U.S. Water and Power Resources Service. Engineering Monograph 381

U.S. Bureau of Reclamation. Mid-Pacific Region. Report (US) 898

U.S. Bureau of the Census. Annual Survey of Manufactures (US ISSN 0082-9307) 226

U.S. Bureau of the Census. Bunker Fuels see Foreign Trade Reports. Bunker Fuels 195

U.S. Bureau of the Census. Census Bureau Methodological Research (US ISSN 0565-0828) 803

U. S. Bureau of the Census. Census of Agriculture (US ISSN 0082-9315) 21

1510 U.S. BUREAU

U.S. Bureau of the Census. Census of Business see U.S. Bureau of the Census. Census of Retail Trade, Wholesale Trade and Selected Service Industries *190*

U. S. Bureau of the Census. Census of Construction Industries (US ISSN 0082-934X) *139*

U. S. Bureau of the Census. Census of Governments (US ISSN 0082-9358) *746*

U. S. Bureau of the Census. Census of Housing (US ISSN 0082-9366) *489*

U. S. Bureau of the Census. Census of Manufactures (US ISSN 0082-9374) *226*

U. S. Bureau of the Census. Census of Mineral Industries (US ISSN 0082-9382) *647*

U. S. Bureau of the Census. Census of Population (US ISSN 0082-9390) *730*

U.S. Bureau of the Census. Census of Retail Trade, Wholesale Trade and Selected Service Industries (US) *190*

U. S. Bureau of the Census. Census of Transportation (US ISSN 0082-9404) *864*

U. S. Bureau of the Census. Census Tract Manual (US ISSN 0082-9412) *730*

U.S. Bureau of the Census. Chart Book on Government Data: Organization, Finances and Employment see Current Governments Reports: Chart Book on Government Data. Organization, Finances and Employment *228*

U.S. Bureau of the Census. City Employment see Current Governments Reports: City Employment *154*

U.S. Bureau of the Census. City Government Finances see Current Governments Reports: City Government Finances *228*

U. S. Bureau of the Census. Congressional District Data Book (US ISSN 0082-9447) *716*

U.S. Bureau of the Census. Consumer Buying Indicators see Current Population Reports: Consumer Buying Indicators *726*

U.S. Bureau of the Census. Consumer Income see Current Population Reports: Consumer Income *726*

U. S. Bureau of the Census. County and City Data Book (US ISSN 0082-9455) *849*

U. S. Bureau of the Census. County Business Patterns (US ISSN 0082-9463) *190*

U.S. Bureau of the Census. County Employment see Current Governments Reports: County Employment *741*

U.S. Bureau of the Census. County Government Finances see Current Governments Reports: County Government Finances *228*

U.S. Bureau of the Census. Current Business Reports see Current Business Reports *184*

U.S. Bureau of the Census. Current Governments Reports see Current Governments Reports *741*

U.S. Bureau of the Census. Current Housing Reports see Current Housing Reports *484*

U.S. Bureau of the Census. Current Industrial Reports see Current Industrial Reports *222*

U.S. Bureau of the Census. Current Population Reports see Current Population Reports *726*

U. S. Bureau of the Census. Current Population Reports: Negro Population see Current Population Reports: Population Characteristics. Social and Economic Characteristics of the Black Population *726*

U. S. Bureau of the Census. Current Population Reports: School Enrollment: October (Year) see Current Population Reports: Population Characteristics. School Enrollment: Social and Economic Characteristics of Students *726*

U.S. Bureau of the Census. Farm Population see Current Population Reports: Farm Population *726*

U.S. Bureau of the Census. Federal-State Cooperative Program for Population Estimates see Current Population Reports: Federal-State Cooperative Program for Population Estimates *726*

U.S. Bureau of the Census. Finances of Employee Retirement Systems of State and Local Governments see Current Governments Reports: Finances of Employee Retirement Systems of State and Local Governments *228*

U.S. Bureau of the Census. Finances of Selected Public Employee Retirement Systems see Current Governments Reports, GR Finances of Selected Public Employee Retirement Systems *228*

U.S. Bureau of the Census. Government Employment see Current Governments Reports, GE-Government Employment *741*

U.S. Bureau of the Census. Government Finance see Current Governments Reports, GF - Government Finance *228*

U.S. Bureau of the Census. Governmental Finances see Current Governments Reports: Governmental Finances *228*

U. S. Bureau of the Census. Guide to Foreign Trade Statistics (US ISSN 0565-0933) *198*

U.S. Bureau of the Census. Household and Family Characteristics see Current Population Reports: Population Characteristics. Household and Family Characteristics *726*

U.S. Bureau of the Census. Housing Characteristics see Current Housing Reports: Housing Characteristics *484*

U.S. Bureau of the Census. Housing Units Authorized for Demolition in Permit-Issuing Places see Current Construction Reports: Housing Units Authorized for Demolition in Permit-Issuing Places *484*

U.S. Bureau of the Census. Housing Vacancies see Current Housing Reports: Housing Vacancies *484*

U. S. Bureau of the Census. Income (in Year) of Families in the United States see Current Population Reports: Consumer Income. Income in (Year) of Families and Persons in the United States *212*

U.S. Bureau of the Census. Local Government Employment in Selected Metropolitan Areas and Large Counties see Current Governments Reports: Local Government Employment in Selected Metropolitan Areas and Large Counties *748*

U.S. Bureau of the Census. Local Government Finances in Selected Metropolitan Areas and Large Counties see Current Governments Reports: Local Government Finances in Selected Metropolitan Areas and Large Counties *228*

U.S. Bureau of the Census. Marital Status and Living Arrangements see Current Population Reports: Populaion Characteristics. Marital Status and Living Arrangements *726*

U.S. Bureau of the Census. Population Characteristics see Current Population Reports: Population Characteristics *726*

U.S. Bureau of the Census. Population Estimates and Projections see Current Population Reports: Population Estimates and Projections *726*

U.S. Bureau of the Census. Public Employment see Current Governments Reports: Public Employment *207*

U.S. Bureau of the Census. Quarterly Summary of State and Local Tax Revenue see Current Governments Reports, GT Quarterly Summary of State and Local Tax Revenue *228*

U.S. Bureau of the Census. Recurrent Reports on Governments (Series G F-7) Chart Book on Government Finances and Employment see Current Governments Reports: Chart Book on Government Data. Organization, Finances and Employment *228*

U.S. Bureau of the Census. Research Document Series (US) *730*

U.S. Bureau of the Census. School Enrollment: Social and Economic Characteristics of Students see Current Population Reports: Population Characteristics. School Enrollment: Social and Economic Characteristics of Students *726*

U.S. Bureau of the Census. Social and Economic Characteristics of the Black Population see Current Population Reports: Population Characteristics. Social and Economic Characteristics of the Black Population *726*

U.S. Bureau of the Census. State Finances see Current Governments Reports: State Government Finances *154*

U.S. Bureau of the Census. State Government Finances see Current Governments Reports: State Government Finances *154*

U.S. Bureau of the Census. State Tax Collections see Current Government Reports: State Tax Collections *228*

U. S. Bureau of the Census. Technical Notes (US ISSN 0082-9536) *849*

U. S. Bureau of the Census. Technical Paper (US ISSN 0082-9544) *849*

U. S. Bureau of the Census. Vessel Entrances and Clearances see Foreign Trade Reports. Vessel Entrances and Clearances *195*

U. S. Bureau of the Census. Working Papers (US ISSN 0082-9552) *849*

U. S. Center for Disease Control. Abortion Surveillance. Annual Summary (US ISSN 0094-0933) *133, 754*

U. S. Center for Disease Control. Brucellosis Surveillance: Annual Summary (US ISSN 0090-1156) *754*

U. S. Center for Disease Control. Diphtheria Surveillance Report (US) *608, 754*

U.S. Center for Disease Control. Family Planning Services: Annual Summary (US ISSN 0094-4424) *133*

U. S. Center for Disease Control. Foodborne & Waterborne Disease Outbreaks. Annual Summary (US ISSN 0098-6623) *754*

U.S. Center for Disease Control. Leprosy Surveillance Report (US) *608, 754*

U.S. Center for Disease Control. Listeriosis Surveillance Report (US) *608, 754*

U.S. Center for Disease Control. Malaria Surveillance Report (US ISSN 0501-8390) *608, 754*

U.S. Center for Disease Control. Neurotropic Viral Diseases Surveillance: Aseptic Meningitis (US) *621*

U.S. Center for Disease Control. Neurotropic Viral Diseases Surveillance: Encephalitis (US) *621*

U.S. Center for Disease Control. Neurotropic Viral Diseases Surveillance: Enterovirus (US) *621*

U.S. Center for Disease Control. Neurotropic Viral Diseases Surveillance: Poliomyelitis (US) *621*

U.S. Center for Disease Control. Reported Tuberculosis Data see U.S. Center for Disease Control. Tuberculosis in the United States *623*

U.S. Center for Disease Control. Salmonella Surveillance. Annual Summary (US) *754*

U.S. Center for Disease Control. Tetanus Surveillance; Report (US ISSN 0094-6605) *754*

U. S. Center for Disease Control. Tuberculosis in the United States (US) *623*

U.S. Center for Disease Control. Tuberculosis Program Reports see U.S. Center for Disease Control. Tuberculosis in the United States *623*

U.S. Center for Disease Control. Tuberculosis: States and Cities see U.S. Center for Disease Control. Tuberculosis Statistics: States and Cities *623*

U.S. Center for Disease Control. Tuberculosis Statistics: States and Cities (US) *623*

U.S. Center for Population Research. Inventory of Federal Population Research (US) *730*

U. S. Civil Aeronautics Board. Aircraft Operating Cost and Performance Report (US ISSN 0082-9609) *869*

U.S. Civil Service Commission. Annual Report (US) *746*

U.S. Civil Service Commission. Bureau of Personnel Management Evaluation. Evaluation Methods Series (US ISSN 0361-6797) *220*

U. S. Civil Service Commission. Personnel Research and Development Center. Technical Study (US ISSN 0093-366X) *220*

U. S. Coast Guard. Oceanographic Reports (CG-373 Series) (US ISSN 0082-9625) *312*

U.S. Coast Guard. Polluting Incidents in and Around U.S. Waters (US ISSN 0092-0320) *389*

U.S. Coast Guard Boating Statistics (US ISSN 0565-1530) *823*

U.S. Coast Guard Technical Report see C G O U Technical Report *309*

U.S. Commission on Civil Rights. Clearinghouse Publications (US ISSN 0082-9641) *719*

U.S. Commodity Futures Trading Commission Databank see C F T C Databank *202*

U.S. Community Services Administration. Annual Report of Community Services Administration (US ISSN 0190-373X) *809*

U. S. Community Services Administration. Federal Outlays in Summary (US ISSN 0091-3553) *233*

U.S. Congress. Congressional Directory (US) *716*

U. S. Copyright Office. Annual Report of the Register of Copyrights (US ISSN 0090-2845) *677*

U.S. Crop Reporting Board. Agricultural Prices (US ISSN 0002-1601) *30*

U.S. Crop Reporting Board. Crop Production (US ISSN 0363-8561) *39*

U.S. Department of Agriculture. Agricultural Economics Report (US ISSN 0083-0445) *30*

U.S. Department of Agriculture. Agricultural Statistics (US ISSN 0082-9714) *21*

U.S. Department of Agriculture. Agriculture Handbook (US ISSN 0065-4612) *21*

U.S. Department of Agriculture. Agriculture Information Bulletin (US ISSN 0065-4639) *21*

U.S. Department of Agriculture. Animal and Plant Health Inspection Service. Cooperative State-Federal Brucellosis Eradication Program: Statistical Tables (US) *26*

U.S. Department of Agriculture. Animal and Plant Health Inspection Service. Cooperative State-Federal Bovine Tuberculosis Eradication Program: Statistical Tables (US) *26*

U.S. Department of Agriculture. Animal and Plant Health Inspection Service. Reported Arthropod-Borne Encephalitides in Horses and Other Equidae (US) *895*

U.S. Department of Agriculture. Animal Science Research Branch. Hatcheries and Dealers Participating in the National Improvement Plan *see* Hatcheries and Dealers Participating in the National Poultry Improvement Plan 45
U.S. Department of Agriculture. Economic Research Service. Agricultural Economics Report *see* U.S. Department of Agriculture. Agricultural Economics Report 30
U.S. Department of Agriculture. Economics, Statistics, and Cooperatives Service. Africa and West Asia Agricultural Situation (US ISSN 0148-7094) 30
U.S. Department of Agriculture. Economics, Statistics, and Cooperatives Service. Agricultural Finance Outlook (US ISSN 0501-9117) 30
U.S. Department of Agriculture. Economics, Statistics, and Cooperatives Service. Agricultural Finance Review (US ISSN 0002-1466) 30
U.S. Department of Agriculture. Economics, Statistics, and Cooperatives Service. Agricultural Finance Statistics (US ISSN 0091-3502) 26
U.S. Department of Agriculture. Economics, Statistics, and Cooperatives Service. Agricultural Situation in Eastern Europe (US ISSN 0098-4000) 31
U.S. Department of Agriculture. Economics, Statistics, and Cooperatives Service. Agricultural Situation in the Far East and Oceania (US ISSN 0566-9502) 31
U.S. Department of Agriculture. Economics, Statistics, and Cooperatives Service. Agricultural Situation in the People's Republic of China (US) 31
U.S. Department of Agriculture. Economics, Statistics, and Cooperatives Service. Agricultural Situation in the Soviet Union (US ISSN 0360-4098) 31
U.S. Department of Agriculture. Economics, Statistics, and Cooperatives Service. Agricultural Situation in the Western Hemisphere(US ISSN 0501-9257) 31
U.S. Department of Agriculture. Economics, Statistics, and Cooperatives Service. Agricultural Situation in Western Europe (US) 31
U.S. Department of Agriculture. Economics, Statistics and Cooperatives Service. Cooperative Information Report (US) 21
U.S. Department of Agriculture. Economics, Statistics and Cooperatives Service. Cost of Storing and Handling Cotton at Public Storage Facilities (US ISSN 0092-9530) 31
U.S. Department of Agriculture. Economics, Statistics, and Cooperatives Service. Fertilizer Situation (US) 31
U.S. Department of Agriculture. Economics, Statistics and Cooperatives Service. Statistics of Farmer Cooperatives (US) 21
U.S. Department of Agriculture. Farmer Cooperative Service. Information (Series) *see* U.S. Department of Agriculture. Economics, Statistics and Cooperatives Service. Cooperative Information Report 21
U.S. Department of Agriculture. Farmer Cooperative Service. Statistics of Farmer Cooperatives *see* U.S. Department of Agriculture. Economics, Statistics and Cooperatives Service. Statistics of Farmer Cooperatives 21
U.S. Department of Agriculture. Home and Garden Bulletin (US ISSN 0073-3075) 416
U.S. Department of Agriculture. Home Economics Research Report (US ISSN 0073-3113) 479
U.S. Department of Agriculture. Marketing Research Report (US ISSN 0082-9781) 31
U.S. Department of Agriculture. Production Research Reports (US ISSN 0082-979X) 31
U. S. Department of Agriculture. Report of the Secretary of Agriculture (US ISSN 0082-9803) 21
U.S. Department of Agriculture. Technical Bulletin (US ISSN 0082-9811) 21
U.S. Department of Agriculture. Yearbook of Agriculture (US ISSN 0084-3628) 21
U. S. Department of Agriculture, Economics, Statistics, and Cooperatives Service. Farm Real Estate Taxes, Recent Trends and Developments (US) 31, 233
U.S. Department of Commerce. Consumer Goods and Services Division. Franchise Opportunities Handbook (US) 219
U.S. Department of Commerce. Effects of Pollution Abatement on International Trade (US ISSN 0093-9692) 915
U.S. Department of Commerce. Library. United States Department of Commerce Publications. Supplement *see* U. S. Department of Commerce. Publications; a Catalog and Index 166
U. S. Department of Commerce. Publications; a Catalog and Index (US ISSN 0091-9039) 166
U. S. Department of Defense. Defense Department Report (US ISSN 0091-6919) 746
U. S. Department of Defense. Defense Program and Defense Budget (US ISSN 0082-9862) 640
U. S. Department of Defense. Report of Secretary of Defense to the Congress(US ISSN 0098-3888) 640
U.S. Department of Energy. Directory of Information Centers (US) 364
U.S. Department of Energy. Fossil Energy Research and Development Program (US ISSN 0190-1141) 364
U.S. Department of Energy. Office of State and Local Programs. Annual Report to the President and the Congress on the State Energy Conservation Program (US ISSN 0161-1674) 364
U.S. Department of Energy. Strategic Petroleum Reserve Office. Annual Report (US) 681
U.S. Department of Health, Education and Welfare. Annual Report to the Congress of the United States on Services Provided to Handicapped Children in Project Head Start (US ISSN 0093-3430) 347
U.S. Department of Health, Education and Welfare. Catalog of Publications (US) 811
U. S. Department of Health, Education and Welfare. Statistics on Public Institutions for Delinquent Children *see* Children in Custody 256
U. S. Department of Housing and Urban Development. Annual Report (US ISSN 0565-2820) 487
U.S. Department of Housing and Urban Development. Community Development Evaluation Series (US) 915
U.S. Department of Housing and Urban Development. Occasional Papers in Housing and Community Affairs (US) 488
U.S. Department of Housing and Urban Development. Office of International Affairs. Foreign Publications Accessions List (US ISSN 0364-0930) 915
U.S. Department of Housing and Urban Development. Office of International Affairs. International Bulletin (US) 488
U.S. Department of Housing and Urban Development. Office of International Affairs. International Review (US) 488
U.S. Department of Housing and Urban Development. Statistical Yearbook (US ISSN 0147-7870) 489, 849
U. S. Department of Justice. Annual Report of the Attorney General of the United States (US ISSN 0082-9943) 519
U. S. Department of Justice. Opinions of Attorney General (US ISSN 0082-9951) 519
U.S. Department of Labor. Employment and Training Administration. Guide to Local Occupational Information (US) 668
U.S. Department of Labor. Employment and Training Administration. Manpower Research and Development Projects (US) 211
U.S. Department of Labor. Register of Reporting Labor Organization (US) 211
U. S. Department of State. African Series (US ISSN 0083-0003) 441
U. S. Department of State. Biographic Register (US ISSN 0083-0011) 98
U. S. Department of State. Commercial Policy Series (US ISSN 0083-002X) 198
U. S. Department of State. Department and Foreign Service Series (US ISSN 0083-0038) 724
U. S. Department of State. East Asian and Pacific Series (US ISSN 0083-0054) 724
U. S. Department of State. Economic Cooperation Series (US ISSN 0083-0062) 201
U. S. Department of State. European and British Commonwealth Series (US ISSN 0083-0070) 464
U. S. Department of State. General Foreign Policy Series (US ISSN 0083-0097) 724
U.S. Department of State. Historical Studies Division. Major Publications: an Annotated Bibliography (US) 724
U. S. Department of State. Inter-American Series (US ISSN 0083-0143) 724
U. S. Department of State. International Information and Cultural Series (US ISSN 0083-0119) 724
U. S. Department of State. International Organization and Conference Series (US ISSN 0083-0127) 724
U. S. Department of State. International Organization Series (US ISSN 0083-0135) 724
U.S. Department of State. Near and Middle Eastern Series *see* U.S. Department of State. Near East and South Asian Series 446
U.S. Department of State. Near East and South Asian Series (US) 446
U. S. Department of State. Treaties and Other International Acts Series (US ISSN 0083-0186) 524
U. S. Department of State. Treaties in Force (US ISSN 0083-0194) 524
U.S. Department of State. World Strength of the Communist Party Organizations. Annual Report. (US ISSN 0084-2257) 915
U.S. Department of the Army. Projects Recommended for Deauthorization, Annual Report (US ISSN 0361-2651) 898
U.S. Department of the Interior.Annual Report *see* U.S. Department of the Interior. Conservation Yearbook 915
U.S. Department of the Interior. Conservation Bulletins (US ISSN 0069-9101) 915
U.S. Department of the Interior. Conservation Yearbook. (US ISSN 0069-9152) 915
U.S. Department of the Interior. Office of Personnel Management. Annual Manpower Personnel Statistics (US ISSN 0093-3716) 915
U.S. Department of the Interior. Oil Shale Environmental Advisory Panel. Annual Report (US ISSN 0360-4543) 389
U. S. Department of the Interior. Safety Conference Guides (US ISSN 0083-0364) 915
U.S. Department of the Navy Journal *see* J A G Journal 513
U. S. Department of Transportation. Annual Report on Highway Safety Improvement Programs (US ISSN 0098-3209) 876
U. S. Department of Transportation. Bibliographic Lists (US ISSN 0083-0380) 95, 867
U.S. Department of Transportation. Energy Statistics *see* U.S. Department of Transportation. National Transportation Statistics. Annual 849
U. S. Department of Transportation. Fiscal Year Budget in Brief (US ISSN 0092-3117) 864
U.S. Department of Transportation. National Transportation Statistics. Annual (US) 364, 849, 864
U. S. Department of Transportation. Office of University Research. Awards to Academic Institutions by the Department of Transportation (US ISSN 0099-2267) 864
U. S. Department of Transportation. Summary of National Transportation Statistics *see* U.S. Department of Transportation. National Transportation Statistics. Annual 849
U.S. Economic Development Administration Research Review *see* E D A Research Review 143
U. S. Energy Information Administration. Annual Report to Congress (US) 364
U.S. Energy Research Administration. Fossil Energy Research Program *see* U.S. Department of Energy. Fossil Energy Research and Development Program 364
U.S. Energy Research and Development Administration. Directory of E R D A Information Centers *see* U.S. Department of Energy. Directory of Information Centers 364
U.S. Environmental Protection Agency. Clean Water; Report to Congress (US ISSN 0092-9433) 278
U.S. Environmental Protection Agency. Eastern Environmental Radiation Facility. Annual Report (US ISSN 0361-9087) 754
U. S. Environmental Protection Agency. Fish Kills Caused by Pollution (US ISSN 0071-5506) 389
U.S. Environmental Protection Agency. Office of General Counsel. a Collection of Legal Opinions (US ISSN 0361-6673) 519
U. S. Environmental Protection Agency. Office of Research and Development. Bibliography of Water Quality Research Reports *see* U. S. Environmental Protection Agency. Office of Research and Development. Indexed Bibliography 390
U. S. Environmental Protection Agency. Office of Research and Development. Indexed Bibliography (US) 390
U.S. Environmental Protection Agency. Office of Research and Development. Program Guide (US) 389
U.S. Environmental Protection Agency. Office of Research and Development. Selected Irrigation Return Flow Quality Abstracts (US ISSN 0090-6808) 390
U. S. Environmental Protection Agency. Pesticides Enforcement Division. Notices of Judgement under Federal Insecticide, Fungicide, and Rodenticide Act (US ISSN 0083-0518) 40
U.S. Environmental Protection Agency. Radiation Protection Activities (US ISSN 0161-7796) 389
U.S. Environmental Protection Agency. Radiation Protection *see* U.S. Environmental Protection Agency. Radiation Protection Activities 389
U.S. Environmental Protection Agency. Radiological Quality of the Environment in the United States (US ISSN 0363-9819) 389

1512   U. S.

U. S. Environmental Protection Agency. Upgrading Metal-Finishing Facilities to Reduce Pollution (US ISSN 0092-9689) *389,* 630
U.S. Environmental Protection Agency. Water Planning Division. Water Quality Strategy Paper (US) 389, *898*
U.S. Environmental Protection Agency Activities Under the Resource Conservation and Recovery Act of 1976 *see* E P A Activities Under the Resource Conservation and Recovery Act of 1976 *385*
U.S. Environmental Protection Agency Research Review *see* E P A Research Review *385*
U.S. Equal Employment Opportunity Commission. Annual Report (US ISSN 0083-0526) *211,* 719
U. S. Excise Tax Guide (US ISSN 0083-0534) *233*
U. S. Executive Office of the President. Economic Report of the President (US) *190*
U.S. Executive Office of the President. International Economic Report of the President (US ISSN 0091-2492) *198,* 201
U.S. Farm Credit Administration. Annual Report of the Farm Credit Administration and the Cooperative Farm Credit System (US) *31,* 181
U.S. Farm Credit Administration. Annual Report of the Farm Credit Administration on the Work of the Cooperative Farm Credit System *see* U.S. Farm Credit Administration. Annual Report of the Farm Credit Administration and the Cooperative Farm Credit System *31*
U.S. Federal Aviation Administration. National Aviation System: Challenges of the Decade Ahead (US) *869*
U.S. Federal Aviation Administration. Systems Research and Development. Report FAA-RD (US) *853*
U. S. Federal Aviation Administration Overview of the F A A Engineering & Development Programs *see* Overview of the F A A Engineering & Development Programs *10*
U.S. Federal Bureau of Investigation. Bomb Summary (US ISSN 0360-3245) *284*
U. S. Federal Communications Commission. Annual Report (US ISSN 0083-0585) *265*
U. S. Federal Communications Commission. I N F Bulletins (US ISSN 0083-0607) *265*
U. S. Federal Communications Commission. Rules and Regulation (US ISSN 0083-0615) *265*
U. S. Federal Council for Science and Technology. Interdepartmental Committee for Atmospheric Sciences. I C A S Reports (US ISSN 0083-0631) *915*
U.S. Federal Crop Insurance Corporation. Annual Report to Congress (US ISSN 0083-064X) *40*
U. S. Federal Deposit Insurance Corporation. Annual Report (US ISSN 0083-0658) *177, 501*
U. S. Federal Deposit Insurance Corporation. Bank Operating Statistics (US ISSN 0083-0666) *166*
U. S. Federal Deposit Insurance Corporation. Changes Among Operating Banks and Branches (US ISSN 0083-0674) *177*
U.S. Federal Deposit Insurance Corporation. Operating Bank Offices (US) *177*
U.S. Federal Deposit Insurance Corporation. Trust. Assets of Insured Commercial Banks (US) *177*
U.S. Federal Election Commission. Annual Report (US) *716*
U.S. Federal Highway Administration. Federally Coordinated Program of Highway Research and Development(US ISSN 0361-4204) *876*
U. S. Federal Highway Administration. Highway and Urban Mass Transportation (US) *864*

U.S. Federal Highway Administration. Highway Planning Technical Reports(US ISSN 0073-2184) *377*
U.S. Federal Highway Administration. Highway Statistics (US) *876*
U.S. Federal Highway Administration. Highway Transportation Research and Development Studies (US ISSN 0092-3389) *377*
U. S. Federal Highway Administration. Motor Vehicle Registrations by Standard Metropolitan Statistical Areas (US ISSN 0091-6056) *872*
U.S. Federal Highway Administration. Research and Development Program *see* U.S. Federal Highway Administration. Federally Coordinated Program of Highway Research and Development *876*
U.S. Federal Highway Administration Research and Development Program (US ISSN 0098-0234) *377*
U.S. Federal Home Loan Bank Board. Report (US ISSN 0083-0720) *177,* 762
U. S. Federal Home Loan Bank Board. Trends in the Savings and Loan Field(US ISSN 0083-0747) *177,* 762
U.S. Federal Housing Administration. F H A Homes (US ISSN 0091-4932) *488*
U. S. Federal Maritime Commission. Annual Report (US ISSN 0083-0755) *881*
U. S. Federal Mediation and Conciliation Service. Annual Report (US ISSN 0083-0771) *211*
U.S. Federal Railroad Administration. Office of Safety. Accident Bulletin *see* U.S. Federal Railroad Administration. Office of Safety. Accident/Incident Bulletin *874*
U.S. Federal Railroad Administration. Office of Safety. Accident/Incident Bulletin (US ISSN 0163-4674) *874*
U. S. Federal Reserve System. Annual Report (US ISSN 0083-0887) *177*
U.S. Federal Reserve System. Annual Statistical Digest (US) *177*
U. S. Federal Trade Commission. Annual Report (US ISSN 0083-0917) *182*
U. S. Federal Trade Commission. Court Decisions Pertaining to the Federal Trade Commission (US ISSN 0083-) *182,* 519
U. S. Federal Trade Commission. Federal Trade Commission Decisions, Findings, Orders and Stipulations (US ISSN 0083-0925) *182,* 519
U.S. Federal Trade Commission. Statutes and Court Decisions Pertaining to the Federal Trade Commission. Supplements *see* U. S. Federal Trade Commission. Court Decisions Pertaining to the Federal Trade Commission *182*
U. S. Fish and Wildlife Service. Investigations in Fish Control (US ISSN 0565-0704) *400*
U.S. Fish and Wildlife Service. National Survey of Hunting, Fishing and Wildlife-Associated Recreation (US) *823, 831, 849*
U. S. Fish and Wildlife Service. Progress in Sport Fishery Research *see* U. S. Fish and Wildlife Service. Sport Fishery and Wildlife Research *831*
U. S. Fish and Wildlife Service. Research Reports (US ISSN 0083-0941) *278, 400*
U.S. Fish and Wildlife Service. Selected List of Federal Laws and Treaties Relating to Sport Fish and Wildlife (US ISSN 0093-4631) *278,* 519
U. S. Fish and Wildlife Service. Sport Fishery and Wildlife Research (US ISSN 0362-0700) *400, 831*
U. S. Fish and Wildlife Service. Wildlife Leaflets (US ISSN 0084-0165) *278*
U.S. Food and Drug Administration. National Drug Code Directory (US ISSN 0077-4235) *686*
U.S. Food and Drug Administration. Pesticide-P C B in Foods Program. Evaluation Report (US ISSN 0361-4522) *755*

U. S. Food and Drug Administration. Clinical Experience Abstracts *see* F D A Clinical Experience Abstracts *684*
U.S. Food and Nutrition Service. Food and Nutrition Programs (US ISSN 0360-4594) *811*
U. S. Foreign Agricultural Service. Food and Agricultural Export Directory (US ISSN 0083-0976) *31,* 198
U. S. Foreign Agricultural Service. Miscellaneous Reports (US ISSN 0083-0992) *31*
U.S. Foreign Agricultural Trade Statistical Report, Calendar Year (US) *26,* 166
U.S. Foreign Agricultural Trade Statistical Report, Fiscal Year (US) *26,* 166
U.S. Forest Service. Annual Fire Report for National Forests (US ISSN 0083-1026) *411*
U.S. Forest Service. Cooperative Fire Protection. Wildfire Statistics (US ISSN 0360-8034) *395, 411*
U.S. Forest Service. Division of Cooperative Fire Protection. Forest Fire Statistics *see* U.S. Forest Service. Cooperative Fire Protection. Wildfire Statistics *411*
U.S. Forest Service. Forest Products Laboratory, Madison, Wisconsin. Annual Report of Research at the Forest Products Laboratory *see* U.S. Forest Service. Forest Products Laboratory, Madison, Wisconsin. Report of Research at the Forest Products Laboratory *413*
U.S. Forest Service. Forest Products Laboratory, Madison, Wisconsin. Report of Research at the Forest Products Laboratory. (US ISSN 0083-1018) *413*
U.S. Forest Service. Forest Service Research Accomplishments (US ISSN 0090-239X) *411*
U.S. Forest Service. General Technical Report INT (US ISSN 0092-9654) *411*
U. S. Forest Service. National Forest Areas *see* U. S. Forest Service. National Forest System Areas *411*
U. S. Forest Service. National Forest System Areas (US) *411*
U.S. Forest Service. North Central Forest Experiment Station. List of Publications (US) *412*
U. S. Forest Service. North Central Forest Experiment Station, St. Paul, Minnesota. Annual Report *see* U.S. Forest Service. North Central Forest Experiment Station. List of Publications *412*
U.S. Forest Service. Pacific Northwest Forest and Range Experiment Station. Annual Report (US ISSN 0083-2987) *915*
U.S. Forest Service. Research Note RM(US ISSN 0502-4994) *411*
U.S. Forest Service. Research Paper RM (US ISSN 0502-5001) *411*
U.S. Forest Service. Resource Bulletin PNW (US) *411*
U.S. Forest Service. Southern Forest Experiment Station. Research Accomplished (US) *411*
U.S. Forest Service. Southern Forest Experiment Station. Recent Publications *see* U.S. Forest Service. Southern Forest Experiment Station. Research Accomplished *411*
U. S. Forest Service. Technical Equipment Reports (US ISSN 0083-1077) *411*
U.S. General Services Administration. Management Improvement and Cost Reduction Goals (US ISSN 0566-5655) *746*
U.S. General Services Administration. Management Report (US ISSN 0091-6242) *809*
U.S. Geological Survey. Annual Report *see* U. S. Geological Survey. Yearbook *301*
U. S. Geological Survey. Bulletin (US ISSN 0083-1093) *300*
U. S. Geological Survey. Circular (US ISSN 0083-1107) *300*

U.S. Geological Survey. Professional Papers (US) *301*
U.S. Geological Survey. Water Resources Investigations (US ISSN 0092-332X) *308*
U. S. Geological Survey. Water Supply Papers (US ISSN 0083-1131) *308*
U. S. Geological Survey. Yearbook (US ISSN 0162-9484) *301*
U. S. Immigration and Naturalization Service. Administrative Decisions under Immigration and Nationality Laws (US ISSN 0083-1220) *730*
U. S. Immigration and Naturalization Service. Administrative Decisions under Immigration and Nationality Laws. Interim Decisions of the Department of Justice (US ISSN 0083-1239) *730*
U. S. Immigration and Naturalization Service. Annual Report (US ISSN 0083-1247) *730*
U. S. Imports for Consumption and General Imports; Tariff Schedules Annotated by Country (US ISSN 0565-1190) *198*
U. S. Industrial College of the Armed Forces. Monograph Series (US ISSN 0083-1328) *640*
U. S. Industrial College of the Armed Forces. Research Project Abstracts (US ISSN 0083-1336) *641*
U. S. Industrial Outlook (US ISSN 0083-1344) *226*
U.S. Institute of Tropical Forestry. Annual Letter (PR) *411*
U. S. Internal Revenue Service. Annual Report (US ISSN 0083-1476) *233*
U. S. Internal Revenue Service. Tax Guide for Small Business (US ISSN 0083-1484) *233,* 234
U.S. International Trade Commission. Annual Report (US) *198*
U.S. International Trade Commission. Imports of Benzenoid Chemicals and Products (US ISSN 0083-3436) *198*
U.S. International Trade Commission. Operation of the Trade Agreements Program (US ISSN 0083-3444) *198*
U. S. Interstate Commerce Commission. Annual Report (US ISSN 0083-1514) *182*
U. S. Interstate Commerce Commission. Interstate Commerce Acts Annotated(US ISSN 0083-1522) *182*
U. S. Interstate Commerce Commission. Interstate Commerce Commission Reports. Decisions of the Interstate Commerce Commission of the United States (US ISSN 0083-1530) *182*
U.S. Judicial Conference of the United States. Report of the Proceedings (US) *519*
U. S. Law Enforcement Assistance Administration. Annual Report (US ISSN 0565-6567) *284*
U.S. Library of Congress. Accessions List: Afghanistan (US ISSN 0148-5644) *915*
U. S. Library of Congress. Annual Report of the Librarian of Congress (US ISSN 0083-1565) *536*
U. S. Library of Congress. Hispanic Foundation. Bibliographic Series (US ISSN 0083-1581) *95*
U. S. Library of Congress. Library of Congress Publications in Print (US ISSN 0083-1603) *539*
U. S. Library of Congress. Manuscript Division. Register of Papers (US ISSN 0083-1611) *436*
U.S. Library of Congress. Processing Department. Newsletter (US ISSN 0092-8429) *536*
U. S. Lodging Industry (US ISSN 0361-2198) *483*
U. S. Maritime Administration. Annual Report (US ISSN 0083-1670) *881*
U. S. Maritime Administration. Technical Report Index, Maritime Administration Research and Development (US ISSN 0083-1697) *881*
U. S. Master Tax Guide (US ISSN 0083-1700) *233*

U.S. Mining Enforcement and Safety Administration. Informational Report(US ISSN 0097-9376) *647*
U.S. National Advisory Council on Extension and Continuing Education. Annual Report (US ISSN 0360-8166) *330*
U.S. National Advisory Council on Indian Education. Annual Report to the Congress of the United States (US ISSN 0093-7924) *324*, 393
U.S. National Aeronautics and Space Administration. Jet Propulsion Laboratory. Technical Memorandum (US ISSN 0068-5682) *915*
U.S. National Aeronautics and Space Administration. Research and Technology Operating Plan (RTOP) Summary (US) *10*, 853
U.S. National Aeronautics and Space Administration. Research and Technology Program Digest. Flash Index *see* U.S. National Aeronautics and Space Administration. Research and Technology Operating Plan (RTOP) Summary *10*
U.S. National Arthritis Advisory Board. Annual Report (US ISSN 0190-5422) *624*
U.S. National Bureau of Standards. Annual Report (US) *637*
U.S. National Bureau of Standards. Applied Mathematics Series (US ISSN 0083-1786) *590*
U. S. National Bureau of Standards. Building Science Series (US ISSN 0083-1794) *139*
U.S. National Bureau of Standards. Commercial Standards *see* U.S. National Bureau of Standards. Voluntary Product Standards *638*
U.S. National Bureau of Standards. Consumer Information Series (US ISSN 0069-9276) *280*
U.S. National Bureau of Standards. Federal Information Processing Standards (US) *637*
U.S. National Bureau of Standards. Methods of Measurement for Semiconductor Materials, Process Control, and Devices; Quarterly Report *see* U.S. National Bureau of Standards. Semiconductor Measurement Technology *638*
U.S. National Bureau of Standards. Monographs (US) *637*
U.S. National Bureau of Standards. National Standard Reference Data Series (US ISSN 0083-1840) *637*
U.S. National Bureau of Standards. Product Standards *see* U.S. National Bureau of Standards. Voluntary Product Standards *638*
U.S. National Bureau of Standards. Semiconductor Measurement Technology (US) 359, *638*
U.S. National Bureau of Standards. Semiconductor Measurement Technology. Quarterly Report *see* U.S. National Bureau of Standards. Semiconductor Measurement Technology *638*
U. S. National Bureau of Standards. Technical Notes (US ISSN 0083-1913) *638*
U.S. National Bureau of Standards. Voluntary Product Standards (US) *638*
U.S. National Cancer Institute. Journal of the National Cancer Institute. Monograph *see* U. S. National Cancer Institute. Monograph *606*
U. S. National Cancer Institute. Monograph (US ISSN 0083-1921) *606*
U.S. National Cancer Institute. Report of the Carcinogenesis Program (US ISSN 0090-2403) *606*
U. S. National Cancer Program. Report of the National Cancer Advisory Board Submitted to the President of the United States for Transmittal to the Congress of the United States (US ISSN 0092-9468) *606*
U.S. National Cartographic Information Center. Newsletter (US ISSN 0364-7064) *426*
U.S. National Center for Education Statistics. Degest of Education Statistics (US) *328*
U.S. National Center for Education Statistics. Digest of Educational Statistics *see* U.S. National Center for Education Statistics. Degest of Education Statistics *328*
U.S. National Center for Education Statistics. Earned Degrees Conferred (US ISSN 0565-744X) *340*
U.S. National Center for Education Statistics. Expenditures and Revenues for Public Elementary and Secondary Education *see* U.S. National Center for Education Statistics. Revenues and Expenditures for Public Elementary and Secondary Education *324*
U.S. National Center for Education Statistics. Fall Enrollment in Higher Education (US) *340*
U.S. National Center for Education Statistics. Financial Statistics of Institutions of Higher Education (US) *340*
U.S. National Center for Education Statistics. Library Statistics of Colleges and Universities (US) *340*
U.S. National Center for Education Statistics. Revenues and Expenditures for Public Elementary and Secondary Education (US) *324*
U.S. National Center for Education Statistics. Statistics of Public Elementary and Secondary Day Schools (US) *324*
U.S. National Center for Health Care Statistics. Vital and Health Statistics. Series 12. Data from the Institutional Population Surveys *see* U.S. National Center for Health Statistics. Vital and Health Statistics. Series 13. Data on Health Resources Utilization O 755n
U.S. National Center for Health Care Statistics. Vital and Health Statistics. Series 13. Data from the Hospital Discharge Survey *see* U.S. National Center for Health Statistics. Vital and Health Statistics. Series 13. Data on Health Resources Utilization z *755*
U.S. National Center for Health Statistics. Advance Data from Vital and Health Statistics (US) *755*
U.S. National Center for Health Statistics. Current Listing and Topical Index to the Vital and Health Statistics Series (US ISSN 0092-7287) 4, 732, *757*
U. S. National Center for Health Statistics. Health Resources Statistics(US ISSN 0083-1956) *755*
U. S. National Center for Health Statistics. Standardized Micro-Data Tape Transcripts (US) 274, *809*
U. S. National Center for Health Statistics. Vital and Health Statistics. Series 1. Programs and Collection Procedures (US ISSN 0083-2014) 730, *755*
U. S. National Center for Health Statistics. Vital and Health Statistics. Series 2. Data Evaluation and Methods Research (US ISSN 0083-2057) 730, *755*
U.S. National Center for Health Statistics. Vital and Health Statistics. Series 3. Analytical Studies (US ISSN 0083-2065) 730, *755*
U.S. National Center for Health Statistics. Vital and Health Statistics. Series 4. Documents and Committee Report (US ISSN 0083-2073) 730, *755*
U. S. National Center for Health Statistics. Vital and Health Statistics. Series 10. Data from the Health Interview Survey (US ISSN 0083-1972) *755*
U.S. National Center for Health Statistics. Vital and Health Statistics. Series 11. Data from the Health and Nutrition Examination Survey (US) *755*
U.S. National Center for Health Statistics. Vital and Health Statistics. Series 11. Data from the Health Examination Survey *see* U.S. National Center for Health Statistics. Vital and Health Statistics. Series 11. Data from the Health and Nutrition Examination Survey 5 *755*
U.S. National Center for Health Statistics. Vital and Health Statistics. Series 13. Data on Health Resources Utilization (US) 481, *755*
U. S. National Center for Health Statistics. Vital and Health Statistics. Series 14. Data on Health Resources: Manpower and Facilities (US ISSN 0083-1999) *755*
U. S. National Center for Health Statistics. Vital and Health Statistics. Series 20. Data on Mortality (US ISSN 0083-2022) 730, *755*
U. S. National Center for Health Statistics. Vital and Health Statistics. Series 21. Data on Natality, Marriage, and Divorce (US ISSN 0083-2030) 730, *755*
U.S. National Center for Health Statistics. Vital and Health Statistics. Series 22. Data on Natality and Mortality Surveys *see* U. S. National Center for Health Statistics. Vital and Health Statistics. Series 20. Data on Mortality *755*
U.S. National Center for Health Statistics. Vital and Health Statistics. Series 22. Date on Natality and Mortality Surveys *see* U. S. National Center for Health Statistics. Vital and Health Statistics. Series 21. Data on Natality, Marriage, and Divorce *755*
U.S. National Center for Health Statistics. Vital and Health Statistics. Series 23: Data from the National Survey of Family Growth (US) *730*
U. S. National Center for Productivity and Quality of Working Life. Annual Report to the President and Congress(US) *211*
U. S. National Clearinghouse for Drug Abuse Information. Report Series (US ISSN 0093-8599) *287*
U.S. National Clearinghouse for Drug Abuse Information. Selected Reference Series (US) *695*
U.S. National Commission for Manpower Policy. Annual Report to the President and the Congress (US ISSN 0361-7440) *211*
U.S. National Credit Union Administration. Annual Report (US) *177*, 181
U. S. National Credit Union Administration. Research Report (US ISSN 0564-9498) *177*, 181
U.S. National Credit Union Administration. Working Papers (US) *177*, 181
U.S. National Diabetes Advisory Board. Annual Report (US ISSN 0163-9609) *612*
U. S. National Endowment for the Arts. Annual Report (US ISSN 0083-2103) *79*
U.S. National Endowment for the Humanities. Education Programs (US) *351*
U.S. National Heart and Lung Advisory Council. Annual Report *see* U. S. National Heart, Lung, and Blood Advisory Council. Report *607*
U.S. National Heart and Lung Institute. Annual Report of the Director of the National Heart and Lung Institute *see* U. S. National Heart, Lung, and Blood Institute. Report of the Director *607*
U. S. National Heart, Lung, and Blood Advisory Council. Report (US) *607*, 623
U. S. National Heart, Lung, and Blood Institute. Report of the Director (US) *607*, 623
U.S. National Highway Traffic Safety Administration.Technical Reports (US) *867*
U. S. National Institute of Child Health and Human Development. Center for Population Research. Federal Program in Population Research *see* U.S. Center for Population Research. Inventory of Federal Population Research *730*
U.S. National Institute of Mental Health. Mental Health Statistical Notes (US ISSN 0098-972X) *603*
U.S. National Institute of Mental Health. Report Series on Mental Health Statistics. Series A: Mental Health Facilities Report (US) *603*
U.S. National Institute of Mental Health. Report Series on Mental Health Statistics. Series B: Analytical and Special Study Reports (US) *603*
U.S. National Institute of Mental Health. Report Series on Mental Health Statistics. Series C: Methodology Reports (US ISSN 0566-7038) *603*
U.S. National Institute of Mental Health. Report Series on Mental Health Statistics. Series D: Conference or Committee Reports, and Analytical Reviews of Literature (US) *849*
U.S. National Institute of Neurological Diseases and Stroke. Research Program Reports (US ISSN 0094-9582) *621*
U. S. National Institute on Drug Abuse. Research Monograph Series (US) *287*
U.S. National Institute on Drug Abuse Supported Drug Treatment Programs *see* N I D A Supported Drug Treatment Programs *287*
U.S. National Institutes of Health Factbook *see* N I H Factbook *753*
U. S. National Labor Relations Board. Annual Report (US ISSN 0083-2200) *211*
U. S. National Labor Relations Board. Court Decisions Relating to the National Labor Relations Act (US ISSN 0083-2219) *211*
U.S. National Library of Medicine. Annual Report *see* National Library of Medicine. Programs and Services *533*
U.S. National Marine Fisheries Service. Grant-in-Aid for Fisheries: Program Activities (US ISSN 0094-7008) *400*
U. S. National Marine Fisheries Service. Imports and Exports of Fishery Products (US) *400*
U.S. National Marine Fisheries Service. Report (US ISSN 0093-9412) *400*
U. S. National Mediation Board. Annual Report (US ISSN 0083-2286) *211*
U. S. National Mediation Board. (Reports of Emergency Boards) (US ISSN 0083-2278) *211*
U.S. National Oceanic and Atmospheric Administration. Annual Climate Diagnostic Workshop. Proceedings (US) *635*
U. S. National Oceanic and Atmospheric Administration. Manned Undersea Science and Technology Program; Report (US ISSN 0092-8917) 312, *370*
U.S. National Oceanic and Atmospheric Administration. National Climatic Center. Marine Climatological Summaries (US ISSN 0091-8512) 312, *635*
U.S. National Oceanic and Atmospheric Administration. Report to the Congress on Ocean Dumping and Other Man-Induced Changes to Ocean Ecosystems *see* U.S. National Oceanic and Atmospheric Administration. Report to the Congress on Ocean Pollution, Overfishing, and Offshore Development O *389c*
U.S. National Oceanic and Atmospheric Administration. Report to the Congress on Ocean Pollution, Overfishing, and Offshore Development (US ISSN 0098-4922) *389*

U.S. NATIONAL

U.S. National Oceanic and Atmospheric Administration. Test and Evaluation Laboratory. Technical Bulletin see U. S. National Oceanic and Atmospheric Administration. Technical Bulletin 312
U. S. National Oceanic and Atmospheric Administration. Technical Bulletin (US) 312
U. S. National Oceanic and Atmospheric Administrationn. Technical Memorandum (US) 312
U. S. National Oceanic and Atmospheric Adminnistration. Test and Evaluation Office. Technical Memorandum see U. S. National Oceanic and Atmospheric Administrationn. Technical Memorandum 312
U. S. National Oceanographic Data Center. Key to Oceanographic Records Documentation (US ISSN 0091-9500) 312
U.S. National Park Service. Archaeological Research Series see Publications in Archaelogy 278
U. S. National Park Service. Historical Handbook Series (US ISSN 0083-2316) 892
U.S. National Park Service. Public Use of the National Park System; Calendar Year Report (US ISSN 0361-9737) 278
U. S. National Park Service. Public Use of the National Park System; Fiscal Year Report (US ISSN 0093-3074) 278
U.S. National Park Service. Research Reports by Service Personnel (US) 831
U. S. National Park Service. Source Books Series (US ISSN 0083-2324) 892
U. S. National Science Foundation. Annual Report (US ISSN 0083-2332) 792
U.S. National Science Foundation. Division of Environmental Systems and Resources. Summary of Awards (US ISSN 0094-7857) 915
U.S. National Science Foundation. Federal Funds for Research, Development, and Other Scientific Activities (US) 792
U.S. National Science Foundation. Federal Funds for Science see U.S. National Science Foundation. Federal Funds for Research, Development, and Other Scientific Activities 792
U.S. National Science Foundation. Graduate Science Education Student Support and Postdoctorals (US ISSN 0094-7881) 340
U.S. National Science Foundation. Guide to Programs (US) 345, 792
U. S. National Science Foundation. N S F Factbook (US ISSN 0083-2375) 792
U. S. National Science Foundation. Research and Development in Industry (US ISSN 0083-2383) 854
U. S. National Science Foundation. Reviews of Data on Science Resources (US ISSN 0080-2026) 792
U. S. National Science Foundation. Surveys of Science Resources Series (US ISSN 0083-2405) 792
U.S. National Transportation Safety Board. Aircraft Accident Reports (US) 869
U. S. National Weather Service. Data Acquisition Division. Marine Surface Observations (US ISSN 0091-8725) 312, 635
U.S. Naval Academy Alumni Association. Register of Alumni (US) 263
U. S. Naval Institute. Naval Review (US ISSN 0077-6238) 640
U. S. Naval Observatory. Astronomical Papers Prepared for Use of American Ephemeris and Nautical Almanac (US ISSN 0083-243X) 84
U. S. Naval Observatory. Publications. Second Series (US ISSN 0083-2448) 84

U. S. Office of Consumer Affairs. Directory: Federal, State, and Local Government Consumer Offices (US ISSN 0190-2962) 280
U. S. Office of Consumer Affairs. Directory: Federal, State, County, and City Government Consumer Offices see U. S. Office of Consumer Affairs. Directory: Federal, State, and Local Government Consumer Offices 280
U.S. Office of Economic Opportunity. Annual Report see U.S. Community Services Administration. Annual Report of Community Services Administration 809
U.S. Office of Economic Opportunity. Federal Outlays in Summary see U. S. Community Services Administration. Federal Outlays in Summary 233
U.S. Office of Education. Opportunities for Teachers Abroad (US) 343
U. S. Office of Federal Coordinator for Meteorological Services and Supporting Research. National Hurricane Operations Plan (US ISSN 0092-2056) 635
U.S. Office of Management and Budget. Special Analysis: Budget of the United States Government (US ISSN 0362-9163) 233
U.S. Office of Minority Business Enterprise. Minority Enterprise Progress Report (US ISSN 0091-4630) 226, 393
U.S. Office of Technology Assessment Annual Report to the Congress (US ISSN 0095-2109) 746
U. S. Office of the Federal Register. Code of Federal Regulations (US ISSN 0083-2960) 519
U.S. Office of the Federal Register. Federal Register: What It Is and How to Use It (US) 519
U. S. Office of the Federal Register. Guide to Record Retention Requirements (US ISSN 0083-2979) 519
U. S. Office of Water Research and Technology. Annual Report (US) 898
U. S. Office of Water Resources Research. Annual Report see U. S. Office of Water Research and Technology. Annual Report 898
U.S. Park Police. Annual Report (US) 284
U. S. Patent and Trademark Office. Annual Report of the Commissioner of Patents (US ISSN 0083-3002) 677
U.S. Patent and Trademark Office. Classification Bulletins (US ISSN 0083-3010) 677
U. S. Patent and Trademark Office. Trademark Rules of Practice of the Patent and Trademark Office with Forms and Statutes (US) 677
U. S. Patent Office. Index of Patents Issued from the United States Patent Office see Index of Patents Issued from the United States Patent and Trademark Office 676
U.S. Patent Office. Trademark Rules of Practice of the Patent Office with Forms and Statutes see U.S. Patent and Trademark Office. Trademark Rules of Practice of the Patent and Trademark Office with Forms and Statutes 677
U. S. Peace Corps. Annual Report (US ISSN 0083-3088) 724
U. S. Postal Service. Support Group. Revenue and Cost Analysis (US ISSN 0092-2765) 266
U.S. Railroad Retirement Board. Annual Report (US) 205, 211
U.S. Rehabilitation Services Administration. Audiovisual Directory of the Research and Training Centers (US) 347
U. S. Rural Electrification Administration. Annual Statistical Report. Rural Electrification Borrowers (US ISSN 0083-3177) 359

U. S. Rural Electrification Administration. Annual Statistical Report. Rural Telephone Program (US ISSN 0083-3185) 359
U. S. Rural Electrification Administration. Report of the Administrator of the Rural Electrification Administration (US ISSN 0083-3193) 359
U. S. Saint Lawrence Seaway Development Corporation. Annual Report (US ISSN 0083-3207) 881
U. S. Securities and Exchange Commission. Annual Report (US ISSN 0083-3215) 205
U. S. Securities and Exchange Commission. Decisions and Reports (US ISSN 0083-3223) 205
U. S. Securities and Exchange Commission. Judicial Decisions (US ISSN 0083-3231) 205
U. S. Small Business Administration. Annual Report (US ISSN 0083-3274) 234
U.S. Small Business Administration. SBIC Digest (US) 234
U.S. Social and Rehabilitation Service. Annual Report of Welfare Programs (US ISSN 0360-487X) 809
U.S. Social and Rehabilitation Service. Juvenile Court Statistics (US ISSN 0082-9900) 257
U.S. Social and Rehabilitation Service. Office of Management. Quality Control, States' Corrective Action Activities (US ISSN 0361-2643) 809
U.S. Social Security Administration. Research and Statistics Notes (US ISSN 0566-0327) 809
U.S. Social Security Administration. Research Report (US ISSN 0566-0335) 809
U. S. Soil Conservation Service. National Engineering Handbook (US ISSN 0083-3304) 40
U. S. Soil Conservation Service. Soil Survey Investigation Reports (US ISSN 0083-3320) 40
U. S. Soil Conservation Service. Technical Publications (US ISSN 0083-3339) 40
U.S. Solicitor for the Department of the Interior. Solicitor's Review (US ISSN 0361-4530) 915
U.S. Tariff Commission. Annual Report see U.S. International Trade Commission. Annual Report 198
U. S. Treasury Department. Bureau of Accounts. Report on Foreign Currencies in the Custody of the United States see U. S. Treasury Department. Bureau of Government Financial Operations. Report on Foreign Currencies Held by the U. S. Government 177
U.S. Treasury Department. Bureau of Government Financial Operations. Annual Report of the Secretary of the Treasury on the State of the Finances (US) 177
U. S. Treasury Department. Bureau of Government Financial Operations. Federal Aid to States (US) 177
U. S. Treasury Department. Bureau of Government Financial Operations. Report on Foreign Currencies Held by the U. S. Government (US ISSN 0098-3896) 177
U.S. Treasury Department. Bureau of the Mint, Annual Report of the Director of the Mint (US) 177
U.S. Treasury Department. Combined Statement of Receipts; Expenditures; and Balance of the United States, Government (US) 233
U.S. Treasury Department. Office of Revenue Sharing. Annual Report (US) 177
U. S. Veterans Administration. Annual Report (US ISSN 0083-3533) 640
U.S. Veterans Administration. Annual Report on Relief from Administrative Error (US ISSN 0360-9464) 747
U. S. Veterans Administration. Medical Research Program. (US ISSN 0083-355X) 600

U. S. Veteran's Administration. Spinal Cord Injury Conference. Conference Proceedings (US ISSN 0083-3568) 621
U. S. Veterans Administration. V A Fact Sheets (US ISSN 0083-3576) 640
U.S. Water and Power Resources Service. Annual Report (US) 278, 898
U.S. Water and Power Resources Service. Engineering and Research Center. Research Reports (US) 898
U.S. Water and Power Resources Service. Engineering and Research Center. Technical Records of Design and Construction (US) 377
U.S. Water and Power Resources Service. Engineering Monograph (US) 381, 898
U.S. Waterborne Exports and General Imports see Foreign Trade Reports. U.S. Waterborne Exports and General Imports 195
United States & Canadian Mailing Lists(US ISSN 0073-2893) 6
United States & the World: Foreign Perspectives (US) 724
United States Animal Health Association. Proceedings of the Annual Meeting (US ISSN 0082-8750) 895
United States Catholic Mission Council. Handbook (US) 775
United States Catholic Missionary Personnel Overseas see United States Catholic Mission Council. Handbook 775
United States Cross-Country and Distance Running Coaches Association. Proceedings see United States Cross-Country Coaches Association. Annual Business Meeting. Minutes 822
United States Cross-Country Coaches Association. Annual Business Meeting. Minutes (US) 822
United States Cross-Country Coaches Association. Proceedings see United States Cross-Country Coaches Association. Annual Business Meeting. Minutes 822
United States Department of Commerce Publications see U. S. Department of Commerce. Publications; a Catalog and Index 166
United States Directory of Federal Regional Structure (US) 747
United States Dispensatory (US) 686
United States Dispensatory and Physicians Pharmacology see United States Dispensatory 686
United States Earthquakes (US ISSN 0091-1429) 306
United States Foamed Plastic Markets and Directory (US ISSN 0083-0968) 707
United States Government Manual (1973) (US ISSN 0092-1904) 716, 747
United States Government Organization Manual see United States Government Manual (1973) 747
United States Import Duties Annotated (US ISSN 0083-1263) 198
United States in World Affairs see American Foreign Relations-a Documentary Record 719
United States Independent Telephone Association. Annual Statistical Volume (US ISSN 0083-1298) 269
United States Independent Telephone Association. Holding Company Report (US) 269
United States - Israel Binational Science Foundation. Annual Report (IS) 792
United States-Israel Binational Science Foundation. Project-Report Abstracts(IS ISSN 0333-5526) 793
United States-Italy Trade Directory (US ISSN 0502-5842) 180
United States Lawn Tennis Association. Yearbook (US ISSN 0083-1557) 826
United States League of Savings Associations. Annals (US ISSN 0098-8944) 177

United States Livestock Sanitary Association. Proceedings see United States Animal Health Association. Proceedings of the Annual Meeting 895
United States Participation in the United Nations. (US ISSN 0083-0208) 724
United States Pharmacopeia see United States Pharmacopeia-National Formulary 686
United States Pharmacopeia-National Formulary (US) 686
United States Political Science Documents (US) 716
United States Polo Association. Yearbook (US ISSN 0083-3118) 822
United States Ski Association. Directory (US ISSN 0083-3258) 822
United States Squash Raquets Association. Official Year Book (US ISSN 0083-3398) 826
United States Statutes at Large (US ISSN 0083-3401) 519
United States Tobacco Journal Supplier Directory (US ISSN 0083-3479) 861
United States Treaties and Other International Agreements (US ISSN 0083-3487) 524
United States Trotting Association Sires and Dams see U S T A Sires and Dams 828
United States Volleyball Association. Official Volleyball Guide and Rule Book (US ISSN 0083-3592) 826
United Way of America. Directory see United Way of America. International Directory 809
United Way of America. International Directory (US) 809
United Way of Canada. Directory of Members (CN) 809
Unites Petrochimiques dans les Pays de l'OPEP et de l'OPAEP/ Petrochemical Units in the OPEC and OAPEC Countries (FR ISSN 0396-2644) 681
Unites Petrochimiques en Europe de l'Ouest/Petrochemical Units in Western Europe (FR ISSN 0339-5081) 682
Unity (AT) 507
Univeritaet Karlsruhe see W B K 371
Univers de la France et des Pays Francophones (FR) 464
Univers Historique (FR ISSN 0083-3673) 436, 793
Universal Business Directories. East Victoria Country Trade Directory see Universal Business Directories, Victoria Country Trade Directory 243
Universal Business Directories, Adelaide and South Australia Country Trade and Business Directory see Universal Business Directories, Adelaide Business and Street Directory 243
Universal Business Directories, Adelaide Business and Street Directory (AT) 243
Universal Business Directories, Brisbane and Suburban Business and Street Directory (AT) 243
Universal Business Directories, Brisbane and Suburban Business and Trade Directory see Universal Business Directories, Brisbane and Suburban Business and Street Directory 243
Universal Business Directories, Combined New England, North and North West New South Wales Business and Trade Directory see Universal Business Directories, New South Wales Business and Street Directory 243
Universal Business Directories Melbourne and Suburban Business and Trade Directory (AT ISSN 0083-3746) 243
Universal Business Directories, New South Wales Business and Street Directory (AT) 243
Universal Business Directories, Northern Queensland Business and Street Directory (AT) 243

Universal Business Directories, Northern Queensland Business and Trade Directory see Universal Business Directories, Northern Queensland Business and Street Directory 243
Universal Business Directories Perth and Fremantle and Suburbs Business and Trade Directory (AT ISSN 0083-3789) 243
Universal Business Directories, Southern Queensland Business and Street Directory (AT) 243
Universal Business Directories, Southern Queensland Business and Trade Directory see Universal Business Directories, Southern Queensland Business and Street Directory 243
Universal Business Directories, Sydney and Suburban Business and Street Directory (AT) 243
Universal Business Directories, Sydney and Suburban Business and Trade Directory see Universal Business Directories, Sydney and Suburban Business and Street Directory 243
Universal Business Directories, Tasmania Business and Street Directory (AT) 243
Universal Business Directories, Tasmania Business and Trade Directory see Universal Business Directories, Tasmania Business and Street Directory 243
Universal Business Directories, Victoria Country Trade Directory (AT) 243
Universal Business Directories Western Australia Country Business and Trade Directory (AT ISSN 0083-3843) 243
Universal Esperanto Association. Kongresa Libro see Kongresa Libro 546
Universidad Autonome de Santo Domingo. Comision para el Desarrollo y Reforma Universitarios (DR) 340
Universidad Boliviana Gabriel Rene Moreno. Revista (BO) 340
Universidad Boliviana Juan Misael Saracho. Informe de Labores. (BO) 340
Universidad Catolica de Chile. Facultad de Teologia. Anales (CL ISSN 0069-3596) 775
Universidad Catolica de Chile. Instituto de Planificacion del Desarrollo Urbano. Documentos de Trabajo (CL) 488
Universidad Catolica de Valparaiso. Revista de Derecho (CL) 519
Universidad Catolica de Valparaiso Imagen U.C.V. see Imagen U.C.V 263
Universidad Central de Venezuela. Consejo de Desarrollo Cientifico y Humanistico. Catalogo de la U. C. V.(VE ISSN 0083-5439) 341
Universidad Central de Venezuela. Facultad de Agronomia. Revista (VE ISSN 0041-8285) 21
Universidad Central de Venezuela. Instituto de Ciencias Penales y Criminologicas. Anuario. (VE ISSN 0507-570X) 284
Universidad Central de Venezuela. Instituto de Estudios Hispanoamericanos. Anuario (VE) 472
Universidad Central de Venezuela. Instituto de Estudios Politicos. Cuadernos (VE ISSN 0083-5420) 716
Universidad de Antioquia. Centro de Investigaciones Economicas. Boletin Bibliografico (CK) 166
Universidad de Antioquia. Departamento de Humanidades. Coleccion Papeles de Trabajo (CK) 493
Universidad de Antioquia. Escuela Interamericana de Bibliotecologia. Publicaciones. Serie: Legislacion Bibliotecaria (CK) 519, 536
Universidad de Antioquia. Extension Cultural. Ediciones (CK) 575

Universidad de Barcelona. Biblioteca Central. Catalogos de la Produccion Editorial Barcelona (SP ISSN 0067-4141) 761
Universidad de Barcelona. Biblioteca. Memoria Anual (SP) 536
Universidad de Barcelona. Facultad de Farmacia. Memoria (SP ISSN 0067-4176) 686
Universidad de Barcelona. Facultad de Filologia. Anuario see Anuario de Filologia 540
Universidad de Barcelona. Instituto de Arqueologia y Prehistoria. Publicaciones Eventuales (SP ISSN 0067-4184) 66
Universidad de Bogota Jorge Tadeo Lozano. Museo del Mar. Boletin (CK) 108, 312
Universidad de Bogota Jorge Tadeo Lozano. Museo del Mar. Informe (CK) 108
Universidad de Buenos Aires. Catedra de Patologia y Clinica de la Tuberculosis. Anales (AG) 623
Universidad de Buenos Aires. Instituto de Arte Americano e Investigaciones Esteticas. Anales (AG) 79
Universidad de Buenos Aires. Instituto de Economia. Bibliografia sobre Economia Nacional (AG) 4, 166
Universidad de Buenos Aires. Instituto de Historia Antigua Oriental. Revista(AG ISSN 0325-1209) 475
Universidad de Buenos Aires Instituto Bibliotecologico. Publicacion (AG ISSN 0068-3493) 536
Universidad de Chile. Departamento de Astronomia. Publicaciones (CL ISSN 0069-3553) 84
Universidad de Chile. Departamento de Geologia. Serie Apartado (CL ISSN 0069-3561) 290
Universidad de Chile. Facultad de Ciencias Economicas y Administrativas. Desarrollo (CL) 149
Universidad de Deusto. Publicaciones. Economia (SP) 149
Universidad de Deusto. Publicaciones. Filosofia (SP) 691
Universidad de Granada. Catedra Francisco Suarez. Anales (SP ISSN 0008-7750) 691
Universidad de Granada. Colleccion Monografica (SP ISSN 0072-5382) 493
Universidad de Guadalajara. Instituto de Botanica. Boletin Informativo (MX) 118
Universidad de Guayaquil. Escuela de Diplomacia. Revista (EC) 724
Universidad de la Habana. Centro de Informacion Cientifica y Tecnica. Serie 4. Ciencias Biologicas (CU) 108
Universidad de la Habana. Centro de Informacion Cientificas y Tecnica. Ciencias. Serie 9. Antropologia y Prehistoria (CU) 54, 66
Universidad de la Laguna. Coleccion Estudios de Historia (SP) 464
Universidad de la Laguna. Facultad de Ciencias. Anales (SP ISSN 0075-7721) 793
Universidad de la Laguna. Facultad de Derecho. Anales (SP ISSN 0075-773X) 519
Universidad de la Republica. Facultad de Agronomia. Publicacion Miscelanea (UY ISSN 0077-1279) 21
Universidad de la Republica. Facultad de Ciencias Economicas y de Administracion. Revista (UY) 149
Universidad de la Republica. Facultad de Humanidades y Ciencias. Publicaciones (UY ISSN 0041-8447) 493, 793
Universidad de la Republica. Facultad de Humanidades y Ciencias. Revista. Serie Ciencias (UY) 108
Universidad de la Republica. Facultad de Humanidades y Ciencias. Revista. Serie Ciencias Antropologicas (UY) 54
Universidad de la Republica. Facultad de Humanidades y Ciencias. Revista. Serie Ciencias de la Tierra (UY) 290

UNIVERSIDAD DE 1515

Universidad de la Republica. Facultad de Humanidades y Ciencias. Revista. Serie Ciencias Exactas (UY) 590
Universidad de la Republica. Facultad de Humanidades y Ciencias. Revista. Serie Filosofia (UY) 691
Universidad de la Republica. Facultad de Humanidades y Ciencias. Revista. Serie Historia (UY) 472
Universidad de la Republica. Facultad de Humanidades y Ciencias. Revista. Serie Linguistica (UY) 553
Universidad de la Republica. Facultad de Humanidades y Ciencias. Revista. Serie Letras (UY) 575
Universidad de la Republica. Facultad de Humanidades y Ciencias. Revista. Serie Musicologia (UY) 664
Universidad de la Republica. Facultad de Odontologia. Anales (UY ISSN 0083-4785) 610
Universidad de la Republica. Hospital de Clinicas. Informe Estatistico (UY ISSN 0041-8455) 482
Universidad de la Republica. Instituto de Administracion. Boletin (UY) 216
Universidad de la Republica. Instituto de Administracion. Cuaderno (UY ISSN 0077-1287) 216
Universidad de los Andes. Centro de Investigaciones Literarias. Serie Bibliografico see Universidad de los Andes. Instituto de Investigaciones Literarias. Serie Bibliografico 95
Universidad de los Andes. Cuadernos de Ciencia Politica (CK) 716
Universidad de los Andes. Cuadernos de Letras (CK) 582
Universidad de los Andes. Escuela de Letras. Anuario (VE) 575
Universidad de los Andes. Facultad de Derecho. Anuario (VE ISSN 0076-6550) 519
Universidad de Los Andes. Instituto de Geografia y Conservacion de Recursos Naturales. Cuadernos Geograficos (VE ISSN 0076-6569) 426
Universidad de los Andes. Instituto de Investigaciones Literarias. Serie Bibliografico (VE) 95
Universidad de Madrid. Departamento de Botanica y Fisiologia Vegetal. Trabajos (SP ISSN 0580-468X) 118
Universidad de Madrid. Seminario de Metafisica. Anales (SP ISSN 0580-8650) 692
Universidad de Medellin. Revista (CK) 341
Universidad de Murcia. Catedra de Teatro. Cuadernos (SP) 860
Universidad de Murcia. Departamento de Derecho Politico. Publicaciones. Serie Monografias (SP) 519
Universidad de Navarra. Departamento de Derecho Canonico. Manuales: Derecho Canonico (SP ISSN 0078-8759) 768
Universidad de Navarra. Departamento de Literatura Espanola. Publicaciones(SP) 575
Universidad de Navarra. Escuela de Arquitectura. Manuales: Arquitectura(SP ISSN 0078-8732) 70
Universidad de Navarra. Escuela de Bibliotecarias. Manuales: Bibliotecarias (SP ISSN 0078-8740) 536
Universidad de Navarra. Facultad de Ciencias de la Informacion. Cuadernos de Trabajo (SP ISSN 0078-8724) 505
Universidad de Navarra. Facultad de Ciencias de la Informacion. Manuales: Periodismo (SP ISSN 0078-8783) 505
Universidad de Navarra. Instituto de Ciencias de la Educacion. Coleccion I C E (SP ISSN 0078-8686) 324
Universidad de Navarra. Instituto de Estudios Superiores de la Empresas. Coleccion I E S E. Serie AC see Empresa y Su Entorno. Serie AC 214

Universidad de Navarra. Instituto de Estudios Superiores de la Empresas. Coleccion I E S E. Serie L *see* Empresa y Su Entorno. Serie L *215*

Universidad de Navarra. Instituto de Periodismo. Cuadernos de Trabajo *see* Universidad de Navarra. Facultad de Ciencias de la Informacion. Cuadernos de Trabajo *505*

Universidad de Navarra. Manuales de Derecho (SP) *519*

Universidad de Navarra. Manuales: Derecho Notarial Espanol *see* Universidad de Navarra. Manuales de Derecho *519*

Universidad de Oriente. Instituto Oceanografico Biblioteca. Boletin Bibliografico (VE ISSN 0590-3343) *290*

Universidad de Oriente. Instituto Oceanografico. Cuadernos Oceanograficos (VE ISSN 0590-3351) *312*

Universidad de Oriente. Instituto Oceanografico. Registro de Datos Oceanograficos y Meteorologicos (VE) *312*

Universidad de Oviedo. Centro de Estudios del Siglo XVIII. Boletin (SP) *464*

Universidad de Oviedo. Departamento de Prehistoria y Arqueologia. Publicaciones (SP) *66*

Universidad de Panama. Centro de Investigacion Juridica. Anuario (PN) *520*

Universidad de Panama. Centro de Investigacion Juridica. Legislacion Panamena. Indices Cronologicos y Analitico de Leyes(o Decretos Ejecutivos) (PN) *520*

Universidad de Panama. Facultad de Derecho y Ciencias Politicas. Cuadernos (PN) *520, 724*

Universidad de Puerto Rico. Centro de Investigaciones Sociales. Informe Anual (PR) *817*

Universidad de Puerto Rico. Graduate School of Planning. Planning Series E (PR) *488*

Universidad de Puerto Rico. Institute of Caribbean Studies. Special Studies (PR ISSN 0079-788X) *472*

Universidad de San Carlos. Facultad de Ingenieria. Escuela Regional de Ingenieria Sanitaria. Carta Periodica (GT) *755*

Universidad de San Carlos Anual (GT) *493*

Universidad de San Carlos de Guatemala. Facultad de Medicina Veterinaria y Zootecnia Revista (GT) *895*

Universidad de Sevilla. Instituto de Desarrollo Regional. Ediciones (SP) *190*

Universidad de Sevilla. Instituto Garcia Oviedo. Cuadernos (SP) *149*

Universidad de Sevilla. Instituto Garcia Oviedo. Publicaciones (SP ISSN 0582-8929) *216, 520, 747*

Universidad de Sevilla. Seminario de Antropologia Americana. Publicaciones (SP ISSN 0080-9101) *54*

Universidad de Uruguay. Departamento de Literatura Iberoamericana Publicaciones (UY ISSN 0077-1252) *575*

Universidad de Uruguay. Facultad de Agronomia. Boletin (UY ISSN 0077-1260) *21*

Universidad de Uruguay. Instituto de Mathematica y Estadistica. Publicaciones Didacticas (UY ISSN 0077-1295) *590*

Universidad del Norte. Museo de Arqueologia. Documentos para la Investigacion (CL) *66*

Universidad del Pacifico. Centro de Investigacion. Serie: Coyuntura Economica (PE) *149*

Universidad del Pacifico. Centro de Investigacion. Serie: Ensayos (PE) *801*

Universidad del Pacifico. Centro de Investigacion. Serie: Monografias (PE) *341*

Universidad del Pacifico. Centro de Investigacion. Serie: Trabajos de Investigacion (PE) *341*

Universidad del Pacifico. Departamento de Ciencias Sociales y Politicas. Serie: Departamentos Academicos (PE) *801*

Universidad del Salvador. Anales (AG ISSN 0068-3485) *493*

Universidad del Zulia. Facultad de Derecho. Revista (VE) *520*

Universidad del Zulia. Facultad de Medicina. Revista (VE ISSN 0542-6375) *600*

Universidad del Zulia. Revista (VE) *341, 575*

Universidad del Zulia. Revista (VE) *493*

Universidad Federal de Pernambuco. Instituto de Geosciencias. Serie B: Estudos e Pesquisas (BL ISSN 0080-0244) *290*

Universidad Hispalense. Anales. Series: Filosofia y Letras, Derecho, Medicina, Ciencias y Veterinaria *see* Anales de la Universidad Hispalense. Serie: Filosofia y Letras *779*

Universidad Industrial de Santander. Boletin de Geologia (CK ISSN 0120-0283) *301*

Universidad Industrial de Santander. Revista *see* Universidad Industrial de Santander. Revista - Investigaciones *370*

Universidad Industrial de Santander. Revista *see* Universidad Industrial de Santander. Revista - Humanidades *493*

Universidad Industrial de Santander. Revista - Humanidades (CK ISSN 0120-095X) *493*

Universidad Industrial de Santander. Revista - Investigaciones (CK ISSN 0120-0852) *370, 493, 600*

Universidad Industrial de Santander. Revista - Ion. (CK ISSN 0120-100X) *374*

Universidad Industrial de Santander. Revista - Medicina (CK ISSN 0120-0909) *600*

Universidad Internacional Menendez Pelayo. Publicaciones (SP ISSN 0080-6145) *341*

Universidad Javeriana. Facultad de Teologia. Coleccion Profesores (CK) *768*

Universidad Mayor Gabriel Rene Moreno. Revista *see* Universidad Boliviana Gabriel Rene Moreno. Revista *340*

Universidad Nacional Agraria. Taller de Estudios Andinos. Serie Andes Centrales (PE) *40*

Universidad Nacional Agraria. Taller de Estudios Andinos. Serie: Costa Central (PE) *40*

Universidad Nacional Autonoma de Mexico. Centro de Estudios Mayas. Cuadernos (MX ISSN 0076-7166) *472*

Universidad Nacional Autonoma de Mexico. Instituto de Biologia. Anales(MX ISSN 0076-7174) *108*

Universidad Nacional Autonoma de Mexico. Instituto de Geofisica. Anales (MX ISSN 0076-7182) *306*

Universidad Nacional Autonoma de Mexico. Instituto de Geofisica. Datos Geofisicos a Tablas de Prediccion de Mareas, Puertos del Golfo de Mexico y Mar Caribe (MX) *308*

Universidad Nacional Autonoma de Mexico. Instituto de Geofisica. Datos Geofisicos a Tablas de Prediccion de Mareas, Puertos del Oceano Pacifico (MX) *308*

Universidad Nacional Autonoma de Mexico. Instituto de Geofisica. Monografias (MX ISSN 0076-7204) *306*

Universidad Nacional Autonoma de Mexico. Instituto de Geografia. Anuario de Geografia (MX) *426*

Universidad Nacional Autonoma de Mexico. Instituto de Geografia. Boletin (MX ISSN 0076-7190) *426*

Universidad Nacional Autonoma de Mexico. Instituto de Geologia. Revista (MX) *301*

Universidad Nacional Autonoma de Mexico. Instituto de Investigaciones Antropologicas. Cuadernos Serie Antropologica (MX ISSN 0076-7263) *54*

Universidad Nacional Autonoma de Mexico. Instituto de Investigaciones Antropoligicas. Serie Antropologica (MX ISSN 0076-7298) *54*

Universidad Nacional Autonoma de Mexico. Instituto de Investigaciones Bibliograficas. Boletin (MX ISSN 0006-1719) *95*

Universidad Nacional Autonoma de Mexico. Instituto de Investigaciones Bibliografica. Instrumenta Bibliographica (MX) *536*

Universidad Nacional Autonoma de Mexico. Instituto de Investigaciones Esteticas. Anales (MX ISSN 0076-7239) *79*

Universidad Nacional Autonoma de Mexico. Instituto de Investigaciones Esteticas. Monografias de Arte (MX) *79*

Universidad Nacional Autonoma de Mexico. Instituto de Investigaciones Esteticas. Monografias. Serie Mayor (MX) *493*

Universidad Nacional Autonoma de Mexico. Instituto de Investigaciones Historicas. Cuadernos Serie Documental (MX ISSN 0076-7271) *472*

Universidad Nacional Autonoma de Mexico. Instituto de Investigaciones Historicas. Cuadernos Serie Historica *see* Devenir. Cuadernos del Seminario de Historia *468*

Universidad Nacional Autonoma de Mexico. Instituto de Investigaciones Historicas. Serie Bibliografica (MX ISSN 0076-7301) *472*

Universidad Nacional Autonoma de Mexico. Instituto de Investigaciones Historicas. Serie Documental (MX ISSN 0076-731X) *472*

Universidad Nacional Autonoma de Mexico. Instituto de Investigaciones Historicas. Serie de Cultures Mesoamericanas (MX ISSN 0076-7328) *472*

Universidad Nacional Autonoma de Mexico. Instituto de Investigaciones Historicas. Serie de Cultura Nahuatl. Estudios de Cultura Nahuatl (MX ISSN 0071-1675) *472*

Universidad Nacional Autonoma de Mexico. Instituto de Investigaciones Historicas. Serie de Cultura Nahuatl. Fuentes (MX ISSN 0076-7212) *472*

Universidad Nacional Autonoma de Mexico. Instituto de Investigaciones Historicas. Serie de Cultura Nahuatl. Monografias (MX ISSN 0076-7344) *473*

Universidad Nacional Autonoma de Mexico. Instituto de Investigaciones Historicas. Serie de Historia General (MX ISSN 0076-7352) *473*

Universidad Nacional Autonoma de Mexico. Instituto de Investigaciones Historicas. Serie de Historia Novohispana *see* Estudios de Historia Novohispana *468*

Universidad Nacional Autonoma de Mexico. Instituto de Investigaciones Historicas. Serie de Historiadores y Cronistas (MX ISSN 0076-7387) *473*

Universidad Nacional Autonoma de Mexico. Instituto de Matematicas. Monografias (MX) *590*

Universidad Nacional Autonoma de Mexico. Seminario de Investigaciones Bibliotecologica. Publicaciones. Serie B. Bibliografia (MX ISSN 0076-7468) *95*

Universidad Nacional de Asuncion. Instituto de Ciencias. Memoria (PY) *793*

Universidad Nacional de Colombia. Biblioteca Central. Boletin de Adquisiciones (CK) *95*

Universidad Nacional de Colombia. Centro de Bibliografia y Documentacion. Boletin Informativo *see* Universidad Nacional de Colombia. Biblioteca Central. Boletin de Adquisiciones *95*

Universidad Nacional de Colombia. Centro de Estudios Folkloricos. Monografias (CK ISSN 0067-9534) *403, 664*

Universidad Nacional de Colombia. Direccion de Divulgacion Cultural. Revista (CK) *801*

Universidad Nacional de Cuyo. Biblioteca Central. Boletin Bibliografico (AG ISSN 0076-6399) *95*

Universidad Nacional de Cuyo. Biblioteca Central. Cuadernos de la Biblioteca (AG ISSN 0076-6402) *536*

Universidad Nacional de la Plata. Facultad de Humanidades y Ciencias de la Educacion. Departamento de Letras. Serie Trabajos. Comunicaciones y Conferencias (AG) *557*

Universidad Nacional de la Plata. Instituto de Estudios Sociales y del Pensamiento Argentino. Cuadernos de Extension Universitaria (AG ISSN 0075-742X) *330*

Universidad Nacional de la Plata. Instituto de la Produccion. Serie Contribuciones (AG ISSN 0457-1673) *226*

Universidad Nacional de Rosario. Facultad de Ciencias, Ingenieria y Arquitectura. Instituto de Fisiografia y Geologia. Publicaciones (AG ISSN 0041-8684) *301, 426*

Universidad Nacional de Tucuman. Facultad de Filosofia y Letras. Cuadernos de Humanitas (AG ISSN 0564-4070) *493*

Universidad Nacional de Tucuman. Instituto de Ingenieria Electrica. Revista (AG ISSN 0082-6693) *359*

Universidad Nacional del Centro del Peru. Anales Cientificos (PE) *341*

Universidad Nacional del Centro del Peru. Cuadernos Universitarios. Serie: Estudios Andinos del Centro (PE) *54*

Universidad Nacional del Litoral. Facultad de Ciencias de la Administracion. Revista (AG) *747*

Universidad Nacional del Litoral. Facultad de Ciencias Economicas Comerciales y Politicas (AG) *149*

Universidad Nacional del Zulia. Facultad de Humanidades y Educacion. Artes y Letras (VE ISSN 0076-4337) *341*

Universidad Nacional del Zulia. Facultad de Humanidades y Educacion. Conferencias y Coloquios(VE ISSN 0076-4345) *493*

Universidad Nacional del Zulia. Facultad de Humanidades y Educacion. Fuera de Serie (VE ISSN 0076-4353) *341*

Universidad Nacional del Zulia. Facultad de Humanidades y Educacion. Manuales de la Escuela de Educacion (VE ISSN 0076-4361) *341*

Universidad Nacional del Zulia. Facultad de Humanidades y Educacion. Monografias y Ensayos (VE ISSN 0076-437X) *341*

Universidad Nacional Federico Villareal. Departamento de Ciencias Historico Sociales. Publicaciones (PE) *473*

Universidad Nacional Mayor de San Marcos. Facultad de Ciencias Economicas y Comerciales. Revista (PE) *149*

Universidad Nacional Mayor de San Marcos. Seminario de Historia Rural Andina. Seminario Arqueologico (PE) *66*

Universidad National Autonoma de Mexico Directorio de Bibliotecas *see* U N A M Directorio de Bibliotecas *536*

Universidad Politecnica de Barcelona. Publicacion (SP) *854*
Universidad Tecnica del Estado. Revista(CL) *801*
Universidad Tecnologica del Choco. Revista (CK) *341, 854*
Universidade Catolica de Goias. Gabinete de Arqueologia. Anuario de Divulgacao Cientifica (BL) *66*
Universidade de Coimbra. Arquivo. Boletim (PO) *537*
Universidade de Coimbra. Departamento de Zoologia. Ciencia Biologica *see* Ciencia Biologica: Biologia Molecular e Celular *127*
Universidade de Coimbra. Museum Zoologico. Memorias e Estudos *see* Ciencia Biologica: Biologia Molecular e Celular *127*
Universidade de Lisboa. Faculdade de Ciencias. Instituto Botanico. Artigo de Divulgacao (PO ISSN 0066-8079) *793*
Universidade de Lisboa. Faculdade de Direito. Revista (PO) *520*
Universidade de Lisboa. Faculdade de Letras. Revista (PO) *557, 575*
Universidade de Mackenzie. Centro de Radio Astronomia e Astrofisica. Relatorio Anual *see* Centro de Radio Astronomia e Astrofisica Mackenzie. Observatoria Nacional. Relatorio Anual *82*
Universidade de Sao Paulo. Centro de Estudos Portugueses. Boletim Informativo (BL) *553*
Universidade de Sao Paulo. Departamento de Botanica. Boletim de Botanica (BL ISSN 0302-2439) *118*
Universidade de Sao Paulo. Departamento de Historia. Boletim (BL) *473*
Universidade de Sao Paulo. Escola Superior de Agricultura "Luis de Queiroz." Anais (BL ISSN 0071-1276) *21*
Universidade de Sao Paulo. Escola Superior de Agricultura "Luis de Queiroz." Boletim de Divulgacao (BL ISSN 0071-1292) *21*
Universidade de Sao Paulo. Faculdade de Ciencias Economicas e Administrativas. Biblioteca. Boletim *see* Universidade de Sao Paulo. Faculdade de Economia e Administracao. Biblioteca. Boletim *95*
Universidade de Sao Paulo. Faculdade de Direito. Revista (BL ISSN 0080-6250) *520*
Universidade de Sao Paulo. Faculdade de Economia e Administracao. Biblioteca. Boletim (Faculdade de Economia e Administracao) (BL) *95*
Universidade de Sao Paulo. Faculdade de Filosofia, Letras e Ciencias Humanas. Departamento de Linguistica e Linguas Orientais. Boletim (BL) *671*
Universidade de Sao Paulo. Instituto Astronomico e Geofisico. Anuario Astronomico (BL) *84*
Universidade de Sao Paulo. Instituto de Estudos Brasileiros. Revista (BL ISSN 0020-3874) *79, 473, 575*
Universidade de Sao Paulo. Instituto de Geociencias. Boletim (BL) *84, 290*
Universidade de Sao Paulo. Instituto de Geociencias y Astronomia. Boletim *see* Universidade de Sao Paulo. Instituto de Geociencias. Boletim *290*
Universidade de Sao Paulo. Instituto de Geografia, Sedimentologia e Pedologia (BL) *301*
Universidade de Sao Paulo. Instituto de Pesquisas Economicas. Trabalho para Discussao (BL) *149*
Universidade de Sao Paulo. Instituto Oceanografico. Boletim (BL ISSN 0373-5524) *312*
Universidade de Sao Paulo. Instituto Oceanografico. Publicacao Especial (BL ISSN 0100-5146) *312*
Universidade de Sao Paulo. Instituto Oceanographico. Relatorio de Cruzeiros (BL ISSN 0100-5197) *313*

Universidade de Sao Paulo. Instituto Oceanografico. Relatorio Interno (BL ISSN 0100-5146) *312*
Universidade de Sao Paulo. Museu Paulista. Anais (BL ISSN 0080-6374) *473*
Universidade de Sao Paulo. Museu Paulista. Colecao. Serie de Arqueologia (BL) *66*
Universidade de Sao Paulo. Museu Paulista. Colecao. Serie de Etnologia (BL) *54*
Universidade de Sao Paulo. Museu Paulista Colecao. Serie de Geografia (BL) *426*
Universidade de Sao Paulo. Museu Paulista. Colecao. Serie de Historia (BL) *473*
Universidade de Sao Paulo. Museu Paulista. Colecao. Serie de Mobiliario(BL) *503, 655*
Universidade de Sao Paulo. Museu Paulista. Colecao. Serie de Numismatica (BL) *478*
Universidade de Sao Paulo. Museu Paulista. Revista (BL ISSN 0080-6390) *54*
Universidade do Amazonas. Centro de Pesquisas Socio-Economicas. Boletim Tecnico Informativo (BL) *801*
Universidade do Parana. Departamento de Historia. Boletim (BL ISSN 0070-1815) *436*
Universidade do Recife. Faculdade de Odontologia. Anais *see* Universidade Federal de Pernambuco. Faculdade de Odontologia. Anais *610*
Universidade do Recife. Instituto Oceanografico. Trabalhos *see* Universidade Federal de Pernambuco. Departamento de Oceanografia. Centro de Tecnologia. Trabalhos Oceanograficas *108*
Universidade do Rio Grande do Sul. Instituto de Ciencias Naturais. Boletim *see* Universidade Federal do Rio Grande do Sul. Instituto de Biociencias. Boletim *793*
Universidade Estadual de Maringa Revista UNIMAR *see* Revista UNIMAR *339*
Universidade Estadual Paulista. Departamento de Educacao. Boletim (BL) *341*
Universidade Estadual Paulista. Departamento de Geografia.Boletim (BL) *426*
Universidade Federal de Minas Gerais. Corpo Discente. Revista Literaria. (BL ISSN 0079-9327) *575*
Universidade Federal de Minas Gerais. Faculdade de Medicina. Anais (BL ISSN 0301-7729) *600*
Universidade Federal de Minas Gerais. Instituto de Pesquisas Radioativas. Relatorios Anuais (BL ISSN 0067-5687) *704*
Universidade Federal de Pernambuco. Anuario Estatistico (BL) *345*
Universidade Federal de Pernambuco. Departamento de Oceanografia. Centro de Tecnologia. Trabalhos Oceanograficas (BL ISSN 0374-0412) *108*
Universidade Federal de Pernambuco. Faculdade de Odontologia. Anais (BL) *610*
Universidade Federal de Pernambuco. Instituto de Antibioticos. Revista (BL ISSN 0080-0228) *686*
Universidade Federal de Pernambuco. Instituto de Biociencias. Memorias (BL) *108*
Universidade Federal de Pernambuco. Instituto Oceanografico. Trabalhos *see* Universidade Federal de Pernambuco. Departamento de Oceanografia. Centro de Tecnologia. Trabalhos Oceanograficas *108*
Universidade Federal de Pernambuco. Jornal (BL) *341*
Universidade Federal de Pernambuco. Relatorio des Attividades Universitarias (BL) *341*
Universidade Federal de Rio de Janeiro. Instituto de Matematica. Memorias de Matematica (BL) *590, 591, 849*

Universidade Federal de Santa Catarina. Museu de Antropologia. Anais (BL ISSN 0581-6076) *54*
Universidade Federal do Ceara. Departamento de Ciencias Sociais e Filosofia. Documentos (BL ISSN 0041-8870) *801*
Universidade Federal do Ceara. Escola de Agronomia. Departamento de Fitotecnia. Relatoria Tecnico (BL ISSN 0084-8646) *21*
Universidade Federal do Ceara. Estacao de Biologia Marinha. Boletim *see* Boletim de Ciencias do Mar *101*
Universidade Federal do Espirito Santo. Comisso de Planejamento. Documentario Estatistico Sobre a Situacao Educacional (BL ISSN 0085-0284) *324*
Universidade Federal do Espirito Santo. Comisson de Planejamento. Documentario Estatistico sobre a Situacao Educacional. Supplemento (BL ISSN 0085-0292) *324*
Universidade Federal do Para. Relatorio Anual (BL) *341*
Universidade Federal do Parana. Museu de Arqueologia e Artes Populares. Cadernos de Artes e Tradicoes Populares (BL) *915*
Universidade Federal do Rio de Janeiro. Instituto de Matematica. Notas de Matematica Fisica *see* Universidade Federal do Rio de Janeiro. Instituto de Matematica. Textos de Metodos Matematicos *590*
Universidade Federal do Rio de Janeiro. Instituto de Matematica. Textos de Metodos Matematicos (BL) *590*
Universidade Federal do Rio Grande do Sul. Faculdade de Agronomia. Boletim Tecnico (BL) *21*
Universidade Federal do Rio Grande do Sul. Faculdade de Medicina. Anais (BL ISSN 0085-042X) *600*
Universidade Federal do Rio Grande do Sul. Gabinete de Pesquisa de Historia. Boletim (BL) *473*
Universidade Federal do Rio Grande do Sul. Instituto Central de Biociencias. Boletim *see* Universidade Federal do Rio Grande do Sul. Instituto de Biociencias. Boletim *793*
Universidade Federal do Rio Grande do Sul. Instituto de Biociencias. Boletim *793*
Universidade Federal do Rio Grande do Sul. Instituto de Filosofia e Ciencias Humanas. Revista (BL) *801*
Universidade Federal do Rio Grande do Sul. Instituto de Geociencias. Pesquisas (BL) *290*
Universita Cattolica del Sacro Cuore. Istituto di Storia Antica. Contributi (IT) *464*
Universita degli Studi Cagliari. Facolta di Lettere-Filosofia. Annali (IT) *493*
Universita degli Studi di Bologna. Osservatorio Astronomico. Pubblicazioni (IT ISSN 0067-9895) *84*
Universita degli Studi di Cagliari. Facolta di Magistero. Annali (IT) *494*
Universita degli Studi di Cagliari. Istituto di Storia Medioevale. Publicazioni (IT ISSN 0068-4805) *436*
Universita degli Studi di Cantania. Istituto di Storia delle Tradizioni Popolari. Studi e Testi (IT ISSN 0069-1186) *403*
Universita degli Studi di Ferrara. Annali. Sezione 14. Fisica Sperimentale e Teorica (IT ISSN 0533-0386) *699*
Universita degli Studi di Ferrara. Istituto di Geologia. Annali. Sezione 9. Scienze Geologiche (IT) *301*
Universita degli Studi di Ferrara. Istituto di Geologia. Annali. Sezione 15. Paleontologia Umana e Paletnologia (IT) *674*

Universita degli Studi di Ferrara. Istituto di Geologia, Paleontologia e Paleontologia Umana. Annali. Sezione 15. Paleontologia Umana e Paleontologia *see* Universita degli Studi di Ferrara. Istituto di Geologia. Annali. Sezione 15. Paleontologia Umana e Paletnologia *674*
Universita degli Studi di Ferrara. Istituto di Geologia, Paleontologia e Paleontologia Umana. Pubblicazioni *see* Universita degli Studi di Ferrara. Istituto di Geologia. Pubblicazioni *301*
Universita degli Studi di Ferrara. Istituto di Geologia. Pubblicazioni (IT) *301, 674*
Universita degli Studi di Ferrara. Istituto di Mineralogia. Annali. Nuova Serie. Sezione 17: Scienze Mineralogiche e Petrografiche (IT) *647*
Universita degli Studi di Firenze. Istituto di Filosofia. Annali (IT) *692*
Universita degli Studi di Genova. Bolletino dei Musei degli Istituti Biologici (IT ISSN 0085-0950) *108*
Universita degli Studi di Genova. Fondazione Nobile Agostino Poggi (Pubblicazione) (IT) *436*
Universita degli Studi di Genova. Istituto di Filologia Classica e Medievale. Pubblicazioni (IT ISSN 0072-0852) *260, 553*
Universita degli Studi di Genova. Istituto di Paleografia e Storia Medievale. Collana. Storica di Fonti e Studi (IT ISSN 0072-0860) *464*
Universita degli Studi di Genova. Istituto di Progettazione Architettonica. Quaderno (IT) *70*
Universita degli Studi di Macerata. Facolta di Lettere e Filosofia. Annali(IT ISSN 0076-1818) *494*
Universita degli Studi di Messina. Istituto di Filologia Moderna. Biblioteca Letteraria (IT ISSN 0076-6623) *575*
Universita degli Studi di Messina. Istituto di Storia Medievale e Moderna. Pubblicazioni (IT ISSN 0076-6631) *464*
Universita degli Studi di Milano. Annuario (IT) *341*
Universita degli Studi di Napoli. Istituto di Geologia Applicata. Memorie e Note (IT) *301*
Universita degli Studi di Padova. Centro per la Storia della Tradizione Aristotelica nel Veneto. Saggi e Testi (IT ISSN 0078-771X) *464*
Universita degli Studi di Padova. Facolta di Lettere e Filosofia. Annali(IT) *494*
Universita degli Studi di Padova. Facolta di Lettere e Filosofia. Opuscoli Accademici (IT ISSN 0078-7728) *79, 575*
Universita degli Studi di Padova. Facolta di Lettere e Filosofia. Pubblicazioni (IT ISSN 0078-7736) *79, 575*
Universita degli Studi di Padova. Facolta di Scienze Statistiche, Demografiche ed Attuariali. Serie Estratti (IT) *732*
Universita degli Studi di Padova. Facolta di Scienze Statistiche, Demografiche ed Attuariali. Serie Pubblicazioni (IT) *732*
Universita degli Studi di Padova. Istituto per la Storia. Contributi (IT ISSN 0078-7752) *341*
Universita degli Studi di Padova. Istituto per la Storia. Quaderni (IT ISSN 0078-7760) *341*
Universita degli Studi di Padova. Scuola di Perfezionamento in Filosofia. Pubblicazioni (IT ISSN 0078-7779) *692*
Universita degli Studi di Padova Istituto di Storia Antica. Pubblicazioni (IT ISSN 0078-7744) *436*
Universita degli Studi di Palermo. Istituto di Entomologia Agraria. Bollettino (IT ISSN 0078-8619) *40*
Universita degli Studi di Palermo. Istituto di Filologia Greca. Quaderni (IT ISSN 0078-8627) *553*

Universita degli Studi di Parma. Facolta di Economia e Commercio. Studi e Ricerche (IT) 149
Universita degli Studi di Parma. Istituto di Storia dell' Arte. Cataloghi (IT) 79
Universita degli Studi di Parma. Rivista di Matematica (IT ISSN 0035-6298) 590
Universita degli Studi di Pavia. Istituto Botanico. Atti (IT ISSN 0079-0265) 118
Universita degli Studi di Roma. Istituto Botanico. Annali di Botanica (IT) 118
Universita degli Studi di Roma. Istituto di Economia Politica. Collana di Studi (IT ISSN 0080-4010) 149
Universita degli Studi di Roma. Scuola di Filologia Moderna. Pubblicazioni (IT ISSN 0080-4029) 553
Universita degli Studi di Roma. Seminario di Archeologia e Storia dell'Arte Greca e Romana. Studi Miscellanei (IT ISSN 0557-3122) 79
Universita degli Studi di Trieste. Facolta di Scienze Politiche. Pubblicazioni (IT) 716
Universita degli Studi di Trieste. Istituto di Pedagogia. Quaderni (IT ISSN 0082-6480) 324
Universita degli Studi di Trieste. Istituto di Ricerche Economico Agrarie. Pubblicazione (IT) 31
Universita degli Studi di Trieste. Istituto di Storia dell'Arte (Pubblicazioni) (IT ISSN 0564-2477) 79
Universita Delgi Studi di Torino. Facolta di Scienze Agrarie. Annali (IT ISSN 0082-6871) 21
Universita di Cagliari. Facolta di Lettere-Filosofia e Magistero. Annali *see* Universita degli Studi Cagliari. Facolta di Lettere-Filosofia. Annali 493
Universita di Cagliari. Facolta di Lettere-Filosofia e Magistero. Annali *see* Universita degli Studi di Cagliari. Facolta di Magistero. Annali 494
Universita J. E. Purkyne. Filosoficka Fakulta. Sbornik Praci (CS ISSN 0068-2705) 793
Universita Palackeho. Filosoficka Fakulta. Slavica (CS) 575
Universita Palackeho. Pedagogicka Fakulta. Sbornik Praci: Rusky Jazyk a Literatura (CS) 553, 575
Universitaet Bonn. Institut fuer Kommunikationsforschung und Phonetik. Forschungsberichte (GW ISSN 0341-3136) 265
Universitaet Bonn. Seminar fuer Orientalische Kunstgeschichte. Veroeffentlichungen. Reihe A. Nimruz (GW) 66
Universitaet Bonn. Seminar fuer orientalische Kunstgeschichte. Veroeffentlichungen. Reihe B. Antiquitates orientales (GW) 79
Universitaet des Saarlandes. Geographisches Institut. Arbeiten (GW ISSN 0563-1491) 426
Universitaet des Saarlandes. Jahresbibliographie (GW ISSN 0080-5173) 95
Universitaet Duesseldorf. Jahrbuch (GW ISSN 0070-7457) 341
Universitaet Frankfurt. Seminar fuer Voelkerkunde. Arbeiten (GW ISSN 0170-3099) 54
Universitaet Frankfurt. Wissenschaftliche Gesellschaft. Sitzungsberichte (GW ISSN 0512-1523) 793
Universitaet fuer Bodenkultur in Wien. Dissertationen (AU) 21
Universitaet Giessen. Bibliothek. Berichte und Arbeiten (GW ISSN 0072-4483) 537
Universitaet Giessen. Bibliothek. Kurzberichte aus den Papyrus-Sammlungen (GW ISSN 0072-4491) 436
Universitaet Giessen. Ergebnisse Landwirtschaftlicher Forschung (GW ISSN 0075-4609) 21
Universitaet Giessen. Mathematisches Institut. Vorlesungen (GW) 590

Universitaet Goettingen. Jahresbericht (GW ISSN 0436-1202) 341
Universitaet Hamburg. Geologisch-Palaeontologisches Institut. Mitteilungen (GW ISSN 0072-1115) 301, 674
Universitaet Hamburg. Institut fuer Internationale Angelegenheiten. Veroeffentlichungen (GW ISSN 0341-3233) 725
Universitaet Hamburg. Institut fuer Internationale Angelegenheiten. Veroeffentlichungen (GW) 725
Universitaet Hamburg. Institut fuer Internationale Angelegenheiten. Werkhefte (GW ISSN 0341-3241) 524, 724
Universitaet Hannover. Institut fuer Statistik. Mitteilungen (GW) 380
Universitaet Hannover. Lehrstuhl fuer Stahlbau. Schriftenreihe (GW) 380
Universitaet Heidelberg. Suedasien-Institut. Schriftenreihe (GW ISSN 0440-601X) 446
Universitaet Innsbruck. Alpenkundliche Studien (AU) 301
Universitaet Innsbruck. Alpin-Biologische Studien (AU) 108
Universitaet Innsbruck. Finanzwissenschaftliche Studien (AU) 177
Universitaet Innsbruck. Kunstgeschichtliche Studien (AU) 79
Universitaet Innsbruck. Mathematische Studien (AU) 590
Universitaet Innsbruck. Medizinische Fakultaet. Arbeiten (AU ISSN 0579-7772) 601
Universitaet Innsbruck. Theologische Fakultaet. Studien und Arbeiten (AU ISSN 0579-7780) 768
Universitaet Kiel. Agrarwissenschaftliche Fakultaet. Schriftenreihe (GW) 21
Universitaet Kiel. Geographisches Institut. Schriften (GW) 426
Universitaet Muenchen. Geophysikalisches Observatorium, Fuerstenfeldbruck. Veroeffentlichungen. Serie A (GW) 306
Universitaet Muenchen. Geophysikalisches Observatorium, Fuerstenfeldbruck. Veroeffentlichungen. Serie B (GW ISSN 0077-2100) 306
Universitaet Muenchen. Wirtschaftsgeographisches Institut. "W G I"-Berichte zur Regionalforschung (GW ISSN 0077-2127) 426
Universitaet Muenster. Astronomisches Institut. Mitteilungen (GW ISSN 0077-1929) 84
Universitaet Muenster. Astronomisches Institut. Sonderdrucke (GW ISSN 0077-1937) 84
Universitaet Muenster. Institut fuer Christliche Sozialwissenschaften. Schriften (GW ISSN 0077-1945) 915
Universitaet Muenster. Institut fuer Missionswissenschaft. Veroeffentlichungen (GW ISSN 0077-197X) 768
Universitaet Salzburg. Dissertationen (AU) 793
Universitaet Stuttgart. Institut fuer Geologie und Palaeontologie Arbeiten Neue Folge (GW ISSN 0585-7856) 290, 674
Universitaet Stuttgart. Institut fuer Steuerungstechnik der Werkzeugmaschinen und Fertigungseinrichtungen. i S W Berichte (US ISSN 0085-6916) 383, 583
Universitaet Wien. Dissertationen (AU) 793
Universitaet zu Koeln. Geologisches Institut. Sonderveroeffentlichungen (GW ISSN 0069-5874) 301
Universitaet zu Koeln. Institut fuer Geophysik und Meteorologie. Mitteilungen (GW ISSN 0069-5882) 306, 635

Universitaet zu Koeln. Institut fuer Handelsforschung. Mitteilungen. Sonderhefte (GW ISSN 0531-0318) 149
Universitaet Zu Koeln. Jahrbuch (GW ISSN 0069-5890) 341
Universitaet zu Koeln. Kunsthistorisches Institut. Abteilung Asien. Publikationen (GW ISSN 0170-3692) 79, 446
Universitaet Zuerich. Institut fuer Betriebswirtschaftliche Forschung. Schriftenreihe (SZ) 216
Universitaet Zuerich. Soziologisches Institut. Bulletin (SZ) 817
Universitaets- und Landesbibliothek Sachsen-Anhalt. Arbeiten (GE) 537
Universitaetssternwarte zu Wien. Annalen (GW ISSN 0342-4030) 84
Universitas Comeniana. Acta Pharmaceuticae (CS ISSN 0041-9087) 686
Universitatea "Al. I. Cuza" din Iasi. Analele Stiintifice. Sectiunea 2B: Geologie (RM ISSN 0075-3521) 301
Universitatea "Al. I. Cuza" din Iasi. Analele Stiintifice. Sectiunea 2c: Geografie (RM) 426
Universitatea "Al. I. Cuza" din Iasi. Analele Stiintifice. Sectiunea 3e: Lingvistica (RM) 553
Universitatea "Al. I. Cuza" din Iasi. Analele Stiintifice. Sectiunea 3f. : Literatura (RM) 575
Universitatea "Al. I. Cuza" din Iasi. Analele Stiintifice. Sectiunea 3c: Stiinte Economice (RM) 149
Universitatea "Al. I. Cuza" din Iasi. Analele Stiintifice. Sectiunea 3b: Stiinte Filozofice (RM ISSN 0075-353X) 692
Universitatea "Al. I. Cuza" din Iasi. Analele Stiintifice. Sectiunea 3d: Stiinte Juridice (RM) 520
Universitatea Bucuresti. Analele. Filologie (RM) 553
Universitatea Bucuresti. Analele. Filozofie. Istorie. Drept (RM) 464, 520, 692
Universitatea Bucuresti. Analele. Stiintele Naturii (RM) 793
Universitatea Bucuresti. Analelf. Acta Logica (RM ISSN 0068-3116) 692
Universitatea din Brasov. Buletinul. Seria A. Mecanica Aplicata-Constructii de Masini (RM) 383
Universitatea din Brasov. Buletinul. Seria a/3. Mecanica Aplicata - Constructii de Masini. Constructia de Masini si Tehnologia Prelucrarii Metalelor (RM) 383
Universitatea din Brasov. Buletinul Seria C. Stiinte Ale Naturii si Pedagogie (RM) 108, 590, 699
Universitatea Din Craiova. Analele: Seria Istorie, Geografie, Filologie (RM) 494
Universitatea din Timisoara. Analele. Stiinte Filologice (RM ISSN 0082-4461) 553
Universitatea din Timisoara. Analele. Stiinte Fizico-Chimice (RM ISSN 0082-4453) 248, 699
Universitatea din Timisoara. Facultatea de Stiinte ale Naturii. Lucrarile Seminarului de Geometrie si Topologie (RM) 590
Universitatea Din Timisoara. Facultatea de Stiinte Ale Naturii. Seminarul de Teoria Functiilor si Matematici Aplicate. A: Spatii Metrice Probabiliste (RM) 590
Universitatea din Timisoara. Facultatea de Stiinte ale Naturii. Seminarul de Teoria Functiilor si Matematici Aplicate. B: Analiza Numerica (RM) 590
Universitatea din Timisoara. Facultatea de Stiinte ale Naturii. Seminarul de Teoria Structurilor (RM) 590
Universite Catholique de Louvain. Centre d'Etudes Politiques. Working Group "American Foreign Policy." Cahier (BE ISSN 0076-1206) 473, 725

Universite Catholique de Louvain. Centre International de Dialectologie Generale. Travaux (BE ISSN 0577-1765) 553
Universite Catholique de Louvain. Facultes de Theologie et de Droit Canonique. Collection des Dissertations Presentees pour l'Obtention du Grade de Maitre a la Faculte de Theologie ou a la Faculte de Droit Canonique (BE) 775
Universite Catholique de Louvain. Facultes de Theologie et de Droit Canonique. Dissertations ad Gradum Magistri in Facultate Theologica Vel in Facultate Iuris Canonici Consequendum Conscriptae *see* Universite Catholique de Louvain. Facultes de Theologie et de Droit Canonique. Collection des Dissertations Presentees pour l'Obtention du Grade de Maitre a la Faculte de Theologie ou a la Faculte de Droit Canonique y 775
Universite Catholique de Louvain. Facultes de Theologie et de Droit Canonique. Travaux de Doctorat en Theologie et en Droit Canonique. Nouvelle Serie (BE ISSN 0076-1230) 775
Universite Catholique de Louvain. Institut de Mathematique Pure et Appliquee. Rapport (BE) 590
Universite Catholique de Louvain. Institut Orientaliste. Publications (BE ISSN 0076-1265) 446, 671
Universite Catholique de Louvain. Laboratoire de Pedagogie Experimentale. Cahiers de Recherches (BE ISSN 0076-1281) 324
Universite Catholique de Louvain. Recueil de Travaux d'Histoire et de Philologie (BE ISSN 0076-1311) 553
Universite d'Abidjan. Annales. Serie F: Ethnosociologie *see* Universite Nationale de Cote d'Ivoire. Annales. Serie F: Ethnosociologie 54
Universite d'Abidjan. Annales. Serie G: Geographie *see* Universite Nationale de Cote d'Ivoire. Annales. Serie G: Geographie 427
Universite d'Aix-Marseille I. Centre d'Etudes des Societes Mediterraneennes. Cahiers (FR ISSN 0065-4949) 801
Universite d'Aix-Marseille I. Centre d'Etudes et de Recherches Helleniques. Publications (FR ISSN 0065-4981) 575
Universite d'Aix-Marseille I. Faculte des Lettres et Sciences Humaines. Annales (FR ISSN 0065-4973) 494
Universite d'Aix-Marseille III. Centre des Hautes Etudes Touristiques. Collection "Essais" (FR) 892
Universite d'Aix-Marseille III. Centre des Hautes Etudes Touristiques. Etudes et Memoires (FR ISSN 0065-4965) 893
Universite d'Aix-Marseille III. Institut d'Histoire des Pays d'Outre-Mer. Etudes et Documents (FR ISSN 0065-5007) 464
Universite d'Alger. Observatoire Astronomique. Annales *see* Observatoire Astronomique d'Alger. Annales 83
Universite d'Etat. Faculte d'Ethnologie. Centre de Recherches en Sciences Humaines et Sociales. Revue (HT) 801
Universite d'Odense. Etudes Romanes (DK) 553, 575
Universite de Besancon. Annales Litteraires *see* Recherches en Linguistique Etrangere 550
Universite de Besancon. Centre de Documentation et de Bibliographie Philosophiques. Travaux (FR) 692
Universite de Bordeaux. Collection Sinologique (FR ISSN 0068-0273) 553
Universite de Bordeaux II. Centre d'Etudes et de Recherches Ethnologiques. Cahiers (FR) 393, 817

Universite de Bordeaux III. Centre de Recherches sur l'Amerique Anglophone. Annales (FR ISSN 0399-0443) 473, 716
Universite de Brazzaville. Annales (CF ISSN 0302-4814) 341
Universite de Bretagne Occidentale. Guide de l'Etudiant (FR) 324
Universite de Clermont-Ferrand II. Annales Scientifique. Serie Biologie Vegetale (FR ISSN 0069-469X) 118
Universite de Clermont-Ferrand II. Annales Scientifique. Serie Chemie (FR ISSN 0069-4703) 248
Universite de Clermont-Ferrand II. Annales Scientifiques. Serie Biologie Animale (FR ISSN 0069-4681) 130
Universite de Clermont-Ferrand II. Annales Scientifiques. Serie Geologie et Mineralogie (FR ISSN 0069-4711) 301, 647
Universite de Clermont-Ferrand II. Annales Scientifiques. Serie Mathematique (FR ISSN 0069-472X) 590
Universite de Clermont-Ferrand II. Annales Scientifiques. Serie Physiologie Animale (FR ISSN 0069-4746) 131
Universite de Clermont-Ferrand II. Annales Scientifiques. Serie Physique(FR ISSN 0069-4738) 699
Universite de Dakar. Faculte des Lettres et Sciences Humaines. Annales (FR) 575, 801
Universite de Fribourg. Historische Schriften (SZ) 464
Universite de Geneve. Institut Universitaire de Hautes Etudes Internationales. Discussion Paper (SZ) 716
Universite de Geneve. Institut Universitaire de Hautes Etudes Internationales. Etudes et Travaux (SZ ISSN 0073-859X) 716
Universite de Geneve. Institut Universitaire de Hautes Etudes Internationales. Publication (SZ ISSN 0073-8603) 716
Universite de Geneve. Section d'Histoire. Documents (SZ ISSN 0072-0836) 464
Universite de Grenoble. Institut de Phonetique. Manuels. Serie A see Universite de Grenoble III. Institut de Phonetique. Travaux: Serie A: Manuals 553
Universite de Grenoble. Institut Francais de Florence. Publication. Serie 1: Collection d'Etudes d'Histoire (IT ISSN 0072-7652) 494
Universite de Grenoble. Institut Francais de Florence. Publication. Serie 2: Collection d'Etudes Bibliographiques (IT ISSN 0072-7660) 578
Universite de Grenoble III. Institut de Phonetique. Bulletin (FR) 553
Universite de Grenoble III. Institut de Phonetique. Travaux: Serie A: Manuals (FR) 553
Universite de Grenoble III. Institut de Phonetique. Travaux. Serie B: Etudes Linguistiques (FR ISSN 0085-1272) 553
Universite de Haute Bretagne. Centre d'Etudes Anglo-Irlandaises. Cahier see Universite de Haute Bretagne. Centre d'Etudes Irlandaises. Cahier 575
Universite de Haute Bretagne. Centre d'Etudes Hispaniques, Hispano-Americaines et Luso-Bresiliennes. Travaux (FR ISSN 0080-0929) 464, 575
Universite de Haute Bretagne. Centre d'Etudes Irlandaises. Cahier (FR ISSN 0181-561X) 575
Universite de l'Etat a Gand. Service de Linguistique Francaise. Travaux de Linguistique see Travaux de Linguistique 553
Universite de Lausanne. Ecole des Sciences Sociales et Politiques. Publications (SZ ISSN 0075-8191) 801

Universite de Lausanne. Faculte des Lettres. Publications (SZ ISSN 0041-915X) 575
Universite de Liege. Association de Classiques Bulletin Semestriel see Otia 260
Universite de Liege. Faculte de Philosophie et Lettres. Publications (BE) 494
Universite de Liege. Institut de Pharmacie. Recueil des Conferences Organisees par le Cercle A. Gilkinet see Journee Scientifique de Mars. Conferences et Communications 685
Universite de Liege. Institut de Pharmacie. Travaux Publies (BE ISSN 0075-935X) 686
Universite de Lyon. Faculte de Droit et des Sciences Economiques. Annales see Universite Jean Moulin. Annales 520
Universite de Lyon III. Faculte de Droit. Annales see Universite Jean Moulin. Annales 520
Universite de Madagascar. Musee d'Art et d'Archeologie. Travaux et Documents (MG) 66, 79
Universite de Metz. Centre de Recherches Relations Internationales. Travaux et Recherches (FR) 725
Universite de Montreal. Ecole de Bibliotheconomie. Publications (CN ISSN 0077-1341) 537
Universite de Montreal. Ecole de Medecine Veterinaire. Annuaire (CN ISSN 0383-8455) 895
Universite de Montreal. Institute Botanique. Contributions (CN ISSN 0041-9168) 118
Universite de Nancy II. Centre de Recherches et d'Applications Pedagogiques en Langues. Melanges (FR ISSN 0077-2712) 351, 553
Universite de Nancy II. Centre Europeen Universitaire. Memoires (FR ISSN 0077-2720) 716
Universite de Nancy II. Faculte de Droit et des Sciences Economiques. Etudes et Travaux. Serie Droit International Public (FR) 524
Universite de Nancy II. Faculte de Droit et des Sciences Economiques. Etudes et Travaux. Serie Droit Prive (FR) 520
Universite de Nancy II. Faculte de Droit et des Sciences Economiques. Etudes et Travaux. Serie Economie Regionale (FR) 716
Universite de Nancy II. Faculte de Droit et des Sciences Economiques. Etudes et Travaux. Serie Science Politique (FR) 716
Universite de Nantes. Centre de Recherches sur l'Histoire de la France Atlantique. Enquetes et Documents (FR) 464
Universite de Neuchatel. Annales (SZ) 341
Universite de Neuchatel. Centre d'Hydrogeologie. Bulletin (SZ) 308
Universite de Neuchatel. Faculte des Lettres. Recueil de Travaux (SZ ISSN 0077-7633) 575
Universite de Neuchatel. Seminaire de Geometrie. Publications. Serie 1. Courtes Publications see Centre de Recherches en Mathematiques Pures. Publications. Serie 1 585
Universite de Neuchatel. Seminaire de Geometrie. Publications. Serie 2. Monographies see Centre de Recherches en Mathematiques Pures. Publications. Serie 2. Monographies 585
Universite de Paris. Faculte des Lettres et Sciences Humaines. Publications. Serie Acta (FR ISSN 0078-9887) 494, 793
Universite de Paris. Faculte des Lettres et Sciences Humaines. Publications. Serie Recherches (FR ISSN 0078-9895) 801
Universite de Paris VI (Pierre et Marie Curie). Institut Henri Poincare. Seminaire Choquet. Initiation a l'Analyse (FR ISSN 0078-9909) 915

Universite de Paris VI (Pierre et Marie Curie). Institut Henri Poincare. Seminaire Lions (FR ISSN 0079-0036) 915
Universite de Paris VII. Groupe de Linguistique Japonaise. Travaux see Travaux de Linguistique Japonaise 553
Universite de Poitiers. Centre d'Etudes Superieures de Civilisation Medievale. Publications (FR ISSN 0079-256X) 464
Universite de Rennes. Institut Armoricain de Recherches Economiques et Humaines. (Publication) (FR) 464
Universite de Saint Etienne. Centre Jean Palerne. Memoires (FR) 494
Universite de Sherbrooke. Departement d'Economie. Dossiers sur les Cooperatives (CN) 181
Universite de Sherbrooke. Revue de Droit (CN) 181
Universite de Skopje. Faculte des Sciences Economiques. Annuaire see Univerzitet vo Skoplje. Ekonomskiot Fakultet. Godisnik 150
Universite de Strasbourg. Centre de Recherche et de Documentation des Institutions Chretiennes. Bulletin du CERDIC (FR ISSN 0081-5926) 537
Universite de Strasbourg. Institut d'Etudes Latino-Americaines. Travaux (FR) 473
Universite de Strasbourg II. Centre de Philologie et Litteratures Romanes. Actes et Colloques (FR ISSN 0081-5918) 553, 575
Universite de Strasbourg II. Institut de Phonetique. Travaux (FR ISSN 0081-5934) 494, 553, 575
Universite de Toulouse II (le Mirail). Institut d'Art Prehistorique. Travaux (FR ISSN 0563-9794) 66, 79
Universite de Tunis. Ecole Normale Superieure. Section A: Lettres et Sciences Humaines. Serie 1: Langue et Litterature (TI) 553, 575
Universite de Yaounde. Faculte de Droit et des Sciences Economiques. Economie Generale (CM) 192
Universite de Yaounde. Faculte des Sciences. Annales (CM ISSN 0566-201X) 793
Universita degli Studi di Ferrara. Istituto di Geologia, Paleontologia e Paleontologia Umana. Annali. Sezione 9. Scienze Geologiche see Universita degli Studi di Ferrara. Istituto di Geologia. Annali. Sezione 9. Scienze Geologiche 301
Universite des Sciences Sociales de Toulouse. Annales (FR ISSN 0563-9727) 801
Universite du Quebec (Province). Rapport Annuel (CN) 341
Universite Federale du Cameroun. Faculte des Sciences. Annales see Universite de Yaounde. Faculte des Sciences. Annales 793
Universite Jean Moulin. Annales (FR) 520
Universite Laval. Archives de Folklore (CN ISSN 0085-5243) 403
Universite Laval. Centre d'Etudes Nordiques. Travaux et Documents (CN ISSN 0079-8347) 473
Universite Laval. Centre de Recherches sur les Atomes et les Molecules. Rapport Annuel (CN) 248, 705
Universite Laval. Departement d'Exploitation et Utilisation des Bois. Note de Recherches (CN ISSN 0079-8355) 413
Universite Laval. Departement d'Exploitation et Utilisation des Bois. Note Technique (CN ISSN 0079-8363) 413
Universite Laval. Departement de Geographie. Travaux (CN) 426
Universite Laval. Fonds de Recherches Forestieres. Contribution (CN ISSN 0079-838X) 411
Universite Laval. Institut d'Histoire. Cahiers (CN ISSN 0079-8398) 436
Universite Libre de Bruxelles. Faculte de Philosophie et Lettres. Sources et Instruments (BE) 494

Universite Libre de Bruxelles. Faculte de Philosophie et Lettres. Travaux (BE) 494
Universite Libre de Bruxelles. Groupe d'Etude du Dix-Huitieme Siecle. Etudes sur le Dix-Huitieme Siecle (BE) 464
Universite Libre de Bruxelles. Institut d'Etudes Europeennes. Enseignement Complementaire. Nouvelle Serie (BE ISSN 0068-2993) 149
Universite Libre de Bruxelles. Institut d'Etudes Europeennes. Theses et Travaux Economiques (BE ISSN 0068-3000) 149
Universite Libre de Bruxelles. Institut d'Etudes Europeennes. Theses et Travaux Juridiques (BE ISSN 0068-3019) 520
Universite Libre de Bruxelles. Institut d'Etudes Europeennes. Theses et Travaux Politiques (BE) 716
Universite Libre de Bruxelles. Institut de Philologie et d'Histoire Orientales et Slaves. Annuaire (BE) 671
Universite Libre de Bruxelles. Institut de Philosophie. Annales (BE) 692
Universite Libre de Bruxelles. Institut de Sociologie. Annee Sociale (BE ISSN 0066-2380) 817
Universite Libre de Bruxelles. Institut de Sociologie. Cahiers (BE ISSN 0068-2985) 817
Universite Libre de Bruxelles. Institut pour l'Etude de la Renaissance et de l'Humanisme. Colloques (BE) 464
Universite Nationale de Cote d'Ivoire. Annales. Serie F: Ethnosociologie (IV) 54, 817
Universite Nationale de Cote d'Ivoire. Annales. Serie G: Geographie (IV) 427
Universite Nationale du Zaire, Kinshasa. Faculte de Droit. Annales (ZR) 520
Universite Nationale du Zaire, Lubumbashi. Centre Linguistique Theorique et Appliquee. Bulletin d'Information (ZR) 553
Universite Saint-Joseph. Faculte de Droit et des Sciences Economiques. Annuaire (LE) 192
Universite Saint-Joseph. Faculte des Lettres et des Sciences Humaines. Recherche. Serie A: Langue Arabe et Pensee Islamique (LE) 553, 770
Universite Saint-Joseph. Faculte des Lettres et des Sciences Humaines. Recherche. Serie B: Orient Chretien (LE) 671, 768
Universite Saint-Joseph. Melanges (LE) 66, 475
Universite Scientifique et Medicale de Grenoble. Institut des Sciences Nucleaires. Rapport Annuel (FR ISSN 0399-127X) 705
Universite Scientifique et Medicale de Grenoble. Institut Fourier. Annales (FR ISSN 0373-0956) 590
Universiteit van Amsterdam. Fysisch Geografisch en Bodemkundig Laboratorium. Publikaties (NE ISSN 0066-1317) 427
Universiteit van Amsterdam. Mathematisch Instituut. Report (NE) 590
Universiteit van Amsterdam. Zoologisch Museum. Bulletin (NE ISSN 0066-1325) 131
Universiteit van Durban-Westville. Tydskrif see University of Durban-Westville. Journal 494
Universiteit van Port Elizabeth. Instituut vir Beplanningsnavorsing. Feitestuk Reeks see University of Port Elizabeth. Institute for Planning Research. Fact Paper Series 190
Universiteit van Port Elizabeth. Instituut vir Beplanningsnavorsing. Inligtingsbulletin Reeks see University of Port Elizabeth. Institute for Planning Research. Information Bulletin Series 190
Universiteit van Port Elizabeth. Instituut vir Beplanningsnavorsing. Jaarverslag see University of Port Elizabeth. Institute for Planning Research. Annual Report 213

Universiteit van Pretoria. Publikasies. Nuwe Reeks (SA) *801*
Universitetet i Trondheim. Biblioteket. Avdeling B. Rapport (NO) *537*
Universitetet i Trondheim. Norges Tekniske Hoegskole. Biblioteket. Literaturliste (NO ISSN 0085-4247) *96*
Universitetet i Trondheim. Norges Tekniske Hoegskole. Biblioteket. Meldinger og Boklister (NO ISSN 0029-1714) *96*
Universitetet i Trondheim. Norges Tekniske Hoegskole. Institutt for Uorganisk Kjemi. Avhandling (NO) *252*
Universitetet i Trondheim. Norges Tekniske Hoegskole. Vassdrags- og Havnelaboratoriet. Meddelelse (NO ISSN 0082-6618) *381*
Universiti Kebangsaan Malaysia. Laporan Tahunan/Annual Report (MY) *324*
Universiti Malaya. Fakulti Kejuruteraan. Jernal *see* University of Malaya. Faculty of Engineering. Journal *371*
Universiti Sains Malaysia Forum Sejarah *see* University of Science of Malaysia History Forum *446*
Universities-National Bureau Conference Series (US ISSN 0083-3940) *149*
University and College Libraries in Canada/Bibliotheques des Universites et des Colleges du Canada (CN ISSN 0318-7179) *915*
University College, Cork Record *see* U. C. C. Record *263*
University College Literary Review *see* U. C. Review *575*
University College London. Institute of Jewish Studies. Bulletin (UK) *393*
University College of Swansea. Centre for Development Studies. Monograph Series (UK ISSN 0144-9486) *201*
University College of Swansea. Centre for Development Studies. Occasional Papers Series (UK ISSN 0144-9494) *201*
University College of Swaziland. Agricultural Research Division. Annual Report (SQ) *21*
University Council for Educational Administration Case Series in Educational Administration *see* U C E A Case Series in Educational Administration *345*
University Geographer (NR ISSN 0083-3975) *427*
University in Crisis (US) *341*
University of Aberdeen. African Studies Group. Occasional Publications (UK) *393, 441*
University of Aberdeen. Department of Forestry. Economic Survey of Private Forestry (UK ISSN 0065-0277) *411*
University of Addis Ababa. Institute of Ethiopian Studies. Ethiopian Publications *see* Ethiopian Publications: Books, Pamphlets, Annuals and Periodical Articles *90*
University of Agricultural Sciences, Bangalore. Annual Report (II ISSN 0067-3455) *21*
University of Agricultural Sciences, Bangalore. Collaborative Series (II) *21*
University of Agricultural Sciences, Bangalore. Educational Series (II) *22*
University of Agricultural Sciences, Bangalore. Information Series (II) *22*
University of Agricultural Sciences, Bangalore. Research Monograph Series (II) *22*
University of Agricultural Sciences, Bangalore. Research Series (II ISSN 0067-3463) *22*
University of Agricultural Sciences, Bangalore. Technical Information Series (II) *22*
University of Agricultural Sciences, Bangalore. Technical Series (II) *22*
University of Agricultural Sciences, Bangalore Extension Series *see* U A S Extension Series *21*
University of Agricultural Sciences, Bangalore Miscellaneous Series *see* U A S Miscellaneous Series *21*

University of Alabama. Center for Business and Economic Research Monograph Series (US) *149*
University of Alaska. Geophysical Institute. Bibliography of Publications(US ISSN 0065-5856) *290*
University of Alaska. Geophysical Institute. Report Series (US ISSN 0041-9362) *306*
University of Alaska. Institute of Marine Science. Occasional Publication (US ISSN 0084-6147) *108*
University of Alaska. Institute of Marine Sciences. Technical Report (US ISSN 0065-5929) *108*
University of Alaska. Institute of Social and Economic Research. Research Summary (US) *149, 817*
University of Alaska. Institute of Water Resources. Annual Report (US ISSN 0065-5953) *898*
University of Alaska. Mineral Industry Research Laboratory. Report (US ISSN 0065-5961) *647*
University of Alaska Museum. Annual Report (US ISSN 0093-7436) *655*
University of Alberta. Department of Agricultural and Rural Sociology. Agricultural Economics Technical Bulletin. *see* University of Alberta. Department of Rural Economy. Bulletin *31*
University of Alberta. Department of Agricultural Economics and Rural Sociology. Agricultural Economics and Rural Sociology Research Bulletin *see* University of Alberta. Department of Rural Economy. Bulletin *31*
University of Alberta. Department of Agricultural Economics and Rural Sociology. Agricultural Economics Special Report *see* University of Alberta. Department of Rural Economy. Bulletin *31*
University of Alberta. Department of Animal Science. Annual Feeders' Day Report (CN ISSN 0084-618X) *46*
University of Alberta. Department of Chemistry. Division of Theoretical Chemistry. Technical Report (CN ISSN 0041-9370) *256*
University of Alberta. Department of Computing Science. Technical Reports (CN ISSN 0316-4683) *274*
University of Alberta. Department of Rural Economy. Bulletin (CN) *31, 817*
University of Alberta. Department of Sociology. Population Research Laboratory. Alberta Series Report (CN ISSN 0317-3119) *730, 817*
University of Alberta. Faculty of Business Administration and Commerce. Research Studies in Business (CN ISSN 0065-6070) *149*
University of Alberta. Nuclear Research Centre. Progress Report (CN) *705*
University of Alberta. Studies in Geography. Monographs (CN) *427*
University of Alberta. Water Resources Centre. Publication (CN) *898*
University of Allahabad. Education Department. Researches and Studies (II ISSN 0084-621X) *324*
University of Arizona. Anthropological Papers (US ISSN 0066-7501) *54, 66*
University of Arizona. College of Business and Public Administration. Department of Public Administration. Publication P W (US) *747*
University of Arizona. College of Education. Monograph Series (US ISSN 0066-751X) *324*
University of Arizona. Department of English. Graduate English Papers (US ISSN 0066-7536) *576*
University of Arizona. Laboratory of Tree-Ring Research. Papers (US ISSN 0066-7587) *118*
University of Arizona. Optical Sciences Center. Newsletter (US ISSN 0066-7609) *915*

University of Arizona. Optical Sciences Center. Technical Report (US ISSN 0066-7617) *915*
University of Arizona Library. Bibliographic Bulletin (US ISSN 0044-8877) *96*
University of Arizona Library. Occasional Papers (US) *537*
University of Arkansas. Industrial Research and Extension Center. Annual Report (US ISSN 0518-6544) *226*
University of Arkansas. Industrial Research and Extension Center. Research Memorandum (US) *226*
University of Auckland. Department of Geography. Occasional Papers (NZ) *427*
University of Auckland. Department of Mathematics. Report Series (NZ) *590*
University of Auckland. Department of Sociology. Papers in Comparative Sociology (NZ) *817*
University of Auckland. Library. Bibliographical Bulletin (NZ ISSN 0067-0499) *96*
University of Auckland Historical Society. Annual (NZ ISSN 0067-0480) *447*
University of Baghdad. Biological Research Centre. Bulletin (IQ ISSN 0067-2890) *108*
University of Benin. Library. Annual Report (NR) *537*
University of Beograd. Faculty of Sciences. Department of Astronomy. Publications (YU ISSN 0350-3283) *84*
University of Bergen. Department of Applied Mathematics. Report (NO ISSN 0084-778X) *590*
University of Bergen. Institute of Psychology. Report (NO) *738*
University of Birmingham. Centre for Urban and Regional Studies. Occasional Papers (UK ISSN 0067-8953) *488, 817*
University of Birmingham. Centre for Urban and Regional Studies. Urban and Regional Studies (UK ISSN 0067-8961) *488, 817*
University of Birmingham. Centre for Urban and Regional Studies. Working Paper (UK) *488, 817*
University of Birmingham. Department of Transportation and Environmental Planning. Research Journal (UK) *389, 864*
University of Botswana, Lesotho and Swaziland. Agricultural Research Division. Annual Report *see* University College of Swaziland. Agricultural Research Division. Annual Report *21*
University of British Columbia. Center for Continuing Education. Occasional Papers in Continuing Education (CN ISSN 0068-1695) *330*
University of British Columbia. Department of Civil Engineering. Report. Soil Mechanics Series (CN ISSN 0068-1709) *377*
University of British Columbia. Department of Civil Engineering. Structural Research Series (CN) *377*
University of British Columbia. Department of Civil Engineering. Transportation Research Series (CN) *377*
University of British Columbia. Department of Economics. Discussion Paper (CN) *149*
University of British Columbia. Department of Economics. Resources Paper (CN ISSN 0381-0410) *149*
University of British Columbia. Department of Geological Sciences. Report (CN) *301*
University of British Columbia. Department of Geology. Report *see* University of British Columbia. Department of Geological Sciences. Report *301*
University of British Columbia. Department of Geophysics and Astronomy. Annual Report (CN ISSN 0068-1725) *84, 306*

University of British Columbia. Faculty of Forestry. Bulletin (CN ISSN 0318-9171) *411*
University of British Columbia. Faculty of Forestry. Research Notes (CN ISSN 0068-1784) *411*
University of British Columbia. Faculty of Forestry. Research Papers (CN ISSN 0068-1792) *411*
University of British Columbia. Faculty of Forestry. Translations (CN ISSN 0068-1806) *411*
University of British Columbia. Faculty of Foresty. Foresty Bulletin *see* University of British Columbia. Faculty of Forestry. Bulletin *411*
University of British Columbia. Forest Club. Research Note (CN ISSN 0407-2294) *411*
University of British Columbia. Research Forest Annual Report (CN ISSN 0084-8069) *411*
University of British Columbia. School of Community and Regional Planning. Occasional Papers *see* B. C. Planning Papers *483*
University of British Columbia. School of Community and Regional Planning. Planning Papers *see* B. C. Planning Papers *483*
University of British Columbia Library. Asian Studies Division. List of Catalogued Books. Supplement (CN ISSN 0068-1687) *446*
University of British Columbia Library. Reference Publication (CN ISSN 0068-1857) *537*
University of Cairo. Herbarium. Publications (UA ISSN 0068-5313) *118*
University of Calcutta. Centre of Advanced Study in Ancient Indian History and Culture. Lectures (II ISSN 0068-5380) *446*
University of Calcutta. Centre of Advanced Study in Ancient Indian History and Culture. Proceedings of Seminars (II ISSN 0068-5399) *446*
University of Calcutta. Department of Philosophy. Journal (II) *692*
University of Calgary. Archaeological Association. Paleo-Environmental Workshop. Proceedings (CN ISSN 0068-5437) *66, 389*
University of Calgary. Department of Civil Engineering Research Report (CN) *377*
University of Calgary. Department of Mathematics and Computing Science. Research Papers *see* University of Calgary. Department of Mathematics and Statistics. Research Papers *590*
University of Calgary. Department of Mathematics and Statistics. Research Papers (CN) *590*
University of Calgary Studies in History(CN) *436*
University of California. Center for South and Southeast Asia Studies. Occasional Papers (US ISSN 0068-600X) *446*
University of California. Center for South and Southeast Asia Studies. Research Monograph Series (US ISSN 0068-6018) *446*
University of California. Institute of Business and Economic Research. Publications (US ISSN 0068-6077) *149*
University of California, Berkeley. Archaeological Research Facility. Contributions (US ISSN 0068-5933) *66*
University of California, Berkeley. Center for Real Estate and Urban Economics. Research Report (US ISSN 0068-5976) *762*
University of California, Berkeley. Center for Real Estate and Urban Economics. Reprint Series (US ISSN 0068-5968) *762*
University of California, Berkeley. Center for Real Estate and Urban Economics. Special Report (US ISSN 0068-5984) *762*
University of California, Berkeley. Center for Real Estate and Urban Economics. Technical Report (US ISSN 0068-5992) *762*

University of California, Berkeley. Institute of Human Development. Annual Report (US ISSN 0068-6085) *817*

University of California, Berkeley. Institute of International Studies. Research Series (US ISSN 0068-6093) *716*

University of California, Berkeley. Institute of Transportation Studies. Library References (US ISSN 0068-6115) *864*

University of California, Berkeley. Language Behavior Research Laboratory. Monograph Series (US) 54, *553*

University of California, Berkeley. Office of Institutional Research. Campus Statistics. (US ISSN 0092-0290) *341*

University of California, Berkeley. School of Criminology. San Francisco Project. Research Report (US ISSN 0068-6174) *284*

University of California, Berkeley, Language Behavior Research Laboratory, Working Paper Series (US) 54, *553*

University of California, Davis. Food Protection and Toxicology Center. Summary Report (US ISSN 0094-7962) *686*

University of California, Davis. Game Bird Workshop. Proceedings (US) *125*

University of California, Davis. Water Resources Center. Annual Report (US ISSN 0068-6298) *898*

University of California, Davis. Water Resources Center. Contributions (US ISSN 0068-6301) *898*

University of California Engineering and Physical Sciences Extension Series (US ISSN 0068-631X) *370*, *699*

University of California, Irvine. Center for Pathobiology. Miscellaneous Publications (US ISSN 0068-6131) *109*

University of California, Irvine. Museum of Systematic Biology. Research Series (US ISSN 0068-614X) *109*

University of California, Los Angeles. African Studies Center. Occasional Paper (US ISSN 0068-6190) *441*

University of California, Los Angeles. Center for Medieval and Renaissance Studies. Contributions (US ISSN 0068-6239) *436*

University of California, Los Angeles. Center for Medieval and Renaissance Studies. Publications (US ISSN 0068-6220) *436*

University of California, Los Angeles. Center for the Study of Comparative Folklore and Mythology. Publications(US ISSN 0068-6247) *403*

University of California, Los Angeles. Chicano Studies Center. Monographs(US ISSN 0045-3994) *473*

University of California, Los Angeles. Graduate School of Management. Annual Report (US ISSN 0146-2571) *217*

University of California, Los Angeles. Institute of Archaeology. Archaeological Survey. Special Monograph Series *see* University of California, Los Angeles. Institute of Archaeology. Monograph Series *66*

University of California, Los Angeles. Institute of Archaeology. Monograph Series (US) *66*

University of California, Los Angeles. Institute of Industrial Relations. Monograph Series (US ISSN 0068-6255) *212*

University of California, Los Angeles. Latin American Center. Latin American Activities and Resources (US ISSN 0092-2242) *915*

University of California, Los Angeles. Latin American Center. Latin American Studies Series (US ISSN 0075-8132) *473*

University of California, Los Angeles. Latin American Center. Reference Series (US ISSN 0068-6263) *473*

University of California, Los Angeles. Museum of Cultural History. Occasional Papers (US ISSN 0068-628X) *79*

University of California, Los Angeles. School of Engineering and Applied Science. Research Development, and Public Service Activities (US ISSN 0084-831X) *793*, *854*

University of California, Los Angeles Business Forecast for the Nation and California *see* U C L A Business Forecast for the Nation and California *149*

University of California, Los Angeles Forum in Medical Sciences *see* U C L A Forum in Medical Sciences *600*

University of California, Los Angeles Music Library Bibliography Series *see* U C L A Music Library Bibliography Series *665*

University of California Publications. Anthropological Records (US ISSN 0068-6336) *54*

University of California Publications. Classical Studies (US ISSN 0068-6344) *260*

University of California Publications. Folklore & Mythology Studies (US) *403*

University of California Publications. Folklore Studies *see* University of California Publications. Folklore & Mythology Studies *403*

University of California Publications. Near Eastern Studies (US ISSN 0068-6514) *446*

University of California Publications. Occasional Papers (US ISSN 0068-6522) *494*

University of California Publications in Anthropology (US ISSN 0068-6379) *54*

University of California Publications in Botany (US ISSN 0068-6395) *118*

University of California Publications in Contemporary Music (US ISSN 0068-6409) *664*

University of California Publications in Entomology (US ISSN 0068-6417) *122*

University of California Publications in Geography (US ISSN 0068-6441) *427*

University of California Publications in Geological Sciences (US ISSN 0068-645X) *290*

University of California Publications in Librarianship (US ISSN 0068-6476) *537*

University of California Publications in Linguistics (US ISSN 0068-6484) *553*

University of California Publications in Modern Philology (US ISSN 0068-6492) *553*

University of California Publications in Zoology (US ISSN 0068-6506) *131*

University of California, San Diego. Institute of Marine Resources. Annual Report *see* University of California, San Diego. Institute of Marine Resources. Biennial Report *109*

University of California, San Diego. Institute of Marine Resources. Biennial Report. (US) *109*

University of California, Santa Barbara. Urban Economics Program. Research Reports in Public Policy (US) *747*

University of California, Santa Cruz. Coastal Marine Laboratory. Special Publication (US) *313*

University of Canterbury. Department of Psychology and Sociology. Research Projects (NZ ISSN 0069-3774) *738*, *817*

University of Cape Town. Centre for African Studies. Communications (SA) *441*

University of Cape Town. Department of Geology. Precambrian Research Unit. Annual Report (SA) *301*

University of Cape Town. Department of Geology. Precambrian Research Unit. Bulletin (SA ISSN 0250-216X) *301*

University of Cape Town. Department of Gynaecology. Annual Report *see* University of Cape Town. Department of Obstetrics and Gynaecology. Annual Report *615*

University of Cape Town. Department of Obstetrics and Gynaecology. Annual Report (SA) *615*

University of Cape Town. Libraries. Bibliographical Series (SA) *96*

University of Cape Town. Libraries. Statistical Report (SA ISSN 0576-6885) *537*

University of Cape Town. Libraries. Varia Series (SA) *537*

University of Cape Town Studies in English *see* U C T Studies in English *553*

University of Chicago. Center for Studies in Criminal Justice. Annual Report (US ISSN 0069-3332) *520*

University of Chicago. Department of Geography. Research Papers (US ISSN 0069-3340) *427*

University of Chicago. Division of the Social Sciences. Reports (US) *801*

University of Chicago. Graduate School of Business. Selected Papers (US ISSN 0069-3359) *150*

University of Chicago . Midwest Administration Center. Monograph Series (US ISSN 0076-857X) *345*

University of Chicago Oriental Institute. Publications (US ISSN 0069-3367) *446*

University of Chicago Press Documents in American History (US) *473*

University of Chicago Record (US ISSN 0362-4706) *263*, *341*

University of Chicago Studies in Anthropology. Series in Social, Cultural, and Linguistic Anthropology (US) *55*

University of Chicago Studies in Library Science (US ISSN 0069-3375) *537*

University of Cochin. Department of Marine Biology and Oceanography. Bulletin *see* University of Cochin. Department of Marine Sciences. Bulletin *313*

University of Cochin. Department of Marine Sciences. Bulletin (II) *313*

University of Colorado. Institute of Arctic and Alpine Research. Occasional Papers (US ISSN 0069-6145) *290*, *427*

University of Colorado Libraries. Report (US ISSN 0069-6161) *537*

University of Connecticut. Center for Real Estate and Urban Economic Studies. Annual Report (US) *762*

University of Connecticut. Center for Real Estate and Urban Economic Studies. General Series (US ISSN 0069-9047) *762*

University of Connecticut. Center for Real Estate and Urban Economic Studies. Working Paper (US) *762*

University of Connecticut. Institute of Water Resources. Report Series (US ISSN 0069-9063) *898*

University of Connecticut. Institute of Water Resources. Wetlands Conference. Proceedings (US) *898*

University of Copenhagen. Institute of Mathematical Statistics. Annual Report (DK) *700*

University of Copenhagen. Institute of Mathematical Statistics. Lecture Notes (DK) *590*

University of Dar es Salaam. Botany Department. Departmental Herbarium Publications (TZ) *118*

University of Dar es Salaam. Bureau of Resource Assessment and Land Use Planning. Annual Report (TZ ISSN 0084-960X) *389*, *730*

University of Dar es Salaam. Bureau of Resource Assessment and Land Use Planning. Research Paper (TZ ISSN 0084-9626) *389*, *730*

University of Dar es Salaam. Bureau of Resource Assessment and Land Use Planning. Research Report (TZ ISSN 0084-9634) *389*, *730*

University of Dar es Salaam. Economic Research Bureau. Occasional Paper (TZ) *150*

University of Dar es Salaam. Economic Research Bureau. Papers (TZ ISSN 0418-3746) *150*

University of Dar es Salaam. Theatre Arts Department. Annual Report (TZ) *860*

University of Dayton. School of Education. Abstracts of Research Projects (US ISSN 0070-3044) *324*

University of Dayton. School of Education. Workshop Proceedings (US ISSN 0070-3052) *776*

University of Delaware. College of Agricultural Sciences. Longwood Program Seminars *see* Longwood Program Seminars *116*

University of Delaware. Water Resources Center. Annual Report (US) *898*

University of Denver. College of Business Administration. Occasional Studies (US ISSN 0070-3761) *150*

University of Denver. College of Business Administration. Special Publication (US ISSN 0070-377X) *150*

University of Durban-Westville. Institute for Social and Economic Research. Annual Report (SA) *801*

University of Durban-Westville. Journal/Universiteit van Durban-Westville. Tydskrif (SA ISSN 0070-7740) *494*

University of East Anglia. Climatic Research Unit. Research Publication (UK) *635*

University of Eastern Philippines. Research Center. Report (PH ISSN 0070-8259) *324*

University of Edinburgh. Architecture Research Unit. Report (UK ISSN 0070-8992) *70*

University of Florida. Center for Gerontology. Studies and Programs. (US ISSN 0071-6103) *428*

University of Florida. Food and Resource Economics Department. Economic Information Report (US) *31*

University of Florida. Food and Resource Economics Department. Economics Report *see* University of Florida. Food and Resource Economics Department. Economic Information Report *31*

University of Florida. Growth Conference. Prepared Papers (US ISSN 0094-0801) *488*

University of Florida. Libraries. Technical Processes Department. Caribbean Acquisitions (US ISSN 0071-6138) *473*, *537*

University of Florida. School of Forest Resources & Conservation. Cooperative Forest Genetics Research Program. Progress Report. (US) *123*, *411*

University of Florida. School of Forestry. Cooperative Forest Genetics Research Program. Progress Report *see* University of Florida. School of Forest Resources & Conservation. Cooperative Forest Genetics Research Program. Progress Report *411*

University of Florida. University College Series (US ISSN 0071-6170) *341*

University of Florida Monographs. Humanities (US ISSN 0071-6189) *494*

University of Florida Monographs. Social Sciences (US ISSN 0071-6197) *801*

University of Georgia. Anthropology Curriculum Project. Occasional Paper Series (US ISSN 0072-1255) *351*

University of Georgia. College of Agriculture Experiment Stations. Bulletin (US ISSN 0072-1271) *22*

University of Georgia. College of Agriculture Experiment Stations. Research Reports (US ISSN 0072-128X) 22

University of Georgia. College of Business Administration. Research Monograph Series (US ISSN 0085-1051) 150

University of Georgia. College of Business Administration. Travel Research Series (US ISSN 0072-1263) 150

University of Georgia. Geography Curriculum Project Publications (US ISSN 0435-5113) 351, 427

University of Georgia. Institute of Ecology. Annual Report (US ISSN 0094-9205) 389

University of Georgia. Institute of Government. Research Papers (US) 747

University of Georgia. School of Pharmacy. Pharmaceutical Services for Small Hospitals and Nursing Homes (US ISSN 0072-1344) 686

University of Ghana. Department of Library and Archival Studies. Occasional Papers (GH) 537

University of Ghana. Department of Sociology. Current Research Report Series (GH) 817

University of Ghana. Institute of African Studies. Collected Language Notes (GH) 553

University of Ghana. Institute of African Studies. Local Studies Series (GH ISSN 0533-8646) 55

University of Ghana. Institute of African Studies. Research Review (GH ISSN 0020-2703) 558

University of Ghana. Institute of Statistical, Social and Economic Research. Technical Publication Series (GH) 166

University of Ghana. Institute of Statistical, Social and Economic Research. Technical Research Monographs see University of Ghana. Institute of Statistical, Social and Economic Research. Technical Publication Series 166

University of Glasgow. Institute of Latin American Studies. Occasional Papers (UK ISSN 0305-8646) 558, 716

University of Glasgow. Social and Economic Research Studies (UK ISSN 0072-4629) 150, 801

University of Glasgow. Social and Economic Studies. Occasional Papers(UK ISSN 0072-4610) 150, 801

University of Guelph. Center for Resources Development. Annual Report (CN) 324

University of Guelph. Department of Geography. Geographical Publication(CN) 301, 427

University of Guelph. Department of Land Resource Science. Progress Report (CN ISSN 0085-1329) 40

University of Hawaii. College of Tropical Agriculture. Cooperative Extension Service. Circular (US ISSN 0073-1161) 22

University of Hawaii. College of Tropical Agriculture. Cooperative Extension Service Leaflet (US ISSN 0073-117X) 22

University of Hawaii. College of Tropical Agriculture. Cooperative Extension Service. Miscellaneous Publication (US ISSN 0073-1188) 22

University of Hawaii. Counseling and Testing Center. Report (US ISSN 0073-1196) 324

University of Hawaii. Industrial Relations Center. Occasional Publications (US ISSN 0073-1226) 212

University of Hawaii. Water Resources Research Center. Collected Reprints (US ISSN 0073-1293) 898

University of Hawaii. Water Resources Research Center. Technical Report (US ISSN 0073-1307) 898

University of Hawaii. Water Resources Research Center. Workshop Series (US) 898

University of Helsinki. Department of Cooperative Studies. Publications (FI ISSN 0356-1364) 181

University of Helsinki. Institute of Education. Research Bulletin (FI ISSN 0073-179X) 324

University of Helsinki. Library. Publication see Helsingin Yliopisto. Kirjasto. Julkaisuja 530

University of Hong Kong. Centre of Asian Studies. Bibliographies and Research Guides (HK ISSN 0441-1900) 672

University of Hong Kong. Centre of Asian Studies. Occasional Papers and Monographs (HK ISSN 0378-2689) 671, 801

University of Hull. Department of Geography. Miscellaneous Series in Geography (UK ISSN 0441-4004) 427

University of Hull. Institute of Education. Aids to Research (UK ISSN 0073-3806) 324

University of Hull. Institute of Education. Research Monographs (UK ISSN 0073-3814) 324

University of Ibadan. Institute of Education. Occasional Publications (NR ISSN 0073-4314) 324

University of Ibadan. Library. Annual Report (NR ISSN 0073-4322) 537

University of Ibadan. Library. Bibliographical Series (NR ISSN 0073-4330) 96

University of Ibadan. Student Affairs Office. Student Handbook of Information on University Policies and Practices (NR) 341

University of Idaho. College of Forestry, Wildlife and Range Sciences.Library Additions (US) 278

University of Idaho. Department of Sociology/Anthropology. Anthropological Monographs (US) 55

University of Idaho. Forest, Wildlife and Range Experiment Station, Moscow. Station Bulletin (US ISSN 0073-4586) 278

University of Idaho. Forest, Wildlife and Range Experiment Station, Moscow. Station Note (US ISSN 0073-4594) 278

University of Idaho. Water Resources Research Institute. Annual Report (US ISSN 0073-4616) 898

University of Ife. Faculty of Agriculture. Annual Research Report(NR ISSN 0579-7195) 22

University of Ife. Faculty of Arts. Lecture Series (NR) 494

University of Illinois. Small Homes Council. Building Research Council. Circulars see University of Illinois. Small Homes Council. Building Research Council. Council Notes 139

University of Illinois. Small Homes Council. Building Research Council. Council Notes (US) 139

University of Illinois. Small Homes Council. Building Research Council. Research Report (US ISSN 0073-540X) 139

University of Illinois. Small Homes Council. Building Research Council. Technical Notes (US ISSN 0073-5426) 139

University of Illinois at Chicago Circle. Center for Urban Studies. Occasional Paper Series see University of Illinois at Chicago Circle. College of Urban Sciences. Occasional Paper Series 488

University of Illinois at Chicago Circle. College of Urban Sciences. Occasional Paper Series (US) 488

University of Illinois at Urbana-Champaign. Agricultural Experiment Station. Research Progress (US) 22

University of Illinois at Urbana-Champaign. Center for International Education and Research in Accounting. Monograph (US ISSN 0073-5191) 168

University of Illinois at Urbana-Champaign. Civil Engineering Studies. Hydraulic Engineering Research Series (US) 377

University of Illinois at Urbana-Champaign. Civil Engineering Studies. Photogrammetry Series (US) 377

University of Illinois at Urbana-Champaign. Civil Engineering Studies. Structural Research Series (US ISSN 0069-4274) 377

University of Illinois at Urbana-Champaign. Civil Engineering Studies. Transportation Engineering Series (US) 377

University of Illinois at Urbana-Champaign. Clinic on Library Applications of Data Processing. Proceedings (US ISSN 0069-4789) 537

University of Illinois at Urbana-Champaign. College of Agriculture. Agricultural Communications Research Report (US ISSN 0073-5299) 22

University of Illinois at Urbana-Champaign. College of Agriculture. Special Publication (US ISSN 0073-5205) 22

University of Illinois at Urbana-Champaign. Department of Agricultural Economics. Agricultural Finance Program Report (US ISSN 0073-5213) 31

University of Illinois at Urbana-Champaign. Department of Agricultural Economics. Landlord and Tenant Shares (US) 31

University of Illinois at Urbana-Champaign. Department of Agricultural Economics. Research Report (US ISSN 0073-523X) 31

University of Illinois at Urbana-Champaign. Department of Art. Newsletter (US ISSN 0073-5256) 79

University of Illinois at Urbana-Champaign. Department of Electrical Engineering. Aeronomy Laboratory. Aeronomy Report (US ISSN 0568-0581) 359

University of Illinois at Urbana - Champaign. Engineering Experiment Station. Bulletin (US ISSN 0073-5272) 370

University of Illinois at Urbana-Champaign. Engineering Experiment Station. Summary of Engineering Research (US ISSN 0073-5280) 371

University of Illinois at Urbana-Champaign. Graduate School of Library Science. Allerton Park Institute. Papers (US ISSN 0536-4604) 537

University of Illinois at Urbana-Champaign. Graduate School of Library Science. Downs Fund Publications Series (US) 537

University of Illinois at Urbana-Champaign. Graduate School of Library Science. Library Research Center. Annual Report (US ISSN 0073-5361) 537

University of Illinois at Urbana-Champaign. Graduate School of Library Science. Monograph Series (US ISSN 0073-5302) 537

University of Illinois at Urbana-Champaign. Graduate School of Library Science. Occasional Papers (US ISSN 0073-5310) 537

University of Illinois at Urbana-Champaign. Institute of Labor and Industrial Relations. Reprint Series (US ISSN 0073-5353) 212

University of Illinois at Urbana-Champaign. Office of Instructional Resources. Measurement and Research Division. Research Report (US ISSN 0073-5388) 324

University of Illinois at Urbana-Champaign. Water Resources Center. Annual Report (US ISSN 0073-5434) 898

University of Illinois at Urbana-Champaign. Water Resources Center. Research Report (US ISSN 0073-5442) 898

University of Iowa. Center for Labor and Management. Monograph Series see University of Iowa. Center for Labor and Management. Research Series 212

University of Iowa. Center for Labor and Management. Research Series. (US ISSN 0578-6371) 212

University of Iowa. Graduate Program in Hospital and Health Administration. Health Care Research Series (US ISSN 0073-1439) 481, 755

University of Iowa. School of Library Science. Newsletter (US ISSN 0041-9648) 537

University of Joensuu. Publications. Series B2 see Joensuun Korkeakoulu. Julkaisuja. Sarja B2 337

University of Kansas. Center for East Asian Studies. International Studies: East Asian Series. Reference Series (US ISSN 0070-8070) 446

University of Kansas. Center for East Asian Studies. International Studies: East Asian Series. Research Series (US ISSN 0070-8062) 446

University of Kansas. Center for Latin American Studies. Graduate Studies on Latin America (US ISSN 0075-4986) 473

University of Kansas. Department of Anthropology. Publications in Anthropology (US ISSN 0085-2457) 55

University of Kansas. Museum of Art. Miscellaneous Publications see University of Kansas. Spencer Museum of Art. Miscellaneous Publications 655

University of Kansas. Museum of Natural History. Miscellaneous Publications (US ISSN 0075-5028) 793

University of Kansas. Museum of Natural History. Monographs (US ISSN 0085-2465) 793

University of Kansas. Museum of Natural History. Occasional Papers. (US ISSN 0091-7958) 793

University of Kansas. Museum of Natural History. Publications (US ISSN 0075-5036) 793

University of Kansas. Paleontological Contributions. Articles (US ISSN 0075-5044) 674

University of Kansas. Paleontological Contributions. Papers (US ISSN 0075-5052) 674

University of Kansas. Spencer Museum of Art. Miscellaneous Publications (US) 655

University of Kansas Humanistic Studies (US ISSN 0085-2473) 494

University of Kansas Law Review (US ISSN 0083-4025) 520

University of Kansas Libraries. Library Series. (US ISSN 0075-5001) 537

University of Kansas Publications in Anthropology see University of Kansas. Department of Anthropology. Publications in Anthropology 55

University of Kansas Science Bulletin (US ISSN 0022-8850) 793

University of Kashmir. Annual Report (II) 341

University of Kensington. School of Librarianship. Occasional Paper (AT) 537

University of Kentucky. Geological Survey. Guidebook to Geological Field Trips (US ISSN 0075-5575) 301

University of Kentucky. Geological Survey. Reprints (US ISSN 0075-5605) 301

University of Kentucky. Geological Survey. Series X. Bulletin (US ISSN 0075-5559) 301

University of Kentucky. Geological Survey. Series X. Report of Investigations (US ISSN 0075-5591) *301*

University of Kentucky. Geological Survey. Series XI. County Report (US ISSN 0075-5567) *301*

University of Kentucky. Geological Survey. Series XI. Information Circular (US ISSN 0075-5583) *301*

University of Kentucky. Geological Survey. Series XI. Special Publication(US ISSN 0075-5613) *301*

University of Kentucky. Geological Survey. Series XI. Thesis Series (US ISSN 0075-5621) *301*

University of Kentucky Research Foundation. Annual Report (US ISSN 0566-8719) *341*

University of Kenya. Bureau of Educational Research. Research Projects (KE) *341*

University of Kerala. Department of Tamil. Journal *see* University of Kerala. Department of Tamil. Research Papers *554*

University of Kerala. Department of Tamil. Research Papers (II) *554*

University of Khartoum. Development Studies and Research Centre. Discussion Papers (SJ) *201*

University of Khartoum. Development Studies and Research Centre. Monograph Series (SJ) *201*

University of Khartoum. Development Studies and Research Centre. Occasional Papers (SJ) *201*

University of Khartoum. Hydrobiological Research Unit. Annual Report (SJ) *109*

University of Kuwait. Journal(Science) (KU) *793*

University of Lagos. Continuing Education Centre. Occasional Papers(NR ISSN 0075-7667) *330*

University of Lagos. Human Resources Research Unit. Monograph (NR) *730, 817*

University of Lagos. Humanities Series (NR ISSN 0075-7675) *494*

University of Lagos. Inaugural Lecture Series (NR ISSN 0075-7659) *494*

University of Lagos. Law Series (UK ISSN 0075-7691) *915*

University of Lagos. Library. Annual Report (NR ISSN 0075-7705) *537*

University of Lagos. Scientific Monograph Series (NR ISSN 0075-7713) *793*

University of Leeds. Institute of Education. Papers (UK ISSN 0075-854X) *324*

University of Leeds. Research Institute of African Geology. Annual Report (UK ISSN 0075-8558) *301*

University of Leiden. Kamerlingh Onnes Laboratory. Communications (NE ISSN 0022-8141) *699*

University of Liberia. A. M. Dogliotti College of Medicine. Annual Report of the Dean (LB) *601*

University of Liverpool. Department of Geography. Research Paper (UK ISSN 0076-0056) *427*

University of London. Contemporary China Institute. Research Notes and Studies (UK ISSN 0308-6119) *802*

University of London. Institute of Archaeology. Bulletin (UK ISSN 0076-0722) *67*

University of London. Institute of Archaeology. Occasional Publication (UK ISSN 0141-8505) *67*

University of London. Institute of Classical Studies. Bulletin (UK ISSN 0076-0730) *260*

University of London. Institute of Classical Studies. Bulletin Supplement (UK ISSN 0076-0749) *260*

University of London. Institute of Commonwealth Studies. Annual Report (UK ISSN 0076-0781) *802*

University of London. Institute of Commonwealth Studies. Collected Seminar Papers (UK ISSN 0076-0773) *802*

University of London. Institute of Commonwealth Studies. Commonwealth Papers (UK ISSN 0076-0765) *802*

University of London. Institute of Education. Library. Education Libraries Bulletin Supplements (UK ISSN 0076-079X) *537*

University of London. Institute of Germanic Studies. Bithell Memorial Lectures (UK ISSN 0144-9850) *576*

University of London. Institute of Germanic Studies. Bithell Series of Dissertations (UK) *576*

University of London. Institute of Germanic Studies. Library Publications (UK ISSN 0076-0803) *576*

University of London. Institute of Germanic Studies. Research in Germanic Studies (UK ISSN 0260-5929) *96*

University of London. Institute of Germanic Studies. Theses in Progress at British Universities *see* University of London. Institute of Germanic Studies. Research in Germanic Studies *96*

University of London. Institute of Historical Research Bulletin. Special Supplement (UK ISSN 0076-082X) *464*

University of London. Institute of Latin American Studies. Monographs (UK ISSN 0076-0846) *473*

University of London. Royal Postgraduate Medical School. Report(UK ISSN 0076-0854) *601*

University of London. School of Oriental and African Studies. Contemporary China Institute. Publications (UK ISSN 0085-2856) *671*

University of London Classical Studies (UK ISSN 0459-7354) *261*

University of London Historical Studies(UK ISSN 0076-0692) *436*

University of London Legal Series (UK ISSN 0076-0714) *520*

University of Louisville. Speed Scientific School. Environmental Engineering and Science Conference. Proceedings (US) *389*

University of Lund. Faculty of Odontology. Annual Publications *see* University of Lund. School of Dentistry. Faculty of Odontology. Annual Publications *610*

University of Lund. School of Dentistry. Faculty of Odontology. Annual Publications (SW ISSN 0076-3438) *610*

University of Madras. Archaeological Series (II ISSN 0076-2202) *67*

University of Madras. Endowment Lectures (II ISSN 0076-2210) *341*

University of Madras. Historical Series (II ISSN 0076-2229) *446*

University of Madras. Kannada Series (II ISSN 0076-2237) *554*

University of Madras. Malayalam Series(II ISSN 0076-2245) *554*

University of Madras. Philosophical Series (II ISSN 0076-2253) *692*

University of Madras. Sanskrit Series (II ISSN 0076-2261) *554*

University of Madras. Tamil Series (II ISSN 0076-227X) *554*

University of Madras. Telugu Series (II ISSN 0076-2288) *554*

University of Madras. Urdu Series (II ISSN 0076-2296) *554*

University of Malawi. Centre for Extension Studies. Annual Report (MW) *341*

University of Malawi.Library. Report to the Senate on the University Libraries (MW ISSN 0085-3038) *537*

University of Malaya. Chinese Language Society. Journal/Majallah Pantai/Pan T'ai Hsueh Pao (MY ISSN 0553-0644) *554*

University of Malaya. Department of Engineering. Journal *see* University of Malaya. Faculty of Engineering. Journal *371*

University of Malaya. Faculty of Engineering. Journal/Universiti Malaya. Fakulti Kejuruteraan. Jernal (MY) *371*

University of Malta. Annual Report (MM) *341*

University of Malta. Faculty of Arts. Journal (MM ISSN 0035-9297) *494*

University of Malta. International Ocean Institute. Occasional Papers (MM) *313*

University of Manchester. School of Education. Gazette (UK ISSN 0305-7984) *324*

University of Manitoba. Center for Transportation Studies. Annual Report (CN) *864*

University of Manitoba. Center for Transportation Studies. Occasional Paper (CN ISSN 0076-3977) *864*

University of Manitoba. Center for Transportation Studies. Research Report (CN ISSN 0316-7984) *864*

University of Manitoba. Center for Transportation Studies. Seminar Series on Transportation. Proceedings(CN ISSN 0076-3993) *864*

University of Manitoba. Department of Agricultural Economics and Farm Management. Occasional Papers (CN ISSN 0076-4000) *31*

University of Manitoba. Department of Slavic Studies. Readings in Slavic Literature (CN ISSN 0076-4035) *576*

University of Manitoba. Faculty of Agriculture. Progress Report on Agricultural Research and Experimentation (CN ISSN 0076-4051) *22*

University of Manitoba. Medical Journal (CN ISSN 0076-4108) *601*

University of Manitoba Anthropology Papers (CN) *55, 67, 554*

University of Maryland. College of Library and Information Services. Conference Proceedings (US ISSN 0076-4833) *537*

University of Maryland. College of Library and Information Services. Student Contribution Series (US ISSN 0076-4841) *537*

University of Maryland. Institute for Fluid Dynamics and Applied Mathematics. Public Lecture Series (US ISSN 0076-4825) *590, 701*

University of Maryland. Natural Resources Institute. N. R. I. Special Report (US ISSN 0090-9750) *109*

University of Massachusetts. Art Acquisitions (US) *655*

University of Massachusetts. Department of Anthropology. Research Reports (US ISSN 0076-5066) *55*

University of Massachusetts. School of Engineering. Annual Report (US ISSN 0542-9307) *371*

University of Mauritius. Annual Report (MF) *341*

University of Melbourne. Department of Civil Engineering. Departmental Report (AT ISSN 0085-3240) *377*

University of Melbourne. Department of Electrical Engineering. Research Report (AT ISSN 0085-3259) *359*

University of Melbourne. Institute of Applied Economic and Social Research. Monographs (AT ISSN 0076-6283) *150, 809*

University of Melbourne. Institute of Applied Economic and Social Research. Technical Papers (AT ISSN 0076-6291) *150, 802*

University of Miami, Coral Gables. Law Center. Annual Institute on Estate Planning (US ISSN 0537-9768) *520*

University of Michigan. Center for Chinese Studies. Occasional Papers *see* Michigan Papers in Chinese Studies *444*

University of Michigan. Center for Japanese Studies. Bibliographical Series (US ISSN 0076-8340) *446*

University of Michigan. Center for Japanese Studies. Occasional Papers (US ISSN 0076-8359) *446*

UNIVERSITY OF   1523

University of Michigan. Center for Population Planning. Annual Report (US) *730*

University of Michigan. Department of Population Planning. Annual Report *see* University of Michigan. Center for Population Planning. Annual Report *730*

University of Michigan. Graduate School of Business Administration. Leadership Award Lecture (US ISSN 0076-8332) *150*

University of Michigan. Graduate School of Business Administration. Proceedings of the Annual Business Conference (US ISSN 0093-4623) *916*

University of Michigan. Great Lakes Research Division. Special Report (US ISSN 0543-940X) *793*

University of Michigan. Herbarium. Contributions (US ISSN 0580-6097) *119*

University of Michigan. Institute of Gerontology. Occasional Papers in Gerontology (US) *428*

University of Michigan. Mental Health Research Institute. Annual Report (US) *738, 755*

University of Michigan. Museum of Anthropology. Anthropological Papers. (US ISSN 0076-8367) *55*

University of Michigan. Museum of Anthropology. Memoirs (US ISSN 0076-8375) *55*

University of Michigan. Museum of Anthropology. Technical Reports (US) *55*

University of Michigan. Museum of Art. Bulletin *see* University of Michigan. Museums of Art and Archaeology. Bulletin *655*

University of Michigan. Museum of Paleontology. Contributions (US ISSN 0041-9834) *674*

University of Michigan. Museum of Paleontology. Papers on Paleontology(US) *674*

University of Michigan. Museum of Zoology. Miscellaneous Publications (US ISSN 0076-8405) *131*

University of Michigan. Museum of Zoology. Occasional Papers (US ISSN 0076-8413) *131*

University of Michigan. Museums of Art and Archaeology. Bulletin (US ISSN 0270-1642) *655*

University of Michigan. Population Studies Center. Annual Report (US) *730*

University of Michigan. School of Dentistry. Alumni Bulletin (US ISSN 0076-843X) *610*

University of Michigan. School of Education. Bulletin (US) *324*

University of Michigan Observatories. Publications (US ISSN 0076-8421) *84*

University of Michigan Papers in Women's Studies *see* Michigan Occasional Papers in Women's Studies *900*

University of Minnesota. Audio-Visual Library Service. Educational Resources Bulletin (US ISSN 0076-9274) *351*

University of Minnesota. Center for Research in Human Learning. Report and Fellowship Offerings (US) *324*

University of Minnesota. Center for Research in Human Learning. Report *see* University of Minnesota. Center for Research in Human Learning. Report and Fellowship Offerings *324*

University of Mississippi Studies in English (US ISSN 0081-7880) *576*

University of Missouri, Columbia. Library Series (US) *537*

University of Missouri, Columbia. Mathematical Sciences Technical Reports (US ISSN 0076-9665) *590*

University of Missouri, Columbia. Museum of Anthropology. Annual Reports (US) *55*

University of Missouri, Columbia. Museum of Anthropology. Museum Briefs (US ISSN 0580-6976) *55*

University of Missouri, Columbia. Veterinary Medical Diagnostic Laboratory. Annual Report (US ISSN 0076-9711) *895*

University of Missouri Monographs in Anthropology (US) *55, 67, 473*

University of Missouri, St. Louis. Center for International Studies. Monograph (University of Missouri-St. Louis) (US ISSN 0076-9657) *725*

University of Missouri- St. Louis University of Missouri, St. Louis. Center for International Studies. Monograph *see* University of Missouri, St. Louis. Center for International Studies. Monograph *725*

University of Missouri Studies (US ISSN 0076-9703) *494*

University of Montana. Department of Antropology. Contributions to Anthropology (US ISSN 0077-118X) *55*

University of Montana. Division of Educational Research and Services. Education Monograph (US) *324*

University of Montana. Forest and Conservation Experiment Station, Missoula. Bulletin. (US ISSN 0077-1155) *411*

University of Montana. Forest and Conservation Experiment Station, Missoula. Research Notes. (US ISSN 0077-1163) *411*

University of Nairobi. Institute for Development Studies. Discussion Papers (KE ISSN 0547-1788) *190, 441*

University of Nairobi. Institute for Development Studies. Occasional Paper (KE) *201, 226*

University of Nairobi. Institute for Development Studies. Research and Publications (KE) *802*

University of Nairobi. Institute for Development Studies. Working Papers (KE) *190, 441*

University of Natal. Institute for Social Research. Annual Report (SA ISSN 0070-7759) *802*

University of Nebraska. Department of Agricultural Education. Report (US ISSN 0548-0906) *22*

University of Nebraska. Institute for International Studies. Occasional Publications (US) *473*

University of Nebraska. School of Journalism. Depth Report (US ISSN 0077-6378) *505*

University of Nebraska State Museum. Bulletin (US) *793*

University of Nebraska Studies. New Series (US ISSN 0077-6386) *494*

University of Nevada. Bureau of Business and Economic Research. Research Report (US ISSN 0077-7943) *150*

University of Nevada. Desert Research Institute. Technical Report (US ISSN 0077-796X) *793*

University of Nevada. Seismological Laboratory. Bulletin (US ISSN 0092-4288) *307*

University of New Brunswick. Law Journal (CN ISSN 0077-8141) *520*

University of New England. Department of Geography. Monograph Series in Geography (AT ISSN 0066-7706) *427*

University of New England. Department of Geography. Studies in Applied Geographical Research (AT) *427*

University of New England. Exploration Society. Report (AT ISSN 0066-7730) *916*

University of New England Convocation Bulletin & Alumni News *see* U N E Convocation Bulletin & Alumni News *340*

University of New Hampshire. Institute of Natural and Environmental Resources. Research Reports (US ISSN 0077-8400) *22*

University of New Mexico. Bureau of Business and Economic Research. Business Information Series (US ISSN 0068-4430) *150*

University of New Mexico. Institute of Meteoritics. Special Publication (US ISSN 0085-3968) *84*

University of New Mexico. Women's Center Newsletter (US) *725*

University of New Mexico Art Museum. Bulletin (US ISSN 0077-8583) *655*

University of New South Wales. Biomedical Library. Newsletter (AT ISSN 0155-0187) *537, 601*

University of New South Wales. Library. Annual Report (AT ISSN 0313-427X) *537*

University of New South Wales. Library. Information Bulletin (AT) *537*

University of New South Wales. Metallurgical Society. Metallurgical Review (AT ISSN 0085-4018) *630*

University of New South Wales. School of Civil Engineering. U N I C I V Reports. Series I (AT ISSN 0077-8796) *377*

University of New South Wales. School of Civil Engineering. U N I C I V Reports. Series R (AT ISSN 0077-880X) *377*

University of New South Wales. Water Research Laboratory, Manly Vale. Laboratory Research Reports (AT ISSN 0077-8818) *898*

University of New South Wales, Kensington. Research and Publications (AT ISSN 0548-6831) *341*

University of Newcastle. Department of Electrical Engineering. Technical Report EE (AT ISSN 0085-4158) *359*

University of Newcastle Historical Journal (AT ISSN 0085-7629) *436*

University of Newcastle-Upon-Tyne. Computing Laboratory. Technical Report (UK) *274*

University of Newcastle-Upon-Tyne. Department of Geography. Research Series (UK ISSN 0078-026X) *427*

University of Newcastle-Upon-Tyne. Exploration Society Journal (UK) *427*

University of Newcastle-Upon-Tyne. Philosophical Society. Proceedings (UK ISSN 0078-0251) *692*

University of Nigeria. Annual Report (NR) *341*

University of North Carolina, Chapel Hill. Graduate School of Business Administration. Technical Papers (US ISSN 0078-1452) *150*

University of North Carolina, Chapel Hill. Institute for Research in Social Science. Technical Papers (US) *802*

University of North Carolina, Chapel Hill. Institute for Research in Social Science. Working Papers in Methodology (US) *802*

University of North Carolina, Greensboro. Faculty Publications (US ISSN 0078-1460) *96*

University of North Dakota. Institute of Ecological Studies. Research Report (US) *389*

University of North Sumatra. Bulletin/Majalah Universitas Sumatera Utara (IO) *341*

University of Northern Colorado. Museum of Anthropology. Occasional Publications in Anthropology. Archaeology Series (US ISSN 0085-1221) *67*

University of Northern Colorado. Museum of Anthropology. Occasional Publications in Anthropology. Ethnology Series (US ISSN 0085-1205) *55*

University of Northern Colorado. Museum of Anthropology. Occasional Publications in Anthropology. Linguistics Series (US ISSN 0085-123X) *554*

University of Northern Colorado. Museum of Anthropology. Occasional Publications in Anthropology. Miscellaneous Series (US ISSN 0085-1213) *55*

University of Notre Dame. Department of Economics. Union-Management Conference. Proceeding (US ISSN 0078-2076) *212*

University of Notre Dame. Department of Theology. Liturgical Studies (US ISSN 0076-003X) *776*

University of Notre Dame. Saint Mary's College. Law School. Department of Economics. Conference on Changing Factors in Collective Bargaining. Proceedings (US) *212*

University of Nottingham. Department of Adult Education. Bulletin of Local History, East Midlands Region (UK ISSN 0141-0008) *464*

University of Oklahoma. Archaeological Research and Management Center. Project Report Series (US ISSN 0160-3078) *67*

University of Oklahoma. Archaeological Research and Management Center. Research Series (US ISSN 0160-3086) *67*

University of Oregon. Bureau of Governmental Research and Service. Information Bulletin (US ISSN 0078-5970) *747*

University of Oregon. Bureau of Governmental Research and Service. Legal Bulletin (US ISSN 0078-5989) *747*

University of Oregon. Bureau of Governmental Research and Service. Local Government Finance (US) *233, 750*

University of Oregon. Bureau of Governmental Research and Service. Local Government Notes and Information: Policy and Practice Series (US ISSN 0078-5997) *747*

University of Oregon. Bureau of Governmental Research and Service. Planning Bulletin (US) *747*

University of Oregon. Center for Educational Policy and Management. Monographs (US) *345*

University of Oregon. Center for the Advanced Study of Educationl Administration. Monographs *see* University of Oregon. Center for Educational Policy and Management. Monographs *345*

University of Oregon. Museum of Natural History. Bulletin (US ISSN 0078-6047) *793*

University of Oregon Anthropological Papers (US ISSN 0078-6071) *55*

University of Osaka Prefecture. Bulletin. Series B: Agriculture and Biology/Osaka-furitsu Daigaku Kiyo, B Nogaku, Seibutsugaku (JA ISSN 0474-7852) *22, 109*

University of Osaka Prefecture. Bulletin. Series D: Sciences of Economy, Commerce and Law (JA ISSN 0473-4637) *150, 182, 520*

University of Ottawa. Department of Geography and Regional Planning. Notes de Recherches/Research Notes (CN) *427*

University of Ottawa. Department of Geography. Occasional Papers (CN) *427, 488*

University of Ottawa. Library. Annual Report (CN ISSN 0078-7027) *537*

University of Ottawa. Vanier Library. List of Serials (CN ISSN 0384-7411) *96*

University of Oxford. School of Geography. Research Papers (UK ISSN 0305-8190) *427*

University of Papua New Guinea. Department of Geography. Occasional Papers in Geography (PP) *427*

University of Papua New Guinea. Department of Physics. Technical Paper (PP ISSN 0085-4735) *699*

University of Pennsylvania. Department of Linguistics. Transformations and Discourse Analysis Papers (US ISSN 0079-0672) *554*

University of Pennsylvania. Institute for Environmental Studies. City Planning Series (US ISSN 0079-0680) *488*

University of Pennsylvania. Institute for Environmental Studies. Report (US ISSN 0079-0699) *389*

University of Pennsylvania. Population Studies Center. Analytical and Technical Report (US ISSN 0553-5816) *730*

University of Pennsylvania. Wharton School of Finance and Commerce. Industrial Research Unit. Studies (US ISSN 0083-9094) *226*

University of Pennsylvania. Wharton School of Finance and Commerce. Labor Relations and Public Policy Series. Reports (US ISSN 0075-7470) *212*

University of Pennsylvania. Wharton School of Finance and Commerce. Studies in Quantitative Economics (US ISSN 0081-8437) *150*

University of Pittsburgh. Center for International Studies: Latin American Studies. Occasional Papers (US ISSN 0075-8140) *473*

University of Pittsburgh. Department of Slavic Languages and Literatures. Slavic Series (US) *554*

University of Pittsburgh. Pymatuning Laboratory of Ecology. Special Publication (US ISSN 0079-8207) *389*

University of Poona. Centre of Advanced Study in Sanskrit. Publications (II ISSN 0079-3809) *554*

University of Port Elizabeth. Institute for Planning Research. Annual Report/Universiteit van Port Elizabeth. Instituut vir Beplanningsnavorsing. Jaarverslag (SA) *213*

University of Port Elizabeth. Institute for Planning Research. Fact Paper Series/Universiteit van Port Elizabeth. Instituut vir Beplanningsnavorsing. Feitestuk Reeks (SA) *190*

University of Port Elizabeth. Institute for Planning Research. Information Bulletin Series/Universiteit van Port Elizabeth. Instituut vir Beplanningsnavorsing. Inligtingsbulletin Reeks (SA) *190*

University of Port Elizabeth. Publications. Bibliographies (SA) *494*

University of Port Elizabeth. Publications. General Series (SA ISSN 0079-3957) *494*

University of Port Elizabeth. Publications. Inaugural and Emeritus Addresses (SA ISSN 0085-5022) *494*

University of Port Elizabeth. Publications. Research Papers (SA ISSN 0079-3965) *494*

University of Port Elizabeth. Publications. Symposia and Seminars *see* University of Port Elizabeth. Publications. Symposia, Seminars, and Lectures *494*

University of Port Elizabeth. Publications. Symposia, Seminars, and Lectures (SA) *494*

University of Punjab. Institute of Geology. Geological Bulletin (PK) *301*

University of Queensland. Combined Faculty Directory (AT) *341*

University of Queensland. Combined Higher Degree Handbook *see* University of Queensland. Higher Degree Handbook *341*

University of Queensland. Computer Centre. Papers (AT ISSN 0079-886X) *274*

University of Queensland. Higher Degree Handbook. (AT) *341*

University of Queensland Inaugural Lectures (AT ISSN 0079-9033) *341*

University of Queensland Law Journal (AT ISSN 0083-4041) *520*

University of Rajasthan. South Asian Studies Centre. Annual Report (II) *671*

UNIVERSITY OF 1525

University of Rajasthan. Studies in Engineering and Technology (II) *854*
University of Rajasthan. Studies in Public Administration (II) *747*
University of Rajasthan. Studies in Sanskrit and Hindi (II ISSN 0448-1712) *554, 576*
University of Reading. Department of Agricultural Economics and Management. Farm Business Data (UK ISSN 0557-6911) *31*
University of Reading. Department of Agricultural Economics. Miscellaneous Studies (UK ISSN 0486-0845) *31*
University of Reading. Graduate School of Contemporary European Studies. Occasional Publication (UK ISSN 0079-9858) *464, 802*
University of Rhode Island. Bureau of Government Research. Information Series (US ISSN 0080-2778) *747*
University of Rhode Island. Bureau of Government Research. Local Government Series (US) *750*
University of Rhode Island. Bureau of Government Research. Research Series (US ISSN 0080-2794) *716*
University of Rhode Island. Graduate School of Oceanography. Collected Reprints (US) *313*
University of Rhode Island. Graduate School of Oceanography. Marine Technical Reports (US) *109, 313*
University of Rhode Island. Library. Library Letter (US) *537*
University of Rhode Island. Narragansett Marine Laboratory. Collected Reprints *see* University of Rhode Island. Graduate School of Oceanography. Collected Reprints *313*
University of Rhode Island. Narragansett Marine Laboratory. Occasional Publication (US ISSN 0077-2828) *313*
University of Rhode Island. Water Resources Center. Annual Report (US) *898*
University of Riyadh. Faculty of Science. Bulletin (SU) *793*
University of Rochester Library Bulletin(US ISSN 0041-9974) *537*
University of San Carlos. Series A: Humanities (PH ISSN 0069-1321) *494*
University of San Carlos. Series D: Occasional Monographs (PH ISSN 0069-1356) *494*
University of Saskatchewan. Institute for Northern Studies. Annual Report (CN ISSN 0080-665X) *793*
University of Science and Technology. Journal (GH ISSN 0075-7225) *793, 854*
University of Science of Malaysia History Forum/Universiti Sains Malaysia Foram Sejarah (MY) *446*
University of Sheffield. Metallurgical Society. Journal (UK ISSN 0080-9209) *630*
University of Sierra Leone. Fourah Bay College. Philosophical Society. Journal (SL) *692*
University of Sind. Research Journal. Arts Series: Humanities and Social Sciences (PK ISSN 0080-9616) *79, 494, 802*
University of Singapore. Chinese Society. Journal (SI ISSN 0080-9667) *446*
University of Singapore. Economic Research Centre. Occasional Papers (SI) *150*
University of Singapore. Faculty of Engineering. Journal *see* Engineering Journal of Singapore *367*
University of Singapore. History Society. Journal (SI ISSN 0085-610X) *446*
University of Singapore Political Science Society. Journal (SI) *716*
University of Singapore Science Journal(SI ISSN 0083-405X) *916*
University of South Carolina. Belle W. Baruch Library in Marine Science and Coastal Research. Collected Papers (US) *313*

University of South Carolina. Bureau of Business and Economic Research. Occasional Studies (US) *150*
University of South Carolina. Institute of Archeology and Anthropology. Annual Report (US) *55, 67*
University of South Carolina. Institute of International Studies. Essay Series(US ISSN 0085-6452) *725*
University of South Carolina. Libraries. Report of the Director of Libraries (US ISSN 0081-2706) *537*
University of South Carolina Governmental Review *see* Public Affairs Bulletin *750*
University of Southampton. Library. Automation Project Report (UK ISSN 0081-2935) *537*
University of Southern California Annual Distinguished Lecture Series Monographs in Special Education and Rehabilitation *see* U S C Annual Distinguished Lecture Series Monographs in Special Education and Rehabilitation *347*
University of Stellenbosch. Bureau for Economic Research. Prospects *see* University of Stellenbosch. Bureau for Economic Research. Survey of Contemporary Economic Conditions and Prospects *150*
University of Stellenbosch. Bureau for Economic Research. Survey of Contemporary Economic Conditions and Prospects (SA ISSN 0081-5454) *150*
University of Stockholm. Institute of Linguistics. Monographs (SW) *554*
University of Strathclyde, Fraser of Allander Institute for Research on the Scottish Economy. Research Monograph (UK ISSN 0306-7408) *150*
University of Sussex. Centre for Continuing Education. Occasional Paper (UK) *341*
University of Sydney. Australian Language Research Centre. Occasional Papers (AT ISSN 0042-0093) *554*
University of Sydney. Basser Department of Computer Science. Technical Report (AT ISSN 0082-0547) *274*
University of Sydney. Department of Agricultural Economics. Agricultural Extension Bulletin (AT ISSN 0313-8704) *31*
University of Sydney. Department of Agricultural Economics. Research Bulletin (AT ISSN 0082-0563) *31*
University of Sydney. Department of Agricultural Economics. Research Report. (AT) *31*
University of Sydney. Department of Agriculture Economics. Mimeographed Report. *see* University of Sydney. Department of Agricultural Economics. Research Report *31*
University of Sydney. Department of Architectural Science. Reports (AT ISSN 0082-0571) *70*
University of Sydney. Department of Government and Public Administration. Occasional Monograph (AT) *747*
University of Sydney. Institute of Criminology. Proceedings (AT ISSN 0085-7033) *284*
University of Sydney Economics Society. Economic Review (AT ISSN 0085-7025) *150*
University of Tasmania Law Review (AT ISSN 0082-2108) *520*
University of Teheran. Central Library. Library Bulletin/Daneshgah-e Tehran. Ketabkhane-Ye Markazi. Nashriye-Ye Ketabkhaneh (IR ISSN 0497-1000) *538*
University of Teheran. Faculty of Letters and Humanities. Bulletin of Iranian Studies/Daneshgah-e Tehran. Daneshkade-Ye Adabiyat va 'olum-e Ensani. Majalle-Ye Iranshenasi (IR) *475*

University of Telecommunications. Research Laboratory of Communication Sciences. Annual Report/Denki Tsushin Daigaku Denki Tsushin Kenkyu Shisetsu Nenpo (JA) *265*
University of Tennessee. Institute for Public Service. MTAS Municipal Technical Report (US) *747*
University of Tennessee. Library Lectures (US ISSN 0270-059X) *538*
University of Tennessee. Report on Research and Publications (US) *328*
University of Texas. Humanities Research Center. Bibliographical Monograph Series (US ISSN 0564-6855) *96*
University of Texas. Humanities Research Center. Tower Bibliographical Series (US ISSN 0563-2595) *96*
University of Texas. Institute of Marine Science. Contributions *see* Contributions in Marine Science *102*
University of Texas. Institute of Marine Science. Publications *see* Contributions in Marine Science *102*
University of Texas at Austin. Institute of Latin American Studies. Technical Papers Series (US) *747*
University of Texas, Austin. Bureau of Business Research. Area Economic Survey (US ISSN 0082-3228) *190*
University of Texas, Austin. Bureau of Business Research. Bibliography (US ISSN 0082-3236) *166*
University of Texas, Austin. Bureau of Business Research. Business Guide (US ISSN 0082-3244) *150*
University of Texas, Austin. Bureau of Business Research. Publications (US ISSN 0495-2634) *150*
University of Texas, Austin. Bureau of Business Research. Research Monograph *see* University of Texas, Austin. Bureau of Business Research. Research Report Series *150*
University of Texas, Austin. Bureau of Business Research. Research Report Series (US) *150*
University of Texas, Austin. Bureau of Business Research. Studies in Accounting (US ISSN 0081-7465) *168*
University of Texas, Austin. Bureau of Business Research. Studies in Banking and Finance (US ISSN 0081-7570) *177*
University of Texas, Austin. Bureau of Business Research. Studies in Latin American Business (US ISSN 0081-8135) *150*
University of Texas, Austin. Bureau of Business Research. Studies in Marketing (US ISSN 0081-8186) *219*
University of Texas, Austin. Bureau of Business Research. Studies in Personnel and Management (US ISSN 0081-8348) *220*
University of Texas, Austin. Bureau of Economic Geology. Annual Report (US ISSN 0082-3287) *301*
University of Texas, Austin. Bureau of Economic Geology. Geological Circular (US ISSN 0082-3309) *301*
University of Texas, Austin. Bureau of Economic Geology. Guidebook (US ISSN 0363-4132) *301*
University of Texas, Austin. Bureau of Economic Geology. Mineral Resource Circulars (US ISSN 0082-3333) *301, 647*
University of Texas, Austin. Bureau of Economic Geology. Report of Investigations (US ISSN 0082-335X) *301*
University of Texas, Austin. County Auditors' Institute. Proceedings (US ISSN 0082-3406) *916*
University of Texas, Austin. Institute for Tax Assessors. Proceedings (US ISSN 0082-3430) *916*
University of Texas, Austin. Lyndon B. Johnson School of Public Affairs. Policy Research Project Report (US) *716*

University of Texas, Austin. Lyndon B. Johnson School of Public Affairs. Seminar Research Report *see* University of Texas, Austin. Lyndon B. Johnson School of Public Affairs. Policy Research Project Report *716*
University of Texas, Austin. Lyndon B. Johnson School of Public Affairs. Working Paper Series (US) *747*
University of Texas, Austin. Natural Fibers Economic Research. Research Report (US ISSN 0082-3384) *31*
University of Texas, Austin. Tarlton Law Library. Legal Bibliography Series (US ISSN 0085-7092) *521*
University of Texas Monographs in Astronomy (US ISSN 0082-3546) *84*
University of Texas Publications in Astronomy (US) *84*
University of the Orange Free State. Institute for Contemporary History. Annual Report (SA) *441*
University of the Orange Free State. Opsommings van Proefskrifte en Verhandelinge. Abstracts of Dissertations and Theses (SA ISSN 0067-9216) *342*
University of the Philippines. Asian Center. Bibliography (PH) *438*
University of the Philippines. Asian Center. Monograph Series (PH ISSN 0079-9238) *446*
University of the Philippines. College of Public Administration. Local Government Studies (PH) *750*
University of the Philippines. College of Public Administration. Public Administration and Special Studies Series (PH) *747*
University of the Philippines. Community Development Research Council. Study Series (PH ISSN 0079-9246) *226*
University of the Philippines. Institute of Public Administration. (Publication) (PH ISSN 0079-9254) *747*
University of the Philippines. Office of Alumni Relations. Alumni Directory (PH) *263*
University of the Philippines at Los Banos. Agrarian Reform Institute. Occasional Papers (PH) *22*
University of the Philippines at Los Banos. Rodent Research Center. Annual Report (PH) *40*
University of the Punjab. Arabic and Persian Society. Journal (PK ISSN 0079-8029) *446*
University of the Punjab. Department of Mathematics. Journal of Mathematics(PK) *590*
University of the Punjab. Department of Zoology. Bulletin. New Series (PK ISSN 0079-8045) *131*
University of the Ryukyus. College of Agriculture. Science Bulletin/Ryukyu Daigaku Nogakubu Gakujutsu Hokoku (JA ISSN 0485-7828) *22*
University of the West Indies. Annual Report on Cacao Research (TR) *40*
University of the West Indies. Institute of Social and Economic Research. Occasional Bibliography Series (JM) *803*
University of the West Indies. Institute of Social and Economic Research. Occasional Paper (BB) *802*
University of the West Indies. Institute of Social and Economic Research. Working Papers (JM) *150, 817*
University of the West Indies Students' Law Review *see* U W I Students' Law Review *519*
University of the West Indies, Trinidad. Institute of Social & Economic Research. Occasional Papers: General Series (TR) *802*
University of the West Indies, Trinidad. Institute of Social & Economic Research. Occasional Papers: Human Resources Series (TR) *212*
University of the Witwatersrand, Johannesburg. Bernard Price Institute for Palaeontological Research. Annals *see* Palaeontologia Africana *674*

University of the Witwatersrand, Johannesburg. Bernard Price Institute for Palaeontological Research. Memoir (SA) *674*
University of the Witwatersrand, Johannesburg. Library. Annual Report of the University Librarian (SA ISSN 0075-3807) *538*
University of the Witwatersrand, Johannesburg. Library. Bibliographical Series (SA) *96*
University of the Witwatersrand, Johannesburg. Library. Historical and Literary Papers: Inventories of Collections (SA) *538*
University of the Witwatersrand, Johannesburg. Library. Occasional Publications (SA) *538*
University of Tokyo. Computer Center. Report (JA ISSN 0564-8742) *274*
University of Tokyo. Department of Geography. Bulletin/Tokyo Daigaku Chirigaku Kyoshitsu Kaiho (JA ISSN 0082-478X) *427*
University of Tokyo. Faculty of Science. Journal. Section 2: Geology, Mineralogy, Geography, Geophysics/ Tokyo Daigaku Rigakubu Kiyo, Dai-2-rui, Chishitsugaku, Kobutsugaku, Chirigaku, Chiyu Butsurigaku (JA ISSN 0040-8999) *290*
University of Tokyo. Faculty of Science. Journal. Section 3: Botany/ Tokyo Daigaku Rigakubu Kiyo, Dai-3-rui, Shokubutsugaku (JA) *119*
University of Tokyo. Faculty of Science. Journal. Section 4: Zoology/ Tokyo Daigaku Rigakubu Kiyo Dai-4-rui, Dobutsugaku (JA) *131*
University of Tokyo. Faculty of Science. Journal. Section 5: Anthropology/Tokyo Daigaku Rigakubu Kiyo, Dai-5-rui, Jinruigaku (JA) *55*
University of Tokyo. Faculty of Science. Misaki Marine Biological Station. Contributions (JA ISSN 0493-4334) *109*
University of Tokyo. Institute for Nuclear Study. Annual Report (JA) *705*
University of Tokyo. Institute for Nuclear Study. INS-J (JA ISSN 0495-7814) *705*
University of Tokyo. Institute for Nuclear Study. INS-PH (JA) *705*
University of Tokyo. Institute for Nuclear Study. INS-PT (JA ISSN 0563-7848) *705*
University of Tokyo. Institute for Nuclear Study. INS-TCH (JA) *705*
University of Tokyo. Institute for Nuclear Study. INS-TEC (JA) *705*
University of Tokyo. Institute for Nuclear Study. INS-TH (JA ISSN 0563-7872) *705*
University of Tokyo. Institute for Nuclear Study. INS-TL (JA ISSN 0563-7880) *705*
University of Tokyo. Institute for Nuclear Study. INS-TS (JA) *705*
University of Tokyo. Institute for Nuclear Study. Report (JA ISSN 0495-7822) *705*
University of Tokyo. Institute for Solid State Physics. Technical Report. Series B (JA ISSN 0082-4801) *699*
University of Tokyo. Institute of Applied Microbiology. Reports (JA ISSN 0082-481X) *124*
University of Tokyo. Institute of Social Science. Annals (JA ISSN 0563-8054) *802*
University of Tokyo. Institute of Space and Aeronautical Science. Report (JA ISSN 0082-4828) *10*
University of Tokyo. Ocean Research Institute. Bulletin/Tokyo Daigaku Kaiyo Kenkyusho (JA ISSN 0564-6898) *313*
University of Tokyo. Research Institute of Logopedics and Phoniatrics. Annual Bulletin (JA ISSN 0564-7630) *126*
University of Toledo. Business Research Center. Bibliographies (US) *96, 150*
University of Toledo. Business Research Center. Hodge Memorial Graduate Lectures (US) *150*
University of Toledo. Business Research Center. Miscellaneous Papers (US) *150*
University of Toledo. Business Research Center. Occasional Papers (US) *150*
University of Toledo. Business Research Center. Regional Research Reports (US) *150*
University of Toledo. Business Research Center. Studies in Financial Institutions (US) *177*
University of Toledo. Business Research Center. Working Papers in Operations Analysis (US ISSN 0094-1565) *217*
University of Toronto. David Dunlap Obervatory. Publications (CN ISSN 0070-2927) *85*
University of Toronto. Department of Electrical Engineering. Research Report (CN ISSN 0082-514X) *359*
University of Toronto. Department of Geography. Discussion Paper Series (CN ISSN 0317-9893) *427*
University of Toronto. Department of Geography. Research Publications (CN ISSN 0082-5174) *427*
University of Toronto. Department of Mechanical Engineering. Technical Publication Series (CN ISSN 0082-5182) *383*
University of Toronto. Department of Urban & Regional Planning. Papers on Planning & Design (CN) *488*
University of Toronto. Faculty of Forestry. Technical Reports (CN ISSN 0082-5190) *411*
University of Toronto. Faculty of Management Studies. Working Paper Series (CN) *217*
University of Toronto. Institute for Aerospace Studies. Progress Report (CN ISSN 0082-5239) *10*
University of Toronto. Institute for Aerospace Studies. Report (CN ISSN 0082-5255) *10*
University of Toronto. Institute for Aerospace Studies. Review (CN ISSN 0082-5247) *10*
University of Toronto. Institute for Aerospace Studies. Technical Note (CN ISSN 0082-5263) *10*
University of Toronto. Institute for Policy Analysis. Annual Report (CN) *150*
University of Toronto. Institute for Policy Analysis. Reprint Series (CN) *150*
University of Toronto. Institute for Policy Analysis. Working Paper Series (CN) *150*
University of Toronto. Institute for the Quantitative Analysis of Social and Economic Policy. News Letter *see* University of Toronto. Institute for Policy Analysis. Annual Report *150*
University of Toronto. Institute for the Quantitative Analysis of Social and Economic Policy. Reprint Series *see* University of Toronto. Institute for Policy Analysis. Reprint Series *150*
University of Toronto. Institute for the Quantitative Analysis of Social and Economic Policy. Working Paper Series *see* University of Toronto. Institute for Policy Analysis. Working Paper Series *150*
University of Toronto. Library. Annual Report (CN ISSN 0082-531X) *538*
University of Toronto Romance Series (CN ISSN 0082-5336) *554, 576*
University of Toronto Undergraduate Dental Journal (CN ISSN 0042-0255) *610*
University of Toronto-York University. Joint Program in Transportation. Annual Report (CN ISSN 0318-1251) *864*
University of Trondheim. Norwegian Institute of Technology. River and Harbour Laboratory. Bulletin *see* Universitetet i Trondheim. Norges Tekniske Hoegskole. Vassdrags- og Havnelaboratoriet. Meddelelse *381*
University of Tulsa. Department of English. Monograph Series (US ISSN 0082-6812) *576*
University of Turku Psychological Reports (FI) *738*
University of Utah. Institute of Industrial Relations. Bulletin (US ISSN 0083-4912) *212*
University of Utah. Office of Institutional Studies. Statistical Summaries (US ISSN 0083-4920) *342*
University of Utah Anthropological Papers (US ISSN 0083-4947) *55*
University of Vaasa. Proceedings. Discussion Papers (FI) *192*
University of Victoria (B.C.) Library. List of Serials *see* University of Victoria (B.C.) Library. Serials Holdings Catalogue *96*
University of Victoria (B.C.) Library. Serials Holdings Catalogue (CN ISSN 0318-174X) *96*
University of Waikato. Antarctic Research Unit. Report (NZ) *301*
University of Wales. Board of Celtic Studies. History and Law Series (UK) *464, 520*
University of Wales. Board of Celtic Studies. Social Science Monographs (UK ISSN 0307-0042) *802*
University of Warwick Library. Occasional Publications. (UK) *538*
University of Washington. Department of Oceanography. Contribution (US ISSN 0083-7520) *313*
University of Washington. Department of Oceanography. Fishery Report (US ISSN 0083-7539) *916*
University of Washington. Department of Oceanography. Special Report (US ISSN 0083-7547) *916*
University of Washington. Office of Public Archaeology. Reconnaissance Reports (US) *67*
University of Washington. Office of Public Archaeology. Reports in Highway Archaeology (US) *67*
University of Washington Publications in Fisheries (US ISSN 0085-7939) *400*
University of Washington Publications on Asia *see* Publications on Asia *445*
University of Waterloo. Division of Environmental Studies. Occasional Paper *see* University of Waterloo. Faculty of Environmental Studies. Occasional Paper *916*
University of Waterloo. Faculty of Environmental Studies. Occasional Paper (CN) *916*
University of Waterloo. Faculty of Environmental Studies. Working Paper Series (CN) *389, 488*
University of Waterloo. Solid Mechanics Division. Studies Series (CN) *380*
University of Waterloo. Solid Mechanics Division. Technical Notes(CN) *380*
University of Waterloo Biology Series (CN ISSN 0317-3348) *109*
University of West Los Angeles Law Review (US ISSN 0083-4068) *520*
University of Western Australia. Department of Music. Music Monograph (AT) *664*
University of Western Australia. Institute of Agriculture. Research Report: Agricultural Economics (AT ISSN 0083-8705) *916*
University of Western Australia. Library. Report on the Library (AT ISSN 0083-8713) *538*
University of Western Ontario. Centre for Radio Science. Annual Report (CN ISSN 0076-0587) *268*
University of Western Ontario. D. B. Weldon Library. Library Bulletin (CN ISSN 0076-0595) *538*
University of Western Ontario. Department of Psychology. Research Bulletin (CN ISSN 0316-4675) *738*
University of Western Ontario. Instructional Media Centre. Newsletter (CN) *351*
University of Western Ontario Journal *see* U W O/D S S Journal *610*
University of Western Ontario Series in Philosophy of Science (NE) *692, 793*
University of Wisconsin. Bureau of Business Research and Service. Monographs *see* Wisconsin Business Monographs *151*
University of Wisconsin. Institute for Research on Poverty. Bibliography Series (US) *802*
University of Wisconsin. Institute for Research on Poverty. Discussion Paper Series (US) *802*
University of Wisconsin. Institute for Research on Poverty. Monograph Series (US) *802*
University of Wisconsin. Institute for Research on Poverty. Special Report Series (US) *802*
University of Wisconsin. Mathematical Research Center Series (US ISSN 0084-0890) *590*
University of Wisconsin, Madison. Applied Population Laboratory. Population Notes (US ISSN 0084-0734) *730*
University of Wisconsin, Madison. Applied Population Laboratory. Population Series (US ISSN 0084-0742) *730*
University of Wisconsin-Madison. Applied Population Laboratory. Technical Series (US) *730*
University of Wisconsin, Madison. Cartographic Laboratory. Paper (US) *427*
University of Wisconsin, Madison. Engineering Experiment Station. Annual Report (US ISSN 0193-9629) *635*
University of Wisconsin, Madison. Institute for Research on Poverty. Reprint Series (US ISSN 0084-0769) *802*
University of Wisconsin, Madison. Institute of Environmental Studies. I E S Reports (US) *389*
University of Wisconsin, Madison. Land Tenure Center. Reprint (US ISSN 0084-0807) *31*
University of Wisconsin, Madison. Land Tenure Center. Training and Methods Series (US ISSN 0084-0823) *31*
University of Wisconsin-Milwaukee. Center for Latin America. Business Series (US) *473*
University of Wisconsin-Milwaukee. Center for Latin America. Conference Series. *see* University of Wisconsin-Milwaukee. Center for Latin America. Business Series *473*
University of Wisconsin, Milwaukee. Center for Latin America. Discussion Papers (US ISSN 0146-258X) *473*
University of Wisconsin, Milwaukee. Center for Latin America. Essay Series (US ISSN 0084-084X) *473*
University of Wisconsin-Milwaukee. Center for Latin America. Special Papers Series (US ISSN 0146-2598) *473*
University of Wisconsin, Milwaukee. Center for Latin America. Special Studies Series (US) *473, 494*
University of Wisconsin, Milwaukee. Language and Area Center for Latin America. Discussion Papers. *see* University of Wisconsin, Milwaukee. Center for Latin America. Discussion Papers *473*
University of Wisconsin, Milwaukee. Language and Area Center for Latin America. Special Studies Series *see* University of Wisconsin, Milwaukee. Center for Latin America. Special Studies Series *473*
University of Witwatersrand, Johannesburg. School of Mechanical Engineering. Reports (SA) *383*
University of Wollongong. Annual Report (AT ISSN 0313-6906) *263*
University of Wollongong. Calendar (AT ISSN 0312-0007) *263*
University of Wollongong. Research Bulletin (AT ISSN 0313-9921) *802*
University of Wyoming. Water Resources Research Institute. Miscellaneous Publications (US) *898*

University of Wyoming. Water Resources Research Institute. Water Resources Series (US ISSN 0084-3210) *898*
University of Wyoming Publications (US ISSN 0084-3199) *494, 793*
University of York. Centre for Southern African Studies. Collected Papers (UK) *441*
University of York. Institute of Advanced Architectural Studies. Research Papers (UK ISSN 0306-0624) *70*
University of Zambia. Centre for Continuing Education. Report of the Annual Resident Tutors' Conference (ZA) *330*
University of Zambia. Centre for Continuing Education. Report of the Annual Staff Conference *see* University of Zambia. Centre for Continuing Education. Report of the Annual Resident Tutors' Conference *330*
University of Zambia. Institute for African Studies. Communication (ZA ISSN 0084-5108) *802*
University of Zambia. School of Humanities and Social Sciences. Annual Report (ZA) *342*
University Resources in the United States and Canada for the Study of Linguistics *see* Guide to Programs in Linguistics *544*
University Resources in the United States for Linguistics and the Teaching of English as a Foreign Language *see* Guide to Programs in Linguistics *544*
University Studies on European Integration *see* Etudes Universitaires sur l'Integration Europeenne *721*
Univerzita Komenskeho. Filozoficka Fakulta. Zbornik: Ethnologia Slavica (CS ISSN 0083-4106) *55, 403*
Univerzita Komenskeho. Filozoficka Fakulta. Zbornik: Graecolatina et Orientalia (CS ISSN 0083-4114) *261, 671*
Univerzita Komenskeho. Filozoficka Fakulta. Zbornik: Historica (CS ISSN 0083-4122) *436*
Univerzita Komenskeho. Filozoficka Fakulta. Zbornik: Informatika (CS) *692*
Univerzita Komenskeho. Filozoficka Fakulta. Zbornik: Marxizmus-Leninizmus (CS) *692, 716*
Univerzita Komenskeho. Filozoficka Fakulta. Zbornik: Musaica (CS ISSN 0083-4130) *67, 79, 664*
Univerzita Komenskeho. Filozoficka Fakulta. Zbornik: Paedagogica (CS ISSN 0083-4165) *324*
Univerzita Komenskeho. Filozoficka Fakulta. Zbornik: Philologica (CS ISSN 0083-4173) *554, 576*
Univerzita Komenskeho. Filozoficka Fakulta. Zbornik: Philosophica (CS ISSN 0083-4181) *692*
Univerzita Komenskeho. Filozoficka Fakulta. Zbornik: Psychologica (CS ISSN 0083-419X) *738*
Univerzita Komenskeho. Filozoficka Fakulta. Zbornik: Zurnalistika (CS ISSN 0083-422X) *505*
Univerzita Komenskeho. Oddelenie Liecebnej a Specialnej Pedagogiky. Zbornik: Paedagogica Specialis (CS ISSN 0083-4211) *347*
Univerzita Komenskeho. Pedagogicka Fakulta v Trnave. Prirodne Vedy: Biologia-Genetika (CS) *123*
Univerzita Komenskeho. Ustav Marxizmu-Leninizmu. Zbornik: Dejiny Robotnickeho Hnutia (CS) *717*
Univerzita Komenskeho. Ustav Marxizmu-Leninizmu. Zbornik: Marxisticka Filozofia (CS) *692, 717*
Univerzita Palackeho. Pedagogicka Fakulta. Sbornik Praci: Cesky Jazyk a Literatura (CS) *554, 576*
Univerzitet u Beogradu. Institut za Botaniku i Botanicke Baste. Glasnik (YU) *119*
Univerzitet u Novom Sadu. Prirodno - Matematicki Fakultet. Zbornik Radova (YU ISSN 0350-140X) *793*

Univerzitet u Sarajevu. Doktorske Disertacije. Rezimei (YU) *328*
Univerzitet vo Skoplje. Ekonomskiot Fakultet. Godisnik/Universite de Skopje. Faculte des Sciences Economique. Annuaire (YU) *150*
Uniwersytet Gdanski. Wydzial Biologii i Nauk o Ziemi. Zeszyty Naukowe. Geografia (PL) *427*
Uniwersytet Gdanski. Wydzial Ekonomiki Produkcji. Zeszyty Naukowe. Zagadnienia Ekonomiki Przemyslu (PL) *226*
Uniwersytet Gdanski. Wydzial Ekonomiki Transportu. Zeszyty Naukowe. Ekonomika Transportu Ladowego (PL) *864*
Uniwersytet Gdanski. Wydzial Ekonomiki Transportu. Zeszyty Naukowe. Ekonomika Transportu Morskiego (PL) *881*
Uniwersytet Gdanski. Wydzial Ekonomiki Transportu. Zeszyty Naukowe. Instytut Ekonomii Politycznej. Prace i Materialy (PL) *150*
Uniwersytet Gdanski. Wydzial Ekonomiki Transportu. Zeszyty Naukowe. Instytut Handlu Zagranicznego. Prace i Materialy (PL) *198*
Uniwersytet Gdanski. Wydzial Humanistyczny. Zeszyty Naukowe. Filozofia i Socjologia (PL ISSN 0072-0453) *692*
Uniwersytet Gdanski. Wydzial Humanistyczny. Zeszyty Naukowe. Historia (PL ISSN 0072-0461) *464*
Uniwersytet Gdanski. Wydzial Humanistyczny. Zeszyty Naukowe. Pedagogika, Psychologia, Historia Wychowania (PL ISSN 0072-047X) *324*
Uniwersytet Gdanski. Wydzial Humanistyczny. Zeszyty Naukowe. Prace Historyczno-Literackie (PL ISSN 0072-0488) *436, 576*
Uniwersytet Gdanski. Wydzial Matematyki, Fizyki, Chemii. Zeszyty Naukowe. Chemia (PL) *248*
Uniwersytet Gdanski. Wydzial Matematyki, Fizyki, Chemii. Zeszyty Naukowe. Fizyka (PL) *699*
Uniwersytet Gdanski. Wydzial Matematyki, Fizyki, Chemii. Zeszyty Naukowe. Matematyka (PL) *590*
Uniwersytet Gdanski. Wydzial Prawa i Administracji. Zeszyty Naukowe. Prawo (PL) *520*
Uniwersytet im. Adama Mickiewicza w Poznaniu. Wydzial Biologii i Nauk o Ziemi. Prace. Seria Geologia (PL ISSN 0083-4238) *301*
Uniwersytet im. Adama Mickiewicza w Poznaniu. Wydzial Biologii i Nauk o Ziemi. Seria Antropologia *see* Antropologia *47*
Uniwersytet im. Adama Mickiewicza w Poznaniu. Wydzial Biologii i Nauk o Ziemi. Seria Biologia *see* Biologia *101*
Uniwersytet im. Adama Mickiewicza w Poznaniu. Wydzial Biologii i Nauk o Ziemi. Seria Zoologia *see* Zoologia *131*
Uniwersytet im. Adama Mickiewicza w Poznaniu. Wydzial Biologii i Nauk o Ziemi. Zeszyty Naukowe. Geografia *see* Geografia *422*
Uniwersytet im. Adama Mickiewicza w Poznaniu. Wydzial Filologiczny. Seria Filologia Angielska *see* Filologia Angielska *543*
Uniwersytet im. Adama Mickiewicza w Poznaniu. Wydzial Filologiczny. Seria Filologia Klasyczna *see* Filologia Klasyczna *543*
Uniwersytet im. Adama Mickiewicza w Poznaniu. Wydzial Filozoficzno-Historyczny. Prace. Seria Filozofia-Logika *see* Filozofia-Logika *688*
Uniwersytet im. Adama Mickiewicza w Poznaniu. Wydzial Filozoficzno-Historyczny. Seria Etnografia *see* Etnografia *401*
Uniwersytet im. Adama Mickiewicza w Poznaniu. Wydzial Historyczny. Prace. Seria Psychologia-Pedagogika *see* Psychologia-Pedagogika *737*

Uniwersytet im. Adama Mickiewicza w Poznaniu. Wydzial Matematyki, Fizyki i Chemii. Prace. Seria Akustyka *see* Akustyka *706*
Uniwersytet im. Adama Mickiewicza w Poznaniu. Wydzial Matematyki, Fizyki i Chemii. Prace. Seria Matematyka *see* Matematyka *587*
Uniwersytet im. Adama Mickiewicza w Poznaniu. Wydzial Matematyki, Fizyki i Chemii. Seria Astronomia *see* Astronomia *81*
Uniwersytet im. Adama Mickiewicza w Poznaniu. Wydzial Matematyki, Fizyki i Chemii. Seria Chemia *see* Chemia *245*
Uniwersytet im. Adama Mickiewicza w Poznaniu. Wydzial Matematyki, Fizyki i Chemii. Seria Fizyka *see* Fizyka *696*
Uniwersytet im. Adama Mickiewicza w Poznaniu. Wydzial Prawa. Prace *see* Prawo *516*
Uniwersytet im. Adama Mickiewicza w Poznaniu. Zeszyty Naukowe. Historia Sztuki *see* Historia Sztuki *75*
Uniwersytet im Adama Mickiewicza w Poznaniu Wydzial Filozoficzno-Historyczny. Prace . Seria Archeologia *see* Archeologia *57*
Uniwersytet Jagiellonski. Zeszyty Naukowe. Prace Archeologiczne (PL ISSN 0083-4300) *67*
Uniwersytet Jagiellonski. Zeszyty Naukowe. Prace Botaniczne (PL ISSN 0302-8585) *119*
Uniwersytet Jagiellonski. Zeszyty Naukowe. Prace Chemiczne (PL ISSN 0083-4319) *248*
Uniwersytet Jagiellonski. Zeszyty Naukowe. Prace Etnograficzne (PL ISSN 0083-4327) *55*
Uniwersytet Jagiellonski. Zeszyty Naukowe. Prace Fizyczne (PL ISSN 0083-4335) *699*
Uniwersytet Jagiellonski. Zeszyty Naukowe. Prace Geograficzne (PL ISSN 0083-4343) *427*
Uniwersytet Jagiellonski. Zeszyty Naukowe. Prace Geograficzne. Prace z Geografii Ekonomicznej (PL ISSN 0083-4289) *151*
Uniwersytet Jagiellonski. Zeszyty Naukowe. Prace Historyczne (PL ISSN 0083-4351) *464*
Uniwersytet Jagiellonski. Zeszyty Naukowe. Prace Historycznoliterackie (PL ISSN 0083-436X) *576*
Uniwersytet Jagiellonski. Zeszyty Naukowe. Prace Jezykoznawcze (PL ISSN 0083-4378) *554*
Uniwersytet Jagiellonski. Zeszyty Naukowe. Prace Matematyczne (PL ISSN 0083-4386) *590*
Uniwersytet Jagiellonski. Zeszyty Naukowe. Prace Prawnicze (PL ISSN 0083-4394) *520*
Uniwersytet Jagiellonski. Zeszyty Naukowe. Prace Psychologiczno-Pedagogiczne (PL ISSN 0083-4408) *324, 739*
Uniwersytet Jagiellonski. Zeszyty Naukowe. Prace z Biologii Molekularnej (PL) *109*
Uniwersytet Jagiellonski. Zeszyty Naukowe. Prace z Historii Sztuki (PL ISSN 0083-4424) *79*
Uniwersytet Jagiellonski. Zeszyty Naukowe. Prace z Nauk Politycznych (PL) *717*
Uniwersytet Jagiellonski. Zeszyty Naukowe. Prace Zoologiczne (PL ISSN 0083-4416) *131*
Uniwersytet Lodzki. Prace (PL ISSN 0076-034X) *494*
Uniwersytet Lodzki. Zeszyty Naukowe. Seria 2: Nauki Matematyczno-Przyrodnicze (PL ISSN 0076-0366) *793*
Uniwersytet Mikolaja Kopernika, Torun. Nauki Humanistyczno-Spoleczne. Archeologia *see* Acta Universitatis Nicolai Copernici. Archeologia *56*

Uniwersytet Mikolaja Kopernika, Torun. Nauki Humanistyczno-Spoleczne. Filozofia *see* Acta Universitatis Nicolai Copernici. Filozofia *687*
Uniwersytet Mikolaja Kopernika, Torun. Nauki Humanistyczno-Spoleczne. Filologia Polska *see* Acta Universitatis Nicolai Copernici. Filologia Polska *540*
Uniwersytet Mikolaja Kopernika, Torun. Nauki Humanistyczno-Spoleczne. Historia *see* Acta Universitatis Nicolai Copernici. Historia *448*
Uniwersytet Mikolaja Kopernika, Torun. Nauki Humanistyczno-Spoleczne. Prawo *see* Acta Universitatis Nicolai Copernici. Prawo *508*
Uniwersytet Mikolaja Kopernika, Torun. Nauki Humanistyczno-Spoleczne. Socjologia *see* Acta Universitatis Nicolai Copernici. Socjologia Wychowania *313*
Uniwersytet Mikolaja Kopernika, Torun. Nauki Matematyczno-Przyrodnicze. Biologia *see* Acta Universitatis Nicolai Copernici. Biologia *100*
Uniwersytet Slaski w Katowicach. Physics Papers (PL) *699*
Uniwersytet Slaski w Katowicach. Prace Chemiczne (PL) *248*
Uniwersytet Slaski w Katowicach. Prace Dydaktyczne (PL) *351*
Uniwersytet Slaski w Katowicach. Prace Historyczne (PL) *436*
Uniwersytet Slaski w Katowicach. Prace Historycznoliterackie (PL) *576*
Uniwersytet Slaski w Katowicach. Prace Jezykoznawcze (PL) *554*
Uniwersytet Slaski w Katowicach. Prace Matematyczne (PL) *590*
Uniwersytet Slaski w Katowicach. Prace Pedagogiczne (PL) *324*
Uniwersytet Slaski W Katowicach. Prace Prawnicze (PL) *520*
Uniwersytet Slaski w Katowicach. Prace Psychologiczne (PL) *324, 739*
Uniwersytet Slaski w Katowicach. Prace z Nauk Spolecznych (PL) *802*
Uniwersytet Slaski w Katowicach. Wydzial Techniki. Prace (PL) *854*
Uniwersytet Warszawski. Instytut Geograficzny. Prace i Studia. (PL ISSN 0083-7326) *427*
Uniwersytet Warszawski. Katedra Klimatologii. Prace i Studia (PL ISSN 0083-7334) *635*
Uniwersytet Warszawski. Roczniki/ Annales Universitatis Varsoviensis (PL ISSN 0083-7342) *342*
Uniwersytet Wroclawski. Instytut Geograficzne. Prace. Seria A: Geografia Fizyczna (PL) *427*
Uniwersytet Wroclawski. Instytut Geograficzne. Prace. Seria B: Geografia Spoleczna i Ekonomiczna (PL) *427*
Uniwersytet Wroclawski. Prace Pedagogiczne i Psychologia *see* Acta Universitatis Wratislaviensis. Prace Pedagogiczne *313*
Unmuzzled Ox (US ISSN 0049-5557) *558, 582*
Unrealist (US) *582*
Unser Krankenhaus *see* Jahrbuch Krankenhaus *481*
Unspeakable Visions of the Individual (US ISSN 0049-559X) *576*
Untei (JA ISSN 0566-2680) *538*
Der Untermieter (GW) *324*
Unternehmung und Unternehmungsfuehrung (SZ ISSN 0083-4548) *217*
Unterrichtswissenschaft (GW) *324*
Untersuchungen zur Deutschen Literaturgeschichte (GW ISSN 0083-4564) *576*
Untersuchungen zur Deutschen Staats- und Rechtsgeschichte. Neue Folge (GW ISSN 0083-4572) *520*
Untersuchungen zur Romanischen Philologie (GW) *554*
Untersuchungen zur Sprach- und Literaturgeschichte der Romanischen Voelker (GW ISSN 0083-4580) *554*
Up-to-Date Civil Reference (BG) *520*

Update (Albany) (US) 717
Update in Clinical Dentistry (US) 916
Update in Endodontics (US) 916
Update in Oral Surgery (US) 916
Update in Orthodontics (US) 916
Update in Periodontics (US) 916
Update in Preventive Dentistry (US) 916
Upgrading Metal Finishing Facilities to Reduce Pollution see U. S. Environmental Protection Agency. Upgrading Metal-Finishing Facilities to Reduce Pollution 389
Upokul (BG) 427
Upper Midwest Economic Study. Progress Report (US ISSN 0083-4610) 190
Upper Midwest Economic Study. Technical Paper (US ISSN 0083-4637) 190
Upper Midwest Economic Study. Urban Report (US ISSN 0083-4645) 190, 488
Upper Volta. Direction de l'Hydraulique et de l'Equipement Rural. Service I.R.H. Rapport d'Activites (UV) 899
Upper Volta. Direction de la Statistique et de la Mecanographie. Bulletin Mensuel d'Information Statistique et Economique see Upper Volta. Institut National de la Statistique et de la Demographie. Bulletin Annuaire d'Information Statistique et Economique 166
Upper Volta. Direction des Eaux et Forets et de la Conservation des Sols. Rapport Annuel (UV) 400, 411
Upper Volta. Institut National de la Statistique et de la Demographie. Bulletin Annuaire d'Information Statistique et Economique (UV) 166
Upper Volta. Service des Statistiques Agricoles. Annuaire (UV) 22
Uppsala Ionospheric Observatory. Rapporter AR (SW) 635
Uppsala Ionospheric Observatory. Rapporter SR (SW) 635
Uppsala Ionospheric Observatory. Rapporter TR (SW) 635
Uppsala Studies in Education (SW ISSN 0347-1314) 324
Uppsala Universitet. Geological Institution. Bulletin (SW) 302
Uppsala Universitet. Institutionen foer Nordiska Spraak. Skrifter (SW ISSN 0083-4661) 916
Uralic and Altaic Series see Indiana University. Research Center for Language and Semiotic Studies. Uralic and Altaic Series 545
Urban Affairs Annual Reviews (US ISSN 0083-4688) 488
Urban Affairs Papers (US) 488
Urban and Regional Planning Series (US) 488
Urban Development Corporation. Annual Report (JM) 488
Urban Environment (US ISSN 0083-4696) 70, 817
Urban Guerilla (US) 717
Urban History Yearbook (UK ISSN 0306-0845) 464, 802
Urban Insights Monograph Series (US) 488
Urban Institute. Annual Report (US ISSN 0092-7481) 488
Urban Institute Report see Urban Institute. Annual Report 488
Urban Issues (AT) 488
Urban Issues (Winnipeg) (CN) 488
Urban Land Institute. Research Report (US ISSN 0083-470X) 916
Urban Land Institute. Technical Bulletin (US ISSN 0083-4718) 916
Urban Life in America (US) 817
Urban Observatory of San Diego. Special Report (US) 817
Urban Planning and Development see American Society of Civil Engineers. Urban Planning and Development Division. Journal 483
Urban Problems and Urban Technology Series (US) 488
Urban Transport Research: Special Series see Forschung Stadtverkehr: Sonderreihe 874

Urbanology (AT ISSN 0310-5601) 488
Uro-Nephro; Annuaire de l'Urologie et de la Nephrologie (FR ISSN 0083-4769) 625
Urthkin (US ISSN 0163-3295) 576
Urthona (US) 576
Uruguay. Administracion Nacional de Telecomunicaciones. Memoria Anual (UY) 265
Uruguay. Centro de Navegacion Transatlantica. Estadistica (UY) 867
Uruguay. Consejo de Estado. Diario de Sessiones (UY) 747
Uruguay. Direccion General de Comercio Exterior. Estadististicas de Comercio Exterior (UY) 198
Uruguay. Direccion General de Estadistica y Censos. Estadisticas Vitales (UY) 730
Uruguay. Instituto Nacional de Carnes. Departamento de Exportaciones. Exportacion de Carnes, Estadisticas (UY) 46
Uruguay. Instituto Nacional de Carnes. Departamento de Exportaciones. Anuario (UY) 406
Uruk-Warka: Abhandlungen der Deutschen Orient-Gesellschaft (GW ISSN 0083-4793) 67
US 1 Worksheets see U S 1 Worksheets 557
Used Book Price Guide (US ISSN 0083-4807) 760
Uspekhi Foroniki (UR) 706
Ustredna Sprava Muzei a Galerii. Vyrocne Spravy o Cinnosti Slovenskych Muzei (CS) 655
Ustredni Ustav Geologicky. Rozpravy (CS) 674
Ustredni Ustav Geologicky. Vyzkumne Prace (CS) 302
Utah. Department of Transportation. Highway Safety Program, Annual Report (US ISSN 0361-5332) 876
Utah. Division of Wildlife Resources. Biennial Report (US ISSN 0360-800X) 278
Utah. Juvenile Court. Annual Report (US ISSN 0566-4152) 257
Utah. State Board of Education. Annual Report of the State Superintendent of Public Instruction (US ISSN 0094-8314) 345
Utah. State Board of Education. Opinions of the Utah State Superintendent of Public Instruction (US ISSN 0093-0040) 345
Utah. State Department of Agriculture. Biennial Report (US) 22
Utah. State Department of Fish and Game. Biennial Report see Utah. Division of Wildlife Resources. Biennial Report 278
Utah Academy of Science, Arts and Letters. Proceedings see Encyclia 782
Utah Agricultural Statistics (US) 26
Utah Bar Journal (US ISSN 0091-9691) 520
Utah Export Directory (US ISSN 0092-2374) 243
Utah Geological and Mineral Survey. Bulletin (US ISSN 0098-4825) 302, 647
Utah Geological Association. Annual Guidebook (US ISSN 0083-484X) 302
Utah Marriage and Divorce Annual Report (US) 849
Utah Public School Directory (US) 332
Utah Public School System see Utah. State Board of Education. Annual Report of the State Superintendent of Public Instruction 345
Utah State Historical Society. Antiquities Section. Selected Papers (US) 473
Utah Vital Statistics Annual Report (US ISSN 0500-7720) 730
Utenrikspolitiske Skrifter/Norwegian Foreign Policy Studies (NO) 725
Utrecht Micropaleontological Bulletins (NE ISSN 0083-4963) 674
Utrechtse Geografische Studies (NE ISSN 0376-4001) 427
Utsaba (BG) 582

Uttar Pradesh. State Mineral Development Corporation. Annual Report and Accounts (II) 647
Uttar Pradesh, India. Scientific Research Committee Monograph Series (II ISSN 0083-5013) 793
V. C. M. File (Victorian Chamber of Manufacturers) (AT ISSN 0311-127X) 180
V D Alert (US) 755
V D E W Arbeitsbericht (Vereinigung Deutscher Elektrizitaetswerke e.V.) (GW) 359
V.I.P. du Conseil (FR) 217
V.I.P. de la Finance et de la Banque (FR) 177
V.I.P. du Marketing et de la Publicite (FR) 6, 219
V K G Jahrbuch (Verband der Kraftfahrzeugteile- und Zweiradgrosshaendler e.V.) (GW) 243, 826, 872
V K G Jahrbuch (Verband der Kraftfahrzeugteile- und Zweiradgrosshaendler e.V.) (GW) 872
V L B see Verzeichnis Lieferbarer Buecher 96
V Mire Muzyki (UR) 664
V O H D see Verzeichnis der Orientalischen Handschriften in Deutschland 671
V O H D Supplementbaende see Verzeichnis der Orientalischen Handschriften in Deutschland. Supplementbaende 671
V T T Symposium (Valtion Teknillinen Tutkimuskeskus) (FI ISSN 0357-9387) 854
V W Z (Verkehrswirtschaftliche Zahlen) (GW ISSN 0083-5021) 876
Vaabenhistoriske Aarboeger (DK) 476
Vaasa School of Economics. Proceedings. Discussion Papers see University of Vaasa. Proceedings. Discussion Papers 192
Vaasan Kauppakorkeakoulu. Julkaisuja. Opetusmonisteita see Vaasan Korkeakoulu. Julkaisuja. Opetusmonisteita 192
Vaasan Kauppakorkeakoulu. Julkaisuja. Tutkimuksia see Vaasan Korkeakoulu. Julkaisuja. Tutkimuksia 192
Vaasan Korkeakoulu. Julkaisuja. Opetusmonisteita (FI) 192
Vaasan Korkeakoulu. Julkaisuja. Tutkimuksia (FI) 192
Vacancy Rates and Characteristics of Housing in the United States see Current Housing Reports: Housing Vacancies 484
Vaccination Certificate Requirements for International Travel/Certificats de Vaccination Exiges dans les Voyages Internationaux (UN ISSN 0512-3011) 755
Vacuum Metallurgy Conference. Proceedings (US) 371, 630
Vacuum Metallurgy Conference. Transactions see Vacuum Metallurgy Conference. Proceedings 630
Vacuum Technology Directory & Buyers Guide (US) 243, 793, 854
Vade-Mecum (FR ISSN 0083-5072) 361
Vade-Mecum for Information Scientists (BE) 538
Vademecum (SZ) 488
Vademecum Deutscher Lehr- und Forschungsstaetten (GW ISSN 0083-5080) 793, 854
Vademecum voor Het Nederlandse Verzekeringswezen; Jaarboek voor Het Assurantie- en Hypotheekwezen see Jaarboek/Vademecum voor het Verzekeringswezen 499
Vaesterbottens Norra Fornminnesfoerening. Skellefteaa Museum. Meddelande (SW) 464
Vaestoentutkimuken Vuosikirja see Yearbook of Population Research in Finland 731
Vaextekologiska Studier (SW) 119
Vaextskydds-Kuriren (SW) 40
Vaextskyddsrapporter (SW ISSN 0347-3236) 109
Vagabond Chapbook (US) 582

Vaikunth Mehta National Institute of Cooperative Management. Publications (II ISSN 0083-5102) 181, 217
Vaincre (Groupe, Union, Defense) (FR) 717
Vakantiebesteding van de Nederlandse Bevolking see Netherlands. Centraal Bureau voor de Statistiek. Vakantieonderzoek 889
Valdres Historielag. Aarbok (NO) 464
Valencia Port (SP) 881, 899
Valhalla (US) 576
Valokuvauksen Vuosikirja/Finnish Photographic Yearbook/Finsk Fotografisk Arsbok (FI ISSN 0356-8075) 694
Valtion Teknillinen Tutkimuskeskus. A T K-Palvelutoimisto. Tiedonanto/Technical Research Centre of Finland. Computing Service. Report (FI ISSN 0356-004X) 274
Valtion Teknillinen Tutkimuskeskus. Betoni- ja Silikaattitekniikan Laboratorio. Tiedonanto/Technical Research Centre of Finland. Concrete Laboratory. Report (FI ISSN 0357-3737) 139
Valtion Teknillinen Tutkimuskeskus. Biotekniikan Labboratorio. Tiedonanto/Technical Research Centre of Finland. Biotechnical Laboratory. Report (FI ISSN 0355-354X) 109
Valtion Teknillinen Tutkimuskeskus. Elintarvikelabboratorio. Tiedonanto/Technical Research Centre of Finland. Food Research Laboratory. Report (FI ISSN 0355-3558) 406
Valtion Teknillinen Tutkimuskeskus. Geotekniikan Laboratorio. Tiedonanto/Technical Research Centre of Finland. Geotechnical Laboratory. Report (FI ISSN 0355-3450) 302
Valtion Teknillinen Tutkimuskeskus. Graafinen Labboratorio. Tiedonanto/Technical Research Centre of Finland. Graphic Arts Laboratory. Report (FI ISSN 0355-3566) 734
Valtion Teknillinen Tutkimuskeskus. Kemian Laboratorio. Tiedonanto/Technical Research Centre of Finland. Chemical Laboratory. Report (FI ISSN 0355-3574) 374
Valtion Teknillinen Tutkimuskeskus. Kojetekniikan Laboratorio. Tiedonanto/Technical Research Centre of Finland. Instrument Laboratory. Report (FI ISSN 0355-3434) 497
Valtion Teknillinen Tutkimuskeskus. Maankayton Laboratorio. Tiedonanto/Technical Research Centre of Finland. Laboratory of Land Use. Report (FI ISSN 0355-3477) 488
Valtion Teknillinen Tutkimuskeskus. Metallilaboratorio. Tiedonanto/Technical Research Centre of Finland. Metals Laboratory. Report (FI ISSN 0355-6395) 631
Valtion Teknillinen Tutkimuskeskus. Metallurgian ja Mineraalitekniikan Laboratorio. Tiedonanto/Technical Research Centre of Finland. Laboratory of Metallurgy and Mineral Engineering. Report (FI ISSN 0357-1831) 630, 647
Valtion Teknillinen Tutkimuskeskus. Palotekniikan Laboratorio. Tiedonanto/Technical Research Centre of Finland. Fire Technology Laboratory. Report (FI ISSN 0355-3485) 395
Valtion Teknillinen Tutkimuskeskus. Polttl- ja Voiteluainelaboratorio. Tiedonanto/Technical Research Centre of Finland. Fuel and Lubricant Research Laboratory. Report (FI ISSN 0355-3590) 682
Valtion Teknillinen Tutkimuskeskus. Rakennetekniikan Laboratorio. Tiedonanto/Technical Research Centre of Finland. Laboratory of Structural Engineering. Report (FI ISSN 0357-7031) 139, 371

VEROEFFENTLICHUNGEN ZUR 1529

Valtion Teknillinen Tutkimuskeskus. Reaktorilaboratorio. Tiedonanto/ Technical Research Centre of Finland. Reactor Laboratory. Report (FI ISSN 0355-3663) *705*
Valtion Teknillinen Tutkimuskeskus. Sahko- ja Atomitekniikka. Julkaisu (FI) *359, 705*
Valtion Teknillinen Tutkimuskeskus. Sahkotekniikan Laboratorio. Tiedonanto/Technical Research Centre of Finland. Electrical Engineering Laboratory. Report (FI ISSN 0355-3671) *359*
Valtion Teknillinen Tutkimuskeskus. Sairaalatekniikan Laboratorio. Tiedonanto/Technical Research Centre of Finland. Biomedical Engineering Laboratory. Report (FI ISSN 0355-9076) *612*
Valtion Teknillinen Tutkimuskeskus. Teknillinen Informaatiopalvelulaitos. Tiedonanto/Technical Research Centre of Finland. Technical Information Service. Report (FI ISSN 0355-3701) *538, 854*
Valtion Teknillinen Tutkimuskeskus. Tekstiililaboratorio. Tiedonanto/ Technical Research Centre of Finland. Textile Laboratory. Report (FI ISSN 0355-3639) *857*
Valtion Teknillinen Tutkimuskeskus. Teletekniikan Laboratorio. Tiedonanto/Technical Research Centre of Finland. Telecommunications Laboratory. Report (FI ISSN 0355-368X) *265*
Valtion Teknillinen Tutkimuskeskus. Ydinvoimatekniikan Laboratorio. Tiedonanto/Technical Research Centre of Finland. Nuclear Engineering Laboratory. Report (FI ISSN 0355-3698) *705*
Valtion Teknillinen Tutkimuskeskus Symposium *see* V T T Symposium *854*
Valtionyhtiot (FI ISSN 0356-8091) *226*
Van Leer Jerusalem Foundation Series (US) *692*
Vancouver. Board of Trade. Annual Report (CN ISSN 0083-517X) *182*
Vancouver Art Gallery. Annual Report (CN ISSN 0083-5161) *655*
Vancouver Community Press. Writing Series (CN) *576*
Vancouver Gastronomic (CN ISSN 0706-5302) *483*
Vancouver Historical Society. Occasional Papers (CN) *473*
Vancouver Neurological Centre. Annual Reports (CN ISSN 0083-5196) *621*
Vancouver Stock Exchange. Annual Report (CN ISSN 0083-520X) *205*
Vanderbilt Rubber Handbook (US ISSN 0083-5218) *777*
Vanderbilt Sociology Conference. Proceedings (US ISSN 0083-5226) *817*
Vanderbilt University. Abstracts of Theses (US) *4, 328*
Vanderbilt University. Center for Latin American Studies. Occasional Papers (US ISSN 0083-5234) *473*
Vanderbilt University. Department of Environmental and Water Resources Engineering. Technical Reports (US ISSN 0093-6332) *389, 899*
Vanderbilt University. Department of Sociology and Anthropology. Publications in Anthropology (US) *55*
Vani (CN ISSN 0705-1867) *394*
Vantage Conference Report (US ISSN 0145-8833) *725*
Varbergs Museum. Aarsbok (SW ISSN 0083-5536) *655*
Varendra Research Museum. Journal (BG) *655, 671*
Varia (US ISSN 0083-5242) *494*
Variety Directory *see* Australian Variety Directory *858*
Varme og Sanitets Nyt Buyers Guide (DK) *916*
VARTA Fuehrer durch Deutschland, Westlicher Teil und Berlin (GW ISSN 0083-5250) *893*
Vascular Flora of Ohio (US ISSN 0083-5269) *119*

Vaskohaszati Enciklopedia (HU ISSN 0083-5277) *374*
Vatican Observatory Publications (VC ISSN 0083-5293) *85*
Vector (CN ISSN 0382-0718) *591*
Veer (SA) *582*
Vegetable Production Recommendations *see* Cornell Recommendations for Commercial Vegetable Production *34*
Vegetables Newsletter (CN ISSN 0042-3092) *416*
Vegetarian Health Food Handbook *see* International Vegetarian Health Food Handbook *666*
Vegetation Ungarischer Landschaften (HU ISSN 0083-5323) *119, 411*
Vehicle Builders & Repairers Association. Directory of Members & Buyers Guide (UK) *383*
Vehicle Builders and Repairers Association. Yearbook *see* Vehicle Builders & Repairers Association. Directory of Members & Buyers Guide *383*
Veiligheidsjaarboek (NE ISSN 0083-534X) *212*
Vejtransporten i Tal og Tekst (DK ISSN 0083-5358) *872*
Velvet Wings (US) *576*
Vending Buyer's Guide *see* International Vending Buyer's Guide and Directory *218*
Vending International Manual (UK ISSN 0143-4381) *219*
Vendsyssel Aarbog (DK ISSN 0085-7645) *464*
Vendsysselske Aarboeger *see* Vendsyssel Aarbog *464*
Venereal Disease Bibliography (US ISSN 0090-8479) *916*
Venereal Diseases in Canada (CN ISSN 0319-0382) *611*
Venezuela. Departamento de Investigaciones Educacionales. Seccion de Estadistica. Estadistica Educacionales (VE) *324*
Venezuela. Instituto de Credito Agricola y Pecuario. Informe Anual (VE) *31*
Venezuela. Ministerio de Agricultura y Cria. Direccion de Economia y Estadistica Agropecuaria. Division de Estadistica. Plan de Trabajo (VE ISSN 0085-7653) *26*
Venezuela. Ministerio de Agricultura y Cria. Direccion de Economia y Estadistica Agropecuaria. Anuario Estadistico Agropecuario (VE ISSN 0083-5366) *22*
Venezuela. Ministerio de Agricultura y Cria. Direccion de Planificacion y Estadistica. Estadisticas Agropecuarias de las Entidades Federales (VE) *32*
Venezuela. Ministerio de Agricultura y Cria. Division de Estadistica. Encuesta Avicola Nacional (VE) *46*
Venezuela. Ministerio de Agricultura y Cria. Division de Estadistica. Encuesta da Ganado Porcino (VE) *46*
Venezuela. Ministerio de Energia y Minas. Apendice Estadistico (VE) *364, 648, 849*
Venezuela. Ministerio de Energia y Minas. Memoria y Cuenta (VE) *647, 682*
Venezuela. Ministerio de Energia y Minas. Petroleo y Otros Datos Estadisticos (VE) *682*
Venezuela. Ministerio de Hacienda. Cuenta General de Ingresos y Gastos Publicos, Bienes Nacionales, Inclusive Materias: Ingresos y Gastos(VE) *213*
Venezuela. Ministerio de Hacienda. Memoria (VE) *177*
Venezuela. Ministerio de Minas e Hidrocarburos *see* Venezuela. Ministerio de Energia y Minas. Memoria y Cuenta *647*
Venezuela. Ministerio de Minas e Hidrocarburos. Oficina de Economia Minera. Hierro y Otros Datos Estadisticos *see* Hierro *648*

Venezuela. Ministerio de Minas e Hidrocarburos. Oficina de Economia Petrolera. Petroleo y Otros Datos Estadisticos *see* Venezuela. Ministerio de Energia y Minas. Petroleo y Otros Datos Estadisticos *682*
Venezuela. Ministerio de Sanidad y Asistencia Social. Memoria y Cuenta(VE) *810*
Venezuela. Ministerio de Energia y Minas. Memoria (VE) *365, 648*
Venezuelan-American Chamber of Commerce and Industry. Yearbook and Membership Directory (VE) *180*
Venezuelan Petroleum Industry. Statistical Data *see* Venezuela. Ministerio de Energia y Minas. Petroleo y Otros Datos Estadisticos *682*
Venga Que le Cuento... (AG) *576*
Ver Sacrum; Neue Hefte fuer Kunst und Literatur (AU ISSN 0083-5463) *79, 576*
Verba Seniorum (IT) *261, 768*
Verbaende, Behoerden, Organisationen der Wirtschaft (GW ISSN 0085-7661) *190*
Verband der Automobilindustrie. Jahresbericht (GW) *872*
Verband der Automobilindustrie. Taetigkeitsbericht *see* Verband der Automobilindustrie. Jahresbericht *872*
Verband der Kraftfahrzeugteile- und Zweiradgrosshaendler e.V. Jahrbuch *see* V K G Jahrbuch *872*
Verband der Kraftfahrzeugteile- und Zweiradgrosshaendler e.V. Jahrbuch *see* V K G Jahrbuch *872*
Verband der Versicherungsunternehmungen Oesterreichs. Bericht ueber das Geschaeftsjahr *see* Verband der Versicherungsunternehmungen Oesterreichs. Geschaeftsbericht *810*
Verband der Versicherungsunternehmungen Oesterreichs. Geschaeftsbericht (AU) *810*
Verde Yerba (SP) *582*
Verdi (IT ISSN 0042-3734) *436, 664*
Vereeniging der Antwerpsche Bibliophielen. Publications (BE) *916*
Verein Deutscher Zementwerke. Forschungsinstitut der Zementindustrie. Taetigkeitsbericht (GW ISSN 0507-6714) *139*
Verein fuer Geschichte der Stadt Nuernberg. Mitteilungen (GW ISSN 0083-5579) *464*
Verein fuer Geschichte der Stadt Wien. Jahrbuch (AU) *464*
Verein fuer Hamburgische Geschichte. Zeitschrift (GW ISSN 0083-5587) *464*
Verein fuer Luebeckische Geschichte und Altertumskunde. Zeitschrift (GW ISSN 0083-5609) *464*
Verein fuer Niedersaechsisches Volkstum. Mitteilungen (GW) *394*
Verein fuer Vaterlaendische Naturkunde in Wuerttemberg. Jahresheft *see* Gesellschaft fuer Naturkunde in Wuerttemberg. Jahreshefte *103*
Verein fuer Volkskunde in Wien. Sonderschriften. (AU) *55, 79, 403*
Verein fuer Wasser-, Boden- und Lufthygiene. Schriftenreihe (GW ISSN 0300-8665) *279, 389*
Verein zum Schutz der Bergwelt. Jahrbuch (GW) *279*
Verein zum Schutze der Alpenpflanzen und Tiere. Jahrbuch *see* Verein zum Schutz der Bergwelt. Jahrbuch *279*
Vereinigte Evangelisch-Lutherische Kirche Deutschlands. Amtsblatt (GW ISSN 0083-5633) *773*
Vereinigung Deutscher Elektrizitaetswerke e.V. Arbeitsbericht *see* V D E W Arbeitsbericht *359*
Vereinigung Freunde der Universitaet Mainz. Jahrbuch (GW ISSN 0083-565X) *342*
Vereinigung Pro Sihltal. Blaetter (SZ ISSN 0083-5641) *464*

Vereinigung Schweizerischer Strassenfachmaenner. Versuchsbericht (SZ) *872*
Vereinigung von Afrikanisten in Deutschland. Schriften (GW ISSN 0341-275X) *441*
Vereniging tot Bevordering der Kennis van de Antieke Beschaving. Bulletin *see* Bulletin Antieke Beschaving *431*
Vereniging van Nederlandse Gemeenten. Blauwe Reeks (NE) *750*
Vereniging van Nederlandse Gemeenten. Groene Reeks (NE) *750*
Vereniging voor Arbeidsrecht. Geschriften (NE) *212*
Verfassung und Verfassungswirklichkeit (GW ISSN 0083-5676) *520, 717*
Verfassungsgeschichte (SZ) *464, 520*
Vergilian Society Newsletter (US) *261*
Vergilius (US ISSN 0506-7294) *261*
Verhandlungen des Deutschen Geographentages (GW ISSN 0083-5684) *427*
Verifiche e Proposte (IT) *494*
Verified Directory of Manufacturers' Representatives (US ISSN 0083-5692) *243*
Verkehrspsychologischer Informationsdienst (AU ISSN 0042-4048) *755, 876*
Verkehrswirtschaftliche Zahlen *see* V W Z *876*
Vermessungs-Informationen/Surveying News/Informations Topografiques (GE) *377*
Vermont. Agricultural Experiment Station, Burlington. Research Report (US ISSN 0083-5706) *22*
Vermont. Agricultural Experiment Station, Burlington. Station Bulletin Series (US ISSN 0083-5714) *22*
Vermont. Agricultural Experiment Station, Burlington. Station Pamphlet Series (US ISSN 0083-5722) *22*
Vermont. Commissioner of Banking and Insurance. Annual Report of the Bank Commissioner (US ISSN 0083-5730) *177*
Vermont. Department of Employment Security. Statistical Tables (US ISSN 0095-1382) *166*
Vermont. Geological Survey. Bulletin (US ISSN 0083-5757) *302*
Vermont. Geological Survey. Special Publication (US ISSN 0083-5765) *302*
Vermont, Agricultural Experiment Station, Burlington. Miscellaneous Publications Series *see* Vermont. Agricultural Experiment Station, Burlington. Research Report *22*
Vermont Children's Magazine (US) *258*
Vermont Directory of Manufacturers (US) *243*
Vermont Educational Directory (US) *325*
Vermont Facts and Figures (US ISSN 0092-5144) *849*
Vermont Industrial Development Authority. Annual Report (US ISSN 0363-2067) *226*
Vermont Media Directory (US) *6, 268, 505*
Vermont Resources Research Center Series (US) *389, 747*
Vermont State Industrial Directory (US ISSN 0098-6208) *243*
Vermont Year Book (US ISSN 0083-5781) *473*
Vermouth (UK) *582*
Vernon's City of Guelph (Ontario) Directory (CN ISSN 0317-2961) *243*
Veroeffentlichungen der Astronomischen Institute der Univeritaet Bonn (GW ISSN 0340-9821) *85*
Veroeffentlichungen des Max-Reger-Institutes (GW ISSN 0543-1735) *664*
Veroeffentlichungen zur Geschichte des Glases und der Glashuetter in Deutschland (GW ISSN 0170-3447) *245*

Veroeffentlichungen zur Musikforschung (GW) 664
Veroeffentlichungen zur Volkskunde und Kulturgeschichte (GE) 403
Verschollene und Vergessene (GW ISSN 0170-3633) 576
Verse Speaking Anthology (UK ISSN 0033-582X) 916
Verstaendliche Wissenschaft (US ISSN 0033-5846) 793
Versuchstierkunde (GW ISSN 0300-1016) 131, 612
Versus (CN ISSN 0384-868X) 576
Vertebrate Pest Conference. Proceedings (US ISSN 0507-6773) 46
Vertebratologicke Zpravy/Notulae Vertebratologicae (CS ISSN 0506-7847) 131
Vervoer- en Padoorsigte see Transport and Road Digest 876
Verzameling van Middelnederlandse Bijbelteksten (NE) 576
Verzeichnis der Orientalischen Handschriften in Deutschland (GW ISSN 0506-7936) 671
Verzeichnis der Orientalischen Handschriften in Deutschland. Supplementbaende (GW ISSN 0506-7944) 671
Verzeichnis Lieferbarer Buecher/German Books in Print (GW ISSN 0057-8899) 96
Vestcijk Kroniek (NE) 576
Vesteuropa Frimaerkekatalog see A F A Vesteuropa Frimaerkekatalog 478
Veter Stranstvii (UR) 576
Veterinaria Tropical (VE) 895
Veterinary College of Norway. Annual Report see Norges Veterinaerhoegskole. Aarsberetning 895
Veterinary Index see Accumulative Veterinary Index 895
Veterinary Surgeons in New Zealand (NZ) 895
Vetus Testamentum. Supplements (NE ISSN 0083-5889) 768
Vetus Testamentum Coptice (GW) 475
Vexilum (CN ISSN 0316-2508) 261
Via (US) 70
Via Domitia (FR ISSN 0563-9786) 554
Viaggi Intorno Alla Tavola (IT) 480
Vialicad Argentina (AG) 747
Viator (US ISSN 0083-5897) 436
Vibrational Spectra and Structure (NE ISSN 0090-1911) 256
Vicino Oriente (IT) 475, 671
Victoria. Ministry of Fuel and Power. the Petroleum and Gas Industries in Victoria: Statistical Review see Victoria, Australia. Department of Minerals and Energy. The Petroleum and Gas Industries in Victoria. Statistical Review 682
Victoria. State Film Centre. New Films (AT) 651
Victoria, Australia. Department of Agriculture. Pig Industry Branch. Pig Farm Management Study (AT ISSN 0083-5951) 46
Victoria, Australia. Department of Agriculture. Poultry Branch. Poultry Farm Management Study (AT ISSN 0083-596X) 46
Victoria, Australia. Department of Minerals and Energy. The Petroleum and Gas Industries in Victoria. Statistical Review (AT) 682
Victoria, Australia. Department of Youth, Sport and Recreation. Report (AT) 822
Victoria, Australia. Directory of Government Departments and Authorities see Victorian Government Directory 747
Victoria, Australia. Education Department. Curriculum and Research Branch. Research Reports (AT ISSN 0085-7726) 351
Victoria, Australia. Forests Commission. Bulletin (AT ISSN 0085-7742) 411
Victoria, Australia. Forests Commission. Forestry Technical Papers (AT ISSN 0083-5978) 411
Victoria, Australia. Geological Survey. Bulletin (AT ISSN 0085-7750) 302

Victoria, Australia. Geological Survey. Memoirs (AT ISSN 0085-7769) 302
Victoria, Australia. Geological Survey. Reports (AT) 302
Victoria, Australia. National Museum of Victoria. Memoirs (AT ISSN 0083-5986) 655
Victoria, Australia. State Electricity Commission. Science Report (AT) 359
Victoria, British Columbia. Dominion Astrophysical Observatory. Publications (CN ISSN 0078-6950) 85, 699
Victoria League for Commonwealth Friendship. Annual Report (UK ISSN 0083-601X) 810
Victoria University of Manchester. Faculty of Arts. Publications (UK ISSN 0083-6028) 79
Victoria University of Wellington. Awards Handbook (NZ ISSN 0083-6036) 325
Victoria University of Wellington. Vice-Chancellor's Report (NZ) 342
Victoria University of Wellington Zoology Publications (NZ ISSN 0083-6060) 131
Victorian Bar Council. Annual Report (AT) 520
Victorian Chamber of Manufacturers File see V. C. M. File 180
Victorian Government Directory (AT ISSN 0158-1589) 747
Victorian Society. Annual (UK ISSN 0083-6079) 70
Victorian Society. Conference Reports (UK ISSN 0083-6087) 436
Victorian Veterinary Proceedings (AT) 895
Victorians Institute Journal (US) 494
Vicus Cuadernos: Arqueologia, Antropologia Cultural, Etnologia (NE) 55, 67
Vicus Cuadernos: Linguistica (NE ISSN 0165-7666) 554
Vida das Artes (BL) 79
Vida Local. Boletin de Informacion (SP) 750
Video Bluebook see Videolog: Programs for Business and Industry 268
Video Bluebook see Videolog: Programs for General Interest and Entertainment 268
Video Directory: Programs for Business and Industry see Videolog: Programs for Business and Industry 268
Video Directory: Programs for General Interest and Entertainment see Videolog: Programs for General Interest and Entertainment 268
Video Directory: Programs for Health Sciences see Videolog: Programs for the Health Sciences 268
Video Exchange Directory (CN) 268
Video Register (US) 243, 651
Videolog: Programs for Business and Industry (US) 268
Videolog: Programs for General Interest and Entertainment (US) 268
Videolog: Programs for the Health Sciences (US) 268
Videoplay Program Source Guide (US) 268
Videorecordings Available in the Public Libraries of Metropolitan Toronto (CN ISSN 0707-2031) 269, 538
Videozine (US) 79
Vie des Affaires (FR ISSN 0083-6095) 217, 747
Vie Montante. Edition Canadienne (CN ISSN 0382-4926) 768
Vie Musicale en France Sous les Rois Bourbons. Serie 1: Etudes (FR ISSN 0083-6109) 664
Vie Musicale en France Sous les Rois Bourbons. Serie 2: Recherches sur la Musique Classique Francaise (FR ISSN 0083-6117) 664
Vie Quotidienne en U.R.S.S. Prise sur le Vif see Sovetskie Ljudi Segodnja 573
Vienna. Universitaet. Institut fuer Theaterwissenschaft. Wissenschaftliche Reihe see Wiener Forschungen zur Theater und Medienwissenschaft 860

Vienna Circle Collection (NE) 98, 464
Viennese Slavonic Yearbook see Wiener Slavistisches Jahrbuch 554
Vierteljahrschrift fuer Sozial-und Wirtschaftsgeschichte. Beihefte (GW ISSN 0341-0846) 192, 436, 802
Vietnam. Directorate of Archives and Libraries. Catalogue of Books (VN) 538
Vietnamese Studies (VN ISSN 0085-7823) 446, 802
A View of University Financing (CN) 328
Viewpoint (US) 719, 817
Viewpoints (US) 394
Viewpoints (Chicago) (US) 274
Viking (NO) 67
Viking (US ISSN 0095-5744) 342
Viking (Northfield) see Viking 342
Viking Critical Library (US) 576
Viking Retrospect see Viking 342
Viking Society for Northern Research. Saga Book (UK ISSN 0305-9219) 465
Viking Society for Northern Research. Text Series (UK ISSN 0083-6257) 576
Vile see Vile International 558
Vile International (US) 558
Villa Guide (UK ISSN 0083-6273) 483
Vilne Slovo Annual (CN) 394
Vincentian Studies (US ISSN 0083-6281) 916
Vinculos (CR) 55
Vinculum (AT) 351, 591
Vintage Aircraft Directory (UK) 10, 476
Vintage Auto Almanac (US ISSN 0363-4639) 476, 872
Viola da Gamba Society of America Journal (US ISSN 0507-0252) 664
Violations of Human Rights in Soviet Occupied Lithuania (US ISSN 0360-7453) 520
Virgil Society. Proceedings (UK ISSN 0083-629X) 261
Virgin Islands (U.S.) Bureau of Libraries, Museums and Archaeological Services. Occasional Paper Series (VI) 473
Virgin Islands Register (US ISSN 0092-1270) 747
Virginia. Agricultural Opportunities Development Program. Annual Report (US ISSN 0362-6490) 916
Virginia. Criminal Justice Officers Training and Standards Commission. Biennial Report see Virginia. Criminal Justice Services Commission. Annual Report 520
Virginia. Criminal Justice Services Commission. Annual Report (US) 284, 520
Virginia. Department of Labor and Industry. Division of Research and Statistics. Occupational Injuries and Illnesses by Industry (US ISSN 0095-8174) 496
Virginia. Division of Mineral Resources. Publications (US) 302, 647
Virginia. Division of Product and Industry Regulation. Inspection Service Section. Annual Report (US ISSN 0362-3661) 22
Virginia. Employment Commission. Annual Planning Report (US) 212
Virginia. Employment Commission. Annual Report (US) 212
Virginia. Employment Commission. Annual Rural Manpower Report (US) 212
Virginia. Employment Commission. Labor Market Trends (US) 212
Virginia. Employment Commission. Manpower Research Division. Economic Assumptions (US ISSN 0095-3075) 190
Virginia. State Library. Publications (US ISSN 0083-6524) 473
Virginia. State Water Control Board. Annual Report (US ISSN 0095-1978) 389, 899
Virginia. State Water Control Board. Basic Data Bulletin (US) 899
Virginia. State Water Control Board. Information Bulletin (US) 899

Virginia. State Water Control Board. Planning Bulletin (US) 899
Virginia. Water Resources Research Center. Bulletin (US) 899
Virginia Baptist Register (US ISSN 0083-6311) 773
Virginia Educational Directory (US ISSN 0083-6354) 325
Virginia Highway and Transportation Conference. Proceedings (US) 377, 876
Virginia Highway Conference. Procceedings see Virginia Highway and Transportation Conference. Proceedings 876
Virginia Historical Society. Documents (US ISSN 0083-6389) 473
Virginia Independence Bicentennial Publications see Revolutionary Virginia: the Road to Independence 471
Virginia Institute of Marine Science, Gloucester Point. Data Reports (US ISSN 0083-6419) 109
Virginia Institute of Marine Science, Gloucester Point. Educational Series (US ISSN 0083-6427) 109
Virginia Institute of Marine Science, Gloucester Point. Marine Resources Advisory Series (US ISSN 0083-6435) 109
Virginia Institute of Marine Science, Gloucester Point. Special Report in Applied Marine Science and Ocean Engineering (US) 313
Virginia Institute of Marine Science, Gloucester Point. Special Scientific Report (US ISSN 0083-6443) 109
Virginia Institute of Marine Science, Gloucester Point. Translation Series. (US ISSN 0083-6397) 109
Virginia Legal Studies (US) 520
Virginia Military Institute, Lexington. Publications, Theses, and Dissertations of the Staff and Faculty(US ISSN 0083-6451) 328, 641
Virginia Outdoors Plan (US) 831
Virginia Place Name Society. Occasional Papers (US ISSN 0083-646X) 554
Virginia Polytechnic Institute and State University. Department of Geological Sciences. Geological Guidebooks. (US ISSN 0507-1259) 302
Virginia Polytechnic Institute and State University. Research Division. Bulletins on Scale Insects (US) 122
Virginia Polytechnic Institute and State University. Research Division. Report (US ISSN 0097-1510) 22
Virginia Polytechnic Institute and State University. Review (US ISSN 0190-3233) 576
Virginia Polytechnic Institute and State University. Wood Research and Wood Construction Laboratory. Special Report (US ISSN 0083-6508) 139, 413
Virginia Polytechnic Institute, Blacksburg, Engineering Extension Division. Geological Guidebook see Virginia Polytechnic Institute and State University. Department of Geological Sciences. Geological Guidebooks 302
Virginia Port Authority. Board of Commissioners. Annual Report (US ISSN 0083-6532) 198, 881
Virginia Port Authority. Foreign Trade Annual Report: The Ports of Virginia(US ISSN 0083-6516) 198, 881
Virginia State Library News (US) 538
Virginia State Publications in Print (US ISSN 0507-102X) 96
Virginia Union List of Biomedical Serials (US ISSN 0083-6540) 603
Virginia's Common Wealth see Virginia Outdoors Plan 831
Virginia's Supply of Public School Instructional Personnel (US ISSN 0083-6575) 342
Virology Monographs/Virusforschung in Einzeldarstellungen (US ISSN 0083-6591) 124, 608
Virusforschung in Einzeldarstellungen see Virology Monographs 124
Vishva Vicharamala (II) 446, 671

Vishveshvaranand Indological Paper Series (II ISSN 0083-6613) 446
Vishveshvaranand Indological Series (II ISSN 0083-6621) 446, 554
Vishveshvaranand Vedic Research Institute. Research and General Publications (II) 446, 672
Vision (CN ISSN 0382-0424) 707
Vision Index (US ISSN 0049-6510) 4, 603
Visit California with Fyfe Robertson (UK ISSN 0260-910X) 893
Visiti Iz Sarseliu (FR ISSN 0083-6672) 802
Vissha Geodeziia (BU) 302
Vistas for Volunteers (CN) 481, 810
Vistas in Plant Sciences (II) 119
Visual Education Yearbook (UK ISSN 0083-6680) 916
Visual Observations of Artificial Earth Satellites in Finland see Finnish Meteorological Institute. Observations of Satellites. Visual Observations of Artificial Earth Satellites in Finland 8
Vita Evangelica (CN ISSN 0507-1690) 768
Vital and Health Statistics Monographs (US) 755
Vital Statistics, Idaho see Idaho. Department of Health and Welfare. Annual Summary of Vital Statistics 841
Vital Statistics Japan see Japan. Ministry of Health and Welfare. Statistics and Information Department. Vital Statistics 842
Vital Statistics of Iowa (US) 849
Vital Statistics of the Province of British Columbia (CN) 849
Vital Statistics of the United States (US ISSN 0083-6710) 730, 755
Vitamins and Hormones: Advances in Research and Applications (US ISSN 0083-6729) 601, 686
Vivaldi Informations (DK) 664
Vivante Eglise (FR) 768
Vivat Hussar (FR) 640
Vivre le Cinema (FR) 651
Vizgazdalkodas es Kornyezetvedelem (HU) 279, 899
Vizminosegi es Viztechnologiai Kutatasi Eredmenyek/Research in Water Quality and Water Technology (HU) 899
Vlastivedny Zbornik (CS) 465, 494
Vocational Education Evaluation Report see Connecticut. Advisory Council on Vocational and Career Education. Vocational Education Evaluation Report 316
Vocational-Technical Education Programs see Pennsylvania State Plan for the Administration of Vocational-Technical Education Programs 329
Vodni Problemi (BU) 381, 899
Voelkerkundliche Abhandlungen (GW ISSN 0073-0270) 55
Voelkerkundliche Veroeffentlichungen (AU) 55
Vogue Beauty & Health Guide (US ISSN 0161-2190) 85, 695
Voice of History (NP) 446
Voices - Israel (IS) 582
Voix dans le Monde (FR ISSN 0083-6826) 576
Vojni Muzej, Belgrade. Vesnik/Military Museum, Belgrade. Bulletin (YU ISSN 0067-5660) 640
Volhynian Bibliographic Center. Publications (US ISSN 0083-6834) 96, 403, 465
Volhynian Bibliographic Center, Proceedings see Volhynian Bibliographic Center. Publications 465
Volkskundliche Studien (AU) 403
Volkslied, Volkstanz, Volksmusik see Oesterreichisches Volksliedwerk. Jahrbuch 662
Volkstum der Schweiz (GW ISSN 0083-6877) 403
Volleyball Guide see N A G W S Guide. Volleyball 825
Volleyball Rules (US) 826
Vollschlank (GE ISSN 0083-6893) 262
Volund (NO ISSN 0048-2277) 655

Voluntary Action Research Series (US) 817
Voluntary Social Services (UK ISSN 0083-6907) 810
Vom Wasser (US ISSN 0083-6915) 248, 899
Von Karman Institute for Fluid Dynamics. Lecture Series (BE) 381
Vooraziatisch-Egyptisch Genootschap "Ex Oriente Lux". Mededelingen en Verhandelingen (NE) 67, 446
Voprosy Bibliografii (UR) 96
Voprosy Ekonomiki Narodnogo Khozyaistva Murmanskoi Oblasti (UR) 151
Voprosy Ekonomiki Sel'skogo Khozyaistva Dal'nego Vostoka (UR) 32
Voprosy Elektroniki Tverdogo Tela (UR) 359
Voprosy Fiziki Tverdogo Tela (UR ISSN 0301-6919) 699
Voprosy Geografii (UR) 427
Voprosy Gidrodinamiki i Teploobmena v Kriogennykh Sistemakh (UR) 700, 701
Voprosy Informatsionnoi Teorii i Praktiki (UR) 538
Voprosy Inzhenernoi Geologii i Gruntovedeniya (UR) 383
Voprosy Istorii Dal'nego Vostoka, Khabarovsk, Gos. Ped. Institut (UR) 465
Voprosy Khimii i Khimicheskoi Tekhnologii (UR) 256
Voprosy Kritiki Burzhuaznoi Politiki i Ideologii. Sbornik Nauchnykh Trudov (UR) 717
Voprosy Radiobiologii i Biologicheskogo Deistviya Tsitostaticheskikh Preparatov (UR) 109, 622
Voprosy Russkogo Yazykoznaniya (UR) 554
Voprosy Statistiki (UR) 849
Voprosy Teatra (UR ISSN 0507-3952) 860
Voprosy Teorii Razrabotki Mestorozhdenii Poleznykh Iskopaemykh (UR) 371
Voprosy Teorii Sistem Avtomaticheskogo Upravleniya (UR) 274
Voprosy Uchebno-vospitatel'noi Raboty v Samodeyatel'nykh Kollektivakh (UR) 664
Vorreformationsgeschichtliche Forschungen (GW ISSN 0083-6923) 768
Vortraege aus der Praktischen Chirurgie see Praktische Chirurgie 625
Vortraege und Aufsaetze see Schriften zur Kooperationsforschung. Vortraege 181
Voyager Series (US) 576
Voyages Entre le Canada et les Autres Pays see Travel Between Canada and Other Countries 893
Voyages to the Inland Sea (US) 582
Vsesoyuznyi Nauchno-Issledovatel'skii Institut Transportnogo Stroitel'stva. Trudy (UR) 864
Vsesoyuznyi Nauchno-Issledovatel'skii Institut Morskogo Rybnogo Khozyaistva i Okeanografii (Vniro). Trudy (UR) 313
Vsesoyuznyi Nauchno-issledovatel'skii Institut Vagonostroeniya. Trudy (UR) 874
Vsesoyuznyi Nauchno-Issledovatel'skii Institut Zernovogo Khozyaistva. Trudy. (UR) 40
Vulkaniseur-Jahrbuch (GW ISSN 0083-694X) 778
Vyberova Anotovana Bibliografie Studijnich Materialu (CS) 266
Vyberova Bibliografia Muzeologickej Literatury (CS) 96, 656
Vysoka Skola Banska. Sbornik Vedeckych Praci: Rada Hutnicka/Institute of Mining and Metallurgy. Transactions: Metallurgical Series (CS ISSN 0042-3726) 630
Vysoka Skola Banska. Sbornik Vedeckych Praci: Rada Strojni (CS) 371
Vysoka Skola Lesnicka a Drevarska vo Zvolene. Lesnicka Fakulta. Zbornik Vedeckych Prac see Acta Facultatis Forestalis, Zvolen 407

Vyzkumny Ustav Spoju. Sbornik Praci (CS) 874
W. A. Cargill Memorial Lectures in Fine Art (UK ISSN 0512-4638) 79
W A P E T Journal (West Australian Petroleum Pty. Ltd.) (AT ISSN 0310-7787) 682
W B K (Univeritaet Karlsruhe, Institut fuer Werkzeugmaschinen und Betriebstechnik) (US) 371
W. C. J. Meredith Memorial Lectures (CN ISSN 0509-5166) 747
W C O T P Annual Report (World Confederation of Organizations of the Teaching Profession) (SZ ISSN 0084-1528) 345
W C O T P Theme Study (World Confederation of Organizations of the Teaching Profession) (SZ ISSN 0512-252X) 325
W. E. L. (Victoria) Papers (Women's Electoral Lobby (Victoria)) (AT ISSN 0310-9496) 901
W E M A Bezugsquellenverzeichnis (GW) 630
W E M A Directory see American Electronics Association Directory 351
W E S C O N Conference Record (Western Electronic Show and Convention) (US) 359
W E S C O N Technical Papers see W E S C O N Conference Record 359
W E S T Newsletter see W E S T Telememo 269
W E S T Telememo (Western Educational Society for Telecommunications) (US) 269
W G A Geschaeftsbericht (Wirtschaftsvereinigung Gross- und Aussenhandel) (GW ISSN 0042-966X) 198
W. H. Irons Memorial Lecture Series (US) 151
W H O Offset Publications (World Health Organization) (UN) 755, 757
W H O Technical Report Series (World Health Organization) (UN ISSN 0512-3054) 601, 755
W-Memo see American Public Welfare Association. W-Memo 803
W P S Professional Handbook Series (Western Psychological Services) (US ISSN 0083-8977) 739
W S N A Mini Journal see Washington Nurse 614
W.V.O.E.S. Annual Report (Office of Emergency Services) (US ISSN 0099-0671) 747
Wadsworth Accounting Series (US) 168
Wadsworth Botany Series (US) 119
Wadsworth Continuing Education Series (US) 330
Wadsworth Developmental Mathematics Series (US) 591
Wadsworth Guides to Literary Study (US) 576
Wadsworth Guides to Science Teaching(US) 351, 793
Wadsworth Music Series (US) 664
Wadsworth Series: Explorations in the Black Experience (US) 394
Wadsworth Series in American Politics (US) 717
Wadsworth Series in Analytic Ethnography (US) 55, 817
Wadsworth Series in Chemistry (US) 248
Wadsworth Series in Curriculum and Instruction (US) 351
Wadsworth Series in Finance (US) 177
Wadsworth Series in Labor Economics and Industrial Relations (US) 212
Wadsworth Series in Sociology (US) 817
Wadsworth Series in Special Education (US) 347
Wadsworth Series in World Politics (US) 725
Wadsworth Studies in Philosophical Criticism (US) 692
Waelzlagertechnik (GW ISSN 0511-0653) 50
Waermelehre und Waermewirtschaft in Einzeldarstellungen (GE ISSN 0083-6982) 916

WAS KOSTET 1531

Wages and Total Labour Costs for Workers: International Survey (SW) 212
Wages for Housewark. Campaign Bulletin (CN) 901
Wagga Wagga and District Historical Society. Journal (AT ISSN 0085-7858) 447
Waigani Seminar. Papers (PP ISSN 0085-7866) 447
Wakayama-ken Kisho Nenpo see Wakayama Prefecture. Annual Report of Meteorology 635
Wakayama Prefecture. Annual Report of Meteorology/Wakayama-ken Kisho Nenpo (JA) 635
Waking and Sleeping (GW ISSN 0340-0905) 621
Waksman Foundation of Japan. Report (JA ISSN 0509-5832) 686
Walch's Tasmanian Almanac see Tasmanian Almanac 447
Walden's A B C Guide and Paper Production Yearbook (US ISSN 0083-7024) 675
Wales. National Library. Handlist on Manuscripts in the National Library of Wales (UK ISSN 0065-0293) 538
Walia (ET ISSN 0083-7059) 279
Walk (AT) 831
Walker-Ames Lectures (US) 436
Walker Art Museum. Bulletin see Bowdoin College. Museum of Art. Occasional Papers 652
Walker's Manual of Western Corporations (US ISSN 0092-749X) 205
Walker's Manual of Western Corporations & Securities see Walker's Manual of Western Corporations 205
Walker's Old Moore's Almanac (UK ISSN 0083-7067) 361
Walks and Trails in Scotland (UK) 893
Wall see Washington and Jefferson Literary Journal 576
Wall Street Journal Index (US ISSN 0083-7075) 177, 205
Wallraf-Richartz-Jahrbuch; Westdeutsches Jahrbuch fuer Kunstgeschichte (GW ISSN 0083-7105) 80
Walter Lynwood Fleming Lectures in Southern History (US ISSN 0083-7121) 473
Walter Neurath Memorial Lectures (US ISSN 0085-7874) 80
Walter Prescott Webb Memorial Lectures (US ISSN 0083-713X) 436
Walter W. S. Cook Alumni Lecture (US ISSN 0083-7148) 80
Walters Art Gallery. Journal (US ISSN 0083-7156) 80
War and Society (US ISSN 0361-0373) 640
War Peace Bibliography Series (US) 718
Warburg Institute. Studies (UK ISSN 0083-7199) 494
Ward-Phillips Lectures in English Language and Literature (US ISSN 0083-7210) 576
Ward's Automotive Yearbook (US ISSN 0083-7229) 872
Ward's Bulletin (US ISSN 0043-0323) 325, 793
Ward's Who's Who Among U.S. Motor Vehicle Manufacturers (US) 872
Warehousing/Distribution Directory (US) 882
Warwick Economic Research Papers (UK ISSN 0083-7350) 151
Warwick Industrial Economic and Business Research Papers (UK) 151
Warwick Research Industrial and Business Studies see Warwick Industrial Economic and Business Research Papers 151
Was Heisst Gut Leben? see Arbeitsgemeinschaft fuer Lebensniveauvergleiche. Schriftenreihe 796
Was Kostet der Geschaeftswagen? (GW) 872
Was Kostet Mein Auto? see Was Kostet der Geschaeftswagen 872

Waseda Business and Economic Studies(JA) *151*
Waseda Daigaku Rikogakubu Kiyo *see* Waseda University. School of Science and Engineering. Memoirs *794*
Waseda Political Studies (JA ISSN 0511-196X) *717*
Waseda University. Casting Research Laboratory. Report (JA ISSN 0511-1927) *630*
Waseda University. School of Science and Engineering. Memoirs/Waseda Daigaku Rikogakubu Kiyo (JA) 371, *794*
Waseda University. Science and Engineering Research Laboratory. Report (JA) 371, *794*
Washington (US ISSN 0083-7393) *473*
Washington (State). Attorney General's Office. Charitable Trust Directory (US) *810*
Washington (State). Attorney General's Office. Directory of Charitable Organizations and Trusts Registered with the Office of Attorney General *see* Washington (State). Attorney General's Office. Charitable Trust Directory *810*
Washington (State). Department of Ecology. Water Quality Assessment Report (US ISSN 0362-6369) *389*
Washington (State). Department of Ecology. Water Supply Bulletins (US) *899*
Washington (State) Department of Fisheries. Technical Report (US ISSN 0083-7474) *400*
Washington (State). Department of Motor Vehicles. Research and Technology. Research Report (US ISSN 0092-3583) *872*
Washington (State). Department of Natural Resources. Annual Fire Statistics (US) *412, 849*
Washington (State). Department of Revenue. Forest Tax Report (US ISSN 0362-7462) *233, 411*
Washington (State). Department of Revenue. Research and Information Division. Comparative State/Local Taxes (US) *233*
Washington (State). Department of Revenue. Research and Information Division. Property Tax Levy and Collection Statistics (US) *233*
Washington (State). Division of Geology and Earth Resources. Bulletin (US) *302*
Washington (State) Division of Geology and Earth Resources. Information Circular (US ISSN 0147-1783) 302, *647*
Washington (State) Game Department. Applied Research Section. Bulletin (US ISSN 0095-3253) *822*
Washington (State). Human Resources Agencies. Annual Report (US ISSN 0091-4312) *810*
Washington (State). Indian Assistance Division. Indian Economic Employment Assistance Program. Annual Report (US ISSN 0360-4837) 212, *394*
Washington (State) Legislature. Pictorial Directory (US ISSN 0091-8253) *747*
Washington (State) Legislature. Transportation Committee. Report (US ISSN 0095-6082) 520, *864*
Washington (State). Natural Areas Advisory Committee. Biennial Report (US ISSN 0362-8906) *279*
Washington (State) Natural Resources and Recreation Agencies. Annual Report (US ISSN 0090-2497) *279, 893*
Washington (State) Office of Financial Management. Forecasting and Support Division. Population Trends (US) *730*
Washington (State) Office of Program Planning and Fiscal Management. Population and Enrollment Section. Population Trends *see* Washington (State) Office of Financial Management. Forecasting and Support Division. Population Trends *730*

Washington (State) Parks and Recreation Commission. Annual Report *see* Washington (State) Natural Resources and Recreation Agencies. Annual Report *279*
Washington (State). Transportation Agencies. Annual Report (US ISSN 0091-4967) *864*
Washington (State). Vocational Rehabilitation Services Division. State Facilities Development Plan (US) *347*
Washington (State). Vocational Rehabilitation Services Division. State Facilities Plan *see* Washington (State). Vocational Rehabilitation Services Division. State Facilities Development Plan *347*
Washington (State) Water Research Center, Pullman. Report (US ISSN 0083-7598) *899*
Washington Agricultural Statistics (US ISSN 0095-4330) *26*
Washington and Jefferson Literary Journal (US ISSN 0043-0455) *576, 582*
Washington Education Directory (US) *325*
Washington Folk Strums (US ISSN 0091-9020) *664*
Washington Information Directory (US) *474*
Washington Letter (US) 394, *717*
Washington Nurse (US) *614*
Washington Report on Federal Legislation for Children (US) *916*
Washington Report on Legislation for Children and What You Can do About It *see* Washington Report on Federal Legislation for Children *916*
Washington Representatives (US) *717*
Washington State Dental Journal (US ISSN 0083-7431) *610*
Washington State Entomological Society Proceedings (US ISSN 0043-0773) *122*
Washington State Horticultural Association. Proceedings (US) *416*
Washington State Industrial Directory (US) *243*
Washington State Traffic Accident Facts (US ISSN 0509-7967) *867*
Washington State University. Bureau of Economic and Business Research. Study (US ISSN 0083-7504) *151*
Washington University. Institute for Urban and Regional Studies. Working Paper (US ISSN 0085-798X) *488*
Washington Want Ads (US) 520, *668*
Wasser-Kalender (GW ISSN 0511-3520) *899*
Wasser und Abwasser in Forschung und Praxis (US ISSN 0512-5030) *899*
Wasserrecht und Wasserwirtschaft (GW ISSN 0508-1254) 520, *899*
Waste Management Research Abstracts(UN ISSN 0083-761X) *757*
Watch It (US) *390*
Watch Review. Curriculum *see* Montre Suisse. Annuaire *503*
Watchmaker, Jeweller and Silversmith Directory of Trade Names and Punch Marks (UK ISSN 0083-7628) *504*
Water (US ISSN 0083-7636) *899*
Water & Pollution Control. Directory and Handbook (CN ISSN 0318-0468) *899*
Water & Pollution Control Directory *see* Water & Pollution Control. Directory and Handbook *899*
Water and Power Development Consultancy Services. Annual Report and Statement of Accounts (II) *899*
Water Development Supply and Management (US) *899*
Water Engineer's Handbook *see* Water Services Handbook *381*
Water in Biological Systems (US ISSN 0083-7652) *109*
Water Japan/Suido Sangyo Shimbun (JA) *899*
Water Pollution: a Series of Monographs (US) *390*
Water Pollution Control Federation Conference. Abstracts of Technical Papers (US) 4, *390*

Water Pollution Control Plan (Springfield) *see* Illinois. Environmental Protection Agency. Water Pollution Control Plan *386*
Water Pollution Research (UK ISSN 0083-7660) *390*
Water Pollution Research *see* Water Research Centre. Annual Report *390*
Water Pollution Research Laboratory, Stevenage, England. Technical Papers(UK ISSN 0083-7679) *390*
Water Quality Assessment Report *see* Washington (State). Department of Ecology. Water Quality Assessment Report *389*
Water Quality Conference.Proceedings *see* Public Water Supply Engineers Conference (Proceedings) *388*
Water Quality Data for Ontario Streams & Lakes (CN ISSN 0383-5472) *390, 899*
Water Quality Instrumentation (US) *497, 899*
Water Quality Monitoring Data for Georgia Streams (US ISSN 0097-7519) *390*
Water Research Association. Report *see* Water Research Centre. Annual Report *390*
Water Research Centre. Annual Report (UK ISSN 0143-2443) *390*
Water Research Foundation of Australia. Bulletin *see* Water Research Foundation of Australia. Reports *899*
Water Research Foundation of Australia. Reports (AT ISSN 0085-8021) *899*
Water Resources Association of the Delaware River Basin. Alerting Bulletin (US) *899*
Water Resources Data for Puerto Rico (PR) *309, 899*
Water Resources Development Series (UN ISSN 0082-8130) *899*
Water-Resources Investigations *see* U. S. Geological Survey. Water Resources Investigations *308*
Water Resources Monographs (US) *899*
Water Resources Report Series (US) *899*
Water Resources Research in Virginia, Annual Report (US ISSN 0095-1250) *309, 899*
Water Resources Summary (US ISSN 0518-6374) *309, 899*
Water Services Handbook (UK ISSN 0307-1782) *381*
Water Transport Statistics of India (II) *881*
Water Works Manual *see* Public Works Manual *750*
Waterborne Commerce of the Port of Boston (US) *867*
Waterborne Commerce of the United States (US ISSN 0083-7725) *881*
Waterloo Historical Society. Report (CN ISSN 0083-7733) *474*
Waterway Guide (US) *827*
Watford and District Industrial History Society. Journal (UK ISSN 0307-5281) *465*
Watford and District Industrial History Society Bulletin *see* Watford and District Industrial History Society. Journal *465*
Watts News *see* T E C Report *359*
Wayne State University. Center for Economic Studies. Monographs (US) *190*
Wayne State University. Center for the Study of Cognitive Processes. Dissertations in Cognitive Processes (US ISSN 0083-7741) *739*
Wayne State University. Medical Library. Report *see* Wayne State University, Detroit. Medical School Library. Report *538*
Wayne State University, Detroit. Medical School Library. Report (US) *538, 601*
We Represent in Israel and Abroad. (IS ISSN 0302-5489) *198*
Weather Almanac (US) *635*
Weather Guide Calendar (US) *635*
Weather Guide Calendar Almanac *see* Weather Guide Calendar *635*

Weatherguide *see* Weather Guide Calendar *635*
Webbia; Raccolta di Scritti Botanici (IT ISSN 0083-7792) *119*
Wedgwood Society of London. Proceedings (UK ISSN 0511-4063) *245*
Weed Control Manual and Herbicide Guide (US ISSN 0511-411X) *40, 416*
Weed Science Society of America. Abstracts (US) *4, 26*
Weed Society of America. Abstracts *see* Weed Science Society of America. Abstracts *26*
Weed Society of New South Wales. Proceedings (AT ISSN 0085-803X) *40, 119*
Weekender (UK ISSN 0260-9061) *893*
Wees Veilig Tuis *see* Be Safe at Home *750*
Wege Vor- und Fruehgeschichtlicher Forschung (GW) *67*
Wehrwissenschaftliche Berichte *see* Bernard und Graefe Aktuell *638*
Weimarer Monographien zur Ur- und Fruehgeschichte (GE) *55, 67*
Weissbuch zur Sicherheit der Bundesrepublik Deutschland und zur Lage der Bundeswehr (GW) *640*
Weizmann Institute of Science, Rehovot, Israel. Scientific Activities (IS ISSN 0083-7849) *794, 854*
Welcome to Finland (DK ISSN 0085-8048) *893*
Welding (UK) *631*
Welding Data Book (US ISSN 0511-4365) *631*
Welfare Services in Nova Scotia *see* Social Services in Nova Scotia *809*
Wellesley Edition (US ISSN 0083-7881) *664*
Wellesley Edition Cantata Index Series (US ISSN 0083-7873) *664*
Wellesley Papers (CN) *725*
Wellsiana (UK) *576*
Welsh Amateur Swimming Association. Handbook (UK) *822*
Welsh Association of Youth Clubs. Yearbook of Activities (UK) *262*
Welsh Bibliographical Society. Journal (UK ISSN 0083-7911) *96*
Welsh Folk-Song Society. Journal *see* Canu Gwerin *658*
Welsh Pony and Cob Society Journal (UK) *828*
Welsh Soils Discussion Group. Report (UK ISSN 0083-7938) *40*
Welsh Studies in Education Series (UK ISSN 0083-7946) *325*
Weltstaedte der Kunst. Edition Leipzig/Great Centers of Art (GE ISSN 0083-7954) *80*
Wenner Gren Center International Symposium Series (US ISSN 0083-7989) *794*
Wenner-Gren Foundation for Anthropological Research. Report (US ISSN 0083-7997) *55*
Wer Baut Maschinen/Who Makes Machinery (GW ISSN 0083-9299) *383*
Wer ist Wer in der Schweiz und im Fuerstentum Liechtenstein? *see* Annuaire Suisse du Monde et des Affaires *70*
Wer Schreibt und Spricht worueber? *see* Journalisten-Handbuch *505*
Wer Schreibt worueber? Journalisten-Handbuch *see* Journalisten-Handbuch *505*
Werbe-Mittel Katalog (GW) *212*
Werbung in Deutschland *see* Jahrbuch der Werbung *653*
Werken und Wohnen (GW ISSN 0083-8047) *70*
Werkstattbuecher fuer Betriebsfachleute Konstrukteure und Studenten *see* Fertigung und Betrieb *222*
Werkstattpapiere (GW) *802*
Werkstoff- Forschung und -Technik *see* Materials Research and Engineering *628*
Werte Unserer Heimat (GE ISSN 0083-8063) *427, 628*
Wertheim Publications in Industrial Relations (US) *212*

Wesley W. Spink Lectures on Comparative Medicine (US) *601*
Wessex Cave Club Occasional Publication (UK ISSN 0083-811X) *302*
Wessex Geographical Year (UK ISSN 0083-8136) *427*
West Africa Annual (NR ISSN 0083-8144) *441*
West Africa Rice Development Association. Annual Report (LB) *40*
West Africa Rice Development Association. Current Bibliography (LB) *26, 96*
West African Archaeological Newsletter *see* West African Journal of Archaeology *67*
West African Institute of Social and Economic Research. Annual Report *see* Nigerian Institute of Social and Economic Research. Annual Report *799*
West African Journal of Archaeology (NR ISSN 0083-8160) *67*
West African Journal of Modern Languages/Revue Ouest Africaine des Langues Vivantes (NR ISSN 0331-0531) *554*
West African Journal of Pharmacology and Drug Research (NR ISSN 0303-691X) *686*
West Australian Petroleum Pty. Ltd. Journal *see* W A P E T Journal *682*
West Bengal. Bureau of Applied Economics and Statistics. Statistical Handbook (II ISSN 0511-5493) *849*
West Bengal Labour Gazette (II ISSN 0043-3071) *212*
West Canadian Research Publications of Geology and Related Sciences (CN ISSN 0083-8195) *290, 302*
West Coast British Columbia Construction Industry Directory. Purchasing Guide (CN) *139, 371*
West Coast Cancer Symposium. Proceedings (US) *606, 622*
West Coast Reliability Symposium (US ISSN 0083-8217) *217*
West European Living Costs (UK ISSN 0142-646X) *198*
West Georgia College Review (US ISSN 0043-3136) *263*
West Georgia College Studies in the Social Sciences (US ISSN 0081-8682) *802*
West Indies and Caribbean Year Book *see* Caribbean Year Book *884*
West Malaysia Annual Statistics of External Trade (MY ISSN 0085-8080) *166*
West Midland Bird Report (UK ISSN 0083-8241) *125, 279*
West Midlands Archives Newsletter (UK ISSN 0143-8158) *465*
West of Scotland Visitor (UK ISSN 0260-4426) *893*
West Tennessee Historical Society. Papers (US) *474*
West Texas Geological Society. Publications (US) *302*
West Virginia. Agricultural and Forestry Experiment Station. Bulletin (US) *22, 412*
West Virginia. Agricultural and Forestry Experiment Station. Resource Management Series (US) *22, 412*
West Virginia. Agricultural Experiment Station, Morgantown. Current Report(US ISSN 0083-8381) *22*
West Virginia. Commission on Aging. Annual Progress Report (US ISSN 0083-8438) *810*
West Virginia. Department of Commerce. Annual Report (US ISSN 0083-8454) *182*
West Virginia. Department of Mines. Annual Report (US) *647*
West Virginia. Department of Mines. Directory of Mines (US ISSN 0083-8462) *647*
West Virginia. Department of Natural Resources. Annual Report on the Comprehensive Water Resources Plan (US ISSN 0095-4659) *899*
West Virginia. Human Rights Commission. Report (US ISSN 0083-8594) *719*

West Virginia. Legislature. Purchasing Practices and Procedures Commission. Report to the West Virginia Legislature (US) *747*
West Virginia Archaeological Investigations *see* West Virginia Reports of Archaeological Investigations *67*
West Virginia Business Index *see* West Virginia Business Index. Annual Review Number *180*
West Virginia Business Index. Annual Review Number (US ISSN 0083-839X) *180*
West Virginia Coal Facts (US ISSN 0091-5513) *647*
West Virginia Coal-Geology Bulletins (US) *302, 647*
West Virginia Coal Mining Institute. Proceedings (US ISSN 0083-842X) *647*
West Virginia Economic Profile (US ISSN 0097-7675) *190*
West Virginia Education Directory (US ISSN 0085-8099) *325*
West Virginia Employment and Earnings Trends: Annual Summary (US) *212*
West Virginia Environmental Geology Bulletins (US) *302, 390*
West Virginia Field Trip Guides (US) *302*
West Virginia Geologic Education Series (US) *302*
West Virginia Geologic Investigations *see* West Virginia Reports of Geologic Investigations *302*
West Virginia Geological Survey. Archaeological Series (US ISSN 0083-8489) *916*
West Virginia Geological Survey. Bulletin (US ISSN 0083-8500) *916*
West Virginia Geological Survey. Circulars (US ISSN 0083-8519) *916*
West Virginia Geological Survey. Coal-Geology Bulletin *see* West Virginia Coal-Geology Bulletins *302*
West Virginia Geological Survey. Educational Series *see* West Virginia Geologic Education Series *302*
West Virginia Geological Survey. Environmental Geology Bulletin *see* West Virginia Environmental Geology Bulletins *390*
West Virginia Geological Survey. Field Trip Guide *see* West Virginia Field Trip Guides *302*
West Virginia Geological Survey. Geological Publications. Volumes (US ISSN 0083-8527) *916*
West Virginia Geological Survey. Mineral Resources Series *see* West Virginia Mineral Resources Series *647*
West Virginia Geological Survey. Newsletter *see* Mountain State Geology *297*
West Virginia Geological Survey. River Basin Basic Data Reports *see* West Virginia River Basin Basic Data Reports *302*
West Virginia Geological Survey. River Basin Bulletins *see* West Virginia River Basin Bulletins *302*
West Virginia Geological Survey. State Park Bulletins *see* West Virginia State Park Geology Bulletins *302*
West Virginia Mineral Resources Series (US) *647*
West Virginia Public Affairs Reporter (US) *747*
West Virginia Reports of Archaeological Investigations (US) *67*
West Virginia Reports of Geologic Investigations (US) *302*
West Virginia Research League. Statistical Handbook (US ISSN 0091-6102) *233*
West Virginia River Basin Basic Data Reports (US) *302*
West Virginia River Basin Bulletins (US) *302, 309*
West Virginia State Park Geology Bulletins (US) *302*
West Virginia Statistical Handbook (US ISSN 0511-6775) *748*
West Virginia Tax Calendar (US) *233*
West Virginia Union List of Serials (US ISSN 0512-4743) *96*

West Virginia University. Business and Economic Studies (US ISSN 0068-4392) *151*
West Virginia University. Center for Appalachian Studies and Development. Research Series *see* West Virginia University. Center for Extension and Continuing Education. Research Series *226*
West Virginia University. Center for Extension and Continuing Education. Research Series (US) *226*
West Virginia University. Engineering Experiment Station. Bulletin (US ISSN 0083-8640) *371*
West Virginia University. Engineering Experiment Station. Report (US ISSN 0083-8659) *371*
West Virginia's State System of Higher Education; Annual Report, Current Operating Revenues and Expenditures (US ISSN 0091-6196) *342*
Western Apparel Industry National Suppliers and Contractors Directory *see* National Apparel Suppliers and Contractors Directory *261*
Western Association of Fish and Wildlife Agencies. Proceedings (US) *279*
Western Association of Graduate Schools. Proceedings of the Annual Meeting (US ISSN 0511-6848) *342*
Western Association of Map Libraries. Occasional Papers (US) *538*
Western Association of State Game and Fish Commissioners. Proceedings *see* Western Association of Fish and Wildlife Agencies. Proceedings *279*
Western Australia. Conservation and Environment Council. Annual Report(AT) *279,* Western Australia. Annual Report(AT)
Western Australia. Department for Community Welfare. Annual Report (AT) *810*
Western Australia. Department of Agriculture. Animal Division. Annual Report (AT) *46*
Western Australia. Department of Agriculture. Bulletin (AT) *22*
Western Australia. Department of Agriculture. Division of Plant Production. Annual Report (AT) *40*
Western Australia. Department of Agriculture. Rangeland Management Section. Rangeland Bulletin (AT ISSN 0310-897X) *40*
Western Australia. Department of Agriculture. Rural Economics and Marketing Section. Report on the Market Milk Industry in Western Australia (AT) *32, 41*
Western Australia. Department of Agriculture. Technical Bulletin (AT ISSN 0083-8675) *23*
Western Australia. Department of Agriculture. Wheat and Sheep Division. Annual Report *see* Western Australia. Department of Agriculture. Division of Plant Production. Annual Report *40*
Western Australia. Department of Corrections. Annual Report (AT) *284*
Western Australia. Department of Fisheries and Wildlife. Fisheries Research Bulletin (AT) *400*
Western Australia. Department of Fisheries & Wildlife. Report (AT) *279, 400*
Western Australia. Department of Fisheries and Wildlife. Wildlife Research Bulletin (AT) *279*
Western Australia. Education Department. Schools & Staffing (AT) *345*
Western Australia. Environmental Protection Council. Annual Report *see* Western Australia. Conservation and Environment Council. Annual Report *279*
Western Australia. Fisheries and Fauna Department. Bulletin *see* Western Australia. Department of Fisheries and Wildlife. Fisheries Research Bulletin *400*
Western Australia. Forests Department. Bulletin (AT ISSN 0085-8129) *412*

Western Australia. Forests Department Research Paper (AT) *412*
Western Australia. Geological Survey. Annual Report (AT ISSN 0511-6996) *302*
Western Australia. Geological Survey. Bulletin (AT ISSN 0085-8137) *302*
Western Australia. Geological Survey. Report (AT ISSN 0085-8145) *302*
Western Australia. Government Chemical Laboratories. Report of Investigations (AT ISSN 0085-8153) *248*
Western Australia. Law Reform Commission. Annual Report (AT) *520*
Western Australia. Main Roads Department. Technical Report (AT ISSN 0310-6330) *876*
Western Australia. Major Investment Projects, Public and Private, Current and Proposed (AT ISSN 0511-6910) *226*
Western Australia. Office of Director General of Transport. Annual Report(AT ISSN 0083-8691) *864*
Western Australia. Public Library, Museum and Art Gallery. Record (AT) *655*
Western Australia. Seed Board. Chairman's Report (AT) *916*
Western Australia. State Energy Commission. Annual Report (AT) *364*
Western Australia. State Health Laboratory Services. Annual Report (AT) *755*
Western Australia. Technical Education Division. Handbook (AT) *342*
Western Australia. Transport Commission. Annual Report of the Commissioner of Transport (AT) *864*
Western Australia Law Almanac (AT ISSN 0085-8161) *520*
Western Australian Museum, Perth. Report of the Museum Board *see* Western Australian Museum, Perth. Annual Report *655*
Western Australia Vegetables (AT) *40, 416*
Western Australian Coastal Shipping Commission. Annual Report (AT) *881*
Western Australian Herbarium. Annual Report (AT) *119*
Western Australian Manufacturers Directory (AT) *243*
Western Australian Museum, Perth. Annual Report (AT) *655*
Western Australian Museum, Perth. Records (AT ISSN 0312-3162) *655*
Western Australian Museum, Perth. Records. Supplement (AT ISSN 0313-122X) *655*
Western Australian Museum, Perth. Special Publication (AT ISSN 0083-873X) *655*
Western Australian Naturalist Scientific Journal (AT) *794*
Western Australian Naturalists' Club, Perth. Handbook *see* Western Australian Naturalist Scientific Journal *794*
Western Australian Pocket Yearbook (AT ISSN 0083-8756) *190, 447*
Western Australian Potato Marketing Board. Annual Report (AT) *32, 40*
Western Australian Reports (AT ISSN 0083-8764) *521*
Western Australian Yearbook. New Series (AT ISSN 0083-8772) *190, 448*
Western Bank Directory (US ISSN 0272-5371) *177*
Western Canada Alaska Campbook (US) *893*
Western Canada and Alaska; Alberta, British Columbia, Manitoba, Saskatchewan, Northwest Territories, Yukon Territory and Alaska TourBook *see* Tourbook: Western Canada and Alaska *892*
Western Canadian Society for Horticulture. Report of Proceedings of Annual Meeting (CN ISSN 0083-8810) *416*

Western Canadian Steam Locomotive Directory (CN ISSN 0085-8188) *874*
Western Conferences on Linguistics. Proceedings of the Annual Meeting (CN) *554*
Western Dry Kiln Clubs. Proceedings (US) *413*
Western Educational Society for Telecommunications Telememo *see* W E S T Telememo *269*
Western Electronic Show and Convention Conference Record *see* W E S C O N Conference Record *359*
Western Europe Report (US) *190, 717*
Western European Airport Association. Statistiques de Trafic (FR) *869*
Western Forest Fire Committee. Proceedings *see* Western Forestry Conference. Executive Summaries of Proceedings *412*
Western Forest Pest Committee. Proceedings *see* Western Forestry Conference. Executive Summaries of Proceedings *412*
Western Forestry Center. Annual Report (US) *412*
Western Forestry Conference. Executive Summaries of Proceedings (US) *412*
Western Forestry Conference. Proceedings *see* Western Forestry Conference. Executive Summaries of Proceedings *412*
Western Frontier Library (US ISSN 0083-887X) *474*
Western Frontiersmen Series (US ISSN 0083-8888) *474*
Western Geographer (AT ISSN 0313-8860) *427*
Western Geographical Series (CN ISSN 0315-2022) *390, 427*
Western Hemisphere Nutrition Congress. Proceedings (US) *666*
Western Historical Series (US ISSN 0513-1545) *474*
Western Industrial Purchasing Guide and Electronic/Sources *see* E I A Guide *218*
Western Lands and Waters Series (US ISSN 0083-8934) *279*
Western Machinery & Steel World Buyer's Directory (US) *630*
Western Michigan University. School of Librarianship. Bulletin (US) *538*
Western Nigeria Development Corporation. Industrial Directory *see* Investments and Credit Corporation of Oyo State. Industrial Directory *238*
Western Ontario Series *see* University of Western Ontario Series in Philosophy of Science *692*
Western Pharmacology Society. Proceedings (US ISSN 0083-8969) *686*
Western Potter (CN ISSN 0049-7495) *245*
Western Psychological Services Professional Handbook Series *see* W P S Professional Handbook Series *739*
Western Reforestation Coordinating Committee. Proceedings *see* Western Forestry Conference. Executive Summaries of Proceedings *412*
Western Regional Solar Energy Directory (US) *364, 699*
Western Reserve Historical Society, Cleveland. Publications (US ISSN 0083-8985) *474*
Western Samoa. Department of Economic Development. Development of Western Samoa (WS) *226*
Western Samoa. Department of Statistics. Migration Report (WS) *730*
Western Snow Conference. Proceedings(US) *635*
Western Social Science Association Monograph Series (US) *802*
Western Society for French History. Proceedings of the Annual Meeting (US ISSN 0099-0329) *465*
Western Society of Malacologists. Annual Report (US ISSN 0361-1175) *131*

Western Society of Malacologists. Echo; Abstracts and Proceedings of the Annual Meeting *see* Western Society of Malacologists. Annual Report *131*
Western Society of Weed Science. Proceedings (US ISSN 0091-4487) *119*
Western Society of Weed Science. Research Progress Report (US ISSN 0511-8107) *119*
Western Stand Management Committee. Proceedings *see* Western Forestry Conference. Executive Summaries of Proceedings *412*
Western State. Estimates Including Budget Speech and Memorandum *see* Oyo State. Estimates Including Budget Speech and Memorandum *745*
Western State. Gazette *see* Oyo State of Nigeria Gazette *745*
Western State. Ministry of Economic Planning and Community Development. Annual Report *see* Oyo State. Ministry of Economic Planning and Community Development. Annual Report *224*
Western Thoroughbred (CN ISSN 0083-9000) *46*
Western Washington State College. Aquatic Studies Program. Technical Report Series (US) *899*
Western Washington State College. Institute for Freshwater Studies. Technical Report Series *see* Western Washington State College. Aquatic Studies Program. Technical Report Series *899*
Western Washington State College. Program in East Asian Studies. Occasional Papers *see* Studies on East Asia *671*
Western Wood Products Association. Statistical Yearbook (US ISSN 0195-931X) *412, 413*
Westernlore Ghost Town Series (US ISSN 0083-9019) *474*
Westfaelische Forschungen (GW ISSN 0083-9027) *403, 465*
Westfaelische Wilhelms-Universitaet Muenster. Institut fuer Kreditwesen. Schriftenreihe (GW ISSN 0077-2119) *177*
Westfaelische Wilhelms-Universitaet Muenster. Slavisch-Baltisches Seminar (GW ISSN 0580-1540) *916*
Westfaelische Zeitschrift (GW ISSN 0083-9043) *465*
Westfalia Sacra (GW) *465, 768*
Westigan Review Chapbooks (US) *576*
Westigan Review of Poetry (US) *582*
Westminster Series (US ISSN 0083-906X) *810*
Westminster Studies in Education (UK ISSN 0140-6728) *325*
Westmorland Historical Society. Newsletter (CN ISSN 0382-0831) *474*
Westpreussen-Jahrbuch (GW ISSN 0511-8484) *465*
Westwater (CN ISSN 0315-3010) *899*
Wetenschap en Technologie Jaarboek *see* Science et Technologie Annuaire *790*
Wetenskaplike en Tegniese Tydskrifte in Suid-Afrika Uitgegee *see* Scientific and Technical Periodicals Published in South Africa *791*
Wetenskaplike en Tegniese Verenigings in Suid-Afrika *see* Scientific and Technical Societies in South Africa *791*
Wetenskaplike Navorsingsorganisasies in Suid-Afrika *see* Scientific Research Organizations in South Africa *791*
Weyers Flottentaschenbuch (GW ISSN 0083-9078) *640*
Whakatane & District Historical Society. Monographs (NZ) *448*
Whales Research Institute, Tokyo, Japan. Scientific Reports/Geirui Kenkyusho Eibun Hokoku (JA ISSN 0083-9086) *131*
What Every Veteran Should Know (US ISSN 0083-9108) *640*
What It Costs to Run an Agency (US) *217*

What Research Says to the Teacher Series (US ISSN 0083-9116) *351*
What They Said (US ISSN 0512-5804) *436*
What You Should Know about Taxes in Puerto Rico (PR ISSN 0083-9132) *233*
What's Developing in Alaska (US) *23*
What's New About London, Jack? (US) *576*
What's New in Forensic Sciences (US ISSN 0511-8662) *613*
What's News in Reinsurance (US ISSN 0043-4612) *501*
What's on North West (UK) *893*
What's the Use of a Library *see* Red Deer College. Learning Resources Centre. What's the Use *350*
Wheat Situation *see* Australia. Bureau of Agricultural Economics. Wheat: Situation and Outlook *42*
Wheats of the World (CN) *43*
Wheel Series (US) *777*
Wheelchair Traveler (US) *810, 893*
Wheelers Recreational Vehicle Resort and Campground Guide: Easterner Edition (US) *831, 893*
Wheelers Recreational Vehicle Resort and Campground Guide: North American Edition (US ISSN 0362-9759) *893*
Wheelers Recreational Vehicle Resort and Campground Guide - Northeasterner Edition *see* Wheelers Recreational Vehicle Resort and Campground Guide: Easterner Edition *893*
Wheelers Recreational Vehicle Resort and Campground Guide - Southeasterner Edition *see* Wheelers Recreational Vehicle Resort and Campground Guide: Easterner Edition *893*
Wheelers Recreational Vehicle Resort and Campground Guide: Westerner Edition (US) *831, 893*
Where America's Large Foundations Make Their Grants (US ISSN 0083-9167) *494, 854*
Where Shall I Go to College to Study Advertising? (US) *6, 332*
Where the Colleges Rank (US) *332*
Where to Build-Where to Repair (NO) *243, 881*
Where to Buy (UK ISSN 0083-9175) *219, 243*
Where to Buy, Board or Train a Dog (US) *682*
Where to Buy Hardwood Plywood *see* Where to Buy Hardwood Plywood and Veneer *141*
Where to Buy Hardwood Plywood and Veneer (US) *141, 413*
Where to Buy Non-Ferrous Metals in the United Kingdom (UK) *630*
Where to Eat & Entertain-Singapore (SI) *483, 893*
Where to Eat in Canada (CN ISSN 0315-3088) *483, 893*
Where to Eat in London (UK ISSN 0083-9205) *483*
Where to Golf in Europe (GW ISSN 0083-9213) *826*
Where to Learn English in Great Britain (UK ISSN 0143-2214) *332, 554*
Where to Retire on a Small Income (US ISSN 0511-8719) *762*
Where-to-Sell-It Directory (US) *476*
Where to Stay in Scotland *see* Scotland: Where to Stay, Hotels and Guest Houses *890*
Where to Stay in Scotland *see* Scotland: Where to Stay, Bed and Breakfast *890*
Where to Stay in Scotland. Bed & Breakfast *see* Scotland: Where to Stay, Bed and Breakfast *890*
Where to Stay in Scotland. Hotels & Guest Houses *see* Scotland: Where to Stay, Hotels and Guest Houses *890*
Where to Write for Birth and Death Records: U.S. and Outlying Areas (US) *730*
Where to Write for Birth and Death Records: U.S. Citizens Who Were Born or Died Outside the United States (US) *730*

Where to Write for Divorce Records: U.S. and Outlying Areas (US ISSN 0565-8454) *730*
Where to Write for Marriage Records *see* Where to Write for Marriage Records: United States and Outlying Areas *730*
Where to Write for Marriage Records: United States and Outlying Areas (US ISSN 0162-0916) *730*
Which Degree (UK) *332*
Which University *see* Which Degree *332*
Whidden Lectures (US ISSN 0083-9248) *342, 494*
Whillan's Tax Tables and Tax Reckoner *see* Whillans's Tax Tables *233*
Whillans's Tax Tables (UK) *233*
Whitaker's Almanack (UK ISSN 0083-9256) *361*
Whitaker's Five-Year Cumulative Book List *see* Whitaker's Three-Year Cumulative Book List *761*
Whitaker's Three-Year Cumulative Book List (UK) *761*
White Book of Ski Areas. U.S. and Canada (US ISSN 0163-9684) *831*
White Book of U.S. Ski Areas *see* White Book of Ski Areas. U.S. and Canada *831*
White Paper on International Trade: Japan (JA) *198*
White Paper on Japanese Economy (JA) *191*
White Paper on Japan's Forest Industries (JA ISSN 0083-9272) *413*
Whiteacre (AT ISSN 0085-820X) *521*
Whites Air Directory & Who's Who in New Zealand Aviation (NZ) *10*
White's Tax Exempt Bond Market Ratings (US) *205*
Whitlock's Wessex (UK) *403, 465*
Whitmark Directory (US ISSN 0511-8794) *243*
Whitney Review (US ISSN 0511-8824) *656*
Whittier Newsletter (US ISSN 0511-8832) *582*
Who Does What: A Guide to National Associations, Service Organizations and Unions Operating in Most Areas of the Arts (CN ISSN 0700-2661) *80, 860*
Who Does What: A Guide to over 800 National Associations, Service Organizations and Unions Operating in Most Areas of the Arts *see* Who Does What: A Guide to National Associations, Service Organizations and Unions Operating in Most Areas of the Arts *80*
Who Is Who (II) *717*
Who Makes Machinery *see* Wer Baut Maschinen *383*
Who Owns Whom. Continental Europe (UK ISSN 0083-9302) *217, 226*
Who Owns Whom. United Kingdom *see* Who Owns Whom. United Kingdom and Republic of Ireland *243*
Who Owns Whom. United Kingdom and Republic of Ireland (UK ISSN 0140-4040) *243*
Who Owns Whom in America *see* Directory of Inter-Corporate Ownership *222*
Who Owns Whom, North America (UK ISSN 0083-9310) *219*
Who Sells Foreign Products in Spain *see* Quien Vende en Espana los Productos Extranjeros *241*
Who Writes What (US) *501*
Whole World Handbook: a Student Guide to Work, Study and Travel Abroad (US ISSN 0070-1165) *343*
Wholesaler Product Directory (US) *430*
Who's Notable in Mexico (MX ISSN 0300-208X) *98*
Who's Where (US ISSN 0508-6795) *269, 860*
Who's Who: A Guide to Federal and Provincial Departments and Agencies and the People Who Head Them *see* Who's Who: A Guide to Federal and Provincial Departments and Agencies, Their Funding Programs, and the People Who Head Them *80*

Who's Who: A Guide to Federal and Provincial Departments and Agencies, Their Funding Programs, and the People Who Head Them (CN ISSN 0384-2355) *80,* 860
Who's Who Among American High School Students (US) *98*
Who's Who Among Black Americans (US ISSN 0362-5753) *98*
Who's Who Among Music Students in American High Schools (US ISSN 0362-3750) *98,* 664
Who's Who Among Professional Insurance Agents (US) *501*
Who's Who Among Students in American Junior Colleges (US ISSN 0511-8891) *98,* 342
Who's Who Among Students in American Universities and Colleges (US) *98,* 342
Who's Who Among Students in American Vocational and Technical Schools see Who's Who Among Vocational and Technical Students in America *347*
Who's Who Among Vocational and Technical Students in America (US ISSN 0148-6381) *347*
Who's Who; an Annual Biographical Dictionary (UK ISSN 0083-937X) *98*
Who's Who and Where in Women's Studies (US) *901*
Who's Who at the Frankfurt Book Fair (GW) *760*
Who's Who in Advertising (US ISSN 0511-8905) 6, *98*
Who's Who in America (US ISSN 0083-9396) *98*
Who's Who in American Art (US ISSN 0000-0191) *98,* 656
Who's Who in American Jewry (US ISSN 0196-8009) *98,* 394
Who's Who in American Law (US) 98, *521*
Who's Who in American Politics (US ISSN 0000-0205) *98,* 717
Who's Who in Banking in Europe (UI) *177*
Who's Who in Baseball (US) *98,* 826
Who's Who in British Columbia Agriculture (CN) *23*
Who's Who in California (US ISSN 0511-8948) *98*
Who's Who in California Business and Finance (US ISSN 0195-539X) *98,* 151
Who's Who in Canada (CN ISSN 0083-9450) *98*
Who's Who in Chiropractic, International (US ISSN 0147-8265) *98*
Who's Who in Communist China (HK ISSN 0083-9477) 99, *446*
Who's Who in Consulting (US ISSN 0083-9485) 99, *217*
Who's Who in Corrugated (UK) *675*
Who's Who in der Politik/Who's Who in German Politics (GW ISSN 0000-0256) 99, *717*
Who's Who in Education (UK) 99, *325*
Who's Who in Engineering (US ISSN 0149-7537) *371*
Who's Who in Finance (UK ISSN 0307-6032) *177*
Who's Who in Finance and Banking in Thailand (TH) *99,* 177
Who's Who in Finance and Industry (US ISSN 0083-9523) *99,* 151
Who's Who in Finland see Kuka Kukin On *97*
Who's Who in Floriculture (US ISSN 0511-8964) *99,* 416
Who's Who in France/Qui Est Qui en France (FR ISSN 0083-9531) *99*
Who's Who in German Politics see Who's Who in der Politik *717*
Who's Who in Ghana (GH) *99*
Who's Who in Government (US) *99,* 717
Who's Who in Hawaii see Men and Women of Hawaii *98*
Who's Who in India (II ISSN 0301-5106) *99*
Who's Who in Indian Engineering and Industry (II ISSN 0083-9558) *99,* 854

Who's Who in Indian Relics (US) 67, *476*
Who's Who in Indian Science (II ISSN 0083-9566) *99,* 794
Who's Who in Industrial Editing see B. A. I. E. Membership Directory *757*
Who's Who in Insurance (US ISSN 0083-9574) *501*
Who's Who in Israel (IS ISSN 0083-9590) *99*
Who's Who in Lebanon (LE ISSN 0083-9612) *99*
Who's Who in Los Angeles County see Who's Who in California *98*
Who's Who in Malaysia and Singapore (MY ISSN 0083-9620) *99*
Who's Who in Movies (US ISSN 0083-9639) 99, *651*
Who's Who in Music and Musicians' International Directory see International Who's Who in Music and Musicians' Directory *660*
Who's Who in National Athletics - High School Football see Who's Who in National High School Football *826*
Who's Who in National High School Football (US ISSN 0091-6935) *826*
Who's Who in New Zealand (NZ ISSN 0083-9655) *99*
Who's Who in Nuclear Energy see Directory: Who's Who in Nuclear Energy *702*
Who's Who in Ocean and Fresh Water Science (UK) *313*
Who's Who in P/M (US ISSN 0361-6304) *630*
Who's Who in Pakistan (PK ISSN 0083-9671) *99*
Who's Who in Public Relations (International) (US ISSN 0511-9022) 6, *99*
Who's Who in Religion (US ISSN 0160-3728) *99,* 768
Who's Who in Risk Management (US) *501*
Who's Who in Saudi Arabia (SU) *99*
Who's Who in Space (US ISSN 0083-9728) 10, *99*
Who's Who in Steel (UK ISSN 0143-6872) *630*
Who's Who in Switzerland (SZ ISSN 0083-9736) *99*
Who's Who in the Agricultural Institute of Canada see Agricultural Institute of Canada. Membership Directory *11*
Who's Who in the Arab World (LE ISSN 0083-9752) *99*
Who's Who in the East (US ISSN 0083-9760) *99*
Who's Who in the Egg and Poultry Industries (US ISSN 0510-4130) 46, *99*
Who's Who in the Gas Industry see Gas Directory and Who's Who *679*
Who's Who in the Labour Movement (MY) *507*
Who's Who in the Midwest (US ISSN 0083-9787) *99*
Who's Who in the Mobile Area (US) *180*
Who's Who in the Securities Industry (US ISSN 0090-418X) *205*
Who's Who in the South and Southwest(US ISSN 0083-9809) *99*
Who's Who in the Theatre (US ISSN 0083-9833) *99,* 826
Who's Who in the Water Industry (UK) *899*
Who's Who in the West (US ISSN 0083-9817) *99*
Who's Who in the World (US ISSN 0083-9825) *99*
Who's Who in Training and Development (US ISSN 0092-4598) 99, *217*
Who's Who in U.S. Business in Australia (AT) *180*
Who's Who in Western Europe (UK) *99*
Who's Who in World Agriculture (UK) *23*
Who's Who of American Women (US ISSN 0083-9841) *99*

Who's Who of Southern Africa Including Mauritius, South West Africa, Rhodesia and Neighboring Countries see Who's Who of Southern Africa Including Mauritius, South West Africa, Zimbabwe-Rhodesia and Neighboring Countries *99*
Who's Who of Southern Africa Including Mauritius, South West Africa, Zimbabwe-Rhodesia and Neighboring Countries (SA) *99*
Who's Who, The Canadian see Canadian Who's Who *97*
Widener Library Shelflist (US ISSN 0083-9892) *538*
Wie Erreiche Ich Wen? (GW) 243, *881*
Wiener Arbeiten zur Deutschen Literatur (AU ISSN 0083-9906) *576*
Wiener Beitraege zur Englischen Philologie (AU ISSN 0083-9914) *554,* 576
Wiener Beitraege zur Kulturgeschichte und Linguistik (AU ISSN 0083-9922) *554*
Wiener Beitraege zur Theologie (AU ISSN 0083-9930) *776*
Wiener Figaro (AU) *664*
Wiener Forschungen zur Theater und Medienwissenschaft (AU) *860*
Wiener Geographische Schriften (AU ISSN 0083-9957) *427*
Wiener Gesellschaft fuer Theaterforschung. Jahrbuch (AU ISSN 0072-4262) *860*
Wiener Gesellschaft fuer Theaterforschung. Jahrbuch (AU) *860*
Wiener-Goethe-Verein. Jahrbuch (AU) *576,* 582
Wiener Humanistische Blaetter (AU ISSN 0083-9965) *494*
Wiener Institut fuer Internationale Wirtschaftsvergleiche. Forschungsberichte (AU) *202*
Wiener Institut fuer Internationale Wirtschaftsvergleiche. Reprint Serie (AU) *202*
Wiener Jahrbuch fuer Kunstgeschichte (AU ISSN 0083-9981) *80*
Wiener Jahrbuch fuer Philosophie (AU ISSN 0083-999X) *692*
Wiener Katholische Akademie. Studien (AU ISSN 0084-0009) *776*
Wiener Mitteilungen: Wasser, Abwasser, Gewaesser (AU) *899*
Wiener Musikhochschule. Publikationen(AU ISSN 0084-0017) *664*
Wiener Rechtswissenschaftliche Studien(AU ISSN 0084-0025) *521,* 524
Wiener Ringstrasse-Bild Einer Epoche (GW) *80,* 465
Wiener Romanistische Arbeiten (AU ISSN 0084-0033) *554,* 576
Wiener Slavistisches Jahrbuch/Viennese Slavonic Yearbook (AU ISSN 0084-0041) *554*
Wiener Studien. Zeitschrift fuer Klassische Philologie und Patristik (AU ISSN 0084-005X) 261, *554*
Wiener Voelkerkundliche Mitteilungen (AU ISSN 0084-0068) 55, *403*
Wiener Zeitschrift fuer die Kunde des Morgenlandes (AU ISSN 0084-0076) *672*
Wiener Zeitschrift fuer Die Kunde Sued- und Ostasiens see Wiener Zeitschrift fuer die Kunde Suedasiens und Archiv fuer Indische Philosphie *692*
Wiener Zeitschrift fuer die Kunde Suedasiens und Archiv fuer Indische Philosphie (AU ISSN 0084-0084) 446, *692*
Wiener Zeitschrift fuer Nervenheilkunde und deren Grenzgebiete. Supplement (US ISSN 0084-0092) *521*
Wijsgerige Teksten en Studies/Philosophical Texts and Studies (NE ISSN 0084-0106) *692*
Wilbour Monographs (US) 67, 80, *436*

Wild Goose Association. Annual Technical Symposium Proceedings (US) *313,* 371
Wilderness Energy Survey (US) *364*
Wildfire Statistics see U.S. Forest Service. Cooperative Fire Protection. Wildfire Statistics *411*
Wildfowl (UK) *125*
Wildlife - a Review (NZ ISSN 0110-604X) 131, *279*
Wildlife Behavior and Ecology (US ISSN 0084-0122) *109*
Wildlife Monographs (US ISSN 0084-0173) *279*
Wildlife Preservation Society of Queensland. Newsletter (AT) *279*
Wiley American Republic Series (US ISSN 0084-0181) *474*
Wiley Monographs in Chemical Physics(US) *256*
Wiley Monographs in Crystallography (US) *251*
Wiley Series in Behavior (US) *739*
Wiley Series in Computing (US) *274*
Wiley Series in Human Factors (US) 371, *739*
Wiley Series in Urban Research (US) *817*
Wiley Series on Systems and Controls for Financial Management (US) *217*
Wiley Series on Systems Engineering and Analysis (US ISSN 0084-019X) *371*
Wiley Series on the Science and Technology of Materials (US ISSN 0084-0203) *380*
Will to Charity: the Charities' Story Book (UK) *810*
Der Wille zur Form (GW ISSN 0043-5570) *80*
William D. Carmichael Jr. Lecture Series (US ISSN 0512-4859) *802*
William-Frederick Poets Series (US ISSN 0084-0238) *582*
William K. McInally Lecture (US ISSN 0084-0246) *151*
William L. Hutcheson Memorial Forest. Bulletin (US ISSN 0511-9723) *412*
William Morris Society. Journal (UK ISSN 0084-0254) *99*
William Morris Society. Report (UK ISSN 0084-0270) *494*
Williamsburg in America Series (US ISSN 0084-0297) *474*
Williamsburg Research Studies (US ISSN 0084-0300) *474*
Willing's Press Guide (UK ISSN 0000-0213) *96*
Wilmington Society of the Fine Arts. Report see Delaware Art Museum. Annual Report *74*
Wilson & Wilson's Comprehensive Analytical Chemistry (NE ISSN 0069-8024) *250*
Wilton Cake Decorating Yearbook see Celebrate *479*
Wiltshire Archaeological and Natural History Magazine see Wiltshire Archaeological Magazine *67*
Wiltshire Archaeological and Natural History Magazine see Wiltshire Natural History Magazine *794*
Wiltshire Archaeological Magazine (UK ISSN 0309-3476) *67*
Wiltshire Natural History Magazine (UK ISSN 0309-3468) *794*
Winchester Studies (UK) *465*
Wind (US ISSN 0361-2481) *576*
Wind Energy Workshop. Proceedings (US) *364*
Wind Engineering Research Digest (US) *371*
Windhaven (US) *576,* 901
Window (US) *576*
Window & Wall Decorating Ideas (US ISSN 0363-5406) *502*
Wine and Spirit Trade Review Directory see Off Licence News Directory *86*
Wine Handbook (US) 86, *219*
Wine Marketing Handbook see Wine Handbook *219*
Wines and Vines-Annual Directory of the Wine Industry see Wines and Vines: Directory of the Wine Industry in North America *86*
Wines and Vines: Directory of the Wine Industry in North America (US) *86*

Winter Sports in Scotland (UK ISSN 0084-0386) *822*
Wintergreen (CN) 96, *558*
Winter's Tales (UK ISSN 0084-0394) *576*
Wir Bauen Unser Haus Selbst (GW) *139*
Die Wirbelsaeule in Forschung und Praxis (GW ISSN 0510-5315) *616*
Wire Industry Machinery Guide (UK) *630*
Wire Industry Yearbook (UK ISSN 0084-0424) *630*
Wire Journal Directory/Catalog (US ISSN 0512-5405) *371*
Wire Review *see* Wire Industry Machinery Guide *630*
Wire Technology Buyer's Guide (US) *854*
Wireless and Electrical Trader Year Book *see* Electrical and Electronic Tracer Year Book *353*
Wireless Pioneer *see* Sparks *268*
Wireless World Diary (UK ISSN 0084-0459) *269*
Wirkung der Literatur (GW ISSN 0084-0467) *576*
Wirtschaft im Ostseeraum *see* Ostseejahrbuch *180*
Wirtschaftspolitische Studien (US) *192*
Wirtschaftsuniversitaet Wien. Dissertationen (AU ISSN 0507-7206) *151*
Wirtschaftsvereinigung Gross- und Aussenhandel Geschaeftsbericht *see* W G A Geschaeftsbericht *198*
Wirtschaftswissenschaftliche Schriften (GW) *151*
Wirtschaftswissenschaftliche und Wirtschaftsrechtliche Untersuchungen(GW ISSN 0083-7113) *151, 521*
Wirtschaftszahl (AU ISSN 0510-5609) *166*
Wisconsin. Commissioner of Securities. Annual Report *see* Wisconsin. Commissioner of Securities. Biennial Report *205*
Wisconsin. Commissioner of Securities. Biennial Report (US) *205*
Wisconsin. Department of Administration. Annual Fiscal Report(US ISSN 0085-8226) *747*
Wisconsin. Department of Natural Resources. Annual Water Quality Report to Congress (US ISSN 0362-5354) *390, 755*
Wisconsin. Department of Natural Resources. Technical Bulletin (US ISSN 0084-0564) *279*
Wisconsin. Department of Transportation. Automatic Traffic Recorder Data *see* Wisconsin Traffic Data - Automatic Traffic Recorder *876*
Wisconsin. Department of Transportation. Division of Planning and Budget. Highway Mileage Data (US ISSN 0084-0572) *876*
Wisconsin. Department of Transportation. Division of Planning. Highway Traffic (US ISSN 0084-0580) *876*
Wisconsin. Department of Veterans Affairs. Biennial Report (US) *641*
Wisconsin. Division of Corrections. Bureau of Planning, Development and Research. Juvenile Probation Admissions *see* Wisconsin. Division of Corrections. Office of Informatiom Management. Juvenile Probation Admissions *284*
Wisconsin. Division of Corrections. Bureau of Planning, Development and Research. Probation and Parole Terminations *see* Wisconsin. Division of Corrections. Office of Information Management. Probation and Parole Terminations *285*
Wisconsin. Division of Corrections. Bureau of Planning, Development and Research. Releases from Juvenile Institutions *see* Wisconsin. Division of Corrections. Office of Information Management. Releases from Juvenile Institutions *285*

Wisconsin. Division of Corrections. Bureau of Planning, Development and Research. Work Release-Study Release Program *see* Wisconsin. Division of Corrections. Office of Information Management. Work Release-Study Release Program *284*
Wisconsin. Division of Corrections. Office of Informatiom Management. Juvenile Probation Admissions (US ISSN 0095-4306) *284*
Wisconsin. Division of Corrections. Office of Information Management. Admissions to Juvenile Institutions (US) *849*
Wisconsin. Division of Corrections. Office of Information Management. Admissions to Juvenile Institutions *see* Wisconsin. Division of Corrections. Office of Information Management. Admissions to Juvenile Institutions *849*
Wisconsin. Division of Corrections. Office of Information Management. Probation and Parole Terminations (US) *285*
Wisconsin. Division of Corrections. Office of Information Management. Releases from Juvenile Institutions (US) *285*
Wisconsin. Division of Corrections. Office of Information Management. Work Release-Study Release Program (US) *284*
Wisconsin. Division of Highway Safety Coordination. Highway Safety Report to the Legislature (US ISSN 0098-5082) *876*
Wisconsin. Division of Highways. System Planning Section. Highway Traffic in Wisconsin Cities *see* Wisconsin. Department of Transportation. Division of Planning. Highway Traffic *876*
Wisconsin. Educational Communications Board. Biennial Report (US ISSN 0361-2120) *325*
Wisconsin. Employment Relations Commission. Reporter (US ISSN 0097-9171) *212*
Wisconsin. Geological and Natural History Survey. Bulletin (US) *302*
Wisconsin. Geological and Natural History Survey. Geoscience Information Series (US) *302*
Wisconsin. Geological and Natural History Survey. Information Circulars (US ISSN 0512-0640) *302*
Wisconsin. Geological and Natural History Survey. Special Report (US ISSN 0512-0659) *302*
Wisconsin. State Elections Board. Annual Report (US) *717*
Wisconsin Academy of Sciences, Arts and Letters, Transactions (US ISSN 0084-0505) *80, 794*
Wisconsin Accident Facts (US) *755, 876*
Wisconsin Blue Book (US) *747*
Wisconsin Business Monographs (US ISSN 0084-0513) *151*
Wisconsin China Series (US ISSN 0084-053X) *446, 672*
Wisconsin Commerce Studies *see* Wisconsin Economy Studies *151*
Wisconsin Council of Teachers of English. Service Bulletin Series (US) *325, 577*
Wisconsin Criminal Justice Information, Crime and Arrests (US) *284*
Wisconsin Economy Studies (US ISSN 0084-0599) *151*
Wisconsin Highway Traffic *see* Wisconsin. Department of Transportation. Division of Planning. Highway Traffic *876*
Wisconsin Library Service Record (US ISSN 0361-2848) *538*
Wisconsin Pharmacy Extension Bulletin(US ISSN 0043-6593) *686*
Wisconsin Poetry (US) *582*
Wisconsin Population Projections (US ISSN 0091-5254) *731*
Wisconsin Public School Directory (US ISSN 0148-5059) *332*

Wisconsin Research and Development Center for Cognitive Learning. Practical Papers *see* Wisconsin Research and Development Center for Individualized Schooling. Practical Papers *325*
Wisconsin Research and Development Center for Cognitive Learning. Theoretical Papers *see* Wisconsin Research and Development Center for Individualized Schooling. Theoretical Papers *325*
Wisconsin Research and Development Center for Cognitive Learning. Technical Reports *see* Wisconsin Research and Development Center for Individualized Schooling. Technical Reports *325*
Wisconsin Research and Development Center for Individualized Schooling. Practical Papers (US) *325*
Wisconsin Research and Development Center for Individualized Schooling. Technical Reports (US) *325*
Wisconsin Research and Development Center for Individualized Schooling. Theoretical Papers (US) *325*
Wisconsin State Historical Society. Urban History Group. Newsletter (US ISSN 0084-067X) *474*
Wisconsin Statistical Abstract (US) *849*
Wisconsin Traffic Data - A T R *see* Wisconsin Traffic Data - Automatic Traffic Recorder *876*
Wisconsin Traffic Data - Automatic Traffic Recorder (US) *876*
Wisconsin Women Newsletter (US ISSN 0085-8242) *719*
Wisdom *see* Kinaadman *444*
Wisdom of Persia (IR) *475*
Wisdom of Tibet Series (US) *916*
Wise Giving Bulletin (US ISSN 0272-0493) *810*
Wissenschaft und Gegenwart. Geisteswissenschaftliche Reihe (GW) *692*
Wissenschaft und Gegenwart. Juristische Reihe (GW) *521*
Wissenschaftliche Alpenvereinshefte (GW ISSN 0084-0912) *427*
Wissenschaftliche Forschungsberichte. Reihe 1. Grundlagenforschung und Grundlegende Methodik. Abt. A. Chemie und Physik/Current Topics in Science. Reihe 1. Basic Research. Abt. A. Chemistry and Physics (GW) *248, 699*
Wissenschaftliche Forschungsberichte. Reihe 1. Grundlagenforschung und Grundlegende Methodik. Abt. B. Biologie und Medizin/Current Topics in Science. Reihe 1. Basic Research. Abt. B. Biology and Medicine (GW) *109, 601*
Wissenschaftliche Forschungsberichte. Reihe 1. Grundlagenforschung und Grundlegende Methodik. Abt. C. Psychologie/Current Topics in Science. Reihe 1. Basic Research Abt. C. Psychology (GW ISSN 0340-031X) *739*
Wissenschaftliche Forschungsberichte. Reihe 2. Anwendungstechnik und Angewandte Wissenschaft/Current Topics in Science. Reihe 2. Engineering (GW ISSN 0340-2703) *371, 374*
Wissenschaftliche Gesellschaft fuer Luft- und Raumfahrt. Jahrbuecher *see* D. G. L. R. Jahrbuecher *8*
Wissenschaftliche Gesellschaft fuer Personenstandswesen und Verwandte Gebiete. Schriftenreihe. Neue Folge (GW ISSN 0084-0939) *521*
Wissenschaftliche Kommission des Theodor-Koerner-Stiftungsfonds und des Leopold-Kunschak-Preises zur Enforschung der Oesterreichischen Geschichte der Jahre 1918 bis 1938. Veroeffentlichungen (AU) *465*
Wissenschaftliche Mitteilungen des Bosnisch-Herzegowinischen Landesmuseums. Archaeologie (YU) *67*
Wissenschaftliche Mitteilungen des Bosnisch-Herzegowinischen Landesmuseums. Naturwissenschaft (YU ISSN 0350-0012) *794*

Wissenschaftliche Paperbacks (GW ISSN 0170-3579) *192, 817*
Wissenschaftliche Redaktion (GW ISSN 0084-0955) *760*
Wissenschaftliche Taschenbuecher. Reihe Biologie (GE ISSN 0084-0963) *109*
Wissenschaftliche Taschenbuecher. Reihe Chemie (GE ISSN 0084-0971) *248*
Wissenschaftliche Taschenbuecher. Reihe Mathematik, Physik (GE ISSN 0084-098X) *591, 699*
Wissenschaftliche und Angewandte Photographie (US ISSN 0084-0998) *694*
Wissenschaftliche Vereinigung der Augenoptiker. Fachvortraege der Jahrestagungen *see* Wissenschaftliche Vereinigung fuer Augenoptik und Optometrie. Fachvortraege des WVAO - Jahreskongresses *706*
Wissenschaftliche Vereinigung fuer Augenoptik und Optometrie. Fachvortraege des WVAO - Jahreskongresses (GW) *706*
Wissenschaftspolitik *see* Politique de la Science *714*
Witchcraft *see* Witchcraft Digest *676*
Witchcraft Digest (US ISSN 0085-8250) *676*
Witches Almanac (US) *676*
Wittenberg Review of Literature and Art (US) 80, *577*
Wizo Review (AT) *394*
Wochenend-, Ferien- und Zweithaus-Katalog (GW) *139*
Wohnen (GE) *502*
Wolfenbuettler Beitraege (GW ISSN 0300-2012) *538*
Wolfman Report on the Photographic Industry in the United States (US ISSN 0084-103X) *694*
Woman's Day Best Ideas for Christmas (US) *429*
Woman's Day Christmas Ideas for Children (US ISSN 0512-5901) *258*
Woman's Day Gifts You Can Make for Christmas *see* Woman's Day Best Ideas for Christmas *429*
Woman's Day Granny Squares (US) *477*
Woman's Day Home Decorating Ideas (US ISSN 0361-638X) *502, 503*
Woman's Day 101 Gardening & Outdoor Ideas (US ISSN 0090-9319) *416*
Woman's Day 101 Sweaters You Can Knit & Crochet (US) *477*
Woman's Day 101 Ways to Lose Weight and Stay Healthy (US) *666, 695*
Women Can *see* Pedestal *900*
Women in a Developing Economy (II) *901*
Women in Context: Development and Stresses (US) *601, 901*
Women in the Working World (US) *212, 901*
Women - Poems (US) *582, 901*
Women Talking, Women Listening (US) *582, 901*
Women's Accessories Directory; New York Metropolitan Area (US ISSN 0084-1056) *261*
Women's Coats and Suits Directory; New York Metropolitan Area (US ISSN 0084-1064) *262*
Women's Collection Newsletter (US) *901*
Women's Education Newsletter *see* Wisconsin Women Newsletter *719*
Women's Electoral Lobby (Victoria) Papers *see* W. E. L. (Victoria) Papers *901*
Women's International Bowling Congress. Playing Rules (US ISSN 0361-3976) *822*
Women's Newsletter (US) *901*
Women's Organizations & Leaders Directory (US ISSN 0092-6639) *901*
Women's Organizations in Great Britain(UK) *901*
Women's Squash Rackets Association. Handbook (UK) *822*
Women's Zionist Council of South Africa. News and Views (SA ISSN 0043-7603) *719, 771*

Woningbouwstudies (NE ISSN 0084-1072) *139*
Wood & Wood Products Reference Buying Guide (US) *413*
Wood & Wood Products Reference Data/Buying Guide *see* Wood & Wood Products Reference Buying Guide *413*
Wood Research/Mokuzai Kenkyu (JA ISSN 0049-7916) *413*
Wood - Woods Family Magazine (US ISSN 0091-6706) *418*
Woodall's Campground Directory. Arizona Edition (US ISSN 0162-7384) *831*
Woodall's Campground Directory. Arkansas/Missouri Edition (US ISSN 0163-5328) *831*
Woodall's Campground Directory. California Edition (US ISSN 0162-7392) *831*
Woodall's Campground Directory. Colorado Edition (US ISSN 0163-5344) *831*
Woodall's Campground Directory. Delaware/Maryland/Virginia/District of Columbia Edition (US) *831*
Woodall's Campground Directory. Eastern Edition (US ISSN 0162-7406) *831*
Woodall's Campground Directory. Florida Campgrounds Edition (US ISSN 0090-5151) *832*
Woodall's Campground Directory. Idaho/Oregon/Washington Edition (US ISSN 0163-2493) *832*
Woodall's Campground Directory. Illinois/Indiana Edition (US ISSN 0163-2485) *832*
Woodall's Campground Directory. Kentucky/Tennessee Edition (US ISSN 0163-5336) *832*
Woodall's Campground Directory. Michigan Edition (US ISSN 0163-0121) *832*
Woodall's Campground Directory. New England States Edition (US ISSN 0163-0083) *832*
Woodall's Campground Directory. New Jersey/New York Edition (US ISSN 0163-0113) *832*
Woodall's Campground Directory. North American/Canadian Edition (US ISSN 0146-1362) *832*
Woodall's Campground Directory. North American Edition *see* Woodall's Campground Directory. North American/Canadian Edition *832*
Woodall's Campground Directory. North Carolina/South Carolina Edition (US ISSN 0163-5352) *832*
Woodall's Campground Directory. Ohio/Pennsylvania Editions (US ISSN 0163-1950) *832*
Woodall's Campground Directory. Ontario Edition (US ISSN 0163-240X) *832*
Woodall's Campground Directory. Texas Edition (US ISSN 0162-7376) *832*
Woodall's Campground Directory. Western Edition (US ISSN 0162-7414) *832*
Woodall's Campground Directory. Wisconsin Edition (US ISSN 0163-0105) *832*
Woodall's Florida & Southern States Retirement & Resort Communities Directory (US ISSN 0163-4313) *810*
Woodall's Retirement and Resort Communites Directory *see* Woodall's Florida & Southern States Retirement & Resort Communities Directory *810*
Woodbridge Lectures, Columbia University (US) *692*
Woodrow Wilson International Center for Scholars. Annual Report (US ISSN 0092-4261) *343*
Woodrow Wilson National Fellowship Foundation. Newsletter (US ISSN 0084-1137) *342*
Woodrow Wilson National Fellowship Foundation. Report (US ISSN 0084-1145) *342*
Woodsman (UG) *412*

Woodstock Papers: Occasional Essays for Theology (US ISSN 0084-117X) *916*
Woodstove, Coalstove, Fireplace & Equipment Directory (US ISSN 0271-5090) *364, 430*
Woodstove Directory *see* Woodstove, Coalstove, Fireplace & Equipment Directory *430*
Woodworker *see* Woodworker Projects & Techniques *476*
Woodworker Annual (UK ISSN 0084-1196) *503*
Woodworker Handbooks (US) *141*
Woodworker Projects & Techniques (US) *476*
Woodworking Industry /Buyers' Guide (UK) *413*
Woodworking Industry /Directory *see* Woodworking Industry /Buyers' Guide *413*
Wool (NZ) *46*
Wool News (AT) *857*
Wool News Digest *see* Wool News *857*
Wool Review (AT ISSN 0084-1218) *857*
Woolhope Naturalists' and Archaeologists Field Club, Herefordshire. Transactions *see* Woolhope Naturalists' Field Club, Herefordshire. Transactions *67*
Woolhope Naturalists' Field Club, Herefordshire. Transactions (UK) *67, 109*
Woolknit Annual (US ISSN 0084-1234) *857*
Woolner Indological Series (II ISSN 0084-1242) *577, 692*
Worcester Art Museum. Journal (US) *656*
Worcester Art Museum Bulletin *see* Worcester Art Museum. Journal *656*
Word (II ISSN 0043-7948) *265*
Word and Deed (IS) *771*
Words from Inside (CN ISSN 0316-8670) *577*
Work Accomplished by the Inter-American Juridicical Committee During Its Meeting (US ISSN 0074-0837) *521*
Work of Aslib: Annual Report (UK ISSN 0084-1285) *538*
Work Related Abstracts Subject Heading List (US) *538*
Work Release-Study Release Program *see* Wisconsin. Division of Corrections. Office of Information Management. Work Release-Study Release Program *284*
Work-Years and Personnel Costs. Executive Branch of the United States Government *see* Federal Civilian Work Force Statistics. Work Years and Personnel Costs. Executive Branch, United States Government *155*
Working Abroad (UK) *177*
Working Conditions in British Columbia Industry *see* British Columbia. Department of Labour. Negotiated Working Conditions *206*
Working Conditions in Canadian Industry/Conditions de Travail dans l'Industrie Canadienne. (CN ISSN 0084-1307) *212*
Working Kelpie Council. National Stud Book (AT) *683*
Working Meeting of Crocodile Specialists. Proceedings *see* Crocodiles *128*
Working Meeting of the Polar Bear Specialist Group. Proceedings *see* Polar Bears *130*
Working Papers in African Studies (US) *441*
Working Papers in Applied Linguistics (US ISSN 0163-0016) *554*
Working Papers in Planning (US) *488*
Working Papers in Yiddish and East European Jewish Studies/In Gang Fun Arbet: Yidish Un Mizrakh Eyropeishe Yidishe Shtudies (US) *394, 771*
Working Papers on the Kapitalistate *see* Kapitalistate *145*
Working Press of the Nation (US ISSN 0084-1323) *506*

Workmen's Compensation Reporter *see* British Columbia. Workers' Compensation Board. Workers' Compensation Reporter *498*
Works in Progress (US ISSN 0512-5472) *760*
Works of Architects (JA) *70*
Workshop Conference Hoechst (NE) *601*
Workshop for Child Care Staff of Florida's Child Caring Facilities. Report (US ISSN 0091-8482) *257, 810*
Workshop Notes Washington, D.C. Textile Museum *see* Textile Museum Journal *857*
World (US ISSN 0043-8154) *582*
World Advertising Expenditures (International Advertising Association.) (US ISSN 0568-0301) *6*
World Aeronautical Records (FR) *11*
World Air Transport Statistics (SZ ISSN 0084-1366) *869*
World Airline Record (US ISSN 0084-1374) *869*
World Airports Conference. Proceedings (UK) *869*
World Alliance of Y M C A's. Annual Report (SZ) *262*
World Alliance of Y M C A's Directory (SZ ISSN 0513-6032) *257, 262*
World Almanac and Book of Facts (US ISSN 0084-1382) *361*
World Almanac Guide to Pro Hockey (US ISSN 0095-7240) *822*
World Archaelogical Society. Special Publication (US) *67*
World Armaments and Disarmament: S I P R I Yearbook (Stockholm International Peace Research Institute) (UK ISSN 0347-2205) *725*
World Aromatics and Derivatives (US) *248*
World Association for Educational Research. Congress Reports (BE) *325*
World Association for the Advancement of Veterinary Parasitology. Proceedings of Conference (GR ISSN 0084-1404) *895*
World Association of Girl Guides and Girl Scouts. Report of Conference (UK ISSN 0084-1412) *257*
World Automotive Market (US) *872*
World Bank. Annual Report (UN) *202*
World Bank. Commodity Trade and Price Trends (UN) *202*
World Bank. Economic Development Institute. E D I Seminar Papers (UN) *202*
World Bank Atlas (UN ISSN 0512-2457) *202*
World Bank Catalog. Accession List *see* Catalog of World Bank Publications *199*
World Bank Catalog of Publications *see* Catalog of World Bank Publications *199*
World Bank Research Program: Abstracts of Current Studies (UN) *166*
World Bank Staff Occasional Papers (UN ISSN 0074-199X) *202*
World Banking (UK) *177*
World Banking Statistical Annual Survey *see* World Banking Survey *166*
World Banking Survey (UK) *166*
World Best SF Short Stories (UK) *4*
World Bibliographical Series (US) *96*
World Book Year Book (US ISSN 0084-1439) *361*
World Bulk Trades (NO) *881*
World Bureau of Metal Statistics. Annual Report (UK) *631*
World Buyers Guide *see* Businessman's Directory of R.O.C *235*
World Cars (US ISSN 0084-1463) *872*
World Cartography (UN ISSN 0084-1471) *428*
World Cement Directory (FR) *139*
World Chronologies Series (US) *436, 717*
World Coal Trade *see* International Coal *644*

World Collectors Annuary (NE ISSN 0084-1498) *80*
World Commerce Annual (II ISSN 0084-1501) *198*
World Confederation for Physical Therapy. Proceedings of the Congress (UK ISSN 0084-151X) *601*
World Confederation of Organizations of the Teaching Profession Annual Report *see* W C O T P Annual Report *345*
World Confederation of Organizations of the Teaching Profession Theme Study *see* W C O T P Theme Study *325*
World Conference on Animal Production. Proceedings (UY ISSN 0084-1552) *46*
World Conference on Tin. Proceedings (UK) *630*
World Conference on Transport Research. Proceedings (NE) *864*
World Congress in Public Park Administration. Programme *see* Congress in Park and Recreation Administration. Programme *626*
World Congress in Public Park Administration. Reports *see* Congress in Park and Recreation Administration. Reports *829*
World Congress of Anaesthesiologists. Proceedings (NE ISSN 0084-1595) *604*
World Congress of Psychiatry. Proceedings (AU ISSN 0084-1609) *621*
World Congress of the Deaf. Lectures and Papers (IT ISSN 0084-1625) *810*
World Congress of the Deaf. Proceedings. (IT ISSN 0510-8292) *286*
World Congress on Fertility and Sterility. Proceedings (AG ISSN 0084-1641) *109*
World Congress on the Prevention of Occupational Accidents and Diseases. Proceedings (SZ ISSN 0084-165X) *496*
World Council of Churches. Faith and Order Papers *see* Faith and Order Papers *765*
World Council of Churches. General Assembly. Assembly-Reports (SZ ISSN 0084-1676) *768*
World Council of Churches. Minutes and Reports of the Central Committee Meeting (SZ ISSN 0084-1684) *768*
World Council of Churches Information *see* P C R Information *766*
World Council of Credit Unions. International Annual Report (US) *177*
World Council of Credit Unions. Yearbook *see* World Council of Credit Unions. International Annual Report *177*
World Council of Young Mens Service Clubs. Minutes of the General Meeting (CN ISSN 0052-2678) *810*
World Crafts Council. General Assembly. Proceedings of the Biennial Meeting (US ISSN 0084-1706) *80*
World Cultural Guides (US) *70, 80, 893*
World Cultural Heritage (UN) *656*
World Currency Charts (US ISSN 0090-2810) *177*
World C4 Hydrocarbons and Derivatives (US) *248*
World Directory of Dental Schools (UN ISSN 0512-2732) *332, 610*
World Directory of Environmental Organizations (US ISSN 0092-0908) *279, 390*
World Directory of Fertilizer Manufacturers (UK) *40*
World Directory of Fertilizer Products (UK) *40*
World Directory of Historians of Mathematics (CN ISSN 0315-1700) *591*
World Directory of Mathematicians (JA ISSN 0512-2740) *591*

World Directory of Medical Schools/ Repertoire Mondial des Ecoles de Medecine (UN ISSN 0512-2759) 332, 601
World Directory of Pharmaceutical Manufacturers (UK) 243, 686
World Directory of Post-Basic and Post-Graduate Schools of Nursing (UN ISSN 0512-2767) 332, 614
World Directory of Schools of Pharmacy (UN ISSN 0512-2775) 332, 686
World Directory of Schools of Public Health (UN ISSN 0512-2783) 332, 755
World Directory of Veterinary Schools (UN ISSN 0512-2791) 332, 895
World Directory of Wood-Based Panel Producers (US) 141
World Economic History (US) 192
World Economic Survey (UN ISSN 0084-1714) 191
World Education Series (Archon) (US) 325
World Energy Conference. Directory of Energy Information Centres in the World (UK) 364
World Energy Conference. Plenary Conferences. Transactions (UK ISSN 0084-1722) 364
World Energy Conference. Survey of Energy Resources (UK ISSN 0084-1730) 364
World Energy Conference. Technical Data on Fuel (UK) 364
World Energy Directory (UK) 364
World Energy Supplies (UN ISSN 0084-1749) 364
World Environmental Directory (US ISSN 0094-4742) 390
World Epidemiology Review see Worldwide Report: Epidemiology 756
World Ethylene and Derivatives (US) 248
World Explorations (US) 428
World Federation for Mental Health. Proceedings of Annual Meetings (CN ISSN 0084-1757) 739, 755
World Fellowship of Buddhists. Book Series (TH ISSN 0084-1781) 771
World Fertility Survey. Basic Documentation (NE) 731
World Fertility Survey. Country Reports (NE) 731
World Fertility Survey. Occasional Papers (NE) 731
World Fertility Survey. Progress Reports (NE) 731
World Fertility Survey. Report see World Fertility Survey. Progress Reports 731
World Fertility Survey. Scientific Reports (NE) 731
World Fertility Survey. Technical Bulletins (NE) 731
World Fertilizer Atlas (UK ISSN 0512-2953) 40
World Food Crisis: an International Directory of Organizations and Information Resources (US) 406
World Food Problems (UN ISSN 0084-179X) 406
World Grain Trade Statistics (UN ISSN 0084-182X) 43
World Guide to Abbreviations of Organizations (US) 538
World Guide to Fertilizer Plant and Equipment (UK) 40
World Guide to Fertilizer Processes and Constructors (UK) 40
World Guide to Libraries see Internationales Bibliotheks-Handbuch 531
World Guide to Pollution Control in the Fertilizer Industry (UK) 40, 390
World Guide to Trade Associations see Internationales Verzeichnis der Wirtschaftsverbaende 238
World Health Organization. Monograph Series (UN ISSN 0512-3038) 755
World Health Organization. Public Health Papers see Public Health Papers 754
World Health Organization. Regional Office for Africa. Report of the Regional Committee. (UN) 755

World Health Organization. Regional Office for Africa. Report of the Regional Committee. Minutes of the Plenary Session see World Health Organization. Regional Office for Africa. Report of the Regional Committee 755
World Health Organization. Regional Office for Africa. Report of the Regional Director (UN ISSN 0510-8837) 755
World Health Organization. Regional Office for the Eastern Mediterranean. Annual Report of the Regional Director see World Health Organization. Regional Office for the Eastern Mediterranean. Biennial Report of the Regional Director 755
World Health Organization. Regional Office for the Eastern Mediterranean. Biennial Report of the Regional Director (UN) 755
World Health Organization. Regional Office for the Western Pacific. Annual Report of the Regional Director to the Regional Committee for the Western Pacific (UN ISSN 0512-4921) 756
World Health Organization. Regional Office for the Western Pacific. Report on the Regional Seminar on the Role of the Hospital in the Public Health Programme (UN ISSN 0510-8845) 481, 755
World Health Organization. Work of W H O (UN ISSN 0085-8285) 756
World Health Organization. World Health Assembly and the Executive Board. Handbook of Resolutions and Decisions. (UN ISSN 0301-0740) 756
World Health Organization Offset Publications see W H O Offset Publications 757
World Health Organization Technical Report Series see W H O Technical Report Series 601
World Health Statistics Annual (UN) 757
World Institute Creative Findings (US) 794
World Jersey Cattle Bureau. Conference Reports (UK ISSN 0084-1854) 46
World License Review (UK) 686
World List of Family Planning Agencies(UK ISSN 0535-1774) 133
World List of Social Science Periodicals(UN ISSN 0084-1870) 803
World List of Universities, Other Institutions of Higher Education and University Organizations (UK ISSN 0084-1889) 333
World Literacy of Canada. Newsletter (CN ISSN 0700-5350) 325
World Literacy of Canada, News and Views see World Literacy of Canada. Newsletter 325
World Medical Association. General Assembly. Proceedings (FR ISSN 0084-1897) 601
World Meteorological Association. Regional Associations. Abridged Final Reports see World Meteorological Organization. Reports of Sessions of Regional Associations 636
World Meteorological Association. Technical Commissions Abridged Final Reports see World Meteorological Organization. Reports of Sessions of Technical Commissions 636
World Meteorological Congress. Abridged Report with Resolutions (UN ISSN 0084-1927) 635
World Meteorological Congress. Proceedings (UN ISSN 0084-1935) 635
World Meteorological Organization. Annual Reports (UN ISSN 0084-1994) 635
World Meteorological Organization. Basic Documents and Official Reports (UN) 635

World Meteorological Organization. Basic Documents, Records and Reports see World Meteorological Organization. Basic Documents and Official Reports 635
World Meteorological Organization. Executive Committee Reports: Abridged Reports with Resolutions (UN) 636
World Meteorological Organization. Executive Committee Sessions: Abridged Reports with Resolutions see World Meteorological Organization. Executive Committee Reports: Abridged Reports with Resolutions 636
World Meteorological Organization. Report on Marine Science Affairs (UN ISSN 0084-2001) 313
World Meteorological Organization. Reports of Sessions of Regional Associations (UN) 636
World Meteorological Organization. Reports of Sessions of Technical Commissions (UN) 636
World Meteorological Organization. Special Environmental Reports (UN) 390, 636
World Meteorological Organization. Technical Notes (UN ISSN 0084-201X) 636
World Military and Social Expenditures(US ISSN 0363-4795) 233
World Military Expenditures see World Military Expenditures and Arms Transfers 640
World Military Expenditures and Arms Transfers (US) 640
World Military Expenditures and Related Data see World Military Expenditures and Arms Transfers 640
World Mineral Statistics (UK) 648, 849
World Mines Register (US ISSN 0095-4322) 647
World Mining. Latin American Edition (US) 647
World Mining Congress. Report (PL) 647
World Motor Vehicle Data (US ISSN 0085-8307) 872
World Movement of Mothers. Reports of Meetings (FR ISSN 0084-2044) 810
World Muslim Conference. Proceedings(PK ISSN 0084-2052) 770
World Muslim Gazetteer (PK ISSN 0084-2060) 770
World Naturalist Series (US) 794
World Nuclear Directory (UK) 705
World O R T Union. Congress Report (Organization for Rehabilitation Through Training) (SZ ISSN 0510-9175) 325
World of Archaeology (Binghamton) (US) 67
World of Church Music (UK) 664
World of Learning (UK ISSN 0084-2117) 333
World of Tennis (US) 826
World of the Future Series (US) 794, 854
World of Yachting see Annee Bateaux 826
World Perspectives (US ISSN 0084-2168) 494
World Phosphate Rock Institute. Proceedings see I M P H O S Congress Proceedings 373
World Plastics (US) 256, 707
World Ploughing Contest. Official Handbook (UK ISSN 0084-2184) 32
World Pop News (NE) 664
World Population Data Sheet (US ISSN 0085-8315) 731
World Propylene and Derivatives (US) 248
World Psychiatric Association. Bulletin (AU ISSN 0084-2206) 916, 916
World Radio & T.V. Handbook (US) 269
World Record Game Fishes (US) 400, 832
World Record Marine Fishes see World Record Game Fishes 400

World Record Markets (UK) 664
World Register of Chambers of Commerce/Associations & Trades see World Register of Trades 243
World Register of Trades (II) 243
World Review of Nutrition and Dietetics (SZ ISSN 0084-2230) 666
World Scout Bureau. Biennial Report (SZ) 257
World Student Chess Team Championship. Results (CS) 822
World Student Christian Federation. Dossier (SZ) 768
World Survey of Climatology (NE ISSN 0084-2265) 636
World Survey of Phosphate Deposits (UK) 40
World Survey of Sulphur Resources (UK) 40
World Tobacco Directory (UK ISSN 0084-2273) 861
World Today Series: Africa (US ISSN 0084-2281) 441
World Today Series: Far East and Southwest Pacific (US ISSN 0084-229X) 446
World Today Series: Latin America (US ISSN 0084-2303) 474
World Today Series: Middle East and South Asia (US ISSN 0084-2311) 447
World Today Series: Soviet Union and Eastern Europe (US ISSN 0084-232X) 465
World Today Series: Western Europe (US ISSN 0084-2338) 465
World Tourism Organization. Collection of Technical Bulletins (SP) 893
World Trade Annual (US ISSN 0512-3739) 198
World Trade Annual Supplement (US ISSN 0512-3747) 198
World Transport Data/Statistiques Mondiales de Transport (SZ ISSN 0302-7902) 867
World Travel Directory see Travel Weekly's World Travel Directory 892
World Travel Statistics/Statistiques du Tourisme Mondial/Estadisticas del Turismo Mundial (SP) 893
World Treaty Index (US) 725
World Trends in Passenger-Car Production and Engines (US) 872
World Union for the Safeguard of Youth. Conference Proceedings (FR) 810
World Union of Organizations for the Safeguard of Youth see World Union for the Safeguard of Youth. Conference Proceedings 810
World University Service. Annual Report (US ISSN 0084-2419) 343
World University Service. Programme of Action (US ISSN 0084-2427) 343
World Veterinary Association. Catalogue of Veterinary Films and Films of Veterinary Interest (SZ ISSN 0084-2435) 895
World Veterinary Congress. Proceedings (SZ ISSN 0084-2443) 895
World Weather Watch Planning Reports (UN ISSN 0084-2451) 636
World Wheat Statistics (UK ISSN 0512-3844) 26
World Who's Who in Commerce and Industry see Who's Who in Finance and Industry 99
World Who's Who of Women (UK) 99, 901
World Who's Who of Women in Education (UK) 99, 325, 901
World Wide Chamber of Commerce Directory (US ISSN 0084-2478) 180
World Wide Register of Adult Education (US ISSN 0084-2486) 330
World Wide Shipping Guide (US ISSN 0162-0088) 881
World-Wide Summer Placement Directory (US ISSN 0512-3879) 325
World Wood. Latin American Edition (US) 413
World Yearbook of Education (UK ISSN 0084-2508) 325

World Zionist Organization. General Council. Addresses, Debates, Resolutions (IS ISSN 0084-2516) *771*
World Zionist Organization. Zionist Congress. Kongres Ha-Tsiyoni. Hahlatot (IS) *717*
World's Poultry Science Association. Report of the Proceedings of International Congress (US ISSN 0084-2532) *46*
World's Telephones (US) *266*
World's Wisdom Series (II) *692, 768*
World's Woman's Christian Temperance Union. Convention Report (SA ISSN 0084-2540) *692, 817*
Worldwatch Papers (US) *390, 817*
Worldwide Chemical Directory (UK) *243, 248*
Worldwide Directory of Computer Companies (US) *274*
Worldwide Directory of Federal Libraries (US) *538*
Worldwide Directory of Pipelines and Contractors (US) *371, 682*
Worldwide Lodging Industry (US ISSN 0361-218X) *483*
Worldwide Offshore Contractors Directory *see* Offshore Contractors and Equipment Directory *680*
Worldwide Petrochemical Directory (US ISSN 0084-2583) *682*
Worldwide Refining and Gas Processing(US ISSN 0084-2591) *682*
Worldwide Report: Environmental Quality (US) *390*
Worldwide Report: Epidemiology (US) *756*
Worldwide Report: Law of the Sea (US) *524*
Worldwide Report: Telecommunications Policy. Research and Development (US) *265*
Wormley, England (Surrey) National Institute of Oceanography. Collected Reprints *see* Institute of Oceanographic Sciences. Collected Reprints *310*
Der Wormsgau (GW ISSN 0084-2613) *465*
Wormsloe Foundation. Publications (US ISSN 0084-2621) *474*
Woroni (AT) *558*
Worrall's Textile & Engineering Directory (II) *243*
Woytinsky Lectures (US ISSN 0084-263X) *717, 747*
Wrestling Officials Manual (US) *823*
Wrestling Rules (US) *823*
Wrightia (US ISSN 0084-2648) *119*
Wrigley's Hotel-Motel Directory (CN) *483*
Writ (CN ISSN 0316-3768) *577*
Writer (UK ISSN 0260-2776) *577*
Writers' and Artists' Yearbook (UK ISSN 0084-2664) *760*
Writers' and Photographers' Marketing Guide; Directory of Australian and New Zealand Literary and Photo Markets (AT ISSN 0084-2680) *694, 760*
Writers Directory (UK ISSN 0084-2699) *760*
Writers Forum (US) *577*
Writer's Handbook (US ISSN 0084-2710) *760*
Writer's Market (US ISSN 0084-2729) *760*
Writers of Wales (UK ISSN 0141-5050) *577*
Writer's Review *see* Writer *577*
Writers Workshop Literary Reader (II) *577*
Writer's Yearbook (US ISSN 0084-2737) *760*
Writing (US ISSN 0084-2745) *577*
Writings of the Left (US) *717*
Writings on American History (US) *438*
Writings on British History (UK ISSN 0084-2753) *438*
Wroclawski Rocznik Ekonomiczny (PL ISSN 0084-2974) *151*
Wroclawskie Towarzystwo Naukowe. Komisja Historii Sztuki. Rozprawy (PL ISSN 0084-2982) *80*

Wroclawskie Towarzystwo Naukowe. Komisja Jezykowa. Rozprawy (PL ISSN 0084-2990) *554*
Wroclawskie Towarzystwo Naukowe. Prace. Seria A. Humanistyka (PL ISSN 0084-3016) *495*
Wroclawskie Towarzystwo Naukowe. Prace. Seria B. Nauki Scisle (PL ISSN 0084-3024) *794*
Wroclawskie Towarzystwo Naukowe. Sprawozdania. Seria A (PL ISSN 0371-4756) *794*
Wspolczesne Malarstwo Wroclawskie (PL ISSN 0084-3032) *80*
Wudd (GW ISSN 0040-8646) *770*
Wuerttembergisch Franken (GW ISSN 0084-3067) *465*
Wuerzburger Dioezesangeschichtsblaetter (GW) *465*
Wuerzburger Geographische Arbeiten (GW ISSN 0510-9833) *428*
Wuerzburger Wehrwissenschaftliche Abhandlungen (GW ISSN 0084-3083) *521, 640*
Wye College (University of London). Agrarian Development Unit. Occasional Paper (UK) *32*
Wye College (University of London). School of Rural Economics & Related Studies. Farm Business Unit. Occasional Paper (UK) *32, 40*
Wykeham Science Series (US ISSN 0084-3113) *794*
Wykeham Technological Series (US ISSN 0084-3121) *854*
Wyoming. Agricultural Experiment Station, Laramie. Bulletin (US ISSN 0084-313X) *23*
Wyoming. Agricultural Experiment Station, Laramie. Research Journal (US ISSN 0084-3148) *23*
Wyoming. Agricultural Experiment Station, Laramie. Science Monograph(US ISSN 0084-3156) *23*
Wyoming. Department of Education. Education Directory (US) *325*
Wyoming. Department of Environmental Quality. Annual Report (US ISSN 0099-1279) *390*
Wyoming. Department of Health and Social Services. Annual Report (US ISSN 0098-6984) *756, 817*
Wyoming. Department of Labor and Statistics. Survey of Occupational Injuries and Illnesses (US ISSN 0093-1241) *496*
Wyoming. Department of Revenue and Taxation. Annual Report (US ISSN 0094-9019) *233*
Wyoming. Division of Planning, Evaluation and Information Services. Statistical Report Series (US ISSN 0093-5530) *849*
Wyoming. Employment Security Commission. Annual Report (US) *212*
Wyoming. Employment Security Commission. Research & Analysis Section. Annual Planning Report (US) *212*
Wyoming. Employment Security Commission. Research and Analysis Section. Farm Labor Report (US ISSN 0095-389X) *212*
Wyoming. Geological Survey. Bulletin (US) *302*
Wyoming. Geological Survey. Report of Investigations (US) *302*
Wyoming. Governor's Office of Highway Safety. Annual Report (US ISSN 0098-5058) *876*
Wyoming. State of Wyoming Annual Report (US ISSN 0094-3924) *747*
Wyoming. Water Quality Division. Wyoming State Plan (US ISSN 0098-0846) *390*
Wyoming Area Manpower Review (US ISSN 0097-739X) *212*
Wyoming Data Handbook (US) *747*
Wyoming Geological Association. Guidebook, Annual Field Conference(US) *302*
Wyoming Geological Association. Publications (US) *302*
Wyoming Mineral Yearbook (US) *302*
Wyoming Nurse (US) *614*

Wyoming Nurses Newsletter *see* Wyoming Nurse *614*
Wyoming State Plan *see* Wyoming. Water Quality Division. Wyoming State Plan *390*
Wyoming Statistical Review (US ISSN 0512-4395) *212*
Wyoming Work Injury Report *see* Wyoming. Department of Labor and Statistics. Survey of Occupational Injuries and Illnesses *496*
Wyzsza Szkola Ekonomiczna. Zeszyty Naukowe *see* Akademia Ekonomiczna, Krakow. Zeszyty Naukowe *141*
Wyzsza Szkola Ekonomiczna we Wroclawiv. Prace Naukowe *see* Akademia Ekonomiczna we Wroclawiu. Prace Naukowe *141*
Wyzsza Szkola Pedagogiczna, Katowice. Zeszyty Naukowe. Sekcja Jezykoznawstwa (PL ISSN 0075-5281) *554*
Wyzsza Szkola Pedagogiczna, Krakow. Prace Jezykoznawcze (PL) *555*
Wyzsza Szkola Pedagogiczna, Krakow. Prace Zoologiczne (PL) *131*
Wyzsza Szkola Pedagogiczna, Opole. Zeszyty Naukowe. Filologia Polska (PL ISSN 0324-9050) *555*
Wyzsza Szkola Rolnicza, Olsztyn. Zeszyty Naukowe *see* Akademia Rolniczo-Techniczna. Zeszyty Naukowe *12*
Wyzsza Szkola Rolnicza, Wroclaw. Rolnictwo *see* Akademia Rolnicza, Wroclaw. Rolnictwo *12*
Xanadu (US) *582*
Xanthippe (US) *577, 901*
Xavier University. Museum and Archives Publications (PH ISSN 0084-3229) *495*
Y Canada (CN ISSN 0315-095X) *257, 262*
Y E R Monograph Series (Yeats Elliot Review) (CN ISSN 0704-5697) *577*
Y M C A Yearbook and Official Roster(US ISSN 0084-4292) *810*
Y M C A's of the World (SZ) *257, 262*
Yachting Belge (BE ISSN 0084-3237) *827*
Yachting Year Book of Northern California (US ISSN 0094-8136) *827*
Yachting's Boat Buyers Guide (US) *827*
Yachtsman's Guide to the Caribbean (US ISSN 0084-3261) *827*
Yachtsman's Guide to the Great Lakes (US ISSN 0084-327X) *827*
Yachtsman's Guide to the Greater Antilles (US ISSN 0162-7635) *827*
Yad Vashem Studies (IS) *771*
Yad Vashem Studies on the European Jewish Catastrophe and Resistance *see* Yad Vashem Studies *771*
Yale Classical Studies (UK ISSN 0084-330X) *261*
Yale College Series (US ISSN 0084-3318) *495*
Yale Fastbacks (US ISSN 0084-3326) *802*
Yale Germanic Studies (US ISSN 0084-3334) *577*
Yale Historical Publications (Miscellany) (US ISSN 0084-3350) *436*
Yale Judaica Series (US ISSN 0084-3369) *771*
Yale Law School Studies (US ISSN 0513-1405) *521, 717*
Yale Linguistic Series (US ISSN 0513-4412) *555*
Yale Mathematical Monographs (US ISSN 0084-3377) *591*
Yale Near Eastern Researches (US ISSN 0084-3385) *475*
Yale Oriental Series. Babylonian Texts (US) *475*
Yale Publications in American Studies (US ISSN 0084-3393) *474*
Yale Publications in Religion (US ISSN 0084-3407) *768*
Yale Publications in the History of Art (US ISSN 0084-3415) *70, 80*
Yale Romanic Studies. Second Series (US ISSN 0084-3423) *577*

Yale Russian and East European Studies (US ISSN 0084-3431) *577*
Yale Scene; University Series (US ISSN 0084-344X) *342*
Yale Series in Economic History (US) *192*
Yale Series in the Sciences (US) *794*
Yale Series of Younger Poets (US ISSN 0084-3458) *582*
Yale Southeast Asia Studies (US ISSN 0084-3466) *447*
Yale Southeast Asia Studies. Monograph Series (US ISSN 0513-4501) *802*
Yale Studies in English (US ISSN 0084-3482) *577*
Yale Studies in Political Science (US ISSN 0084-3490) *717*
Yale Studies in the History of Music (US ISSN 0084-3504) *664*
Yale Studies in the History of Science and Medicine (US ISSN 0084-3512) *601, 794*
Yale Studies of the City (US ISSN 0084-3520) *488*
Yale University. Department of Anthropology. Publications in Anthropology (US) *55*
Yale University. Economic Growth Center. Discussion Papers (US) *151*
Yale University. School of Forestry. Bulletin (US ISSN 0361-4425) *412*
Yale University Art Gallery. Bulletin (US ISSN 0084-3539) *656*
Yale Western Americana Series (US ISSN 0084-3563) *474*
Yamagata University. Bulletin (JA ISSN 0085-834X) *495*
Yamaguchi University. Faculty of Engineering. Technology Reports (JA) *854*
Yankee Ingenuity (US) *265, 274*
Yapi ve Kredi Bankasi. Annual Report (TU) *178*
Yardsticks for Costing (CN) *70*
Year-End Regulatory Review (US) *217*
Year-End Summary of the Electric Power Situation in the United States (US ISSN 0424-480X) *359*
Year in Hematology *see* Contemporary Hematology/Oncology *613*
Year in Review *see* Malawi. Department of Information. Year in Review *440*
Yearbook and Church Directory of the Orthodox Church in America *see* Orthodox Church in America. Yearbook and Church Directory *776*
Year Book and Directory for the Dental Technician (UK) *610*
Yearbook and Directory of Osteopathic Physicians (US ISSN 0084-358X) *607*
Year Book Color Atlas Series *see* Color Atlas Series *594*
Yearbook - Geological Society of America *see* Geological Society of America. Yearbook *294*
Yearbook Geomagnetism: Paramaribo, Surinam (NE ISSN 0077-7587) *307*
Yearbook in Education (US) *325*
Yearbook in Women's Policy Studies (US) *901*
Yearbook of Adult and Continuing Education (US) *330*
Yearbook of Adult Education (UK ISSN 0084-3601) *330*
Yearbook of Adult Education in Scotland *see* Handbook of Adult Education in Scotland *329*
Year Book of Agricultural Co-Operation (UK ISSN 0142-498X) *32, 219*
Yearbook of American and Canadian Churches (US ISSN 0084-3644) *768*
Yearbook of American Churches *see* Yearbook of American and Canadian Churches *768*
Year Book of Anesthesia (US ISSN 0084-3652) *604*
Yearbook of Astronomy (US ISSN 0084-3660) *85*
Year Book of Cancer (US ISSN 0084-3679) *4, 603*
Year Book of Cardiology (US ISSN 0145-4145) *607*

Yearbook of Cardiovascular and Renal Disease see Year Book of Cardiology 607
Yearbook of Cardiovascular Medicine see Year Book of Cardiology 607
Yearbook of Cardiovascular Medicine and Surgery see Year Book of Cardiology 607
Yearbook of Common Carrier Telecommunication Statistics/Annuaire Statistique des Telecommunications du Secteur Public (UN) 265
Yearbook of Comparative and General Literature (US ISSN 0084-3695) 577
Yearbook of Comparative Criticism (US ISSN 0084-3709) 577
Yearbook of Cultural & Artistic Activities/Munyeyungam (KO) 80, 860
Yearbook of Danish Medical History see Dansk Medicinhistorisk Aarbog 594
Year Book of Dentistry (US ISSN 0084-3717) 610
Year Book of Dermatology (US ISSN 0093-3619) 611
Yearbook of Dermatology and Syphilology see Year Book of Dermatology 611
Year Book of Diagnostic Radiology (US ISSN 0098-1672) 622
Yearbook of Drug Abuse. (US ISSN 0090-662X) 287
Year Book of Drug Therapy (US ISSN 0084-3733) 686
Yearbook of East-European Economics see Jahrbuch der Wirtschaft Osteuropas 186
Year Book of Endocrinology (US ISSN 0084-3741) 612
Yearbook of English Studies (UK ISSN 0306-2473) 495, 577
Yearbook of Equal Educational Opportunity see Sourcebook of Equal Educational Opportunity 323
Year Book of Family Practice (US ISSN 0147-1996) 601
Yearbook of Finnish Foreign Policy (FI ISSN 0355-0079) 725
Yearbook of Fishery Statistics (UN ISSN 0084-375X) 400
Yearbook of Forest Products (UN ISSN 0084-3768) 413
Yearbook of Forest Statistics see Metsatilastollinen Vuosikirja 409
Year Book of General Surgery see Year Book of Surgery 625
Yearbook of Greek Press (GR) 506
Yearbook of Herpetology (Herpetological Information Search Systems) (US ISSN 0098-2644) 131
Yearbook of Higher Education (US ISSN 0084-3784) 342
Yearbook of Higher Education Law (US) 325, 521
Yearbook of Human Rights (NE) 719
Yearbook of International Congress Proceedings (BE ISSN 0084-3806) 725
Yearbook of International Organizations (BE ISSN 0084-3814) 725
Yearbook of International Trade Statistics (UN ISSN 0084-3822) 166
Yearbook of Israel Ports Statistics/Shenaton Statisti: Le Nemlei Israel (IS ISSN 0084-3830) 198
Yearbook of Italian Studies (IT) 465
Year Book of Labour Statistics. (UN ISSN 0084-3857) 166
Yearbook of Manitoba Agriculture (CN ISSN 0084-3865) 23
Year Book of Medicine (US ISSN 0084-3873) 601
Yearbook of National Accounts Statistics (UN ISSN 0084-3881) 166
Year Book of Neurology & Neurosurgery (US) 621, 625
Year Book of Neurology, Psychiatry and Neurosurgery see Year Book of Neurology & Neurosurgery 621
Yearbook of Neurology, Psychiatry and Neurosurgery see Year Book of Psychiatry and Applied Mental Health 622

Yearbook of Nordic Statistics see Nordisk Statistisk Aarsbok 843
Year Book of Nuclear Medicine (US ISSN 0084-3903) 623
Year Book of Obstetrics and Gynecology (US ISSN 0084-3911) 615
Year Book of Ophthalmology (US ISSN 0084-392X) 616
Year Book of Orthopedics and Traumatic Surgery (US ISSN 0084-3938) 616
Year Book of Otolaryngology (US) 617
Year Book of Pathology and Clinical Pathology (US ISSN 0084-3946) 601
Year Book of Pediatrics (US ISSN 0084-3954) 618
Year Book of Physical Anthropology (Washington) (US ISSN 0096-848X) 55
Year Book of Plastic and Reconstructive Surgery (US ISSN 0084-3962) 625
Yearbook of Population Research in Finland/Vaestoentutkimuken Vuosikirja (FI ISSN 0506-3590) 731
Year Book of Psychiatry and Applied Mental Health (US ISSN 0084-3970) 622
Yearbook of Pulp and Paper Statistics/Kami Parupu Tokei Nenpo (JA ISSN 0453-1515) 675
Year Book of Radiology see Year Book of Diagnostic Radiology 622
Yearbook of Railroad Facts (US ISSN 0084-3997) 874
Yearbook of Romanian Studies (US) 465, 577
Yearbook of Scandinavian Shipowners see Skandinaviske Skipsrederier 880
Yearbook of School Law (US) 325, 521
Yearbook of Science and the Future (US ISSN 0096-3291) 794
Yearbook of Selected Osteopathic Papers see American Academy of Osteopathy Yearbook 607
Yearbook of Special Education (US) 347
Year Book of Sports Medicine (US ISSN 0162-0908) 601, 823
Year Book of Surgery (US ISSN 0090-3671) 625
Yearbook of Symbolic Anthropology (CN) 55
Yearbook of Technical and Further Education see Directory of Technical and Further Education 667
Yearbook of the American Baptist Churches in the U. S. A. see American Baptist Churches in the U. S. A. Yearbook 771
Yearbook of the Brazilian Industry of Automotive Parts see Anuario da Industria Brasileira de Autopecas 869
Yearbook of the Commonwealth (UK ISSN 0084-4047) 465
Year Book of the Ear, Nose and Throat see Year Book of Otolaryngology 617
Yearbook of the Italian Rubber Industry see Annuario dell' Industria Italiana della Gomma 777
Year-Book of the Lebanese Joint-Stock Companies/Annuaire des Societes Libanaises Par Action (LE ISSN 0075-8361) 205
Year-Book of the Lebanese Limited Liability Companies/Annuaire der Societes Libanaises a Responsibilite Limitee (LE) 205
Yearbook of Tidal Records see Choi Nenpo 309
Year Book of Urology (US ISSN 0084-4071) 625
Yearbook of Works re Appalachia (US) 582
Yearbook of World Affairs (UK ISSN 0084-408X) 428
Yearbook of World Problems and Human Potential (BE ISSN 0304-0089) 725, 810
Yearbook on Human Rights (UN ISSN 0084-4098) 495, 719
Yearbook on International Communist Affairs (US ISSN 0084-4101) 725

Yearbook on Jute (BG ISSN 0084-411X) 857
Yearbook- Society of Wireless Pioneers see Society of Wireless Pioneers. Yearbook 269
Yearbook - Supreme Court Historical Society see Supreme Court Historical Society. Yearbook 519
Yearbooks in Christian Education (US ISSN 0084-4128) 768
Yearly All India Criminal Digest. (II) 284
Yearly Supreme Court Digest (II) 521
Year's Work in English Studies (US ISSN 0084-4144) 577
Year's Work in Modern Language Studies (UK ISSN 0084-4152) 555, 578
Yeats Centenary Papers see New Yeats Papers 569
Yeats Elliot Review Monograph Series see Y E R Monograph Series 577
Yeh Ko see Evensongs 556
Yellow Book of Funeral Directors & Services (US ISSN 0098-3322) 414
Yemen. Central Statistical Office. Statistical Yearbook (YE) 849
Yerusholaymer Almanakh. (IS) 577
Yes see Chien d'Or 561
Yes! Capra Chapbook Series (US) 577
Yiddish Language see Yidishe Shprakh 555
Yidishe Shprakh/Yiddish Language (US ISSN 0044-0442) 555
Yivo Annual of Jewish Social Science (US ISSN 0084-4209) 802
Yivo Bleter/Yivo Pages (US ISSN 0084-4217) 802
Yivo Pages see Yivo Bleter 802
Ymer (SW ISSN 0044-0477) 55, 428
Yokohama Kokuritsu Daigaku Jimbun Kiyo Dai-1-rui, Tetsugaku, Shakai Kagaku see Yokohama National University. Humanities. Section 1: Philosophy and Social Sciences 802
Yokohama Kokuritsu Daigaku Kogakubu Kiyo see Yokohama National University. Faculty of Engineering. Bulletin 371
Yokohama Kokuritsu Daigaku Rika Kiyo, Dai-1-rui, Sugaku, Butsurigaku, Kagaku see Yokohama National University. Science Reports. Section I: Mathematics, Physics, Chemistry 794
Yokohama Kokuritu Daigaku Kyoiku Kiyo see Yokohama National University. Educational Sciences 325
Yokohama National University. Educational Sciences/Yokohama Kokuritu Daigaku Kyoiku Kiyo (JA ISSN 0513-5656) 325
Yokohama National University. Faculty of Engineering. Bulletin/Yokohama Kokuritsu Daigaku Kogakubu Kiyo (JA ISSN 0513-2592) 371
Yokohama National University. Humanities. Section 1: Philosophy and Social Sciences/Yokohama Kokuritsu Daigaku Jimbun Kiyo Dai-1-rui, Tetsugaku, Shakai Kagaku (JA ISSN 0513-5621) 692, 802
Yokohama National University. Science Reports. Section I: Mathematics, Physics, Chemistry/Yokohama Kokuritsu Daigaku Rika Kiyo, Dai-1-rui, Sugaku, Butsurigaku, Kagaku (JA ISSN 0085-8366) 794
Yokohama National University. Science Reports. Section II: Biological and Geological Sciences (JA) 109
Yokohama National University. Science Reports. Section II: Biological Sciences see Yokohama National University. Science Reports. Section II: Biological and Geological Sciences 109
Yokufukai Chosa Kenkyu Kiyo see Yokufukai Geriatric Journal 428
Yokufukai Geriatric Journal/Yokufukai Chosa Kenkyu Kiyo (JA) 428
Yonsei Reports on Tropical Medicine (KO) 608
Yonsei University. Graduate School. Abstracts of Faculty Research Reports (KO) 4, 328
York Georgian Society. Annual Report (UK) 70

York Journal of Convocation (UK ISSN 0085-8374) 768
York-Simcoe Ontario Construction Industry Directory. Purchasing Guide (CN ISSN 0704-8785) 139, 371
Yorker (1976) (US) 474
Yorker Annual see Yorker (1976) 474
Yorkshire Archaeological Journal (UK ISSN 0084-4276) 67
Yorkshire Archaeological Society Parish Register Series (UK) 418
Yorkshire Archaeological Society Record Series (UK) 465
Yorkshire Dialect Society. Summer Bulletin (UK ISSN 0513-2762) 555
Yorkshire Dialect Society Transactions (UK) 555
Young Adult Alternative Newsletter (US) 258
Young Buddhist (SI) 771
Young Communist see Young Worker 717
Young Fabian Pamphlet (UK ISSN 0513-5982) 717
Young Socialist (CN ISSN 0044-0884) 717
Young Socialist Forum see Young Socialist 717
Young Students Encyclopedia Yearbook (US ISSN 0094-9027) 436
Young Women's Christian Association of the United States of America. National Board. Annual Report (US) 262
Young Women's Christian Association of the United States of America. The Printout (US ISSN 0084-4306) 768
Young Worker (CN ISSN 0382-4047) 717
Young Worker (SA) 768
Your Australian Garden (AT ISSN 0085-8382) 416
Your Friendly Fascist (AT) 582
Your Investments; How to Increase Your Capital and Income see Dun & Bradstreet's Guide to Your Investments 203
Your Texas Ancestors (US ISSN 0085-8390) 418
Your United Nations (UN ISSN 0084-4322) 436, 725
Youth Correctional Institution, Bordentown, N.J. Annual Report (US ISSN 0092-4539) 257
Youth Info Digest (US) 258
Youth International (UK) 343
Youth-Serving Organizations Directory (US) 810
Yrke och Framtid (SW) 668
Yugoslav Export-Import Directory (YU ISSN 0084-4349) 199, 243
Yugoslav Serbo-Croatian-English Contrastive Project. Series B: studies (YU) 555
Yugoslavia. Savezni Zavod za Statistiku. Anketa O Ostvarivanju Prava Radnika Iz Radnog Odnosa (YU) 166
Yugoslavia. Savezni Zavod za Statistiku. Anketa O Porodicnim Budzetima Radnickih Domacinstava (YU) 166
Yugoslavia. Savezni Zavod za Statistiku. Industrijske Organizacije (YU) 166
Yugoslavia. Savezni Zavod za Statistiku. Komunalni Fondovi u Gradskim Naseljima (YU) 748
Yugoslavia. Savezni Zavod za Statistiku. Osnovna i Srednje (YU) 328
Yugoslavia. Savezni Zavod za Statistiku. Samoupravljanje u Privredi (YU) 166
Yugoslavia. Savezni Zavod za Statistiku. Samoupravljanje u Ustanovama Drustvenih Sluzbi (YU) 166
Yugoslavia. Savezni Zavod za Statistiku. Saobracaj i Veze (YU ISSN 0513-0794) 867
Yugoslavia. Savezni Zavod za Statistiku. Turizam (YU) 893
Yugoslavia. Savezni Zavod za Statistiku. Ucenici u Privredi (YU ISSN 0513-0832) 328
Yugoslavia. Savezni Zavod za Statistiku. Zaposleno Osoblje (YU ISSN 0513-0883) 166

Yugoslavia. Savezni Zavod za Statistiku. Vitalna Statistika *see* Demografska Statistika 727
Yugoslavia; Hotel and Tourist Directory(YU) 483
Yukijirushi Nyugyo Gijutsu Kenkyusho Hokoku *see* Snow Brand Milk Products Co., Ltd. Research Laboratory. Reports 41
Yuval (IS ISSN 0084-439X) 664
Z.A.S.E. Bulletin *see* Science Education in Zambia 322
Z.C.L.A. Journal *see* Zen Writings 771
Z Dziejow Form Artystycznych w Literaturze Polskiej (PL ISSN 0084-4411) 577
Z Dziejow Muzyki Polskiej (PL ISSN 0084-442X) 664
Z F I-Mitteilungen (Zentralinstitut fuer Isotopen- und Strahlenforschung) (GE ISSN 0323-8776) 699
Z G A Bibliographic Series (Zambia Geographical Association) (ZA) 96, 428
Z G A Magazine *see* Zambian Geographical Journal 428
Z G A Occasional Studies (Zambia Geographical Association) (ZA) 428
Z G A Regional Handbook *see* Zambia Geographical Association. Regional Handbook 428
Z M P Bilanz Getreide-Futtermittel (GW ISSN 0170-7809) 43
Z 6 A Occasional Studies and Special Publications *see* Z G A Occasional Studies 428
Zagadnienia Drgan Nieliniowych (PL ISSN 0044-1597) 700
Zahlestafeln der Physikalisch-Chemischen Untersuchungen des Rheins sowie der Mosel/Tableaux Numeriques des Analyses Physico-Chimiques des Eaux du Rhin Ainsi Que de la Moselle. (GW ISSN 0539-1539) 390
Zahnaerztliche Fortbildung (GE ISSN 0084-4462) 610
Zahranicne Periodika v C S S R (CS) 96
Zaidan Hojin Toyo Bunko *see* Oriental Library. Research Department. Memoirs 445
Zaire. Assemblee Nationale. Compte Rendu Analytique *see* Zaire. Conseil Legislatif National. Compte Rendu Analytique 521
Zaire. Bibliotheque Nationale. Bibliographie Nationale (ZR) 96
Zaire. Conseil Legislatif National. Compte Rendu Analytique (ZR) 521
Zaire. Direction de la Statistique et des Etudes Economiques. Annuaire des Statistiques du Commerce Exterieur *see* Zaire. Institut National de la Statistique. Annuaire des Statistiques du Commerce Exterieur 166
Zaire. Institut National de la Statistique. Annuaire des Statistiques du Commerce Exterieur (ZR ISSN 0304-5692) 166
Zairyo Kenkyu Rengo Koenkai Ronbunshu *see* Japan Congress on Materials Research. Proceedings 380
Zambia. Central Statistical Office. Agricultural and Pastoral Production (Commercial and Non-Commercial) (ZA) 26
Zambia. Central Statistical Office. Agricultural and Pastoral Production (Commercial Farms) (ZA) 26, 849
Zambia. Central Statistical Office. Agricultural and Pastoral Production (Non-Commercial) (ZA) 26, 849
Zambia. Central Statistical Office. Agricultural and Pastoral Production *see* Zambia. Central Statistical Office. Agricultural and Pastoral Production (Commercial and Non-Commercial) 26
Zambia. Central Statistical Office. Agricultural and Pastoral Production *see* Zambia. Central Statistical Office. Agricultural and Pastoral Production (Non-Commercial) 26
Zambia. Central Statistical Office. Agricultural and Pastoral Production *see* Zambia. Central Statistical Office. Agricultural and Pastoral Production (Commercial Farms) 26

Zambia. Central Statistical Office. Annual Statement of External Trade (ZA ISSN 0084-4489) 166
Zambia. Central Statistical Office. Balance of Payments Statistics (ZA) 166
Zambia. Central Statistical Office. Employment and Earnings (ZA ISSN 0084-4500) 166
Zambia. Central Statistical Office. Financial Statistics of Government Sector (Economic and Functional Analysis) (ZA) 748
Zambia. Central Statistical Office. Financial Statistics of Public Corporations (ZA ISSN 0084-4519) 166
Zambia. Central Statistical Office. Fisheries Statistics (Natural Waters) (ZA ISSN 0514-8731) 400
Zambia. Central Statistical Office. Government Sector Accounts (Economic and Functional Analysis) *see* Zambia. Central Statistical Office. Financial Statistics of Government Sector (Economic and Functional Analysis) 748
Zambia. Central Statistical Office. Industry Monographs (ZA) 151
Zambia. Central Statistical Office. Migration Statistics (ZA ISSN 0084-4543) 731
Zambia. Central Statistical Office. Migration Statistics: Immigrants and Visitors *see* Zambia. Central Statistical Office. Migration Statistics 731
Zambia. Central Statistical Office. National Accounts (ZA) 233, 747
Zambia. Central Statistical Office. Quarterly Agricultural Statistical Bulletin (ZA) 26, 849
Zambia. Central Statistical Office. Registered Births, Marriages and Deaths (Vital Statistics) *see* Zambia. Central Statistical Office. Vital Statistics 849
Zambia. Central Statistical Office. Statistical Year Book (ZA ISSN 0084-4551) 849
Zambia. Central Statistical Office. Vital Statistics (ZA ISSN 0084-456X) 849
Zambia. Commission for Investigations. Annual Report (ZA) 747
Zambia. Commission for the Preservation of Natural and Historical Monuments and Relics. Annual Report (ZA ISSN 0084-4586) 279
Zambia. Department of Community Development. Report (ZA ISSN 0084-4608) 810
Zambia. Department of Cooperatives. Annual Report (ZA ISSN 0514-5430) 181
Zambia. Department of Forestry. Report (ZA ISSN 0084-4616) 412
Zambia. Department of Labour. Report (ZA ISSN 0084-4632) 212
Zambia. Department of Social Welfare. Report (ZA ISSN 0084-4667) 810
Zambia. Department of Social Welfare. Social Welfare Research Monographs(ZA ISSN 0081-0533) 810
Zambia. Department of Taxes. Annual Report of the Commissioner of Taxes(ZA ISSN 0084-4675) 233
Zambia. Department of the Administrator-General and Official Receiver. Report (ZA ISSN 0084-4683) 233
Zambia. Department of Water Affairs. Report (ZA ISSN 0084-4705) 899
Zambia. Educational and Occupational Assessment Service. Annual Report (ZA ISSN 0514-5457) 668
Zambia. General Post Office. Annual Report of the Postmaster-General *see* Zambia. Posts and Telecommunications Corporation. Annual Report 266
Zambia. Geological Survey. Annual Reports (ZA ISSN 0084-473X) 302
Zambia. Geological Survey. Economic Reports (ZA ISSN 0084-4748) 303
Zambia. Geological Survey. Occasional Papers (ZA ISSN 0084-4756) 303

Zambia. Geological Survey. Reports (ZA ISSN 0084-4764) 303
Zambia. Geological Survey. Technical Reports (ZA) 303
Zambia. Immigration Department. Report (ZA ISSN 0084-4802) 731
Zambia. Information Services. Annual Report (ZA ISSN 0084-4810) 441
Zambia. Ministry of Agriculture and Water Development. Land Use Branch. Soil Survey Report (ZA) 40
Zambia. Ministry of Agriculture. Annual Report (ZA ISSN 0084-4853) 23
Zambia. Ministry of Development and National Guidance. Annual Report *see* Zambia. Ministry of Planning and Finance. Annual Report 226
Zambia. Ministry of Education. Annual Report (ZA ISSN 0084-487X) 325
Zambia. Ministry of Finance. Annual Report *see* Zambia. Ministry of Planning and Finance. Annual Report 226
Zambia. Ministry of Lands and Agriculture. Land Use Branch. Soil Survey Report *see* Zambia. Ministry of Agriculture and Water Development. Land Use Branch. Soil Survey Report 40
Zambia. Ministry of Planning and Finance. Annual Report (ZA) 226
Zambia. National Commission for Development Planning. Economic Report (ZA) 191
Zambia. National Council for Scientific Research. Annual Report (ZA ISSN 0084-4950) 794
Zambia. National Council for Scientific Research. N C S R Bibliography (ZA) 96, 795
Zambia. National Food and Nutrition Commission. Annual Report (ZA ISSN 0084-4969) 406, 666
Zambia. National Museums Board. Occasional Paper Series (ZA) 55, 441
Zambia. National Museums Board. Report (ZA ISSN 0084-4977) 656
Zambia. Natural Resources Advisory Board. Annual Report *see* Zambia. Natural Resources Department. Annual Report 279
Zambia. Natural Resources Department. Annual Report (ZA) 279
Zambia. Office of the Auditor-General. Report of the Auditor-General (ZA ISSN 0084-4497) 233
Zambia. Pneumoconiosis Medical and Research Bureau and Pneumoconiosis Compensation Board. Annual Reports (ZA ISSN 0084-5000) 623
Zambia. Posts and Telecommunications Corporation. Annual Report (ZA) 266
Zambia. Prisons Department. Report (ZA ISSN 0084-4659) 284
Zambia. Public Service Commission. Report (ZA ISSN 0084-5035) 810
Zambia. Sports Directorate. Report (ZA ISSN 0084-506X) 823
Zambia. Survey Department. Report (ZA ISSN 0084-5078) 428
Zambia. Teaching Service Commission. Annual Report (ZA ISSN 0084-5086) 325
Zambia Directory (ZA) 243
Zambia Educational Journal (ZA) 325
Zambia Electricity Supply Corporation. Annual Report (ZA) 359
Zambia Geographical Association. Conference Handbook *see* Zambia Geographical Association. Regional Handbook 428
Zambia Geographical Association. Regional Handbook (ZA) 428
Zambia Geographical Association Bibliographic Series *see* Z G A Bibliographic Series 428
Zambia Geographical Association Occasional Studies *see* Z G A Occasional Studies 428
Zambia Law Reports (ZA) 521
Zambia Mining Yearbook (ZA ISSN 0076-9010) 648
Zambia Museums Journal (ZA) 656
Zambia Museums Papers Series (ZA) 67, 441
Zambia Science Abstracts (ZA) 4, 795

ZEITSCHRIFT FUER   1541

Zambia State Insurance Corporation. Report and Accounts (ZA) 501
Zambian Geographical Journal (ZA) 428
Zambian Industrial Directory. (ZA ISSN 0084-5116) 243
Zambian Ornithological Society Occasional Papers (ZA) 125
Zambian Papers (ZA ISSN 0084-5124) 441
Zaposleni po Obcinah (YU) 212
Zbornik Istorije Knjizevnosti/Recueil des Travaux de l'Histoire de la Litterature (YU ISSN 0084-5183) 577
Zbornik za Istoriju, Jezik i Knjizevnost Srpskog Naroda. Fontes Rerum Slavorum Meridionalium (YU ISSN 0084-5191) 465
Zbornik za Istoriju, Jezik i Knjizevnost Srpskog Naroda. Spomenici na Srpskom Jeziku (YU ISSN 0084-5205) 577
Zbornik za Istoriju, Jezik i Knjizevnost Srpskog Naroda. Spomenici na Tudjim Jezicima (YU ISSN 0084-5213) 465
Zbornik Zagrebacke Slavisticke Skole (YU) 555
Zbornik Zastite Spomenika Kulture/Recueil des Travaux sur la Protection des Monuments Historiques (YU ISSN 0514-616X) 80
Ze Skarbca Kultury (PL ISSN 0084-5221) 495
Zeichenwerk (GW ISSN 0084-523X) 80
Zeimu Tokei Kara Mita Hojin Kigyo No Jittai (JA) 233
Zeirei Forum (US) 394
Zeiss Information (GW ISSN 0044-2054) 706
Zeitschrift fuer Alternsforschung. Supplementbaende (GE ISSN 0084-5272) 428
Zeitschrift fuer Archaeologie des Mittelalters (GW ISSN 0340-0824) 67
Zeitschrift fuer Bibliothekswesen und Bibliographie. Sonderhefte (GW ISSN 0514-6364) 538
Zeitschrift fuer Celtische Philologie (GW ISSN 0084-5302) 555, 577
Zeitschrift fuer Dialektologie und Linguistik. Beihefte (GW ISSN 0341-0838) 555
Zeitschrift fuer die Alttestamentliche Wissenschaft. Beihefte (GW) 769
Zeitschrift fuer die Geschichte des Oberrheins (GW) 465
Zeitschrift fuer Ernaehrungswissenschaft. Supplementa (GW ISSN 0084-5337) 666
Zeitschrift fuer Franzoesische Sprache und Literatur. Beihefte.Neue Folge (GW ISSN 0341-0811) 555
Zeitschrift fuer Geschichte der Naturwissenschaften, der Technik und der Medizin *see* Zeitschrift fuer Geschichte der Naturwissenschaften, Technik und Medizin. Schriftenreihe 783
Zeitschrift fuer Immunitaetsforschung-Immunobiology (GW ISSN 0340-904X) 604
Zeitschrift fuer Immunitaetsforschung - Immunologie *see* Zeitschrift fuer Immunitaetsforschung-Immunobiology 604
Zeitschrift fuer Literaturwissenschaft und Linguistik LiLi. Beihefte *see* LiLi. Beihefte 546
Zeitschrift fuer Orgelbau *see* Organ Building Periodical 662
Zeitschrift fuer Papyrologie und Epigraphik (GW ISSN 0084-5388) 67
Zeitschrift fuer Philosophische Forschung. Beihefte (GW ISSN 0514-2733) 692
Zeitschrift fuer Psychosomatische Medizin und Psychoanalyse. Beihefte(GW ISSN 0085-8412) 622, 739
Zeitschrift fuer Romanische Philologie. Beihefte (GW ISSN 0084-5396) 555

Zeitschrift fuer Schweizerisches Recht/ Revue de Droit Suisse (SZ ISSN 0084-540X) *521*
Zeitschrift fuer Tierzuechtung und Zuechtungsbiologie/Journal of Animal Breeding and Genetics (GW ISSN 0044-3581) *46*
Zeitschrift fuer Unternehmensgeschichte. Beihefte (GW ISSN 0342-3956) *192*
Zemaljski Muzej Bosne i Hercegovine. Glasnik. Arheologija (YU ISSN 0581-7501) *67*
Zemaljski Muzej Bosne i Hercegovine. Glasnik. Etnologija (YU ISSN 0581-751X) *55, 403*
Zemaljski Muzej Bosne i Hercegovine. Glasnik. Prirodne Nauke (YU ISSN 0581-7528) *794*
Zement-Taschenbuch (GW ISSN 0514-2938) *139*
Zement und Beton (AU) *140*
Zen Center of Los Angeles Zen Writings *see* Zen Writings *771*
Zen Nihon Shuppanbutsu Somokuroku *see* Japanese National Bibliography *92*
Zen Writings (Zen Center of Los Angeles) (US) *771*
Zentai Fuzetek (YU) *465*
Zentralasiatische Studien (GW ISSN 0514-857X) *447*
Zentralblatt fuer Bakteriologie, Parasitenkunde, Infektionskrankheiten und Hygiene. Originale Reihe A: Medizinische Mikrobiologie und Parasitologie (GW ISSN 0172-5599) *124, 608*
Zentralblatt fuer Bakteriologie, Parasitenkunde, Infektionskrankheiten und Hygiene. Orginale Reihe B: Hygiene - Preventive Medizin *see* Zentralblatt fuer Bakteriologie, Parasitenkunnde, Infektionskrankheiten und Hygiene-Krankenhaushygiene-Praeventive Medizin-Betriebshygiene *756*
Zentralblatt fuer Bakteriologie, Parasitenkunnde, Infektionskrankheiten und Hygiene-Krankenhaushygiene-Praeventive Medizin-Betriebshygiene (GW ISSN 0172-5602) *756*
Zentrales Geologisches Institut. Palaeontologische Abhandlungen (GE ISSN 0078-8600) *674*
Zentralinstitut fuer Mathematik und Mechanik. Schriftenreihe (GE) *591, 701*
Zentralinstitut fuer Physik der Erde. Seismologischer Dienst Jena. Seismologische Bulletin (GE ISSN 0065-5023) *307*
Zerowork (US) *151*
Zeszyty Problemowe Postepow Nauk Rolniczych (PL ISSN 0084-5477) *23*
Zidis (GE) *166, 700*

Zidis-Information *see* Zidis *166*
Ziegeleitechnisches Jahrbuch (GW ISSN 0084-5485) *245*
Ziema Kozielska. Studia i Materialy (PL ISSN 0084-5493) *465*
Ziemie Zachodnie. Studia i Materialy (PL ISSN 0084-5507) *465*
Ziemniak/Kartofel/Potato (PL) *40*
Zimbabwe. Central Statistical Office. Agricultural Production in European Areas: Livestock. National and Provincial Totals (RH) *46*
Zimbabwe. Central Statistical Office. Agricultural Production in Purchase Lands: National and Provincial Totals (RH) *40*
Zimbabwe. Central Statistical Office. Agricultural Production in Tribal Trust Land Irrigation Schemes and Tilcor Estates (RH) *23*
Zimbabwe. Central Statistical Office. Census of Population. (RH ISSN 0085-5685) *731*
Zimbabwe. Central Statistical Office. Census of Production (RH) *226, 849*
Zimbabwe. Central Statistical Office. Income Tax Statistics (RH) *166, 233, 849*
Zimbabwe. Cotton Research Institue. Annual Report (RH) *40*
Zimbabwe. Department of Meteorological Services. Rainfall Report (RH ISSN 0085-5693) *636*
Zimbabwe. Department of Meteorological Services. Report (RH ISSN 0085-5707) *636*
Zimbabwe. Department of Works. Report of the Controller of Works (RH) *747*
Zimbabwe. Estimates of Expenditure (RH) *234*
Zimbabwe. Ministry of Education. African Education Report (RH ISSN 0080-2859) *325*
Zimbabwe. Ministry of Finance. Financial Statement (RH) *234*
Zimbabwe. Ministry of Lands and Natural Resources. Report of the Secretary for Lands and Natural Resources (RH) *279, 648*
Zimbabwe. Ministry of Water Development. Hydrological Summaries (RH ISSN 0080-2832) *303, 381*
Zimbabwe. Ministry of Water Development. Hydrological Year Book (RH ISSN 0080-2840) *303, 381*
Zimbabwe. National Archives. Annual Report (RH) *441*
Zimbabwe. National Archives. Occasional Papers (RH ISSN 0035-4716) *441*
Zimbabwe. Registrar of Insurance. Report (RH ISSN 0556-8692) *501*
Zimbabwe National Bibliography(RH) *96*

Zimbabwe-Rhodesia. Tobacco Research Board. Annual Report and Accounts (RH ISSN 0080-2875) *861*
Zion (IS) *394*
Zionism; Studies in the History of the Zionist Movement and of the Jews in Palestine/Ha-Tsiyonut (IS ISSN 0084-5523) *770, 771*
Zionist Year Book (UK ISSN 0084-5531) *717*
Zip/Area Code Directory (US) *266, 269*
Zip Code Business Patterns (US ISSN 0275-7451) *219*
Zitteliana (GW ISSN 0373-9627) *303, 674*
Zodchestvo (UR) *70*
Zollkalender (GW) *234*
Zonarida (CL ISSN 0084-554X) *109*
Zondervan Pastor's Annual (US ISSN 0084-5558) *769*
La Zone Franc (FR) *178*
Zoologia (PL) *131*
Zoologia (BL ISSN 0084-5582) *917*
Zoological Parks & Aquariums in the Americas (US) *131*
Zoological Record (UK ISSN 0084-5604) *110*
Zoological Society of London. Symposia(UK ISSN 0084-5612) *131*
Zoological Society of London. Transactions (UK ISSN 0084-5620) *131*
Zoological Society of Southern Africa. Newsletter (SA) *131*
Zoological Society of Southern Africa. Occasional Bulletin *see* Zoological Society of Southern Africa. Newsletter *131*
Zoological Survey of India. Memoirs (II) *131*
Zoologicka Zahrada v Praze. Vyrocni Zprava/Annual Report (CS) *131*
Zoologisch-Botanische Gesellschaft, Vienna. Abhandlungen (AU ISSN 0084-5639) *119, 131*
Zoologisch-Botanische Gesellschaft, Vienna. Verhandlungen (AU ISSN 0084-5647) *119, 131*
Zoologische Staatssammlung, Muenchen. Veroeffentlichungen (GW ISSN 0077-2135) *131*
Zoology of Iceland (DK ISSN 0084-5655) *131*
Zoon (SA ISSN 0044-5274) *131*
Zoophysiology (US) *109*
Zoophysiology and Ecology *see* Zoophysiology *109*
Zoos & Aquariums in the Americas *see* Zoological Parks & Aquariums in the Americas *131*
Zrodla do Dziejow Bydgoszczy (PL ISSN 0084-568X) *465*
Zrodla do Dziejow Mysli Pedagogicznej(PL ISSN 0084-5698) *325*

Zrodla do Dziejow Nauki i Techniki (PL ISSN 0084-5701) *794, 854*
Zrodla do Historii Muzyki Polskiej (PL ISSN 0084-571X) *664*
Zshurnalist (IS) *506*
Zuckerwirtschaftliches Taschenbuch/ Sugar Economy/Economie Sucriere (GW ISSN 0084-5736) *406*
Zuercher Archaeologische Hefte (SZ) *67*
Zuercher Boerse. Jahresbericht (SZ) *205*
Zuerl's Adressbuch der Deutschen Luft- und Raumfahrt (GW ISSN 0065-2024) *11*
Zulassungsarbet (GW) *325*
Zumbambico (CK) *495*
Zur Lage der Schweiz (SZ ISSN 0084-5809) *465*
Zurich Stock Exchange. Handbook (SZ) *205*
Zusammenstelung Studieneinfuehrender Schriften (GW) *325*
Zweisprachige Reihe (GW ISSN 0084-5817) *577*
Zwischen Hausmannsturm und Walbecker Warte (NE) *465*
3 D Film Gids (NE) *651*
8 X 10 Art Portfolios (US) *80*
13th Moon (US ISSN 0094-3320) *577, 901*
18 Almanac (US ISSN 0163-1640) *258*
36 Manieres (CN ISSN 0708-2495) *577*
37 Design & Environment Projects (US ISSN 0363-9525) *70, 390*
50 State Legislative Review (US ISSN 0164-0356) *717*
99 Basic Advertising Layout Designs (US) *6*
100 European Banks (SZ) *178*
101 Gardening and Outdoor Ideas *see* Woman's Day 101 Gardening & Outdoor Ideas *416*
101 Gardening and Outdoor Ideas *see* Woman's Day 101 Gardening & Outdoor Ideas *416*
132 Expres (SP) *226*
0312-9012 James Cook University of North Queensland. Research and Publications Report *see* James Cook University of North Queensland. Research and Publications Report *794*
1000 Largest Companies in Sweden *see* Sveriges 1000 Stoersta Foeretag *225*
1040 Preparation (US) *234*
1745 Association and National Military History Society. Quarterly Notes. (UK) *465*
1810 Overture (US ISSN 0093-0288) *664*
2000 Largest Companies in Denmark *see* Danmarks 2000 Stoerste Virksomheder *222*